Digest of Education Statistics 2014
50th Edition

April 2016

Thomas D. Snyder
Cristobal de Brey
National Center for Education Statistics

Sally A. Dillow
American Institutes for Research

NCES 2016-006
U.S. DEPARTMENT OF EDUCATION

NATIONAL CENTER FOR EDUCATION STATISTICS

Institute of Education Sciences

U.S. Department of Education
John B. King, Jr.
Secretary

Institute of Education Sciences
Ruth Neild
Deputy Director for Policy and Research
Delegated Duties of the Director

National Center for Education Statistics
Peggy G. Carr
Acting Commissioner

The National Center for Education Statistics (NCES) is the primary federal entity for collecting, analyzing, and reporting data related to education in the United States and other nations. It fulfills a congressional mandate to collect, collate, analyze, and report full and complete statistics on the condition of education in the United States; conduct and publish reports and specialized analyses of the meaning and significance of such statistics; assist state and local education agencies in improving their statistical systems; and review and report on education activities in foreign countries.

NCES activities are designed to address high-priority education data needs; provide consistent, reliable, complete, and accurate indicators of education status and trends; and report timely, useful, and high-quality data to the U.S. Department of Education, the Congress, the states, other education policymakers, practitioners, data users, and the general public. Unless specifically noted, all information contained herein is in the public domain.

We strive to make our products available in a variety of formats and in language that is appropriate to a variety of audiences. You, as our customer, are the best judge of our success in communicating information effectively. If you have any comments or suggestions about this or any other NCES product or report, we would like to hear from you. Please direct your comments to

> NCES, IES, U.S. Department of Education
> Potomac Center Plaza (PCP)
> 550 12th Street SW
> Washington, DC 20202

April 2016

The NCES Home Page address is http://nces.ed.gov.
The NCES Publications and Products address is http://nces.ed.gov/pubsearch.

This report was prepared for the National Center for Education Statistics under Contract No. ED-IES-12-D-0002 with American Institutes for Research. Mention of trade names, commercial products, or organizations does not imply endorsement by the U.S. Government.

Suggested Citation

Snyder, T.D., de Brey, C., and Dillow, S.A. (2016). *Digest of Education Statistics 2014* (NCES 2016-006). National Center for Education Statistics, Institute of Education Sciences, U.S. Department of Education. Washington, DC.

Content Contact

Thomas D. Snyder
(202) 245-7165
tom.snyder@ed.gov

FOREWORD

The 2014 edition of the *Digest of Education Statistics* is the 50th in a series of publications initiated in 1962. The *Digest* has been issued annually except for combined editions for the years 1977–78, 1983–84, and 1985–86. Its primary purpose is to provide a compilation of statistical information covering the broad field of American education from prekindergarten through graduate school. The *Digest* includes a selection of data from many sources, both government and private, and draws especially on the results of surveys and activities carried out by the National Center for Education Statistics (NCES). To qualify for inclusion in the *Digest*, material must be nationwide in scope and of current interest and value. The publication contains information on a variety of subjects in the field of education statistics, including the number of schools and colleges, teachers, enrollments, and graduates, in addition to data on educational attainment, finances, federal funds for education, libraries, and international comparisons. Supplemental information on population trends, attitudes on education, education characteristics of the labor force, government finances, and economic trends provides background for evaluating education data. Although the *Digest* contains important information on federal education funding, more detailed information on federal activities is available from federal education program offices.

The *Digest* contains seven chapters: All Levels of Education, Elementary and Secondary Education, Postsecondary Education, Federal Funds for Education and Related Activities, Outcomes of Education, International Comparisons of Education, and Libraries and Technology. Each chapter is divided into a number of topical subsections. Preceding the seven chapters is an Introduction that provides a brief overview of current trends in American education, which supplements the tabular materials in chapters 1 through 7. The *Digest* concludes with three appendixes. The first appendix, Guide to Sources, provides a brief synopsis of the surveys used to generate the *Digest* tables; the second, Definitions, is included to help readers understand terms used in the *Digest*; and the third, Index of Table Numbers, allows readers to quickly locate tables on specific topics.

In addition to providing updated versions of many statistics that have appeared in previous years, this edition incorporates new material on the following topics:

- Number and percentage distribution of children under age 18 and under age 6, by living arrangements, race/ethnicity, and selected racial/ethnic subgroups (table 102.20)

- Number and percentage distribution of spring 2002 high school sophomores, by highest level of education completed through 2012, and socioeconomic status and selected student characteristics while in high school (table 104.91)

- Number and percentage distribution of spring 2002 high school sophomores, by highest level of education completed through 2012, socioeconomic status and educational expectations while in high school, and college enrollment status 2 years after high school (table 104.92)

- Sources of college information for spring 2002 high school sophomores who expected to attend a postsecondary institution, by highest level of education completed through 2012 and socioeconomic status while in high school (table 104.93)

- Primary child care arrangements of 4- and 5-year-old children who are not yet enrolled in kindergarten, by selected child and family characteristics (table 202.35)

- Public school students participating in programs for English language learners, by race/ethnicity (table 204.25)

- Percentage distribution of students enrolled in grades 1 through 12, by public school type and charter status, private school type, and selected household characteristics (table 206.30)

- Percentage of students enrolled in grades 1 through 12 whose parents reported having public school choice, considered other schools, reported current school was their first choice, or moved to their current neighborhood for the public school, by school type and selected child and household characteristics (table 206.40)

- Percentage of students enrolled in grades 3 through 12 whose parents were satisfied or dissatisfied with various aspects of their children's schools, by public and private school type (table 206.50)

- Number and percentage distribution of principals in public and private elementary and secondary schools, by selected characteristics (table 212.08)

- Mobility of public elementary and secondary principals, by selected principal and school characteristics (table 212.20)

- Number and percentage distribution of public and private school principals who left the profession during the past year, by total years of experience as a principal and occupational status (table 212.30)

- Among 18- to 24-year-olds who are not enrolled in high school, percentage who are high school completers (status completion rate), by sex and race/ethnicity (table 219.65)

- Among 18- to 24-year-olds who are not enrolled in high school, number and percentage who are high school completers (status completers), and percentage distribution, by selected characteristics (table 219.67)

- Average National Assessment of Educational Progress (NAEP) mathematics scale score of 12th-graders with various attitudes toward mathematics and percentage reporting these attitudes, by selected student characteristics (table 222.35)
- Percentage of public school students in grades 9–12 who reported having been bullied on school property or electronically bullied during the previous 12 months, by state (table 230.62)
- Number of incidents of students bringing firearms to or possessing firearms at a public school and ratio of incidents per 100,000 students, by state (table 231.65)
- Number and percentage of undergraduate students taking distance education or online classes and degree programs, by selected characteristics (table 311.22)
- Number and percentage of graduate students taking distance education or online classes and degree programs, by selected characteristics (table 311.32)

- On-campus hate crimes at degree-granting postsecondary institutions, by level and control of institution, type of crime, and category of bias motivating the crime (table 329.30)
- Percentage of full-time, full-year undergraduates receiving financial aid, and average annual amount received, by source of aid and selected student characteristics (table 331.35)
- Percentage of part-time or part-year undergraduates receiving financial aid, and average annual amount received, by source of aid and selected student characteristics (table 331.37)
- Percentage of 3- and 4-year-olds and 5- to 14-year-olds enrolled in school, by country (table 601.35)

The *Digest* can be accessed from http://nces.ed.gov/programs/digest.

Thomas D. Snyder
Supervisor
Annual Reports and Information Staff

Contents

List of Figures

List of Text Tables

List of Reference Tables

Chapter 2. Elementary and Secondary Education

Historical

Enrollment Status and Child Care Arrangements of Young Children

Enrollment in Public Schools

Reading Achievement

Mathematics Achievement

Science Achievement

Achievement in Other Subjects

Coursetaking and Grades

College Admission Tests

Student Activities, Homework, and Attendance

School Crime Victims

School Crime Incidents

School Environment

Fights and Weapons

Chapter 3. Postsecondary Education

Overview and Historical

Enrollment Rates

Total Fall Enrollment—General

Faculty and Instructional Staff

Faculty Salaries and Benefits

Institutions

Completion Rates

Achievement and Admissions Testing

Security and Crime

Student Charges

Financial Aid for Undergraduates

Financial Aid for Postbaccalaureate Students

Revenues

Chapter 6. International Comparisons of Education

Population, Enrollment, and Teachers

Achievement and Instruction

READER'S GUIDE

Data Sources

The data in this edition of the *Digest of Education Statistics* were obtained from many different sources—including students and teachers, state education agencies, local elementary and secondary schools, and colleges and universities—using surveys and compilations of administrative records. Users should be cautious when comparing data from different sources. Differences in aspects such as procedures, timing, question phrasing, and interviewer training can affect the comparability of results across data sources.

Most of the tables present data from surveys conducted by the National Center for Education Statistics (NCES) or conducted by other agencies and organizations with support from NCES. Some tables also include other data published by federal and state agencies, private research organizations, or professional organizations. Totals reported in the *Digest* are for the 50 states and the District of Columbia unless otherwise noted. Brief descriptions of the surveys and other data sources used in this volume can be found in Appendix A: Guide to Sources. For each NCES and non-NCES data source, the Guide to Sources also provides information on where to obtain further details about that source.

Data are obtained primarily from two types of surveys: universe surveys and sample surveys. In universe surveys, information is collected from every member of the population. For example, in a survey regarding certain expenditures of public elementary and secondary schools, data would be obtained from each school district in the United States. When data from an entire population are available, estimates of the total population or a subpopulation are made by simply summing the units in the population or subpopulation. As a result, there is no sampling error, and observed differences are reported as true.

Since a universe survey is often expensive and time consuming, many surveys collect data from a sample of the population of interest (sample survey). For example, the National Assessment of Educational Progress (NAEP) assesses a representative sample of students rather than the entire population of students. When a sample survey is used, statistical uncertainty is introduced, because the data come from only a portion of the entire population. This statistical uncertainty must be considered when reporting estimates and making comparisons. For information about how NCES accounts for statistical uncertainty when reporting sample survey results, see "Data Analysis and Interpretation," later in this Reader's Guide.

Common Measures and Indexes

Various types of statistics derived from universe and sample surveys are reported. Many tables report the size of a population or a subpopulation, and often the size of a subpopulation is expressed as a percentage of the total population.

In addition, the average (or *mean*) value of some characteristic of the population or subpopulation may be reported. The average is obtained by summing the values for all members of the population and dividing the sum by the size of the population. An example is the average annual salary of full-time instructional faculty at degree-granting postsecondary institutions. Another measure that is sometimes used is the *median*. The median is the midpoint value of a characteristic at or above which 50 percent of the population is estimated to fall, and at or below which 50 percent of the population is estimated to fall. An example is the median annual earnings of young adults who are full-time year-round workers. Some tables also present an *average per capita,* or per person, which represents an average computed for every person in a specified group or population. It is derived by dividing the total for an item (such as income or expenditures) by the number of persons in the specified population. An example is the per capita expenditure on education in each state.

Many tables report financial data in dollar amounts. Unless otherwise noted, all financial data are in *current dollars,* meaning not adjusted for changes in the purchasing power of the dollar over time due to inflation. For example, 1993–94 teacher salaries in current dollars are the amounts that the teachers earned in 1993–94, without any adjustments to account for inflation. *Constant dollar* adjustments attempt to remove the effects of price changes (inflation) from statistical series reported in dollars. For example, if teacher salaries over a 20-year period are adjusted to constant 2013–14 dollars, the salaries for all years are adjusted to the dollar values that presumably would exist if prices in each year were the same as in 2013–14, in other words, as if the dollar had constant purchasing power over the entire period. Any changes in the constant dollar amounts would reflect only changes in real values. Constant dollar amounts are computed using *price indexes*. Price indexes for inflation adjustments can be found in table 106.70. Each table that presents constant dollars includes a note indicating which index was used for the inflation adjustments; in most cases, the Consumer Price Index was used.

When presenting data for a time series, some tables include both *actual* and *projected* data. Actual data are data that have already been collected. Projected data can be used when data for a recent or future year are not yet available. Projections are estimates that are based on recent trends in relevant statistics and patterns associated with correlated variables. Unless otherwise noted, all data in this volume are actual.

Standard Errors

Using estimates calculated from data based on a sample of the population requires consideration of several factors before the estimates become meaningful. When using data from a sample, some margin of error will always be present in estimations of characteristics of the total population or subpopulation because the data are available from only a portion of the total population. Consequently, data from samples can provide only an approximation of the true or actual value. The margin of error of an estimate, or the range of potential true or actual values, depends on several factors such as the amount of variation in the responses, the size and representativeness of the sample, and the size of the subgroup for which the estimate is computed. The magnitude of this margin of error is measured by what statisticians call the "standard error" of an estimate.

When data from sample surveys are reported, the standard error is calculated for each estimate. In the tables, the standard error for each estimate generally appears in parentheses next to the estimate to which it applies. In order to caution the reader when interpreting findings, estimates from sample surveys are flagged with a "!" when the standard error is between 30 and 50 percent of the estimate, and suppressed with a "‡" when the standard error is 50 percent of the estimate or greater. The term "coefficient of variation (CV)" refers to the ratio of the standard error to the estimate; for example, if an estimate has a CV of 30 percent, this means that the standard error is equal to 30 percent of the value of the estimate.

Nonsampling Errors

In addition to standard errors, which apply only to sample surveys, all surveys are subject to nonsampling errors. Nonsampling errors may arise when individual respondents or interviewers interpret questions differently; when respondents must estimate values, or when coders, keyers, and other processors handle answers differently; when people who should be included in the universe are not; or when people fail to respond, either totally or partially. Total nonresponse means that people do not respond to the survey at all, while partial nonresponse (or item nonresponse) means that people fail to respond to specific survey items. To compensate for nonresponse, adjustments are often made. For universe surveys, an adjustment made for either type of nonresponse, total or partial, is often referred to as an imputation, which is often a substitution of the "average" questionnaire response for the nonresponse. For universe surveys, imputations are usually made separately within various groups of sample members that have similar survey characteristics. For sample surveys, total nonresponse is handled through nonresponse adjustments to the sample weights. For sample surveys, imputation for item nonresponse is usually made by substituting for a missing item the response to that item of a respondent having characteristics that are similar to those of the nonrespondent. For additional general information about imputations, see the *NCES Statistical Standards* (NCES 2014-097). Appendix A: Guide to Sources includes some information about specific surveys' response rates, nonresponse adjustments, and other efforts to reduce nonsampling error. Although the magnitude of nonsampling error is frequently unknown, idiosyncrasies that have been identified are noted in the appropriate tables.

Data Analysis and Interpretation

When estimates are from a sample, caution is warranted when drawing conclusions about one estimate in comparison to another, or about whether a time series of estimates is increasing, decreasing, or staying the same. Although one estimate may appear to be larger than another, a statistical test may find that the apparent difference between them is not reliably measurable due to the uncertainty around the estimates. In this case, the estimates will be described as having no measurable difference, meaning that the difference between them is not statistically significant.

Whether differences in means or percentages are statistically significant can be determined using the standard errors of the estimates. In reports produced by NCES, when differences are statistically significant, the probability that the difference occurred by chance is less than 5 percent, according to NCES standards.

Data presented in the text do not investigate more complex hypotheses, account for interrelationships among variables, or support causal inferences. We encourage readers who are interested in more complex questions and in-depth analysis to explore other NCES resources, including publications, online data tools, and public- and restricted-use datasets at http://nces.ed.gov.

In text that reports estimates based on samples, differences between estimates (including increases and decreases) are stated only when they are statistically significant. To determine whether differences reported are statistically significant, two-tailed t tests at the .05 level are typically used. The t test formula for determining statistical significance is adjusted when the samples being compared are dependent. The t test formula is not adjusted for multiple comparisons, with the exception of statistical tests conducted using the NAEP Data Explorer (http://nces.ed.gov/nationsreportcard/naepdata/). When the variables to be tested are postulated to form a trend, the relationship may be tested using linear regression, logistic regression, or ANOVA trend analysis instead of a series of t tests. These alternate methods of analysis test for specific relationships (e.g., linear, quadratic, or cubic) among variables. For more information on data analysis, please see the NCES Statistical Standards, Standard 5-1, available at http://nces.ed.gov/statprog/2012/pdf/Chapter5.pdf.

A number of considerations influence the ultimate selection of the data years to include in the tables and to feature in the text. To make analyses as timely as possible, the latest year of available data is shown. The choice of comparison years is often also based on the need to show the earliest available survey year, as in the case of NAEP and the international assessment surveys. The text typically compares the most current year's data with those from the initial year and then with those from a more recent year. In the case of surveys with long time frames, such as surveys measuring enrollment, changes over the course of a decade may be noted in the text. Where applicable, the text may also note years in which the data begin to diverge from previous trends. In figures and tables, intervening years are selected in increments in order to show the general trend.

Rounding and Other Considerations

All calculations are based on unrounded estimates. Therefore, the reader may find that a calculation, such as a difference or a percentage change, cited in the text or a figure may not be identical to the calculation obtained by using the rounded values shown in the accompanying tables. Although values reported in the tables are generally rounded to one decimal place (e.g., 76.5 percent), values reported in the text are generally rounded to whole numbers (with any value of 0.50 or above rounded to the next highest whole number). Due to rounding, cumulative percentages may sometimes equal 99 or 101 percent rather than 100 percent.

Race and Ethnicity

The Office of Management and Budget (OMB) is responsible for the standards that govern the categories used to collect and present federal data on race and ethnicity. The OMB revised the guidelines on racial/ethnic categories used by the federal government in October 1997, with a January 2003 deadline for implementation. The revised standards require a minimum of these five categories for data on race: American Indian or Alaska Native, Asian, Black or African American, Native Hawaiian or Other Pacific Islander, and White. The standards also require the collection of data on the ethnicity categories Hispanic or Latino and Not Hispanic or Latino. It is important to note that Hispanic origin is an ethnicity rather than a race, and therefore persons of Hispanic origin may be of any race. Origin can be viewed as the heritage, nationality group, lineage, or country of birth of the person or the person's parents or ancestors before their arrival in the United States. The race categories White, Black, Asian, Native Hawaiian or Other Pacific Islander, and American Indian or Alaska Native exclude persons of Hispanic origin unless otherwise noted.

For a description of each racial/ethnic category, please see the "Racial/ethnic group" entry in Appendix B: Definitions. Some of the category labels are shortened for more concise presentation in text, tables, and figures. American Indian or Alaska Native is denoted as American Indian/Alaska Native (except when separate estimates are available for American Indians alone or Alaska Natives alone); Black or African American is shortened to Black; and Hispanic or Latino is shortened to Hispanic. When discussed separately from Asian estimates, Native Hawaiian or Other Pacific Islander is shortened to Pacific Islander.

Many of the data sources used for this volume are federal surveys that collect data using the OMB standards for racial/ethnic classification described above; however, some sources have not fully adopted the standards, and some tables include historical data collected prior to the adoption of the OMB standards. Asians and Pacific Islanders are combined into a single category for years in which the data were not collected separately for the two groups. The combined category can sometimes mask significant differences between the two subgroups. For example, prior to 2011, NAEP collected data that did not allow for separate reporting of estimates for Asians and Pacific Islanders. The population counts presented in table 101.20, based on the U.S. Census Bureau's Current Population Reports, indicate that 96 percent of all Asian/Pacific Islander 5- to 17-year-olds were Asian in 2013. Thus, the combined category for Asians/Pacific Islanders is more representative of Asians than of Pacific Islanders.

Some surveys give respondents the option of selecting more than one race category, an "other" race category, or a "Two or more races" or "multiracial" category. Where possible, tables present data on the "Two or more races" category; however, in some cases this category may not be separately shown because the information was not collected or due to other data issues. Some tables include the "other" category. Any comparisons made between persons of one racial/ethnic group and persons of "all other racial/ethnic groups" include only the racial/ethnic groups shown in the reference table. In some surveys, respondents are not given the option to select more than one race category and also are not given an option such as "other" or "multiracial." In these surveys, respondents of Two or more races must select a single race category. Any comparisons between data from surveys that give the option to select more than one race and surveys that do not offer such an option should take into account the fact that there is a potential for bias if members of one racial group are more likely than members of the others to identify themselves as "Two or more races."[1] For postsecondary data, foreign students are counted separately and are therefore not included in any racial/ethnic category.

In addition to the major racial/ethnic categories, several tables include Hispanic ancestry subgroups (such as Mexican, Puerto Rican, Cuban, Dominican, Salvadoran, Other Central American, and South American) and Asian ancestry subgroups (such as Asian Indian, Chinese, Filipino, Japanese, Korean, and Vietnamese). In addition, selected tables include "Two or more races" subgroups (such as White and Black, White and Asian, and White and American Indian/Alaska Native).

---

[1]For discussion of such bias in responses to the 2000 Census, see Parker, J. et al. (2004). Bridging Between Two Standards for Collecting Information on Race and Ethnicity: An Application to Census 2000 and Vital Rates. *Public Health Reports, 119*(2): 192–205. Available at http://www.pubmed central.nih.gov/articlerender.fcgi?artid=1497618.

Limitations of the Data

Due to large standard errors, some differences that seem substantial are not statistically significant and, therefore, are not cited in the text. This situation often applies to estimates involving American Indians/Alaska Natives and Pacific Islanders. The relatively small sizes of these populations pose many measurement difficulties when conducting statistical analysis. Even in larger surveys, the numbers of American Indians/Alaska Natives and Pacific Islanders included in a sample are often small. Researchers studying data on these two populations often face small sample sizes that increase the size of standard errors and reduce the reliability of results. Readers should keep these limitations in mind when comparing estimates presented in the tables.

As mentioned, caution should be exercised when comparing data from different sources. Differences in sampling, data collection procedures, coverage of target population, timing, phrasing of questions, scope of nonresponse, interviewer training, and data processing and coding mean that results from different sources may not be strictly comparable. For example, the racial/ethnic categories presented to a respondent, and the way in which the question is asked, can influence the response, especially for individuals who consider themselves of mixed race or ethnicity. In addition, data on American Indians/Alaska Natives are often subject to inaccuracies that can result from respondents self-identifying their race/ethnicity. Research on the collection of race/ethnicity data suggests that the categorization of American Indian and Alaska Native is the least stable self-identification (for example, the same individual may identify as American Indian when responding to one survey, but may not do so on a subsequent survey).[2]

---

[2]See U.S. Department of Labor, Bureau of Labor Statistics (1995). *A Test of Methods for Collecting Racial and Ethnic Information* (USDL 95-428). Washington DC: Author.

INTRODUCTION

The Introduction provides a brief overview of current trends in American education, highlighting key data that are presented in more detail later in this volume. Topics outlined include the participation of students, teachers, and faculty in U.S. educational institutions; the performance of U.S. elementary/secondary students overall and in comparison to students in other countries; the numbers of high school graduates and postsecondary degrees; and the amounts of expenditures on education at the elementary/secondary and postsecondary levels.

In fall 2014, about 75.2 million people were enrolled in American schools and colleges (table 105.10). About 4.6 million people were employed as elementary and secondary school teachers or as college faculty, in full-time equivalents (FTE). Other professional, administrative, and support staff at educational institutions totaled 5.3 million. All data for 2014 in this Introduction are projected, except for data on educational attainment. Some data for other years are projected or estimated as noted. In discussions of historical trends, different time periods and specific years are cited, depending on the timing of important changes as well as the availability of relevant data.

Elementary/Secondary Education

Enrollment

A pattern of annual increases in total public elementary and secondary school enrollment began in 1985, but enrollment stabilized at 49.3 million between 2006 and 2008, before beginning to increase again (table 105.30). Overall, public school enrollment rose 27 percent, from 39.4 million to 50.0 million, between 1985 and 2014. Private school enrollment fluctuated during this period, with the fall 2014 enrollment of 5.0 million being 10 percent lower than the enrollment of 5.6 million in 1985. About 9 percent of elementary and secondary school students were enrolled in private schools in 2014, reflecting a decrease from 12 percent in 1985.

In public schools between 1985 and 2014, there was a 30 percent increase in elementary enrollment (prekindergarten through grade 8), compared with a 20 percent increase in secondary enrollment (grades 9 through 12) (table 105.30). Part of the higher growth in public elementary school enrollment resulted from the expansion of prekindergarten enrollment (table 203.10). Between fall 1985 and fall 2012, enrollment in prekindergarten increased 764 percent, while enrollment in other elementary grades (including kindergarten through grade 8 plus ungraded elementary programs) increased 25 percent. The number of children enrolled in prekindergarten increased

from 0.2 million in 1985 to 1.3 million in 2012, and the number enrolled in other elementary grades increased from 26.9 million to 33.7 million. Public secondary school enrollment declined 8 percent from 1985 to 1990, but then increased 33 percent from 1990 to 2007, before declining 2 percent from 2007 to 2014 (table 105.30). Between 1990 and 2014, the net increase in public secondary school enrollment was 31 percent, compared with an 18 percent increase in public elementary school enrollment. Over the most recent 10-year period (between 2004 and 2014), public school enrollment rose 2 percent. Elementary enrollment increased 3 percent over this period, while secondary enrollment was 1 percent higher in 2014 than in 2004.

Since the enrollment rates of 5- and 6-year-olds, 7- to 13-year-olds, and 14- to 17-year-olds changed by less than 3 percentage points from 1985 to 2013, increases in public elementary and secondary school enrollment primarily reflect increases in the number of children in the population in these age groups (tables 101.10 and 103.20). For example, the enrollment rate of 7- to 13-year-olds decreased from 99 to 98 percent between 1985 and 2013, but the number of 7- to 13-year-olds increased by 25 percent. Increases in both the enrollment rate of 3- and 4-year-old children (from 39 percent in 1985 to 55 percent in 2013) and the number of children in this age group (from 7.1 million to 8.0 million) also contributed to overall enrollment increases.

The National Center for Education Statistics (NCES) projects record levels of total public elementary and secondary enrollment from 2014 (50.0 million) through at least 2024 (52.9 million) (table 105.30). The total public school enrollment projected for fall 2014 is a record-high number, and new records are expected every year through 2024, the last year for which NCES enrollment projections have been developed. Public elementary school enrollment (prekindergarten through grade 8) is projected to increase 7 percent between 2014 and 2024. Public secondary school enrollment (grades 9 through 12) is expected to increase 3 percent between 2014 and 2024. Overall, total public school enrollment is expected to increase 6 percent between 2014 and 2024.

Teachers

About 3.5 million full-time-equivalent (FTE) elementary and secondary school teachers were engaged in classroom instruction in fall 2014 (table 105.40). This number is less than 1 percent lower than in fall 2004. The 2014 number of FTE teachers includes 3.1 million public school teachers and 0.4 million private school teachers.

Public school enrollment was about 2 percent higher in 2014 than in 2004, while the number of public school teachers was about 1 percent higher (table 208.20). In fall 2014, the number of public school pupils per teacher was 16.0, which was higher than the ratio of 15.8 in 2004.

The average salary for public school teachers in 2013–14 was $56,689 in current dollars (i.e., dollars that are not adjusted for inflation) (table 211.50). In constant (i.e., inflation-adjusted) dollars, the average salary for teachers was 2 percent lower in 2013–14 than in 1990–91.

Student Performance

Most of the student performance data in the *Digest* are drawn from the National Assessment of Educational Progress (NAEP). The NAEP assessments have been conducted using three basic designs: the national main NAEP, state NAEP, and long-term trend NAEP. The national main NAEP and state NAEP provide current information about student performance in subjects including reading, mathematics, science, and writing, while long-term trend NAEP provides information on performance since the early 1970s in reading and mathematics only. Results from long-term trend NAEP are included in the discussion in chapter 2 of the *Digest*, while the information in this Introduction includes only selected results from the national main and state NAEP. Readers should keep in mind that comparisons of NAEP scores in the text (like all comparisons of estimates in the *Digest*) are based on statistical testing of unrounded values.

The main NAEP reports current information for the nation and specific geographic regions of the country. The assessment program includes students drawn from both public and private schools and reports results for student achievement at grades 4, 8, and 12. The main NAEP assessments follow the frameworks developed by the National Assessment Governing Board and use the latest advances in assessment methodology. The state NAEP is identical in content to the national main NAEP, but the state NAEP reports information only for public school students. Chapter 2 presents more information on the NAEP designs and methodology, and additional details appear in Appendix A: Guide to Sources.

Reading

The main NAEP reading assessment data are reported on a scale of 0 to 500. In 2013, the average reading score for 4th-grade students (222) was not measurably different from the 2011 score, but it was higher than the scores on assessments between 1992 (217) and 2009 (221) (table 221.10). At grade 4, only the average reading scores for White students were higher in 2013 (232) than in both 2011 (231) and 1992 (224). The 2013 scores for Black (206), Hispanic (207), and Asian/Pacific Islander (235) 4th-graders were not measurably different from the 2011 scores, but the 2013 scores were higher than the 1992 scores (192, 197, and 216, respectively). For 8th-grade students, the average reading score in 2013 (268) was more than 2 points higher than in 2011 (265), was 8 points higher than in 1992 (260), and was

higher than the average scores in all previous years. At grade 8, the average reading scores for White (276), Black (250), Hispanic (256), and Asian/Pacific Islander (280) students were higher in 2013 than in 2011 and 1992. For 12th-grade students, the average reading score in 2013 (288) was not measurably different from the score in 2009 (12th-graders were not assessed in 2011), but was lower than the score in 1992 (292). At grade 12, the 2013 average reading scores for White (297), Hispanic (276), and Asian/Pacific Islander (296) students were not measurably different from either the 2009 scores or the 1992 scores. The 2013 reading score for Black students (268) was not measurably different from the score in 2009, but was lower than the score in 1992 (273).

From 2011 to 2013, there was no measurable change in the average reading score for 4th-grade public school students nationally. However, average scores at grade 4 were higher in 2013 than in 2011 in 7 states (Colorado, Indiana, Iowa, Maine, Minnesota, Tennessee, and Washington) plus the District of Columbia and the Department of Defense dependents schools; scores were lower in 2013 than in 2011 in 3 states (Massachusetts, Montana, and North Dakota) (table 221.40). At grade 8, the average reading score for public school students nationally was 2 points higher in 2013 than in 2011, and 12 states (Arkansas, California, Florida, Hawaii, Iowa, Nevada, New Hampshire, Oregon, Pennsylvania, Tennessee, Utah, and Washington) plus the District of Columbia and the Department of Defense dependents schools had higher scores in 2013 than in 2011 (table 221.60). In the other states, scores did not change measurably from 2011 to 2013.

Mathematics

The main NAEP mathematics assessment data for 4th- and 8th-graders are reported on a scale of 0 to 500. In 2013, the average NAEP mathematics scores for 4th-grade and 8th-grade students were higher than the average scores in all previous assessment years (table 222.10). The average 4th-grade NAEP mathematics score increased from 213 in 1990 (the first assessment year) to 242 in 2013, an increase of 28 points (based on unrounded scores). During that same period, the average 8th-grade score increased by 22 points, from 263 to 285. At grade 4, the average mathematics scores in 2013 for White (250) and Hispanic students (231) were higher than the scores in both 2011 and 1990. The 2013 score for Black 4th-graders (224) was not measurably different from the 2011 score, but it was higher than the 1990 score. The 2013 score for Asian 4th-graders (259) was also not measurably different from the 2011 score; prior to 2011, separate data on Asians were not available. At grade 8, the average mathematics scores in 2013 for all racial/ethnic groups were not measurably different from the 2011 scores. However, the 2013 scores for White (294), Black (263), and Hispanic (272) 8th-graders were higher than the scores in 1990. Due to changes in the 12th-grade mathematics assessment framework, a new trend line started in 2005, with data reported on a scale of 0 to 300. The average 12th-grade mathematics score in 2013 (153) was not measurably different from the score in 2009, but was higher than the score in 2005 (150).

NAEP results also permit state-level comparisons of the mathematics achievement of 4th- and 8th-grade students in public schools (tables 222.50 and 222.60). The average mathematics scores for 4th-grade public school students increased from 2011 to 2013 in 14 states (Arizona, Colorado, Delaware, Hawaii, Indiana, Iowa, Minnesota, Nebraska, New York, North Dakota, Tennessee, Washington, West Virginia, and Wyoming) and the District of Columbia and did not decrease for any states. At grade 8, scores were higher in 2013 than in 2011 in five states (Florida, Hawaii, New Hampshire, Pennsylvania, and Tennessee), the District of Columbia, and the Department of Defense dependents schools, and scores decreased in three states (Montana, Oklahoma, and South Dakota).

Science

NAEP has assessed the science abilities of students in grades 4, 8, and 12 in both public and private schools since 1996. As of 2009, however, NAEP science assessments are based on a new framework, so results from these assessments cannot be compared to results from earlier science assessments. The main NAEP science assessment data are reported on a scale of 0 to 300. The average 8th-grade science score increased from 150 in 2009 to 152 in 2011 (table 223.10). Average scores for both male and female students were higher in 2011 than in 2009. Male students scored 5 points higher on average than female students in 2011, which was not significantly different from the 4-point gap in 2009. Score gaps between White and Black students and between White and Hispanic students narrowed from 2009 to 2011. The 5-point gain from 2009 to 2011 for Hispanic students was larger than the 1-point gain for White students, narrowing the score gap from 30 points to 27 points. Black students scored 3 points higher in 2011 than in 2009. The 35-point score gap between White and Black students in 2011 was smaller than the 36-point gap in 2009. The average scores of Asian/Pacific Islander and American Indian/Alaska Native students were not significantly different in 2011 from their scores in 2009.

International Comparisons

The 2011 Trends in International Mathematics and Science Study (TIMSS) assessed students' mathematics and science performance at grade 4 in 45 countries and at grade 8 in 38 countries. In addition to countries, a number of subnational entities—including the public school systems in several U.S. states—also participated in TIMSS as separate education systems. Results for the participating states are included in the discussion in chapter 6 of the *Digest*, while this Introduction includes only results for the United States and other countries. TIMSS assessments are curriculum based and measure what students have actually learned against the subject matter that is expected to be taught in the participating countries by the end of grades 4 and 8. At both grades, TIMSS scores are reported on a scale of 0 to 1,000, with the scale average set at 500.

On the 2011 TIMSS, the average mathematics scores of U.S. 4th-graders (541) and 8th-graders (509) were higher than the scale average (tables 602.20 and 602.30). U.S. 4th-graders scored higher in mathematics, on average, than their counterparts in 37 countries and lower than those in 3 countries (table 602.20). Average mathematics scores in the other 4 countries were not measurably different from the U.S. average. At grade 8, the average U.S. mathematics score was higher than the average scores of students in 27 countries in 2011 and below the average scores of students in 4 countries (table 602.30). Average 8th-grade mathematics scores in the other 6 countries were not measurably different from the U.S. average. The average science scores of both U.S. 4th-graders (544) and U.S. 8th-graders (525) were higher than the TIMSS scale average of 500 in 2011. The average U.S. 4th-grade science score was higher than the average scores of students in 39 countries and lower than those of students in 5 countries. At grade 8, the average U.S. science score was higher than the average scores of students in 28 countries, lower than those in 6 countries, and not measurably different from those in the other 3 countries.

The Program for International Student Assessment (PISA), coordinated by the Organization for Economic Cooperation and Development (OECD), has measured the performance of 15-year-old students in reading, mathematics, and science literacy every 3 years since 2000. PISA assesses 15-year-old students' application of reading, mathematics, and science literacy to problems within a real-life context. In 2012, PISA assessed students in the 34 OECD countries as well as in a number of other education systems. Some subnational entities participated as separate education systems, including public school systems in the U.S. states of Connecticut, Florida, and Massachusetts. Results for the participating U.S. states are included in the discussion in chapter 6, while this Introduction includes only results for the United States in comparison with other OECD countries. PISA scores are reported on a scale of 0 to 1,000.

On the 2012 PISA assessment, U.S. 15-year-olds' average score in reading literacy was 498, which was not measurably different from the OECD average of 496 (table 602.50). The average reading literacy score in the United States was lower than the average score in 13 of the 33 other OECD countries, higher than the average score in 10 of the other OECD countries, and not measurably different from the average score in 10 of the OECD countries. In all countries, females outperformed males in reading (table 602.40). The U.S. gender gap in reading (31 points) was smaller than the OECD average gap (38 points) and smaller than the gaps in 14 of the OECD countries.

In mathematics literacy, U.S. 15-year-olds' average score of 481 on the 2012 PISA assessment was lower than the OECD average score of 494 (table 602.60). The average mathematics literacy score in the United States was lower than the average in 21 of the 33 other OECD countries, higher than the average in 5 OECD countries, and not measurably different from the average in 7 OECD countries. In 25 of the OECD countries, males outperformed females in mathematics literacy (table 602.40). In the United States, however, the average score of males (484) was not measurably different from that of females (479).

In science literacy, U.S. 15-year-olds' average score of 497 was not measurably different from the OECD average score of 501 (table 602.70). The average science literacy score in the United States was lower than the average in 15 OECD countries, higher than the average in 8 OECD countries, and not measurably different from the average in 10 OECD countries.

The Progress in International Reading Literacy Study (PIRLS) measures the reading knowledge and skills of 4th-graders over time. PIRLS scores are reported on a scale from 0 to 1,000, with the scale average set at 500. On the 2011 PIRLS, U.S. 4th-graders had an average reading literacy score of 556 (table 602.10). The U.S. average score in 2011 was 14 points higher than in 2001 and 16 points higher than in 2006. In all three assessment years, the U.S. average score was higher than the PIRLS scale average. In 2011, PIRLS assessed 4th-grade reading literacy in 40 countries. The average reading literacy score of 4th-graders in the United States was higher than the average score in 33 of the 39 other participating countries, lower than the average score in 3 countries, and not measurably different from the average in the remaining 3 countries.

High School Graduates and Dropouts

About 3,323,000 U.S. high school students are expected to graduate during the 2014–15 school year (table 219.10), including about 3,031,000 public school graduates and 291,000 private school graduates. High school graduates include only recipients of diplomas, not recipients of equivalency credentials. The number of high school graduates projected for 2014–15 is lower than the record high in 2011–12, but exceeds the baby boom era's high point in 1975–76, when 3,142,000 students earned diplomas. In 2011–12, an estimated 80.8 percent of public high school students graduated on time—that is, received a diploma 4 years after beginning their freshman year.

The number of GED credentials issued by the states to GED test passers rose from 330,000 in 1977 to 487,000 in 2000 (table 219.60). A record number of 648,000 GED credentials were issued in 2001. In 2002, there were revisions to the GED test and to the data reporting procedures. In 2001, test takers were required to successfully complete all five components of the GED or else begin the five-part series again with the new test that was introduced in 2002. Prior to 2002, reporting was based on summary data from the states on the number of GED credentials issued. As of 2002, reporting has been based on individual GED candidate- and test-level records collected by the GED Testing Service.[1] Between 2003 and 2013, the number of persons passing the GED tests increased by 40 percent, from 387,000 to 541,000.

The percentage of dropouts among 16- to 24-year-olds (known as the status dropout rate) has decreased over the past 20 years (table 219.70). The status dropout rate is the percentage of the civilian noninstitutionalized 16- to 24-year-old population who are not enrolled in school and who have not completed a high school program, regardless of when they left school. (People who left school but went on to receive a GED credential are not treated as dropouts in this measure.) Between 1990 and 2013, the status dropout rate declined from 12.1 percent to 6.8 percent (table 219.70). Although the status dropout rate declined for both Blacks and Hispanics during this period, their rates in 2013 (7.3 and 11.7 percent, respectively) remained higher than the rate for Whites (5.1 percent).

Postsecondary Education

College Enrollment

College enrollment was 20.4 million in fall 2013, which was 3 percent lower than the record enrollment in fall 2010 (table 105.30). College enrollment is expected to set new records from fall 2018 through fall 2024, the last year for which NCES enrollment projections have been developed. Between fall 2013 and fall 2024, enrollment is expected to increase by 14 percent. Despite decreases in the size of the traditional college-age population (18 to 24 years old) during the late 1980s and early 1990s, total enrollment increased during this period (tables 101.10 and 105.30). The traditional college-age population rose 9 percent between 2003 and 2013, and total college enrollment increased 20 percent during the same period. Between 2003 and 2013, the number of full-time students increased by 22 percent, compared with an 18 percent increase in part-time students (table 303.10). During the same time period, the number of males enrolled increased 22 percent, and the number of females enrolled increased 19 percent.

Faculty

In fall 2013, degree-granting institutions—defined as postsecondary institutions that grant an associate's or higher degree and are eligible for Title IV federal financial aid programs—employed 1.5 million faculty members, including 0.8 million full-time and 0.8 million part-time faculty (table 314.30). In addition, degree-granting institutions employed 0.4 million graduate assistants.

Postsecondary Degrees

During the 2014–15 academic year, postsecondary degrees conferred were projected to number 949,000 associate's degrees, 1,852,000 bachelor's degrees, 778,000 master's degrees, and 178,000 doctor's degrees (table 318.10). The doctor's degree total includes most degrees formerly classified as first-professional, such as M.D., D.D.S., and law degrees. Between 2002–03 and 2012–13 (the last year of actual data), the number of degrees conferred increased at all levels. The number of associate's degrees was 59 percent higher in 2012–13 than in 2002–03, the number of bachelor's degrees was 36 percent higher, the number of master's degrees was 45 percent higher, and the number of doctor's degrees was 44 percent higher.

---

[1]Information on changes in GED test series and reporting is based on the 2003 edition of *Who Passed the GED Tests?*, by the GED Testing Service of the American Council on Education, as well as communication with staff of the GED Testing Service.

Between 2002–03 and 2012–13, the number of bachelor's degrees awarded to males increased 37 percent, while the number of bachelor's degrees awarded to females increased 36 percent. Females earned 57 percent of all bachelor's degrees in 2012–13, the same percentage as in 2002–03. Between 2002–03 and 2012–13, the number of White students earning bachelor's degrees increased 23 percent, compared with larger increases of 54 percent for Black students, 110 percent for Hispanic students, and 48 percent for Asian/Pacific Islander students (table 322.20). The number of American Indian/Alaska Native students earning bachelor's degrees increased 16 percent over the same period. In 2012–13, White students earned 69 percent of all bachelor's degrees awarded (vs. 76 percent in 2002–03), Black students earned 11 percent (vs. 10 percent in 2002–03), Hispanic students earned 11 percent (vs. 7 percent in 2002–03), and Asian/Pacific Islander students earned about 7 percent (increasing their share of the degrees from 6.7 percent in 2002–03 to 7.3 percent in 2012–13). American Indian/Alaska Native students earned less than 1 percent of the degrees in both years.

Undergraduate Prices

For the 2013–14 academic year, annual prices for undergraduate tuition, fees, room, and board were estimated to be $15,640 at public institutions, $40,614 at private nonprofit institutions, and $23,135 at private for-profit institutions in current dollars (table 330.10). Between 2003–04 and 2013–14, prices for undergraduate tuition, fees, room, and board at public institutions rose 34 percent, and prices at private nonprofit institutions rose 25 percent, after adjustment for inflation. Prices for total tuition, fees, room, and board at private for-profit institutions decreased 16 percent between 2003–04 and 2013–14.

Educational Attainment

The U.S. Census Bureau collects annual statistics on the educational attainment of the population. Between 2004 and 2014, the percentage of the adult population 25 years of age and over who had completed high school rose from 85 percent to 88 percent, and the percentage of adults with a bachelor's degree increased from 28 percent to 32 percent (table 104.10). High school completers include those people who graduated from high school with a diploma, as well as those who completed high school through equivalency programs. The percentage of young adults (25- to 29-year-olds) who had completed high school increased from 87 percent in 2004 to 91 percent in 2014 (table 104.20). The percentage of young adults who had completed a bachelor's degree increased from 29 percent in 2004 to 34 percent in 2014.

Education Expenditures

Expenditures for public and private education, from pre-kindergarten through graduate school (excluding postsecondary schools not awarding associate's or higher degrees), were an estimated $1.2 trillion for 2013–14 (table 106.10). Expenditures of elementary and secondary schools totaled an estimated $682 billion, while those of degree-granting postsecondary institutions totaled an estimated $512 billion. Total expenditures for education were an estimated 7.1 percent of the gross domestic product in 2013–14. The percentage of GDP was higher in 2009–10 (7.6) than in 2003–04 (7.2); however, the percentage has declined since 2009–10.

CHAPTER 1
All Levels of Education

This chapter provides a broad overview of education in the United States. It brings together material from preprimary, elementary, secondary, and postsecondary education, as well as from the general population, to present a composite picture of the American educational system. Tables feature data on the total number of people enrolled in school, the number of teachers, the number of schools, and total expenditures for education at all levels. This chapter also includes statistics on education-related topics such as educational attainment, family characteristics, and population. Economic indicators and price indexes have been added to facilitate analyses.

Many of the statistics in this chapter are derived from the statistical activities of the National Center for Education Statistics (NCES). In addition, substantial contributions have been drawn from the work of other groups, both governmental and nongovernmental, as shown in the source notes of the tables. Information on survey methodologies is contained in Appendix A: Guide to Sources and in the publications cited in the table source notes.

The U.S. System of Education

The U.S. system of education can be described as having three levels of formal education (elementary, secondary, and postsecondary) (figure 1). Students may spend 1 to 3 years in preprimary programs (prekindergarten [PK] and kindergarten [K]), which may be offered either in separate schools or in elementary schools that also offer higher grades. (In *Digest of Education Statistics* tables, prekindergarten and kindergarten are generally defined as a part of elementary education.) Following kindergarten, students ordinarily spend from 6 to 8 years in elementary school. The elementary school program is followed by a 4- to 6-year program in secondary school. Students typically complete the entire program through grade 12 by age 18. Education at the elementary and secondary levels is provided in a range of institutional settings—including elementary schools (preprimary schools, middle schools, and schools offering broader ranges of elementary grades); secondary schools (junior high schools, high schools, and senior high schools); and combined elementary/secondary schools—that vary in structure from locality to locality.

High school graduates who decide to continue their education may enter a specialized career/technical institution, a 2-year community or junior college, or a 4-year college or university. A 2-year college typically offers the first 2 years of a standard 4-year college curriculum and a selection of terminal career and technical education programs. Academic courses completed at a 2-year college are usually transferable for credit at a 4-year college or university. A career/technical institution offers postsecondary technical training programs of varying lengths leading to a specific career.

An associate's degree requires at least 2 years of postsecondary coursework, and a bachelor's degree typically requires 4 years of postsecondary coursework. At least 1 year of coursework beyond the bachelor's is necessary for a master's degree, while a doctor's degree usually requires a minimum of 3 or 4 years beyond the bachelor's.

Professional schools differ widely in admission requirements and program length. Medical students, for example, generally complete a bachelor's program of premedical studies at a college or university before they can enter the 4-year program at a medical school. Law programs typically involve 3 years of coursework beyond the bachelor's degree level.

Enrollment

Total enrollment in public and private elementary and secondary schools (prekindergarten through grade 12) grew rapidly during the 1950s and 1960s, reaching a peak year in 1971 (table A, table 105.30, and figure 2). This enrollment rise reflected what is known as the "baby boom," a dramatic increase in births following World War II. Between 1971 and 1984, total elementary and secondary school enrollment decreased every year, reflecting the decline in the size of the school-age population over that period. After these years of decline, enrollment in elementary and secondary schools started increasing in fall 1985, began hitting new record levels in the mid-1990s, and continued to reach new record levels every year through 2006. Enrollment in fall 2012 (55.0 million) was slightly higher than in fall 2010 (54.9 million), but was slightly lower than in fall 2006 (55.3 million). However, a pattern of annual enrollment increases is projected to begin with a slight increase in fall 2015 (no substantial change since 2012) and continue at least through fall 2024 (the last year for which NCES has projected school enrollment), when enrollment is expected to reach 57.9 million.

Table A. Total elementary and secondary school enrollment, by overall trends: Selected years, 1949–50 through fall 2024

Trend and year	Number of students (in millions)
"Baby boom" increases	
1949–50 school year	28.5
Fall 1959	40.9
Fall 1969	51.1
Fall 1971 (peak)	51.3
13 years with annual declines	
Fall 1972 (first year of decline)	50.7
Fall 1984 (final year of decline)	44.9
Annual increases from 1985 to 2006	
Fall 1985	45.0
Fall 1996 (new record highs begin)	51.5
Fall 2006 (final year of record highs)	55.3
Slight declines or stable enrollment	
Fall 2007	55.2
Fall 2010	54.9
Fall 2012	55.0
Fall 2014	55.0
Annual increases projected to start again	
Fall 2015	55.0
Fall 2024	57.9

SOURCE: U.S. Department of Education, National Center for Education Statistics, *Biennial Survey of Education in the United States*, 1949–50; *Statistics of Public Elementary and Secondary School Systems*, 1959 through 1972; Common Core of Data (CCD), 1984 through 2012; Private School Universe Survey (PSS), 1997–98 through 2011–12; and National Elementary and Secondary Enrollment Projection Model, 1972 through 2024.

Between 1985 and 2013, the total public and private school enrollment rate for 5- and 6-year-olds decreased from 96 percent to 94 percent, while the enrollment rate for 7- to 13-year-olds decreased from 99 percent to 98 percent (table 103.20). However, the enrollment rate for 14- to 17-year-olds increased from 95 to 96 percent during this period. Since these enrollment rates changed by 2 or fewer percentage points between 1985 and 2013, increases in public and private elementary and secondary school enrollment primarily reflect increases in the number of children in these age groups. Between 1985 and 2013, the number of 5- and 6-year-olds increased by 19 percent, the number of 7- to 13-year-olds increased by 25 percent, and the number of 14- to 17-year-olds increased by 12 percent (table 101.10). Increases in the enrollment rate of prekindergarten-age children (ages 3 and 4) from 39 percent in 1985 to 55 percent in 2013 (table 103.20) and in the number of 3- and 4-year-olds from 7.1 million to 8.0 million (table 101.10) also contributed to overall prekindergarten through grade 12 enrollment increases.

Public school enrollment at the elementary level (prekindergarten through grade 8) rose from 29.9 million in fall 1990 to 34.2 million in fall 2003 (table 105.30). Elementary enrollment was less than 1 percent lower in fall 2004 than in fall 2003 and then generally increased to a projected total of 35.2 million for fall 2014. Public elementary enrollment is projected to increase 7 percent between 2014 and 2024. Public school enrollment at the secondary level (grades 9 through 12) rose from 11.3 million in 1990 to 15.1 million in 2007, but then declined 2 percent to a projected enrollment of 14.8 million in 2014. Public secondary enrollment is pro-

jected to increase 3 percent between 2014 and 2024. Total public elementary and secondary enrollment is projected to increase every year from 2014 to 2024.

The percentage of students in private elementary and secondary schools declined from 11.7 percent in fall 2001 to 9.6 percent in fall 2011 (table 105.30). In fall 2014, an estimated 5.0 million students were enrolled in private schools at the elementary and secondary levels.

Total enrollment in public and private degree-granting postsecondary institutions reached 14.5 million in fall 1992, but decreased every year through fall 1995 (table 105.30). Total enrollment increased 47 percent between 1995 and 2010 (to 21.0 million), but declined 3 percent between 2010 and 2013 (to 20.4 million). Total enrollment is expected to increase 14 percent between fall 2013 and fall 2024, reaching 23.1 million. The percentage of students who attended private institutions rose from 24 to 28 percent between 2003 and 2013. In fall 2013, about 5.6 million students attended private institutions, with about 4.0 million in nonprofit institutions and 1.7 million in for-profit institutions (table 303.10). Enrollment increases in degree-granting postsecondary institutions have been driven by increases in population, as well as by increases in enrollment rates for some age groups. The percentage of 18- and 19-year-olds enrolled in degree-granting postsecondary institutions was 47 percent in both 2003 and 2013; however, the number of 18- and 19-year-olds rose 4 percent (tables 101.10 and 103.20). The enrollment rate of 20- to 24-year-olds rose from 36 to 39 percent, and the number of 20- to 24-year-olds rose 11 percent during the same period.

Educational Attainment

The percentages of adults 25 years old and over completing high school and higher education have been rising. Between 2004 and 2014, the percentage of the population 25 years old and over who had completed at least high school increased from 85 to 88 percent, and the percentage who had completed a bachelor's or higher degree increased from 28 to 32 percent (table 104.10 and figure 3). In 2014, about 8 percent of people 25 years old or over held a master's degree as their highest degree and 3 percent held a doctor's or first-professional degree (table 104.30).

Among young adults (25- to 29-year-olds), the percentage who had completed at least high school increased from 87 percent in 2004 to 91 percent in 2014 (table 104.20 and figure 4). The percentage of young adults who had completed a bachelor's or higher degree increased from 29 percent in 2004 to 34 percent in 2014. In 2014, about 6 percent of young adults held a master's degree as their highest degree and 2 percent held a doctor's or first-professional degree (table 104.30 and figure 5). Overall, the percentage of young adults who had a master's or higher degree rose from 6 percent in 2004 to 8 percent in 2014.

Between 2004 and 2014, changes occurred in the educational attainment of young adults (25- to 29-year-olds) by race/ethnicity. During this period, the percentages who had completed at least high school increased for Hispanic, White, and Black young adults, but there was no measurable change in the percentage for Asian young adults (97 percent in both years) (table 104.20 and figure 6). The percentage of Hispanic young adults who had completed at least high school rose from 62 percent in 2004 to 75 percent in 2014, an increase of 12 percentage points. During the same period, the percentage of White young adults who had completed at least high school rose from 93 to 96 percent, an increase of 2 percentage points (based on unrounded data). Since the increase for White young adults was smaller than the increase for Hispanic young adults, the gap between the high school completion percentages for these two groups decreased from 31 percentage points in 2004 to 21 percentage points in 2014. Between 2004 and 2014, the percentage of Black young adults who had completed high school increased from 89 percent to 92 percent, but there was no measurable change in the gap between the White and Black high school completion percentages. In 2014, the percentage of young adults who had completed at least high school was higher for Whites and Asians than for Blacks, and the percentage for Hispanics was lower than for Whites, Asians, and Blacks.

The percentage of bachelor's degree holders also varied among young adults of different racial/ethnic groups, with 63 percent of Asians in the 25- to 29-year-old age group holding a bachelor's or higher degree in 2014, compared with 41 percent of Whites, 22 percent of Blacks, and 15 percent of Hispanics. Between 2004 and 2014, the percentages who had completed a bachelor's or higher degree increased for White, Black, and Hispanic young adults, but showed no measurable change for Asian young adults. During this period, the percentage of young adults who held a bachelor's or higher degree increased from 34 to 41 percent among Whites, from 17 to 22 percent among Blacks, and from 11 to 15 percent among Hispanics. With these increases for all three groups, the gaps in bachelor's degree attainment percentages between Whites and Blacks and between Whites and Hispanics did not change measurably from 2004 to 2014.

Teachers and Faculty

A projected 3.5 million elementary and secondary school full-time-equivalent (FTE) teachers were engaged in classroom instruction in the fall of 2014 (table 105.40), which was not substantially different from the number in 2004. The number of FTE public school teachers in 2014 was 3.1 million, and the number of FTE private school teachers was 0.4 million. FTE faculty at degree-granting postsecondary institutions totaled a projected 1.0 million in 2014, including 0.7 million at public institutions and 0.4 million at private institutions (table 105.10).

Expenditures

Expenditures of educational institutions were an estimated $1.2 trillion for the 2013–14 school year (table 106.20 and figure 2). Elementary and secondary schools spent 57 percent of this total ($682 billion), and colleges and universities spent the remaining 43 percent ($512 billion). After adjustment for inflation, total expenditures of all educational institutions rose by an estimated 14 percent between 2003–04 and 2013–14. Inflation-adjusted expenditures of degree-granting postsecondary institutions rose by an estimated 28 percent. Expenditures of elementary and secondary schools were about 5 percent higher in 2013–14 than in 2003–04. In 2013–14, expenditures of educational institutions were an estimated 7.1 percent of the gross domestic product (table 106.10).

Figure 1. The structure of education in the United States

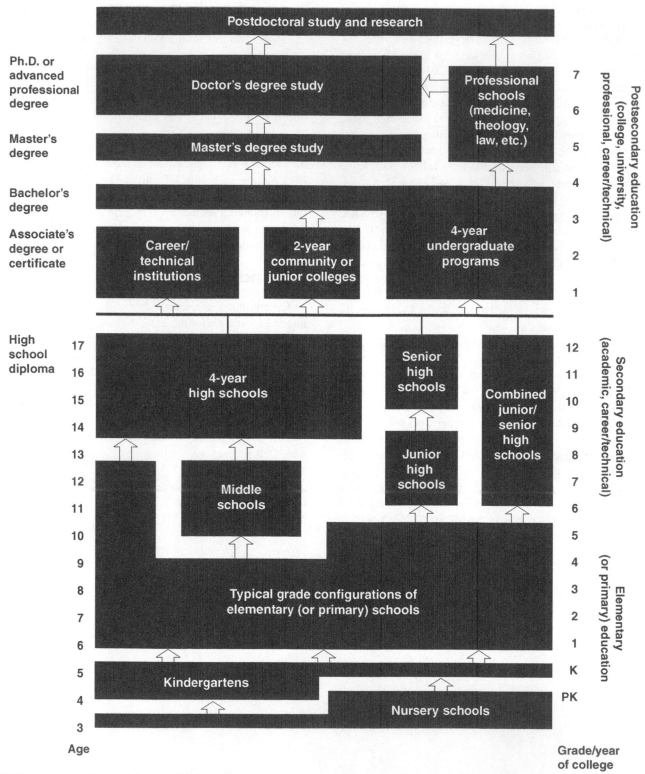

NOTE: Figure is not intended to show relative number of institutions nor relative size of enrollment for the different levels of education. Figure reflects typical patterns of progression rather than all possible variations. Adult education programs, while not separately delineated above, may provide instruction at the adult basic, adult secondary, or postsecondary education levels.
SOURCE: U.S. Department of Education, National Center for Education Statistics, Annual Reports Program.

Figure 2. Enrollment, total expenditures in constant dollars, and expenditures as a percentage of the gross domestic product (GDP), by level of education: Selected years, 1965–66 through 2013–14

Enrollment, in millions

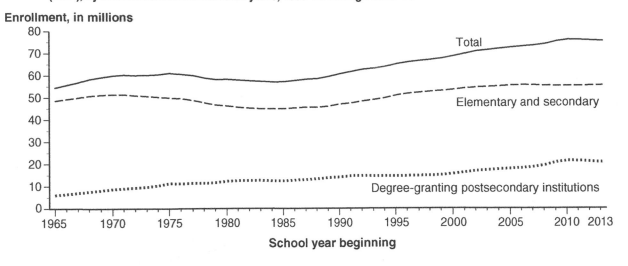

Expenditures, in billions of constant 2013–14 dollars

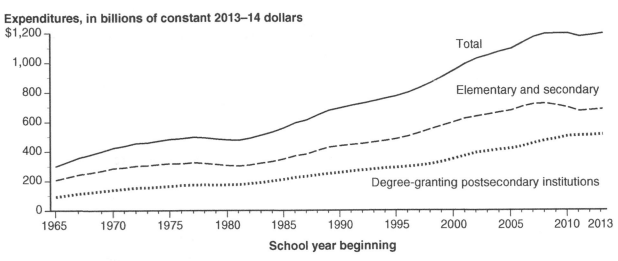

Percent of GDP

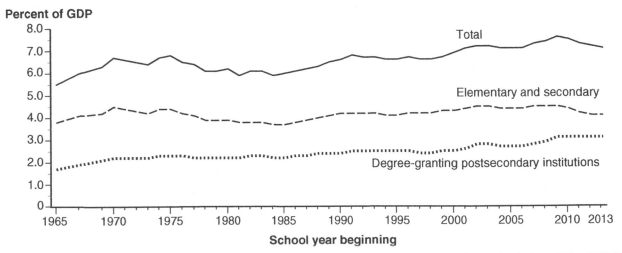

NOTE: Elementary and secondary enrollment data for school year 2013 (2013–14) are projected. Elementary and secondary expenditure data for school years 2012 and 2013 (2012–13 and 2013–14) are estimated. Postsecondary expenditure data for school year 2013 (2013–14) are estimated.
SOURCE: U.S. Department of Education, National Center for Education Statistics, *Statistics of State School Systems*, 1965–66 through 1969–70; *Statistics of Public Elementary and Secondary School Systems*, 1965 through 1980; *Revenues and Expenditures for Public Elementary and Secondary Education*, 1970–71 through 1986–87; Common Core of Data (CCD), "State Nonfiscal Survey of Public Elementary and Secondary Education," 1981–82 through 2012–13, and "National Public Education Financial Survey," 1987–88 through 2011–12; Private School Universe Survey (PSS), 1989–90 through 2011–12; National Elementary and Secondary Enrollment Projection Model, 1972 through 2024; Higher Education General Information Survey (HEGIS), "Fall Enrollment in Institutions of Higher Education" and "Financial Statistics of Institutions of Higher Education" surveys, 1965–66 through 1985–86; Integrated Postsecondary Education Data System (IPEDS), "Fall Enrollment Survey" (IPEDS-EF:86–99) and "Finance Survey" (IPEDS-F:FY87–99); and IPEDS Spring 2001 through Spring 2014, Enrollment and Finance components. U.S. Department of Commerce, Bureau of Economic Analysis, National Income and Product Accounts Tables, retrieved May 1, 2015, from http://www.bea.gov/iTable/index_nipa.cfm.

Figure 3. Percentage of persons 25 years old and over, by highest level of educational attainment: Selected years, 1940 through 2014

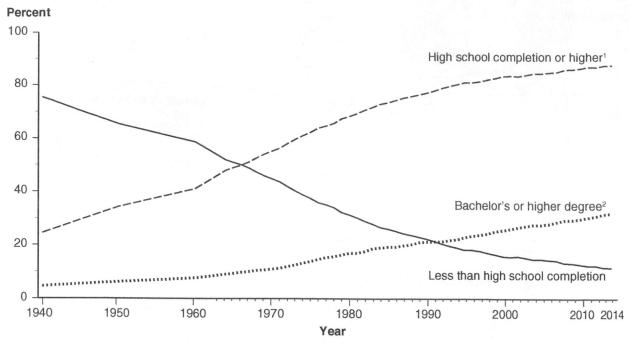

[1]Includes high school completion through equivalency programs, such as a GED program. For years prior to 1993, includes all persons with 4 or more years of high school.
[2]For years prior to 1993, includes all persons with 4 or more years of college.
SOURCE: U.S. Department of Commerce, Census Bureau, *U.S. Census of Population: 1960*, Vol. I, Part 1; J.K. Folger and C.B. Nam, *Education of the American Population* (1960 Census Monograph); Current Population Reports, Series P-20, various years; and Current Population Survey (CPS), March 1961 through March 2014.

Figure 4. Percentage of persons 25 through 29 years old, by highest level of educational attainment: Selected years, 1940 through 2014

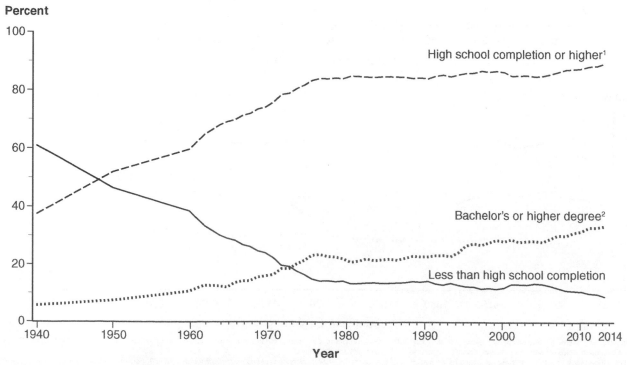

[1]Includes high school completion through equivalency programs, such as a GED program. For years prior to 1993, includes all persons with 4 or more years of high school.
[2]For years prior to 1993, includes all persons with 4 or more years of college.
SOURCE: U.S. Department of Commerce, Census Bureau, *U.S. Census of Population: 1960*, Vol. I, Part 1; J.K. Folger and C.B. Nam, *Education of the American Population* (1960 Census Monograph); Current Population Reports, Series P-20, various years; and Current Population Survey (CPS), March 1961 through March 2014.

Figure 5. Highest level of education attained by persons 25 through 29 years old: 2014

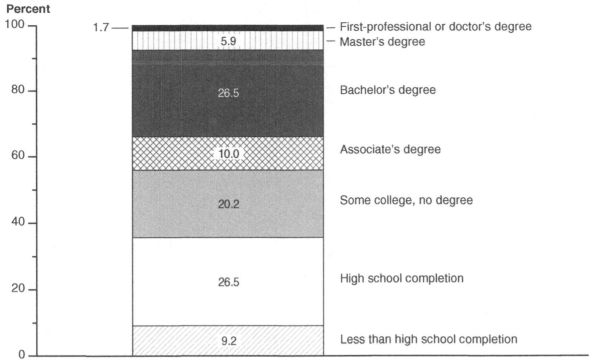

Highest level of education attained

NOTE: High school completion includes equivalency programs, such as a GED program. Detail may not sum to totals because of rounding.
SOURCE: U.S. Department of Commerce, Census Bureau, Current Population Survey (CPS), March 2014.

Figure 6. Percentage of persons 25 through 29 years old, by selected levels of educational attainment and race/ethnicity: 2004 and 2014

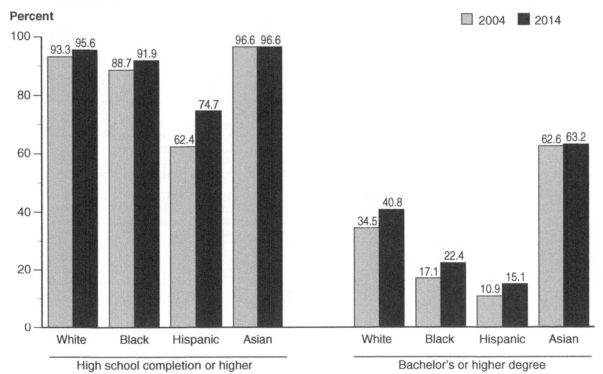

Selected levels of educational attainment and race/ethnicity

NOTE: High school completion includes equivalency programs, such as a GED program. Race categories exclude persons of Hispanic ethnicity.
SOURCE: U.S. Department of Commerce, Census Bureau, Current Population Survey (CPS), March 2004 and March 2014.

Table 101.10. Estimates of resident population, by age group: 1970 through 2013

[In thousands]

Year	Total, all ages	Total, 3 to 34 years old	3 and 4 years old	5 and 6 years old	7 to 13 years old	14 to 17 years old	18 and 19 years old	20 and 21 years old	22 to 24 years old	25 to 29 years old	30 to 34 years old
1	2	3	4	5	6	7	8	9	10	11	12
1970	205,052	109,592	6,961	7,703	28,969	15,924	7,510	7,210	9,992	13,736	11,587
1971	207,661	111,202	6,805	7,344	28,892	16,328	7,715	7,350	10,809	14,041	11,917
1972	209,896	112,807	6,789	7,051	28,628	16,639	7,923	7,593	10,560	15,240	12,383
1973	211,909	114,426	6,938	6,888	28,158	16,867	8,114	7,796	10,725	15,786	13,153
1974	213,854	116,075	7,117	6,864	27,600	17,035	8,257	8,003	10,972	16,521	13,704
1975	215,973	117,435	6,912	7,013	26,905	17,128	8,478	8,196	11,331	17,280	14,191
1976	218,035	118,474	6,436	7,195	26,321	17,119	8,659	8,336	11,650	18,274	14,485
1977	220,239	119,261	6,190	6,978	25,877	17,045	8,675	8,550	11,949	18,277	15,721
1978	222,585	119,833	6,208	6,500	25,594	16,946	8,677	8,730	12,216	18,683	16,280
1979	225,055	120,544	6,252	6,256	25,175	16,611	8,751	8,754	12,542	19,178	17,025
1980	227,225	121,132	6,366	6,291	24,800	16,143	8,718	8,669	12,716	19,686	17,743
1981	229,466	121,999	6,535	6,315	24,396	15,609	8,582	8,759	12,903	20,169	18,731
1982	231,664	121,823	6,658	6,407	24,121	15,057	8,480	8,768	12,914	20,704	18,714
1983	233,792	122,302	6,877	6,572	23,709	14,740	8,290	8,652	12,981	21,414	19,067
1984	235,825	122,254	7,045	6,694	23,367	14,725	7,932	8,567	12,962	21,459	19,503
1985	237,924	122,512	7,134	6,916	22,976	14,888	7,637	8,370	12,895	21,671	20,025
1986	240,133	122,688	7,187	7,086	22,992	14,824	7,483	8,024	12,720	21,893	20,479
1987	242,289	122,672	7,132	7,178	23,325	14,502	7,502	7,742	12,450	21,857	20,984
1988	244,499	122,713	7,176	7,238	23,791	14,023	7,701	7,606	12,048	21,739	21,391
1989	246,819	122,655	7,315	7,184	24,228	13,536	7,898	7,651	11,607	21,560	21,676
1990	249,623	122,787	7,359	7,244	24,785	13,329	7,702	7,886	11,264	21,277	21,939
1991	252,981	123,210	7,444	7,393	25,216	13,491	7,208	8,029	11,205	20,923	22,301
1992	256,514	123,722	7,614	7,447	25,752	13,775	6,949	7,797	11,391	20,503	22,494
1993	259,919	124,371	7,887	7,549	26,212	14,096	6,985	7,333	11,657	20,069	22,584
1994	263,126	124,976	8,089	7,725	26,492	14,637	7,047	7,071	11,585	19,740	22,590
1995	266,278	125,478	8,107	8,000	26,825	15,013	7,182	7,103	11,197	19,680	22,372
1996	269,394	125,924	8,022	8,206	27,168	15,443	7,399	7,161	10,715	19,864	21,945
1997	272,647	126,422	7,915	8,232	27,683	15,769	7,569	7,309	10,601	19,899	21,446
1998	275,854	126,939	7,841	8,152	28,302	15,829	7,892	7,520	10,647	19,804	20,953
1999	279,040	127,446	7,772	8,041	28,763	16,007	8,094	7,683	10,908	19,575	20,603
2000	282,162	128,041	7,724	7,972	29,082	16,144	8,199	7,995	11,122	19,280	20,524
2001	284,969	128,467	7,630	7,883	29,210	16,280	8,235	8,290	11,467	18,819	20,652
2002	287,625	128,955	7,617	7,750	29,251	16,506	8,237	8,342	11,902	18,691	20,658
2003	290,108	129,346	7,678	7,661	29,153	16,694	8,325	8,324	12,267	18,772	20,472
2004	292,805	129,965	7,885	7,652	28,806	17,054	8,457	8,312	12,534	19,107	20,160
2005	295,517	130,280	7,973	7,721	28,527	17,358	8,482	8,392	12,568	19,535	19,724
2006	298,380	130,754	7,937	7,942	28,327	17,549	8,567	8,507	12,529	20,110	19,285
2007	301,231	131,417	8,002	8,040	28,256	17,597	8,730	8,500	12,578	20,543	19,171
2008	304,094	132,269	8,033	8,012	28,426	17,395	9,014	8,555	12,626	20,903	19,305
2009	306,772	133,202	8,059	8,088	28,569	17,232	9,146	8,691	12,693	21,078	19,645
2010[1]	309,326	134,094	8,189	8,138	28,729	17,064	9,061	8,955	12,747	21,144	20,068
2011[1]	311,583	134,866	8,224	8,162	28,752	16,865	8,913	9,188	12,967	21,282	20,512
2012[1]	313,874	135,463	8,093	8,230	28,775	16,714	8,774	9,169	13,410	21,391	20,906
2013	316,129	136,001	7,981	8,264	28,810	16,644	8,662	9,014	13,781	21,580	21,264

[1]Revised from previously published figures.
NOTE: Resident population includes civilian population and armed forces personnel residing within the United States; it excludes armed forces personnel residing overseas. Detail may not sum to totals because of rounding. Population estimates as of July 1 of the indicated reference year.

SOURCE: U.S. Department of Commerce, Census Bureau, Current Population Reports, Series P-25, Nos. 1000, 1022, 1045, 1057, 1059, 1092, and 1095; 2000 through 2009 Population Estimates, retrieved August 14, 2012, from http://www.census.gov/popest/data/national/asrh/2011/index.html; and 2010 through 2013 Population Estimates, retrieved October 3, 2014, from http://www.census.gov/popest/data/national/asrh/2013/2013-nat-res.html. (This table was prepared October 2014.)

Table 101.20. Estimates of resident population, by race/ethnicity and age group: Selected years, 1980 through 2013

Year and age group	Number (in thousands)								Percentage distribution							
	Total	White	Black	His-panic	Asian	Pacific Islander	American Indian/ Alaska Native	Two or more races	Total	White	Black	His-panic	Asian	Pacific Islander	American Indian/ Alaska Native	Two or more races
1	2	3	4	5	6	7	8	9	10	11	12	13	14	15	16	17
Total																
1980	227,225	181,140	26,215	14,869	3,665	(1)	1,336	—	100.0	79.7	11.5	6.5	1.6	(1)	0.6	—
1990	249,623	188,725	29,439	22,573	7,092	(1)	1,793	—	100.0	75.6	11.8	9.0	2.8	(1)	0.7	—
1995	266,278	194,389	32,500	28,158	9,188	(1)	2,044	—	100.0	73.0	12.2	10.6	3.5	(1)	0.8	—
2000[2]	282,162	195,702	34,406	35,662	10,469	370	2,102	3,452	100.0	69.4	12.2	12.6	3.7	0.1	0.7	1.2
2005[2]	295,517	196,621	36,147	43,024	12,658	434	2,186	4,447	100.0	66.5	12.2	14.6	4.3	0.1	0.7	1.5
2007[2]	301,231	197,011	36,906	46,197	13,527	461	2,220	4,909	100.0	65.4	12.3	15.3	4.5	0.2	0.7	1.6
2008[2]	304,094	197,184	37,291	47,794	13,956	475	2,237	5,158	100.0	64.8	12.3	15.7	4.6	0.2	0.7	1.7
2009[2]	306,772	197,275	37,657	49,327	14,361	488	2,252	5,411	100.0	64.3	12.3	16.1	4.7	0.2	0.7	1.8
2010[2]	309,326	197,391	38,008	50,747	14,764	500	2,268	5,649	100.0	63.8	12.3	16.4	4.8	0.2	0.7	1.8
2011[2]	311,583	197,534	38,362	51,868	15,194	510	2,289	5,827	100.0	63.4	12.3	16.6	4.9	0.2	0.7	1.9
2012[2]	313,874	197,701	38,726	52,968	15,642	520	2,309	6,007	100.0	63.0	12.3	16.9	5.0	0.2	0.7	1.9
2013[2]	316,129	197,836	39,076	54,071	16,094	531	2,330	6,190	100.0	62.6	12.4	17.1	5.1	0.2	0.7	2.0
Under 5 years old																
1980	16,451	11,904	2,413	1,677	319	(1)	137	—	100.0	72.4	14.7	10.2	1.9	(1)	0.8	—
1990	18,856	12,757	2,825	2,497	593	(1)	184	—	100.0	67.7	15.0	13.2	3.1	(1)	1.0	—
1995	19,627	12,415	3,050	3,245	734	(1)	182	—	100.0	63.3	15.5	16.5	3.7	(1)	0.9	—
2000[2]	19,178	11,253	2,753	3,748	686	30	171	538	100.0	58.7	14.4	19.5	3.6	0.2	0.9	2.8
2005[2]	19,917	10,847	2,706	4,607	839	35	171	712	100.0	54.5	13.6	23.1	4.2	0.2	0.9	3.6
2007[2]	20,126	10,645	2,716	4,899	868	37	174	787	100.0	52.9	13.5	24.3	4.3	0.2	0.9	3.9
2008[2]	20,271	10,557	2,753	5,032	885	38	176	831	100.0	52.1	13.6	24.8	4.4	0.2	0.9	4.1
2009[2]	20,245	10,395	2,776	5,101	890	39	176	868	100.0	51.3	13.7	25.2	4.4	0.2	0.9	4.3
2010[2]	20,189	10,276	2,780	5,125	894	39	176	899	100.0	50.9	13.8	25.4	4.4	0.2	0.9	4.5
2011[2]	20,122	10,157	2,776	5,151	908	39	174	917	100.0	50.5	13.8	25.6	4.5	0.2	0.9	4.6
2012[2]	19,990	10,034	2,759	5,137	922	40	171	928	100.0	50.2	13.8	25.7	4.6	0.2	0.9	4.6
2013[2]	19,868	9,937	2,737	5,119	931	40	169	935	100.0	50.0	13.8	25.8	4.7	0.2	0.9	4.7
5 to 17 years old																
1980	47,232	35,220	6,840	4,005	790	(1)	377	—	100.0	74.6	14.5	8.5	1.7	(1)	0.8	—
1990	45,359	—	—	—	—	—	—	—	—	—	—	—	—	—	—	—
1995	49,838	—	—	—	—	—	—	—	—	—	—	—	—	—	—	—
2000[2]	53,198	33,008	7,994	8,700	1,829	85	522	1,059	100.0	62.0	15.0	16.4	3.4	0.2	1.0	2.0
2005[2]	53,606	31,379	7,987	10,207	2,047	92	499	1,396	100.0	58.5	14.9	19.0	3.8	0.2	0.9	2.6
2007[2]	53,893	30,679	7,916	10,988	2,166	96	489	1,559	100.0	56.9	14.7	20.4	4.0	0.2	0.9	2.9
2008[2]	53,833	30,226	7,813	11,346	2,227	98	483	1,641	100.0	56.1	14.5	21.1	4.1	0.2	0.9	3.0
2009[2]	53,890	29,851	7,726	11,717	2,290	99	478	1,729	100.0	55.4	14.3	21.7	4.2	0.2	0.9	3.2
2010[2]	53,930	29,496	7,643	12,057	2,349	101	475	1,809	100.0	54.7	14.2	22.4	4.4	0.2	0.9	3.4
2011[2]	53,780	29,174	7,543	12,236	2,392	101	470	1,863	100.0	54.2	14.0	22.8	4.4	0.2	0.9	3.5
2012[2]	53,718	28,882	7,477	12,432	2,438	102	467	1,920	100.0	53.8	13.9	23.1	4.5	0.2	0.9	3.6
2013[2]	53,718	28,606	7,443	12,632	2,490	102	465	1,980	100.0	53.3	13.9	23.5	4.6	0.2	0.9	3.7
18 to 24 years old																
1980	30,103	23,278	3,872	2,284	468	(1)	201	—	100.0	77.3	12.9	7.6	1.6	(1)	0.7	—
1990	26,853	—	—	—	—	—	—	—	—	—	—	—	—	—	—	—
1995	25,482	—	—	—	—	—	—	—	—	—	—	—	—	—	—	—
2000[2]	27,315	16,913	3,780	4,786	1,158	50	239	389	100.0	61.9	13.8	17.5	4.2	0.2	0.9	1.4
2005[2]	29,442	17,741	4,092	5,406	1,351	57	263	531	100.0	60.3	13.9	18.4	4.6	0.2	0.9	1.8
2007[2]	29,808	17,668	4,189	5,636	1,408	60	266	581	100.0	59.3	14.1	18.9	4.7	0.2	0.9	2.0
2008[2]	30,194	17,712	4,283	5,813	1,445	62	266	613	100.0	58.7	14.2	19.3	4.8	0.2	0.9	2.0
2009[2]	30,530	17,705	4,363	6,006	1,481	64	266	645	100.0	58.0	14.3	19.7	4.9	0.2	0.9	2.1
2010[2]	30,762	17,617	4,435	6,183	1,518	66	266	678	100.0	57.3	14.4	20.1	4.9	0.2	0.9	2.2
2011[2]	31,068	17,614	4,559	6,302	1,542	66	272	714	100.0	56.7	14.7	20.3	5.0	0.2	0.9	2.3
2012[2]	31,353	17,610	4,655	6,427	1,566	65	276	753	100.0	56.2	14.8	20.5	5.0	0.2	0.9	2.4
2013[2]	31,458	17,520	4,691	6,536	1,578	65	277	791	100.0	55.7	14.9	20.8	5.0	0.2	0.9	2.5
25 years old and over																
1980	133,438	110,737	13,091	6,903	2,088	(1)	620	—	100.0	83.0	9.8	5.2	1.6	(1)	0.5	—
1990	158,555	125,653	16,322	11,447	4,190	(1)	944	—	100.0	79.2	10.3	7.2	2.6	(1)	0.6	—
1995	171,332	131,839	18,250	14,519	5,628	(1)	1,096	—	100.0	76.9	10.7	8.5	3.3	(1)	0.6	—
2000[2]	182,471	134,529	19,879	18,427	6,796	205	1,170	1,465	100.0	73.7	10.9	10.1	3.7	0.1	0.6	0.8
2005[2]	192,551	136,655	21,361	22,804	8,421	250	1,253	1,808	100.0	71.0	11.1	11.8	4.4	0.1	0.7	0.9
2007[2]	197,404	138,020	22,083	24,674	9,086	268	1,292	1,981	100.0	69.9	11.2	12.5	4.6	0.1	0.7	1.0
2008[2]	199,795	138,689	22,441	25,603	9,400	277	1,312	2,074	100.0	69.4	11.2	12.8	4.7	0.1	0.7	1.0
2009[2]	202,107	139,324	22,792	26,504	9,700	285	1,332	2,170	100.0	68.9	11.3	13.1	4.8	0.1	0.7	1.1
2010[2]	204,445	140,001	23,150	27,383	10,003	294	1,352	2,262	100.0	68.5	11.3	13.4	4.9	0.1	0.7	1.1
2011[2]	206,612	140,589	23,484	28,179	10,352	304	1,373	2,332	100.0	68.0	11.4	13.6	5.0	0.1	0.7	1.1
2012[2]	208,812	141,175	23,835	28,972	10,716	313	1,395	2,406	100.0	67.6	11.4	13.9	5.1	0.2	0.7	1.2
2013[2]	211,085	141,774	24,205	29,784	11,095	324	1,418	2,484	100.0	67.2	11.5	14.1	5.3	0.2	0.7	1.2

—Not available.
[1]Included under Asian.
[2]Data on persons of two or more races were collected beginning in 2000. Direct comparability of the data (other than Hispanic) prior to 2000 with the data for 2000 and later years is limited by the extent to which people reporting more than one race in later years had been reported in specific race groups in earlier years.
NOTE: Resident population includes civilian population and armed forces personnel residing within the United States; it excludes armed forces personnel residing overseas. Race catego-ries exclude persons of Hispanic ethnicity. Detail may not sum to totals because of rounding. Some data have been revised from previously published figures. Population estimates as of July 1 of the indicated reference year.
SOURCE: U.S. Department of Commerce, Census Bureau, Current Population Reports, Series P 25, Nos. 1092 and 1095; 2000 through 2009 Population Estimates, retrieved August 14, 2012, from http://www.census.gov/popest/data/national/asrh/2011/index.html; and 2010 through 2013 Population Estimates, retrieved October 3, 2014, from http://www.census.gov/popest/data/national/asrh/2013/2013-nat-res.html. (This table was prepared October 2014.)

Table 101.30. Number, percentage, and percentage distribution of total resident population and population under 18 years old, by nativity, race/ethnicity, and selected subgroups: 2003, 2008, and 2013

[Numbers in thousands. Standard errors appear in parentheses]

Year and race/ethnicity	Total, all ages						Under 18					
	Total number	U.S.-born[1]		Foreign-born			Total number	U.S.-born[1]		Foreign-born		
		Number	Percent	Number	Percent	Percentage distribution		Number	Percent	Number	Percent	Percentage distribution
1	2	3	4	5	6	7	8	9	10	11	12	13
2003												
Total[2]	283,051 (#)	249,384 (225.9)	88.1 (0.08)	33,668 (225.9)	11.9 (0.08)	100.0 (†)	72,760 (304.9)	69,771 (300.7)	95.9 (0.10)	2,989 (71.3)	4.1 (0.10)	100.0 (†)
White	191,784 (326.1)	184,494 (332.4)	96.2 (0.06)	7,290 (110.5)	3.8 (0.06)	21.7 (0.29)	43,206 (250.9)	42,679 (249.7)	98.8 (0.09)	527 (30.1)	1.2 (0.09)	17.6 (0.91)
Black	33,719 (226.0)	31,300 (218.8)	92.8 (0.18)	2,420 (64.2)	7.2 (0.18)	7.2 (0.18)	10,618 (132.6)	10,378 (131.1)	97.7 (0.19)	240 (20.3)	2.3 (0.19)	8.0 (0.65)
Hispanic	39,274 (241.2)	23,758 (193.5)	60.5 (0.32)	15,516 (158.8)	39.5 (0.32)	46.1 (0.36)	13,561 (149.0)	12,001 (140.6)	88.5 (0.36)	1,559 (51.6)	11.5 (0.36)	52.2 (1.20)
Asian	11,610 (138.4)	3,670 (78.9)	31.6 (0.57)	7,939 (115.2)	68.4 (0.57)	23.6 (0.30)	2,646 (67.1)	2,025 (58.8)	76.5 (1.08)	621 (32.6)	23.5 (1.08)	20.8 (0.97)
Pacific Islander	362 (24.9)	279 (21.9)	76.9 (2.90)	84 (12.0)	23.1 (2.90)	0.2 ! (0.04)	95 (12.8)	87 (12.2)	90.9 (3.86)	9 ! (3.9)	9.1 ! (3.86)	‡ (†)
American Indian/Alaska Native	1,855 (56.3)	1,831 (55.9)	98.7 (0.43)	24 (6.4)	1.3 ! (0.43)	‡ (†)	539 (30.4)	538 (30.4)	99.8 (0.79)	‡ (4.9)	‡ (†)	‡ (†)
Some other race[3]	576 (31.4)	373 (25.3)	64.8 (2.61)	203 (18.7)	35.2 (2.61)	0.6 (0.10)	228 (19.8)	215 (19.2)	94.0 (2.06)	14 ! (4.9)	6.0 ! (2.06)	‡ (†)
Two or more races	3,871 (81.0)	3,679 (79.0)	95.1 (0.46)	191 (18.1)	4.9 (0.46)	0.6 (0.10)	1,866 (56.5)	1,848 (56.2)	99.0 (0.43)	18 ! (5.6)	1.0 ! (0.43)	‡ (†)
White and Black	976 (40.9)	951 (40.4)	97.5 (0.65)	24 (6.5)	2.5 (0.65)	‡ (†)	711 (34.9)	710 (34.9)	99.9 (0.69)	‡ (†)	‡ (0.69)	‡ (†)
White and Asian	805 (37.2)	734 (35.5)	91.3 (1.31)	70 (11.0)	8.7 (1.31)	0.2 ! (0.10)	458 (28.0)	449 (27.8)	98.0 (0.86)	9 ! (3.9)	2.0 ! (0.86)	‡ (†)
White and American Indian/Alaska Native	1,125 (43.9)	1,123 (43.9)	99.8 (0.55)	‡ (†)	‡ (†)	‡ (†)	297 (22.6)	297 (22.6)	100.0 (1.07)	‡ (3.9)	‡ (†)	‡ (†)
Other two or more races	965 (40.7)	871 (38.6)	90.2 (1.25)	94 (12.7)	9.8 (1.25)	0.3 ! (0.10)	401 (26.2)	392 (25.9)	97.8 (0.95)	9 ! (3.9)	2.2 ! (0.95)	‡ (†)
2008												
Total[2]	304,060 (8.9)	266,044 (98.8)	87.5 (0.03)	38,016 (95.7)	12.5 (0.03)	100.0 (†)	73,891 (62.2)	71,088 (66.7)	96.2 (0.04)	2,802 (28.0)	3.8 (0.04)	100.0 (†)
White	198,964 (83.7)	191,190 (93.8)	96.1 (0.03)	7,773 (50.6)	3.9 (0.03)	20.4 (0.11)	41,403 (43.3)	40,917 (44.3)	98.8 (0.03)	486 (11.1)	1.2 (0.03)	17.3 (0.34)
Black	36,774 (66.5)	33,954 (68.8)	92.3 (0.07)	2,821 (27.2)	7.7 (0.07)	7.4 (0.07)	10,249 (36.4)	10,007 (37.3)	97.6 (0.08)	242 (8.3)	2.4 (0.08)	8.6 (0.28)
Hispanic	46,822 (71.0)	28,985 (67.1)	61.9 (0.12)	17,837 (63.3)	38.1 (0.12)	46.9 (0.13)	16,002 (36.3)	14,600 (36.3)	91.2 (0.10)	1,402 (17.2)	8.8 (0.10)	50.0 (0.42)
Mexican	30,746 (78.8)	19,375 (61.6)	63.0 (0.15)	11,372 (58.5)	37.0 (0.15)	29.9 (0.14)	11,358 (37.6)	10,372 (35.6)	91.3 (0.13)	985 (16.0)	8.7 (0.13)	35.2 (0.48)
Puerto Rican	4,151 (38.9)	4,105 (38.5)	98.9 (0.08)	46 (3.5)	1.1 (0.08)	0.1 (0.01)	1,368 (18.3)	1,365 (18.2)	99.8 (0.06)	‡ (†)	0.2 (0.06)	0.1 (0.03)
Cuban	1,631 (22.8)	652 (13.3)	39.9 (0.46)	979 (13.7)	60.1 (0.46)	2.6 (0.04)	335 (8.1)	293 (7.6)	87.4 (0.78)	42 (2.8)	12.6 (0.78)	1.5 (0.10)
Dominican	1,334 (24.9)	570 (14.9)	42.7 (0.67)	764 (15.7)	57.3 (0.67)	2.0 (0.04)	418 (11.5)	361 (10.1)	86.2 (0.69)	58 (3.4)	13.8 (0.69)	2.1 (0.12)
Salvadoran	1,560 (26.2)	551 (11.9)	35.3 (0.55)	1,010 (19.8)	64.7 (0.55)	2.7 (0.05)	457 (11.4)	407 (9.9)	89.1 (0.77)	50 (4.0)	10.9 (0.77)	1.8 (0.15)
Other Central American	2,264 (37.0)	765 (17.6)	33.8 (0.52)	1,498 (26.7)	66.2 (0.52)	3.9 (0.07)	628 (16.6)	525 (14.9)	83.6 (0.73)	103 (5.1)	16.4 (0.73)	3.7 (0.17)
South American	2,729 (31.7)	891 (15.6)	32.7 (0.41)	1,838 (23.6)	67.3 (0.41)	4.8 (0.06)	669 (12.5)	526 (6.1)	78.6 (0.79)	143 (6.1)	21.4 (0.79)	5.1 (0.21)
Other Hispanic or Latino	2,407 (30.0)	2,077 (26.5)	86.3 (0.35)	330 (9.7)	13.7 (0.35)	0.9 (0.03)	770 (14.7)	751 (14.6)	97.6 (0.23)	18 (1.8)	2.4 (0.23)	0.7 (0.06)
Asian	13,227 (45.6)	4,277 (31.1)	32.3 (0.20)	8,950 (38.2)	67.7 (0.20)	23.5 (0.10)	2,897 (19.1)	2,280 (18.0)	78.7 (0.37)	617 (11.7)	21.3 (0.37)	22.0 (0.34)
Asian Indian	2,482 (31.7)	659 (12.9)	26.6 (0.38)	1,822 (24.5)	73.4 (0.38)	4.8 (0.07)	599 (10.5)	465 (10.5)	77.6 (0.82)	134 (4.9)	22.4 (0.82)	4.8 (0.18)
Chinese[4]	3,014 (32.5)	917 (14.0)	30.4 (0.31)	2,097 (23.9)	69.6 (0.31)	5.5 (0.06)	606 (11.3)	469 (9.4)	77.3 (0.63)	138 (4.7)	22.7 (0.63)	4.9 (0.16)
Filipino	2,360 (25.3)	771 (14.0)	32.7 (0.50)	1,589 (21.3)	67.3 (0.50)	4.2 (0.06)	452 (9.0)	356 (8.7)	78.7 (1.09)	96 (5.3)	21.3 (1.09)	3.4 (0.18)
Japanese	692 (13.4)	391 (9.2)	56.6 (0.90)	300 (9.0)	43.4 (0.90)	0.8 (0.02)	80 (3.9)	59 (3.3)	73.5 (2.31)	21 (2.2)	26.5 (2.31)	0.8 (0.08)
Korean	1,360 (20.5)	376 (10.0)	27.6 (0.51)	984 (14.7)	72.4 (0.51)	2.6 (0.04)	280 (7.8)	192 (6.3)	68.5 (1.33)	88 (4.6)	31.5 (1.33)	3.1 (0.16)
Vietnamese	1,410 (23.6)	425 (10.7)	30.1 (0.55)	985 (18.0)	69.9 (0.55)	2.6 (0.05)	332 (8.7)	284 (8.1)	85.6 (0.75)	48 (2.6)	14.4 (0.75)	1.7 (0.09)
Other Asian	1,910 (29.5)	737 (15.3)	38.6 (0.45)	1,173 (18.8)	61.4 (0.45)	3.1 (0.05)	548 (12.6)	456 (12.0)	83.3 (0.93)	91 (5.3)	16.7 (0.93)	3.3 (0.18)
Pacific Islander	399 (10.6)	302 (9.0)	75.7 (1.22)	97 (5.7)	24.3 (1.22)	0.3 (0.02)	103 (5.2)	91 (4.7)	88.9 (1.87)	11 (2.1)	11.1 (1.87)	0.4 (0.07)
American Indian/Alaska Native	2,003 (19.4)	1,982 (19.6)	98.9 (0.10)	21 (2.0)	1.1 (0.10)	0.1 (0.01)	543 (9.5)	541 (9.6)	99.6 (0.14)	‡ (†)	0.4 ! (0.14)	0.1 ! (0.03)
Some other race[3]	696 (20.4)	432 (13.6)	62.1 (0.78)	264 (9.6)	37.9 (0.78)	0.7 (0.03)	243 (9.6)	222 (9.0)	91.5 (0.73)	21 (1.9)	8.5 (0.73)	0.7 (0.07)
Two or more races	5,174 (37.5)	4,922 (36.7)	95.1 (0.13)	252 (6.7)	4.9 (0.13)	0.7 (0.02)	2,451 (24.4)	2,430 (24.8)	99.1 (0.09)	21 (2.1)	0.9 (0.09)	0.8 (0.07)
White and Black	1,393 (22.5)	1,360 (22.4)	97.6 (0.20)	34 (2.8)	2.4 (0.20)	0.1 (0.01)	970 (19.7)	967 (19.8)	99.7 (0.08)	‡ (†)	0.3 (0.08)	0.1 (0.03)
White and Asian	1,110 (15.7)	1,015 (14.6)	91.4 (0.37)	95 (4.5)	8.6 (0.37)	0.3 (0.01)	608 (9.9)	598 (10.0)	98.2 (0.21)	11 (1.3)	1.8 (0.21)	0.4 (0.04)
White and American Indian/Alaska Native	1,404 (17.9)	1,400 (17.9)	99.7 (0.05)	4 (0.7)	0.3 (0.05)	# (0.01)	378 (7.8)	377 (7.8)	100.0 (0.04)	‡ (1.2)	‡ (0.24)	‡ (†)
Other two or more races	1,266 (17.2)	1,148 (16.6)	90.7 (0.37)	118 (4.9)	9.3 (0.37)	0.3 (0.01)	495 (11.0)	488 (11.1)	98.6 (0.24)	7 (1.2)	1.4 (0.24)	0.2 (0.04)

See notes at end of table.

Table 101.30. Number, percentage, and percentage distribution of total resident population and population under 18 years old, by nativity, race/ethnicity, and selected subgroups: 2003, 2008, and 2013—Continued

[Numbers in thousands. Standard errors appear in parentheses]

Year and race/ethnicity	Total, all ages						Under 18					
	Total number	U.S.-born[1] Number	U.S.-born[1] Percent	Foreign-born Number	Foreign-born Percent	Foreign-born Percentage distribution	Total number	U.S.-born[1] Number	U.S.-born[1] Percent	Foreign-born Number	Foreign-born Percent	Foreign-born Percentage distribution
1	2	3	4	5	6	7	8	9	10	11	12	13
2013												
Total[2]	316,129 (1.8)	274,788 (96.6)	86.9 (0.03)	41,341 (95.8)	13.1 (0.03)	100.0 (†)	73,502 (24.4)	70,982 (34.4)	96.6 (0.04)	2,520 (26.4)	3.4 (0.04)	100.0 (†)
White	197,392 (17.3)	189,707 (39.6)	96.1 (0.02)	7,685 (41.1)	3.9 (0.02)	18.6 (0.09)	38,399 (8.9)	38,008 (12.0)	99.0 (0.03)	391 (10.4)	1.0 (0.03)	15.5 (0.38)
Black	38,851 (39.0)	35,579 (47.4)	91.6 (0.09)	3,272 (35.9)	8.4 (0.09)	7.9 (0.08)	10,060 (24.3)	9,807 (25.0)	97.5 (0.07)	253 (7.3)	2.5 (0.07)	10.0 (0.27)
Hispanic	53,964 (10.9)	34,981 (60.4)	64.8 (0.11)	18,983 (60.8)	35.2 (0.11)	45.9 (0.09)	17,688 (8.5)	16,578 (19.4)	93.7 (0.10)	1,110 (17.8)	6.3 (0.10)	44.1 (0.46)
Mexican	34,582 (66.9)	23,081 (53.8)	66.7 (0.15)	11,502 (65.5)	33.3 (0.15)	27.8 (0.13)	12,299 (19.7)	11,609 (29.0)	94.4 (0.12)	690 (14.5)	5.6 (0.12)	27.4 (0.44)
Puerto Rican	5,122 (43.2)	5,041 (42.5)	98.4 (0.08)	81 (4.1)	1.6 (0.08)	0.2 (0.01)	1,588 (19.7)	1,584 (19.7)	99.7 (0.05)	4 (0.9)	0.3 (0.05)	0.2 (0.03)
Cuban	1,986 (20.6)	851 (14.2)	42.9 (0.53)	1,135 (15.3)	57.1 (0.53)	2.7 (0.04)	396 (9.5)	346 (9.0)	87.6 (0.75)	49 (3.2)	12.4 (0.75)	2.0 (0.12)
Dominican	1,788 (31.1)	806 (18.8)	45.1 (0.67)	982 (20.5)	54.9 (0.67)	2.4 (0.05)	524 (12.7)	450 (11.9)	85.9 (0.82)	74 (4.6)	14.1 (0.82)	2.9 (0.18)
Salvadoran	1,975 (33.1)	802 (19.5)	40.6 (0.51)	1,173 (18.4)	59.4 (0.51)	2.8 (0.04)	585 (16.9)	527 (15.5)	90.2 (0.59)	57 (3.9)	9.8 (0.59)	2.3 (0.15)
Other Central American	2,832 (39.6)	1,112 (17.9)	39.3 (0.33)	1,720 (25.9)	60.7 (0.33)	4.2 (0.06)	787 (16.4)	687 (14.5)	87.3 (0.55)	100 (5.0)	12.7 (0.55)	4.0 (0.20)
South American	3,266 (42.2)	1,233 (21.5)	37.8 (0.39)	2,033 (28.0)	62.2 (0.39)	4.9 (0.07)	793 (18.0)	680 (15.7)	85.8 (0.60)	113 (5.7)	14.2 (0.60)	4.5 (0.22)
Other Hispanic or Latino	2,413 (29.2)	2,054 (25.8)	85.1 (0.36)	359 (9.9)	14.9 (0.36)	0.9 (0.02)	716 (14.0)	693 (13.7)	96.8 (0.32)	23 (2.3)	3.2 (0.32)	0.9 (0.09)
Asian	15,825 (26.6)	5,283 (28.4)	33.4 (0.16)	10,543 (26.2)	66.6 (0.16)	25.5 (0.08)	3,304 (16.5)	2,607 (18.3)	78.9 (0.32)	697 (10.7)	21.1 (0.32)	27.7 (0.37)
Asian Indian	3,177 (28.7)	904 (13.6)	28.4 (0.33)	2,273 (22.5)	71.6 (0.33)	5.5 (0.05)	765 (11.1)	608 (9.7)	79.4 (0.65)	157 (5.7)	20.6 (0.65)	6.2 (0.22)
Chinese[4]	3,559 (31.0)	1,098 (16.7)	30.9 (0.34)	2,461 (22.6)	69.1 (0.34)	6.0 (0.06)	649 (11.9)	505 (11.7)	77.8 (0.85)	144 (5.7)	22.2 (0.85)	5.7 (0.22)
Filipino	2,631 (31.1)	880 (17.8)	33.4 (0.43)	1,752 (19.9)	66.6 (0.43)	4.2 (0.05)	467 (9.9)	365 (9.5)	78.2 (0.83)	102 (3.9)	21.8 (0.83)	4.0 (0.16)
Japanese	787 (14.0)	466 (10.6)	59.2 (0.80)	321 (8.3)	40.8 (0.80)	0.8 (0.02)	74 (3.5)	53 (3.2)	71.4 (2.71)	21 (2.3)	28.6 (2.71)	0.8 (0.09)
Korean	1,448 (21.5)	392 (10.6)	27.1 (0.54)	1,056 (16.0)	72.9 (0.54)	2.6 (0.04)	253 (8.1)	176 (6.7)	69.5 (1.27)	77 (3.8)	30.5 (1.27)	3.1 (0.15)
Vietnamese	1,708 (26.3)	557 (11.8)	32.6 (0.50)	1,151 (20.0)	67.4 (0.50)	2.8 (0.05)	394 (10.2)	337 (9.5)	85.4 (0.74)	57 (3.1)	14.6 (0.74)	2.3 (0.12)
Other Asian	2,516 (31.5)	987 (16.6)	39.2 (0.44)	1,529 (22.0)	60.8 (0.44)	3.7 (0.05)	701 (14.1)	563 (12.8)	80.3 (0.88)	138 (6.8)	19.7 (0.88)	5.5 (0.27)
Pacific Islander	468 (9.1)	375 (8.7)	80.2 (1.05)	93 (5.2)	19.8 (1.05)	0.2 (0.01)	122 (5.1)	114 (5.2)	93.1 (1.26)	8 (1.5)	6.9 (1.26)	0.3 (0.06)
American Indian/Alaska Native	2,081 (14.0)	2,058 (13.7)	98.9 (0.11)	23 (2.2)	1.1 (0.11)	0.1 (0.01)	574 (8.2)	572 (8.2)	99.8 (0.07)	‡ (†)	0.2 ! (0.07)	0.1 ! (0.02)
Some other race[3]	640 (17.6)	417 (12.2)	65.2 (0.99)	223 (9.4)	34.8 (0.99)	0.5 (0.02)	219 (8.9)	206 (8.5)	93.8 (0.80)	14 (1.8)	6.2 (0.80)	0.5 (0.07)
Two or more races	6,907 (44.6)	6,387 (44.1)	92.5 (0.16)	520 (11.4)	7.5 (0.16)	1.3 (0.03)	3,135 (23.7)	3,089 (23.1)	98.5 (0.12)	46 (3.7)	1.5 (0.12)	1.8 (0.14)
White and Black	2,008 (25.4)	1,968 (24.9)	98.0 (0.17)	40 (3.5)	2.0 (0.17)	0.1 (0.01)	1,297 (17.1)	1,293 (17.2)	99.6 (0.10)	5 (1.3)	0.4 (0.10)	0.2 (0.05)
White and Asian	1,704 (22.4)	1,476 (22.1)	86.6 (0.45)	228 (7.8)	13.4 (0.45)	0.6 (0.02)	845 (14.7)	821 (14.3)	97.1 (0.25)	24 (2.2)	2.9 (0.25)	1.0 (0.09)
White and American Indian/Alaska Native	1,460 (15.4)	1,454 (15.4)	99.6 (0.06)	6 (0.9)	0.4 (0.06)	# (†)	385 (9.0)	385 (9.0)	100.0 (0.02)	‡ (†)	‡ (†)	‡ (†)
Other two or more races	1,735 (23.6)	1,489 (22.1)	85.8 (0.44)	246 (8.1)	14.2 (0.44)	0.6 (0.02)	607 (13.1)	591 (12.9)	97.3 (0.38)	16 (2.4)	2.7 (0.38)	0.6 (0.09)

†Not applicable.
#Rounds to zero.
!Interpret data with caution. The coefficient of variation (CV) for this estimate is between 30 and 50 percent.
‡Reporting standards not met. Either there are too few cases for a reliable estimate or the coefficient of variation (CV) is 50 percent or greater.
[1]Includes those born in the 50 states, the District of Columbia, Puerto Rico, American Samoa, Guam, the U.S. Virgin Islands, and the Northern Marianas, as well as those born abroad to U.S.-citizen parents.
[2]Total includes other racial/ethnic groups not shown separately.
[3]Respondents who wrote in some other race that was not included as an option on the questionnaire.
[4]In 2008 only, includes Taiwanese. As of 2013, excludes Taiwanese, which is included in "Other Asian."
NOTE: Resident population includes civilian population and armed forces personnel residing within the United States; it excludes armed forces personnel residing overseas. Data are from the American Community Survey and may differ from data shown in other tables obtained from the Current Population Survey. Race categories exclude persons of Hispanic ethnicity. Detail may not sum to totals because of rounding.
SOURCE: U.S. Department of Commerce, Census Bureau, American Community Survey (ACS), 2003, 2008, and 2013. (This table was prepared January 2015.)

Table 101.40. Estimated total and school-age resident populations, by state: Selected years, 1970 through 2013

[In thousands]

State	Total, all ages								5- to 17-year-olds							
	1970[1]	1980[1]	1990[1]	2000[2]	2010[2]	2011[2]	2012[2]	2013[2]	1970[1]	1980[1]	1990[1]	2000[2]	2010[2]	2011[2]	2012[2]	2013[2]
1	2	3	4	5	6	7	8	9	10	11	12	13	14	15	16	17
United States	203,302	226,546	248,765	282,162	309,326	311,583	313,874	316,129	52,540	47,407	45,178	53,198	53,930	53,780	53,718	53,718
Alabama	3,444	3,894	4,040	4,452	4,786	4,802	4,818	4,834	934	866	774	828	826	822	817	814
Alaska..................	303	402	550	628	714	723	730	735	88	92	117	143	134	133	133	133
Arizona	1,775	2,718	3,665	5,161	6,409	6,469	6,551	6,627	486	578	686	989	1,174	1,171	1,179	1,185
Arkansas...............	1,923	2,286	2,351	2,679	2,922	2,939	2,950	2,959	498	496	455	500	515	514	516	517
California	19,971	23,668	29,786	33,988	37,334	37,669	38,000	38,333	4,999	4,681	5,344	6,775	6,751	6,715	6,688	6,667
Colorado	2,210	2,890	3,294	4,327	5,048	5,118	5,189	5,268	589	592	607	808	883	889	895	903
Connecticut............	3,032	3,108	3,287	3,412	3,579	3,589	3,592	3,596	768	638	520	619	613	607	601	594
Delaware...............	548	594	666	786	900	908	917	926	148	125	114	143	150	149	148	147
District of Columbia	757	638	607	572	605	620	633	646	164	109	80	82	68	68	69	71
Florida..................	6,791	9,746	12,938	16,048	18,846	19,083	19,321	19,553	1,609	1,789	2,011	2,709	2,925	2,927	2,935	2,948
Georgia.................	4,588	5,463	6,478	8,227	9,713	9,810	9,916	9,992	1,223	1,231	1,230	1,581	1,805	1,808	1,813	1,821
Hawaii..................	770	965	1,108	1,214	1,364	1,377	1,390	1,404	204	198	196	217	216	216	216	216
Idaho...................	713	944	1,007	1,299	1,571	1,584	1,596	1,612	200	213	228	272	308	310	311	314
Illinois..................	11,110	11,427	11,431	12,434	12,840	12,856	12,868	12,882	2,859	2,401	2,095	2,369	2,288	2,267	2,246	2,224
Indiana.................	5,195	5,490	5,544	6,092	6,490	6,516	6,538	6,571	1,386	1,200	1,056	1,152	1,173	1,169	1,166	1,165
Iowa....................	2,825	2,914	2,777	2,929	3,050	3,064	3,075	3,090	743	604	525	544	526	526	527	529
Kansas.................	2,249	2,364	2,478	2,694	2,859	2,870	2,885	2,894	573	468	472	525	522	522	524	524
Kentucky...............	3,221	3,661	3,687	4,049	4,348	4,367	4,380	4,395	844	800	703	730	741	741	739	739
Louisiana...............	3,645	4,206	4,222	4,472	4,545	4,575	4,602	4,625	1,041	969	891	902	804	802	803	805
Maine...................	994	1,125	1,228	1,277	1,327	1,328	1,329	1,328	260	243	223	231	204	201	199	196
Maryland...............	3,924	4,217	4,781	5,311	5,787	5,840	5,885	5,929	1,038	895	803	1,004	987	981	979	977
Massachusetts..............	5,689	5,737	6,016	6,361	6,563	6,606	6,645	6,693	1,407	1,153	940	1,104	1,049	1,041	1,034	1,028
Michigan................	8,882	9,262	9,295	9,952	9,876	9,875	9,883	9,896	2,450	2,067	1,754	1,924	1,740	1,714	1,691	1,672
Minnesota..............	3,806	4,076	4,376	4,934	5,310	5,347	5,380	5,420	1,051	865	829	958	928	927	928	932
Mississippi.............	2,217	2,521	2,575	2,848	2,970	2,978	2,986	2,991	635	599	550	571	544	540	540	539
Missouri................	4,678	4,917	5,117	5,607	5,996	6,010	6,025	6,044	1,183	1,008	944	1,059	1,034	1,029	1,024	1,021
Montana................	694	787	799	904	991	998	1,005	1,015	197	167	163	175	161	161	161	163
Nebraska...............	1,485	1,570	1,578	1,714	1,830	1,842	1,855	1,869	389	324	309	333	328	329	332	334
Nevada.................	489	800	1,202	2,019	2,703	2,718	2,754	2,790	127	160	204	369	477	476	479	483
New Hampshire...............	738	921	1,109	1,240	1,317	1,318	1,322	1,323	189	196	194	235	216	213	209	205
New Jersey.............	7,171	7,365	7,748	8,431	8,803	8,837	8,868	8,899	1,797	1,528	1,269	1,526	1,521	1,510	1,499	1,489
New Mexico.............	1,017	1,303	1,515	1,821	2,065	2,078	2,084	2,085	311	303	320	378	374	373	371	369
New York...............	18,241	17,558	17,991	19,002	19,398	19,503	19,576	19,651	4,358	3,552	3,000	3,451	3,160	3,126	3,094	3,066
North Carolina..........	5,084	5,882	6,632	8,082	9,560	9,651	9,748	9,848	1,323	1,254	1,147	1,429	1,651	1,657	1,664	1,673
North Dakota	618	653	639	642	674	685	701	723	175	136	127	121	106	107	110	114
Ohio....................	10,657	10,798	10,847	11,364	11,545	11,550	11,553	11,571	2,820	2,307	2,012	2,133	2,005	1,985	1,970	1,959
Oklahoma..............	2,559	3,025	3,146	3,454	3,759	3,786	3,816	3,851	640	622	609	656	667	671	675	683
Oregon.................	2,092	2,633	2,842	3,430	3,837	3,868	3,900	3,930	534	525	521	624	628	627	628	628
Pennsylvania...........	11,801	11,864	11,883	12,284	12,710	12,741	12,764	12,774	2,925	2,376	1,996	2,192	2,057	2,037	2,018	2,000
Rhode Island	950	947	1,003	1,050	1,053	1,050	1,050	1,052	225	186	159	184	166	164	161	159
South Carolina.........	2,591	3,122	3,486	4,024	4,636	4,674	4,723	4,775	720	703	662	746	778	777	782	787
South Dakota...........	666	691	696	756	816	824	834	845	187	147	144	152	143	144	146	148
Tennessee	3,926	4,591	4,877	5,704	6,357	6,398	6,455	6,496	1,002	972	882	1,025	1,088	1,088	1,090	1,092
Texas	11,199	14,229	16,986	20,944	25,245	25,641	26,061	26,448	3,002	3,137	3,437	4,278	4,947	4,992	5,044	5,101
Utah....................	1,059	1,461	1,723	2,245	2,774	2,815	2,855	2,901	312	350	457	511	610	620	631	643
Vermont................	445	511	563	610	626	626	626	627	118	109	102	113	97	95	94	92
Virginia.................	4,651	5,347	6,189	7,106	8,024	8,106	8,187	8,260	1,197	1,114	1,060	1,281	1,345	1,346	1,349	1,352
Washington.............	3,413	4,132	4,867	5,911	6,742	6,821	6,895	6,971	881	826	893	1,121	1,141	1,141	1,144	1,151
West Virginia...........	1,744	1,950	1,793	1,807	1,854	1,855	1,857	1,854	442	414	337	300	283	282	281	279
Wisconsin..............	4,418	4,706	4,892	5,374	5,689	5,709	5,725	5,743	1,203	1,011	927	1,027	979	973	968	963
Wyoming................	332	470	454	494	564	567	577	583	92	101	101	98	95	96	98	99

[1]As of April 1.
[2]Estimates as of July 1.
NOTE: Resident population includes civilian population and armed forces personnel residing within the United States and within each state; it excludes armed forces personnel residing overseas. Some data have been revised from previously published figures. Detail may not sum to totals because of rounding.

SOURCE: U.S. Department of Commerce, Census Bureau, Current Population Reports, Series P-25, No. 1095; CPH-L-74 (1990 data); 2000 through 2009 Population Estimates, retrieved August 17, 2012, from http://www.census.gov/popest/data/state/asrh/2011/index.html; and 2010 through 2013 Population Estimates, retrieved October 3, 2014, from http://www.census.gov/popest/data/state/asrh/2013/SC-EST2013-ALLDATA6.html. (This table was prepared October 2014.)

Table 102.10. Number and percentage distribution of family households, by family structure and presence of own children under 18: Selected years, 1970 through 2014

[Standard errors appear in parentheses]

Family structure and presence of own children	1970	1980	1990	2000	2010	2011	2012	2013	2014	Change, 2000 to 2010	Change, 2010 to 2014
1	2	3	4	5	6	7	8	9	10	11	12

Number (in thousands)

Family structure and presence of own children	1970	1980	1990	2000	2010	2011	2012	2013	2014	Change, 2000 to 2010	Change, 2010 to 2014
All families	51,456 (257.3)	59,550 (271.4)	66,090 (307.8)	72,025 (311.6)	78,833 (241.0)	78,613 (240.8)	80,506 (242.4)	80,902 (242.8)	81,353 (311.8)	9.5 (0.58)	3.2 (0.51)
Married-couple families	44,728 (243.6)	49,112 (252.7)	52,317 (283.3)	55,311 (289.5)	58,410 (218.6)	58,036 (218.1)	58,949 (219.3)	59,204 (219.7)	59,629 (281.1)	5.6 (0.68)	2.1 (0.61)
Without own children under 18	19,196 (168.7)	24,151 (187.3)	27,780 (218.1)	30,062 (230.5)	33,835 (176.1)	34,098 (176.7)	35,245 (179.2)	35,333 (179.4)	35,697 (229.0)	12.6 (1.04)	5.5 (0.87)
With own children under 18	25,532 (192.0)	24,961 (190.1)	24,537 (206.4)	25,248 (214.1)	24,575 (153.1)	23,938 (151.3)	23,704 (150.6)	23,870 (151.1)	23,933 (191.9)	-2.7! (1.02)	-2.6! (0.99)
One own child under 18	8,163 (112.5)	9,671 (122.0)	9,583 (133.0)	9,402 (136.2)	9,567 (98.5)	9,300 (97.1)	9,215 (96.7)	9,157 (96.4)	9,298 (123.0)	‡ (†)	‡ (†)
Two own children under 18	8,045 (111.7)	9,488 (120.9)	9,784 (134.3)	10,274 (142.1)	9,658 (98.9)	9,527 (98.3)	9,442 (97.9)	9,597 (98.6)	9,536 (124.5)	-6.0 (1.62)	‡ (†)
Three or more own children under 18	9,325 (119.9)	5,802 (95.3)	5,170 (98.5)	5,572 (105.9)	5,351 (74.3)	5,111 (72.6)	5,047 (72.2)	5,117 (72.7)	5,099 (91.8)	‡ (†)	-4.7! (2.17)
Families with male householder, no spouse present	1,228 (44.2)	1,733 (52.5)	2,884 (73.9)	4,028 (90.4)	5,580 (75.8)	5,559 (75.7)	5,888 (77.8)	6,229 (80.0)	6,304 (101.8)	38.5 (3.63)	13.0 (2.38)
Without own children under 18	887 (37.6)	1,117 (42.2)	1,731 (57.4)	2,242 (67.7)	3,356 (59.0)	3,334 (58.8)	3,473 (60.0)	3,669 (61.7)	3,832 (79.8)	49.7 (5.23)	14.2 (3.11)
With own children under 18	341 (23.3)	616 (31.3)	1,153 (46.9)	1,786 (60.5)	2,224 (48.2)	2,225 (48.2)	2,415 (50.2)	2,560 (51.6)	2,472 (64.2)	24.5 (5.01)	11.2! (3.76)
One own child under 18	179 (16.9)	374 (24.4)	723 (37.2)	1,131 (48.2)	1,375 (38.5)	1,337 (37.4)	1,419 (38.5)	1,482 (39.4)	1,445 (49.2)	21.6 (6.17)	‡ (†)
Two own children under 18	87 (11.8)	165 (16.2)	307 (24.2)	483 (31.6)	576 (24.6)	627 (25.7)	704 (27.2)	766 (28.3)	731 (35.0)	19.3! (9.31)	26.9! (8.14)
Three or more own children under 18	75 (10.9)	77 (11.1)	123 (15.3)	171 (18.8)	273 (16.9)	262 (16.6)	293 (17.5)	312 (18.1)	296 (22.3)	59.6! (20.15)	‡ (†)
Families with female householder, no spouse present	5,500 (92.8)	8,705 (116.0)	10,890 (141.4)	12,687 (156.9)	14,843 (121.4)	15,019 (122.1)	15,669 (124.5)	15,469 (123.8)	15,420 (156.6)	17.0 (1.73)	3.9! (1.35)
Without own children under 18	2,642 (64.7)	3,261 (71.8)	4,290 (89.9)	5,116 (101.6)	6,424 (81.2)	6,422 (81.2)	6,799 (83.5)	6,842 (83.7)	6,870 (106.2)	25.6 (2.96)	6.9! (2.14)
With own children under 18	2,858 (67.2)	5,445 (92.3)	6,599 (111.0)	7,571 (122.8)	8,419 (92.6)	8,597 (93.5)	8,869 (95.0)	8,627 (93.7)	8,550 (118.1)	11.2 (2.18)	‡ (†)
One own child under 18	1,008 (40.1)	2,398 (61.6)	3,225 (78.1)	3,777 (87.6)	4,207 (66.0)	4,375 (67.3)	4,399 (67.5)	4,144 (65.5)	4,167 (83.1)	11.4 (3.12)	‡ (†)
Two own children under 18	810 (35.9)	1,817 (53.7)	2,173 (64.2)	2,458 (70.9)	2,714 (53.2)	2,681 (52.8)	2,853 (54.5)	2,825 (54.2)	2,778 (68.0)	10.4! (3.85)	‡ (†)
Three or more own children under 18	1,040 (40.7)	1,230 (44.2)	1,202 (47.9)	1,336 (52.4)	1,499 (39.6)	1,541 (40.1)	1,618 (41.1)	1,658 (41.6)	1,605 (51.8)	12.2! (5.31)	‡ (†)

Percentage distribution of all families

Family structure and presence of own children	1970	1980	1990	2000	2010	2011	2012	2013	2014	Change in percentage points, 2000 to 2010	Change in percentage points, 2010 to 2014
All families	100.0 (†)	100.0 (†)	100.0 (†)	100.0 (†)	100.0 (†)	100.0 (†)	100.0 (†)	100.0 (†)	100.0 (†)	† (†)	† (†)
Married-couple families	86.9 (0.19)	82.5 (0.20)	79.2 (0.22)	76.8 (0.23)	74.1 (0.16)	73.8 (0.16)	73.2 (0.16)	73.2 (0.16)	73.3 (0.20)	-2.7 (0.28)	-0.8! (0.26)
Without own children under 18	37.3 (0.27)	40.6 (0.25)	42.0 (0.27)	41.7 (0.26)	42.9 (0.18)	43.4 (0.18)	43.8 (0.18)	43.7 (0.18)	43.9 (0.23)	1.2 (0.32)	1.0! (0.29)
With own children under 18	49.6 (0.28)	41.9 (0.26)	37.1 (0.26)	35.1 (0.26)	31.2 (0.17)	30.5 (0.17)	29.4 (0.16)	29.5 (0.16)	29.4 (0.21)	-3.9 (0.31)	-1.8 (0.27)
One own child under 18	15.9 (0.20)	16.2 (0.19)	14.5 (0.19)	13.1 (0.18)	12.1 (0.12)	11.8 (0.12)	11.4 (0.12)	11.3 (0.11)	11.4 (0.14)	-0.9 (0.22)	-0.7 (0.19)
Two own children under 18	15.6 (0.20)	15.9 (0.19)	14.8 (0.19)	14.3 (0.19)	12.3 (0.12)	12.1 (0.12)	11.7 (0.12)	11.9 (0.12)	11.7 (0.15)	-2.0 (0.22)	-0.5! (0.19)
Three or more own children under 18	18.1 (0.21)	9.7 (0.15)	7.8 (0.14)	7.7 (0.14)	6.8 (0.09)	6.5 (0.09)	6.3 (0.09)	6.3 (0.09)	6.3 (0.11)	-0.9 (0.17)	-0.5 (0.14)
Families with male householder, no spouse present	2.4 (0.09)	2.9 (0.09)	4.4 (0.11)	5.6 (0.12)	7.1 (0.09)	7.1 (0.09)	7.3 (0.09)	7.7 (0.10)	7.7 (0.12)	1.5 (0.15)	0.7 (0.15)
Without own children under 18	1.7 (0.07)	1.9 (0.07)	2.6 (0.09)	3.1 (0.09)	4.3 (0.07)	4.2 (0.07)	4.3 (0.07)	4.5 (0.08)	4.7 (0.10)	1.1 (0.12)	0.5 (0.12)
With own children under 18	0.7 (0.05)	1.0 (0.05)	1.7 (0.07)	2.5 (0.08)	2.8 (0.06)	2.8 (0.06)	3.0 (0.06)	3.2 (0.06)	3.0 (0.08)	0.3! (0.10)	0.2! (0.10)
One own child under 18	0.3 (0.03)	0.6 (0.04)	1.1 (0.06)	1.6 (0.07)	1.7 (0.05)	1.7 (0.05)	1.8 (0.05)	1.8 (0.05)	1.8 (0.06)	‡ (0.08)	‡ (†)
Two own children under 18	0.2 (0.02)	0.3 (0.03)	0.5 (0.04)	0.7 (0.04)	0.7 (0.03)	0.8 (0.03)	0.9 (0.03)	0.9 (0.03)	0.9 (0.04)	0.2! (0.04)	0.2! (0.05)
Three or more own children under 18	0.1 (0.02)	0.1 (0.02)	0.2 (0.02)	0.2 (0.03)	0.3 (0.02)	0.3 (0.02)	0.4 (0.02)	0.4 (0.02)	0.4 (0.03)	0.1! (0.03)	‡ (†)
Families with female householder, no spouse present	10.7 (0.17)	14.6 (0.18)	16.5 (0.20)	17.6 (0.20)	18.8 (0.14)	19.1 (0.14)	19.5 (0.14)	19.1 (0.14)	19.0 (0.18)	1.2 (0.25)	† (†)
Without own children under 18	5.1 (0.12)	5.5 (0.12)	6.5 (0.13)	7.1 (0.14)	8.1 (0.10)	8.2 (0.10)	8.4 (0.10)	8.5 (0.10)	8.4 (0.13)	1.0 (0.17)	† (†)
With own children under 18	5.6 (0.13)	9.1 (0.15)	10.0 (0.16)	10.5 (0.16)	10.7 (0.11)	10.9 (0.11)	11.0 (0.11)	10.7 (0.11)	10.5 (0.14)	‡ (†)	‡ (†)
One own child under 18	2.0 (0.08)	4.0 (0.10)	4.9 (0.12)	5.2 (0.12)	5.3 (0.08)	5.6 (0.08)	5.5 (0.08)	5.1 (0.08)	5.1 (0.10)	‡ (†)	‡ (†)
Two own children under 18	1.6 (0.07)	3.1 (0.09)	3.3 (0.10)	3.4 (0.10)	3.4 (0.07)	3.4 (0.07)	3.5 (0.07)	3.5 (0.07)	3.4 (0.08)	‡ (†)	‡ (†)
Three or more own children under 18	2.0 (0.08)	2.1 (0.07)	1.8 (0.07)	1.9 (0.07)	1.9 (0.05)	2.0 (0.05)	2.0 (0.05)	2.0 (0.05)	2.0 (0.06)	‡ (†)	‡ (†)

†Not applicable.
!Interpret data with caution. The coefficient of variation (CV) for this estimate is between 30 and 50 percent.
‡Reporting standards not met. The coefficient of variation (CV) for this estimate is 50 percent or greater.
NOTE: A family household consists of two or more people who are related by birth, marriage, or adoption and are residing together. Own children are never-married sons and daughters, including stepchildren and adopted children, of the householder or married couple. Detail may not sum to totals because of rounding.

SOURCE: U.S. Department of Commerce, Census Bureau, Current Population Reports, Series P20, *Household and Family Characteristics: 1995*; and *America's Families and Living Arrangements: 2000 and 2008–2014*, Current Population Survey (CPS), Annual Social and Economic Supplement, retrieved April 28, 2015, from http://www.census.gov/hhes/families/data/cps2014.html. (This table was prepared April 2015.)

Table 102.20.   Number and percentage distribution of children under age 18 and under age 6, by living arrangements, race/ethnicity, and selected racial/ethnic subgroups: 2013

[Standard errors appear in parentheses]

Age and race/ethnicity	Number of children (in thousands)		Percentage distribution of children		Percentage distribution of children, by living arrangements							
					Total		Children living with parent(s) or related to householder[1]						All other children[2]	
							Married parents		Female parent, no spouse present		Male parent, no spouse present			
1	2		3		4		5		6		7		8	
Under 18 years old														
Total	73,502	(24.4)	100.0	(†)	100.0	(†)	62.8	(0.12)	27.5	(0.10)	7.6	(0.06)	2.1	(0.03)
White	38,399	(8.9)	52.2	(0.02)	100.0	(†)	72.8	(0.15)	18.2	(0.12)	6.9	(0.08)	2.0	(0.04)
Black	10,060	(24.3)	13.7	(0.03)	100.0	(†)	32.1	(0.33)	57.8	(0.35)	7.6	(0.15)	2.5	(0.08)
Hispanic	17,688	(8.5)	24.1	(0.01)	100.0	(†)	56.6	(0.23)	31.8	(0.20)	9.5	(0.15)	2.1	(0.06)
Mexican	12,299	(29.5)	16.7	(0.04)	100.0	(†)	58.5	(0.25)	29.9	(0.22)	9.6	(0.18)	2.0	(0.07)
Puerto Rican	1,588	(19.7)	2.2	(0.03)	100.0	(†)	42.7	(0.69)	46.1	(0.74)	8.8	(0.47)	2.4	(0.19)
Cuban	396	(9.5)	0.5	(0.01)	100.0	(†)	61.9	(1.31)	27.8	(1.19)	8.4	(0.68)	1.8	(0.28)
Dominican	524	(12.7)	0.7	(0.02)	100.0	(†)	38.2	(1.41)	49.2	(1.38)	10.9	(0.88)	1.7	(0.27)
Salvadoran	585	(16.9)	0.8	(0.02)	100.0	(†)	53.8	(1.35)	31.9	(1.20)	12.4	(0.86)	1.9	(0.31)
Other Central American	787	(16.4)	1.1	(0.02)	100.0	(†)	53.5	(1.31)	32.5	(1.18)	11.2	(0.64)	2.8	(0.33)
South American	793	(18.0)	1.1	(0.02)	100.0	(†)	66.9	(0.96)	25.0	(0.86)	6.5	(0.48)	1.6	(0.25)
Other Hispanic or Latino	716	(14.0)	1.0	(0.02)	100.0	(†)	59.6	(0.97)	30.2	(0.92)	8.0	(0.52)	2.2	(0.24)
Asian	3,304	(16.5)	4.5	(0.02)	100.0	(†)	83.5	(0.39)	10.8	(0.34)	4.3	(0.19)	1.5	(0.10)
Asian Indian	765	(11.1)	1.0	(0.02)	100.0	(†)	93.8	(0.49)	3.9	(0.36)	1.9	(0.28)	0.4	(0.08)
Chinese[3]	649	(11.9)	0.9	(0.02)	100.0	(†)	83.7	(0.67)	11.5	(0.60)	3.1	(0.28)	1.8	(0.21)
Filipino	467	(9.9)	0.6	(0.01)	100.0	(†)	76.9	(1.04)	14.5	(0.90)	6.5	(0.67)	2.1	(0.33)
Japanese	74	(3.5)	0.1	(0.00)	100.0	(†)	84.9	(2.28)	8.4	(1.74)	4.7	(1.16)	2.0 !	(0.69)
Korean	253	(8.1)	0.3	(0.01)	100.0	(†)	87.5	(0.95)	8.7	(0.87)	2.3	(0.40)	1.5	(0.32)
Vietnamese	394	(10.2)	0.5	(0.01)	100.0	(†)	78.6	(1.19)	14.2	(0.89)	5.2	(0.57)	1.9	(0.42)
Other Asian	701	(14.1)	1.0	(0.02)	100.0	(†)	77.5	(0.84)	14.2	(0.83)	6.7	(0.45)	1.6	(0.22)
Pacific Islander	122	(5.1)	0.2	(0.01)	100.0	(†)	60.3	(2.76)	29.5	(2.33)	6.3	(1.32)	3.9	(0.81)
American Indian/Alaska Native	574	(8.2)	0.8	(0.01)	100.0	(†)	43.9	(0.99)	40.4	(0.90)	12.4	(0.57)	3.4	(0.36)
Some other race[4]	219	(8.9)	0.3	(0.01)	100.0	(†)	58.7	(1.85)	30.0	(1.87)	7.2	(1.09)	4.0	(0.77)
Two or more races	3,135	(23.7)	4.3	(0.03)	100.0	(†)	56.6	(0.47)	34.0	(0.47)	7.2	(0.22)	2.2	(0.10)
White and Black	1,297	(17.1)	1.8	(0.02)	100.0	(†)	40.3	(0.83)	49.3	(0.81)	7.3	(0.38)	3.1	(0.21)
White and Asian	845	(14.7)	1.2	(0.02)	100.0	(†)	80.4	(0.64)	13.1	(0.53)	5.3	(0.35)	1.1	(0.16)
White and American Indian/ Alaska Native	385	(9.0)	0.5	(0.01)	100.0	(†)	60.2	(1.24)	26.6	(1.08)	10.9	(0.77)	2.3	(0.31)
Other Two or more races	607	(13.1)	0.8	(0.02)	100.0	(†)	55.9	(1.28)	35.2	(1.16)	6.9	(0.52)	1.9	(0.25)
Under 6 years old														
Total	23,855	(35.3)	100.0	(†)	100.0	(†)	62.0	(0.15)	28.2	(0.15)	8.1	(0.10)	1.7	(0.04)
White	11,958	(18.6)	50.1	(0.06)	100.0	(†)	74.0	(0.19)	17.7	(0.16)	6.8	(0.11)	1.6	(0.04)
Black	3,243	(17.1)	13.6	(0.07)	100.0	(†)	29.0	(0.44)	60.6	(0.49)	8.5	(0.29)	2.0	(0.13)
Hispanic	6,128	(19.2)	25.7	(0.06)	100.0	(†)	53.7	(0.31)	33.4	(0.30)	10.9	(0.21)	1.9	(0.10)
Mexican	4,255	(18.0)	17.8	(0.07)	100.0	(†)	55.1	(0.35)	31.9	(0.35)	11.1	(0.26)	1.9	(0.11)
Puerto Rican	539	(8.9)	2.3	(0.04)	100.0	(†)	40.9	(1.00)	47.7	(1.15)	8.9	(0.64)	2.6	(0.38)
Cuban	136	(5.4)	0.6	(0.02)	100.0	(†)	59.8	(1.88)	27.7	(1.66)	11.1	(1.37)	1.4	(0.41)
Dominican	176	(6.2)	0.7	(0.03)	100.0	(†)	39.2	(2.24)	47.0	(2.39)	12.1	(1.53)	1.7	(0.50)
Salvadoran	218	(9.2)	0.9	(0.04)	100.0	(†)	50.2	(1.72)	33.5	(1.77)	14.9	(1.29)	1.3	(0.38)
Other Central American	291	(9.2)	1.2	(0.04)	100.0	(†)	50.5	(1.81)	33.3	(1.53)	13.3	(1.14)	2.9	(0.47)
South American	277	(9.6)	1.2	(0.04)	100.0	(†)	65.0	(1.43)	26.1	(1.29)	7.5	(0.78)	1.4	(0.33)
Other Hispanic or Latino	237	(7.2)	1.0	(0.03)	100.0	(†)	59.3	(1.53)	29.3	(1.34)	9.6	(0.92)	1.8	(0.36)
Asian	1,062	(9.1)	4.5	(0.04)	100.0	(†)	86.2	(0.48)	8.4	(0.41)	4.5	(0.29)	0.8	(0.13)
Asian Indian	302	(6.5)	1.3	(0.03)	100.0	(†)	95.7	(0.58)	2.3	(0.36)	1.9	(0.39)	‡	(†)
Chinese[3]	187	(5.6)	0.8	(0.02)	100.0	(†)	87.2	(1.01)	8.7	(0.95)	3.6	(0.55)	0.5 !	(0.17)
Filipino	126	(4.9)	0.5	(0.02)	100.0	(†)	77.5	(1.70)	13.3	(1.52)	8.1	(1.15)	1.1 !	(0.40)
Japanese	24	(2.1)	0.1	(0.01)	100.0	(†)	89.6	(2.80)	6.3 !	(2.38)	3.6 !	(1.62)	‡	(†)
Korean	74	(4.2)	0.3	(0.02)	100.0	(†)	92.8	(1.37)	5.5	(1.36)	1.6	(0.43)	‡	(†)
Vietnamese	113	(5.0)	0.5	(0.02)	100.0	(†)	78.3	(1.95)	13.1	(1.36)	6.2	(1.04)	2.3 !	(0.75)
Other Asian	237	(6.6)	1.0	(0.03)	100.0	(†)	79.3	(1.15)	12.4	(1.02)	7.0	(0.70)	1.3	(0.32)
Pacific Islander	39	(2.3)	0.2	(0.01)	100.0	(†)	58.8	(4.18)	29.2	(3.28)	7.8 !	(2.95)	4.1 !	(1.37)
American Indian/Alaska Native	177	(3.8)	0.7	(0.02)	100.0	(†)	39.6	(1.35)	43.7	(1.39)	13.9	(1.03)	2.7	(0.48)
Some other race[4]	79	(4.2)	0.3	(0.02)	100.0	(†)	61.0	(2.69)	29.0	(2.52)	6.4	(1.29)	3.6	(1.04)
Two or more races	1,169	(13.6)	4.9	(0.06)	100.0	(†)	56.0	(0.72)	34.2	(0.75)	7.9	(0.37)	1.9	(0.18)
White and Black	512	(10.3)	2.1	(0.04)	100.0	(†)	37.7	(1.16)	50.7	(1.23)	8.7	(0.53)	2.9	(0.38)
White and Asian	329	(7.2)	1.4	(0.03)	100.0	(†)	84.6	(0.95)	11.1	(0.88)	3.8	(0.39)	0.4	(0.12)
White and American Indian/ Alaska Native	119	(4.9)	0.5	(0.02)	100.0	(†)	57.4	(2.02)	26.4	(1.83)	14.5	(1.71)	1.7 !	(0.52)
Other Two or more races	209	(6.3)	0.9	(0.03)	100.0	(†)	55.1	(1.90)	34.7	(1.71)	8.4	(0.97)	1.8	(0.51)

†Not applicable.
!Interpret data with caution. The coefficient of variation (CV) for this estimate is between 30 and 50 percent.
‡Reporting standards not met. Either there are too few cases for a reliable estimate or the coefficient of variation (CV) is 50 percent or greater.
[1]Includes all children who live either with their parent(s) or with a householder to whom they are related by birth, marriage, or adoption (except a child who is the spouse of the householder). Children are classified by their parents' marital status or, if no parents are present in the household, by the marital status of the householder who is related to the children. Living arrangements with only a "female parent" or "male parent" are those in which the parent or the householder who is related to the child does not have a spouse living in the household. The householder is the person (or one of the people) who owns or rents (maintains) the housing unit.
[2]Includes foster children, children in unrelated subfamilies, children living in group quarters, and children who were reported as the householder or spouse of the householder.
[3]Excludes Taiwanese. Taiwanese is included in "Other Asian."
[4]Respondents who wrote in some other race that was not included as an option on the questionnaire.
NOTE: Race categories exclude persons of Hispanic ethnicity. Detail may not sum to totals because of rounding.
SOURCE: U.S. Department of Commerce, Census Bureau, American Community Survey (ACS), 2013. (This table was prepared April 2015.)

Table 102.30. Median household income, by state: Selected years, 1990 through 2013
[In constant 2013 dollars. Standard errors appear in parentheses]

State	1990[1]	2000[2]	2005		2008		2009		2010		2011		2012		2013	
1	2	3	4		5		6		7		8		9		10	
United States	$54,518	$58,709	$55,200	($80)	$56,300	($50)	$54,500	($50)	$53,500	($40)	$52,300	($50)	$52,100	($30)	$52,300	($40)
Alabama	42,802	47,722	44,000	(380)	46,200	(450)	44,000	(350)	43,200	(310)	42,900	(350)	42,200	(290)	42,800	(390)
Alaska...	75,110	72,098	67,100	(1,310)	74,100	(1,260)	72,700	(1,540)	69,000	(1,350)	70,200	(1,230)	68,700	(1,170)	72,200	(1,150)
Arizona	49,955	56,702	52,800	(470)	55,100	(340)	52,900	(320)	50,000	(340)	48,400	(350)	48,500	(370)	48,500	(360)
Arkansas.....................................	38,358	44,992	41,800	(430)	42,000	(460)	41,100	(420)	40,900	(420)	40,100	(480)	40,700	(310)	40,500	(430)
California	64,934	66,397	64,000	(240)	66,000	(160)	64,000	(180)	61,700	(230)	59,300	(180)	59,200	(220)	60,200	(160)
Colorado.....................................	54,671	65,992	60,400	(400)	61,700	(410)	60,200	(460)	57,700	(470)	57,400	(380)	57,600	(370)	58,800	(490)
Connecticut................................	75,677	75,403	72,700	(590)	74,200	(740)	72,800	(660)	68,400	(710)	68,100	(540)	68,300	(530)	67,100	(640)
Delaware.....................................	63,259	66,240	62,600	(1,030)	62,700	(1,050)	61,800	(1,150)	59,700	(970)	60,900	(1,000)	59,300	(980)	57,800	(1,140)
District of Columbia....................	55,735	56,099	56,300	(1,400)	62,700	(1,580)	64,400	(1,130)	65,100	(1,000)	65,400	(1,520)	67,600	(1,260)	67,600	(2,060)
Florida..	49,851	54,270	50,600	(200)	51,700	(230)	48,600	(190)	47,400	(210)	45,900	(260)	45,700	(210)	46,000	(190)
Georgia.......................................	52,641	59,323	54,400	(320)	55,000	(270)	51,700	(270)	49,600	(310)	47,700	(290)	47,900	(230)	47,800	(380)
Hawaii...	70,432	69,650	69,300	(1,430)	72,700	(1,230)	69,600	(1,040)	67,300	(1,010)	64,000	(650)	67,200	(1,000)	68,000	(930)
Idaho..	45,813	52,527	49,500	(610)	51,500	(630)	48,800	(630)	46,500	(650)	44,900	(830)	46,200	(570)	46,800	(570)
Illinois..	58,502	65,135	60,000	(250)	60,800	(240)	58,600	(270)	56,600	(290)	55,100	(320)	55,900	(250)	56,200	(240)
Indiana..	52,235	58,112	52,500	(360)	51,900	(350)	49,300	(300)	47,700	(290)	48,100	(290)	47,700	(260)	47,500	(310)
Iowa..	47,577	55,179	52,000	(380)	53,000	(420)	52,200	(280)	51,200	(420)	51,200	(440)	51,700	(270)	52,200	(320)
Kansas..	49,503	56,794	51,200	(530)	54,300	(310)	51,900	(440)	51,600	(570)	50,700	(480)	51,000	(320)	51,000	(370)
Kentucky.....................................	40,874	47,075	44,600	(350)	44,900	(290)	43,500	(350)	42,800	(330)	42,600	(290)	42,300	(260)	43,400	(400)
Louisiana....................................	39,813	45,529	43,800	(420)	47,300	(420)	46,100	(420)	45,400	(460)	43,200	(330)	43,600	(420)	44,200	(530)
Maine..	50,524	52,063	51,100	(700)	50,400	(590)	49,700	(620)	48,900	(620)	47,700	(500)	47,400	(550)	47,000	(480)
Maryland.....................................	71,442	73,911	73,500	(430)	76,300	(410)	75,200	(460)	73,600	(600)	72,500	(510)	72,200	(360)	72,500	(440)
Massachusetts............................	67,027	70,604	68,200	(500)	70,800	(390)	69,600	(450)	66,300	(260)	65,100	(570)	66,300	(400)	66,800	(430)
Michigan.....................................	56,267	62,446	54,900	(330)	52,600	(280)	49,100	(240)	48,500	(200)	47,600	(210)	47,500	(200)	48,300	(230)
Minnesota...................................	56,066	65,863	62,100	(270)	62,000	(340)	60,400	(360)	59,300	(300)	59,000	(310)	59,800	(410)	60,700	(260)
Mississippi..................................	36,525	43,801	39,300	(450)	40,900	(440)	39,800	(460)	39,400	(410)	38,200	(370)	37,600	(360)	38,000	(630)
Missouri......................................	47,818	53,033	50,100	(260)	50,700	(250)	49,100	(340)	47,300	(330)	46,900	(330)	46,000	(260)	46,900	(260)
Montana......................................	41,698	46,169	46,900	(700)	47,200	(830)	46,000	(710)	45,600	(730)	45,800	(680)	45,700	(670)	47,000	(690)
Nebraska.....................................	47,190	54,873	52,300	(550)	53,800	(530)	51,400	(530)	51,700	(590)	52,100	(430)	51,500	(360)	51,400	(300)
Nevada..	56,251	62,326	58,700	(650)	61,000	(520)	57,900	(650)	54,500	(510)	50,700	(640)	50,500	(510)	51,200	(360)
New Hampshire...........................	65,897	69,157	67,700	(720)	69,000	(1,080)	65,800	(910)	65,200	(740)	64,900	(890)	64,200	(950)	64,200	(820)
New Jersey..................................	74,237	77,096	73,600	(380)	76,100	(340)	74,200	(440)	72,300	(500)	69,900	(450)	70,700	(440)	70,200	(330)
New Mexico.................................	43,691	47,719	44,700	(540)	47,100	(600)	46,700	(680)	45,000	(480)	43,500	(510)	43,200	(560)	43,900	(580)
New York.....................................	59,795	60,665	59,000	(310)	60,600	(250)	59,400	(260)	57,900	(240)	57,200	(250)	57,300	(230)	57,400	(260)
North Carolina	48,335	54,781	48,600	(230)	50,400	(280)	47,400	(250)	46,300	(240)	45,500	(330)	45,800	(240)	45,900	(260)
North Dakota	42,106	48,378	49,000	(510)	49,400	(640)	51,900	(660)	52,000	(1,020)	53,600	(790)	54,400	(950)	55,800	(880)
Ohio..	52,070	57,258	51,900	(250)	51,900	(210)	49,300	(230)	48,200	(190)	47,400	(200)	47,500	(180)	48,100	(250)
Oklahoma....................................	42,766	46,694	44,200	(410)	46,300	(470)	45,200	(330)	44,900	(260)	44,800	(380)	45,000	(280)	45,700	(320)
Oregon..	49,429	57,202	51,200	(420)	54,300	(340)	52,600	(410)	49,700	(350)	48,500	(450)	49,900	(500)	50,300	(320)
Pennsylvania...............................	52,728	56,070	53,100	(280)	54,900	(170)	53,800	(190)	52,700	(280)	52,000	(180)	52,000	(160)	52,000	(160)
Rhode Island	58,373	58,843	61,400	(1,000)	60,300	(1,180)	58,800	(1,000)	55,800	(810)	55,600	(1,070)	55,300	(1,100)	55,900	(1,160)
South Carolina............................	47,626	51,842	46,900	(450)	48,300	(420)	46,100	(370)	44,900	(280)	43,900	(350)	43,700	(410)	44,200	(400)
South Dakota..............................	40,818	49,326	48,100	(650)	49,800	(770)	48,900	(800)	49,000	(790)	50,000	(1,010)	49,100	(600)	48,900	(660)
Tennessee...................................	44,997	50,833	46,400	(350)	47,200	(280)	45,300	(290)	44,300	(260)	43,200	(270)	43,400	(360)	44,300	(300)
Texas	49,004	55,819	50,300	(180)	54,100	(140)	52,400	(160)	51,900	(230)	51,200	(250)	51,500	(160)	51,700	(140)
Utah..	53,455	63,927	57,200	(690)	61,300	(460)	59,900	(530)	58,500	(410)	57,900	(510)	57,900	(450)	59,800	(460)
Vermont......................................	54,039	57,118	54,500	(870)	56,400	(640)	56,100	(630)	52,800	(960)	54,700	(890)	53,700	(780)	52,600	(950)
Virginia.......................................	60,453	65,256	64,700	(390)	66,200	(290)	64,400	(320)	64,800	(300)	64,100	(320)	62,600	(250)	62,700	(400)
Washington.................................	56,563	63,997	58,800	(470)	62,800	(380)	61,400	(350)	59,400	(360)	58,900	(360)	58,400	(370)	58,400	(410)
West Virginia...............................	37,720	41,516	39,900	(580)	41,100	(670)	40,700	(470)	40,800	(580)	39,900	(550)	40,800	(430)	41,300	(450)
Wisconsin	53,405	61,222	56,200	(290)	56,400	(230)	54,300	(270)	52,400	(320)	52,200	(270)	51,800	(200)	51,500	(220)
Wyoming.....................................	49,149	52,974	55,100	(1,100)	57,600	(1,310)	57,200	(1,240)	57,200	(1,230)	58,300	(1,190)	55,700	(920)	58,800	(1,090)

[1]Based on 1989 incomes collected in the 1990 census.
[2]Based on 1999 incomes collected in the 2000 census.
NOTE: Constant dollars adjusted by the Consumer Price Index research series using current methods (CPI-U-RS).
SOURCE: U.S. Department of Commerce, Census Bureau, 1990 Summary Tape File 3 (STF 3), "Median Household Income in 1989," retrieved May 12, 2005, from https://www.census.gov/hhes/ www/income/data/historical/state/state1.html; Decennial Census, 2000, *Summary Social, Economic, and Housing Characteristics*; Census 2000 Summary File 4 (SF 4), retrieved March 28, 2005, from http://factfinder2.census.gov/faces/tableservices/jsf/pages/ productview.xhtml?pid= DEC_00_SF4_PCT089&prodType=table; and American Community Survey (ACS), selected years, 2005 through 2013. (This table was prepared April 2015.)

Table 102.40. Poverty rates for all persons and poverty status of 5- to 17-year-olds, by region and state: Selected years, 1990 through 2013

[Standard errors appear in parentheses]

Region and state	Percent of persons in poverty				Poverty status of related children[1] 5 through 17 years old						
								2012[4]		2013[4]	
	1990[2]	2000[3]	2012[4]	2013[4]	1990,[2] percent in poverty	2000,[3] percent in poverty	2010,[4] percent in poverty	Number in poverty (in thousands)	Percent in poverty	Number in poverty (in thousands)	Percent in poverty
1	2	3	4	5	6	7	8	9	10	11	12
United States	13.1	12.4	15.8 (0.07)	15.4 (0.06)	17.0 (0.02)	15.4 (0.01)	19.7 (0.12)	11,060 (77.8)	21.0 (0.14)	10,892 (73.1)	20.7 (0.13)
Region											
Northeast	10.6	11.4	13.6 (0.11)	13.3 (0.11)	14.3 (0.54)	14.3 (0.39)	16.3 (0.24)	1,567 (21.6)	17.9 (0.25)	1,544 (20.9)	17.9 (0.24)
South	15.7	13.9	17.3 (0.09)	16.8 (0.08)	20.5 (0.90)	17.6 (0.64)	22.2 (0.20)	4,644 (43.8)	23.3 (0.22)	4,595 (39.3)	23.0 (0.19)
Midwest	12.0	10.2	14.9 (0.10)	14.4 (0.11)	14.9 (0.58)	12.0 (0.37)	18.4 (0.25)	2,160 (26.2)	19.0 (0.22)	2,112 (28.0)	18.7 (0.24)
West	12.6	13.0	16.1 (0.10)	15.7 (0.09)	16.2 (0.79)	16.2 (0.54)	19.4 (0.21)	2,689 (27.9)	21.2 (0.22)	2,641 (27.9)	20.8 (0.22)
Alabama	18.3	16.1	18.7 (0.36)	18.4 (0.31)	23.2 (0.16)	20.3 (0.11)	26.1 (0.90)	203 (6.3)	24.9 (0.77)	204 (6.5)	25.5 (0.79)
Alaska	9.0	9.4	11.3 (0.77)	8.7 (0.63)	9.6 (0.27)	10.3 (0.18)	11.2 (1.38)	18 (2.1)	13.7 (1.59)	14 (2.1)	10.5 (1.70)
Arizona	15.7	13.9	18.3 (0.27)	18.1 (0.31)	20.3 (0.15)	17.8 (0.11)	22.4 (0.77)	285 (7.1)	24.7 (0.59)	291 (8.1)	25.2 (0.69)
Arkansas	19.1	15.8	19.0 (0.46)	18.7 (0.44)	23.8 (0.20)	20.1 (0.13)	24.7 (1.00)	129 (5.3)	25.5 (1.04)	132 (5.3)	26.2 (1.03)
California	12.5	14.2	16.8 (0.13)	16.4 (0.12)	17.2 (0.06)	18.5 (0.04)	20.7 (0.30)	1,505 (19.5)	22.9 (0.30)	1,448 (19.1)	22.2 (0.29)
Colorado	11.7	9.3	13.6 (0.28)	12.6 (0.28)	13.7 (0.13)	10.0 (0.08)	14.9 (0.72)	155 (6.1)	17.7 (0.69)	141 (6.3)	15.9 (0.71)
Connecticut	6.8	7.9	10.8 (0.34)	10.2 (0.32)	9.8 (0.15)	9.6 (0.10)	11.2 (0.70)	82 (4.5)	13.9 (0.76)	76 (4.2)	13.1 (0.71)
Delaware	8.7	9.2	12.2 (0.70)	12.6 (0.75)	11.0 (0.27)	10.9 (0.22)	16.2 (1.55)	21 (2.5)	14.2 (1.66)	25 (2.7)	17.1 (1.89)
District of Columbia	16.9	20.2	17.4 (0.90)	18.3 (0.89)	24.1 (0.59)	30.4 (0.44)	30.2 (2.50)	19 (1.8)	27.7 (2.55)	21 (1.9)	30.7 (2.73)
Florida	12.7	12.5	17.1 (0.14)	16.6 (0.20)	17.5 (0.10)	16.6 (0.07)	21.7 (0.40)	687 (12.4)	23.9 (0.43)	662 (15.2)	23.0 (0.52)
Georgia	14.7	13.0	19.1 (0.27)	18.3 (0.26)	18.9 (0.14)	16.1 (0.09)	22.6 (0.48)	453 (11.2)	25.2 (0.61)	443 (11.7)	24.6 (0.65)
Hawaii	8.3	10.7	11.8 (0.59)	10.3 (0.51)	10.5 (0.25)	12.9 (0.18)	11.2 (1.28)	34 (3.3)	16.5 (1.60)	25 (2.9)	11.9 (1.38)
Idaho	13.3	11.8	15.5 (0.63)	15.5 (0.75)	14.4 (0.23)	12.6 (0.14)	15.0 (0.89)	59 (4.7)	19.2 (1.52)	61 (5.8)	19.7 (1.86)
Illinois	11.9	10.7	14.7 (0.19)	14.2 (0.21)	15.9 (0.08)	13.4 (0.05)	18.1 (0.41)	430 (11.1)	19.4 (0.51)	413 (11.7)	18.9 (0.53)
Indiana	10.7	9.5	15.6 (0.28)	15.3 (0.27)	12.8 (0.10)	10.6 (0.08)	20.0 (0.68)	224 (7.7)	19.7 (0.67)	221 (7.0)	19.6 (0.61)
Iowa	11.5	9.1	12.6 (0.38)	12.6 (0.41)	12.6 (0.14)	9.5 (0.09)	15.6 (0.95)	74 (4.8)	14.4 (0.92)	81 (5.5)	15.6 (1.07)
Kansas	11.5	9.9	13.7 (0.33)	13.2 (0.45)	12.8 (0.15)	10.4 (0.10)	15.7 (0.97)	85 (4.4)	16.7 (0.87)	84 (4.9)	16.7 (0.94)
Kentucky	19.0	15.8	19.2 (0.41)	17.8 (0.34)	23.2 (0.16)	19.4 (0.10)	23.3 (0.79)	178 (6.7)	24.7 (0.96)	165 (6.6)	22.8 (0.89)
Louisiana	23.6	19.6	19.8 (0.36)	19.1 (0.37)	30.4 (0.19)	25.3 (0.11)	24.2 (0.77)	216 (7.4)	27.3 (0.93)	207 (7.1)	26.2 (0.90)
Maine	10.8	10.9	14.9 (0.66)	13.0 (0.51)	12.3 (0.20)	12.0 (0.15)	17.0 (1.42)	33 (3.4)	17.2 (1.76)	29 (2.9)	15.5 (1.53)
Maryland	8.3	8.5	10.1 (0.27)	10.1 (0.23)	10.5 (0.12)	9.8 (0.09)	11.6 (0.50)	119 (5.4)	12.4 (0.57)	124 (6.6)	12.9 (0.67)
Massachusetts	8.9	9.3	12.0 (0.24)	11.5 (0.28)	12.2 (0.12)	11.4 (0.08)	12.6 (0.57)	153 (5.9)	15.0 (0.58)	150 (6.0)	14.9 (0.60)
Michigan	13.1	10.5	17.5 (0.26)	16.4 (0.23)	16.7 (0.09)	12.7 (0.05)	20.5 (0.58)	381 (9.6)	23.1 (0.59)	349 (8.9)	21.4 (0.53)
Minnesota	10.2	7.9	11.4 (0.29)	11.0 (0.32)	11.4 (0.10)	8.7 (0.06)	13.7 (0.81)	118 (6.3)	12.9 (0.68)	120 (7.2)	13.2 (0.79)
Mississippi	25.2	19.9	23.7 (0.54)	23.6 (0.49)	32.6 (0.21)	26.0 (0.13)	29.0 (1.03)	170 (6.9)	31.7 (1.26)	172 (5.7)	32.8 (1.08)
Missouri	13.3	11.7	16.3 (0.29)	15.8 (0.32)	16.2 (0.12)	14.4 (0.08)	18.1 (0.64)	207 (8.0)	20.7 (0.77)	214 (7.9)	21.5 (0.78)
Montana	16.1	14.6	14.9 (0.64)	16.9 (0.78)	18.4 (0.30)	17.1 (0.20)	17.8 (1.57)	28 (2.8)	18.0 (1.75)	34 (3.1)	21.6 (1.94)
Nebraska	11.1	9.7	11.6 (0.48)	12.6 (0.48)	12.0 (0.18)	11.1 (0.12)	16.4 (1.31)	45 (3.2)	14.0 (0.99)	45 (3.6)	13.7 (1.11)
Nevada	10.2	10.5	15.7 (0.48)	15.4 (0.51)	11.7 (0.26)	12.3 (0.16)	19.8 (1.08)	97 (5.0)	20.7 (1.06)	97 (5.9)	20.5 (1.22)
New Hampshire	6.4	6.5	9.6 (0.64)	8.5 (0.50)	6.4 (0.16)	6.7 (0.12)	8.1 (1.14)	26 (2.7)	12.8 (1.35)	18 (2.2)	9.3 (1.11)
New Jersey	7.6	8.5	10.7 (0.21)	11.1 (0.23)	10.8 (0.10)	10.5 (0.07)	12.9 (0.45)	204 (6.6)	13.7 (0.45)	217 (7.4)	14.8 (0.50)
New Mexico	20.6	18.4	20.6 (0.58)	22.8 (0.57)	26.3 (0.25)	23.6 (0.17)	28.2 (1.37)	98 (4.6)	26.6 (1.25)	115 (4.5)	31.6 (1.19)
New York	13.0	14.6	16.0 (0.15)	15.7 (0.16)	18.1 (0.09)	19.1 (0.06)	20.0 (0.39)	662 (11.3)	21.9 (0.36)	661 (11.5)	22.0 (0.38)
North Carolina	13.0	12.3	17.9 (0.26)	17.4 (0.23)	16.0 (0.11)	14.9 (0.07)	22.3 (0.55)	385 (9.5)	23.4 (0.58)	388 (10.0)	23.6 (0.61)
North Dakota	14.4	11.9	10.6 (0.63)	11.5 (0.71)	15.9 (0.30)	12.2 (0.17)	13.1 (1.76)	12 (1.7)	11.0 (1.56)	11 (1.9)	9.7 (1.70)
Ohio	12.5	10.6	16.3 (0.21)	15.1 (0.21)	16.2 (0.08)	12.9 (0.05)	21.0 (0.54)	415 (9.7)	21.6 (0.50)	388 (9.9)	20.4 (0.51)
Oklahoma	16.7	14.7	17.2 (0.41)	16.2 (0.32)	19.9 (0.16)	17.7 (0.11)	23.2 (1.04)	151 (6.8)	22.7 (1.03)	151 (5.4)	22.6 (0.80)
Oregon	12.4	11.6	16.8 (0.40)	16.2 (0.38)	13.4 (0.15)	12.8 (0.11)	19.5 (0.80)	121 (6.4)	19.6 (1.04)	116 (5.5)	19.0 (0.90)
Pennsylvania	11.1	11.0	13.9 (0.24)	13.3 (0.24)	14.5 (0.08)	13.6 (0.05)	17.3 (0.49)	368 (11.4)	18.6 (0.56)	349 (10.6)	17.9 (0.54)
Rhode Island	9.6	11.9	13.8 (0.58)	13.5 (0.60)	12.3 (0.30)	15.6 (0.25)	17.9 (1.57)	28 (2.4)	17.7 (1.50)	29 (2.4)	18.7 (1.52)
South Carolina	15.4	14.1	18.2 (0.32)	18.0 (0.36)	20.0 (0.19)	17.9 (0.12)	22.9 (0.86)	193 (6.7)	25.0 (0.86)	192 (6.3)	25.0 (0.81)
South Dakota	15.9	13.2	13.3 (0.69)	13.2 (0.73)	18.7 (0.33)	15.5 (0.21)	17.5 (2.26)	21 (2.1)	15.3 (1.46)	22 (2.6)	15.4 (1.76)
Tennessee	15.7	13.5	18.0 (0.30)	17.7 (0.28)	19.5 (0.13)	16.6 (0.10)	23.7 (0.76)	260 (8.6)	24.4 (0.78)	261 (6.0)	24.4 (0.56)
Texas	18.1	15.4	17.8 (0.17)	17.1 (0.17)	23.4 (0.09)	19.3 (0.06)	23.8 (0.32)	1,208 (18.5)	24.3 (0.37)	1,194 (19.0)	23.7 (0.38)
Utah	11.4	9.4	12.3 (0.45)	12.6 (0.41)	10.9 (0.16)	8.9 (0.09)	15.2 (0.91)	86 (5.5)	14.0 (0.90)	87 (5.8)	13.8 (0.91)
Vermont	9.9	9.4	11.3 (0.92)	12.4 (0.86)	10.7 (0.26)	9.9 (0.16)	12.4 (2.04)	11 (2.0)	12.0 (2.21)	14 (2.1)	14.8 (2.23)
Virginia	10.2	9.6	11.8 (0.21)	11.3 (0.22)	12.4 (0.12)	11.4 (0.08)	13.6 (0.46)	197 (6.9)	14.8 (0.52)	191 (6.9)	14.4 (0.52)
Washington	10.9	10.6	13.5 (0.31)	13.6 (0.30)	12.8 (0.10)	12.2 (0.09)	16.2 (0.59)	188 (7.8)	16.9 (0.70)	199 (8.0)	17.7 (0.72)
West Virginia	19.7	17.9	17.3 (0.58)	17.6 (0.53)	24.0 (0.23)	22.9 (0.17)	24.4 (1.50)	56 (4.1)	20.7 (1.50)	64 (3.9)	23.5 (1.43)
Wisconsin	10.7	8.7	12.9 (0.29)	13.3 (0.31)	13.3 (0.10)	10.0 (0.07)	17.0 (0.73)	148 (6.9)	15.8 (0.72)	163 (7.5)	17.3 (0.77)
Wyoming	11.9	11.4	12.6 (0.74)	10.3 (0.74)	12.6 (0.33)	12.5 (0.24)	11.7 (1.71)	15 (1.6)	15.9 (1.69)	11 (1.7)	11.0 (1.65)

[1]Related children in a family include all children in the household who are related to the householder by birth, marriage, or adoption (except a child who is the spouse of the householder). The householder is the person (or one of the people) who owns or rents (maintains) the housing unit.

[2]Based on 1989 incomes and family sizes collected in the 1990 census. May differ from Current Population Survey data that are shown in other tables.

[3]Based on 1999 incomes and family sizes collected in the 2000 census. May differ from Current Population Survey data that are shown in other tables.

[4]Based on income and family size data from the American Community Survey (ACS). May differ from Current Population Survey data that are shown in other tables. ACS respondents were interviewed throughout the given year and reported the income they received during the previous 12 months.

NOTE: For information about how the Census Bureau determines who is in poverty, see http://www.census.gov/hhes/www/poverty/about/overview/measure.html. Detail may not sum to totals because of rounding.
SOURCE: U.S. Department of Commerce, Census Bureau, 1990 Summary Tape File 3 (STF 3), "Median Household Income in 1989" and "Poverty Status in 1989 by Family Type and Age"; Decennial Census, 1990, Minority Economic Profiles, unpublished data; Decennial Census, 2000, Summary Social, Economic, and Housing Characteristics; Census 2000 Summary File 4 (SF 4), "Poverty Status in 1999 of Related Children Under 18 Years by Family Type and Age"; and American Community Survey, 2010, 2012, and 2013. (This table was prepared October 2014.)

Table 102.50. Official and supplemental measures of poverty status for all persons, persons in families, and related children under age 18, by race/ethnicity: Selected years, 1960 through 2013

[Standard errors appear in parentheses]

Race/ethnicity, type of poverty measure,[1] and year	Number below the poverty level (in thousands)						Percent below the poverty level					
		In all families			In families with female householder, no husband present			In all families			In families with female householder, no husband present	
	All persons	Total	Householder[2]	Related children under 18[3]	Total	Related children under 18[3]	All persons	Total	Householder[2]	Related children under 18[3]	Total	Related children under 18[3]
1	2	3	4	5	6	7	8	9	10	11	12	13
Total, official poverty measure[4]												
1960	39,851 (644.0)	34,925 (493.6)	8,243 (177.2)	17,288 (290.6)	7,247 (163.6)	4,095 (116.6)	22.2 (0.34)	20.7 (0.17)	18.1 (0.30)	26.5 (0.29)	48.9 (0.69)	68.4 (1.01)
1965	33,185 (595.4)	28,358 (419.2)	6,721 (156.2)	14,388 (255.6)	7,524 (167.4)	4,562 (124.1)	17.3 (0.30)	15.8 (0.14)	13.9 (0.26)	20.7 (0.26)	46.0 (0.66)	64.2 (0.96)
1970	25,420 (431.8)	20,330 (266.6)	5,260 (110.1)	10,235 (166.2)	7,503 (136.5)	4,689 (102.9)	12.6 (0.21)	10.9 (0.10)	10.1 (0.18)	14.9 (0.19)	38.1 (0.48)	53.0 (0.73)
1975	25,877 (435.2)	20,789 (271.0)	5,450 (112.4)	10,882 (173.4)	8,846 (151.3)	5,597 (114.2)	12.3 (0.20)	10.9 (0.10)	9.7 (0.17)	16.8 (0.20)	37.5 (0.43)	52.7 (0.67)
1980	29,272 (460.0)	22,601 (288.2)	6,217 (121.7)	11,114 (175.4)	10,120 (165.0)	5,866 (117.5)	13.0 (0.20)	11.5 (0.11)	10.3 (0.17)	17.9 (0.21)	36.7 (0.40)	50.8 (0.64)
1985	33,064 (513.3)	25,729 (336.0)	7,223 (141.0)	12,483 (200.4)	11,600 (190.8)	6,716 (134.8)	14.0 (0.21)	12.6 (0.11)	11.4 (0.18)	20.1 (0.23)	37.6 (0.40)	53.6 (0.65)
1990	33,585 (534.4)	25,232 (342.9)	7,098 (144.4)	12,715 (210.0)	12,578 (262.9)	7,363 (147.7)	13.5 (0.21)	12.0 (0.11)	10.7 (0.18)	19.9 (0.24)	37.2 (0.40)	53.4 (0.64)
1995	36,425 (553.5)	27,501 (366.1)	7,532 (149.8)	13,998 (224.2)	14,205 (226.5)	8,362 (159.9)	13.8 (0.21)	12.3 (0.10)	10.8 (0.18)	20.2 (0.23)	36.5 (0.37)	50.3 (0.58)
2000	31,581 (538.4)	22,347 (324.8)	6,400 (140.7)	11,005 (198.1)	10,926 (197.1)	6,300 (139.4)	11.3 (0.19)	9.6 (0.10)	8.7 (0.16)	15.6 (0.21)	28.5 (0.36)	40.1 (0.61)
2001	32,907 (548.1)	23,215 (334.2)	6,813 (146.2)	11,175 (260.1)	11,223 (320.6)	6,341 (140.0)	11.7 (0.20)	9.9 (0.10)	9.2 (0.17)	15.8 (0.21)	28.6 (0.36)	39.3 (0.60)
2002	34,570 (399.9)	24,534 (248.6)	7,229 (108.2)	11,646 (146.7)	11,657 (146.8)	6,564 (102.0)	12.1 (0.14)	10.4 (0.07)	9.6 (0.12)	16.3 (0.15)	28.8 (0.25)	39.6 (0.42)
2003	35,861 (407.8)	25,684 (257.4)	7,607 (111.6)	12,340 (152.5)	12,413 (153.1)	7,085 (106.9)	12.5 (0.14)	10.8 (0.07)	10.0 (0.12)	17.2 (0.16)	30.0 (0.25)	41.8 (0.42)
2004	37,040 (465.3)	26,544 (405.3)	7,835 (128.6)	12,473 (203.6)	12,832 (262.7)	7,210 (153.5)	12.7 (0.16)	11.0 (0.17)	10.2 (0.16)	17.3 (0.28)	30.5 (0.56)	41.9 (0.73)
2005	36,950 (466.0)	26,068 (410.7)	7,657 (124.4)	12,335 (215.0)	13,153 (303.2)	7,210 (178.4)	12.6 (0.16)	10.8 (0.15)	9.9 (0.15)	17.1 (0.30)	31.1 (0.62)	42.8 (0.86)
2006	36,450 (421.7)	25,915 (378.2)	7,668 (113.2)	12,299 (205.6)	13,199 (290.2)	7,341 (170.5)	12.3 (0.14)	10.6 (0.15)	9.8 (0.14)	16.9 (0.28)	30.5 (0.53)	42.1 (0.70)
2007	37,276 (511.9)	26,509 (441.4)	7,623 (136.3)	12,802 (241.1)	13,478 (317.4)	7,546 (193.5)	12.5 (0.17)	10.8 (0.18)	9.8 (0.17)	17.6 (0.33)	30.7 (0.61)	43.0 (0.87)
2008	39,829 (479.0)	28,564 (422.6)	8,147 (127.9)	13,507 (224.3)	13,812 (291.9)	7,587 (180.9)	13.2 (0.16)	11.5 (0.17)	10.3 (0.16)	18.5 (0.31)	31.4 (0.58)	43.5 (0.81)
2009	43,559 (487.0)	31,197 (439.7)	8,792 (131.7)	14,774 (233.1)	14,746 (307.2)	7,942 (178.2)	14.3 (0.16)	12.5 (0.18)	11.1 (0.16)	20.1 (0.32)	32.5 (0.61)	44.4 (0.80)
2010	46,180 (511.9)	33,007 (442.0)	9,221 (130.6)	15,730 (233.9)	15,895 (290.2)	8,648 (174.9)	15.1 (0.17)	13.2 (0.18)	11.7 (0.16)	21.5 (0.31)	34.2 (0.55)	46.9 (0.71)
2011	46,247 (462.7)	33,126 (442.9)	9,497 (132.7)	15,539 (229.0)	16,451 (326.0)	9,026 (196.8)	15.0 (0.15)	13.1 (0.18)	11.8 (0.16)	21.4 (0.32)	34.2 (0.59)	47.6 (0.80)
2012	46,496 (546.4)	33,198 (500.1)	9,520 (140.0)	15,435 (262.1)	15,957 (384.6)	8,664 (224.6)	15.0 (0.18)	13.1 (0.20)	11.8 (0.17)	21.3 (0.36)	33.9 (0.65)	47.2 (0.87)
2013	45,318 (616.6)	31,530 (513.4)	9,130 (150.1)	14,142 (270.3)	15,606 (375.3)	8,305 (217.6)	14.5 (0.20)	12.4 (0.21)	11.2 (0.18)	19.5 (0.37)	33.2 (0.71)	45.8 (0.89)
Total, Supplemental Poverty Measure[5]												
2009	45,927 (529.5)	34,003 (482.0)	10,133 (139.0)	12,331 (233.6)	12,912 (323.0)	5,843 (168.8)	15.1 (0.17)	13.6 (0.20)	12.8 (0.17)	16.8 (0.32)	28.5 (0.65)	32.6 (0.82)
2010	48,631 (560.3)	35,603 (491.9)	10,535 (144.1)	12,965 (225.2)	14,133 (307.9)	6,507 (159.7)	15.9 (0.18)	14.2 (0.20)	13.4 (0.18)	17.7 (0.31)	30.4 (0.56)	35.3 (0.73)
2011	49,603 (541.1)	36,709 (506.3)	11,075 (152.7)	12,945 (220.0)	14,926 (302.0)	6,833 (164.2)	16.1 (0.18)	14.5 (0.20)	13.8 (0.18)	17.9 (0.30)	31.0 (0.57)	36.1 (0.77)
2012	49,690 (555.1)	36,709 (505.3)	11,118 (148.3)	12,945 (216.8)	14,105 (348.3)	6,477 (184.1)	16.0 (0.18)	14.5 (0.20)	13.7 (0.18)	17.8 (0.30)	30.0 (0.62)	35.3 (0.79)
2013	48,603 (629.7)	35,550 (549.9)	10,778 (155.0)	11,827 (233.1)	13,694 (378.8)	6,080 (188.6)	15.5 (0.20)	13.9 (0.22)	13.3 (0.19)	16.3 (0.32)	29.1 (0.73)	33.6 (0.88)
White, official poverty measure[4]												
1970[6]	17,484 (363.3)	13,323 (198.0)	3,708 (90.0)	6,138 (120.7)	3,761 (90.7)	2,247 (68.2)	9.9 (0.20)	8.1 (0.09)	8.0 (0.17)	10.5 (0.17)	28.4 (0.54)	43.1 (0.94)
1975[6]	17,770 (366.1)	13,799 (202.8)	3,838 (91.7)	6,748 (127.9)	4,577 (101.5)	2,813 (77.1)	9.7 (0.20)	8.3 (0.09)	7.7 (0.16)	12.5 (0.20)	29.4 (0.50)	44.2 (0.86)
1980[6]	19,699 (384.1)	14,587 (210.7)	4,195 (96.5)	6,817 (128.7)	4,940 (106.1)	2,813 (77.1)	10.2 (0.21)	8.6 (0.09)	8.0 (0.16)	13.4 (0.21)	28.0 (0.46)	41.6 (0.82)
1985[6]	22,850 (435.1)	17,125 (249.2)	4,983 (112.8)	7,838 (148.3)	5,990 (125.8)	3,372 (90.2)	11.4 (0.21)	9.9 (0.10)	9.1 (0.18)	15.6 (0.24)	29.8 (0.47)	45.2 (0.84)
1990	16,622 (388.2)	11,086 (191.7)	3,442 (94.4)	5,106 (118.4)	4,284 (106.9)	2,411 (77.5)	8.8 (0.20)	7.0 (0.10)	6.6 (0.16)	11.6 (0.23)	25.0 (0.50)	39.6 (0.94)
1995	16,257 (384.2)	10,599 (186.1)	3,384 (93.5)	4,745 (113.5)	4,183 (105.5)	2,299 (75.5)	8.5 (0.20)	6.6 (0.09)	6.4 (0.16)	10.6 (0.22)	22.8 (0.47)	33.5 (0.86)
2000	14,336 (375.9)	8,664 (169.7)	2,896 (89.0)	3,715 (102.4)	3,412 (097.6)	1,832 (69.4)	7.4 (0.19)	5.5 (0.09)	5.4 (0.15)	8.5 (0.21)	18.8 (0.45)	28.0 (0.87)
2001	15,271 (386.8)	9,122 (175.4)	3,051 (91.7)	3,887 (105.0)	3,661 (101.5)	1,953 (71.8)	7.8 (0.20)	5.7 (0.09)	5.7 (0.16)	8.9 (0.21)	19.9 (0.46)	29.0 (0.87)
2002	15,567 (278.6)	9,389 (127.5)	3,208 (67.3)	3,848 (74.5)	3,733 (73.2)	1,949 (51.2)	8.0 (0.14)	5.9 (0.07)	6.0 (0.11)	9.0 (0.15)	20.0 (0.33)	29.2 (0.62)
2003	15,902 (281.9)	9,658 (129.8)	3,270 (68.0)	3,957 (75.7)	3,959 (75.7)	2,033 (52.4)	8.2 (0.14)	6.1 (0.07)	6.1 (0.11)	9.3 (0.16)	20.7 (0.33)	30.7 (0.63)
2004	16,908 (303.2)	10,323 (254.5)	3,505 (92.4)	4,190 (120.4)	4,116 (154.0)	2,114 (84.1)	8.7 (0.16)	6.5 (0.16)	6.5 (0.17)	9.9 (0.28)	21.7 (0.70)	31.5 (1.02)
2005	16,227 (303.1)	10,323 (247.5)	3,285 (80.6)	3,973 (127.3)	4,278 (163.7)	2,158 (93.8)	8.3 (0.16)	6.0 (0.15)	6.1 (0.14)	9.5 (0.30)	22.6 (0.77)	33.1 (1.17)
2006	16,227 (280.1)	9,676 (239.5)	3,372 (79.5)	3,930 (123.5)	4,353 (151.2)	2,206 (85.3)	8.2 (0.14)	6.1 (0.15)	6.2 (0.14)	9.5 (0.30)	22.5 (0.66)	32.9 (1.17)
2007	16,032 (329.9)	9,553 (257.4)	3,184 (86.4)	3,996 (132.7)	4,099 (172.5)	2,101 (100.7)	8.2 (0.17)	5.9 (0.16)	5.9 (0.16)	9.7 (0.32)	21.4 (0.79)	32.4 (1.27)
2008	17,024 (313.4)	10,138 (255.5)	3,383 (83.7)	4,059 (130.7)	4,046 (154.6)	1,985 (88.5)	8.6 (0.16)	6.4 (0.16)	6.2 (0.15)	10.0 (0.32)	21.5 (0.73)	31.7 (1.17)
2009	18,530 (358.3)	11,211 (298.4)	3,797 (101.4)	4,518 (137.4)	4,532 (158.8)	2,144 (89.4)	9.4 (0.18)	7.1 (0.19)	7.0 (0.18)	11.2 (0.34)	23.8 (0.71)	33.5 (1.11)
2010	19,539 (342.7)	11,740 (281.8)	3,922 (96.1)	4,675 (134.0)	4,802 (165.2)	2,269 (83.1)	9.9 (0.17)	7.4 (0.18)	7.3 (0.17)	11.7 (0.33)	24.8 (0.78)	34.8 (1.03)
2011	19,171 (333.4)	11,562 (287.9)	3,955 (92.2)	4,554 (149.5)	4,746 (160.0)	2,321 (89.9)	9.8 (0.17)	7.4 (0.19)	7.3 (0.17)	11.9 (0.39)	23.8 (0.66)	35.5 (1.03)
2012	18,940 (361.6)	11,387 (298.3)	3,835 (93.5)	4,510 (140.5)	4,655 (164.0)	2,245 (91.8)	9.7 (0.19)	7.3 (0.20)	7.1 (0.18)	11.8 (0.37)	24.3 (0.75)	36.5 (1.17)
2013	18,796 (438.9)	10,710 (339.9)	3,717 (114.6)	3,833 (150.1)	4,325 (217.6)	2,001 (111.3)	9.6 (0.23)	6.9 (0.22)	6.9 (0.21)	10.1 (0.40)	22.9 (0.98)	33.6 (1.45)

See notes at end of table.

Table 102.50. Official and supplemental measures of poverty status for all persons, persons in families, and related children under age 18, by race/ethnicity: Selected years, 1960 through 2013—Continued
[Standard errors appear in parentheses]

Race/ethnicity, type of poverty measure,[1] and year	Number below the poverty level (in thousands)						Percent below the poverty level					
	All persons	In all families			In families with female householder, no husband present		All persons	In all families			In families with female householder, no husband present	
		Total	Householder[2]	Related children under 18[3]	Total	Related children under 18[3]		Total	Householder[2]	Related children under 18[3]	Total	Related children under 18[3]
1	2	3	4	5	6	7	8	9	10	11	12	13
White, Supplemental Poverty Measure[5]												
2009	20,422 (351.3)	13,393 (299.8)	4,796 (104.0)	3,810 (122.2)	4,046 (164.4)	1,572 (77.5)	10.4 (0.18)	8.4 (0.19)	8.8 (0.19)	9.4 (0.30)	21.3 (0.76)	24.6 (1.05)
2010	21,746 (371.8)	13,972 (303.9)	4,917 (109.0)	3,894 (122.4)	4,242 (162.1)	1,660 (72.1)	11.0 (0.19)	8.9 (0.20)	9.1 (0.20)	9.8 (0.31)	21.9 (0.73)	25.5 (0.99)
2011	21,436 (344.0)	13,972 (305.6)	4,993 (105.1)	3,788 (122.9)	4,299 (156.4)	1,675 (75.3)	11.0 (0.18)	9.0 (0.19)	9.2 (0.19)	9.9 (0.32)	21.6 (0.66)	25.6 (0.96)
2012	20,923 (357.6)	13,561 (289.1)	4,870 (102.4)	3,582 (113.1)	3,972 (147.3)	1,510 (69.0)	10.7 (0.18)	8.7 (0.19)	9.0 (0.19)	9.4 (0.30)	20.7 (0.70)	24.6 (0.98)
2013	20,894 (396.1)	13,203 (336.3)	4,765 (116.7)	3,226 (128.2)	3,988 (201.2)	1,409 (83.9)	10.7 (0.20)	8.5 (0.22)	8.9 (0.21)	8.5 (0.34)	21.1 (0.95)	23.7 (1.26)
Black, official poverty measure[4]												
1970[6]	7,548 (219.8)	6,683 (219.3)	1,481 (55.3)	3,922 (96.3)	3,656 (92.3)	2,383 (72.0)	33.5 (0.89)	32.2 (0.89)	29.5 (0.88)	41.5 (0.70)	58.7 (0.86)	67.7 (1.08)
1975[6]	7,545 (219.8)	6,533 (132.3)	1,513 (56.0)	3,884 (95.7)	4,168 (99.9)	2,724 (77.7)	31.3 (0.85)	30.1 (0.85)	27.1 (0.82)	41.4 (0.70)	54.3 (0.78)	66.0 (1.01)
1980[6]	8,579 (230.2)	7,190 (140.8)	1,826 (62.1)	3,906 (96.0)	4,984 (111.4)	2,944 (81.3)	32.5 (0.82)	31.1 (0.82)	28.9 (0.78)	42.1 (0.70)	53.4 (0.71)	64.8 (0.97)
1985[6]	8,926 (246.7)	7,504 (153.2)	1,983 (68.7)	4,057 (103.9)	5,342 (123.1)	3,181 (89.9)	31.3 (0.82)	30.5 (0.82)	28.7 (0.79)	43.1 (0.74)	53.2 (0.72)	66.9 (0.99)
1990	9,653 (262.0)	7,993 (165.4)	2,153 (74.4)	4,309 (111.5)	5,877 (133.5)	3,460 (97.8)	31.8 (0.83)	30.9 (0.83)	29.3 (0.80)	44.0 (0.75)	50.4 (0.70)	64.6 (0.98)
1995	9,562 (261.2)	7,924 (164.4)	2,063 (72.7)	4,481 (114.2)	6,391 (142.8)	3,848 (104.2)	28.2 (0.78)	28.2 (0.78)	26.2 (0.75)	41.1 (0.71)	48.1 (0.65)	61.3 (0.92)
2000	7,680 (249.9)	5,957 (134.8)	1,617 (64.9)	3,342 (96.4)	4,593 (115.6)	2,793 (87.3)	22.4 (0.73)	21.0 (0.73)	19.1 (0.67)	30.7 (0.69)	38.2 (0.69)	49.0 (1.03)
2001	7,752 (251.1)	6,076 (136.4)	1,744 (67.6)	3,248 (94.9)	4,490 (114.1)	2,610 (84.1)	22.4 (0.72)	21.1 (0.72)	20.4 (0.68)	29.7 (0.68)	37.0 (0.68)	46.1 (1.04)
2002	8,259 (183.3)	6,464 (101.0)	1,837 (49.6)	3,420 (69.7)	4,799 (84.6)	2,762 (61.9)	24.0 (0.53)	22.6 (0.53)	21.3 (0.49)	32.1 (0.50)	38.1 (0.48)	47.5 (0.73)
2003	8,463 (194.7)	6,609 (102.4)	1,921 (50.8)	3,599 (71.7)	4,947 (86.2)	2,927 (63.9)	24.3 (0.53)	24.0 (0.53)	22.3 (0.50)	33.5 (0.51)	38.8 (0.48)	49.7 (0.73)
2004	8,697 (207.2)	6,891 (192.5)	1,956 (58.6)	3,562 (107.3)	5,076 (171.6)	2,864 (102.9)	24.7 (0.59)	23.8 (0.59)	22.7 (0.65)	33.4 (0.99)	39.4 (1.06)	49.0 (1.34)
2005	8,850 (236.5)	6,917 (227.2)	1,922 (63.9)	3,615 (124.6)	5,127 (200.0)	2,897 (118.9)	24.9 (0.66)	23.8 (0.66)	22.0 (0.70)	34.2 (1.15)	39.3 (1.33)	50.2 (1.63)
2006	8,653 (196.5)	6,749 (184.3)	1,914 (56.2)	3,531 (107.1)	4,945 (162.5)	2,859 (103.1)	24.1 (0.55)	22.9 (0.55)	21.4 (0.62)	33.0 (0.99)	38.9 (1.00)	49.9 (1.30)
2007	8,821 (220.6)	6,966 (207.3)	1,941 (63.5)	3,646 (119.6)	5,181 (181.3)	2,950 (115.4)	24.3 (0.61)	23.5 (0.61)	21.7 (0.64)	34.1 (1.09)	39.3 (1.20)	49.9 (1.53)
2008	8,979 (225.8)	7,003 (221.1)	1,971 (70.4)	3,586 (124.7)	5,278 (198.0)	2,961 (119.8)	24.6 (0.62)	23.6 (0.62)	21.8 (0.72)	34.4 (1.17)	40.3 (1.22)	51.8 (1.50)
Black, Supplemental Poverty Measure[5]												
2009	9,419 (239.9)	7,223 (207.8)	2,036 (67.4)	3,682 (114.2)	5,179 (192.2)	2,853 (115.1)	25.5 (0.64)	24.2 (0.70)	22.5 (0.67)	35.3 (1.08)	39.6 (1.18)	50.8 (1.51)
2010	10,122 (240.9)	7,681 (217.0)	2,173 (69.1)	4,021 (119.7)	5,546 (171.4)	3,103 (106.3)	27.3 (0.64)	25.8 (0.74)	24.0 (0.69)	39.3 (1.17)	40.7 (1.15)	53.2 (1.51)
2011	10,108 (245.0)	7,665 (235.9)	2,175 (75.3)	3,872 (124.5)	5,540 (200.1)	3,053 (116.6)	27.3 (0.66)	25.9 (0.78)	23.8 (0.77)	38.7 (1.21)	41.9 (1.24)	54.2 (1.55)
2012	10,148 (245.0)	7,636 (245.4)	2,169 (78.0)	3,797 (132.4)	5,344 (211.9)	2,936 (123.5)	27.0 (0.66)	25.5 (0.80)	23.4 (0.78)	38.0 (1.30)	41.1 (1.28)	53.5 (1.61)
2013	10,264 (292.7)	7,761 (257.9)	2,116 (72.0)	3,863 (143.2)	5,439 (218.4)	2,972 (133.7)	27.2 (0.78)	25.8 (0.87)	22.7 (0.75)	38.9 (1.43)	42.5 (1.41)	54.6 (1.73)
Hispanic, official poverty measure[4]												
1975	2,991 (176.8)	2,755 (90.2)	627 (41.3)	1,619 (67.7)	1,053 (54.0)	694 (43.5)	26.9 (1.41)	26.3 (1.41)	25.1 (1.41)	33.1 (1.09)	57.2 (1.88)	68.4 (2.37)
1980	3,491 (189.8)	3,143 (97.0)	751 (45.3)	1,718 (69.8)	1,319 (60.7)	809 (47.1)	25.7 (1.26)	25.1 (1.26)	23.2 (1.21)	33.0 (1.06)	54.5 (1.65)	65.0 (2.20)
1985	5,236 (202.8)	4,605 (107.7)	1,074 (48.7)	2,512 (76.6)	1,983 (67.4)	1,247 (52.7)	29.0 (1.01)	28.3 (1.01)	25.5 (0.98)	39.6 (0.89)	55.7 (1.21)	72.4 (1.57)
1990	6,006 (222.4)	5,091 (118.2)	1,244 (54.4)	2,750 (83.3)	2,115 (72.2)	1,314 (56.0)	28.1 (0.95)	26.9 (0.95)	25.0 (0.92)	37.7 (0.85)	53.0 (1.19)	68.4 (1.60)
1995	8,574 (256.1)	7,341 (147.4)	1,695 (64.1)	3,936 (101.9)	3,053 (88.3)	1,870 (60.3)	30.3 (0.85)	29.2 (0.85)	27.0 (0.84)	39.3 (0.73)	52.8 (0.99)	65.7 (1.34)
2000	7,747 (247.8)	6,430 (141.1)	1,540 (63.3)	3,342 (96.4)	2,444 (81.1)	1,407 (60.3)	21.5 (0.70)	20.3 (0.70)	19.2 (0.69)	27.6 (0.63)	37.8 (0.94)	49.8 (1.47)
2001	7,997 (251.7)	6,674 (144.4)	1,649 (65.6)	3,433 (97.9)	2,585 (83.6)	1,508 (62.6)	21.4 (0.68)	20.2 (0.68)	19.4 (0.67)	27.4 (0.62)	37.8 (0.92)	49.3 (1.41)
2002	8,555 (186.7)	7,184 (107.8)	1,792 (48.9)	3,653 (72.3)	2,554 (59.3)	1,501 (44.5)	21.8 (0.48)	20.8 (0.48)	19.7 (0.47)	28.2 (0.44)	36.4 (0.64)	47.9 (0.99)
2003	9,051 (192.6)	7,637 (111.9)	1,925 (50.8)	3,982 (76.0)	2,861 (63.1)	1,727 (48.0)	22.5 (0.48)	21.8 (0.48)	20.8 (0.47)	29.5 (0.44)	38.4 (0.63)	50.6 (0.95)
2004	9,122 (215.6)	7,705 (205.4)	1,953 (54.5)	3,985 (115.8)	3,072 (135.0)	1,840 (85.4)	21.9 (0.52)	21.1 (0.52)	20.5 (0.54)	28.6 (0.83)	39.3 (1.39)	50.9 (1.67)
2005	9,368 (202.4)	7,767 (192.2)	1,948 (51.0)	3,977 (113.4)	3,069 (120.9)	1,774 (76.7)	21.8 (0.47)	20.6 (0.47)	19.7 (0.48)	27.7 (0.78)	39.0 (1.22)	50.2 (1.59)
2006	9,243 (216.1)	7,650 (214.8)	1,922 (61.3)	3,959 (115.1)	3,189 (152.6)	1,848 (88.9)	20.6 (0.48)	19.5 (0.48)	18.9 (0.56)	26.6 (0.76)	36.9 (1.41)	47.2 (1.66)
2007	9,890 (244.8)	8,248 (229.3)	2,045 (60.4)	4,348 (134.9)	3,527 (158.7)	2,092 (98.1)	21.5 (0.53)	20.6 (0.53)	19.7 (0.56)	28.3 (0.87)	39.6 (1.32)	51.6 (1.59)
2008	10,987 (249.6)	9,303 (237.9)	2,239 (60.3)	4,888 (129.2)	3,751 (144.1)	2,218 (86.9)	23.2 (0.53)	22.3 (0.57)	21.3 (0.54)	30.3 (0.79)	40.5 (1.24)	51.9 (1.48)

See notes at end of table.

Table 102.50. Official and supplemental measures of poverty status for all persons, persons in families, and related children under age 18, by race/ethnicity: Selected years, 1960 through 2013—Continued

[Standard errors appear in parentheses]

Race/ethnicity, type of poverty measure,[1] and year	Number below the poverty level (in thousands)						Percent below the poverty level					
		In all families			In families with female householder, no husband present			In all families			In families with female householder, no husband present	
	All persons	Total	Householder[2]	Related children under 18[3]	Total	Related children under 18[3]	All persons	Total	Householder[2]	Related children under 18[3]	Total	Related children under 18[3]
1	2	3	4	5	6	7	8	9	10	11	12	13
2009	12,350 (267.3)	10,345 (254.8)	2,369 (62.7)	5,419 (138.6)	4,176 (169.1)	2,437 (100.1)	25.3 (0.55)	24.2 (0.59)	22.7 (0.56)	32.5 (0.83)	40.6 (1.33)	52.2 (1.61)
2010	13,243 (254.4)	11,188 (242.8)	2,557 (64.4)	5,881 (139.4)	4,643 (167.5)	2,715 (107.1)	26.6 (0.51)	25.6 (0.55)	24.0 (0.54)	34.5 (0.81)	44.5 (1.24)	57.0 (1.49)
2011	13,244 (263.5)	11,143 (253.2)	2,651 (59.5)	5,820 (146.1)	4,996 (182.1)	2,955 (120.5)	25.3 (0.50)	24.3 (0.56)	22.9 (0.50)	33.7 (0.84)	44.0 (1.22)	56.8 (1.57)
2012	13,616 (278.2)	11,358 (276.3)	2,807 (71.8)	5,773 (145.5)	4,816 (187.7)	2,809 (114.9)	25.6 (0.52)	24.6 (0.59)	23.5 (0.54)	33.3 (0.84)	42.8 (1.19)	54.7 (1.49)
2013	12,744 (312.0)	10,536 (293.3)	2,613 (78.6)	5,273 (155.7)	4,860 (197.6)	2,763 (114.5)	23.5 (0.58)	22.3 (0.63)	21.6 (0.63)	30.0 (0.89)	41.6 (1.47)	52.3 (1.65)
Hispanic, Supplemental Poverty Measure[5]												
2009	13,329 (281.7)	11,239 (271.8)	2,674 (64.6)	4,879 (132.5)	3,842 (168.4)	1,953 (89.5)	27.3 (0.58)	26.3 (0.63)	25.7 (0.59)	29.3 (0.80)	37.4 (1.36)	41.9 (1.58)
2010	13,845 (279.4)	11,669 (262.5)	2,791 (63.3)	5,109 (136.5)	4,331 (160.6)	2,227 (94.3)	27.8 (0.56)	26.7 (0.59)	26.2 (0.53)	30.0 (0.80)	41.5 (1.19)	46.8 (1.51)
2011	14,571 (303.9)	12,397 (284.6)	2,907 (71.5)	5,210 (132.0)	4,907 (180.7)	2,473 (99.6)	27.9 (0.58)	27.1 (0.63)	26.6 (0.62)	30.2 (0.77)	43.2 (1.25)	47.5 (1.45)
2012	14,799 (273.5)	12,443 (264.0)	3,170 (69.8)	5,212 (127.6)	4,492 (172.7)	2,315 (99.3)	27.9 (0.52)	26.9 (0.56)	26.5 (0.52)	30.1 (0.74)	39.9 (1.16)	45.1 (1.49)
2013	14,062 (338.9)	11,883 (318.0)	3,032 (80.7)	4,747 (143.6)	4,371 (193.5)	2,175 (103.4)	26.0 (0.62)	25.1 (0.68)	25.0 (0.65)	27.0 (0.82)	37.4 (1.46)	41.2 (1.70)
Asian, official poverty measure[4]												
1990[7]	851 (88.5)	706 (40.5)	167 (19.5)	352 (28.4)	127 (17.0)	77 (13.2)	12.2 (1.22)	11.3 (0.60)	11.0 (1.20)	16.9 (1.24)	20.1 (2.40)	31.2 (4.45)
1995[7]	1,379 (111.1)	1,087 (50.7)	258 (24.3)	520 (34.7)	253 (24.1)	139 (17.8)	14.6 (1.12)	12.9 (0.55)	12.3 (1.08)	18.5 (1.10)	28.7 (2.29)	41.8 (4.07)
2000[7]	1,210 (108.8)	863 (46.8)	227 (23.7)	390 (31.2)	272 (26.0)	151 (19.3)	9.8 (0.86)	8.0 (0.41)	7.8 (0.77)	12.3 (0.91)	22.8 (1.90)	37.0 (3.74)
2001	1,242 (110.2)	854 (46.5)	225 (23.6)	344 (29.2)	190 (21.6)	99 (15.6)	10.2 (0.89)	8.1 (0.42)	7.7 (0.77)	11.2 (0.89)	14.7 (1.54)	26.3 (3.54)
2002	1,143 (75.4)	751 (31.0)	207 (16.1)	297 (19.3)	152 (13.8)	83 (10.2)	10.1 (0.65)	7.7 (0.30)	7.4 (0.55)	11.4 (0.69)	15.3 (1.28)	30.3 (3.07)
2003	1,372 (82.1)	992 (35.8)	305 (19.6)	313 (19.9)	226 (16.9)	107 (11.5)	11.7 (0.68)	9.7 (0.33)	10.0 (0.61)	11.7 (0.70)	22.6 (1.48)	35.5 (3.07)
2004	1,184 (76.3)	799 (70.5)	228 (21.4)	256 (32.4)	126 (23.6)	47 (11.9)	9.8 (0.64)	7.5 (0.67)	7.3 (0.69)	9.2 (1.16)	12.6 (2.20)	17.0 (4.09)
2005	1,391 (85.4)	960 (80.0)	286 (23.6)	309 (34.1)	182 (30.1)	65 (15.1)	11.2 (0.68)	8.9 (0.73)	7.9 (0.69)	11.1 (1.19)	17.9 (2.77)	26.2 (5.06)
2006	1,301 (95.4)	881 (86.5)	252 (24.1)	335 (42.0)	186 (34.5)	89 (20.7)	10.0 (0.73)	7.8 (0.76)	7.6 (0.72)	11.7 (1.45)	18.0 (2.99)	36.8 (6.58)
2007	1,329 (80.5)	916 (79.6)	255 (23.2)	340 (39.2)	205 (36.6)	95 (21.5)	10.2 (0.62)	8.1 (0.70)	7.8 (0.70)	11.8 (1.33)	16.8 (2.77)	32.2 (5.77)
2008	1,528 (89.1)	1,154 (88.6)	334 (24.8)	410 (41.7)	205 (34.2)	85 (18.7)	11.8 (0.68)	10.1 (0.76)	9.8 (0.71)	14.1 (1.41)	16.1 (2.38)	25.5 (4.53)
2009	1,634 (96.8)	1,201 (87.4)	327 (23.6)	434 (39.7)	227 (36.1)	88 (16.0)	12.3 (0.70)	10.0 (0.72)	9.3 (0.65)	13.7 (1.24)	17.4 (2.64)	25.8 (4.25)
2010	1,672 (95.0)	1,211 (90.2)	323 (23.4)	434 (42.0)	281 (45.4)	118 (19.6)	11.9 (0.68)	9.9 (0.74)	9.3 (0.66)	13.7 (1.31)	21.7 (3.09)	35.1 (4.61)
2011	1,871 (114.8)	1,317 (99.8)	385 (29.4)	422 (44.2)	295 (58.4)	124 (34.0)	12.2 (0.74)	9.9 (0.74)	9.6 (0.72)	12.7 (1.32)	20.6 (3.53)	34.4 (6.88)
2012	1,813 (113.6)	1,268 (109.7)	361 (29.4)	422 (46.4)	257 (45.0)	95 (21.9)	11.4 (0.70)	9.2 (0.78)	9.0 (0.69)	12.5 (1.37)	18.3 (2.81)	28.8 (5.46)
2013	1,733 (103.7)	1,134 (89.7)	374 (30.2)	346 (34.3)	227 (43.3)	89 (18.9)	10.4 (0.61)	7.8 (0.61)	8.7 (0.69)	9.9 (0.97)	14.2 (2.54)	24.2 (4.87)
Asian, Supplemental Poverty Measure[5]												
2009	2,403 (109.7)	1,894 (102.8)	529 (28.1)	547 (42.3)	308 (43.0)	107 (17.7)	17.6 (0.78)	15.8 (0.84)	15.0 (0.76)	17.3 (1.30)	23.5 (3.00)	31.5 (4.46)
2010	2,262 (113.2)	1,747 (113.4)	504 (29.8)	440 (42.4)	346 (50.0)	105 (17.1)	16.1 (0.80)	14.3 (0.91)	14.5 (0.84)	13.9 (1.31)	26.7 (3.25)	31.1 (4.30)
2011	2,618 (125.6)	2,006 (114.5)	620 (34.5)	475 (40.5)	357 (52.5)	94 (21.3)	16.5 (0.80)	14.9 (0.84)	15.5 (0.84)	14.2 (1.20)	25.0 (3.27)	26.1 (5.25)
2012	2,628 (127.7)	2,018 (123.4)	556 (33.6)	556 (48.0)	368 (49.0)	122 (23.4)	16.5 (0.79)	14.7 (0.88)	13.9 (0.78)	16.5 (1.43)	26.2 (2.80)	37.1 (5.47)
2013	2,750 (160.0)	2,138 (149.5)	658 (42.9)	494 (51.7)	360 (58.4)	94 (21.2)	16.6 (0.93)	14.7 (1.00)	15.4 (0.94)	14.2 (1.45)	22.5 (3.40)	25.7 (5.46)

[1] All data for 2008 and earlier years are based on the official poverty measure. Supplemental Poverty Measure (SPM) data are available only for 2009 and later years.
[2] Refers to the person who owns or rents (maintains) the housing unit.
[3] Refers to all children in the household who are related to the householder by birth, marriage, or adoption (except a child who is the spouse of the householder). For 1960 and 1965 only, the data exclude related children who have ever been married.
[4] The official poverty measure consists of a set of thresholds for families of different sizes and compositions that are compared to before-tax cash income to determine a family's poverty status. For more information about how the Census Bureau determines who is in poverty, see http://www.census.gov/hhes/www/poverty/about/overview/measure.html.
[5] The Supplemental Poverty Measure (SPM) extends the information provided by the official poverty measure by adding to family income the value of benefits from many government programs designed to assist low-income families, subtracting taxes and necessary expenses such as child care costs (for working families) and medical expenses, and adjusting poverty thresholds for differences in housing costs. To match the population included in the current official poverty measure,

SPM estimates presented in this table exclude unrelated children under age 15. For more information about the SPM, see http://www.census.gov/hhes/povmeas/methodology/supplemental/research/Short_ResearchSPM2011.pdf.
[6] Includes persons of Hispanic ethnicity, because data for the White, non-Hispanic and Black, non-Hispanic populations are not available for the indicated years.
[7] Includes Pacific Islanders as well as Asians.
NOTE: Data are from the Current Population Survey and may differ from data shown in other tables obtained from the Decennial Census and the American Community Survey. Race categories exclude persons of Hispanic ethnicity except where otherwise noted. Some data have been revised from previously published figures.
SOURCE: U.S. Department of Commerce, Census Bureau, Current Population Reports, Series P-60, Poverty in the United States, selected years, 1960 through 2002; Current Population Survey (CPS), Annual Social and Economic Supplement, 1991 through 2014; and Supplemental Poverty Measure (SPM) Research Files, 2009 through 2013. (This table was prepared November 2014.)

Table 102.60. Number and percentage of children under age 18 living in poverty, by family structure, race/ethnicity, and selected subgroups: 2008 and 2013

[Standard errors appear in parentheses]

Year and race/ethnicity	Number of related children[1] living in poverty (in thousands)		Percent of related children[1] living in poverty, by family structure							
			Total, all families		Married-couple household[2]		Mother-only household, no spouse present[2]		Father-only household, no spouse present[2]	
1	2		3		4		5		6	
2008										
Total	12,901	(92.9)	17.8	(0.12)	8.4	(0.09)	40.9	(0.25)	24.5	(0.31)
White	4,301	(41.9)	10.6	(0.10)	5.1	(0.08)	32.4	(0.34)	17.3	(0.37)
Black	3,301	(40.7)	33.0	(0.36)	10.8	(0.40)	47.1	(0.49)	34.9	(0.73)
Hispanic	4,342	(43.2)	27.7	(0.25)	18.3	(0.27)	47.7	(0.48)	29.4	(0.70)
Mexican	3,289	(39.5)	29.6	(0.31)	21.1	(0.35)	50.1	(0.60)	30.4	(0.76)
Puerto Rican	397	(12.2)	29.7	(0.83)	9.9	(0.76)	48.6	(1.21)	33.5	(2.41)
Cuban	42	(3.2)	12.7	(0.90)	6.4	(0.87)	29.0	(2.35)	20.8	(3.96)
Dominican	127	(7.7)	30.7	(1.48)	10.7	(1.32)	50.2	(2.28)	20.0	(3.89)
Salvadoran	92	(6.7)	20.7	(1.32)	13.9	(1.46)	38.0	(2.51)	18.8	(3.28)
Other Central American	142	(7.4)	24.9	(1.14)	16.6	(1.24)	40.2	(2.54)	29.3	(3.24)
South American	89	(5.8)	13.5	(0.85)	8.0	(0.82)	28.8	(2.16)	17.7	(2.72)
Other Hispanic or Latino	162	(6.8)	20.5	(0.71)	8.8	(0.76)	41.9	(1.81)	27.6	(3.24)
Asian	303	(10.7)	10.6	(0.37)	8.1	(0.37)	27.6	(1.53)	16.1	(1.72)
Asian Indian	43	(3.3)	7.2	(0.54)	6.2	(0.54)	22.9	(4.63)	17.9 !	(7.86)
Chinese[3]	57	(3.8)	9.5	(0.58)	7.3	(0.63)	23.2	(2.68)	22.1	(3.99)
Filipino	20	(2.6)	4.5	(0.57)	2.3	(0.42)	15.5	(2.80)	7.9 !	(2.41)
Japanese	6	(1.1)	7.5	(1.34)	5.4	(1.21)	17.7 !	(5.62)	28.9 !	(11.80)
Korean	34	(3.6)	12.2	(1.20)	8.9	(1.09)	36.3	(5.25)	25.3	(5.61)
Vietnamese	46	(3.3)	14.0	(1.01)	10.1	(1.18)	35.2	(3.75)	10.3 !	(3.48)
Other Asian	98	(6.7)	18.1	(1.16)	15.2	(1.18)	36.1	(3.90)	17.3	(3.27)
Pacific Islander	21	(2.8)	21.2	(2.66)	13.8	(2.64)	44.3	(6.06)	18.0 !	(6.30)
American Indian/Alaska Native	151	(6.6)	29.1	(1.20)	15.2	(1.22)	45.0	(2.11)	34.8	(2.60)
Some other race[4]	48	(4.8)	20.2	(1.77)	8.4	(1.19)	46.5	(4.00)	17.3 !	(5.27)
Two or more races	434	(12.2)	18.1	(0.48)	6.1	(0.37)	37.6	(1.00)	24.6	(1.56)
White and Black	266	(10.9)	26.2	(0.91)	9.0	(0.83)	41.5	(1.39)	26.7	(2.65)
White and Asian	35	(2.7)	5.6	(0.42)	2.8	(0.30)	21.5	(2.39)	11.5	(2.06)
White and American Indian/Alaska Native	64	(3.5)	17.5	(0.85)	8.0	(0.82)	35.0	(2.24)	31.6	(2.79)
Other Two or more races	68	(4.6)	17.5	(1.06)	6.3	(1.00)	34.4	(2.32)	24.0	(3.48)
2013										
Total	15,649	(103.2)	21.7	(0.14)	11.0	(0.12)	44.9	(0.29)	29.1	(0.35)
White	4,897	(46.2)	13.0	(0.12)	6.7	(0.10)	35.7	(0.34)	20.8	(0.40)
Black	3,825	(32.9)	39.0	(0.31)	15.6	(0.46)	52.3	(0.45)	41.2	(0.79)
Hispanic	5,581	(48.8)	32.2	(0.27)	21.8	(0.33)	50.1	(0.40)	35.6	(0.79)
Mexican	4,075	(39.4)	33.8	(0.30)	24.2	(0.37)	52.4	(0.45)	36.1	(0.92)
Puerto Rican	520	(12.6)	33.6	(0.70)	14.7	(1.04)	50.1	(1.05)	40.1	(2.54)
Cuban	89	(5.1)	22.9	(1.12)	11.8	(1.16)	43.2	(2.40)	37.8	(3.94)
Dominican	180	(8.2)	34.9	(1.27)	17.6	(1.75)	47.5	(1.97)	39.9	(4.44)
Salvadoran	151	(8.0)	26.3	(1.24)	17.6	(1.50)	40.0	(2.49)	29.8	(3.93)
Other Central American	246	(10.7)	33.9	(1.12)	24.6	(1.33)	49.6	(2.12)	35.3	(3.47)
South American	140	(7.6)	18.0	(0.83)	11.8	(1.11)	34.2	(2.37)	19.5	(3.09)
Other Hispanic or Latino	180	(7.7)	24.3	(0.89)	14.7	(1.06)	41.9	(1.89)	29.8	(2.66)
Asian	412	(11.6)	12.6	(0.34)	10.3	(0.33)	28.1	(1.47)	21.0	(1.98)
Asian Indian	48	(3.8)	6.3	(0.47)	5.5	(0.45)	25.1	(4.29)	7.7 !	(3.56)
Chinese[3]	78	(4.2)	11.8	(0.60)	9.5	(0.61)	24.1	(2.48)	28.4	(3.87)
Filipino	34	(3.2)	7.4	(0.68)	4.7	(0.65)	17.0	(2.46)	17.7	(4.02)
Japanese	4	(0.9)	5.5	(1.18)	4.2	(1.19)	16.7 !	(6.90)	‡	(†)
Korean	27	(2.9)	11.0	(1.05)	9.1	(0.97)	28.9	(4.99)	15.9 !	(6.18)
Vietnamese	57	(4.1)	14.7	(1.00)	12.2	(1.11)	27.6	(3.53)	18.0	(4.23)
Other Asian	164	(7.8)	24.5	(1.01)	21.4	(1.10)	40.3	(3.43)	26.4	(3.93)
Pacific Islander	32	(3.2)	27.0	(2.32)	15.1	(2.52)	46.9	(4.65)	47.2	(9.07)
American Indian/Alaska Native	200	(5.8)	36.1	(0.91)	18.2	(1.05)	55.3	(1.53)	40.5	(2.33)
Some other race[4]	53	(4.4)	25.3	(1.82)	13.2	(1.83)	49.3	(3.90)	26.4	(5.02)
Two or more races	650	(15.4)	21.2	(0.47)	8.5	(0.36)	41.5	(0.90)	27.4	(1.65)
White and Black	366	(10.0)	29.1	(0.78)	11.3	(0.66)	43.8	(1.28)	31.2	(2.80)
White and Asian	64	(4.1)	8.1	(0.51)	4.9	(0.46)	23.8	(2.08)	18.1	(2.99)
White and American Indian/Alaska Native	77	(3.7)	20.6	(0.90)	10.9	(0.94)	40.5	(1.98)	26.6	(3.14)
Other Two or more races	142	(7.4)	22.3	(0.96)	9.4	(0.88)	43.6	(1.70)	28.0	(3.23)

†Not applicable.
!Interpret data with caution. The coefficient of variation (CV) for this estimate is between 30 and 50 percent.
‡Reporting standards not met. Either there are too few cases for a reliable estimate or the coefficient of variation (CV) is 50 percent or greater.
[1]Related children in a family include all children in the household who are related to the householder by birth, marriage, or adoption (except a child who is the spouse of the householder). The householder is the person (or one of the people) who owns or rents (maintains) the housing unit. This table includes only children related to the householder. It excludes unrelated children and householders who are themselves under the age of 18.
[2]To determine family structure, children are classified by their parents' marital status or, if no parents are present in the household, by the marital status of the householder who is related to the children. Mother-only households are those that have only a female householder, and father-only households are those that have only a male householder.

[3]In 2008 only, includes Taiwanese. As of 2013, excludes Taiwanese, which is included in "Other Asian."
[4]Respondents who wrote in some other race that was not included as an option on the questionnaire.
NOTE: Data may differ from Current Population Survey data that are shown in other tables. American Community Survey respondents were interviewed throughout the given year and reported the income they received during the previous 12 months. For information about how the Census Bureau determines who is in poverty, see http://www.census.gov/hhes/www/poverty/about/overview/measure.html. Detail may not sum to totals because of rounding. Race categories exclude persons of Hispanic ethnicity.
SOURCE: U.S. Department of Commerce, Census Bureau, American Community Survey, 2008 and 2013. (This table was prepared October 2014.)

Table 103.10. Percentage of the population 3 to 34 years old enrolled in school, by sex, race/ethnicity, and age group: Selected years, 1980 through 2013

[Standard errors appear in parentheses]

Year and age group	Total				Male				Female			
	Total	White	Black	Hispanic	Total	White	Black	Hispanic	Total	White	Black	Hispanic
1	2	3	4	5	6	7	8	9	10	11	12	13
1980												
Total, 3 to 34 years old	49.7 (0.21)	48.8 (0.24)	54.0 (0.69)	49.8 (1.40)	50.9 (0.30)	50.0 (0.34)	56.2 (0.99)	49.9 (2.00)	48.5 (0.30)	47.7 (0.34)	52.1 (0.95)	49.8 (1.98)
3 and 4 years old	36.7 (0.95)	37.4 (1.12)	38.2 (2.85)	28.5 (5.13)	37.8 (1.34)	39.2 (1.59)	36.4 (3.98)	30.1 (7.03)	35.5 (1.35)	35.5 (1.59)	40.0 (4.08)	26.6 (7.48)
5 and 6 years old	95.7 (0.40)	95.9 (0.46)	95.5 (1.23)	94.5 (2.79)	95.0 (0.61)	95.4 (0.68)	94.1 (1.97)	94.0 (4.21)	96.4 (0.53)	96.5 (0.62)	97.0 (1.45)	94.9 (3.70)
7 to 9 years old	99.1 (0.15)	99.1 (0.18)	99.4 (0.36)	98.4 (1.19)	99.0 (0.22)	99.0 (0.26)	99.5 (0.46)	97.7 (2.05)	99.2 (0.20)	99.2 (0.24)	99.3 (0.55)	99.0 (1.29)
10 to 13 years old	99.4 (0.10)	99.4 (0.12)	99.4 (0.31)	99.7 (0.47)	99.4 (0.14)	99.4 (0.16)	99.4 (0.43)	99.7 (0.86)	99.4 (0.15)	99.3 (0.18)	99.3 (0.46)	99.9 (0.32)
14 and 15 years old	98.2 (0.22)	98.7 (0.22)	97.9 (0.73)	94.3 (2.46)	98.7 (0.27)	98.9 (0.28)	98.4 (0.89)	96.7 (2.74)	97.7 (0.36)	98.5 (0.34)	97.3 (1.16)	92.1 (3.91)
16 and 17 years old	89.0 (0.51)	89.2 (0.57)	90.7 (1.46)	81.8 (4.25)	89.1 (0.71)	89.4 (0.80)	90.7 (2.06)	81.5 (6.15)	89.0 (0.73)	89.0 (0.83)	90.6 (2.06)	82.2 (5.88)
18 and 19 years old	46.4 (0.80)	47.0 (0.91)	45.8 (2.58)	37.8 (5.16)	48.5 (1.15)	48.5 (1.30)	42.9 (3.76)	36.9 (7.12)	45.8 (1.12)	45.7 (1.27)	48.3 (3.55)	38.8 (7.47)
20 and 21 years old	31.0 (0.75)	33.0 (0.86)	23.3 (2.23)	19.5 (4.31)	32.6 (1.09)	34.8 (1.24)	22.8 (3.32)	21.4 (6.39)	29.5 (1.02)	31.3 (1.18)	23.7 (3.02)	17.6 ! (5.80)
22 to 24 years old	16.3 (0.49)	16.8 (0.56)	13.6 (1.54)	11.7 (2.96)	17.8 (0.73)	18.7 (0.84)	13.4 (2.31)	10.7 ! (4.11)	14.9 (0.66)	15.0 (0.75)	13.7 (2.07)	12.6 ! (4.25)
25 to 29 years old	9.3 (0.31)	9.4 (0.35)	8.8 (1.05)	6.9 (1.88)	9.8 (0.46)	9.8 (0.51)	10.6 (1.71)	6.8 ! (2.70)	8.8 (0.42)	9.1 (0.48)	7.5 (1.31)	6.9 ! (2.61)
30 to 34 years old	6.4 (0.27)	6.4 (0.30)	6.9 (1.01)	5.1 ! (1.77)	5.9 (0.38)	5.6 (0.40)	7.2 (1.56)	6.2 ! (2.72)	7.0 (0.39)	7.2 (0.45)	6.6 (1.33)	‡ (†)
1990												
Total, 3 to 34 years old	50.2 (0.23)	49.8 (0.27)	52.2 (0.71)	47.2 (1.06)	50.9 (0.32)	50.4 (0.38)	54.3 (1.02)	46.8 (1.48)	49.5 (0.32)	49.2 (0.38)	50.3 (0.99)	47.7 (1.52)
3 and 4 years old	44.4 (0.99)	47.2 (1.19)	41.8 (2.97)	30.7 (4.08)	43.9 (1.38)	47.9 (1.66)	38.1 (4.14)	28.0 (5.57)	44.9 (1.41)	46.6 (1.70)	45.5 (4.25)	33.6 (5.95)
5 and 6 years old	96.5 (0.37)	96.7 (0.43)	96.5 (1.05)	94.9 (1.96)	96.5 (0.51)	96.8 (0.59)	96.2 (1.53)	95.8 (2.48)	96.4 (0.53)	96.7 (0.62)	96.9 (1.43)	93.9 (3.05)
7 to 9 years old	99.7 (0.09)	99.7 (0.11)	99.8 (0.19)	98.5 (0.52)	99.8 (0.13)	99.7 (0.16)	99.9 (0.24)	99.5 (0.70)	99.6 (0.14)	99.7 (0.15)	99.8 (0.31)	99.4 (0.79)
10 to 13 years old	99.6 (0.09)	99.7 (0.10)	99.9 (0.15)	99.1 (0.64)	99.6 (0.13)	99.6 (0.14)	99.9 (0.19)	99.0 (0.93)	99.7 (0.12)	99.7 (0.13)	99.8 (0.24)	99.1 (0.87)
14 and 15 years old	99.0 (0.19)	99.0 (0.23)	99.4 (0.46)	99.0 (0.90)	99.1 (0.25)	99.2 (0.30)	99.7 (0.48)	99.1 (1.10)	98.9 (0.29)	98.9 (0.35)	99.1 (0.79)	98.8 (1.47)
16 and 17 years old	92.5 (0.52)	93.5 (0.58)	91.7 (1.59)	85.4 (3.22)	92.6 (0.72)	93.4 (0.82)	93.0 (2.09)	85.5 (4.39)	92.4 (0.74)	93.7 (0.81)	90.5 (2.41)	85.3 (4.73)
18 and 19 years old	57.2 (0.94)	59.1 (1.11)	55.0 (2.83)	44.0 (4.36)	58.2 (1.33)	59.7 (1.56)	60.4 (3.99)	40.7 (6.23)	56.3 (1.32)	58.5 (1.57)	49.8 (3.96)	47.2 (6.08)
20 and 21 years old	39.7 (0.92)	43.1 (1.10)	28.3 (2.56)	27.2 (3.82)	40.3 (1.32)	44.2 (1.59)	31.0 (3.81)	21.7 (4.94)	39.2 (1.28)	42.0 (1.53)	25.8 (3.45)	33.1 (5.79)
22 to 24 years old	21.0 (0.63)	21.9 (0.75)	19.7 (2.01)	9.9 (2.05)	22.3 (0.92)	23.7 (1.11)	19.3 (3.03)	11.2 (2.98)	19.9 (0.86)	20.3 (1.02)	20.0 (2.68)	8.4 ! (2.77)
25 to 29 years old	9.7 (0.33)	10.4 (0.39)	6.1 (0.87)	6.3 (1.29)	9.2 (0.46)	10.0 (0.55)	4.7 (1.14)	4.6 ! (1.55)	10.2 (0.47)	10.7 (0.56)	7.3 (1.27)	8.1 (2.05)
30 to 34 years old	5.8 (0.25)	6.2 (0.30)	4.5 (0.75)	3.6 (0.99)	4.8 (0.33)	5.0 (0.38)	2.3 ! (0.80)	4.0 ! (1.45)	6.9 (0.38)	7.4 (0.46)	6.3 (1.19)	3.1 ! (1.32)
1995												
Total, 3 to 34 years old[1]	53.7 (0.21)	53.8 (0.25)	56.3 (0.58)	49.7 (0.65)	54.3 (0.30)	54.2 (0.36)	58.6 (0.83)	49.1 (0.90)	53.2 (0.30)	53.4 (0.36)	54.1 (0.81)	50.3 (0.93)
3 and 4 years old	48.7 (0.87)	52.2 (1.09)	47.8 (2.29)	36.9 (2.36)	49.4 (1.22)	51.1 (1.53)	52.4 (3.27)	40.8 (3.35)	48.1 (1.24)	53.5 (1.56)	43.4 (3.18)	32.7 (3.29)
5 and 6 years old	96.0 (0.34)	96.6 (0.39)	95.4 (0.97)	93.9 (1.23)	95.3 (0.52)	95.9 (0.60)	94.6 (1.48)	93.6 (1.75)	96.8 (0.44)	97.4 (0.49)	96.3 (1.24)	94.3 (1.72)
7 to 9 years old	98.7 (0.17)	98.8 (0.18)	97.7 (0.59)	98.5 (0.55)	98.8 (0.22)	99.0 (0.24)	98.1 (0.74)	98.8 (0.72)	98.5 (0.25)	98.6 (0.27)	97.2 (0.92)	98.2 (0.83)
10 to 13 years old	99.1 (0.12)	99.0 (0.15)	99.2 (0.30)	99.2 (0.36)	99.1 (0.17)	99.0 (0.21)	98.8 (0.34)	99.1 (0.59)	99.0 (0.18)	98.9 (0.22)	99.8 (0.50)	99.5 (0.39)
14 and 15 years old	98.9 (0.18)	98.8 (0.22)	99.0 (0.46)	98.8 (0.56)	98.8 (0.24)	98.8 (0.30)	99.6 (0.40)	98.3 (0.93)	98.8 (0.27)	98.7 (0.33)	98.3 (0.83)	99.4 (0.59)
16 and 17 years old	93.6 (0.42)	94.4 (0.47)	93.0 (1.16)	88.2 (1.83)	95.6 (0.55)	95.0 (0.63)	95.6 (1.30)	88.4 (2.59)	92.6 (0.64)	93.8 (0.72)	90.3 (1.94)	88.0 (2.58)
18 and 19 years old	59.4 (0.86)	61.8 (1.03)	57.5 (2.38)	46.1 (2.63)	59.2 (1.21)	61.9 (1.45)	59.2 (3.48)	47.4 (3.63)	59.2 (1.22)	61.8 (1.46)	56.1 (3.27)	44.8 (3.83)
20 and 21 years old	44.9 (0.90)	49.7 (1.10)	37.8 (2.47)	27.1 (2.37)	44.7 (1.29)	50.0 (1.57)	36.7 (3.67)	24.8 (3.30)	45.1 (1.25)	49.3 (1.54)	38.7 (3.35)	29.2 (3.40)
22 to 24 years old	23.2 (0.60)	24.4 (0.74)	20.0 (1.62)	15.6 (1.52)	22.8 (0.84)	24.1 (1.04)	20.6 (2.42)	14.8 (2.00)	23.6 (0.85)	24.8 (1.04)	19.5 (2.18)	16.6 (2.34)
25 to 29 years old	11.6 (0.34)	12.3 (0.42)	10.0 (0.95)	7.1 (0.88)	11.0 (0.48)	12.2 (0.59)	6.3 (1.16)	5.6 (1.10)	12.2 (0.49)	12.3 (0.59)	13.0 (1.41)	8.7 (1.38)
30 to 34 years old	5.9 (0.24)	5.7 (0.28)	7.7 (0.80)	4.7 (0.70)	5.4 (0.33)	5.0 (0.37)	6.9 (1.14)	4.5 (0.95)	6.5 (0.35)	6.3 (0.41)	8.3 (1.13)	4.9 (1.03)
2000												
Total, 3 to 34 years old[1]	55.9 (0.22)	56.0 (0.27)	59.3 (0.59)	51.3 (0.63)	55.8 (0.31)	55.8 (0.38)	59.7 (0.85)	50.5 (0.88)	56.0 (0.31)	56.1 (0.38)	59.0 (0.83)	52.2 (0.89)
3 and 4 years old	52.1 (0.93)	54.6 (1.19)	59.8 (2.50)	35.9 (2.36)	50.8 (1.30)	54.1 (1.66)	58.0 (3.53)	31.9 (3.23)	53.4 (1.32)	55.2 (1.70)	61.8 (3.55)	40.0 (3.43)
5 and 6 years old	95.6 (0.38)	95.5 (0.49)	96.7 (0.89)	94.3 (1.13)	95.1 (0.56)	94.5 (0.76)	96.0 (1.38)	95.4 (1.41)	96.1 (0.51)	96.4 (0.63)	97.5 (1.12)	93.1 (1.79)
7 to 9 years old	98.1 (0.20)	98.4 (0.24)	97.5 (0.61)	97.5 (0.65)	98.1 (0.29)	98.1 (0.36)	98.2 (0.72)	96.6 (1.09)	98.2 (0.28)	98.6 (0.32)	96.7 (1.01)	98.4 (0.74)
10 to 13 years old	98.3 (0.17)	98.5 (0.19)	98.5 (0.42)	97.4 (0.59)	98.3 (0.23)	98.2 (0.30)	98.8 (0.52)	98.4 (0.65)	98.3 (0.24)	98.8 (0.25)	98.1 (0.66)	96.4 (1.01)
14 and 15 years old	98.7 (0.20)	98.9 (0.22)	99.6 (0.30)	96.2 (0.99)	98.8 (0.27)	98.8 (0.33)	99.6 (0.42)	96.9 (1.26)	98.6 (0.29)	99.0 (0.31)	99.6 (0.42)	95.4 (1.54)
16 and 17 years old	92.8 (0.45)	94.0 (0.50)	91.7 (1.32)	87.0 (1.77)	92.7 (0.63)	94.7 (0.66)	88.9 (2.09)	85.7 (2.60)	92.9 (0.64)	93.3 (0.76)	94.1 (1.54)	88.3 (2.40)
18 and 19 years old	61.2 (0.84)	63.9 (1.02)	57.2 (2.34)	49.5 (2.47)	58.3 (1.19)	61.2 (1.46)	51.5 (3.45)	48.0 (3.40)	64.2 (1.16)	66.7 (1.42)	62.2 (3.14)	51.1 (3.59)
20 and 21 years old	44.1 (0.88)	49.2 (1.10)	37.4 (2.38)	26.1 (2.22)	41.0 (1.23)	45.8 (1.54)	31.3 (3.42)	24.2 (3.02)	47.3 (1.26)	52.7 (1.09)	42.3 (3.26)	28.1 (3.26)
22 to 24 years old	24.6 (0.63)	24.9 (0.78)	24.0 (1.76)	18.2 (1.64)	23.9 (0.88)	25.0 (1.12)	22.0 (2.46)	15.2 (2.08)	25.3 (0.89)	24.8 (1.09)	25.8 (2.51)	21.6 (2.55)
25 to 29 years old	11.4 (0.37)	11.1 (0.45)	14.5 (1.18)	7.4 (0.88)	10.0 (0.50)	10.5 (0.62)	11.6 (1.63)	5.1 (1.06)	12.7 (0.53)	11.8 (0.65)	16.7 (1.66)	9.5 (1.38)
30 to 34 years old	6.7 (0.27)	6.1 (0.32)	9.9 (0.97)	5.6 (0.75)	5.6 (0.36)	4.7 (0.41)	8.5 (1.34)	5.7 (1.06)	7.7 (0.41)	7.4 (0.50)	11.2 (1.39)	5.5 (1.05)

See notes at end of table.

Table 103.10. Percentage of the population 3 to 34 years old enrolled in school, by sex, race/ethnicity, and age group: Selected years, 1980 through 2013—Continued

[Standard errors appear in parentheses]

Year and age group	Total				Male				Female			
	Total	White	Black	Hispanic	Total	White	Black	Hispanic	Total	White	Black	Hispanic
1	2	3	4	5	6	7	8	9	10	11	12	13
2005												
Total, 3 to 34 years old[1]	56.5 (0.20)	57.6 (0.26)	58.5 (0.57)	50.9 (0.53)	55.8 (0.28)	57.1 (0.37)	58.8 (0.82)	48.4 (0.73)	58.0 (0.29)	58.0 (0.37)	58.1 (0.80)	53.7 (0.76)
3 and 4 years old[1]	53.6 (0.86)	58.5 (1.14)	52.4 (2.39)	43.0 (2.07)	52.8 (1.21)	56.8 (1.61)	54.8 (3.42)	43.0 (2.91)	54.4 (1.23)	60.3 (1.63)	50.1 (3.32)	43.0 (2.96)
5 and 6 years old	95.4 (0.37)	95.9 (0.47)	95.9 (0.97)	93.8 (1.06)	94.8 (0.54)	95.4 (0.68)	94.8 (1.50)	92.4 (1.62)	96.1 (0.50)	96.3 (0.63)	97.1 (1.18)	95.3 (1.34)
7 to 9 years old	98.6 (0.17)	99.0 (0.19)	98.7 (0.45)	97.4 (0.58)	98.0 (0.27)	98.9 (0.27)	98.0 (0.81)	96.0 (1.00)	99.0 (0.20)	99.0 (0.27)	99.5 (0.41)	98.8 (0.57)
10 to 13 years old	98.6 (0.14)	99.0 (0.16)	98.5 (0.40)	97.3 (0.46)	98.4 (0.22)	99.1 (0.21)	97.6 (0.70)	97.2 (0.72)	98.8 (0.18)	98.8 (0.24)	99.5 (0.33)	98.6 (0.54)
14 and 15 years old	98.0 (0.22)	98.6 (0.24)	96.1 (0.83)	97.2 (0.70)	97.5 (0.34)	98.4 (0.35)	93.3 (1.52)	97.8 (0.90)	98.7 (0.33)	98.7 (0.33)	98.8 (0.66)	96.7 (1.09)
16 and 17 years old	95.1 (0.33)	96.1 (0.38)	93.6 (1.05)	92.6 (1.14)	95.9 (0.47)	95.9 (0.55)	93.6 (1.51)	92.5 (1.61)	94.3 (0.53)	96.3 (0.53)	93.6 (1.05)	92.6 (1.60)
18 and 19 years old	67.6 (0.79)	71.6 (0.95)	62.0 (2.30)	54.3 (2.33)	66.5 (1.11)	69.8 (1.35)	66.9 (3.20)	51.8 (3.22)	68.7 (1.34)	73.5 (1.34)	57.4 (3.27)	57.2 (3.37)
20 and 21 years old	48.7 (0.80)	54.4 (1.01)	37.9 (2.25)	30.0 (1.96)	45.3 (1.11)	50.5 (1.42)	35.5 (3.12)	25.2 (2.56)	52.1 (1.15)	58.5 (1.43)	40.4 (3.23)	35.3 (2.99)
22 to 24 years old	27.3 (0.59)	27.8 (0.76)	28.6 (1.75)	19.5 (1.41)	25.2 (0.83)	26.4 (1.07)	24.0 (2.45)	17.5 (1.85)	29.4 (0.85)	29.1 (1.09)	32.5 (2.45)	21.8 (2.17)
25 to 29 years old	11.9 (0.34)	12.5 (0.45)	11.9 (1.00)	7.8 (0.70)	9.6 (0.43)	10.2 (0.58)	9.1 (1.32)	5.6 (0.82)	14.2 (0.51)	14.7 (0.67)	14.2 (1.47)	10.4 (1.19)
30 to 34 years old	6.9 (0.27)	6.9 (0.34)	9.8 (0.94)	4.2 (0.54)	5.9 (0.35)	6.5 (0.47)	6.3 (1.15)	2.6 (0.58)	7.9 (0.40)	7.4 (0.50)	12.7 (1.42)	6.1 (0.94)
2010[2]												
Total, 3 to 34 years old[1]	56.6 (0.17)	56.1 (0.25)	58.7 (0.58)	55.1 (0.35)	55.9 (0.23)	55.5 (0.29)	58.4 (0.78)	52.9 (0.45)	57.4 (0.26)	56.7 (0.36)	58.9 (0.77)	57.4 (0.49)
3 and 4 years old[1]	53.2 (0.89)	56.1 (1.17)	57.2 (2.78)	44.2 (1.84)	53.0 (1.21)	55.9 (1.64)	57.0 (3.79)	43.3 (2.60)	53.4 (1.27)	56.3 (1.53)	57.4 (3.79)	45.0 (2.68)
5 and 6 years old	94.5 (0.46)	94.2 (0.66)	94.1 (1.12)	94.3 (0.96)	93.7 (0.69)	93.3 (1.04)	93.5 (1.94)	93.4 (1.31)	95.3 (0.54)	95.2 (0.77)	94.7 (1.38)	95.2 (1.20)
7 to 9 years old	97.7 (0.25)	97.4 (0.37)	96.9 (0.77)	98.5 (0.37)	97.6 (0.36)	97.1 (0.54)	97.3 (0.88)	98.1 (0.60)	98.0 (0.35)	97.7 (0.53)	96.5 (1.23)	98.9 (0.40)
10 to 13 years old	98.2 (0.21)	98.3 (0.26)	99.2 (0.41)	97.3 (0.54)	97.9 (0.30)	97.7 (0.42)	99.6 (0.37)	96.9 (0.77)	98.6 (0.26)	98.9 (0.24)	98.8 (0.74)	97.7 (0.61)
14 and 15 years old	98.1 (0.25)	98.0 (0.37)	98.8 (0.58)	97.9 (0.69)	98.0 (0.37)	98.0 (0.52)	98.4 (0.92)	97.5 (0.98)	98.3 (0.34)	98.1 (0.49)	99.3 (0.46)	98.3 (0.85)
16 and 17 years old	96.1 (0.33)	96.2 (0.47)	95.7 (0.82)	96.0 (0.83)	94.9 (0.51)	94.7 (0.74)	93.7 (1.41)	96.0 (1.17)	97.6 (0.47)	97.8 (0.47)	96.0 (0.95)	96.0 (1.10)
18 and 19 years old	69.2 (0.92)	71.0 (1.28)	62.9 (2.42)	66.2 (2.03)	66.9 (1.25)	67.8 (1.63)	62.3 (3.88)	64.9 (3.02)	71.5 (1.38)	74.3 (2.01)	63.4 (3.44)	67.6 (2.78)
20 and 21 years old	52.4 (1.08)	55.5 (1.28)	51.1 (2.93)	37.0 (2.34)	49.2 (1.31)	52.1 (1.76)	45.7 (4.18)	34.0 (3.08)	56.0 (1.47)	59.2 (1.78)	56.0 (3.84)	40.5 (3.36)
22 to 24 years old	28.9 (0.79)	29.1 (1.01)	29.8 (2.13)	23.8 (1.57)	27.0 (1.15)	27.8 (1.44)	29.5 (3.12)	18.6 (2.08)	30.8 (1.10)	30.4 (1.46)	30.4 (2.99)	29.2 (2.16)
25 to 29 years old	14.6 (0.47)	14.6 (0.64)	16.5 (1.34)	11.4 (0.90)	13.5 (0.65)	13.8 (0.84)	13.9 (2.06)	9.6 (1.21)	15.8 (0.66)	15.4 (0.88)	18.8 (1.97)	13.6 (1.44)
30 to 34 years old	8.3 (0.39)	8.5 (0.50)	11.0 (1.14)	5.7 (0.65)	6.7 (0.44)	7.2 (0.62)	6.6 (1.20)	4.9 (0.87)	9.9 (0.58)	9.8 (0.77)	14.8 (1.80)	6.6 (0.95)
2012[2]												
Total, 3 to 34 years old[1]	56.6 (0.22)	55.6 (0.30)	58.9 (0.63)	56.4 (0.46)	55.9 (0.26)	55.0 (0.37)	58.8 (0.87)	54.7 (0.60)	57.4 (0.28)	56.2 (0.36)	59.1 (0.83)	58.2 (0.57)
3 and 4 years old[1]	53.5 (1.11)	56.5 (1.39)	54.8 (3.19)	46.3 (2.24)	52.7 (1.40)	55.6 (1.77)	51.7 (4.37)	45.4 (2.80)	54.4 (1.60)	57.4 (1.96)	57.8 (4.12)	47.1 (3.17)
5 and 6 years old	93.2 (0.49)	93.8 (0.61)	91.9 (1.43)	92.1 (1.11)	93.2 (0.68)	93.6 (0.95)	92.4 (2.03)	92.2 (1.38)	93.3 (0.71)	94.0 (0.83)	92.1 (2.15)	92.1 (1.56)
7 to 9 years old	98.0 (0.22)	98.1 (0.28)	96.8 (0.99)	98.1 (0.49)	97.7 (0.32)	97.7 (0.43)	96.7 (1.28)	98.2 (0.70)	98.4 (0.29)	98.5 (0.37)	98.1 (1.24)	98.1 (0.68)
10 to 13 years old	98.0 (0.20)	97.5 (0.32)	99.1 (0.36)	98.3 (0.39)	98.2 (0.25)	97.7 (0.40)	99.3 (0.42)	98.6 (0.48)	97.8 (0.30)	97.3 (0.48)	98.8 (0.57)	98.0 (0.58)
14 and 15 years old	98.2 (0.31)	98.2 (0.36)	97.4 (1.35)	98.5 (0.51)	98.3 (0.37)	97.9 (0.50)	98.4 (0.98)	98.9 (0.70)	98.0 (0.43)	98.4 (0.52)	96.4 (1.97)	98.1 (0.74)
16 and 17 years old	95.8 (0.40)	96.4 (0.55)	94.5 (1.10)	94.8 (0.96)	95.7 (0.51)	96.0 (0.70)	96.5 (1.32)	95.1 (1.34)	96.0 (0.55)	96.8 (0.71)	92.4 (1.89)	94.5 (1.34)
18 and 19 years old	69.0 (0.98)	68.8 (1.20)	68.9 (2.77)	68.1 (1.64)	65.8 (1.28)	65.4 (1.62)	62.0 (3.93)	65.7 (2.60)	72.3 (1.40)	72.3 (1.73)	75.7 (3.74)	70.7 (2.85)
20 and 21 years old	54.0 (1.04)	55.9 (1.27)	50.7 (3.09)	49.5 (2.28)	49.5 (1.54)	49.7 (1.96)	51.3 (4.14)	44.4 (3.07)	58.3 (1.50)	61.7 (1.84)	55.0 (4.21)	55.0 (3.18)
22 to 24 years old	30.7 (0.84)	30.2 (1.10)	28.4 (2.22)	27.1 (1.76)	29.6 (1.10)	29.6 (1.44)	26.2 (3.04)	24.7 (2.20)	32.1 (1.15)	30.8 (1.48)	30.3 (3.01)	29.7 (2.53)
25 to 29 years old	14.0 (0.48)	14.6 (0.58)	16.6 (1.45)	9.4 (0.88)	13.0 (0.66)	13.0 (0.80)	11.4 (1.86)	7.4 (1.04)	16.0 (0.64)	16.2 (0.82)	20.9 (2.11)	11.5 (1.31)
30 to 34 years old	7.5 (0.33)	6.6 (0.40)	12.4 (1.36)	6.2 (0.70)	5.8 (0.37)	6.1 (0.44)	7.9 (1.68)	3.3 (0.83)	9.2 (0.51)	7.1 (0.63)	16.0 (1.94)	9.3 (1.20)
2013[2]												
Total, 3 to 34 years old[1]	55.8 (0.18)	54.7 (0.26)	57.8 (0.60)	55.5 (0.37)	55.2 (0.23)	54.1 (0.34)	57.3 (0.80)	54.0 (0.54)	56.4 (0.26)	55.4 (0.34)	58.3 (0.83)	57.0 (0.51)
3 and 4 years old[1]	54.9 (1.00)	57.4 (1.50)	61.1 (2.54)	45.4 (2.14)	53.2 (1.46)	55.2 (2.09)	58.2 (4.15)	44.2 (2.78)	56.7 (1.48)	59.7 (1.92)	63.8 (4.13)	46.7 (3.18)
5 and 6 years old	93.8 (0.45)	93.6 (0.63)	94.7 (1.54)	93.9 (0.91)	93.7 (0.64)	93.7 (0.92)	95.2 (1.77)	93.6 (1.17)	93.5 (0.73)	93.5 (0.88)	94.1 (2.68)	94.1 (1.45)
7 to 9 years old	97.9 (0.26)	97.9 (0.34)	96.4 (1.03)	98.4 (0.34)	97.9 (0.34)	97.8 (0.42)	96.2 (1.55)	98.6 (0.43)	97.9 (0.37)	98.0 (0.51)	96.6 (1.35)	98.2 (0.61)
10 to 13 years old	98.2 (0.20)	98.5 (0.24)	96.4 (0.66)	97.7 (0.52)	98.1 (0.28)	98.4 (0.31)	96.2 (0.94)	97.7 (0.58)	98.2 (0.25)	98.5 (0.31)	97.1 (0.88)	97.7 (0.67)
14 and 15 years old	98.4 (0.27)	98.4 (0.38)	98.6 (0.58)	98.3 (0.56)	98.4 (0.40)	98.4 (0.50)	98.7 (0.91)	97.9 (0.90)	98.4 (0.32)	98.4 (0.47)	98.5 (0.81)	98.8 (0.60)
16 and 17 years old	93.7 (0.50)	93.6 (0.64)	92.7 (1.42)	93.9 (1.02)	92.8 (0.70)	92.8 (0.98)	93.7 (1.68)	93.5 (1.44)	94.5 (0.68)	94.5 (0.79)	91.7 (2.41)	94.3 (1.51)
18 and 19 years old	67.1 (1.24)	69.6 (1.62)	64.2 (3.07)	59.3 (1.98)	65.1 (1.31)	68.6 (1.49)	60.8 (4.26)	55.4 (2.99)	69.2 (1.40)	70.8 (1.72)	67.5 (3.92)	63.2 (2.96)
20 and 21 years old	52.8 (1.24)	55.2 (1.62)	48.7 (3.07)	43.9 (2.38)	48.5 (1.62)	50.0 (2.13)	43.5 (4.32)	38.0 (3.16)	57.3 (1.62)	59.6 (2.05)	53.5 (4.26)	50.6 (3.09)
22 to 24 years old	29.7 (0.81)	29.1 (1.02)	28.0 (2.18)	26.7 (1.66)	26.2 (1.14)	26.2 (1.42)	25.7 (3.27)	24.4 (2.18)	33.5 (1.01)	31.9 (1.31)	30.2 (3.01)	29.1 (2.39)
25 to 29 years old	13.3 (0.44)	12.9 (0.57)	17.1 (1.62)	10.4 (0.93)	11.4 (0.61)	11.4 (0.74)	13.2 (2.16)	10.8 (1.39)	14.4 (0.59)	14.3 (0.82)	20.5 (2.06)	10.0 (1.24)
30 to 34 years old	6.7 (0.32)	6.5 (0.37)	9.1 (1.12)	5.7 (0.61)	5.7 (0.37)	5.6 (0.46)	5.7 (1.37)	3.9 (0.75)	8.1 (0.53)	7.4 (0.60)	11.8 (1.71)	7.6 (0.97)

†Not applicable.
!Interpret data with caution. The coefficient of variation (CV) for this estimate is between 30 and 50 percent.
‡Reporting standards not met. The coefficient of variation (CV) for this estimate is 50 percent or greater.
[1]Beginning in 1994, preprimary enrollment data were collected using new procedures. Data may not be comparable to figures for earlier years.
[2]Beginning in 2010, standard errors were computed using replicate weights, which produced more precise values than the generalized variance function methodology used in prior years.

NOTE: Includes enrollment in any type of graded public, parochial, or other private schools. Includes nursery schools, preschools, kindergartens, elementary schools, high schools, colleges, universities, and professional schools. Attendance may be on either a full-time or part-time basis and during the day or night. Total includes persons from other racial/ethnic groups not shown separately. Race categories exclude persons of Hispanic ethnicity.
SOURCE: U.S. Department of Commerce, Census Bureau, Current Population Survey (CPS), October, selected years, 1980 through 2013. (This table was prepared July 2014.)

Table 103.20. Percentage of the population 3 to 34 years old enrolled in school, by age group: Selected years, 1940 through 2013

[Standard errors appear in parentheses]

Year	Total, 3 to 34 years old	3 and 4 years old	5 and 6 years old	7 to 13 years old	14 to 17 years old — Total	14 and 15	16 and 17	18 and 19 years old — Total	In elementary and secondary	In higher education	20 to 24 years old — Total	20 and 21	22 to 24	25 to 29 years old	30 to 34 years old
1	2	3	4	5	6	7	8	9	10	11	12	13	14	15	16
1940	— (†)	(†)	— (†)	95.0 (—)	— (—)	— (†)	— (†)	28.9 (—)	— (—)	— (—)	6.6 (—)	— (†)	— (†)	— (†)	(†)
1945	— (†)	(†)	— (†)	98.1 (—)	— (—)	— (†)	— (†)	20.7 (—)	— (—)	— (—)	3.9 (—)	— (†)	— (†)	— (†)	(†)
1947	— (†)	(†)	73.8 (—)	98.5 (—)	— (—)	91.6 (—)	67.6 (—)	24.3 (—)	— (—)	— (—)	10.2 (—)	— (†)	— (†)	3.0 (—)	1.0 (—)
1948	— (†)	(†)	74.7 (—)	98.1 (—)	— (—)	92.7 (—)	71.2 (—)	26.9 (—)	— (—)	— (—)	9.7 (—)	— (†)	— (†)	2.6 (—)	0.9 (—)
1949	— (†)	(†)	76.2 (—)	98.6 (—)	— (—)	93.5 (—)	69.5 (—)	25.3 (—)	— (—)	— (—)	9.2 (—)	— (†)	— (†)	3.8 (—)	1.1 (—)
1950	— (†)	(†)	74.4 (—)	98.7 (—)	— (—)	94.7 (—)	71.3 (—)	29.4 (—)	— (—)	— (—)	9.0 (—)	— (†)	— (†)	3.0 (—)	0.9 (—)
1951	— (†)	(†)	73.6 (—)	99.1 (—)	— (—)	94.8 (—)	75.1 (—)	26.2 (—)	— (—)	— (—)	8.6 (—)	— (†)	— (†)	2.5 (—)	0.7 (—)
1952	— (†)	(†)	75.2 (—)	98.8 (—)	— (—)	96.2 (—)	73.4 (—)	28.8 (—)	— (—)	— (—)	9.7 (—)	— (†)	— (†)	2.6 (—)	1.2 (—)
1953	— (†)	(†)	78.6 (—)	99.4 (—)	— (—)	96.5 (—)	74.7 (—)	31.2 (—)	— (—)	— (—)	11.1 (—)	— (†)	— (†)	2.9 (—)	1.7 (—)
1954	— (†)	(†)	77.3 (—)	99.4 (—)	— (—)	95.8 (—)	78.0 (—)	32.4 (—)	— (—)	— (—)	11.2 (—)	— (†)	— (†)	4.1 (—)	1.5 (—)
1955	— (†)	(†)	78.1 (—)	99.2 (—)	— (—)	95.9 (—)	77.4 (—)	31.5 (—)	— (—)	— (—)	11.1 (—)	— (†)	— (†)	4.2 (—)	1.6 (—)
1956	— (†)	(†)	77.6 (—)	99.3 (—)	— (—)	96.9 (—)	78.4 (—)	35.4 (—)	— (—)	— (—)	12.8 (—)	— (†)	— (†)	5.1 (—)	1.9 (—)
1957	— (†)	(†)	78.6 (—)	99.5 (—)	— (—)	97.1 (—)	80.5 (—)	34.9 (—)	— (—)	— (—)	14.0 (—)	— (†)	— (†)	5.5 (—)	1.8 (—)
1958	— (†)	(†)	80.4 (—)	99.5 (—)	— (—)	96.9 (—)	80.6 (—)	37.6 (—)	— (—)	— (—)	13.4 (—)	— (†)	— (†)	5.7 (—)	2.2 (—)
1959	— (†)	9.5 (—)	80.0 (—)	99.4 (—)	— (—)	97.5 (—)	82.9 (—)	36.8 (—)	— (—)	— (—)	12.7 (—)	18.8 (—)	8.6 (—)	5.1 (—)	2.2 (—)
1960	— (†)	10.6 (—)	80.7 (—)	99.5 (—)	— (—)	97.8 (—)	82.6 (—)	38.4 (—)	— (—)	— (—)	13.1 (—)	19.4 (—)	8.7 (—)	4.9 (—)	2.4 (—)
1961	— (†)	12.5 (—)	81.7 (—)	99.3 (—)	— (—)	97.6 (—)	83.6 (—)	38.0 (—)	— (—)	— (—)	13.7 (—)	21.5 (—)	8.4 (—)	4.4 (—)	2.0 (—)
1962	— (†)	14.2 (—)	82.2 (—)	99.3 (—)	— (—)	98.0 (—)	84.3 (—)	41.8 (—)	— (—)	— (—)	15.6 (—)	23.0 (—)	10.3 (—)	5.0 (—)	2.6 (—)
1963	— (†)	15.7 (—)	82.7 (—)	99.3 (—)	— (—)	98.4 (—)	87.1 (—)	40.9 (—)	10.9 (—)	29.8 (—)	17.3 (—)	25.0 (—)	11.4 (—)	4.9 (—)	2.5 (—)
1964	— (†)	16.1 (—)	83.3 (—)	99.0 (—)	— (—)	98.6 (—)	87.7 (—)	41.6 (—)	11.0 (—)	30.6 (—)	16.8 (—)	26.3 (—)	9.9 (—)	5.2 (—)	2.6 (—)
1965	55.5 (—)	— (—)	84.9 (—)	99.4 (—)	— (—)	98.9 (—)	87.4 (—)	46.3 (—)	11.2 (—)	35.0 (—)	19.0 (—)	27.6 (—)	13.2 (—)	6.1 (—)	3.2 (—)
1966	56.1 (—)	— (—)	85.8 (—)	99.3 (—)	— (—)	98.6 (—)	88.5 (—)	47.2 (—)	10.8 (—)	36.3 (—)	19.9 (—)	29.9 (—)	13.2 (—)	6.5 (—)	2.7 (—)
1967	56.6 (—)	— (—)	87.4 (—)	99.3 (—)	— (—)	98.2 (—)	88.8 (—)	47.6 (—)	11.7 (—)	36.0 (—)	22.0 (—)	33.3 (—)	13.6 (—)	6.6 (—)	4.0 (—)
1968	56.7 (—)	— (—)	87.6 (—)	99.1 (—)	— (—)	98.0 (—)	90.2 (—)	50.4 (—)	12.4 (—)	38.0 (—)	21.4 (—)	31.2 (—)	13.8 (—)	7.0 (—)	3.9 (—)
1969	57.0 (—)	— (—)	88.4 (—)	99.2 (—)	— (—)	98.1 (—)	89.7 (—)	50.2 (—)	11.2 (—)	39.0 (—)	23.0 (—)	34.1 (—)	15.4 (—)	7.9 (—)	4.8 (—)
1970	56.4 (0.22)	20.5 (0.74)	89.5 (0.54)	99.2 (0.07)	94.1 (0.27)	98.1 (0.22)	90.0 (0.50)	47.7 (0.87)	10.5 (0.53)	37.3 (0.84)	21.5 (0.48)	31.9 (0.87)	14.9 (0.53)	7.5 (0.33)	4.2 (0.27)
1971	56.2 (0.22)	21.2 (0.76)	91.6 (0.50)	99.1 (0.08)	94.5 (0.26)	98.6 (0.19)	90.2 (0.49)	49.2 (0.85)	11.5 (0.54)	37.7 (0.83)	21.9 (0.47)	32.2 (0.85)	15.4 (0.52)	8.0 (0.33)	4.9 (0.29)
1972	54.9 (0.22)	24.4 (0.81)	91.9 (0.51)	99.2 (0.08)	93.3 (0.28)	97.6 (0.24)	88.9 (0.51)	46.3 (0.84)	10.4 (0.51)	35.9 (0.81)	21.6 (0.46)	31.4 (0.81)	14.8 (0.51)	8.6 (0.34)	4.6 (0.28)
1973	53.5 (0.22)	24.2 (0.80)	92.5 (0.50)	99.2 (0.08)	92.9 (0.29)	97.5 (0.25)	88.3 (0.52)	42.9 (0.82)	10.0 (0.50)	32.9 (0.78)	20.8 (0.44)	30.1 (0.79)	14.5 (0.50)	8.5 (0.33)	4.5 (0.27)
1974	53.6 (0.22)	28.8 (0.85)	94.2 (0.44)	99.3 (0.07)	92.9 (0.29)	97.9 (0.23)	87.9 (0.52)	43.1 (0.81)	9.9 (0.49)	33.2 (0.77)	21.4 (0.45)	30.2 (0.77)	15.1 (0.51)	9.6 (0.34)	5.7 (0.29)
1975	53.7 (0.22)	31.5 (0.89)	94.7 (0.42)	99.3 (0.08)	93.6 (0.27)	98.2 (0.21)	89.0 (0.50)	46.9 (0.81)	10.2 (0.49)	36.7 (0.78)	22.4 (0.45)	31.2 (0.77)	16.2 (0.52)	10.1 (0.34)	6.6 (0.31)
1976	53.1 (0.21)	31.3 (0.91)	95.5 (0.38)	99.2 (0.08)	93.7 (0.27)	98.2 (0.21)	89.1 (0.50)	46.2 (0.80)	10.2 (0.49)	36.0 (0.77)	23.3 (0.45)	32.0 (0.77)	17.1 (0.52)	10.0 (0.33)	6.0 (0.29)
1977	52.5 (0.21)	32.0 (0.94)	95.8 (0.38)	99.4 (0.07)	93.7 (0.28)	98.5 (0.20)	88.9 (0.50)	46.2 (0.80)	10.4 (0.49)	35.7 (0.77)	22.9 (0.44)	31.8 (0.76)	16.5 (0.51)	10.8 (0.34)	6.9 (0.30)
1978	51.2 (0.21)	34.2 (0.95)	95.3 (0.42)	99.1 (0.09)	93.7 (0.28)	98.4 (0.20)	89.1 (0.50)	45.4 (0.80)	9.8 (0.48)	35.6 (0.77)	21.8 (0.43)	29.5 (0.74)	16.3 (0.50)	9.4 (0.32)	6.4 (0.28)
1979	50.3 (0.21)	35.1 (0.95)	95.8 (0.40)	99.2 (0.08)	93.6 (0.28)	98.1 (0.22)	89.2 (0.50)	45.0 (0.80)	10.3 (0.49)	34.6 (0.76)	21.7 (0.43)	30.2 (0.74)	15.8 (0.49)	9.6 (0.32)	6.4 (0.28)
1980	49.7 (0.21)	36.7 (0.95)	95.7 (0.40)	99.3 (0.08)	93.4 (0.29)	98.2 (0.22)	89.0 (0.51)	46.4 (0.80)	13.5 (0.49)	35.9 (0.77)	22.3 (0.43)	31.0 (0.75)	16.3 (0.49)	9.3 (0.31)	6.4 (0.27)
1981	48.9 (0.21)	36.0 (0.93)	94.0 (0.46)	99.2 (0.08)	94.1 (0.28)	98.0 (0.24)	90.6 (0.47)	49.0 (0.81)	11.5 (0.51)	37.5 (0.78)	22.5 (0.42)	31.6 (0.74)	16.5 (0.48)	9.0 (0.30)	6.9 (0.27)
1982	48.6 (0.22)	36.4 (0.97)	95.0 (0.45)	99.2 (0.09)	94.4 (0.29)	98.5 (0.22)	90.6 (0.51)	47.8 (0.86)	11.3 (0.54)	36.5 (0.83)	23.5 (0.45)	34.0 (0.81)	16.8 (0.51)	9.6 (0.32)	6.3 (0.28)
1983	48.4 (0.22)	37.5 (0.96)	95.4 (0.43)	99.2 (0.09)	95.0 (0.28)	98.3 (0.23)	91.7 (0.50)	50.4 (0.87)	12.8 (0.58)	37.6 (0.84)	22.7 (0.45)	32.5 (0.80)	16.6 (0.51)	9.6 (0.32)	6.4 (0.28)
1984	47.9 (0.22)	36.3 (0.94)	94.5 (0.46)	99.2 (0.09)	94.7 (0.29)	97.8 (0.26)	91.5 (0.51)	50.1 (0.89)	11.5 (0.57)	38.6 (0.87)	23.7 (0.46)	33.9 (0.82)	17.3 (0.52)	9.1 (0.30)	6.3 (0.27)

See notes at end of table.

Table 103.20. Percentage of the population 3 to 34 years old enrolled in school, by age group: Selected years, 1940 through 2013—Continued

[Standard errors appear in parentheses]

Year	Total, 3 to 34 years old	3 and 4 years old	5 and 6 years old	7 to 13 years old	14 to 17 years old			18 and 19 years old			20 to 24 years old			25 to 29 years old	30 to 34 years old
					Total	14 and 15	16 and 17	Total	In elementary and secondary	In higher education	Total	20 and 21	22 to 24		
1	2	3	4	5	6	7	8	9	10	11	12	13	14	15	16
1985	48.3 (0.22)	38.9 (0.95)	96.1 (0.38)	99.2 (0.09)	94.9 (0.28)	98.1 (0.24)	91.7 (0.50)	51.6 (0.91)	11.2 (0.57)	40.4 (0.89)	24.0 (0.47)	35.3 (0.84)	16.9 (0.52)	9.2 (0.31)	6.1 (0.26)
1986	48.2 (0.22)	38.9 (0.95)	95.3 (0.41)	99.2 (0.09)	94.9 (0.28)	97.6 (0.28)	92.3 (0.48)	54.6 (0.91)	13.1 (0.62)	41.5 (0.90)	23.6 (0.47)	33.0 (0.84)	17.9 (0.54)	8.8 (0.30)	6.0 (0.25)
1987	48.6 (0.22)	38.3 (0.95)	95.1 (0.42)	99.5 (0.07)	95.0 (0.28)	98.6 (0.22)	91.7 (0.49)	55.6 (0.90)	13.1 (0.61)	42.5 (0.90)	25.5 (0.49)	38.7 (0.89)	17.5 (0.54)	9.0 (0.30)	5.8 (0.25)
1988	48.7 (0.24)	38.2 (1.02)	96.0 (0.41)	99.7 (0.06)	95.1 (0.31)	98.9 (0.22)	91.6 (0.55)	55.6 (0.98)	13.9 (0.68)	41.8 (0.97)	26.1 (0.54)	39.1 (0.98)	18.2 (0.60)	8.3 (0.32)	5.9 (0.27)
1989	49.0 (0.23)	39.1 (0.97)	95.2 (0.43)	99.3 (0.08)	95.7 (0.28)	98.8 (0.21)	92.7 (0.50)	56.0 (0.92)	14.4 (0.65)	41.6 (0.91)	27.0 (0.53)	38.5 (0.94)	19.9 (0.60)	9.3 (0.32)	5.7 (0.25)
1990	50.2 (0.23)	44.4 (0.99)	96.5 (0.37)	99.6 (0.06)	95.8 (0.28)	99.0 (0.19)	92.5 (0.52)	57.2 (0.94)	14.5 (0.67)	42.7 (0.94)	28.6 (0.54)	39.7 (0.92)	21.0 (0.63)	9.7 (0.33)	5.8 (0.25)
1991	50.7 (0.23)	40.5 (0.96)	95.4 (0.41)	99.6 (0.06)	96.0 (0.27)	98.8 (0.22)	93.3 (0.49)	59.6 (0.96)	15.6 (0.71)	44.0 (0.97)	30.2 (0.55)	42.0 (0.92)	22.2 (0.64)	10.2 (0.34)	6.2 (0.26)
1992	51.4 (0.23)	39.7	95.5 (0.41)	99.4 (0.08)	96.7 (0.25)	99.1 (0.18)	94.1 (0.46)	61.4 (0.96)	17.1 (0.74)	44.3 (0.98)	31.6 (0.56)	44.0 (0.95)	23.7 (0.65)	9.8 (0.34)	6.1 (0.26)
1993	51.8 (0.23)	40.4 (0.93)	95.4 (0.41)	99.5 (0.07)	96.5 (0.25)	98.9 (0.20)	94.0 (0.46)	61.6 (0.95)	17.2 (0.74)	44.4 (0.97)	30.8 (0.56)	42.7 (0.97)	23.6 (0.65)	10.2 (0.35)	5.9 (0.25)
1994	53.3 (0.23)	47.3[1] (0.94)	96.7 (0.34)	99.4 (0.08)	96.6 (0.24)	98.8 (0.20)	94.4 (0.43)	60.2 (0.94)	16.2 (0.70)	43.9 (0.95)	32.0 (0.55)	44.9 (0.95)	24.0 (0.64)	10.8 (0.36)	6.7 (0.27)
1995	53.7 (0.21)	48.7[1] (0.87)	96.0 (0.34)	98.9 (0.09)	96.3 (0.23)	98.9 (0.18)	93.6 (0.42)	59.4 (0.86)	16.3 (0.64)	43.1 (0.86)	31.5 (0.52)	44.9 (0.90)	23.2 (0.60)	11.6 (0.34)	5.9 (0.24)
1996	54.1 (0.22)	48.3[1] (0.91)	94.0 (0.43)	97.7 (0.14)	95.4 (0.26)	98.0 (0.24)	92.8 (0.45)	61.5 (0.87)	16.7 (0.67)	44.9 (0.89)	32.5 (0.55)	44.4 (0.93)	24.8 (0.65)	11.9 (0.36)	6.1 (0.25)
1997	55.6 (0.22)	52.6[1] (0.92)	96.5 (0.33)	99.1 (0.09)	96.6 (0.22)	98.9 (0.18)	94.3 (0.40)	61.5 (0.86)	16.7 (0.66)	44.7 (0.88)	34.3 (0.55)	45.9 (0.91)	26.4 (0.66)	11.8 (0.36)	5.7 (0.25)
1998	55.8 (0.22)	52.1[1] (0.92)	95.6 (0.37)	98.9 (0.10)	96.1 (0.24)	98.4 (0.22)	93.9 (0.41)	62.2 (0.84)	15.7 (0.63)	46.4 (0.86)	33.0 (0.54)	44.8 (0.91)	24.9 (0.65)	11.9 (0.36)	6.6 (0.27)
1999	56.0 (0.22)	54.2[1] (0.93)	96.0 (0.36)	98.7 (0.10)	95.8 (0.24)	98.2 (0.23)	93.6 (0.42)	60.6 (0.84)	16.5 (0.64)	44.1 (0.85)	32.8 (0.54)	45.3 (0.90)	24.5 (0.64)	11.1 (0.36)	6.2 (0.27)
2000	55.9 (0.22)	52.1[1] (0.93)	95.6 (0.38)	98.2 (0.12)	95.7 (0.25)	98.7 (0.20)	92.8 (0.45)	61.2 (0.84)	16.5 (0.64)	44.7 (0.85)	32.5 (0.53)	44.1 (0.88)	24.6 (0.63)	11.4 (0.37)	6.7 (0.27)
2001	56.4 (0.20)	52.4[1] (0.88)	95.3 (0.37)	98.3 (0.11)	95.8 (0.23)	98.1 (0.22)	93.4 (0.40)	61.1 (0.79)	17.1 (0.61)	44.0 (0.80)	34.1 (0.50)	46.1 (0.82)	25.5 (0.61)	11.8 (0.36)	6.9 (0.26)
2002	56.2 (0.20)	56.3[1] (0.89)	95.5 (0.37)	98.3 (0.11)	96.4 (0.21)	98.4 (0.20)	94.3 (0.37)	63.3 (0.79)	18.0 (0.63)	45.3 (0.82)	34.4 (0.50)	47.8 (0.83)	25.6 (0.59)	12.1 (0.35)	6.6 (0.25)
2003	56.2 (0.20)	55.1[1] (0.85)	94.5 (0.40)	98.3 (0.11)	96.2 (0.21)	97.5 (0.25)	94.9 (0.34)	64.5 (0.80)	17.9 (0.64)	46.6 (0.84)	35.6 (0.50)	48.3 (0.83)	27.8 (0.59)	11.8 (0.34)	6.8 (0.26)
2004	56.2 (0.20)	54.0[1] (0.85)	95.4 (0.37)	98.4 (0.11)	96.5 (0.21)	98.5 (0.19)	94.5 (0.36)	64.4 (0.80)	16.6 (0.62)	47.8 (0.83)	35.2 (0.49)	48.9 (0.82)	26.3 (0.58)	13.0 (0.35)	6.6 (0.26)
2005	56.5 (0.20)	53.6[1] (0.86)	95.4 (0.37)	98.6 (0.10)	96.5 (0.20)	98.0 (0.22)	95.1 (0.33)	67.6 (0.79)	18.3 (0.65)	49.3 (0.84)	36.1 (0.49)	48.7 (0.80)	27.3 (0.59)	11.9 (0.34)	6.9 (0.27)
2006	56.0 (0.20)	55.7[1] (0.86)	94.6 (0.39)	98.3 (0.11)	96.4 (0.21)	98.3 (0.21)	94.6 (0.36)	65.5 (0.77)	19.3 (0.64)	46.2 (0.81)	35.0 (0.49)	47.5 (0.81)	26.7 (0.58)	11.7 (0.33)	7.2 (0.27)
2007	56.1 (0.20)	54.5[1] (0.86)	94.7 (0.39)	98.4 (0.11)	96.4 (0.21)	98.7 (0.18)	94.3 (0.36)	66.8 (0.75)	17.9 (0.61)	48.9 (0.80)	35.7 (0.49)	48.4 (0.81)	27.3 (0.59)	12.4 (0.33)	7.2 (0.27)
2008	56.2 (0.20)	52.8[1] (0.85)	93.8 (0.42)	98.7 (0.10)	96.8 (0.20)	98.6 (0.19)	95.2 (0.34)	66.0 (0.75)	17.4 (0.60)	48.6 (0.79)	36.9 (0.49)	50.1 (0.81)	28.2 (0.59)	13.2 (0.34)	7.3 (0.27)
2009	56.5 (0.20)	52.4[1] (0.85)	94.1 (0.40)	98.2 (0.12)	96.3 (0.22)	98.0 (0.23)	94.6 (0.36)	68.9 (0.73)	19.1 (0.62)	49.8 (0.79)	38.7 (0.50)	51.7 (0.81)	30.4 (0.60)	13.5 (0.34)	8.1 (0.28)
2010[2]	56.6 (0.17)	53.2[1] (0.89)	94.5 (0.46)	98.0 (0.16)	97.1 (0.21)	98.1 (0.25)	96.1 (0.33)	69.2 (0.92)	18.1 (0.71)	51.2 (1.05)	38.6 (0.71)	52.4 (1.08)	28.9 (0.79)	14.6 (0.47)	8.3 (0.39)
2011[2]	56.8 (0.19)	52.4[1] (0.90)	95.1 (0.43)	98.3 (0.14)	97.1 (0.22)	98.6 (0.21)	95.7 (0.38)	71.1 (0.95)	21.0 (0.78)	50.1 (1.08)	39.9 (0.68)	52.7 (1.05)	31.1 (0.82)	14.8 (0.44)	7.7 (0.32)
2012[2]	56.6 (0.22)	53.5[1] (1.11)	93.2 (0.49)	98.0 (0.17)	97.0 (0.28)	98.2 (0.31)	95.8 (0.40)	69.0 (0.98)	21.7 (0.77)	47.3 (0.96)	40.2 (0.72)	54.0 (1.04)	30.7 (0.84)	14.0 (0.48)	7.5 (0.33)
2013[2]	55.8 (0.18)	54.9[1] (1.00)	93.8 (0.45)	98.1 (0.16)	96.1 (0.28)	98.4 (0.27)	93.7 (0.50)	67.1 (0.97)	20.5 (0.80)	46.6 (1.00)	38.7 (0.76)	52.8 (1.24)	29.7 (0.81)	13.3 (0.44)	6.7 (0.32)

—Not available.
†Not applicable.
[1]Beginning in 1994, preprimary enrollment data were collected using new procedures. Data may not be comparable to figures for earlier years.
[2]Beginning in 2010, standard errors were computed using replicate weights, which produced more precise values than the generalized variance function methodology used in prior years.

NOTE: Data for 1940 are for April. Data for all other years are as of October. Includes enrollment in any type of graded public, parochial, or other private schools. Includes nursery schools, kindergartens, elementary schools, high schools, colleges, universities, and professional schools. Attendance may be on either a full-time or part-time basis and during the day or night.
SOURCE: U.S. Department of Commerce, Census Bureau, *Historical Statistics of the United States, Colonial Times to 1970: Current Population Reports,* Series P-20, various years; CPS Historical Time Series Tables on School Enrollment, retrieved June 6, 2012, from http://www.census.gov/hhes/school/data/cps/historical/index.html; and Current Population Survey, October, 1970 through 2013. (This table was prepared July 2014.)

Table 104.10. Rates of high school completion and bachelor's degree attainment among persons age 25 and over, by race/ethnicity and sex: Selected years, 1910 through 2014

[Standard errors appear in parentheses]

Sex, high school or bachelor's degree attainment, and year	Total, percent of all persons age 25 and over		White[1]		Black[1]		Hispanic		Asian/Pacific Islander Total		Asian		Pacific Islander		American Indian/ Alaska Native		Two or more races	
1	2		3		4		5		6		7		8		9		10	
Total																		
High school completion or higher[2]																		
1910[3]	13.5	(—)	—	(†)	—	(†)	—	(†)	—	(†)	—	(†)	—	(†)	—	(†)	—	(†)
1920[3]	16.4	(—)	—	(†)	—	(†)	—	(†)	—	(†)	—	(†)	—	(†)	—	(†)	—	(†)
1930[3]	19.1	(—)	—	(†)	—	(†)	—	(†)	—	(†)	—	(†)	—	(†)	—	(†)	—	(†)
1940	24.5	(—)	26.1	(—)	7.7	(—)	—	(†)	—	(†)	—	(†)	—	(†)	—	(†)	—	(†)
1950	34.3	(—)	36.4	(—)	13.7	(—)	—	(†)	—	(†)	—	(†)	—	(†)	—	(†)	—	(†)
1960	41.1	(—)	43.2	(—)	21.7	(—)	—	(†)	—	(†)	—	(†)	—	(†)	—	(†)	—	(†)
1970	55.2	(—)	57.4	(—)	36.1	(—)	—	(†)	—	(†)	—	(†)	—	(†)	—	(†)	—	(†)
1975	62.5	(—)	65.8	(—)	42.6	(—)	38.5	(—)	—	(†)	—	(†)	—	(†)	—	(†)	—	(†)
1980	68.6	(0.20)	71.9	(0.21)	51.4	(0.81)	44.5	(1.18)	—	(†)	—	(†)	—	(†)	—	(†)	—	(†)
1985	73.9	(0.18)	77.5	(0.19)	59.9	(0.74)	47.9	(0.99)	—	(†)	—	(†)	—	(†)	—	(†)	—	(†)
1986	74.7	(0.18)	78.2	(0.19)	62.5	(0.72)	48.5	(0.96)	—	(†)	—	(†)	—	(†)	—	(†)	—	(†)
1987	75.6	(0.17)	79.0	(0.18)	63.6	(0.71)	50.9	(0.94)	—	(†)	—	(†)	—	(†)	—	(†)	—	(†)
1988	76.2	(0.17)	79.8	(0.18)	63.5	(0.70)	51.0	(0.92)	—	(†)	—	(†)	—	(†)	—	(†)	—	(†)
1989	76.9	(0.17)	80.7	(0.18)	64.7	(0.69)	50.9	(0.89)	82.3	(1.17)	—	(†)	—	(†)	—	(†)	—	(†)
1990	77.6	(0.17)	81.4	(0.17)	66.2	(0.67)	50.8	(0.88)	84.2	(1.09)	—	(†)	—	(†)	—	(†)	—	(†)
1991	78.4	(0.16)	82.4	(0.17)	66.8	(0.66)	51.3	(0.86)	84.2	(1.05)	—	(†)	—	(†)	—	(†)	—	(†)
1992	79.4	(0.16)	83.4	(0.16)	67.7	(0.65)	52.6	(0.85)	83.7	(1.02)	—	(†)	—	(†)	—	(†)	—	(†)
1993	80.2	(0.16)	84.1	(0.16)	70.5	(0.63)	53.1	(0.83)	84.2	(1.00)	—	(†)	—	(†)	—	(†)	—	(†)
1994	80.9	(0.15)	84.9	(0.16)	73.0	(0.61)	53.3	(0.78)	84.8	(0.98)	—	(†)	—	(†)	—	(†)	—	(†)
1995	81.7	(0.15)	85.9	(0.16)	73.8	(0.61)	53.4	(0.78)	83.8	(1.06)	—	(†)	—	(†)	—	(†)	—	(†)
1996	81.7	(0.16)	86.0	(0.16)	74.6	(0.53)	53.1	(0.68)	83.5	(0.82)	—	(†)	—	(†)	—	(†)	—	(†)
1997	82.1	(0.14)	86.3	(0.15)	75.3	(0.52)	54.7	(0.54)	85.2	(0.75)	—	(†)	—	(†)	—	(†)	—	(†)
1998	82.8	(0.14)	87.1	(0.14)	76.4	(0.50)	55.5	(0.53)	84.9	(0.74)	—	(†)	—	(†)	—	(†)	—	(†)
1999	83.4	(0.14)	87.7	(0.14)	77.4	(0.49)	56.1	(0.52)	84.7	(0.73)	—	(†)	—	(†)	—	(†)	—	(†)
2000	84.1	(0.13)	88.4	(0.14)	78.9	(0.48)	57.0	(0.51)	85.7	(0.71)	—	(†)	—	(†)	—	(†)	—	(†)
2001	84.3	(0.13)	88.7	(0.13)	79.5	(0.47)	56.5	(0.50)	87.8	(0.60)	—	(†)	—	(†)	—	(†)	—	(†)
2002	84.1	(0.09)	88.7	(0.10)	79.2	(0.34)	57.0	(0.34)	87.7	(0.44)	—	(†)	—	(†)	—	(†)	—	(†)
2003	84.6	(0.09)	89.4	(0.09)	80.3	(0.33)	57.0	(0.33)	87.8	(0.43)	87.8	(0.44)	88.2	(1.87)	77.2	(1.64)	86.1	(0.97)
2004	85.2	(0.09)	90.0	(0.09)	81.1	(0.32)	58.4	(0.32)	86.9	(0.43)	86.9	(0.44)	88.5	(1.91)	77.8	(1.61)	87.2	(0.91)
2005	85.2	(0.14)	90.1	(0.16)	81.4	(0.44)	58.5	(0.35)	87.8	(0.62)	87.7	(0.62)	90.1	(2.69)	75.6	(2.02)	88.6	(0.83)
2006	85.5	(0.15)	90.5	(0.15)	81.2	(0.43)	59.3	(0.58)	87.5	(0.71)	87.5	(0.71)	85.7	(2.51)	78.5	(2.11)	88.1	(0.90)
2007	85.7	(0.15)	90.6	(0.15)	82.8	(0.39)	60.3	(0.56)	88.0	(0.79)	87.9	(0.81)	88.6	(2.30)	80.3	(2.27)	89.3	(0.87)
2008	86.6	(0.15)	91.5	(0.15)	83.3	(0.40)	62.3	(0.58)	89.0	(0.62)	88.8	(0.64)	94.4	(1.00)	78.4	(2.74)	89.5	(1.12)
2009	86.7	(0.15)	91.6	(0.15)	84.2	(0.44)	61.9	(0.56)	88.4	(0.61)	88.3	(0.63)	90.8	(1.76)	81.5	(1.83)	87.4	(0.96)
2010	87.1	(0.13)	92.1	(0.14)	84.6	(0.41)	62.9	(0.53)	89.1	(0.67)	89.1	(0.68)	90.2	(1.95)	80.8	(1.76)	88.9	(0.90)
2011	87.6	(0.13)	92.4	(0.14)	84.8	(0.41)	64.3	(0.54)	88.8	(0.55)	88.7	(0.57)	90.4	(1.61)	82.3	(1.77)	89.4	(1.00)
2012	87.6	(0.15)	92.5	(0.14)	85.7	(0.40)	65.0	(0.59)	89.2	(0.59)	89.0	(0.61)	91.6	(1.33)	81.8	(1.69)	91.0	(0.89)
2013	88.2	(0.14)	92.9	(0.13)	85.9	(0.42)	66.2	(0.52)	90.2	(0.51)	90.2	(0.53)	89.5	(1.72)	82.2	(1.68)	92.6	(0.75)
2014	88.3	(0.15)	93.1	(0.17)	86.7	(0.45)	66.5	(0.57)	89.5	(0.62)	89.5	(0.64)	88.8	(2.15)	81.0	(2.01)	93.3	(0.88)
Bachelor's or higher degree[4]																		
1910[3]	2.7	(—)	—	(†)	—	(†)	—	(†)	—	(†)	—	(†)	—	(†)	—	(†)	—	(†)
1920[3]	3.3	(—)	—	(†)	—	(†)	—	(†)	—	(†)	—	(†)	—	(†)	—	(†)	—	(†)
1930[3]	3.9	(—)	—	(†)	—	(†)	—	(†)	—	(†)	—	(†)	—	(†)	—	(†)	—	(†)
1940	4.6	(—)	4.9	(—)	1.3	(—)	—	(†)	—	(†)	—	(†)	—	(†)	—	(†)	—	(†)
1950	6.2	(—)	6.6	(—)	2.2	(—)	—	(†)	—	(†)	—	(†)	—	(†)	—	(†)	—	(†)
1960	7.7	(—)	8.1	(—)	3.5	(—)	—	(†)	—	(†)	—	(†)	—	(†)	—	(†)	—	(†)
1970	11.0	(—)	11.6	(—)	6.1	(—)	—	(†)	—	(†)	—	(†)	—	(†)	—	(†)	—	(†)
1975	13.9	(—)	14.9	(—)	6.4	(—)	6.6	(—)	—	(†)	—	(†)	—	(†)	—	(†)	—	(†)
1980	17.0	(0.16)	18.4	(0.18)	7.9	(0.44)	7.6	(0.63)	—	(†)	—	(†)	—	(†)	—	(†)	—	(†)
1985	19.4	(0.16)	20.8	(0.19)	11.1	(0.47)	8.5	(0.55)	—	(†)	—	(†)	—	(†)	—	(†)	—	(†)
1986	19.4	(0.16)	20.9	(0.19)	10.9	(0.47)	8.4	(0.53)	—	(†)	—	(†)	—	(†)	—	(†)	—	(†)
1987	19.9	(0.16)	21.4	(0.19)	10.8	(0.46)	8.6	(0.53)	—	(†)	—	(†)	—	(†)	—	(†)	—	(†)
1988	20.3	(0.16)	21.8	(0.19)	11.2	(0.46)	10.0	(0.55)	—	(†)	—	(†)	—	(†)	—	(†)	—	(†)
1989	21.1	(0.16)	22.8	(0.19)	11.7	(0.46)	9.9	(0.53)	41.5	(1.51)	—	(†)	—	(†)	—	(†)	—	(†)
1990	21.3	(0.16)	23.1	(0.19)	11.3	(0.45)	9.2	(0.51)	41.7	(1.47)	—	(†)	—	(†)	—	(†)	—	(†)
1991	21.4	(0.16)	23.3	(0.19)	11.5	(0.45)	9.7	(0.51)	40.3	(1.42)	—	(†)	—	(†)	—	(†)	—	(†)
1992	21.4	(0.16)	23.2	(0.19)	11.9	(0.45)	9.3	(0.49)	39.3	(1.35)	—	(†)	—	(†)	—	(†)	—	(†)
1993	21.9	(0.16)	23.8	(0.19)	12.2	(0.45)	9.0	(0.48)	42.1	(1.35)	—	(†)	—	(†)	—	(†)	—	(†)
1994	22.2	(0.16)	24.3	(0.19)	12.9	(0.46)	9.1	(0.45)	41.3	(1.34)	—	(†)	—	(†)	—	(†)	—	(†)
1995	23.0	(0.16)	25.4	(0.19)	13.3	(0.47)	9.3	(0.45)	38.5	(1.40)	—	(†)	—	(†)	—	(†)	—	(†)
1996	23.6	(0.17)	25.9	(0.20)	13.8	(0.42)	9.3	(0.40)	42.3	(1.09)	—	(†)	—	(†)	—	(†)	—	(†)
1997	23.9	(0.16)	26.2	(0.19)	13.3	(0.41)	10.3	(0.33)	42.6	(1.04)	—	(†)	—	(†)	—	(†)	—	(†)
1998	24.4	(0.16)	26.6	(0.19)	14.8	(0.42)	11.0	(0.33)	42.3	(1.02)	—	(†)	—	(†)	—	(†)	—	(†)
1999	25.2	(0.16)	27.7	(0.19)	15.5	(0.43)	10.9	(0.33)	42.4	(1.01)	—	(†)	—	(†)	—	(†)	—	(†)
2000	25.6	(0.16)	28.1	(0.19)	16.6	(0.44)	10.6	(0.32)	44.4	(1.00)	—	(†)	—	(†)	—	(†)	—	(†)
2001	26.1	(0.16)	28.6	(0.19)	16.1	(0.43)	11.2	(0.32)	48.0	(0.92)	—	(†)	—	(†)	—	(†)	—	(†)
2002	26.7	(0.11)	29.4	(0.14)	17.2	(0.31)	11.1	(0.21)	47.7	(0.66)	—	(†)	—	(†)	—	(†)	—	(†)
2003	27.2	(0.11)	30.0	(0.14)	17.4	(0.31)	11.4	(0.21)	48.8	(0.65)	50.0	(0.67)	27.0	(2.56)	12.6	(1.30)	22.0	(1.17)
2004	27.7	(0.11)	30.6	(0.14)	17.7	(0.31)	12.1	(0.21)	48.9	(0.64)	49.7	(0.66)	32.4	(2.81)	14.3	(1.36)	21.8	(1.13)
2005	27.7	(0.23)	30.6	(0.29)	17.6	(0.45)	12.0	(0.31)	49.3	(0.91)	50.4	(0.93)	24.6	(3.67)	14.5	(1.51)	23.2	(1.19)

See notes at end of table.

Table 104.10.   Rates of high school completion and bachelor's degree attainment among persons age 25 and over, by race/ethnicity and sex: Selected years, 1910 through 2014—Continued

[Standard errors appear in parentheses]

Sex, high school or bachelor's degree attainment, and year	Total, percent of all persons age 25 and over		White[1]		Black[1]		Hispanic		Asian/Pacific Islander Total		Asian		Pacific Islander		American Indian/ Alaska Native		Two or more races	
1	2		3		4		5		6		7		8		9		10	
2006	28.0	(0.20)	31.0	(0.25)	18.6	(0.47)	12.4	(0.32)	49.1	(1.04)	50.0	(1.06)	26.9	(3.42)	12.9	(1.60)	23.1	(1.28)
2007	28.7	(0.21)	31.8	(0.27)	18.7	(0.51)	12.7	(0.31)	51.2	(1.02)	52.5	(1.03)	23.8	(3.30)	13.1	(1.24)	23.7	(1.30)
2008	29.4	(0.21)	32.6	(0.26)	19.7	(0.51)	13.3	(0.29)	51.9	(0.95)	52.9	(0.97)	28.4	(2.86)	14.9	(1.52)	24.4	(1.36)
2009	29.5	(0.21)	32.9	(0.26)	19.4	(0.45)	13.2	(0.34)	51.6	(0.91)	52.8	(0.95)	28.3	(2.68)	17.5	(2.08)	25.5	(1.34)
2010	29.9	(0.19)	33.2	(0.24)	20.0	(0.51)	13.9	(0.31)	51.6	(1.04)	52.8	(1.09)	25.6	(2.89)	16.0	(1.77)	25.3	(1.30)
2011	30.4	(0.19)	34.0	(0.24)	20.2	(0.50)	14.1	(0.34)	49.5	(0.92)	50.8	(0.96)	22.1	(2.73)	16.1	(1.73)	27.4	(1.27)
2012	30.9	(0.21)	34.5	(0.27)	21.4	(0.53)	14.5	(0.35)	50.7	(0.92)	51.9	(0.94)	24.5	(2.75)	16.7	(1.82)	27.1	(1.34)
2013	31.7	(0.21)	35.2	(0.26)	22.0	(0.49)	15.1	(0.34)	52.5	(0.92)	53.9	(0.93)	25.6	(2.66)	15.4	(1.72)	30.6	(1.35)
2014	32.0	(0.27)	35.6	(0.35)	22.8	(0.66)	15.2	(0.39)	51.3	(1.00)	52.7	(1.02)	22.3	(3.27)	13.8	(1.43)	31.2	(1.81)
Males																		
High school completion or higher[2]																		
1940	22.7	(—)	24.2	(—)	6.9	(—)	—	(†)	—	(†)	—	(†)	—	(†)	—	(†)	—	(†)
1950	32.6	(—)	34.6	(—)	12.6	(—)	—	(†)	—	(†)	—	(†)	—	(†)	—	(†)	—	(†)
1960	39.5	(—)	41.6	(—)	20.0	(—)	—	(†)	—	(†)	—	(†)	—	(†)	—	(†)	—	(†)
1970	55.0	(—)	57.2	(—)	35.4	(—)	—	(†)	—	(†)	—	(†)	—	(†)	—	(†)	—	(†)
1980	69.2	(0.29)	72.4	(0.31)	51.2	(1.21)	44.9	(1.71)	—	(†)	—	(†)	—	(†)	—	(†)	—	(†)
1990	77.7	(0.24)	81.6	(0.25)	65.8	(1.01)	50.3	(1.49)	86.0	(1.49)	—	(†)	—	(†)	—	(†)	—	(†)
1995	81.7	(0.22)	86.0	(0.22)	73.5	(0.91)	52.9	(1.11)	85.8	(1.46)	—	(†)	—	(†)	—	(†)	—	(†)
1996	81.9	(0.23)	86.1	(0.23)	74.6	(0.80)	53.0	(0.97)	86.2	(1.10)	—	(†)	—	(†)	—	(†)	—	(†)
1997	82.0	(0.21)	86.3	(0.21)	73.8	(0.79)	54.9	(0.76)	87.5	(1.00)	—	(†)	—	(†)	—	(†)	—	(†)
1998	82.8	(0.20)	87.1	(0.21)	75.4	(0.77)	55.7	(0.74)	87.9	(0.98)	—	(†)	—	(†)	—	(†)	—	(†)
1999	83.4	(0.20)	87.7	(0.20)	77.2	(0.74)	56.0	(0.75)	86.9	(1.00)	—	(†)	—	(†)	—	(†)	—	(†)
2000	84.2	(0.19)	88.5	(0.20)	79.1	(0.72)	56.6	(0.73)	88.4	(0.94)	—	(†)	—	(†)	—	(†)	—	(†)
2001	84.4	(0.19)	88.6	(0.19)	80.6	(0.69)	55.6	(0.72)	90.6	(0.78)	—	(†)	—	(†)	—	(†)	—	(†)
2002	83.8	(0.14)	88.5	(0.14)	79.0	(0.51)	56.1	(0.48)	89.8	(0.58)	—	(†)	—	(†)	—	(†)	—	(†)
2003	84.1	(0.13)	89.0	(0.14)	79.9	(0.50)	56.3	(0.46)	89.8	(0.58)	89.8	(0.59)	89.8	(2.61)	76.5	(2.33)	87.2	(1.36)
2004	84.8	(0.13)	89.9	(0.13)	80.8	(0.49)	57.3	(0.45)	88.8	(0.59)	88.8	(0.60)	88.9	(2.65)	77.1	(2.31)	87.8	(1.29)
2005	84.9	(0.19)	89.9	(0.20)	81.4	(0.60)	57.9	(0.69)	90.4	(0.65)	90.5	(0.66)	88.5	(3.62)	75.6	(2.57)	89.0	(1.19)
2006	85.0	(0.20)	90.2	(0.21)	80.7	(0.63)	58.5	(0.77)	89.5	(0.84)	89.7	(0.86)	85.8	(3.10)	78.1	(2.77)	88.0	(1.36)
2007	85.0	(0.21)	90.2	(0.22)	82.5	(0.55)	58.2	(0.80)	90.0	(0.81)	90.1	(0.82)	88.1	(2.75)	78.3	(3.58)	89.4	(1.28)
2008	85.9	(0.19)	91.1	(0.20)	82.1	(0.61)	60.9	(0.72)	91.0	(0.66)	90.8	(0.69)	95.8	(1.40)	77.3	(3.37)	89.6	(1.21)
2009	86.2	(0.19)	91.4	(0.20)	84.2	(0.60)	60.6	(0.72)	90.8	(0.66)	90.7	(0.68)	92.1	(2.18)	80.0	(2.33)	87.3	(1.26)
2010	86.6	(0.17)	91.8	(0.19)	84.2	(0.57)	61.4	(0.68)	91.4	(0.78)	91.5	(0.79)	89.3	(2.84)	78.9	(2.46)	88.1	(1.36)
2011	87.1	(0.18)	92.0	(0.17)	84.2	(0.55)	63.6	(0.71)	90.6	(0.68)	90.6	(0.69)	91.5	(2.22)	80.6	(2.35)	88.1	(1.40)
2012	87.3	(0.19)	92.2	(0.18)	85.1	(0.56)	64.0	(0.73)	90.6	(0.68)	90.5	(0.70)	93.3	(1.84)	81.8	(2.39)	90.2	(1.45)
2013	87.6	(0.17)	92.7	(0.17)	84.9	(0.62)	64.6	(0.66)	91.6	(0.57)	91.7	(0.57)	89.3	(2.48)	81.0	(2.11)	93.3	(1.03)
2014	87.7	(0.19)	92.5	(0.22)	86.3	(0.58)	65.1	(0.74)	91.8	(0.70)	91.9	(0.72)	90.0	(2.68)	80.2	(2.30)	93.8	(1.08)
Bachelor's or higher degree[4]																		
1940	5.5	(—)	5.9	(—)	1.4	(—)	—	(†)	—	(†)	—	(†)	—	(†)	—	(†)	—	(†)
1950	7.3	(—)	7.9	(—)	2.1	(—)	—	(†)	—	(†)	—	(†)	—	(†)	—	(†)	—	(†)
1960	9.7	(—)	10.3	(—)	3.5	(—)	—	(†)	—	(†)	—	(†)	—	(†)	—	(†)	—	(†)
1970	14.1	(—)	15.0	(—)	6.8	(—)	—	(†)	—	(†)	—	(†)	—	(†)	—	(†)	—	(†)
1980	20.9	(0.26)	22.7	(0.29)	7.7	(0.65)	9.2	(0.99)	—	(†)	—	(†)	—	(†)	—	(†)	—	(†)
1990	24.4	(0.25)	26.7	(0.28)	11.9	(0.69)	9.8	(0.74)	45.9	(2.14)	—	(†)	—	(†)	—	(†)	—	(†)
1995	26.0	(0.25)	28.9	(0.29)	13.7	(0.71)	10.1	(0.67)	42.3	(2.06)	—	(†)	—	(†)	—	(†)	—	(†)
1996	26.0	(0.26)	28.8	(0.30)	12.5	(0.61)	10.3	(0.59)	46.9	(1.59)	—	(†)	—	(†)	—	(†)	—	(†)
1997	26.2	(0.24)	29.0	(0.28)	12.5	(0.60)	10.6	(0.47)	48.0	(1.51)	—	(†)	—	(†)	—	(†)	—	(†)
1998	26.5	(0.24)	29.3	(0.28)	14.0	(0.62)	11.1	(0.47)	46.0	(1.50)	—	(†)	—	(†)	—	(†)	—	(†)
1999	27.5	(0.24)	30.6	(0.28)	14.3	(0.62)	10.7	(0.46)	46.3	(1.48)	—	(†)	—	(†)	—	(†)	—	(†)
2000	27.8	(0.24)	30.8	(0.28)	16.4	(0.65)	10.7	(0.45)	48.1	(1.47)	—	(†)	—	(†)	—	(†)	—	(†)
2001	28.0	(0.24)	30.9	(0.28)	15.9	(0.64)	11.1	(0.45)	52.9	(1.33)	—	(†)	—	(†)	—	(†)	—	(†)
2002	28.5	(0.17)	31.7	(0.20)	16.5	(0.47)	11.0	(0.30)	51.5	(0.96)	—	(†)	—	(†)	—	(†)	—	(†)
2003	28.9	(0.17)	32.3	(0.20)	16.8	(0.47)	11.2	(0.29)	52.8	(0.96)	54.2	(0.98)	25.7	(3.76)	13.1	(1.85)	21.9	(1.69)
2004	29.4	(0.17)	32.9	(0.20)	16.6	(0.46)	11.8	(0.30)	52.9	(0.93)	54.0	(0.95)	31.9	(3.94)	15.6	(1.99)	20.7	(1.60)
2005	28.9	(0.29)	32.4	(0.37)	16.0	(0.64)	11.8	(0.43)	53.0	(1.10)	54.3	(1.13)	25.1	(4.70)	17.0	(2.30)	23.1	(1.67)
2006	29.2	(0.24)	32.8	(0.31)	17.5	(0.63)	11.9	(0.40)	51.9	(1.33)	53.1	(1.35)	26.6	(4.67)	13.7	(2.07)	22.6	(1.75)
2007	29.5	(0.25)	33.2	(0.33)	18.1	(0.62)	11.8	(0.37)	54.2	(1.31)	55.8	(1.32)	19.2	(4.14)	12.7	(1.89)	21.5	(1.81)
2008	30.1	(0.25)	33.8	(0.33)	18.7	(0.67)	12.6	(0.39)	54.9	(1.24)	56.1	(1.24)	27.5	(3.64)	14.6	(2.15)	22.7	(1.62)
2009	30.1	(0.28)	33.9	(0.36)	17.9	(0.57)	12.5	(0.41)	54.8	(1.14)	56.5	(1.17)	23.0	(3.35)	16.1	(2.96)	24.4	(1.92)
2010	30.3	(0.23)	34.2	(0.30)	17.9	(0.59)	12.9	(0.37)	54.6	(1.26)	56.2	(1.30)	18.0	(3.74)	13.5	(2.61)	24.8	(1.86)
2011	30.8	(0.23)	35.0	(0.29)	18.4	(0.64)	13.1	(0.44)	52.4	(1.15)	54.0	(1.21)	19.1	(3.55)	14.1	(1.98)	25.7	(1.91)
2012	31.4	(0.27)	35.5	(0.33)	19.5	(0.62)	13.3	(0.45)	53.1	(1.26)	54.4	(1.29)	24.1	(3.34)	16.1	(2.27)	25.2	(1.85)
2013	32.0	(0.25)	36.0	(0.31)	20.2	(0.64)	13.9	(0.43)	55.1	(1.17)	56.9	(1.20)	23.1	(3.32)	14.0	(2.13)	29.0	(1.78)
2014	31.9	(0.32)	35.9	(0.41)	21.0	(0.88)	14.2	(0.51)	53.7	(1.33)	55.5	(1.34)	16.7	(3.42)	14.8	(2.46)	29.2	(2.56)
Females																		
High school completion or higher[2]																		
1940	26.3	(—)	28.1	(—)	8.4	(—)	—	(†)	—	(†)	—	(†)	—	(†)	—	(†)	—	(†)
1950	36.0	(—)	38.2	(—)	14.7	(—)	—	(†)	—	(†)	—	(†)	—	(†)	—	(†)	—	(†)
1960	42.5	(—)	44.7	(—)	23.1	(—)	—	(†)	—	(†)	—	(†)	—	(†)	—	(†)	—	(†)
1970	55.4	(—)	57.7	(—)	36.6	(—)	—	(†)	—	(†)	—	(†)	—	(†)	—	(†)	—	(†)
1980	68.1	(0.28)	71.5	(0.30)	51.5	(1.08)	44.2	(1.63)	—	(†)	—	(†)	—	(†)	—	(†)	—	(†)
1990	77.5	(0.23)	81.3	(0.24)	66.5	(0.90)	51.3	(1.23)	82.5	(1.57)	—	(†)	—	(†)	—	(†)	—	(†)
1995	81.6	(0.21)	85.8	(0.22)	74.1	(0.81)	53.8	(1.09)	81.9	(1.54)	—	(†)	—	(†)	—	(†)	—	(†)

See notes at end of table.

Table 104.10. Rates of high school completion and bachelor's degree attainment among persons age 25 and over, by race/ethnicity and sex: Selected years, 1910 through 2014—Continued

[Standard errors appear in parentheses]

Sex, high school or bachelor's degree attainment, and year	Total, percent of all persons age 25 and over		White[1]		Black[1]		Hispanic		Asian/Pacific Islander Total		Asian		Pacific Islander		American Indian/ Alaska Native		Two or more races	
1	2		3		4		5		6		7		8		9		10	
1996	81.6	(0.22)	85.9	(0.22)	74.6	(0.71)	53.3	(0.97)	81.0	(1.21)	—	(†)	—	(†)	—	(†)	—	(†)
1997	82.2	(0.20)	86.3	(0.20)	76.5	(0.68)	54.6	(0.76)	82.9	(1.11)	—	(†)	—	(†)	—	(†)	—	(†)
1998	82.9	(0.19)	87.1	(0.20)	77.1	(0.67)	55.3	(0.75)	82.3	(1.09)	—	(†)	—	(†)	—	(†)	—	(†)
1999	83.3	(0.19)	87.6	(0.19)	77.5	(0.66)	56.3	(0.73)	82.8	(1.06)	—	(†)	—	(†)	—	(†)	—	(†)
2000	84.0	(0.19)	88.4	(0.19)	78.7	(0.64)	57.5	(0.71)	83.4	(1.03)	—	(†)	—	(†)	—	(†)	—	(†)
2001	84.2	(0.18)	88.8	(0.19)	78.6	(0.64)	57.4	(0.70)	85.2	(0.91)	—	(†)	—	(†)	—	(†)	—	(†)
2002	84.4	(0.13)	88.9	(0.13)	79.4	(0.45)	57.9	(0.48)	85.7	(0.64)	—	(†)	—	(†)	—	(†)	—	(†)
2003	85.0	(0.13)	89.7	(0.13)	80.7	(0.44)	57.8	(0.46)	86.1	(0.62)	86.1	(0.64)	86.9	(2.63)	77.9	(2.30)	85.1	(1.38)
2004	85.4	(0.12)	90.1	(0.12)	81.2	(0.43)	59.5	(0.46)	85.3	(0.63)	85.1	(0.64)	88.1	(2.76)	78.6	(2.24)	86.5	(1.29)
2005	85.5	(0.15)	90.3	(0.18)	81.5	(0.53)	59.1	(0.63)	85.4	(0.76)	85.2	(0.78)	91.7	(2.46)	75.6	(2.29)	88.1	(1.12)
2006	85.9	(0.16)	90.8	(0.17)	81.5	(0.51)	60.1	(0.59)	85.6	(0.82)	85.6	(0.81)	85.7	(3.08)	78.9	(2.18)	88.2	(1.11)
2007	86.4	(0.15)	91.0	(0.16)	83.0	(0.49)	62.5	(0.56)	86.1	(0.93)	86.0	(0.97)	89.1	(2.40)	81.9	(1.91)	89.2	(1.22)
2008	87.2	(0.17)	91.8	(0.18)	84.2	(0.49)	63.7	(0.61)	87.2	(0.75)	87.0	(0.78)	93.0	(1.57)	79.2	(2.95)	89.5	(1.53)
2009	87.1	(0.16)	91.9	(0.17)	84.2	(0.48)	63.3	(0.59)	86.4	(0.73)	86.3	(0.75)	89.7	(2.33)	82.7	(1.96)	87.6	(1.16)
2010	87.6	(0.15)	92.3	(0.17)	85.0	(0.46)	64.4	(0.59)	87.2	(0.72)	87.1	(0.75)	90.9	(2.41)	82.5	(1.95)	89.7	(1.13)
2011	88.0	(0.15)	92.8	(0.16)	85.3	(0.50)	65.1	(0.57)	87.1	(0.64)	87.0	(0.66)	89.5	(2.25)	83.8	(2.00)	90.7	(1.22)
2012	88.0	(0.17)	92.7	(0.18)	86.1	(0.46)	66.0	(0.65)	87.9	(0.64)	87.8	(0.66)	90.1	(2.11)	81.8	(1.84)	91.6	(1.13)
2013	88.6	(0.16)	93.2	(0.16)	86.6	(0.46)	67.9	(0.55)	89.0	(0.61)	88.9	(0.63)	89.6	(2.01)	83.1	(2.16)	92.0	(0.95)
2014	88.9	(0.17)	93.7	(0.20)	87.0	(0.55)	67.9	(0.61)	87.4	(0.76)	87.4	(0.77)	87.8	(2.98)	81.6	(2.78)	92.8	(1.28)
Bachelor's or higher degree[4]																		
1940	3.8	(—)	4.0	(—)	1.2	(—)	—	(†)	—	(†)	—	(†)	—	(†)	—	(†)	—	(†)
1950	5.2	(—)	5.4	(—)	2.4	(—)	—	(†)	—	(†)	—	(†)	—	(†)	—	(†)	—	(†)
1960	5.8	(—)	6.0	(—)	3.6	(—)	—	(†)	—	(†)	—	(†)	—	(†)	—	(†)	—	(†)
1970	8.2	(—)	8.6	(—)	5.6	(—)	—	(†)	—	(†)	—	(†)	—	(†)	—	(†)	—	(†)
1980	13.6	(0.20)	14.4	(0.23)	8.1	(0.59)	6.2	(0.79)	—	(†)	—	(†)	—	(†)	—	(†)	—	(†)
1990	18.4	(0.21)	19.8	(0.25)	10.8	(0.59)	8.7	(0.69)	37.8	(2.01)	—	(†)	—	(†)	—	(†)	—	(†)
1995	20.2	(0.22)	22.1	(0.26)	13.0	(0.62)	8.4	(0.61)	35.0	(1.90)	—	(†)	—	(†)	—	(†)	—	(†)
1996	21.4	(0.23)	23.2	(0.27)	14.8	(0.58)	8.3	(0.53)	38.0	(1.50)	—	(†)	—	(†)	—	(†)	—	(†)
1997	21.7	(0.21)	23.7	(0.25)	14.0	(0.56)	10.1	(0.46)	37.4	(1.43)	—	(†)	—	(†)	—	(†)	—	(†)
1998	22.4	(0.21)	24.1	(0.25)	15.4	(0.58)	10.9	(0.47)	38.9	(1.39)	—	(†)	—	(†)	—	(†)	—	(†)
1999	23.1	(0.22)	25.0	(0.26)	16.5	(0.59)	11.0	(0.46)	39.0	(1.37)	—	(†)	—	(†)	—	(†)	—	(†)
2000	23.6	(0.22)	25.5	(0.26)	16.8	(0.59)	10.6	(0.44)	41.0	(1.37)	—	(†)	—	(†)	—	(†)	—	(†)
2001	24.3	(0.22)	26.5	(0.26)	16.3	(0.58)	11.3	(0.45)	43.4	(1.26)	—	(†)	—	(†)	—	(†)	—	(†)
2002	25.1	(0.15)	27.3	(0.19)	17.7	(0.42)	11.2	(0.31)	44.2	(0.91)	—	(†)	—	(†)	—	(†)	—	(†)
2003	25.7	(0.15)	27.9	(0.19)	18.0	(0.43)	11.6	(0.30)	45.3	(0.89)	46.3	(0.92)	28.0	(3.50)	12.2	(1.81)	22.2	(1.61)
2004	26.1	(0.15)	28.4	(0.19)	18.5	(0.43)	12.3	(0.31)	45.2	(0.88)	45.7	(0.90)	32.9	(4.01)	13.1	(1.84)	22.7	(1.59)
2005	26.5	(0.23)	28.9	(0.30)	18.9	(0.51)	12.1	(0.42)	46.0	(1.08)	46.8	(1.10)	24.1	(4.08)	12.2	(2.00)	23.3	(1.43)
2006	26.9	(0.22)	29.3	(0.28)	19.5	(0.55)	12.9	(0.39)	46.6	(1.11)	47.3	(1.15)	27.2	(4.03)	12.3	(1.81)	23.6	(1.70)
2007	28.0	(0.23)	30.6	(0.29)	19.2	(0.59)	13.7	(0.44)	48.6	(1.07)	49.5	(1.10)	27.9	(4.16)	13.4	(1.53)	25.8	(1.58)
2008	28.8	(0.24)	31.5	(0.29)	20.5	(0.58)	14.1	(0.37)	49.3	(0.99)	50.1	(1.02)	29.3	(3.82)	15.1	(1.75)	26.1	(1.92)
2009	29.1	(0.21)	31.9	(0.26)	20.6	(0.56)	14.0	(0.41)	48.8	(0.98)	49.7	(1.02)	32.9	(3.74)	18.8	(1.91)	26.6	(1.67)
2010	29.6	(0.21)	32.4	(0.26)	21.6	(0.63)	14.9	(0.42)	49.1	(1.12)	49.9	(1.19)	32.2	(4.11)	18.2	(1.83)	25.7	(1.59)
2011	30.1	(0.22)	33.1	(0.28)	21.7	(0.60)	15.2	(0.43)	47.0	(1.04)	48.0	(1.07)	24.7	(3.52)	17.9	(2.17)	28.9	(1.70)
2012	30.6	(0.23)	33.5	(0.30)	22.9	(0.61)	15.8	(0.45)	48.6	(0.93)	49.7	(0.94)	24.9	(3.70)	17.2	(2.13)	28.8	(1.88)
2013	31.4	(0.24)	34.4	(0.31)	23.4	(0.61)	16.2	(0.42)	50.2	(0.94)	51.3	(0.96)	28.0	(3.44)	16.6	(2.05)	32.0	(1.89)
2014	32.0	(0.32)	35.3	(0.42)	24.2	(0.75)	16.1	(0.50)	49.3	(1.12)	50.4	(1.15)	27.1	(4.38)	13.1	(1.92)	33.1	(2.08)

—Not available.
†Not applicable.
[1]Includes persons of Hispanic ethnicity for years prior to 1980.
[2]Data for years prior to 1993 are for persons with 4 or more years of high school. Data for later years are for high school completers—i.e., those persons who graduated from high school with a diploma as well as those who completed high school through equivalency programs, such as a GED program.
[3]Estimates based on Census Bureau reverse projection of 1940 census data on education by age.
[4]Data for years prior to 1993 are for persons with 4 or more years of college.

NOTE: Beginning in 2005, standard errors were computed using replicate weights, which produced more precise values than the generalized variance function methodology used in prior years. For 1960 and prior years, data were collected in April. For all other years, data were collected in March. Race categories exclude persons of Hispanic ethnicity except where otherwise noted.
SOURCE: U.S. Department of Commerce, Census Bureau, *U.S. Census of Population: 1960*, Vol. I, Part 1; J.K. Folger and C.B. Nam, *Education of the American Population* (1960 Census Monograph); Current Population Reports, Series P-20, various years; and Current Population Survey (CPS), March 1970 through March 2014. (This table was prepared October 2014.)

Table 104.20. Percentage of persons 25 to 29 years old with selected levels of educational attainment, by race/ethnicity and sex: Selected years, 1920 through 2014

[Standard errors appear in parentheses]

Sex, selected level of educational attainment, and year	Total		White[1]		Black[1]		Hispanic		Asian/Pacific Islander						American Indian/ Alaska Native		Two or more races	
									Total		Asian		Pacific Islander					
1	2		3		4		5		6		7		8		9		10	
Total																		
High school completion or higher[2]																		
1920[3]	—	(†)	22.0	(—)	6.3	(—)	—	(†)	—	(†)	—	(†)	—	(†)	—	(†)	—	(†)
1940	38.1	(—)	41.2	(—)	12.3	(—)	—	(†)	—	(†)	—	(†)	—	(†)	—	(†)	—	(†)
1950	52.8	(—)	56.3	(—)	23.6	(—)	—	(†)	—	(†)	—	(†)	—	(†)	—	(†)	—	(†)
1960	60.7	(—)	63.7	(—)	38.6	(—)	—	(†)	—	(†)	—	(†)	—	(†)	—	(†)	—	(†)
1970	75.4	(—)	77.8	(—)	58.4	(—)	—	(†)	—	(†)	—	(†)	—	(†)	—	(†)	—	(†)
1980	85.4	(0.40)	89.2	(0.40)	76.7	(1.64)	58.0	(2.59)	—	(†)	—	(†)	—	(†)	—	(†)	—	(†)
1990	85.7	(0.38)	90.1	(0.37)	81.7	(1.37)	58.2	(1.94)	91.5	(2.09)	—	(†)	—	(†)	—	(†)	—	(†)
1995	86.8	(0.39)	92.5	(0.36)	86.7	(1.23)	57.1	(1.80)	90.8	(2.26)	—	(†)	—	(†)	—	(†)	—	(†)
2000	88.1	(0.37)	94.0	(0.33)	86.8	(1.13)	62.8	(1.22)	93.7	(1.27)	—	(†)	—	(†)	—	(†)	—	(†)
2004	86.6	(0.27)	93.3	(0.26)	88.7	(0.76)	62.4	(0.75)	96.4	(0.67)	96.6	(0.67)	‡	(†)	77.3	(4.82)	91.2	(2.02)
2005	86.2	(0.42)	92.8	(0.39)	87.0	(1.03)	63.3	(1.32)	95.6	(0.88)	95.5	(0.92)	‡	(†)	80.2	(4.77)	91.4	(3.91)
2006	86.4	(0.36)	93.4	(0.35)	86.3	(1.09)	63.2	(1.17)	96.4	(0.88)	96.6	(0.86)	‡	(†)	79.8	(5.19)	89.3	(3.96)
2007	87.0	(0.36)	93.5	(0.33)	87.7	(1.16)	65.0	(1.06)	96.8	(0.91)	97.5	(0.73)	‡	(†)	84.5	(4.41)	90.5	(4.30)
2008	87.8	(0.36)	93.7	(0.38)	87.5	(1.29)	68.3	(1.16)	95.9	(0.86)	95.8	(0.91)	‡	(†)	86.7	(3.36)	94.2	(3.82)
2009	88.6	(0.36)	94.6	(0.33)	88.9	(0.98)	68.9	(1.16)	95.4	(0.91)	95.8	(0.95)	91.6	(3.46)	81.1	(4.26)	88.5	(3.61)
2010	88.8	(0.32)	94.5	(0.31)	89.6	(0.93)	69.4	(1.22)	93.7	(1.18)	94.0	(1.24)	89.7	(5.05)	89.9	(2.98)	88.5	(3.86)
2011	89.0	(0.34)	94.4	(0.34)	88.1	(0.98)	71.5	(1.12)	95.4	(0.87)	95.3	(0.91)	‡	(†)	84.9	(3.95)	90.7	(3.79)
2012	89.7	(0.38)	94.6	(0.37)	88.5	(0.96)	75.0	(1.16)	96.2	(0.73)	96.1	(0.77)	98.6	(0.83)	84.5	(3.94)	92.8	(2.22)
2013	89.9	(0.35)	94.1	(0.35)	90.3	(0.92)	75.8	(1.10)	95.4	(0.77)	95.4	(0.81)	95.5	(2.72)	84.7	(3.47)	97.4	(1.11)
2014	90.8	(0.39)	95.6	(0.41)	91.9	(0.93)	74.7	(1.31)	96.6	(0.76)	96.6	(0.79)	‡	(†)	83.9	(4.67)	96.0	(2.01)
Bachelor's or higher degree[4]																		
1920[3]	—	(†)	4.5	(—)	1.2	(—)	—	(†)	—	(†)	—	(†)	—	(†)	—	(†)	—	(†)
1940	5.9	(—)	6.4	(—)	1.6	(—)	—	(†)	—	(†)	—	(†)	—	(†)	—	(†)	—	(†)
1950	7.7	(—)	8.2	(—)	2.8	(—)	—	(†)	—	(†)	—	(†)	—	(†)	—	(†)	—	(†)
1960	11.0	(—)	11.8	(—)	5.4	(—)	—	(†)	—	(†)	—	(†)	—	(†)	—	(†)	—	(†)
1970	16.4	(—)	17.3	(—)	10.0	(—)	—	(†)	—	(†)	—	(†)	—	(†)	—	(†)	—	(†)
1980	22.5	(0.47)	25.0	(0.55)	11.6	(1.24)	7.7	(1.39)	—	(†)	—	(†)	—	(†)	—	(†)	—	(†)
1990	23.2	(0.46)	26.4	(0.55)	13.4	(1.20)	8.1	(1.07)	43.0	(3.71)	—	(†)	—	(†)	—	(†)	—	(†)
1995	24.7	(0.49)	28.8	(0.62)	15.4	(1.31)	8.9	(1.04)	43.1	(3.87)	—	(†)	—	(†)	—	(†)	—	(†)
2000	29.1	(0.52)	34.0	(0.67)	17.8	(1.28)	9.7	(0.75)	54.3	(2.60)	—	(†)	—	(†)	—	(†)	—	(†)
2004	28.7	(0.36)	34.5	(0.49)	17.1	(0.90)	10.9	(0.48)	60.9	(1.74)	62.6	(1.78)	‡	(†)	9.1 !	(3.31)	21.2	(2.92)
2005	28.8	(0.55)	34.5	(0.78)	17.6	(1.21)	11.2	(0.81)	60.0	(2.20)	62.1	(2.25)	‡	(†)	16.4	(3.56)	28.0	(3.79)
2006	28.4	(0.52)	34.3	(0.78)	18.7	(1.33)	9.5	(0.66)	59.6	(2.39)	61.9	(2.44)	‡	(†)	9.5 !	(4.26)	23.3	(3.14)
2007	29.6	(0.54)	35.5	(0.75)	19.5	(1.21)	11.6	(0.61)	59.4	(2.24)	61.5	(2.26)	‡	(†)	6.4 !	(2.99)	26.3	(3.44)
2008	30.8	(0.51)	37.1	(0.70)	20.4	(1.35)	12.4	(0.69)	57.9	(2.26)	60.2	(2.32)	‡	(†)	14.3	(3.17)	26.6	(3.75)
2009	30.6	(0.57)	37.2	(0.85)	18.9	(1.36)	12.2	(0.80)	56.4	(2.25)	60.3	(2.28)	12.5 !	(4.44)	15.9	(3.73)	29.7	(3.84)
2010	31.7	(0.51)	38.6	(0.72)	19.4	(1.20)	13.5	(0.80)	52.5	(2.32)	55.8	(2.47)	10.0 !	(4.40)	18.6	(4.80)	29.8	(3.22)
2011	32.2	(0.62)	39.2	(0.88)	20.1	(1.25)	12.8	(0.73)	56.0	(2.50)	57.2	(2.52)	‡	(†)	17.3	(4.45)	32.4	(3.85)
2012	33.5	(0.58)	39.8	(0.78)	23.2	(1.38)	14.8	(0.90)	59.6	(2.17)	61.7	(2.24)	25.5	(6.12)	10.4	(2.87)	32.9	(3.72)
2013	33.6	(0.55)	40.4	(0.77)	20.5	(1.38)	15.7	(0.82)	58.0	(2.16)	60.1	(2.18)	24.7 !	(7.54)	16.6	(4.89)	29.6	(3.45)
2014	34.0	(0.75)	40.8	(1.05)	22.4	(1.82)	15.1	(0.97)	60.8	(2.44)	63.2	(2.50)	‡	(†)	5.6 !	(2.24)	32.4	(4.12)
Master's or higher degree																		
1995	4.5	(0.24)	5.3	(0.31)	1.8	(0.48)	1.6	(0.46)	10.9	(1.85)	—	(†)	‡	(†)	—	(†)	—	(†)
2000	5.4	(0.26)	5.8	(0.33)	3.7	(0.63)	2.1	(0.36)	15.5	(1.70)	—	(†)	‡	(†)	—	(†)	—	(†)
2004	5.8	(0.19)	6.5	(0.25)	3.0	(0.41)	1.6	(0.20)	20.2	(1.43)	21.1	(1.50)	‡	(†)	5.5 !	(2.63)	3.8 !	(1.37)
2005	6.3	(0.31)	7.5	(0.45)	2.6	(0.44)	2.1	(0.38)	16.9	(1.93)	17.5	(2.01)	‡	(†)	‡	(†)	7.0 !	(2.49)
2006	6.4	(0.29)	7.5	(0.42)	3.2	(0.58)	1.5	(0.25)	20.1	(2.00)	21.1	(2.10)	‡	(†)	‡	(†)	7.1	(1.83)
2007	6.3	(0.30)	7.6	(0.42)	3.5	(0.59)	1.5	(0.25)	17.5	(1.84)	18.5	(1.93)	‡	(†)	‡	(†)	6.2 !	(2.38)
2008	7.0	(0.28)	8.2	(0.40)	4.4	(0.64)	2.0	(0.28)	19.9	(1.84)	21.0	(1.96)	‡	(†)	‡	(†)	6.9 !	(2.57)
2009	7.4	(0.30)	8.9	(0.45)	4.2	(0.54)	1.9	(0.26)	21.1	(1.98)	22.9	(2.16)	‡	(†)	‡	(†)	6.5 !	(2.02)
2010	6.8	(0.26)	7.7	(0.38)	4.7	(0.60)	2.5	(0.37)	17.9	(1.87)	19.2	(1.99)	‡	(†)	‡	(†)	5.3 !	(1.63)
2011	6.9	(0.32)	8.1	(0.45)	4.0	(0.52)	2.7	(0.37)	16.7	(1.78)	17.5	(1.85)	‡	(†)	‡	(†)	6.1	(1.59)
2012	7.2	(0.35)	8.2	(0.51)	5.1	(0.66)	2.7	(0.36)	17.8	(1.85)	18.9	(1.92)	‡	(†)	2.6 !	(1.28)	4.1 !	(1.49)
2013	7.4	(0.31)	8.6	(0.50)	3.3	(0.50)	3.0	(0.37)	20.6	(1.73)	21.8	(1.79)	‡	(†)	‡	(†)	4.8 !	(1.54)
2014	7.6	(0.41)	9.0	(0.58)	3.9	(0.77)	2.9	(0.43)	17.9	(1.84)	18.8	(1.92)	‡	(†)	#	(†)	7.1 !	(2.32)
Males																		
High school completion or higher[2]																		
1980	85.4	(0.49)	89.1	(0.48)	74.7	(1.97)	57.0	(3.45)	—	(†)	—	(†)	—	(†)	—	(†)	—	(†)
1990	84.4	(0.56)	88.6	(0.57)	81.4	(2.03)	56.6	(2.69)	95.3	(1.78)	—	(†)	—	(†)	—	(†)	—	(†)
1995	86.3	(0.56)	92.0	(0.53)	88.4	(1.72)	55.7	(2.51)	90.5	(2.37)	—	(†)	—	(†)	—	(†)	—	(†)
2000	86.7	(0.55)	92.9	(0.51)	87.6	(1.67)	59.2	(1.76)	92.1	(1.83)	—	(†)	—	(†)	—	(†)	—	(†)
2004	85.2	(0.40)	92.1	(0.39)	91.2	(1.01)	60.1	(1.03)	96.7	(0.91)	96.9	(0.91)	‡	(†)	‡	(†)	91.8	(2.66)
2005	85.0	(0.58)	91.8	(0.53)	86.6	(1.76)	63.2	(1.72)	96.8	(1.09)	96.7	(1.15)	‡	(†)	‡	(†)	89.1	(3.07)
2006	84.4	(0.54)	92.3	(0.52)	84.2	(2.02)	60.5	(1.64)	97.2	(1.01)	97.2	(1.06)	‡	(†)	‡	(†)	89.2	(3.81)
2007	84.9	(0.50)	92.7	(0.48)	87.4	(1.65)	60.5	(1.59)	95.9	(1.13)	96.3	(1.10)	‡	(†)	‡	(†)	92.9	(2.64)
2008	85.8	(0.54)	92.6	(0.58)	85.7	(1.99)	65.6	(1.55)	95.6	(1.23)	95.4	(1.31)	‡	(†)	‡	(†)	92.7	(2.68)
2009	87.5	(0.51)	94.4	(0.46)	88.8	(1.56)	66.2	(1.54)	96.4	(1.17)	96.2	(1.25)	‡	(†)	‡	(†)	92.0	(3.01)
2010	87.4	(0.44)	94.6	(0.42)	87.9	(1.52)	65.7	(1.52)	93.8	(1.83)	93.5	(1.95)	‡	(†)	93.2	(3.47)	87.9	(4.32)
2011	87.5	(0.49)	93.4	(0.48)	88.0	(1.43)	69.2	(1.62)	94.2	(1.30)	93.9	(1.36)	‡	(†)	84.5	(5.28)	86.2	(4.41)
2012	88.4	(0.51)	93.8	(0.50)	86.2	(1.58)	73.3	(1.57)	96.1	(1.04)	96.0	(1.09)	‡	(†)	‡	(†)	91.0	(3.58)
2013	88.3	(0.52)	93.3	(0.53)	87.8	(1.60)	73.1	(1.64)	94.4	(1.13)	94.3	(1.21)	‡	(†)	‡	(†)	96.8	(1.77)
2014	90.1	(0.53)	95.4	(0.60)	93.5	(1.18)	72.4	(1.76)	96.1	(1.10)	96.1	(1.14)	‡	(†)	‡	(†)	96.9	(2.02)
Bachelor's or higher degree[4]																		
1980	24.0	(0.59)	26.8	(0.69)	10.5	(1.39)	8.4	(1.94)	—	(†)	—	(†)	—	(†)	—	(†)	—	(†)
1990	23.7	(0.65)	26.6	(0.79)	15.1	(1.87)	7.3	(1.41)	47.6	(4.19)	—	(†)	—	(†)	—	(†)	—	(†)
1995	24.5	(0.70)	28.4	(0.88)	17.4	(2.04)	7.8	(1.35)	42.0	(3.98)	—	(†)	—	(†)	—	(†)	—	(†)
2000	27.9	(0.73)	32.3	(0.93)	18.4	(1.96)	8.3	(0.98)	55.5	(3.37)	—	(†)	—	(†)	—	(†)	—	(†)
2004	26.1	(0.49)	31.4	(0.68)	13.5	(1.23)	9.6	(0.62)	61.7	(2.46)	63.1	(2.52)	‡	(†)	‡	(†)	20.8	(3.95)

See notes at end of table.

Table 104.20. Percentage of persons 25 to 29 years old with selected levels of educational attainment, by race/ethnicity and sex: Selected years, 1920 through 2014—Continued

[Standard errors appear in parentheses]

Sex, selected level of educational attainment, and year	Total	White[1]	Black[1]	Hispanic	Asian/Pacific Islander — Total	Asian/Pacific Islander — Asian	Pacific Islander	American Indian/ Alaska Native	Two or more races
1	2	3	4	5	6	7	8	9	10
2005	25.5 (0.68)	30.7 (0.98)	14.2 (1.57)	10.2 (0.99)	58.5 (3.11)	61.0 (3.17)	‡ (†)	‡ (†)	24.5 (4.13)
2006	25.3 (0.67)	31.4 (0.98)	15.2 (1.66)	6.9 (0.70)	58.7 (3.46)	60.9 (3.52)	‡ (†)	‡ (†)	20.8 (4.65)
2007	26.3 (0.72)	31.9 (0.98)	18.9 (1.86)	8.6 (0.71)	58.5 (3.45)	60.4 (3.54)	‡ (†)	‡ (†)	23.3 (4.88)
2008	26.8 (0.64)	32.6 (0.89)	19.0 (1.94)	10.0 (0.86)	54.1 (3.41)	55.8 (3.53)	‡ (†)	‡ (†)	25.7 (4.45)
2009	26.6 (0.66)	32.6 (1.04)	14.8 (1.82)	11.0 (1.04)	55.2 (3.07)	59.2 (3.24)	‡ (†)	‡ (†)	24.6 (5.77)
2010	27.8 (0.68)	34.8 (0.96)	15.0 (1.72)	10.8 (1.06)	49.0 (3.12)	52.3 (3.31)	‡ (†)	18.9! (7.12)	24.9 (4.91)
2011	28.4 (0.82)	35.5 (1.16)	17.0 (1.83)	9.6 (0.90)	50.8 (3.42)	52.1 (3.55)	‡ (†)	15.4! (4.80)	34.1 (6.62)
2012	29.8 (0.82)	36.0 (1.06)	19.1 (1.74)	12.5 (1.20)	55.0 (3.15)	56.9 (3.16)	‡ (†)	‡ (†)	30.4 (5.44)
2013	30.2 (0.68)	37.1 (1.00)	17.4 (1.63)	13.1 (1.06)	53.0 (3.03)	55.1 (3.13)	‡ (†)	‡ (†)	29.3 (4.61)
2014	30.9 (0.93)	37.7 (1.36)	20.8 (2.40)	12.4 (1.22)	56.9 (3.55)	59.0 (3.59)	‡ (†)	‡ (†)	26.4 (6.13)
Master's or higher degree									
1995	4.9 (0.35)	5.6 (0.45)	2.2! (0.80)	2.0! (0.70)	12.6 (2.68)	— (†)	— (†)	— (†)	— (†)
2000	4.7 (0.34)	4.9 (0.43)	2.1! (0.72)	1.5 (0.43)	17.2 (2.56)	— (†)	— (†)	— (†)	— (†)
2004	4.9 (0.24)	5.4 (0.33)	2.1 (0.51)	1.6 (0.27)	20.2 (2.03)	21.1 (2.13)	‡ (†)	‡ (†)	‡ (†)
2005	5.2 (0.38)	6.2 (0.55)	1.1! (0.43)	1.7 (0.46)	19.7 (3.13)	20.5 (3.30)	‡ (†)	‡ (†)	‡ (†)
2006	5.1 (0.37)	5.8 (0.51)	1.7! (0.52)	1.1 (0.32)	20.5 (2.68)	21.8 (2.83)	‡ (†)	‡ (†)	5.9! (2.66)
2007	5.0 (0.39)	5.7 (0.50)	3.3 (0.99)	0.6! (0.19)	18.4 (2.89)	19.3 (3.00)	‡ (†)	‡ (†)	9.8! (4.28)
2008	5.3 (0.34)	5.9 (0.49)	3.4 (0.90)	1.2 (0.32)	20.9 (2.94)	22.1 (3.07)	‡ (†)	‡ (†)	7.8! (2.85)
2009	6.1 (0.37)	7.4 (0.60)	3.2 (0.73)	1.2 (0.28)	20.4 (2.48)	22.0 (2.69)	‡ (†)	‡ (†)	5.0! (2.38)
2010	5.2 (0.32)	6.3 (0.50)	2.9 (0.69)	1.5 (0.39)	15.0 (2.19)	16.2 (2.36)	‡ (†)	‡ (†)	# (†)
2011	5.1 (0.38)	5.9 (0.49)	1.9 (0.54)	1.8 (0.41)	18.0 (2.58)	19.1 (2.71)	‡ (†)	‡ (†)	‡ (†)
2012	5.6 (0.42)	6.3 (0.59)	2.7 (0.72)	2.4 (0.50)	16.2 (2.46)	17.2 (2.60)	‡ (†)	‡ (†)	‡ (†)
2013	5.7 (0.38)	6.3 (0.53)	1.5! (0.56)	2.1 (0.43)	20.8 (2.49)	22.1 (2.60)	‡ (†)	‡ (†)	5.9! (2.47)
2014	5.9 (0.51)	7.0 (0.72)	2.6! (0.82)	2.2 (0.52)	15.9 (2.56)	16.6 (2.65)	‡ (†)	‡ (†)	‡ (†)
Females									
High school completion or higher[2]									
1980	85.5 (0.48)	89.2 (0.48)	78.3 (1.71)	58.9 (3.38)	— (†)	— (†)	— (†)	— (†)	— (†)
1990	87.0 (0.51)	91.7 (0.49)	82.0 (1.85)	59.9 (2.79)	85.1 (2.82)	— (†)	— (†)	— (†)	— (†)
1995	87.4 (0.54)	93.0 (0.50)	85.3 (1.75)	58.7 (2.60)	91.2 (2.50)	— (†)	— (†)	— (†)	— (†)
2000	89.4 (0.49)	95.2 (0.43)	86.2 (1.53)	66.4 (1.69)	95.2 (1.39)	— (†)	— (†)	— (†)	— (†)
2004	88.0 (0.37)	94.5 (0.33)	86.6 (1.10)	65.2 (1.10)	96.1 (0.98)	96.3 (0.98)	‡ (†)	‡ (†)	90.4 (3.09)
2005	87.4 (0.44)	93.8 (0.47)	87.3 (1.22)	63.4 (1.54)	94.6 (1.36)	94.4 (1.41)	‡ (†)	‡ (†)	94.2 (2.26)
2006	88.5 (0.44)	94.6 (0.41)	88.0 (1.14)	66.6 (1.41)	95.6 (1.44)	96.0 (1.31)	‡ (†)	‡ (†)	89.4 (3.81)
2007	89.1 (0.45)	94.2 (0.44)	87.9 (1.46)	70.7 (1.30)	97.7 (1.05)	98.5 (0.68)	‡ (†)	90.2 (4.49)	87.9 (3.82)
2008	89.9 (0.39)	94.7 (0.44)	89.2 (1.43)	71.9 (1.34)	96.1 (1.12)	96.2 (1.18)	‡ (†)	84.2 (4.68)	95.9 (2.44)
2009	89.8 (0.41)	94.8 (0.44)	89.0 (1.12)	72.5 (1.34)	94.5 (1.20)	95.3 (1.18)	‡ (†)	83.4 (4.81)	84.8 (3.57)
2010	90.2 (0.39)	94.4 (0.42)	91.1 (0.96)	74.1 (1.53)	93.6 (1.25)	94.5 (1.27)	‡ (†)	86.8 (4.80)	89.1 (3.55)
2011	90.7 (0.36)	95.5 (0.42)	88.2 (1.24)	74.3 (1.26)	96.6 (0.89)	96.6 (0.92)	‡ (†)	85.3 (6.02)	94.0 (2.52)
2012	91.1 (0.44)	95.3 (0.46)	90.6 (1.11)	76.9 (1.39)	96.3 (0.98)	96.1 (1.04)	‡ (†)	85.8 (4.53)	94.7 (2.35)
2013	91.5 (0.38)	94.9 (0.43)	92.5 (0.95)	78.8 (1.17)	96.2 (0.96)	96.3 (1.01)	‡ (†)	82.0 (5.40)	98.2 (1.15)
2014	91.5 (0.50)	95.9 (0.54)	90.5 (1.62)	77.4 (1.56)	97.1 (0.96)	97.1 (0.99)	‡ (†)	84.1 (6.05)	95.2 (3.44)
Bachelor's or higher degree[4]									
1980	21.0 (0.56)	23.2 (0.65)	12.4 (1.36)	6.9 (1.74)	— (†)	— (†)	— (†)	— (†)	— (†)
1990	22.8 (0.64)	26.2 (0.78)	11.9 (1.56)	9.1 (1.64)	37.4 (3.83)	— (†)	— (†)	— (†)	— (†)
1995	24.9 (0.70)	29.2 (0.89)	13.7 (1.70)	10.1 (1.59)	44.5 (4.38)	— (†)	— (†)	— (†)	— (†)
2000	30.1 (0.73)	35.8 (0.96)	17.4 (1.69)	11.0 (1.12)	53.1 (3.26)	— (†)	— (†)	— (†)	— (†)
2004	31.4 (0.52)	37.5 (0.70)	20.0 (1.29)	12.4 (0.76)	60.1 (2.47)	62.1 (2.52)	‡ (†)	‡ (†)	21.7 (4.32)
2005	32.2 (0.75)	38.2 (1.00)	20.5 (1.68)	12.4 (1.07)	61.4 (3.06)	63.1 (3.11)	‡ (†)	‡ (†)	32.1 (5.70)
2006	31.6 (0.70)	37.2 (0.99)	21.7 (1.77)	12.8 (1.05)	60.4 (2.76)	62.8 (2.82)	‡ (†)	‡ (†)	25.7 (4.72)
2007	33.0 (0.72)	39.2 (1.03)	20.0 (1.38)	15.4 (1.10)	60.3 (2.83)	62.5 (2.88)	‡ (†)	‡ (†)	29.6 (5.17)
2008	34.9 (0.71)	41.7 (0.98)	21.6 (1.57)	15.5 (1.11)	61.6 (2.67)	64.4 (2.71)	‡ (†)	12.2! (3.69)	27.7 (5.57)
2009	34.8 (0.78)	42.0 (1.12)	22.6 (1.75)	13.8 (1.09)	57.6 (3.00)	61.3 (3.03)	‡ (†)	16.3 (4.42)	35.0 (5.07)
2010	35.7 (0.68)	42.4 (0.96)	23.3 (1.72)	16.8 (1.20)	55.8 (2.93)	58.9 (3.00)	‡ (†)	18.4! (6.68)	34.0 (4.96)
2011	36.1 (0.71)	43.0 (1.03)	22.9 (1.62)	16.8 (1.10)	61.0 (2.74)	62.0 (2.75)	‡ (†)	19.7! (6.64)	31.2 (4.36)
2012	37.2 (0.69)	43.6 (0.97)	26.7 (1.78)	17.4 (1.10)	64.0 (2.38)	66.2 (2.46)	‡ (†)	14.0! (4.55)	35.5 (5.50)
2013	37.0 (0.71)	43.8 (0.95)	23.2 (2.03)	18.6 (1.10)	62.4 (2.51)	64.3 (2.54)	‡ (†)	16.4! (6.57)	30.0 (5.26)
2014	37.2 (1.00)	43.9 (1.36)	23.8 (2.61)	18.3 (1.40)	64.3 (3.23)	66.9 (3.29)	‡ (†)	‡ (†)	38.4 (5.96)
Master's or higher degree									
1995	4.1 (0.32)	5.0 (0.42)	1.4! (0.59)	1.2! (0.58)	8.9 (2.50)	— (†)	— (†)	— (†)	— (†)
2000	6.2 (0.38)	6.7 (0.50)	4.9 (0.96)	2.7 (0.58)	13.9 (2.26)	— (†)	— (†)	— (†)	— (†)
2004	6.6 (0.28)	7.6 (0.38)	3.7 (0.61)	1.6 (0.29)	20.2 (2.02)	21.1 (2.12)	‡ (†)	‡ (†)	5.6! (2.40)
2005	7.3 (0.44)	8.8 (0.64)	4.0 (0.70)	2.6 (0.51)	14.4 (2.08)	15.0 (2.15)	‡ (†)	‡ (†)	10.0! (4.26)
2006	7.8 (0.42)	9.2 (0.63)	4.5 (0.93)	2.0 (0.41)	19.7 (2.33)	20.4 (2.44)	‡ (†)	‡ (†)	8.3! (2.89)
2007	7.6 (0.43)	9.4 (0.63)	3.7 (0.66)	2.6 (0.53)	16.5 (2.39)	17.7 (2.54)	‡ (†)	‡ (†)	‡ (†)
2008	8.7 (0.44)	10.4 (0.64)	5.2 (0.87)	2.9 (0.46)	18.9 (2.30)	19.9 (2.44)	‡ (†)	‡ (†)	‡ (†)
2009	8.8 (0.45)	10.4 (0.66)	5.1 (0.80)	2.7 (0.43)	21.7 (2.45)	23.7 (2.70)	‡ (†)	‡ (†)	7.9! (2.84)
2010	8.5 (0.39)	9.2 (0.56)	6.2 (0.94)	3.8 (0.56)	20.6 (2.60)	21.8 (2.75)	‡ (†)	‡ (†)	10.0! (3.06)
2011	8.8 (0.48)	10.4 (0.72)	5.8 (0.85)	3.8 (0.63)	15.4 (1.98)	15.9 (2.03)	‡ (†)	‡ (†)	9.9 (2.61)
2012	8.8 (0.45)	10.0 (0.67)	7.1 (1.00)	3.0 (0.45)	19.3 (2.23)	20.4 (2.31)	‡ (†)	‡ (†)	6.3! (2.49)
2013	9.2 (0.44)	10.8 (0.71)	4.8 (0.74)	4.0 (0.59)	20.4 (1.91)	21.6 (2.00)	‡ (†)	‡ (†)	3.3! (1.56)
2014	9.3 (0.56)	11.1 (0.84)	5.0 (1.17)	3.6 (0.63)	19.7 (2.33)	20.8 (2.47)	‡ (†)	# (†)	7.5! (3.00)

—Not available.
†Not applicable.
#Rounds to zero.
!Interpret data with caution. The coefficient of variation (CV) for this estimate is between 30 and 50 percent.
‡Reporting standards not met. Either there are too few cases for a reliable estimate or the coefficient of variation (CV) is 50 percent or greater.
[1]Includes persons of Hispanic ethnicity for years prior to 1980.
[2]Data for years prior to 1993 are for persons with 4 or more years of high school. Data for later years are for high school completers—i.e., those persons who graduated from high school with a diploma as well as those who completed high school through equivalency programs, such as a GED program.

[3]Estimates based on Census Bureau reverse projection of 1940 census data on education by age.
[4]Data for years prior to 1993 are for persons with 4 or more years of college.
NOTE: Beginning in 2005, standard errors were computed using replicate weights, which produced more precise values than the generalized variance function methodology used in prior years. For 1960 and prior years, data were collected in April. For all other years, data were collected in March. Race categories exclude persons of Hispanic ethnicity except where otherwise noted.
SOURCE: U.S. Department of Commerce, Census Bureau, U.S. Census of Population: 1960, Vol. I, Part 1; J.K. Folger and C.B. Nam, Education of the American Population (1960 Census Monograph); Current Population Reports, Series P-20, various years; and Current Population Survey (CPS), March 1970 through March 2014. (This table was prepared October 2014.)

Table 104.30. Number of persons age 18 and over, by highest level of educational attainment, sex, race/ethnicity, and age: 2014

[Numbers in thousands. Standard errors appear in parentheses]

Sex, race/ethnicity, and age	Total	Elementary school (kindergarten–8th grade)	1 to 3 years	High school: 4 years, no completion	Completion	Some college, no degree	Postsecondary education: Associate's degree	Bachelor's degree	Master's degree	First-professional or doctor's degree
1	2	3	4	5	6	7	8	9	10	11
Total, 18 and over	239,341 (128.3)	10,379 (218.9)	15,414 (241.1)	3,716 (123.9)	70,919 (481.0)	46,484 (387.1)	22,400 (305.3)	45,176 (450.3)	17,960 (278.2)	6,893 (195.5)
18 and 19 years old	7,783 (96.4)	100 (20.4)	2,474 (70.0)	676 (40.8)	2,082 (72.0)	2,329 (78.0)	67 (15.1)	‡ (124.0)	‡ (†)	‡ (†)
20 to 24 years old	22,271 (26.0)	366 (37.4)	1,062 (68.2)	373 (41.2)	6,597 (155.1)	9,236 (175.1)	1,543 (75.5)	2,885 (148.3)	171 (27.4)	‡ (28.2)
25 years old and over	209,287 (60.4)	9,913 (214.9)	11,878 (214.3)	2,667 (110.1)	62,240 (448.9)	34,919 (358.2)	20,790 (298.3)	42,256 (416.1)	17,772 (277.4)	6,851 (194.3)
25 to 29 years old	21,486 (45.4)	516 (46.2)	1,123 (64.0)	330 (34.6)	5,699 (138.7)	4,345 (120.9)	2,158 (83.6)	5,687 (119.6)	1,262 (72.3)	366 (42.8)
30 to 34 years old	20,980 (36.7)	716 (51.1)	1,287 (66.6)	279 (27.0)	5,342 (106.1)	3,438 (106.2)	2,237 (87.7)	4,869 (99.4)	2,136 (86.4)	678 (43.7)
35 to 39 years old	19,411 (43.0)	889 (49.9)	1,101 (56.4)	229 (27.7)	4,994 (106.5)	3,126 (87.0)	2,184 (76.1)	4,236 (155.9)	1,947 (78.2)	705 (50.5)
40 to 49 years old	41,044 (50.7)	1,674 (70.0)	2,063 (73.2)	561 (48.1)	11,389 (176.0)	6,553 (143.5)	4,459 (104.5)	9,286 (177.2)	3,768 (108.6)	1,291 (70.0)
50 to 59 years old	43,389 (76.9)	1,725 (72.4)	2,240 (96.8)	570 (46.2)	13,757 (189.5)	7,251 (151.7)	4,817 (121.1)	8,123 (110.6)	3,425 (99.5)	1,482 (83.6)
60 to 64 years old	18,470 (73.5)	888 (50.0)	837 (55.0)	159 (23.0)	5,721 (131.6)	3,106 (104.1)	1,864 (82.2)	3,430 (154.6)	1,761 (84.1)	704 (52.9)
65 years old and over	44,508 (29.2)	3,505 (109.2)	3,228 (112.5)	539 (47.0)	15,339 (209.5)	7,099 (147.5)	3,072 (112.8)	6,624 (154.6)	3,474 (118.9)	1,626 (83.7)
Males, 18 and over	115,880 (104.7)	5,252 (145.8)	7,998 (162.1)	1,990 (83.2)	35,514 (330.8)	22,085 (250.9)	9,665 (208.5)	21,300 (266.2)	7,898 (168.9)	4,177 (139.6)
18 and 19 years old	4,055 (68.0)	‡ (†)	1,399 (53.3)	372 (30.9)	1,106 (49.3)	1,065 (55.9)	‡ (†)	‡ (†)	‡ (†)	‡ (†)
20 to 24 years old	11,234 (25.4)	245 (32.4)	593 (50.7)	221 (31.8)	3,690 (104.9)	4,563 (110.8)	667 (54.2)	1,180 (69.7)	119 (24.5)	‡ (†)
25 years old and over	100,592 (57.9)	4,945 (137.2)	6,005 (146.5)	1,398 (71.5)	30,718 (307.9)	16,457 (228.9)	8,973 (196.7)	20,099 (257.7)	7,846 (169.3)	4,150 (139.3)
25 to 29 years old	10,831 (45.0)	287 (34.2)	606 (45.1)	174 (26.5)	3,295 (100.1)	2,202 (82.4)	915 (57.1)	2,710 (94.2)	478 (42.8)	164 (28.4)
30 to 34 years old	10,386 (36.5)	376 (33.4)	660 (46.0)	171 (25.1)	3,029 (77.6)	1,764 (74.0)	1,029 (63.2)	2,192 (82.0)	829 (55.0)	337 (32.3)
35 to 39 years old	9,562 (42.5)	480 (35.5)	616 (41.4)	148 (22.5)	2,821 (83.0)	1,525 (62.9)	942 (51.3)	1,850 (68.5)	833 (54.0)	347 (37.4)
40 to 49 years old	20,175 (50.8)	964 (49.1)	1,135 (55.0)	325 (37.1)	5,955 (131.1)	3,052 (88.8)	1,929 (72.1)	4,361 (112.8)	1,679 (68.4)	776 (52.8)
50 to 59 years old	21,039 (62.6)	910 (53.7)	1,203 (72.1)	292 (31.0)	6,915 (132.7)	3,406 (92.4)	2,117 (75.8)	3,743 (108.6)	1,555 (69.6)	898 (58.3)
60 to 64 years old	8,836 (57.7)	396 (30.5)	435 (36.0)	88 (18.3)	2,652 (86.3)	1,446 (66.1)	839 (54.2)	1,790 (76.3)	768 (55.0)	421 (38.4)
65 years old and over	19,763 (29.2)	1,531 (71.3)	1,350 (70.3)	201 (25.3)	6,053 (144.1)	3,062 (93.0)	1,201 (73.2)	3,453 (110.8)	1,704 (85.5)	1,207 (74.5)
Females, 18 and over	123,461 (77.4)	5,127 (121.7)	7,416 (150.8)	1,726 (76.5)	35,405 (306.7)	24,399 (263.6)	12,735 (191.9)	23,876 (291.7)	10,061 (192.1)	2,717 (107.2)
18 and 19 years old	3,729 (75.8)	‡ (†)	1,075 (54.2)	304 (28.1)	975 (49.5)	1,264 (57.6)	‡ (†)	‡ (†)	‡ (†)	‡ (†)
20 to 24 years old	11,037 (5.5)	121 (19.0)	469 (41.6)	152 (23.7)	2,907 (94.0)	4,673 (110.4)	876 (53.9)	1,705 (90.6)	119 (24.5)	‡ (24.5)
25 years old and over	108,695 (11.3)	4,968 (122.3)	5,873 (131.5)	1,270 (66.4)	31,522 (290.1)	18,462 (240.6)	11,818 (190.5)	22,157 (263.8)	9,926 (193.2)	2,701 (106.3)
25 to 29 years old	10,655 (7.5)	229 (25.9)	517 (40.5)	156 (23.4)	2,404 (85.7)	2,143 (86.8)	1,243 (55.5)	2,977 (99.9)	784 (53.4)	202 (29.1)
30 to 34 years old	10,594 (4.6)	340 (33.5)	627 (33.4)	108 (16.7)	2,313 (73.4)	1,674 (66.3)	1,208 (55.6)	2,677 (78.6)	1,307 (59.3)	340 (31.3)
35 to 39 years old	9,848 (3.7)	408 (29.2)	485 (33.4)	81 (13.7)	2,173 (60.5)	1,601 (60.3)	1,242 (52.6)	2,386 (67.2)	1,113 (53.8)	358 (29.6)
40 to 49 years old	20,869 (5.0)	710 (39.1)	927 (47.8)	237 (24.4)	5,434 (101.0)	3,501 (98.2)	2,530 (70.4)	4,925 (99.6)	2,089 (71.4)	515 (37.8)
50 to 59 years old	22,350 (54.4)	815 (40.4)	1,036 (57.7)	278 (29.8)	6,842 (124.5)	3,845 (104.5)	2,700 (86.9)	4,381 (116.4)	1,870 (74.1)	584 (44.1)
60 to 64 years old	9,635 (54.5)	492 (36.6)	402 (38.7)	71 (13.2)	3,069 (93.4)	1,660 (71.2)	1,025 (64.3)	1,639 (72.4)	993 (61.3)	283 (31.6)
65 years old and over	24,745 (0.3)	1,973 (70.9)	1,879 (76.7)	338 (35.5)	9,286 (145.6)	4,037 (112.3)	1,871 (77.8)	3,171 (96.9)	1,770 (79.4)	419 (44.8)
White, 18 and over	156,773 (154.3)	2,972 (141.8)	7,301 (183.0)	1,648 (93.3)	46,138 (434.6)	30,694 (313.7)	15,842 (254.4)	33,391 (388.5)	13,506 (248.6)	5,282 (164.3)
18 and 19 years old	4,204 (75.1)	‡ (†)	1,329 (58.4)	337 (28.9)	1,075 (52.8)	1,326 (56.6)	‡ (†)	‡ (†)	‡ (†)	‡ (†)
20 to 24 years old	12,445 (44.1)	103 (25.5)	338 (37.8)	134 (26.1)	3,393 (114.3)	5,242 (139.9)	978 (64.3)	2,123 (108.7)	113 (22.6)	‡ (22.6)
25 years old and over	140,124 (130.8)	2,815 (135.2)	5,633 (162.4)	1,176 (82.5)	41,670 (412.9)	24,126 (288.8)	14,824 (245.1)	31,239 (358.7)	13,384 (248.2)	5,256 (164.9)
25 to 29 years old	12,357 (48.8)	117 (22.6)	356 (35.4)	111 (19.8)	2,953 (99.5)	2,451 (90.0)	1,375 (66.4)	3,925 (118.4)	861 (62.6)	252 (35.4)
30 to 34 years old	12,124 (49.9)	115 (21.1)	409 (42.6)	98 (17.9)	2,820 (83.6)	1,971 (73.5)	1,454 (75.0)	3,330 (97.0)	1,475 (76.9)	449 (37.4)
35 to 39 years old	11,249 (48.7)	143 (21.1)	362 (33.8)	82 (17.3)	2,716 (69.6)	1,921 (65.6)	1,399 (58.7)	2,827 (77.1)	1,313 (65.0)	514 (43.2)
40 to 49 years old	25,580 (67.0)	266 (35.7)	803 (51.5)	195 (31.6)	6,792 (143.8)	4,214 (119.3)	3,094 (93.7)	6,666 (124.3)	2,646 (92.5)	905 (60.8)
50 to 59 years old	30,529 (63.9)	396 (39.5)	1,045 (72.9)	285 (35.7)	9,812 (169.2)	5,313 (138.5)	3,640 (108.0)	6,244 (156.4)	2,653 (92.5)	1,139 (76.9)
60 to 64 years old	13,504 (51.1)	278 (34.0)	419 (41.7)	75 (18.9)	4,153 (118.5)	2,391 (92.7)	1,392 (71.5)	2,720 (101.7)	1,471 (78.5)	605 (51.3)
65 years old and over	34,781 (56.3)	1,569 (88.5)	2,239 (98.8)	330 (38.0)	12,425 (196.7)	5,865 (136.4)	2,471 (101.3)	5,526 (149.6)	2,965 (109.5)	1,391 (78.0)
Black, 18 and over	27,670 (99.7)	791 (58.1)	2,508 (97.0)	629 (48.3)	9,419 (147.0)	6,242 (144.6)	2,559 (100.9)	3,644 (122.1)	1,496 (68.0)	382 (39.3)
18 and 19 years old	1,115 (41.2)	‡ (†)	384 (29.6)	104 (18.1)	333 (29.3)	285 (30.2)	‡ (†)	‡ (†)	‡ (†)	‡ (†)
20 to 24 years old	3,203 (29.1)	‡ (†)	226 (29.5)	‡ (†)	1,211 (58.8)	1,307 (62.1)	156 (26.3)	182 (29.1)	‡ (†)	‡ (†)
25 years old and over	23,352 (78.0)	758 (55.1)	1,899 (83.2)	454 (41.1)	7,875 (130.3)	4,650 (120.1)	2,400 (95.2)	3,462 (114.9)	1,473 (65.7)	382 (39.3)
25 to 29 years old	2,698 (30.9)	‡ (†)	137 (21.4)	‡ (†)	927 (49.1)	691 (44.2)	259 (27.4)	499 (45.1)	90 (19.1)	91 (17.5)
30 to 34 years old	2,553 (32.1)	117 (22.6)	221 (32.2)	‡ (†)	830 (47.2)	554 (46.2)	234 (28.2)	424 (36.7)	164 (19.1)	101 (20.0)
35 to 39 years old	2,343 (22.9)	115 (21.1)	143 (24.2)	101 (17.4)	772 (42.1)	492 (37.7)	253 (28.2)	427 (35.6)	172 (21.8)	‡ (†)
40 to 49 years old	4,966 (32.7)	80 (18.0)	242 (27.0)	118 (22.6)	1,705 (54.7)	944 (47.7)	566 (40.9)	854 (53.4)	382 (33.5)	‡ (†)
50 to 59 years old	4,955 (65.8)	91 (17.0)	454 (39.9)	‡ (†)	1,715 (69.7)	950 (51.0)	575 (42.7)	629 (43.6)	322 (33.1)	91 (17.5)
60 to 64 years old	1,995 (63.3)	76 (15.5)	201 (23.5)	101 (17.4)	686 (40.0)	378 (34.9)	204 (27.8)	272 (26.8)	118 (17.8)	101 (20.0)
65 years old and over	3,841 (32.5)	434 (37.8)	500 (35.1)	74 (13.0)	1,239 (46.5)	641 (45.8)	308 (28.3)	355 (31.8)	225 (26.9)	66 (13.0)

See notes at end of table.

Table 104.30. Number of persons age 18 and over, by highest level of educational attainment, sex, race/ethnicity, and age: 2014—Continued

[Numbers in thousands. Standard errors appear in parentheses]

Sex, race/ethnicity, and age	Total	Elementary school (kindergarten–8th grade)	High school: 1 to 3 years	High school: 4 years, no completion	High school: Completion	Postsecondary education: Some college, no degree	Associate's degree	Bachelor's degree	Master's degree	First-professional or doctor's degree
1	2	3	4	5	6	7	8	9	10	11
Hispanic, 18 and over...	**36,307** (46.0)	**5,784** (159.6)	**4,651** (121.4)	**1,151** (64.7)	**10,984** (149.9)	**6,327** (121.4)	**2,605** (75.4)	**3,417** (110.2)	**1,052** (50.9)	**337** (27.3)
18 and 19 years old............	1,736 (44.1)	‡ (†)	560 (30.6)	168 (18.5)	484 (27.9)	467 (35.5)	‡ (†)	‡ (†)	‡ (†)	‡ (†)
20 to 24 years old...............	4,652 (8.6)	220 (25.9)	438 (38.9)	145 (25.5)	1,544 (56.7)	1,722 (60.8)	314 (27.2)	254 (27.3)	‡ (†)	‡ (†)
25 years old and over..........	29,919 (13.2)	5,525 (153.1)	3,652 (98.2)	838 (52.1)	8,957 (139.2)	4,138 (95.0)	2,275 (73.0)	3,162 (104.7)	1,037 (50.8)	334 (27.1)
25 to 29 years old...............	4,429 (32.5)	405 (38.2)	583 (44.5)	132 (19.5)	1,422 (56.8)	848 (46.0)	369 (32.1)	542 (37.2)	96 (15.6)	‡ (†)
30 to 34 years old...............	4,281 (29.9)	518 (40.8)	571 (38.2)	123 (17.6)	1,357 (47.7)	660 (38.1)	377 (30.7)	473 (34.7)	163 (19.1)	‡ (†)
35 to 39 years old...............	3,984 (36.4)	690 (44.1)	533 (33.6)	111 (17.8)	1,141 (47.6)	535 (38.1)	376 (29.3)	407 (33.5)	145 (19.2)	46 (9.4)
40 to 49 years old...............	7,057 (48.1)	1,210 (56.0)	889 (49.2)	228 (30.2)	2,129 (59.0)	939 (44.8)	494 (32.7)	814 (43.8)	272 (25.3)	82 (14.3)
50 to 59 years old...............	5,027 (60.9)	1,101 (57.5)	571 (38.8)	128 (16.3)	1,469 (54.1)	644 (35.9)	364 (26.1)	521 (35.3)	166 (17.8)	64 (10.4)
60 to 64 years old...............	1,736 (49.7)	455 (33.6)	166 (23.2)	‡ (†)	483 (35.4)	203 (21.1)	146 (17.6)	152 (16.8)	64 (11.0)	‡ (†)
65 years old and over..........	3,405 (7.2)	1,146 (45.2)	339 (25.1)	81 (14.4)	955 (38.1)	309 (28.3)	150 (19.7)	254 (25.8)	131 (16.6)	‡ (†)
Asian, 18 and over........	**13,143** (138.2)	**708** (57.4)	**476** (46.5)	**191** (26.8)	**2,637** (89.9)	**1,899** (77.6)	**846** (55.0)	**3,909** (112.6)	**1,690** (79.0)	**787** (52.2)
18 and 19 years old............	386 (25.2)	‡ (†)	70 (13.5)	‡ (†)	92 (14.9)	172 (19.8)	‡ (†)	‡ (†)	‡ (†)	‡ (†)
20 to 24 years old...............	1,184 (39.9)	‡ (†)	‡ (†)	‡ (†)	183 (26.2)	627 (39.6)	‡ (†)	252 (28.9)	‡ (†)	‡ (†)
25 years old and over..........	11,573 (121.1)	699 (57.6)	370 (41.4)	146 (23.7)	2,363 (86.0)	1,099 (62.6)	794 (53.2)	3,652 (106.7)	1,668 (77.7)	782 (52.3)
25 to 29 years old...............	1,335 (35.9)	‡ (†)	‡ (†)	‡ (†)	173 (22.6)	179 (26.0)	94 (18.2)	592 (39.9)	201 (23.8)	122 (20.7)
30 to 34 years old...............	1,465 (41.6)	‡ (†)	‡ (†)	‡ (†)	185 (22.0)	134 (19.4)	110 (19.2)	516 (41.3)	316 (34.1)	100 (19.3)
35 to 39 years old...............	1,360 (42.9)	‡ (†)	‡ (†)	‡ (†)	213 (29.8)	99 (17.2)	87 (15.3)	469 (32.3)	289 (29.3)	100 (19.3)
40 to 49 years old...............	2,574 (63.6)	109 (21.8)	66 (12.8)	‡ (†)	511 (44.4)	249 (29.2)	204 (24.0)	805 (51.5)	419 (39.5)	192 (24.5)
50 to 59 years old...............	2,085 (53.4)	122 (19.1)	83 (17.1)	‡ (†)	495 (38.6)	198 (22.3)	134 (21.4)	620 (45.2)	232 (25.0)	167 (27.3)
60 to 64 years old...............	885 (40.5)	67 (15.2)	‡ (†)	‡ (†)	275 (26.6)	83 (15.7)	78 (13.9)	225 (26.8)	82 (13.7)	‡ (†)
65 years old and over..........	1,870 (44.8)	292 (30.9)	102 (20.0)	‡ (†)	511 (38.9)	157 (23.3)	87 (15.1)	424 (32.8)	129 (16.5)	119 (20.6)

†Not applicable.
‡Reporting standards not met. Either there are too few cases for a reliable estimate or the coefficient of variation (CV) is 50 percent or greater.

NOTE: Total includes other racial/ethnic groups not shown separately. Race categories exclude persons of Hispanic ethnicity. Detail may not sum to totals because of rounding. Standard errors were computed using replicate weights.
SOURCE: U.S. Department of Commerce, Census Bureau, Current Population Survey (CPS), March 2014. (This table was prepared October 2014.)

Table 104.40. Percentage of persons 18 to 24 years old and age 25 and over, by educational attainment, race/ethnicity, and selected subgroups: 2008 and 2013

[Standard errors appear in parentheses]

Year and race/ethnicity	18 to 24 years old							Age 25 and over					
	High school completion[1] or higher			At least some college				Less than high school completion	High school completion[1] or higher				
	Less than high school completion	Total, high school or higher	High school only	Total, at least some college	Some college, no degree	Associate's degree	Bachelor's or higher degree		Total, high school or higher	High school only	Some college, no degree	Associate's degree	Bachelor's or higher degree
1	2	3	4	5	6	7	8	9	10	11	12	13	14
2008													
Total[2]	17.0 (0.11)	83.0 (0.11)	30.7 (0.13)	52.3 (0.13)	38.4 (0.13)	4.7 (0.06)	9.2 (0.08)	15.0 (0.04)	85.0 (0.04)	28.5 (0.04)	21.3 (0.04)	7.5 (0.02)	27.7 (0.05)
White	12.3 (0.10)	87.7 (0.10)	30.0 (0.17)	57.7 (0.16)	41.0 (0.17)	5.4 (0.08)	11.2 (0.11)	9.9 (0.04)	90.1 (0.04)	29.3 (0.04)	22.1 (0.05)	7.9 (0.03)	30.7 (0.06)
Black	22.3 (0.32)	77.7 (0.32)	34.1 (0.35)	43.6 (0.39)	35.9 (0.43)	3.1 (0.14)	4.7 (0.14)	19.1 (0.12)	80.9 (0.12)	31.6 (0.15)	24.3 (0.11)	7.4 (0.08)	17.5 (0.12)
Hispanic	30.3 (0.29)	69.7 (0.29)	32.5 (0.24)	37.2 (0.28)	29.9 (0.26)	3.5 (0.10)	3.7 (0.10)	39.2 (0.15)	60.8 (0.15)	26.0 (0.13)	16.6 (0.10)	5.3 (0.06)	12.9 (0.11)
Mexican	32.9 (0.35)	67.1 (0.35)	33.8 (0.32)	33.3 (0.32)	27.7 (0.31)	3.0 (0.11)	2.6 (0.10)	45.2 (0.20)	54.8 (0.20)	25.5 (0.18)	15.7 (0.13)	4.5 (0.06)	9.1 (0.10)
Puerto Rican	24.2 (0.89)	75.8 (0.89)	33.9 (0.89)	41.8 (1.07)	33.0 (0.89)	4.2 (0.46)	4.6 (0.35)	26.8 (0.36)	73.2 (0.36)	28.8 (0.40)	20.6 (0.33)	7.8 (0.26)	16.0 (0.31)
Cuban	14.7 (1.30)	85.3 (1.30)	29.9 (1.43)	55.4 (1.66)	38.9 (1.72)	7.0 (0.74)	9.5 (1.11)	24.2 (0.48)	75.8 (0.48)	27.6 (0.60)	15.3 (0.41)	7.8 (0.31)	25.1 (0.52)
Dominican	24.6 (1.58)	75.4 (1.58)	29.3 (1.72)	46.1 (1.86)	35.3 (1.75)	4.7 (0.72)	6.0 (0.74)	36.3 (0.79)	63.7 (0.79)	25.7 (0.64)	16.3 (0.58)	6.0 (0.40)	15.6 (0.59)
Salvadoran	35.6 (1.53)	64.4 (1.53)	28.1 (1.48)	36.3 (1.60)	28.5 (1.55)	3.1 (0.51)	4.7 (0.71)	52.8 (0.87)	47.2 (0.87)	23.4 (0.66)	11.9 (0.50)	3.6 (0.29)	8.4 (0.36)
Other Central American	41.7 (1.48)	58.3 (1.48)	25.4 (1.23)	32.9 (1.21)	24.5 (1.15)	3.2 (0.47)	5.2 (0.61)	43.0 (0.59)	57.0 (0.59)	23.5 (0.50)	15.0 (0.42)	5.0 (0.25)	13.6 (0.37)
South American	14.8 (0.80)	85.2 (0.80)	25.9 (1.15)	59.3 (1.34)	43.1 (1.23)	6.7 (0.71)	9.4 (0.64)	17.2 (0.48)	82.8 (0.48)	26.6 (0.49)	19.0 (0.35)	7.2 (0.27)	30.0 (0.47)
Other Hispanic or Latino	17.9 (1.01)	82.1 (1.01)	32.2 (0.97)	49.9 (1.27)	39.9 (1.26)	4.9 (0.54)	5.1 (0.51)	20.6 (0.53)	79.4 (0.53)	28.4 (0.47)	23.5 (0.47)	7.2 (0.29)	20.4 (0.46)
Asian	8.4 (0.34)	91.6 (0.34)	20.5 (0.48)	71.1 (0.52)	46.0 (0.67)	4.9 (0.23)	20.2 (0.46)	14.9 (0.20)	85.1 (0.20)	15.8 (0.17)	12.7 (0.14)	6.7 (0.10)	50.0 (0.21)
Asian Indian	6.8 (0.73)	93.2 (0.73)	14.9 (1.01)	78.3 (1.18)	39.4 (1.44)	4.2 (0.62)	34.7 (1.60)	9.4 (0.32)	90.6 (0.32)	10.1 (0.35)	6.6 (0.28)	4.0 (0.19)	69.9 (0.47)
Chinese[3]	6.9 (0.52)	93.1 (0.52)	18.6 (0.93)	74.5 (0.97)	44.6 (1.20)	3.3 (0.36)	26.6 (1.02)	19.8 (0.37)	80.2 (0.37)	14.0 (0.29)	8.3 (0.24)	5.6 (0.17)	52.4 (0.45)
Filipino	6.9 (0.68)	93.1 (0.68)	23.2 (1.27)	69.9 (1.47)	50.1 (1.63)	6.9 (0.72)	12.9 (0.86)	8.1 (0.24)	91.9 (0.24)	14.7 (0.37)	19.5 (0.36)	8.8 (0.23)	48.8 (0.47)
Japanese	6.6 (1.55)	93.4 (1.55)	23.2 (2.38)	70.1 (2.61)	48.9 (2.96)	7.8 (1.58)	13.5 (1.76)	6.3 (0.39)	93.7 (0.39)	21.2 (0.71)	15.7 (0.56)	9.9 (0.59)	46.9 (0.78)
Korean	7.6 (1.11)	92.4 (1.11)	21.0 (1.41)	71.4 (1.78)	52.6 (2.11)	4.1 (0.64)	14.8 (1.29)	10.3 (0.47)	89.7 (0.47)	19.4 (0.55)	13.6 (0.45)	6.5 (0.29)	50.2 (0.69)
Vietnamese	11.6 (1.33)	88.4 (1.33)	19.0 (1.48)	69.3 (1.68)	49.2 (1.82)	5.5 (0.90)	14.7 (1.37)	27.2 (0.66)	72.8 (0.66)	21.8 (0.71)	15.7 (0.51)	7.5 (0.35)	27.7 (0.60)
Other Asian	12.3 (0.90)	87.7 (0.90)	25.7 (1.13)	61.9 (1.22)	44.3 (1.20)	5.2 (0.55)	12.4 (0.81)	21.8 (0.63)	78.2 (0.63)	18.2 (0.52)	14.6 (0.40)	7.3 (0.31)	38.1 (0.59)
Pacific Islander	15.0 (1.90)	85.0 (1.90)	39.2 (3.02)	45.8 (2.85)	39.1 (2.76)	2.8 ! (1.32)	3.8 (1.06)	13.4 (0.86)	86.6 (0.86)	33.7 (1.49)	27.4 (1.42)	10.5 (0.91)	15.0 (1.14)
American Indian/Alaska Native	28.9 (1.17)	71.1 (1.17)	34.6 (1.18)	36.6 (1.26)	29.7 (1.23)	3.3 (0.53)	3.5 (0.68)	20.5 (0.55)	79.5 (0.55)	31.6 (0.59)	26.4 (0.51)	8.0 (0.28)	13.5 (0.42)
Two or more races	16.1 (0.57)	83.9 (0.57)	32.2 (0.77)	51.7 (0.86)	39.6 (0.82)	4.3 (0.38)	7.8 (0.46)	12.1 (0.29)	87.9 (0.29)	25.2 (0.34)	28.0 (0.39)	9.1 (0.22)	25.6 (0.35)
White and Black	21.2 (1.33)	78.8 (1.33)	34.3 (1.79)	44.5 (1.57)	35.2 (1.63)	3.0 (0.58)	6.3 (0.85)	10.4 (0.78)	89.6 (0.78)	25.3 (0.97)	29.9 (1.03)	7.4 (0.60)	27.0 (1.04)
White and Asian	8.1 (0.81)	91.9 (0.81)	28.5 (1.50)	63.4 (1.69)	46.1 (1.70)	4.1 (0.59)	13.2 (1.12)	6.0 (0.42)	94.0 (0.42)	18.0 (0.83)	25.2 (0.95)	9.8 (0.56)	41.0 (0.90)
White and American Indian/Alaska Native	19.1 (1.12)	80.9 (1.12)	34.0 (1.42)	46.9 (1.55)	38.1 (1.46)	4.5 (0.66)	4.3 (0.61)	15.3 (0.45)	84.7 (0.45)	29.3 (0.55)	27.8 (0.57)	8.8 (0.31)	18.8 (0.52)
Other Two or more races	14.9 (1.12)	85.1 (1.12)	31.3 (1.58)	53.8 (1.73)	39.8 (1.63)	5.7 (0.96)	8.3 (0.95)	11.9 (0.58)	88.1 (0.58)	23.8 (0.66)	29.2 (0.76)	9.7 (0.56)	25.3 (0.60)

See notes at end of table.

Table 104.40. Percentage of persons 18 to 24 years old and age 25 and over, by educational attainment, race/ethnicity, and selected subgroups: 2008 and 2013—Continued
[Standard errors appear in parentheses]

Year and race/ethnicity	18 to 24 years old							Age 25 and over					
	Less than high school completion	High school completion or higher						Less than high school completion	High school completion or higher				
		Total, high school or higher	High school only	At least some college					Total, high school or higher	High school only	Some college, no degree	Associate's degree	Bachelor's or higher degree
				Total, at least some college	Some college, no degree	Associate's degree	Bachelor's or higher degree						
1	2	3	4	5	6	7	8	9	10	11	12	13	14
2013													
Total[2]	14.7 (0.09)	85.3 (0.09)	29.7 (0.11)	55.7 (0.12)	40.8 (0.14)	5.0 (0.06)	9.8 (0.08)	13.4 (0.04)	86.6 (0.04)	27.9 (0.05)	21.1 (0.04)	8.1 (0.03)	29.6 (0.06)
White	11.1 (0.09)	88.9 (0.09)	28.3 (0.14)	60.1 (0.19)	42.2 (0.19)	5.7 (0.09)	12.2 (0.11)	8.3 (0.03)	91.7 (0.03)	28.4 (0.05)	21.6 (0.04)	8.6 (0.03)	33.0 (0.07)
Black	19.2 (0.32)	80.8 (0.32)	32.2 (0.28)	48.5 (0.36)	39.9 (0.34)	3.5 (0.12)	5.1 (0.16)	16.1 (0.10)	83.9 (0.10)	31.4 (0.16)	25.4 (0.10)	7.9 (0.08)	19.3 (0.13)
Hispanic	22.4 (0.27)	77.6 (0.27)	32.5 (0.24)	45.1 (0.29)	36.3 (0.27)	4.4 (0.11)	4.4 (0.12)	35.3 (0.15)	64.7 (0.15)	27.1 (0.11)	17.7 (0.10)	5.8 (0.06)	14.0 (0.11)
Mexican	24.0 (0.34)	76.0 (0.34)	34.0 (0.31)	42.0 (0.35)	35.2 (0.33)	3.7 (0.12)	3.1 (0.09)	40.8 (0.19)	59.2 (0.19)	27.2 (0.14)	17.0 (0.13)	4.9 (0.07)	10.2 (0.11)
Puerto Rican	18.6 (0.63)	81.4 (0.63)	34.5 (0.89)	46.9 (0.90)	36.5 (0.81)	5.1 (0.36)	5.3 (0.41)	23.0 (0.39)	77.0 (0.39)	29.6 (0.38)	21.5 (0.30)	8.3 (0.21)	17.6 (0.32)
Cuban	12.6 (0.93)	87.4 (0.93)	28.9 (1.38)	58.5 (1.36)	38.9 (1.48)	9.7 (0.87)	9.9 (0.92)	21.2 (0.47)	78.8 (0.47)	29.8 (0.55)	16.1 (0.43)	8.0 (0.29)	24.9 (0.51)
Dominican	17.2 (0.99)	82.8 (0.99)	29.2 (1.16)	53.6 (1.37)	40.5 (1.54)	5.8 (0.69)	7.3 (0.73)	32.3 (0.75)	67.7 (0.75)	25.6 (0.69)	18.6 (0.50)	6.9 (0.37)	16.6 (0.58)
Salvadoran	25.7 (1.41)	74.3 (1.41)	31.1 (1.55)	43.2 (1.51)	34.4 (1.36)	4.1 (0.51)	4.7 (0.68)	48.3 (0.64)	51.7 (0.64)	25.7 (0.50)	13.8 (0.43)	3.8 (0.24)	8.4 (0.36)
Other Central American	30.7 (1.13)	69.3 (1.13)	29.0 (0.97)	40.4 (1.24)	31.4 (1.09)	4.0 (0.50)	5.0 (0.53)	42.3 (0.66)	57.7 (0.66)	24.0 (0.48)	15.3 (0.42)	5.3 (0.24)	13.2 (0.39)
South American	12.5 (0.84)	87.5 (0.84)	22.7 (1.00)	64.8 (1.22)	47.5 (1.20)	7.6 (0.60)	9.8 (0.61)	15.4 (0.46)	84.6 (0.46)	24.5 (0.43)	20.0 (0.41)	8.6 (0.24)	31.5 (0.51)
Other Hispanic or Latino	17.8 (0.99)	82.2 (0.99)	28.2 (1.19)	54.0 (1.40)	41.4 (1.23)	5.0 (0.54)	7.7 (0.74)	18.6 (0.44)	81.4 (0.44)	27.4 (0.46)	23.2 (0.47)	7.9 (0.28)	22.9 (0.48)
Asian	7.2 (0.28)	92.8 (0.28)	19.5 (0.44)	73.4 (0.47)	46.9 (0.54)	4.8 (0.24)	21.7 (0.42)	13.8 (0.14)	86.2 (0.14)	15.3 (0.16)	12.3 (0.13)	7.1 (0.09)	51.5 (0.20)
Asian Indian	4.7 (0.51)	95.3 (0.51)	14.6 (0.97)	80.7 (1.02)	42.5 (1.37)	4.2 (0.56)	34.0 (1.32)	7.6 (0.19)	92.4 (0.19)	8.3 (0.29)	6.5 (0.22)	4.1 (0.17)	73.5 (0.45)
Chinese[3]	5.3 (0.45)	94.7 (0.45)	17.8 (0.68)	77.0 (0.84)	44.3 (1.00)	4.1 (0.40)	28.6 (0.88)	18.7 (0.37)	81.3 (0.37)	14.7 (0.32)	8.4 (0.21)	6.0 (0.21)	52.2 (0.46)
Filipino	5.8 (0.49)	94.2 (0.49)	21.1 (1.15)	73.1 (1.17)	49.8 (1.43)	7.4 (0.65)	15.8 (1.11)	7.4 (0.28)	92.6 (0.28)	14.6 (0.37)	19.7 (0.38)	10.2 (0.29)	48.2 (0.48)
Japanese	5.3 (1.44)	94.7 (1.44)	24.9 (2.52)	69.8 (2.90)	48.3 (2.78)	6.5 (1.39)	15.0 (1.90)	4.8 (0.30)	95.2 (0.30)	19.5 (0.69)	15.9 (0.42)	10.9 (0.56)	48.9 (0.84)
Korean	7.6 (0.93)	92.4 (0.93)	15.0 (1.19)	77.4 (1.60)	54.5 (1.85)	3.8 (0.72)	19.1 (1.10)	7.4 (0.38)	92.6 (0.38)	18.3 (0.65)	13.9 (0.53)	6.5 (0.32)	54.0 (0.74)
Vietnamese	8.7 (1.11)	91.3 (1.11)	20.2 (1.23)	71.0 (1.41)	50.8 (1.69)	5.8 (0.75)	14.4 (1.11)	27.0 (0.58)	73.0 (0.58)	22.5 (0.52)	14.0 (0.49)	8.3 (0.32)	28.1 (0.53)
Other Asian	12.1 (0.79)	87.9 (0.79)	25.5 (1.05)	62.4 (1.23)	45.4 (1.19)	3.8 (0.42)	13.2 (0.80)	21.3 (0.47)	78.7 (0.47)	17.7 (0.46)	13.8 (0.38)	6.9 (0.24)	40.4 (0.56)
Pacific Islander	13.1 (1.93)	86.9 (1.93)	38.1 (2.61)	48.8 (2.66)	38.5 (2.65)	4.7 (1.34)	5.6 (1.20)	12.6 (0.71)	87.4 (0.71)	36.5 (1.13)	27.8 (1.11)	7.2 (0.55)	15.9 (0.86)
American Indian/Alaska Native	24.9 (1.12)	75.1 (1.12)	35.7 (1.02)	39.4 (1.36)	32.2 (1.22)	3.1 (0.48)	4.1 (0.60)	18.2 (0.44)	81.8 (0.44)	32.0 (0.49)	26.4 (0.41)	8.7 (0.25)	14.7 (0.37)
Two or more races	13.9 (0.53)	86.1 (0.53)	29.2 (0.63)	56.9 (0.66)	43.8 (0.60)	4.5 (0.28)	8.7 (0.33)	9.9 (0.22)	90.1 (0.22)	23.0 (0.33)	26.3 (0.33)	9.3 (0.21)	31.5 (0.39)
White and Black	17.8 (1.19)	82.2 (1.19)	33.7 (1.36)	48.5 (1.49)	39.8 (1.29)	3.3 (0.44)	5.4 (0.52)	9.2 (0.58)	90.8 (0.58)	24.4 (0.90)	27.8 (0.88)	9.2 (0.44)	29.5 (0.77)
White and Asian	8.6 (0.76)	91.4 (0.76)	23.2 (1.07)	68.2 (1.11)	47.4 (1.08)	5.4 (0.57)	15.5 (0.90)	6.8 (0.47)	93.2 (0.47)	14.7 (0.59)	20.9 (0.65)	8.5 (0.46)	49.1 (0.86)
White and American Indian/Alaska Native	16.1 (1.29)	83.9 (1.29)	32.8 (1.34)	51.1 (1.66)	39.8 (1.64)	4.9 (0.66)	6.4 (0.77)	12.1 (0.39)	87.9 (0.39)	27.1 (0.55)	28.4 (0.64)	10.0 (0.36)	22.5 (0.48)
Other Two or more races	12.9 (0.93)	87.1 (0.93)	27.2 (1.28)	59.9 (1.33)	47.7 (1.35)	4.7 (0.53)	7.5 (0.72)	10.2 (0.42)	89.8 (0.42)	24.0 (0.54)	27.4 (0.57)	9.1 (0.41)	29.3 (0.64)

‡Interpret data with caution. The coefficient of variation (CV) for this estimate is between 30 and 50 percent.
[1]High school completers include diploma recipients and those completing high school through alternative credentials, such as a GED.
[2]Total includes other racial/ethnic groups not shown separately.
[3]In 2008 only, includes Taiwanese. As of 2013, excludes Taiwanese, which is included in "Other Asian."

NOTE: Race categories exclude persons of Hispanic ethnicity. Detail may not sum to totals because of rounding.
SOURCE: U.S. Department of Commerce, Census Bureau, American Community Survey, 2008 and 2013. (This table was prepared January 2015.)

Table 104.50. Persons age 25 and over who hold a bachelor's or higher degree, by sex, race/ethnicity, age group, and field of bachelor's degree: 2013

[Standard errors appear in parentheses]

Field of bachelor's degree	Total[1]		Sex			Race/ethnicity[1]					Age		
			Males	Females	White	Black	Hispanic	Asian/Pacific Islander	American Indian/Alaska Native	25 to 29 years old	30 to 49 years old	50 years old and over
1	2		3	4	5	6	7	8	9	10	11	12
Total population, 25 and over (in thousands)	210,991	(52.9)	101,749 (34.8)	109,243 (30.7)	141,461 (14.8)	24,112 (27.2)	29,685 (23.6)	11,244 (18.3)	1,267 (11.0)	21,371 (20.8)	83,156 (26.2)	106,465 (36.4)
Percent of population, 25 and over with bachelor's degree	29.6	(0.02)	29.5 (0.07)	29.7 (0.07)	33.0 (0.07)	19.3 (0.13)	14.0 (0.11)	50.6 (0.19)	14.7 (0.37)	32.0 (0.16)	32.5 (0.09)	26.9 (0.06)
Bachelor's degree holders												
						Number (in thousands)						
Total	62,454	(142.7)	30,060 (72.0)	32,394 (84.5)	46,747 (95.4)	4,648 (32.8)	4,169 (34.5)	5,690 (24.3)	186 (5.0)	6,830 (34.1)	27,033 (81.2)	28,592 (66.8)
Agriculture/forestry	650	(10.9)	457 (8.4)	194 (4.9)	544 (9.2)	28 (2.4)	32 (2.0)	38 (2.2)	‡ (†)	61 (3.1)	240 (6.7)	349 (6.2)
Art/architecture	2,987	(21.3)	1,297 (13.3)	1,690 (14.8)	2,326 (18.2)	131 (5.3)	220 (5.3)	244 (5.7)	7 (1.0)	444 (10.0)	1,352 (16.5)	1,191 (12.2)
Business/management	12,756	(41.1)	7,155 (29.7)	5,601 (28.0)	9,327 (35.2)	1,122 (14.7)	967 (15.6)	1,112 (14.0)	35 (2.3)	1,313 (14.2)	6,012 (23.6)	5,431 (28.3)
Communications	2,270	(17.9)	940 (10.6)	1,330 (14.2)	1,784 (15.7)	191 (5.4)	143 (4.5)	103 (3.6)	4 (0.7)	377 (7.8)	1,232 (13.3)	661 (9.5)
Computer and information sciences	1,798	(16.7)	1,271 (14.6)	527 (8.8)	1,074 (13.4)	157 (4.9)	127 (5.9)	399 (7.5)	4 (0.7)	227 (5.3)	1,117 (13.8)	454 (8.9)
Education	8,530	(32.1)	2,111 (15.6)	6,420 (28.2)	7,003 (28.1)	622 (10.6)	482 (9.1)	298 (7.2)	36 (2.2)	558 (10.4)	2,640 (18.8)	5,332 (26.4)
Engineering	4,888	(29.3)	4,197 (26.4)	691 (10.9)	3,261 (23.5)	209 (6.9)	357 (9.3)	969 (12.4)	9 (1.0)	479 (8.9)	2,094 (18.1)	2,315 (17.7)
English/literature	2,059	(17.9)	698 (10.3)	1,361 (13.6)	1,686 (15.0)	108 (4.0)	89 (4.0)	136 (4.6)	4 (0.7)	203 (5.9)	850 (10.0)	1,006 (12.5)
Foreign languages	668	(9.5)	188 (4.8)	481 (8.2)	498 (8.5)	28 (2.3)	67 (3.5)	62 (3.3)	‡ (†)	65 (3.5)	254 (6.8)	349 (5.9)
Health sciences	4,442	(24.7)	805 (9.8)	3,638 (20.5)	3,215 (20.2)	391 (9.3)	252 (6.6)	509 (8.5)	12 (1.2)	478 (10.1)	1,854 (15.5)	2,110 (17.0)
Liberal arts/humanities	938	(11.0)	379 (7.1)	558 (9.3)	689 (10.5)	74 (4.1)	80 (3.9)	76 (4.3)	3 (0.7)	90 (3.9)	403 (8.5)	445 (7.7)
Mathematics/statistics	951	(13.4)	550 (9.1)	401 (8.2)	721 (10.8)	55 (3.1)	39 (2.3)	118 (4.1)	‡ (†)	78 (3.5)	343 (8.6)	531 (8.1)
Natural sciences (biological and physical)	4,832	(26.3)	2,773 (18.3)	2,058 (16.6)	3,518 (20.6)	276 (7.4)	258 (7.1)	677 (9.3)	14 (1.4)	584 (9.2)	2,092 (18.2)	2,155 (14.3)
Philosophy/religion/theology	854	(10.9)	599 (9.2)	254 (5.8)	681 (10.0)	61 (3.2)	46 (3.0)	48 (2.6)	4 (0.7)	79 (3.8)	315 (7.7)	459 (7.2)
Pre-professional	1,002	(11.9)	613 (9.4)	389 (8.0)	694 (10.1)	155 (5.7)	105 (4.9)	26 (2.2)	5 (0.8)	157 (5.0)	557 (9.0)	288 (6.7)
Psychology	2,922	(20.2)	915 (10.4)	2,008 (14.9)	2,208 (17.2)	253 (6.4)	229 (6.7)	164 (5.2)	8 (0.9)	405 (8.5)	1,367 (14.9)	1,151 (11.9)
Social sciences/history	6,061	(30.6)	3,439 (23.2)	2,623 (16.8)	4,659 (24.9)	428 (8.3)	397 (8.9)	449 (8.9)	20 (1.5)	703 (10.5)	2,517 (21.1)	2,841 (20.2)
Other fields	3,845	(23.8)	1,675 (14.3)	2,171 (17.2)	2,858 (20.6)	359 (7.9)	278 (7.1)	259 (5.9)	17 (1.6)	528 (10.9)	1,793 (17.3)	1,525 (13.6)
						Percentage distribution, by field						
Total	100.0	(†)	100.0 (†)	100.0 (†)	100.0 (†)	100.0 (†)	100.0 (†)	100.0 (†)	100.0 (†)	100.0 (†)	100.0 (†)	100.0 (†)
Agriculture/forestry	1.0	(0.02)	1.5 (0.03)	0.6 (0.01)	1.2 (0.02)	0.6 (0.05)	0.8 (0.05)	0.7 (0.04)	0.8 (0.17)	0.9 (0.04)	0.9 (0.02)	1.2 (0.02)
Art/architecture	4.8	(0.03)	4.3 (0.04)	5.2 (0.04)	5.0 (0.04)	2.8 (0.11)	5.3 (0.13)	4.3 (0.10)	3.7 (0.52)	6.5 (0.15)	5.0 (0.06)	4.2 (0.04)
Business/management	20.4	(0.05)	23.8 (0.09)	17.3 (0.08)	20.0 (0.07)	24.1 (0.28)	23.2 (0.30)	19.6 (0.23)	18.9 (1.15)	19.2 (0.19)	22.2 (0.07)	19.0 (0.09)
Communications	3.6	(0.03)	3.1 (0.03)	4.1 (0.04)	3.8 (0.03)	4.1 (0.11)	3.4 (0.11)	1.8 (0.06)	2.2 (0.37)	5.5 (0.11)	4.6 (0.05)	2.3 (0.03)
Computer and information sciences	2.9	(0.03)	4.2 (0.05)	1.6 (0.03)	2.3 (0.03)	3.4 (0.11)	3.0 (0.14)	7.0 (0.13)	2.1 (0.37)	3.3 (0.08)	4.1 (0.05)	1.6 (0.03)
Education	13.7	(0.05)	7.0 (0.05)	19.8 (0.08)	15.0 (0.05)	13.4 (0.21)	11.6 (0.21)	5.2 (0.13)	19.2 (0.71)	8.2 (0.14)	9.8 (0.06)	18.6 (0.08)
Engineering	7.8	(0.04)	14.0 (0.08)	2.1 (0.03)	7.0 (0.05)	4.5 (0.15)	8.6 (0.21)	17.0 (0.20)	4.8 (0.55)	7.0 (0.13)	7.7 (0.06)	8.1 (0.06)
English/literature	3.3	(0.03)	2.3 (0.03)	4.2 (0.04)	3.6 (0.03)	2.3 (0.08)	2.1 (0.09)	2.4 (0.08)	2.3 (0.35)	3.0 (0.09)	3.1 (0.03)	3.5 (0.04)
Foreign languages	1.1	(0.01)	0.6 (0.02)	1.5 (0.02)	1.1 (0.02)	0.6 (0.05)	1.6 (0.08)	1.1 (0.06)	0.4 ! (0.13)	1.0 (0.05)	0.9 (0.02)	1.2 (0.02)
Health sciences	7.1	(0.04)	2.7 (0.03)	11.2 (0.06)	6.9 (0.04)	8.4 (0.20)	6.0 (0.16)	9.0 (0.15)	6.7 (0.64)	7.0 (0.14)	6.9 (0.05)	7.4 (0.06)
Liberal arts/humanities	1.5	(0.02)	1.3 (0.02)	1.7 (0.03)	1.5 (0.02)	1.6 (0.09)	1.9 (0.09)	1.3 (0.07)	1.8 (0.38)	1.3 (0.06)	1.5 (0.03)	1.6 (0.03)
Mathematics/statistics	1.5	(0.02)	1.8 (0.03)	1.2 (0.02)	1.5 (0.02)	1.2 (0.07)	0.9 (0.06)	2.1 (0.07)	1.0 (0.27)	1.1 (0.05)	1.3 (0.03)	1.9 (0.03)
Natural sciences (biological and physical)	7.7	(0.04)	9.2 (0.06)	6.4 (0.05)	7.5 (0.04)	5.9 (0.15)	6.2 (0.16)	11.9 (0.17)	7.3 (0.71)	8.6 (0.13)	7.7 (0.06)	7.5 (0.05)
Philosophy/religion/theology	1.4	(0.02)	2.0 (0.03)	0.8 (0.02)	1.5 (0.02)	1.3 (0.07)	1.1 (0.07)	0.8 (0.04)	2.0 (0.39)	1.2 (0.06)	1.2 (0.03)	1.6 (0.03)
Pre-professional	1.6	(0.02)	2.0 (0.03)	1.2 (0.02)	1.5 (0.02)	3.3 (0.12)	2.5 (0.11)	0.5 (0.04)	2.8 (0.43)	2.3 (0.07)	2.1 (0.03)	1.0 (0.02)
Psychology	4.7	(0.03)	3.0 (0.03)	6.2 (0.05)	4.7 (0.04)	5.4 (0.13)	5.5 (0.15)	2.9 (0.09)	4.2 (0.50)	5.9 (0.12)	5.1 (0.05)	4.0 (0.04)
Social sciences/history	9.7	(0.04)	11.4 (0.07)	8.1 (0.05)	10.0 (0.05)	9.2 (0.17)	9.5 (0.19)	7.9 (0.15)	10.6 (0.76)	10.3 (0.14)	9.3 (0.07)	9.9 (0.06)
Other fields	6.2	(0.03)	5.6 (0.04)	6.7 (0.05)	6.1 (0.04)	7.7 (0.15)	6.7 (0.17)	4.6 (0.10)	9.4 (0.83)	7.7 (0.15)	6.6 (0.06)	5.3 (0.05)

†Not applicable.
!Interpret data with caution. The coefficient of variation (CV) for this estimate is between 30 and 50 percent.
‡Reporting standards not met (too few cases for a reliable estimate).
[1]Totals include other racial/ethnic groups not separately shown.

NOTE: Race categories exclude persons of Hispanic ethnicity. Detail may not sum to totals because of rounding.
SOURCE: U.S. Department of Commerce, Census Bureau, American Community Survey (ACS), 2013. (This table was prepared March 2015.)

Table 104.60. Number of persons 25 to 34 years old and percentage with a bachelor's or higher degree, by undergraduate field of study, sex, race/ethnicity, and U.S. nativity and citizenship status: 2013
[Standard errors appear in parentheses]

Sex, race/ethnicity, and U.S. nativity and citizenship status	Total population ages 25 to 34 (in thousands)	Percent of population with bachelor's or higher degree	Total, all fields	STEM total	Agriculture/ natural resources	Architecture	Computer and information sciences	Engineering/ engineering technologies	Biology/ biomedical sciences	Mathematics/ statistics	Physical/ social sciences	Health studies	Non-STEM total	Business	Education	All other fields of study
1	2	3	4	5	6	7	8	9	10	11	12	13	14	15	16	17
Total¹	42,538 (34.0)	32.8 (0.13)	100.0 (†)	40.5 (0.17)	1.6 (0.04)	0.7 (0.03)	4.0 (0.06)	7.8 (0.09)	5.6 (0.08)	1.2 (0.04)	13.0 (0.13)	6.6 (0.09)	59.5 (0.17)	19.9 (0.13)	8.5 (0.09)	31.0 (0.16)
Sex																
Male	21,443 (24.2)	28.8 (0.15)	100.0 (†)	43.8 (0.27)	1.9 (0.07)	1.0 (0.05)	6.8 (0.12)	13.8 (0.17)	5.1 (0.12)	1.4 (0.06)	11.2 (0.18)	2.6 (0.08)	56.2 (0.27)	22.7 (0.23)	4.1 (0.11)	29.4 (0.23)
Female	21,095 (22.3)	36.9 (0.16)	100.0 (†)	38.0 (0.20)	1.3 (0.05)	0.5 (0.03)	1.9 (0.06)	3.1 (0.07)	6.0 (0.12)	1.0 (0.05)	14.4 (0.16)	9.8 (0.13)	62.0 (0.20)	17.7 (0.15)	12.0 (0.14)	32.3 (0.21)
Race/ethnicity																
White	24,409 (13.5)	39.0 (0.15)	100.0 (†)	37.3 (0.21)	1.9 (0.05)	0.7 (0.04)	3.0 (0.07)	6.2 (0.10)	5.4 (0.09)	1.2 (0.05)	12.6 (0.15)	6.5 (0.09)	62.7 (0.21)	19.5 (0.15)	10.0 (0.11)	33.2 (0.20)
Black	5,459 (22.3)	20.1 (0.26)	100.0 (†)	38.8 (0.72)	0.8 (0.13)	0.6 (0.10)	3.8 (0.25)	5.4 (0.35)	4.7 (0.27)	0.7 (0.11)	15.0 (0.45)	7.9 (0.43)	61.2 (0.72)	23.0 (0.61)	6.5 (0.43)	31.6 (0.78)
Hispanic	8,669 (19.0)	14.6 (0.19)	100.0 (†)	37.5 (0.60)	1.1 (0.12)	0.8 (0.10)	3.2 (0.22)	7.3 (0.34)	4.0 (0.24)	0.9 (0.13)	14.5 (0.43)	5.7 (0.30)	62.5 (0.60)	21.4 (0.49)	8.1 (0.35)	33.0 (0.58)
Asian	2,649 (14.6)	63.7 (0.39)	100.0 (†)	61.4 (0.45)	0.8 (0.08)	0.8 (0.09)	10.7 (0.31)	19.2 (0.44)	8.0 (0.25)	1.8 (0.15)	12.5 (0.32)	7.6 (0.30)	38.6 (0.45)	19.5 (0.38)	2.6 (0.15)	16.6 (0.40)
Pacific Islander	80 (3.5)	16.3 (1.73)	100.0 (†)	41.7 (5.57)	‡	‡	6.0 (2.72)	8.7 (3.95)	4.0 ! (1.81)	‡	15.3 (3.56)	7.1 (2.07)	58.3 (5.57)	20.6 (3.98)	10.2 ! (3.13)	27.4 (5.82)
American Indian/Alaska Native²	295 (6.0)	12.5 (0.72)	100.0 (†)	40.4 (3.34)	‡	‡	2.3 ! (1.03)	5.8 (1.40)	8.7 (1.67)	‡	14.3 (2.27)	6.5 (1.39)	59.6 (3.34)	16.8 (2.55)	10.9 (1.89)	32.0 (2.95)
American Indian	246 (5.9)	12.2 (0.88)	100.0 (†)	39.0 (3.63)	‡	‡	2.9 ! (1.28)	4.7 (1.38)	7.7 (2.06)	‡	15.0 (2.68)	5.5 (1.33)	61.0 (3.63)	15.2 (2.29)	10.1 (2.06)	35.6 (3.44)
Alaska Native	18 (1.5)	4.4 ! (1.64)	100.0 (†)	‡	‡	‡	‡	‡	‡	‡	‡	‡	‡	‡	‡	‡
Two or more races	877 (14.1)	35.9 (0.75)	100.0 (†)	42.3 (1.28)	1.4 (0.25)	0.6 (0.14)	3.9 (0.44)	7.3 (0.55)	6.1 (0.49)	1.1 (0.21)	15.7 (0.86)	6.1 (0.57)	57.7 (1.28)	18.2 (0.93)	4.9 (0.50)	34.6 (1.12)
Race/ethnicity by sex																
Male																
White	12,330 (9.3)	34.5 (0.18)	100.0 (†)	39.9 (0.33)	2.3 (0.09)	1.0 (0.06)	5.6 (0.14)	11.3 (0.20)	5.0 (0.13)	1.5 (0.08)	10.9 (0.21)	2.3 (0.09)	60.1 (0.33)	23.6 (0.24)	4.7 (0.14)	31.8 (0.30)
Black	2,629 (16.1)	16.1 (0.35)	100.0 (†)	39.3 (1.29)	1.1 (0.24)	1.0 (0.22)	6.0 (0.52)	10.5 (0.71)	3.8 (0.47)	1.0 (0.24)	12.6 (0.74)	3.4 (0.44)	60.7 (1.29)	25.0 (1.11)	4.1 (0.39)	31.6 (1.14)
Hispanic	4,560 (13.8)	11.8 (0.22)	100.0 (†)	39.6 (0.90)	1.1 (0.16)	1.2 (0.20)	5.7 (0.42)	13.3 (0.65)	3.4 (0.33)	1.0 (0.21)	11.5 (0.64)	2.5 (0.32)	60.4 (0.90)	23.0 (0.76)	4.5 (0.42)	32.9 (0.95)
Asian	1,259 (8.7)	62.6 (0.62)	100.0 (†)	69.0 (0.65)	0.8 (0.12)	0.7 (0.11)	14.0 (0.46)	28.7 (0.69)	7.2 (0.36)	1.8 (0.19)	14.8 (0.47)	4.3 (0.30)	31.0 (0.65)	17.3 (0.53)	1.0 (0.13)	12.7 (0.46)
Pacific Islander	40 (2.3)	12.3 (2.34)	100.0 (†)	37.5 (10.00)	‡	‡	14.0 ‡	28.7 ‡	7.2 ‡	‡	14.8 (5.61)	‡	62.5 (10.00)	15.6 ! (6.62)	‡	46.5 (11.34)
American Indian/Alaska Native²	149 (4.3)	10.6 (1.05)	100.0 (†)	43.8 (4.89)	‡	‡	‡	12.1 (3.29)	9.7 ! (3.09)	‡	11.2 (2.98)	‡	56.2 (4.89)	15.4 (3.72)	6.8 ! (2.60)	33.9 (4.34)
American Indian	122 (4.2)	10.8 (1.16)	100.0 (†)	41.8 (5.55)	‡	‡	‡	9.3 ! (3.06)	9.3 ! (3.62)	‡	10.7 ! (3.26)	‡	58.2 (5.55)	14.5 (3.84)	7.0 ! (2.97)	36.7 (5.07)
Alaska Native	9 (0.8)	‡	100.0 (†)	‡	‡	‡	‡	‡	‡	‡	‡	‡	‡	‡	‡	‡
Two or more races	430 (9.5)	32.3 (1.08)	100.0 (†)	44.8 (1.86)	1.6 (0.40)	0.6 (0.18)	6.2 (0.87)	13.8 (1.18)	5.2 (0.70)	1.4 (0.34)	13.2 (1.22)	2.8 (0.62)	55.2 (1.86)	20.7 (1.44)	3.1 (0.68)	31.4 (1.51)
Female																
White	12,079 (8.3)	43.5 (0.19)	100.0 (†)	35.2 (0.24)	1.5 (0.06)	0.5 (0.04)	0.9 (0.05)	2.0 (0.06)	5.7 (0.13)	0.9 (0.06)	13.9 (0.20)	9.8 (0.15)	64.8 (0.24)	16.2 (0.19)	14.2 (0.27)	34.3 (0.27)
Black	2,829 (14.9)	23.9 (0.37)	100.0 (†)	38.5 (0.86)	0.5 (0.16)	0.3 (0.08)	2.5 (0.26)	2.1 (0.25)	5.3 (0.31)	0.6 (0.09)	16.5 (0.54)	10.8 (0.56)	61.5 (0.86)	21.7 (0.75)	8.1 (0.63)	31.7 (0.85)
Hispanic	4,109 (11.5)	17.7 (0.25)	100.0 (†)	36.0 (0.76)	1.1 (0.16)	0.5 (0.11)	1.4 (0.16)	2.8 (0.24)	4.4 (0.33)	0.8 (0.15)	17.0 (0.61)	8.1 (0.43)	64.0 (0.76)	20.2 (0.59)	10.8 (0.52)	33.0 (0.73)
Asian	1,390 (10.1)	64.7 (0.47)	100.0 (†)	54.6 (0.62)	0.7 (0.10)	0.9 (0.13)	7.7 (0.33)	10.8 (0.41)	8.8 (0.37)	1.8 (0.19)	13.4 (0.46)	10.5 (0.47)	45.4 (0.62)	21.5 (0.55)	3.9 (0.27)	20.0 (0.57)
Pacific Islander	40 (2.1)	20.4 (2.48)	100.0 (†)	44.3 (5.53)	‡	‡	‡	10.8 ! ‡	6.5 ! (2.94)	‡	15.7 (2.94)	10.3 ! (3.19)	55.7 (5.53)	23.6 (4.97)	16.2 (4.54)	15.9 (4.74)
American Indian/Alaska Native²	146 (4.3)	14.4 (1.03)	100.0 (†)	37.8 (4.40)	‡	‡	0.9 ! ‡	‡	8.0 (2.35)	‡	16.5 (3.15)	9.9 (2.10)	62.2 (4.40)	17.8 (3.55)	14.0 (2.54)	30.5 (3.97)
American Indian	124 (4.0)	13.6 (1.21)	100.0 (†)	36.8 (4.82)	‡	‡	‡	‡	6.5 ! (2.33)	‡	18.4 (3.85)	8.0 (2.02)	63.2 (4.82)	15.8 (3.40)	12.6 (2.57)	34.8 (4.47)
Alaska Native	9 (1.3)	‡	100.0 (†)	‡	‡	‡	‡	‡	‡	‡	‡	‡	‡	‡	‡	‡
Two or more races	447 (8.6)	39.4 (0.91)	100.0 (†)	40.4 (1.68)	1.3 (0.35)	0.5 ! (0.20)	2.0 (0.40)	2.3 (0.30)	6.9 (0.79)	0.9 (0.23)	17.8 (1.22)	8.7 (0.92)	59.6 (1.68)	16.1 (1.10)	6.4 (0.62)	37.1 (1.47)
Nativity																
Hispanic																
U.S.-born³	4,606 (24.9)	19.1 (0.25)	100.0 (†)	35.6 (0.64)	1.0 (0.12)	0.6 (0.10)	2.4 (0.24)	5.2 (0.35)	4.1 (0.28)	0.9 (0.16)	15.5 (0.56)	5.9 (0.34)	64.4 (0.64)	20.5 (0.57)	8.5 (0.40)	35.4 (0.68)
Foreign-born³	4,063 (24.3)	9.5 (0.24)	100.0 (†)	41.9 (1.24)	1.3 (0.25)	1.2 (0.25)	5.0 (0.43)	11.9 (0.74)	3.8 (0.43)	1.0 (0.24)	12.3 (0.79)	5.3 (0.52)	58.1 (1.24)	23.5 (0.97)	7.2 (0.62)	27.4 (1.12)
Asian																
U.S.-born³	809 (10.9)	60.5 (0.71)	100.0 (†)	51.0 (0.87)	0.5 (0.13)	0.7 (0.17)	4.1 (0.32)	9.0 (0.52)	11.0 (0.53)	1.5 (0.21)	16.9 (0.68)	7.2 (0.50)	49.0 (0.87)	21.4 (0.73)	2.8 (0.30)	24.8 (0.85)
Foreign-born³	1,840 (15.1)	65.1 (0.45)	100.0 (†)	65.6 (0.49)	0.7 (0.10)	0.8 (0.11)	13.4 (0.40)	23.3 (0.55)	6.9 (0.28)	1.9 (0.18)	10.7 (0.35)	7.8 (0.36)	34.4 (0.49)	18.7 (0.45)	2.5 (0.18)	13.2 (0.41)
Citizenship status																
U.S.-born citizen	34,876 (40.9)	33.3 (0.13)	100.0 (†)	37.2 (0.19)	1.7 (0.05)	0.7 (0.03)	2.9 (0.06)	5.8 (0.09)	5.4 (0.08)	1.1 (0.04)	13.2 (0.13)	6.5 (0.10)	62.8 (0.19)	19.8 (0.14)	9.5 (0.10)	33.5 (0.17)
Naturalized citizen	2,255 (19.3)	39.2 (0.41)	100.0 (†)	48.4 (0.66)	0.7 (0.11)	1.0 (0.14)	6.0 (0.33)	9.2 (0.38)	7.9 (0.30)	1.3 (0.14)	13.2 (0.47)	9.2 (0.46)	51.6 (0.66)	24.9 (0.58)	3.9 (0.30)	22.8 (0.62)
Noncitizen	5,407 (32.9)	27.1 (0.29)	100.0 (†)	62.0 (0.48)	1.2 (0.13)	1.0 (0.09)	11.8 (0.37)	23.0 (0.46)	5.3 (0.23)	2.0 (0.15)	11.5 (0.35)	6.2 (0.26)	38.0 (0.48)	17.5 (0.38)	3.8 (0.21)	16.7 (0.40)

†Not applicable.
!Interpret data with caution. The coefficient of variation (CV) for this estimate is between 30 and 50 percent.
‡Reporting standards not met. Either there are too few cases for a reliable estimate or the coefficient of variation (CV) is 50 percent or greater.
¹Total includes other racial/ethnic groups not shown separately.
²Includes persons reporting American Indian alone, persons reporting Alaska Native alone, and persons from American Indian and/or Alaska Native tribes specified or not specified.
³Includes those born in the 50 states, the District of Columbia, Puerto Rico, American Samoa, Guam, the U.S. Virgin Islands, and the Northern Marianas, as well as those born abroad to U.S.-citizen parents.

NOTE: Estimates are for the entire population in the indicated age range, including persons living in households and persons living in group quarters (such as college residence halls, residential treatment centers, military barracks, and correctional facilities). The first bachelor's degree major reported by respondents was used to classify their field of study, even though they were able to report a second bachelor's degree major and may possess advanced degrees in other fields. STEM fields, as defined here, consist of the fields specified in columns 6 through 13. Data were assembled based on major field aggregations, except that management of STEM activities was counted as a STEM field instead of a business field. Detail may not sum to totals because of rounding. Race categories exclude persons of Hispanic ethnicity.
SOURCE: U.S. Department of Commerce, Census Bureau, American Community Survey (ACS), 2013. (This table was prepared February 2015.)

Table 104.70. Number and percentage distribution of 6- to 18-year-olds, by parent's highest level of educational attainment, household type, and child's race/ethnicity: 2008 and 2013

[Standard errors appear in parentheses]

Year, household type, and race/ethnicity	Number (in thousands)	Percentage distribution	Total, all levels	Less than high school completion	High school completion[2]	Some college, no degree	Associate's degree	Bachelor's or higher degree — Total	Bachelor's degree	Master's degree	Doctor's degree
1	2	3	4	5	6	7	8	9	10	11	12
2008											
Total, both household types	49,454 (59.8)	100.0 (†)	100.0 (†)	10.9 (0.09)	20.8 (0.10)	23.3 (0.11)	10.3 (0.07)	34.7 (0.13)	20.5 (0.09)	9.4 (0.07)	4.8 (0.04)
White	28,920 (47.0)	58.5 (0.08)	100.0	3.9 (0.06)	18.5 (0.13)	22.9 (0.13)	11.5 (0.09)	43.3 (0.15)	25.2 (0.12)	12.0 (0.09)	6.1 (0.06)
Black	6,719 (31.0)	13.6 (0.06)	100.0	11.6 (0.27)	27.6 (0.36)	30.5 (0.32)	10.3 (0.23)	20.0 (0.29)	13.0 (0.24)	5.2 (0.15)	1.7 (0.09)
Hispanic	9,858 (28.3)	19.9 (0.05)	100.0	32.1 (0.25)	25.0 (0.25)	20.6 (0.23)	6.9 (0.14)	15.4 (0.18)	10.2 (0.16)	3.5 (0.11)	1.8 (0.06)
Asian	1,929 (15.1)	3.9 (0.03)	100.0	10.0 (0.41)	12.8 (0.45)	12.0 (0.37)	7.1 (0.35)	58.2 (0.54)	30.3 (0.49)	16.3 (0.35)	11.6 (0.31)
Pacific Islander	69 (3.9)	0.1 (0.01)	100.0	5.6 (1.62)	25.1 (3.02)	36.0 (3.50)	13.3 (2.61)	20.1 (2.69)	13.6 (2.51)	5.1 (1.27)	1.3 ! (0.48)
American Indian/Alaska Native	348 (7.5)	0.7 (0.02)	100.0	11.8 (0.90)	24.7 (1.30)	33.2 (1.28)	11.8 (0.78)	18.5 (1.00)	12.3 (0.83)	4.9 (0.56)	1.3 (0.28)
Some other race	152 (6.2)	0.3 (0.01)	100.0	12.7 (1.63)	20.8 (1.76)	22.5 (2.06)	10.7 (1.69)	33.2 (2.19)	16.7 (1.49)	11.7 (1.28)	4.8 (0.79)
Two or more races	1,458 (17.4)	2.9 (0.04)	100.0	5.9 (0.41)	18.2 (0.53)	28.1 (0.59)	12.1 (0.48)	35.8 (0.62)	20.2 (0.52)	10.0 (0.35)	5.5 (0.28)
Two-parent household	33,492 (68.6)	100.0 (†)	100.0 (†)	7.4 (0.08)	16.8 (0.13)	21.4 (0.12)	10.8 (0.09)	43.6 (0.17)	24.9 (0.12)	12.2 (0.09)	6.5 (0.06)
White	21,968 (55.1)	65.6 (0.10)	100.0	2.0 (0.05)	14.9 (0.13)	21.4 (0.13)	11.7 (0.11)	50.1 (0.18)	28.4 (0.14)	14.2 (0.11)	7.4 (0.08)
Black	2,473 (25.4)	7.4 (0.07)	100.0	3.6 (0.23)	19.4 (0.53)	29.6 (0.55)	13.0 (0.38)	34.5 (0.57)	20.9 (0.45)	9.7 (0.33)	3.8 (0.21)
Hispanic	6,264 (29.8)	18.7 (0.08)	100.0	28.7 (0.32)	24.2 (0.30)	20.4 (0.28)	7.4 (0.16)	19.3 (0.26)	12.4 (0.21)	4.6 (0.12)	2.4 (0.09)
Asian	1,604 (15.2)	4.8 (0.04)	100.0	8.1 (0.41)	11.2 (0.43)	10.9 (0.37)	6.7 (0.35)	63.1 (0.58)	32.2 (0.57)	17.9 (0.39)	13.0 (0.36)
Pacific Islander	49 (3.8)	0.1 (0.01)	100.0	2.8 ! (1.23)	19.9 (3.06)	41.0 (3.97)	14.6 (3.44)	21.8 (3.45)	14.1 (3.06)	6.4 (1.78)	1.3 ! (0.64)
American Indian/Alaska Native	181 (6.0)	0.5 (0.02)	100.0	6.0 (0.94)	22.7 (1.64)	32.0 (1.70)	13.6 (1.16)	25.7 (1.54)	16.0 (1.28)	7.3 (0.87)	2.4 (0.56)
Some other race	96 (5.4)	0.3 (0.02)	100.0	10.0 (1.78)	15.6 (2.04)	18.8 (2.30)	9.8 (1.95)	45.8 (2.96)	21.9 (1.94)	16.9 (1.95)	7.0 (1.19)
Two or more races	857 (15.2)	2.6 (0.04)	100.0	1.5 (0.22)	12.6 (0.57)	25.0 (0.69)	12.1 (0.50)	48.9 (0.84)	26.2 (0.76)	14.2 (0.51)	8.5 (0.44)
Single-parent household	15,962 (69.9)	100.0 (†)	100.0 (†)	18.3 (0.19)	29.3 (0.19)	27.1 (0.19)	9.1 (0.12)	16.1 (0.16)	11.2 (0.12)	3.6 (0.08)	1.3 (0.04)
White	6,951 (48.1)	43.5 (0.18)	100.0	10.0 (0.19)	29.7 (0.33)	27.7 (0.29)	10.7 (0.18)	21.9 (0.27)	14.9 (0.21)	4.9 (0.14)	2.0 (0.08)
Black	4,247 (30.8)	26.6 (0.17)	100.0	16.3 (0.38)	32.4 (0.41)	31.1 (0.35)	8.8 (0.27)	11.5 (0.30)	8.5 (0.25)	2.6 (0.14)	0.4 (0.05)
Hispanic	3,594 (30.8)	22.5 (0.17)	100.0	38.0 (0.46)	26.4 (0.42)	20.9 (0.37)	6.0 (0.23)	8.7 (0.28)	6.4 (0.25)	1.5 (0.10)	0.8 (0.07)
Asian	325 (8.5)	2.0 (0.05)	100.0	19.2 (1.26)	20.5 (1.24)	17.3 (1.09)	8.9 (0.92)	34.2 (1.34)	21.0 (1.09)	8.2 (0.71)	4.9 (0.46)
Pacific Islander	20 (2.5)	0.1 (0.02)	100.0	12.3 ! (4.94)	37.5 (6.12)	23.9 (4.72)	10.3 ! (3.43)	15.9 (4.59)	12.5 ! (4.35)	2.3 ! (1.07)	‡ (†)
American Indian/Alaska Native	167 (5.9)	1.0 (0.04)	100.0	18.1 (1.45)	26.8 (1.78)	34.5 (1.84)	10.0 (1.08)	10.7 (1.27)	8.2 (1.07)	2.3 (0.64)	‡ (†)
Some other race	56 (4.0)	0.4 (0.03)	100.0	17.3 (3.05)	29.7 (2.94)	28.8 (3.57)	12.4 (3.00)	11.8 (2.16)	7.8 (1.84)	2.9 (0.74)	‡ (†)
Two or more races	601 (11.7)	3.8 (0.08)	100.0	12.1 (0.89)	26.2 (0.80)	32.5 (1.11)	12.0 (0.75)	17.2 (0.79)	11.8 (0.67)	4.0 (0.32)	1.3 (0.20)
2013											
Total, both household types	50,064 (47.6)	100.0 (†)	100.0 (†)	10.8 (0.08)	19.3 (0.12)	22.0 (0.11)	10.6 (0.07)	37.3 (0.15)	21.3 (0.12)	11.1 (0.09)	4.9 (0.06)
White	26,921 (28.4)	53.8 (0.05)	100.0	3.6 (0.08)	16.0 (0.15)	20.9 (0.15)	11.9 (0.09)	47.7 (0.19)	27.0 (0.16)	14.3 (0.12)	6.3 (0.07)
Black	6,647 (26.4)	13.3 (0.05)	100.0	10.2 (0.23)	24.6 (0.32)	30.6 (0.37)	11.4 (0.22)	23.2 (0.34)	14.1 (0.25)	7.1 (0.16)	2.0 (0.09)
Hispanic	11,668 (24.5)	23.3 (0.04)	100.0	29.0 (0.28)	25.8 (0.25)	20.8 (0.22)	7.6 (0.14)	16.8 (0.21)	10.9 (0.18)	4.2 (0.11)	1.7 (0.07)
Asian	2,279 (16.0)	4.6 (0.03)	100.0	9.1 (0.32)	12.0 (0.34)	10.8 (0.31)	6.8 (0.28)	61.3 (0.44)	29.2 (0.40)	20.0 (0.36)	12.1 (0.30)
Pacific Islander	82 (4.3)	0.2 (0.01)	100.0	6.0 (1.33)	30.1 (2.43)	31.8 (2.62)	12.7 (1.98)	19.3 (2.12)	13.2 (1.89)	5.5 (1.24)	‡ (†)
American Indian/Alaska Native	376 (7.4)	0.8 (0.01)	100.0	11.7 (0.68)	25.0 (1.08)	29.8 (1.30)	13.2 (0.84)	20.3 (0.83)	13.4 (0.69)	5.1 (0.42)	1.7 (0.33)
Some other race	136 (6.5)	0.3 (0.01)	100.0	13.5 (1.59)	19.0 (2.02)	21.3 (1.75)	8.4 (1.32)	37.9 (2.59)	19.7 (2.33)	10.0 (1.16)	8.1 (1.34)
Two or more races	1,956 (18.6)	3.9 (0.04)	100.0	4.9 (0.25)	15.8 (0.48)	26.0 (0.54)	12.2 (0.38)	41.2 (0.54)	21.8 (0.47)	13.4 (0.38)	6.0 (0.23)
Two-parent household	32,770 (68.1)	100.0 (†)	100.0 (†)	7.2 (0.09)	15.0 (0.12)	19.3 (0.12)	10.8 (0.08)	47.7 (0.17)	26.2 (0.14)	14.7 (0.11)	6.8 (0.08)
White	20,032 (48.1)	61.1 (0.10)	100.0	1.8 (0.06)	12.2 (0.14)	18.5 (0.16)	11.9 (0.11)	55.6 (0.19)	30.6 (0.17)	17.2 (0.14)	7.8 (0.10)
Black	2,333 (28.4)	7.1 (0.08)	100.0	2.6 (0.21)	15.9 (0.47)	27.8 (0.59)	13.3 (0.40)	40.4 (0.60)	22.4 (0.50)	13.3 (0.34)	4.6 (0.25)
Hispanic	7,019 (34.6)	21.4 (0.08)	100.0	24.9 (0.35)	24.5 (0.28)	20.6 (0.26)	8.0 (0.17)	21.8 (0.30)	13.7 (0.24)	5.6 (0.18)	2.5 (0.10)
Asian	1,916 (17.2)	5.8 (0.05)	100.0	7.4 (0.28)	10.5 (0.30)	9.5 (0.34)	6.3 (0.26)	66.3 (0.42)	30.6 (0.43)	22.0 (0.42)	13.7 (0.35)
Pacific Islander	54 (3.9)	0.2 (0.01)	100.0	2.5 ! (0.76)	29.2 (3.40)	31.4 (3.14)	12.2 (2.04)	24.7 (2.91)	15.9 (2.52)	7.9 (1.75)	‡ (†)
American Indian/Alaska Native	182 (5.8)	0.6 (0.02)	100.0	4.7 (0.66)	19.6 (1.08)	29.2 (1.30)	16.3 (1.17)	30.2 (1.42)	19.2 (1.28)	7.9 (0.77)	3.1 (0.65)
Some other race	82 (4.9)	0.3 (0.01)	100.0	9.1 (1.62)	19.7 (2.66)	13.6 (1.97)	8.6 (1.61)	49.0 (3.34)	23.9 (2.76)	13.2 (1.69)	11.9 (2.13)
Two or more races	1,152 (15.4)	3.5 (0.05)	100.0	1.3 (0.16)	10.0 (0.56)	22.1 (0.69)	11.2 (0.49)	55.3 (0.70)	27.7 (0.62)	18.4 (0.53)	9.2 (0.39)
Single-parent household	17,295 (73.4)	100.0 (†)	100.0 (†)	17.6 (0.16)	27.5 (0.20)	27.0 (0.19)	10.2 (0.13)	17.7 (0.21)	12.0 (0.17)	4.3 (0.10)	1.3 (0.05)
White	6,889 (43.0)	39.8 (0.16)	100.0	8.6 (0.19)	27.0 (0.28)	27.8 (0.28)	11.9 (0.21)	24.6 (0.32)	16.7 (0.29)	5.9 (0.16)	2.0 (0.08)
Black	4,314 (31.8)	24.9 (0.16)	100.0	14.3 (0.32)	29.4 (0.41)	32.1 (0.45)	10.3 (0.40)	13.9 (0.32)	9.6 (0.29)	3.7 (0.15)	0.6 (0.06)
Hispanic	4,649 (36.1)	26.9 (0.17)	100.0	35.2 (0.44)	27.7 (0.43)	20.9 (0.32)	6.9 (0.21)	9.3 (0.23)	6.7 (0.21)	1.9 (0.09)	0.6 (0.06)
Asian	363 (10.1)	2.1 (0.06)	100.0	18.2 (1.17)	20.0 (1.13)	17.9 (1.07)	9.0 (0.91)	34.8 (1.32)	21.8 (1.08)	9.4 (0.74)	3.7 (0.45)
Pacific Islander	27 (2.8)	0.2 (0.02)	100.0	12.9 (3.46)	31.9 (4.21)	32.7 (4.80)	13.8 (3.75)	8.7 ! (2.62)	7.9 ! (2.62)	2.4 (0.77)	0.5 ! (0.21)
American Indian/Alaska Native	194 (5.6)	1.1 (0.03)	100.0	12.9 (1.12)	30.1 (1.57)	30.4 (1.58)	10.3 (0.97)	11.0 (0.95)	8.1 (0.87)	5.3 (1.32)	2.3 ! (1.04)
Some other race	54 (4.2)	0.3 (0.02)	100.0	20.1 (2.93)	17.9 (3.32)	32.8 (3.86)	8.1 (2.03)	21.1 (3.44)	13.6 (3.10)	5.3 (1.32)	‡ (†)
Two or more races	805 (12.6)	4.7 (0.07)	100.0	9.9 (0.59)	24.0 (0.80)	31.5 (0.87)	13.6 (0.63)	21.0 (0.81)	13.2 (0.57)	6.1 (0.51)	1.6 (0.21)

†Not applicable.

!Interpret data with caution. The coefficient of variation (CV) for this estimate is between 30 and 50 percent.

‡Reporting standards not met. Either there are too few cases for a reliable estimate or the coefficient of variation (CV) is 50 percent or greater.

[1]Includes adoptive and stepparents, but excludes parents not residing in the same household as their children.

[2]Includes parents who completed high school through equivalency programs, such as a GED program.

NOTE: Table includes only 6- to 18-year-olds who resided with at least one of their parents (including an adoptive or stepparent). The 6- to 18-year-olds in single-parent households resided with only one parent, while those in two-parent households resided with two parents. Race categories exclude persons of Hispanic ethnicity. Detail may not sum to totals because of rounding. SOURCE: U.S. Department of Commerce, Census Bureau, American Community Survey, 2008 and 2013. (This table was prepared January 2015.)

Table 104.80. Percentage of persons 18 to 24 years old and age 25 and over, by educational attainment and state: 2000 and 2013

[Standard errors appear in parentheses]

State	Percent of 18- to 24-year-olds who were high school completers[1]		Percent of population 25 years old and over, by educational attainment											
			2000					2013						
			Less than high school completion	High school completion or higher	Bachelor's or higher degree			Less than high school completion	High school completion or higher		Bachelor's or higher degree			
	2000	2013			Total	Bachelor's degree	Graduate degree		Total	High school only	Total	Bachelor's degree	Graduate degree
1	2	3	4	5	6	7	8	9	10	11	12	13	14
United States	**74.7 (0.02)**	**85.3 (0.09)**	**19.6 (0.01)**	**80.4 (0.01)**	**24.4 (0.01)**	**15.5 (0.01)**	**8.9 (#)**	**13.4 (0.04)**	**86.6 (0.04)**	**27.9 (0.05)**	**29.6 (0.06)**	**18.4 (0.04)**	**11.2 (0.04)**
Alabama	72.2 (0.15)	81.9 (0.75)	24.7 (0.06)	75.3 (0.06)	19.0 (0.05)	12.1 (0.04)	6.9 (0.03)	15.1 (0.29)	84.9 (0.29)	31.4 (0.37)	23.5 (0.31)	14.7 (0.25)	8.8 (0.18)
Alaska	76.9 (0.40)	83.1 (2.32)	11.7 (0.12)	88.3 (0.12)	24.7 (0.16)	16.1 (0.13)	8.6 (0.10)	8.4 (0.67)	91.6 (0.67)	26.5 (1.06)	29.2 (1.14)	18.8 (0.94)	10.4 (0.72)
Arizona	69.2 (0.19)	81.8 (0.60)	19.0 (0.06)	81.0 (0.06)	23.5 (0.07)	15.1 (0.06)	8.4 (0.04)	14.2 (0.22)	85.8 (0.22)	24.8 (0.26)	27.5 (0.25)	17.2 (0.20)	10.3 (0.18)
Arkansas	75.4 (0.19)	85.7 (0.95)	24.7 (0.07)	75.3 (0.07)	16.7 (0.06)	11.0 (0.05)	5.7 (0.04)	15.5 (0.29)	84.5 (0.29)	35.7 (0.43)	20.6 (0.43)	13.2 (0.32)	7.4 (0.27)
California	70.7 (0.07)	85.7 (0.24)	23.2 (0.03)	76.8 (0.03)	26.6 (0.03)	17.1 (0.02)	9.5 (0.02)	18.3 (0.11)	81.7 (0.11)	20.9 (0.11)	31.1 (0.10)	19.5 (0.09)	11.5 (0.07)
Colorado	75.1 (0.15)	84.4 (0.62)	13.1 (0.05)	86.9 (0.05)	32.7 (0.06)	21.6 (0.06)	11.1 (0.04)	9.5 (0.23)	90.5 (0.23)	21.4 (0.27)	37.7 (0.27)	23.8 (0.26)	13.9 (0.21)
Connecticut	78.2 (0.21)	86.7 (0.79)	16.0 (0.06)	84.0 (0.06)	31.4 (0.08)	18.1 (0.07)	13.3 (0.06)	10.3 (0.27)	89.7 (0.27)	27.5 (0.33)	37.5 (0.36)	20.6 (0.29)	16.9 (0.27)
Delaware	77.6 (0.41)	84.7 (1.47)	17.4 (0.14)	82.6 (0.14)	25.0 (0.16)	15.6 (0.14)	9.4 (0.11)	11.9 (0.53)	88.1 (0.53)	31.2 (0.72)	29.6 (0.76)	17.1 (0.63)	12.5 (0.48)
District of Columbia	79.4 (0.40)	88.8 (1.56)	22.2 (0.18)	77.8 (0.18)	39.1 (0.21)	18.1 (0.17)	21.0 (0.18)	10.1 (0.54)	89.9 (0.54)	19.1 (0.62)	54.5 (0.72)	22.2 (0.85)	32.3 (0.80)
Florida	71.7 (0.11)	83.2 (0.44)	20.1 (0.04)	79.9 (0.04)	22.3 (0.04)	14.2 (0.03)	8.1 (0.02)	13.2 (0.12)	86.8 (0.12)	29.4 (0.15)	27.2 (0.15)	17.6 (0.13)	9.7 (0.10)
Georgia	70.0 (0.15)	82.0 (0.51)	21.4 (0.05)	78.6 (0.05)	24.3 (0.05)	16.0 (0.05)	8.3 (0.04)	14.4 (0.17)	85.6 (0.17)	28.6 (0.26)	28.4 (0.22)	17.8 (0.19)	10.6 (0.13)
Hawaii	85.8 (0.25)	91.9 (0.77)	15.4 (0.10)	84.6 (0.10)	26.2 (0.12)	17.8 (0.10)	8.4 (0.08)	9.0 (0.42)	91.0 (0.42)	26.9 (0.63)	31.4 (0.66)	21.2 (0.51)	10.2 (0.40)
Idaho	77.3 (0.25)	85.7 (1.27)	15.3 (0.09)	84.7 (0.09)	21.7 (0.10)	14.9 (0.09)	6.8 (0.06)	10.6 (0.37)	89.4 (0.37)	27.5 (0.65)	26.2 (0.65)	18.1 (0.57)	8.1 (0.31)
Illinois	76.0 (0.09)	86.5 (0.37)	18.6 (0.03)	81.4 (0.03)	26.1 (0.03)	16.6 (0.03)	9.5 (0.02)	12.1 (0.13)	87.9 (0.13)	27.1 (0.21)	32.3 (0.24)	19.8 (0.21)	12.5 (0.14)
Indiana	76.5 (0.15)	82.9 (0.56)	17.9 (0.05)	82.1 (0.05)	19.4 (0.05)	12.2 (0.04)	7.2 (0.04)	12.4 (0.19)	87.6 (0.19)	34.5 (0.26)	23.7 (0.28)	15.1 (0.21)	8.6 (0.15)
Iowa	81.4 (0.16)	88.8 (0.78)	13.9 (0.06)	86.1 (0.06)	21.2 (0.07)	14.7 (0.06)	6.5 (0.04)	8.4 (0.25)	91.6 (0.25)	33.2 (0.49)	26.0 (0.43)	17.9 (0.40)	8.1 (0.27)
Kansas	78.3 (0.18)	87.2 (0.75)	14.0 (0.06)	86.0 (0.06)	25.8 (0.08)	17.1 (0.06)	8.7 (0.05)	9.7 (0.31)	90.3 (0.31)	26.8 (0.40)	30.9 (0.40)	19.7 (0.37)	11.2 (0.28)
Kentucky	74.9 (0.15)	84.8 (0.68)	25.9 (0.06)	74.1 (0.06)	17.1 (0.05)	10.2 (0.04)	6.9 (0.03)	16.1 (0.26)	83.9 (0.26)	32.9 (0.33)	22.6 (0.29)	13.1 (0.23)	9.5 (0.20)
Louisiana	72.3 (0.15)	79.2 (0.88)	25.2 (0.06)	74.8 (0.06)	18.7 (0.05)	12.2 (0.04)	6.5 (0.03)	17.0 (0.29)	83.0 (0.29)	33.7 (0.36)	22.7 (0.31)	15.1 (0.26)	7.6 (0.20)
Maine	78.9 (0.28)	90.5 (1.22)	14.6 (0.08)	85.4 (0.08)	22.9 (0.10)	15.0 (0.09)	7.9 (0.06)	7.9 (0.36)	92.1 (0.36)	34.7 (0.85)	28.0 (0.68)	18.2 (0.54)	9.8 (0.45)
Maryland	79.6 (0.16)	88.4 (0.53)	16.2 (0.05)	83.8 (0.05)	31.4 (0.07)	18.0 (0.06)	13.4 (0.05)	10.7 (0.18)	89.3 (0.18)	26.0 (0.28)	37.3 (0.30)	20.1 (0.26)	17.2 (0.24)
Massachusetts	82.2 (0.13)	89.0 (0.48)	15.2 (0.05)	84.8 (0.05)	33.2 (0.06)	19.5 (0.05)	13.7 (0.04)	9.9 (0.14)	90.1 (0.14)	26.0 (0.27)	40.1 (0.30)	22.2 (0.22)	17.9 (0.21)
Michigan	76.5 (0.10)	86.5 (0.51)	16.6 (0.03)	83.4 (0.03)	21.8 (0.04)	13.7 (0.03)	8.1 (0.02)	10.6 (0.16)	89.4 (0.16)	29.4 (0.25)	26.9 (0.23)	16.5 (0.18)	10.4 (0.15)
Minnesota	79.3 (0.13)	86.4 (0.67)	12.1 (0.04)	87.9 (0.04)	27.4 (0.06)	19.1 (0.05)	8.3 (0.03)	7.8 (0.20)	92.2 (0.20)	26.4 (0.36)	33.6 (0.40)	22.6 (0.33)	11.0 (0.22)
Mississippi	71.3 (0.18)	80.6 (1.09)	27.1 (0.08)	72.9 (0.08)	16.9 (0.06)	11.1 (0.05)	5.8 (0.04)	17.7 (0.33)	82.3 (0.33)	30.3 (0.40)	20.5 (0.35)	13.1 (0.25)	7.4 (0.25)
Missouri	76.5 (0.13)	87.6 (0.58)	18.7 (0.05)	81.3 (0.05)	21.6 (0.05)	14.0 (0.04)	7.6 (0.03)	11.0 (0.18)	89.0 (0.18)	31.9 (0.30)	27.0 (0.28)	17.1 (0.24)	10.0 (0.17)
Montana	78.6 (0.31)	82.1 (1.79)	12.8 (0.10)	87.2 (0.10)	24.4 (0.13)	17.2 (0.11)	7.2 (0.08)	6.8 (0.35)	93.2 (0.35)	28.0 (0.67)	29.3 (0.81)	19.9 (0.61)	9.4 (0.49)
Nebraska	80.0 (0.21)	89.9 (0.92)	13.4 (0.07)	86.6 (0.07)	23.7 (0.09)	16.4 (0.08)	7.3 (0.06)	9.4 (0.32)	90.6 (0.32)	26.9 (0.54)	30.3 (0.61)	20.3 (0.47)	10.0 (0.39)
Nevada	66.7 (0.32)	79.7 (1.16)	19.3 (0.10)	80.7 (0.10)	18.2 (0.10)	12.1 (0.08)	6.1 (0.06)	14.8 (0.31)	85.2 (0.31)	28.6 (0.50)	22.4 (0.39)	15.1 (0.32)	7.3 (0.23)
New Hampshire	77.8 (0.29)	90.8 (1.09)	12.6 (0.08)	87.4 (0.08)	28.7 (0.11)	18.7 (0.10)	10.0 (0.07)	7.4 (0.36)	92.6 (0.36)	28.9 (0.63)	35.1 (0.71)	22.2 (0.53)	12.9 (0.40)
New Jersey	76.3 (0.14)	87.7 (0.50)	17.9 (0.04)	82.1 (0.04)	29.8 (0.05)	18.8 (0.04)	11.0 (0.04)	11.6 (0.18)	88.4 (0.18)	29.0 (0.23)	36.4 (0.22)	22.5 (0.20)	13.9 (0.19)
New Mexico	70.5 (0.24)	82.4 (1.09)	21.1 (0.09)	78.9 (0.09)	23.5 (0.09)	13.7 (0.07)	9.8 (0.06)	16.3 (0.38)	83.7 (0.38)	26.6 (0.47)	26.3 (0.46)	14.5 (0.41)	11.8 (0.29)
New York	76.1 (0.09)	86.6 (0.32)	20.9 (0.03)	79.1 (0.03)	27.4 (0.04)	15.6 (0.03)	11.8 (0.03)	14.6 (0.15)	85.4 (0.15)	26.8 (0.18)	33.9 (0.18)	19.2 (0.14)	14.7 (0.14)
North Carolina	74.2 (0.11)	84.0 (0.59)	21.9 (0.04)	78.1 (0.04)	22.5 (0.04)	15.3 (0.04)	7.2 (0.03)	14.3 (0.20)	85.7 (0.20)	26.6 (0.21)	28.3 (0.25)	18.3 (0.20)	10.0 (0.13)
North Dakota	84.4 (0.24)	87.9 (1.91)	16.1 (0.10)	83.9 (0.10)	22.0 (0.12)	16.5 (0.10)	5.5 (0.06)	8.1 (0.47)	91.9 (0.47)	27.2 (0.95)	27.8 (0.86)	20.5 (0.81)	7.3 (0.55)
Ohio	76.8 (0.09)	86.0 (0.43)	17.0 (0.03)	83.0 (0.03)	21.1 (0.03)	13.7 (0.03)	7.4 (0.02)	10.9 (0.15)	89.1 (0.15)	34.2 (0.25)	26.0 (0.18)	16.3 (0.16)	9.7 (0.11)
Oklahoma	74.8 (0.16)	82.8 (0.67)	19.4 (0.06)	80.6 (0.06)	20.3 (0.06)	13.5 (0.05)	6.8 (0.04)	13.3 (0.27)	86.7 (0.27)	32.0 (0.39)	24.0 (0.39)	16.2 (0.31)	7.8 (0.22)
Oregon	74.2 (0.17)	85.6 (0.98)	14.9 (0.05)	85.1 (0.05)	25.1 (0.06)	16.4 (0.06)	8.7 (0.04)	10.4 (0.24)	89.6 (0.24)	24.3 (0.33)	30.4 (0.33)	19.0 (0.31)	11.4 (0.21)
Pennsylvania	79.8 (0.09)	87.9 (0.42)	18.1 (0.03)	81.9 (0.03)	22.4 (0.03)	14.0 (0.03)	8.4 (0.02)	10.8 (0.14)	89.2 (0.14)	36.4 (0.23)	28.6 (0.24)	17.3 (0.18)	11.3 (0.16)
Rhode Island	81.3 (0.32)	89.5 (1.10)	22.0 (0.13)	78.0 (0.13)	25.6 (0.14)	15.9 (0.12)	9.7 (0.10)	13.7 (0.56)	86.3 (0.56)	26.4 (0.76)	32.7 (0.63)	20.1 (0.57)	12.7 (0.44)
South Carolina	74.3 (0.18)	83.4 (0.72)	23.7 (0.07)	76.3 (0.07)	20.4 (0.07)	13.5 (0.06)	6.9 (0.04)	14.6 (0.31)	85.4 (0.31)	29.2 (0.35)	25.9 (0.32)	16.3 (0.27)	9.6 (0.20)
South Dakota	78.2 (0.33)	86.5 (1.71)	15.4 (0.12)	84.6 (0.12)	21.5 (0.13)	15.5 (0.12)	6.0 (0.08)	8.7 (0.52)	91.3 (0.52)	31.9 (0.92)	25.9 (0.82)	18.8 (0.69)	7.1 (0.43)
Tennessee	75.1 (0.16)	86.9 (0.53)	24.1 (0.06)	75.9 (0.06)	19.6 (0.06)	12.8 (0.05)	6.8 (0.03)	14.4 (0.20)	85.6 (0.20)	33.1 (0.27)	24.7 (0.28)	15.5 (0.22)	9.1 (0.17)
Texas	68.6 (0.08)	82.9 (0.38)	24.3 (0.03)	75.7 (0.03)	23.2 (0.03)	15.6 (0.03)	7.6 (0.02)	18.1 (0.12)	81.9 (0.12)	25.2 (0.15)	27.5 (0.15)	18.3 (0.13)	9.3 (0.10)
Utah	80.3 (0.16)	87.3 (0.83)	12.3 (0.07)	87.7 (0.07)	26.1 (0.09)	17.8 (0.08)	8.3 (0.06)	8.4 (0.29)	91.6 (0.29)	23.1 (0.42)	31.3 (0.42)	20.8 (0.34)	10.5 (0.30)
Vermont	83.0 (0.28)	91.2 (1.41)	13.6 (0.10)	86.4 (0.10)	29.4 (0.13)	18.3 (0.11)	11.1 (0.09)	8.5 (0.57)	91.5 (0.57)	30.5 (0.98)	34.2 (1.18)	20.5 (0.92)	13.7 (0.74)
Virginia	79.4 (0.13)	88.6 (0.46)	18.5 (0.05)	81.5 (0.05)	29.5 (0.06)	17.9 (0.05)	11.6 (0.04)	11.7 (0.19)	88.3 (0.19)	24.9 (0.27)	36.1 (0.26)	20.9 (0.20)	15.2 (0.19)
Washington	75.3 (0.16)	85.0 (0.56)	12.9 (0.05)	87.1 (0.05)	27.7 (0.06)	18.4 (0.05)	9.3 (0.04)	9.8 (0.18)	90.2 (0.18)	23.1 (0.31)	32.8 (0.27)	21.0 (0.25)	11.8 (0.18)
West Virginia	78.2 (0.22)	85.7 (1.28)	24.8 (0.09)	75.2 (0.09)	14.8 (0.07)	8.9 (0.06)	5.9 (0.05)	15.4 (0.38)	84.6 (0.38)	40.3 (0.52)	18.8 (0.48)	11.3 (0.39)	7.5 (0.32)
Wisconsin	78.9 (0.13)	87.1 (0.53)	14.9 (0.04)	85.1 (0.04)	22.4 (0.05)	15.2 (0.04)	7.2 (0.03)	9.4 (0.21)	90.6 (0.21)	31.8 (0.30)	27.8 (0.34)	18.7 (0.32)	9.1 (0.20)
Wyoming	79.0 (0.41)	88.9 (1.65)	12.1 (0.13)	87.9 (0.13)	21.9 (0.16)	14.9 (0.14)	7.0 (0.10)	6.4 (0.49)	93.6 (0.49)	28.1 (0.86)	27.1 (1.09)	18.3 (0.86)	8.8 (0.61)

#Rounds to zero.

[1]High school completers include diploma recipients and those completing high school through alternative credentials, such as a GED.

NOTE: Detail may not sum to totals because of rounding.

SOURCE: U.S. Department of Commerce, Census Bureau, Census 2000 Summary File 3, retrieved October 11, 2006, from http://factfinder2.census.gov/faces/tableservices/jsf/pages/productview.xhtml?pid=DEC_00_SF3_QTP20&prodType=table; Census Briefs, *Educational Attainment: 2000*; and 2013 American Community Survey (ACS) 1-Year Public Use Microdata Sample (PUMS) data. (This table was prepared May 2015.)

Table 104.85. Rates of high school completion and bachelor's degree attainment among persons age 25 and over, by race/ethnicity and state: 2013

[Standard errors appear in parentheses]

	Percent with high school completion or higher						Percent with bachelor's degree or higher					
State	Total¹	White	Black	Hispanic	Asian	Two or more races	Total¹	White	Black	Hispanic	Asian	Two or more races
1	2	3	4	5	6	7	8	9	10	11	12	13
United States	86.6 (0.04)	91.7 (0.03)	83.9 (0.10)	64.7 (0.15)	86.2 (0.14)	90.1 (0.22)	29.6 (0.06)	33.0 (0.07)	19.3 (0.13)	14.0 (0.11)	51.5 (0.20)	31.5 (0.39)
Alabama	84.9 (0.29)	87.0 (0.36)	81.2 (0.51)	61.7 (2.36)	90.7 (2.11)	88.7 (2.11)	23.5 (0.31)	25.8 (0.35)	16.0 (0.61)	15.3 (1.95)	56.2 (3.35)	29.5 (3.52)
Alaska	91.6 (0.67)	95.4 (0.60)	78.2 (6.60)	90.3 (3.34)	81.0 (4.93)	92.7 (3.58)	29.2 (1.14)	34.0 (1.46)	19.6 (4.97)	26.8 (5.37)	20.2 (5.11)	35.7 (7.37)
Arizona	85.8 (0.22)	94.1 (0.18)	87.8 (1.10)	64.4 (0.71)	86.8 (1.33)	92.0 (1.57)	27.5 (0.25)	34.0 (0.36)	22.0 (1.51)	10.0 (0.36)	50.5 (1.74)	34.2 (2.51)
Arkansas	84.5 (0.29)	86.9 (0.31)	82.2 (0.91)	51.3 (2.65)	85.3 (2.83)	92.1 (1.65)	20.6 (0.43)	22.2 (0.50)	13.7 (0.93)	7.7 (1.24)	50.2 (3.63)	23.8 (3.45)
California	81.7 (0.11)	94.3 (0.09)	88.5 (0.33)	60.4 (0.29)	86.5 (0.25)	91.4 (0.50)	31.1 (0.10)	40.5 (0.16)	22.8 (0.52)	11.3 (0.16)	48.9 (0.31)	36.5 (0.97)
Colorado	90.5 (0.23)	95.7 (0.17)	87.7 (1.34)	68.3 (0.98)	87.3 (1.17)	93.2 (1.39)	37.7 (0.27)	43.8 (0.33)	23.3 (1.84)	12.4 (0.58)	51.5 (2.01)	36.5 (2.62)
Connecticut	89.7 (0.27)	93.4 (0.25)	85.9 (1.07)	69.4 (1.26)	89.2 (1.43)	91.5 (1.90)	37.5 (0.36)	41.8 (0.39)	18.6 (1.19)	15.3 (0.98)	67.2 (2.06)	39.1 (3.56)
Delaware	88.1 (0.53)	91.1 (0.62)	86.2 (1.41)	63.5 (3.16)	89.5 (2.90)	81.4 (7.13)	29.6 (0.76)	31.7 (0.87)	20.6 (1.86)	14.5 (2.38)	67.6 (4.29)	15.4! (5.01)
District of Columbia	89.9 (0.54)	99.5 (0.19)	84.2 (0.87)	75.5 (3.78)	93.6 (2.63)	96.0 (2.53)	54.5 (0.72)	90.9 (0.76)	23.4 (1.27)	46.7 (3.21)	70.1 (4.92)	68.0 (7.22)
Florida	86.8 (0.12)	91.5 (0.11)	81.0 (0.37)	77.0 (0.41)	87.3 (0.76)	89.7 (0.96)	27.2 (0.15)	30.5 (0.22)	17.2 (0.34)	21.6 (0.28)	49.3 (1.20)	29.9 (1.76)
Georgia	85.6 (0.17)	89.4 (0.20)	84.6 (0.35)	57.0 (1.11)	86.0 (0.91)	92.9 (1.13)	28.4 (0.22)	32.3 (0.26)	21.3 (0.43)	12.7 (0.72)	52.1 (1.33)	38.5 (2.78)
Hawaii	91.0 (0.42)	96.8 (0.39)	98.2 (0.96)	90.0 (1.61)	87.4 (0.75)	92.9 (0.89)	31.4 (0.66)	43.7 (1.31)	43.7 (5.10)	20.9 (2.21)	33.5 (0.97)	19.1 (1.26)
Idaho	89.4 (0.37)	93.0 (0.33)	‡ (†)	58.2 (2.61)	79.5 (4.44)	84.4 (3.82)	26.2 (0.65)	27.7 (0.70)	‡ (†)	11.3 (1.46)	34.5 (4.00)	22.7 (4.48)
Illinois	87.9 (0.13)	90.9 (0.12)	85.2 (0.43)	62.2 (0.71)	91.6 (0.62)	91.1 (1.30)	32.3 (0.24)	35.9 (0.29)	20.2 (0.53)	13.3 (0.48)	62.5 (1.00)	41.2 (2.32)
Indiana	87.6 (0.19)	89.1 (0.21)	85.0 (0.85)	64.8 (1.58)	90.3 (1.39)	87.6 (2.06)	23.7 (0.28)	24.9 (0.29)	15.1 (0.92)	11.7 (1.22)	59.4 (3.08)	19.6 (2.06)
Iowa	91.6 (0.25)	93.1 (0.24)	85.2 (2.35)	61.6 (2.86)	83.9 (2.60)	94.0 (2.25)	26.0 (0.43)	26.3 (0.44)	18.0 (4.19)	10.9 (2.12)	56.2 (4.33)	10.9 (2.93)
Kansas	90.3 (0.31)	93.6 (0.26)	87.1 (1.37)	60.8 (2.31)	82.0 (2.22)	92.8 (1.88)	30.9 (0.40)	33.1 (0.43)	19.4 (1.85)	12.5 (1.23)	46.0 (3.71)	30.1 (3.79)
Kentucky	83.9 (0.26)	84.1 (0.29)	85.4 (1.02)	66.5 (2.57)	83.6 (2.56)	90.6 (2.19)	22.8 (0.29)	22.8 (0.31)	16.1 (1.05)	16.2 (1.89)	58.1 (3.63)	25.9 (3.31)
Louisiana	83.0 (0.29)	86.9 (0.35)	77.1 (0.66)	72.7 (1.52)	72.2 (2.70)	82.0 (3.42)	22.7 (0.31)	26.3 (0.42)	14.7 (0.52)	18.8 (1.22)	40.8 (2.72)	21.6 (2.59)
Maine	92.1 (0.36)	92.5 (0.38)	73.7 (6.96)	83.9 (5.57)	76.2 (6.32)	93.3 (2.42)	28.0 (0.68)	27.9 (0.69)	13.0! (6.11)	33.1 (7.07)	47.7 (7.23)	27.3 (5.20)
Maryland	89.3 (0.18)	92.8 (0.22)	88.6 (0.37)	65.7 (1.13)	89.3 (0.93)	91.5 (1.75)	37.3 (0.30)	42.8 (0.36)	25.5 (0.61)	21.7 (1.23)	59.2 (1.30)	37.9 (3.13)
Massachusetts	90.1 (0.14)	93.9 (0.19)	83.0 (1.10)	69.9 (1.11)	86.8 (0.77)	89.2 (1.73)	40.1 (0.30)	42.5 (0.31)	24.2 (1.02)	17.8 (0.82)	60.1 (1.28)	34.8 (2.51)
Michigan	89.4 (0.16)	94.7 (0.15)	83.7 (0.60)	70.4 (1.39)	87.9 (1.19)	88.3 (1.43)	26.9 (0.23)	28.2 (0.25)	15.7 (0.54)	16.6 (1.16)	60.1 (1.84)	24.6 (1.88)
Minnesota	92.2 (0.20)	95.8 (0.18)	79.9 (1.88)	63.2 (2.86)	82.2 (1.79)	84.7 (2.56)	33.6 (0.23)	34.6 (0.40)	17.8 (1.74)	19.4 (1.97)	47.3 (2.56)	30.2 (3.12)
Mississippi	82.3 (0.33)	86.2 (0.38)	76.8 (0.68)	65.0 (3.36)	82.2 (3.79)	85.2 (3.93)	20.5 (0.35)	24.0 (0.44)	14.4 (0.55)	13.6 (2.16)	37.9 (4.39)	20.5 (4.40)
Missouri	89.0 (0.18)	90.2 (0.20)	85.8 (0.75)	70.2 (1.85)	87.5 (1.81)	86.4 (1.86)	27.0 (0.28)	28.2 (0.32)	15.8 (0.73)	18.9 (1.62)	55.9 (2.47)	25.2 (2.42)
Montana	93.0 (0.35)	93.9 (0.36)	‡ (†)	85.6 (3.82)	‡ (†)	96.9 (2.14)	29.3 (0.81)	30.7 (0.86)	‡ (†)	14.5 (4.06)	‡ (†)	36.4 (8.64)
Nebraska	90.6 (0.32)	94.7 (0.31)	88.4 (1.96)	45.1 (2.43)	82.8 (3.72)	92.2 (4.12)	30.3 (0.61)	32.6 (0.65)	16.2 (2.46)	8.9 (1.49)	46.2 (6.30)	31.7 (6.74)
Nevada	85.2 (0.31)	92.6 (0.28)	86.5 (1.38)	63.7 (1.17)	86.8 (1.14)	92.3 (1.48)	22.4 (0.39)	26.5 (0.58)	15.8 (1.22)	9.0 (0.58)	36.6 (1.41)	30.0 (2.96)
New Hampshire	92.6 (0.36)	93.2 (0.35)	83.0 (8.01)	75.0 (6.17)	89.0 (3.68)	85.7 (3.99)	35.1 (0.71)	35.0 (0.73)	23.4! (7.48)	21.9 (4.33)	59.1 (4.64)	34.0 (6.09)
New Jersey	88.4 (0.18)	93.0 (0.17)	86.3 (0.58)	70.7 (0.74)	92.5 (0.44)	87.8 (2.14)	36.4 (0.18)	39.7 (0.28)	21.8 (0.61)	16.7 (0.49)	70.0 (0.89)	39.4 (2.29)
New Mexico	83.7 (0.38)	93.5 (0.50)	92.5 (2.58)	72.9 (0.79)	89.3 (2.35)	97.4 (1.27)	26.3 (0.46)	38.5 (0.75)	29.6 (4.34)	15.0 (0.57)	52.7 (4.72)	34.9 (4.80)
New York	85.4 (0.15)	92.3 (0.19)	82.6 (0.65)	66.4 (0.49)	78.3 (0.60)	86.9 (1.24)	33.9 (0.18)	39.7 (0.23)	22.1 (0.40)	16.7 (0.37)	45.8 (0.63)	37.9 (1.64)
North Carolina	85.7 (0.20)	89.5 (0.22)	83.1 (0.40)	54.6 (1.22)	83.8 (1.13)	86.1 (1.39)	28.3 (0.25)	32.0 (0.29)	18.2 (0.46)	12.8 (0.74)	52.5 (1.99)	28.1 (1.97)
North Dakota	91.9 (0.47)	92.3 (0.47)	‡ (†)	85.9 (4.87)	‡ (†)	92.3 (4.77)	27.8 (0.86)	28.3 (0.96)	‡ (†)	‡ (†)	‡ (†)	34.0 (4.39)
Ohio	89.1 (0.15)	90.5 (0.13)	83.0 (0.57)	71.3 (1.64)	87.2 (1.12)	86.6 (1.24)	26.0 (0.18)	27.0 (0.21)	15.2 (0.59)	16.4 (1.33)	61.9 (1.72)	27.8 (1.72)
Oklahoma	86.7 (0.27)	89.4 (0.27)	87.9 (1.22)	59.1 (1.84)	75.2 (3.19)	89.2 (0.94)	24.0 (0.30)	26.5 (0.35)	17.5 (1.36)	9.0 (0.92)	38.9 (3.19)	25.4 (1.51)
Oregon	89.6 (0.24)	93.2 (0.21)	86.9 (2.37)	59.5 (1.47)	82.3 (1.29)	89.8 (1.51)	30.4 (0.33)	32.2 (0.37)	19.2 (2.16)	13.8 (1.11)	43.1 (1.89)	25.4 (2.02)
Pennsylvania	89.2 (0.14)	91.1 (0.13)	84.6 (0.65)	68.6 (1.19)	82.2 (1.35)	89.5 (1.85)	28.6 (0.24)	29.9 (0.26)	16.5 (0.63)	14.5 (0.85)	54.6 (1.59)	30.5 (2.50)
Rhode Island	86.3 (0.56)	88.9 (0.52)	80.1 (3.10)	64.1 (2.60)	79.8 (3.30)	91.5 (3.56)	32.7 (0.63)	35.8 (0.76)	21.1 (3.77)	11.4 (1.37)	46.8 (4.04)	31.0 (7.33)
South Carolina	85.4 (0.31)	89.1 (0.33)	79.9 (0.58)	59.7 (2.11)	86.5 (2.16)	84.8 (2.94)	25.9 (0.32)	30.5 (0.38)	15.0 (0.61)	13.7 (1.09)	40.9 (3.09)	23.1 (3.78)
South Dakota	91.3 (0.52)	93.3 (0.50)	83.5 (10.10)	75.3 (5.79)	72.6 (8.07)	82.1 (5.58)	25.9 (0.82)	27.6 (0.86)	37.8! (15.66)	8.8! (3.04)	38.7 (10.15)	10.1! (4.30)
Tennessee	85.6 (0.20)	87.5 (0.19)	82.3 (0.68)	58.2 (2.06)	85.9 (1.82)	85.6 (2.24)	24.7 (0.15)	26.0 (0.32)	17.9 (0.60)	12.0 (1.10)	49.6 (3.18)	26.4 (2.28)
Texas	81.9 (0.12)	93.0 (0.09)	87.7 (0.24)	61.9 (0.30)	88.8 (0.45)	86.1 (0.89)	27.5 (0.15)	35.8 (0.22)	22.3 (0.41)	12.4 (0.22)	57.8 (0.80)	35.9 (1.68)
Utah	91.6 (0.29)	95.3 (0.23)	86.2 (4.43)	67.0 (1.79)	84.9 (2.57)	93.9 (1.95)	31.3 (0.42)	33.7 (0.47)	22.8 (4.43)	11.7 (0.99)	50.3 (3.41)	31.9 (5.08)
Vermont	91.5 (0.57)	91.8 (0.58)	‡ (†)	90.6 (4.08)	89.7 (5.63)	85.0 (5.63)	34.0 (1.18)	34.0 (1.18)	‡ (†)	34.7 (8.36)	53.7 (12.02)	36.5 (8.55)
Virginia	88.3 (0.19)	91.2 (0.18)	87.9 (0.42)	71.9 (1.18)	89.8 (0.30)	90.1 (0.94)	36.1 (0.26)	39.4 (0.30)	21.8 (0.57)	22.8 (1.10)	58.2 (1.15)	39.3 (2.00)
Washington	90.2 (0.18)	93.8 (0.15)	88.3 (1.12)	62.1 (1.14)	85.7 (0.76)	92.9 (1.12)	32.8 (0.27)	34.4 (0.30)	21.0 (1.40)	13.9 (0.79)	46.7 (1.09)	30.5 (1.79)
West Virginia	84.6 (0.38)	84.5 (0.40)	88.7 (2.03)	71.5 (4.13)	97.0 (1.90)	84.0 (3.98)	18.6 (0.48)	18.6 (0.50)	16.8 (2.28)	12.5 (1.30)	70.5 (7.06)	22.1 (5.03)
Wisconsin	90.6 (0.21)	93.0 (0.19)	78.8 (1.34)	65.2 (1.97)	82.3 (1.87)	91.1 (1.99)	29.2 (0.34)	29.2 (0.36)	12.8 (1.29)	12.5 (1.30)	46.4 (2.78)	24.2 (3.33)
Wyoming	93.6 (0.49)	94.5 (0.46)	‡ (†)	81.6 (3.09)	‡ (†)	98.1 (1.81)	27.1 (1.09)	27.9 (1.15)	‡ (†)	13.0 (2.77)	‡ (†)	26.4 (7.32)

†Not applicable.
!Interpret data with caution. The coefficient of variation (CV) for this estimate is between 30 and 50 percent.
‡Reporting standards not met. Either there are too few cases for a reliable estimate or the coefficient of variation (CV) is 50 percent or greater.
¹Total includes racial/ethnic groups not shown separately.
NOTE: Race categories exclude persons of Hispanic ethnicity.
SOURCE: U.S. Department of Commerce, Census Bureau, 2013 American Community Survey (ACS) 1-Year Public Use Microdata Sample (PUMS) data. (This table was prepared March 2015.)

Table 104.88. Rates of high school completion and bachelor's degree attainment among persons age 25 and over, by sex and state: 2013

[Standard errors appear in parentheses]

State	Number of persons age 25 and over (in thousands)						Percent with high school completion or higher						Percent with bachelor's or higher degree					
	Total		Male		Female		Total		Male		Female		Total		Male		Female	
1	2		3		4		5		6		7		8		9		10	
United States	210,991	(53.6)	101,749	(35.4)	109,243	(30.8)	86.6	(0.04)	85.9	(0.04)	87.2	(0.04)	29.6	(0.06)	29.5	(0.07)	29.7	(0.07)
Alabama	3,226	(4.4)	1,525	(3.6)	1,701	(2.8)	84.9	(0.29)	84.0	(0.43)	85.7	(0.35)	23.5	(0.31)	23.4	(0.35)	23.5	(0.44)
Alaska	462	(3.1)	239	(2.2)	222	(2.3)	91.6	(0.67)	91.0	(0.90)	92.3	(0.90)	29.2	(1.14)	25.5	(1.49)	33.2	(1.43)
Arizona	4,350	(4.1)	2,133	(3.2)	2,216	(3.0)	85.8	(0.22)	85.5	(0.25)	86.2	(0.29)	27.5	(0.25)	28.2	(0.32)	26.8	(0.32)
Arkansas	1,962	(3.0)	944	(2.8)	1,018	(2.3)	84.5	(0.29)	83.9	(0.37)	85.0	(0.46)	20.6	(0.43)	20.5	(0.51)	20.7	(0.55)
California	25,150	(7.9)	12,279	(6.6)	12,871	(6.0)	81.7	(0.11)	81.4	(0.13)	82.0	(0.13)	31.1	(0.10)	31.2	(0.11)	30.9	(0.14)
Colorado	3,516	(4.1)	1,741	(3.3)	1,774	(2.6)	90.5	(0.23)	89.8	(0.34)	91.2	(0.25)	37.7	(0.27)	37.9	(0.39)	37.5	(0.35)
Connecticut	2,469	(2.4)	1,176	(2.7)	1,293	(1.7)	89.7	(0.27)	89.1	(0.33)	90.2	(0.35)	37.5	(0.36)	37.7	(0.56)	37.4	(0.44)
Delaware	631	(1.8)	299	(1.6)	333	(1.4)	88.1	(0.53)	87.8	(0.75)	88.4	(0.66)	29.6	(0.76)	30.0	(0.96)	29.3	(0.99)
District of Columbia	454	(0.9)	211	(0.8)	243	(0.8)	88.9	(0.54)	88.9	(0.69)	90.0	(0.72)	54.5	(0.72)	55.6	(0.96)	53.5	(0.90)
Florida	13,731	(7.0)	6,575	(5.1)	7,156	(5.2)	86.8	(0.12)	86.0	(0.17)	87.5	(0.13)	27.2	(0.15)	27.9	(0.22)	26.7	(0.16)
Georgia	6,475	(6.2)	3,083	(5.0)	3,392	(4.2)	85.6	(0.17)	84.4	(0.25)	86.7	(0.21)	28.4	(0.22)	28.2	(0.30)	28.7	(0.27)
Hawaii	961	(1.9)	475	(1.5)	486	(1.7)	91.0	(0.42)	91.8	(0.58)	90.3	(0.53)	31.4	(0.66)	30.1	(0.84)	32.6	(0.82)
Idaho	1,025	(2.0)	504	(1.8)	520	(1.5)	89.4	(0.37)	88.8	(0.46)	90.0	(0.55)	26.2	(0.65)	27.0	(0.84)	25.4	(0.72)
Illinois	8,594	(6.0)	4,129	(4.2)	4,464	(4.6)	87.9	(0.13)	87.2	(0.18)	88.6	(0.17)	32.3	(0.24)	31.8	(0.30)	32.7	(0.26)
Indiana	4,315	(5.1)	2,078	(3.8)	2,237	(3.3)	87.6	(0.19)	86.9	(0.25)	88.3	(0.26)	23.7	(0.28)	23.5	(0.31)	23.9	(0.36)
Iowa	2,051	(3.3)	996	(2.3)	1,054	(2.5)	91.6	(0.25)	91.1	(0.31)	92.0	(0.34)	26.0	(0.43)	25.2	(0.63)	26.7	(0.43)
Kansas	1,874	(3.2)	913	(2.8)	961	(2.7)	90.3	(0.31)	89.5	(0.50)	91.1	(0.34)	30.9	(0.40)	30.5	(0.50)	31.2	(0.59)
Kentucky	2,956	(3.2)	1,422	(3.2)	1,534	(2.6)	83.9	(0.26)	82.5	(0.36)	85.2	(0.32)	22.6	(0.29)	22.4	(0.34)	22.7	(0.39)
Louisiana	3,033	(4.0)	1,453	(3.2)	1,580	(2.8)	83.0	(0.29)	80.9	(0.40)	85.0	(0.35)	22.7	(0.31)	21.5	(0.41)	23.8	(0.41)
Maine	952	(2.2)	457	(2.1)	495	(1.5)	92.1	(0.36)	90.8	(0.55)	93.2	(0.43)	28.0	(0.68)	26.0	(0.87)	29.9	(0.82)
Maryland	4,021	(3.6)	1,899	(2.7)	2,121	(2.5)	89.3	(0.18)	88.4	(0.27)	90.1	(0.23)	37.3	(0.30)	36.4	(0.38)	38.1	(0.37)
Massachusetts	4,607	(3.2)	2,184	(2.9)	2,423	(2.4)	90.1	(0.14)	89.6	(0.19)	90.4	(0.21)	40.1	(0.30)	39.9	(0.40)	40.3	(0.33)
Michigan	6,653	(5.5)	3,197	(4.4)	3,456	(3.8)	89.4	(0.16)	88.6	(0.22)	90.1	(0.21)	26.9	(0.23)	27.0	(0.28)	26.9	(0.28)
Minnesota	3,638	(4.6)	1,775	(4.4)	1,862	(4.0)	92.2	(0.20)	91.8	(0.26)	92.7	(0.28)	33.6	(0.40)	33.2	(0.51)	34.0	(0.47)
Mississippi	1,933	(3.4)	916	(3.1)	1,017	(2.7)	82.3	(0.33)	80.4	(0.50)	84.0	(0.47)	20.5	(0.35)	19.2	(0.44)	21.6	(0.50)
Missouri	4,052	(4.1)	1,947	(3.5)	2,105	(3.3)	89.0	(0.18)	88.5	(0.25)	89.5	(0.25)	27.0	(0.28)	27.0	(0.39)	27.1	(0.33)
Montana	688	(1.6)	340	(1.5)	349	(1.3)	93.2	(0.35)	93.1	(0.52)	93.3	(0.48)	29.3	(0.81)	28.7	(0.92)	30.0	(0.99)
Nebraska	1,213	(2.4)	591	(2.3)	622	(2.2)	90.6	(0.32)	89.5	(0.43)	91.5	(0.43)	30.3	(0.61)	29.8	(0.67)	30.7	(0.76)
Nevada	1,871	(2.5)	931	(2.1)	939	(1.8)	85.2	(0.31)	84.9	(0.44)	85.5	(0.42)	22.4	(0.39)	22.6	(0.60)	22.2	(0.45)
New Hampshire	924	(1.7)	449	(1.6)	475	(1.2)	92.6	(0.36)	92.0	(0.56)	93.1	(0.45)	35.1	(0.71)	34.6	(0.87)	35.6	(0.81)
New Jersey	6,085	(3.9)	2,897	(2.8)	3,188	(3.1)	88.4	(0.18)	88.0	(0.22)	88.7	(0.20)	36.4	(0.22)	37.1	(0.26)	35.8	(0.29)
New Mexico	1,361	(2.7)	664	(2.4)	697	(1.8)	83.7	(0.38)	83.2	(0.59)	84.1	(0.49)	26.3	(0.46)	25.6	(0.57)	27.0	(0.65)
New York	13,429	(7.0)	6,366	(6.1)	7,063	(4.7)	85.4	(0.15)	85.1	(0.18)	85.8	(0.17)	33.9	(0.18)	33.2	(0.22)	34.5	(0.22)
North Carolina	6,567	(5.8)	3,107	(4.4)	3,460	(4.0)	85.7	(0.20)	84.0	(0.26)	87.2	(0.23)	28.3	(0.25)	28.0	(0.32)	28.5	(0.28)
North Dakota	466	(2.0)	236	(1.8)	230	(1.4)	91.9	(0.47)	91.3	(0.62)	92.5	(0.66)	27.8	(0.86)	27.4	(1.16)	28.2	(1.09)
Ohio	7,810	(5.1)	3,740	(4.3)	4,070	(4.1)	89.1	(0.15)	88.6	(0.20)	89.6	(0.16)	26.0	(0.18)	26.2	(0.25)	25.9	(0.23)
Oklahoma	2,507	(4.2)	1,213	(3.8)	1,294	(2.8)	86.7	(0.27)	85.7	(0.43)	87.6	(0.39)	24.0	(0.39)	24.0	(0.48)	24.0	(0.49)
Oregon	2,703	(3.2)	1,318	(2.7)	1,385	(2.7)	89.6	(0.24)	88.9	(0.30)	90.2	(0.36)	30.4	(0.33)	30.8	(0.40)	30.0	(0.47)
Pennsylvania	8,813	(5.6)	4,227	(4.6)	4,586	(4.0)	89.2	(0.14)	88.8	(0.18)	89.5	(0.19)	28.6	(0.24)	28.7	(0.31)	28.6	(0.28)
Rhode Island	719	(1.3)	343	(1.1)	376	(1.0)	86.3	(0.56)	85.8	(0.69)	86.8	(0.74)	32.7	(0.63)	33.6	(0.85)	32.0	(0.73)
South Carolina	3,194	(3.7)	1,514	(2.9)	1,681	(2.6)	85.4	(0.31)	84.3	(0.43)	86.5	(0.35)	25.9	(0.32)	26.2	(0.45)	25.5	(0.44)
South Dakota	555	(1.8)	275	(1.6)	280	(1.4)	91.3	(0.52)	91.2	(0.80)	91.4	(0.60)	25.9	(0.82)	25.4	(0.94)	26.4	(1.18)
Tennessee	4,371	(4.2)	2,090	(3.7)	2,281	(2.8)	85.6	(0.20)	84.4	(0.30)	86.7	(0.26)	24.7	(0.28)	24.5	(0.32)	24.8	(0.35)
Texas	16,679	(8.3)	8,132	(6.9)	8,547	(5.3)	81.9	(0.12)	81.4	(0.15)	82.5	(0.15)	27.5	(0.15)	27.6	(0.19)	27.4	(0.18)
Utah	1,670	(2.4)	830	(2.2)	840	(2.0)	91.6	(0.29)	91.2	(0.43)	92.1	(0.34)	31.3	(0.42)	33.7	(0.57)	28.9	(0.61)
Vermont	437	(1.4)	211	(1.1)	226	(1.0)	91.5	(0.57)	89.4	(0.88)	93.5	(0.67)	34.2	(1.18)	31.1	(1.41)	37.2	(1.27)
Virginia	5,564	(5.7)	2,677	(3.9)	2,886	(4.0)	88.3	(0.19)	87.5	(0.24)	89.1	(0.21)	36.1	(0.26)	36.4	(0.35)	35.8	(0.32)
Washington	4,713	(4.3)	2,322	(4.0)	2,391	(3.3)	90.2	(0.18)	89.5	(0.24)	90.8	(0.21)	32.8	(0.27)	33.2	(0.34)	32.4	(0.34)
West Virginia	1,296	(1.7)	632	(1.5)	664	(1.3)	84.6	(0.38)	83.3	(0.53)	85.8	(0.49)	18.8	(0.48)	18.5	(0.56)	19.1	(0.56)
Wisconsin	3,883	(4.9)	1,898	(4.4)	1,985	(3.6)	90.6	(0.21)	89.7	(0.27)	91.5	(0.26)	27.8	(0.34)	26.7	(0.41)	28.8	(0.45)
Wyoming	383	(1.7)	192	(1.6)	191	(1.2)	93.6	(0.49)	93.0	(0.83)	94.2	(0.65)	27.1	(1.09)	27.3	(1.32)	26.9	(1.28)

NOTE: Detail may not sum to totals because of rounding.

SOURCE: U.S. Department of Commerce, Census Bureau, 2013 American Community Survey (ACS) 1-Year Public Use Microdata Sample (PUMS) data. (This table was prepared April 2015.)

Table 104.90. Percentage distribution of spring 2002 high school sophomores, by highest level of education completed through 2012 and selected student characteristics: 2012

[Standard errors appear in parentheses]

Selected student characteristic	Total		Less than high school completion		High school completion		Some post-secondary (no credential)		Postsecondary certificate		Associate's degree		Bachelor's degree		Master's or higher degree	
1	2		3		4		5		6		7		8		9	
Total, all students	100.0	(†)	3.1	(0.23)	12.6	(0.44)	32.3	(0.47)	10.1	(0.32)	8.7	(0.35)	26.6	(0.65)	6.7	(0.26)
Sex																
Male	100.0	(†)	3.7	(0.31)	16.0	(0.67)	33.9	(0.72)	8.4	(0.43)	8.0	(0.46)	25.1	(0.87)	4.9	(0.31)
Female	100.0	(†)	2.5	(0.26)	9.3	(0.51)	30.7	(0.68)	11.8	(0.46)	9.4	(0.50)	28.1	(0.80)	8.3	(0.42)
Race/ethnicity																
White	100.0	(†)	1.8	(0.22)	11.7	(0.51)	28.9	(0.60)	8.7	(0.40)	9.1	(0.47)	31.6	(0.80)	8.2	(0.36)
Black	100.0	(†)	4.7	(0.70)	13.2	(1.10)	40.2	(1.31)	14.6	(0.93)	7.5	(0.80)	16.1	(1.07)	3.7	(0.56)
Hispanic	100.0	(†)	6.6	(0.75)	14.6	(1.10)	38.7	(1.27)	12.3	(0.84)	9.1	(0.87)	15.8	(1.26)	2.8	(0.49)
Asian	100.0	(†)	1.6	(0.46)	5.9	(0.96)	27.6	(1.60)	8.5	(0.93)	5.6	(0.87)	39.8	(2.08)	11.1	(0.97)
Pacific Islander	100.0	(†)	#	(†)	22.7 !	(8.56)	35.0	(8.93)	‡	(†)	‡	(†)	29.5 !	(10.00)	‡	(†)
American Indian/Alaska Native	100.0	(†)	8.1 !	(3.31)	22.7	(5.00)	33.7	(4.82)	11.3 !	(3.57)	7.1 !	(2.59)	13.7 !	(4.28)	‡	(†)
Two or more races	100.0	(†)	3.4	(0.89)	18.5	(2.00)	32.6	(2.69)	9.0	(1.51)	8.6	(1.60)	22.2	(2.12)	5.7	(1.20)
Parents' educational attainment in 2002																
High school completion or less	100.0	(†)	6.4	(0.53)	21.1	(0.80)	33.5	(0.81)	12.5	(0.72)	9.3	(0.63)	14.7	(0.80)	2.5	(0.32)
Some college	100.0	(†)	2.2	(0.27)	13.4	(0.65)	36.8	(0.83)	12.1	(0.57)	9.5	(0.53)	21.7	(0.82)	4.3	(0.38)
Bachelor's degree	100.0	(†)	1.6	(0.30)	6.6	(0.58)	30.2	(1.13)	7.5	(0.58)	8.5	(0.74)	36.4	(1.21)	9.2	(0.76)
Master's or higher degree	100.0	(†)	1.3	(0.30)	4.4	(0.62)	23.5	(1.24)	5.5	(0.64)	6.1	(0.65)	44.0	(1.41)	15.1	(0.85)
Parents' socioeconomic status in 2012[1]																
Low quartile	100.0	(†)	7.0	(0.58)	21.3	(0.92)	36.2	(1.03)	12.8	(0.72)	8.2	(0.63)	12.3	(0.86)	2.2	(0.30)
Middle two quartiles	100.0	(†)	2.4	(0.26)	12.9	(0.54)	34.7	(0.68)	11.1	(0.48)	9.9	(0.52)	24.2	(0.78)	4.9	(0.32)
High quartile	100.0	(†)	0.5	(0.15)	3.1	(0.41)	23.6	(1.07)	5.4	(0.51)	6.7	(0.58)	45.9	(1.13)	14.7	(0.70)
Student's educational expectation in 10th grade																
High school completion or less	100.0	(†)	12.3	(1.44)	36.0	(1.88)	31.5	(1.94)	11.3	(1.38)	5.3	(0.92)	3.3	(0.70)	‡	(†)
Some college	100.0	(†)	5.7	(0.88)	22.8	(1.45)	37.5	(1.70)	14.5	(1.31)	10.7	(1.16)	7.9	(0.91)	1.0 !	(0.36)
Bachelor's degree	100.0	(†)	1.7	(0.27)	10.3	(0.66)	33.3	(0.88)	10.6	(0.57)	10.0	(0.64)	29.0	(0.92)	5.0	(0.37)
Master's or higher degree	100.0	(†)	1.0	(0.19)	4.1	(0.40)	29.3	(0.79)	8.0	(0.53)	7.7	(0.47)	37.9	(0.88)	12.1	(0.57)
Don't know	100.0	(†)	5.0	(0.88)	21.2	(1.58)	36.7	(1.92)	11.5	(1.06)	7.7	(0.98)	14.7	(1.38)	3.2	(0.66)
2002 high school type																
Public	100.0	(†)	3.3	(0.25)	13.4	(0.47)	33.0	(0.49)	10.4	(0.35)	8.8	(0.37)	25.0	(0.69)	6.1	(0.28)
Catholic	100.0	(†)	‡	(†)	1.6	(0.45)	23.7	(1.26)	6.4	(0.66)	6.2	(0.68)	47.3	(1.76)	14.6	(1.15)
Other private	100.0	(†)	‡	(†)	3.9	(0.98)	23.9	(2.00)	6.4	(1.01)	8.5	(1.26)	44.3	(2.44)	12.8	(1.38)
Cumulative high school grade point average																
0.00–1.99	100.0	(†)	11.3	(0.90)	25.7	(1.22)	41.8	(1.29)	12.5	(0.79)	5.4	(0.58)	3.1	(0.46)	‡	(†)
2.00–2.49	100.0	(†)	2.4	(0.47)	18.3	(1.00)	44.5	(1.11)	12.5	(0.77)	9.9	(0.79)	11.4	(0.83)	1.0	(0.24)
2.50–2.99	100.0	(†)	0.6	(0.17)	11.1	(0.91)	35.8	(1.21)	12.4	(0.86)	12.5	(0.90)	24.1	(1.13)	3.5	(0.50)
3.00–3.49	100.0	(†)	‡	(†)	5.0	(0.54)	25.9	(1.06)	9.0	(0.66)	9.8	(0.83)	41.9	(1.22)	8.2	(0.69)
3.50+	100.0	(†)	‡	(†)	1.6	(0.32)	13.1	(0.85)	2.9	(0.42)	5.7	(0.61)	55.0	(1.34)	21.7	(0.99)
Students with subsequent postsecondary enrollment																
Timing of first postsecondary enrollment																
Within 3 months of high school completion	100.0	(†)	†	(†)	†	(†)	28.8	(0.65)	8.5	(0.40)	10.2	(0.48)	41.9	(0.80)	10.7	(0.42)
Between 4 and 12 months of high school completion	100.0	(†)	†	(†)	†	(†)	45.2	(1.65)	17.8	(1.52)	10.7	(1.05)	21.2	(1.41)	5.1	(0.80)
13 or more months after high school completion	100.0	(†)	†	(†)	†	(†)	65.7	(1.27)	18.4	(1.05)	9.9	(0.85)	5.5	(0.74)	0.5 !	(0.17)
Type of postsecondary institution first attended																
Public	100.0	(†)	†	(†)	†	(†)	40.1	(0.67)	10.6	(0.43)	10.9	(0.50)	31.5	(0.75)	6.9	(0.33)
Private nonprofit	100.0	(†)	†	(†)	†	(†)	24.2	(1.31)	5.1	(0.65)	4.7	(0.65)	49.1	(1.42)	17.0	(0.98)
Private for-profit	100.0	(†)	†	(†)	†	(†)	46.8	(2.13)	30.4	(2.13)	15.5	(1.59)	6.6	(1.01)	0.7 !	(0.35)
Selectivity and level of postsecondary institution first attended																
Highly selective 4-year	100.0	(†)	†	(†)	†	(†)	14.8	(1.02)	2.5	(0.45)	1.7	(0.37)	60.7	(1.39)	20.3	(0.98)
Moderately selective 4-year	100.0	(†)	†	(†)	†	(†)	26.1	(1.17)	5.0	(0.42)	5.7	(0.62)	49.4	(1.19)	13.7	(0.91)
Inclusive 4-year	100.0	(†)	†	(†)	†	(†)	40.9	(2.01)	7.3	(1.04)	10.9	(1.51)	33.0	(2.06)	7.8	(1.08)
2-year	100.0	(†)	†	(†)	†	(†)	51.7	(0.92)	15.8	(0.71)	16.1	(0.79)	15.2	(0.78)	1.3	(0.20)
Less-than-2-year	100.0	(†)	†	(†)	†	(†)	41.8	(3.14)	51.9	(3.19)	4.9	(1.07)	1.3 !	(0.64)	‡	(†)

†Not applicable.
#Rounds to zero.
!Interpret data with caution. The coefficient of variation (CV) for this estimate is between 30 and 50 percent.
‡Reporting standards not met. Either there are too few cases for a reliable estimate or the coefficient of variation (CV) is 50 percent or greater.

[1]Socioeconomic status (SES) was measured by a composite score on parental education and occupations, and family income.
NOTE: Race categories exclude persons of Hispanic ethnicity. Detail may not sum to totals because of rounding.
SOURCE: U.S. Department of Education, National Center for Education Statistics, Education Longitudinal Study of 2002 (ELS:2002), Third Follow-up. (This table was prepared May 2014.)

Table 104.91. Number and percentage distribution of spring 2002 high school sophomores, by highest level of education completed, and socioeconomic status and selected student characteristics while in high school: 2012

[Standard errors appear in parentheses]

Socioeconomic status (SES) and selected student characteristic	Total Number (in thousands)	Total Percentage distribution	All levels	Less than high school completion	High school completion	Some post-secondary education (no credential)	Postsecondary certificate	Associate's degree	Bachelor's or higher degree
1	2	3	4	5	6	7	8	9	10
Total, all SES¹ groups	3,242 (49.0)	100.0 (†)	100.0 (†)	3.1 (0.23)	12.5 (0.44)	32.3 (0.47)	10.1 (0.33)	8.7 (0.35)	33.3 (0.74)
Low SES¹	810 (24.4)	100.0 (†)	100.0 (†)	7.5 (0.61)	21.4 (0.91)	36.0 (1.02)	12.7 (0.71)	8.2 (0.62)	14.2 (0.89)
Sex									
Male	370 (12.9)	45.7 (0.94)	100.0 (†)	10.0 (1.06)	26.5 (1.48)	35.8 (1.49)	8.7 (0.95)	6.9 (0.85)	12.2 (1.15)
Female	440 (15.8)	54.3 (0.94)	100.0 (†)	5.4 (0.64)	17.1 (1.10)	36.2 (1.45)	16.0 (1.03)	9.3 (0.83)	15.9 (1.16)
Race/ethnicity									
White	311 (15.1)	38.4 (1.53)	100.0 (†)	5.5 (0.77)	26.0 (1.49)	31.9 (1.61)	12.5 (1.22)	9.7 (1.16)	14.4 (1.36)
Black	162 (10.6)	20.1 (1.26)	100.0 (†)	8.6 (1.51)	18.3 (1.98)	41.0 (2.57)	13.5 (1.54)	6.0 (1.00)	12.6 (1.75)
Hispanic	251 (16.9)	30.9 (1.71)	100.0 (†)	9.6 (1.18)	18.1 (1.97)	39.3 (2.20)	12.2 (1.28)	8.1 (1.15)	12.6 (1.68)
Asian	38 (3.5)	4.7 (0.45)	100.0 (†)	4.6 (1.32)	10.9 (2.23)	33.5 (3.19)	12.9 (2.03)	7.2 (1.62)	30.8 (3.18)
Pacific Islander	‡ (†)	0.2 ! (0.07)	100.0 (†)	‡ (†)	‡ (†)	‡ (†)	‡ (†)	‡ (†)	‡ (†)
American Indian/Alaska Native	11 ! (3.4)	1.4 ! (0.43)	100.0 (†)	‡ (†)	‡ (†)	38.1 (9.76)	22.4 ! (10.82)	‡ (†)	‡ (†)
Two or more races	35 (3.8)	4.3 (0.45)	100.0 (†)	7.1 ! (2.69)	32.7 (5.06)	28.5 (5.37)	10.0 ! (3.45)	8.2 ! (3.30)	13.5 (3.72)
Reading achievement quartile²									
First (lowest)	324 (14.0)	40.6 (1.16)	100.0 (†)	11.8 (1.17)	27.0 (1.59)	35.3 (1.72)	11.7 (1.09)	7.7 (0.77)	6.5 (1.02)
Second	246 (10.8)	30.8 (1.05)	100.0 (†)	5.9 (0.88)	20.2 (1.76)	38.5 (1.84)	15.7 (1.48)	7.5 (1.10)	12.3 (1.27)
Third	140 (8.6)	17.6 (0.89)	100.0 (†)	3.5 (0.94)	15.6 (1.78)	37.7 (2.24)	12.2 (1.77)	10.1 (1.64)	20.9 (2.30)
Fourth (highest)	88 (5.8)	11.0 (0.70)	100.0 (†)	‡ (†)	11.5 (2.25)	31.2 (3.09)	8.2 (1.96)	9.1 (2.03)	38.4 (3.25)
Math achievement quartile²									
First (lowest)	320 (14.1)	40.2 (1.17)	100.0 (†)	11.4 (1.15)	27.8 (1.55)	35.7 (1.77)	13.5 (1.07)	6.7 (0.78)	5.0 (0.81)
Second	239 (12.0)	30.0 (1.09)	100.0 (†)	6.7 (1.00)	18.3 (1.51)	40.4 (2.08)	13.7 (1.33)	8.7 (1.22)	12.1 (1.35)
Third	160 (8.7)	20.1 (1.01)	100.0 (†)	3.5 (1.03)	16.6 (1.90)	36.4 (2.34)	10.9 (1.52)	9.4 (1.67)	23.2 (2.11)
Fourth (highest)	78 (5.4)	9.8 (0.68)	100.0 (†)	‡ (†)	12.4 (2.06)	25.6 (2.92)	9.4 (2.29)	10.4 (2.35)	41.3 (3.39)
Middle SES¹	1,631 (31.5)	100.0 (†)	100.0 (†)	2.5 (0.28)	13.1 (0.55)	34.7 (0.68)	11.1 (0.48)	9.8 (0.51)	28.8 (0.82)
Sex									
Male	810 (20.1)	49.6 (0.83)	100.0 (†)	2.7 (0.37)	17.3 (0.88)	36.5 (1.10)	10.1 (0.66)	8.6 (0.72)	24.8 (1.11)
Female	822 (21.3)	50.4 (0.83)	100.0 (†)	2.4 (0.39)	8.9 (0.68)	32.9 (1.00)	12.1 (0.70)	11.0 (0.72)	32.8 (1.09)
Race/ethnicity									
White	1,027 (26.7)	62.9 (1.14)	100.0 (†)	1.8 (0.31)	13.0 (0.68)	32.2 (0.82)	9.9 (0.56)	10.3 (0.63)	32.9 (1.03)
Black	241 (14.2)	14.7 (0.82)	100.0 (†)	3.7 (0.80)	12.2 (1.45)	40.6 (1.92)	16.6 (1.50)	8.5 (1.12)	18.5 (1.64)
Hispanic	215 (12.3)	13.2 (0.70)	100.0 (†)	4.9 (1.01)	12.8 (1.45)	39.8 (1.97)	13.1 (1.48)	10.5 (1.53)	18.8 (1.65)
Asian	53 (4.2)	3.2 (0.26)	100.0 (†)	‡ (†)	6.1 (1.49)	31.1 (2.46)	7.0 (1.45)	6.3 (1.34)	48.8 (2.96)
Pacific Islander	‡ (†)	0.2 (0.06)	100.0 (†)	‡ (†)	‡ (†)	‡ (†)	‡ (†)	‡ (†)	‡ (†)
American Indian/Alaska Native	16 (3.3)	1.0 (0.20)	100.0 (†)	‡ (†)	32.6 (7.74)	33.2 (6.95)	‡ (†)	8.6 ! (3.68)	14.8 ! (6.32)
Two or more races	77 (5.9)	4.7 (0.36)	100.0 (†)	2.7 ! (1.02)	17.2 (3.05)	37.9 (3.41)	8.9 (2.04)	8.6 (2.09)	24.6 (3.31)
Reading achievement quartile²									
First (lowest)	358 (14.4)	22.0 (0.82)	100.0 (†)	5.9 (0.82)	21.8 (1.44)	38.7 (1.73)	16.0 (1.17)	9.2 (1.03)	8.4 (0.84)
Second	427 (15.5)	26.3 (0.72)	100.0 (†)	2.7 (0.56)	14.8 (1.02)	37.3 (1.50)	12.5 (1.00)	11.7 (1.08)	21.1 (1.26)
Third	462 (15.0)	28.4 (0.73)	100.0 (†)	1.1 ! (0.32)	10.1 (1.04)	34.2 (1.47)	10.8 (0.88)	9.6 (0.84)	34.2 (1.65)
Fourth (highest)	379 (13.5)	23.3 (0.76)	100.0 (†)	0.8 ! (0.29)	5.6 (0.68)	28.9 (1.46)	5.5 (0.73)	8.6 (0.95)	50.6 (1.73)
Math achievement quartile²									
First (lowest)	353 (14.8)	21.7 (0.83)	100.0 (†)	6.3 (0.86)	22.5 (1.32)	38.9 (1.57)	15.6 (1.10)	8.9 (1.05)	7.9 (0.93)
Second	448 (15.5)	27.5 (0.71)	100.0 (†)	2.7 (0.55)	14.7 (1.07)	38.2 (1.39)	13.6 (1.01)	11.8 (0.96)	18.9 (1.14)
Third	443 (13.5)	27.2 (0.69)	100.0 (†)	1.1 (0.31)	10.0 (0.89)	33.8 (1.44)	9.7 (0.94)	10.1 (0.87)	35.2 (1.58)
Fourth (highest)	382 (13.9)	23.5 (0.76)	100.0 (†)	‡ (†)	5.0 (0.78)	28.1 (1.51)	5.8 (0.77)	8.0 (0.94)	52.8 (1.73)
High SES¹	801 (27.1)	100.0 (†)	100.0 (†)	0.5 (0.16)	3.1 (0.41)	23.7 (1.07)	5.5 (0.51)	6.7 (0.58)	60.4 (1.17)
Sex									
Male	411 (17.3)	51.3 (1.19)	100.0 (†)	0.8 ! (0.29)	4.4 (0.63)	27.1 (1.51)	4.8 (0.65)	7.5 (0.84)	55.3 (1.54)
Female	390 (15.7)	48.7 (1.19)	100.0 (†)	‡ (†)	1.8 (0.39)	20.1 (1.18)	6.2 (0.80)	5.9 (0.77)	65.7 (1.50)
Race/ethnicity									
White	616 (23.3)	76.9 (1.08)	100.0 (†)	0.4 ! (0.16)	2.8 (0.41)	22.3 (1.14)	4.7 (0.55)	6.7 (0.64)	63.2 (1.26)
Black	61 (5.9)	7.7 (0.70)	100.0 (†)	‡ (†)	5.1 ! (2.01)	36.6 (4.64)	8.5 (2.44)	7.2 ! (2.26)	42.5 (4.53)
Hispanic	53 (5.3)	6.6 (0.63)	100.0 (†)	‡ (†)	6.1 ! (1.98)	30.6 (3.99)	9.3 (2.38)	7.6 (1.94)	44.6 (4.24)
Asian	39 (3.7)	4.9 (0.46)	100.0 (†)	‡ (†)	‡ (†)	17.8 (1.87)	6.5 (1.48)	3.1 ! (1.18)	70.8 (2.47)
Pacific Islander	‡ (†)	‡ (†)	100.0 (†)	‡ (†)	‡ (†)	‡ (†)	‡ (†)	‡ (†)	‡ (†)
American Indian/Alaska Native	‡ (†)	‡ (†)	100.0 (†)	‡ (†)	‡ (†)	‡ (†)	‡ (†)	‡ (†)	‡ (†)
Two or more races	27 (3.0)	3.4 (0.38)	100.0 (†)	‡ (†)	‡ (†)	21.8 (4.40)	7.4 ! (2.96)	8.7 ! (3.55)	57.2 (5.63)
Reading achievement quartile²									
First (lowest)	70 (5.8)	8.7 (0.70)	100.0 (†)	4.9 ! (1.67)	14.1 (2.68)	34.7 (3.13)	17.3 (2.83)	7.7 (2.05)	21.4 (3.00)
Second	120 (7.9)	15.0 (0.86)	100.0 (†)	‡ (†)	4.0 (1.10)	31.7 (2.74)	8.9 (1.56)	11.0 (1.97)	44.4 (2.82)
Third	239 (11.9)	29.9 (0.99)	100.0 (†)	‡ (†)	2.7 (0.69)	24.9 (1.93)	4.3 (0.90)	8.1 (1.15)	59.8 (2.14)
Fourth (highest)	370 (15.3)	46.4 (1.18)	100.0 (†)	‡ (†)	0.9 ! (0.30)	18.3 (1.25)	3.0 (0.51)	4.2 (0.68)	73.5 (1.43)
Math achievement quartile²									
First (lowest)	68 (6.6)	8.5 (0.79)	100.0 (†)	4.0 ! (1.58)	14.1 (2.97)	36.3 (3.57)	17.2 (2.71)	7.4 (2.17)	21.0 (3.12)
Second	125 (7.3)	15.6 (0.81)	100.0 (†)	‡ (†)	3.8 ! (1.21)	32.4 (2.92)	9.4 (1.70)	13.1 (2.00)	40.5 (2.92)
Third	222 (10.0)	27.9 (0.90)	100.0 (†)	‡ (†)	3.0 (0.72)	23.1 (1.69)	4.7 (0.89)	8.1 (1.16)	60.9 (2.03)
Fourth (highest)	383 (17.0)	48.0 (1.18)	100.0 (†)	‡ (†)	0.9 ! (0.28)	19.0 (1.23)	2.6 (0.45)	3.7 (0.59)	73.7 (1.34)

†Not applicable.

!Interpret data with caution. The coefficient of variation (CV) for this estimate is between 30 and 50 percent.

‡Reporting standards not met. Either there are too few cases for a reliable estimate or the coefficient of variation (CV) is 50 percent or greater.

¹Socioeconomic status (SES) was measured by a composite score on parental education and occupations, and family income in 2002. The "low" SES group is the lowest quartile; the middle SES group is the "middle" two quartiles; and the "high" SES group is the upper quartile.

²Reading and math achievement quartiles reflect students' scores on assessments conducted in 2002.

NOTE: Race categories exclude persons of Hispanic ethnicity. Detail may not sum to totals because of rounding and survey item nonresponse.

SOURCE: U.S. Department of Education, National Center for Education Statistics, Education Longitudinal Study of 2002 (ELS:2002), Base Year and Third Follow-up. (This table was prepared January 2015.)

Table 104.92. Number and percentage distribution of spring 2002 high school sophomores, by highest level of education completed, socioeconomic status and educational expectations while in high school, and college enrollment status 2 years after high school: 2012

[Standard errors appear in parentheses]

Socioeconomic status (SES), educational expectations, and college enrollment status	Total Number (in thousands)	Total Percentage distribution	Highest level of education completed through 2012 All levels	Less than high school completion	High school completion	Some post-secondary education (no credential)	Postsecondary certificate	Associate's degree	Bachelor's or higher degree
1	2	3	4	5	6	7	8	9	10
Low SES[1]	810 (24.4)	100.0 (†)	100.0 (†)	7.5 (0.61)	21.4 (0.91)	36.0 (1.02)	12.7 (0.71)	8.2 (0.62)	14.2 (0.89)
Educational expectations in 2002									
Don't know	94 (6.5)	12.6 (0.75)	100.0 (†)	7.7 (2.02)	28.6 (2.80)	35.6 (3.02)	11.6 (1.96)	7.2 (1.71)	9.3 (1.90)
Less than high school	13 (2.1)	1.7 (0.26)	100.0 (†)	21.3! (7.71)	42.0 (8.08)	34.6 (7.92)	‡ (†)	‡ (†)	‡ (†)
High school diploma or GED	92 (6.5)	12.4 (0.71)	100.0 (†)	16.2 (2.36)	41.0 (3.39)	27.1 (2.97)	10.3 (2.27)	4.3 (1.25)	1.0! (0.49)
Attend or complete 2-year college	66 (5.2)	8.8 (0.60)	100.0 (†)	9.5 (2.39)	28.4 (3.44)	35.0 (3.75)	15.3 (2.75)	5.9 (1.52)	6.0 (1.59)
Attend college, 4-year degree incomplete	43 (4.0)	5.7 (0.48)	100.0 (†)	10.7 (2.88)	24.2 (4.55)	36.5 (5.26)	10.8 (2.82)	10.5 (3.02)	7.3! (2.25)
Bachelor's degree	247 (10.9)	33.1 (0.94)	100.0 (†)	4.6 (0.98)	17.2 (1.50)	39.0 (2.06)	14.9 (1.44)	9.3 (1.14)	15.0 (1.44)
Advanced degree	191 (9.7)	25.6 (1.06)	100.0 (†)	3.8 (0.88)	9.7 (1.32)	38.3 (2.24)	11.3 (1.51)	9.8 (1.29)	27.0 (1.98)
Educational expectations in 2004									
Don't know	114 (7.5)	14.3 (0.82)	100.0 (†)	13.9 (2.24)	33.2 (3.28)	33.5 (2.80)	10.2 (2.05)	6.7 (1.61)	2.6! (0.98)
Less than high school	‡ (†)	0.7 (0.21)	100.0 (†)	‡ (†)	‡ (†)	‡ (†)	‡ (†)	‡ (†)	‡ (†)
High school diploma or GED	88 (6.6)	11.0 (0.77)	100.0 (†)	17.1 (2.54)	46.9 (3.47)	22.2 (2.62)	6.9 (1.61)	5.0! (1.60)	1.8! (0.86)
Attend or complete 2-year college	176 (10.6)	22.0 (1.08)	100.0 (†)	6.3 (1.37)	25.0 (2.04)	39.4 (2.38)	17.5 (1.80)	8.9 (1.38)	2.9 (0.79)
Attend college, 4-year degree incomplete	40 (4.1)	5.0 (0.51)	100.0 (†)	‡ (†)	22.3 (4.44)	41.2 (5.30)	14.1 (3.98)	11.3! (3.66)	8.2! (3.01)
Bachelor's degree	202 (10.0)	25.2 (1.02)	100.0 (†)	2.3! (0.68)	8.6 (1.25)	41.6 (2.19)	12.2 (1.38)	11.3 (1.42)	24.1 (2.07)
Advanced degree	173 (8.8)	21.6 (0.93)	100.0 (†)	2.9! (1.02)	7.7 (1.19)	37.7 (2.78)	12.6 (1.79)	8.2 (1.29)	30.9 (2.42)
College enrollment status in 2006									
Enrolled in a 4-year college	152 (7.7)	21.0 (1.00)	100.0 (†)	‡ (†)	‡ (†)	34.7 (2.52)	7.5 (1.13)	8.1 (1.44)	49.7 (2.70)
Enrolled in a 2-year college	207 (12.4)	28.6 (1.36)	100.0 (†)	‡ (†)	‡ (†)	48.6 (2.18)	19.7 (1.76)	17.0 (1.80)	14.8 (1.52)
Enrolled in a less-than-2-year college	25 (3.2)	3.5 (0.43)	100.0 (†)	‡ (†)	‡ (†)	42.9 (7.21)	50.3 (6.97)	‡ (†)	‡ (†)
Not enrolled	340 (14.3)	46.9 (1.39)	100.0 (†)	15.2 (1.30)	44.4 (1.62)	28.0 (1.51)	8.5 (0.94)	3.1 (0.58)	0.7! (0.23)
Middle SES[1]	1,631 (31.5)	100.0 (†)	100.0 (†)	2.5 (0.28)	13.1 (0.55)	34.7 (0.68)	11.1 (0.48)	9.8 (0.51)	28.8 (0.82)
Educational expectations in 2002									
Don't know	149 (7.5)	9.8 (0.44)	100.0 (†)	5.2 (1.16)	21.1 (2.23)	37.8 (2.78)	13.1 (1.68)	6.6 (1.37)	16.3 (2.00)
Less than high school	14 (2.6)	0.9 (0.16)	100.0 (†)	19.1! (7.19)	34.2 (8.99)	23.0! (7.26)	‡ (†)	‡ (†)	‡ (†)
High school diploma or GED	105 (6.7)	6.9 (0.41)	100.0 (†)	9.1 (1.82)	32.9 (2.84)	35.1 (3.68)	13.2 (2.02)	5.1 (1.19)	4.6 (1.19)
Attend or complete 2-year college	110 (7.0)	7.2 (0.39)	100.0 (†)	3.2! (1.19)	22.7 (2.64)	37.7 (3.10)	15.4 (2.18)	13.9 (2.36)	7.1 (1.56)
Attend college, 4-year degree incomplete	59 (4.8)	3.9 (0.28)	100.0 (†)	‡ (†)	17.5 (2.95)	39.9 (4.35)	17.5 (2.81)	9.4 (2.33)	11.4 (2.35)
Bachelor's degree	562 (15.3)	36.9 (0.74)	100.0 (†)	1.2 (0.30)	10.9 (0.95)	34.7 (1.13)	10.8 (0.77)	11.4 (0.93)	31.0 (1.31)
Advanced degree	523 (15.8)	34.4 (0.74)	100.0 (†)	0.8! (0.27)	4.7 (0.61)	33.0 (1.32)	9.3 (0.77)	9.1 (0.73)	43.1 (1.30)
Educational expectations in 2004									
Don't know	150 (8.8)	9.2 (0.50)	100.0 (†)	8.7 (1.54)	24.8 (2.27)	34.4 (2.39)	11.5 (1.71)	9.4 (1.56)	11.2 (1.89)
Less than high school	‡ (†)	‡ (†)	100.0 (†)	‡ (†)	‡ (†)	‡ (†)	‡ (†)	‡ (†)	‡ (†)
High school diploma or GED	97 (7.2)	5.9 (0.42)	100.0 (†)	7.6 (1.96)	44.1 (3.48)	28.2 (3.03)	12.0 (1.94)	4.2! (1.36)	3.8! (1.41)
Attend or complete 2-year college	281 (11.7)	17.2 (0.62)	100.0 (†)	3.1 (0.70)	22.4 (1.76)	37.9 (1.83)	20.0 (1.80)	12.4 (1.44)	4.2 (0.77)
Attend college, 4-year degree incomplete	68 (6.0)	4.2 (0.35)	100.0 (†)	‡ (†)	14.8 (2.85)	48.1 (3.91)	10.1 (2.42)	11.6 (2.74)	14.0 (3.00)
Bachelor's degree	547 (15.7)	33.5 (0.73)	100.0 (†)	0.8 (0.22)	6.4 (0.74)	35.9 (1.39)	8.6 (0.79)	12.1 (0.99)	36.1 (1.45)
Advanced degree	489 (14.8)	29.9 (0.78)	100.0 (†)	‡ (†)	3.3 (0.57)	30.7 (1.39)	7.7 (0.70)	7.5 (0.71)	50.3 (1.48)
College enrollment status in 2006									
Enrolled in a 4-year college	574 (16.7)	39.4 (1.00)	100.0 (†)	‡ (†)	‡ (†)	27.3 (1.06)	5.5 (0.56)	7.3 (0.71)	59.9 (1.27)
Enrolled in a 2-year college	451 (16.7)	30.9 (0.94)	100.0 (†)	‡ (†)	‡ (†)	45.2 (1.39)	15.3 (1.06)	18.3 (1.19)	21.2 (1.19)
Enrolled in a less-than-2-year college	32 (3.8)	2.2 (0.26)	100.0 (†)	‡ (†)	‡ (†)	39.7 (6.54)	45.1 (6.32)	11.4 (3.31)	‡ (†)
Not enrolled	402 (15.5)	27.5 (0.87)	100.0 (†)	8.5 (0.93)	42.5 (1.49)	30.6 (1.31)	11.3 (0.86)	5.3 (0.74)	1.7 (0.41)
High SES[1]	801 (27.1)	100.0 (†)	100.0 (†)	0.5 (0.16)	3.1 (0.41)	23.7 (1.07)	5.5 (0.51)	6.7 (0.58)	60.4 (1.17)
Educational expectations in 2002									
Don't know	42 (4.0)	5.6 (0.48)	100.0 (†)	‡ (†)	5.8! (2.18)	34.9 (4.35)	5.9! (2.07)	12.3 (2.87)	40.8 (4.56)
Less than high school	‡ (†)	0.3! (0.10)	100.0 (†)	‡ (†)	‡ (†)	‡ (†)	‡ (†)	‡ (†)	‡ (†)
High school diploma or GED	14 (2.4)	1.9 (0.29)	100.0 (†)	‡ (†)	25.3 (7.29)	33.3 (8.48)	‡ (†)	‡ (†)	15.7! (7.60)
Attend or complete 2-year college	19 (2.8)	2.5 (0.35)	100.0 (†)	‡ (†)	20.7 (7.21)	41.4 (7.62)	9.2! (3.87)	16.1 (4.45)	11.5! (3.85)
Attend college, 4-year degree incomplete	13 (2.2)	1.7 (0.28)	100.0 (†)	‡ (†)	17.5! (7.75)	37.1 (8.34)	‡ (†)	‡ (†)	26.7 (7.42)
Bachelor's degree	262 (12.2)	35.0 (1.01)	100.0 (†)	‡ (†)	2.8 (0.63)	24.8 (1.77)	6.3 (0.90)	7.8 (0.99)	58.0 (2.06)
Advanced degree	396 (14.8)	52.9 (1.06)	100.0 (†)	‡ (†)	0.7 (0.22)	20.3 (1.12)	4.6 (0.67)	4.7 (0.63)	69.4 (1.38)
Educational expectations in 2004									
Don't know	37 (4.2)	4.6 (0.51)	100.0 (†)	4.2! (1.98)	13.1 (3.70)	30.7 (4.66)	11.2 (3.00)	17.2 (4.15)	23.7 (4.30)
Less than high school	‡ (†)	‡ (†)	100.0 (†)	‡ (†)	‡ (†)	‡ (†)	‡ (†)	‡ (†)	‡ (†)
High school diploma or GED	13 (2.4)	1.7 (0.30)	100.0 (†)	‡ (†)	23.2! (9.42)	37.6 (11.14)	‡ (†)	‡ (†)	‡ (†)
Attend or complete 2-year college	43 (4.3)	5.3 (0.50)	100.0 (†)	‡ (†)	10.0! (3.48)	49.8 (4.98)	19.8 (3.54)	12.2 (3.15)	7.6 (2.15)
Attend college, 4-year degree incomplete	22 (3.3)	2.7 (0.40)	100.0 (†)	‡ (†)	14.8! (7.01)	45.0 (8.82)	9.1! (4.52)	16.6! (6.16)	14.4! (5.06)
Bachelor's degree	268 (12.1)	33.2 (1.06)	100.0 (†)	‡ (†)	1.7 (0.39)	25.4 (1.71)	5.6 (0.85)	6.5 (0.89)	60.6 (1.88)
Advanced degree	423 (17.6)	52.4 (1.15)	100.0 (†)	‡ (†)	0.5! (0.20)	17.3 (1.27)	3.1 (0.48)	4.7 (0.67)	74.4 (1.39)
College enrollment status in 2006									
Enrolled in a 4-year college	527 (21.4)	70.5 (1.27)	100.0 (†)	‡ (†)	‡ (†)	16.6 (1.02)	3.2 (0.45)	3.4 (0.50)	76.8 (1.11)
Enrolled in a 2-year college	150 (9.1)	20.1 (1.06)	100.0 (†)	‡ (†)	‡ (†)	38.0 (2.61)	10.7 (1.60)	16.9 (1.89)	34.4 (2.37)
Enrolled in a less-than-2-year college	6 (1.6)	0.8 (0.21)	100.0 (†)	‡ (†)	‡ (†)	37.0! (13.03)	38.9! (11.73)	‡ (†)	‡ (†)
Not enrolled	64 (5.4)	8.6 (0.70)	100.0 (†)	6.2! (1.98)	33.3 (4.16)	40.3 (4.37)	5.2 (1.46)	‡ (†)	11.8 (2.38)

†Not applicable.
!Interpret data with caution. The coefficient of variation (CV) for this estimate is between 30 and 50 percent.
‡Reporting standards not met. Either there are too few cases for a reliable estimate or the coefficient of variation (CV) is 50 percent or greater.

[1]Socioeconomic status (SES) was measured by a composite score on parental education and occupations, and family income in 2002. The "low" SES group is the lowest quartile; the "middle" SES group is the middle two quartiles; and the "high" SES group is the upper quartile.
NOTE: Detail may not sum to totals because of rounding and survey item nonresponse.
SOURCE: U.S. Department of Education, National Center for Education Statistics, Education Longitudinal Study of 2002 (ELS:2002), Base Year, First Follow-up, Second Follow-up, and Third Follow-up. (This table was prepared January 2015.)

Table 104.93. Sources of college information for spring 2002 high school sophomores who expected to attend a postsecondary institution, by highest level of education completed and socioeconomic status while in high school: 2012

[Standard errors appear in parentheses]

Socioeconomic status (SES) and sources of college information	All students who expected to attend a postsecondary institution	Less than high school completion	High school completion	Some postsecondary education (no credential)	Postsecondary certificate	Associate's degree	Bachelor's or higher degree
1	2	3	4	5	6	7	8
Low SES[1]							
Information sources as of 2002							
School counselor	40.8 (1.43)	‡ (†)	36.2 (3.34)	39.4 (2.25)	38.6 (3.98)	46.8 (4.88)	50.6 (2.68)
Teacher	35.5 (1.29)	31.2 (5.69)	30.4 (2.73)	36.6 (2.11)	34.5 (3.76)	38.1 (4.50)	38.6 (3.27)
Coach	7.5 (0.68)	‡ (†)	6.7 (1.60)	9.5 (1.28)	5.4 ! (1.69)	6.0 ! (2.09)	6.9 (1.44)
Parent	42.0 (1.28)	30.0 (5.53)	37.8 (3.14)	42.2 (2.23)	44.2 (3.34)	46.2 (4.28)	45.1 (3.01)
Friend	39.5 (1.18)	31.1 (5.42)	36.8 (3.15)	41.8 (2.08)	39.0 (3.56)	31.8 (3.88)	44.1 (3.14)
Sibling	23.4 (1.13)	8.5 ! (2.98)	21.8 (2.78)	24.1 (1.95)	23.5 (3.33)	23.8 (3.64)	27.6 (2.65)
Other relative	27.2 (1.22)	26.7 (5.33)	22.9 (2.60)	29.5 (2.04)	28.2 (3.12)	26.8 (4.21)	26.2 (2.58)
College publication or website	29.9 (1.20)	13.3 ! (4.25)	21.2 (2.77)	30.8 (2.13)	24.0 (3.36)	36.0 (3.62)	42.4 (3.16)
College representative	15.2 (1.07)	‡ (†)	13.2 (1.79)	15.8 (1.68)	14.6 (2.50)	21.8 (3.83)	15.4 (2.58)
College search guide	28.7 (1.23)	18.9 (5.08)	21.4 (2.60)	29.2 (2.13)	21.1 (3.12)	30.8 (3.59)	42.3 (3.13)
Information sources as of 2004							
School counselor	77.7 (1.41)	‡ (†)	67.8 (4.03)	74.0 (2.38)	77.0 (3.18)	84.9 (4.12)	90.8 (1.83)
Teacher	46.1 (1.66)	‡ (†)	40.6 (3.71)	44.8 (2.80)	48.0 (4.57)	36.5 (4.88)	55.2 (3.69)
Coach	9.0 (0.89)	‡ (†)	‡ (†)	12.6 (1.65)	8.5 ! (3.88)	4.8 ! (2.26)	9.5 (1.80)
Parent	42.8 (1.41)	‡ (†)	35.0 (3.82)	42.3 (2.20)	48.9 (3.79)	39.5 (5.14)	46.0 (3.43)
Friend	25.9 (1.47)	‡ (†)	18.2 (2.87)	24.4 (2.16)	29.5 (4.49)	29.8 (5.14)	29.6 (2.91)
Sibling	32.6 (1.44)	‡ (†)	22.2 (3.40)	31.7 (2.20)	33.5 (3.72)	33.8 (4.93)	41.4 (3.25)
Other relative	53.1 (1.53)	‡ (†)	43.1 (4.43)	53.0 (2.61)	49.3 (4.30)	46.5 (5.42)	66.1 (3.04)
College publication or website	53.9 (1.50)	‡ (†)	36.3 (4.11)	54.5 (2.46)	56.2 (4.00)	49.9 (5.10)	67.3 (2.91)
College representative	50.7 (1.58)	‡ (†)	29.5 (3.82)	50.4 (2.62)	42.3 (4.31)	46.8 (4.77)	73.9 (3.16)
College search guide	43.0 (1.73)	‡ (†)	26.5 (3.48)	43.8 (2.68)	34.0 (4.22)	42.1 (4.87)	59.7 (2.93)
Middle SES[1]							
Information sources as of 2002							
School counselor	44.3 (1.06)	26.5 (6.75)	40.8 (2.91)	42.1 (1.41)	45.2 (2.70)	38.8 (2.54)	49.8 (1.72)
Teacher	31.6 (0.91)	42.2 (7.46)	32.4 (2.69)	32.1 (1.35)	27.5 (2.28)	23.6 (2.21)	34.3 (1.54)
Coach	9.3 (0.55)	‡ (†)	12.1 (1.92)	9.3 (0.79)	7.7 (1.38)	7.3 (1.58)	9.6 (1.00)
Parent	55.2 (0.90)	50.1 (8.26)	47.7 (3.05)	54.7 (1.38)	54.5 (2.84)	51.8 (2.51)	59.5 (1.56)
Friend	39.2 (0.86)	36.8 (9.38)	38.6 (3.05)	37.0 (1.37)	41.8 (2.49)	34.3 (2.72)	42.6 (1.42)
Sibling	23.6 (0.71)	21.2 ! (7.12)	17.2 (2.23)	21.4 (1.15)	26.1 (2.31)	21.7 (2.22)	27.8 (1.31)
Other relative	26.5 (0.84)	25.0 (7.01)	27.9 (2.65)	26.6 (1.37)	27.4 (2.29)	22.9 (2.29)	26.7 (1.30)
College publication or website	33.5 (0.86)	22.5 (5.83)	23.0 (2.77)	31.0 (1.35)	30.0 (2.57)	30.3 (2.41)	42.1 (1.49)
College representative	14.3 (0.67)	16.3 ! (6.43)	14.2 (1.97)	14.1 (1.02)	15.0 (1.84)	15.2 (2.25)	14.0 (1.08)
College search guide	31.0 (0.80)	31.0 (7.27)	21.2 (2.39)	29.6 (1.25)	27.3 (2.21)	27.6 (2.43)	37.6 (1.37)
Information sources as of 2004							
School counselor	79.6 (0.97)	‡ (†)	67.5 (3.45)	78.5 (1.50)	72.8 (3.02)	78.5 (2.65)	85.3 (1.23)
Teacher	43.6 (1.03)	‡ (†)	36.8 (3.60)	43.0 (1.95)	45.9 (3.05)	37.2 (2.90)	47.0 (1.76)
Coach	12.1 (0.77)	‡ (†)	8.7 (2.17)	11.6 (1.23)	8.7 (1.86)	12.8 (2.10)	13.9 (1.40)
Parent	58.5 (1.04)	‡ (†)	43.4 (3.58)	56.6 (1.87)	62.6 (2.96)	56.0 (3.06)	63.2 (1.51)
Friend	25.2 (0.81)	‡ (†)	22.8 (2.76)	22.4 (1.43)	22.0 (2.36)	23.4 (2.44)	29.6 (1.31)
Sibling	28.6 (1.00)	‡ (†)	28.1 (3.30)	27.4 (1.53)	35.8 (3.32)	26.9 (2.66)	28.5 (1.59)
Other relative	52.0 (0.97)	‡ (†)	46.2 (3.85)	51.5 (1.74)	49.0 (3.09)	46.2 (3.00)	56.4 (1.56)
College publication or website	59.3 (1.16)	‡ (†)	36.6 (3.50)	56.9 (1.76)	51.5 (3.45)	57.6 (3.00)	69.1 (1.79)
College representative	65.1 (1.01)	‡ (†)	37.9 (3.48)	59.5 (1.61)	55.2 (3.41)	61.7 (2.96)	79.9 (1.52)
College search guide	48.2 (1.11)	‡ (†)	32.2 (3.40)	43.6 (1.97)	40.2 (3.35)	42.5 (2.90)	59.7 (1.49)
High SES[1]							
Information sources as of 2002							
School counselor	46.3 (1.24)	‡ (†)	49.8 (8.33)	46.8 (2.27)	51.8 (5.41)	39.4 (5.03)	46.4 (1.46)
Teacher	30.7 (1.10)	‡ (†)	37.5 (8.63)	30.3 (2.14)	26.0 (4.87)	28.0 (4.07)	31.2 (1.37)
Coach	10.8 (0.70)	‡ (†)	13.3 ! (6.11)	10.3 (1.40)	10.8 ! (3.46)	8.4 (2.31)	11.1 (0.89)
Parent	68.4 (1.10)	‡ (†)	58.9 (8.68)	62.9 (2.22)	64.8 (4.76)	68.2 (4.40)	71.2 (1.32)
Friend	42.1 (1.09)	‡ (†)	41.1 (9.11)	38.8 (2.35)	40.4 (5.00)	44.4 (4.29)	43.3 (1.43)
Sibling	29.2 (0.94)	‡ (†)	23.7 ! (7.41)	25.4 (2.00)	21.5 (4.10)	31.7 (4.17)	31.2 (1.21)
Other relative	26.3 (0.97)	‡ (†)	34.8 (9.10)	28.1 (2.04)	27.3 (4.57)	23.0 (4.06)	25.6 (1.15)
College publication or website	44.4 (1.18)	‡ (†)	27.5 (8.19)	38.5 (2.44)	36.5 (5.40)	39.3 (4.66)	48.5 (1.42)
College representative	15.3 (0.78)	‡ (†)	11.3 ! (5.45)	18.6 (1.67)	20.1 (4.39)	13.6 (3.02)	14.0 (0.94)
College search guide	39.7 (1.13)	‡ (†)	17.5 ! (6.74)	37.5 (2.16)	31.6 (5.26)	30.1 (4.32)	43.1 (1.53)
Information sources as of 2004							
School counselor	80.9 (1.12)	‡ (†)	72.7 (9.01)	80.7 (2.11)	82.0 (4.60)	82.1 (4.09)	81.0 (1.33)
Teacher	42.7 (1.23)	‡ (†)	41.4 (10.31)	39.8 (2.69)	44.5 (5.72)	39.3 (5.32)	43.8 (1.51)
Coach	14.9 (0.88)	‡ (†)	‡ (†)	12.5 (1.83)	11.3 (3.17)	11.2 (3.15)	16.4 (1.12)
Parent	72.7 (1.29)	‡ (†)	64.4 (10.16)	66.0 (2.93)	66.0 (6.01)	66.3 (5.46)	76.0 (1.38)
Friend	30.0 (1.09)	‡ (†)	24.6 ! (8.24)	25.9 (2.16)	29.0 (5.50)	27.9 (4.87)	31.7 (1.23)
Sibling	28.0 (1.09)	‡ (†)	25.0 ! (8.94)	27.4 (2.58)	29.1 (5.09)	24.7 (4.15)	28.4 (1.32)
Other relative	53.2 (1.28)	‡ (†)	40.5 (9.56)	51.5 (2.74)	50.7 (6.15)	43.3 (5.11)	55.1 (1.50)
College publication or website	64.0 (1.23)	‡ (†)	36.5 (9.54)	55.9 (2.77)	51.8 (5.85)	46.4 (5.44)	69.6 (1.42)
College representative	79.5 (1.03)	‡ (†)	41.9 (10.05)	72.8 (2.54)	60.7 (5.78)	67.7 (5.03)	85.1 (1.15)
College search guide	59.6 (1.38)	‡ (†)	28.3 ! (8.61)	55.1 (2.92)	43.7 (5.55)	54.4 (5.55)	63.6 (1.66)

†Not applicable.

!Interpret data with caution. The coefficient of variation (CV) for this estimate is between 30 and 50 percent.

‡Reporting standards not met. Either there are too few cases for a reliable estimate or the coefficient of variation (CV) is 50 percent or greater.

[1]Socioeconomic status (SES) was measured by a composite score on parental education and occupations, and family income in 2002. The "low" SES group is the lowest quartile; the "middle" SES group is the middle two quartiles; and the "high" SES group is the upper quartile.

NOTE. Students who reported that they planned to attend postsecondary education were asked, "Where have you gone for information about the entrance requirements of various colleges?" Because each student could indicate multiple sources, percentages do not sum to 100. SOURCE: U.S. Department of Education, National Center for Education Statistics, Education Longitudinal Study of 2002 (ELS:2002), Base Year, First Follow-up, and Third Follow-up. (This table was prepared January 2015.)

Table 104.95.   Number of persons age 25 and over in metropolitan areas with populations greater than 1 million and rates of high school completion and bachelor's degree attainment among persons in this age group, by sex: 2014

[Standard errors appear in parentheses]

Metropolitan area	Number of persons 25 years old and over (in thousands)			Percent with high school completion or higher			Percent with bachelor's or higher degree		
	Total	Males	Females	Total	Male	Female	Total	Male	Female
1	2	3	4	5	6	7	8	9	10
Atlanta-Sandy Springs-Marietta, GA CBSA	3,591 (259.9)	1,719 (126.0)	1,873 (143.8)	90.9 (1.42)	88.9 (2.10)	92.8 (1.30)	38.7 (2.82)	39.9 (3.18)	37.6 (3.20)
Austin-Round Rock, TX CBSA	1,370 (133.2)	729 (76.4)	641 (65.8)	90.1 (2.68)	89.8 (3.21)	90.3 (2.50)	50.0 (4.08)	48.3 (5.10)	51.8 (4.06)
Birmingham-Hoover, AL CBSA	887 (93.5)	429 (52.4)	458 (46.0)	87.5 (2.32)	83.2 (4.42)	91.5 (2.49)	30.1 (4.53)	27.9 (5.18)	32.1 (5.16)
Boston-Worcester-Manchester, MA-NH-CT-ME CSA[1]	3,820 (132.2)	1,795 (77.1)	2,025 (69.7)	91.6 (1.32)	91.5 (1.74)	91.7 (1.31)	44.8 (2.31)	45.7 (2.54)	44.0 (2.67)
Buffalo-Niagara Falls, NY CBSA	759 (84.3)	354 (42.8)	405 (47.2)	92.3 (1.81)	89.1 (3.00)	95.0 (2.02)	24.4 (3.49)	23.9 (6.69)	24.9 (4.15)
Charlotte-Gastonia-Concord, NC-SC CBSA	1,291 (133.7)	602 (68.6)	689 (71.7)	82.5 (2.71)	81.7 (3.32)	83.2 (3.47)	30.9 (3.67)	32.3 (4.64)	29.6 (4.50)
Chicago-Naperville-Michigan City, IL-IN-WI CSA	6,218 (318.7)	2,993 (163.7)	3,224 (165.9)	89.0 (0.99)	87.7 (1.36)	90.3 (0.94)	38.2 (1.79)	37.2 (2.11)	39.1 (1.91)
Cincinnati-Middletown, OH-KY-IN CBSA[1]	1,344 (123.8)	668 (63.6)	676 (69.0)	89.0 (2.37)	92.0 (2.69)	86.1 (3.08)	29.3 (3.08)	31.8 (4.23)	26.9 (3.16)
Cleveland-Akron-Elyria, OH CSA	1,908 (145.4)	926 (81.0)	982 (77.2)	87.8 (1.63)	87.8 (2.43)	91.8 (1.60)	30.5 (3.09)	33.5 (3.98)	27.7 (2.91)
Columbus, OH CSA	1,174 (134.8)	565 (72.3)	608 (69.9)	90.9 (2.28)	89.9 (3.02)	91.8 (2.63)	32.3 (4.57)	34.3 (5.55)	30.5 (4.98)
Dallas-Fort Worth-Arlington, TX CBSA	4,565 (177.5)	2,248 (103.2)	2,317 (92.3)	85.6 (1.63)	84.2 (1.89)	86.9 (1.63)	33.7 (2.04)	35.4 (2.70)	32.1 (2.16)
Denver-Aurora-Boulder, CO CSA	2,086 (90.9)	1,042 (52.9)	1,044 (44.5)	93.1 (0.96)	92.7 (1.27)	93.6 (1.04)	48.7 (3.31)	47.2 (3.71)	50.2 (3.45)
Detroit-Warren-Flint, MI CSA	3,849 (249.4)	1,876 (132.9)	1,973 (123.8)	89.3 (1.35)	89.6 (1.65)	89.1 (1.56)	30.4 (2.06)	28.3 (2.63)	32.5 (2.38)
Fresno-Madera, CA CSA	688 (155.1)	345 (84.1)	342 (71.8)	84.5 (2.56)	86.0 (3.45)	83.0 (3.22)	18.4 (4.20)	17.0 (4.52)	19.8 (4.83)
Grand Rapids-Muskegon-Holland, MI CSA	895 (180.2)	418 (72.9)	477 (109.6)	96.7 (0.91)	96.7 (1.78)	96.7 (1.43)	33.2 (4.45)	30.3 (5.68)	35.7 (4.79)
Greensboro-Winston-Salem-High Point, NC CSA	1,040 (111.1)	488 (60.2)	551 (61.3)	86.8 (2.52)	84.7 (4.20)	88.7 (2.95)	21.4 (3.55)	22.3 (5.34)	20.7 (3.19)
Hartford-West Hartford, CT CBSA	789 (60.4)	384 (32.3)	406 (31.1)	89.7 (1.57)	87.7 (2.24)	91.6 (1.47)	38.5 (3.10)	37.3 (3.76)	39.7 (3.32)
Houston-Baytown-Sugarland, TX CBSA	4,044 (217.8)	1,944 (106.9)	2,100 (127.9)	83.0 (1.47)	81.1 (1.89)	84.8 (1.53)	31.8 (2.31)	30.5 (2.56)	32.9 (2.80)
Indianapolis-Anderson-Columbus, IN CSA	1,299 (108.4)	588 (54.0)	711 (61.4)	92.2 (2.00)	90.4 (2.69)	93.7 (1.81)	32.4 (4.20)	29.8 (5.06)	34.5 (4.22)
Jacksonville, FL CBSA	995 (99.7)	454 (49.3)	541 (55.4)	93.1 (1.87)	96.3 (1.89)	90.3 (2.19)	36.2 (4.26)	38.6 (5.45)	34.2 (4.69)
Kansas City, MO-KS CSBA	1,369 (92.3)	637 (49.1)	732 (49.7)	95.5 (0.96)	93.4 (1.44)	97.4 (0.92)	37.7 (3.03)	38.7 (3.92)	36.8 (3.39)
Las Vegas-Paradise, NV CBSA	1,259 (55.4)	630 (34.2)	630 (25.9)	89.9 (1.43)	90.6 (1.44)	89.1 (1.92)	23.4 (1.81)	22.5 (2.32)	24.4 (2.19)
Los Angeles-Long Beach-Riverside, CA CSA	11,824 (184.4)	5,696 (117.5)	6,128 (95.1)	80.7 (1.01)	80.7 (1.28)	80.6 (0.99)	32.4 (1.09)	33.0 (1.38)	31.8 (1.25)
Louisville, KY-IN CBSA	883 (112.4)	437 (74.5)	446 (44.4)	93.0 (1.37)	92.8 (2.01)	93.2 (2.21)	29.9 (2.87)	32.7 (5.19)	27.1 (4.31)
Memphis, TN-MS-AR CBSA[1]	896 (87.3)	396 (44.4)	500 (51.7)	84.8 (3.34)	87.7 (4.58)	82.6 (5.17)	31.6 (4.59)	26.8 (6.88)	35.4 (4.69)
Miami-Fort Lauderdale-Miami Beach, FL CBSA	3,893 (183.7)	1,822 (97.6)	2,071 (99.6)	88.9 (1.10)	89.7 (1.59)	88.2 (1.21)	31.7 (1.86)	32.7 (2.41)	30.8 (1.95)
Milwaukee-Racine-Waukesha, WI CSA	1,174 (243.7)	569 (119.6)	606 (126.4)	91.3 (1.68)	90.2 (2.54)	92.4 (1.44)	30.8 (3.49)	25.9 (4.42)	35.5 (3.41)
Minneapolis-St. Paul-St. Cloud, MN-WI CSA[1]	2,254 (97.4)	1,081 (54.3)	1,173 (50.9)	93.4 (0.90)	93.4 (1.10)	93.4 (1.07)	39.2 (1.97)	37.1 (2.17)	41.2 (2.34)
Nashville-Davidson-Murfreesboro, TN CBSA	1,159 (191.4)	552 (94.2)	607 (101.7)	87.5 (2.85)	89.6 (3.25)	85.6 (3.59)	37.2 (4.15)	39.5 (4.59)	35.1 (4.50)
New Orleans-Metairie-Kenner, LA CBSA	789 (88.1)	372 (46.0)	417 (47.9)	86.9 (2.95)	85.2 (4.23)	88.5 (3.02)	32.3 (4.08)	37.2 (5.40)	27.8 (5.40)
New York-Newark, NY-NJ-PA CSA	14,815 (254.8)	6,872 (160.0)	7,943 (128.1)	87.9 (0.72)	88.2 (0.92)	87.7 (0.74)	40.3 (1.12)	38.8 (1.44)	41.7 (1.19)
Oklahoma City, OK CBSA	937 (66.4)	412 (35.8)	524 (36.4)	89.5 (2.39)	88.0 (2.93)	90.7 (2.57)	29.4 (3.35)	32.1 (4.61)	27.4 (3.39)
Orlando, FL CBSA	1,496 (134.5)	750 (75.9)	746 (67.4)	92.7 (1.81)	91.0 (2.56)	94.5 (1.73)	29.4 (3.36)	28.4 (4.36)	30.4 (3.57)
Philadelphia-Camden-Vineland, PA-NJ-DE-MD CSA	4,274 (161.6)	2,029 (91.3)	2,244 (87.0)	93.1 (0.85)	92.6 (1.05)	93.6 (1.05)	36.6 (2.25)	37.4 (2.77)	35.9 (2.28)
Phoenix-Mesa-Scottsdale, AZ CBSA[1]	2,805 ! (1,357.4)	1,425 ! (681.2)	1,380 ! (676.3)	85.0 (0.32)	83.1 (0.48)	86.9 (0.22)	31.3 (0.34)	33.3 (0.55)	29.2 (0.36)
Pittsburgh-New Castle, PA CBSA	1,742 (130.9)	818 (72.1)	923 (71.5)	93.2 (1.33)	90.1 (2.12)	96.0 (1.50)	37.7 (3.53)	37.6 (4.37)	37.7 (3.97)
Portland-Vancouver-Beaverton, OR-WA CBSA	1,552 (231.7)	773 (116.2)	779 (117.7)	92.7 (1.13)	95.4 (1.12)	90.1 (1.95)	36.2 (2.73)	34.6 (3.08)	37.7 (3.21)
Providence-Fall River-Warwick, RI-MA CBSA	876 (50.5)	419 (27.5)	457 (25.3)	84.8 (1.59)	86.0 (1.62)	83.8 (2.02)	35.8 (2.53)	38.5 (3.29)	33.4 (2.81)
Raleigh-Durham-Cary, NC CSA	1,382 (125.4)	648 (70.0)	734 (63.9)	86.3 (3.12)	83.6 (4.04)	88.7 (2.87)	44.7 (4.76)	45.6 (5.38)	44.0 (5.27)
Richmond, VA CBSA	976 (102.6)	466 (50.1)	510 (58.7)	90.4 (2.32)	89.3 (2.98)	91.4 (2.74)	34.5 (4.67)	30.4 (4.92)	38.3 (5.77)
Rochester, NY CBSA	806 (81.1)	398 (46.3)	408 (43.1)	93.6 (2.38)	92.3 (2.84)	94.9 (2.58)	34.7 (5.11)	34.1 (6.06)	35.2 (5.04)
Sacramento-Arden-Arcade-Roseville, CA CBSA	1,462 (86.0)	704 (49.0)	758 (51.2)	88.1 (2.25)	88.1 (3.27)	88.1 (2.28)	30.9 (2.92)	35.0 (3.58)	27.1 (2.93)
Salt Lake City-Ogden-Clearfield, UT CSA	1,053 (64.3)	521 (37.5)	532 (32.0)	91.5 (1.75)	90.5 (1.68)	92.5 (1.65)	32.5 (3.11)	35.4 (4.20)	29.7 (2.84)
San Antonio, TX CBSA	1,433 (121.2)	748 (66.4)	685 (65.5)	78.9 (2.50)	75.5 (3.18)	82.5 (2.45)	24.1 (3.01)	24.5 (3.68)	23.7 (3.46)
San Diego-Carlsbad-San Marcos, CA CBSA	2,087 (111.4)	1,018 (60.0)	1,069 (61.6)	90.7 (1.59)	92.7 (1.83)	88.8 (1.93)	41.3 (2.82)	43.4 (3.69)	39.2 (3.14)
San Jose-San Francisco-Oakland, CA CSA	5,604 (233.3)	2,838 (124.4)	2,766 (123.1)	89.0 (1.09)	89.6 (1.33)	88.4 (1.10)	45.7 (1.99)	47.1 (2.19)	44.3 (2.34)
Seattle-Tacoma-Olympia, WA CSA	2,808 (124.6)	1,331 (68.7)	1,477 (67.8)	92.6 (1.19)	92.2 (1.42)	92.9 (1.29)	41.5 (2.46)	39.7 (2.85)	43.2 (2.70)
St. Louis, MO-IL CBSA	1,951 (124.6)	954 (69.0)	997 (65.3)	91.8 (1.57)	90.8 (1.68)	92.6 (1.95)	32.2 (2.63)	30.4 (3.12)	34.0 (3.03)
Tampa-St. Petersburg-Clearwater, FL CBSA	2,321 (220.5)	1,120 (114.2)	1,202 (114.4)	90.1 (1.47)	92.3 (1.88)	88.2 (1.99)	30.4 (3.15)	32.3 (3.61)	28.6 (3.69)
Virginia Beach-Norfolk-Newport News, VA-NC CBSA[1]	1,114 (85.2)	515 (42.1)	598 (50.6)	91.7 (1.82)	88.9 (2.79)	94.2 (1.55)	27.4 (3.15)	25.6 (3.96)	29.0 (3.40)
Washington-Baltimore-Northern Virginia, DC-MD-VA-WV CSA[1]	5,989 (143.3)	2,890 (78.8)	3,099 (81.6)	92.0 (0.82)	91.5 (0.99)	92.5 (0.96)	49.1 (1.42)	49.9 (1.53)	48.3 (1.75)

! Interpret data with caution. The coefficient of variation (CV) for this estimate is between 30 and 50 percent.
[1] Information on metropolitan status was suppressed for a small portion of sample observations. As a result, population estimates for these areas may be slightly underestimated.
NOTE: A Core Based Statistical Area (CBSA) consists of one or more counties associated with at least one population core of at least 10,000 people, plus adjacent counties having a high degree of social and economic integration with the core as measured through commuting ties. A Combined Statistical Area (CSA) consists of two or more adjacent CBSAs that have social and economic ties as measured by commuting, but at lower levels than are found within each component CBSA. Detail may not sum to totals because of rounding. Standard errors were computed using replicate weights.
SOURCE: U.S. Department of Commerce, Census Bureau, Current Population Survey (CPS), March 2014. (This table was prepared March 2015.)

Table 105.10. Projected number of participants in educational institutions, by level and control of institution: Fall 2014

[In millions]

Participants	All levels (elementary, secondary, and degree-granting postsecondary)	Elementary and secondary schools			Degree-granting postsecondary institutions		
		Total	Public	Private	Total	Public	Private
1	2	3	4	5	6	7	8
Total..	**85.1**	**61.9**	**56.2**	**5.7**	**23.2**	**16.6**	**6.7**
Enrollment	75.2	55.0	50.0	5.0	20.3	14.7	5.6
Teachers and faculty.........................	4.6	3.5	3.1	0.4	1.0	0.7	0.4
Other professional, administrative, and support staff............................	5.3	3.4	3.1	0.3	1.9	1.2	0.7

NOTE: Includes enrollments in local public school systems and in most private schools (religiously affiliated and nonsectarian). Excludes federal Bureau of Indian Education schools and Department of Defense schools. Excludes private preprimary enrollment in schools that do not offer kindergarten or above. Degree-granting institutions grant associate's or higher degrees and participate in Title IV federal financial aid programs. Data for teachers and other staff in public and private elementary and secondary schools and colleges and universities are reported in terms of full-time equivalents. Detail may not sum to totals because of rounding.
SOURCE: U.S. Department of Education, National Center for Education Statistics, National Elementary and Secondary Enrollment Projection Model, 1972 through 2024; Enrollment in Degree-Granting Institutions Projection Model, 1980 through 2024; Elementary and Secondary Teacher Projection Model, 1973 through 2024; and unpublished projections and estimates. (This table was prepared March 2015.)

Table 105.20.   Enrollment in elementary, secondary, and degree-granting postsecondary institutions, by level and control of institution, enrollment level, and attendance status and sex of student: Selected years, fall 1990 through fall 2024

[In thousands]

Level and control of institution, enrollment level, and attendance status and sex of student	Actual				Projected											
	1990	2000	2010	2012	2013	2014	2015	2016	2017	2018	2019	2020	2021	2022	2023	2024
1	2	3	4	5	6	7	8	9	10	11	12	13	14	15	16	17
All levels..............	60,683	68,685	75,886	75,595	75,412	75,219	75,227	75,563	76,372	77,049	77,661	78,263	78,948	79,662	80,405	81,007
Elementary and secondary schools[1].............	46,864	53,373	54,867	54,952	55,036	54,965	54,994	55,077	55,447	55,719	56,031	56,404	56,779	57,151	57,524	57,872
Public........................	41,217	47,204	49,484	49,771	49,942	49,986	50,094	50,229	50,584	50,871	51,183	51,547	51,910	52,260	52,601	52,920
Private.........................	5,648 [2]	6,169 [2]	5,382 [2]	5,181 [3]	5,094	4,979	4,899	4,848	4,863	4,848	4,848	4,856	4,869	4,891	4,922	4,952
Prekindergarten to grade 8....	34,388	38,592	38,708	38,924	39,045	38,938	38,926	39,010	39,363	39,642	39,937	40,204	40,450	40,728	41,147	41,574
Public[4]......................	29,876	33,686	34,625	35,018	35,188	35,159	35,182	35,282	35,595	35,856	36,125	36,366	36,587	36,839	37,223	37,615
Private.....................	4,512 [2]	4,906 [2]	4,084 [2]	3,906 [3]	3,858	3,779	3,744	3,728	3,768	3,786	3,813	3,839	3,863	3,889	3,924	3,959
Grades 9 to 12..................	12,476	14,781	16,159	16,028	15,990	16,026	16,067	16,067	16,084	16,078	16,094	16,199	16,330	16,424	16,377	16,298
Public[4]......................	11,341	13,517	14,860	14,753	14,754	14,826	14,912	14,947	14,989	15,015	15,058	15,182	15,324	15,421	15,378	15,304
Private.....................	1,136 [2]	1,264 [2]	1,299 [2]	1,275 [3]	1,236	1,200	1,155	1,120	1,095	1,063	1,035	1,017	1,006	1,003	998	994
Degree-granting postsecondary institutions..........	13,819	15,312	21,019	20,643	20,376 [5]	20,255	20,234	20,486	20,925	21,330	21,630	21,859	22,168	22,511	22,881	23,135
Undergraduate..................	11,959	13,155	18,082	17,732	17,475 [5]	17,322	17,280	17,472	17,823	18,156	18,404	18,591	18,843	19,119	19,423	19,640
Full-time..................	6,976	7,923	11,457	11,098	10,938 [5]	10,966	10,904	11,033	11,261	11,463	11,601	11,708	11,857	12,019	12,211	12,345
Part-time	4,983	5,232	6,625	6,635	6,536 [5]	6,356	6,376	6,439	6,562	6,693	6,804	6,883	6,986	7,100	7,211	7,295
Male........................	5,380	5,778	7,836	7,714	7,660 [5]	7,466	7,446	7,490	7,612	7,745	7,836	7,898	7,998	8,113	8,236	8,330
Female......................	6,579	7,377	10,246	10,019	9,815 [5]	9,855	9,834	9,982	10,210	10,412	10,569	10,692	10,845	11,006	11,187	11,310
2-year..................	5,240	5,948	7,684	7,164	6,969 [5]	7,009	7,011	7,090	7,235	7,378	7,487	7,562	7,664	7,782	7,907	7,996
4-year..................	6,719	7,207	10,399	10,568	10,506 [5]	10,313	10,269	10,381	10,587	10,778	10,917	11,029	11,179	11,337	11,516	11,645
Public......................	9,710	10,539	13,703	13,474	13,347 [5]	13,245	13,221	13,366	13,633	13,890	14,083	14,225	14,418	14,631	14,863	15,029
Private......................	2,250	2,616	4,379	4,259	4,128 [5]	4,077	4,059	4,106	4,189	4,266	4,321	4,365	4,425	4,488	4,560	4,611
Postbaccalaureate	1,860	2,157	2,937	2,910	2,901 [5]	2,933	2,953	3,013	3,102	3,173	3,225	3,268	3,325	3,391	3,458	3,495
Full-time..................	845	1,087	1,630	1,639	1,659 [5]	1,698	1,710	1,749	1,804	1,842	1,866	1,888	1,917	1,953	1,991	2,007
Part-time	1,015	1,070	1,307	1,271	1,242 [5]	1,234	1,243	1,264	1,298	1,331	1,359	1,381	1,408	1,438	1,467	1,488
Male........................	904	944	1,209	1,205	1,201 [5]	1,260	1,271	1,293	1,329	1,360	1,382	1,399	1,424	1,454	1,483	1,500
Female......................	955	1,213	1,728	1,705	1,700 [5]	1,673	1,682	1,720	1,773	1,813	1,843	1,869	1,901	1,937	1,975	1,994

[1]Includes enrollments in local public school systems and in most private schools (religiously affiliated and nonsectarian). Excludes homeschooled children who were not also enrolled in public and private schools. Private elementary enrollment includes preprimary students in schools offering kindergarten or higher grades.
[2]Estimated.
[3]Projected.
[4]Includes prorated proportion of students classified as ungraded.
[5]Data are actual.
NOTE: Postsecondary data for 1990 are for institutions of higher education, while later data are for degree-granting institutions. Degree-granting institutions grant associate's or higher degrees and participate in Title IV federal financial aid programs. The degree-granting clas-

sification is very similar to the earlier higher education classification, but it includes more 2-year colleges and excludes a few higher education institutions that did not grant degrees. Detail may not sum to totals because of rounding. Some data have been revised from previously published figures.
SOURCE: U.S. Department of Education, National Center for Education Statistics, Common Core of Data (CCD), "State Nonfiscal Survey of Public Elementary and Secondary Education," 1990–91 through 2012–13; Private School Universe Survey (PSS), 1995–96 through 2011–12; National Elementary and Secondary Enrollment Projection Model, 1972 through 2024; Integrated Postsecondary Education Data System (IPEDS), "Fall Enrollment Survey" (IPEDS-EF:90-99); and IPEDS Spring 2001 through Spring 2014, Enrollment component. (This table was prepared March 2015.)

Table 105.30. Enrollment in elementary, secondary, and degree-granting postsecondary institutions, by level and control of institution: Selected years, 1869–70 through fall 2024

[In thousands]

Year	Total enrollment, all levels	Elementary and secondary, total	Public elementary and secondary schools			Private elementary and secondary schools[1]			Degree-granting postsecondary institutions[2]		
			Total	Prekindergarten through grade 8	Grades 9 through 12	Total	Prekindergarten through grade 8	Grades 9 through 12	Total	Public	Private
1	2	3	4	5	6	7	8	9	10	11	12
1869–70	—	—	6,872	6,792	80	—	—	—	52	—	—
1879–80	—	—	9,868	9,757	110	—	—	—	116	—	—
1889–90	14,491	14,334	12,723	12,520	203	1,611	1,516	95	157	—	—
1899–1900	17,092	16,855	15,503	14,984	519	1,352	1,241	111	238	—	—
1909–10	19,728	19,372	17,814	16,899	915	1,558	1,441	117	355	—	—
1919–20	23,876	23,278	21,578	19,378	2,200	1,699	1,486	214	598	—	—
1929–30	29,430	28,329	25,678	21,279	4,399	2,651	2,310	341	1,101	—	—
1939–40	29,539	28,045	25,434	18,832	6,601	2,611	2,153	458	1,494	797	698
1949–50	31,151	28,492	25,111	19,387	5,725	3,380	2,708	672	2,659	1,355	1,304
Fall 1959	44,497	40,857	35,182	26,911	8,271	5,675	4,640	1,035	3,640	2,181	1,459
Fall 1969	59,055	51,050	45,550	32,513	13,037	5,500 [3]	4,200 [3]	1,300 [3]	8,005	5,897	2,108
Fall 1979	58,221	46,651	41,651	28,034	13,616	5,000 [3]	3,700 [3]	1,300 [3]	11,570	9,037	2,533
Fall 1985	57,226	44,979	39,422	27,034	12,388	5,557	4,195	1,362	12,247	9,479	2,768
Fall 1990	60,683	46,864	41,217	29,876	11,341	5,648 [3]	4,512 [3]	1,136 [3]	13,819	10,845	2,974
Fall 1991	62,087	47,728	42,047	30,503	11,544	5,681	4,550	1,131	14,359	11,310	3,049
Fall 1992	63,181	48,694	42,823	31,086	11,737	5,870 [3]	4,746 [3]	1,125 [3]	14,487	11,385	3,103
Fall 1993	63,837	49,532	43,465	31,502	11,963	6,067	4,950	1,118	14,305	11,189	3,116
Fall 1994	64,385	50,106	44,111	31,896	12,215	5,994 [3]	4,856 [3]	1,138 [3]	14,279	11,134	3,145
Fall 1995	65,020	50,759	44,840	32,338	12,502	5,918	4,756	1,163	14,262	11,092	3,169
Fall 1996	65,911	51,544	45,611	32,762	12,849	5,933 [3]	4,755 [3]	1,178 [3]	14,368	11,120	3,247
Fall 1997	66,574	52,071	46,127	33,071	13,056	5,944	4,759	1,185	14,502	11,196	3,306
Fall 1998	67,033	52,526	46,539	33,344	13,195	5,988 [3]	4,776 [3]	1,212 [3]	14,507	11,138	3,369
Fall 1999	67,725	52,875	46,857	33,486	13,371	6,018	4,789	1,229	14,850	11,376	3,474
Fall 2000	68,685	53,373	47,204	33,686	13,517	6,169 [3]	4,906 [3]	1,264 [3]	15,312	11,753	3,560
Fall 2001	69,920	53,992	47,672	33,936	13,736	6,320	5,023	1,296	15,928	12,233	3,695
Fall 2002	71,015	54,403	48,183	34,114	14,069	6,220 [3]	4,915 [3]	1,306 [3]	16,612	12,752	3,860
Fall 2003	71,551	54,639	48,540	34,201	14,339	6,099	4,788	1,311	16,911	12,859	4,053
Fall 2004	72,154	54,882	48,795	34,178	14,618	6,087 [3]	4,756 [3]	1,331 [3]	17,272	12,980	4,292
Fall 2005	72,674	55,187	49,113	34,204	14,909	6,073	4,724	1,349	17,487	13,022	4,466
Fall 2006	73,066	55,307	49,316	34,235	15,081	5,991 [3]	4,631 [3]	1,360 [3]	17,759	13,180	4,579
Fall 2007	73,449	55,201	49,291	34,204	15,086	5,910	4,546	1,364	18,248	13,491	4,757
Fall 2008	74,076	54,973	49,266	34,286	14,980	5,707 [3]	4,365 [3]	1,342 [3]	19,103	13,972	5,131
Fall 2009	75,163	54,849	49,361	34,409	14,952	5,488	4,179	1,309	20,314	14,811	5,503
Fall 2010	75,886	54,867	49,484	34,625	14,860	5,382 [3]	4,084 [3]	1,299 [3]	21,019	15,142	5,877
Fall 2011	75,800	54,790	49,522	34,773	14,749	5,268	3,977	1,291	21,011	15,116	5,894
Fall 2012	75,595	54,952	49,771	35,018	14,753	5,181 [4]	3,906 [4]	1,275 [4]	20,643	14,880	5,762
Fall 2013[4]	75,412	55,036	49,942	35,188	14,754	5,094	3,858	1,236	20,376	14,746	5,630
Fall 2014[4]	75,219	54,965	49,986	35,159	14,826	4,979	3,779	1,200	20,255	14,660	5,595
Fall 2015[4]	75,227	54,994	50,094	35,182	14,912	4,899	3,744	1,155	20,234	14,646	5,588
Fall 2016[4]	75,563	55,077	50,229	35,282	14,947	4,848	3,728	1,120	20,486	14,820	5,666
Fall 2017[4]	76,372	55,447	50,584	35,595	14,989	4,863	3,768	1,095	20,925	15,129	5,796
Fall 2018[4]	77,049	55,719	50,871	35,856	15,015	4,848	3,786	1,063	21,330	15,421	5,909
Fall 2019[4]	77,661	56,031	51,183	36,125	15,058	4,848	3,813	1,035	21,630	15,639	5,991
Fall 2020[4]	78,263	56,404	51,547	36,366	15,182	4,856	3,839	1,017	21,859	15,802	6,057
Fall 2021[4]	78,948	56,779	51,910	36,587	15,324	4,869	3,863	1,006	22,168	16,022	6,146
Fall 2022[4]	79,662	57,151	52,260	36,839	15,421	4,891	3,889	1,003	22,511	16,267	6,243
Fall 2023[4]	80,405	57,524	52,601	37,223	15,378	4,922	3,924	998	22,881	16,531	6,350
Fall 2024[4]	81,007	57,872	52,920	37,615	15,304	4,952	3,959	994	23,135	16,716	6,419

—Not available.

[1]Beginning in fall 1985, data include estimates for an expanded universe of private schools. Therefore, direct comparisons with earlier years should be avoided.

[2]Data for 1869–70 through 1949–50 include resident degree-credit students enrolled at any time during the academic year. Beginning in 1959, data include all resident and extension students enrolled at the beginning of the fall term.

[3]Estimated.

[4]Projected data. Fall 2013 data for degree-granting institutions are actual.

NOTE: Data for 1869–70 through 1949–50 reflect enrollment for the entire school year. Elementary and secondary enrollment includes students in local public school systems and in most private schools (religiously affiliated and nonsectarian), but generally excludes homeschooled children and students in subcollegiate departments of colleges and in federal schools. Excludes preprimary pupils in private schools that do not offer kindergarten or above. Postsecondary data through 1995 are for institutions of higher education, while later data are for degree-granting institutions. Degree-granting institutions grant associate's or higher degrees and participate in Title IV federal financial aid programs. The degree-granting classification is very similar to the earlier higher education classification, but it includes more 2-year colleges and excludes a few higher education institutions that did not grant degrees. Some data have been revised from previously published figures. Detail may not sum to totals because of rounding.

SOURCE: U.S. Department of Education, National Center for Education Statistics, Annual Report of the Commissioner of Education, 1870 to 1910; Biennial Survey of Education in the United States, 1919–20 through 1949–50; Statistics of Public Elementary and Secondary School Systems, 1959 through 1979; Common Core of Data (CCD), "State Nonfiscal Survey of Public Elementary and Secondary Education," 1989–90 through 2012–13; Private School Universe Survey (PSS), 1991–92 through 2011–12; National Elementary and Secondary Enrollment Projection Model, 1972 through 2024; Opening (Fall) Enrollment in Higher Education, 1959; Higher Education General Information Survey (HEGIS), "Fall Enrollment in Institutions of Higher Education" surveys, 1969, 1979, and 1985; Integrated Postsecondary Education Data System (IPEDS), "Fall Enrollment Survey" (IPEDS-EF:90–99); IPEDS Spring 2001 through Spring 2014, Enrollment component; and Enrollment in Degree-Granting Institutions Projection Model, 1980 through 2024. (This table was prepared March 2015.)

Table 105.40. Number of teachers in elementary and secondary schools, and faculty in degree-granting postsecondary institutions, by control of institution: Selected years, fall 1970 through fall 2024

[In thousands]

Year	All levels			Elementary and secondary teachers[1]			Degree-granting institutions instructional staff[2]		
	Total	Public	Private	Total	Public	Private	Total	Public	Private
1	2	3	4	5	6	7	8	9	10
1970	2,766	2,373	393	2,292	2,059	233	474	314	160
1975	3,081	2,641	440	2,453	2,198	255[3]	628	443	185
1980	3,171	2,679	492	2,485	2,184	301	686[3,4]	495[3,4]	191[3,4]
1981	3,145	2,636	509	2,440	2,127	313[3]	705	509	196
1982	3,168	2,639	529	2,458	2,133	325[3]	710[3,4]	506[3,4]	204[3,4]
1983	3,200	2,651	549	2,476	2,139	337	724	512	212
1984	3,225	2,673	552	2,508	2,168	340[3]	717[3,4]	505[3,4]	212[3,4]
1985	3,264	2,709	555	2,549	2,206	343	715[3,4]	503[3,4]	212[3,4]
1986	3,314	2,754	560	2,592	2,244	348[3]	722[3,4]	510[3,4]	212[3,4]
1987	3,424	2,832	592	2,631	2,279	352	793	553	240
1988	3,472	2,882	590	2,668	2,323	345	804[3]	559[3]	245[3]
1989	3,537	2,934	603	2,713	2,357	356	824	577	247
1990	3,577	2,972	604	2,759	2,398	361[3]	817[3]	574[3]	244[3]
1991	3,623	3,013	610	2,797	2,432	365	826	581	245
1992	3,700	3,080	621	2,823	2,459	364[3]	877[3]	621[3]	257[3]
1993	3,784	3,154	629	2,868	2,504	364	915	650	265
1994	3,846	3,205	640	2,922	2,552	370[3]	923[3]	653[3]	270[3]
1995	3,906	3,255	651	2,974	2,598	376	932	657	275
1996	4,006	3,339	666	3,051	2,667	384[3]	954[3]	672[3]	282[3]
1997	4,127	3,441	687	3,138	2,746	391	990	695	295
1998	4,230	3,527	703	3,230	2,830	400[3]	999[3]	697[3]	303[3]
1999	4,347	3,624	723	3,319	2,911	408	1,028	713	315
2000	4,433	3,682	750	3,366	2,941	424	1,067[3]	741[3]	325[3]
2001	4,554	3,771	783	3,440	3,000	441	1,113	771	342
2002	4,631	3,829	802	3,476	3,034	442[3]	1,155[3]	794[3]	361[3]
2003	4,663	3,840	823	3,490	3,049	441	1,174	792	382
2004	4,774	3,909	865	3,538	3,091	447[3]	1,237[3]	818[3]	418[3]
2005	4,883	3,984	899	3,593	3,143	450	1,290	841	449
2006	4,944	4,021	924	3,622	3,166	456[3]	1,322[3]	854[3]	468[3]
2007	5,028	4,077	951	3,656	3,200	456	1,371	877	494
2008	5,065	4,107	958	3,670	3,222	448[3]	1,395[3]	885[3]	510[3]
2009	5,086	4,123	963	3,647	3,210	437	1,439	914	525
2010	5,038	4,044	994	3,529	3,099	429[3]	1,510[3]	945[3]	565[3]
2011	5,049	4,057	991	3,524	3,103	421	1,524	954	570
2012	5,054	4,067	987	3,523	3,109	414[5]	1,531[3]	958[3]	573[3]
2013[6]	5,071	4,087	983	3,527	3,120	407	1,544	968	576
2014[5]	—	—	—	3,520	3,122	398	—	—	—
2015[5]	—	—	—	3,521	3,129	391	—	—	—
2016[5]	—	—	—	3,525	3,138	387	—	—	—
2017[5]	—	—	—	3,577	3,185	392	—	—	—
2018[5]	—	—	—	3,617	3,224	393	—	—	—
2019[5]	—	—	—	3,660	3,264	395	—	—	—
2020[5]	—	—	—	3,700	3,302	398	—	—	—
2021[5]	—	—	—	3,743	3,342	401	—	—	—
2022[5]	—	—	—	3,788	3,383	405	—	—	—
2023[5]	—	—	—	3,840	3,429	410	—	—	—
2024[5]	—	—	—	3,881	3,466	415	—	—	—

—Not available.
[1]Includes teachers in local public school systems and in most private schools (religiously affiliated and nonsectarian). Teachers are reported in terms of full-time equivalents.
[2]Data through 1995 are for institutions of higher education, while later data are for degree-granting institutions. Degree-granting institutions grant associate's or higher degrees and participate in Title IV federal financial aid programs. The degree-granting classification is very similar to the earlier higher education classification, but it includes more 2-year colleges and excludes a few higher education institutions that did not grant degrees. Includes full-time and part-time faculty with the rank of instructor or above in colleges, universities, professional schools, and 2-year colleges. Excludes teaching assistants.
[3]Estimated.
[4]Inclusion of institutions is not consistent with surveys for 1987 and later years.
[5]Projected.
[6]Data for elementary and secondary teachers are projected and data for degree-granting institutions faculty are actual.

NOTE: Detail may not sum to totals because of rounding. Some data have been revised from previously published figures. Headcounts are used to report data for degree-granting institutions faculty.
SOURCE: U.S. Department of Education, National Center for Education Statistics, *Statistics of Public Elementary and Secondary Day Schools*, 1970 and 1975; Common Core of Data (CCD), "State Nonfiscal Survey of Public Elementary/Secondary Education," 1980 through 2012; Private School Universe Survey (PSS), 1989–90 through 2011–12; Elementary and Secondary Teacher Projection Model, 1973 through 2024; Higher Education General Information Survey (HEGIS), "Fall Staff" survey, 1970 and 1975; Integrated Postsecondary Education Data System (IPEDS), "Fall Staff Survey" (IPEDS-S:87–99); IPEDS Winter 2001–02 through Winter 2011–12, Human Resources component, Fall Staff section; IPEDS Spring 2014, Human Resources component, Fall Staff section; U.S. Equal Opportunity Commission, EEO-6, 1981 and 1983; and unpublished data. (This table was prepared March 2015.)

Table 105.50. Number of educational institutions, by level and control of institution: Selected years, 1980–81 through 2012–13

Level and control of institution	1980–81	1990–91	1999–2000	2000–01	2003–04	2004–05	2005–06	2006–07	2007–08	2008–09	2009–10	2010–11	2011–12	2012–13
1	2	3	4	5	6	7	8	9	10	11	12	13	14	15
All institutions	—	—	131,414	—	136,819	—	138,899	—	139,207	—	138,925	—	136,423	—
Elementary and secondary schools	106,746	109,228	125,007	—	130,407	—	132,436	—	132,656	—	132,183	—	129,189	—
Elementary	72,659	74,716	86,433	—	89,252	—	88,896	—	88,982	—	88,565	—	86,386	—
Secondary	24,856	23,602	24,903	—	25,476	—	26,925	—	27,575	—	27,427	—	27,034	—
Combined	5,202	8,847	12,197	—	13,931	—	14,964	—	14,837	—	14,895	—	14,799	—
Other[1]	4,029	2,063	1,474	—	1,749	—	1,651	—	1,262	—	1,296	—	971	—
Public schools	85,982	84,538	92,012	93,273	95,726	96,513	97,382	98,793	98,916	98,706	98,817	98,817	98,328	98,454
Elementary	59,326	59,015	64,131	64,601	65,758	65,984	66,026	66,458	67,112	67,148	67,140	67,086	66,689	66,718
Secondary	22,619	21,135	22,365	21,994	22,782	23,445	23,998	23,920	24,643	24,348	24,651	24,544	24,357	24,280
Combined	1,743	2,325	4,042	5,096	5,437	5,572	5,707	5,984	5,899	5,623	5,730	6,137	6,311	6,371
Other[1]	2,294	2,063	1,474	1,582	1,749	1,512	1,651	2,431	1,262	1,587	1,296	1,050	971	1,085
Private schools[2]	20,764	24,690	32,995	—	34,681	—	35,054	—	33,740	—	33,366	—	30,861	—
Elementary	13,333	15,701	22,302	—	23,494	—	22,870	—	21,870	—	21,425	—	19,697	—
Schools with highest grade of kindergarten	†	†	5,952	—	6,297	—	6,059	—	5,522	—	5,275	—	4,658	—
Secondary	2,237	2,467	2,538	—	2,694	—	2,927	—	2,932	—	2,776	—	2,677	—
Combined	3,459	6,522	8,155	—	8,494	—	9,257	—	8,938	—	9,165	—	8,488	—
Other[1]	1,735	(3)	(3)	—	(3)	—	(3)	—	(3)	—	(3)	—	(3)	—
Postsecondary Title IV institutions	—	—	6,407	6,479	6,412	6,383	6,463	6,536	6,551	6,632	6,742	7,021	7,234	7,253
Public	—	—	2,078	2,084	2,047	2,027	2,013	2,009	2,004	1,997	1,989	2,015	2,011	1,981
Private	—	—	4,329	4,395	4,365	4,356	4,450	4,527	4,547	4,635	4,753	5,006	5,223	5,272
Nonprofit	—	—	1,936	1,950	1,913	1,875	1,866	1,848	1,815	1,809	1,809	1,812	1,830	1,820
For-profit	—	—	2,393	2,445	2,452	2,481	2,584	2,679	2,732	2,826	2,944	3,194	3,393	3,452
Title IV non-degree-granting institutions	—	—	2,323	2,297	2,176	2,167	2,187	2,222	2,199	2,223	2,247	2,422	2,528	2,527
Public	—	—	396	386	327	327	320	321	319	321	317	359	362	358
Private	—	—	1,927	1,911	1,849	1,840	1,867	1,901	1,880	1,902	1,930	2,063	2,166	2,169
Nonprofit	—	—	255	255	249	238	219	208	191	180	185	182	177	168
For-profit	—	—	1,672	1,656	1,600	1,602	1,648	1,693	1,689	1,722	1,745	1,881	1,989	2,001
Title IV degree-granting institutions	3,231	3,559	4,084	4,182	4,236	4,216	4,276	4,314	4,352	4,409	4,495	4,599	4,706	4,726
2-year colleges	1,274	1,418	1,721	1,732	1,706	1,683	1,694	1,685	1,677	1,690	1,721	1,729	1,738	1,700
Public	945	972	1,068	1,076	1,086	1,061	1,053	1,045	1,032	1,024	1,000	978	967	934
Private	329	446	653	656	620	622	641	640	645	666	721	751	771	766
Nonprofit	182	167	150	144	118	112	113	107	92	92	85	87	100	97
For-profit	147	279	503	512	502	510	528	533	553	574	636	664	671	669
4-year colleges	1,957	2,141	2,363	2,450	2,530	2,533	2,582	2,629	2,675	2,719	2,774	2,870	2,968	3,026
Public	552	595	614	622	634	639	640	643	653	652	672	678	682	689
Private	1,405	1,546	1,749	1,828	1,896	1,894	1,942	1,986	2,022	2,067	2,102	2,192	2,286	2,337
Nonprofit	1,387	1,482	1,531	1,551	1,546	1,525	1,534	1,533	1,532	1,537	1,539	1,543	1,553	1,555
For-profit	18	64	218	277	350	369	408	453	490	530	563	649	733	782

—Not available.

†Not applicable.

[1]Includes special education, alternative, and other schools not classified by grade span. Because of changes in survey definitions, figures for "other" schools are not comparable from year to year.

[2]Data for 1980–81 and 1990–91 include schools with first or higher grades. Data for 1997–98 and later years include schools with kindergarten or higher grades.

[3]Included in the elementary, secondary, and combined categories.

NOTE: Postsecondary data for 1980–81 and 1990–91 are for institutions of higher education, while later data are for Title IV degree-granting and non-degree-granting institutions. Degree-granting institutions grant associate's or higher degrees and participate in Title IV federal financial aid programs. The degree-granting classification is very similar to the ear-

lier higher education classification, but it includes more 2-year colleges and excludes a few higher education institutions that did not grant degrees.

SOURCE: U.S. Department of Education, National Center for Education Statistics, Common Core of Data (CCD), "Public Elementary/Secondary School Universe Survey," 1989–90 through 2012–13; Private Schools in American Education; Statistics of Public Elementary and Secondary Day Schools, 1980–81; Schools and Staffing Survey (SASS), "Private School Data File," 1990–91; Private School Universe Survey (PSS), 1995–96 through 2011–12; Higher Education General Information Survey (HEGIS), "Institutional Characteristics of Colleges and Universities" survey, 1980–81; Integrated Postsecondary Education Data System (IPEDS), "Institutional Characteristics Survey" (IPEDS-IC:90–99); and IPEDS Fall 2001 through Fall 2012, Institutional Characteristics component. (This table was prepared March 2015.)

Table 106.10. Expenditures of educational institutions related to the gross domestic product, by level of institution: Selected years, 1929–30 through 2013–14

Year	Gross domestic product (GDP) (in billions of current dollars)	School year	Expenditures for education in current dollars					
			All educational institutions		All elementary and secondary schools		All degree-granting postsecondary institutions	
			Amount (in millions)	As a percent of GDP	Amount (in millions)	As a percent of GDP	Amount (in millions)	As a percent of GDP
1	2	3	4	5	6	7	8	9
1929	$104.6	1929–30	—	—	—	—	$632	0.6
1939	93.5	1939–40	—	—	—	—	758	0.8
1949	272.8	1949–50	$8,494	3.1	$6,249	2.3	2,246	0.8
1959	522.5	1959–60	22,314	4.3	16,713	3.2	5,601	1.1
1961	563.3	1961–62	26,828	4.8	19,673	3.5	7,155	1.3
1963	638.6	1963–64	32,003	5.0	22,825	3.6	9,178	1.4
1965	743.7	1965–66	40,558	5.5	28,048	3.8	12,509	1.7
1967	861.7	1967–68	51,558	6.0	35,077	4.1	16,481	1.9
1969	1,019.9	1969–70	64,227	6.3	43,183	4.2	21,043	2.1
1970	1,075.9	1970–71	71,575	6.7	48,200	4.5	23,375	2.2
1971	1,167.8	1971–72	76,510	6.6	50,950	4.4	25,560	2.2
1972	1,282.4	1972–73	82,908	6.5	54,952	4.3	27,956	2.2
1973	1,428.5	1973–74	91,084	6.4	60,370	4.2	30,714	2.2
1974	1,548.8	1974–75	103,903	6.7	68,846	4.4	35,058	2.3
1975	1,688.9	1975–76	114,004	6.8	75,101	4.4	38,903	2.3
1976	1,877.6	1976–77	121,793	6.5	79,194	4.2	42,600	2.3
1977	2,086.0	1977–78	132,515	6.4	86,544	4.1	45,971	2.2
1978	2,356.6	1978–79	143,733	6.1	93,012	3.9	50,721	2.2
1979	2,632.1	1979–80	160,075	6.1	103,162	3.9	56,914	2.2
1980	2,862.5	1980–81	176,378	6.2	112,325	3.9	64,053	2.2
1981	3,211.0	1981–82	190,825	5.9	120,486	3.8	70,339	2.2
1982	3,345.0	1982–83	204,661	6.1	128,725	3.8	75,936	2.3
1983	3,638.1	1983–84	220,993	6.1	139,000	3.8	81,993	2.3
1984	4,040.7	1984–85	239,351	5.9	149,400	3.7	89,951	2.2
1985	4,346.7	1985–86	259,336	6.0	161,800	3.7	97,536	2.2
1986	4,590.2	1986–87	280,964	6.1	175,200	3.8	105,764	2.3
1987	4,870.2	1987–88	301,786	6.2	187,999	3.9	113,787	2.3
1988	5,252.6	1988–89	333,245	6.3	209,377	4.0	123,867	2.4
1989	5,657.7	1989–90	365,825	6.5	231,170	4.1	134,656	2.4
1990	5,979.6	1990–91	395,318	6.6	249,230	4.2	146,088	2.4
1991	6,174.0	1991–92	417,944	6.8	261,755	4.2	156,189	2.5
1992	6,539.3	1992–93	439,676	6.7	274,435	4.2	165,241	2.5
1993	6,878.7	1993–94	460,756	6.7	287,407	4.2	173,351	2.5
1994	7,308.8	1994–95	485,169	6.6	302,200	4.1	182,969	2.5
1995	7,664.1	1995–96	508,523	6.6	318,046	4.1	190,476	2.5
1996	8,100.2	1996–97	538,854	6.7	338,951	4.2	199,903 [1]	2.5
1997	8,608.5	1997–98	570,471	6.6	361,615	4.2	208,856 [1]	2.4
1998	9,089.2	1998–99	603,847	6.6	384,638	4.2	219,209	2.4
1999	9,660.6	1999–2000	649,322	6.7	412,538	4.3	236,784	2.5
2000	10,284.8	2000–01	705,017	6.9	444,811	4.3	260,206	2.5
2001	10,621.8	2001–02	752,780	7.1	472,064	4.4	280,715	2.6
2002	10,977.5	2002–03	795,691	7.2	492,807	4.5	302,884	2.8
2003	11,510.7	2003–04	830,293	7.2	513,542	4.5	316,751	2.8
2004	12,274.9	2004–05	875,988	7.1	540,969	4.4	335,019	2.7
2005	13,093.7	2005–06	925,246	7.1	571,669	4.4	353,577	2.7
2006	13,855.9	2006–07	984,034	7.1	608,495	4.4	375,539	2.7
2007	14,477.6	2007–08	1,054,904	7.3	646,414	4.5	408,490	2.8
2008	14,718.6	2008–09	1,089,670	7.4	658,926	4.5	430,744	2.9
2009	14,418.7	2009–10	1,100,902	7.6	654,418	4.5	446,484	3.1
2010	14,964.4	2010–11	1,123,565	7.5	652,356	4.4	471,209	3.1
2011	15,517.9	2011–12	1,137,011	7.3	648,567	4.2	488,444	3.1
2012	16,163.2	2012–13 [2]	1,165,000	7.2	666,000	4.1	498,939	3.1
2013	16,768.1	2013–14 [3]	1,194,000	7.1	682,000	4.1	512,000	3.1

—Not available.

[1]Estimated by the National Center for Education Statistics based on enrollment data for the given year and actual expenditures for prior years.

[2]Data for elementary and secondary education are estimated; data for degree-granting institutions are actual.

[3]Estimated by the National Center for Education Statistics based on teacher and enrollment data, and actual expenditures for prior years.

NOTE: Total expenditures for public elementary and secondary schools include current expenditures, interest on school debt, and capital outlay. Data for private elementary and secondary schools are estimated. Expenditures for colleges and universities in 1929–30 and 1939–40 include current-fund expenditures and additions to plant value. Public and private degree-granting institutions data for 1949–50 through 1995–96 are for current-fund expenditures. Data for private degree-granting institutions for 1996–97 and later years are for total expenditures. Postsecondary data through 1995–96 are for institutions of higher education, while later data are for degree-granting institutions. Degree-granting institutions grant associate's or higher degrees and participate in Title IV federal financial aid pro-grams. The degree-granting classification is very similar to the earlier higher education classification, but it includes more 2-year colleges and excludes a few higher education institutions that did not grant degrees. Some data have been revised from previously published figures. Detail may not sum to totals because of rounding.

SOURCE: U.S. Department of Education, National Center for Education Statistics, *Biennial Survey of Education in the United States*, 1929–30 through 1949–50; *Statistics of State School Systems*, 1959–60 through 1969–70; *Revenues and Expenditures for Public Elementary and Secondary Education*, 1970–71 through 1986–87; Common Core of Data (CCD), "National Public Education Financial Survey," 1987–88 through 2011–12; Higher Education General Information Survey (HEGIS), Financial Statistics of Institutions of Higher Education, 1965–66 through 1985–86; Integrated Postsecondary Education Data System (IPEDS), "Finance Survey" (IPEDS-F:FY87–99); and IPEDS Spring 2001 through Spring 2014, Finance component. U.S. Department of Commerce, Bureau of Economic Analysis, National Income and Product Accounts Tables, retrieved May 1, 2015, from http://www.bea.gov/iTable/index_nipa.cfm. (This table was prepared May 2015.)

Table 106.20. Expenditures of educational institutions, by level and control of institution: Selected years, 1899–1900 through 2013–14

[In millions]

School year	Current dollars							Constant 2013–14 dollars[1]			
	Total	Elementary and secondary schools			Degree-granting postsecondary institutions			Total	Elementary and secondary schools		Degree-granting post-secondary institutions
		Total	Public	Private[2]	Total	Public	Private		Total	Public	
1	2	3	4	5	6	7	8	9	10	11	12
1899–1900	—	—	$215	—	—	—	—	—	—	—	—
1909–10	—	—	426	—	—	—	—	—	—	—	—
1919–20	—	—	1,036	—	—	—	—	—	—	$12,775	—
1929–30	—	—	2,317	—	$632	$292	$341	—	—	31,803	$8,679
1939–40	—	—	2,344	—	758	392	367	—	—	39,411	12,752
1949–50	$8,494	$6,249	5,838	$411	2,246	1,154	1,092	$84,274	$61,995	57,917	22,280
1959–60	22,314	16,713	15,613	1,100	5,601	3,131	2,470	178,438	133,650	124,854	44,787
1969–70	64,227	43,183	40,683	2,500	21,043	13,250	7,794	399,498	268,607	253,057	130,891
1970–71	71,575	48,200	45,500	2,700	23,375	14,996	8,379	423,353	285,093	269,123	138,260
1971–72	76,510	50,950	48,050	2,900	25,560	16,484	9,075	436,870	290,925	274,367	145,945
1972–73	82,908	54,952	51,852	3,100	27,956	18,204	9,752	455,068	301,624	284,608	153,444
1973–74	91,084	60,370	56,970	3,400	30,714	20,336	10,377	459,016	304,236	287,101	154,781
1974–75	103,903	68,846	64,846	4,000	35,058	23,490	11,568	471,381	312,335	294,188	159,046
1975–76	114,004	75,101	70,601	4,500	38,903	26,184	12,719	483,014	318,188	299,122	164,826
1976–77	121,793	79,194	74,194	5,000	42,600	28,635	13,965	487,585	317,042	297,025	170,543
1977–78	132,515	86,544	80,844	5,700	45,971	30,725	15,246	497,127	324,669	303,285	172,458
1978–79	143,733	93,012	86,712	6,300	50,721	33,733	16,988	493,026	319,045	297,435	173,981
1979–80	160,075	103,162	95,962	7,200	56,914	37,768	19,146	484,487	312,231	290,440	172,256
1980–81	176,378	112,325	104,125	8,200	64,053	42,280	21,773	478,416	304,676	282,434	173,740
1981–82	190,825	120,486	111,186	9,300	70,339	46,219	24,120	476,447	300,826	277,606	175,621
1982–83	204,661	128,725	118,425	10,300	75,936	49,573	26,363	489,947	308,161	283,503	181,786
1983–84	220,993	139,000	127,500	11,500	81,993	53,087	28,907	510,163	320,881	294,334	189,282
1984–85	239,351	149,400	137,000	12,400	89,951	58,315	31,637	531,729	331,899	304,351	199,831
1985–86	259,336	161,800	148,600	13,200	97,536	63,194	34,342	559,978	349,371	320,869	210,607
1986–87	280,964	175,200	160,900	14,300	105,764	67,654	38,110	593,501	370,088	339,881	223,412
1987–88	301,786	187,999	172,699	15,300	113,787	72,641	41,145	612,123	381,324	350,291	230,799
1988–89	333,245	209,377	192,977	16,400	123,867	78,946	44,922	646,092	405,939	374,143	240,153
1989–90	365,825	231,170	212,770	18,400	134,656	85,771	48,885	676,956	427,777	393,728	249,179
1990–91	395,318	249,230	229,430	19,800	146,088	92,961	53,127	693,610	437,290	402,549	256,321
1991–92	417,944	261,755	241,055	20,700	156,189	98,847	57,342	710,542	445,007	409,815	265,536
1992–93	439,676	274,435	252,935	21,500	165,241	104,570	60,671	724,848	452,432	416,987	272,416
1993–94	460,757	287,407	265,307	22,100	173,351	109,310	64,041	740,422	461,853	426,339	278,569
1994–95	485,169	302,200	279,000	23,200	182,969	115,465	67,504	757,926	472,095	435,852	285,832
1995–96	508,523	318,046	293,646	24,400	190,476	119,525	70,952	773,369	483,690	446,582	289,679
1996–97	538,854	338,951	313,151	25,800	199,903 [2]	125,978	73,925 [2]	796,765	501,183	463,034	295,582 [2]
1997–98	570,471	361,615	334,315	27,300	208,856 [2]	132,846	76,010 [2]	828,735	525,326	485,666	303,410 [2]
1998–99	603,847	384,638	355,838	28,800	219,209	140,539	78,670	862,293	549,263	508,136	313,030
1999–2000	649,322	412,538	381,838	30,700	236,784	152,325	84,459	901,216	572,575	529,966	328,641
2000–01	705,017	444,811	410,811	34,000	260,206	170,345	89,861	946,103	596,918	551,291	349,185
2001–02	752,780	472,064	435,364	36,700	280,715	183,436	97,280	992,624	622,469	574,076	370,154
2002–03	795,691	492,807	454,907	37,900	302,884	197,026	105,858	1,026,646	635,847	586,947	390,798
2003–04	830,293	513,542	474,242	39,300	316,751	205,069	111,682	1,048,355	648,415	598,793	399,940
2004–05	875,988	540,969	499,569	41,400	335,019	215,794	119,225	1,073,740	663,091	612,345	410,649
2005–06	925,246	571,669	528,269	43,400	353,577	226,550	127,027	1,092,513	675,016	623,770	417,497
2006–07	984,034	608,495	562,195	46,300	375,539	238,829	136,710	1,132,638	700,387	647,095	432,251
2007–08	1,054,904	646,414	597,314	49,100	408,490	261,046	147,444	1,170,827	717,448	662,953	453,379
2008–09	1,089,670	658,926	610,326	48,600	430,744	273,030	157,714	1,192,760	721,265	668,067	471,495
2009–10	1,100,902	654,418	607,018	47,400	446,484	281,368	165,115	1,193,506	709,466	658,079	484,040
2010–11	1,123,565	652,356	604,356	48,000	471,209	296,114	175,095	1,194,098	693,308	642,295	500,790
2011–12	1,137,011	648,567	601,767	46,800	488,444	305,534	182,910	1,173,990	669,660	621,338	504,330
2012–13[3]	1,165,000	666,000	619,000	47,000	498,939	311,425	187,514	1,183,000	676,000	629,000	507,000
2013–14[2]	1,194,000	682,000	635,000	47,000	512,000	319,000	193,000	1,194,000	682,000	635,000	512,000

—Not available.
[1]Constant dollars based on the Consumer Price Index, prepared by the Bureau of Labor Statistics, U.S. Department of Labor, adjusted to a school-year basis.
[2]Estimated by the National Center for Education Statistics based on enrollment data for the given year and actual expenditures for prior years.
[3]Data for elementary and secondary education are estimated; data for degree-granting institutions are actual.
NOTE: Total expenditures for public elementary and secondary schools include current expenditures, interest on school debt, and capital outlay. Expenditures for public and private colleges and universities in 1929–30 and 1939–40 include current-fund expenditures and additions to plant value. Public and private degree-granting institutions data for 1949–50 through 1995–96 are for current-fund expenditures. Data for private degree-granting institutions for 1996–97 and later years are for total expenditures. Data for public degree-granting institutions for 1996–97 through 2000–01 are for current expenditures; data for later years are for total expenditures. Postsecondary data through 1995–96 are for institutions of higher education, while later data are for degree-granting institutions.

Degree-granting institutions grant associate's or higher degrees and participate in Title IV federal financial aid programs. The degree-granting classification is very similar to the earlier higher education classification, but it includes more 2-year colleges and excludes a few higher education institutions that did not grant degrees. Some data have been revised from previously published figures. Detail may not sum to totals because of rounding.
SOURCE: U.S. Department of Education, National Center for Education Statistics, *Annual Report of the Commissioner of Education,* 1899–1900 and 1909–10; *Biennial Survey of Education in the United States,* 1919–20 through 1949–50; *Statistics of State School Systems,* 1959–60 and 1969–70; *Revenues and Expenditures for Public Elementary and Secondary Education,* 1970–71 through 1986–87; Common Core of Data (CCD), "National Public Education Financial Survey," 1987–88 through 2011–12; Higher Education General Information Survey (HEGIS), Financial Statistics of Institutions of Higher Education, 1965–66 through 1985–86; Integrated Postsecondary Education Data System (IPEDS), "Finance Survey," (IPEDS-F:FY87–99); IPEDS Spring 2001 through Spring 2014, Finance component; and unpublished tabulations. (This table was prepared May 2015.)

Table 106.30. Amount and percentage distribution of direct general expenditures of state and local governments, by function: Selected years, 1970–71 through 2011–12

Function	1970–71	1980–81	1990–91	2000–01	2006–07	2007–08	2008–09	2009–10	2010–11	2011–12
1	2	3	4	5	6	7	8	9	10	11
	Amount (in millions of current dollars)									
Total direct general expenditures	$150,674	$407,449	$908,108	$1,621,757	$2,259,364	$2,401,417	$2,495,901	$2,537,892	$2,579,509	$2,587,317
Education and public libraries	60,174	147,649	313,744	571,374	784,936	837,582	862,819	871,109	872,969	880,642
Education	59,413	145,784	309,302	563,572	774,170	826,061	851,689	860,118	862,271	869,196
Public libraries	761	1,865	4,442	7,802	10,766	11,521	11,130	10,991	10,699	11,447
Social services and income maintenance	30,376	92,555	214,919	396,086	583,532	619,237	661,111	689,435	729,846	731,695
Public welfare	18,226	54,121	130,402	257,380	384,634	404,198	432,428	456,200	490,645	485,588
Hospitals and health	11,205	36,101	81,110	134,010	193,885	209,904	223,180	227,285	233,018	240,153
Social insurance administration	945	2,276	3,250	4,359	3,983	4,055	4,570	5,157	5,256	5,116
Veterans' services	†	57	157	337	1,031	1,080	933	794	927	838
Transportation[1]	19,819	39,231	75,410	130,422	171,653	181,607	184,166	187,073	183,282	187,292
Public safety	9,416	31,233	79,932	146,544	202,969	216,471	225,735	224,346	225,202	225,532
Police and fire protection	7,531	21,283	46,568	84,554	120,690	128,768	135,904	137,106	138,147	139,377
Correction	1,885	7,393	27,356	52,370	68,030	72,753	75,096	73,100	73,243	72,577
Protective inspection and regulation	†	2,557	6,008	9,620	14,250	14,951	14,735	14,139	13,812	13,578
Environment and housing	11,832	35,223	76,167	124,203	179,645	191,828	196,750	198,223	200,491	195,513
Natural resources, parks, and recreation	5,191	13,239	28,505	50,082	66,180	70,380	71,714	68,680	67,053	66,413
Housing and community development	2,554	7,086	16,648	27,402	46,593	51,071	49,885	53,923	56,284	53,141
Sewerage and sanitation	4,087	14,898	31,014	46,718	66,872	70,378	75,152	75,620	77,154	75,959
Governmental administration	6,703	20,001	48,461	85,910	119,385	125,789	128,350	126,719	123,851	123,932
Financial administration	2,271	7,230	16,995	30,007	39,745	40,350	40,576	40,241	39,351	38,984
General control[2]	4,432	12,771	31,466	55,903	79,640	85,439	87,775	86,479	84,500	84,948
Interest on general debt	5,089	17,131	52,234	73,836	93,658	101,008	104,449	105,715	108,478	109,118
Other direct general expenditures	7,265	24,426	47,242	93,382	123,585	127,895	132,521	135,273	135,388	133,592
	Amount (in millions of constant 2013–14 dollars)[3]									
Total direct general expenditures	$891,208	$1,105,185	$1,593,337	$2,176,333	$2,600,564	$2,665,307	$2,732,031	$2,751,369	$2,741,438	$2,671,466
Education and public libraries	355,918	400,490	550,485	766,761	903,474	929,623	944,448	944,383	927,770	909,284
Education	351,417	395,432	542,691	756,291	891,082	916,836	932,265	932,467	916,400	897,465
Public libraries	4,501	5,059	7,794	10,470	12,392	12,787	12,183	11,916	11,370	11,819
Social services and income maintenance	179,668	251,051	377,090	531,531	671,654	687,284	723,657	747,427	775,663	755,493
Public welfare	107,803	146,800	228,799	345,394	442,720	448,615	473,339	494,573	521,445	501,381
Hospitals and health	66,275	97,922	142,313	179,836	223,164	232,970	244,295	246,403	247,646	247,964
Social insurance administration	5,589	6,174	5,702	5,849	4,584	4,500	5,002	5,590	5,586	5,283
Veterans' services	†	155	275	452	1,186	1,199	1,022	860	985	865
Transportation[1]	117,226	106,412	132,312	175,021	197,576	201,564	201,589	202,809	194,788	193,384
Public safety	55,694	84,718	140,246	196,657	233,621	240,259	247,091	243,217	239,339	232,867
Police and fire protection	44,544	57,729	81,707	113,468	138,916	142,918	148,761	148,639	146,819	143,910
Correction	11,149	20,053	47,998	70,279	78,303	80,747	82,201	79,249	77,841	74,937
Protective inspection and regulation	†	6,936	10,541	12,910	16,402	16,594	16,129	15,328	14,679	14,020
Environment and housing	69,984	95,541	133,640	166,675	206,774	212,908	215,364	214,897	213,077	201,872
Natural resources, parks, and recreation	30,704	35,910	50,014	67,209	76,174	78,114	78,498	74,457	71,263	68,573
Housing and community development	15,106	19,220	29,210	36,773	53,630	56,683	54,604	58,459	59,817	54,870
Sewerage and sanitation	24,174	40,410	54,416	62,694	76,970	78,111	82,261	81,981	81,998	78,429
Governmental administration	39,647	54,252	85,028	115,287	137,414	139,612	140,493	137,378	131,626	127,963
Financial administration	13,433	19,611	29,819	40,268	45,747	44,784	44,414	43,625	41,821	40,252
General control[2]	26,214	34,641	55,209	75,019	91,667	94,828	96,079	93,753	89,804	87,711
Interest on general debt	30,100	46,467	91,648	99,085	107,802	112,107	114,331	114,607	115,288	112,667
Other direct general expenditures	42,971	66,254	82,889	125,315	142,249	141,949	145,059	146,651	143,887	137,937
	Percentage distribution									
Total direct general expenditures	100.0	100.0	100.0	100.0	100.0	100.0	100.0	100.0	100.0	100.0
Education and public libraries	39.9	36.2	34.5	35.2	34.7	34.9	34.6	34.3	33.8	34.0
Education	39.4	35.8	34.1	34.8	34.3	34.4	34.1	33.9	33.4	33.6
Public libraries	0.5	0.5	0.5	0.5	0.5	0.5	0.4	0.4	0.4	0.4
Social services and income maintenance	20.2	22.7	23.7	24.4	25.8	25.8	26.5	27.2	28.3	28.3
Public welfare	12.1	13.3	14.4	15.9	17.0	16.8	17.3	18.0	19.0	18.8
Hospitals and health	7.4	8.9	8.9	8.3	8.6	8.7	8.9	9.0	9.0	9.3
Social insurance administration	0.6	0.6	0.4	0.3	0.2	0.2	0.2	0.2	0.2	0.2
Veterans' services	†	#	#	#	#	#	#	#	#	#
Transportation[1]	13.2	9.6	8.3	8.0	7.6	7.6	7.4	7.4	7.1	7.2
Public safety	6.2	7.7	8.8	9.0	9.0	9.0	9.0	8.8	8.7	8.7
Police and fire protection	5.0	5.2	5.1	5.2	5.3	5.4	5.4	5.4	5.4	5.4
Correction	1.3	1.8	3.0	3.2	3.0	3.0	3.0	2.9	2.8	2.8
Protective inspection and regulation	†	0.6	0.7	0.6	0.6	0.6	0.6	0.6	0.5	0.5
Environment and housing	7.9	8.6	8.4	7.7	8.0	8.0	7.9	7.8	7.8	7.6
Natural resources, parks, and recreation	3.4	3.2	3.1	3.1	2.9	2.9	2.9	2.7	2.6	2.6
Housing and community development	1.7	1.7	1.8	1.7	2.1	2.1	2.0	2.1	2.2	2.1
Sewerage and sanitation	2.7	3.7	3.4	2.9	3.0	2.9	3.0	3.0	3.0	2.9
Governmental administration	4.4	4.9	5.3	5.3	5.3	5.2	5.1	5.0	4.8	4.8
Financial administration	1.5	1.8	1.9	1.9	1.8	1.7	1.6	1.6	1.5	1.5
General control[2]	2.9	3.1	3.5	3.4	3.5	3.6	3.5	3.4	3.3	3.3
Interest on general debt	3.4	4.2	5.8	4.6	4.1	4.2	4.2	4.2	4.2	4.2
Other direct general expenditures	4.8	6.0	5.2	5.8	5.5	5.3	5.3	5.3	5.2	5.2

†Not applicable.
#Rounds to zero.
[1]As of 2006–07, no longer includes transit subsidies.
[2]Includes judicial and legal expenditures, expenditures on general public buildings, and other governmental administration expenditures.
[3]Constant dollars based on the Consumer Price Index, prepared by the Bureau of Labor Statistics, U.S. Department of Labor, adjusted to a school-year basis.

NOTE: Excludes monies paid by states to the federal government. Some data have been revised from previously published figures. Detail may not sum to totals because of rounding.
SOURCE: U.S. Department of Commerce, Census Bureau, Governmental Finances. Retrieved January 13, 2015, from http://www.census.gov/govs/local/. (This table was prepared January 2015.)

Table 106.40. Direct general expenditures of state and local governments for all functions and for education, by level of education and state: 2010–11 and 2011–12

[In millions of current dollars. Standard errors appear in parentheses]

State	Direct general expenditures,[1] 2010–11 Total	For education	Direct general expenditures,[1] 2011–12 For education Total	Elementary and secondary education Total for education	Total for elementary and secondary	Current expenditure	Capital outlay	Colleges and universities Total for colleges and universities	Current expenditure	Capital outlay	Other education[2]
1	2	3	4	5	6	7	8	9	10	11	12
United States	$2,579,509 (2,063.6)	$862,271 (431.1)	$2,587,317	$869,196	$565,403	$514,340	$51,063	$259,736	$228,709	$31,027	$44,057
Alabama	35,559 (145.8)	13,322 (37.3)	34,900	12,645	7,258	6,676	581	4,601	3,875	726	786
Alaska	12,683 (34.2)	3,367 (20.9)	12,648	3,304	2,290	2,144	146	895	691	204	119
Arizona	42,733 (166.7)	13,385 (#)	41,567	13,519	7,897	7,199	698	4,765	4,055	710	856
Arkansas	20,768 (72.7)	8,446 (#)	21,321	8,275	4,985	4,373	612	2,643	2,277	365	647
California	353,057 (1,059.2)	103,055 (154.6)	348,787	107,730	66,954	60,240	6,714	35,845	31,554	4,290	4,931
Colorado	39,561 (482.6)	13,204 (#)	39,745	13,213	7,989	7,292	697	4,590	4,056	534	633
Connecticut	33,098 (79.4)	11,653 (46.6)	34,372	12,255	8,991	8,025	966	2,605	2,217	388	660
Delaware	8,602 (9.5)	3,134 (#)	9,043	3,339	1,839	1,690	150	1,152	963	189	348
District of Columbia	10,678 (#)	2,342 (#)	10,765	2,372	2,201	1,983	219	170	143	27	0
Florida	136,982 (561.6)	38,691 (#)	134,653	37,372	24,741	22,895	1,845	9,565	8,560	1,005	3,067
Georgia	64,502 (212.9)	25,349 (#)	64,594	25,277	17,117	15,551	1,566	6,274	5,473	801	1,885
Hawaii	12,206 (#)	3,345 (#)	12,315	3,503	1,896	1,706	190	1,507	1,092	414	100
Idaho	10,441 (44.9)	3,131 (#)	9,975	3,116	1,853	1,784	69	1,111	999	111	152
Illinois	103,386 (579.0)	34,669 (#)	102,728	35,372	24,846	22,814	2,033	8,978	8,182	797	1,548
Indiana	45,880 (183.5)	16,270 (#)	45,832	16,913	9,812	8,914	898	6,021	5,389	632	1,080
Iowa	26,455 (121.7)	9,636 (#)	27,930	9,803	5,904	5,004	901	3,485	3,050	434	414
Kansas	22,956 (121.7)	8,366 (#)	22,953	8,427	5,089	4,426	663	3,083	2,836	248	255
Kentucky	32,298 (96.9)	11,466 (#)	32,742	11,632	6,931	6,144	787	3,751	3,469	282	950
Louisiana	43,026 (129.1)	12,119 (#)	42,526	12,804	8,730	7,855	875	3,171	2,889	283	903
Maine	11,238 (49.4)	3,437 (36.4)	11,271	3,353	2,342	2,210	132	799	732	67	212
Maryland	49,980 (100.0)	18,258 (#)	53,848	18,751	12,117	10,978	1,139	5,945	5,239	706	688
Massachusetts	62,217 (248.9)	19,039 (125.7)	63,393	19,633	13,581	12,269	1,313	5,062	3,901	1,161	990
Michigan	73,762 (317.2)	28,697 (#)	73,792	28,695	17,082	15,881	1,201	10,608	9,025	1,583	1,004
Minnesota	47,256 (179.6)	15,391 (#)	48,666	15,438	10,089	9,055	1,034	4,391	3,975	416	957
Mississippi	23,874 (152.8)	7,254 (#)	24,136	7,445	4,352	4,023	329	2,673	2,404	270	419
Missouri	41,614 (208.1)	13,779 (#)	42,820	14,534	9,503	8,612	891	4,292	3,902	390	739
Montana	8,126 (21.9)	2,596 (#)	8,199	2,578	1,618	1,501	117	788	731	57	172
Nebraska	14,446 (106.9)	5,701 (#)	14,867	5,940	3,773	3,398	375	1,902	1,709	193	265
Nevada	18,728 (5.6)	5,577 (#)	18,537	5,406	3,867	3,546	321	1,211	1,126	84	328
New Hampshire	10,261 (18.5)	3,773 (#)	10,034	3,840	2,759	2,599	160	928	840	88	153
New Jersey	81,617 (236.7)	30,551 (#)	83,030	31,483	23,935	22,821	1,114	5,902	5,098	805	1,646
New Mexico	19,037 (62.8)	6,345 (#)	18,140	6,290	3,544	2,929	615	2,367	1,976	391	378
New York	235,691 (518.5)	71,545 (71.5)	237,735	71,490	55,473	51,400	4,073	13,986	12,907	1,079	2,031
North Carolina	67,523 (216.1)	23,735 (83.1)	70,264	23,692	12,837	12,083	754	9,545	8,466	1,079	1,311
North Dakota	6,479 (36.3)	2,232 (0.9)	7,210	2,353	1,310	1,149	161	936	851	85	108
Ohio	93,267 (373.1)	33,309 (#)	91,423	32,530	22,425	20,007	2,417	8,700	7,528	1,172	1,406
Oklahoma	25,825 (87.8)	9,297 (#)	26,589	9,446	5,496	4,999	496	3,421	3,040	381	529
Oregon	31,742 (152.4)	10,492 (#)	32,064	10,339	5,985	5,537	449	3,961	3,383	578	393
Pennsylvania	107,545 (397.9)	35,400 (#)	107,002	35,323	24,176	22,436	1,740	9,179	8,351	828	1,968
Rhode Island	9,245 (7.4)	3,049 (#)	9,292	3,133	2,194	2,149	45	675	631	44	264
South Carolina	35,349 (130.8)	12,067 (#)	34,487	12,134	7,502	6,650	852	3,491	3,134	357	1,141
South Dakota	6,220 (34.2)	2,086 (#)	6,101	2,001	1,257	1,085	172	641	569	72	103
Tennessee	42,144 (387.7)	13,125 (303.2)	42,863	13,680	8,928	8,226	702	3,806	3,495	311	946
Texas	185,608 (631.1)	73,484 (#)	183,968	70,749	44,772	39,234	5,538	23,929	21,249	2,680	2,048
Utah	20,388 (95.8)	7,773 (#)	21,256	8,207	4,215	3,549	667	3,635	3,153	482	357
Vermont	6,180 (15.5)	2,378 (#)	6,237	2,375	1,477	1,431	46	728	694	34	170
Virginia	61,168 (269.1)	22,718 (202.2)	62,781	23,191	14,732	13,592	1,140	7,510	6,165	1,345	950
Washington	58,209 (349.3)	18,786 (#)	58,364	19,284	11,755	10,203	1,552	5,901	5,154	747	1,628
West Virginia	14,449 (43.3)	5,596 (#)	14,567	5,507	3,198	2,953	245	1,685	1,493	192	624
Wisconsin	47,927 (186.9)	17,350 (1.7)	47,265	16,989	10,131	9,681	450	6,212	5,394	819	646
Wyoming	7,523 (34.6)	2,496 (#)	7,721	2,519	1,653	1,440	213	716	623	93	150

#Rounds to zero.
[1]Includes state and local government expenditures for education services, social services and income maintenance, transportation, public safety, environment and housing, governmental administration, interest on general debt, and other general expenditures.
[2]Includes assistance and subsidies to individuals, private elementary and secondary schools, and private colleges and universities, as well as miscellaneous education expenditures. Does not include expenditures for public libraries.

NOTE: Current expenditure data in this table differ from figures appearing in other tables because of slightly varying definitions used in the Governmental Finances and Common Core of Data surveys. In 2011–12, a census of state and local governments was conducted; therefore, standard errors are not applicable. Detail may not sum to totals because of rounding. Some data have been revised from previously published figures.
SOURCE: U.S. Department of Commerce, Census Bureau, Governmental Finances. Retrieved January 13, 2015, from http://www.census.gov/govs/local/. (This table was prepared January 2015.)

Table 106.50.   Direct general expenditures of state and local governments per capita for all functions and for education, by level of education and state: 2010–11 and 2011–12

[Amounts in current dollars]

State	Direct general expenditures,[1] 2010–11			Direct general expenditures,[1] 2011–12									
		For education			For education								
					All education		Elementary and secondary education		Colleges and universities		Other education[2]		
	Total amount per capita	Amount per capita	As a percent of all functions	Total amount per capita	Amount per capita	As a percent of all functions	Amount per capita	As a percent of all functions	Amount per capita	As a percent of all functions	Amount per capita	As a percent of all functions	
1	2	3	4	5	6	7	8	9	10	11	12	13	
United States	$8,278	$2,767	33.4	$8,242	$2,769	33.6	$1,801	21.9	$827	10.0	$140	1.7	
Alabama	7,404	2,774	37.5	7,238	2,622	36.2	1,505	20.8	954	13.2	163	2.3	
Alaska	17,549	4,659	26.5	17,292	4,517	26.1	3,131	18.1	1,223	7.1	163	0.9	
Arizona	6,592	2,065	31.3	6,343	2,063	32.5	1,205	19.0	727	11.5	131	2.1	
Arkansas	7,069	2,875	40.7	7,229	2,806	38.8	1,690	23.4	896	12.4	219	3.0	
California	9,367	2,734	29.2	9,169	2,832	30.9	1,760	19.2	942	10.3	130	1.4	
Colorado	7,732	2,580	33.4	7,662	2,547	33.2	1,540	20.1	885	11.5	122	1.6	
Connecticut	9,243	3,254	35.2	9,574	3,413	35.7	2,504	26.2	725	7.6	184	1.9	
Delaware	9,482	3,455	36.4	9,860	3,641	36.9	2,005	20.3	1,256	12.7	379	3.8	
District of Columbia	17,279	3,790	21.9	17,025	3,751	22.0	3,481	20.4	270	1.6	0	0.0	
Florida	7,188	2,030	28.2	6,970	1,935	27.8	1,281	18.4	495	7.1	159	2.3	
Georgia	6,572	2,583	39.3	6,512	2,548	39.1	1,726	26.5	632	9.7	190	2.9	
Hawaii	8,878	2,433	27.4	8,845	2,516	28.4	1,362	15.4	1,082	12.2	72	0.8	
Idaho	6,587	1,975	30.0	6,251	1,953	31.2	1,161	18.6	696	11.1	95	1.5	
Illinois	8,034	2,694	33.5	7,979	2,747	34.4	1,930	24.2	697	8.7	120	1.5	
Indiana	7,040	2,497	35.5	7,011	2,587	36.9	1,501	21.4	921	13.1	165	2.4	
Iowa	8,639	3,147	36.4	9,085	3,189	35.1	1,921	21.1	1,133	12.5	135	1.5	
Kansas	7,995	2,914	36.4	7,953	2,920	36.7	1,763	22.2	1,068	13.4	88	1.1	
Kentucky	7,392	2,624	35.5	7,475	2,655	35.5	1,582	21.2	856	11.5	217	2.9	
Louisiana	9,405	2,649	28.2	9,241	2,782	30.1	1,897	20.5	689	7.5	196	2.1	
Maine	8,461	2,588	30.6	8,480	2,523	29.7	1,762	20.8	601	7.1	160	1.9	
Maryland	8,575	3,133	36.5	9,151	3,186	34.8	2,059	22.5	1,010	11.0	117	1.3	
Massachusetts	9,445	2,890	30.6	9,538	2,954	31.0	2,043	21.4	762	8.0	149	1.6	
Michigan	7,469	2,906	38.9	7,466	2,903	38.9	1,728	23.1	1,073	14.4	102	1.4	
Minnesota	8,841	2,880	32.6	9,047	2,870	31.7	1,876	20.7	816	9.0	178	2.0	
Mississippi	8,016	2,436	30.4	8,086	2,494	30.8	1,458	18.0	896	11.1	140	1.7	
Missouri	6,923	2,292	33.1	7,111	2,414	33.9	1,578	22.2	713	10.0	123	1.7	
Montana	8,141	2,601	32.0	8,157	2,565	31.4	1,610	19.7	784	9.6	171	2.1	
Nebraska	7,840	3,094	39.5	8,012	3,201	40.0	2,033	25.4	1,025	12.8	143	1.8	
Nevada	6,877	2,048	29.8	6,719	1,959	29.2	1,402	20.9	439	6.5	119	1.8	
New Hampshire	7,784	2,862	36.8	7,597	2,907	38.3	2,089	27.5	702	9.2	116	1.5	
New Jersey	9,252	3,463	37.4	9,367	3,552	37.9	2,700	28.8	666	7.1	186	2.0	
New Mexico	9,143	3,047	33.3	8,698	3,016	34.7	1,699	19.5	1,135	13.1	181	2.1	
New York	12,108	3,676	30.4	12,148	3,653	30.1	2,835	23.3	715	5.9	104	0.9	
North Carolina	6,993	2,458	35.2	7,205	2,429	33.7	1,316	18.3	979	13.6	134	1.9	
North Dakota	9,474	3,263	34.4	10,305	3,363	32.6	1,872	18.2	1,338	13.0	154	1.5	
Ohio	8,079	2,885	35.7	7,919	2,818	35.6	1,942	24.5	754	9.5	122	1.5	
Oklahoma	6,811	2,452	36.0	6,970	2,476	35.5	1,441	20.7	897	12.9	139	2.0	
Oregon	8,198	2,710	33.1	8,223	2,652	32.2	1,535	18.7	1,016	12.4	101	1.2	
Pennsylvania	8,440	2,778	32.9	8,383	2,768	33.0	1,894	22.6	719	8.6	154	1.8	
Rhode Island	8,794	2,900	33.0	8,847	2,983	33.7	2,089	23.6	643	7.3	251	2.8	
South Carolina	7,554	2,579	34.1	7,301	2,569	35.2	1,588	21.8	739	10.1	242	3.3	
South Dakota	7,547	2,532	33.5	7,321	2,401	32.8	1,509	20.6	769	10.5	123	1.7	
Tennessee	6,581	2,050	31.1	6,639	2,119	31.9	1,383	20.8	590	8.9	146	2.2	
Texas	7,229	2,862	39.6	7,060	2,715	38.5	1,718	24.3	918	13.0	79	1.1	
Utah	7,237	2,759	38.1	7,444	2,874	38.6	1,476	19.8	1,273	17.1	125	1.7	
Vermont	9,865	3,796	38.5	9,963	3,795	38.1	2,360	23.7	1,164	11.7	271	2.7	
Virginia	7,555	2,806	37.1	7,669	2,833	36.9	1,800	23.5	917	12.0	116	1.5	
Washington	8,523	2,750	32.3	8,462	2,796	33.0	1,704	20.1	856	10.1	236	2.8	
West Virginia	7,788	3,016	38.7	7,851	2,968	37.8	1,724	22.0	908	11.6	336	4.3	
Wisconsin	8,391	3,038	36.2	8,254	2,967	35.9	1,769	21.4	1,085	13.1	113	1.4	
Wyoming	13,241	4,393	33.2	13,394	4,369	32.6	2,868	21.4	1,241	9.3	260	1.9	

[1]Includes state and local government expenditures for education services, social services and income maintenance, transportation, public safety, environment and housing, governmental administration, interest on general debt, and other general expenditures.
[2]Includes assistance and subsidies to individuals, private elementary and secondary schools, and private colleges and universities, as well as miscellaneous education expenditures. Does not include expenditures for public libraries.
NOTE: Per capita amounts for 2011–12 are based on population estimates for July 2012. Per capita amounts for 2010–11 are based on the latest population estimates for July 2011

and have been revised from previously published figures. Detail may not sum to totals because of rounding.
SOURCE: U.S. Department of Commerce, Census Bureau, Governmental Finances, retrieved January 13, 2015, from http://www.census.gov/govs/local/; and GCT-T1 Population Estimates, retrieved January 13, 2015, from http://www.census.gov/popest/data/national/totals/2013/index.html. (This table was prepared January 2015).

Table 106.60. Gross domestic product, state and local expenditures, national income, personal income, disposable personal income, median family income, and population: Selected years, 1929 through 2014

Year	Gross domestic product (in billions)		State and local direct general expenditures (in millions)[1]		National income (in billions)	Personal income (in billions)	Disposable personal income (in billions of chained 2009 dollars)[2]	Disposable personal income per capita		Median family income		Population (in thousands)	
	Current dollars	Chained 2009 dollars[2]	All direct general expenditures	Education expenditures	National income (in billions)	Personal income (in billions)		Current dollars	Chained 2009 dollars[2]	Current dollars	Constant 2013 dollars[3]	Midyear data[4]	Resident as of July 1[5]
1	2	3	4	5	6	7	8	9	10	11	12	13	14
1929	$104.6	$1,056.6	—	—	$94.2	$85.3	$843.0	$685	$6,917	—	—	121,878	121,767
1939	93.5	1,163.6	—	—	82.5	73.6	923.2	551	7,046	—	—	131,028	130,880
1940	102.9	1,266.1	$9,229	$2,638	91.6	79.4	986.2	588	7,464	—	—	132,122	132,122
1950	300.2	2,184.0	22,787	7,177	267.0	233.9	1,521.9	1,417	10,033	$3,319	—	151,684	152,271
1960	543.3	3,108.7	51,876	18,719	479.9	422.5	2,146.9	2,083	11,877	5,620	$38,684	180,760	180,671
1970	1,075.9	4,722.0	131,332	52,718	940.1	864.6	3,413.2	3,713	16,643	9,867	52,825	205,089	205,052
1971	1,167.8	4,877.6	150,674	59,413	1,017.0	932.1	3,570.4	3,998	17,191	10,285	52,751	207,692	207,661
1972	1,282.4	5,134.3	168,550	65,814	1,123.0	1,023.6	3,741.2	4,287	17,821	11,116	55,353	209,924	209,896
1973	1,428.5	5,424.1	181,357	69,714	1,257.0	1,138.5	3,968.6	4,747	18,725	12,051	56,475	211,939	211,909
1974	1,548.8	5,396.0	198,959	75,833	1,350.8	1,249.3	3,923.6	5,135	18,343	12,902	54,966	213,898	213,854
1975	1,688.9	5,385.4	230,721	87,858	1,451.1	1,366.9	4,020.0	5,645	18,613	13,719	54,008	215,981	215,973
1976	1,877.6	5,675.4	256,731	97,216	1,614.8	1,498.1	4,144.0	6,079	19,002	14,958	55,682	218,086	218,035
1977	2,086.0	5,937.0	274,215	102,780	1,798.7	1,654.2	4,274.8	6,613	19,406	16,009	56,056	220,289	220,239
1978	2,356.6	6,267.2	296,984	110,758	2,029.9	1,859.5	4,470.5	7,322	20,080	17,640	57,803	222,629	222,585
1979	2,632.1	6,466.2	327,517	119,448	2,248.2	2,077.9	4,557.8	8,037	20,248	19,587	58,573	225,106	225,055
1980	2,862.5	6,450.4	369,086	133,211	2,426.8	2,316.8	4,590.5	8,861	20,158	21,023	56,585	227,726	227,225
1981	3,211.0	6,617.7	407,449	145,784	2,722.1	2,595.9	4,705.6	9,785	20,458	22,388	55,021	230,008	229,466
1982	3,345.0	6,491.3	436,733	154,282	2,840.4	2,778.8	4,803.3	10,442	20,685	23,433	54,312	232,218	231,664
1983	3,638.1	6,792.0	466,516	163,876	3,060.5	2,969.7	4,971.0	11,170	21,214	24,580	54,638	234,333	233,792
1984	4,040.7	7,285.0	505,008	176,108	3,444.0	3,281.3	5,314.0	12,284	22,480	26,433	56,447	236,394	235,825
1985	4,346.7	7,593.8	553,899	192,686	3,684.2	3,515.9	5,476.2	12,991	22,960	27,735	57,261	238,506	237,924
1986	4,590.2	7,860.5	605,623	210,819	3,848.2	3,725.1	5,687.8	13,661	23,632	29,458	59,737	240,683	240,133
1987	4,870.2	8,132.6	657,134	226,619	4,119.2	3,955.3	5,811.0	14,274	23,929	30,970	60,750	242,843	242,289
1988	5,252.6	8,474.5	704,921	242,683	4,493.4	4,275.3	6,083.9	15,386	24,826	32,191	60,910	245,061	244,499
1989	5,657.7	8,786.4	762,360	263,898	4,782.2	4,618.2	6,268.7	16,380	25,340	34,213	62,059	247,387	246,819
1990	5,979.6	8,955.0	834,818	288,148	5,036.1	4,904.5	6,393.5	17,235	25,555	35,353	61,082	250,181	249,623
1991	6,174.0	8,948.4	908,108	309,302	5,186.1	5,071.1	6,438.4	17,688	25,395	35,939	59,945	253,530	252,981
1992	6,539.3	9,266.6	981,253	324,652	5,499.7	5,410.8	6,714.2	18,684	26,133	36,573	59,494	256,922	256,514
1993	6,878.7	9,521.0	1,033,167	342,287	5,754.8	5,646.8	6,823.6	19,211	26,216	36,959	58,671	260,282	259,919
1994	7,308.8	9,905.4	1,077,665	353,287	6,140.2	5,934.7	7,010.7	19,906	26,611	38,782	60,279	263,455	263,126
1995	7,664.1	10,174.8	1,146,188	378,273	6,479.5	6,276.5	7,245.8	20,753	27,180	40,611	61,637	266,588	266,278
1996	8,100.2	10,561.0	1,189,356	398,859	6,899.4	6,661.9	7,476.1	21,615	27,719	42,300	62,536	269,714	269,394
1997	8,608.5	11,034.9	1,247,436	419,053	7,380.4	7,075.0	7,751.3	22,527	28,397	44,568	64,495	272,958	272,647
1998	9,089.2	11,525.9	1,314,496	450,365	7,857.3	7,587.7	8,208.1	23,759	29,723	46,737	66,703	276,154	275,854
1999	9,660.6	12,065.9	1,398,533	483,259	8,324.4	7,983.8	8,477.7	24,617	30,350	48,831	68,268	279,328	279,040
2000	10,284.8	12,559.7	1,502,768	521,612	8,907.0	8,632.8	8,902.2	26,206	31,524	50,732	68,626	282,398	282,162
2001	10,621.8	12,682.2	1,621,757	563,572	9,184.6	8,987.1	9,148.7	27,179	32,075	51,407	67,640	285,225	284,969
2002	10,977.5	12,908.8	1,732,478	594,694	9,436.8	9,149.5	9,431.6	28,127	32,754	51,680	66,918	287,955	287,625
2003	11,510.7	13,271.1	1,817,513	621,335	9,864.2	9,486.6	9,690.1	29,198	33,342	52,680	66,723	290,626	290,108
2004	12,274.9	13,773.5	1,903,915	655,182	10,540.9	10,048.3	10,035.7	30,697	34,221	54,061	66,670	293,262	292,805
2005	13,093.7	14,234.2	2,007,490	688,314	11,239.8	10,609.3	10,189.4	31,760	34,424	56,194	67,053	295,993	295,517
2006	13,855.9	14,613.8	2,117,161	728,917	12,004.8	11,389.0	10,595.4	33,589	35,458	58,407	67,481	298,818	298,380
2007	14,477.6	14,873.7	2,259,364	774,170	12,321.4	11,994.9	10,820.6	34,826	35,866	61,355	68,931	301,696	301,231
2008	14,718.6	14,830.4	2,401,417	826,061	12,427.8	12,429.6	10,987.3	36,101	36,078	61,521	66,560	304,543	304,094
2009	14,418.7	14,418.7	2,495,901	851,689	12,126.1	12,087.5	10,942.5	35,616	35,616	60,088	65,257	307,240	306,772
2010	14,964.4	14,783.8	2,537,892	860,118	12,739.5	12,429.3	11,055.1	36,274	35,684	60,236	64,356	309,808	309,326
2011	15,517.9	15,020.6	2,579,509	862,271	13,352.3	13,202.0	11,331.2	37,804	36,298	60,974	63,152	312,172	311,583
2012	16,163.2	15,369.2	2,587,317	869,196	14,069.5	13,887.7	11,676.2	39,377	37,126	62,241	63,145	314,499	313,874
2013	16,768.1	15,710.3	—	—	14,577.1	14,166.9	11,650.8	39,468	36,772	63,815	63,815	316,839	316,129
2014	17,418.9	16,085.6	—	—	15,076.5	14,733.9	11,943.3	40,699	37,420	—	—	319,173	—

—Not available.

[1]Data for years prior to 1963 include expenditures for government fiscal years ending during that particular calendar year. Data for 1963 and later years are the aggregations of expenditures for government fiscal years that ended on June 30 of the stated year. General expenditures exclude expenditures of publicly owned utilities and liquor stores, and of insurance-trust activities. Intergovernmental payments between state and local governments are excluded. Payments to the federal government are included.

[2]Constant dollars based on a chain-price index, which uses the geometric mean of output weights of adjacent time periods compiled over a time series. Chain-price indexes reflect changes in prices, while implicit price deflators reflect both changes in prices and in the composition of output. More information is available at https://www.bea.gov/scb/account_articles/national/0597od/maintext.htm.

[3]Data adjusted by the CPU-RS, which is a price index of inflation that incorporates most of the improvements in methodology made to the current CPI-U since 1978 into a single, uniform series. See Census Bureau, *Money Income in the United States: 1999* (www.census.gov/prod/2000pubs/p60-209.pdf).

[4]Population of the United States including armed forces overseas. Includes Alaska and Hawaii beginning in 1960.

[5]Resident population of the United States. Includes Alaska and Hawaii beginning in 1958. Data for 1990 and later years include revisions based on the 2000 census. Excludes overseas armed forces personnel.

NOTE: Gross domestic product (GDP) data are adjusted by the GDP chained weight price deflator. Personal income data are adjusted by the personal consumption deflator. Some data have been revised from previously published figures.

SOURCE: Department of Commerce, Census Bureau, Current Population Survey, Income, retrieved June 2, 2015, from http://www.census.gov/hhes/www/income/data/historical/families/; Population Estimates, retrieved June 2, 2015, from http://www.census.gov/popest/data/historical/2010s/vintage_2013/national.html; and State and Local Government Finances, retrieved June 2, 2015, from http://www.census.gov/govs/local/. U.S. Department of Commerce, Bureau of Economic Analysis, National Income and Product Accounts Tables, retrieved June 2, 2015, from http://www.bea.gov/iTable/index_nipa.cfm. (This table was prepared June 2015.)

Table 106.70. Gross domestic product price index, Consumer Price Index, education price indexes, and federal budget composite deflator: Selected years, 1919 through 2014

Calendar year			School year					Federal fiscal year	
Year	Gross domestic product price index	Consumer Price Index[1]	Year	Consumer Price Index[2]	Higher Education Price Index[3]	Research and Development Index	Academic Library Operations Index	Year	Federal budget composite deflator
1	2	3	4	5	6	7	8	9	10
1919	—	17.3	1919–20	19.1	—	—	—	1919	—
1929	9.899	17.1	1929–30	17.1	—	—	—	1929	—
1939	8.049	13.9	1939–40	14.0	—	—	—	1939	—
1949	13.622	23.8	1949–50	23.7	—	—	—	1949	0.0958
1950	13.746	24.1	1950–51	25.1	—	—	—	1950	0.1005
1951	14.675	26.0	1951–52	26.3	—	—	—	1951	0.1009
1952	14.996	26.5	1952–53	26.7	—	—	—	1952	0.1006
1953	15.190	26.7	1953–54	26.9	—	—	—	1953	0.1080
1954	15.346	26.9	1954–55	26.8	—	—	—	1954	0.1113
1955	15.566	26.8	1955–56	26.9	—	—	—	1955	0.1151
1956	16.101	27.2	1956–57	27.7	—	—	—	1956	0.1202
1957	16.663	28.1	1957–58	28.6	—	—	—	1957	0.1261
1958	17.050	28.9	1958–59	29.0	—	—	—	1958	0.1336
1959	17.277	29.1	1959–60	29.4	—	—	—	1959	0.1391
1960	17.516	29.6	1960–61	29.8	25.6	26.7	—	1960	0.1411
1961	17.709	29.9	1961–62	30.1	26.5	27.5	—	1961	0.1443
1962	17.927	30.2	1962–63	30.4	27.6	28.5	—	1962	0.1446
1963	18.129	30.6	1963–64	30.8	28.6	29.5	—	1963	0.1507
1964	18.407	31.0	1964–65	31.2	29.8	30.7	—	1964	0.1531
1965	18.744	31.5	1965–66	31.9	31.3	32.0	—	1965	0.1553
1966	19.271	32.4	1966–67	32.9	32.9	33.8	—	1966	0.1596
1967	19.831	33.4	1967–68	34.0	34.9	35.7	—	1967	0.1632
1968	20.674	34.8	1968–69	35.7	37.1	38.0	—	1968	0.1692
1969	21.691	36.7	1969–70	37.8	39.5	40.3	—	1969	0.1798
1970	22.836	38.8	1970–71	39.7	42.1	42.7	—	1970	0.1899
1971	23.996	40.5	1971–72	41.2	44.3	45.0	—	1971	0.2031
1972	25.035	41.8	1972–73	42.8	46.7	47.1	—	1972	0.2166
1973	26.396	44.4	1973–74	46.6	49.9	50.1	—	1973	0.2267
1974	28.760	49.3	1974–75	51.8	54.3	54.8	—	1974	0.2455
1975	31.431	53.8	1975–76	55.5	57.8	59.0	57.3	1975	0.2696
1976	33.157	56.9	1976–77	58.7	61.5	62.7	61.6	1976	0.2890
1977	35.209	60.6	1977–78	62.6	65.7	66.8	65.8	1977	0.3099
1978	37.680	65.2	1978–79	68.5	70.5	71.7	71.4	1978	0.3294
1979	40.790	72.6	1979–80	77.6	77.5	78.3	78.5	1979	0.3578
1980	44.480	82.4	1980–81	86.6	85.8	86.6	86.1	1980	0.3953
1981	48.658	90.9	1981–82	94.1	93.9	94.0	94.0	1981	0.4393
1982	51.624	96.5	1982–83	98.2	100.0	100.0	100.0	1982	0.4722
1983	53.658	99.6	1983–84	101.8	104.8	104.3	105.1	1983	0.4958
1984	55.564	103.9	1984–85	105.8	110.8	109.8	111.2	1984	0.5185
1985	57.341	107.6	1985–86	108.8	116.3	115.2	117.6	1985	0.5373
1986	58.504	109.6	1986–87	111.2	120.9	120.0	124.2	1986	0.5487
1987	59.935	113.6	1987–88	115.8	126.2	126.8	130.0	1987	0.5644
1988	62.036	118.3	1988–89	121.2	132.8	132.1	138.6	1988	0.5835
1989	64.448	124.0	1989–90	127.0	140.8	139.0	147.4	1989	0.6059
1990	66.841	130.7	1990–91	133.9	148.2	145.8	155.7	1990	0.6238
1991	69.057	136.2	1991–92	138.2	153.5	150.6	163.3	1991	0.6527
1992	70.632	140.3	1992–93	142.5	157.9	155.2	169.8	1992	0.6772
1993	72.315	144.5	1993–94	146.2	163.3	160.1	176.7	1993	0.6973
1994	73.851	148.2	1994–95	150.4	168.1	165.4	183.9	1994	0.7100
1995	75.393	152.4	1995–96	154.5	173.0	170.8	192.6	1995	0.7307
1996	76.767	156.9	1996–97	158.9	178.4	—	—	1996	0.7460
1997	78.088	160.5	1997–98	161.7	184.7	—	—	1997	0.7612
1998	78.935	163.0	1998–99	164.5	189.1	—	—	1998	0.7681
1999	80.065	166.6	1999–2000	169.3	196.9	—	—	1999	0.7778
2000	81.890	172.2	2000–01	175.1	208.7	—	—	2000	0.7971
2001	83.755	177.1	2001–02	178.2	212.7	—	—	2001	0.8184
2002	85.040	179.9	2002–03	182.1	223.5	—	—	2002	0.8320
2003	86.735	184.0	2003–04	186.1	231.7	—	—	2003	0.8555
2004	89.118	188.9	2004–05	191.7	240.8	—	—	2004	0.8779
2005	91.985	195.3	2005–06	199.0	253.1	—	—	2005	0.9083
2006	94.812	201.6	2006–07	204.1	260.3	—	—	2006	0.9396
2007	97.340	207.3	2007–08	211.7	273.2	—	—	2007	0.9644
2008	99.218	215.3	2008–09	214.7	279.3	—	—	2008	0.9981
2009	100.000	214.5	2009–10	216.7	281.8	—	—	2009	1.0000
2010	101.226	218.1	2010–11	221.1	288.4	—	—	2010	1.0119
2011	103.315	224.9	2011–12	227.6	293.2	—	—	2011	1.0318
2012	105.174	229.6	2012–13	231.4	297.8	—	—	2012	1.0512
2013	106.739	233.0	2013–14	235.0	—	—	—	2013	1.0659
2014	108.320	236.7	2014–15	—	—	—	—	2014	1.0825

—Not available.

[1]Index for urban wage earners and clerical workers through 1977; 1978 and later figures are for all urban consumers.
[2]Consumer Price Index adjusted to a school-year basis (July through June).
[3]Beginning in 2001–02, components of index were weighted through a regression methodology.
NOTE: Some data have been revised from previously published figures.
SOURCE: U.S. Department of Commerce, Bureau of Economic Analysis, National Income and Product Accounts, retrieved June 3, 2015, from http://www.bea.gov/iTable/iTable.cfm?ReqID=9 &step=1#reqid=9&step=3&isuri=1&904=2013&903=4&906=a&905=2015&910=x&911=1. U.S. Department of Labor, Bureau of Labor Statistics, Consumer Price Index, retrieved June 3, 2015, from http://www.bls.gov/data/. Commonfund Institute, retrieved June 3, 2015, from https://www.commonfund.org/CommonfundInstitute/HEPI/Pages/default.aspx. U.S. Office of Management and Budget, Composite Deflator, retrieved June 3, 2015, from http://www.whitehouse.gov/omb/budget/Historicals. (This table was prepared June 2015.)

CHAPTER 2
Elementary and Secondary Education

This chapter contains a variety of statistics on public and private elementary and secondary education. Data are presented for enrollments, teachers and other school staff, schools, dropouts, achievement, school violence, and revenues and expenditures. These data are derived from surveys, censuses, and administrative data collections conducted by the National Center for Education Statistics (NCES) and other public and private organizations. The information ranges from counts of students and schools to state graduation requirements.

Enrollments

Public elementary and secondary school enrollment rose from 49.3 million in 2007 to 49.8 million in 2012, an increase of 1 percent (table 203.10 and figure 7). Public elementary enrollment (prekindergarten through grade 8) was 2 percent higher in 2012 (35.0 million) than in 2007 (34.2 million), while public secondary enrollment (grades 9 through 12) was 2 percent lower in 2012 (14.8 million) than in 2007 (15.1 million). Although public school enrollment increased slightly overall between 2007 and 2012, there were increases in enrollment for some racial/ethnic groups and decreases for other groups (table 203.50). Between 2007 and 2012, the enrollment of Hispanic students increased 16 percent and the enrollment of Asian/Pacific Islander students increased 6 percent. In contrast, the enrollment of White students decreased 8 percent, the enrollment of Black students decreased 7 percent, and the enrollment of American Indian/Alaska Native students decreased 10 percent.

From 2007 to 2012, changes in public school enrollment varied from state to state. Thirty-four states had higher enrollment in 2012 than in 2007, while 16 states and the District of Columbia had lower enrollment in 2012 than in 2007 (table 203.20 and figure 8). The largest public school enrollment increases occurred in Texas (9 percent) and Colorado (8 percent), and 5 other states had increases of at least 5 percent. The largest decrease in public school enrollment occurred in Michigan (a decrease of 8 percent), and 3 other states had decreases of at least 5 percent.

Enrollment in private elementary and secondary schools decreased by an estimated 12 percent between 2007 and 2012, from 5.9 million to 5.2 million (table 208.20). In 2012, private school students made up 9.4 percent of all elementary and secondary school students.

In 2013, about 65 percent of 3- to 5-year-olds were enrolled in preprimary education (nursery school and kindergarten), the same as the percentage in 2003 (table 202.10 and figure 9). However, the percentage of children in full-day programs increased from 2003 to 2013. In 2013, about 60 percent of the children enrolled in preprimary education attended a full-day preprimary program, compared with 56 percent in 2003.

A higher percentage of 4-year-old children (57 percent) were cared for primarily in center-based programs during the day in 2005–06 than had no regular nonparental care (20 percent) or were cared for primarily in home-based settings by relatives (13 percent) or by nonrelatives (8 percent) (table 202.50). There were differences in the average quality of care children received in these settings. A higher percentage of children in Head Start and other center-based programs (35 percent) received high-quality care than those in home-based relative and nonrelative care (9 percent), according to the ratings of trained observers (table 202.60).

The Individuals with Disabilities Education Act (IDEA), enacted in 1975, mandates that children and youth ages 3–21 with disabilities be provided a free and appropriate public school education. The percentage of total public school enrollment that represents children served by federally supported special education programs increased from 8.3 percent to 13.8 percent between 1976–77 and 2004–05 (table 204.30). Much of this overall increase can be attributed to a rise in the percentage of students identified as having specific learning disabilities from 1976–77 (1.8 percent) to 2004–05 (5.7 percent). The overall percentage of students being served in programs for those with disabilities decreased between 2004–05 (13.8 percent) and 2012–13 (12.9 percent). However, there were different patterns of change in the percentages served with some specific conditions between 2004–05 and 2012–13. The percentage of children identified as having other health impairments (limited strength, vitality, or alertness due to chronic or acute health problems such as a heart condition, tuberculosis, rheumatic fever, nephritis, asthma, sickle cell anemia, hemophilia, epilepsy, lead poisoning, leukemia, or diabetes) rose from 1.1 to 1.6 percent of total public school enrollment, the percentage with autism rose from 0.4 to 1.0 percent, and the percentage with developmental delay rose from 0.7 to 0.8 percent. The percentage of children with specific learning disabilities declined from 5.7 percent to 4.6 percent of total public school enrollment during this period. In fall 2012, some 95 percent of 6- to 21-year-old students with disabilities were served in regular schools; 3 percent were served in a separate school for students with disabilities; 1 percent were placed in regular private schools by their parents; and less than 1 percent each were served in one of the following environments: in a separate residential facility, homebound or in a hospital, or in a correctional facility (table 204.60).

Teachers and Other School Staff

During the 1970s and early 1980s, public school enrollment decreased, while the number of teachers generally increased. For public schools, the number of pupils per teacher—that is, the pupil/teacher ratio[1]—declined from 22.3 in 1970 to 17.9 in 1985 (table 208.20 and figure 7). After enrollment started increasing in 1985, the public school pupil/teacher ratio continued to decline, reaching 17.2 in 1989. After a period of relative stability during the late 1980s through the mid-1990s, the ratio declined from 17.3 in 1995 to 15.3 in 2008. The public school pupil/teacher ratio increased from 15.3 in 2008 to 16.0 in 2012. By comparison, the pupil/teacher ratio for private schools was estimated at 12.5 in 2012. The average class size in 2011–12 was 21.2 pupils for public elementary schools and 26.8 pupils for public secondary schools (table 209.30).

In 2011–12, some 76 percent of public school teachers were female, 44 percent were under age 40, and 56 percent had a master's or higher degree (table 209.10). Compared with public school teachers, a lower percentage of private school teachers had a master's or higher degree (43 percent).

Public school principals tend to be older and have more advanced credentials than public school teachers. In 2011–12, some 20 percent of public school principals were under age 40, and 98 percent of public school principals had a master's or higher degree (table 212.10). Compared with public school principals, a lower percentage of private school principals had a master's or higher degree (69 percent). A lower percentage of principals than of teachers were female: About 52 percent of public school principals were female, compared with 76 percent of teachers. At private schools, 55 percent of principals were female in 2011–12, compared with 75 percent of teachers.

From 1969–70 to 1980, there was an 8 percent increase in the number of public school teachers, compared with a 48 percent increase in the number of all other public school staff [2] (table B and table 213.10). Consequently, the percentage of staff who were teachers declined from 60 percent in 1969–70 to 52 percent in 1980. From 1980 to 2012, the number of

teachers and the number of all other staff grew at more similar rates (42 and 55 percent, respectively) than they did in the 1970s. As a result, the proportion of teachers among total staff was 2 percentage points lower in 2012 than in 1980, in contrast to the decrease of 8 percentage points during the 1970s. Two staff categories increased more than 100 percent between 1980 and 2012—instructional aides, which rose 124 percent, and instruction coordinators, which rose 245 percent. Taken together, the percentage of staff with direct instructional responsibilities (teachers and instructional aides) increased from 60 to 62 percent between 1980 and 2012. In 2012, there were 8 pupils per staff member (total staff) at public schools, compared with 10 pupils per staff member in 1980 (table 213.10). At private schools in 2011–12, the number of pupils per staff member was 6 (table 205.60).

Table B. Number of public school staff, by selected categories: 1969–70, 1980, and 2012

[In thousands]

Selected staff category	1969–70	1980	2012
Total	3,361	4,168	6,181
Teachers	2,016	2,184	3,109
Instructional aides	57	326	730
Instruction coordinators	32	21	71

SOURCE: U.S. Department of Education, National Center for Education Statistics, *Statistics of State School Systems, 1969–70; Statistics of Public Elementary and Secondary Schools, 1980;* and Common Core of Data (CCD), "State Nonfiscal Survey of Public Elementary/Secondary Education," 2012–13.

Schools

During most of the last century, the trend to consolidate small schools brought declines in the total number of public schools in the United States. In 1929–30, there were approximately 248,000 public schools, compared with about 98,000 in 2012–13 (table 214.10). However, the number of public schools has increased in recent decades: between 1988–89 and 2006–07, there was an increase of approximately 15,600 schools. Since 2006–07, the number of public schools has remained relatively stable, varying by about 500 schools or less from year to year.

While the total number of public schools in the country has remained between 98,000 and 99,000 in recent years, new schools have opened and some schools have closed. In 2012–13, there were 1,493 school closures (table 216.95). The schools that closed had enrolled about 241,000 students in the prior school year (2011–12). Of the schools that closed, 1,075 were regular schools, 83 were special education schools, 66 were vocational schools, and 269 were alternative schools. The number of schools that closed in 2012–13 was higher than the number in 2000–01 (1,193); however, the number of annual school closures has fluctuated during this period, ranging from around 1,200 to 2,200. School closures do not necessarily reflect the number of school buildings that have been closed, since a school may share a building with another school, or one school may have multiple buildings.

Since the early 1970s, public school systems have been shifting away from junior high schools (schools consisting of either grades 7 and 8 or grades 7 to 9) and moving toward

---

[1] The pupil/teacher ratio is based on all teachers—including teachers for students with disabilities and other special teachers—and all students enrolled in the fall of the school year. Unlike the pupil/teacher ratio, the average class size excludes students and teachers in classes that are exclusively for special education students. Class size averages are based on surveys of teachers reporting on the counts of students in their classes.

[2] "All other public school staff" includes administrative staff, principals, librarians, guidance counselors, secretaries, custodial staff, food service workers, school bus drivers, and other professional and nonprofessional staff.

middle schools (a subset of elementary schools beginning with grade 4, 5, or 6 and ending with grade 6, 7, or 8) (table 216.10). Although the number of all elementary schools (schools beginning with grade 6 or below and having no grade higher than 8) was similar in 1970–71 and 2000–01 (64,000 in 1970–71 and 64,600 in 2000–01), the number of middle schools was 462 percent higher in 2000–01 than in 1970–71 (11,700 vs. 2,100). During the same period, the number of junior high schools declined by 57 percent (from 7,800 in 1970–71 to 3,300 in 2000–01). Between 2002–03 and 2012–13, the number of all elementary schools rose by 2 percent to 66,700, while the subset of middle schools rose by 7 percent to 13,100. During the same period, the number of junior high schools declined by 14 percent to 2,800.

The average number of students in public elementary schools in 2012–13 (481) was higher than in 2002–03 (476) (table 216.45). The average enrollment size of public secondary schools decreased from 720 in 2002–03 to an average of 689 students in 2012–13. The average size of regular public secondary schools—which exclude alternative, special education, and vocational education schools—decreased from 813 in 2002–03 to 785 in 2012–13.

School Choice

Over the past 2 decades, the range of options that parents have for the education of their children has expanded. Private schools have been a traditional alternative to public school education, but there are now more options for parents to choose public charter schools, and more parents are also homeschooling their children. Between 1999–2000 and 2012–13, enrollment in private schools decreased from 6.0 million to an estimated 5.2 million, a decline of 0.8 million or 14 percent (table 105.30). During the same period, the percentage of elementary and secondary students who were enrolled in private schools declined from 11.4 percent to 9.4 percent. In contrast, enrollment in public charter schools increased between 1999–2000 and 2012–13, rising from 0.3 million to 2.3 million, an increase of 1.9 million students (table 216.30). During this period, the percentage of public elementary and secondary school children who were in charter schools increased from 0.7 percent to 4.6 percent. In addition, there has been an increase in the number and percentage of 5- to 17-year-olds who are homeschooled (tables 206.10 and 206.20). About 1.8 million children were homeschooled in 2012, compared to 0.9 million in 1999.[3] Also, the percentage of 5- to 17-year-olds who were homeschooled in 2012 (3.4 percent) was higher than in 1999 (1.7 percent).

[3]The number of homeschooled children in 1999 is from *Homeschooling in the United States: 1999* (NCES 2001-033), available at http://nces.ed.gov/pubsearch/pubsinfo.asp?pubid=2001033. While National Household Education Surveys Program (NHES) administrations prior to 2012 were administered via telephone with an interviewer, NHES:2012 used self-administered paper-and-pencil questionnaires that were mailed to respondents. Measurable differences in estimates between 1999 and 2012 could reflect actual changes in the population, or the changes could be due to the mode change from telephone to mail.

Charter schools are the typical form of choice within the public education sector; however, some parental selection also can be found among traditional public schools. In 2012, the parents of 37 percent of all 1st- through 12th-grade students indicated that public school choice was available to them (table 206.40). Also in 2012, 13 percent of the students in traditional public schools were in a school chosen by their parents rather than an assigned school (table 206.30). There were differences in the characteristics of students attending their local assigned public schools in 2012 compared to those in public schools chosen by their parents. For example, White students made up a higher percentage of those in assigned schools (53 percent) than of those in chosen schools (40 percent). In contrast, Black students made up a higher percentage of those in chosen schools (22 percent) than of those in assigned schools (14 percent). Hispanic students also made up a higher percentage of those in chosen schools (27 percent) than of those in assigned schools (23 percent). Students in cities made up a higher percentage of those in chosen schools (46 percent) than of those in assigned schools (25 percent). In contrast, students in rural areas made up a higher percentage of those in assigned schools (26 percent) than of those in chosen schools (14 percent).

Compared with students in assigned public schools, a higher percentage of students in chosen public schools had parents who were very satisfied with some elements of their children's education in 2012 (table 206.50). Among students in grades 3 through 12, the percentage of students whose parents were very satisfied with their school was higher for students in chosen schools (56 percent) than for students in assigned schools (52 percent). Similarly, the percentage of students whose parents were very satisfied with academic standards was higher for students in chosen schools (59 percent) than for students in assigned schools (53 percent). Also, higher percentages of students in chosen schools had parents who were very satisfied with school order and discipline as well as with staff interaction with parents. However, there was no measurable difference between the percentages of students in chosen and assigned public schools whose parents were highly satisfied with the teachers in their school (52 percent each).

High School Graduates and Dropouts

About 3,323,000 high school students are expected to graduate during the 2015–16 school year (table 219.10), including about 3,048,000 public school graduates and 275,000 private school graduates. High school graduates include only recipients of diplomas, not recipients of equivalency credentials. The 2015–16 projection of high school graduates is lower than the record high of 3,452,000 graduates for 2011–12, but exceeds the baby boom era's high point in 1975–76, when 3,142,000 students earned diplomas. In 2011–12, an estimated 80.8 percent of public high school students graduated on time—that is, received a diploma 4 years after beginning their freshman (9th-grade) year.

The number of GED credentials issued by the states to GED test passers rose from 330,000 in 1977 to 487,000 in 2000 (table 219.60). A record number of 648,000 GED credentials were issued in 2001. In 2002, there were revisions to the GED test and to the data reporting procedures. In 2001, test takers were required to successfully complete all five components of the GED or else begin the five-part series again with the new test that was introduced in 2002. Prior to 2002, reporting was based on summary data from the states on the number of GED credentials issued. As of 2002, reporting has been based on individual GED candidate- and test-level records collected by the GED Testing Service.[4] In 2013, some 541,000 people passed the GED tests, up from 387,000 in 2003.

The percentage of dropouts among 16- to 24-year-olds (known as the status dropout rate) has decreased over the past 20 years (table 219.70). The status dropout rate is the percentage of the civilian noninstitutionalized 16- to 24-year-old population who are not enrolled in school and who have not completed a high school program, regardless of when they left school. (People who left school but went on to receive a GED credential are not treated as dropouts.) Between 1990 and 2013, the status dropout rate declined from 12.1 to 6.8 percent. Although the status dropout rate declined for both Blacks and Hispanics during this period, their rates (7.3 and 11.7 percent, respectively) remained higher than the rate for Whites (5.1 percent) in 2013.

Achievement

Most of the student performance data in the *Digest* are drawn from the National Assessment of Educational Progress (NAEP). The NAEP assessments have been conducted using three basic designs: the national main NAEP, state NAEP (which includes the Trial Urban District Assessment), and national long-term trend NAEP. The main NAEP reports current information for the nation and specific geographic regions of the country. The assessment program includes students drawn from both public and private schools and reports results for student achievement at grades 4, 8, and 12. The main NAEP assessments follow the frameworks developed by the National Assessment Governing Board and use the latest advances in assessment methodology. Because the assessment items reflect curricula associated with specific grade levels, the main NAEP uses samples of students at those grade levels.

Since 1990, NAEP assessments have also been conducted at the state level. Each participating state receives assessment results that report on the performance of students in that state. In its content, the state assessment is identical to the assessment conducted nationally. From 1990 through 2001, the national sample was a subset of the combined sample of students assessed in each participating state along with an additional sample from the states that did not participate in the state assessment. For mathematics, reading, science, and writing assessments since 2002, a combined sample of public schools has been selected for 4th- and 8th-grade national NAEP and state NAEP (including the Trial Urban District Assessment).

NAEP long-term trend assessments are designed to give information on the changes in the basic achievement level of America's youth since the early 1970s. They are administered nationally and report student performance in reading and mathematics at ages 9, 13, and 17. Measuring long-term trends of student achievement requires the precise replication of past procedures. For example, students of specific ages are sampled in order to maintain consistency with the original sample design. Similarly, the long-term trend instrument does not evolve based on changes in curricula or in educational practices. The differences in procedures between the main NAEP and the long-term trend NAEP mean that their results cannot be compared directly.

The following paragraphs discuss results for the national main NAEP, state NAEP, and long-term trend NAEP. Readers should keep in mind that comparisons of NAEP scores in the text (like all comparisons of estimates in the *Digest*) are based on statistical testing of unrounded values.

Reading

The main NAEP reading assessment data are reported on a scale of 0 to 500 (table 221.10). In 2013, the average reading score for 4th-grade students (222) was not measurably different from the 2011 score, but it was higher than the scores on assessments between 1992 (217) and 2009 (221). At grade 4, only the average reading scores for White students were higher in 2013 (232) than in both 2011 (231) and 1992 (224). The 2013 scores for Black (206), Hispanic (207), and Asian/Pacific Islander (235) 4th-graders were not measurably different from the 2011 scores, but the 2013 scores were higher than the 1992 scores (192, 197, and 216, respectively). The difference in the reading scale scores of White and Black 4th- graders decreased from 32 points in 1992 to 26 points in 2013. For 8th-grade students, the average reading score in 2013 (268) was more than 2 points higher than in 2011 (265), was 8 points higher than in 1992 (260), and was higher than the average scores in all previous years. At grade 8, the average reading scores for White (276), Black (250), Hispanic (256), and Asian/Pacific Islander (280) students were higher in 2013 than in 2011 and 1992. The difference in the reading scale scores of White and Hispanic 8th- graders decreased from 26 points in 1992 to 21 points in 2013. For 12th-grade students, the average reading score in 2013 (288) was not measurably different from the score in 2009 (12th-graders were not assessed in 2011), but was lower than the score in 1992 (292). At grade 12, the 2013 average reading scores for White (297), Hispanic (276), and Asian/Pacific Islander (296) students were not measurably different from either the 2009 scores or the

---

[4]Information on changes in GED test series and reporting is based on the 2003 edition of *Who Passed the GED Tests?*, by the GED Testing Service of the American Council on Education, as well as communication with staff of the GED Testing Service.

1992 scores. The 2013 reading score for Black students (268) was not measurably different from the score in 2009, but was lower than the score in 1992 (273). The difference in the reading scale scores of White and Black 12th- graders increased from 24 points in 1992 to 30 points in 2013.

While there was no measurable change from 2011 to 2013 in the average score for 4th-grade public school students nationally, average scores were higher in 2013 than in 2011 in Colorado, the Department of Defense dependents schools, Indiana, Iowa, Maine, Minnesota, Tennessee, Washington, and the District of Columbia; scores were lower in 2013 than in 2011 in Massachusetts, Montana, and North Dakota (table 221.40). At grade 8, the average reading score for public school students nationally was 2 points higher in 2013 than in 2011, and 12 states (Arkansas, California, Florida, Hawaii, Iowa, Nevada, New Hampshire, Oregon, Pennsylvania, Tennessee, Utah, and Washington) plus the District of Columbia and the Department of Defense dependents schools had higher scores in 2013 than in 2011 (table 221.60). In the other states, scores did not change measurably from 2011 to 2013.

Reported on a scale of 0 to 500, NAEP long-term trend results in reading are available for 13 assessment years going back to the first in 1971. The average reading score for 9-year-olds was higher in 2012 (221) than in assessment years prior to 2008, increasing 5 points since 2004 and 13 points in comparison to 1971 (table 221.85). The average score for 13-year-olds in 2012 (263) was higher than in all previous assessment years, except for 1992. The average reading score for 17-year-olds was higher in 2012 (287) than in 2004 (283), but was not significantly different from the score in 1971 (285).

White, Black, and Hispanic 9-, 13-, and 17-year-olds all had higher average reading scores in 2012 than they did in the first assessment year (which is 1975 for Hispanic students because separate data for Hispanics were not collected in 1971). Average reading scores were higher in 2012 than in 2004 for White, Black, and Hispanic students at all three ages (table 221.85). Reading results for 2012 continued to show gaps in scores between White and Black students (ranging from 23 to 26 points, depending on age) and between White and Hispanic students (about 21 points at all three ages). The White-Black and the White-Hispanic reading gaps were smaller in 2012 than in 1971 (1975 for Hispanic students) at all three ages. For example, the White-Black reading gap for 17-year-olds was 53 points in 1971 compared with 26 points in 2012. Similarly the White-Hispanic reading gap for 17-year-olds narrowed from 41 points in 1975 to 21 points in 2012.

In 2012, female 9-, 13-, and 17-year-old students continued to have higher average reading scores than male students at all three ages (table 221.85). The gap between male and female 9-year-olds was 5 points in 2012; this was narrower than the gap in 1971 (13 points). The 8-point gender gap for 13-year-olds in 2012 was not significantly different from the gap in 1971. At age 17, the 8-point gap between males and females in 2012 was not significantly different from the gap in 1971.

Mathematics

The main NAEP mathematics assessment data for 4th- and 8th-graders are reported on a scale of 0 to 500. In 2013, the average NAEP mathematics scores for 4th-grade and 8th-grade students were higher than the average scores in all previous assessment years (table 222.10). From 1990 (the first assessment year) to 2013, the average 4th-grade NAEP mathematics score increased by 28 points, from 213 to 242. During that same period, the average 8th-grade score increased by 22 points, from 263 to 285. At grade 4, the average mathematics scores in 2013 for White (250) and Hispanic students (231) were higher than the scores in both 2011 and 1990. The 2013 score for Black 4th-graders (224) was not measurably different from the 2011 score, but it was higher than the 1990 score. Prior to 2011, separate data on Asians were not available; the 2013 score for Asian 4th-graders (259) was also not measurably different from the 2011 score. The difference in the mathematics scale scores of White and Black 4th-graders decreased from 32 points in 1990 to 26 points in 2013. At grade 8, the mathematics scores of White (294), Black (263), and Hispanic (272) students were higher in 2013 than in 1990. However, the 31-point gap between the mathematics scores of White and Black 8th-graders in 2013 was not significantly different from the 33-point gap in 1990. Due to changes in the 12th-grade mathematics assessment framework, a new trend line started in 2005, with data reported on a scale of 0 to 300. The average 12th-grade mathematics score in 2013 (153) was not measurably different from the score in 2009, but was higher than the score in 2005 (150). Scores were higher in 2013 than in 2005 for White, Black, Hispanic, and Asian/Pacific Islander 12th-graders, as well as for those of Two or more races. The 2013 mathematics score for American Indian/Alaska Native 12th-graders was not measurably different from the 2005 score. The mathematics score gap in favor of Asian/Pacific Islander 12th-graders compared with White 12th-graders was higher in 2013 (11 points) than in 2005 (5 points). There were no other measurable changes in the size of gaps between 12th-grade mathematics scores for White students compared with scores for students of other racial/ethnic groups.

NAEP results also permit state-level comparisons of the mathematics achievement of 4th- and 8th-grade students in public schools (tables 222.50 and 222.60). The average mathematics scores for 4th-grade public school students increased from 2011 to 2013 in 14 states (Arizona, Colorado, Delaware, Hawaii, Indiana, Iowa, Minnesota, Nebraska, New York, North Dakota, Tennessee, Washington, West Virginia, and Wyoming), the District of Columbia, and the Department of Defense dependents schools, and scores did not decrease for any states. At grade 8, scores were higher in 2013 than in 2011 in five states (Florida, Hawaii, New Hampshire, Pennsylvania, and Tennessee), the District of Columbia, and the Department of Defense dependents schools, and scores decreased in three states (Montana, Oklahoma, and South Dakota).

NAEP long-term trend mathematics results, reported on a scale of 0 to 500, are available for 12 assessment years, going back to the first in 1973. In 2012, the average mathematics score for 9-year-olds (244) was higher than in all previous assessment years prior to 2008 (table 222.85). The average score for 9-year-olds in 2012 was 5 points higher than in 2004 and 25 points higher than in 1973. The average mathematics score for 13-year-olds in 2012 (285) was higher than in all previous assessment years. For 13-year-olds, the average score in 2012 was 6 points higher than in 2004 and 19 points higher than in 1973. In contrast, the average score for 17-year-olds in 2012 (306) was not significantly different from the scores in 2004 and 1973.

White, Black, and Hispanic 9-, 13-, and 17-year-olds all had higher average mathematics scores in 2012 than in 1973 (table 222.85). In comparison to 2004, average mathematics scores were higher in 2012 for White 9-, 13-, and 17-year-olds, Hispanic 9- and 13-year-olds, and Black 13-year-olds. Mathematics results for 2012 continued to show score gaps between White and Hispanic students (ranging from 17 to 21 points [based on unrounded scores], depending on age) and between White and Black students (ranging from 25 to 28 points). Across all three age groups, both the White-Black and White-Hispanic gaps in mathematics scores were lower in 2012 than in 1973. For example, among 17-year-olds, the White-Black gap was 40 points in 1973 compared to 26 points in 2012, and the White-Hispanic gap was 33 points in 1973 compared to 19 points in 2012.

While there was no significant difference between the average mathematics scores of male and female 9- and 13-year-olds in 2012, male students did score higher than female students at age 17 (table 222.85). At both age 9 and age 13, the gap between males and females in 2012 was not significantly different from the gap in 1973. At age 17, the 4-point gender score gap in 2012 was smaller than the gap in 1973 (8 points).

Science

NAEP has assessed the science abilities of students in grades 4, 8, and 12 in both public and private schools since 1996. As of 2009, however, NAEP science assessments are based on a new framework, so results from these assessments cannot be compared to results from earlier science assessments. Scores are based on a scale ranging from 0 to 300. In 2009, White 4th-graders had a higher average science score (163) than did Black (127), Hispanic (131), Asian/Pacific Islander (160), and American Indian/Alaska Native (135) 4th-graders (table 223.10). The average science score was higher for male 4th-graders (151) than for female 4th-graders (149). In 2009, the pattern of differences in average science scores by students' race/ethnicity at grade 8 was similar to the pattern at grade 4. The average science score also was higher for male 8th-graders (152) than for female 8th-graders (148). At grade 12, average scores for White (159) and Asian/Pacific Islander (164) students were higher than the scores for Black (125), Hispanic (134), and American Indian/Alaska Native (144) students. The average science score in 2009 for male 12th-graders (153) was higher than the score for female 12th-graders (147). In 2011, a science assessment was conducted at grade 8 only. The average 8th-grade science score increased from 150 in 2009 to 152 in 2011. While there were no significant changes from 2009 to 2011 in the average scores for Asian/Pacific Islander or American Indian/Alaska Native 8th-graders, average scores increased 1 point for White 8th-graders, 3 points for Black 8th-graders, and 5 points for Hispanic 8th-graders. The average science score of White 8th-graders continued to be higher than the average scores of 8th-graders in all other racial/ethnic groups in 2011, but score gaps between White and Black 8th-graders and between White and Hispanic 8th-graders narrowed from 2009 to 2011. Average scores for both male and female 8th-graders were higher in 2011 than in 2009. In 2011, the average score was 5 points higher for male 8th-graders than for female 8th-graders, which was not significantly different from the 4-point gap in 2009.

Skills of Young Children

In addition to student performance data available through NAEP, the *Digest* presents data from other surveys to provide additional perspectives on student achievement. Differences among demographic groups in the acquisition of cognitive skills have been demonstrated at relatively early ages in the Early Childhood Longitudinal Survey's Birth Cohort (ECLS-B) study as well as its Kindergarten Class (ECLS-K) studies.

In 2003–04, about 64 percent of 2-year-olds demonstrated proficiency in expressive vocabulary, which measured toddlers' ability to communicate using gestures, words, and sentences (table 220.20). The percentage of 2-year-olds demonstrating expressive vocabulary was higher for females (69 percent) than for males (59 percent). Also, a higher percentage of White (71 percent) and Asian (62 percent) 2-year-olds demonstrated expressive vocabulary than of Black, Hispanic, or American Indian/Alaska Native 2-year-olds (56, 54, and 50 percent, respectively). The percentage of 2-year-olds from families with high socioeconomic status (SES) who demonstrated expressive vocabulary (75 percent) was higher than the percentage of children from low-SES families who did so (52 percent).

Patterns of differences were also observed by race/ethnicity and SES for children at about 4 years of age (48 to 57 months old). In 2005–06, average early reading scores were higher for White (27) and Asian (31) 48- to 57-month-old children than for Black (23), Hispanic (21), and American Indian/Alaska Native (20) children (table 220.30). Also, high-SES children (33) had higher average early reading scores than low-SES children (19) at this age. These same patterns were observed among 48- to 57-month-old children with respect to average mathematics scores. White (32) and Asian (35) 48- to 57-month-old children had higher mathematics scores than Black (27), Hispanic (26), and American Indian/Alaska Native children (23). High-SES 48- to 57-month-old children (36) had higher average mathematics scores than low-SES children (24).

Children who enrolled in kindergarten for the first time in 2010–11 showed similar patterns of score differences by race/ethnicity and SES. In fall 2010, average mathematics scores were higher for first-time kindergartners from high-SES families (37) than for those from low-SES families (24) (table 220.40). White (33) and Asian (36) first-time kindergartners had higher mathematics scores than their Black (27), Hispanic (26), and American Indian/Alaska Native (27) counterparts. Similarly, reading scores in fall 2010 were higher for White (39) and Asian (42) first-time kindergartners than for their Black (36), Hispanic (35), and American Indian/Alaska Native (34) counterparts. High-SES children (43) had higher average early reading scores than low-SES children (32). These same patterns were observed among these children during 1st grade in spring 2012. White (67) and Asian (68) 1st-graders had higher mathematics scores than their Black (57), Hispanic (58), and American Indian/ Alaska Native (61) counterparts. Average mathematics scores were higher for 1st-graders from high-SES families (70) than for those from low-SES families (55). Average reading scores were also higher for White (72) and Asian (74) 1st-graders than for their Black (67), Hispanic (66), and American Indian/Alaska Native (67) counterparts; and 1st-graders from high-SES families (77) had higher average reading scores than those from low-SES families (62).

SAT Scores of College-Bound Seniors

The SAT (formerly known as the Scholastic Assessment Test and the Scholastic Aptitude Test) is not designed as an indicator of student achievement, but rather as an aid for predicting how well students will do in college. Between 1998–99 and 2004–05, the mathematics SAT average score increased by 9 points, but it decreased 7 points between 2004–05 (520) and 2013–14 (513) (table 226.20). The critical reading average score decreased 11 points between 2004–05 (508) and 2013–14 (497). The writing average score in 2013–14 (487) was 10 points lower than in 2005–06 (497), the year in which the SAT writing section was introduced.

Coursetaking in High School

The average number of science and mathematics courses completed by public high school graduates increased between 1982 and 2009. The average number of mathematics courses (Carnegie units) completed in high school rose from 2.6 in 1982 to 3.9 in 2009, and the number of science courses rose from 2.2 to 3.5 (table 225.10). The average number of courses in career/technical areas completed by public high school graduates was lower in 2009 (2.5 units) than in 2000 (2.9 units). As a result of the increased academic course load, the percentage of public and private high school graduates completing the 1983 National Commission on Excellence recommendations (4 units of English, 3 units of social studies, 3 units of science, 3 units of mathematics, and 2 units of foreign language) rose from 10 percent in 1982 to 62 percent in 2009 (table 225.50).

School Violence

In 2009–10, about 85 percent of public schools had a criminal incident, which is defined as theft, vandalism, drug possession, weapons possession, a serious violent crime, or a less serious violent crime such as a fight without weapons (table 229.20). In 2009–10, some 74 percent of schools reported one or more violent incidents, 44 percent of schools reported one or more thefts/larcenies, and 46 percent reported vandalism. The percentage of schools reporting a serious violent crime in 2009–10 (16 percent) was lower than the percentage of schools reporting a serious violent crime in 1999–2000 (20 percent). Also, the percentage of schools reporting an incident of vandalism was lower in 2009–10 (46 percent) than in 1999–2000 (51 percent). Overall, there were 4 criminal incidents reported per 100 students in 2009–10, which was lower than the 5 criminal incidents per 100 students reported in 1999–2000.

In 2013, data from the National Crime Victimization Survey showed that students ages 12–18 experienced more nonfatal victimizations at school than away from school. Nonfatal victimizations consist of theft and violent victimizations, which include serious violent crimes as well as simple assault. Students ages 12–18 experienced 1,420,900 nonfatal victimizations at school, compared with 778,500 away from school (table 228.20). These figures represent total victimization rates of 55 nonfatal victimizations per 1,000 students at school, compared with 30 per 1,000 students away from school. Between 1992 and 2013, the total victimization rates for students ages 12–18 generally declined both at and away from school. At school, the total victimization rate declined 70 percent, from 181 victimizations per 1,000 students in 1992 to 55 victimizations per 1,000 students in 2013. Away from school, the total rate declined 83 percent, from 173 victimizations per 1,000 students in 1992 to 30 victimizations per 1,000 students in 2013. This pattern of decline also held for thefts, all violent victimizations, and serious violent victimizations between 1992 and 2013. Thefts at school declined from a rate of 114 per 1,000 students to 18 per 1,000 students, and thefts away from school declined from 79 per 1,000 students to 16 per 1,000 students. The rate of violent victimization at school declined overall from 1992 (68 per 1,000 students) to 2013 (37 per 1,000 students); however, this rate increased between 2010 and 2013 (from 17 to 37 per 1,000 students). Away from school, the rate of violent victimization declined from 94 victimizations per 1,000 students in 1992 to 15 victimizations per 1,000 students in 2013. Serious violent victimization is a subcategory of violent victimization that includes the crimes of rape, sexual assault, robbery, and aggravated assault. Serious violent victimizations at school declined from 8 per 1,000 students in 1992 to 5 per 1,000 in 2013. The rate of serious violent victimization away from school declined from 43 victimizations per 1,000 students in 1992 to 6 per 1,000 in 2013.

Revenues and Expenditures

The state share of revenues for public elementary and secondary schools generally grew from the 1930s through the mid-1980s, while the local share declined during the same time period (table 235.10 and figure 10).[5] However, this pattern changed in the late 1980s, when the local share began to increase at the same time the state share decreased. Between 1986–87 and 1993–94, the state share declined from 49.7 percent to 45.2 percent, while the local share rose from 43.9 percent to 47.8 percent. Between 1993–94 and 2000–01, the state share rose again to 49.7 percent, the highest share since 1986–87, but declined every school year thereafter until 2005–06, when the state share was 46.5 percent. Overall, between 2001–02 and 2011–12, the federal share increased from 7.9 percent to 10.2 percent, while the

state share decreased from 49.2 to 45.2 percent. The local share in 2011–12 (44.6) was higher than the percentage in 2001–02 (42.9).

After adjustment for inflation, current expenditures per student in fall enrollment at public schools rose during the 1980s, remained stable during the first part of the 1990s, and then rose again until 2011 (table 236.55 and figure 11). There was an increase of 37 percent from 1980–81 to 1990–91, followed by minor fluctuations from 1990–91 to 1994–95. Although there was an overall increase of 28 percent from 1994–95 to 2011–12; the expenditure per student in 2011–12 was 5 percent lower than in 2008–09. In 2011–12, current expenditures per student in fall enrollment were $10,667 in unadjusted dollars. The expenditure for public school student transportation was $904 per student transported in 2011–12 (also in unadjusted dollars), and 55 percent of students were transported at public expense in 2007–08 (table 236.90).

[5]For data on individual years from 1980–81 through 1988–89, see *Digest of Education Statistics 2011* (NCES 2012-001), table 180.

Figure 7. Enrollment, number of teachers, pupil/teacher ratio, and expenditures in public elementary and secondary schools: 1960–61 through 2012–13

Fall enrollment, in millions

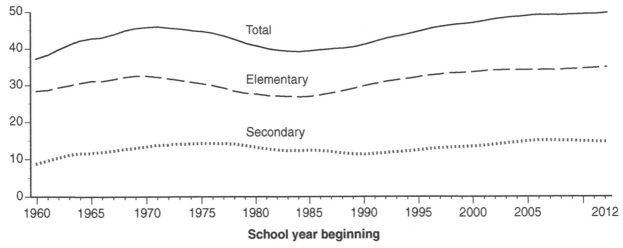

Teachers, in millions   Pupil/teacher ratio

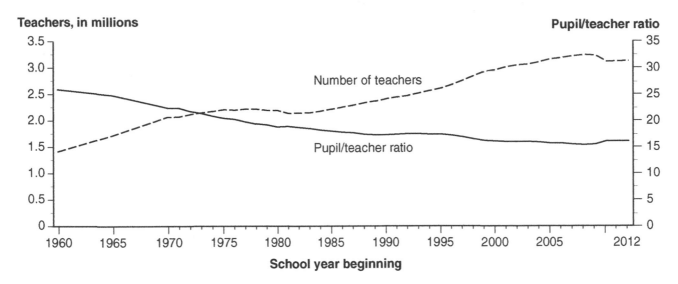

Current expenditures, in billions

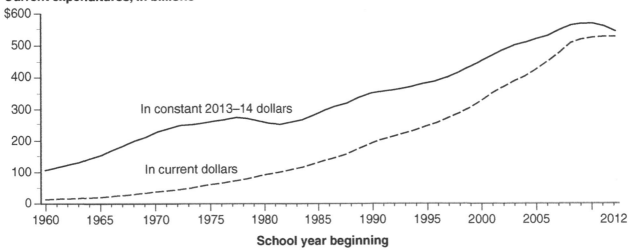

SOURCE: U.S. Department of Education, National Center for Education Statistics, *Statistics of State School Systems*, 1959–60 through 1969–70; *Statistics of Public Elementary and Secondary Day Schools*, 1959–60 through 1980–81; *Revenues and Expenditures for Public Elementary and Secondary Education*, 1970–71 through 1980–81; and Common Core of Data (CCD), "State Nonfiscal Survey of Public Elementary/Secondary Education," 1981–82 through 2012–13, and "National Public Education Financial Survey," 1989–90 through 2011–12.

Figure 8. Percentage change in public elementary and secondary enrollment, by state: Fall 2007 to fall 2012

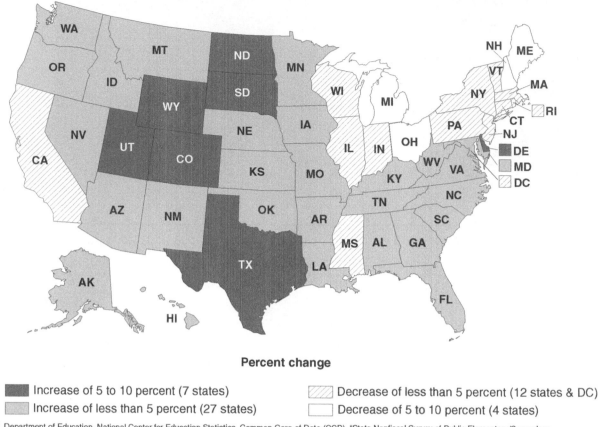

Percent change

■ Increase of 5 to 10 percent (7 states)   ▨ Decrease of less than 5 percent (12 states & DC)

▨ Increase of less than 5 percent (27 states)   □ Decrease of 5 to 10 percent (4 states)

SOURCE: U.S. Department of Education, National Center for Education Statistics, Common Core of Data (CCD), "State Nonfiscal Survey of Public Elementary/Secondary Education," 2007–08 and 2012–13.

Figure 9. Total and full-day preprimary enrollment of 3- to 5-year-olds: October 1970 through October 2013

Enrollment, in millions

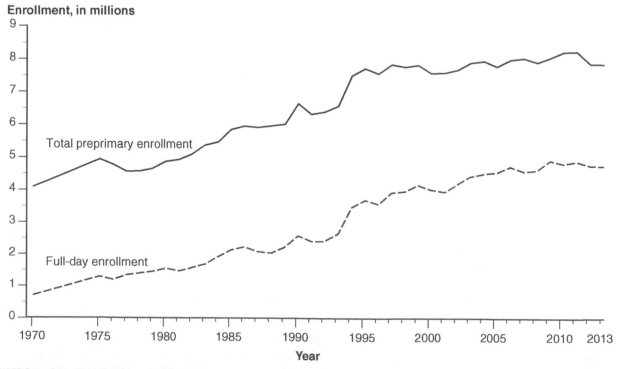

NOTE: Data prior to 1994 may not be comparable to later years.
SOURCE: U.S. Department of Education, National Center for Education Statistics, *Preprimary Enrollment*, 1970 and 1975. U.S. Department of Commerce, Census Bureau, Current Population Survey (CPS), October 1976 through October 2013.

Figure 10. Percentage of revenue for public elementary and secondary schools, by source of funds: 1970–71 through 2011–12

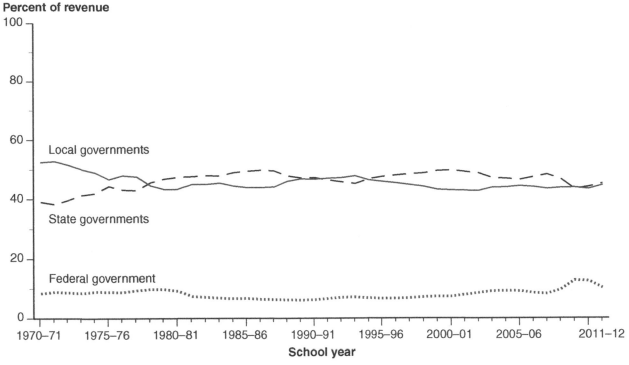

SOURCE: U.S. Department of Education, National Center for Education Statistics, *Revenues and Expenditures for Public Elementary and Secondary Education*, 1970–71 through 1986–87; and Common Core of Data (CCD), "National Public Education Financial Survey," 1987–88 through 2011–12.

Figure 11. Current expenditure per pupil in fall enrollment in public elementary and secondary schools: 1970–71 through 2011–12

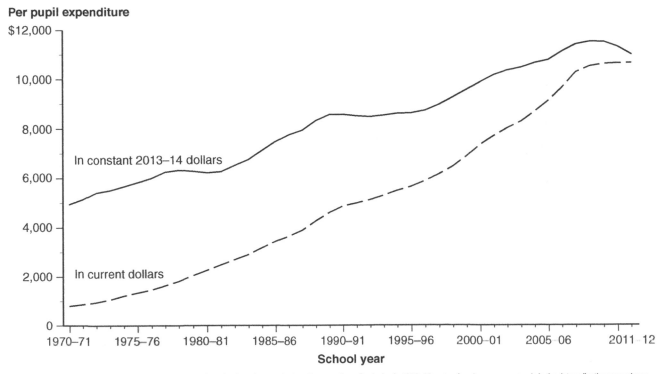

NOTE: Current expenditures include instruction, support services, food services, and enterprise operations. Beginning in 1988–89, extensive changes were made in the data collection procedures.
SOURCE: U.S. Department of Education, National Center for Education Statistics, *Revenues and Expenditures for Public Elementary and Secondary Education*, 1970–71 through 1986–87; and Common Core of Data (CCD), "National Public Education Financial Survey," 1987–88 through 2011–12.

Table 201.10. Historical summary of public elementary and secondary school statistics: Selected years, 1869–70 through 2011–12

Selected characteristic	1869–70	1879–80	1889–90	1899–1900	1909–10	1919–20	1929–30	1939–40	1949–50	1959–60	1969–70	1979–80	1989–90	1999–2000	2007–08	2008–09	2009–10	2010–11	2011–12
1	2	3	4	5	6	7	8	9	10	11	12	13	14	15	16	17	18	19	20
Population, pupils, and instructional staff																			
Total population (in thousands)[1]	38,558	50,156	62,622	75,995	90,490	104,514	121,878	131,028	149,188	177,830	201,385	225,055	246,819	279,040	301,231	304,094	306,772	309,326	311,583
5- to 17-year-olds (in thousands)[1]	11,683	15,066	18,473	21,573	24,011	27,571	31,414	30,151	30,223	43,881	52,386	48,043	44,947	52,811	53,893	53,833	53,890	53,930	53,780
5- to 17-year-olds as a percent of total population	30.3	30.0	29.5	28.4	26.5	26.4	25.8	23.0	20.3	24.7	26.0	21.3	18.2	18.9	17.9	17.7	17.6	17.4	17.3
Total enrollment in elementary and secondary schools (in thousands)[2]	7,562[3]	9,867	12,723	15,503	17,814	21,578	25,678	25,434	25,112	36,087	45,550	41,651	40,543	46,857	49,291	49,266	49,361	49,484	49,522
Prekindergarten through grade 8 (in thousands)	7,481[3]	9,757	12,520	14,984	16,899	19,378	21,279	18,833	19,387	27,602	32,513	28,034	29,152	33,486	34,204	34,286	34,409	34,625	34,773
Grades 9–12 (in thousands)	80[3]	110	203	519	915	2,200	4,399	6,601	5,725	8,485	13,037	13,616	11,390	13,371	15,086	14,980	14,952	14,860	14,749
Enrollment as a percent of total population	19.6[3]	19.7	20.3	20.4	19.7	20.6	21.1	19.4	16.8	20.3	22.6	18.5	16.4	16.8	16.4	16.2	16.1	16.0	15.9
Enrollment as a percent of 5- to 17-year-olds	64.7[3]	65.5	68.9	71.9	74.2	78.3	81.7	84.4	83.1	82.2	87.0	86.7	90.2	88.7	91.5	91.5	91.6	91.8	92.1
Percent of total enrollment in grades 9–12	1.1[3]	1.1	1.6	3.3	5.1	10.2	17.1	26.0	22.8	23.5	28.6	32.7	28.1	28.5	30.6	30.4	30.3	30.0	29.8
High school graduates (in thousands)	—	—	22	62	111	231	592	1,143	1,063	1,627	2,589	2,748	2,320	2,554	3,001	3,039	3,128	3,144	3,148
Average daily attendance (in thousands)	4,077	6,144	8,154	10,633	12,827	16,150	21,265	22,042	22,284	32,477	41,934	38,289	37,799	43,807	46,156	46,173	45,919	46,119	46,388
Total number of days attended by pupils enrolled (in millions)	539	801	1,098	1,535	2,011	2,615	3,673	3,858	3,964	5,782	7,501	6,835[4]	—	7,858	8,261	8,264	8,199	8,235	8,296
Percent of enrolled pupils attending daily	59.3	62.3	64.1	68.6	72.1	74.8	82.8	86.7	88.7	90.0	90.4	90.1[4]	—	94.3	93.1	—	—	—	93.9
Average length of school term, in days	132.2	130.3	134.7	144.3	157.5	161.9	172.7	175.0	177.9	178.0	178.9	178.5[4]	—	179.4	179.0	179.0	178.6	178.6	178.8
Average number of days attended per pupil[5]	78.4	81.1	86.3	99.0	113.0	121.2	143.0	151.7	157.9	160.2	161.7	160.8[4]	—	169.2	166.6	—	—	—	167.9
Total full-time equivalent (FTE) instructional staff (in thousands)	—	—	—	—	—	678	880	912	963	1,457	2,286	2,406	2,996	3,819	4,214	4,278	4,279	4,151	4,134
Supervisors (in thousands)	—	—	—	—	—	7	7	5	—	—	—	—	—	—	—	—	—	—	—
Principals (in thousands)	—	—	—	—	—	14	31	32	43	64	91	106	126	137	158	160	168	165	166
Teachers, teacher aides, librarians, and guidance counselors																			
(in thousands)	201	287	364	423	523	657	843	875	920	1,393	2,195	2,300	2,860	3,682	4,056	4,118	4,111	3,996	3,967
Males (in thousands)	78	123	126	127	110	93	140	195	196	404[4]	711[4]	782[4]	—	—	—	—	—	—	—
Females (in thousands)	123	164	238	296	413	585	703	681	724	989[4]	1,484[4]	1,518[4]	—	—	—	—	—	—	—
Percent male	38.7	42.8	34.5	29.9	21.1	14.1	16.6	22.2	21.3	29.0[4]	32.4[4]	34.0[4]	—	—	—	—	—	—	—
Amounts in current dollars																			
Total revenues and expenditures																			
Total revenue receipts (in millions)	—	—	$143	$220	$433	$970	$2,089	$2,261	$5,437	$14,747	$40,267	$96,881	$208,548	$372,944	$584,684	$592,422	$596,391	$604,229	$600,489
Federal government	—	—	—	—	—	2	7	40	156	652	3,220	9,504	12,701	27,098	47,788	56,670	75,998	75,549	61,043
State governments	—	—	—	—	—	160	354	684	2,166	5,768	16,063	45,349	98,239	184,613	282,623	276,526	258,864	266,786	271,453
Local sources, including intermediate	—	—	—	—	—	808	1,728	1,536	3,116	8,327	20,985	42,029	97,608	161,233	254,273	259,226	261,529	261,883	267,993
Percentage distribution of revenue receipts																			
Federal government	—	—	—	—	—	0.3	0.4	1.8	2.9	4.4	8.0	9.8	6.1	7.3	8.2	9.6	12.7	12.5	10.2
State governments	—	—	—	—	—	16.5	16.9	30.3	39.8	39.1	39.9	46.8	47.1	49.5	48.3	46.7	43.4	44.2	45.2
Local sources, including intermediate	—	—	—	—	—	83.2	82.7	68.0	57.3	56.5	52.1	43.4	46.8	43.2	43.5	43.8	43.9	43.3	44.6
Total expenditures for public schools (in millions)	$63	$78	$141	$215	$426	$1,036	$2,317	$2,344	$5,838	$15,613	$40,683	$95,962	$212,770	$381,838	$597,314	$610,526	$607,018	$604,356	$601,767
Current expenditures[8]	—	—	$114	180	356	861	1,844	1,942	4,687	12,329[7]	34,218[7]	86,984[7]	188,229[7]	323,889[7]	506,884[7]	518,923[7]	524,715[7]	527,291[7]	527,096[7]
Capital outlay[8]	—	—	26	35	70	154	371	258	1,014	2,662	4,659	6,506	17,781	43,357	66,426	65,690	56,715	50,969	48,773
Interest on school debt	—	—	—	—	—	18	93	131	101	490	1,171	1,874	3,776	9,135	15,695	17,049	17,934	17,994	17,701
Other current expenditures[9]	—	—	—	—	—	3	10	13	36	133	636	598[10]	2,983	5,457	8,308	8,464	8,356	8,161	8,195
Percentage distribution of total expenditures																			
Current expenditures[8]	—	—	81.3	83.5	83.6	83.1	79.6	82.8	80.3	79.0[7]	84.1[7]	90.6[7]	88.5[7]	84.8[7]	84.9[7]	85.0[7]	86.4[7]	87.2[7]	87.6[7]
Capital outlay[8]	—	—	18.7	16.5	16.4	14.8	16.0	11.0	17.4	17.0	11.5	6.8	8.4	11.4	11.1	10.8	9.3	8.4	8.1
Interest on school debt	—	—	—	—	—	1.8	4.0	5.6	1.7	3.1	2.9	2.0	1.8	2.4	2.6	2.8	2.8	3.0	2.9
Other current expenditures[9]	—	—	—	—	—	0.3	0.4	0.6	0.6	0.8	1.6	0.6[10]	1.4	1.4	1.4	1.4	1.4	1.4	1.4

See notes at end of table.

Table 201.10. Historical summary of public elementary and secondary school statistics: Selected years, 1869–70 through 2011–12—Continued

Selected characteristic	1869–70	1879–80	1889–90	1899–1900	1909–10	1919–20	1929–30	1939–40	1949–50	1959–60	1969–70	1979–80	1989–90	1999–2000	2007–08	2008–09	2009–10	2010–11	2011–12
1	2	3	4	5	6	7	8	9	10	11	12	13	14	15	16	17	18	19	20
Teacher salaries; income and expenditures per pupil and per capita																			
Annual salary of classroom teachers[11]	$189	$195	$252	$325	$485	$871	$1,420	$1,441	$3,010	$4,995	$8,626	$15,970	$31,367	$41,807	$52,800	$54,319	$55,202	$55,623	$55,418
Personal income per member of labor force[1]	—	—	—	—	—	—	1,734	1,333	3,446	5,897	9,913	19,797	37,283	57,286	78,335	80,562	78,418	80,768	86,941
Total school expenditures per capita of total population[1]	2	2	2	3	5	10	19	18	39	88	202	426	862	1,368	1,983	2,007	1,979	1,954	1,931
National income per capita[1]	—	—	—	—	—	—	773	630	1,609	2,584	4,467	9,990	19,375	29,832	40,903	40,868	39,528	41,185	42,853
Current expenditure per pupil in ADA[6,12,13]	16	13	14	17	28	53	87	88	210	375	816	2,272	4,990	7,394	10,982	11,239	11,427	11,453	11,363
Total expenditure per pupil in ADA[13,14]	16	13	17	20	33	64	108	106	260	471	955	2,491	5,547	8,589	12,759	13,033	13,035	12,926	12,794
National income per pupil in ADA[13]	—	—	—	—	—	—	4,430	3,743	10,770	14,152	21,450	58,717	126,516	190,026	266,962	269,155	264,075	276,233	287,837
Current expenditure per day per pupil in ADA[6,13,15]	0.12	0.10	0.10	0.12	0.18	0.33	0.50	0.50	1.17	2.11	4.56	12.73	—	41.22	61.36	62.79	64.00	64.03	63.54
Total expenditure per day per pupil in ADA[13]	—	—	0.13	0.14	0.21	0.40	0.63	0.60	1.46	2.65	5.34	13.95	—	47.90	71.30	72.83	73.02	72.39	71.55
Amounts in constant 2013–14 dollars[16]																			
Annual salary of classroom teachers[11]	—	—	—	—	—	$10,739	$19,492	$24,228	$29,863	$39,943	$53,655	$48,335	$58,044	$58,025	$58,602	$59,458	$59,845	$59,115	$57,220
Personal income per member of labor force[1]	—	—	—	—	—	—	23,809	22,406	34,190	47,160	61,659	59,917	68,992	79,509	86,943	88,183	85,014	85,838	88,736
Total school expenditures per capita of total population[1]	—	—	—	—	—	122	261	301	388	702	1,257	1,291	1,595	1,899	2,201	2,197	2,145	2,076	1,994
National income per capita[1]	—	—	—	—	—	—	10,610	10,596	15,960	20,667	27,783	30,235	35,854	41,405	45,398	44,735	42,853	43,770	44,247
Current expenditure per pupil in ADA[6,12,13]	—	—	—	—	—	657	1,190	1,481	2,087	3,000	5,076	6,876	9,215	10,262	12,189	12,302	12,388	12,151	11,732
Total expenditure per pupil in ADA[13,14]	—	—	—	—	—	788	1,489	1,778	2,583	3,766	5,940	7,538	10,265	11,921	14,161	14,266	14,132	13,737	13,210
National income per pupil in ADA[13]	—	—	—	—	—	—	60,808	62,930	106,863	113,165	133,424	177,714	234,116	263,743	296,287	294,618	286,288	293,573	297,198
Current expenditure per day per pupil in ADA[6,13,15]	—	—	—	—	—	4.1	6.9	8.4	11.6	16.9	28.4	38.5	53.2	53.2	68.1	68.7	69.4	68.0	65.6
Total expenditure per day per pupil in ADA[13]	—	—	—	—	—	4.9	8.6	10.1	14.5	21.2	33.2	42.2	—	61.8	79.1	79.7	79.2	76.9	73.9

—Not available.

[1] Data on population and labor force are from the Census Bureau, and data on personal income and national income are from the Bureau of Economic Analysis, U.S. Department of Commerce. Population data through 1900 are based on total population from the decennial census. From 1909–10 to 1959–60, population data are total population, including armed forces overseas, as of July 1. Data for later years are for resident population that excludes armed forces overseas.

[2] Data for 1869–70 through 1959–60 are school year enrollment. Data for later years are fall enrollment. Total counts of ungraded students were prorated to prekindergarten through grade 8 and grades 9 through 12 based on prior reports.

[3] Data for 1870–71.

[4] Estimated by the National Center for Education Statistics.

[5] Prior to 1919–20, data are for the number of different persons employed rather than number of positions.

[6] Prior to 1919–20, includes interest on school debt.

[7] Because of the modification of the scope of "current expenditures for elementary and secondary schools," data for 1959–60 and later years are not entirely comparable with prior years.

[8] Beginning in 1969–70, includes capital outlay by state and local school building authorities.

[9] Includes summer schools, community colleges, and adult education. Beginning in 1959–60, also includes community services, formerly classified with "current expenditures for elementary and secondary schools."

[10] Excludes community colleges and adult education.

[11] Prior to 1959–60, average includes supervisors, principals, teachers, and other nonsupervisory instructional staff. Data for 1959–60 and later years are estimated by the National Education Association.

[12] Excludes current expenditures not allocable to pupil costs.

[13] "ADA" means average daily attendance in elementary and secondary schools.

[14] Expenditure figure is the sum of current expenditures allocable to pupil costs, capital outlay, and interest on school debt.

[15] Per-day rates derived by dividing annual rates by average length of term.

[16] Constant dollars based on the Consumer Price Index, prepared by the Bureau of Labor Statistics, U.S. Department of Labor, adjusted to a school-year basis.

NOTE: Some data have been revised from previously published figures. Beginning in 1959–60, data include Alaska and Hawaii. Detail may not sum to totals because of rounding.

SOURCE: U.S. Department of Education, National Center for Education Statistics, Annual Report of the United States Commissioner of Education, 1869–70 through 1909–10; Biennial Survey of Education in the United States, 1919–20 through 1949–50; Statistics of State School Systems, 1959–60 and 1969–70; Statistics of Public Elementary and Secondary Education, 1979–80; Revenues and Expenditures for Public Elementary and Secondary Education, FY 1980; Schools and Staffing Survey (SASS), "Public School Questionnaire," 1999–2000 and 2007–08; Common Core of Data (CCD), "State Nonfiscal Survey of Public Elementary/Secondary Education," 1989–90 through 2012–13, and "National Public Education Financial Survey," 1989–90 through 2011–12. U.S. Department of Commerce, Census Bureau, retrieved October 3, 2014, from http://www.census.gov/popest/data/national/asrh/2013/2013-nat-res.html. U.S. Department of Commerce, Bureau of Economic Analysis, retrieved May 6, 2015, from http://www.bea.gov/iTable/. U.S. Department of Labor, Bureau of Labor Statistics, retrieved May 6, 2015, from http://stats.bls.gov/cpi/cpifiles/cpiai.txt. (This table was prepared May 2015.)

Table 201.20.   Enrollment in grades 9 through 12 in public and private schools compared with population 14 to 17 years of age: Selected years, 1889–90 through fall 2014

[In thousands]

Year	All schools	Enrollment, grades 9 to 12[1]												Population 14 to 17 years of age[2]	Enrollment as a ratio of population 14 to 17 years of age[3]
		Public schools						Private schools							
		Total	9th grade	10th grade	11th grade	12th grade	Secondary ungraded	Total	9th grade	10th grade	11th grade	12th grade	Secondary ungraded		
1	2	3	4	5	6	7	8	9	10	11	12	13	14	15	16
1889–90............	298	203	—	—	—	—	—	95	—	—	—	—	—	5,355	5.6
1899–1900.........	630	519	—	—	—	—	—	111	—	—	—	—	—	6,152	10.2
1909–10.............	1,032	915	—	—	—	—	—	117	—	—	—	—	—	7,220	14.3
1919–20.............	2,414	2,200	917	576	396	312	0	214	—	—	—	—	—	7,736	31.2
1929–30.............	4,741	4,399	1,627	1,192	880	701	0	341 [4]	—	—	—	—	—	9,341	50.7
1939–40.............	7,059	6,601	2,011	1,767	1,486	1,282	55	458 [5]	—	—	—	—	—	9,720	72.6
1949–50.............	6,397	5,725	1,761	1,513	1,275	1,134	42	672	—	—	—	—	—	8,405	76.1
Fall 1959............	9,306	8,271	—	—	—	—	—	1,035	—	—	—	—	—	11,155	83.4
Fall 1963............	12,170	10,883	—	—	—	—	—	1,287	—	—	—	—	—	13,492	90.2
Fall 1965............	13,002	11,602	3,215	2,993	2,741	2,477	176	1,400 [6]	—	—	—	—	—	14,146	91.9
Fall 1966............	13,280	11,880	3,318	3,111	2,756	2,508	187	1,400 [6]	—	—	—	—	—	14,398	92.2
Fall 1967............	13,647	12,247	3,395	3,221	2,879	2,525	226	1,400 [6]	—	—	—	—	—	14,727	92.7
Fall 1968............	14,123	12,723	3,508	3,310	2,986	2,650	268	1,400 [6]	—	—	—	—	—	15,170	93.1
Fall 1969............	14,337	13,037	3,568	3,405	3,047	2,732	285	1,300 [6]	—	—	—	—	—	15,549	92.2
Fall 1970............	14,647	13,336	3,654	3,458	3,128	2,775	321	1,311	—	—	—	—	—	15,924	92.0
Fall 1971............	15,053	13,753	3,781	3,571	3,200	2,864	337	1,300 [6]	—	—	—	—	—	16,328	92.2
Fall 1972............	15,148	13,848	3,779	3,648	3,248	2,873	299	1,300 [6]	—	—	—	—	—	16,639	91.0
Fall 1973............	15,344	14,044	3,801	3,650	3,323	2,918	352	1,300 [6]	—	—	—	—	—	16,867	91.0
Fall 1974............	15,403	14,103	3,832	3,675	3,302	2,955	339	1,300 [6]	—	—	—	—	—	17,035	90.4
Fall 1975............	15,604	14,304	3,879	3,723	3,354	2,986	362	1,300 [6]	—	—	—	—	—	17,128	91.1
Fall 1976............	15,656	14,314	3,825	3,738	3,373	3,015	363	1,342	—	—	—	—	—	17,119	91.5
Fall 1977............	15,546	14,203	3,779	3,686	3,388	3,026	324	1,343	—	—	—	—	—	17,045	91.2
Fall 1978............	15,441	14,088	3,726	3,610	3,312	3,023	416	1,353	—	—	—	—	—	16,946	91.1
Fall 1979............	14,916	13,616	3,526	3,532	3,241	2,969	348	1,300 [6]	—	—	—	—	—	16,611	89.8
Fall 1980............	14,570	13,231	3,377	3,368	3,195	2,925	366	1,339	—	—	—	—	—	16,143	90.3
Fall 1981............	14,164	12,764	3,286	3,218	3,039	2,907	314	1,400 [6]	—	—	—	—	—	15,609	90.7
Fall 1982............	13,805	12,405	3,248	3,137	2,917	2,787	315	1,400 [6]	—	—	—	—	—	15,057	91.7
Fall 1983............	13,671	12,271	3,330	3,103	2,861	2,678	299	1,400	—	—	—	—	—	14,740	92.7
Fall 1984............	13,704	12,304	3,440	3,145	2,819	2,599	300	1,400 [6]	—	—	—	—	—	14,725	93.1
Fall 1985............	13,750	12,388	3,439	3,230	2,866	2,550	303	1,362	—	—	—	—	—	14,888	92.4
Fall 1986............	13,669	12,333	3,256	3,215	2,954	2,601	308	1,336 [6]	—	—	—	—	—	14,824	92.2
Fall 1987............	13,323	12,076	3,143	3,020	2,936	2,681	296	1,247	—	—	—	—	—	14,502	91.9
Fall 1988............	12,893	11,687	3,106	2,895	2,749	2,650	288	1,206 [6]	—	—	—	—	—	14,023	91.9
Fall 1989............	12,524	11,393	3,141	2,868	2,629	2,473	281	1,131	303	284	267	273	5	13,536	92.5
Fall 1990............	12,476	11,341	3,169	2,896	2,612	2,381	284	1,136 [6]	—	—	—	—	—	13,329	93.6
Fall 1991............	12,675	11,544	3,313	2,915	2,645	2,392	278	1,131	309	286	272	260	4	13,491	94.0
Fall 1992............	12,862	11,737	3,352	3,027	2,656	2,431	272	1,125 [6]	—	—	—	—	—	13,775	93.4
Fall 1993............	13,081	11,963	3,487	3,050	2,751	2,424	250	1,118	312	286	266	249	5	14,096	92.8
Fall 1994............	13,354	12,215	3,604	3,131	2,748	2,488	244	1,138 [6]	—	—	—	—	—	14,637	91.2
Fall 1995............	13,665	12,502	3,704	3,237	2,826	2,487	247	1,163	325	304	276	255	2	15,013	91.0
Fall 1996............	14,027	12,849	3,801	3,323	2,930	2,586	208	1,178 [6]	—	—	—	—	—	15,443	90.8
Fall 1997............	14,241	13,056	3,819	3,376	2,972	2,673	216	1,185	326	306	283	266	4	15,769	90.3
Fall 1998............	14,407	13,195	3,856	3,382	3,021	2,722	214	1,212 [6]	—	—	—	—	—	15,829	91.0
Fall 1999............	14,600	13,371	3,935	3,415	3,034	2,782	205	1,229	336	313	295	280	5	16,007	91.2
Fall 2000............	14,781	13,517	3,963	3,491	3,083	2,803	177	1,264 [6]	—	—	—	—	—	16,144	91.6
Fall 2001............	15,032	13,736	4,012	3,528	3,174	2,863	159	1,296	350	333	316	293	3	16,280	92.3
Fall 2002............	15,374	14,069	4,105	3,584	3,229	2,990	161	1,306 [6]	—	—	—	—	—	16,506	93.1
Fall 2003............	15,651	14,339	4,190	3,675	3,277	3,046	150	1,311	351	334	317	304	5	16,694	93.8
Fall 2004............	15,949	14,618	4,281	3,750	3,369	3,094	122	1,331 [6]	—	—	—	—	—	17,054	93.5
Fall 2005............	16,258	14,909	4,287	3,866	3,454	3,180	121	1,349	356	348	326	315	3	17,358	93.7
Fall 2006............	16,441	15,081	4,260	3,882	3,551	3,277	110	1,360 [6]	—	—	—	—	—	17,549	93.7
Fall 2007............	16,451	15,086	4,200	3,863	3,557	3,375	92	1,364 [6]	357	347	334	324	2	17,597	93.5
Fall 2008............	16,322	14,980	4,123	3,822	3,548	3,400	87	1,342 [6]	—	—	—	—	—	17,395	93.8
Fall 2009............	16,261	14,952	4,080	3,809	3,541	3,432	90	1,309	333	330	324	319	3	17,232	94.4
Fall 2010............	16,159	14,860	4,008	3,800	3,533	3,472	42	1,299 [6]	—	—	—	—	—	17,064	94.7
Fall 2011............	16,040	14,749	3,957	3,751	3,546	3,452	43	1,291	330	325	318	315	4	16,865	95.1
Fall 2012............	16,028	14,753	3,975	3,730	3,528	3,477	43	1,275 [7]	—	—	—	—	—	16,714	95.9
Fall 2013[7].........	15,990	14,754	3,997	3,747	3,508	3,460	42	1,236	—	—	—	—	—	16,644	96.1
Fall 2014[7].........	16,026	14,826	4,052	3,767	3,524	3,440	42	1,200	—	—	—	—	—	—	—

—Not available.

[1]Includes a relatively small number of secondary ungraded students.
[2]Data for 1890 through 1950 are from the decennial censuses of population. Later data are Census Bureau estimates as of July 1 preceding the opening of the school year.
[3]Gross enrollment ratio based on school enrollment of all ages in grades 9 to 12 divided by the 14- to 17-year-old population. Differs from enrollment rates in other tables, which are based on the enrollment of persons in the given age group only.
[4]Data are for 1927–28.
[5]Data are for 1940–41.
[6]Estimated.
[7]Projected.
NOTE: Includes enrollment in public schools that are a part of state and local school systems and also in most private schools, both religiously affiliated and nonsectarian. The enrollment for ungraded public school students was estimated based on the secondary proportion of ungraded students in prior years. The enrollment of ungraded private school students was estimated based on the secondary proportion of ungraded students in individual high schools. Some data have been revised from previously published figures. Detail may not sum to totals because of rounding.
SOURCE: U.S. Department of Education, National Center for Education Statistics, *Annual Report of the Commissioner of Education*, 1890 through 1910; *Biennial Survey of Education in the United States*, 1919–20 through 1949–50; *Statistics of State School Systems*, 1951–52 through 1957–58; *Statistics of Public Elementary and Secondary School Systems*, 1959 through 1980; *Statistics of Nonpublic Elementary and Secondary Schools*, 1959 through 1980; Common Core of Data (CCD), "State Nonfiscal Survey of Public Elementary/Secondary Education," 1981–82 through 2012–13; Schools and Staffing Survey, Private School Data File, 1987–88; Private School Universe Survey (PSS), 1989–90 through 2011–12; National Elementary and Secondary Enrollment Projection Model, 1972 through 2024; and unpublished data. U.S. Department of Commerce, Census Bureau, Current Population Reports, Series P-25, Nos. 1000, 1022, 1045, 1057, 1059, 1092, and 1095; 2000 through 2009 Population Estimates, retrieved August 14, 2012, from http://www.census.gov/popest/data/national/asrh/2011/index.html; and 2010 through 2013 Population Estimates, retrieved October 3, 2014, from http://www.census.gov/popest/data/national/asrh/2013/2013-nat-res.html. (This table was prepared April 2015.)

Table 202.10. Enrollment of 3-, 4-, and 5-year-old children in preprimary programs, by age of child, level of program, control of program, and attendance status: Selected years, 1970 through 2013

[Standard errors appear in parentheses]

Age of child, level and control of program, and attendance status	1970	1980	1990	1995[1]	2000[1]	2003[1]	2005[1]	2010[1,2]	2011[1,2]	2012[1,2]	2013[1,2]
1	2	3	4	5	6	7	8	9	10	11	12
3 to 5 years old[3]											
Total population (in thousands)	10,949 (131.4)	9,284 (121.0)	11,207 (145.5)	12,518 (153.7)	11,858 (155.3)	12,204 (149.6)	12,134 (149.1)	12,949 (80.4)	12,965 (81.8)	12,259 (114.8)	12,166 (151.1)
Enrollment of 3- to 5-year-olds (in thousands)											
Total	4,104 (78.9)	4,878 (75.0)	6,659 (88.8)	7,739 (86.4)	7,592 (86.2)	7,921 (82.6)	7,801 (82.7)	8,246 (107.3)	8,260 (105.0)	7,883 (101.5)	7,878 (129.1)
Level											
Preschool	1,094 (48.9)	1,981 (61.5)	3,379 (83.0)	4,331 (84.6)	4,326 (86.5)	4,859 (84.7)	4,529 (83.4)	4,797 (94.5)	4,911 (98.5)	4,602 (98.5)	4,625 (115.4)
Kindergarten	3,010 (72.8)	2,897 (69.6)	3,280 (82.3)	3,408 (79.2)	3,266 (80.3)	3,062 (75.0)	3,272 (76.6)	3,449 (75.9)	3,349 (76.2)	3,281 (74.9)	3,254 (72.0)
Control											
Public	2,830 (71.4)	3,066 (70.6)	3,971 (86.5)	4,750 (86.3)	4,847 (88.3)	5,051 (85.2)	5,213 (85.4)	5,829 (105.5)	5,823 (100.6)	5,638 (94.4)	5,448 (104.8)
Private	1,274 (52.3)	1,812 (59.5)	2,688 (77.2)	2,989 (75.8)	2,745 (75.8)	2,870 (73.4)	2,588 (70.7)	2,417 (77.1)	2,438 (82.9)	2,245 (78.9)	2,430 (84.9)
Attendance status											
Full-day	698 (39.8)	1,551 (56.0)	2,577 (76.1)	3,689 (81.1)	4,008 (85.0)	4,429 (83.2)	4,548 (83.5)	4,813 (98.5)	4,884 (107.6)	4,760 (97.2)	4,753 (100.4)
Part-day	3,406 (75.5)	3,327 (72.0)	4,082 (87.0)	4,051 (83.2)	3,584 (82.5)	3,492 (78.2)	3,253 (76.4)	3,432 (88.5)	3,376 (87.0)	3,123 (85.1)	3,125 (100.4)
Percent of 3- to 5-year-olds enrolled											
Total	37.5 (0.72)	52.5 (0.81)	59.4 (0.79)	61.8 (0.69)	64.0 (0.73)	64.9 (0.68)	64.3 (0.68)	63.7 (0.66)	63.7 (0.72)	64.3 (0.85)	64.8 (0.78)
Full-day as a percent of total enrollment	17.0 (0.91)	31.8 (1.04)	38.7 (1.02)	47.7 (0.90)	52.8 (0.95)	55.9 (0.87)	58.3 (0.87)	58.4 (0.92)	59.1 (0.98)	60.4 (0.95)	60.3 (0.99)
3 and 4 years old											
Total population (in thousands)	7,135 (106.1)	6,215 (99.0)	7,415 (118.3)	8,294 (125.1)	7,869 (126.5)	8,336 (123.6)	8,179 (122.4)	8,850 (63.8)	8,765 (81.5)	8,014 (124.2)	8,101 (126.7)
3 years old	3,516 (74.4)	3,143 (70.4)	3,692 (83.5)	4,148 (88.5)	3,929 (89.4)	4,260 (88.4)	4,151 (87.2)	4,492 (59.4)	4,292 (96.0)	3,983 (218.7)	4,000 (128.8)
4 years old	3,620 (75.5)	3,072 (69.6)	3,723 (83.8)	4,145 (88.5)	3,940 (89.5)	4,076 (86.4)	4,028 (85.9)	4,358 (57.7)	4,473 (76.0)	4,031 (124.6)	4,101 (67.1)
Enrollment of 3- and 4-year-olds (in thousands)											
Total	1,461 (53.1)	2,280 (59.2)	3,292 (73.1)	4,043 (72.4)	4,097 (73.1)	4,590 (71.1)	4,383 (70.6)	4,706 (84.1)	4,597 (84.0)	4,289 (89.1)	4,449 (104.4)
Age											
3 years old	454 (31.0)	857 (38.9)	1,205 (48.7)	1,489 (49.1)	1,541 (50.5)	1,806 (50.5)	1,715 (49.7)	1,718 (59.5)	1,651 (67.8)	1,614 (97.2)	1,674 (87.2)
4 years old	1,007 (42.0)	1,423 (43.1)	2,087 (51.7)	2,553 (49.8)	2,556 (49.4)	2,785 (46.5)	2,668 (47.0)	2,988 (67.2)	2,946 (76.8)	2,675 (87.8)	2,775 (69.5)
Level											
Preschool	1,003 (45.8)	1,889 (56.5)	3,026 (72.3)	3,720 (72.0)	3,762 (73.1)	4,198 (71.5)	4,024 (70.8)	4,245 (85.3)	4,169 (84.4)	3,978 (89.1)	4,022 (106.3)
Kindergarten	458 (32.3)	391 (29.8)	266 (27.3)	322 (28.0)	335 (29.6)	392 (30.3)	359 (29.0)	462 (44.6)	428 (33.4)	312 (28.5)	427 (37.2)
Control											
Public	617 (37.0)	838 (42.0)	1,211 (64.4)	1,787 (59.5)	2,042 (64.2)	2,374 (64.5)	2,341 (64.0)	2,795 (82.2)	2,732 (69.5)	2,578 (75.9)	2,499 (80.2)
Private	844 (42.5)	1,441 (51.9)	2,081 (66.1)	2,256 (64.4)	2,055 (64.3)	2,216 (63.2)	2,042 (61.3)	1,911 (64.0)	1,865 (69.2)	1,711 (69.3)	1,950 (77.9)
Attendance status											
Full-day	373 (29.3)	788 (40.9)	1,163 (53.5)	1,858 (60.4)	1,944 (63.1)	2,380 (64.6)	2,233 (63.1)	2,265 (69.0)	2,320 (79.0)	2,174 (75.9)	2,250 (76.4)
Part-day	1,088 (47.3)	1,492 (52.5)	2,129 (66.6)	2,184 (63.8)	2,153 (65.3)	2,211 (63.1)	2,150 (62.4)	2,441 (76.5)	2,276 (68.5)	2,115 (68.7)	2,199 (83.1)
Percent of 3- and 4-year-olds enrolled											
Total	20.5 (1.65)	36.7 (1.57)	44.4 (1.48)	48.7 (1.25)	52.1 (1.29)	55.1 (1.15)	53.6 (1.18)	53.2 (0.89)	52.4 (0.90)	53.5 (1.11)	54.9 (1.00)
Age											
3 years old	12.9 (2.45)	27.3 (2.37)	32.6 (2.31)	35.9 (1.98)	39.2 (2.05)	42.4 (1.82)	41.3 (1.86)	38.2 (1.25)	38.5 (1.19)	40.5 (1.52)	41.8 (1.40)
4 years old	27.8 (2.20)	46.3 (2.06)	56.1 (1.86)	61.6 (1.53)	64.9 (1.56)	68.3 (1.38)	66.2 (1.43)	68.6 (1.25)	65.9 (1.28)	66.4 (1.31)	67.7 (1.37)
Full-day as a percent of total enrollment	25.5 (1.78)	34.5 (1.55)	35.3 (1.42)	46.0 (1.25)	47.4 (1.29)	51.8 (1.16)	50.9 (1.18)	48.1 (1.26)	50.5 (1.32)	50.7 (1.33)	50.6 (1.35)
5 years old[3]											
Total population (in thousands)	3,814 (77.5)	3,069 (69.6)	3,792 (84.6)	4,224 (89.3)	3,989 (90.1)	3,867 (84.2)	3,955 (85.1)	4,099 (57.9)	4,201 (69.1)	4,245 (77.0)	4,064 (69.1)
Enrollment of 5-year-olds (in thousands)[3]											
Total	2,643 (44.4)	2,598 (31.1)	3,367 (33.2)	3,697 (34.1)	3,495 (34.3)	3,331 (33.7)	3,418 (33.7)	3,540 (56.2)	3,663 (67.6)	3,594 (71.1)	3,429 (72.1)
Level											
Preschool	91 (14.7)	93 (14.8)	352 (30.5)	611 (36.3)	565 (36.3)	661 (36.7)	505 (32.9)	552 (35.8)	742 (46.5)	624 (45.1)	602 (42.0)
Kindergarten	2,552 (45.3)	2,505 (33.4)	3,015 (42.5)	3,086 (45.8)	2,931 (46.0)	2,670 (45.0)	2,913 (43.4)	2,987 (59.8)	2,921 (67.4)	2,970 (70.5)	2,827 (68.5)
Control											
Public	2,214 (47.5)	2,228 (38.5)	2,760 (46.8)	2,963 (47.3)	2,806 (47.6)	2,677 (45.0)	2,872 (43.9)	3,034 (57.8)	3,090 (71.2)	3,060 (70.8)	2,949 (68.2)
Private	429 (30.4)	370 (28.1)	607 (38.6)	733 (39.1)	690 (39.4)	654 (36.5)	546 (34.0)	506 (35.0)	573 (40.4)	534 (37.1)	480 (34.7)
Attendance status											
Full-day	326 (26.9)	763 (37.3)	1,414 (50.9)	1,830 (51.2)	2,065 (52.1)	2,050 (48.6)	2,316 (48.5)	2,548 (60.1)	2,564 (67.6)	2,585 (72.9)	2,503 (67.3)
Part-day	2,317 (47.0)	1,835 (42.3)	1,953 (52.6)	1,867 (51.3)	1,431 (50.0)	1,281 (45.8)	1,102 (44.2)	992 (44.6)	1,099 (54.3)	1,008 (50.4)	926 (46.2)
Percent of 5-year-olds enrolled											
Total	69.3 (1.16)	84.7 (1.01)	88.8 (0.88)	87.5 (0.81)	87.6 (0.86)	86.1 (0.87)	86.4 (0.85)	86.3 (0.92)	87.2 (0.85)	84.6 (0.94)	84.4 (1.04)
Full-day as a percent of total enrollment	12.3 (1.00)	29.4 (1.39)	42.0 (1.45)	49.5 (1.31)	59.1 (1.37)	61.5 (1.32)	67.7 (1.25)	72.0 (1.20)	70.0 (1.36)	71.9 (1.34)	73.0 (1.22)

[1] Beginning in 1994, preprimary enrollment data were collected using new procedures. Data may not be comparable to figures for earlier years.

[2] Beginning in 2010, standard errors were computed using replicate weights, which produced more precise values than the generalized variance function methodology used in prior years.

[3] Enrollment data for 5-year-olds include only those students in preprimary programs and do not include those enrolled in primary programs.

NOTE: Preprimary programs include kindergarten and preschool (or nursery school) programs. "Preschool," which was referred to as "nursery school" in previous versions of this table, is defined as a group or class that is organized to provide educational experiences for children during the year or years preceding kindergarten. Data are based on sample surveys of the civilian noninstitutional population. Detail may not sum to totals because of rounding. Some data have been revised from previously published figures.
SOURCE: U.S. Department of Commerce, Census Bureau, Current Population Survey (CPS), October, 1970 through 2013. (This table was prepared August 2014.)

Table 202.20. Percentage of 3-, 4-, and 5-year-old children enrolled in preprimary programs, by attendance status, level of program, and selected child and family characteristics: 2013

[Standard errors appear in parentheses]

Selected child and family characteristics	Total 3- to 5-year-old population (in thousands)	Total enrollment (in thousands)	Percent of 3- to 5-year-old population enrolled							Percentage distribution of enrollment	
			Total	Preschool			Kindergarten			Full-day	Part-day
				Total	Full-day	Part-day	Total	Full-day	Part-day		
	2	3	4	5	6	7	8	9	10	11	12
Total	12,166 (151.1)	7,878 (129.1)	64.8 (0.78)	38.0 (0.74)	18.7 (0.56)	19.3 (0.64)	26.7 (0.62)	20.3 (0.62)	6.4 (0.37)	60.3 (0.99)	39.7 (0.99)
Sex											
Male	6,240 (122.3)	4,007 (86.4)	64.2 (1.13)	37.6 (0.96)	18.2 (0.80)	19.3 (0.90)	26.7 (0.84)	20.2 (0.84)	6.4 (0.49)	59.9 (1.38)	40.1 (1.38)
Female	5,925 (57.7)	3,871 (80.9)	65.3 (1.15)	38.5 (1.11)	19.3 (0.89)	19.2 (0.91)	26.8 (0.78)	20.5 (0.87)	6.4 (0.52)	60.8 (1.45)	39.2 (1.45)
Age of child											
3 and 4 years old	8,101 (126.7)	4,449 (104.4)	54.9 (1.00)	49.7 (1.01)	24.7 (0.87)	24.9 (0.84)	5.3 (0.47)	3.1 (0.36)	2.2 (0.31)	50.6 (1.35)	49.4 (1.35)
3 years old	4,000 (128.8)	1,674 (87.2)	41.8 (1.40)	40.1 (1.41)	20.2 (1.16)	19.8 (1.14)	1.8 (0.34)	0.8 ‡ (0.25)	1.0 (0.25)	50.3 (2.16)	49.7 (2.16)
4 years old	4,101 (67.1)	2,775 (69.5)	67.7 (1.37)	59.0 (1.45)	29.1 (1.29)	29.9 (1.25)	8.7 (0.81)	5.3 (0.64)	3.4 (0.58)	50.8 (1.73)	49.2 (1.73)
5 years old	4,064 (69.1)	3,429 (72.1)	84.4 (1.04)	14.8 (0.98)	6.8 (0.68)	8.0 (0.72)	69.6 (1.27)	54.8 (1.42)	14.8 (0.92)	73.0 (1.22)	27.0 (1.22)
Race/ethnicity of child											
White	6,028 (130.4)	4,033 (93.5)	66.9 (1.10)	41.5 (1.01)	18.4 (0.89)	23.1 (0.84)	25.4 (0.70)	19.6 (0.71)	5.8 (0.48)	56.8 (1.21)	43.2 (1.21)
Black	1,647 (54.1)	1,148 (51.6)	69.7 (1.98)	36.9 (2.01)	25.3 (1.63)	11.6 (1.53)	32.8 (1.91)	25.8 (1.72)	7.0 (1.18)	73.4 (2.28)	26.6 (2.28)
Hispanic	3,202 (48.8)	1,837 (55.6)	57.4 (1.49)	30.7 (1.91)	15.5 (1.29)	15.2 (1.32)	26.6 (1.54)	19.7 (1.34)	6.9 (0.78)	61.4 (2.17)	38.6 (2.17)
Asian	581 (31.4)	370 (26.9)	63.7 (3.28)	40.8 (3.31)	16.5 (2.59)	24.2 (2.66)	22.9 (2.66)	15.0 (2.14)	7.9 (1.73)	49.6 (3.87)	50.4 (3.87)
Native Hawaiian/Pacific Islander	‡ (†)	‡ (†)	‡ (†)	‡ (†)	‡ (†)	‡ (†)	‡ (†)	‡ (†)	‡ (†)	‡ (†)	‡ (†)
American Indian/Alaska Native	115 (20.0)	73 (15.0)	63.5 (8.59)	34.9 (7.80)	15.0 ! (5.82)	19.8 ! (7.70)	28.7 (6.41)	22.8 (6.76)	‡ (†)	59.6 (12.15)	40.4 ! (12.15)
Two or more races	563 (38.4)	402 (34.2)	71.4 (3.68)	44.0 (4.16)	25.5 (3.86)	18.5 (3.24)	27.4 (3.52)	20.3 (2.90)	7.1 ! (2.23)	64.2 (4.58)	35.8 (4.58)
Number of parents or guardians in household											
One parent or guardian	3,565 (97.6)	2,362 (81.5)	66.3 (1.54)	36.1 (1.45)	21.1 (1.21)	15.0 (1.12)	30.2 (1.32)	22.8 (1.19)	7.4 (0.85)	66.2 (1.76)	33.8 (1.76)
Two parents or guardians	8,601 (148.2)	5,516 (119.6)	64.1 (0.91)	38.8 (0.95)	17.8 (0.74)	21.0 (0.78)	25.3 (0.69)	19.3 (0.73)	6.0 (0.39)	57.8 (1.15)	42.2 (1.15)
Mother's current employment status[1]											
Employed	6,751 (135.9)	4,668 (109.4)	69.1 (1.01)	41.4 (1.00)	22.4 (0.93)	18.9 (0.80)	27.8 (0.98)	21.2 (0.94)	6.5 (0.52)	63.2 (1.25)	36.8 (1.25)
Unemployed	635 (51.2)	409 (37.7)	64.4 (3.26)	38.4 (3.15)	16.8 (2.27)	21.6 (2.84)	25.9 (3.27)	22.6 (3.09)	3.3 ! (1.26)	61.2 (4.24)	38.8 (4.24)
Not in the labor force	4,248 (124.9)	2,431 (96.5)	57.2 (1.46)	33.0 (1.30)	12.9 (0.96)	20.1 (1.09)	24.2 (1.12)	17.7 (1.06)	6.5 (0.66)	53.4 (1.86)	46.6 (1.86)
No mother in household	532 (41.0)	371 (36.4)	69.8 (4.17)	34.7 (3.61)	20.9 (3.41)	13.8 (2.87)	35.1 (3.38)	27.2 (3.33)	7.8 (2.06)	68.9 (4.43)	31.1 (4.43)
Father's current employment status[1]											
Employed	8,110 (137.2)	5,270 (106.5)	65.0 (0.97)	39.0 (0.91)	18.2 (0.72)	20.8 (0.82)	26.0 (0.74)	19.6 (0.79)	6.4 (0.41)	58.1 (1.21)	41.9 (1.21)
Unemployed	399 (42.9)	250 (29.6)	62.6 (4.14)	37.6 (4.44)	21.5 (3.75)	16.1 (3.18)	24.9 (4.00)	21.9 (3.88)	3.1 ! (1.35)	69.3 (5.04)	30.7 (5.04)
Not in the labor force	624 (47.5)	367 (35.0)	58.9 (3.77)	33.9 (3.61)	12.9 (2.70)	21.0 (3.11)	25.0 (3.30)	21.0 (3.05)	4.0 ! (1.23)	57.5 (4.95)	42.5 (4.95)
No father in household	3,033 (93.9)	1,991 (104.4)	65.6 (1.64)	36.3 (1.68)	21.1 (1.34)	15.2 (1.25)	29.3 (1.43)	22.0 (1.31)	7.3 (0.92)	65.7 (1.95)	34.3 (1.95)
Every parent or guardian employed[1]	6,679 (126.4)	4,672 (104.4)	70.0 (1.05)	41.2 (0.95)	22.8 (0.92)	18.4 (0.79)	28.7 (0.97)	22.1 (0.97)	6.7 (0.55)	64.1 (1.22)	35.9 (1.22)
No parent or guardian employed[1]	1,747 (78.3)	1,010 (62.1)	57.8 (2.34)	32.3 (2.22)	16.5 (1.67)	15.8 (1.59)	25.6 (2.02)	21.9 (2.01)	3.7 (0.86)	66.3 (2.77)	33.7 (2.77)
Highest educational attainment of parents or guardians[1]											
Less than high school	1,210 (67.8)	662 (47.1)	54.7 (2.68)	27.1 (2.41)	13.3 (1.82)	13.7 (1.72)	27.7 (2.39)	19.1 (1.86)	8.5 (1.55)	59.3 (3.38)	40.7 (3.38)
High school/GED	2,738 (99.6)	1,623 (83.9)	59.3 (1.78)	31.0 (1.73)	17.5 (1.44)	13.5 (1.14)	28.3 (1.53)	22.2 (1.40)	6.0 (0.82)	67.0 (1.94)	33.0 (1.94)
Vocational/technical or some college	2,124 (86.9)	1,316 (61.9)	62.0 (1.83)	35.0 (1.58)	16.7 (1.30)	18.2 (1.33)	27.0 (1.58)	21.3 (1.52)	5.7 (0.92)	61.4 (2.37)	38.6 (2.37)
Associate's degree	1,278 (76.5)	816 (58.3)	63.9 (2.43)	36.3 (2.39)	16.5 (2.08)	19.8 (1.89)	27.6 (2.06)	20.7 (1.95)	6.9 (1.11)	58.3 (2.94)	41.7 (2.94)
Bachelor's degree	2,665 (104.5)	1,853 (84.6)	69.5 (1.49)	44.7 (1.64)	20.1 (1.32)	24.6 (1.45)	24.8 (1.36)	19.2 (1.26)	5.6 (0.78)	56.6 (2.02)	43.4 (2.02)
Graduate or professional degree	2,151 (84.2)	1,607 (67.2)	74.7 (1.75)	48.8 (1.86)	24.9 (1.65)	23.8 (1.65)	25.9 (1.59)	18.8 (1.54)	7.2 (0.92)	58.5 (2.23)	41.5 (2.23)

†Not applicable.
‡Reporting standards not met. Either there are too few cases for a reliable estimate or the coefficient of variation (CV) is 50 percent or greater.
!Interpret data with caution. The coefficient of variation (CV) for this estimate is between 30 and 50 percent.
[1]Data pertain only to parents or guardians who live in the household with the child.

NOTE: Preprimary programs provide educational experiences for children and include kindergarten, preschool, and nursery school programs. Enrollment data for 5-year-olds include only those students in preprimary programs and do not include those enrolled in primary programs. Race categories exclude persons of Hispanic ethnicity. Data are based on sample surveys of the civilian noninstitutional population. Detail may not sum to totals because of rounding.
SOURCE: U.S. Department of Commerce, Census Bureau, Current Population Survey (CPS), October 2013. (This table was prepared August 2014.)

Table 202.30.   Number of children under 6 years old and not yet enrolled in kindergarten, percentage in center-based programs, average weekly hours in nonparental care, and percentage in various types of primary care arrangements, by selected child and family characteristics: 2012

[Standard errors appear in parentheses]

Selected child or family characteristic	Number of children, ages 0 to 5 (in thousands)	Percent in center-based programs[2]	Average hours per week in nonparental care[3]	Percentage distribution, by type of primary care arrangement[1]							
				Parental care only	Center-based care	Nonparental care					
						Nonrelative home-based care			Relative	Multiple arrangements[4]	
						Total	In another home	In child's home			
1	2	3	4	5	6	7	8	9	10	11	
Total children	21,674 (1.0)	34.3 (0.66)	30.0 (0.37)	39.6 (0.78)	28.2 (0.62)	11.1 (0.49)	7.8 (0.43)	3.4 (0.27)	19.6 (0.62)	1.4 (0.15)	
Age											
Under 1 year	4,794 (130.9)	11.0 (1.11)	29.1 (0.98)	54.1 (1.92)	9.1 (0.90)	11.6 (1.11)	7.2 (0.80)	4.4 (0.72)	24.1 (1.48)	1.2 ! (0.38)	
1 year old	4,468 (114.7)	17.9 (1.25)	31.0 (0.94)	49.3 (1.86)	15.4 (1.14)	13.3 (1.17)	10.0 (1.16)	3.3 (0.54)	21.0 (1.36)	1.0 (0.25)	
2 years old	4,167 (133.9)	26.5 (1.43)	32.2 (0.88)	42.6 (1.57)	20.4 (1.30)	14.1 (1.13)	10.2 (1.12)	4.0 (0.61)	21.3 (1.38)	1.5 (0.39)	
3 years old	3,674 (89.8)	48.8 (1.47)	29.7 (0.75)	30.5 (1.43)	40.0 (1.42)	9.4 (0.87)	6.3 (0.61)	3.1 (0.69)	18.5 (1.25)	1.6 (0.31)	
4 years old	3,508 (90.4)	70.6 (1.57)	28.5 (0.65)	19.8 (1.68)	58.4 (1.50)	6.6 (0.65)	4.8 (0.57)	1.8 (0.37)	13.2 (1.15)	1.9 (0.36)	
5 years old	1,062 (59.6)	68.3 (3.48)	29.7 (1.42)	18.5 (2.38)	58.4 (3.43)	9.0 (2.09)	6.7 (1.91)	2.3 ! (0.92)	12.1 (1.85)	2.0 ! (0.90)	
Race/ethnicity of child and poverty status of household[5]											
White	10,893 (99.5)	35.5 (0.90)	29.2 (0.38)	38.3 (0.95)	29.3 (0.84)	13.9 (0.78)	9.6 (0.72)	4.3 (0.33)	17.2 (0.73)	1.3 (0.20)	
Poor	1,544 (63.3)	16.7 (1.72)	27.7 (1.65)	62.5 (2.84)	14.3 (1.52)	6.0 (1.36)	4.1 ! (1.24)	2.0 ! (0.73)	16.8 (1.78)	0.4 ! (0.15)	
Near-poor	2,190 (82.6)	26.5 (1.83)	27.2 (1.20)	49.7 (2.35)	20.9 (1.72)	6.9 (0.91)	4.8 (0.73)	2.1 (0.57)	21.3 (1.79)	1.1 ! (0.37)	
Nonpoor	7,159 (69.5)	42.4 (1.14)	29.9 (0.45)	29.5 (1.18)	35.2 (1.03)	17.7 (1.05)	12.3 (0.99)	5.4 (0.47)	16.1 (0.82)	1.5 (0.27)	
Black	2,890 (#)	42.1 (2.28)	32.9 (1.21)	31.1 (2.46)	34.2 (2.39)	8.5 (1.66)	5.9 (1.29)	2.6 ! (1.07)	24.6 (1.94)	1.5 ! (0.50)	
Poor	1,245 (34.2)	34.5 (3.33)	34.4 (1.68)	39.1 (3.99)	26.7 (3.16)	7.7 ! (2.62)	4.7 ! (2.22)	‡ (†)	25.2 (2.98)	1.3 ! (0.51)	
Near-poor	729 (43.4)	44.0 (4.62)	33.4 (2.36)	29.2 (4.89)	36.3 (4.55)	8.2 (2.27)	7.2 ! (2.24)	‡ (†)	24.8 (3.93)	‡ (†)	
Nonpoor	916 (24.9)	51.0 (3.92)	31.0 (2.34)	21.8 (3.32)	42.8 (4.39)	10.0 ! (3.45)	6.5 ! (2.29)	‡ (†)	23.5 (3.34)	‡ (†)	
Hispanic	5,469 (1.0)	27.7 (1.15)	30.2 (0.80)	44.9 (1.62)	22.3 (1.13)	8.1 (0.97)	6.3 (0.71)	1.8 (0.54)	22.9 (1.58)	1.8 (0.44)	
Poor	1,914 (42.0)	21.6 (1.81)	26.3 (1.54)	54.6 (2.57)	17.7 (1.78)	4.1 (0.80)	3.5 (0.75)	‡ (†)	21.0 (2.40)	2.5 ! (0.94)	
Near-poor	1,575 (56.1)	24.3 (2.24)	31.5 (1.64)	47.1 (3.32)	20.0 (2.15)	7.7 (1.80)	6.1 (1.52)	‡ (†)	23.1 (2.47)	2.0 ! (0.68)	
Nonpoor	1,980 (39.7)	36.3 (2.52)	32.0 (1.06)	33.8 (2.76)	28.4 (2.24)	12.3 (1.87)	9.2 (1.47)	3.1 (0.93)	24.6 (2.71)	0.9 ! (0.34)	
Asian	1,030 (60.5)	37.3 (2.74)	28.8 (1.47)	44.9 (3.21)	32.9 (2.63)	5.2 (1.11)	3.1 (0.83)	2.1 ! (0.80)	15.7 (1.95)	1.3 ! (0.44)	
Other[6]	1,393 (80.8)	31.5 (2.31)	29.1 (1.14)	42.9 (2.84)	26.9 (2.28)	11.1 (1.62)	6.5 (1.25)	4.7 (1.02)	18.1 (1.88)	1.0 ! (0.39)	
Number of parents in the household[7]											
Two parents	15,428 (139.0)	33.4 (0.73)	28.3 (0.36)	41.6 (0.87)	28.6 (0.68)	11.8 (0.61)	8.3 (0.55)	3.5 (0.27)	16.5 (0.68)	1.4 (0.18)	
One parent	5,629 (131.2)	36.0 (1.36)	33.1 (0.79)	35.5 (1.55)	27.5 (1.31)	9.8 (1.00)	6.8 (0.84)	3.0 (0.62)	25.7 (1.36)	1.5 (0.31)	
Mother in household											
Yes	19,989 (91.0)	33.9 (0.70)	29.6 (0.37)	40.0 (0.84)	28.3 (0.62)	11.4 (0.51)	8.2 (0.47)	3.2 (0.24)	18.9 (0.63)	1.4 (0.16)	
No	1,685 (91.0)	38.4 (2.65)	34.3 (1.68)	34.6 (2.74)	27.6 (2.38)	8.0 (1.93)	3.2 ! (1.00)	4.9 ! (1.68)	27.6 (2.85)	2.2 ! (0.69)	
Mother's employment status[8]											
Currently employed	10,801 (136.5)	43.1 (1.06)	32.2 (0.38)	17.9 (0.94)	34.9 (0.93)	18.1 (0.87)	13.7 (0.78)	4.4 (0.40)	26.9 (0.98)	2.2 (0.29)	
35 or more hours per week	7,615 (148.0)	44.7 (1.25)	35.1 (0.44)	15.2 (1.13)	36.3 (1.13)	19.2 (0.99)	15.0 (0.93)	4.2 (0.46)	26.8 (1.14)	2.4 (0.38)	
Less than 35 hours per week	3,186 (102.7)	39.4 (1.79)	24.6 (0.67)	24.5 (1.59)	31.4 (1.58)	15.3 (1.41)	10.5 (1.35)	4.8 (0.74)	27.0 (1.45)	1.7 (0.40)	
Looking for work	1,478 (83.0)	26.8 (3.03)	29.4 (2.03)	55.1 (3.50)	22.2 (2.92)	3.8 ! (1.29)	2.4 ! (1.17)	1.4 ! (0.70)	18.5 (2.79)	‡ (†)	
Not in labor force	7,710 (130.4)	22.3 (0.93)	20.1 (0.70)	68.1 (1.15)	20.2 (0.90)	3.5 (0.40)	1.5 (0.32)	1.9 (0.33)	7.9 (0.77)	0.3 ! (0.12)	
Mother's highest education[8]											
Less than high school	2,991 (71.5)	20.5 (1.83)	28.9 (1.69)	56.4 (2.74)	17.8 (1.75)	6.4 (1.40)	4.8 (1.27)	1.6 ! (0.59)	17.8 (2.06)	1.6 ! (0.65)	
High school/GED	4,041 (96.1)	25.7 (1.75)	29.1 (1.11)	48.2 (2.24)	22.2 (1.68)	7.6 (1.32)	6.4 (1.26)	1.2 ! (0.39)	21.6 (1.68)	0.4 ! (0.16)	
Vocational/technical or some college	4,084 (104.5)	31.4 (1.31)	28.6 (0.76)	42.7 (1.47)	26.0 (1.37)	9.2 (0.94)	7.4 (0.74)	1.8 (0.44)	20.4 (1.35)	1.7 (0.36)	
Associate's degree	1,795 (80.2)	35.9 (2.30)	31.9 (1.14)	34.3 (2.49)	28.0 (2.04)	14.3 (1.96)	11.3 (1.85)	3.0 (0.77)	21.0 (2.04)	2.4 ! (0.77)	
Bachelor's degree	5,056 (102.6)	43.4 (1.39)	29.4 (0.53)	31.3 (1.34)	36.1 (1.33)	14.3 (0.93)	9.9 (0.82)	4.4 (0.50)	17.3 (1.04)	1.1 (0.24)	
Graduate/professional degree	2,022 (40.2)	49.7 (1.79)	31.0 (0.61)	21.2 (1.55)	41.2 (1.71)	21.1 (1.38)	11.2 (0.98)	9.8 (1.08)	14.7 (1.20)	1.8 (0.43)	
Language spoken most at home by mother[8]											
English	16,057 (127.9)	35.8 (0.83)	29.7 (0.35)	37.5 (0.91)	29.6 (0.75)	12.6 (0.63)	9.0 (0.57)	3.6 (0.26)	19.0 (0.67)	1.3 (0.15)	
Non-English	3,932 (108.8)	26.1 (1.44)	28.9 (1.05)	50.3 (2.03)	22.7 (1.39)	6.6 (0.94)	4.9 (0.80)	1.7 (0.44)	18.7 (1.88)	1.7 ! (0.53)	
Mother's age when first became parent[8]											
Less than 18	1,628 (86.3)	28.9 (2.94)	31.3 (1.81)	48.3 (2.95)	23.3 (2.80)	5.5 ! (1.81)	4.9 ! (1.79)	‡ (†)	21.8 (2.36)	1.1 ! (0.44)	
18 or 19	2,285 (110.7)	24.3 (2.03)	30.7 (1.49)	49.2 (2.78)	20.3 (1.92)	7.4 (1.64)	5.9 (1.25)	1.6 ! (0.59)	22.5 (2.18)	0.6 ! (0.26)	
20 or older	15,935 (142.3)	35.7 (0.78)	29.3 (0.39)	37.9 (0.89)	29.8 (0.68)	12.6 (0.58)	8.9 (0.53)	3.8 (0.29)	18.1 (0.60)	1.5 (0.19)	
Household income											
$20,000 or less	3,955 (#)	24.6 (1.40)	29.7 (0.98)	52.0 (1.92)	19.3 (1.21)	6.7 (1.00)	4.5 (0.88)	2.2 (0.58)	20.6 (1.47)	1.4 ! (0.45)	
$20,001 to $50,000	6,246 (1.0)	28.5 (1.20)	28.8 (0.80)	46.8 (1.46)	23.5 (1.18)	6.4 (0.62)	5.1 (0.54)	1.2 (0.28)	21.6 (1.18)	1.7 (0.29)	
$50,001 to $75,000	3,881 (#)	34.3 (1.75)	29.4 (0.94)	38.7 (2.00)	28.9 (1.61)	10.4 (1.14)	8.6 (1.03)	1.8 (0.44)	20.9 (1.22)	1.0 (0.26)	
$75,001 to $100,000	2,745 (#)	40.6 (1.86)	31.0 (0.98)	28.4 (1.89)	33.9 (1.73)	16.4 (1.66)	13.9 (1.64)	2.5 (0.63)	20.1 (1.73)	1.3 ! (0.46)	
Over $100,000	4,847 (#)	45.9 (1.49)	31.2 (0.57)	27.3 (1.66)	37.8 (1.37)	18.5 (1.20)	9.8 (0.90)	8.8 (0.86)	14.9 (1.17)	1.5 (0.31)	
Poverty status of household[5]											
Poor	5,213 (75.9)	23.7 (1.31)	29.0 (0.86)	53.2 (1.73)	19.5 (1.24)	5.7 (0.76)	3.9 (0.69)	1.7 (0.45)	20.3 (1.21)	1.3 (0.37)	
Near-poor	4,996 (96.6)	28.1 (1.41)	29.5 (0.92)	46.3 (1.66)	23.0 (1.29)	6.8 (0.80)	5.2 (0.68)	1.6 (0.35)	22.4 (1.26)	1.6 (0.31)	
Nonpoor	11,464 (56.5)	41.7 (0.96)	30.5 (0.44)	30.5 (1.02)	34.5 (0.83)	15.5 (0.78)	10.6 (0.69)	4.9 (0.41)	18.1 (0.82)	1.4 (0.20)	

See notes at end of table.

Table 202.30. Number of children under 6 years old and not yet enrolled in kindergarten, percentage in center-based programs, average weekly hours in nonparental care, and percentage in various types of primary care arrangements, by selected child and family characteristics: 2012—Continued

Selected child or family characteristic	Number of children, ages 0 to 5 (in thousands)		Percent in center-based programs[2]		Average hours per week in nonparental care[3]		Percentage distribution, by type of primary care arrangement[1]											
							Parental care only		Nonparental care									
									Center-based care		Nonrelative home-based care						Relative		Multiple arrangements[4]	
											Total		In another home		In child's home					
1	2		3		4		5		6		7		8		9		10		11	
Household size																				
2 or 3 persons	5,427	(96.1)	37.4	(1.13)	32.5	(0.60)	33.2	(1.33)	30.2	(1.08)	13.1	(0.79)	9.4	(0.66)	3.7	(0.51)	21.7	(0.95)	1.8	(0.26)
4 persons	7,435	(96.1)	38.0	(1.21)	28.5	(0.55)	36.1	(1.18)	32.2	(1.12)	12.6	(0.94)	9.4	(0.85)	3.2	(0.43)	18.3	(0.93)	0.9	(0.18)
5 persons	4,243	(107.2)	34.0	(1.46)	28.8	(0.91)	43.5	(1.72)	27.7	(1.29)	9.6	(1.22)	6.4	(1.03)	3.2	(0.58)	17.8	(1.40)	1.4	(0.41)
6 or more persons	4,569	(107.1)	24.7	(1.48)	30.5	(1.13)	49.4	(2.00)	19.9	(1.44)	7.8	(0.95)	4.5	(0.70)	3.3	(0.70)	21.0	(1.54)	1.9	(0.49)
Locale																				
City	7,165	(154.8)	34.3	(1.16)	30.4	(0.66)	38.3	(1.42)	28.3	(1.12)	11.3	(0.90)	7.1	(0.68)	4.3	(0.56)	20.5	(1.25)	1.5	(0.25)
Suburban	7,682	(173.4)	35.7	(1.18)	29.7	(0.56)	38.2	(1.23)	29.8	(1.12)	10.6	(0.68)	7.4	(0.61)	3.2	(0.38)	20.0	(0.95)	1.4	(0.29)
Town	2,208	(119.2)	29.4	(1.80)	29.5	(1.19)	45.1	(2.10)	23.4	(1.86)	10.0	(1.13)	7.1	(0.97)	2.9	(0.79)	19.6	(1.81)	2.0 !	(0.67)
Rural	4,619	(121.6)	34.0	(1.58)	30.1	(0.66)	41.4	(1.50)	27.7	(1.42)	12.2	(1.19)	9.8	(1.00)	2.5	(0.46)	17.6	(1.04)	1.1	(0.23)

†Not applicable.
#Rounds to zero.
!Interpret data with caution. The coefficient of variation (CV) for this estimate is between 30 and 50 percent.
‡Reporting standards not met. The coefficient of variation (CV) for this estimate is 50 percent or greater.
[1]A child's primary arrangement is the regular nonparental care arrangement or early childhood education program in which the child spent the most time per week.
[2]Center-based arrangements include day care centers, Head Start programs, preschools, prekindergartens, and other early childhood programs.
[3]Mean hours per week per child, among preschool children enrolled in any type of nonparental care arrangement. For children with more than one arrangement, the hours of each weekly arrangement were summed to calculate the total amount of time in child care per week.
[4]Children who spent an equal number of hours per week in multiple nonparental care arrangements.
[5]Poor children are those whose family incomes were below the Census Bureau's poverty threshold in the year prior to data collection; near-poor children are those whose family

incomes ranged from the poverty threshold to 199 percent of the poverty threshold; and non-poor children are those whose family incomes were at or above 200 percent of the poverty threshold. The poverty threshold is a dollar amount that varies depending on a family's size and composition and is updated annually to account for inflation. In 2011, for example, the poverty threshold for a family of four with two children was $22,811. Survey respondents are asked to select the range within which their income falls, rather than giving the exact amount of their income; therefore, the measure of poverty status is an approximation.
[6]Includes persons of all other races and Two or more races.
[7]Excludes children living apart from their parents.
[8]Excludes children living in households with no mother or female guardian present.
NOTE: Race categories exclude persons of Hispanic ethnicity. Detail may not sum to totals because of rounding.
SOURCE: U.S. Department of Education, National Center for Education Statistics, Early Childhood Program Participation Survey of the National Household Education Surveys Program (ECPP-NHES:2012). (This table was prepared April 2015.)

Table 202.35. Primary child care arrangements of 4- and 5-year-old children who are not yet enrolled in kindergarten, by selected child and family characteristics: Selected years, 1995 through 2012

[Standard errors appear in parentheses]

Year and primary child care arrangement	Total	Race/ethnicity					Poverty status[1]			Mother's highest education[2]				
		White	Black	Hispanic	Asian/Pacific Islander	Other[3]	Poor	Near-poor	Nonpoor	Less than high school	High school/GED	Vocational/technical or some college	Associate's degree	Bachelor's or higher degree
1	2	3	4	5	6	7	8	9	10	11	12	13	14	15
1995														
Percent of all children	100.0 (†)	69.2 (1.09)	14.8 (0.79)	10.8 (0.53)	2.4 (0.36)	2.9 (0.46)	25.9 (1.11)	22.5 (1.11)	51.7 (1.28)	12.3 (0.97)	35.3 (1.31)	21.7 (1.10)	7.8 (0.68)	22.9 (0.95)
Percent in all types of care	100.0 (†)	100.0 (†)	100.0 (†)	100.0 (†)	100.0 (†)	100.0 (†)	100.0 (†)	100.0 (†)	100.0 (†)	100.0 (†)	100.0 (†)	100.0 (†)	100.0 (†)	100.0 (†)
Parental care only	21.7 (1.09)	20.9 (1.27)	15.8 (3.24)	33.7 (2.55)	15.5! (5.61)	30.0 (7.78)	28.4 (3.03)	32.1 (2.52)	13.8 (1.16)	40.2 (3.32)	26.2 (2.11)	18.9 (2.16)	17.4 (2.87)	9.0 (1.51)
Nonparental care	78.3 (1.09)	79.1 (1.27)	84.2 (3.24)	66.3 (2.55)	84.5 (5.61)	70.0 (7.78)	71.6 (3.03)	67.9 (2.52)	86.2 (1.16)	59.8 (3.32)	73.8 (2.11)	81.1 (2.16)	82.6 (2.87)	91.0 (1.51)
Primary arrangement[4]														
Center-based care[5]	55.1 (1.08)	55.0 (1.38)	59.7 (4.21)	44.3 (2.69)	73.7 (7.32)	58.3 (9.02)	51.4 (3.10)	45.4 (2.73)	61.0 (1.72)	41.2 (3.88)	50.0 (2.07)	57.5 (1.85)	57.7 (4.30)	67.4 (2.58)
Nonrelative care	11.0 (0.86)	12.7 (1.02)	7.8 (1.71)	6.6 (1.72)	‡ (†)	‡ (†)	5.8 (1.18)	9.4 (1.27)	14.3 (1.25)	5.7 (1.69)	9.5 (1.15)	11.1 (1.64)	13.5 (3.15)	14.8 (1.94)
Relative care	10.8 (0.70)	10.0 (0.75)	14.2 (2.82)	14.7 (1.86)	7.1! (3.49)	‡ (†)	11.8 (1.94)	12.3 (1.59)	9.7 (0.93)	11.6 (2.61)	12.1 (0.94)	12.1 (1.87)	10.6 (2.74)	7.1 (1.20)
Multiple arrangements[6]	1.4! (0.48)	1.4! (0.48)	‡ (†)	‡ (†)	‡ (†)	‡ (†)	‡ (†)	0.8! (0.38)	1.2 (0.33)	‡ (†)	2.2! (0.93)	‡ (†)	‡ (†)	1.7! (0.60)
2001														
Percent of all children	100.0 (†)	62.6 (0.89)	14.5 (0.82)	17.1 (0.73)	2.2 (0.41)	3.7 (0.47)	23.6 (1.26)	20.6 (1.15)	55.8 (1.21)	10.2 (0.67)	32.7 (1.44)	23.8 (1.23)	7.0 (0.66)	26.3 (1.20)
Percent in all types of care	100.0 (†)	100.0 (†)	100.0 (†)	100.0 (†)	100.0 (†)	100.0 (†)	100.0 (†)	100.0 (†)	100.0 (†)	100.0 (†)	100.0 (†)	100.0 (†)	100.0 (†)	100.0 (†)
Parental care only	20.5 (1.00)	20.3 (1.32)	10.6 (2.45)	31.6 (2.35)	22.6! (7.97)	10.7! (4.34)	25.1 (2.69)	30.0 (2.60)	15.1 (1.35)	35.0 (3.90)	25.0 (2.28)	17.3 (1.98)	14.0 (3.86)	13.3 (1.94)
Nonparental care	79.5 (1.00)	79.7 (1.32)	89.4 (2.45)	68.4 (2.35)	77.4 (7.97)	89.3 (4.34)	74.9 (2.69)	70.0 (2.60)	84.9 (1.35)	65.0 (3.90)	75.0 (2.28)	82.7 (1.98)	86.0 (3.86)	86.7 (1.94)
Primary arrangement[4]														
Center-based care[5]	56.2 (1.17)	57.3 (1.48)	63.4 (3.66)	44.1 (2.42)	59.6 (9.47)	62.4 (6.73)	47.4 (3.00)	50.8 (2.33)	61.9 (1.74)	42.6 (3.71)	49.5 (2.64)	59.3 (2.74)	68.0 (4.08)	66.0 (2.68)
Nonrelative care	9.6 (0.72)	11.5 (1.03)	4.3! (1.70)	8.4 (1.59)	‡ (†)	8.5! (3.71)	5.2 (1.17)	8.3 (1.48)	12.0 (1.07)	7.0 (1.92)	8.6 (1.39)	8.3 (1.40)	9.7! (3.03)	13.1 (1.67)
Relative care	12.1 (0.95)	10.1 (0.99)	17.4 (3.64)	13.8 (1.98)	12.6! (5.47)	17.0! (5.95)	19.5 (3.28)	8.7 (2.02)	10.2 (0.95)	12.5 (3.10)	15.5 (2.02)	12.5 (1.79)	7.8 (2.32)	6.7 (1.26)
Multiple arrangements[6]	1.6 (0.40)	0.7! (0.32)	‡ (†)	2.1! (0.76)	‡ (†)	‡ (†)	2.9! (1.31)	‡ (†)	0.8! (0.24)	‡ (†)	1.3! (0.61)	2.6! (1.27)	‡ (†)	0.9! (0.40)
2005														
Percent of all children	100.0 (†)	57.9 (1.14)	14.1 (1.02)	19.1 (0.94)	3.2 (0.58)	5.7 (0.65)	22.2 (1.15)	25.9 (1.48)	51.9 (1.42)	9.3 (0.89)	31.6 (1.61)	20.7 (1.44)	7.4 (0.68)	31.1 (1.25)
Percent in all types of care	100.0 (†)	100.0 (†)	100.0 (†)	100.0 (†)	100.0 (†)	100.0 (†)	100.0 (†)	100.0 (†)	100.0 (†)	100.0 (†)	100.0 (†)	100.0 (†)	100.0 (†)	100.0 (†)
Parental care only	21.1 (1.37)	19.3 (1.69)	13.8 (3.72)	32.6 (2.91)	14.7! (5.84)	21.2 (6.06)	25.8 (3.40)	29.7 (2.77)	14.7 (1.60)	36.2 (4.03)	27.4 (3.35)	22.5 (2.94)	14.7 (3.87)	11.2 (1.57)
Nonparental care	78.9 (1.37)	80.7 (1.69)	86.2 (3.72)	67.4 (2.91)	85.3 (5.84)	78.8 (6.06)	74.2 (3.40)	70.3 (2.77)	85.3 (1.60)	63.8 (4.03)	72.6 (3.35)	77.5 (2.94)	85.3 (3.87)	88.8 (1.57)
Primary arrangement[4]														
Center-based care[5]	59.2 (1.34)	60.2 (1.86)	66.1 (4.75)	49.7 (3.00)	70.2 (8.60)	57.5 (6.98)	51.8 (3.98)	48.4 (3.21)	67.7 (1.96)	50.6 (3.84)	48.1 (3.15)	57.1 (3.02)	65.7 (5.07)	72.4 (2.17)
Nonrelative care	5.5 (0.89)	7.3 (1.29)	2.6! (1.14)	3.2 (0.80)	3.6! (1.70)	‡ (†)	4.7! (2.14)	3.0 (0.75)	7.1 (1.26)	‡ (†)	5.1 (1.64)	5.1 (1.48)	9.5 (2.63)	6.1 (1.52)
Relative care	12.0 (1.16)	10.7 (1.20)	15.7! (4.72)	13.6 (2.22)	12.0! (4.59)	‡ (†)	16.0 (3.18)	15.1 (2.98)	8.8 (1.12)	9.6! (3.27)	15.9 (2.42)	13.9 (2.62)	6.5! (2.68)	8.8 (1.52)
Multiple arrangements[6]	2.2 (0.44)	2.4 (0.51)	1.8! (0.86)	0.9! (0.40)	‡ (†)	‡ (†)	‡ (†)	3.8 (1.07)	1.7 (0.38)	‡ (†)	3.0! (0.94)	1.5! (0.66)	3.5! (1.73)	1.5 (0.44)
2012														
Percent of all children	100.0 (†)	50.6 (1.50)	14.6 (1.05)	23.9 (1.26)	5.2 (0.55)	5.7 (0.68)	22.9 (1.22)	23.6 (1.28)	53.5 (1.30)	16.9 (1.44)	21.3 (1.17)	21.8 (1.28)	8.1 (0.84)	31.9 (1.16)
Percent in all types of care	100.0 (†)	100.0 (†)	100.0 (†)	100.0 (†)	100.0 (†)	100.0 (†)	100.0 (†)	100.0 (†)	100.0 (†)	100.0 (†)	100.0 (†)	100.0 (†)	100.0 (†)	100.0 (†)
Parental care only	19.5 (1.43)	18.5 (1.83)	15.3 (3.50)	24.3 (3.38)	19.4 (5.00)	18.9 (5.51)	29.0 (2.87)	23.9 (2.66)	13.5 (1.96)	35.1 (5.53)	23.5 (3.23)	22.0 (2.23)	15.0 (3.11)	7.7 (1.12)
Nonparental care	80.5 (1.43)	81.5 (1.83)	84.7 (3.50)	75.7 (3.38)	80.6 (5.00)	81.1 (5.51)	71.0 (2.87)	76.1 (2.66)	86.5 (1.96)	64.9 (5.53)	76.5 (3.23)	78.0 (2.23)	85.0 (3.11)	92.3 (1.12)
Primary arrangement[4]														
Center-based care[5]	58.4 (1.32)	58.5 (1.82)	65.3 (4.10)	52.9 (3.60)	67.0 (5.41)	55.6 (6.52)	49.4 (3.05)	51.4 (3.04)	65.4 (1.88)	45.9 (5.65)	51.9 (3.68)	54.2 (2.93)	63.4 (4.02)	71.1 (1.88)
Nonrelative care	7.2 (0.72)	9.7 (1.19)	2.4! (0.93)	5.5 (1.47)	‡ (†)	‡ (†)	5.2! (1.67)	5.9 (1.46)	8.6 (1.04)	‡ (†)	7.9 (1.98)	6.4 (1.33)	7.3! (2.24)	9.8 (1.36)
Relative care	13.0 (0.96)	11.3 (1.14)	16.3 (3.17)	14.4 (2.36)	10.2! (3.64)	15.4! (4.69)	14.9 (2.19)	15.1 (2.78)	11.0 (1.37)	12.3! (3.01)	16.4 (2.63)	15.2 (2.26)	9.7 (2.45)	9.3 (1.35)
Multiple arrangements[6]	1.9 (0.33)	1.9 (0.44)	‡ (†)	2.9! (1.04)	‡ (†)	‡ (†)	‡ (†)	3.2! (1.09)	1.5 (0.37)	‡ (†)	2.2 (0.61)	2.2 (0.63)	4.6! (1.72)	2.2 (0.63)

†Not applicable.

!Interpret data with caution. The coefficient of variation (CV) for this estimate is between 30 and 50 percent.

‡Reporting standards not met. Either there are too few cases for a reliable estimate or the coefficient of variation (CV) is 50 percent or greater.

[1]Poor children are those whose family incomes were below the Census Bureau's poverty threshold in the year prior to data collection; near-poor children are those whose family incomes ranged from the poverty threshold to 199 percent of the poverty threshold; and nonpoor children are those whose family incomes were at or above 200 percent of the poverty threshold. The poverty threshold is a dollar amount that varies depending on a family's size and composition and is updated annually to account for inflation. In 2011, for example, the poverty threshold for a family of four with two children was $22,811. Survey respondents are asked to select the range within which their income falls, rather than giving the exact amount of their income; therefore, the measure of poverty status is an approximation.

[2]Excludes children living in households with no mother or female guardian present.

[3]Includes persons of all other races and Two or more races.

[4]A child's primary arrangement is the regular nonparental care arrangement or early childhood education program in which the child spent the most time per week.

[5]Center-based arrangements include day care centers, Head Start programs, preschools, prekindergartens, and other early childhood programs.

[6]Refers to children who spent an equal number of hours per week in multiple nonparental care arrangements.

NOTE: While National Household Education Surveys Program (NHES) administrations prior to 2012 were administered via telephone with an interviewer, NHES:2012 used self-administered paper-and-pencil questionnaires that were mailed to respondents. Measurable differences in estimates between 2012 and prior years could reflect actual changes in the population, or the changes could be due to the mode change from telephone to mail. Race categories exclude persons of Hispanic ethnicity. Detail may not sum to totals because of rounding.
SOURCE: U.S. Department of Education, National Center for Education Statistics, Early Childhood Program Participation Survey of the National Household Education Surveys Program (ECPP-NHES:1995, 2001, 2005, and 2012). (This table was prepared November 2014.)

Table 202.40.   Child care arrangements of 3- to 5-year-old children who are not yet in kindergarten, by age and race/ethnicity: Selected years, 1991 through 2012

[Standard errors appear in parentheses]

Year and child care arrangement	Total	Age			Race/ethnicity				
		3 years old	4 years old	5 years old	White	Black	Hispanic	Asian/ Pacific Islander	Other[1]
1	2	3	4	5	6	7	8	9	10
1991									
All 3- to 5-year-olds									
In thousands	8,402 (40.9)	3,733 (7.1)	3,627 (14.6)	1,042 (38.6)	5,850 (59.9)	1,236 (41.0)	999 (31.3)	147 (19.0)	170 (29.9)
Percent	100.0 (†)	44.4 (0.21)	43.2 (0.24)	12.4 (0.40)	69.6 (0.67)	14.7 (0.47)	11.9 (0.37)	1.7 (0.23)	2.0 (0.35)
Percent in nonparental arrangements[2]	69.0 (0.80)	62.2 (1.19)	74.0 (1.05)	75.7 (2.10)	69.4 (0.87)	75.2 (2.02)	59.3 (2.35)	73.5 (4.94)	61.7 (6.08)
Relative care	16.9 (0.60)	16.2 (0.72)	18.0 (0.85)	15.6 (1.34)	14.8 (0.66)	24.1 (2.09)	19.6 (2.08)	22.5 (4.03)	16.6 ! (6.52)
Nonrelative care	14.8 (0.56)	14.8 (0.76)	14.7 (0.79)	14.9 (1.81)	17.3 (0.76)	7.9 (1.20)	9.4 (1.27)	11.2 (3.19)	12.9 (3.60)
Center-based programs[3]	52.8 (0.89)	42.3 (1.44)	60.4 (1.04)	63.9 (2.12)	54.0 (0.95)	58.3 (2.49)	38.8 (2.20)	56.4 (5.76)	49.9 (6.09)
Percent with parental care only	31.0 (0.80)	37.8 (1.19)	26.0 (1.05)	24.3 (2.10)	30.6 (0.87)	24.8 (2.02)	40.7 (2.35)	26.5 (4.94)	38.3 (6.08)
1995									
All 3- to 5-year-olds									
In thousands	9,222 (52.9)	4,123 (8.3)	4,061 (12.5)	1,038 (48.3)	6,334 (94.0)	1,389 (56.1)	1,042 (38.8)	208 (25.0)	249 (31.0)
Percent	100.0 (†)	44.7 (0.25)	44.0 (0.24)	11.3 (0.46)	68.7 (0.94)	15.1 (0.60)	11.3 (0.42)	2.3 (0.27)	2.7 (0.34)
Percent in nonparental arrangements[2]	74.1 (1.01)	68.0 (1.95)	77.9 (1.24)	83.8 (1.78)	74.8 (1.39)	80.1 (2.50)	61.6 (2.33)	80.1 (4.78)	72.2 (5.53)
Relative care	19.4 (0.64)	21.4 (1.23)	18.4 (0.95)	15.2 (2.14)	16.5 (0.84)	28.7 (2.78)	22.8 (2.01)	24.3 (5.61)	21.2 (4.73)
Nonrelative care	16.9 (0.84)	18.5 (1.35)	15.3 (1.03)	17.2 (2.19)	19.4 (1.04)	11.3 (1.65)	12.5 (1.64)	8.8 ! (3.96)	11.8 (3.40)
Center-based programs[3]	55.1 (0.97)	40.7 (1.55)	64.8 (1.45)	74.5 (2.35)	56.9 (1.44)	59.8 (3.19)	37.4 (2.15)	59.4 (6.51)	54.5 (6.96)
Percent with parental care only	25.9 (1.01)	32.0 (1.95)	22.1 (1.24)	16.2 (1.78)	25.2 (1.39)	19.9 (2.50)	38.4 (2.33)	19.9 (4.78)	27.8 (5.53)
1999									
All 3- to 5-year-olds									
In thousands	8,518 (139.7)	3,809 (79.1)	3,703 (79.9)	1,006 (54.2)	5,384 (77.4)	1,214 (59.2)	1,376 (52.3)	204 (25.5)	341 (33.5)
Percent	100.0 (†)	44.7 (0.93)	43.5 (0.93)	11.8 (0.64)	63.2 (0.91)	14.2 (0.69)	16.2 (0.61)	2.4 (0.30)	4.0 (0.39)
Percent in nonparental arrangements[2]	76.9 (0.72)	69.2 (1.42)	82.3 (0.99)	86.5 (1.78)	76.8 (0.91)	86.3 (1.97)	66.6 (2.04)	84.0 (5.25)	83.0 (4.28)
Relative care	22.8 (0.77)	24.3 (1.28)	22.0 (1.14)	20.2 (2.06)	18.7 (0.90)	33.4 (2.58)	26.5 (1.86)	22.5 ! (6.85)	34.4 (4.81)
Nonrelative care	16.1 (0.67)	16.3 (1.02)	15.9 (1.07)	16.1 (2.08)	19.4 (0.88)	7.4 (1.37)	12.7 (1.29)	9.1 ! (3.95)	11.2 (2.22)
Center-based programs[3]	59.7 (0.63)	45.7 (1.28)	69.6 (1.19)	76.5 (2.40)	60.0 (0.81)	73.2 (2.40)	44.2 (2.19)	61.1 (7.05)	68.9 (5.19)
Percent with parental care only	23.1 (0.72)	30.8 (1.42)	17.7 (0.99)	13.5 (1.78)	23.2 (0.91)	13.7 (1.97)	33.4 (2.04)	16.0 ! (5.25)	17.0 (4.28)
2001									
All 3- to 5-year-olds									
In thousands	8,551 (11.0)	3,795 (91.4)	3,861 (89.0)	896 (47.0)	5,313 (68.0)	1,251 (55.1)	1,506 (43.5)	202 (29.0)	280 (28.2)
Percent	100.0 (†)	44.4 (1.06)	45.1 (1.04)	10.5 (0.55)	62.1 (0.79)	14.6 (0.64)	17.6 (0.51)	2.4 (0.34)	3.3 (0.33)
Percent in nonparental arrangements[2]	73.9 (0.67)	66.2 (1.29)	79.6 (1.11)	82.0 (2.49)	74.7 (0.99)	84.9 (2.22)	61.0 (2.03)	69.9 (7.18)	80.9 (4.11)
Relative care	22.8 (0.89)	23.6 (1.39)	22.5 (1.33)	20.9 (2.66)	19.6 (1.01)	36.7 (3.42)	22.8 (1.89)	19.6 (4.42)	25.2 (5.16)
Nonrelative care	14.0 (0.65)	14.7 (1.17)	13.6 (0.95)	13.1 (2.13)	16.5 (0.98)	8.5 (1.65)	11.3 (1.43)	‡ (†)	14.0 (4.09)
Center-based programs[3]	56.4 (0.55)	42.8 (1.21)	65.9 (1.25)	73.0 (2.69)	59.1 (0.89)	63.1 (2.93)	39.9 (1.86)	63.4 (7.13)	60.6 (4.85)
Percent with parental care only	26.1 (0.67)	33.8 (1.29)	20.4 (1.11)	18.0 (2.49)	25.3 (0.99)	15.1 (2.22)	39.0 (2.03)	30.1 (7.18)	19.1 (4.11)
2005									
All 3- to 5-year-olds									
In thousands	9,066 (9.0)	4,070 (93.0)	3,873 (92.0)	1,123 (67.3)	5,177 (80.2)	1,233 (57.1)	1,822 (50.0)	282 (31.7)	552 (48.3)
Percent	100.0 (†)	44.9 (1.03)	42.7 (1.01)	12.4 (0.74)	57.1 (0.89)	13.6 (0.63)	20.1 (0.56)	3.1 (0.35)	6.1 (0.53)
Percent in nonparental arrangements[2]	73.7 (0.92)	66.6 (1.48)	79.4 (1.42)	79.6 (3.15)	75.9 (1.22)	80.5 (2.85)	62.0 (2.10)	79.8 (4.41)	72.9 (4.62)
Relative care	22.6 (1.02)	24.0 (1.44)	20.8 (1.56)	23.8 (3.17)	21.4 (1.34)	25.0 (3.42)	22.6 (1.79)	15.9 (4.68)	31.7 (4.49)
Nonrelative care	11.6 (0.73)	14.4 (1.12)	9.2 (1.03)	9.9 (2.00)	15.0 (1.13)	5.2 (1.31)	8.1 (1.36)	7.0 ! (3.34)	8.7 (2.41)
Center-based programs[3]	57.2 (0.83)	42.5 (1.67)	69.2 (1.36)	68.7 (3.51)	59.1 (1.32)	66.5 (3.41)	43.4 (2.10)	72.5 (4.99)	55.9 (4.89)
Percent with parental care only	26.3 (0.92)	33.4 (1.48)	20.6 (1.42)	20.4 (3.15)	24.1 (1.22)	19.5 (2.85)	38.0 (2.10)	20.2 (4.41)	27.1 (4.62)
2012									
All 3- to 5-year-olds									
In thousands	8,244 (85.1)	3,674 (89.8)	3,508 (90.4)	1,062 (59.6)	4,062 (97.4)	1,154 (63.4)	2,100 (76.1)	423 (32.7)	505 (44.4)
Percent	100.0 (†)	44.6 (0.97)	42.5 (1.01)	12.9 (0.72)	49.3 (1.12)	14.0 (0.75)	25.5 (0.84)	5.1 (0.38)	6.1 (0.55)
Percent in nonparental arrangements[2]	77.9 (1.02)	72.7 (1.32)	81.8 (1.62)	83.1 (2.32)	78.7 (1.41)	83.5 (2.97)	73.7 (2.24)	79.5 (3.76)	74.8 (4.21)
Relative care	26.2 (0.98)	27.9 (1.45)	25.1 (1.44)	24.6 (2.72)	24.0 (1.17)	30.2 (3.23)	29.3 (2.12)	21.7 (3.50)	26.6 (3.92)
Nonrelative care	13.3 (0.75)	15.4 (1.09)	11.0 (0.88)	13.9 (2.41)	16.1 (1.20)	11.4 (2.18)	10.8 (1.16)	5.9 (1.57)	12.1 (2.77)
Center-based programs[3]	60.6 (1.05)	48.8 (1.47)	70.6 (1.57)	68.3 (3.48)	63.0 (1.54)	68.0 (3.10)	51.5 (2.12)	67.8 (3.98)	55.5 (4.57)
Percent with parental care only	22.1 (1.02)	27.3 (1.32)	18.2 (1.62)	16.9 (2.32)	21.3 (1.41)	16.5 (2.97)	26.3 (2.24)	20.5 (3.76)	25.2 (4.21)

†Not applicable.

!Interpret data with caution. The coefficient of variation (CV) for this estimate is between 30 and 50 percent.

‡Reporting standards not met. The coefficient of variation (CV) for this estimate is 50 percent or greater.

[1]Includes persons of all other races and Two or more races.

[2]The total percentage of children who participated in nonparental arrangements. Counts each child only once, even if the child participated in more than one type of nonparental care.

[3]Center-based programs include day care centers, nursery schools, prekindergartens, preschools, and Head Start programs.

NOTE: While National Household Education Surveys Program (NHES) administrations prior to 2012 were administered via telephone with an interviewer, NHES:2012 used self-administered paper-and-pencil questionnaires that were mailed to respondents. Measurable differences in estimates between 2012 and prior years could reflect actual changes in the population, or the changes could be due to the mode change from telephone to mail. Race categories exclude persons of Hispanic ethnicity. Detail may not sum to totals because of rounding.

SOURCE: U.S. Department of Education, National Center for Education Statistics, Early Childhood Education Survey, Parent Survey, and Early Childhood Program Participation Survey of the National Household Education Surveys Program (ECE-NHES:1991; Parent-NHES:1999; ECPP-NHES:1995, 2001, 2005, and 2012). (This table was prepared September 2014.)

Table 202.50. Percentage distribution of children at about 2 and 4 years of age, by type of child care arrangement and selected child and family characteristics: 2003–04 and 2005–06

[Standard errors appear in parentheses]

Selected child and family characteristics	Children at about 2 years of age in 2003–04						Children at about 4 years of age in 2005–06							
	Percentage distribution of children[1]	No regular nonparental care	Home-based care[2] Relative care[3]	Nonrelative care[4]	Center-based care[5]	Multiple arrangements[6]	Percentage distribution of children[7]	No regular nonparental care	Home-based care Relative care[3]	Nonrelative care[4]	Center-based care[5] Total	Head Start	Other than Head Start	Multiple arrangements[6]
1	2	3	4	5	6	7	8	9	10	11	12	13	14	15
Total	100.0 (†)	50.5 (0.74)	18.5 (0.62)	14.6 (0.51)	15.8 (0.50)	0.5 (0.10)	100.0 (†)	20.0 (0.65)	13.1 (0.61)	7.6 (0.32)	57.4 (0.81)	12.6 (0.64)	44.8 (0.71)	1.9 (0.21)
Sex of child														
Male	51.2 (0.08)	50.0 (0.96)	19.1 (0.79)	14.3 (0.61)	16.3 (0.65)	0.3 (0.07)	51.2 (0.11)	19.3 (0.80)	13.1 (0.79)	7.5 (0.51)	58.0 (0.98)	12.9 (0.80)	45.1 (1.02)	2.1 (0.33)
Female	48.8 (0.08)	51.1 (1.01)	18.0 (0.78)	14.9 (0.71)	15.2 (0.63)	0.8 (0.19)	48.8 (0.11)	20.7 (0.90)	13.2 (0.86)	7.7 (0.52)	56.8 (1.02)	12.4 (0.74)	44.4 (0.92)	1.7 (0.20)
Race/ethnicity of child														
White	53.6 (0.54)	50.8 (1.08)	14.9 (0.88)	17.0 (0.74)	16.9 (0.74)	0.5 (0.13)	53.8 (0.59)	17.9 (0.98)	11.0 (0.74)	9.2 (0.49)	60.0 (1.04)	6.8 (0.61)	53.3 (1.00)	1.8 (0.28)
Black	13.7 (0.24)	37.3 (1.39)	25.8 (1.51)	12.0 (1.30)	24.2 (1.15)	0.8! (0.24)	13.8 (0.26)	16.3 (1.38)	13.9 (1.49)	4.4 (0.73)	62.1 (2.08)	25.1 (1.98)	37.0 (1.88)	3.3 (0.65)
Hispanic	25.3 (0.37)	57.5 (1.39)	21.4 (1.14)	11.5 (0.94)	9.2 (0.94)	† (†)	25.1 (0.42)	27.3 (1.36)	15.9 (1.14)	6.2 (0.78)	49.3 (1.57)	18.6 (1.23)	30.7 (1.64)	1.2 (0.29)
Asian	2.7 (0.09)	55.3 (2.17)	23.8 (1.44)	10.8 (1.05)	9.6 (1.39)	† (†)	2.6 (0.05)	17.1 (1.71)	16.1 (1.44)	3.6 (0.70)	60.9 (2.02)	5.5 (0.90)	55.3 (2.12)	2.3! (1.05)
Pacific Islander	0.2 (0.04)	73.2 (9.89)	23.8! (9.95)	‡ (†)	‡ (†)	‡ (†)	0.2 (0.05)	22.3! (6.82)	45.0! (14.27)	‡ (†)	19.9! (7.94)	‡ (†)	14.9! (6.47)	‡ (†)
American Indian/Alaska Native	0.5 (0.06)	57.3 (3.16)	17.4 (3.10)	11.6! (3.85)	13.8 (2.72)	† (†)	0.5 (0.05)	19.9 (2.40)	14.0 (2.06)	5.2 (1.45)	59.7 (3.57)	31.0 (4.71)	28.7 (5.61)	‡ (†)
Two or more races	4.0 (0.28)	46.3 (2.87)	20.0 (1.71)	13.2 (2.23)	19.3 (2.18)	1.1! (0.54)	4.0 (0.28)	17.9 (2.14)	17.6 (2.43)	9.1 (2.16)	53.6 (3.47)	11.1 (2.35)	42.5 (3.22)	1.8! (0.85)
Age of child														
22 or fewer months	1.9 (0.29)	58.6 (4.73)	21.0 (4.62)	11.0! (3.41)	9.4 (2.77)	† (†)	‡ (†)	‡ (†)	‡ (†)	‡ (†)	‡ (†)	‡ (†)	‡ (†)	‡ (†)
23 months	38.3 (1.22)	54.1 (1.16)	17.0 (0.93)	13.6 (0.91)	14.5 (0.85)	0.7 (0.16)	‡ (†)	‡ (†)	‡ (†)	‡ (†)	‡ (†)	‡ (†)	‡ (†)	‡ (†)
24 months	38.0 (0.89)	49.1 (1.02)	18.5 (0.95)	15.6 (0.80)	16.6 (0.87)	0.2! (0.10)	‡ (†)	‡ (†)	‡ (†)	‡ (†)	‡ (†)	‡ (†)	‡ (†)	‡ (†)
25 months	12.4 (0.46)	44.9 (1.91)	23.1 (1.44)	14.7 (1.41)	16.8 (1.44)	† (†)	‡ (†)	‡ (†)	‡ (†)	‡ (†)	‡ (†)	‡ (†)	‡ (†)	‡ (†)
26 or more months	9.4 (0.60)	47.7 (2.37)	18.6 (1.82)	14.8 (1.39)	17.9 (1.60)	1.1! (0.54)	‡ (†)	‡ (†)	‡ (†)	‡ (†)	‡ (†)	‡ (†)	‡ (†)	‡ (†)
Less than 48 months	‡ (†)	‡ (†)	‡ (†)	‡ (†)	‡ (†)	‡ (†)	16.4 (0.57)	27.3 (1.63)	13.9 (1.48)	8.7 (0.95)	47.9 (1.77)	10.6 (1.25)	37.3 (1.91)	2.2 (0.55)
48 to 52 months	‡ (†)	‡ (†)	‡ (†)	‡ (†)	‡ (†)	‡ (†)	38.1 (0.55)	19.9 (1.01)	13.0 (0.87)	8.3 (0.60)	56.8 (1.29)	12.0 (0.79)	44.8 (1.31)	2.0 (0.37)
53 to 57 months	‡ (†)	‡ (†)	‡ (†)	‡ (†)	‡ (†)	‡ (†)	36.5 (0.42)	16.5 (0.93)	13.1 (0.83)	6.7 (0.52)	62.2 (1.33)	14.4 (1.01)	47.8 (1.23)	1.5 (0.25)
58 or more months	‡ (†)	‡ (†)	‡ (†)	‡ (†)	‡ (†)	‡ (†)	9.0 (0.41)	21.1 (1.98)	12.1 (1.66)	6.4 (1.09)	57.8 (2.80)	12.0 (1.70)	45.8 (2.50)	2.7 (0.75)
Mother's employment status[8]														
Employed full-time	34.7 (0.73)	15.7 (0.89)	30.4 (1.10)	26.0 (0.86)	27.1 (0.96)	0.8 (0.21)	34.7 (0.77)	11.3 (0.96)	16.2 (0.91)	12.1 (0.77)	58.7 (1.56)	11.5 (1.03)	47.2 (1.29)	1.7 (0.27)
Employed part-time	20.2 (0.62)	35.4 (1.53)	26.4 (1.53)	20.5 (1.37)	16.7 (1.23)	1.0! (0.34)	20.3 (0.63)	16.4 (1.33)	14.1 (1.20)	9.1 (0.86)	57.3 (1.70)	8.7 (1.00)	48.6 (1.65)	3.1 (0.57)
Looking for work	6.3 (0.35)	71.1 (2.30)	11.5 (1.58)	3.8 (0.95)	13.4 (2.02)	† (†)	6.3 (0.36)	22.3 (2.33)	18.5 (2.33)	5.4 (1.23)	52.4 (2.83)	25.9 (2.87)	26.5 (2.33)	1.4! (0.56)
Not in labor force	38.4 (0.78)	86.8 (0.75)	4.8 (0.48)	3.0 (0.35)	5.4 (0.46)	† (†)	38.3 (0.38)	29.4 (0.97)	8.6 (0.63)	3.3 (0.38)	57.1 (0.96)	13.7 (0.80)	43.5 (1.10)	1.6 (0.32)
No mother in household	0.4 (0.09)	21.2! (7.28)	33.5 (8.60)	19.5! (9.29)	25.9! (8.01)	‡ (†)	0.4 (0.10)	11.0! (6.13)	36.2 (9.59)	‡ (†)	52.5 (9.42)	21.0! (8.49)	31.5 (8.19)	‡ (†)
Parents' highest level of education														
Less than high school	12.8 (0.36)	67.6 (1.98)	17.5 (1.45)	6.8 (1.08)	7.7 (0.98)	† (†)	10.5 (0.36)	34.2 (2.10)	16.4 (1.77)	3.7 (1.04)	43.5 (2.59)	22.4 (2.13)	21.1 (2.06)	2.1! (0.80)
High school completion	25.7 (0.46)	50.1 (1.47)	23.1 (1.27)	12.3 (0.97)	14.1 (0.87)	0.4! (0.15)	23.1 (0.57)	22.0 (1.24)	17.0 (1.20)	6.9 (0.69)	52.1 (1.87)	21.6 (1.41)	30.6 (1.49)	1.9 (0.34)
Some college/vocational	29.7 (0.48)	46.9 (1.51)	21.6 (1.22)	15.1 (0.92)	15.7 (0.94)	0.7! (0.21)	33.4 (0.64)	21.0 (1.24)	15.2 (0.95)	7.1 (0.56)	54.9 (1.41)	13.3 (0.99)	41.6 (1.26)	1.8 (0.33)
Bachelor's degree	16.9 (0.46)	48.6 (1.14)	14.4 (1.18)	17.8 (1.18)	18.6 (1.14)	0.7! (0.23)	16.8 (0.45)	16.0 (1.57)	8.4 (1.02)	8.2 (0.93)	65.6 (1.88)	3.2 (0.75)	62.4 (2.00)	1.8 (0.48)
Any graduate education	14.9 (0.35)	46.0 (1.91)	10.5 (1.05)	20.7 (1.57)	22.4 (1.49)	0.4 (0.16)	16.2 (0.37)	9.7 (0.83)	6.2 (0.90)	11.3 (1.16)	70.8 (1.57)	2.0 (0.52)	68.8 (1.67)	2.0 (0.52)
Poverty status[9]														
Below poverty threshold	23.9 (0.75)	61.8 (1.40)	18.0 (1.15)	7.8 (0.79)	11.7 (0.92)	0.7! (0.24)	24.8 (0.64)	27.5 (1.27)	15.1 (1.19)	4.4 (0.54)	51.0 (1.61)	26.3 (1.45)	24.7 (1.20)	2.0 (0.40)
At or above poverty threshold	76.1 (0.75)	47.0 (0.90)	18.7 (0.68)	16.7 (0.62)	17.1 (0.60)	0.5 (0.11)	75.2 (0.64)	17.5 (0.71)	12.5 (0.64)	8.6 (0.39)	59.5 (0.86)	8.1 (0.57)	51.4 (0.85)	1.9 (0.22)
Socioeconomic status[10]														
Lowest 20 percent	20.0 (0.48)	66.7 (1.43)	17.2 (1.20)	6.8 (0.75)	8.9 (0.72)	0.4! (0.18)	20.0 (0.52)	30.5 (1.31)	14.9 (1.33)	5.0 (0.69)	47.2 (1.84)	24.9 (1.58)	22.4 (1.47)	2.3 (0.58)
Middle 60 percent	60.0 (0.67)	48.8 (0.98)	21.8 (0.78)	15.1 (0.63)	15.8 (0.58)	0.6 (0.15)	60.0 (0.67)	19.7 (0.86)	15.1 (0.82)	7.4 (0.49)	56.0 (1.09)	12.4 (0.80)	43.6 (0.90)	1.8 (0.23)
Highest 20 percent	20.0 (0.48)	45.9 (1.75)	10.2 (0.85)	20.8 (1.52)	22.6 (1.45)	0.5! (0.21)	20.0 (0.48)	10.4 (0.93)	5.4 (0.73)	10.7 (0.91)	71.6 (1.39)	1.0 (0.23)	70.5 (1.42)	1.9 (0.42)

†Not applicable.
!Interpret data with caution. The coefficient of variation (CV) for this estimate is between 30 and 50 percent.
‡Reporting standards not met. Either there are too few cases for a reliable estimate or the coefficient of variation (CV) is 50 percent or greater.
[1]Distribution of weighted Early Childhood Longitudinal Study, Birth Cohort survey population with data on primary care arrangements.
[2]Primary type of care arrangement is the type of nonparental care in which the child spent the most hours.
[3]Care provided in the child's home or in another private home by a relative (excluding parents).
[4]Care provided in the child's home or in another private home by a person unrelated to the child.
[5]Care provided in places such as early learning centers, nursery schools, and preschools.
[6]Children who spent an equal amount of time in each of two or more arrangements.
[7]Distribution of weighted Early Childhood Longitudinal Study, Birth Cohort survey population between 44 and 65 months of age with data on primary care arrangements.

[8]Mothers who reported working at least 35 hours per week are defined as employed full time, while those who reported working less than 35 hours per week are defined as employed part time. Those neither employed nor looking for work are not in the labor force.
[9]Poverty status based on Census Bureau guidelines from 2002 (for 2-year-olds in 2003–04) and 2005 (for 4-year-olds in 2005–06), which identify a dollar amount determined to meet a household's needs, given its size and composition. In 2002, a family of four was considered to live below the poverty threshold if its income was less than or equal to $18,392 (in current dollars).
[10]Socioeconomic status (SES) was measured by a composite score on parental education and occupations, and family income.
NOTE: Data are based on a representative sample of children born in 2001. Estimates for children at about 2 years of age weighted by W2R0. Estimates for children at about 4 years of age weighted by W3R0. Race categories exclude persons of Hispanic ethnicity. Detail may not sum to totals because of rounding and suppression of cells that do not meet standards. Some data have been revised from previously published figures.
SOURCE: U.S. Department of Education, National Center for Education Statistics, Early Childhood Longitudinal Study, Birth Cohort, 9-month–Kindergarten Restricted-Use Data File and Electronic Codebook. (This table was prepared December 2010.)

Table 202.60. Percentage distribution of quality rating of child care arrangements of children at about 4 years of age, by type of arrangement and selected child and family characteristics: 2005–06

Selected child and family characteristics	Quality rating of primary type of child care arrangement[1] — Home-based relative and nonrelative care[2,3] Low	Medium	High	Head Start and other center-based programs[4] Low	Medium	High	All center-based programs — Head Start[4] Low	Medium	High	Center-based care other than Head Start[4,5] Low	Medium	High
1	2	3	4	5	6	7	8	9	10	11	12	13
Total	42.6 (4.01)	47.9 (4.22)	9.5 (2.37)	9.5 (1.40)	55.9 (2.44)	34.6 (2.58)	3.2 (0.78)	56.7 (3.27)	40.1 (3.34)	11.6 (1.74)	55.6 (3.05)	32.8 (3.10)
Sex of child												
Male	45.5 (5.48)	44.1 (5.58)	10.4! (3.88)	6.3 (1.47)	53.5 (3.35)	40.2 (3.29)	2.2! (0.97)	56.5 (3.94)	41.2 (3.95)	7.7 (1.82)	52.4 (4.07)	39.8 (4.08)
Female	39.3 (5.23)	52.2 (5.83)	8.5 (2.45)	12.7 (2.32)	58.2 (3.33)	29.1 (3.24)	4.3 (1.14)	56.8 (4.83)	38.9 (4.88)	15.2 (2.84)	58.7 (3.98)	26.2 (3.71)
Race/ethnicity of child												
White	29.9 (4.72)	55.3 (5.34)	14.9 (4.09)	9.3 (1.79)	54.7 (3.77)	36.0 (3.69)	4.0! (1.93)	47.5 (8.27)	48.5 (8.29)	10.2 (1.95)	55.8 (4.01)	34.0 (3.84)
Black	52.8 (8.64)	47.2 (8.64)	‡ (†)	14.8 (3.75)	59.9 (4.55)	25.3 (3.91)	6.9 (1.60)	67.0 (4.49)	26.1 (4.70)	20.8 (6.22)	54.6 (6.76)	24.6 (4.24)
Hispanic	62.5 (8.53)	33.4 (8.03)	‡ (†)	7.2! (2.79)	52.9 (4.25)	39.8 (4.77)	‡ (†)	56.2 (5.54)	43.4 (5.47)	11.7! (4.47)	50.8 (6.82)	37.6 (7.31)
Asian	‡ (†)	‡ (†)	‡ (†)	‡ (†)	61.7 (8.22)	32.8 (8.15)	‡ (†)	‡ (†)	‡ (†)	‡ (†)	64.8 (8.25)	29.3 (8.02)
Pacific Islander	‡ (†)	‡ (†)	‡ (†)	‡ (†)	‡ (†)	‡ (†)	‡ (†)	‡ (†)	‡ (†)	‡ (†)	‡ (†)	‡ (†)
American Indian/Alaska Native	‡ (†)	‡ (†)	‡ (†)	‡ (†)	73.5 (7.69)	23.5 (7.02)	‡ (†)	‡ (†)	‡ (†)	‡ (†)	68.4 (8.83)	19.7! (6.84)
Two or more races	‡ (†)	‡ (†)	‡ (†)	‡ (†)	66.0 (7.63)	25.5 (6.61)	‡ (†)	59.7 (10.79)	40.3 (10.79)	‡ (†)	‡ (†)	‡ (†)
Age of child												
Less than 48 months	31.8 (7.35)	64.3 (7.24)	‡ (†)	9.8 (2.35)	57.1 (5.33)	33.1 (5.51)	‡ (†)	62.3 (8.56)	35.3 (8.44)	12.5 (3.49)	55.2 (7.31)	32.3 (7.22)
48 to 52 months	40.3 (6.19)	47.2 (6.86)	12.5! (4.19)	12.3 (2.59)	54.9 (4.12)	32.8 (3.72)	‡ (†)	55.5 (6.29)	43.6 (6.31)	16.2 (3.23)	54.7 (5.00)	29.1 (4.37)
53 to 57 months	46.6 (6.49)	42.5 (6.69)	10.9 (3.14)	7.3 (1.67)	56.5 (3.22)	36.2 (3.36)	3.8! (1.34)	57.5 (4.02)	38.7 (4.06)	8.4 (2.08)	56.2 (4.22)	35.4 (4.29)
58 or more months	‡ (†)	‡ (†)	‡ (†)	‡ (†)	55.1 (4.81)	37.7 (4.57)	‡ (†)	46.7 (13.27)	38.4 (11.42)	‡ (†)	57.5 (5.77)	37.5 (5.88)
Mother's employment status[6]												
Full-time (35 hours or more)	36.6 (4.34)	56.6 (4.50)	6.9! (2.52)	14.9 (2.84)	55.5 (3.74)	29.6 (3.67)	4.9 (1.16)	47.7 (5.16)	47.4 (5.53)	17.6 (3.47)	57.6 (4.47)	24.8 (3.72)
Part-time (less than 35 hours)	48.9 (7.47)	35.1 (7.08)	16.0 (4.61)	5.7! (1.80)	60.9 (4.64)	33.4 (4.72)	‡ (†)	59.8 (8.26)	37.0 (7.97)	6.5! (2.17)	61.2 (6.14)	32.3 (5.97)
Looking for work	‡ (†)	‡ (†)	‡ (†)	14.0! (5.19)	53.4 (6.27)	32.5 (6.64)	‡ (†)	73.1 (8.42)	24.5! (8.27)	22.4! (8.52)	39.2 (8.58)	38.4 (9.45)
Not in labor force	‡ (†)	‡ (†)	‡ (†)	3.5! (1.31)	53.3 (4.81)	43.2 (4.98)	‡ (†)	59.0 (5.59)	39.2 (5.61)	4.2! (1.73)	51.2 (6.71)	44.7 (7.02)
No mother in household	‡ (†)	‡ (†)	‡ (†)	‡ (†)	‡ (†)	‡ (†)	‡ (†)	‡ (†)	‡ (†)	‡ (†)	‡ (†)	‡ (†)
Parents' highest level of education												
Less than high school	62.0 (6.10)	‡ (†)	‡ (†)	12.6! (4.52)	59.6 (7.01)	27.8 (5.88)	5.4 (1.47)	57.4 (7.36)	40.4 (7.28)	20.8! (7.99)	61.3 (10.74)	17.9! (7.65)
High school completion	32.8 (6.20)	‡ (†)	‡ (†)	6.3 (1.81)	49.2 (3.34)	44.5 (4.07)	‡ (†)	51.8 (6.12)	42.9 (6.28)	6.7! (2.48)	47.9 (4.55)	45.4 (5.62)
Some college/vocational	41.7 (6.68)	50.9 (6.75)	7.4! (3.39)	15.3 (2.78)	59.0 (2.92)	25.7 (2.68)	‡ (†)	62.0 (4.22)	35.3 (4.12)	21.5 (3.69)	57.5 (3.97)	21.0 (3.62)
Bachelor's degree	29.9 (8.51)	62.1 (8.63)	‡ (†)	6.7! (2.43)	59.8 (6.64)	33.4 (6.78)	‡ (†)	‡ (†)	‡ (†)	7.3! (2.64)	60.2 (7.18)	32.6 (7.32)
Any graduate education	‡ (†)	61.3 (8.63)	28.3 (7.99)	‡ (†)	53.6 (7.44)	41.4 (7.48)	‡ (†)	‡ (†)	‡ (†)	‡ (†)	54.5 (7.46)	40.2 (7.46)
Poverty status[7]												
Below poverty threshold	68.1 (6.76)	28.3 (6.86)	‡ (†)	9.0 (2.36)	59.2 (3.18)	31.8 (3.48)	2.6! (1.10)	57.8 (4.16)	39.7 (4.35)	15.0 (4.14)	60.6 (5.68)	24.4 (5.14)
At or above poverty threshold	35.8 (4.32)	53.2 (4.79)	11.1 (2.70)	9.7 (1.46)	54.8 (3.18)	35.6 (3.30)	3.8! (1.35)	55.6 (4.74)	40.5 (4.70)	10.8 (1.73)	54.6 (3.61)	34.6 (3.73)
Socioeconomic status[8]												
Lowest 20 percent	71.2 (7.12)	26.4 (7.02)	‡ (†)	6.7! (2.21)	58.6 (4.39)	34.7 (4.46)	3.5! (1.27)	53.0 (5.31)	43.6 (5.65)	9.8! (3.98)	63.9 (7.34)	26.4 (6.60)
Middle 60 percent	43.3 (5.26)	49.7 (5.50)	7.0! (2.57)	11.2 (1.83)	56.5 (2.69)	32.3 (2.68)	3.2! (1.22)	59.7 (4.07)	37.1 (4.05)	14.0 (2.28)	55.4 (3.37)	30.6 (3.37)
Highest 20 percent	‡ (†)	66.3 (7.41)	25.9 (6.85)	7.3! (2.54)	52.2 (6.27)	40.5 (6.19)	‡ (†)	‡ (†)	‡ (†)	7.5! (2.61)	52.7 (6.33)	39.8 (6.21)

†Not applicable.
!Interpret data with caution. The coefficient of variation (CV) for this estimate is between 30 and 50 percent.
‡Reporting standards not met. Either there are too few cases for a reliable estimate or the coefficient of variation (CV) is 50 percent or greater.
[1]Primary type of care arrangement is the type of nonparental care in which the child spent the most hours.
[2]Care provided in the child's home or in another private home by a relative (excluding parents) or by a person unrelated to the child.
[3]Quality rating based on the Family Day Care Rating Scale (FDCRS). Low quality = score of 1 but less than 3. Medium quality = score of 3 but less than 5. High quality = score of 5 to 7.
[4]Quality rating based on the Early Childhood Environment Rating Scale (ECERS). Low quality = score of 1 but less than 3. Medium quality = score of 3 but less than 5. High quality = score of 5 to 7.
[5]Care provided in places such as early learning centers, nursery schools, and preschools, not classified as Head Start.
[6]Mothers who reported working at least 35 hours per week are defined as employed full time, while those who reported working less than 35 hours per week are defined as employed part time. Those neither employed nor looking for work are not in the labor force.

[7]Poverty status based on Census Bureau guidelines from 2002, which identify a dollar amount determined to meet a household's needs, given its size and composition. In 2002, a family of four was considered to live below the poverty threshold if its income was less than or equal to $18,392 (in current dollars).
[8]Socioeconomic status (SES) was measured by a composite score based on parental education and occupations, and family income.
NOTE: Estimates weighted by W33P0. Estimates pertain to children assessed between 44 months and 65 months of age. Rating is for child's primary type of care arrangement, which was the type of nonparental care in which the child spent the most hours. Children who were primarily cared for by parents or in multiple arrangements are not included in this table. Ratings of care arrangement quality using both the FDCRS and ECERS scales were based on interviewer observations of children's interactions with adults and peers, children's exposure to materials and activities, the extent to which and the manner in which routine care needs were met, and the furnishings and displays in the classroom. The FDCRS and ECERS metrics are designed to be equivalent. Race categories exclude persons of Hispanic ethnicity. Detail may not sum to totals because of rounding and suppression of cells that do not meet standards.
SOURCE: U.S. Department of Education, National Center for Education Statistics, Early Childhood Longitudinal Study, Birth Cohort, Longitudinal 9-month–Kindergarten Restricted-Use Data File. (This table was prepared January 2013.)

Table 202.65. Percentage distribution of first-time kindergartners, by primary type of child care arrangement during the year prior to kindergarten entry and selected child, family, and school characteristics: 2010–11

[Standard errors appear in parentheses]

Selected child, family, or school characteristic	Total, all children		No regular nonparental care	Total, any regular nonparental care	Home-based care — Relative care	Home-based care — Nonrelative care	Center-based care	Multiple arrangements
1	2		3	4	5	6	7	8
Total....................................	100.0	(†)	20.9 (0.82)	79.1 (0.82)	14.9 (0.46)	6.3 (0.36)	55.3 (0.97)	2.5 (0.18)
Sex of child								
Male......................................	100.0	(†)	21.0 (0.91)	79.0 (0.91)	14.3 (0.51)	6.6 (0.38)	55.6 (1.01)	2.6 (0.23)
Female...................................	100.0	(†)	20.8 (0.88)	79.2 (0.88)	15.6 (0.67)	6.0 (0.46)	55.1 (1.13)	2.4 (0.25)
Age of child at kindergarten entry, fall 2010								
Less than 5 years old................	100.0	(†)	19.5 (1.88)	80.5 (1.88)	14.4 (1.39)	4.3 (1.19)	59.3 (2.53)	2.5 (0.53)
5 years old to 5 1/2 years old.......	100.0	(†)	21.5 (0.92)	78.5 (0.92)	15.8 (0.64)	5.9 (0.39)	54.5 (1.09)	2.3 (0.21)
More than 5 1/2 years old to 6 years old................	100.0	(†)	20.5 (0.89)	79.5 (0.89)	14.8 (0.62)	6.4 (0.45)	55.6 (1.05)	2.7 (0.26)
More than 6 years old................	100.0	(†)	21.1 (1.56)	78.9 (1.56)	11.8 (1.15)	8.6 (1.15)	55.8 (2.26)	2.6 (0.63)
Race/ethnicity of child								
White.....................................	100.0	(†)	18.1 (0.86)	81.9 (0.86)	12.9 (0.57)	8.5 (0.65)	57.8 (1.15)	2.7 (0.25)
Black.....................................	100.0	(†)	19.9 (1.93)	80.1 (1.93)	17.8 (1.29)	3.9 (0.59)	55.5 (2.06)	2.8 (0.47)
Hispanic.................................	100.0	(†)	28.3 (1.28)	71.7 (1.28)	18.1 (0.70)	4.0 (0.43)	47.8 (1.41)	1.8 (0.21)
Asian.....................................	100.0	(†)	19.6 (2.37)	80.4 (2.37)	14.6 (1.43)	2.3 (0.57)	61.6 (3.25)	1.8 (0.52)
Pacific Islander.......................	100.0	(†)	38.8 (6.02)	61.2 (6.02)	27.2 (7.27)	‡ (†)	27.6 (6.59)	‡ (†)
American Indian/Alaska Native.....	100.0	(†)	23.5 (3.93)	76.5 (3.93)	13.2 ! (4.58)	‡ (†)	56.7 (2.41)	‡ (†)
Two or more races....................	100.0	(†)	17.2 (2.03)	82.8 (2.03)	13.8 (1.53)	5.2 (0.97)	60.9 (2.51)	2.9 ! (0.93)
Parents' employment status, fall 2010[2]								
Two parents								
Both employed full time.............	100.0	(†)	8.4 (0.67)	91.6 (0.67)	17.6 (0.89)	12.9 (1.12)	57.1 (1.35)	4.0 (0.47)
One employed full time, one part time..............	100.0	(†)	16.5 (1.19)	83.5 (1.19)	14.7 (0.85)	7.1 (0.75)	58.8 (1.40)	2.8 (0.38)
One employed full time, one looking for work......	100.0	(†)	23.6 (2.19)	76.4 (2.19)	16.2 (1.87)	4.6 (0.86)	52.9 (2.82)	2.8 (0.80)
One employed full time, one not in labor force.....	100.0	(†)	33.7 (1.63)	66.3 (1.63)	4.7 (0.49)	1.6 (0.25)	58.9 (1.59)	1.0 (0.22)
Other combination....................	100.0	(†)	36.8 (1.48)	63.2 (1.48)	11.7 (1.29)	4.3 (0.90)	45.8 (1.92)	1.5 (0.43)
Single parent								
Employed full time....................	100.0	(†)	9.5 (0.97)	90.5 (0.97)	29.0 (1.23)	7.9 (0.95)	49.4 (1.39)	4.2 (0.41)
Employed part time...................	100.0	(†)	16.3 (1.75)	83.7 (1.75)	26.6 (1.99)	5.0 (1.14)	49.4 (2.56)	2.7 ! (0.97)
Looking for work......................	100.0	(†)	23.0 (2.23)	77.0 (2.23)	17.9 (2.32)	2.8 ! (1.19)	54.7 (2.38)	1.5 ! (0.72)
Not in labor force.....................	100.0	(†)	35.2 (2.53)	64.8 (2.53)	14.2 (1.70)	‡ (†)	48.1 (2.69)	‡ (†)
No parent in household.............	100.0	(†)	23.4 (2.65)	76.6 (2.65)	16.9 (3.28)	3.7 ! (1.29)	52.8 (4.15)	3.3 ! (1.45)
Parents' highest level of education[3]								
Less than high school...............	100.0	(†)	37.7 (2.11)	62.3 (2.11)	15.8 (1.21)	3.1 (0.68)	42.5 (2.04)	0.9 ! (0.27)
High school completion..............	100.0	(†)	28.3 (1.22)	71.7 (1.22)	19.1 (0.96)	5.1 (0.40)	45.5 (1.25)	1.9 (0.33)
Some college/vocational............	100.0	(†)	20.2 (0.90)	79.8 (0.90)	18.1 (0.81)	7.0 (0.54)	51.6 (1.30)	3.0 (0.35)
Bachelor's degree....................	100.0	(†)	14.7 (0.96)	85.3 (0.96)	10.9 (0.69)	6.5 (0.71)	64.8 (1.23)	3.1 (0.31)
Any graduate education.............	100.0	(†)	12.9 (1.14)	87.1 (1.14)	8.7 (0.70)	7.6 (0.67)	68.3 (1.38)	2.4 (0.33)
Household type, fall 2010								
Two-parent household...............	100.0	(†)	21.5 (0.94)	78.5 (0.94)	12.4 (0.45)	6.9 (0.49)	56.7 (1.14)	2.5 (0.21)
Mother-only household..............	100.0	(†)	17.5 (0.87)	82.5 (0.87)	23.9 (0.90)	5.2 (0.58)	50.4 (1.08)	3.1 (0.32)
Father-only household...............	100.0	(†)	17.5 (2.96)	82.5 (2.96)	30.8 (3.51)	5.8 (1.69)	43.4 (3.66)	2.4 ! (1.16)
Other household type................	100.0	(†)	23.4 (2.65)	76.6 (2.65)	16.9 (3.28)	3.7 ! (1.29)	52.8 (4.15)	3.3 ! (1.45)
Primary home language								
English...................................	100.0	(†)	18.4 (0.72)	81.6 (0.72)	14.9 (0.56)	7.0 (0.41)	57.1 (0.98)	2.7 (0.21)
Non-English............................	100.0	(†)	35.6 (2.10)	64.4 (2.10)	14.7 (0.95)	2.9 (0.48)	45.3 (1.84)	1.5 (0.25)
Primary language not identified...	100.0	(†)	22.1 (4.09)	77.9 (4.09)	18.2 (3.74)	‡ (†)	54.2 (4.62)	‡ (†)
Poverty status[4]								
Below poverty threshold............	100.0	(†)	30.4 (1.46)	69.6 (1.46)	16.4 (0.90)	2.6 (0.36)	48.9 (1.46)	1.7 (0.30)
100 to 199 percent of poverty threshold.......	100.0	(†)	24.9 (1.20)	75.1 (1.20)	16.5 (0.90)	5.0 (0.49)	51.8 (1.40)	1.7 (0.25)
200 percent or more of poverty threshold..............	100.0	(†)	13.5 (0.69)	86.5 (0.69)	12.3 (0.64)	8.7 (0.58)	62.3 (1.12)	3.2 (0.29)
Socioeconomic status[5]								
Lowest 20 percent....................	100.0	(†)	35.2 (1.52)	64.8 (1.52)	15.6 (0.75)	3.4 (0.44)	44.3 (1.28)	1.6 (0.27)
Middle 60 percent....................	100.0	(†)	19.6 (0.71)	80.4 (0.71)	16.9 (0.54)	6.9 (0.45)	53.9 (1.09)	2.7 (0.23)
Highest 20 percent...................	100.0	(†)	12.3 (1.13)	87.7 (1.13)	8.7 (0.67)	7.1 (0.56)	69.1 (1.29)	2.7 (0.29)
School type								
Public....................................	100.0	(†)	21.8 (0.80)	78.2 (0.80)	15.8 (0.51)	6.2 (0.35)	53.7 (0.98)	2.5 (0.20)
Private...................................	100.0	(†)	14.5 (1.98)	85.5 (1.98)	8.3 (0.78)	7.0 (0.88)	67.9 (1.69)	2.3 (0.32)

†Not applicable.

!Interpret data with caution. The coefficient of variation (CV) for this estimate is between 30 and 50 percent.

‡Reporting standards not met. Either there are too few cases for a reliable estimate or the coefficient of variation (CV) is 50 percent or greater.

[1]The type of nonparental care in which the child spent the most hours. Multiple arrangements refers to children who spent an equal amount of time in each of two or more types of arrangements.

[2]Parents who reported working at least 35 hours per week are defined as employed full time, while those who reported working less than 35 hours per week are defined as employed part time. Those neither employed nor looking for work are not in the labor force.

[3]Parents highest level of education is the highest level of education achieved by either of the parents or guardians in a two-parent household, by the only parent in a single-parent household, or by any guardian in a household with no parents.

[4]Poverty status is based on preliminary U.S. Census income thresholds for 2010, which identify incomes determined to meet household needs, given family size and composition.

For example, a family of three with one child was below the poverty threshold if its annual income was less than $17,552 in 2010.

[5]Socioeconomic status (SES) was measured by a composite score based on parental education and occupations and household income at the time of data collection.

NOTE: Estimates weighted by W1_2P0. Estimates pertain to a sample of children who were enrolled in kindergarten for the first time in the 2010–11 school year. Two parents may refer to two biological parents, two adoptive parents, or one biological/adoptive parent and one other parent/partner. Single parent refers to one biological or adoptive parent only. In households without parents, the guardian or guardians may be related or unrelated to the child. Race categories exclude persons of Hispanic ethnicity. Detail may not sum to totals because of rounding and survey item nonresponse. Some data have been revised from previously published figures.

SOURCE: U.S. Department of Education, National Center for Education Statistics, Early Childhood Longitudinal Study, Kindergarten Class of 2010–11 (ECLS-K:2011), Kindergarten–First Grade Restricted-Use Data File. (This table was prepared November 2014.)

Table 202.70. Number and percentage distribution of 3- to 5-year-olds not enrolled in school and all children enrolled in prekindergarten through second grade, by grade level and selected maternal and household characteristics: 2001, 2005, and 2012

[Standard errors appear in parentheses]

Selected maternal or household characteristic	3- to 5-year-olds, not enrolled in school			Enrolled in nursery school or prekindergarten			Enrolled in kindergarten			Enrolled in first grade			Enrolled in second grade		
	2001	2005	2012	2001	2005	2012	2001	2005	2012	2001	2005	2012	2001	2005	2012
1	2	3	4	5	6	7	8	9	10	11	12	13	14	15	16
Number of children (in thousands)	3,990 (3.2)	4,156 (5.0)	3,250 (90.6)	4,586 (#)	4,926 (#)	4,994 (103.8)	3,831 (#)	3,717 (#)	5,710 (115.2)	4,333 (#)	4,118 (#)	3,944 (136.3)	3,934 (#)	3,900 (#)	4,192 (151.8)
Percentage distribution															
Mother's highest level of education[1]	100.0 (†)	100.0 (†)	100.0 (†)	100.0 (†)	100.0 (†)	100.0 (†)	100.0 (†)	100.0 (†)	100.0 (†)	100.0 (†)	100.0 (†)	100.0 (†)	100.0 (†)	100.0 (†)	100.0 (†)
Less than high school	16.4 (1.26)	13.8 (1.24)	24.4 (1.60)	8.0 (0.76)	6.8 (0.76)	11.4 (1.06)	10.7 (1.31)	9.5 (1.16)	16.9 (1.83)	11.7 (1.28)	10.0 (1.20)	11.1 (1.56)	13.5 (1.21)	10.3 (1.21)	10.1 (1.93)
High school/GED	39.7 (1.59)	37.2 (2.17)	26.8 (1.61)	26.1 (1.34)	24.6 (1.34)	16.7 (1.04)	30.3 (1.86)	27.5 (1.92)	21.6 (1.92)	30.3 (2.17)	31.1 (2.13)	16.4 (1.45)	32.8 (2.11)	29.5 (1.77)	27.0 (2.94)
Vocational/technical or some college	19.1 (1.30)	21.2 (1.43)	24.1 (1.41)	24.6 (1.28)	19.2 (1.32)	19.5 (1.21)	23.5 (1.84)	20.7 (1.70)	21.3 (2.12)	24.3 (1.87)	19.9 (1.93)	25.4 (1.96)	22.5 (2.18)	19.8 (1.64)	20.0 (1.60)
Associate's degree	5.9 (0.67)	6.8 (0.82)	7.7 (0.82)	7.7 (0.71)	8.4 (0.71)	9.4 (0.86)	7.6 (1.18)	7.7 (0.96)	8.0 (1.06)	7.5 (1.01)	10.3 (1.22)	8.4 (0.81)	7.5 (0.92)	8.0 (0.98)	12.0 (1.50)
Bachelor's degree	13.0 (1.05)	14.9 (1.20)	13.9 (1.10)	20.4 (1.03)	25.5 (1.13)	30.6 (1.15)	18.8 (1.51)	21.3 (1.42)	23.4 (1.73)	18.5 (1.71)	18.0 (1.23)	28.1 (1.78)	14.9 (1.66)	18.7 (1.46)	20.7 (1.59)
Graduate/professional degree	6.0 (0.73)	6.1 (0.73)	3.1 (0.38)	13.2 (0.99)	15.5 (0.94)	12.4 (0.70)	9.1 (1.16)	13.4 (1.43)	8.7 (0.87)	7.7 (1.03)	10.6 (1.22)	10.6 (0.99)	8.8 (1.25)	13.6 (1.62)	10.1 (0.94)
Mother's employment status[1]	100.0 (†)	100.0 (†)	100.0 (†)	100.0 (†)	100.0 (†)	100.0 (†)	100.0 (†)	100.0 (†)	100.0 (†)	100.0 (†)	100.0 (†)	100.0 (†)	100.0 (†)	100.0 (†)	100.0 (†)
Working 35 hours/week or more	36.7 (1.55)	33.5 (1.92)	34.2 (2.03)	43.7 (1.18)	39.4 (1.42)	45.3 (1.23)	38.9 (1.99)	36.9 (2.25)	40.4 (2.32)	46.1 (2.33)	40.7 (2.35)	44.2 (1.98)	42.3 (2.30)	41.2 (2.19)	42.6 (2.26)
Working less than 35 hours/week	19.2 (1.30)	21.1 (1.50)	14.3 (1.34)	22.8 (1.00)	24.4 (1.36)	18.3 (0.94)	22.6 (1.57)	21.5 (1.62)	16.8 (1.63)	19.7 (1.59)	20.7 (1.42)	17.8 (1.68)	20.1 (1.60)	22.7 (1.72)	19.6 (1.65)
Looking for work	5.7 (0.75)	8.7 (1.37)	7.6 (1.01)	3.9 (0.55)	4.0 (0.59)	6.7 (0.90)	3.9 (0.87)	7.3 (1.06)	8.2 (1.59)	4.1 (0.89)	5.7 (1.07)	5.7 (1.01)	5.1 (1.09)	4.9 (0.82)	3.5 (0.58)
Not in labor force	38.4 (1.48)	36.8 (1.79)	43.9 (2.00)	29.6 (1.27)	32.2 (1.35)	29.7 (1.18)	34.7 (2.16)	34.3 (1.99)	34.6 (2.31)	30.1 (2.05)	32.8 (1.97)	32.3 (2.06)	32.5 (1.99)	31.2 (1.99)	34.4 (2.42)
Household income	100.0 (†)	100.0 (†)	100.0 (†)	100.0 (†)	100.0 (†)	100.0 (†)	100.0 (†)	100.0 (†)	100.0 (†)	100.0 (†)	100.0 (†)	100.0 (†)	100.0 (†)	100.0 (†)	100.0 (†)
$20,000 or less	28.6 (1.24)	22.2 (1.29)	24.0 (1.74)	21.2 (0.93)	17.3 (1.07)	14.0 (0.80)	22.6 (1.56)	19.3 (1.26)	20.8 (1.52)	23.1 (1.79)	18.2 (1.45)	12.6 (1.12)	21.8 (1.71)	20.1 (1.54)	14.8 (1.41)
$20,001 to $50,000	40.5 (1.50)	42.4 (1.65)	34.8 (1.92)	28.9 (1.20)	27.6 (1.39)	24.9 (1.07)	37.8 (1.95)	31.9 (1.76)	30.4 (1.86)	36.4 (2.18)	33.0 (1.95)	25.1 (1.52)	36.3 (2.11)	32.9 (2.10)	28.7 (1.90)
$50,001 to $75,000	18.8 (1.31)	19.9 (1.24)	17.4 (1.46)	21.2 (1.09)	20.8 (0.97)	18.9 (1.02)	20.9 (1.68)	18.4 (1.84)	13.9 (1.34)	18.3 (1.41)	20.4 (1.84)	19.5 (1.73)	19.6 (1.80)	20.3 (1.56)	18.5 (1.51)
$75,001 to $100,000	7.2 (0.76)	9.0 (1.08)	10.2 (1.08)	13.0 (0.92)	14.7 (0.93)	15.1 (0.88)	9.0 (1.04)	14.1 (1.29)	13.4 (1.02)	11.1 (1.41)	10.8 (1.22)	15.1 (1.26)	12.0 (1.33)	13.9 (1.41)	10.8 (1.08)
Over $100,000	4.9 (0.61)	6.4 (0.93)	13.7 (1.60)	15.7 (0.83)	19.7 (1.11)	27.1 (1.02)	9.6 (0.98)	16.3 (1.29)	21.5 (1.63)	11.0 (1.30)	17.6 (1.36)	27.8 (1.90)	10.3 (1.27)	12.8 (1.39)	27.3 (1.68)
Poverty status of household[2]	100.0 (†)	100.0 (†)	100.0 (†)	100.0 (†)	100.0 (†)	100.0 (†)	100.0 (†)	100.0 (†)	100.0 (†)	100.0 (†)	100.0 (†)	100.0 (†)	100.0 (†)	100.0 (†)	100.0 (†)
Poor	27.5 (1.24)	25.9 (1.53)	33.0 (1.79)	19.3 (0.94)	17.2 (1.10)	17.7 (1.00)	22.2 (1.67)	21.2 (1.53)	28.9 (2.16)	23.1 (2.00)	20.8 (1.47)	17.1 (1.46)	21.2 (1.70)	22.1 (1.50)	22.0 (1.76)
Near-poor	23.9 (1.27)	31.3 (1.73)	29.6 (1.78)	17.9 (0.99)	20.9 (1.24)	20.0 (1.18)	22.6 (1.86)	23.1 (2.05)	21.4 (1.84)	22.8 (1.93)	20.9 (1.35)	20.9 (1.39)	22.1 (1.92)	23.4 (1.66)	23.0 (1.81)
Nonpoor	48.6 (1.39)	42.8 (1.66)	37.5 (1.62)	62.8 (1.18)	61.9 (1.34)	62.3 (1.32)	55.2 (1.91)	55.7 (1.82)	49.7 (1.77)	56.0 (1.74)	56.4 (1.74)	62.1 (1.89)	56.7 (1.97)	54.5 (1.82)	55.0 (2.14)

†Not applicable.
#Rounds to zero.
[1]Excludes children living in households with no mother or female guardian present.
[2]Poor children are those whose family incomes were below the Census Bureau's poverty threshold in the year prior to data collection; near-poor children are those whose family incomes ranged from the poverty threshold to 199 percent of the poverty threshold; and nonpoor children are those whose family incomes were at or above 200 percent of the poverty threshold. The poverty threshold is a dollar amount that varies depending on a family's size and composition and is updated annually to account for inflation. In 2011, for example, the poverty threshold for a family of four with two children was $22,811. Survey respondents are asked to select the range within which their income falls, rather than giving the exact amount of their income; therefore, the measure of poverty status is an approximation.

NOTE: Enrollment data include homeschooled students and ungraded students if a grade equivalent was available. For 2001 and 2005, excludes students for whom no grade equivalent was available. For 2012, all students had a known grade level and were included. While National Household Education Surveys Program (NHES) administrations prior to 2012 were administered via telephone with an interviewer, NHES:2012 used self-administered paper-and-pencil questionnaires that were mailed to respondents. Measurable differences in estimates between 2012 and prior years could reflect actual changes in the population, or the changes could be due to the mode change from telephone to mail. Detail may not sum to totals because of rounding.
SOURCE: U.S. Department of Education, National Center for Education Statistics, Early Childhood Program Participation Survey, Before- and After-School Programs and Activities Survey, and Parent and Family Involvement in Education Survey of the National Household Education Surveys Program (ECPP-NHES:2001, 2005, and 2012; ASPA-NHES:2001 and 2005; and PFI-NHES:2012). (This table was prepared October 2014.)

Table 203.10. Enrollment in public elementary and secondary schools, by level and grade: Selected years, fall 1980 through fall 2024

[In thousands]

Year	All grades	Elementary												Secondary					
		Total	Pre-kinder-garten	Kinder-garten	1st grade	2nd grade	3rd grade	4th grade	5th grade	6th grade	7th grade	8th grade	Un-graded	Total	9th grade	10th grade	11th grade	12th grade	Un-graded
1	2	3	4	5	6	7	8	9	10	11	12	13	14	15	16	17	18	19	20
1980	40,877	27,647	96	2,593	2,894	2,800	2,893	3,107	3,130	3,038	3,085	3,086	924	13,231	3,377	3,368	3,195	2,925	366
1985	39,422	27,034	151	3,041	3,239	2,941	2,895	2,771	2,776	2,789	2,938	2,982	511	12,388	3,439	3,230	2,866	2,550	303
1990	41,217	29,876	303	3,306	3,499	3,327	3,297	3,248	3,197	3,110	3,067	2,979	541	11,341	3,169	2,896	2,612	2,381	284
1991	42,047	30,503	375	3,311	3,556	3,360	3,334	3,315	3,268	3,239	3,181	3,020	542	11,544	3,313	2,915	2,645	2,392	278
1992	42,823	31,086	505	3,313	3,542	3,431	3,361	3,342	3,325	3,303	3,299	3,129	536	11,737	3,352	3,027	2,656	2,431	272
1993	43,465	31,502	545	3,377	3,529	3,429	3,437	3,361	3,350	3,356	3,355	3,249	513	11,963	3,487	3,050	2,751	2,424	250
1994	44,111	31,896	603	3,444	3,593	3,440	3,439	3,426	3,372	3,381	3,404	3,302	492	12,215	3,604	3,131	2,748	2,488	244
1995	44,840	32,338	637	3,536	3,671	3,507	3,445	3,431	3,438	3,395	3,422	3,356	500	12,502	3,704	3,237	2,826	2,487	247
1996	45,611	32,762	670	3,532	3,770	3,600	3,524	3,454	3,453	3,494	3,464	3,403	399	12,849	3,801	3,323	2,930	2,586	208
1997	46,127	33,071	695	3,503	3,755	3,689	3,597	3,507	3,458	3,492	3,520	3,415	440	13,056	3,819	3,376	2,972	2,673	216
1998	46,539	33,344	729	3,443	3,727	3,681	3,696	3,592	3,520	3,497	3,530	3,480	449	13,195	3,856	3,382	3,021	2,722	214
1999	46,857	33,486	751	3,397	3,684	3,656	3,691	3,686	3,604	3,564	3,541	3,497	415	13,371	3,935	3,415	3,034	2,782	205
2000	47,204	33,686	776	3,382	3,636	3,634	3,676	3,711	3,707	3,663	3,629	3,538	334	13,517	3,963	3,491	3,083	2,803	177
2001	47,672	33,936	865	3,379	3,614	3,593	3,653	3,695	3,727	3,769	3,720	3,616	304	13,736	4,012	3,528	3,174	2,863	159
2002	48,183	34,114	915	3,434	3,594	3,565	3,623	3,669	3,711	3,788	3,821	3,709	285	14,069	4,105	3,584	3,229	2,990	161
2003	48,540	34,201	950	3,503	3,613	3,544	3,611	3,619	3,685	3,772	3,841	3,809	255	14,339	4,190	3,675	3,277	3,046	150
2004	48,795	34,178	990	3,544	3,663	3,560	3,580	3,612	3,635	3,735	3,818	3,825	215	14,618	4,281	3,750	3,369	3,094	122
2005	49,113	34,204	1,036	3,619	3,691	3,606	3,586	3,578	3,633	3,670	3,777	3,802	205	14,909	4,287	3,866	3,454	3,180	121
2006	49,316	34,235	1,084	3,631	3,751	3,641	3,627	3,586	3,602	3,660	3,716	3,766	170	15,081	4,260	3,882	3,551	3,277	110
2007	49,291	34,204	1,081	3,609	3,750	3,704	3,659	3,624	3,600	3,628	3,700	3,709	139	15,086	4,200	3,863	3,557	3,375	92
2008	49,266	34,286	1,180	3,640	3,708	3,699	3,708	3,647	3,629	3,614	3,653	3,692	117	14,980	4,123	3,822	3,548	3,400	87
2009	49,361	34,409	1,223	3,678	3,729	3,665	3,707	3,701	3,652	3,644	3,641	3,651	119	14,952	4,080	3,809	3,541	3,432	90
2010	49,484	34,625	1,279	3,682	3,754	3,701	3,686	3,711	3,718	3,682	3,676	3,659	77	14,860	4,008	3,800	3,538	3,472	42
2011	49,522	34,773	1,291	3,746	3,773	3,713	3,703	3,672	3,699	3,724	3,696	3,679	77	14,749	3,957	3,751	3,546	3,452	43
2012	49,771	35,018	1,307	3,831	3,824	3,729	3,719	3,690	3,673	3,723	3,746	3,699	76	14,753	3,975	3,730	3,528	3,477	43
Projected																			
2013	49,942	35,188	1,304	3,822	3,865	3,780	3,736	3,719	3,696	3,694	3,745	3,750	76	14,754	3,997	3,747	3,508	3,460	42
2014	49,986	35,159	1,266	3,711	3,855	3,821	3,787	3,736	3,725	3,717	3,715	3,749	76	14,826	4,052	3,767	3,524	3,440	42
2015	50,094	35,182	1,269	3,720	3,744	3,811	3,828	3,787	3,743	3,746	3,739	3,719	75	14,912	4,051	3,820	3,543	3,456	42
2016	50,229	35,282	1,281	3,756	3,753	3,701	3,818	3,828	3,793	3,764	3,768	3,743	75	14,947	4,019	3,819	3,593	3,475	42
2017	50,584	35,595	1,344	3,940	3,790	3,711	3,708	3,818	3,834	3,815	3,786	3,772	76	14,989	4,044	3,788	3,591	3,523	42
2018	50,871	35,856	1,354	3,970	3,976	3,747	3,717	3,708	3,825	3,856	3,837	3,790	76	15,015	4,076	3,812	3,563	3,522	42
2019	51,183	36,125	1,364	3,997	4,006	3,930	3,754	3,717	3,714	3,846	3,879	3,841	77	15,058	4,095	3,842	3,585	3,494	42
2020	51,547	36,366	1,372	4,022	4,033	3,960	3,938	3,754	3,724	3,735	3,869	3,883	77	15,182	4,150	3,860	3,614	3,516	42
2021	51,910	36,587	1,380	4,044	4,058	3,987	3,967	3,938	3,760	3,744	3,757	3,873	78	15,324	4,195	3,912	3,630	3,543	42
2022	52,260	36,839	1,387	4,065	4,081	4,012	3,994	3,967	3,944	3,781	3,767	3,761	78	15,421	4,185	3,955	3,680	3,560	43
2023	52,601	37,223	1,394	4,085	4,103	4,035	4,019	3,995	3,974	3,966	3,803	3,771	79	15,378	4,064	3,944	3,719	3,608	42
2024	52,920	37,615	1,399	4,102	4,122	4,056	4,042	4,019	4,001	3,996	3,990	3,807	80	15,304	4,074	3,831	3,710	3,647	42

NOTE: Due to changes in reporting and imputation practices, prekindergarten enrollment for years prior to 1992 represent an undercount compared to later years. The total ungraded counts of students were prorated to the elementary and secondary levels based on prior reports. Detail may not sum to totals because of rounding.

SOURCE: U.S. Department of Education, National Center for Education Statistics, *Statistics of Public Elementary and Secondary School Systems, 1980–81*; Common Core of Data (CCD), "State Nonfiscal Survey of Public Elementary/Secondary Education," 1985–86 through 2012–13; and National Elementary and Secondary Enrollment Projection Model, 1972 through 2024. (This table was prepared March 2015.)

Table 203.20. Enrollment in public elementary and secondary schools, by region, state, and jurisdiction: Selected years, fall 1990 through fall 2024

Region, state, and jurisdiction	Actual total enrollment													Percent change in total enrollment, 2007 to 2012	Projected total enrollment						Percent change in total enrollment, 2012 to 2024
	Fall 1990	Fall 2000	Fall 2002	Fall 2003	Fall 2004	Fall 2005	Fall 2006	Fall 2007	Fall 2008	Fall 2009	Fall 2010	Fall 2011	Fall 2012		Fall 2013	Fall 2014	Fall 2015	Fall 2016	Fall 2020	Fall 2024	
1	2	3	4	5	6	7	8	9	10	11	12	13	14	15	16	17	18	19	20	21	22
United States	**41,216,683**	**47,203,539**	**48,183,086**	**48,540,215**	**48,795,465**	**49,113,298**	**49,315,842**	**49,290,559**	**49,265,572**	**49,360,982**	**49,484,181**	**49,521,669**	**49,771,118**	**1.0**	**49,941,900**	**49,985,600**	**50,094,400**	**50,229,000**	**51,547,400**	**52,919,600**	**6.3**
Region																					
Northeast	7,281,763	8,222,127	8,296,621	8,292,315	8,271,259	8,240,160	8,257,889	8,122,022	8,052,985	8,092,029	8,071,335	7,953,981	7,959,128	-2.0	7,928,100	7,887,700	7,861,000	7,839,300	7,899,500	7,958,400	#
Midwest	9,943,761	10,729,987	10,818,970	10,808,977	10,775,409	10,818,815	10,819,248	10,770,210	10,742,973	10,672,171	10,609,604	10,573,792	10,559,230	-2.0	10,549,500	10,512,200	10,493,800	10,479,700	10,536,700	10,553,800	-0.1
South	14,807,016	17,007,261	17,471,440	17,672,745	17,891,987	18,103,166	18,293,633	18,422,773	18,490,770	18,651,889	18,805,000	18,955,932	19,128,376	3.8	19,283,200	19,359,300	19,449,800	19,542,100	20,187,900	20,899,600	9.3
West	9,184,143	11,244,164	11,596,055	11,766,178	11,856,810	11,951,157	11,945,072	11,975,554	11,978,844	11,944,893	11,998,242	12,037,964	12,124,384	1.2	12,181,100	12,226,400	12,289,800	12,367,900	12,923,300	13,507,900	11.4
State																					
Alabama	721,806	739,992	739,366	731,220	730,140	741,761	743,632	742,919	745,668	748,889	755,552	744,621	744,637	0.2	743,500	739,500	735,000	731,000	724,100	723,900	-2.8
Alaska	113,903	133,356	134,364	133,933	132,970	133,288	132,608	131,029	130,662	131,661	132,104	131,167	131,489	0.4	131,800	132,700	133,900	135,400	144,500	153,800	17.0
Arizona	639,853	877,696	937,755	1,012,068	1,043,298	1,094,454	1,068,249	1,087,447	1,087,817	1,077,831	1,071,751	1,080,319	1,089,384	0.2	1,097,600	1,105,700	1,116,900	1,132,900	1,222,300	1,320,000	21.2
Arkansas	436,286	449,959	450,985	454,523	463,115	474,206	476,409	479,016	478,965	480,559	482,114	483,114	486,157	1.5	486,300	484,100	481,600	479,600	478,800	482,800	-0.7
California	4,950,474	6,140,814	6,353,667	6,413,867	6,441,557	6,437,202	6,406,750	6,343,471	6,322,528	6,263,438	6,289,578	6,287,834	6,299,451	-0.7	6,311,800	6,314,700	6,328,400	6,351,400	6,586,000	6,833,200	8.5
Colorado	574,213	724,508	751,862	757,693	765,976	779,826	794,026	801,867	818,443	832,368	843,316	854,265	863,561	7.7	873,100	879,900	887,600	894,400	929,300	961,200	11.3
Connecticut	469,123	562,179	570,023	577,203	577,390	575,059	575,100	570,626	567,198	563,968	560,546	554,437	550,954	-3.4	543,500	535,900	530,300	525,300	521,000	524,400	-4.8
Delaware	99,658	114,676	116,342	117,668	119,091	120,937	122,254	122,574	125,430	126,801	129,403	128,946	129,026	5.3	129,800	130,200	130,800	131,700	136,500	138,300	7.2
District of Columbia	80,694	68,925	76,166	78,057	76,714	76,876	72,850	78,422	68,681	69,433	71,284	73,911	76,140	-2.9	77,700	77,800	78,200	78,400	80,100	78,300	2.8
Florida	1,861,592	2,434,821	2,539,929	2,587,628	2,639,336	2,675,024	2,671,513	2,666,811	2,631,020	2,634,522	2,643,347	2,668,156	2,692,162	1.0	2,707,400	2,717,000	2,727,000	2,742,300	2,868,200	3,040,900	13.0
Georgia	1,151,687	1,444,937	1,496,012	1,522,611	1,553,437	1,598,461	1,629,157	1,649,589	1,655,792	1,667,685	1,677,067	1,685,016	1,703,332	3.3	1,716,100	1,722,100	1,729,500	1,735,600	1,788,600	1,858,300	9.1
Hawaii	171,708	184,360	183,829	183,609	183,185	182,818	180,728	179,897	179,478	180,196	179,601	182,706	184,760	2.7	186,500	187,000	187,400	188,000	190,900	189,300	2.5
Idaho	220,840	245,117	248,604	252,120	256,084	261,982	267,380	272,119	275,051	276,299	275,859	279,873	284,834	4.7	288,300	290,400	293,000	295,400	305,900	313,000	9.9
Illinois	1,821,407	2,048,792	2,084,187	2,100,961	2,097,503	2,111,706	2,118,276	2,112,805	2,119,707	2,104,175	2,091,654	2,083,097	2,072,880	-1.9	2,069,800	2,059,400	2,055,500	2,052,800	2,052,200	2,037,000	-1.7
Indiana	954,525	989,267	1,003,875	1,011,130	1,021,348	1,035,074	1,045,940	1,046,764	1,046,147	1,046,661	1,047,232	1,040,765	1,041,369	-0.5	1,039,100	1,032,900	1,028,500	1,023,600	1,017,400	1,029,800	-1.1
Iowa	483,652	495,080	482,210	481,226	478,319	483,482	483,122	485,115	487,559	491,842	495,775	495,870	499,825	3.0	502,800	502,800	503,600	504,400	510,300	506,400	1.3
Kansas	437,034	470,610	470,957	470,490	469,136	467,525	469,506	468,295	471,060	474,489	483,701	486,108	489,043	4.4	491,000	490,900	492,000	492,500	498,800	499,800	2.2
Kentucky	636,401	665,850	660,782	663,369	674,796	679,878	683,152	666,225	670,030	680,089	673,128	681,987	685,167	2.8	687,700	686,500	686,700	686,300	689,400	689,200	0.6
Louisiana	784,757	743,089	730,464	727,709	724,281	654,526	675,851	681,038	684,873	690,915	696,558	703,390	710,903	4.4	714,800	714,400	714,700	714,900	715,700	707,400	-0.5
Maine	215,149	207,037	204,337	202,084	198,820	195,498	193,986	196,245	192,935	189,225	189,077	188,969	185,739	-5.4	183,300	181,100	179,400	177,700	175,700	173,100	-6.8
Maryland	715,176	852,920	866,743	869,113	865,561	860,020	851,640	845,700	843,861	848,412	852,211	854,086	859,638	1.6	864,600	869,100	875,900	884,800	941,100	989,800	15.1
Massachusetts	834,314	975,150	982,989	980,459	975,574	971,909	968,661	962,958	958,910	957,053	955,563	953,369	954,773	-0.8	952,800	947,000	941,900	936,900	936,000	944,000	-1.1
Michigan	1,584,431	1,720,626	1,785,160	1,757,604	1,751,290	1,742,282	1,722,656	1,692,739	1,659,921	1,649,082	1,587,067	1,573,537	1,555,370	-8.1	1,542,100	1,527,100	1,513,600	1,502,800	1,483,100	1,474,600	-5.2
Minnesota	756,374	854,340	846,891	842,854	838,503	839,243	840,565	837,578	836,048	837,053	838,037	839,738	845,404	0.9	854,600	861,300	868,800	877,900	925,100	961,600	13.7
Mississippi	502,417	497,871	492,645	493,540	495,376	494,954	495,026	494,122	491,962	492,481	490,526	490,619	493,650	-0.1	494,000	493,200	492,000	490,400	485,900	478,900	-3.0
Missouri	816,558	912,744	906,499	905,941	905,449	917,705	920,353	917,188	917,871	917,982	918,710	916,584	917,900	0.1	916,500	912,800	910,400	908,000	914,700	919,000	0.1
Montana	152,974	154,875	149,995	148,356	146,705	145,416	144,418	142,823	141,899	141,807	141,693	142,349	142,908	0.1	144,400	145,300	146,400	147,400	152,700	154,100	7.8
Nebraska	274,081	286,199	285,402	285,542	285,761	286,646	287,580	291,244	292,590	295,368	298,500	301,296	303,505	4.2	307,000	307,800	309,100	310,700	317,000	316,400	4.2
Nevada	201,316	340,706	369,498	385,401	400,083	412,395	424,766	429,362	433,371	428,947	437,149	439,634	445,707	3.8	447,900	452,900	458,600	464,900	505,300	560,900	25.8
New Hampshire	172,785	208,461	207,671	207,417	206,852	205,767	203,572	200,772	197,934	197,140	194,711	191,900	188,974	-5.9	185,900	183,600	181,500	180,000	180,300	185,000	-2.1
New Jersey	1,089,646	1,313,405	1,367,438	1,380,753	1,393,347	1,395,602	1,388,850	1,382,348	1,381,420	1,396,029	1,402,548	1,356,431	1,372,203	-0.7	1,367,500	1,362,200	1,357,400	1,353,200	1,361,200	1,374,200	0.1
New Mexico	301,881	320,306	320,234	323,066	326,102	326,758	328,220	329,040	330,245	334,419	338,122	337,225	338,220	2.8	339,900	340,500	341,300	341,900	344,800	340,800	0.8
New York	2,598,337	2,882,188	2,888,233	2,864,775	2,836,337	2,815,581	2,809,649	2,765,435	2,740,592	2,766,052	2,734,955	2,704,718	2,710,703	-2.0	2,710,500	2,704,900	2,702,000	2,701,100	2,741,800	2,762,300	1.9
North Carolina	1,086,871	1,293,638	1,335,954	1,360,209	1,385,754	1,416,436	1,444,481	1,489,492	1,488,645	1,483,397	1,490,605	1,507,864	1,518,465	1.9	1,530,600	1,538,600	1,546,800	1,555,100	1,617,500	1,717,900	13.1
North Dakota	117,825	109,201	104,225	102,233	100,513	98,283	96,670	95,059	94,728	95,073	96,323	97,646	101,111	6.4	104,300	106,600	109,100	111,300	121,100	124,200	22.9
Ohio	1,771,089	1,835,049	1,838,285	1,845,428	1,840,032	1,839,683	1,836,722	1,827,184	1,817,163	1,764,297	1,754,191	1,740,030	1,729,916	-5.3	1,719,600	1,708,800	1,699,600	1,690,100	1,671,500	1,651,900	-4.5
Oklahoma	579,087	623,110	624,548	626,160	629,476	634,739	639,391	642,065	645,108	654,802	659,911	666,120	673,483	4.9	679,600	682,400	685,600	688,100	703,600	711,500	5.6
Oregon	472,394	546,231	554,071	551,273	552,505	552,194	562,574	565,586	575,393	582,839	570,720	568,208	587,564	3.9	583,000	584,300	587,200	590,200	616,900	649,900	10.6
Pennsylvania	1,667,834	1,814,311	1,816,747	1,821,146	1,828,089	1,830,684	1,871,060	1,801,971	1,775,029	1,785,993	1,793,284	1,771,395	1,763,677	-2.1	1,754,900	1,745,600	1,742,400	1,739,900	1,755,200	1,764,700	0.1
Rhode Island	138,813	157,347	159,205	159,375	156,498	153,422	151,612	147,629	145,342	145,118	143,793	142,854	142,481	-3.5	140,700	139,200	138,100	137,400	137,900	137,800	-3.3
South Carolina	622,112	677,411	694,389	699,198	703,736	701,544	708,021	712,317	718,113	723,143	725,838	727,186	735,998	3.3	743,600	749,100	754,700	759,500	784,600	805,400	9.4
South Dakota	129,164	128,603	130,048	125,537	122,798	122,012	121,158	121,606	126,429	123,713	126,128	128,016	130,471	7.3	131,100	132,000	133,100	134,300	139,500	140,600	7.8
Tennessee	824,595	909,161	927,608	936,682	941,091	953,928	978,368	964,259	971,950	972,549	987,422	999,693	993,496	3.0	998,000	999,100	1,001,800	1,004,800	1,034,400	1,071,900	7.9
Texas	3,382,887	4,059,619	4,259,823	4,331,751	4,405,215	4,525,394	4,599,509	4,674,832	4,752,148	4,850,210	4,935,715	5,000,470	5,077,659	8.6	5,154,100	5,200,200	5,250,300	5,297,300	5,540,000	5,766,300	13.6
Utah	446,652	481,485	489,262	495,981	503,607	508,430	523,386	576,244	559,778	571,586	585,552	598,832	613,279	6.4	626,100	636,400	646,000	654,100	688,800	719,400	17.3

See notes at end of table.

Table 203.20. Enrollment in public elementary and secondary schools, by region, state, and jurisdiction: Selected years, fall 1990 through fall 2024—Continued

Region, state, and jurisdiction	Actual total enrollment													Percent change in total enrollment, 2007 to 2012	Projected total enrollment						Percent change in total enrollment, 2012 to 2024
	Fall 1990	Fall 2000	Fall 2002	Fall 2003	Fall 2004	Fall 2005	Fall 2006	Fall 2007	Fall 2008	Fall 2009	Fall 2010	Fall 2011	Fall 2012		Fall 2013	Fall 2014	Fall 2015	Fall 2016	Fall 2020	Fall 2024	
1	2	3	4	5	6	7	8	9	10	11	12	13	14	15	16	17	18	19	20	21	22
Vermont	95,762	102,049	99,978	99,103	98,352	96,638	95,399	94,038	93,625	91,451	96,858	89,908	89,624	-4.7	89,000	88,300	88,000	87,900	90,400	92,900	3.6
Virginia	998,601	1,144,915	1,177,229	1,192,092	1,204,739	1,213,616	1,220,440	1,230,857	1,235,795	1,245,340	1,251,440	1,257,883	1,265,419	2.8	1,273,200	1,277,200	1,283,000	1,289,100	1,336,600	1,388,100	9.7
Washington	839,709	1,004,770	1,014,798	1,021,349	1,020,005	1,031,985	1,026,774	1,030,247	1,037,018	1,035,347	1,043,788	1,045,453	1,051,694	2.1	1,057,500	1,062,300	1,068,200	1,076,100	1,138,100	1,216,900	15.7
West Virginia	322,389	286,367	282,455	281,215	280,129	280,866	281,939	282,535	282,729	282,662	282,879	282,870	283,044	0.2	282,000	279,000	276,100	273,100	282,800	250,700	-11.4
Wisconsin	797,621	879,476	881,231	880,031	864,757	875,174	876,700	874,633	873,750	872,436	872,286	871,105	872,436	-0.3	871,700	869,800	870,500	871,400	885,900	892,300	2.3
Wyoming	98,226	89,940	88,116	87,462	84,733	84,409	85,193	86,422	87,161	88,155	89,009	90,099	91,533	5.9	93,400	94,400	95,200	95,800	97,800	95,300	4.1
Jurisdiction																					
Bureau of Indian Education	—	46,938	46,126	45,828	45,828	50,938	—	—	40,927	41,351	41,962	—	—	—	—	—	—	—	—	—	—
DoD, overseas	—	73,581	72,889	71,053	68,327	62,543	60,891	57,247	56,768	—	—	—	—	—	—	—	—	—	—	—	—
DoD, domestic	—	34,174	32,115	30,603	29,151	28,329	26,631	27,548	28,013	—	—	—	—	—	—	—	—	—	—	—	—
Other jurisdictions																					
American Samoa	12,463	15,702	15,984	15,893	16,126	16,438	16,400	—	—	—	—	—	—	—	—	—	—	—	—	—	—
Guam	26,391	32,473	—	31,572	30,605	30,986	—	—	—	—	31,618	31,243	31,186	—	—	—	—	—	—	—	—
Northern Marianas	6,449	10,004	11,251	11,244	11,601	11,601	11,695	11,299	10,913	10,961	11,105	11,011	10,646	-5.8	—	—	—	—	—	—	—
Puerto Rico	644,734	612,725	596,502	584,916	575,648	563,490	544,138	526,565	503,635	493,393	473,735	452,740	434,609	-17.5	—	—	—	—	—	—	—
U.S. Virgin Islands	21,750	19,459	18,333	17,716	16,429	16,750	16,284	15,903	15,768	15,493	15,495	15,711	15,192	-4.5	—	—	—	—	—	—	—

—Not available.
#Rounds to zero.
NOTE: DoD = Department of Defense. Detail may not sum to totals because of rounding. Some data have been revised from previously published figures.

SOURCE: U.S. Department of Education, National Center for Education Statistics, Common Core of Data (CCD), "State Nonfiscal Survey of Public Elementary/Secondary Education," 1990–91 through 2012–13; and State Public Elementary and Secondary Enrollment Projection Model, 1980 through 2024. (This table was prepared August 2015.)

Table 203.25. Public school enrollment in prekindergarten through grade 8, by region, state, and jurisdiction: Selected years, fall 1990 through fall 2024

Region, state, and jurisdiction	Actual enrollment													Percent change in enrollment, 2007 to 2012	Projected enrollment						Percent change in enrollment, 2012 to 2024
	Fall 1990	Fall 2000	Fall 2002	Fall 2003	Fall 2004	Fall 2005	Fall 2006	Fall 2007	Fall 2008	Fall 2009	Fall 2010	Fall 2011	Fall 2012		Fall 2013	Fall 2014	Fall 2015	Fall 2016	Fall 2020	Fall 2024	
1	2	3	4	5	6	7	8	9	10	11	12	13	14	15	16	17	18	19	20	21	22
United States	**29,875,914**	**33,686,421**	**34,114,245**	**34,200,741**	**34,177,565**	**34,203,962**	**34,234,751**	**34,204,081**	**34,285,564**	**34,409,260**	**34,624,530**	**34,772,751**	**35,017,893**	**2.4**	**35,187,700**	**35,159,200**	**35,181,900**	**35,282,300**	**36,365,600**	**37,615,400**	**7.4**
Region																					
Northeast	5,188,795	5,839,970	5,809,545	5,751,561	5,689,094	5,622,955	5,573,729	5,504,400	5,476,224	5,494,080	5,540,276	5,479,174	5,493,308	-0.2	5,487,900	5,458,400	5,436,900	5,427,600	5,485,000	5,587,800	1.7
Midwest	7,129,501	7,523,246	7,534,620	7,501,579	7,438,674	7,425,308	7,404,578	7,359,028	7,373,391	7,361,959	7,349,334	7,358,792	7,368,484	0.1	7,371,200	7,330,100	7,299,400	7,284,100	7,335,700	7,405,800	0.5
South	10,858,800	12,314,176	12,573,054	12,675,179	12,780,160	12,881,836	12,989,696	13,085,045	13,166,980	13,300,643	13,434,553	13,578,211	13,711,284	4.8	13,821,000	13,827,800	13,852,400	13,914,300	14,450,200	15,048,400	9.8
West	6,698,818	8,009,029	8,197,026	8,272,422	8,269,637	8,273,863	8,266,748	8,255,608	8,268,969	8,252,578	8,300,367	8,356,574	8,444,817	2.3	8,507,600	8,542,900	8,593,300	8,656,300	9,094,600	9,573,500	13.4
State																					
Alabama	527,097	538,634	533,207	525,313	521,757	529,347	528,664	525,978	528,078	529,394	533,612	527,006	527,434	0.3	526,400	521,400	517,100	514,300	514,600	516,800	-2.0
Alaska	85,297	94,442	94,380	93,695	91,981	91,225	90,167	88,980	89,263	90,824	91,990	92,057	93,069	4.6	93,800	94,600	95,700	97,300	104,900	112,100	20.5
Arizona	479,046	640,564	660,359	704,322	722,203	739,535	759,656	771,056	771,749	760,420	751,992	759,494	767,734	-0.4	778,800	789,500	800,300	812,400	876,600	957,400	24.7
Arkansas	313,505	318,023	318,826	321,508	328,187	335,746	336,552	339,920	341,603	344,209	345,808	346,022	347,631	2.3	346,500	343,600	340,900	338,800	339,900	347,700	#
California	3,613,734	4,407,035	4,525,385	4,539,777	4,507,355	4,465,615	4,410,105	4,328,968	4,306,258	4,264,022	4,293,968	4,308,447	4,331,807	0.1	4,355,900	4,361,500	4,379,200	4,402,600	4,602,600	4,809,500	11.0
Colorado	419,910	516,566	534,465	536,325	540,695	549,875	559,041	565,726	580,304	591,378	601,077	610,854	617,510	9.2	623,900	626,100	628,300	630,700	651,900	682,200	10.5
Connecticut	347,396	406,445	405,998	407,794	404,169	399,705	398,063	394,034	392,218	389,964	387,475	383,377	380,709	-3.4	375,500	370,400	366,300	363,700	365,200	377,300	-0.9
Delaware	72,606	80,801	82,221	82,898	83,599	84,639	84,996	85,019	86,811	87,710	90,279	90,624	91,004	7.0	92,000	92,400	93,100	93,700	95,700	97,500	7.2
District of Columbia	61,282	53,692	58,802	59,489	57,118	55,646	52,391	55,836	50,779	51,656	53,548	56,195	58,273	4.4	60,300	60,300	60,700	61,300	62,300	58,600	0.6
Florida	1,369,934	1,759,902	1,809,279	1,832,376	1,857,798	1,873,395	1,866,562	1,855,859	1,849,295	1,850,901	1,858,498	1,876,102	1,892,560	2.0	1,903,500	1,907,300	1,914,400	1,931,300	2,055,200	2,194,200	15.9
Georgia	849,082	1,059,983	1,088,561	1,103,181	1,118,379	1,145,446	1,166,508	1,178,577	1,185,684	1,194,751	1,202,479	1,211,250	1,222,289	3.7	1,228,400	1,227,300	1,227,900	1,232,600	1,282,000	1,343,900	9.9
Hawaii	122,840	132,293	130,862	130,054	128,788	127,472	126,008	125,556	125,910	127,477	127,525	131,005	133,590	6.4	135,400	135,300	135,800	135,700	136,100	134,700	0.9
Idaho	160,091	170,421	173,249	175,424	178,221	182,829	187,005	191,171	193,554	194,728	194,144	198,064	202,203	5.8	204,200	205,500	206,400	207,400	213,700	219,500	8.6
Illinois	1,309,516	1,473,933	1,487,650	1,492,725	1,483,644	1,480,320	1,477,679	1,472,909	1,479,195	1,463,713	1,454,793	1,453,156	1,448,201	-1.7	1,448,300	1,436,600	1,428,700	1,421,200	1,412,900	1,427,000	-1.5
Indiana	675,804	703,261	714,003	716,819	720,006	724,467	730,108	729,550	730,021	730,599	729,414	724,605	725,040	-0.6	722,500	716,100	708,100	704,100	712,300	728,000	0.4
Iowa	344,804	333,750	325,843	326,831	324,169	326,160	326,218	329,504	335,566	341,333	348,112	350,152	355,041	7.8	357,700	356,900	356,900	357,200	358,600	353,600	-0.4
Kansas	319,648	323,157	321,795	322,491	321,176	320,513	326,201	326,771	331,079	332,997	342,927	347,129	349,695	7.0	351,500	350,600	350,000	350,100	353,500	355,100	1.5
Kentucky	459,200	471,429	476,751	478,254	485,794	487,429	487,165	469,373	472,204	484,466	480,334	488,456	491,065	4.6	493,600	491,300	488,700	487,600	488,500	490,300	-0.2
Louisiana	586,202	546,579	536,882	536,390	533,751	482,082	492,116	499,549	504,213	509,883	512,266	518,802	524,792	5.1	528,800	526,100	524,300	522,500	522,000	512,700	-2.3
Maine	155,203	145,701	141,776	139,420	136,275	133,491	132,338	130,742	129,324	128,646	128,929	130,046	127,924	-2.2	126,600	125,200	124,200	123,500	122,800	122,500	-4.2
Maryland	526,744	609,043	610,337	605,862	597,417	588,571	579,065	576,479	576,473	581,785	588,156	594,216	602,802	4.6	611,200	616,400	624,200	631,100	671,500	708,900	17.6
Massachusetts	604,234	702,575	701,050	692,130	682,175	675,398	670,628	666,926	666,538	666,551	666,402	666,314	667,267	0.1	665,800	660,000	654,800	651,100	653,200	671,500	0.6
Michigan	1,144,878	1,222,482	1,253,811	1,229,121	1,211,698	1,191,397	1,170,558	1,136,823	1,118,569	1,114,611	1,075,584	1,070,873	1,061,930	-6.6	1,053,300	1,040,900	1,031,000	1,024,200	1,024,600	1,030,700	-2.9
Minnesota	545,556	577,766	567,701	564,049	558,447	557,757	558,445	558,180	560,184	564,661	569,963	575,544	583,363	4.5	591,700	596,600	601,600	608,100	637,700	666,800	14.3
Mississippi	371,641	363,873	360,254	360,881	361,057	358,030	356,382	353,512	351,807	351,652	350,885	352,999	356,364	0.8	357,000	354,400	352,600	351,300	349,500	341,000	-4.3
Missouri	588,070	644,766	634,667	632,227	628,667	635,142	634,275	631,746	635,411	638,082	642,991	645,376	647,530	2.5	646,600	643,100	641,000	640,400	646,700	654,000	1.0
Montana	111,169	105,226	101,177	100,160	98,673	97,770	97,021	96,354	96,869	97,868	98,491	99,725	100,819	4.6	102,200	103,400	104,200	105,100	108,200	107,100	6.3
Nebraska	198,080	195,486	195,113	195,417	194,816	195,055	195,769	200,095	202,912	206,860	210,292	213,504	215,432	7.7	218,900	219,200	219,400	219,400	220,100	220,300	2.3
Nevada	149,881	250,720	270,940	280,734	288,753	295,989	302,953	307,573	308,328	305,512	307,297	309,360	313,730	2.0	316,900	320,300	324,400	329,400	365,600	410,700	30.9
New Hampshire	126,301	147,121	143,616	142,031	140,241	138,584	136,188	134,359	132,995	132,768	131,576	129,632	128,169	-4.6	126,400	125,000	124,000	123,200	126,200	132,700	3.5
New Jersey	783,422	967,533	978,609	978,440	975,856	970,592	963,418	954,418	956,765	968,332	981,255	947,576	956,070	0.2	953,100	947,300	942,500	939,900	949,400	971,200	1.6
New Mexico	208,087	224,879	224,497	226,032	227,900	229,552	230,091	229,718	231,415	235,343	239,345	239,481	240,978	4.9	242,100	242,100	241,700	241,600	242,600	238,900	-0.8
New York	1,827,418	2,028,906	2,016,282	1,978,181	1,942,575	1,909,028	1,887,284	1,856,315	1,843,080	1,847,003	1,869,150	1,857,574	1,868,561	0.7	1,876,300	1,872,100	1,871,200	1,872,700	1,898,500	1,921,000	2.8
North Carolina	783,132	945,470	963,967	974,019	985,740	1,003,118	1,027,067	1,072,324	1,058,926	1,053,801	1,058,409	1,074,063	1,080,090	0.7	1,086,100	1,086,500	1,087,600	1,093,000	1,157,300	1,243,600	15.1
North Dakota	84,943	72,421	69,089	67,870	67,122	65,638	64,395	63,492	63,955	64,576	66,035	67,888	70,995	11.8	73,900	76,100	78,100	79,900	84,200	82,800	16.6
Ohio	1,257,580	1,293,646	1,283,795	1,278,202	1,267,088	1,261,331	1,253,193	1,241,322	1,239,494	1,225,346	1,222,808	1,217,226	1,211,299	-2.4	1,206,500	1,195,500	1,185,400	1,178,200	1,169,700	1,165,200	-3.8
Oklahoma	424,899	445,402	449,030	450,310	452,942	456,954	459,944	462,629	467,960	476,962	483,464	490,196	496,144	7.2	500,100	499,800	500,400	501,300	509,300	515,100	3.8
Oregon	340,243	379,264	381,988	378,052	376,933	379,680	380,576	383,598	395,421	404,451	392,601	391,310	409,325	6.7	404,700	406,000	408,300	411,800	435,900	462,200	12.9
Pennsylvania	1,172,164	1,257,824	1,241,636	1,235,624	1,234,828	1,227,625	1,220,074	1,205,351	1,194,327	1,200,446	1,209,766	1,204,850	1,204,732	-0.1	1,204,500	1,199,400	1,195,700	1,195,800	1,209,600	1,226,600	1.8
Rhode Island	101,797	113,545	112,544	111,209	107,040	103,870	101,996	99,159	97,983	98,184	97,734	97,659	97,809	-1.4	97,600	97,100	96,100	95,300	95,000	97,900	0.1
South Carolina	452,033	493,226	500,427	500,743	504,264	498,030	501,273	504,566	507,602	512,124	515,581	519,389	527,350	4.5	532,500	534,100	536,100	539,400	559,000	570,600	8.2
South Dakota	95,165	87,838	89,450	86,015	83,891	83,530	83,137	83,424	87,477	85,745	87,936	90,529	93,204	11.7	93,800	94,700	95,700	96,600	98,600	98,100	5.2
Tennessee	598,111	668,123	673,337	675,277	670,880	676,576	691,971	681,751	684,549	686,668	701,707	712,749	711,525	4.4	716,100	715,700	716,400	719,100	744,600	778,300	9.4
Texas	2,510,955	2,943,047	3,079,665	3,132,584	3,184,235	3,268,339	3,319,782	3,374,684	3,446,511	3,520,348	3,586,609	3,636,852	3,690,146	9.3	3,740,000	3,755,100	3,772,200	3,799,500	3,972,300	4,164,100	12.8
Utah	324,982	333,104	342,607	348,840	355,445	357,644	371,272	410,258	404,469	413,343	424,979	434,536	444,202	8.3	452,200	456,600	460,700	464,700	483,700	507,600	14.3

See notes at end of table.

Table 203.25. Public school enrollment in prekindergarten through grade 8, by region, state, and jurisdiction: Selected years, fall 1990 through fall 2024—Continued

Region, state, and jurisdiction	Actual enrollment													Percent change in enrollment, 2007 to 2012	Projected enrollment						Percent change in enrollment, 2012 to 2024
	Fall 1990	Fall 2000	Fall 2002	Fall 2003	Fall 2004	Fall 2005	Fall 2006	Fall 2007	Fall 2008	Fall 2009	Fall 2010	Fall 2011	Fall 2012		Fall 2013	Fall 2014	Fall 2015	Fall 2016	Fall 2020	Fall 2024	
1	2	3	4	5	6	7	8	9	10	11	12	13	14	15	16	17	18	19	20	21	22
Vermont	70,860	70,320	68,034	66,732	65,935	64,662	63,740	63,096	62,994	62,186	67,999	62,146	62,067	-1.6	62,000	61,800	62,000	62,300	65,100	67,200	8.3
Virginia	728,280	815,748	831,504	837,258	839,687	841,299	841,685	850,444	855,008	864,020	871,446	881,225	889,444	4.6	896,600	897,500	900,000	904,700	942,000	988,500	11.1
Washington	612,597	694,367	697,191	699,248	695,405	699,482	694,858	697,407	704,794	705,387	714,172	718,184	724,560	3.9	731,000	734,800	740,400	749,400	805,200	867,200	19.7
West Virginia	224,097	201,201	200,004	198,836	197,555	197,189	197,573	198,545	199,477	200,313	201,472	202,065	202,371	1.9	201,900	198,600	195,900	192,900	184,500	176,700	-12.7
Wisconsin	565,457	594,740	591,703	589,812	577,950	583,998	584,600	585,212	589,528	593,436	598,479	602,810	606,754	3.7	606,400	603,800	603,500	604,600	616,800	624,100	2.9
Wyoming	70,941	60,148	59,926	59,759	57,285	57,195	57,995	59,243	60,635	61,825	62,786	64,057	65,290	10.2	66,700	67,300	67,800	68,200	67,700	64,300	-1.5
Jurisdiction																					
Bureau of Indian Education	—	35,746	34,392	33,671	33,671	36,133	—	—	30,612	31,381	31,985	—	—	—	—	—	—	—	—	—	—
DoD, overseas	—	59,299	58,214	56,226	53,720	48,691	47,589	44,418	43,931	—	—	—	—	—	—	—	—	—	—	—	—
DoD, domestic	—	30,697	28,759	27,500	26,195	25,558	24,062	24,807	25,255	—	—	—	—	—	—	—	—	—	—	—	—
Other jurisdictions																					
American Samoa	9,390	11,895	11,838	11,772	11,873	11,766	11,763	—	—	—	—	—	—	—	—	—	—	—	—	—	—
Guam	19,276	23,698	—	22,551	21,686	21,946	—	—	—	—	21,561	21,223	21,166	—	—	—	—	—	—	—	—
Northern Marianas	4,918	7,809	8,379	8,192	8,416	8,427	8,504	8,140	7,816	7,743	7,688	7,703	7,396	-9.1	—	—	—	—	—	—	—
Puerto Rico	480,356	445,524	429,413	418,649	408,671	399,447	382,647	372,514	355,115	347,638	334,613	318,924	305,048	-18.1	—	—	—	—	—	—	—
U.S. Virgin Islands	16,249	13,910	12,933	12,738	11,650	11,728	11,237	10,770	10,567	10,409	10,518	10,576	10,302	-4.3	—	—	—	—	—	—	—

—Not available.
#Rounds to zero.
NOTE: DoD = Department of Defense. Detail may not sum to totals because of rounding. Some data have been revised from previously published figures.

SOURCE: U.S. Department of Education, National Center for Education Statistics, Common Core of Data (CCD), State Nonfiscal Survey of Public Elementary/Secondary Education, 1990–91 through 2012–13; and State Public Elementary and Secondary Enrollment Projection Model, 1980 through 2024. (This table was prepared August 2015.)

Table 203.30. Public school enrollment in grades 9 through 12, by region, state, and jurisdiction: Selected years, fall 1990 through fall 2024

Region, state, and jurisdiction	Actual enrollment													Percent change in enrollment, 2007 to 2012	Projected enrollment						Percent change in enrollment, 2012 to 2024
	Fall 1990	Fall 2000	Fall 2002	Fall 2003	Fall 2004	Fall 2005	Fall 2006	Fall 2007	Fall 2008	Fall 2009	Fall 2010	Fall 2011	Fall 2012		Fall 2013	Fall 2014	Fall 2015	Fall 2016	Fall 2020	Fall 2024	
1	2	3	4	5	6	7	8	9	10	11	12	13	14	15	16	17	18	19	20	21	22
United States	11,340,769	13,517,118	14,068,841	14,339,474	14,617,900	14,909,336	15,081,091	15,086,478	14,980,008	14,951,722	14,859,651	14,748,918	14,753,225	-2.2	14,754,200	14,826,400	14,912,500	14,946,700	15,181,900	15,304,200	3.7
Region																					
Northeast	2,092,968	2,382,157	2,487,076	2,540,754	2,582,165	2,617,205	2,684,160	2,617,622	2,576,761	2,597,949	2,531,059	2,474,807	2,465,820	-5.8	2,440,300	2,429,300	2,424,200	2,411,700	2,414,500	2,370,600	-3.9
Midwest	2,814,260	3,206,741	3,284,350	3,307,398	3,336,735	3,393,507	3,414,670	3,411,182	3,389,582	3,310,212	3,260,270	3,215,000	3,190,746	-6.5	3,178,300	3,182,100	3,194,400	3,195,600	3,201,000	3,148,000	-1.3
South	3,948,216	4,693,085	4,898,386	4,997,566	5,111,827	5,221,330	5,303,937	5,337,728	5,323,790	5,351,246	5,370,447	5,377,721	5,417,092	1.5	5,462,200	5,531,500	5,597,400	5,627,700	5,737,700	5,851,200	8.0
West	2,485,325	3,235,135	3,399,029	3,493,756	3,587,173	3,677,294	3,678,324	3,719,946	3,709,875	3,692,315	3,697,875	3,681,390	3,679,567	-1.1	3,673,400	3,683,500	3,696,600	3,711,600	3,828,700	3,934,400	6.9
State																					
Alabama	194,709	201,358	206,159	205,907	208,383	212,414	214,968	216,941	217,590	219,495	221,940	217,615	217,203	0.1	217,000	218,100	218,000	216,700	209,500	207,100	-4.7
Alaska	28,606	38,914	39,984	40,238	40,989	42,063	42,441	42,049	41,399	40,837	40,114	39,110	38,420	-8.6	38,000	38,100	38,100	38,100	39,700	41,700	8.6
Arizona	160,807	237,132	277,396	307,746	321,095	354,919	308,563	316,391	316,068	317,411	319,759	320,825	321,650	1.7	318,800	316,200	316,600	320,500	345,700	362,700	12.8
Arkansas	122,781	131,306	132,159	133,015	134,928	138,460	139,861	139,096	136,360	136,350	136,306	137,092	138,526	-0.4	139,800	140,500	140,700	140,900	138,900	135,100	-2.5
California	1,336,740	1,733,779	1,828,282	1,874,090	1,934,202	1,971,587	1,996,845	2,014,503	2,016,270	1,999,416	1,995,610	1,979,387	1,967,644	-2.3	1,955,800	1,953,200	1,949,100	1,948,900	1,983,500	2,023,700	2.8
Colorado	154,303	207,942	217,397	221,368	225,281	229,951	234,985	236,141	238,139	240,990	242,239	243,411	246,051	4.2	249,100	253,700	259,300	263,800	277,400	279,100	13.4
Connecticut	121,727	155,734	164,025	169,409	173,221	175,354	177,037	176,592	174,980	174,004	173,071	171,060	170,245	-3.6	168,000	165,500	163,900	161,500	155,800	147,100	-13.6
Delaware	27,052	33,875	34,121	34,770	35,492	36,298	37,258	37,555	38,619	39,091	39,124	38,322	37,867	1.2	37,800	37,500	37,700	38,000	40,800	40,800	7.3
District of Columbia	19,412	15,233	17,364	18,568	19,596	21,230	20,459	22,586	17,902	17,777	17,736	17,716	17,867	-20.9	17,500	17,500	17,500	17,100	17,800	19,700	10.1
Florida	491,658	674,919	730,650	755,252	781,538	801,629	804,951	810,952	781,725	783,621	784,849	792,054	799,602	-1.4	803,900	809,700	812,600	811,000	813,000	846,700	5.9
Georgia	302,605	384,954	407,451	419,430	435,058	453,015	462,649	471,012	470,108	472,934	474,588	473,766	481,043	2.1	487,800	494,800	501,600	503,000	506,600	514,400	6.9
Hawaii	48,868	52,067	52,967	53,555	54,397	55,346	54,720	54,341	53,568	52,719	52,076	51,701	51,170	-5.8	51,100	51,700	51,600	52,300	54,800	54,600	6.7
Idaho	60,749	74,696	75,355	76,696	77,863	79,153	80,375	80,948	81,497	81,571	81,715	81,809	82,631	2.1	84,100	84,900	86,500	87,900	92,100	93,500	13.2
Illinois	511,891	574,859	596,537	608,236	613,889	631,386	640,597	639,896	640,512	640,462	636,861	629,941	624,679	-2.4	621,500	622,800	626,800	631,600	639,400	610,000	-2.4
Indiana	278,721	286,006	289,872	294,311	301,342	310,607	315,832	317,214	316,126	316,062	317,818	316,160	316,329	-0.3	316,600	316,700	320,500	319,400	305,100	301,800	-4.6
Iowa	138,848	161,330	156,367	154,995	154,150	157,322	156,904	155,611	151,993	150,509	147,663	145,718	144,784	-7.0	145,100	145,900	146,700	147,200	151,700	152,600	5.6
Kansas	117,386	147,453	149,162	147,999	147,960	147,012	143,305	141,524	139,981	139,492	140,774	138,979	139,948	-1.5	139,500	140,400	142,000	142,300	145,400	144,700	3.9
Kentucky	177,201	194,421	184,031	185,115	189,002	192,449	195,987	196,852	197,826	195,623	192,794	193,531	194,102	-1.4	194,100	195,200	198,000	198,700	200,900	198,900	2.5
Louisiana	198,555	196,510	193,582	191,319	190,530	172,444	183,735	181,489	180,660	181,032	184,292	184,588	186,111	2.5	186,100	188,400	190,400	192,500	193,800	194,700	4.6
Maine	59,946	61,336	62,561	62,664	62,545	62,007	61,648	65,503	63,611	60,579	60,148	58,923	57,815	-11.7	56,800	55,900	55,200	54,100	52,900	50,600	-12.5
Maryland	188,432	243,877	256,406	263,251	268,144	271,449	272,575	269,221	267,388	266,627	264,055	259,870	256,836	-4.6	253,400	252,600	251,800	253,600	269,600	280,900	9.4
Massachusetts	230,080	272,575	281,939	288,329	293,399	296,511	298,033	296,032	292,372	290,502	289,161	287,055	287,506	-2.9	287,000	287,000	287,100	285,800	282,700	272,500	-5.2
Michigan	439,553	498,144	531,349	528,483	539,592	550,885	552,098	555,916	541,352	534,471	511,483	502,664	493,440	-11.2	488,800	486,200	482,600	478,600	458,500	443,900	-10.0
Minnesota	210,818	276,574	279,190	278,805	280,056	281,496	282,120	279,998	275,864	272,392	268,074	264,194	262,041	-6.2	262,800	264,600	267,200	269,800	287,400	294,800	12.5
Mississippi	130,776	133,998	132,391	132,689	134,319	138,924	138,644	140,155	140,155	140,829	139,641	137,620	137,286	-2.4	137,000	138,700	139,400	139,200	136,400	137,900	0.5
Missouri	228,488	267,978	271,832	273,714	276,782	282,563	286,078	285,442	282,460	279,900	275,719	271,208	270,370	-5.3	269,900	269,700	269,500	267,700	268,000	265,000	-2.0
Montana	41,805	49,649	48,818	48,196	48,032	47,646	47,397	46,469	45,030	43,939	43,202	42,624	42,089	-9.4	42,200	41,900	42,100	42,300	44,500	47,000	11.6
Nebraska	76,001	90,713	90,289	90,125	90,945	91,591	91,811	91,149	89,678	88,508	88,208	87,792	88,073	-3.4	88,000	88,600	89,700	91,300	96,900	96,000	9.0
Nevada	51,435	89,986	98,558	104,667	111,330	116,406	121,813	121,789	125,043	123,435	129,852	130,274	131,977	8.4	131,000	132,600	134,200	135,500	139,700	150,200	13.8
New Hampshire	46,484	61,340	64,055	65,386	66,611	67,183	67,384	66,413	64,939	64,372	63,135	62,268	60,805	-8.4	59,500	58,600	57,600	56,800	54,200	52,300	-14.0
New Jersey	306,224	345,872	388,829	402,313	417,491	425,010	425,432	427,930	424,655	427,697	421,293	408,855	416,133	-2.8	414,300	414,800	414,900	413,200	411,800	403,000	-3.1
New Mexico	93,794	95,427	95,737	97,034	98,202	97,206	98,129	99,922	98,830	99,076	98,777	97,744	97,242	-2.1	97,700	98,400	99,600	100,300	102,200	101,800	4.7
New York	770,919	853,282	871,951	886,594	893,762	906,553	922,365	909,120	897,512	919,049	865,805	847,144	842,142	-7.4	834,200	832,800	830,700	828,400	843,300	841,400	-0.1
North Carolina	303,739	348,188	371,987	386,190	400,014	413,318	417,414	417,188	429,719	429,596	432,196	433,801	438,375	5.1	444,600	452,100	459,100	462,100	460,300	474,400	8.2
North Dakota	32,882	36,780	35,136	34,363	33,391	32,645	32,275	31,567	30,773	30,497	30,288	29,758	30,116	-4.6	30,400	30,500	31,000	31,400	36,900	41,500	37.7
Ohio	513,509	541,403	554,490	567,226	572,944	578,352	583,529	585,862	577,669	539,951	531,383	522,804	518,617	-11.5	513,100	513,300	514,100	511,900	501,900	486,700	-6.2
Oklahoma	154,188	177,708	175,518	175,850	176,534	177,785	179,447	179,436	177,148	177,840	176,447	175,924	177,339	-1.2	179,500	182,700	185,200	186,800	194,300	196,500	10.8
Oregon	132,151	166,967	172,083	173,221	175,572	172,514	181,998	181,988	179,972	178,388	178,119	176,898	178,239	-2.1	178,300	178,300	178,900	178,400	181,000	187,600	5.3
Pennsylvania	495,670	556,487	575,111	585,522	593,261	603,059	650,986	596,620	580,702	585,547	583,518	566,545	558,945	-6.3	550,400	546,100	546,700	544,100	545,600	538,100	-3.7
Rhode Island	37,016	43,802	46,661	48,166	49,458	49,552	49,616	48,470	47,359	46,934	46,059	45,195	44,672	-7.8	43,100	42,100	42,000	42,100	42,900	39,900	-10.6
South Carolina	170,079	184,185	193,962	198,455	199,472	203,514	206,748	207,751	210,511	211,019	210,257	207,797	208,648	0.4	211,100	215,000	218,700	220,000	225,500	234,800	12.6
South Dakota	33,999	40,765	40,598	39,522	38,807	38,482	38,021	38,182	38,952	37,968	38,192	37,487	37,267	-2.4	37,200	37,300	37,400	37,800	40,900	42,500	14.1
Tennessee	226,484	241,038	254,271	261,405	270,211	277,352	286,397	282,508	287,401	285,881	285,715	286,944	281,971	-0.2	281,900	283,400	285,300	285,700	289,800	293,600	4.1
Texas	871,932	1,116,572	1,180,158	1,199,167	1,220,980	1,257,055	1,279,727	1,300,148	1,305,637	1,329,862	1,349,106	1,363,618	1,387,513	6.7	1,414,100	1,445,100	1,478,100	1,497,900	1,567,700	1,602,200	15.5
Utah	121,670	148,381	146,655	147,141	148,162	150,796	152,114	165,986	155,309	158,243	160,573	164,296	169,077	1.9	173,900	179,800	185,300	189,400	205,100	211,800	25.3

See notes at end of table.

Table 203.30. Public school enrollment in grades 9 through 12, by region, state, and jurisdiction: Selected years, fall 1990 through fall 2024—Continued

Region, state, and jurisdiction	Fall 1990	Fall 2000	Fall 2002	Fall 2003	Fall 2004	Fall 2005	Fall 2006	Fall 2007	Fall 2008	Fall 2009	Fall 2010	Fall 2011	Fall 2012	Percent change in enrollment, 2007 to 2012	Fall 2013	Fall 2014	Fall 2015	Fall 2016	Fall 2020	Fall 2024	Percent change in enrollment, 2012 to 2024
1	2	3	4	5	6	7	8	9	10	11	12	13	14	15	16	17	18	19	20	21	22
Vermont	24,902	31,729	31,944	32,371	32,417	31,976	31,669	30,942	30,631	29,285	28,869	27,762	27,557	-10.9	27,000	26,500	26,000	25,600	25,300	25,700	-6.9
Virginia	270,321	329,167	345,725	354,834	365,052	372,317	378,755	380,413	380,787	381,320	379,994	376,658	375,975	-1.2	376,600	379,800	383,000	384,400	394,500	399,600	6.3
Washington	227,112	310,403	317,607	322,101	324,600	332,503	331,916	332,840	332,224	329,960	329,616	327,289	327,134	-1.7	326,500	327,500	327,800	326,700	332,900	349,700	6.9
West Virginia	98,292	85,166	82,451	82,379	82,574	83,677	84,366	83,990	83,252	82,349	81,407	80,805	80,673	-3.9	80,100	80,400	80,300	80,100	78,300	73,900	-8.3
Wisconsin	232,164	284,736	289,528	290,219	296,807	291,176	292,100	289,421	284,222	279,000	273,807	268,295	265,682	-8.2	265,300	266,000	267,000	266,800	269,000	268,200	1.0
Wyoming	27,285	29,792	28,190	27,703	27,448	27,214	27,198	27,179	26,526	26,330	26,223	26,042	26,243	-3.4	26,700	27,100	27,400	27,600	30,100	31,000	18.0
Jurisdiction																					
Bureau of Indian Education	—	11,192	11,734	12,157	12,157	14,805	—	—	10,315	9,970	9,977	—	—	—	—	—	—	—	—	—	—
DoD, overseas	—	14,282	14,675	14,827	14,607	13,852	13,302	12,829	12,837	—	—	—	—	—	—	—	—	—	—	—	—
DoD, domestic	—	3,477	3,356	3,103	2,956	2,771	2,579	2,741	2,758	—	—	—	—	—	—	—	—	—	—	—	—
Other jurisdictions																					
American Samoa	3,073	3,807	4,146	4,121	4,253	4,672	4,637	—	—	—	—	—	—	—	—	—	—	—	—	—	—
Guam	7,115	8,775	—	9,021	8,919	9,040	—	—	—	—	10,057	10,020	10,020	—	—	—	—	—	—	—	—
Northern Marianas	1,531	2,195	2,872	3,052	3,185	3,291	3,191	3,159	3,097	3,218	3,417	3,308	3,250	2.9	—	—	—	—	—	—	—
Puerto Rico	164,378	167,201	167,089	166,287	166,977	164,043	161,491	154,051	148,520	145,755	139,122	133,816	129,561	-15.9	—	—	—	—	—	—	—
U.S. Virgin Islands	5,501	5,549	5,400	4,978	4,779	5,022	5,047	5,133	5,201	5,084	4,977	5,135	4,890	-4.7	—	—	—	—	—	—	—

—Not available.

NOTE: DoD = Department of Defense. Detail may not sum to totals because of rounding. Some data have been revised from previously published figures.

SOURCE: U.S. Department of Education, National Center for Education Statistics, Common Core of Data (CCD), "State Nonfiscal Survey of Public Elementary/Secondary Education," 1990–91 through 2012–13; and State Public Elementary and Secondary Enrollment Projection Model, 1980 through 2024. (This table was prepared August 2015.)

Table 203.40. Enrollment in public elementary and secondary schools, by level, grade, and state or jurisdiction: Fall 2012

State or jurisdiction	Total, all grades	Elementary												Secondary					
		Total	Prekinder-garten	Kinder-garten	Grade 1	Grade 2	Grade 3	Grade 4	Grade 5	Grade 6	Grade 7	Grade 8	Elementary ungraded	Total	Grade 9	Grade 10	Grade 11	Grade 12	Secondary ungraded
1	2	3	4	5	6	7	8	9	10	11	12	13	14	15	16	17	18	19	20
United States	49,771,118	35,017,893	1,306,991	3,830,982	3,823,604	3,729,465	3,719,135	3,690,224	3,672,977	3,723,354	3,746,485	3,698,977	75,699	14,753,225	3,975,264	3,729,960	3,528,256	3,477,025	42,720
Alabama	744,637	527,434	9,032	59,428	58,287	56,361	55,868	55,859	56,523	58,240	59,685	58,151	0	217,203	61,642	56,229	50,387	48,945	0
Alaska	131,489	93,069	3,131	10,569	10,393	10,109	9,950	9,756	9,677	9,844	9,834	9,806	0	38,420	9,724	9,415	9,585	9,696	0
Arizona	1,089,384	767,734	9,304	86,265	86,474	84,763	83,883	83,892	83,093	83,540	83,568	82,769	183	321,650	82,291	80,074	77,518	81,751	16
Arkansas	486,157	347,631	14,290	40,463	37,093	36,450	36,362	36,140	36,569	36,727	36,693	36,607	237	138,526	37,978	36,343	33,373	30,734	98
California	6,299,451	4,331,807	74,360	489,274	489,420	474,656	470,243	468,007	462,439	463,024	470,054	465,967	4,363	1,967,644	497,945	487,566	482,903	496,754	2,476
Colorado	863,561	617,510	30,375	66,951	67,369	66,134	65,667	65,921	64,727	64,448	63,658	62,260	0	246,051	63,859	60,842	58,847	62,503	0
Connecticut	550,954	380,709	16,393	39,410	39,558	39,858	39,867	40,895	40,196	40,979	41,533	42,020	0	170,245	45,166	42,144	42,192	40,743	0
Delaware	129,026	91,004	1,291	10,128	10,393	10,123	9,963	10,089	9,619	9,699	9,983	9,716	0	38,022	11,056	9,670	8,931	8,365	0
District of Columbia	76,140	58,273	11,428	6,980	6,163	5,629	4,991	4,631	4,575	4,627	4,559	4,202	488	17,867	6,275	4,245	3,740	3,317	290
Florida	2,692,162	1,892,560	55,124	210,489	208,344	202,517	209,027	195,358	197,412	204,704	205,469	204,116	0	799,602	215,693	206,662	194,054	183,193	0
Georgia	1,703,332	1,222,289	45,252	136,837	133,482	130,176	129,257	128,538	129,054	130,803	130,458	128,432	0	481,043	146,953	124,928	108,084	101,078	0
Hawaii	184,760	133,590	1,509	17,497	15,555	15,264	14,810	14,572	14,383	13,315	13,772	12,791	122	51,170	14,786	13,307	12,255	10,721	101
Idaho	284,834	202,203	2,683	22,409	22,535	22,508	22,247	21,884	22,000	22,304	21,963	21,670	0	82,631	21,987	20,812	20,702	19,130	0
Illinois	2,072,880	1,448,201	81,475	147,315	150,312	150,336	154,232	151,409	151,508	154,031	155,078	152,505	0	624,679	165,536	160,924	151,946	146,273	0
Indiana	1,041,369	725,040	9,114	80,681	80,151	77,465	80,476	75,678	78,450	82,158	80,959	79,908	0	316,329	82,545	80,253	78,645	74,886	0
Iowa	499,825	355,041	27,729	41,381	36,730	35,891	35,455	35,492	35,142	35,469	36,058	35,694	0	144,784	36,752	36,240	35,538	36,254	0
Kansas	489,043	349,695	18,475	38,379	37,304	36,399	36,000	36,167	35,546	35,962	35,963	35,447	4,044	139,348	37,060	34,486	33,499	32,810	1,493
Kentucky	685,167	491,065	26,753	53,875	54,028	51,296	51,215	50,583	49,999	51,550	51,154	50,259	353	194,102	53,562	49,561	46,806	44,032	141
Louisiana	710,903	524,792	29,426	58,691	58,085	54,765	53,691	57,434	51,799	53,866	54,528	52,507	0	186,111	55,745	46,920	43,267	40,179	0
Maine	185,739	127,924	4,890	13,727	13,449	13,575	13,628	13,345	13,427	13,778	13,978	14,127	0	57,815	14,684	14,421	14,248	14,462	0
Maryland	859,638	602,802	29,671	66,896	66,274	64,595	64,272	63,703	63,204	61,120	62,159	60,908	0	256,836	71,360	64,841	60,657	59,978	0
Massachusetts	954,773	667,267	28,245	69,669	70,629	69,549	70,673	70,952	70,826	71,588	72,012	72,048	1,076	287,506	77,458	72,264	69,928	67,856	0
Michigan	1,555,370	1,061,930	36,769	107,986	113,035	110,939	113,332	112,068	112,720	116,465	118,538	117,640	2,438	493,440	128,111	128,144	117,453	118,564	1,168
Minnesota	845,404	583,363	14,695	65,745	64,520	63,357	63,659	62,523	61,355	62,547	62,627	62,335	0	262,041	63,743	64,278	63,510	70,510	0
Mississippi	493,650	356,364	4,026	43,208	40,851	38,001	37,735	36,663	37,336	37,646	39,034	36,745	5,119	137,286	37,825	34,874	31,434	29,676	3,477
Missouri	917,900	647,530	29,684	71,778	70,072	68,570	68,043	67,493	67,269	67,959	68,605	68,057	0	270,370	72,240	68,242	65,737	64,151	0
Montana	142,908	100,819	1,321	11,709	11,678	11,031	11,036	10,861	10,822	10,842	10,624	10,895	0	42,089	11,256	10,676	10,373	9,784	0
Nebraska	303,505	215,432	13,831	22,095	23,331	22,836	23,057	22,583	22,370	21,998	21,893	21,438	0	88,073	21,796	21,725	21,400	23,152	0
Nevada	445,707	313,730	4,599	35,008	35,429	34,266	33,557	33,462	33,787	34,364	34,373	34,192	693	131,977	34,025	33,462	32,527	31,939	24
New Hampshire	188,974	128,169	3,260	11,892	13,692	13,531	13,861	13,907	14,253	14,284	14,705	14,784	0	60,805	16,321	15,243	14,641	14,600	0
New Jersey	1,372,203	956,070	35,128	94,830	98,464	97,499	98,305	98,152	97,328	98,744	99,624	100,052	37,944	416,133	105,857	101,466	96,504	97,048	15,258
New Mexico	338,220	240,978	7,509	27,662	26,932	26,208	25,818	25,474	25,573	25,490	25,135	25,177	0	97,242	29,217	25,711	21,755	20,559	0
New York	2,710,703	1,868,561	48,712	202,670	205,963	199,600	199,088	198,361	196,709	198,595	202,583	200,642	15,638	842,142	225,291	215,312	193,257	192,112	16,170
North Carolina	1,518,465	1,080,090	30,329	121,389	120,038	116,691	107,832	116,264	116,351	118,514	117,535	115,147	0	438,375	126,694	113,605	103,428	94,648	0
North Dakota	101,111	70,995	1,848	8,578	8,367	7,710	7,725	7,380	7,292	7,339	7,256	7,500	0	30,116	7,801	7,536	7,432	7,347	0
Ohio	1,729,916	1,211,299	27,558	131,874	131,637	128,867	129,079	129,295	130,392	133,468	135,174	133,955	0	518,617	148,752	133,301	118,941	117,623	0
Oklahoma	673,483	496,115	42,154	55,115	54,039	50,660	49,840	49,274	48,675	48,486	48,640	47,856	1,405	177,339	49,577	45,628	42,200	39,407	527
Oregon	587,564	409,325	23,850	42,642	43,438	42,436	42,532	42,401	42,235	42,916	43,297	43,578	0	178,239	44,662	43,751	43,103	46,723	0
Pennsylvania	1,763,677	1,204,732	10,109	129,624	131,691	129,861	131,638	131,315	130,592	134,359	137,172	136,775	1,596	558,945	144,396	140,180	136,531	136,357	1,481
Rhode Island	142,481	97,809	2,068	10,786	10,429	10,737	10,968	10,831	10,820	10,900	10,299	9,971	0	44,672	12,014	11,330	10,819	10,509	0

See notes at end of table.

Table 203.40. Enrollment in public elementary and secondary schools, by level, grade, and state or jurisdiction: Fall 2012—Continued

State or jurisdiction	Total, all grades	Elementary — Total	Prekindergarten	Kindergarten	Grade 1	Grade 2	Grade 3	Grade 4	Grade 5	Grade 6	Grade 7	Grade 8	Elementary ungraded	Secondary — Total	Grade 9	Grade 10	Grade 11	Grade 12	Secondary ungraded
1	2	3	4	5	6	7	8	9	10	11	12	13	14	15	16	17	18	19	20
South Carolina	735,998	527,350	23,786	58,641	58,030	55,275	54,354	54,058	54,541	56,493	56,807	55,365	0	208,648	61,897	54,033	47,963	44,755	0
South Dakota	130,471	93,204	3,117	11,901	10,546	10,316	9,874	9,657	9,458	9,377	9,550	9,408	0	37,267	10,018	9,548	8,885	8,816	0
Tennessee	933,496	711,525	27,096	81,186	79,010	75,716	74,934	74,425	74,311	75,116	75,272	74,459	0	281,971	76,794	71,810	67,068	66,299	0
Texas	5,077,659	3,690,146	250,911	390,636	396,903	389,225	382,990	378,750	376,426	380,202	377,246	366,857	0	1,387,513	403,136	350,949	328,003	305,425	0
Utah	613,279	444,202	12,329	50,378	50,171	48,872	48,926	48,362	46,991	46,540	46,246	45,387	0	169,077	44,379	42,760	41,164	40,774	0
Vermont	89,624	62,067	5,705	6,273	6,096	6,269	6,196	6,133	6,190	6,291	6,373	6,541	0	27,557	7,004	6,980	6,817	6,756	0
Virginia	1,265,419	889,444	32,852	96,935	97,267	95,231	95,405	94,005	93,941	94,874	95,147	93,787	0	375,975	101,867	94,931	90,206	88,971	0
Washington	1,051,694	724,560	12,466	80,789	80,494	78,904	78,723	78,244	77,331	78,966	79,371	79,272	0	327,134	82,972	80,696	78,485	84,981	0
West Virginia	283,044	202,371	15,781	21,785	20,788	20,459	20,483	20,181	20,698	20,623	21,052	20,521	0	80,673	22,741	20,397	18,832	18,703	0
Wisconsin	872,436	606,754	55,008	62,422	61,037	60,585	61,243	60,670	60,253	61,369	62,310	61,857	0	265,682	67,699	64,507	66,346	67,130	0
Wyoming	91,533	65,290	540	8,131	7,628	7,394	7,116	7,127	6,790	6,811	6,879	6,874	0	26,243	7,122	6,738	6,337	6,046	0
Bureau of Indian Education	—	—	—	—	—	—	—	—	—	—	—	—	—	—	—	—	—	—	—
DoD, overseas	—	—	—	—	—	—	—	—	—	—	—	—	—	—	—	—	—	—	—
DoD, domestic	—	—	—	—	—	—	—	—	—	—	—	—	—	—	—	—	—	—	—
Other jurisdictions																			
American Samoa	31,186	21,166	13	2,207	2,329	2,317	2,408	2,325	2,348	2,364	2,383	2,472	0	10,020	3,101	3,269	2,089	1,561	0
Guam	10,646	7,396	462	582	745	686	740	776	799	825	934	792	55	3,250	1,078	794	748	630	0
Northern Marianas																			
Puerto Rico	434,609	305,048	1,050	27,887	33,453	32,372	31,647	31,345	32,116	33,811	36,096	35,547	9,724	129,561	34,414	32,839	30,216	27,169	4,923
U.S. Virgin Islands	15,192	10,302	—	1,052	1,146	1,118	1,108	1,144	1,243	1,129	1,278	1,084	0	4,890	1,651	1,193	1,051	995	0

—Not available.

NOTE: DoD = Department of Defense. The total ungraded counts of students were prorated to the elementary and secondary levels based on prior reports.

SOURCE: U.S. Department of Education, National Center for Education Statistics, Common Core of Data (CCD), "State Non-fiscal Survey of Public Elementary/Secondary Education," 2012–13. (This table was prepared October 2014.)

Table 203.45. Enrollment in public elementary and secondary schools, by level, grade, and state or jurisdiction: Fall 2011

State or jurisdiction	Total, all grades	Elementary												Secondary					
		Total	Prekindergarten	Kindergarten	Grade 1	Grade 2	Grade 3	Grade 4	Grade 5	Grade 6	Grade 7	Grade 8	Elementary ungraded	Total	Grade 9	Grade 10	Grade 11	Grade 12	Secondary ungraded
1	2	3	4	5	6	7	8	9	10	11	12	13	14	15	16	17	18	19	20
United States	49,521,669	34,772,751	1,290,977	3,746,415	3,772,639	3,713,225	3,703,314	3,671,865	3,699,119	3,723,575	3,695,995	3,679,111	76,516	14,748,918	3,956,990	3,751,378	3,545,841	3,451,876	42,833
Alabama	744,621	527,006	8,282	57,602	57,859	56,315	55,991	56,491	58,415	59,082	59,050	57,919	0	217,615	61,412	55,908	50,785	49,510	0
Alaska	131,167	92,057	2,755	10,453	10,143	9,961	9,835	9,667	9,891	9,901	9,924	9,527	0	39,110	9,833	9,546	9,813	9,918	0
Arizona	1,080,319	759,494	8,860	84,433	85,535	83,843	83,546	82,566	83,185	83,150	82,879	81,294	203	320,825	82,089	80,788	76,751	81,179	18
Arkansas	483,114	346,022	14,466	37,305	37,491	36,702	36,452	36,662	36,856	36,592	36,832	36,339	325	137,092	38,078	35,729	32,711	30,441	133
California	6,287,834	4,308,447	73,630	488,070	489,961	471,993	467,539	462,082	452,305	466,942	464,260	467,626	4,039	1,979,387	501,073	494,739	487,113	494,144	2,318
Colorado	854,265	610,854	31,091	66,361	66,398	65,598	65,956	64,560	64,089	63,492	62,153	61,156	0	243,411	62,358	60,662	58,993	61,398	0
Connecticut	554,437	383,377	16,022	38,840	40,396	40,051	40,946	40,138	41,078	41,431	41,964	42,511	0	171,060	45,140	43,145	42,098	40,677	0
Delaware	128,946	90,624	1,402	10,116	10,220	9,943	10,138	9,691	9,900	9,887	9,758	9,569	0	38,322	11,168	9,809	8,775	8,570	0
District of Columbia	73,911	56,195	10,831	6,358	5,757	5,102	4,805	4,643	4,816	4,560	4,248	4,328	747	17,716	6,050	4,313	3,708	3,190	455
Florida	2,668,156	1,876,102	54,938	203,302	203,496	200,381	206,732	195,625	202,733	204,229	204,288	200,378	0	792,054	218,469	203,907	195,307	174,371	0
Georgia	1,685,016	1,211,250	45,353	133,372	131,044	128,319	128,647	128,827	131,075	130,164	127,664	126,785	0	473,766	144,204	124,998	105,939	98,625	0
Hawaii	182,706	131,005	1,492	16,827	15,156	14,810	14,672	14,353	13,598	13,919	13,274	12,783	121	51,701	14,830	13,443	12,241	11,084	103
Idaho	279,873	198,064	1,338	21,901	22,557	22,068	21,845	21,835	21,818	21,765	21,765	21,172	0	81,809	21,479	20,996	19,911	19,423	0
Illinois	2,083,097	1,453,156	80,723	145,489	151,937	153,299	153,362	151,811	153,769	155,517	153,362	153,828	0	629,941	165,849	163,897	155,148	145,047	0
Indiana	1,040,765	724,605	9,540	78,166	79,365	79,264	77,866	78,627	81,987	80,259	79,945	79,586	0	316,160	81,801	82,495	77,793	74,071	0
Iowa	495,870	350,152	26,930	40,187	35,807	35,364	35,320	34,951	35,116	35,509	35,470	35,498	0	145,718	36,726	36,333	35,590	37,069	0
Kansas	486,108	347,129	18,110	37,557	36,798	36,180	36,215	35,608	35,992	35,816	35,455	35,291	4,107	138,979	36,197	35,081	33,699	32,478	1,524
Kentucky	681,987	488,456	28,107	52,325	52,552	51,269	51,309	49,894	51,330	51,087	50,194	50,043	346	193,531	52,499	49,938	47,027	43,928	139
Louisiana	703,390	518,802	29,422	56,037	56,214	54,202	53,607	58,304	51,709	55,279	51,739	52,289	0	184,588	54,775	48,355	42,370	39,088	0
Maine	188,969	130,046	5,048	13,644	13,826	13,714	13,457	13,533	13,885	14,038	14,317	14,584	0	58,923	14,695	14,686	14,655	14,887	0
Maryland	854,086	594,216	28,850	64,727	64,300	63,976	63,421	63,118	61,111	61,901	60,895	61,917	0	259,870	71,862	65,895	61,824	60,289	0
Massachusetts	953,369	666,314	18,116	67,956	69,906	70,561	70,826	70,404	71,355	71,483	71,950	72,758	999	287,055	76,690	72,220	70,685	67,460	0
Michigan	1,573,537	1,070,873	37,020	107,852	112,451	113,884	111,984	112,465	115,681	117,691	117,802	118,628	5,415	502,664	129,661	130,276	119,607	120,498	2,622
Minnesota	839,738	575,544	14,568	64,133	63,117	63,340	62,311	60,917	61,972	61,580	62,032	61,574	0	264,194	64,074	63,908	64,629	71,583	0
Mississippi	490,619	352,999	3,842	41,048	39,291	38,456	37,067	37,715	37,983	38,800	37,689	36,071	5,037	137,620	37,856	35,235	31,952	29,115	3,462
Missouri	916,584	645,376	29,931	69,864	69,325	68,320	67,473	67,274	68,154	68,500	68,122	68,413	0	271,208	71,813	69,041	65,879	64,475	0
Montana	142,349	99,725	1,475	11,697	11,013	11,015	10,825	10,739	10,780	10,566	10,842	10,773	0	42,624	11,326	10,841	10,249	10,208	0
Nebraska	301,296	213,504	12,907	23,795	22,951	23,099	22,428	22,279	21,949	21,738	21,243	21,115	0	87,792	21,965	21,986	21,509	22,332	22
Nevada	439,634	309,360	4,408	33,502	34,405	33,644	33,316	33,608	34,001	33,911	34,177	33,745	643	130,274	33,511	33,402	33,017	30,322	22
New Hampshire	191,900	129,632	3,228	11,915	13,680	13,859	13,902	14,190	14,237	14,607	14,850	15,164	0	62,268	16,641	15,537	15,179	14,911	0
New Jersey	1,356,431	947,576	36,581	90,955	96,939	98,784	97,569	96,459	98,000	97,384	99,004	98,968	36,933	408,855	104,553	98,853	96,668	94,059	14,722
New Mexico	337,225	239,481	7,652	26,954	26,643	26,175	25,639	25,703	25,786	25,270	25,223	24,436	0	97,744	29,325	25,734	22,014	20,671	0
New York	2,704,718	1,857,574	49,569	197,458	199,702	199,594	199,611	196,082	198,007	201,429	200,192	201,190	14,740	847,144	226,304	218,032	196,644	190,732	15,432
North Carolina	1,507,864	1,074,063	33,603	117,944	117,693	107,431	117,223	116,325	118,534	117,223	115,038	113,238	0	433,801	125,149	111,972	102,663	94,017	0
North Dakota	97,646	67,888	1,706	8,236	7,521	7,490	7,229	7,028	7,029	6,887	7,326	7,436	0	29,758	7,483	7,551	7,376	7,348	0
Ohio	1,740,030	1,217,226	29,015	131,323	130,527	129,983	129,674	130,406	133,152	134,459	134,468	134,219	0	522,804	148,538	135,373	121,027	117,866	0
Oklahoma	666,120	490,196	42,145	53,053	53,145	50,090	49,523	48,690	48,456	48,469	47,869	47,321	1,435	175,924	48,154	45,332	42,450	39,447	541
Oregon	568,208	391,310	7,262	41,478	42,402	42,474	42,463	42,072	42,885	43,193	43,428	43,653	0	176,898	43,968	44,249	42,783	45,898	0
Pennsylvania	1,771,395	1,204,850	12,887	128,804	129,881	131,128	130,624	129,845	133,069	135,198	136,390	135,598	1,426	566,545	144,339	144,453	138,146	138,265	1,342
Rhode Island	142,854	97,659	1,979	10,164	10,762	10,989	10,799	10,827	10,841	10,222	9,930	11,146	0	45,195	12,277	11,492	10,868	10,558	0

See notes at end of table.

Table 203.45. Enrollment in public elementary and secondary schools, by level, grade, and state or jurisdiction: Fall 2011—Continued

State or jurisdiction	Total, all grades	Elementary												Secondary					
		Total	Prekinder-garten	Kinder-garten	Grade 1	Grade 2	Grade 3	Grade 4	Grade 5	Grade 6	Grade 7	Grade 8	Elementary ungraded	Total	Grade 9	Grade 10	Grade 11	Grade 12	Secondary ungraded
1	2	3	4	5	6	7	8	9	10	11	12	13	14	15	16	17	18	19	20
South Carolina	727,186	519,389	23,551	56,065	55,995	54,373	53,730	54,157	55,713	56,312	55,250	54,243	0	207,797	60,710	54,075	48,328	44,684	0
South Dakota	128,016	90,529	2,996	11,375	10,326	9,787	9,531	9,364	9,207	9,437	9,367	9,139	0	37,487	10,209	9,740	8,876	8,662	0
Tennessee	999,693	712,749	27,982	79,803	77,853	75,660	75,220	75,146	76,079	75,908	75,373	73,725	0	286,944	76,970	73,216	69,121	67,637	0
Texas	5,000,470	3,636,852	249,524	379,446	392,291	383,411	379,421	375,756	377,729	372,846	366,149	360,279	0	1,363,618	394,326	347,268	323,387	298,637	0
Utah	598,832	434,536	11,972	48,953	48,829	48,768	48,039	46,758	46,198	45,951	45,097	43,971	0	164,296	42,540	41,498	40,565	39,693	0
Vermont	89,908	62,146	5,559	6,062	6,232	6,185	6,165	6,158	6,304	6,283	6,552	6,646	0	27,762	7,017	6,869	6,946	6,930	0
Virginia	1,257,883	881,225	31,805	95,574	95,019	95,322	93,829	93,770	94,316	94,863	93,366	93,361	0	376,658	100,701	95,596	91,037	89,324	0
Washington	1,045,453	718,184	12,268	78,014	78,889	78,338	77,865	77,051	78,848	79,109	78,911	78,891	0	327,269	83,237	80,316	79,627	84,089	0
West Virginia	282,870	202,065	15,280	21,172	21,026	20,623	20,225	20,748	20,491	21,085	20,637	20,778	0	80,805	22,569	20,479	19,259	18,498	0
Wisconsin	871,105	602,810	54,438	60,875	60,572	60,984	60,216	60,094	60,958	61,818	61,442	61,413	0	268,295	67,542	65,510	66,851	68,392	0
Wyoming	90,099	64,057	518	7,873	7,441	7,104	7,115	6,790	6,747	6,833	6,840	6,796	0	26,042	6,955	6,661	6,248	6,178	0
Bureau of Indian Education	—	—	—	—	—	—	—	—	—	—	—	—	—	—	—	—	—	—	—
DoD, overseas	—	—	—	—	—	—	—	—	—	—	—	—	—	—	—	—	—	—	—
DoD, domestic	—	—	—	—	—	—	—	—	—	—	—	—	—	—	—	—	—	—	—
Other jurisdictions																			
American Samoa	—	—	—	—	—	—	—	—	—	—	—	—	—	—	—	—	—	—	—
Guam	31,243	21,223	13	2,216	2,337	2,328	2,418	2,334	2,358	2,364	2,383	2,472	0	10,020	3,101	3,269	2,089	1,561	0
Northern Marianas	11,011	7,703	462	608	736	762	792	814	851	849	944	841	44	3,308	962	950	742	654	0
Puerto Rico	452,740	318,924	1,060	29,287	35,333	32,808	31,990	33,638	34,920	35,415	37,989	36,488	9,996	133,816	35,472	34,152	30,914	28,278	5,000
U.S. Virgin Islands	15,711	10,576	—	1,114	1,101	1,145	1,148	1,251	1,217	1,200	1,274	1,126	0	5,135	1,746	1,215	1,056	1,118	0

—Not available.
NOTE: DoD = Department of Defense. The total ungraded counts of students were prorated to the elementary and secondary levels based on prior reports.

SOURCE: U.S. Department of Education, National Center for Education Statistics, Common Core of Data (CCD), "State Non-fiscal Survey of Public Elementary/Secondary Education," 2011–12. (This table was prepared August 2013.)

Table 203.50. Enrollment and percentage distribution of enrollment in public elementary and secondary schools, by race/ethnicity and region: Selected years, fall 1995 through fall 2024

Region and year	Enrollment (in thousands)							Percentage distribution						
	Total	White	Black	Hispanic	Asian/ Pacific Islander	American Indian/ Alaska Native	Two or more races	Total	White	Black	Hispanic	Asian/ Pacific Islander	American Indian/ Alaska Native	Two or more races
1	2	3	4	5	6	7	8	9	10	11	12	13	14	15
United States														
1995	44,840	29,044	7,551	6,072	1,668	505	—	100.0	64.8	16.8	13.5	3.7	1.1	†
2000	47,204	28,878	8,100	7,726	1,950	550	—	100.0	61.2	17.2	16.4	4.1	1.2	†
2001	47,672	28,735	8,177	8,169	2,028	564	—	100.0	60.3	17.2	17.1	4.3	1.2	†
2002	48,183	28,618	8,299	8,594	2,088	583	—	100.0	59.4	17.2	17.8	4.3	1.2	†
2003	48,540	28,442	8,349	9,011	2,145	593	—	100.0	58.6	17.2	18.6	4.4	1.2	†
2004	48,795	28,318	8,386	9,317	2,183	591	—	100.0	58.0	17.2	19.1	4.5	1.2	†
2005	49,113	28,005	8,445	9,787	2,279	598	—	100.0	57.0	17.2	19.9	4.6	1.2	†
2006	49,316	27,801	8,422	10,166	2,332	595	—	100.0	56.4	17.1	20.6	4.7	1.2	†
2007	49,291	27,454	8,392	10,454	2,396	594	—	100.0	55.7	17.0	21.2	4.9	1.2	†
2008	49,266	27,057	8,358	10,563	2,451	589	247 [1]	100.0	54.9	17.0	21.4	5.0	1.2	0.5 [1]
2009	49,361	26,702	8,245	10,991	2,484	601	338 [1]	100.0	54.1	16.7	22.3	5.0	1.2	0.7 [1]
2010	49,484	25,933	7,917	11,439	2,466	566	1,164	100.0	52.4	16.0	23.1	5.0	1.1	2.4
2011	49,522	25,602	7,827	11,759	2,513	547	1,272	100.0	51.7	15.8	23.7	5.1	1.1	2.6
2012	49,771	25,386	7,803	12,104	2,552	534	1,393	100.0	51.0	15.7	24.3	5.1	1.1	2.8
2013[2]	49,942	25,194	7,787	12,497	2,571	530	1,362	100.0	50.4	15.6	25.0	5.1	1.1	2.7
2014[2]	49,986	24,913	7,740	12,812	2,585	524	1,412	100.0	49.8	15.5	25.6	5.2	1.0	2.8
2015[2]	50,094	24,665	7,700	13,150	2,604	520	1,456	100.0	49.2	15.4	26.2	5.2	1.0	2.9
2016[2]	50,229	24,437	7,671	13,476	2,630	516	1,499	100.0	48.7	15.3	26.8	5.2	1.0	3.0
2017[2]	50,584	24,326	7,679	13,845	2,672	513	1,549	100.0	48.1	15.2	27.4	5.3	1.0	3.1
2018[2]	50,871	24,214	7,678	14,176	2,699	510	1,594	100.0	47.6	15.1	27.9	5.3	1.0	3.1
2019[2]	51,183	24,179	7,673	14,438	2,745	503	1,645	100.0	47.2	15.0	28.2	5.4	1.0	3.2
2020[2]	51,547	24,158	7,694	14,702	2,791	498	1,705	100.0	46.9	14.9	28.5	5.4	1.0	3.3
2021[2]	51,910	24,142	7,734	14,939	2,837	495	1,763	100.0	46.5	14.9	28.8	5.5	1.0	3.4
2022[2]	52,260	24,131	7,778	15,152	2,887	492	1,819	100.0	46.2	14.9	29.0	5.5	0.9	3.5
2023[2]	52,601	24,142	7,821	15,328	2,944	491	1,875	100.0	45.9	14.9	29.1	5.6	0.9	3.6
2024[2]	52,920	24,157	7,862	15,473	3,010	489	1,929	100.0	45.6	14.9	29.2	5.7	0.9	3.6
Northeast														
1995	7,894	5,497	1,202	878	295	21	—	100.0	69.6	15.2	11.1	3.7	0.3	†
2000	8,222	5,545	1,270	1,023	361	24	—	100.0	67.4	15.4	12.4	4.4	0.3	†
2002	8,297	5,503	1,287	1,091	390	26	—	100.0	66.3	15.5	13.2	4.7	0.3	†
2005	8,240	5,317	1,282	1,189	425	27	—	100.0	64.5	15.6	14.4	5.2	0.3	†
2006	8,258	5,281	1,279	1,230	440	28	—	100.0	64.0	15.5	14.9	5.3	0.3	†
2007	8,122	5,148	1,250	1,246	451	27	—	100.0	63.4	15.4	15.3	5.6	0.3	†
2008	8,053	5,041	1,226	1,267	467	27	25 [1]	100.0	62.6	15.2	15.7	5.8	0.3	0.3 [1]
2009	8,092	5,010	1,230	1,308	487	27	30 [1]	100.0	61.9	15.2	16.2	6.0	0.3	0.4 [1]
2010	8,071	4,876	1,208	1,364	500	27	96	100.0	60.4	15.0	16.9	6.2	0.3	1.2
2011	7,954	4,745	1,166	1,394	510	27	113	100.0	59.7	14.7	17.5	6.4	0.3	1.4
2012	7,959	4,665	1,161	1,444	523	27	138	100.0	58.6	14.6	18.1	6.6	0.3	1.7
Midwest														
1995	10,512	8,335	1,450	438	197	92	—	100.0	79.3	13.8	4.2	1.9	0.9	†
2000	10,730	8,208	1,581	610	239	92	—	100.0	76.5	14.7	5.7	2.2	0.9	†
2002	10,819	8,118	1,638	704	255	104	—	100.0	75.0	15.1	6.5	2.4	1.0	†
2005	10,819	7,950	1,654	836	283	96	—	100.0	73.5	15.3	7.7	2.6	0.9	†
2006	10,819	7,894	1,655	883	290	97	—	100.0	73.0	15.3	8.2	2.7	0.9	†
2007	10,770	7,808	1,642	922	300	99	—	100.0	72.5	15.2	8.6	2.8	0.9	†
2008	10,743	7,734	1,632	963	314	99	—	100.0	72.0	15.2	9.0	2.9	0.9	†
2009	10,672	7,622	1,606	1,000	318	98	29 [1]	100.0	71.4	15.0	9.4	3.0	0.9	0.3 [1]
2010	10,610	7,327	1,505	1,077	312	94	294	100.0	69.1	14.2	10.2	2.9	0.9	2.8
2011	10,574	7,240	1,485	1,127	321	90	311	100.0	68.5	14.0	10.7	3.0	0.9	2.9
2012	10,559	7,175	1,464	1,167	330	89	334	100.0	68.0	13.9	11.1	3.1	0.8	3.2
South														
1995	16,118	9,565	4,236	1,890	280	148	—	100.0	59.3	26.3	11.7	1.7	0.9	†
2000	17,007	9,501	4,516	2,468	352	170	—	100.0	55.9	26.6	14.5	2.1	1.0	†
2002	17,471	9,457	4,617	2,822	394	180	—	100.0	54.1	26.4	16.2	2.3	1.0	†
2005	18,103	9,381	4,738	3,334	456	194	—	100.0	51.8	26.2	18.4	2.5	1.1	†
2006	18,294	9,358	4,729	3,522	485	200	—	100.0	51.2	25.9	19.3	2.6	1.1	†
2007	18,423	9,286	4,750	3,674	511	201	—	100.0	50.4	25.8	19.9	2.8	1.1	†
2008	18,491	9,190	4,771	3,790	537	203	—	100.0	49.7	25.8	20.5	2.9	1.1	†
2009	18,652	9,074	4,710	4,039	555	219	55 [1]	100.0	48.6	25.3	21.7	3.0	1.2	0.3 [1]
2010	18,805	8,869	4,545	4,206	555	207	424	100.0	47.2	24.2	22.4	3.0	1.1	2.3
2011	18,956	8,830	4,535	4,353	577	198	463	100.0	46.6	23.9	23.0	3.0	1.0	2.4
2012	19,128	8,780	4,545	4,513	595	191	504	100.0	45.9	23.8	23.6	3.1	1.0	2.6
West														
1995	10,316	5,648	662	2,866	896	244	—	100.0	54.7	6.4	27.8	8.7	2.4	†
2000	11,244	5,624	733	3,625	998	264	—	100.0	50.0	6.5	32.2	8.9	2.4	†
2002	11,596	5,541	757	3,976	1,049	273	—	100.0	47.8	6.5	34.3	9.0	2.4	†
2005	11,951	5,356	771	4,428	1,115	281	—	100.0	44.8	6.5	37.1	9.3	2.4	†
2006	11,945	5,268	759	4,531	1,117	270	—	100.0	44.1	6.4	37.9	9.4	2.3	†
2007	11,976	5,213	750	4,611	1,134	267	—	100.0	43.5	6.3	38.5	9.5	2.2	†
2008	11,979	5,092	728	4,543	1,133	261	222 [1]	100.0	42.5	6.1	37.9	9.5	2.2	1.9 [1]
2009	11,945	4,997	699	4,645	1,124	256	223 [1]	100.0	41.8	5.9	38.9	9.4	2.1	1.9 [1]
2010	11,998	4,861	659	4,792	1,100	237	349	100.0	40.5	5.5	39.9	9.2	2.0	2.9
2011	12,038	4,787	642	4,886	1,105	233	385	100.0	39.8	5.3	40.6	9.2	1.9	3.2
2012	12,124	4,766	632	4,978	1,104	227	417	100.0	39.3	5.2	41.1	9.1	1.9	3.4

—Not available.
†Not applicable.
[1]For this year, data on students of two or more races were reported by only a small number of states. Therefore, the data are not comparable to figures for 2010 and later years.
[2]Projected.
NOTE: Race categories exclude persons of Hispanic ethnicity. Enrollment data for students not reported by race/ethnicity were prorated by state and grade to match state totals. Prior to 2008, data on students of two or more races were not collected. Some data have been revised from previously published figures. Detail may not sum to totals because of rounding.
SOURCE: U.S. Department of Education, National Center for Education Statistics, Common Core of Data (CCD), "State Nonfiscal Survey of Public Elementary and Secondary Education," 1995–96 through 2012–13; and National Elementary and Secondary Enrollment by Race/Ethnicity Projection Model, 1972 through 2024. (This table was prepared March 2015.)

Table 203.60. Enrollment and percentage distribution of enrollment in public elementary and secondary schools, by race/ethnicity and level of education: Fall 1999 through fall 2024

Level of education and year	Enrollment (in thousands)									Percentage distribution								
	Total	White	Black	His-panic	Asian/Pacific Islander			American Indian/ Alaska Native	Two or more races	Total	White	Black	His-panic	Asian/Pacific Islander			American Indian/ Alaska Native	Two or more races
					Total	Asian	Pacific Islander							Total	Asian	Pacific Islander		
1	2	3	4	5	6	7	8	9	10	11	12	13	14	15	16	17	18	19
Total																		
1999	46,857	29,035	8,066	7,327	1,887	—	—	542	—	100.0	62.0	17.2	15.6	4.0	†	†	1.2	†
2000	47,204	28,878	8,100	7,726	1,950	—	—	550	—	100.0	61.2	17.2	16.4	4.1	†	†	1.2	†
2001	47,672	28,735	8,177	8,169	2,028	—	—	564	—	100.0	60.3	17.2	17.1	4.3	†	†	1.2	†
2002	48,183	28,618	8,299	8,594	2,088	—	—	583	—	100.0	59.4	17.2	17.8	4.3	†	†	1.2	†
2003	48,540	28,442	8,349	9,011	2,145	—	—	593	—	100.0	58.6	17.2	18.6	4.4	†	†	1.2	†
2004	48,795	28,318	8,386	9,317	2,183	—	—	591	—	100.0	58.0	17.2	19.1	4.5	†	†	1.2	†
2005	49,113	28,005	8,445	9,787	2,279	—	—	598	—	100.0	57.0	17.2	19.9	4.6	†	†	1.2	†
2006	49,316	27,801	8,422	10,166	2,332	—	—	595	—	100.0	56.4	17.1	20.6	4.7	†	†	1.2	†
2007	49,291	27,454	8,392	10,454	2,396	—	—	594	—	100.0	55.7	17.0	21.2	4.9	†	†	1.2	†
2008	49,266	27,057	8,358	10,563	2,451	2,405	46	589	247 [1]	100.0	54.9	17.0	21.4	5.0	4.9	0.1	1.2	0.5 [1]
2009	49,361	26,702	8,245	10,991	2,484	2,435	49	601	338 [1]	100.0	54.1	16.7	22.3	5.0	4.9	0.1	1.2	0.7 [1]
2010	49,484	25,933	7,917	11,439	2,466	2,296	171	566	1,164	100.0	52.4	16.0	23.1	5.0	4.6	0.3	1.1	2.4
2011	49,522	25,602	7,827	11,759	2,513	2,334	179	547	1,272	100.0	51.7	15.8	23.7	5.1	4.7	0.4	1.1	2.6
2012	49,771	25,386	7,803	12,104	2,552	2,372	180	534	1,393	100.0	51.0	15.7	24.3	5.1	4.8	0.4	1.1	2.8
2013 [2]	49,942	25,194	7,787	12,497	2,571	2,388	183	530	1,362	100.0	50.4	15.6	25.0	5.1	4.8	0.4	1.1	2.7
2014 [2]	49,986	24,913	7,740	12,812	2,585	2,399	186	524	1,412	100.0	49.8	15.5	25.6	5.2	4.8	0.4	1.0	2.8
2015 [2]	50,094	24,665	7,700	13,150	2,604	2,416	188	520	1,456	100.0	49.2	15.4	26.2	5.2	4.8	0.4	1.0	2.9
2016 [2]	50,229	24,437	7,671	13,476	2,630	2,440	190	516	1,499	100.0	48.7	15.3	26.8	5.2	4.9	0.4	1.0	3.0
2017 [2]	50,584	24,326	7,679	13,845	2,672	2,479	193	513	1,549	100.0	48.1	15.2	27.4	5.3	4.9	0.4	1.0	3.1
2018 [2]	50,871	24,214	7,678	14,176	2,699	2,503	195	510	1,594	100.0	47.6	15.1	27.9	5.3	4.9	0.4	1.0	3.1
2019 [2]	51,183	24,179	7,673	14,438	2,745	2,548	196	503	1,645	100.0	47.2	15.0	28.2	5.4	5.0	0.4	1.0	3.2
2020 [2]	51,547	24,158	7,694	14,702	2,791	2,594	197	498	1,705	100.0	46.9	14.9	28.5	5.4	5.0	0.4	1.0	3.3
2021 [2]	51,910	24,142	7,734	14,939	2,837	2,639	198	495	1,763	100.0	46.5	14.9	28.8	5.5	5.1	0.4	1.0	3.4
2022 [2]	52,260	24,131	7,778	15,152	2,887	2,689	198	492	1,819	100.0	46.2	14.9	29.0	5.5	5.1	0.4	0.9	3.5
2023 [2]	52,601	24,142	7,821	15,328	2,944	2,746	198	491	1,875	100.0	45.9	14.9	29.1	5.6	5.2	0.4	0.9	3.6
2024 [2]	52,920	24,157	7,862	15,473	3,010	2,810	200	489	1,929	100.0	45.6	14.9	29.2	5.7	5.3	0.4	0.9	3.6
Prekindergarten through grade 8																		
1999	33,486	20,327	5,952	5,512	1,303	—	—	391	—	100.0	60.7	17.8	16.5	3.9	†	†	1.2	†
2000	33,686	20,130	5,981	5,830	1,349	—	—	397	—	100.0	59.8	17.8	17.3	4.0	†	†	1.2	†
2001	33,936	19,960	6,004	6,159	1,409	—	—	405	—	100.0	58.8	17.7	18.1	4.2	†	†	1.2	†
2002	34,114	19,764	6,042	6,446	1,447	—	—	415	—	100.0	57.9	17.7	18.9	4.2	†	†	1.2	†
2003	34,201	19,558	6,015	6,729	1,483	—	—	415	—	100.0	57.2	17.6	19.7	4.3	†	†	1.2	†
2004	34,178	19,368	5,983	6,909	1,504	—	—	413	—	100.0	56.7	17.5	20.2	4.4	†	†	1.2	†
2005	34,204	19,051	5,954	7,216	1,569	—	—	412	—	100.0	55.7	17.4	21.1	4.6	†	†	1.2	†
2006	34,235	18,863	5,882	7,465	1,611	—	—	414	—	100.0	55.1	17.2	21.8	4.7	†	†	1.2	†
2007	34,204	18,679	5,821	7,632	1,660	—	—	412	—	100.0	54.6	17.0	22.3	4.9	†	†	1.2	†
2008	34,286	18,501	5,793	7,689	1,705	1,674	31	410	187 [1]	100.0	54.0	16.9	22.4	5.0	4.9	0.1	1.2	0.5 [1]
2009	34,409	18,316	5,713	7,977	1,730	1,697	33	419	254 [1]	100.0	53.2	16.6	23.2	5.0	4.9	0.1	1.2	0.7 [1]
2010	34,625	17,823	5,495	8,314	1,711	1,589	122	394	887	100.0	51.5	15.9	24.0	4.9	4.6	0.4	1.1	2.6
2011	34,773	17,654	5,470	8,558	1,744	1,616	128	384	963	100.0	50.8	15.7	24.6	5.0	4.6	0.4	1.1	2.8
2012	35,018	17,535	5,473	8,804	1,773	1,644	129	375	1,057	100.0	50.1	15.6	25.1	5.1	4.7	0.4	1.1	3.0
2013 [2]	35,188	17,409	5,475	9,103	1,796	1,665	131	373	1,032	100.0	49.5	15.6	25.9	5.1	4.7	0.4	1.1	2.9
2014 [2]	35,159	17,182	5,432	9,309	1,800	1,668	132	368	1,069	100.0	48.9	15.4	26.5	5.1	4.7	0.4	1.0	3.0
2015 [2]	35,182	16,987	5,398	9,521	1,813	1,680	133	364	1,100	100.0	48.3	15.3	27.1	5.2	4.8	0.4	1.0	3.1
2016 [2]	35,282	16,839	5,392	9,729	1,829	1,695	134	360	1,133	100.0	47.7	15.3	27.6	5.2	4.8	0.4	1.0	3.2
2017 [2]	35,595	16,803	5,442	9,961	1,854	1,718	136	360	1,174	100.0	47.2	15.3	28.0	5.2	4.8	0.4	1.0	3.3
2018 [2]	35,856	16,771	5,480	10,158	1,876	1,740	137	360	1,211	100.0	46.8	15.3	28.3	5.2	4.9	0.4	1.0	3.4
2019 [2]	36,125	16,825	5,503	10,275	1,919	1,783	136	355	1,248	100.0	46.6	15.2	28.4	5.3	4.9	0.4	1.0	3.5
2020 [2]	36,366	16,864	5,528	10,362	1,967	1,831	136	353	1,292	100.0	46.4	15.2	28.5	5.4	5.0	0.4	1.0	3.6
2021 [2]	36,587	16,903	5,546	10,437	2,017	1,880	137	350	1,334	100.0	46.2	15.2	28.5	5.5	5.1	0.4	1.0	3.6
2022 [2]	36,839	16,963	5,567	10,523	2,064	1,926	137	347	1,374	100.0	46.0	15.1	28.6	5.6	5.2	0.4	0.9	3.7
2023 [2]	37,223	17,074	5,613	10,655	2,120	1,982	138	347	1,414	100.0	45.9	15.1	28.6	5.7	5.3	0.4	0.9	3.8
2024 [2]	37,615	17,188	5,667	10,783	2,175	2,035	139	346	1,457	100.0	45.7	15.1	28.7	5.8	5.4	0.4	0.9	3.9
Grades 9 through 12																		
1999	13,371	8,708	2,114	1,815	584	—	—	151	—	100.0	65.1	15.8	13.6	4.4	†	†	1.1	†
2000	13,517	8,747	2,119	1,896	601	—	—	153	—	100.0	64.7	15.7	14.0	4.4	†	†	1.1	†
2001	13,736	8,774	2,173	2,011	619	—	—	159	—	100.0	63.9	15.8	14.6	4.5	†	†	1.2	†
2002	14,069	8,854	2,257	2,148	642	—	—	168	—	100.0	62.9	16.0	15.3	4.6	†	†	1.2	†
2003	14,339	8,884	2,334	2,282	663	—	—	177	—	100.0	62.0	16.3	15.9	4.6	†	†	1.2	†
2004	14,618	8,950	2,403	2,408	679	—	—	178	—	100.0	61.2	16.4	16.5	4.6	†	†	1.2	†
2005	14,909	8,954	2,490	2,570	709	—	—	186	—	100.0	60.1	16.7	17.2	4.8	†	†	1.2	†
2006	15,081	8,938	2,540	2,701	720	—	—	181	—	100.0	59.3	16.8	17.9	4.8	†	†	1.2	†
2007	15,086	8,775	2,571	2,821	736	—	—	183	—	100.0	58.2	17.0	18.7	4.9	†	†	1.2	†
2008	14,980	8,556	2,565	2,874	746	731	15	179	59 [1]	100.0	57.1	17.1	19.2	5.0	4.9	0.1	1.2	0.4 [1]
2009	14,952	8,385	2,532	3,014	754	738	16	182	84 [1]	100.0	56.1	16.9	20.2	5.0	4.9	0.1	1.2	0.6 [1]
2010	14,860	8,109	2,422	3,125	755	707	49	171	277	100.0	54.6	16.3	21.0	5.1	4.8	0.3	1.2	1.9
2011	14,749	7,948	2,357	3,202	769	719	50	163	309	100.0	53.9	16.0	21.7	5.2	4.9	0.3	1.1	2.1
2012	14,753	7,851	2,330	3,300	779	727	51	158	335	100.0	53.2	15.8	22.4	5.3	4.9	0.3	1.1	2.3
2013 [2]	14,754	7,786	2,312	3,394	776	723	53	157	329	100.0	52.8	15.7	23.0	5.3	4.9	0.4	1.1	2.2

See notes at end of table.

Table 203.60. Enrollment and percentage distribution of enrollment in public elementary and secondary schools, by race/ethnicity and level of education: Fall 1999 through fall 2024—Continued

Level of education and year	Enrollment (in thousands)				Asian/Pacific Islander			American Indian/ Alaska Native	Two or more races	Percentage distribution				Asian/Pacific Islander			American Indian/ Alaska Native	Two or more races
	Total	White	Black	His-panic	Total	Asian	Pacific Islander			Total	White	Black	His-panic	Total	Asian	Pacific Islander		
1	2	3	4	5	6	7	8	9	10	11	12	13	14	15	16	17	18	19
2014[2]	14,826	7,731	2,308	3,503	785	731	54	156	343	100.0	52.1	15.6	23.6	5.3	4.9	0.4	1.1	2.3
2015[2]	14,912	7,678	2,302	3,629	791	736	55	156	356	100.0	51.5	15.4	24.3	5.3	4.9	0.4	1.0	2.4
2016[2]	14,947	7,598	2,279	3,747	801	745	56	156	366	100.0	50.8	15.2	25.1	5.4	5.0	0.4	1.0	2.5
2017[2]	14,989	7,523	2,237	3,883	818	760	57	154	374	100.0	50.2	14.9	25.9	5.5	5.1	0.4	1.0	2.5
2018[2]	15,015	7,443	2,198	4,018	822	764	59	151	383	100.0	49.6	14.6	26.8	5.5	5.1	0.4	1.0	2.6
2019[2]	15,058	7,354	2,170	4,163	826	765	61	148	397	100.0	48.8	14.4	27.6	5.5	5.1	0.4	1.0	2.6
2020[2]	15,182	7,294	2,166	4,339	824	763	61	146	413	100.0	48.0	14.3	28.6	5.4	5.0	0.4	1.0	2.7
2021[2]	15,324	7,238	2,189	4,502	820	759	61	145	429	100.0	47.2	14.3	29.4	5.4	5.0	0.4	0.9	2.8
2022[2]	15,421	7,168	2,211	4,629	823	762	61	145	445	100.0	46.5	14.3	30.0	5.3	4.9	0.4	0.9	2.9
2023[2]	15,378	7,069	2,208	4,672	824	764	60	144	461	100.0	46.0	14.4	30.4	5.4	5.0	0.4	0.9	3.0
2024[2]	15,304	6,969	2,195	4,690	836	775	61	143	472	100.0	45.5	14.3	30.6	5.5	5.1	0.4	0.9	3.1

—Not available.
†Not applicable.
[1]For this year, data on students of two or more races were reported by only a small number of states. Therefore, the data are not comparable to figures for 2010 and later years.
[2]Projected.
NOTE: Race categories exclude persons of Hispanic ethnicity. Enrollment data for students not reported by race/ethnicity were prorated by state and grade to match state totals. Prior to 2008, data on students of two or more races were not collected separately. Total counts

of ungraded students were prorated to prekindergarten through grade 8 and grades 9 through 12 based on prior reports. Some data have been revised from previously published figures. Detail may not sum to totals because of rounding.
SOURCE: U.S. Department of Education, National Center for Education Statistics, Common Core of Data (CCD), "State Nonfiscal Survey of Public Elementary and Secondary Education," 1998–99 through 2012–13; and National Elementary and Secondary Enrollment by Race/Ethnicity Projection Model, 1972 through 2024. (This table was prepared March 2015.)

Table 203.70. Percentage distribution of enrollment in public elementary and secondary schools, by race/ethnicity and state or jurisdiction: Fall 2002 and fall 2012

State or jurisdiction	Percentage distribution, fall 2002						Percentage distribution, fall 2012							
	Total	White	Black	Hispanic	Asian/Pacific Islander	American Indian/Alaska Native	Total	White	Black	Hispanic	Asian	Pacific Islander	American Indian/Alaska Native	Two or more races
1	2	3	4	5	6	7	8	9	10	11	12	13	14	15
United States	100.0	59.5	17.3	17.8	4.3	1.2	100.0	51.0	15.7	24.3	4.8	0.4	1.1	2.8
Alabama	100.0	60.2	36.3	1.8	0.9	0.8	100.0	57.6	33.9	5.1	1.3	0.1	0.8	1.2
Alaska	100.0	59.4	4.7	3.7	6.3	25.9	100.0	50.1	3.6	6.4	6.2	2.4	23.5	7.9
Arizona	100.0	50.0	4.8	36.5	2.1	6.6	100.0	41.6	5.3	43.3	2.8	0.3	4.9	1.9
Arkansas	100.0	70.5	23.2	4.8	1.0	0.5	100.0	63.9	21.0	10.6	1.5	0.5	0.7	1.8
California	100.0	34.0	8.3	45.5	11.3	0.9	100.0	25.5	6.3	52.7	11.1	0.5	0.7	3.1
Colorado	100.0	65.7	5.7	24.3	3.0	1.2	100.0	55.6	4.7	32.3	3.2	0.2	0.8	3.3
Connecticut	100.0	69.0	13.6	14.1	3.0	0.3	100.0	59.6	13.0	20.4	4.6	0.1	0.3	2.1
Delaware	100.0	58.4	31.4	7.2	2.6	0.3	100.0	48.6	31.4	13.9	3.5	0.1	0.5	2.1
District of Columbia	100.0	4.3	83.7	10.4	1.6	0.1	100.0	8.4	74.6	13.9	1.4	0.1	0.1	1.5
Florida	100.0	51.6	24.7	21.4	2.0	0.3	100.0	41.6	23.0	29.3	2.6	0.1	0.4	3.1
Georgia	100.0	53.0	38.2	6.2	2.5	0.2	100.0	43.5	36.9	12.7	3.5	0.1	0.2	3.1
Hawaii	100.0	20.4	2.4	4.6	72.2	0.5	100.0	13.9	2.2	8.3	33.0	32.8	0.5	9.3
Idaho	100.0	85.9	0.8	10.8	1.2	1.2	100.0	77.7	1.0	16.5	1.3	0.3	1.3	1.8
Illinois	100.0	58.3	21.1	16.9	3.5	0.2	100.0	50.5	17.6	24.1	4.3	0.1	0.3	3.0
Indiana	100.0	82.2	12.2	4.3	1.0	0.3	100.0	71.7	12.3	9.6	1.8	0.1	0.3	4.4
Iowa	100.0	89.0	4.3	4.4	1.8	0.5	100.0	79.8	5.2	9.3	2.1	0.2	0.4	2.9
Kansas	100.0	76.8	9.1	10.4	2.3	1.4	100.0	66.7	7.2	17.8	2.6	0.2	1.1	4.5
Kentucky	100.0	86.9	10.8	1.4	0.8	0.2	100.0	80.3	10.7	4.8	1.4	0.1	0.1	2.5
Louisiana	100.0	48.5	47.8	1.7	1.3	0.7	100.0	47.0	45.0	4.3	1.5	0.1	0.8	1.4
Maine	100.0	96.1	1.6	0.7	1.1	0.5	100.0	91.4	3.0	1.7	1.5	0.1	0.8	1.4
Maryland	100.0	51.5	37.5	5.8	4.7	0.4	100.0	41.8	35.1	12.9	6.0	0.1	0.3	3.9
Massachusetts	100.0	75.1	8.8	11.2	4.6	0.3	100.0	66.0	8.6	16.4	5.9	0.1	0.2	2.7
Michigan	100.0	72.4	20.3	3.8	2.0	1.5	100.0	68.9	18.4	6.5	2.8	0.1	0.8	2.5
Minnesota	100.0	81.1	7.4	4.2	5.3	2.1	100.0	72.0	9.4	7.7	6.3	0.1	1.8	2.8
Mississippi	100.0	47.3	50.9	1.0	0.7	0.2	100.0	45.7	49.5	2.7	1.0	#	0.2	0.9
Missouri	100.0	77.9	18.2	2.3	1.3	0.3	100.0	73.7	16.6	5.1	1.9	0.2	0.4	2.1
Montana	100.0	85.4	0.7	2.0	1.1	10.9	100.0	80.5	1.0	3.9	0.8	0.2	11.4	2.1
Nebraska	100.0	80.6	7.0	9.2	1.6	1.6	100.0	69.6	6.7	16.8	2.2	0.1	1.4	3.2
Nevada	100.0	52.7	10.5	28.7	6.4	1.7	100.0	36.8	9.7	40.0	5.7	1.3	1.1	5.4
New Hampshire	100.0	94.4	1.5	2.2	1.6	0.3	100.0	88.6	1.9	4.1	2.9	0.1	0.3	2.1
New Jersey	100.0	58.6	17.8	16.6	6.8	0.2	100.0	49.8	16.3	23.4	9.1	0.2	0.1	1.0
New Mexico	100.0	33.6	2.4	51.7	1.1	11.2	100.0	25.5	2.0	59.9	1.2	0.1	10.0	1.3
New York	100.0	54.2	20.0	19.0	6.3	0.4	100.0	47.2	18.3	24.0	8.5	0.2	0.6	1.2
North Carolina	100.0	59.2	31.4	5.9	2.0	1.5	100.0	51.9	26.2	14.2	2.6	0.1	1.4	3.6
North Dakota	100.0	88.6	1.1	1.3	0.9	8.1	100.0	82.1	2.9	3.3	1.3	0.2	9.0	1.2
Ohio	100.0	79.7	16.9	2.0	1.2	0.1	100.0	73.3	16.2	4.2	1.8	0.1	0.1	4.3
Oklahoma	100.0	62.6	10.9	7.0	1.5	17.9	100.0	52.6	9.4	14.1	1.8	0.3	15.7	6.0
Oregon	100.0	78.1	3.0	12.5	4.2	2.2	100.0	64.5	2.5	22.0	3.9	0.7	1.7	4.9
Pennsylvania	100.0	77.1	15.5	5.2	2.2	0.1	100.0	69.9	15.2	9.1	3.4	0.1	0.2	2.3
Rhode Island	100.0	72.2	8.4	15.6	3.3	0.5	100.0	62.8	8.2	22.4	2.9	0.2	0.6	2.9
South Carolina	100.0	54.4	41.5	2.7	1.1	0.3	100.0	52.9	35.4	7.0	1.4	0.1	0.3	2.9
South Dakota	100.0	85.3	1.5	1.6	1.0	10.6	100.0	77.6	2.7	4.3	1.7	0.1	11.5	2.1
Tennessee	100.0	71.3	24.8	2.4	1.2	0.2	100.0	66.3	23.0	7.3	1.7	0.1	0.2	1.4
Texas	100.0	39.8	14.3	42.7	2.9	0.3	100.0	30.0	12.7	51.3	3.6	0.1	0.4	1.8
Utah	100.0	84.1	1.1	10.4	2.9	1.5	100.0	76.9	1.3	15.7	1.7	1.5	1.2	1.7
Vermont	100.0	95.8	1.3	0.7	1.6	0.6	100.0	91.9	2.0	1.5	1.8	0.1	0.3	2.4
Virginia	100.0	61.8	27.2	6.2	4.5	0.3	100.0	52.9	23.5	12.5	6.2	0.1	0.3	4.5
Washington	100.0	72.6	5.6	11.6	7.6	2.6	100.0	59.2	4.6	20.4	7.2	0.9	1.4	6.3
West Virginia	100.0	94.4	4.5	0.5	0.6	0.1	100.0	91.4	4.9	1.3	0.7	#	0.1	1.6
Wisconsin	100.0	79.5	10.4	5.4	3.3	1.5	100.0	73.1	9.8	10.1	3.6	0.1	1.3	2.2
Wyoming	100.0	86.7	1.3	7.7	0.9	3.3	100.0	80.1	1.1	12.8	0.8	0.2	3.3	1.6
Bureau of Indian Education	100.0	0.0	0.0	0.0	0.0	100.0	—	—	—	—	—	—	—	—
DoD, overseas	100.0	56.5	19.8	12.9	9.9	0.8	—	—	—	—	—	—	—	—
DoD, domestic	100.0	49.2	24.2	22.2	3.7	0.7	—	—	—	—	—	—	—	—
Other jurisdictions														
American Samoa	100.0	0.0	0.0	0.0	100.0	0.0	—	—	—	—	—	—	—	—
Guam	—	—	—	—	—	—	100.0	0.7	0.2	0.1	23.7	73.2	#	2.1
Northern Marianas	100.0	0.4	0.0	0.0	99.5	0.0	100.0	0.6	0.0	0.1	40.5	58.3	0.0	0.5
Puerto Rico	100.0	0.0	0.0	100.0	0.0	0.0	100.0	0.1	#	99.8	#	#	0.1	0.0
U.S. Virgin Islands	100.0	0.7	84.7	14.1	0.2	0.2	100.0	1.5	78.9	18.2	0.3	0.1	0.1	0.8

—Not available.
#Rounds to zero.
NOTE: Percentage distribution based on students for whom race/ethnicity was reported, which may be less than the total number of students in the state. Race categories exclude persons of Hispanic ethnicity. DoD = Department of Defense. Detail may not sum to totals because of rounding.

SOURCE: U.S. Department of Education, National Center for Education Statistics, Common Core of Data (CCD), "State Nonfiscal Survey of Public Elementary/Secondary Education," 2002–03 and 2012–13. (This table was prepared November 2014.)

Table 203.80. Average daily attendance (ADA) in public elementary and secondary schools, by state or jurisdiction: Selected years, 1969–70 through 2011–12

State or jurisdiction	1969–70	1979–80	1989–90	1999–2000	2003–04	2004–05	2005–06	2006–07	2007–08	2008–09	2009–10	2010–11	2011–12
1	2	3	4	5	6	7	8	9	10	11	12	13	14
United States	41,934,376	38,288,911	37,799,296	43,806,726	45,325,731	45,625,458	45,931,617	46,132,663	46,155,880	46,173,477	45,919,206	46,118,737	46,388,428
Alabama	777,123	711,432	683,833	725,212	706,446	706,588	714,197	714,302	731,161	712,179	698,208	709,225	715,402
Alaska	72,489	79,945	98,213	122,412	122,341	121,699	122,010	120,988	119,882	119,330	120,118	119,949	119,799
Arizona	391,526	481,905	557,252	782,851	878,891	911,640	933,663	972,404	973,689	999,386	968,764	964,683	969,825
Arkansas	414,158	423,610	403,025	422,958	425,571	430,290	435,278	436,804	439,347	439,432	435,676	443,118	443,125
California[1]	4,418,423	4,044,736	4,893,341	5,957,216	6,384,882	6,373,959	6,349,270	6,351,774	6,365,266	6,365,278	6,017,381 [2]	6,029,786 [2]	6,034,192 [2]
Colorado	500,388	513,475	519,419	656,700	673,285	700,485	712,476	722,168	735,549	747,845	762,190	763,147	779,747
Connecticut	618,881	507,362	439,524	533,779	561,530	559,478	558,423	555,428	553,445	549,776	548,787	537,104	534,846
Delaware	120,819	94,058	89,838	106,444	108,751	110,393	113,986	113,992	116,472	119,092	119,879	121,959	122,864
District of Columbia	138,600	91,576	71,468	65,371	65,625	70,817	59,137	61,799	61,636	68,447	68,217	69,575	71,910
Florida	1,312,693	1,464,461	1,646,583	2,175,453	2,418,329	2,463,323	2,494,778	2,527,431	2,494,397	2,468,060	2,493,694	2,541,022	2,575,910
Georgia	1,019,427	989,433	1,054,097	1,326,713	1,424,004	1,460,767	1,499,317	1,542,305	1,561,935	1,569,767	1,596,180	1,621,397	1,646,051
Hawaii	168,140	151,563	157,360	171,180	167,739	169,825	168,009	165,415	166,179	166,118	165,766	169,926	171,763
Idaho	170,920	189,199	203,987	230,828	237,095	241,590	247,009	251,278	255,523	258,712	262,238	263,001	263,377
Illinois	2,084,844	1,770,435	1,587,733	1,789,089	1,862,274	1,862,046	1,871,619	1,879,288	1,881,810	1,881,276	1,887,561	1,863,017	1,858,409
Indiana	1,111,043	983,444	884,568	929,281	943,735	944,944	966,967	976,373	969,976	973,342	976,503	976,225	976,337
Iowa	624,403	510,081	450,224	471,384	457,771	456,559	477,491	481,528	492,922	451,403	455,579	459,613	462,585
Kansas	470,296	382,019	388,986	426,853	415,529	411,455	407,812	422,142	418,751	418,495	435,745	443,131	454,740
Kentucky	647,970	619,868	569,795	565,693	570,911	574,380	580,937	583,102	585,775	585,556	587,102	593,323	594,440
Louisiana	776,555	727,601	727,125	701,957	674,333	670,238	648,243	625,916	631,163	637,764	643,374	654,093	664,640
Maine	225,146	211,400	195,089	194,554	187,492	184,374	180,223	178,870	175,161	173,357	168,213	165,067	166,483
Maryland	785,989	686,336	620,617	791,133	808,557	804,696	800,553	795,473	793,881	793,333	795,577	798,953	803,656
Massachusetts	1,056,207	935,960	763,231	913,502	932,417	930,338	930,151	933,697	917,181	913,976	912,792	910,568	906,736
Michigan	1,991,235	1,758,427	1,446,996	1,574,894	1,590,555	1,583,496	1,574,023	1,556,297	1,528,815	1,498,107	1,477,312	1,452,125	1,438,279
Minnesota	864,595	748,606	699,001	818,819	792,896	788,354	787,521	791,417	790,206	791,427	785,455	786,838	792,437
Mississippi	524,623	454,401	476,048	468,746	463,470	463,816	461,112	462,251	461,459	460,797	460,327	460,894	460,703
Missouri	906,132	777,269	729,693	836,105	851,749	851,114	859,441	858,821	852,106	853,580	852,460	839,997	840,917
Montana	162,664	144,608	135,446	142,313	132,356	130,998	129,948	128,872	132,104	131,982	130,704	130,949	133,266
Nebraska	314,516	270,524	254,754	261,767	260,352	260,725	262,805	263,800	264,810	266,536	269,590	271,468	273,722
Nevada	113,421	134,995	173,149	305,067	364,409	378,186	383,403	395,536	395,355	406,792	405,097	406,965	411,919
New Hampshire	140,203	154,187	154,915	200,283	202,352	201,242	199,952	198,004	195,383	192,890	191,969	188,913	185,947
New Jersey	1,322,124	1,140,111	997,561	1,222,438	1,336,869	1,341,156	1,358,562	1,348,279	1,340,220	1,342,419	1,343,405	1,339,012	1,340,367
New Mexico	259,997	253,453	290,245	323,963	319,637	322,046	323,964	327,244	326,034	327,562	331,152	334,272	335,243
New York	3,099,192	2,530,289	2,244,110	2,595,070	2,599,902	2,581,772	2,556,705	2,542,259	2,520,932	2,510,519	2,516,922	2,513,770	2,512,327
North Carolina	1,104,295	1,072,150	1,012,274	1,185,737	1,264,266	1,289,444	1,319,335	1,343,357	1,364,608	1,374,267	1,366,164	1,377,899	1,393,621
North Dakota	141,961	118,986	109,659	105,123	96,231	94,823	92,843	91,078	91,972	91,816	91,114	92,440	94,310
Ohio	2,246,282	1,849,283	1,584,735	1,659,903	1,700,533	1,719,566	1,730,080	1,691,206	1,660,981	1,628,515	1,609,008	1,601,188	1,605,571
Oklahoma	560,993	548,065	543,170	586,266	583,932	587,188	591,486	596,172	596,450	603,375	610,019	616,775	624,410
Oregon	436,736	418,593	419,771	479,321	486,073	506,638	513,650	516,258	515,834	518,119	515,644	517,373	518,896
Pennsylvania	2,169,225	1,808,630	1,524,839	1,684,913	1,701,096	1,698,795	1,702,566	1,701,044	1,693,569	1,680,772	1,661,990	1,668,916	1,659,616
Rhode Island	163,205	139,195	125,934	144,422	143,792	143,939	139,001	138,993	134,737	131,963	131,538	131,494	131,379
South Carolina	600,292	569,612	569,029	624,456	635,750	639,950	647,703	652,803	656,996	662,231	664,136	664,133	673,850
South Dakota	158,543	124,934	119,823	122,252	116,651	115,148	114,673	114,863	114,723	114,209	115,242	119,449	120,950
Tennessee	836,010	806,696	761,766	844,878	859,522	868,129	881,414	889,312	891,430	895,335	896,130	899,382	903,695
Texas	2,432,420	2,608,817	3,075,333	3,706,550	4,016,791	4,084,792	4,186,812	4,255,963	4,322,975	4,393,893	4,473,236	4,551,084	4,634,133
Utah	287,405	312,813	408,917	448,096	456,183	464,645	478,233	488,514	503,562	513,884	528,608	540,683	556,885
Vermont	97,772	95,045	87,832	98,894	95,160	93,608	92,508	91,437	89,880	87,931	86,378	85,501	85,184
Virginia	995,580	955,105	989,197	1,195,123	1,118,446	1,133,882	1,141,790	1,142,342	1,150,316	1,154,689	1,159,105	1,165,907	1,177,274
Washington	764,735	710,929	755,141	925,696	937,656	941,238	946,824	947,857	947,791	953,719	960,084	965,191	964,255
West Virginia	372,278	353,264	301,947	273,277	266,078	271,197	271,780	272,045	267,989	269,623	268,872	270,961	273,355
Wisconsin	880,609	770,554	711,466	825,699	826,864	831,809	834,177	835,072	823,754	823,595	817,284	825,622	825,949
Wyoming	81,293	89,471	91,277	86,092	78,652	77,878	77,757	79,090	79,788	81,006	80,717	81,654	83,131
Other jurisdictions													
American Samoa	—	—	11,448	15,102	15,123	15,302	15,237	14,606	14,646	14,646	14,403	15,451	15,541
Guam	20,315	—	23,883	—	28,301	—	29,617	29,515	28,358	28,521	28,075	28,765	28,735
Northern Marianas	—	—	6,809	8,712	10,047	10,301	10,871	10,277	9,927	9,815	9,900	9,965	9,731
Puerto Rico	—	656,709	597,436	540,676	534,941	540,365	522,655	531,273	494,880	477,918	466,483	411,164	429,799
U.S. Virgin Islands	—	—	18,924	18,676	15,878	15,841	15,241	14,927	15,903	15,768	15,493	15,747	15,711

—Not available.
[1]Data for California for 1989–90 and earlier years are not strictly comparable with those for other states because California's attendance figures included excused absences.
[2]Excludes average daily attendance for regional occupational programs and summer school programs that were reported in prior years.

NOTE: Some data have been revised from previously published figures.
SOURCE: U.S. Department of Education, National Center for Education Statistics, *Statistics of State School Systems, 1969–70; Revenues and Expenditures for Public Elementary and Secondary Education, 1979–80;* and Common Core of Data (CCD), "National Public Education Financial Survey," 1989–90 through 2011–12. (This table was prepared March 2015.)

Table 203.90. Average daily attendance (ADA) as a percentage of total enrollment, school day length, and school year length in public schools, by school level and state: 2007–08 and 2011–12

[Standard errors appear in parentheses]

State	2007–08 ADA as percent of enrollment	2007–08 Average hours in school day	2011–12 Total elementary, secondary, and combined elementary/secondary schools — ADA as percent of enrollment	Average hours in school day	Average days in school year	Average hours in school year	Elementary schools — ADA as percent of enrollment	Average hours in school day	Secondary schools — ADA as percent of enrollment	Average hours in school day
1	2	3	4	5	6	7	8	9	10	11
United States.............	93.1 (0.22)	6.6 (0.02)	93.9 (0.12)	6.7 (0.01)	179 (0.1)	1,203 (2.0)	94.9 (0.12)	6.7 (0.01)	91.7 (0.34)	6.7 (0.02)
Alabama	93.8 (1.24)	7.0 (0.07)	94.4 (0.94)	7.0 (0.04)	181 (0.8)	1,271 (8.5)	95.3 (0.92)	7.1 (0.04)	94.6 (0.65)	6.9 (0.13)
Alaska...............................	89.9 (1.22)	6.5 (0.05)	91.4 (1.19)	6.7 (0.17)	177 (1.3)	1,183 (37.3)	‡ (†)	‡ (†)	‡ (†)	‡ (†)
Arizona.............................	89.0 (2.95)	6.4 (0.09)	91.7 (0.99)	6.7 (0.08)	179 (1.3)	1,201 (12.5)	93.5 (0.53)	6.9 (0.06)	87.9 (2.40)	6.5 (0.26)
Arkansas...........................	91.8 (1.35)	6.9 (0.06)	94.2 (0.58)	7.0 (0.07)	180 (0.5)	1,261 (14.1)	94.7 (0.36)	7.0 (0.08)	92.9 (1.93)	6.9 (0.14)
California	93.2 (0.71)	6.2 (0.07)	93.1 (0.46)	6.2 (0.05)	180 (0.3)	1,121 (9.0)	94.7 (0.51)	6.3 (0.06)	89.7 (1.08)	6.3 (0.08)
Colorado...........................	93.9 (0.44)	7.0 (0.05)	93.1 (0.71)	7.1 (0.06)	172 (1.4)	1,215 (7.7)	94.6 (0.59)	7.0 (0.07)	88.0 (2.57)	7.1 (0.10)
Connecticut.......................	87.9 (2.98)	6.5 (0.09)	94.9 (0.47)	6.6 (0.04)	181 (0.1)	1,201 (7.5)	95.4 (0.61)	6.6 (0.05)	94.3 (0.33)	6.7 (0.09)
Delaware...........................	89.8 (1.75)	6.7 (0.09)	93.5 (0.50)	7.0 (0.10)	182 (1.2)	1,269 (23.7)	94.1 (0.50)	7.0 (0.12)	93.8 (0.71)	7.0 (0.09)
District of Columbia	91.2 (1.27)	6.9 (0.21)	‡ (†)	‡ (†)	‡ (†)	‡ (†)	‡ (†)	‡ (†)	‡ (†)	‡ (†)
Florida...............................	92.7 (0.74)	6.4 (0.08)	93.2 (0.52)	6.6 (0.06)	181 (1.2)	1,193 (14.2)	94.3 (0.49)	6.6 (0.08)	90.7 (0.84)	6.7 (0.09)
Georgia.............................	93.3 (1.28)	6.8 (0.06)	94.3 (0.53)	7.0 (0.04)	178 (0.4)	1,242 (8.5)	95.0 (0.59)	6.9 (0.05)	‡ (†)	‡ (†)
Hawaii...............................	90.7 (4.58)	6.3 (0.10)	‡ (†)	‡ (†)	‡ (†)	‡ (†)	‡ (†)	‡ (†)	‡ (†)	‡ (†)
Idaho.................................	92.4 (2.27)	6.6 (0.09)	94.1 (1.01)	6.7 (0.13)	166 (5.1)	1,110 (21.7)	94.4 (0.75)	6.7 (0.08)	93.1 (0.83)	6.7 (0.20)
Illinois...............................	94.0 (0.71)	6.5 (0.05)	94.1 (0.40)	6.5 (0.04)	176 (0.4)	1,151 (7.7)	95.1 (0.29)	6.5 (0.05)	92.4 (1.29)	6.8 (0.08)
Indiana..............................	95.7 (0.51)	6.8 (0.06)	95.9 (0.20)	6.8 (0.05)	180 (0.1)	1,226 (9.1)	96.1 (0.25)	6.7 (0.05)	95.5 (0.31)	7.0 (0.07)
Iowa..................................	94.8 (0.65)	6.9 (0.09)	95.7 (0.36)	6.7 (0.12)	180 (0.2)	1,213 (21.8)	96.4 (0.21)	6.9 (0.05)	93.6 (1.39)	6.3 (0.47)
Kansas..............................	95.4 (0.52)	7.0 (0.07)	94.9 (0.42)	7.0 (0.03)	177 (2.6)	1,245 (17.9)	95.5 (0.53)	7.0 (0.04)	94.0 (0.42)	7.1 (0.04)
Kentucky...........................	93.1 (1.89)	6.7 (0.06)	93.2 (1.33)	6.8 (0.06)	179 (1.0)	1,211 (11.6)	95.9 (0.22)	6.8 (0.07)	87.0 (4.87)	6.8 (0.14)
Louisiana...........................	90.3 (2.31)	7.1 (0.08)	92.8 (0.70)	7.2 (0.07)	178 (1.1)	1,283 (10.7)	93.0 (0.88)	7.3 (0.07)	93.5 (0.42)	7.1 (0.14)
Maine................................	90.3 (2.41)	6.5 (0.06)	94.2 (0.73)	6.6 (0.06)	176 (0.2)	1,156 (10.7)	94.4 (1.00)	6.6 (0.07)	93.8 (0.45)	6.3 (0.08)
Maryland...........................	94.1 (0.44)	6.6 (0.07)	‡ (†)	‡ (†)	‡ (†)	‡ (†)	‡ (†)	‡ (†)	‡ (†)	‡ (†)
Massachusetts..................	94.6 (0.58)	6.5 (0.05)	93.5 (0.62)	6.4 (0.07)	180 (0.2)	1,157 (13.3)	94.4 (0.63)	6.4 (0.07)	90.3 (2.55)	6.6 (0.05)
Michigan............................	93.0 (1.01)	6.6 (0.08)	91.6 (0.71)	6.8 (0.03)	177 (0.5)	1,196 (5.9)	92.3 (0.99)	6.8 (0.03)	89.4 (1.28)	6.7 (0.07)
Minnesota..........................	93.1 (0.91)	6.3 (0.12)	93.1 (0.49)	6.4 (0.08)	173 (1.3)	1,111 (14.0)	96.1 (0.19)	6.6 (0.07)	89.5 (1.21)	6.0 (0.20)
Mississippi........................	92.1 (2.00)	7.0 (0.12)	94.4 (0.47)	7.2 (0.09)	181 (0.4)	1,312 (16.4)	94.9 (0.57)	7.3 (0.06)	93.7 (0.86)	7.2 (0.24)
Missouri............................	94.8 (0.26)	6.7 (0.05)	95.1 (0.20)	6.9 (0.03)	175 (0.3)	1,197 (5.3)	95.6 (0.24)	6.9 (0.04)	94.3 (0.24)	6.8 (0.11)
Montana............................	91.3 (1.39)	6.8 (0.05)	93.9 (0.81)	6.6 (0.06)	179 (0.4)	1,189 (11.2)	94.3 (0.79)	6.6 (0.09)	93.0 (0.48)	6.7 (0.08)
Nebraska	94.9 (1.21)	6.9 (0.08)	94.8 (0.60)	7.1 (0.05)	177 (1.0)	1,257 (9.6)	96.0 (0.53)	7.1 (0.04)	94.5 (0.66)	6.8 (0.19)
Nevada	93.5 (1.27)	6.3 (0.06)	93.9 (0.39)	6.5 (0.07)	180 (1.1)	1,164 (10.9)	94.5 (0.30)	6.4 (0.10)	93.9 (0.70)	6.5 (0.07)
New Hampshire	92.2 (1.75)	6.5 (0.06)	91.1 (2.86)	6.6 (0.05)	180 (0.3)	1,181 (10.3)	95.9 (0.45)	6.5 (0.07)	75.1 (12.63)	6.7 (0.05)
New Jersey........................	94.6 (0.59)	6.4 (0.05)	93.5 (1.13)	6.6 (0.06)	181 (0.2)	1,201 (11.8)	93.7 (1.40)	6.6 (0.07)	92.6 (1.29)	6.7 (0.07)
New Mexico	91.9 (1.76)	6.8 (0.08)	92.8 (0.80)	6.9 (0.09)	177 (0.6)	1,216 (15.7)	93.8 (0.80)	6.7 (0.08)	88.5 (2.41)	7.1 (0.14)
New York............................	92.7 (1.30)	6.6 (0.09)	92.7 (0.94)	6.6 (0.06)	182 (0.2)	1,206 (10.6)	93.6 (1.28)	6.6 (0.07)	90.0 (1.32)	6.8 (0.07)
North Carolina	92.6 (1.73)	6.7 (0.06)	94.7 (0.37)	6.9 (0.04)	181 (0.2)	1,240 (7.4)	95.2 (0.23)	6.8 (0.04)	‡ (†)	‡ (†)
North Dakota	95.9 (0.59)	6.6 (0.04)	95.2 (0.46)	6.5 (0.06)	177 (0.3)	1,159 (10.0)	96.4 (0.35)	6.4 (0.08)	95.5 (0.45)	6.6 (0.14)
Ohio..................................	91.8 (2.01)	6.6 (0.10)	93.8 (0.48)	6.6 (0.03)	180 (0.5)	1,191 (6.2)	95.0 (0.30)	6.6 (0.04)	91.0 (1.45)	6.7 (0.07)
Oklahoma..........................	92.1 (2.24)	6.6 (0.06)	94.4 (0.32)	6.7 (0.04)	174 (0.7)	1,176 (8.6)	94.9 (0.38)	6.7 (0.04)	93.3 (0.74)	6.8 (0.10)
Oregon..............................	94.4 (0.59)	6.6 (0.06)	94.2 (0.40)	6.6 (0.05)	170 (0.9)	1,118 (7.9)	95.1 (0.29)	6.5 (0.06)	91.1 (1.41)	6.7 (0.06)
Pennsylvania.....................	94.9 (0.39)	6.4 (0.12)	94.4 (0.29)	6.7 (0.05)	181 (0.3)	1,212 (9.5)	94.9 (0.38)	6.7 (0.06)	92.9 (0.56)	6.9 (0.14)
Rhode Island	93.7 (1.27)	6.3 (0.03)	94.6 (0.36)	6.4 (0.05)	180 (0.1)	1,150 (8.2)	95.1 (0.38)	6.3 (0.05)	‡ (†)	‡ (†)
South Carolina	94.9 (0.71)	6.9 (0.07)	95.6 (0.26)	7.0 (0.04)	181 (0.4)	1,263 (7.3)	96.2 (0.27)	6.9 (0.05)	93.9 (0.84)	7.1 (0.05)
South Dakota.....................	93.6 (2.53)	6.8 (0.08)	96.1 (0.24)	7.0 (0.07)	170 (1.1)	1,180 (6.7)	96.7 (0.30)	6.9 (0.08)	93.6 (0.53)	6.9 (0.17)
Tennessee	94.9 (0.23)	7.0 (0.05)	94.6 (0.30)	7.1 (0.03)	179 (0.4)	1,272 (7.8)	95.0 (0.28)	7.1 (0.04)	94.2 (0.45)	7.0 (0.02)
Texas	94.1 (1.34)	7.2 (0.11)	95.2 (0.43)	7.3 (0.04)	179 (0.7)	1,297 (8.8)	95.9 (0.41)	7.3 (0.03)	94.8 (0.29)	7.3 (0.06)
Utah..................................	91.4 (1.56)	6.3 (0.29)	93.3 (0.80)	6.5 (0.08)	179 (0.3)	1,165 (13.5)	94.4 (0.80)	6.5 (0.08)	93.6 (0.74)	6.6 (0.09)
Vermont............................	92.7 (3.39)	6.7 (0.07)	94.0 (0.95)	6.7 (0.04)	178 (0.3)	1,183 (7.2)	93.7 (1.30)	6.8 (0.04)	94.7 (0.35)	6.2 (0.12)
Virginia.............................	94.7 (0.46)	6.6 (0.05)	95.0 (0.32)	6.6 (0.03)	185 (3.4)	1,222 (18.8)	95.8 (0.32)	6.7 (0.03)	93.3 (0.65)	6.6 (0.10)
Washington........................	82.9 (3.06)	6.2 (0.08)	92.2 (0.67)	6.3 (0.06)	179 (0.3)	1,129 (11.3)	94.3 (0.55)	6.4 (0.04)	88.0 (2.00)	6.1 (0.19)
West Virginia......................	94.0 (0.99)	6.9 (0.07)	94.9 (0.46)	7.0 (0.05)	181 (0.4)	1,272 (9.8)	96.2 (0.27)	7.0 (0.07)	89.8 (1.98)	7.3 (0.09)
Wisconsin	95.0 (0.57)	6.9 (0.04)	94.9 (0.31)	6.9 (0.11)	179 (0.2)	1,234 (19.2)	95.7 (0.21)	7.0 (0.03)	91.9 (1.08)	7.0 (0.12)
Wyoming...........................	92.4 (1.15)	6.9 (0.05)	93.6 (0.81)	7.0 (0.04)	174 (0.5)	1,209 (6.5)	94.8 (0.78)	6.9 (0.05)	89.9 (2.19)	7.0 (0.08)

†Not applicable.
‡Reporting standards not met. Either the response rate is under 50 percent or there are too few cases for a reliable estimate.
NOTE: Averages reflect data reported by schools rather than state requirements. School-reported length of day may exceed state requirements, and there is a range of statistical error in reported estimates.

SOURCE: U.S. Department of Education, National Center for Education Statistics, Schools and Staffing Survey (SASS), "Public School Data File," 2007–08 and 2011–12. (This table was prepared May 2013.)

Table 204.10. Number and percentage of public school students eligible for free or reduced-price lunch, by state: Selected years, 2000–01 through 2012–13

State	Number of students				Number of students eligible for free/reduced-price lunch				Percent of students eligible for free/reduced-price lunch			
	2000–01	2010–11	2011–12	2012–13	2000–01	2010–11	2011–12	2012–13	2000–01	2010–11	2011–12	2012–13
1	2	3	4	5	6	7	8	9	10	11	12	13
United States	46,579,068 [1]	48,941,267	48,995,812 [1]	49,084,316	17,839,867 [1]	23,544,479	24,291,646 [1]	25,188,294	38.3 [1]	48.1	49.6 [1]	51.3
Alabama	728,351	730,427	731,556	740,475	335,143	402,386	420,447	429,604	46.0	55.1	57.5	58.0
Alaska	105,333	132,104	131,166	131,483	32,468	50,701	53,238	53,082	30.8	38.4	40.6	40.4
Arizona	877,696 [2]	1,067,210	1,024,454	990,378	274,277 [2]	482,044	511,885	514,193	31.2 [2]	45.2	50.0	51.9
Arkansas	449,959	482,114	483,114	486,157	205,058	291,608	294,324	298,573	45.6	60.5	60.9	61.4
California	6,050,753	6,169,427	6,202,862 [2]	6,178,788	2,820,611	3,335,885	3,353,964 [2]	3,478,407	46.6	54.1	54.1 [2]	56.3
Colorado	724,349	842,864	853,610	863,121	195,148	336,426	348,896	358,876	26.9	39.9	40.9	41.6
Connecticut	562,179 [2]	552,919	543,883	549,295	143,030 [2]	190,554	194,339	201,085	25.4 [2]	34.5	35.7	36.6
Delaware	114,676	128,342	128,470	127,791	37,766	61,564	62,774	66,413	32.9	48.0	48.9	52.0
District of Columbia	68,380	71,263	72,329	75,411	47,839	52,027	45,199	46,416	70.0	73.0	62.5	61.6
Florida	2,434,755	2,641,555	2,668,037	2,691,881	1,079,009	1,479,519	1,535,670	1,576,379	44.3	56.0	57.6	58.6
Georgia	1,444,937	1,676,419	1,682,447	1,702,766	624,511	961,954	986,865	1,017,193	43.2	57.4	58.7	59.7
Hawaii	184,357	179,601	182,705	184,760	80,657	84,106	90,021	93,457	43.8	46.8	49.3	50.6
Idaho	244,755	275,815	276,969	279,277	85,824	124,104	135,642	134,560	35.1	45.0	49.0	48.2
Illinois	2,048,792 [2]	1,973,401	2,068,926	2,031,835	759,973 [2]	921,471	1,014,713	1,027,336	37.1 [2]	46.7	49.0	50.6
Indiana	977,219	1,038,817	1,037,779	1,039,797	285,267	485,728	497,663	509,604	29.2	46.8	48.0	49.0
Iowa	492,021	484,856	485,358	490,630	131,553	188,486	194,146	200,417	26.7	38.9	40.0	40.8
Kansas	462,594	479,953	481,519	470,283	154,693	228,852	235,362	233,322	33.4	47.7	48.9	49.6
Kentucky	626,723	673,128	677,628	675,167	298,334	380,773	368,355	373,837	47.6	56.6	54.4	55.4
Louisiana	741,162	695,772	702,301	693,980	433,068	460,546	471,347	459,617	58.4	66.2	67.1	66.2
Maine	198,532	183,477	178,989 [2]	179,323	60,162	78,915	76,985 [2]	80,636	30.3	43.0	43.0 [2]	45.0
Maryland	852,911	852,202	854,060	856,775	255,872	341,557	356,631	366,695	30.0	40.1	41.8	42.8
Massachusetts	979,590	955,301	952,044	952,970	237,871	326,849	334,511	352,988	24.3	34.2	35.1	37.0
Michigan	1,703,260	1,551,861	1,532,809	1,511,030	504,044	719,800	735,010	724,340	29.6	46.4	48.0	47.9
Minnesota	854,154	837,930	839,645	845,291	218,867	306,136	311,645	323,459	25.6	36.5	37.1	38.3
Mississippi	497,421	489,462	487,870	491,220	319,670	345,734	348,664	352,084	64.3	70.6	71.5	71.7
Missouri	912,247	902,375	885,138	898,402	315,608	406,358	411,750	408,726	34.6	45.0	46.5	45.5
Montana	154,438	140,497	142,349	142,908	47,415	57,836	57,349	60,262	30.7	41.2	40.3	42.2
Nebraska	286,138	298,276	301,296	303,332	87,045	127,114	132,010	133,912	30.4	42.6	43.8	44.1
Nevada	282,621	436,840	438,745	443,158	92,978	219,904	237,212	228,660	32.9	50.3	54.1	51.6
New Hampshire	206,919	194,001	190,784	187,940	31,212	48,904	50,123	50,596	15.1	25.2	26.3	26.9
New Jersey	1,312,983	1,356,882	1,316,792	1,363,967	357,728	444,735	467,798	501,804	27.2	32.8	35.5	36.8
New Mexico	320,303	335,810	333,331	335,922	174,939	227,077	228,227	229,249	54.6	67.6	68.5	68.2
New York	2,859,927	2,722,761	2,685,751	2,708,341	1,236,945	1,315,564	1,334,698	1,297,148	43.3	48.3	49.7	47.9
North Carolina	1,194,371	1,487,699	1,497,711	1,506,080	470,316	747,978	784,268	809,732	39.4	50.3	52.4	53.8
North Dakota	109,201	94,273	94,018	98,993	31,840	29,929	30,870	30,330	29.2	31.7	32.8	30.6
Ohio	1,745,237	1,747,851	1,738,642	1,656,390	494,829	745,121	758,106	674,438	28.4	42.6	43.6	40.7
Oklahoma	623,110	659,376	665,243	665,404	300,179	398,917	406,908	410,378	48.2	60.5	61.2	61.7
Oregon	535,617	553,468	540,266	533,966	186,203	280,174	287,214	286,635	34.8	50.6	53.2	53.7
Pennsylvania	1,798,977	1,742,608	1,732,035	1,716,262	510,121	686,641	696,531	712,584	28.4	39.4	40.2	41.5
Rhode Island	157,347	142,575	141,456	141,124	52,209	61,127	62,082	65,184	33.2	42.9	43.9	46.2
South Carolina	677,411	722,203	726,003	735,998	320,254	395,033	412,345	427,396	47.3	54.7	56.8	58.1
South Dakota	128,598	125,883	128,016	130,294	37,857	46,718	49,469	51,678	29.4	37.1	38.6	39.7
Tennessee	909,161 [2]	987,078	964,832	982,312	436,298 [2]	542,953	554,768	575,522	48.0 [2]	55.0	57.5	58.6
Texas	4,059,353	4,916,401	5,000,193	5,077,507	1,823,029	2,471,212	2,552,819	3,059,657	44.9	50.3	51.1	60.3
Utah	470,265	585,552	598,294	600,146	135,428	223,943	284,910	362,933	28.8	38.2	47.6	60.5
Vermont	102,049	85,144	83,451	83,568	23,986	31,339	32,748	32,581	23.5	36.8	39.2	39.0
Virginia	1,067,710	1,250,206	1,227,099	1,235,561	320,233	458,879	480,821	487,463	30.0	36.7	39.2	39.5
Washington	1,004,770 [2]	1,043,466	1,041,934	1,050,904	326,295 [2]	418,065	463,246	474,940	32.5 [2]	40.1	44.5	45.2
West Virginia	286,285	282,879	282,870	283,044	143,446	145,605	149,407	148,493	50.1	51.5	52.8	52.5
Wisconsin	859,276	872,164	869,670	871,376	219,276	342,660	354,527	360,803	25.5	39.3	40.8	41.4
Wyoming	89,895	88,779	89,363	91,533	43,483	32,968	33,145	34,617	48.4	37.1	37.1	37.8

[1]U.S. total includes imputation for nonreporting states.
[2]Imputation for survey nonresponse. State-level imputations for 2000–01 were based on the reported percentages for 2001–02 applied to the 2000–01 enrollments. State-level imputations for 2011–12 were based on the reported percentages for 2010–11 applied to the 2011–12 enrollments.

NOTE: Table reflects counts of students enrolled in all schools for which both enrollment data and free/reduced-price lunch eligibility data were reported. Some data have been revised from previously published figures.
SOURCE: U.S. Department of Education, National Center for Education Statistics, Common Core of Data (CCD), "Public Elementary/Secondary School Universe Survey," 2000–01, 2010–11, 2011–12, and 2012–13. (This table was prepared December 2014.)

Table 204.20. Number and percentage of public school students participating in programs for English language learners, by state: Selected years, 2002–03 through 2012–13

State	Number of public school students participating in programs for English language learners							Percent of students participating in programs for English language learners						
	2002–03	2007–08	2008–09	2009–10	2010–11	2011–12	2012–13	2002–03	2007–08	2008–09	2009–10	2010–11	2011–12	2012–13
1	2	3	4	5	6	7	8	9	10	11	12	13	14	15
United States.............	4,118,918 [1]	4,153,870 [1]	4,439,514 [1]	4,364,510 [1]	4,370,004 [1]	4,389,325	4,397,318 [1]	8.7 [1]	8.6 [1]	9.2 [1]	9.1 [1]	9.1 [1]	9.1	9.2 [1]
Alabama..........................	10,568	20,943	19,523	19,497	17,559	17,895	17,837 [2]	1.5	2.8	2.6	2.6	2.4	2.4	2.4 [2]
Alaska.............................	16,351	16,752	11,937	14,581	14,894	14,538	14,824	12.3	12.8	9.2	11.1	11.3	11.1	11.3
Arizona............................	140,664	143,482	118,868	78,793	70,716	70,527	58,512	15.9	14.6	12.1	8.2	7.5	7.5	6.2
Arkansas.........................	15,146	25,896	27,629	29,735	31,457	32,671	33,745	3.4	5.4	5.8	6.3	6.6	6.9	7.1
California.........................	1,587,771	1,517,559 [2]	1,498,660	1,468,815 [3]	1,445,496 [2]	1,415,623	1,391,913	25.7	24.5 [2]	24.3	24.1 [3]	23.6 [2]	23.2	22.8
Colorado.........................	86,118	84,900	88,254	94,391	98,809	101,262	101,913	11.5	10.7	10.9	11.4	11.8	12.0	12.0
Connecticut.....................	21,970	29,424	28,886	29,266	29,671	29,318	30,077	4.0	5.4	5.4	5.4	5.6	5.6	5.8
Delaware.........................	3,445	7,179	7,111	7,615	6,766	6,972	7,280	3.1	6.3	6.1	6.5	5.6	5.9	6.1
District of Columbia	5,363	4,092	4,370	4,203	3,741	3,745	4,530	7.9	7.0	9.9	9.6	8.4	8.4	10.3
Florida.............................	203,659	231,326	226,037	230,440	229,659	234,347	242,133	8.0	8.7	8.6	8.8	8.7	8.8	9.0
Georgia...........................	70,464	81,008	82,000	86,668	80,965	83,400	87,104	4.7	4.9	5.0	5.2	4.9	5.0	5.2
Hawaii.............................	12,853	16,959	18,564	18,097	19,092	24,750	16,474	7.0	9.4	10.3	10.0	10.6	13.5	8.9
Idaho...............................	18,747	16,660	17,657	15,931	15,361	15,143	16,615	7.5	6.3	6.6	6.0	5.8	5.7	6.1
Illinois.............................	168,591	156,673	204,737	179,850	174,335	170,626	191,738	8.2	7.5	9.7	8.6	8.4	8.2	9.4
Indiana............................	42,560	46,092	45,527	48,364	48,574	50,082	50,750	4.3	4.5	4.4	4.7	4.7	5.0	5.0
Iowa................................	13,961	19,442	20,334	20,867	21,733	22,503	21,839	2.9	4.0	4.2	4.2	4.4	4.5	4.4
Kansas............................	17,942	31,760	34,095	38,011	39,323	41,052	42,590	3.8	6.8	7.2	8.0	8.1	8.5	8.7
Kentucky.........................	6,343	12,896	14,589	14,244	16,351	16,878	18,761	1.0	1.9	2.2	2.1	2.4	2.5	2.7
Louisiana........................	11,042	8,545	12,223	12,499	11,617	12,348	13,105	1.5	1.3	1.9	1.9	1.7	1.9	2.0
Maine..............................	2,575	3,803	4,128 [2]	4,467	4,792	5,104	4,980	1.2	2.0	2.2 [2]	2.4	2.5	2.7	2.7
Maryland..........................	27,311	36,971 [2]	39,919 [2]	43,179	45,500	51,574	55,343	3.2	4.4 [2]	4.7 [2]	5.1	5.3	6.0	6.4
Massachusetts.................	50,578	53,788	47,198	49,612	52,610	62,354	63,917	6.1	6.7	5.9	6.3	6.7	7.9	8.1
Michigan..........................	54,961	47,139	55,593	53,565	50,773	52,811	56,865	3.2	3.0	3.6	3.5	3.5	3.7	4.1
Minnesota.......................	51,224	55,377	55,738	54,349	40,778	54,034	50,837	6.1	6.9	7.0	6.8	5.1	6.8	6.3
Mississippi......................	2,250	5,428	6,543	6,061	5,617	6,175	8,485	0.5	1.1	1.3	1.2	1.1	1.3	1.7
Missouri..........................	13,121	16,472 [2]	15,468	19,393	20,411	23,169	24,455	1.4	1.8 [2]	1.7	2.2	2.3	2.6	2.7
Montana..........................	6,642	6,721	4,549	3,806	3,299	3,318	3,750	4.4	4.7	3.2	2.7	2.3	2.3	2.6
Nebraska.........................	13,803	19,128	18,388	19,323	20,062	17,532	16,895	4.9	6.6	6.3	6.6	6.7	5.8	5.6
Nevada............................	58,753	46,602	75,952	67,868	83,351	84,125	67,970	15.9	10.9	17.6	16.0	19.4	19.6	15.7
New Hampshire	3,270	3,201	3,496	3,821	3,965	3,892	3,709	1.6	1.6	1.8	1.9	2.0	2.0	2.0
New Jersey......................	57,548	52,559 [2]	53,960	55,450	52,580	53,543	57,838	4.3	3.9 [2]	4.0	4.1	3.8	4.0	4.3
New Mexico	65,317	61,173	55,978 [2]	51,257	52,029	53,071	51,554	20.4	18.6	17.0 [2]	15.5	15.7	16.1	15.8
New York..........................	178,704	209,449	183,736	200,433	207,708	204,898	197,594	6.2	7.7	6.8	7.4	7.8	7.8	7.5
North Carolina	59,712	126,792	113,155	105,651	102,397	98,264	97,338	4.5	8.9	7.8	7.3	7.1	6.7	6.6
North Dakota	883	2,645	3,540	3,031	2,788	2,589	2,667	0.9	2.8	3.7	3.3	3.0	2.7	2.7
Ohio................................	25,610	34,167	35,362	36,527	35,170	35,729	37,207	1.4	2.0	2.0	2.2	2.1	2.2	2.3
Oklahoma........................	40,179	37,744	38,314 [2]	39,259	41,431	44,593	46,155	6.4	5.9	5.9 [2]	6.0	6.3	6.7	6.9
Oregon............................	52,331	61,999	62,857	61,625	58,662	63,790	50,181	9.5	11.0	11.2	11.0	10.5	11.3	8.9
Pennsylvania....................	30,731 [2]	44,564	44,853	44,359	44,729	44,242	44,017	1.7 [2]	2.6	2.7	2.6	2.7	2.7	2.7
Rhode Island	10,050	6,672	6,466 [2]	6,340	7,161	7,724	7,856	6.4	5.0	4.9 [2]	4.9	5.5	6.1	6.2
South Carolina.................	7,467	13,531	31,422	34,661	36,360	38,986	40,876	1.1	1.9	4.4	4.8	5.1	5.4	5.7
South Dakota...................	4,522	3,994 [2]	3,580	4,005	4,383	4,736	4,999	3.5	3.3 [2]	2.8	3.2	3.5	3.7	3.8
Tennessee	26,808 [2]	25,670	27,433	27,550	29,680	30,996	32,331	3.0 [2]	2.7	2.8	2.8	3.0	3.1	3.3
Texas	625,946	445,334	704,142	708,615	718,350	722,043	739,639	14.9	9.7	15.2	15.0	15.0	14.9	15.1
Utah................................	43,269	46,398	43,957	46,591	41,805	32,423	31,810	9.0	8.3	8.3	8.5	7.7	5.9	5.7
Vermont	1,057	1,675 [2]	1,645 [2]	1,525	1,510	1,447	1,427	1.1	1.9 [2]	1.9 [2]	1.7	1.6	1.6	1.6
Virginia............................	49,780	84,080	86,745	86,475	87,752	91,431	92,937	4.3	6.9	7.1	7.0	7.1	7.4	7.4
Washington......................	70,431	80,694	82,711	65,101	90,282	82,070	93,940	6.9	7.8	8.0	6.3	8.7	7.9	8.9
West Virginia....................	1,281	2,335	1,617	1,605	1,786	1,914	2,084	0.5	0.8	0.6	0.6	0.6	0.7	0.7
Wisconsin	25,764	43,782	47,798	45,041	43,562	44,362	43,189	2.9	5.0	5.5	5.2	5.0	5.1	5.0
Wyoming..........................	3,483	2,395	2,271	2,098	2,602	2,706	2,733	4.1	2.8	2.6	2.4	2.9	3.0	3.0

[1]U.S. total includes imputation for nonreporting states.
[2]Imputation for survey nonresponse. State-level imputations were based on the percentages reported by the state for other years applied to the enrollment for the given year.
[3]Based on data reported by the California Education Agency (http://www.cde.ca.gov/ds/sd/cb/cefelfacts.asp).
NOTE: Includes students served in regular school districts, excluding regional education service agencies and supervisory union administrative centers, state-operated agencies, federally operated agencies, and other types of local education agencies, such as independent charter schools.
SOURCE: U.S. Department of Education, National Center for Education Statistics, Common Core of Data (CCD), Local Education Agency Universe Survey, 2002–03 through 2012–13. (This table was prepared March 2015.)

Table 204.25. Public school students participating in programs for English language learners, by race/ethnicity: Fall 2009 through fall 2013

Year	Total	White	Black	Hispanic	Asian/Pacific Islander			American Indian/ Alaska Native[1]	Two or more races
					Total	Asian	Pacific Islander		
1	2	3	4	5	6	7	8	9	10
Total enrollment in public schools									
2009....................	49,360,982	26,701,772	8,245,375	10,991,275	2,484,305	—	—	600,526	337,729
2010....................	49,484,181	25,932,691	7,917,019	11,438,797	2,466,199	2,435,232	49,073	565,629	1,163,846
2011....................	49,521,669	25,602,197	7,827,305	11,759,474	2,512,779	2,295,692	170,507	547,435	1,272,479
2012....................	49,771,118	25,385,841	7,803,273	12,103,504	2,552,088	2,334,144	178,635	533,583	1,392,829
2013[2]..................	49,941,000	25,194,000	7,787,000	12,497,000	2,571,000	2,388,000	183,000	530,000	1,362,000
Number of students participating in English language learner (ELL) programs									
2009....................	4,437,388	218,285	142,626	3,406,735	509,540	—	—	38,148	(3)
2010....................	4,464,734	228,897	148,256	3,512,240	509,846	478,620	31,226	39,947	20,928
2011[4]..................	4,454,824	230,434	153,168	3,491,411	515,613	492,182	23,431	38,816	25,371
2012....................	4,505,849	242,341	155,625	3,534,292	511,310	486,946	24,364	36,820	25,461
2013....................	4,580,409	251,553	161,075	3,591,423	512,263	487,194	25,069	36,629	27,466
Percentage distribution of ELL program participants									
2009....................	100.0	4.9	3.2	76.8	11.5	—	—	0.9	(3)
2010....................	100.0	5.1	3.3	78.7	11.4	10.7	0.7	0.9	0.5
2011[4]..................	100.0	5.2	3.4	78.4	11.6	11.0	0.5	0.9	0.6
2012....................	100.0	5.4	3.5	78.4	11.3	10.8	0.5	0.8	0.6
2013....................	100.0	5.5	3.5	78.4	11.2	10.6	0.5	0.8	0.6
Number of ELL program participants as a percent of total enrollment									
2009....................	9.0	0.8	1.7	31.0	20.5	—	—	6.4	(3)
2010....................	9.0	0.9	1.9	30.7	20.7	20.8	18.3	7.1	1.8
2011[4]..................	9.0	0.9	2.0	29.7	20.5	21.1	13.1	7.1	2.0
2012....................	9.1	1.0	2.0	29.2	20.0	20.5	13.5	6.9	1.8
2013[5]..................	9.2	1.0	2.1	28.7	19.9	20.4	13.7	6.9	2.0

—Not available.

[1]National totals do not include data for Bureau of Indian Education (BIE) schools. In fall 2010, the most recent year for which BIE data are available, there were 12,130 American Indian/Alaska Native ELL program participants in BIE schools.

[2]Projected.

[3]For 2009, data on students of Two or more races are included in the totals but are not shown separately. Only a small number of states reported these data, and they are not comparable to data for 2010 and later years.

[4]Includes imputations for missing data.

[5]Enrollment base for percentage of enrollment is projected.

NOTE: Race categories exclude persons of Hispanic ethnicity. Detail may not sum to totals because racial/ethnic categories were not reported for some students and because of rounding. SOURCE: U.S. Department of Education, National Center for Education Statistics, ED*Facts* file 046, Data Group 123, extracted March 6, 2015, from the ED*Facts* Data Warehouse (internal U.S. Department of Education source); Common Core of Data (CCD), "State Nonfiscal Survey of Public Elementary and Secondary Education," 2009–10 through 2012–13; and National Elementary and Secondary Enrollment Projection Model, 1972 through 2024. (This table was prepared March 2015.)

Table 204.30. Children 3 to 21 years old served under Individuals with Disabilities Education Act (IDEA), Part B, by type of disability: Selected years, 1976–77 through 2012–13

Type of disability	1976–77	1980–81	1990–91	2000–01	2002–03	2003–04	2004–05	2005–06	2006–07	2007–08[1]	2008–09[1]	2009–10	2010–11	2011–12	2012–13
1	2	3	4	5	6	7	8	9	10	11	12	13	14	15	16
	Number served (in thousands)														
All disabilities	3,694	4,144	4,710	6,296	6,523	6,634	6,720	6,718	6,687	6,597	6,483	6,481	6,436	6,401	6,429
Autism	—	—	—	93	137	163	191	223	258	296	336	378	417	455	498
Deaf-blindness	—	3	1	1	2	2	2	2	2	2	2	2	2	2	1
Developmental delay	—	—	—	213	283	305	332	339	333	357	354	368	382	393	402
Emotional disturbance	283	347	389	480	485	489	489	477	464	442	420	407	390	373	362
Hearing impairment	88	79	58	77	78	79	79	79	80	79	78	79	78	78	77
Intellectual disability	961	830	534	624	602	593	578	556	534	500	478	463	448	435	430
Multiple disabilities	—	68	96	131	138	140	140	141	142	138	130	131	130	132	133
Orthopedic impairment	87	58	49	82	83	77	73	71	69	67	70	65	63	61	59
Other health impairment[2]	141	98	55	303	403	464	521	570	610	641	659	689	716	743	779
Preschool disabled[3]	†	†	390	†	†	†	†	†	†	†	†	†	†	†	†
Specific learning disability	796	1,462	2,129	2,860	2,848	2,831	2,798	2,740	2,665	2,569	2,476	2,431	2,361	2,303	2,277
Speech or language impairment	1,302	1,168	985	1,388	1,412	1,441	1,463	1,468	1,475	1,454	1,426	1,416	1,396	1,373	1,356
Traumatic brain injury	—	—	—	16	22	23	24	24	25	25	26	25	26	26	26
Visual impairment	38	31	23	29	29	28	29	29	29	29	29	29	28	28	28
	Percentage distribution of children served														
All disabilities	100.0	100.0	100.0	100.0	100.0	100.0	100.0	100.0	100.0	100.0	100.0	100.0	100.0	100.0	100.0
Autism	—	—	—	1.5	2.1	2.5	2.8	3.3	3.9	4.5	5.2	5.8	6.5	7.1	7.8
Deaf-blindness	—	0.1	#	#	#	#	#	#	#	#	#	#	#	#	#
Developmental delay	—	—	—	3.4	4.3	4.6	4.9	5.0	5.0	5.4	5.5	5.7	5.9	6.1	6.2
Emotional disturbance	7.7	8.4	8.3	7.6	7.4	7.4	7.3	7.1	6.9	6.7	6.5	6.3	6.1	5.8	5.6
Hearing impairment	2.4	1.9	1.2	1.2	1.2	1.2	1.2	1.2	1.2	1.2	1.2	1.2	1.2	1.2	1.2
Intellectual disability	26.0	20.0	11.3	9.9	9.2	8.9	8.6	8.3	8.0	7.6	7.4	7.1	7.0	6.8	6.7
Multiple disabilities	—	1.6	2.0	2.1	2.1	2.1	2.1	2.1	2.1	2.1	2.0	2.0	2.0	2.1	2.1
Orthopedic impairment	2.4	1.4	1.0	1.3	1.3	1.2	1.1	1.1	1.0	1.0	1.1	1.0	1.0	1.0	0.9
Other health impairment[2]	3.8	2.4	1.2	4.8	6.2	7.0	7.7	8.5	9.1	9.7	10.2	10.6	11.1	11.6	12.1
Preschool disabled[3]	†	†	8.3	†	†	†	†	†	†	†	†	†	†	†	†
Specific learning disability	21.5	35.3	45.2	45.4	43.7	42.7	41.6	40.8	39.9	38.9	38.2	37.5	36.7	36.0	35.4
Speech or language impairment	35.2	28.2	20.9	22.0	21.6	21.7	21.8	21.8	22.1	22.0	22.0	21.8	21.7	21.4	21.1
Traumatic brain injury	—	—	—	0.2	0.3	0.4	0.4	0.4	0.4	0.4	0.4	0.4	0.4	0.4	0.4
Visual impairment	1.0	0.7	0.5	0.5	0.4	0.4	0.4	0.4	0.4	0.4	0.4	0.4	0.4	0.4	0.4
	Number served as a percent of total enrollment[4]														
All disabilities	8.3	10.1	11.4	13.3	13.5	13.7	13.8	13.7	13.6	13.4	13.2	13.1	13.0	12.9	12.9
Autism	—	—	—	0.2	0.3	0.3	0.4	0.5	0.5	0.6	0.7	0.8	0.8	0.9	1.0
Deaf-blindness	—	#	#	#	#	#	#	#	#	#	#	#	#	#	#
Developmental delay	—	—	—	0.5	0.6	0.6	0.7	0.7	0.7	0.7	0.7	0.7	0.8	0.8	0.8
Emotional disturbance	0.6	0.8	0.9	1.0	1.0	1.0	1.0	1.0	0.9	0.9	0.9	0.8	0.8	0.8	0.7
Hearing impairment	0.2	0.2	0.1	0.2	0.2	0.2	0.2	0.2	0.2	0.2	0.2	0.2	0.2	0.2	0.2
Intellectual disability	2.2	2.0	1.3	1.3	1.2	1.2	1.2	1.1	1.1	1.0	1.0	0.9	0.9	0.9	0.9
Multiple disabilities	—	0.2	0.2	0.3	0.3	0.3	0.3	0.3	0.3	0.3	0.3	0.3	0.3	0.3	0.3
Orthopedic impairment	0.2	0.1	0.1	0.2	0.2	0.2	0.2	0.1	0.1	0.1	0.1	0.1	0.1	0.1	0.1
Other health impairment[2]	0.3	0.2	0.1	0.6	0.8	1.0	1.1	1.2	1.2	1.3	1.3	1.4	1.4	1.5	1.6
Preschool disabled[3]	†	†	0.9	†	†	†	†	†	†	†	†	†	†	†	†
Specific learning disability	1.8	3.6	5.2	6.1	5.9	5.8	5.7	5.6	5.4	5.2	5.0	4.9	4.8	4.7	4.6
Speech or language impairment	2.9	2.9	2.4	2.9	2.9	3.0	3.0	3.0	3.0	2.9	2.9	2.9	2.8	2.8	2.7
Traumatic brain injury	—	—	—	#	#	#	#	#	0.1	0.1	0.1	0.1	0.1	0.1	0.1
Visual impairment	0.1	0.1	0.1	0.1	0.1	0.1	0.1	0.1	0.1	0.1	0.1	0.1	0.1	0.1	0.1

—Not available.
†Not applicable.
#Rounds to zero.
[1]Data do not include Vermont, for which 2007–08 and 2008–09 data were not available. In 2006–07, the total number of 3- to 21-year-olds served in Vermont was 14,010.
[2]Other health impairments include having limited strength, vitality, or alertness due to chronic or acute health problems such as a heart condition, tuberculosis, rheumatic fever, nephritis, asthma, sickle cell anemia, hemophilia, epilepsy, lead poisoning, leukemia, or diabetes.
[3]For 1990–91, preschool children are not included in the counts by disability condition but are separately reported. For other years, preschool children are included in the counts by disability condition.
[4]Based on the total enrollment in public schools, prekindergarten through 12th grade. For total enrollment in public schools, see table 203.20.
NOTE: Prior to October 1994, children and youth with disabilities were served under Chapter 1 of the Elementary and Secondary Education Act as well as under the Individuals with Disabilities

Education Act (IDEA), Part B. Data reported in this table for years prior to 1994–95 include children ages 0–21 served under Chapter 1. Data are for the 50 states and the District of Columbia only. Increases since 1987–88 are due in part to new legislation enacted in fall 1986, which added a mandate for public school special education services for 3- to 5-year-old children with disabilities. Detail may not sum to totals because of rounding.
SOURCE: U.S. Department of Education, Office of Special Education Programs, *Annual Report to Congress on the Implementation of the Individuals with Disabilities Education Act*, selected years, 1979 through 2006; and Individuals with Disabilities Education Act (IDEA) database, retrieved October 3, 2014, from https://inventory.data.gov/dataset/8715a3e8-bf48-4eef-9deb-fd9bb76a196e/resource/a68a23f3-3981-47db-ac75-98a167b65259. National Center for Education Statistics, *Statistics of Public Elementary and Secondary School Systems*, 1977–78 and 1980–81; and Common Core of Data (CCD), "State Nonfiscal Survey of Public Elementary/Secondary Education," 1990–91 through 2012–13. (This table was prepared October 2014.)

Table 204.40. Children 3 to 21 years old served under Individuals with Disabilities Education Act (IDEA), Part B, by race/ethnicity and age group: 2000–01 through 2012–13

Age group and year	Total	White	Black	Hispanic	Asian[1]	Pacific Islander	American Indian/ Alaska Native	Two or more races
1	2	3	4	5	6	7	8	9
				Number of children served				
3 to 21 years old								
2000–01	6,295,709	3,957,589	1,259,348	877,655	121,044	—	80,073	—
2001–02	6,407,417	3,989,528	1,281,803	928,776	123,434	—	83,876	—
2002–03	6,522,977	4,014,340	1,311,270	980,590	130,252	—	86,525	—
2003–04	6,633,902	4,035,880	1,334,666	1,035,463	137,544	—	90,349	—
2004–05	6,718,630	4,044,491	1,355,550	1,081,697	144,339	—	92,553	—
2005–06	6,712,614	4,003,865	1,346,177	1,119,140	149,954	—	93,478	—
2006–07	6,686,386	3,948,853	1,335,870	1,154,217	153,265	—	94,181	—
2007–08[2]	6,574,368	3,833,922	1,307,462	1,181,130	158,623	—	93,231	—
2008–09[2]	6,461,938	3,725,896	1,273,996	1,200,290	162,630	—	93,672	5,454 [3]
2009–10	6,461,226	3,659,194	1,262,799	1,252,493	167,144	—	92,646	26,950 [3]
2010–11	6,435,141	3,518,169	1,214,849	1,310,031	145,896	19,581	91,258	135,357
2011–12	6,401,238	3,436,105	1,196,679	1,352,435	147,697	19,203	88,665	160,458
2012–13[4]	6,429,331	3,396,135	1,189,148	1,406,540	150,913	20,343	86,884	180,268
3 to 5 years old								
2000–01	592,090	400,650	93,281	78,070	13,203	—	6,886	—
2005–06	698,608	453,531	102,310	112,883	20,791	—	9,093	—
2010–11	723,793	416,034	102,097	153,033	23,189	2,159	9,141	18,140
2011–12	730,558	408,973	103,051	158,507	23,023	2,146	8,729	26,133
2012–13[4]	735,890	399,019	102,677	163,997	23,101	2,087	8,291	36,774
6 to 21 years old								
2000–01	5,703,619	3,556,939	1,166,067	799,585	107,841	—	73,187	—
2005–06	6,014,006	3,550,334	1,243,867	1,006,257	129,163	—	84,385	—
2010–11	5,711,348	3,102,135	1,112,752	1,156,998	122,707	17,422	82,117	117,217
2011–12	5,670,680	3,027,132	1,093,628	1,193,928	124,674	17,057	79,936	134,325
2012–13[4]	5,693,441	2,997,116	1,086,471	1,242,543	127,812	18,256	78,593	143,494
				Percentage distribution of children served				
3 to 21 years old								
2000–01	100.0	62.9	20.0	13.9	1.9	†	1.3	†
2001–02	100.0	62.3	20.0	14.5	1.9	†	1.3	†
2002–03	100.0	61.5	20.1	15.0	2.0	†	1.3	†
2003–04	100.0	60.8	20.1	15.6	2.1	†	1.4	†
2004–05	100.0	60.2	20.2	16.1	2.1	†	1.4	†
2005–06	100.0	59.6	20.1	16.7	2.2	†	1.4	†
2006–07	100.0	59.1	20.0	17.3	2.3	†	1.4	†
2007–08[2]	100.0	58.3	19.9	18.0	2.4	†	1.4	†
2008–09[2]	100.0	57.7	19.7	18.6	2.5	†	1.4	0.1 [3]
2009–10	100.0	56.6	19.5	19.4	2.6	†	1.4	0.4 [3]
2010–11	100.0	54.7	18.9	20.4	2.3	0.3	1.4	2.1
2011–12	100.0	53.7	18.7	21.1	2.3	0.3	1.4	2.5
2012–13	100.0	52.8	18.5	21.9	2.3	0.3	1.4	2.8
				Number served as a percent of total enrollment[5]				
3 to 21 years old								
2000–01	13.3	13.7	15.5	11.4	6.2	†	14.6	†
2001–02	13.4	13.9	15.7	11.4	6.1	†	14.9	†
2002–03	13.5	14.0	15.8	11.4	6.2	†	14.8	†
2003–04	13.7	14.2	16.0	11.5	6.4	†	15.2	†
2004–05	13.8	14.3	16.1	11.5	6.5	†	15.7	†
2005–06	13.7	14.3	15.9	11.4	6.6	†	15.6	†
2006–07	13.6	14.2	15.9	11.3	6.6	†	15.8	†
2007–08[2]	13.3	14.0	15.6	11.3	6.6	†	15.7	†
2008–09[2]	13.1	13.8	15.2	11.4	6.6	†	15.9	2.2 [3]
2009–10	13.1	13.7	15.2	11.5	6.7	†	15.6	8.0 [3]
2010–11	13.0	13.6	15.4	11.5	6.4	11.5	16.2	11.7
2011–12	12.9	13.4	15.3	11.5	6.4	10.8	16.2	12.6
2012–13	12.9	13.4	15.2	11.7	6.4	11.3	16.3	13.0

—Not available.
†Not applicable.
[1]For years prior to 2010–11, Asian data include Pacific Islanders.
[2]Data do not include Vermont, for which 2007–08 and 2008–09 data were not available.
[3]For 2008–09 and 2009–10, data on children of two or more races were reported by only a small number of states. Therefore, these data are not comparable to figures for later years.
[4]For 2012–13, the total column shows the overall counts of children as reported by the 50 states and the District of Columbia rather than the sum of counts reported for individual racial/ethnic groups. (Due to data limitations, summing the data for the racial/ethnic groups results in a total overcount of 56 children in the 3- to 5-year-old age group and 844 children in the 6- to 21-year-old age group.)

[5]Based on the total enrollment in public schools, prekindergarten through 12th grade, by race/ethnicity. For total enrollment in public schools by race/ethnicity, see table 203.50.
NOTE: Data include only those children served for whom race/ethnicity was reported. Race categories exclude persons of Hispanic ethnicity. Detail may not sum to totals because of rounding.
SOURCE: U.S. Department of Education, Office of Special Education Programs, Individuals with Disabilities Education Act (IDEA) database, retrieved October 3, 2014, from https://inventory.data.gov/dataset/8715a3e8-bf48-4eef-9deb-fd9bb76a196e/resource/a68a23f3-3981-47db-ac75-98a167b65259; and National Center for Education Statistics, Common Core of Data (CCD), "State Nonfiscal Survey of Public Elementary and Secondary Education," 2000–01 through 2012–13. (This table was prepared October 2014.)

Table 204.50. Children 3 to 21 years old served under Individuals with Disabilities Education Act (IDEA), Part B, by race/ethnicity and type of disability: 2011–12 and 2012–13

Number of children served

Type of disability	2011–12 White	Black	Hispanic	Asian	Pacific Islander	American Indian/Alaska Native	Two or more races	2012–13 White	Black	Hispanic	Asian	Pacific Islander	American Indian/Alaska Native	Two or more races
1	2	3	4	5	6	7	8	9	10	11	12	13	14	15
All disabilities	3,436,115	1,196,695	1,355,780	147,704	19,203	88,675	160,458	3,396,133	1,189,148	1,406,536	150,913	20,343	86,884	180,268
Autism	274,355	61,628	77,714	24,592	1,151	3,418	12,491	292,713	67,760	91,192	26,980	1,238	3,723	14,786
Deaf-blindness	890	158	397	65	16	26	31	866	165	334	54	13	27	28
Developmental delay	215,164	73,250	68,045	10,578	1,806	7,830	16,465	212,872	74,060	69,300	10,364	1,775	7,702	25,739
Emotional disturbance	199,929	100,412	51,698	3,224	980	5,381	11,530	192,562	95,790	52,463	3,218	988	5,025	12,300
Hearing impairment	38,409	11,412	21,617	4,156	402	841	1,611	37,679	11,130	21,461	4,187	460	805	1,786
Intellectual disability	203,247	120,492	85,206	10,018	1,239	5,679	8,705	197,797	116,641	89,518	10,445	1,258	5,517	9,117
Multiple disabilities	76,726	24,901	22,483	3,681	471	1,952	2,772	76,039	24,974	22,594	3,872	510	1,971	2,839
Orthopedic impairment	33,919	7,430	15,875	2,289	180	534	1,489	32,539	7,069	15,139	2,236	186	486	1,472
Other health impairment[1]	465,223	134,232	102,785	10,083	2,032	8,771	19,740	478,940	141,714	114,078	10,704	2,109	9,065	22,197
Specific learning disability	1,118,435	464,337	591,664	34,192	8,064	36,988	49,281	1,085,488	455,428	605,684	34,359	8,871	36,200	51,333
Speech or language impairment	778,171	189,926	307,379	43,075	2,692	16,570	35,057	757,210	186,038	314,260	42,698	2,735	15,678	37,257
Traumatic brain injury	16,006	4,041	4,254	609	77	329	653	16,015	4,009	4,351	636	81	328	707
Visual impairment	15,641	4,476	6,663	1,142	93	356	633	15,413	4,370	6,162	1,160	119	357	707

Percentage distribution of children served

Type of disability	2011–12 White	Black	Hispanic	Asian	Pacific Islander	American Indian/Alaska Native	Two or more races	2012–13 White	Black	Hispanic	Asian	Pacific Islander	American Indian/Alaska Native	Two or more races
All disabilities	100.0	100.0	100.0	100.0	100.0	100.0	100.0	100.0	100.0	100.0	100.0	100.0	100.0	100.0
Autism	8.0	5.1	5.7	16.6	6.0	3.9	7.8	8.6	5.7	6.5	17.9	6.1	4.3	8.2
Deaf-blindness	#	#	#	#	0.1	#	#	#	#	#	#	0.1	#	#
Developmental delay	6.3	6.1	5.0	7.2	9.4	8.8	10.3	6.3	6.2	4.9	6.9	8.7	8.9	14.3
Emotional disturbance	5.8	8.4	3.8	2.2	5.1	6.1	7.2	5.7	8.1	3.7	2.1	4.9	5.8	6.8
Hearing impairment	1.1	1.0	1.6	2.8	2.1	0.9	1.0	1.1	0.9	1.5	2.8	2.3	0.9	1.0
Intellectual disability	5.9	10.1	6.3	6.8	6.5	6.4	5.4	5.8	9.8	6.4	6.9	6.2	6.3	5.1
Multiple disabilities	2.2	2.1	1.7	2.5	2.5	2.2	1.7	2.2	2.1	1.6	2.6	2.5	2.3	1.6
Orthopedic impairment	1.0	0.6	1.2	1.5	0.9	0.6	0.9	1.0	0.6	1.1	1.5	0.9	0.6	0.8
Other health impairment[1]	13.5	11.2	7.6	6.8	10.6	9.9	12.3	14.1	11.9	8.1	7.1	10.4	10.4	12.3
Specific learning disability	32.5	38.8	43.6	23.1	42.0	41.7	30.7	32.0	38.3	43.1	22.8	43.6	41.7	28.5
Speech or language impairment	22.6	15.9	22.7	29.2	14.0	18.7	21.8	22.3	15.6	22.3	28.3	13.4	18.0	20.7
Traumatic brain injury	0.5	0.3	0.3	0.4	0.4	0.4	0.4	0.5	0.3	0.3	0.4	0.4	0.4	0.4
Visual impairment	0.5	0.4	0.5	0.8	0.5	0.4	0.4	0.5	0.4	0.4	0.8	0.6	0.4	0.4

Number served as a percent of total enrollment[2]

Type of disability	2011–12 White	Black	Hispanic	Asian	Pacific Islander	American Indian/Alaska Native	Two or more races	2012–13 White	Black	Hispanic	Asian	Pacific Islander	American Indian/Alaska Native	Two or more races
All disabilities	13.4	15.3	11.6	6.4	10.8	16.2	12.6	13.4	15.2	11.7	6.4	11.3	16.3	13.0
Autism	1.1	0.8	0.7	1.1	0.6	0.6	1.0	1.2	0.9	0.8	1.1	0.7	0.7	1.1
Deaf-blindness	#	#	#	#	#	#	#	#	#	#	#	#	#	#
Developmental delay	0.8	0.9	0.6	0.5	1.0	1.4	1.3	0.8	0.9	0.6	0.4	1.0	1.4	1.9
Emotional disturbance	0.8	1.3	0.4	0.1	0.5	1.0	0.9	0.8	1.2	0.4	0.1	0.5	0.9	0.9
Hearing impairment	0.2	0.1	0.2	0.2	0.2	0.2	0.1	0.1	0.1	0.2	0.2	0.3	0.2	0.1
Intellectual disability	0.8	1.5	0.7	0.4	0.7	1.0	0.7	0.8	1.5	0.7	0.4	0.7	1.0	0.7
Multiple disabilities	0.3	0.3	0.2	0.2	0.3	0.4	0.2	0.3	0.3	0.2	0.2	0.3	0.4	0.2
Orthopedic impairment	0.1	0.1	0.1	0.1	0.1	0.1	0.1	0.1	0.1	0.1	0.1	0.1	0.1	0.1
Other health impairment[1]	1.8	1.7	0.9	0.4	1.1	1.6	1.6	1.9	1.8	0.9	0.5	1.2	1.7	1.6
Specific learning disability	4.4	5.9	5.0	1.5	4.5	6.8	3.9	4.3	5.8	5.0	1.5	4.9	6.8	3.7
Speech or language impairment	3.0	2.4	2.6	1.9	1.5	3.0	2.8	3.0	2.4	2.6	1.8	1.5	2.9	2.7
Traumatic brain injury	0.1	0.1	#	#	#	0.1	0.1	0.1	0.1	#	#	#	0.1	0.1
Visual impairment	0.1	0.1	0.1	#	0.1	0.1	#	0.1	0.1	0.1	#	0.1	0.1	0.1

#Rounds to zero.
[1] Other health impairments include having limited strength, vitality, or alertness due to chronic or acute health problems such as a heart condition, tuberculosis, rheumatic fever, nephritis, asthma, sickle cell anemia, hemophilia, epilepsy, lead poisoning, leukemia, or diabetes.
[2] Based on the total enrollment in public schools, prekindergarten through 12th grade, by race/ethnicity. For total enrollment in public schools by race/ethnicity, see table 203.50.
NOTE: Data include only those children served for whom race/ethnicity and type of disability were reported. Although data are for the 50 states and the District of Columbia, data limitations result in inclusion of a small (but unknown) number of students

from Bureau of Indian Education and Puerto Rican schools. For these reasons, totals may differ from those shown in other tables. Race categories exclude persons of Hispanic ethnicity. Detail may not sum to totals because of rounding.
SOURCE: U.S. Department of Education, Office of Special Education Programs, Individuals with Disabilities Education Act (IDEA) database, retrieved October 3, 2014, from https://inventory.data.gov/dataset/8715a3e8-bf48-4eef-9deb-b89b76a196c/resource/a68a23f3-3981-47db-ac75-98a167b6525e; and National Center for Education Statistics, Common Core of Data (CCD), "State Nonfiscal Survey of Public Elementary/Secondary Education," 2011–12 and 2012–13. (This table was prepared October 2014.)

Table 204.60. Percentage distribution of students 6 to 21 years old served under Individuals with Disabilities Education Act (IDEA), Part B, by educational environment and type of disability: Selected years, fall 1989 through fall 2012

Type of disability	All environments	Regular school, time inside general class			Separate school for students with disabilities	Separate residential facility	Parentally placed in regular private schools[1]	Homebound/ hospital placement	Correctional facility
		Less than 40 percent	40–79 percent	80 percent or more					
1	2	3	4	5	6	7	8	9	10
All students with disabilities									
1989	100.0	24.9	37.5	31.7	4.5	1.0	—	0.6	—
1990	100.0	25.0	36.4	33.1	4.2	0.9	—	0.5	—
1994	100.0	22.4	28.5	44.8	3.0	0.7	—	0.6	—
1995	100.0	21.5	28.5	45.7	3.1	0.7	—	0.5	—
1996	100.0	21.4	28.3	46.1	3.0	0.7	—	0.5	—
1997	100.0	20.4	28.8	46.8	2.9	0.7	—	0.5	—
1998	100.0	20.0	29.9	46.0	2.9	0.7	—	0.5	—
1999	100.0	20.3	29.8	45.9	2.9	0.7	—	0.5	—
2000	100.0	19.5	29.8	46.5	3.0	0.7	—	0.5	—
2001	100.0	19.2	28.5	48.2	2.9	0.7	—	0.4	—
2002	100.0	19.0	28.7	48.2	2.9	0.7	—	0.5	—
2003	100.0	18.5	27.7	49.9	2.8	0.7	—	0.5	—
2004	100.0	17.9	26.5	51.5	3.0	0.6	—	0.4	—
2005	100.0	16.7	25.1	54.2	2.9	0.6	—	0.4	—
2006	100.0	16.4	23.8	54.8	2.9	0.4	1.0	0.4	0.4
2007	100.0	15.4	22.4	56.8	3.0	0.4	1.1	0.4	0.4
2008	100.0	14.9	21.4	58.5	2.9	0.4	1.1	0.4	0.4
2009	100.0	14.6	20.7	59.4	3.0	0.4	1.2	0.4	0.4
2010									
All students with disabilities	100.0	14.2	20.0	60.5	3.0	0.4	1.2	0.4	0.3
Autism	100.0	34.1	18.1	38.5	7.9	0.5	0.6	0.3	#
Deaf-blindness	100.0	33.4	11.9	22.9	18.2	9.6	0.7	3.3	#
Developmental delay	100.0	16.1	19.6	62.5	0.9	0.1	0.6	0.2	#
Emotional disturbance	100.0	21.3	18.3	42.2	13.1	2.0	0.2	1.1	1.9
Hearing impairment	100.0	14.1	16.7	56.2	8.2	3.4	1.2	0.2	0.1
Intellectual disability	100.0	47.7	26.8	17.9	6.2	0.4	0.2	0.5	0.3
Multiple disabilities	100.0	46.0	15.9	13.0	19.7	1.8	0.4	3.1	0.2
Orthopedic impairment	100.0	22.9	16.2	53.3	4.9	0.2	0.8	1.7	0.1
Other health impairment[2]	100.0	10.6	23.0	62.5	1.6	0.2	1.0	0.9	0.3
Specific learning disability	100.0	7.4	25.5	65.2	0.6	0.1	0.9	0.2	0.3
Speech or language impairment	100.0	4.7	5.5	86.5	0.3	#	2.9	0.1	#
Traumatic brain injury	100.0	20.9	23.6	47.4	5.1	0.5	0.7	1.7	0.1
Visual impairment	100.0	11.8	13.3	63.8	5.5	3.7	1.3	0.6	#
2011									
All students with disabilities	100.0	14.0	19.8	61.1	3.0	0.3	1.1	0.4	0.3
Autism	100.0	33.7	18.2	39.0	7.7	0.5	0.6	0.3	#
Deaf-blindness	100.0	32.5	10.5	27.0	18.1	8.4	0.7	2.8	#
Developmental delay	100.0	16.3	19.6	62.5	0.8	0.1	0.6	0.2	#
Emotional disturbance	100.0	20.6	18.0	43.2	13.2	1.9	0.2	1.1	1.8
Hearing impairment	100.0	13.0	16.8	56.7	8.6	3.4	1.3	0.2	0.1
Intellectual disability	100.0	48.8	26.6	17.0	6.2	0.4	0.3	0.5	0.2
Multiple disabilities	100.0	46.2	16.4	13.0	19.2	1.7	0.3	3.0	0.1
Orthopedic impairment	100.0	22.2	16.3	54.0	4.7	0.2	0.8	1.7	0.1
Other health impairment[2]	100.0	10.0	22.7	63.5	1.6	0.2	1.0	0.9	0.3
Specific learning disability	100.0	6.8	25.1	66.2	0.5	0.1	0.8	0.1	0.3
Speech or language impairment	100.0	4.5	5.5	86.9	0.3	#	2.6	0.1	#
Traumatic brain injury	100.0	20.5	22.8	48.5	5.2	0.5	0.8	1.7	0.1
Visual impairment	100.0	11.3	13.1	64.3	5.9	3.8	1.1	0.6	#
2012									
All students with disabilities	100.0	13.9	19.7	61.2	3.0	0.3	1.2	0.4	0.3
Autism	100.0	33.3	18.1	39.5	7.7	0.5	0.7	0.3	#
Deaf-blindness	100.0	34.7	11.4	21.0	19.8	8.2	1.5	2.7	0.7
Developmental delay	100.0	16.6	19.5	62.3	0.8	0.1	0.6	0.2	#
Emotional disturbance	100.0	20.4	17.8	44.0	13.0	1.8	0.2	1.1	1.7
Hearing impairment	100.0	12.6	16.4	57.6	8.3	3.4	1.4	0.2	0.1
Intellectual disability	100.0	49.1	27.0	16.5	6.1	0.4	0.3	0.5	0.2
Multiple disabilities	100.0	46.4	16.3	12.9	19.1	1.7	0.4	3.1	0.1
Orthopedic impairment	100.0	21.8	16.2	54.6	4.5	0.2	0.9	1.7	0.1
Other health impairment[2]	100.0	9.8	22.4	63.7	1.7	0.2	1.1	0.8	0.3
Specific learning disability	100.0	6.4	25.0	66.7	0.5	0.1	0.9	0.1	0.3
Speech or language impairment	100.0	4.3	5.4	86.8	0.3	#	3.0	#	#
Traumatic brain injury	100.0	20.1	22.4	49.0	5.3	0.6	0.8	1.8	0.1
Visual impairment	100.0	11.3	13.3	64.0	6.0	3.6	1.2	0.6	0.1

—Not available.
#Rounds to zero.
[1]Students who are enrolled by their parents or guardians in regular private schools and have their basic education paid through private resources, but receive special education services at public expense. These students are not included under "Regular school, time inside general class" (columns 3 through 5).
[2]Other health impairments include having limited strength, vitality, or alertness due to chronic or acute health problems such as a heart condition, tuberculosis, rheumatic fever, nephritis, asthma, sickle cell anemia, hemophilia, epilepsy, lead poisoning, leukemia, or diabetes.

NOTE: Data are for the 50 United States, the District of Columbia, and the Bureau of Indian Education schools. Detail may not sum to totals because of rounding.
SOURCE: U.S. Department of Education, Office of Special Education Programs, Individuals with Disabilities Education Act (IDEA) database, retrieved October 3, 2014, from https://inventory.data.gov/dataset/8715a3e8-bf48-4eef-9deb-fd9bb76a196e/resource/a68a23f3-3981-47db-ac75-98a167b65259. (This table was prepared October 2014.)

Table 204.70. Number and percentage of children served under Individuals with Disabilities Education Act (IDEA), Part B, by age group and state or jurisdiction: Selected years, 1990–91 through 2012–13

State or jurisdiction	3- to 21-year-olds served								3- to 5-year-olds served					
	1990–91	2000–01	2005–06	2010–11	2011–12	2012–13	As a percent of public school enrollment, 2012–13[1]	Percent change in number served, 2000–01 to 2012–13	1990–91	2000–01	2005–06	2010–11	2011–12	2012–13
1	2	3	4	5	6	7	8	9	10	11	12	13	14	15
United States	4,710,089	6,295,816	6,712,605	6,434,916	6,401,238	6,429,331	12.9	2.1	389,751	592,087	698,608	723,738	730,558	735,890
Alabama	94,601	99,828	92,635	82,286	80,149	79,705	10.7	-20.2	7,154	7,554	8,218	7,492	7,355	7,344
Alaska	14,390	17,691	17,997	18,048	18,055	17,959	13.7	1.5	1,458	1,637	2,082	2,104	2,166	2,116
Arizona	56,629	96,442	124,504	125,816	127,198	128,281	11.8	33.0	4,330	9,144	14,062	14,756	15,235	15,386
Arkansas	47,187	62,222	67,314	64,881	64,790	64,698	13.3	4.0	4,626	9,376	10,286	13,034	13,275	12,789
California	468,420	645,287	676,318	672,174	679,269	688,346	10.9	6.7	39,627	57,651	66,653	72,404	73,720	75,285
Colorado	56,336	78,715	83,498	84,710	87,233	89,280	10.3	13.4	4,128	8,202	10,540	11,797	12,348	12,799
Connecticut	63,886	73,886	71,968	68,167	68,280	69,730	12.7	-5.6	5,466	7,172	7,881	7,933	7,956	8,025
Delaware	14,208	16,760	18,857	18,608	19,166	19,224	14.9	14.7	1,493	1,652	2,073	2,123	2,230	2,304
District of Columbia	6,290	10,559	11,738	11,947	12,536	12,585	16.5	19.2	411	374	507	957	1,431	1,550
Florida	234,509	367,335	398,916	368,808	358,922	354,352	13.2	-3.5	14,883	30,660	34,350	36,027	37,445	37,470
Georgia	101,762	171,292	197,596	177,544	179,423	185,037	10.9	8.0	7,098	16,560	20,728	15,911	16,539	17,395
Hawaii	12,705	23,951	21,963	19,716	19,605	19,696	10.7	-17.8	809	1,919	2,423	2,398	2,449	2,554
Idaho	21,703	29,174	29,021	27,388	26,864	27,086	9.5	-7.2	2,815	3,591	4,043	3,596	3,379	3,283
Illinois	236,060	297,316	323,444	302,830	292,956	292,430	14.1	-1.6	22,997	28,787	35,454	36,488	36,943	37,211
Indiana	112,949	156,320	177,826	166,073	164,147	168,815	16.2	8.0	7,243	15,101	19,228	18,725	18,172	18,476
Iowa	59,787	72,461	72,457	68,501	67,990	65,882	13.2	-9.1	5,421	5,580	6,118	7,378	7,467	7,109
Kansas	44,785	61,267	65,595	66,873	65,809	67,369	13.8	10.0	3,881	7,728	9,267	10,604	10,598	10,850
Kentucky	78,853	94,572	108,798	102,370	98,785	97,555	14.2	3.2	10,440	16,372	21,317	17,963	17,422	17,455
Louisiana	72,825	97,938	90,453	82,943	82,301	81,238	11.4	-17.1	6,703	9,957	10,597	10,427	11,206	11,209
Maine	27,987	35,633	36,522	32,261	32,078	32,194	17.3	-9.7	2,895	3,978	4,348	3,824	3,831	3,793
Maryland	88,017	112,077	110,959	103,490	103,563	103,429	12.0	-7.7	7,163	10,003	12,148	12,821	13,114	13,062
Massachusetts	149,743	162,216	162,654	167,526	166,236	166,437	17.4	2.6	12,141	14,328	15,195	16,662	16,491	16,583
Michigan	166,511	221,456	243,607	218,957	210,034	203,427	13.1	-8.1	14,547	19,937	24,290	23,183	21,086	20,831
Minnesota	79,013	109,880	116,511	122,850	123,353	123,785	14.6	12.7	8,646	11,522	13,402	15,076	15,361	15,289
Mississippi	60,872	62,281	68,099	64,038	64,334	64,860	13.1	4.1	5,642	6,944	8,319	10,191	10,498	10,244
Missouri	101,166	137,381	143,204	127,164	125,075	123,655	13.5	-10.0	4,100	11,307	15,268	15,891	15,984	16,040
Montana	16,955	19,313	19,259	16,761	16,032	16,450	11.5	-14.8	1,751	1,635	1,925	1,656	1,696	1,697
Nebraska	32,312	42,793	45,239	44,299	44,829	45,564	15.0	6.5	2,512	3,724	4,665	5,050	5,175	5,379
Nevada	18,099	38,160	47,794	48,148	49,117	50,332	11.3	31.9	1,401	3,676	5,492	6,947	7,598	8,047
New Hampshire	19,049	30,077	31,782	29,920	29,422	29,329	15.5	-2.5	1,468	2,387	2,902	3,135	3,158	3,227
New Jersey	178,870	221,715	249,385	232,002	223,935	232,317	16.9	4.8	14,741	16,361	19,329	17,073	16,925	17,954
New Mexico	36,000	52,256	50,322	46,628	46,555	46,498	13.7	-11.0	2,210	4,970	6,441	5,224	5,021	4,494
New York	307,366	441,333	447,422	454,542	452,319	450,794	16.6	2.1	26,266	51,665	58,297	64,923	64,082	65,031
North Carolina	122,942	173,067	192,820	185,107	187,767	190,098	12.5	9.8	10,516	17,361	20,543	18,433	18,787	18,665
North Dakota	12,294	13,652	13,883	13,170	13,093	13,234	13.1	-3.1	1,164	1,247	1,520	1,714	1,791	1,804
Ohio	205,440	237,643	266,447	259,454	259,064	255,953	14.8	7.7	12,487	18,664	22,702	22,454	23,904	23,401
Oklahoma	65,457	85,577	96,601	97,250	98,960	100,893	15.0	17.9	5,163	6,393	8,149	8,298	8,480	8,500
Oregon	54,422	75,204	77,376	81,050	81,718	82,183	14.0	9.3	2,854	6,926	8,167	9,392	9,913	10,052
Pennsylvania	214,254	242,655	288,733	295,080	294,963	295,502	16.8	21.8	17,982	21,477	25,964	31,072	32,722	33,041
Rhode Island	20,646	30,727	30,681	25,332	24,826	24,165	17.0	-21.4	1,682	2,614	2,815	2,945	2,984	2,910
South Carolina	77,367	105,922	110,219	100,289	99,624	99,530	13.5	-6.0	7,948	11,775	11,603	11,083	10,862	10,626
South Dakota	14,726	16,825	17,631	18,026	18,005	18,316	14.0	8.9	2,105	2,286	2,747	2,738	2,726	2,659
Tennessee	104,853	125,863	120,122	120,263	124,070	127,407	12.8	1.2	7,487	10,699	12,008	13,096	13,381	13,067
Texas	344,529	491,642	507,405	442,019	439,675	439,635	8.7	-10.6	24,848	36,442	40,236	41,494	40,756	43,981
Utah	46,606	53,921	60,526	70,278	71,233	78,270	12.8	45.2	3,424	5,785	7,462	8,990	8,856	9,890
Vermont	12,160	13,623	13,917	13,936	13,833	13,873	15.5	1.8	1,097	1,237	1,556	1,762	1,752	1,831
Virginia	112,072	162,212	174,640	162,338	161,198	161,498	12.8	-0.4	9,892	14,444	17,480	17,081	16,677	16,611
Washington	83,545	118,851	124,498	127,978	129,346	130,778	12.4	10.0	9,558	11,760	13,429	14,275	14,588	14,763
West Virginia	42,428	50,333	49,677	45,007	44,259	44,487	15.7	-11.6	2,923	5,445	5,833	5,607	5,488	5,483
Wisconsin	85,651	125,358	130,076	124,722	123,825	123,287	14.1	-1.7	10,934	14,383	16,077	16,079	16,106	16,325
Wyoming	10,852	13,154	13,696	15,348	15,419	11,883	13.0	-9.7	1,221	1,695	2,469	3,398	3,429	—
Bureau of Indian Education	6,997	8,448	7,795	6,801	—	6,504	—	-23.0	1,092	338	330	396	—	305
Other jurisdictions	38,986	70,670	93,256	131,847	134,600	135,431	—	91.6	3,892	8,168	5,149	14,505	15,396	13,785
American Samoa	363	697	1,211	935	932	870	—	33.7	48	48	80	142	161	102
Guam	1,750	2,267	2,480	2,003	2,013	2,017	6.5	-11.2	198	205	171	165	179	161
Northern Marianas	411	569	750	944	931	895	8.4	63.6	211	53	70	104	104	86
Palau	—	131	—	—	—	119	—	—	—	10	—	—	—	9
Puerto Rico	35,129	65,504	87,125	126,560	129,314	130,212	30.0	97.4	3,345	7,746	4,677	13,952	14,791	13,276
U.S. Virgin Islands	1,333	1,502	1,690	1,405	1,410	1,318	8.7	-6.1	90	106	151	142	161	151

—Not available.
[1]Based on the total enrollment in public schools, prekindergarten through 12th grade. For total enrollment in public schools, see table 203.10.
NOTE: Prior to October 1994, children and youth with disabilities were served under Chapter 1 of the Elementary and Secondary Education Act as well as under the Individuals with Disabilities Education Act (IDEA), Part B. Data reported in this table for 1990–91 include children ages 0–21 served under Chapter 1.

SOURCE: U.S. Department of Education, Office of Special Education Programs, *Annual Report to Congress on the Implementation of the Individuals with Disabilities Education Act,* selected years, 1992 through 2006, and Individuals with Disabilities Education Act (IDEA) database, retrieved October 3, 2014, from https://inventory.data.gov/dataset/8715a3e8-bf48-4eef-9deb-fd9bb76a196e/resource/a68a23f3-3981-47db-ac75-98a167b65259. National Center for Education Statistics, Common Core of Data (CCD), "State Nonfiscal Survey of Public Elementary/Secondary Education," 2012–13. (This table was prepared October 2014.)

Table 204.80. Number of gifted and talented students in public elementary and secondary schools, by sex, race/ethnicity, and state: 2004 and 2006

[Standard errors appear in parentheses]

State	2004, total	2006							
		Total	Male	Female	White	Black	Hispanic	Asian/Pacific Islander	American Indian/Alaska Native
1	2	3	4	5	6	7	8	9	10
United States	3,202,760 (24,248)	3,236,990 (21,177)	1,579,000 (10,460)	1,657,990 (10,859)	2,191,210 (15,896)	296,150 (3,375)	414,060 (3,350)	304,220 (6,195)	31,360 (1,179)
Alabama	35,680 (798)	40,610 (361)	19,970 (184)	20,650 (184)	31,450 (338)	7,260 (109)	660 (14)	820 (6)	420 (6)
Alaska	5,390 (166)	5,620 (192)	2,810 (102)	2,810 (91)	4,390 (143)	160 (#)	160 (5)	490 (31)	420 (29)
Arizona	57,570 (1,275)	60,060 (711)	30,770 (412)	29,290 (306)	38,830 (544)	1,730 (20)	13,940 (178)	3,620 (29)	1,940 (394)
Arkansas	50,340 (3,219)	45,600 (1,870)	21,110 (924)	24,490 (967)	34,900 (1,253)	7,470 (677)	2,200 ! (860)	760 (26)	270 (41)
California	527,370 (10,256)	523,450 (13,209)	260,010 (6,688)	263,440 (6,567)	230,220 (7,405)	21,150 (559)	147,040 (2,827)	121,410 (5,930)	3,630 (276)
Colorado	50,350 (747)	54,000 (620)	27,770 (314)	26,240 (319)	40,420 (543)	2,280 (6)	8,190 (93)	2,730 (14)	400 (11)
Connecticut	15,980 (1,572)	20,170 (2,183)	9,660 (1,094)	10,510 (1,097)	15,470 (1,515)	1,710 (404)	1,350 (295)	1,560 (192)	‡ (†)
Delaware	5,260 (†)	6,240 (†)	2,830 (†)	3,410 (†)	4,120 (†)	1,290 (†)	390 (†)	430 (†)	10 (†)
District of Columbia	—	—	—	—	—	—	—	—	—
Florida	114,400 (1,095)	132,440 (893)	66,740 (462)	65,700 (438)	81,710 (761)	13,170 (92)	31,020 (106)	6,130 (23)	400 (6)
Georgia	136,620 (3,954)	150,680 (5,291)	71,110 (2,572)	79,560 (2,725)	110,350 (4,419)	26,370 (796)	4,470 (187)	9,250 (265)	240 (14)
Hawaii[2]	10,290 (993)	11,140 (†)	4,680 (†)	6,460 (†)	2,570 (†)	120 (†)	220 (†)	8,180 (†)	30 (†)
Idaho	9,920 (528)	10,650 (475)	5,570 (242)	5,070 (237)	9,850 (425)	50 (3)	450 (38)	240 (18)	40 (8)
Illinois	112,570 (4,554)	118,480 (5,016)	56,230 (2,375)	62,250 (2,674)	76,680 (3,996)	18,240 (1,697)	12,720 (225)	10,610 (667)	230 (24)
Indiana	74,780 (5,219)	82,830 (4,222)	37,930 (1,896)	44,900 (2,350)	72,400 (3,880)	5,320 (644)	2,560 (222)	2,450 (272)	110 (14)
Iowa	41,460 (1,657)	39,300 (1,030)	19,490 (516)	19,820 (533)	36,060 (970)	1,000 (21)	910 (86)	1,250 (71)	80 (6)
Kansas	15,150 (389)	14,430 (487)	7,810 (280)	6,610 (218)	12,760 (445)	390 (17)	500 (25)	650 (54)	120 (11)
Kentucky	85,660 (3,179)	96,600 (2,885)	45,310 (1,384)	51,290 (1,528)	89,170 (2,781)	5,150 (394)	890 (43)	1,310 (54)	70 (8)
Louisiana	28,020 (2,300)	22,010 (721)	10,710 (362)	11,300 (369)	15,740 (591)	4,590 (107)	510 (15)	1,010 (18)	160 (30)
Maine	5,640 (619)	6,030 (304)	2,960 (147)	3,060 (168)	5,750 (297)	50 (5)	40 (10)	160 (15)	20 ! (9)
Maryland[1]	117,010 (†)	137,410 (†)	65,760 (†)	71,650 (†)	86,470 (†)	22,510 (†)	10,480 (†)	17,520 (†)	430 (†)
Massachusetts	7,440 (1,190)	6,130 (908)	2,550 (348)	3,580 (631)	4,240 (820)	540 (30)	510 (26)	820 (106)	30 (6)
Michigan	65,970 (6,408)	54,950 (4,750)	26,470 (2,312)	28,480 (2,467)	44,610 (3,918)	5,510 (1,255)	1,050 (117)	3,600 (507)	190 (21)
Minnesota	73,940 (2,585)	72,280 (2,154)	35,550 (1,043)	36,740 (1,120)	56,970 (2,047)	4,590 (24)	2,460 (62)	7,560 (62)	710 (54)
Mississippi	30,510 (837)	31,070 (1,015)	15,110 (496)	15,970 (534)	22,580 (806)	7,520 (253)	410 (23)	530 (51)	40 (6)
Missouri	34,470 (898)	33,070 (831)	16,110 (424)	16,960 (425)	28,780 (767)	2,350 (93)	440 (18)	1,420 (47)	80 (6)
Montana	8,760 (401)	7,490 (251)	3,770 (133)	3,720 (122)	6,800 (235)	30 (3)	140 (10)	130 (3)	390 (31)
Nebraska	32,160 (824)	32,650 (604)	16,200 (307)	16,450 (305)	29,100 (581)	1,080 (11)	1,390 (57)	960 (12)	130 (7)
Nevada[2]	7,640 (23)	8,270 (†)	4,220 (†)	4,050 (†)	5,100 (†)	410 (†)	1,210 (†)	1,010 (†)	70 ! (†)
New Hampshire	4,450 (1,089)	4,700 (1,005)	2,350 (540)	2,350 (469)	4,380 (969)	40 (7)	50 (6)	220 (39)	‡ (†)
New Jersey	88,960 (4,851)	97,260 (4,904)	43,920 (2,190)	53,350 (2,764)	64,810 (3,890)	8,620 (808)	9,360 (787)	14,390 (1,327)	90 (9)
New Mexico	36,410 (404)	12,950 (399)	6,890 (219)	6,050 (185)	7,180 (256)	240 (8)	4,280 (137)	510 (53)	740 (36)
New York	61,350 (5,223)	81,520 (3,741)	38,090 (1,799)	43,440 (1,955)	49,010 (3,322)	12,900 (358)	8,480 (177)	10,900 (342)	230 (24)
North Carolina	155,330 (10,613)	149,700 (4,678)	72,600 (2,261)	77,100 (2,429)	120,700 (3,981)	18,090 (639)	4,040 (168)	5,150 (155)	1,710 ! (777)
North Dakota	3,320 (305)	2,770 (162)	1,450 (87)	1,320 (76)	2,560 (100)	160 (#)	20 (#)	50 (2)	300 ! (123)
Ohio	133,690 (7,411)	127,610 (5,925)	64,720 (3,150)	62,900 (2,829)	108,200 (5,477)	13,890 (949)	1,540 (70)	3,860 (386)	130 (13)
Oklahoma	87,620 (2,447)	87,320 (2,151)	42,570 (990)	44,760 (1,192)	61,980 (1,581)	5,050 (93)	4,010 (94)	2,460 (46)	13,820 (692)
Oregon	39,440 (903)	38,570 (666)	20,600 (357)	17,970 (318)	32,590 (603)	640 (10)	1,750 (63)	3,110 (26)	480 (33)
Pennsylvania	85,070 (3,170)	75,990 (2,881)	38,830 (1,414)	37,090 (1,297)	63,480 (2,415)	6,680 (292)	1,370 (60)	4,350 (362)	‡ (†)
Rhode Island	2,780 (531)	2,060 (300)	920 (134)	1,150 (168)	1,560 (252)	160 (41)	230 (30)	110 (13)	# (†)
South Carolina	88,070 (6,564)	77,520 (3,781)	36,580 (1,772)	40,940 (2,022)	59,580 (2,832)	14,660 (964)	1,510 (118)	1,620 (164)	160 (31)
South Dakota	2,940 (241)	3,070 (175)	1,680 (92)	1,390 (87)	2,790 (139)	20 (#)	20 (1)	50 (3)	190 ! (93)
Tennessee	32,630 (1,451)	17,100 (904)	8,810 (493)	8,290 (416)	14,540 (827)	1,650 (63)	260 (15)	620 (43)	30 (4)
Texas	344,500 (3,483)	344,640 (2,413)	167,640 (1,243)	177,000 (1,234)	175,730 (1,923)	28,260 (618)	115,950 (1,189)	23,630 (134)	1,070 (30)
Utah	23,510 (1,218)	25,660 (170)	12,090 (79)	13,570 (91)	20,380 (152)	320 (1)	2,880 (19)	1,890 (#)	190 (#)
Vermont	740 (151)	730 (129)	390 (70)	340 (61)	690 (121)	10 (10)	10 ! (5)	20 (6)	# (†)
Virginia	142,140 (3,772)	160,140 (3,319)	77,980 (1,608)	82,160 (1,732)	116,360 (2,709)	18,410 (1,070)	7,310 (117)	17,510 (165)	560 (107)
Washington	38,520 (843)	39,010 (1,289)	19,050 (573)	19,960 (726)	30,390 (1,170)	850 (12)	2,430 (89)	4,970 (90)	380 (17)
West Virginia	6,040 (493)	6,630 (559)	3,500 (305)	3,130 (262)	6,120 (504)	230 (35)	30 (4)	240 (40)	10 ! (3)
Wisconsin	62,000 ! (4,348)	56,450 (3,095)	27,340 (1,478)	29,100 (1,628)	48,560 (2,821)	3,370 (210)	2,180 (125)	1,900 (129)	440 (151)
Wyoming	2,910 ! (944)	2,030 (314)	990 (152)	1,040 (164)	1,830 (295)	30 (2)	80 (8)	70 (13)	30 (#)

—Not available.
†Not applicable.
#Rounds to zero.
!Interpret data with caution. The coefficient of variation (CV) for this estimate is between 30 and 50 percent.
‡Reporting standards not met. Either there are too few cases for a reliable estimate or the coefficient of variation (CV) is 50 percent or greater.

[1]Data are based on universe counts of schools and school districts; therefore, these figures do not have standard errors.
[2]Data for 2006 are based on universe counts of schools and school districts; therefore, these figures do not have standard errors.
NOTE: Race categories exclude persons of Hispanic ethnicity. Detail may not sum to totals because of rounding.
SOURCE: U.S. Department of Education, Office for Civil Rights, Civil Rights Data Collection: 2004 and 2006. (This table was revised May 2008.)

Table 204.90. Percentage of gifted and talented students in public elementary and secondary schools, by sex, race/ethnicity, and state: 2004 and 2006

[Standard errors appear in parentheses]

State	Total 2004	Total 2006	Sex: Male 2004	Sex: Male 2006	Sex: Female 2004	Sex: Female 2006	Race/ethnicity: White 2004	White 2006	Black 2004	Black 2006	Hispanic 2004	Hispanic 2006	Asian/Pacific Islander 2004	Asian/Pacific Islander 2006	American Indian/Alaska Native 2004	American Indian/Alaska Native 2006
1	2	3	4	5	6	7	8	9	10	11	12	13	14	15	16	17
United States	**6.7 (0.05)**	**6.7 (0.04)**	**6.3 (0.05)**	**6.3 (0.04)**	**7.0 (0.06)**	**7.0 (0.05)**	**7.9 (0.07)**	**8.0 (0.07)**	**3.5 (0.05)**	**3.6 (0.05)**	**4.3 (0.05)**	**4.2 (0.04)**	**11.9 (0.20)**	**13.1 (0.29)**	**5.2 (0.20)**	**5.2 (0.24)**
Alabama	4.8 (0.11)	5.5 (0.06)	4.6 (0.11)	5.2 (0.06)	4.9 (0.11)	5.7 (0.07)	6.3 (0.16)	7.1 (0.11)	2.4 (0.09)	2.8 (0.06)	2.3 (0.17)	2.9 (0.09)	9.4 (0.50)	10.2 (0.45)	4.9 (0.54)	6.1 (0.43)
Alaska	4.1 (0.19)	4.1 (0.19)	3.9 (0.19)	4.0 (0.19)	4.2 (0.19)	4.3 (0.19)	5.8 (0.22)	5.8 (0.22)	2.1 (0.03)	2.5 (0.02)	2.3 (0.11)	2.5 (0.13)	4.5 (0.45)	5.0 (0.52)	1.0 (0.08)	1.1 (0.12)
Arizona	5.9 (0.17)	6.3 (0.11)	5.9 (0.17)	6.3 (0.12)	5.9 (0.17)	6.3 (0.11)	8.4 (0.26)	9.1 (0.21)	3.5 (0.14)	3.4 (0.06)	3.3 (0.13)	3.5 (0.07)	13.9 (0.54)	14.2 (0.21)	4.0 (1.09)	3.7 (0.92)
Arkansas	9.9 (0.65)	9.5 (0.43)	8.8 (0.63)	8.6 (0.41)	11.0 (0.67)	10.5 (0.50)	11.2 (0.80)	10.7 (0.53)	7.1 (0.90)	7.3 (0.73)	5.8 ! (2.39)	5.8 ! (2.29)	10.6 (0.78)	10.3 (0.62)	4.7 (1.21)	8.2 (1.35)
California	8.4 (0.18)	8.3 (0.21)	8.0 (0.16)	8.0 (0.21)	8.8 (0.20)	8.6 (0.23)	12.0 (0.36)	11.9 (0.42)	4.6 (0.16)	4.3 (0.16)	5.1 (0.13)	4.8 (0.11)	14.6 (0.56)	16.1 (0.89)	6.5 (0.56)	5.8 (0.62)
Colorado	6.7 (0.11)	6.8 (0.11)	6.6 (0.11)	6.9 (0.11)	6.8 (0.12)	6.8 (0.11)	7.9 (0.14)	8.2 (0.16)	5.2 (0.03)	5.0 (0.02)	3.9 (0.14)	3.8 (0.07)	9.6 (0.11)	10.4 (0.09)	4.5 (0.39)	4.3 (0.29)
Connecticut	3.0 (0.32)	3.8 (0.41)	2.9 (0.31)	3.5 (0.40)	3.2 (0.34)	4.0 (0.44)	3.5 (0.38)	4.3 (0.44)	1.7 (0.44)	2.3 (0.59)	1.4 (0.33)	1.8 (0.42)	5.7 (0.68)	7.3 (0.95)	1.7 (0.44)	‡ (†)
Delaware[1]	4.6 (†)	5.6 (†)	4.0 (†)	4.9 (†)	5.3 (†)	6.3 (†)	6.1 (†)	6.8 (†)	2.2 (†)	3.6 (†)	1.7 (†)	3.5 (†)	11.5 (†)	13.2 (†)	3.4 (†)	3.7 (†)
District of Columbia	— (†)	— (†)	— (†)	— (†)	— (†)	— (†)	— (†)	— (†)	— (†)	— (†)	— (†)	— (†)	— (†)	— (†)	— (†)	— (†)
Florida	4.5 (0.06)	4.7 (0.05)	4.5 (0.06)	4.7 (0.05)	4.5 (0.05)	4.8 (0.05)	5.7 (0.11)	6.1 (0.10)	2.0 (0.02)	2.0 (0.02)	4.0 (0.02)	4.4 (0.03)	8.8 (0.08)	9.3 (0.06)	4.6 (0.12)	5.0 (0.15)
Georgia	8.9 (0.30)	9.3 (0.35)	8.3 (0.29)	8.6 (0.33)	9.5 (0.31)	10.0 (0.39)	13.6 (0.59)	14.1 (0.69)	3.7 (0.15)	4.1 (0.15)	2.6 (0.25)	3.1 (0.17)	18.8 (0.41)	19.3 (0.71)	7.6 (0.49)	9.6 (0.65)
Hawaii[2]	5.7 (0.57)	6.2 (†)	4.4 (0.42)	5.1 (†)	7.0 (0.74)	7.5 (†)	7.7 (0.95)	9.7 (†)	2.9 (0.53)	2.9 (†)	2.6 (0.36)	3.9 (†)	5.5 (0.59)	5.8 (†)	4.3 (0.76)	4.8 (†)
Idaho	3.9 (0.23)	4.2 (0.20)	3.9 (0.21)	4.3 (0.20)	3.9 (0.24)	4.1 (0.21)	4.4 (0.26)	4.7 (0.23)	1.7 (0.20)	2.0 (0.14)	0.9 (0.13)	1.3 (0.12)	6.9 (0.38)	6.1 (0.46)	1.2 (0.28)	1.0 (0.23)
Illinois	5.4 (0.22)	5.8 (0.24)	5.0 (0.20)	5.4 (0.23)	5.8 (0.24)	6.3 (0.28)	6.7 (0.33)	7.0 (0.39)	2.5 (0.18)	4.2 (0.40)	2.8 (0.13)	3.1 (0.08)	13.1 (0.98)	13.3 (0.97)	5.4 (1.15)	5.1 (0.83)
Indiana	7.1 (0.49)	7.9 (0.40)	6.3 (0.44)	7.0 (0.36)	7.9 (0.55)	8.8 (0.49)	7.7 (0.52)	8.7 (0.50)	3.8 (0.78)	4.1 (0.54)	3.8 (0.66)	3.9 (0.39)	15.5 (2.71)	14.1 (2.08)	6.7 (1.64)	3.9 (0.56)
Iowa	8.5 (0.38)	8.2 (0.26)	8.2 (0.37)	7.9 (0.25)	8.9 (0.40)	8.5 (0.29)	9.0 (0.41)	8.8 (0.30)	4.6 (0.33)	3.9 (0.11)	3.7 (0.61)	3.1 (0.38)	13.5 (1.10)	12.2 (0.97)	3.6 (0.35)	2.9 (0.25)
Kansas	3.3 (0.11)	3.0 (0.12)	3.5 (0.11)	3.2 (0.13)	3.1 (0.11)	2.9 (0.12)	3.9 (0.15)	3.6 (0.16)	1.1 (0.05)	1.0 (0.04)	1.0 (0.08)	0.8 (0.04)	5.5 (0.17)	5.4 (0.25)	1.5 (0.19)	1.8 (0.20)
Kentucky	13.0 (0.54)	14.6 (0.50)	11.9 (0.51)	13.2 (0.47)	14.2 (0.57)	16.1 (0.60)	14.2 (0.62)	15.8 (0.64)	5.2 (0.54)	7.0 (0.60)	4.6 (0.46)	5.7 (0.38)	20.2 (1.48)	21.3 (1.14)	6.6 (1.24)	7.2 (0.96)
Louisiana	3.9 (0.32)	3.4 (0.13)	3.8 (0.31)	3.2 (0.13)	4.0 (0.34)	3.5 (0.14)	5.5 (0.60)	4.8 (0.26)	1.9 (0.07)	1.6 (0.04)	4.2 (0.34)	3.3 (0.12)	11.7 (0.91)	11.7 (0.34)	2.6 ! (1.04)	2.7 (0.78)
Maine	3.0 (0.36)	3.2 (0.19)	2.9 (0.33)	3.1 (0.18)	3.2 (0.39)	3.4 (0.22)	3.1 (0.37)	3.3 (0.20)	1.3 (0.22)	1.1 (0.12)	1.2 (0.27)	2.3 (0.54)	3.8 (0.80)	5.6 (0.60)	0.8 ! (0.35)	3.1 ! (1.29)
Maryland[1]	13.8 (†)	16.1 (†)	12.9 (†)	15.0 (†)	14.7 (†)	17.2 (†)	17.0 (†)	21.1 (†)	6.7 (†)	7.0 (†)	14.5 (†)	14.7 (†)	33.8 (†)	37.8 (†)	9.8 (†)	12.6 (†)
Massachusetts	0.8 (0.13)	0.7 (0.10)	0.7 (0.12)	0.6 (0.08)	0.9 (0.14)	0.8 (0.15)	0.8 (0.14)	0.6 (0.12)	0.7 (0.13)	0.7 (0.05)	0.8 ! (0.21)	0.5 (0.04)	1.9 (0.30)	1.7 (0.24)	0.9 ! (0.25)	0.5 (0.13)
Michigan	3.9 (0.37)	3.4 (0.29)	3.6 (0.35)	3.2 (0.28)	4.3 (0.40)	3.7 (0.32)	4.1 (0.41)	3.8 (0.34)	3.0 (0.62)	1.9 (0.44)	2.7 (0.54)	1.4 (0.18)	10.1 (1.56)	8.1 (1.30)	1.4 (0.25)	1.2 (0.19)
Minnesota	8.1 (0.37)	8.8 (0.28)	7.7 (0.36)	8.4 (0.26)	8.6 (0.38)	9.2 (0.32)	8.3 (0.44)	8.8 (0.36)	5.2 (0.34)	6.7 (0.11)	4.5 (0.20)	5.4 (0.18)	13.7 (0.33)	16.5 (0.25)	3.8 (0.57)	4.6 (0.54)
Mississippi	6.0 (0.19)	6.1 (0.20)	5.7 (0.18)	5.8 (0.19)	6.3 (0.22)	6.4 (0.22)	9.1 (0.38)	9.6 (0.41)	3.3 (0.21)	2.9 (0.11)	5.0 (0.43)	4.5 (0.37)	10.7 (0.48)	13.5 (1.47)	3.7 (0.93)	3.7 (0.64)
Missouri	3.8 (0.12)	3.6 (0.11)	3.8 (0.12)	3.5 (0.11)	3.8 (0.13)	3.6 (0.11)	4.3 (0.15)	4.0 (0.14)	1.7 (0.05)	1.5 (0.08)	1.4 (0.10)	1.3 (0.09)	9.0 (0.33)	9.1 (0.36)	2.0 (0.22)	2.4 (0.20)
Montana	5.6 (0.28)	5.2 (0.20)	5.4 (0.26)	5.0 (0.20)	5.9 (0.31)	5.3 (0.21)	6.0 (0.31)	5.7 (0.24)	2.8 (0.21)	2.2 (0.22)	3.3 (0.22)	3.9 (0.29)	9.9 (0.77)	8.2 (0.62)	2.9 (0.38)	2.1 (0.23)
Nebraska	11.4 (0.31)	11.4 (0.24)	10.9 (0.30)	11.0 (0.24)	11.9 (0.32)	11.8 (0.27)	12.8 (0.38)	13.3 (0.33)	6.4 (0.06)	4.8 (0.05)	4.5 (0.32)	3.9 (0.24)	17.0 (0.25)	18.2 (0.28)	4.6 (0.94)	3.1 (0.36)
Nevada[2]	1.9 (0.01)	1.9 (†)	2.1 (0.01)	1.9 (†)	1.8 (0.01)	1.9 (†)	2.8 (0.01)	3.0 (†)	0.8 (#)	0.9 (†)	0.8 (0.01)	0.8 (†)	2.8 (0.02)	3.1 (†)	1.0 (0.07)	1.1 (†)
New Hampshire	2.3 (0.55)	2.6 (0.54)	2.1 (0.49)	2.5 (0.56)	2.5 ! (0.62)	2.7 (0.54)	2.3 (0.56)	2.6 (0.58)	0.6 (0.11)	1.1 (0.19)	1.0 (0.20)	0.9 (0.10)	5.8 (1.25)	5.9 (1.07)	0.9 (0.09)	‡ (†)
New Jersey	6.9 (0.38)	7.0 (0.35)	6.2 (0.34)	6.1 (0.31)	7.7 (0.42)	7.9 (0.43)	8.4 (0.53)	8.4 (0.55)	3.3 (0.35)	3.5 (0.36)	3.4 (0.39)	3.5 (0.33)	12.2 (1.13)	13.9 (1.50)	3.3 (0.59)	4.8 (0.61)
New Mexico	10.7 (0.26)	4.0 (0.14)	10.9 (0.27)	4.1 (0.15)	10.5 (0.26)	3.8 (0.14)	12.6 (0.42)	7.1 (0.31)	9.6 (0.18)	2.8 (0.11)	11.4 (0.37)	2.4 (0.11)	13.6 (1.09)	12.0 (1.34)	2.2 (0.17)	2.1 (0.15)
New York	2.2 (0.18)	2.9 (0.13)	2.0 (0.17)	2.6 (0.12)	2.3 (0.19)	3.2 (0.15)	3.4 (0.31)	3.3 (0.23)	0.8 (0.07)	2.4 (0.09)	0.4 (0.04)	1.5 (0.04)	1.7 (0.18)	5.5 (0.19)	1.4 (0.29)	1.5 (0.25)
North Carolina	10.9 (0.83)	10.8 (0.42)	10.3 (0.81)	10.2 (0.40)	11.6 (0.85)	11.3 (0.47)	15.7 (1.17)	15.4 (0.68)	3.9 (0.27)	4.3 (0.20)	3.0 (0.29)	3.1 (0.18)	16.5 (2.76)	17.3 (0.98)	6.3 (1.39)	‡ (†)
North Dakota	3.1 (0.30)	2.8 (0.18)	3.0 (0.30)	2.9 (0.19)	3.2 (0.32)	2.8 (0.18)	2.8 (0.23)	2.8 (0.15)	2.3 (0.05)	1.7 (0.09)	1.5 (0.23)	1.4 (0.13)	8.1 (0.38)	5.4 (0.26)	7.0 ! (3.34)	3.3 ! (1.46)
Ohio	7.4 (0.40)	7.3 (0.33)	7.3 (0.40)	7.2 (0.34)	7.6 (0.40)	7.4 (0.35)	7.6 (0.48)	7.8 (0.42)	6.5 (0.37)	4.7 (0.37)	3.5 (0.26)	3.3 (0.28)	13.6 (1.44)	14.0 (1.64)	5.6 (0.62)	5.4 (0.60)
Oklahoma	14.0 (0.45)	13.7 (0.39)	13.1 (0.41)	13.0 (0.36)	15.0 (0.50)	14.4 (0.47)	16.6 (0.56)	16.2 (0.55)	7.7 (0.22)	7.4 (0.23)	7.0 (0.27)	6.8 (0.23)	23.6 (0.56)	21.5 (0.60)	11.3 (0.67)	11.8 (0.72)
Oregon	7.1 (0.20)	6.9 (0.16)	7.3 (0.20)	7.2 (0.17)	6.9 (0.21)	6.6 (0.16)	8.0 (0.24)	8.0 (0.22)	3.6 (0.05)	3.5 (0.09)	1.8 (0.10)	2.0 (0.09)	11.6 (0.14)	11.1 (0.21)	3.6 (0.42)	3.9 (0.31)
Pennsylvania	4.8 (0.19)	4.5 (0.17)	4.9 (0.20)	4.5 (0.17)	4.8 (0.19)	4.5 (0.18)	5.3 (0.23)	5.0 (0.22)	2.7 (0.16)	2.4 (0.15)	1.8 (0.38)	1.7 (0.12)	9.5 (0.87)	9.7 (0.96)	2.2 (0.35)	1.9 (0.36)
Rhode Island	1.8 (0.38)	1.4 (0.21)	1.6 (0.35)	1.2 (0.18)	2.1 (0.41)	1.6 (0.24)	2.0 (0.44)	1.5 (0.25)	1.5 (0.47)	1.2 ! (0.34)	1.2 (0.48)	1.0 (0.13)	2.2 (0.60)	2.3 (0.30)	0.9 ! (0.34)	0.3 ! (0.10)
South Carolina	12.7 (0.98)	11.0 (0.57)	11.7 (0.89)	10.1 (0.52)	13.9 (1.07)	11.9 (0.68)	17.8 (1.29)	15.9 (0.95)	5.9 (0.70)	5.1 (0.39)	5.1 (0.93)	4.6 (0.56)	21.6 (3.32)	19.3 (2.33)	8.3 (1.29)	8.2 (2.52)
South Dakota	2.2 (0.20)	2.7 (0.17)	2.3 (0.20)	2.8 (0.18)	2.1 (0.20)	2.5 (0.18)	2.4 (0.21)	2.9 (0.19)	1.2 (0.16)	0.9 (0.03)	0.6 (0.12)	0.7 (0.04)	3.3 (0.37)	4.2 (0.31)	‡ (†)	1.4 ! (0.70)
Tennessee	3.3 (0.18)	1.7 (0.10)	3.1 (0.18)	1.7 (0.10)	3.5 (0.18)	1.7 (0.09)	2.9 (0.21)	2.0 (0.13)	4.5 (0.15)	0.7 (0.03)	1.6 (0.15)	0.6 (0.04)	7.9 (0.77)	4.2 (0.37)	2.9 (0.41)	1.4 (0.20)
Texas	8.0 (0.10)	7.6 (0.07)	7.5 (0.10)	7.2 (0.07)	8.5 (0.11)	8.0 (0.08)	11.2 (0.21)	10.8 (0.17)	4.9 (0.14)	4.4 (0.11)	5.6 (0.12)	5.5 (0.07)	16.4 (0.28)	16.0 (0.13)	7.1 (0.27)	7.1 (0.24)
Utah	4.6 (0.29)	5.0 (0.05)	4.3 (0.28)	4.6 (0.05)	5.0 (0.29)	5.5 (0.06)	4.5 (0.29)	4.9 (0.06)	5.1 (0.26)	4.6 (0.03)	4.4 (0.37)	4.1 (0.05)	11.7 (0.81)	12.0 (0.06)	2.6 (0.36)	2.7 (0.03)
Vermont	0.8 (0.17)	0.8 (0.15)	0.8 (0.17)	0.9 (0.16)	0.9 (0.17)	0.8 (0.15)	0.8 (0.17)	0.8 (0.15)	0.4 ! (0.16)	0.5 ! (0.16)	# (†)	1.3 ! (0.57)	0.2 ! (0.10)	1.4 ! (0.41)	# (†)	# (†)
Virginia	12.1 (0.38)	12.6 (0.32)	11.5 (0.36)	12.0 (0.30)	12.8 (0.40)	13.3 (0.37)	14.9 (0.55)	15.6 (0.50)	4.6 (0.21)	5.2 (0.35)	6.7 (0.65)	7.5 (0.23)	24.5 (0.83)	26.4 (0.46)	8.3 (2.41)	13.3 (2.61)
Washington	3.8 (0.10)	3.9 (0.13)	3.6 (0.10)	3.7 (0.12)	3.9 (0.10)	4.1 (0.16)	4.2 (0.14)	4.4 (0.19)	1.4 (0.02)	1.4 (0.02)	1.8 (0.12)	1.7 (0.09)	5.0 (0.09)	5.8 (0.12)	1.6 (0.28)	1.4 (0.10)
West Virginia	2.2 (0.19)	2.2 (0.21)	2.3 (0.20)	2.2 (0.22)	2.0 (0.18)	2.1 (0.21)	2.2 (0.19)	2.2 (0.21)	1.4 (0.17)	1.6 (0.32)	1.6 (0.37)	0.9 (0.23)	9.3 (1.90)	10.9 (2.21)	3.9 ! (1.25)	2.9 ! (0.82)
Wisconsin	6.8 (0.47)	6.4 (0.35)	6.4 (0.44)	6.1 (0.33)	7.3 (0.51)	6.8 (0.41)	7.8 (0.55)	7.1 (0.45)	2.0 (0.21)	3.7 (0.25)	2.4 (0.23)	3.5 (0.21)	6.7 (0.55)	6.1 (0.44)	4.6 ! (2.04)	3.2 ! (1.23)
Wyoming	3.2 ! (1.04)	2.2 (0.35)	2.8 ! (0.90)	2.0 (0.32)	3.7 ! (1.19)	2.3 (0.39)	3.5 ! (1.14)	2.3 (0.39)	1.5 ! (0.47)	2.0 (0.19)	1.2 (0.29)	0.9 (0.11)	3.6 (0.31)	6.7 (1.35)	‡ (†)	1.0 (0.16)

—Not available.
†Not applicable.
#Rounds to zero.
!Interpret data with caution. The coefficient of variation (CV) for this estimate is between 30 and 50 percent.
‡Reporting standards not met. Either there are too few cases for a reliable estimate or the coefficient of variation (CV) is 50 percent or greater.

[1]Data are based on universe counts of schools and school districts; therefore, these figures do not have standard errors.
[2]Data for 2006 are based on universe counts of schools and school districts; therefore, these figures do not have standard errors.
NOTE: Race categories exclude persons of Hispanic ethnicity.
SOURCE: U.S. Department of Education, Office for Civil Rights, Civil Rights Data Collection: 2004 and 2006. (This table was prepared June 2008.)

Table 205.10. Private elementary and secondary school enrollment and private enrollment as a percentage of total enrollment in public and private schools, by region and grade level: Selected years, fall 1995 through fall 2011

[Standard errors appear in parentheses]

Grade level and year	Total private enrollment		Private enrollment, by region								
			Northeast		Midwest		South		West	
	In thousands	Percent of total enrollment	In thousands	Percent of total enrollment in Northeast	In thousands	Percent of total enrollment in Midwest	In thousands	Percent of total enrollment in South	In thousands	Percent of total enrollment in West
1	2	3	4	5	6	7	8	9	10	11
Total, all grades										
1995	5,918 (31.8)	11.7 (0.06)	1,509 (18.8)	16.0 (0.20)	1,525 (14.2)	12.7 (0.12)	1,744 (12.8)	9.8 (0.07)	1,141 (11.5)	10.0 (0.10)
1997	5,944 (18.5)	11.4 (0.04)	1,496 (8.3)	15.6 (0.09)	1,528 (11.6)	12.5 (0.10)	1,804 (11.3)	9.8 (0.06)	1,116 (5.2)	9.4 (0.04)
1999	6,018 (30.2)	11.4 (0.06)	1,507 (7.9)	15.5 (0.08)	1,520 (10.3)	12.4 (0.09)	1,863 (26.7)	10.0 (0.14)	1,127 (5.4)	9.2 (0.04)
2001	6,320 (40.3)	11.7 (0.08)	1,581 (9.5)	16.1 (0.10)	1,556 (22.9)	12.6 (0.19)	1,975 (21.4)	10.3 (0.11)	1,208 (23.4)	9.6 (0.19)
2003	6,099 (41.2)	11.2 (0.08)	1,513 (25.8)	15.4 (0.27)	1,460 (15.1)	11.9 (0.12)	1,944 (21.0)	9.9 (0.11)	1,182 (19.1)	9.1 (0.15)
2005	6,073 (42.4)	11.0 (0.08)	1,430 (7.7)	14.8 (0.08)	1,434 (21.0)	11.7 (0.17)	1,976 (24.7)	9.8 (0.12)	1,234 (26.3)	9.4 (0.20)
2007	5,910 (28.4)	10.7 (0.05)	1,426 (11.0)	14.9 (0.12)	1,352 (8.3)	11.2 (0.07)	1,965 (21.5)	9.6 (0.11)	1,167 (12.3)	8.9 (0.09)
2009	5,488 (35.9)	10.0 (0.07)	1,310 (15.7)	14.0 (0.17)	1,296 (25.9)	10.8 (0.22)	1,842 (17.6)	9.1 (0.09)	1,041 (8.0)	8.0 (0.06)
2011	5,268 (24.9)	9.7 (0.04)	1,252 (18.0)	13.7 (0.17)	1,263 (17.1)	10.7 (0.13)	1,747 (2.6)	8.5 (0.01)	1,006 (0.4)	7.8 (#)
Prekindergarten through grade 8										
1995	4,756 (28.4)	12.8 (0.08)	1,174 (16.8)	17.2 (0.25)	1,238 (13.5)	14.3 (0.16)	1,413 (11.9)	10.7 (0.09)	931 (9.2)	11.1 (0.11)
1997	4,759 (17.3)	12.6 (0.05)	1,165 (8.3)	16.8 (0.12)	1,235 (11.0)	14.1 (0.13)	1,449 (10.0)	10.8 (0.07)	909 (4.4)	10.5 (0.05)
1999	4,789 (23.1)	12.5 (0.06)	1,168 (7.5)	16.7 (0.11)	1,222 (8.4)	13.9 (0.10)	1,487 (19.6)	10.9 (0.14)	913 (4.4)	10.4 (0.05)
2001	5,023 (36.1)	12.9 (0.09)	1,216 (9.4)	17.3 (0.14)	1,253 (21.2)	14.3 (0.24)	1,584 (17.8)	11.3 (0.13)	969 (21.2)	10.6 (0.23)
2003	4,788 (30.3)	12.3 (0.08)	1,131 (7.8)	16.4 (0.11)	1,167 (13.6)	13.5 (0.16)	1,547 (18.6)	10.9 (0.13)	944 (18.1)	10.2 (0.20)
2005	4,724 (33.0)	12.1 (0.09)	1,063 (6.6)	15.9 (0.10)	1,142 (19.3)	13.3 (0.23)	1,551 (21.2)	10.7 (0.15)	969 (15.0)	10.5 (0.16)
2007	4,546 (21.9)	11.7 (0.06)	1,047 (6.3)	16.0 (0.10)	1,065 (7.7)	12.6 (0.09)	1,525 (17.7)	10.4 (0.12)	909 (8.1)	9.9 (0.09)
2009	4,179 (33.2)	10.8 (0.09)	938 (12.6)	14.6 (0.20)	1,016 (25.1)	12.1 (0.30)	1,424 (16.2)	9.8 (0.11)	802 (7.2)	8.8 (0.08)
2011	3,977 (18.2)	10.3 (0.04)	898 (12.8)	14.1 (0.17)	967 (12.8)	11.7 (0.14)	1,337 (1.8)	9.0 (0.01)	774 (0.3)	8.6 (#)
Grades 9 through 12										
1995	1,163 (4.6)	8.5 (0.03)	335 (2.9)	13.0 (0.11)	287 (0.9)	8.6 (0.03)	331 (2.1)	7.1 (0.04)	209 (2.3)	6.8 (0.08)
1997	1,185 (2.4)	8.3 (0.02)	331 (0.5)	12.5 (0.02)	293 (0.7)	8.5 (0.02)	354 (1.7)	7.2 (0.03)	207 (1.2)	6.4 (0.04)
1999	1,229 (8.3)	8.4 (0.06)	340 (1.1)	12.6 (0.04)	299 (2.5)	8.6 (0.07)	376 (7.6)	7.5 (0.15)	215 (1.8)	6.3 (0.05)
2001	1,296 (6.7)	8.6 (0.04)	365 (0.8)	13.1 (0.03)	302 (2.0)	8.6 (0.06)	390 (4.4)	7.5 (0.08)	239 (4.5)	6.8 (0.13)
2003	1,311 (24.7)	8.4 (0.16)	382 (24.0)	13.1 (0.83)	294 (4.1)	8.2 (0.11)	397 (3.0)	7.4 (0.06)	238 (3.5)	6.4 (0.09)
2005	1,349 (18.1)	8.3 (0.11)	367 (1.7)	12.3 (0.06)	292 (5.0)	7.9 (0.14)	425 (7.2)	7.5 (0.13)	265 (15.7)	6.7 (0.40)
2007	1,364 (12.0)	8.3 (0.07)	379 (8.8)	12.7 (0.30)	287 (1.3)	7.8 (0.04)	440 (5.5)	7.6 (0.10)	257 (5.7)	6.5 (0.14)
2009	1,309 (6.5)	8.0 (0.04)	372 (5.7)	12.6 (0.20)	280 (2.2)	7.7 (0.06)	418 (1.7)	7.3 (0.03)	239 (1.1)	6.1 (0.03)
2011	1,291 (15.4)	8.1 (0.09)	353 (5.2)	12.6 (0.16)	295 (14.4)	8.4 (0.38)	411 (1.8)	7.1 (0.03)	232 (0.1)	5.9 (#)

#Rounds to zero.
NOTE: Includes enrollment in prekindergarten through grade 12 in schools that offer kindergarten or higher grade. Ungraded students are prorated into prekindergarten through grade 8 and grades 9 through 12. Detail may not sum to totals because of rounding.

SOURCE: U.S. Department of Education, National Center for Education Statistics, Private School Universe Survey (PSS), 1995–96 through 2011–12; and Common Core of Data (CCD), "State Nonfiscal Survey of Public Elementary/Secondary Education," 1995–96 through 2011–12. (This table was prepared May 2014.)

Table 205.20. Enrollment and percentage distribution of students enrolled in private elementary and secondary schools, by school orientation and grade level: Selected years, fall 1995 through fall 2011

[Standard errors appear in parentheses]

Grade level and year	Total private enrollment	Catholic				Other religious				Nonsectarian
		Total	Parochial	Diocesan	Private (independent)	Total	Conservative Christian	Affiliated[1]	Unaffiliated[1]	
1	2	3	4	5	6	7	8	9	10	11

Enrollment

Grade level and year	Total private enrollment	Catholic Total	Parochial	Diocesan	Private (independent)	Other religious Total	Conservative Christian	Affiliated[1]	Unaffiliated[1]	Nonsectarian
Total, all grades										
1995	5,918,040 (31,815)	2,660,450 (6,878)	1,458,990 (2,079)	850,560 (5,674)	350,900 (1,176)	2,094,690 (16,956)	786,660 (8,815)	697,280 (4,886)	610,750 (11,831)	1,162,900 (18,443)
1997	5,944,320 (18,543)	2,665,630 (5,472)	1,438,860 (5,331)	873,780 (761)	352,990 (1,405)	2,097,190 (13,733)	823,610 (7,342)	646,500 (3,104)	627,080 (11,133)	1,181,510 (12,013)
1999	6,018,280 (30,179)	2,660,420 (4,831)	1,397,570 (4,421)	880,650 (†)	382,190 (1,945)	2,193,370 (27,176)	871,060 (4,827)	646,280 (4,894)	676,030 (24,593)	1,164,500 (8,156)
2001	6,319,650 (40,272)	2,672,650 (12,460)	1,309,890 (5,626)	979,050 (6,976)	383,710 (3,152)	2,328,160 (17,281)	937,420 (6,070)	663,190 (8,636)	727,550 (13,303)	1,318,840 (27,300)
2003	6,099,220 (41,219)	2,520,120 (10,580)	1,183,250 (9,937)	963,140 (4,754)	373,740 (3,996)	2,228,230 (19,674)	889,710 (8,852)	650,530 (5,860)	688,000 (14,805)	1,350,870 (29,197)
2005	6,073,240 (42,446)	2,402,800 (9,293)	1,062,950 (6,355)	956,610 (6,325)	383,230 (3,996)	2,303,330 (22,368)	957,360 (9,561)	696,910 (6,677)	649,050 (14,200)	1,367,120 (27,558)
2007	5,910,210 (28,363)	2,308,150 (6,083)	945,860 (5,361)	969,940 (1,788)	392,340 (3,432)	2,283,210 (20,628)	883,180 (6,616)	527,040 (3,512)	872,990 (18,217)	1,318,850 (18,235)
2009	5,488,490 (35,857)	2,160,220 (3,494)	856,440 (3,088)	909,010 (4,393)	394,770 (1,087)	2,076,220 (32,751)	737,020 (1,891)	516,310 (4,366)	822,890 (31,180)	1,252,050 (8,849)
2011	5,268,090 (24,908)	2,087,870 (14,426)	804,410 (3,686)	899,810 (14,320)	383,650 (459)	1,991,950 (21,814)	730,570 (4,721)	565,340 (2,990)	696,040 (20,419)	1,188,270 (5,376)
Prekindergarten through grade 8										
1995	4,755,540 (28,435)	2,041,990 (5,249)	1,368,340 (2,079)	575,190 (3,528)	98,460 (1,176)	1,752,510 (14,834)	651,050 (7,219)	574,820 (4,581)	526,630 (11,121)	961,040 (17,471)
1997	4,759,060 (17,323)	2,046,620 (5,469)	1,352,620 (5,331)	598,380 (761)	95,620 (1,393)	1,744,500 (12,194)	678,660 (5,957)	529,050 (2,504)	536,790 (10,120)	967,940 (11,050)
1999	4,788,990 (23,055)	2,033,900 (4,830)	1,317,300 (4,421)	607,860 (†)	108,740 (1,943)	1,818,260 (19,897)	713,020 (3,748)	529,280 (3,866)	575,970 (17,632)	936,820 (7,302)
2001	5,023,160 (36,096)	2,032,080 (10,751)	1,226,960 (4,494)	687,540 (6,976)	117,580 (2,978)	1,926,870 (15,459)	765,080 (5,110)	535,850 (7,370)	625,940 (12,240)	1,064,210 (24,703)
2003	4,788,070 (30,338)	1,886,530 (11,055)	1,108,320 (9,937)	670,910 (4,754)	107,300 (337)	1,835,930 (16,931)	722,460 (6,517)	519,310 (4,134)	594,160 (13,504)	1,065,620 (15,379)
2005	4,724,310 (33,034)	1,779,830 (9,318)	993,390 (6,355)	673,110 (6,286)	113,330 (2,896)	1,865,430 (19,380)	764,920 (8,028)	561,320 (5,730)	539,190 (12,633)	1,079,050 (15,497)
2007	4,545,910 (21,853)	1,685,220 (5,288)	878,830 (4,562)	688,260 (1,640)	118,130 (3,104)	1,833,540 (18,364)	698,930 (5,885)	417,610 (3,218)	717,000 (16,573)	1,027,150 (11,379)
2009	4,179,060 (33,168)	1,541,830 (3,250)	782,050 (3,085)	642,720 (846)	117,050 (578)	1,665,680 (30,216)	579,190 (1,685)	401,430 (3,952)	685,050 (28,928)	971,550 (8,113)
2011	3,976,960 (18,241)	1,481,620 (3,867)	737,090 (3,675)	630,970 (321)	113,560 (459)	1,583,610 (16,558)	568,150 (3,607)	443,780 (2,604)	571,690 (15,197)	911,730 (3,469)
Grades 9 through 12										
1995	1,162,500 (4,625)	618,460 (2,786)	90,650 (2,079)	275,370 (2,786)	252,440 (†)	342,180 (3,174)	135,610 (2,338)	122,460 (645)	84,120 (1,720)	201,860 (1,495)
1997	1,185,260 (2,374)	619,010 (96)	86,240 (†)	275,400 (†)	257,370 (96)	352,690 (2,261)	144,950 (1,660)	117,450 (848)	90,290 (1,221)	213,560 (1,860)
1999	1,229,290 (8,260)	626,520 (70)	80,270 (†)	272,790 (†)	273,460 (70)	375,100 (7,920)	158,040 (1,640)	117,000 (1,237)	100,060 (7,461)	227,670 (2,208)
2001	1,296,480 (6,669)	640,570 (2,317)	82,930 (2,293)	291,520 (†)	266,130 (338)	401,290 (3,527)	172,340 (2,633)	127,340 (1,625)	101,600 (1,852)	254,620 (4,465)
2003	1,311,150 (24,733)	633,590 (3,888)	74,930 (†)	292,230 (†)	266,430 (3,888)	392,310 (4,195)	167,250 (1,924)	131,220 (2,031)	93,840 (2,031)	285,250 (23,952)
2005	1,348,930 (18,073)	622,970 (1,538)	69,560 (†)	283,510 (700)	269,900 (1,341)	437,900 (6,541)	192,440 (3,404)	135,590 (1,493)	109,860 (5,190)	288,070 (16,551)
2007	1,364,300 (11,958)	622,930 (1,377)	67,030 (1,201)	281,680 (566)	274,210 (364)	449,680 (3,796)	184,260 (1,768)	109,430 (374)	156,000 (3,052)	291,700 (11,156)
2009	1,309,430 (6,480)	618,390 (4,409)	74,380 (42)	266,290 (4,311)	277,720 (920)	410,540 (4,285)	157,830 (362)	114,880 (1,074)	137,840 (4,111)	280,500 (1,880)
2011	1,291,130 (15,396)	606,250 (14,313)	67,320 (10)	268,840 (14,313)	270,090 (†)	408,330 (5,747)	162,420 (1,349)	121,560 (513)	124,350 (5,792)	276,550 (3,485)

Percentage distribution

Grade level and year	Total private enrollment	Catholic Total	Parochial	Diocesan	Private (independent)	Other religious Total	Conservative Christian	Affiliated[1]	Unaffiliated[1]	Nonsectarian
Total, all grades										
1995	100.0 (†)	45.0 (0.19)	24.7 (0.13)	14.4 (0.08)	5.9 (0.03)	35.4 (0.19)	13.3 (0.12)	11.8 (0.08)	10.3 (0.18)	19.7 (0.23)
1997	100.0 (†)	44.8 (0.13)	24.2 (0.09)	14.7 (0.05)	5.9 (0.03)	35.3 (0.18)	13.9 (0.12)	10.9 (0.06)	10.5 (0.17)	19.9 (0.17)
1999	100.0 (†)	44.2 (0.24)	23.2 (0.14)	14.6 (0.07)	6.4 (0.04)	36.4 (0.28)	14.5 (0.09)	10.7 (0.08)	11.2 (0.36)	19.3 (0.11)
2001	100.0 (†)	42.3 (0.25)	20.7 (0.14)	15.5 (0.12)	6.1 (0.04)	36.8 (0.22)	14.8 (0.13)	10.5 (0.13)	11.5 (0.18)	20.9 (0.33)
2003	100.0 (†)	41.3 (0.27)	19.4 (0.17)	15.8 (0.14)	6.1 (0.07)	36.5 (0.25)	14.6 (0.13)	10.7 (0.10)	11.3 (0.22)	22.1 (0.36)
2005	100.0 (†)	39.6 (0.26)	17.5 (0.13)	15.8 (0.14)	6.3 (0.07)	37.9 (0.25)	15.8 (0.14)	11.5 (0.09)	10.7 (0.20)	22.5 (0.34)
2007	100.0 (†)	39.1 (0.20)	16.0 (0.11)	16.4 (0.09)	6.6 (0.06)	38.6 (0.25)	14.9 (0.12)	8.9 (0.06)	14.8 (0.26)	22.3 (0.25)
2009	100.0 (†)	39.4 (0.25)	15.6 (0.11)	16.6 (0.13)	7.2 (0.05)	37.8 (0.37)	13.4 (0.09)	9.4 (0.07)	15.0 (0.48)	22.8 (0.16)
2011	100.0 (†)	39.6 (0.25)	15.3 (0.09)	17.1 (0.25)	7.3 (0.04)	37.8 (0.28)	13.9 (0.09)	10.7 (0.08)	13.2 (0.34)	22.6 (0.15)
Prekindergarten through grade 8										
1995	100.0 (†)	42.9 (0.20)	28.8 (0.17)	12.1 (0.06)	2.1 (0.02)	36.9 (0.22)	13.7 (0.13)	12.1 (0.09)	11.1 (0.21)	20.2 (0.28)
1997	100.0 (†)	43.0 (0.15)	28.4 (0.12)	12.6 (0.05)	2.0 (0.03)	36.7 (0.20)	14.3 (0.13)	11.1 (0.06)	11.3 (0.19)	20.3 (0.19)
1999	100.0 (†)	42.5 (0.23)	27.5 (0.16)	12.7 (0.06)	2.3 (0.04)	38.0 (0.26)	14.9 (0.09)	11.1 (0.07)	12.0 (0.32)	19.6 (0.12)
2001	100.0 (†)	40.5 (0.27)	24.4 (0.17)	13.7 (0.14)	2.3 (0.05)	38.4 (0.25)	15.2 (0.15)	10.7 (0.14)	12.5 (0.20)	21.2 (0.37)
2003	100.0 (†)	39.4 (0.25)	23.1 (0.18)	14.0 (0.13)	2.2 (0.01)	38.3 (0.23)	15.1 (0.12)	10.8 (0.09)	12.4 (0.24)	22.3 (0.22)

See notes at end of table.

Table 205.20. Enrollment and percentage distribution of students enrolled in private elementary and secondary schools, by school orientation and grade level: Selected years, fall 1995 through fall 2011—Continued

[Standard errors appear in parentheses]

Grade level and year	Total private enrollment	Catholic				Other religious				Nonsectarian
		Total	Parochial	Diocesan	Private (independent)	Total	Conservative Christian	Affiliated[1]	Unaffiliated[1]	
1	2	3	4	5	6	7	8	9	10	11
2005	100.0 (†)	37.7 (0.25)	21.0 (0.14)	14.2 (0.15)	2.4 (0.06)	39.5 (0.21)	16.2 (0.16)	11.9 (0.09)	11.4 (0.22)	22.8 (0.23)
2007	100.0 (†)	37.1 (0.20)	19.3 (0.13)	15.1 (0.09)	2.6 (0.07)	40.3 (0.27)	15.4 (0.14)	9.2 (0.07)	15.8 (0.30)	22.6 (0.21)
2009	100.0 (†)	36.9 (0.29)	18.7 (0.15)	15.4 (0.12)	2.8 (0.03)	39.9 (0.43)	13.9 (0.11)	9.6 (0.10)	16.4 (0.57)	23.2 (0.20)
2011	100.0 (†)	37.3 (0.18)	18.5 (0.11)	15.9 (0.08)	2.9 (0.02)	39.8 (0.24)	14.3 (0.08)	11.2 (0.08)	14.4 (0.32)	22.9 (0.11)
Grades 9 through 12										
1995	100.0 (†)	53.2 (0.20)	7.8 (0.03)	23.7 (0.20)	21.7 (0.09)	29.4 (0.20)	11.7 (0.18)	10.5 (0.06)	7.2 (0.14)	17.4 (0.12)
1997	100.0 (†)	52.2 (0.10)	7.3 (0.01)	23.2 (0.05)	21.7 (0.04)	29.8 (0.16)	12.2 (0.13)	9.9 (0.08)	7.6 (0.10)	18.0 (0.14)
1999	100.0 (†)	51.0 (0.34)	6.5 (0.04)	22.2 (0.15)	22.2 (0.15)	30.5 (0.45)	12.9 (0.14)	9.5 (0.11)	8.1 (0.56)	18.5 (0.19)
2001	100.0 (†)	49.4 (0.26)	6.4 (0.17)	22.5 (0.12)	20.5 (0.10)	31.0 (0.19)	13.3 (0.17)	9.8 (0.12)	7.8 (0.13)	19.6 (0.28)
2003	100.0 (†)	48.3 (0.91)	5.7 (0.11)	22.3 (0.42)	20.3 (0.44)	29.9 (0.59)	12.8 (0.32)	10.0 (0.23)	7.2 (0.20)	21.8 (1.43)
2005	100.0 (†)	46.2 (0.60)	5.2 (0.07)	21.0 (0.28)	20.0 (0.27)	32.5 (0.52)	14.3 (0.28)	10.1 (0.16)	8.1 (0.37)	21.4 (0.97)
2007	100.0 (†)	45.7 (0.40)	4.9 (0.09)	20.6 (0.18)	20.1 (0.17)	33.0 (0.33)	13.5 (0.16)	8.0 (0.07)	11.4 (0.22)	21.4 (0.65)
2009	100.0 (†)	47.2 (0.25)	5.7 (0.03)	20.3 (0.27)	21.2 (0.12)	31.4 (0.25)	12.1 (0.06)	8.8 (0.08)	10.5 (0.28)	21.4 (0.15)
2011	100.0 (†)	47.0 (0.63)	5.2 (0.06)	20.8 (0.88)	20.9 (0.25)	31.6 (0.49)	12.6 (0.18)	9.4 (0.13)	9.6 (0.43)	21.4 (0.35)

†Not applicable.
[1]Affiliated schools belong to associations of schools with a specific religious orientation other than Catholic or conservative Christian. Unaffiliated schools have a religious orientation or purpose but are not classified as Catholic, conservative Christian, or affiliated.

NOTE: Includes enrollment in prekindergarten through grade 12 in schools that offer kindergarten or higher grade. Ungraded students are prorated into prekindergarten through grade 8 and grades 9 through 12. Detail may not sum to totals because of rounding.
SOURCE: U.S. Department of Education, National Center for Education Statistics, Private School Universe Survey (PSS), 1995–96 through 2011–12. (This table was prepared April 2013.)

Table 205.30. Percentage distribution of students enrolled in private elementary and secondary schools, by school orientation and selected characteristics: Fall 2009 and fall 2011

[Standard errors appear in parentheses]

Selected characteristic	Total	Catholic				Other religious				Nonsectarian
		Total	Parochial	Diocesan	Private (independent)	Total	Conservative Christian	Affiliated[1]	Unaffiliated[1]	
1	2	3	4	5	6	7	8	9	10	11
Fall 2009										
Total	100.0 (†)	39.4 (0.25)	15.6 (0.11)	16.6 (0.13)	7.2 (0.05)	37.8 (0.37)	13.4 (0.09)	9.4 (0.07)	15.0 (0.48)	22.8 (0.16)
School level[2]										
Elementary	100.0 (†)	49.5 (0.44)	25.9 (0.24)	20.9 (0.19)	2.7 (0.03)	30.1 (0.58)	7.1 (0.08)	8.4 (0.12)	14.6 (0.68)	20.4 (0.22)
Secondary	100.0 (†)	74.7 (0.25)	8.5 (0.05)	33.2 (0.38)	33.0 (0.22)	13.6 (0.22)	2.3 (0.01)	5.5 (0.03)	5.8 (0.23)	11.7 (0.13)
Combined	100.0 (†)	6.7 (0.06)	1.6 (0.02)	2.0 (0.02)	3.1 (0.03)	61.5 (0.35)	28.9 (0.26)	12.8 (0.15)	19.7 (0.68)	31.8 (0.31)
Student race/ethnicity[3]										
White	100.0 (†)	41.7 (0.38)	16.2 (0.16)	17.9 (0.20)	7.6 (0.07)	39.2 (0.54)	13.7 (0.13)	10.1 (0.11)	15.5 (0.72)	19.0 (0.18)
Black	100.0 (†)	35.1 (0.21)	13.1 (0.08)	13.8 (0.08)	8.2 (0.05)	41.8 (0.20)	18.0 (0.14)	8.9 (0.09)	14.8 (0.27)	23.1 (0.24)
Hispanic	100.0 (†)	60.3 (0.55)	25.1 (0.24)	23.5 (0.22)	11.7 (0.11)	24.3 (0.14)	10.4 (0.11)	6.2 (0.10)	7.7 (0.21)	15.4 (0.53)
Asian	100.0 (†)	38.1 (0.29)	15.1 (0.12)	15.5 (0.12)	7.5 (0.06)	30.3 (0.25)	11.5 (0.09)	9.7 (0.08)	9.1 (0.14)	31.6 (0.52)
Pacific Islander	100.0 (†)	40.3 (1.28)	17.7 (0.56)	16.7 (0.53)	5.9 (0.19)	44.6 (1.75)	12.5 (0.40)	5.4 (0.17)	26.7 (2.32)	15.1 (0.48)
American Indian/Alaska Native	100.0 (†)	41.0 (0.32)	10.3 (0.08)	18.2 (0.14)	12.5 (0.10)	34.1 (0.40)	17.1 (0.32)	5.6 (0.25)	11.4 (0.29)	24.9 (0.43)
Two or more races	100.0 (†)	44.8 (0.26)	16.5 (0.10)	19.7 (0.11)	8.7 (0.09)	27.0 (0.39)	9.8 (0.07)	8.0 (0.05)	9.2 (0.48)	28.2 (0.21)
School enrollment										
Less than 50	100.0 (†)	2.3 (0.26)	0.7 (0.10)	0.7 (0.06)	0.9 (0.19)	57.7 (3.20)	12.1 (0.97)	6.9 (0.86)	38.8 (4.56)	40.0 (3.04)
50 to 149	100.0 (†)	15.6 (0.21)	6.9 (0.09)	6.6 (0.12)	2.1 (0.06)	47.2 (0.42)	16.3 (0.21)	9.2 (0.12)	21.7 (0.65)	37.2 (0.36)
150 to 299	100.0 (†)	44.8 (0.32)	21.8 (0.15)	19.6 (0.14)	3.5 (0.06)	36.5 (0.40)	12.8 (0.12)	9.2 (0.14)	14.4 (0.51)	18.7 (0.25)
300 to 499	100.0 (†)	50.0 (0.46)	23.3 (0.33)	20.1 (0.38)	6.7 (0.06)	32.6 (0.58)	12.7 (0.12)	9.4 (0.26)	10.6 (0.71)	17.3 (0.27)
500 to 749	100.0 (†)	53.7 (#)	19.7 (#)	23.3 (#)	10.7 (#)	30.4 (#)	13.4 (#)	9.3 (#)	7.8 (#)	15.9 (#)
750 or more	100.0 (†)	42.0 (0.31)	6.6 (0.05)	17.3 (0.13)	18.2 (0.13)	36.5 (0.46)	12.7 (0.09)	11.0 (0.08)	12.8 (0.64)	21.5 (0.16)
Region										
Northeast	100.0 (†)	45.6 (0.57)	19.4 (0.28)	16.8 (0.38)	9.4 (0.13)	28.0 (0.80)	4.9 (0.09)	9.5 (0.11)	13.6 (0.77)	26.4 (0.28)
Midwest	100.0 (†)	56.1 (1.08)	23.3 (0.44)	24.3 (0.49)	8.5 (0.18)	32.3 (1.26)	9.2 (0.19)	8.0 (0.22)	15.1 (1.58)	11.6 (0.35)
South	100.0 (†)	26.8 (0.25)	9.9 (0.09)	12.0 (0.11)	5.0 (0.05)	48.7 (0.42)	19.4 (0.19)	11.3 (0.11)	18.0 (0.65)	24.5 (0.25)
West	100.0 (†)	32.9 (0.25)	11.4 (0.09)	14.7 (0.11)	6.8 (0.05)	37.8 (0.35)	18.9 (0.15)	7.7 (0.13)	11.3 (0.39)	29.2 (0.34)
School locale										
City	100.0 (†)	44.2 (0.23)	16.0 (0.10)	18.2 (0.10)	10.0 (0.06)	33.8 (0.09)	10.8 (0.07)	10.2 (0.07)	12.8 (0.11)	21.9 (0.26)
Suburban	100.0 (†)	40.6 (0.38)	17.0 (0.16)	17.0 (0.24)	6.6 (0.06)	35.4 (0.48)	13.2 (0.13)	9.2 (0.12)	13.0 (0.54)	23.9 (0.28)
Town	100.0 (†)	47.1 (1.16)	22.5 (0.56)	22.4 (0.55)	2.2 (0.05)	39.6 (1.45)	15.1 (0.40)	7.7 (0.40)	16.7 (1.94)	13.3 (0.72)
Rural	100.0 (†)	15.8 (0.59)	6.2 (0.23)	6.8 (0.25)	2.9 (0.11)	56.7 (1.50)	21.6 (0.81)	8.2 (0.36)	26.9 (2.56)	27.5 (0.97)
Fall 2011										
Total	100.0 (†)	39.6 (0.25)	15.3 (0.09)	17.1 (0.25)	7.3 (0.04)	37.8 (0.28)	13.9 (0.09)	10.7 (0.08)	13.2 (0.34)	22.6 (0.15)
School level[2]										
Elementary	100.0 (†)	49.8 (0.16)	25.7 (0.12)	21.5 (0.07)	2.7 (0.02)	29.5 (0.19)	7.1 (0.05)	9.5 (0.05)	12.9 (0.23)	20.6 (0.12)
Secondary	100.0 (†)	74.0 (0.52)	8.1 (0.15)	34.3 (1.24)	31.6 (0.60)	14.1 (0.28)	2.6 (0.05)	5.9 (0.11)	5.7 (0.12)	11.9 (0.31)
Combined	100.0 (†)	8.3 (0.11)	1.7 (0.02)	2.6 (0.05)	4.1 (0.04)	61.4 (0.48)	29.6 (0.34)	14.8 (0.24)	17.1 (0.89)	30.3 (0.39)
Student race/ethnicity[3]										
White	100.0 (†)	41.9 (0.35)	15.9 (0.14)	18.3 (0.33)	7.7 (0.06)	39.5 (0.45)	14.3 (0.13)	11.5 (0.12)	13.7 (0.55)	18.7 (0.19)
Black	100.0 (†)	35.4 (0.15)	11.9 (0.05)	14.9 (0.08)	8.6 (0.03)	41.8 (0.18)	17.7 (0.08)	10.5 (0.10)	13.6 (0.06)	22.8 (0.30)
Hispanic	100.0 (†)	60.2 (0.22)	24.3 (0.12)	24.5 (0.32)	11.4 (0.05)	24.4 (0.19)	11.1 (0.19)	6.9 (0.04)	6.4 (0.06)	15.4 (0.10)
Asian	100.0 (†)	36.6 (0.10)	13.8 (0.02)	15.2 (0.11)	7.5 (0.01)	31.2 (0.05)	12.3 (0.04)	10.1 (0.01)	8.9 (0.01)	32.2 (0.07)
Pacific Islander	100.0 (†)	46.3 (0.33)	16.2 (0.08)	20.9 (0.36)	9.2 (0.04)	38.1 (0.28)	12.2 (0.18)	13.0 (0.06)	12.9 (0.06)	15.6 (0.30)
American Indian/Alaska Native	100.0 (†)	43.9 (0.18)	11.0 (0.05)	18.0 (0.08)	15.0 (0.06)	30.4 (0.29)	16.1 (0.35)	7.2 (0.03)	7.2 (0.06)	25.7 (0.11)
Two or more races	100.0 (†)	44.1 (0.14)	15.5 (0.04)	19.9 (0.14)	8.7 (0.06)	27.6 (0.10)	11.0 (0.04)	9.4 (0.02)	7.3 (0.09)	28.3 (0.12)
School enrollment										
Less than 50	100.0 (†)	2.9 (0.21)	0.8 (0.03)	0.8 (0.02)	1.4 (0.19)	54.4 (1.45)	14.5 (0.57)	8.2 (0.30)	31.7 (1.65)	42.7 (1.38)
50 to 149	100.0 (†)	15.4 (0.15)	6.7 (0.06)	6.5 (0.08)	2.2 (0.02)	46.9 (0.78)	16.1 (0.37)	11.1 (0.11)	19.7 (0.52)	37.7 (0.69)
150 to 299	100.0 (†)	44.0 (0.10)	21.2 (0.08)	19.5 (0.05)	3.3 (0.01)	37.3 (0.10)	14.4 (0.03)	10.8 (0.11)	12.2 (0.03)	18.7 (0.12)
300 to 499	100.0 (†)	51.2 (0.10)	23.1 (0.15)	21.6 (0.08)	6.5 (0.02)	31.9 (0.12)	12.9 (0.05)	9.6 (0.17)	9.4 (0.03)	16.8 (0.06)
500 to 749	100.0 (†)	55.6 (0.80)	18.6 (0.34)	24.9 (1.36)	12.2 (0.22)	29.7 (0.54)	12.5 (0.23)	9.5 (0.17)	7.7 (0.14)	14.7 (0.27)
750 or more	100.0 (†)	38.4 (0.80)	5.7 (0.12)	15.7 (0.33)	16.9 (0.35)	39.6 (1.25)	13.0 (0.27)	13.5 (0.28)	13.0 (1.80)	22.1 (0.46)

See notes at end of table.

Table 205.30. Percentage distribution of students enrolled in private elementary and secondary schools, by school orientation and selected characteristics: Fall 2009 and fall 2011—Continued

[Standard errors appear in parentheses]

Selected characteristic	Total	Catholic				Other religious				
		Total	Parochial	Diocesan	Private (independent)	Total	Conservative Christian	Affiliated[1]	Unaffiliated[1]	Nonsectarian
1	2	3	4	5	6	7	8	9	10	11
Region										
Northeast..........	100.0 (†)	43.3 (0.66)	17.0 (0.25)	16.5 (0.27)	9.8 (0.14)	30.9 (0.89)	4.7 (0.07)	11.9 (0.30)	14.2 (1.24)	25.8 (0.28)
Midwest..........	100.0 (†)	56.8 (0.79)	24.3 (0.38)	24.5 (0.94)	8.0 (0.13)	31.5 (0.90)	10.2 (0.32)	8.9 (0.18)	12.4 (0.66)	11.6 (0.43)
South..........	100.0 (†)	27.8 (0.04)	9.8 (0.01)	12.9 (0.02)	5.1 (0.01)	47.9 (0.07)	20.2 (0.06)	12.2 (0.02)	15.5 (0.02)	24.3 (0.09)
West..........	100.0 (†)	34.0 (0.01)	11.2 (0.01)	15.8 (0.01)	7.0 (0.00)	36.8 (0.02)	18.8 (0.01)	9.0 (0.01)	9.0 (0.02)	29.2 (0.01)
School locale										
City..........	100.0 (†)	44.2 (0.37)	15.4 (0.10)	19.3 (0.53)	9.5 (0.06)	33.9 (0.23)	10.4 (0.07)	11.1 (0.10)	12.4 (0.08)	21.9 (0.17)
Suburban..........	100.0 (†)	40.9 (0.14)	16.8 (0.15)	17.0 (0.06)	7.2 (0.02)	35.0 (0.08)	13.8 (0.05)	11.1 (0.10)	10.2 (0.04)	24.0 (0.15)
Town..........	100.0 (†)	49.4 (0.43)	23.9 (0.21)	23.4 (0.20)	2.1 (0.02)	39.3 (0.53)	16.8 (0.36)	8.6 (0.08)	14.0 (0.67)	11.3 (0.10)
Rural..........	100.0 (†)	16.7 (0.47)	6.3 (0.18)	7.2 (0.20)	3.2 (0.09)	57.2 (1.41)	23.4 (0.76)	9.7 (0.28)	24.1 (2.10)	26.2 (0.98)

†Not applicable.
#Rounds to zero.
[1]Affiliated schools belong to associations of schools with a specific religious orientation other than Catholic or conservative Christian. Unaffiliated schools have a religious orientation or purpose but are not classified as Catholic, conservative Christian, or affiliated.
[2]Elementary schools have grade 6 or lower and no grade higher than 8. Secondary schools have no grade lower than 7. Combined schools include those that have grades lower than 7 and higher than 8, as well as those that do not classify students by grade level.

[3]Race/ethnicity was not collected for prekindergarten students (788,370 out of 5,488,490 students in 2009 and 773,240 out of 5,268,090 students in 2011). Percentage distribution is based on the students for whom race/ethnicity was reported.
NOTE: Includes enrollment in prekindergarten through grade 12 in schools that offer kindergarten or higher grade. Detail may not sum to totals because of rounding.
SOURCE: U.S. Department of Education, National Center for Education Statistics, Private School Universe Survey (PSS), 2009–10 and 2011–12. (This table was prepared April 2013.)

Table 205.40. Number and percentage distribution of private elementary and secondary students, teachers, and schools, by orientation of school and selected characteristics: Fall 1999, fall 2009, and fall 2011

[Standard errors appear in parentheses]

Selected characteristic	Fall 1999, total number	Fall 2009, total number	Fall 2011 Total Number	Percent	Catholic Number	Percent	Other religious Number	Percent	Nonsectarian Number	Percent
1	2	3	4	5	6	7	8	9	10	11
Students[1]										
Total	6,018,280 (30,179)	5,488,490 (35,857)	5,268,090 (24,908)	100.0 (†)	2,087,870 (14,426)	100.0 (†)	1,991,950 (21,814)	100.0 (†)	1,188,270 (5,376)	100.0 (†)
School level[2]										
Elementary	3,595,020 (11,516)	2,937,090 (26,807)	2,775,270 (9,594)	52.7 (0.23)	1,383,420 (3,829)	66.3 (0.47)	819,070 (7,697)	41.1 (0.37)	572,790 (3,263)	48.2 (0.22)
Secondary	806,640 (2,395)	785,810 (4,810)	757,620 (14,401)	14.4 (0.25)	560,280 (14,312)	26.8 (0.51)	106,970 (444)	5.4 (0.06)	90,370 (1,827)	7.6 (0.14)
Combined	1,616,620 (23,949)	1,765,590 (15,909)	1,735,200 (16,892)	32.9 (0.21)	144,170 (475)	6.9 (0.05)	1,065,910 (18,183)	53.5 (0.41)	525,120 (3,824)	44.2 (0.23)
School enrollment										
Less than 50	238,980 (5,691)	296,000 (22,889)	242,910 (7,660)	4.6 (0.14)	7,030 (473)	0.3 (0.02)	132,200 (7,447)	6.6 (0.35)	103,690 (1,771)	8.7 (0.14)
50 to 149	939,110 (10,717)	950,050 (12,053)	886,240 (7,898)	16.8 (0.15)	136,680 (498)	6.5 (0.05)	415,450 (10,139)	20.9 (0.43)	334,110 (4,582)	28.1 (0.29)
150 to 299	1,615,970 (7,315)	1,423,220 (9,951)	1,379,070 (3,193)	26.2 (0.15)	606,670 (1,318)	29.1 (0.19)	514,970 (1,773)	25.9 (0.34)	257,430 (2,046)	21.7 (0.16)
300 to 499	1,419,360 (13,203)	1,154,950 (10,730)	1,104,910 (4,050)	21.0 (0.11)	566,000 (2,400)	27.1 (0.19)	352,970 (2,234)	17.7 (0.21)	185,950 (†)	15.6 (0.07)
500 to 749	917,670 (2,330)	768,540 (†)	790,830 (14,312)	15.0 (0.25)	439,990 (14,312)	21.1 (0.55)	234,500 (†)	11.8 (0.13)	116,340 (†)	9.8 (0.04)
750 or more	887,190 (18,232)	895,720 (6,538)	864,120 (17,908)	16.4 (0.29)	331,500 (†)	15.9 (0.11)	341,860 (17,908)	17.2 (0.77)	190,760 (†)	16.1 (0.07)
Student race/ethnicity[3]										
White	4,061,870 (24,242)	3,410,360 (31,067)	3,208,730 (23,933)	71.4 (0.14)	1,342,980 (11,961)	69.6 (0.09)	1,266,580 (21,804)	75.5 (0.32)	599,160 (3,387)	67.3 (0.15)
Black	494,530 (5,079)	430,970 (2,579)	400,260 (1,601)	8.9 (0.06)	141,670 (239)	7.3 (0.04)	167,280 (472)	10.0 (0.13)	91,310 (1,532)	10.3 (0.15)
Hispanic	435,890 (1,592)	443,290 (4,113)	441,680 (2,016)	9.8 (0.05)	265,880 (1,805)	13.8 (0.02)	107,860 (925)	6.4 (0.10)	67,930 (379)	7.6 (0.02)
Asian	239,510 (877)	239,320 (1,894)	245,640 (281)	5.5 (0.03)	89,810 (297)	4.7 (0.02)	76,710 (89)	4.6 (0.06)	79,130 (203)	8.9 (0.04)
Pacific Islander	[4] (†)	28,020 (884)	26,810 (117)	0.6 (#)	12,410 (108)	0.6 (#)	10,210 (39)	0.6 (0.01)	4,190 (94)	0.5 (0.01)
American Indian/Alaska Native	22,690 (164)	21,080 (162)	21,430 (91)	0.5 (#)	9,420 (5)	0.5 (#)	6,510 (90)	0.4 (0.01)	5,500 (5)	0.6 (#)
Two or more races	— (†)	127,090 (781)	150,300 (370)	3.3 (0.01)	66,220 (300)	3.4 (0.01)	41,490 (141)	2.5 (0.03)	42,590 (216)	4.8 (0.03)
School locale										
City	— (†)	2,252,780 (12,708)	2,186,170 (14,689)	41.5 (0.27)	966,990 (14,322)	46.3 (0.39)	740,520 (1,602)	37.2 (0.46)	478,660 (2,558)	40.3 (0.21)
Suburban	— (†)	2,137,800 (20,891)	2,018,570 (6,493)	38.3 (0.20)	826,400 (3,857)	39.6 (0.30)	707,340 (2,728)	35.5 (0.39)	484,840 (3,400)	40.8 (0.22)
Town	— (†)	387,920 (9,565)	358,600 (3,130)	6.8 (0.05)	177,140 (113)	8.5 (0.06)	141,060 (3,128)	7.1 (0.13)	40,400 (31)	3.4 (0.02)
Rural	— (†)	709,990 (26,462)	704,750 (19,874)	13.4 (0.33)	117,350 (†)	5.6 (0.04)	403,030 (21,029)	20.2 (0.84)	184,370 (3,228)	15.5 (0.24)
Teachers[5]										
Total	408,400 (2,977)	437,410 (3,222)	420,880 (1,836)	100.0 (†)	138,070 (1,069)	100.0 (.00)	163,140 (1,568)	100.0 (†)	119,670 (567)	100.0 (†)
School level[2]										
Elementary	200,910 (735)	194,480 (1,878)	184,130 (855)	43.7 (0.16)	84,340 (224)	61.1 (0.47)	57,310 (731)	35.1 (0.26)	42,480 (373)	35.5 (0.23)
Secondary	62,740 (229)	67,530 (553)	65,180 (1,055)	15.5 (0.22)	41,290 (1,051)	29.9 (0.54)	10,850 (72)	6.7 (0.07)	13,030 (95)	10.9 (0.09)
Combined	144,750 (2,682)	175,410 (1,853)	171,570 (918)	40.8 (0.14)	12,440 (49)	9.0 (0.08)	94,980 (1,049)	58.2 (0.26)	64,160 (388)	53.6 (0.22)
School enrollment										
Less than 50	25,970 (488)	34,120 (1,642)	30,960 (1,104)	7.4 (0.24)	1,000 (72)	0.7 (0.05)	16,700 (1,080)	10.2 (0.59)	13,260 (241)	11.1 (0.18)
50 to 149	70,800 (983)	82,460 (1,102)	76,830 (766)	18.3 (0.16)	11,960 (48)	8.7 (0.07)	35,720 (918)	21.9 (0.45)	29,150 (415)	24.4 (0.27)
150 to 299	102,240 (486)	107,490 (1,873)	103,940 (376)	24.7 (0.14)	39,210 (69)	28.4 (0.22)	39,730 (285)	24.4 (0.32)	25,000 (221)	20.9 (0.15)
300 to 499	90,010 (1,316)	86,850 (751)	83,150 (295)	19.8 (0.10)	36,100 (124)	26.1 (0.20)	27,590 (244)	16.9 (0.20)	19,460 (†)	16.3 (0.08)
500 to 749	57,930 (79)	56,920 (†)	58,070 (1,051)	13.8 (0.22)	27,770 (1,051)	20.1 (0.61)	17,840 (†)	10.9 (0.11)	12,460 (†)	10.4 (0.05)
750 or more	61,440 (2,143)	69,570 (566)	67,930 (696)	16.1 (0.16)	22,030 (†)	16.0 (0.12)	25,570 (696)	15.7 (0.41)	20,330 (†)	17.0 (0.08)
School locale										
City	— (†)	176,740 (799)	173,390 (1,121)	41.2 (0.24)	62,980 (1,051)	45.6 (0.42)	60,890 (283)	37.3 (0.44)	49,530 (248)	41.4 (0.20)
Suburban	— (†)	166,170 (2,463)	155,630 (591)	37.0 (0.18)	53,660 (240)	38.9 (0.32)	55,960 (324)	34.3 (0.34)	46,010 (423)	38.4 (0.23)
Town	— (†)	30,390 (663)	28,270 (598)	6.7 (0.13)	12,620 (8)	9.1 (0.07)	11,730 (598)	7.2 (0.31)	3,920 (1)	3.3 (0.02)
Rural	— (†)	64,120 (1,960)	63,590 (1,123)	15.1 (0.23)	8,810 (†)	6.4 (0.05)	34,560 (1,203)	21.2 (0.56)	20,210 (241)	16.9 (0.18)
Schools										
Total	33,000 (301)	33,370 (834)	30,860 (542)	100.0 (†)	6,870 (31)	100.0 (.00)	14,210 (551)	100.0 (†)	9,770 (87)	100.0 (†)
School level[2]										
Elementary	22,300 (242)	21,420 (745)	19,700 (414)	63.8 (0.43)	5,420 (23)	78.9 (0.35)	7,930 (407)	55.8 (1.04)	6,350 (66)	64.9 (0.42)
Secondary	2,540 (62)	2,780 (39)	2,680 (30)	8.7 (0.18)	1,050 (27)	15.2 (0.36)	760 (13)	5.3 (0.22)	870 (10)	8.9 (0.12)
Combined	8,150 (160)	9,160 (153)	8,490 (188)	27.5 (0.38)	410 (9)	5.9 (0.11)	5,530 (204)	38.9 (0.95)	2,560 (53)	26.1 (0.43)
School enrollment										
Less than 50	9,160 (210)	11,070 (801)	9,660 (520)	31.3 (1.15)	250 (20)	3.7 (0.28)	5,600 (517)	39.4 (2.21)	3,810 (54)	39.0 (0.41)
50 to 149	10,260 (134)	10,470 (154)	9,720 (120)	31.5 (0.58)	1,310 (7)	19.0 (0.12)	4,540 (151)	32.0 (1.32)	3,860 (64)	39.5 (0.46)
150 to 299	7,440 (34)	6,690 (46)	6,460 (16)	20.9 (0.37)	2,770 (6)	40.3 (0.14)	2,440 (9)	17.2 (0.67)	1,240 (10)	12.7 (0.13)
300 to 499	3,730 (41)	3,010 (30)	2,900 (10)	9.4 (0.17)	1,470 (5)	21.4 (0.07)	940 (6)	6.6 (0.26)	490 (†)	5.0 (0.04)
500 to 749	1,530 (3)	1,280 (†)	1,320 (27)	4.3 (0.12)	740 (27)	10.8 (0.37)	390 (†)	2.7 (0.11)	190 (†)	2.0 (0.02)
750 or more	870 (20)	850 (7)	800 (10)	2.6 (0.06)	330 (†)	4.7 (0.02)	300 (10)	2.1 (0.11)	180 (†)	1.8 (0.02)
School locale										
City	— (†)	10,810 (171)	10,000 (52)	32.4 (0.59)	2,830 (27)	41.2 (0.33)	3,830 (9)	26.9 (1.05)	3,350 (41)	34.2 (0.37)
Suburban	— (†)	11,610 (176)	10,910 (70)	35.4 (0.63)	2,490 (27)	36.3 (0.33)	3,960 (24)	27.8 (1.08)	4,460 (56)	45.6 (0.41)
Town	— (†)	3,340 (154)	2,900 (104)	9.4 (0.22)	930 (1)	13.6 (0.06)	1,530 (104)	10.8 (0.43)	430 (1)	4.4 (0.04)
Rural	— (†)	7,610 (799)	7,050 (453)	22.8 (1.07)	610 (†)	8.9 (0.04)	4,900 (463)	34.4 (1.94)	1,540 (46)	15.7 (0.41)

—Not available.
†Not applicable.
#Rounds to zero.
[1]Includes students in prekindergarten through grade 12 in schools that offer kindergarten or higher grade.
[2]Elementary schools have grade 6 or lower and no grade higher than 8. Secondary schools have no grade lower than 7. Combined schools include those that have grades lower than 7 and higher than 8, as well as those that do not classify students by grade level.
[3]Race/ethnicity was not collected for prekindergarten students (773,000 in fall 2011). Percentage distribution is based on the students for whom race/ethnicity was reported.

[4]For 1999, Pacific Islander students are included under Asian. Prior to 2009, data were not collected on Pacific Islander students as a separate category.
[5]Reported in full-time equivalents (FTE). Excludes teachers who teach only prekindergarten students.
NOTE: Tabulation includes schools that offer kindergarten or higher grade. Detail may not sum to totals because of rounding.
SOURCE: U.S. Department of Education, National Center for Education Statistics, Private School Universe Survey (PSS), 1999–2000, 2009–10, and 2011–12. (This table was prepared April 2013.)

Table 205.50. Private elementary and secondary enrollment, number of schools, and average tuition, by school level, orientation, and tuition: Selected years, 1999–2000 through 2011–12

[Standard errors appear in parentheses]

School orientation and tuition	Kindergarten through 12th-grade enrollment[1]				Total schools	Average tuition charged[2] (in current dollars)				Average tuition charged[2] (in constant 2013–14 dollars), total
	Total	Elementary	Secondary	Combined		Total	Elementary	Secondary	Combined	
1	2	3	4	5	6	7	8	9	10	11
1999–2000										
Total	5,262,850 (131,001)	2,920,680 (55,057)	818,920 (34,102)	1,523,240 (88,816)	27,220 (239)	$4,980 (157)	$3,740 (249)	$6,080 (175)	$6,760 (261)	$6,910 (218)
Catholic	2,548,710 (29,352)	1,810,330 (18,134)	616,200 (25,935)	122,190 (15,613)	8,100 (24)	3,340 (57)	2,600 (47)	4,830 (92)	6,890 (690)	4,640 (79)
Other religious	1,871,850 (36,782)	831,060 (41,035)	115,010 (10,981)	925,780 (66,926)	13,270 (237)	4,440 (153)	4,070 (130)	6,400 (456)	4,520 (280)	6,160 (213)
Nonsectarian	842,290 (61,373)	279,290 (28,987)	87,720 (11,774)	475,270 (43,377)	5,850 (76)	11,120 (775)	10,130 (1,921)	14,450 (1,461)	11,090 (801)	15,430 (1,075)
2003–04										
Total	5,059,450 (104,287)	2,675,960 (55,714)	832,320 (54,051)	1,551,170 (82,059)	28,380 (262)	$6,600 (145)	$5,050 (120)	$8,410 (433)	$8,300 (290)	$8,330 (182)
Catholic	2,320,040 (49,156)	1,645,680 (41,231)	584,250 (32,236)	90,110 (14,746)	7,920 (35)	4,250 (96)	3,530 (106)	6,050 (131)	5,800 (883)	5,370 (121)
Other religious	1,746,460 (63,090)	714,860 (28,935)	107,980 ! (33,776)	923,630 (48,379)	13,660 (203)	5,840 (144)	5,400 (161)	9,540 (963)	5,750 (230)	7,370 (182)
Nonsectarian	992,940 (71,519)	315,430 (30,820)	140,080 (27,556)	537,440 (59,332)	6,810 (136)	13,420 (379)	12,170 (468)	17,410 (1,988)	13,110 (480)	16,940 (479)
2007–08										
Total	5,165,280 (104,435)	2,462,980 (58,830)	850,750 (38,553)	1,851,550 (91,348)	28,220 (328)	$8,550 (176)	$6,730 (181)	$10,550 (356)	$10,050 (372)	$9,490 (195)
Less than $3,500	1,122,300 (50,988)	750,020 (35,402)	143,510 (19,815)	342,100 (35,615)	10,030 (344)	2,710 (61)	2,900 (54)	‡ (†)	2,350 (134)	3,010 (68)
$3,500 to $5,999	1,790,410 (77,850)	1,066,750 (45,444)	455,840 (33,376)	580,150 (53,528)	9,110 (341)	5,210 (42)	5,220 (49)	5,080 (80)	5,210 (89)	5,780 (46)
$6,000 to $9,999	1,155,290 (60,342)	366,470 (37,396)	125,660 (15,623)	237,850 (37,089)	4,460 (232)	8,260 (101)	9,230 (287)	7,660 (105)	8,030 (192)	9,170 (112)
$10,000 to $14,999	503,380 (45,776)	169,970 (26,731)	‡ (†)	358,470 (43,060)	1,980 (154)	13,640 (319)	15,730 (696)	12,910 (318)	12,910 (318)	15,140 (355)
$15,000 or more	593,900 (50,049)	109,770 (19,266)	‡ (†)	‡ (†)	2,650 (187)	25,890 (768)	25,360 (1,940)	28,400 (1,327)	25,180 (1,061)	28,740 (852)
Catholic	2,224,470 (49,385)	1,457,960 (32,114)	620,840 (32,581)	145,680 (25,445)	7,400 (34)	6,020 (180)	4,940 (212)	7,830 (232)	9,070 (964)	6,680 (200)
Less than $3,500	619,410 (37,867)	571,560 (34,303)	‡ (†)	‡ (†)	2,810 (132)	2,980 (55)	3,010 (57)	‡ (†)	‡ (†)	3,310 (61)
$3,500 to $5,999	826,120 (37,974)	683,980 (32,576)	111,770 (16,043)	‡ (†)	3,040 (131)	4,900 (49)	4,860 (57)	5,150 (80)	‡ (†)	5,440 (54)
$6,000 to $9,999	607,980 (49,329)	165,120 (28,123)	395,900 (30,158)	‡ (†)	1,170 (102)	7,680 (116)	7,790 (240)	7,650 (117)	‡ (†)	8,520 (129)
$10,000 to $14,999	‡ (†)	‡ (†)	‡ (†)	‡ (†)	‡ (†)	‡ (†)	‡ (†)	‡ (†)	‡ (†)	‡ (†)
$15,000 or more	‡ (†)	‡ (†)	‡ (†)	‡ (†)	‡ (†)	‡ (†)	‡ (†)	‡ (†)	‡ (†)	‡ (†)
Other religious	1,975,980 (81,216)	709,730 (36,666)	128,550 (15,136)	1,137,700 (75,038)	13,950 (282)	7,120 (237)	6,580 (241)	10,490 (1,336)	7,070 (359)	7,900 (263)
Less than $3,500	430,010 (31,875)	172,660 (14,154)	‡ (†)	252,490 (29,920)	6,180 (291)	2,520 (106)	2,550 (167)	‡ (†)	2,510 (133)	2,800 (118)
$3,500 to $5,999	860,370 (59,588)	340,150 (27,800)	57,150 (10,809)	489,390 (49,116)	5,030 (257)	5,370 (75)	5,570 (111)	‡ (†)	5,270 (101)	5,960 (83)
$6,000 to $9,999	384,850 (39,687)	103,280 (15,561)	‡ (†)	224,420 (33,273)	1,640 (137)	8,050 (155)	8,810 (430)	7,680 (188)	7,790 (164)	8,930 (172)
$10,000 to $14,999	167,770 (25,960)	‡ (†)	‡ (†)	‡ (†)	620 (83)	13,230 (401)	‡ (†)	‡ (†)	‡ (†)	14,680 (445)
$15,000 or more	132,980 (24,657)	‡ (†)	‡ (†)	‡ (†)	480 (91)	22,880 (1,053)	‡ (†)	‡ (†)	‡ (†)	25,390 (1,169)
Nonsectarian	964,830 (55,074)	295,280 (25,191)	101,370 (12,739)	568,180 (48,321)	6,860 (119)	17,320 (555)	15,940 (702)	27,300 (1,506)	16,250 (795)	19,220 (616)
Less than $3,500	72,890 (10,998)	42,610 (7,809)	‡ (†)	59,910 (10,584)	1,030 (125)	1,610 (387)	‡ (†)	‡ (†)	1,640 (467)	1,790 (429)
$3,500 to $5,999	103,930 (18,494)	98,070 (16,434)	‡ (†)	‡ (†)	1,040 (143)	6,290 (352)	8,090 (687)	‡ (†)	‡ (†)	6,980 (391)
$6,000 to $9,999	162,450 (24,872)	77,450 (15,769)	‡ (†)	‡ (†)	1,650 (168)	10,960 (530)	12,110 (792)	‡ (†)	‡ (†)	12,160 (589)
$10,000 to $14,999	208,670 (29,194)	‡ (†)	‡ (†)	126,610 (25,784)	1,150 (124)	14,890 (567)	17,750 (1,501)	13,230 (336)	13,230 (336)	16,530 (630)
$15,000 or more	416,900 (39,779)	71,360 (14,776)	85,870 (13,205)	259,670 (38,826)	2,000 (157)	26,500 (943)	25,010 (1,422)	25,350 (1,647)	25,350 (1,334)	29,410 (1,047)
2011–12										
Total	4,479,530 (105,651)	2,133,810 (59,964)	731,620 (53,646)	1,614,100 (98,602)	26,230 (541)	$10,740 (316)	$7,770 (211)	$13,030 (727)	$13,640 (753)	$11,090 (326)
Less than $3,500	618,710 (45,753)	404,700 (36,956)	42,580 ! (13,642)	171,430 (23,140)	7,950 (581)	2,190 (112)	2,410 (139)	1,370 (392)	1,870 (182)	2,260 (116)
$3,500 to $5,999	1,351,550 (64,739)	946,810 (56,403)	‡ (†)	364,520 (30,056)	7,800 (326)	5,300 (58)	5,350 (67)	‡ (†)	5,250 (118)	5,470 (60)
$6,000 to $9,999	1,167,820 (80,517)	467,040 (41,842)	275,980 (29,528)	424,800 (62,852)	5,070 (279)	8,560 (124)	9,090 (230)	7,980 (172)	8,360 (251)	8,840 (128)
$10,000 to $14,999	534,560 (45,926)	143,500 (18,976)	208,750 (38,977)	182,310 (36,985)	1,840 (150)	13,400 (207)	15,050 (454)	11,960 (225)	13,750 (348)	13,840 (214)
$15,000 or more	806,380 (69,846)	171,760 (25,237)	164,090 (32,298)	471,040 (65,345)	3,570 (194)	27,820 (951)	24,020 (960)	28,000 (2,487)	29,140 (1,274)	28,720 (982)
Catholic	1,892,480 (59,899)	1,244,480 (36,762)	511,870 (43,761)	136,130 (19,283)	6,760 (39)	6,890 (185)	5,330 (128)	9,790 (405)	10,230 (1,230)	7,110 (191)
Less than $3,500	307,610 (35,036)	259,330 (33,704)	‡ (†)	‡ (†)	1,730 (170)	2,580 (123)	2,690 (122)	‡ (†)	‡ (†)	2,660 (127)
$3,500 to $5,999	781,420 (53,974)	716,630 (50,260)	‡ (†)	‡ (†)	3,070 (187)	5,110 (68)	5,120 (72)	‡ (†)	‡ (†)	5,280 (70)
$6,000 to $9,999	516,660 (48,765)	243,570 (35,924)	234,460 (29,418)	‡ (†)	1,320 (126)	7,850 (139)	7,820 (210)	7,970 (199)	‡ (†)	8,110 (143)
$10,000 to $14,999	243,570 (36,032)	‡ (†)	177,560 (34,919)	‡ (†)	440 (68)	12,290 (240)	‡ (†)	12,020 (252)	‡ (†)	12,690 (248)
$15,000 or more	‡ (†)	‡ (†)	‡ (†)	‡ (†)	‡ (†)	‡ (†)	‡ (†)	‡ (†)	‡ (†)	‡ (†)

See notes at end of table.

Table 205.50. Private elementary and secondary enrollment, number of schools, and average tuition, by school level, orientation, and tuition: Selected years, 1999–2000 through 2011–12—Continued

[Standard errors appear in parentheses]

School orientation and tuition	Kindergarten through 12th-grade enrollment[1]				Total schools	Average tuition charged[2] (in current dollars)				Average tuition charged[2] (in constant 2013–14 dollars), total
	Total	Elementary	Secondary	Combined		Total	Elementary	Secondary	Combined	
1	2	3	4	5	6	7	8	9	10	11
Other religious	1,604,900 (84,424)	609,930 (38,479)	116,660 (31,187)	878,320 (77,923)	13,040 (550)	8,690 (397)	7,960 (447)	16,520 (2,288)	8,160 (518)	8,970 (410)
Less than $3,500	243,840 (25,511)	136,240 (19,015)	† (†)	103,980 (13,231)	5,190 (518)	2,090 (156)	1,860 (245)	† (†)	2,440 (169)	2,160 (162)
$3,500 to $5,999	507,660 (38,017)	214,270 (23,446)	† (†)	286,370 (28,337)	4,280 (259)	5,540 (101)	5,980 (183)	† (†)	5,220 (123)	5,720 (105)
$6,000 to $9,999	532,720 (61,948)	144,110 (26,978)	40,740 (7,928)	347,870 (59,370)	2,220 (228)	8,460 (186)	9,010 (269)	8,030 (196)	8,280 (260)	8,740 (192)
$10,000 to $14,999	165,130 (32,486)	‡ (‡)	‡ (‡)	‡ (†)	630 (89)	13,490 (359)	‡ (†)	‡ (†)	‡ (†)	13,930 (371)
$15,000 or more	155,550 (33,317)	‡ (‡)	‡ (‡)	‡ (†)	720 (126)	25,000 (2,243)	‡ (†)	‡ (†)	‡ (†)	25,810 (2,316)
Nonsectarian	982,140 (67,032)	279,400 (21,508)	103,090 (19,049)	599,650 (61,512)	6,430 (68)	21,510 (1,018)	18,170 (906)	25,180 (2,907)	22,440 (1,503)	22,210 (1,051)
Less than $3,500	67,260 (15,092)	‡ (‡)	‡ (‡)	47,370 ! (14,470)	1,040 (140)	740 ! (285)	‡ (†)	‡ (†)	490 ! (244)	760 ! (294)
$3,500 to $5,999	‡ (†)	‡ (‡)	‡ (‡)	‡ (†)	‡ (†)	‡ (†)	‡ (†)	‡ (†)	‡ (†)	‡ (†)
$6,000 to $9,999	118,440 (21,597)	79,370 (7,976)	‡ (‡)	‡ (†)	1,530 (119)	12,130 (628)	13,140 (683)	‡ (†)	‡ (†)	12,520 (649)
$10,000 to $14,999	148,280 (33,642)	59,130 (11,788)	‡ (‡)	‡ (†)	770 (106)	14,950 (418)	15,960 (908)	‡ (†)	‡ (†)	15,440 (432)
$15,000 or more	585,680 (66,696)	115,850 (20,781)	74,630 (16,406)	395,200 (61,972)	2,640 (165)	29,160 (1,092)	25,490 (1,219)	32,120 (3,206)	29,670 (1,368)	30,110 (1,127)

†Not applicable.

!Interpret data with caution. The coefficient of variation (CV) for this estimate is between 30 and 50 percent.

‡Reporting standards not met. Either there are too few cases for a reliable estimate or the coefficient of variation (CV) is 50 percent or greater.

[1]Only includes kindergarten students who attend schools that offer first or higher grade.

[2]Each school reports the highest annual tuition charged for a full-time student; this amount does not take into account discounts that individual students may receive. This amount is weighted by the number of students enrolled in each school and averaged.

NOTE: Excludes schools not offering first or higher grade. Elementary schools have grade 6 or lower and no grade higher than 8. Secondary schools have no grade lower than 7. Combined schools include those that have grades lower than 7 and higher than 8, as well as those that do not classify students by grade level. Excludes prekindergarten students. Includes a small percentage of schools reporting tuition of 0; these private schools are often under contract to public school districts to provide special education services. Detail may not sum to totals because of rounding and cell suppression. Some data have been revised from previously published figures.
SOURCE: U.S. Department of Education, National Center for Education Statistics, Schools and Staffing Survey (SASS), "Private School Data File," 1999–2000, 2003–04, 2007–08, and 2011–12. (This table was prepared in March 2015.)

Table 205.60. Private elementary and secondary school full-time-equivalent (FTE) staff and student to FTE staff ratios, by orientation of school, school level, and type of staff: 2007–08 and 2011–12

[Standard errors appear in parentheses]

Type of staff	Total, 2007–08	2011–12 Total				2011–12 Catholic[1]			
		Total	Elementary[1]	Secondary[2]	Combined[3]	Total	Elementary[1]	Secondary[2]	Combined[3]
1	2	3	4	5	6	7	8	9	10
Number of schools	28,220 (328)	26,230 (541)	15,000 (434)	2,820 (153)	8,400 (220)	6,760 (39)	5,300 (24)	1,040 (37)	410 (26)
Enrollment (in thousands)	5,165 (104)	4,480 (106)	2,134 (60)	732 (54)	1,614 (99)	1,892 (60)	1,244 (37)	512 (44M)	136 (19)
Number of FTE staff									
Total FTE staff	786,250 (16,261)	733,560 (17,373)	296,720 (8,627)	118,740 (8,321)	318,100 (17,125)	224,790 (7,201)	138,980 (3,830)	62,650 (5,069)	23,160 (2,739)
Principals	30,550 (463)	26,290 (497)	12,670 (319)	3,040 (159)	10,580 (410)	7,070 (115)	5,240 (83)	1,250 (50)	580 (66)
Assistant principals	13,120 (487)	11,280 (418)	4,160 (274)	2,510 (253)	4,610 (326)	3,270 (208)	1,470 (147)	1,460 (138)	350 (68)
Other managers	26,110 (952)	25,950 (872)	9,710 (511)	5,160 (479)	11,070 (707)	6,690 (410)	3,010 (252)	2,710 (312)	970 (142)
Instruction coordinators	7,850 (538)	7,630 (733)	2,310 (296)	1,440 ! (443)	3,880 (572)	1,280 (176)	550 (124)	500 (107)	230 (54)
Teachers	436,910 (8,665)	413,140 (9,516)	174,930 (4,690)	64,390 (4,936)	173,810 (10,001)	130,210 (3,981)	82,300 (2,281)	36,000 (2,853)	11,900 (1,567)
Teacher aides	53,740 (2,591)	52,440 (3,563)	25,210 (1,664)	2,370 (384)	24,860 (2,940)	14,260 (1,102)	11,350 (720)	450 ! (136)	2,460 ! (763)
Other aides	11,350 (1,251)	11,060 (2,290)	3,480 (374)	1,250 ! (400)	6,330 ! (2,122)	2,040 (281)	1,800 (260)	70 ! (28)	‡ (†)
Guidance counselors	11,780 (506)	11,040 (501)	2,140 (188)	3,590 (288)	5,310 (390)	4,220 (259)	1,390 (146)	2,320 (209)	500 (86)
Librarians/media specialists	12,190 (351)	11,190 (393)	5,230 (228)	1,610 (134)	4,350 (319)	4,300 (164)	3,080 (147)	900 (78)	320 (51)
Library/media center aides	4,150 (261)	2,650 (443)	1,320 (246)	‡ (†)	900 (152)	1,210 (215)	910 (220)	200 (46)	100 ! (30)
Nurses	8,340 (399)	7,600 (372)	3,010 (203)	1,680 (246)	2,900 (279)	2,890 (180)	2,070 (158)	600 (122)	230 (51)
Student support staff[4]	24,920 (1,236)	23,010 (1,629)	5,510 (482)	4,190 (617)	13,300 (1,516)	4,420 (468)	2,210 (230)	1,350 (254)	860 ! (298)
Secretaries/clerical staff	50,360 (1,441)	42,730 (1,382)	15,420 (586)	8,210 (753)	19,090 (1,203)	13,460 (584)	7,080 (208)	5,160 (471)	1,220 (186)
Food service personnel	28,080 (1,019)	25,040 (1,196)	9,620 (549)	5,220 (583)	10,210 (998)	10,470 (625)	6,530 (435)	3,000 (383)	940 (142)
Custodial and maintenance	45,660 (1,469)	38,300 (1,482)	14,450 (614)	7,230 (527)	16,630 (1,369)	12,820 (576)	7,410 (325)	4,210 (393)	1,210 (185)
Other employees[5]	21,140 (2,717)	24,230 (3,023)	7,550 (1,820)	6,420 (1,602)	10,260 ! (1,975)	6,180 (1,381)	2,570 ! (921)	2,480 (735)	1,120 ! (508)
Students per FTE staff member									
Total FTE staff	7 (0.1)	6 (0.1)	7 (0.1)	6 (0.3)	5 (0.2)	8 (0.1)	9 (0.1)	8 (0.2)	6 (0.6)
Principals	169 (2.9)	170 (3.4)	168 (4.1)	241 (16.1)	153 (6.4)	268 (7.7)	237 (7.2)	409 (28.9)	235 (23.1)
Assistant principals	394 (12.3)	397 (14.5)	512 (30.9)	292 (20.2)	350 (23.5)	579 (28.4)	847 (77.4)	352 (19.1)	394 (69.0)
Other managers	198 (6.0)	173 (6.0)	220 (11.2)	142 (11.0)	146 (9.3)	283 (14.1)	413 (33.4)	189 (15.0)	140 (21.5)
Instruction coordinators	658 (43.1)	587 (54.5)	925 (125.5)	507 (128.0)	416 (64.9)	1,480 (198.3)	2,253 (653.7)	1,022 (226.7)	605 ! (223.6)
Teachers	12 (0.1)	11 (0.2)	12 (0.2)	11 (0.5)	9 (0.2)	15 (0.2)	15 (0.3)	14 (0.3)	11 (0.5)
Teacher aides	96 (4.8)	85 (5.9)	85 (5.0)	308 (57.9)	65 (8.9)	133 (10.6)	110 (6.3)	‡ (†)	‡ (†)
Other aides	455 (52.2)	405 (78.2)	614 (64.7)	‡ (†)	255 ! (80.4)	929 (144.9)	692 (107.9)	‡ (†)	‡ (†)
Guidance counselors	439 (16.1)	406 (15.0)	998 (84.7)	204 (9.3)	304 ! (16.0)	448 (21.0)	894 (96.6)	220 (7.9)	270 (34.6)
Librarians/media specialists	424 (9.5)	400 (13.0)	408 (15.7)	455 (35.2)	371 (20.6)	440 (17.9)	404 (22.0)	571 (30.4)	421 (46.3)
Library/media center aides	1,243 (75.1)	1,692 (229.0)	1,615 (281.5)	1,696 ! (636.7)	1,803 (329.9)	1,570 (259.6)	1,374 (328.5)	2,512 (665.0)	1,416 ! (510.9)
Nurses	619 (26.1)	590 (31.8)	709 (41.8)	434 (83.1)	556 (55.8)	654 (45.4)	602 (39.8)	860 ! (269.8)	594 (152.5)
Student support staff[4]	207 (9.9)	195 (14.1)	387 (32.3)	174 (26.7)	121 (12.7)	428 (49.0)	562 (61.8)	380 (98.6)	‡ (†)
Secretaries/clerical staff	103 (2.1)	105 (2.6)	138 (4.2)	89 (4.9)	85 (3.5)	141 (4.6)	176 (5.9)	99 (5.2)	112 (13.1)
Food service personnel	184 (6.2)	179 (7.8)	222 (12.1)	140 (15.9)	158 (13.9)	181 (9.1)	191 (12.0)	171 (17.8)	144 (26.5)
Custodial and maintenance	113 (2.8)	117 (3.8)	148 (5.0)	101 (5.4)	97 (6.2)	148 (4.5)	168 (5.8)	122 (6.2)	113 (15.5)
Other employees[5]	244 (29.0)	185 (24.0)	283 (62.5)	114 (32.0)	157 (37.1)	306 (71.6)	‡ (†)	206 ! (66.7)	‡ (†)

See notes at end of table.

Table 205.60. Private elementary and secondary school full-time-equivalent (FTE) staff and student to FTE staff ratios, by orientation of school, school level, and type of staff: 2007–08 and 2011–12—Continued

[Standard errors appear in parentheses]

2011–12

Type of staff	Other religious orientation				Nonsectarian			
	Total	Elementary¹	Secondary²	Combined³	Total	Elementary¹	Secondary²	Combined³
	11	12	13	14	15	16	17	18
Number of FTE staff								
Number of schools	13,040 (550)	6,860 (433)	890 (146)	5,290 (226)	6,430 (68)	2,840 (48)	890 (19)	2,700 (65)
Enrollment (in thousands)	1,605 (84)	610 (38)	117 (31)	878 (78)	982 (67)	279 (22)	103 (19)	600 (62)
Total FTE staff	254,000 (11,431)	92,610 (6,078)	25,040 (6,246)	136,350 (10,252)	254,770 (14,961)	65,140 (3,983)	31,050 (4,110)	158,590 (13,610)
Principals	11,990 (419)	4,760 (291)	840 (141)	6,390 (350)	7,230 (249)	2,670 (106)	950 (63)	3,610 (215)
Assistant principals	4,000 (300)	1,320 (177)	540 ! (228)	2,140 (221)	4,020 (338)	1,380 (165)	510 (108)	2,130 (278)
Other managers	8,790 (592)	3,230 (280)	1,120 ! (377)	4,440 (375)	10,470 (734)	3,470 (322)	1,330 (238)	5,670 (620)
Instruction coordinators	2,790 (470)	790 (135)	‡ (†)	1,470 (236)	3,560 (529)	960 (200)	410 ! (125)	2,190 (487)
Teachers	154,650 (6,944)	56,490 (3,508)	13,990 (3,896)	84,170 (6,547)	128,280 (8,136)	36,140 (2,384)	14,400 (2,231)	77,740 (7,508)
Teacher aides	12,200 (1,070)	7,250 (987)	310 ! (132)	4,630 (522)	25,980 (3,077)	6,610 (809)	1,610 (354)	17,760 (2,705)
Other aides	2,990 (585)	780 (158)	320 ! (140)	1,900 (512)	6,020 ! (2,194)	900 (203)	870 ! (384)	4,260 ! (2,068)
Guidance counselors	3,080 (276)	370 (67)	600 ! (183)	2,120 (208)	3,740 (370)	380 (104)	670 (112)	2,690 (328)
Librarians/media specialists	3,630 (240)	1,290 (134)	390 (112)	1,960 (199)	3,260 (283)	870 (98)	320 (63)	2,070 (252)
Library/media center aides	730 ! (330)	240 (63)	‡ (†)	320 (88)	710 (146)	170 ! (60)	‡ (†)	470 (132)
Nurses	1,740 (182)	530 (71)	400 ! (121)	810 (115)	2,960 (310)	410 (74)	690 (190)	1,860 (258)
Student support staff	4,050 (436)	1,550 (245)	810 ! (405)	1,680 (335)	14,540 (1,529)	1,750 (342)	2,030 (448)	10,760 (1,372)
Secretaries/clerical staff	16,000 (966)	5,510 (457)	1,610 ! (593)	8,890 (730)	13,270 (1,017)	2,830 (293)	1,450 (333)	8,980 (900)
Food service personnel	8,290 (813)	2,300 (238)	1,050 (264)	4,940 (718)	6,280 (886)	790 (155)	1,170 ! (392)	4,320 (756)
Custodial and maintenance	13,150 (904)	4,250 (358)	1,410 (323)	7,480 (804)	12,330 (1,101)	2,790 (347)	1,600 (348)	7,930 (998)
Other employees⁵	5,910 (1,690)	‡ (†)	970 ! (450)	2,990 (762)	12,130 (2,194)	3,020 (831)	2,970 ! (1,293)	6,150 (1,810)
Students per FTE staff member								
Total FTE staff	6 (0.2)	7 (0.2)	5 (0.5)	6 (0.2)	4 (0.1)	4 (0.2)	3 (0.4)	4 (0.2)
Principals	134 (5.5)	128 (6.4)	140 (26.9)	137 (8.9)	136 (7.6)	105 (7.9)	108 (21.6)	166 (13.0)
Assistant principals	402 (30.3)	464 (58.8)	217 (49.8)	410 (44.2)	245 (18.1)	203 (23.1)	202 (42.8)	282 (30.8)
Other managers	183 (11.8)	189 (16.7)	104 (17.1)	198 (16.3)	94 (6.1)	80 (5.5)	78 (16.8)	106 (11.1)
Instruction coordinators	575 (88.4)	769 (136.5)	‡ (†)	598 (107.7)	276 (40.2)	291 (64.2)	250 ! (116.8)	274 (66.3)
Teachers	10 (0.3)	11 (0.3)	8 (1.1)	10 (0.4)	8 (0.2)	8 (0.3)	7 (0.7)	8 (0.3)
Teacher aides	132 (12.6)	84 (9.7)	‡ (†)	190 (23.3)	38 (4.8)	42 (5.9)	64 (16.6)	34 (6.1)
Other aides	536 (110.3)	785 (171.8)	‡ (†)	462 ! (141.0)	163 ! (64.9)	310 (82.7)	‡ (†)	‡ (†)
Guidance counselors	520 (36.9)	1,653 (313.9)	195 (46.5)	415 (24.6)	263 (20.3)	743 (219.1)	154 (22.6)	223 (20.8)
Librarians/media specialists	442 (26.3)	475 (37.3)	301 ! (99.7)	448 (39.1)	301 (15.9)	322 (29.6)	319 (44.4)	290 (20.1)
Library/media center aides	2,196 (593.2)	2,512 (626.7)	‡ (†)	2,711 ! (866.0)	1,381 (257.5)	‡ (†)	‡ (†)	1,262 (352.2)
Nurses	922 (107.2)	1,154 (131.9)	143 ! (65.7)	1,080 (160.3)	331 (34.0)	679 (160.0)	149 ! (54.5)	322 (46.9)
Student support staff	396 (43.6)	394 (51.9)	73 (11.9)	521 (105.2)	68 (7.4)	160 (33.7)	51 (14.7)	56 (7.4)
Secretaries/clerical staff	100 (4.6)	111 (6.7)	‡ (†)	99 (6.0)	74 (3.5)	99 (7.3)	71 (11.0)	67 (4.6)
Food service personnel	194 (17.2)	265 (27.7)	82 (16.4)	178 (21.3)	156 (19.4)	354 (82.1)	88 ! (32.9)	139 (24.1)
Custodial and maintenance	122 (6.7)	143 (10.7)	‡ (†)	117 (9.1)	80 (4.6)	100 (9.0)	64 (11.3)	76 (6.7)
Other employees⁵	271 (64.9)	311 ! (131.9)	‡ (†)	294 ! (90.0)	81 (18.5)	93 ! (36.7)	‡ (†)	98 ! (45.5)

†Not applicable.
‡Reporting standards not met. The coefficient of variation (CV) for this estimate is 50 percent or greater.
! Interpret data with caution. The coefficient of variation (CV) for this estimate is between 30 and 50 percent.
¹Includes schools beginning with grade 6 or below and with no grade higher than 8.
²Schools with no grade lower than 7.
³Schools with grades lower than 7 and higher than 8, as well as schools that do not classify students by grade level.
⁴Includes student support services professional staff, such as school psychologists, social workers, and speech therapists or pathologists.

⁵Includes other employees not identified by function.
NOTE: FTE staff consists of the total number of full-time staff, plus 48 percent of the part-time staff; this percentage was estimated based on the number of hours that part-time staff reported working. Data are based on a sample survey and may not be strictly comparable with data reported elsewhere. Excludes all prekindergarten students from calculations, but includes kindergarten students attending schools that offer first or higher grade. Includes only schools that offer first or higher grade. Detail may not sum to totals because of rounding. Some data have been revised from previously published figures.
SOURCE: U.S. Department of Education, National Center for Education Statistics, Schools and Staffing Survey (SASS), "Private School Data File," 2007–08 and 2011–12. (This table was prepared June 2013.)

Table 205.70. Enrollment and instructional staff in Catholic elementary and secondary schools, by level: Selected years, 1919–20 through 2013–14

School year	Number of schools			Enrollment[1]				Instructional staff[2]		
	Total	Elementary[3]	Secondary	Total	Pre-kindergarten	Elementary	Secondary	Total	Elementary[3]	Secondary
1	2	3	4	5	6	7	8	9	10	11
1919–20	8,103	6,551	1,552	1,925,521	([4])	1,795,673	129,848	49,516	41,592	7,924
1929–30	10,046	7,923	2,123	2,464,467	([4])	2,222,598	241,869	72,552	58,245	14,307
1939–40	10,049	7,944	2,105	2,396,305	([4])	2,035,182	361,123	81,057	60,081	20,976
1949–50	10,778	8,589	2,189	3,066,387	([4])	2,560,815	505,572	94,295	66,525	27,770
Fall 1960	12,893	10,501	2,392	5,253,791	([4])	4,373,422	880,369	151,902	108,169	43,733
1969–70	11,352	9,366	1,986	4,367,000	([4])	3,359,000	1,008,000	195,400 [5]	133,200 [5]	62,200 [5]
1970–71	11,350	9,370	1,980	4,363,566	([4])	3,355,478	1,008,088	166,208	112,750	53,458
1974–75	10,127	8,437	1,690	3,504,000	([4])	2,602,000	902,000	150,179	100,011	50,168
1975–76	9,993	8,340	1,653	3,415,000	([4])	2,525,000	890,000	149,276	99,319	49,957
1979–80	9,640	8,100	1,540	3,139,000	([4])	2,293,000	846,000	147,294	97,724	49,570
1980–81	9,559	8,043	1,516	3,106,000	([4])	2,269,000	837,000	145,777	96,739	49,038
1981–82	9,494	7,996	1,498	3,094,000	([4])	2,266,000	828,000	146,172	96,847	49,325
1982–83	9,432	7,950	1,482	3,007,189	([4])	2,211,412	795,777	146,460	97,337	49,123
1983–84	9,401	7,937	1,464	2,969,000	([4])	2,179,000	790,000	146,913	98,591	48,322
1984–85	9,325	7,876	1,449	2,903,000	([4])	2,119,000	784,000	149,888	99,820	50,068
1985–86	9,220	7,790	1,430	2,821,000	([4])	2,061,000	760,000	146,594	96,741	49,853
1986–87	9,102	7,693	1,409	2,726,000	([4])	1,998,000	728,000	141,930	93,554	48,376
1987–88	8,992	7,601	1,391	2,690,668	67,637	1,942,148	680,883	139,887	93,199	46,688
1988–89	8,867	7,505	1,362	2,627,745	76,626	1,911,911	639,208	137,700	93,154	44,546
1989–90	8,719	7,395	1,324	2,588,893	90,023	1,892,913	605,957	136,900	94,197	42,703
1990–91	8,587	7,291	1,296	2,575,815	100,376	1,883,906	591,533	131,198	91,039	40,159
1991–92	8,508	7,239	1,269	2,550,863	107,939	1,856,302	586,622	153,334	109,084	44,250
1992–93	8,423	7,174	1,249	2,567,630	122,788	1,860,937	583,905	154,816	109,825	44,991
1993–94	8,345	7,114	1,231	2,576,845	132,236	1,859,947	584,662	157,201	112,199	45,002
1994–95	8,293	7,055	1,238	2,618,567	143,360	1,877,782	597,425	164,219	117,620	46,599
1995–96	8,250	7,022	1,228	2,635,210	144,099	1,884,461	606,650	166,759	118,753	48,006
1996–97	8,231	7,005	1,226	2,645,462	148,264	1,885,037	612,161	153,276	107,548	45,728
1997–98	8,223	7,004	1,219	2,648,859	150,965	1,879,737	618,157	152,259	105,717	46,542
1998–99	8,217	6,990	1,227	2,648,844	152,356	1,876,211	620,277	153,081	105,943	47,138
1999–2000	8,144	6,923	1,221	2,653,038	152,622	1,877,236	623,180	157,134	109,404	47,730
2000–01	8,146	6,920	1,226	2,647,301	155,742	1,863,682	627,877	160,731	111,937	48,794
2001–02	8,114	6,886	1,228	2,616,330	159,869	1,827,319	629,142	155,658	108,485	47,173
2002–03	8,000	6,785	1,215	2,553,277	157,250	1,765,893	630,134	163,004	112,884	50,120
2003–04	7,955	6,727	1,228	2,484,252	150,422	1,708,501	625,329	162,337	112,303	50,034
2004–05	7,799	6,574	1,225	2,420,590	150,905	1,642,868	626,817	160,153	107,764	52,389
2005–06	7,589	6,386	1,203	2,325,220	146,327	1,568,687	610,206	152,502 [6]	103,481 [6]	49,021 [6]
2006–07	7,498	6,288	1,210	2,320,651	152,429	1,544,695	623,527	159,135	107,682	51,453
2007–08	7,378	6,165	1,213	2,270,913	152,980	1,494,979	622,954	160,075	107,217	52,858
2008–09	7,248	6,028	1,220	2,192,531	153,325	1,434,949	604,257	157,615	105,518	52,097
2009–10	7,094	5,889	1,205	2,119,341	150,262	1,375,982	593,097	154,316	103,460	50,856
2010–11	6,980	5,774	1,206	2,065,872	152,846	1,336,560	576,466	151,473	102,365	49,108
2011–12	6,841	5,636	1,205	2,031,455	154,282	1,303,028	574,145	151,395	100,365	51,030
2012–13	6,685	5,472	1,213	2,001,740	156,233	1,278,010	567,497	151,405	100,633	50,772
2013–14	6,594	5,399	1,195	1,974,578	158,537	1,252,397	563,644	151,351	100,244	51,107

[1]Elementary enrollment is for kindergarten through grade 8, and secondary enrollment is for grades 9 through 12.
[2]From 1919–20 through fall 1960, includes part-time teachers. From 1969–70 through 1993–94, excludes part-time teachers. Beginning in 1994–95, reported in full-time equivalents (FTE). Prekindergarten teachers not counted separately but may be included with elementary teachers.
[3]Includes middle schools.
[4]Prekindergarten enrollment was not reported separately, but may be included in elementary enrollment.
[5]Includes estimates for the nonreporting schools.

[6]Excludes the Archdiocese of New Orleans.
NOTE: Data collected by the National Catholic Educational Association and data collected by the National Center for Education Statistics are not directly comparable because survey procedures and definitions differ.
SOURCE: National Catholic Educational Association, *A Statistical Report on Catholic Elementary and Secondary Schools for the Years 1967–68 to 1969–70; A Report on Catholic Schools*, 1970–71 through 1973–74; *A Statistical Report on U.S. Catholic Schools*, 1974–75 through 1980–81; and *United States Catholic Elementary and Secondary Schools*, 1981–82 through 2013–14, retrieved November 19, 2014, from http://www.ncea.org/data-information/catholic-school-data. (This table was prepared November 2014.)

Table 205.80. Private elementary and secondary schools, enrollment, teachers, and high school graduates, by state: Selected years, 2001 through 2011

[Standard errors appear in parentheses]

State	Schools, fall 2011		Enrollment in prekindergarten through grade 12												Teachers,[1] fall 2011		High school graduates, 2010–11	
			Fall 2001		Fall 2003		Fall 2005		Fall 2007		Fall 2009		Fall 2011					
1	2		3		4		5		6		7		8		9		10	
United States	30,860	(542)	6,319,650	(40,272)	6,099,220	(41,219)	6,073,240	(42,446)	5,910,210	(28,363)	5,488,490	(35,857)	5,268,090	(24,908)	420,880	(1,836)	305,840	(3,479)
Alabama	400	(1)	92,380	(3,926)	99,580	(12,130)	92,280	(5,892)	83,840	(103)	95,570	(11,745)	81,070	(49)	6,210	(1)	4,720	(†)
Alaska	50	(†)	7,420	(†)	7,370	(424)	7,500	(1,028)	4,990	(†)	7,510 !	(2,740)	5,170	(†)	420	(†)	220	(†)
Arizona	340	(5)	78,660	(18,218)	75,360	(16,426)	66,840	(†)	64,910	(†)	55,390	(†)	53,120	(229)	3,810	(16)	2,650	(†)
Arkansas	230 !	(73)	32,570	(†)	31,300	(†)	35,390	(5,858)	40,120	(11,961)	28,900	(1,371)	29,930	(1,245)	2,640	(337)	1,490	(†)
California	3,480	(2)	757,750	(8,415)	740,460	(8,703)	737,490	(15,529)	703,810	(6,129)	623,150	(4,185)	608,070	(69)	44,270	(12)	34,380	(1)
Colorado	410	(2)	64,700	(†)	62,080	(476)	70,770	(1,160)	64,740	(†)	63,720	(3,486)	61,140	(148)	4,880	(4)	2,890	(†)
Connecticut	410	(18)	82,320	(†)	102,960	(25,024)	76,220	(1,619)	85,150	(9,241)	72,540	(464)	66,320	(142)	7,080	(68)	5,960	(†)
Delaware	120	(†)	31,690	(1,023)	33,020	(2,649)	29,830	(†)	32,520	(2,701)	26,640	(†)	25,090	(†)	2,060	(†)	1,770	(†)
District of Columbia	80	(†)	33,660 !	(14,373)	23,510	(6,121)	19,880	(†)	19,640	(†)	17,810	(†)	16,950	(†)	1,960	(†)	1,510	(†)
Florida	1,880	(2)	365,890	(8,301)	398,720	(14,590)	396,790	(7,429)	391,660	(6,123)	343,990	(1,023)	340,960	(230)	26,430	(37)	20,060	(†)
Georgia	710	(†)	137,060	(4,550)	144,850	(6,527)	152,600	(10,394)	157,430	(9,185)	150,300	(6,251)	138,080	(†)	13,010	(†)	7,760	(†)
Hawaii	130	(†)	42,980	(220)	39,940	(†)	32,810	(†)	37,300	(290)	37,130	(†)	37,530	(†)	3,010	(†)	2,760	(†)
Idaho	120	(4)	12,050	(†)	12,570	(†)	15,320	(2,518)	24,700 !	(11,608)	18,680	(4,814)	13,670	(193)	990	(17)	580	(4)
Illinois	1,570	(53)	357,390	(19,293)	316,430	(1,698)	317,940	(4,263)	312,270	(6,638)	289,720	(9,237)	271,030	(1,289)	19,150	(221)	14,500	(49)
Indiana	970	(198)	129,240	(326)	124,500	(455)	139,370	(17,870)	119,910	(2,284)	120,770	(5,919)	129,120	(12,177)	8,900	(995)	5,620	(374)
Iowa	300	(51)	51,540	(†)	53,850	(4,634)	60,960	(8,311)	47,820	(†)	45,160	(†)	63,840	(14,665)	4,700	(1,078)	‡	(†)
Kansas	400 !	(193)	51,540	(8,341)	47,710	(2,151)	47,130	(1,654)	47,780	(2,414)	44,680	(1,668)	43,100	(1,640)	3,530	(446)	2,260	(†)
Kentucky	330	(1)	85,230	(3,227)	82,100	(1,525)	78,880	(1,228)	76,140	(2,074)	70,590	(2,132)	69,410	(12)	5,240	(1)	4,130	(†)
Louisiana	390	(2)	159,910	(11,381)	155,780	(3,515)	138,270	(525)	137,460	(†)	147,040	(9,890)	125,720	(108)	8,830	(5)	7,510	(†)
Maine	160	(†)	20,820	(174)	24,740	(3,629)	20,680	(337)	21,260	(143)	18,310	(†)	18,350	(†)	2,000	(†)	2,600	(†)
Maryland	740	(8)	175,740	(†)	172,360	(†)	170,350	(4,201)	165,760	(1,160)	145,690	(160)	137,450	(564)	12,430	(42)	8,830	(†)
Massachusetts	800	(44)	177,490	(9,836)	164,390	(6,636)	157,770	(3,273)	151,640	(2,516)	137,110	(1,169)	130,940	(1,596)	14,060	(323)	10,130	(†)
Michigan	790	(7)	198,380	(†)	180,080	(†)	166,950	(407)	159,100	(2,047)	153,230	(5,828)	135,580	(544)	9,290	(52)	7,290	(†)
Minnesota	500	(†)	112,310	(2,993)	106,010	(3,011)	104,730	(3,467)	101,740	(3,903)	89,530	(†)	87,620	(†)	6,420	(†)	4,710	(†)
Mississippi	220	(†)	67,380	(10,106)	57,110	(2,981)	57,930	(4,104)	55,270	(†)	54,650	(2,458)	52,060	(†)	4,120	(†)	3,250	(†)
Missouri	1,270 !	(468)	138,140	(4,321)	141,530	(9,966)	137,810	(10,580)	125,610	(3,685)	117,970	(2,065)	130,130	(8,715)	10,510	(951)	7,530	(89)
Montana	110	(†)	12,930	(1,895)	12,510	(2,091)	‡	(†)	15,030 !	(5,465)	10,390	(1,221)	10,550	(†)	980	(†)	430	(†)
Nebraska	220	(†)	45,590	(618)	41,650	(†)	42,420	(†)	40,320	(†)	39,040	(†)	40,750	(†)	2,840	(†)	2,300	(†)
Nevada	160	(†)	20,370	(385)	23,930	(†)	29,120	(†)	29,820	(2,009)	25,060	(†)	26,130	(†)	1,590	(†)	900	(†)
New Hampshire	280	(†)	38,650	(†)	33,780	(†)	33,220	(†)	30,920	(†)	26,470	(†)	27,350	(†)	2,670	(†)	2,520	(†)
New Jersey	1,290	(18)	282,450	(4,182)	269,530	(7,577)	256,160	(8,439)	253,250	(5,016)	232,020	(16,536)	210,220	(1,211)	16,850	(208)	12,980	(71)
New Mexico	170	(1)	26,510	(†)	29,310	(3,928)	25,030	(141)	27,290	(1,388)	23,730	(507)	22,680	(10)	1,940	(2)	1,280	(†)
New York	1,930	(31)	559,670	(1,669)	515,620	(4,071)	510,750	(3,596)	518,850	(7,196)	486,310	(5,211)	487,810	(19,574)	41,450	(821)	30,440	(1,462)
North Carolina	640	(†)	116,500	(4,112)	126,230	(11,439)	117,280	(11,681)	121,660	(2,226)	110,740	(1,851)	119,070	(†)	10,680	(†)	6,310	(†)
North Dakota	50	(†)	7,180	(†)	6,840	(†)	7,290	(†)	7,430	(†)	7,750	(†)	7,770	(†)	590	(†)	410	(†)
Ohio	970	(59)	290,370	(7,180)	270,660	(7,094)	254,530	(9,821)	239,520	(2,741)	246,250	(24,214)	213,990	(3,419)	15,270	(396)	12,860	(124)
Oklahoma	180	(10)	46,570	(8,723)	34,300	(2,013)	35,350	(1,194)	40,320	(5,032)	34,000	(716)	35,750	(847)	3,000	(72)	1,760	(17)
Oregon	430	(†)	71,500	(15,519)	54,320	(†)	69,620	(14,139)	66,260	(5,188)	56,820	(3,502)	53,200	(†)	3,820	(†)	2,970	(†)
Pennsylvania	2,320	(60)	374,490	(†)	357,580	(3,364)	332,740	(3,918)	324,020	(6,253)	301,640	(5,036)	276,300	(3,668)	21,960	(468)	16,370	(90)
Rhode Island	140	(†)	30,970	(†)	31,960	(†)	30,600	(†)	28,260	(1,096)	24,940	(†)	25,420	(†)	2,360	(†)	2,020	(†)
South Carolina	380	(†)	70,950	(†)	73,800	(†)	70,240	(1,797)	71,430	(1,043)	62,320	(311)	60,890	(†)	5,000	(†)	2,960	(†)
South Dakota	70	(†)	11,740	(†)	11,980	(†)	12,700	(†)	12,280	(†)	11,470	(†)	12,490	(†)	970	(†)	650	(†)
Tennessee	510	(1)	98,790	(†)	93,390	(†)	105,240	(2,531)	117,540	(12,851)	98,310	(4,176)	92,430	(34)	8,150	(2)	5,860	(†)
Texas	1,500	(18)	314,210	(12,244)	271,380	(2,758)	304,170	(20,453)	296,540	(4,132)	313,360	(11,968)	285,320	(2,046)	23,360	(101)	12,840	(489)
Utah	160	(2)	20,040	(†)	19,990	(†)	21,220	(†)	20,860	(†)	21,990	(1,558)	18,660	(55)	1,620	(6)	1,210	(1)
Vermont	110	(†)	14,090	(†)	12,730	(†)	11,530	(†)	12,600	(232)	10,350	(†)	9,030	(†)	1,200	(†)	1,000	(†)
Virginia	750	(2)	129,470	(†)	131,160	(6,936)	155,220	(14,290)	143,140	(7,988)	128,140	(2,581)	123,780	(82)	10,980	(11)	6,400	(1)
Washington	630	(5)	91,150	(2,028)	101,130	(7,935)	119,640	(13,187)	104,070	(3,054)	94,340	(625)	93,630	(234)	7,130	(21)	4,210	(30)
West Virginia	120	(1)	16,560	(†)	15,300	(†)	16,120	(†)	14,980	(†)	13,860	(†)	13,430	(1)	1,130	(†)	660	(1)
Wisconsin	840	(†)	162,220	(9,080)	159,240	(11,743)	142,280	(137)	138,290	(1,597)	130,510	(†)	127,250	(†)	9,150	(†)	5,420	(†)
Wyoming	40	(†)	2,430	(†)	2,600	(†)	2,310	(†)	2,930	(†)	2,910	(†)	2,740	(†)	260	(†)	30	(†)

†Not applicable.
!Interpret data with caution. The coefficient of variation (CVV) for this estimate is between 30 and 50 percent.
‡Reporting standards not met. The coefficient of variation (CV) for this estimate is 50 percent or greater.
[1]Reported in full-time equivalents (FTE). Excludes teachers who teach only prekindergarten students.

NOTE: Includes special education, vocational/technical education, and alternative schools. Tabulation includes schools that offer kindergarten or higher grade. Includes enrollment of students in prekindergarten through grade 12 in schools that offer kindergarten or higher grade. Detail may not sum to totals because of rounding.
SOURCE: U.S. Department of Education, National Center for Education Statistics, Private School Universe Survey (PSS), 2001–02 through 2011–12. (This table was prepared May 2013.)

Table 206.10. Number and percentage of homeschooled students ages 5 through 17 with a grade equivalent of kindergarten through 12th grade, by selected child, parent, and household characteristics: 2003, 2007, and 2012

[Standard errors appear in parentheses]

Selected child, parent, or household characteristic	2003 Number of students[1] (in thousands)	2003 Number homeschooled[2] (in thousands)	2003 Percent homeschooled[2]	2007 Number of students[1] (in thousands)	2007 Number homeschooled[2] (in thousands)	2007 Percent homeschooled[2]	2012 Number of students[1] (in thousands)	2012 Number homeschooled[2] (in thousands)	2012 Percent homeschooled[2]
1	2	3	4	5	6	7	8	9	10
Total	50,707 (89.3)	1,096 (92.3)	2.2 (0.18)	51,135 (155.3)	1,520 (118.0)	3.0 (0.23)	51,657 (98.7)	1,773[3] (115.7)	3.4[3] (0.23)
Sex of child									
Male	25,819 (286.8)	569 (61.9)	2.2 (0.24)	26,286 (355.6)	639 (75.1)	2.4 (0.28)	26,620 (318.2)	499 (48.0)	1.9 (0.18)
Female	24,888 (277.7)	527 (58.2)	2.1 (0.23)	24,849 (386.9)	881 (97.4)	3.5 (0.39)	25,037 (314.0)	583 (63.4)	2.3 (0.25)
Race/ethnicity of child									
White	31,584 (187.2)	843 (77.5)	2.7 (0.25)	29,815 (197.9)	1,171 (102.2)	3.9 (0.34)	26,978 (161.7)	893 (81.2)	3.3 (0.30)
Black	7,985 (45.7)	‡ (†)	‡ (†)	7,523 (114.0)	‡ (†)	‡ (†)	7,191 (45.8)	‡ (†)	‡ (†)
Hispanic	8,075 (35.1)	‡ (†)	‡ (†)	9,589 (84.8)	147 (27.5)	1.5 (0.29)	11,814 (55.1)	72 (17.3)	0.6 (0.15)
Asian/Pacific Islander	1,432 (114.5)	‡ (†)	‡ (†)	1,580 (122.9)	‡ (†)	‡ (†)	2,849 (118.4)	‡ (†)	‡ (†)
Other	1,631 (127.7)	‡ (†)	‡ (†)	2,629 (141.0)	‡ (†)	‡ (†)	2,825 (120.0)	‡ (†)	‡ (†)
Grade equivalent[4]									
Kindergarten through grade 5	24,269 (24.7)	472 (55.3)	1.9 (0.23)	23,529 (68.1)	717 (83.8)	3.0 (0.36)	25,842 (141.1)	423 (61.1)	1.6 (0.24)
Kindergarten	3,643 (24.7)	‡ (†)	‡ (†)	3,669 (67.9)	‡ (†)	‡ (†)	5,295 (136.2)	‡ (†)	‡ (†)
Grades 1 through 3	12,098 (#)	214 (33.3)	1.8 (0.28)	11,965 (2.4)	406 (64.5)	3.4 (0.54)	12,101 (135.0)	203 (45.6)	1.7 (0.38)
Grades 4 through 5	8,528 (#)	160 (30.1)	1.9 (0.35)	7,895 (0.7)	197 (41.4)	2.5 (0.52)	8,446 (128.1)	142 (26.1)	1.7 (0.31)
Grades 6 through 8	12,472 (6.5)	302 (44.9)	2.4 (0.36)	12,435 (0.7)	371 (65.3)	3.0 (0.53)	12,006 (139.1)	317 (44.3)	2.6 (0.37)
Grades 9 through 12	13,958 (81.8)	315 (47.0)	2.3 (0.33)	15,161 (129.3)	422 (58.2)	2.8 (0.38)	13,808 (112.0)	341 (42.8)	2.5 (0.31)
Number of children in the household									
One child	8,033 (218.1)	110 (22.3)	1.4 (0.27)	8,463 (227.1)	197 (32.5)	2.3 (0.38)	10,899 (182.6)	179 (21.4)	1.6 (0.19)
Two children	20,530 (319.4)	306 (45.1)	1.5 (0.22)	20,694 (295.3)	414 (67.2)	2.0 (0.32)	20,337 (251.8)	314 (44.5)	1.5 (0.22)
Three or more children	22,144 (362.8)	679 (80.2)	3.1 (0.36)	21,979 (331.0)	909 (102.4)	4.1 (0.46)	20,421 (209.6)	589 (63.5)	2.9 (0.30)
Number of parents in the household									
Two parents	35,936 (315.1)	886 (82.7)	2.5 (0.23)	37,219 (300.7)	1,357 (111.5)	3.6 (0.30)	34,252 (254.7)	908 (79.2)	2.7 (0.23)
One parent	13,260 (319.2)	196 (42.6)	1.5 (0.32)	11,777 (296.8)	118 (28.4)	1.0 (0.24)	15,436 (250.8)	137 (34.5)	0.9 (0.22)
Nonparental guardians	1,511 (100.1)	‡ (†)	‡ (†)	2,139 (203.2)	‡ (†)	‡ (†)	1,968 (112.5)	‡ (†)	‡ (†)
Parent participation in the labor force									
Two parents—both in labor force	25,108 (373.1)	274 (44.1)	1.1 (0.18)	26,055 (318.3)	518 (76.2)	2.0 (0.29)	22,884 (293.3)	295 (41.3)	1.3 (0.18)
Two parents—one in labor force	10,545 (297.2)	594 (73.7)	5.6 (0.67)	10,754 (286.1)	808 (94.3)	7.5 (0.82)	11,581 (275.2)	618 (70.1)	5.3 (0.60)
One parent—in labor force	12,045 (267.9)	174 (39.8)	1.4 (0.33)	10,020 (277.1)	127 (29.5)	1.3 (0.30)	13,083 (238.6)	96 (19.2)	0.7 (0.15)
No parent participation in labor force	3,008 (171.4)	‡ (†)	‡ (†)	4,308 (228.9)	‡ (†)	‡ (†)	4,108 (187.3)	74 ! (26.9)	1.8 ! (0.65)
Highest education level of parents									
High school diploma or less	16,106 (272.3)	269 (51.6)	1.7 (0.32)	14,306 (292.9)	208 (35.5)	1.5 (0.24)	16,762 (83.8)	270 (53.3)	1.6 (0.32)
Vocational/technical or some college	16,068 (323.4)	338 (57.7)	2.1 (0.36)	14,581 (326.5)	559 (77.5)	3.8 (0.52)	15,621 (173.9)	344 (38.4)	2.2 (0.24)
Bachelor's degree/some graduate school	10,849 (275.0)	309 (48.5)	2.8 (0.45)	11,448 (276.5)	444 (64.7)	3.9 (0.57)	11,675 (168.4)	275 (41.9)	2.4 (0.36)
Graduate/professional degree	7,683 (239.5)	180 (41.6)	2.3 (0.55)	10,800 (236.0)	309 (50.0)	2.9 (0.46)	7,599 (34.1)	192 (26.5)	2.5 (0.35)
Household income									
$20,000 or less	9,079 (146.2)	164 (38.9)	1.8 (0.43)	8,488 (201.2)	186 (42.1)	2.2 (0.50)	7,593 (39.6)	59 (12.1)	0.8 (0.16)
$20,001 to $50,000	16,515 (336.1)	430 (60.3)	2.6 (0.36)	13,648 (306.1)	420 (59.8)	3.1 (0.42)	13,973 (84.7)	321 (44.2)	2.3 (0.32)
$50,001 to $75,000	10,961 (282.2)	264 (51.1)	2.4 (0.46)	10,289 (292.9)	414 (58.8)	4.0 (0.57)	9,406 (23.9)	278 (40.8)	3.0 (0.44)
$75,001 to $100,000	6,432 (238.0)	169 (42.9)	2.6 (0.66)	6,899 (210.8)	264 (57.2)	3.8 (0.83)	6,916 (29.5)	211 (42.4)	3.0 (0.61)
Over $100,000	7,718 (212.6)	‡ (†)	‡ (†)	11,811 (228.2)	236 (57.5)	2.0 (0.49)	13,769 (56.5)	214 (34.4)	1.6 (0.25)
Locale									
City	— (†)	— (†)	— (†)	15,998 (292.3)	327 (40.4)	2.0 (0.26)	15,191 (236.0)	226 (28.0)	1.5 (0.18)
Suburb	— (†)	— (†)	— (†)	18,988 (291.3)	503 (78.8)	2.6 (0.41)	19,356 (330.6)	303 (44.6)	1.6 (0.22)
Town	— (†)	— (†)	— (†)	5,574 (209.4)	168 (37.1)	3.0 (0.65)	4,839 (197.9)	112 (30.8)	2.3 (0.63)
Rural	— (†)	— (†)	— (†)	10,576 (110.9)	523 (75.9)	4.9 (0.71)	12,271 (249.1)	441 (65.0)	3.6 (0.52)

—Not available.
†Not applicable.
#Rounds to zero.
‡Reporting standards not met (too few cases for a reliable estimate).
!Interpret data with caution.
[1]Refers to all students in public and private schools and homeschooled students.
[2]Numbers and percentages of homeschoolers exclude students who were enrolled in school for more than 25 hours a week or who were homeschooled only due to a temporary illness.
[3]The National Center for Education Statistics uses a statistical adjustment for estimates of total homeschoolers in 2012. For more information about this adjustment, please see *Homeschooling in the United States: 2012* (NCES 2015-019, forthcoming). All other estimates about homeschoolers do not use a statistical adjustment.

[4]Students whose grade equivalent was "ungraded" were excluded from the grade analysis. The percentage of students with an "ungraded" grade equivalent was 0.02 percent in 2003 and 2007. There were no students with an "ungraded" grade equivalent in 2012.
NOTE: While National Household Education Surveys Program (NHES) administrations prior to 2012 were administered via telephone with an interviewer, NHES:2012 used self-administered paper-and-pencil questionnaires that were mailed to respondents. Measurable differences in estimates between 2012 and prior years could reflect actual changes in the population, or the changes could be due to the mode change from telephone to mail. Race categories exclude persons of Hispanic ethnicity. Detail may not sum to totals because of rounding. Some data have been revised from previously published figures.
SOURCE: U.S. Department of Education, National Center for Education Statistics, Parent and Family Involvement in Education Survey of the National Household Education Surveys Program (PFI-NHES:2003, 2007, and 2012). (This table was prepared November 2014.)

Table 206.20. Percentage distribution of students ages 5 through 17 attending kindergarten through 12th grade, by school type or participation in homeschooling and selected child, parent, and household characteristics: 1999, 2003, and 2007

[Standard errors appear in parentheses]

Selected child, parent, or household characteristic	1999				2003				2007			
	Public school		Private school	Homeschooled[1]	Public school		Private school	Homeschooled[1]	Public school		Private school	Homeschooled[1]
	Assigned	Chosen			Assigned	Chosen			Assigned	Chosen		
1	2	3	4	5	6	7	8	9	10	11	12	13
Total	74.1 (0.45)	14.3 (0.33)	10.0 (0.28)	1.7 (0.14)	72.1 (0.57)	15.0 (0.41)	10.8 (0.39)	2.2 (0.18)	70.6 (0.70)	15.0 (0.55)	11.4 (0.45)	2.9 (0.23)
Sex of child												
Male	74.8 (0.60)	13.9 (0.44)	9.7 (0.34)	1.6 (0.17)	72.1 (0.70)	15.0 (0.56)	10.7 (0.48)	2.2 (0.24)	70.7 (1.05)	15.3 (0.79)	11.5 (0.73)	2.4 (0.28)
Female	73.4 (0.61)	14.6 (0.45)	10.3 (0.41)	1.8 (0.19)	72.1 (0.78)	14.9 (0.54)	10.8 (0.51)	2.1 (0.23)	70.5 (0.88)	14.7 (0.64)	11.2 (0.54)	3.5 (0.39)
Race/ethnicity of child												
White	75.0 (0.54)	11.2 (0.35)	11.8 (0.39)	2.0 (0.19)	72.7 (0.67)	12.4 (0.47)	12.2 (0.48)	2.7 (0.25)	69.9 (0.80)	12.0 (0.46)	14.2 (0.61)	3.9 (0.34)
Black	70.2 (1.24)	22.6 (1.22)	6.2 (0.47)	1.0 (0.31)	66.6 (1.49)	23.4 (1.45)	8.6 (0.85)	1.3! (0.42)	68.4 (2.30)	23.0 (2.20)	7.8 (1.33)	0.8! (0.28)
Hispanic	76.0 (1.02)	17.6 (0.91)	5.2 (0.40)	1.1 (0.25)	77.2 (1.17)	15.0 (0.99)	7.1 (0.66)	0.7! (0.26)	74.6 (1.41)	17.5 (1.25)	6.3 (0.57)	1.5 (0.29)
Other	69.5 (2.20)	17.6 (1.99)	11.0 (1.35)	1.9! (0.65)	67.1 (2.59)	18.7 (1.94)	11.3 (1.61)	3.0! (1.02)	70.4 (2.23)	16.7 (1.79)	9.4 (1.12)	3.3 (0.86)
Disability status of child as reported by parent												
Has a disability	74.8 (0.93)	15.3 (0.78)	8.0 (0.49)	1.8 (0.27)	72.4 (1.12)	16.2 (0.75)	9.2 (0.70)	2.2 (0.35)	72.7 (1.35)	14.0 (0.91)	10.5 (0.96)	2.6 (0.48)
Does not have a disability	73.9 (0.51)	14.0 (0.36)	10.5 (0.34)	1.7 (0.16)	72.0 (0.67)	14.5 (0.51)	11.3 (0.44)	2.1 (0.21)	69.9 (0.76)	15.3 (0.63)	11.7 (0.48)	3.1 (0.28)
Grade equivalent[2]												
Kindergarten through 5th grade	71.5 (0.61)	15.1 (0.43)	11.6 (0.41)	1.8 (0.20)	70.1 (0.70)	16.2 (0.56)	11.8 (0.53)	1.9 (0.23)	68.5 (1.16)	16.2 (1.04)	12.2 (0.69)	3.0 (0.36)
Kindergarten	66.2 (1.67)	15.4 (1.13)	15.9 (1.29)	2.4 (0.52)	69.0 (1.50)	15.5 (1.18)	12.8 (1.21)	2.7 (0.64)	66.4 (2.20)	14.7 (1.60)	15.8 (1.61)	3.1! (0.96)
Grades 1 through 3	72.2 (0.87)	15.3 (0.67)	10.9 (0.53)	1.6 (0.29)	70.0 (1.18)	16.2 (0.96)	12.1 (0.73)	1.8 (0.28)	68.4 (1.68)	15.9 (1.63)	12.3 (0.93)	3.4 (0.54)
Grades 4 through 5	72.9 (1.17)	14.6 (0.79)	10.7 (0.77)	1.7 (0.28)	70.7 (1.12)	16.5 (0.96)	10.9 (0.76)	1.9 (0.35)	69.7 (1.62)	17.5 (1.34)	10.3 (1.08)	2.5 (0.52)
Grades 6 through 8	77.4 (0.79)	11.5 (0.65)	9.5 (0.47)	1.6 (0.24)	73.3 (1.03)	14.1 (0.81)	10.2 (0.59)	2.4 (0.36)	74.4 (1.44)	11.6 (0.81)	11.0 (1.14)	2.9 (0.52)
Grades 9 through 12	75.7 (0.75)	15.1 (0.60)	7.5 (0.44)	1.7 (0.24)	74.6 (0.97)	13.6 (0.76)	9.5 (0.63)	2.3 (0.33)	70.8 (1.07)	15.9 (0.84)	10.5 (0.75)	2.8 (0.38)
Number of parents in the household												
Two parents	74.5 (0.54)	12.0 (0.35)	11.5 (0.37)	2.1 (0.21)	71.8 (0.67)	13.6 (0.51)	12.1 (0.47)	2.5 (0.23)	69.5 (0.73)	13.8 (0.49)	12.9 (0.52)	3.6 (0.30)
One parent	73.5 (0.78)	18.2 (0.55)	7.3 (0.47)	0.9 (0.16)	72.9 (1.09)	18.0 (0.98)	7.6 (0.67)	1.5 (0.32)	73.6 (1.39)	17.2 (1.14)	8.1 (1.18)	1.0 (0.24)
Nonparental guardians	71.6 (2.70)	21.9 (2.72)	5.1 (0.84)	‡ (†)	73.2 (3.05)	20.1 (2.59)	5.8 (1.36)	‡ (†)	72.2 (5.91)	23.0 (6.19)	2.6 (0.74)	2.1! (0.81)
Highest education level of parents												
Less than a high school diploma	79.1 (1.38)	18.0 (1.46)	2.7 (0.51)	0.2! (0.10)	76.9 (2.06)	18.9 (1.76)	2.9! (1.18)	‡ (†)	83.3 (2.03)	12.7 (1.53)	3.5! (1.81)	0.5! (0.23)
High school diploma or GED	79.0 (0.84)	14.3 (0.72)	5.6 (0.44)	1.1 (0.19)	77.8 (1.01)	15.5 (0.89)	4.9 (0.45)	1.8 (0.34)	78.8 (1.90)	15.1 (1.84)	4.1 (0.63)	1.9 (0.36)
Vocational/technical or some college	75.8 (0.72)	14.7 (0.63)	7.7 (0.40)	1.9 (0.24)	74.0 (0.97)	15.5 (0.74)	8.3 (0.58)	2.1 (0.36)	72.0 (1.03)	15.3 (0.99)	8.8 (0.70)	3.8 (0.52)
Bachelor's degree/some graduate school	68.6 (1.06)	13.2 (0.75)	15.8 (0.75)	2.4 (0.37)	67.1 (1.00)	13.2 (0.84)	16.8 (0.90)	2.8 (0.45)	66.8 (1.24)	14.8 (1.02)	14.3 (0.87)	4.1 (0.57)
Graduate/professional degree	65.0 (1.14)	12.4 (0.77)	20.2 (0.91)	2.4 (0.54)	63.6 (1.50)	13.5 (1.14)	20.5 (1.28)	2.3 (0.55)	59.2 (1.37)	15.9 (1.01)	22.4 (1.22)	2.5 (0.41)
Poverty status of household												
Below poverty	74.8 (1.16)	19.2 (1.06)	4.3 (0.50)	1.7 (0.34)	76.3 (1.28)	17.7 (1.10)	3.7 (0.67)	2.3 (0.58)	76.6 (2.48)	17.8 (2.35)	3.7 (1.04)	1.8 (0.40)
Between poverty and 200 percent of poverty	76.8 (0.79)	15.3 (0.70)	5.9 (0.48)	2.0 (0.31)	75.1 (1.17)	16.0 (0.87)	5.9 (0.69)	3.1 (0.50)	74.4 (1.45)	16.2 (1.15)	5.2 (0.69)	4.1 (0.69)
At or above 200 percent of poverty	72.5 (0.57)	11.8 (0.34)	14.0 (0.47)	1.6 (0.18)	69.8 (0.70)	13.8 (0.54)	14.6 (0.54)	1.8 (0.21)	67.6 (0.75)	13.8 (0.48)	15.7 (0.54)	2.9 (0.30)
Urbanicity												
City	— (†)	—	—	— (†)	— (†)	—	—	— (†)	61.7 (1.46)	22.1 (1.38)	14.2 (0.97)	2.0 (0.26)
Suburb	— (†)	—	—	— (†)	— (†)	—	—	— (†)	72.7 (0.95)	11.8 (0.67)	12.8 (0.68)	2.6 (0.41)
Town	— (†)	—	—	— (†)	— (†)	—	—	— (†)	77.3 (1.77)	12.4 (1.43)	7.1 (0.75)	3.0 (0.66)
Rural	— (†)	—	—	— (†)	— (†)	—	—	— (†)	76.7 (1.36)	11.5 (1.03)	6.8 (1.09)	4.9 (0.71)
Region												
Northeast	72.8 (1.06)	13.4 (0.78)	12.6 (0.63)	1.1 (0.30)	71.6 (1.42)	11.9 (1.02)	14.6 (1.03)	1.8! (0.58)	72.5 (1.42)	11.8 (1.11)	13.6 (0.98)	2.1 (0.47)
South	75.4 (0.65)	13.2 (0.52)	9.3 (0.43)	2.0 (0.28)	74.2 (0.88)	14.9 (0.72)	8.3 (0.58)	2.6 (0.39)	71.9 (1.15)	13.6 (0.96)	10.8 (0.58)	3.7 (0.46)
Midwest	74.3 (0.80)	13.4 (0.72)	10.9 (0.61)	1.4 (0.24)	69.9 (1.27)	14.4 (0.92)	13.8 (1.04)	2.0 (0.37)	70.8 (1.54)	14.2 (1.06)	12.8 (1.14)	2.2 (0.53)
West	72.7 (0.95)	17.7 (0.73)	7.5 (0.49)	2.0 (0.34)	71.9 (1.07)	17.9 (0.97)	8.3 (0.59)	2.0 (0.34)	67.0 (1.40)	20.3 (1.17)	9.4 (0.75)	3.1 (0.42)

—Not available.
†Not applicable.
!Interpret data with caution. The coefficient of variation (CV) for this estimate is between 30 and 50 percent.
‡Reporting standards not met. The coefficient of variation (CV) for this estimate is 50 percent or greater.
[1]Excludes students who were enrolled in school for more than 25 hours a week; also excluded in 1999 and 2003 are students who were homeschooled only due to a temporary illness and, in 2007, students who were homeschooled primarily due to a temporary illness.

[2]Students whose grade equivalent was "ungraded" were excluded from the grade analysis. The percentage of students with an "ungraded" grade equivalent was 0.03 percent in 1999 and 0.02 percent in 2003 and 2007.
NOTE: Data are based on parent reports. Race categories exclude persons of Hispanic ethnicity. Detail may not sum to totals because of rounding. Some data have been revised from previously published figures.
SOURCE: U.S. Department of Education, National Center for Education Statistics, Parent Survey (Parent:1999) and Parent and Family Involvement in Education Survey (PFI:2003 and PFI:2007) of the National Household Education Surveys Program. (This table was prepared July 2010.)

Table 206.30. Percentage distribution of students enrolled in grades 1 through 12, by public school type and charter status, private school type, and selected child and household characteristics: 2012

[Standard errors appear in parentheses]

Selected child or household characteristic and public school type	Total		Public school								Private school					
			Total		Assigned or chosen type[1]				Traditional or charter status				Total		Religious		Nonsectarian
					Assigned		Chosen		Traditional[2]		Charter						
1	2		3		4		5		6		7		8		9		10
Total	100.0	(†)	100.0	(†)	100.0	(†)	100.0	(†)	100.0	(†)	100.0	(†)	100.0	(†)	100.0	(†)	100.0	(†)
Sex of child																		
Male	51.6	(0.60)	51.5	(0.63)	51.9	(0.68)	50.2	(1.48)	51.7	(0.63)	45.4	(3.46)	52.7	(1.89)	52.8	(2.24)	51.8	(3.71)
Female	48.4	(0.60)	48.5	(0.63)	48.1	(0.68)	49.8	(1.48)	48.3	(0.63)	54.6	(3.46)	47.3	(1.89)	47.2	(2.24)	48.2	(3.71)
Race/ethnicity of child																		
White	52.3	(0.39)	51.3	(0.43)	53.1	(0.49)	40.2	(1.36)	51.9	(0.43)	31.5	(2.85)	65.0	(1.77)	63.3	(1.94)	72.8	(3.35)
Black	14.4	(0.19)	14.7	(0.24)	13.5	(0.31)	21.6	(1.19)	14.3	(0.26)	29.9	(3.24)	10.2	(1.05)	11.0	(1.18)	6.6	(1.82)
Hispanic	22.7	(0.26)	23.3	(0.28)	22.7	(0.37)	27.4	(1.21)	23.1	(0.31)	30.8	(3.13)	15.2	(1.38)	16.8	(1.57)	7.6	(1.93)
Asian/Pacific Islander	5.2	(0.22)	5.2	(0.23)	5.1	(0.25)	5.5	(0.68)	5.2	(0.23)	5.4 !	(1.83)	5.2	(0.62)	5.1	(0.73)	6.0	(1.40)
Other	5.4	(0.26)	5.5	(0.27)	5.5	(0.30)	5.3	(0.55)	5.6	(0.28)	2.4 !	(0.84)	4.4	(0.70)	3.8	(0.79)	7.0	(1.95)
Disability status of child as reported by parent																		
Has a disability	17.3	(0.46)	17.7	(0.47)	17.7	(0.55)	17.7	(0.98)	17.8	(0.49)	15.5	(2.04)	12.2	(1.16)	11.1	(1.14)	17.7	(2.78)
Does not have a disability	82.7	(0.46)	82.3	(0.47)	82.3	(0.55)	82.3	(0.98)	82.2	(0.49)	84.5	(2.04)	87.8	(1.16)	88.9	(1.14)	82.3	(2.78)
Grade level																		
Grades 1 through 5	43.4	(0.26)	43.2	(0.32)	43.5	(0.40)	40.6	(1.19)	43.0	(0.33)	47.0	(3.65)	46.7	(1.73)	47.2	(1.84)	44.0	(3.84)
Grades 6 through 8	25.2	(0.33)	25.4	(0.34)	25.2	(0.42)	27.2	(1.05)	25.2	(0.36)	32.5	(3.12)	22.7	(1.42)	22.7	(1.60)	23.0	(3.26)
Grades 9 through 12	31.3	(0.23)	31.4	(0.30)	31.3	(0.34)	32.2	(1.13)	31.7	(0.30)	20.5	(2.41)	30.6	(1.74)	30.1	(1.84)	33.0	(3.77)
Number of parents in the household																		
Two parents	65.7	(0.50)	64.6	(0.54)	65.0	(0.62)	61.5	(1.29)	64.8	(0.55)	57.8	(3.61)	78.9	(1.18)	79.0	(1.33)	78.7	(2.54)
One parent	30.6	(0.49)	31.6	(0.53)	31.2	(0.63)	34.3	(1.37)	31.4	(0.55)	38.0	(3.61)	18.4	(1.19)	18.3	(1.35)	19.0	(2.40)
Nonparental guardians	3.8	(0.18)	3.8	(0.20)	3.8	(0.22)	4.2	(0.53)	3.8	(0.20)	4.2 !	(1.31)	2.7	(0.47)	2.8	(0.57)	2.3 !	(0.89)
Highest education level of parents																		
Less than a high school diploma	11.7	(0.21)	12.3	(0.23)	12.1	(0.28)	12.4	(1.06)	12.3	(0.24)	12.3	(3.08)	4.8	(1.09)	4.9	(1.11)	‡	(†)
High school diploma or GED	20.3	(0.22)	21.2	(0.26)	21.9	(0.33)	18.1	(1.26)	21.0	(0.27)	25.8	(3.53)	9.8	(1.30)	10.5	(1.44)	6.6 !	(2.24)
Vocational/technical or some college	30.4	(0.39)	31.3	(0.42)	31.6	(0.46)	30.4	(1.25)	31.4	(0.43)	26.4	(2.75)	20.0	(1.44)	20.7	(1.69)	16.8	(2.68)
Bachelor's degree/some graduate school	22.7	(0.34)	21.6	(0.35)	21.1	(0.41)	23.9	(1.27)	21.6	(0.36)	22.9	(2.72)	36.1	(1.68)	37.6	(1.92)	29.4	(3.97)
Graduate/professional degree	14.8	(0.13)	13.6	(0.17)	13.3	(0.21)	15.3	(0.65)	13.7	(0.18)	12.6	(1.82)	29.3	(1.38)	26.3	(1.48)	43.2	(3.30)
Poverty status of household[3]																		
Poor	18.6	(0.29)	19.5	(0.32)	19.6	(0.42)	19.3	(1.08)	19.4	(0.34)	25.2	(3.62)	7.1	(1.07)	6.9	(1.24)	8.1 !	(2.82)
Near-poor	22.1	(0.39)	23.0	(0.43)	23.1	(0.49)	22.9	(1.00)	22.9	(0.44)	27.7	(3.14)	10.7	(1.23)	11.2	(1.39)	8.0	(1.93)
Nonpoor	59.3	(0.30)	57.4	(0.37)	57.3	(0.42)	57.9	(1.21)	57.8	(0.39)	47.2	(3.19)	82.2	(1.54)	81.8	(1.71)	83.9	(3.18)
Locale																		
City	29.0	(0.49)	28.5	(0.48)	25.3	(0.49)	45.9	(1.41)	27.7	(0.46)	51.6	(3.10)	34.8	(1.81)	33.8	(2.03)	39.2	(3.41)
Suburban	38.0	(0.63)	37.7	(0.65)	38.5	(0.71)	33.8	(1.41)	37.9	(0.64)	30.8	(3.45)	41.6	(1.44)	42.8	(1.75)	35.7	(3.36)
Town	9.4	(0.34)	9.8	(0.36)	10.6	(0.43)	5.9	(0.82)	9.9	(0.37)	5.2 !	(2.08)	5.0	(0.65)	4.8	(0.72)	5.9	(1.63)
Rural	23.6	(0.49)	24.0	(0.50)	25.6	(0.57)	14.4	(1.03)	24.4	(0.50)	12.3	(2.18)	18.7	(1.50)	18.5	(1.68)	19.2	(2.99)
Region																		
Northeast	17.5	(0.39)	17.0	(0.39)	18.2	(0.44)	10.0	(0.79)	17.1	(0.41)	13.1	(2.05)	24.7	(1.53)	23.9	(1.88)	28.4	(4.04)
South	35.9	(0.57)	36.3	(0.60)	36.2	(0.69)	37.1	(1.36)	36.5	(0.61)	30.3	(3.20)	30.6	(1.52)	28.6	(1.69)	39.6	(3.32)
Midwest	22.2	(0.53)	22.1	(0.54)	22.4	(0.58)	20.0	(1.16)	22.0	(0.53)	23.8	(3.26)	23.2	(1.61)	26.6	(1.93)	7.2	(1.73)
West	24.4	(0.51)	24.7	(0.55)	23.2	(0.57)	33.0	(1.32)	24.4	(0.55)	32.8	(3.01)	21.5	(1.48)	20.8	(1.67)	24.8	(3.71)
Public school type[1]																		
Assigned	84.6 [4]	(0.46)	84.6	(0.46)	100.0	(†)	†	(†)	87.3	(0.40)	†	(†)	†	(†)	†	(†)	†	(†)
Chosen	15.4 [4]	(0.46)	15.4	(0.46)	†	(†)	100.0	(†)	12.7	(0.40)	100.0	(†)	†	(†)	†	(†)	†	(†)

†Not applicable.
!Interpret data with caution. The coefficient of variation (CV) for this estimate is between 30 and 50 percent.
‡Reporting standards not met. The coefficient of variation (CV) for this estimate is 50 percent or greater.
[1]In 160 cases, questions about whether the school was assigned were not asked because parents reported the school as a private school, and it was only later found to be a public school. These cases were excluded from the analysis of assigned versus chosen public schools, but were included in the charter school analysis as well as in the public school and overall totals.
[2]Includes all types of public noncharter schools.
[3]Poor children are those whose family incomes were below the Census Bureau's poverty threshold in the year prior to data collection; near-poor children are those whose family incomes ranged from the poverty threshold to 199 percent of the poverty threshold; and nonpoor chil-

dren are those whose family incomes were at or above 200 percent of the poverty threshold. The poverty threshold is a dollar amount that varies depending on a family's size and composition and is updated annually to account for inflation. In 2011, for example, the poverty threshold for a family of four with two children was $22,811. Survey respondents are asked to select the range within which their income falls, rather than giving the exact amount of their income; therefore, the measure of poverty status is an approximation.
[4]Includes only students enrolled in public schools.
NOTE: Data exclude homeschooled children. Race categories exclude persons of Hispanic ethnicity. Detail may not sum to totals because of rounding.
SOURCE: U.S. Department of Education, National Center for Education Statistics, Parent and Family Involvement in Education Survey of the National Household Education Surveys Program (PFI-NHES:2012). (This table was prepared September 2014.)

Table 206.40. Percentage of students enrolled in grades 1 through 12 whose parents reported having public school choice, considered other schools, reported current school was their first choice, or moved to their current neighborhood for the public school, by school type and selected child and household characteristics: 2012

[Standard errors appear in parentheses]

School type and selected child or household characteristic	Public choice available		Considered other schools		School was parent's first choice		Moved to neighborhood for public school[1]	
1	2		3		4		5	
Total..	37.3	(0.54)	30.5	(0.51)	78.6	(0.43)	18.6	(0.54)
School type[2]								
Public, assigned........................	27.8	(0.58)	24.2	(0.59)	77.5	(0.50)	20.3	(0.64)
Public, chosen[3]........................	100.0	(†)	53.1	(1.49)	79.3	(1.05)	9.8	(0.97)
Private, religious........................	20.7	(1.57)	46.5	(1.92)	87.2	(1.51)	†	(†)
Private, nonsectarian..................	21.2	(3.58)	61.5	(3.63)	88.9	(2.37)	†	(†)
Sex of child								
Male..	36.3	(0.78)	29.9	(0.78)	79.0	(0.56)	17.6	(0.67)
Female.....................................	38.5	(0.71)	31.2	(0.81)	78.1	(0.71)	19.7	(0.79)
Race/ethnicity of child								
White.......................................	34.2	(0.64)	26.5	(0.67)	83.4	(0.60)	20.5	(0.60)
Black.......................................	43.2	(1.56)	40.1	(1.56)	69.4	(1.69)	15.0	(1.70)
Hispanic...................................	38.9	(1.25)	31.5	(1.20)	74.3	(1.04)	16.5	(1.33)
Asian/Pacific Islander.................	42.8	(2.51)	33.2	(2.50)	77.2	(2.12)	24.4	(1.75)
Other.......................................	40.5	(2.33)	36.4	(2.55)	75.6	(1.99)	14.9	(1.55)
Disability status of child as reported by parent								
Has a disability.........................	37.8	(1.25)	32.5	(1.32)	75.4	(1.15)	18.3	(1.22)
Does not have a disability...........	37.2	(0.56)	30.1	(0.55)	79.2	(0.50)	18.7	(0.62)
Grade level								
Grades 1 through 5....................	35.0	(0.87)	30.9	(0.94)	78.4	(0.81)	18.7	(0.86)
Grades 6 through 8....................	39.0	(1.11)	30.3	(0.92)	78.1	(0.83)	19.4	(1.05)
Grades 9 through 12...................	39.2	(0.86)	30.1	(0.80)	79.1	(0.73)	17.9	(1.06)
Number of parents in the household								
Two parents..............................	37.2	(0.62)	30.7	(0.61)	81.3	(0.45)	19.2	(0.57)
One parent................................	37.4	(1.01)	30.4	(0.97)	73.1	(1.04)	18.5	(1.08)
Nonparental guardians...............	38.5	(2.63)	27.9	(2.67)	75.3	(2.87)	10.6	(1.74)
Highest education level of parents								
Less than a high school diploma...	37.3	(1.71)	25.8	(1.63)	75.7	(1.65)	16.3	(1.89)
High school diploma or GED........	34.7	(1.45)	23.9	(1.46)	77.9	(1.10)	13.5	(1.03)
Vocational/technical or some college...	37.5	(0.90)	28.5	(0.74)	75.3	(0.87)	17.0	(0.85)
Bachelor's degree/some graduate school...	38.4	(1.17)	35.1	(1.22)	81.9	(0.85)	21.6	(0.97)
Graduate/professional degree......	39.0	(0.93)	40.2	(0.99)	83.3	(0.67)	27.8	(0.84)
Poverty status of household[4]								
Poor..	37.7	(1.35)	26.8	(1.32)	72.5	(1.18)	14.8	(1.06)
Near-poor.................................	39.2	(1.14)	28.4	(1.13)	76.6	(1.01)	14.6	(0.92)
Nonpoor...................................	36.5	(0.67)	32.4	(0.75)	81.2	(0.56)	21.5	(0.69)
Locale								
City...	48.8	(1.07)	39.7	(1.05)	73.6	(0.77)	17.0	(0.80)
Suburban..................................	32.0	(0.88)	30.0	(0.72)	78.1	(0.80)	22.5	(0.90)
Town.......................................	33.1	(1.91)	19.6	(1.46)	82.2	(1.33)	14.0	(1.77)
Rural.......................................	33.6	(1.15)	24.3	(1.02)	84.0	(0.88)	16.4	(0.96)
Region								
Northeast.................................	22.4	(1.01)	29.5	(1.08)	76.5	(1.13)	18.4	(1.10)
South.......................................	34.2	(0.93)	28.9	(0.90)	78.3	(0.79)	18.3	(0.96)
Midwest....................................	41.8	(1.01)	28.5	(1.24)	80.1	(1.08)	21.1	(1.13)
West..	48.6	(1.21)	35.3	(0.98)	79.2	(0.80)	17.1	(0.89)

†Not applicable.
[1]This column shows percentages of public school students only. Private school students are excluded from the analysis.
[2]There were 160 cases excluded from the school type analysis because parents reported the school as a private school when it was later found to be a public school, and therefore questions about whether the school was assigned were not asked.
[3]Students who attended chosen public schools were automatically coded as yes for whether or not their district allowed public school choice.
[4]Poor children are those whose family incomes were below the Census Bureau's poverty threshold in the year prior to data collection; near-poor children are those whose family incomes ranged from the poverty threshold to 199 percent of the poverty threshold; and nonpoor children are those whose family incomes were at or above 200 per-

cent of the poverty threshold. The poverty threshold is a dollar amount that varies depending on a family's size and composition and is updated annually to account for inflation. In 2011, for example, the poverty threshold for a family of four with two children was $22,811. Survey respondents are asked to select the range within which their income falls, rather than giving the exact amount of their income; therefore, the measure of poverty status is an approximation.
NOTE: Data exclude homeschooled children. Race categories exclude persons of Hispanic ethnicity.
SOURCE: U.S. Department of Education, National Center for Education Statistics, Parent and Family Involvement in Education Survey of the National Household Education Surveys Program (PFI-NHES:2012). (This table was prepared September 2014.)

Table 206.50. Percentage of students enrolled in grades 3 through 12 whose parents were satisfied or dissatisfied with various aspects of their children's schools, by public and private school type: 2003, 2007, and 2012

[Standard errors appear in parentheses]

Parent satisfaction	2003 Public school Assigned	2003 Public school Chosen	2003 Private school Religious	2003 Private school Nonsectarian	2007 Public school Assigned	2007 Public school Chosen	2007 Private school Religious	2007 Private school Nonsectarian	2012 Public school Assigned	2012 Public school Chosen	2012 Private school Religious	2012 Private school Nonsectarian
1	2	3	4	5	6	7	8	9	10	11	12	13
Very satisfied												
School...........	53.7 (0.79)	64.2 (1.72)	77.0 (2.01)	71.7 (3.65)	52.1 (0.96)	62.1 (2.34)	78.7 (1.97)	78.6 (3.57)	52.5 (0.58)	56.2 (1.30)	80.0 (1.44)	77.8 (3.36)
Teachers...........	56.4 (0.74)	64.5 (1.62)	72.5 (1.88)	70.3 (3.68)	56.6 (0.88)	63.5 (2.32)	76.3 (1.96)	74.0 (3.67)	52.3 (0.65)	51.7 (1.48)	72.1 (1.80)	76.3 (3.23)
Academic standards...........	54.5 (0.78)	63.8 (1.75)	79.5 (1.77)	77.3 (3.32)	56.3 (0.84)	65.9 (2.09)	81.9 (1.70)	78.8 (3.81)	52.7 (0.58)	58.8 (1.48)	79.2 (1.76)	83.5 (2.89)
Order and discipline...........	55.9 (0.78)	64.8 (1.81)	81.2 (1.81)	80.5 (3.23)	55.0 (0.97)	60.9 (2.21)	82.7 (1.95)	80.5 (3.15)	52.4 (0.64)	57.9 (1.64)	82.2 (1.49)	79.8 (3.68)
Staff interaction with parents...........	— (†)	— (†)	— (†)	— (†)	47.7 (1.00)	56.7 (2.24)	75.4 (1.85)	73.0 (4.03)	44.7 (0.72)	48.8 (1.67)	72.2 (1.66)	72.8 (3.53)
Somewhat satisfied												
School...........	35.3 (0.74)	27.6 (1.40)	18.7 (1.84)	22.6 (3.33)	34.9 (0.82)	30.5 (2.01)	18.4 (1.82)	17.8 (3.40)	37.6 (0.68)	34.0 (1.57)	16.4 (1.42)	19.4 (3.16)
Teachers...........	35.4 (0.71)	29.3 (1.57)	23.4 (1.69)	23.6 (3.25)	34.1 (0.84)	29.8 (1.87)	21.1 (1.90)	23.1 (3.78)	38.4 (0.64)	38.7 (1.47)	23.6 (1.70)	20.4 (3.16)
Academic standards...........	35.4 (0.79)	29.1 (1.59)	16.4 (1.52)	17.7 (2.97)	32.7 (0.84)	28.2 (1.99)	15.8 (1.58)	18.6 (3.67)	38.0 (0.67)	33.0 (1.49)	17.2 (1.56)	14.0 (2.70)
Order and discipline...........	30.5 (0.72)	26.0 (1.67)	14.7 (1.70)	15.6 (3.13)	30.1 (0.85)	27.6 (2.57)	14.6 (1.83)	16.8 (2.89)	35.3 (0.67)	30.8 (1.50)	15.2 (1.53)	16.9 (3.37)
Staff interaction with parents...........	— (†)	— (†)	— (†)	— (†)	36.4 (0.92)	33.5 (2.03)	21.1 (1.83)	22.9 (3.92)	40.1 (0.79)	35.4 (1.69)	23.6 (1.54)	23.4 (3.40)
Somewhat dissatisfied												
School...........	7.4 (0.37)	5.6 (0.75)	3.2 (0.69)	4.5 ! (1.98)	8.4 (0.45)	5.5 (0.98)	2.6 (0.58)	3.3 ! (1.50)	7.4 (0.37)	7.6 (0.95)	2.9 (0.68)	‡ (†)
Teachers...........	6.2 (0.38)	4.1 (0.52)	3.4 (0.69)	3.8 ! (1.67)	6.6 (0.48)	5.6 (1.11)	1.7 (0.50)	2.9 ! (1.35)	7.2 (0.33)	7.7 (0.84)	4.0 (0.84)	2.0 ! (0.88)
Academic standards...........	6.6 (0.37)	4.3 (0.56)	3.3 (0.77)	4.5 ! (1.94)	6.8 (0.47)	4.9 (0.83)	2.0 ! (0.74)	‡ (†)	7.0 (0.40)	6.3 (0.77)	3.5 (0.92)	‡ (†)
Order and discipline...........	7.8 (0.42)	5.0 (0.69)	2.1 (0.52)	3.7 ! (1.45)	8.6 (0.50)	7.0 (1.00)	2.1 (0.52)	‡ (†)	8.6 (0.36)	7.3 (0.75)	1.8 (0.48)	‡ (†)
Staff interaction with parents...........	— (†)	— (†)	— (†)	— (†)	10.7 (0.59)	6.7 (0.93)	2.3 (0.57)	‡ (†)	11.0 (0.41)	11.9 (1.03)	3.0 (0.58)	1.9 ! (0.77)
Very dissatisfied												
School...........	3.6 (0.26)	2.6 (0.54)	1.1 ! (0.50)	‡ (†)	4.6 (0.44)	1.8 (0.51)	0.4 ! (0.20)	‡ (†)	2.5 (0.21)	2.3 (0.39)	0.7 ! (0.33)	‡ (†)
Teachers...........	2.0 (0.16)	2.1 (0.45)	‡ (†)	‡ (†)	2.7 (0.39)	1.1 ! (0.34)	0.9 ! (0.32)	# (†)	2.0 (0.18)	2.0 (0.47)	‡ (†)	‡ (†)
Academic standards...........	3.4 (0.28)	2.7 (0.59)	‡ (†)	‡ (†)	4.3 (0.43)	1.0 ! (0.30)	‡ (†)	‡ (†)	2.3 (0.21)	1.8 (0.33)	‡ (†)	‡ (†)
Order and discipline...........	5.8 (0.38)	4.2 (0.72)	2.0 ! (0.80)	‡ (†)	8.6 (0.50)	4.5 (0.82)	‡ (†)	‡ (†)	3.6 (0.22)	4.1 (0.59)	0.7 ! (0.35)	‡ (†)
Staff interaction with parents...........	— (†)	— (†)	— (†)	— (—)	5.3 (0.48)	3.2 (0.62)	1.2 ! (0.38)	‡ (†)	4.3 (0.28)	3.9 (0.55)	1.2 ! (0.42)	‡ (†)

—Not available.
†Not applicable.
#Rounds to zero.
!Interpret data with caution. The coefficient of variation (CV) for this estimate is between 30 and 50 percent.
‡Reporting standards not met. Either there are too few cases for a reliable estimate or the coefficient of variation (CV) is 50 percent or greater.
NOTE: Data exclude homeschooled children. While National Household Education Surveys Program (NHES) administrations prior to 2012 were administered via telephone with an interviewer, NHES:2012 used self-administered paper-and-pencil ques-

tionnaires that were mailed to respondents. Measurable differences in estimates between 2012 and prior years could reflect actual changes in the population, or the changes could be due to the mode change from telephone to mail. Detail may not sum to totals because of rounding.
SOURCE: U.S. Department of Education, National Center for Education Statistics. Parent and Family Involvement in Education Survey of the National Household Education Surveys Program (PFI-NHES:2003, 2007, and 2012). (This table was prepared September 2014.)

Table 207.10. Number of 3- to 5-year-olds not yet enrolled in kindergarten and percentage participating in home literacy activities with a family member, by type and frequency of activity and selected child and family characteristics: 2001, 2007, and 2012

[Standard errors appear in parentheses]

Selected child or family characteristic	Number of children (in thousands) 2001	2007	2012	Percent of children participating in activity with family member[1] — Read by family member three or more times in past week 2001	2007	2012	Told a story by family member 2001	2007	2012	At least once in past week — Taught letters, words, or numbers 2001	2007	2012	Did arts and crafts 2001	2007	2012	Visited a library at least once in past month 2001	2007	2012
1	2	3	4	5	6	7	8	9	10	11	12	13	14	15	16	17	18	19
Total	8,551 (11.0)	8,686 (18.1)	8,244 (85.1)	84 (0.8)	83 (1.1)	83 (0.8)	84 (0.8)	79 (1.1)	83 (0.8)	94 (0.6)	87 (1.1)	98 (0.3)	79 (0.9)	90 (1.1)	86 (0.8)	36 (1.1)	36 (1.2)	42 (1.2)
Age																		
3 years old	3,795 (91.4)	3,755 (108.1)	3,674 (89.8)	84 (1.1)	84 (1.5)	82 (1.3)	83 (1.2)	80 (2.0)	82 (1.3)	93 (1.0)	87 (1.4)	97 (0.5)	77 (1.3)	91 (1.3)	85 (1.1)	35 (1.9)	36 (2.0)	38 (1.6)
4 years old	3,861 (89.0)	3,738 (123.5)	3,508 (90.4)	85 (1.2)	83 (1.6)	84 (1.3)	84 (1.1)	76 (2.0)	84 (1.3)	95 (0.7)	86 (1.9)	98 (0.3)	82 (1.2)	89 (2.0)	87 (1.2)	37 (1.4)	35 (1.6)	43 (1.8)
5 years old	896 (47.0)	1,193 (78.0)	1,062 (59.6)	81 (2.7)	83 (3.0)	80 (2.7)	82 (2.4)	86 (2.6)	80 (2.7)	93 (1.8)	89 (2.2)	98 (0.7)	80 (2.4)	89 (2.7)	88 (1.9)	37 (3.4)	39 (3.4)	49 (3.8)
Sex																		
Male	4,292 (79.9)	4,364 (101.1)	4,251 (103.9)	82 (1.2)	81 (1.7)	82 (1.2)	82 (1.0)	77 (1.9)	82 (1.2)	94 (0.7)	86 (1.6)	97 (0.4)	76 (1.3)	87 (1.8)	84 (1.1)	35 (1.4)	34 (1.8)	41 (1.7)
Female	4,260 (79.6)	4,322 (100.8)	3,993 (104.2)	86 (1.0)	86 (1.2)	84 (1.4)	85 (1.0)	81 (1.6)	85 (1.0)	94 (0.8)	88 (1.5)	98 (0.4)	83 (1.3)	93 (1.1)	88 (1.1)	37 (1.6)	38 (1.8)	42 (1.4)
Race/ethnicity																		
White	5,313 (68.0)	4,664 (66.3)	4,062 (97.4)	89 (0.8)	91 (1.3)	90 (1.0)	86 (1.0)	85 (1.4)	90 (1.0)	95 (0.7)	88 (1.3)	98 (0.4)	85 (1.0)	92 (1.3)	90 (0.9)	39 (1.3)	41 (1.6)	44 (1.4)
Black	1,251 (55.1)	1,311 (6.0)	1,154 (63.4)	77 (2.6)	78 (4.0)	77 (3.3)	81 (2.1)	61 (5.0)	77 (3.3)	94 (1.8)	81 (5.2)	99 (0.6)	70 (3.1)	82 (5.1)	83 (2.8)	31 (2.6)	25 (3.6)	41 (3.8)
Hispanic	1,506 (43.5)	1,899 (13.6)	2,100 (76.1)	71 (1.9)	68 (2.4)	71 (2.0)	75 (2.2)	75 (2.2)	71 (2.0)	92 (1.1)	86 (1.6)	97 (0.7)	67 (2.2)	91 (1.4)	80 (1.9)	30 (2.0)	27 (2.2)	34 (2.2)
Asian/Pacific Islander	202 (29.0)	368 (44.3)	423 (32.7)	87 (4.1)	87 (3.7)	77 (3.2)	81 (5.8)	73 (7.2)	77 (3.2)	96 (2.2)	92 (2.7)	98 (1.1)	74 (6.9)	84 (5.8)	86 (2.6)	47 (7.5)	48 (7.2)	55 (4.4)
Other	280 (28.2)	444 (46.3)	505 (44.4)	87 (3.4)	86 (5.8)	87 (2.9)	92 (2.4)	95 (1.6)	87 (2.9)	94 (2.7)	90 (4.7)	99 (0.7)	85 (4.3)	90 (4.2)	88 (3.4)	31 (5.4)	43 (6.7)	46 (4.4)
Mother's highest level of education[2]																		
Less than high school	996 (54.5)	808 (71.6)	1,291 (71.9)	69 (2.8)	56 (5.1)	73 (3.1)	72 (2.7)	66 (4.5)	73 (3.1)	91 (2.0)	84 (3.3)	98 (0.8)	62 (3.0)	86 (4.4)	82 (2.6)	21 (2.4)	20 (3.7)	26 (3.1)
High school/GED	2,712 (89.0)	2,048 (108.7)	1,614 (64.0)	81 (1.6)	74 (2.8)	75 (2.5)	83 (1.3)	74 (3.2)	75 (2.5)	95 (0.9)	82 (3.3)	97 (0.9)	77 (1.8)	89 (2.3)	84 (1.8)	30 (1.9)	29 (2.9)	38 (2.8)
Vocational/technical or some college	1,833 (73.9)	1,838 (107.2)	1,663 (77.3)	85 (1.8)	84 (2.3)	85 (1.7)	85 (1.7)	75 (3.5)	85 (1.7)	94 (1.2)	85 (3.2)	97 (0.8)	81 (1.9)	87 (3.4)	86 (1.6)	38 (2.2)	28 (2.5)	40 (2.0)
Associate's degree	573 (40.9)	821 (59.4)	678 (50.0)	89 (2.5)	90 (2.1)	85 (2.3)	84 (2.7)	84 (2.8)	85 (2.3)	92 (2.3)	91 (2.1)	98 (0.7)	82 (3.2)	92 (2.2)	86 (2.3)	42 (4.3)	45 (4.5)	43 (3.9)
Bachelor's degree	1,553 (68.4)	1,990 (92.4)	1,870 (65.9)	93 (1.2)	95 (0.9)	92 (1.2)	88 (1.5)	86 (1.7)	92 (1.2)	95 (1.1)	90 (1.3)	99 (0.3)	89 (1.4)	92 (1.7)	92 (1.0)	46 (2.4)	43 (2.5)	49 (2.2)
Graduate/professional degree	685 (45.7)	1,053 (63.7)	680 (30.8)	96 (1.1)	95 (1.6)	95 (1.0)	89 (2.3)	90 (1.7)	95 (1.0)	95 (1.3)	93 (1.4)	97 (0.8)	86 (2.2)	92 (1.8)	91 (1.5)	55 (3.8)	54 (3.5)	64 (2.5)
Mother's employment status[2]																		
Employed	5,148 (84.2)	4,985 (130.1)	4,491 (88.6)	86 (1.0)	85 (1.2)	84 (1.1)	84 (1.0)	80 (1.4)	84 (1.1)	94 (0.7)	86 (1.5)	98 (0.3)	80 (1.2)	90 (1.3)	86 (0.9)	36 (1.2)	35 (1.7)	42 (1.5)
Unemployed	396 (36.9)	467 (61.5)	550 (52.0)	77 (5.0)	69 (7.5)	80 (4.4)	80 (4.7)	69 (7.9)	80 (4.4)	94 (3.3)	94 (2.0)	98 (1.1)	69 (5.5)	88 (7.1)	89 (4.0)	37 (4.8)	26 (5.8)	33 (4.2)
Not in labor force	2,809 (73.3)	3,105 (128.9)	2,756 (86.9)	83 (1.4)	83 (1.7)	84 (1.7)	82 (1.5)	79 (2.2)	84 (1.7)	94 (0.9)	87 (2.1)	97 (0.7)	80 (1.3)	89 (2.1)	87 (1.4)	38 (1.9)	38 (2.0)	43 (1.9)
Number of parents in the household																		
Two parents	6,416 (75.1)	6,826 (82.0)	5,702 (95.5)	87 (0.8)	85 (1.1)	86 (0.9)	84 (0.9)	82 (1.2)	86 (0.9)	94 (0.6)	88 (1.0)	98 (0.3)	81 (0.9)	91 (1.0)	88 (0.9)	38 (1.2)	37 (1.4)	42 (1.4)
None or one parent	2,135 (75.1)	1,859 (83.9)	2,542 (86.2)	76 (2.0)	78 (3.2)	76 (2.0)	82 (1.6)	70 (3.6)	76 (2.0)	93 (1.2)	83 (3.7)	97 (0.6)	74 (2.3)	84 (3.5)	82 (1.7)	30 (2.1)	30 (3.1)	40 (2.3)
Poverty status[3]																		
Poor	2,008 (60.4)	1,934 (72.9)	1,958 (77.8)	74 (2.1)	71 (3.4)	74 (2.2)	81 (1.7)	69 (3.4)	74 (2.2)	92 (1.6)	86 (3.1)	96 (0.8)	73 (2.3)	85 (3.2)	83 (1.7)	27 (2.1)	28 (2.8)	39 (2.2)
Near-poor	1,782 (70.5)	1,939 (109.5)	1,960 (86.5)	81 (0.9)	81 (1.9)	81 (2.1)	76 (2.8)	76 (2.8)	81 (2.1)	95 (1.0)	81 (3.4)	98 (0.5)	76 (1.9)	84 (2.0)	82 (2.1)	34 (2.8)	34 (3.3)	38 (2.6)
Nonpoor	4,762 (71.9)	4,812 (83.0)	4,327 (87.6)	90 (0.8)	89 (1.3)	90 (1.0)	85 (2.0)	84 (1.2)	88 (1.0)	95 (0.6)	90 (0.9)	98 (0.4)	85 (1.0)	92 (1.1)	89 (1.0)	41 (1.4)	40 (1.7)	44 (1.5)

[1] The respondent was the parent most knowledgeable about the child's care and education. Responding parents reported on their own activities and the activities of their spouse/other adults in the household.
[2] Excludes children living in households with no mother or female guardian present.
[3] Poor children are those whose family incomes were below the Census Bureau's poverty threshold in the year prior to data collection; near-poor children are those whose family incomes ranged from the poverty threshold to 199 percent of the poverty threshold; and nonpoor children are those whose family incomes were at or above 200 percent of the poverty threshold. The poverty threshold is a dollar amount that varies depending on a family's size and composition and is updated annually to account for inflation. In 2011, for example, the poverty threshold for a family of four with two children was $22,811. Survey respondents are asked to select the range within which their income falls, rather than giving the exact amount of their income; therefore, the measure of poverty status is an approximation.

NOTE: While National Household Education Surveys Program (NHES) administrations prior to 2012 were administered via telephone with an interviewer, NHES:2012 used self-administered paper-and-pencil questionnaires that were mailed to respondents. Measurable differences in estimates between 2012 and prior years could reflect actual changes in the population, or the changes could be due to the mode change from telephone to mail. Totals include other racial/ethnic groups not separately shown. Race categories exclude persons of Hispanic ethnicity. Detail may not sum to totals because of rounding.
SOURCE: U.S. Department of Education, National Center for Education Statistics, Early Childhood Program Participation Survey (ECPP:2001 and 2012) and Parent and Family Involvement in Education Survey (PFI:2007) of the National Household Education Surveys Program. (This table was prepared October 2014.)

Table 207.20. Percentage of kindergartners through fifth-graders whose parents reported doing education-related activities with their children in the past month, by selected child, parent, and school characteristics: 2003, 2007, and 2012

[Standard errors appear in parentheses]

Selected child, parent, or school characteristic	Visited a library			Went to a play, concert, or other live show			Visited an art gallery, museum, or historical site			Visited a zoo or aquarium			Attended an event sponsored by a community, religious, or ethnic group[1]		
	2003	2007	2012	2003	2007	2012	2003	2007	2012	2003	2007	2012	2003	2007	2012
1	2	3	4	5	6	7	8	9	10	11	12	13	14	15	16
Total	50.2 (0.80)	48.8 (1.12)	46.5 (0.88)	35.5 (0.87)	31.4 (0.87)	32.0 (0.88)	22.2 (0.83)	26.3 (1.09)	25.9 (0.77)	16.5 (0.69)	19.0 (0.80)	24.6 (0.86)	62.0 (0.80)	58.9 (1.14)	57.3 (0.79)
Sex of child															
Male	47.3 (1.08)	46.8 (1.66)	44.8 (1.40)	33.6 (1.09)	28.7 (1.06)	30.0 (1.25)	23.1 (1.12)	27.1 (1.80)	25.6 (1.11)	16.3 (0.88)	18.5 (0.95)	24.1 (1.07)	61.0 (1.08)	57.3 (1.48)	57.2 (1.24)
Female	53.1 (1.11)	50.9 (1.52)	48.3 (1.37)	37.5 (1.09)	34.5 (1.57)	34.1 (1.16)	21.2 (1.07)	25.4 (1.30)	26.2 (1.09)	16.7 (0.87)	19.6 (1.41)	25.2 (1.18)	63.0 (1.09)	60.6 (1.49)	57.5 (1.15)
Race/ethnicity of child															
White	49.1 (1.03)	48.5 (1.22)	45.3 (1.14)	37.2 (1.26)	32.8 (1.13)	33.6 (1.10)	21.2 (1.09)	25.4 (1.18)	27.4 (1.00)	13.6 (0.85)	15.3 (0.85)	20.8 (0.99)	64.6 (1.12)	63.1 (1.19)	56.8 (1.13)
Black	52.3 (2.50)	56.1 (3.95)	50.2 (2.97)	36.7 (2.23)	34.5 (3.02)	35.9 (2.65)	24.4 (1.97)	32.7 (5.13)	25.1 (2.05)	18.9 (1.55)	24.2 (2.72)	27.5 (2.69)	66.3 (2.35)	61.7 (4.59)	68.7 (2.10)
Hispanic	48.2 (1.77)	44.6 (2.14)	43.5 (2.11)	28.0 (1.53)	25.1 (1.67)	26.8 (1.80)	20.8 (1.38)	23.5 (2.13)	23.3 (1.66)	23.7 (1.32)	25.4 (1.97)	29.3 (2.04)	49.3 (1.75)	44.9 (2.17)	53.5 (2.28)
Asian/Pacific Islander	70.9 (5.11)	58.8 (5.81)	58.6 (3.93)	36.0 (4.44)	34.8 (5.45)	36.9 (3.75)	34.3 (4.22)	30.8 (5.21)	34.5 (3.35)	22.3 (3.97)	22.2 (3.51)	32.8 (3.86)	65.4 (4.25)	56.7 (5.49)	51.2 (4.28)
Other	51.9 (4.57)	41.8 (5.09)	47.2 (3.48)	38.6 (4.28)	31.1 (4.18)	25.3 (2.76)	25.8 (3.65)	27.1 (4.05)	27.0 (3.19)	14.7 (3.13)	17.3 (3.02)	22.5 (3.13)	59.5 (5.41)	62.4 (4.60)	55.9 (3.54)
Grade of child															
Kindergarten and grade 1	48.7 (1.28)	48.0 (2.19)	46.0 (1.44)	34.2 (1.32)	29.8 (1.53)	31.9 (1.69)	21.1 (1.04)	25.7 (2.12)	28.5 (1.44)	18.2 (1.10)	21.5 (1.69)	28.7 (1.78)	59.3 (1.29)	55.9 (1.87)	55.9 (1.41)
Grades 2 and 3	50.5 (1.45)	46.9 (1.64)	48.6 (1.59)	33.2 (1.41)	31.5 (1.71)	32.8 (1.52)	22.2 (1.13)	25.3 (1.65)	27.1 (1.59)	17.5 (1.13)	16.7 (1.11)	26.1 (1.49)	61.5 (1.41)	60.5 (1.72)	59.0 (1.57)
Grades 4 and 5	51.2 (1.32)	51.4 (1.68)	45.0 (1.59)	38.9 (1.18)	33.0 (1.57)	31.3 (1.30)	23.1 (1.28)	27.8 (1.74)	21.8 (1.28)	14.0 (0.90)	18.8 (1.58)	18.5 (1.04)	65.0 (1.28)	60.2 (1.86)	57.3 (1.48)
Language spoken most at home by child[2]															
English	50.2 (0.86)	49.7 (1.23)	46.6 (1.00)	37.0 (0.93)	32.7 (0.93)	32.7 (0.91)	22.6 (0.90)	27.1 (1.20)	26.8 (0.76)	15.5 (0.71)	17.9 (0.80)	23.3 (0.87)	63.9 (0.85)	61.3 (1.20)	57.8 (0.78)
Spanish	41.8 (3.21)	37.5 (3.62)	33.8 (4.10)	16.4 (1.95)	16.7 (2.55)	20.0 (3.13)	14.9 (2.25)	16.2 (2.61)	12.8 (2.11)	26.0 (2.87)	27.0 (3.14)	30.4 (3.61)	34.7 (2.76)	33.4 (3.67)	54.9 (3.69)
English and Spanish equally	51.1 (4.40)	51.3 (5.65)	48.7 (4.14)	24.2 (3.77)	28.5 (5.18)	24.2 (3.38)	19.6 (3.35)	27.8 (5.45)	23.3 (4.60)	28.3 (4.06)	31.4 (5.49)	34.5 (4.78)	53.5 (4.92)	43.1 (5.88)	53.0 (5.31)
English and other language equally	‡ (†)	‡ (†)	61.5 (5.01)	‡ (†)	‡ (†)	42.8 (4.44)	‡ (†)	‡ (†)	31.2 (5.01)	‡ (†)	‡ (†)	38.7 (4.85)	‡ (†)	‡ (†)	64.2 (3.82)
Other language	69.8 (6.74)	41.4 (11.41)	47.0 (10.39)	30.5 (7.05)	28.8 (8.24)	32.0 (9.29)	26.3 (5.28)	22.5 ! (7.32)	17.6 ! (7.68)	27.8 (6.45)	14.5 ! (5.37)	21.9 ! (9.08)	55.8 (8.96)	66.0 (9.17)	42.5 (11.31)
Highest education level of parents/guardians in the household															
Less than high school	36.1 (3.39)	36.5 (4.20)	37.4 (3.31)	20.0 (3.10)	19.7 (3.46)	18.5 (2.69)	9.3 (1.75)	16.2 (2.82)	18.1 (3.19)	15.3 (2.05)	19.2 (3.08)	27.7 (3.58)	34.3 (3.06)	35.9 (4.70)	48.0 (2.88)
High school/GED	44.5 (1.64)	41.2 (3.13)	45.0 (2.43)	28.6 (1.83)	21.9 (2.08)	26.3 (2.17)	17.8 (1.73)	22.2 (3.16)	21.2 (2.12)	16.5 (1.18)	17.0 (2.00)	23.3 (1.90)	50.5 (1.81)	44.6 (2.88)	53.8 (2.41)
Vocational/technical or some college	44.3 (2.04)	43.5 (2.46)	41.0 (1.74)	32.8 (1.89)	29.6 (2.15)	30.7 (1.76)	19.1 (1.32)	18.6 (2.00)	23.7 (1.55)	15.2 (1.29)	16.4 (1.95)	23.8 (1.70)	62.1 (1.64)	58.2 (2.61)	54.0 (1.64)
Associate's degree	47.4 (3.04)	46.6 (2.74)	43.7 (3.08)	41.1 (3.24)	31.0 (2.46)	28.0 (2.74)	22.0 (2.40)	22.3 (2.72)	24.9 (2.39)	15.4 (2.09)	19.3 (2.56)	25.8 (2.72)	67.0 (2.85)	58.7 (2.84)	58.2 (2.38)
Bachelor's degree/some graduate school	57.7 (1.74)	51.9 (1.89)	51.2 (1.53)	40.1 (1.61)	37.1 (1.85)	38.3 (1.45)	27.6 (1.70)	32.1 (2.07)	30.2 (1.47)	16.0 (1.32)	21.1 (1.79)	24.3 (1.50)	71.3 (1.63)	66.7 (2.07)	61.5 (1.37)
Graduate/professional degree	65.2 (2.04)	62.2 (1.86)	57.8 (1.56)	47.2 (2.53)	40.0 (2.20)	45.0 (1.68)	31.7 (2.02)	34.7 (1.96)	35.6 (1.72)	20.7 (1.82)	20.3 (1.61)	24.7 (1.23)	75.6 (1.55)	72.3 (1.63)	67.0 (1.56)
Family income (in current dollars)															
$20,000 or less	44.2 (2.14)	42.5 (4.09)	43.6 (2.48)	29.0 (2.07)	20.4 (2.46)	22.1 (1.72)	19.4 (2.02)	20.6 (4.29)	19.4 (1.87)	20.1 (1.73)	16.8 (1.99)	25.7 (2.05)	51.3 (2.32)	44.4 (3.74)	51.5 (2.11)
$20,001 to $50,000	48.9 (1.45)	46.5 (2.05)	44.1 (2.11)	31.0 (1.51)	29.6 (1.75)	27.7 (1.58)	18.9 (1.25)	22.9 (2.06)	18.9 (1.47)	15.2 (2.01)	21.0 (2.19)	25.4 (1.84)	61.5 (1.65)	55.1 (2.06)	56.7 (2.01)
$50,001 to $75,000	50.0 (1.65)	49.2 (2.28)	47.1 (2.14)	39.0 (1.59)	31.9 (1.80)	33.7 (2.39)	23.1 (1.42)	23.9 (1.64)	29.7 (1.88)	14.9 (1.27)	15.8 (1.50)	27.4 (1.96)	64.5 (1.42)	61.2 (2.02)	56.3 (2.05)
$75,001 to $100,000	49.9 (2.36)	49.5 (2.44)	46.8 (2.16)	39.4 (2.27)	33.9 (2.03)	34.4 (2.01)	23.0 (2.22)	29.7 (2.25)	28.2 (2.07)	15.3 (1.52)	18.5 (2.17)	26.2 (2.03)	66.2 (2.25)	63.0 (2.18)	60.1 (2.18)
Over $100,000	60.9 (2.14)	56.0 (1.87)	50.1 (1.76)	45.3 (2.10)	40.7 (1.91)	40.0 (1.39)	30.9 (1.66)	35.2 (1.69)	31.2 (1.63)	18.3 (1.88)	21.4 (1.41)	20.5 (1.21)	69.4 (1.84)	70.5 (1.86)	60.7 (1.59)

See notes at end of table.

Table 207.20. Percentage of kindergartners through fifth-graders whose parents reported doing education-related activities with their children in the past month, by selected child, parent, and school characteristics: 2003, 2007, and 2012—Continued

[Standard errors appear in parentheses]

Selected child, parent, or school characteristic	Visited a library			Went to a play, concert, or other live show			Visited an art gallery, museum, or historical site			Visited a zoo or aquarium			Attended an event sponsored by a community, religious, or ethnic group[1]		
	2003	2007	2012	2003	2007	2012	2003	2007	2012	2003	2007	2012	2003	2007	2012
1	2	3	4	5	6	7	8	9	10	11	12	13	14	15	16
Poverty status[3]															
Poor..........	43.3 (2.30)	42.1 (3.38)	45.0 (2.53)	26.3 (1.98)	19.4 (2.18)	22.5 (1.63)	18.9 (1.97)	20.4 (3.83)	18.3 (1.55)	19.5 (1.67)	17.0 (2.04)	24.3 (2.09)	52.0 (2.14)	45.8 (3.76)	54.0 (2.18)
Near-poor..........	48.9 (1.63)	47.1 (2.40)	41.8 (1.86)	31.6 (2.10)	31.7 (2.15)	28.5 (2.10)	17.7 (1.50)	20.6 (1.96)	21.9 (1.77)	16.1 (1.28)	21.9 (2.17)	26.2 (1.99)	61.6 (2.24)	57.4 (2.28)	57.1 (2.10)
Nonpoor..........	52.8 (1.02)	51.7 (1.14)	48.8 (1.14)	39.8 (1.17)	35.7 (1.07)	36.9 (1.00)	24.9 (1.06)	30.2 (1.08)	30.4 (1.04)	15.8 (0.87)	18.8 (0.90)	24.1 (0.91)	65.2 (0.99)	64.0 (1.14)	58.7 (0.96)
Control of school															
Public..........	49.2 (0.87)	47.6 (1.22)	46.2 (0.94)	34.9 (0.88)	31.0 (0.93)	30.9 (0.96)	21.2 (0.92)	24.9 (1.12)	25.0 (0.82)	16.3 (0.71)	19.1 (0.88)	24.1 (0.94)	60.6 (0.85)	56.9 (1.25)	55.9 (0.87)
Private..........	57.0 (2.31)	57.0 (2.86)	49.0 (2.51)	40.0 (2.55)	34.3 (2.65)	41.8 (2.56)	29.0 (2.04)	35.6 (2.82)	34.4 (2.49)	17.9 (1.85)	18.5 (2.05)	28.8 (2.43)	72.2 (2.15)	71.8 (2.77)	70.0 (2.30)

†Not applicable.
‡Interpret data with caution. The coefficient of variation (CV) for this estimate is between 30 and 50 percent.
‡Reporting standards not met (too few cases for a reliable estimate).
[1]In 2007 and 2012, a single item asked parents if they had attended an event sponsored by a community, ethnic, or religious group. In 2003, attendance at an event sponsored by a religious group was asked separately about separately from attendance at an event sponsored by a community or ethnic group.
[2]Excludes children who were not able to speak.
[3]Poor children are those whose family incomes were below the Census Bureau's poverty threshold in the year prior to data collection; near-poor children are those whose family incomes ranged from the poverty threshold to 199 percent of the poverty threshold; and nonpoor children are those whose family incomes were at or above 200 percent of the poverty threshold. The poverty threshold is a dollar amount that varies depending on a family's size and composition and is updated annually to account for inflation. In 2011, for example, the poverty threshold for a family of four with two children was $22,811. Survey respondents

are asked to select the range within which their income falls, rather than giving the exact amount of their income; therefore, the measure of poverty status is an approximation.
NOTE: While National Household Education Surveys Program (NHES) administrations prior to 2012 were administered via telephone with an interviewer, NHES:2012 used self-administered paper-and-pencil questionnaires that were mailed to respondents. Measurable differences in estimates between 2012 and prior years could reflect actual changes in the population, or the changes could be due to the mode change from telephone to mail. The respondent was the parent most knowledgeable about the child's education. Responding parents reported on their own activities and the activities of their spouse/other adults in the household. All information, including control of school, is based on parent reports. Excludes homeschooled children. Race categories exclude persons of Hispanic ethnicity. Some data have been revised from previously published figures.
SOURCE: U.S. Department of Education, National Center for Education Statistics, Parent and Family Involvement in Education Survey (PFI:2003, 2007, and 2012) of the National Household Education Surveys Program. (This table was prepared September 2014.)

Table 207.30. Percentage of kindergartners through fifth-graders whose parents reported doing education-related activities with their children in the past week, by selected child, parent, and school characteristics: 2003, 2007, and 2012

[Standard errors appear in parentheses]

Selected child, parent, or school characteristic	Told child a story			Did arts and crafts			Discussed family history/ethnic heritage			Played board games or did puzzles		
	2003	2007	2012	2003	2007	2012	2003	2007	2012	2003	2007	2012
1	2	3	4	5	6	7	8	9	10	11	12	13
Total	74.9 (0.66)	70.3 (1.11)	68.8 (0.91)	74.9 (0.70)	75.7 (1.00)	67.0 (0.84)	53.1 (0.89)	53.5 (1.10)	49.4 (1.00)	72.9 (0.68)	69.0 (0.99)	64.0 (0.94)
Sex of child												
Male	73.3 (0.86)	68.7 (1.51)	68.2 (1.27)	69.7 (0.98)	70.3 (1.32)	60.7 (1.19)	51.1 (1.16)	52.9 (1.48)	47.6 (1.10)	71.8 (0.92)	69.0 (1.49)	63.0 (1.20)
Female	76.6 (0.96)	72.0 (1.47)	69.5 (1.22)	80.2 (1.01)	81.7 (1.33)	73.8 (1.25)	55.1 (1.28)	54.3 (1.45)	51.2 (1.47)	74.1 (1.05)	69.0 (1.43)	65.2 (1.14)
Race/ethnicity of child												
White	76.0 (0.96)	73.2 (1.20)	71.9 (0.98)	75.4 (0.89)	74.9 (1.23)	67.5 (1.08)	44.7 (1.13)	45.6 (1.28)	37.3 (1.21)	73.8 (0.87)	69.0 (1.19)	66.6 (1.03)
Black	69.6 (2.00)	61.6 (3.81)	64.3 (2.40)	68.1 (2.14)	73.0 (3.53)	64.0 (2.76)	66.6 (2.45)	66.9 (3.59)	67.4 (2.44)	72.9 (1.92)	72.8 (3.14)	60.1 (2.94)
Hispanic	74.2 (1.55)	67.6 (2.46)	65.4 (2.15)	79.6 (1.45)	81.2 (1.66)	67.7 (1.69)	64.5 (1.71)	61.1 (2.22)	58.1 (2.09)	68.5 (1.82)	67.5 (2.33)	62.2 (1.88)
Asian/Pacific Islander	75.8 (3.73)	71.4 (4.75)	70.9 (3.19)	70.9 (4.34)	70.4 (4.64)	65.0 (3.53)	68.2 (4.83)	74.6 (4.32)	69.3 (3.67)	77.0 (3.82)	63.7 (4.79)	61.1 (3.94)
Other	83.6 (4.37)	72.4 (4.43)	65.2 (3.20)	76.2 (3.58)	73.5 (4.00)	69.4 (2.66)	67.5 (5.02)	59.7 (4.90)	51.7 (3.72)	76.7 (3.81)	68.7 (4.34)	62.6 (3.64)
Grade of child												
Kindergarten through grade 1	84.5 (0.93)	74.1 (1.81)	78.0 (1.60)	89.3 (0.84)	89.1 (1.08)	81.2 (1.14)	47.7 (1.38)	45.7 (2.03)	44.4 (1.89)	77.5 (1.17)	73.5 (1.71)	69.3 (1.56)
Grades 2 through 3	74.5 (1.21)	70.7 (1.94)	66.9 (1.51)	74.0 (1.12)	75.4 (1.84)	66.7 (1.54)	54.7 (1.34)	55.7 (1.93)	52.1 (1.53)	72.7 (1.09)	68.9 (1.70)	65.5 (1.44)
Grades 4 through 5	66.4 (1.20)	66.1 (1.60)	60.2 (1.55)	62.2 (1.36)	62.6 (1.80)	51.2 (1.45)	56.5 (1.42)	59.3 (1.78)	52.3 (1.44)	68.9 (1.18)	64.6 (1.83)	56.6 (1.50)
Language spoken most at home by child[1]												
English	75.4 (0.73)	71.0 (1.22)	69.4 (0.98)	74.4 (0.72)	74.6 (1.04)	67.2 (0.81)	51.5 (0.93)	52.0 (1.10)	46.8 (1.13)	73.7 (0.73)	68.8 (1.06)	64.0 (1.06)
Spanish	65.6 (2.85)	60.7 (3.74)	56.4 (2.40)	81.7 (2.16)	84.5 (2.84)	70.7 (3.63)	60.2 (3.11)	62.2 (3.48)	64.7 (4.04)	58.1 (3.10)	69.2 (3.62)	60.2 (4.36)
English and Spanish equally	76.6 (3.83)	67.5 (4.69)	68.7 (2.15)	78.7 (3.88)	85.7 (3.23)	64.5 (4.01)	77.3 (4.18)	63.2 (3.98)	72.2 (4.54)	75.2 (3.73)	76.9 (4.06)	67.0 (3.51)
English and other language equally	‡ (†)	‡ (†)	74.6 (3.94)	‡ (†)	‡ (†)	66.9 (4.78)	‡ (†)	‡ (†)	72.2 (4.54)	‡ (†)	‡ (†)	68.2 (3.67)
Other language	81.7 (6.95)	80.3 (8.34)	66.1 (9.93)	76.7 (4.81)	84.4 (5.61)	55.2 (10.98)	75.1 (6.13)	74.8 (8.83)	63.1 (11.51)	74.8 (7.43)	66.3 (10.40)	65.5 (11.12)
Highest education level of parents/guardians in the household												
Less than high school	68.6 (2.73)	58.4 (3.93)	65.0 (3.19)	75.7 (2.63)	75.7 (3.55)	67.2 (3.32)	59.1 (3.11)	54.2 (3.05)	60.7 (3.45)	70.1 (2.69)	65.7 (3.57)	61.7 (3.09)
High school/GED	71.2 (1.56)	68.4 (2.75)	65.7 (2.45)	75.1 (1.41)	79.2 (2.57)	70.3 (2.50)	54.7 (2.01)	55.9 (3.56)	50.8 (2.04)	72.6 (1.39)	74.5 (2.61)	64.8 (2.32)
Vocational/technical or some college	75.9 (1.54)	70.0 (2.56)	69.1 (1.56)	76.2 (1.51)	76.2 (2.15)	64.4 (1.87)	50.8 (1.75)	53.1 (2.69)	47.0 (1.90)	71.6 (1.58)	69.0 (2.44)	63.9 (1.72)
Associate's degree	76.0 (2.00)	68.9 (2.58)	67.0 (3.80)	73.6 (2.47)	72.3 (3.13)	66.0 (2.45)	50.9 (3.16)	48.7 (3.17)	44.6 (3.22)	70.1 (2.50)	64.9 (2.77)	57.9 (3.69)
Bachelor's degree/some graduate school	77.3 (1.60)	70.6 (2.11)	71.3 (1.37)	74.0 (1.48)	74.2 (1.31)	66.8 (1.47)	47.3 (1.74)	51.8 (2.06)	45.6 (1.49)	75.8 (1.27)	69.4 (1.65)	65.1 (1.67)
Graduate/professional degree	78.6 (1.64)	77.9 (1.91)	72.7 (1.41)	73.9 (1.72)	74.1 (1.99)	67.3 (1.41)	60.1 (2.16)	55.9 (1.87)	51.9 (1.74)	74.9 (1.82)	66.8 (1.88)	67.8 (1.39)
Family income (in current dollars)												
$20,000 or less	73.9 (1.61)	64.9 (4.03)	68.7 (1.81)	76.0 (1.87)	79.8 (2.93)	71.4 (2.08)	61.6 (2.05)	57.8 (3.43)	54.3 (2.17)	73.9 (1.70)	73.9 (2.57)	61.7 (2.22)
$20,001 to $50,000	74.0 (1.31)	69.5 (2.19)	68.6 (1.87)	75.3 (1.05)	77.2 (1.86)	68.1 (1.86)	53.5 (1.59)	57.9 (2.05)	53.6 (2.07)	72.3 (1.45)	66.6 (2.01)	63.6 (1.80)
$50,001 to $75,000	74.9 (1.53)	69.1 (2.00)	68.5 (2.31)	75.3 (1.55)	77.5 (1.94)	67.5 (1.86)	49.6 (1.99)	44.4 (2.27)	47.7 (2.35)	72.1 (1.51)	66.6 (2.26)	63.3 (2.35)
$75,001 to $100,000	74.7 (2.02)	72.4 (2.29)	68.4 (2.03)	71.2 (1.98)	64.7 (2.03)	64.7 (1.83)	48.8 (2.28)	49.4 (2.77)	46.3 (2.46)	73.3 (2.30)	70.5 (2.41)	65.6 (2.29)
Over $100,000	78.6 (1.52)	75.3 (1.86)	69.4 (1.35)	75.1 (1.87)	73.9 (1.89)	64.1 (1.62)	50.1 (1.93)	55.4 (2.09)	44.5 (1.48)	74.7 (1.81)	69.1 (1.69)	65.5 (1.50)
Poverty status[2]												
Poor	73.2 (1.67)	65.5 (3.24)	68.6 (2.15)	76.9 (1.85)	77.3 (3.19)	72.0 (2.01)	60.9 (2.13)	59.8 (3.15)	57.6 (2.64)	72.4 (1.88)	72.5 (2.77)	61.7 (2.29)
Near-poor	74.3 (1.30)	68.5 (2.28)	68.3 (1.88)	76.7 (1.24)	81.3 (1.81)	67.5 (1.63)	53.3 (1.79)	56.0 (2.53)	49.8 (2.18)	73.6 (1.85)	68.7 (2.22)	63.3 (1.71)
Nonpoor	75.7 (0.85)	72.6 (1.07)	69.0 (1.07)	73.6 (0.92)	73.2 (1.13)	64.9 (0.98)	50.6 (1.11)	50.5 (1.26)	46.1 (1.09)	72.8 (0.87)	67.8 (1.05)	65.2 (1.16)
Control of school												
Public	75.0 (0.68)	69.6 (1.19)	68.2 (1.04)	75.2 (0.72)	75.9 (0.99)	67.0 (0.89)	52.4 (0.98)	54.0 (1.16)	49.6 (1.07)	73.4 (0.74)	68.9 (1.06)	63.7 (1.04)
Private	74.2 (2.09)	75.2 (2.51)	73.7 (2.08)	72.1 (1.94)	74.8 (2.76)	72.1 (2.45)	58.1 (2.17)	50.6 (2.72)	47.0 (2.75)	69.1 (1.99)	69.6 (2.40)	67.2 (2.25)

†Not applicable.
‡Reporting standards not met (too few cases for a reliable estimate).
[1]Excludes children who were not able to speak.
[2]Poor children are those whose family incomes were below the Census Bureau's poverty threshold in the year prior to data collection; near-poor children are those whose family incomes ranged from the poverty threshold to 199 percent of the poverty threshold; and nonpoor children are those whose family incomes were at or above 200 percent of the poverty threshold. The poverty threshold is a dollar amount that varies depending on a family's size and composition and is updated annually to account for inflation. In 2011, for example, the poverty threshold for a family of four with two children was $22,811. Survey respondents are asked to select the range within which their income falls, rather than giving the exact amount of their income; therefore, the measure of poverty status is an approximation.

NOTE: While National Household Education Surveys Program (NHES) administrations prior to 2012 were administered via telephone with an interviewer, NHES:2012 used self-administered paper-and-pencil questionnaires that were mailed to respondents. Measurable differences in estimates between 2012 and prior years could reflect actual changes in the population, or the changes could be due to the mode change from telephone to mail. The respondent was the parent most knowledgeable about the child's education. Responding parents reported on their own activities and the activities of their spouse/other adults in the household. All information, including control of school, is based on parent reports. Excludes homeschooled children. Race categories exclude persons of Hispanic ethnicity. Some data have been revised from previously published figures.
SOURCE: U.S. Department of Education, National Center for Education Statistics, Parent and Family Involvement in Education Survey (PFI:2003, 2007, and 2012) of the National Household Education Surveys Program. (This table was prepared October 2014.)

Table 207.40. Percentage of elementary and secondary school children whose parents were involved in school activities, by selected child, parent, and school characteristics: 2003, 2007, and 2012

[Standard errors appear in parentheses]

Percent of children whose parents report the following types of involvement in school activities

Selected child, parent, or school characteristic	2003 Attended a general school meeting	2003 Attended parent-teacher conference	2003 Attended a class event	2003 Volunteered at school	2007 Attended a general school meeting	2007 Attended parent-teacher conference	2007 Attended a class event	2007 Volunteered at school	2012 Attended a general school meeting	2012 Attended parent-teacher conference	2012 Attended a class event	2012 Volunteered at school
1	2	3	4	5	6	7	8	9	10	11	12	13
Total	87.7 (0.37)	77.1 (0.42)	69.9 (0.42)	41.8 (0.60)	89.4 (0.48)	78.1 (0.52)	74.5 (0.57)	46.4 (0.63)	87.4 (0.41)	75.8 (0.43)	74.4 (0.45)	41.7 (0.49)
Sex of child												
Male	87.4 (0.49)	77.7 (0.63)	67.4 (0.75)	41.2 (0.87)	89.3 (0.70)	79.2 (0.65)	71.5 (0.90)	44.8 (0.95)	87.1 (0.66)	76.4 (0.61)	72.3 (0.65)	40.0 (0.71)
Female	87.9 (0.55)	76.5 (0.63)	72.6 (0.63)	42.4 (0.83)	89.6 (0.59)	76.8 (0.94)	77.7 (0.82)	48.1 (1.01)	87.7 (0.50)	75.1 (0.61)	76.7 (0.68)	43.5 (0.88)
Race/ethnicity of child												
White	88.7 (0.50)	76.4 (0.62)	74.1 (0.65)	48.3 (0.82)	90.9 (0.52)	77.8 (0.64)	80.1 (0.68)	54.2 (0.85)	89.1 (0.50)	77.2 (0.56)	81.5 (0.54)	49.6 (0.72)
Black	88.7 (0.85)	78.7 (1.35)	63.3 (1.54)	31.9 (1.64)	86.7 (1.77)	77.3 (1.98)	64.7 (2.31)	35.0 (1.89)	85.0 (1.35)	76.1 (1.35)	68.0 (1.66)	30.3 (1.33)
Hispanic	82.6 (1.05)	78.1 (1.10)	60.9 (1.36)	27.7 (1.23)	86.7 (1.14)	80.2 (1.05)	65.0 (1.46)	31.8 (1.34)	85.7 (0.98)	72.8 (1.08)	64.0 (1.34)	31.7 (1.14)
Asian/Pacific Islander	88.5 (2.14)	77.7 (3.03)	65.1 (3.65)	33.9 (2.69)	90.5 (1.98)	80.1 (2.80)	72.5 (2.86)	45.9 (3.78)	83.5 (1.73)	72.3 (1.91)	65.4 (2.56)	36.9 (2.30)
Asian	— (†)	— (†)	— (†)	— (†)	91.0 (2.06)	79.9 (2.87)	71.4 (2.89)	45.8 (3.78)	82.5 (1.80)	71.5 (2.03)	65.0 (2.30)	34.0 (2.33)
Pacific Islander	— (†)	— (†)	— (†)	— (†)	‡ (‡)	‡ (‡)	‡ (‡)	‡ (‡)	90.7 (3.96)	71.4 (8.97)	79.0 (6.32)	54.3 (11.37)
American Indian/Alaska Native[1]	— (†)	— (†)	— (†)	— (†)	94.2 (2.96)	79.7 (7.16)	80.8 (9.63)	58.4 (12.64)	85.1 (4.91)	79.9 (6.85)	75.6 (6.61)	42.3 (8.61)
Other	86.7 (2.22)	77.6 (3.17)	71.6 (2.95)	40.3 (3.86)	89.2 (1.76)	73.6 (3.48)	75.7 (2.83)	44.8 (3.13)	88.8 (1.30)	78.4 (2.31)	76.0 (2.52)	45.3 (2.57)
Highest education level of parents/guardians in the household												
Less than high school	73.5 (1.76)	70.2 (1.94)	47.0 (2.07)	17.5 (1.65)	77.1 (1.83)	72.0 (2.16)	49.8 (2.41)	20.2 (2.68)	77.0 (1.79)	63.3 (1.88)	48.0 (2.04)	18.3 (1.72)
High school/GED[3]	84.0 (0.93)	75.3 (1.03)	62.7 (1.30)	31.4 (1.25)	84.8 (1.28)	73.8 (1.25)	66.6 (1.63)	34.5 (1.71)	82.1 (1.42)	72.2 (1.23)	62.3 (1.45)	27.6 (1.38)
Vocational/technical or some college	88.5 (0.67)	78.0 (1.02)	69.1 (0.94)	38.8 (1.25)	87.5 (1.56)	75.7 (1.48)	69.3 (1.60)	40.3 (1.66)	87.5 (0.62)	75.4 (1.02)	76.1 (0.99)	39.0 (1.14)
Associate's degree	88.6 (1.27)	76.6 (1.68)	73.0 (1.76)	39.8 (1.67)	91.9 (1.18)	80.2 (1.75)	76.9 (2.14)	45.3 (2.32)	88.9 (0.91)	79.5 (1.13)	80.5 (1.37)	44.9 (1.77)
Bachelor's degree/some graduate school	92.0 (0.73)	79.8 (0.89)	80.1 (0.94)	53.9 (1.30)	93.6 (0.75)	81.4 (1.00)	83.2 (0.95)	57.1 (1.44)	92.1 (0.53)	79.9 (0.62)	85.0 (0.63)	55.0 (1.11)
Graduate/professional degree	94.6 (0.74)	79.5 (1.00)	80.8 (1.10)	61.7 (1.57)	95.6 (0.64)	82.3 (1.13)	87.3 (0.95)	64.1 (1.33)	95.1 (0.47)	83.0 (0.68)	90.1 (0.59)	61.8 (1.30)
Family income (in current dollars)												
$20,000 or less	79.8 (1.43)	74.6 (1.33)	56.6 (1.42)	26.1 (1.45)	78.9 (1.87)	75.1 (1.90)	54.8 (2.11)	24.8 (1.87)	79.9 (1.15)	69.4 (1.36)	57.2 (1.31)	24.1 (1.18)
$20,001 to $50,000	85.1 (0.67)	77.3 (0.85)	66.2 (0.94)	34.6 (1.14)	86.7 (1.02)	77.1 (1.21)	68.6 (1.15)	34.8 (1.10)	84.3 (0.73)	74.5 (1.04)	67.2 (1.28)	31.1 (1.22)
$50,001 to $75,000	89.9 (0.79)	76.9 (0.96)	74.5 (1.03)	46.0 (1.26)	92.0 (0.73)	78.6 (0.96)	79.0 (1.15)	51.7 (1.18)	88.7 (0.97)	77.3 (1.23)	77.3 (1.19)	43.7 (1.40)
$75,001 to $100,000	94.0 (0.80)	79.4 (1.28)	77.7 (1.34)	51.5 (1.71)	92.9 (0.85)	79.6 (1.47)	83.2 (1.20)	57.3 (1.90)	89.9 (0.88)	77.3 (1.15)	81.9 (1.13)	47.8 (1.24)
Over $100,000	93.9 (0.71)	77.9 (1.21)	80.7 (1.03)	61.1 (1.19)	96.1 (0.39)	80.1 (1.06)	86.7 (0.80)	64.7 (1.39)	92.5 (0.92)	79.0 (0.80)	85.5 (0.96)	57.6 (1.05)
Poverty status[2]												
Poor	79.4 (1.55)	74.5 (1.37)	56.7 (1.57)	26.8 (1.55)	80.9 (1.81)	76.8 (1.76)	55.8 (2.01)	26.5 (1.84)	82.5 (1.08)	71.3 (1.29)	60.0 (1.52)	26.8 (1.28)
Near-poor	85.1 (0.89)	77.9 (1.05)	64.8 (0.98)	32.5 (1.31)	86.2 (1.28)	76.8 (1.58)	68.1 (1.32)	35.2 (1.31)	83.7 (0.78)	75.2 (0.97)	66.5 (1.22)	31.2 (1.35)
Nonpoor	91.0 (0.46)	77.6 (0.58)	75.7 (0.51)	49.5 (0.76)	93.1 (0.34)	78.9 (0.58)	82.3 (0.57)	56.1 (0.77)	90.4 (0.51)	77.5 (0.55)	82.2 (0.61)	50.6 (0.71)
Control of school and enrollment level of child												
Public school	86.7 (0.40)	75.9 (0.45)	68.0 (0.47)	38.5 (0.64)	88.5 (0.53)	76.9 (0.59)	72.6 (0.66)	42.7 (0.69)	86.5 (0.43)	74.8 (0.45)	72.9 (0.50)	39.0 (0.52)
Elementary (kindergarten to grade 8)	90.9 (0.40)	85.1 (0.42)	71.7 (0.57)	42.8 (0.74)	91.7 (0.59)	85.1 (0.69)	76.1 (0.79)	48.5 (1.00)	90.0 (0.42)	82.4 (0.47)	76.0 (0.64)	44.1 (0.69)
Secondary (grades 9 to 12)	76.9 (1.06)	54.8 (1.02)	59.4 (1.06)	28.5 (0.98)	82.0 (1.12)	59.9 (1.14)	65.5 (1.20)	30.6 (1.05)	77.8 (0.92)	55.5 (1.04)	65.1 (0.90)	26.2 (0.71)
Private school	95.7 (0.61)	86.6 (1.03)	85.6 (1.23)	68.7 (1.57)	96.3 (1.08)	88.1 (1.84)	88.1 (1.27)	74.1 (1.75)	96.2 (0.58)	86.9 (1.13)	90.1 (1.13)	69.5 (1.63)
Elementary (kindergarten to grade 8)	96.6 (0.69)	91.6 (0.92)	88.4 (1.22)	73.4 (1.90)	96.8 (1.46)	92.5 (1.61)	89.2 (1.65)	80.3 (1.87)	97.4 (0.63)	91.2 (1.47)	91.8 (1.39)	74.4 (1.87)
Secondary (grades 9 to 12)	93.0 (1.56)	72.2 (2.54)	77.6 (2.93)	55.2 (2.78)	95.2 (1.11)	71.2 (4.05)	85.2 (2.21)	58.6 (3.50)	92.5 (1.20)	73.6 (2.19)	84.9 (2.08)	54.6 (2.44)

—Not available.
†Not applicable.
‡Reporting standards not met (too few cases for a reliable estimate).
[1]Included in "Other" in 2003 data.
[2]Poor children are those whose family incomes were below the Census Bureau's poverty threshold in the year prior to data collection; near-poor children are those whose family incomes ranged from the poverty threshold to 199 percent of the poverty threshold; and nonpoor children are those whose family incomes were at or above 200 percent of the poverty threshold. The poverty threshold is a dollar amount that varies depending on a family's size and composition and is updated annually to account for inflation. In 2011, for example, the poverty threshold for a family of four with two children was $22,811. Survey respondents are asked to select the range within which their income falls, rather than giving the exact amount of their income; therefore, the measure of poverty status is an approximation.

NOTE: While National Household Education Surveys Program (NHES) administrations prior to 2012 were administered via telephone with an interviewer, NHES:2012 used self-administered paper-and-pencil questionnaires that were mailed to respondents. Measurable differences in estimates between 2012 and prior years could reflect actual changes in the population, or the changes could be due to the mode change from telephone to mail. Includes children enrolled in kindergarten through grade 12 and ungraded students. Excludes homeschooled children. The respondent was the parent most knowledgeable about the child's education. Responding parents reported on their own activities and the activities of their spouse/other adults in the household. Race categories exclude persons of Hispanic ethnicity. Asian and Pacific Islander data were not collected separately prior to 2007. Some data have been revised from previously published figures.
SOURCE: U.S. Department of Education, National Center for Education Statistics, Parent and Family Involvement in Education: 2002–03 and Parent and Family Involvement in Education Survey (PFI:2003, 2007, and 2012) of the National Household Education Surveys Program. (This table was prepared October 2014.)

Table 208.10. Public elementary and secondary pupil/teacher ratios, by selected school characteristics: Selected years, fall 1990 through fall 2012

Selected school characteristic	1990	1993	1994	1995	1996	1997	1998	1999	2000	2001	2002	2003	2004	2005	2006	2007	2008	2009	2010[1]	2011	2012
1	2	3	4	5	6	7	8	9	10	11	12	13	14	15	16	17	18	19	20	21	22
All schools	17.4	17.8	17.7	17.8	17.6	17.2	16.9	16.6	16.4	16.3	16.2	16.4	16.2	16.0	15.8	15.7	15.7	16.0	16.4	16.3	16.2
Enrollment size of school																					
Under 300	14.0	14.3	14.1	14.1	14.0	13.7	13.6	13.3	13.1	12.9	12.8	13.0	12.8	12.7	12.7	12.7	12.5	12.6	12.9	12.8	12.7
300 to 499	17.0	17.3	17.2	17.1	16.9	16.5	16.2	15.8	15.5	15.4	15.3	15.5	15.2	15.0	14.9	15.0	14.8	15.2	15.4	15.4	15.3
500 to 999	18.0	18.2	18.1	18.2	17.9	17.5	17.1	16.8	16.7	16.5	16.5	16.6	16.4	16.2	15.9	15.9	15.9	16.3	16.7	16.7	16.6
1,000 to 1,499	17.9	18.5	18.6	18.7	18.5	18.1	17.7	17.6	17.4	17.4	17.4	17.6	17.3	16.9	16.7	16.5	16.5	16.8	17.3	17.1	17.0
1,500 or more	19.2	19.7	19.9	20.0	20.0	19.7	19.3	19.3	19.1	19.0	18.9	19.2	19.1	18.8	18.6	18.1	18.3	18.7	19.5	19.0	18.8
Type																					
Regular schools	17.6	17.9	17.8	17.9	17.7	17.3	17.0	16.7	16.5	16.4	16.3	16.5	16.3	16.1	15.9	15.8	15.8	16.1	16.5	16.4	16.4
Alternative....................	14.2	17.4	18.0	16.6	16.6	16.5	16.4	15.8	15.2	14.9	14.9	15.0	14.4	14.0	14.7	13.5	14.2	14.3	14.8	14.7	14.7
Special education	6.5	7.4	6.9	7.2	7.4	7.6	7.3	7.2	7.0	6.4	7.0	7.3	7.4	6.2	6.6	7.1	6.8	7.1	6.9	7.1	6.9
Vocational	13.0	13.1	12.9	12.7	12.9	12.9	13.1	13.0	12.7	12.7	9.9	10.3	11.5	12.0	13.3	11.3	10.7	10.2	11.7	11.8	11.6
Percent of students eligible for free or reduced-price lunch																					
25 percent or less	—	—	—	—	—	—	—	—	—	—	—	—	16.8	16.4	16.4	16.3	16.1	16.5	16.9	17.5	16.4
26 percent to 50 percent..	—	—	—	—	—	—	—	—	—	—	—	—	16.2	16.1	15.8	15.7	15.7	16.1	16.5	16.2	16.3
51 percent to 75 percent..	—	—	—	—	—	—	—	—	—	—	—	—	15.9	15.6	15.3	15.2	15.4	15.8	16.2	15.8	16.1
More than 75 percent.....	—	—	—	—	—	—	—	—	—	—	—	—	15.9	15.5	15.4	15.0	15.1	15.6	16.0	15.5	16.2
Level and size																					
Elementary schools	18.1	18.2	18.0	18.1	17.8	17.4	17.0	16.7	16.5	16.3	16.2	16.3	16.0	15.8	15.6	15.6	15.5	15.9	16.3	16.3	16.3
Regular	18.2	18.3	18.0	18.1	17.9	17.4	17.0	16.7	16.5	16.3	16.2	16.3	16.0	15.8	15.6	15.6	15.5	15.9	16.3	16.3	16.3
Under 300..............	16.0	16.0	15.7	15.7	15.6	15.3	15.1	14.6	14.4	14.1	13.9	14.0	13.7	13.6	13.5	13.7	13.5	13.7	14.0	14.0	13.9
300 to 499	17.6	17.7	17.5	17.5	17.2	16.8	16.4	16.1	15.8	15.6	15.5	15.6	15.3	15.2	15.1	15.2	15.0	15.4	15.6	15.7	15.6
500 to 999	18.8	18.8	18.5	18.6	18.3	17.8	17.4	17.1	16.9	16.8	16.7	16.8	16.5	16.3	16.0	16.0	16.0	16.5	16.9	16.9	16.9
1,000 to 1,499	19.5	19.7	19.6	19.7	19.4	18.8	18.4	18.3	18.1	18.0	18.0	18.1	17.7	17.2	17.0	16.7	16.8	17.2	17.8	17.7	17.7
1,500 or more........	19.9	21.2	20.4	20.9	21.2	20.7	19.9	20.0	20.5	20.2	20.3	20.8	20.5	19.6	19.4	18.0	18.1	18.5	19.3	19.0	18.7
Secondary schools	16.6	17.3	17.5	17.6	17.5	17.3	17.0	16.8	16.6	16.6	16.7	16.9	16.8	16.6	16.4	16.3	16.2	16.4	16.8	16.5	16.5
Regular	16.7	17.4	17.6	17.7	17.6	17.4	17.1	16.9	16.7	16.7	16.8	17.0	16.9	16.8	16.6	16.4	16.3	16.6	16.9	16.7	16.6
Under 300..............	12.3	12.6	12.7	12.8	12.7	12.5	12.5	12.0	12.0	11.9	12.0	12.3	12.0	12.2	12.0	12.1	11.9	11.9	12.2	12.0	12.0
300 to 499	14.9	15.5	15.7	15.7	15.5	15.3	15.1	14.6	14.5	14.4	14.4	14.7	14.7	14.6	14.4	14.4	14.3	14.3	14.6	14.6	14.5
500 to 999	16.1	16.7	16.8	16.9	16.7	16.4	16.2	16.0	15.8	15.7	15.8	16.0	15.9	15.8	15.6	15.4	15.4	15.6	15.8	15.7	15.6
1,000 to 1,499	17.2	17.8	17.9	18.0	17.9	17.5	17.2	17.1	16.8	16.8	16.9	17.2	17.0	16.8	16.5	16.5	16.3	16.6	16.9	16.6	16.5
1,500 or more........	19.3	19.6	19.9	20.0	20.0	19.7	19.3	19.2	18.9	18.8	18.8	19.0	19.0	18.8	18.5	18.2	18.2	18.6	19.3	18.8	18.7
Combined schools	14.5	15.3	15.1	15.0	14.7	14.4	13.4	13.4	13.7	13.4	13.5	13.8	13.9	14.1	14.7	13.4	13.9	14.0	15.4	14.4	14.3
Under 300	8.9	9.6	9.3	9.0	8.7	8.6	8.9	9.1	9.2	9.1	9.1	9.5	9.2	9.5	10.1	9.2	8.9	9.1	9.2	9.4	9.1
300 to 499	14.2	14.8	14.4	14.7	14.3	14.0	13.6	13.8	13.5	13.1	13.1	14.4	13.4	13.9	14.3	13.7	13.9	13.8	13.6	13.3	13.2
500 to 999	16.3	16.5	16.6	16.6	16.6	16.2	15.5	14.9	15.8	15.6	16.0	15.4	15.8	15.9	16.0	15.2	15.6	15.8	16.9	15.6	15.5
1,000 to 1,499	17.8	18.6	18.3	18.2	18.4	18.0	16.9	16.9	17.5	18.1	17.7	17.5	17.4	16.4	17.3	15.9	16.7	17.9	19.2	18.1	17.8
1,500 or more..............	17.7	18.8	19.5	19.6	19.3	19.3	18.7	19.2	18.6	18.9	19.1	19.2	18.7	20.0	20.3	18.0	21.7	21.7	25.7	23.4	23.0
Ungraded	6.4	7.1	6.7	6.9	5.9	6.2	5.9	5.3	7.0	6.3	6.8	9.6	8.0	7.7	7.2	7.3	5.5	8.5	5.3	6.0	5.6
Level, type, and percent of students eligible for free or reduced-price lunch																					
Elementary, regular																					
25 percent or less	—	—	—	—	—	—	—	—	—	—	—	—	16.6	16.4	16.2	16.2	16.0	16.4	16.8	17.4	16.4
26 to 50 percent........	—	—	—	—	—	—	—	—	—	—	—	—	16.0	15.8	15.5	15.6	15.6	16.0	16.4	16.3	16.3
51 to 75 percent.........	—	—	—	—	—	—	—	—	—	—	—	—	15.7	15.5	15.1	15.2	15.2	15.7	16.0	15.9	16.1
More than 75 percent...	—	—	—	—	—	—	—	—	—	—	—	—	16.0	15.6	15.4	15.1	15.2	15.8	16.1	15.7	16.4
Secondary, regular																					
25 percent or less	—	—	—	—	—	—	—	—	—	—	—	—	17.5	17.0	16.9	16.8	16.6	16.8	17.2	17.8	16.6
26 to 50 percent........	—	—	—	—	—	—	—	—	—	—	—	—	16.9	16.8	16.4	16.4	16.2	16.5	16.8	16.4	16.6
51 to 75 percent.........	—	—	—	—	—	—	—	—	—	—	—	—	16.9	16.7	16.3	16.1	16.4	16.5	17.1	16.1	16.7
More than 75 percent...	—	—	—	—	—	—	—	—	—	—	—	—	16.2	16.7	16.2	15.7	15.9	16.0	16.5	15.5	16.5

—Not available.
[1]Includes imputations for California and Wyoming.
NOTE: Pupil/teacher ratios are based on data reported by types of schools rather than by instructional programs within schools. Only includes schools that reported both enrollment and teacher data. Ratios are based on data reported by schools and may differ from data reported in other tables that reflect aggregate totals reported by states.

SOURCE: U.S. Department of Education, National Center for Education Statistics, Common Core of Data (CCD), "Public Elementary/Secondary School Universe Survey," 1990–91 through 2012–13. (This table was prepared March 2015.)

Table 208.20. Public and private elementary and secondary teachers, enrollment, pupil/teacher ratios, and new teacher hires: Selected years, fall 1955 through fall 2024

Year	Teachers (in thousands)			Enrollment (in thousands)			Pupil/teacher ratio			Number of new teacher hires (in thousands)[1]		
	Total	Public	Private	Total	Public	Private	Total	Public	Private	Total	Public	Private
1	2	3	4	5	6	7	8	9	10	11	12	13
1955	1,286	1,141	145 [2]	35,280	30,680	4,600 [2]	27.4	26.9	31.7 [2]	—	—	—
1960	1,600	1,408	192 [2]	42,181	36,281	5,900 [2]	26.4	25.8	30.7 [2]	—	—	—
1965	1,933	1,710	223	48,473	42,173	6,300	25.1	24.7	28.3	—	—	—
1970	2,292	2,059	233	51,257	45,894	5,363	22.4	22.3	23.0	—	—	—
1971	2,293	2,063	230 [2]	51,271	46,071	5,200 [2]	22.4	22.3	22.6 [2]	—	—	—
1972	2,337	2,106	231 [2]	50,726	45,726	5,000 [2]	21.7	21.7	21.6 [2]	—	—	—
1973	2,372	2,136	236 [2]	50,445	45,445	5,000 [2]	21.3	21.3	21.2 [2]	—	—	—
1974	2,410	2,165	245 [2]	50,073	45,073	5,000 [2]	20.8	20.8	20.4 [2]	—	—	—
1975	2,453	2,198	255 [2]	49,819	44,819	5,000 [2]	20.3	20.4	19.6 [2]	—	—	—
1976	2,457	2,189	268	49,478	44,311	5,167	20.1	20.2	19.3	—	—	—
1977	2,488	2,209	279	48,717	43,577	5,140	19.6	19.7	18.4	—	—	—
1978	2,479	2,207	272	47,637	42,551	5,086	19.2	19.3	18.7	—	—	—
1979	2,461	2,185	276 [2]	46,651	41,651	5,000 [2]	19.0	19.1	18.1 [2]	—	—	—
1980	2,485	2,184	301	46,208	40,877	5,331	18.6	18.7	17.7			
1981	2,440	2,127	313 [2]	45,544	40,044	5,500 [2]	18.7	18.8	17.6 [2]	—	—	—
1982	2,458	2,133	325 [2]	45,166	39,566	5,600 [2]	18.4	18.6	17.2 [2]	—	—	—
1983	2,476	2,139	337	44,967	39,252	5,715	18.2	18.4	17.0	—	—	—
1984	2,508	2,168	340 [2]	44,908	39,208	5,700 [2]	17.9	18.1	16.8 [2]	—	—	—
1985	2,549	2,206	343	44,979	39,422	5,557	17.6	17.9	16.2	—	—	—
1986	2,592	2,244	348 [2]	45,205	39,753	5,452 [2]	17.4	17.7	15.7 [2]	—	—	—
1987	2,631	2,279	352	45,488	40,008	5,479	17.3	17.6	15.6	—	—	—
1988	2,668	2,323	345 [2]	45,430	40,189	5,242 [2]	17.0	17.3	15.2 [2]	—	—	—
1989	2,713	2,357	356	46,141	40,543	5,599	17.0	17.2	15.7	—	—	—
1990	2,759	2,398	361 [2]	46,864	41,217	5,648 [2]	17.0	17.2	15.6 [2]	—	—	—
1991	2,797	2,432	365	47,728	42,047	5,681	17.1	17.3	15.6	—	—	—
1992	2,823	2,459	364 [2]	48,694	42,823	5,870 [2]	17.2	17.4	16.1 [2]	—	—	—
1993	2,868	2,504	364	49,532	43,465	6,067	17.3	17.4	16.7	—	—	—
1994	2,922	2,552	370 [2]	50,106	44,111	5,994 [2]	17.1	17.3	16.2 [2]	—	—	—
1995	2,974	2,598	376	50,759	44,840	5,918	17.1	17.3	15.7	—	—	—
1996	3,051	2,667	384 [2]	51,544	45,611	5,933 [2]	16.9	17.1	15.5 [2]	—	—	—
1997	3,138	2,746	391	52,071	46,127	5,944	16.6	16.8	15.2	—	—	—
1998	3,230	2,830	400 [2]	52,526	46,539	5,988 [2]	16.3	16.4	15.0 [2]	—	—	—
1999	3,319	2,911	408	52,875	46,857	6,018	15.9	16.1	14.7	305	222	83
2000	3,366	2,941	424 [2]	53,373	47,204	6,169 [2]	15.9	16.0	14.5 [2]	—	—	—
2001	3,440	3,000	441	53,992	47,672	6,320	15.7	15.9	14.3	—	—	—
2002	3,476	3,034	442 [2]	54,403	48,183	6,220 [2]	15.7	15.9	14.1 [2]	—	—	—
2003	3,490	3,049	441	54,639	48,540	6,099	15.7	15.9	13.8	311	236	74
2004	3,536	3,091	445 [2]	54,882	48,795	6,087 [2]	15.5	15.8	13.7 [2]	—	—	—
2005	3,593	3,143	450	55,187	49,113	6,073	15.4	15.6	13.5	—	—	—
2006	3,622	3,166	456 [2]	55,307	49,316	5,991 [2]	15.3	15.6	13.2 [2]	—	—	—
2007	3,656	3,200	456	55,201	49,291	5,910	15.1	15.4	13.0	327	246	80
2008	3,670	3,222	448 [2]	54,973	49,266	5,707 [2]	15.0	15.3	12.8 [2]	—	—	—
2009	3,647	3,210	437	54,849	49,361	5,488	15.0	15.4	12.5	—	—	—
2010	3,529	3,099	429 [2]	54,867	49,484	5,382 [2]	15.5	16.0	12.5 [2]	—	—	—
2011	3,524	3,103	421	54,790	49,522	5,268	15.5	16.0	12.5	241	173	68
2012	3,523	3,109	414 [3]	54,952	49,771	5,181 [3]	15.6	16.0	12.5 [3]	321	247	74
2013[3]	3,527	3,120	407	55,036	49,942	5,094	15.6	16.0	12.5	319	250	69
2014[3]	3,520	3,122	398	54,965	49,986	4,979	15.6	16.0	12.5	310	244	66
2015[3]	3,521	3,129	391	54,994	50,094	4,899	15.6	16.0	12.5	316	249	67
2016[3]	3,525	3,138	387	55,077	50,229	4,848	15.6	16.0	12.5	318	250	68
2017[3]	3,577	3,185	392	55,447	50,584	4,863	15.5	15.9	12.4	364	288	76
2018[3]	3,617	3,224	393	55,719	50,871	4,848	15.4	15.8	12.3	358	283	74
2019[3]	3,660	3,264	395	56,031	51,183	4,848	15.3	15.7	12.3	361	286	76
2020[3]	3,700	3,302	398	56,404	51,547	4,856	15.2	15.6	12.2	362	285	76
2021[3]	3,743	3,342	401	56,779	51,910	4,869	15.2	15.5	12.1	367	289	77
2022[3]	3,788	3,383	405	57,151	52,260	4,891	15.1	15.4	12.1	371	292	79
2023[3]	3,840	3,429	410	57,524	52,601	4,922	15.0	15.3	12.0	381	300	81
2024[3]	3,881	3,466	415	57,872	52,920	4,952	14.9	15.3	11.9	375	293	81

—Not available.

[1] A teacher is considered to be a new hire for a public or private school if the teacher had not taught in that control of school in the previous year. A teacher who moves from a public to private or a private to public school is considered a new teacher hire, but a teacher who moves from one public school to another public school or one private school to another private school is not considered a new teacher hire.

[2] Estimated.

[3] Projected.

NOTE: Data for teachers are expressed in full-time equivalents (FTE). Counts of private school teachers and enrollment include prekindergarten through grade 12 in schools offering kindergarten or higher grades. Counts of public school teachers and enrollment include prekindergarten through grade 12. The pupil/teacher ratio includes teachers for students with disabilities and other special teachers, while these teachers are generally excluded from class size calculations. Ratios for public schools reflect totals reported by states and differ from totals reported for schools or school districts. Some data have been revised from previously published figures. Detail may not sum to totals because of rounding.

SOURCE: U.S. Department of Education, National Center for Education Statistics, *Statistics of Public Elementary and Secondary Day Schools*, 1955–56 through 1980–81; Common Core of Data (CCD), "State Nonfiscal Survey of Public Elementary/Secondary Education," 1981–82 through 2012–13; Private School Universe Survey (PSS), 1989–90 through 2011–12; Schools and Staffing Survey (SASS), "Public School Teacher Data File" and "Private School Teacher Data File," 1999–2000 through 2011–12; Elementary and Secondary Teacher Projection Model, 1973 through 2024; and New Teacher Hires Projection Model, 1988 through 2024. (This table was prepared March 2015.)

Table 208.30. Public elementary and secondary teachers, by level and state or jurisdiction: Selected years, fall 2000 through fall 2012

State or jurisdiction	Fall 2000	Fall 2005	Fall 2008	Fall 2009	Fall 2010	Fall 2011				Fall 2012			
						Total	Elementary	Secondary	Ungraded	Total	Elementary	Secondary	Ungraded
1	2	3	4	5	6	7	8	9	10	11	12	13	14
United States	2,941,461 [1]	3,143,003 [1]	3,222,154 [1]	3,209,672 [1]	3,099,095 [1]	3,103,263 [1]	1,734,606 [1]	1,194,504	174,153	3,109,101 [1]	1,719,764 [1]	1,215,042 [1]	174,295
Alabama	48,194 [2]	57,757	47,818	47,492	49,363	47,723	26,963	20,759	0	51,877	30,428	21,450	0
Alaska	7,880	7,912	7,927	8,083	8,171	8,088	4,309	3,779	0	7,682	4,191	3,491	0
Arizona	44,438	51,376	54,696	51,947	50,031	50,800	36,058	14,742	0	48,866	34,248	14,619	0
Arkansas	31,947	32,997	37,162	37,240	34,273	33,983	17,407	13,974	2,601	34,131	17,619	13,929	2,583
California	298,021 [2]	309,222 [2]	303,647 [2]	316,299 [2]	260,806 [2]	268,689 [2]	174,194 [2]	85,727	8,768	266,255 [2]	172,533 [2]	87,675	6,048
Colorado	41,983	45,841	48,692	49,060	48,543	48,078	27,656	20,421	0	48,922	28,033	20,889	0
Connecticut	41,044	39,687	48,463	43,593	42,951	43,805	29,185	13,310	1,310	43,931	29,256	13,365	1,311
Delaware	7,469	7,998	8,322	8,640	8,933	8,587	4,255	4,332	0	9,257	4,661	4,596	0
District of Columbia	4,949	5,481 [3]	5,321	5,854	5,925	6,278	3,781	1,930	568	5,925	2,975	2,295	655
Florida	132,030	158,962	186,361	183,827	175,609	175,006	76,703	65,633	32,670	176,537	76,564	66,930	33,043
Georgia	91,043	108,535	118,839	115,918	112,460	111,133	52,141	43,441	15,551	109,365	50,808	42,795	15,763
Hawaii	10,927	11,226	11,295	11,472	11,396	11,458	6,278	5,113	68	11,608	6,378	5,149	81
Idaho	13,714	14,521	15,148	15,201	15,673	15,990	7,640	8,351	0	14,563	6,997	7,566	0
Illinois	127,620	133,857	135,704	138,483	132,983	131,777	89,868	41,910	0	135,701 [4]	92,561 [5]	42,044 [3]	1,095
Indiana	59,226	60,592	62,668	62,258	58,121 [2]	62,339	42,599	19,740	0	59,863	31,187	28,676	0
Iowa	34,636	35,181	35,961	35,842	34,642	34,658	24,093	10,565	0	35,080	24,443	10,637	0
Kansas	32,742	33,608	35,883	34,700	34,644	37,407	19,700	17,024	684	41,243	20,833	19,608	802
Kentucky	39,589	42,413	43,451	41,981	42,042	41,860	21,169	9,907	10,783	42,769	21,874	10,120	10,776
Louisiana	49,915	44,660	49,377	49,646	48,655	48,657	33,214	15,443	0	46,493	31,715	14,778	0
Maine	16,559	16,684	15,912	16,331	15,384	14,888	10,286	4,602	0	15,222	10,561	4,661	0
Maryland	52,433	56,685	58,940	58,463	58,428	57,589	34,188	23,401	0	57,718	34,453	23,266	0
Massachusetts	67,432	73,596	70,398	69,909	68,754	69,342	45,772	23,571	0	70,636	46,678	23,958	0
Michigan	97,031	98,069	94,754	92,691	88,615	86,997	35,137	34,385	17,475	86,154	35,430	33,967	16,757
Minnesota	53,457	51,107	53,083	52,839	52,672	52,832	27,991	23,338	1,503	53,585	28,561	23,413	1,611
Mississippi	31,006	31,433	33,358	33,103	32,255	32,007	15,391	12,557	4,058	32,613	15,401	13,187	4,026
Missouri	64,735	67,076	68,015	67,796	66,735	66,252	34,141	32,111	0	66,248	34,219	32,029	0
Montana	10,411	10,369	10,467	10,521	10,361	10,153	6,981	3,172	0	10,200	7,079	3,121	0
Nebraska	20,983	21,359	22,057	22,256	22,345	22,182	13,842	8,340	0	22,103	13,805	8,298	0
Nevada	18,293	21,744	21,993	22,104	21,839	21,132	10,317	7,769	3,046	20,695	10,088	7,683	2,924
New Hampshire	14,341	15,536	15,661	15,491	15,365	15,049	10,180	4,869	0	14,925	9,983	4,941	0
New Jersey	99,061	112,673	114,713	115,248	110,202	109,719	58,767	37,691	13,262	110,929	58,569	37,481	14,879
New Mexico	21,042	22,021	22,825	22,724	22,437	21,957	9,739	8,182	4,035	22,201	9,806	8,339	4,056
New York	206,961	218,989	217,944	214,804	211,606	209,527	121,569	87,687	271	207,060	109,082	97,751	227
North Carolina	83,680	95,664	109,634	105,036 [6]	98,357	97,308	64,599	31,706	1,003	98,590	68,745	28,772	1,073
North Dakota	8,141	8,003	8,181	8,366	8,417	8,525	5,499	3,026	0	8,677	5,595	3,082	0
Ohio	118,361	117,982	112,845	111,378	109,282	107,972	52,065	49,614	6,292	106,000	50,217	47,953	7,830
Oklahoma	41,318	41,833	46,571	42,615	41,278	41,349	22,545	18,804	0	41,775	22,948	18,827	0
Oregon	28,094	28,346	30,152	28,768	28,109	26,791	18,801	7,990	0	26,410	18,541	7,869	0
Pennsylvania	116,963	122,397	129,708	130,984	129,911	124,646	59,431	55,684	9,530	123,147	58,769	54,682	9,696
Rhode Island	10,645	14,180 [2]	11,316	11,366	11,212	11,414	5,472	5,942	0	9,871	5,359	4,512	0
South Carolina	45,380	48,212	49,941	46,980	45,210	46,782	32,577	14,205	0	48,072	33,640	14,432	0
South Dakota	9,397	9,129	9,244	9,326	9,512	9,247	5,890	2,514	843	9,334	5,967	2,505	862
Tennessee	57,164	59,596	64,926	65,361	66,558	66,382	45,212	19,066	2,104	66,406	45,229	19,103	2,075
Texas	274,826	302,425	327,905	333,164	334,997	324,282	162,768	130,424	31,090	327,357	165,006	133,053	29,298
Utah	22,008	22,993	23,657	25,615	25,677	25,970	13,032	10,333	2,605	26,610	13,318	10,642	2,649
Vermont	8,414	8,851	8,766	8,734	8,382	8,364	3,360	3,206	1,798	8,403	3,377	3,186	1,840
Virginia	86,977 [2]	103,944	71,415	70,827	70,947	90,832	41,909	48,923	0	89,389	41,852	47,536	0
Washington	51,098	53,508	54,428	53,448	53,934	53,119	28,113	22,934	2,072	53,699	28,139	23,575	1,985
West Virginia	20,930	19,940	20,209	20,299	20,338	20,247	9,483	10,765	0	20,101	9,433	10,668	0
Wisconsin	60,165	60,127	59,401	58,426	57,625	56,245	27,873	28,209	163	57,551	28,658	28,543	350
Wyoming	6,783	6,706	7,000	7,166	7,127	7,847	4,461	3,385	0	7,350	3,952	3,397	0
Bureau of Indian Education	—	—	—	—	—	—	—	—	—	5,308	4,282	1,027	0
DoD, overseas	5,105	5,726	4,551	—	—	—	—	—	—	—	—	—	—
DoD, domestic	2,399	2,033	2,145	—	—	—	—	—	—	—	—	—	—
Other jurisdictions													
American Samoa	820	989	—	—	—	—	—	—	—	—	—	—	—
Guam	1,975	1,804	—	—	1,843	2,291	925	991	375	2,291	925	991	375
Northern Marianas	526	614	514	552	607	496	292	200	4	409	249	156	4
Puerto Rico	37,620	42,036	39,356	39,102	36,506	33,079	15,140	12,618	5,321	30,986	14,293	11,765	4,928
U.S. Virgin Islands	1,511	1,434	1,331	1,425	1,457	1,217	522	399	296	1,129	489	351	289

—Not available.
[1]Includes imputed values for states.
[2]Includes imputations for underreporting of prekindergarten teachers.
[3]Imputed.
[4]Includes imputations for underreporting of prekindergarten, kindergarten, and secondary teachers.
[5]Includes imputations for underreporting of prekindergarten and kindergarten teachers.
[6]Includes imputations for underreporting of kindergarten teachers.
NOTE: Distribution of elementary and secondary teachers determined by reporting units. Teachers reported in full-time equivalents (FTE). DoD = Department of Defense.
SOURCE: U.S. Department of Education, National Center for Education Statistics, Common Core of Data (CCD), "State Nonfiscal Survey of Public Elementary/Secondary Education," 2000–01 through 2012–13. (This table was prepared October 2014.)

Table 208.40. Public elementary and secondary teachers, enrollment, and pupil/teacher ratios, by state or jurisdiction: Selected years, fall 2000 through fall 2012

State or jurisdiction	Pupil/teacher ratio				Fall 2010			Fall 2011			Fall 2012		
	Fall 2000	Fall 2007	Fall 2008	Fall 2009	Teachers	Enrollment	Pupil/teacher ratio	Teachers	Enrollment	Pupil/teacher ratio	Teachers	Enrollment	Pupil/teacher ratio
1	2	3	4	5	6	7	8	9	10	11	12	13	14
United States	16.0 [1]	15.4 [1]	15.3 [1]	15.4 [1]	3,099,095 [1]	49,484,181	16.0 [1]	3,103,263 [1]	49,521,669	16.0 [1]	3,109,101 [1]	49,771,118	16.0 [1]
Alabama	15.4 [2]	14.7	15.6	15.8	49,363	755,552	15.3	47,723	744,621	15.6	51,877	744,637	14.4
Alaska........................	16.9	17.2	16.5	16.3	8,171	132,104	16.2	8,088	131,167	16.2	7,682	131,489	17.1
Arizona.......................	19.8	20.1	19.9	20.7	50,031	1,071,751	21.4	50,800	1,080,319	21.3	48,866	1,089,384	22.3
Arkansas....................	14.1	14.1	12.9	12.9	34,273	482,114	14.1	33,983	483,114	14.2	34,131	486,157	14.2
California	20.6 [2]	20.8 [2]	20.8 [2]	19.8 [2]	260,806 [2]	6,289,578	24.1 [2]	268,689 [2]	6,287,834	23.4 [2]	266,255 [2]	6,299,451	23.7 [2]
Colorado.....................	17.3	16.8	16.8	17.0	48,543	843,316	17.4	48,078	854,265	17.8	48,922	863,561	17.7
Connecticut.................	13.7	14.5	11.7	12.9	42,951	560,546	13.1	43,805	554,437	12.7	43,931	550,954	12.5
Delaware.....................	15.4	15.0	15.1	14.7	8,933	129,403	14.5	8,587	128,946	15.0	9,257	129,026	13.9
District of Columbia	13.9	12.4	12.9	11.9	5,925	71,284	12.0	6,278	73,911	11.8	5,925	76,140	12.9
Florida........................	18.4	14.0	14.1	14.3	175,609	2,643,347	15.1	175,006	2,668,156	15.2	176,537	2,692,162	15.2
Georgia.......................	15.9	14.1	13.9	14.4	112,460	1,677,067	14.9	111,133	1,685,016	15.2	109,365	1,703,332	15.6
Hawaii.........................	16.9	15.8	15.9	15.7	11,396	179,601	15.8	11,458	182,706	15.9	11,608	184,760	15.9
Idaho..........................	17.9	18.1	18.2	18.2	15,673	275,859	17.6	15,990	279,873	17.5	14,563	284,834	19.6
Illinois........................	16.1	15.5	15.6	15.2	132,983	2,091,654	15.7	131,777	2,083,097	15.8	135,701 [3]	2,072,880	15.3
Indiana........................	16.7	16.8	16.7	16.8	58,121 [2]	1,047,232	18.0 [2]	62,339	1,040,765	16.7	59,863	1,041,369	17.4
Iowa...........................	14.3	13.4	13.6	13.7	34,642	495,775	14.3	34,658	495,870	14.3	35,080	499,825	14.2
Kansas........................	14.4	13.2	13.1	13.7	34,644	483,701	14.0	37,407	486,108	13.0	41,243	489,043	11.9
Kentucky.....................	16.8	15.3	15.4	16.2	42,042	673,128	16.0	41,860	681,987	16.3	42,769	685,167	16.0
Louisiana.....................	14.9	14.0	13.9	13.9	48,655	696,558	14.3	48,657	703,390	14.5	46,493	710,903	15.3
Maine..........................	12.5	11.9	12.1	11.6	15,384	189,077	12.3	14,888	188,969	12.7	15,222	185,739	12.2
Maryland......................	16.3	14.3	14.3	14.5	58,428	852,211	14.6	57,589	854,086	14.8	57,718	859,638	14.9
Massachusetts..............	14.5	13.6	13.6	13.7	68,754	955,563	13.9	69,342	953,369	13.7	70,636	954,773	13.5
Michigan......................	17.7 [2]	17.6	17.5	17.8	88,615	1,587,067	17.9	86,997	1,573,537	18.1	86,154	1,555,370	18.1
Minnesota....................	16.0	15.8	15.7	15.8	52,672	838,037	15.9	52,832	839,738	15.9	53,585	845,404	15.8
Mississippi...................	16.1	14.7	14.7	14.9	32,255	490,526	15.2	32,007	490,619	15.3	32,613	493,650	15.1
Missouri......................	14.1	13.4	13.5	13.5	66,735	918,710	13.8	66,252	916,584	13.8	66,248	917,900	13.9
Montana......................	14.9	13.6	13.6	13.5	10,361	141,693	13.7	10,153	142,349	14.0	10,200	142,908	14.0
Nebraska.....................	13.6	13.3	13.3	13.3	22,345	298,500	13.4	22,182	301,296	13.6	22,103	303,505	13.7
Nevada........................	18.6	18.3	19.7	19.4	21,839	437,149	20.0	21,132	439,634	20.8	20,695	445,707	21.5
New Hampshire.............	14.5	13.0	12.6	12.7	15,365	194,711	12.7	15,049	191,900	12.8	14,925	188,974	12.7
New Jersey...................	13.3	12.4	12.0	12.1	110,202	1,402,548	12.7	109,719	1,356,431	12.4	110,929	1,372,203	12.4
New Mexico..................	15.2	14.8	14.5	14.7	22,437	338,122	15.1	21,957	337,225	15.4	22,201	338,220	15.2
New York......................	13.9	13.1	12.6	12.9	211,606	2,734,955	12.9	209,527	2,704,718	12.9	207,060	2,710,703	13.1
North Carolina	15.5	14.0	13.6	14.1 [4]	98,357	1,490,605	15.2	97,308	1,507,864	15.5	98,590	1,518,465	15.4
North Dakota	13.4	11.8	11.6	11.4	8,417	96,323	11.4	8,525	97,646	11.5	8,677	101,111	11.7
Ohio...........................	15.5	16.6	16.1	15.8	109,282	1,754,191	16.1	107,972	1,740,030	16.1	106,000	1,729,916	16.3
Oklahoma....................	15.1	13.7	13.9	15.4	41,278	659,911	16.0	41,349	666,120	16.1	41,775	673,483	16.1
Oregon........................	19.4	18.8	19.1	20.3	28,109	570,720	20.3	26,791	568,208	21.2	26,410	587,564	22.2
Pennsylvania.................	15.5	13.3	13.7	13.6	129,911	1,793,284	13.8	124,646	1,771,395	14.2	123,147	1,763,677	14.3
Rhode Island	14.8	13.1	12.8	12.8	11,212	143,793	12.8	11,414	142,854	12.5	9,871	142,481	14.4
South Carolina..............	14.9	15.0	14.4	15.4	45,210	725,838	16.1	46,782	727,186	15.5	48,072	735,998	15.3
South Dakota................	13.7	12.9	13.7	13.3	9,512	126,128	13.3	9,247	128,016	13.8	9,334	130,471	14.0
Tennessee	15.9 [2]	14.9	15.0	14.9	66,558	987,422	14.8	66,382	999,693	15.1	66,406	993,496	15.0
Texas	14.8	14.5	14.5	14.6	334,997	4,935,715	14.7	324,282	5,000,470	15.4	327,357	5,077,659	15.5
Utah...........................	21.9	23.7	23.7	22.3	25,677	585,552	22.8	25,970	598,832	23.1	26,610	613,279	23.0
Vermont.......................	12.1	10.7	10.7	10.5	8,382	96,858	11.6	8,364	89,908	10.7	8,403	89,624	10.7
Virginia........................	13.2 [2]	17.1	17.3	17.6	70,947	1,251,440	17.6	90,832	1,257,883	13.8	89,389	1,265,419	14.2
Washington...................	19.7	19.1	19.1	19.4	53,934	1,043,788	19.4	53,119	1,045,453	19.7	53,699	1,051,694	19.6
West Virginia.................	13.7	13.9	14.0	13.9	20,338	282,879	13.9	20,247	282,870	14.0	20,101	283,044	14.1
Wisconsin	14.6	14.8	14.7	14.9	57,625	872,286	15.1	56,245	871,105	15.5	57,551	872,436	15.2
Wyoming......................	13.3	12.5	12.5	12.3	7,127	89,009	12.5	7,847	90,099	11.5	7,350	91,533	12.5
Bureau of Indian Education	—	—	—	—	—	41,962	—	—	—	—	5,308	—	—
DoD, overseas	14.4	13.8	12.5	—	—	—	—	—	—	—	—	—	—
DoD, domestic	14.2	12.3	13.1	—	—	—	—	—	—	—	—	—	—
Other jurisdictions													
American Samoa	19.1	—	—	—	—	—	—	—	—	—	—	—	—
Guam........................	16.4	—	—	—	1,843	31,618	17.2	2,291	31,243	13.6	2,291	31,186	13.6
Northern Marianas.......	19.0	20.5	21.2	19.9	607	11,105	18.3	496	11,011	22.2	409	10,646	26.0
Puerto Rico.................	16.3	12.9	12.8	12.6	36,506	473,735	13.0	33,079	452,740	13.7	30,986	434,609	14.0
U.S. Virgin Islands.......	12.9	10.5	11.8	10.9	1,457	15,495	10.6	1,217	15,711	12.9	1,129	15,192	13.5

—Not available.
[1]Includes imputed values for states.
[2]Includes imputations to correct for underreporting of prekindergarten teachers/enrollment.
[3]Includes imputations to correct for underreporting of prekindergarten, kindergarten, and secondary teachers.
[4]Includes imputations to correct for underreporting of kindergarten teachers.
NOTE: Teachers reported in full-time equivalents (FTE). DoD = Department of Defense. The pupil/teacher ratio includes teachers for students with disabilities and other special teachers, while these teachers are generally excluded from class size calculations. Ratios reflect totals reported by states and differ from totals reported for schools or school districts.
SOURCE: U.S. Department of Education, National Center for Education Statistics, Common Core of Data (CCD), "State Nonfiscal Survey of Public Elementary/Secondary Education," 2000–01 through 2012–13. (This table was prepared October 2014.)

Table 209.10. Number and percentage distribution of teachers in public and private elementary and secondary schools, by selected teacher characteristics: Selected years, 1987–88 through 2011–12

[Standard errors appear in parentheses]

Selected teacher characteristic	Number of teachers (in thousands)							Percentage distribution of teachers						
	1987–88	1990–91	1993–94	1999–2000	2003–04	2007–08	2011–12	1987–88	1990–91	1993–94	1999–2000	2003–04	2007–08	2011–12
1	2	3	4	5	6	7	8	9	10	11	12	13	14	15
Public schools Total	2,323 (13.2)	2,559 (20.7)	2,561 (20.8)	3,002 (19.4)	3,251 (29.2)	3,405 (44.0)	3,385 (41.4)	100.0 (†)	100.0 (†)	100.0 (†)	100.0 (†)	100.0 (†)	100.0 (†)	100.0 (†)
Sex														
Male	685 (6.8)	719 (11.2)	694 (11.8)	754 (10.7)	813 (13.3)	821 (20.4)	802 (22.2)	29.5 (0.22)	28.1 (0.31)	27.1 (0.36)	25.1 (0.30)	25.0 (0.32)	24.1 (0.47)	23.7 (0.49)
Female	1,638 (10.1)	1,840 (14.7)	1,867 (16.2)	2,248 (16.0)	2,438 (23.5)	2,584 (34.6)	2,584 (30.5)	70.5 (0.22)	71.9 (0.31)	72.9 (0.36)	74.9 (0.30)	75.0 (0.32)	75.9 (0.47)	76.3 (0.49)
Race/ethnicity														
White[1]	2,018 (12.6)	2,214 (20.0)	2,217 (19.5)	2,532 (17.2)	2,702 (30.1)	2,829 (38.7)	2,773 (30.5)	86.9 (0.24)	86.5 (0.29)	86.5 (0.33)	84.3 (0.30)	83.1 (0.53)	83.1 (0.53)	81.9 (0.53)
Black[1]	191 (4.6)	212 (6.4)	188 (5.4)	228 (6.0)	257 (11.0)	239 (15.8)	231 (12.1)	8.2 (0.19)	8.3 (0.25)	7.4 (0.21)	7.6 (0.19)	7.9 (0.34)	7.0 (0.45)	6.8 (0.31)
Hispanic[1]	69 (2.6)	87 (4.5)	109 (6.2)	169 (6.4)	202 (11.3)	240 (16.6)	264 (13.4)	3.0 (0.11)	3.4 (0.17)	4.2 (0.20)	5.6 (0.20)	6.2 (0.34)	7.1 (0.46)	7.8 (0.37)
Asian[1,2]	21 (1.1)	27 (1.7)	28 (1.2)	48 (2.7)	42 (2.5)	42 (7.2)	61 (7.3)	0.9 (0.05)	1.0 (0.06)	1.1 (0.05)	1.6 (0.09)	1.3 (0.08)	1.2 (0.21)	1.8 (0.21)
Pacific Islander	— (†)	— (†)	— (†)	— (†)	6 (0.8)	6 (1.3)	5 (1.4)	— (†)	— (†)	— (†)	— (†)	0.2 (0.03)	0.2 (0.04)	0.1 (0.04)
American Indian/Alaska Native[1]	24 (1.3)	20 (1.4)	20 (1.4)	26 (1.9)	17 (1.2)	17 (1.9)	17 (2.9)	1.0 (0.06)	0.8 (0.05)	0.8 (0.06)	0.9 (0.06)	0.5 (0.04)	0.5 (0.06)	0.5 (0.08)
Two or more races	— (†)	— (†)	— (†)	— (†)	24 (2.2)	31 (2.9)	35 (3.7)	— (†)	— (†)	— (†)	— (†)	0.7 (0.07)	0.9 (0.09)	1.0 (0.11)
Age														
Under 30	313 (5.0)	257 (5.7)	280 (4.5)	509 (9.2)	540 (27.4)	612 (22.4)	518 (15.9)	13.5 (0.19)	10.0 (0.23)	10.9 (0.16)	17.0 (0.28)	16.6 (0.84)	18.0 (0.61)	15.3 (0.44)
30 to 39	823 (7.7)	684 (10.8)	573 (8.0)	661 (9.8)	798 (14.5)	898 (16.8)	979 (19.3)	35.4 (0.30)	26.7 (0.35)	22.4 (0.30)	22.0 (0.29)	24.5 (0.38)	26.4 (0.39)	28.9 (0.53)
40 to 49	762 (7.4)	1,034 (13.3)	1,070 (12.5)	953 (10.3)	840 (14.3)	808 (19.2)	849 (19.2)	32.8 (0.25)	40.4 (0.37)	41.8 (0.33)	31.8 (0.32)	25.9 (0.38)	23.7 (0.47)	25.1 (0.51)
50 to 59	357 (5.7)	477 (8.6)	540 (10.1)	786 (12.6)	942 (26.0)	879 (21.1)	783 (20.5)	15.4 (0.23)	18.7 (0.29)	21.1 (0.29)	26.2 (0.35)	29.0 (0.74)	25.8 (0.51)	23.1 (0.49)
60 and over	68 (2.5)	107 (4.1)	97 (3.5)	93 (4.0)	131 (4.8)	207 (10.3)	256 (13.2)	2.9 (0.11)	4.2 (0.16)	3.8 (0.14)	3.1 (0.13)	4.0 (0.14)	6.1 (0.29)	7.6 (0.34)
Highest degree earned														
Less than bachelor's	15 (1.0)	17 (1.2)	18 (1.4)	20 (1.3)	35 (2.5)	27 (2.1)	128 (8.6)	0.7 (0.04)	0.7 (0.05)	0.7 (0.06)	0.7 (0.04)	1.1 (0.08)	0.8 (0.06)	3.8 (0.24)
Bachelor's	1,214 (9.8)	1,327 (11.7)	1,331 (13.4)	1,560 (15.8)	1,651 (22.8)	1,612 (28.8)	1,350 (21.1)	52.3 (0.28)	51.9 (0.31)	52.0 (0.33)	52.0 (0.40)	50.8 (0.56)	47.4 (0.59)	39.9 (0.52)
Master's	932 (8.5)	1,077 (13.5)	1,075 (12.0)	1,257 (13.9)	1,331 (21.7)	1,517 (27.8)	1,614 (29.1)	40.1 (0.30)	42.1 (0.34)	42.0 (0.33)	41.9 (0.38)	40.9 (0.56)	44.5 (0.55)	47.7 (0.57)
Education specialist[3]	146 (3.4)	118 (3.8)	117 (3.8)	143 (5.2)	195 (6.8)	218 (8.6)	257 (9.7)	6.3 (0.14)	4.6 (0.20)	4.6 (0.14)	4.7 (0.17)	6.0 (0.19)	6.4 (0.25)	7.6 (0.27)
Doctor's	16 (1.2)	20 (1.7)	19 (1.7)	22 (1.8)	38 (3.5)	30 (2.7)	37 (4.0)	0.7 (0.05)	0.8 (0.07)	0.7 (0.07)	0.7 (0.06)	1.2 (0.11)	0.9 (0.08)	1.1 (0.11)
Years of full-time teaching experience														
Less than 3	188 (3.3)	223 (4.8)	249 (5.2)	387 (8.7)	396 (39.8)	457 (21.8)	305 (10.2)	8.1 (0.15)	8.7 (0.19)	9.7 (0.20)	12.9 (0.27)	12.2 (1.23)	13.4 (0.59)	9.0 (0.29)
3 to 9	605 (6.1)	634 (9.8)	653 (9.7)	865 (12.0)	1,070 (15.3)	1,143 (19.7)	1,128 (19.9)	26.0 (0.20)	24.8 (0.31)	25.5 (0.32)	28.8 (0.36)	32.9 (0.34)	33.6 (0.52)	33.3 (0.52)
10 to 20	1,034 (8.2)	1,025 (11.7)	898 (9.2)	854 (10.3)	924 (21.6)	997 (23.2)	1,232 (21.0)	44.5 (0.25)	40.0 (0.35)	35.0 (0.33)	28.5 (0.33)	28.4 (0.59)	29.3 (0.55)	36.4 (0.51)
Over 20	497 (5.8)	678 (10.4)	762 (12.4)	896 (12.8)	860 (26.6)	808 (22.9)	720 (23.7)	21.4 (0.21)	26.5 (0.30)	29.8 (0.32)	29.8 (0.34)	26.5 (0.77)	23.7 (0.60)	21.3 (0.54)
Level														
Elementary	1,292 (9.5)	1,442 (11.8)	1,331 (17.0)	1,602 (13.5)	1,716 (25.8)	1,725 (37.1)	1,726 (20.2)	55.6 (0.33)	56.3 (0.40)	52.0 (0.57)	53.3 (0.42)	52.8 (0.66)	50.7 (0.91)	51.0 (0.65)
General	788 (7.4)	887 (10.6)	881 (13.5)	1,042 (12.5)	1,130 (29.8)	1,100 (26.5)	1,078 (22.1)	33.9 (0.29)	34.6 (0.39)	34.4 (0.46)	34.7 (0.41)	34.8 (0.86)	32.3 (0.70)	31.8 (0.71)
Arts/music	116 (3.0)	110 (4.3)	83 (3.1)	99 (3.7)	101 (5.3)	103 (6.6)	82 (5.4)	5.0 (0.13)	4.3 (0.17)	3.2 (0.12)	3.3 (0.12)	3.1 (0.17)	3.0 (0.19)	2.4 (0.16)
English	60 (2.3)	72 (3.8)	49 (3.2)	66 (3.8)	70 (5.1)	104 (9.9)	92 (6.9)	2.6 (0.10)	2.8 (0.14)	1.9 (0.12)	2.2 (0.13)	2.2 (0.16)	3.0 (0.29)	2.7 (0.21)
ESL/bilingual	18 (1.1)	20 (1.3)	27 (2.2)	28 (1.8)	25 (3.6)	24 (3.3)	51 (6.8)	0.8 (0.05)	0.8 (0.05)	1.1 (0.09)	0.9 (0.06)	0.8 (0.11)	0.7 (0.10)	1.5 (0.20)
Health/physical ed.	56 (2.0)	66 (3.2)	58 (3.0)	57 (3.5)	73 (5.0)	63 (6.0)	79 (8.1)	2.4 (0.09)	2.6 (0.12)	2.3 (0.12)	1.9 (0.12)	2.2 (0.15)	1.8 (0.18)	2.3 (0.23)
Mathematics	31 (1.5)	30 (1.9)	24 (2.2)	23 (2.4)	19 (2.3)	28 (3.8)	32 (6.5)	1.3 (0.06)	1.2 (0.08)	0.9 (0.08)	0.8 (0.08)	0.6 (0.07)	0.8 (0.11)	0.9 (0.19)
Science	18 (1.5)	21 (1.9)	10 (1.2)	11 (1.3)	19 (3.0)	15 (3.4)	18 (3.3)	0.8 (0.06)	0.8 (0.07)	0.4 (0.05)	0.4 (0.04)	0.6 (0.09)	0.4 (0.10)	0.5 (0.10)
Special education	168 (3.9)	176 (5.9)	158 (4.2)	227 (5.6)	240 (20.6)	230 (13.0)	239 (10.3)	7.2 (0.16)	6.9 (0.23)	6.2 (0.16)	7.6 (0.18)	7.4 (0.63)	6.7 (0.37)	7.1 (0.31)
Other elementary	37 (2.4)	60 (3.2)	42 (2.9)	49 (3.5)	40 (3.5)	58 (4.2)	55 (5.2)	1.6 (0.10)	2.4 (0.12)	1.7 (0.11)	1.6 (0.12)	1.2 (0.10)	1.7 (0.12)	1.6 (0.15)
Secondary	1,031 (10.5)	1,118 (16.5)	1,230 (18.9)	1,401 (17.7)	1,534 (26.0)	1,680 (39.0)	1,659 (37.8)	44.4 (0.33)	43.7 (0.40)	48.0 (0.57)	46.7 (0.42)	47.2 (0.66)	49.3 (0.91)	49.0 (0.65)
Arts/music	73 (2.0)	74 (2.3)	92 (2.5)	110 (3.4)	112 (4.1)	121 (5.6)	121 (5.6)	3.1 (0.09)	2.9 (0.08)	3.6 (0.10)	3.7 (0.11)	3.4 (0.12)	3.6 (0.18)	3.6 (0.14)
English	171 (3.2)	195 (5.1)	209 (5.0)	245 (5.1)	269 (9.0)	306 (10.0)	289 (9.9)	7.4 (0.12)	7.6 (0.18)	8.2 (0.18)	8.2 (0.15)	8.3 (0.27)	9.0 (0.27)	8.5 (0.25)
ESL/bilingual	6 (0.5)	10 (0.7)	12 (1.3)	16 (1.2)	18 (2.5)	21 (2.5)	20 (2.4)	0.3 (0.02)	0.4 (0.03)	0.5 (0.05)	0.5 (0.04)	0.6 (0.08)	0.6 (0.07)	0.6 (0.07)
Foreign language	43 (1.2)	52 (2.4)	59 (2.0)	71 (2.4)	73 (3.3)	78 (5.0)	88 (4.5)	1.9 (0.05)	2.0 (0.09)	2.3 (0.07)	2.4 (0.08)	2.3 (0.10)	2.3 (0.14)	2.6 (0.12)
Health/physical ed.	76 (2.4)	76 (2.2)	88 (2.7)	99 (3.1)	102 (4.3)	119 (5.7)	101 (3.9)	3.3 (0.10)	3.0 (0.08)	3.4 (0.10)	3.3 (0.10)	3.1 (0.12)	3.5 (0.16)	3.0 (0.11)
Mathematics	139 (2.5)	155 (4.3)	174 (3.7)	207 (4.5)	213 (5.5)	252 (9.1)	250 (7.5)	6.0 (0.10)	6.0 (0.15)	6.8 (0.13)	6.9 (0.14)	6.5 (0.17)	7.4 (0.25)	7.4 (0.19)
Science	115 (2.9)	128 (4.0)	143 (3.4)	169 (4.0)	189 (6.8)	195 (8.3)	209 (6.1)	4.9 (0.11)	5.0 (0.15)	5.6 (0.11)	5.6 (0.12)	5.8 (0.20)	5.7 (0.24)	6.2 (0.16)
Social studies	118 (2.4)	124 (3.3)	138 (3.3)	163 (4.4)	178 (5.7)	209 (9.9)	197 (6.3)	5.1 (0.10)	4.8 (0.12)	5.4 (0.12)	5.4 (0.14)	5.5 (0.16)	6.1 (0.27)	5.8 (0.16)
Special education	100 (2.2)	113 (3.5)	126 (3.1)	113 (2.8)	174 (7.5)	165 (9.7)	191 (12.2)	4.3 (0.09)	4.4 (0.13)	4.9 (0.11)	3.8 (0.09)	5.4 (0.23)	4.9 (0.28)	5.7 (0.32)
Vocational/technical	166 (3.0)	160 (3.7)	153 (3.5)	161 (3.5)	169 (5.7)	164 (6.3)	147 (5.7)	7.1 (0.12)	6.3 (0.12)	6.0 (0.12)	5.4 (0.10)	5.2 (0.17)	4.8 (0.17)	4.3 (0.16)
Other secondary	25 (1.3)	30 (1.5)	36 (1.4)	47 (2.0)	36 (2.1)	47 (3.4)	46 (4.0)	1.1 (0.06)	1.2 (0.06)	1.4 (0.06)	1.6 (0.07)	1.1 (0.06)	1.4 (0.10)	1.4 (0.12)

See notes at end of table.

Table 209.10. Number and percentage distribution of teachers in public and private elementary and secondary schools, by selected teacher characteristics: Selected years, 1987–88 through 2011–12—Continued

[Standard errors appear in parentheses]

Selected teacher characteristic	Number of teachers (in thousands)							Percentage distribution of teachers						
	1987–88	1990–91	1993–94	1999–2000	2003–04	2007–08	2011–12	1987–88	1990–91	1993–94	1999–2000	2003–04	2007–08	2011–12
1	2	3	4	5	6	7	8	9	10	11	12	13	14	15
Private schools														
Total	307 (8.5)	356 (7.2)	378 (5.6)	449 (10.6)	467 (10.3)	490 (9.2)	465 (11.1)	100.0 (†)	100.0 (†)	100.0 (†)	100.0 (†)	100.0 (†)	100.0 (†)	100.0 (†)
Sex														
Male	67 (3.3)	82 (3.3)	93 (2.3)	107 (3.8)	110 (8.4)	127 (4.6)	117 (6.9)	21.8 (0.86)	22.9 (0.74)	24.6 (0.43)	23.9 (0.48)	23.6 (1.93)	26.0 (0.78)	25.2 (1.33)
Female	240 (7.2)	275 (5.8)	285 (4.2)	342 (7.7)	357 (14.3)	362 (7.7)	348 (10.1)	78.2 (0.86)	77.1 (0.74)	75.4 (0.43)	76.1 (0.48)	76.4 (1.93)	74.0 (0.78)	74.8 (1.33)
Race/ethnicity														
White[1]	285 (8.3)	329 (7.0)	348 (5.1)	402 (9.6)	411 (12.0)	423 (8.8)	411 (11.1)	92.8 (0.50)	92.2 (0.46)	91.9 (0.41)	89.5 (0.42)	88.0 (0.99)	86.4 (0.80)	88.3 (0.69)
Black[1]	7 (0.8)	9 (1.0)	9 (1.0)	17 (1.4)	19 (2.9)	20 (2.2)	17 (2.4)	2.3 (0.27)	2.7 (0.28)	3.1 (0.27)	3.7 (0.29)	4.0 (0.65)	4.0 (0.44)	3.6 (0.54)
Hispanic[1]	9 (1.1)	12 (1.0)	12 (1.0)	21 (1.5)	23 (3.1)	29 (2.1)	24 (2.4)	2.8 (0.36)	3.3 (0.26)	3.2 (0.26)	4.7 (0.30)	4.8 (0.71)	5.9 (0.38)	5.2 (0.51)
Asian[1,2]	4 (0.8)	5 (0.6)	5 (0.6)	7 (0.6)	9 (1.0)	11 (1.5)	9 (1.4)	1.2 (0.26)	1.5 (0.18)	1.4 (0.16)	1.6 (0.14)	1.8 (0.20)	2.2 (0.29)	1.8 (0.31)
Pacific Islander[2]	— (†)	—	—	—	‡	‡	‡	— (†)	—	— (†)	—	0.2! (0.07)	0.3! (0.14)	‡ (†)
American Indian/Alaska Native[1]	3 (0.4)	1 (0.3)	2 (0.3)	2 (0.4)	‡ (†)	‡ (†)	‡ (†)	0.9 (0.12)	0.4 (0.09)	0.4 (0.07)	0.6 (0.08)	‡ (†)	‡ (†)	‡ (†)
Two or more races	— (†)	—	—	—	3! (1.4)	4	4 (0.9)	— (†)	—	— (†)	—	0.6! (0.28)	0.7 (0.12)	0.8 (0.19)
Age														
Under 30	67 (2.6)	60 (2.2)	65 (1.7)	87 (3.1)	88 (3.7)	80 (3.9)	78 (6.8)	21.8 (0.77)	16.7 (0.61)	17.2 (0.39)	19.3 (0.43)	18.9 (0.78)	16.3 (0.67)	16.7 (1.48)
30 to 39	106 (3.6)	100 (4.0)	94 (2.1)	101 (3.2)	103 (5.8)	109 (5.2)	112 (6.2)	34.5 (0.81)	28.1 (0.78)	24.8 (0.48)	22.4 (0.50)	22.0 (1.36)	22.3 (0.91)	24.0 (1.07)
40 to 49	84 (3.4)	121 (3.1)	131 (3.3)	131 (4.2)	119 (7.1)	116 (3.6)	110 (6.3)	27.4 (0.78)	33.9 (0.74)	34.8 (0.60)	29.2 (0.62)	25.4 (1.41)	23.8 (0.65)	23.8 (1.06)
50 to 59	34 (2.2)	53 (2.3)	66 (2.1)	106 (3.2)	121 (11.1)	128 (4.5)	99 (5.0)	11.1 (0.57)	14.8 (0.55)	17.4 (0.48)	23.5 (0.46)	25.8 (2.07)	26.2 (0.87)	21.3 (1.06)
60 and over	16 (1.7)	23 (1.6)	22 (1.1)	25 (1.2)	37 (4.7)	56 (3.1)	66 (5.0)	5.3 (0.49)	6.4 (0.41)	5.8 (0.27)	5.7 (0.24)	8.0 (0.99)	11.5 (0.62)	14.2 (1.05)
Highest degree earned														
Less than bachelor's	13 (1.4)	23 (1.6)	25 (1.8)	33 (2.3)	43! (21.5)	40 (2.9)	39 (5.2)	4.4 (0.42)	6.4 (0.45)	6.7 (0.46)	7.3 (0.46)	9.2! (4.41)	8.1 (0.58)	8.4 (1.07)
Bachelor's	189 (5.1)	221 (5.7)	223 (3.3)	258 (5.8)	259 (11.2)	264 (6.8)	225 (6.7)	61.4 (0.75)	61.9 (0.90)	59.0 (0.63)	57.5 (0.64)	55.5 (2.90)	53.9 (0.95)	48.5 (1.37)
Master's	92 (3.8)	96 (3.1)	113 (3.6)	136 (4.5)	138 (6.1)	161 (6.3)	166 (7.5)	29.8 (0.73)	27.0 (0.71)	29.8 (0.69)	30.3 (0.58)	29.5 (1.35)	32.8 (0.84)	35.8 (1.16)
Education specialist[3]	9 (0.9)	11 (0.9)	11 (0.7)	14 (1.0)	17 (2.4)	14 (1.3)	23 (2.3)	3.0 (0.30)	2.9 (0.24)	2.9 (0.19)	3.1 (0.19)	3.6 (0.54)	2.8 (0.25)	5.0 (0.48)
Doctor's	4 (0.7)	6 (0.8)	6 (0.6)	8 (0.8)	10 (1.2)	12 (1.9)	11 (2.0)	1.5 (0.23)	1.8 (0.22)	1.7 (0.15)	1.8 (0.16)	2.2 (0.26)	2.4 (0.38)	2.3 (0.41)
Years of full-time teaching experience														
Less than 3	59 (2.1)	73 (2.8)	79 (2.1)	108 (3.8)	116 (14.6)	116 (5.4)	91 (8.4)	19.0 (0.60)	20.4 (0.72)	20.9 (0.54)	23.9 (0.52)	24.8 (2.75)	23.6 (0.99)	19.5 (1.76)
3 to 9	115 (4.1)	123 (4.0)	128 (3.1)	139 (4.2)	154 (6.0)	152 (5.2)	145 (5.7)	37.6 (0.88)	34.6 (0.69)	33.9 (0.60)	31.0 (0.55)	33.0 (1.23)	31.0 (0.82)	31.3 (0.94)
10 to 20	92 (3.8)	107 (3.5)	112 (3.0)	122 (3.6)	112 (5.8)	120 (4.7)	129 (5.8)	29.8 (0.80)	30.0 (0.78)	29.6 (0.60)	27.2 (0.52)	23.9 (1.19)	24.6 (0.86)	27.7 (1.06)
Over 20	42 (2.4)	53 (2.5)	59 (2.1)	80 (2.6)	86 (8.0)	102 (4.0)	100 (7.2)	13.6 (0.62)	14.9 (0.67)	15.6 (0.51)	17.8 (0.45)	18.3 (1.87)	20.8 (0.75)	21.4 (1.47)
Level														
Elementary	179 (5.6)	225 (4.7)	221 (3.6)	261 (5.8)	263 (17.5)	258 (6.5)	245 (9.3)	58.3 (0.92)	63.2 (0.72)	58.4 (0.57)	58.1 (0.66)	56.4 (3.06)	52.8 (1.03)	52.8 (1.67)
Secondary	128 (4.7)	131 (4.0)	157 (3.4)	188 (6.2)	204 (13.4)	231 (7.1)	219 (9.9)	41.7 (0.92)	36.8 (0.72)	41.6 (0.57)	41.9 (0.66)	43.6 (3.06)	47.2 (1.03)	47.2 (1.67)

—Not available.
†Not applicable.
‡Reporting standards not met. Either there are too few cases for a reliable estimate or the coefficient of variation (CV) is 50 percent or greater.
!Interpret data with caution. The coefficient of variation (CV) for this estimate is between 30 and 50 percent.
[1]Data for years 1987–88 through 1999–2000 are only roughly comparable to data for later years, because the new category of two or more races was introduced in 2003–04.
[2]Includes Pacific Islander for years 1987–88 through 1999–2000.

[3]Education specialist degrees or certificates are generally awarded for 1 year's work beyond the master's level. Includes certificate of advanced graduate studies.
NOTE: Excludes prekindergarten teachers. Data are based on a head count of full-time and part-time teachers rather than on the number of full-time-equivalent teachers reported in other tables. Detail may not sum to totals because of rounding, missing data, and cell suppression. Race categories exclude persons of Hispanic ethnicity.
SOURCE: U.S. Department of Education, National Center for Education Statistics, Schools and Staffing Survey (SASS), "Public School Teacher Data File," 1987–88 through 2011–12; "Private School Teacher Data File," 1987–88 through 2011–12; and "Charter School Teacher Data File," 1999–2000. (This table was prepared July 2013.)

Table 209.20.   Number, highest degree, and years of full-time teaching experience of teachers in public and private elementary and secondary schools, by selected teacher characteristics: 1999–2000 through 2011–12

[Standard error appears in parentheses]

Selected teacher characteristic	Number of teachers (in thousands)				Percent of teachers, by highest degree earned, 2011–12					Percent of teachers, by years of full-time teaching experience, 2011–12			
	1999–2000	2003–04	2007–08	2011–12	Less than bachelor's	Bachelor's	Master's	Education specialist[1]	Doctor's	Less than 3	3 to 9	10 to 20	Over 20
1	2	3	4	5	6	7	8	9	10	11	12	13	14
Public schools													
Total	3,002 (19.4)	3,251 (29.2)	3,405 (44.0)	3,385 (41.4)	3.8 (0.24)	39.9 (0.52)	47.7 (0.57)	7.6 (0.27)	1.1 (0.11)	9.0 (0.29)	33.3 (0.52)	36.4 (0.51)	21.3 (0.54)
Sex													
Males	754 (10.7)	813 (13.3)	821 (20.4)	802 (22.2)	5.7 (0.58)	39.7 (1.03)	46.3 (1.04)	6.6 (0.51)	1.7 (0.20)	9.7 (0.52)	32.3 (1.11)	38.3 (0.98)	19.7 (1.01)
Females	2,248 (16.0)	2,438 (23.5)	2,584 (34.6)	2,584 (30.5)	3.2 (0.22)	39.9 (0.59)	48.1 (0.64)	7.9 (0.33)	0.9 (0.13)	8.8 (0.34)	33.7 (0.59)	35.8 (0.61)	21.8 (0.61)
Race/ethnicity													
White	2,532[2] (17.2)	2,702 (30.1)	2,829 (38.7)	2,773 (30.5)	3.7 (0.23)	39.3 (0.57)	48.7 (0.61)	7.4 (0.28)	0.9 (0.12)	8.7 (0.33)	32.5 (0.54)	36.5 (0.56)	22.3 (0.64)
Black	228[2] (6.0)	257 (11.0)	239 (15.8)	231 (12.1)	4.2 (0.91)	39.6 (2.36)	45.0 (3.06)	8.7 (1.39)	2.5 (0.52)	9.5 (1.25)	32.4 (2.85)	34.7 (2.46)	23.4 (2.54)
Hispanic	169[2] (6.4)	202 (11.3)	240 (16.6)	263 (13.4)	4.5 (1.16)	48.1 (2.31)	39.0 (2.18)	6.9 (0.98)	1.5 (0.41)	10.8 (2.05)	40.4 (2.44)	36.4 (2.54)	12.4 (1.63)
Asian	48[3] (2.7)	42 (2.5)	42 (7.2)	61 (7.3)	1.8 ! (0.76)	27.9 (4.51)	53.4 (5.32)	15.8 (4.91)	1.1 ! (0.50)	10.1 (2.13)	45.0 (6.77)	33.7 (6.51)	11.2 (3.19)
Pacific Islander	— (†)	6 (0.8)	6 (1.3)	5 (1.4)	‡ (†)	39.2 ! (12.26)	39.2 ! (13.35)	‡ (†)	‡ (†)	‡ (†)	30.0 ! (13.01)	46.0 (12.75)	‡ (†)
American Indian/Alaska Native	26[2] (1.9)	17 (1.2)	17 (1.9)	17 (2.9)	‡ (†)	48.0 (8.20)	30.7 (6.60)	7.6 ! (3.45)	‡ (†)	‡ (†)	24.3 (4.72)	49.5 (6.77)	18.0 ! (5.46)
Two or more races	— (†)	24 (2.2)	31 (2.9)	35 (3.8)	2.3 ! (0.84)	45.0 (5.56)	44.2 (5.15)	6.8 ! (2.58)	‡ (†)	17.6 (3.95)	37.6 (5.52)	35.0 (5.32)	9.8 (2.70)
Age													
Under 30	509 (9.2)	540 (27.4)	612 (22.4)	518 (15.9)	2.7 (0.36)	61.6 (1.27)	33.7 (1.27)	1.9 (0.33)	‡ (†)	35.9 (1.16)	64.1 (1.16)	‡ (†)	‡ (†)
30 to 39	661 (9.8)	798 (14.5)	898 (16.8)	979 (19.3)	3.3 (0.36)	37.0 (1.04)	51.1 (1.07)	7.8 (0.49)	0.9 (0.23)	6.3 (0.46)	51.5 (1.07)	42.2 (1.08)	‡ (†)
40 to 49	953 (10.3)	840 (14.3)	808 (19.2)	849 (19.2)	4.1 (0.42)	35.2 (1.15)	51.2 (1.17)	8.1 (0.64)	1.4 (0.23)	4.0 (0.41)	21.2 (0.88)	55.9 (1.08)	18.8 (0.98)
50 to 59	786 (12.6)	942 (26.0)	879 (21.1)	783 (20.5)	4.5 (0.52)	36.3 (1.18)	48.7 (1.06)	9.3 (0.56)	1.2 (0.19)	2.6 (0.31)	11.8 (0.74)	34.4 (1.31)	51.1 (1.25)
60 and over	93 (4.0)	131 (4.8)	207 (10.3)	256 (13.2)	4.8 (0.85)	33.6 (2.08)	48.1 (2.17)	11.3 (1.15)	2.2 (0.42)	1.4 (0.39)	7.3 (1.09)	28.8 (1.83)	62.5 (1.86)
Level of instruction[4]													
Elementary	1,602 (13.5)	1,716 (25.8)	1,725 (37.1)	1,726 (20.2)	3.2 (0.35)	41.3 (0.80)	47.1 (0.90)	7.9 (0.47)	0.4 (0.10)	8.3 (0.46)	33.6 (0.91)	36.1 (1.00)	22.0 (0.83)
General	1,019 (13.6)	1,130 (29.8)	1,100 (26.5)	1,078 (22.1)	3.3 (0.42)	43.5 (1.12)	46.0 (1.20)	6.8 (0.57)	0.3 ! (0.12)	8.0 (0.56)	33.8 (1.19)	36.9 (1.21)	21.3 (1.09)
Arts/music	[5] (†)	101 (5.3)	103 (6.6)	82 (5.4)	3.5 ! (1.24)	42.9 (3.71)	44.8 (3.76)	7.1 (2.12)	1.7 ! (0.75)	12.9 (2.56)	28.7 (3.00)	36.1 (3.60)	22.3 (3.98)
English	33 (2.8)	70 (5.1)	104 (9.9)	92 (6.9)	‡ (†)	35.4 (3.93)	48.4 (3.71)	13.5 (2.88)	‡ (†)	7.5 (1.94)	20.7 (2.70)	41.2 (3.37)	30.6 (3.64)
ESL/bilingual	[5] (†)	25 (3.6)	24 (3.3)	51 (6.8)	‡ (†)	42.9 (5.52)	37.6 (6.42)	16.2 (4.09)	‡ (†)	‡ (†)	44.7 (6.79)	26.8 (5.75)	20.8 (5.95)
Health/physical ed. ..	[5] (†)	73 (5.0)	63 (6.0)	79 (8.1)	‡ (†)	48.4 (5.08)	42.7 (4.67)	4.3 ! (1.78)	‡ (†)	10.1 (2.24)	28.4 (4.53)	33.3 (4.84)	28.2 (4.70)
Mathematics	26 (2.5)	19 (2.3)	28 (3.8)	32 (6.5)	4.2 ! (2.04)	31.8 (5.90)	59.4 (6.33)	4.6 ! (1.79)	‡ (†)	5.9 ! (1.96)	29.9 (7.56)	41.0 (8.18)	23.1 (5.80)
Science	[5] (†)	19 (3.0)	15 (3.4)	18 (3.3)	‡ (†)	42.0 (6.99)	46.6 (7.72)	‡ (†)	‡ (†)	‡ (†)	42.6 (9.63)	38.5 (8.31)	12.6 ! (4.48)
Special education	210 (5.8)	240 (20.6)	230 (13.0)	239 (10.3)	2.7 ! (1.00)	33.6 (2.18)	53.0 (2.52)	10.6 (1.45)	‡ (†)	8.8 (1.39)	39.1 (2.38)	32.1 (2.16)	20.0 (1.72)
Other elementary	314 (8.4)	40 (3.5)	58 (4.2)	55 (5.2)	4.4 ! (2.11)	33.6 (4.12)	52.8 (4.77)	9.2 (2.31)	‡ (†)	7.1 (1.68)	30.6 (4.28)	39.4 (4.33)	22.9 (3.67)
Secondary	1,401 (17.7)	1,534 (26.0)	1,680 (39.0)	1,659 (37.8)	4.4 (0.26)	38.4 (0.60)	48.2 (0.61)	7.2 (0.32)	1.8 (0.20)	9.8 (0.31)	33.0 (0.59)	36.7 (0.53)	20.5 (0.61)
Arts/music	[5] (†)	112 (4.1)	121 (6.2)	121 (5.6)	4.1 (0.59)	44.6 (2.01)	44.7 (1.87)	5.8 (1.23)	0.8 ! (0.29)	10.0 (1.01)	30.2 (1.79)	34.7 (1.84)	25.1 (1.64)
English	235 (5.0)	269 (9.0)	306 (10.0)	289 (9.9)	3.4 (0.52)	36.6 (1.44)	49.0 (1.43)	9.1 (0.75)	1.9 (0.44)	9.6 (0.82)	33.3 (1.21)	38.3 (1.39)	18.7 (0.95)
ESL/bilingual	[5] (†)	18 (2.5)	21 (2.5)	20 (2.4)	8.0 ! (3.15)	27.6 (6.21)	51.4 (5.76)	11.1 (2.98)	‡ (†)	6.9 ! (2.86)	41.4 (5.52)	35.7 (4.77)	16.1 (3.19)
Foreign language	[5] (†)	73 (3.3)	78 (5.0)	88 (4.5)	3.0 (0.76)	37.0 (2.42)	51.3 (2.48)	7.1 (1.08)	1.6 ! (0.52)	11.6 (1.24)	31.7 (2.14)	37.5 (2.35)	19.2 (1.70)
Health/physical ed. ..	191 (4.3)	102 (4.3)	119 (5.7)	101 (3.9)	4.9 (0.91)	44.6 (1.92)	44.9 (2.03)	4.9 (1.11)	0.6 ! (0.28)	9.2 (1.34)	25.6 (2.06)	37.7 (2.04)	27.5 (2.04)
Mathematics	159 (3.7)	213 (5.5)	252 (9.1)	250 (7.5)	2.7 (0.43)	41.4 (1.50)	48.9 (1.27)	5.6 (0.62)	1.4 ! (0.70)	12.0 (1.05)	33.9 (1.21)	35.0 (1.00)	19.1 (1.25)
Science	147 (4.3)	189 (6.8)	195 (8.3)	209 (6.1)	3.2 (0.51)	37.8 (1.57)	49.7 (1.51)	6.3 (0.73)	3.0 (0.54)	9.7 (0.95)	36.0 (1.75)	35.9 (1.34)	18.4 (1.40)
Social studies	99 (3.7)	178 (5.7)	209 (9.9)	197 (6.3)	3.2 (0.57)	39.2 (1.62)	49.1 (1.62)	5.8 (0.62)	2.8 (0.54)	8.8 (0.79)	34.4 (1.54)	38.5 (1.94)	18.3 (1.31)
Special education	125 (3.2)	174 (7.5)	165 (9.7)	191 (12.2)	3.1 ! (0.99)	31.3 (1.53)	52.7 (1.72)	11.8 (1.09)	1.1 ! (0.41)	8.1 (0.93)	35.5 (2.14)	35.3 (2.25)	21.1 (1.13)
Vocational/technical ..	443 (8.5)	169 (5.7)	164 (6.3)	147 (5.7)	12.8 (1.28)	38.7 (1.56)	41.2 (1.57)	5.7 (0.78)	1.6 ! (0.60)	9.8 (0.88)	30.2 (1.62)	35.8 (1.68)	24.2 (1.53)
Other secondary		36 (2.1)	47 (3.4)	46 (4.0)	9.8 (2.15)	37.9 (3.80)	42.2 (3.68)	8.2 (2.46)	1.8 ! (0.87)	8.6 ! (2.76)	28.4 (3.32)	40.5 (3.04)	22.6 (3.04)

See notes at end of table.

Table 209.20. Number, highest degree, and years of full-time teaching experience of teachers in public and private elementary and secondary schools, by selected teacher characteristics: 1999–2000 through 2011–12—Continued

[Standard error appears in parentheses]

Selected teacher characteristic	Number of teachers (in thousands)				Percent of teachers, by highest degree earned, 2011–12					Percent of teachers, by years of full-time teaching experience, 2011–12			
	1999–2000	2003–04	2007–08	2011–12	Less than bachelor's	Bachelor's	Master's	Education specialist[1]	Doctor's	Less than 3	3 to 9	10 to 20	Over 20
1	2	3	4	5	6	7	8	9	10	11	12	13	14
Private schools													
Total	449 (10.6)	467 (10.3)	490 (9.2)	465 (11.1)	8.4 (1.07)	48.5 (1.37)	35.8 (1.16)	5.0 (0.48)	2.3 (0.41)	19.5 (1.76)	31.3 (0.94)	27.7 (1.06)	21.4 (1.47)
Sex													
Males	107 (3.8)	110 (8.4)	127 (4.6)	117 (6.9)	10.0! (3.00)	40.0 (2.90)	40.1 (3.26)	5.4 (1.09)	4.6 (1.23)	18.3 (2.98)	31.2 (2.36)	25.4 (2.15)	25.0 (3.18)
Females	342 (7.7)	357 (14.3)	362 (7.7)	348 (10.1)	7.9 (0.97)	51.3 (1.53)	34.3 (1.21)	4.9 (0.56)	1.5 (0.41)	19.9 (1.67)	31.3 (1.28)	28.5 (1.29)	20.2 (1.28)
Race/ethnicity													
White	402 (9.6)[2]	411 (12.0)	423 (8.8)	411 (11.1)	8.0 (1.23)	48.1 (1.34)	36.7 (1.20)	5.0 (0.52)	2.2 (0.39)	18.5 (1.73)	30.7 (1.07)	27.9 (1.09)	22.9 (1.53)
Black	17 (1.4)[2]	19 (2.9)	20 (2.2)	17 (2.4)	10.5 (2.50)	53.4 (5.90)	29.1 (5.81)	4.8! (1.50)	‡ (†)	22.9 (6.38)	31.7 (5.60)	32.0 (5.94)	13.5 (3.97)
Hispanic	21 (1.5)[2]	23 (3.1)	29 (2.1)	24 (2.4)	13.3 (2.67)	47.0 (4.62)	29.5 (5.29)	6.0 (1.79)	‡ (†)	24.4 (3.44)	40.6 (4.88)	26.1 (5.05)	9.0! (3.01)
Asian[3]	‡ (†)	‡ (†)	11 (1.5)	9 (1.4)	‡ (†)	55.5 (10.22)	27.3 (7.53)	‡ (†)	‡ (†)	42.4 (10.10)	26.6 (7.95)	24.8 (6.50)	‡ (†)
Pacific Islander	— (†)	‡ (†)	‡ (†)	‡ (†)	‡ (†)	‡ (†)	‡ (†)	‡ (†)	‡ (†)	‡ (†)	‡ (†)	‡ (†)	‡ (†)
American Indian/Alaska Native	‡ (†)	‡ (†)	‡ (†)	‡ (†)	‡ (†)	‡ (†)	‡ (†)	‡ (†)	‡ (†)	‡ (†)	‡ (†)	‡ (†)	‡ (†)
Two or more races	— (†)	‡ (†)	4 (0.6)	4 (0.9)	12.5! (5.87)	60.2 (11.13)	24.2! (10.48)	‡ (†)	‡ (†)	35.0! (11.38)	40.6! (12.49)	‡ (†)	‡ (†)
Age													
Under 30	87 (3.1)	88 (3.7)	80 (3.9)	78 (6.8)	10.4 (2.29)	63.0 (3.25)	24.7 (2.55)	1.7! (0.59)	‡ (†)	53.9 (4.80)	46.1 (4.80)	‡ (†)	‡ (†)
30 to 39	101 (3.2)	103 (5.8)	109 (5.2)	112 (6.2)	9.2 (2.51)	47.9 (2.57)	38.0 (2.56)	3.9 (0.80)	‡ (†)	18.0 (2.10)	55.0 (2.74)	27.0 (2.71)	‡ (†)
40 to 49	131 (4.2)	119 (7.1)	116 (3.6)	110 (6.3)	8.6 (1.57)	45.3 (2.66)	37.7 (2.47)	5.3 (1.26)	3.1! (0.99)	13.4 (1.63)	25.3 (2.34)	48.7 (2.38)	12.7 (1.87)
50 to 59	106 (3.2)	121 (11.1)	128 (4.5)	99 (5.0)	8.1 (1.16)	48.7 (2.50)	33.4 (2.47)	6.1 (1.07)	3.6 (0.82)	10.3 (1.51)	14.9 (1.47)	32.5 (2.08)	42.3 (2.31)
60 and over	25 (1.2)	37 (4.7)	56 (3.1)	66 (5.0)	5.0 (1.23)	37.2 (2.54)	45.5 (3.34)	9.0 (1.84)	3.4! (1.43)	5.7! (1.85)	8.2 (1.96)	19.5 (2.55)	66.6 (3.49)
Level of instruction[4]													
Elementary	261 (5.8)	263 (17.5)	258 (6.5)	245 (9.3)	11.1 (1.88)	53.0 (1.60)	29.3 (1.41)	5.7 (0.67)	0.9! (0.36)	20.0 (1.69)	31.5 (1.46)	28.3 (1.55)	20.2 (1.43)
General	168 (4.0)	174 (17.1)	163 (3.9)	151 (7.0)	12.5 (2.49)	55.4 (2.01)	26.1 (1.64)	5.3 (0.70)	‡ (†)	15.1 (1.68)	33.1 (1.99)	29.2 (1.81)	22.5 (1.77)
Arts/music	[5]	21 (2.5)	20 (1.6)	20 (1.8)	10.7 (3.04)	59.9 (4.34)	18.6 (2.90)	10.0! (3.66)	‡ (†)	39.5 (5.51)	23.9 (4.04)	23.5 (6.09)	13.7 (3.17)
English	[5]	8 (1.1)	13 (1.2)	11 (1.2)	‡ (†)	39.3 (9.17)	43.9 (8.21)	3.2! (1.57)	‡ (†)	17.6! (8.52)	25.9 (6.21)	31.1 (6.92)	25.5 (6.17)
Health/physical ed.	[5]	14 (1.8)	14 (1.7)	11 (1.2)	8.7! (3.21)	57.1 (6.06)	30.1 (5.80)	‡ (†)	‡ (†)	29.3 (6.66)	31.3 (4.58)	24.7 (7.14)	14.7 (4.19)
Mathematics	[5]	6 (0.7)	7 (1.0)	6 (1.1)	‡ (†)	51.2 (9.03)	38.8 (8.87)	‡ (†)	‡ (†)	24.6 (7.35)	35.3 (7.24)	29.0 (8.25)	11.1! (4.46)
Science	[5]	5 (0.8)	6 (0.8)	5 (1.0)	‡ (†)	49.7 (9.14)	39.9 (10.37)	15.1! (6.05)	‡ (†)	17.0! (5.96)	25.7! (7.80)	35.6 (8.32)	21.6! (9.24)
Special education	16 (1.6)	12 (2.3)	9 (1.0)	10 (1.9)	‡ (†)	29.7 (6.55)	58.3 (7.50)	‡ (†)	‡ (†)	21.2 (6.23)	33.0 (8.47)	30.3 (7.24)	15.5! (5.20)
Other elementary	77 (2.2)	24 (3.5)	27 (2.3)	25 (2.8)	11.7 (3.14)	50.8 (4.16)	30.5 (3.48)	4.3! (1.98)	2.7! (1.22)	30.4 (4.23)	31.9 (5.04)	23.8 (3.64)	13.9 (3.01)
Secondary	188 (6.2)	204 (13.4)	231 (7.1)	219 (9.9)	5.4 (0.66)	43.3 (2.28)	43.1 (2.14)	4.4 (0.85)	3.8 (0.73)	19.0 (2.58)	31.0 (1.58)	27.1 (1.52)	22.9 (2.13)
Arts/music	[6]	18 (1.9)	19 (1.8)	21 (2.2)	10.6! (4.00)	36.8 (5.86)	40.6 (7.37)	5.9! (2.68)	‡ (†)	24.7 (5.27)	35.7 (6.25)	33.8 (7.11)	14.3 (3.87)
English	33 (1.7)	38 (2.8)	39 (2.8)	39 (4.1)	3.1! (0.96)	46.0 (3.81)	41.6 (4.36)	7.5! (2.57)	1.8! (0.87)	12.8 (2.57)	35.7 (4.90)	29.7 (4.01)	21.9 (3.73)
Foreign language	[6]	18 (2.1)	22 (2.6)	22 (3.5)	5.3! (2.42)	34.0 (6.40)	49.9 (5.92)	‡ (†)	‡ (†)	24.0 (5.59)	34.9 (7.22)	23.6 (7.03)	17.5 (3.50)
Health/physical ed.	[6]	9 (1.0)	12 (1.8)	10 (1.8)	8.6! (3.75)	47.2 (10.06)	44.1 (9.51)	‡ (†)	‡ (†)	23.6! (9.69)	28.0 (9.59)	27.0! (8.24)	21.4! (9.03)
Mathematics	33 (1.6)	31 (3.2)	36 (2.6)	38 (5.1)	3.5! (1.09)	41.6 (4.57)	48.6 (5.38)	‡ (†)	4.8! (2.03)	16.9 (4.18)	27.8 (3.96)	28.6 (5.57)	27.8 (5.20)
Science	23 (1.3)	27 (1.8)	31 (1.9)	28 (2.6)	5.0! (2.23)	42.1 (5.15)	45.2 (4.66)	2.5! (1.22)	5.2! (1.97)	14.6 (3.18)	33.3 (5.88)	28.6 (5.57)	23.6 (4.64)
Social studies	19 (1.1)	27 (2.4)	31 (2.6)	28 (2.9)	‡ (†)	45.4 (5.22)	43.5 (5.25)	3.4! (1.25)	5.4! (2.50)	16.8 (4.16)	24.3 (3.63)	26.7 (5.51)	32.2 (5.76)
Special education	7 (1.0)	7 (1.5)	6 (1.0)	9 (1.5)	2.3! (1.12)	61.0 (6.98)	25.8 (5.34)	9.7! (3.69)	‡ (†)	18.9 (5.39)	50.9 (6.28)	19.8 (4.31)	10.3! (3.73)
Vocational/technical	4 (0.6)	5 (0.9)	6 (0.8)	5 (1.2)	‡ (†)	48.1 (11.53)	26.3! (9.50)	‡ (†)	‡ (†)	20.3! (9.08)	35.8! (11.28)	‡ (†)	37.8! (11.69)
Other secondary	69 (2.6)	24 (2.7)	29 (2.3)	20 (2.2)	10.8 (3.10)	45.6 (5.04)	38.7 (5.24)	‡ (†)	‡ (†)	29.9 (6.17)	25.4 (3.33)	24.8 (5.33)	19.9 (5.33)

—Not available.
†Not applicable.
!Interpret data with caution. The coefficient of variation (CV) for this estimate is between 30 and 50 percent.
‡Reporting standards not met. Either there are too few cases for a reliable estimate or the coefficient of variation (CV) is 50 percent or greater.
[1]Education specialist degrees or certificates are generally awarded for 1 year's work beyond the master's level. Includes certificate of advanced graduate studies.
[2]Data for 1999–2000 are only roughly comparable to data for later years, because the new category of two or more races was introduced in 2003–04.
[3]Includes Pacific Islander.
[4]Teachers were classified as elementary or secondary on the basis of the grades they taught, rather than on the level of the school in which they taught. In general, elementary teachers include those teaching prekindergarten through grade 5 and those teaching multiple grades, with a preponderance of grades taught being kindergarten through grade 6. In general, secondary teachers include those teaching any of grades 7 through 12 and those teaching multiple grades, with a preponderance of grades taught being grades 7 through 12 and usually with no grade taught lower than grade 5.
[5]Included under Other elementary.
[6]Included under Other secondary.
NOTE: Excludes prekindergarten teachers. Data are based on a head count of full-time and part-time teachers rather than on the number of full-time-equivalent teachers reported in other tables. Detail may not sum to totals because of rounding and cell suppression. Race categories exclude persons of Hispanic ethnicity.
SOURCE: U.S. Department of Education, National Center for Education Statistics, Schools and Staffing Survey (SASS), "Public School Teacher Data File," 1999–2000, 2003–04, 2007–08, and 2011–12; "Private School Teacher Data File," 1999–2000, 2003–04, 2007–08, and 2011–12; and "Charter School Teacher Data File," 1999–2000. (This table was prepared May 2013.)

Table 209.30. Highest degree earned, years of full-time teaching experience, and average class size for teachers in public elementary and secondary schools, by state: 2011–12

[Standard errors appear in parentheses]

State	Total number of teachers (in thousands)	Percent of teachers, by highest degree earned				Percent of teachers, by years of full-time teaching experience				Average class size, by level of instruction[1]	
		Less than bachelor's	Bachelor's	Master's	Education specialist[2] or doctor's	Less than 3	3 to 9	10 to 20	Over 20	Elementary	Secondary
1	2	3	4	5	6	7	8	9	10	11	12
United States	3,385.2 (41.42)	3.8 (0.24)	39.9 (0.52)	47.7 (0.57)	8.7 (0.28)	9.0 (0.29)	33.3 (0.52)	36.4 (0.51)	21.3 (0.54)	21.2 (0.18)	26.8 (0.22)
Alabama	45.0 (2.61)	3.8! (1.51)	34.5 (2.69)	52.8 (2.81)	8.9 (1.64)	8.0 (1.28)	30.9 (2.75)	39.9 (2.85)	21.3 (2.34)	19.2 (0.42)	27.4 (0.94)
Alaska	7.5 (0.70)	4.4! (1.78)	45.6 (4.44)	41.9 (4.01)	8.2 (2.37)	12.9 (3.30)	30.8 (4.15)	39.6 (4.16)	16.7 (3.76)	18.3 (1.35)	18.7 (1.22)
Arizona	61.7 (2.61)	4.6! (1.16)	44.4 (3.67)	44.1 (3.49)	6.9 (1.71)	16.4 (2.29)	38.0 (2.75)	28.5 (2.60)	17.2 (2.02)	24.1 (0.67)	27.7 (0.96)
Arkansas	37.7 (2.01)	3.7! (1.45)	54.7 (3.36)	35.0 (3.13)	6.6 (1.72)	11.5 (2.03)	28.9 (3.38)	32.3 (3.93)	27.3 (3.37)	20.4 (0.73)	25.4 (1.69)
California	285.5 (7.27)	4.8 (0.91)	43.4 (2.33)	39.2 (2.18)	12.7 (1.56)	9.4 (1.29)	29.1 (2.13)	42.3 (2.25)	19.1 (1.89)	25.0 (0.52)	32.0 (0.53)
Colorado	55.9 (3.14)	2.8! (1.00)	36.1 (3.51)	49.9 (4.26)	11.2 (2.79)	10.8 (2.25)	33.4 (3.50)	42.9 (3.96)	12.9 (2.51)	22.8 (1.29)	29.1 (1.25)
Connecticut	44.9 (2.51)	‡ (†)	15.3 (1.86)	64.4 (3.01)	17.7 (2.37)	10.0 (1.43)	29.1 (2.66)	37.1 (2.43)	23.8 (3.34)	19.6 (0.68)	22.0 (0.71)
Delaware	9.3 (0.70)	4.0! (1.50)	34.5 (4.36)	49.7 (4.55)	11.8 (2.85)	12.6 (3.31)	35.0 (3.59)	33.8 (4.04)	18.6 (2.75)	20.3 (0.82)	25.8 (2.09)
District of Columbia	‡ (†)	‡ (†)	‡ (†)	‡ (†)	‡ (†)	‡ (†)	‡ (†)	‡ (†)	‡ (†)	‡ (†)	‡ (†)
Florida	‡ (†)	‡ (†)	‡ (†)	‡ (†)	‡ (†)	‡ (†)	‡ (†)	‡ (†)	‡ (†)	‡ (†)	‡ (†)
Georgia	123.3 (3.97)	3.4! (1.15)	29.5 (3.48)	43.5 (3.79)	23.6 (3.00)	6.3 (1.70)	34.2 (3.42)	39.8 (3.34)	19.7 (2.58)	21.0 (0.91)	27.5 (1.42)
Hawaii	‡ (†)	‡ (†)	‡ (†)	‡ (†)	‡ (†)	‡ (†)	‡ (†)	‡ (†)	‡ (†)	‡ (†)	‡ (†)
Idaho	16.3 (1.83)	4.6 (0.81)	55.6 (3.30)	35.3 (3.18)	4.4 (1.20)	10.4 (1.93)	30.4 (3.18)	35.2 (3.02)	24.0 (2.89)	24.5 (0.63)	25.4 (2.13)
Illinois	140.9 (9.09)	2.7 (0.91)	32.6 (2.53)	57.8 (2.44)	7.0 (1.34)	9.3 (1.56)	36.4 (2.59)	34.4 (2.85)	20.0 (2.51)	22.9 (1.26)	27.7 (1.26)
Indiana	64.0 (2.98)	2.2 (0.52)	43.6 (3.04)	47.4 (3.29)	6.9 (1.45)	10.0 (1.92)	26.1 (2.42)	35.6 (3.01)	28.3 (3.02)	21.4 (0.45)	27.3 (1.07)
Iowa	36.1 (2.28)	3.5 (1.22)	52.8 (3.89)	39.7 (3.60)	4.1! (1.26)	8.8 (1.85)	29.0 (2.98)	33.0 (2.77)	29.2 (2.55)	20.3 (0.93)	27.4 (1.35)
Kansas	36.5 (2.27)	3.8 (0.83)	43.8 (3.52)	47.0 (3.66)	5.4 (1.38)	12.5 (2.98)	27.4 (3.00)	32.7 (3.15)	27.4 (2.83)	20.4 (0.86)	24.6 (1.21)
Kentucky	46.8 (2.51)	5.1 (1.22)	17.5 (2.24)	57.5 (2.58)	20.0 (2.11)	10.1 (1.83)	32.2 (2.82)	38.5 (2.81)	19.2 (2.02)	23.3 (1.92)	26.6 (1.09)
Louisiana	44.5 (2.39)	3.5! (1.72)	61.9 (3.12)	27.0 (2.68)	7.6 (1.55)	8.6 (1.51)	31.2 (3.13)	33.4 (3.31)	26.8 (3.10)	19.0 (0.80)	23.4 (0.78)
Maine	18.4 (0.90)	4.9! (1.60)	46.3 (3.41)	42.8 (3.30)	6.0 (1.36)	5.8 (1.47)	24.1 (2.57)	39.4 (3.32)	30.6 (2.81)	17.6 (0.64)	19.9 (1.76)
Maryland	79.2 (4.42)	3.9 (1.08)	21.8 (2.33)	67.5 (2.54)	6.8 (1.48)	12.4 (1.96)	33.4 (3.04)	36.8 (3.02)	17.4 (3.09)	19.9 (1.72)	24.5 (1.18)
Massachusetts	96.7 (3.73)	2.3 (0.55)	29.8 (2.50)	62.9 (2.52)	5.0 (1.40)	7.3 (1.00)	31.4 (2.68)	42.7 (2.44)	18.7 (2.12)	23.8 (0.93)	28.9 (0.81)
Michigan	62.3 (2.99)	4.4 (0.77)	35.3 (2.06)	50.1 (1.87)	10.2 (1.40)	9.5 (1.20)	27.4 (2.05)	40.3 (2.14)	22.9 (2.00)	22.8 (0.70)	29.9 (0.86)
Minnesota	‡ (†)	‡ (†)	‡ (†)	‡ (†)	‡ (†)	‡ (†)	‡ (†)	‡ (†)	‡ (†)	‡ (†)	‡ (†)
Mississippi	37.6 (2.11)	5.3 (1.45)	54.4 (3.87)	35.2 (3.57)	5.1 (1.51)	10.3 (1.97)	41.0 (3.45)	30.5 (3.35)	18.2 (3.18)	21.6 (1.01)	22.8 (1.07)
Missouri	68.7 (2.34)	4.4 (0.91)	33.3 (2.90)	57.5 (2.96)	4.8 (0.94)	10.4 (1.90)	35.3 (2.21)	35.2 (2.31)	19.2 (2.31)	20.2 (0.83)	26.8 (1.18)
Montana	12.4 (0.90)	6.4 (1.52)	55.2 (3.34)	34.6 (3.39)	3.7 (1.66)	9.6 (2.33)	31.3 (3.17)	32.7 (3.04)	28.6 (3.65)	18.9 (0.80)	21.7 (1.81)
Nebraska	23.9 (1.73)	5.5 (1.31)	44.9 (3.29)	45.9 (3.15)	3.8 (0.98)	10.6 (1.74)	27.2 (2.52)	34.6 (2.63)	27.6 (2.54)	17.9 (0.72)	23.5 (0.99)
Nevada	25.2 (2.63)	4.5 (1.85)	25.1 (3.92)	49.8 (4.26)	20.6 (3.23)	6.5! (2.17)	39.0 (4.02)	36.2 (4.29)	18.2 (3.55)	25.3 (1.41)	34.5 (1.54)
New Hampshire	15.7 (1.05)	3.0 (1.12)	40.2 (3.49)	48.7 (3.55)	8.1 (1.82)	8.1 (1.54)	32.8 (3.41)	31.5 (3.57)	27.5 (3.54)	20.4 (3.09)	21.7 (1.16)
New Jersey	125.2 (4.16)	3.0 (0.74)	48.5 (2.47)	40.8 (2.30)	7.6 (1.60)	7.3 (1.24)	35.4 (2.45)	37.4 (2.66)	20.0 (2.03)	18.5 (0.81)	23.9 (0.68)
New Mexico	21.7 (2.83)	4.3 (2.01)	43.3 (3.80)	42.1 (3.52)	10.3 (2.82)	8.0 (2.46)	30.9 (3.73)	40.3 (5.11)	20.8 (5.19)	19.8 (0.76)	23.7 (1.58)
New York	241.4 (14.58)	2.8! (1.00)	4.4 (1.09)	84.2 (1.56)	8.6 (1.32)	5.3 (1.38)	30.0 (2.81)	45.5 (2.35)	19.1 (2.41)	20.7 (1.36)	25.1 (0.96)
North Carolina	104.3 (5.71)	4.1 (1.57)	54.2 (3.16)	33.8 (2.80)	7.8 (1.84)	8.4 (1.52)	35.8 (3.13)	34.8 (3.05)	21.1 (2.74)	18.8 (0.65)	25.8 (1.25)
North Dakota	10.3 (0.74)	6.9 (1.94)	59.2 (3.96)	30.1 (3.88)	3.9 (1.13)	12.2 (2.09)	24.6 (3.06)	30.6 (3.28)	32.6 (3.45)	17.8 (0.60)	19.2 (1.41)
Ohio	122.1 (4.29)	5.3 (1.17)	24.0 (1.79)	64.5 (2.16)	6.2 (1.28)	7.1 (1.11)	28.8 (2.48)	40.8 (2.67)	23.3 (2.00)	21.3 (0.99)	26.7 (0.85)
Oklahoma	46.2 (2.49)	4.3 (1.04)	65.6 (2.66)	26.9 (2.56)	3.2 (1.12)	9.8 (1.84)	30.1 (2.58)	36.9 (2.93)	23.3 (2.27)	20.7 (0.56)	23.7 (0.88)
Oregon	31.8 (1.28)	4.2 (1.53)	26.3 (3.18)	59.8 (3.62)	9.7 (1.94)	7.2 (1.54)	37.0 (3.58)	35.6 (3.58)	20.2 (2.45)	26.4 (0.96)	30.0 (1.05)
Pennsylvania	148.8 (7.48)	4.5! (1.94)	32.9 (2.52)	53.9 (3.34)	8.7! (1.77)	6.2 (1.78)	37.0 (2.55)	35.8 (2.17)	21.0 (2.30)	22.4 (0.99)	25.2 (1.25)
Rhode Island	10.3 (0.74)	‡ (†)	‡ (†)	‡ (†)	‡ (†)	‡ (†)	‡ (†)	‡ (†)	‡ (†)	‡ (†)	‡ (†)
South Carolina	51.8 (1.76)	3.0 (1.34)	28.8 (3.14)	57.9 (3.95)	10.3 (2.15)	8.4 (1.58)	30.5 (3.22)	32.3 (3.54)	28.9 (3.38)	19.1 (0.75)	26.0 (1.98)
South Dakota	10.8 (0.92)	3.3! (0.73)	68.8 (3.52)	26.6 (3.13)	2.3! (1.14)	8.6 (1.65)	24.6 (2.76)	32.9 (3.48)	33.7 (3.28)	20.7 (0.66)	22.3 (1.31)
Tennessee	76.5 (2.91)	4.4! (1.52)	35.1 (3.54)	46.3 (3.44)	14.2 (2.83)	10.6 (1.80)	34.0 (3.66)	34.1 (3.48)	21.3 (3.03)	17.7 (0.52)	26.9 (1.60)
Texas	350.8 (22.99)	3.3 (0.65)	66.4 (2.09)	25.8 (2.12)	4.6 (0.77)	8.9 (0.95)	40.4 (2.05)	31.1 (1.88)	19.7 (1.74)	18.2 (0.82)	26.9 (1.07)
Utah	27.9 (1.67)	4.2 (1.10)	56.8 (3.96)	27.3 (3.88)	11.7! (3.94)	15.0 (2.43)	39.9 (4.49)	25.6 (4.52)	19.5 (3.12)	27.4 (2.09)	31.5 (1.29)
Vermont	9.4 (0.34)	6.6 (1.46)	35.4 (2.78)	52.0 (2.87)	6.0 (1.59)	12.9 (1.60)	22.1 (2.38)	37.0 (2.56)	28.0 (2.73)	16.6 (0.40)	19.8 (1.25)
Virginia	88.5 (3.35)	3.3! (1.07)	47.5 (3.08)	41.6 (3.17)	7.6 (1.26)	9.1 (1.68)	31.5 (3.20)	34.8 (2.73)	24.8 (2.43)	20.4 (1.27)	23.8 (0.90)
Washington	55.5 (3.15)	2.9 (0.59)	23.1 (2.61)	62.9 (2.92)	11.1 (1.96)	6.2 (1.45)	32.2 (3.00)	34.8 (2.82)	26.8 (3.03)	23.7 (0.60)	29.7 (0.99)
West Virginia	24.2 (0.79)	3.1 (0.90)	46.6 (4.82)	43.2 (4.71)	7.1 (1.73)	6.2 (2.26)	31.2 (4.12)	30.5 (3.82)	32.1 (3.24)	18.7 (1.00)	29.7 (1.60)
Wisconsin	66.8 (3.42)	2.7 (0.79)	36.7 (2.96)	55.1 (2.98)	5.5 (1.41)	10.5 (2.62)	26.2 (3.12)	42.1 (3.24)	21.3 (3.73)	20.8 (0.55)	24.0 (1.65)
Wyoming	8.5 (0.57)	7.0! (3.08)	44.3 (4.47)	41.2 (4.18)	7.5! (2.74)	7.6! (2.62)	25.2 (4.09)	35.1 (3.73)	32.1 (4.30)	17.0 (1.05)	19.6 (1.22)

†Not applicable.
!Interpret data with caution. The coefficient of variation (CV) for this estimate is between 30 and 50 percent.
‡Reporting standards not met. Data may be suppressed because the response rate is under 50 percent, there are too few cases for a reliable estimate, or the coefficient of variation (CV) is 50 percent or greater.
[1]Elementary teachers are those who taught self-contained classes at the elementary level, and secondary teachers are those who taught departmentalized classes (e.g., science, art, social science, or other course subjects) at the secondary level. Teachers were classified as elementary or secondary on the basis of the grades they taught, rather than on the level of the school in which they taught. In general, elementary teachers include those teaching prekindergarten through grade 5 and those teaching multiple grades, with a preponderance of grades taught being kindergarten through grade 6. In general, sec-ondary teachers include those teaching any of grades 7 through 12 and those teaching multiple grades, with a preponderance of grades taught being grades 7 through 12 and usually with no grade taught being lower than grade 5.
[2]Education specialist degrees or certificates are generally awarded for 1 year's work beyond the master's level. Includes certificate of advanced graduate studies.
NOTE: Data are based on a head count of all teachers rather than on the number of full-time-equivalent teachers appearing in other tables. Excludes prekindergarten teachers. Detail may not sum to totals because of rounding and cell suppression.
SOURCE: U.S. Department of Education, National Center for Education Statistics, Schools and Staffing Survey (SASS), "Public School Teacher Data File," 2011–12. (This table was prepared May 2013.)

Table 209.50. Percentage of public school teachers of grades 9 through 12, by field of main teaching assignment and selected demographic and educational characteristics: 2011–12

[Standard errors appear in parentheses]

Selected demographic or educational characteristic	Total		Arts and music		English or language arts		Foreign languages		Health and physical education		Mathematics		Natural sciences		Social sciences		Special education		Vocational/ technical		All other	
1	2		3		4		5		6		7		8		9		10		11		12	
Number of teachers (in thousands)	1,108.2	(32.76)	87.3	(4.85)	166.0	(7.03)	74.0	(4.18)	65.6	(3.47)	152.8	(6.67)	132.9	(5.35)	126.2	(5.35)	130.3	(10.33)	125.6	(5.49)	47.5	(3.92)
Total	100.0	(†)	100.0	(†)	100.0	(†)	100.0	(†)	100.0	(†)	100.0	(†)	100.0	(†)	100.0	(†)	100.0	(†)	100.0	(†)	100.0	(†)
Sex																						
Male	41.9	(0.66)	43.3	(2.45)	23.2	(1.73)	24.5	(2.38)	63.5	(2.62)	42.7	(1.88)	46.4	(2.16)	63.4	(1.79)	29.0	(2.10)	48.9	(1.99)	47.4	(3.75)
Female	58.1	(0.66)	56.7	(2.45)	76.8	(1.73)	75.5	(2.38)	36.5	(2.62)	57.3	(1.88)	53.6	(2.16)	36.6	(1.79)	71.0	(2.10)	51.1	(1.99)	52.6	(3.75)
Race/ethnicity																						
White	83.0	(0.75)	89.8	(2.53)	84.8	(1.55)	67.5	(2.43)	83.3	(2.44)	81.5	(1.90)	84.5	(1.50)	86.5	(1.30)	84.0	(1.83)	85.9	(1.81)	69.6	(3.48)
Black	6.2	(0.60)	4.4 !	(2.16)	6.1	(1.47)	2.1 !	(0.68)	9.2	(1.89)	6.4	(1.40)	5.4	(0.97)	4.4	(0.88)	8.4	(1.85)	6.2	(1.05)	11.2	(2.31)
Hispanic	6.8	(0.46)	3.5	(1.01)	6.3	(1.15)	25.5	(2.55)	4.5	(1.34)	6.2	(0.82)	5.1	(1.01)	5.9	(0.93)	4.4	(0.96)	4.0 !	(1.31)	12.6	(2.49)
Asian	2.0	(0.25)	0.8 !	(0.39)	0.9	(0.23)	3.1 !	(0.93)	‡	(†)	4.1	(1.01)	3.7	(0.93)	1.0 !	(0.38)	1.7 !	(0.52)	1.1 !	(0.41)	2.4 !	(0.97)
Pacific Islander	‡	(†)	‡	(†)	‡	(†)	‡	(†)	‡	(†)	‡	(†)	‡	(†)	‡	(†)	‡	(†)	‡	(†)	‡	(†)
American Indian/Alaska Native	0.6 !	(0.17)	‡	(†)	‡	(†)	‡	(†)	‡	(†)	0.6 !	(0.21)	0.4 !	(0.15)	‡	(†)	0.5 !	(0.20)	‡	(†)	‡	(†)
Two or more races	1.2	(0.15)	1.2 !	(0.38)	1.3	(0.27)	1.0 !	(0.46)	1.1	(0.32)	1.1	(0.31)	0.8	(0.23)	1.7 !	(0.51)	0.7 !	(0.23)	‡	(†)	1.9 !	(0.93)
Age																						
Under 30	15.4	(0.63)	17.2	(1.33)	17.4	(1.29)	15.3	(1.90)	13.0	(1.61)	20.9	(2.04)	16.0	(1.78)	16.5	(1.62)	12.2	(1.36)	10.5	(0.97)	8.0	(1.58)
30 to 39	28.1	(0.66)	27.2	(2.08)	29.4	(1.59)	28.8	(2.36)	29.6	(2.68)	28.1	(1.75)	29.6	(1.94)	33.8	(1.80)	27.0	(2.27)	21.3	(1.63)	22.8	(3.22)
40 to 49	25.0	(0.57)	21.1	(1.97)	24.6	(1.69)	25.8	(2.35)	29.1	(2.40)	24.7	(1.59)	25.7	(1.74)	25.4	(1.71)	23.1	(1.56)	26.6	(1.68)	25.1	(2.76)
50 to 59	22.8	(0.82)	26.2	(2.10)	20.1	(1.39)	20.9	(2.27)	22.2	(1.95)	18.1	(1.81)	21.5	(1.67)	16.7	(1.37)	28.3	(2.26)	30.3	(1.75)	30.8	(3.54)
60 and over	8.8	(0.43)	8.4	(1.43)	8.5	(0.87)	9.3	(1.39)	6.1	(1.33)	8.3	(1.31)	7.2	(1.39)	7.6	(0.98)	9.5	(1.12)	11.3	(1.00)	13.4	(2.31)
Age at which first began to teach full time or part time																						
25 or under	51.8	(0.66)	56.7	(2.46)	54.0	(1.75)	53.5	(2.42)	61.8	(2.57)	61.3	(1.79)	49.0	(1.86)	50.2	(1.89)	48.2	(2.54)	41.9	(1.78)	35.3	(3.21)
26 to 35	30.2	(0.55)	29.1	(2.50)	29.2	(1.48)	30.9	(2.26)	31.9	(2.54)	24.1	(1.49)	35.3	(1.73)	34.4	(1.84)	28.7	(1.84)	29.8	(1.81)	31.5	(3.82)
36 to 45	12.6	(0.51)	9.5	(1.40)	12.7	(1.19)	12.1	(1.68)	4.6	(1.03)	10.0	(1.05)	10.6	(1.20)	11.8	(1.28)	14.5	(1.86)	20.0	(1.62)	21.6	(3.23)
46 to 55	4.8	(0.32)	4.6 !	(1.42)	3.9	(0.79)	3.2 !	(0.98)	‡	(†)	4.2	(1.10)	4.5	(0.79)	3.0	(0.54)	8.2	(1.47)	6.6	(1.11)	9.4	(2.38)
56 or over	0.6	(0.12)	‡	(†)	‡	(†)	‡	(†)	‡	(†)	‡	(†)	‡	(†)	‡	(†)	0.4 !	(0.16)	1.7	(0.39)	2.2 !	(1.03)
Years of full-time teaching experience																						
Less than 3 years	9.9	(0.36)	10.8	(1.16)	9.7	(0.87)	11.2	(1.39)	10.1	(1.90)	11.6	(1.12)	10.0	(1.24)	8.8	(0.98)	7.9	(0.96)	10.4	(0.96)	7.4	(2.01)
3 to 9 years	32.7	(0.76)	30.7	(2.48)	34.3	(1.56)	31.1	(2.50)	23.9	(2.33)	33.8	(1.69)	33.5	(1.88)	34.7	(1.89)	34.8	(2.69)	30.9	(1.75)	34.0	(3.80)
10 to 20 years	36.7	(0.62)	34.4	(2.12)	37.1	(1.61)	37.2	(2.63)	38.4	(2.53)	34.5	(1.58)	35.8	(1.82)	40.2	(2.23)	37.3	(3.04)	35.2	(1.81)	38.6	(3.37)
Over 20 years	20.7	(0.68)	24.1	(1.82)	18.9	(1.42)	20.4	(2.04)	27.6	(2.37)	20.1	(1.49)	20.7	(1.77)	16.3	(1.31)	19.9	(1.53)	23.5	(1.74)	19.9	(2.97)
Highest degree earned																						
Less than bachelor's degree	4.9	(0.36)	4.2	(0.77)	3.4	(0.72)	3.3	(0.88)	5.4	(1.25)	2.6	(0.55)	2.9	(0.62)	3.1	(0.80)	3.3 !	(1.37)	14.2	(1.43)	11.4	(2.38)
Bachelor's degree	38.2	(0.73)	46.5	(2.67)	35.8	(1.99)	37.9	(2.64)	44.9	(2.41)	41.0	(2.03)	35.6	(1.86)	37.9	(1.70)	31.8	(1.97)	38.9	(1.76)	38.2	(3.72)
Master's degree	47.9	(0.74)	42.6	(2.41)	50.3	(2.26)	50.6	(2.77)	43.5	(2.31)	49.8	(1.74)	51.8	(1.96)	49.6	(1.79)	52.3	(2.08)	39.7	(1.82)	40.4	(3.48)
Education specialist[1]	6.8	(0.39)	5.8	(1.56)	8.6	(0.91)	6.8	(1.15)	5.3	(1.42)	4.8	(0.67)	5.6	(0.71)	5.9	(0.85)	11.2	(1.16)	5.6	(0.86)	8.1	(2.02)
Doctor's degree	2.1	(0.28)	0.9 !	(0.34)	1.9 !	(0.71)	1.4 !	(0.57)	0.8 !	(0.39)	‡	(†)	4.0	(0.85)	3.4	(0.78)	1.5 !	(0.58)	1.7 !	(0.64)	1.8 !	(0.88)
Major field of study in bachelor's or higher degree[2]																						
Arts and music	9.2	(0.42)	87.6	(1.37)	4.9	(0.84)	3.5	(0.78)	1.0 !	(0.51)	1.2	(0.34)	1.1 !	(0.36)	1.7 !	(0.52)	3.5	(0.79)	2.1 !	(0.93)	3.5 !	(1.49)
Education, elementary instruction	6.4	(0.32)	2.9	(0.77)	5.0	(0.63)	5.2 !	(1.62)	2.6	(0.65)	4.9	(0.68)	3.2	(0.66)	2.6	(0.52)	21.7	(1.81)	3.1	(0.56)	14.9	(2.17)
Education, secondary instruction	20.7	(0.64)	11.1	(1.83)	29.1	(1.68)	19.7	(1.91)	9.5	(1.38)	27.1	(1.36)	29.9	(1.76)	29.5	(2.00)	8.1 !	(2.96)	11.2	(1.06)	15.5	(2.80)
Education, special education	11.4	(0.58)	1.3	(0.36)	5.8	(0.81)	1.7 !	(0.68)	2.9 !	(1.19)	3.5 !	(1.20)	3.0 !	(0.98)	3.6	(0.65)	70.9	(1.84)	2.4 !	(0.89)	7.9	(1.75)
Education, other	17.7	(0.54)	12.8	(1.83)	17.4	(1.19)	17.3	(1.91)	20.5	(1.94)	18.2	(1.54)	17.8	(1.34)	21.5	(1.84)	17.0	(1.57)	17.2	(1.77)	16.3	(2.29)
English and language arts	17.1	(0.54)	6.7	(1.39)	77.9	(1.22)	15.0	(1.73)	2.3 !	(0.82)	3.8	(0.62)	1.6	(0.35)	6.4	(1.03)	11.5	(2.11)	2.4	(0.52)	15.4	(2.92)
Foreign languages	6.2	(0.32)	1.1 !	(0.50)	2.4	(0.47)	75.1	(2.32)	‡	(†)	1.2 !	(0.41)	‡	(†)	1.2 !	(0.43)	1.4	(0.38)	‡	(†)	3.9	(1.05)
Health and physical education	10.0	(0.43)	2.4 !	(0.80)	3.1	(0.61)	3.2 !	(1.20)	82.9	(2.11)	4.9	(0.83)	6.5	(0.96)	5.7	(0.96)	9.0	(1.38)	5.4	(0.99)	11.7	(2.79)
Mathematics	10.0	(0.31)	‡	(†)	‡	(†)	‡	(†)	‡	(†)	64.5	(2.00)	3.0	(0.58)	0.3 !	(0.09)	1.6 !	(0.52)	1.5	(0.40)	3.1 !	(1.03)
Natural sciences	12.0	(0.46)	0.5 !	(0.24)	0.7	(0.20)	0.9 !	(0.35)	3.2	(0.89)	8.4	(1.10)	78.3	(2.04)	1.1	(0.31)	2.0	(0.54)	4.1	(0.71)	4.8	(1.10)
Social sciences	18.6	(0.55)	4.0	(0.94)	10.6	(1.07)	15.9	(1.92)	6.8	(1.72)	9.2	(1.31)	7.3	(1.31)	78.6	(1.55)	21.5	(1.53)	6.4	(1.19)	20.1	(2.71)
Vocational/technical education	14.6	(0.51)	3.1	(0.85)	4.4	(0.78)	4.9	(1.15)	5.5	(1.26)	11.3	(1.55)	7.1	(1.18)	7.1	(1.10)	8.2	(1.07)	70.8	(1.81)	20.2	(3.24)
Other field	5.9	(0.31)	2.2	(0.49)	5.7	(0.88)	10.6	(1.80)	3.3	(0.85)	5.7	(0.65)	3.5	(0.65)	6.3	(0.93)	5.3	(1.15)	4.3	(0.66)	21.4	(2.77)
No degree	4.9	(0.36)	4.2	(0.77)	3.4	(0.72)	3.3	(0.88)	5.4	(1.25)	2.6	(0.55)	2.9	(0.62)	3.1	(0.80)	3.3 !	(1.37)	14.2	(1.43)	11.4	(2.38)

†Not applicable.
!Interpret data with caution. The coefficient of variation (CV) for this estimate is between 30 and 50 percent.
‡Reporting standards not met. Either there are too few cases for a reliable estimate or the coefficient of variation (CV) is 50 percent or greater.
[1]Education specialist degrees or certificates are generally awarded for 1 year's work beyond the master's level. Includes certificates of advanced graduate studies.

[2]Data may sum to more than 100 percent because (1) a teacher who reported more than one major is represented in more than one field of study and (2) a teacher with multiple degrees in different fields of study is represented in more than one field of study.
NOTE: Race categories exclude persons of Hispanic ethnicity. Detail may not sum to totals because of rounding.
SOURCE: U.S. Department of Education, National Center for Education Statistics, Schools and Staffing Survey (SASS), "Public School Teacher Data File," 2011–12. (This table was prepared May 2013.)

Table 210.10. Percentage of teachers indicating that certain issues are serious problems in their schools, by level and control of school: Selected years, 1987–88 through 2011–12

[Standard errors appear in parentheses]

Control of school and issue	1987–88 total	1993–94 total	1999–2000 total	2003–04 Total[1]	2003–04 Elementary schools	2003–04 Secondary schools	2007–08 Total	2007–08 Elementary schools	2007–08 Secondary schools	2007–08 Combined schools	2011–12 Total	2011–12 Elementary schools	2011–12 Secondary schools	2011–12 Combined schools
1	2	3	4	5	6	7	8	9	10	11	12	13	14	15
Public schools														
Student tardiness	10.5 (0.18)	10.5 (0.28)	10.2 (0.22)	13.8 (0.29)	9.8 (0.38)	23.1 (0.58)	9.8 (0.33)	5.8 (0.37)	17.9 (0.65)	9.0 (1.36)	11.9 (0.33)	8.5 (0.49)	17.6 (0.55)	16.4 (1.11)
Student absenteeism	16.4 (0.23)	14.4 (0.29)	13.9 (0.26)	13.1 (0.31)	8.3 (0.36)	23.7 (0.59)	11.7 (0.36)	6.5 (0.42)	21.4 (0.63)	14.2 (0.95)	13.9 (0.35)	8.6 (0.49)	22.6 (0.63)	21.9 (1.48)
Teacher absenteeism	2.3 (0.09)	1.5 (0.09)	2.2 (0.10)	1.1 (0.08)	0.9 (0.12)	1.7 (0.15)	1.5 (0.15)	1.2 (0.20)	2.0 (0.20)	2.3 (0.48)	1.6 (0.14)	1.3 (0.16)	1.8 (0.20)	3.3 (0.58)
Students cutting class	5.9 (0.16)	5.1 (0.12)	4.7 (0.12)	5.5 (0.23)	1.5 (0.17)	14.5 (0.59)	4.0 (0.20)	0.5 (0.12)	10.9 (0.52)	4.0 (0.64)	4.9 (0.22)	1.2 (0.16)	10.8 (0.47)	10.4 (1.05)
Physical conflicts among students	5.8 (0.18)	8.2 (0.25)	4.8 (0.19)	12.1 (0.29)	13.7 (0.43)	9.3 (0.38)	— (†)	— (†)	— (†)	— (†)	— (†)	— (†)	— (†)	— (†)
Robbery or theft	3.7 (0.12)	4.1 (0.17)	2.4 (0.11)	3.7 (0.17)	2.9 (0.23)	5.9 (0.24)	— (†)	— (†)	— (†)	— (†)	— (†)	— (†)	— (†)	— (†)
Vandalism of school property	6.1 (0.15)	6.7 (0.23)	3.4 (0.15)	3.7 (0.16)	2.5 (0.21)	6.3 (0.33)	— (†)	— (†)	— (†)	— (†)	— (†)	— (†)	— (†)	— (†)
Student pregnancy	6.9 (0.17)	7.3 (0.24)	3.7 (0.12)	2.4 (0.12)	‡ (†)	7.0 (0.34)	— (†)	— (†)	— (†)	— (†)	— (†)	— (†)	— (†)	— (†)
Student use of alcohol	11.4 (0.18)	9.3 (0.17)	7.4 (0.14)	3.0 (0.10)	0.3 (0.07)	9.0 (0.28)	— (†)	— (†)	— (†)	— (†)	— (†)	— (†)	— (†)	— (†)
Student drug abuse	8.0 (0.14)	5.7 (0.14)	6.0 (0.11)	4.5 (0.14)	0.5 (0.10)	13.0 (0.35)	— (†)	— (†)	— (†)	— (†)	— (†)	— (†)	— (†)	— (†)
Student possession of weapons	1.7 (0.06)	2.8 (0.12)	0.8 (0.06)	0.5 (0.05)	‡ (†)	1.2 (0.12)	— (†)	— (†)	— (†)	— (†)	— (†)	— (†)	— (†)	— (†)
Verbal abuse of teachers	8.1 (0.21)	11.1 (0.26)	— (†)	11.8 (0.31)	9.3 (0.39)	17.1 (0.50)	— (†)	— (†)	— (†)	— (†)	— (†)	— (†)	— (†)	— (†)
Student disrespect for teachers	— (†)	18.5 (0.35)	17.2 (0.34)	21.6 (0.45)	18.6 (0.62)	28.3 (0.58)	— (†)	— (†)	— (†)	— (†)	— (†)	— (†)	— (†)	— (†)
Students dropping out	— (†)	5.8 (0.16)	4.6 (0.11)	3.3 (0.13)	0.4 (0.08)	9.6 (0.41)	3.5 (0.19)	0.8 (0.19)	8.7 (0.41)	5.3 (0.77)	3.1 (0.17)	0.9 (0.16)	6.3 (0.39)	7.7 (0.85)
Student apathy	— (†)	23.6 (0.35)	20.6 (0.30)	16.6 (0.34)	9.9 (0.40)	30.4 (0.56)	16.5 (0.45)	10.0 (0.55)	28.5 (0.67)	21.4 (1.16)	20.0 (0.44)	13.4 (0.61)	31.4 (0.74)	27.3 (1.41)
Lack of parental involvement	— (†)	27.6 (0.45)	23.7 (0.36)	21.6 (0.42)	19.3 (0.58)	26.3 (0.59)	19.5 (0.49)	16.8 (0.68)	24.0 (0.69)	23.5 (1.42)	24.6 (0.54)	22.1 (0.77)	28.3 (0.65)	29.4 (1.55)
Poverty	— (†)	19.5 (0.52)	19.2 (0.43)	21.4 (0.45)	22.4 (0.64)	19.0 (0.57)	22.1 (0.59)	22.8 (0.83)	20.2 (0.68)	26.7 (1.36)	29.0 (0.59)	29.5 (0.86)	26.8 (0.79)	32.4 (2.00)
Students come unprepared to learn	— (†)	28.8 (0.39)	29.5 (0.36)	26.8 (0.46)	23.7 (0.68)	33.5 (0.69)	24.2 (0.56)	20.7 (0.84)	30.5 (0.77)	28.5 (1.45)	30.2 (0.59)	27.1 (0.86)	35.4 (0.85)	34.9 (1.54)
Poor student health	— (†)	— (†)	— (†)	— (†)	— (†)	— (—)	3.3 (0.20)	3.4 (0.30)	2.8 (0.21)	4.2 (0.50)	5.0 (0.25)	5.1 (0.38)	4.4 (0.37)	6.3 (0.63)
Private schools														
Student tardiness	3.6 (0.38)	2.6 (0.23)	2.9 (0.21)	2.8 (0.40)	2.1 (0.45)	5.0 (0.83)	2.5 (0.28)	2.3 (0.37)	3.0 (0.83)	2.6 (0.47)	2.7 (0.32)	1.8 (0.34)	3.2 (0.80)	‡ (†)
Student absenteeism	3.7 (0.39)	2.2 (0.19)	2.5 (0.22)	1.9 (0.23)	0.9 (0.17)	4.0 (0.75)	2.0 (0.23)	0.9 (0.23)	3.9 (0.99)	2.3 (0.40)	2.6 (0.33)	2.7 (0.52)	2.8 (0.79)	‡ (†)
Teacher absenteeism	0.8 (0.13)	0.8 (0.10)	0.8 (0.11)	0.5 (0.11)	‡ (†)	‡ (†)	0.5 (0.13)	0.3 ! (0.08)	‡ (†)	1.0 ! (0.32)	0.3 ! (0.13)	‡ (†)	0.7 ! (0.28)	‡ (†)
Students cutting class	0.9 (0.16)	0.7 (0.11)	0.8 (0.12)	0.3 ! (0.11)	‡ (†)	‡ (†)	0.5 ! (0.18)	‡ (†)	1.1 ! (0.41)	‡ (†)	‡ (†)	‡ (†)	‡ (†)	‡ (†)
Physical conflicts among students	1.3 (0.19)	1.5 (0.15)	1.0 (0.18)	2.4 (0.31)	2.7 (0.55)	1.3 ! (0.40)	— (†)	— (†)	— (†)	— (†)	— (†)	— (†)	— (†)	— (†)
Robbery or theft	1.3 (0.18)	0.8 (0.10)	0.9 (0.11)	0.4 (0.10)	‡ (†)	‡ (†)	— (†)	— (†)	— (†)	— (†)	— (†)	— (†)	— (†)	— (†)
Vandalism of school property	1.3 (0.19)	1.2 (0.11)	0.7 (0.11)	0.5 (0.11)	‡ (†)	‡ (†)	— (†)	— (†)	— (†)	— (†)	— (†)	— (†)	— (†)	— (†)
Student pregnancy	0.6 (0.12)	0.4 (0.06)	0.4 (0.09)	‡ (†)	# (†)	3.3 (0.86)	— (†)	— (†)	— (†)	— (†)	— (†)	— (†)	— (†)	— (†)
Student use of alcohol	3.6 (0.30)	3.1 (0.19)	3.1 (0.16)	0.7 (0.17)	# (†)	3.3 (0.86)	— (†)	— (†)	— (†)	— (†)	— (†)	— (†)	— (†)	— (†)
Student drug abuse	1.8 (0.24)	1.3 (0.15)	1.8 (0.14)	1.1 (0.25)	# (†)	5.2 (1.31)	— (†)	— (†)	— (†)	— (†)	— (†)	— (†)	— (†)	— (†)
Student possession of weapons	0.4 (0.11)	0.3 (0.06)	0.3 (0.06)	# (†)	# (†)	# (†)	— (†)	— (†)	— (†)	— (†)	— (†)	— (†)	— (†)	— (†)
Verbal abuse of teachers	2.0 (0.24)	2.3 (0.25)	— (†)	2.4 (0.40)	1.1 (0.29)	4.0 (0.84)	— (†)	— (†)	— (†)	— (†)	— (†)	— (†)	— (†)	— (†)
Student disrespect for teachers	— (†)	3.4 (0.27)	3.8 (0.31)	5.1 (0.37)	3.6 (0.54)	6.3 (1.05)	— (†)	— (†)	— (†)	— (†)	— (†)	— (†)	— (†)	— (†)
Students dropping out	— (†)	0.6 (0.09)	0.5 (0.11)	0.3 (0.09)	‡ (†)	6.6 (0.95)	0.4 ! (0.20)	0.4 (0.13)	0.5 ! (0.22)	0.3 ! (0.22)	0.3 ! (0.13)	‡ (†)	‡ (†)	‡ (†)
Student apathy	— (†)	4.5 (0.28)	4.3 (0.29)	3.0 (0.39)	1.4 (0.23)	6.6 (0.95)	3.9 (0.34)	1.7 (0.30)	6.9 (1.06)	5.1 (0.74)	3.6 (0.38)	1.7 (0.42)	7.1 (1.32)	‡ (†)
Lack of parental involvement	— (†)	4.0 (0.26)	3.4 (0.30)	2.5 (0.37)	1.6 (0.28)	3.6 (0.77)	2.5 (0.24)	1.9 (0.36)	2.8 (0.56)	3.0 (0.46)	2.7 (0.32)	1.8 (0.34)	3.2 (0.80)	‡ (†)
Poverty	— (†)	2.7 (0.23)	2.1 (0.21)	2.2 (0.26)	1.7 (0.31)	3.4 (0.78)	2.0 (0.21)	1.4 (0.28)	2.0 (0.56)	2.6 (0.44)	2.6 (0.33)	2.7 (0.52)	2.8 (0.79)	‡ (†)
Students come unprepared to learn	— (†)	4.1 (0.28)	4.9 (0.36)	3.5 (0.30)	2.1 (0.53)	6.8 (0.99)	3.6 (0.34)	1.9 (0.33)	6.2 (1.51)	4.4 (0.85)	3.9 (0.41)	2.0 (0.41)	6.7 (1.07)	‡ (†)
Poor student health	— (†)	— (†)	— (†)	— (†)	— (†)	— (—)	0.7 (0.13)	0.3 ! (0.12)	‡ (†)	1.0 (0.25)	0.8 (0.21)	0.4 ! (0.17)	0.5 ! (0.25)	‡ (†)

—Not available.
†Not applicable.
#Rounds to zero.
!Interpret data with caution. The coefficient of variation (CV) for this estimate is between 30 and 50 percent.
‡Reporting standards not met. Data may be suppressed because the response rate is under 50 percent, there are too few cases for a reliable estimate, or the coefficient of variation (CV) is 50 percent or greater.
[1]For 2003–04, combined schools are included in the total but not shown separately.

NOTE: Elementary schools are those with any of grades kindergarten through grade 6 and none of grades 9 through 12. Secondary schools have any of grades 7 through 12, and none of grades kindergarten through grade 6. Combined schools have both elementary and secondary grades, or have all students in ungraded classrooms.
SOURCE: U.S. Department of Education, National Center for Education Statistics, Schools and Staffing Survey (SASS), "Public School Teacher Data File," selected years, 1987–88 through 2011–12; "Private School Teacher Data File," selected years, 1987–88 through 2011–12; and "Charter School Teacher Data File," 1999–2000. (This table was prepared May 2013.)

Table 210.20. Percentage of teachers agreeing with statements about teaching and school conditions, by control and level of school: Selected years, 1993–94 through 2011–12

[Standard errors appear in parentheses]

Statement about conditions	Public school teachers								Private school teachers						
					2011–12								2011–12[1]		
	1993–94 total	1999–2000 total	2003–04 total	2007–08 total	Total	Elementary schools	Secondary schools	Combined schools	1993–94 total	1999–2000 total	2003–04 total	2007–08 total	Total	Elementary schools	Secondary schools
1	2	3	4	5	6	7	8	9	10	11	12	13	14	15	16
	Percent of teachers somewhat agreeing or strongly agreeing with statement														
The school administration's behavior toward the staff is supportive.	79.2 (0.36)	78.8 (0.38)	85.2 (0.33)	87.7 (0.39)	83.6 (0.44)	84.0 (0.67)	83.2 (0.57)	82.0 (1.18)	88.2 (0.42)	87.3 (0.45)	91.1 (0.78)	93.1 (0.43)	88.5 (0.90)	88.1 (1.20)	85.5 (2.41)
My principal enforces school rules for student conduct and backs me up when I need it.	80.8 (0.35)	82.2 (0.33)	87.2 (0.34)	88.0 (0.37)	83.7 (0.43)	84.5 (0.64)	82.2 (0.59)	83.1 (1.27)	88.4 (0.41)	88.3 (0.39)	92.2 (0.75)	92.2 (0.57)	89.4 (0.98)	90.1 (1.00)	87.0 (2.21)
In this school, staff members are recognized for a job well done.	67.9 (0.39)	68.3 (0.42)	75.5 (0.38)	76.7 (0.56)	74.3 (0.45)	75.6 (0.69)	72.5 (0.58)	71.0 (1.60)	81.1 (0.40)	78.9 (0.50)	83.8 (1.14)	84.0 (0.66)	80.6 (1.04)	80.7 (1.48)	79.9 (2.27)
Principal knows what kind of school he/she wants and has communicated it to the staff.	80.5 (0.36)	83.2 (0.28)	87.3 (0.30)	88.4 (0.33)	84.7 (0.41)	85.8 (0.60)	83.1 (0.54)	82.7 (1.20)	88.6 (0.38)	88.4 (0.43)	91.9 (0.68)	91.7 (0.53)	87.6 (0.96)	88.2 (0.91)	85.7 (1.55)
Most of my colleagues share my beliefs and values about what the central mission of the school should be.	84.2 (0.22)	84.7 (0.26)	88.1 (0.26)	88.3 (0.35)	87.7 (0.38)	90.1 (0.52)	83.5 (0.49)	84.5 (1.47)	93.2 (0.37)	92.2 (0.31)	93.8 (0.49)	93.7 (0.44)	92.9 (0.66)	93.0 (0.82)	89.6 (1.75)
There is a great deal of cooperative effort among staff.	77.5 (0.31)	78.4 (0.32)	83.2 (0.36)	84.3 (0.33)	82.3 (0.41)	84.3 (0.61)	78.9 (0.53)	80.2 (1.11)	90.5 (0.29)	89.0 (0.42)	91.2 (0.77)	91.7 (0.63)	88.8 (0.83)	88.8 (1.05)	87.0 (1.45)
I receive a great deal of support from parents for the work I do.	52.5 (0.38)	57.9 (0.40)	61.1 (0.50)	64.3 (0.52)	58.6 (0.63)	61.9 (0.87)	52.8 (0.69)	55.1 (2.04)	84.6 (0.41)	84.0 (0.49)	86.1 (2.33)	87.7 (0.60)	85.0 (0.97)	85.8 (1.18)	80.2 (2.73)
I make a conscious effort to coordinate the content of my courses with that of other teachers.	85.0 (0.25)	84.1 (0.24)	86.3 (0.31)	— (†)	90.0 (0.32)	92.7 (0.39)	85.8 (0.48)	85.8 (1.25)	85.2 (0.44)	81.4 (0.55)	84.6 (0.90)	— (†)	87.3 (0.90)	89.9 (0.96)	83.4 (1.59)
Routine duties and paperwork interfere with my job of teaching.	70.8 (0.38)	71.1 (0.30)	70.8 (0.44)	69.0 (0.53)	69.2 (0.53)	70.5 (0.70)	67.3 (0.66)	65.9 (2.10)	40.1 (0.65)	44.5 (0.57)	40.7 (2.70)	42.7 (0.97)	41.1 (1.50)	43.9 (1.64)	46.2 (3.22)
Level of student misbehavior in this school interferes with my teaching.	44.1 (0.40)	40.8 (0.42)	37.2 (0.52)	36.0 (0.57)	40.7 (0.65)	40.1 (0.96)	41.9 (0.82)	41.3 (1.58)	22.4 (0.43)	24.1 (0.61)	20.7 (2.47)	20.6 (0.72)	22.0 (1.05)	23.7 (1.39)	20.4 (2.78)
Amount of student tardiness and class cutting in this school interferes with my teaching.	27.9 (0.32)	31.5 (0.35)	33.4 (0.45)	33.4 (0.64)	37.6 (0.51)	32.3 (0.76)	47.1 (0.69)	42.4 (1.56)	8.6 (0.42)	15.0 (0.43)	16.9 (1.11)	17.9 (0.72)	18.8 (1.06)	17.8 (1.05)	21.4 (2.45)
Rules for student behavior are consistently enforced by teachers in this school, even for students who are not in their classes.	61.8 (0.42)	62.6 (0.39)	71.1 (0.46)	70.6 (0.55)	67.6 (0.51)	75.2 (0.76)	53.4 (0.71)	62.0 (2.06)	77.6 (0.50)	75.9 (0.51)	81.0 (1.52)	80.1 (0.81)	77.4 (1.49)	80.2 (1.72)	68.3 (2.78)
I am satisfied with my teaching salary.	44.9 (0.45)	39.4 (0.36)	45.9 (0.46)	50.9 (0.64)	47.0 (0.50)	45.0 (0.71)	50.7 (0.70)	49.0 (1.67)	41.6 (0.59)	42.6 (0.73)	50.6 (1.76)	51.7 (0.86)	49.5 (1.44)	41.8 (1.84)	56.5 (2.28)
Necessary materials are available as needed by staff.	73.1 (0.42)	75.0 (0.32)	79.0 (0.42)	82.2 (0.55)	79.4 (0.45)	79.6 (0.68)	78.9 (0.59)	79.5 (1.42)	85.7 (0.44)	89.0 (0.38)	91.8 (0.74)	92.1 (0.54)	90.8 (0.68)	90.3 (0.84)	91.9 (1.25)
I worry about the security of my job because of the performance of my students on state or local tests.	— (†)	28.8 (0.37)	31.2 (0.43)	30.9 (0.58)	44.0 (0.54)	45.3 (0.78)	41.1 (0.60)	43.8 (2.05)	— (†)	6.7 (0.29)	7.8 (0.68)	7.6 (0.46)	9.8 (0.75)	11.0 (0.96)	9.8 (1.38)
State or district content standards have had a positive influence on my satisfaction with teaching.	— (†)	— (†)	— (†)	49.3 (0.62)	47.5 (0.52)	50.8 (0.74)	41.0 (0.63)	46.2 (1.86)	— (†)	— (†)	— (†)	41.1 (0.80)	38.9 (1.19)	46.9 (1.35)	33.8 (2.53)
I am given the support I need to teach students with special needs.	— (†)	60.9 (0.33)	64.5 (0.47)	67.2 (0.57)	65.5 (0.51)	63.9 (0.73)	68.2 (0.61)	67.6 (1.74)	— (†)	67.1 (0.58)	71.8 (2.00)	68.4 (0.84)	66.9 (1.22)	63.5 (1.71)	67.6 (2.70)
Stress and disappointments involved in teaching at this school aren't really worth it.	— (†)	— (†)	— (†)	18.9 (0.38)	22.0 (0.49)	21.9 (0.72)	21.4 (0.62)	25.5 (2.10)	— (†)	— (†)	— (†)	10.1 (0.52)	11.9 (0.82)	12.5 (1.12)	12.9 (1.93)
Teachers at this school like being here; I would describe us as a satisfied group.	— (†)	— (†)	— (†)	79.4 (0.47)	75.7 (0.53)	76.0 (0.75)	75.7 (0.71)	74.5 (1.66)	— (†)	— (†)	— (†)	89.0 (0.55)	87.5 (0.93)	85.2 (1.22)	87.7 (1.88)
I like the way things are run at this school.	— (†)	— (†)	— (†)	77.1 (0.55)	72.9 (0.51)	73.6 (0.73)	72.4 (0.62)	69.6 (2.22)	— (†)	— (†)	— (†)	84.5 (0.66)	79.6 (1.12)	78.6 (1.32)	79.0 (2.35)
If I could get a higher paying job I'd leave teaching as soon as possible.	— (†)	— (†)	— (†)	26.0 (0.45)	29.6 (0.59)	29.3 (0.83)	29.7 (0.61)	32.0 (1.52)	— (†)	— (†)	— (†)	18.3 (0.73)	21.6 (1.05)	23.6 (1.29)	19.1 (1.77)
I think about transferring to another school.	— (†)	— (†)	— (†)	28.5 (0.53)	29.1 (0.51)	29.0 (0.76)	28.2 (0.71)	33.6 (1.87)	— (†)	— (†)	— (†)	23.8 (0.92)	25.6 (1.31)	28.2 (1.58)	24.1 (2.27)
I am generally satisfied with being a teacher at this school.	— (†)	89.7 (0.24)	90.9 (0.29)	92.8 (0.31)	90.2 (0.33)	90.1 (0.48)	90.4 (0.42)	89.8 (1.39)	— (†)	93.3 (0.26)	95.2 (0.56)	95.7 (0.43)	94.2 (0.60)	94.1 (0.78)	93.0 (1.37)

—Not available.
†Not applicable.
[1]Data for combined private schools in 2011–12 are included in the total, but not shown separately due to low response rates (under 50 percent).

NOTE: Elementary schools are those with any of grades kindergarten through grade 6 and none of grades 7 through 12. Secondary schools have any of grades 7 through 12, and none of grades kindergarten through grade 6. Combined schools have both elementary and secondary grades, or have all students in ungraded classrooms.
SOURCE: U.S. Department of Education, National Center for Education Statistics, Schools and Staffing Survey (SASS), "Public School Teacher Data File," selected years 1993–94 through 2011–12; "Private School Teacher Data File," selected years 1993–94 through 2011–12; and "Charter School Teacher Data File," 1999–2000. (This table was prepared May 2013.)

Table 210.30. Mobility of public elementary and secondary teachers, by selected teacher and school characteristics: Selected years, 1987–88 through 2012–13

[Standard errors appear in parentheses]

	Percent of public school teachers											
	Left teaching					2011–12 to 2012–13						
								Moved to another school				
									Teachers who moved, by destination			
Selected teacher or school characteristic	1987–88 to 1988–89	1993–94 to 1994–95	1999–2000 to 2000–01	2003–04 to 2004–05	2007–08 to 2008–09	Remained in same school	Total moving to another school	Public school in same school district	Public school in different district	Private school	Left teaching
1	2	3	4	5	6	7	8	9	10	11	12
Total................	5.6 (0.30)	6.6 (0.34)	7.4 (0.37)	8.4 (0.44)	8.0 (0.55)	84.3 (0.98)	8.1 (0.65)	58.8 (3.56)	38.2 (3.63)	2.9 (0.67)	7.7 (0.64)
Sex											
Male.........................	5.1 (0.52)	5.2 (0.32)	7.4 (0.67)	7.7 (0.68)	7.9 (1.13)	85.7 (2.17)	7.9 (1.53)	46.4 (8.74)	51.2 (8.87)	2.3 ! (0.92)	6.4 (1.13)
Female.....................	5.8 (0.39)	7.1 (0.44)	7.4 (0.45)	8.6 (0.50)	8.0 (0.65)	83.8 (1.03)	8.1 (0.70)	62.6 (3.80)	34.3 (3.85)	3.1 (0.86)	8.1 (0.70)
Race/ethnicity											
White......................	5.7 (0.32)	6.5 (0.36)	7.5 (0.45)	8.2 (0.50)	8.0 (0.67)	85.0 (0.86)	7.5 (0.63)	58.7 (3.94)	37.7 (3.93)	3.6 (0.90)	7.5 (0.56)
Black......................	5.1 ! (1.84)	6.6 (1.48)	7.4 (1.60)	11.0 (2.31)	9.0 (2.27)	78.2 (5.97)	11.7 ! (4.43)	64.2 (14.00)	35.2 ! (14.01)	‡ (†)	10.1 ! (3.47)
Hispanic.................	2.9 (0.84)	9.1 (2.14)	7.5 (1.67)	9.3 (1.89)	5.6 ! (1.81)	79.4 (5.00)	12.6 (3.13)	57.9 (10.56)	41.4 (10.56)	‡ (†)	8.0 ! (3.73)
Asian/Pacific Islander .	‡ (†)	2.4 (0.71)	2.1 ! (0.87)	‡ (†)	8.0 ! (3.84)	95.5 (7.98)	‡ (†)	‡ (†)	‡ (†)	‡ (†)	‡ (†)
Asian............	— (†)	— (†)	— (†)	‡ (†)	9.6 ! (4.38)	95.8 (7.75)	‡ (†)	‡ (†)	‡ (†)	‡ (†)	‡ (†)
Pacific Islander.......	— (†)	— (†)	— (†)	‡ (†)	‡ (†)	‡ (†)	‡ (†)	‡ (†)	‡ (†)	‡ (†)	‡ (†)
American Indian/ Alaska Native.......	‡ (†)	3.5 ! (1.06)	7.6 ! (3.68)	1.9 ! (0.77)	‡ (†)	‡ (†)	‡ (†)	‡ (†)	‡ (†)	‡ (†)	‡ (†)
Two or more races	— (†)	— (†)	— (†)	‡ (†)	‡ (†)	88.8 (6.09)	‡ (†)	‡ (†)	‡ (†)	‡ (†)	‡ (†)
Age											
Less than 25.............	4.3 (0.91)	3.8 (1.05)	9.3 (2.20)	4.8 (1.24)	8.7 ! (3.11)	73.8 (6.02)	17.1 (3.97)	35.1 (9.35)	60.0 (8.85)	‡ (†)	‡ (†)
25 to 29...................	9.0 (1.18)	10.0 (1.25)	9.7 (1.39)	10.6 (1.98)	9.4 (2.09)	80.0 (2.93)	12.9 (2.59)	50.9 (9.17)	43.9 (9.14)	5.2 ! (1.88)	7.1 (1.26)
30 to 39...................	5.8 (0.59)	6.7 (0.94)	6.5 (0.88)	6.8 (0.87)	8.4 (1.46)	86.3 (1.50)	8.5 (0.98)	59.0 (6.36)	39.7 (6.42)	1.3 ! (0.78)	5.3 (1.10)
40 to 49...................	2.4 (0.32)	3.9 (0.54)	4.6 (0.62)	5.3 (0.73)	3.9 (0.91)	90.1 (1.46)	5.9 (1.00)	65.9 (6.57)	33.3 (6.52)	‡ (†)	4.0 (0.88)
50 to 59...................	5.7 (0.82)	6.3 (0.77)	8.1 (0.80)	9.8 (0.82)	8.4 (1.26)	83.0 (1.96)	6.6 (1.24)	67.5 (8.28)	29.0 (8.22)	‡ (†)	10.5 (1.44)
60 to 64...................	23.4 (4.90)	30.5 (4.78)	25.7 (5.44)	28.0 (4.35)	17.5 (5.10)	73.3 (6.04)	7.0 ! (2.77)	52.9 ! (20.56)	‡ (†)	‡ (†)	19.7 (4.44)
65 and over..............	‡ (†)	34.1 (7.79)	16.6 ! (5.44)	21.2 (5.95)	10.4 ! (4.84)	70.0 (14.55)	‡ (†)	‡ (†)	‡ (†)	‡ (†)	24.8 ! (11.73)
Full- and part-time teaching experience											
1 year or less	7.9 (0.96)	5.7 (0.82)	10.5 (1.93)	9.6 (1.66)	11.4 ! (3.94)	79.0 (6.34)	13.4 ! (4.63)	43.2 (8.33)	52.6 (7.94)	‡ (†)	7.6 ! (3.14)
2 years.....................	7.3 (1.81)	9.1 (1.51)	8.5 (1.94)	6.4 (1.43)	8.8 ! (2.93)	78.0 (4.02)	14.5 (2.53)	26.0 (7.02)	68.1 (7.62)	5.9 ! (2.44)	7.5 ! (2.31)
3 years.....................	9.3 (1.50)	9.8 (1.42)	7.5 (1.60)	7.7 (1.55)	9.0 ! (3.11)	84.0 (3.13)	9.8 (2.54)	46.1 (11.39)	48.0 (11.80)	‡ (†)	6.2 (1.56)
4 to 10 years.............	6.4 (0.89)	6.8 (0.94)	7.3 (0.72)	8.1 (0.98)	8.1 (1.27)	81.3 (1.95)	11.3 (1.33)	62.0 (6.39)	36.3 (6.42)	1.8 ! (0.72)	7.4 (1.48)
11 to 20 years...........	3.5 (0.42)	4.9 (0.64)	5.2 (0.74)	5.5 (0.70)	4.3 (0.89)	89.5 (1.51)	5.3 (1.04)	63.1 (6.55)	35.6 (6.48)	‡ (†)	5.2 (0.88)
21 to 25 years...........	3.5 (0.87)	4.0 (0.81)	4.2 (0.68)	6.6 (1.23)	5.8 ! (2.31)	87.5 (2.74)	6.6 ! (2.16)	63.1 (16.69)	35.1 ! (16.83)	‡ (†)	5.9 (1.33)
More than 25 years.....	11.3 (1.63)	12.0 (1.04)	11.4 (1.05)	14.3 (1.13)	12.6 (2.12)	79.4 (2.26)	4.5 (1.10)	73.5 (12.38)	‡ (†)	‡ (†)	16.1 (2.06)
Grade level taught											
Elementary (preK–grade 8)	5.5 (0.39)	6.4 (0.53)	6.8 (0.45)	8.4 (0.68)	7.9 (1.01)	84.1 (1.27)	8.9 (0.99)	66.5 (4.90)	30.5 (4.98)	3.0 ! (1.12)	7.1 (0.77)
Secondary (grades 9–12)	5.6 (0.42)	6.7 (0.53)	8.6 (0.71)	8.4 (0.59)	8.0 (0.75)	84.5 (1.37)	7.2 (0.82)	48.8 (5.19)	48.4 (5.16)	2.8 (0.74)	8.3 (0.94)
School size											
Less than 150............	7.3 (1.36)	6.4 (1.15)	9.5 (2.29)	12.1 (2.92)	‡ (†)	85.4 (3.62)	7.6 ! (2.31)	36.5 (7.43)	59.0 (7.59)	‡ (†)	7.0 (1.97)
150 to 349................	4.8 (0.45)	7.8 (1.03)	6.7 (0.99)	10.3 (1.58)	7.3 (1.26)	84.2 (2.66)	8.1 (1.83)	49.1 (8.80)	47.1 (8.52)	3.7 ! (1.64)	7.7 (1.60)
350 to 499................	6.1 (0.98)	5.8 (0.73)	7.4 (0.85)	8.6 (1.16)	9.4 (2.28)	84.2 (1.93)	8.0 (1.17)	66.0 (5.53)	30.8 (5.13)	‡ (†)	7.8 (1.45)
500 to 749................	5.6 (0.77)	7.6 (0.67)	7.1 (0.78)	7.0 (0.75)	5.3 (0.79)	82.9 (1.78)	9.2 (1.40)	68.6 (6.24)	28.2 (6.65)	‡ (†)	7.8 (1.24)
750 or more..............	5.0 (0.48)	5.7 (0.57)	7.7 (0.74)	8.2 (0.79)	8.9 (1.01)	85.1 (1.89)	7.3 (1.12)	51.9 (6.90)	45.9 (7.01)	2.2 ! (0.77)	7.5 (1.07)
Percent of students who are Black, Hispanic, Asian, Pacific Islander, American Indian/Alaska Native or Two or more races[1]											
Less than 5 percent....	5.1 (0.56)	8.0 (0.93)	6.8 (0.96)	7.6 (1.13)	8.6 (1.97)	85.9 (3.16)	7.6 ! (2.83)	79.2 (11.49)	‡ (†)	‡ (†)	6.5 (1.30)
5 to 19 percent..........	5.8 (0.74)	6.0 (0.71)	6.8 (0.65)	7.5 (0.75)	7.8 (1.75)	87.6 (1.37)	5.4 (0.86)	46.8 (6.94)	50.6 (7.02)	2.6 ! (1.17)	7.0 (1.04)
20 to 49 percent.........	5.2 (0.64)	6.2 (0.82)	9.4 (0.96)	6.5 (0.60)	8.1 (1.42)	86.4 (1.13)	7.3 (0.93)	62.0 (4.66)	34.2 (4.33)	3.8 ! (1.86)	6.3 (0.80)
50 percent or more	5.3 (0.66)	6.8 (0.72)	6.8 (0.62)	10.3 (0.84)	7.9 (0.82)	80.5 (1.88)	10.4 (1.26)	62.7 (4.94)	34.1 (5.04)	3.2 ! (1.00)	9.1 (1.23)
Percent of students approved for free or reduced-price lunch											
0 to 25.0 percent....	— (†)	— (†)	— (†)	8.1 (0.69)	8.4 (1.06)	87.8 (1.79)	6.2 (1.30)	61.4 (7.11)	36.3 (6.82)	‡ (†)	6.0 (0.98)
25.1 to 50.0 percent....	— (†)	— (†)	— (†)	7.3 (0.63)	9.8 (1.55)	85.8 (1.78)	6.2 (0.95)	58.4 (6.96)	39.1 (6.68)	‡ (†)	7.9 (1.36)
50.1 to 75.0 percent....	— (†)	— (†)	— (†)	9.0 (1.21)	8.8 (1.77)	84.1 (1.75)	8.7 (1.23)	55.9 (7.11)	40.5 (7.05)	‡ (†)	7.1 (1.20)
More than 75.0 percent.................	— (†)	— (†)	— (†)	10.4 (1.49)	5.5 (0.90)	77.9 (2.88)	12.3 (1.79)	60.8 (6.16)	36.7 (6.16)	2.5 ! (1.14)	9.9 (1.85)
School did not respond or did not participate in program..............	— (†)	— (†)	— (†)	14.3 (2.44)	14.3 (1.73)	85.8 (4.95)	‡ (†)	40.0 ! (15.95)	36.7 ! (16.68)	‡ (†)	10.7 ! (3.67)
Locale											
City.......................	— (†)	— (†)	— (†)	10.1 (1.05)	7.5 (1.01)	82.3 (2.35)	9.7 (1.54)	66.2 (6.58)	30.9 (6.59)	2.9 ! (1.20)	7.9 (1.44)
Suburban..................	— (†)	— (†)	— (†)	8.3 (0.83)	8.3 (1.08)	84.9 (1.43)	7.8 (1.12)	60.0 (6.03)	36.9 (6.33)	3.1 ! (1.52)	7.3 (0.90)
Town.......................	— (†)	— (†)	— (†)	6.5 (0.76)	7.5 ! (2.51)	86.3 (2.15)	7.3 (1.56)	55.0 (9.53)	39.9 (8.77)	‡ (†)	6.4 (1.10)
Rural......................	— (†)	— (†)	— (†)	7.9 (0.99)	8.4 (1.44)	84.6 (1.69)	7.0 (1.08)	48.9 (7.30)	49.3 (7.18)	‡ (†)	8.4 (1.23)

—Not available.
†Not applicable.
!Interpret data with caution. The coefficient of variation (CV) for this estimate is between 30 and 50 percent.
‡Reporting standards not met. Either there are too few cases for a reliable estimate or the coefficient of variation (CV) is 50 percent or greater.
[1]Data were not available for approximately 4 percent of teachers for 2011–12 to 2012–13.
NOTE: Race categories exclude persons of Hispanic ethnicity. Detail may not sum to totals because of rounding.

SOURCE: U.S. Department of Education, National Center for Education Statistics, Schools and Staffing Survey (SASS), *Characteristics of Stayers, Movers, and Leavers: Results From the Teacher Follow-up Survey 1994–95; Teacher Attrition and Mobility: Results From the Teacher Follow-up Survey: 2000–01;* "Public School Teacher Data File" 2003–04, 2007–08, and 2011–12; and Teacher Follow-up Survey (TFS), "Current and Former Teacher Data Files," 1988–89, 2004–05, 2008–09, and 2012–13. (This table was prepared October 2014.)

Table 210.31. Mobility of private elementary and secondary teachers, by selected teacher and school characteristics: Selected years, 1987–88 through 2008–09

[Standard errors appear in parentheses]

Selected teacher or school characteristic	Percent of private school teachers													
	Left teaching								2007–08 to 2008–09					
	1987–88 to 1988–89		1993–94 to 1994–95		1999–2000 to 2000–01		2003–04 to 2004–05		Remained in same school		Changed schools		Left teaching	
1	2		3		4		5		6		7		8	
Total	12.7	(0.85)	11.9	(0.70)	12.5	(0.69)	13.6	(2.18)	79.2	(1.72)	4.9	(0.60)	15.9	(1.53)
Sex														
Male	10.2	(1.72)	13.1	(1.20)	11.7	(1.48)	14.2	(2.06)	80.0	(3.42)	5.7	(1.29)	14.3	(3.11)
Female	13.4	(0.92)	11.6	(0.78)	12.8	(0.76)	13.4	(2.88)	78.9	(1.84)	4.7	(0.68)	16.4	(1.63)
Race/ethnicity														
White	12.1	(0.90)	11.7	(0.69)	12.3	(0.73)	13.0	(2.33)	80.7	(1.82)	4.6	(0.59)	14.7	(1.59)
Black	34.7	(8.35)	12.6 !	(4.52)	14.8 !	(5.09)	‡	(†)	67.2	(10.90)	8.6 !	(3.78)	24.2 !	(10.11)
Hispanic	21.3 !	(6.46)	14.6	(4.31)	9.6	(2.85)	22.1	(5.72)	69.2	(8.37)	‡	(†)	23.7 !	(7.18)
Asian/Pacific Islander	‡	(†)	17.5 !	(8.67)	‡	(†)	7.6 !	(2.84)	‡	(†)	‡	(†)	‡	(†)
Asian	—	(†)	—	(†)	—	(†)	7.8 !	(3.01)	‡	(†)	‡	(†)	‡	(†)
Pacific Islander	—	(†)	—	(†)	—	(†)	‡	(†)	‡	(†)	‡	(†)	‡	(†)
American Indian/Alaska Native	‡	(†)	‡	(†)	‡	(†)	‡	(†)	‡	(†)	‡	(†)	‡	(†)
Two or more races	—	(†)	—	(†)	—	(†)	‡	(†)	‡	(†)	‡	(†)	‡	(†)
Age														
Less than 25	19.0	(3.79)	20.0	(4.19)	29.9	(4.24)	18.0	(3.41)	67.0	(8.95)	6.5 !	(2.81)	26.5 !	(8.04)
25 to 29	17.6	(2.42)	13.1	(1.35)	18.6	(2.07)	21.2	(4.00)	69.7	(5.70)	11.6	(3.14)	18.7	(5.07)
30 to 39	12.4	(1.59)	14.9	(1.54)	13.7	(1.52)	14.2	(1.81)	76.9	(3.73)	4.9	(1.42)	18.2	(3.35)
40 to 49	10.5	(1.63)	8.7	(1.02)	8.5	(1.34)	10.7	(2.08)	83.7	(2.93)	5.4	(1.22)	10.9	(2.81)
50 to 59	11.3	(2.45)	8.2	(1.53)	5.9	(0.90)	‡	(†)	85.2	(2.11)	2.4	(0.63)	12.4	(2.06)
60 to 64	16.9 !	(5.93)	13.1	(2.74)	18.1	(3.72)	20.7	(5.27)	79.2	(6.44)	‡	(†)	17.6 !	(5.93)
65 and over	7.9 !	(3.16)	41.9	(8.67)	29.4	(7.60)	21.2 !	(7.31)	74.7	(9.34)	‡	(†)	23.3 !	(8.67)
Full- and part-time teaching experience														
1 year or less	15.9	(2.73)	18.2	(2.12)	28.9	(3.95)	20.2	(4.36)	66.1	(8.45)	‡	(†)	29.8	(7.86)
2 years	18.2	(3.32)	23.6	(2.72)	22.5	(3.24)	‡	(†)	72.8	(8.46)	6.5 !	(2.18)	20.7 !	(8.57)
3 years	15.4	(3.80)	12.8	(2.15)	17.8	(2.49)	15.3	(2.47)	73.9	(6.77)	9.6	(2.75)	16.5 !	(6.35)
4 to 10 years	14.0	(1.91)	13.1	(1.51)	12.6	(1.37)	16.0	(2.54)	76.9	(2.63)	6.9	(1.44)	16.3	(2.13)
11 to 20 years	11.5	(1.73)	7.1	(0.93)	6.9	(1.13)	8.2	(1.75)	83.4	(3.12)	3.1	(0.90)	13.5	(2.88)
21 to 25 years	5.2 !	(2.36)	6.0	(1.64)	5.5	(1.32)	8.9 !	(4.25)	88.7	(3.19)	2.7 !	(1.23)	8.6 !	(2.88)
More than 25 years	8.4	(2.03)	12.7	(2.53)	10.0	(1.40)	8.5	(1.77)	84.4	(3.25)	2.9 !	(1.01)	12.7	(2.95)
Level taught														
Elementary	12.5	(0.99)	11.5	(0.96)	13.4	(0.84)	14.4	(3.64)	79.8	(1.91)	5.9	(0.88)	14.3	(1.80)
Secondary	12.9	(2.38)	12.6	(1.51)	8.5	(0.90)	12.5	(1.35)	78.6	(2.64)	3.8	(0.93)	17.6	(2.44)
School size														
Less than 150	16.6	(1.72)	14.8	(1.43)	14.6	(1.45)	22.7	(6.32)	72.8	(3.77)	6.2	(1.43)	21.0	(3.32)
150 to 349	10.9	(1.62)	12.6	(1.21)	13.1	(1.24)	12.4	(1.40)	78.9	(2.92)	5.5	(1.35)	15.7	(2.38)
350 to 499	10.7	(2.63)	12.1	(1.95)	10.3	(1.26)	9.8	(1.40)	85.4	(2.87)	‡	(†)	11.5	(2.59)
500 to 749	9.6	(2.07)	7.1	(1.27)	11.1	(1.91)	9.8	(2.63)	86.7	(3.74)	3.8	(1.09)	9.6 !	(3.36)
750 or more	12.9	(3.14)	6.2	(1.18)	10.8	(1.64)	4.9	(0.90)	79.8	(5.61)	‡	(†)	16.6	(4.87)
Percent of students who are Black, Hispanic, Asian, Pacific Islander, American Indian/Alaska Native or Two or more races														
Less than 5 percent	13.2	(1.67)	11.0	(1.06)	12.3	(1.07)	‡	(†)	81.4	(3.29)	5.4	(1.40)	13.2	(2.87)
5 to 19 percent	10.3	(1.37)	11.1	(1.07)	11.4	(1.10)	12.5	(1.54)	78.9	(2.43)	5.0	(0.91)	16.1	(2.22)
20 to 49 percent	18.9	(4.18)	15.6	(2.28)	13.8	(1.82)	15.6	(2.00)	79.0	(3.19)	3.0	(0.84)	18.0	(2.97)
50 percent or more	13.6	(2.85)	13.2	(2.15)	14.7	(2.34)	18.5	(4.47)	77.0	(4.01)	7.3 !	(2.41)	15.6	(3.44)
Locale														
City	—	(†)	—	(†)	—	(†)	11.4	(1.42)	78.6	(2.81)	5.2	(0.96)	16.2	(2.55)
Suburban	—	(†)	—	(†)	—	(†)	12.4	(1.34)	79.1	(2.96)	4.8	(0.98)	16.2	(2.71)
Town	—	(†)	—	(†)	—	(†)	18.0	(3.63)	82.1	(4.47)	7.5 !	(2.43)	10.3	(3.08)
Rural	—	(†)	—	(†)	—	(†)	15.2	(3.30)	80.4	(4.50)	3.4 !	(1.59)	16.3	(3.86)

—Not available.
†Not applicable.
!Interpret data with caution. The coefficient of variation (CV) for this estimate is between 30 and 50 percent.
‡Reporting standards not met. Either there are too few cases for a reliable estimate or the coefficient of variation (CV) is 50 percent or greater.
NOTE: Race categories exclude persons of Hispanic ethnicity. Detail may not sum to totals because of rounding.

SOURCE: U.S. Department of Education, National Center for Education Statistics, Schools and Staffing Survey (SASS), *Characteristics of Stayers, Movers, and Leavers: Results From the Teacher Follow-up Survey 1994–95; Teacher Attrition and Mobility: Results From the Teacher Follow-up Survey: 2000–01;* "Private School Teacher Data File," 2003–04 and 2007–08; and Teacher Follow-up Survey (TFS), "Current and Former Teacher Data Files," 2004–05 and 2008–09. (This table was prepared October 2014.)

Table 211.10.   Average salaries for full-time teachers in public and private elementary and secondary schools, by selected characteristics: 2011–12

[Amounts in current dollars. Standard errors appear in parentheses]

Selected characteristic	Number of full-time teachers (in thousands)	Total school-year and summer earned income from school and non-school sources[1]	Base salary	School year supplemental contract[2] — Percent of teachers	Average supplement	Merit pay bonus — Percent of teachers	Average amount	State supplements — Percent of teachers	Average amount	Job outside school system during school year — Percent of teachers	Average income	Supplemental school system contract during summer[3] — Percent of teachers	Average supplement	Employed in nonschool summer job — Percent of teachers	Average income
1	2	3	4	5	6	7	8	9	10	11	12	13	14	15	16
Public schools Total	3,139.2 (38.34)	$56,410 (251)	$53,070 (213)	41.8 (0.53)	$2,530 (74)	4.4 (0.23)	$1,400 (85)	7.9 (0.31)	$2,070 (96)	16.1 (0.39)	$4,820 (172)	17.8 (0.41)	$2,510 (69)	15.0 (0.41)	$3,430 (112)
Sex															
Males	754.6 (20.70)	60,360 (464)	54,430 (385)	56.6 (0.92)	3,920 (134)	3.9 (0.35)	1,450 (101)	8.0 (0.54)	2,440 (189)	23.3 (0.76)	6,060 (309)	21.4 (0.90)	2,880 (86)	23.2 (0.75)	4,560 (201)
Females	2,384.6 (28.89)	55,160 (267)	52,640 (237)	37.1 (0.58)	1,860 (61)	4.6 (0.29)	1,390 (101)	7.9 (0.34)	1,950 (105)	13.9 (0.50)	4,150 (208)	16.6 (0.49)	2,360 (87)	12.4 (0.48)	2,770 (108)
Race/ethnicity															
White	2,556.2 (28.29)	56,400 (265)	53,020 (225)	42.8 (0.57)	2,560 (75)	4.1 (0.24)	1,390 (101)	7.9 (0.30)	2,130 (100)	17.0 (0.44)	4,740 (183)	16.7 (0.43)	2,410 (67)	16.1 (0.48)	3,310 (96)
Black	221.0 (10.15)	55,790 (985)	52,370 (901)	36.2 (2.58)	2,690 (371)	5.4 (1.28)	1,470 (263)	9.6 (1.52)	1,970 (339)	15.5 (2.23)	4,740 (775)	26.2 (1.85)	2,920 (274)	9.5 (1.40)	4,540 (727)
Hispanic	252.2 (12.62)	56,240 (891)	53,620 (872)	39.3 (2.29)	2,150 (219)	7.2 (1.29)	1,280 (202)	7.4 (1.23)	1,570 (367)	9.5 (1.13)	4,600 (456)	20.7 (3.75)	2,710 (233)	9.4 (1.19)	3,640 (509)
Asian	57.5 (7.30)	62,480 (2,702)	58,860 (2,253)	28.4 (5.19)	2,110 (477)	3.3 ! (1.42)	2,320 ! (725)	‡ (†)	‡ (†)	7.9 (1.89)	7,000 (1,520)	19.7 (3.75)	3,080 (743)	7.0 (1.68)	5,400 ! (2,166)
Pacific Islander	4.4 (1.24)	57,280 (3,301)	52,920 (2,692)	‡ (†)	‡ (†)	‡ (†)	‡ (†)	‡ (†)	‡ (†)	‡ (†)	‡ (†)	‡ (†)	‡ (†)	‡ (†)	‡ (†)
American Indian/ Alaska Native	15.4 (2.79)	53,000 (3,354)	46,630 (2,005)	43.9 (7.72)	2,360 (414)	‡ (†)	‡ (†)	‡ (†)	‡ (†)	22.4 (5.49)	‡ (†)	19.2 (3.74)	2,640 (639)	21.5 (6.15)	4,470 ! (1,464)
Two or more races	31.2 (3.64)	53,750 (1,306)	50,230 (1,195)	45.9 (6.50)	2,230 (293)	‡ (†)	‡ (†)	9.0 ! (3.13)	2,020 (537)	16.0 (3.39)	5,690 ! (1,977)	14.5 (2.76)	2,610 (268)	16.1 (3.24)	3,550 (1,648)
Age															
Less than 30	487.4 (15.04)	45,160 (393)	41,720 (405)	49.0 (1.53)	2,340 (86)	5.2 (0.61)	1,150 (134)	8.3 (0.76)	1,560 (143)	18.7 (1.05)	3,360 (239)	21.5 (1.10)	2,430 (150)	24.5 (1.16)	2,980 (181)
30 to 39	921.9 (19.46)	53,120 (392)	50,020 (350)	43.8 (0.96)	2,810 (182)	4.3 (0.41)	1,240 (113)	7.6 (0.63)	1,870 (148)	15.7 (0.73)	4,380 (340)	18.4 (0.90)	2,420 (83)	14.8 (0.86)	3,320 (218)
40 to 49	783.7 (18.62)	58,660 (394)	55,420 (368)	41.9 (1.12)	2,490 (81)	4.2 (0.45)	1,410 (135)	7.7 (0.58)	2,210 (183)	16.8 (0.79)	5,070 (339)	17.4 (0.77)	2,490 (108)	14.6 (0.70)	3,720 (199)
50 or more	946.2 (25.68)	63,550 (410)	59,940 (351)	36.1 (1.06)	2,370 (100)	4.2 (0.43)	1,710 (206)	8.3 (0.56)	2,390 (181)	14.6 (0.72)	6,000 (413)	15.6 (0.80)	2,680 (140)	10.6 (0.62)	3,800 (211)
Years of full-time teaching experience															
1 year or less	144.2 (7.55)	44,610 (519)	40,540 (512)	37.6 (2.48)	2,140 (137)	5.6 (1.29)	1,120 (271)	6.4 (1.10)	2,070 (420)	16.9 (1.67)	4,380 (668)	18.7 (2.01)	2,980 (390)	31.2 (1.90)	4,860 (524)
2 to 4 years	395.9 (12.54)	44,490 (305)	41,480 (244)	44.1 (1.42)	2,100 (85)	4.5 (0.52)	1,280 (127)	7.7 (0.76)	1,800 (179)	17.3 (1.02)	3,970 (275)	20.2 (0.86)	2,260 (116)	20.6 (0.89)	2,800 (181)
5 to 9 years	784.6 (18.32)	50,370 (360)	47,300 (312)	43.3 (1.10)	2,520 (96)	5.1 (0.59)	1,270 (129)	8.2 (0.70)	1,640 (137)	16.6 (0.94)	4,250 (321)	19.4 (0.97)	2,380 (113)	14.7 (1.00)	3,110 (208)
10 to 14 years	652.1 (16.57)	58,040 (412)	54,860 (596)	42.5 (1.28)	2,740 (178)	3.6 (0.38)	1,820 (135)	8.4 (0.68)	2,060 (166)	15.7 (0.81)	4,830 (318)	17.2 (0.83)	2,670 (152)	12.2 (0.76)	3,450 (213)
15 to 19 years	426.2 (14.56)	62,050 (602)	58,880 (593)	41.3 (1.51)	2,550 (179)	4.3 (0.76)	1,800 (332)	7.7 (1.05)	2,300 (230)	15.4 (1.13)	5,940 (861)	17.2 (1.34)	2,430 (124)	13.0 (0.84)	3,390 (277)
20 to 24 years	295.8 (10.26)	64,210 (602)	60,930 (593)	40.9 (1.51)	2,500 (146)	4.4 (0.85)	1,610 (365)	7.6 (0.94)	1,980 (230)	15.2 (1.07)	5,730 (612)	13.4 (1.09)	2,460 (158)	13.8 (1.29)	4,220 (498)
25 to 29 years	217.9 (11.00)	67,440 (1,044)	63,780 (838)	39.8 (2.37)	2,810 (278)	5.0 (0.90)	1,500 (274)	9.0 (1.30)	2,530 (304)	15.9 (1.49)	5,000 (781)	16.8 (1.62)	2,550 (214)	12.8 (1.42)	3,010 (316)
30 or more years	222.5 (11.58)	69,790 (763)	64,820 (646)	37.0 (1.98)	2,730 (186)	3.1 (0.58)	1,680 (270)	7.3 (1.14)	3,360 (558)	15.6 (1.35)	5,400 (433)	16.5 (1.57)	2,920 (376)	11.0 (1.12)	3,700 (401)
Highest degree earned															
Less than bachelor's degree	118.9 (8.32)	55,430 (960)	51,330 (794)	41.5 (2.79)	2,460 (199)	6.1 (1.29)	1,190 (353)	9.4 (2.00)	2,030 (420)	20.1 (1.76)	7,340 (1,356)	16.6 (2.16)	2,360 (200)	20.9 (2.38)	3,750 (469)
Bachelor's degree	1,278.2 (20.53)	49,410 (262)	46,340 (225)	42.4 (0.85)	2,370 (66)	5.2 (0.39)	1,350 (100)	8.6 (0.56)	1,790 (99)	14.5 (0.62)	4,600 (295)	16.8 (0.61)	2,360 (97)	16.2 (0.68)	3,400 (191)
Master's degree	1,479.3 (27.00)	61,230 (408)	57,830 (352)	41.5 (0.71)	2,650 (125)	3.6 (0.38)	1,500 (148)	7.1 (0.38)	2,250 (178)	16.6 (0.61)	4,570 (160)	18.1 (0.67)	2,600 (104)	13.8 (0.58)	3,380 (146)
Education specialist[4]	228.7 (9.17)	63,420 (727)	59,680 (642)	39.4 (1.51)	2,640 (184)	3.6 (0.83)	1,450 (270)	9.0 (1.05)	2,480 (297)	17.7 (1.62)	5,330 (536)	20.4 (1.67)	2,650 (198)	12.2 (1.45)	3,620 (361)
Doctor's degree	34.2 (3.97)	66,140 (1,718)	60,230 (1,775)	49.2 (4.70)	3,110 (748)	‡ (†)	‡ (†)	‡ (†)	‡ (†)	30.8 (3.99)	6,610 (1,139)	26.9 (3.97)	2,810 (397)	18.8 (3.00)	3,940 (825)
Instructional level[5]															
Elementary	1,572.3 (22.63)	54,820 (349)	52,620 (303)	30.9 (0.87)	1,530 (104)	4.2 (0.37)	1,310 (157)	7.4 (0.41)	1,720 (127)	12.8 (0.62)	4,350 (313)	16.6 (0.68)	2,270 (113)	12.6 (0.67)	2,930 (178)
Secondary	1,566.9 (35.32)	58,000 (280)	53,520 (261)	52.8 (0.57)	3,110 (77)	4.6 (0.26)	1,480 (82)	8.5 (0.41)	2,370 (109)	19.5 (0.48)	5,130 (186)	19.0 (0.48)	2,720 (87)	17.4 (0.49)	3,790 (129)
School locale															
City	‡ (†)	‡ (†)	‡ (†)	‡ (†)	‡ (†)	‡ (†)	‡ (†)	‡ (†)	‡ (†)	‡ (†)	‡ (†)	‡ (†)	‡ (†)	‡ (†)	‡ (†)
Suburban	1,016.9 (30.46)	61,610 (476)	58,470 (427)	42.4 (1.09)	2,750 (136)	4.0 (0.43)	1,450 (140)	6.6 (0.53)	1,870 (148)	15.6 (0.65)	4,300 (188)	17.4 (0.75)	2,450 (94)	13.8 (0.63)	3,350 (161)
Town	382.9 (13.34)	51,050 (475)	47,780 (431)	43.6 (1.43)	2,580 (101)	3.0 (0.55)	1,110 (194)	7.4 (0.72)	1,940 (169)	16.3 (0.93)	4,910 (474)	15.6 (1.21)	2,030 (127)	16.0 (0.85)	3,520 (240)
Rural	853.0 (21.06)	50,670 (275)	47,130 (237)	44.3 (1.07)	2,520 (81)	3.7 (0.42)	1,390 (151)	10.0 (0.71)	2,070 (138)	16.3 (0.61)	5,340 (393)	15.1 (0.63)	2,290 (129)	16.9 (0.69)	3,600 (193)

See notes at end of table.

Table 211.10. Average salaries for full-time teachers in public and private elementary and secondary schools, by selected characteristics: 2011–12—Continued

[Amounts in current dollars. Standard errors appear in parentheses]

Selected characteristic	Number of full-time teachers (in thousands)	Total school-year and summer earned income from school and nonschool sources[1]	Base salary	School year supplemental contract[2] — Percent of teachers	— Average supplement	School year income from merit pay bonus — Percent of teachers	— Average amount	School year income from state supplements — Percent of teachers	— Average amount	Job outside the school system during the school year — Percent of teachers	— Average income	Supplemental school system contract during summer[3] — Percent of teachers	— Average supplement	Employed in a nonschool job during the summer — Percent of teachers	— Average income
	2	3	4	5	6	7	8	9	10	11	12	13	14	15	16
Private schools Total	368.4 (10.95)	$44,130 (803)	$40,200 (732)	28.9 (1.30)	$2,730 (168)	‡ (†)	‡ (†)	1.8 (0.48)	$1,960 ! (615)	19.6 (1.08)	$5,440 (373)	20.8 (1.15)	$3,370 (361)	17.1 (1.01)	$3,780 (484)
Sex															
Males	92.9 (6.50)	51,150 (1,829)	44,470 (1,264)	42.7 (2.52)	3,850 (254)	‡ (†)	‡ (†)	‡ (†)	‡ (†)	26.9 (2.86)	6,550 (661)	29.3 (2.61)	3,600 (471)	23.3 (3.12)	4,650 (508)
Females	275.5 (9.40)	41,760 (887)	38,760 (864)	24.3 (.54)	2,070 (201)	‡ (†)	‡ (†)	1.8 (0.52)	2,200 ! (806)	17.1 (1.14)	4,850 (431)	17.9 (1.27)	3,240 (483)	15.0 (1.03)	3,320 (665)
Race/ethnicity															
White	326.0 (11.07)	44,390 (826)	40,450 (778)	29.1 (.43)	2,750 (174)	‡ (†)	‡ (†)	1.6 (0.47)	1,690 (252)	19.4 (1.21)	5,350 (378)	20.2 (1.25)	3,410 (408)	17.5 (1.06)	3,710 (519)
Black	13.0 (1.83)	41,790 (2,813)	37,080 (2,201)	23.0 (5.65)	2,360 (414)	‡ (†)	‡ (†)	‡ (†)	‡ (†)	‡ (†)	‡ (†)	29.6 (4.67)	3,560 ! (1,145)	‡ (†)	‡ (†)
Hispanic	19.8 (2.35)	42,850 (2,307)	39,530 (2,271)	27.2 (4.96)	2,180 (397)	‡ (†)	‡ (†)	‡ (†)	‡ (†)	15.3 (3.28)	6,090 (1,617)	18.0 (3.33)	2,590 (464)	‡ (†)	3,070 (765)
Asian	6.3 (1.25)	40,170 (3,767)	36,720 (3,796)	‡ (†)	‡ (†)	‡ (†)	‡ (†)	‡ (†)	‡ (†)	‡ (†)	‡ (†)	‡ (†)	‡ (†)	‡ (†)	‡ (†)
Pacific Islander	‡ (†)	‡ (†)	‡ (†)	‡ (†)	‡ (†)	‡ (†)	‡ (†)	‡ (†)	‡ (†)	‡ (†)	‡ (†)	‡ (†)	‡ (†)	‡ (†)	‡ (†)
American Indian/ Alaska Native	‡ (†)	42,860 (7,642)	‡ (†)	‡ (†)	‡ (†)	‡ (†)	‡ (†)	‡ (†)	‡ (†)	‡ (†)	19,000 (0)	‡ (†)	‡ (†)	‡ (†)	‡ (†)
Two or more races	2.3 ! (0.86)	46,660 (4,580)	39,640 (2,908)	‡ (†)	‡ (†)	‡ (†)	‡ (†)	‡ (†)	‡ (†)	‡ (†)	‡ (†)	‡ (†)	‡ (†)	‡ (†)	‡ (†)
Age															
Less than 30	63.2 (5.13)	34,340 (710)	31,010 (680)	34.1 (2.76)	1,980 (298)	‡ (†)	‡ (†)	‡ (†)	‡ (†)	23.6 (2.55)	4,170 (575)	24.0 (2.23)	2,050 (141)	32.7 (2.70)	3,460 (454)
30 to 39	94.3 (5.59)	42,110 (1,051)	38,420 (922)	34.6 (3.07)	3,080 (258)	‡ (†)	‡ (†)	‡ (†)	‡ (†)	19.4 (2.08)	4,950 (522)	23.9 (2.44)	4,270 ! (1,293)	15.4 (2.05)	3,580 (548)
40 to 49	87.3 (5.74)	45,740 (1,316)	42,860 (1,282)	26.2 (2.96)	2,940 (486)	‡ (†)	‡ (†)	‡ (†)	‡ (†)	19.2 (2.09)	4,980 (966)	20.2 (2.75)	3,460 (451)	12.3 (1.91)	2,690 (403)
50 or more	123.0 (6.67)	49,580 (1,439)	44,420 (1,203)	23.8 (1.87)	2,750 (263)	‡ (†)	‡ (†)	‡ (†)	‡ (†)	18.5 (2.14)	7,000 (712)	17.1 (1.56)	3,280 (644)	13.9 (1.88)	5,000 (1,398)
Years of full-time teaching experience															
1 year or less	30.9 (4.65)	33,980 (1,386)	29,940 (1,139)	29.6 (5.24)	2,440 ! (768)	‡ (†)	‡ (†)	‡ (†)	‡ (†)	24.5 (4.12)	5,100 (1,103)	21.4 (5.20)	2,330 (511)	30.9 (4.68)	4,390 (1,170)
2 to 4 years	61.5 (4.73)	36,760 (1,024)	33,540 (948)	31.6 (2.80)	2,760 (347)	‡ (†)	‡ (†)	‡ (†)	‡ (†)	22.0 (2.63)	4,250 (550)	23.9 (2.96)	2,540 (196)	23.5 (2.80)	2,820 (400)
5 to 9 years	85.0 (4.57)	40,990 (1,036)	37,220 (830)	30.8 (2.80)	2,560 (299)	‡ (†)	‡ (†)	‡ (†)	‡ (†)	19.3 (2.34)	5,760 (734)	24.8 (3.29)	4,170 ! (1,277)	16.1 (1.92)	4,080 (637)
10 to 14 years	58.8 (4.67)	43,570 (1,203)	40,440 (1,095)	27.4 (3.19)	3,050 (563)	‡ (†)	‡ (†)	‡ (†)	‡ (†)	19.3 (3.11)	5,310 (915)	18.6 (2.26)	3,740 (607)	14.2 (2.73)	3,340 (615)
15 to 19 years	43.9 (3.38)	47,190 (2,185)	44,820 (2,218)	23.2 (4.60)	2,560 (478)	‡ (†)	‡ (†)	‡ (†)	‡ (†)	15.1 (3.05)	5,110 ! (2,128)	20.5 (3.62)	3,180 (768)	10.6 (2.21)	2,400 (528)
20 to 24 years	27.7 (2.85)	52,380 (2,991)	48,170 (2,386)	30.8 (4.37)	2,990 (214)	‡ (†)	‡ (†)	‡ (†)	‡ (†)	20.3 (4.78)	6,230 (1,740)	16.0 (3.19)	1,790 (370)	15.4 (4.00)	3,860 ! (1,393)
25 to 29 years	24.3 (2.53)	52,040 (2,524)	47,070 (2,091)	25.3 (4.04)	3,660 (999)	‡ (†)	‡ (†)	‡ (†)	‡ (†)	17.6 (4.16)	5,340 (1,069)	17.6 (4.29)	3,230 (628)	‡ (†)	‡ (†)
30 or more years	36.5 (4.19)	57,950 (3,772)	50,390 (3,772)	29.4 (3.83)	3,200 (460)	‡ (†)	‡ (†)	‡ (†)	‡ (†)	18.4 (3.58)	7,420 (1,820)	15.1 (3.03)	4,700 ! (1,783)	14.8 (3.29)	2,410 (474)
Highest degree earned															
Less than bachelor's degree	27.9 (4.18)	30,160 (1,733)	27,690 (1,749)	21.3 (5.09)	3,210 (653)	‡ (†)	‡ (†)	‡ (†)	‡ (†)	15.3 (4.03)	3,820 ! (1,216)	19.5 (3.96)	2,760 (363)	15.5 (4.10)	3,750 ! (1,158)
Bachelor's degree	180.9 (5.98)	39,450 (887)	36,270 (830)	27.2 (1.73)	2,490 (251)	‡ (†)	‡ (†)	1.3 (0.36)	1,970 (540)	18.2 (1.32)	5,420 (522)	19.6 (1.36)	2,880 (333)	18.7 (1.16)	4,000 (840)
Master's degree	134.3 (7.12)	50,670 (1,074)	46,460 (830)	32.9 (2.25)	2,850 (228)	‡ (†)	‡ (†)	‡ (†)	‡ (†)	20.7 (1.77)	5,070 (584)	21.8 (2.35)	4,160 (807)	16.3 (1.60)	3,470 (357)
Education specialist[4]	17.7 (1.95)	55,230 (3,542)	47,450 (2,839)	22.5 (5.57)	3,230 ! (1,570)	‡ (†)	‡ (†)	‡ (†)	‡ (†)	25.2 (4.61)	7,280 (1,580)	24.6 (4.78)	2,820 (598)	‡ (†)	‡ (†)
Doctor's degree	7.7 (1.84)	64,890 (11,118)	52,590 (6,259)	‡ (†)	‡ (†)	‡ (†)	‡ (†)	‡ (†)	‡ (†)	18.4	‡ (†)	‡ (†)	‡ (†)	‡ (†)	‡ (†)
Instructional level[5]															
Elementary	196.8 (8.15)	39,310 (794)	36,260 (632)	19.2 (1.39)	2,130 (251)	‡ (†)	‡ (†)	‡ (†)	‡ (†)	16.0 (1.21)	5,190 (720)	17.1 (1.23)	2,770 (349)	15.8 (1.37)	3,730 (853)
Secondary	171.6 (8.24)	49,640 (1,319)	44,720 (1,174)	40.0 (2.23)	3,070 (224)	‡ (†)	‡ (†)	2.6 ! (0.85)	1,600 (308)	23.7 (1.70)	5,640 (499)	25.0 (2.03)	3,840 (602)	18.7 (1.39)	3,820 (439)
School locale															
City	157.9 (9.51)	48,980 (1,569)	44,770 (1,436)	29.3 (1.75)	30,100 (314)	‡ (†)	‡ (†)	‡ (†)	‡ (†)	19.2 (1.59)	59,700 (555)	21.1 (1.68)	39,400 (722)	16.3 (1.58)	3,750 (991)
Suburban	‡ (†)	42,860 (7,642)	‡ (†)	‡ (†)	‡ (†)	‡ (†)	‡ (†)	‡ (†)	‡ (†)	‡ (†)	19,000 (1,535)	‡ (†)	‡ (†)	‡ (†)	3,820 (439)
Town	20.7 (2.54)	33,080 (1,479)	29,980 (1,134)	20.8 (3.66)	12,500 (257)	‡ (†)	‡ (†)	‡ (†)	‡ (†)	18.4 (3.49)	55,600 (1,535)	16.0 (2.82)	35,900 (1,418)	19.5 (3.41)	3,010 (670)
Rural	‡ (†)	‡ (†)	‡ (†)	‡ (†)	‡ (†)	‡ (†)	‡ (†)	‡ (†)	‡ (†)	‡ (†)	‡ (†)	‡ (†)	‡ (†)	‡ (†)	‡ (†)

†Not applicable.

!Interpret data with caution. The coefficient of variation (CV) for this estimate is between 30 and 50 percent.

‡Reporting standards not met. Data may be suppressed because the response rate is under 50 percent, there are too few cases for a reliable estimate, or the coefficient of variation (CV) is 50 percent or greater.

[1]Includes retirement pension funds paid during the school year.

[2]Includes compensation for extracurricular or additional activities such as coaching, student activity sponsorship, or teaching evening classes.

[3]Includes teaching summer sessions and other non-teaching jobs at any school.

[4]Education specialist degrees or certificates are generally awarded for 1 year's work beyond the master's level. Includes certificates of advanced graduate studies.

[5]Teachers were classified as elementary or secondary on the basis of the grades they taught, rather than on the level of the school in which they taught. In general, elementary teachers include those teaching prekindergarten through grade 5 and those teaching multiple grades, with a preponderance of grades taught being kindergarten through grade 6. In general, secondary teachers include those teaching any of grades 7 through 12 and those teaching multiple grades, with a preponderance of grades taught being grades 7 through 12 and usually with no grade taught being lower than grade 5.

NOTE: This table includes regular full-time teachers only; it excludes other staff even when they have full-time teaching duties (regular part-time teachers, itinerant teachers, long-term substitutes, administrators, library media specialists, other professional staff, and support staff). Race categories exclude persons of Hispanic ethnicity. Detail may not sum to totals because of rounding and missing values in cells with too few cases to report.

SOURCE: U.S. Department of Education, National Center for Education Statistics, Schools and Staffing Survey (SASS), "Public School Teacher Data File" and "Private School Teacher Data File," 2011–12. (This table was prepared May 2013.)

Table 211.20. Average base salary for full-time teachers in public elementary and secondary schools, by highest degree earned and years of full-time teaching: Selected years, 1990–91 through 2011–12

[Standard errors appear in parentheses]

Years of full-time teaching experience	Number of full-time teachers	Salary (current dollars) Highest degree earned					Salary (constant 2013–14 dollars)[1] Highest degree earned				
		All teachers[2]	Bachelor's degree	Master's degree	Education specialist[3]	Doctor's degree	All teachers[2]	Bachelor's degree	Master's degree	Education specialist[3]	Doctor's degree
1	2	3	4	5	6	7	8	9	10	11	12
1990–91											
Total...........	2,336,750 (20,958)	$31,330 (97)	$27,740 (103)	$34,960 (125)	$34,960 (391)	$40,070 (817)	$54,970 (170)	$48,670 (180)	$61,330 (220)	$65,320 (685)	$70,300 (1,433)
1 year or less........	94,000 (3,014)	22,210 (200)	21,510 (207)	26,440 (863)	26,630 (982)	‡ (†)	38,970 (351)	37,740 (363)	46,380 (1,515)	46,720 (1,723)	‡ (†)
2 years...............	86,900 (2,963)	22,120 (162)	21,650 (147)	25,060 (505)	‡ (†)	‡ (†)	38,810 (285)	37,980 (259)	43,980 (886)	‡ (†)	‡ (†)
3 years...............	80,340 (2,542)	23,010 (177)	22,440 (174)	25,960 (695)	‡ (†)	‡ (†)	40,370 (311)	39,380 (306)	45,550 (1,219)	‡ (†)	‡ (†)
4 years...............	79,610 (3,271)	23,960 (236)	23,150 (246)	26,340 (526)	29,160 (1,489)	‡ (†)	42,040 (415)	40,620 (431)	46,210 (923)	51,170 (2,613)	‡ (†)
5 years...............	83,540 (3,238)	25,080 (202)	24,070 (240)	27,220 (436)	29,870 (2,195)	‡ (†)	44,010 (354)	42,230 (422)	47,750 (766)	52,410 (3,851)	‡ (†)
6 to 9 years.........	316,210 (6,805)	26,500 (109)	25,010 (135)	28,800 (237)	30,210 (761)	‡ (†)	46,500 (190)	43,890 (237)	50,520 (417)	53,000 (1,335)	‡ (†)
10 to 14 years......	408,300 (7,843)	29,620 (161)	27,320 (172)	31,760 (299)	33,640 (592)	37,900 (1,943)	51,970 (282)	47,930 (302)	55,720 (525)	59,020 (1,039)	66,510 (3,409)
15 to 19 years......	444,930 (7,580)	33,590 (209)	30,820 (253)	35,240 (248)	37,800 (842)	40,340 (1,548)	58,930 (367)	54,080 (443)	61,840 (436)	66,320 (1,477)	70,770 (2,717)
20 to 24 years......	392,330 (8,038)	36,960 (202)	34,050 (274)	38,460 (243)	39,520 (838)	43,740 (1,391)	64,840 (355)	59,750 (481)	67,470 (426)	69,340 (1,471)	76,740 (2,441)
25 to 29 years......	219,140 (6,214)	38,100 (305)	34,770 (409)	39,830 (370)	42,460 (1,257)	43,110 (2,179)	66,860 (536)	61,010 (718)	69,880 (649)	74,500 (2,206)	75,640 (3,824)
30 to 34 years......	100,460 (4,766)	38,530 (380)	35,040 (451)	40,660 (489)	40,900 (1,596)	‡ (†)	67,600 (666)	61,470 (791)	71,340 (859)	71,770 (2,800)	‡ (†)
35 years or more...	30,980 (2,515)	39,150 (888)	34,120 (1,258)	41,730 (1,116)	‡ (†)	‡ (†)	68,700 (1,559)	59,860 (2,208)	73,230 (1,958)	‡ (†)	‡ (†)
1999–2000											
Total...........	2,742,210 (20,301)	$39,890 (118)	$35,310 (116)	$44,700 (174)	$47,990 (439)	$48,180 (1,418)	$55,370 (164)	$49,000 (161)	$62,050 (241)	$66,600 (610)	$66,870 (1,968)
1 year or less........	172,710 (5,492)	29,280 (166)	28,110 (150)	34,010 (446)	33,360 (1,009)	‡ (†)	40,640 (230)	39,020 (208)	47,200 (619)	46,300 (1,400)	‡ (†)
2 years...............	161,220 (5,678)	29,670 (179)	28,800 (165)	33,030 (404)	‡ (†)	‡ (†)	41,180 (249)	39,970 (229)	45,840 (561)	‡ (†)	‡ (†)
3 years...............	145,290 (4,630)	30,690 (169)	29,650 (199)	34,360 (370)	34,540 (1,341)	‡ (†)	42,590 (235)	41,150 (276)	47,690 (513)	47,940 (1,861)	‡ (†)
4 years...............	133,840 (5,657)	32,380 (258)	30,810 (232)	35,870 (665)	37,130 (1,354)	‡ (†)	44,940 (358)	42,760 (323)	49,780 (923)	51,530 (1,880)	‡ (†)
5 years...............	120,490 (4,300)	32,440 (253)	31,040 (287)	34,880 (392)	35,800 (1,915)	‡ (†)	45,030 (352)	43,080 (398)	48,420 (544)	49,690 (2,658)	‡ (†)
6 to 9 years.........	385,840 (8,205)	34,960 (167)	32,630 (190)	37,800 (240)	40,170 (836)	41,260 (2,302)	48,530 (232)	45,290 (264)	52,460 (333)	55,760 (1,161)	57,260 (3,194)
10 to 14 years......	382,730 (6,298)	39,340 (257)	36,160 (386)	42,070 (334)	44,840 (988)	36,500 (2,313)	54,600 (357)	50,190 (536)	58,390 (464)	62,230 (1,371)	50,660 (3,210)
15 to 19 years......	321,740 (8,067)	43,400 (225)	40,280 (318)	45,930 (356)	47,270 (916)	34,890 (872)	60,230 (312)	55,900 (442)	63,740 (495)	65,600 (1,272)	48,430 (1,211)
20 to 24 years......	351,730 (6,993)	45,650 (264)	41,260 (279)	48,480 (383)	49,000 (1,055)	33,430 (1,319)	63,360 (366)	57,260 (387)	67,290 (532)	68,010 (1,464)	46,390 (1,830)
25 to 29 years......	329,170 (7,167)	48,540 (276)	44,750 (333)	50,170 (399)	54,230 (968)	38,150 (2,437)	67,370 (383)	62,110 (462)	69,630 (553)	75,270 (1,344)	52,950 (3,383)
30 to 34 years......	185,470 (5,488)	52,150 (346)	47,270 (634)	54,240 (441)	55,990 (1,126)	‡ (†)	72,390 (480)	65,600 (880)	75,290 (612)	77,720 (1,563)	‡ (†)
35 years or more...	51,990 (3,006)	50,620 (673)	46,690 (1,359)	52,270 (923)	56,200 (2,797)	‡ (†)	70,260 (934)	64,800 (1,887)	72,550 (1,281)	78,010 (3,882)	‡ (†)
2003–04											
Total...........	2,948,230 (28,203)	$44,360 (245)	$39,200 (300)	$49,440 (202)	$52,940 (458)	$53,750 (1,295)	$56,010 (309)	$49,490 (378)	$62,420 (255)	$66,840 (578)	$67,860 (1,635)
1 year or less........	177,920 (17,391)	33,160 (381)	31,820 (342)	38,600 (732)	44,280 (5,030)	37,320 (1,690)	41,870 (481)	40,180 (432)	48,740 (924)	55,910 (6,351)	47,120 (2,134)
2 years...............	153,950 (17,695)	34,060 (284)	32,720 (334)	37,940 (646)	33,960 (1,299)	‡ (†)	43,000 (359)	41,320 (422)	47,910 (815)	42,880 (1,640)	‡ (†)
3 years...............	168,140 (9,009)	35,230 (349)	33,420 (282)	40,230 (683)	40,340 (3,173)	‡ (†)	44,480 (441)	42,200 (356)	50,790 (862)	50,940 (4,006)	‡ (†)
4 years...............	159,490 (6,723)	36,260 (265)	34,560 (279)	40,280 (530)	38,530 (1,799)	‡ (†)	45,790 (335)	43,640 (352)	50,860 (669)	48,650 (2,271)	‡ (†)
5 years...............	153,180 (6,194)	37,370 (403)	34,950 (324)	40,830 (763)	42,810 (1,957)	‡ (†)	47,180 (509)	44,130 (410)	51,560 (963)	54,050 (2,471)	‡ (†)
6 to 9 years.........	498,590 (13,859)	40,340 (201)	37,070 (209)	43,700 (300)	45,810 (1,308)	44,270 (2,321)	50,940 (253)	46,810 (264)	55,180 (378)	57,840 (1,652)	55,890 (2,930)
10 to 14 years......	433,530 (14,595)	44,330 (257)	39,730 (267)	47,900 (393)	50,000 (956)	55,040 (3,584)	55,980 (325)	50,170 (338)	60,480 (496)	63,140 (1,207)	69,490 (4,526)
15 to 19 years......	343,970 (9,606)	49,200 (356)	44,310 (482)	52,290 (469)	56,250 (1,349)	58,350 (3,443)	62,120 (450)	55,940 (608)	66,020 (592)	71,030 (1,704)	73,680 (4,347)
20 to 24 years......	285,980 (8,436)	50,810 (362)	46,390 (374)	53,980 (583)	54,900 (999)	53,580 (3,551)	64,150 (457)	58,570 (473)	68,160 (736)	69,320 (1,261)	67,650 (4,458)
25 to 29 years......	283,460 (11,809)	52,790 (281)	48,650 (488)	55,000 (411)	55,870 (975)	65,210 (3,524)	66,660 (354)	61,420 (616)	69,440 (519)	70,540 (1,231)	82,340 (4,450)
30 to 34 years......	223,710 (11,435)	56,280 (428)	51,310 (606)	58,070 (566)	62,450 (1,389)	60,830 (2,664)	71,060 (540)	64,790 (765)	73,320 (714)	78,850 (1,754)	76,800 (3,363)
35 years or more...	66,310 (3,427)	58,220 (755)	55,360 (1,296)	59,150 (978)	61,260 (2,224)	‡ (†)	73,520 (953)	69,900 (1,637)	74,680 (1,235)	77,350 (2,808)	‡ (†)

See notes at end of table.

Table 211.20. Average base salary for full-time teachers in public elementary and secondary schools, by highest degree earned and years of full-time teaching: Selected years, 1990–91 through 2011–12—Continued

[Standard errors appear in parentheses]

Years of full-time teaching experience	Number of full-time teachers	Salary (current dollars) Highest degree earned					Salary (constant 2013–14 dollars)[1] Highest degree earned				
		All teachers[2]	Bachelor's degree	Master's degree	Education specialist[3]	Doctor's degree	All teachers[2]	Bachelor's degree	Master's degree	Education specialist[3]	Doctor's degree
1	2	3	4	5	6	7	8	9	10	11	12
2007–08											
Total.............	3,114,690 (41,111)	$49,630 (203)	$43,650 (220)	$54,810 (281)	$58,420 (722)	$59,150 (1,620)	$55,080 (225)	$48,440 (244)	$60,830 (312)	$64,840 (801)	$65,660 (1,798)
1 year or less.........	211,500 (12,029)	38,210 (332)	36,670 (308)	42,840 (807)	47,410 (3,584)	‡ (†)	42,400 (368)	40,700 (341)	47,550 (895)	52,630 (3,978)	‡ (†)
2 years.........	185,130 (10,587)	38,640 (334)	36,900 (340)	42,640 (717)	47,420 (4,082)	‡ (†)	42,890 (370)	40,960 (377)	47,320 (795)	52,630 (4,531)	‡ (†)
3 years.........	177,230 (7,735)	40,070 (374)	37,740 (358)	44,430 (864)	52,230 (4,612)	‡ (†)	44,480 (415)	41,880 (397)	49,320 (959)	57,970 (5,119)	‡ (†)
4 years.........	174,350 (7,951)	41,180 (377)	38,550 (428)	45,490 (577)	47,590 (2,293)	‡ (†)	45,710 (418)	42,780 (475)	50,490 (641)	52,820 (2,545)	‡ (†)
5 years.........	148,540 (7,995)	42,830 (534)	39,690 (476)	46,470 (869)	46,670 (2,690)	‡ (†)	47,540 (593)	44,050 (529)	51,580 (965)	51,800 (2,985)	‡ (†)
6 to 9 years.........	557,050 (14,475)	46,330 (252)	41,800 (379)	50,190 (441)	51,740 (1,128)	52,850 (2,349)	51,420 (279)	46,390 (421)	55,710 (490)	57,420 (1,252)	58,660 (2,607)
10 to 14 years.........	508,300 (14,867)	50,470 (377)	45,380 (436)	53,430 (559)	56,550 (1,220)	60,400 (4,124)	56,010 (419)	50,370 (484)	59,300 (621)	62,760 (1,354)	67,040 (4,577)
15 to 19 years.........	350,690 (12,953)	55,000 (484)	48,500 (553)	59,180 (722)	59,620 (1,353)	63,280 (3,462)	61,040 (537)	53,830 (614)	65,680 (801)	66,170 (1,501)	70,230 (3,842)
20 to 24 years.........	288,110 (11,954)	57,830 (636)	52,760 (783)	60,640 (794)	65,300 (2,162)	67,960 (6,394)	64,180 (706)	58,560 (869)	67,300 (881)	72,480 (2,399)	75,430 (7,097)
25 to 29 years.........	221,950 (8,609)	60,260 (740)	54,420 (830)	63,280 (1,068)	66,830 (3,306)	‡ (†)	66,880 (822)	60,410 (921)	70,230 (1,185)	74,170 (3,669)	‡ (†)
30 to 34 years.........	197,490 (8,304)	61,120 (754)	54,860 (997)	64,280 (998)	63,820 (1,555)	‡ (†)	67,840 (837)	60,890 (1,106)	71,350 (1,107)	70,830 (1,726)	‡ (†)
35 years or more.........	94,340 (7,055)	61,920 (1,067)	55,350 (1,561)	64,400 (1,499)	68,780 (3,364)	‡ (†)	68,720 (1,184)	61,440 (1,733)	71,470 (1,664)	76,340 (3,733)	‡ (†)
2011–12											
Total.............	3,139,250 (38,342)	$53,070 (213)	$46,340 (225)	$57,830 (352)	$59,680 (642)	$60,230 (1,775)	$54,790 (220)	$47,850 (232)	$59,710 (364)	$61,620 (662)	$62,190 (1,833)
1 year or less.........	144,240 (7,545)	40,540 (512)	38,490 (578)	45,240 (1,122)	49,140 (3,732)	‡ (†)	41,850 (529)	39,750 (597)	46,720 (1,158)	50,740 (3,854)	‡ (†)
2 years.........	118,520 (5,799)	39,740 (356)	38,140 (381)	42,930 (725)	47,570 (4,451)	‡ (†)	41,040 (368)	39,380 (394)	44,330 (749)	49,120 (4,596)	‡ (†)
3 years.........	126,030 (7,109)	41,470 (450)	39,150 (478)	45,590 (800)	47,850 (2,277)	‡ (†)	42,820 (465)	40,420 (494)	47,080 (826)	49,400 (2,351)	‡ (†)
4 years.........	151,350 (8,219)	42,840 (422)	40,280 (461)	45,940 (637)	46,360 (2,122)	‡ (†)	44,240 (435)	41,590 (476)	47,430 (658)	47,870 (2,191)	‡ (†)
5 years.........	174,140 (8,549)	43,830 (789)	40,600 (422)	47,420 (1,610)	45,950 (2,262)	‡ (†)	45,260 (814)	41,920 (436)	48,960 (1,662)	47,450 (2,335)	‡ (†)
6 to 9 years.........	610,420 (16,507)	48,290 (327)	43,450 (419)	51,400 (457)	52,780 (1,237)	51,340 (2,507)	49,870 (338)	44,860 (432)	53,080 (472)	54,500 (1,278)	53,010 (2,589)
10 to 14 years.........	652,140 (16,569)	54,860 (369)	48,620 (537)	58,260 (541)	58,070 (1,044)	61,190 (2,548)	56,640 (381)	50,200 (554)	60,150 (559)	59,960 (1,078)	63,180 (2,631)
15 to 19 years.........	426,250 (14,564)	58,880 (596)	51,290 (749)	62,460 (775)	65,430 (1,673)	64,420 (3,910)	60,790 (615)	52,960 (773)	64,490 (801)	67,560 (1,727)	66,510 (4,037)
20 to 24 years.........	295,760 (10,256)	60,930 (593)	54,110 (849)	65,340 (871)	64,560 (1,665)	67,630 (4,095)	62,910 (612)	55,870 (877)	66,660 (899)	66,660 (1,719)	69,830 (4,228)
25 to 29 years.........	217,870 (11,000)	63,780 (838)	56,890 (1,046)	67,550 (1,253)	69,410 (2,890)	‡ (†)	65,850 (865)	58,740 (1,080)	69,750 (1,294)	71,670 (2,984)	‡ (†)
30 to 34 years.........	142,630 (9,117)	65,610 (791)	58,510 (1,069)	69,420 (1,083)	67,260 (2,406)	‡ (†)	67,750 (816)	60,420 (1,104)	71,680 (1,118)	69,450 (2,484)	‡ (†)
35 years or more.........	79,900 (5,008)	63,400 (947)	59,560 (1,548)	66,120 (1,133)	64,660 (2,385)	‡ (†)	65,470 (977)	61,500 (1,598)	68,270 (1,169)	66,770 (2,462)	‡ (†)

†Not applicable.
‡Reporting standards not met (too few cases for a reliable estimate).
[1]Constant dollars based on the Consumer Price Index, prepared by the Bureau of Labor Statistics, U.S. Department of Labor, adjusted to a school-year basis.
[2]Includes teachers with levels of education below the bachelor's degree (not shown separately).
[3]Education specialist degrees or certificates are generally awarded for 1 year's work beyond the master's level. Includes certificate of advanced graduate studies.

NOTE: This table includes regular full-time teachers only; it excludes other staff even when they have full-time teaching duties (regular part-time teachers, itinerant teachers, long-term substitutes, administrators, library media specialists, other professional staff, and support staff). Some data have been revised from previously published figures. Detail may not sum to totals because of rounding.
SOURCE: U.S. Department of Education, National Center for Education Statistics, Schools and Staffing Survey (SASS), "Public School Teacher Data File," 1990–91, 1999–2000, 2003–04, 2007–08, and 2011–12; and "Charter School Teacher Data File," 1999–2000. (This table was prepared March 2015.)

Table 211.30. Average base salary for full-time public elementary and secondary school teachers with a bachelor's degree as their highest degree, by years of full-time teaching experience and state: 1993–94 through 2011–12

[Amounts in current dollars. Standard errors appear in parentheses]

State	1993–94, total	1999–2000, total	2003–04, total	2007–08			2011–12					
				Total	2 or fewer years	Over 20 years	Total	2 or fewer years	3 to 5 years	6 to 10 years	11 to 20 years	Over 20 years
1	2	3	4	5	6	7	8	9	10	11	12	13
United States	$30,150 (97)	$35,310 (116)	$39,200 (300)	$43,650 (220)	$36,780 (262)	$54,170 (463)	$46,340 (225)	$38,330 (341)	$40,030 (256)	$44,040 (456)	$50,440 (456)	$56,620 (604)
Alabama	24,450 (151)	31,300 (210)	32,750 (256)	39,210 (381)	34,810 (465)	44,220 (1,210)	41,010 (641)	35,030 (692)	39,070 (1,329)	40,150 (594)	43,490 (1,250)	46,810 (978)
Alaska	42,620 (308)	42,170 (269)	46,160 (720)	51,950 (747)	40,100 (746)	63,600 (1,932)	58,800 (2,016)	47,930 (1,664)	50,790 (2,385)	‡ (†)	65,020 (2,320)	‡ (†)
Arizona	28,050 (347)	30,110 (491)	33,370 (556)	36,880 (571)	33,640 (388)	45,670 (1,770)	36,960 (644)	32,850 (515)	35,170 (857)	35,650 (770)	41,010 (807)	46,640 (3,131)
Arkansas	24,970 (199)	29,810 (345)	32,710 (328)	40,220 (418)	33,090 (626)	44,610 (984)	41,830 (1,073)	37,390 (1,481)	36,200 (1,204)	39,540 (1,153)	43,390 (942)	48,000 (3,092)
California	37,330 (412)	41,930 (301)	51,210 (704)	56,950 (966)	44,770 (997)	72,680 (1,235)	62,010 (1,031)	47,310 (3,537)	48,930 (966)	58,570 (2,253)	66,030 (1,129)	73,980 (1,820)
Colorado	27,590 (391)	32,180 (428)	36,140 (699)	38,090 (884)	32,600 (621)	‡ (†)	40,770 (1,284)	33,270 (750)	35,140 (763)	40,420 (1,206)	49,250 (2,841)	‡ (†)
Connecticut	40,510 (645)	38,530 (883)	48,380 (1,997)	49,700 (1,286)	42,830 (1,348)	‡ (†)	53,300 (1,578)	‡ (†)	45,860 (1,365)	‡ (†)	‡ (†)	‡ (†)
Delaware	31,400 (375)	37,620 (893)	41,210 (991)	45,880 (960)	‡ (†)	‡ (†)	47,000 (1,504)	39,020 (1,497)	‡ (†)	‡ (†)	‡ (†)	‡ (†)
District of Columbia	37,690 (645)	40,980 (593)	48,350 (1,290)	54,970 (2,025)	42,180 (425)	55,480 (1,182)	‡ (†)	‡ (†)	‡ (†)	‡ (†)	‡ (†)	‡ (†)
Florida	28,970 (229)	33,650 (407)	36,460 (624)	41,640 (554)	36,030 (473)	‡ (†)	‡ (†)	‡ (†)	‡ (†)	‡ (†)	‡ (†)	‡ (†)
Georgia	25,650 (215)	33,610 (373)	37,160 (490)	41,640 (760)	34,580 (573)	54,330 (1,192)	42,490 (1,032)	38,060 (4,530)	37,820 (858)	40,760 (922)	46,140 (1,243)	47,650 (1,002)
Hawaii	34,060 (460)	36,710 (533)	39,250 (887)	45,380 (922)	38,650 (496)	48,450 (1,122)	38,680 (794)	32,230 (1,010)	‡ (†)	32,270 (491)	43,270 (1,178)	54,690 (2,716)
Idaho	24,610 (252)	31,500 (208)	36,150 (627)	39,870 (609)	31,110 (619)	52,950 (1,857)	45,660 (1,156)	37,380 (1,287)	33,770 (2,284)	46,120 (1,710)	52,480 (2,868)	‡ (†)
Illinois	29,480 (277)	35,250 (563)	38,730 (791)	42,740 (836)	36,030 (926)	‡ (†)	42,900 (1,489)	34,240 (701)	41,570 (1,299)	39,960 (1,273)	47,630 (1,457)	‡ (†)
Indiana	25,400 (329)	30,760 (296)	34,600 (640)	38,670 (786)	32,850 (452)	‡ (†)	‡ (†)	‡ (†)	37,420 (996)	‡ (†)	‡ (†)	‡ (†)
Iowa	24,950 (319)	28,910 (279)	33,600 (696)	35,240 (500)	28,580 (827)	40,400 (903)	41,040 (759)	33,900 (1,926)	36,410 (850)	39,280 (1,164)	45,250 (1,378)	45,100 (1,920)
Kansas	25,930 (135)	29,430 (264)	32,290 (326)	37,160 (476)	34,390 (523)	42,250 (880)	38,120 (438)	35,670 (955)	35,560 (445)	37,610 (872)	39,190 (659)	42,730 (1,282)
Kentucky	24,910 (457)	27,720 (358)	31,610 (468)	35,640 (608)	33,460 (1,011)	‡ (†)	38,840 (896)	36,060 (716)	36,670 (496)	‡ (†)	‡ (†)	‡ (†)
Louisiana	22,520 (159)	28,020 (476)	32,590 (489)	39,880 (462)	36,300 (825)	44,800 (1,061)	43,040 (614)	39,120 (798)	39,560 (1,105)	42,510 (1,134)	44,130 (980)	47,540 (961)
Maine	28,550 (330)	34,690 (775)	36,650 (606)	38,770 (651)	31,260 (573)	46,260 (1,321)	43,710 (1,023)	‡ (†)	34,180 (1,538)	38,000 (1,033)	45,230 (891)	52,570 (1,385)
Maryland	33,520 (476)	37,760 (683)	42,960 (1,313)	50,680 (1,213)	41,270 (492)	66,640 (1,644)	56,360 (2,123)	46,220 (3,395)	38,070 (839)	46,250 (1,873)	58,540 (2,167)	‡ (†)
Massachusetts	34,340 (309)	40,410 (464)	43,930 (964)	50,880 (917)	37,720 (970)	58,510 (2,309)	47,260 (1,588)	36,620 (1,186)	39,570 (1,387)	41,950 (1,915)	48,040 (1,229)	‡ (†)
Michigan	37,170 (670)	39,950 (838)	45,230 (682)	47,440 (1,612)	35,930 (664)	59,330 (1,506)	45,250 (1,184)	35,830 (2,261)	33,470 (490)	43,080 (658)	49,220 (802)	60,850 (2,504)
Minnesota	31,010 (419)	35,270 (685)	39,030 (566)	41,760 (593)	33,830 (574)	51,890 (924)	‡ (†)	‡ (†)	‡ (†)	‡ (†)	‡ (†)	56,320 (2,294)
Mississippi	22,640 (106)	28,000 (186)	31,890 (425)	36,610 (344)	32,770 (434)	43,690 (850)	36,030 (520)	31,890 (761)	‡ (†)	‡ (†)	‡ (†)	44,490 (1,504)
Missouri	23,510 (286)	28,020 (378)	31,340 (547)	34,730 (553)	31,200 (632)	39,320 (1,512)	36,640 (941)	36,210 (2,581)	34,100 (891)	35,460 (1,290)	38,370 (1,733)	42,550 (2,022)
Montana	24,070 (199)	27,920 (256)	31,870 (522)	35,880 (597)	27,090 (591)	44,080 (1,045)	38,470 (1,155)	28,560 (1,128)	31,410 (1,454)	35,040 (1,442)	41,240 (1,713)	48,570 (1,719)
Nebraska	22,580 (388)	26,090 (254)	30,300 (435)	34,190 (805)	29,400 (379)	36,690 (1,524)	38,670 (912)	33,970 (1,111)	34,240 (775)	34,980 (1,238)	41,330 (1,354)	44,090 (2,004)
Nevada	29,350 (285)	34,470 (434)	35,970 (700)	40,060 (619)	34,040 (462)	48,800 (2,143)	45,100 (1,913)	‡ (†)	‡ (†)	43,260 (1,505)	51,190 (2,994)	‡ (†)
New Hampshire	31,280 (437)	34,210 (542)	38,800 (644)	43,910 (843)	33,810 (1,139)	52,430 (1,050)	48,320 (1,394)	‡ (†)	34,240 (†)	44,300 (1,527)	51,260 (1,568)	56,980 (1,956)
New Jersey	41,330 (744)	46,720 (653)	49,780 (1,049)	54,580 (1,091)	45,370 (977)	72,840 (2,642)	61,120 (1,391)	50,880 (1,517)	49,590 (920)	54,610 (1,178)	66,830 (2,276)	78,660 (3,520)
New Mexico	25,260 (224)	29,290 (363)	34,310 (470)	39,830 (596)	32,520 (844)	48,430 (885)	41,460 (747)	34,900 (1,856)	36,750 (1,639)	42,620 (851)	42,480 (1,418)	46,950 (1,045)
New York	39,650 (1,152)	41,600 (1,094)	42,630 (1,074)	48,520 (2,004)	43,670 (1,652)	‡ (†)	60,460 (2,704)	‡ (†)	‡ (†)	‡ (†)	‡ (†)	‡ (†)
North Carolina	26,010 (220)	31,920 (331)	33,650 (479)	37,050 (469)	30,930 (499)	48,070 (843)	37,660 (545)	32,770 (895)	31,620 (913)	35,090 (613)	39,660 (832)	46,430 (1,154)
North Dakota	22,450 (193)	25,910 (279)	30,870 (490)	34,790 (695)	27,770 (579)	38,920 (1,069)	40,470 (1,666)	33,570 (722)	35,190 (720)	38,220 (1,096)	43,230 (2,102)	45,570 (2,866)
Ohio	30,370 (399)	35,120 (583)	41,600 (891)	41,670 (1,567)	35,350 (1,976)	54,890 (2,001)	46,070 (1,116)	34,980 (1,085)	36,990 (878)	43,670 (1,507)	51,930 (1,642)	59,950 (2,284)
Oklahoma	24,880 (108)	27,400 (224)	31,190 (211)	35,880 (226)	32,390 (458)	41,410 (477)	36,700 (371)	33,260 (868)	33,360 (469)	33,750 (416)	38,100 (409)	42,860 (1,104)
Oregon	31,310 (440)	38,370 (613)	42,430 (865)	46,930 (1,282)	32,050 (655)	52,750 (1,869)	51,260 (1,653)	‡ (†)	44,250 (1,367)	‡ (†)	54,330 (2,170)	57,940 (1,849)
Pennsylvania	37,260 (523)	42,620 (826)	44,250 (963)	47,780 (1,162)	38,950 (780)	64,470 (1,680)	54,210 (1,485)	41,180 (1,073)	44,250 (†)	47,540 (1,414)	58,910 (2,455)	72,350 (2,919)
Rhode Island	38,000 (522)	43,900 (357)	49,360 (834)	56,680 (1,362)	‡ (†)	‡ (†)	‡ (†)	‡ (†)	‡ (†)	‡ (†)	‡ (†)	‡ (†)
South Carolina	25,120 (280)	29,820 (300)	34,950 (483)	37,150 (606)	31,670 (625)	45,920 (1,013)	39,380 (1,077)	32,760 (668)	33,280 (601)	36,080 (1,103)	34,950 (900)	38,820 (1,345)
South Dakota	22,000 (186)	26,000 (230)	29,360 (301)	32,180 (445)	27,730 (422)	36,250 (784)	34,870 (601)	32,890 (2,513)	30,760 (639)	32,100 (490)	41,650 (2,085)	45,900 (1,820)
Tennessee	25,650 (291)	30,830 (378)	34,310 (432)	37,420 (553)	32,990 (481)	43,350 (1,430)	39,420 (877)	34,490 (2,730)	37,380 (1,322)	38,120 (1,301)	52,600 (2,364)	54,600 (1,206)
Texas	26,950 (295)	34,770 (386)	38,140 (278)	42,890 (480)	39,150 (706)	48,800 (753)	46,820 (440)	41,200 (935)	43,630 (571)	44,900 (590)	47,820 (639)	53,220 (1,206)
Utah	25,800 (195)	31,810 (375)	35,160 (525)	38,570 (863)	30,430 (745)	48,750 (1,469)	39,740 (1,087)	30,000 (1,831)	34,230 (411)	38,680 (1,059)	45,660 (1,248)	55,230 (1,500)
Vermont	29,750 (494)	33,470 (733)	39,040 (840)	43,430 (1,005)	37,170 (974)	52,160 (1,253)	48,240 (1,416)	38,080 (850)	38,200 (710)	41,220 (1,203)	50,670 (2,079)	55,660 (2,233)
Virginia	29,410 (378)	34,060 (424)	37,520 (583)	43,440 (569)	37,220 (2,053)	54,320 (1,391)	44,860 (999)	37,360 (2,125)	39,280 (†)	42,010 (878)	46,500 (2,085)	54,290 (1,561)
Washington	33,150 (490)	36,330 (359)	40,040 (916)	44,650 (905)	29,030 (491)	53,950 (1,445)	45,590 (1,439)	34,240 (1,737)	34,120 (1,702)	36,830 (775)	52,600 (2,364)	53,220 (4,347)
West Virginia	26,980 (183)	30,040 (246)	32,980 (344)	34,410 (475)	32,020 (651)	40,660 (581)	38,360 (646)	34,180 (637)	38,830 (595)	42,470 (1,338)	46,880 (1,598)	46,740 (1,211)
Wisconsin	31,490 (351)	35,470 (331)	37,150 (634)	41,390 (859)	38,230 (863)	49,630 (1,457)	42,790 (840)	43,440 (1,162)	38,830 (1,124)	48,910 (1,480)	52,180 (1,212)	54,890 (1,714)
Wyoming	27,310 (247)	29,470 (248)	34,080 (576)	45,750 (543)	‡ (†)	51,210 (1,119)	50,610 (1,105)	43,440 (†)	47,530 (1,083)	48,910 (†)	52,180 (†)	55,710 (2,807)

†Not applicable.

‡Reporting standards not met. Data may be suppressed because the response rate is under 50 percent, there are too few cases for a reliable estimate, or the coefficient of variation (CV) is 50 percent or greater.

NOTE: This table includes regular full-time teachers only; it excludes other staff even when they have full-time teaching duties (regular part-time teachers, itinerant teachers, long-term substitutes, administrators, library media specialists, other professional staff, and support staff).

SOURCE: U.S. Department of Education, National Center for Education Statistics, Schools and Staffing Survey (SASS), "Public School Teacher Data File," 1993–94, 1999–2000, 2003–04, 2007–08, and 2011–12; and "Public Charter School Teacher Data File," 1999–2000. (This table was prepared June 2013.)

Table 211.40. Average base salary for full-time public elementary and secondary school teachers with a master's degree as their highest degree, by years of full-time teaching experience and state: 1993–94 through 2011–12

[Amounts in current dollars. Standard errors appear in parentheses]

State	1993–94, total	1999–2000, total	2003–04, total	2007–08 Total	2007–08 6 to 10 years	2007–08 11 to 20 years	2007–08 Over 20 years	2011–12 Total	2011–12 5 or fewer years	2011–12 6 to 10 years	2011–12 11 to 20 years	2011–12 Over 20 years
1	2	3	4	5	6	7	8	9	10	11	12	13
United States	$38,480 (154)	$44,700 (174)	$49,440 (202)	$54,810 (281)	$50,540 (380)	$56,770 (493)	$63,050 (576)	$57,830 (352)	$45,880 (650)	$52,260 (514)	$60,810 (504)	$67,150 (604)
Alabama	28,920 (156)	36,930 (145)	39,730 (383)	46,980 (436)	45,050 (828)	48,150 (480)	50,960 (1,102)	48,410 (367)	44,830 (666)	45,940 (757)	49,500 (483)	51,910 (557)
Alaska	50,900 (373)	51,170 (662)	53,720 (1,005)	58,640 (800)	54,480 (1,141)	61,530 (965)	65,260 (1,456)	64,240 (2,039)	53,330 (1,643)	‡ (†)	68,130 (3,724)	‡ (†)
Arizona	35,280 (302)	38,150 (465)	41,310 (531)	43,910 (701)	39,600 (877)	44,910 (853)	52,300 (1,381)	42,560 (660)	36,780 (723)	39,270 (976)	45,220 (1,043)	48,420 (1,191)
Arkansas	29,070 (322)	34,830 (483)	39,480 (639)	45,460 (678)	42,450 (1,355)	45,130 (1,150)	50,260 (971)	47,100 (921)	41,060 (937)	42,230 (1,199)	49,350 (1,574)	53,850 (1,869)
California	43,420 (636)	50,800 (537)	59,160 (761)	65,040 (982)	59,930 (1,076)	68,830 (1,477)	78,710 (1,186)	67,830 (981)	50,170 (1,334)	61,100 (1,091)	70,260 (1,776)	81,310 (1,116)
Colorado	35,580 (364)	41,200 (445)	47,960 (641)	50,140 (1,069)	46,050 (1,719)	54,760 (1,692)	60,770 (1,920)	52,760 (1,280)	42,580 (2,262)	45,800 (1,598)	54,990 (1,512)	67,830 (3,875)
Connecticut	49,310 (416)	56,140 (590)	57,340 (934)	62,480 (762)	57,870 (1,079)	68,270 (1,430)	72,230 (868)	67,040 (996)	52,510 (1,560)	59,060 (1,602)	72,890 (1,058)	77,630 (1,366)
Delaware	42,350 (535)	48,120 (910)	54,670 (913)	56,930 (1,117)	52,280 (1,679)	62,270 (2,243)	69,340 (1,947)	57,730 (1,420)	45,820 (1,361)	52,090 (1,343)	63,840 (1,647)	71,640 (1,769)
District of Columbia	45,360 (828)	51,040 (472)	55,450 (1,568)	66,250 (1,933)	41,600 (920)	70,100 (2,147)	81,410 (1,654)	‡ (†)	‡ (†)	‡ (†)	‡ (†)	‡ (†)
Florida	33,150 (487)	39,330 (476)	42,120 (784)	48,680 (985)	‡ (†)	45,760 (937)	61,650 (1,329)	‡ (†)	‡ (†)	‡ (†)	‡ (†)	‡ (†)
Georgia	31,890 (227)	41,950 (524)	47,540 (752)	51,600 (799)	48,020 (1,214)	53,320 (863)	57,920 (1,278)	50,700 (1,002)	43,240 (1,809)	46,510 (934)	53,010 (1,253)	60,350 (2,025)
Hawaii	36,430 (731)	39,280 (524)	42,910 (967)	49,380 (1,513)	41,150 (1,707)	51,410 (1,249)	53,120 (1,855)	45,920 (1,724)	‡ (†)	37,300 (1,627)	49,020 (2,067)	54,210 (2,258)
Idaho	31,590 (440)	38,150 (772)	47,020 (857)	47,020 (981)	‡ (†)	‡ (†)	‡ (†)	‡ (†)	49,030 (2,082)	‡ (†)	‡ (†)	‡ (†)
Illinois	42,400 (588)	47,770 (953)	54,110 (1,253)	61,330 (1,503)	53,930 (1,513)	62,610 (1,854)	74,860 (2,895)	64,670 (1,520)	‡ (†)	57,570 (1,787)	66,730 (2,353)	60,650 (2,944)
Indiana	38,040 (292)	45,480 (413)	51,640 (670)	51,640 (686)	43,470 (1,128)	49,100 (883)	58,370 (655)	55,360 (735)	39,610 (943)	45,570 (1,258)	54,370 (908)	61,760 (753)
Iowa	32,220 (571)	38,010 (494)	41,880 (608)	44,770 (829)	39,040 (1,073)	43,130 (1,487)	50,980 (1,111)	49,630 (1,509)	39,350 (1,318)	42,010 (1,819)	51,650 (2,543)	53,420 (2,764)
Kansas	32,560 (314)	36,140 (428)	40,400 (755)	46,220 (955)	41,240 (1,390)	46,160 (1,036)	50,260 (1,519)	47,940 (1,090)	45,830 (1,882)	41,890 (638)	48,730 (1,461)	53,720 (1,554)
Kentucky	31,390 (396)	36,380 (310)	40,570 (457)	46,220 (578)	42,750 (762)	48,430 (1,162)	51,540 (866)	50,080 (751)	41,670 (1,457)	46,240 (922)	51,520 (975)	56,590 (1,585)
Louisiana	27,300 (262)	33,120 (806)	38,000 (558)	44,090 (854)	‡ (†)	46,060 (1,135)	47,470 (974)	46,790 (986)	‡ (†)	45,420 (1,824)	48,690 (1,524)	50,220 (1,492)
Maine	33,060 (499)	38,770 (458)	42,460 (677)	44,820 (733)	38,970 (871)	45,960 (1,030)	51,680 (1,138)	48,890 (1,145)	‡ (†)	42,190 (769)	48,160 (1,394)	57,530 (1,506)
Maryland	42,340 (406)	45,930 (1,055)	53,190 (1,307)	59,130 (1,422)	51,950 (1,240)	62,770 (2,878)	70,570 (1,880)	63,420 (1,002)	49,650 (1,399)	58,840 (1,673)	68,450 (1,821)	73,440 (1,603)
Massachusetts	39,710 (254)	47,630 (370)	53,500 (714)	58,680 (894)	57,660 (960)	62,000 (1,225)	68,590 (1,404)	64,130 (962)	54,060 (3,458)	55,250 (1,916)	67,590 (962)	70,610 (1,269)
Michigan	47,660 (488)	53,050 (651)	59,680 (906)	63,100 (1,116)	56,030 (1,790)	67,540 (1,494)	69,980 (1,434)	57,200 (700)	43,830 (1,531)	49,380 (640)	60,860 (847)	64,270 (1,098)
Minnesota	40,710 (552)	46,050 (674)	49,590 (731)	55,040 (1,503)	49,930 (1,041)	56,750 (900)	61,800 (1,203)	‡ (†)	35,860 (749)	40,180 (1,742)	43,290 (841)	50,860 (1,612)
Mississippi	26,600 (200)	34,170 (326)	38,460 (479)	44,170 (617)	40,110 (537)	44,090 (798)	50,570 (804)	43,110 (767)	‡ (†)	‡ (†)	‡ (†)	‡ (†)
Missouri	33,180 (625)	37,400 (747)	40,880 (761)	45,830 (1,020)	41,260 (978)	46,150 (1,385)	54,300 (2,175)	47,480 (989)	39,240 (817)	43,430 (1,422)	47,790 (1,067)	58,230 (2,342)
Montana	32,270 (423)	35,960 (536)	39,650 (885)	45,970 (908)	39,360 (1,161)	45,700 (1,589)	51,300 (1,290)	49,060 (1,393)	39,320 (1,722)	42,210 (1,213)	47,620 (1,652)	50,160 (1,685)
Nebraska	30,290 (538)	33,540 (429)	39,620 (1,083)	40,410 (913)	37,490 (1,008)	38,420 (1,330)	43,880 (1,677)	47,260 (1,310)	46,770 (2,914)	44,950 (1,798)	48,880 (2,290)	50,660 (2,253)
Nevada	38,570 (353)	41,350 (689)	45,770 (558)	50,050 (906)	47,280 (840)	53,010 (757)	60,420 (1,560)	52,960 (1,713)	‡ (†)	45,770 (891)	58,850 (3,067)	63,590 (1,751)
New Hampshire	36,970 (505)	41,310 (505)	45,140 (677)	51,320 (1,002)	46,650 (1,397)	55,020 (1,528)	59,610 (1,134)	54,350 (1,169)	‡ (†)	48,480 (1,329)	58,180 (1,303)	63,000 (987)
New Jersey	50,950 (883)	57,410 (709)	60,200 (1,571)	62,580 (1,901)	54,270 (2,691)	66,070 (2,656)	81,170 (2,065)	68,910 (1,227)	56,040 (1,008)	59,390 (983)	72,360 (1,596)	85,460 (2,549)
New Mexico	28,400 (281)	35,570 (539)	40,100 (810)	47,200 (833)	44,420 (854)	48,890 (553)	53,050 (1,393)	47,360 (1,492)	37,280 (2,051)	44,620 (1,343)	50,160 (2,096)	53,570 (3,476)
New York	47,440 (840)	53,130 (923)	56,650 (746)	64,300 (1,698)	58,520 (2,054)	67,830 (2,458)	83,090 (3,081)	73,180 (1,462)	55,820 (2,523)	67,940 (1,897)	74,960 (1,693)	89,350 (2,861)
North Carolina	29,180 (306)	36,810 (542)	42,720 (641)	45,470 (1,321)	40,790 (1,636)	46,800 (1,948)	52,660 (2,098)	42,290 (1,149)	33,070 (985)	39,020 (2,025)	44,700 (912)	48,870 (2,335)
North Dakota	28,520 (730)	32,920 (559)	39,710 (789)	44,090 (885)	40,400 (1,690)	43,610 (1,629)	49,560 (1,644)	52,090 (1,471)	‡ (†)	43,410 (1,130)	53,160 (2,149)	59,920 (1,552)
Ohio	37,960 (550)	43,420 (585)	50,090 (689)	55,680 (982)	49,420 (1,058)	58,470 (1,779)	63,100 (1,473)	57,430 (1,025)	42,660 (1,403)	49,940 (1,492)	61,280 (1,215)	65,380 (1,169)
Oklahoma	28,510 (186)	35,610 (261)	43,580 (319)	40,220 (486)	36,550 (718)	39,350 (769)	44,400 (592)	39,490 (727)	41,170 (840)	39,890 (1,301)	39,220 (639)	44,610 (1,204)
Oregon	36,930 (471)	42,180 (588)	45,850 (647)	48,170 (914)	46,830 (721)	53,310 (1,396)	57,740 (1,375)	51,520 (936)	45,940 (1,778)	54,790 (1,157)	57,300 (1,863)	61,040 (1,615)
Pennsylvania	44,830 (816)	50,790 (1,027)	54,800 (925)	62,340 (1,667)	52,120 (1,628)	64,360 (2,553)	74,360 (2,998)	62,650 (1,408)	‡ (†)	‡ (†)	67,650 (1,850)	75,380 (2,112)
Rhode Island	41,630 (303)	48,610 (204)	55,110 (909)	65,180 (1,137)	‡ (†)	67,950 (1,212)	69,950 (1,244)	‡ (†)	‡ (†)	‡ (†)	‡ (†)	‡ (†)
South Carolina	31,860 (208)	38,390 (528)	42,910 (625)	46,480 (529)	41,280 (1,209)	47,160 (812)	52,970 (892)	46,770 (966)	38,250 (1,216)	41,190 (1,777)	48,850 (851)	54,960 (1,263)
South Dakota	28,110 (449)	32,800 (443)	37,670 (801)	39,880 (764)	35,110 (1,125)	39,180 (1,199)	44,110 (1,224)	41,730 (910)	38,260 (947)	40,540 (949)	41,160 (1,285)	45,840 (1,731)
Tennessee	30,270 (350)	35,610 (414)	43,620 (543)	43,730 (694)	39,840 (999)	44,370 (1,197)	49,150 (964)	44,550 (984)	44,300 (989)	46,340 (854)	48,770 (2,096)	49,660 (1,879)
Texas	31,610 (355)	40,280 (453)	43,370 (723)	47,520 (1,092)	44,490 (2,023)	48,340 (1,242)	51,960 (2,138)	49,390 (593)	‡ (†)	42,530 (1,558)	50,120 (1,102)	56,520 (1,316)
Utah	32,590 (277)	38,770 (586)	43,370 (636)	47,200 (1,092)	41,020 (748)	49,140 (866)	54,170 (1,687)	48,750 (1,772)	36,970 (1,495)	‡ (†)	54,440 (1,724)	58,620 (1,332)
Vermont	36,770 (594)	37,260 (668)	44,500 (926)	51,320 (987)	44,780 (1,742)	51,310 (1,494)	58,040 (1,387)	56,190 (1,158)	44,410 (1,916)	50,380 (1,587)	56,450 (1,679)	64,460 (1,418)
Virginia	33,740 (579)	40,230 (668)	43,860 (948)	50,910 (1,572)	43,090 (1,865)	52,520 (2,135)	62,310 (2,889)	51,130 (1,408)	45,110 (2,671)	45,780 (1,317)	51,120 (1,603)	60,390 (3,502)
Washington	38,270 (398)	43,160 (364)	47,970 (500)	51,800 (649)	47,380 (1,210)	55,970 (831)	58,670 (882)	57,670 (1,077)	44,030 (1,130)	52,050 (3,153)	61,510 (1,406)	63,780 (785)
West Virginia	32,130 (195)	36,590 (226)	40,440 (500)	43,090 (477)	37,120 (580)	41,910 (762)	47,700 (513)	45,460 (805)	36,640 (1,543)	41,530 (1,333)	45,730 (1,133)	51,600 (1,012)
Wisconsin	40,920 (486)	46,420 (512)	47,750 (713)	52,210 (873)	46,650 (1,245)	53,120 (1,604)	58,010 (1,380)	55,430 (791)	‡ (†)	‡ (†)	57,280 (924)	61,410 (1,797)
Wyoming	32,490 (371)	36,120 (497)	41,610 (1,014)	52,990 (932)	49,530 (1,444)	52,550 (1,243)	57,580 (1,495)	59,390 (817)	‡ (†)	48,360 (1,235)	59,700 (1,074)	63,230 (1,803)

† Not applicable.
‡ Reporting standards not met. Data may be suppressed because the response rate is under 50 percent, there are too few cases for a reliable estimate, or the coefficient of variation (CV) is 50 percent or greater.
NOTE: This table includes regular full-time teachers only; it excludes other staff even when they have full-time teaching duties (regular part-time teachers, itinerant teachers, long-term substitutes, administrators, library media specialists, other professional staff, and support staff.

SOURCE: U.S. Department of Education, National Center for Education Statistics, Schools and Staffing Survey (SASS), "Public School Teacher Data File," 1993–94, 1999–2000, 2003–04, 2007–08, and 2011–12; and "Public Charter School Teacher Data File," 1999–2000. (This table was prepared June 2013.)

Table 211.50. Estimated average annual salary of teachers in public elementary and secondary schools: Selected years, 1959–60 through 2013–14

School year	Current dollars					Average public school teachers' salary in constant 2013–14 dollars[1]		
	Average public school teachers' salary			Wage and salary accruals per full-time-equivalent (FTE) employee[2]	Ratio of average teachers' salary to accruals per FTE employee			
	All teachers	Elementary teachers	Secondary teachers			All teachers	Elementary teachers	Secondary teachers
1	2	3	4	5	6	7	8	9
1959–60	$4,995	$4,815	$5,276	$4,749	1.05	$39,943	$38,504	$42,190
1961–62	5,515	5,340	5,775	5,063	1.09	43,111	41,743	45,144
1963–64	5,995	5,805	6,266	5,478	1.09	45,672	44,225	47,737
1965–66	6,485	6,279	6,761	5,934	1.09	47,755	46,238	49,787
1967–68	7,423	7,208	7,692	6,533	1.14	51,287	49,801	53,145
1969–70	8,626	8,412	8,891	7,486	1.15	53,655	52,324	55,303
1970–71	9,268	9,021	9,568	7,998	1.16	54,818	53,358	56,593
1971–72	9,705	9,424	10,031	8,521	1.14	55,415	53,811	57,277
1972–73	10,174	9,893	10,507	9,056	1.12	55,843	54,301	57,671
1973–74	10,770	10,507	11,077	9,667	1.11	54,275	52,950	55,822
1974–75	11,641	11,334	12,000	10,411	1.12	52,812	51,419	54,441
1975–76	12,600	12,280	12,937	11,194	1.13	53,384	52,028	54,812
1976–77	13,354	12,989	13,776	11,971	1.12	53,461	52,000	55,150
1977–78	14,198	13,845	14,602	12,811	1.11	53,263	51,939	54,779
1978–79	15,032	14,681	15,450	13,807	1.09	51,562	50,358	52,996
1979–80	15,970	15,569	16,459	15,050	1.06	48,335	47,122	49,815
1980–81	17,644	17,230	18,142	16,461	1.07	47,858	46,736	49,209
1981–82	19,274	18,853	19,805	17,795	1.08	48,123	47,072	49,449
1982–83	20,695	20,227	21,291	18,873	1.10	49,543	48,422	50,970
1983–84	21,935	21,487	22,554	19,781	1.11	50,637	49,603	52,066
1984–85	23,600	23,200	24,187	20,694	1.14	52,428	51,540	53,732
1985–86	25,199	24,718	25,846	21,685	1.16	54,412	53,373	55,809
1986–87	26,569	26,057	27,244	22,700	1.17	56,124	55,042	57,550
1987–88	28,034	27,519	28,798	23,777	1.18	56,862	55,818	58,412
1988–89	29,564	29,022	30,218	24,752	1.19	57,318	56,268	58,586
1989–90	31,367	30,832	32,049	25,762	1.22	58,044	57,054	59,306
1990–91	33,084	32,490	33,896	26,935	1.23	58,048	57,006	59,473
1991–92	34,063	33,479	34,827	28,169	1.21	57,910	56,917	59,209
1992–93	35,029	34,350	35,880	29,245	1.20	57,749	56,629	59,152
1993–94	35,737	35,233	36,566	30,030	1.19	57,428	56,618	58,760
1994–95	36,675	36,088	37,523	30,857	1.19	57,293	56,376	58,618
1995–96	37,642	37,138	38,397	31,822	1.18	57,247	56,480	58,395
1996–97	38,443	38,039	39,184	33,058	1.16	56,843	56,246	57,939
1997–98	39,350	39,002	39,944	34,635	1.14	57,165	56,659	58,027
1998–99	40,544	40,165	41,203	36,277	1.12	57,897	57,356	58,838
1999–2000	41,807	41,306	42,546	38,144	1.10	58,025	57,330	59,051
2000–01	43,378	42,910	44,053	39,727	1.09	58,211	57,583	59,117
2001–02	44,655	44,177	45,310	40,589	1.10	58,883	58,252	59,746
2002–03	45,686	45,408	46,106	41,629	1.10	58,947	58,588	59,489
2003–04	46,542	46,187	46,976	43,259	1.08	58,765	58,317	59,313
2004–05	47,516	47,122	47,688	44,908	1.06	58,243	57,760	58,453
2005–06	49,086	48,573	49,496	46,626	1.05	57,960	57,354	58,444
2006–07	51,052	50,740	51,529	48,713	1.05	58,762	58,403	59,311
2007–08	52,800	52,385	53,262	50,504	1.05	58,602	58,142	59,115
2008–09	54,319	53,998	54,552	51,409	1.06	59,458	59,107	59,713
2009–10	55,202	54,918	55,595	52,413	1.05	59,845	59,537	60,271
2010–11	55,623	55,217	56,225	53,975	1.03	59,115	58,683	59,755
2011–12	55,418	54,704	56,226	55,435	1.00	57,220	56,483	58,055
2012–13	56,103	55,344	57,077	56,361	1.00	56,979	56,208	57,969
2013–14	56,689	56,015	57,593	—	—	56,689	56,015	57,593

—Not available.
[1]Constant dollars based on the Consumer Price Index, prepared by the Bureau of Labor Statistics, U.S. Department of Labor, adjusted to a school-year basis.
[2]The average monetary remuneration earned by FTE employees across all industries in a given year, including wages, salaries, commissions, tips, bonuses, voluntary employee contributions to certain deferred compensation plans, and receipts in kind that represent income. Calendar-year data from the U.S. Department of Commerce, Bureau of Economic Analysis, have been converted to a school-year basis by averaging the two appropriate calendar years in each case.

NOTE: Some data have been revised from previously published figures. Standard errors are not available for these estimates, which are based on state reports.
SOURCE: National Education Association, *Estimates of School Statistics*, 1959–60 through 2013–14; and unpublished tabulations. U.S. Department of Commerce, Bureau of Economic Analysis, National Income and Product Accounts, tables 6.6B-D, retrieved August 26, 2014, from http://www.bea.gov/iTable/iTable.cfm?ReqID=9&step=1#reqid=9&step=3&isuri=1&904=2001&903=201&906=q&905=2006&910=x&911=0. (This table was prepared August 2014.)

Table 211.60. Estimated average annual salary of teachers in public elementary and secondary schools, by state: Selected years, 1969–70 through 2013–14

State	Current dollars							Constant 2013–14 dollars[1]							Percent change, 1999–2000 to 2013–14
	1969–70	1979–80	1989–90	1999–2000	2009–10	2012–13	2013–14	1969–70	1979–80	1989–90	1999–2000	2009–10	2012–13	2013–14	
1	2	3	4	5	6	7	8	9	10	11	12	13	14	15	16
United States...	$8,626	$15,970	$31,367	$41,807	$55,202	$56,103	$56,689	$53,655	$48,335	$58,044	$58,025	$59,845	$56,979	$56,689	-2.3
Alabama	6,818	13,060	24,828	36,689	47,571	47,949	48,413	42,409	39,528	45,944	50,922	51,572	48,698	48,413	-4.9
Alaska....................	10,560	27,210	43,153	46,462	59,672	65,468	66,739	65,685	82,354	79,854	64,486	64,691	66,491	66,739	3.5
Arizona	8,711	15,054	29,402	36,902	46,952	49,885	51,109	54,184	45,563	54,408	51,218	50,901	50,664	51,109	-0.2
Arkansas...............	6,307	12,299	22,352	33,386	46,700	46,631	46,950	39,230	37,224	41,362	46,338	50,628	47,359	46,950	1.3
California	10,315	18,020	37,998	47,680	68,203	69,324	70,126	64,161	54,540	70,315	66,177	73,940	70,407	70,126	6.0
Colorado	7,761	16,205	30,758	38,163	49,202	49,844	50,651	48,275	49,046	56,917	52,968	53,341	50,623	50,651	-4.4
Connecticut............	9,262	16,229	40,461	51,780	64,350	69,397	70,584	57,611	49,119	74,873	71,867	69,763	70,481	70,584	-1.8
Delaware................	9,015	16,148	33,377	44,435	57,080	59,679	60,571	56,075	48,874	61,764	61,673	61,881	60,611	60,571	-1.8
District of Columbia..	10,285	22,190	38,402	47,076	64,548	70,906	73,162	63,974	67,161	71,063	65,338	69,978	72,014	73,162	12.0
Florida...................	8,412	14,149	28,803	36,722	46,708	46,598	46,691	52,324	42,824	53,300	50,968	50,637	47,326	46,691	-8.4
Georgia..................	7,276	13,853	28,006	41,023	53,112	52,880	52,924	45,258	41,928	51,825	56,937	57,580	53,706	52,924	-7.0
Hawaii....................	9,453	19,920	32,047	40,578	55,063	54,300	56,291	58,799	60,290	59,303	56,320	59,695	55,148	56,291	-0.1
Idaho.....................	6,890	13,611	23,861	35,547	46,283	49,734	50,945	42,857	41,195	44,155	49,337	50,176	50,511	50,945	3.3
Illinois...................	9,569	17,601	32,794	46,486	62,077	59,113	60,124	59,521	53,271	60,685	64,520	67,299	60,036	60,124	-6.8
Indiana..................	8,833	15,599	30,902	41,850	49,986	50,065	50,644	54,943	47,212	57,184	58,085	54,191	50,847	50,644	-12.8
Iowa......................	8,355	15,203	26,747	35,678	49,626	50,946	51,662	51,969	46,014	49,495	49,519	53,800	51,742	51,662	4.3
Kansas...................	7,612	13,690	28,744	34,981	46,657	47,464	48,221	47,348	41,434	53,190	48,551	50,582	48,205	48,221	-0.7
Kentucky	6,953	14,520	26,292	36,380	49,543	50,203	50,705	43,249	43,946	48,653	50,493	53,710	50,987	50,705	0.4
Louisiana	7,028	13,760	24,300	33,109	48,903	51,381	52,259	43,715	41,646	44,967	45,953	53,017	52,184	52,259	13.7
Maine....................	7,572	13,071	26,881	35,561	46,106	48,430	49,232	47,099	39,561	49,743	49,356	49,984	49,186	49,232	-0.3
Maryland................	9,383	17,558	36,319	44,048	63,971	64,248	64,868	58,364	53,141	67,208	61,136	69,352	65,252	64,868	6.1
Massachusetts.......	8,764	17,253	34,712	46,580	69,273	72,334	73,736	54,513	52,218	64,234	64,650	75,100	73,464	73,736	14.1
Michigan	9,826	19,663	37,072	49,044	57,958	61,560	61,866	61,119	59,512	68,601	68,070	62,833	62,522	61,866	-9.1
Minnesota..............	8,658	15,912	32,190	39,802	52,431	56,268	57,230	53,854	48,159	59,567	55,243	56,841	57,147	57,230	3.6
Mississippi............	5,798	11,850	24,292	31,857	45,644	41,814	42,187	36,064	35,865	44,952	44,215	49,483	42,467	42,187	-4.6
Missouri.................	7,799	13,682	27,094	35,656	45,317	47,517	48,329	48,511	41,410	50,137	49,488	49,129	48,259	48,329	-2.3
Montana.................	7,606	14,537	25,081	32,121	45,759	48,855	49,893	47,310	43,998	46,412	44,582	49,608	49,618	49,893	11.9
Nebraska	7,375	13,516	25,522	33,237	46,227	48,997	49,545	45,874	40,908	47,228	46,131	50,115	49,762	49,545	7.4
Nevada	9,215	16,295	30,590	39,390	51,524	55,957	57,391	57,319	49,319	56,606	54,671	55,858	56,831	57,391	5.0
New Hampshire......	7,771	13,017	28,986	37,734	51,443	55,599	57,057	48,337	39,397	53,638	52,372	55,770	56,467	57,057	8.9
New Jersey............	9,130	17,161	35,676	52,015	65,130	68,797	70,060	56,790	51,940	66,018	72,193	70,608	69,872	70,060	-3.0
New Mexico	7,796	14,887	24,756	32,554	46,258	45,453	45,727	48,492	45,057	45,811	45,183	50,149	46,163	45,727	1.2
New York................	10,336	19,812	38,925	51,020	71,633	75,279	76,566	64,291	59,963	72,030	70,812	77,658	76,455	76,566	8.1
North Carolina	7,494	14,117	27,883	39,404	46,850	45,737	45,355	46,614	42,727	51,597	54,690	50,791	46,451	45,355	-17.1
North Dakota	6,696	13,263	23,016	29,863	42,964	47,344	48,666	41,650	40,142	42,591	41,448	46,578	48,083	48,666	17.4
Ohio......................	8,300	15,269	31,218	41,436	55,958	56,307	57,270	51,627	46,213	57,769	57,510	60,665	57,186	57,270	-0.4
Oklahoma	6,882	13,107	23,070	31,298	47,691	44,373	44,277	42,807	39,670	42,691	43,440	51,703	45,066	44,277	1.9
Oregon...................	8,818	16,266	30,840	42,336	55,224	57,612	58,597	54,849	49,231	57,069	58,760	59,869	58,512	58,597	-0.3
Pennsylvania..........	8,858	16,515	33,338	48,321	59,156	62,994	64,072	55,098	49,984	61,692	67,066	64,132	63,978	64,072	-4.5
Rhode Island	8,776	18,002	36,057	47,041	59,686	63,474	64,696	54,588	54,485	66,723	65,290	64,707	64,465	64,696	-0.9
South Carolina.......	6,927	13,063	27,217	36,081	47,508	48,375	48,425	43,087	39,537	50,365	50,078	51,504	49,131	48,425	-3.3
South Dakota.........	6,403	12,348	21,300	29,071	38,837	39,018	40,023	39,828	37,373	39,415	40,349	42,104	39,627	40,023	-0.8
Tennessee	7,050	13,972	27,052	36,328	46,290	47,563	48,049	43,852	42,288	50,059	50,421	50,184	48,306	48,049	-4.7
Texas	7,255	14,132	27,496	37,567	48,261	48,819	49,270	45,127	42,772	50,881	52,141	52,321	49,582	49,270	-5.5
Utah......................	7,644	14,909	23,686	34,946	45,885	49,393	50,659	47,547	45,124	43,831	48,503	49,745	50,164	50,659	4.4
Vermont.................	7,968	12,484	29,012	37,758	49,084	52,526	53,656	49,562	37,784	53,686	52,406	53,213	53,346	53,656	2.4
Virginia..................	8,070	14,060	30,938	38,744	50,015	48,670	49,233	50,197	42,554	57,250	53,774	54,222	49,430	49,233	-8.4
Washington............	9,225	18,820	30,457	41,043	53,003	52,234	52,236	57,381	56,961	56,360	56,965	57,461	53,050	52,236	-8.3
West Virginia..........	7,650	13,710	22,842	35,009	45,959	45,453	45,583	47,584	41,495	42,269	48,590	49,825	46,163	45,583	-6.2
Wisconsin	8,963	16,006	31,921	41,153	51,264	53,797	54,717	55,751	48,444	59,069	57,118	55,576	54,637	54,717	-4.2
Wyoming................	8,232	16,012	28,141	34,127	55,861	56,775	57,910	51,204	48,462	52,075	47,366	60,560	57,662	57,910	22.3

[1]Constant dollars based on the Consumer Price Index (CPI), prepared by the Bureau of Labor Statistics, U.S. Department of Labor, adjusted to a school-year basis. The CPI does not account for differences in inflation rates from state to state.

NOTE: Some data have been revised from previously published figures. Standard errors are not available for these estimates, which are based on state reports.

SOURCE: National Education Association, *Estimates of School Statistics*, 1969–70 through 2013–14. (This table was prepared August 2014.)

Table 212.08. Number and percentage distribution of principals in public and private elementary and secondary schools, by selected characteristics: Selected years, 1993–94 through 2011–12

[Standard errors appear in parentheses]

Selected characteristic	Number of principals 1993–94	2003–04	2007–08	2011–12	Percentage distribution of principals 1993–94	2003–04	2007–08	2011–12
1	2	3	4	5	6	7	8	9
Public schools								
Total	79,620 (235)	87,620 (307)	90,470 (544)	89,810 (406)	100.0 (†)	100.0 (†)	100.0 (†)	100.0 (†)
Sex								
Male	52,110 (613)	45,930 (707)	44,950 (1,129)	43,450 (901)	65.5 (0.70)	52.4 (0.79)	49.7 (1.21)	48.4 (0.92)
Female	27,500 (542)	41,690 (708)	45,520 (1,129)	46,360 (801)	34.5 (0.70)	47.6 (0.79)	50.3 (1.21)	51.6 (0.92)
Race/ethnicity								
White[1]	67,080 (540)	72,200 (509)	73,160 (1,008)	72,070 (723)	84.3 (0.54)	82.4 (0.52)	80.9 (0.92)	80.3 (0.66)
Black[1]	8,020 (351)	9,250 (377)	9,620 (659)	9,110 (394)	10.1 (0.45)	10.6 (0.43)	10.6 (0.73)	10.1 (0.43)
Hispanic[1]	3,270 (258)	4,680 (355)	5,870 (540)	6,130 (404)	4.1 (0.33)	5.3 (0.40)	6.5 (0.60)	6.8 (0.46)
Asian[1,2]	620 (109)	460 (87)	570 (146)	820 (154)	0.8 (0.14)	0.5 (0.10)	0.6 (0.16)	0.9 (0.17)
Pacific Islander	— (†)	80 (18)	130 ! (52)	20 ! (9)	— (†)	0.1 (0.02)	0.1 ! (0.06)	# (†)
American Indian/Alaska Native[1]	630 (67)	600 (80)	620 (179)	650 (123)	0.8 (0.08)	0.7 (0.09)	0.7 (0.20)	0.7 (0.14)
Two or more races	— (†)	350 (82)	490 ! (155)	1,010 (183)	— (†)	0.4 (0.09)	0.5 ! (0.17)	1.1 (0.20)
Age								
Under 40	5,940 (273)	12,840 (477)	17,290 (785)	18,040 (523)	7.5 (0.34)	14.7 (0.55)	19.1 (0.84)	20.1 (0.58)
40 to 44	14,570 (496)	9,540 (449)	13,330 (706)	17,650 (565)	18.3 (0.61)	10.9 (0.51)	14.7 (0.78)	19.7 (0.62)
45 to 49	25,430 (429)	16,120 (526)	13,690 (767)	14,700 (541)	31.9 (0.55)	18.4 (0.59)	15.1 (0.86)	16.4 (0.60)
50 to 54	18,870 (539)	24,170 (669)	17,570 (746)	15,060 (668)	23.7 (0.68)	27.6 (0.75)	19.4 (0.82)	16.8 (0.73)
55 or over	14,820 (441)	24,960 (679)	28,590 (1,000)	24,350 (655)	18.6 (0.55)	28.5 (0.76)	31.6 (1.06)	27.1 (0.74)
School level								
Elementary	53,680 [4] (294)	61,480 (361)	62,340 (584)	61,250 (443)	71.9 (0.21)	70.2 (0.32)	68.9 (0.54)	68.2 (0.38)
Secondary	18,260 [4] (161)	19,700 (272)	21,550 (460)	20,470 (537)	24.4 (0.20)	22.5 (0.32)	23.8 (0.46)	22.8 (0.56)
Combined	2,750 [4] (143)	6,450 (263)	6,580 (364)	8,090 (658)	3.7 (0.19)	7.4 (0.30)	7.3 (0.40)	9.0 (0.74)
Highest degree earned								
Bachelor's or less	1,150 (167)	1,650 (213)	1,320 (207)	1,960 (272)	1.4 (0.21)	1.9 (0.24)	1.5 (0.23)	2.2 (0.30)
Master's	50,470 (536)	51,840 (657)	55,250 (906)	55,420 (678)	63.4 (0.65)	59.2 (0.71)	61.1 (1.01)	61.7 (0.71)
Education specialist[3]	20,570 (459)	26,570 (619)	26,270 (930)	23,560 (492)	25.8 (0.57)	30.3 (0.69)	29.0 (0.97)	26.2 (0.54)
Doctor's or first professional	7,430 (263)	7,560 (376)	7,630 (512)	8,870 (442)	9.3 (0.33)	8.6 (0.43)	8.4 (0.57)	9.9 (0.49)
Number of years as a principal								
3 or fewer	24,450 (451)	30,400 (695)	31,500 (1,033)	29,520 (758)	30.7 (0.56)	34.7 (0.78)	34.8 (1.11)	32.9 (0.84)
4 to 9	26,600 (548)	29,160 (710)	32,140 (989)	35,500 (886)	33.4 (0.68)	33.3 (0.80)	35.5 (1.09)	39.5 (0.96)
10 to 19	19,730 (412)	21,330 (663)	20,470 (926)	19,870 (634)	24.8 (0.52)	24.3 (0.76)	22.6 (1.01)	22.1 (0.70)
20 or more	8,840 (377)	6,740 (314)	6,350 (414)	4,920 (273)	11.1 (0.47)	7.7 (0.35)	7.0 (0.46)	5.5 (0.31)
Years of full-time teaching experience prior to becoming a principal								
3 or fewer	5,690 (251)	4,820 (280)	4,150 (384)	4,040 (264)	7.1 (0.31)	5.5 (0.32)	4.6 (0.42)	4.5 (0.30)
4 to 9	29,500 (516)	26,260 (603)	30,260 (958)	34,240 (792)	37.1 (0.63)	30.0 (0.70)	33.4 (1.03)	38.1 (0.84)
10 to 19	36,680 (558)	39,790 (676)	40,200 (992)	39,160 (752)	46.1 (0.70)	45.4 (0.73)	44.4 (1.09)	43.6 (0.82)
20 or more	7,740 (275)	16,760 (552)	15,850 (781)	12,380 (519)	9.7 (0.34)	19.1 (0.62)	17.5 (0.86)	13.8 (0.58)
School locale								
City	— (†)	22,690 (425)	21,560 (731)	23,440 (274)	27.4 (0.34)	25.9 (0.49)	23.8 (0.81)	26.1 (0.28)
Suburban	— (†)	25,600 (506)	25,880 (921)	24,520 (356)	25.9 (0.45)	29.2 (0.56)	28.6 (1.01)	27.3 (0.36)
Town	— (†)	13,700 (424)	13,860 (669)	12,330 (341)	22.0 (0.43)	15.6 (0.48)	15.3 (0.74)	13.7 (0.40)
Rural	— (†)	25,640 (492)	29,170 (1,012)	29,520 (430)	24.7 (0.43)	29.3 (0.55)	32.2 (1.07)	32.9 (0.43)
Private schools								
Total	25,020 (198)	27,690 (677)	27,960 (328)	25,730 (605)	100.0 (†)	100.0 (†)	100.0 (†)	100.0 (†)
Sex								
Male	11,610 (301)	12,110 (552)	13,070 (457)	11,490 (501)	46.4 (1.10)	43.7 (1.43)	46.7 (1.38)	44.6 (1.48)
Female	13,410 (283)	15,580 (491)	14,890 (369)	14,240 (462)	53.6 (1.10)	56.3 (1.43)	53.3 (1.38)	55.4 (1.48)
Race/ethnicity								
White[1]	23,130 (270)	24,850 (715)	24,400 (409)	22,470 (628)	92.5 (0.70)	89.8 (0.88)	87.3 (0.91)	87.3 (1.08)
Black[1]	1,060 (124)	1,440 (155)	1,820 (184)	1,750 (193)	4.2 (0.50)	5.2 (0.57)	6.5 (0.67)	6.8 (0.75)
Hispanic[1]	520 (91)	820 (116)	1,110 (149)	860 (141)	2.1 (0.37)	3.0 (0.41)	4.0 (0.52)	3.3 (0.56)
Asian[1,2]	170 (43)	330 (82)	330 (77)	460 (101)	0.7 (0.17)	1.2 (0.29)	1.2 (0.28)	1.8 (0.38)
Pacific Islander	— (†)	‡ (†)	‡ (†)	‡ (†)	— (†)	‡ (†)	‡ (†)	‡ (†)
American Indian/Alaska Native[1]	130 (37)	160 ! (77)	‡ (†)	‡ (†)	0.5 (0.15)	0.6 ! (0.27)	‡ (†)	‡ (†)
Two or more races	— (†)	60 ! (28)	200 ! (62)	90 ! (45)	— (†)	0.2 ! (0.10)	0.7 ! (0.22)	0.4 ! (0.17)
Age								
Under 40	4,790 (302)	4,420 (267)	4,750 (318)	4,360 (392)	19.2 (1.21)	16.0 (0.94)	17.0 (1.09)	16.9 (1.44)
40 to 44	4,400 (217)	3,040 (250)	3,250 (277)	3,130 (300)	17.6 (0.83)	11.0 (0.85)	11.6 (1.00)	12.2 (1.05)
45 to 49	5,140 (216)	4,020 (250)	3,420 (246)	2,630 (281)	20.6 (0.87)	14.5 (0.82)	12.2 (0.86)	10.2 (1.00)
50 to 54	4,120 (228)	5,820 (337)	4,390 (263)	3,480 (247)	16.5 (0.90)	21.0 (1.00)	15.7 (0.94)	13.5 (0.93)
55 or over	6,550 (043)	10,390 (82)	12,150 (77)	12,120 (101)	26.2 (0.17)	37.5 (0.29)	43.5 (0.28)	47.1 (0.38)
School level								
Elementary	13,350 [4] (244)	16,750 (327)	16,110 (297)	14,510 (505)	59.5 (0.74)	60.5 (1.07)	57.6 (0.81)	56.4 (0.90)
Secondary	2,300 [4] (115)	2,510 (364)	2,930 (168)	2,660 (138)	10.3 (0.52)	9.1 (1.14)	10.5 (0.59)	10.3 (0.57)
Combined	6,770 [4] (174)	8,430 (281)	8,920 (271)	8,570 (210)	30.2 (0.77)	30.4 (0.77)	31.9 (0.88)	33.3 (0.71)
Highest degree earned								
Bachelor's or less	8,590 (337)	9,170 (422)	9,120 (427)	7,990 (570)	34.3 (1.23)	33.1 (1.27)	32.6 (1.37)	31.0 (1.73)
Master's	12,900 (292)	13,720 (458)	14,030 (344)	12,800 (363)	51.6 (1.28)	49.5 (1.20)	50.2 (1.20)	49.7 (1.49)
Education specialist[3]	2,050 (103)	2,950 (183)	2,800 (203)	2,610 (200)	8.2 (0.41)	10.7 (0.61)	10.0 (0.75)	10.1 (0.80)
Doctor's or first professional	1,480 (138)	1,850 (190)	2,010 (177)	2,340 (224)	5.9 (0.54)	6.7 (0.63)	7.2 (0.63)	9.1 (0.87)

See notes at end of table.

Table 212.08. Number and percentage distribution of principals in public and private elementary and secondary schools, by selected characteristics: Selected years, 1993–94 through 2011–12—Continued

[Standard errors appear in parentheses]

Selected characteristic	Number of principals								Percentage distribution of principals							
	1993–94		2003–04		2007–08		2011–12		1993–94		2003–04		2007–08		2011–12	
1	2		3		4		5		6		7		8		9	
Number of years as a principal																
3 or fewer	8,270	(341)	8,990	(395)	9,190	(351)	7,100	(516)	33.1	(1.32)	32.5	(1.23)	32.9	(1.20)	27.6	(1.74)
4 to 9	7,080	(269)	6,830	(283)	7,230	(345)	6,750	(415)	28.3	(1.03)	24.6	(0.95)	25.9	(1.19)	26.2	(1.45)
10 to 19	6,950	(310)	7,260	(381)	6,430	(298)	6,910	(350)	27.8	(1.23)	26.2	(1.03)	23.0	(1.04)	26.8	(1.33)
20 or more	2,710	(189)	4,610	(275)	5,110	(260)	4,970	(318)	10.8	(0.77)	16.7	(0.88)	18.3	(0.91)	19.3	(1.27)
Years of full-time teaching experience prior to becoming a principal																
3 or fewer	6,290	(335)	7,350	(359)	7,850	(381)	6,820	(473)	25.2	(1.27)	26.6	(1.19)	28.1	(1.24)	26.5	(1.48)
4 to 9	6,940	(268)	6,690	(357)	7,030	(287)	6,810	(363)	27.8	(1.05)	24.2	(1.15)	25.1	(1.00)	26.5	(1.36)
10 to 19	9,240	(251)	9,110	(394)	8,510	(306)	7,790	(403)	36.9	(1.03)	32.9	(1.09)	30.4	(1.09)	30.3	(1.50)
20 or more	2,540	(136)	4,530	(275)	4,580	(247)	4,310	(249)	10.1	(0.54)	16.4	(0.83)	16.4	(0.89)	16.7	(0.99)
School locale																
City	—	(†)	9,670	(374)	9,610	(268)	8,590	(267)	—	(†)	34.9	(1.05)	34.4	(0.90)	33.4	(1.28)
Suburban	—	(†)	11,690	(370)	9,510	(229)	8,110	(298)	—	(†)	42.2	(1.14)	34.0	(0.83)	31.5	(1.27)
Town	—	(†)	1,980	(179)	2,780	(205)	2,630	(323)	—	(†)	7.2	(0.59)	10.0	(0.72)	10.2	(1.16)
Rural	—	(†)	4,350	(293)	6,060	(296)	6,390	(510)	—	(†)	15.7	(0.85)	21.7	(0.95)	24.8	(1.57)

—Not available.
†Not applicable.
#Rounds to zero.
!Interpret data with caution. The coefficient of variation (CV) for this estimate is between 30 and 50 percent.
‡Reporting standards not met. Either there are too few cases for a reliable estimate or the coefficient of variation (CV) is 50 percent or greater.
[1]Data for 1993–94 are only roughly comparable to data for later years, because the new category of Two or more races was introduced in 2003–04.
[2]Includes Pacific Islander for 1993–94.
[3]Education specialist degrees or certificates are generally awarded for 1 year's work beyond the master's level. Includes certificate of advanced graduate studies.

[4]Excludes data for 4,930 public and 2,690 private school principals whose school level could not be determined.
NOTE: Data are based on a head count of full-time and part-time principals rather than on the number of full-time-equivalent principals reported in other tables. Detail may not sum to totals because of rounding, missing data, and cell suppression. Race categories exclude persons of Hispanic ethnicity.
SOURCE: U.S. Department of Education, National Center for Education Statistics, Schools and Staffing Survey (SASS), "Public School Principal Data File" and "Private School Principal Data File," 1993–94, 2003–04, 2007–08, and 2011–12. (This table was prepared October 2014.)

Table 212.10. Number, highest degree, average years of experience, and salaries of principals in public and private elementary and secondary schools, by selected characteristics: Selected years, 1993–94 through 2011–12

[Standard errors appear in parentheses]

Selected characteristic	Bachelor's or less	Master's	Education specialist[2]	Doctor's and first-professional	As a principal 1993–94	As a principal 2003–04	As a principal 2007–08	As a principal 2011–12	Teaching experience, 2011–12	Salary 1993–94	Salary 2003–04	Salary 2007–08	Salary 2011–12
1	2	3	4	5	6	7	8	9	10	11	12	13	14
Public schools Total	2.2 (0.30)	61.7 (0.71)	26.2 (0.54)	9.9 (0.49)	8.7 (0.10)	7.8 (0.10)	7.5 (0.14)	7.2 (0.09)	12.2 (0.12)	$88,150 (203)	$95,330 (234)	$95,170 (426)	$93,450 (256)
Sex													
Males	2.2 (0.37)	64.2 (0.95)	24.9 (0.77)	8.7 (0.57)	10.3 (0.16)	9.1 (0.16)	8.2 (0.20)	7.7 (0.12)	11.0 (0.17)	88,260 (257)	95,490 (366)	95,560 (737)	94,190 (451)
Females	2.1 (0.43)	59.4 (1.08)	27.5 (0.93)	11.0 (0.80)	5.6 (0.12)	6.3 (0.13)	6.8 (0.19)	6.6 (0.15)	13.3 (0.20)	87,960 (443)	95,150 (422)	94,780 (692)	92,760 (491)
Race/ethnicity													
White	1.8 (0.29)	62.0 (0.68)	26.9 (0.58)	9.3 (0.46)	9.0 (0.12)	8.0 (0.12)	7.8 (0.17)	7.3 (0.10)	12.4 (0.13)	87,520 (222)	94,800 (279)	94,160 (488)	92,860 (329)
Black	2.8 (0.74)	52.7 (2.67)	29.5 (2.17)	14.9 (1.89)	7.1 (0.21)	6.9 (0.33)	6.2 (0.38)	6.2 (0.30)	11.8 (0.39)	92,670 (730)	97,680 (840)	97,490 (1,438)	95,440 (1,179)
Hispanic	4.9! (1.70)	70.6 (3.73)	15.9 (2.69)	8.5 (2.18)	6.3 (0.37)	6.1 (0.43)	6.5 (0.62)	7.7 (0.42)	10.5 (0.45)	89,770 (1,283)	100,310 (1,728)	103,140 (2,946)	96,720 (1,458)
Asian	‡ (†)	62.8 (10.48)	‡ (†)	‡ (†)	6.0³ (0.60)	6.8 (1.17)	6.3 (0.97)	7.7 (1.13)	10.6 (1.16)	95,530³ (2,290)	104,350 (2,111)	114,810 (7,401)	105,870 (4,399)
Pacific Islander	—	—	—	—	—	—	—	—	—	—	—	—	—
American Indian/Alaska Native	‡ (†)	75.7 (7.38)	13.1! (4.29)	10.9! (3.44)	12.6 (0.67)	6.9 (0.63)	6.4 (1.30)	9.2! (1.67)	13.7‡ (1.92)	82,140 (2,786)	78,290 (2,686)	110,640 (6,762)	83,160 (3,871)
Two or more races	‡ (†)	59.0 (8.49)	30.1 (8.48)	‡ (†)	— (†)	5.6 (1.12)	5.8 (1.50)	7.8 (0.77)	11.3 (0.95)	— (†)	95,710 (4,756)	90,650 (6,244)	94,640 (3,746)
Age													
Under 40	3.0 (0.63)	67.2 (1.67)	21.7 (1.26)	8.2 (0.99)	2.8 (0.13)	2.4 (0.10)	2.9 (0.14)	3.0 (0.10)	7.6 (0.11)	74,790 (760)	86,890 (687)	88,230 (1,005)	88,560 (722)
40 to 44	2.4 (0.60)	62.3 (1.69)	25.0 (1.48)	10.3 (1.30)	5.0 (0.12)	4.5 (0.18)	4.8 (0.22)	4.8 (0.18)	9.8 (0.14)	83,620 (620)	91,300 (836)	92,960 (1,240)	90,960 (670)
45 to 49	1.7 (0.52)	63.4 (2.01)	24.9 (1.54)	9.9 (1.11)	7.1 (0.13)	6.1 (0.16)	6.1 (0.26)	6.5 (0.18)	11.7 (0.23)	89,060 (419)	92,530 (665)	94,180 (1,067)	92,760 (885)
50 to 54	2.8! (0.93)	59.2 (2.13)	28.4 (1.70)	9.6 (1.39)	10.3 (0.18)	8.7 (0.19)	8.2 (0.28)	8.1 (0.24)	14.8 (0.27)	90,890 (586)	97,290 (551)	96,400 (1,023)	94,550 (920)
55 or over	1.3 (0.29)	57.7 (1.32)	30.0 (1.15)	11.0 (0.82)	15.1 (0.35)	11.9 (0.23)	11.8 (0.29)	11.8 (0.22)	16.0 (0.26)	92,920 (795)	101,120 (601)	100,120 (1,036)	98,620 (624)
School level													
Elementary	1.7 (0.30)	62.6 (0.93)	26.4 (0.72)	9.3 (0.68)	8.9 (0.14)	7.9 (0.13)	7.7 (0.17)	7.2 (0.15)	12.4 (0.16)	87,040 (271)	95,200 (284)	94,600 (543)	92,490 (312)
Secondary	2.2 (0.44)	59.6 (1.14)	26.2 (1.07)	12.0 (0.78)	8.0 (0.12)	7.5 (0.19)	7.1 (0.19)	7.1 (0.29)	11.5 (0.14)	90,950 (269)	100,210 (558)	100,180 (780)	99,440 (631)
Combined	5.5 (1.45)	60.3 (2.26)	25.4 (2.09)	8.9 (1.45)	7.5 (0.29)	7.4 (0.36)	7.1 (0.43)	7.1 (0.51)	12.2 (0.51)	84,890 (820)	81,640 (777)	84,090 (1,374)	85,630 (1,385)
School locale													
City	3.6 (0.76)	59.4 (1.76)	24.7 (1.42)	12.3 (1.15)	— (†)	7.3 (0.17)	7.0 (0.25)	6.8 (0.21)	12.0 (0.24)	— (†)	101,260 (475)	101,220 (825)	98,990 (584)
Suburban	1.2 (0.27)	59.6 (1.42)	26.9 (1.15)	12.9 (0.99)	— (†)	7.9 (0.23)	7.8 (0.28)	7.3 (0.21)	11.6 (0.21)	— (†)	107,800 (597)	107,570 (1,025)	104,910 (475)
Town	2.5! (0.79)	61.4 (1.94)	29.1 (1.74)	7.0 (0.81)	— (†)	8.1 (0.28)	7.8 (0.34)	7.5 (0.30)	12.5 (0.30)	— (†)	87,050 (635)	86,040 (789)	85,580 (572)
Rural	1.7 (0.33)	65.9 (0.99)	25.8 (0.91)	6.6 (0.66)	— (†)	7.9 (0.22)	7.5 (0.27)	7.3 (0.15)	12.7 (0.20)	— (†)	82,050 (444)	84,020 (729)	82,830 (370)
Private schools Total	31.0 (1.73)	49.7 (1.49)	10.1 (0.80)	9.1 (0.87)	8.8 (0.20)	10.0 (0.24)	10.0 (0.22)	10.8 (0.31)	13.9 (0.38)	$51,540 (584)	$63,360 (771)	$63,790 (889)	$67,400 (1,200)
Sex													
Males	32.7 (2.87)	45.9 (2.41)	8.8 (1.24)	12.6 (1.62)	9.0 (0.26)	11.0 (0.35)	10.6 (0.37)	11.4 (0.43)	12.7 (0.62)	57,200 (907)	69,940 (1,266)	69,880 (1,498)	76,310 (2,553)
Females	29.7 (1.93)	52.9 (1.84)	11.2 (1.10)	6.2 (0.81)	8.6 (0.27)	9.2 (0.28)	9.5 (0.26)	10.4 (0.41)	14.8 (0.43)	46,900 (976)	58,410 (1,064)	58,820 (1,068)	61,020 (1,299)
Race/ethnicity													
White	31.5 (1.81)	49.2 (1.61)	10.0 (0.79)	9.2 (0.94)	8.7 (0.22)	10.3 (0.24)	10.4 (0.25)	10.9 (0.31)	13.9 (0.42)	51,370 (644)	63,880 (762)	65,160 (974)	68,470 (1,380)
Black	24.0 (5.62)	50.5 (5.71)	12.4 (3.67)	13.0! (4.43)	8.3 (1.04)	7.1 (1.08)	7.1 (0.87)	11.3 (1.12)	14.9 (1.23)	55,250 (3,979)	55,950 (4,370)	54,820 (2,385)	60,260 (4,900)
Hispanic	41.1 (7.82)	43.1 (6.95)	10.7! (5.11)	‡ (†)	10.1 (1.43)	6.6 (1.29)	7.8 (0.93)	9.2 (0.93)	11.7 (1.34)	50,380 (3,146)	50,620 (4,974)	53,450 (3,657)	64,000 (6,195)
Age													
Under 40	53.7 (4.95)	36.4 (4.27)	4.8! (1.59)	5.1 (1.23)	3.5 (0.22)	2.9 (0.20)	3.0 (0.22)	3.3 (0.36)	6.4 (0.45)	42,280 (1,396)	51,680 (1,997)	51,800 (1,536)	50,600 (1,898)
40 to 44	35.4 (6.03)	47.0 (5.24)	10.6 (2.46)	‡ (†)	5.3 (0.24)	5.4 (0.38)	5.3 (0.35)	5.9 (0.56)	9.8 (0.82)	48,990 (1,492)	55,090 (2,171)	59,940 (2,969)	69,410 (7,319)
45 to 49	35.3 (5.89)	47.3 (4.78)	9.9 (2.36)	7.5 (2.32)	8.3 (0.27)	7.6 (0.38)	6.2 (0.38)	6.6 (0.50)	11.7 (1.08)	55,670 (1,183)	65,220 (1,852)	60,210 (2,286)	68,560 (3,876)
50 to 54	27.3 (3.71)	54.2 (3.78)	7.6 (1.88)	10.9! (3.33)	9.6 (0.34)	10.1 (0.45)	9.0 (0.45)	6.7 (0.59)	14.1 (0.75)	60,630 (1,605)	66,250 (1,979)	60,860 (2,029)	70,860 (3,769)
55 or over	21.9 (1.80)	54.5 (1.71)	12.7 (1.20)	10.9 (1.22)	14.8 (0.40)	15.2 (0.40)	15.4 (0.43)	16.1 (0.44)	18.0 (0.50)	51,070 (1,216)	68,180 (1,400)	69,770 (1,591)	70,790 (1,958)
School level													
Elementary	34.8 (2.23)	50.3 (1.92)	9.2 (1.06)	5.7 (0.80)	9.4 (0.27)	9.9 (0.30)	9.9 (0.30)	10.6 (0.39)	13.4 (0.47)	46,250 (714)	59,660 (850)	61,550 (1,076)	62,410 (1,199)
Secondary	9.1 (2.23)	57.1 (4.60)	15.4 (2.71)	18.3 (4.83)	7.8 (0.36)	9.3 (0.77)	9.9 (0.58)	11.0 (0.89)	15.4 (1.04)	70,200 (1,260)	82,080 (3,274)	83,350 (2,633)	87,630 (7,162)
Combined	31.5 (2.43)	46.6 (2.33)	10.0 (1.65)	11.9 (1.42)	8.0 (0.34)	10.3 (0.39)	10.2 (0.44)	11.2 (0.57)	14.2 (0.62)	54,050 (1,784)	65,120 (1,914)	61,100 (1,641)	69,090 (2,369)
School locale													
City	20.9 (2.16)	56.7 (2.60)	10.1 (1.39)	12.3 (2.05)	— (†)	— (†)	10.8 (0.36)	11.0 (0.53)	15.0 (0.58)	— (†)	— (†)	72,060 (1,437)	74,810 (2,160)
Suburban	26.3 (2.27)	52.4 (2.20)	11.1 (1.34)	10.2 (1.94)	— (†)	— (†)	10.5 (0.36)	11.8 (0.49)	14.8 (0.48)	— (†)	— (†)	68,350 (1,579)	70,260 (2,527)
Town	38.2 (5.31)	47.6 (5.43)	9.5! (3.17)	4.8! (2.19)	— (†)	— (†)	9.4 (0.80)	14.3 (1.00)	14.3 (1.01)	— (†)	— (†)	49,130 (2,386)	46,560 (2,367)
Rural	47.7 (3.97)	37.8 (3.29)	9.3 (1.77)	5.1 (1.18)	— (†)	— (†)	8.1 (0.53)	9.7 (0.76)	10.9 (0.93)	— (†)	— (†)	47,570 (1,822)	59,860 (2,801)

—Not available.
†Not applicable.
!Interpret data with caution. The coefficient of variation (CV) for this estimate is between 30 and 50 percent.
‡Reporting standards not met (too few cases for a reliable estimate).
[1]Constant dollars based on the Consumer Price Index, prepared by the Bureau of Labor Statistics, U.S. Department of Labor, adjusted to a school-year basis. Excludes principals reporting a salary of $0.
[2]Education specialist degrees or certificates are generally awarded for 1 year's work beyond the master's level. Includes certificate of advanced graduate studies.
[3]Data include Pacific Islanders.
NOTE: Race categories exclude persons of Hispanic ethnicity. Detail may not sum to totals because of rounding and survey item nonresponse.
SOURCE: U.S. Department of Education, National Center for Education Statistics, Schools and Staffing Survey (SASS), "Public School Principal Data File" and "Private School Principal Data File," 2003–04, 2007–08, and 2011–12. (This table was prepared January 2015.)

Table 212.20. Mobility of public elementary and secondary principals, by selected principal and school characteristics: 2007–08 to 2008–09 and 2011–12 to 2012–13

[Standard errors appear in parentheses]

Percent of public school principals

Selected principal or school characteristic	2007–08 to 2008–09 Remained in same school	Moved to another school — Total moving to another school[2]	Moved to another school — Public school in same school district	Moved to another school — Public school in different district	Stopped working as a principal — Working at a different type of job	Stopped working as a principal — Other[1]	2011–12 to 2012–13 Remained in same school	Moved to another school — Total moving to another school[2]	Moved to another school — Public school in same school district	Moved to another school — Public school in different district	Stopped working as a principal — Working at a different type of job	Stopped working as a principal — Other[1]
1	2	3	4	5	6	7	8	9	10	11	12	13
Total	79.5 (1.85)	6.9 (1.25)	4.3 (0.99)	2.5! (0.77)	11.9 (1.35)	1.8! (0.64)	77.4 (1.23)	7.0 (0.92)	4.4 (0.79)	2.4 (0.47)	11.5 (1.00)	4.1 (0.72)
Sex												
Male	77.6 (2.57)	7.5! (1.69)	4.0! (1.38)	3.3! (1.00)	13.0 (2.10)	† (†)	77.1 (1.73)	7.0 (1.15)	3.8 (0.82)	3.1! (0.81)	11.6 (1.57)	4.3 (0.81)
Female	81.3 (2.55)	6.4 (1.71)	4.6! (1.39)	† (†)	10.8 (0.96)	† (†)	77.8 (2.01)	6.9 (1.33)	5.1 (1.33)	1.8! (0.55)	11.4 (1.48)	4.0 (1.08)
Race/ethnicity												
White	80.1 (2.14)	6.8! (1.37)	4.1 (0.98)	2.6! (0.87)	11.9 (1.60)	1.3! (0.55)	78.6 (1.15)	6.4 (0.92)	4.0 (0.76)	2.4 (0.50)	11.7 (1.05)	3.3 (0.68)
Black	77.4 (5.57)	‡ (†)	‡ (†)	‡ (†)	11.3! (4.32)	‡ (†)	72.2 (5.08)	9.7! (3.22)	6.6! (2.69)	‡ (†)	10.4! (3.30)	7.7! (3.10)
Hispanic	79.1 (8.27)	‡ (†)	‡ (†)	‡ (†)	‡ (†)	‡ (†)	73.6 (8.19)	‡ (†)	‡ (†)	‡ (†)	‡ (†)	‡ (†)
Age												
Under 40	81.6 (4.40)	9.5! (3.27)	5.2! (2.47)	‡ (†)	7.1 (2.78)	‡ (†)	81.1 (3.44)	7.5 (2.01)	3.7 (1.51)	3.8! (1.25)	7.9! (2.70)	3.5! (1.60)
40 to 44	83.7 (4.27)	7.5! (2.58)	4.6! (2.18)	2.9! (1.42)	6.9 (2.85)	‡ (†)	77.3 (3.75)	9.6 (2.60)	6.2! (2.21)	3.3! (1.41)	8.0 (2.29)	5.0! (2.28)
45 to 49	83.0 (4.64)	6.8! (3.23)	‡ (†)	‡ (†)	8.3! (3.43)	‡ (†)	82.8 (2.91)	7.4 (2.02)	5.2! (1.87)	2.0! (0.81)	6.9 (1.81)	‡ (†)
50 to 54	80.7 (3.38)	6.6! (2.49)	‡ (†)	‡ (†)	10.5 (2.82)	‡ (†)	80.4 (3.01)	6.8! (2.26)	5.0! (2.20)	‡ (†)	9.8 (2.06)	3.0! (1.33)
55 or over	73.7 (3.94)	5.3! (2.33)	3.1! (1.46)	‡ (†)	19.7 (3.35)	‡ (†)	69.7 (3.06)	4.5 (1.30)	2.9! (1.16)	1.4! (0.68)	20.5 (2.60)	5.4 (1.50)
Years of experience as a principal at any school												
Less than 3	81.3 (3.41)	8.5! (2.56)	5.4! (1.91)	3.0! (1.48)	8.0 (2.30)	‡ (†)	80.8 (2.30)	6.6 (1.34)	4.0! (1.29)	2.5! (0.70)	8.3 (1.68)	4.2! (1.43)
3 to 5	81.1 (5.55)	‡ (†)	‡ (†)	2.3! (1.07)	9.8! (3.91)	‡ (†)	76.9 (3.88)	8.8! (2.65)	4.9! (1.99)	3.8! (1.78)	10.2 (2.39)	4.1! (1.79)
6 to 9	82.1 (3.88)	5.7! (1.89)	3.3! (1.50)	‡ (†)	10.8 (3.01)	‡ (†)	77.1 (2.81)	7.5! (1.96)	5.2! (1.90)	2.2! (0.85)	11.4 (1.85)	4.0! (1.31)
10 or more	74.5 (3.68)	5.6! (1.94)	3.3! (1.59)	‡ (†)	18.2 (3.11)	‡ (†)	74.0 (2.67)	5.8 (1.62)	4.1! (1.47)	1.6! (0.62)	16.1 (2.44)	4.2! (1.44)
School level												
Elementary	80.4 (2.58)	7.0 (1.66)	4.5 (1.25)	2.4! (1.00)	11.0 (1.90)	1.5! (0.71)	77.9 (1.64)	7.1 (1.22)	5.0 (1.08)	2.0 (0.49)	10.9 (1.30)	4.1 (1.02)
Secondary	78.6 (2.62)	6.3! (1.98)	‡ (†)	2.7! (1.18)	13.1 (2.81)	‡ (†)	77.1 (2.32)	6.3 (1.34)	3.1! (1.04)	3.1 (0.92)	12.8 (1.77)	3.8 (1.04)
Combined	73.4 (5.74)	7.5! (3.13)	‡ (†)	‡ (†)	15.9! (5.15)	‡ (†)	74.7 (3.91)	7.2! (2.42)	3.4 (1.34)	‡ (†)	12.8 (2.73)	5.2! (1.87)
School size												
Less than 150	75.8 (6.40)	‡ (†)	‡ (†)	‡ (†)	12.6! (4.66)	‡ (†)	76.1 (4.43)	6.5 (1.91)	5.7! (2.10)	3.6! (1.60)	11.9! (3.56)	5.5! (1.98)
150 to 349	80.2 (4.27)	7.0! (2.60)	4.4! (1.99)	‡ (†)	11.0 (3.15)	‡ (†)	74.8 (3.31)	8.6 (2.20)	4.4! (1.63)	2.8! (0.93)	11.3 (2.45)	5.3! (1.98)
350 to 499	77.0 (4.78)	7.6! (3.22)	‡ (†)	‡ (†)	13.4 (3.59)	‡ (†)	78.0 (3.24)	6.6 (1.88)	4.4! (1.59)	2.1! (0.82)	11.4 (2.21)	4.1! (1.76)
500 to 749	82.2 (4.38)	5.8! (2.45)	3.4! (1.66)	‡ (†)	10.9 (3.22)	‡ (†)	78.1 (3.26)	7.4 (2.13)	4.8! (1.59)	‡ (†)	10.7 (2.20)	3.8! (1.53)
750 or more	80.5 (3.27)	6.3! (2.10)	4.2! (1.89)	1.8! (0.84)	12.0 (2.53)	‡ (†)	79.6 (2.40)	5.3 (1.56)	3.5! (1.28)	1.6! (0.80)	12.4 (1.87)	2.6! (0.92)
Percent of students who are Black, Hispanic, Asian, Pacific Islander, American Indian/Alaska Native, or Two or more races												
Less than 5 percent	81.3 (4.15)	5.8! (2.79)	‡ (†)	‡ (†)	12.2 (3.20)	‡ (†)	80.0 (3.65)	4.4 (1.03)	‡ (†)	3.3 (0.92)	12.0 (2.94)	‡ (†)
5 to 19 percent	80.4 (4.44)	7.1! (3.41)	‡ (†)	‡ (†)	11.3 (2.59)	‡ (†)	79.5 (2.45)	5.9 (1.52)	3.6! (1.27)	2.2! (0.89)	11.7 (2.18)	2.9! (1.14)
20 to 49 percent	82.8 (3.41)	5.5! (1.80)	3.8! (1.53)	‡ (†)	10.7 (2.77)	‡ (†)	79.4 (2.57)	6.9 (1.55)	4.5! (1.37)	2.2! (0.89)	10.8 (1.94)	2.9! (1.14)
50 percent or more	75.9 (3.13)	8.3 (2.20)	6.0! (1.97)	2.1! (0.98)	12.9 (2.56)	3.0! (1.42)	74.3 (2.44)	8.3 (1.82)	5.8 (1.64)	2.4! (0.80)	11.6 (1.76)	5.8 (1.39)
Percent of students approved for free or reduced-price lunch												
0 to 25.0 percent	81.9 (3.34)	6.1! (2.03)	‡ (†)	2.8! (1.34)	11.1 (2.83)	‡ (†)	79.2 (2.77)	6.4! (2.07)	4.4! (1.80)	1.7! (0.83)	11.4 (2.28)	‡ (†)
25.1 to 50.0 percent	81.8 (3.25)	6.8! (2.34)	4.1! (1.64)	‡ (†)	10.3 (2.14)	‡ (†)	79.8 (2.35)	5.4 (1.54)	3.2! (1.02)	2.1! (0.90)	11.7 (1.86)	3.1! (1.13)
50.1 to 75.0 percent	80.4 (3.92)	6.1! (1.93)	4.1 (1.55)	‡ (†)	12.2 (3.53)	‡ (†)	78.4 (2.80)	7.1 (1.62)	4.3! (1.43)	2.9! (0.98)	10.4 (2.02)	4.0! (1.53)
More than 75.0 percent	74.0 (4.56)	9.1! (3.29)	7.1 (3.11)	‡ (†)	13.4 (3.90)	‡ (†)	72.5 (2.89)	9.3 (2.29)	6.2! (2.06)	2.9! (0.94)	11.9 (2.52)	4.0! (1.53)
Locale												
City	78.3 (4.25)	7.6! (2.71)	5.6! (2.41)	‡ (†)	11.4 (2.98)	‡ (†)	74.4 (3.35)	8.5 (2.50)	6.7! (2.28)	1.8! (0.75)	11.8 (2.72)	5.3 (1.51)
Suburban	82.0 (3.21)	5.5! (1.78)	3.7! (1.51)	‡ (†)	10.8 (2.61)	‡ (†)	78.3 (2.39)	7.0 (1.77)	4.5! (1.52)	2.3! (0.95)	10.9 (1.89)	3.8 (1.58)
Town	77.9 (4.88)	6.5! (2.70)	‡ (†)	‡ (†)	14.0! (4.59)	‡ (†)	79.5 (3.65)	6.3! (2.08)	4.1! (1.64)	‡ (†)	10.3 (2.19)	3.8 (1.80)
Rural	78.8 (3.17)	7.9! (2.45)	4.0! (1.69)	3.9! (1.76)	12.3 (2.30)	‡ (†)	78.3 (1.77)	5.9 (1.11)	2.8 (0.73)	3.1 (0.78)	12.2 (1.46)	3.6! (1.18)

†Not applicable.
!Interpret data with caution. The coefficient of variation (CV) for this estimate is between 30 and 50 percent.
‡Reporting standards not met. Either there are too few cases for a reliable estimate or the coefficient of variation (CV) is 50 percent or greater.
[1]Includes retired, on leave (e.g., maternity/paternity or disability), deceased, and "other."
[2]Includes principals who moved from a public school to a private school, a category that is not shown separately.

NOTE: Race categories exclude persons of Hispanic ethnicity. Totals include other racial/ethnic groups not separately shown. Detail may not sum to totals because of rounding.
SOURCE: U.S. Department of Education, National Center for Education Statistics, Schools and Staffing Survey (SASS), "Public School Principal Data File," 2007–08 and 2011–12; and Principal Follow-up Survey (PFS), "Public School Principal Status Data File," 2008–09 and 2012–13. (This table was prepared January 2015.)

Table 212.30. Number and percentage distribution of public and private school principals who left the profession during the past year, by total years of experience as a principal and occupational status: 2012–13

[Standard errors appear in parentheses]

Occupational status	Total Number		Percent		Less than 3 years		3 to 5 years		6 to 9 years		10 or more years	
1	2		3		4		5		6		7	
All school principal leavers................	13,160	(1,041)	100.0	(†)	18.3	(4.39)	22.2	(4.19)	20.3	(3.63)	39.2	(3.79)
Public school principal leavers................	10,270	(875)	100.0	(†)	16.3	(4.23)	22.2	(4.36)	23.0	(4.30)	38.6	(4.54)
Private school principal leavers	2,880	(592)	100.0	(†)	25.3 !	(10.18)	22.3 !	(8.66)	‡	(†)	41.4	(10.35)
	Principals who left public schools											
All public school principal leavers...............	10,270	(875)	100.0	(†)	100.0	(†)	100.0	(†)	100.0	(†)	100.0	(†)
Retired, not working outside of home................	3,860	(533)	37.6	(3.96)	15.5 !	(7.53)	22.1 !	(9.48)	35.3	(8.14)	57.1	(7.01)
Deceased....................................	‡	(†)	‡	(†)	‡	(†)	‡	(†)	‡	(†)	‡	(†)
On leave (e.g., maternity/paternity or disability)	‡	(†)	‡	(†)	‡	(†)	‡	(†)	‡	(†)	‡	(†)
Working in a kindergarten through grade 12 school, but not as a principal ...	2,530	(440)	24.6	(3.89)	49.5	(11.42)	31.0 !	(9.72)	24.8 !	(9.95)	10.3 !	(3.99)
Working in current school, but not as a principal	890 !	(293)	8.6 !	(2.86)	21.7 !	(9.98)	‡	(†)	‡	(†)	‡	(†)
Working in a different public school, but not as a principal	1,440	(352)	14.0	(3.21)	‡	(†)	23.7 !	(9.08)	‡	(†)	5.9 !	(2.88)
Working in a private school, but not as a principal	‡	(†)	‡	(†)	‡	(†)	‡	(†)	‡	(†)	‡	(†)
Working in a different (not identified) school, but not as a principal.........	‡	(†)	‡	(†)	‡	(†)	‡	(†)	‡	(†)	‡	(†)
Working in kindergarten through grade 12 education, but not in a school....	3,070	(538)	29.9	(4.44)	24.9 !	(9.97)	37.5 !	(11.37)	33.6	(8.28)	25.3	(7.06)
Working in a district or administrative office as a superintendent, assistant superintendent, or other higher level administrator	1,900	(424)	18.5	(3.95)	‡	(†)	20.3 !	(8.18)	24.9 !	(7.87)	16.2 !	(6.05)
Working in a district or administrative office, in a position other than that of a superintendent, assistant superintendent, or other higher level administrator	820 !	(315)	8.0 !	(2.87)	‡	(†)	‡	(†)	8.1 !	(3.84)	5.7 !	(2.45)
Working at a job associated with kindergarten through grade 12 education, but not directly associated with any schools or school systems	‡	(†)	‡	(†)	‡	(†)	‡	(†)	‡	(†)	‡	(†)
Position unknown	‡	(†)	‡	(†)	‡	(†)	‡	(†)	‡	(†)	‡	(†)
Working at a job outside of kindergarten through grade 12 education	710 !	(287)	6.9 !	(2.75)	‡	(†)	‡	(†)	‡	(†)	‡	(†)
Other.................................	‡	(†)	‡	(†)	‡	(†)	‡	(†)	‡	(†)	‡	(†)
	Principals who left private schools											
All private school principal leavers...............	2,880	(592)	100.0	(†)	100.0	(†)	100.0	(†)	100.0	(†)	100.0	(†)
Retired, not working outside of home................	860 !	(264)	29.9 !	(9.06)	‡	(†)	‡	(†)	‡	(†)	43.3 !	(15.36)
Deceased....................................	‡	(†)	‡	(†)	‡	(†)	‡	(†)	‡	(†)	‡	(†)
On leave (e.g., maternity/paternity or disability)	‡	(†)	‡	(†)	‡	(†)	‡	(†)	‡	(†)	‡	(†)
Working in a kindergarten through grade 12 school, but not as a principal ...	1,100 !	(399)	38.2	(10.26)	60.3 !	(20.13)	‡	(†)	‡	(†)	30.0 !	(13.57)
Working in current school, but not as a principal	660 !	(281)	23.0 !	(7.77)	‡	(†)	‡	(†)	‡	(†)	‡	(†)
Working in a different public school, but not as a principal	‡	(†)	‡	(†)	‡	(†)	‡	(†)	‡	(†)	‡	(†)
Working in a private school, but not as a principal	‡	(†)	‡	(†)	‡	(†)	‡	(†)	‡	(†)	‡	(†)
Working in a different (not identified) school, but not as a principal.........	‡	(†)	‡	(†)	‡	(†)	‡	(†)	‡	(†)	‡	(†)
Working in kindergarten through grade 12 education, but not in a school....	‡	(†)	‡	(†)	‡	(†)	‡	(†)	‡	(†)	‡	(†)
Working in a district or administrative office as a superintendent, assistant superintendent, or other higher level administrator	‡	(†)	‡	(†)	‡	(†)	‡	(†)	‡	(†)	‡	(†)
Working in a district or administrative office, in a position other than that of a superintendent, assistant superintendent, or other higher level administrator	‡	(†)	‡	(†)	‡	(†)	‡	(†)	‡	(†)	‡	(†)
Working at a job associated with kindergarten through grade 12 education, but not directly associated with any schools or school systems	‡	(†)	‡	(†)	‡	(†)	‡	(†)	‡	(†)	‡	(†)
Position unknown	‡	(†)	‡	(†)	‡	(†)	‡	(†)	‡	(†)	‡	(†)
Working at a job outside of kindergarten through grade 12 education	‡	(†)	20.3 !	(8.98)	‡	(†)	‡	(†)	‡	(†)	‡	(†)
Other.................................	‡	(†)	‡	(†)	‡	(†)	‡	(†)	‡	(†)	‡	(†)

†Not applicable.
!Interpret data with caution. The coefficient of variation (CV) for this estimate is between 30 and 50 percent.
‡Reporting standards not met. Either there are too few cases for a reliable estimate or the coefficient of variation (CV) is 50 percent or greater.
NOTE: Detail may not sum to totals because of rounding.

SOURCE: U.S. Department of Education, National Center for Education Statistics, Schools and Staffing Survey (SASS), "Public School Principal Data File" and "Private School Principal Data File," 2011–12; and Principal Follow-up Survey (PFS), "Public School Principal Status Data File" and "Private School Principal Status Data File," 2012–13. (This table was prepared November 2014.)

Table 213.10. Staff employed in public elementary and secondary school systems, by type of assignment: Selected years, 1949–50 through fall 2012

[In full-time equivalents]

School year	Total	School district administrative staff			Instructional staff						Support staff[1]
		Total	Officials and administrators	Instruction coordinators	Total	Principals and assistant principals	Teachers	Instructional aides	Librarians	Guidance counselors	
1	2	3	4	5	6	7	8	9	10	11	12
					Number						
1949–50[2]	1,300,031	33,642	23,868	9,774	956,808	43,137	913,671	(3)	(3)	(3)	309,582
1959–60[2]	2,089,283	42,423	28,648	13,775	1,448,931	63,554	1,353,372	(3)	17,363	14,643	597,929
1969–70[2]	3,360,763	65,282	33,745	31,537	2,255,707	90,593	2,016,244	57,418	42,689	48,763	1,039,774
Fall 1980[2]	4,168,286	78,784	58,230	20,554	2,729,023	107,061	2,184,216	325,755	48,018	63,973	1,360,479
Fall 1990	4,494,076	75,868	—	—	3,051,404	127,417	2,398,169	395,959	49,909	79,950	1,366,804
Fall 1996	5,091,205	81,975	48,480	33,495	3,447,580	123,734	2,667,419	516,356	51,464	88,607	1,561,650
Fall 1997	5,266,415	85,267	50,432	34,835	3,572,955	126,129	2,746,157	557,453	52,142	91,074	1,608,193
Fall 1998	5,419,181	88,939	52,975	35,964	3,693,630	129,317	2,830,286	588,108	52,805	93,114	1,636,612
Fall 1999	5,632,004	94,134	55,467	38,667	3,819,057	137,199	2,910,633	621,942	53,659	95,624	1,718,813
Fall 2000	5,709,753	97,270	57,837	39,433	3,876,628	141,792	2,941,461	641,392	54,246	97,737	1,735,855
Fall 2001	5,904,195	109,526	63,517	46,009	3,989,211	160,543	2,999,528	674,741	54,350	100,049	1,805,458
Fall 2002	5,954,661	110,777	62,781	47,996	4,016,963	164,171	3,034,123	663,552	54,205	100,912	1,826,921
Fall 2003	5,953,667	107,483	63,418	44,065	4,052,739	165,233	3,048,652	685,118	54,349	99,387	1,793,445
Fall 2004	6,058,174	111,832	64,101	47,731	4,120,063	165,657	3,090,925	707,514	54,145	101,822	1,826,279
Fall 2005	6,130,686	121,164	62,464	58,700	4,151,236	156,454	3,143,003	693,792	54,057	103,930	1,858,286
Fall 2006	6,153,735	118,707	53,722	64,985	4,186,968	153,673	3,166,391	709,715	54,444	102,745	1,848,060
Fall 2007	6,232,911	130,044	59,361	70,683	4,235,238	157,539	3,199,995	717,806	54,386	105,512	1,867,629
Fall 2008	6,326,702	135,706	62,153	73,553	4,277,674	159,897	3,222,154	734,010	53,805	107,808	1,913,322
Fall 2009	6,351,157	138,471	63,969	74,502	4,279,488	168,450	3,209,672	741,337	52,545	107,484	1,933,198
Fall 2010	6,195,207	133,833	64,597	69,236	4,151,225	165,047	3,099,095	731,705	50,300	105,079	1,910,150
Fall 2011	6,138,890	130,595	62,884	67,711	4,133,767	166,416	3,103,263	710,335	48,402	105,351	1,874,528
Fall 2012	6,181,238	136,387	65,420	70,967	4,158,000	169,240	3,109,101	729,756	46,685	103,218	1,886,851
					Percentage distribution						
1949–50[2]	100.0	2.6	1.8	0.8	73.6	3.3	70.3	(3)	(3)	(3)	23.8
1959–60[2]	100.0	2.0	1.4	0.7	69.4	3.0	64.8	(3)	0.8	0.7	28.6
1969–70[2]	100.0	1.9	1.0	0.9	67.1	2.7	60.0	1.7	1.3	1.5	30.9
Fall 1980[2]	100.0	1.9	1.4	0.5	65.5	2.6	52.4	7.8	1.2	1.5	32.6
Fall 1990	100.0	1.7	—	—	67.9	2.8	53.4	8.8	1.1	1.8	30.4
Fall 1996	100.0	1.6	1.0	0.7	67.7	2.4	52.4	10.1	1.0	1.7	30.7
Fall 1997	100.0	1.6	1.0	0.7	67.8	2.4	52.1	10.6	1.0	1.7	30.5
Fall 1998	100.0	1.6	1.0	0.7	68.2	2.4	52.2	10.9	1.0	1.7	30.2
Fall 1999	100.0	1.7	1.0	0.7	67.8	2.4	51.7	11.0	1.0	1.7	30.5
Fall 2000	100.0	1.7	1.0	0.7	67.9	2.5	51.5	11.2	1.0	1.7	30.4
Fall 2001	100.0	1.9	1.1	0.8	67.6	2.7	50.8	11.4	0.9	1.7	30.6
Fall 2002	100.0	1.9	1.1	0.8	67.5	2.8	51.0	11.1	0.9	1.7	30.7
Fall 2003	100.0	1.8	1.1	0.7	68.1	2.8	51.2	11.5	0.9	1.7	30.1
Fall 2004	100.0	1.8	1.1	0.8	68.0	2.7	51.0	11.7	0.9	1.7	30.1
Fall 2005	100.0	2.0	1.0	1.0	67.7	2.6	51.3	11.3	0.9	1.7	30.3
Fall 2006	100.0	1.9	0.9	1.1	68.0	2.5	51.5	11.5	0.9	1.7	30.0
Fall 2007	100.0	2.1	1.0	1.1	67.9	2.5	51.3	11.5	0.9	1.7	30.0
Fall 2008	100.0	2.1	1.0	1.2	67.6	2.5	50.9	11.6	0.9	1.7	30.2
Fall 2009	100.0	2.2	1.0	1.2	67.4	2.7	50.5	11.7	0.8	1.7	30.4
Fall 2010	100.0	2.2	1.0	1.1	67.0	2.7	50.0	11.8	0.8	1.7	30.8
Fall 2011	100.0	2.1	1.0	1.1	67.3	2.7	50.6	11.6	0.8	1.7	30.5
Fall 2012	100.0	2.2	1.1	1.1	67.3	2.7	50.3	11.8	0.8	1.7	30.5
					Pupils per staff member						
1949–50[2]	19.3	746.4	1,052.1	2,569.2	26.2	582.1	27.5	(3)	(3)	(3)	81.1
1959–60[2]	16.8	829.3	1,228.1	2,554.1	24.3	553.6	26.0	(3)	2,026.3	2,402.7	58.8
1969–70[2]	13.6	697.7	1,349.8	1,444.3	20.2	502.8	22.6	793.3	1,067.0	934.1	43.8
Fall 1980[2]	9.8	518.9	702.0	1,988.8	15.0	381.8	18.7	125.5	851.3	639.0	30.0
Fall 1990	9.2	543.3	—	—	13.5	323.5	17.2	104.1	825.8	515.5	30.2
Fall 1996	9.0	556.4	940.8	1,361.7	13.2	368.6	17.1	88.3	886.3	514.8	29.2
Fall 1997	8.8	541.0	914.6	1,324.2	12.9	365.7	16.8	82.7	884.6	506.5	28.7
Fall 1998	8.6	523.3	878.5	1,294.0	12.6	359.9	16.4	79.1	881.3	499.8	28.4
Fall 1999	8.3	497.8	844.8	1,211.8	12.3	341.5	16.1	75.3	873.2	490.0	27.3
Fall 2000	8.3	485.3	816.1	1,197.1	12.2	332.9	16.0	73.6	870.2	483.0	27.2
Fall 2001	8.1	435.3	750.5	1,036.1	12.0	296.9	15.9	70.7	877.1	476.5	26.4
Fall 2002	8.1	435.0	767.5	1,003.9	12.0	293.5	15.9	72.6	888.9	477.5	26.4
Fall 2003	8.2	451.6	765.4	1,101.6	12.0	293.8	15.9	70.8	893.1	488.4	27.1
Fall 2004	8.1	436.3	761.2	1,022.3	11.8	294.6	15.8	69.0	901.2	479.2	26.7
Fall 2005	8.0	405.3	786.3	836.7	11.8	313.9	15.6	70.8	908.5	472.6	26.4
Fall 2006	8.0	415.4	918.0	758.9	11.8	320.9	15.6	69.5	905.8	480.0	26.7
Fall 2007	7.9	379.0	830.4	697.3	11.6	312.9	15.4	68.7	906.3	467.2	26.4
Fall 2008	7.8	363.0	792.6	669.8	11.5	308.1	15.3	67.1	915.6	457.0	25.7
Fall 2009	7.8	356.5	771.6	662.5	11.5	293.0	15.4	66.6	939.4	459.2	25.5
Fall 2010	8.0	369.7	766.0	714.7	11.9	299.8	16.0	67.6	983.8	470.9	25.9
Fall 2011	8.1	379.2	787.5	731.4	12.0	297.6	16.0	69.7	1,023.1	470.1	26.4
Fall 2012	8.1	364.9	760.8	701.3	12.0	294.1	16.0	68.2	1,066.1	482.2	26.4

—Not available.
[1]Includes school district administrative support staff, school and library support staff, student support staff, and other support services staff.
[2]Because of classification revisions, categories other than teachers, principals, librarians, and guidance counselors are only roughly comparable to figures for years after 1980.
[3]Data included in column 8.

NOTE: Data for 1949–50 through 1969–70 are cumulative for the entire school year, rather than counts as of the fall of the year. Detail may not sum to totals because of rounding.
SOURCE: U.S. Department of Education, National Center for Education Statistics, *Statistics of State School Systems*, various years; *Statistics of Public Elementary and Secondary Schools*, various years; and Common Core of Data (CCD), "State Nonfiscal Survey of Public Elementary/Secondary Education," 1986–87 through 2012–13. (This table was prepared October 2014.)

Table 213.20. Staff employed in public elementary and secondary school systems, by type of assignment and state or jurisdiction: Fall 2012
[In full-time equivalents]

		School district staff			School staff							Other
State or jurisdiction	Total	Officials and administrators	Administrative support staff	Instruction coordinators	Principals and assistant principals	School and library support staff	Teachers	Instructional aides	Guidance counselors	Librarians	Student support staff	Other support services staff
1	2	3	4	5	6	7	8	9	10	11	12	13
United States[1]	6,181,238	65,420	186,118	70,967	169,240	285,055	3,109,101	729,756	103,218	46,685	280,358	1,135,319
Alabama[2,3,4,5,6,7,8,9,10,11]	96,485	796	1,615	996	2,569	3,840	51,877	6,191	1,767	1,345	2,354	23,135
Alaska[4]	17,116	637	799	195	647	1,205	7,682	2,442	310	135	651	2,413
Arizona	103,228	1,230	4,161	592	2,497	3,903	48,866	14,804	1,238	595	11,527	13,813
Arkansas	71,279	612	2,410	969	1,651	4,005	34,131	7,519	1,264	964	8,194	9,559
California[6,12]	544,875	2,777	19,874	15,772	16,343	34,702	266,255	62,890	7,623	769	16,627	101,244
Colorado	102,480	1,158	4,417	2,579	2,940	5,540	48,922	15,137	2,198	630	5,696	13,264
Connecticut	91,264	1,919	2,860	3,618	2,462	2,088	43,931	13,703	1,111	742	2,678	16,151
Delaware	17,554	406	448	257	451	361	9,257	1,696	291	133	1,031	3,223
District of Columbia	12,480	260	1,147	304	595	584	5,925	1,494	258	82	1,020	811
Florida	335,100	1,925	14,670	695	8,237	16,504	176,537	29,900	5,517	2,266	10,572	68,276
Georgia	220,603	2,360	2,428	2,524	6,084	10,105	109,365	24,087	3,506	2,176	7,934	50,035
Hawaii	22,238	233	587	680	590	1,367	11,608	2,399	629	192	1,734	2,219
Idaho[3,4,10,11]	26,319	44	611	231	636	1,121	14,563	2,901	454	62	819	4,878
Illinois[2,4,5,9,10,12,13,14]	263,565	2,743	4,754	501	7,456	15,290	135,701	34,126	2,716	1,872	9,681	48,724
Indiana	147,936	1,267	727	3,200	3,147	8,278	59,863	16,648	1,925	781	13,115	38,985
Iowa	71,089	1,326	1,972	423	1,767	2,743	35,080	11,399	1,176	479	4,213	10,510
Kansas	73,020	508	1,349	1,103	1,969	2,602	41,243	9,327	1,123	742	2,474	10,579
Kentucky	99,176	892	2,243	1,049	3,290	5,962	42,769	13,630	1,511	1,087	2,848	23,893
Louisiana	95,585	340	2,614	2,003	2,874	3,622	46,493	10,658	1,708	1,066	4,718	19,486
Maine	32,859	446	732	315	913	1,550	15,222	5,906	580	219	1,395	5,581
Maryland	113,093	3,425	2,219	1,485	3,534	6,056	57,718	11,021	2,305	1,136	4,720	19,473
Massachusetts	125,347	2,605	3,006	404	4,621	6,465	70,636	24,255	2,231	752	8,888	1,483
Michigan	186,065	4,036	1,120	1,248	6,643	11,568	86,154	20,699	2,137	561	13,034	38,865
Minnesota	111,069	2,138	2,285	2,187	2,155	4,610	53,585	17,473	1,120	665	12,124	12,728
Mississippi	68,215	995	2,014	653	1,952	2,495	32,613	8,214	1,106	846	3,066	14,259
Missouri	126,937	1,354	7,847	1,110	3,113	372	66,248	13,445	2,569	1,394	4,368	25,116
Montana[3,6,7,11]	18,896	174	479	156	528	171	10,200	2,319	454	365	673	3,377
Nebraska	45,426	591	1,088	885	1,037	1,924	22,103	6,425	778	545	1,443	8,608
Nevada[3,4,6,7,8]	32,702	188	956	1,402	1,009	1,619	20,695	4,145	882	345	74	1,387
New Hampshire	31,734	721	716	223	554	793	14,925	6,853	805	312	704	5,131
New Jersey[6]	223,279	1,369	5,186	3,464	4,773	10,135	110,929	33,966	3,645	1,486	12,608	35,719
New Mexico	46,222	846	108	618	1,284	3,824	22,201	6,002	787	255	3,295	7,003
New York	370,214	2,485	19,266	1,666	9,144	9,536	207,060	42,866	6,443	2,610	10,025	59,114
North Carolina	191,732	1,607	5,216	1,026	5,368	7,290	98,590	24,474	3,988	2,198	10,495	31,479
North Dakota	16,713	475	261	197	450	733	8,677	2,174	321	195	804	2,425
Ohio	242,806	2,389	13,944	1,537	5,220	13,301	106,000	19,254	3,655	1,025	22,437	54,045
Oklahoma	84,380	544	2,975	318	2,286	4,405	41,775	9,006	1,619	1,054	4,724	15,676
Oregon	59,771	428	2,792	446	1,510	4,485	26,410	9,190	967	144	2,187	11,212
Pennsylvania	252,179	2,531	7,179	1,502	5,120	12,015	123,147	32,168	4,480	1,842	7,467	54,729
Rhode Island	16,934	177	491	102	477	700	9,871	2,211	353	193	489	1,868
South Carolina	72,511	765	1,720	1,879	2,689	1,451	48,072	9,263	1,930	1,110	3,332	301
South Dakota	19,146	757	380	177	417	595	9,334	2,511	327	126	1,001	3,520
Tennessee	127,643	172	977	844	3,494	5,183	66,406	16,090	2,912	1,911	1,387	28,266
Texas	644,442	6,042	21,598	3,300	22,027	26,422	327,357	60,362	10,828	4,644	23,950	137,911
Utah	53,730	397	730	1,958	1,366	2,732	26,610	8,396	887	259	1,322	9,074
Vermont	18,422	140	492	230	482	883	8,403	4,197	417	213	924	2,042
Virginia	177,357	1,751	4,470	1,675	4,058	8,891	89,389	19,477	3,306	1,727	4,713	37,901
Washington	102,540	2,326	1,869	290	2,852	4,982	53,699	10,139	2,035	1,056	3,282	20,011
West Virginia[6]	39,267	757	1,104	369	1,145	773	20,101	3,699	736	324	1,672	8,588
Wisconsin	101,644	984	2,730	1,261	2,439	4,283	57,551	10,229	1,880	935	5,207	14,144
Wyoming	16,573	373	481	346	373	996	7,350	2,377	409	122	661	3,085
Bureau of Indian Education	12,373 [15]	—	—	244	558	1,128	5,308	1,654	317	182	1,014	1,968
DoD, overseas	—	—	—	—	—	—	—	—	—	—	—	—
DoD, domestic	—	—	—	—	—	—	—	—	—	—	—	—
Other jurisdictions												
American Samoa	—	—	—	—	—	—	—	—	—	—	—	—
Guam	3,923	18	251	128	92	215	2,291	606	87	37	36	162
Northern Marianas	891	9	76	8	34	64	409	164	23	1	24	79
Puerto Rico	54,381	400	1,710	1,883	1,401	2,159	30,986	81	728	1,004	4,865	9,164
U.S. Virgin Islands	2,208	7	76	30	97	87	1,129	280	60	29	68	345

—Not available.
[1]Includes imputations for undercounts in states as designated in footnotes 2 through 14.
[2]Includes imputations for officials and administrators.
[3]Includes imputations for administrative support staff.
[4]Includes imputations for instruction coordinators.
[5]Includes imputations for principals and assistant principals.
[6]Includes imputations for library support staff.
[7]Includes imputations for school support staff.
[8]Includes imputations for instructional aides.
[9]Includes imputations for librarians.
[10]Includes imputations for student support staff.

[11]Includes imputations for other support services staff.
[12]Includes imputations for prekindergarten teachers.
[13]Includes imputations for kindergarten teachers.
[14]Includes imputations for secondary teachers.
[15]Excludes counts for officials and administrators and for administrative support staff, which were not reported.
NOTE: DoD = Department of Defense.
SOURCE: U.S. Department of Education, National Center for Education Statistics, Common Core of Data (CCD), "State Nonfiscal Survey of Public Elementary/Secondary Education," 2012–13. (This table was prepared October 2014.)

Table 213.30. Staff employed in public elementary and secondary school systems, by type of assignment and state or jurisdiction: Fall 2011

[In full-time equivalents]

State or jurisdiction	Total	School district staff			School staff						Student support staff	Other support services staff
		Officials and administrators	Administrative support staff	Instruction coordinators	Principals and assistant principals	School and library support staff	Teachers	Instructional aides	Guidance counselors	Librarians		
1	2	3	4	5	6	7	8	9	10	11	12	13
United States[1]	6,138,890	62,884	187,959	67,711	166,416	272,178	3,103,263	710,335	105,351	48,402	275,704	1,138,687
Alabama	92,289	792	1,605	956	2,537	3,824	47,723	6,146	1,773	1,379	2,316	23,238
Alaska[2]	17,747	668	777	187	659	1,259	8,088	2,458	323	165	654	2,508
Arizona	98,712	425	881	96	2,576	5,840	50,800	15,183	1,252	515	7,649	13,495
Arkansas	72,650	675	2,390	806	1,781	4,965	33,983	8,052	1,530	1,095	7,644	9,729
California[3,4]	547,188	3,212	21,543	12,540	16,148	34,681	268,689	63,886	7,683	797	16,214	101,796
Colorado	100,349	1,156	4,390	2,505	2,829	5,511	48,078	14,118	2,159	659	5,520	13,423
Connecticut	92,955	1,893	3,275	3,585	2,199	2,233	43,805	14,253	1,103	757	2,906	16,946
Delaware	15,449	67	79	244	445	367	8,587	1,672	290	136	717	2,844
District of Columbia	11,541	240	185	134	584	512	6,278	1,404	247	119	1,026	812
Florida	328,709	1,923	14,359	678	8,191	16,340	175,006	29,659	5,555	2,377	10,377	64,244
Georgia	224,207	2,257	2,520	2,417	6,129	10,250	111,133	25,119	3,577	2,226	7,375	51,204
Hawaii	22,065	226	563	640	580	1,360	11,458	2,446	627	199	1,705	2,262
Idaho	28,065	62	607	222	662	1,196	15,990	3,001	547	71	806	4,900
Illinois[3,5,6,7,8]	213,578	2,729	2,395	481	7,362	3,618	131,777	29,951	3,132	1,920	9,522	20,692
Indiana	150,191	1,207	688	3,230	3,126	8,271	62,339	16,078	1,946	868	12,845	39,593
Iowa	69,901	1,221	1,916	302	1,789	2,696	34,658	10,907	1,168	496	4,207	10,541
Kansas	70,631	499	1,349	999	1,874	2,602	37,407	9,327	1,071	735	4,193	10,575
Kentucky	92,287	902	2,009	995	3,159	5,033	41,860	12,149	1,496	1,105	2,512	21,067
Louisiana	100,880	380	2,811	2,078	2,879	3,836	48,657	11,448	1,918	1,157	4,856	20,860
Maine[5,6]	39,946	45	760	205	1,655	1,858	14,888	8,894	1,097	386	1,703	8,455
Maryland	113,351	3,410	2,185	1,526	3,577	6,175	57,589	11,099	2,345	1,153	4,732	19,559
Massachusetts	122,880	2,477	2,919	388	4,538	6,282	69,342	23,672	2,195	730	8,873	1,465
Michigan	188,428	3,091	1,166	3,372	4,680	11,796	86,997	21,264	2,196	631	13,310	39,924
Minnesota	109,119	2,074	2,285	1,992	2,120	4,640	52,832	16,841	1,096	675	11,905	12,658
Mississippi	67,850	991	2,041	632	1,955	2,495	32,007	8,286	1,106	854	3,016	14,469
Missouri	132,167	1,403	12,398	1,031	3,117	411	66,252	13,010	2,573	1,422	4,197	26,353
Montana[3,5,6,8]	18,790	173	476	159	519	173	10,153	2,262	452	356	676	3,392
Nebraska	45,290	591	1,037	975	1,034	1,894	22,182	6,345	796	540	1,435	8,462
Nevada[2,3,5,6,7]	32,533	31	950	1,346	978	1,614	21,132	4,115	886	362	46	1,074
New Hampshire	31,971	737	729	238	549	810	15,049	6,964	808	313	707	5,067
New Jersey[3]	202,928	1,388	5,657	3,147	4,709	7,992	109,719	26,780	3,870	1,550	11,756	26,359
New Mexico	45,907	883	103	600	1,331	3,778	21,957	5,919	801	260	3,173	7,101
New York	406,625	2,952	21,141	1,750	9,226	8,473	209,527	35,677	6,757	2,729	11,860	96,533
North Carolina	188,553	1,555	5,173	992	5,238	7,260	97,308	24,036	3,925	2,193	9,751	31,121
North Dakota	16,401	473	256	158	451	719	8,525	2,081	314	194	809	2,420
Ohio	243,586	2,406	14,052	1,708	5,295	13,998	107,972	19,845	3,673	1,115	22,528	50,994
Oklahoma	82,719	547	2,891	299	2,194	4,359	41,349	8,462	1,629	1,047	4,496	15,445
Oregon	60,715	433	3,060	389	1,558	4,302	26,791	9,193	975	203	2,160	11,652
Pennsylvania	254,297	2,633	7,180	1,588	5,295	12,015	124,646	32,169	4,581	1,934	7,462	54,795
Rhode Island	18,743	87	517	85	451	718	11,414	2,248	379	286	525	2,033
South Carolina	69,272	734	1,426	1,744	2,587	1,179	46,782	8,471	1,829	1,100	3,180	240
South Dakota	19,059	737	388	155	413	563	9,247	2,418	324	125	1,026	3,663
Tennessee	127,781	176	963	838	3,410	5,065	66,382	16,335	2,887	1,912	1,325	28,489
Texas	640,166	5,781	22,120	3,338	21,515	26,262	324,282	58,460	10,821	4,749	23,707	139,132
Utah	51,994	403	657	1,745	1,330	2,531	25,970	8,074	840	275	1,273	8,898
Vermont	18,385	137	466	227	478	879	8,364	4,171	416	217	902	2,129
Virginia	180,086	1,590	4,271	1,751	4,016	8,633	90,832	19,736	3,338	1,789	4,178	39,953
Washington	101,914	2,286	1,903	317	2,802	4,962	53,119	10,176	2,025	1,078	3,226	20,020
West Virginia[3]	39,380	769	1,143	375	1,129	768	20,247	3,657	740	344	1,682	8,525
Wisconsin	101,533	997	2,801	1,164	2,394	4,166	56,245	10,014	1,852	979	6,363	14,558
Wyoming	17,128	360	503	385	363	1,014	7,847	2,403	428	125	679	3,021
Bureau of Indian Education	—	—	—	—	—	—	—	—	—	—	—	—
DoD, overseas	—	—	—	—	—	—	—	—	—	—	—	—
DoD, domestic	—	—	—	—	—	—	—	—	—	—	—	—
Other jurisdictions												
American Samoa	—	—	—	—	—	—	—	—	—	—	—	—
Guam	3,923	18	251	128	92	215	2,291	606	87	37	36	162
Northern Marianas	1,042	9	74	12	40	67	496	184	36	1	30	93
Puerto Rico	55,797	457	1,910	1,549	1,108	1,846	33,079	79	756	1,047	4,688	9,278
U.S. Virgin Islands	2,391	6	67	41	79	84	1,217	313	59	27	83	415

—Not available.
[1]Includes imputations for undercounts in states as designated in footnotes 2 through 8.
[2]Includes imputations for instruction coordinators.
[3]Includes imputations for library support staff.
[4]Includes imputations for prekindergarten teachers.
[5]Includes imputations for administrative support staff.
[6]Includes imputations for school support staff.
[7]Includes imputations for instructional aides.
[8]Includes imputations for other support services staff.
NOTE: DoD = Department of Defense.
SOURCE: U.S. Department of Education, National Center for Education Statistics, Common Core of Data (CCD), "State Nonfiscal Survey of Public Elementary/Secondary Education," 2011–12. (This table was prepared August 2013.)

Table 213.40. Staff, teachers, and teachers as a percentage of staff in public elementary and secondary school systems, by state or jurisdiction: Selected years, fall 2000 through fall 2012

[In full-time equivalents]

State or jurisdiction	Teachers as a percent of staff						Fall 2010			Fall 2011			Fall 2012		
	Fall 2000	Fall 2005	Fall 2006	Fall 2007	Fall 2008	Fall 2009	All staff	Teachers	Teachers as a percent of staff	All staff	Teachers	Teachers as a percent of staff	All staff	Teachers	Teachers as a percent of staff
1	2	3	4	5	6	7	8	9	10	11	12	13	14	15	16
United States[1]	51.5	51.3	51.5	51.3	50.9	50.5	6,195,207	3,099,095	50.0	6,138,890	3,103,263	50.6	6,181,238	3,109,101	50.3
Alabama	53.7[2]	55.7	51.1	45.2[2]	50.1	50.5	95,144	49,363	51.9	92,289	47,723	51.7	96,485[2]	51,877	53.8[2]
Alaska	49.3[2]	44.1[2]	46.9[2]	45.9[2]	46.2[2]	45.6[2]	18,102[2]	8,171	45.1[2]	17,747[2]	8,088	45.6[2]	17,116[2]	7,682	44.9[2]
Arizona	49.3	51.3	51.4	51.6	51.8	51.8	96,622	50,031	51.8	98,712	50,800	51.5	103,228	48,866	47.3
Arkansas	50.6	46.7	49.0	48.2	52.1	50.1	72,185	34,273	47.5	72,650	33,983	46.8	71,279	34,131	47.9
California	54.1[2]	53.4[2]	53.0[2]	52.3[2]	51.5[2]	51.9[2]	530,337[2]	260,806[2]	49.2[2]	547,188[2]	268,689[2]	49.1[2]	544,875[2]	266,255[2]	48.9[2]
Colorado	50.7	49.2	48.2	48.1	47.5	47.5	101,426	48,543	47.9	100,349	48,078	47.9	102,480	48,922	47.7
Connecticut	50.0	46.9	45.1	45.3	52.4	46.9	93,088	42,951	46.1	92,955	43,805	47.1	91,264	43,931	48.1
Delaware	59.2	51.7	52.2	52.8	56.2	50.9	16,478	8,933	54.2	15,449	8,587	55.6	17,554	9,257	52.7
District of Columbia	46.2	44.3[2]	44.2[2]	50.6	43.9	50.1	11,381	5,925	52.1	11,541	6,278	54.4	12,480	5,925	47.5
Florida	47.8	50.6	50.6	54.9	54.7	54.8	333,183	175,609	52.7	328,709	175,006	53.2	335,100	176,537	52.7
Georgia	49.2	49.6	49.9	49.7	49.7	49.4	227,188	112,460	49.5	224,207	111,133	49.6	220,603	109,365	49.6
Hawaii	59.5	53.3	53.5	52.6	52.3	52.9	21,704	11,396	52.5	22,065	11,458	51.9	22,238	11,608	52.2
Idaho	56.2	55.8	56.1	55.3	55.6	54.9	27,783	15,673	56.4	28,065	15,990	57.0	26,319[2]	14,563	55.3[2]
Illinois	51.1[2]	53.2[2]	63.6[2]	63.7[2]	61.4[2]	62.4[2]	215,764[2]	132,983	61.6[2]	213,578[2]	131,777	61.7[2]	263,565[2]	135,701[2]	51.5[2]
Indiana	46.7	45.5	45.6	44.7	44.1	43.6	138,802[2]	58,121[2]	41.9[2]	150,191	62,339	41.5	147,936	59,863	40.5
Iowa	51.1	50.9	51.2	50.3	49.7	49.4	69,615	34,642	49.8	69,901	34,658	49.6	71,089	35,080	49.3
Kansas	50.9	51.3	65.7	65.2	64.8	51.4	67,751	34,644	51.1	70,631	37,407	53.0	73,020	41,243	56.5
Kentucky	44.1	43.3	43.9	43.4	43.4	42.3	99,225	42,042	42.4	92,287	41,860	45.4	99,176	42,769	43.1
Louisiana	49.3	48.2	48.3	48.8	48.9	48.3	100,881	48,655	48.2	100,880	48,657	48.2	95,585	46,493	48.6
Maine	49.7	47.3	45.7	41.5	43.6	43.8	32,549	15,384	47.3	39,946[2]	14,888	37.3[2]	32,859	15,222	46.3
Maryland	54.3	51.0	51.5	50.8	50.4	50.7	115,367	58,428	50.6	113,351	57,589	50.8	113,093	57,718	51.0
Massachusetts	55.1	53.0[2]	53.6[2]	57.4	56.9	56.8	122,057	68,754	56.3	122,880	69,342	56.4	125,347	70,636	56.4
Michigan	46.1	47.9[2]	46.2	46.0	45.5	45.3	193,487	88,615	45.8	188,428	86,997	46.2	186,065	86,154	46.3
Minnesota	51.6[2]	48.9	48.6	48.9	48.6	48.4	108,993	52,672	48.3	109,119	52,832	48.4	111,069	53,585	48.2
Mississippi	47.9	46.5	47.0	47.2	46.3	46.8	67,866	32,255	47.5	67,850	32,007	47.2	68,215	32,613	47.8
Missouri	53.2	52.1	51.3	51.2	51.3	51.3	128,289	66,735	52.0	132,167	66,252	50.1	126,937	66,248	52.2
Montana	53.5[2]	52.9[2]	54.7[2]	54.8[2]	54.5[2]	54.1[2]	19,249[2]	10,361	53.8[2]	18,790[2]	10,153	54.0[2]	18,896[2]	10,200	54.0[2]
Nebraska	52.6	51.9	50.0	50.2	48.8	48.6	45,509	22,345	49.1	45,290	22,182	49.0	45,426	22,103	48.7
Nevada	58.6	67.2[2]	67.5[2]	65.8[2]	65.6[2]	65.5[2]	33,400[2]	21,839	65.4[2]	32,533[2]	21,132	65.0[2]	32,702[2]	20,695	63.3[2]
New Hampshire	51.1	48.5	48.2	47.5	47.7	47.1	32,955	15,365	46.6	31,971	15,049	47.1	31,734	14,925	47.0
New Jersey	53.4	53.2[2]	54.7[2]	55.3[2]	55.8[2]	53.9[2]	202,634[2]	110,202	54.4[2]	202,928[2]	109,719	54.1[2]	223,279[2]	110,929	49.7[2]
New Mexico	46.8	45.9	47.3	47.8	47.7	47.8	46,519	22,437	48.2	45,907	21,957	47.8	46,222	22,201	48.0
New York	49.7	58.6	58.6	56.6	50.9	50.9	413,971	211,606	51.1	406,625	209,527	51.5	370,214	207,060	55.9
North Carolina	51.5	52.5	54.9	52.4	52.7	52.4[2]	193,039	98,357	51.0	188,553	97,308	51.6	191,732	98,590	51.4
North Dakota	53.9	52.9	52.8	52.4	52.3	52.3	16,239	8,417	51.8	16,401	8,525	52.0	16,713	8,677	51.9
Ohio	53.1	49.4	45.5	45.1	46.1	45.6	241,212	109,282	45.3	243,586	107,972	44.3	242,806	106,000	43.7
Oklahoma	55.0	51.1	51.6	53.9	53.2	50.3	82,262	41,278	50.2	82,719	41,349	50.0	84,380	41,775	49.5
Oregon	50.0	47.0	48.1	46.4	46.3	45.7	63,603	28,109	44.2	60,715	26,791	44.1	59,771	26,410	44.2
Pennsylvania	52.2	50.9	51.2	53.1	51.5	51.6	266,796	129,911	48.7	254,297	124,646	49.0	252,179	123,147	48.8
Rhode Island	60.0	58.4[2]	63.5[2]	64.2	60.8	60.4	18,632	11,222	60.2	18,743	11,414	60.9	16,934	9,871	58.3
South Carolina	65.7[2]	70.9[2]	71.6[2]	71.7	71.6	69.7	65,508	45,210	69.0	69,272	46,782	67.5	72,511	48,072	66.3
South Dakota	52.0	48.0	52.4	55.3	50.3	50.1	19,545	9,512	48.7	19,059	9,247	48.5	19,146	9,334	48.8
Tennessee	52.1	52.2	50.5	51.1	51.2	51.2	128,197	66,558	51.9	127,781	66,382	51.9	127,643	66,406	52.0
Texas	50.6	50.5	50.6	50.6	50.5	50.3	665,419	334,997	50.3	640,166	324,282	50.7	644,442	327,357	50.8
Utah	54.1	50.2	49.9	50.2	48.2	49.4	52,341	25,677	49.1	51,994	25,970	49.9	53,730	26,610	49.5
Vermont	47.3	46.5	46.1	45.6	45.3	45.2	18,485	8,382	45.3	18,385	8,364	45.5	18,422	8,403	45.6
Virginia	54.1[2]	44.4	37.2	35.2	35.1	34.8	201,047	70,947	35.3	180,086	90,832	50.4	177,357	89,389	50.4
Washington	52.3	47.0	52.2	52.0	52.0	51.4	103,783	53,934	52.0	101,914	53,119	52.1	102,540	53,699	52.4
West Virginia	54.3	52.3	53.5[2]	53.0[2]	52.4	51.8[2]	39,270[2]	20,338	51.8[2]	39,380[2]	20,247	51.4[2]	39,267[2]	20,101	51.2[2]
Wisconsin	56.3	57.0	56.3	56.1	55.7	55.5	103,901	57,625	55.5	101,533	56,245	55.4	101,644	57,551	56.6
Wyoming	48.6	46.2	44.6	44.7	44.2	43.5	16,424	7,127	43.4	17,128	7,847	45.8	16,573	7,350	44.3
Bureau of Indian Education	—	—	—	—	—	—	—	—	—	—	—	—	12,373	5,308	42.9[3]
DoD, overseas	66.0	62.9	62.4	66.2	60.5	—	—	—	—	—	—	—	—	—	—
DoD, domestic	59.2	55.4	56.9	56.2	55.8	—	—	—	—	—	—	—	—	—	—
Other jurisdictions															
American Samoa	50.0	68.4	52.0	—	—	—	—	—	—	—	—	—	—	—	—
Guam	51.5	52.2	—	—	—	—	3,383	1,843	54.5	3,923	2,291	58.4	3,923	2,291	58.4
Northern Marianas	50.2	49.8	49.9	49.5	49.3	47.8	1,215	607	50.0	1,042	496	47.6	891	409	45.9
Puerto Rico	54.4	56.0	55.8	56.8	56.2	61.9	59,261	36,506	61.6	55,797	33,079	59.3	54,381	30,986	57.0
U.S. Virgin Islands	52.1	53.8	50.7	48.4	53.8	49.9	2,918	1,457	49.9	2,391	1,217	50.9	2,208	1,129	51.1

—Not available.
[1]U.S. totals include imputations for underreporting and nonreporting states.
[2]Includes imputations for underreporting.
[3]Total staff count excludes officials and administrators and administrative support staff, so computed percentage of teachers may be overstated.

NOTE: DoD = Department of Defense.
SOURCE: U.S. Department of Education, National Center for Education Statistics, Common Core of Data (CCD), "State Nonfiscal Survey of Public Elementary/Secondary Education," 2000–01 through 2012–13. (This table was prepared October 2014.)

Table 213.50. Staff, enrollment, and pupil/staff ratios in public elementary and secondary school systems, by state or jurisdiction: Selected years, fall 2000 through fall 2012

State or jurisdiction	Pupil/staff ratio						Fall 2010			Fall 2011			Fall 2012		
	Fall 2000	Fall 2005	Fall 2006	Fall 2007	Fall 2008	Fall 2009	Staff	Enrollment	Pupil/ staff ratio	Staff	Enrollment	Pupil/ staff ratio	Staff	Enrollment	Pupil/ staff ratio
1	2	3	4	5	6	7	8	9	10	11	12	13	14	15	16
United States[1]....	8.3	8.0	8.0	7.9	7.8	7.8	6,195,207	49,484,181	8.0	6,138,890	49,521,669	8.1	6,181,238	49,771,118	8.1
Alabama	8.2 [2]	7.1	6.8	6.7 [2]	7.8	8.0	95,144	755,552	7.9	92,289	744,621	8.1	96,485 [2]	744,637	7.7 [2]
Alaska	8.3 [2]	7.4 [2]	7.9 [2]	7.9 [2]	7.6 [2]	7.4 [2]	18,102 [2]	132,104	7.3 [2]	17,747 [2]	131,167	7.4 [2]	17,116 [2]	131,489	7.7 [2]
Arizona	9.7	10.9	10.4	10.4	10.3	10.7	96,622	1,071,751	11.1	98,712	1,080,319	10.9	103,228	1,089,384	10.6
Arkansas	7.1	6.7	6.7	6.8	6.7	6.5	72,185	482,114	6.7	72,650	483,114	6.6	71,279	486,157	6.8
California	11.1 [2]	11.1 [2]	11.0 [2]	10.9 [2]	10.7 [2]	10.3 [2]	530,337 [2]	6,289,578	11.9 [2]	547,188 [2]	6,287,834	11.5 [2]	544,875 [2]	6,299,451	11.6 [2]
Colorado	8.7	8.4	8.2	8.1	8.0	8.1	101,426	843,316	8.3	100,349	854,265	8.5	102,480	863,561	8.4
Connecticut	6.8	6.8	6.6	6.6	6.1	6.1	93,088	560,546	6.0	92,955	554,437	6.0	91,264	550,954	6.0
Delaware	9.1	7.8	7.9	7.9	8.5	7.5	16,478	129,403	7.9	15,449	128,946	8.3	17,554	129,026	7.4
District of Columbia	6.4	6.2 [2]	6.0 [2]	6.3	5.7	5.9	11,381	71,284	6.3	11,541	73,911	6.4	12,480	76,140	6.1
Florida	8.8	8.5	8.3	7.7	7.7	7.9	333,183	2,643,347	7.9	328,709	2,668,156	8.1	335,100	2,692,162	8.0
Georgia	7.8	7.3	7.2	7.0	6.9	7.1	227,188	1,677,067	7.4	224,207	1,685,016	7.5	220,603	1,703,332	7.7
Hawaii	10.0	8.7	8.6	8.3	8.3	8.3	21,704	179,601	8.3	22,065	182,706	8.3	22,238	184,760	8.3
Idaho	10.1	10.1	10.2	10.0	10.1	10.0	27,783	275,859	9.9	28,065	279,873	10.0	26,319 [2]	284,834	10.8 [2]
Illinois	8.2 [2]	8.4 [2]	9.6 [2]	9.9 [2]	9.6 [2]	9.5 [2]	215,764 [2]	2,091,654	9.7 [2]	213,578 [2]	2,083,097	9.8 [2]	263,565 [2]	2,072,880	7.9 [2]
Indiana	7.8	7.8	7.8	7.5	7.4	7.3	138,802 [2]	1,047,232	7.5 [2]	150,191	1,040,765	6.9	147,936	1,041,369	7.0
Iowa	7.3	7.0	6.9	6.8	6.7	6.8	69,615	495,775	7.1	69,901	495,870	7.1	71,089	499,825	7.0
Kansas	7.3	7.1	8.7	8.6	8.5	7.0	67,751	483,701	7.1	70,631	486,108	6.9	73,020	489,043	6.7
Kentucky	7.4	6.9	6.9 [2]	6.6 [2]	6.7	6.9	99,225	673,128	6.8	92,287	681,987	7.4	99,176	685,167	6.9
Louisiana	7.3	7.1	7.1	6.8	6.8	6.7	100,881	696,558	6.9	100,880	703,390	7.0	95,585	710,903	7.4
Maine	6.2	5.5	5.3	4.9	5.3	5.1	32,549	189,077	5.8	39,946 [2]	188,969	4.7 [2]	32,859	185,739	5.7
Maryland	8.8	7.7	7.5	7.2	7.2	7.4	115,367	852,211	7.4	113,351	854,086	7.5	113,093	859,638	7.6
Massachusetts	8.0	7.0 [2]	7.1 [2]	7.8	7.8	7.8	122,057	955,563	7.8	122,880	953,369	7.8	125,347	954,773	7.6
Michigan	8.2 [2]	8.5 [2]	8.1	8.1	8.0	8.1	193,487	1,587,067	8.2	188,428	1,573,537	8.4	186,065	1,555,370	8.4
Minnesota	8.2 [2]	8.0	7.9	7.7	7.7	7.7	108,993	838,037	7.7	109,119	839,738	7.7	111,069	845,404	7.6
Mississippi	7.7	7.3	7.2	6.9	6.8	7.0	67,866	490,526	7.2	67,850	490,619	7.2	68,215	493,650	7.2
Missouri	7.5	7.1	7.0	6.9	6.9	7.0	128,289	918,710	7.2	132,167	916,584	6.9	126,937	917,900	7.2
Montana	8.0 [2]	7.4 [2]	7.6 [2]	7.4 [2]	7.4 [2]	7.3 [2]	19,249 [2]	141,693	7.4 [2]	18,790 [2]	142,349	7.6 [2]	18,896 [2]	142,908	7.6 [2]
Nebraska	7.2	7.0	6.7	6.7	6.5	6.4	45,509	298,500	6.6	45,290	301,296	6.7	45,426	303,505	6.7
Nevada	10.9	12.7 [2]	12.5 [2]	12.1 [2]	12.9 [2]	12.7 [2]	33,400 [2]	437,149	13.1 [2]	32,533 [2]	439,634	13.5 [2]	32,702 [2]	445,707	13.6 [2]
New Hampshire	7.4	6.4	6.3	6.2	6.0	6.0	32,955	194,711	5.9	31,971	191,900	6.0	31,734	188,974	6.0
New Jersey	7.1	6.6 [2]	6.8 [2]	6.9 [2]	6.7 [2]	6.5 [2]	202,634 [2]	1,402,548	6.9 [2]	202,928 [2]	1,356,431	6.7 [2]	223,279 [2]	1,372,203	6.1 [2]
New Mexico	7.1	6.8	7.1	7.0	6.9	7.0	46,519	338,122	7.3	45,907	337,225	7.3	46,222	338,220	7.3
New York	6.9	7.5	7.5	7.4	6.4	6.6	413,971	2,734,955	6.6	406,625	2,704,718	6.7	370,214	2,710,703	7.3
North Carolina	8.0	7.8	7.1	7.3	7.2	7.4 [2]	193,039	1,490,605	7.7	188,553	1,507,864	8.0	191,732	1,518,465	7.9
North Dakota	7.2	6.5	6.4	6.2	6.1	5.9	16,239	96,323	5.9	16,401	97,646	6.0	16,713	101,111	6.0
Ohio	8.2	7.7	7.6	7.5	7.4	7.2	241,212	1,754,191	7.3	243,586	1,740,030	7.1	242,806	1,729,916	7.1
Oklahoma	8.3	7.8	7.8	7.4	7.4	7.7	82,262	659,911	8.0	82,719	666,120	8.1	84,380	673,483	8.0
Oregon	9.7	9.2	9.0	8.8	8.8	9.3	63,603	570,720	9.0	60,715	568,208	9.4	59,771	587,564	9.8
Pennsylvania	8.1	7.6	7.8	7.1	7.0	7.0	266,796	1,793,284	6.7	254,297	1,771,395	7.0	252,179	1,763,677	7.0
Rhode Island	8.9	6.3 [2]	8.5 [2]	8.4	7.8	7.7	18,632	143,793	7.7	18,743	142,854	7.6	16,934	142,481	8.4
South Carolina	9.8 [2]	10.3 [2]	10.3 [2]	10.8	10.3	10.7	65,508	725,838	11.1	69,272	727,186	10.5	72,511	735,998	10.2
South Dakota	7.1	6.4	7.0	7.1	6.9	6.6	19,545	126,128	6.5	19,059	128,016	6.7	19,146	130,471	6.8
Tennessee	8.3 [2]	8.4	7.9	7.6	7.7	7.6	128,197	987,422	7.7	127,781	999,693	7.8	127,643	993,496	7.8
Texas	7.5	7.6	7.5	7.4	7.3	7.3	665,419	4,935,715	7.4	640,166	5,000,470	7.8	644,442	5,077,659	7.9
Utah	11.8	11.1	11.1	11.9	11.4	11.0	52,341	585,552	11.2	51,994	598,832	11.5	53,730	613,279	11.4
Vermont	5.7	5.1	5.0	4.9	4.8	4.7	18,485	96,858	5.2	18,385	89,908	4.9	18,422	89,624	4.9
Virginia	7.1 [2]	5.2	5.7	6.0	6.1	6.1	201,047	1,251,440	6.2	180,086	1,257,883	7.0	177,357	1,265,419	7.1
Washington	10.3	9.1	10.0	9.9	9.9	10.0	103,783	1,043,788	10.1	101,914	1,045,453	10.3	102,540	1,051,694	10.3
West Virginia	7.4	7.4	7.7 [2]	7.4 [2]	7.3	7.2 [2]	39,270 [2]	282,879	7.2 [2]	39,380 [2]	282,870	7.2 [2]	39,267 [2]	283,044	7.2 [2]
Wisconsin	8.2	8.3	8.3	8.3	8.2	8.3	103,901	872,286	8.4	101,533	871,105	8.6	101,644	872,436	8.6
Wyoming	6.4	5.8	5.6	5.6	5.5	5.4	16,424	89,009	5.4	17,128	90,099	5.3	16,573	91,533	5.5
Bureau of Indian Education	—	—	—	—	—	—	—	41,962	—	—	—	—	12,373 [3]	—	—
DoD, overseas	9.5	6.9	7.3	9.1	7.5	—	—	—	—	—	—	—	—	—	—
DoD, domestic	8.4	7.7	7.5	6.9	7.3	—	—	—	—	—	—	—	—	—	—
Other jurisdictions															
American Samoa	9.6	11.4	8.8	—	—	—	—	—	—	—	—	—	—	—	—
Guam	8.5	9.0	—	—	—	—	3,383	31,618	9.3	3,923	31,243	8.0	3,923	31,186	7.9
Northern Marianas..	9.6	9.5	10.1	10.2	10.5	9.5	1,215	11,105	9.1	1,042	11,011	10.6	891	10,646	11.9
Puerto Rico	8.9	7.5	7.6	7.3	7.2	7.8	59,261	473,735	8.0	55,797	452,740	8.1	54,381	434,609	8.0
U.S. Virgin Islands...	6.7	6.3	5.4	5.1	6.4	5.4	2,918	15,495	5.3	2,391	15,711	6.6	2,208	15,192	6.9

—Not available.
[1]U.S. totals include imputations for underreporting and nonreporting states.
[2]Includes imputations for underreporting.
[3]Excludes counts for officials and administrators and for administrative support staff, which were not reported.

NOTE: Staff reported in full-time equivalents. DoD = Department of Defense.
SOURCE: U.S. Department of Education, National Center for Education Statistics, Common Core of Data (CCD), "State Nonfiscal Survey of Public Elementary/Secondary Education," 2000–01 through 2012–13. (This table was prepared November 2014.)

Table 214.10. Number of public school districts and public and private elementary and secondary schools: Selected years, 1869–70 through 2012–13

School year	Regular public school districts[1]	Total, all public and private schools	Total, all public schools[4]	Total, schools with reported grade spans[5]	Schools with elementary grades — Total	Schools with elementary grades — One-teacher	Schools with secondary grades	Total, all private schools	Schools with elementary grades	Schools with secondary grades
1	2	3	4	5	6	7	8	9	10	11
1869–70	—	—	116,312	—	—	—	—	—	—	—
1879–80	—	—	178,122	—	—	—	—	—	—	—
1889–90	—	—	224,526	—	—	—	—	—	—	—
1899–1900	—	—	248,279	—	—	—	—	—	—	—
1909–10	—	—	265,474	—	—	212,448	—	—	—	—
1919–20	—	—	271,319	—	—	187,948	—	—	—	—
1929–30	—	—	248,117	—	238,306	148,712	23,930	—	9,275 [6]	3,258 [6]
1939–40	117,108 [7]	—	226,762	—	—	113,600	—	—	11,306 [6]	3,568 [6]
1949–50	83,718 [7]	—	—	—	128,225	59,652	24,542	—	10,375 [6]	3,331 [6]
1951–52	71,094 [7]	—	—	—	123,763	50,742	23,746	—	10,666 [6]	3,322 [6]
1959–60	40,520 [7]	—	—	—	91,853	20,213	25,784	—	13,574 [6]	4,061 [6]
1961–62	35,676 [7]	125,634	107,260	—	81,910	13,333	25,350	18,374	14,762 [6]	4,129 [6]
1963–64	31,705 [7]	—	104,015	—	77,584	9,895	26,431	—	—	4,451 [6]
1965–66	26,983 [7]	117,662	99,813	—	73,216	6,491	26,597	17,849 [6]	15,340 [6]	4,606 [6]
1967–68	22,010 [7]	—	—	94,197	70,879	4,146	27,011	—	—	—
1970–71	17,995 [7]	—	—	89,372	65,800	1,815	25,352	—	14,372 [6]	3,770 [6]
1973–74	16,730 [7]	—	—	88,655	65,070	1,365	25,906	—	—	—
1975–76	16,376 [7]	—	88,597	87,034	63,242	1,166	25,330	—	—	—
1976–77	16,271 [7]	—	—	86,501	62,644	1,111	25,378	19,910 [6]	16,385 [6]	5,904 [6]
1978–79	16,014 [7]	—	—	84,816	61,982	1,056	24,504	19,489 [6]	16,097 [6]	5,766 [6]
1979–80	15,944 [7]	—	87,004	—	—	—	—	—	—	—
1980–81	15,912 [7]	106,746	85,982	83,688	61,069	921	24,362	20,764 [6]	16,792 [6]	5,678 [6]
1982–83	15,824 [7]	—	84,740	82,039	59,656	798	23,988	—	—	—
1983–84	15,747 [7]	111,872	84,178	81,418	59,082	838	23,947	27,694	20,872	7,862
1984–85	—	—	84,007	81,147	58,827	825	23,916	—	—	—
1985–86	—	—	—	—	—	—	—	25,616	20,252	7,387
1986–87	15,713	—	83,421	82,316	60,811	763	23,481	—	—	—
1987–88	15,577	110,055	83,248	81,416	59,754	729	23,841	26,807	22,959	8,418
1988–89	15,376	—	83,165	81,579	60,176	583	23,638	—	—	—
1989–90	15,367	110,137	83,425	81,880	60,699	630	23,461	26,712	24,221	10,197
1990–91	15,358	109,228	84,538	82,475	61,340	617	23,460	24,690	22,223	8,989
1991–92	15,173	110,576	84,578	82,506	61,739	569	23,248	25,998	23,523	9,282
1992–93	15,025	—	84,497	82,896	62,225	430	23,220	—	—	—
1993–94	14,881	111,486	85,393	83,431	62,726	442	23,379	26,093	23,543	10,555
1994–95	14,772	—	86,221	84,476	63,572	458	23,668	—	—	—
1995–96	14,766	121,519	87,125	84,958	63,961	474	23,793	34,394	32,401	10,942
1996–97	14,841	—	88,223	86,092	64,785	487	24,287	—	—	—
1997–98	14,805	123,403	89,508	87,541	65,859	476	24,802	33,895	31,408	10,779
1998–99	14,891	—	90,874	89,259	67,183	463	25,797	—	—	—
1999–2000	14,928	125,007	92,012	90,538	68,173	423	26,407	32,995	30,457	10,693
2000–01	14,859	—	93,273	91,691	69,697	411	27,090	—	—	—
2001–02	14,559	130,007	94,112	92,696	70,516	408	27,468	35,895	33,191	11,846
2002–03	14,465	—	95,615	93,869	71,270	366	28,151	—	—	—
2003–04	14,383	130,407	95,726	93,977	71,195	376	28,219	34,681	31,988	11,188
2004–05	14,205	—	96,513	95,001	71,556	338	29,017	—	—	—
2005–06	14,166	132,436	97,382	95,731	71,733	326	29,705	35,054	32,127	12,184
2006–07	13,856	—	98,793	96,362	72,442	313	29,904	—	—	—
2007–08	13,838	132,656	98,916	97,654	73,011	288	30,542	33,740	30,808	11,870
2008–09	13,809	—	98,706	97,119	72,771	237	29,971	—	—	—
2009–10	13,625	132,183	98,817	97,521	72,870	217	30,381	33,366	30,590	11,491
2010–11	13,588	—	98,817	97,767	73,323	224	30,681	—	—	—
2011–12	13,567	129,189	98,328	97,357	73,000	205	30,668	30,861	28,184	11,165
2012–13	13,515	—	98,454	97,369	73,089	196	30,651	—	—	—

—Not available.

[1]Regular districts exclude regional education service agencies and supervisory union administrative centers, state-operated agencies, federally operated agencies, and other types of local education agencies, such as independent charter schools.

[2]Schools with both elementary and secondary programs are included under elementary schools and also under secondary schools.

[3]Data for most years prior to 1976–77 are partly estimated. Prior to 1995–96, excludes schools with highest grade of kindergarten.

[4]Includes regular schools and special schools not classified by grade span.

[5]Includes elementary, secondary, and combined elementary/secondary schools.

[6]These data cannot be compared directly with the data for years after 1980–81.

[7]Because of expanded survey coverage, data are not directly comparable with figures after 1983–84.

SOURCE: U.S. Department of Education, National Center for Education Statistics, *Annual Report of the Commissioner of Education*, 1870 through 1910; *Biennial Survey of Education in the United States*, 1919–20 through 1949–50; *Statistics of State School Systems*, 1951–52 through 1967–68; *Statistics of Public Elementary and Secondary School Systems*, 1970–71 through 1980–81; *Statistics of Public and Nonpublic Elementary and Secondary Day Schools*, 1968–69; *Statistics of Nonpublic Elementary and Secondary Schools*, 1970–71; *Private Schools in American Education*; Schools and Staffing Survey (SASS), "Private School Questionnaire," 1987–88 and 1990–91; Private School Universe Survey (PSS), 1989–90 through 2009–10; and Common Core of Data (CCD), "Local Education Agency Universe Survey" and "Public Elementary/Secondary School Universe Survey," 1982–83 through 2012–13. (This table was prepared March 2015.)

Table 214.20. Number and percentage distribution of regular public school districts and students, by enrollment size of district: Selected years, 1979–80 through 2012–13

Year	Total	25,000 or more	10,000 to 24,999	5,000 to 9,999	2,500 to 4,999	1,000 to 2,499	600 to 999	300 to 599	1 to 299	Size not reported
1	2	3	4	5	6	7	8	9	10	11
Number of districts										
1979–80	15,944	181	478	1,106	2,039	3,475	1,841	2,298	4,223	303
1989–90	15,367	179	479	913	1,937	3,547	1,801	2,283	3,910	318
1999–2000	14,928	238	579	1,036	2,068	3,457	1,814	2,081	3,298	357
2000–01	14,859	240	581	1,036	2,060	3,448	1,776	2,107	3,265	346
2001–02	14,559	243	573	1,067	2,031	3,429	1,744	2,015	3,127	330
2002–03	14,465	248	587	1,062	2,033	3,411	1,745	1,987	3,117	275
2003–04	14,383	256	594	1,058	2,031	3,421	1,728	1,981	2,994	320
2004–05	14,205	264	589	1,056	2,018	3,391	1,739	1,931	2,881	336
2005–06	14,166	269	594	1,066	2,015	3,335	1,768	1,895	2,857	367
2006–07	13,856	275	598	1,066	2,006	3,334	1,730	1,898	2,685	264
2007–08	13,838	281	589	1,062	2,006	3,292	1,753	1,890	2,692	273
2008–09	13,809	280	594	1,049	1,995	3,272	1,766	1,886	2,721	246
2009–10	13,625	284	598	1,044	1,985	3,242	1,750	1,891	2,707	124
2010–11	13,588	282	600	1,052	1,975	3,224	1,738	1,887	2,687	143
2011–12	13,567	286	592	1,044	1,952	3,222	1,755	1,911	2,676	129
2012–13	13,515	290	588	1,048	1,924	3,227	1,751	1,908	2,678	101
Percentage distribution of districts										
1979–80	100.0	1.1	3.0	6.9	12.8	21.8	11.5	14.4	26.5	1.9
1989–90	100.0	1.2	3.1	5.9	12.6	23.1	11.7	14.9	25.4	2.1
1999–2000	100.0	1.6	3.9	6.9	13.9	23.2	12.2	13.9	22.1	2.4
2000–01	100.0	1.6	3.9	7.0	13.9	23.2	12.0	14.2	22.0	2.3
2001–02	100.0	1.7	3.9	7.3	14.0	23.6	12.0	13.8	21.5	2.3
2002–03	100.0	1.7	4.1	7.3	14.1	23.6	12.1	13.7	21.5	1.9
2003–04	100.0	1.8	4.1	7.4	14.1	23.8	12.0	13.8	20.8	2.2
2004–05	100.0	1.9	4.1	7.4	14.2	23.9	12.2	13.6	20.3	2.4
2005–06	100.0	1.9	4.2	7.5	14.2	23.5	12.5	13.4	20.2	2.6
2006–07	100.0	2.0	4.3	7.7	14.5	24.1	12.5	13.7	19.4	1.9
2007–08	100.0	2.0	4.3	7.7	14.5	23.8	12.7	13.7	19.5	2.0
2008–09	100.0	2.0	4.3	7.6	14.4	23.7	12.8	13.7	19.7	1.8
2009–10	100.0	2.1	4.4	7.7	14.6	23.8	12.8	13.9	19.9	0.9
2010–11	100.0	2.1	4.4	7.7	14.5	23.7	12.8	13.9	19.8	1.1
2011–12	100.0	2.1	4.4	7.7	14.4	23.7	12.9	14.1	19.7	1.0
2012–13	100.0	2.1	4.4	7.8	14.2	23.9	13.0	14.1	19.8	0.7
Number of students										
1979–80	41,882,000	11,415,000	7,004,000	7,713,000	7,076,000	5,698,000	1,450,000	1,005,000	521,000	†
1989–90	40,069,756	11,209,889	7,107,362	6,347,103	6,731,334	5,763,282	1,402,623	997,434	510,729	†
1999–2000	46,318,635	14,886,636	8,656,672	7,120,704	7,244,407	5,620,962	1,426,280	911,127	451,847	†
2000–01	46,588,307	15,083,671	8,750,743	7,144,242	7,235,089	5,597,023	1,400,732	927,146	449,661	†
2001–02	46,906,607	15,356,867	8,756,777	7,393,237	7,129,358	5,576,508	1,375,571	885,061	433,228	†
2002–03	47,379,395	15,690,805	8,957,891	7,348,643	7,150,205	5,547,189	1,375,070	874,163	435,429	†
2003–04	47,685,982	15,939,776	9,039,697	7,342,745	7,160,367	5,558,125	1,355,563	867,599	422,110	†
2004–05	47,800,967	16,182,672	8,980,096	7,346,960	7,134,861	5,533,156	1,368,546	851,455	403,221	†
2005–06	48,013,931	16,376,213	9,055,547	7,394,010	7,114,942	5,442,588	1,391,314	835,430	403,887	†
2006–07	48,105,666	16,496,573	9,083,944	7,395,889	7,092,532	5,433,770	1,363,287	840,032	399,639	†
2007–08	48,096,140	16,669,611	8,946,432	7,408,553	7,103,274	5,358,492	1,381,342	834,295	394,141	†
2008–09	48,033,126	16,634,807	9,043,665	7,324,565	7,079,061	5,329,406	1,392,110	832,262	397,250	†
2009–10	48,021,335	16,788,789	9,053,144	7,265,111	7,034,640	5,266,945	1,381,415	835,035	396,256	†
2010–11	48,059,830	16,803,247	9,150,912	7,318,413	6,973,720	5,215,389	1,372,759	833,764	391,626	†
2011–12	47,973,834	16,934,369	9,031,528	7,266,770	6,907,658	5,218,533	1,381,289	842,134	391,553	†
2012–13	48,033,002	17,101,040	8,967,874	7,300,285	6,817,724	5,232,487	1,377,490	841,150	394,952	†
Percentage distribution of students										
1979–80	100.0	27.3	16.7	18.4	16.9	13.6	3.5	2.4	1.2	†
1989–90	100.0	28.0	17.7	15.8	16.8	14.4	3.5	2.5	1.3	†
1999–2000	100.0	32.1	18.7	15.4	15.6	12.1	3.1	2.0	1.0	†
2000–01	100.0	32.4	18.8	15.3	15.5	12.0	3.0	2.0	1.0	†
2001–02	100.0	32.7	18.7	15.8	15.2	11.9	2.9	1.9	0.9	†
2002–03	100.0	33.1	18.9	15.5	15.1	11.7	2.9	1.8	0.9	†
2003–04	100.0	33.4	19.0	15.4	15.0	11.7	2.8	1.8	0.9	†
2004–05	100.0	33.9	18.8	15.4	14.9	11.6	2.9	1.8	0.8	†
2005–06	100.0	34.1	18.9	15.4	14.8	11.3	2.9	1.7	0.8	†
2006–07	100.0	34.3	18.9	15.4	14.7	11.3	2.8	1.7	0.8	†
2007–08	100.0	34.7	18.6	15.4	14.8	11.1	2.9	1.7	0.8	†
2008–09	100.0	34.6	18.8	15.2	14.7	11.1	2.9	1.7	0.8	†
2009–10	100.0	35.0	18.9	15.1	14.6	11.0	2.9	1.7	0.8	†
2010–11	100.0	35.0	19.0	15.2	14.5	10.9	2.9	1.7	0.8	†
2011–12	100.0	35.3	18.8	15.1	14.4	10.9	2.9	1.8	0.8	†
2012–13	100.0	35.6	18.7	15.2	14.2	10.9	2.9	1.8	0.8	†

†Not applicable.
NOTE: Size not reported (column 11) includes school districts reporting enrollment of zero. Regular districts exclude regional education service agencies and supervisory union administrative centers, state-operated agencies, federally operated agencies, and other types of local education agencies, such as independent charter schools. Enrollment totals differ from other tables because this table represents data reported by regular school districts rather than states or schools. Detail may not sum to totals because of rounding.
SOURCE: U.S. Department of Education, National Center for Education Statistics, Common Core of Data (CCD), "Local Education Agency Universe Survey," 1979–80 through 2012–13. (This table was prepared March 2015.)

Table 214.30. Number of public elementary and secondary education agencies, by type of agency and state or jurisdiction: 2011–12 and 2012–13

State or jurisdiction	Total agencies		Regular school districts[1]		Regional education service agencies and supervisory union administrative centers		State-operated agencies		Federally operated agencies		Independent charter schools and other agencies	
	2011–12	2012–13	2011–12	2012–13	2011–12	2012–13	2011–12	2012–13	2011–12	2012–13	2011–12	2012–13
1	2	3	4	5	6	7	8	9	10	11	12	13
United States	17,992	18,087	13,567	13,515	1,540	1,540	280	265	1	3	2,604	2,764
Alabama	170	173	133	135	0	0	37	38	0	0	0	0
Alaska	54	54	53	53	0	0	1	1	0	0	0	0
Arizona	662	665	224	223	19	19	10	10	0	0	409	413
Arkansas	289	288	239	238	15	15	5	5	0	0	30	30
California	1,187	1,181	951	948	198	198	8	4	0	0	30	31
Colorado	259	259	178	178	79	79	1	1	0	0	1	1
Connecticut	200	200	169	169	6	6	7	7	0	0	18	18
Delaware	44	44	19	19	1	1	2	2	0	0	22	22
District of Columbia	56	60	1	1	0	0	2	2	0	0	53	57
Florida	76	76	67	67	0	0	3	3	0	0	6	6
Georgia	216	218	179	180	16	16	4	7	0	0	17	15
Hawaii	1	1	1	1	0	0	0	0	0	0	0	0
Idaho	149	149	116	116	0	0	4	3	0	0	29	30
Illinois	1,075	1,070	866	863	199	197	5	5	0	0	5	5
Indiana	394	407	292	297	31	32	4	4	0	0	67	74
Iowa	361	357	351	348	9	9	0	0	0	0	1	0
Kansas	321	321	309	309	0	0	12	12	0	0	0	0
Kentucky	194	194	174	174	18	18	2	2	0	0	0	0
Louisiana	132	131	70	70	0	0	6	6	0	0	56	55
Maine	260	255	237	231	19	18	4	4	0	0	0	2
Maryland	25	25	24	24	0	0	1	1	0	0	0	0
Massachusetts	401	404	242	237	86	89	1	1	0	0	72	77
Michigan	869	890	550	550	57	56	6	6	0	0	256	278
Minnesota	555	553	337	336	67	66	3	3	0	0	148	148
Mississippi	163	162	152	151	0	0	11	11	0	0	0	0
Missouri	572	567	524	521	0	0	5	5	0	0	43	41
Montana	500	496	414	410	77	77	4	4	0	0	5	5
Nebraska	288	286	249	249	34	32	5	5	0	0	0	0
Nevada	18	18	17	17	0	0	0	0	0	0	1	1
New Hampshire	281	288	178	178	93	93	0	0	0	0	10	17
New Jersey	700	691	616	601	1	1	3	3	0	0	80	86
New Mexico	135	146	89	89	0	0	6	6	0	0	40	51
New York[2]	923	950	696	696	37	37	6	6	0	0	184	211
North Carolina	236	244	115	115	0	0	7	4	0	2	114	123
North Dakota	223	223	179	177	41	43	3	3	0	0	0	0
Ohio	1,079	1,093	615	616	105	105	4	4	0	0	355	368
Oklahoma	575	584	522	521	0	0	3	3	0	0	50	60
Oregon	221	220	184	180	20	19	4	4	0	0	13	17
Pennsylvania	784	799	500	500	103	103	18	19	0	0	163	177
Rhode Island	54	54	32	32	4	4	5	5	0	0	13	13
South Carolina	105	103	86	84	12	12	4	4	0	0	3	3
South Dakota	171	170	152	151	15	15	4	4	0	0	0	0
Tennessee	140	141	137	141	0	0	3	0	0	0	0	0
Texas	1,262	1,254	1,031	1,029	20	20	13	3	0	0	198	202
Utah	126	132	41	41	4	4	3	3	0	0	78	84
Vermont	369	361	303	294	59	60	2	2	0	0	5	5
Virginia	221	227	130	134	70	71	20	21	1	1	0	0
Washington	316	322	295	295	9	9	2	2	0	0	10	16
West Virginia	57	57	55	55	0	0	2	2	0	0	0	0
Wisconsin	462	464	424	423	16	16	3	3	0	0	19	22
Wyoming	61	60	49	48	0	0	12	12	0	0	0	0
Bureau of Indian Education .	195	196	173	174	22	22	0	0	0	0	0	0
DoD, domestic and overseas	16	16	0	0	0	0	0	0	16	16	0	0
Other jurisdictions American Samoa	1	1	1	1	0	0	0	0	0	0	0	0
Guam	1	1	1	1	0	0	0	0	0	0	0	0
Northern Marianas	1	1	1	1	0	0	0	0	0	0	0	0
Puerto Rico	1	1	1	1	0	0	0	0	0	0	0	0
U.S. Virgin Islands	2	2	2	2	0	0	0	0	0	0	0	0

[1]Regular school districts include both independent districts and those that are a dependent segment of a local government. Also includes components of supervisory unions that operate schools, but share superintendent services with other districts.
[2]New York City counted as one school district.

NOTE: DoD = Department of Defense.
SOURCE: U.S. Department of Education, National Center for Education Statistics, Common Core of Data (CCD), "Local Education Agency Universe Survey," 2011–12 and 2012–13. (This table was prepared March 2015.)

Table 214.40. Public elementary and secondary school enrollment, number of schools, and other selected characteristics, by locale: 2009–10 through 2012–13

Enrollment, number of schools and other characteristics	Total	City				Suburban				Town				Rural				Locale unknown
		Total	Large[1]	Midsize[2]	Small[3]	Total	Large[4]	Midsize[5]	Small[6]	Total	Fringe[7]	Distant[8]	Remote[9]	Total	Fringe[10]	Distant[11]	Remote[12]	
1	2	3	4	5	6	7	8	9	10	11	12	13	14	15	16	17	18	19
Fall 2009																		
Enrollment (in thousands)	49,082	14,377	7,511	3,174	3,692	16,873	14,296	1,574	1,003	5,899	956	3,089	1,854	11,932	7,267	3,495	1,171	#
Percentage distribution of enrollment, by race/ethnicity	100.0	100.0	100.0	100.0	100.0	100.0	100.0	100.0	100.0	100.0	100.0	100.0	100.0	100.0	100.0	100.0	100.0	100.0
White	54.1	31.4	21.2	34.9	49.3	55.5	53.7	64.5	66.7	68.0	71.7	69.2	64.0	72.6	67.8	81.5	76.0	44.4
Black	16.8	26.5	29.7	27.9	18.8	14.9	15.6	11.0	10.7	11.1	6.5	12.4	11.5	10.6	12.3	8.4	7.2	16.2
Hispanic	22.2	33.5	39.8	29.3	24.1	22.0	22.7	18.6	16.7	16.3	18.4	14.9	17.5	11.7	14.6	7.0	7.9	34.8
Asian/Pacific Islander	5.0	7.1	7.9	6.2	6.2	6.3	6.7	4.3	3.7	1.9	1.7	1.4	2.9	2.4	3.4	0.8	0.7	2.8
American Indian/Alaska Native	1.2	0.8	0.8	0.7	1.0	0.6	0.5	0.7	0.9	2.2	1.2	1.6	3.6	2.1	1.2	2.1	7.7	0.6
Other	0.7	0.8	0.7	1.0	0.7	0.8	0.7	1.0	1.2	0.5	0.5	0.6	0.5	0.6	0.7	0.3	0.4	1.1
Schools	98,817	25,767	13,234	5,705	6,828	27,041	22,395	2,771	1,875	13,986	1,926	7,069	4,991	31,946	13,156	11,687	7,103	77
Average school size[13]	516	578	583	582	566	642	656	583	555	447	513	462	399	388	579	308	170	13
Pupil/teacher ratio[14]	16.0	16.3	16.4	16.4	16.1	16.4	16.4	16.4	16.6	15.5	16.5	15.5	15.1	15.2	16.2	14.5	12.5	5.0
Enrollment (percentage distribution)	100.0	29.3	15.3	6.5	7.5	34.4	29.1	3.2	2.0	12.0	1.9	6.3	3.8	24.3	14.8	7.1	2.4	#
Schools (percentage distribution)	100.0	26.1	13.4	5.8	6.9	27.4	22.7	2.8	1.9	14.2	1.9	7.2	5.1	32.3	13.3	11.8	7.2	0.1
Fall 2010																		
Enrollment (in thousands)	49,178	14,425	7,545	3,186	3,694	16,872	14,290	1,580	1,001	5,841	939	3,066	1,835	12,032	7,418	3,460	1,154	8
Percentage distribution of enrollment, by race/ethnicity	100.0	100.0	100.0	100.0	100.0	100.0	100.0	100.0	100.0	100.0	100.0	100.0	100.0	100.0	100.0	100.0	100.0	100.0
White	52.5	30.3	20.4	34.1	47.0	53.5	51.7	62.8	64.7	66.3	70.0	67.6	62.5	70.8	65.7	80.3	75.3	62.1
Black	16.0	25.2	28.4	25.7	18.3	14.3	15.0	10.2	10.0	10.5	6.2	11.6	10.9	10.0	11.6	7.8	6.8	16.4
Hispanic	23.1	34.3	40.5	30.3	25.1	22.9	23.6	19.4	18.5	17.1	18.8	15.8	18.4	12.8	15.9	7.6	8.5	12.9
Asian	4.6	6.6	7.5	5.8	5.6	5.8	6.2	3.3	3.5	1.5	1.5	1.2	1.9	2.2	3.2	0.6	0.5	4.2
Pacific Islander	0.3	0.3	0.4	0.4	0.3	0.4	0.4	0.6	0.2	0.5	0.1	0.2	1.1	0.2	0.2	0.1	0.2	0.1
American Indian/Alaska Native	1.1	0.8	0.8	0.7	0.9	0.5	0.5	0.7	0.8	2.0	1.0	1.5	3.3	2.0	1.1	2.0	7.4	0.9
Two or more races	2.4	2.5	2.0	3.1	2.8	2.6	2.5	3.1	2.3	2.2	2.4	2.2	2.1	2.0	2.3	1.6	1.4	3.4
Schools	98,817	25,879	13,279	5,737	6,863	27,108	22,425	2,805	1,878	13,838	1,906	7,004	4,928	31,952	13,348	11,593	7,011	40
Average school size[13]	517	579	584	583	568	640	655	579	555	447	511	462	400	391	583	307	170	481
Pupil/teacher ratio[14]	16.4	16.9	17.1	17.0	16.6	16.8	16.8	16.8	17.1	15.8	16.8	15.8	15.4	15.5	16.6	14.6	12.7	16.2
Enrollment (percentage distribution)	100.0	29.3	15.3	6.5	7.5	34.3	29.1	3.2	2.0	11.9	1.9	6.2	3.7	24.5	15.1	7.0	2.3	#
Schools (percentage distribution)	100.0	26.2	13.4	5.8	6.9	27.4	22.7	2.8	1.9	14.0	1.9	7.1	5.0	32.3	13.5	11.7	7.1	#
Fall 2011																		
Enrollment (in thousands)	49,256	14,457	7,559	3,180	3,718	16,709	14,193	1,549	967	5,671	907	2,953	1,812	12,418	7,859	3,416	1,143	†
Percentage distribution of enrollment, by race/ethnicity	100.0	100.0	100.0	100.0	100.0	100.0	100.0	100.0	100.0	100.0	100.0	100.0	100.0	100.0	100.0	100.0	100.0	100.0
White	51.7	29.7	20.2	33.3	46.1	52.5	50.7	61.9	63.9	65.5	69.1	66.8	61.6	70.0	65.0	79.9	75.0	75.0
Black	15.8	24.8	27.9	25.4	18.2	14.2	14.9	9.9	9.7	10.4	6.1	11.5	10.8	10.0	11.5	7.5	6.8	6.8
Hispanic	23.7	34.9	41.0	31.0	25.8	23.8	24.4	20.3	19.3	17.7	19.8	16.4	19.0	13.4	16.4	8.1	8.7	8.7
Asian	4.7	6.7	7.5	5.9	5.6	5.9	6.4	3.4	3.5	1.5	1.6	1.2	1.9	2.2	3.2	0.6	0.5	0.5
Pacific Islander	0.4	0.4	0.4	0.4	0.3	0.4	0.4	0.6	0.2	0.5	0.1	0.2	1.1	0.2	0.3	0.2	0.2	0.2
American Indian/Alaska Native	1.1	0.8	0.8	0.6	0.9	0.5	0.4	0.6	0.8	2.0	1.0	1.5	3.4	1.9	1.1	2.0	7.3	7.3
Two or more races	2.6	2.7	2.2	3.3	3.1	2.8	2.7	3.3	2.7	2.4	2.3	2.5	2.3	2.2	2.5	1.8	1.6	1.6
Schools	98,328	25,800	13,266	5,666	6,868	26,840	22,263	2,760	1,817	13,387	1,844	6,720	4,823	32,301	13,904	11,445	6,952	†
Average school size[13]	520	581	585	588	568	641	656	577	552	448	509	463	402	399	592	307	170	†
Pupil/teacher ratio[14]	16.3	16.9	17.1	17.0	16.4	16.6	16.5	16.6	17.0	15.9	16.9	15.9	15.4	15.5	16.5	14.6	12.5	†
Enrollment (percentage distribution)	100.0	29.4	15.3	6.5	7.5	33.9	28.8	3.1	2.0	11.5	1.8	6.0	3.7	25.2	16.0	6.9	2.3	†
Schools (percentage distribution)	100.0	26.2	13.5	5.8	7.0	27.3	22.6	2.8	1.8	13.6	1.9	6.8	4.9	32.9	14.1	11.6	7.1	†
English language learners (in thousands)[15]	4,389	2,035	1,211	430	394	1,604	1,439	97	68	336	63	159	114	414	294	77	42	†
English language learners as a percent of enrollment[16]	9.1	14.2	16.7	12.6	10.9	9.0	9.4	6.4	7.6	6.2	8.4	5.7	6.1	3.9	4.7	2.5	3.9	†

See notes at end of table.

Table 214.40. Public elementary and secondary school enrollment, number of schools, and other selected characteristics, by locale: 2009–10 through 2012–13—Continued

Enrollment, number of schools, and other characteristics	Total	City				Suburban				Town				Rural				Locale unknown
		Total	Large[1]	Midsize[2]	Small[3]	Total	Large[4]	Midsize[5]	Small[6]	Total	Fringe[7]	Distant[8]	Remote[9]	Total	Fringe[10]	Distant[11]	Remote[12]	
1	2	3	4	5	6	7	8	9	10	11	12	13	14	15	16	17	18	19
Fall 2012																		
Enrollment (in thousands)	49,474	15,018	7,976	3,368	3,674	19,641	16,851	1,807	983	5,672	1,435	2,499	1,738	9,143	5,189	2,918	1,036	†
Percentage distribution of enrollment, by race/ethnicity	100.0	100.0	100.0	100.0	100.0	100.0	100.0	100.0	100.0	100.0	100.0	100.0	100.0	100.0	100.0	100.0	100.0	†
White	51.0	30.4	20.9	33.6	48.1	52.4	50.6	62.4	65.7	65.4	69.2	66.4	60.9	73.1	68.7	80.5	73.9	†
Black	15.7	24.2	26.8	24.8	17.9	13.6	14.3	10.3	8.4	10.3	7.2	11.8	10.6	9.4	10.8	7.6	7.1	†
Hispanic	24.3	34.6	41.0	31.8	23.3	24.2	25.0	19.6	19.0	17.8	17.8	16.4	19.9	11.6	14.5	7.4	9.0	†
Asian	4.8	6.7	7.5	5.4	5.9	5.9	6.4	3.0	3.2	1.3	1.5	1.0	1.5	1.4	2.1	0.5	0.5	†
Pacific Islander	0.4	0.4	0.4	0.4	0.4	0.4	0.4	0.5	0.2	0.4	0.5	0.1	0.9	0.2	0.2	0.1	0.3	†
American Indian/Alaska Native	1.1	0.7	0.8	0.6	0.8	0.5	0.4	0.7	0.7	2.2	1.2	1.7	3.7	2.2	1.1	2.1	7.5	†
Two or more races	2.8	3.0	2.5	3.5	3.5	3.0	2.9	3.6	2.8	2.6	2.7	2.6	2.5	2.2	2.5	1.9	1.8	†
English language learners (in thousands)[15]	4,397	2,063	1,293	430	340	1,753	1,581	108	64	334	75	147	112	248	153	59	36	†
English language learners as a percent of enrollment[15]	9.2	14.0	16.7	12.6	9.4	8.5	8.9	5.9	7.0	6.0	6.0	5.9	6.2	3.5	4.4	2.2	3.6	†
Schools	98,454	26,545	13,873	5,916	6,756	30,922	25,780	3,226	1,916	13,530	2,973	5,916	4,641	27,457	10,368	10,545	6,544	†
Average school size[13]	522	588	590	601	571	655	674	578	534	444	500	447	404	345	522	285	164	†
Pupil/teacher ratio[14]	16.2	16.8	17.1	16.9	16.2	16.6	16.6	16.7	16.7	15.8	16.5	15.7	15.4	14.9	15.8	14.2	12.6	†
Enrollment (percentage distribution)	100.0	30.4	16.1	6.8	7.4	39.7	34.1	3.7	2.0	11.5	2.9	5.1	3.5	18.5	10.5	5.9	2.1	†
Schools (percentage distribution)	100.0	27.0	14.1	6.0	6.9	31.4	26.2	3.3	1.9	13.7	3.0	6.0	4.7	27.9	10.5	10.7	6.6	†

†Not applicable.
#Rounds to zero.
[1]Located inside an urbanized area and inside a principal city with a population of at least 250,000.
[2]Located inside an urbanized area and inside a principal city with a population of at least 100,000, but less than 250,000.
[3]Located inside an urbanized area and inside a principal city with a population less than 100,000.
[4]Located inside an urbanized area and outside a principal city with a population of 250,000 or more.
[5]Located inside an urbanized area and outside a principal city with a population of at least 100,000, but less than 250,000.
[6]Located inside an urbanized area and outside a principal city with a population less than 100,000.
[7]Located inside an urban cluster that is 10 miles or less from an urbanized area.
[8]Located inside an urban cluster that is more than 10 but less than or equal to 35 miles from an urbanized area.
[9]Located inside an urban cluster that is more than 35 miles from an urbanized area.
[10]Located outside any urbanized area or urban cluster, but 5 miles or less from an urbanized area or 2.5 miles or less from an urban cluster.
[11]Located outside any urbanized area or urban cluster and more than 5 miles but less than or equal to 25 miles from an urbanized area, or more than 2.5 miles but less than or equal to 10 miles from an urban cluster.

[12]Located outside any urbanized area or urban cluster, more than 25 miles from an urbanized area, and more than 10 miles from an urban cluster.
[13]Average for schools reporting enrollment. Enrollment data were available for 95,222 out of 98,817 schools in 2009–10, 95,111 out of 98,817 schools in 2010–11, 94,743 out of 98,328 schools in 2011–12, and 94,771 out of 98,454 schools in 2012–13.
[14]Ratio for schools reporting both full-time-equivalent teachers and fall enrollment data.
[15]Data are based on locales of school districts, rather than locales of schools as in the rest of the table. Includes imputed data for California and Vermont.
NOTE: Detail may not sum to totals because of rounding. Race categories exclude persons of Hispanic ethnicity. Enrollment and ratios are based on data reported by schools and may differ from data reported in other tables that reflect aggregate totals reported by states. Some data have been revised from previously published figures.
SOURCE: U.S. Department of Education, National Center for Education Statistics, Common Core of Data (CCD), "Public Elementary/Secondary School Universe Survey," 2009–10, 2010–11, 2011–12 and 2012–13; and "Local Education Agency Universe Survey," 2011–12 and 2012–13. (This table was prepared January 2015.)

Table 215.10. Selected statistics on enrollment, teachers, dropouts, and graduates in public school districts enrolling more than 15,000 students: Selected years, 1990 through 2012

Name of district	State	Enrollment, fall 1990	Enrollment, fall 2000	Enrollment, fall 2010	Enrollment, fall 2012	Number of English language learners, 2012	Percent eligible for free or reduced-price lunch, 2012[1]	Percentage distribution of enrollment, by race/ethnicity, fall 2012							Number of classroom teachers	Pupil/ teacher ratio	Total number of staff	Student/ staff ratio	Teachers as a percentage of total staff	Percent dropping out of grades 9-12	Averaged freshman graduation rate (AFGR)[2]	Number of high school graduates[3]	Number of schools, fall 2012
								White	Black	Hispanic	Asian	Pacific Islander	American Indian/ Alaska Native	Two or more races									
1	2	3	4	5	6	7	8	9	10	11	12	13	14	15	16	17	18	19	20	21	22	23	24
Districts with more than 15,000 students[4]	†	16,951,837	20,374,040	21,896,958	22,030,570	2,717,023	56.3	35.2	21.0	33.2	6.4	0.6	0.6	3.0	—	—	—	—	—	—	—	—	32,897
Baldwin County	AL	17,479	22,656	28,199	29,419	—	42.7	78.0	13.6	5.1	0.9	0.1	0.6	1.7	1,853	15.9	—	—	—	0.7	72.5	1,549	47
Birmingham City	AL	41,710	37,843	25,914	25,104	—	87.6	0.9	94.7	3.7	0.2	#	#	0.4	1,579	15.9	—	—	—	4.3	47.4	1,210	83
Huntsville City	AL	24,024	22,832	23,364	23,437	—	49.5	45.8	41.9	6.8	2.2	0.3	0.5	2.5	1,691	13.9	—	—	—	1.5	68.1	1,351	50
Jefferson County	AL	40,752	40,726	35,860	36,069	—	55.7	48.1	44.2	5.9	0.5	#	0.1	1.1	2,542	14.2	—	—	—	1.5	68.9	2,194	62
Madison County	AL	13,861	15,675	19,897	19,764	—	35.8	68.8	19.1	2.7	1.6	0.1	6.0	1.9	1,357	14.6	—	—	—	1.9	71.7	1,142	29
Mobile County	AL	67,286	64,976	62,016	58,625	—	73.4	43.2	50.6	2.1	2.3	#	1.1	0.6	3,963	14.8	—	—	—	1.4	65.2	3,369	111
Montgomery County	AL	35,973	33,267	31,464	31,359	—	72.1	12.9	78.2	4.4	3.1	#	0.1	1.2	2,047	15.3	—	—	—	0.6	52.4	1,279	65
Shelby County	AL	16,096	20,129	28,063	28,655	—	32.8	72.3	14.9	9.4	1.9	#	0.1	1.4	2,018	14.2	—	—	—	0.6	83.3	1,597	42
Tuscaloosa County	AL	14,514	15,666	17,785	17,763	—	53.9	66.2	27.9	4.0	0.7	#	0.2	1.0	1,205	14.7	—	—	—	2.9	69.4	878	34
Anchorage	AK	41,992	49,526	49,206	48,790	5,654	40.9	45.1	6.3	10.9	10.8	4.7	8.6	13.6	2,872	17.0	5,894	8.3	48.7	4.7	74.9	2,967	97
Matanuska-Susitna Borough	AK	9,810	13,008	17,079	17,484	465	33.2	73.5	2.3	3.3	2.6	1.3	17.1	0.1	640	27.3	1,583	11.0	40.4	7.0	76.4	1,012	45
Carwright Elementary	AZ	14,368	17,746	17,672	18,928	4,045	99.7	4.2	3.9	89.3	0.4	0.1	1.1	0.9	963	19.7	1,935	9.8	49.8	—	—	—	20
Chandler Unified	AZ	11,041	21,703	38,876	40,163	1,303	29.5	56.7	6.1	25.9	8.4	0.1	1.7	1.1	2,045	19.6	3,876	10.4	52.8	4.1	85.6	2,083	42
Deer Valley Unified	AZ	15,899	27,158	35,190	34,028	643	25.2	71.8	3.0	17.9	3.3	0.4	0.8	2.8	1,779	19.1	3,555	9.6	50.1	2.7	76.3	2,182	38
Dysart Unified	AZ	3,804	5,459	34,175	25,971	730	49.2	50.1	7.5	35.6	2.5	0.3	0.9	3.1	1,268	20.5	2,278	11.4	55.7	3.7	88.4	1,084	25
Gilbert Unified	AZ	10,862	29,188	38,086	38,007	400	1.1	69.8	3.8	19.0	4.6	0.3	0.9	1.7	2,045	18.6	4,176	9.1	49.0	4.1	84.8	2,503	42
Glendale Union High	AZ	12,189	13,453	14,839	15,022	314	63.9	32.5	8.1	52.1	3.8	0.1	2.5	0.9	708	21.2	1,483	10.1	47.7	2.5	—	2,802	10
Kyrene Elementary	AZ	10,483	19,446	17,815	17,786	285	26.9	53.1	9.7	22.5	7.2	#	3.4	3.8	951	18.7	1,706	10.4	55.7	—	—	—	26
Mesa Unified	AZ	62,748	73,587	65,123	64,161	4,020	57.5	48.6	4.3	39.5	2.3	0.2	4.3	1.0	3,264	19.7	7,333	8.7	44.5	5.3	68.8	4,068	81
Paradise Valley Unified	AZ	26,695	34,882	33,017	32,919	1,601	43.7	61.4	2.8	27.5	3.3	0.1	1.1	3.7	1,749	18.8	3,264	10.1	53.6	2.0	78.7	2,263	49
Peoria Unified	AZ	20,850	32,608	36,873	36,736	834	40.1	60.1	4.7	28.1	2.6	0.4	1.0	3.2	1,850	19.9	3,520	10.4	52.6	2.1	80.9	2,679	41
Phoenix Union High	AZ	18,297	22,192	25,854	25,246	1,112	53.6	5.6	9.2	79.3	2.4	0.1	2.6	0.9	1,435	18.0	2,765	9.4	51.9	4.1	89.1	4,260	15
Scottsdale Unified	AZ	19,752	26,938	26,235	25,246	667	24.3	68.8	3.8	19.1	4.7	0.1	2.2	1.1	1,387	18.2	2,791	9.0	49.7	2.2	57.0	1,924	32
Sunnyside Unified	AZ	13,067	14,518	17,323	17,470	2,294	6.7	4.5	2.4	88.3	0.4	0.1	3.9	0.4	917	19.0	2,056	8.5	44.6	8.0	69.0	746	23
Tucson Unified	AZ	56,174	61,869	53,275	50,771	3,203	64.8	23.5	5.5	62.1	1.9	0.4	3.8	2.8	2,698	18.8	6,085	8.3	44.3	4.5	†	3,317	104
Washington Elementary	AZ	22,446	24,723	22,349	22,895	3,015	78.8	32.5	7.6	50.6	2.7	0.2	4.3	2.0	1,201	19.1	2,769	8.3	43.4	†	—	—	32
Little Rock	AR	25,813	25,502	25,685	25,097	2,292	71.9	19.3	66.3	10.9	2.3	#	0.3	0.9	1,769	14.2	3,903	6.4	45.3	3.0	65.6	1,355	49
Pulaski County Special	AR	21,495	18,735	17,501	17,937	477	57.6	45.4	43.0	6.3	2.0	0.1	0.5	2.7	1,126	15.9	2,499	7.2	45.1	5.5	59.6	875	36
Springdale	AR	7,877	11,422	19,411	20,741	8,805	67.9	40.0	2.2	44.6	1.7	9.5	0.5	1.5	1,274	16.3	2,496	8.3	51.0	4.0	74.2	868	27
ABC Unified	CA	20,972	22,303	20,682	20,835	4,554	51.2	7.2	9.4	43.9	35.9	0.8	0.3	2.7	862	24.2	1,768	11.8	48.7	—	—	—	30
Alhambra Unified	CA	20,313	19,776	18,413	18,076	5,354	73.1	2.2	0.6	43.3	51.6	0.1	0.2	2.1	652	27.7	1,302	13.9	50.1	—	—	—	18
Alvord Unified	CA	14,853	17,664	19,803	19,634	8,351	77.6	11.1	4.0	78.2	4.9	0.4	0.3	1.2	731	26.9	1,403	14.0	52.1	—	—	—	23
Anaheim City	CA	14,972	22,275	19,095	19,126	11,770	87.2	4.6	1.4	86.3	6.1	0.5	0.1	0.9	743	25.7	1,442	13.3	51.6	—	—	—	24
Anaheim Union High	CA	23,086	29,363	33,156	32,085	6,987	66.4	12.4	2.7	64.2	16.1	0.7	0.5	3.3	1,265	25.4	2,500	12.8	50.6	—	—	—	24
Antelope Valley Union High	CA	10,937	19,056	26,084	24,816	2,819	57.6	19.9	18.6	53.1	3.1	0.2	1.0	4.2	1,028	24.1	2,139	11.6	48.0	—	—	—	15
Antioch Unified	CA	13,045	20,018	19,081	18,852	3,014	61.7	19.8	24.7	39.2	9.3	1.0	0.8	5.3	754	25.0	1,529	12.3	49.3	—	—	—	28
Bakersfield City	CA	24,911	27,674	27,590	28,987	7,345	87.6	10.5	8.7	77.5	1.3	0.2	0.6	1.3	1,322	21.9	2,636	11.0	50.2	—	—	—	41
Baldwin Park Unified	CA	15,878	17,473	19,923	18,845	5,036	86.1	3.4	3.3	86.8	5.6	0.2	0.3	0.6	895	21.1	1,520	12.4	58.9	—	—	—	22
Burbank Unified	CA	12,057	16,170	16,630	16,481	1,846	41.2	44.4	2.6	39.3	9.8	0.1	0.2	3.5	685	24.1	1,267	13.0	53.9	—	—	—	22
Cajon Valley Union	CA	17,328	16,059	16,065	16,231	5,203	68.5	46.5	7.2	36.4	2.8	0.5	0.4	6.3	671	24.2	1,327	12.2	50.6	—	—	—	30
Capistrano Unified	CA	26,852	45,074	53,192	53,785	5,416	24.2	60.2	1.3	25.1	7.0	0.1	0.3	6.0	1,920	28.0	3,673	14.6	52.3	—	—	—	63
Central Unified	CA	5,070	10,290	14,817	15,262	1,943	65.6	18.8	10.1	54.3	14.1	0.2	0.7	1.8	611	25.0	1,300	11.7	47.0	—	—	—	21
Chaffey Joint Union High	CA	13,505	19,851	15,427	15,020	2,802	52.1	18.9	8.7	62.5	6.9	0.5	0.4	2.1	946	26.4	1,756	14.3	53.9	—	—	—	11
Chino Valley Unified	CA	23,257	31,763	31,608	30,705	4,322	44.8	44.0	3.4	44.8	15.7	0.2	0.1	1.7	1,144	26.9	2,167	14.2	52.8	—	—	—	36
Chula Vista Elementary	CA	17,604	23,132	27,723	28,524	8,535	38.2	14.0	4.2	67.2	12.9	0.6	0.7	0.3	1,392	20.5	2,253	12.7	61.8	—	†	†	47
Clovis Unified	CA	23,224	32,717	38,495	39,894	2,682	48.9	45.3	3.3	32.6	14.5	0.2	0.8	3.1	1,503	26.5	3,391	11.8	44.3	—	—	—	47
Coachella Valley Unified	CA	9,091	12,636	18,464	18,720	10,155	96.7	1.3	0.2	96.7	0.2	0.0	0.3	1.2	843	22.2	1,653	11.3	51.0	—	—	—	23
Colton Joint Unified	CA	16,415	22,118	23,382	23,172	6,347	82.1	7.9	5.6	82.1	2.9	0.4	0.3	0.8	1,021	22.7	1,948	11.9	52.4	—	—	—	27
Compton Unified	CA	27,585	31,037	24,224	24,710	10,317	74.4	0.3	19.7	78.7	0.1	0.7	0.1	0.3	1,036	23.9	2,807	8.8	36.9	—	—	—	38

See notes at end of table.

Table 215.10. Selected statistics on enrollment, teachers, dropouts, and graduates in public school districts enrolling more than 15,000 students: Selected years, 1990 through 2012—Continued

Name of district	State	Enrollment, fall 1990	Enrollment, fall 2000	Enrollment, fall 2010	Enrollment, fall 2012	Number of English language learners, 2012	Percent eligible for free or reduced-price lunch, 2012[1]	White	Black	Hispanic	Asian	Pacific Islander	American Indian/Alaska Native	Two or more races	Number of classroom teachers	Pupil/teacher ratio	Total number of staff	Student/staff ratio	Teachers as a percentage of total staff	Percent dropping out of grades 9-12	Averaged freshman graduation rate (AFGR)[2]	Number of high school graduates[3]	Number of schools, fall 2012
								Percentage distribution of enrollment, by race/ethnicity, fall 2012							Teachers and staff, fall 2012					Dropouts and graduates, 2008-09			
1	2	3	4	5	6	7	8	9	10	11	12	13	14	15	16	17	18	19	20	21	22	23	24
Conejo Valley Unified	CA	17,209	20,999	21,091	20,595	2,236	22.6	61.6	1.5	22.8	10.3	0.3	0.5	3.0	861	23.9	1,484	13.9	58.0	—	—	—	27
Corona-Norco Unified	CA	23,036	37,487	53,149	53,437	7,382	43.6	29.7	6.3	51.2	10.5	0.4	0.3	1.6	2,102	25.4	3,630	14.7	57.9	—	—	—	52
Cupertino Union	CA	12,227	15,670	18,370	19,035	2,204	5.3	18.2	0.9	5.3	73.7	0.2	0.2	1.6	785	24.2	1,396	13.6	56.3	†	†	†	25
Desert Sands Unified	CA	16,058	23,500	29,123	29,159	7,097	68.2	22.6	2.0	70.5	2.7	0.1	0.3	1.8	1,102	26.5	2,056	14.2	53.6	—	—	—	34
Downey Unified	CA	15,418	21,474	22,848	22,844	3,215	70.4	6.3	3.0	86.9	3.0	0.2	0.3	0.3	870	26.3	1,583	14.4	54.9	—	—	—	20
East Side Union High	CA	21,973	24,282	25,676	26,297	5,306	42.4	7.2	3.0	50.4	36.6	0.7	0.4	1.7	1,093	24.1	1,849	14.2	59.1	—	—	—	22
Elk Grove Unified	CA	27,246	47,736	62,465	62,137	10,779	55.2	23.2	15.3	25.7	26.9	1.8	0.5	6.6	3,173	19.6	5,443	11.4	58.3	—	—	—	66
Escondido Union	CA	14,663	19,312	19,242	19,365	8,569	67.7	20.1	2.0	66.4	4.1	1.2	0.3	6.8	815	23.8	1,704	11.4	47.8	†	†	†	29
Fairfield-Suisun Unified	CA	20,227	22,263	21,534	21,400	3,153	55.5	19.9	17.8	37.3	13.6	0.8	1.0	9.3	834	25.7	1,545	13.8	54.0	—	—	—	34
Folsom-Cordova Unified	CA	12,656	16,277	18,893	19,117	2,365	34.9	57.1	7.1	17.4	13.7	0.8	0.7	3.2	777	24.6	1,469	13.0	52.9	—	—	—	43
Fontana Unified	CA	27,043	37,244	40,841	40,374	14,979	87.0	4.8	6.1	85.8	2.3	0.2	0.2	0.6	1,634	24.7	3,373	12.0	48.4	—	—	—	43
Fremont Unified	CA	27,172	31,078	32,607	33,308	5,717	21.6	16.4	3.7	16.0	59.3	0.4	0.4	3.6	1,390	24.0	2,208	15.1	62.9	—	—	—	42
Fresno Unified	CA	71,500	79,007	74,833	73,689	17,586	89.5	12.0	9.4	64.7	12.1	0.3	0.6	0.9	3,030	24.3	6,598	11.2	45.9	—	—	—	107
Garden Grove Unified	CA	37,969	48,742	48,659	47,599	19,960	71.5	9.9	0.8	53.5	34.2	0.7	0.2	0.7	1,780	26.7	3,508	13.6	50.7	—	—	—	67
Glendale Unified	CA	25,459	30,329	26,371	26,179	6,849	51.1	54.7	1.3	23.1	18.8	0.1	0.2	1.7	1,066	24.6	2,081	12.6	51.2	—	—	—	34
Grossmont Union High	CA	18,647	23,639	24,224	22,965	2,688	44.6	47.2	6.9	33.9	3.0	0.7	0.7	7.6	894	25.7	1,847	12.4	48.4	—	—	—	16
Hacienda La Puente Unified	CA	23,267	24,646	20,942	20,358	4,208	73.9	4.0	1.1	80.2	13.3	0.4	0.4	0.8	888	22.9	1,887	10.8	47.0	—	—	—	36
Hayward Unified	CA	19,122	24,205	21,744	21,937	7,022	67.8	6.5	12.5	60.1	14.4	3.7	0.4	2.5	800	27.4	1,759	12.5	45.5	—	—	—	34
Hemet Unified	CA	12,811	17,451	22,294	21,689	2,993	76.9	33.8	7.7	51.4	2.2	0.5	1.1	3.3	873	24.8	1,880	11.5	46.4	—	—	—	27
Hesperia Unified	CA	13,113	15,360	23,137	23,448	4,163	72.2	27.6	7.8	59.5	1.7	0.4	0.5	2.5	879	26.7	1,840	12.7	47.8	—	—	—	30
Huntington Beach Union High	CA	14,039	14,359	16,320	16,400	1,380	28.1	40.4	1.2	24.7	23.6	3.7	0.7	3.5	635	25.8	1,214	13.5	52.3	—	—	—	9
Irvine Unified	CA	20,735	23,961	27,262	29,072	4,442	13.1	34.1	2.3	10.5	46.4	0.5	0.3	6.0	1,002	29.0	2,066	14.1	48.5	—	—	—	35
Jurupa Unified	CA	15,419	19,839	20,088	19,577	7,333	73.6	12.0	2.2	83.1	1.4	0.4	0.2	0.8	820	23.9	1,583	12.4	51.8	—	—	—	26
Kern Union High	CA	20,183	29,333	37,070	37,070	3,156	58.8	25.3	6.3	62.1	3.6	0.3	0.8	1.8	1,505	24.6	3,292	11.3	45.7	—	—	—	25
Lake Elsinore Unified	CA	11,000	17,178	22,065	22,137	3,306	60.2	34.3	4.5	54.0	2.7	0.5	0.6	3.4	885	25.0	1,849	12.0	47.9	—	—	—	26
Lodi Unified	CA	23,954	27,339	30,528	30,222	7,913	68.0	25.5	7.3	41.9	21.3	0.7	0.5	2.8	1,323	22.8	2,484	12.2	53.2	—	—	—	54
Long Beach Unified	CA	71,342	93,694	84,812	82,256	17,512	62.2	14.7	15.2	54.4	11.0	1.7	0.2	2.9	3,006	27.4	6,973	11.8	43.1	—	—	—	88
Los Angeles Unified	CA	625,073	721,346	667,273	655,465	186,593	59.8	9.2	9.4	73.8	6.1	0.4	0.2	0.8	27,887	23.5	61,235	10.7	45.5	—	—	—	978
Lynwood Unified	CA	15,469	18,237	16,360	15,029	6,040	88.7	0.6	4.9	93.9	0.2	0.3	#	#	570	26.4	1,212	12.4	47.0	—	—	—	19
Madera Unified	CA	13,728	15,957	19,576	19,984	6,919	84.4	8.4	2.2	86.8	1.4	0.1	0.5	0.6	768	26.0	1,488	13.4	51.6	—	—	—	27
Manteca Unified	CA	13,356	19,746	23,406	23,235	4,959	59.6	24.0	8.0	50.8	13.6	1.0	0.7	1.9	924	25.2	1,632	14.2	56.6	—	—	—	30
Modesto City Elementary	CA	17,405	18,740	15,088	15,237	5,976	84.5	18.9	3.2	66.6	4.1	0.7	0.6	5.9	617	24.7	1,353	11.3	45.6	†	†	†	26
Montebello Unified	CA	32,938	34,794	32,046	30,564	9,136	88.3	1.6	0.3	95.2	2.4	0.1	0.2	0.3	1,117	27.4	2,434	12.6	45.9	—	—	—	30
Moreno Valley Unified	CA	29,064	32,730	36,901	34,922	8,504	81.3	9.6	17.1	65.2	3.7	0.9	0.3	2.0	1,389	25.1	2,602	13.4	53.4	—	—	—	39
Mount Diablo Unified	CA	32,840	36,648	34,116	32,001	7,437	45.2	37.2	4.4	39.3	11.4	0.6	0.4	6.3	1,444	22.2	2,492	12.8	58.0	—	—	—	52
Murrieta Valley Unified	CA	3,990	12,065	22,318	22,929	863	33.5	46.8	5.5	33.5	8.0	0.6	0.4	5.3	800	28.7	1,667	13.8	48.0	—	—	—	20
Napa Valley Unified	CA	13,705	16,392	18,003	18,326	4,128	43.8	30.6	2.3	52.1	8.2	0.4	0.5	6.0	755	24.3	1,491	12.3	50.6	—	—	—	32
Newport-Mesa Unified	CA	16,434	21,658	21,811	22,003	5,505	45.6	47.7	1.3	43.5	5.2	0.7	0.3	1.4	929	23.7	2,016	10.9	46.1	—	—	—	31
Norwalk-La Mirada Unified	CA	19,179	23,610	20,421	19,770	3,693	73.6	10.0	2.7	78.5	6.1	0.5	0.2	2.0	801	24.7	1,625	12.2	49.3	—	—	—	29
Oakland Unified	CA	52,095	54,863	46,586	46,463	14,324	77.3	9.2	28.9	42.0	14.4	1.1	0.2	4.1	2,134	21.8	4,164	11.2	51.2	—	—	—	124
Oceanside Unified	CA	17,034	22,354	21,082	21,215	3,324	57.9	28.9	6.2	54.0	5.3	2.3	0.5	2.7	825	25.7	1,750	12.1	47.1	—	—	—	25
Ontario-Montclair Elementary	CA	21,033	26,407	22,591	22,735	10,695	85.8	4.2	2.6	88.3	2.4	0.4	0.3	1.5	1,057	21.5	1,931	11.8	54.8	†	†	†	32
Orange Unified	CA	25,224	31,097	30,373	29,854	7,456	46.6	32.2	1.4	46.6	11.5	0.1	0.4	2.4	1,140	26.2	2,251	13.3	50.7	—	—	—	41
Oxnard	CA	12,212	16,249	15,870	16,533	8,903	78.7	4.1	1.6	90.8	2.6	0.3	0.1	0.7	654	25.3	1,291	12.8	50.7	—	—	—	21
Oxnard Union High	CA	11,512	14,552	16,676	16,780	3,201	59.6	16.0	2.2	73.5	6.5	0.3	0.1	1.2	630	26.6	1,157	14.5	54.5	—	—	—	10
Pajaro Valley Unified	CA	16,355	19,864	19,542	20,001	9,689	75.5	16.7	0.5	80.5	1.9	0.2	0.5	0.1	774	25.8	2,102	9.5	36.8	—	—	—	33
Palm Springs Unified	CA	14,427	20,847	23,626	23,581	7,373	75.7	15.0	5.5	74.1	3.4	0.2	0.7	1.3	889	26.5	1,715	13.7	51.8	—	—	—	30
Palmdale Elementary	CA	13,199	20,853	21,049	21,264	6,181	81.8	7.9	16.2	70.7	2.0	0.2	0.5	2.3	824	25.8	1,498	14.2	55.0	†	†	†	28
Panama-Buena Vista Union	CA	10,066	12,843	16,562	17,325	2,475	61.1	26.5	10.7	52.3	8.7	0.2	0.7	1.0	659	26.3	1,576	11.0	41.8	†	†	†	23
Paramount Unified	CA	12,855	16,862	15,792	15,846	5,868	92.4	1.3	8.7	87.3	1.3	0.7	#	0.5	582	27.2	1,192	13.3	48.8	—	—	—	19
Pasadena Unified	CA	21,802	23,559	19,803	19,540	4,102	65.2	15.6	15.6	59.3	5.7	0.2	0.3	3.3	847	23.1	1,931	10.1	43.9	—	—	—	32
Placentia-Yorba Linda Unified	CA	21,438	26,046	25,821	25,622	3,570	27.1	42.7	1.6	39.2	13.9	0.1	0.2	2.2	994	25.8	1,968	13.0	50.5	—	—	—	34
Pomona Unified	CA	26,918	34,479	28,298	27,186	10,438	80.9	3.9	5.5	83.8	5.2	0.1	0.1	1.3	1,420	19.1	2,596	10.5	54.7	—	—	—	43
Poway Unified	CA	24,662	32,532	34,135	35,196	4,298	13.9	52.4	2.7	13.7	25.3	0.5	0.3	5.1	1,249	28.2	2,621	13.4	47.7	—	—	—	37

See notes at end of table.

Table 215.10. Selected statistics on enrollment, teachers, dropouts, and graduates in public school districts enrolling more than 15,000 students: Selected years, 1990 through 2012—Continued

Name of district	State	Enrollment, fall 1990	Enrollment, fall 2000	Enrollment, fall 2010	Enrollment, fall 2012	Number of English language learners, 2012	Percent eligible for free or reduced-price lunch, 2012[1]	White	Black	Hispanic	Asian	Pacific Islander	American Indian/ Alaska Native	Two or more races	Number of classroom teachers	Pupil/ teacher ratio	Total number of staff	Student/ staff ratio	Teachers as a percentage of total staff	Percent dropping out of grades 9–12	Averaged freshman graduation rate (AFGR)[2]	Number of high school graduates[3]	Number of schools, fall 2012
1	2	3	4	5	6	7	8	9	10	11	12	13	14	15	16	17	18	19	20	21	22	23	24
Redlands Unified	CA	16,002	19,411	21,398	21,379	2,058	54.3	32.4	6.8	45.0	10.9	0.5	0.5	4.0	864	24.7	1,522	14.0	56.8	—	—	—	25
Rialto Unified	CA	19,794	28,060	27,026	26,596	7,224	73.4	4.3	12.3	80.4	1.4	0.5	0.3	0.7	1,069	24.9	2,130	12.5	50.2	—	—	—	30
Riverside Unified	CA	31,326	38,124	42,532	42,560	7,393	64.3	25.4	7.5	58.9	4.4	0.5	0.4	2.9	1,599	26.6	3,138	13.6	51.0	—	—	—	50
Rowland Unified	CA	19,143	18,972	15,711	15,501	4,640	66.8	3.7	2.3	64.0	28.1	0.3	0.1	1.6	658	23.6	1,435	10.8	45.9	—	—	—	23
Sacramento City Unified	CA	49,557	52,734	47,897	47,616	11,306	72.2	18.7	17.6	37.2	18.6	1.7	0.8	5.4	1,809	26.3	3,458	13.8	52.3	—	—	—	87
Saddleback Valley Unified	CA	25,130	35,199	31,724	30,355	4,465	26.1	52.0	1.5	30.6	10.1	0.3	0.3	5.3	1,119	27.1	2,024	15.0	55.3	—	—	—	35
San Bernardino City Unified	CA	40,589	52,031	54,518	54,102	14,800	91.6	7.9	14.0	72.7	2.0	0.6	0.5	2.4	2,303	23.5	4,809	11.3	47.9	—	—	—	85
San Diego Unified	CA	121,107	141,804	131,785	130,271	29,524	65.6	23.2	10.2	46.6	13.8	0.6	0.3	5.3	6,571	19.8	12,787	10.2	51.4	—	—	—	224
San Francisco Unified	CA	61,688	59,979	55,571	56,970	14,196	57.5	10.8	9.5	25.9	39.3	1.6	0.4	12.4	2,872	19.8	5,068	11.2	56.7	—	—	—	126
San Jose Unified	CA	29,630	33,015	33,018	33,184	8,406	44.2	25.8	2.9	52.4	14.3	0.4	0.5	3.6	1,471	22.6	2,723	12.2	54.0	—	—	—	53
San Juan Unified	CA	47,690	50,266	47,752	47,116	4,554	46.4	61.2	7.6	20.1	6.2	0.9	1.2	2.7	1,891	25.3	4,256	11.2	44.4	—	—	—	74
San Marcos Unified	CA	9,108	12,804	18,642	19,617	4,127	45.6	41.1	2.6	45.9	7.5	0.6	0.4	1.8	703	27.9	1,581	12.4	44.4	—	—	—	19
San Ramon Valley Unified	CA	16,119	20,742	28,987	30,757	1,599	3.4	50.4	1.8	8.3	31.9	0.2	0.1	7.2	1,302	23.6	2,262	13.6	57.6	—	—	—	36
Santa Ana Unified	CA	45,964	60,643	57,319	57,410	28,580	84.4	3.7	0.4	93.2	2.9	0.1	0.1	0.5	2,145	26.8	4,082	14.1	52.5	—	—	—	60
Santa Barbara Unified	CA	13,370	16,957	16,003	15,489	4,939	52.1	33.6	1.1	58.6	3.2	0.1	0.1	2.8	642	24.1	1,299	11.9	49.4	—	—	—	27
Santa Clara Unified	CA	14,043	14,107	15,383	15,151	4,402	44.4	22.2	3.8	36.4	31.6	1.1	0.3	4.3	624	24.3	1,172	12.9	53.2	—	—	—	25
Santa Maria-Bonita	CA	8,904	11,312	15,050	15,050	9,686	86.3	3.9	0.8	92.5	2.1	0.3	0.3	0.3	581	25.9	1,095	13.7	53.1	—	—	—	19
Simi Valley Unified	CA	18,262	21,181	19,953	18,857	1,673	28.4	55.9	1.1	30.7	9.0	0.1	0.5	2.6	776	24.3	1,545	12.2	50.2	—	—	—	29
Stockton Unified	CA	32,687	37,573	38,252	38,435	11,069	85.6	7.5	11.4	61.8	14.7	0.6	2.9	1.2	1,385	27.7	3,401	11.3	40.7	—	—	—	60
Sweetwater Union High	CA	27,894	35,330	41,426	40,916	9,163	49.2	7.8	3.2	74.8	10.2	0.5	0.4	3.1	1,557	26.3	3,435	11.9	45.3	—	—	—	30
Temecula Valley Unified	CA	7,596	18,980	30,272	30,337	1,434	20.2	47.2	3.9	30.6	9.0	0.4	1.4	7.5	1,147	26.4	2,262	13.4	50.7	—	—	—	31
Torrance Unified	CA	19,645	24,118	24,370	24,324	3,390	29.7	27.7	4.3	24.7	34.6	0.7	0.4	7.6	924	26.3	1,853	13.1	49.9	—	—	—	32
Tracy Joint Unified	CA	7,626	13,816	17,530	17,405	4,015	44.6	25.1	7.2	47.0	15.5	1.0	0.4	3.6	722	24.1	1,375	12.7	52.5	—	—	—	24
Tustin Unified	CA	10,831	16,963	23,093	23,771	5,661	42.7	29.8	2.2	46.4	18.4	0.4	0.2	2.5	807	29.5	1,504	15.8	53.7	—	—	—	29
Twin Rivers Unified	CA	—	—	31,632	31,420	8,859	75.9	30.4	14.9	38.0	9.2	1.5	1.0	5.0	1,378	22.8	2,945	10.7	46.8	—	—	—	53
Val Verde Unified	CA	—	11,242	19,687	19,832	4,935	83.0	5.8	14.5	72.8	3.2	0.3	0.3	3.1	750	26.4	1,300	13.8	52.3	—	—	—	22
Vallejo City Unified	CA	19,049	20,270	15,604	15,157	2,646	65.4	9.8	30.5	34.9	19.9	1.9	0.4	2.6	614	24.7	1,474	11.7	47.3	—	—	—	26
Ventura Unified	CA	15,383	17,527	17,509	17,402	2,748	47.2	43.1	1.4	48.1	3.3	0.2	0.5	3.3	682	25.5	1,023	11.8	46.3	—	—	—	29
Visalia Unified	CA	21,309	23,989	27,118	27,617	4,629	65.2	25.3	2.1	63.6	5.1	1.3	0.4	2.2	1,062	27.0	2,150	12.8	49.4	—	—	—	40
Vista Unified	CA	18,489	27,651	25,843	25,642	6,564	56.9	27.1	4.0	60.4	3.7	1.1	0.2	3.3	1,265	24.2	2,612	11.9	48.4	—	—	—	33
West Contra Costa Unified	CA	31,292	34,499	29,842	30,398	10,283	70.1	10.8	20.2	51.3	15.9	0.8	0.2	0.9	1,265	24.0	2,612	11.6	49.4	—	—	—	59
William S. Hart Union High	CA	10,278	17,001	26,161	26,373	2,377	23.1	45.8	5.0	34.7	10.4	0.2	0.4	3.6	1,067	24.7	1,941	13.6	55.0	—	—	—	20
Academy, No. 20	CO	10,986	17,628	23,119	23,973	353	12.5	75.0	3.1	12.1	3.8	0.4	0.4	5.3	1,440	16.6	2,944	8.1	48.9	1.1	93.1	1,554	32
Adams 12 Five Star Schools	CO	20,838	30,079	41,957	43,268	5,256	37.0	56.9	2.3	33.2	5.2	0.2	0.7	1.7	2,086	20.7	4,228	10.2	49.3	10.3	69.1	1,950	55
Aurora, Joint District No. 28	CO	25,897	30,453	38,605	39,835	13,956	67.8	19.2	17.6	53.7	4.3	0.5	0.7	3.9	2,012	19.8	4,412	9.0	45.6	13.2	52.6	1,360	59
Boulder Valley School, No. RE2	CO	21,502	27,508	29,526	30,041	2,451	18.8	70.3	0.8	17.4	6.0	0.1	0.4	4.9	1,711	17.6	3,683	8.2	46.5	2.4	92.5	2,114	56
Brighton, No. 27J	CO	3,953	5,796	15,089	16,184	2,007	33.5	48.2	1.8	44.0	2.6	0.1	0.5	2.6	743	21.8	1,497	10.8	49.7	8.6	72.5	554	60
Cherry Creek, No. 5	CO	29,210	42,320	52,232	53,422	4,032	25.1	56.2	11.8	18.0	8.2	0.3	0.6	5.0	2,928	18.2	6,359	8.4	46.0	5.4	86.9	3,337	60
Colorado Springs, No. 11	CO	30,009	32,699	29,498	29,032	2,434	53.4	52.8	7.2	29.3	2.0	0.3	0.9	7.4	1,706	17.0	3,796	7.6	44.9	6.3	78.3	1,872	60
Denver	CO	59,013	70,847	78,339	83,377	26,685	71.4	20.6	14.1	58.2	3.3	0.2	0.7	2.9	4,941	16.9	10,594	7.9	46.6	14.0	55.1	2,893	173
Douglas County, No. RE1	CO	13,125	34,918	61,465	64,657	2,055	11.5	76.2	1.7	13.5	4.0	0.1	0.4	4.0	3,103	20.8	6,524	9.9	47.6	2.8	97.5	3,347	82
Falcon, No. 49	CO	2,488	6,026	14,708	15,478	415	21.2	64.9	6.7	17.8	3.1	0.4	0.6	6.5	817	18.9	1,547	10.0	52.8	3.7	80.7	659	21
Greeley, No. 6	CO	11,657	15,998	19,623	19,821	3,865	61.5	36.4	1.9	58.4	1.6	0.2	0.3	1.3	1,116	17.8	2,213	9.0	50.4	5.7	69.8	980	32
Jefferson County, No. R1	CO	76,275	87,703	85,542	85,542	5,166	33.7	67.8	1.2	23.8	3.1	0.2	0.7	3.3	4,785	17.9	10,374	8.2	46.1	3.6	81.2	5,767	163
Littleton, No. 6	CO	15,524	16,516	15,733	15,754	631	20.8	74.2	1.4	16.6	3.3	0.1	0.5	3.8	829	19.0	1,816	8.7	45.6	1.7	91.7	1,222	23
Mesa County Valley, No. 51	CO	17,024	19,688	22,109	21,746	872	44.4	77.1	0.7	17.7	0.8	0.1	0.9	3.2	1,228	17.7	2,485	8.7	49.4	6.2	81.8	1,336	46
Poudre, No. R1	CO	18,599	24,052	26,923	27,909	1,655	29.5	73.9	1.3	22.2	3.2	0.1	0.5	3.2	1,620	17.2	3,440	8.1	47.1	2.7	89.3	1,813	51
Pueblo, No. 60	CO	18,364	17,636	18,443	17,711	916	69.7	27.1	2.1	68.4	0.6	0.1	0.6	1.0	1,036	17.1	1,990	8.9	52.1	8.7	69.7	978	34
Saint Vrain Valley, No. RE1J	CO	15,070	19,620	27,379	29,382	3,676	32.5	65.3	1.0	28.4	3.3	0.2	0.6	1.3	1,643	17.9	3,134	9.4	52.4	4.8	81.0	1,394	53
Thompson, No. R2J	CO	12,019	14,766	15,310	16,042	401	37.4	76.0	0.9	18.9	1.3	0.2	0.6	2.1	849	18.9	1,913	8.4	44.4	4.1	87.6	1,106	35

See notes at end of table.

Table 215.10. Selected statistics on enrollment, teachers, dropouts, and graduates in public school districts enrolling more than 15,000 students: Selected years, 1990 through 2012—Continued

Name of district	State	Enrollment, fall 1990	Enrollment, fall 2000	Enrollment, fall 2010	Enrollment, fall 2012	Number of English language learners, 2012	Percent eligible for free or reduced-price lunch, 2012[1]	White	Black	Hispanic	Asian	Pacific Islander	American Indian/Alaska Native	Two or more races	Number of classroom teachers	Pupil/teacher ratio	Total number of staff	Student/staff ratio	Teachers as a percentage of total staff	Percent dropping out of grades 9–12	Averaged freshman graduation rate (AFGR)[2]	Number of high school graduates[3]	Number of schools, fall 2012
1	2	3	4	5	6	7	8	9	10	11	12	13	14	15	16	17	18	19	20	21	22	23	24
Bridgeport	CT	19,687	22,432	20,205	20,155	2,667	99.5	8.8	38.6	48.8	2.9	0.1	0.6	0.3	1,363	14.8	2,891	7.0	47.1	9.8	53.4	937	36
Hartford	CT	25,418	22,543	21,021	21,545	3,733	84.9	11.2	31.6	50.0	2.9	0.1	0.4	3.7	1,649	13.1	3,348	6.4	49.3	10.8	50.6	909	48
New Haven	CT	17,881	19,549	20,003	21,150	2,627	78.2	15.1	43.5	38.7	2.2	#	0.2	0.4	1,664	12.7	1,986	10.6	83.8	8.7	59.7	911	47
Stamford	CT	11,574	14,791	15,309	15,758	2,005	50.0	34.4	19.7	36.4	8.4	#	#	1.0	1,240	12.7	2,124	7.4	58.4	2.5	88.6	1,018	21
Waterbury	CT	13,323	16,282	18,152	18,391	2,059	81.0	21.8	24.7	48.3	1.7	0.1	0.4	2.9	1,426	12.9	2,950	6.2	48.3	6.3	68.9	857	31
Christina	DE	17,872	19,882	17,190	16,384	1,332	61.2	35.1	39.1	18.7	4.4	0.1	0.3	2.3	1,238	13.2	2,844	5.8	43.5	10.8	51.7	877	31
Red Clay Consolidated	DE	14,551	15,827	15,954	16,157	1,682	52.4	45.3	22.8	25.3	5.1	#	0.2	1.2	1,143	14.1	2,104	7.7	54.3	5.3	60.9	814	27
District of Columbia	DC	80,694	68,925	44,199	44,179	4,530	53.8	11.5	68.6	16.1	2.0	0.1	0.1	1.7	3,313	13.3	6,955	6.4	47.6	8.6	65.0	2,679	127
Alachua	FL	26,387	29,712	27,513	27,826	502	49.0	45.7	36.1	8.2	4.3	0.1	0.2	5.3	1,783	15.6	4,236	6.6	42.1	3.0	76.2	1,864	70
Bay	FL	21,875	25,755	25,935	26,634	428	57.2	72.5	15.3	5.1	2.2	0.1	0.4	4.5	1,773	15.0	3,525	7.6	50.3	0.9	69.5	1,532	50
Brevard	FL	56,639	70,597	71,866	71,228	2,053	45.4	63.4	14.5	12.9	2.1	#	0.2	6.8	4,918	14.5	9,301	7.7	52.9	0.7	79.8	4,931	124
Broward	FL	161,100	251,129	256,472	260,226	25,022	56.9	24.9	39.5	29.0	3.5	0.1	0.3	2.6	14,931	17.4	27,425	9.5	54.4	2.4	70.9	15,663	337
Charlotte	FL	13,030	17,170	16,640	16,355	245	62.5	72.8	9.0	12.3	1.4	0.1	0.3	4.1	1,389	11.8	2,747	6.0	50.5	3.3	90.0	1,402	25
Citrus	FL	11,697	15,199	15,675	15,307	136	63.1	82.2	4.7	7.3	1.8	0.1	0.4	3.6	1,143	13.4	2,420	6.3	47.2	1.6	73.8	1,056	23
Clay	FL	21,933	28,115	35,812	35,244	550	36.0	69.5	13.4	9.9	2.6	0.3	0.2	4.2	2,495	14.1	4,718	7.5	52.9	1.3	84.8	2,469	46
Collier	FL	20,878	34,203	42,919	43,789	5,734	61.2	38.1	12.1	45.6	1.1	0.1	0.9	2.1	2,961	14.8	5,474	8.0	54.1	2.4	69.3	2,477	69
Dade	FL	292,000	368,625	347,366	354,262	69,880	73.1	8.0	23.6	66.6	1.2	#	0.1	0.5	21,475	16.5	38,755	9.1	55.4	4.7	61.6	19,207	529
Duval	FL	111,100	125,846	123,997	125,686	4,173	49.1	38.5	44.1	8.9	4.4	0.2	0.2	3.7	7,619	16.5	12,149	10.3	62.7	5.9	59.9	5,958	197
Escambia	FL	43,091	45,012	40,227	40,670	484	61.0	49.5	35.1	5.1	2.6	0.2	0.9	6.5	2,725	14.9	5,113	8.0	53.3	2.7	56.6	2,116	73
Hernando	FL	12,861	17,215	22,684	22,218	583	59.6	71.2	7.3	15.7	1.7	0.1	0.4	3.6	1,516	14.7	2,879	7.7	52.7	3.1	68.8	1,338	35
Hillsborough	FL	123,900	164,311	194,525	200,466	23,876	57.5	37.7	21.5	33.1	3.4	0.2	0.3	3.9	13,819	14.5	25,733	9.4	53.7	1.1	69.1	10,415	311
Indian River	FL	11,838	14,979	17,740	18,011	1,107	56.6	57.9	16.4	20.8	1.4	0.1	0.4	3.1	994	18.1	1,916	9.4	51.9	1.6	76.6	1,108	29
Lake	FL	21,065	29,293	41,110	41,495	1,686	57.3	56.9	15.4	21.0	2.7	#	0.5	3.5	2,580	16.1	5,546	7.5	46.5	3.2	78.0	2,354	60
Lee	FL	43,240	58,401	81,967	85,765	5,760	65.3	46.4	15.2	34.2	1.6	0.1	0.3	2.3	5,461	15.7	10,901	6.9	50.1	1.7	71.2	4,258	125
Leon	FL	27,241	32,050	33,326	33,432	543	44.6	45.7	42.6	4.7	3.5	0.1	0.3	3.2	2,134	15.7	4,821	6.9	44.3	3.6	73.6	1,857	61
Manatee	FL	26,326	36,569	44,249	46,165	4,223	55.1	50.9	14.4	29.9	1.7	0.1	0.2	2.8	3,009	15.3	6,221	7.4	48.4	4.3	71.6	2,438	81
Marion	FL	29,577	38,562	41,955	41,990	1,899	67.1	54.7	19.8	18.6	1.3	0.1	0.6	4.9	2,756	15.2	5,883	7.1	46.8	3.1	64.5	2,421	65
Martin	FL	11,808	16,308	18,170	18,687	2,281	41.4	62.6	7.8	25.1	1.7	0.1	0.3	2.5	1,207	15.5	2,550	7.3	47.3	0.7	76.8	1,242	38
Okaloosa	FL	26,140	30,344	28,695	29,786	703	39.7	69.0	12.6	8.3	2.3	0.2	0.5	7.1	1,830	16.3	3,307	9.0	55.3	0.8	80.7	2,089	53
Orange	FL	103,000	150,681	176,008	183,066	25,021	62.1	30.5	27.4	34.7	4.5	0.2	0.4	2.4	11,450	16.0	22,343	8.2	51.2	1.2	70.0	9,946	249
Osceola	FL	19,570	34,566	53,357	56,411	9,752	71.7	27.0	11.6	55.9	2.4	0.1	0.5	2.5	3,433	16.4	6,920	8.2	49.6	1.2	75.7	3,202	68
Palm Beach	FL	106,000	153,871	174,663	179,514	20,248	54.7	35.0	28.9	29.7	2.9	0.1	0.7	2.7	12,094	14.8	21,617	8.3	55.9	2.9	73.3	10,654	258
Pasco	FL	33,891	49,704	66,994	67,153	2,436	55.1	66.8	6.1	19.9	2.5	0.1	0.4	4.1	4,587	14.6	9,248	7.3	49.6	1.4	65.9	3,611	110
Pinellas	FL	94,364	113,027	104,001	103,590	5,059	53.7	58.7	19.0	13.9	4.1	0.1	0.3	3.8	7,047	14.7	13,941	7.4	50.5	2.6	68.4	6,711	172
Polk	FL	65,218	79,477	95,178	96,937	10,058	66.6	45.1	21.2	28.3	1.6	0.1	0.6	3.1	6,704	14.5	13,190	7.3	50.8	5.0	68.4	4,884	166
Saint Johns	FL	12,080	20,090	30,710	32,447	294	22.5	80.1	7.5	6.9	3.1	0.1	0.2	2.0	2,228	14.6	4,132	7.9	53.9	1.2	84.9	1,840	48
Saint Lucie	FL	22,224	29,540	39,259	39,641	2,643	61.2	38.7	29.6	26.0	1.7	0.2	0.2	3.4	2,486	15.9	4,902	8.1	50.7	1.8	67.6	2,052	51
Santa Rosa	FL	15,741	22,633	25,533	25,878	153	40.5	80.2	5.4	5.4	1.5	0.2	0.5	6.8	1,657	15.6	2,590	10.0	64.0	2.1	80.9	1,664	39
Sarasota	FL	27,888	35,533	40,899	41,096	2,359	52.1	66.0	9.0	17.9	2.2	0.1	0.5	4.3	3,463	11.9	6,401	6.4	54.1	2.1	74.5	2,607	59
Seminole	FL	49,027	60,669	64,259	64,463	2,278	44.8	55.5	14.1	22.2	4.3	0.2	0.2	3.3	4,942	13.0	8,230	7.8	60.0	0.4	76.1	4,373	75
Volusia	FL	48,403	61,517	61,559	61,064	3,148	58.5	61.1	15.2	17.8	1.8	0.1	0.3	3.7	3,784	16.1	7,779	7.8	48.6	1.4	63.9	3,633	91
Atlanta	GA	60,795	58,230	49,796	49,558	1,624	75.3	14.1	77.0	6.5	0.9	#	0.1	1.5	3,690	13.4	6,620	7.5	55.7	9.5	53.3	2,033	103
Bibb County	GA	24,413	24,739	24,961	24,508	410	79.7	19.7	72.9	3.7	1.6	#	0.1	1.8	1,586	15.5	3,490	7.0	45.4	7.1	49.0	979	45
Chatham County	GA	34,100	35,344	35,246	36,610	703	64.6	28.7	57.7	5.7	1.9	0.1	0.2	5.6	2,550	14.4	4,639	7.9	55.0	4.7	55.3	1,528	56
Cherokee County	GA	16,086	26,043	38,760	39,270	1,704	31.8	73.4	7.1	14.6	1.7	0.1	0.3	2.9	2,328	16.9	4,504	8.7	51.7	4.2	70.2	1,880	41
Clayton County	GA	34,754	46,930	50,366	51,757	3,824	86.5	3.3	70.8	18.3	4.6	0.1	0.2	2.7	2,958	17.5	6,146	8.4	48.1	5.8	45.8	1,944	63
Cobb County	GA	69,441	95,781	107,315	108,452	8,236	45.4	42.6	31.3	17.9	4.9	0.1	0.2	3.2	7,090	15.3	13,274	8.2	53.4	3.5	77.9	6,833	114
Columbia County	GA	14,096	18,756	23,722	24,431	303	33.0	64.6	18.7	7.6	4.0	0.2	0.3	4.7	1,393	17.5	2,924	8.4	47.7	3.6	74.1	1,380	31
Coweta County	GA	10,430	16,766	22,490	22,691	477	45.0	65.1	21.3	7.6	1.9	#	0.4	3.7	1,422	16.0	3,021	7.5	47.1	3.3	74.1	1,217	29
DeKalb County	GA	74,404	95,958	98,115	98,910	10,540	71.4	11.1	67.7	13.6	5.8	#	0.2	1.5	6,149	16.1	12,174	8.1	50.5	6.0	63.1	5,129	134
Dougherty County	GA	18,877	16,799	15,906	15,816	210	82.3	7.9	88.4	2.0	0.5	0.1	0.1	0.9	1,019	15.5	2,340	6.8	43.5	3.3	59.1	752	27
Douglas County	GA	14,002	17,489	24,601	25,175	1,257	60.4	32.5	49.6	12.1	1.3	0.2	0.1	4.1	1,607	15.7	3,306	7.6	48.6	2.7	77.6	1,459	36

See notes at end of table.

Table 215.10. Selected statistics on enrollment, teachers, dropouts, and graduates in public school districts enrolling more than 15,000 students: Selected years, 1990 through 2012—Continued

Name of district	State	Enrollment, fall 1990	Enrollment, fall 2000	Enrollment, fall 2010	Enrollment, fall 2012	Number of English language learners, 2012	Percent eligible for free or reduced-price lunch, 2012[1]	Percentage distribution of enrollment, by race/ethnicity, fall 2012							Teachers and staff, fall 2012					Dropouts and graduates, 2008-09			
								White	Black	Hispanic	Asian	Pacific Islander	American Indian/ Alaska Native	Two or more races	Number of classroom teachers	Pupil/ teacher ratio	Total number of staff	Student/ staff ratio	Teachers as a percentage of total staff	Percent dropping out of grades 9-12	Averaged freshman graduation rate (AFGR)[2]	Number of high school graduates[3]	Number of schools, fall 2012
1	2	3	4	5	6	7	8	9	10	11	12	13	14	15	16	17	18	19	20	21	22	23	24
Fayette County	GA	13,105	19,590	21,274	20,301	515	24.8	55.1	24.5	9.6	4.8	0.1	0.4	5.5	1,402	14.5	2,761	7.4	50.8	1.0	90.1	1,829	28
Forsyth County	GA	7,742	17,131	35,920	38,850	1,644	19.4	73.3	2.6	12.3	8.6	0.1	0.4	2.5	2,280	17.0	4,201	9.2	54.3	2.1	83.7	1,555	36
Fulton County	GA	41,935	68,583	91,864	93,907	5,351	45.2	32.1	42.1	13.4	9.5	#	0.1	2.8	6,279	15.0	11,920	7.9	52.7	4.6	81.5	5,090	104
Gwinnett County	GA	64,980	110,075	160,744	164,976	18,646	55.7	29.4	30.5	25.8	10.2	0.1	0.3	3.7	10,100	16.3	19,379	8.5	52.1	3.4	71.5	8,327	132
Hall County	GA	13,833	20,330	25,946	26,675	4,130	61.4	53.5	4.6	38.3	1.4	0.1	0.1	2.0	1,666	16.0	3,087	8.6	54.0	3.3	62.2	1,273	33
Henry County	GA	10,929	23,601	40,909	40,180	599	51.6	38.2	47.0	7.9	2.7	0.1	0.2	3.9	2,516	16.0	4,848	8.3	51.9	5.1	77.8	2,395	50
Houston County	GA	16,249	21,529	27,061	27,610	771	53.6	49.0	36.1	7.5	2.7	0.1	0.2	4.4	1,836	15.0	3,828	7.2	48.0	3.6	76.8	1,523	39
Muscogee County	GA	30,125	32,916	32,288	32,172	533	66.7	28.7	57.6	6.6	2.2	0.2	0.1	4.6	2,268	14.2	4,980	6.5	45.6	3.3	64.7	1,791	59
Newton County	GA	8,054	11,734	19,478	19,181	483	66.9	37.5	51.5	6.2	0.9	0.1	0.1	3.8	1,284	14.9	2,519	7.6	51.0	2.9	62.4	858	25
Paulding County	GA	7,604	16,587	28,407	28,408	383	42.2	67.2	20.1	7.6	0.8	0.1	0.3	3.9	1,675	17.0	3,250	8.7	51.5	3.5	71.8	1,349	33
Richmond County	GA	33,660	35,424	32,322	32,052	172	77.9	19.7	72.7	3.4	0.8	0.8	0.1	2.4	2,074	15.5	4,338	7.4	47.8	3.7	52.9	1,529	61
Rockdale County	GA	10,942	13,519	15,864	15,871	612	66.2	20.6	61.4	12.5	1.9	0.2	0.1	3.2	1,038	15.3	2,080	7.6	49.9	2.9	69.5	1,033	18
Hawaii Department of Education	HI	159,285	184,360	179,601	184,760	16,474	50.6	13.9	2.2	8.3	33.0	32.8	0.5	9.3	11,608	15.9	22,238	8.3	52.2	4.9	75.3	11,508	286
Boise Independent	ID	23,394	26,598	25,039	25,750	2,936	43.6	78.2	3.0	11.5	4.2	0.6	0.5	2.0	1,465	17.6	1,959	13.1	74.8	1.2	86.9	1,809	50
Meridian Joint	ID	14,802	23,854	35,537	36,838	1,943	30.5	84.0	1.3	8.5	2.3	0.3	0.6	3.0	1,770	20.8	2,306	16.0	76.7	1.4	80.7	1,887	54
Nampa	ID	7,878	11,403	15,181	16,073	2,369	64.9	63.6	1.3	32.0	1.0	0.8	0.9	0.3	772	20.8	1,010	15.9	76.4	0.8	70.4	761	31
Carpentersville (CUSD 300)	IL	11,196	16,711	20,678	20,775	2,411	44.2	52.6	4.9	33.6	5.8	0.1	0.1	2.9	—	—	—	—	—	8.7	91.4	1,326	27
City of Chicago (SD 299)	IL	408,830	435,261	405,644	395,948	64,260	84.9	9.2	40.4	45.1	3.4	0.1	0.3	1.5	—	—	—	—	—	15.0	60.8	20,082	635
Elgin (SDU-46)	IL	27,726	36,767	40,683	40,340	9,692	60.9	31.3	6.7	50.4	8.5	0.1	0.5	2.4	—	—	—	—	—	9.1	80.2	2,455	57
Indian Prairie (CUSD 204)	IL	7,670	23,173	29,522	28,996	1,651	19.1	54.7	9.2	10.4	21.4	0.1	0.2	4.1	—	—	—	—	—	5.5	—	—	33
Naperville (CUSD 203)	IL	16,212	18,762	17,834	17,544	773	13.5	67.2	5.1	8.8	15.3	0.1	0.1	3.3	—	—	—	—	—	5.4	100.0[5]	1,579	22
Oswego (CUSD 308)	IL	4,108	6,846	16,729	17,595	719	27.6	62.1	7.6	18.6	6.5	#	0.2	5.0	—	—	—	—	—	6.0	93.3	795	23
Plainfield (SD 202)	IL	3,324	11,986	28,921	28,777	1,799	20.6	59.0	9.0	22.7	5.4	0.1	0.4	3.4	—	—	—	—	—	8.1	96.9	1,643	30
Rockford (SD 205)	IL	27,255	27,399	28,961	28,777	3,328	78.8	33.8	29.8	25.9	4.0	#	0.2	6.2	—	—	—	—	—	22.7	55.0	1,367	51
Springfield (SD 186)	IL	15,813	15,387	15,176	15,044	105	60.8	48.2	38.0	2.6	1.9	0.1	0.2	9.0	—	—	—	—	—	11.0	59.6	684	36
Valley View (CUSD 365U)	IL	11,781	13,558	17,874	17,819	2,283	62.1	28.0	20.7	40.6	6.4	0.3	0.3	3.7	—	—	—	—	—	13.7	84.6	1,140	36
Waukegan (CUSD 60)	IL	12,116	15,510	16,462	16,812	4,977	26.9	4.2	14.8	77.2	1.4	0.2	0.4	1.8	—	—	—	—	—	17.8	65.2	811	24
Carmel Clay	IN	8,449	12,073	15,550	15,724	502	10.1	77.6	3.4	2.4	11.0	0.4	0.2	5.1	836	18.8	2,010	7.8	41.6	0.5	90.9	916	15
Evansville Vanderburgh	IN	22,918	22,875	23,440	23,020	436	57.7	71.8	14.1	3.3	1.3	0.2	0.2	9.1	1,519	15.2	3,514	6.6	43.2	1.8	75.7	1,416	37
Fort Wayne	IN	31,611	31,843	31,401	30,407	2,488	70.5	47.9	24.2	14.7	4.4	0.5	0.5	8.2	1,871	16.3	4,165	7.3	44.9	0.8	70.8	1,898	50
Hamilton Southeastern	IN	3,113	8,777	18,687	20,209	504	14.5	77.4	7.2	5.2	5.5	0.1	0.2	4.4	999	20.2	2,308	8.8	43.3	0.5	94.6	863	21
Indianapolis	IN	48,140	41,008	33,079	29,806	4,045	83.9	21.2	52.8	20.4	0.6	#	0.1	4.8	2,417	12.3	5,936	5.0	40.7	5.1	35.0	1,159	66
MSD Lawrence Township	IN	11,066	15,692	15,456	15,118	1,688	58.9	33.9	40.8	16.8	1.3	0.1	0.1	7.1	850	17.8	1,667	9.1	51.0	1.6	77.6	1,079	17
MSD Wayne Township	IN	12,229	13,263	16,002	15,742	2,310	73.9	41.2	30.9	20.7	0.9	0.1	0.2	6.1	1,106	14.2	2,155	7.3	51.3	2.4	67.6	786	18
South Bend	IN	21,425	21,536	19,998	19,476	2,225	72.3	36.7	34.7	17.8	1.4	#	0.4	9.0	952	20.5	2,697	7.2	35.3	3.2	66.3	1,109	38
Vigo County	IN	16,982	16,545	15,891	15,404	182	54.9	83.0	5.3	2.8	1.7	#	0.2	7.0	861	17.9	1,700	9.1	50.6	0.1	71.6	952	28
Cedar Rapids	IA	17,003	17,780	17,272	17,120	371	46.9	72.8	13.9	5.6	1.9	0.2	0.4	5.3	1,157	14.8	2,540	6.7	45.6	5.6	76.3	1,071	31
Davenport	IA	17,846	16,874	17,096	16,766	486	59.1	57.9	18.9	13.2	2.0	0.1	0.4	7.6	1,079	15.5	2,076	8.1	52.0	9.4	72.7	930	33
Des Moines Independent	IA	30,888	32,435	33,091	34,092	5,466	72.5	46.0	17.2	23.1	6.8	0.2	0.4	6.3	2,308	14.8	4,573	7.5	50.5	7.6	64.9	1,607	61
Blue Valley	KS	9,433	17,111	21,641	22,162	380	8.1	78.5	3.1	4.6	9.9	0.1	0.3	3.5	1,428	15.5	2,635	8.4	54.2	0.5	94.4	1,412	34
Kansas City	KS	22,118	21,173	20,229	20,914	6,013	89.5	13.1	34.8	44.5	5.0	0.4	0.4	1.9	1,513	13.8	2,737	7.6	55.3	3.3	53.9	911	43
Olathe	KS	14,870	20,703	27,882	28,745	1,735	27.3	71.3	6.9	13.3	4.6	0.2	0.4	3.3	2,050	14.0	3,659	7.9	56.0	0.8	95.0	1,788	47
Shawnee Mission	KS	30,619	30,765	27,822	27,435	2,276	36.9	66.0	8.6	16.8	3.0	0.2	0.3	5.0	1,782	15.4	3,075	8.9	57.9	2.2	87.1	2,061	43
Wichita	KS	47,222	48,228	49,329	50,339	8,146	77.3	35.1	18.1	32.2	4.6	0.2	1.4	8.6	3,228	15.6	5,783	8.7	55.8	2.9	72.0	2,635	90
Boone County	KY	9,911	13,445	19,306	19,827	931	34.0	85.3	3.3	6.0	2.3	0.2	0.2	2.7	1,220	16.3	2,721	7.3	44.8	1.5	80.9	1,079	25
Fayette County	KY	32,083	33,130	37,819	39,250	3,421	46.8	56.2	22.8	12.9	4.1	0.1	0.2	3.9	2,779	14.1	5,723	6.9	48.6	3.5	78.0	2,101	76
Jefferson County	KY	91,450	96,860	97,331	100,316	5,850	59.4	49.7	36.8	7.4	3.2	0.1	0.1	2.7	6,348	15.8	14,624	6.9	43.4	5.7	69.5	5,506	173
Ascension Parish	LA	13,001	15,038	19,953	21,003	347	49.1	60.8	30.7	5.7	1.5	0.1	0.4	1.3	1,353	15.5	2,653	7.9	51.0	4.8	78.9	1,083	27
Bossier Parish	LA	17,804	18,797	20,656	21,459	536	45.7	60.3	27.4	6.7	2.0	0.2	0.4	3.5	1,352	15.9	2,784	7.7	48.5	5.3	71.2	1,041	33
Caddo Parish	LA	51,375	45,119	41,894	41,323	439	64.6	32.5	62.6	2.4	1.2	#	0.2	1.1	2,593	15.9	5,832	7.1	44.5	10.0	60.5	2,126	65

See notes at end of table.

Table 215.10. Selected statistics on enrollment, teachers, dropouts, and graduates in public school districts enrolling more than 15,000 students: Selected years, 1990 through 2012—Continued

Name of district	State	Enrollment, fall 1990	Enrollment, fall 2000	Enrollment, fall 2010	Enrollment, fall 2012	Number of English language learners, 2012	Percent eligible for free or reduced-price lunch, 2012[1]	White	Black	Hispanic	Asian	Pacific Islander	American Indian/Alaska Native	Two or more races	Number of classroom teachers	Pupil/teacher ratio	Total number of staff	Student/staff ratio	Teachers as a percentage of total staff	Percent dropping out of grades 9–12	Averaged freshman graduation rate (AFGR)[2]	Number of high school graduates[3]	Number of schools, fall 2012
1	2	3	4	5	6	7	8	9	10	11	12	13	14	15	16	17	18	19	20	21	22	23	24
Calcasieu Parish	LA	32,917	32,261	33,063	32,265	289	58.8	61.0	33.3	2.8	1.2	#	0.2	1.5	2,343	13.8	4,736	6.8	49.5	3.5	69.9	1,695	58
East Baton Rouge Parish	LA	61,669	54,246	42,723	42,982	1,525	81.5	10.9	80.7	4.5	3.0	0.1	0.1	0.7	2,843	15.1	5,686	7.6	50.0	9.9	51.7	1,839	81
Jefferson Parish	LA	58,177	50,891	45,290	46,100	4,077	76.7	28.9	44.9	18.3	4.7	0.4	0.7	2.1	2,896	15.9	5,768	8.0	50.2	8.1	59.7	2,093	80
Lafayette Parish	LA	29,403	28,931	30,218	30,723	853	61.2	49.2	43.3	4.6	2.1	#	0.3	0.5	2,018	15.2	4,210	7.3	47.9	6.6	70.9	1,652	41
Livingston Parish	LA	16,310	19,723	24,468	25,294	236	50.8	88.2	7.2	3.3	0.7	#	0.2	0.4	1,516	16.7	3,139	8.1	48.3	4.0	73.1	1,203	44
Ouachita Parish	LA	17,667	17,479	19,680	20,043	142	33.6	62.8	33.8	2.0	0.8	#	0.1	0.4	1,239	16.2	2,847	7.0	43.5	6.8	68.9	1,057	36
Rapides Parish	LA	24,765	23,467	23,989	24,065	360	68.9	52.3	42.7	2.7	1.4	#	0.6	0.3	1,652	14.6	3,240	7.4	51.0	7.7	64.2	1,134	49
Saint Tammany Parish	LA	27,522	32,392	36,651	37,513	556	47.3	73.6	19.0	4.3	1.5	#	0.4	1.2	2,501	15.0	5,123	7.3	48.8	4.6	77.2	2,132	55
Tangipahoa Parish	LA	16,724	18,197	19,400	19,834	284	75.9	46.7	47.4	3.6	0.7	#	0.1	1.5	1,182	16.8	2,362	8.4	50.0	5.4	65.5	995	33
Terrebonne Parish	LA	21,116	19,774	18,722	18,642	281	66.3	55.3	27.9	4.7	1.0	#	9.1	1.9	1,107	16.8	2,216	8.4	49.9	6.7	69.6	1,003	38
Anne Arundel County	MD	65,011	74,491	75,481	77,770	3,209	30.2	60.3	20.3	10.1	3.5	0.3	0.3	5.2	5,269	14.8	9,590	8.1	54.9	—	81.2	4,908	121
Baltimore City	MD	108,663	99,859	83,800	84,747	3,043	84.1	8.0	84.7	5.4	0.9	0.3	0.4	0.4	5,380	15.8	10,165	8.3	52.9	—	56.4	4,285	194
Baltimore County	MD	86,737	106,898	104,160	106,927	4,092	46.0	44.4	38.6	6.6	6.3	0.1	0.4	3.6	7,262	14.7	14,168	7.5	51.3	—	81.1	7,299	174
Calvert County	MD	10,398	16,170	16,795	16,323	157	22.5	74.2	14.1	4.3	1.5	0.1	0.2	5.5	1,026	15.9	2,108	7.7	48.7	—	89.4	1,356	26
Carroll County	MD	21,835	27,528	27,334	26,687	205	17.8	87.7	3.6	4.0	2.2	0.1	0.2	2.2	1,865	14.3	3,461	7.7	53.9	—	93.5	2,359	47
Cecil County	MD	12,868	15,905	15,937	15,634	148	40.5	80.4	8.4	5.2	0.9	0.1	0.3	4.7	1,138	13.7	2,091	7.5	54.4	—	78.1	1,080	29
Charles County	MD	18,708	23,468	26,850	26,644	220	31.6	32.7	52.3	5.7	3.0	0.1	0.5	5.7	1,703	15.6	3,259	8.2	52.3	—	93.4	2,172	37
Frederick County	MD	26,848	36,885	40,188	40,456	1,629	25.0	66.6	10.9	11.9	4.9	0.1	0.4	5.1	2,651	15.3	5,417	7.5	48.9	—	92.3	3,022	66
Harford County	MD	31,500	39,520	38,394	37,868	400	28.4	67.4	17.8	5.7	3.2	0.2	0.3	5.5	2,703	14.0	5,185	7.3	52.1	—	90.7	2,666	54
Howard County	MD	29,949	44,946	50,994	52,053	2,158	17.9	46.1	21.1	8.7	17.6	0.1	0.2	6.2	3,821	13.6	7,601	6.8	50.3	—	90.4	3,711	74
Montgomery County	MD	103,757	134,180	144,023	148,780	21,367	33.1	33.0	21.3	26.6	14.3	0.1	0.2	4.6	9,885	15.1	20,190	7.4	49.0	—	89.0	10,129	207
Prince George's County	MD	108,868	133,723	126,671	123,737	16,604	59.9	4.5	66.1	24.2	2.9	0.2	0.4	1.7	7,811	15.8	15,795	7.8	49.4	—	69.5	8,266	208
Saint Mary's County	MD	12,549	15,151	17,271	17,453	163	31.2	68.3	18.6	5.6	2.5	0.2	0.4	4.3	1,071	16.3	2,056	8.5	52.1	—	79.7	1,093	27
Washington County	MD	17,778	19,782	22,206	22,403	354	46.5	73.4	12.3	6.1	1.8	0.1	0.2	6.3	1,514	14.8	2,907	7.7	52.1	—	88.4	1,546	46
Boston	MA	60,543	63,024	56,037	55,114	15,649	71.7	13.2	35.6	39.9	8.6	0.2	0.3	2.2	4,592	12.0	7,607	7.2	60.4	7.2	71.3	3,549	119
Brockton	MA	14,529	16,791	15,828	16,595	3,140	77.1	24.7	54.0	14.4	2.5	0.2	0.4	3.8	1,065	15.6	1,998	8.3	53.3	5.4	69.8	909	23
Springfield	MA	24,194	26,526	25,213	25,283	3,911	87.5	13.5	20.2	60.9	2.4	#	0.1	2.8	2,119	11.9	3,695	6.8	57.3	9.6	52.7	1,099	53
Worcester	MA	21,066	25,828	24,192	24,740	6,372	73.1	35.8	14.2	38.1	8.1	#	0.3	3.5	1,581	15.6	3,151	7.9	50.2	5.1	78.7	1,535	45
Ann Arbor	MI	14,190	16,539	16,764	16,654	684	25.1	55.4	14.3	6.4	14.8	#	0.4	8.6	962	17.3	3,004	5.5	32.0	1.7	92.8	1,289	32
Chippewa Valley	MI	9,340	12,329	16,088	16,422	1,011	26.1	81.6	8.9	3.1	2.7	0.1	0.2	3.4	804	20.4	1,358	12.1	59.2	1.7	90.5	1,124	20
Dearborn City	MI	13,380	17,129	18,663	18,915	8,055	67.0	92.1	4.4	2.2	0.9	#	0.2	0.2	1,147	16.5	1,903	9.9	60.2	1.9	75.4	1,220	33
Detroit City	MI	168,956	162,194	77,757	49,239	5,190	81.0	2.6	83.6	12.2	1.2	#	0.3	0.1	3,142	15.7	7,046	7.0	44.6	6.0	45.1	5,634	97
Grand Rapids	MI	26,871	25,625	18,125	17,038	3,860	82.8	20.1	35.8	35.8	1.0	#	0.5	6.6	1,195	14.3	2,804	6.1	42.6	6.5	45.7	808	63
Livonia	MI	16,543	18,347	15,617	15,176	1	27.7	80.0	8.8	3.3	3.3	0.0	0.3	3.8	813	18.7	1,673	9.1	48.6	1.0	89.9	1,393	26
Plymouth-Canton	MI	14,955	16,518	18,905	17,997	658	16.4	72.8	9.6	3.2	10.4	0.0	0.3	3.6	892	20.2	1,790	10.1	49.8	2.0	93.7	1,379	25
Rochester Community	MI	11,350	13,862	14,890	15,007	528	14.9	76.4	5.3	3.7	11.1	0.1	0.3	3.1	825	18.2	1,583	9.5	52.1	0.4	97.2	1,182	22
Utica	MI	23,960	27,786	28,985	28,415	1,525	29.7	88.5	4.8	2.1	3.2	0.3	0.3	0.9	1,392	20.4	2,616	10.9	53.2	0.9	93.1	2,236	38
Walled Lake Consolidated	MI	9,555	14,438	15,455	15,177	1,526	26.6	79.5	9.5	3.6	5.6	#	0.3	1.5	775	19.6	1,516	10.0	51.2	2.4	90.1	1,193	20
Warren Consolidated	MI	14,336	14,602	15,820	15,193	2,583	57.6	74.1	12.5	1.4	9.0	0.2	0.3	2.4	728	20.9	1,410	10.8	51.6	2.2	88.8	1,136	25
Anoka-Hennepin	MN	34,524	41,314	39,158	38,467	2,466	32.3	77.1	9.2	4.3	6.0	0.1	1.0	2.3	2,199	17.5	4,505	8.5	48.8	1.6	85.0	2,870	50
Minneapolis	MN	41,050	48,834	34,934	35,842	8,227	65.7	36.4	35.6	14.8	7.3	0.1	4.6	1.1	2,427	14.8	5,680	6.3	42.7	5.8	55.1	1,724	91
Osseo Public	MN	19,579	22,017	21,053	20,843	1,904	40.2	49.0	21.8	7.7	15.9	0.1	0.4	5.2	1,219	17.1	2,684	7.8	45.4	0.7	78.2	1,353	34
Rochester	MN	14,045	15,929	16,353	16,451	1,733	37.3	65.2	11.4	8.8	10.3	0.2	0.4	3.7	976	16.9	1,977	8.3	49.4	1.4	84.2	1,194	38
Rosemount-Apple Valley-Eagan	MN	20,547	28,330	27,590	27,243	1,393	23.2	71.5	9.4	7.2	7.9	0.1	0.4	3.5	1,571	17.3	3,216	8.5	48.8	0.8	92.7	2,109	35
Saint Paul	MN	35,932	45,115	38,316	38,419	8,851	73.2	23.4	27.6	14.0	30.9	#	1.3	2.8	2,511	15.3	5,533	6.9	45.4	3.9	73.0	2,409	97
South Washington County	MN	11,417	14,953	17,456	18,048	431	19.4	72.7	7.4	6.7	9.1	#	0.3	3.9	1,105	16.3	2,093	8.6	52.8	0.6	97.7	1,248	26
Desoto County	MS	13,470	19,812	31,916	32,759	1,286	52.1	59.6	32.3	6.0	1.5	0.1	0.1	0.3	1,875	17.5	3,873	8.5	48.4	1.4	70.7	1,551	41
Jackson	MS	33,546	31,351	30,366	29,738	218	91.3	1.5	96.9	1.1	0.1	0.0	0.4	0.4	1,800	16.5	4,416	6.7	40.8	5.9	51.6	1,274	63
Rankin County	MS	12,824	15,013	18,937	19,448	372	40.7	73.6	22.1	1.9	1.4	#	0.1	0.8	1,330	14.6	2,146	9.1	62.0	3.0	66.9	890	27
Columbia, 93	MO	12,786	16,178	17,550	17,719	854	36.9	62.4	20.5	5.8	5.1	0.0	0.4	5.8	1,273	13.9	2,553	7.0	50.3	4.1	91.5	1,213	31
Fort Zumwalt, R-II	MO	10,110	16,521	18,951	18,871	382	22.2	84.2	5.4	3.8	3.1	0.1	0.2	3.1	1,218	15.5	2,431	7.8	50.1	3.2	87.0	1,297	24

See notes at end of table.

Table 215.10. Selected statistics on enrollment, teachers, dropouts, and graduates in public school districts enrolling more than 15,000 students: Selected years, 1990 through 2012—Continued

Name of district	State	Enrollment, fall 1990	Enrollment, fall 2000	Enrollment, fall 2010	Enrollment, fall 2012	Number of English language learners, 2012	Percent eligible for free or reduced-price lunch, 2012[1]	Percentage distribution of enrollment, by race/ethnicity, fall 2012							Teachers and staff, fall 2012					Dropouts and graduates, 2008-09		Number of high school graduates[3]	Number of schools, fall 2012
								White	Black	Hispanic	Asian	Pacific Islander	American Indian/ Alaska Native	Two or more races	Number of classroom teachers	Pupil/ teacher ratio	Total number of staff	Student/ staff ratio	Teachers as a percentage of total staff	Percent dropping out of grades 9-12	Averaged freshman graduation rate (AFGR)[2]		
1	2	3	4	5	6	7	8	9	10	11	12	13	14	15	16	17	18	19	20	21	22	23	24
Francis Howell, R-III	MO	13,391	19,497	19,981	19,835	284	15.8	85.2	6.8	2.7	3.7	0.2	0.1	1.4	1,147	17.3	1,987	10.0	57.7	1.8	96.5	1,488	23
Hazelwood	MO	16,985	18,855	18,655	18,325	349	55.3	24.1	71.8	2.1	1.1	0.1	0.1	0.8	1,110	16.5	1,210	15.1	91.7	2.6	75.1	1,386	33
Kansas City, 33	MO	34,486	37,298	17,326	16,832	3,625	0.0	9.0	59.7	27.2	3.4	0.1	0.3	0.3	1,101	15.3	2,310	7.3	47.7	5.4	43.3	1,032	34
Lee's Summit, R-VII	MO	7,182	14,340	17,803	17,783	164	19.9	77.0	14.1	5.4	2.7	0.3	0.5	0.0	1,105	16.1	2,373	7.5	46.6	3.1	90.1	1,189	27
North Kansas City, 74	MO	15,732	17,258	18,764	19,443	1,260	46.8	64.2	12.1	12.8	3.6	0.6	0.7	0.0	1,287	15.1	2,994	6.5	43.0	3.1	93.4	1,268	32
Parkway, C-2	MO	21,542	20,433	17,458	16,192	629	15.3	69.4	9.2	4.9	12.2	0.1	0.2	4.1	1,205	13.4	2,572	6.3	46.8	1.4	92.0	1,418	28
Rockwood, R-VI	MO	15,608	21,203	22,823	20,460	397	8.1	87.3	2.0	2.7	6.7	#	0.2	1.1	1,453	14.1	3,181	6.4	45.7	1.3	94.5	1,721	31
Saint Louis City	MO	43,284	44,412	25,084	32,364	1,681	68.4	9.9	85.3	2.6	2.1	0.0	0.2	0.0	2,006	16.1	3,603	9.0	55.7	25.9	51.9	1,643	77
Springfield, R-XII	MO	23,631	24,630	24,730	25,545	720	51.6	82.0	7.9	4.5	2.6	0.4	0.5	2.2	1,631	15.7	3,246	7.9	50.2	4.9	82.7	1,673	55
Lincoln	NE	27,986	31,354	35,896	36,943	2,120	43.1	69.2	6.3	12.1	4.7	0.1	0.8	6.8	2,647	14.0	5,218	7.1	50.7	3.9	79.4	1,954	70
Millard	NE	16,764	19,160	22,783	23,395	286	18.1	81.8	2.9	7.0	4.8	0.2	0.3	2.9	1,500	15.6	2,653	8.8	56.5	0.9	96.8	1,583	37
Omaha	NE	41,699	45,197	49,405	50,559	6,319	73.0	32.3	26.0	31.4	3.4	0.1	1.1	5.6	3,103	16.3	6,683	7.6	46.4	5.6	57.7	2,293	101
Clark County	NV	121,984	231,655	314,059	316,778	53,155	54.9	29.4	12.5	43.5	6.6	1.5	0.5	6.0	14,292	22.2	17,246	18.4	82.9	—	—	—	372
Washoe County	NV	38,466	56,268	64,380	64,995	10,341	46.0	47.0	2.5	38.3	4.5	0.9	1.7	5.1	3,129	20.8	3,583	18.1	87.3	—	—	—	106
Elizabeth	NJ	15,266	19,674	24,258	23,988	3,084	88.0	8.1	21.3	68.6	1.8	0.1	#	0.0	1,904	12.6	2,288	10.5	83.2	6.7	62.2	928	33
Jersey City	NJ	28,585	31,347	34,505	27,028	2,708	74.8	10.9	32.7	38.1	16.9	0.7	0.4	0.2	2,561	10.6	4,669	5.8	54.9	6.4	71.1	1,471	38
Newark	NJ	48,433	42,150	41,235	35,588	3,410	89.0	8.6	48.2	42.1	0.9	0.1	0.2	0.0	3,158	11.3	6,333	5.6	49.9	4.2	75.4	2,421	72
Paterson	NJ	22,109	24,629	31,350	24,571	4,270	84.7	5.8	27.8	62.3	3.9	0.1	0.1	0.0	2,108	11.7	4,157	5.9	50.7	4.3	52.7	991	45
Toms River Regional	NJ	16,002	17,621	17,285	16,760	174	23.6	77.9	5.0	11.4	3.9	0.1	0.1	1.6	1,180	14.2	2,161	7.8	54.6	2.2	89.2	1,315	18
Albuquerque	NM	88,295	85,276	95,415	94,083	16,209	65.3	21.8	2.4	66.5	2.1	0.1	4.4	2.9	6,201	15.2	12,334	7.6	50.3	2.7	61.9	4,784	161
Las Cruces	NM	19,216	22,185	25,488	25,384	3,313	65.0	20.2	2.5	75.0	0.9	0.3	0.9	0.2	1,610	15.8	3,311	7.7	48.6	6.6	63.3	1,268	42
Rio Rancho	NM	—	10,219	16,751	16,884	600	43.7	39.8	3.1	48.6	2.0	0.1	3.7	2.8	1,046	16.1	2,086	8.1	50.1	3.9	75.8	915	19
Brentwood Union Free	NY	11,749	15,565	16,833	17,492	4,901	75.4	6.4	13.0	78.1	2.1	#	0.2	0.2	1,074	16.3	2,228	7.9	48.2	2.0	73.1	1,029	17
Buffalo City	NY	47,224	45,721	33,543	32,762	3,879	74.9	22.2	50.5	17.0	6.5	#	1.2	2.6	2,835	11.6	5,169	6.3	54.8	9.3	61.4	1,538	57
New York City	NY	943,969	1,066,516	995,336	989,391	—	66.1	15.0	27.1	40.4	15.8	0.4	0.7	0.6	65,914	15.0	78,540	12.6	83.9	7.4	—	56,655	1,596
Rochester City	NY	32,730	36,294	30,145	30,622	2,979	82.7	10.4	61.4	24.9	3.0	0.1	0.2	0.1	2,604	11.6	5,289	5.7	49.2	11.3	43.9	1,406	67
Syracuse City	NY	22,561	23,015	21,247	20,622	2,674	74.6	25.0	50.2	12.8	6.7	0.1	1.4	3.8	2,108	14.2	3,249	6.3	44.8	11.0	52.3	847	32
Yonkers City	NY	18,621	26,237	25,568	25,529	2,961	75.6	18.0	20.6	54.5	5.5	#	0.3	1.0	1,509	16.9	3,115	8.2	48.4	4.7	64.3	1,361	39
Alamance-Burlington	NC	10,322	20,729	22,811	22,872	2,258	56.5	51.0	21.1	22.7	1.3	0.1	0.4	3.4	1,468	15.6	2,766	8.3	53.1	8.0	72.3	1,349	36
Burcombe County	NC	22,026	24,708	25,572	25,824	1,696	55.5	74.9	6.1	12.8	1.4	0.2	0.3	4.2	1,666	15.5	3,645	7.1	45.7	4.7	75.2	1,628	42
Cabarrus County	NC	12,853	19,115	28,980	30,418	1,839	42.7	60.9	18.6	13.7	2.8	0.1	0.4	3.5	1,886	16.1	3,787	8.0	49.8	5.0	80.4	1,591	38
Catawba County	NC	12,770	16,250	17,370	17,256	1,178	51.7	71.1	5.2	12.8	6.7	0.1	0.2	4.0	1,064	16.2	2,039	8.5	52.2	4.2	81.8	1,166	28
Charlotte-Mecklenburg	NC	77,069	103,336	135,954	144,478	14,468	55.9	31.7	41.7	18.4	5.2	0.0	0.5	2.5	8,646	16.7	17,363	8.3	49.8	6.3	69.2	7,052	159
Cleveland County	NC	8,131	9,663	15,951	15,951	251	61.9	63.6	26.2	4.8	0.8	#	0.1	4.4	1,130	14.1	2,215	7.2	51.0	8.1	68.6	1,027	29
Craven County	NC	14,239	14,829	15,048	15,028	681	55.2	53.3	29.1	8.8	3.4	0.2	0.3	4.8	962	15.6	1,806	8.3	53.3	5.0	74.2	867	25
Cumberland County	NC	44,612	50,850	53,307	52,925	936	58.5	33.1	44.6	11.5	1.7	0.4	1.9	6.7	3,607	14.7	7,094	7.5	50.8	3.8	76.4	3,327	88
Davidson County	NC	16,426	19,136	20,648	20,259	391	45.0	87.3	3.1	6.5	1.0	0.1	0.3	1.8	1,198	16.9	2,338	8.7	51.2	6.4	77.7	1,289	35
Durham	NC	18,517	29,728	32,479	33,079	4,487	63.9	19.3	50.5	24.4	2.4	0.1	0.2	2.9	2,262	14.6	4,501	7.3	50.3	5.1	70.1	1,813	56
Forsyth County	NC	37,625	44,769	53,367	53,881	6,150	54.5	42.8	28.9	21.8	2.3	0.1	0.2	3.9	3,646	14.8	6,771	8.0	53.8	6.0	78.3	3,150	80
Gaston County	NC	29,631	30,603	32,326	31,804	1,544	60.2	64.4	20.4	9.8	1.4	0.1	0.2	3.8	1,873	17.0	3,647	8.7	51.4	6.1	72.6	2,035	55
Guilford County	NC	24,575	63,417	73,205	74,161	5,721	57.7	37.0	40.8	12.1	5.8	0.2	0.6	3.7	4,931	15.0	9,859	7.5	50.0	3.1	80.4	4,616	123
Harnett County	NC	11,890	16,338	19,704	20,569	1,320	57.5	51.1	25.1	17.2	0.5	0.2	0.9	5.0	1,273	16.2	2,303	8.9	55.3	6.3	73.1	1,108	27
Iredall-Statesville	NC	10,610	17,235	21,393	21,400	1,038	43.9	59.6	13.9	11.1	2.8	#	0.2	3.6	1,342	15.9	2,543	8.4	52.8	3.6	85.9	1,407	36
Johnston County	NC	14,647	21,334	32,454	33,711	2,934	44.2	59.8	16.0	19.8	0.7	0.2	0.5	3.2	2,177	15.5	3,930	8.6	55.4	5.3	74.0	1,625	44
Nash-Rocky Mount	NC	11,653	18,342	17,448	16,770	813	67.7	34.4	49.8	10.5	0.8	0.1	0.5	4.0	1,000	16.8	2,122	7.9	47.1	7.0	70.8	1,049	27
New Hanover County	NC	19,090	21,605	24,806	25,836	1,007	46.6	62.5	21.9	9.8	1.6	0.1	0.5	3.6	1,664	15.5	3,366	8.7	49.4	5.8	72.1	1,462	41
Onslow County	NC	18,605	20,984	23,890	25,533	315	43.2	62.5	19.3	11.4	1.1	0.4	0.6	6.9	1,561	16.4	3,063	8.3	51.0	4.7	81.9	1,472	36
Pitt County	NC	17,693	20,040	23,630	23,791	953	58.6	37.8	47.9	9.8	1.3	#	0.2	3.0	1,608	14.8	3,054	7.8	52.7	6.6	69.2	1,298	31
Randolph County	NC	13,572	17,271	18,935	18,628	1,108	55.1	72.4	3.7	14.4	1.2	0.1	0.6	2.8	1,151	16.2	2,238	8.3	51.4	6.3	69.2	1,035	36
Robeson County	NC	23,251	23,911	23,933	24,651	1,508	83.4	15.4	25.3	12.4	0.8	0.1	42.7	3.4	1,511	16.3	3,048	8.1	49.6	6.7	70.3	1,389	42
Rowan-Salisbury	NC	16,403	20,472	20,460	20,165	1,343	62.1	63.8	18.6	13.3	1.1	0.1	0.3	2.8	1,372	14.7	2,662	7.6	51.5	6.1	75.9	1,352	35

See notes at end of table.

Table 215.10. Selected statistics on enrollment, teachers, dropouts, and graduates in public school districts enrolling more than 15,000 students: Selected years, 1990 through 2012—Continued

Name of district	State	Enrollment, fall 1990	Enrollment, fall 2000	Enrollment, fall 2010	Enrollment, fall 2012	Number of English language learners, 2012	Percent eligible for free or reduced-price lunch, 2012[1]	White	Black	Hispanic	Asian	Pacific Islander	American Indian/Alaska Native	Two or more races	Number of classroom teachers	Pupil/teacher ratio	Total number of staff	Student/staff ratio	Teachers as a percentage of total staff	Percent dropping out of grades 9-12	Averaged freshman graduation rate (AFGR)[2]	Number of high school graduates[3], 2008–09	Number of schools, fall 2012
1	2	3	4	5	6	7	8	9	10	11	12	13	14	15	16	17	18	19	20	21	22	23	24
Union County	NC	12,864	22,862	40,153	40,659	2,211	34.8	67.4	13.2	14.9	2.0	#	0.2	2.3	2,561	15.9	4,899	8.3	52.3	3.3	87.6	2,136	52
Wake County	NC	64,266	98,950	144,173	150,956	11,344	35.1	49.0	24.5	15.6	6.5	#	0.3	4.2	9,668	15.6	17,033	8.9	56.8	4.3	84.7	8,186	169
Wayne County	NC	13,653	19,279	19,471	19,761	1,530	63.7	40.9	34.6	17.8	1.0	0.1	0.2	5.5	1,268	15.6	2,504	7.9	50.6	5.6	75.5	1,170	31
Akron City	OH	33,213	31,464	23,113	22,394	1,012	42.4	38.9	46.0	3.1	4.4	0.1	0.1	7.3	1,422	15.7	2,979	7.5	47.7	6.3	65.0	1,484	54
Cincinnati City	OH	51,148	46,562	33,783	31,615	1,313	65.3	26.8	62.7	3.3	1.1	0.1	0.1	5.8	1,684	18.8	4,315	7.3	39.0	5.3	52.7	1,723	56
Cleveland Municipal	OH	70,019	75,684	44,974	39,813	2,737	8.7	14.8	66.9	14.3	0.8	0.1	0.2	2.9	2,864	13.9	7,506	5.3	38.2	12.9	42.3	2,187	100
Columbus City	OH	64,280	64,511	51,134	50,384	5,464	72.6	27.1	57.3	7.9	2.4	#	0.2	5.2	2,957	17.0	6,779	7.4	43.6	2.2	55.0	2,709	117
Hilliard City	OH	6,533	12,423	15,455	15,435	1,013	23.2	77.0	5.7	5.8	6.6	0.1	0.1	4.6	834	18.5	1,760	8.8	47.4	1.1	86.4	968	23
Lakota Local	OH	9,356	14,659	18,185	16,526	791	18.0	74.5	10.3	4.9	5.8	0.1	0.2	4.3	723	22.8	1,558	10.6	46.4	1.6	95.1	1,232	20
Olentangy Local	OH	2,140	5,417	15,815	17,383	297	7.3	81.6	3.9	2.5	8.1	#	0.1	3.7	920	18.9	1,889	9.2	48.7	0.4	100.0 [5]	733	23
South-Western City	OH	16,605	19,216	20,725	20,906	2,488	53.2	68.4	12.1	12.9	2.3	#	0.1	4.2	1,116	18.7	2,485	8.4	44.9	3.7	70.4	1,220	33
Toledo City	OH	40,452	37,738	24,283	22,107	342	65.4	39.8	41.2	10.5	0.6	#	0.1	7.8	1,350	16.4	2,944	7.5	45.9	4.2	48.9	1,276	52
Broken Arrow	OK	13,872	14,990	16,732	17,207	715	42.4	67.3	4.4	9.9	2.7	0.2	7.0	8.5	957	18.0	2,039	8.4	46.9	3.6	78.7	921	23
Edmond	OK	13,041	17,084	21,344	22,489	696	26.6	66.5	10.5	8.5	4.8	0.1	2.2	7.3	1,245	18.1	2,504	9.0	49.7	0.6	89.2	1,331	23
Lawton	OK	17,727	17,338	16,199	15,684	667	60.8	41.5	27.7	15.6	2.0	0.6	6.4	6.2	1,001	15.7	2,273	6.9	44.0	3.4	77.5	1,013	32
Moore	OK	16,630	18,101	22,226	23,173	578	41.0	54.7	6.8	12.9	4.9	0.7	6.8	13.6	1,342	17.3	2,622	8.8	51.2	3.4	80.0	1,233	31
Norman	OK	11,572	12,596	14,644	15,129	776	48.9	64.2	6.0	11.1	2.9	0.2	5.9	9.7	935	16.2	1,800	8.4	51.9	1.2	82.4	811	25
Oklahoma City	OK	36,066	39,750	42,989	44,720	13,472	86.3	17.8	26.6	47.4	2.2	0.2	3.8	2.0	2,591	17.3	5,245	8.5	49.4	4.9	58.3	1,657	93
Putnam City	OK	18,071	19,506	19,068	19,257	2,218	75.3	38.0	25.1	22.4	4.4	0.2	3.4	6.5	1,237	15.6	2,197	8.8	56.3	2.1	73.6	1,182	27
Tulsa	OK	40,732	42,812	41,930	41,076	6,916	83.5	28.1	28.2	27.4	1.5	0.2	7.0	7.6	2,413	17.0	5,698	7.2	42.3	0.4	58.0	1,652	82
Union	OK	9,563	13,054	14,931	15,298	2,526	62.2	40.4	14.3	26.1	6.9	0.1	5.3	7.0	812	18.8	1,808	8.5	44.9	4.1	81.8	919	17
Beaverton, 48J	OR	24,874	33,600	38,902	39,691	5,043	36.2	51.6	2.7	23.8	13.6	0.7	0.5	7.1	1,704	23.3	3,515	11.3	48.5	2.8	83.0	2,459	53
Bend-Lapine, SD1	OR	9,481	13,128	16,173	16,586	583	44.8	84.9	0.8	10.5	1.2	0.2	0.9	1.5	719	23.1	1,468	11.3	49.0	2.6	86.1	1,131	28
Eugene, SD4J	OR	17,904	18,432	17,379	17,029	362	43.7	69.8	1.9	13.4	3.5	0.4	1.6	9.4	726	23.5	1,669	10.2	43.5	1.5	91.3	1,353	36
Hillsboro, SD1J	OR	10,396	18,315	20,923	21,158	2,889	45.9	51.0	2.1	34.6	6.7	0.7	0.8	4.2	896	23.6	2,097	10.1	42.7	2.0	85.3	1,293	31
North Clackamas, SD12	OR	12,403	14,876	17,420	17,048	1,930	47.8	67.6	2.1	16.3	6.9	0.6	0.8	5.6	686	24.9	1,623	10.5	42.2	3.7	81.8	1,113	31
Portland, SD1J	OR	53,042	53,141	45,818	46,748	3,948	44.4	56.5	11.1	15.8	8.1	0.9	1.0	6.7	2,435	19.2	5,262	8.9	46.3	8.6	68.4	2,320	86
Salem-Keizer, SD24J	OR	27,756	35,108	40,403	40,360	6,317	60.8	50.3	0.9	39.1	2.1	2.0	1.1	4.5	1,818	22.2	4,193	9.6	43.4	4.5	81.7	2,474	65
Allentown City	PA	13,519	16,424	17,637	16,966	1,901	86.1	14.0	15.7	66.0	1.5	0.1	0.2	2.5	1,054	16.1	2,272	7.5	46.4	9.1	67.3	1,068	21
Central Bucks	PA	10,286	17,305	20,432	19,814	117	8.9	88.2	1.6	3.1	5.6	#	0.1	1.5	1,151	17.2	2,239	8.9	51.4	0.4	96.2	1,529	23
Philadelphia City	PA	190,979	201,190	166,233	143,898	11,502	85.5	14.3	54.6	18.5	7.8	#	0.2	4.6	8,624	16.7	19,577	7.4	44.1	7.0	53.5	8,377	242
Pittsburgh	PA	39,896	38,560	27,982	26,292	629	69.4	33.6	54.7	1.9	3.1	#	0.1	6.5	1,893	13.9	3,831	6.9	49.4	5.6	64.8	1,716	60
Reading	PA	11,965	15,487	18,194	17,651	3,344	88.7	7.4	9.6	79.7	0.6	#	0.1	2.7	1,034	17.1	2,080	8.5	49.7	10.0	55.5	760	19
Providence	RI	20,908	26,937	23,573	23,872	4,239	83.7	8.7	18.1	64.0	5.2	0.1	0.9	3.0	1,344	17.8	2,641	9.0	50.9	7.5	66.9	1,462	40
Aiken, 01	SC	23,970	25,147	24,632	24,686	1,408	60.0	55.4	33.3	7.3	0.7	0.1	0.3	2.9	1,529	16.1	2,405	10.3	63.6	4.7	62.5	1,276	40
Beaufort, 01	SC	12,518	16,721	19,648	20,443	3,304	57.9	43.8	30.5	21.3	0.9	0.2	0.3	3.0	1,414	14.5	2,148	9.5	65.8	0.9	63.7	995	30
Berkeley, 01	SC	27,384	26,635	29,400	30,942	1,826	60.3	53.5	31.1	7.8	1.7	0.2	0.4	5.2	1,861	16.6	2,852	10.9	65.3	5.5	64.6	1,422	40
Charleston, 01	SC	43,637	44,767	43,654	44,599	2,482	50.3	45.8	43.5	6.9	1.4	0.1	0.1	2.2	3,290	13.6	4,947	9.0	66.5	2.8	60.2	2,158	78
Dorchester, 02	SC	13,735	16,678	22,762	23,741	661	52.1	57.8	29.6	5.6	1.7	0.3	0.1	4.6	1,445	16.4	2,029	11.7	71.2	4.2	67.4	1,136	21
Florence, 01	SC	14,731	13,930	15,919	16,146	384	61.6	41.8	51.5	2.5	1.9	0.1	0.2	2.0	1,069	15.1	1,804	9.0	59.3	2.2	67.3	900	24
Greenville, 01	SC	51,434	59,875	71,930	73,649	7,834	49.1	58.0	23.4	12.6	2.2	0.1	0.2	3.4	4,440	16.6	7,066	10.4	62.8	3.5	69.0	3,805	96
Horry, 01	SC	24,080	29,894	38,534	39,998	2,782	63.3	64.4	20.5	8.8	1.2	0.2	0.3	4.6	2,638	15.2	4,140	9.7	63.7	4.8	72.1	2,091	53
Lexington, 01	SC	11,202	17,285	22,694	23,556	925	38.9	78.8	10.4	5.7	1.7	0.1	0.3	3.0	1,578	14.9	2,396	9.8	65.8	1.4	73.7	1,206	28
Lexington, 05	SC	11,683	15,064	16,699	16,435	408	33.3	62.6	27.7	3.2	2.6	0.3	0.3	3.4	1,210	13.6	1,551	10.6	78.0	1.7	80.8	1,186	20
Pickens, 01	SC	14,289	15,938	16,319	16,735	590	49.1	82.6	6.8	5.2	1.1	#	0.1	4.1	1,034	16.2	1,375	12.2	75.2	4.0	62.9	855	26
Richland, 01	SC	27,051	27,061	24,220	24,138	733	69.9	18.4	73.2	3.8	1.1	0.1	0.1	3.3	1,831	13.2	2,502	9.6	73.2	2.9	58.8	1,251	50
Richland, 02	SC	12,788	19,063	17,060	16,796	247	48.6	28.0	59.1	6.7	2.9	0.2	0.2	2.9	1,762	16.4	2,280	11.6	77.3		74.4	1,347	31
Sumter, 01	SC	18,531	19,063	17,343	17,524	883	71.8	31.9	61.4	3.2	0.9	0.2	0.2	2.3	1,023	15.1	1,708	9.8	59.9	—	—	—	27
York, 03	SC	12,685	14,925	17,343	17,524		55.2	50.9	36.6	6.9	1.7	0.1	1.6	2.3	1,164	15.1	1,537	11.4	75.7	2.8	67.5	997	28
Sioux Falls	SD	16,092	19,097	21,390	23,227	2,106	45.9	69.6	10.3	8.5	3.6	0.1	5.2	2.7	1,363	17.0	2,675	8.7	51.0	0.6	75.6	1,289	50

See notes at end of table.

Table 215.10. Selected statistics on enrollment, teachers, dropouts, and graduates in public school districts enrolling more than 15,000 students: Selected years, 1990 through 2012—Continued

Name of district	State	Enrollment, fall 1990	Enrollment, fall 2000	Enrollment, fall 2010	Enrollment, fall 2012	Number of English language learners, 2012	Percent eligible for free or reduced-price lunch, 2012	White	Black	Hispanic	Asian	Pacific Islander	American Indian/Alaska Native	Two or more races	Number of classroom teachers	Pupil/teacher ratio	Total number of staff	Student/staff ratio	Teachers as a percentage of total staff	Percent dropping out of grades 9-12	Averaged freshman graduation rate (AFGR)[2]	Number of high school graduates, 2008–09[3]	Number of schools, fall 2012
1	2	3	4	5	6	7	8	9	10	11	12	13	14	15	16	17	18	19	20	21	22	23	24
Davidson County	TN	68,452	67,669	78,782	81,134	9,013	72.4	32.9	44.6	17.7	3.9	0.1	0.2	0.7	5,523	14.7	10,356	7.8	53.3	5.7	70.4	3,978	155
Hamilton County	TN	22,785	39,915	42,589	43,707	1,509	58.8	58.5	30.7	7.8	2.2	0.1	0.2	0.6	2,995	14.6	5,063	8.6	59.1	4.9	71.8	2,367	79
Knox County	TN	50,750	51,944	57,977	58,929	1,699	47.2	75.4	14.2	5.8	2.0	0.1	0.2	2.3	3,903	15.1	7,209	8.2	54.1	4.0	79.2	3,500	88
Memphis	TN	107,103	113,730	111,834	107,594	6,662	84.2	7.1	81.0	9.7	1.3	0.1	0.1	0.7	7,070	15.2	12,224	8.8	57.8	10.5	67.3	6,559	217
Montgomery County	TN	16,591	23,339	29,780	30,622	606	46.7	57.5	23.5	10.6	1.5	0.6	0.4	6.0	2,021	15.2	3,913	7.8	51.6	1.1	86.3	1,826	37
Rutherford County	TN	17,996	25,356	38,846	40,400	1,574	42.1	67.6	16.1	10.2	4.2	0.1	0.2	1.8	2,680	15.1	4,295	9.4	62.4	1.4	88.7	2,649	46
Shelby County	TN	37,675	46,972	47,706	46,552	970	36.9	50.6	36.9	5.4	5.0	0.1	0.3	1.7	2,919	15.9	5,367	8.7	54.4	0.3	76.1	2,727	52
Sumner County	TN	19,630	22,347	27,907	28,448	448	40.0	82.3	9.4	5.5	1.5	0.1	0.2	1.0	1,926	14.8	3,646	7.8	52.8	1.4	82.6	1,689	46
Williamson County	TN	11,472	19,545	31,616	33,312	405	11.6	86.2	4.2	4.0	4.3	0.3	0.1	0.8	2,111	15.8	3,868	8.6	54.6	0.8	100.0[5]	2,300	41
Wilson County	TN	10,175	11,430	15,705	16,312	203	29.5	85.7	7.0	3.9	1.9	0.2	0.2	1.0	1,005	16.2	2,000	8.2	50.2	1.6	91.4	1,175	21
Abilene ISD	TX	18,217	18,118	17,161	17,152	495	65.6	40.7	11.9	41.3	1.9	0.1	0.4	3.8	1,109	15.5	2,257	7.6	49.2	2.7	69.7	879	37
Aldine ISD	TX	41,372	52,520	63,154	65,684	16,680	84.7	1.1	25.6	70.1	1.3	0.1	0.1	0.7	3,848	17.1	8,010	8.2	48.0	5.6	59.0	2,652	76
Alief ISD	TX	29,774	42,151	45,768	45,783	14,366	81.7	3.5	31.2	51.2	12.7	0.2	0.6	0.6	3,102	14.8	5,969	7.7	52.0	5.0	64.6	2,270	46
Allen ISD	TX	5,240	10,604	18,888	19,894	1,092	16.7	56.9	10.4	13.3	14.2	0.1	0.4	4.3	1,246	16.0	2,185	9.1	57.0	0.3	98.5	1,230	23
Alvin ISD	TX	9,323	11,324	17,367	18,886	2,758	51.6	30.9	13.9	44.7	8.4	0.1	0.4	1.6	1,146	16.5	2,319	8.1	49.4	3.2	79.6	808	24
Amarillo ISD	TX	27,374	28,908	32,682	33,327	4,178	66.9	37.2	10.0	44.6	5.0	0.3	0.5	2.4	2,240	14.9	4,095	8.1	54.7	3.1	73.8	1,706	54
Arlington ISD	TX	44,958	58,866	64,484	65,001	11,589	68.3	23.8	23.5	43.9	6.5	0.1	0.2	1.8	4,051	16.0	7,969	8.2	50.8	2.9	68.1	3,441	76
Austin ISD	TX	65,885	77,816	85,697	86,516	21,728	62.9	24.8	8.7	60.4	3.4	0.1	0.2	2.4	5,893	14.7	11,468	7.5	51.4	4.9	68.6	3,914	129
Beaumont ISD	TX	20,627	20,696	19,893	19,850	1,177	74.2	13.5	60.9	20.3	2.9	0.1	0.2	2.1	1,407	14.1	2,857	6.9	49.2	3.1	70.2	1,091	30
Birdville ISD	TX	18,477	21,246	23,545	24,190	2,838	57.6	46.2	7.6	38.1	4.9	0.1	0.2	2.4	1,527	15.8	2,928	8.3	52.1	3.6	70.7	1,297	32
Brownsville ISD	TX	37,489	40,898	49,879	49,190	14,133	95.9	0.3	0.1	98.6	0.3	#	0.6	#	3,201	15.4	7,256	6.8	44.1	2.3	68.7	2,524	60
Bryan ISD	TX	11,413	13,501	15,751	15,624	2,935	73.2	25.8	20.1	52.4	0.3	0.1	0.2	1.1	1,032	15.1	2,172	7.2	47.5	4.4	72.1	747	27
Carrollton-Farmers Branch ISD	TX	17,561	24,134	26,159	26,385	5,836	62.3	17.3	16.3	53.8	10.9	0.1	0.4	1.3	1,628	16.2	3,026	8.7	53.8	1.6	73.7	1,553	40
Clear Creek ISD	TX	22,372	29,875	36,406	36,635	2,683	28.0	51.3	8.2	27.0	9.8	0.1	0.2	3.3	2,453	16.2	4,809	8.2	51.0	0.9	83.5	2,412	44
Comal ISD	TX	5,883	10,695	17,239	18,693	729	31.2	56.9	2.2	36.4	1.2	0.2	0.3	2.7	1,116	16.7	2,265	8.3	49.3	1.3	100.0[5]	1,072	30
Conroe ISD	TX	23,288	34,928	51,170	53,934	5,244	35.7	53.7	6.0	33.7	3.2	0.1	0.5	2.7	3,216	16.8	6,174	8.7	52.1	0.9	84.2	2,931	55
Corpus Christi ISD	TX	41,881	39,138	38,409	39,213	1,757	68.5	14.0	4.1	79.0	1.7	0.1	0.2	0.8	2,251	17.4	4,633	8.5	48.6	2.8	69.4	2,079	58
Crowley ISD	TX	5,832	9,137	15,240	15,060	1,214	59.3	23.1	41.2	24.2	4.3	0.1	5.4	1.7	906	16.6	1,494	10.1	60.6	3.1	74.1	808	22
Cypress-Fairbanks ISD	TX	41,196	63,497	106,097	110,013	13,629	49.7	29.0	16.3	43.5	8.1	0.1	0.3	2.6	6,392	17.2	12,718	8.7	50.3	1.2	85.9	5,614	83
Dallas ISD	TX	135,000	161,548	157,162	158,932	57,446	88.9	4.8	23.7	69.4	1.2	0.1	0.4	0.5	9,921	16.0	18,030	8.8	55.0	6.0	57.1	6,671	234
Denton ISD	TX	10,690	13,645	23,994	25,775	3,438	43.0	51.6	12.0	31.2	2.5	0.1	0.9	1.7	1,795	14.4	3,127	8.2	57.4	0.8	78.8	1,081	36
Donna ISD	TX	7,906	10,332	15,028	15,276	7,240	97.0	0.3	0.1	99.6	#	0.0	0.7	#	944	16.2	2,324	6.6	40.6	5.4	69.5	586	23
Eagle Mt.-Saginaw ISD	TX	4,691	6,567	16,709	17,728	1,087	40.2	47.8	9.3	35.2	3.9	0.2	0.7	2.9	1,087	16.3	2,081	8.5	52.2	1.7	93.9	821	26
Eagle Pass ISD	TX	10,584	12,515	15,094	15,094	4,965	79.1	1.0	0.1	97.3	0.1	#	0.4	0.1	909	16.6	2,074	7.3	43.9	3.5	76.6	797	24
Ector County ISD	TX	26,993	26,831	28,126	29,649	3,777	51.9	22.7	3.9	70.9	0.8	0.2	0.2	1.0	1,716	17.3	3,306	9.0	51.9	4.4	61.6	1,270	39
Edinburg CISD	TX	15,645	22,005	33,223	33,673	9,853	85.2	1.1	0.2	98.0	0.6	#	0.2	1.0	2,193	15.4	4,476	7.5	49.0	3.7	74.9	1,494	45
El Paso ISD	TX	64,092	62,325	64,330	63,210	12,866	69.4	10.6	4.1	82.6	1.1	0.3	0.2	1.2	4,145	15.2	7,872	8.0	52.7	4.8	66.0	3,396	96
Fort Bend ISD	TX	36,286	53,999	68,948	69,591	8,769	38.5	19.1	29.3	26.5	22.2	0.1	0.3	2.4	4,030	17.3	7,959	8.7	50.6	1.5	83.5	4,636	73
Fort Worth ISD	TX	69,163	79,661	81,651	83,503	23,472	77.0	13.3	22.8	60.5	1.9	0.1	0.4	1.1	4,958	16.8	9,556	8.7	51.9	6.5	62.4	3,568	144
Frisco ISD	TX	1,419	7,234	37,279	42,707	1,502	12.0	57.0	10.5	15.0	13.9	0.1	0.2	2.8	2,828	15.1	5,119	8.3	55.3	0.2	100.0[5]	1,270	55
Galena Park ISD	TX	15,593	18,885	21,680	22,113	6,121	82.9	5.9	16.3	75.6	0.8	0.2	0.4	0.6	1,480	14.9	2,940	7.5	50.4	4.0	81.1	1,298	24
Garland ISD	TX	37,978	50,312	57,833	58,059	11,007	61.0	22.5	17.2	49.6	8.1	0.2	0.6	2.0	3,636	16.0	7,172	8.1	50.7	2.7	80.0	3,562	72
Goose Creek CISD	TX	17,654	18,003	21,283	21,821	6,217	64.3	24.0	16.0	56.6	1.3	#	0.5	1.5	1,372	15.9	2,805	7.8	48.9	2.8	68.1	1,103	26
Grand Prairie ISD	TX	16,482	20,257	26,541	26,921	2,223	73.2	13.5	17.2	63.6	3.1	#	0.4	1.4	1,660	16.2	2,885	9.3	57.5	4.4	67.2	1,266	39
Harlandale ISD	TX	15,089	14,468	14,895	15,175	2,410	87.6	2.2	0.3	97.3	0.1	0.1	0.1	0.1	976	15.5	2,085	7.3	46.8	4.3	66.4	734	30
Harlingen CISD	TX	14,863	15,857	18,422	18,509	2,443	78.0	7.1	0.4	91.5	0.6	0.1	0.2	0.2	1,203	15.4	2,640	7.0	45.6	4.2	68.9	960	32
Hays CISD	TX	4,166	7,402	15,325	16,568	1,650	46.0	32.0	3.3	61.8	0.7	#	0.4	1.9	1,035	16.0	2,183	7.6	47.4	4.3	80.5	662	23
Houston ISD	TX	194,000	208,462	204,245	203,354	53,722	79.7	8.2	24.6	62.7	3.4	0.1	0.2	0.8	10,958	18.6	22,152	9.2	49.5	4.6	59.2	8,595	276
Humble ISD	TX	19,560	24,684	35,913	37,095	1,650	33.7	44.7	18.0	31.2	3.0	0.4	0.3	2.2	2,334	15.9	4,559	8.1	51.2	1.7	90.3	2,140	43
Hurst-Euless-Bedford ISD	TX	18,740	19,203	21,046	21,814	1,650	53.1	42.9	12.9	28.8	6.8	0.1	0.3	2.4	1,294	16.9	2,433	9.0	53.2	0.9	90.3	1,323	32
Irving ISD	TX	23,509	29,097	34,243	35,030	12,774	81.3	10.1	13.8	71.5	3.3	0.1	0.3	0.6	2,304	15.2	3,954	8.9	58.3	3.0	68.9	1,648	40
Judson ISD	TX	13,145	16,603	22,040	22,606	1,586	62.3	17.8	24.0	52.8	1.7	0.2	0.6	3.1	1,302	17.4	2,753	8.2	47.3	4.5	75.0	1,154	30
Katy ISD	TX	19,507	34,503	60,803	64,562	7,396	30.0	41.8	9.6	34.3	11.6	0.1	0.3	2.4	4,068	15.9	7,742	8.3	52.6	1.0	93.3	3,539	60
Keller ISD	TX	8,212	17,083	32,746	33,367	1,600	22.2	61.0	7.9	19.4	7.9	0.2	1.1	2.6	1,941	17.2	3,446	9.7	56.3	1.4	87.8	1,736	39

See notes at end of table.

Table 215.10. Selected statistics on enrollment, teachers, dropouts, and graduates in public school districts enrolling more than 15,000 students: Selected years, 1990 through 2012—Continued

Name of district	State	Enrollment, fall 1990	Enrollment, fall 2000	Enrollment, fall 2010	Enrollment, fall 2012	Number of English language learners, 2012	Percent eligible for free or reduced-price lunch, 2012[1]	White	Black	Hispanic	Asian	Pacific Islander	American Indian/Alaska Native	Two or more races	Number of classroom teachers	Pupil/teacher ratio	Total number of staff	Student/staff ratio	Teachers as a percentage of total staff	Percent dropping out of grades 9–12	Averaged freshman graduation rate (AFGR)[2]	Number of high school graduates[3]	Number of schools, fall 2012
1	2	3	4	5	6	7	8	9	10	11	12	13	14	15	16	17	18	19	20	21	22	23	24
Killeen ISD	TX	22,131	29,687	40,231	41,756	2,830	56.2	27.9	33.0	27.6	2.7	1.4	0.8	6.6	2,733	15.3	5,733	7.3	47.7	2.6	69.1	1,660	55
Klein ISD	TX	26,220	32,376	45,310	47,045	5,109	41.3	37.1	14.2	37.0	8.5	0.1	0.4	2.7	2,998	15.7	5,719	8.2	52.4	2.8	79.7	2,760	47
La Joya ISD	TX	9,844	17,641	28,846	29,235	12,936	95.2	0.2	#	99.7	0.0	#	#	#	1,957	14.9	4,063	7.2	48.2	4.0	69.7	1,190	38
Lamar CISD	TX	12,335	15,159	24,637	26,135	2,818	52.2	28.2	18.5	46.1	5.7	0.0	0.3	1.2	1,481	17.6	2,953	8.9	50.2	2.7	82.7	1,228	36
Laredo ISD	TX	23,304	22,547	24,706	24,823	14,482	97.4	0.4	0.1	99.4	0.1	0.0	0.3	0.0	1,454	17.1	3,535	7.0	41.1	2.9	62.3	1,068	30
Leander ISD	TX	5,419	14,499	32,152	34,381	1,425	21.9	63.3	3.9	23.8	5.1	0.2	0.3	3.4	2,231	15.4	4,137	8.3	53.9	2.5	92.7	1,477	40
Lewisville ISD	TX	20,776	39,096	51,484	52,528	6,721	30.0	49.6	9.0	26.8	11.1	0.1	0.4	2.9	3,746	14.0	6,255	8.4	59.9	1.2	82.8	3,158	68
Lubbock ISD	TX	30,991	29,026	28,905	29,219	797	66.1	26.6	13.2	56.3	1.7	0.1	0.4	1.8	1,913	15.3	3,310	8.8	57.8	6.2	75.2	1,603	54
Mansfield ISD	TX	7,570	14,888	32,251	32,879	3,049	38.5	38.4	26.5	24.2	6.4	0.1	0.5	3.9	1,990	16.5	3,958	8.3	50.3	2.1	81.1	1,666	42
McAllen ISD	TX	21,120	21,747	25,622	24,931	6,682	55.6	4.5	0.4	93.0	1.5	0.2	0.2	0.4	1,603	15.6	3,297	7.6	48.6	4.2	68.9	1,306	34
McKinney ISD	TX	5,052	12,000	24,422	24,443	2,132	29.6	53.9	12.6	26.6	3.3	0.3	0.6	2.9	1,631	15.0	2,546	9.6	64.1	1.5	88.3	1,234	32
Mesquite ISD	TX	25,920	32,334	37,747	39,127	6,359	70.2	19.4	24.9	51.2	1.9	0.1	0.6	1.9	2,482	15.8	4,826	8.1	51.4	1.4	78.4	2,265	47
Midland ISD	TX	21,082	20,522	21,736	23,319	2,027	46.6	30.0	8.4	58.6	1.5	0.0	0.3	1.2	1,430	16.3	2,672	8.7	53.5	4.8	73.1	1,212	35
Mission CISD	TX	11,032	12,464	15,841	15,534	4,516	84.0	0.8	0.1	98.9	0.1	0.0	#	#	1,003	15.5	2,131	7.3	47.1	1.4	70.1	756	77
North East ISD	TX	39,909	50,875	66,604	67,901	4,928	46.0	29.9	7.2	56.1	3.5	0.2	0.3	2.9	4,286	15.8	8,391	8.1	51.1	1.3	81.0	3,961	112
Northside ISD	TX	50,229	63,739	95,581	100,159	6,299	53.2	19.1	6.1	68.7	2.9	0.3	0.2	2.8	5,952	16.8	12,111	8.3	49.1	1.1	80.4	5,000	26
Northwest ISD	TX	3,197	5,356	15,370	17,811	578	23.2	68.1	6.2	19.7	2.8	0.1	0.6	2.4	1,120	15.9	1,763	10.1	63.5	2.0	85.0	597	65
Pasadena ISD	TX	37,643	42,577	52,218	53,665	12,861	79.4	7.4	6.7	82.1	2.8	0.1	0.2	0.6	3,430	15.6	7,186	7.5	47.7	5.0	63.8	2,428	25
Pearland ISD	TX	6,739	10,618	18,769	19,650	1,177	27.3	42.8	16.7	27.7	9.5	0.1	0.2	2.5	1,120	17.5	2,182	9.0	51.3	1.6	90.6	991	28
Pflugerville ISD	TX	6,482	14,545	22,763	23,347	3,603	52.7	24.7	18.8	44.8	7.7	0.0	0.4	3.4	1,557	15.0	2,687	8.7	57.9	4.0	84.3	1,271	24
Pharr-San Juan-Alamo ISD	TX	18,773	22,537	31,508	32,050	12,775	89.0	0.8	0.1	98.9	0.2	0.1	0.0	#	2,017	15.9	4,305	7.4	46.9	1.6	78.6	1,594	80
Plano ISD	TX	30,585	47,161	55,568	55,185	5,654	27.3	41.4	11.3	22.6	20.9	0.1	0.3	3.4	3,813	14.5	6,538	8.4	58.3	0.8	86.6	3,449	58
Richardson ISD	TX	32,555	35,138	36,070	38,043	6,375	57.9	28.1	23.0	39.4	6.8	0.1	0.3	2.4	2,405	15.8	4,695	8.1	51.2	1.9	75.6	1,922	54
Round Rock ISD	TX	19,636	31,536	44,776	45,749	3,236	29.7	44.1	9.0	30.2	11.9	#	0.4	4.2	3,088	14.8	5,661	8.1	54.6	1.9	88.2	2,545	99
San Antonio ISD	TX	60,161	57,273	55,116	54,268	8,545	92.9	2.0	6.3	91.1	0.2	0.1	0.1	0.3	3,367	16.1	7,521	7.2	44.8	9.0	55.7	2,270	45
Socorro ISD	TX	14,350	26,711	42,569	44,259	7,806	71.9	5.3	2.3	91.0	0.6	0.1	0.1	0.4	2,296	19.3	4,568	9.7	50.3	2.0	77.7	2,336	49
Spring Branch ISD	TX	26,495	31,659	32,948	34,857	9,944	58.4	27.9	5.5	58.3	6.2	0.1	0.7	1.0	2,181	16.0	4,239	8.2	51.5	2.3	78.0	1,818	39
Spring ISD	TX	18,537	23,034	36,323	36,098	5,983	73.1	12.1	39.8	42.6	3.8	0.1	0.5	1.0	2,149	16.8	4,663	7.7	46.1	3.5	76.1	1,718	27
Tyler ISD	TX	16,182	16,626	18,549	18,263	3,413	70.7	23.6	29.7	43.4	1.3	#	0.5	1.6	1,278	14.3	2,469	7.4	51.8	3.7	66.5	901	41
United ISD	TX	12,553	27,556	41,876	42,891	16,625	73.9	1.0	0.1	98.4	0.3	#	0.6	0.1	2,514	17.1	6,044	7.1	41.6	0.4	80.4	2,140	26
Waco ISD	TX	14,304	15,433	15,905	15,221	1,677	86.9	10.5	30.2	56.9	0.3	#	0.6	1.4	906	16.8	1,391	10.9	65.1	7.5	66.9	722	22
Weslaco ISD	TX	11,903	13,407	17,839	17,936	4,548	85.6	1.4	0.1	98.2	0.2	#	0.2	0.0	1,082	16.6	2,325	7.7	46.5	2.3	67.6	801	63
Ysleta ISD	TX	49,974	46,394	44,746	43,680	9,110	80.9	2.7	1.0	95.7	0.2	0.1	0.1	0.3	3,054	14.3	6,369	6.9	47.9	4.0	77.9	2,915	52
Alpine	UT	38,854	47,117	67,076	72,452	2,073	38.3	86.2	0.7	9.0	1.0	1.3	0.5	1.2	2,961	24.5	5,377	13.5	55.1	2.2	76.4	3,032	80
Cache	UT	12,280	13,026	15,648	16,116	475	56.5	88.6	0.6	8.2	0.6	0.4	0.3	1.3	634	25.4	1,651	9.8	38.4	1.3	90.0	904	27
Canyons	UT	—	—	33,714	33,951	1,479	51.7	76.6	1.2	13.9	2.4	1.2	0.7	4.1	1,478	23.0	2,710	12.5	54.5	—	—	—	49
Davis	UT	54,558	59,578	67,452	70,192	1,255	43.1	84.9	1.4	8.9	1.6	1.1	0.5	1.7	2,839	24.7	5,953	11.8	47.7	2.9	83.9	3,837	89
Granite	UT	78,554	71,328	70,083	69,312	10,440	77.8	55.5	3.1	31.4	4.3	3.7	1.5	0.5	2,906	23.9	6,057	11.4	48.0	4.9	67.2	3,601	92
Jordan	UT	64,991	73,158	50,048	52,481	1,549	44.9	79.3	1.1	12.9	1.7	1.6	0.4	3.0	2,159	24.3	4,146	12.7	52.1	2.1	85.0	4,982	54
Nebo	UT	16,393	21,094	29,848	31,241	795	78.1	86.6	0.6	9.9	0.5	0.7	0.5	1.2	1,264	24.7	2,681	11.7	47.1	2.2	86.2	1,540	42
Salt Lake	UT	24,766	25,367	24,647	24,680	3,647	81.7	41.6	4.2	41.9	4.2	4.0	1.2	2.9	1,151	21.5	2,604	9.5	44.2	7.6	66.7	1,117	42
Washington	UT	13,264	18,374	26,091	27,271	1,439	76.3	81.6	0.9	12.4	0.6	1.8	1.8	0.8	1,233	22.1	2,489	11.0	49.5	2.8	76.7	1,280	46
Weber	UT	25,661	27,783	30,431	30,895	813	58.7	82.6	0.9	11.8	1.2	0.6	0.5	2.5	1,345	23.0	2,614	11.8	51.5	2.3	82.5	1,816	48
Arlington County	VA	14,825	18,870	21,485	22,543	5,186	31.1	45.8	10.9	28.6	9.4	0.1	0.4	4.8	1,887	11.9	3,750	6.0	50.3	2.7	82.3	1,124	37
Chesapeake City	VA	29,533	37,645	39,748	39,630	675	31.5	50.6	33.1	6.6	2.7	0.1	0.3	6.5	2,653	14.9	5,477	7.2	48.4	1.8	78.5	2,871	47
Chesterfield County	VA	44,480	51,212	59,243	58,859	2,943	30.3	52.6	26.3	10.8	3.5	0.1	0.3	3.8	3,936	15.0	7,269	8.1	54.1	1.7	85.7	4,103	62
Fairfax County	VA	128,840	156,412	174,479	180,616	36,049	26.5	42.5	10.4	22.6	19.4	0.1	0.2	4.8	14,247	12.7	30,264	6.0	47.1	2.0	89.6	12,003	218
Hampton City	VA	21,383	23,290	21,568	21,350	363	55.7	27.0	59.9	5.6	2.3	0.3	0.3	4.8	1,632	13.1	3,218	6.6	50.7	4.2	65.6	1,357	31
Hanover County	VA	11,328	16,611	18,628	18,370	137	20.1	82.5	6.9	5.3	1.7	0.1	0.4	2.4	1,392	13.2	2,660	6.9	52.3	1.1	88.1	1,446	26
Henrico County	VA	32,638	41,655	49,405	50,083	2,703	36.4	44.5	36.1	7.2	8.5	0.1	0.3	3.4	2,913	17.2	3,919	12.8	74.3	3.3	86.2	3,090	80
Loudoun County	VA	14,485	31,804	63,142	68,205	5,234	17.2	56.0	6.9	15.4	16.3	0.1	0.6	4.8	4,377	15.6	8,995	7.6	48.7	1.0	95.1	3,389	83
Newport News City	VA	28,925	33,008	30,488	29,786	919	58.5	27.5	54.3	11.2	2.7	0.1	0.4	3.7	2,051	14.5	3,041	9.8	67.4	4.7	68.0	1,852	44
Norfolk City	VA	36,541	37,349	33,787	32,862	599	64.5	22.6	61.9	6.2	2.2	0.4	0.5	6.3	2,173	15.1	4,412	7.4	49.3	5.6	52.9	1,560	52

See notes at end of table.

Table 215.10. Selected statistics on enrollment, teachers, dropouts, and graduates in public school districts enrolling more than 15,000 students: Selected years, 1990 through 2012—Continued

Name of district	State	Enrollment, fall 1990	Enrollment, fall 2000	Enrollment, fall 2010	Enrollment, fall 2012	Number of English language learners, 2012	Percent eligible for free or reduced-price lunch, 2012[1]	White	Black	Hispanic	Asian	Pacific Islander	American Indian/Alaska Native	Two or more races	Number of classroom teachers	Pupil/teacher ratio	Total number of staff	Student/staff ratio	Teachers as a percentage of total staff	Percent dropping out of grades 9–12	Averaged freshman graduation rate (AFGR)[2]	Number of high school graduates[3]	Number of schools, fall 2012
1	2	3	4	5	6	7	8	9	10	11	12	13	14	15	16	17	18	19	20	21	22	23	24
Portsmouth City	VA	18,405	16,473	15,126	15,256	78	60.4	21.5	70.8	3.0	0.8	0.2	0.3	3.4	952	16.0	2,051	7.4	46.4	7.4	57.9	826	25
Prince William County	VA	41,888	54,646	79,358	83,865	13,610	37.6	35.1	20.6	29.5	7.6	0.2	0.3	6.7	5,207	16.1	9,722	8.6	53.6	2.2	78.5	4,590	89
Richmond City	VA	27,021	27,237	23,454	23,649	1,273	75.1	9.3	79.9	8.8	0.7	0.1	0.2	1.0	1,922	12.3	3,576	6.6	53.7	5.1	52.2	991	53
Spotsylvania County	VA	12,227	18,876	23,585	23,768	872	34.4	62.4	18.3	11.4	2.8	0.1	0.3	4.7	1,448	16.4	2,553	9.3	56.7	2.2	83.1	1,669	34
Stafford County	VA	12,555	21,124	27,257	27,463	1,192	24.8	56.9	18.4	14.6	2.7	0.2	0.4	6.7	1,790	15.3	3,504	7.8	51.1	1.5	88.4	1,960	30
Virginia Beach City	VA	70,266	76,586	71,185	70,259	932	31.8	51.8	24.0	9.9	5.6	0.5	0.3	7.9	4,046	17.4	8,775	8.0	46.1	1.9	75.7	4,789	85
Bellevue	WA	14,971	15,431	18,330	19,009	1,875	20.5	45.9	2.9	11.2	31.3	0.1	0.2	8.3	965	19.7	1,838	10.3	52.5	1.1	87.1	1,219	29
Bethel	WA	11,319	16,029	17,779	18,031	283	39.0	60.7	9.4	13.7	5.9	2.5	1.8	6.0	846	21.3	1,666	10.8	50.7	6.6	66.6	981	40
Edmonds	WA	18,452	22,067	20,757	20,741	2,091	38.5	53.8	5.8	16.6	13.3	0.6	0.6	9.3	954	21.7	1,869	11.1	51.0	5.5	75.5	1,355	40
Everett	WA	14,846	18,683	18,992	18,909	1,871	41.4	60.4	3.9	15.9	12.0	1.2	0.8	5.8	886	21.3	1,671	11.3	53.0	2.2	75.8	1,102	33
Evergreen (Clark)	WA	14,242	21,650	25,750	26,495	2,477	49.2	64.9	3.3	15.9	6.7	1.6	0.7	7.0	1,426	18.6	2,445	10.8	58.3	7.4	70.7	1,317	37
Federal Way	WA	17,263	22,623	22,258	22,231	2,909	57.6	35.3	11.4	24.4	12.5	4.1	0.8	11.5	1,186	18.7	2,160	10.3	54.9	3.4	64.0	1,291	47
Highline	WA	15,900	18,024	17,992	18,372	3,983	70.6	25.0	11.0	36.5	14.7	4.0	1.1	7.8	975	18.8	1,953	9.4	49.9	4.0	56.8	847	42
Issaquah	WA	8,533	14,259	17,358	18,455	758	10.2	62.7	2.0	7.3	22.5	0.3	0.4	4.7	865	21.3	1,600	11.5	54.0	1.5	88.7	1,146	27
Kennewick	WA	11,147	13,629	16,467	16,580	2,081	54.1	65.4	2.4	27.1	2.4	0.3	0.7	1.7	802	20.7	1,512	11.0	53.0	4.0	74.8	886	28
Kent	WA	20,212	26,535	27,079	27,518	4,512	48.8	39.6	11.9	19.8	17.1	2.4	0.7	8.6	1,369	20.1	2,566	10.7	53.4	5.8	64.3	1,533	43
Lake Washington	WA	22,431	23,662	24,677	25,522	1,536	12.6	63.6	1.6	9.7	18.8	0.2	0.3	5.9	1,313	19.4	2,271	11.2	57.8	1.6	86.0	1,597	53
Northshore	WA	17,213	20,255	19,750	20,328	1,087	18.7	65.2	1.7	12.0	13.3	0.4	0.5	6.9	985	20.6	1,819	11.2	54.2	1.9	88.8	1,491	34
Pasco	WA	6,677	8,850	15,164	16,067	5,687	58.6	26.1	1.9	68.5	1.2	0.2	0.1	1.9	851	18.9	1,567	10.3	54.3	8.7	62.1	615	19
Puyallup	WA	14,325	19,757	20,986	20,625	681	36.4	65.2	3.9	13.4	4.6	1.2	1.0	10.7	1,028	20.1	1,907	10.8	53.9	7.1	81.9	1,419	37
Seattle	WA	40,917	47,575	47,735	50,655	4,583	40.1	44.0	17.7	12.6	17.5	0.5	1.0	11.2	2,780	18.2	5,140	9.9	54.1	6.7	77.0	2,661	62
Spokane	WA	27,965	31,725	29,446	29,032	1,322	58.1	71.2	2.8	8.9	2.5	1.5	1.9	1.8	1,661	17.5	3,061	9.5	54.3	8.3	62.7	1,622	64
Tacoma	WA	29,465	34,093	27,407	28,957	2,475	63.2	46.1	21.6	16.5	10.3	2.2	1.5	5.9	1,585	18.3	3,007	9.6	52.7	6.3	54.3	1,460	41
Vancouver	WA	15,943	21,892	22,669	22,925	2,356	53.7	63.9	3.3	20.8	0.5	3.6	0.7	2.6	1,089	21.0	2,171	10.6	50.2	4.7	72.8	1,285	28
Yakima	WA	12,076	13,985	14,927	15,387	4,576	84.8	19.8	1.0	75.1	0.5	#	1.0	2.6	802	19.2	1,526	10.1	52.6	4.5	54.2	677	28
Berkeley County	WV	10,415	13,076	17,720	18,171	419	51.6	79.1	9.4	5.7	0.9	0.1	0.2	4.5	1,269	14.3	2,516	7.2	50.4	4.2	79.2	1,018	30
Kanawha County	WV	34,284	29,250	28,458	28,548	191	48.3	83.8	12.6	0.8	1.4	#	0.1	1.3	1,972	14.5	3,829	7.5	51.5	5.3	75.4	1,656	69
Appleton Area	WI	12,876	14,793	15,194	15,231	1,127	32.8	75.5	4.5	7.9	11.2	0.0	0.9	#	949	16.0	1,577	9.7	60.2	2.1	94.6	1,159	38
Green Bay Area	WI	18,048	20,104	20,376	20,685	3,637	59.5	53.4	7.8	24.7	6.7	#	4.0	3.3	1,431	14.5	2,390	8.7	59.9	5.8	83.8	1,381	39
Kenosha	WI	16,219	20,099	22,986	22,570	1,897	50.6	54.6	15.5	24.6	1.5	0.1	0.2	3.5	1,199	18.8	2,129	10.6	56.3	3.7	82.1	1,482	42
Madison Metropolitan	WI	23,214	25,087	24,806	27,112	4,743	48.6	45.2	19.1	18.6	9.3	0.1	0.4	7.3	2,193	12.4	4,028	6.7	54.4	3.6	82.5	1,674	54
Milwaukee	WI	92,789	97,985	80,934	78,363	7,666	82.3	13.9	55.4	24.0	5.5	#	0.8	0.4	4,191	18.7	8,751	9.0	47.9	8.9	65.0	4,745	166
Racine Unified	WI	22,159	21,102	21,100	20,577	2,373	64.2	43.9	26.2	25.4	1.4	#	0.3	2.8	1,386	14.8	2,476	8.3	56.0	5.6	73.9	1,250	35

—Not available.
†Not applicable.
#Rounds to zero.
[1]Percentages are for those schools that reported on free and reduced-price lunch eligibility.
[2]The averaged freshman graduation rate provides an estimate of the percentage of students who receive a regular diploma within 4 years of entering ninth grade. The rate uses aggregate student enrollment data to estimate the size of an incoming freshman class and aggregate counts of the number of diplomas awarded 4 years later.
[3]Includes regular diplomas only.
[4]Total for districts reporting data.

[5]Reported data indicated an averaged freshman graduation rate of greater than 100.0 percent.
NOTE: Total enrollment, staff, and teacher data in this table reflect totals reported by school districts and may differ from data derived from summing school-level data to school district aggregates. ISD = independent school district. CISD = consolidated independent school district. Race categories exclude persons of Hispanic ethnicity. Detail may not sum to totals because of rounding.
SOURCE: U.S. Department of Education, National Center for Education Statistics, Common Core of Data (CCD), "Public Elementary/Secondary School Universe Survey," 2012–13; "Local Education Agency Universe Survey," 1990–91, 2000–01, 2010–11, and 2012–13; and "Local Education Agency-Level Public-Use Data File on Public School Dropouts: School Year 2008–09." (This table was prepared May 2015.)

Table 215.20. Revenues, expenditures, poverty rate, and Title I allocations of public school districts enrolling more than 15,000 students: 2011–12 and fiscal year 2014

Name of district	State	Revenues by source of funds, 2011–12 (in thousands of current dollars)				Percentage distribution of revenues, 2011–12				Expenditures, 2011–12 (in thousands of current dollars)					Poverty rate of 5- to 17-year-olds, 2013[1]	Current expenditure per pupil,[2] 2011–12 (in current dollars)	Title I allocations, federal fiscal year 2014	
		Total	Federal	State	Local	Total	Federal	State	Local	Total[3]	Current expenditures Total	Instruction	Capital outlay	Interest on school debt			Total[4] (in thousands of current dollars)	Per poverty child[5] (in current dollars)
1	2	3	4	5	6	7	8	9	10	11	12	13	14	15	16	17	18	19
Districts with more than 15,000 students.........	†	$254,369,215	$28,371,763	$116,334,186	$109,663,266	100.0	11.2	45.7	43.1	$258,977,518	$220,679,942	$137,826,069	$23,555,177	$9,029,596	22.8	$10,048	$7,420,255	$1,307
Baldwin County.............	AL	277,787	22,367	113,823	141,597	100.0	8.1	41.0	51.0	252,178	233,055	136,576	3,767	10,496	19.2	8,120	6,173	1,010
Birmingham City............	AL	260,231	41,840	125,544	92,847	100.0	16.1	48.2	35.7	341,911	258,124	141,643	72,902	3,460	43.7	10,288	15,582	1,162
Huntsville City..............	AL	249,354	22,333	113,178	113,843	100.0	9.0	45.4	45.7	266,632	229,176	138,350	34,288	1,026	22.4	9,975	5,950	1,003
Jefferson County..........	AL	331,052	33,308	187,927	109,817	100.0	10.1	56.8	33.2	349,170	306,995	176,941	32,000	4,653	19.0	8,532	7,577	1,021
Madison County............	AL	176,055	13,313	104,596	58,146	100.0	7.6	59.4	33.0	172,746	157,495	91,824	4,822	6,202	11.7	7,870	2,202	811
Mobile County...............	AL	585,089	83,326	323,217	178,526	100.0	14.2	55.2	30.5	573,397	522,840	286,383	34,307	10,601	28.3	8,507	23,719	1,177
Montgomery County.......	AL	276,560	42,979	161,583	71,998	100.0	15.5	58.4	26.0	277,110	256,131	144,770	15,254	2,605	29.8	8,168	13,140	1,106
Shelby County...............	AL	273,082	15,400	142,147	115,535	100.0	5.6	52.1	42.3	293,703	232,100	137,386	45,593	10,143	12.1	8,200	3,491	873
Tuscaloosa County........	AL	168,443	14,533	93,219	60,691	100.0	8.6	55.3	36.0	164,608	136,873	78,153	22,615	2,149	19.4	7,763	3,521	958
Anchorage....................	AK	746,315	94,110	438,433	213,772	100.0	12.6	58.7	28.6	777,227	729,654	419,466	18,495	25,639	10.8	14,963	13,517	2,372
Matanuska-Susitna Borough...	AK	256,100	19,503	185,486	51,111	100.0	7.6	72.4	20.0	274,716	247,240	141,523	20,771	6,633	10.5	14,144	3,867	1,910
Cartwright Elementary....	AZ	118,075	26,092	62,627	29,356	100.0	22.1	53.0	24.9	134,201	128,980	79,776	4,536	685	42.4	7,025	10,257	1,143
Chandler Unified............	AZ	284,984	19,495	118,221	147,268	100.0	6.8	41.5	51.7	334,245	282,436	171,807	40,957	10,852	12.8	7,140	5,180	883
Deer Valley Unified........	AZ	276,561	19,867	98,216	158,478	100.0	7.2	35.5	57.3	279,953	244,229	144,353	34,988	736	12.3	7,046	5,312	906
Dysart Unified...............	AZ	190,457	16,884	80,076	93,497	100.0	8.9	42.0	49.1	195,859	185,828	102,976	710	9,171	16.6	7,506	5,492	999
Gilbert Unified...............	AZ	263,476	21,294	116,833	125,349	100.0	8.1	44.3	47.6	287,070	268,527	159,310	8,590	9,353	10.0	7,009	3,735	868
Glendale Union High......	AZ	133,999	17,664	47,857	68,478	100.0	13.2	35.7	51.1	139,404	121,863	68,170	13,385	3,620	28.2	8,125	5,549	999
Kyrene Elementary........	AZ	159,381	10,863	48,369	100,149	100.0	6.8	30.3	62.8	157,075	130,141	78,853	20,319	6,611	9.7	7,299	1,393	773
Mesa Unified................	AZ	565,143	67,494	214,838	282,811	100.0	11.9	38.0	50.0	517,772	492,352	291,827	15,126	10,269	25.6	7,606	24,355	1,175
Paradise Valley Unified...	AZ	284,222	26,813	66,603	190,806	100.0	9.4	23.4	67.1	286,994	245,622	136,006	28,165	12,815	17.0	7,439	6,986	1,027
Peoria Unified..............	AZ	250,023	21,793	118,542	109,688	100.0	8.7	47.4	43.9	281,785	262,356	150,627	8,409	10,699	15.2	7,164	6,005	1,013
Phoenix Union High.......	AZ	287,988	37,187	45,887	204,914	100.0	12.9	15.9	71.2	301,078	271,902	141,087	17,002	11,097	36.3	10,506	17,424	1,136
Scottsdale Unified.........	AZ	247,761	16,097	36,018	195,646	100.0	6.5	14.5	79.0	300,056	206,273	126,262	78,783	14,766	12.7	8,007	3,453	864
Sunnyside Unified..........	AZ	137,034	26,181	61,192	49,661	100.0	19.1	44.7	36.2	142,079	121,025	63,106	20,243	735	43.7	6,871	10,319	1,185
Tucson Unified..............	AZ	501,632	77,010	153,134	271,488	100.0	15.4	30.5	54.1	494,649	439,422	206,838	40,204	14,999	29.9	8,496	26,534	1,203
Washington Elementary...	AZ	205,700	38,163	76,710	90,827	100.0	18.6	37.3	44.2	189,236	169,445	92,210	8,817	10,945	34.0	7,546	10,273	1,075
Little Rock...................	AR	371,708	46,667	271,413	53,628	100.0	12.6	73.0	14.4	365,395	308,718	170,305	11,580	6,878	27.6	12,089	10,282	1,236
Pulaski County Special...	AR	227,534	22,932	168,823	35,779	100.0	10.1	74.2	15.7	252,364	192,311	107,648	23,999	6,316	18.6	10,904	5,706	1,148
Springdale..................	AR	204,286	19,951	160,513	23,802	100.0	9.8	78.6	11.7	233,662	167,215	101,166	30,805	5,891	26.0	8,371	6,078	1,139
ABC Unified.................	CA	196,710	23,448	137,977	35,285	100.0	11.9	70.1	17.9	197,212	175,435	107,499	8,741	1,055	18.8	8,480	3,498	993
Alhambra Unified...........	CA	244,951	36,155	157,240	51,556	100.0	14.8	64.2	21.0	252,260	169,554	95,419	18,457	5,565	26.8	9,270	5,005	1,025
Alvord Unified..............	CA	168,561	19,516	111,543	37,502	100.0	11.6	66.2	22.2	178,868	154,653	96,057	18,880	5,132	25.6	7,834	6,092	1,041
Anaheim City...............	CA	185,235	26,044	93,498	65,693	100.0	14.1	50.5	35.5	207,209	156,422	97,995	34,206	4,236	31.3	8,100	6,919	1,036
Anaheim Union High.......	CA	327,952	40,639	215,905	71,408	100.0	12.4	65.8	21.8	330,347	306,461	192,634	5,617	5,645	24.3	9,371	8,533	1,054
Antelope Valley Union High...	CA	224,788	30,784	156,576	37,428	100.0	13.7	69.7	16.7	233,009	217,353	134,111	7,203	4,772	24.3	8,509	7,421	1,050
Antioch Unified.............	CA	153,981	19,443	97,096	37,442	100.0	12.6	63.1	24.3	168,929	148,328	96,776	16,924	2,776	17.1	7,858	3,862	1,007
Bakersfield City............	CA	282,698	48,830	205,922	27,946	100.0	17.3	72.8	9.9	278,162	259,777	159,875	15,280	1,731	44.3	9,173	15,291	1,185
Baldwin Park Unified......	CA	176,805	20,865	116,952	38,988	100.0	11.8	66.1	22.1	190,557	147,719	90,083	21,034	3,480	28.9	7,679	4,732	1,020
Burbank Unified............	CA	143,170	12,063	80,892	50,215	100.0	8.4	56.5	35.1	143,107	126,330	80,879	11,990	2,231	14.7	7,578	2,043	927
Cajon Valley Union........	CA	148,649	18,634	81,352	48,663	100.0	12.5	54.7	32.7	157,852	138,385	89,773	14,036	5,225	28.5	8,618	5,555	1,025
Capistrano Unified.........	CA	437,617	34,955	134,886	267,766	100.0	8.0	30.8	61.2	411,168	391,870	262,769	2,713	2,592	8.9	7,370	5,137	909
Central Unified.............	CA	128,021	15,583	81,923	30,515	100.0	12.2	64.0	23.8	134,585	114,096	62,247	12,016	6,173	28.2	7,660	4,597	1,014
Chaffey Joint Union High...	CA	242,746	19,181	151,444	72,121	100.0	7.9	62.4	29.7	225,463	197,373	125,766	15,732	3,210	18.2	7,874	5,135	1,033
Chino Valley Unified.......	CA	276,120	27,963	163,364	84,793	100.0	10.1	59.2	30.7	252,585	226,160	145,447	14,115	5,841	14.4	7,223	4,494	915

See notes at end of table.

Table 215.20. Revenues, expenditures, poverty rate, and Title I allocations of public school districts enrolling more than 15,000 students: 2011–12 and fiscal year 2014—Continued

Name of district	State	Revenues by source of funds, 2011–12 (in thousands of current dollars)				Percentage distribution of revenues, 2011–12				Expenditures, 2011–12 (in thousands of current dollars)					Poverty rate of 5- to 17-year-olds, 2013[1]	Current expenditure per pupil,[2] 2011–12 (in current dollars)	Title I allocations, federal fiscal year 2014	
		Total	Federal	State	Local	Total	Federal	State	Local	Total[3]	Current expenditures		Capital outlay	Interest on school debt			Total[4] (in thousands of current dollars)	Per poverty child[5] (in current dollars)
											Total	Instruction						
1	2	3	4	5	6	7	8	9	10	11	12	13	14	15	16	17	18	19
Chula Vista Elementary	CA	265,424	23,305	122,154	119,965	100.0	8.8	46.0	45.2	246,595	228,009	142,526	6,657	8,981	19.0	8,114	5,671	1,027
Clovis Unified	CA	371,031	28,626	227,731	114,674	100.0	7.7	61.4	30.9	354,804	310,971	186,478	29,689	8,729	16.4	7,965	6,562	1,044
Coachella Valley Unified	CA	195,534	33,767	121,416	40,351	100.0	17.3	62.1	20.6	188,886	174,600	105,261	6,722	6,050	41.3	9,486	10,313	1,160
Colton Joint Unified	CA	208,443	22,889	146,122	39,432	100.0	11.0	70.1	18.9	291,549	191,215	117,073	90,010	8,125	26.6	8,245	7,006	1,053
Compton Unified	CA	256,065	45,994	185,410	24,661	100.0	18.0	72.4	9.6	262,478	245,485	143,556	3,225	4,165	34.5	9,906	13,949	1,146
Conejo Valley Unified	CA	188,249	9,931	62,056	116,262	100.0	5.3	33.0	61.8	183,607	166,408	110,512	3,513	2,934	8.6	8,030	1,703	805
Corona-Norco Unified	CA	481,844	35,106	315,947	130,791	100.0	7.3	65.6	27.1	471,474	402,657	259,862	53,823	13,385	15.2	7,531	9,200	1,080
Cupertino Union	CA	157,688	4,525	39,858	113,285	100.0	2.9	25.3	71.9	152,263	144,233	98,151	4,415	3,473	4.9	7,734	496	492
Desert Sands Unified	CA	311,080	29,990	145,947	135,143	100.0	9.6	46.9	43.4	323,454	249,061	151,714	51,910	22,308	25.1	8,530	7,924	1,055
Downey Unified	CA	212,392	23,145	143,012	46,235	100.0	10.9	67.3	21.8	194,768	184,782	121,770	2,246	3,293	20.9	8,111	4,981	1,024
East Side Union High	CA	284,154	18,747	120,317	145,090	100.0	6.6	42.3	51.1	309,311	204,586	127,761	66,391	30,124	16.2	7,980	5,024	1,019
Elk Grove Unified	CA	541,376	63,320	368,394	109,662	100.0	11.7	68.0	20.3	518,944	492,254	321,255	10,091	8,473	20.7	7,923	16,608	1,161
Escondido Union	CA	166,997	24,180	84,900	57,917	100.0	14.5	50.8	34.7	156,375	150,356	93,167	2,161	3,778	23.0	7,875	4,830	1,015
Fairfield-Suisun Unified	CA	184,949	19,676	118,498	46,775	100.0	10.6	64.1	25.3	170,569	157,302	91,575	2,238	6,065	17.0	7,290	4,201	1,016
Folsom-Cordova Unified	CA	169,528	14,437	92,540	62,551	100.0	8.5	54.6	36.9	179,148	145,627	90,402	24,700	7,682	15.0	7,603	3,304	986
Fontana Unified	CA	384,764	52,280	284,195	48,289	100.0	13.6	73.9	12.6	373,824	345,066	210,349	11,633	16,390	27.4	8,501	13,296	1,142
Fremont Unified	CA	303,053	25,060	167,507	110,486	100.0	8.3	55.3	36.5	304,388	263,544	177,481	4,724	13,918	9.4	8,028	3,118	869
Fresno Unified	CA	759,074	139,111	511,214	108,749	100.0	18.3	67.3	14.3	775,662	660,284	392,514	89,068	14,690	46.8	8,895	46,058	1,240
Garden Grove Unified	CA	433,419	53,814	282,484	97,121	100.0	12.4	65.2	22.4	427,642	410,289	264,388	5,048	7,431	24.7	8,548	14,241	1,132
Glendale Unified	CA	250,152	33,797	142,442	73,913	100.0	13.5	56.9	29.5	266,626	231,595	157,126	19,383	5,766	20.3	8,830	6,331	1,040
Grossmont Union High	CA	270,101	20,635	113,740	135,726	100.0	7.6	42.1	50.3	327,701	200,414	109,869	97,181	5,741	16.1	8,465	4,359	1,016
Hacienda La Puente Unified	CA	220,776	28,762	156,197	35,817	100.0	13.0	70.7	16.2	217,274	192,072	111,375	6,875	4,271	22.6	9,213	5,080	1,026
Hayward Unified	CA	215,645	36,136	116,272	63,237	100.0	16.8	53.9	29.3	286,188	195,094	126,491	73,076	11,608	20.2	9,017	5,843	1,026
Hemet Unified	CA	215,083	28,922	122,421	63,740	100.0	13.4	56.9	29.6	215,065	186,654	108,162	18,539	9,275	27.5	8,493	7,391	1,052
Hesperia Unified	CA	178,131	22,615	128,939	26,577	100.0	12.7	72.4	14.9	172,070	159,889	94,351	6,417	4,893	28.0	6,820	6,846	1,052
Huntington Beach Union High	CA	197,567	17,415	78,582	101,570	100.0	8.8	39.8	51.4	192,667	143,834	84,579	5,704	11,157	13.7	8,748	1,908	812
Irvine Unified	CA	283,371	15,716	56,523	211,132	100.0	5.5	19.9	74.5	229,599	229,007	142,344	51,402	6,373	9.1	8,148	2,234	833
Jurupa Unified	CA	176,515	26,041	117,790	32,684	100.0	14.8	66.7	18.5	172,057	164,309	104,405	4,582	2,476	26.6	8,263	6,015	1,040
Kern Union High	CA	404,653	35,735	234,008	134,910	100.0	8.8	57.8	33.3	424,420	364,151	197,042	36,596	12,272	27.9	9,709	13,468	1,125
Lake Elsinore Unified	CA	182,452	18,848	117,596	46,008	100.0	10.3	64.5	25.2	211,070	179,692	110,047	26,005	2,109	20.4	8,105	5,403	1,033
Lodi Unified	CA	265,018	32,430	175,731	56,857	100.0	12.2	66.3	21.5	268,202	243,773	154,663	13,832	8,994	19.9	8,040	7,246	1,055
Long Beach Unified	CA	837,323	144,082	540,531	152,710	100.0	17.2	64.6	18.2	876,917	733,732	464,208	81,639	25,587	26.5	8,767	28,366	1,209
Los Angeles Unified	CA	8,314,608	1,251,529	5,002,708	2,060,371	100.0	15.1	60.2	24.8	8,898,332	6,993,429	4,250,633	1,141,293	598,235	30.9	10,602	338,423	1,454
Lynwood Unified	CA	145,481	21,546	107,476	16,459	100.0	14.8	73.9	11.3	145,592	131,160	74,510	4,309	1,776	31.6	8,454	5,284	1,029
Madera Unified	CA	163,790	20,394	112,261	31,135	100.0	12.5	68.5	19.0	161,261	149,873	87,421	6,408	2,891	35.8	7,518	8,096	1,073
Manteca Unified	CA	197,816	19,439	124,756	53,621	100.0	9.8	63.1	27.1	179,810	166,798	104,218	6,138	4,859	16.1	7,156	4,285	1,019
Modesto City[6]	CA	289,866	37,381	181,985	70,500	100.0	12.9	62.8	24.3	265,429	248,294	146,040	4,270	1,346	30.8	8,280	11,213	1,097
Montebello Unified	CA	312,474	48,845	202,324	61,305	100.0	15.6	64.7	19.6	326,382	284,221	168,133	20,114	7,032	29.8	9,075	10,886	1,105
Moreno Valley Unified	CA	308,053	35,696	227,683	44,674	100.0	11.6	73.9	14.5	302,399	284,533	176,673	1,982	10,754	27.9	7,972	12,526	1,128
Mount Diablo Unified	CA	330,755	33,179	156,822	140,754	100.0	10.0	47.4	42.6	402,851	300,630	190,691	76,677	21,666	14.1	8,848	5,887	1,017
Murrieta Valley Unified	CA	191,193	9,710	106,993	74,490	100.0	5.1	56.0	39.0	204,929	173,021	112,692	22,966	7,232	11.7	7,624	2,398	851
Napa Valley Unified	CA	177,674	18,273	50,480	108,921	100.0	10.3	28.4	61.3	179,658	137,836	86,241	25,287	12,877	12.8	7,625	2,176	840
Newport-Mesa Unified	CA	255,848	22,156	34,407	199,285	100.0	8.7	13.4	77.9	259,058	237,964	141,191	11,459	5,032	16.0	10,887	4,480	1,007
Norwalk-La Mirada Unified	CA	210,922	28,326	147,005	35,591	100.0	13.4	69.7	16.9	212,672	183,797	112,339	5,200	3,088	18.9	9,095	4,470	1,016
Oakland Unified	CA	556,623	83,946	289,622	183,055	100.0	15.1	52.0	32.9	592,071	430,804	240,145	101,940	39,254	27.9	9,289	18,688	1,166
Oceanside Unified	CA	193,117	30,213	93,331	69,573	100.0	15.6	48.3	36.0	210,776	170,052	104,671	33,521	6,451	21.4	8,103	4,851	1,016
Ontario-Montclair Elementary	CA	219,443	34,034	147,941	37,468	100.0	15.5	67.4	17.1	210,100	199,009	128,629	8,070	2,639	31.2	8,818	8,094	1,061
Orange Unified	CA	264,091	26,348	100,197	137,546	100.0	10.0	37.9	52.1	238,684	220,201	141,854	10,217	3,727	15.1	7,307	5,809	1,026
Oxnard	CA	151,091	17,479	95,141	38,471	100.0	11.6	63.0	25.5	150,816	136,190	89,426	6,731	5,551	26.2	8,450	4,607	1,014

See notes at end of table.

Table 215.20. Revenues, expenditures, poverty rate, and Title I allocations of public school districts enrolling more than 15,000 students: 2011–12 and fiscal year 2014—Continued

Name of district	State	Revenues by source of funds, 2011–12 (in thousands of current dollars)				Percentage distribution of revenues, 2011–12				Expenditures, 2011–12 (in thousands of current dollars)					Poverty rate of 5- to 17-year-olds, 2013[1]	Current expenditure per pupil,[2] 2011–12 (in current dollars)	Title I allocations, federal fiscal year 2014	
											Current expenditures							
		Total	Federal	State	Local	Total	Federal	State	Local	Total[3]	Total	Instruction	Capital outlay	Interest on school debt			Total[4] (in thousands of current dollars)	Per poverty child[5] (in current dollars)
1	2	3	4	5	6	7	8	9	10	11	12	13	14	15	16	17	18	19
Oxnard Union High	CA	156,410	15,445	77,441	63,524	100.0	9.9	49.5	40.6	177,852	142,852	86,034	24,131	6,614	18.0	8,508	3,481	989
Pajaro Valley Unified	CA	212,478	44,334	110,365	57,779	100.0	20.9	51.9	27.2	203,542	198,171	115,585	1,094	2,057	23.6	9,951	5,404	1,030
Palm Springs Unified	CA	275,803	28,128	156,886	90,789	100.0	10.2	56.9	32.9	287,530	199,837	119,839	73,809	13,749	32.6	8,440	9,325	1,082
Palmdale Elementary	CA	242,213	53,080	170,141	18,992	100.0	21.9	70.2	7.8	249,446	186,749	108,565	4,959	3,593	30.3	9,072	6,643	1,043
Panama-Buena Vista Union	CA	138,245	11,223	107,215	19,807	100.0	8.1	77.6	14.3	140,552	126,647	76,155	2,919	1,638	22.3	7,534	3,912	995
Paramount Unified	CA	143,660	22,224	99,621	21,815	100.0	15.5	69.3	15.2	174,621	135,456	80,585	31,146	3,448	28.0	8,504	5,013	1,025
Pasadena Unified	CA	230,034	34,275	99,956	95,803	100.0	14.9	43.5	41.6	225,574	192,812	108,888	16,532	15,428	20.4	9,737	5,866	1,036
Placentia-Yorba Linda Unified	CA	248,159	21,590	116,088	110,481	100.0	8.7	46.8	44.5	273,641	212,897	132,292	39,252	15,447	11.7	8,269	2,961	864
Pomona Unified	CA	327,584	65,554	211,952	50,078	100.0	20.0	64.7	15.3	340,341	276,095	156,488	24,713	11,302	28.8	9,954	10,612	1,101
Poway Unified	CA	361,235	12,593	142,285	206,357	100.0	3.5	39.4	57.1	324,861	282,893	167,836	6,317	33,961	6.5	8,183	1,927	815
Redlands Unified	CA	193,750	18,548	124,766	50,436	100.0	9.6	64.4	26.0	186,475	165,299	102,614	11,875	4,951	17.1	7,721	3,816	1,012
Rialto Unified	CA	245,341	33,170	177,430	34,741	100.0	13.5	72.3	14.2	251,689	233,103	132,657	14,896	2,378	28.1	8,710	8,543	1,071
Riverside Unified	CA	385,057	44,104	246,374	94,579	100.0	11.5	64.0	24.6	368,850	337,328	212,209	19,566	7,484	21.5	7,955	10,990	1,109
Rowland Unified	CA	196,283	29,871	135,893	30,519	100.0	15.2	69.2	15.5	202,330	134,998	82,979	28,256	6,794	24.0	8,577	4,516	1,017
Sacramento City Unified	CA	498,462	80,477	307,271	110,714	100.0	16.1	61.6	22.2	516,542	463,600	285,612	27,283	17,640	33.5	9,670	20,755	1,185
Saddleback Valley Unified	CA	280,113	18,730	102,689	158,694	100.0	6.7	36.7	56.7	258,271	225,604	157,043	7,682	6,410	8.9	7,305	2,721	856
San Bernardino City Unified	CA	614,746	101,866	461,395	51,485	100.0	16.6	75.1	8.4	619,086	494,951	279,644	101,676	8,190	41.1	9,102	28,309	1,217
San Diego Unified	CA	1,408,787	162,054	508,108	738,625	100.0	11.5	36.1	52.4	1,428,904	1,210,667	724,011	159,838	55,521	23.6	9,239	40,642	1,233
San Francisco Unified	CA	746,702	92,837	195,653	458,212	100.0	12.4	26.2	61.4	772,453	554,190	277,945	124,165	28,264	16.6	9,842	13,991	1,134
San Jose Unified	CA	356,268	32,584	104,828	218,856	100.0	9.1	29.4	61.4	340,997	300,396	177,674	15,938	23,479	13.9	9,019	5,691	1,007
San Juan Unified	CA	446,540	56,544	268,832	121,164	100.0	12.7	60.2	27.1	450,680	408,642	247,791	21,947	14,920	22.7	8,649	13,034	1,151
San Marcos Unified	CA	177,838	14,089	87,812	75,937	100.0	7.9	49.4	42.7	208,012	149,883	94,612	41,450	11,058	15.0	7,840	3,045	977
San Ramon Valley Unified	CA	270,383	7,299	86,690	176,394	100.0	2.7	32.1	65.2	291,380	239,727	156,234	32,764	17,131	4.3	8,022	669	501
Santa Ana Unified	CA	615,303	103,610	392,106	119,587	100.0	16.8	63.7	19.4	643,235	524,758	330,547	101,033	14,176	29.1	9,166	18,586	1,162
Santa Barbara Unified	CA	208,715	13,563	29,797	165,355	100.0	6.5	14.3	79.2	161,161	127,459	76,897	23,852	4,311	15.3	8,317	2,410	948
Santa Clara Unified	CA	190,795	13,568	20,929	156,298	100.0	7.1	11.0	81.9	245,556	139,121	85,449	85,646	16,428	9.4	9,099	1,446	798
Santa Maria-Bonita	CA	122,477	20,008	84,167	18,302	100.0	16.3	68.7	14.9	117,865	115,983	71,601	895	947	30.3	7,931	4,442	1,013
Simi Valley Unified	CA	189,548	13,022	106,745	69,781	100.0	6.9	56.3	36.8	183,538	158,111	102,792	13,319	5,948	9.0	8,137	1,708	805
Stockton Unified	CA	394,213	63,361	272,213	58,639	100.0	16.1	69.1	14.9	389,586	332,201	203,239	40,112	14,223	35.5	8,561	17,937	1,178
Sweetwater Union High	CA	438,734	42,392	252,357	143,985	100.0	9.7	57.5	32.8	427,224	359,612	210,491	28,887	24,067	21.6	8,853	10,616	1,101
Temecula Valley Unified	CA	257,588	18,518	133,884	105,186	100.0	7.2	52.0	40.8	237,470	218,793	151,679	14,935	1,560	9.7	7,229	2,837	877
Torrance Unified	CA	224,099	19,176	128,581	76,342	100.0	8.6	57.4	34.1	261,628	176,293	118,985	62,884	8,646	10.3	7,276	2,008	826
Tracy Joint Unified	CA	148,527	12,604	100,745	35,178	100.0	8.5	67.8	23.7	163,394	128,739	80,589	21,673	3,215	14.4	7,389	2,413	957
Tustin Unified	CA	212,192	14,069	88,893	109,230	100.0	6.6	41.9	51.5	229,589	166,506	105,719	44,369	14,878	13.5	7,083	2,913	863
Twin Rivers Unified	CA	303,002	43,389	199,644	59,969	100.0	14.3	65.9	19.8	303,124	263,769	150,147	20,062	12,726	35.9	8,337	13,868	1,137
Val Verde Unified	CA	355,529	68,864	241,802	44,863	100.0	19.4	68.0	12.6	378,525	168,329	104,670	10,655	4,459	26.1	8,582	5,579	1,035
Vallejo City Unified	CA	146,246	17,891	93,793	34,562	100.0	12.2	64.1	23.6	150,300	132,241	76,524	8,884	7,051	21.2	8,636	4,182	1,015
Ventura Unified	CA	163,378	19,439	73,419	70,520	100.0	11.9	44.9	43.2	161,402	147,456	84,375	4,817	3,181	14.6	8,460	2,381	845
Visalia Unified	CA	251,048	33,120	159,331	58,597	100.0	13.2	63.5	23.3	233,559	199,908	123,684	28,085	1,067	31.2	7,331	10,511	1,089
Vista Unified	CA	226,584	27,409	109,519	89,656	100.0	12.1	48.3	39.6	213,315	195,515	126,544	7,441	6,401	19.8	7,596	5,337	1,026
West Contra Costa Unified	CA	375,705	50,788	185,837	139,080	100.0	13.5	49.5	37.0	422,591	283,153	161,918	104,189	32,297	18.3	9,475	7,743	1,059
William S. Hart Union High	CA	231,289	11,342	155,164	64,783	100.0	4.9	67.1	28.0	213,235	188,637	110,136	9,300	8,314	9.9	7,132	2,163	836
Academy, No. 20	CO	223,284	10,684	104,808	107,792	100.0	4.8	46.9	48.3	207,182	188,729	113,015	5,777	11,048	6.4	7,978	1,098	784
Adams 12 Five Star Schools	CO	400,452	22,740	218,966	158,746	100.0	5.7	54.7	39.6	389,846	347,648	219,897	16,301	24,401	13.7	8,087	5,475	930
Aurora, Joint District No. 28	CO	374,369	41,058	209,935	123,376	100.0	11.0	56.1	33.0	393,628	329,428	188,980	43,396	18,198	26.8	8,299	12,216	1,128
Boulder Valley, No. RE2	CO	339,356	15,782	69,642	253,932	100.0	4.7	20.5	74.8	362,869	288,934	176,811	50,622	17,666	8.6	9,702	2,166	826
Brighton, No. 27J	CO	133,309	7,844	74,935	50,530	100.0	5.9	56.2	37.9	128,246	110,849	61,102	8,893	7,773	11.6	7,074	1,566	795
Cherry Creek, No. 5	CO	528,040	27,338	216,417	284,285	100.0	5.2	41.0	53.8	521,506	470,768	318,987	27,798	21,755	9.1	8,941	4,607	913

See notes at end of table.

Table 215.20. Revenues, expenditures, poverty rate, and Title I allocations of public school districts enrolling more than 15,000 students: 2011–12 and fiscal year 2014—Continued

Name of district	State	Revenues by source of funds, 2011–12 (in thousands of current dollars)				Percentage distribution of revenues, 2011–12				Expenditures, 2011–12 (in thousands of current dollars)					Poverty rate of 5- to 17-year-olds, 2013[1]	Current expenditure per pupil,[2] 2011–12 (in current dollars)	Title I allocations, federal fiscal year 2014	
		Total	Federal	State	Local	Total	Federal	State	Local	Total[3]	Current expenditures		Capital outlay	Interest on school debt			Total[4] (in thousands of current dollars)	Per poverty child[5] (in current dollars)
											Total	Instruction						
1	2	3	4	5	6	7	8	9	10	11	12	13	14	15	16	17	18	19
Colorado Springs, No. 11	CO	280,725	28,989	124,972	126,764	100.0	10.3	44.5	45.2	273,646	253,891	150,929	8,512	9,651	22.3	8,594	8,343	1,063
Denver	CO	967,307	140,975	270,703	555,629	100.0	14.6	28.0	57.4	1,052,787	814,951	430,808	100,357	96,647	29.0	10,075	32,758	1,243
Douglas County, No. RE1	CO	584,330	13,899	260,462	309,969	100.0	2.4	44.6	53.0	532,576	468,702	276,423	30,079	31,994	3.8	7,426	1,193	465
Falcon, No. 49	CO	123,805	5,683	73,591	44,531	100.0	4.6	59.4	36.0	111,729	98,290	53,722	5,382	7,528	9.6	6,525	1,273	792
Greeley, No. 6	CO	168,630	19,743	98,356	50,531	100.0	11.7	58.3	30.0	163,615	151,371	89,312	6,529	5,712	24.2	7,630	5,441	1,024
Jefferson County, No. R1	CO	823,580	55,926	338,935	428,719	100.0	6.8	41.2	52.1	790,472	723,994	416,885	39,187	27,025	11.3	8,439	11,261	1,130
Littleton, No. 6	CO	161,526	8,139	62,761	90,626	100.0	5.0	38.9	56.1	147,552	139,331	83,729	4,410	3,806	9.9	8,948	1,223	787
Mesa County Valley, No. 51	CO	184,510	16,656	88,350	79,504	100.0	9.0	47.9	43.1	178,822	166,953	101,255	5,622	3,898	17.5	7,615	4,228	1,016
Poudre, No. R1	CO	274,031	17,367	99,402	157,262	100.0	6.3	36.3	57.4	279,335	243,297	135,024	20,980	13,737	12.4	8,844	2,971	871
Pueblo, No. 60	CO	156,630	27,057	86,985	42,588	100.0	17.3	55.5	27.2	153,650	146,800	80,729	1,604	3,983	32.8	8,200	6,242	1,037
Saint Vrain Valley, No. RE1J	CO	273,946	16,093	111,994	145,859	100.0	5.9	40.9	53.2	284,228	220,791	128,294	36,287	24,379	12.0	7,855	3,173	878
Thompson, No. R2J	CO	142,094	10,056	63,911	68,127	100.0	7.1	45.0	47.9	139,912	126,154	70,662	3,371	8,361	11.1	8,058	1,626	799
Bridgeport	CT	358,388	47,148	259,387	51,853	100.0	13.2	72.4	14.5	365,919	307,649	193,966	37,835	5,944	27.0	15,286	11,435	1,672
Hartford	CT	471,500	54,956	326,159	90,385	100.0	11.7	69.2	19.2	502,538	416,041	242,657	57,904	5,545	38.2	19,877	16,265	1,923
New Haven	CT	454,550	46,039	288,079	119,432	100.0	10.1	63.6	26.3	478,085	367,952	233,331	81,167	14,836	36.5	17,902	12,601	1,740
Stamford	CT	310,110	11,515	54,256	244,339	100.0	3.7	17.5	78.8	297,380	288,698	180,838	1,722	5,179	12.9	18,634	3,014	1,285
Waterbury	CT	335,722	29,792	207,014	98,916	100.0	8.9	61.7	29.5	383,233	295,007	169,272	82,650	933	33.0	16,334	10,964	1,680
Christina	DE	266,079	30,390	125,846	109,843	100.0	11.4	47.3	41.3	303,963	279,159	175,108	3,635	2,623	15.3	17,123	7,701	1,880
Red Clay Consolidated	DE	235,122	27,103	112,355	95,664	100.0	11.5	47.8	40.7	245,176	229,339	149,467	768	2,597	15.5	14,361	6,337	1,833
District of Columbia	DC	1,331,006	137,742	0	1,193,264	100.0	10.3	0.0	89.7	1,189,542	899,032	594,156	283,890	0	29.1	20,150	43,206	2,103
Alachua	FL	252,314	36,143	91,363	124,808	100.0	14.3	36.2	49.5	273,986	237,189	131,371	29,710	3,178	25.5	8,631	7,790	993
Bay	FL	234,725	27,326	68,827	138,572	100.0	11.6	29.3	59.0	251,605	205,306	128,533	36,121	4,789	23.9	7,793	6,290	994
Brevard	FL	587,566	61,891	277,166	248,509	100.0	10.5	47.2	42.3	602,642	560,048	347,040	14,433	25,764	20.9	7,801	17,666	1,078
Broward	FL	2,221,054	269,571	835,872	1,115,611	100.0	12.1	37.6	50.2	2,317,961	2,073,343	1,277,974	80,326	93,967	19.6	8,021	66,711	1,181
Charlotte	FL	153,844	21,360	26,916	105,568	100.0	13.9	17.5	68.6	184,603	151,830	81,626	26,407	3,659	22.2	9,244	3,520	947
Citrus	FL	143,189	18,522	35,549	89,118	100.0	12.9	24.8	62.2	166,450	136,683	77,889	24,859	823	28.1	8,796	4,331	961
Clay	FL	284,218	25,599	166,048	92,571	100.0	9.0	58.4	32.6	296,337	277,806	179,193	14,711	3,015	14.0	7,791	4,492	1,044
Collier	FL	481,571	55,720	74,366	351,485	100.0	11.6	15.4	73.0	508,093	436,937	260,761	41,115	23,287	23.3	10,105	11,246	1,097
Dade	FL	3,188,967	457,537	1,011,288	1,720,142	100.0	14.3	31.7	53.9	3,407,559	3,043,425	1,947,976	162,694	108,430	28.7	8,690	137,361	1,220
Duval	FL	1,084,243	156,609	457,677	469,957	100.0	14.4	42.2	43.3	1,131,916	1,033,432	619,856	78,978	16,660	24.9	8,239	39,875	1,119
Escambia	FL	355,483	51,647	155,015	148,821	100.0	14.5	43.6	41.9	368,927	335,126	192,789	26,994	2,295	25.8	8,276	12,261	1,049
Hernando	FL	189,268	23,259	86,632	79,377	100.0	12.3	45.8	41.9	195,150	175,217	101,769	11,414	7,994	26.0	7,747	6,476	983
Hillsborough	FL	1,803,776	291,908	847,219	664,649	100.0	16.2	47.0	36.8	1,916,730	1,639,082	990,247	117,715	51,986	24.5	8,318	62,216	1,176
Indian River	FL	169,065	16,691	30,793	121,581	100.0	9.9	18.2	71.9	186,840	143,335	87,370	34,930	7,388	20.5	7,979	3,780	950
Lake	FL	335,544	38,690	148,796	148,058	100.0	11.5	44.3	44.1	359,790	314,984	189,605	28,043	16,590	22.5	7,623	10,610	1,030
Lee	FL	765,065	91,712	199,089	474,264	100.0	12.0	26.0	62.0	852,347	707,461	422,929	105,594	20,468	24.5	8,433	24,467	1,097
Leon	FL	307,854	36,707	115,050	156,097	100.0	11.9	37.4	50.7	325,439	263,447	147,419	42,609	7,322	19.4	7,931	7,388	998
Manatee	FL	425,709	56,195	120,513	249,001	100.0	13.2	28.3	58.5	459,108	389,778	238,002	43,920	16,321	21.0	8,664	10,707	1,033
Marion	FL	361,447	53,799	157,228	150,420	100.0	14.9	43.5	41.6	382,755	346,937	201,044	20,691	7,068	30.4	8,206	15,061	1,063
Martin	FL	178,061	17,307	32,189	128,565	100.0	9.7	18.1	72.2	195,862	155,471	89,031	32,766	2,204	20.9	8,464	3,886	953
Okaloosa	FL	252,094	27,612	93,022	131,460	100.0	11.0	36.9	52.1	255,189	235,728	153,982	10,561	2,956	18.6	8,022	5,372	980
Orange	FL	1,827,011	202,082	612,677	1,012,252	100.0	11.1	33.5	55.4	1,768,303	1,443,975	859,216	226,144	71,400	25.8	8,022	60,584	1,161
Osceola	FL	468,040	57,912	229,871	180,257	100.0	12.4	49.1	38.5	502,154	431,325	260,122	46,777	15,521	25.8	7,873	15,049	1,066
Palm Beach	FL	1,710,762	180,910	324,304	1,205,548	100.0	10.6	19.0	70.5	1,777,058	1,560,528	989,179	68,576	86,782	20.5	8,935	47,155	1,140
Pasco	FL	582,449	61,671	286,001	234,777	100.0	10.6	49.1	40.3	593,276	533,474	310,347	38,696	17,855	18.0	8,003	13,856	1,063
Pinellas	FL	922,370	117,146	270,159	535,065	100.0	12.7	29.3	58.0	998,382	885,130	545,199	89,323	2,195	19.2	8,529	24,958	1,106
Polk	FL	891,269	116,482	431,022	343,765	100.0	13.1	48.4	38.6	924,557	835,993	550,360	57,987	20,208	25.8	8,702	29,861	1,114

See notes at end of table.

Table 215.20. Revenues, expenditures, poverty rate, and Title I allocations of public school districts enrolling more than 15,000 students: 2011–12 and fiscal year 2014—Continued

Name of district	State	Revenues by source of funds, 2011–12 (in thousands of current dollars)				Percentage distribution of revenues, 2011–12				Expenditures, 2011–12 (in thousands of current dollars)					Poverty rate of 5- to 17-year-olds, 2013[1]	Current expenditure per pupil,[2] 2011–12 (in current dollars)	Title I allocations, federal fiscal year 2014	
											Current expenditures								
		Total	Federal	State	Local	Total	Federal	State	Local	Total[3]	Total	Instruction	Capital outlay	Interest on school debt			Total[4] (in thousands of current dollars)	Per poverty child[5] (in current dollars)
1	2	3	4	5	6	7	8	9	10	11	12	13	14	15	16	17	18	19
Saint Johns	FL	270,901	17,143	77,138	176,620	100.0	6.3	28.5	65.2	292,268	248,345	145,643	34,394	6,501	10.2	7,864	2,970	830
Saint Lucie	FL	358,633	44,521	150,408	163,704	100.0	12.4	41.9	45.6	374,783	331,572	192,564	26,342	15,771	25.7	8,406	12,241	1,046
Santa Rosa	FL	207,528	22,838	99,212	85,478	100.0	11.0	47.8	41.2	226,310	197,050	113,536	20,425	2,341	15.9	7,613	4,172	965
Sarasota	FL	469,978	46,994	69,884	353,100	100.0	10.0	14.9	75.1	520,726	407,325	258,289	95,326	10,188	19.2	9,915	8,685	1,010
Seminole	FL	513,064	52,192	232,046	228,826	100.0	10.2	45.2	44.6	518,329	487,144	308,409	18,139	10,898	15.3	7,571	11,503	1,040
Volusia	FL	547,213	63,123	211,407	272,683	100.0	11.5	38.6	49.8	562,932	500,586	300,711	35,555	22,300	28.8	8,136	21,283	1,095
Atlanta	GA	800,352	95,495	143,264	561,593	100.0	11.9	17.9	70.2	753,355	700,437	327,349	49,176	2,808	36.9	14,006	33,189	1,583
Bibb County	GA	279,214	54,001	107,038	118,175	100.0	19.3	38.3	42.3	267,058	239,829	142,912	25,923	1,306	37.8	9,698	12,348	1,153
Chatham County	GA	395,048	48,060	122,442	224,546	100.0	12.2	31.0	56.8	418,995	338,097	219,155	77,389	3,473	30.5	9,433	14,497	1,123
Cherokee County	GA	395,067	19,430	177,421	198,216	100.0	4.9	44.9	50.2	386,063	326,923	217,936	41,806	15,443	11.9	8,432	4,767	903
Clayton County	GA	487,526	70,677	226,538	190,311	100.0	14.5	46.5	39.0	493,833	431,646	272,062	61,664	0	38.6	8,461	24,405	1,166
Cobb County	GA	1,102,087	83,131	423,821	595,135	100.0	7.5	38.5	54.0	1,181,875	978,017	656,789	198,826	118	17.4	9,116	24,611	1,173
Columbia County	GA	211,207	11,204	97,591	102,412	100.0	5.3	46.2	48.5	214,562	195,224	125,591	17,411	1,739	10.4	8,205	2,208	810
Coweta County	GA	208,377	14,651	96,070	97,656	100.0	7.0	46.1	46.9	211,323	185,884	119,137	23,120	1,241	17.7	8,259	4,487	987
DeKalb County	GA	1,041,282	113,519	373,258	554,505	100.0	10.9	35.8	53.3	1,054,536	990,224	613,704	55,524	8,788	31.9	10,095	42,439	1,205
Dougherty County	GA	165,543	27,756	76,963	60,824	100.0	16.8	46.5	36.7	162,519	149,826	87,992	11,980	156	42.9	9,396	8,297	1,133
Douglas County	GA	256,399	27,599	119,145	109,655	100.0	10.8	46.5	42.8	274,410	222,499	140,106	42,055	9,856	21.9	8,993	6,230	1,028
Fayette County	GA	214,938	8,724	80,817	125,397	100.0	4.1	37.6	58.3	211,137	194,340	128,818	9,970	4,464	9.1	9,462	1,534	782
Forsyth County	GA	356,970	15,069	136,826	205,075	100.0	4.2	38.3	57.4	333,757	299,689	204,816	15,350	16,966	7.1	8,043	2,507	838
Fulton County	GA	1,134,739	73,056	327,708	733,975	100.0	6.4	28.9	64.7	1,002,318	890,691	563,004	102,020	8,304	17.1	9,618	21,788	1,158
Gwinnett County	GA	1,574,463	138,288	686,817	749,358	100.0	8.8	43.6	47.6	1,590,201	1,464,055	890,294	73,575	52,341	18.5	9,017	38,605	1,196
Hall County	GA	251,117	25,472	118,812	106,833	100.0	10.1	47.3	42.5	250,202	223,127	142,534	25,115	1,466	24.4	8,497	7,478	1,025
Henry County	GA	496,741	27,320	292,559	176,862	100.0	5.5	58.9	35.6	355,368	332,785	218,614	9,210	11,182	19.0	8,338	8,862	1,041
Houston County	GA	269,423	24,718	136,925	107,780	100.0	9.2	50.8	40.0	258,922	252,926	162,165	3,557	1,651	23.7	9,219	6,588	1,010
Muscogee County	GA	368,463	49,950	167,628	150,885	100.0	13.6	45.5	40.9	384,582	315,405	188,650	64,976	2,346	27.1	9,786	9,822	1,072
Newton County	GA	198,327	18,419	116,351	63,557	100.0	9.3	58.7	32.0	204,912	161,040	102,897	39,036	3,337	22.0	8,402	4,564	987
Paulding County	GA	244,394	18,569	142,031	83,794	100.0	7.6	58.1	34.3	237,709	221,351	143,409	12,745	3,520	13.3	7,839	4,068	965
Richmond County	GA	351,383	59,801	148,030	143,552	100.0	17.0	42.1	40.9	344,970	305,385	186,354	34,857	4,566	41.6	9,595	16,437	1,155
Rockdale County	GA	167,858	17,480	67,771	82,607	100.0	10.4	40.4	49.2	167,980	156,533	92,984	11,447	0	24.2	10,029	3,976	982
Hawaii Department of Education	HI	2,535,038	318,728	2,161,254	55,056	100.0	12.6	85.3	2.2	2,344,733	2,202,298	1,262,938	124,096	0	15.9	12,054	53,163	1,568
Boise Independent	ID	219,821	24,579	112,643	82,599	100.0	11.2	51.2	37.6	213,270	202,151	125,010	4,564	4,864	16.3	7,935	5,176	1,074
Meridian Joint	ID	222,959	17,258	158,373	47,328	100.0	7.7	71.0	21.2	205,937	191,413	116,081	4,617	9,708	10.2	5,273	4,166	951
Nampa	ID	99,667	16,041	70,684	12,942	100.0	16.1	70.9	13.0	96,976	90,175	56,405	692	6,109	27.6	5,797	5,732	1,079
Carpentersville (CUSD 300)	IL	239,374	15,099	54,118	170,157	100.0	6.3	22.6	71.1	227,877	194,694	111,743	4,564	14,563	12.8	9,356	3,399	1,177
City of Chicago (SD 299)	IL	5,760,419	892,899	2,245,498	2,622,022	100.0	15.5	39.0	45.5	5,741,225	4,826,426	3,040,082	579,993	276,013	32.4	11,976	273,393	1,981
Elgin (SDU-46)	IL	496,205	33,847	157,715	304,643	100.0	6.8	31.8	61.4	449,776	411,254	235,657	14,649	12,944	17.0	10,108	11,104	1,475
Indian Prairie (CUSD 204)	IL	355,694	9,327	81,431	264,936	100.0	2.6	22.9	74.5	336,366	315,542	214,281	4,621	15,289	5.2	10,774	1,678	1,097
Naperville (CUSD 203)	IL	283,129	6,855	53,768	222,506	100.0	2.4	19.0	78.6	274,635	244,212	147,827	21,605	1,808	5.1	13,744	1,022	1,042
Oswego (CUSD 308)	IL	195,656	6,752	62,038	126,866	100.0	3.5	31.7	64.8	185,507	149,179	85,316	9,573	12,233	6.3	8,698	1,228	1,082
Plainfield (SD 202)	IL	293,104	15,488	119,130	158,486	100.0	5.3	40.6	54.1	279,789	257,308	170,065	1,622	15,888	6.4	8,902	2,188	1,127
Rockford (SD 205)	IL	390,873	48,815	166,674	175,384	100.0	12.5	42.6	44.9	352,484	315,570	176,816	14,198	2,527	26.1	11,223	14,310	1,648
Springfield (SD 186)	IL	208,390	27,389	84,178	96,823	100.0	13.1	40.4	46.5	226,100	196,589	107,483	16,078	4,680	26.5	13,130	6,972	1,458
Valley View (CUSD 365U)	IL	235,724	13,183	71,451	151,090	100.0	5.6	30.3	64.1	232,349	214,146	127,219	12,649	5,451	13.7	12,005	3,109	1,178
Waukegan (CUSD 60)	IL	210,910	18,422	117,085	75,403	100.0	8.7	55.5	35.8	194,578	188,585	102,786	3,370	1,353	26.2	11,363	6,420	1,423
Carmel Clay	IN	204,515	15,463	101,434	87,618	100.0	7.6	49.6	42.8	179,397	153,729	97,512	15,100	7,858	3.2	9,761	371	597
Evansville Vanderburgh	IN	264,367	36,239	172,159	55,969	100.0	13.7	65.1	21.2	266,955	235,427	131,553	20,968	7,250	19.4	10,326	6,571	1,196

See notes at end of table.

Table 215.20. Revenues, expenditures, poverty rate, and Title I allocations of public school districts enrolling more than 15,000 students: 2011–12 and fiscal year 2014—Continued

Name of district	State	Revenues by source of funds, 2011–12 (in thousands of current dollars)				Percentage distribution of revenues, 2011–12				Expenditures, 2011–12 (in thousands of current dollars)					Poverty rate of 5- to 17-year-olds, 2013[1]	Current expenditure per pupil,[2] 2011–12 (in current dollars)	Title I allocations, federal fiscal year 2014	
		Total	Federal	State	Local	Total	Federal	State	Local	Total[3]	Current expenditures						Total[4] (in thousands of current dollars)	Per poverty child[5] (in current dollars)
											Total	Instruction	Capital outlay	Interest on school debt				
1	2	3	4	5	6	7	8	9	10	11	12	13	14	15	16	17	18	19
Fort Wayne	IN	358,078	48,579	238,965	70,534	100.0	13.6	66.7	19.7	333,075	303,873	189,275	21,660	4,083	27.5	9,859	13,926	1,303
Hamilton Southeastern	IN	198,933	6,150	116,975	75,808	100.0	3.1	58.8	38.1	165,003	149,552	89,222	12,594	38	3.9	7,849	434	510
Indianapolis	IN	512,019	74,919	331,965	105,135	100.0	14.6	64.8	20.5	591,308	459,843	242,318	88,489	27,807	45.7	14,371	32,427	1,445
MSD Lawrence Township	IN	193,244	16,091	113,383	63,770	100.0	8.3	58.7	33.0	159,338	143,545	95,628	13,798	1,405	19.3	9,648	4,013	1,124
MSD Wayne Township	IN	219,294	27,599	129,798	61,897	100.0	12.6	59.2	28.2	205,621	183,238	109,465	7,302	1,120	30.4	11,258	5,169	1,154
South Bend	IN	325,933	50,339	169,190	106,404	100.0	15.4	51.9	32.6	267,277	238,385	139,863	14,967	9,081	29.4	11,874	9,509	1,210
Vigo County	IN	166,738	14,006	117,137	35,595	100.0	8.4	70.3	21.3	164,259	144,996	92,714	16,130	62	25.3	9,294	4,813	1,153
Cedar Rapids	IA	220,532	15,453	95,202	109,877	100.0	7.0	43.2	49.8	240,405	180,462	116,922	42,513	5,839	11.8	10,510	3,023	1,264
Davenport	IA	200,930	19,805	92,697	88,428	100.0	9.9	46.1	44.0	191,657	169,925	113,905	17,673	0	20.9	10,022	4,803	1,270
Des Moines Independent	IA	430,610	59,869	202,951	167,790	100.0	13.9	47.1	39.0	415,927	341,175	222,405	54,255	3,418	23.2	10,199	11,455	1,403
Blue Valley	KS	297,081	6,073	100,302	190,706	100.0	2.0	33.8	64.2	269,594	208,711	129,104	46,299	14,463	3.1	9,519	497	602
Kansas City	KS	247,126	26,608	165,917	54,601	100.0	10.8	67.1	22.1	239,763	224,222	132,424	10,317	4,204	36.5	10,938	11,593	1,385
Olathe	KS	321,643	15,936	173,761	131,946	100.0	5.0	54.0	41.0	296,221	289,783	176,099	11,842	14,559	7.5	9,573	2,309	1,005
Shawnee Mission	KS	318,585	18,720	116,381	183,484	100.0	5.9	36.5	57.6	313,762	260,313	171,572	43,333	10,104	9.9	9,377	3,645	1,082
Wichita	KS	578,456	70,782	345,915	161,759	100.0	12.2	59.8	28.0	638,760	506,209	289,116	110,054	22,495	28.0	10,249	23,901	1,500
Boone County	KY	194,630	15,185	83,006	96,439	100.0	7.8	42.6	49.5	195,221	163,122	94,777	23,053	8,368	10.8	8,332	2,561	996
Fayette County	KY	443,314	44,626	167,029	231,659	100.0	10.1	37.7	52.3	492,400	415,256	249,484	61,377	13,255	18.3	10,747	10,323	1,250
Jefferson County	KY	1,218,406	188,192	479,204	551,010	100.0	15.4	39.3	45.2	1,258,019	1,131,376	588,596	97,827	19,481	23.4	11,406	41,823	1,462
Ascension Parish	LA	233,660	21,215	100,987	111,458	100.0	9.1	43.2	47.7	235,729	208,758	123,193	22,675	4,092	14.7	10,201	3,891	1,146
Bossier Parish	LA	224,526	21,839	105,044	97,643	100.0	9.7	46.8	43.5	221,778	214,713	132,848	4,152	2,063	18.9	10,206	5,121	1,228
Caddo Parish	LA	503,432	71,514	227,474	204,444	100.0	14.2	45.2	40.6	519,007	479,521	281,104	33,451	4,923	28.9	11,508	17,827	1,382
Calcasieu Parish	LA	365,328	45,892	166,811	152,625	100.0	12.6	45.7	41.8	353,035	329,914	189,332	14,533	8,122	22.8	10,132	10,308	1,291
East Baton Rouge Parish	LA	589,856	95,276	191,035	303,545	100.0	16.2	32.4	51.5	627,759	543,944	300,144	69,215	327	30.4	12,693	26,406	1,435
Jefferson Parish	LA	625,708	164,551	195,487	265,670	100.0	26.3	31.2	42.5	647,475	544,439	303,251	93,122	6,474	24.2	11,916	23,496	1,421
Lafayette Parish	LA	346,064	45,979	132,892	167,193	100.0	13.3	38.4	48.3	329,592	315,885	190,315	10,449	2,575	21.7	10,373	10,866	1,287
Livingston Parish	LA	239,483	26,203	155,971	57,309	100.0	10.9	65.1	23.9	246,029	221,480	136,363	20,818	3,291	18.3	8,940	5,875	1,235
Ouachita Parish	LA	224,983	28,356	127,490	69,137	100.0	12.6	56.7	30.7	229,877	211,468	114,648	11,427	5,541	25.7	10,725	6,290	1,235
Rapides Parish	LA	245,281	33,795	138,111	73,375	100.0	13.8	56.3	29.9	251,654	230,750	141,284	17,427	2,986	29.7	9,603	9,406	1,285
Saint Tammany Parish	LA	479,133	64,343	219,363	195,427	100.0	13.4	45.8	40.8	470,886	434,885	249,830	24,123	10,657	16.6	11,735	9,540	1,266
Tangipahoa Parish	LA	194,959	39,881	113,351	41,727	100.0	20.5	58.1	21.4	204,793	191,982	113,290	12,249	430	30.2	9,840	8,359	1,262
Terrebonne Parish	LA	188,676	33,874	94,157	60,645	100.0	18.0	49.9	32.1	185,800	179,331	104,482	5,789	142	22.9	9,647	5,812	1,239
Anne Arundel County	MD	1,088,736	55,614	402,917	630,205	100.0	5.1	37.0	57.9	1,128,315	973,747	613,482	114,515	19,413	8.1	12,762	11,289	1,533
Baltimore City	MD	1,459,517	203,999	983,161	272,357	100.0	14.0	67.4	18.7	1,478,108	1,287,343	751,045	115,390	7,152	31.8	15,287	52,034	1,788
Baltimore County	MD	1,589,273	90,954	676,250	822,069	100.0	5.7	42.6	51.7	1,560,907	1,360,714	837,765	150,059	14,445	12.2	12,940	26,974	1,730
Calvert County	MD	244,940	10,271	106,263	128,406	100.0	4.2	43.4	52.4	247,024	217,759	138,323	15,227	1,927	7.8	13,155	1,621	1,204
Carroll County	MD	399,621	19,852	180,518	199,251	100.0	5.0	45.2	49.9	386,306	340,686	209,313	35,146	4,960	6.4	12,580	2,359	1,191
Cecil County	MD	209,828	13,993	114,337	81,498	100.0	6.7	54.5	38.8	201,088	188,681	119,133	5,809	2,599	13.9	11,921	3,206	1,262
Charles County	MD	379,886	23,686	183,253	172,947	100.0	6.2	48.2	45.5	358,993	341,802	199,963	8,191	3,000	9.6	12,764	3,482	1,307
Frederick County	MD	618,540	20,512	271,775	326,253	100.0	3.3	43.9	52.7	558,687	504,501	319,554	34,492	11,333	7.8	12,484	4,478	1,333
Harford County	MD	562,869	28,187	259,493	275,189	100.0	5.0	46.1	48.9	544,760	487,653	296,826	29,514	13,775	8.5	12,758	5,018	1,280
Howard County	MD	889,422	23,875	282,270	583,277	100.0	2.7	31.7	65.6	858,194	760,263	504,862	71,887	15,366	5.9	14,747	4,295	1,657
Montgomery County	MD	2,854,888	109,485	759,591	1,985,812	100.0	3.8	26.6	69.6	2,646,912	2,178,319	1,387,437	391,146	39,143	7.6	14,873	21,478	1,700
Prince George's County	MD	2,065,364	145,794	1,017,616	901,954	100.0	7.1	49.3	43.7	1,845,509	1,676,111	973,389	98,263	18,474	13.5	13,535	33,155	1,218
Saint Mary's County	MD	218,360	15,847	108,864	93,649	100.0	7.3	49.9	42.9	220,955	208,619	123,004	8,776	1,827	10.6	11,956	2,602	1,503
Washington County	MD	298,631	21,794	175,811	101,026	100.0	7.3	58.9	33.8	296,808	279,839	168,897	12,239	1,872	17.2	12,583	6,402	

See notes at end of table.

Table 215.20. Revenues, expenditures, poverty rate, and Title I allocations of public school districts enrolling more than 15,000 students: 2011–12 and fiscal year 2014—Continued

Name of district	State	Revenues by source of funds, 2011–12 (in thousands of current dollars)				Percentage distribution of revenues, 2011–12				Expenditures, 2011–12 (in thousands of current dollars)					Poverty rate of 5- to 17-year-olds, 2013[1]	Current expenditure per pupil,[2] 2011–12 (in current dollars)	Title I allocations, federal fiscal year 2014	
											Current expenditures								
		Total	Federal	State	Local	Total	Federal	State	Local	Total[3]	Total	Instruction	Capital outlay	Interest on school debt			Total[4] (in thousands of current dollars)	Per poverty child[5] (in current dollars)
1	2	3	4	5	6	7	8	9	10	11	12	13	14	15	16	17	18	19
Boston	MA	1,262,395	131,642	319,499	811,254	100.0	10.4	25.3	64.3	1,252,519	1,185,502	716,062	44,087	11,993	27.2	21,544	37,617	1,888
Brockton	MA	235,360	14,311	160,665	60,384	100.0	6.1	68.3	25.7	234,335	227,320	147,563	2,265	1,184	22.0	14,065	5,711	1,542
Springfield	MA	507,171	64,086	374,808	68,277	100.0	12.6	73.9	13.5	491,799	430,052	261,826	46,199	9,604	40.2	17,076	21,488	1,828
Worcester	MA	410,096	45,125	253,792	111,179	100.0	11.0	61.9	27.1	425,511	379,363	265,772	23,256	9,008	26.6	15,541	12,269	1,688
Ann Arbor	MI	222,110	5,012	87,882	129,216	100.0	2.3	39.6	58.2	227,627	192,987	115,638	13,261	8,503	11.2	11,601	2,149	964
Chippewa Valley	MI	162,723	5,058	105,362	52,303	100.0	3.1	64.7	32.1	191,917	135,175	87,818	30,529	24,005	9.4	8,355	1,595	957
Dearborn City	MI	228,113	19,980	132,396	75,737	100.0	8.8	58.0	33.2	217,965	200,527	119,672	7,783	7,039	44.6	10,703	13,769	1,415
Detroit City	MI	1,035,068	271,358	499,995	263,715	100.0	26.2	48.3	25.5	1,231,375	893,986	515,473	213,384	116,464	53.5	13,330	147,012	2,082
Grand Rapids	MI	262,739	47,192	124,676	90,871	100.0	18.0	47.5	34.6	262,794	227,179	125,747	4,546	6,023	36.2	12,903	14,712	1,340
Livonia	MI	183,134	5,777	112,911	64,446	100.0	3.2	61.7	35.2	183,156	167,405	102,990	7,154	4,349	10.5	10,852	1,746	957
Plymouth-Canton	MI	187,309	3,990	120,015	63,304	100.0	2.1	64.1	33.8	180,715	162,180	98,084	3,527	9,213	7.5	8,802	1,607	950
Rochester Community	MI	180,028	2,511	111,035	66,482	100.0	1.4	61.7	36.9	175,474	159,193	97,150	3,342	8,245	6.4	10,668	1,015	913
Utica	MI	288,927	16,778	198,026	74,123	100.0	5.8	68.5	25.7	288,797	258,839	178,656	14,995	9,540	11.4	9,048	3,766	1,046
Walled Lake Consolidated	MI	176,100	4,694	103,795	67,611	100.0	2.7	58.9	38.4	167,267	155,282	101,747	3,224	6,645	10.9	10,040	1,812	950
Warren Consolidated	MI	183,486	12,636	108,329	62,521	100.0	6.9	59.0	34.1	210,034	174,925	104,703	25,909	7,817	19.7	11,348	3,950	1,171
Anoka-Hennepin	MN	471,942	27,692	313,974	130,276	100.0	5.9	66.5	27.6	430,596	383,012	257,674	20,534	4,261	8.7	9,885	4,621	1,200
Minneapolis	MN	618,494	62,347	361,522	194,625	100.0	10.1	58.5	31.5	623,918	495,183	336,036	75,826	20,909	29.3	14,130	23,472	1,550
Osseo Public	MN	279,769	16,232	172,739	90,798	100.0	5.8	61.7	32.5	279,524	235,837	163,594	15,095	8,317	12.3	11,275	3,657	1,127
Rochester	MN	189,943	13,716	126,918	49,309	100.0	7.2	66.8	26.0	180,445	152,615	98,920	12,520	5,453	11.1	9,353	2,430	1,051
Rosemount-Apple Valley-Eagan	MN	335,707	16,572	218,969	100,166	100.0	4.9	65.2	29.8	315,802	284,279	203,649	16,479	3,782	7.0	10,332	2,103	1,032
Saint Paul	MN	626,518	76,265	402,820	147,433	100.0	12.2	64.3	23.5	619,394	528,489	362,596	41,458	17,715	29.2	13,795	22,725	1,552
South Washington County	MN	212,229	9,112	130,985	72,132	100.0	4.3	61.7	34.0	216,158	163,186	107,297	21,541	15,331	4.4	9,138	516	585
DeSoto County	MS	243,669	25,121	129,196	89,352	100.0	10.3	53.0	36.7	220,366	201,905	117,268	11,173	6,692	14.5	6,249	4,294	857
Jackson	MS	291,507	70,976	129,200	91,331	100.0	24.3	44.3	31.3	289,523	263,370	146,889	15,718	9,685	43.3	8,809	15,694	1,119
Rankin County	MS	160,129	14,730	78,230	67,169	100.0	9.2	48.9	41.9	151,633	141,962	85,301	5,092	3,562	16.2	7,327	3,312	932
Columbia, 93.	MO	203,458	16,699	78,350	108,409	100.0	8.2	38.5	53.3	220,793	160,768	92,472	47,006	7,157	15.7	9,078	3,457	1,131
Fort Zumwalt, R-II.	MO	198,817	9,620	82,974	106,223	100.0	4.8	41.7	53.4	199,268	177,484	110,817	11,966	7,197	6.7	9,353	1,350	888
Francis Howell, R-III.	MO	203,538	8,935	76,525	118,078	100.0	4.4	37.6	58.0	205,388	166,219	106,304	22,329	8,805	6.5	8,469	1,243	885
Hazelwood	MO	227,843	17,625	88,218	122,000	100.0	7.7	38.7	53.5	229,452	185,392	107,268	24,619	6,586	19.9	10,432	5,016	1,185
Kansas City, 33.	MO	231,853	41,920	56,288	133,645	100.0	18.1	24.3	57.6	214,923	186,315	90,042	14,446	2,641	38.0	11,217	14,495	1,294
Lee's Summit, R-VII.	MO	216,612	12,821	85,226	118,565	100.0	5.9	39.3	54.7	185,075	160,021	100,877	6,796	12,668	9.4	8,977	1,624	895
North Kansas City, 74	MO	223,786	14,446	81,252	128,088	100.0	6.5	36.3	57.2	219,578	184,280	109,172	13,430	16,096	14.5	9,632	3,216	1,060
Parkway, C-2.	MO	225,901	6,501	48,843	170,557	100.0	2.9	21.6	75.5	250,159	214,304	122,582	23,707	7,601	6.4	12,343	1,281	876
Rockwood, R-VI.	MO	258,754	8,197	72,791	177,766	100.0	3.2	28.1	68.7	282,079	205,979	122,828	25,471	10,216	4.8	9,153	622	517
Saint Louis City	MO	370,420	72,381	99,292	198,747	100.0	19.5	26.8	53.7	390,955	327,424	173,232	31,050	18,029	40.3	13,275	30,343	1,649
Springfield, R-XII.	MO	244,686	29,164	82,186	133,336	100.0	11.9	33.6	54.5	250,279	207,949	125,513	23,641	16,316	22.8	8,260	7,763	1,215
Lincoln	NE	395,725	46,610	113,305	235,810	100.0	11.8	28.6	59.6	428,752	366,370	253,874	45,549	16,806	14.7	10,030	9,027	1,465
Millard	NE	236,437	16,961	92,012	127,464	100.0	7.2	38.9	53.9	236,625	215,194	138,016	14,350	5,463	6.2	9,326	2,039	1,311
Omaha	NE	611,657	102,834	205,033	303,790	100.0	16.8	33.5	49.7	613,168	562,446	373,110	40,293	8,350	24.4	11,173	26,252	1,705
Clark County	NV	2,863,675	282,471	1,687,290	893,914	100.0	9.9	58.9	31.2	2,889,780	2,462,255	1,454,066	192,306	190,033	21.5	7,857	90,187	1,186
Washoe County	NV	606,096	86,385	367,101	172,610	100.0	11.0	60.6	28.5	636,000	554,333	306,839	42,888	35,341	22.0	8,562	16,437	1,045
Elizabeth	NJ	528,622	37,981	438,604	52,037	100.0	7.2	83.0	9.8	514,198	491,669	296,632	7,933	0	26.9	21,024	9,426	1,585
Jersey City	NJ	700,922	63,831	522,498	114,593	100.0	9.1	74.5	16.3	598,442	579,436	377,689	7,522	3,907	30.2	21,150	18,464	1,742

See notes at end of table.

Table 215.20. Revenues, expenditures, poverty rate, and Title I allocations of public school districts enrolling more than 15,000 students: 2011–12 and fiscal year 2014—Continued

Name of district	State	Revenues by source of funds, 2011–12 (in thousands of current dollars)				Percentage distribution of revenues, 2011–12				Expenditures, 2011–12 (in thousands of current dollars)					Poverty rate of 5- to 17-year-olds, 2013[1]	Current expenditure per pupil,[2] 2011–12 (in current dollars)[1]	Title I allocations, federal fiscal year 2014	
		Total	Federal	State	Local	Total	Federal	State	Local	Total[3]	Current expenditures						Total[4] (in thousands of current dollars)	Per poverty child[5] (in current dollars)
											Total	Instruction	Capital outlay	Interest on school debt				
1	2	3	4	5	6	7	8	9	10	11	12	13	14	15	16	17	18	19
Newark	NJ	1,094,167	104,857	863,005	126,305	100.0	9.6	78.9	11.5	1,092,654	1,059,603	644,467	5,834	3,525	36.7	29,812	34,372	1,896
Paterson	NJ	590,806	58,743	488,973	43,090	100.0	9.9	82.8	7.3	567,978	523,675	333,033	7,725	363	31.4	21,493	17,763	1,981
Toms River Regional	NJ	241,397	11,667	83,147	146,583	100.0	4.8	34.4	60.7	233,776	227,216	137,056	1,550	3,157	8.9	13,381	2,032	1,251
Albuquerque	NM	963,715	97,699	688,092	177,924	100.0	10.1	71.4	18.5	983,498	802,693	482,085	159,710	19,937	22.4	8,510	30,674	1,192
Las Cruces	NM	246,254	28,307	178,479	39,468	100.0	11.5	72.5	16.0	261,969	208,132	123,447	48,743	3,082	32.3	8,209	8,577	1,022
Rio Rancho	NM	148,251	7,614	108,757	31,880	100.0	5.1	73.4	21.5	142,572	122,383	74,318	14,327	4,764	11.2	7,254	1,595	773
Brentwood Union Free	NY	334,185	17,018	222,186	94,981	100.0	5.1	66.5	28.4	333,292	311,995	217,346	14,832	3,980	17.7	18,200	3,815	1,345
Buffalo City	NY	925,386	117,988	644,965	162,433	100.0	12.8	69.7	17.6	949,724	748,663	512,818	130,811	58,701	38.1	22,879	28,570	1,762
New York City	NY	23,517,452	2,237,047	8,648,188	12,632,217	100.0	9.5	36.8	53.7	24,814,225	21,993,233	17,125,980	2,111,295	483,008	30.7	22,212	716,620	1,884
Rochester City	NY	690,922	93,565	480,435	116,922	100.0	13.5	69.5	16.9	682,173	631,229	383,966	34,294	7,168	41.0	20,082	23,890	1,665
Syracuse City	NY	425,283	55,429	297,649	72,205	100.0	13.0	70.0	17.0	471,499	391,052	277,302	62,545	9,105	40.4	19,084	13,884	1,538
Yonkers City	NY	533,720	36,323	300,612	196,785	100.0	6.8	56.3	36.9	512,352	494,428	337,747	6,307	4,894	19.6	19,523	8,926	1,460
Alamance-Burlington	NC	182,461	23,017	117,739	41,705	100.0	12.6	64.5	22.9	195,284	184,237	123,653	5,598	3,831	26.3	8,063	7,031	1,020
Buncombe County	NC	228,213	29,073	130,500	68,640	100.0	12.7	57.2	30.1	240,793	212,951	129,798	19,019	7,420	22.5	8,300	7,365	1,041
Cabarrus County	NC	231,763	22,938	144,961	63,864	100.0	9.9	62.5	27.6	249,084	216,180	135,289	10,474	19,727	14.9	7,267	4,890	1,001
Catawba County	NC	142,730	21,926	87,531	33,273	100.0	15.4	61.3	23.3	148,346	135,136	86,418	5,508	6,924	23.9	7,783	4,485	1,000
Charlotte-Mecklenburg	NC	1,209,892	156,055	670,885	382,952	100.0	12.9	55.4	31.7	1,241,903	1,104,932	702,565	36,282	82,491	20.8	7,796	41,820	1,170
Cleveland County	NC	149,603	24,027	91,555	34,021	100.0	16.1	61.2	22.7	148,816	139,132	89,163	7,494	1,360	33.0	8,573	5,573	1,018
Craven County	NC	120,961	22,973	75,347	22,641	100.0	19.0	62.3	18.7	122,781	116,165	72,595	2,742	3,228	25.6	7,628	4,098	987
Cumberland County	NC	446,774	83,302	263,276	100,196	100.0	18.6	58.9	22.4	475,034	427,720	270,505	33,136	7,740	24.0	8,062	14,649	1,121
Davidson County	NC	157,373	20,318	102,095	34,960	100.0	12.9	64.9	22.2	169,010	141,961	90,644	20,288	6,062	16.7	6,980	3,722	987
Durham	NC	349,845	47,453	171,275	131,117	100.0	13.6	49.0	37.5	396,771	330,655	204,770	43,278	16,683	25.6	9,943	11,736	1,077
Forsyth County	NC	462,134	70,974	263,463	127,697	100.0	15.4	57.0	27.6	528,982	447,091	292,732	46,934	31,928	30.1	8,382	21,110	1,127
Gaston County	NC	247,411	38,137	156,760	52,514	100.0	15.4	63.4	21.2	278,155	237,617	147,728	27,867	11,401	25.2	7,497	9,547	1,056
Guilford County	NC	769,588	90,219	382,738	296,631	100.0	11.7	49.7	38.5	778,610	652,679	404,251	88,051	34,112	23.4	8,810	22,537	1,136
Harnett County	NC	160,368	24,392	107,295	28,681	100.0	15.2	66.9	17.9	161,248	143,484	91,743	11,184	6,173	24.4	7,290	5,987	1,012
Iredell-Statesville	NC	175,672	24,910	105,768	44,994	100.0	14.2	60.2	25.6	187,158	160,962	99,118	8,478	15,132	17.8	7,489	4,465	1,004
Johnston County	NC	264,723	34,468	170,801	59,454	100.0	13.0	64.5	22.5	288,569	282,600	170,429	3,969	21,114	23.0	7,934	8,395	1,034
Nash-Rocky Mount	NC	149,396	25,038	97,232	27,126	100.0	16.8	65.1	18.2	153,819	148,000	90,949	2,521	2,552	29.4	8,731	5,485	1,010
New Hanover County	NC	229,372	25,182	129,634	74,556	100.0	11.0	56.5	32.5	234,294	212,055	126,690	9,214	12,462	19.4	8,438	5,830	1,022
Onslow County	NC	193,181	32,792	113,326	47,063	100.0	17.0	58.7	24.4	193,437	182,326	114,045	2,283	7,053	21.9	7,296	5,589	1,015
Pitt County	NC	197,786	31,449	124,269	42,068	100.0	15.9	62.8	21.3	209,522	191,018	125,675	8,784	7,566	29.3	7,986	8,225	1,032
Randolph County	NC	144,822	20,396	95,641	28,785	100.0	14.1	66.0	19.9	150,174	139,800	87,938	2,821	6,676	22.1	7,472	4,553	999
Robeson County	NC	204,665	42,139	135,845	26,681	100.0	20.6	66.4	13.0	207,276	197,615	122,903	7,445	793	44.4	7,906	13,066	1,131
Rowan-Salisbury	NC	176,167	28,365	104,907	42,895	100.0	16.1	59.5	24.3	181,422	171,197	107,171	4,817	4,488	23.0	8,417	5,169	1,011
Union County	NC	325,357	39,189	191,672	94,496	100.0	12.0	58.9	29.0	358,366	308,459	194,525	12,421	32,201	13.2	7,690	5,721	908
Wake County	NC	1,202,796	135,729	709,165	357,902	100.0	11.3	59.0	29.8	1,353,430	1,128,321	735,593	108,167	104,238	13.7	7,616	28,029	1,151
Wayne County	NC	165,768	35,467	105,683	24,618	100.0	21.4	63.8	14.9	165,403	152,574	104,691	12,195	0	31.4	7,662	6,989	1,020
Akron City	OH	400,504	47,707	206,660	146,137	100.0	11.9	51.6	36.5	383,840	327,005	195,108	47,888	0	36.7	14,419	16,454	1,503
Cincinnati City	OH	611,847	80,388	213,261	318,198	100.0	13.1	34.9	52.0	712,448	481,635	268,354	163,147	35,549	43.7	14,979	33,777	1,606
Cleveland Municipal	OH	839,400	135,087	494,139	210,174	100.0	16.1	58.9	25.0	793,657	709,364	465,054	31,413	8,448	44.5	16,572	54,694	1,840
Columbus City	OH	949,275	141,562	339,022	468,691	100.0	14.9	35.7	49.4	936,473	805,774	459,657	75,767	22,631	36.7	15,960	47,072	1,823
Hilliard City	OH	193,300	8,101	57,613	127,586	100.0	4.2	29.8	66.0	184,384	170,973	110,052	5,763	5,121	8.8	11,056	1,604	1,041
Lakota Local	OH	169,076	8,179	59,064	101,833	100.0	4.8	34.9	60.2	175,408	159,593	89,085	4,697	9,656	7.3	9,191	1,607	1,042
Olentangy Local	OH	192,485	3,835	26,464	162,186	100.0	2.0	13.7	84.3	191,261	161,698	101,467	11,545	17,536	3.2	9,688	359	604
South-Western City	OH	264,684	26,534	116,604	121,546	100.0	10.0	44.1	45.9	230,720	213,660	131,116	8,037	2,989	22.8	10,225	7,987	1,400
Toledo City	OH	415,983	47,543	253,965	114,475	100.0	11.4	61.1	27.5	361,692	278,349	142,989	68,573	7,568	41.3	12,042	24,386	1,542

See notes at end of table.

Table 215.20. Revenues, expenditures, poverty rate, and Title I allocations of public school districts enrolling more than 15,000 students: 2011–12 and fiscal year 2014—Continued

Name of district	State	Revenues by source of funds, 2011–12 (in thousands of current dollars)				Percentage distribution of revenues, 2011–12				Expenditures, 2011–12 (in thousands of current dollars)					Poverty rate of 5- to 17-year-olds, 2013[1]	Current expenditure per pupil,[2] 2011–12 (in current dollars)	Title I allocations, federal fiscal year 2014	
		Total	Federal	State	Local	Total	Federal	State	Local	Total[3]	Current expenditures Total	Instruction	Capital outlay	Interest on school debt			Total[4] (in thousands of current dollars)	Per poverty child[5] (in current dollars)
1	2	3	4	5	6	7	8	9	10	11	12	13	14	15	16	17	18	19
Broken Arrow	OK	139,004	11,294	64,807	62,903	100.0	8.1	46.6	45.3	137,818	119,980	59,760	14,513	2,481	10.9	7,064	1,703	811
Edmond	OK	188,302	13,719	60,252	114,331	100.0	7.3	32.0	60.7	182,069	152,103	81,025	25,324	3,053	9.8	6,918	2,126	861
Lawton	OK	136,491	24,169	78,301	34,021	100.0	17.7	57.4	24.9	141,630	129,644	65,415	10,391	630	22.3	8,167	3,588	1,012
Moore	OK	171,969	13,759	88,677	69,533	100.0	8.0	51.6	40.4	189,796	161,068	91,683	26,515	1,688	11.2	7,104	2,371	880
Norman	OK	125,111	9,688	53,534	61,889	100.0	7.7	42.8	49.5	134,096	107,648	61,247	24,402	1,575	13.8	7,166	2,109	993
Oklahoma City	OK	466,306	74,790	185,756	205,760	100.0	16.0	39.8	44.1	387,147	359,891	182,342	19,813	5,239	36.3	8,328	23,022	1,239
Putnam City	OK	164,242	19,472	75,644	69,126	100.0	11.9	46.1	42.1	158,543	143,350	78,619	12,961	1,883	25.0	7,461	5,249	1,039
Tulsa	OK	411,118	80,511	160,802	169,805	100.0	19.6	39.1	41.3	399,538	347,922	171,582	43,070	3,407	31.6	8,445	18,003	1,199
Union	OK	136,261	13,660	58,518	64,083	100.0	10.0	42.9	47.0	138,520	109,191	52,988	22,904	1,600	17.3	7,284	2,638	964
Beaverton, 48J	OR	385,781	24,967	182,189	178,625	100.0	6.5	47.2	46.3	381,625	345,259	217,497	7,051	28,097	12.9	8,689	6,430	1,082
Bend-Lapine, SD1	OR	162,733	13,073	61,067	88,593	100.0	8.0	37.5	54.4	152,203	136,446	79,509	3,855	11,023	16.6	8,301	3,401	1,153
Eugene, SD4J	OR	180,188	13,658	67,955	98,575	100.0	7.6	37.7	54.7	182,640	165,962	98,125	6,967	8,827	19.4	9,556	4,304	1,171
Hillsboro, SD1J	OR	210,435	16,815	101,918	91,702	100.0	8.0	48.4	43.6	207,083	182,589	107,494	8,066	15,776	15.4	8,578	4,353	1,164
North Clackamas, SD12	OR	179,239	12,385	85,690	81,164	100.0	6.9	47.8	45.3	172,612	143,107	78,336	6,808	19,981	11.6	8,205	2,583	1,170
Portland, SD1J	OR	525,852	55,577	174,246	296,029	100.0	10.6	33.1	56.3	568,932	524,713	303,873	15,303	25,607	17.0	11,181	12,632	1,332
Salem-Keizer, SD24J	OR	407,544	42,703	248,020	116,821	100.0	10.5	60.9	28.7	461,612	373,916	231,292	66,631	19,661	24.0	9,175	14,432	1,327
Allentown City	PA	233,150	32,102	121,433	79,615	100.0	13.8	52.1	34.1	236,823	189,494	122,316	7,341	6,779	30.6	10,791	10,582	1,623
Central Bucks	PA	287,968	2,927	45,421	239,620	100.0	1.0	15.8	83.2	257,796	212,957	135,157	21,105	12,018	3.5	10,605	544	700
Philadelphia City	PA	2,681,763	452,562	1,292,598	936,603	100.0	16.9	48.2	34.9	2,813,912	1,683,739	993,871	89,663	89,892	36.4	10,915	178,387	2,031
Pittsburgh	PA	606,111	78,468	242,595	285,048	100.0	12.9	40.0	47.0	602,348	416,186	234,089	27,596	22,297	29.3	15,615	17,863	1,777
Reading	PA	211,083	27,098	146,780	37,205	100.0	12.8	69.5	17.6	233,545	186,504	113,535	17,927	14,088	48.4	10,327	16,352	1,822
Providence	RI	419,516	61,644	227,740	130,132	100.0	14.7	54.3	31.0	403,115	377,488	216,760	2,921	15,419	36.1	16,051	20,520	1,978
Aiken, 01	SC	228,609	32,001	113,336	83,272	100.0	14.0	49.6	36.4	221,214	202,707	123,460	16,516	1,300	25.5	8,197	7,568	1,086
Beaufort, 01	SC	277,076	25,739	73,159	178,178	100.0	9.3	26.4	64.3	259,486	221,171	122,967	20,527	16,993	21.6	11,063	5,490	1,062
Berkeley, 01	SC	297,716	36,647	147,609	113,460	100.0	12.3	49.6	38.1	314,205	249,257	139,854	39,362	22,272	19.8	8,285	7,162	1,090
Charleston, 01	SC	631,466	72,130	190,979	368,357	100.0	11.4	30.2	58.3	554,043	438,197	257,047	65,422	42,182	27.1	9,946	17,007	1,213
Dorchester, 02	SC	208,414	15,992	119,910	72,512	100.0	7.7	57.5	34.8	203,681	183,027	108,246	8,456	9,216	14.7	7,840	3,881	1,059
Florence, 01	SC	158,773	17,974	81,514	59,285	100.0	11.3	51.3	37.3	164,854	140,546	80,690	22,178	431	23.7	8,769	4,099	1,037
Greenville, 01	SC	685,904	67,024	335,785	283,095	100.0	9.8	49.0	41.3	674,602	563,389	322,530	55,348	53,332	21.3	7,808	22,134	1,258
Horry, 01	SC	471,819	43,888	158,030	269,901	100.0	9.3	33.5	57.2	459,446	394,645	237,356	44,512	17,541	29.4	10,130	14,159	1,186
Lexington, 01	SC	264,338	13,127	136,664	114,547	100.0	5.0	51.7	43.3	329,625	218,172	121,074	92,945	18,354	15.5	9,490	3,873	1,034
Lexington, 05	SC	205,223	9,715	106,681	88,827	100.0	4.7	52.0	43.3	243,319	171,270	97,343	66,443	4,334	12.8	10,342	1,872	833
Pickens, 01	SC	158,863	15,879	79,527	63,457	100.0	10.0	50.1	39.9	230,927	126,422	74,926	87,103	16,460	18.8	7,641	3,439	1,036
Richland, 01	SC	362,627	35,955	115,508	211,164	100.0	9.9	31.9	58.2	354,130	299,161	167,728	14,983	38,727	29.9	12,495	9,473	1,136
Richland, 02	SC	305,356	23,683	149,398	132,275	100.0	7.8	48.9	43.3	332,861	260,529	147,010	47,843	22,528	15.3	10,038	4,247	1,041
Sumter, 01	SC	153,275	23,773	80,333	49,169	100.0	15.5	52.4	32.1	150,120	137,442	73,408	4,342	5,920	30.2	8,125	6,252	1,073
York, 03	SC	180,567	14,878	91,592	74,097	100.0	8.2	50.7	41.0	166,983	152,155	89,396	6,487	7,438	18.6	8,837	3,902	1,073
Sioux Falls	SD	202,945	22,293	64,077	116,575	100.0	11.0	31.6	57.4	205,598	173,023	109,591	25,832	4,495	12.7	7,580	5,112	1,655
Davidson County	TN	852,377	124,758	237,139	490,480	100.0	14.6	27.8	57.5	874,304	787,272	450,044	54,449	29,758	27.5	9,793	31,378	1,189
Hamilton County	TN	402,575	55,347	129,679	217,549	100.0	13.7	32.2	54.0	389,623	376,823	241,943	5,261	4,625	21.4	8,703	12,778	1,122
Knox County	TN	517,620	66,212	166,759	284,649	100.0	12.8	32.2	55.0	501,983	458,063	280,341	34,206	8,882	20.0	7,812	15,791	1,147
Memphis	TN	1,194,046	247,241	463,916	482,889	100.0	20.7	38.9	40.4	1,190,720	1,085,345	649,243	88,992	0	37.6	9,782	55,123	1,261
Montgomery County	TN	255,693	37,627	127,006	91,060	100.0	14.7	49.7	35.6	283,358	241,710	145,968	31,244	9,850	24.7	7,895	8,454	1,041
Rutherford County	TN	314,474	29,698	156,628	128,148	100.0	9.4	49.8	40.7	367,387	304,058	197,446	49,221	13,484	14.2	7,677	5,207	894
Shelby County	TN	408,303	39,752	185,148	183,403	100.0	9.7	45.3	44.9	438,607	398,616	251,426	30,941	0	11.1	8,587	7,143	1,103
Sumner County	TN	222,870	19,544	114,682	88,644	100.0	8.8	51.5	39.8	227,765	217,592	142,154	2,225	5,860	14.0	7,672	4,093	961

See notes at end of table.

Table 215.20. Revenues, expenditures, poverty rate, and Title I allocations of public school districts enrolling more than 15,000 students: 2011–12 and fiscal year 2014—Continued

Name of district	State	Revenues by source of funds, 2011–12 (in thousands of current dollars)				Percentage distribution of revenues, 2011–12				Expenditures, 2011–12 (in thousands of current dollars)					Poverty rate of 5- to 17-year-olds, 2013[1]	Current expenditure per pupil[2] 2011–12 (in current dollars)	Title I allocations, federal fiscal year 2014	
		Total	Federal	State	Local	Total	Federal	State	Local	Total[3]	Current expenditures						Total[4] (in thousands of current dollars)	Per poverty child[5] (in current dollars)
											Total	Instruction	Capital outlay	Interest on school debt				
1	2	3	4	5	6	7	8	9	10	11	12	13	14	15	16	17	18	19
Williamson County	TN	271,659	12,286	102,765	156,608	100.0	4.5	37.8	57.6	303,203	263,910	173,025	20,736	16,180	5.6	8,001	1,671	779
Wilson County	TN	129,248	10,906	58,774	59,568	100.0	8.4	45.5	46.1	164,831	119,377	78,963	27,828	13,945	10.8	5,947	1,524	781
Abilene ISD	TX	155,982	29,149	77,540	49,273	100.0	18.7	49.7	31.6	153,467	137,113	81,155	10,646	3,566	26.0	7,982	4,265	971
Aldine ISD	TX	610,147	97,303	324,058	188,786	100.0	15.9	53.1	30.9	553,073	497,038	309,275	32,541	21,749	38.1	7,730	27,038	1,140
Alief ISD	TX	443,391	68,621	226,065	148,705	100.0	15.5	51.0	33.5	407,976	382,978	240,833	13,096	8,035	35.7	8,434	20,576	1,119
Allen ISD	TX	194,652	4,591	53,955	136,106	100.0	2.4	27.7	69.9	232,630	142,094	89,068	69,145	20,571	6.2	7,285	927	734
Alvin ISD	TX	176,341	16,596	102,019	57,726	100.0	9.4	57.9	32.7	183,589	140,213	85,118	28,657	13,834	19.0	7,700	3,180	958
Amarillo ISD	TX	287,021	44,754	143,890	98,377	100.0	15.6	50.1	34.3	274,728	263,568	170,767	3,581	4,885	24.0	7,988	7,963	1,009
Arlington ISD	TX	566,407	63,788	242,020	260,599	100.0	11.3	42.7	46.0	531,090	460,939	297,929	45,456	20,127	23.8	7,124	17,764	1,103
Austin ISD	TX	1,070,061	130,188	169,928	769,945	100.0	12.2	15.9	72.0	1,002,664	768,411	445,203	57,139	36,942	29.6	8,880	33,205	1,152
Beaumont ISD	TX	218,982	32,490	55,688	130,774	100.0	14.8	25.4	59.7	296,350	193,058	108,208	80,024	19,198	31.2	9,716	6,545	984
Birdville ISD	TX	233,992	28,940	97,660	107,392	100.0	12.4	41.7	45.9	210,480	184,829	120,736	4,545	15,963	18.7	7,795	4,372	954
Brownsville ISD	TX	501,603	112,894	328,109	60,600	100.0	22.5	65.4	12.1	486,144	443,428	264,062	24,504	10,664	47.5	8,930	26,207	1,155
Bryan ISD	TX	148,979	24,009	56,168	68,802	100.0	16.1	37.7	46.2	140,912	128,471	77,505	4,913	7,064	30.4	8,230	4,994	973
Carrollton-Farmers Branch ISD	TX	282,031	22,873	66,095	193,063	100.0	8.1	23.4	68.5	245,324	211,084	125,216	18,982	13,682	18.2	7,989	4,959	965
Clear Creek ISD	TX	361,101	24,638	113,516	222,947	100.0	6.8	31.4	61.7	329,565	289,863	185,005	9,283	29,243	9.9	7,393	3,409	837
Comal ISD	TX	192,954	12,077	38,349	142,528	100.0	6.3	19.9	73.9	203,240	134,671	78,797	28,551	27,647	11.6	7,559	1,785	815
Conroe ISD	TX	454,374	27,519	141,663	285,192	100.0	6.1	31.2	62.8	495,365	358,995	227,046	90,736	44,718	12.9	6,817	7,074	992
Corpus Christi ISD	TX	355,763	61,886	149,602	144,275	100.0	17.4	42.1	40.6	380,469	309,649	180,796	48,784	15,922	24.5	8,006	12,005	1,125
Crowley ISD	TX	136,553	13,778	47,872	74,903	100.0	10.1	35.1	54.9	125,297	107,264	67,642	2,773	14,687	16.8	7,103	2,947	919
Cypress-Fairbanks ISD	TX	930,535	72,251	366,723	491,561	100.0	7.8	39.4	52.8	894,600	737,107	483,511	46,917	104,966	15.8	6,828	19,589	1,115
Dallas ISD	TX	1,677,871	251,377	466,566	959,928	100.0	15.0	27.8	57.2	1,900,501	1,349,783	792,087	386,544	152,173	36.8	8,566	88,388	1,273
Denton ISD	TX	270,498	21,275	89,288	159,935	100.0	7.9	33.0	59.1	247,317	206,226	131,093	13,734	26,003	12.0	8,301	2,746	825
Donna ISD	TX	164,347	33,727	116,424	14,196	100.0	20.5	70.8	8.6	178,005	129,104	77,778	42,671	4,391	52.1	8,641	10,018	1,190
Eagle Mt.-Saginaw ISD	TX	169,326	9,804	60,879	98,643	100.0	5.8	36.0	58.3	203,193	132,991	80,010	44,869	25,168	12.0	7,752	1,621	757
Eagle Pass ISD	TX	133,903	21,256	90,450	22,197	100.0	15.9	67.5	16.6	131,575	120,444	71,627	5,841	3,111	39.3	8,023	7,320	1,402
Ector County ISD	TX	233,319	26,807	82,367	124,145	100.0	11.5	35.3	53.2	218,999	203,389	121,643	7,953	5,874	18.9	7,128	6,033	1,097
Edinburg CISD	TX	329,234	54,379	204,422	70,433	100.0	16.5	62.1	21.4	310,009	273,211	170,471	23,896	9,858	41.1	8,177	15,424	1,083
El Paso ISD	TX	618,764	108,474	312,306	197,984	100.0	17.5	50.5	32.0	581,392	527,127	325,863	28,872	22,486	31.1	8,209	28,008	1,384
Fort Bend ISD	TX	619,643	54,351	219,685	345,607	100.0	8.8	35.5	55.8	597,592	512,646	320,568	32,031	45,082	11.5	7,382	9,573	1,051
Fort Worth ISD	TX	826,247	145,549	318,191	362,507	100.0	17.6	38.5	43.9	864,878	734,644	430,484	82,987	34,429	34.2	8,840	36,104	1,173
Frisco ISD	TX	394,088	13,564	118,441	262,083	100.0	3.4	30.1	66.5	454,621	292,080	187,518	98,190	60,862	5.8	7,280	1,768	766
Galena Park ISD	TX	217,110	27,835	102,211	87,064	100.0	12.8	47.1	40.1	205,165	181,606	106,550	7,853	13,149	27.2	8,307	5,256	969
Garland ISD	TX	515,646	59,297	273,440	182,909	100.0	11.5	53.0	35.5	481,473	431,666	267,515	31,860	15,009	21.7	7,423	14,198	1,080
Goose Creek CISD	TX	235,372	26,023	87,169	122,180	100.0	11.1	37.0	51.9	213,069	186,874	109,324	9,366	14,639	23.6	8,622	4,829	964
Grand Prairie ISD	TX	260,610	31,855	153,797	74,958	100.0	12.2	59.0	28.8	265,227	200,417	118,393	40,306	22,169	22.9	7,532	6,475	980
Harlandale ISD	TX	161,611	23,323	116,971	21,317	100.0	14.4	72.4	13.2	148,913	125,356	73,959	13,103	9,547	38.0	8,385	5,545	1,135
Harlingen CISD	TX	176,295	31,199	103,117	41,979	100.0	17.7	58.5	23.8	202,529	150,704	91,113	41,631	6,208	42.5	8,100	8,450	1,092
Hays CISD	TX	155,832	14,001	81,585	60,246	100.0	9.0	52.4	38.7	148,328	123,844	72,905	10,095	13,900	14.2	7,773	1,814	778
Houston ISD	TX	2,046,214	248,401	509,806	1,288,007	100.0	12.1	24.9	62.9	2,355,857	1,874,685	1,000,287	322,985	140,778	33.9	9,232	99,095	1,311
Humble ISD	TX	348,681	23,302	148,673	176,706	100.0	6.7	42.6	50.7	324,553	269,589	171,791	22,799	31,186	11.1	7,473	3,382	837
Hurst-Euless-Bedford ISD	TX	215,181	20,021	68,918	126,242	100.0	9.3	32.0	58.7	221,160	162,246	103,184	39,204	19,177	18.1	7,522	3,921	945
Irving ISD	TX	352,084	47,201	168,787	136,096	100.0	13.4	47.9	38.7	351,142	277,684	176,986	41,196	29,034	28.9	7,986	10,176	1,036
Judson ISD	TX	208,689	22,499	95,920	90,270	100.0	10.8	46.0	43.3	193,218	164,937	103,030	8,241	18,561	21.0	7,330	5,189	987
Katy ISD	TX	590,635	41,823	205,720	343,092	100.0	7.1	34.8	58.1	717,715	463,897	293,139	202,321	50,163	10.6	7,433	6,484	985
Keller ISD	TX	306,279	15,726	101,614	188,939	100.0	5.1	33.2	61.7	275,498	219,999	143,760	10,236	44,193	7.0	6,640	2,066	793
Killeen ISD	TX	372,275	86,995	206,019	79,261	100.0	23.4	55.3	21.3	351,024	320,142	200,339	22,150	4,570	19.9	7,809	8,341	1,023
Klein ISD	TX	418,202	35,099	183,388	199,715	100.0	8.4	43.9	47.8	513,141	343,415	213,613	136,474	31,695	15.2	7,465	7,247	988

See notes at end of table.

Table 215.20. Revenues, expenditures, poverty rate, and Title I allocations of public school districts enrolling more than 15,000 students: 2011–12 and fiscal year 2014—Continued

Name of district	State	Revenues by source of funds, 2011–12 (in thousands of current dollars)				Percentage distribution of revenues, 2011–12				Expenditures, 2011–12 (in thousands of current dollars)					Poverty rate of 5- to 17-year-olds, 2013[1]	Current expenditure per pupil,[2] 2011–12 (in current dollars)	Title I allocations, federal fiscal year 2014	
										Total[3]	Current expenditure						Total[4] (in thousands of current dollars)	Per poverty child[5] (in current dollars)
		Total	Federal	State	Local	Total	Federal	State	Local		Total	Instruction	Capital outlay	Interest on school debt				
1	2	3	4	5	6	7	8	9	10	11	12	13	14	15	16	17	18	19
La Joya ISD	TX	309,488	62,888	214,578	32,022	100.0	20.3	69.3	10.3	298,878	265,065	155,159	15,992	15,020	54.1	9,151	17,476	1,208
Lamar CISD	TX	247,839	23,943	78,060	145,836	100.0	9.7	31.5	58.8	243,351	199,187	127,469	20,650	22,562	15.0	7,880	3,886	968
Laredo ISD	TX	265,786	56,692	177,034	32,060	100.0	21.3	66.6	12.1	253,851	215,726	129,600	22,318	12,176	57.4	8,703	16,164	1,297
Leander ISD	TX	333,093	16,082	103,972	213,039	100.0	4.8	31.2	64.0	319,819	250,615	154,180	30,750	34,857	6.8	7,524	1,878	779
Lewisville ISD	TX	532,667	33,972	139,514	359,181	100.0	6.4	26.2	67.4	517,474	416,307	269,805	48,832	47,479	8.3	8,018	4,247	857
Lubbock ISD	TX	262,242	37,513	100,036	124,693	100.0	14.3	38.1	47.5	286,816	227,827	139,405	46,810	6,359	30.3	7,913	9,577	1,053
Mansfield ISD	TX	303,754	20,886	126,928	155,940	100.0	6.9	41.8	51.3	334,594	238,909	151,758	61,275	33,723	12.4	7,337	3,593	840
McAllen ISD	TX	237,645	41,308	120,493	75,844	100.0	17.4	50.7	31.9	227,478	200,798	123,479	17,521	5,269	37.4	7,952	10,359	1,037
McKinney ISD	TX	250,586	15,282	81,772	153,532	100.0	6.1	32.6	61.3	243,583	190,822	121,798	30,068	19,738	10.2	7,715	2,186	792
Mesquite ISD	TX	369,526	39,255	229,553	100,718	100.0	10.6	62.1	27.3	340,095	287,679	182,426	33,992	16,988	23.5	7,514	9,285	1,021
Midland ISD	TX	192,152	23,129	31,464	137,559	100.0	12.0	16.4	71.6	175,978	165,186	99,120	4,058	4,584	16.3	7,300	4,569	1,063
Mission CISD	TX	165,027	33,151	106,907	24,969	100.0	20.1	64.8	15.1	147,206	131,914	77,399	5,923	7,252	48.5	8,413	8,463	1,156
North East ISD	TX	682,125	62,851	212,338	406,936	100.0	9.2	31.1	59.7	667,846	540,210	337,383	66,352	60,030	17.6	8,010	14,552	1,096
Northside ISD	TX	931,113	95,055	349,773	486,285	100.0	10.2	37.6	52.2	955,210	730,208	463,442	147,226	68,441	18.6	7,443	21,662	1,136
Northwest ISD	TX	205,412	8,325	38,527	158,560	100.0	4.1	18.8	77.2	233,842	136,326	80,571	43,543	32,088	6.3	8,200	798	726
Pasadena ISD	TX	499,925	74,268	282,576	143,081	100.0	14.9	56.5	28.6	495,172	446,262	273,099	28,794	17,110	27.8	8,429	16,722	1,100
Pearland ISD	TX	164,356	8,982	69,966	85,408	100.0	5.5	42.6	52.0	147,196	127,319	73,320	5,066	13,780	8.3	6,629	1,285	755
Pflugerville ISD	TX	222,471	21,252	88,477	112,742	100.0	9.6	39.8	50.7	227,678	174,357	107,971	35,398	15,572	18.3	7,558	4,504	957
Pharr-San Juan-Alamo ISD	TX	339,751	64,318	224,929	50,504	100.0	18.9	66.2	14.9	401,417	269,544	162,611	108,414	18,509	42.7	8,521	14,564	1,115
Plano ISD	TX	630,492	27,978	102,983	499,531	100.0	4.4	16.3	79.2	595,680	446,069	290,380	59,836	47,692	9.5	8,014	5,242	869
Richardson ISD	TX	366,469	36,867	109,340	220,262	100.0	10.1	29.8	60.1	359,424	287,029	186,625	52,770	16,838	24.9	7,748	9,828	1,030
Round Rock ISD	TX	449,842	36,216	123,411	290,215	100.0	8.1	27.4	64.5	480,444	349,782	213,962	77,443	49,262	8.7	7,767	3,719	856
San Antonio ISD	TX	561,919	131,088	268,440	162,391	100.0	23.3	47.8	28.9	574,466	490,556	296,038	43,252	31,925	41.7	9,019	29,156	1,205
Socorro ISD	TX	385,448	51,798	238,934	94,716	100.0	13.4	62.0	24.6	376,607	324,028	195,514	28,790	20,830	23.9	7,420	11,220	1,044
Spring Branch ISD	TX	359,810	43,173	59,669	256,968	100.0	12.0	16.6	71.4	427,588	282,102	166,156	94,833	39,402	27.8	8,374	10,014	1,035
Spring ISD	TX	354,704	39,991	191,976	122,737	100.0	11.3	54.1	34.6	314,025	271,681	163,820	7,159	33,057	25.4	7,441	9,700	1,031
Tyler ISD	TX	187,052	25,960	57,807	103,285	100.0	13.9	30.9	55.2	164,898	149,734	92,787	5,444	8,467	25.4	8,141	5,516	1,006
United ISD	TX	395,797	47,684	213,976	134,137	100.0	12.0	54.1	33.9	384,076	349,030	203,760	23,274	10,057	31.8	8,275	14,424	1,079
Waco ISD	TX	156,523	28,406	73,851	54,266	100.0	18.1	47.2	34.7	162,631	125,975	68,946	22,694	10,631	34.7	8,218	7,556	1,301
Weslaco ISD	TX	170,226	32,957	113,570	23,699	100.0	19.4	66.7	13.9	169,435	153,388	88,789	9,466	4,209	48.8	8,623	9,952	1,220
Ysleta ISD	TX	438,835	71,049	278,556	89,230	100.0	16.2	63.5	20.3	440,107	398,150	245,662	16,095	21,020	34.6	8,972	16,624	1,220
Alpine	UT	473,421	46,224	273,197	154,000	100.0	9.8	57.7	32.5	436,267	376,888	252,901	37,649	15,283	11.1	5,412	9,642	1,099
Cache	UT	110,568	10,343	68,590	31,635	100.0	9.4	62.0	28.6	103,343	93,563	60,834	4,714	3,450	10.1	5,897	1,421	797
Canyons	UT	274,481	20,111	116,438	137,932	100.0	7.3	42.4	50.3	333,699	217,424	128,824	99,023	9,788	10.8	6,405	4,160	899
Davis	UT	488,488	42,301	278,010	168,177	100.0	8.7	56.9	34.4	499,424	403,749	256,380	64,456	18,397	9.4	5,827	7,561	1,047
Granite	UT	487,404	64,405	258,193	164,806	100.0	13.2	53.0	33.8	588,361	425,085	272,950	141,743	6,967	19.3	6,138	18,297	1,178
Jordan	UT	350,709	20,903	191,136	138,670	100.0	6.0	54.5	39.5	348,394	283,231	177,631	54,975	4,113	9.0	5,558	4,963	924
Nebo	UT	217,551	16,579	135,370	65,602	100.0	7.6	62.2	30.2	226,388	174,493	101,987	38,656	8,462	10.3	5,724	3,243	901
Salt Lake	UT	226,228	30,168	76,551	119,509	100.0	13.3	33.8	52.8	233,711	182,536	115,909	28,944	4,085	24.2	7,297	7,145	1,035
Washington	UT	215,472	22,402	100,683	92,387	100.0	10.4	46.7	42.9	210,345	166,842	104,427	30,916	9,320	20.7	6,206	6,632	1,032
Weber	UT	200,004	18,062	118,100	63,842	100.0	9.0	59.0	31.9	203,882	185,747	124,151	12,964	3,852	9.7	6,077	2,917	878
Arlington County	VA	445,338	14,688	51,261	379,389	100.0	3.3	11.5	85.2	493,756	379,591	231,539	81,258	10,898	9.5	17,339	2,190	1,008
Chesapeake City	VA	464,144	51,462	198,985	213,697	100.0	11.1	42.9	46.0	477,645	418,338	264,559	37,640	11,454	12.8	10,599	6,227	1,144
Chesterfield County	VA	626,131	42,011	267,399	316,721	100.0	6.7	42.7	50.6	555,196	503,052	308,423	31,518	15,786	8.7	8,498	6,121	1,141
Fairfax County	VA	2,398,065	128,140	488,170	1,781,755	100.0	5.3	20.4	74.3	2,574,460	2,295,411	1,418,386	192,120	67,839	7.6	12,924	21,311	1,460
Hampton City	VA	227,183	31,233	117,795	78,155	100.0	13.7	51.9	34.4	234,018	214,331	125,229	11,010	6,571	23.0	9,928	6,344	1,266
Hanover County	VA	187,698	12,595	77,821	97,282	100.0	6.7	41.5	51.8	183,442	167,446	113,281	9,796	5,093	6.2	9,036	1,114	952
Henrico County	VA	519,170	44,871	214,524	259,775	100.0	8.6	41.3	50.0	523,534	441,519	288,856	62,430	15,056	11.8	8,892	8,120	1,265

See notes at end of table.

Table 215.20. Revenues, expenditures, poverty rate, and Title I allocations of public school districts enrolling more than 15,000 students: 2011–12 and fiscal year 2014—Continued

Name of district	State	Revenues by source of funds, 2011–12 (in thousands of current dollars)				Percentage distribution of revenues, 2011–12				Expenditures, 2011–12 (in thousands of current dollars)					Poverty rate of 5- to 17-year-olds, 2013[1]	Current expenditure per pupil,[2] 2011–12 (in current dollars)	Title I allocations, federal fiscal year 2014	
		Total	Federal	State	Local	Total	Federal	State	Local	Total[3]	Current expenditures Total	Current expenditures Instruction	Capital outlay	Interest on school debt			Total[4] (in thousands of current dollars)	Per poverty child[5] (in current dollars)
1	2	3	4	5	6	7	8	9	10	11	12	13	14	15	16	17	18	19
Loudoun County	VA	969,001	37,030	222,755	709,216	100.0	3.8	23.0	73.2	919,047	790,985	504,858	86,689	38,525	3.7	12,060	1,584	580
Newport News City	VA	343,415	52,195	161,547	129,673	100.0	15.2	47.0	37.8	340,390	308,469	176,096	22,258	0	24.0	10,300	9,273	1,304
Norfolk City	VA	387,018	67,605	179,133	140,280	100.0	17.5	46.3	36.2	378,632	331,854	203,265	36,251	32	26.8	9,918	12,924	1,431
Portsmouth City	VA	177,469	28,402	86,914	62,153	100.0	16.0	49.0	35.0	190,603	158,015	91,085	26,239	437	29.0	10,354	5,779	1,268
Prince William County	VA	960,967	64,039	394,638	502,290	100.0	6.7	41.1	52.3	975,843	826,992	469,058	87,254	27,639	8.9	10,093	10,101	1,308
Richmond City	VA	320,820	66,205	119,317	135,298	100.0	20.6	37.2	42.2	335,268	317,495	183,667	8,479	4,826	35.9	13,605	16,874	1,760
Spotsylvania County	VA	254,805	16,579	111,948	126,278	100.0	6.5	43.9	49.6	235,527	221,039	128,594	4,338	9,450	10.3	9,281	2,682	1,036
Stafford County	VA	285,996	21,885	126,556	137,555	100.0	7.7	44.3	48.1	282,533	261,426	165,209	20,230	82	5.9	9,564	1,656	993
Virginia Beach City	VA	754,661	83,828	316,409	354,424	100.0	11.1	41.9	47.0	854,836	747,056	434,432	71,513	16,104	12.5	10,525	12,643	1,367
Bellevue	WA	246,457	10,989	106,410	129,058	100.0	4.5	43.2	52.4	286,083	177,424	108,536	75,899	25,568	9.5	9,603	1,774	941
Bethel	WA	194,933	12,970	126,584	55,379	100.0	6.7	64.9	28.4	210,227	161,231	89,005	37,421	10,111	13.1	8,976	2,666	1,023
Edmonds	WA	234,032	12,514	128,847	92,671	100.0	5.3	55.1	39.6	216,679	185,687	112,006	15,765	14,092	13.0	8,990	3,142	1,014
Everett	WA	232,480	13,667	130,969	87,844	100.0	5.9	56.3	37.8	247,210	183,682	109,344	43,560	19,166	13.4	9,783	3,222	1,119
Evergreen (Clark)	WA	265,719	19,361	176,110	70,248	100.0	7.3	66.3	26.4	273,641	234,378	142,157	28,202	9,890	15.3	8,901	5,134	1,196
Federal Way	WA	230,397	18,154	140,327	71,916	100.0	7.9	60.9	31.2	253,483	204,234	120,204	38,473	10,221	18.6	9,167	5,419	1,185
Highline	WA	216,712	22,385	118,516	75,811	100.0	10.3	54.7	35.0	225,067	185,068	106,361	24,146	14,850	26.4	10,195	6,468	1,204
Issaquah	WA	216,628	5,781	100,571	110,276	100.0	2.7	46.4	50.9	239,261	151,354	93,799	66,966	16,023	4.8	8,491	525	534
Kennewick	WA	168,400	13,004	119,945	35,451	100.0	7.7	71.2	21.1	168,284	144,540	88,951	16,950	6,542	22.8	8,708	4,636	1,172
Kent	WA	290,469	20,968	165,888	103,613	100.0	7.2	57.1	35.7	266,077	242,419	147,334	12,607	10,362	16.7	8,926	6,075	1,198
Lake Washington	WA	297,692	13,433	152,102	132,157	100.0	4.5	51.1	44.4	409,300	223,829	137,414	161,027	22,336	6.2	8,980	1,749	951
Northshore	WA	252,515	10,989	118,497	123,029	100.0	4.4	46.9	48.7	254,890	187,480	116,293	49,700	16,851	7.6	9,463	1,580	946
Pasco	WA	159,269	17,129	109,140	33,000	100.0	10.8	68.5	20.7	151,962	141,354	81,340	4,570	5,865	22.9	8,999	5,297	1,296
Puyallup	WA	218,783	13,017	133,874	71,892	100.0	5.9	61.2	32.9	213,540	194,961	113,879	7,634	10,126	9.6	9,369	2,180	990
Seattle	WA	684,501	56,340	307,249	320,912	100.0	8.2	44.9	46.9	624,241	548,092	325,689	65,040	9,956	14.0	11,124	11,225	1,274
Spokane	WA	343,546	35,944	202,922	104,680	100.0	10.5	59.1	30.5	380,431	293,929	168,496	64,658	14,659	22.4	10,122	9,474	1,256
Tacoma	WA	382,734	45,143	197,416	140,175	100.0	11.8	51.6	36.6	378,484	321,903	178,886	43,340	12,812	22.8	11,279	9,391	1,241
Vancouver	WA	232,007	19,721	143,450	68,836	100.0	8.5	61.8	29.7	223,172	207,259	115,769	7,974	7,059	19.7	9,125	5,787	1,205
Yakima	WA	187,806	31,896	132,532	23,378	100.0	17.0	70.6	12.4	228,103	158,854	96,215	64,827	4,315	34.2	10,506	6,488	1,215
Berkeley County	WV	238,620	17,666	121,783	99,171	100.0	7.4	51.0	41.6	217,152	189,728	112,144	23,989	1,703	16.6	10,539	4,443	1,381
Kanawha County	WV	384,864	44,638	183,766	156,460	100.0	11.6	47.7	40.7	335,378	315,364	194,593	10,205	0	20.7	11,093	8,983	1,527
Appleton Area	WI	176,154	15,145	82,830	78,179	100.0	8.6	47.0	44.4	170,114	160,828	100,024	3,191	1,716	11.4	10,637	1,999	1,081
Green Bay Area	WI	256,609	29,080	140,523	87,006	100.0	11.3	54.8	33.9	252,490	223,298	134,751	15,913	1,831	18.3	10,821	5,744	1,356
Kenosha	WI	290,492	26,543	155,206	108,743	100.0	9.1	53.4	37.4	281,460	264,430	165,458	6,145	6,609	18.6	11,545	6,087	1,362
Madison Metropolitan	WI	377,899	38,826	74,352	264,721	100.0	10.3	19.7	70.1	367,320	333,726	198,981	9,794	1,517	19.1	12,445	6,941	1,371
Milwaukee	WI	1,189,747	221,083	633,933	334,731	100.0	18.6	53.3	28.1	1,187,745	1,028,504	584,266	31,836	17,165	39.0	12,998	75,042	1,707
Racine Unified	WI	256,639	25,094	144,484	87,061	100.0	9.8	56.3	33.9	235,026	217,984	133,851	8,342	1,231	23.0	10,475	7,666	1,375

†Not applicable.
[1]Poverty is defined based on the number of persons and related children in the family and their income. For information on poverty thresholds, see http://www.census.gov/hhes/www/poverty/data/threshld/
[2]Current expenditure per pupil based on fall enrollment collected through the "Local Education Agency (School District) Finance Survey (F33)."
[3]Includes other expenditures not shown separately.
[4]Fiscal year 2014 Department of Education funds available for spending by school districts beginning with the 2014–15 school year.

[5]Fiscal year 2014 Department of Education funds available for spending by school districts beginning with the 2014–15 school year divided by number of poverty children in 2013.
[6]Includes data for both Modesto City Elementary and Modesto City High.
NOTE: Detail may not sum to totals because of rounding. ISD = independent school district. CISD = consolidated independent school district.
SOURCE: U.S. Department of Education, National Center for Education Statistics, Common Core of Data (CCD), "Local Education Agency Universe Survey," 2012–13; "Local Education Agency (School District) Finance Survey (F33)," 2011–12; and unpublished Department of Education budget data. (This table was prepared May 2015.)

Table 215.30. Enrollment, poverty, and federal funds for the 100 largest school districts, by enrollment size in 2012: Selected years, 2011–12 through 2014

Name of district	State	Rank order	Enrollment, fall 2012	5- to 17-year-old population, 2013	5- to 17-year-olds in poverty, 2013[1]	Poverty rate of 5- to 17-year-olds, 2013[1]	Revenues by source of funds, 2011–12				Revenue from selected federal programs (in thousands), 2011–12						Federal Title I allocations (in thousands), federal fiscal year 2014[2]				
							Total (in thousands)	Federal (in thousands)	Federal as a percent of total	Federal revenue per student[3]	Title I basic and concentration grants	School lunch	Individuals with Disabilities Education Act (IDEA)	Eisenhower math and science	Vocational education	Drug-free schools	Total	Basic grants	Concentration grants	Targeted grants	Education finance incentive grants
1	2	3	4	5	6	7	8	9	10	11	12	13	14	15	16	17	18	19	20	21	22
New York City	NY	1	989,391	1,240,307	380,296	30.7	$23,517,452	$2,237,047	9.5	$2,259	$858,833	$361,201	$322,786	$49,926	$16,145	$2,657	$716,620	$267,134	$66,534	$205,085	$177,867
Los Angeles Unified	CA	2	655,455	752,855	232,786	30.9	8,314,608	1,251,529	15.1	1,897	443,698	240,598	157,315	—	8,073	96	338,423	117,099	27,715	93,071	100,538
City of Chicago (SD 299)	IL	3	395,948	426,511	137,986	32.4	5,760,419	892,899	15.5	2,216	325,057	182,835	93,229	31,703	5,501	92	273,393	94,749	22,425	73,494	82,725
Dade	FL	4	354,262	392,194	112,616	28.7	3,188,967	457,537	14.3	1,306	144,610	112,963	78,012	—	5,275	4	137,361	51,435	12,174	39,352	34,400
Clark County	NV	5	316,778	354,042	76,039	21.5	2,863,675	282,471	9.9	901	82,280	80,232	50,748	8,811	3,821	84	90,187	35,126	8,314	25,963	20,784
Broward	FL	6	260,226	287,643	56,476	19.6	2,221,054	269,571	12.1	1,043	79,066	67,987	52,895	7,568	2,870	—	66,711	25,979	6,149	18,453	16,131
Houston ISD	TX	7	203,354	223,209	75,570	33.9	2,046,214	248,401	12.1	1,223	111,886	1,975	40,373	4,960	3,214	238	99,095	35,609	8,685	26,340	28,462
Hillsborough	FL	8	200,466	215,831	52,911	24.5	1,803,776	291,908	16.2	1,481	66,290	64,738	48,526	7,833	3,758	—	62,216	24,359	5,765	17,123	14,969
Hawaii Department of Education	HI	9	184,760	213,862	33,910	15.9	2,535,038	318,728	12.6	1,744	59,405	51,160	41,724	872	2,779	800	53,163	22,194	5,253	12,318	13,398
Orange	FL	10	183,066	202,058	52,198	25.8	1,827,011	202,082	11.1	1,123	60,532	58,569	38,815	6,174	1,704	5	60,584	23,771	5,626	16,641	14,547
Fairfax County	VA	11	180,616	192,302	14,596	7.6	2,398,065	128,140	5.3	721	22,202	28,828	34,627	3,830	1,530	—	21,311	8,431	1,996	4,920	5,964
Palm Beach	FL	12	179,514	202,243	41,374	20.5	1,710,762	180,910	10.6	1,023	61,111	47,956	38,208	1,667	1,045	—	47,155	18,932	4,481	12,668	11,074
Gwinnett County	GA	13	164,976	174,192	32,286	18.5	1,574,463	138,288	8.8	852	30,741	54,861	26,735	2,633	1,045	240	38,605	15,213	3,601	9,716	10,075
Dallas ISD	TX	14	158,932	188,720	69,449	36.8	1,677,871	251,377	15.0	1,595	88,086	72,697	27,235	9,348	2,732	—	88,388	31,848	7,538	23,272	25,729
Wake County	NC	15	150,956	177,724	24,344	13.7	1,202,796	135,729	11.3	916	2,203	29,599	1,112	2,887	—	—	28,029	11,148	2,639	6,957	7,286
Montgomery County	MD	16	148,780	171,187	12,960	7.6	2,854,888	109,485	3.8	748	20,301	27,269	31,700	3,666	1,199	—	21,478	8,994	2,129	5,147	5,208
Charlotte-Mecklenburg	NC	17	144,478	172,047	35,754	20.8	1,209,892	156,055	12.9	1,101	3,797	42,805	576	3,907	—	—	41,820	16,351	3,870	10,550	11,049
Philadelphia City	PA	18	143,898	241,283	87,824	36.4	2,681,763	462,562	16.9	2,994	264,375	71,760	—	21,275	5,414	141	178,387	61,155	14,474	45,895	56,862
San Diego Unified	CA	19	130,271	139,538	32,965	23.6	1,408,787	162,054	11.5	1,237	46,663	44,182	27,442	7,077	1,229	16	40,642	16,335	3,866	10,461	9,981
Duval	FL	20	125,686	143,363	35,645	24.9	1,084,243	156,609	14.4	1,249	45,153	36,093	39,764	5,498	1,149	—	39,875	16,309	3,860	10,515	9,191
Prince George's County	MD	21	123,737	144,245	19,505	13.5	2,065,364	145,794	7.1	1,177	37,217	41,036	29,999	4,345	990	—	33,155	13,463	3,186	8,205	8,301
Cypress-Fairbanks ISD	TX	22	110,013	111,340	17,572	15.8	930,535	72,251	7.8	669	10,660	28,663	12,449	1,243	718	8	19,589	8,065	1,909	4,847	4,768
Cobb County	GA	23	108,452	120,565	20,976	17.4	1,102,087	83,131	7.5	775	17,176	26,053	22,663	2,227	645	1,553	24,611	9,947	2,354	6,113	6,197
Memphis	TN	24	107,594	116,157	43,707	37.6	1,194,046	247,241	20.7	2,228	82,926	49,512	27,715	—	2,783	877	55,123	20,135	4,766	13,656	16,565
Baltimore County	MD	25	106,927	128,270	15,590	12.2	1,589,273	90,954	5.7	865	17,502	23,587	25,855	3,815	918	—	26,974	11,098	2,627	6,587	6,664
Pinellas	FL	26	103,590	117,817	22,567	19.2	922,370	117,146	12.7	1,129	35,943	25,867	32,071	4,637	2,462	7	24,958	10,407	2,463	6,450	5,638
Jefferson County	KY	27	100,316	122,213	28,610	23.4	1,218,406	188,192	15.4	1,897	49,423	34,716	24,116	—	—	—	41,823	15,590	3,690	9,881	12,663
Northside ISD	TX	28	100,159	102,392	19,069	18.6	931,113	95,055	10.2	969	17,302	27,723	11,772	2,065	795	8	21,662	8,849	2,094	5,384	5,334
DeKalb County	GA	29	98,910	110,367	35,214	31.9	1,041,282	113,519	10.9	1,157	35,292	38,534	12,737	3,410	1,011	255	42,439	16,656	3,942	10,707	11,133
Polk	FL	30	96,937	103,892	26,816	25.8	891,269	116,482	13.1	1,212	33,903	31,469	19,990	4,724	1,167	15	29,861	12,354	2,924	7,781	6,802
Albuquerque	NM	31	94,083	114,582	25,723	22.4	963,715	97,699	10.1	1,036	30,623	4	18,564	3,337	932	237	30,674	12,018	2,844	7,551	8,261
Fulton County	GA	32	93,907	110,033	18,811	17.1	1,134,739	73,056	6.4	789	21,441	21,644	16,592	2,748	573	24	21,788	8,881	2,102	5,384	5,420
Austin ISD	TX	33	86,516	97,332	28,829	29.6	1,070,061	130,188	12.2	1,505	34,178	27,785	11,699	3,313	1,296	—	33,205	13,217	3,128	8,372	8,488
Lee	FL	34	85,765	90,999	22,307	24.5	765,065	91,712	12.0	1,093	22,710	27,616	18,737	—	1,021	—	24,467	10,212	2,417	6,316	5,521
Jefferson County, No. R1	CO	35	85,542	87,870	9,969	11.3	823,580	55,926	6.8	652	11,541	12,485	15,653	2,510	402	—	11,261	4,697	1,112	2,537	2,915
Baltimore City	MD	36	84,747	91,479	29,103	31.8	1,459,517	203,999	14.0	2,422	74,748	34,816	30,089	8,011	2,149	0	52,034	20,688	4,896	13,148	13,302
Prince William County	VA	37	83,865	86,363	7,721	8.9	960,967	64,039	6.7	782	9,467	18,676	24,113	1,591	725	75	10,101	4,459	1,055	2,208	2,378
Fort Worth ISD	TX	38	83,503	90,073	30,781	34.2	826,247	145,549	17.6	1,751	46,234	33,348	14,993	5,002	1,439	0	36,104	14,332	3,495	9,135	9,142
Denver	CO	39	83,377	90,920	26,358	29.0	967,307	140,975	14.6	1,743	54,942	26,459	17,656	5,339	1,283	19	32,758	12,306	2,913	7,743	9,796
Long Beach Unified	CA	40	82,256	88,452	23,468	26.5	837,323	144,082	17.2	1,722	40,111	27,661	15,721	4,559	769	72	28,366	11,606	2,747	7,226	6,787
Davidson County	TN	41	81,134	95,913	26,385	27.5	852,377	124,758	14.6	1,552	39,012	29,942	25,791	—	1,761	61	31,378	12,101	2,864	7,608	8,805
Milwaukee	WI	42	78,363	112,571	43,952	39.0	1,189,747	221,083	18.6	2,794	106,849	35,133	26,957	—	1,996	—	75,042	26,689	6,600	18,265	23,488
Anne Arundel County	MD	43	77,770	90,637	7,363	8.1	1,088,736	55,614	5.1	715	10,544	11,165	20,385	2,368	640	—	11,289	5,066	1,199	2,498	2,527
Guilford County	NC	44	74,161	84,691	19,843	23.4	769,588	90,219	11.7	1,218	5,346	23,368	338	2,897	—	—	22,537	9,066	2,146	5,532	5,794
Fresno Unified	CA	45	73,689	79,344	37,152	46.8	759,074	139,111	18.3	1,874	66,664	33,321	15,516	6,692	997	—	46,058	18,267	4,323	11,934	11,535

See notes at end of table.

Table 215.30. Enrollment, poverty, and federal funds for the 100 largest school districts, by enrollment size in 2012: Selected years, 2011–12 through 2014—Continued

Name of district	State	Rank order	Enroll- ment, fall 2012	5- to 17- year-old population, 2013	5- to 17- year-olds in poverty, 2013[1]	Poverty rate of 5- to 17- year-olds, 2013[1]	Revenues by source of funds, 2011–12				Revenue from selected federal programs (in thousands), 2011–12						Federal Title I allocations (in thousands), federal fiscal year 2014[2]				
							Total (in thousands)	Federal (in thousands)	Federal as a percent of total	Federal revenue per student[3]	Title I basic and concen- tration grants	School lunch	Individuals with Disabilities Education Act (IDEA)	Eisen- hower math and science	Vocational education	Drug-free schools	Total	Basic grants	Concen- tration grants	Targeted grants	Education finance incentive grants
1	2	3	4	5	6	7	8	9	10	11	12	13	14	15	16	17	18	19	20	21	22
Greenville, 01	SC	46	73,649	82,644	17,591	21.3	685,904	67,024	9.8	929	23,288	18,819	15,705	2,559	962	13	22,134	8,636	2,044	5,197	6,256
Alpine	UT	47	72,452	79,291	8,770	11.1	473,421	46,224	9.8	664	6,758	11,455	15,436	1,167	668	—	9,642	4,101	971	2,135	2,434
Brevard	FL	48	71,228	78,356	16,380	20.9	587,566	61,891	10.5	862	15,743	16,712	16,279	2,761	607	—	17,666	7,512	1,778	4,469	3,907
Virginia Beach City	VA	49	70,259	74,032	9,249	12.5	754,661	83,828	11.1	1,181	13,960	12,465	22,094	2,641	892	—	12,643	5,365	1,270	2,822	3,186
Davis	UT	50	70,192	76,728	7,219	9.4	488,488	42,301	8.7	611	3,126	11,474	10,465	1,395	681	—	7,561	3,334	789	1,642	1,796
Fort Bend ISD	TX	51	69,591	79,132	9,105	11.5	619,643	54,351	8.8	783	7,871	11,513	9,233	1,043	577	—	9,573	4,275	1,012	2,254	2,032
Granite	UT	52	69,312	80,301	15,529	19.3	487,404	64,405	13.2	930	13,275	17,886	18,167	2,325	1,532	13	18,297	7,146	1,691	4,218	5,241
Loudoun County	VA	53	68,205	72,923	2,729	3.7	989,001	37,030	3.8	565	1,184	5,832	13,469	705	161	—	1,584	1,584	0	0	0
North East ISD	TX	54	67,901	75,236	13,277	17.6	682,125	62,851	9.2	932	10,602	15,782	10,870	1,465	642	—	14,552	6,159	1,458	3,543	3,392
Pasco	FL	55	67,153	72,396	13,029	18.0	582,449	61,671	10.6	925	15,727	19,945	12,169	—	600	1,811	13,856	6,000	1,420	3,434	3,002
Aldine ISD	TX	56	65,684	62,208	23,713	38.1	610,147	97,303	15.9	1,513	22,805	34,869	9,454	2,190	907	3	27,038	10,883	2,576	6,775	6,803
Arlington ISD	TX	57	65,001	67,530	16,101	23.8	566,407	63,788	11.3	986	15,321	20,899	11,812	2,088	814	—	17,764	7,374	1,745	4,375	4,269
Washoe County	NV	58	64,995	71,448	15,726	22.0	606,096	66,385	11.0	1,025	17,510	14,445	11,530	2,320	813	112	16,437	7,321	1,733	4,338	3,044
Douglas County No. RE1	CO	59	64,657	67,455	2,564	3.8	584,330	13,899	2.4	220	1,058	2,713	6,446	592	174	—	1,193	1,193	0	0	0
Katy ISD	TX	60	64,562	62,239	6,582	10.6	590,635	41,823	7.1	670	4,348	9,939	6,000	834	338	—	6,484	3,031	717	1,475	1,261
Seminole	FL	61	64,463	72,084	11,057	15.3	513,064	52,192	10.2	811	11,653	14,794	16,035	2,082	511	161	11,503	5,066	1,199	2,795	2,443
Mesa Unified	AZ	62	64,161	81,109	20,727	25.6	565,143	67,494	11.9	1,043	20,745	21,468	10,365	2,523	1,299	—	24,355	9,800	2,319	6,034	6,201
El Paso ISD	TX	63	63,210	64,983	20,236	31.1	618,764	108,474	17.5	1,689	39,363	22,998	6,919	3,730	1,054	1	28,008	11,026	2,810	7,332	6,840
Elk Grove Unified	CA	64	62,137	69,018	14,299	20.7	541,376	63,320	11.7	1,019	15,072	14,861	11,706	2,373	368	—	16,608	7,077	1,675	4,127	3,728
Volusia	FL	65	61,064	67,519	19,435	28.8	547,213	63,123	11.5	1,026	19,446	17,299	14,008	2,490	643	9	21,283	8,948	2,118	5,451	4,765
Knox County	TN	66	58,929	68,899	13,766	20.0	517,620	66,212	12.8	1,129	14,046	15,771	15,183	—	1,307	335	15,791	6,430	1,522	3,728	4,112
Chesterfield County	VA	67	58,859	61,694	5,366	8.7	626,131	42,011	6.7	710	5,992	7,284	12,926	1,528	609	—	6,121	3,099	1,464	1,557	1,557
Mobile County	AL	68	58,625	71,282	20,155	28.3	585,069	83,326	14.2	1,356	31,104	22,773	21,981	4,294	1,320	400	23,719	9,263	2,192	5,667	6,596
Garland ISD	TX	69	58,059	60,711	13,147	21.7	515,646	59,297	11.5	1,020	13,903	16,613	10,612	1,428	674	1	14,198	6,025	1,426	3,451	3,295
Santa Ana Unified	CA	70	57,410	54,879	15,995	29.1	615,303	103,610	16.8	1,810	34,710	27,250	11,778	3,575	401	24	18,586	7,839	1,855	4,649	4,243
San Francisco Unified	CA	71	56,970	74,087	12,334	16.6	746,702	92,837	12.4	1,649	31,359	13,062	—	3,705	359	104	13,991	6,069	1,436	3,438	3,048
Osceola	FL	72	56,411	54,731	14,118	25.8	468,040	57,912	12.4	1,057	16,674	19,735	11,765	—	584	21	15,049	6,474	1,532	3,758	3,285
Plano ISD	TX	73	55,185	63,737	6,032	9.5	630,492	27,978	4.4	503	5,138	7,407	7,758	1,258	460	—	5,242	2,772	0	1,334	1,136
Boston	MA	74	55,114	73,240	19,920	27.2	1,262,395	131,642	10.4	2,392	45,498	17,515	23,358	—	1,393	—	37,617	13,867	3,282	8,481	11,986
San Antonio ISD	TX	75	54,268	58,017	24,186	41.7	561,919	131,088	23.3	2,410	34,760	31,753	13,802	4,368	992	—	29,156	11,769	2,931	7,378	7,077
San Bernardino City Unified	CA	76	54,102	56,603	23,270	41.1	614,746	101,866	16.6	1,873	46,520	23,318	12,828	3,608	575	43	28,309	11,584	2,742	7,211	6,772
Conroe ISD	TX	77	53,934	55,259	7,130	12.9	454,374	27,519	6.1	523	7,020	7,912	7,452	1,247	419	—	7,074	3,291	779	1,618	1,386
Forsyth County	NC	78	53,881	62,218	18,732	30.1	462,134	70,974	15.4	1,331	3,596	15,597	222	2,010	0	—	21,110	8,525	2,018	5,162	5,406
Capistrano Unified	CA	79	53,785	63,755	5,648	8.9	437,617	34,955	8.0	657	4,912	4,445	11,136	931	185	—	5,137	2,768	0	1,320	1,049
Pasadena ISD	TX	80	53,665	54,651	15,208	27.8	499,925	74,268	14.9	1,403	19,600	23,446	8,792	1,815	626	—	16,722	6,980	1,652	4,105	3,985
Corona-Norco Unified	CA	81	53,437	56,070	8,519	15.2	481,844	35,106	7.3	657	6,941	10,643	9,123	1,701	199	—	9,200	4,224	1,000	2,175	1,801
Cherry Creek, No. 5	CO	82	53,422	55,276	5,048	9.1	528,040	27,338	5.2	519	6,577	7,151	9,180	714	227	18	4,607	2,345	0	1,099	1,164
Cumberland County	NC	83	52,925	54,461	13,064	24.0	446,774	83,302	18.6	1,570	2,190	17,663	290	2,149	—	—	14,649	6,075	1,438	3,486	3,650
Lewisville ISD	TX	84	52,528	59,696	4,953	8.3	532,667	33,972	6.4	654	3,479	8,497	8,198	610	424	4	4,247	2,281	0	1,065	900
Jordan	UT	85	52,481	59,395	5,368	9.0	350,709	20,903	6.0	410	—	7,733	7,510	856	337	—	4,963	2,497	0	1,184	1,282
Howard County	MD	86	52,053	56,897	3,357	5.9	888,422	23,875	2.7	463	2,140	4,493	10,672	728	285	—	4,295	2,308	0	988	1,000
Clayton County	GA	87	51,757	54,215	20,926	38.6	487,526	70,677	14.5	1,385	20,610	24,559	10,674	1,340	365	—	24,405	9,867	2,335	6,059	6,144
Tucson Unified	AZ	88	50,771	73,691	22,053	29.9	501,632	77,010	15.4	1,489	28,287	16,392	10,044	2,792	1,358	1,766	26,534	10,618	2,513	6,593	6,810
Seattle	WA	89	50,655	62,845	8,810	14.0	684,501	56,340	8.2	1,144	14,675	9,462	11,825	21	384	—	11,225	4,694	1,111	2,446	2,973
Omaha	MO	90	50,559	63,020	15,398	24.4	611,657	102,834	16.8	2,043	23,718	20,460	4,244	1,977	770	133	26,252	9,873	2,337	5,872	8,171

See notes at end of table.

Table 215.30. Enrollment, poverty, and federal funds for the 100 largest school districts, by enrollment size in 2012: Selected years, 2011–12 through 2014—Continued

Name of district	State	Rank order	Enrollment, fall 2012	5- to 17-year-old population, 2013	5- to 17-year-olds in poverty, 2013[1]	Poverty rate of 5- to 17-year-olds, 2013[1]	Revenues by source of funds, 2011–12				Revenue from selected federal programs (in thousands), 2011–12						Federal Title I allocations (in thousands), federal fiscal year 2014[2]				
							Total (in thousands)	Federal (in thousands)	Federal as a percent of total	Federal revenue per student[3]	Title I basic and concentration grants	School lunch	Individuals with Disabilities Education Act (IDEA)	Eisenhower math and science	Vocational education	Drug-free schools	Total	Basic grants	Concentration grants	Targeted grants	Education finance incentive grants
1	2	3	4	5	6	7	8	9	10	11	12	13	14	15	16	17	18	19	20	21	22
Columbus City	OH	91	50,384	70,385	25,815	36.7	949,275	141,562	14.9	2,804	70,484	24,128	17,225	—	2,302	10	47,072	17,302	4,220	10,980	14,570
Wichita	KS	92	50,339	56,978	15,932	28.0	578,456	70,782	12.2	1,433	24,596	18,052		—	—	234	23,901	8,966	2,122	5,342	7,471
Henrico County	VA	93	50,083	54,194	6,417	11.8	519,170	44,871	8.6	904	9,261	9,725	8,609	797	1,001	1	8,120	3,714	676	1,801	1,929
Atlanta	GA	94	49,558	56,872	20,967	36.9	800,352	95,495	11.9	1,910	38,039	21,487	10,100	4,251	586	1,813	33,189	12,873	3,140	8,066	9,111
Detroit City	MI	95	49,239	132,044	70,613	53.5	1,035,068	271,358	26.2	4,046	157,079	37,238	—	37,406	3,849	790	147,012	48,300	12,311	38,287	48,115
Brownsville ISD	TX	96	49,190	47,720	22,683	47.5	501,603	112,894	22.5	2,274	27,591	33,098	8,993	4,067	883	74	26,207	10,349	2,529	6,693	6,637
Anchorage	AK	97	48,790	52,747	5,698	10.8	746,315	94,110	12.6	1,930	15,445	14,510	13,486	4,011	1,060	—	13,517	5,427	766	3,633	3,691
San Juan Unified	CA	98	47,752	49,862	11,327	22.7	446,540	56,544	12.7	1,197	15,064	9,559	11,050	1,895	405	34	13,034	5,701	1,349	3,186	2,799
Sacramento City Unified	CA	99	47,616	52,283	17,521	33.5	498,462	80,477	16.1	1,679	24,796	17,400	10,435	3,587	598	49	20,755	8,674	2,055	5,219	4,807
Garden Grove Unified	CA	100	47,599	50,907	12,580	24.7	433,419	53,814	12.4	1,121	16,043	17,346	9,150	3,577	315	21	14,241	6,165	1,459	3,504	3,113

—Not available.
[1]Poverty is defined based on the number of persons and related children in the family and their income. For information on poverty thresholds, see http://www.census.gov/hhes/www/poverty/data/threshld/.
[2]Fiscal year 2014 Department of Education funds available for spending by school districts in the 2014–15 school year.
[3]Federal revenue per student is based on fall enrollment collected through the "Local Education Agency (School District) Finance Survey (F33)."

NOTE: Detail may not sum to totals because of rounding. ISD = independent school district.
SOURCE: U.S. Department of Education, National Center for Education Statistics, Common Core of Data (CCD), "Local Education Agency Universe Survey," 2012–13; "Local Education Agency (School District) Finance Survey (F33)," 2011–12; and unpublished Department of Education budget data. U.S. Department of Commerce, Census Bureau, Small Area Income and Poverty Estimates (SAIPE) Program, 2013 Poverty Estimates for School Districts. (This table was prepared May 2015.)

Table 216.10. Public elementary and secondary schools, by level of school: Selected years, 1967–68 through 2012–13

		Schools with reported grade spans											
			Elementary schools				Secondary schools					Combined elementary/ secondary schools[2]	Other schools[1]
Year	Total, all public schools	Total	Total[3]	Middle schools[4]	One-teacher schools	Other elementary schools	Total[5]	Junior high[6]	3-year or 4-year high schools	5-year or 6-year high schools	Other secondary schools		
1	2	3	4	5	6	7	8	9	10	11	12	13	14
1967–68	—	94,197	67,186	—	4,146	63,040	23,318	7,437	10,751	4,650	480	3,693	—
1970–71	—	89,372	64,020	2,080	1,815	60,125	23,572	7,750	11,265	3,887	670	1,780	—
1972–73	—	88,864	62,942	2,308	1,475	59,159	23,919	7,878	11,550	3,962	529	2,003	—
1974–75	—	87,456	61,759	3,224	1,247	57,288	23,837	7,690	11,480	4,122	545	1,860	—
1975–76	88,597	87,034	61,704	3,916	1,166	56,622	23,792	7,521	11,572	4,113	586	1,538	1,563
1976–77	—	86,501	61,123	4,180	1,111	55,832	23,857	7,434	11,658	4,130	635	1,521	—
1978–79	—	84,816	60,312	5,879	1,056	53,377	22,834	6,282	11,410	4,429	713	1,670	—
1980–81	85,982	83,688	59,326	6,003	921	52,402	22,619	5,890	10,758	4,193	1,778	1,743	2,294
1982–83	84,740	82,039	58,051	6,875	798	50,378	22,383	5,948	11,678	4,067	690	1,605	2,701
1983–84	84,178	81,418	57,471	6,885	838	49,748	22,336	5,936	11,670	4,046	684	1,611	2,760
1984–85	84,007	81,147	57,231	6,893	825	49,513	22,320	5,916	11,671	4,021	712	1,596	2,860
1986–87	83,421	82,316	58,835	7,483	763	50,589	21,505	5,109	11,430	4,196	770	1,976	1,105[7]
1987–88	83,248	81,416	57,575	7,641	729	49,205	21,662	4,900	11,279	4,048	1,435	2,179	1,832[7]
1988–89	83,165	81,579	57,941	7,957	583	49,401	21,403	4,687	11,350	3,994	1,372	2,235	1,586[7]
1989–90	83,425	81,880	58,419	8,272	630	49,517	21,181	4,512	11,492	3,812	1,365	2,280	1,545[7]
1990–91	84,538	82,475	59,015	8,545	617	49,853	21,135	4,561	11,537	3,723	1,314	2,325	2,063
1991–92	84,578	82,506	59,258	8,829	569	49,860	20,767	4,298	11,528	3,699	1,242	2,481	2,072
1992–93	84,497	82,896	59,676	9,152	430	50,094	20,671	4,115	11,651	3,613	1,292	2,549	1,601
1993–94	85,393	83,431	60,052	9,573	442	50,037	20,705	3,970	11,858	3,595	1,282	2,674	1,962
1994–95	86,221	84,476	60,808	9,954	458	50,396	20,904	3,859	12,058	3,628	1,359	2,764	1,745
1995–96	87,125	84,958	61,165	10,205	474	50,486	20,997	3,743	12,168	3,621	1,465	2,796	2,167
1996–97	88,223	86,092	61,805	10,499	487	50,819	21,307	3,707	12,424	3,614	1,562	2,980	2,131
1997–98	89,508	87,541	62,739	10,944	476	51,319	21,682	3,599	12,734	3,611	1,738	3,120	1,967
1998–99	90,874	89,259	63,462	11,202	463	51,797	22,076	3,607	13,457	3,707	1,305	3,721	1,615
1999–2000	92,012	90,538	64,131	11,521	423	52,187	22,365	3,566	13,914	3,686	1,199	4,042	1,474
2000–01	93,273	91,691	64,601	11,696	411	52,494	21,994	3,318	13,793	3,974	909	5,096	1,582
2001–02	94,112	92,696	65,228	11,983	408	52,837	22,180	3,285	14,070	3,917	908	5,288	1,416
2002–03	95,615	93,869	65,718	12,174	366	53,178	22,599	3,263	14,330	4,017	989	5,552	1,746
2003–04	95,726	93,977	65,758	12,341	376	53,041	22,782	3,251	14,595	3,840	1,096	5,437	1,749
2004–05	96,513	95,001	65,984	12,530	338	53,116	23,445	3,250	14,854	3,945	1,396	5,572	1,512
2005–06	97,382	95,731	66,026	12,545	326	53,155	23,998	3,249	15,103	3,910	1,736	5,707	1,651
2006–07	98,793	96,362	66,458	12,773	313	53,372	23,920	3,112	15,043	4,048	1,717	5,984	2,431
2007–08	98,916	97,654	67,112	13,014	288	53,810	24,643	3,117	16,146	3,981	1,399	5,899	1,262
2008–09	98,706	97,119	67,148	13,060	237	53,760	24,348	3,037	16,246	3,761	1,304	5,623	1,587
2009–10	98,817	97,521	67,140	13,163	217	53,760	24,651	2,953	16,706	3,778	1,214	5,730	1,296
2010–11	98,817	97,767	67,086	13,045	224	53,817	24,544	2,855	16,321	4,047	1,321	6,137	1,050
2011–12	98,328	97,357	66,689	12,963	205	53,521	24,357	2,865	16,586	3,899	1,007	6,311	971
2012–13	98,454	97,369	66,718	13,061	196	53,461	24,280	2,810	16,657	3,871	942	6,371	1,085

—Not available.
[1]Includes special education, alternative, and other schools not reported by grade span.
[2]Includes schools beginning with grade 6 or below and ending with grade 9 or above.
[3]Includes schools beginning with grade 6 or below and with no grade higher than 8.
[4]Includes schools with grade spans beginning with 4, 5, or 6 and ending with 6, 7, or 8.
[5]Includes schools with no grade below 7, and at least one higher grade.
[6]Includes schools with grades 7 and 8 or grades 7 through 9.

[7]Because of revision in data collection procedures, figures not comparable to data for other years.
SOURCE: U.S. Department of Education, National Center for Education Statistics, *Statistics of State School Systems*, 1967–68 and 1975–76; *Statistics of Public Elementary and Secondary Day Schools*, 1970–71, 1972–73, 1974–75, and 1976–77 through 1980–81; and Common Core of Data (CCD), "Public Elementary/Secondary School Universe Survey," 1982–83 through 2012–13. (This table was prepared November 2014.)

Table 216.20. Number and enrollment of public elementary and secondary schools, by school level, type, and charter and magnet status: Selected years, 1990–91 through 2012–13

School level, type, and charter and magnet status	Number of schools										Enrollment									
	1990–91	2000–01	2005–06	2006–07	2007–08	2008–09	2009–10	2010–11	2011–12	2012–13	1990–91	2000–01	2005–06	2006–07	2007–08	2008–09	2009–10	2010–11	2011–12	2012–13
1	2	3	4	5	6	7	8	9	10	11	12	13	14	15	16	17	18	19	20	21
Total, all schools	84,538	93,273	97,382	98,793	98,916	98,706	98,817	98,817	98,328	98,454	41,141,366	47,060,714	48,912,085	49,065,594	48,910,025	49,053,786	49,081,519	49,177,617	49,256,120	49,474,030
School type																				
Regular	80,395	85,422	87,585	88,273	88,274	88,801	89,018	88,929	88,663	89,031	40,599,943	46,194,730	47,957,375	48,098,781	47,962,492	48,168,727	48,186,142	48,259,245	48,273,539	48,539,891
Special education	1,932	2,008	2,128	2,325	2,267	2,289	2,089	2,206	2,087	2,034	209,145	174,577	222,497	221,728	207,030	164,874	192,989	190,910	195,161	198,417
Vocational	1,060	1,025	1,221	1,289	1,409	1,409	1,417	1,485	1,434	1,403	198,117	199,669	217,621	204,101	163,003	156,380	129,840	164,013	159,905	159,917
Alternative[1]	1,151	4,818	6,448	6,906	6,966	6,207	6,293	6,197	6,144	5,986	134,161	491,738	514,592	540,984	577,500	563,795	572,548	563,449	627,515	575,805
School level and type																				
Elementary[2]	59,015	64,601	66,026	66,458	67,112	67,148	67,140	67,086	66,689	66,718	26,503,677	30,673,453	31,104,018	31,273,476	31,225,474	31,446,040	31,547,988	31,581,751	31,724,573	31,993,347
Regular	58,440	63,674	64,996	65,232	65,721	65,999	65,947	65,874	65,461	65,581	26,400,740	30,582,610	31,003,942	31,151,419	31,093,502	31,325,566	31,413,221	31,441,027	31,545,886	31,747,440
Special education	419	496	508	545	583	538	520	587	544	540	58,204	42,127	49,652	63,253	63,371	49,661	56,959	59,987	58,844	59,537
Vocational	31	8	8	10		1	24	16	17	15	17,686	2,409	1,713	2,719	1,634	16	1,892	3,495	4,558	3,734
Alternative[1]	125	423	514	671	801	610	649	609	667	582	27,047	46,307	48,711	56,085	66,967	70,797	75,916	78,242	115,285	82,636
Secondary[3]	21,135	21,994	23,998	23,920	24,643	24,348	24,651	24,544	24,357	24,280	13,569,787	15,038,171	16,219,309	16,068,448	16,184,724	16,055,123	15,930,401	15,692,610	15,708,815	15,644,214
Regular	19,459	18,456	19,252	19,152	19,371	19,349	19,604	19,449	19,441	19,470	13,313,097	14,567,999	15,685,032	15,549,702	15,568,507	15,568,281	15,454,043	15,197,786	15,194,153	15,137,814
Special education	165	219	368	365	375	325	354	359	339	330	11,913	12,607	42,696	39,232	30,680	24,266	30,443	27,990	27,905	27,731
Vocational	1,010	997	1,185	1,213	1,366	1,326	1,343	1,387	1,349	1,324	174,105	193,981	209,762	198,071	159,270	154,522	126,827	154,088	154,187	154,275
Alternative[1]	501	2,322	3,193	3,190	3,541	3,348	3,350	3,349	3,228	3,156	70,672	263,614	281,819	281,443	314,267	308,054	319,088	312,746	332,570	324,394
Combined elementary/secondary[4]	2,325	5,096	5,707	5,984	5,899	5,623	5,730	6,137	6,311	6,371	925,887	1,266,778	1,526,186	1,672,583	1,472,248	1,520,246	1,542,734	1,897,712	1,818,020	1,934,697
Regular	1,784	2,780	3,121	3,058	2,786	2,793	3,028	3,363	3,435	3,572	855,814	1,007,368	1,283,952	1,393,546	1,187,281	1,253,785	1,288,109	1,620,031	1,533,002	1,654,266
Special education	376	715	735	850	904	938	847	964	970	960	43,992	86,253	91,966	87,018	88,000	80,245	76,691	99,120	104,344	109,992
Vocational	19	20	28	66	46	82	50	82	68	64	6,326	3,279	6,146	3,311	2,099	1,852	1,121	6,430	1,160	1,908
Alternative[1]	146	1,581	1,823	2,010	2,163	1,810	1,805	1,728	1,838	1,775	19,755	169,878	164,122	188,708	194,868	184,364	176,813	172,131	179,514	168,541
Other (not classified by grade span)	2,063	1,582	1,651	2,431	1,262	1,587	1,296	1,050	971	1,085	142,015	82,312	62,572	51,087	27,579	32,377	60,396	5,544	4,712	1,772
Regular	712	512	216	831	396	660	439	243	326	408	30,292	36,783	4,449	4,114	1,202	21,095	30,769	401	498	381
Special education	972	578	517	565	405	488	368	296	234	204	95,036	33,590	38,183	32,225	24,979	10,702	28,896	4,813	4,068	1,157
Vocational	0	0	0	0	0	0	0	0	0	0	0	0	0	0	0	0	0	0	0	0
Alternative[1]	379	492	918	1,035	461	439	489	511	411	473	16,687	11,939	19,940	14,748	1,398	580	731	330	146	234
Charter status and level																				
All charter schools[5]	—	1,993	3,780	4,132	4,388	4,694	4,952	5,274	5,696	6,079	—	448,343	1,012,906	1,157,359	1,276,731	1,433,116	1,610,285	1,787,091	2,057,599	2,267,814
Elementary[2]	—	1,011	1,999	2,150	2,340	2,513	2,679	2,966	3,127	3,391	—	249,101	532,217	611,095	674,990	746,950	824,297	905,575	1,045,492	1,156,384
Secondary[3]	—	467	1,057	1,110	1,218	1,255	1,329	1,368	1,418	1,463	—	79,588	219,627	235,912	264,402	291,016	327,289	341,534	386,482	398,430
Combined elementary/secondary[4]	—	448	704	762	803	865	929	1,027	1,112	1,204	—	117,377	259,837	309,480	337,195	395,122	458,075	539,653	625,429	712,634
Other (not classified by grade span)[5]	—	67	50	110	27	61	15	13	39	21	—	2,277	1,225	872	144	28	624	329	196	366
Magnet status and level																				
All magnet schools[5]	—	1,469	2,736	2,266	2,793	3,021	2,213	2,722	2,949	3,151	—	1,213,976	2,103,013	1,592,614	2,132,395	2,307,712	1,515,562	2,055,133	2,248,177	2,479,188
Elementary[2]	—	1,111	1,994	1,666	2,015	2,193	1,530	1,849	2,012	2,150	—	704,763	1,186,160	904,536	1,157,470	1,267,944	799,546	1,035,288	1,158,405	1,287,589
Secondary[3]	—	328	643	510	688	728	582	746	802	862	—	484,684	869,010	618,349	926,314	976,483	668,832	944,434	1,015,267	1,119,969
Combined elementary/secondary[4]	—	29	80	81	83	92	79	103	116	121	—	24,529	47,509	69,476	48,593	63,285	46,467	75,411	74,505	72,192
Other (not classified by grade span)[5]	—	1	19	9	7	8	22	24	19	18	—	1	334	253	18		717	329	0	38

—Not available.

[1]Includes schools that provide nontraditional education, address needs of students that typically cannot be met in regular schools, serve as adjuncts to regular schools, or fall outside the categories of regular, special education, or vocational education.

[2]Includes schools beginning with grade 6 or below and with no grade higher than 8.

[3]Includes schools with no grade lower than 7.

[4]Includes schools beginning with grade 6 or below and ending with grade 9 or above.

[5]Magnet and charter schools are also included under regular, special education, vocational, or alternative schools as appropriate.

SOURCE: U.S. Department of Education, National Center for Education Statistics, Common Core of Data (CCD), "Public Elementary/Secondary School Universe Survey," 1990–91 through 2012–13. (This table was prepared January 2015.)

Table 216.30. Number and percentage distribution of public elementary and secondary students and schools, by traditional or charter school status and selected characteristics: Selected years, 1999–2000 through 2012–13

Selected characteristic	1999–2000 Total, all public schools	1999–2000 Traditional (noncharter) schools	1999–2000 Charter schools	Charter schools 2001–02	2003–04	2005–06	2007–08	2009–10	2010–11	2011–12	2012–13 Total, all public schools	2012–13 Traditional (noncharter) schools	2012–13 Charter schools
1	2	3	4	5	6	7	8	9	10	11	12	13	14
Enrollment (in thousands)............	46,689	46,350	340	571	789	1,013	1,277	1,610	1,787	2,058	49,474	47,206	2,268
Percentage distribution of students													
Sex........	100.0	100.0	100.0	100.0	100.0	100.0	100.0	100.0	100.0	100.0	100.0	100.0	100.0
Male........	51.4	51.4	51.0	50.8	50.3	49.9	49.5	49.5	49.5	49.6	51.4	51.4	49.6
Female........	48.6	48.6	49.0	49.2	49.7	50.1	50.5	50.5	50.5	50.4	48.6	48.6	50.4
Race/ethnicity........	100.0	100.0	100.0	100.0	100.0	100.0	100.0	100.0	100.0	100.0	100.0	100.0	100.0
White........	61.8	61.9	42.5	42.6	41.8	40.5	38.8	37.3	36.2	35.6	51.0	51.8	35.4
Black........	17.1	16.9	33.5	32.5	31.9	32.1	31.8	30.3	28.9	28.7	15.7	15.1	27.6
Hispanic........	15.9	15.9	19.6	20.1	21.5	22.4	24.5	26.0	27.3	28.0	24.3	24.1	29.1
Asian/Pacific Islander........	4.1	4.1	2.8	3.1	3.2	3.6	3.8	3.9	3.7	4.0	5.1	5.2	4.2
American Indian/Alaska Native........	1.2	1.2	1.5	1.7	1.5	1.4	1.2	1.0	0.9	0.9	1.1	1.1	0.8
Two or more races........	—	—	—	—	—	—	—	1.4	2.9	2.8	2.8	2.8	2.9
Percent of students eligible for free or reduced-price lunch program[1]........	100.0	100.0	100.0	100.0	100.0	100.0	100.0	100.0	100.0	100.0	100.0	100.0	100.0
0 to 25.0........	44.9	45.0	36.9	42.5	33.2	36.1	19.8	20.6	26.7	21.9	20.6	20.6	19.5
25.1 to 50.0........	25.4	25.5	12.7	14.3	17.1	15.9	16.5	18.8	18.9	18.4	27.8	28.2	19.8
50.1 to 75.0........	16.0	16.1	13.0	14.7	16.1	17.4	18.9	20.2	20.4	21.0	27.1	27.4	22.0
More than 75.0........	12.2	12.2	14.3	15.2	18.4	22.0	21.2	30.7	30.7	30.8	23.7	23.1	35.5
Missing/school does not participate........	1.4	1.2	23.2	13.3	15.2	8.6	23.6	9.7	3.2	7.9	0.8	0.7	3.1
Number of teachers[2]........	2,636,277	2,622,678	13,599	23,415	36,406	49,142	69,725	84,983	91,126	107,929	3,030,435	2,913,398	117,037
Pupil/teacher ratio[2]........	16.6	16.6	18.8	17.7	17.6	17.3	15.9	17.3	18.0	17.6	16.2	16.2	17.7
Total number of schools........	92,012	90,488	1,524	2,348	2,977	3,780	4,388	4,952	5,274	5,696	98,454	92,375	6,079
Percentage distribution of schools													
School level........	100.0	100.0	100.0	100.0	100.0	100.0	100.0	100.0	100.0	100.0	100.0	100.0	100.0
Elementary[3]........	69.7	70.0	54.6	50.6	52.0	52.1	53.3	54.1	54.3	54.9	67.8	68.6	55.8
Secondary[4]........	24.3	24.3	25.9	24.2	26.2	28.0	27.8	26.8	25.9	24.9	24.7	24.7	24.1
Combined[5]........	4.4	4.2	18.6	21.6	21.0	18.6	18.3	18.8	19.5	19.5	6.5	5.6	19.8
Other........	1.6	1.6	0.9	3.6	0.8	1.3	0.6	0.3	0.2	0.7	1.1	1.2	0.3
Size of enrollment........	100.0	100.0	100.0	100.0	100.0	100.0	100.0	100.0	100.0	100.0	100.0	100.0	100.0
Less than 300........	31.4	30.7	77.1	73.6	71.1	69.6	65.6	61.5	59.0	55.8	30.4	28.8	54.1
300 to 499........	26.4	26.7	12.0	13.6	15.6	16.5	19.3	20.8	22.3	23.1	27.5	27.7	23.5
500 to 999........	32.6	33.0	8.6	9.9	10.1	10.9	12.0	14.0	14.8	17.0	33.1	34.1	18.0
1,000 or more........	9.5	9.7	2.4	2.8	3.2	3.0	3.1	3.7	3.9	4.2	9.1	9.4	4.4
Racial/ethnic concentration													
More than 50 percent White........	70.9	71.2	51.1	50.9	48.7	46.5	43.2	40.3	38.4	37.5	58.9	60.4	36.6
More than 50 percent Black........	11.1	10.8	26.5	23.8	24.5	26.4	26.5	25.8	25.4	25.3	10.3	9.3	24.9
More than 50 percent Hispanic........	8.8	8.7	11.4	12.5	13.6	15.1	17.8	19.8	20.8	21.8	15.4	14.9	22.6
Percent of students eligible for free or reduced-price lunch program[1]........	100.0	100.0	100.0	100.0	100.0	100.0	100.0	100.0	100.0	100.0	100.0	100.0	100.0
0 to 25.0........	42.3	42.3	44.5	47.8	28.7	32.7	20.2	19.3	27.7	18.7	17.9	17.8	18.3
25.1 to 50.0........	25.6	25.9	11.1	11.7	16.0	15.2	15.5	17.2	17.4	17.9	25.9	26.3	18.7
50.1 to 75.0........	16.8	16.9	10.2	12.0	16.0	16.9	18.8	20.9	20.1	19.9	27.3	27.7	20.9
More than 75.0........	11.9	11.9	12.4	13.5	19.9	22.7	22.4	32.8	33.1	33.8	24.2	23.4	36.9
Missing/school does not participate........	3.3	3.0	21.9	14.9	19.5	12.5	23.0	9.8	1.7	9.7	4.8	4.7	5.2
Locale........	—	—	—	—	100.0	100.0	100.0	100.0	100.0	100.0	100.0	100.0	100.0
City........	—	—	—	—	52.7	52.5	54.3	54.8	55.5	55.4	27.0	25.0	56.7
Suburban........	—	—	—	—	22.0	22.2	22.0	21.1	21.3	21.2	31.4	31.8	25.5
Town........	—	—	—	—	9.6	9.4	8.5	8.0	7.6	7.4	13.7	14.2	7.0
Rural........	—	—	—	—	15.8	16.0	15.2	16.1	15.6	16.0	27.9	29.0	10.8
Region........	100.0	100.0	100.0	100.0	100.0	100.0	100.0	100.0	100.0	100.0	100.0	100.0	100.0
Northeast........	16.1	16.3	7.2	10.1	9.2	9.0	8.6	9.1	9.5	9.7	15.5	15.9	10.0
Midwest........	28.9	29.0	24.9	22.6	23.7	27.4	26.5	24.0	23.1	22.3	25.9	26.2	21.9
South........	33.1	33.2	28.9	28.4	26.7	26.5	28.2	29.5	29.5	30.8	34.9	35.2	30.7
West........	21.8	21.6	38.9	38.9	40.3	37.2	36.6	37.4	37.9	37.2	23.6	22.7	37.3

—Not available.

[1]The National School Lunch Program is a federally assisted meal program. To be eligible for free lunch under the program, a student must be from a household with an income at or below 130 percent of the poverty threshold; to be eligible for reduced-price lunch, a student must be from a household with an income between 130 percent and 185 percent of the poverty threshold.
[2]Pupil/teacher ratio based on schools that reported both enrollment and teacher data. Data for 2010 include imputations for teachers in California and Vermont.

[3]Includes schools beginning with grade 6 or below and with no grade higher than 8.
[4]Includes schools with no grade lower than 7.
[5]Includes schools beginning with grade 6 or below and ending with grade 9 or above.
NOTE: Detail may not sum to totals because of rounding. Race categories exclude persons of Hispanic ethnicity.
SOURCE: U.S. Department of Education, National Center for Education Statistics, Common Core of Data (CCD), "Public Elementary/Secondary School Universe Survey," 1999–2000 through 2012–13. (This table was prepared November 2014.)

Table 216.40. Number and percentage distribution of public elementary and secondary schools and enrollment, by level, type, and enrollment size of school: 2010–11, 2011–12, and 2012–13

Enrollment size of school	Number and percentage distribution of schools, by level and type						Enrollment totals and percentage distribution, by level and type of school[1]					
			Secondary[4]		Combined elementary/ secondary[5]				Secondary[4]		Combined elementary/ secondary[5]	
	Total[2]	Elementary[3]	All schools	Regular schools[7]		Other[6]	Total[2]	Elementary[3]	All schools	Regular schools[7]		Other[6]
1	2	3	4	5	6	7	8	9	10	11	12	13
2010–11												
Total	98,817	67,086	24,544	19,449	6,137	1,050	49,177,617	31,581,751	15,692,610	15,197,786	1,897,712	5,544
Percent[8]	100.00	100.00	100.00	100.00	100.00	100.00	100.00	100.00	100.00	100.00	100.00	100.00
Under 100	10.51	5.51	18.27	9.30	37.19	81.44	0.91	0.59	1.12	0.66	4.36	49.35
100 to 199	9.25	7.96	11.49	10.57	15.47	15.46	2.67	2.55	2.46	1.98	6.45	34.74
200 to 299	11.01	11.84	9.08	9.33	9.30	2.06	5.36	6.31	3.29	2.94	6.68	7.95
300 to 399	13.86	16.34	8.02	8.87	8.45	0.00	9.39	12.08	4.07	3.91	8.53	0.00
400 to 499	13.94	17.07	6.61	7.54	6.86	1.03	12.09	16.14	4.30	4.26	8.98	7.95
500 to 599	11.51	13.97	5.87	6.72	5.41	0.00	12.18	16.11	4.70	4.66	8.60	0.00
600 to 699	8.50	10.12	4.98	5.74	3.69	0.00	10.62	13.78	4.71	4.71	6.96	0.00
700 to 799	5.94	6.84	4.02	4.67	3.22	0.00	8.57	10.75	4.40	4.43	6.97	0.00
800 to 999	6.51	6.69	6.69	7.83	3.73	0.00	11.14	12.43	8.72	8.86	9.70	0.00
1,000 to 1,499	5.32	3.33	11.40	13.36	4.16	0.00	12.31	8.11	20.48	20.81	14.61	0.00
1,500 to 1,999	2.02	0.28	7.24	8.56	1.36	0.00	6.74	0.98	18.35	18.81	6.72	0.00
2,000 to 2,999	1.36	0.03	5.37	6.37	0.76	0.00	6.21	0.16	18.48	18.97	5.29	0.00
3,000 or more	0.26	0.00	0.97	1.14	0.42	0.00	1.80	0.00	4.89	5.00	6.14	0.00
Average enrollment[8]	517	475	684	790	343	57	517	475	684	790	343	57
2011–12												
Total	98,328	66,689	24,357	19,441	6,311	971	49,256,120	31,724,573	15,708,815	15,194,153	1,818,020	4,712
Percent[8]	100.00	100.00	100.00	100.00	100.00	100.00	100.00	100.00	100.00	100.00	100.00	100.00
Under 100	10.32	5.46	17.47	9.31	37.92	67.86	0.89	0.57	1.08	0.65	4.80	35.93
100 to 199	9.09	7.65	11.57	10.59	15.72	28.57	2.62	2.43	2.47	2.00	7.05	49.79
200 to 299	10.96	11.68	9.12	9.36	10.02	1.79	5.31	6.18	3.29	2.96	7.68	4.69
300 to 399	13.79	16.20	8.12	8.88	8.45	0.00	9.29	11.88	4.10	3.93	9.10	0.00
400 to 499	13.92	17.08	6.56	7.40	6.55	1.79	12.00	16.00	4.26	4.21	9.16	9.59
500 to 599	11.65	14.14	5.87	6.68	5.90	0.00	12.27	16.17	4.66	4.64	10.01	0.00
600 to 699	8.58	10.23	4.92	5.56	4.04	0.00	10.67	13.82	4.61	4.56	8.12	0.00
700 to 799	6.13	6.98	4.48	5.12	2.96	0.00	8.80	10.88	4.85	4.85	6.80	0.00
800 to 999	6.56	6.77	6.79	7.87	3.13	0.00	11.17	12.49	8.80	8.94	8.65	0.00
1,000 to 1,499	5.40	3.48	11.51	13.30	3.28	0.00	12.42	8.42	20.53	20.76	12.20	0.00
1,500 to 1,999	2.02	0.29	7.26	8.53	1.24	0.00	6.71	1.02	18.24	18.77	6.49	0.00
2,000 to 2,999	1.33	0.03	5.36	6.29	0.44	0.00	6.03	0.13	18.26	18.78	3.27	0.00
3,000 or more	0.25	#	0.97	1.13	0.35	0.00	1.80	0.01	4.85	4.93	6.67	0.00
Average enrollment[8]	520	479	690	788	322	84	520	479	690	788	322	84
2012–13												
Total	98,454	66,718	24,280	19,470	6,371	1,085	49,474,030	31,893,347	15,644,214	15,137,814	1,934,697	1,772
Percent[8]	100.00	100.00	100.00	100.00	100.00	100.00	100.00	100.00	100.00	100.00	100.00	100.00
Under 100	10.14	5.34	17.35	9.30	36.73	86.21	0.88	0.56	1.08	0.65	4.42	57.73
100 to 199	9.20	7.74	11.66	10.60	16.30	6.90	2.63	2.44	2.48	1.99	6.94	12.64
200 to 299	10.90	11.50	9.30	9.66	10.23	6.90	5.28	6.08	3.36	3.07	7.52	29.63
300 to 399	13.62	16.05	7.95	8.65	8.11	0.00	9.15	11.71	4.02	3.84	8.37	0.00
400 to 499	13.86	16.93	6.87	7.72	6.07	0.00	11.91	15.80	4.46	4.40	8.06	0.00
500 to 599	11.72	14.24	5.85	6.63	5.93	0.00	12.28	16.19	4.64	4.62	9.63	0.00
600 to 699	8.64	10.35	4.91	5.54	3.71	0.00	10.70	13.90	4.62	4.57	7.13	0.00
700 to 799	6.14	7.06	4.23	4.87	3.21	0.00	8.78	10.94	4.59	4.64	7.10	0.00
800 to 999	6.70	6.94	6.70	7.76	3.87	0.00	11.36	12.74	8.69	8.84	10.13	0.00
1,000 to 1,499	5.47	3.52	11.60	13.37	3.68	0.00	12.53	8.47	20.74	20.97	13.08	0.00
1,500 to 1,999	2.04	0.29	7.38	8.64	1.17	0.00	6.77	1.00	18.63	19.13	5.88	0.00
2,000 to 2,999	1.30	0.03	5.23	6.12	0.49	0.00	5.86	0.14	17.85	18.34	3.29	0.00
3,000 or more	0.27	#	0.97	1.14	0.51	0.00	1.87	0.02	4.84	4.95	8.44	0.00
Average enrollment[8]	522	481	689	785	337	61	522	481	689	785	337	61

#Rounds to zero.
[1] Totals differ from those reported in other tables because this table represents data reported by schools rather than by states or school districts. Percentage distribution and average enrollment calculations exclude data for schools not reporting enrollment.
[2] Includes elementary, secondary, combined elementary/secondary, and other schools.
[3] Includes schools beginning with grade 6 or below and with no grade higher than 8.
[4] Includes schools with no grade lower than 7.
[5] Includes schools beginning with grade 6 or below and ending with grade 9 or above.
[6] Includes special education, alternative, and other schools not reported by grade span.

[7] Excludes special education schools, vocational schools, and alternative schools.
[8] Data are for schools reporting enrollments greater than zero. Enrollments greater than zero were reported for 95,111 out of 98,817 schools in 2010–11, 94,743 out of 98,328 in 2011–12, and 94,771 out of 98,454 in 2012–13.
NOTE: Detail may not sum to totals because of rounding.
SOURCE: U.S. Department of Education, National Center for Education Statistics, Common Core of Data (CCD), "Public Elementary/Secondary School Universe Survey," 2010–11, 2011–12, 2012–13. (This table was prepared November 2014.)

Table 216.45. Average enrollment and percentage distribution of public elementary and secondary schools, by level, type, and enrollment size: Selected years, 1982–83 through 2012–13

Year	Average enrollment in schools, by level and type						Percentage distribution of schools, by enrollment size							
	Total[1]	Elementary[2]	Secondary[3]		Combined elementary/ secondary[4]	Other[5]	Under 200	200 to 299	300 to 399	400 to 499	500 to 599	600 to 699	700 to 999	1,000 or more
			All schools	Regular schools[6]										
1	2	3	4	5	6	7	8	9	10	11	12	13	14	15
1982–83	478	399	719	—	478	142	21.9	13.8	15.5	13.1	10.2	7.1	10.2	8.3
1983–84	480	401	720	—	475	145	21.7	13.7	15.5	13.2	10.2	7.1	10.3	8.3
1984–85	482	403	721	—	476	146	21.5	13.6	15.5	13.2	10.3	7.1	10.4	8.4
1986–87	489	416	707	714	426	118	21.1	13.1	15.0	13.5	10.8	7.5	10.7	8.1
1987–88	490	424	695	711	420	122	20.3	12.9	14.9	13.8	11.1	7.8	11.2	8.0
1988–89	494	433	689	697	412	142	20.0	12.5	14.7	13.8	11.4	8.0	11.6	8.0
1989–90	493	441	669	689	402	142	19.8	12.2	14.5	13.7	11.5	8.3	12.0	7.9
1990–91	497	449	663	684	398	150	19.7	11.9	14.2	13.6	11.7	8.5	12.3	8.1
1991–92	507	458	677	717	407	152	19.1	11.7	14.1	13.5	11.8	8.6	12.8	8.5
1992–93	513	464	688	733	423	135	18.6	11.6	13.9	13.5	11.9	8.7	13.1	8.7
1993–94	518	468	693	748	418	136	18.6	11.5	13.6	13.5	11.7	8.8	13.3	9.0
1994–95	520	471	696	759	412	131	18.6	11.4	13.6	13.4	11.8	8.7	13.3	9.2
1995–96	525	476	703	771	401	136	18.5	11.2	13.5	13.4	11.8	8.8	13.4	9.4
1996–97	527	478	703	777	387	135	18.7	11.3	13.2	13.2	11.8	8.8	13.6	9.5
1997–98	525	478	699	779	374	121	19.3	11.2	13.1	13.3	11.6	8.6	13.4	9.6
1998–99	524	478	707	786	290	135	19.6	11.2	13.1	13.2	11.5	8.5	13.3	9.6
1999–2000	521	477	706	785	282	123	20.0	11.3	13.3	13.2	11.2	8.4	13.1	9.5
2000–01	519	477	714	795	274	136	20.4	11.4	13.2	13.3	11.0	8.2	12.9	9.6
2001–02	520	477	718	807	270	138	20.5	11.5	13.3	13.1	10.9	8.1	12.7	9.7
2002–03	519	476	720	813	265	136	20.7	11.6	13.4	13.0	10.9	8.1	12.4	9.8
2003–04	521	476	722	816	269	142	20.7	11.6	13.5	13.2	10.8	8.0	12.3	9.9
2004–05	521	474	713	815	298	143	20.7	11.6	13.5	13.2	10.8	8.1	12.2	9.9
2005–06	521	473	709	819	318	128	20.7	11.5	13.6	13.2	11.0	8.1	12.2	9.8
2006–07	521	473	711	818	325	138	20.3	11.5	13.8	13.4	11.0	8.2	12.2	9.6
2007–08	516	469	704	816	292	136	20.4	11.5	13.9	13.6	11.1	8.1	12.0	9.3
2008–09	517	470	704	807	308	177	20.0	11.4	13.8	13.9	11.3	8.3	12.2	9.1
2009–10	516	473	692	796	300	191	20.0	11.3	13.7	13.9	11.4	8.5	12.3	9.0
2010–11	517	475	684	790	343	57	19.8	11.0	13.9	13.9	11.5	8.5	12.5	9.0
2011–12	520	479	690	788	322	84	19.4	11.0	13.8	13.9	11.7	8.6	12.7	9.0
2012–13	522	481	689	785	337	61	19.3	10.9	13.6	13.9	11.7	8.6	12.8	9.1

—Not available.
[1]Includes elementary, secondary, combined elementary/secondary, and other schools.
[2]Includes schools beginning with grade 6 or below and with no grade higher than 8.
[3]Includes schools with no grade lower than 7.
[4]Includes schools beginning with grade 6 or below and ending with grade 9 or above.
[5]Includes special education, alternative, and other schools not reported by grade span.
[6]Excludes special education schools, vocational schools, and alternative schools.

NOTE: Data reflect reports by schools rather than by states or school districts. Percentage distribution and average enrollment calculations include data only for schools reporting enrollments data. Enrollment data were reported for 94,771 out of 98,454 schools in 2012–13. Detail may not sum to totals because of rounding.
SOURCE: U.S. Department of Education, National Center for Education Statistics, Common Core of Data (CCD), "Public Elementary/Secondary School Universe Survey," 1982–83 through 2012–13. (This table was prepared November 2014.)

Table 216.50. Number and percentage distribution of public elementary and secondary school students, by percentage of minority enrollment in the school and student's racial/ethnic group: Selected years, fall 1995 through fall 2012

Year and racial/ethnic group	Total	Number of students in racial/ethnic group, by percent minority enrollment in the school — Less than 10 percent	10 to 24 percent	25 to 49 percent	50 to 74 percent	75 to 89 percent	90 percent or more	Total	Percentage distribution of students in racial/ethnic group, by percent minority enrollment in the school — Less than 10 percent	10 to 24 percent	25 to 49 percent	50 to 74 percent	75 to 89 percent	90 percent or more
1	2	3	4	5	6	7	8	9	10	11	12	13	14	15
Total, 1995	44,424,467	14,508,573	8,182,484	8,261,110	5,467,784	2,876,302	5,128,214	100.0	32.7	18.4	18.6	12.3	6.5	11.5
White	28,736,961	13,939,633	6,812,196	5,246,785	2,094,440	499,884	144,023	100.0	48.5	23.7	18.3	7.3	1.7	0.5
Minority	15,687,506	568,940	1,370,288	3,014,325	3,373,344	2,376,418	4,984,191	100.0	3.6	8.7	19.2	21.5	15.1	31.8
Black	7,510,678	198,386	598,716	1,588,850	1,622,448	941,335	2,560,943	100.0	2.6	8.0	21.2	21.6	12.5	34.1
Hispanic	6,016,293	174,140	415,761	932,949	1,289,184	1,099,109	2,105,150	100.0	2.9	6.9	15.5	21.4	18.3	35.0
Asian/Pacific Islander	1,656,787	142,886	259,335	367,888	379,110	297,680	209,888	100.0	8.6	15.7	22.2	22.9	18.0	12.7
American Indian/Alaska Native	503,748	53,528	96,476	124,638	82,602	38,294	108,210	100.0	10.6	19.2	24.7	16.4	7.6	21.5
Total, 2000	46,120,425	12,761,478	8,736,252	8,760,300	6,013,131	3,472,083	6,377,181	100.0	27.7	18.9	19.0	13.0	7.5	13.8
White	28,146,613	12,218,862	7,271,285	5,566,681	2,303,106	596,478	190,201	100.0	43.4	25.8	19.8	8.2	2.1	0.7
Minority	17,973,812	542,616	1,464,967	3,193,619	3,710,025	2,875,605	6,186,980	100.0	3.0	8.2	17.8	20.6	16.0	34.4
Black	7,854,032	178,185	561,488	1,485,130	1,652,393	1,043,907	2,932,929	100.0	2.3	7.1	18.9	21.0	13.3	37.3
Hispanic	7,649,728	181,685	505,612	1,121,809	1,542,982	1,432,639	2,865,001	100.0	2.4	6.6	14.7	20.2	18.7	37.5
Asian/Pacific Islander	1,924,875	132,813	295,437	441,769	423,175	353,395	278,286	100.0	6.9	15.3	23.0	22.0	18.4	14.5
American Indian/Alaska Native	545,177	49,933	102,430	144,911	91,475	45,664	110,764	100.0	9.2	18.8	26.6	16.8	8.4	20.3
Total, 2005	48,584,980	10,711,307	9,283,783	9,865,121	6,839,850	4,149,802	7,735,117	100.0	22.0	19.1	20.3	14.1	8.5	15.9
White	27,742,612	10,208,608	7,720,632	6,259,485	2,604,846	707,603	241,438	100.0	36.8	27.8	22.6	9.4	2.6	0.9
Minority	20,842,368	502,699	1,563,151	3,605,636	4,235,004	3,442,199	7,493,679	100.0	2.4	7.5	17.3	20.3	16.5	36.0
Black	8,366,722	162,455	560,928	1,513,020	1,752,207	1,176,649	3,201,463	100.0	1.9	6.7	18.1	20.9	14.1	38.3
Hispanic	9,638,712	182,039	581,533	1,388,496	1,873,877	1,803,567	3,809,200	100.0	1.9	6.0	14.4	19.4	18.7	39.5
Asian/Pacific Islander	2,242,628	115,084	319,524	543,952	496,515	406,788	360,765	100.0	5.1	14.2	24.3	22.1	18.1	16.1
American Indian/Alaska Native	594,306	43,121	101,166	160,168	112,405	55,195	122,251	100.0	7.3	17.0	27.0	18.9	9.3	20.6
Total, 2009	48,634,893	8,732,585	9,061,653	10,466,589	7,419,977	4,502,052	8,452,037	100.0	18.0	18.6	21.5	15.3	9.3	17.4
White	26,311,473	8,295,175	7,532,475	6,627,227	2,814,575	768,359	273,662	100.0	31.5	28.6	25.2	10.7	2.9	1.0
Minority	22,323,420	437,410	1,529,178	3,839,362	4,605,402	3,733,693	8,178,375	100.0	2.0	6.9	17.2	20.6	16.7	36.6
Black	8,166,410	131,097	507,800	1,448,683	1,735,281	1,203,375	3,140,174	100.0	1.6	6.2	17.7	21.2	14.7	38.5
Hispanic	10,775,975	165,220	586,701	1,529,688	2,095,878	1,981,911	4,416,577	100.0	1.5	5.4	14.2	19.4	18.4	41.0
Asian/Pacific Islander	2,461,820	94,593	310,703	614,990	578,595	441,613	421,326	100.0	3.8	12.6	25.0	23.5	17.9	17.1
American Indian/Alaska Native	584,756	34,079	89,843	166,648	118,637	56,413	119,136	100.0	5.8	15.4	28.5	20.3	9.6	20.4
Other[1]	334,459	12,421	34,131	79,353	77,011	50,381	81,162	100.0	3.7	10.2	23.7	23.0	15.1	24.3
Total, 2010	49,212,031	7,395,549	9,177,649	11,236,328	7,904,340	4,718,126	8,780,039	100.0	15.0	18.6	22.8	16.1	9.6	17.8
White	25,801,021	6,987,898	7,614,557	7,097,284	3,003,599	808,637	289,046	100.0	27.1	29.5	27.5	11.6	3.1	1.1
Minority	23,411,010	407,651	1,563,092	4,139,044	4,900,741	3,909,489	8,490,993	100.0	1.7	6.7	17.7	20.9	16.7	36.3
Black	7,873,809	95,108	415,807	1,335,674	1,697,727	1,236,333	3,093,160	100.0	1.2	5.3	17.0	21.6	15.7	39.3
Hispanic	11,367,157	142,927	583,019	1,654,084	2,238,071	2,063,492	4,685,564	100.0	1.3	5.1	14.6	19.7	18.2	41.2
Asian	2,281,908	63,974	259,910	585,447	552,633	390,731	429,213	100.0	2.8	11.4	25.7	24.2	17.1	18.8
Pacific Islander	169,678	4,958	13,772	27,478	32,241	41,652	49,577	100.0	2.9	8.1	16.2	19.0	24.5	29.2
American Indian/Alaska Native	561,126	26,066	77,990	157,300	116,787	58,476	124,507	100.0	4.6	13.9	28.0	20.8	10.4	22.2
Two or more races	1,157,332	74,618	212,594	379,061	263,282	118,805	108,972	100.0	6.4	18.4	32.8	22.7	10.3	9.4
Total, 2011	49,246,537	6,943,209	9,090,845	11,325,084	8,087,862	4,909,344	8,890,193	100.0	14.1	18.5	23.0	16.4	10.0	18.1
White	25,464,162	6,549,257	7,535,852	7,154,879	3,086,247	842,317	295,610	100.0	25.7	29.6	28.1	12.1	3.3	1.2
Minority	23,782,375	393,952	1,554,993	4,170,205	5,001,615	4,067,027	8,594,583	100.0	1.7	6.5	17.5	21.0	17.1	36.1
Black	7,782,146	85,682	393,118	1,302,027	1,686,653	1,255,240	3,059,426	100.0	1.1	5.1	16.7	21.7	16.1	39.3
Hispanic	11,693,788	141,593	594,874	1,678,320	2,302,100	2,161,819	4,815,082	100.0	1.2	5.1	14.4	19.7	18.5	41.2
Asian	2,321,362	58,414	249,943	587,291	570,921	415,832	438,961	100.0	2.5	10.8	25.3	24.6	17.9	18.9
Pacific Islander	177,871	5,170	13,635	27,828	34,546	42,851	53,841	100.0	2.9	7.7	15.6	19.4	24.1	30.3
American Indian/Alaska Native	541,986	23,215	69,953	152,088	112,568	58,106	126,056	100.0	4.3	12.9	28.1	20.8	10.7	23.3
Two or more races	1,265,222	79,878	233,470	422,651	294,827	133,179	101,217	100.0	6.3	18.5	33.4	23.3	10.5	8.0
Total, 2012	49,460,399	6,512,145	9,106,399	11,465,619	8,280,130	4,994,550	9,101,556	100.0	13.2	18.4	23.2	16.7	10.1	18.4
White	25,238,825	6,136,381	7,549,183	7,233,482	3,153,892	859,415	306,472	100.0	24.3	29.9	28.7	12.5	3.4	1.2
Minority	24,221,574	375,764	1,557,216	4,232,137	5,126,238	4,135,135	8,795,084	100.0	1.6	6.4	17.5	21.2	17.1	36.3
Black	7,745,244	76,614	377,613	1,275,975	1,690,994	1,260,621	3,063,427	100.0	1.0	4.9	16.5	21.8	16.3	39.6
Hispanic	12,028,116	137,254	601,847	1,721,620	2,374,944	2,210,057	4,982,394	100.0	1.1	5.0	14.3	19.7	18.4	41.4
Asian	2,358,015	52,671	244,691	595,541	589,235	417,742	458,135	100.0	2.2	10.4	25.3	25.0	17.7	19.4
Pacific Islander	179,353	4,899	13,819	28,583	34,480	40,876	56,696	100.0	2.7	7.7	15.9	19.2	22.8	31.6
American Indian/Alaska Native	528,024	20,847	65,566	147,080	110,908	59,210	124,413	100.0	3.9	12.4	27.9	21.0	11.2	23.6
Two or more races	1,382,822	83,479	253,680	463,338	325,677	146,629	110,019	100.0	6.0	18.3	33.5	23.6	10.6	8.0

[1]Includes data for Two or more races reported by 14 states.
NOTE: Data reflect racial/ethnic data reported by schools. Because some schools do not report complete racial/ethnic data, totals may differ from figures in other tables. Excludes 1995 data for Idaho and 2000 data for Tennessee because racial/ethnic data were not reported. Race categories exclude persons of Hispanic ethnicity. Detail may not sum to totals because of rounding.
SOURCE: U.S. Department of Education, National Center for Education Statistics, Common Core of Data (CCD), "Public Elementary/Secondary School Universe Survey," 1995–96 through 2012–13. (This table was prepared March 2015.)

Table 216.55. Number and percentage distribution of public elementary and secondary school students, by percentage of student's racial/ethnic group enrolled in the school and student's racial/ethnic group: Selected years, fall 1995 through fall 2012

| Year and racial/ethnic group | Number of students in each racial/ethnic group, by percent of that racial/ethnic group in the school | | | | | | | Percentage distribution of students in each racial/ethnic group, by percent of that racial/ethnic group in the school | | | | | | |
	Total	Less than 10 percent of group	10 to 24 percent of group	25 to 49 percent of group	50 to 74 percent of group	75 to 89 percent of group	90 percent or more of group	Total	Less than 10 percent of group	10 to 24 percent of group	25 to 49 percent of group	50 to 74 percent of group	75 to 89 percent of group	90 percent or more of group
1	2	3	4	5	6	7	8	9	10	11	12	13	14	15
1995														
White	28,736,961	143,787	498,649	2,084,689	5,244,015	6,813,804	13,952,017	100.0	0.5	1.7	7.3	18.2	23.7	48.6
Black	7,510,678	657,403	1,119,556	1,873,303	1,386,802	811,898	1,661,716	100.0	8.8	14.9	24.9	18.5	10.8	22.1
Hispanic	6,016,293	646,364	847,792	1,359,649	1,360,020	874,878	927,590	100.0	10.7	14.1	22.6	22.6	14.5	15.4
Asian/Pacific Islander	1,656,787	703,101	435,495	301,984	135,001	67,558	13,648	100.0	42.4	26.3	18.2	8.1	4.1	0.8
American Indian/Alaska Native	503,748	223,244	75,019	63,070	39,200	15,084	88,131	100.0	44.3	14.9	12.5	7.8	3.0	17.5
2000														
White	28,146,613	189,779	595,137	2,294,232	5,556,108	7,279,301	12,232,056	100.0	0.7	2.1	8.2	19.7	25.9	43.5
Black	7,854,032	735,459	1,199,865	1,899,982	1,366,363	871,399	1,780,964	100.0	9.4	15.3	24.2	17.4	11.1	22.7
Hispanic	7,649,728	738,509	1,054,396	1,696,944	1,739,038	1,134,466	1,286,375	100.0	9.7	13.8	22.2	22.7	14.8	16.8
Asian/Pacific Islander	1,924,875	799,220	524,279	331,576	171,739	81,461	16,600	100.0	41.5	27.2	17.2	8.9	4.2	0.9
American Indian/Alaska Native	545,177	251,983	81,119	75,831	39,944	15,363	80,937	100.0	46.2	14.9	13.9	7.3	2.8	14.8
2005														
White	27,742,612	240,614	705,300	2,596,310	6,256,109	7,718,175	10,226,104	100.0	0.9	2.5	9.4	22.6	27.8	36.9
Black	8,366,722	849,399	1,396,670	2,004,856	1,453,759	884,663	1,777,375	100.0	10.2	16.7	24.0	17.4	10.6	21.2
Hispanic	9,638,712	848,160	1,316,558	2,071,303	2,218,616	1,545,322	1,638,753	100.0	8.8	13.7	21.5	23.0	16.0	17.0
Asian/Pacific Islander	2,242,628	925,411	616,762	363,562	214,304	100,845	21,744	100.0	41.3	27.5	16.2	9.6	4.5	1.0
American Indian/Alaska Native	594,306	276,846	86,978	84,665	43,272	21,275	81,270	100.0	46.6	14.6	14.2	7.3	3.6	13.7
2009														
White	26,311,473	273,285	766,093	2,802,435	6,623,809	7,537,266	8,308,585	100.0	1.0	2.9	10.7	25.2	28.6	31.6
Black	8,166,410	885,911	1,469,582	1,984,384	1,387,212	858,152	1,581,169	100.0	10.8	18.0	24.3	17.0	10.5	19.4
Hispanic	10,775,975	875,979	1,475,714	2,312,508	2,557,263	1,710,475	1,844,036	100.0	8.1	13.7	21.5	23.7	15.9	17.1
Asian/Pacific Islander	2,461,820	990,104	680,770	422,114	233,733	109,671	25,428	100.0	40.2	27.7	17.1	9.5	4.5	1.0
American Indian/Alaska Native	584,756	280,738	79,981	89,944	40,595	21,274	72,224	100.0	48.0	13.7	15.4	6.9	3.6	12.4
2010														
White	25,801,021	288,136	807,107	2,991,928	7,090,581	7,620,071	7,003,198	100.0	1.1	3.1	11.6	27.5	29.5	27.1
Black	7,873,809	904,777	1,453,068	1,907,158	1,328,164	859,843	1,420,799	100.0	11.5	18.5	24.2	16.9	10.9	18.0
Hispanic	11,367,157	896,796	1,603,546	2,473,080	2,657,108	1,791,161	1,945,466	100.0	7.9	14.1	21.8	23.4	15.8	17.1
Asian	2,281,908	944,657	633,149	431,446	219,381	43,509	9,766	100.0	41.4	27.7	18.9	9.6	1.9	0.4
Pacific Islander	169,678	104,646	15,170	27,558	14,860	5,146	2,298	100.0	61.7	8.9	16.2	8.8	3.0	1.4
American Indian/Alaska Native	561,126	276,859	76,874	78,978	38,349	21,156	68,910	100.0	49.3	13.7	14.1	6.8	3.8	12.3
Two or more races	1,157,332	996,181	128,813	15,347	6,709	3,286	6,996	100.0	86.1	11.1	1.3	0.6	0.3	0.6
2011														
White	25,464,162	294,998	840,764	3,072,182	7,153,778	7,543,427	6,559,013	100.0	1.2	3.3	12.1	28.1	29.6	25.8
Black	7,782,146	909,399	1,448,983	1,912,335	1,301,165	864,856	1,345,408	100.0	11.7	18.6	24.6	16.7	11.1	17.3
Hispanic	11,693,788	909,247	1,658,024	2,543,266	2,720,777	1,877,108	1,985,366	100.0	7.8	14.2	21.7	23.3	16.1	17.0
Asian	2,321,362	946,520	644,479	441,656	232,408	43,530	12,769	100.0	40.8	27.8	19.0	10.0	1.9	0.6
Pacific Islander	177,871	112,805	14,759	28,211	15,688	4,471	1,937	100.0	63.4	8.3	15.9	8.8	2.5	1.1
American Indian/Alaska Native	541,986	267,993	72,148	77,142	36,010	22,095	66,598	100.0	49.4	13.3	14.2	6.6	4.1	12.3
Two or more races	1,265,222	1,107,727	139,250	8,444	3,484	5,324	993	100.0	87.6	11.0	0.7	0.3	0.4	0.1
2012														
White	25,238,825	306,146	857,049	3,139,878	7,229,221	7,552,960	6,153,571	100.0	1.2	3.4	12.4	28.6	29.9	24.4
Black	7,745,244	912,607	1,458,854	1,902,995	1,326,005	854,903	1,289,880	100.0	11.8	18.8	24.6	17.1	11.0	16.7
Hispanic	12,028,116	918,483	1,709,042	2,610,291	2,818,279	1,916,973	2,055,048	100.0	7.6	14.2	21.7	23.4	15.9	17.1
Asian	2,358,015	954,868	649,405	460,219	235,915	44,832	12,776	100.0	40.5	27.5	19.5	10.0	1.9	0.5
Pacific Islander	179,353	115,282	14,614	28,687	14,860	4,542	1,368	100.0	64.3	8.1	16.0	8.3	2.5	0.8
American Indian/Alaska Native	528,024	260,268	70,477	77,044	33,558	20,767	65,910	100.0	49.3	13.3	14.6	6.4	3.9	12.5
Two or more races	1,382,822	1,205,382	164,423	7,702	1,229	3,114	972	100.0	87.2	11.9	0.6	0.1	0.2	0.1

NOTE: Data reflect racial/ethnic data reported by schools. Because some schools do not report complete racial/ethnic data, totals may differ from figures in other tables. Excludes 1995 data for Idaho and 2000 data for Tennessee because racial/ethnic data were not reported. Race categories exclude persons of Hispanic ethnicity. Detail may not sum to totals because of rounding.

SOURCE: U.S. Department of Education, National Center for Education Statistics, Common Core of Data (CCD), "Public Elementary/Secondary School Universe Survey," 1995–96 through 2012–13. (This table was prepared March 2015.)

Table 216.60. Number and percentage distribution of public school students, by percentage of students in school who are eligible for free or reduced-price lunch, school level, locale, and student race/ethnicity: 2012–13

School level, locale, and student race/ethnicity	Number of students, by percent of students in school eligible for free or reduced-price lunch						Percentage distribution of students, by percent of students in school eligible for free or reduced-price lunch					
	Total[1]	0 to 25.0 percent	25.1 to 50.0 percent	50.1 to 75.0 percent	More than 75.0 percent	Missing/ school does not participate	Total[1]	0 to 25.0 percent	25.1 to 50.0 percent	50.1 to 75.0 percent	More than 75.0 percent	Missing/ school does not participate
1	2	3	4	5	6	7	8	9	10	11	12	13
Total[2]	49,460,400	10,168,747	13,775,260	13,422,528	11,705,070	388,795	100.0	20.6	27.9	27.1	23.7	0.8
White	25,238,826	7,357,513	9,113,924	6,631,280	1,935,989	200,120	100.0	29.2	36.1	26.3	7.7	0.8
Black	7,745,244	563,321	1,299,845	2,293,251	3,519,281	69,546	100.0	7.3	16.8	29.6	45.4	0.9
Hispanic	12,028,116	984,852	2,152,154	3,392,301	5,412,186	86,623	100.0	8.2	17.9	28.2	45.0	0.7
Asian	2,358,015	889,757	610,835	476,139	368,439	12,845	100.0	37.7	25.9	20.2	15.6	0.5
Pacific Islander	179,353	20,740	48,516	63,398	45,827	872	100.0	11.6	27.1	35.3	25.6	0.5
American Indian/ Alaska Native	528,024	44,583	118,037	167,857	190,600	6,947	100.0	8.4	22.4	31.8	36.1	1.3
Two or more races	1,382,822	307,981	431,949	398,302	232,748	11,842	100.0	22.3	31.2	28.8	16.8	0.9
School level[3]												
Elementary[4]	31,884,623	6,041,786	7,807,072	8,698,853	9,118,969	217,943	100.0	18.9	24.5	27.3	28.6	0.7
White	15,835,631	4,377,965	5,206,629	4,565,921	1,577,539	107,577	100.0	27.6	32.9	28.8	10.0	0.7
Black	5,002,578	296,581	677,951	1,319,711	2,671,209	37,126	100.0	5.9	13.6	26.4	53.4	0.7
Hispanic	8,116,562	566,852	1,202,014	2,081,648	4,209,749	56,299	100.0	7.0	14.8	25.6	51.9	0.7
Asian	1,509,084	560,187	360,118	297,327	285,920	5,532	100.0	37.1	23.9	19.7	18.9	0.4
Pacific Islander	114,147	11,792	25,735	39,653	36,483	484	100.0	10.3	22.5	34.7	32.0	0.4
American Indian/ Alaska Native	329,118	22,555	59,540	104,661	138,493	3,869	100.0	6.9	18.1	31.8	42.1	1.2
Two or more races	977,503	205,854	275,085	289,932	199,576	7,056	100.0	21.1	28.1	29.7	20.4	0.7
Secondary[5]	15,640,768	3,792,857	5,475,980	4,108,112	2,134,906	128,913	100.0	24.2	35.0	26.3	13.6	0.8
White	8,385,889	2,747,671	3,570,868	1,727,759	272,283	67,308	100.0	32.8	42.6	20.6	3.2	0.8
Black	2,356,184	232,459	575,796	856,361	665,001	26,567	100.0	9.9	24.4	36.3	28.2	1.1
Hispanic	3,521,681	380,521	877,394	1,187,634	1,051,218	24,914	100.0	10.8	24.9	33.7	29.8	0.7
Asian	793,635	314,672	233,386	166,408	74,617	4,552	100.0	39.6	29.4	21.0	9.4	0.6
Pacific Islander	57,227	7,984	20,903	20,823	7,246	271	100.0	14.0	36.5	36.4	12.7	0.5
American Indian/ Alaska Native	165,802	18,699	53,172	53,595	38,249	2,087	100.0	11.3	32.1	32.3	23.1	1.3
Two or more races	360,350	90,851	144,461	95,532	26,292	3,214	100.0	25.2	40.1	26.5	7.3	0.9
School locale												
City	15,013,618	1,967,769	3,053,312	3,835,501	5,996,218	160,818	100.0	13.1	20.3	25.5	39.9	1.1
White	4,563,312	1,104,514	1,545,655	1,208,967	638,933	65,243	100.0	24.2	33.9	26.5	14.0	1.4
Black	3,629,084	182,773	421,497	898,141	2,080,615	46,058	100.0	5.0	11.6	24.7	57.3	1.3
Hispanic	5,200,559	296,980	700,188	1,316,877	2,850,825	35,689	100.0	5.7	13.5	25.3	54.8	0.7
Asian	999,089	284,489	228,677	233,514	246,528	5,881	100.0	28.5	22.9	23.4	24.7	0.6
Pacific Islander	61,822	6,128	12,939	21,201	21,161	393	100.0	9.9	20.9	34.3	34.2	0.6
American Indian/ Alaska Native	112,122	12,400	25,533	31,432	41,356	1,401	100.0	11.1	22.8	28.0	36.9	1.2
Two or more races	447,630	80,485	118,823	125,369	116,800	6,153	100.0	18.0	26.5	28.0	26.1	1.4
Suburban	19,636,540	6,288,500	5,663,282	4,182,027	3,381,008	121,723	100.0	32.0	28.8	21.3	17.2	0.6
White	10,288,900	4,642,581	3,438,874	1,647,708	499,865	59,872	100.0	45.1	33.4	16.0	4.9	0.6
Black	2,677,398	314,620	636,420	865,986	842,815	17,557	100.0	11.8	23.8	32.3	31.5	0.7
Hispanic	4,755,390	568,590	1,018,896	1,295,855	1,837,953	34,096	100.0	12.0	21.4	27.3	38.6	0.7
Asian	1,160,049	547,341	315,262	188,342	103,020	6,084	100.0	47.2	27.2	16.2	8.9	0.5
Pacific Islander	75,122	12,155	24,542	21,908	16,190	327	100.0	16.2	32.7	29.2	21.6	0.4
American Indian/ Alaska Native	94,281	18,515	32,800	25,600	16,639	727	100.0	19.6	34.8	27.2	17.6	0.8
Two or more races	585,400	184,698	196,488	136,628	64,526	3,060	100.0	31.6	33.6	23.3	11.0	0.5
Town	5,670,361	437,339	1,833,627	2,270,349	1,085,023	44,023	100.0	7.7	32.3	40.0	19.1	0.8
White	3,708,893	375,100	1,491,523	1,483,619	331,333	27,318	100.0	10.1	40.2	40.0	8.9	0.7
Black	581,543	11,966	63,784	226,297	277,452	2,044	100.0	2.1	11.0	38.9	47.7	0.4
Hispanic	1,009,795	27,179	173,026	405,819	393,255	10,516	100.0	2.7	17.1	40.2	38.9	1.0
Asian	73,472	8,259	26,159	28,755	9,949	350	100.0	11.2	35.6	39.1	13.5	0.5
Pacific Islander	24,704	704	6,353	13,163	4,407	77	100.0	2.8	25.7	53.3	17.8	0.3
American Indian/ Alaska Native	124,680	4,932	27,260	47,793	42,130	2,565	100.0	4.0	21.9	38.3	33.8	2.1
Two or more races	147,274	9,199	45,522	64,903	26,497	1,153	100.0	6.2	30.9	44.1	18.0	0.8
Rural	9,139,881	1,475,139	3,225,039	3,134,651	1,242,821	62,231	100.0	16.1	35.3	34.3	13.6	0.7
White	6,677,721	1,235,318	2,637,872	2,290,986	465,858	47,687	100.0	18.5	39.5	34.3	7.0	0.7
Black	857,219	53,962	178,144	302,827	318,399	3,887	100.0	6.3	20.8	35.3	37.1	0.5
Hispanic	1,062,372	92,103	260,044	373,750	330,153	6,322	100.0	8.7	24.5	35.2	31.1	0.6
Asian	125,405	49,668	40,737	25,528	8,942	530	100.0	39.6	32.5	20.4	7.1	0.4
Pacific Islander	17,705	1,753	4,682	7,126	4,069	75	100.0	9.9	26.4	40.2	23.0	0.4
American Indian/ Alaska Native	196,941	8,736	32,444	63,032	90,475	2,254	100.0	4.4	16.5	32.0	45.9	1.1
Two or more races	202,518	33,599	71,116	71,402	24,925	1,476	100.0	16.6	35.1	35.3	12.3	0.7

[1]Includes students enrolled in schools that did not report free or reduced-price lunch eligibility.
[2]Excludes 13,630 students whose race/ethnicity was not available. Includes students who attended combined elementary/secondary schools and schools not reported by grade span, which are not shown separately.
[3]Combined elementary/secondary schools and schools not reported by grade span are not shown separately.
[4]Includes schools beginning with grade 6 or below and with no grade higher than 8.
[5]Includes schools with no grade lower than 7.
NOTE: Students with household incomes under 185 percent of the poverty threshold are eligible for free or reduced price lunch under the National School Lunch Program (NSLP). In addition, some groups of children—such as foster children, children participating in the Head Start and Migrant Education programs, and children receiving services under the Runaway and Homeless Youth Act—are assumed to be categorically eligible to participate in the NSLP. Also, under the Community Eligibility option, some nonpoor children who attend school in a low-income area may participate if the district decides that it would be more efficient to provide free lunch to all children in the school. For more information, see http://www.fns.usda.gov/nslp/national-school-lunch-program-nslp. Race categories exclude persons of Hispanic ethnicity. Detail may not sum to totals because of rounding.
SOURCE: U.S. Department of Education, National Center for Education Statistics, Common Core of Data (CCD), "Public Elementary/Secondary School Universe Survey," 2012–13. (This table was prepared December 2014.)

Table 216.70. Public elementary and secondary schools, by level, type, and state or jurisdiction: 1990–91, 2000–01, 2010–11, and 2012–13

State or jurisdiction	Total, all schools, 1990–91	Total, all schools, 2000–01	Total, all schools, 2010–11	Schools by level, 2012–13								Selected types of schools, 2012–13		
				Total, all schools	Elemen-tary[1]	Second-ary[2]	Combined elementary/secondary[3]					Alter-native[5]	Special education[5]	One-teacher schools[5]
							Total	Prekinder-garten, kindergar-ten, or 1st grade to grade 12	Other schools ending with grade 12	Other combined schools	Other[4]			
1	2	3	4	5	6	7	8	9	10	11	12	13	14	15
United States	84,538	93,273	98,817	98,454	66,718	24,280	6,371	3,104	2,400	867	1,085	5,986	2,034	196
Alabama........................	1,297	1,517	1,600	1,637	721	420	465	125	65	275	31	119	44	0
Alaska...........................	498	515	509	509	199	83	227	210	14	3	0	67	3	10
Arizona	1,049	1,724	2,265	2,267	1,342	741	161	90	47	24	23	65	22	2
Arkansas.......................	1,098	1,138	1,110	1,102	720	371	11	3	6	2	0	11	4	0
California	7,913	8,773	10,124	10,315	6,953	2,648	594	450	131	13	120	1,293	149	35
Colorado	1,344	1,632	1,796	1,825	1,294	393	138	60	62	16	0	87	7	1
Connecticut...................	985	1,248	1,157	1,148	808	284	40	12	15	13	16	50	47	0
Delaware.......................	173	191	214	224	161	39	16	11	5	0	8	6	21	0
District of Columbia	181	198	228	230	169	35	8	1	3	4	18	12	7	0
Florida..........................	2,516	3,316	4,131	4,269	2,804	703	626	244	357	25	136	424	185	2
Georgia.........................	1,734	1,946	2,449	2,387	1,784	469	57	15	26	16	77	74	59	0
Hawaii...........................	235	261	289	286	205	52	29	22	3	4	0	1	1	1
Idaho............................	582	673	748	719	444	216	59	38	15	6	0	69	11	10
Illinois	4,239	4,342	4,361	4,266	3,154	954	156	44	98	14	2	148	140	0
Indiana	1,915	1,976	1,936	1,925	1,367	451	107	55	40	12	0	9	29	0
Iowa.............................	1,588	1,534	1,436	1,390	970	381	39	4	35	0	0	30	6	3
Kansas..........................	1,477	1,430	1,378	1,351	944	360	43	12	31	0	4	2	10	0
Kentucky.......................	1,400	1,526	1,554	1,568	997	439	120	37	79	4	12	135	6	0
Louisiana	1,533	1,530	1,471	1,407	952	270	151	91	55	5	34	152	28	0
Maine............................	747	714	631	617	452	151	11	10	1	0	3	0	3	0
Maryland........................	1,220	1,383	1,449	1,449	1,132	254	49	20	21	8	14	57	39	1
Massachusetts................	1,842	1,905	1,829	1,854	1,429	373	46	13	29	4	6	20	21	2
Michigan........................	3,313	3,998	3,877	3,550	2,237	959	342	184	134	24	12	294	193	4
Minnesota......................	1,590	2,362	2,392	2,403	1,264	851	286	135	134	17	2	487	279	0
Mississippi.....................	972	1,030	1,083	1,063	623	324	108	66	41	1	8	61	4	0
Missouri........................	2,199	2,368	2,410	2,406	1,584	646	156	75	79	2	20	105	64	0
Montana........................	900	879	827	824	482	342	0	0	0	0	0	4	2	58
Nebraska.......................	1,506	1,326	1,096	1,090	718	307	12	10	1	1	53	53	26	5
Nevada..........................	354	511	645	664	476	130	38	13	25	0	20	52	12	13
New Hampshire	439	526	480	481	377	104	0	0	0	0	0	0	0	1
New Jersey....................	2,272	2,410	2,607	2,598	1,951	549	63	36	22	5	35	117	59	0
New Mexico....................	681	765	862	877	611	239	27	9	14	4	0	39	8	0
New York.......................	4,010	4,336	4,757	4,822	3,286	1,123	318	124	142	52	95	26	123	0
North Carolina	1,955	2,207	2,567	2,557	1,876	533	133	57	61	15	15	81	25	0
North Dakota	663	579	516	517	298	187	0	0	0	0	32	0	33	6
Ohio	3,731	3,916	3,758	3,685	2,500	1,018	152	50	66	36	15	6	54	1
Oklahoma......................	1,880	1,821	1,785	1,784	1,218	559	7	2	3	2	0	4	4	0
Oregon..........................	1,199	1,273	1,296	1,251	885	282	84	56	25	3	0	38	2	11
Pennsylvania..................	3,260	3,252	3,233	3,127	2,199	817	107	56	40	11	4	11	8	0
Rhode Island	309	328	317	304	226	73	5	3	1	1	0	5	2	0
South Carolina	1,097	1,127	1,214	1,239	917	284	31	8	19	4	7	21	10	0
South Dakota.................	802	769	710	697	434	239	24	10	14	0	0	34	9	11
Tennessee	1,543	1,624	1,784	1,817	1,343	376	79	37	36	6	19	21	16	0
Texas............................	5,991	7,519	8,732	8,731	5,951	2,084	690	290	227	173	6	999	22	1
Utah..............................	714	793	1,016	995	634	266	95	48	6	41	0	26	69	7
Vermont........................	397	393	320	318	234	68	16	11	5	0	0	1	0	1
Virginia..........................	1,811	1,969	2,175	2,182	1,503	408	37	24	12	1	234	196	54	0
Washington....................	1,936	2,305	2,338	2,370	1,521	631	218	147	66	5	0	322	98	5
West Virginia..................	1,015	840	757	755	566	125	64	44	15	5	0	30	3	0
Wisconsin......................	2,018	2,182	2,238	2,238	1,560	572	102	31	68	3	4	98	10	5
Wyoming........................	415	393	360	364	243	97	24	11	6	7	0	24	3	0
Bureau of Indian Education.................	—	189	173	174	110	19	45	39	3	3	0	0	0	1
DoD, domestic and overseas	—	227	191	191	142	35	14	10	4	0	0	0	0	0
Other jurisdictions														
American Samoa	30	31	28	28	22	6	0	0	0	0	0	0	0	0
Guam.........................	35	38	40	39	34	5	0	0	0	0	0	0	0	0
Northern Marianas......	26	29	30	29	21	7	0	0	0	0	1	0	0	0
Puerto Rico	1,619	1,543	1,473	1,457	860	396	170	2	2	166	31	9	23	0
U.S. Virgin Islands.......	33	36	32	31	22	9	0	0	0	0	0	0	0	0

—Not available.
[1]Includes schools beginning with grade 6 or below and with no grade higher than 8.
[2]Includes schools with no grade lower than 7.
[3]Includes schools beginning with grade 6 or below and ending with grade 9 or above.
[4]Includes schools not reported by grade span.
[5]Schools are also included under elementary, secondary, combined, or other as appropriate.
NOTE: DoD = Department of Defense.
SOURCE: U.S. Department of Education, National Center for Education Statistics, Common Core of Data (CCD), "Public Elementary/Secondary School Universe Survey," 1990–91, 2000–01, 2010–11, and 2012–13. (This table was prepared November 2014.)

Table 216.75. Public elementary schools, by grade span, average school enrollment, and state or jurisdiction: 2012–13

State or jurisdiction	Total, all elementary schools	Total, all regular elementary schools[1]	Prekindergarten, kindergarten, or 1st grade to grades 3 or 4	Prekindergarten, kindergarten, or 1st grade to grade 5	Prekindergarten, kindergarten, or 1st grade to grade 6	Prekindergarten, kindergarten, or 1st grade to grade 8	Grade 4, 5, or 6 to grade 6, 7, or 8	Other grade spans	Average school enrollment[2] All elementary schools	Average school enrollment[2] Regular elementary schools[1]
1	2	3	4	5	6	7	8	9	10	11
United States	66,718	65,581	5,104	25,257	10,415	6,444	13,061	6,437	481	486
Alabama	721	712	83	313	177	6	33	109	494	497
Alaska	199	190	3	47	88	25	24	12	332	327
Arizona	1,342	1,321	49	248	352	459	168	66	515	517
Arkansas	720	717	127	155	164	4	163	107	429	430
California	6,953	6,741	137	2,446	2,152	1,001	1,038	179	560	571
Colorado	1,294	1,289	30	606	217	117	248	76	434	435
Connecticut	808	798	96	244	74	98	151	145	436	440
Delaware	161	156	15	79	5	10	38	14	556	562
District of Columbia	169	165	8	69	4	37	25	26	327	326
Florida	2,804	2,739	31	1,678	140	220	590	145	652	665
Georgia	1,784	1,779	41	1,064	27	31	466	155	668	669
Hawaii	205	205	0	82	86	9	27	1	569	569
Idaho	444	433	35	144	136	30	75	24	392	399
Illinois	3,154	3,114	287	799	321	696	583	468	432	436
Indiana	1,367	1,365	167	475	303	42	261	119	475	475
Iowa	970	967	130	336	140	12	232	120	333	334
Kansas	944	940	90	351	174	63	199	67	338	339
Kentucky	997	987	30	478	110	74	205	100	472	476
Louisiana	952	889	73	336	110	107	200	126	482	486
Maine	452	452	65	94	54	84	86	69	264	264
Maryland	1,132	1,116	13	667	81	92	223	56	523	528
Massachusetts	1,429	1,415	188	488	119	98	293	243	437	438
Michigan	2,237	2,194	246	796	215	223	481	276	419	421
Minnesota	1,264	1,109	109	351	318	72	236	178	429	470
Mississippi	623	620	64	141	97	37	160	124	513	514
Missouri	1,584	1,573	144	504	295	113	314	214	380	381
Montana	482	479	17	56	207	112	58	32	186	186
Nebraska	718	711	57	165	279	29	100	88	277	278
Nevada	476	468	9	264	79	23	89	12	629	639
New Hampshire	377	377	57	115	36	53	82	34	331	331
New Jersey	1,951	1,932	274	563	145	289	366	314	464	468
New Mexico	611	600	18	249	124	28	130	62	364	369
New York	3,286	3,267	295	1,247	374	261	717	392	522	523
North Carolina	1,876	1,865	78	1,082	66	115	455	80	547	550
North Dakota	298	297	12	57	127	62	27	13	213	214
Ohio	2,500	2,476	386	612	340	272	548	342	432	435
Oklahoma	1,218	1,214	74	319	148	289	239	149	383	384
Oregon	885	879	28	408	129	118	174	28	403	404
Pennsylvania	2,199	2,198	287	669	422	199	416	206	481	481
Rhode Island	226	225	37	77	42	4	39	27	402	403
South Carolina	917	914	41	462	48	38	229	99	553	555
South Dakota	434	430	16	134	68	95	98	23	207	209
Tennessee	1,343	1,333	168	530	62	180	321	82	514	517
Texas	5,951	5,802	616	2,741	481	133	1,334	646	565	576
Utah	634	598	13	84	427	30	34	46	549	572
Vermont	234	234	12	26	104	63	18	11	231	231
Virginia	1,503	1,503	49	839	151	12	314	138	566	566
Washington	1,521	1,437	54	639	340	75	271	142	437	453
West Virginia	566	566	69	266	36	37	116	42	348	348
Wisconsin	1,560	1,549	153	599	144	154	323	187	367	369
Wyoming	243	241	23	63	77	13	44	23	229	230
Bureau of Indian Education	110	110	6	5	26	67	4	2	—	—
DoD, domestic and overseas	142	142	20	43	26	9	28	16	—	—
Other jurisdictions										
American Samoa	22	22	0	0	0	22	0	0	—	—
Guam	34	34	0	24	0	0	8	2	—	—
Northern Marianas	21	21	0	0	12	0	0	9	267	267
Puerto Rico	860	860	41	1	786	0	18	14	232	232
U.S. Virgin Islands	22	22	1	1	17	1	2	0	386	386

—Not available.
[1]Excludes special education and alternative schools.
[2]Average for schools reporting enrollment data. Enrollment data were available for 66,296 out of 66,718 public elementary schools in 2012–13.

NOTE: Includes schools beginning with grade 6 or below and with no grade higher than 8. Excludes schools not reported by grade level, such as some special education schools for the disabled. DoD = Department of Defense.
SOURCE: U.S. Department of Education, National Center for Education Statistics, Common Core of Data (CCD), "Public Elementary/Secondary School Universe Survey," 2012–13. (This table was prepared November 2014.)

Table 216.80. Public secondary schools, by grade span, average school enrollment, and state or jurisdiction: 2012–13

State or jurisdiction	Total, all secondary schools	Total, all regular secondary schools[1]	Grades 7 to 8 and 7 to 9	Grades 7 to 12	Grades 8 to 12	Grades 9 to 12	Grades 10 to 12	Other spans ending with grade 12	Other grade spans	Vocational schools[2]	Average school enrollment[3] — All secondary schools	Average school enrollment[3] — Regular secondary schools[1]
1	2	3	4	5	6	7	8	9	10	11	12	13
United States	24,280	19,470	2,810	3,088	783	15,995	662	343	599	1,403	689	785
Alabama	420	316	30	87	244	13	30	3	13	72	705	717
Alaska	83	61	13	21	1	46	1	1	0	3	448	558
Arizona	741	502	73	45	7	588	10	6	12	225	605	697
Arkansas	371	335	43	127	8	139	34	0	20	26	499	510
California	2,648	1,647	384	312	9	1,838	63	27	15	87	858	1,245
Colorado	393	339	43	46	2	290	5	1	6	6	631	708
Connecticut	284	203	31	19	6	189	13	20	6	16	654	847
Delaware	39	31	2	1	12	23	0	0	1	6	971	992
District of Columbia	35	31	1	1	1	27	3	0	2	3	430	452
Florida	703	506	17	39	39	581	7	13	7	51	1,199	1,502
Georgia	469	437	22	7	8	395	3	2	32	1	1,040	1,106
Hawaii	52	51	12	7	0	33	0	0	0	0	1,141	1,161
Idaho	216	143	37	48	1	119	10	0	1	10	445	606
Illinois	954	826	147	75	22	665	12	11	22	0	706	794
Indiana	451	434	75	90	3	268	4	4	7	27	827	831
Iowa	381	352	42	71	0	252	8	3	5	0	419	449
Kansas	360	354	42	84	2	228	1	2	1	1	441	446
Kentucky	439	257	26	37	10	353	4	6	3	126	654	780
Louisiana	270	217	28	47	93	85	13	0	4	9	701	747
Maine	151	122	11	13	2	119	3	2	1	27	466	472
Maryland	254	192	7	4	4	222	2	10	5	26	1,060	1,252
Massachusetts	373	322	32	38	11	284	2	4	2	39	820	835
Michigan	959	699	70	109	34	681	32	17	16	6	548	684
Minnesota	851	456	47	283	26	389	52	47	7	11	402	609
Mississippi	324	229	25	59	3	211	22	2	2	90	642	645
Missouri	646	563	61	185	1	357	19	10	13	64	527	531
Montana	342	339	171	0	0	171	0	0	0	0	157	158
Nebraska	307	300	28	164	1	109	1	4	0	0	365	365
Nevada	130	116	19	8	2	95	1	5	0	1	1,024	1,124
New Hampshire	104	104	13	0	0	87	1	0	3	0	616	616
New Jersey	549	407	52	43	14	406	7	7	20	62	827	1,041
New Mexico	239	209	37	33	0	155	8	0	6	1	469	511
New York	1,123	1,055	71	142	23	803	22	1	61	29	753	761
North Carolina	533	505	28	7	8	474	2	6	8	7	832	864
North Dakota	187	175	10	95	0	76	3	1	2	12	206	206
Ohio	1,018	933	140	133	42	662	17	14	10	70	583	596
Oklahoma	559	555	88	0	0	427	30	2	12	0	358	359
Oregon	282	261	28	49	4	197	2	2	0	0	628	667
Pennsylvania	817	721	115	147	9	472	58	6	10	87	802	814
Rhode Island	73	58	13	0	1	58	1	0	0	12	739	787
South Carolina	284	229	19	9	1	234	8	4	9	42	888	930
South Dakota	239	221	62	0	0	175	1	1	0	3	171	177
Tennessee	376	355	14	18	2	321	11	3	7	16	825	841
Texas	2,084	1,539	287	161	63	1,282	41	49	201	0	744	972
Utah	266	238	87	43	2	72	46	3	13	3	835	905
Vermont	68	52	7	19	0	27	0	0	15	15	504	513
Virginia	408	341	32	7	30	333	3	0	3	58	1,152	1,181
Washington	631	444	92	52	26	405	28	18	10	18	631	818
West Virginia	125	103	2	26	1	92	2	1	1	30	620	735
Wisconsin	572	505	56	63	4	405	14	25	5	5	487	532
Wyoming	97	80	18	14	1	62	2	0	0	0	330	380
Bureau of Indian Education	19	19	1	5	0	13	0	0	0	0	—	—
DoD, domestic and overseas	35	35	3	11	0	21	0	0	0	0	—	—
Other jurisdictions												
American Samoa	6	5	0	0	0	6	0	0	0	1	—	—
Guam	5	5	0	0	0	5	0	0	0	0	—	—
Northern Marianas	7	7	2	2	0	3	0	0	0	0	711	711
Puerto Rico	396	365	194	26	1	6	158	0	11	30	439	425
U.S. Virgin Islands	9	8	4	0	0	5	0	0	0	1	837	837

—Not available.
[1]Excludes vocational, special education, and alternative schools.
[2]Vocational schools are also included under appropriate grade span. Includes vocational schools not classified as secondary schools.
[3]Average for schools reporting enrollment data. Enrollment data were available for 22,710 out of 24,280 public secondary schools in 2012–13.

NOTE: Includes schools with no grade lower than 7. Excludes schools not reported by grade level, such as some special education schools for the disabled. DoD = Department of Defense.
SOURCE: U.S. Department of Education, National Center for Education Statistics, Common Core of Data (CCD), "Public Elementary/Secondary School Universe Survey," 2012–13. (This table was prepared November 2014.)

Table 216.90. Public elementary and secondary charter schools and enrollment, by state: Selected years, 1999–2000 through 2012–13

State	Number of charter schools					Charter school enrollment					Charter schools as a percent of total public schools				Charter school enrollment as a percent of total public school enrollment			
	1999–2000	2002–03	2009–10	2011–12	2012–13	1999–2000	2002–03	2009–10	2011–12	2012–13	1999–2000	2002–03	2009–10	2012–13	1999–2000	2002–03	2009–10	2012–13
1	2	3	4	5	6	7	8	9	10	11	12	13	14	15	16	17	18	19
United States	1,524	2,575	4,952	5,696	6,079	339,678	666,038	1,610,285	2,057,599	2,267,814	1.7	2.7	5.0	6.2	0.7	1.4	3.3	4.6
Alabama	0	0	0	0	0	0	0	0	0	0	0.0	0.0	0.0	0.0	0.0	0.0	0.0	0.0
Alaska	18	15	25	27	27	2,300	2,577	5,196	5,922	5,869	3.6	2.9	4.9	5.3	1.7	1.9	3.9	4.5
Arizona	245	325	504	531	542	31,176	56,636	113,974	136,323	151,086	14.9	17.2	22.4	23.9	3.7	6.1	10.6	13.9
Arkansas	0	7	38	41	45	0	899	8,662	11,395	13,261	0.0	0.6	3.4	4.1	0.0	0.2	1.8	2.7
California	238	409	813	985	1,085	104,730	156,696	316,658	413,124	470,880	2.8	4.5	8.1	10.5	1.8	2.5	5.1	7.6
Colorado	69	93	158	178	187	17,822	28,785	66,826	83,478	89,451	4.3	5.5	8.8	10.2	2.5	3.8	8.0	10.4
Connecticut	16	13	18	17	17	2,148	2,198	5,215	6,098	6,518	1.5	1.0	1.5	1.5	0.4	0.4	0.9	1.2
Delaware	1	11	18	22	22	115	5,060	9,173	10,322	9,942	0.5	5.5	8.3	9.8	0.1	4.3	7.3	7.8
District of Columbia	27	35	99	100	102	6,432	8,644	25,813	29,002	31,580	14.3	17.2	42.5	44.3	8.3	11.3	37.3	41.7
Florida	113	226	412	519	581	17,251	51,708	137,887	180,880	204,132	3.5	6.5	10.2	13.6	0.7	2.0	5.2	7.6
Georgia	18	48	63	128	93	11,005	25,732	37,545	79,989	64,233	1.0	2.1	2.6	3.9	0.8	1.7	2.3	3.8
Hawaii	8	25	31	31	32	790	3,354	7,869	9,165	9,635	0.8	8.8	10.7	11.2	0.4	1.8	4.4	5.2
Idaho	8	16	36	45	47	915	3,058	14,529	17,257	18,188	1.2	2.3	4.9	6.5	0.4	1.2	5.3	6.4
Illinois	17	23	39	52	58	6,152	7,466	35,836	49,070	53,829	0.4	0.5	0.9	1.4	0.3	0.4	1.7	2.6
Indiana	0	11	53	65	72	0	1,271	18,488	28,270	33,297	0.0	0.6	2.7	3.7	0.0	0.1	1.8	3.2
Iowa	0	0	9	7	3	0	0	593	403	352	0.0	0.0	0.6	0.2	0.0	0.0	0.1	0.1
Kansas	0	18	35	17	16	0	1,944	4,684	3,122	2,888	0.0	1.3	2.5	1.2	0.0	0.4	1.0	0.6
Kentucky	0	0	0	0	0	0	0	0	0	0	0.0	0.0	0.0	0.0	0.0	0.0	0.0	0.0
Louisiana	16	20	77	99	104	2,449	4,730	31,467	44,330	45,293	1.0	1.3	5.2	7.4	0.3	0.6	4.6	6.5
Maine	0	0	0	0	2	0	0	0	0	106	0.0	0.0	0.0	0.3	0.0	0.0	0.0	0.1
Maryland	0	0	42	50	52	0	0	11,995	17,273	18,943	0.0	0.0	2.9	3.6	0.0	0.0	1.4	2.2
Massachusetts	40	47	62	72	77	12,518	15,912	27,393	30,595	31,830	2.1	2.5	3.4	4.2	1.3	1.6	2.9	3.3
Michigan	193	198	294	306	346	46,078	68,081	110,504	118,177	126,602	4.9	4.9	7.6	9.7	2.8	3.8	6.8	8.4
Minnesota	62	94	181	174	176	7,794	12,144	35,375	39,143	41,615	2.6	3.8	7.4	7.3	0.9	1.4	4.2	4.9
Mississippi	1	1	1	0	0	347	335	375	0	0	0.1	0.1	0.1	0.0	0.1	0.1	0.1	0.0
Missouri	15	25	48	61	57	4,303	9,743	18,415	21,472	17,925	0.6	1.0	2.0	2.4	0.5	1.1	2.0	2.0
Montana	0	0	0	0	0	0	0	0	0	0	0.0	0.0	0.0	0.0	0.0	0.0	0.0	0.0
Nebraska	0	0	0	0	0	0	0	0	0	0	0.0	0.0	0.0	0.0	0.0	0.0	0.0	0.0
Nevada	5	13	35	39	40	898	2,788	11,613	18,255	22,199	1.0	2.4	5.5	6.0	0.3	0.8	2.7	5.0
New Hampshire	0	0	15	15	22	0	0	816	1,169	1,739	0.0	0.0	3.1	4.6	0.0	0.0	0.4	0.9
New Jersey	0	50	70	86	86	0	12,526	22,981	29,007	29,540	0.0	2.0	2.7	3.3	0.0	0.9	1.7	2.2
New Mexico	1	27	72	84	94	22	4,404	13,090	16,864	19,916	0.1	3.3	8.4	10.7	#	1.4	3.9	5.9
New York	5	44	140	183	211	0	10,410	43,963	60,137	78,139	0.1	0.9	3.0	4.4	—	0.4	1.6	2.9
North Carolina	82	93	96	100	108	12,691	20,420	38,973	45,496	50,060	3.8	4.1	3.8	4.2	1.0	1.5	2.6	3.3
North Dakota	0	0	0	0	0	0	0	375	0	0	0.0	0.0	0.0	0.0	0.0	0.0	0.0	0.0
Ohio	48	134	323	355	368	9,809	34,028	90,989	107,089	114,459	1.2	3.4	8.5	10.0	0.5	1.9	5.2	6.6
Oklahoma	0	10	18	21	23	0	2,712	6,315	9,229	12,037	0.0	0.6	1.0	1.3	0.0	0.4	1.0	1.8
Oregon	1	21	102	115	123	109	1,959	18,334	24,205	27,077	0.1	1.7	7.8	9.8	#	0.4	3.3	4.9
Pennsylvania	47	91	134	162	175	11,413	32,862	79,167	104,967	118,430	1.5	2.8	4.1	5.6	0.6	1.8	4.5	6.8
Rhode Island	2	7	12	18	18	446	705	3,233	4,662	5,131	0.6	2.1	3.7	5.9	0.3	0.4	2.3	3.6
South Carolina	7	13	39	47	55	327	1,132	13,035	17,034	20,067	0.6	1.1	3.2	4.4	#	0.2	1.8	2.7
South Dakota	0	0	0	0	0	0	0	0	0	0	0.0	0.0	0.0	0.0	0.0	0.0	0.0	0.0
Tennessee	0	0	20	40	51	0	0	4,343	9,104	11,698	0.0	0.0	1.1	2.8	0.0	0.0	0.4	1.2
Texas	176	263	536	581	628	25,687	53,988	148,392	189,654	215,082	2.4	3.3	6.2	7.2	0.6	1.3	3.1	4.2
Utah	6	12	72	81	88	390	1,558	33,968	44,687	50,694	0.8	1.5	6.9	8.8	0.1	0.3	5.8	8.3
Vermont	0	0	0	0	0	0	0	0	0	0	0.0	0.0	0.0	0.0	0.0	0.0	0.0	0.0
Virginia	0	7	3	4	4	0	466	179	393	399	0.0	0.3	0.1	0.2	0.0	#	#	#
Washington	0	0	0	0	0	0	0	0	0	0	0.0	0.0	0.0	0.0	0.0	0.0	0.0	0.0
West Virginia	0	0	0	0	0	0	0	0	0	0	0.0	0.0	0.0	0.0	0.0	0.0	0.0	0.0
Wisconsin	45	129	206	234	238	3,561	19,005	36,153	40,531	43,323	2.1	5.8	9.2	10.6	0.4	2.2	4.1	5.0
Wyoming	0	1	3	4	4	0	102	269	306	369	0.0	0.3	0.8	1.1	0.0	0.1	0.3	0.4

—Not available.
#Rounds to zero.

SOURCE: U.S. Department of Education, National Center for Education Statistics, Common Core of Data (CCD), "Public Elementary/Secondary School Universe Survey," 1999–2000 through 2012–13. (This table was prepared December 2014.)

Table 216.95. Number and enrollment of public elementary and secondary schools that have closed, by school level, type, and charter status: Selected years, 1995–96 through 2012–13

School level, type, and charter status	1995–96	1999–2000	2000–01	2001–02	2002–03	2003–04	2004–05	2005–06	2006–07	2007–08	2008–09	2009–10	2010–11	2011–12	2012–13
1	2	3	4	5	6	7	8	9	10	11	12	13	14	15	16
	Number of schools that closed														
Total, all schools....................	954	1,180	1,193	1,412	1,368	2,168	1,913	1,553	1,877	2,120	1,515	1,822	1,929	1,840	1,493
School type															
Regular...............................	686	970	908	1,018	985	1,248	1,190	1,171	1,348	1,450	1,059	1,321	1,486	1,340	1,075
Special education	110	86	84	118	91	114	271	88	160	195	99	235	72	87	83
Vocational................................	17	18	17	90	27	33	18	28	14	30	15	11	7	11	66
Alternative[1]...............................	141	106	184	186	265	773	434	266	355	445	342	255	364	402	269
School level and type															
Elementary[2]............................	497	559	601	697	721	947	901	770	846	844	769	936	1,073	1,020	776
Regular............................	449	529	563	648	660	870	847	725	771	804	713	893	1,010	959	726
Special education.......................	28	16	20	21	26	23	25	13	53	20	22	13	18	18	18
Vocational............................	0	0	2	0	0	0	0	1	1	0	1	0	0	0	0
Alternative[1].............................	20	14	16	28	35	54	29	31	21	20	33	30	45	43	32
Secondary[3]............................	199	300	302	313	245	347	302	342	308	394	368	346	436	451	421
Regular............................	114	235	173	141	127	144	177	192	171	233	186	212	237	238	204
Special education.......................	12	8	19	12	9	10	4	11	24	19	21	12	15	15	24
Vocational............................	17	18	14	89	27	33	18	27	13	29	13	11	7	10	64
Alternative[1].............................	56	39	96	71	82	160	103	112	100	113	148	111	177	188	129
Combined elementary/secondary[4]....	42	143	146	168	124	158	321	184	193	172	164	91	157	207	170
Regular............................	10	96	83	76	57	54	68	82	65	65	50	42	74	82	64
Special education.......................	13	17	22	29	22	30	28	38	45	48	34	16	24	34	34
Vocational............................	0	0	1	1	0	0	0	0	0	1	1	0	0	1	2
Alternative[1].............................	19	30	40	62	45	74	225	64	83	58	79	33	59	90	70
Other (not classified by grade span).	216	178	144	234	278	716	389	257	530	710	214	449	263	162	126
Regular............................	113	110	89	153	141	180	98	172	341	348	110	174	165	61	81
Special education.......................	57	45	23	56	34	51	214	26	38	108	22	194	15	20	7
Vocational............................	0	0	0	0	0	0	0	0	0	0	0	0	0	0	0
Alternative[1].............................	46	23	32	25	103	485	77	59	151	254	82	81	83	81	38
All charter schools[5].............................	—	24	72	111	85	74	171	206	267	133	161	189	216	202	183
	Prior year enrollment of schools that have closed														
Total, enrollment..................	173,766	187,493	209,228	171,669	195,033	262,183	297,487	229,259	242,388	268,212	243,166	306,806	321,246	300,764	240,704
School type															
Regular...............................	151,574	175,083	198,699	161,663	185,536	242,383	282,432	216,360	227,260	253,409	227,714	292,915	304,001	281,961	227,444
Special education	4,475	2,873	1,665	2,840	1,789	4,144	2,799	3,068	4,745	4,060	1,916	2,173	1,709	3,765	1,168
Vocational................................	1,613	1,021	632	75	223	719	2,975	73	429	183	1,665	767	22	26	289
Alternative[1]...............................	16,104	8,516	8,232	7,091	7,485	14,937	9,281	9,758	9,954	10,560	11,871	10,951	15,514	15,012	11,803
School level and type															
Elementary[2]............................	112,328	128,426	134,934	125,753	146,709	194,752	213,607	161,649	172,403	179,554	171,722	221,681	242,193	225,205	174,885
Regular............................	108,440	126,944	134,060	124,170	144,013	192,117	211,822	158,744	169,895	176,862	169,815	219,469	239,913	222,186	173,272
Special education.......................	2,991	734	338	591	1,020	1,040	1,153	1,158	1,892	2,131	651	727	404	1,539	272
Vocational............................	0	0	2	0	0	0	0	0	9	0	569	0	0	0	0
Alternative[1].............................	897	748	534	992	1,676	1,595	632	1,747	607	561	687	1,485	1,876	1,480	1,341
Secondary[3]............................	48,074	44,371	47,950	30,817	33,243	52,437	60,029	54,489	55,834	66,163	55,261	68,548	56,935	54,558	51,820
Regular............................	39,307	39,919	42,666	27,752	30,271	42,750	51,547	49,335	48,797	60,085	45,800	60,734	48,430	46,345	43,775
Special education.......................	398	509	121	175	357	172	108	83	1,126	440	501	508	520	404	500
Vocational............................	1,613	1,021	592	72	223	719	2,975	73	420	183	1,096	767	22	19	202
Alternative[1].............................	6,756	2,922	4,571	2,818	2,392	8,796	5,399	4,998	5,491	5,455	7,864	6,539	7,963	7,790	7,343
Combined elementary/secondary[4]....	12,418	13,083	25,031	12,622	12,957	13,150	22,022	12,993	12,157	19,349	16,093	12,151	21,360	20,931	13,963
Regular............................	3,743	8,044	21,973	8,999	9,451	7,484	18,415	8,281	7,682	16,295	12,081	8,342	14,941	13,430	10,361
Special education.......................	326	515	701	410	365	1,328	840	1,791	1,293	1,008	692	882	744	1,752	396
Vocational............................	0	0	38	3	0	0	0	0	0	0	0	0	0	7	87
Alternative[1].............................	8,349	4,524	2,319	3,210	3,141	4,338	2,767	2,921	3,182	2,046	3,320	2,927	5,675	5,742	3,119
Other (not classified by grade span).	946	1,613	1,313	2,477	2,124	1,844	1,829	128	1,994	3,146	90	4,426	758	70	36
Regular............................	84	176	0	742	1,801	32	648	0	886	167	18	4,370	717	0	36
Special education.......................	760	1,115	505	1,664	47	1,604	698	36	434	481	72	56	41	70	0
Vocational............................	0	0	0	0	0	0	0	0	0	0	0	0	0	0	0
Alternative[1].............................	102	322	808	71	276	208	483	92	674	2,498	0	0	0	0	0
All charter schools[5].............................	—	7,141	5,925	11,134	11,894	6,797	21,505	14,118	15,340	12,226	20,537	17,954	24,165	29,095	24,437

—Not available.
[1]Includes schools that provide nontraditional education, address needs of students that typically cannot be met in regular schools, serve as adjuncts to regular schools, or fall outside the categories of regular, special education, or vocational education.
[2]Includes schools beginning with grade 6 or below and with no grade higher than 8.
[3]Includes schools with no grade lower than 7.
[4]Includes schools beginning with grade 6 or below and ending with grade 9 or above.
[5]Charter schools are also included under the school level and type categories, as appropriate.

NOTE: This table indicates the school year by which the school no longer operated (generally it closed between that school year and the prior school year). The closure of a school does not necessarily mean that a building is no longer used for educational purposes. A single school may share a building with another school, or one school may be housed in several buildings.
SOURCE: U.S. Department of Education, National Center for Education Statistics, Common Core of Data (CCD), "Public Elementary/Secondary School Universe Survey," 1995–96 through 2012–13. (This table was prepared May 2015.)

Table 217.10. Functional age of public schools' main instructional buildings and percentage of schools with permanent and portable (temporary) buildings, by selected school characteristics and condition of permanent and portable buildings: 2012

[Standard errors appear in parentheses]

Functional age of main instructional building; presence and condition of permanent and portable buildings	All public schools[1]	Instructional level			Community type				Percent of students eligible for free or reduced-price lunch			
		Elementary	Secondary	Combined	City	Suburban	Town	Rural	Less than 35 percent	35 to 49 percent	50 to 74 percent	75 percent or more
1	2	3	4	5	6	7	8	9	10	11	12	13
Estimated number of schools	84,000 (†)	62,600 (†)	18,900 (†)	2,400 (†)	21,200 (†)	23,500 (†)	10,900 (†)	28,400 (†)	31 (†)	18 (†)	27 (†)	23 (†)
Main instructional building												
Percent of schools, by functional age[2]												
Less than 5 years old	21 (1.1)	19 (1.2)	25 (2.2)	27 (6.8)	24 (2.6)	23 (2.2)	19 (2.9)	17 (1.9)	20 (2.1)	23 (2.9)	18 (2.0)	24 (2.5)
5 to 14 years old	38 (1.2)	37 (1.4)	39 (2.3)	34 (7.2)	33 (2.5)	39 (2.7)	37 (4.1)	40 (2.3)	40 (2.2)	34 (3.3)	39 (2.6)	35 (3.0)
15 to 34 years old	23 (1.2)	25 (1.6)	17 (1.8)	28 (7.5)	20 (2.3)	20 (1.8)	27 (2.3)	28 (2.3)	25 (2.1)	22 (2.9)	25 (2.3)	20 (2.7)
35 or more years old	18 (1.2)	19 (1.4)	18 (1.7)	11 ! (4.3)	22 (2.4)	19 (2.2)	17 (3.0)	15 (1.9)	15 (2.0)	21 (2.9)	17 (2.1)	21 (2.8)
Average years												
Since construction[3]	44 (0.7)	45 (0.9)	43 (1.2)	50 (4.2)	50 (1.7)	43 (1.2)	48 (1.8)	40 (1.2)	42 (1.3)	46 (1.8)	43 (1.4)	48 (1.9)
Since major renovation[3]	12 (0.4)	12 (0.5)	11 (0.7)	12 (2.0)	11 (0.7)	11 (0.7)	14 (1.2)	12 (0.8)	11 (0.6)	12 (1.1)	12 (0.8)	11 (0.8)
Permanent buildings (percent of schools)												
School has permanent buildings[4]	99 (0.2)	99 (0.3)	100 (0.3)	100 (#)	99 (0.7)	100 (0.4)	99 (0.6)	100 (0.3)	100 (0.4)	99 (0.6)	100 (#)	98 (0.8)
Overall condition of buildings[4]												
Excellent	20 (1.1)	20 (1.4)	20 (1.5)	15 ! (5.5)	17 (2.0)	23 (2.2)	18 (3.3)	20 (1.8)	24 (2.0)	18 (2.3)	20 (2.1)	16 (2.0)
Good	56 (1.4)	57 (1.7)	57 (2.2)	44 (7.0)	55 (2.6)	56 (2.6)	57 (3.8)	57 (2.5)	56 (2.3)	63 (3.5)	56 (2.7)	52 (3.2)
Fair	21 (1.0)	21 (1.3)	20 (2.0)	38 (7.4)	23 (2.3)	20 (2.1)	23 (3.2)	20 (2.0)	18 (1.9)	17 (2.0)	22 (2.0)	28 (2.7)
Poor	3 (0.5)	3 (0.6)	2 ! (0.7)	‡ (†)	5 (1.3)	‡ (†)	‡ (†)	2 ! (0.8)	2 ! (0.8)	2 ! (0.9)	2 ! (1.0)	4 (1.3)
Environmental factors are unsatisfactory[5]												
Lighting, artificial	8 (0.9)	8 (1.1)	7 (1.4)	‡ (†)	9 (1.6)	7 (1.4)	8 (2.1)	9 (1.4)	6 (1.4)	7 (1.8)	8 (1.8)	11 (1.9)
Lighting, natural	16 (1.1)	17 (1.4)	16 (1.7)	15 ! (5.3)	16 (2.2)	15 (2.0)	20 (3.2)	16 (1.9)	14 (1.7)	17 (2.7)	17 (2.0)	19 (2.6)
Heating	14 (0.9)	13 (1.2)	16 (2.1)	20 ! (6.2)	16 (2.1)	10 (1.6)	14 (2.4)	14 (1.7)	12 (1.6)	14 (2.4)	14 (2.2)	15 (2.3)
Air conditioning	17 (1.1)	16 (1.4)	20 (2.3)	21 (6.7)	21 (2.5)	13 (1.9)	18 (3.2)	17 (2.0)	17 (1.9)	16 (2.7)	15 (2.5)	19 (2.7)
Ventilation	17 (1.2)	16 (1.4)	16 (1.8)	28 (7.3)	18 (1.8)	12 (1.9)	16 (2.2)	20 (2.1)	15 (1.9)	16 (2.6)	16 (1.8)	20 (2.7)
Indoor air quality	9 (0.8)	9 (1.0)	9 (1.4)	13 ! (5.0)	11 (1.8)	4 (1.0)	7 (1.7)	12 (1.7)	7 (1.2)	9 (2.1)	11 (1.8)	10 (1.9)
Water quality	5 (0.6)	5 (0.8)	6 (1.1)	16 ! (6.4)	6 (1.5)	3 (0.9)	5 (1.6)	7 (1.3)	4 (1.0)	5 (1.5)	6 (1.4)	7 (1.4)
Acoustics or noise control	14 (1.0)	14 (1.3)	12 (1.5)	25 (6.2)	14 (2.1)	10 (1.5)	15 (3.0)	16 (2.0)	12 (1.7)	13 (2.4)	13 (1.8)	17 (2.3)
Portable (temporary) buildings (percent of schools)												
School has portable buildings[6]	31 (1.4)	33 (1.8)	24 (2.0)	29 (6.8)	40 (2.8)	32 (2.2)	27 (3.6)	25 (2.1)	25 (2.0)	30 (2.9)	31 (2.2)	39 (3.4)
Overall condition of buildings[6]												
Excellent	6 (1.1)	6 (1.4)	5 ! (1.5)	‡ (†)	4 ! (1.8)	5 ! (1.8)	10 ! (4.7)	7 ! (2.3)	8 ! (2.7)	7 ! (3.0)	4 ! (1.9)	5 ! (2.0)
Good	49 (2.8)	49 (3.2)	46 (4.4)	56 (14.2)	53 (4.2)	51 (4.9)	43 (7.7)	44 (5.0)	51 (4.8)	53 (6.1)	45 (4.4)	48 (5.0)
Fair	36 (2.4)	36 (2.9)	43 (4.8)	‡ (†)	34 (4.1)	38 (4.8)	38 (7.5)	36 (4.8)	29 (4.1)	36 (5.9)	41 (4.2)	38 (4.6)
Poor	9 (1.4)	9 (1.7)	7 ! (2.3)	‡ (†)	8 ! (2.6)	6 ! (2.0)	9 ! (4.1)	13 (3.5)	12 (3.2)	‡ (†)	10 ! (3.2)	8 ! (3.0)
Environmental factors are unsatisfactory[7]												
Lighting, artificial	11 (1.8)	11 (2.1)	12 (3.3)	‡ (†)	10 (2.9)	6 ! (2.6)	14 ! (5.7)	15 (4.0)	10 ! (3.0)	8 ! (3.5)	12 (3.3)	12 (3.3)
Lighting, natural	28 (2.5)	29 (3.0)	28 (4.3)	‡ (†)	26 (4.2)	26 (4.4)	41 (8.0)	28 (4.4)	26 (4.1)	28 (4.9)	29 (4.8)	30 (4.5)
Heating	12 (1.8)	11 (2.0)	16 (3.5)	‡ (†)	11 (2.4)	7 ! (2.4)	17 ! (5.3)	16 (4.0)	13 (3.5)	8 ! (3.5)	15 (3.5)	10 (3.1)
Air conditioning	15 (2.2)	16 (2.6)	14 (3.3)	‡ (†)	15 (3.6)	12 (3.1)	14 ! (5.3)	18 (4.3)	17 (3.9)	13 ! (4.1)	16 (3.9)	14 (3.7)
Ventilation	19 (2.2)	19 (2.6)	22 (3.9)	‡ (†)	18 (3.7)	14 (3.1)	26 (6.7)	24 (4.4)	18 (3.9)	18 ! (5.7)	23 (4.6)	18 (4.0)
Indoor air quality	16 (2.0)	17 (2.3)	14 (3.0)	‡ (†)	17 (3.6)	11 (2.8)	18 ! (5.5)	19 (4.2)	18 (3.4)	15 ! (4.4)	19 (4.1)	16 (3.6)
Water quality	10 (1.7)	10 (2.0)	8 ! (3.1)	‡ (†)	7 ! (2.7)	7 ! (2.9)	16 ! (6.7)	14 ! (4.6)	9 ! (3.8)	‡ (†)	11 ! (3.8)	14 (3.8)
Acoustics or noise control	21 (2.5)	21 (2.9)	21 (4.1)	‡ (†)	19 (3.6)	17 (3.9)	24 ! (7.1)	26 (4.6)	19 (4.2)	11 ! (4.2)	26 (4.6)	23 (4.7)

†Not applicable.
#Rounds to zero.
!Interpret data with caution. The coefficient of variation (CV) for this estimate is between 30 and 50 percent.
‡Reporting standards not met. Either there are too few cases for a reliable estimate or the coefficient of variation (CV) for this estimate is 50 percent or greater.
[1]Excludes special education, vocational, and alternative schools; schools without enrollment data; and schools offering only prekindergarten–preprimary education.
[2]The functional age of the main instructional building is the number of years since its most recent major renovation or since its construction if no major renovation has ever occurred.
[3]Based on schools whose main instructional building has undergone a major renovation.

[4]Based on the 99 percent of public schools with permanent buildings.
[5]Based on schools with the specified environmental factor in their permanent buildings. Includes ratings of "unsatisfactory" and "very unsatisfactory."
[6]Based on the 31 percent of public schools with portable (temporary) buildings.
[7]Based on schools with the specified environmental factor in their portable (temporary) buildings. Includes ratings of "unsatisfactory" and "very unsatisfactory."
NOTE: Detail may not sum to totals because of rounding.
SOURCE: U.S. Department of Education, National Center for Education Statistics, Fast Response Survey System (FRSS), "Condition of Public School Facilities: 2012–13," FRSS 105, 2013. (This table was prepared June 2014.)

Table 217.15. Percentage of public schools with plans for major repair, renovation, or replacement of building systems or features in the next 2 years and percentage distribution of schools with such plans, by selected school characteristics, type of system or feature, and main reason for the plans: 2012–13

[Standard errors appear in parentheses]

Type of system or feature and main reason for major repair, renovation, or replacement plans	All public schools	Instructional level			Community type				Percent of students eligible for free or reduced-priced lunch			
		Elementary	Secondary	Combined	City	Suburban	Town	Rural	Less than 35 percent	35 to 49 percent	50 to 74 percent	75 percent or more
1	2	3	4	5	6	7	8	9	10	11	12	13
Roofs—percent of schools with plans	19 (1.1)	17 (1.3)	25 (1.8)	25 (6.8)	19 (2.1)	19 (2.0)	20 (3.0)	19 (1.9)	22 (1.8)	18 (2.4)	17 (2.0)	18 (2.3)
Percentage distribution by main reason for the plans	100 (†)	100 (†)	100 (†)	100 (†)	100 (†)	100 (†)	100 (†)	100 (†)	100 (†)	100 (†)	100 (†)	100 (†)
Functional problem in existing system or feature	39 (3.1)	38 (3.9)	41 (4.4)	31! (14.2)	35 (6.0)	40 (5.6)	50 (10.0)	35 (5.3)	33 (4.5)	45 (7.5)	40 (5.8)	42 (7.1)
Improve operational or energy efficiency	9 (1.7)	8 (2.1)	9 (2.6)	30! (15.1)	6! (2.9)	8! (3.0)	‡ (†)	13! (4.1)	6! (2.2)	‡ (†)	8! (3.2)	17! (5.4)
Replacement cycle	46 (3.1)	47 (4.2)	45 (4.7)	38! (12.3)	50 (5.9)	46 (5.3)	36 (9.0)	49 (5.8)	55 (5.0)	46 (7.6)	49 (5.4)	30 (6.5)
Other reason	6 (1.5)	7! (2.2)	5! (1.7)	# (†)	8! (3.7)	‡ (†)	‡ (†)	‡ (†)	7! (2.9)	‡ (†)	‡ (†)	11! (4.9)
Framing, floors, foundations—percent of schools with plans	7 (0.7)	5 (0.9)	8 (1.4)	22! (6.8)	7 (1.2)	7 (1.3)	7 (2.0)	5 (1.1)	6 (1.1)	5 (1.3)	6 (1.4)	8 (1.6)
Percentage distribution by main reason for the plans	100 (†)	100 (†)	100 (†)	100 (†)	100 (†)	100 (†)	100 (†)	100 (†)	100 (†)	100 (†)	100 (†)	100 (†)
Functional problem in existing system or feature	41 (4.9)	40 (6.2)	42 (7.1)	48! (19.9)	37 (9.4)	38 (9.9)	53 (15.6)	41 (11.6)	27! (8.1)	58 (12.6)	37! (11.3)	51 (9.8)
Improve operational or energy efficiency	16 (3.8)	12! (4.7)	17! (6.6)	43! (18.9)	19! (8.9)	14! (6.8)	20! (9.6)	‡ (†)	15! (6.7)	‡ (†)	21! (9.0)	‡ (†)
Replacement cycle	27 (4.5)	30 (6.0)	26 (6.9)	‡ (†)	27 (7.5)	23! (9.4)	‡ (†)	32! (10.6)	38 (9.7)	‡ (†)	33! (11.0)	17! (7.5)
Other reason	16 (3.9)	19! (5.7)	15! (7.1)	# (†)	16! (7.4)	24! (9.1)	24! (11.5)	‡ (†)	20! (8.9)	‡ (†)	‡ (†)	16! (7.5)
Exterior walls, finishes—percent of schools with plans	9 (0.7)	8 (0.9)	10 (1.3)	17! (6.0)	9 (1.5)	8 (1.3)	9 (1.9)	8 (1.3)	9 (1.3)	9 (1.7)	8 (1.3)	10 (1.8)
Percentage distribution by main reason for the plans	100 (†)	100 (†)	100 (†)	100 (†)	100 (†)	100 (†)	100 (†)	100 (†)	100 (†)	100 (†)	100 (†)	100 (†)
Functional problem in existing system or feature	38 (4.5)	36 (5.6)	46 (7.5)	‡ (†)	33 (7.1)	39 (9.5)	53 (11.8)	35 (8.9)	38 (8.1)	37! (11.4)	46 (10.5)	31 (8.8)
Improve operational or energy efficiency	21 (3.6)	19 (4.5)	23! (7.1)	‡ (†)	20! (7.0)	17! (6.6)	18! (7.3)	26! (8.5)	14! (5.4)	20! (7.7)	23! (9.3)	29! (8.8)
Replacement cycle	23 (3.7)	26 (5.1)	18 (4.9)	‡ (†)	31! (7.7)	25! (7.7)	‡ (†)	23! (8.1)	32 (8.1)	18! (8.8)	21! (7.6)	19! (8.0)
Other reason	18 (3.9)	20 (5.2)	14! (5.9)	‡ (†)	16! (7.3)	19! (8.1)	24! (11.5)	15! (6.6)	16! (7.4)	25! (10.5)	‡ (†)	20! (8.3)
Windows, doors—percent of schools with plans	15 (0.9)	13 (1.1)	21 (2.1)	21! (6.7)	15 (2.1)	14 (1.8)	18 (2.7)	16 (1.8)	15 (1.8)	15 (2.2)	15 (1.9)	16 (2.2)
Percentage distribution by main reason for the plans	100 (†)	100 (†)	100 (†)	100 (†)	100 (†)	100 (†)	100 (†)	100 (†)	100 (†)	100 (†)	100 (†)	100 (†)
Functional problem in existing system or feature	30 (3.4)	29 (4.5)	31 (4.8)	40! (16.8)	24 (5.4)	30 (7.0)	40 (9.6)	31 (6.3)	28 (6.2)	27 (7.7)	37 (7.5)	30 (6.4)
Improve operational or energy efficiency	43 (3.9)	41 (4.7)	45 (6.1)	60 (16.8)	34 (6.7)	36 (7.2)	43 (9.8)	54 (7.1)	39 (6.9)	52 (9.2)	46 (7.3)	36 (8.0)
Replacement cycle	17 (2.6)	19 (3.4)	14 (3.8)	# (†)	31 (6.7)	21 (5.8)	‡ (†)	10! (3.9)	20 (4.9)	12! (5.5)	13! (4.4)	22! (6.6)
Other reason	10 (2.3)	11 (2.9)	10! (3.3)	# (†)	11! (5.1)	13! (4.8)	14! (6.3)	‡ (†)	13! (4.8)	‡ (†)	‡ (†)	12! (4.9)
Interior finishes, trim—percent of schools with plans	12 (0.8)	11 (1.0)	13 (1.5)	25 (6.8)	13 (1.7)	13 (1.6)	12 (2.3)	11 (1.3)	14 (1.6)	9 (1.7)	11 (1.7)	12 (1.9)
Percentage distribution by main reason for the plans	100 (†)	100 (†)	100 (†)	100 (†)	100 (†)	100 (†)	100 (†)	100 (†)	100 (†)	100 (†)	100 (†)	100 (†)
Functional problem in existing system or feature	19 (3.1)	17 (3.7)	27 (5.3)	‡ (†)	19 (5.5)	20! (6.1)	32! (11.5)	13! (5.7)	17! (5.4)	16! (6.2)	27 (7.0)	16! (5.8)
Improve operational or energy efficiency	20 (3.2)	17 (3.7)	24! (6.2)	33! (16.4)	18 (5.4)	17! (5.2)	33! (10.9)	19! (6.2)	14! (4.8)	‡ (†)	20 (5.7)	31 (8.0)
Replacement cycle	44 (3.9)	48 (5.1)	31 (5.1)	49! (15.3)	45 (7.6)	46 (6.9)	30! (10.8)	47 (7.7)	50 (6.9)	44 (9.0)	39 (7.8)	39 (9.0)
Other reason	17 (3.0)	18 (4.0)	19! (5.7)	# (†)	18! (6.5)	18! (5.7)	‡ (†)	22 (6.2)	19! (5.9)	26! (8.4)	13! (5.8)	14! (5.7)

See notes at end of table.

Table 217.15.   Percentage of public schools with plans for major repair, renovation, or replacement of building systems or features in the next 2 years and percentage distribution of schools with such plans, by selected school characteristics, type of system or feature, and main reason for the plans: 2012–13—Continued

[Standard errors appear in parentheses]

Type of system or feature and main reason for major repair, renovation, or replacement plans	All public schools	Instructional level			Community type				Percent of students eligible for free or reduced-priced lunch			
		Elementary	Secondary	Combined	City	Suburban	Town	Rural	Less than 35 percent	35 to 49 percent	50 to 74 percent	75 percent or more
1	2	3	4	5	6	7	8	9	10	11	12	13
Plumbing/lavatories—percent of schools with plans	13 (1.0)	12 (1.2)	17 (1.8)	28 (7.2)	15 (2.0)	13 (1.9)	16 (2.4)	11 (1.5)	13 (1.8)	13 (2.0)	13 (1.7)	13 (2.2)
Percentage distribution by main reason for the plans	100 (†)	100 (†)	100 (†)	100 (†)	100 (†)	100 (†)	100 (†)	100 (†)	100 (†)	100 (†)	100 (†)	100 (†)
Functional problem in existing system or feature	25 (3.7)	25 (4.6)	21 (3.8)	46! (16.6)	29 (7.0)	22 (6.1)	26! (7.9)	24 (7.2)	26 (7.4)	29 (8.6)	27 (6.1)	20! (6.5)
Improve operational or energy efficiency	35 (3.8)	32 (4.7)	41 (5.9)	44! (15.0)	27 (6.4)	33 (6.9)	49 (9.6)	39 (7.7)	24 (5.7)	29 (8.0)	47 (7.6)	42 (7.6)
Replacement cycle	26 (3.1)	28 (4.4)	25 (5.0)	‡ (†)	34 (6.7)	22 (4.8)	19! (7.7)	27 (6.5)	29 (5.8)	25! (7.6)	23 (6.3)	28 (7.3)
Other reason	13 (2.5)	14 (3.5)	13! (4.1)	# (†)	10! (4.5)	24 (5.6)	‡ (†)	10! (4.8)	22 (5.5)	16! (6.6)	‡ (†)	10! (4.9)
Heating system—percent of schools with plans	16 (1.1)	14 (1.2)	21 (2.1)	29 (6.8)	15 (2.0)	17 (1.9)	15 (2.5)	16 (1.8)	18 (1.7)	15 (2.0)	16 (1.9)	15 (2.2)
Percentage distribution by main reason for the plans	100 (†)	100 (†)	100 (†)	100 (†)	100 (†)	100 (†)	100 (†)	100 (†)	100 (†)	100 (†)	100 (†)	100 (†)
Functional problem in existing system or feature	26 (2.9)	23 (3.7)	31 (4.7)	33! (14.0)	24 (6.1)	24 (6.0)	32 (8.8)	27 (6.0)	23 (5.3)	31 (8.1)	23 (5.3)	30 (7.6)
Improve operational or energy efficiency	41 (3.1)	34 (3.7)	54 (5.4)	54 (14.1)	34 (6.8)	37 (5.4)	38 (9.6)	51 (6.8)	31 (5.0)	38 (8.1)	53 (6.8)	45 (7.6)
Replacement cycle	27 (2.9)	35 (4.0)	13! (4.4)	‡ (†)	35 (6.5)	31 (6.0)	23! (8.4)	20 (5.1)	38 (7.9)	30 (7.9)	20 (5.5)	17! (6.4)
Other reason	6 (1.7)	8! (2.7)	‡ (†)	# (†)	‡ (†)	8! (3.5)	‡ (†)	‡ (†)	8! (3.8)	‡ (†)	‡ (†)	‡ (†)
Air conditioning system—percent of schools with plans	16 (1.1)	14 (1.3)	22 (2.2)	17! (5.2)	18 (2.4)	16 (2.0)	14 (2.7)	16 (1.9)	14 (1.7)	18 (2.6)	17 (2.3)	16 (2.5)
Percentage distribution by main reason for the plans	100 (†)	100 (†)	100 (†)	100 (†)	100 (†)	100 (†)	100 (†)	100 (†)	100 (†)	100 (†)	100 (†)	100 (†)
Functional problem in existing system or feature	28 (3.5)	26 (4.4)	34 (4.9)	‡ (†)	25 (6.2)	29 (6.7)	31! (10.4)	30 (6.4)	28 (6.0)	31 (7.9)	22 (6.2)	34 (7.7)
Improve operational or energy efficiency	44 (3.5)	39 (4.6)	52 (5.0)	57! (19.0)	44 (7.4)	43 (5.7)	39 (11.1)	46 (7.1)	36 (5.9)	44 (8.0)	54 (6.4)	40 (7.5)
Replacement cycle	23 (2.8)	29 (3.9)	11! (3.6)	‡ (†)	26 (6.0)	21 (5.6)	27! (9.6)	20 (5.9)	31 (6.0)	19! (6.4)	23 (5.9)	16! (5.9)
Other reason	5 (1.5)	6! (2.2)	4! (1.8)	# (†)	‡ (†)	8! (3.4)	‡ (†)	‡ (†)	‡ (†)	‡ (†)	‡ (†)	10! (4.4)
Ventilation/filtration system—percent of schools with plans	11 (0.8)	10 (0.9)	15 (1.7)	13! (4.3)	11 (1.6)	11 (1.6)	11 (2.6)	11 (1.5)	13 (1.4)	11 (1.9)	11 (1.5)	9 (1.7)
Percentage distribution by main reason for the plans	100 (†)	100 (†)	100 (†)	100 (†)	100 (†)	100 (†)	100 (†)	100 (†)	100 (†)	100 (†)	100 (†)	100 (†)
Functional problem in existing system or feature	31 (4.3)	30 (5.6)	32 (5.6)	‡ (†)	30 (7.4)	26 (7.5)	37! (13.5)	33 (7.3)	27 (6.5)	37 (10.8)	26 (7.4)	38 (10.7)
Improve operational or energy efficiency	38 (4.3)	30 (5.3)	55 (6.1)	41! (19.2)	39 (8.4)	39 (7.2)	28! (10.5)	41 (7.8)	33 (6.1)	36! (10.0)	49 (8.3)	35 (10.1)
Replacement cycle	23 (3.4)	29 (5.0)	8! (3.0)	‡ (†)	19! (5.7)	24 (7.0)	32! (11.6)	22 (6.4)	30 (6.7)	25! (8.8)	22! (6.8)	‡ (†)
Other reason	8 (2.4)	10! (3.5)	5! (2.4)	# (†)	‡ (†)	11! (4.9)	‡ (†)	‡ (†)	‡ (†)	‡ (†)	‡ (†)	18! (7.3)
Electrical system—percent of schools with plans	9 (0.8)	9 (0.9)	10 (1.4)	17! (6.1)	11 (1.5)	10 (1.6)	9 (2.1)	8 (1.4)	11 (1.5)	8 (1.6)	8 (1.3)	10 (1.7)
Percentage distribution by main reason for the plans	100 (†)	100 (†)	100 (†)	100 (†)	100 (†)	100 (†)	100 (†)	100 (†)	100 (†)	100 (†)	100 (†)	100 (†)
Functional problem in existing system or feature	28 (4.0)	28 (5.0)	27 (5.8)	‡ (†)	31 (8.2)	32 (7.6)	25! (12.3)	21! (8.4)	23 (6.2)	46 (12.9)	24! (8.2)	28! (8.3)
Improve operational or energy efficiency	37 (4.5)	31 (6.0)	51 (7.7)	52! (19.2)	29 (7.1)	35 (8.5)	42! (13.5)	45 (9.7)	37 (7.4)	29! (11.1)	42 (9.6)	38 (9.4)
Replacement cycle	22 (3.5)	26 (4.9)	11! (4.5)	‡ (†)	33 (8.3)	16! (5.7)	19! (9.2)	18! (7.5)	32 (7.0)	‡ (†)	23! (7.5)	15! (7.5)
Other reason	13 (3.2)	15 (4.2)	11! (5.4)	# (†)	‡ (†)	17! (6.2)	‡ (†)	15! (7.0)	‡ (†)	‡ (†)	‡ (†)	19! (7.7)

See notes at end of table.

Table 217.15. Percentage of public schools with plans for major repair, renovation, or replacement of building systems or features in the next 2 years and percentage distribution of schools with such plans, by selected school characteristics, type of system or feature, and main reason for the plans: 2012–13—Continued

[Standard errors appear in parentheses]

Type of system or feature and main reason for major repair, renovation, or replacement plans	All public schools	Instructional level			Community type				Percent of students eligible for free or reduced-priced lunch			
		Elementary	Secondary	Combined	City	Suburban	Town	Rural	Less than 35 percent	35 to 49 percent	50 to 74 percent	75 percent or more
1	2	3	4	5	6	7	8	9	10	11	12	13
Interior lighting—percent of schools with plans	13 (0.9)	13 (1.1)	13 (1.4)	18! (6.5)	14 (1.9)	14 (1.7)	10 (2.3)	12 (1.6)	15 (1.6)	10 (1.9)	13 (1.7)	12 (2.1)
Percentage distribution by main reason for the plans	100 (†)	100 (†)	100 (†)	100 (†)	100 (†)	100 (†)	100 (†)	100 (†)	100 (†)	100 (†)	100 (†)	100 (†)
Functional problem in existing system or feature	12 (2.6)	13 (3.4)	11! (3.8)	‡ (†)	12! (4.5)	12! (5.3)	22! (9.5)	‡ (†)	11! (4.4)	‡ (†)	13! (5.4)	19! (6.5)
Improve operational or energy efficiency	70 (3.9)	68 (4.9)	74 (5.6)	73 (17.7)	66 (7.2)	67 (7.4)	62 (11.2)	78 (6.1)	65 (7.1)	78 (8.6)	78 (5.9)	60 (8.4)
Replacement cycle	9 (2.0)	10 (2.6)	6! (2.8)	‡ (†)	13! (5.5)	8! (3.4)	‡ (†)	8! (3.5)	13! (4.3)	‡ (†)	7! (3.2)	‡ (†)
Other reason	9 (2.3)	10! (2.9)	‡ (†)	‡ (†)	‡ (†)	13! (4.9)	‡ (†)	‡ (†)	10! (4.6)	‡ (†)	‡ (†)	11! (5.4)
Exterior lighting—percent of schools with plans	10 (0.8)	9 (1.0)	10 (1.3)	18! (6.0)	9 (1.5)	10 (1.5)	9 (2.1)	10 (1.6)	12 (1.6)	8 (1.7)	7 (1.2)	10 (1.8)
Percentage distribution by main reason for the plans	100 (†)	100 (†)	100 (†)	100 (†)	100 (†)	100 (†)	100 (†)	100 (†)	100 (†)	100 (†)	100 (†)	100 (†)
Functional problem in existing system or feature	19 (3.5)	20 (4.6)	19! (5.8)	‡ (†)	12! (5.2)	14! (6.3)	39! (14.2)	22! (7.2)	13! (5.5)	‡ (†)	29! (9.9)	21! (8.1)
Improve operational or energy efficiency	56 (4.7)	53 (5.9)	62 (6.9)	73 (17.2)	50 (9.2)	67 (8.8)	47 (13.9)	56 (8.5)	57 (7.8)	66 (10.9)	48 (10.2)	56 (10.2)
Replacement cycle	14 (3.0)	15 (3.9)	10! (3.9)	‡ (†)	27! (8.6)	8! (†)	‡ (†)	15! (6.2)	17! (5.1)	‡ (†)	17! (7.5)	‡ (†)
Other reason	11 (3.2)	12! (3.8)	‡ (†)	# (†)	‡ (†)	14! (6.1)	‡ (†)	‡ (†)	13! (5.7)	‡ (†)	‡ (†)	‡ (†)
Energy management system—percent of schools with plans	14 (0.9)	13 (1.2)	16 (1.9)	34 (7.9)	13 (2.0)	14 (1.9)	17 (2.9)	15 (1.9)	17 (1.9)	12 (2.0)	14 (1.9)	14 (2.0)
Percentage distribution by main reason for the plans	100 (†)	100 (†)	100 (†)	100 (†)	100 (†)	100 (†)	100 (†)	100 (†)	100 (†)	100 (†)	100 (†)	100 (†)
Functional problem in existing system or feature	14 (2.4)	13 (3.2)	15 (4.1)	‡ (†)	19! (5.9)	‡ (†)	21! (7.9)	11! (4.2)	16 (4.4)	‡ (†)	16! (5.7)	11! (5.2)
Improve operational or energy efficiency	65 (3.6)	64 (4.5)	66 (6.0)	68 (14.8)	59 (8.7)	63 (7.3)	64 (10.3)	71 (5.6)	58 (6.8)	68 (8.4)	72 (6.3)	67 (8.4)
Replacement cycle	14 (2.7)	16 (3.5)	9! (4.3)	‡ (†)	13! (5.6)	16! (6.2)	13! (5.1)	14! (5.0)	20 (5.8)	15! (6.7)	8! (3.4)	‡ (†)
Other reason	7 (2.0)	7! (2.6)	9! (4.1)	# (†)	‡ (†)	12! (4.8)	‡ (†)	‡ (†)	‡ (†)	‡ (†)	‡ (†)	11! (5.3)
Life safety features[1]—percent of schools with plans	12 (0.8)	11 (1.0)	12 (1.5)	16! (5.8)	11 (1.6)	13 (1.8)	16 (2.7)	10 (1.5)	13 (1.8)	12 (2.0)	11 (1.8)	9 (1.7)
Percentage distribution by main reason for the plans	100 (†)	100 (†)	100 (†)	100 (†)	100 (†)	100 (†)	100 (†)	100 (†)	100 (†)	100 (†)	100 (†)	100 (†)
Functional problem in existing system or feature	24 (3.7)	23 (4.4)	23 (5.8)	‡ (†)	22! (7.5)	30 (7.8)	21! (7.7)	21! (6.6)	26 (6.2)	36 (9.4)	20! (6.3)	12! (4.7)
Improve operational or energy efficiency	37 (4.2)	34 (4.9)	41 (6.9)	60! (22.4)	42 (8.3)	33 (7.6)	40 (8.5)	35 (8.1)	31 (6.9)	29 (7.9)	41 (8.2)	51 (9.6)
Replacement cycle	21 (3.0)	22 (4.0)	19 (4.9)	‡ (†)	24! (7.5)	19! (6.6)	24! (8.7)	18! (6.0)	23 (6.0)	17! (6.2)	20! (6.2)	20! (8.6)
Other reason	19 (3.5)	21 (4.2)	16! (5.5)	# (†)	‡ (†)	19! (5.8)	16! (6.7)	26! (8.2)	19! (6.0)	19! (8.1)	19! (6.7)	17! (7.2)
Security systems—percent of schools with plans	21 (1.2)	20 (1.5)	20 (1.9)	32 (7.4)	16 (2.1)	19 (2.0)	24 (3.1)	24 (2.2)	23 (2.2)	19 (2.7)	21 (2.2)	17 (2.3)
Percentage distribution by main reason for the plans	100 (†)	100 (†)	100 (†)	100 (†)	100 (†)	100 (†)	100 (†)	100 (†)	100 (†)	100 (†)	100 (†)	100 (†)
Functional problem in existing system or feature	22 (2.8)	22 (3.5)	25 (4.4)	‡ (†)	19! (5.7)	16 (4.7)	33 (7.5)	24 (4.6)	17 (3.8)	33 (7.7)	22 (4.9)	21 (6.1)
Improve operational or energy efficiency	46 (3.0)	44 (3.7)	50 (5.5)	67 (12.3)	43 (7.2)	53 (6.2)	51 (7.6)	41 (5.3)	48 (5.2)	36 (7.2)	48 (5.7)	48 (8.0)
Replacement cycle	9 (1.8)	10 (2.3)	10! (3.1)	# (†)	14! (5.1)	8! (2.5)	‡ (†)	9! (3.1)	13 (3.6)	‡ (†)	7! (3.0)	‡ (†)
Other reason	22 (3.0)	25 (3.9)	15 (4.3)	‡ (†)	24 (6.9)	22 (5.5)	9! (4.2)	26 (4.8)	21 (4.7)	25 (6.9)	22 (4.8)	22 (6.6)

See notes at end of table.

Table 217.15. Percentage of public schools with plans for major repair, renovation, or replacement of building systems or features in the next 2 years and percentage distribution of schools with such plans, by selected school characteristics, type of system or feature, and main reason for the plans: 2012–13—Continued

[Standard errors appear in parentheses]

Type of system or feature and main reason for major repair, renovation, or replacement plans	All public schools	Instructional level			Community type				Percent of students eligible for free or reduced-priced lunch			
		Elementary	Secondary	Combined	City	Suburban	Town	Rural	Less than 35 percent	35 to 49 percent	50 to 74 percent	75 percent or more
1	2	3	4	5	6	7	8	9	10	11	12	13
Internal communication systems— percent of schools with plans	**14** (1.0)	**13** (1.2)	**16** (2.1)	**23 !** (7.0)	**13** (2.0)	**13** (1.7)	**16** (2.6)	**14** (1.7)	**15** (1.8)	**12** (2.1)	**14** (1.8)	**14** (2.5)
Percentage distribution by main reason for the plans	100 (†)	100 (†)	100 (†)	100 (†)	100 (†)	100 (†)	100 (†)	100 (†)	100 (†)	100 (†)	100 (†)	100 (†)
Functional problem in existing system or feature	24 (3.3)	21 (4.2)	28 (5.5)	37 ! (18.4)	24 (6.4)	19 ! (5.9)	17 ! (6.7)	30 (6.2)	21 (5.2)	31 (8.0)	23 (6.3)	24 (7.0)
Improve operational or energy efficiency	43 (3.5)	39 (4.7)	49 (6.9)	63 (18.4)	41 (7.3)	50 (8.1)	42 (9.1)	39 (7.0)	43 (6.3)	47 (9.5)	39 (7.5)	44 (7.1)
Replacement cycle	21 (3.1)	25 (4.2)	12 ! (3.8)	# (†)	21 (6.4)	15 ! (5.2)	34 (9.3)	19 ! (5.7)	25 (6.2)	‡ (†)	22 (6.5)	19 ! (6.3)
Other reason	13 (2.7)	15 (3.5)	11 ! (4.6)	# (†)	14 ! (6.2)	16 ! (5.7)	‡ (†)	12 ! (4.8)	12 ! (4.8)	‡ (†)	16 ! (5.3)	13 ! (5.5)
Technology infrastructure—percent of schools with plans	**20** (1.0)	**19** (1.2)	**23** (2.2)	**33** (7.4)	**17** (2.1)	**20** (2.1)	**23** (2.8)	**21** (2.0)	**23** (2.0)	**20** (2.6)	**18** (2.1)	**19** (2.6)
Percentage distribution by main reason for the plans	100 (†)	100 (†)	100 (†)	100 (†)	100 (†)	100 (†)	100 (†)	100 (†)	100 (†)	100 (†)	100 (†)	100 (†)
Functional problem in existing system or feature	17 (2.4)	16 (3.0)	19 (4.1)	‡ (†)	16 ! (5.0)	11 ! (4.1)	16 ! (5.6)	22 (4.7)	14 (3.8)	17 ! (5.9)	16 (4.6)	23 (5.3)
Improve operational or energy efficiency	51 (3.3)	46 (4.2)	59 (5.0)	71 (14.0)	53 (6.5)	51 (6.5)	65 (7.3)	44 (5.3)	44 (4.9)	53 (7.3)	59 (6.6)	51 (6.5)
Replacement cycle	21 (2.6)	25 (3.4)	14 (3.4)	‡ (†)	21 (5.5)	21 (4.5)	10 ! (4.6)	26 (5.1)	28 (5.1)	19 ! (6.0)	19 (5.4)	15 ! (4.8)
Other reason	11 (2.0)	13 (2.7)	8 ! (2.9)	# (†)	9 ! (4.3)	17 (4.5)	‡ (†)	8 ! (3.6)	13 (3.7)	11 ! (4.5)	6 ! (2.9)	12 ! (4.8)

†Not applicable.
#Rounds to zero.
!Interpret data with caution. The coefficient of variation (CV) for this estimate is between 30 and 50 percent.
‡Reporting standards not met. Either there are too few cases for a reliable estimate or the coefficient of variation (CV) for this estimate is 50 percent or greater.

¹Life safety features include sprinklers, fire alarms, and smoke detectors.
NOTE: Percentage of schools with major repair, renovation, or replacement plans is based on schools having the specified building system or feature. Detail may not sum to totals because of rounding.
SOURCE: U.S. Department of Education, National Center for Education Statistics, Fast Response Survey System (FRSS), "Condition of Public School Facilities: 2012–13," FRSS 105, 2013. (This table was prepared April 2014.)

Table 217.20. Percentage of public schools with enrollment under, at, or over capacity, by selected school characteristics: 1999 and 2005
[Standard errors appear in parentheses]

School enrollment versus design capacity	All public schools[1]		Instructional level				Size of school enrollment						Percent of students eligible for free or reduced-price lunch							
			Elementary		Secondary/combined		Less than 350		350 to 699		700 or more		Less than 35 percent		35 to 49 percent		50 to 74 percent		75 percent or more	
1	2		3		4		5		6		7		8		9		10		11	
1999, total	100	(†)	100	(†)	100	(†)	100	(†)	100	(†)	100	(†)	100	(†)	100	(†)	100	(†)	100	(†)
Underenrolled by more than 25 percent	19	(1.5)	17	(1.7)	22	(2.5)	39	(4.0)	11	(2.0)	8	(1.7)	16	(2.0)	18	(3.1)	17	(4.1)	27	(4.4)
Underenrolled by 6 to 25 percent	33	(1.7)	31	(2.1)	39	(2.9)	32	(3.8)	36	(2.4)	31	(2.8)	38	(2.6)	32	(4.6)	29	(4.6)	25	(4.5)
Enrollment within 5 percent of capacity	26	(1.5)	28	(2.0)	20	(2.2)	16	(2.9)	34	(2.6)	25	(2.0)	25	(2.2)	26	(4.4)	32	(4.5)	23	(4.1)
Overenrolled by 6 to 25 percent	14	(1.2)	15	(1.5)	11	(1.8)	10	(2.4)	14	(2.0)	20	(1.8)	14	(2.1)	18	(3.6)	14	(3.3)	11	(3.0)
Overenrolled by more than 25 percent	8	(0.9)	8	(1.1)	8	(1.6)	3 !	(1.3)	6	(1.3)	16	(2.4)	6	(1.2)	6	(1.8)	7 !	(2.4)	14	(3.4)
2005, total	100	(†)	100	(†)	100	(†)	100	(†)	100	(†)	100	(†)	100	(†)	100	(†)	100	(†)	100	(†)
Underenrolled by more than 25 percent	21	(1.4)	20	(1.7)	24	(2.6)	41	(3.3)	14	(1.7)	6	(1.4)	19	(2.6)	25	(4.6)	24	(2.7)	19	(3.0)
Underenrolled by 6 to 25 percent	38	(1.8)	39	(2.1)	36	(2.6)	39	(3.4)	44	(2.9)	29	(2.4)	38	(2.7)	43	(4.0)	37	(2.8)	36	(4.1)
Enrollment within 5 percent of capacity	22	(1.5)	23	(1.9)	21	(1.9)	14	(2.3)	27	(2.5)	26	(2.4)	27	(2.5)	19	(3.3)	18	(3.1)	22	(2.9)
Overenrolled by 6 to 25 percent	10	(1.0)	10	(1.4)	11	(1.2)	4	(1.1)	9	(1.9)	20	(2.1)	11	(1.8)	6 !	(2.0)	12	(2.6)	9	(1.6)
Overenrolled by more than 25 percent	8	(1.0)	8	(1.3)	8	(1.0)	2 !	(0.9)	6	(1.4)	19	(2.5)	5	(1.0)	7 !	(2.3)	8	(2.2)	14	(2.9)

†Not applicable.
!Interpret data with caution. The coefficient of variation (CV) for this estimate is between 30 and 50 percent.
[1]Excludes special education, vocational, and alternative schools; schools without enrollment data; and schools offering only preprimary education.

NOTE: Detail may not sum to totals because of rounding.
SOURCE: U.S. Department of Education, National Center for Education Statistics, Fast Response Survey System (FRSS), "Condition of America's Public School Facilities, 1999," FRSS 73, 1999, and "Public School Principals' Perceptions of Their School Facilities: Fall 2005," FRSS 88, 2005. (This table was prepared July 2007.)

Table 218.10. Number and internet access of instructional computers and rooms in public schools, by selected school characteristics: Selected years, 1995 through 2008

[Standard errors appear in parentheses]

Instructional computers and rooms, and access	All public schools	Instructional level[1]		Size of school enrollment			Community type[2]				Percent of students eligible for free or reduced-price lunch[3]			
		Elementary	Secondary	Less than 300	300 to 999	1,000 or more	City	Suburban	Town	Rural	Less than 35 percent	35 to 49 percent	50 to 74 percent	75 percent or more
1	2	3	4	5	6	7	8	9	10	11	12	13	14	15
Computers for instructional purposes														
Number (in thousands)														
1995[4]	5,621 (—)	3,453 (—)	2,021 (—)	850 (—)	3,600 (—)	1,171 (—)	1,497 (—)	1,526 (—)	1,404 (—)	1,195 (—)	2,905 (—)	806 (—)	950 (—)	882 (—)
2000	8,776 (174)	5,296 (149)	3,271 (113)	1,135 (73)	5,524 (121)	2,117 (103)	2,537 (179)	3,396 (213)	1,155 (132)	1,689 (131)	4,394 (147)	1,373 (93)	1,606 (112)	1,384 (107)
2005	12,672 (281)	7,701 (251)	4,783 (148)	1,566 (98)	7,966 (243)	3,139 (163)	3,132 (177)	4,058 (242)	1,819 (193)	3,663 (255)	5,352 (261)	2,193 (185)	2,687 (244)	2,440 (152)
2008	15,434 (193)	9,711 (159)	5,415 (125)	1,746 (68)	9,486 (144)	4,202 (130)	3,611 (155)	5,787 (255)	2,062 (159)	3,974 (180)	6,195 (174)	2,364 (155)	3,805 (190)	3,070 (175)
Average number per school														
1995[4]	72 (—)	60 (—)	112 (—)	41 (—)	72 (—)	164 (—)	84 (—)	83 (—)	72 (—)	54 (—)	78 (—)	59 (—)	74 (—)	67 (—)
2000	110 (2.0)	89 (2.4)	178 (5.3)	57 (3.1)	106 (2.3)	259 (9.0)	120 (4.9)	128 (4.3)	97 (5.6)	82 (3.6)	120 (3.4)	111 (5.9)	94 (5.7)	99 (5.5)
2005	154 (3.4)	124 (3.8)	253 (6.8)	75 (4.2)	149 (4.2)	388 (13.5)	165 (7.2)	170 (6.3)	154 (13.4)	132 (5.9)	166 (5.5)	153 (9.3)	147 (6.9)	139 (7.4)
2008	189 (2.9)	157 (2.8)	301 (6.5)	87 (3.4)	179 (2.9)	486 (10.4)	205 (7.5)	221 (6.1)	189 (8.0)	147 (4.2)	209 (5.6)	182 (7.7)	181 (6.8)	170 (8.2)
Number with internet access (in thousands)														
1995[4]	447 (—)	232 (—)	187 (—)	59 (—)	315 (—)	73 (—)	96 (—)	131 (—)	126 (—)	94 (—)	286 (—)	46 (—)	57 (—)	36 (—)
2000	6,759 (174)	3,813 (136)	2,779 (113)	882 (69)	4,191 (114)	1,686 (97)	1,782 (148)	2,688 (178)	955 (111)	1,335 (91)	3,608 (139)	1,064 (80)	1,215 (93)	858 (87)
2005	12,245 (274)	7,361 (246)	4,706 (151)	1,515 (98)	7,642 (239)	3,089 (162)	3,009 (173)	3,912 (238)	1,784 (193)	3,541 (239)	5,239 (259)	2,090 (176)	2,583 (228)	2,332 (146)
2008	15,162 (204)	9,508 (169)	5,356 (128)	1,710 (69)	9,308 (153)	4,144 (130)	3,517 (154)	5,716 (253)	2,028 (154)	3,901 (178)	6,131 (174)	2,321 (153)	3,739 (188)	2,971 (175)
Percent with internet access														
1995[4]	8 (—)	7 (—)	9 (—)	7 (—)	9 (—)	6 (—)	6 (—)	9 (—)	9 (—)	8 (—)	10 (—)	6 (—)	6 (—)	4 (—)
2000	77 (1.1)	72 (1.5)	85 (1.2)	78 (2.6)	76 (1.3)	80 (1.8)	70 (2.1)	79 (1.7)	83 (2.5)	79 (2.1)	82 (1.2)	77 (2.9)	76 (2.6)	62 (3.1)
2005	97 (0.4)	96 (0.5)	98 (0.4)	97 (0.7)	96 (0.5)	98 (0.5)	96 (0.7)	96 (1.1)	98 (0.6)	97 (0.7)	98 (0.6)	95 (1.0)	96 (1.0)	96 (0.8)
2008	98 (0.2)	98 (0.3)	99 (0.2)	98 (0.7)	98 (0.3)	99 (0.4)	97 (0.5)	99 (0.3)	98 (0.7)	98 (0.4)	99 (0.3)	98 (0.5)	98 (0.4)	97 (0.7)
Ratio of students to instructional computers with internet access														
2000	6.6 (0.10)	7.8 (0.20)	5.2 (0.20)	3.9 (0.30)	7.0 (0.20)	7.2 (0.20)	8.2 (0.40)	6.6 (0.20)	6.2 (0.30)	5.0 (0.30)	6.0 (0.20)	6.3 (0.40)	7.2 (0.40)	9.1 (0.70)
2005	3.8 (0.10)	4.1 (0.10)	3.3 (0.10)	2.4 (0.10)	3.9 (0.10)	4.0 (0.10)	4.2 (0.20)	4.1 (0.10)	3.4 (0.20)	3.0 (0.10)	3.8 (0.10)	3.4 (0.20)	3.6 (0.20)	4.0 (0.20)
2008	3.1 (0.04)	3.2 (0.05)	2.9 (0.05)	2.2 (0.07)	3.2 (0.05)	3.2 (0.06)	3.4 (0.12)	3.2 (0.08)	2.7 (0.09)	2.9 (0.07)	3.1 (0.06)	3.2 (0.08)	2.9 (0.08)	3.2 (0.14)
Instructional rooms[5]														
Number (in thousands)														
2000	2,905 (35)	1,864 (28)	972 (24)	377 (22)	1,871 (23)	657 (23)	866 (56)	1,086 (61)	413 (47)	541 (39)	1,380 (46)	465 (28)	570 (36)	482 (29)
2005	3,283 (71)	2,152 (70)	1,078 (27)	426 (23)	2,152 (70)	705 (30)	849 (62)	1,050 (61)	439 (41)	945 (67)	1,339 (50)	593 (51)	695 (56)	655 (39)
2008[5]	2,663 (21)	1,723 (20)	887 (15)	282 (9)	1,692 (20)	689 (18)	639 (26)	1,003 (35)	338 (24)	683 (28)	1,053 (27)	425 (26)	653 (27)	532 (22)
Percent with internet access[6]														
1995	8 (0.7)	8 (1.0)	8 (1.0)	9 (1.6)	8 (1.0)	4 (1.0)	6 (1.3)	8 (1.4)	8 (2.0)	8 (1.5)	10 (1.2)	6 (1.4)	6 ! (1.9)	3 ! (1.0)
2000	77 (1.1)	76 (1.5)	79 (1.6)	83 (2.8)	78 (1.5)	70 (2.2)	66 (2.2)	78 (2.0)	87 (2.6)	85 (1.7)	82 (1.5)	81 (2.9)	77 (2.8)	60 (3.3)
2005	94 (1.3)	93 (1.9)	95 (0.9)	92 (1.9)	94 (1.9)	94 (1.5)	88 (3.7)	96 (0.8)	98 (0.7)	95 (1.8)	96 (0.8)	88 (4.3)	96 (0.8)	91 (2.5)
2008	— (†)	— (†)	— (†)	— (†)	— (†)	— (†)	— (†)	— (†)	— (†)	— (†)	— (†)	— (†)	— (†)	— (†)

—Not available.
†Not applicable.
!Interpret data with caution. The coefficient of variation (CV) for this estimate is between 30 and 50 percent.
[1]Data for combined schools are included in the totals and in analyses by other school characteristics, but are not shown separately.
[2]Due to definitional changes for community type, estimates for years prior to 2005 may not be directly comparable with estimates for later years.
[3]Free or reduced-price lunch information was obtained on the questionnaire and supplemented, if necessary, with data from the Common Core of Data (CCD).
[4]Includes computers used for instructional or administrative purposes.

[5]In 2008, instructional rooms included classrooms only and excluded computer labs and library/media centers. Prior to 2008, instructional rooms included classrooms, computer labs and other labs, library/media centers, and other rooms used for instructional purposes.
[6]Some data differ slightly (e.g., by 1 percent) from previously published figures.
NOTE: Detail may not sum to totals because of rounding.
SOURCE: U.S. Department of Education, National Center for Education Statistics, Fast Response Survey System (FRSS), *Internet Access in U.S. Public Schools and Classrooms: 1994–2005* and *Educational Technology in U.S. Public Schools: Fall 2008*; and unpublished tabulations. (This table was prepared August 2010.)

Table 218.20. Percentage of public school districts with students enrolled in technology-based distance education courses and number of enrollments in such courses, by instructional level and district characteristics: 2002–03, 2004–05, and 2009–10

[Standard errors appear in parentheses]

District characteristic	Percent of districts enrolling distance education students		Number of enrollments in technology-based distance education courses,[1] by instructional level									
			All instructional levels		Elementary schools		Middle or junior high schools		High schools		Combined or ungraded schools[2]	
1	2		3		4		5		6		7	
2002–03												
Total	36	(1.2)	317,070	(27,437)	2,780 !	(977)	6,390	(1,067)	214,140	(16,549)	93,760	(22,593)
District enrollment size												
Less than 2,500	37	(1.5)	116,300	(21,698)	‡	(†)	1,250 !	(450)	72,730	(6,924)	42,240 !	(20,502)
2,500 to 9,999	32	(1.8)	82,370	(6,384)	230 !	(109)	1,870 !	(642)	44,170	(5,832)	36,110	(1,210)
10,000 or more	50	(2.1)	118,390	(15,703)	2,480 !	(968)	3,270	(723)	97,240	(13,853)	‡	(†)
Region												
Northeast	21	(2.2)	41,950 !	(20,821)	100 !	(49)	‡	(†)	17,300	(3,656)	‡	(†)
Southeast	45	(2.6)	59,240	(6,251)	‡	(†)	2,530	(632)	50,640	(5,698)	4,680	(1,254)
Central	46	(2.3)	106,690	(7,726)	940 !	(441)	1,050 !	(412)	59,110	(6,455)	45,590	(2,529)
West	32	(2.2)	109,190	(16,010)	350 !	(165)	2,620	(782)	87,090	(14,825)	19,130 !	(8,619)
Poverty concentration												
Less than 10 percent	33	(2.1)	75,740	(11,177)	‡	(†)	2,020	(564)	55,670	(7,556)	17,470 !	(8,591)
10 to 19 percent	42	(2.1)	95,510	(7,962)	‡	(†)	1,830	(392)	78,680	(7,050)	13,560	(2,446)
20 percent or more	42	(2.5)	86,110	(13,518)	760 !	(249)	2,540 !	(837)	75,930	(13,532)	6,880	(1,557)
2004–05												
Total	37	(1.2)	506,950	(56,959)	12,540 !	(6,107)	15,150	(3,367)	309,630	(24,350)	169,630 !	(51,753)
District enrollment size												
Less than 2,500	37	(1.6)	210,200	(54,063)	610 !	(275)	‡	(†)	103,190	(17,659)	‡	(†)
2,500 to 9,999	35	(1.6)	102,730	(13,404)	‡	(†)	2,570	(731)	48,420	(5,136)	45,080	(9,429)
10,000 or more	50	(2.5)	193,440	(16,415)	5,280 !	(2,202)	6,520	(1,101)	157,440	(16,044)	24,210	(5,298)
Region												
Northeast	22	(2.0)	108,300 !	(49,777)	570 !	(206)	‡	(†)	16,860	(2,621)	‡	(†)
Southeast	46	(3.2)	112,830	(6,341)	‡	(†)	5,030	(732)	89,800	(5,276)	16,090	(1,913)
Central	45	(2.4)	128,650	(22,055)	‡	(†)	2,130 !	(953)	70,450	(13,024)	46,190 !	(15,067)
West	35	(2.1)	157,180	(22,608)	200 !	(161)	4,110 !	(1,732)	132,520	(21,287)	20,350 !	(7,587)
Poverty concentration												
Less than 10 percent	35	(1.9)	112,320	(16,778)	‡	(†)	4,070	(1,123)	80,150	(10,651)	‡	(†)
10 to 19 percent	42	(2.2)	151,050	(12,379)	‡	(†)	4,800	(602)	124,540	(10,283)	19,700	(5,835)
20 percent or more	43	(2.7)	106,610	(14,709)	‡	(†)	6,280 !	(3,111)	78,590	(13,367)	21,340	(2,905)
2009–10												
Total	55	(1.4)	1,816,390	(251,054)	78,040 !	(25,180)	154,970	(30,828)	1,348,920	(135,979)	‡	(†)
District enrollment size												
Less than 2,500	51	(1.8)	509,030 !	(167,570)	‡	(†)	‡	(†)	408,030 !	(123,883)	6,570 !	2,753
2,500 to 9,999	66	(1.5)	579,250 !	(185,243)	‡	(†)	23,960 !	(9,196)	312,130	(50,963)	‡	(†)
10,000 or more	74	(0.8)	728,110	(27,105)	11,540	(1,862)	77,750	(4,730)	628,760	(23,545)	10,060	2,756
Metropolitan status												
City	37	(4.0)	653,660 !	(201,665)	‡	(†)	40,400 !	(15,671)	405,740	(79,507)	‡	(†)
Suburban	47	(2.6)	527,250	(34,188)	22,900 !	(11,293)	62,210	(4,106)	434,260	(30,904)	7,880	2,347
Town	67	(2.7)	306,840 !	(145,000)	‡	(†)	‡	(†)	246,850 !	(107,079)	9,310 !	3,908
Rural	59	(2.5)	328,640	(36,233)	‡	(†)	15,360	(2,420)	262,070	(27,077)	‡	(†)
Region												
Northeast	39	(3.3)	77,670	(7,358)	‡	(†)	4,970	(989)	71,330	(6,651)	‡	(†)
Southeast	78	(3.7)	518,770	(63,187)	12,070 !	(4,154)	57,500	(9,828)	443,770	(50,079)	5,440 !	1,678
Central	62	(2.2)	697,140 !	(235,103)	37,920 !	(18,915)	‡	(†)	416,550	(122,633)	‡	(†)
West	51	(2.4)	522,810	(42,673)	‡	(†)	41,620	(3,384)	417,270	(33,400)	36,510 !	14,278
Poverty concentration												
Less than 10 percent	54	(2.5)	287,680	(34,577)	‡	(†)	12,620	(2,997)	231,890	(27,672)	‡	(†)
10 to 19 percent	56	(2.1)	1,009,290	(193,646)	23,540 !	(11,116)	97,220	(16,126)	682,380	(78,795)	‡	(†)
20 percent or more	56	(2.4)	519,420	(146,507)	‡	(†)	‡	(†)	434,640	(108,046)	5,750 !	2,484

†Not applicable.
!Interpret data with caution. The coefficient of variation (CV) for this estimate is between 30 and 50 percent.
‡Reporting standards not met. Either there are too few cases for a reliable estimate or the coefficient of variation (CV) is 50 percent or greater.
[1]Based on students regularly enrolled in the districts. Enrollments may include duplicated counts of students, since districts were instructed to count a student enrolled in multiple courses for each course in which he or she was enrolled.
[2]Combined or ungraded schools are those in which the grades offered in the school span both elementary and secondary grades or that are not divided into grade levels.

NOTE: Percentages are based on unrounded numbers. For the 2002–03 FRSS study sample, there were 3 cases for which district enrollment size was missing and 112 cases for which poverty concentration was missing. For the 2004–05 FRSS study sample, there were 7 cases for which district enrollment size was missing and 103 cases for which poverty concentration was missing. Detail may not sum to totals because of rounding or missing data.
SOURCE: U.S. Department of Education, National Center for Education Statistics, Fast Response Survey System (FRSS), *Technology-Based Distance Education Courses for Public Elementary and Secondary Schools: 2002–03 and 2004–05* and "Distance Education Courses for Public Elementary and Secondary School Students: 2009–10," FRSS 98. (This table was prepared November 2011.)

Table 219.10. High school graduates, by sex and control of school: Selected years, 1869–70 through 2024–25

School year	High school graduates							Averaged freshman graduation rate for public schools[3]	Population 17 years old[4]	Graduates as a ratio of 17-year-old population
	Total[1]	Sex		Control						
		Males	Females	Public[2]			Private			
				Total	Males	Females				
1	2	3	4	5	6	7	8	9	10	11
1869–70	16,000	7,064	8,936	—	—	—	—	—	815,000	2.0
1879–80	23,634	10,605	13,029	—	—	—	—	—	946,026	2.5
1889–90	43,731	18,549	25,182	21,882	—	—	21,849 [5]	—	1,259,177	3.5
1899–1900	94,883	38,075	56,808	61,737	—	—	33,146 [5]	—	1,489,146	6.4
1909–10	156,429	63,676	92,753	111,363	—	—	45,066 [5]	—	1,786,240	8.8
1919–20	311,266	123,684	187,582	230,902	—	—	80,364 [5]	—	1,855,173	16.8
1929–30	666,904	300,376	366,528	591,719	—	—	75,185 [5]	—	2,295,822	29.0
1939–40	1,221,475	578,718	642,757	1,143,246	538,273	604,973	78,229 [5]	—	2,403,074	50.8
1949–50	1,199,700	570,700	629,000	1,063,444	505,394	558,050	136,256 [5]	—	2,034,450	59.0
1959–60	1,858,023	895,000	963,000	1,627,050	791,426	835,624	230,973	—	2,672,000	69.5
1969–70	2,888,639	1,430,000	1,459,000	2,588,639	1,285,895	1,302,744	300,000 [5]	78.7	3,757,000	76.9
1974–75	3,132,502	1,542,000	1,591,000	2,822,502	1,391,519	1,430,983	310,000 [5]	74.9	4,256,000	73.6
1975–76	3,142,120	1,552,000	1,590,000	2,837,129	1,401,064	1,436,065	304,991	74.9	4,272,000	73.6
1976–77	3,139,536	1,551,000	1,589,000	2,837,340	—	—	302,196	74.4	4,272,000	73.5
1977–78	3,128,824	1,546,000	1,583,000	2,824,636	—	—	304,188	73.2	4,286,000	73.0
1978–79	3,101,152	1,532,000	1,569,000	2,801,152	—	—	300,000 [5]	71.9	4,327,000	71.7
1979–80	3,042,214	1,503,000	1,539,000	2,747,678	—	—	294,536	71.5	4,262,000	71.4
1980–81	3,020,285	1,492,000	1,528,000	2,725,285	—	—	295,000 [5]	72.2	4,212,000	71.7
1981–82	2,994,758	1,479,000	1,515,000	2,704,758	—	—	290,000 [5]	72.9	4,134,000	72.4
1982–83	2,887,604	1,426,000	1,461,000	2,597,604	—	—	290,000 [5]	73.8	3,962,000	72.9
1983–84	2,766,797	—	—	2,494,797	—	—	272,000 [5]	74.5	3,784,000	73.1
1984–85	2,676,917	—	—	2,413,917	—	—	263,000 [5]	74.2	3,699,000	72.4
1985–86	2,642,616	—	—	2,382,616	—	—	260,000 [5]	74.3	3,670,000	72.0
1986–87	2,693,803	—	—	2,428,803	—	—	265,000 [5]	74.3	3,754,000	71.8
1987–88	2,773,020	—	—	2,500,020	—	—	273,000 [5]	74.2	3,849,000	72.0
1988–89	2,743,743	—	—	2,458,800	—	—	284,943	73.4	3,842,000	71.4
1989–90[6]	2,574,162	—	—	2,320,337	—	—	253,825 [7]	73.6	3,505,000	73.4
1990–91	2,492,988	—	—	2,234,893	—	—	258,095	73.7	3,417,913	72.9
1991–92	2,480,399	—	—	2,226,016	—	—	254,383 [7]	74.2	3,398,884	73.0
1992–93	2,480,519	—	—	2,233,241	—	—	247,278	73.8	3,449,143	71.9
1993–94	2,463,849	—	—	2,220,849	—	—	243,000 [5]	73.1	3,442,521	71.6
1994–95	2,519,084	—	—	2,273,541	—	—	245,543	71.8	3,635,803	69.3
1995–96	2,518,109	—	—	2,273,109	—	—	245,000 [5]	71.0	3,640,132	69.2
1996–97	2,611,988	—	—	2,358,403	—	—	253,585	71.3	3,792,207	68.9
1997–98	2,704,050	—	—	2,439,050	1,187,647	1,251,403	265,000 [5]	71.3	4,008,416	67.5
1998–99	2,758,655	—	—	2,485,630	1,212,924	1,272,706	273,025	71.1	3,917,885	70.4
1999–2000	2,832,844	—	—	2,553,844	1,241,631	1,312,213	279,000 [5]	71.7	4,056,639	69.8
2000–01	2,847,973	—	—	2,569,200	1,251,931	1,317,269	278,773	71.7	4,023,686	70.8
2001–02	2,906,534	—	—	2,621,534	1,275,813	1,345,721	285,000 [5]	72.6	4,023,968	72.2
2002–03	3,015,735	—	—	2,719,947	1,330,973	1,388,974	295,788	73.9	4,125,087	73.1
2003–04[6,8]	3,054,438	—	—	2,753,438	1,347,800	1,405,638	301,000 [5]	74.3	4,113,074	74.3
2004–05[6]	3,106,499	—	—	2,799,250	1,369,749	1,429,501	307,249	74.7	4,120,073	75.4
2005–06[6]	3,122,544	—	—	2,815,544	1,376,458	1,439,086	307,000 [5]	73.4	4,200,554	74.3
2006–07	3,199,650	—	—	2,893,045	1,414,069	1,478,976	306,605	73.9	4,297,239	74.5
2007–08	3,312,337	—	—	3,001,337	1,467,180	1,534,157	311,000 [5]	74.7	4,436,955	74.7
2008–09[6]	3,347,828	—	—	3,039,015	1,490,317	1,548,698	308,813	75.5	4,336,950	77.2
2009–10	3,439,102	—	—	3,128,022	1,542,684 [9]	1,585,338 [9]	311,080 [5]	78.2	4,311,831	79.8
2010–11	3,449,719	—	—	3,143,879	—	—	305,840	79.6	4,368,154	79.0
2011–12	3,454,010	—	—	3,147,790	—	—	306,220 [5]	80.8	4,294,956	80.4
2012–13[10]	3,470,660	—	—	3,170,700	—	—	299,960	—	—	—
2013–14[10]	3,451,590	—	—	3,154,960	—	—	296,630	—	—	—
2014–15[10]	3,429,770	—	—	3,136,920	—	—	292,850	—	—	—
2015–16[10]	3,427,660	—	—	3,151,390	—	—	276,270	—	—	—
2016–17[10]	3,432,890	—	—	3,168,410	—	—	264,490	—	—	—
2017–18[10]	3,475,330	—	—	3,212,490	—	—	262,840	—	—	—
2018–19[10]	3,462,200	—	—	3,211,480	—	—	250,720	—	—	—
2019–20[10]	3,429,870	—	—	3,185,810	—	—	244,060	—	—	—
2020–21[10]	3,446,760	—	—	3,206,080	—	—	240,680	—	—	—
2021–22[10]	3,464,070	—	—	3,231,310	—	—	232,760	—	—	—
2022–23[10]	3,471,880	—	—	3,246,200	—	—	225,690	—	—	—
2023–24[10]	3,517,300	—	—	3,290,220	—	—	227,070	—	—	—
2024–25[10]	3,555,400	—	—	3,325,870	—	—	229,530	—	—	—

—Not available.

[1]Includes graduates of public and private schools.

[2]Data for 1929–30 and preceding years are from *Statistics of Public High Schools* and exclude graduates from high schools that failed to report to the Office of Education. Includes estimates for jurisdictions not reporting counts of graduates by sex.

[3]The averaged freshman graduation rate provides an estimate of the percentage of students who receive a regular diploma within 4 years of entering ninth grade. The rate uses aggregate student enrollment data to estimate the size of an incoming freshman class and aggregate counts of the number of diplomas awarded 4 years later. Averaged freshman graduation rates in this table are based on reported totals of enrollment by grade and high school graduates, rather than on details reported by race/ethnicity.

[4]Derived from Current Population Reports, Series P-25. For years 1869–70 through 1989–90, 17-year-old population is an estimate of the October 17-year-old population based on July data. Data for 1990–91 and later years are October resident population estimates prepared by the Census Bureau.

[5]Estimated.

[6]Includes imputations for nonreporting states.

[7]Projected by private schools responding to the Private School Universe Survey.

[8]Includes estimates for public schools in New York and Wisconsin. Without estimates for these two states, the averaged freshman graduation rate for the remaining 48 states and the District of Columbia is 75.0 percent.

[9]Includes estimate for Connecticut, which did not report graduates by sex.

[10]Projected by NCES.

NOTE: Includes graduates of regular day school programs. Excludes graduates of other programs, when separately reported, and recipients of high school equivalency certificates. Some data have been revised from previously published figures. Detail may not sum to totals because of rounding.

SOURCE: U.S. Department of Education, National Center for Education Statistics, *Annual Report of the Commissioner of Education*, 1870 through 1910; *Biennial Survey of Education in the United States*, 1919–20 through 1949–50; *Statistics of State School Systems*, 1951–52 through 1957–58; *Statistics of Public Elementary and Secondary School Systems*, 1958–59 through 1980–81; *Statistics of Nonpublic Elementary and Secondary Schools*, 1959 through 1980; Common Core of Data (CCD), "State Nonfiscal Survey of Public Elementary/Secondary Education," 1981–82 through 2009–10; "State Dropout and Completion Data File," 2005–06 through 2011–12; *Public School Graduates and Dropouts From the Common Core of Data*, 2007–08 and 2008–09; Private School Universe Survey (PSS), 1989 through 2011; and National High School Graduates Projection Model, 1972–73 through 2024–25. U.S. Department of Commerce, Census Bureau, Population Estimates, retrieved August 11, 2011, from http://www.census.gov/popest/national/asrh/2009-nat-res.html and Population Estimates, retrieved August 18, 2015, from http://www.census.gov/popest/data/national/asrh/2014/2014-nat-res.html. (This table was prepared August 2015.)

Table 219.20. Public high school graduates, by region, state, and jurisdiction: Selected years, 1980–81 through 2024–25

Region, state, and jurisdiction	1980–81	1989–90	1999–2000	2005–06	2006–07	2007–08	2008–09	2009–10	2010–11	2011–12	2012–13	2013–14	2014–15	2015–16	2016–17	2017–18	2018–19	2019–20	2020–21	2021–22	2022–23	2023–24	2024–25	Percent change, 2011–12 to 2024–25
1	2	3	4	5	6	7	8	9	10	11	12	13	14	15	16	17	18	19	20	21	22	23	24	25
United States	2,725,285	2,320,337 [1]	2,553,844 [1]	2,815,544 [1]	2,893,045	3,001,337	3,039,015 [1]	3,128,022	3,143,879	3,147,790	3,170,700	3,154,960	3,136,920	3,151,390	3,168,410	3,212,490	3,211,480	3,165,810	3,206,080	3,231,310	3,246,200	3,290,220	3,325,870	5.7
Region																								
Northeast	593,727	446,045	463,814	521,015	536,697	552,289	552,973	556,400	556,620	554,770	554,060	544,390	535,500	535,210	532,570	534,290	530,990	524,630	530,120	532,010	527,360	534,460	534,070	-3.7
Midwest	794,071	616,700	648,020	684,049	702,987	721,220	717,536	726,844	718,540	716,080	713,900	705,900	695,640	696,020	700,840	708,400	707,040	698,430	700,690	710,250	703,910	706,610	709,720	-0.9
South	869,088	796,385	861,498	962,327	986,801	1,031,773	1,068,270	1,104,770	1,119,420	1,119,870	1,136,850	1,142,740	1,148,550	1,162,440	1,175,040	1,200,060	1,205,870	1,192,880	1,196,610	1,202,490	1,222,070	1,244,760	1,263,430	12.8
West	473,419	461,207	590,512	648,153	666,560	696,055	700,236	740,008	749,300	757,070	766,880	761,930	757,240	757,710	759,960	769,760	767,590	769,860	778,670	786,550	792,880	804,400	818,640	8.1
State																								
Alabama	44,894	40,485	37,819	37,918	38,912	41,346	42,082	43,166	46,030	45,420	44,960	44,380	44,610	44,280	44,740	45,210	44,550	43,480	42,870	42,860	42,930	43,180	43,930	-3.3
Alaska	5,343	5,396	6,615	7,361	7,666	7,855	8,008	8,245	8,070	7,990	7,900	7,430	7,390	7,330	7,540	7,480	7,440	7,300	7,450	7,650	7,810	8,040	8,060	0.9
Arizona	28,416	32,103	38,304	54,091	55,954	61,667	62,374	61,145	64,480	63,210	65,420	65,430	64,080	62,040	63,040	63,240	64,400	65,090	67,030	68,240	69,940	70,660	72,220	14.2
Arkansas	23,577	26,475	27,336	28,790	27,166	28,725	28,057	28,276	28,210	28,430	28,730	29,340	29,910	29,750	29,910	29,960	30,070	29,910	29,580	29,750	29,580	29,300	29,680	4.4
California	242,172	236,291	309,886	343,515	356,641	374,561	372,310 [2]	404,987	410,470	418,670	421,270	419,180	414,790	413,440	410,860	416,990	411,330	413,160	415,780	419,050	421,050	425,530	432,530	3.3
Colorado	35,897	32,967	38,924	44,424	45,628	46,082	47,459	49,321	50,120	50,090	51,130	51,200	51,560	52,940	53,760	55,100	56,190	56,720	57,980	57,840	58,270	59,130	59,610	19.0
Connecticut	38,399	27,878	31,562	36,222	37,541	38,419	34,968	34,495	38,860	38,680	37,680	37,460	36,230	36,220	35,720	35,280	34,890	34,140	34,700	33,830	33,660	32,980	32,490	-16.0
Delaware	7,349	5,550	6,108	7,275	7,205	7,988	7,839	8,133	8,040	8,240	8,060	8,230	7,930	7,860	7,880	8,080	7,950	8,040	8,530	8,460	8,590	8,710	8,740	6.0
District of Columbia[3]	4,848	3,626	2,695	3,150 [4]	2,944	3,352	3,517	3,602	3,480	3,860	3,540	3,480	3,340	3,530	3,280	3,420	3,410	3,220	3,190	3,270	3,490	3,680	3,980	3.0
Florida	88,755	88,934	106,708	134,686	142,284	149,046	153,461	156,130	155,500	151,970	160,090	159,610	162,420	160,840	163,420	164,400	164,640	160,110	159,830	162,020	163,750	167,700	171,200	12.7
Georgia	62,963	56,605	62,563	73,498	77,829	83,505	88,003	91,561	92,340	90,580	93,090	95,320	95,420	97,490	98,500	100,670	101,060	99,290	98,990	99,360	100,710	102,580	103,690	14.5
Hawaii	11,472	10,325	10,437	10,922	11,063	11,613	11,508	10,998	10,720	11,360	10,950	11,000	10,870	10,810	10,870	11,410	10,830	11,390	11,460	11,550	11,770	11,860	12,040	5.9
Idaho	12,679	11,971	16,170	16,096	16,242	16,567	16,807	17,793	17,520	17,570	17,390	18,190	17,920	18,240	18,650	18,890	19,350	19,450	19,490	19,910	20,290	20,300	20,510	16.7
Illinois	136,735	108,119	111,835	126,817	130,220	135,143	131,670	139,035	134,960	139,580	139,130	138,970	134,300	134,050	136,030	139,410	137,800	138,530	140,520	141,780	140,140	136,670	136,740	-2.0
Indiana	73,381	60,012	57,012	57,920	59,887	61,901	63,663	64,551	66,140	65,670	66,570	67,550	66,000	66,810	66,810	67,610	66,100	66,010	63,490	65,840	63,740	64,370	65,220	-0.7
Iowa	42,636	31,796	33,926	33,693	34,127	34,573	33,926	34,462	31,370	33,230	32,590	32,660	32,630	32,670	32,900	33,400	33,300	33,160	33,610	33,760	34,260	33,970	35,530	6.9
Kansas	29,397	25,367	29,102	29,818	30,139	30,737	30,368	31,642	31,370	31,900	32,310	32,200	31,530	32,350	32,440	32,970	33,110	32,680	33,310	33,250	33,490	33,970	34,220	7.3
Kentucky	41,714	38,005	36,830	38,449	39,099	39,339	41,851	42,664	43,030	42,640	42,630	42,430	41,350	42,060	42,500	43,260	43,780	42,750	43,230	43,230	43,210	44,490	44,820	5.1
Louisiana	46,199	36,053	38,430	33,275	34,274	39,401	35,622	36,573	35,850	36,670	37,130	37,690	36,860	36,810	37,060	39,010	38,560	38,660	37,830	38,340	38,470	39,520	40,470	10.4
Maine	15,554	13,839	12,211	12,950	13,151	14,350 [5]	14,093 [5]	14,069	13,650	13,470	13,120	12,780	12,560	12,590	12,190	12,050	11,920	11,660	11,550	11,850	11,780	11,500	11,340	-15.8
Maryland	54,050	41,566	47,849	55,536	57,564	59,171	58,304	59,078	58,750	58,810	58,670	57,590	56,770	56,540	55,560	56,750	56,000	57,930	58,530	59,620	60,140	62,050	62,940	7.0
Massachusetts	74,831	55,941 [6]	52,950	61,272	63,903	65,197	65,258	64,462	64,730	65,160	66,000	64,470	64,430	65,000	64,520	64,530	64,550	63,920	64,030	64,050	63,020	63,630	63,230	-3.0
Michigan	124,372	93,807	97,679	102,582	111,838	115,183	112,742	110,682	105,750	105,450	103,880	101,580	101,090	99,050	99,550	99,310	98,120	95,950	94,920	95,710	92,880	92,940	92,710	-12.1
Minnesota	64,166	49,087	57,372	58,898	59,497	60,409	59,729	59,667	59,360	57,500	56,880	56,130	56,410	56,130	57,080	57,680	58,700	58,290	60,010	61,840	62,140	63,030	63,630	10.7
Mississippi	28,083	25,182	24,232	23,848	24,186	24,795	24,505	25,478	27,320	26,150	26,910	26,490	26,210	26,270	26,690	27,640	26,790	26,300	25,650	26,210	26,030	27,070	27,830	6.4
Missouri	60,359	48,957	52,848	58,417	60,275	61,717	62,969	63,994	63,000	61,310	61,200	61,190	60,640	61,180	60,790	61,010	60,480	59,590	59,750	60,410	60,570	61,280	61,340	#
Montana	11,634	9,370	10,903	10,283	10,122	10,396	10,077	10,075	9,730	9,760	9,320	9,490	9,370	9,340	9,440	9,250	9,500	9,590	9,610	9,820	9,820	10,410	10,700	9.7
Nebraska	21,411	17,664	20,149	19,764	19,873	20,035	19,501	19,370	20,330	20,460	21,240	21,190	21,000	20,930	21,190	21,800	22,060	22,450	22,750	23,420	23,150	23,560	23,720	15.9
Nevada	9,009	9,477	14,551	16,455	17,149	18,815	19,904 [2]	20,956	21,180	21,930	23,160	21,680	21,810	22,160	22,420	22,690	22,890	23,060	22,960	23,140	23,530	24,230	24,950	13.8
New Hampshire	11,552	10,766	11,829	13,988	14,452	14,982	14,757	15,034	14,500	14,430	14,150	13,730	13,540	13,340	12,990	12,920	12,620	12,610	12,330	12,340	12,040	12,050	11,840	-17.9
New Jersey	93,168	69,824	74,420	90,049	93,013	94,994	95,085	96,225	95,180	93,820	97,060	94,780	95,040	95,580	95,930	95,300	95,200	94,080	95,040	95,240	93,830	95,010	95,300	1.6
New Mexico	17,915	14,884	18,031	17,822	16,131	18,264	17,931	18,586	19,350	20,310	19,760	19,400	19,360	19,410	19,990	19,940	20,290	20,080	20,050	20,390	20,490	20,760	20,860	2.7
New York	198,465	143,318	141,731	161,817	166,333	176,310	180,917	183,826	182,760	181,050	182,970	180,480	178,720	177,710	176,780	179,000	176,590	175,560	178,550	179,330	179,070	184,170	185,060	2.2
North Carolina	69,356	64,782	62,140	76,710	76,031	83,307	86,712	88,704	89,900	93,980	94,420	95,450	96,940	98,410	99,840	102,030	103,160	101,460	101,980	94,650	102,990	104,790	105,400	12.1
North Dakota	9,924	7,680	8,606	7,192	7,159	6,999	7,232	7,155	7,160	6,940	6,650	7,020	6,940	7,250	7,230	7,090	7,400	7,610	7,900	8,440	8,600	9,550	10,000	44.1
Ohio	143,503	114,513	111,668	117,356	117,658	120,758	122,203	123,437	124,230	123,140	123,210	117,880	116,410	116,660	117,270	117,870	117,300	115,110	114,700	114,700	114,020	114,600	114,440	-7.1
Oklahoma	38,875	35,606	37,646	36,497	37,100	37,630	37,219	38,503	37,740	37,310	37,480	37,250	37,630	38,780	39,290	39,920	39,900	40,230	40,750	41,140	41,520	42,220	43,330	16.1
Oregon	28,729	25,473	30,151	32,394	33,446	34,949	35,138	34,671	34,720	34,260	35,040	34,940	34,880	35,110	35,080	35,000	35,050	34,660	34,880	35,310	35,400	36,260	36,850	7.6
Pennsylvania	144,645	110,527	113,959	127,830 [4]	128,603	130,298	130,658	131,182	130,290	131,740	127,590	124,360	118,900	118,990	119,700	120,310	119,450	116,930	118,630	119,890	118,660	120,320	120,020	-8.9
Rhode Island	10,719	7,825	8,477	10,108	10,384	10,347	10,028	9,908	9,730	9,560	9,860	9,840	9,680	9,440	8,610	8,900	9,480	9,430	9,430	9,540	9,280	9,000	8,770	-8.3

See notes at end of table.

Table 219.20. Public high school graduates, by region, state, and jurisdiction: Selected years, 1980–81 through 2024–25—Continued

Region, state, and jurisdiction	Actual data										Projected data													Percent change, 2011–12 to 2024–25
	1980–81	1989–90	1999–2000	2005–06	2006–07	2007–08	2008–09	2009–10	2010–11	2011–12	2012–13	2013–14	2014–15	2015–16	2016–17	2017–18	2018–19	2019–20	2020–21	2021–22	2022–23	2023–24	2024–25	
1	2	3	4	5	6	7	8	9	10	11	12	13	14	15	16	17	18	19	20	21	22	23	24	25
South Carolina	38,347	32,483	31,617	34,970 [4]	35,108	35,303	39,114	40,438	40,710	41,850	41,460	41,300	41,400	42,340	43,210	44,300	44,470	43,740	43,690	44,170	45,100	46,700	48,060	14.8
South Dakota	10,385	7,650	9,278	8,589	8,346	8,582	8,123	8,162	8,250	8,200	8,230	8,180	8,040	7,970	8,210	8,240	8,150	8,230	8,460	8,750	9,090	9,250	9,520	16.1
Tennessee	50,648	46,094	41,568	50,880	54,502	57,486	60,368	62,408	61,860	62,320	61,250	60,030	59,480	60,130	60,970	61,260	61,240	60,580	60,740	61,410	61,910	63,180	63,940	2.6
Texas	171,665	172,480	212,925	240,485	241,193	252,121	264,275	280,894	290,470	290,700	297,500	304,090	308,460	316,310	321,240	331,100	337,700	334,920	339,020	343,800	349,770	353,890	359,090	23.5
Utah	19,886	21,196	32,501	29,050	28,276	28,167	30,463	31,481	30,890	31,160	32,240	32,390	33,370	34,900	36,060	37,020	37,670	38,140	39,370	40,130	40,280	41,480	42,530	36.5
Vermont	6,424	6,127	6,675	6,779	7,317	7,392	7,209	7,199	6,930	6,860	6,650	6,510	6,400	6,270	6,140	6,000	5,980	5,890	5,850	5,940	6,020	5,890	6,020	-12.2
Virginia	67,126	60,635	65,596	69,597	73,997	77,369	79,651	81,511	82,900	83,340	83,170	82,730	82,490	83,530	83,690	85,450	85,390	84,890	85,300	87,050	86,940	88,870	89,380	7.2
Washington	50,046	45,941	57,597	60,213	62,801	61,625	62,764	66,046	66,450	65,210	66,850	66,060	66,490	66,170	66,380	66,870	66,740	65,330	66,340	67,240	67,660	69,040	70,860	8.7
West Virginia	23,580	21,854	19,437	16,763	17,407	17,489	17,690	17,651	17,310	17,600	17,790	17,340	17,380	17,520	17,270	17,620	17,230	17,390	16,910	17,160	17,020	16,820	16,980	-3.6
Wisconsin	67,743	52,038	58,545	63,003	63,968	65,183	65,410	64,687	64,140	62,710	61,670	61,350	60,610	60,980	61,350	62,010	61,540	60,760	61,270	62,370	61,850	62,250	62,650	-0.1
Wyoming	6,161	5,823	6,462	5,527	5,441	5,494	5,493	5,695	5,600	5,550	5,460	5,550	5,640	5,820	5,880	5,900	5,910	5,960	6,270	6,280	6,540	6,710	6,930	24.8
Jurisdiction																								
Bureau of Indian Education	—	—	—	—	—	—	—	—	—	—	—	—	—	—	—	—	—	—	—	—	—	—	—	—
DoD, overseas	—	—	2,642	—	—	—	—	—	—	—	—	—	—	—	—	—	—	—	—	—	—	—	—	—
DoD, domestic	—	—	560	—	—	—	—	—	—	—	—	—	—	—	—	—	—	—	—	—	—	—	—	—
Other jurisdictions																								
American Samoa	—	703	698	879	954	—	—	—	—	—	—	—	—	—	—	—	—	—	—	—	—	—	—	—
Guam	—	1,033	1,406	—	—	—	—	—	—	—	—	—	—	—	—	—	—	—	—	—	—	—	—	—
Northern Marianas	—	227	360	670	643	—	—	—	—	—	—	—	—	—	—	—	—	—	—	—	—	—	—	—
Puerto Rico	—	29,049	30,856	31,896	31,718	30,016	29,286	25,514	—	—	—	—	—	—	—	—	—	—	—	—	—	—	—	—
U.S. Virgin Islands	—	1,260	1,050	—	820	820	940	958	—	—	—	—	—	—	—	—	—	—	—	—	—	—	—	—

—Not available.
#Rounds to zero.
[1]U.S. total includes estimates for nonreporting states.
[2]Estimated high school graduates from NCES 2011-312, *Public School Graduates and Dropouts from the Common Core of Data: School Year 2008–09.*
[3]Beginning in 1989–90, graduates from adult programs are excluded.
[4]Projected data from NCES 2009-062, *Projections of Education Statistics to 2018.*
[5]Includes 1,161 graduates in 2007–08 and 1,169 graduates in 2008–09 from private high schools that received a majority of their funding from public sources.

[6]Projected data from NCES 91-490, *Projections of Education Statistics to 2002.*
NOTE: Data include regular diploma recipients, but exclude students receiving a certificate of attendance and persons receiving high school equivalency certificates. DoD = Department of Defense. Some data have been revised from previously published figures. Detail may not sum to totals because of rounding.
SOURCE: U.S. Department of Education, National Center for Education Statistics, Common Core of Data (CCD), "State Nonfiscal Survey of Public Elementary/Secondary Education," 1981–82 through 2005–06; "State Dropout and Completion Data File," 2005–06 through 2009–10; *Public School Graduates and Dropouts from the Common Core of Data,* 2007–08 and 2008–09; and State High School Graduates Projection Model, 1980–81 through 2024–25. (This table was prepared August 2015.)

Table 219.30. Public high school graduates, by race/ethnicity: 1998–99 through 2024–25

Year	Number of high school graduates							Percentage distribution of graduates						
	Total	White	Black	Hispanic	Asian/ Pacific Islander	American Indian/ Alaska Native	Two or more races	Total	White	Black	Hispanic	Asian/ Pacific Islander	American Indian/ Alaska Native	Two or more races
1	2	3	4	5	6	7	8	9	10	11	12	13	14	15
1998–99	2,485,630	1,749,561	325,708	270,836	115,216	24,309	—	100.0	70.4	13.1	10.9	4.6	1.0	†
1999–2000	2,553,844	1,778,370	338,116	289,139	122,344	25,875	—	100.0	69.6	13.2	11.3	4.8	1.0	†
2000–01	2,569,200	1,775,036	339,578	301,740	126,465	26,381	—	100.0	69.1	13.2	11.7	4.9	1.0	†
2001–02	2,621,534	1,796,110	348,969	317,197	132,182	27,076	—	100.0	68.5	13.3	12.1	5.0	1.0	†
2002–03	2,719,947	1,856,454	359,920	340,182	135,588	27,803	—	100.0	68.3	13.2	12.5	5.0	1.0	†
2003–04	2,753,438	1,829,177	383,443	374,492	137,496	28,830	—	100.0	66.4	13.9	13.6	5.0	1.0	†
2004–05	2,799,250	1,855,198	385,987	383,714	143,729	30,622	—	100.0	66.3	13.8	13.7	5.1	1.1	†
2005–06	2,815,544	1,838,765	399,406	396,820	150,925	29,628	—	100.0	65.3	14.2	14.1	5.4	1.1	†
2006–07	2,893,045	1,868,056	418,113	421,036	154,837	31,003	—	100.0	64.6	14.5	14.6	5.4	1.1	†
2007–08	3,001,337	1,898,367	429,840	448,887	159,410	32,036	32,797 [1]	100.0	63.3	14.3	15.0	5.3	1.1	1.1 [1]
2008–09	3,039,015	1,883,382	451,384	481,698	163,575	32,213	26,763 [1]	100.0	62.0	14.9	15.9	5.4	1.1	0.9 [1]
2009–10	3,128,022	1,871,980	472,261	545,518	167,840	34,131	36,292 [1]	100.0	59.8	15.1	17.4	5.4	1.1	1.2 [1]
2010–11	3,143,879	1,835,156	471,410	583,907	168,880	32,778	51,748	100.0	58.4	15.0	18.6	5.4	1.0	1.6
2011–12	3,147,790	1,807,104	467,419	605,674	173,762	32,423	61,408	100.0	57.4	14.8	19.2	5.5	1.0	2.0
2012–13 [2]	3,170,700	1,794,490	460,680	636,100	180,300	31,060	68,070	100.0	56.6	14.5	20.1	5.7	1.0	2.1
2013–14 [2]	3,154,960	1,775,000	448,730	655,330	179,950	29,830	66,120	100.0	56.3	14.2	20.8	5.7	0.9	2.1
2014–15 [2]	3,136,920	1,747,580	439,490	672,100	180,030	28,780	68,940	100.0	55.7	14.0	21.4	5.7	0.9	2.2
2015–16 [2]	3,151,390	1,739,520	439,690	695,250	176,750	28,250	71,930	100.0	55.2	14.0	22.1	5.6	0.9	2.3
2016–17 [2]	3,168,410	1,733,160	443,830	712,300	175,940	29,380	73,800	100.0	54.7	14.0	22.5	5.6	0.9	2.3
2017–18 [2]	3,212,490	1,729,800	445,100	743,880	188,080	29,610	76,020	100.0	53.8	13.9	23.2	5.9	0.9	2.4
2018–19 [2]	3,211,480	1,706,400	437,760	775,350	185,290	28,900	77,770	100.0	53.1	13.6	24.1	5.8	0.9	2.4
2019–20 [2]	3,185,810	1,672,230	425,850	792,700	186,150	28,480	80,400	100.0	52.5	13.4	24.9	5.8	0.9	2.5
2020–21 [2]	3,206,080	1,666,820	413,890	823,390	191,440	27,680	82,870	100.0	52.0	12.9	25.7	6.0	0.9	2.6
2021–22 [2]	3,231,310	1,658,810	414,030	854,140	191,560	27,360	85,410	100.0	51.3	12.8	26.4	5.9	0.8	2.6
2022–23 [2]	3,246,200	1,633,360	415,730	895,040	187,680	26,660	87,730	100.0	50.3	12.8	27.6	5.8	0.8	2.7
2023–24 [2]	3,290,220	1,626,920	421,950	938,580	185,110	27,120	90,550	100.0	49.4	12.8	28.5	5.6	0.8	2.8
2024–25 [2]	3,325,870	1,623,940	432,000	961,270	187,850	27,420	93,390	100.0	48.8	13.0	28.9	5.6	0.8	2.8

—Not available.
†Not applicable.
[1]Data on students of Two or more races were not reported by all states; therefore, the data are not comparable to figures for 2010–11 and later years.
[2]Projected.
NOTE: Race categories exclude persons of Hispanic ethnicity. Prior to 2007–08, data on students of Two or more races were not collected separately. Some data have been revised from previously published figures. Detail may not sum to totals because of rounding.

SOURCE: U.S. Department of Education, National Center for Education Statistics, Common Core of Data (CCD), "State Nonfiscal Survey of Public Elementary/Secondary Education," 1999–2000 through 2005–06; "State Dropout and Completion Data File," 2005–06 through 2011–12; and National Public High School Graduates by Race/Ethnicity Projection Model, 1995–96 through 2024–25. (This table was prepared August 2015.)

Table 219.35. Averaged freshman graduation rates for public secondary schools, by state or jurisdiction: Selected years, 1990–91 through 2009–10

State or jurisdiction	1990–91	1995–96	1997–98	1998–99	1999–2000	2000–01	2001–02	2002–03	2003–04	2004–05	2005–06	2006–07	2007–08	2008–09	2009–10
1	2	3	4	5	6	7	8	9	10	11	12	13	14	15	16
United States	73.7	71.0	71.3	71.1	71.7	71.7	72.6	73.9	74.3 [1]	74.7	73.4 [2]	73.9	74.7	75.5 [2]	78.2
Alabama	69.8	62.7	64.4	61.3	64.1	63.7	62.1	64.7	65.0	65.9	66.2	67.1	69.0	69.9	71.8
Alaska	74.6	68.3	68.9	70.0	66.7	68.0	65.9	68.0	67.2	64.1	66.5	69.0	69.1	72.6	75.5
Arizona	76.7	60.8	65.6	62.3	63.6	74.2	74.7	75.9	66.8	84.7	70.5	69.6	70.7	72.5	74.7
Arkansas	76.6	74.2	73.9	73.7	74.6	73.9	74.8	76.6	76.8	75.7	80.4	74.4	76.4	74.0	75.0
California	69.6	67.6	69.6	71.1	71.7	71.6	72.7	74.1	73.9	74.6	69.2	70.7	71.2	71.0 [3]	78.2
Colorado	76.3	74.8	73.9	73.4	74.1	73.2	74.7	76.4	78.7	76.7	75.5	76.6	75.4	77.6	79.8
Connecticut	80.2	76.1	76.9	76.0	81.9	77.5	79.7	80.9	80.7	80.9	80.9	81.8	82.2	75.4	75.1
Delaware	72.5	70.4	74.1	70.4	66.8	71.0	69.5	73.0	72.9	73.0	76.3	71.9	72.1	73.7	75.5
District of Columbia	54.5	49.7	53.9	52.0	54.5	60.2	68.4	59.6	68.2	66.3	65.4 [4]	54.8	56.0	62.4	59.9
Florida	65.6	62.3	62.1	61.4	61.0	61.2	63.4	66.7	66.4	64.6	63.6	65.0	66.9	68.9	70.8
Georgia	70.3	61.9	58.2	57.5	59.7	58.7	61.1	60.8	61.2	61.7	62.4	64.1	65.4	67.8	69.9
Hawaii	75.9	74.5	68.8	67.5	70.9	68.3	72.1	71.3	72.6	75.1	75.5	75.4	76.0	75.3	75.4
Idaho	79.6	80.5	79.7	79.5	79.4	79.6	79.3	81.4	81.5	81.0	80.5	80.4	80.1	80.6	84.0
Illinois	76.6	75.2	76.8	76.0	76.3	75.6	77.1	75.9	80.3	79.4	79.7	79.5	80.4	77.7	81.9
Indiana	76.9	73.6	73.8	74.3	71.8	72.1	73.1	75.5	73.5	73.2	73.3	73.9	74.1	75.2	77.2
Iowa	84.4	84.3	83.9	83.3	83.1	82.8	84.1	85.3	85.8	86.6	86.9	86.5	86.4	85.7	87.9
Kansas	80.8	77.1	76.0	76.7	77.1	76.5	77.1	76.9	77.9	79.2	77.5	78.8	79.0	80.2	84.5
Kentucky	72.9	71.3	70.2	70.0	69.7	69.8	69.8	71.7	73.0	75.9	77.2	76.4	74.4	77.6	79.9
Louisiana	57.5	61.7	61.3	61.1	62.2	63.7	64.4	64.1	69.4	63.9	59.5	61.3	63.5	67.3	68.8
Maine	80.7	73.7	78.5	74.7	75.9	76.4	75.6	76.3	77.6	78.6	76.3	78.5	79.1 [5]	79.9 [5]	82.8 [6]
Maryland	77.5	78.3	76.2	76.6	77.6	78.7	79.7	79.2	79.5	79.3	79.9	80.0	80.4	80.1	82.2
Massachusetts	79.1	78.0	78.3	77.9	78.0	78.9	77.6	75.7	79.3	78.7	79.5	80.8	81.5	83.3	82.6
Michigan	72.1	71.4	74.6	73.9	75.3	75.4	72.9	74.0	72.5	73.0	72.2	77.0	76.3	75.3	75.9
Minnesota	90.8	86.1	85.0	86.0	84.9	83.6	83.9	84.8	84.7	85.9	86.2	86.5	86.4	87.4	88.2
Mississippi	63.3	59.7	59.8	59.2	59.4	59.7	61.2	62.7	62.7	63.3	63.5	63.5	63.9	62.0	63.8
Missouri	76.0	75.0	75.2	75.8	76.3	75.5	76.8	78.3	80.4	80.6	81.0	81.9	82.4	83.1	83.7
Montana	84.4	83.9	82.2	81.3	80.8	80.0	79.8	81.0	80.4	81.5	81.9	81.5	82.0	82.0	81.9
Nebraska	86.7	85.6	85.6	87.3	85.7	83.8	83.9	85.2	87.6	87.8	87.0	86.3	83.8	82.9	83.8
Nevada	77.0	65.8	70.6	71.0	69.7	70.0	71.9	72.3	57.4	55.8	55.8	54.2	56.3	56.3 [3]	57.8
New Hampshire	78.6	77.5	76.7	75.3	76.1	77.8	77.8	78.2	78.7	80.1	81.1	81.7	83.3	84.3	86.3
New Jersey	81.4	82.8	76.3	77.5	83.6	85.4	85.8	87.0	86.3	85.1	84.8	84.4	84.6	85.3	87.2
New Mexico	70.1	63.7	61.6	63.3	64.7	65.9	67.4	63.1	67.0	65.4	67.3	59.1	66.8	64.8	67.3
New York	66.1	63.6	63.4	62.5	61.8	61.5	60.5	60.9	60.9 [7]	65.3	67.4	68.9	70.9	73.5	76.0
North Carolina	71.3	66.5	65.6	65.4	65.8	66.5	68.2	70.1	71.4	72.6	71.8	68.6	72.8	75.1	76.9
North Dakota	87.6	89.5	86.7	85.6	86.0	85.4	85.0	86.4	86.1	86.3	82.2	83.1	83.8	87.4	88.4
Ohio	77.5	74.5	77.0	75.0	75.2	76.5	77.5	79.0	81.3	80.2	79.2	78.7	79.0	79.6	81.4
Oklahoma	76.5	75.6	75.1	76.4	75.8	75.8	76.0	76.0	77.0	76.9	77.8	77.8	78.0	77.3	78.5
Oregon	72.7	68.3	69.0	68.2	69.6	68.3	71.0	73.7	74.2	74.2	73.0	73.8	76.7	76.5	76.3
Pennsylvania	79.7	80.0	79.4	79.1	78.7	79.0	80.2	81.7	82.2	82.5	83.5 [4]	83.0	82.7	80.5	84.1
Rhode Island	75.0	72.7	72.5	72.2	72.8	73.5	75.7	77.7	75.9	78.4	77.8	78.4	76.4	75.3	76.4
South Carolina	66.6	60.9	59.3	59.1	58.6	56.5	57.9	59.7	60.6	60.1	61.0 [4]	58.9	62.2	66.0	68.2
South Dakota	83.8	84.5	77.7	74.2	77.6	77.4	79.0	83.0	83.7	82.3	84.5	82.5	84.4	81.7	81.8
Tennessee	69.8	66.6	58.4	58.5	59.5	59.0	59.6	63.4	66.1	68.5	70.7	72.6	74.9	77.4	80.4
Texas	72.2	66.1	69.4	69.2	71.0	70.8	73.5	75.5	76.7	74.0	72.5	71.9	73.1	75.4	78.8
Utah	77.5	76.9	80.7	81.6	82.5	81.6	80.5	80.2	83.0	84.4	78.6	76.6	74.3	79.4	78.6
Vermont	79.5	85.3	83.9	81.9	81.0	80.2	82.0	83.6	85.4	86.5	82.3	88.5	89.3	89.6	91.4
Virginia	76.2	76.2	76.6	76.3	76.9	77.5	76.7	80.6	79.3	79.6	74.5	75.5	77.0	78.4	81.2
Washington	75.7	75.5	73.3	73.2	73.7	69.2	72.2	74.2	74.6	75.0	72.9	74.8	71.9	73.7	77.2
West Virginia	76.6	77.0	77.4	77.9	76.7	75.9	74.2	75.7	76.9	77.3	76.9	78.2	77.3	77.0	78.3
Wisconsin	85.2	83.6	83.1	82.6	82.7	83.3	84.8	85.8	85.8 [7]	86.7	87.5	88.5	89.6	90.7	91.1
Wyoming	81.1	77.7	77.1	76.6	76.3	73.4	74.4	73.9	76.0	76.7	76.1	75.8	76.0	75.2	80.3
Other jurisdictions															
American Samoa	85.3	79.7	76.6	80.4	71.9	77.0	82.9	81.0	80.2	81.1	81.0	84.6	—	—	—
Guam	48.2	44.6	39.5	54.7	52.9	51.7	—	56.3	48.4	—	—	—	—	—	—
Northern Marianas	—	63.3	63.4	63.5	61.1	62.7	65.2	65.2	75.3	75.4	80.3	73.6	—	—	—
Puerto Rico	60.9	60.8	61.9	63.6	64.7	65.7	66.2	67.8	64.8	61.7	68.6	66.7	64.5	67.2	60.2
U.S. Virgin Islands	53.2	54.2	58.6	58.6	53.8	57.3	48.7	53.5	—	—	—	57.8	58.3	63.1	65.5

—Not available.

[1] Includes estimates for New York and Wisconsin. Without estimates for these two states, the averaged freshman graduation rate for the remaining 48 states and the District of Columbia is 75.0 percent.

[2] U.S. total includes estimates for nonreporting states.

[3] Estimated high school graduates from NCES 2011-312, *Public School Graduates and Dropouts From the Common Core of Data: School Year 2008–09*.

[4] Projected high school graduates from NCES 2009-062, *Projections of Education Statistics to 2018*.

[5] Includes 1,161 graduates in 2007–08 and 1,169 graduates in 2008–09 from private high schools that received a majority of their funding from public sources.

[6] Includes 1,419 fall 2006 9th-graders who attended publicly funded private schools that were not reported in the 2006–07 Common Core of Data, but were reported in data for later years.

[7] Estimated high school graduates from NCES 2006-606rev, *The Averaged Freshman Graduation Rate for Public High Schools From the Common Core of Data: School Years 2002–03 and 2003–04*.

NOTE: The averaged freshman graduation rate provides an estimate of the percentage of students who receive a regular diploma within 4 years of entering ninth grade. The rate uses aggregate student enrollment data to estimate the size of an incoming freshman class and aggregate counts of the number of diplomas awarded 4 years later. Averaged freshman graduation rates in this table are based on reported totals of enrollment by grade and high school graduates, rather than on details reported by race/ethnicity. Some data have been revised from previously published figures.
SOURCE: U.S. Department of Education, National Center for Education Statistics, Common Core of Data (CCD), "State Nonfiscal Survey of Public Elementary/Secondary Education," 1986–87 through 2007–08; "State Dropout and Completion Data File," 2005–06 through 2009–10; *The Averaged Freshman Graduation Rate for Public High Schools From the Common Core of Data: School Years 2002–03 and 2003–04*; *Public School Graduates and Dropouts From the Common Core of Data*, 2007–08 and 2008–09; and *Projections of Education Statistics to 2018*. (This table was prepared October 2012.)

Table 219.40. Public high school averaged freshman graduation rate (AFGR), by sex, race/ethnicity, and state or jurisdiction: 2010–11

State or jurisdiction	Total, male and female						Male						Female					
	Total[1]	White	Black	Hispanic	Asian/ Pacific Islander	American Indian/ Alaska Native	Total[1]	White	Black	Hispanic	Asian/ Pacific Islander	American Indian/ Alaska Native	Total[1]	White	Black	Hispanic	Asian/ Pacific Islander	American Indian/ Alaska Native
1	2	3	4	5	6	7	8	9	10	11	12	13	14	15	16	17	18	19
United States	79.6	84.0	66.6	74.6	92.6	68.2	76.3	81.7	61.1	70.2	90.6	65.4	83.2	86.4	72.4	79.4	94.8	71.1
Alabama	76.1	79.8	70.1	73.3	87.1	87.0	72.8	77.8	64.6	72.1	85.9	86.8	79.6	82.1	75.8	74.8	88.5	87.2
Alaska	77.9	83.2	70.0	79.8	98.7	56.6	74.6	81.1	67.6	76.8	93.1	51.2	81.3	85.4	72.5	83.4	100.0	62.6
Arizona	78.9	83.1	79.8	73.5	94.5	65.7	75.9	80.8	77.2	69.5	92.4	62.7	82.1	85.5	82.5	77.7	96.5	68.8
Arkansas	77.0	77.8	69.7	79.1	98.4	77.0	74.0	75.7	64.0	74.7	97.8	76.7	80.3	80.0	75.6	83.9	99.1	77.2
California	79.7	86.7	66.6	74.7	95.2	75.1	75.8	83.7	61.9	69.7	93.0	71.0	84.0	90.0	71.5	79.9	97.7	79.4
Colorado	82.0	83.7	68.6	75.3	84.2	57.1	78.8	81.4	65.1	70.7	82.5	48.3	85.3	86.2	72.0	80.2	86.0	66.1
Connecticut	84.7	89.0	72.9	71.5	98.0	100.0	82.1	87.3	67.0	68.0	99.1	100.0 [2]	87.5	90.8	79.4	75.2	96.9	100.0 [2]
Delaware	76.1	79.5	68.9	73.3	93.3	98.2 [2]	71.9	75.6	63.4	68.8	94.7	‡	80.6	83.8	74.5	77.8	93.8	‡
District of Columbia	64.9	97.5	63.0	69.5	61.8 [2]	‡	60.2	97.2 [2]	58.1	67.3	56.0 [2]	‡	69.4	97.7 [2]	67.9	71.7	‡	‡
Florida	72.0	74.7	63.0	74.9	91.5	93.6	68.3	71.9	58.0	70.4	90.0	88.3	76.0	77.7	68.3	79.8	93.2	99.5
Georgia	69.6	74.5	62.5	66.4	93.2	100.0	65.6	72.0	56.5	62.6	91.5	100.0 [2]	73.8	77.1	68.7	70.6	95.1	100.0 [2]
Hawaii	73.7	52.9	79.5	56.0	73.4	47.9 [2]	71.4	52.2	75.7	52.8	71.2	49.9 [2]	76.3	53.7	83.9	59.2	76.0	45.5 [2]
Idaho	83.2	83.2	67.0	77.2	93.5	75.3	80.4	80.5	64.9	74.2	88.4	75.1	86.1	86.0	69.9	80.6	99.2	75.4
Illinois	80.0	87.5	62.6	74.2	97.1	96.7	78.1	87.8	56.9	70.0	99.2	100.0	82.0	87.2	68.6	78.4	95.0	89.1
Indiana	79.9	81.6	66.5	83.3	99.8	86.4	76.1	78.1	61.1	76.9	100.0	85.3	84.0	85.2	72.3	90.5	97.3	87.4
Iowa	89.0	89.2	65.5	89.1	87.5	60.6	86.5	87.4	62.1	79.9	86.1	56.6	91.6	91.2	69.0	99.7	88.8	66.7 [2]
Kansas	86.5	86.8	68.7	84.2	92.9	61.2	83.4	84.6	64.9	77.1	89.4	63.8	89.9	89.2	73.0	92.1	96.7	58.6
Kentucky	80.9	81.7	76.3	89.2	100.0	62.7 [2]	78.7	79.1	71.0	85.0	100.0	65.5 [2]	84.9	84.5	82.1	94.4	100.0	60.5 [2]
Louisiana	71.2	75.6	63.7	89.8	97.8	66.1	65.5	71.6	55.9	82.1	96.1	60.1	77.2	79.9	71.6	97.1	99.6	72.9
Maine[3]	85.7	84.9	78.2	100.0	95.3	88.7	84.1	83.1	78.5	100.0 [2]	100.0 [2]	78.8 [2]	87.3	86.7	77.8	100.0 [2]	89.2	99.4 [2]
Maryland	83.8	86.3	74.6	84.7	96.4	75.5	79.3	84.0	68.0	77.5	95.2	68.9	88.6	88.7	81.6	92.9	97.7	82.8
Massachusetts	85.4	89.2	76.7	68.5	96.5	68.2	82.9	87.2	71.3	65.0	94.8	59.9	88.1	91.3	82.6	72.1	98.4	74.6
Michigan	74.7	80.4	57.3	51.2	91.9	59.4	70.3	76.7	50.0	47.7	90.0	55.0	79.5	84.3	65.1	55.2	93.9	63.9
Minnesota	89.2	92.5	69.9	73.3	90.1	48.7	87.0	90.6	68.1	68.3	87.9	48.1	91.5	94.6	71.7	78.7	92.4	49.2
Mississippi	68.5	72.2	65.1	68.1	93.4	55.9 [2]	63.3	68.7	58.2	65.2	83.5	50.8 [2]	74.0	75.9	72.0	71.6	100.0	‡
Missouri	84.7	86.4	72.7	88.2	98.2	87.7	81.9	84.4	66.6	84.7	99.0	90.6	87.6	88.5	79.2	92.0	97.4	84.8
Montana	83.7	85.7	92.0 [2]	92.7	87.0	61.5	82.5	84.4	83.2 [2]	94.6	83.5 [2]	61.2	85.0	87.0	100.0 [2]	90.7	90.2 [2]	62.0
Nebraska	89.8	91.3	58.4	87.6	96.3	57.9	87.1	90.0	53.4	81.4	90.0	53.4	92.6	92.7	63.9	94.7	100.0	62.6
Nevada	58.7	64.3	39.7	49.9	67.9	39.6	53.7	59.7	34.5	44.7	63.4	37.0	64.3	69.2	45.2	55.7	72.8	42.2
New Hampshire	86.6	85.9	78.5	87.3	100.0	78.7 [2]	84.0	83.5	73.3	81.5	100.0	‡	89.4	88.4	84.2	93.5	100.0	‡
New Jersey[3]	86.6	91.5	73.5	78.3	97.3	100.0	83.3	89.8	67.4	72.5	96.1	100.0 [2]	90.0	93.2	79.9	84.7	98.6	100.0 [2]
New Mexico	70.7	73.3	59.9	69.5	80.5	66.1	66.8	69.5	57.6	65.8	82.0	61.6	74.8	77.3	62.4	73.5	78.7	70.9
New York	77.6	87.7	63.9	63.1	93.8	64.3	74.8	85.9	59.1	59.0	89.7	62.2	81.0	89.5	69.0	67.5	98.5	66.4
North Carolina	76.8	80.6	68.0	74.2	83.8	71.4	73.1	78.3	62.0	70.2	83.8	67.0	80.7	83.1	74.3	78.7	83.8	76.1
North Dakota	90.2	92.9	100.0	78.7	100.0 [2]	62.0	88.5	91.2	100.0 [2]	80.9 [2]	100.0 [2]	59.1	92.0	94.7	96.3 [2]	76.4 [2]	100.0 [2]	65.1
Ohio	82.3	87.4	61.3	79.2	97.5	82.8	79.9	85.6	56.9	74.6	94.5	80.7	85.0	89.4	66.2	84.5	100.0	84.9
Oklahoma	79.9	81.5	67.5	74.4	100.0	74.3	77.0	78.4	64.2	69.1	100.0	73.3	82.9	84.9	70.9	80.0	100.0	75.5
Oregon	78.1	78.2	65.0	79.9	81.5	62.5	74.4	74.9	62.2	74.0	80.0	56.1	82.1	81.7	67.9	86.3	83.0	68.7
Pennsylvania	85.8	89.6	69.6	72.5	100.0	74.1	83.1	87.8	64.2	67.3	100.0	71.3	88.6	91.5	75.4	78.1	100.0	77.1
Rhode Island	76.6	78.8	66.1	70.2	69.8	55.2 [2]	71.5	75.0	61.7	62.3	67.1	50.5 [2]	81.8	82.8	71.0	78.3	72.7	58.2 [2]
South Carolina	69.0	73.3	61.6	69.7	79.2	61.5	63.4	69.3	53.7	63.4	78.8	57.0 [2]	75.0	77.6	69.8	76.5	79.5	66.3 [2]
South Dakota	81.6	85.9	79.2	80.6	100.0 [2]	42.9	79.2	83.4	81.4 [2]	72.3	100.0 [2]	39.3	84.2	88.6	77.5	91.3 [2]	100.0 [2]	46.4
Tennessee	81.1	83.5	75.2	74.3	97.0	98.8	77.8	81.4	68.6	71.0	94.9	100.0 [2]	84.6	85.7	82.0	77.8	99.2	97.2 [2]
Texas	81.4	83.1	71.4	79.7	94.7	100.0	78.7	81.7	67.7	76.4	93.0	99.4	84.3	84.5	75.3	83.3	96.6	100.0
Utah	78.5	81.5	64.8	61.6	80.7	56.0	75.9	79.1	66.0	58.0	78.4	51.1	81.2	84.1	63.5	65.7	83.3	61.0
Vermont	92.7	91.4	100.0	100.0 [2]	100.0	‡	90.8	89.3	96.7 [2]	100.0 [2]	100.0	‡	94.6	93.6	100.0 [2]	97.3 [2]	100.0 [2]	‡
Virginia	82.7	84.1	69.8	91.3	99.0	86.8	78.6	81.2	63.9	84.6	97.6	85.3	87.1	87.2	76.1	98.7	100.0	88.5
Washington	79.0	79.8	58.1	78.2	80.6	41.5	75.8	76.6	55.0	72.4	78.4	40.3	83.3	83.4	61.5	84.3	82.9	42.7
West Virginia	78.1	78.0	74.5	81.1	98.0	55.4 [2]	76.3	76.1	73.5	75.7	100.0 [2]	‡	80.1	80.0	75.5	88.3 [2]	94.5 [2]	‡
Wisconsin	92.2	95.4	67.2	83.3	99.3	70.0	89.5	93.5	61.0	79.0	98.3	69.0	95.0	97.4	74.0	88.2	100.0	71.0
Wyoming	80.4	80.9	52.2 [2]	82.4	86.7 [2]	46.3	78.2	79.3	56.0 [2]	76.3	78.5 [2]	44.1	82.7	82.5	47.2 [2]	88.5	‡	48.5
Bureau of Indian Education	—	—	—	—	—	—	—	—	—	—	—	—	—	—	—	—	—	—
DoD, overseas	—	—	—	—	—	—	—	—	—	—	—	—	—	—	—	—	—	—
DoD, domestic	—	—	—	—	—	—	—	—	—	—	—	—	—	—	—	—	—	—
Other jurisdictions																		
American Samoa	—	—	—	—	—	—	—	—	—	—	—	—	—	—	—	—	—	—
Guam	—	—	—	—	—	—	—	—	—	—	—	—	—	—	—	—	—	—
Northern Marianas	—	—	—	—	—	—	—	—	—	—	—	—	—	—	—	—	—	—
Puerto Rico	61.6	‡	‡	61.4	‡	‡	55.3	‡	‡	55.1	‡	‡	68.0	‡	‡	67.7	‡	‡
U.S. Virgin Islands	96.8	‡	92.4	100.0	‡	‡	82.5	‡	78.9	99.4 [2]	‡	‡	100.0	‡	100.0	100.0 [2]	‡	‡

—Not available.

‡Reporting standards not met (too few cases).

[1]Total averaged freshman graduation rate (AFGR) is based on reported totals of enrollment by grade and high school graduates, rather than on details reported by race/ethnicity.

[2]AFGR is based on an estimate of 30 to 99 students entering ninth grade and may show large variation from year to year.

[3]AFGR by sex is based on an estimated distribution of male and female graduates.

NOTE: The AFGR provides an estimate of the percentage of students who receive a regular diploma within 4 years of entering ninth grade. The rate uses aggregate student enrollment data to estimate the size of an incoming freshman class and aggregate counts of the number of diplomas awarded 4 years later. The enrollment data used in computing the AFGR for race/ethnicity categories include only students for whom race/ethnicity was reported. Race categories exclude persons of Hispanic ethnicity. DoD = Department of Defense.

SOURCE: U.S. Department of Education, National Center for Education Statistics, Common Core of Data (CCD), "State Dropout and Completion Data File," 2010–11. (This table was prepared January 2016.)

Table 219.50. Number and percentage of 9th- to 12th-graders who dropped out of public schools, by race/ethnicity, grade, and state or jurisdiction: 2009–10

State or jurisdiction	Percent of 9th- to 12th-graders who dropped out (event dropout rate), by race/ethnicity							Number and percent of 9th- to 12th-graders who dropped out (event dropout rate), by grade							
								Grade 9		Grade 10		Grade 11		Grade 12	
	Total	White	Black	Hispanic	Asian/ Pacific Islander	American Indian/ Alaska Native	Two or more races	Number of dropouts	Event dropout rate	Number of dropouts	Event dropout rate	Number of dropouts	Event dropout rate	Number of dropouts	Event dropout rate
1	2	3	4	5	6	7	8	9	10	11	12	13	14	15	16
United States	3.4	2.3	5.5	5.0	1.9	6.7	‡	104,756	2.6	113,370	3.0	117,536	3.3	175,806	5.1
Alabama	1.8	1.6	2.0	0.9	1.4	1.3	—	864	1.4	1,128	2.0	1,048	2.1	862	1.8
Alaska	6.9	5.1	6.4	6.1	4.8	11.6	9.6	404	4.0	551	5.5	1,014	9.3	851	8.7
Arizona	7.8	6.8	8.8	8.1	4.9	14.6	—	4,207	5.1	4,594	5.7	5,269	7.0	10,795	13.6
Arkansas	3.6	3.1	5.0	4.1	2.0	4.9	3.1	720	1.9	1,130	3.2	1,427	4.4	1,613	5.3
California	4.6	2.8	8.4	5.8	2.0	6.5	5.0	13,849	2.6	15,518	3.1	20,625	4.2	42,587	8.9
Colorado	5.3	3.2	8.6	9.9	2.4	10.1	—	1,957	3.1	2,216	3.7	3,045	5.3	5,673	9.7
Connecticut	3.0	1.4	6.8	6.9	1.1	3.0	—	1,316	2.8	1,127	2.6	1,452	3.4	1,299	3.2
Delaware	3.9	3.1	4.9	4.7	3.2	10.3	—	546	4.7	386	3.7	299	3.4	288	3.5
District of Columbia[1]	7.0	4.9	6.9	8.3	5.4	#	—	501	8.1	262	5.9	153	4.2	133	4.0
Florida	2.3	1.6	3.5	2.8	0.8	2.7	—	4,189	1.9	4,348	2.2	4,678	2.4	4,816	2.8
Georgia	3.8	3.1	4.6	4.3	1.5	4.2	3.4	5,800	4.0	5,095	4.2	4,074	3.8	2,800	2.9
Hawaii	5.2	6.4	7.9	5.9	4.7	9.0	—	562	3.7	816	5.7	726	5.8	632	6.0
Idaho	1.4	1.2	1.9	2.2	1.2	2.5	—	211	1.0	235	1.1	301	1.5	386	2.0
Illinois	2.9	1.8	5.7	3.8	0.9	3.0	—	3,482	2.0	5,287	3.1	3,970	2.7	5,801	4.0
Indiana	1.6	1.3	3.1	2.4	1.1	2.2	—	373	0.4	945	1.2	1,349	1.7	2,346	3.2
Iowa	3.4	2.8	9.1	6.9	2.1	8.9	4.9	363	1.0	713	1.9	1,276	3.5	2,747	7.1
Kansas	2.1	1.8	3.7	2.9	0.7	4.1	2.0	442	1.2	661	1.9	765	2.3	1,105	3.3
Kentucky	3.2	2.9	5.5	5.6	2.0	1.9	—	1,076	2.0	1,769	3.5	1,762	3.8	1,615	3.7
Louisiana	4.8	3.2	6.8	3.9	2.0	4.8	—	3,229	5.7	1,920	4.2	1,663	4.1	1,892	4.9
Maine	4.2	4.2	4.9	5.0	3.8	8.6	—	252	1.7	349	2.3	703	4.8	1,260	8.3
Maryland	2.7	2.0	3.4	4.2	0.9	3.2	—	1,998	2.7	2,029	3.0	1,686	2.7	1,369	2.2
Massachusetts	2.8	1.7	5.0	7.3	1.7	3.3	3.1	2,356	3.0	2,045	2.8	1,837	2.6	1,847	2.7
Michigan	4.3	2.7	9.2	6.2	3.1	5.4	—	4,305	3.1	6,661	4.9	5,318	4.2	6,699	5.3
Minnesota	1.6	1.0	3.9	4.2	1.6	5.7	—	337	0.5	453	0.7	796	1.2	2,752	3.7
Mississippi	7.4	5.6	9.3	5.9	2.8	4.6	#	2,399	6.0	2,651	7.3	2,339	7.3	2,023	7.0
Missouri	3.5	2.4	8.4	4.1	1.5	3.0	—	2,139	2.9	2,009	2.9	2,449	3.6	3,245	4.8
Montana	4.3	3.5	7.0	6.2	2.0	10.3	—	340	2.9	435	3.9	527	4.9	599	5.7
Nebraska	2.2	1.6	4.1	4.0	1.8	7.0	—	186	0.8	372	1.7	538	2.5	825	3.7
Nevada	4.5	3.4	6.5	5.4	3.1	4.7	—	790	2.3	1,389	4.0	1,294	4.4	2,071	8.0
New Hampshire	1.2	1.1	1.6	2.9	1.1	1.5	1.0	3	#	6	#	90	0.6	667	4.3
New Jersey	1.6	0.9	3.5	2.8	0.4	1.5	3.4	1,696	1.6	1,667	1.6	1,522	1.5	1,594	1.6
New Mexico	6.9	5.3	9.0	7.2	4.6	8.8	4.7	2,229	7.5	2,075	7.8	1,484	6.6	1,021	5.1
New York	3.6	1.7	6.5	5.9	2.4	5.6	—	7,354	3.1	8,222	3.5	6,674	3.4	8,931	4.7
North Carolina	4.7	4.0	5.4	6.1	2.0	6.1	—	6,553	5.1	5,535	4.9	4,769	4.8	3,338	3.8
North Dakota	2.2	1.7	2.6	3.5	0.9	7.5	—	40	0.5	174	2.3	207	2.7	259	3.4
Ohio	4.2	2.8	9.4	7.4	1.4	7.8	—	6,968	4.4	3,853	2.8	4,574	3.7	7,011	5.9
Oklahoma	2.4	2.1	3.3	3.5	1.1	2.5	—	949	1.9	1,062	2.3	1,188	2.8	1,086	2.7
Oregon	3.4	2.9	6.2	4.7	1.4	6.7	—	465	1.0	771	1.7	1,451	3.3	3,299	7.2
Pennsylvania	2.1	1.5	3.7	5.1	1.3	2.2	—	1,643	1.1	3,029	2.0	3,268	2.3	4,302	3.1
Rhode Island	4.6	3.8	6.6	6.8	4.5	8.5	—	573	4.4	613	5.0	509	4.7	471	4.4
South Carolina	3.0	2.7	3.3	3.6	1.3	5.6	—	1,691	2.7	1,811	3.3	1,547	3.2	1,220	2.7
South Dakota	2.6	1.6	3.4	5.2	2.7	10.5	—	184	1.8	267	2.7	258	2.8	291	3.3
Tennessee	2.7	1.8	4.9	3.3	1.2	2.7	—	1,370	1.8	1,579	2.1	1,790	2.6	2,843	4.3
Texas	2.7	1.2	4.2	3.6	0.5	3.6	—	6,945	1.8	8,253	2.5	6,824	2.2	14,048	4.8
Utah	2.6	2.1	3.8	5.5	2.8	5.7	—	207	0.5	555	1.4	927	2.3	2,444	6.1
Vermont	2.4	2.4	1.5	2.6	2.0	#	4.1	76	1.0	180	2.4	215	3.0	250	3.4
Virginia	2.1	1.4	3.0	4.6	1.2	1.6	—	1,741	1.7	1,857	1.9	1,934	2.1	2,467	2.8
Washington	4.2	3.6	6.1	5.8	3.0	8.2	—	2,881	3.4	2,792	3.4	3,472	4.4	4,815	5.8
West Virginia	4.0	4.0	4.6	4.6	0.5	3.6	1.9	809	3.4	848	4.1	839	4.4	798	4.3
Wisconsin	2.2	1.2	7.5	4.7	1.6	5.2	—	971	1.4	611	0.9	1,222	1.7	3,260	4.6
Wyoming	6.0	5.0	13.1	#	1.7	20.8	94.9	215	3.2	516	7.3	389	6.1	460	7.5
Bureau of Indian Education	—	—	—	—	—	—	—	—	—	—	—	—	—	—	—
DoD, overseas	—	—	—	—	—	—	—	—	—	—	—	—	—	—	—
DoD, domestic	—	—	—	—	—	—	—	—	—	—	—	—	—	—	—
Other jurisdictions															
American Samoa	—	—	—	—	—	—	—	—	—	—	—	—	—	—	—
Guam	—	—	—	—	—	—	—	—	—	—	—	—	—	—	—
Northern Marianas	—	—	—	—	—	—	—	—	—	—	—	—	—	—	—
Puerto Rico	—	—	—	—	—	—	—	—	—	—	—	—	—	—	—
U.S. Virgin Islands	5.5	#	5.3	7.4	#	#	—	122	7.2	68	5.5	53	4.7	38	3.7

—Not available.
#Rounds to zero.
‡Reporting standards not met (too few cases for a reliable estimate).
[1]Data were imputed based on prior year rates.
NOTE: Race categories exclude persons of Hispanic ethnicity. Event dropout rates measure the percentage of public school students in grades 9 through 12 who dropped out of school between one October and the next. Enrollment and dropout data for ungraded students were prorated into grades 9 through 12 based on the counts for graded students. DoD stands for Department of Defense.
SOURCE: U.S. Department of Education, National Center for Education Statistics, Common Core of Data (CCD), "State Dropout and Completion Data File," 2009–10. (This table was prepared November 2012.)

Table 219.60. Number of people taking the general educational development (GED) test and percentage distribution of those who passed, by age group: 1971 through 2013

Year	Number of test takers (in thousands)			Percentage distribution of test passers, by age group[1]				
	Total[2]	Completing test battery[3]	Passing tests[4]	16 to 18 years old	19 to 24 years old	25 to 29 years old	30 to 34 years old	35 years old or over
1	2	3	4	5	6	7	8	9
1971[5]	377	—	227	—	—	—	—	—
1972[5]	419	—	245	—	—	—	—	—
1973[5]	423	—	249	—	—	—	—	—
1974	—	—	294	35 [6]	27 [6]	13	9	17
1975	—	—	340	33 [6]	26 [6]	14	9	18
1976	—	—	333	31 [6]	28 [6]	14	10	17
1977	—	—	330	40 [6]	24 [6]	13	8	14
1978	—	—	381	31 [6]	27 [6]	13	10	18
1979	—	—	426	37 [6]	28 [6]	12	13	11
1980	—	—	479	37 [6]	27 [6]	13	8	15
1981	—	—	489	37 [6]	27 [6]	13	8	14
1982	—	—	486	37 [6]	28 [6]	13	8	15
1983	—	—	465	34 [6]	29 [6]	14	8	15
1984	—	—	427	32 [6]	28 [6]	15	9	16
1985	—	—	413	32 [6]	26 [6]	15	10	16
1986	—	—	428	32 [6]	26 [6]	15	10	17
1987	—	—	444	33 [6]	24 [6]	15	10	18
1988	—	—	410	35 [6]	22 [6]	14	10	18
1989	632	541	357	22	37	13	—	—
1990	714	615	410	22	39	13	10	15
1991	755	657	462	20	40	13	10	16
1992	739	639	457	22	39	13	9	17
1993	746	651	469	22	38	13	10	16
1994	774	668	491	25	37	13	10	15
1995	787	682	504	27	36	13	9	15
1996	824	716	488	27	37	13	9	14
1997	785	681	460	31	36	12	8	13
1998	776	673	481	32	36	11	7	13
1999	808	702	498	32	37	11	7	13
2000	811	699	487	33	37	11	7	13
2001[7]	1,016	928	648	29	38	11	8	14
2002[7]	557	467	330	38	36	10	6	11
2003	657	552	387	35	37	10	7	11
2004	666	570	406	35	38	11	6	10
2005	681	588	424	34	37	12	7	11
2006	676	580	398	35	36	12	6	11
2007	692	600	429	35	35	12	7	11
2008	737	642	469	34	35	13	7	11
2009	748	645	448	31	36	13	8	12
2010	720	623	452	27	37	14	9	14
2011	691	602	434	27	37	13	9	14
2012	674	581	401	26	37	14	9	13
2013	816	714	541	22	35	15	11	17

—Not available.

[1]Age data for 1988 and prior years are for all test takers and may not be comparable to data for later years. For 1989 and later years, age data are only for test passers. The less than 1 percent of people who failed to report their date of birth—2,948 of the 540,535 test passers in 2013—were excluded from the calculation.
[2]All people taking the GED tests (one or more subtests).
[3]People completing the entire GED battery of five tests.
[4]Data for 2002 and later years are for people passing the GED tests (i.e., earning both a passing total score on the test battery and a passing score on each individual test). Data for 2001 and prior years are for high school equivalency credentials issued by the states to GED test passers. In order to receive high school equivalency credentials in some states, GED test passers must meet additional state requirements (e.g., complete an approved course in civics or government).

[5]Includes other jurisdictions, such as Puerto Rico, Guam, and American Samoa.
[6]For 1988 and prior years, 19-year-olds are included with the 16- to 18-year-olds instead of the 19- to 24-year-olds.
[7]A revised GED test was introduced in 2002. In 2001, test takers were required to successfully complete all five components of the GED or else begin the five-part series again with the new test that was introduced in 2002.
NOTE: Data are for the United States only and exclude other jurisdictions, except where noted. Detail may not sum to totals because of rounding.
SOURCE: American Council on Education, General Educational Development Testing Service, the GED annual *Statistical Report*, 1971 through 1992; *Who Took the GED?* 1993 through 2001; *Who Passed the GED Tests?* 2002 through 2005; and *GED Testing Program Statistical Report*, 2006 through 2013, retrieved November 5, 2014, from http://www.gedtesting service.com/educators/historical-testing-data. (This table was prepared November 2014.)

Table 219.65. Among 18- to 24-year-olds who are not enrolled in high school, percentage who are high school completers (status completion rate), by sex and race/ethnicity: 1972 through 2013

[Standard errors appear in parentheses]

Year	Total		Sex				Race/ethnicity[2]							
			Male		Female		White		Black		Hispanic		Asian	
1	2		3		4		5		6		7		8	
1972	82.8	(0.35)	83.0	(0.51)	82.7	(0.48)	86.0	(0.35)	72.1	(1.41)	56.2	(2.78)	—	(†)
1973	83.7	(0.34)	84.0	(0.49)	83.4	(0.47)	87.0	(0.34)	71.6	(1.39)	58.7	(2.79)	—	(†)
1974	83.6	(0.34)	83.4	(0.49)	83.8	(0.46)	86.7	(0.34)	72.9	(1.38)	60.1	(2.58)	—	(†)
1975	83.8	(0.33)	84.1	(0.47)	83.6	(0.46)	87.2	(0.33)	70.2	(1.40)	62.2	(2.61)	—	(†)
1976	83.5	(0.33)	83.0	(0.48)	84.0	(0.45)	86.4	(0.34)	73.5	(1.33)	60.3	(2.55)	—	(†)
1977	83.6	(0.33)	82.8	(0.49)	84.4	(0.45)	86.7	(0.34)	73.9	(1.33)	58.6	(2.52)	—	(†)
1978	83.6	(0.33)	82.8	(0.48)	84.2	(0.45)	86.9	(0.33)	73.4	(1.32)	58.8	(2.45)	—	(†)
1979	83.1	(0.33)	82.1	(0.49)	84.0	(0.45)	86.5	(0.34)	72.6	(1.32)	58.5	(2.40)	—	(†)
1980	83.9	(0.32)	82.3	(0.48)	85.3	(0.43)	87.5	(0.33)	75.2	(1.27)	57.1	(2.28)	—	(†)
1981	83.8	(0.32)	82.0	(0.48)	85.4	(0.42)	87.1	(0.33)	76.7	(1.20)	59.1	(2.22)	—	(†)
1982	83.8	(0.33)	82.7	(0.49)	84.9	(0.45)	87.0	(0.35)	76.4	(1.26)	60.9	(2.37)	—	(†)
1983	83.9	(0.34)	82.1	(0.50)	85.6	(0.45)	87.4	(0.35)	76.8	(1.25)	59.4	(2.40)	—	(†)
1984	84.7	(0.33)	83.3	(0.49)	85.9	(0.45)	87.5	(0.35)	80.3	(1.17)	63.7	(2.33)	—	(†)
1985	85.4	(0.33)	84.0	(0.49)	86.7	(0.44)	88.2	(0.35)	81.0	(1.18)	66.6	(2.39)	—	(†)
1986	85.5	(0.33)	84.2	(0.50)	86.7	(0.45)	88.8	(0.35)	81.8	(1.17)	63.5	(2.29)	—	(†)
1987	84.7	(0.35)	83.6	(0.51)	85.8	(0.47)	87.7	(0.37)	81.9	(1.19)	65.1	(2.23)	—	(†)
1988	84.5	(0.38)	83.2	(0.57)	85.8	(0.51)	88.6	(0.39)	80.9	(1.33)	58.2	(2.70)	—	(†)
1989	84.7	(0.38)	83.2	(0.57)	86.2	(0.51)	89.0	(0.39)	81.9	(1.30)	59.4	(2.62)	89.3	(2.56)
1990	85.6	(0.36)	85.1	(0.53)	86.0	(0.50)	89.6	(0.37)	83.2	(1.23)	59.1	(2.35)	94.2	(1.72)
1991	84.9	(0.37)	83.8	(0.55)	85.9	(0.51)	89.4	(0.38)	82.5	(1.26)	56.5	(2.32)	95.2	(1.42)
1992	86.4	(0.36)	85.3	(0.53)	87.4	(0.49)	90.7	(0.36)	82.0	(1.27)	62.1	(2.32)	93.1	(1.73)
1993	86.2	(0.36)	85.4	(0.53)	86.9	(0.50)	90.1	(0.37)	81.9	(1.27)	64.4	(2.26)	93.9	(1.66)
1994	85.8	(0.33)	84.5	(0.49)	87.0	(0.45)	90.7	(0.34)	83.3	(1.01)	61.8	(1.43)	92.4	(1.56)
1995	85.0	(0.34)	84.3	(0.50)	85.7	(0.47)	89.5	(0.36)	84.1	(1.01)	62.6	(1.40)	94.8	(1.43)
1996	86.2	(0.35)	85.7	(0.50)	86.8	(0.48)	91.5	(0.34)	83.0	(1.08)	61.9	(1.49)	93.5	(1.25)
1997	85.9	(0.35)	84.6	(0.51)	87.2	(0.47)	90.5	(0.36)	82.0	(1.10)	66.7	(1.42)	90.6	(1.58)
1998	84.8	(0.36)	82.6	(0.53)	87.0	(0.47)	90.2	(0.36)	81.4	(1.11)	62.8	(1.37)	94.2	(1.22)
1999	85.9	(0.34)	84.8	(0.50)	87.0	(0.46)	91.2	(0.34)	83.5	(1.04)	63.4	(1.39)	94.0	(1.19)
2000	86.5	(0.33)	84.9	(0.49)	88.1	(0.44)	91.8	(0.33)	83.7	(1.01)	64.1	(1.36)	94.6	(1.13)
2001	86.5	(0.33)	84.6	(0.50)	88.3	(0.43)	91.1	(0.34)	85.7	(0.97)	65.7	(1.31)	96.1	(0.96)
2002	86.6	(0.31)	84.8	(0.46)	88.4	(0.41)	91.8	(0.31)	84.7	(0.95)	67.3	(1.15)	95.7	(0.89)
2003	87.1	(0.30)	85.1	(0.46)	89.2	(0.40)	91.9	(0.31)	85.0	(0.96)	69.2	(1.15)	94.8	(1.06)
2004	86.9	(0.30)	84.9	(0.46)	88.8	(0.40)	91.7	(0.31)	83.5	(0.98)	69.9	(1.12)	95.2	(1.00)
2005	87.6	(0.30)	85.4	(0.45)	89.8	(0.38)	92.3	(0.30)	86.0	(0.91)	70.3	(1.12)	96.0	(0.93)
2006	87.8	(0.29)	86.5	(0.43)	89.2	(0.39)	92.6	(0.30)	84.9	(0.93)	70.9	(1.11)	95.8	(0.95)
2007	89.0	(0.28)	87.4	(0.42)	90.6	(0.37)	93.5	(0.28)	88.8	(0.80)	72.7	(1.07)	92.8	(1.23)
2008	89.9	(0.27)	89.3	(0.39)	90.5	(0.37)	94.2	(0.26)	86.9	(0.86)	75.5	(1.03)	95.5	(1.01)
2009	89.8	(0.27)	88.3	(0.40)	91.2	(0.35)	93.8	(0.27)	87.1	(0.84)	76.8	(1.00)	97.6	(0.72)
2010	90.4	(0.35)	89.2	(0.53)	91.6	(0.38)	93.7	(0.38)	89.2	(1.08)	79.4	(1.21)	95.3	(1.26)
2011	90.8	(0.35)	89.9	(0.50)	91.8	(0.46)	93.8	(0.39)	90.1	(0.98)	82.2	(1.04)	94.1	(1.48)
2012	91.3	(0.33)	90.3	(0.47)	92.3	(0.45)	94.6	(0.38)	90.0	(1.01)	82.8	(1.02)	95.3	(1.24)
2013	92.0	(0.35)	91.4	(0.47)	92.6	(0.45)	94.3	(0.38)	91.5	(1.13)	85.0	(0.98)	96.3	(1.27)

—Not available.
†Not applicable.
[1]The status completion rate is the number of 18- to 24-year-olds who are high school completers as a percentage of the total number of 18- to 24-year-olds who are not enrolled in high school or a lower level of education. High school completers include those with a high school diploma, as well as those with an alternative credential, such as a GED.
[2]Race categories exclude persons of Hispanic ethnicity. Prior to 2003, Asian data include Pacific Islanders, because Asian and Pacific Islander data were collected as a single, combined race category. Beginning in 2003, Asians and Pacific Islanders have been separately categorized. Also beginning in 2003, respondents have been able to select more than one race category and can therefore be categorized as of Two or more races. As of 2003, the

Pacific Islander and Two or more races categories are included in the totals but are not separately shown due to small sample sizes. The American Indian/Alaska Native category is included in the totals for all years.
NOTE: Data are based on sample surveys of the civilian noninstitutionalized population, which excludes persons in prisons, persons in the military, and other persons not living in households. Because of changes in data collection procedures, data for 1992 and later years may not be comparable with figures for prior years. Beginning in 2010, standard errors were computed using replicate weights, which produced more precise values than the generalized variance function methodology used in prior years.
SOURCE: U.S. Department of Commerce, Census Bureau, Current Population Survey (CPS), October, 1972 through 2013. (This table was prepared May 2015.)

Table 219.67. Among 18- to 24-year-olds who are not enrolled in high school, number and percentage who are high school completers (status completers), and percentage distribution, by selected characteristics: 2013
[Standard errors appear in parentheses]

	18- to 24-year-olds not enrolled in high school or lower level of education									
	Number (in thousands)						Percentage distribution			
Selected characteristic	Total population[1]		Status completers[2]		Status completion rate[3]		Of total population[1]		Of status completers[2]	
1	2		3		4		5		6	
Total	28,532	(212.2)	26,257	(209.3)	92.0	(0.35)	100.0	(†)	100.0	(†)
Sex										
Male	14,234	(133.4)	13,017	(138.2)	91.4	(0.47)	49.9	(0.19)	49.6	(0.25)
Female	14,298	(101.5)	13,240	(104.8)	92.6	(0.45)	50.1	(0.19)	50.4	(0.25)
Race/ethnicity										
White	16,010	(178.4)	15,094	(176.1)	94.3	(0.38)	56.1	(0.33)	57.5	(0.39)
Black	3,975	(58.8)	3,638	(72.6)	91.5	(1.13)	13.9	(0.20)	13.9	(0.27)
Hispanic	6,007	(65.2)	5,104	(78.5)	85.0	(0.98)	21.1	(0.29)	19.4	(0.34)
Asian	1,490	(54.2)	1,435	(59.2)	96.3	(1.27)	5.2	(0.17)	5.5	(0.20)
Pacific Islander	127	(34.3)	126	(34.3)	99.3	(0.79)	0.4	(0.12)	0.5	(0.13)
American Indian/Alaska Native	198	(29.9)	181	(29.8)	91.7	(2.97)	0.7	(0.10)	0.7	(0.11)
Two or more races	725	(45.9)	679	(45.2)	93.6	(1.83)	2.5	(0.16)	2.6	(0.17)
Race/ethnicity by sex										
Male										
White	7,988	(126.9)	7,495	(125.0)	93.8	(0.48)	56.1	(0.50)	57.6	(0.57)
Black	1,928	(40.5)	1,742	(45.0)	90.3	(1.41)	13.5	(0.24)	13.4	(0.30)
Hispanic	3,054	(60.2)	2,560	(67.3)	83.8	(1.35)	21.5	(0.54)	19.7	(0.59)
Asian	762	(32.4)	744	(33.8)	97.6	(1.17)	5.4	(0.21)	5.7	(0.24)
Pacific Islander	‡	(†)	‡	(†)	‡	(†)	‡	(†)	‡	(†)
American Indian/Alaska Native	82	(14.7)	74	(15.7)	90.5	(6.44)	0.6	(0.10)	0.6	(0.12)
Two or more races	352	(27.9)	333	(28.8)	94.7	(2.65)	2.5	(0.20)	2.6	(0.22)
Female										
White	8,023	(75.2)	7,599	(75.6)	94.7	(0.45)	56.1	(0.37)	57.4	(0.44)
Black	2,047	(44.0)	1,896	(50.4)	92.6	(1.39)	14.3	(0.32)	14.3	(0.38)
Hispanic	2,953	(43.4)	2,544	(52.4)	86.2	(1.30)	20.7	(0.26)	19.2	(0.35)
Asian	728	(34.5)	691	(38.9)	94.9	(1.94)	5.1	(0.22)	5.2	(0.28)
Pacific Islander	‡	(†)	‡	(†)	‡	(†)	‡	(†)	‡	(†)
American Indian/Alaska Native	116	(22.7)	107	(22.4)	92.5	(4.02)	0.8	(0.16)	0.8	(0.17)
Two or more races	373	(33.2)	345	(32.0)	92.5	(2.88)	2.6	(0.23)	2.6	(0.24)
Age										
18–19	6,737	(79.1)	6,158	(80.9)	91.4	(0.69)	23.6	(0.28)	23.5	(0.32)
20–21	8,372	(163.2)	7,738	(153.2)	92.4	(0.63)	29.3	(0.49)	29.5	(0.50)
22–24	13,423	(168.8)	12,361	(172.2)	92.1	(0.51)	47.0	(0.49)	47.1	(0.52)
Recency of immigration[4]										
Born outside the United States										
Hispanic	1,627	(83.2)	1,188	(72.3)	73.0	(2.36)	5.7	(0.30)	4.5	(0.28)
Non-Hispanic	1,727	(82.2)	1,611	(79.1)	93.3	(1.34)	6.1	(0.28)	6.1	(0.29)
First generation										
Hispanic	2,503	(88.7)	2,230	(85.3)	89.1	(1.36)	8.8	(0.31)	8.5	(0.33)
Non-Hispanic	1,785	(88.9)	1,701	(85.3)	95.3	(1.22)	6.3	(0.30)	6.5	(0.32)
Second generation or higher										
Hispanic	1,877	(89.6)	1,685	(78.0)	89.8	(1.46)	6.6	(0.32)	6.4	(0.31)
Non-Hispanic	19,013	(192.4)	17,842	(195.1)	93.8	(0.38)	66.6	(0.37)	68.0	(0.42)
Disability[5]										
With a disability	1,068	(67.8)	869	(60.8)	81.3	(2.27)	3.7	(0.24)	3.3	(0.23)
Without a disability	27,464	(213.7)	25,389	(212.1)	92.4	(0.33)	96.3	(0.24)	96.7	(0.23)
Region										
Northeast	5,369	(158.4)	5,014	(151.5)	93.4	(0.79)	18.8	(0.51)	19.1	(0.54)
Midwest	5,714	(126.2)	5,328	(128.9)	93.2	(0.71)	20.0	(0.45)	20.3	(0.50)
South	10,370	(173.7)	9,462	(172.1)	91.2	(0.60)	36.3	(0.58)	36.0	(0.60)
West	7,079	(160.7)	6,453	(155.0)	91.2	(0.70)	24.8	(0.52)	24.6	(0.55)

†Not applicable.
‡Reporting standards not met (too few cases for a reliable estimate).
[1]Includes all 18- to 24-year-olds who are not enrolled in high school or a lower level of education.
[2]Status completers are 18- to 24-year-olds who are not enrolled in high school or a lower level of education and who also are high school completers—that is, have either a high school diploma or an alternative credential, such as a GED.
[3]The status completion rate is the number of 18- to 24-year-olds who are high school completers as a percentage of the total number of 18- to 24-year-olds who are not enrolled in high school or a lower level of education. High school completers include those with a high school diploma, as well as those with an alternative credential, such as a GED.
[4]The United States includes the 50 states and the District of Columbia. Individuals defined as "first generation" were born in the United States, but one or both of their parents were born out-

side the United States. Individuals defined as "second generation or higher" were born in the United States, as were both of their parents.
[5]Individuals identified as having a disability reported difficulty in at least one of the following: hearing, seeing even when wearing glasses, walking or climbing stairs, dressing or bathing, doing errands alone, concentrating, remembering, or making decisions.
NOTE: Data are based on sample surveys of the civilian noninstitutionalized population, which excludes persons in prisons, persons in the military, and other persons not living in households. Race categories exclude persons of Hispanic ethnicity. Detail may not sum to totals because of rounding.
SOURCE: U.S. Department of Commerce, Census Bureau, Current Population Survey (CPS), October 2013. (This table was prepared February 2015.)

Table 219.70. Percentage of high school dropouts among persons 16 through 24 years old (status dropout rate), by sex and race/ethnicity: Selected years, 1960 through 2013

[Standard errors appear in parentheses]

Year	Total status dropout rate				Male status dropout rate				Female status dropout rate			
	All races[1]	White	Black	Hispanic	All races[1]	White	Black	Hispanic	All races[1]	White	Black	Hispanic
1	2	3	4	5	6	7	8	9	10	11	12	13
1960[2]	27.2 (—)	— (†)	— (†)	— (†)	27.8 (—)	— (†)	— (†)	— (†)	26.7 (—)	— (†)	— (†)	— (†)
1967[3]	17.0 (—)	15.4 (—)	28.6 (—)	— (†)	16.5 (—)	14.7 (—)	30.6 (—)	— (†)	17.3 (—)	16.1 (—)	26.9 (—)	— (†)
1968[3]	16.2 (—)	14.7 (—)	27.4 (—)	— (†)	15.8 (—)	14.4 (—)	27.1 (—)	— (†)	16.5 (—)	15.0 (—)	27.6 (—)	— (†)
1969[3]	15.2 (—)	13.6 (—)	26.7 (—)	— (†)	14.3 (—)	12.6 (—)	26.9 (—)	— (†)	16.0 (—)	14.6 (—)	26.7 (—)	— (†)
1970[3]	15.0 (0.29)	13.2 (0.30)	27.9 (1.22)	— (†)	14.2 (0.42)	12.2 (0.42)	29.4 (1.82)	— (†)	15.7 (0.41)	14.1 (0.42)	26.6 (1.65)	— (†)
1971[3]	14.7 (0.28)	13.4 (0.29)	24.0 (1.14)	— (†)	14.2 (0.41)	12.6 (0.41)	25.5 (1.70)	— (†)	15.2 (0.40)	14.2 (0.42)	22.6 (1.54)	— (†)
1972	14.6 (0.28)	12.3 (0.29)	21.3 (1.07)	34.3 (2.22)	14.1 (0.40)	11.6 (0.40)	22.3 (1.59)	33.7 (3.23)	15.1 (0.39)	12.8 (0.41)	20.5 (1.44)	34.8 (3.05)
1973	14.1 (0.27)	11.6 (0.28)	22.2 (1.06)	33.5 (2.24)	13.7 (0.38)	11.5 (0.39)	21.5 (1.53)	30.4 (3.16)	14.5 (0.38)	11.8 (0.39)	22.8 (1.47)	36.4 (3.16)
1974	14.3 (0.27)	11.9 (0.28)	21.2 (1.05)	33.0 (2.08)	14.2 (0.39)	12.0 (0.40)	20.1 (1.51)	33.8 (2.99)	14.3 (0.38)	11.8 (0.39)	22.1 (1.45)	32.2 (2.90)
1975	13.9 (0.27)	11.4 (0.27)	22.9 (1.06)	29.2 (2.02)	13.3 (0.37)	11.0 (0.38)	23.0 (1.56)	26.7 (2.84)	14.5 (0.38)	11.8 (0.39)	22.9 (1.44)	31.6 (2.86)
1976	14.1 (0.27)	12.0 (0.28)	20.5 (1.00)	31.4 (2.01)	14.1 (0.38)	12.1 (0.39)	21.2 (1.49)	30.3 (2.94)	14.2 (0.37)	11.8 (0.39)	19.9 (1.35)	32.3 (2.76)
1977	14.1 (0.27)	11.9 (0.28)	19.8 (0.99)	33.0 (2.02)	14.5 (0.38)	12.6 (0.40)	19.5 (1.45)	31.6 (2.89)	13.8 (0.37)	11.2 (0.38)	20.0 (1.36)	34.3 (2.83)
1978	14.2 (0.27)	11.9 (0.28)	20.2 (1.00)	33.3 (2.00)	14.6 (0.38)	12.2 (0.40)	22.5 (1.52)	33.6 (2.88)	13.9 (0.37)	11.6 (0.39)	18.3 (1.31)	33.1 (2.78)
1979	14.6 (0.27)	12.0 (0.28)	21.1 (1.01)	33.8 (1.98)	15.0 (0.39)	12.6 (0.40)	22.4 (1.52)	33.0 (2.83)	14.2 (0.37)	11.5 (0.38)	20.0 (1.35)	34.5 (2.77)
1980	14.1 (0.26)	11.4 (0.27)	19.1 (0.97)	35.2 (1.89)	15.1 (0.39)	12.3 (0.40)	20.8 (1.47)	37.2 (2.72)	13.1 (0.36)	10.5 (0.37)	17.7 (1.28)	33.2 (2.61)
1981	13.9 (0.26)	11.3 (0.27)	18.4 (0.93)	33.2 (1.80)	15.1 (0.38)	12.5 (0.40)	19.9 (1.40)	36.0 (2.61)	12.8 (0.35)	10.2 (0.36)	17.1 (1.24)	30.4 (2.48)
1982	13.9 (0.27)	11.4 (0.29)	18.4 (0.97)	31.7 (1.93)	14.5 (0.40)	12.0 (0.42)	21.2 (1.50)	30.5 (2.73)	13.3 (0.38)	10.8 (0.40)	15.9 (1.26)	32.8 (2.71)
1983	13.7 (0.27)	11.1 (0.29)	18.0 (0.97)	31.6 (1.93)	14.9 (0.41)	12.2 (0.43)	19.9 (1.46)	34.3 (2.84)	12.5 (0.37)	10.1 (0.39)	16.2 (1.28)	29.1 (2.61)
1984	13.1 (0.27)	11.0 (0.29)	15.5 (0.91)	29.8 (1.91)	14.0 (0.40)	11.9 (0.43)	16.8 (1.37)	30.6 (2.78)	12.3 (0.37)	10.1 (0.39)	14.3 (1.22)	29.0 (2.63)
1985	12.6 (0.27)	10.4 (0.29)	15.2 (0.92)	27.6 (1.93)	13.4 (0.40)	11.1 (0.42)	16.1 (1.37)	29.9 (2.76)	11.8 (0.37)	9.8 (0.39)	14.3 (1.23)	25.2 (2.68)
1986	12.2 (0.27)	9.7 (0.28)	14.2 (0.90)	30.1 (1.88)	13.1 (0.40)	10.3 (0.42)	15.0 (1.33)	32.8 (2.66)	11.4 (0.37)	9.1 (0.39)	13.5 (1.21)	27.2 (2.63)
1987	12.6 (0.28)	10.4 (0.30)	14.1 (0.90)	28.6 (1.84)	13.2 (0.40)	10.8 (0.43)	15.0 (1.35)	29.1 (2.57)	12.1 (0.38)	10.0 (0.41)	13.3 (1.21)	28.1 (2.64)
1988	12.9 (0.30)	9.6 (0.31)	14.5 (1.00)	35.8 (2.30)	13.5 (0.44)	10.3 (0.46)	15.0 (1.48)	36.0 (3.19)	12.2 (0.42)	8.9 (0.43)	14.0 (1.36)	35.4 (3.31)
1989	12.6 (0.31)	9.4 (0.32)	13.9 (0.98)	33.0 (2.19)	13.6 (0.45)	10.3 (0.47)	14.9 (1.46)	34.4 (3.08)	11.7 (0.42)	8.5 (0.43)	13.0 (1.32)	31.6 (3.11)
1990	12.1 (0.29)	9.0 (0.30)	13.2 (0.94)	32.4 (1.91)	12.3 (0.42)	9.3 (0.44)	11.9 (1.30)	34.3 (2.71)	11.8 (0.41)	8.7 (0.42)	14.4 (1.34)	30.3 (2.70)
1991	12.5 (0.30)	8.9 (0.31)	13.6 (0.95)	35.3 (1.93)	13.0 (0.43)	8.9 (0.44)	13.5 (1.37)	39.2 (2.74)	11.9 (0.41)	8.9 (0.43)	13.7 (1.31)	31.1 (2.70)
1992[4]	11.0 (0.28)	7.7 (0.29)	13.7 (0.95)	29.4 (1.86)	11.3 (0.41)	8.0 (0.42)	12.5 (1.32)	32.1 (2.67)	10.7 (0.39)	7.4 (0.40)	14.8 (1.36)	26.6 (2.56)
1993[4]	11.0 (0.28)	7.9 (0.29)	13.6 (0.94)	27.5 (1.79)	11.2 (0.40)	8.2 (0.42)	12.6 (1.32)	28.1 (2.54)	10.9 (0.40)	7.6 (0.41)	14.4 (1.34)	26.9 (2.52)
1994[4]	11.4 (0.26)	7.7 (0.27)	12.6 (0.75)	30.0 (1.16)	12.3 (0.38)	8.0 (0.38)	14.1 (1.14)	31.6 (1.60)	10.6 (0.36)	7.5 (0.37)	11.3 (0.99)	28.1 (1.66)
1995[4]	12.0 (0.27)	8.6 (0.28)	12.1 (0.74)	30.0 (1.15)	12.2 (0.38)	9.0 (0.40)	11.1 (1.05)	30.0 (1.59)	11.7 (0.37)	8.2 (0.39)	12.9 (1.05)	30.0 (1.66)
1996[4]	11.1 (0.27)	7.3 (0.27)	13.0 (0.80)	29.4 (1.19)	11.4 (0.38)	7.3 (0.38)	13.5 (1.18)	30.3 (1.67)	10.9 (0.38)	7.3 (0.39)	12.5 (1.08)	28.3 (1.69)
1997[4]	11.0 (0.27)	7.6 (0.28)	13.4 (0.80)	25.3 (1.11)	11.9 (0.39)	8.5 (0.41)	13.3 (1.16)	27.0 (1.55)	10.1 (0.36)	6.7 (0.37)	13.5 (1.11)	23.4 (1.59)
1998[4]	11.8 (0.27)	7.7 (0.28)	13.8 (0.81)	29.5 (1.12)	13.3 (0.40)	8.6 (0.41)	15.5 (1.24)	33.5 (1.59)	10.3 (0.36)	6.9 (0.37)	12.2 (1.05)	25.0 (1.56)
1999[4]	11.2 (0.26)	7.3 (0.27)	12.6 (0.77)	28.6 (1.11)	11.9 (0.38)	7.7 (0.39)	12.1 (1.10)	31.0 (1.58)	10.5 (0.36)	6.9 (0.37)	13.0 (1.08)	26.0 (1.54)
2000[4]	10.9 (0.26)	6.9 (0.26)	13.1 (0.78)	27.8 (1.08)	12.0 (0.38)	7.0 (0.37)	15.3 (1.20)	31.8 (1.56)	9.9 (0.35)	6.9 (0.37)	11.1 (1.00)	23.5 (1.48)
2001[4]	10.7 (0.25)	7.3 (0.26)	10.9 (0.71)	27.0 (1.06)	12.2 (0.38)	7.9 (0.39)	13.0 (1.12)	31.6 (1.55)	9.3 (0.34)	6.7 (0.36)	9.0 (0.90)	22.1 (1.42)
2002[4]	10.5 (0.24)	6.5 (0.24)	11.3 (0.70)	25.7 (0.93)	11.8 (0.35)	6.7 (0.35)	12.8 (1.07)	29.6 (1.32)	9.2 (0.32)	6.3 (0.34)	9.9 (0.91)	21.2 (1.27)
2003[4,5]	9.9 (0.23)	6.3 (0.24)	10.9 (0.69)	23.5 (0.90)	11.3 (0.34)	7.1 (0.35)	12.5 (1.05)	26.7 (1.29)	8.4 (0.30)	5.6 (0.32)	9.5 (0.89)	20.1 (1.23)
2004[4,5]	10.3 (0.23)	6.8 (0.24)	11.8 (0.70)	23.8 (0.89)	11.6 (0.34)	7.1 (0.35)	13.5 (1.08)	28.5 (1.30)	9.0 (0.31)	6.4 (0.34)	10.2 (0.92)	18.5 (1.18)
2005[4,5]	9.4 (0.22)	6.0 (0.23)	10.4 (0.66)	22.4 (0.87)	10.8 (0.33)	6.6 (0.34)	12.0 (1.02)	26.4 (1.26)	8.0 (0.29)	5.3 (0.31)	9.0 (0.86)	18.1 (1.16)
2006[4,5]	9.3 (0.22)	5.8 (0.23)	10.7 (0.66)	22.1 (0.86)	10.3 (0.33)	6.4 (0.33)	9.7 (0.91)	25.7 (1.25)	8.3 (0.30)	5.3 (0.31)	11.7 (0.96)	18.1 (1.15)
2007[4,5]	8.7 (0.21)	5.3 (0.22)	8.4 (0.59)	21.4 (0.83)	9.8 (0.32)	6.0 (0.32)	8.0 (0.82)	24.7 (1.22)	7.7 (0.29)	4.5 (0.28)	8.8 (0.84)	18.0 (1.13)
2008[4,5]	8.0 (0.20)	4.8 (0.21)	9.9 (0.63)	18.3 (0.78)	8.5 (0.30)	5.4 (0.30)	8.7 (0.85)	19.9 (1.12)	7.5 (0.28)	4.2 (0.28)	11.1 (0.93)	16.7 (1.08)
2009[4,5]	8.1 (0.20)	5.2 (0.21)	9.3 (0.61)	17.6 (0.76)	9.1 (0.31)	6.3 (0.33)	10.6 (0.93)	19.0 (1.10)	7.0 (0.27)	4.1 (0.27)	8.1 (0.80)	16.1 (1.06)
2010[4,5,6]	7.4 (0.27)	5.1 (0.30)	8.0 (0.76)	15.1 (0.87)	8.5 (0.40)	5.9 (0.42)	9.5 (1.11)	17.3 (1.24)	6.3 (0.28)	4.2 (0.35)	6.7 (0.85)	12.8 (0.97)
2011[4,5,6]	7.1 (0.26)	5.0 (0.31)	7.3 (0.67)	13.6 (0.78)	7.7 (0.36)	5.4 (0.41)	8.3 (0.98)	14.6 (1.09)	6.5 (0.34)	4.6 (0.38)	6.4 (0.94)	12.4 (0.97)
2012[4,5,6]	6.6 (0.25)	4.3 (0.31)	7.5 (0.76)	12.7 (0.72)	7.3 (0.36)	4.8 (0.40)	8.1 (1.15)	13.9 (1.04)	5.9 (0.33)	3.8 (0.37)	7.0 (1.01)	11.3 (1.00)
2013[4,5,6]	6.8 (0.28)	5.1 (0.31)	7.3 (0.87)	11.7 (0.74)	7.2 (0.37)	5.5 (0.39)	8.2 (1.11)	12.6 (1.01)	6.3 (0.34)	4.7 (0.36)	6.6 (1.07)	10.8 (0.98)

—Not available.
†Not applicable.
[1]Includes other racial/ethnic categories not separately shown.
[2]Based on the April 1960 decennial census.
[3]For 1967 through 1971, White and Black include persons of Hispanic ethnicity.
[4]Because of changes in data collection procedures, data may not be comparable with figures for years prior to 1992.
[5]White and Black exclude persons identifying themselves as two or more races.
[6]Beginning in 2010, standard errors were computed using replicate weights, which produced more precise values than the generalized variance function methodology used in prior years.

NOTE: "Status" dropouts are 16- to 24-year-olds who are not enrolled in school and who have not completed a high school program, regardless of when they left school. People who have received GED credentials are counted as high school completers. All data except for 1960 are based on October counts. Data are based on sample surveys of the civilian noninstitutionalized population, which excludes persons in prisons, persons in the military, and other persons not living in households. Race categories exclude persons of Hispanic ethnicity except where otherwise noted.
SOURCE: U.S. Department of Commerce, Census Bureau, Current Population Survey (CPS), October, 1967 through 2013. (This table was prepared July 2014.)

Table 219.71. Population 16 through 24 years old and number of 16- to 24-year-old high school dropouts (status dropouts), by sex and race/ethnicity: 1970 through 2013

[Standard errors appear in parentheses]

Population 16 through 24 years old (in thousands)

Year	Total				Males				Females			
	All races[1]	White	Black	Hispanic	All races[1]	White	Black	Hispanic	All races[1]	White	Black	Hispanic
1	2	3	4	5	6	7	8	9	10	11	12	13
1970[2]	30,251 (260.7)	26,241 (245.8)	3,669 (93.6)	— (†)	14,260 (175.6)	12,403 (165.7)	1,703 (62.5)	— (†)	15,991 (177.3)	13,838 (167.3)	1,966 (63.7)	— (†)
1971[2]	31,538 (265.1)	27,299 (249.9)	3,871 (95.5)	— (†)	15,060 (179.5)	13,076 (169.4)	1,809 (64.0)	— (†)	16,478 (179.4)	14,223 (169.2)	2,062 (64.8)	— (†)
1972	32,643 (268.8)	26,502 (246.8)	4,024 (96.9)	1,774 (81.5)	15,787 (183.0)	12,913 (168.5)	1,878 (64.8)	830 (55.2)	16,856 (181.0)	13,589 (166.1)	2,145 (65.7)	944 (55.3)
1973	33,430 (271.4)	27,100 (249.1)	4,190 (98.3)	1,718 (80.4)	16,248 (185.1)	13,259 (170.4)	1,976 (66.0)	821 (54.9)	17,182 (182.3)	13,841 (167.4)	2,214 (66.4)	896 (54.1)
1974	33,968 (273.1)	27,301 (249.9)	4,153 (98.0)	1,981 (85.6)	16,508 (186.2)	13,361 (171.0)	1,921 (65.3)	972 (59.2)	17,460 (183.4)	13,941 (167.8)	2,232 (66.6)	1,009 (57.0)
1975	34,700 (275.4)	27,867 (252.0)	4,310 (99.3)	1,962 (85.3)	16,925 (188.0)	13,711 (172.8)	1,992 (66.2)	940 (58.3)	17,775 (184.7)	14,157 (168.9)	2,319 (67.4)	1,022 (57.3)
1976	35,222 (277.0)	28,146 (253.1)	4,429 (100.2)	2,060 (87.1)	17,210 (189.3)	13,925 (173.9)	2,054 (66.9)	944 (58.4)	18,012 (185.6)	14,221 (169.2)	2,375 (67.9)	1,115 (59.4)
1977	35,658 (278.3)	28,393 (254.0)	4,516 (100.9)	2,123 (88.3)	17,431 (190.2)	14,027 (174.4)	2,086 (67.2)	1,018 (60.4)	18,227 (186.4)	14,366 (169.9)	2,430 (68.4)	1,106 (59.2)
1978	35,931 (279.1)	28,490 (254.3)	4,584 (101.4)	2,183 (89.3)	17,582 (190.8)	14,084 (174.7)	2,113 (67.5)	1,059 (61.5)	18,349 (186.9)	14,406 (170.1)	2,471 (68.8)	1,123 (59.6)
1979	36,131 (279.7)	28,602 (254.8)	4,618 (101.7)	2,242 (90.4)	17,708 (191.4)	14,172 (175.2)	2,128 (67.7)	1,085 (62.1)	18,423 (187.2)	14,430 (170.2)	2,490 (69.0)	1,157 (60.3)
1980	36,143 (279.7)	28,253 (253.5)	4,651 (101.9)	2,518 (95.0)	17,715 (191.4)	13,979 (174.2)	2,148 (67.9)	1,240 (65.8)	18,428 (187.2)	14,274 (169.5)	2,503 (69.1)	1,277 (62.8)
1981	36,945 (282.1)	28,483 (254.3)	4,895 (103.7)	2,684 (97.5)	18,167 (193.2)	14,111 (174.9)	2,286 (69.2)	1,333 (67.8)	18,778 (188.5)	14,372 (169.9)	2,608 (69.9)	1,352 (64.3)
1982	36,452 (296.5)	27,979 (266.7)	4,912 (109.6)	2,598 (103.0)	17,938 (203.2)	13,841 (183.3)	2,303 (73.3)	1,263 (70.9)	18,514 (198.1)	14,139 (178.4)	2,609 (73.9)	1,335 (64.0)
1983	35,884 (294.7)	27,385 (264.3)	4,907 (109.6)	2,587 (101.9)	17,712 (202.2)	13,616 (182.0)	2,329 (73.6)	1,242 (69.8)	18,172 (196.7)	13,769 (176.4)	2,578 (73.6)	1,345 (68.1)
1984	35,204 (292.6)	26,758 (261.8)	4,890 (109.5)	2,558 (101.4)	17,387 (200.8)	13,325 (180.4)	2,329 (73.6)	1,226 (69.4)	17,817 (195.3)	13,433 (174.7)	2,561 (73.5)	1,332 (67.8)
1985	34,382 (289.9)	25,772 (257.7)	4,749 (108.4)	2,887 (86.4)	16,892 (198.5)	12,715 (176.9)	2,239 (72.7)	1,472 (60.7)	17,490 (193.9)	13,057 (172.6)	2,510 (73.0)	1,415 (69.4)
1986	33,945 (288.4)	24,959 (254.2)	4,698 (108.0)	3,206 (93.7)	16,709 (197.7)	12,276 (174.3)	2,222 (72.5)	1,667 (66.4)	17,236 (192.9)	12,684 (170.5)	2,476 (72.7)	1,538 (60.5)
1987	33,452 (286.8)	24,479 (252.1)	4,631 (107.5)	3,234 (94.1)	16,458 (196.5)	12,058 (173.0)	2,176 (72.0)	1,680 (66.6)	16,994 (191.8)	12,420 (169.2)	2,455 (72.5)	1,554 (60.7)
1988	32,893 (310.4)	23,908 (272.0)	4,584 (116.5)	3,267 (107.8)	16,134 (212.5)	11,725 (186.3)	2,156 (78.2)	1,696 (76.3)	16,759 (207.9)	12,184 (182.7)	2,429 (78.7)	1,571 (61.0)
1989	32,007 (291.9)	22,947 (254.0)	4,593 (111.1)	3,459 (98.1)	15,783 (200.2)	11,314 (174.4)	2,193 (74.8)	1,783 (69.1)	16,224 (195.2)	11,634 (170.3)	2,399 (74.6)	1,676 (69.8)
1990	31,443 (289.8)	22,360 (251.1)	4,487 (110.2)	3,443 (99.8)	15,502 (198.8)	11,059 (172.7)	2,117 (73.9)	1,773 (70.4)	15,941 (193.8)	11,302 (168.2)	2,370 (74.3)	1,669 (64.6)
1991	31,171 (288.8)	21,883 (248.8)	4,475 (110.1)	3,519 (100.7)	15,408 (198.3)	10,819 (171.0)	2,126 (74.0)	1,829 (71.2)	15,763 (193.0)	11,064 (166.7)	2,350 (74.1)	1,690 (64.9)
1992[3]	30,944 (287.5)	21,697 (247.9)	4,527 (110.6)	3,476 (100.2)	15,375 (198.1)	10,826 (171.1)	2,169 (74.6)	1,760 (70.2)	15,569 (192.0)	10,871 (165.5)	2,358 (74.2)	1,716 (65.3)
1993[3]	30,845 (287.5)	21,499 (246.9)	4,536 (110.7)	3,595 (101.5)	15,355 (198.0)	10,742 (170.5)	2,179 (74.6)	1,802 (70.8)	15,490 (191.6)	10,757 (164.7)	2,357 (74.2)	1,793 (66.3)
1994[3]	32,560 (293.9)	22,080 (249.8)	4,805 (112.8)	4,411 (109.3)	16,304 (202.8)	11,016 (172.4)	2,298 (75.9)	2,355 (77.9)	16,257 (195.3)	11,064 (166.7)	2,507 (75.7)	2,056 (69.5)
1995[3]	32,379 (293.2)	21,991 (249.3)	4,732 (112.2)	4,485 (109.9)	16,208 (202.3)	11,062 (172.7)	2,236 (75.3)	2,338 (77.7)	16,170 (194.9)	10,929 (165.8)	2,496 (75.6)	2,147 (70.5)
1996[3]	32,452 (304.7)	21,527 (256.4)	4,745 (116.6)	4,481 (115.4)	16,296 (210.5)	10,836 (177.7)	2,251 (78.2)	2,313 (81.4)	16,156 (202.3)	10,690 (170.5)	2,494 (78.4)	2,168 (70.7)
1997[3]	32,960 (306.6)	21,800 (257.8)	4,847 (117.4)	4,660 (115.6)	16,619 (212.1)	11,001 (178.8)	2,308 (78.9)	2,487 (82.3)	16,341 (203.2)	10,799 (171.3)	2,540 (78.8)	2,173 (73.4)
1998[3]	33,445 (308.3)	21,920 (258.4)	4,893 (117.7)	5,034 (118.5)	16,854 (213.3)	11,067 (179.3)	2,305 (78.8)	2,683 (84.2)	16,592 (204.4)	10,854 (171.6)	2,588 (79.3)	2,351 (75.2)
1999[3]	34,169 (310.9)	22,408 (260.9)	4,939 (118.1)	5,060 (118.7)	17,106 (214.5)	11,325 (181.1)	2,336 (79.2)	2,603 (83.5)	17,063 (206.6)	11,084 (173.2)	2,603 (79.4)	2,457 (76.2)
2000[3]	34,568 (312.4)	22,574 (261.8)	5,058 (119.0)	5,237 (120.0)	17,402 (215.9)	11,390 (181.5)	2,417 (80.0)	2,725 (84.6)	17,166 (207.0)	11,184 (173.9)	2,641 (79.7)	2,513 (76.7)
2001[3]	35,167 (298.5)	22,874 (249.9)	5,119 (113.3)	5,344 (112.0)	17,663 (206.1)	11,598 (173.6)	2,418 (75.9)	2,744 (78.6)	17,504 (198.0)	11,276 (165.6)	2,701 (76.2)	2,601 (77.4)
2002[3]	35,495 (299.6)	22,358 (247.4)	4,991 (112.4)	6,120 (118.8)	17,893 (207.2)	11,183 (170.9)	2,375 (75.5)	3,281 (84.3)	17,602 (198.4)	11,175 (165.0)	2,617 (75.5)	2,888 (75.0)
2003[3,4]	36,017 (301.3)	22,565 (248.4)	4,973 (115.6)	6,103 (118.8)	18,099 (208.1)	11,329 (171.9)	2,385 (78.1)	3,214 (83.9)	17,918 (199.7)	11,236 (165.4)	2,588 (77.7)	2,888 (75.3)
2004[3,4]	36,504 (302.8)	22,654 (248.8)	5,048 (116.3)	6,301 (119.8)	18,406 (209.4)	11,395 (172.3)	2,425 (78.5)	3,326 (84.6)	18,097 (200.5)	11,259 (165.5)	2,623 (78.0)	2,975 (75.8)
2005[3,4]	36,761 (303.6)	22,806 (249.6)	5,111 (116.8)	6,364 (120.1)	18,547 (210.0)	11,492 (173.0)	2,457 (78.9)	3,341 (84.6)	18,214 (201.0)	11,314 (165.9)	2,654 (78.4)	3,023 (76.0)
2006[3,4]	37,047 (304.5)	22,863 (249.8)	5,260 (118.0)	6,439 (120.4)	18,707 (210.7)	11,537 (173.3)	2,573 (80.1)	3,357 (84.7)	18,340 (201.5)	11,327 (165.9)	2,688 (78.7)	3,083 (76.3)
2007[3,4]	37,480 (305.9)	22,962 (250.3)	5,363 (118.7)	6,632 (121.2)	18,940 (211.6)	11,641 (173.9)	2,639 (80.7)	3,447 (85.2)	18,541 (202.3)	11,320 (165.9)	2,724 (79.1)	3,186 (76.8)
2008[3,4]	37,569 (306.2)	22,956 (250.3)	5,387 (118.9)	6,721 (121.5)	18,948 (211.7)	11,628 (173.8)	2,616 (80.5)	3,472 (85.3)	18,621 (202.6)	11,328 (165.9)	2,771 (79.5)	3,249 (77.1)
2009[3,4]	37,616 (306.3)	22,809 (249.6)	5,445 (119.4)	6,809 (121.9)	18,949 (211.7)	11,542 (173.3)	2,633 (80.7)	3,497 (85.4)	18,667 (202.8)	11,267 (165.6)	2,812 (79.9)	3,313 (77.3)
2010[3,4,5]	37,949 (#)	22,607 (38.0)	5,450 (33.5)	7,193 (10.0)	19,126 (#)	11,437 (27.6)	2,609 (24.1)	3,714 (5.8)	18,823 (#)	11,170 (24.6)	2,841 (20.2)	3,479 (8.6)
2011[3,4,5]	38,205 (133.8)	22,359 (138.0)	5,444 (86.7)	7,656 (59.0)	19,430 (40.3)	11,290 (36.9)	2,627 (58.2)	4,123 (41.9)	18,775 (135.4)	11,068 (133.6)	2,817 (36.2)	3,533 (23.1)
2012[4,5]	38,800 (306.3)	21,708 (137.5)	5,540 (64.1)	8,201 (73.5)	19,557 (266.3)	10,963 (120.5)	2,699 (47.9)	4,241 (85.8)	19,243 (54.1)	10,745 (44.8)	2,841 (35.0)	3,959 (22.9)
2013[3,4,5]	38,804 (210.7)	21,542 (196.8)	5,570 (48.4)	8,263 (43.2)	19,561 (150.8)	10,911 (119.0)	2,708 (40.5)	4,248 (30.3)	19,243 (71.7)	10,631 (89.5)	2,863 (33.1)	4,015 (22.0)

See notes at end of table.

Table 219.71. Population 16 through 24 years old and number of 16- to 24-year-old high school dropouts (status dropouts), by sex and race/ethnicity: 1970 through 2013—Continued

[Standard errors appear in parentheses]

	Total				Number of 16- to 24-year-old (status) dropouts (in thousands)							
					Males				Females			
Year	All races[1]	White	Black	Hispanic	All races[1]	White	Black	Hispanic	All races[1]	White	Black	Hispanic
1	2	3	4	5	6	7	8	9	10	11	12	13
1970[2]	4,525 (108.5)	3,459 (95.1)	1,022 (53.6)	— (†)	2,022 (71.1)	1,508 (61.6)	500 (36.8)	— (†)	2,503 (76.3)	1,951 (67.6)	522 (36.0)	— (†)
1971[2]	4,641 (109.8)	3,663 (97.8)	919 (50.9)	— (†)	2,137 (73.0)	1,649 (64.3)	462 (35.5)	— (†)	2,504 (76.3)	2,013 (68.6)	456 (33.8)	— (†)
1972	4,770 (111.3)	3,250 (92.2)	858 (49.3)	609 (49.4)	2,226 (74.5)	1,504 (61.5)	419 (33.9)	280 (33.1)	2,545 (76.9)	1,745 (64.0)	439 (33.2)	329 (34.0)
1973	4,716 (110.7)	3,150 (90.8)	930 (51.2)	576 (48.1)	2,220 (74.4)	1,519 (61.8)	425 (34.1)	250 (31.3)	2,496 (76.2)	1,631 (61.9)	504 (35.4)	326 (33.9)
1974	4,849 (112.2)	3,240 (92.1)	878 (49.9)	653 (51.1)	2,343 (76.4)	1,601 (63.4)	386 (32.6)	328 (35.7)	2,505 (76.3)	1,638 (62.0)	493 (35.0)	325 (33.9)
1975	4,824 (111.9)	3,185 (91.3)	987 (52.7)	573 (48.0)	2,248 (74.9)	1,509 (61.6)	457 (35.3)	251 (31.3)	2,577 (77.4)	1,676 (62.7)	530 (36.3)	323 (33.7)
1976	4,981 (113.7)	3,366 (93.8)	908 (50.7)	646 (50.8)	2,432 (77.8)	1,688 (65.1)	435 (34.5)	286 (33.4)	2,549 (77.0)	1,678 (62.8)	473 (34.4)	360 (35.5)
1977	5,031 (114.2)	3,374 (94.0)	893 (50.3)	701 (52.9)	2,519 (79.1)	1,767 (66.5)	407 (33.4)	322 (35.4)	2,512 (76.4)	1,607 (61.5)	487 (34.8)	379 (36.4)
1978	5,114 (115.1)	3,384 (94.1)	928 (51.2)	728 (53.8)	2,572 (79.9)	1,715 (65.6)	475 (36.0)	356 (37.1)	2,541 (76.9)	1,670 (62.6)	453 (33.7)	371 (36.1)
1979	5,265 (116.8)	3,433 (94.8)	975 (52.4)	758 (54.9)	2,650 (81.1)	1,779 (66.8)	477 (36.0)	358 (37.2)	2,614 (77.9)	1,653 (62.3)	499 (35.2)	400 (37.4)
1980	5,085 (114.8)	3,211 (91.7)	889 (50.2)	885 (59.1)	2,672 (81.4)	1,715 (65.6)	446 (34.9)	462 (42.0)	2,413 (75.0)	1,496 (59.3)	444 (33.3)	424 (38.4)
1981	5,143 (115.4)	3,232 (92.0)	901 (50.5)	891 (59.3)	2,746 (82.5)	1,762 (66.5)	454 (35.2)	480 (42.8)	2,397 (74.7)	1,470 (58.8)	447 (33.4)	411 (37.9)
1982	5,055 (121.0)	3,202 (96.7)	902 (53.4)	823 (60.7)	2,601 (84.9)	1,668 (68.3)	488 (38.5)	386 (41.0)	2,454 (76.9)	1,534 (63.5)	414 (34.1)	437 (38.0)
1983	4,905 (119.2)	3,053 (94.5)	882 (52.8)	816 (60.3)	2,631 (85.4)	1,661 (68.2)	463 (37.6)	426 (42.9)	2,274 (76.9)	1,392 (60.5)	418 (34.2)	391 (39.2)
1984	4,626 (115.8)	2,952 (92.9)	758 (49.1)	762 (58.4)	2,438 (82.3)	1,592 (66.8)	391 (34.7)	375 (40.4)	2,188 (75.5)	1,360 (59.8)	367 (32.2)	387 (39.0)
1985	4,324 (112.1)	2,688 (88.8)	719 (47.9)	797 (49.8)	2,264 (79.4)	1,406 (62.8)	360 (33.3)	440 (36.4)	2,060 (73.3)	1,282 (58.1)	360 (31.9)	357 (37.6)
1986	4,142 (109.8)	2,418 (84.2)	667 (46.2)	966 (55.1)	2,183 (78.0)	1,260 (59.5)	333 (32.1)	547 (40.7)	1,959 (70.7)	1,158 (55.2)	334 (30.7)	419 (34.2)
1987	4,230 (110.9)	2,538 (86.3)	653 (45.7)	926 (54.0)	2,169 (77.7)	1,299 (60.4)	326 (31.8)	490 (38.7)	2,061 (73.3)	1,239 (57.1)	327 (30.4)	437 (34.8)
1988	4,232 (120.9)	2,301 (89.6)	664 (50.2)	1,168 (67.8)	2,184 (85.0)	1,214 (63.7)	323 (34.5)	611 (48.3)	2,049 (79.7)	1,087 (58.4)	341 (33.9)	557 (39.0)
1989	4,038 (112.3)	2,152 (82.4)	639 (46.9)	1,142 (61.4)	2,145 (80.1)	1,160 (59.2)	327 (32.9)	613 (44.2)	1,893 (72.9)	991 (53.0)	312 (30.8)	529 (42.6)
1990	3,797 (108.9)	2,007 (79.6)	594 (45.2)	1,114 (61.0)	1,909 (75.6)	1,027 (55.8)	252 (29.1)	608 (44.3)	1,887 (72.8)	980 (52.7)	342 (32.2)	506 (38.7)
1991	3,881 (110.1)	1,953 (78.5)	609 (45.8)	1,241 (64.2)	2,001 (77.4)	967 (54.1)	288 (31.0)	717 (47.8)	1,880 (72.6)	985 (52.8)	321 (31.3)	525 (39.3)
1992[3]	3,410 (103.4)	1,676 (72.8)	621 (46.2)	1,022 (58.6)	1,742 (72.3)	866 (51.3)	271 (30.1)	565 (42.8)	1,668 (68.5)	810 (48.0)	350 (32.6)	457 (36.9)
1993[3]	3,396 (115.2)	1,707 (73.4)	615 (46.0)	989 (57.7)	1,715 (71.8)	884 (51.8)	275 (30.3)	507 (40.7)	1,681 (68.7)	823 (48.1)	340 (32.1)	483 (37.8)
1994[3]	3,727 (113.6)	1,709 (73.5)	607 (45.7)	1,322 (66.1)	2,000 (77.4)	1,160 (59.2)	324 (32.8)	744 (48.6)	1,727 (69.7)	991 (53.0)	284 (29.4)	578 (41.1)
1995[3]	3,876 (110.1)	1,887 (77.2)	571 (44.4)	1,345 (66.6)	1,978 (77.0)	996 (54.9)	249 (28.9)	701 (47.3)	1,898 (73.0)	891 (50.3)	322 (31.3)	644 (43.2)
1996[3]	3,611 (106.9)	1,569 (73.1)	615 (47.8)	1,315 (68.6)	1,854 (77.4)	792 (50.9)	304 (33.0)	701 (49.3)	1,757 (72.9)	777 (48.8)	312 (32.0)	614 (42.3)
1997[3]	3,624 (110.6)	1,656 (75.1)	649 (49.0)	1,180 (65.1)	1,970 (79.7)	934 (55.2)	306 (33.2)	671 (48.2)	1,654 (70.8)	722 (47.0)	343 (33.5)	509 (41.3)
1998[3]	3,942 (115.2)	1,697 (76.0)	675 (50.0)	1,487 (72.4)	2,241 (84.9)	950 (55.7)	358 (35.7)	899 (55.0)	1,701 (71.8)	747 (47.8)	317 (32.2)	587 (40.6)
1999[3]	3,829 (113.6)	1,636 (74.7)	621 (48.0)	1,445 (71.5)	2,032 (81.0)	873 (53.4)	282 (31.9)	807 (52.4)	1,797 (73.7)	763 (48.3)	338 (33.3)	638 (39.6)
2000[3]	3,776 (112.8)	1,564 (73.0)	663 (49.5)	1,456 (71.7)	2,082 (81.9)	795 (51.0)	369 (36.3)	866 (54.1)	1,694 (71.6)	769 (48.5)	294 (31.1)	590 (43.1)
2001[3]	3,766 (106.2)	1,668 (71.6)	557 (43.2)	1,442 (67.5)	2,151 (79.0)	916 (51.9)	314 (31.8)	865 (51.0)	1,615 (66.4)	752 (45.6)	243 (26.9)	577 (42.7)
2002[3]	3,721 (106.3)	1,457 (66.9)	564 (43.5)	1,572 (70.5)	2,108 (78.2)	752 (47.1)	305 (31.4)	971 (54.0)	1,612 (66.4)	705 (44.1)	259 (27.7)	601 (41.3)
2003[3,4]	3,552 (106.9)	1,431 (66.3)	544 (42.8)	1,437 (67.7)	2,045 (77.1)	802 (48.6)	298 (31.2)	858 (51.1)	1,506 (64.2)	630 (41.7)	246 (27.1)	579 (40.6)
2004[3,4]	3,766 (106.9)	1,530 (68.5)	594 (44.7)	1,499 (69.0)	2,140 (78.8)	808 (48.8)	326 (32.6)	949 (53.5)	1,626 (66.6)	722 (44.6)	268 (28.3)	549 (39.6)
2005[3,4]	3,458 (102.5)	1,358 (64.6)	534 (42.4)	1,429 (67.5)	2,009 (76.4)	760 (47.3)	295 (31.0)	883 (51.8)	1,449 (63.0)	599 (40.7)	239 (26.7)	546 (39.5)
2006[3,4]	3,462 (102.6)	1,337 (64.1)	565 (43.6)	1,421 (67.3)	1,935 (75.0)	739 (46.7)	250 (28.6)	864 (51.3)	1,527 (64.6)	598 (40.7)	315 (30.6)	557 (39.8)
2007[3,4]	3,278 (99.9)	1,210 (61.0)	451 (39.1)	1,422 (67.3)	1,859 (73.6)	704 (45.6)	212 (26.4)	850 (50.9)	1,419 (62.3)	507 (37.4)	239 (26.8)	572 (40.3)
2008[3,4]	3,010 (95.8)	1,103 (58.3)	535 (42.5)	1,232 (63.0)	1,606 (68.5)	623 (42.9)	227 (27.3)	690 (46.3)	1,403 (62.0)	480 (36.5)	308 (30.3)	541 (39.3)
2009[3,4]	3,030 (96.1)	1,188 (60.5)	508 (41.4)	1,199 (62.2)	1,731 (71.0)	725 (46.2)	280 (30.2)	665 (45.5)	1,299 (59.7)	464 (35.8)	228 (26.2)	534 (39.1)
2010[3,4,5]	2,816 (100.8)	1,147 (67.9)	437 (41.5)	1,090 (62.3)	1,625 (77.3)	675 (48.4)	247 (29.2)	644 (46.2)	1,192 (53.0)	472 (38.7)	190 (24.1)	446 (33.9)
2011[3,4,5]	2,714 (99.1)	1,118 (68.1)	400 (37.5)	1,040 (60.1)	1,501 (69.9)	614 (46.0)	218 (26.4)	602 (44.9)	1,213 (64.6)	505 (42.9)	182 (27.2)	439 (34.0)
2012[3,4,5]	2,562 (101.1)	930 (67.7)	418 (42.3)	1,040 (59.0)	1,427 (74.2)	526 (43.8)	219 (31.2)	591 (46.1)	1,135 (63.8)	404 (39.4)	199 (28.9)	449 (39.6)
2013[3,4,5]	2,622 (109.3)	1,100 (66.7)	409 (48.4)	969 (61.2)	1,406 (73.6)	596 (42.8)	221 (29.9)	536 (43.1)	1,216 (66.0)	504 (38.5)	188 (31.1)	432 (39.5)

—Not available.
†Not applicable.
#Rounds to zero.
[1]Includes other racial/ethnic categories not separately shown.
[2]For 1970 and 1971, White and Black include persons of Hispanic ethnicity.
[3]Because of changes in data collection procedures, data may not be comparable with figures for years prior to 1992.
[4]White and Black exclude persons who selected more than one race category. These persons are classified as Two or more races and included only in the "All races" columns. Prior to 2003, respondents could select only a single race category.
[5]Beginning in 2010, standard errors were computed using replicate weights, which produced more precise values than the generalized variance function methodology used in prior years.

NOTE: "Status" dropouts are 16- to 24-year-olds who are not enrolled in school and who have not completed a high school program, regardless of when they left school. People who have received GED credentials are counted as high school completers. All data are based on October counts. Data are based on sample surveys of the civilian noninstitutionalized population, which excludes persons in prisons, persons in the military, and other persons not living in households. Race categories exclude persons of Hispanic ethnicity except where otherwise noted. Detail may not sum to totals because of rounding.
SOURCE: U.S. Department of Commerce, Census Bureau, Current Population Survey (CPS), October, 1970 through 2013. (This table was prepared March 2015.)

Table 219.75. Percentage of high school dropouts among persons 16 through 24 years old (status dropout rate), by income level, and percentage distribution of status dropouts, by labor force status and years of school completed: 1970 through 2013

[Standard errors appear in parentheses]

Year	Status dropout rate	Status dropout rate, by family income quartile				Percentage distribution of status dropouts, by labor force status				Percentage distribution of status dropouts, by years of school completed					
		Lowest quartile	Middle low quartile	Middle high quartile	Highest quartile	Total	Employed[1]	Unemployed	Not in labor force	Total	Less than 9 years	9 years	10 years	11 or 12 years
1	2	3	4	5	6	7	8	9	10	11	12	13	14	15
1970	15.0 (0.29)	28.0 (0.92)	21.2 (0.65)	11.7 (0.50)	5.2 (0.34)	100.0 (†)	49.8 (1.06)	10.3 (0.65)	39.9 (1.04)	100.0 (†)	28.5 (0.96)	20.6 (0.86)	26.8 (0.94)	24.0 (0.91)
1971	14.7 (0.28)	28.8 (0.90)	20.7 (0.63)	10.9 (0.49)	5.1 (0.32)	100.0 (†)	49.5 (1.05)	10.9 (0.65)	39.6 (1.02)	100.0 (†)	27.9 (0.94)	21.7 (0.86)	27.8 (0.94)	22.7 (0.88)
1972	14.6 (0.28)	27.6 (0.85)	20.8 (0.62)	10.2 (0.46)	5.4 (0.33)	100.0 (†)	51.2 (1.03)	10.2 (0.63)	38.6 (1.01)	100.0 (†)	27.5 (0.92)	20.8 (0.84)	29.0 (0.94)	22.7 (0.87)
1973	14.1 (0.27)	28.0 (†)	19.6 (0.60)	9.9 (0.45)	4.9 (0.31)	100.0 (†)	53.2 (1.04)	9.2 (0.60)	37.5 (1.01)	100.0 (†)	26.5 (0.92)	20.9 (0.84)	27.4 (0.93)	25.3 (0.90)
1974	14.3 (0.27)	— (†)	— (†)	— (†)	—	100.0 (†)	51.8 (1.02)	12.3 (0.67)	35.9 (0.98)	100.0 (†)	25.4 (0.89)	20.1 (0.82)	28.7 (0.93)	25.8 (0.90)
1975	13.9 (0.27)	28.8 (0.82)	18.0 (0.58)	10.2 (0.45)	5.0 (0.30)	100.0 (†)	46.0 (1.02)	15.6 (0.74)	38.4 (1.00)	100.0 (†)	23.5 (0.87)	21.1 (0.84)	27.5 (0.92)	27.9 (0.92)
1976	14.1 (0.27)	28.1 (0.79)	19.2 (0.60)	10.1 (0.45)	4.9 (0.29)	100.0 (†)	48.8 (1.01)	16.0 (0.74)	35.2 (0.97)	100.0 (†)	24.3 (0.87)	20.1 (0.81)	27.8 (0.91)	27.8 (0.91)
1977	14.1 (0.27)	28.5 (0.80)	19.0 (0.60)	10.4 (0.46)	4.5 (0.29)	100.0 (†)	52.9 (1.02)	13.6 (0.70)	33.6 (0.96)	100.0 (†)	24.3 (0.85)	21.7 (0.84)	27.3 (0.91)	26.6 (0.90)
1978	14.2 (0.27)	28.2 (0.80)	18.9 (0.60)	10.5 (0.46)	5.5 (0.31)	100.0 (†)	54.3 (1.01)	12.4 (0.67)	33.3 (0.95)	100.0 (†)	22.9 (0.85)	20.2 (0.81)	28.2 (0.91)	28.8 (0.91)
1979	14.6 (0.27)	28.1 (0.79)	18.5 (0.60)	11.5 (0.47)	5.6 (0.32)	100.0 (†)	54.0 (0.99)	12.7 (0.66)	33.3 (0.94)	100.0 (†)	22.6 (0.83)	21.0 (0.81)	28.6 (0.90)	27.8 (0.89)
1980	14.1 (0.26)	27.0 (0.77)	18.1 (0.60)	10.7 (0.46)	5.7 (0.32)	100.0 (†)	50.4 (1.01)	17.0 (0.76)	32.6 (0.95)	100.0 (†)	23.6 (0.86)	19.7 (0.80)	29.8 (0.93)	27.0 (0.90)
1981	13.9 (0.26)	26.4 (0.75)	17.8 (0.57)	11.1 (0.47)	5.2 (0.30)	100.0 (†)	49.8 (1.01)	18.3 (0.78)	31.9 (0.94)	100.0 (†)	24.3 (0.86)	18.6 (0.78)	30.2 (0.92)	26.9 (0.89)
1982	13.9 (0.27)	27.2 (0.78)	18.3 (0.63)	10.2 (0.48)	4.4 (0.29)	100.0 (†)	45.2 (1.06)	21.1 (0.87)	33.7 (1.01)	100.0 (†)	22.9 (0.90)	20.8 (0.87)	28.8 (0.96)	27.6 (0.95)
1983	13.7 (0.27)	26.5 (0.77)	17.8 (0.62)	10.5 (0.50)	4.1 (0.29)	100.0 (†)	48.4 (1.08)	18.2 (0.83)	33.4 (1.02)	100.0 (†)	23.0 (0.91)	19.3 (0.85)	28.8 (0.98)	28.8 (0.98)
1984	13.1 (0.27)	25.9 (0.76)	16.5 (0.61)	9.9 (0.48)	3.8 (0.29)	100.0 (†)	49.7 (1.11)	17.3 (0.84)	32.9 (1.05)	100.0 (†)	23.6 (0.95)	21.4 (0.91)	27.5 (1.00)	27.5 (0.99)
1985	12.6 (0.27)	27.1 (0.78)	14.7 (0.60)	8.3 (0.46)	4.0 (0.29)	100.0 (†)	50.1 (1.15)	17.5 (0.88)	32.4 (1.08)	100.0 (†)	23.9 (0.98)	21.0 (0.94)	27.9 (1.03)	27.2 (1.03)
1986	12.2 (0.27)	25.4 (0.75)	14.8 (0.60)	8.0 (0.45)	3.4 (0.28)	100.0 (†)	51.1 (1.18)	16.4 (0.87)	32.5 (1.10)	100.0 (†)	25.4 (1.02)	21.5 (0.97)	25.7 (1.03)	27.4 (1.05)
1987	12.6 (0.28)	25.5 (0.76)	16.6 (0.63)	8.0 (0.46)	3.6 (0.28)	100.0 (†)	52.4 (1.16)	13.6 (0.80)	34.0 (1.10)	100.0 (†)	25.9 (1.02)	20.7 (0.94)	26.0 (1.02)	27.5 (1.04)
1988	12.9 (0.30)	27.2 (0.85)	15.4 (0.68)	8.2 (0.51)	3.4 (0.30)	100.0 (†)	52.9 (1.27)	— (†)	— (†)	100.0 (†)	28.9 (1.15)	19.3 (1.00)	25.1 (1.10)	26.8 (1.12)
1989	12.6 (0.31)	25.0 (0.84)	16.2 (0.71)	8.7 (0.52)	3.3 (0.31)	100.0 (†)	53.2 (1.30)	13.8 (0.90)	33.0 (1.22)	100.0 (†)	29.4 (1.18)	20.8 (1.05)	24.9 (1.12)	25.0 (1.13)
1990	12.1 (0.29)	24.3 (0.82)	15.1 (0.65)	8.7 (0.51)	2.9 (0.28)	100.0 (†)	52.5 (1.29)	13.3 (0.88)	34.2 (1.23)	100.0 (†)	28.6 (1.17)	20.9 (1.05)	24.4 (1.11)	26.1 (1.14)
1991	12.5 (0.30)	25.9 (0.83)	15.5 (0.66)	7.7 (0.49)	3.0 (0.29)	100.0 (†)	47.5 (1.28)	15.8 (0.93)	36.7 (1.23)	100.0 (†)	28.6 (1.15)	20.5 (1.03)	26.1 (1.12)	24.9 (1.10)
1992[2]	11.0 (0.28)	23.4 (0.79)	12.9 (0.62)	7.3 (0.48)	2.4 (0.26)	100.0 (†)	47.6 (1.36)	15.0 (0.97)	37.4 (1.32)	100.0 (†)	21.6 (1.12)	17.5 (1.04)	24.4 (1.17)	36.5 (1.31)
1993	11.0 (0.28)	22.9 (0.77)	12.7 (0.62)	6.6 (0.46)	2.9 (0.29)	100.0 (†)	48.7 (1.37)	12.8 (0.91)	38.5 (1.33)	100.0 (†)	20.5 (1.10)	16.6 (1.02)	24.1 (1.17)	38.8 (1.33)
1994	11.4 (0.26)	20.7 (0.70)	13.7 (0.58)	8.7 (0.45)	4.9 (0.33)	100.0 (†)	49.5 (1.21)	13.0 (0.81)	37.5 (1.17)	100.0 (†)	23.9 (1.03)	16.2 (0.89)	20.3 (0.97)	39.6 (1.18)
1995[2]	12.0 (0.27)	23.2 (0.82)	13.8 (0.59)	8.3 (0.46)	3.6 (0.29)	100.0 (†)	48.9 (1.19)	14.2 (0.83)	37.0 (1.14)	100.0 (†)	22.2 (1.06)	17.0 (0.99)	22.5 (0.99)	38.3 (1.15)
1996[2]	11.1 (0.27)	22.0 (0.83)	13.6 (0.60)	7.0 (0.45)	3.2 (0.28)	100.0 (†)	47.3 (1.28)	15.4 (0.91)	37.3 (1.24)	100.0 (†)	22.0 (1.09)	17.7 (1.06)	22.6 (1.07)	39.4 (1.25)
1997[2]	11.0 (0.27)	21.8 (0.79)	13.5 (0.59)	6.2 (0.42)	3.4 (0.29)	100.0 (†)	53.3 (1.28)	13.2 (0.86)	33.5 (1.21)	100.0 (†)	19.9 (1.02)	15.7 (1.01)	22.3 (1.06)	42.1 (1.26)
1998[2]	11.8 (0.27)	22.3 (0.77)	14.9 (0.62)	7.7 (0.45)	3.5 (0.29)	100.0 (†)	55.1 (1.22)	10.3 (0.74)	34.6 (1.17)	100.0 (†)	21.0 (1.00)	14.9 (1.04)	21.4 (1.01)	42.6 (1.21)
1999[2]	11.2 (0.26)	21.0 (0.70)	14.3 (0.60)	7.4 (0.44)	3.9 (0.30)	100.0 (†)	55.6 (1.24)	10.0 (0.75)	34.4 (1.18)	100.0 (†)	22.2 (1.03)	16.3 (1.04)	22.5 (1.04)	39.0 (1.21)
2000[2]	10.9 (0.26)	20.7 (0.70)	12.8 (0.56)	8.3 (0.46)	3.5 (0.29)	100.0 (†)	56.9 (1.24)	12.3 (0.82)	30.8 (1.16)	100.0 (†)	21.5 (1.03)	15.3 (0.90)	23.1 (1.06)	40.0 (1.23)
2001[2]	10.7 (0.25)	19.3 (0.68)	13.4 (0.57)	9.0 (0.47)	3.2 (0.27)	100.0 (†)	58.3 (1.24)	14.8 (0.89)	26.9 (1.11)	100.0 (†)	18.4 (0.97)	16.8 (0.94)	23.8 (1.07)	40.9 (1.23)
2002[2]	10.5 (0.24)	18.8 (0.62)	12.3 (0.53)	8.4 (0.43)	3.8 (0.28)	100.0 (†)	57.4 (1.18)	13.3 (0.81)	29.2 (1.09)	100.0 (†)	22.8 (1.00)	17.1 (0.90)	21.3 (0.98)	38.9 (1.17)
2003[2]	9.9 (0.23)	19.5 (0.64)	10.8 (0.49)	7.3 (0.40)	3.4 (0.26)	100.0 (†)	53.5 (1.22)	13.7 (0.84)	32.9 (1.15)	100.0 (†)	21.2 (1.00)	18.2 (0.94)	20.7 (0.99)	40.3 (1.20)
2004[2]	10.3 (0.23)	18.0 (0.60)	12.7 (0.52)	8.2 (0.42)	3.7 (0.27)	100.0 (†)	53.0 (1.19)	14.3 (0.83)	32.7 (1.12)	100.0 (†)	21.4 (0.97)	15.9 (0.87)	22.5 (0.99)	40.3 (1.17)
2005[2]	9.4 (0.22)	17.9 (0.60)	11.5 (0.51)	7.1 (0.39)	2.7 (0.23)	100.0 (†)	56.9 (1.23)	11.9 (0.80)	31.2 (1.15)	100.0 (†)	18.9 (0.97)	16.8 (0.93)	21.4 (1.02)	42.9 (1.23)
2006[2]	9.3 (0.22)	16.5 (0.58)	12.1 (0.51)	6.3 (0.37)	3.8 (0.27)	100.0 (†)	56.4 (1.23)	11.7 (0.80)	32.0 (1.16)	100.0 (†)	22.1 (1.03)	13.4 (0.85)	20.7 (1.01)	43.9 (1.23)
2007[2]	8.7 (0.21)	16.7 (0.59)	10.5 (0.48)	6.4 (0.36)	3.2 (0.25)	100.0 (†)	55.5 (1.27)	11.2 (0.80)	33.3 (1.20)	100.0 (†)	21.2 (1.04)	16.9 (0.96)	22.9 (1.07)	39.0 (1.24)
2008[2]	8.0 (0.20)	16.4 (0.58)	9.4 (0.45)	5.4 (0.34)	2.2 (0.21)	100.0 (†)	46.8 (1.33)	16.3 (0.98)	36.9 (1.28)	100.0 (†)	18.4 (1.03)	15.2 (0.96)	23.8 (1.13)	42.6 (1.32)
2009[2]	8.1 (0.20)	15.8 (0.57)	9.7 (0.45)	5.4 (0.34)	2.5 (0.22)	100.0 (†)	43.2 (1.31)	19.9 (1.06)	36.9 (1.28)	100.0 (†)	17.7 (1.01)	13.6 (0.91)	24.4 (1.14)	44.3 (1.32)
2010[2,3]	7.4 (0.27)	13.8 (0.83)	8.9 (0.54)	5.1 (0.48)	2.5 (0.31)	100.0 (†)	45.8 (1.64)	18.7 (1.38)	35.5 (1.70)	100.0 (†)	19.2 (1.48)	13.1 (1.07)	22.5 (1.59)	45.2 (1.89)
2011[2,3]	7.1 (0.26)	13.0 (0.73)	9.0 (0.53)	4.8 (0.45)	2.3 (0.32)	100.0 (†)	49.8 (1.77)	16.0 (1.33)	34.2 (1.69)	100.0 (†)	18.1 (1.72)	12.9 (1.15)	21.2 (1.39)	47.7 (1.87)
2012[2,3]	6.6 (0.25)	11.8 (0.70)	8.7 (0.65)	4.1 (0.44)	1.9 (0.31)	100.0 (†)	44.8 (2.07)	18.1 (1.49)	37.1 (1.83)	100.0 (†)	18.3 (1.76)	10.3 (1.21)	21.9 (1.57)	49.6 (2.20)
2013[2,3]	6.8 (0.28)	10.7 (0.73)	8.8 (0.67)	5.0 (0.44)	3.2 (0.36)	100.0 (†)	41.1 (2.01)	16.8 (1.58)	42.1 (1.84)	100.0 (†)	18.3 (1.70)	13.3 (1.34)	21.1 (1.63)	47.4 (2.31)

—Not available.
†Not applicable.
[1]Includes persons who were employed but not at work during the survey week.
[2]Because of changes in data collection procedures, data may not be comparable with figures for years prior to 1992.
[3]Beginning in 2010, standard errors were computed using replicate weights, which produced more precise values than the generalized variance function methodology used in prior years.

NOTE: "Status" dropouts are 16- to 24-year-olds who are not enrolled in school and who have not completed a high school program, regardless of when they left school. People who have received GED credentials are counted as high school completers. Data are based on sample surveys of the civilian noninstitutionalized population, which excludes persons in prisons, persons in the military, and other persons not living in households. Detail may not sum to totals because of rounding.
SOURCE: U.S. Department of Commerce, Census Bureau, Current Population Survey (CPS), October, 1970 through 2013. (This table was prepared July 2014.)

Table 219.80. Percentage of high school dropouts among persons 16 through 24 years old (status dropout rate) and number of status dropouts, by noninstitutionalized or institutionalized status, birth in or outside of the United States, and selected characteristics: 2011 and 2012
[Standard errors appear in parentheses]

Selected characteristic	Total status dropout rate		Noninstitutionalized population[1]						Institutionalized population[2]	
	2011	2012	2012 Number of status dropouts	Percentage distribution of status dropouts	Status dropout rate: Total for noninstitutionalized population	For those born in the United States[3]	For those born outside of the United States[3]		Number of status dropouts	Status dropout rate
1	2	3	4	5	6	7	8		9	10
Total	7.7 (0.06)	7.0 (0.07)	2,611,450 (26,882)	100.0 (†)	6.6 (0.07)	5.8 (0.06)	13.8 (0.25)		172,870 (4,254)	35.4 (0.73)
Sex										
Male	9.0 (0.09)	8.2 (0.08)	1,509,880 (17,216)	57.8 (0.39)	7.6 (0.09)	6.6 (0.08)	16.0 (0.35)		160,100 (3,945)	36.8 (0.78)
Female	6.2 (0.07)	5.7 (0.08)	1,101,570 (16,400)	42.2 (0.39)	5.7 (0.08)	5.0 (0.08)	11.4 (0.32)		12,770 (1,275)	23.9 (2.02)
Race/ethnicity										
White	5.1 (0.07)	4.7 (0.06)	1,004,120 (13,891)	38.5 (0.39)	4.5 (0.06)	4.6 (0.07)	3.6 (0.31)		39,130 (1,872)	25.9 (0.97)
Black	9.6 (0.18)	9.0 (0.18)	441,300 (10,334)	16.9 (0.37)	7.9 (0.18)	8.1 (0.18)	5.4 (0.61)		80,330 (2,692)	41.1 (1.17)
Hispanic	14.5 (0.19)	12.8 (0.18)	1,007,430 (15,680)	38.6 (0.40)	12.4 (0.19)	8.6 (0.18)	24.2 (0.48)		47,640 (2,276)	40.9 (1.55)
Asian	2.7 (0.14)	2.6 (0.14)	48,610 (2,628)	1.9 (0.10)	2.6 (0.14)	1.8 (0.15)	3.4 (0.25)		(†)	17.5 ! (7.42)
Pacific Islander	8.8 (1.62)	9.1 (1.45)	6,280 (1,065)	0.2 (0.04)	8.8 (1.45)	6.6 (1.33)	20.2 (5.60)		‡	‡
American Indian/Alaska Native	13.1 (0.75)	12.8 (0.71)	37,440 (2,192)	1.4 (0.08)	12.4 (0.72)	12.4 (0.73)	12.0 ! (5.80)		2,040 (441)	31.4 (5.39)
Two or more races	6.0 (0.33)	5.6 (0.25)	60,630 (2,836)	2.3 (0.11)	5.5 (0.25)	5.5 (0.27)	5.2 (0.78)		2,860 (526)	19.0 (3.16)
Race/ethnicity by sex										
Male										
White	5.8 (0.10)	5.4 (0.09)	577,190 (10,251)	38.2 (0.49)	5.1 (0.09)	5.2 (0.10)	4.0 (0.44)		34,170 (1,700)	26.7 (1.07)
Black	11.8 (0.25)	10.9 (0.26)	243,060 (7,319)	16.1 (0.46)	8.9 (0.27)	9.2 (0.27)	5.2 (0.84)		75,400 (2,540)	42.0 (1.21)
Hispanic	17.0 (0.27)	15.0 (0.23)	600,260 (10,332)	39.8 (0.50)	14.3 (0.24)	9.7 (0.24)	27.3 (0.61)		45,100 (2,120)	42.2 (1.60)
Asian	3.1 (0.19)	2.8 (0.24)	25,910 (2,284)	1.7 (0.15)	2.7 (0.24)	2.0 (0.23)	3.5 (0.41)		‡	19.9 ! (8.44)
Pacific Islander	9.2 (2.10)	10.0 (1.74)	‡	0.2 (0.05)	9.5 (1.73)	7.1 (2.02)	22.1 ! (7.13)		(†)	‡
American Indian/Alaska Native	14.8 (1.11)	14.8 (1.06)	21,370 (1,576)	1.4 (0.10)	14.0 (1.08)	13.9 (1.06)	‡		1,920 (420)	35.2 (5.94)
Two or more races	7.4 (0.57)	6.7 (0.43)	34,230 (2,433)	2.3 (0.16)	6.3 (0.42)	6.3 (0.43)	6.1 (1.35)		2,650 (514)	22.0 (3.80)
Female										
White	4.3 (0.08)	4.0 (0.08)	426,930 (9,070)	38.8 (0.66)	3.9 (0.08)	4.0 (0.09)	3.2 (0.38)		4,970 (711)	21.4 (2.64)
Black	7.3 (0.22)	7.0 (0.21)	198,240 (5,941)	18.0 (0.48)	6.9 (0.20)	7.0 (0.21)	5.7 (0.85)		4,930 (734)	31.0 (3.98)
Hispanic	11.7 (0.23)	10.4 (0.23)	407,160 (9,421)	37.0 (0.57)	10.4 (0.24)	7.4 (0.23)	20.4 (0.60)		2,540 (538)	26.1 (4.73)
Asian	2.4 (0.18)	2.4 (0.20)	22,700 (1,877)	2.1 (0.17)	2.4 (0.20)	1.6 (0.22)	3.2 (0.32)		‡	‡
Pacific Islander	8.4 (2.11)	8.0 ! (2.41)	‡	0.2 ! (0.08)	8.0 ! (2.41)	6.1 ! (2.55)	18.0 ! (8.06)		‡	‡
American Indian/Alaska Native	11.4 (0.86)	10.8 (0.95)	16,070 (1,438)	1.5 (0.13)	10.8 (0.95)	10.9 (0.96)	‡		‡	‡
Two or more races	4.6 (0.41)	4.7 (0.34)	26,400 (1,956)	2.4 (0.17)	4.6 (0.34)	4.7 (0.36)	4.1 (1.07)		‡	‡
Age										
16	2.2 (0.09)	2.1 (0.08)	82,960 (3,316)	3.2 (0.12)	2.0 (0.08)	1.9 (0.08)	3.0 (0.38)		3,340 (508)	10.2 (1.50)
17	3.8 (0.11)	3.3 (0.12)	133,560 (4,693)	5.1 (0.17)	3.2 (0.12)	3.1 (0.12)	4.9 (0.48)		4,450 (514)	13.1 (1.45)
18	6.2 (0.15)	5.4 (0.14)	235,580 (6,064)	9.0 (0.21)	5.2 (0.13)	4.9 (0.14)	8.0 (0.57)		12,170 (1,090)	32.1 (2.50)
19	7.7 (0.15)	6.8 (0.13)	273,760 (5,767)	10.5 (0.20)	6.4 (0.13)	6.0 (0.12)	10.5 (0.76)		19,430 (1,278)	42.7 (2.32)
20–24	9.8 (0.10)	9.0 (0.09)	1,885,590 (20,667)	72.2 (0.34)	8.5 (0.09)	7.3 (0.09)	17.4 (0.32)		133,470 (3,757)	39.4 (0.90)
Region										
Northeast	6.1 (0.13)	5.6 (0.11)	370,020 (7,747)	14.2 (0.27)	5.4 (0.11)	4.7 (0.11)	9.8 (0.53)		23,650 (1,293)	30.7 (1.52)
Midwest	6.8 (0.12)	6.0 (0.12)	479,780 (9,820)	18.4 (0.30)	5.7 (0.12)	5.4 (0.12)	11.2 (0.65)		30,340 (1,603)	31.6 (1.38)
South	8.7 (0.11)	7.8 (0.10)	1,076,320 (15,066)	41.2 (0.36)	7.4 (0.13)	6.5 (0.09)	15.5 (0.49)		83,370 (2,952)	39.1 (1.13)
West	8.0 (0.12)	7.6 (0.10)	685,340 (9,795)	26.2 (0.31)	7.3 (0.10)	6.0 (0.11)	15.6 (0.43)		35,500 (1,983)	34.8 (1.55)

†Not applicable.
!Interpret data with caution. The coefficient of variation (CV) for this estimate is between 30 and 50 percent.
‡Reporting standards not met. Either there are too few cases for a reliable estimate or the coefficient of variation (CV) is 50 percent or greater.
[1]Persons living in households as well as persons living in noninstitutionalized group quarters. Noninstitutionalized group quarters include college and university housing, military quarters, facilities for workers and religious groups, and temporary shelters for the homeless.
[2]Persons living in institutionalized group quarters, including adult and juvenile correctional facilities, nursing facilities, and other health care facilities.

[3]United States refers to the 50 states and the District of Columbia.
NOTE: "Status" dropouts are 16- to 24-year-olds who are not enrolled in school and who have not completed a high school program, regardless of when they left school and whether they ever attended school in the United States. People who have received GED credentials are counted as high school completers. Detail may not sum to totals because of rounding. Race categories exclude persons of Hispanic ethnicity. Status dropout rates in this table may differ from those in tables based on the Current Population Survey (CPS) because of differences in survey design and target populations.
SOURCE: U.S. Department of Commerce, Census Bureau, American Community Survey (ACS), 2011 and 2012. (This table was prepared August 2014.)

Table 219.90. Number and percentage distribution of 14- through 21-year-old students served under Individuals with Disabilities Education Act, Part B, who exited school, by exit reason, age, and type of disability: 2010–11 and 2011–12

Year, age, and type of disability	Total	Exiting school					Transferred to regular education[3]	Moved, known to be continuing[4]
		Graduated with diploma	Received a certificate of attendance	Reached maximum age[1]	Dropped out[2]	Died		
1	2	3	4	5	6	7	8	9
2010–11								
Total number.................................	402,038	255,512	58,938	5,245	80,839	1,504	61,102	181,554
Percentage distribution of total	100.0	63.6	14.7	1.3	20.1	0.4	†	†
Number by age								
14..	3,023	1	4	†	2,808	210	15,836	35,708
15..	6,051	35	29	†	5,735	252	13,769	38,361
16..	18,118	3,429	658	†	13,743	288	13,386	40,515
17..	145,037	105,110	16,384	†	23,225	318	10,996	35,885
18..	152,198	107,659	23,017	0	21,323	199	5,160	21,103
19..	47,013	28,176	9,102	29	9,589	117	1,346	6,899
20..	18,595	7,845	5,659	1,548	3,458	85	441	2,251
21..	12,003	3,257	4,085	3,668	958	35	168	832
Number by type of disability								
Autism......................................	14,162	9,179	3,366	685	892	40	1,366	4,297
Deaf-blindness.........................	93	48	21	8	14	2	6	35
Emotional disturbance..............	42,889	22,423	4,160	308	15,866	132	6,207	34,844
Hearing impairment..................	4,707	3,439	737	42	479	10	620	1,469
Intellectual disability................	40,439	16,137	14,446	2,122	7,480	254	1,556	15,383
Multiple disabilities..................	8,523	4,019	2,456	665	1,116	267	267	3,133
Orthopedic impairment.............	3,605	2,243	673	172	416	101	458	1,141
Other health impairment[5].......	52,682	36,883	5,598	238	9,683	280	9,806	23,862
Specific learning disability........	220,902	150,974	25,806	861	42,894	367	31,676	91,302
Speech or language impairment..	9,795	7,111	1,060	45	1,564	15	8,776	4,899
Traumatic brain injury...............	2,536	1,717	431	73	289	26	178	706
Visual impairment.....................	1,705	1,339	184	26	146	10	186	483
2011–12								
Total number.................................	386,385	247,763	53,575	5,505	77,986	1,556	64,063	174,960
Percentage distribution of total	100.0	64.1	13.9	1.4	20.2	0.4	†	†
Number by age								
14..	—	—	—	†	—	—	—	—
15..	—	—	—	†	—	—	—	—
16..	—	—	—	†	—	—	—	—
17..	—	—	—	†	—	—	—	—
18..	—	—	—	—	—	—	—	—
19..	—	—	—	—	—	—	—	—
20..	—	—	—	—	—	—	—	—
21..	—	—	—	—	—	—	—	—
Number by type of disability								
Autism......................................	16,714	10,802	3,791	840	1,217	64	1,815	4,947
Deaf-blindness.........................	82	39	15	12	12	4	6	27
Emotional disturbance..............	40,634	20,909	3,671	362	15,538	154	6,050	32,485
Hearing impairment..................	4,692	3,443	696	60	479	14	726	1,504
Intellectual disability................	37,989	15,421	13,248	2,163	6,914	243	2,176	14,098
Multiple disabilities..................	8,669	4,220	2,118	708	1,363	260	334	3,038
Orthopedic impairment.............	3,731	2,305	731	183	422	90	502	1,181
Other health impairment[5].......	54,117	37,868	5,431	268	10,270	280	9,688	24,977
Specific learning disability........	205,606	142,240	22,352	760	39,850	404	33,695	87,031
Speech or language impairment..	9,815	7,365	907	49	1,483	11	8,682	4,625
Traumatic brain injury...............	2,583	1,771	412	60	319	21	204	671
Visual impairment.....................	1,727	1,337	220	40	119	11	185	453

—Not available.
†Not applicable.
[1]Students may exit special education services due to maximum age beginning at age 18, depending on state law or practice or order of any court.
[2]"Dropped out" is defined as the total who were enrolled at some point in the reporting year, were not enrolled at the end of the reporting year, and did not exit for any of the other reasons described. Includes students previously categorized as "moved, not known to continue."
[3]"Transferred to regular education" was previously labeled "no longer receives special education."
[4]"Moved, known to be continuing" is the total number of students who moved out of the administrative area or transferred to another district and are known to be continuing in an educational program.

[5]Other health impairments include having limited strength, vitality, or alertness due to chronic or acute health problems such as a heart condition, tuberculosis, rheumatic fever, nephritis, asthma, sickle cell anemia, hemophilia, epilepsy, lead poisoning, leukemia, or diabetes.
NOTE: Data are for the 50 states, the District of Columbia, and the Bureau of Indian Education schools. Detail may not sum to totals because of rounding.
SOURCE: U.S. Department of Education, Office of Special Education Programs, Individuals with Disabilities Education Act (IDEA) database. Retrieved October 3, 2014, from https://inventory.data.gov/dataset/737e9eb8-8fdf-4f50-b903-b9724afb10ab/resource/3887a286-d6c1-4c5a-a211-cc18b34254e9. (This table was prepared November 2014.)

Table 220.10. Percentage of children demonstrating specific cognitive and motor skills at about 9 months of age, by child's age and selected characteristics: 2001–02

[Standard errors appear in parentheses]

Age and selected characteristic	Number of children (in thousands)	Percentage distribution of children	Percent of children who demonstrate skills[1]										
			Specific cognitive skills						Specific motor skills				
			Explores objects[2]	Explores purposefully[3]	Jabbers expressively[4]	Early problem solving[5]	Names objects[6]	Eye-hand coordination[7]	Sitting[8]	Prewalking[9]	Stands alone[10]	Skillful walking[11]	Balance[12]
1	2	3	4	5	6	7	8	9	10	11	12	13	14
8 through 10 months													
Total	2,882 (39.1)	100.0 (†)	98.6 (0.06)	83.2 (0.54)	29.6 (0.57)	3.7 (0.13)	0.6 (0.03)	89.1 (0.26)	86.8 (0.24)	64.7 (0.60)	18.6 (0.50)	8.4 (0.21)	1.7 (0.09)
Sex of child													
Male	1,460 (23.0)	50.7 (0.38)	98.6 (0.06)	82.7 (0.51)	28.8 (0.56)	3.5 (0.14)	0.6 (0.03)	89.3 (0.30)	87.0 (0.27)	65.1 (0.69)	18.5 (0.55)	8.3 (0.23)	1.7 (0.10)
Female	1,422 (22.0)	49.3 (0.38)	98.7 (0.09)	83.8 (0.68)	30.4 (0.71)	3.9 (0.18)	0.7 (0.05)	88.9 (0.36)	86.6 (0.33)	64.4 (0.78)	18.7 (0.67)	8.4 (0.29)	1.8 (0.14)
Race/ethnicity of child													
White	1,569 (29.2)	54.5 (0.63)	98.8 (0.07)	84.0 (0.69)	30.4 (0.72)	3.9 (0.17)	0.7 (0.04)	88.8 (0.37)	86.5 (0.33)	63.8 (0.81)	18.0 (0.66)	8.1 (0.27)	1.6 (0.10)
Black	381 (11.1)	13.3 (0.38)	98.1 (0.16)	80.8 (0.92)	27.8 (0.99)	3.3 (0.25)	0.6 (0.07)	91.0 (0.33)	88.6 (0.32)	69.7 (0.94)	22.8 (1.15)	10.4 (0.58)	2.6 (0.35)
Hispanic	717 (18.5)	24.9 (0.54)	98.5 (0.13)	82.9 (0.82)	29.0 (0.84)	3.4 (0.21)	0.6 (0.05)	88.4 (0.47)	86.1 (0.43)	63.4 (1.00)	17.0 (0.77)	7.8 (0.32)	1.6 (0.15)
Asian	79 (3.1)	2.7 (0.10)	98.8 (0.13)	83.3 (0.96)	28.2 (0.92)	3.1 (0.20)	0.5 (0.04)	89.5 (0.53)	87.1 (0.49)	65.2 (1.21)	18.2 (1.00)	8.2 (0.39)	1.6 (0.14)
Pacific Islander	6 (1.5)	0.2 (0.05)	98.9 (0.23)	81.8 (3.58)	23.8 (3.22)	2.0 (0.47)	0.3 (0.07)	95.4 (0.97)	93.0 (1.13)	79.9 (3.81)	34.8 (8.69)	15.1 (3.90)	3.9 ! (1.67)
American Indian/Alaska Native	10 (1.1)	0.4 (0.04)	98.4 (0.30)	80.3 (2.72)	27.2 (2.49)	3.4 (0.70)	0.6 (0.18)	90.2 (0.99)	87.8 (0.91)	66.8 (2.15)	19.6 (2.08)	8.4 (0.80)	1.5 (0.29)
Two or more races	115 (9.8)	4.0 (0.33)	98.6 (0.14)	83.0 (1.24)	29.8 (1.51)	3.9 (0.55)	0.8 (0.21)	90.0 (0.94)	87.8 (0.87)	67.7 (2.20)	22.1 (2.03)	9.6 (0.79)	2.0 (0.30)
Months of age													
8 months	642 (32.8)	29.5 (0.90)	97.5 (0.14)	67.9 (1.04)	15.7 (0.53)	1.1 (0.09)	0.1 (0.02)	84.0 (0.52)	82.0 (0.46)	52.7 (1.08)	8.8 (0.63)	4.5 (0.22)	0.5 (0.05)
9 months	1,389 (28.2)	22.3 (0.99)	98.7 (0.06)	84.5 (0.43)	27.5 (0.44)	2.7 (0.09)	0.4 (0.02)	89.1 (0.32)	86.7 (0.30)	64.2 (0.74)	16.1 (0.55)	7.2 (0.21)	1.2 (0.07)
10 months	851 (24.2)	48.2 (0.76)	99.3 (0.07)	92.7 (0.33)	43.5 (0.74)	7.1 (0.27)	1.4 (0.08)	92.8 (0.26)	90.5 (0.25)	74.6 (0.63)	30.1 (0.85)	13.3 (0.42)	3.6 (0.25)
Primary type of nonparental care arrangement[13]													
No regular nonparental arrangement	1,459 (28.0)	50.7 (0.90)	98.5 (0.09)	82.4 (0.59)	28.7 (0.55)	3.4 (0.14)	0.6 (0.04)	88.2 (0.34)	86.0 (0.30)	63.1 (0.70)	17.7 (0.52)	8.0 (0.22)	1.6 (0.10)
Home-based care													
Relative care[14]	759 (27.1)	26.4 (0.81)	98.8 (0.08)	84.3 (0.67)	30.6 (0.79)	3.9 (0.22)	0.7 (0.06)	90.3 (0.35)	87.9 (0.33)	67.3 (0.84)	20.4 (0.81)	9.2 (0.38)	2.0 (0.19)
Nonrelative care[15]	430 (17.1)	14.9 (0.53)	98.8 (0.08)	84.7 (0.80)	31.3 (1.00)	4.3 (0.29)	0.8 (0.08)	90.0 (0.45)	87.6 (0.45)	66.1 (1.14)	19.3 (1.35)	8.7 (0.58)	1.8 (0.23)
Center-based care[16]	211 (13.9)	7.3 (0.48)	98.6 (0.19)	82.8 (1.43)	29.3 (1.54)	3.5 (0.39)	0.6 (0.09)	89.0 (0.77)	86.7 (0.71)	64.0 (1.72)	18.0 (1.51)	8.3 (0.66)	1.9 (0.32)
Multiple arrangements[17]	19 (4.0)	0.7 (0.14)	98.1 (0.36)	77.5 (3.54)	24.8 (3.12)	2.8 (0.65)	0.4 (0.12)	86.8 (2.89)	84.6 (2.55)	61.8 (5.09)	14.4 (2.71)	6.4 (0.94)	0.9 (0.19)
Parents' highest level of education													
Less than high school	388 (12.4)	13.5 (0.42)	98.4 (0.11)	80.0 (0.87)	25.9 (0.79)	2.8 (0.20)	0.5 (0.06)	88.9 (0.62)	86.5 (0.58)	64.4 (1.20)	17.3 (0.96)	8.0 (0.42)	1.7 (0.20)
High school completion	702 (19.8)	24.4 (0.60)	98.4 (0.13)	82.6 (0.89)	29.2 (0.81)	3.6 (0.21)	0.7 (0.06)	89.6 (0.45)	87.3 (0.42)	66.8 (0.91)	20.6 (0.84)	9.1 (0.36)	1.9 (0.17)
Some college/vocational	847 (24.8)	29.4 (0.68)	98.7 (0.08)	84.4 (0.60)	30.8 (0.69)	3.9 (0.20)	0.7 (0.05)	90.0 (0.35)	87.7 (0.33)	66.7 (0.84)	20.8 (0.82)	9.3 (0.35)	2.0 (0.16)
Bachelor's degree	497 (16.2)	17.3 (0.54)	98.8 (0.07)	83.9 (0.60)	30.2 (0.71)	3.8 (0.20)	0.7 (0.05)	88.4 (0.46)	86.1 (0.41)	62.5 (1.05)	16.3 (0.85)	7.4 (0.34)	1.4 (0.12)
Any graduate education	446 (15.7)	15.5 (0.52)	98.8 (0.11)	84.0 (0.94)	30.4 (0.88)	3.8 (0.22)	0.7 (0.06)	87.5 (0.58)	85.4 (0.52)	60.5 (1.23)	15.2 (0.91)	7.0 (0.40)	1.4 (0.18)
Poverty status[18]													
Below poverty threshold	682 (23.0)	23.7 (0.74)	98.3 (0.13)	80.9 (0.75)	27.1 (0.79)	3.1 (0.21)	0.5 (0.05)	89.1 (0.47)	86.8 (0.43)	65.5 (0.98)	19.2 (0.86)	8.7 (0.42)	1.9 (0.24)
At or above poverty threshold	2,200 (37.2)	76.3 (0.74)	98.7 (0.07)	84.0 (0.58)	30.4 (0.63)	3.8 (0.15)	0.7 (0.04)	89.1 (0.27)	86.8 (0.25)	64.5 (0.66)	18.4 (0.56)	8.3 (0.23)	1.7 (0.10)
Socioeconomic status[19]													
Lowest 20 percent	557 (16.8)	19.3 (0.58)	98.3 (0.13)	80.7 (0.72)	26.8 (0.69)	3.0 (0.17)	0.5 (0.04)	89.1 (0.46)	86.7 (0.43)	65.4 (0.90)	18.8 (0.83)	8.5 (0.35)	1.8 (0.18)
Middle 60 percent	1,719 (38.2)	59.7 (0.83)	98.6 (0.08)	83.5 (0.63)	30.2 (0.67)	3.8 (0.18)	0.7 (0.05)	89.5 (0.30)	87.2 (0.28)	65.6 (0.73)	19.6 (0.67)	8.8 (0.28)	1.9 (0.11)
Highest 20 percent	606 (18.4)	21.0 (0.63)	98.8 (0.09)	84.8 (0.73)	30.5 (0.79)	3.8 (0.18)	0.6 (0.04)	88.0 (0.45)	85.8 (0.40)	61.5 (0.96)	15.6 (0.66)	7.1 (0.28)	1.3 (0.13)

See notes at end of table.

Table 220.10. Percentage of children demonstrating specific cognitive and motor skills at about 9 months of age, by child's age and selected characteristics: 2001–02—Continued
[Standard errors appear in parentheses]

Age and selected characteristic	Number of children (in thousands)	Percentage distribution of children	Percent of children who demonstrate skills[1]											
			Specific cognitive skills					Specific motor skills					
			Explores objects[2]	Explores purposefully[3]	Jabbers expressively[4]	Early problem solving[5]	Names objects[6]	Eye-hand coordination[7]	Sitting[8]	Prewalking[9]	Stands alone[10]	Skillful walking[11]	Balance[12]
1	2	3	4	5	6	7	8	9	10	11	12	13	14
11 through 13 months													
Total	839 (32.2)	100.0 (†)	99.7 (0.05)	97.3 (0.15)	67.9 (0.54)	22.5 (0.55)	8.2 (0.37)	97.1 (0.17)	95.6 (0.19)	89.0 (0.54)	62.5 (1.29)	34.9 (0.95)	19.1 (0.84)
Months of age													
11 months	425 (19.6)	50.6 (1.54)	99.5 (0.10)	95.8 (0.28)	57.6 (0.77)	14.2 (0.59)	4.0 (0.33)	95.8 (0.28)	93.9 (0.29)	84.4 (0.86)	49.0 (1.74)	24.3 (1.05)	10.5 (0.77)
12 months	251 (14.8)	30.0 (1.29)	99.8 (0.03)	98.4 (0.13)	74.3 (0.83)	26.9 (0.94)	10.2 (0.65)	98.1 (0.21)	96.8 (0.26)	92.6 (0.71)	70.9 (2.09)	40.2 (1.65)	22.9 (1.50)
13 months	163 (12.1)	19.4 (1.16)	100.0 (†)	99.5 (0.08)	85.0 (0.62)	37.7 (1.04)	16.0 (0.87)	99.0 (0.27)	98.2 (0.30)	95.8 (0.85)	84.8 (2.24)	54.4 (1.81)	36.0 (1.83)
14 through 22 months	260 (19.7)	100.0 (†)	100.0 (†)	99.5 (0.14)	90.0 (0.60)	58.4 (1.44)	40.8 (1.71)	99.5 (0.12)	99.1 (0.13)	98.3 (0.28)	94.1 (0.91)	74.0 (1.35)	61.7 (1.82)

†Not applicable.

!Interpret data with caution. The coefficient of variation (CV) for this estimate is between 30 and 50 percent.

[1]Based on assessments collected using the Bayley Short Form Research Edition (BSF-R), a shortened field method of administering the Bayley Scales of Infant Development-II (BSID-II) (Bayley 1993). The scores are fully equated with the BSID-II; for more information, see NCES's *Early Childhood Longitudinal Study, Birth Cohort (ECLS-B) Psychometric Report for the 2-year Data Collection*. The proficiency probabilities indicate mastery of a specific skill or ability within cognitive or physical domains.

[2]Ability to explore objects, for example, reaching for and holding objects. The child may have no specific purpose except to play or discover.

[3]Ability to explore objects with a purpose, such as to explore a bell to understand the source of the sound.

[4]Measures proficiency in communication through diverse nonverbal sounds and gestures, such as vowel and vowel-consonant sounds.

[5]Measures proficiency in engaging in early problem solving, such as using a tool to reach an out-of-reach toy or locating a hidden toy.

[6]Measures proficiency in early communication skills, such as saying simple words like "mama" and "dada."

[7]Measures proficiency in being able to use visual tracking to guide hand movements to pick up a small object.

[8]Measures proficiency in ability to maintain control of the muscles used in sitting with and without support.

[9]Measures proficiency in ability to engage in various prewalking types of mobility, with and without support, such as shifting weight from one foot to the other.

[10]Measures proficiency in ability to walk with help and to stand independently.

[11]Measures proficiency in being able to walk independently.

[12]Measures proficiency in ability to maintain balance while changing position.

[13]The type of nonparental care in which the child spent the most hours.

[14]Care provided in the child's home or in another private home by a relative (excluding parents).

[15]Care provided in the child's home or in another private home by a person unrelated to the child.

[16]Care provided in places such as early learning centers, nursery schools, and preschools.

[17]Children who spent an equal amount of time in each of two or more types of arrangements.

[18]Poverty status based on Census Bureau guidelines from 2002, which identify a dollar amount determined to meet a household's needs, given its size and composition. In 2002, a family of four was considered to live below the poverty threshold if its income was less than or equal to $18,392.

[19]Socioeconomic status (SES) was measured by a composite score based on parental education and occupations, and family income.

NOTE: Estimates weighted by W1C0. This table is based on a survey that sampled children born in 2001 and was designed to collect information about them for the first time when the children were about 9 months of age (i.e., 8 to 10 months). As shown in the table, some children were older than this at the time data were collected, although only 6.5 percent were over 13 months of age. Race categories exclude persons of Hispanic ethnicity. Detail may not sum to totals because of rounding and survey item nonresponse. Some data have been revised from previously published figures.

SOURCE: U.S. Department of Education, National Center for Education Statistics, Early Childhood Longitudinal Study, Birth Cohort 9-month–Kindergarten 2007 Restricted-Use Data File and Electronic Codebook. (This table was prepared December 2010.)

Table 220.20. Percentage of children demonstrating specific cognitive skills, motor skills, and secure emotional attachment to parents at about 2 years of age, by selected characteristics: 2003–04

[Standard errors appear in parentheses]

Selected characteristic	Percentage distribution of children[1]	Specific cognitive skills[2]						Specific motor skills[2]					Secure emotional attachment to parent[3]
		Receptive vocabulary[4]	Expressive vocabulary[5]	Listening comprehension[6]	Matching/ discrimination[7]	Early counting[8]	Skillful walking[9]	Balance[10]	Fine motor control[11]	Uses stairs[12]	Alternating balance[13]	Motor planning[14]	
1	2	3	4	5	6	7	8	9	10	11	12	13	14
Total	100.0 (†)	84.5 (0.38)	63.9 (0.53)	36.6 (0.42)	31.9 (0.39)	3.9 (0.14)	92.6 (0.20)	89.4 (0.33)	55.5 (0.48)	48.1 (0.41)	30.0 (0.47)	10.2 (0.21)	61.6 (1.12)
Sex of child													
Male	51.1 (0.21)	81.4 (0.56)	59.3 (0.75)	32.9 (0.58)	28.4 (0.53)	3.0 (0.16)	92.0 (0.26)	88.4 (0.43)	54.2 (0.53)	46.9 (0.44)	28.7 (0.48)	9.6 (0.20)	55.0 (1.23)
Female	48.9 (0.21)	87.7 (0.38)	68.9 (0.59)	40.6 (0.50)	35.6 (0.48)	4.8 (0.20)	93.2 (0.20)	90.5 (0.32)	56.8 (0.53)	49.3 (0.47)	31.3 (0.55)	10.9 (0.26)	68.4 (1.27)
Race/ethnicity of child													
White	54.6 (0.61)	88.7 (0.40)	70.7 (0.63)	42.2 (0.52)	37.1 (0.49)	5.2 (0.21)	92.8 (0.23)	89.9 (0.38)	55.8 (0.58)	48.4 (0.50)	30.2 (0.58)	10.4 (0.26)	65.7 (1.41)
Black	13.4 (0.29)	79.4 (0.93)	55.7 (1.18)	29.9 (0.86)	25.5 (0.75)	2.2 (0.21)	93.3 (0.40)	90.6 (0.66)	58.0 (0.94)	50.2 (0.79)	32.5 (0.87)	11.2 (0.37)	53.3 (2.13)
Hispanic	24.5 (0.45)	78.3 (0.99)	53.7 (1.19)	28.2 (0.83)	24.1 (0.73)	1.9 (0.16)	91.6 (0.42)	87.9 (0.69)	53.5 (0.76)	46.3 (0.65)	28.2 (0.66)	9.4 (0.27)	57.3 (1.84)
Asian	2.7 (0.10)	82.5 (1.23)	61.8 (1.40)	35.2 (0.93)	20.5 (0.82)	3.6 (0.27)	92.4 (0.39)	89.2 (0.65)	54.7 (0.91)	47.4 (0.72)	29.2 (0.76)	9.9 (0.29)	61.1 (2.29)
Pacific Islander	0.2 (0.05)	78.8 (4.16)	54.1 (5.83)	27.8 (4.30)	23.2 (3.61)	1.1 ! (0.36)	92.8 (1.34)	90.0 (2.29)	54.0 (4.00)	46.5 (2.99)	27.4 (3.24)	8.9 (1.22)	61.9 (12.63)
American Indian/Alaska Native	0.5 (0.06)	75.3 (3.99)	50.5 (4.17)	25.9 (2.69)	22.0 (2.23)	1.5 (0.27)	92.4 (0.70)	89.1 (1.28)	55.1 (1.14)	47.9 (0.90)	29.8 (1.05)	10.1 (0.45)	46.3 (5.14)
Two or more races	4.1 (0.31)	85.1 (0.91)	64.7 (1.47)	37.2 (1.26)	32.3 (1.26)	3.7 (0.55)	92.4 (0.54)	89.1 (0.93)	54.4 (1.35)	47.2 (1.11)	28.9 (1.22)	9.7 (0.53)	61.4 (3.03)
Age of child													
22 months	2.0 (0.30)	78.1 (2.15)	53.1 (2.77)	28.4 (2.34)	24.5 (2.31)	2.9 ! (1.01)	90.9 (1.68)	86.5 (2.78)	53.4 (3.05)	46.5 (2.70)	29.2 (2.77)	10.6 (1.58)	65.1 (5.06)
23 months	42.3 (1.22)	81.9 (0.54)	60.1 (0.66)	33.4 (0.47)	28.8 (0.41)	2.9 (0.13)	92.2 (0.27)	88.7 (0.45)	54.3 (0.59)	47.0 (0.49)	28.8 (0.53)	9.7 (0.22)	62.7 (1.40)
24 months	42.0 (1.02)	86.5 (0.42)	66.9 (0.65)	39.1 (0.56)	34.3 (0.54)	4.6 (0.23)	92.9 (0.22)	90.0 (0.37)	56.1 (0.57)	48.6 (0.48)	30.4 (0.57)	10.4 (0.25)	60.8 (1.65)
25 months	13.7 (0.54)	87.4 (0.58)	68.3 (0.91)	40.3 (0.78)	35.4 (0.77)	5.0 (0.35)	93.0 (0.35)	90.2 (0.56)	57.5 (0.79)	50.0 (0.68)	32.4 (0.81)	11.4 (0.40)	59.8 (1.90)
Primary type of nonparental care arrangement[15]													
No regular nonparental arrangement	50.8 (0.75)	83.4 (0.50)	62.0 (0.70)	34.8 (0.56)	30.2 (0.52)	3.3 (0.17)	92.2 (0.26)	88.8 (0.43)	54.5 (0.55)	47.2 (0.47)	29.0 (0.52)	9.7 (0.22)	62.1 (1.35)
Home-based care													
Relative care[16]	18.6 (0.63)	83.2 (0.70)	61.6 (1.04)	34.7 (0.84)	30.1 (0.78)	3.6 (0.29)	92.7 (0.30)	89.7 (0.49)	55.8 (0.79)	48.3 (0.67)	30.1 (0.77)	10.3 (0.35)	57.5 (1.94)
Nonrelative care[17]	14.5 (0.57)	86.7 (0.72)	67.8 (1.00)	39.8 (0.81)	34.8 (0.76)	4.4 (0.29)	93.3 (0.27)	90.6 (0.46)	57.1 (0.73)	49.5 (0.63)	31.5 (0.74)	10.8 (0.35)	61.1 (2.23)
Center-based care[18]	15.6 (0.51)	87.5 (0.69)	69.4 (0.99)	41.6 (0.84)	36.8 (0.82)	5.5 (0.47)	93.0 (0.31)	90.2 (0.50)	56.9 (0.70)	49.5 (0.61)	31.8 (0.74)	11.2 (0.37)	64.6 (1.87)
Multiple arrangements[19]	0.5 (0.09)	81.7 (5.66)	63.1 (7.07)	38.0 (5.92)	33.8 (5.68)	6.2 ! (2.87)	91.3 (1.70)	87.1 (2.97)	52.4 (3.41)	45.8 (2.92)	27.9 (3.29)	9.8 (1.62)	72.2 (8.48)
Mother's employment status													
Full-time (35 hours or more)	34.3 (0.76)	85.6 (0.56)	65.8 (0.83)	38.2 (0.66)	33.4 (0.62)	4.2 (0.24)	93.0 (0.25)	90.1 (0.43)	56.6 (0.65)	49.1 (0.57)	31.2 (0.66)	10.8 (0.31)	59.8 (1.58)
Part-time (less than 35 hours)	20.3 (0.69)	86.6 (0.64)	67.6 (0.98)	39.7 (0.84)	34.8 (0.80)	4.7 (0.37)	92.8 (0.28)	89.8 (0.47)	55.5 (0.70)	48.1 (0.58)	29.8 (0.66)	10.1 (0.30)	65.2 (1.53)
Looking for work	6.3 (0.33)	80.1 (1.28)	56.6 (1.77)	30.2 (1.33)	25.8 (1.20)	1.9 (0.24)	92.0 (0.48)	88.4 (0.81)	53.8 (1.04)	46.7 (0.85)	28.5 (0.91)	9.6 (0.37)	58.8 (3.07)
Not in labor force	38.8 (0.82)	83.1 (0.56)	61.6 (0.77)	34.7 (0.63)	30.1 (0.60)	3.4 (0.21)	92.2 (0.26)	88.8 (0.43)	54.6 (0.56)	47.3 (0.49)	29.2 (0.54)	9.9 (0.24)	61.4 (1.41)
No mother in household	0.4 (0.09)	82.1 (4.44)	58.8 (6.94)	33.5 (6.05)	29.3 (5.73)	‡ (†)	94.4 (1.25)	92.4 (2.19)	59.7 (3.58)	51.6 (2.90)	33.5 (3.30)	11.3 (1.37)	62.1 (9.92)
Parents' highest level of education													
Less than high school	12.2 (0.37)	76.6 (1.00)	50.5 (1.32)	25.4 (0.95)	21.6 (0.81)	1.3 (0.14)	91.2 (0.43)	87.3 (0.70)	52.7 (0.84)	45.8 (0.69)	27.4 (0.71)	9.0 (0.28)	51.8 (2.90)
High school completion	25.2 (0.52)	81.9 (0.61)	58.7 (0.88)	31.8 (0.68)	27.2 (0.62)	2.3 (0.18)	92.4 (0.29)	89.3 (0.47)	55.2 (0.66)	47.8 (0.56)	29.7 (0.63)	10.0 (0.27)	54.3 (1.78)
Some college/vocational	29.7 (0.53)	84.4 (0.62)	64.0 (0.85)	36.6 (0.68)	31.8 (0.65)	3.7 (0.21)	92.5 (0.31)	89.4 (0.51)	55.6 (0.70)	48.2 (0.60)	30.2 (0.67)	10.4 (0.30)	62.6 (1.77)
Bachelor's degree	17.5 (0.46)	88.6 (0.66)	71.1 (1.11)	42.6 (0.99)	37.4 (0.98)	5.3 (0.47)	93.2 (0.30)	90.5 (0.52)	56.7 (0.79)	49.1 (0.67)	31.0 (0.78)	10.7 (0.37)	67.2 (2.09)
Any graduate education	15.4 (0.39)	90.4 (0.60)	74.8 (0.93)	46.5 (0.79)	41.4 (0.78)	7.1 (0.37)	93.0 (0.36)	90.2 (0.61)	56.5 (0.80)	48.9 (0.68)	30.9 (0.77)	10.6 (0.35)	72.8 (1.90)
Poverty status[20]													
Below poverty threshold	23.0 (0.80)	78.7 (0.85)	54.6 (1.11)	29.0 (0.81)	24.8 (0.72)	2.1 (0.18)	91.8 (0.32)	88.1 (0.53)	54.1 (0.70)	46.8 (0.60)	28.8 (0.67)	9.6 (0.28)	52.7 (1.73)
At or above poverty threshold	77.0 (0.80)	86.2 (0.37)	66.7 (0.53)	38.9 (0.44)	34.0 (0.42)	4.4 (0.18)	92.8 (0.21)	89.8 (0.35)	55.9 (0.53)	48.4 (0.45)	30.3 (0.51)	10.4 (0.23)	64.2 (1.22)

See notes at end of table.

Table 220.20. Percentage of children demonstrating specific cognitive skills, motor skills, and secure emotional attachment to parents at about 2 years of age, by selected characteristics: 2003–04—Continued

[Standard errors appear in parentheses]

Selected characteristic	Percentage distribution of children[1]	Percent of children who demonstrate skills or secure emotional attachment											Secure emotional attachment to parent[8]
		Specific cognitive skills[2]					Specific motor skills[2]						
		Receptive vocabulary[4]	Expressive vocabulary[5]	Listening comprehension[6]	Matching/ discrimination[7]	Early counting[8]	Skillful walking[9]	Balance[10]	Fine motor control[11]	Uses stairs[12]	Alternating balance[13]	Motor planning[14]	
1	2	3	4	5	6	7	8	9	10	11	12	13	14
Socioeconomic status[21]													
Lowest 20 percent...........	19.1 (0.53)	77.3 (0.89)	51.7 (1.12)	26.5 (0.78)	22.5 (0.67)	1.5 (0.12)	91.7 (0.37)	88.1 (0.60)	53.7 (0.75)	46.5 (0.63)	28.3 (0.66)	9.4 (0.26)	51.5 (1.90)
Middle 60 percent...........	60.3 (0.73)	84.5 (0.47)	63.8 (0.69)	36.3 (0.56)	31.5 (0.53)	3.5 (0.17)	92.5 (0.24)	89.4 (0.41)	55.4 (0.60)	48.0 (0.52)	30.0 (0.60)	10.2 (0.27)	61.3 (1.49)
Highest 20 percent...........	20.6 (0.56)	91.1 (0.43)	75.4 (0.80)	46.7 (0.70)	41.5 (0.70)	7.0 (0.38)	93.4 (0.24)	90.9 (0.40)	57.2 (0.64)	49.5 (0.54)	31.5 (0.63)	10.9 (0.29)	71.7 (1.86)

†Not applicable.
‡Interpret data with caution. The coefficient of variation (CV) for this estimate is between 30 and 50 percent.
‡Reporting standards not met. The coefficient of variation (CV) for this estimate is 50 percent or greater.
[1]Weighted distribution of Early Childhood Longitudinal Study, Birth Cohort survey population between 22 and 25 months of age.
[2]Based on assessments collected using the Bayley Short Form Research Edition (BSF-R), a shortened field method of administering the Bayley Scales of Infant Development-II (BSID-II) (Bayley 1993). The scores are fully equated with the BSID-II; for more information, see NCES's *Early Childhood Longitudinal Study, Birth Cohort (ECLS-B) Psychometric Report for the 2-year Data Collection*. The proficiency probabilities indicate mastery of a specific skill or ability within cognitive or physical domains.
[3]Attachment was measured by trained observers using the Toddler Attachment Sort-45 Item (TAS-45) assessment. The formation of secure attachments in early childhood is an indicator that the child is able to use the parent as a secure base from which to explore novel stimuli in the environment freely and acquire a sense of self-confidence and adaptability to new and challenging situations. Other possible attachment classifications were avoidant, ambivalent, and disorganized/disoriented.
[4]Ability to recognize and understand spoken words or to indicate a named object by pointing.
[5]Verbal expressiveness using gestures, words, and sentences.
[6]Ability to understand actions depicted by a story, in pictures, or by verbal instructions.
[7]Ability to match objects by their properties (e.g., color) or differentiate one object from another.
[8]Knowledge of counting words, knowledge of ordinality, and understanding of simple quantities.
[9]Ability to walk independently.
[10]Ability to maintain balance when changing position.
[11]Ability to use fine motor control with hands, such as grasping a pencil or holding a piece of paper while scribbling.

[12]Ability to walk up and down stairs, with or without alternating feet.
[13]Ability to maintain balance when changing position or when in motion, such as jumping.
[14]Ability to anticipate, regulate, and execute motor movements, such as being able to replicate the motions of others.
[15]The type of nonparental care in which the child spent the most hours.
[16]Care provided in the child's home or in another private home by a relative (excluding parents).
[17]Care provided in the child's home or in another private home by a person unrelated to the child.
[18]Care provided in places such as early learning centers, nursery schools, and preschools.
[19]Children who spent an equal amount of time in each of two or more types of arrangements.
[20]Poverty status based on Census Bureau guidelines from 2002, which identify a dollar amount determined to meet a household's needs, given its size and composition. In 2002, a family of four was considered to live below the poverty threshold if its income was less than or equal to $18,392.
[21]Socioeconomic status (SES) was measured by a composite score based on parental education and occupations, and family income.
NOTE: Estimates weighted by W2R0. Estimates pertain to sample of children born in 2001 and assessed between 22 months and 25 months of age. Children younger than 22 months (less than 1 percent of the survey population) and children older than 25 months (approximately 9 percent of the survey population) are excluded from this table. Race categories exclude persons of Hispanic ethnicity. Detail may not sum to totals because of rounding and survey item nonresponse. Some data have been revised from previously published figures.
SOURCE: U.S. Department of Education, National Center for Education Statistics, Early Childhood Longitudinal Study, Birth Cohort 9-month–Kindergarten 2007 Restricted-Use Data File and Electronic Codebook. (This table was prepared December 2010.)

Table 220.30. Children's reading, language, mathematics, color knowledge, and fine motor skills at about 4 years of age, by child's age and selected characteristics: 2005–06

[Standard errors appear in parentheses]

Age and selected characteristic	Number of children (in thousands)		Percentage distribution of children		Average early reading scale score[1]		Expressive vocabulary (telling stories) score[2]		Average mathematics scale score[3]		Color knowledge— percent scoring 10 out of 10[4]		Fine motor score[5]	
1	2		3		4		5		6		7		8	
Less than 48 months														
Total	645	(22.3)	100.0	(†)	21.5	(0.32)	2.1	(0.04)	24.5	(0.31)	49.0	(1.89)	2.5	(0.05)
Sex of child														
Male	324	(15.8)	50.3	(1.79)	20.7	(0.48)	1.9	(0.05)	23.5	(0.44)	41.8	(3.03)	2.3	(0.07)
Female	321	(16.3)	49.7	(1.79)	22.4	(0.43)	2.2	(0.06)	25.5	(0.45)	56.1	(2.40)	2.8	(0.06)
Socioeconomic status[6]														
Lowest 20 percent	121	(11.3)	18.7	(1.50)	16.7	(0.35)	1.8	(0.09)	19.1	(0.52)	16.2	(3.65)	2.0	(0.10)
Middle 60 percent	380	(16.7)	58.9	(1.67)	21.0	(0.39)	2.1	(0.04)	24.2	(0.39)	50.9	(2.57)	2.6	(0.06)
Highest 20 percent	144	(10.7)	22.4	(1.59)	26.3	(0.67)	2.2	(0.07)	29.2	(0.64)	67.8	(2.97)	2.9	(0.09)
48 through 57 months														
Total	2,939	(23.2)	100.0	(†)	25.5	(0.22)	2.4	(0.02)	29.7	(0.20)	63.6	(0.84)	3.4	(0.02)
Sex of child														
Male	1,516	(18.2)	51.6	(0.48)	24.6	(0.26)	2.3	(0.03)	29.2	(0.25)	61.2	(1.12)	3.1	(0.04)
Female	1,423	(18.4)	48.4	(0.48)	26.4	(0.29)	2.6	(0.02)	30.3	(0.24)	66.1	(1.29)	3.7	(0.04)
Race/ethnicity of child														
White	1,604	(22.9)	54.7	(0.69)	27.4	(0.30)	2.6	(0.03)	31.6	(0.28)	71.0	(1.11)	3.5	(0.03)
Black	391	(11.5)	13.3	(0.37)	22.9	(0.46)	2.4	(0.04)	26.9	(0.44)	55.3	(2.44)	3.2	(0.06)
Hispanic	729	(18.1)	24.9	(0.56)	21.2	(0.36)	2.1	(0.04)	26.2	(0.34)	50.2	(1.79)	3.3	(0.06)
Asian	74	(3.6)	2.5	(0.12)	30.5	(0.56)	2.1	(0.05)	34.7	(0.42)	70.7	(2.37)	4.5	(0.09)
Pacific Islander	4	(0.7)	0.1	(0.03)	22.2	(2.24)	2.1	(0.18)	26.3	(3.41)	39.0	(9.21)	3.0	(0.34)
American Indian/Alaska Native	15	(1.5)	0.5	(0.05)	20.1	(0.89)	2.1	(0.09)	23.2	(0.98)	44.1	(3.83)	3.0	(0.18)
Two or more races	115	(9.0)	3.9	(0.31)	27.3	(0.89)	2.5	(0.06)	30.2	(0.82)	62.7	(3.04)	3.5	(0.12)
Primary type of nonparental care arrangement[7]														
No regular nonparental arrangement	535	(20.8)	18.2	(0.69)	22.9	(0.41)	2.3	(0.04)	26.9	(0.41)	51.6	(2.04)	3.1	(0.05)
Home-based care														
Relative care[8]	384	(18.8)	13.1	(0.65)	23.0	(0.44)	2.3	(0.05)	27.3	(0.42)	53.4	(2.58)	3.2	(0.07)
Nonrelative care[9]	220	(11.8)	7.5	(0.40)	25.1	(0.51)	2.5	(0.07)	30.2	(0.58)	63.8	(2.72)	3.3	(0.09)
Head Start	386	(22.3)	13.2	(0.73)	22.2	(0.35)	2.3	(0.05)	26.8	(0.40)	52.8	(2.55)	3.2	(0.07)
Other center-based care[10]	1,358	(26.2)	46.3	(0.83)	28.0	(0.32)	2.6	(0.03)	32.2	(0.27)	73.5	(1.19)	3.6	(0.04)
Multiple arrangements[11]	52	(6.8)	1.8	(0.23)	24.6	(0.93)	2.5	(0.10)	29.3	(0.92)	67.1	(5.44)	3.2	(0.23)
Mother's employment status														
Full-time (35 hours or more)	1,149	(26.5)	39.4	(0.85)	25.6	(0.30)	2.5	(0.03)	30.3	(0.24)	67.5	(1.09)	3.5	(0.05)
Part-time (less than 35 hours)	573	(17.7)	19.6	(0.60)	26.3	(0.35)	2.5	(0.04)	30.6	(0.35)	63.5	(2.06)	3.5	(0.05)
Looking for work	163	(9.9)	5.6	(0.34)	21.7	(0.57)	2.2	(0.07)	25.8	(0.74)	47.1	(3.83)	3.0	(0.11)
Not in labor force	1,010	(27.1)	34.6	(0.88)	25.5	(0.39)	2.4	(0.03)	29.3	(0.35)	62.1	(1.42)	3.3	(0.04)
No mother in household	22	(4.0)	0.8	(0.14)	21.6	(1.35)	2.3	(0.24)	26.3	(1.25)	57.3	(8.79)	3.0	(0.21)
Parents' highest level of education														
Less than high school	292	(11.9)	9.9	(0.41)	18.7	(0.41)	1.9	(0.06)	23.6	(0.47)	37.3	(2.74)	3.1	(0.09)
High school completion	672	(24.1)	22.9	(0.79)	21.6	(0.28)	2.3	(0.03)	25.9	(0.30)	52.0	(1.64)	3.1	(0.04)
Some college/vocational	998	(23.5)	34.0	(0.76)	24.3	(0.30)	2.5	(0.03)	28.9	(0.28)	63.4	(1.29)	3.4	(0.04)
Bachelor's degree	498	(17.6)	17.0	(0.57)	28.8	(0.40)	2.7	(0.04)	33.2	(0.28)	75.6	(1.69)	3.7	(0.08)
Any graduate education	475	(14.6)	16.2	(0.49)	33.0	(0.43)	2.7	(0.04)	36.2	(0.33)	81.0	(1.48)	3.9	(0.05)
Poverty status[12]														
Below poverty threshold	732	(21.0)	24.9	(0.71)	20.5	(0.26)	2.1	(0.03)	24.6	(0.28)	46.9	(1.76)	3.1	(0.05)
At or above poverty threshold	2,207	(28.4)	75.1	(0.71)	27.0	(0.24)	2.5	(0.02)	31.3	(0.21)	68.8	(0.91)	3.5	(0.03)
Socioeconomic status[6]														
Lowest 20 percent	576	(17.2)	19.6	(0.57)	19.3	(0.31)	2.0	(0.04)	23.6	(0.35)	43.1	(2.15)	3.0	(0.06)
Middle 60 percent	1,768	(27.3)	60.2	(0.77)	24.7	(0.22)	2.5	(0.03)	29.3	(0.23)	63.5	(1.07)	3.4	(0.03)
Highest 20 percent	594	(20.4)	20.2	(0.68)	32.7	(0.43)	2.8	(0.03)	36.2	(0.33)	81.6	(1.51)	3.9	(0.05)
58 months or more														
Total	356	(16.4)	100.0	(†)	29.7	(0.58)	2.6	(0.04)	34.5	(0.44)	71.1	(2.09)	4.1	(0.07)
Sex of child														
Male	179	(12.1)	50.3	(2.21)	29.0	(0.77)	2.6	(0.06)	34.2	(0.64)	66.5	(3.05)	3.7	(0.10)
Female	177	(10.5)	49.7	(2.21)	30.4	(0.76)	2.7	(0.06)	34.8	(0.51)	75.9	(2.49)	4.4	(0.10)
Socioeconomic status[6]														
Lowest 20 percent	91	(8.0)	25.5	(2.26)	22.3	(0.91)	2.1	(0.11)	28.4	(0.97)	47.4	(5.25)	3.6	(0.14)
Middle 60 percent	215	(14.7)	60.5	(2.47)	30.0	(0.75)	2.7	(0.05)	34.9	(0.54)	76.0	(2.63)	4.1	(0.10)
Highest 20 percent	50	(6.9)	14.0	(1.84)	40.3	(2.31)	2.9	(0.10)	42.8	(1.15)	88.5	(2.89)	4.7	(0.18)

†Not applicable.
[1]Reflects performance on language and literacy items (e.g., conventions of print, letter recognition, understanding of letter-sound relationships, phonological awareness, sight word recognition, and understanding words in the context of simple sentences). Potential score ranges from 0 to 85.
[2]Verbal expressiveness using gestures, words, and sentences. Potential score ranges from 0 to 5.
[3]Includes number sense, geometry, counting, operations, and patterns. Potential score ranges from 0 to 71.
[4]Percentage of children who scored 10 on a test with a potential score range of 0 to 10. These children were able to name the colors of five pictured objects (2 points per correct answer).
[5]Measures the ability to use fine motor skills in drawing basic forms and shapes. Potential score ranges from 0 to 7.
[6]Socioeconomic status (SES) was measured by a composite score based on parental education and occupations, and family income.
[7]The type of nonparental care in which the child spent the most hours.
[8]Care provided in the child's home or in another private home by a relative (excluding parents).
[9]Care provided in the child's home or in another private home by a person unrelated to the child.

[10]Care provided in places such as early learning centers, nursery schools, and preschools, excluding Head Start.
[11]Children who spent an equal amount of time in each of two or more types of arrangements.
[12]Poverty status based on Census Bureau guidelines from 2005, which identify a dollar amount determined to meet a household's needs, given its size and composition. In 2005, a family of four was considered to live below the poverty threshold if its income was less than or equal to $19,971.
NOTE: Estimates weighted by W3R0. Estimates pertain to a sample of children who were born in 2001. This table was designed to present data collected when the children were about 4 years of age (i.e., 48 to 57 months old). As shown in the table, some children were younger or older than this at the time data were collected, although 75 percent were within the target age range. Race categories exclude persons of Hispanic ethnicity. Detail may not sum to totals because of rounding and survey item nonresponse. Some data have been revised from previously published figures.
SOURCE: U.S. Department of Education, National Center for Education Statistics, Early Childhood Longitudinal Study, Birth Cohort (ECLS-B), Longitudinal 9-Month–Kindergarten 2007 Restricted-Use Data File. (This table was prepared December 2010.)

Table 220.40. Fall 2010 first-time kindergartners' reading, mathematics, and science scale scores, by selected child, family, and school characteristics: Fall 2010, spring 2011, and spring 2012

[Standard errors appear in parentheses]

Selected child, family, or school characteristic	Number of children (in thousands)	Percentage distribution of children	Mean reading score[1]			Mean mathematics score[2]			Mean science score[3]	
			Kindergarten		First grade, spring 2012	Kindergarten		First grade, spring 2012	Kindergarten, spring 2011	First grade, spring 2012
			Fall 2010	Spring 2011		Fall 2010	Spring 2011			
1	2	3	4	5	6	7	8	9	10	11
Total	3,765 (31.3)	100.0 (†)	37.4 (0.23)	49.9 (0.31)	69.9 (0.31)	30.6 (0.27)	43.5 (0.31)	63.1 (0.31)	21.2 (0.14)	26.8 (0.17)
Sex of child										
Male	1,921 (22.2)	51.0 (0.45)	37.0 (0.26)	49.1 (0.34)	68.7 (0.37)	30.8 (0.33)	43.6 (0.36)	63.6 (0.39)	21.2 (0.15)	27.0 (0.19)
Female	1,843 (23.9)	49.0 (0.45)	38.0 (0.25)	50.8 (0.33)	71.2 (0.33)	30.4 (0.29)	43.5 (0.31)	62.7 (0.32)	21.1 (0.16)	26.6 (0.19)
Age of child at kindergarten entry, fall 2010										
Less than 5 years old	142 (18.3)	3.8 (0.49)	35.0 (0.56)	45.8 (0.75)	65.9 (0.91)	26.0 (0.61)	38.4 (0.73)	57.8 (0.84)	19.2 (0.38)	24.7 (0.41)
5 years old to 5 1/2 years old	1,594 (28.2)	42.3 (0.57)	36.1 (0.27)	48.4 (0.35)	68.6 (0.37)	28.2 (0.32)	41.4 (0.36)	61.1 (0.39)	20.2 (0.17)	25.7 (0.21)
More than 5 1/2 years old to 6 years old	1,681 (26.6)	44.7 (0.66)	38.4 (0.27)	51.1 (0.33)	71.0 (0.37)	32.3 (0.31)	45.1 (0.33)	64.7 (0.34)	21.9 (0.14)	27.6 (0.19)
More than 6 years old	347 (16.5)	9.2 (0.44)	40.2 (0.43)	53.2 (0.56)	72.9 (0.52)	35.4 (0.57)	47.8 (0.63)	67.4 (0.56)	22.7 (0.29)	28.9 (0.31)
Race/ethnicity of child										
White	1,957 (66.6)	52.0 (1.67)	38.8 (0.30)	51.7 (0.38)	72.4 (0.36)	33.1 (0.34)	46.2 (0.38)	66.7 (0.34)	23.2 (0.14)	29.0 (0.16)
Black	491 (43.5)	13.1 (1.16)	36.0 (0.32)	47.6 (0.55)	67.0 (0.68)	27.0 (0.34)	38.5 (0.37)	56.7 (0.46)	18.6 (0.30)	23.6 (0.36)
Hispanic	934 (46.2)	24.8 (1.24)	34.5 (0.26)	46.5 (0.30)	65.5 (0.44)	26.3 (0.30)	39.7 (0.35)	58.3 (0.49)	18.3 (0.19)	23.8 (0.23)
Asian	157 (23.8)	4.2 (0.63)	42.2 (0.62)	54.5 (0.73)	74.2 (0.79)	35.8 (0.62)	47.4 (0.45)	67.8 (0.48)	19.8 (0.22)	26.6 (0.28)
Pacific Islander	29 (4.9)	0.8 (0.13)	36.1 (1.59)	49.0 (1.93)	70.0 (1.36)	30.1 (1.78)	44.9 (2.28)	62.1 (2.06)	18.9 (0.87)	24.8 (1.10)
American Indian/Alaska Native	42 ! (19.6)	1.1 ! (0.52)	34.4 (0.54)	45.7 (0.79)	67.2 (1.02)	27.4 (1.06)	41.3 (1.06)	61.4 (1.28)	21.7 (0.91)	27.1 (1.07)
Two or more races	154 (9.3)	4.1 (0.24)	39.2 (0.62)	51.7 (0.75)	71.4 (0.88)	32.5 (0.60)	45.2 (0.70)	64.2 (0.86)	22.5 (0.31)	28.4 (0.38)
How often child exhibited positive learning behaviors, fall 2010[4]										
Never	50 (5.3)	1.4 (0.15)	29.3 (0.48)	37.1 (0.78)	51.8 (1.22)	18.5 (0.67)	28.8 (0.90)	45.1 (1.23)	16.5 (0.51)	20.5 (0.62)
Sometimes	915 (23.7)	25.3 (0.52)	33.4 (0.29)	44.7 (0.35)	63.3 (0.44)	25.3 (0.34)	37.9 (0.38)	56.8 (0.45)	19.3 (0.18)	24.3 (0.22)
Often	1,716 (27.0)	47.5 (0.70)	37.4 (0.23)	50.3 (0.35)	70.9 (0.34)	31.0 (0.32)	44.3 (0.36)	64.2 (0.35)	21.4 (0.16)	27.3 (0.17)
Very often	933 (28.7)	25.8 (0.69)	41.8 (0.38)	55.3 (0.46)	75.9 (0.39)	35.7 (0.38)	48.7 (0.39)	68.8 (0.38)	23.0 (0.15)	29.0 (0.23)
Primary type of nonparental care arrangement prior to kindergarten entry[5]										
No regular nonparental arrangement	747 (31.8)	20.6 (0.84)	35.7 (0.32)	48.1 (0.42)	67.7 (0.46)	28.1 (0.38)	41.6 (0.40)	60.8 (0.40)	20.0 (0.18)	25.7 (0.22)
Home-based care										
Relative care	555 (18.6)	15.3 (0.50)	35.6 (0.30)	48.5 (0.37)	68.4 (0.46)	28.3 (0.38)	41.6 (0.39)	61.4 (0.46)	20.5 (0.21)	26.2 (0.27)
Nonrelative care	228 (15.1)	6.3 (0.41)	37.8 (0.46)	51.0 (0.63)	72.5 (0.53)	32.6 (0.59)	45.8 (0.70)	66.4 (0.59)	22.5 (0.29)	28.3 (0.33)
Center-based care	2,007 (41.2)	55.4 (1.04)	38.6 (0.25)	50.9 (0.35)	71.0 (0.35)	32.0 (0.30)	44.6 (0.35)	64.1 (0.35)	21.6 (0.17)	27.3 (0.20)
Multiple arrangements	88 (6.7)	2.4 (0.18)	38.8 (0.53)	51.8 (0.79)	72.0 (0.88)	32.2 (0.56)	44.9 (0.72)	65.9 (0.68)	22.6 (0.39)	28.6 (0.38)
Parents' employment status, fall 2010[6]										
Two parents										
Both employed full time	878 (26.2)	26.1 (0.73)	39.4 (0.26)	52.4 (0.33)	72.8 (0.35)	33.3 (0.32)	46.3 (0.37)	66.2 (0.37)	22.3 (0.15)	28.2 (0.17)
One employed full time, one part time	563 (19.7)	16.7 (0.53)	39.2 (0.44)	52.4 (0.50)	73.2 (0.53)	33.3 (0.49)	46.4 (0.47)	66.5 (0.47)	22.6 (0.18)	28.7 (0.23)
One employed full time, one looking for work	143 (10.3)	4.2 (0.30)	36.4 (0.55)	49.2 (0.78)	68.4 (0.86)	29.4 (0.62)	42.3 (0.67)	62.3 (0.70)	20.6 (0.38)	26.3 (0.40)
One employed full time, one not in labor force	799 (28.5)	23.7 (0.82)	38.0 (0.39)	50.4 (0.50)	70.6 (0.55)	31.2 (0.44)	44.2 (0.46)	64.2 (0.47)	21.6 (0.20)	27.3 (0.24)
Other combination	205 (13.1)	6.1 (0.36)	35.9 (0.54)	48.0 (0.64)	66.6 (0.74)	27.5 (0.46)	44.1 (0.49)	59.9 (0.73)	19.7 (0.25)	25.2 (0.33)
Single parent										
Employed full time	361 (17.6)	10.7 (0.52)	35.8 (0.34)	47.7 (0.48)	67.7 (0.58)	28.1 (0.39)	40.6 (0.50)	60.2 (0.55)	19.9 (0.27)	25.3 (0.31)
Employed part time	130 (8.1)	3.9 (0.24)	34.9 (0.39)	47.0 (0.57)	67.6 (0.70)	27.7 (0.57)	40.0 (0.65)	59.9 (0.81)	20.2 (0.33)	25.6 (0.34)
Looking for work	102 (9.0)	3.0 (0.27)	33.2 (0.52)	44.7 (0.78)	62.9 (1.21)	24.8 (0.63)	37.0 (0.56)	55.3 (1.10)	18.9 (0.46)	24.1 (0.56)
Not in labor force	120 (10.9)	3.5 (0.33)	34.4 (0.50)	45.5 (0.61)	64.1 (0.88)	25.8 (0.62)	39.0 (0.79)	56.7 (0.91)	19.4 (0.40)	24.4 (0.56)
No parent in household	67 (5.9)	2.0 (0.18)	33.7 (0.54)	45.1 (0.71)	64.7 (1.15)	24.9 (0.71)	37.6 (0.81)	55.3 (1.24)	19.7 (0.45)	24.2 (0.57)
Parents' highest level of education[7]										
Less than high school	298 (17.4)	7.9 (0.47)	31.2 (0.33)	42.5 (0.33)	60.1 (0.50)	22.0 (0.44)	35.6 (0.51)	53.5 (0.51)	16.2 (0.21)	21.0 (0.25)
High school completion	725 (20.3)	19.3 (0.51)	34.0 (0.26)	45.9 (0.33)	65.2 (0.43)	26.2 (0.34)	39.0 (0.32)	58.3 (0.32)	19.0 (0.18)	24.4 (0.19)
Some college/vocational	1,342 (30.8)	35.8 (0.77)	36.4 (0.21)	49.0 (0.34)	69.4 (0.31)	29.7 (0.29)	42.6 (0.34)	62.3 (0.38)	21.1 (0.14)	26.7 (0.17)
Bachelor's degree	756 (27.8)	20.1 (0.71)	40.3 (0.31)	53.1 (0.36)	73.8 (0.39)	34.3 (0.29)	47.3 (0.34)	67.3 (0.34)	22.9 (0.16)	28.8 (0.21)
Any graduate education	633 (27.0)	16.9 (0.71)	43.1 (0.40)	56.1 (0.43)	76.5 (0.38)	37.1 (0.36)	49.9 (0.39)	69.9 (0.36)	24.0 (0.14)	30.3 (0.22)
Household type, fall 2010										
Two-parent household	2,662 (45.8)	76.6 (0.92)	38.4 (0.26)	51.2 (0.32)	71.4 (0.34)	31.9 (0.31)	45.0 (0.32)	64.8 (0.31)	21.8 (0.13)	27.6 (0.16)
Mother-only household	696 (29.8)	20.0 (0.85)	35.0 (0.25)	46.7 (0.38)	66.5 (0.49)	27.3 (0.33)	39.7 (0.37)	59.0 (0.45)	19.6 (0.25)	25.0 (0.29)
Father-only household	48 (4.5)	1.4 (0.13)	34.9 (0.69)	46.9 (1.07)	66.3 (1.25)	27.6 (0.74)	40.2 (0.74)	59.3 (1.20)	21.8 (0.45)	25.9 (0.53)
Other household type	67 (5.9)	1.9 (0.17)	33.7 (0.54)	45.1 (0.71)	64.7 (1.15)	24.9 (0.71)	37.6 (0.81)	55.3 (1.24)	19.7 (0.45)	24.2 (0.57)

See notes at end of table.

Table 220.40. Fall 2010 first-time kindergartners' reading, mathematics, and science scale scores, by selected child, family, and school characteristics: Fall 2010, spring 2011, and spring 2012—Continued

[Standard errors appear in parentheses]

Selected child, family, or school characteristic	Number of children (in thousands)	Percentage distribution of children	Mean reading score[1]			Mean mathematics score[2]			Mean science score[3]	
			Kindergarten		First grade, spring 2012	Kindergarten		First grade, spring 2012	Kindergarten, spring 2011	First grade, spring 2012
			Fall 2010	Spring 2011		Fall 2010	Spring 2011			
1	2	3	4	5	6	7	8	9	10	11
Primary home language										
English	3,140 (40.0)	83.6 (0.70)	38.1 (0.23)	50.8 (0.33)	71.0 (0.32)	31.6 (0.27)	44.4 (0.32)	64.2 (0.32)	22.0 (0.14)	27.8 (0.18)
Non-English	567 (24.0)	15.1 (0.64)	34.0 (0.43)	45.5 (0.51)	64.5 (0.69)	25.4 (0.52)	38.9 (0.53)	57.8 (0.62)	16.4 (0.21)	22.0 (0.28)
Primary language not identified	48 (6.1)	1.3 (0.16)	34.9 (0.91)	46.8 (1.25)	65.7 (1.74)	27.9 (1.27)	40.3 (1.07)	58.2 (1.59)	18.1 (0.57)	23.8 (0.46)
Poverty status[8]										
Below poverty threshold	723 (31.8)	22.7 (0.95)	33.6 (0.27)	45.2 (0.34)	63.6 (0.43)	25.4 (0.37)	38.4 (0.41)	56.9 (0.45)	18.3 (0.23)	23.4 (0.28)
100 to 199 percent of poverty threshold	766 (20.7)	24.0 (0.61)	36.2 (0.23)	48.7 (0.43)	69.0 (0.48)	29.2 (0.35)	42.2 (0.42)	61.9 (0.46)	20.6 (0.19)	26.3 (0.23)
200 percent or more of poverty threshold	1,702 (41.8)	53.3 (1.16)	40.3 (0.28)	53.1 (0.34)	73.9 (0.33)	34.3 (0.30)	47.1 (0.35)	67.3 (0.33)	23.1 (0.13)	29.1 (0.15)
Socioeconomic status[9]										
Lowest 20 percent	694 (26.9)	18.5 (0.71)	32.4 (0.27)	43.6 (0.30)	62.0 (0.42)	23.7 (0.38)	36.8 (0.40)	55.3 (0.42)	17.4 (0.20)	22.5 (0.22)
Middle 60 percent	2,279 (34.5)	60.7 (0.73)	37.0 (0.19)	49.7 (0.31)	70.1 (0.30)	30.4 (0.26)	43.4 (0.31)	63.1 (0.31)	21.3 (0.13)	27.0 (0.16)
Highest 20 percent	782 (33.0)	20.8 (0.86)	43.1 (0.39)	56.1 (0.42)	76.5 (0.35)	37.1 (0.31)	49.9 (0.36)	70.1 (0.33)	24.1 (0.14)	30.4 (0.22)
School type										
Public	3,361 (23.4)	89.3 (0.25)	37.2 (0.25)	49.6 (0.34)	69.6 (0.34)	30.2 (0.30)	43.1 (0.33)	62.8 (0.34)	21.0 (0.16)	26.6 (0.19)
Private	404 (11.7)	10.7 (0.25)	39.9 (0.55)	52.3 (0.71)	72.8 (0.81)	34.1 (0.53)	47.3 (0.71)	66.3 (0.74)	22.9 (0.25)	28.5 (0.38)

†Not applicable.
!Interpret data with caution. The coefficient of variation (CV) for this estimate is between 30 and 50 percent.
[1]Reflects performance on questions measuring basic skills (print familiarity, letter recognition, beginning and ending sounds, rhyming words, and word recognition); vocabulary knowledge; and reading comprehension, including identifying information specifically stated in text (e.g., definitions, facts, and supporting details), making complex inferences from texts, and considering the text objectively and judging its appropriateness and quality. Possible scores for the reading assessment range from 0 to 100.
[2]Reflects performance on questions on number sense, properties, and operations; measurement; geometry and spatial sense; data analysis, statistics, and probability (measured with a set of simple questions assessing children's ability to read a graph); and prealgebra skills such as identification of patterns. Possible scores for the mathematics assessment range from 0 to 96.
[3]Science was not assessed in the fall of kindergarten. Reflects performance on questions on physical sciences, life sciences, environmental sciences, and scientific inquiry. Possible scores for the science assessment range from 0 to 47.
[4]Derived from child's approaches to learning scale score in fall of the kindergarten year. This score is based on teachers' reports on how often students exhibit positive learning behaviors in seven areas: attentiveness, task persistence, eagerness to learn, learning independence, ability to adapt easily to changes in routine, organization, and ability to follow classroom rules. Possible scores range from 1 to 4, with higher scores indicating that a child exhibits positive learning behaviors more often. Fall 2010 scores were categorized into the four anchor points on the original scale—1 (never), 2 (sometimes), 3 (often), and 4 (very often)—by rounding the mean score to the nearest whole number.
[5]The type of nonparental care in which the child spent the most hours. "Multiple arrangements" refers to children who spent an equal amount of time in each of two or more arrangements.

[6]Parents who reported working at least 35 hours per week are defined as employed full time, while those who reported working less than 35 hours per week are defined as employed part time. Those neither employed nor looking for work are not in the labor force.
[7]Parents' highest level of education is the highest level of education achieved by either of the parents or guardians in a two-parent household, by the only parent in a single-parent household, or by any guardian in a household with no parents.
[8]Poverty status is based on preliminary U.S. Census income thresholds for 2010, which identify incomes determined to meet household needs, given family size and composition. For example, a family of three with one child was below the poverty threshold if its income was less than $17,552 in 2010.
[9]Socioeconomic status (SES) was measured by a composite score based on parental education and occupations and household income at the time of data collection.
NOTE: Estimates weighted by W4C4P_2T0. Estimates pertain to a sample of children who were enrolled in kindergarten for the first time in the 2010–11 school year. Most of the children were in first grade in 2011–12, but 4 percent were in kindergarten or other grades (e.g., second grade, ungraded classrooms). Two parents may refer to two biological parents, two adoptive parents, or one biological/adoptive parent and one other parent/partner. Single parent refers to one biological or adoptive parent only. In households without parents, the guardian or guardians may be related or unrelated to the child. Estimates differ from previously published figures because scores were recalibrated to represent the kindergarten through first-grade assessment item pools and weights were adjusted to account for survey nonresponse at each data collection wave. Race categories exclude persons of Hispanic ethnicity. Detail may not sum to totals because of rounding and survey item nonresponse.
SOURCE: U.S. Department of Education, National Center for Education Statistics, Early Childhood Longitudinal Study, Kindergarten Class of 2010–11 (ECLS-K:2011), Kindergarten–First Grade Restricted-Use Data File. (This table was prepared September 2014.)

Table 220.45. Fall 2010 first-time kindergartners' cognitive flexibility, approaches to learning, interpersonal skills, and self-control scale scores, by selected child, family, and school characteristics: Fall 2010, spring 2011, and spring 2012

[Standard errors appear in parentheses]

Selected child, family, or school characteristic	Mean cognitive flexibility score[1]			Mean approaches to learning score[2]			Mean interpersonal skills score[3]			Mean self-control score[4]		
	Kindergarten		First grade, spring 2012	Kindergarten		First grade, spring 2012	Kindergarten		First grade, spring 2012	Kindergarten		First grade, spring 2012
	Fall 2010	Spring 2011		Fall 2010	Spring 2011		Fall 2010	Spring 2011		Fall 2010	Spring 2011	
1	2	3	4	5	6	7	8	9	10	11	12	13
Total	14.3 (0.07)	15.2 (0.07)	16.1 (0.05)	3.0 (0.01)	3.1 (0.01)	3.1 (0.01)	3.0 (0.01)	3.2 (0.01)	3.1 (0.01)	3.1 (0.01)	3.2 (0.01)	3.2 (0.01)
Sex of child												
Male	14.2 (0.09)	15.0 (0.09)	16.0 (0.06)	2.8 (0.01)	3.0 (0.01)	2.9 (0.01)	2.9 (0.01)	3.0 (0.01)	3.0 (0.01)	3.0 (0.01)	3.1 (0.01)	3.1 (0.01)
Female	14.4 (0.07)	15.4 (0.06)	16.2 (0.05)	3.1 (0.01)	3.3 (0.01)	3.2 (0.01)	3.1 (0.01)	3.3 (0.01)	3.3 (0.01)	3.2 (0.01)	3.3 (0.01)	3.3 (0.01)
Age of child at kindergarten entry, fall 2010												
Less than 5 years old	13.2 (0.25)	14.6 (0.17)	15.6 (0.14)	2.8 (0.04)	3.0 (0.03)	3.0 (0.04)	3.0 (0.04)	3.1 (0.04)	3.2 (0.04)	3.1 (0.04)	3.1 (0.03)	3.2 (0.03)
5 years old to 5 1/2 years old	14.0 (0.10)	15.1 (0.10)	15.9 (0.07)	2.9 (0.01)	3.1 (0.01)	3.0 (0.01)	3.0 (0.02)	3.1 (0.02)	3.1 (0.01)	3.1 (0.01)	3.2 (0.01)	3.2 (0.01)
More than 5 1/2 years old to 6 years old	14.6 (0.06)	15.4 (0.08)	16.2 (0.06)	3.0 (0.01)	3.2 (0.01)	3.1 (0.01)	3.0 (0.01)	3.2 (0.01)	3.2 (0.01)	3.1 (0.01)	3.2 (0.01)	3.2 (0.01)
More than 6 years old	14.7 (0.15)	15.5 (0.15)	16.5 (0.09)	3.1 (0.03)	3.3 (0.03)	3.2 (0.02)	3.1 (0.03)	3.2 (0.03)	3.2 (0.03)	3.1 (0.03)	3.3 (0.03)	3.2 (0.03)
Race/ethnicity of child												
White	14.8 (0.07)	15.6 (0.09)	16.4 (0.05)	3.0 (0.02)	3.2 (0.02)	3.1 (0.01)	3.1 (0.02)	3.2 (0.02)	3.2 (0.01)	3.1 (0.01)	3.2 (0.01)	3.3 (0.01)
Black	13.5 (0.18)	14.3 (0.12)	15.4 (0.15)	2.8 (0.02)	3.0 (0.02)	2.9 (0.03)	2.9 (0.02)	3.0 (0.03)	3.0 (0.02)	3.0 (0.02)	3.0 (0.02)	3.0 (0.03)
Hispanic	13.6 (0.16)	14.8 (0.08)	15.7 (0.09)	2.9 (0.02)	3.1 (0.02)	3.1 (0.02)	3.0 (0.02)	3.2 (0.02)	3.1 (0.02)	3.1 (0.02)	3.2 (0.02)	3.2 (0.02)
Asian	14.2 (0.16)	15.4 (0.13)	16.3 (0.09)	3.1 (0.04)	3.2 (0.04)	3.3 (0.04)	3.0 (0.04)	3.1 (0.04)	3.2 (0.04)	3.1 (0.05)	3.2 (0.04)	3.3 (0.04)
Pacific Islander	13.4 (0.71)	13.9 (0.51)	16.1 (0.46)	2.9 (0.11)	3.1 (0.09)	3.0 (0.11)	3.1 (0.11)	3.1 (0.11)	3.2 (0.11)	3.0 (0.13)	3.2 (0.08)	3.3 (0.10)
American Indian/Alaska Native	14.6 (0.51)	16.0 (0.10)	16.3 (0.19)	3.0 (0.07)	3.1 (0.06)	3.0 (0.05)	3.1 (0.04)	3.2 (0.08)	3.2 (0.06)	3.1 (0.04)	3.2 (0.07)	3.2 (0.05)
Two or more races	14.6 (0.15)	15.3 (0.18)	16.2 (0.11)	3.0 (0.03)	3.1 (0.03)	3.1 (0.03)	3.0 (0.04)	3.2 (0.03)	3.1 (0.03)	3.1 (0.03)	3.2 (0.02)	3.2 (0.03)
How often child exhibited positive learning behaviors, fall 2010[5]												
Never	11.1 (0.53)	13.1 (0.44)	14.0 (0.33)	† (†)	1.8 (0.05)	2.2 (0.08)	1.9 (0.06)	2.2 (0.07)	2.6 (0.08)	2.0 (0.05)	2.4 (0.07)	2.7 (0.08)
Sometimes	13.5 (0.13)	14.7 (0.10)	15.6 (0.08)	† (†)	2.5 (0.01)	2.6 (0.02)	2.4 (0.01)	2.7 (0.02)	2.8 (0.01)	2.5 (0.01)	2.8 (0.02)	2.9 (0.02)
Often	14.5 (0.07)	15.3 (0.06)	15.6 (0.05)	† (†)	3.2 (0.01)	3.1 (0.01)	3.0 (0.01)	3.2 (0.01)	3.1 (0.01)	3.1 (0.01)	3.2 (0.01)	3.1 (0.01)
Very often	15.0 (0.06)	15.7 (0.08)	16.5 (0.06)	† (†)	3.7 (0.01)	3.5 (0.01)	3.6 (0.01)	3.6 (0.01)	3.4 (0.01)	3.6 (0.01)	3.6 (0.01)	3.5 (0.01)
Primary type of nonparental care arrangement prior to kindergarten entry[6]												
No regular nonparental arrangement	13.9 (0.10)	14.9 (0.14)	15.9 (0.07)	2.9 (0.02)	3.1 (0.02)	3.1 (0.02)	3.0 (0.02)	3.2 (0.02)	3.1 (0.02)	3.1 (0.02)	3.2 (0.02)	3.2 (0.02)
Home-based care												
Relative care	14.0 (0.13)	15.0 (0.11)	15.8 (0.11)	2.9 (0.02)	3.1 (0.02)	3.0 (0.02)	3.0 (0.02)	3.2 (0.03)	3.2 (0.02)	3.1 (0.02)	3.2 (0.02)	3.2 (0.02)
Nonrelative care	14.4 (0.23)	15.3 (0.19)	16.3 (0.08)	3.0 (0.03)	3.2 (0.03)	3.1 (0.03)	3.0 (0.03)	3.2 (0.03)	3.2 (0.02)	3.1 (0.02)	3.2 (0.02)	3.2 (0.02)
Center-based care	14.5 (0.07)	15.4 (0.06)	16.2 (0.05)	3.0 (0.01)	3.1 (0.01)	3.1 (0.01)	3.0 (0.01)	3.2 (0.01)	3.1 (0.01)	3.1 (0.01)	3.2 (0.01)	3.3 (0.01)
Multiple arrangements	14.9 (0.24)	15.5 (0.22)	16.5 (0.11)	3.0 (0.04)	3.1 (0.04)	3.1 (0.04)	3.0 (0.05)	3.2 (0.03)	3.1 (0.05)	3.1 (0.04)	3.2 (0.03)	3.2 (0.04)
Parents' employment status, fall 2010[7]												
Two parents												
Both employed full time	14.8 (0.07)	15.6 (0.07)	16.4 (0.06)	3.0 (0.02)	3.2 (0.02)	3.2 (0.02)	3.1 (0.02)	3.2 (0.02)	3.2 (0.01)	3.1 (0.02)	3.2 (0.02)	3.3 (0.01)
One employed full time, one part time	14.6 (0.10)	15.5 (0.08)	16.4 (0.07)	3.1 (0.02)	3.2 (0.02)	3.2 (0.02)	3.1 (0.02)	3.2 (0.03)	3.3 (0.02)	3.2 (0.02)	3.3 (0.02)	3.3 (0.02)
One employed full time, one looking for work	13.9 (0.21)	15.3 (0.14)	15.9 (0.15)	2.9 (0.05)	3.1 (0.05)	3.1 (0.04)	3.0 (0.04)	3.1 (0.04)	3.2 (0.03)	3.1 (0.04)	3.2 (0.04)	3.3 (0.03)
One employed full time, one not in labor force	13.9 (0.10)	15.3 (0.10)	16.2 (0.08)	3.0 (0.02)	3.2 (0.02)	3.2 (0.02)	3.1 (0.01)	3.2 (0.02)	3.2 (0.02)	3.1 (0.02)	3.2 (0.02)	3.3 (0.02)
Other combination	13.9 (0.16)	15.1 (0.12)	15.9 (0.12)	2.9 (0.03)	3.1 (0.03)	3.0 (0.03)	3.0 (0.03)	3.1 (0.03)	3.1 (0.03)	3.1 (0.03)	3.2 (0.03)	3.1 (0.03)
Single parent												
Employed full time	14.1 (0.18)	14.8 (0.12)	15.9 (0.12)	2.8 (0.03)	3.0 (0.02)	2.9 (0.03)	2.9 (0.02)	3.1 (0.03)	3.0 (0.03)	3.0 (0.03)	3.1 (0.03)	3.1 (0.04)
Employed part time	14.0 (0.25)	14.9 (0.16)	15.7 (0.17)	2.9 (0.04)	3.0 (0.05)	2.9 (0.05)	3.0 (0.04)	3.0 (0.05)	3.0 (0.05)	3.1 (0.05)	3.1 (0.04)	3.1 (0.04)
Looking for work	13.7 (0.35)	14.7 (0.32)	15.3 (0.28)	2.7 (0.06)	2.9 (0.06)	2.7 (0.05)	2.8 (0.06)	3.0 (0.05)	2.8 (0.06)	2.9 (0.06)	3.0 (0.06)	3.0 (0.05)
Not in labor force	13.5 (0.22)	14.6 (0.25)	15.3 (0.23)	2.7 (0.05)	2.8 (0.05)	2.9 (0.05)	2.8 (0.06)	2.9 (0.05)	3.0 (0.05)	2.9 (0.04)	3.0 (0.05)	3.0 (0.05)
No parent in household	13.4 (0.25)	14.4 (0.28)	15.6 (0.16)	2.7 (0.05)	2.9 (0.05)	2.7 (0.08)	2.8 (0.05)	2.9 (0.06)	2.9 (0.08)	2.8 (0.05)	2.9 (0.06)	2.9 (0.07)
Parents' highest level of education[8]												
Less than high school	13.0 (0.16)	14.3 (0.15)	15.2 (0.13)	2.8 (0.03)	3.0 (0.03)	2.9 (0.02)	2.9 (0.03)	3.1 (0.03)	3.0 (0.03)	3.0 (0.03)	3.2 (0.03)	3.2 (0.03)
High school completion	13.8 (0.09)	14.9 (0.08)	15.8 (0.07)	2.8 (0.02)	3.0 (0.02)	3.0 (0.02)	2.9 (0.02)	3.0 (0.02)	3.1 (0.02)	3.1 (0.02)	3.1 (0.02)	3.1 (0.02)
Some college/vocational	14.2 (0.08)	15.1 (0.10)	16.0 (0.07)	2.9 (0.01)	3.1 (0.02)	3.0 (0.02)	3.0 (0.01)	3.1 (0.02)	3.1 (0.02)	3.1 (0.01)	3.3 (0.02)	3.3 (0.02)
Bachelor's degree	14.8 (0.09)	15.6 (0.07)	16.4 (0.07)	3.1 (0.02)	3.2 (0.02)	3.2 (0.02)	3.1 (0.02)	3.2 (0.02)	3.2 (0.02)	3.2 (0.02)	3.3 (0.02)	3.3 (0.02)
Any graduate education	15.1 (0.08)	15.9 (0.08)	16.6 (0.06)	3.1 (0.02)	3.3 (0.02)	3.3 (0.02)	3.1 (0.02)	3.3 (0.02)	3.3 (0.02)	3.2 (0.02)	3.3 (0.02)	3.3 (0.02)
Household type, fall 2010												
Two-parent household	14.5 (0.06)	15.4 (0.07)	16.2 (0.04)	3.0 (0.01)	3.2 (0.01)	3.2 (0.01)	3.1 (0.01)	3.2 (0.01)	3.2 (0.01)	3.2 (0.01)	3.3 (0.01)	3.3 (0.01)
Mother-only household	13.9 (0.12)	14.7 (0.11)	15.7 (0.10)	2.8 (0.02)	3.0 (0.02)	2.9 (0.02)	2.9 (0.02)	3.0 (0.03)	3.0 (0.02)	3.0 (0.02)	3.1 (0.02)	3.0 (0.02)
Father-only household	14.3 (0.32)	14.8 (0.34)	15.7 (0.25)	2.8 (0.06)	2.9 (0.05)	2.8 (0.07)	2.9 (0.07)	3.0 (0.06)	2.9 (0.08)	2.9 (0.07)	2.9 (0.06)	2.9 (0.07)
Other household type	13.4 (0.25)	14.4 (0.28)	15.6 (0.16)	2.7 (0.05)	2.9 (0.05)	2.7 (0.08)	2.8 (0.05)	2.9 (0.06)	2.9 (0.08)	2.8 (0.05)	2.9 (0.06)	2.9 (0.07)

See notes at end of table.

Table 220.45. Fall 2010 first-time kindergartners' cognitive flexibility, approaches to learning, interpersonal skills, and self-control scale scores, by selected child, family, and school characteristics: Fall 2010, spring 2011, and spring 2012—Continued

[Standard errors appear in parentheses]

Selected child, family, or school characteristic	Mean cognitive flexibility score[1]			Mean approaches to learning score[2]			Mean interpersonal skills score[3]			Mean self-control score[4]		
	Kindergarten Fall 2010	Kindergarten Spring 2011	First grade, spring 2012	Kindergarten Fall 2010	Kindergarten Spring 2011	First grade, spring 2012	Kindergarten Fall 2010	Kindergarten Spring 2011	First grade, spring 2012	Kindergarten Fall 2010	Kindergarten Spring 2011	First grade, spring 2012
1	2	3	4	5	6	7	8	9	10	11	12	13
Primary home language												
English	14.5 (0.06)	15.3 (0.07)	16.2 (0.05)	3.0 (0.01)	3.1 (0.01)	3.1 (0.01)	3.0 (0.01)	3.2 (0.01)	3.2 (0.01)	3.1 (0.01)	3.2 (0.01)	3.2 (0.01)
Non-English	13.2 (0.16)	14.6 (0.10)	15.6 (0.09)	2.9 (0.03)	3.1 (0.02)	3.1 (0.02)	3.0 (0.03)	3.1 (0.02)	3.1 (0.02)	3.1 (0.03)	3.2 (0.02)	3.2 (0.02)
Primary language not identified	13.8 (0.37)	15.2 (0.22)	15.7 (0.34)	2.8 (0.06)	3.0 (0.06)	3.1 (0.08)	3.0 (0.06)	3.1 (0.06)	3.2 (0.08)	3.0 (0.06)	3.2 (0.07)	3.3 (0.09)
Poverty status[9]												
Below poverty threshold	13.5 (0.11)	14.6 (0.08)	15.6 (0.08)	2.8 (0.02)	3.0 (0.02)	2.9 (0.02)	2.9 (0.02)	3.1 (0.02)	3.0 (0.02)	3.0 (0.02)	3.1 (0.02)	3.1 (0.02)
100 to 199 percent of poverty threshold	14.2 (0.11)	15.2 (0.09)	16.0 (0.08)	2.9 (0.02)	3.1 (0.02)	3.1 (0.02)	3.0 (0.02)	3.2 (0.02)	3.1 (0.02)	3.1 (0.02)	3.2 (0.02)	3.2 (0.02)
200 percent or more of poverty threshold	14.8 (0.06)	15.6 (0.08)	16.4 (0.04)	3.1 (0.01)	3.2 (0.02)	3.2 (0.01)	3.1 (0.02)	3.2 (0.02)	3.2 (0.01)	3.2 (0.01)	3.3 (0.01)	3.3 (0.01)
Socioeconomic status[10]												
Lowest 20 percent	13.3 (0.11)	14.6 (0.11)	15.4 (0.06)	2.8 (0.02)	3.0 (0.02)	2.9 (0.02)	2.9 (0.02)	3.1 (0.02)	3.0 (0.02)	3.0 (0.02)	3.1 (0.01)	3.1 (0.02)
Middle 60 percent	14.3 (0.08)	15.2 (0.09)	16.1 (0.05)	3.0 (0.01)	3.1 (0.01)	3.1 (0.01)	3.0 (0.01)	3.2 (0.01)	3.1 (0.01)	3.1 (0.01)	3.2 (0.01)	3.2 (0.01)
Highest 20 percent	15.1 (0.06)	15.9 (0.06)	16.7 (0.05)	3.1 (0.02)	3.3 (0.02)	3.3 (0.02)	3.1 (0.02)	3.3 (0.02)	3.3 (0.01)	3.2 (0.02)	3.3 (0.01)	3.4 (0.01)
School type												
Public	14.3 (0.07)	15.2 (0.07)	16.1 (0.05)	3.0 (0.01)	3.1 (0.01)	3.1 (0.01)	3.0 (0.01)	3.2 (0.01)	3.1 (0.01)	3.1 (0.01)	3.2 (0.01)	3.2 (0.01)
Private	14.4 (0.15)	15.6 (0.07)	16.3 (0.10)	3.1 (0.03)	3.2 (0.03)	3.2 (0.03)	3.1 (0.03)	3.2 (0.03)	3.2 (0.03)	3.1 (0.04)	3.2 (0.03)	3.2 (0.03)

†Not applicable.

[1] To measure cognitive flexibility, children were administered the Dimensional Change Card Sort (DCCS) (developed by Philip Zelazo in 2006). Children were asked to sort a series of picture cards into one of two trays according to different rules (e.g., by color, by shape). Possible scores range from 0 to 18.

[2] The approaches to learning scale is based on teachers' reports on how students rate in seven areas: attentiveness, task persistence, eagerness to learn, learning independence, ability to adapt easily to changes in routine, organization, and ability to follow classroom rules. Possible scores on the scale range from 1 to 4, with higher scores indicating that a child exhibits positive learning behaviors more often.

[3] The interpersonal skills scale is based on teachers' reports on the student's skill in forming and maintaining friendships; getting along with people who are different; comforting or helping other children; expressing feelings, ideas, and opinions in positive ways; and showing sensitivity to the feelings of others. Possible scores on the scale range from 1 to 4, with higher scores indicating that a child interacted with others in a positive way more often.

[4] The self-control scale is based on teachers' reports on the student's ability to control behavior by respecting the property rights of others, controlling temper, accepting peer ideas for group activities, and responding appropriately to pressure from peers. Possible scores on the scale range from 1 to 4, with higher scores indicating that a child exhibited behaviors indicative of self-control more often.

[5] Derived from child's approaches to learning scale score in fall of the kindergarten year. This score is based on teachers' reports on how often students exhibit positive learning behaviors in seven areas: attentiveness, task persistence, eagerness to learn, learning independence, ability to adapt easily to changes in routine, organization, and ability to follow classroom rules. Possible scores range from 1 to 4. Fall 2010 scores were categorized into the four anchor points on the original scale— 1 (never), 2 (sometimes), 3 (often), and 4 (very often)—by rounding the mean score to the nearest whole number.

[6] The type of nonparental care in which the child spent the most hours. Multiple arrangements refers to children who spent an equal amount of time in each of two or more arrangements.

[7] Parents who reported working at least 35 hours per week are defined as employed full time, while those who reported working less than 35 hours per week are defined as employed part time. Those neither employed nor looking for work are not in the labor force.

[8] Parents' highest level of education is the highest level of education achieved by either of the parents or guardians in a two-parent household, by the only parent in a single-parent household, or by any guardian in a household with no parents.

[9] Poverty status is based on preliminary U.S. Census income thresholds for 2010, which identify incomes determined to meet household needs, given family size and composition. For example, a family of three with one child was below the poverty threshold if its income was less than $17,552 in 2010.

[10] Socioeconomic status (SES) was measured by a composite score based on parental education and occupations and household income at the time of data collection.

NOTE: Estimates weighted by W4C4P_2T0. Estimates pertain to a sample of children who were enrolled in kindergarten for the first time in the 2010–11 school year. Most of the children were in first grade in 2011–12, but 4 percent were in kindergarten or other grades (e.g., second grade, ungraded classrooms). Two parents may refer to two biological parents, two adoptive parents, or one biological/adoptive parent and one other parent/partner. Single parent refers to one biological or adoptive parent only. In households without parents, the guardian or guardians may be related or unrelated to the child. Race categories exclude persons of Hispanic ethnicity. Detail may not sum to totals because of rounding and survey item nonresponse.

SOURCE: U.S. Department of Education, National Center for Education Statistics, Early Childhood Longitudinal Study, Kindergarten Class of 2010–11 (ECLS-K:2011), Kindergarten–First Grade Restricted-Use Data File. (This table was prepared September 2014.)

Table 220.50. Number and percentage distribution of kindergartners, by fall 2010 kindergarten entry status and selected child, family, and school characteristics: 2010–11

[Standard errors appear in parentheses]

Selected child, family, or school characteristic	All kindergartners[1] Number (in thousands)		Percentage distribution, by selected characteristics		Percentage distribution of kindergartners, by entry status[2] Total[1]		Early kindergarten entrants		On-time kindergarten entrants		Delayed kindergarten entrants		Kindergarten repeaters	
1	2		3		4		5		6		7		8	
Total	4,054	(5.7)	100.0	(†)	100.0	(†)	1.5	(0.17)	86.6	(0.91)	5.9	(0.41)	6.0	(0.87)
Sex of child														
Male	2,097	(18.9)	51.7	(0.47)	100.0	(†)	1.1	(0.16)	85.0	(1.03)	6.8	(0.63)	7.1	(0.90)
Female	1,957	(19.7)	48.3	(0.47)	100.0	(†)	1.9	(0.24)	88.3	(0.96)	4.9	(0.35)	4.9	(0.90)
Age of child at first kindergarten entry[3]														
Less than 5 years old	234	(33.2)	6.4	(0.90)	100.0	(†)	12.3	(2.57)	47.2	(7.36)	1.2	(0.32)	39.3	(8.87)
5 years old to 5 1/2 years old	1,557	(31.0)	42.3	(0.62)	100.0	(†)	1.0	(0.18)	92.3	(0.56)	1.3	(0.18)	5.4	(0.42)
More than 5 1/2 years old to 6 years old	1,572	(31.6)	42.7	(0.68)	100.0	(†)	0.5	(0.11)	92.3	(0.49)	4.7	(0.48)	2.5	(0.29)
More than 6 years old	315	(15.7)	8.6	(0.41)	100.0	(†)	‡	(†)	60.4	(3.20)	38.3	(3.14)	1.1 !	(0.47)
Race/ethnicity of child														
White	2,080	(70.5)	51.3	(1.75)	100.0	(†)	1.0	(0.17)	86.5	(0.75)	7.4	(0.64)	5.1	(0.59)
Black	547	(52.2)	13.5	(1.29)	100.0	(†)	1.8 !	(0.64)	85.4	(3.29)	3.1	(0.40)	9.7 !	(3.26)
Hispanic	1,004	(54.0)	24.8	(1.33)	100.0	(†)	1.7	(0.32)	88.3	(0.93)	3.7	(0.40)	6.3	(0.84)
Asian	186	(28.4)	4.6	(0.70)	100.0	(†)	5.1 !	(1.55)	84.0	(2.27)	6.1	(1.15)	4.8 !	(1.70)
Pacific Islander	17	(3.0)	0.4	(0.07)	100.0	(†)	‡	(†)	90.3	(4.38)	‡	(†)	‡	(†)
American Indian/Alaska Native	49 !	(21.4)	1.2 !	(0.53)	100.0	(†)	‡	(†)	81.3	(2.01)	8.0	(1.87)	8.2	(2.37)
Two or more races	169	(9.2)	4.2	(0.23)	100.0	(†)	1.5 !	(0.49)	86.4	(1.85)	6.6	(1.28)	5.5	(1.19)
Primary type of nonparental care arrangement prior to kindergarten entry[4]														
No regular nonparental arrangement	815	(29.3)	21.5	(0.75)	100.0	(†)	1.3	(0.25)	85.1	(1.21)	5.6	(0.55)	8.1	(1.12)
Home-based care														
Relative care	560	(17.3)	14.8	(0.44)	100.0	(†)	1.6	(0.31)	87.3	(1.06)	4.7	(0.51)	6.5	(0.85)
Nonrelative care	225	(12.7)	5.9	(0.33)	100.0	(†)	0.9 !	(0.35)	87.9	(1.46)	7.4	(1.26)	3.8	(0.74)
Center-based care	2,103	(33.3)	55.4	(0.90)	100.0	(†)	1.7	(0.25)	87.0	(1.02)	6.2	(0.53)	5.1	(0.96)
Multiple arrangements	90	(6.5)	2.4	(0.17)	100.0	(†)	0.7 !	(0.34)	86.6	(1.87)	5.9	(1.51)	6.7	(1.87)
Parents' employment status, fall 2010[5]														
Two parents														
Both employed full time	824	(24.5)	25.0	(0.68)	100.0	(†)	1.8	(0.25)	87.3	(0.97)	6.4	(0.75)	4.5	(0.59)
One employed full time, one part time	524	(20.1)	15.9	(0.51)	100.0	(†)	1.5	(0.35)	88.1	(0.77)	6.8	(0.59)	3.5	(0.65)
One employed full time, one looking for work	141	(8.0)	4.3	(0.23)	100.0	(†)	2.4 !	(0.87)	86.8	(2.08)	3.5 !	(1.31)	7.3	(1.51)
One employed full time, one not in labor force	779	(28.2)	23.6	(0.81)	100.0	(†)	1.1	(0.22)	86.8	(1.11)	6.7	(0.64)	5.4	(0.90)
Other combination	220	(12.5)	6.7	(0.35)	100.0	(†)	1.7	(0.46)	84.8	(1.56)	5.8	(1.05)	7.7	(1.41)
Single parent														
Employed full time	348	(17.0)	10.5	(0.47)	100.0	(†)	1.6	(0.41)	88.4	(1.49)	4.1	(0.53)	5.9	(1.46)
Employed part time	135	(8.3)	4.1	(0.24)	100.0	(†)	1.0 !	(0.45)	87.6	(2.03)	5.5	(1.16)	5.8	(1.51)
Looking for work	116	(8.9)	3.5	(0.26)	100.0	(†)	‡	(†)	84.3	(2.53)	6.1	(1.48)	8.8	(2.31)
Not in labor force	137	(10.1)	4.1	(0.30)	100.0	(†)	‡	(†)	83.0	(2.42)	5.7	(1.14)	9.9	(2.02)
No parent in household	79	(5.6)	2.4	(0.17)	100.0	(†)	‡	(†)	82.2	(2.26)	3.8 !	(1.52)	12.1	(2.28)
Parents' highest level of education[6]														
Less than high school	388	(18.6)	9.6	(0.46)	100.0	(†)	2.0	(0.50)	82.7	(1.48)	4.7	(0.85)	10.7	(1.58)
High school completion	852	(23.0)	21.1	(0.56)	100.0	(†)	1.1	(0.26)	86.3	(1.20)	4.4	(0.53)	8.1	(1.15)
Some college/vocational	1,292	(27.3)	32.0	(0.67)	100.0	(†)	1.0	(0.18)	88.4	(1.23)	4.8	(0.55)	5.9	(1.09)
Bachelor's degree	792	(24.6)	19.6	(0.60)	100.0	(†)	1.8	(0.34)	85.3	(0.98)	8.4	(0.67)	4.5	(0.79)
Any graduate education	711	(29.2)	17.6	(0.73)	100.0	(†)	2.2	(0.44)	87.0	(0.75)	7.4	(0.64)	3.4	(0.60)
Household type, fall 2010														
Two-parent household	2,563	(50.1)	75.1	(0.92)	100.0	(†)	1.5	(0.19)	87.1	(0.75)	6.3	(0.50)	5.1	(0.65)
Mother-only household	719	(31.1)	21.1	(0.84)	100.0	(†)	1.2	(0.27)	86.8	(1.59)	4.6	(0.48)	7.3	(1.57)
Father-only household	51	(3.5)	1.5	(0.10)	100.0	(†)	‡	(†)	83.5	(2.75)	9.7 !	(2.96)	4.6 !	(2.04)
Other household type	79	(5.6)	2.3	(0.17)	100.0	(†)	‡	(†)	82.2	(2.26)	3.8 !	(1.52)	12.1	(2.28)
Primary home language														
English	3,338	(36.8)	82.6	(0.89)	100.0	(†)	1.3	(0.17)	86.8	(0.90)	6.3	(0.45)	5.7	(0.84)
Non-English	663	(33.7)	16.4	(0.84)	100.0	(†)	2.6	(0.67)	85.1	(1.64)	4.0	(0.53)	8.3	(1.56)
Primary language not identified	42	(4.9)	1.0	(0.12)	100.0	(†)	1.9 !	(0.89)	90.6	(2.55)	‡	(†)	5.6 !	(2.18)
Poverty status[7]														
Below poverty threshold	893	(35.8)	26.3	(1.03)	100.0	(†)	1.2	(0.30)	84.5	(1.64)	4.4	(0.53)	9.9	(1.63)
100 to 199 percent of poverty threshold	762	(18.1)	22.5	(0.51)	100.0	(†)	0.9	(0.20)	87.1	(1.31)	5.7	(0.64)	6.3	(1.07)
200 percent or more of poverty threshold	1,736	(44.5)	51.2	(1.25)	100.0	(†)	1.8	(0.26)	87.2	(0.64)	7.3	(0.57)	3.8	(0.52)
Socioeconomic status[8]														
Lowest 20 percent	799	(29.9)	19.8	(0.75)	100.0	(†)	1.5	(0.33)	84.1	(1.46)	4.3	(0.51)	10.1	(1.55)
Middle 60 percent	2,429	(30.6)	60.2	(0.73)	100.0	(†)	1.2	(0.16)	87.1	(1.01)	5.9	(0.52)	5.7	(0.88)
Highest 20 percent	808	(33.5)	20.0	(0.83)	100.0	(†)	2.4	(0.47)	87.2	(0.70)	7.2	(0.61)	3.2	(0.59)
School type														
Public	3,329	(48.4)	88.5	(0.18)	100.0	(†)	0.8	(0.11)	87.8	(0.86)	5.6	(0.42)	5.8	(0.77)
Private	432	(5.1)	11.5	(0.18)	100.0	(†)	6.8	(1.12)	78.0	(1.87)	7.8	(0.90)	7.5	(2.18)

†Not applicable.

!Interpret data with caution. The coefficient of variation (CV) for this estimate is between 30 and 50 percent.

‡Reporting standards not met. Either there are too few cases for a reliable estimate or the coefficient of variation (CV) is 50 percent or greater.

[1]Includes students with missing kindergarten entry status information.

[2]A child who enrolled in kindergarten for the first time in 2010–11 is classified as an early, on-time, or delayed kindergarten entrant depending on whether the parent reported enrolling the child early, enrolling the child when he or she was old enough, or waiting until the child was older relative to school guidelines about when children can start school based on their birth date. A child is classified as a kindergarten repeater if the parent reported that 2010–11 was the child's second (or third or more) year of kindergarten.

[3]Most of the children first entered kindergarten in 2010–11, but the children who were repeating kindergarten in 2010–11—that is, the "Kindergarten repeaters" shown in column 8—had first entered kindergarten in an earlier school year.

[4]The type of nonparental care in which the child spent the most hours. "Multiple arrangements" refers to children who spent an equal amount of time in each of two or more arrangements.

[5]Parents who reported working at least 35 hours per week are defined as employed full time, while those who reported working less than 35 hours per week are defined as employed part time. Those neither employed nor looking for work are not in the labor force.

[6]Parents' highest level of education is the highest level of education achieved by either of the parents or guardians in a two-parent household, by the only parent in a single-parent household, or by any guardian in a household with no parents.

[7]Poverty status is based on preliminary U.S. Census income thresholds for 2010, which identify incomes determined to meet household needs, given family size and composition. For example, a family of three with one child was below the poverty threshold if its income was less than $17,552 in 2010.

[8]Socioeconomic status (SES) was measured by a composite score based on parental education and occupations and household income at the time of data collection.

NOTE: Estimates weighted by W1_2P0. Estimates pertain to a sample of children who were enrolled in kindergarten in the 2010–11 school year. Two parents may refer to two biological parents, two adoptive parents, or one biological/adoptive parent and one other parent/partner. Single parent refers to one biological or adoptive parent only. In households without parents, the guardian or guardians may be related or unrelated to the child. Race categories exclude persons of Hispanic ethnicity. Detail may not sum to totals because of rounding and survey item nonresponse. Some data have been revised from previously published figures.

SOURCE: U.S. Department of Education, National Center for Education Statistics, Early Childhood Longitudinal Study, Kindergarten Class of 2010–11 (ECLS-K:2011), Kindergarten-First Grade Restricted-Use Data File. (This table was prepared February 2015.)

Table 220.60. Fall 2010 kindergartners' reading, mathematics, science, cognitive flexibility, and approaches to learning scale scores, by kindergarten entry status and time of assessment: Fall 2010, spring 2011, and spring 2012

[Standard errors appear in parentheses]

Type and time of assessment	Overall mean score[1]	Mean score by fall 2010 kindergarten entry status[2]			
		Early kindergarten entrants	On-time kindergarten entrants	Delayed kindergarten entrants	Kindergarten repeaters
1	2	3	4	5	6
Reading scale score[3]					
Kindergarten					
Fall 2010..	37.6 (0.21)	36.8 (0.78)	37.6 (0.23)	38.8 (0.55)	39.0 (0.60)
Spring 2011......................................	49.8 (0.29)	47.1 (1.51)	50.1 (0.30)	51.0 (0.61)	48.7 (0.76)
First grade, spring 2012...................	69.5 (0.29)	66.2 (1.66)	70.1 (0.31)	71.1 (0.59)	65.0 (0.99)
Mathematics scale score[4]					
Kindergarten					
Fall 2010..	30.6 (0.26)	27.4 (0.95)	30.6 (0.28)	34.2 (0.69)	31.1 (0.62)
Spring 2011......................................	43.4 (0.30)	39.9 (1.41)	43.6 (0.32)	46.4 (0.69)	42.5 (0.71)
First grade, spring 2012...................	62.9 (0.29)	58.0 (1.56)	63.2 (0.31)	66.3 (0.73)	59.5 (0.86)
Science scale score[5]					
Kindergarten, spring 2011	21.1 (0.14)	19.2 (0.58)	21.3 (0.15)	22.7 (0.27)	20.8 (0.39)
First grade, spring 2012...................	26.7 (0.17)	24.8 (0.78)	26.9 (0.18)	28.5 (0.28)	25.7 (0.49)
Cognitive flexibility score[6]					
Kindergarten					
Fall 2010..	14.3 (0.07)	13.0 (0.53)	14.3 (0.06)	14.6 (0.17)	13.9 (0.21)
Spring 2011......................................	15.2 (0.07)	14.7 (0.31)	15.2 (0.07)	15.5 (0.10)	14.8 (0.21)
First grade, spring 2012...................	16.0 (0.05)	16.0 (0.29)	16.1 (0.05)	16.4 (0.11)	15.5 (0.19)
Approaches to learning score[7]					
Kindergarten					
Fall 2010..	3.0 (0.01)	2.9 (0.07)	3.0 (0.01)	3.0 (0.03)	2.9 (0.05)
Spring 2011......................................	3.1 (0.01)	3.0 (0.08)	3.1 (0.01)	3.2 (0.03)	2.9 (0.05)
First grade, spring 2012...................	3.1 (0.01)	3.1 (0.11)	3.1 (0.01)	3.1 (0.04)	2.8 (0.04)

[1]Includes students with missing kindergarten entry status information.

[2]A child who enrolled in kindergarten for the first time in 2010–11 is classified as an early, on-time, or delayed kindergarten entrant depending on whether the parent reported enrolling the child early, enrolling the child when he or she was old enough, or waiting until the child was older relative to school guidelines about when children can start school based on their birth date. A child is classified as a kindergarten repeater if the parent reported that 2010–11 was the child's second (or third or more) year of kindergarten.

[3]Reflects performance on questions measuring basic skills (print familiarity, letter recognition, beginning and ending sounds, rhyming words, and word recognition); vocabulary knowledge; and reading comprehension, including identifying information specifically stated in text (e.g., definitions, facts, and supporting details), making complex inferences from texts, and considering the text objectively and judging its appropriateness and quality. Possible scores for the reading assessment range from 0 to 100.

[4]Reflects performance on questions on number sense, properties, and operations; measurement; geometry and spatial sense; data analysis, statistics, and probability (measured with a set of simple questions assessing children's ability to read a graph); and prealgebra skills such as identification of patterns. Possible scores for the mathematics assessment range from 0 to 96.

[5]Science was not assessed in the fall of kindergarten. Reflects performance on questions on physical sciences, life sciences, environmental sciences, and scientific inquiry. Possible scores for the science assessment range from 0 to 47.

[6]To measure cognitive flexibility, children were administered the Dimensional Change Card Sort (DCCS) (developed by Philip Zelazo in 2006). Children were asked to sort a series of picture cards into one of two trays according to different rules (e.g., by color, by shape). Possible scores range from 0 to 18.

[7]The approaches to learning scale is based on teachers' reports on how students rate in seven areas: attentiveness, task persistence, eagerness to learn, learning independence, ability to adapt easily to changes in routine, organization, and ability to follow classroom rules. Possible scores on the scale range from 1 to 4, with higher scores indicating that a child exhibits positive learning behaviors more often.

NOTE: Estimates weighted by W4C4P_20. Estimates pertain to a sample of children who were enrolled in kindergarten in the 2010–11 school year. Estimates differ from previously published figures because reading, mathematics, and science scores were recalibrated to represent the kindergarten through first-grade assessment item pools and because weights were adjusted to account for survey nonresponse at each data collection wave, including the latest round of data collection (spring 2012).

SOURCE: U.S. Department of Education, National Center for Education Statistics, Early Childhood Longitudinal Study, Kindergarten Class of 2010–11 (ECLS-K:2011), Kindergarten-First Grade Restricted-Use Data File. (This table was prepared February 2015.)

Table 220.70. Mean reading scale scores and specific reading skills of fall 1998 first-time kindergartners, by time of assessment and selected characteristics: Selected years, fall 1998 through spring 2007

[Standard errors appear in parentheses]

Selected characteristic	Mean reading scale score						Percentage of children with specific reading skills, eighth grade, spring 2007			
	Kindergarten		First grade, spring 2000	Third grade, spring 2002	Fifth grade, spring 2004	Eighth grade, spring 2007	Deriving meaning from text	Interpreting beyond text	Evaluating nonfiction	Evaluating complex syntax
	Fall 1998	Spring 1999								
1	2	3	4	5	6	7	8	9	10	11
Total	36 (0.2)	47 (0.3)	79 (0.6)	128 (0.8)	151 (0.7)	169 (0.8)	83 (0.8)	66 (0.8)	29 (0.9)	6 (0.3)
Sex										
Male	35 (0.3)	46 (0.4)	77 (0.9)	126 (1.0)	149 (1.0)	166 (1.2)	80 (1.1)	63 (1.2)	26 (1.3)	5 (0.4)
Female	36 (0.3)	48 (0.5)	81 (0.8)	131 (1.0)	153 (0.9)	172 (0.9)	85 (0.8)	69 (1.0)	31 (1.2)	7 (0.4)
Race/ethnicity										
White	37 (0.3)	48 (0.4)	83 (0.8)	135 (0.9)	158 (0.8)	176 (0.8)	89 (0.7)	74 (0.8)	36 (1.1)	8 (0.4)
Black	32 (0.5)	42 (0.8)	70 (1.3)	114 (2.0)	135 (1.9)	149 (2.4)	66 (2.6)	45 (2.4)	10 (1.6)	2 (0.3)
Hispanic	33 (0.5)	44 (0.8)	72 (1.1)	118 (1.3)	142 (1.1)	160 (1.3)	76 (1.3)	57 (1.4)	18 (1.4)	3 (0.3)
Asian	41 (1.3)	53 (1.7)	90 (2.0)	135 (2.3)	157 (1.8)	178 (2.0)	89 (1.6)	75 (2.2)	41 (3.3)	10 (1.2)
Other[1]	34 (1.4)	46 (1.7)	76 (2.4)	125 (3.9)	150 (4.3)	167 (3.8)	82 (3.3)	64 (4.1)	25 (3.6)	5 (0.8)
Parents' highest level of education[2]										
Less than high school	30 (0.5)	39 (0.7)	64 (1.5)	103 (1.7)	128 (1.8)	141 (2.2)	58 (2.5)	37 (2.1)	5 (0.7)	1 (0.1)
High school	32 (0.3)	42 (0.5)	71 (1.0)	118 (1.2)	140 (1.2)	159 (1.3)	75 (1.3)	55 (1.4)	16 (1.3)	3 (0.3)
Some college	35 (0.4)	46 (0.4)	78 (0.8)	128 (1.1)	151 (1.0)	169 (1.1)	84 (1.1)	66 (1.2)	25 (1.1)	4 (0.3)
Bachelor's or higher degree	40 (0.5)	52 (0.7)	89 (1.1)	143 (0.8)	165 (0.8)	183 (0.8)	93 (0.6)	81 (0.8)	49 (1.3)	12 (0.6)
Primary home language[2]										
English	36 (0.2)	47 (0.3)	80 (0.7)	130 (0.8)	152 (0.7)	170 (0.9)	84 (0.8)	67 (0.9)	30 (0.9)	6 (0.3)
Non-English	33 (0.6)	44 (0.8)	70 (1.1)	113 (1.3)	138 (1.4)	157 (1.6)	73 (1.6)	54 (1.6)	17 (1.4)	4 (0.5)
Socioeconomic status[2]										
Lowest 20 percent	30 (0.3)	39 (0.5)	64 (1.1)	105 (1.3)	129 (1.3)	145 (1.5)	62 (1.7)	41 (1.5)	8 (0.9)	1 (0.2)
Middle 60 percent	35 (0.3)	46 (0.3)	78 (0.7)	128 (0.8)	151 (0.7)	169 (0.8)	84 (0.8)	66 (0.9)	26 (0.9)	5 (0.3)
Highest 20 percent	41 (0.6)	54 (0.8)	92 (1.4)	145 (0.9)	167 (0.9)	186 (0.8)	95 (0.6)	84 (0.9)	52 (1.5)	14 (0.8)
Grade level in spring 2007										
Eighth grade or above	36 (0.2)	48 (0.4)	82 (0.6)	133 (0.7)	155 (0.7)	173 (0.9)	86 (0.8)	70 (0.9)	32 (1.0)	7 (0.3)
Below eighth grade	30 (0.5)	37 (0.6)	57 (1.4)	100 (1.9)	126 (2.2)	143 (2.5)	58 (2.7)	39 (2.5)	9 (2.0)	2! (0.7)
School type across all waves of the study										
Public school all years	35 (0.3)	46 (0.4)	77 (0.6)	126 (0.9)	149 (0.8)	166 (0.9)	80 (0.9)	63 (1.0)	25 (1.0)	5 (0.2)
Private school all years	39 (0.6)	52 (0.9)	88 (1.5)	140 (1.4)	163 (1.0)	184 (1.2)	94 (0.7)	81 (1.4)	47 (2.5)	10 (0.8)
Change in school type during study	38 (0.8)	51 (1.1)	84 (1.9)	134 (1.8)	158 (1.4)	177 (1.8)	89 (1.4)	74 (1.9)	38 (2.7)	9 (1.1)

!Interpret data with caution. The coefficient of variation (CV) for this estimate is between 30 and 50 percent.
[1]Includes persons of all other races and two or more races.
[2]Status during kindergarten year.
NOTE: Reading scale ranges from 0 to 209. Estimates for each assessment round include all children assessed in English in that round, even if they were not assessed in English in a previous round. In fall 1998, 8 percent of the kindergarten sample was not administered the English battery because of nonpassing scores on the OLDS (Oral Language Development Scale) English proficiency assessment. By spring of first grade, this percentage had decreased to 2 percent. In the third grade and subsequent years, the OLDS was not administered and all children were assessed in English. Most of the children were in first grade in 1999–2000, but 5 percent were in kindergarten or other grades (e.g., second grade, ungraded classrooms); most were in third grade in 2001–02, but 11 percent were in second grade or other grades (e.g., fourth grade, ungraded classrooms); most were in fifth grade in 2003–04, but 14 percent were in fourth grade or other grades (e.g., sixth grade, ungraded classrooms); most were in eighth grade in 2006–07, but 14 percent were in seventh grade or other grades (e.g., ninth grade or ungraded classrooms). Data were calculated using C1_7FC0 weight. Estimates differ from previously published figures because the data were recalibrated to represent the kindergarten through eighth-grade reading assessment item pool. Race categories exclude persons of Hispanic ethnicity.
SOURCE: U.S. Department of Education, National Center for Education Statistics, Early Childhood Longitudinal Study, Kindergarten Class of 1998–99 (ECLS-K), Longitudinal Kindergarten–Eighth Grade Full Sample Public-Use Data File, fall 1998, spring 1999, spring 2000, spring 2002, spring 2004, and spring 2007. (This table was prepared September 2009.)

Table 220.80. Mean mathematics and science scale scores and specific mathematics skills of fall 1998 first-time kindergartners, by time of assessment and selected characteristics: Selected years, fall 1998 through spring 2007

[Standard errors appear in parentheses]

Selected characteristic	Mathematics									Science		
	Mean scale score						Percentage of children with specific skills, eighth grade, spring 2007			Mean scale score		
	Kindergarten		First grade, spring 2000	Third grade, spring 2002	Fifth grade, spring 2004	Eighth grade, spring 2007	Rate and measurement	Fractions	Area and volume	Third grade, spring 2002	Fifth grade, spring 2004	Eighth grade, spring 2007
	Fall 1998	Spring 1999										
1	2	3	4	5	6	7	8	9	10	11	12	13
Total	26 (0.2)	37 (0.3)	62 (0.4)	100 (0.7)	124 (0.7)	140 (0.6)	68 (0.9)	38 (1.0)	16 (0.8)	51 (0.4)	65 (0.4)	84 (0.5)
Sex												
Male	26 (0.3)	37 (0.4)	63 (0.6)	103 (0.8)	126 (0.9)	141 (0.8)	70 (1.3)	40 (1.3)	18 (1.0)	53 (0.6)	67 (0.6)	85 (0.7)
Female	26 (0.3)	37 (0.4)	61 (0.5)	97 (0.9)	121 (1.0)	139 (0.8)	65 (1.3)	35 (1.4)	14 (1.0)	49 (0.6)	63 (0.6)	82 (0.6)
Race/ethnicity												
White	29 (0.3)	40 (0.4)	67 (0.6)	106 (0.8)	130 (0.8)	146 (0.6)	77 (1.0)	46 (1.3)	21 (1.1)	56 (0.5)	70 (0.4)	89 (0.5)
Black	22 (0.4)	31 (0.6)	52 (0.8)	84 (1.8)	105 (1.8)	123 (1.6)	40 (2.3)	13 (1.8)	4 (1.2)	40 (1.1)	52 (1.1)	69 (1.3)
Hispanic	22 (0.4)	32 (0.5)	57 (0.9)	93 (1.1)	119 (1.1)	136 (1.0)	62 (1.7)	29 (2.1)	10 (1.1)	44 (0.7)	60 (0.7)	78 (0.8)
Asian	30 (1.0)	40 (1.2)	65 (1.7)	107 (2.7)	135 (2.4)	150 (2.3)	81 (3.1)	59 (3.8)	38 (3.7)	53 (1.5)	67 (1.6)	89 (1.1)
Other[1]	25 (1.0)	36 (1.3)	60 (2.1)	97 (3.3)	122 (3.6)	138 (3.2)	65 (5.2)	34 (4.7)	15 (3.2)	49 (2.0)	63 (2.2)	82 (2.6)
Parents' highest level of education[2]												
Less than high school	20 (0.4)	28 (0.6)	49 (1.1)	81 (1.4)	105 (1.9)	122 (2.1)	41 (2.9)	14 (1.9)	3 (0.8)	37 (0.9)	50 (1.0)	68 (1.2)
High school	23 (0.3)	33 (0.5)	56 (0.7)	91 (1.0)	114 (1.0)	131 (0.8)	53 (1.4)	21 (1.2)	7 (0.7)	45 (0.6)	59 (0.7)	77 (0.7)
Some college	26 (0.3)	37 (0.4)	62 (0.6)	100 (1.0)	124 (0.9)	141 (0.8)	70 (1.3)	35 (1.5)	13 (1.0)	51 (0.6)	65 (0.6)	84 (0.6)
Bachelor's or higher degree	31 (0.3)	42 (0.4)	70 (0.6)	111 (0.9)	136 (0.8)	152 (0.7)	85 (1.2)	59 (1.5)	30 (1.4)	59 (0.6)	73 (0.5)	92 (0.4)
Primary home language[2]												
English	27 (0.2)	38 (0.3)	63 (0.4)	101 (0.7)	125 (0.8)	141 (0.6)	69 (1.0)	38 (1.0)	16 (0.8)	52 (0.4)	66 (0.5)	84 (0.5)
Non-English	21 (0.4)	30 (0.6)	55 (0.8)	91 (1.1)	117 (1.2)	135 (1.1)	58 (1.7)	30 (1.9)	13 (1.2)	41 (0.8)	57 (0.8)	77 (0.9)
Socioeconomic status[2]												
Lowest 20 percent	20 (0.3)	28 (0.4)	50 (0.8)	83 (1.1)	105 (1.3)	123 (1.2)	42 (1.8)	14 (1.1)	4 (0.5)	38 (0.4)	51 (0.9)	70 (0.9)
Middle 60 percent	26 (0.2)	37 (0.3)	62 (0.4)	99 (0.7)	123 (0.7)	140 (0.6)	67 (0.9)	35 (1.0)	13 (0.8)	51 (0.4)	65 (0.4)	84 (0.5)
Highest 20 percent	32 (0.4)	43 (0.5)	72 (0.7)	115 (0.9)	139 (0.9)	154 (0.7)	88 (1.0)	63 (1.8)	33 (1.8)	60 (0.6)	75 (0.6)	94 (0.5)
Grade level in spring 2007												
Eighth grade or above	27 (0.2)	38 (0.3)	65 (0.4)	103 (0.7)	127 (0.8)	143 (0.6)	73 (1.0)	41 (1.1)	18 (0.8)	53 (0.4)	67 (0.4)	86 (0.5)
Below eighth grade	20 (0.4)	27 (0.6)	47 (1.2)	79 (1.6)	103 (1.9)	121 (1.8)	37 (2.5)	14 (2.5)	5 (1.5)	40 (1.1)	53 (1.3)	69 (1.4)
School type across all waves of the study												
Public school all years	26 (0.2)	36 (0.4)	61 (0.5)	99 (0.9)	122 (0.9)	139 (0.7)	66 (1.1)	35 (1.2)	15 (0.8)	50 (0.5)	64 (0.5)	82 (0.6)
Private school all years	31 (0.6)	43 (0.8)	69 (1.0)	107 (1.7)	133 (1.5)	149 (1.3)	82 (2.4)	50 (3.0)	22 (1.9)	56 (1.0)	71 (0.9)	90 (0.8)
Change in school type during study	28 (0.7)	39 (0.8)	66 (1.1)	103 (1.5)	128 (1.6)	144 (1.3)	73 (2.0)	44 (2.6)	20 (2.1)	55 (1.0)	69 (1.0)	88 (0.9)

[1]Includes persons of all other races and two or more races.

[2]Status during kindergarten year.

NOTE: Mathematics scale ranges from 0 to 172, and science scale ranges from 0 to 108. Estimates for each assessment round include all children assessed in that round, including children assessed in Spanish. In kindergarten and first grade, the mathematics assessment was administered in Spanish for Spanish-speaking children who did not pass the English OLDS (Oral Language Development Scale). All assessments were administered in English in third grade through eighth grade. Most of the children were in first grade in 1999–2000, but 5 percent were in kindergarten or other grades (e.g., second grade, ungraded classrooms); most were in third grade in 2001–02, but 11 percent were in second grade or other grades (e.g., fourth grade, ungraded classrooms); most were in fifth grade in 2003–04, but 14 percent were in fourth grade or other grades (e.g., sixth grade, ungraded classrooms); most were in eighth grade in 2006–07, but 14 percent were in seventh grade or other grades (e.g., ninth grade or ungraded classrooms). Data were calculated using C1_7FC0 weight. Estimates differ from previously published figures because the data were recalibrated to represent the kindergarten through eighth-grade mathematics assessment item pool and the third-grade through eighth-grade science assessment item pool. Race categories exclude persons of Hispanic ethnicity.
SOURCE: U.S. Department of Education, National Center for Education Statistics, Early Childhood Longitudinal Study, Kindergarten Class of 1998–99 (ECLS-K), Longitudinal Kindergarten–Eighth Grade Full Sample Public-Use Data File, fall 1998, spring 1999, spring 2000, spring 2002, spring 2004, and spring 2007. (This table was prepared September 2009.)

Table 221.10. Average National Assessment of Educational Progress (NAEP) reading scale score, by sex, race/ethnicity, and grade: Selected years, 1992 through 2013

[Standard errors appear in parentheses]

Grade and year	All students	Sex — Average reading scale score: Male	Female	Gap between female and male score	Race/ethnicity — Average reading scale score: White	Black	Hispanic	Asian/Pacific Islander: Total	Asian[1]	Pacific Islander[1]	American Indian/Alaska Native	Two or more races[1]	Gap between White and Black score	Gap between White and Hispanic score
1	2	3	4	5	6	7	8	9	10	11	12	13	14	15
Grade 4														
1992[2]	217 (0.9)	213 (1.2)	221 (1.0)	8 (1.6)	224 (1.2)	192 (1.7)	197 (2.6)	216 (2.9)	— (†)	— (†)	‡ (†)	— (†)	32 (2.1)	27 (2.9)
1994[2]	214 (1.0)	209 (1.3)	220 (1.1)	10 (1.7)	224 (1.3)	185 (1.8)	188 (3.4)	220 (3.8)	— (†)	— (†)	211 (6.6)	— (†)	38 (2.2)	35 (3.6)
1998	215 (1.1)	212 (1.3)	217 (1.3)	5 (1.8)	225 (1.0)	193 (1.9)	193 (3.2)	215 (5.6)	— (†)	— (†)	‡ (†)	— (†)	32 (2.2)	32 (3.3)
2000	213 (1.3)	208 (1.3)	219 (1.4)	11 (1.9)	224 (1.1)	190 (1.8)	190 (2.9)	225 (5.2)	— (†)	— (†)	214 (6.0)	— (†)	34 (2.1)	35 (3.1)
2002	219 (0.4)	215 (0.4)	222 (0.5)	6 (0.7)	229 (0.3)	199 (0.5)	201 (1.3)	224 (1.6)	— (†)	— (†)	207 (2.0)	— (†)	30 (0.6)	28 (1.4)
2003	218 (0.3)	215 (0.3)	222 (0.3)	7 (0.5)	229 (0.2)	198 (0.4)	200 (0.6)	226 (1.2)	— (†)	— (†)	202 (1.4)	— (†)	31 (0.5)	28 (0.6)
2005	219 (0.2)	216 (0.2)	222 (0.3)	6 (0.4)	229 (0.2)	200 (0.3)	203 (0.5)	229 (0.7)	— (†)	— (†)	204 (1.3)	— (†)	29 (0.4)	26 (0.5)
2007	221 (0.3)	218 (0.3)	224 (0.3)	7 (0.4)	231 (0.2)	203 (0.4)	205 (0.5)	232 (1.0)	— (†)	— (†)	203 (1.2)	— (†)	27 (0.5)	26 (0.6)
2009	221 (0.3)	218 (0.3)	224 (0.3)	7 (0.4)	230 (0.3)	205 (0.5)	205 (0.5)	235 (1.0)	— (†)	— (†)	204 (1.3)	— (†)	26 (0.6)	25 (0.6)
2011	221 (0.3)	218 (0.3)	225 (0.3)	7 (0.5)	231 (0.2)	205 (0.5)	206 (0.5)	235 (1.2)	236 (1.3)	216 (1.9)	202 (1.3)	227 (1.2)	25 (0.5)	24 (0.6)
2013	222 (0.3)	219 (0.3)	225 (0.3)	7 (0.5)	232 (0.3)	206 (0.5)	207 (0.5)	235 (1.1)	237 (1.1)	212 (2.5)	205 (1.3)	227 (1.0)	26 (0.6)	25 (0.6)
Grade 8														
1992[2]	260 (0.9)	254 (1.1)	267 (1.0)	13 (1.5)	267 (1.1)	237 (1.7)	241 (1.6)	268 (3.9)	— (†)	— (†)	‡ (†)	— (†)	30 (2.0)	26 (2.0)
1994[2]	260 (0.8)	252 (1.0)	267 (1.0)	15 (1.4)	267 (1.0)	236 (1.8)	243 (1.2)	265 (3.0)	— (†)	— (†)	248 (4.7)	— (†)	30 (2.1)	24 (1.5)
1998	263 (0.8)	256 (1.0)	270 (0.8)	14 (1.3)	270 (0.9)	244 (1.2)	243 (1.7)	264 (7.1)	— (†)	— (†)	‡ (†)	— (†)	26 (1.5)	27 (1.9)
2000	— (†)	— (†)	— (†)	— (†)	— (†)	— (†)	— (†)	— (†)	— (†)	— (†)	— (†)	— (†)	— (†)	— (†)
2002	264 (0.4)	260 (0.5)	269 (0.5)	9 (0.7)	272 (0.4)	245 (0.7)	247 (0.8)	267 (1.7)	— (†)	— (†)	250 (3.5)	— (†)	27 (0.9)	26 (0.9)
2003	263 (0.2)	258 (0.3)	269 (0.2)	11 (0.4)	272 (0.2)	244 (0.5)	245 (0.7)	270 (1.1)	— (†)	— (†)	246 (3.0)	— (†)	28 (0.5)	27 (0.7)
2005	262 (0.2)	257 (0.2)	267 (0.2)	10 (0.3)	271 (0.2)	243 (0.4)	246 (0.4)	271 (0.8)	— (†)	— (†)	249 (1.4)	— (†)	28 (0.5)	25 (0.5)
2007	263 (0.2)	258 (0.3)	268 (0.3)	10 (0.4)	272 (0.2)	245 (0.4)	247 (0.4)	271 (1.1)	— (†)	— (†)	247 (1.2)	— (†)	27 (0.4)	25 (0.5)
2009	264 (0.3)	259 (0.3)	269 (0.3)	9 (0.5)	273 (0.2)	246 (0.4)	249 (0.6)	274 (1.1)	— (†)	— (†)	251 (1.2)	— (†)	26 (0.5)	24 (0.7)
2011	265 (0.2)	261 (0.3)	270 (0.2)	9 (0.4)	274 (0.2)	249 (0.5)	252 (0.5)	275 (1.0)	277 (1.0)	254 (2.2)	252 (1.2)	269 (1.2)	25 (0.5)	22 (0.5)
2013	268 (0.3)	263 (0.3)	273 (0.3)	10 (0.4)	276 (0.3)	250 (0.4)	256 (0.5)	280 (0.9)	282 (0.9)	259 (2.6)	251 (1.0)	271 (0.9)	26 (0.5)	21 (0.5)
Grade 12														
1992[2]	292 (0.6)	287 (0.7)	297 (0.7)	10 (1.0)	297 (0.6)	273 (1.4)	279 (2.7)	290 (3.2)	— (†)	— (†)	‡ (†)	— (†)	24 (1.5)	19 (2.7)
1994[2]	287 (0.7)	280 (0.8)	294 (0.8)	14 (1.2)	293 (0.7)	265 (1.6)	270 (1.7)	278 (2.4)	— (†)	— (†)	274 (5.8)	— (†)	29 (1.8)	23 (1.9)
1998	290 (0.6)	282 (0.8)	298 (0.8)	16 (1.1)	297 (0.7)	269 (1.4)	275 (1.5)	287 (2.7)	— (†)	— (†)	‡ (†)	— (†)	27 (1.6)	22 (1.6)
2000	— (†)	— (†)	— (†)	— (†)	— (†)	— (†)	— (†)	— (†)	— (†)	— (†)	— (†)	— (†)	— (†)	— (†)
2002	287 (0.7)	279 (0.9)	295 (0.7)	16 (1.1)	292 (0.7)	267 (1.3)	273 (1.5)	286 (2.0)	— (†)	— (†)	‡ (†)	— (†)	25 (1.5)	20 (1.6)
2003	— (†)	— (†)	— (†)	— (†)	— (†)	— (†)	— (†)	— (†)	— (†)	— (†)	— (†)	— (†)	— (†)	— (†)
2005	286 (0.6)	279 (0.8)	292 (0.7)	13 (1.1)	293 (0.7)	267 (1.2)	272 (1.2)	287 (1.9)	— (†)	— (†)	279 (6.3)	— (†)	26 (1.4)	21 (1.4)
2007	— (†)	— (†)	— (†)	— (†)	— (†)	— (†)	— (†)	— (†)	— (†)	— (†)	— (†)	— (†)	— (†)	— (†)
2009	288 (0.7)	282 (0.7)	294 (0.8)	12 (1.1)	296 (0.6)	269 (1.1)	274 (1.0)	298 (2.4)	— (†)	— (†)	283 (3.7)	— (†)	27 (1.3)	22 (1.2)
2011	— (†)	— (†)	— (†)	— (†)	— (†)	— (†)	— (†)	— (†)	— (†)	— (†)	— (†)	— (†)	— (†)	— (†)
2013	288 (0.6)	284 (0.6)	293 (0.7)	10 (0.9)	297 (0.6)	268 (0.9)	276 (0.9)	296 (1.9)	296 (2.0)	289 (6.0)	277 (3.5)	291 (2.5)	30 (1.0)	22 (1.0)

—Not available.
†Not applicable.
‡Reporting standards not met (too few cases for a reliable estimate).
[1]Prior to 2011, separate data for Asians, Pacific Islanders, and those of Two or more races were not collected.
[2]Accommodations were not permitted for this assessment.
NOTE: Scale ranges from 0 to 500. Includes public and private schools. For 1998 and later years, includes students tested with accommodations (1 to 11 percent of all students, depending on grade level and year); excludes only those students with disabilities and English language learners who were unable to be tested even with accommodations (2 to 6 percent of all students). Data on race/ethnicity are based on school reports. Race categories exclude persons of Hispanic ethnicity.
SOURCE: U.S. Department of Education, National Center for Education Statistics, National Assessment of Educational Progress (NAEP), 1992, 1994, 1998, 2000, 2002, 2003, 2005, 2007, 2009, 2011, and 2013 Reading Assessments, retrieved June 16, 2014, from the Main NAEP Data Explorer (http://nces.ed.gov/nationsreportcard/naepdata/). (This table was prepared September 2014.)

Table 221.12. Average National Assessment of Educational Progress (NAEP) reading scale score and percentage of students attaining selected NAEP reading achievement levels, by selected school and student characteristics and grade: Selected years, 1992 through 2013

[Standard errors appear in parentheses]

Grade and year	Percent of students in school eligible for free or reduced-price lunch					English language learner (ELL) status			Disability status[1]			Percent of all students attaining reading achievement levels		
	Average reading scale score[2]				Gap between low-poverty and high-poverty score	Average reading scale score[2]		Gap between non-ELL and ELL score	Average reading scale score[2]		Gap between non-SD and SD score	Below Basic[3]	At or above Basic[3]	At or above Proficient[4]
	0–25 percent eligible (low poverty)	26–50 percent eligible	51–75 percent eligible	76–100 percent eligible (high poverty)		ELL	Non-ELL		Identified as student with disability (SD)	Not identified as SD				
1	2	3	4	5	6	7	8	9	10	11	12	13	14	15
Grade 4														
1992[5]	— (†)	— (†)	— (†)	— (†)	— (†)	‡ (†)	‡ (†)	‡ (†)	‡ (†)	‡ (†)	‡ (†)	38 (1.1)	62 (1.1)	29 (1.2)
1994[5]	— (†)	— (†)	— (†)	— (†)	— (†)	‡ (†)	‡ (†)	‡ (†)	‡ (†)	‡ (†)	‡ (†)	40 (1.0)	60 (1.0)	30 (1.1)
1998	231 (1.4)	218 (1.6)	205 (1.8)	187 (3.1)	44 (3.4)	174 (5.2)	217 (1.0)	43 (5.3)	176 (4.6)	217 (1.1)	41 (4.7)	40 (1.2)	60 (1.2)	29 (0.9)
2000	231 (1.5)	218 (1.3)	205 (2.1)	184 (2.8)	48 (3.2)	167 (5.2)	216 (1.1)	49 (5.3)	167 (4.8)	217 (1.2)	50 (4.9)	41 (1.4)	59 (1.4)	29 (1.1)
2002	233 (0.4)	221 (0.5)	210 (0.7)	196 (0.7)	37 (0.9)	183 (2.1)	221 (0.3)	38 (2.1)	187 (0.8)	221 (0.5)	34 (0.9)	36 (0.5)	64 (0.5)	31 (0.4)
2003	233 (0.4)	221 (0.5)	211 (0.5)	194 (0.5)	39 (0.7)	186 (0.8)	221 (0.3)	35 (0.8)	185 (0.6)	221 (0.3)	36 (0.6)	37 (0.3)	63 (0.3)	31 (0.3)
2005	234 (0.3)	221 (0.3)	211 (0.4)	197 (0.4)	37 (0.5)	187 (0.5)	222 (0.2)	35 (0.6)	190 (0.5)	222 (0.2)	32 (0.6)	36 (0.3)	64 (0.3)	31 (0.2)
2007	235 (0.4)	223 (0.4)	212 (0.4)	200 (0.5)	35 (0.5)	188 (0.6)	224 (0.3)	36 (0.6)	191 (0.6)	224 (0.3)	33 (0.7)	33 (0.3)	67 (0.3)	33 (0.3)
2009	237 (0.4)	223 (0.5)	215 (0.5)	202 (0.5)	35 (0.6)	188 (0.8)	224 (0.3)	36 (0.8)	190 (0.7)	224 (0.3)	35 (0.7)	33 (0.3)	67 (0.3)	33 (0.4)
2011	238 (0.5)	226 (0.5)	217 (0.4)	203 (0.5)	35 (0.7)	188 (0.8)	225 (0.3)	36 (0.9)	186 (0.5)	225 (0.3)	39 (0.6)	33 (0.3)	67 (0.3)	34 (0.4)
2013	240 (0.4)	227 (0.5)	218 (0.6)	203 (0.4)	37 (0.6)	187 (0.7)	226 (0.3)	38 (0.7)	184 (0.6)	227 (0.3)	42 (0.7)	32 (0.3)	68 (0.3)	35 (0.3)
Grade 8														
1992[5]	— (†)	— (†)	— (†)	— (†)	— (†)	‡ (†)	‡ (†)	‡ (†)	‡ (†)	‡ (†)	‡ (†)	31 (1.0)	69 (1.0)	29 (1.1)
1994[5]	— (†)	— (†)	— (†)	— (†)	— (†)	‡ (†)	‡ (†)	‡ (†)	‡ (†)	‡ (†)	‡ (†)	30 (0.9)	70 (0.9)	30 (0.9)
1998	273 (1.1)	262 (1.3)	252 (2.1)	240 (1.8)	33 (2.1)	218 (2.5)	264 (0.7)	46 (2.6)	224 (3.7)	266 (0.7)	42 (3.7)	27 (0.8)	73 (0.8)	32 (1.1)
2000	— (†)	— (†)	— (†)	— (†)	— (†)	— (†)	— (†)	— (†)	— (†)	— (†)	— (†)	— (†)	— (†)	— (†)
2002	276 (0.6)	264 (0.6)	254 (0.8)	240 (1.1)	36 (1.3)	224 (1.4)	266 (0.4)	42 (1.4)	228 (1.0)	268 (0.4)	39 (1.0)	25 (0.5)	75 (0.5)	33 (0.5)
2003	275 (0.4)	263 (0.4)	253 (0.6)	239 (1.0)	36 (1.1)	222 (1.5)	265 (0.3)	43 (1.5)	225 (0.6)	267 (0.3)	42 (0.6)	26 (0.3)	74 (0.3)	32 (0.3)
2005	274 (0.3)	262 (0.3)	252 (0.4)	240 (0.6)	34 (0.7)	224 (0.9)	264 (0.2)	40 (0.9)	227 (0.5)	266 (0.2)	39 (0.5)	27 (0.2)	73 (0.2)	31 (0.2)
2007	275 (0.4)	263 (0.4)	253 (0.5)	241 (0.7)	34 (0.8)	223 (1.1)	265 (0.2)	42 (1.1)	227 (0.6)	266 (0.2)	39 (0.6)	26 (0.2)	74 (0.2)	31 (0.2)
2009	277 (0.5)	265 (0.4)	256 (0.4)	243 (0.7)	34 (0.8)	219 (1.0)	266 (0.2)	47 (1.0)	230 (0.6)	267 (0.3)	37 (0.7)	25 (0.3)	75 (0.3)	32 (0.4)
2011	279 (0.4)	268 (0.4)	258 (0.5)	247 (0.5)	32 (0.7)	224 (1.0)	267 (0.2)	44 (1.0)	231 (0.5)	269 (0.3)	38 (0.6)	24 (0.3)	76 (0.3)	34 (0.3)
2013	282 (0.5)	270 (0.5)	261 (0.4)	249 (0.5)	33 (0.7)	225 (0.9)	270 (0.2)	45 (1.0)	232 (0.6)	272 (0.2)	39 (0.7)	22 (0.3)	78 (0.3)	36 (0.3)
Grade 12														
1992[5]	— (†)	— (†)	— (†)	— (†)	— (†)	‡ (†)	‡ (†)	‡ (†)	‡ (†)	‡ (†)	‡ (†)	20 (0.6)	80 (0.6)	40 (0.8)
1994[5]	— (†)	— (†)	— (†)	— (†)	— (†)	‡ (†)	‡ (†)	‡ (†)	‡ (†)	‡ (†)	‡ (†)	25 (0.7)	75 (0.7)	36 (1.0)
1998	296 (0.9)	284 (1.7)	275 (2.0)	272 (3.3)	23 (3.4)	244 (2.6)	291 (0.6)	46 (2.7)	244 (3.2)	292 (0.6)	48 (3.2)	24 (0.7)	76 (0.7)	40 (0.7)
2000	— (†)	— (†)	— (†)	— (†)	— (†)	— (†)	— (†)	— (†)	— (†)	— (†)	— (†)	— (†)	— (†)	— (†)
2002	293 (0.9)	282 (1.6)	275 (2.6)	268 (2.4)	25 (2.6)	245 (2.4)	288 (0.7)	43 (2.5)	247 (2.0)	289 (0.7)	42 (2.1)	26 (0.8)	74 (0.8)	36 (0.8)
2003	— (†)	— (†)	— (†)	— (†)	— (†)	— (†)	— (†)	— (†)	— (†)	— (†)	— (†)	— (†)	— (†)	— (†)
2005	292 (1.1)	282 (1.1)	273 (1.8)	266 (2.0)	26 (2.3)	247 (2.4)	288 (0.6)	40 (2.4)	244 (1.8)	289 (0.6)	45 (1.9)	27 (0.8)	73 (0.8)	35 (0.7)
2007	— (†)	— (†)	— (†)	— (†)	— (†)	— (†)	— (†)	— (†)	— (†)	— (†)	— (†)	— (†)	— (†)	— (†)
2009	299 (1.1)	286 (0.8)	276 (1.1)	266 (1.0)	33 (1.5)	240 (2.1)	290 (0.7)	50 (2.2)	253 (1.4)	291 (0.7)	38 (1.6)	26 (0.6)	74 (0.6)	38 (0.8)
2011	— (†)	— (†)	— (†)	— (†)	— (†)	— (†)	— (†)	— (†)	— (†)	— (†)	— (†)	— (†)	— (†)	— (†)
2013	302 (1.1)	289 (0.9)	280 (0.9)	268 (1.5)	35 (1.9)	237 (1.9)	290 (0.5)	53 (2.0)	252 (1.4)	292 (0.6)	40 (1.5)	25 (0.6)	75 (0.6)	38 (0.7)

—Not available.
†Not applicable.
‡Reporting standards not met (too few cases for a reliable estimate).
[1]The student with disability (SD) variable used in this table includes students who have a 504 plan, even if they do not have an Individualized Education Plan (IEP).
[2]Scale ranges from 0 to 500.
[3]Basic denotes partial mastery of the knowledge and skills that are fundamental for proficient work at a given grade.
[4]Proficient represents solid academic performance. Students reaching this level have demonstrated competency over challenging subject matter.
[5]Accommodations were not permitted for this assessment.
NOTE: Includes public and private schools. For 1998 and later years, includes students tested with accommodations (1 to 11 percent of all students, depending on grade level and year); excludes only those students with disabilities and English language learners who were unable to be tested even with accommodations (2 to 6 percent of all students).
SOURCE: U.S. Department of Education, National Center for Education Statistics, National Assessment of Educational Progress (NAEP), 1992, 1994, 1998, 2000, 2002, 2003, 2005, 2007, 2009, 2011, and 2013 Reading Assessments, retrieved June 16, 2014, from the Main NAEP Data Explorer (http://nces.ed.gov/nationsreportcard/naepdata/). (This table was prepared September 2014.)

Table 221.20. Percentage of students at or above selected National Assessment of Educational Progress (NAEP) reading achievement levels, by grade and selected student characteristics: Selected years, 1998 through 2013

[Standard errors appear in parentheses]

Grade and selected student characteristic	1998 Basic[1]	1998 Proficient[2]	2000 Basic[1]	2000 Proficient[2]	2003 Basic[1]	2003 Proficient[2]	2005 Basic[1]	2005 Proficient[2]	2007 Basic[1]	2007 Proficient[2]	2009 Basic[1]	2009 Proficient[2]	2011 Basic[1]	2011 Proficient[2]	2013 Basic[1]	2013 Proficient[2]
1	2	3	4	5	6	7	8	9	10	11	12	13	14	15	16	17
4th grade, all students	60 (1.2)	29 (0.9)	59 (1.4)	29 (1.1)	63 (0.3)	31 (0.3)	64 (0.3)	31 (0.2)	67 (0.3)	33 (0.3)	67 (0.3)	33 (0.4)	67 (0.3)	34 (0.4)	68 (0.3)	35 (0.3)
Sex																
Male	57 (1.3)	27 (1.1)	55 (1.4)	25 (1.2)	60 (0.4)	28 (0.3)	61 (0.4)	29 (0.3)	64 (0.4)	30 (0.3)	64 (0.4)	30 (0.4)	64 (0.4)	31 (0.4)	65 (0.3)	32 (0.4)
Female	62 (1.5)	32 (1.2)	64 (1.6)	34 (1.4)	67 (0.4)	35 (0.4)	67 (0.3)	34 (0.3)	70 (0.3)	36 (0.4)	70 (0.4)	36 (0.4)	71 (0.4)	37 (0.5)	72 (0.4)	38 (0.4)
Race/ethnicity																
White	70 (1.3)	37 (1.2)	70 (1.2)	38 (1.2)	75 (0.3)	41 (0.4)	76 (0.3)	41 (0.3)	78 (0.3)	43 (0.4)	78 (0.3)	42 (0.4)	78 (0.3)	44 (0.4)	79 (0.3)	46 (0.4)
Black	36 (1.8)	10 (1.1)	35 (1.6)	10 (1.0)	40 (0.5)	13 (0.4)	42 (0.5)	13 (0.3)	46 (0.6)	14 (0.4)	48 (0.5)	16 (0.5)	49 (0.6)	17 (0.5)	50 (0.6)	18 (0.5)
Hispanic	37 (3.2)	13 (1.7)	37 (3.0)	13 (1.8)	44 (0.7)	15 (0.5)	46 (0.7)	16 (0.5)	50 (0.6)	17 (0.6)	49 (0.7)	17 (0.5)	51 (0.8)	18 (0.5)	53 (0.6)	20 (0.6)
Asian/Pacific Islander	58 (6.1)	30 (4.5)	70 (5.0)	41 (5.7)	70 (1.5)	38 (1.4)	73 (0.9)	42 (0.9)	77 (1.0)	46 (1.4)	80 (1.0)	49 (1.3)	80 (1.2)	49 (1.7)	82 (1.0)	51 (1.2)
Asian	— (†)	— (†)	—	—	— (†)	— (†)	— (†)	— (†)	— (†)	— (†)	— (†)	— (†)	81 (1.0)	50 (1.5)	82 (1.0)	53 (1.2)
Pacific Islander	— (†)	— (†)	—	—	— (†)	— (†)	— (†)	— (†)	— (†)	— (†)	— (†)	— (†)	61 (2.4)	28 (3.2)	57 (3.2)	28 (3.0)
American Indian/Alaska Native	‡ (†)	‡ (†)	63 (10.9)	28 (8.9)	47 (2.0)	16 (1.5)	48 (1.5)	18 (1.0)	49 (1.4)	18 (1.1)	50 (1.7)	20 (1.4)	47 (1.7)	18 (1.4)	51 (1.6)	21 (1.4)
Two or more races	— (†)	— (†)	—	—	—	—	—	—	—	—	—	—	50 (1.7)	20 (1.4)	73 (1.2)	40 (1.4)
Eligibility for free or reduced-price lunch																
Eligible	39 (1.8)	13 (1.0)	38 (1.8)	13 (1.1)	45 (0.4)	15 (0.3)	46 (0.4)	16 (0.4)	46 (0.4)	17 (0.4)	51 (0.4)	17 (0.3)	52 (0.4)	18 (0.3)	53 (0.4)	20 (0.4)
Not eligible	73 (0.9)	40 (1.2)	73 (1.4)	39 (1.5)	76 (0.3)	40 (0.3)	77 (0.2)	42 (0.2)	79 (0.3)	44 (0.4)	80 (0.3)	45 (0.3)	82 (0.3)	48 (0.5)	83 (0.4)	51 (0.5)
Unknown	69 (3.0)	37 (3.8)	71 (2.4)	40 (2.4)	76 (0.9)	43 (0.9)	77 (1.1)	45 (1.1)	80 (1.3)	46 (1.4)	81 (1.9)	50 (1.9)	82 (1.0)	48 (1.3)	83 (1.6)	51 (2.1)
8th grade, all students	73 (0.8)	32 (1.1)	— (†)	— (†)	74 (0.3)	32 (0.3)	73 (0.2)	31 (0.2)	74 (0.2)	31 (0.2)	75 (0.3)	32 (0.4)	76 (0.3)	34 (0.3)	78 (0.3)	36 (0.3)
Sex																
Male	67 (1.2)	26 (1.2)	—	—	69 (0.3)	27 (0.3)	68 (0.3)	26 (0.3)	69 (0.4)	26 (0.3)	71 (0.4)	28 (0.4)	72 (0.4)	29 (0.3)	74 (0.4)	31 (0.4)
Female	80 (0.9)	39 (1.3)	—	—	79 (0.3)	38 (0.3)	78 (0.2)	36 (0.2)	79 (0.3)	36 (0.3)	79 (0.4)	37 (0.5)	80 (0.3)	38 (0.4)	82 (0.3)	42 (0.4)
Race/ethnicity																
White	81 (0.9)	39 (1.3)	—	—	83 (0.2)	41 (0.3)	82 (0.2)	39 (0.2)	84 (0.3)	40 (0.3)	84 (0.2)	41 (0.4)	85 (0.2)	43 (0.4)	86 (0.2)	46 (0.4)
Black	53 (1.8)	13 (1.5)	—	—	54 (0.6)	13 (0.6)	52 (0.6)	12 (0.6)	55 (0.5)	13 (0.5)	57 (0.6)	14 (0.6)	59 (0.7)	15 (0.5)	61 (0.6)	17 (0.6)
Hispanic	53 (2.4)	14 (1.7)	—	—	56 (0.9)	15 (0.6)	56 (0.6)	15 (0.6)	58 (0.5)	15 (0.5)	61 (0.8)	17 (0.6)	64 (1.0)	19 (0.7)	68 (0.7)	22 (0.6)
Asian/Pacific Islander	75 (8.8)	33 (5.6)	—	—	79 (1.2)	40 (1.2)	80 (0.8)	40 (0.8)	80 (1.1)	41 (1.1)	83 (1.1)	45 (1.1)	83 (1.0)	47 (1.4)	86 (0.7)	52 (0.7)
Asian	— (†)	— (†)	—	—	— (†)	— (†)	— (†)	— (†)	— (†)	— (†)	— (†)	— (†)	84 (1.0)	49 (1.5)	87 (0.7)	54 (1.3)
Pacific Islander	— (†)	— (†)	—	—	— (†)	— (†)	— (†)	— (†)	— (†)	— (†)	— (†)	— (†)	63 (2.7)	24 (3.2)	70 (3.5)	27 (3.7)
American Indian/Alaska Native	‡ (†)	‡ (†)	—	—	57 (3.3)	17 (1.7)	59 (2.1)	17 (†)	56 (1.9)	18 (†)	62 (2.0)	21 (1.2)	63 (1.4)	22 (1.4)	62 (1.8)	19 (1.6)
Two or more races	— (†)	— (†)	—	—	—	—	—	—	—	—	—	—	79 (1.7)	39 (1.5)	81 (1.1)	40 (1.4)
Eligibility for free or reduced-price lunch																
Eligible	56 (1.3)	14 (1.0)	—	—	57 (0.5)	16 (0.5)	57 (0.4)	16 (0.4)	58 (0.4)	15 (0.2)	60 (0.5)	16 (0.3)	63 (0.5)	18 (0.4)	66 (0.4)	20 (0.4)
Not eligible	80 (1.0)	38 (1.5)	—	—	82 (0.3)	40 (0.6)	81 (0.3)	39 (0.3)	83 (0.3)	40 (0.3)	85 (0.3)	45 (0.3)	86 (0.3)	45 (0.4)	87 (0.3)	48 (0.4)
Unknown	80 (1.9)	43 (2.5)	—	—	81 (0.9)	42 (1.2)	84 (1.0)	45 (1.3)	86 (1.0)	48 (1.6)	89 (1.3)	51 (1.8)	90 (0.8)	54 (1.4)	92 (0.9)	59 (2.4)
12th grade, all students	76 (0.7)	40 (0.7)	— (†)	— (†)	— (†)	— (†)	73 (0.8)	35 (0.7)	— (†)	— (†)	74 (0.6)	38 (0.8)	— (†)	— (†)	75 (0.6)	38 (0.7)
Sex																
Male	70 (0.9)	32 (0.9)	—	—	—	—	67 (0.9)	29 (0.9)	—	—	69 (0.8)	32 (0.9)	—	—	70 (0.7)	33 (0.7)
Female	83 (0.8)	48 (1.1)	—	—	—	—	78 (0.9)	41 (0.9)	—	—	80 (0.6)	43 (1.0)	—	—	79 (0.7)	42 (0.9)
Race/ethnicity																
White	82 (0.7)	47 (0.9)	—	—	—	—	79 (0.8)	43 (0.9)	—	—	81 (0.5)	46 (0.8)	—	—	83 (0.6)	47 (0.8)
Black	57 (1.9)	17 (1.4)	—	—	—	—	54 (1.5)	16 (1.2)	—	—	57 (1.3)	17 (1.1)	—	—	56 (1.2)	16 (0.9)
Hispanic	62 (2.5)	24 (2.5)	—	—	—	—	60 (1.9)	20 (1.3)	—	—	61 (1.1)	22 (1.1)	—	—	64 (1.2)	23 (1.0)
Asian/Pacific Islander	74 (3.1)	38 (2.9)	—	—	—	—	74 (2.3)	36 (2.3)	—	—	81 (1.5)	49 (2.9)	—	—	80 (1.8)	47 (2.5)
Asian	— (†)	— (†)	—	—	—	—	— (†)	— (†)	—	—	— (†)	— (†)	—	—	80 (1.9)	48 (2.6)
Pacific Islander	— (†)	— (†)	—	—	—	—	— (†)	— (†)	—	—	— (†)	— (†)	—	—	75 (8.2)	39 (8.4)
American Indian/Alaska Native	‡ (†)	‡ (†)	—	—	—	—	67 (10.1)	26 (8.6)	—	—	70 (6.4)	29 (5.5)	—	—	65 (5.0)	26 (4.8)
Two or more races	— (†)	— (†)	—	—	—	—	—	—	—	—	—	—	—	—	77 (2.9)	38 (3.4)

—Not available.
†Not applicable.
‡Reporting standards not met (too few cases for a reliable estimate).
[1] Basic denotes partial mastery of the knowledge and skills that are fundamental for proficient work at a given grade.
[2] Proficient represents solid academic performance. Students reaching this level have demonstrated solid competency over challenging subject matter.

NOTE: Includes public and private schools. Includes students tested with accommodations (1 to 12 percent of all students, depending on grade level and year); excludes only those students with disabilities and English language learners who were unable to be tested even with accommodations (2 to 6 percent of all students). Race categories exclude persons of Hispanic ethnicity. Prior to 2011, separate data for Asians, Pacific Islanders, and those of two or more races were not collected.
SOURCE: U.S. Department of Education, National Center for Education Statistics, National Assessment of Educational Progress (NAEP), 1998, 2000, 2003, 2005, 2007, 2009, 2011, and 2013 Reading Assessments, retrieved June 9, 2014, from the Main NAEP Data Explorer (http://nces.ed.gov/nationsreportcard/naepdata/). (This table was prepared June 2014.)

Table 221.30. Average National Assessment of Educational Progress (NAEP) reading scale score and percentage distribution of students, by age, amount of reading for school and for fun, and time spent on homework and watching TV/video: Selected years, 1984 through 2012

[Standard errors appear in parentheses]

Amount of reading for school and for fun, time spent on homework and watching TV/video	9-year-olds 1984	9-year-olds 1994	9-year-olds 1999	9-year-olds 2008	9-year-olds 2012	13-year-olds 1984	13-year-olds 1994	13-year-olds 1999	13-year-olds 2008	13-year-olds 2012	17-year-olds 1984	17-year-olds 1994	17-year-olds 1999	17-year-olds 2008	17-year-olds 2012
1	2	3	4	5	6	7	8	9	10	11	12	13	14	15	16
Average scale score¹															
Pages read daily in school and for homework															
5 or fewer	208 (0.9)	203 (2.3)	202 (1.8)	210 (1.1)	207 (1.1)	250 (0.8)	249 (1.7)	249 (2.0)	250 (1.2)	251 (1.8)	273 (0.8)	271 (1.9)	273 (2.7)	271 (1.3)	274 (1.1)
6–10	215 (1.0)	214 (1.7)	212 (1.7)	219 (1.3)	219 (1.5)	261 (0.6)	261 (1.4)	262 (1.7)	258 (1.2)	261 (1.5)	287 (0.9)	284 (2.1)	285 (2.1)	284 (1.4)	283 (1.2)
11–15	220 (1.4)	217 (2.3)	221 (2.4)	224 (1.4)	225 (1.3)	264 (1.0)	266 (1.8)	263 (2.1)	263 (1.1)	266 (1.8)	294 (0.9)	288 (1.9)	292 (2.1)	290 (1.6)	289 (1.5)
16–20	215 (1.4)	209 (2.9)	214 (2.0)	225 (1.5)	226 (1.3)	263 (1.1)	263 (2.3)	264 (2.6)	267 (1.6)	268 (1.8)	296 (1.1)	298 (2.8)	292 (2.9)	296 (1.5)	297 (1.5)
More than 20	215 (1.6)	217 (2.4)	217 (2.1)	226 (1.2)	227 (1.0)	261 (1.5)	261 (2.0)	265 (2.0)	267 (1.4)	271 (1.3)	300 (1.2)	304 (2.2)	302 (1.9)	303 (1.3)	301 (1.5)
Frequency of reading for fun															
Almost every day	214 (1.1)	215 (2.3)	215 (2.4)	225 (1.2)	226 (0.9)	264 (1.4)	272 (3.2)	272 (3.2)	274 (1.4)	276 (1.4)	297 (1.5)	302 (4.2)	301 (4.9)	302 (1.3)	302 (1.3)
Once or twice a week	212 (1.7)	214 (3.1)	215 (2.6)	225 (1.3)	226 (1.5)	255 (1.4)	255 (3.1)	263 (3.2)	264 (1.1)	267 (1.4)	290 (1.7)	286 (4.1)	289 (4.9)	291 (1.7)	294 (1.4)
Once or twice a month	204 (3.3)	213 (5.8)	211 (4.2)	221 (1.7)	219 (2.0)	255 (2.1)	255 (5.7)	260 (3.7)	261 (1.3)	264 (1.7)	290 (1.8)	286 (4.5)	286 (4.8)	288 (1.3)	288 (1.5)
A few times a year	197 (4.2)	‡ (†)	‡ (†)	212 (2.0)	212 (1.9)	252 (3.6)	252 (5.4)	253 (4.4)	254 (2.0)	258 (1.3)	279 (2.7)	281 (8.2)	283 (4.4)	287 (1.5)	288 (1.3)
Never or hardly ever	198 (2.7)	193 (3.9)	195 (3.3)	211 (1.2)	208 (1.9)	239 (2.5)	237 (5.1)	242 (5.3)	247 (0.9)	249 (1.3)	269 (2.4)	258 (5.2)	262 (5.0)	269 (1.1)	272 (1.4)
TV/video watched on school day															
None	212 (3.4)	212 (4.8)	221 (4.6)	223 (3.0)	222 (3.1)	264 (2.7)	270 (5.1)	265 (6.0)	267 (3.0)	276 (3.5)	300 (1.6)	299 (3.4)	300 (2.8)	292 (2.4)	292 (2.5)
1 hour or less	217 (1.5)	216 (1.8)	218 (2.1)	225 (1.1)	229 (1.2)	269 (1.1)	270 (1.5)	270 (1.6)	266 (1.2)	269 (1.2)	300 (1.2)	299 (2.0)	298 (2.0)	293 (1.2)	292 (1.3)
2 hours	222 (1.1)	219 (2.1)	221 (1.7)	229 (1.1)	227 (1.1)	268 (0.8)	268 (1.4)	268 (1.6)	266 (1.1)	266 (1.5)	295 (0.9)	292 (1.8)	292 (2.1)	290 (1.1)	290 (1.3)
3 hours	220 (1.2)	218 (2.2)	218 (2.3)	227 (1.1)	226 (1.4)	264 (0.7)	262 (2.2)	263 (1.5)	262 (1.3)	261 (1.5)	288 (1.0)	284 (2.0)	282 (2.3)	284 (1.3)	284 (1.2)
4 hours	219 (1.0)	212 (1.8)	214 (2.4)	223 (1.4)	224 (1.4)	262 (0.9)	254 (2.2)	254 (2.4)	255 (1.5)	259 (1.5)	284 (1.0)	276 (4.1)	273 (4.1)	276 (2.3)	277 (2.1)
5 hours	214 (1.4)	209 (2.7)	208 (3.0)	219 (2.2)	213 (2.1)	257 (1.0)	250 (3.1)	253 (3.2)	255 (2.6)	255 (2.1)	277 (1.5)	269 (4.0)	275 (3.8)	273 (2.4)	275 (3.9)
6 hours or more	199 (0.8)	192 (2.7)	191 (1.7)	205 (1.2)	205 (1.2)	245 (1.0)	234 (3.1)	238 (1.8)	238 (1.4)	241 (1.4)	269 (1.5)	256 (3.7)	256 (5.2)	256 (2.3)	261 (2.6)
Percentage distribution															
Pages read daily in school and for homework															
5 or fewer	36 (0.8)	28 (1.4)	28 (1.4)	25 (0.9)	22 (0.7)	27 (0.7)	26 (0.9)	23 (1.0)	26 (0.8)	23 (0.8)	21 (0.8)	21 (1.2)	23 (1.4)	30 (0.9)	29 (0.7)
6–10	25 (0.4)	26 (0.6)	24 (0.9)	20 (0.5)	17 (0.6)	34 (0.5)	31 (0.6)	31 (1.1)	24 (0.6)	22 (0.6)	26 (0.6)	25 (0.9)	24 (0.8)	23 (0.5)	22 (0.6)
11–15	14 (0.4)	16 (0.5)	15 (0.7)	14 (0.5)	12 (0.4)	18 (0.4)	17 (0.5)	18 (0.8)	17 (0.5)	17 (0.5)	18 (0.5)	18 (0.6)	17 (0.8)	16 (0.4)	15 (0.4)
16–20	13 (0.4)	14 (0.9)	14 (0.7)	14 (0.6)	15 (0.6)	11 (0.2)	13 (0.5)	13 (0.7)	13 (0.4)	14 (0.5)	14 (0.4)	13 (0.6)	14 (0.8)	12 (0.4)	12 (0.5)
More than 20	13 (0.5)	17 (1.0)	19 (1.0)	28 (0.8)	34 (1.1)	11 (0.5)	14 (0.8)	16 (1.0)	22 (0.9)	24 (1.1)	21 (0.9)	23 (1.5)	22 (1.2)	19 (0.7)	22 (0.7)
Frequency of reading for fun															
Almost every day	53 (1.0)	58 (1.6)	54 (1.7)	48 (0.7)	53 (0.8)	35 (1.0)	32 (1.8)	28 (1.7)	26 (0.7)	27 (0.7)	31 (0.8)	30 (2.6)	25 (1.7)	20 (0.6)	19 (0.6)
Once or twice a week	28 (0.8)	25 (1.5)	25 (1.5)	23 (0.6)	23 (0.6)	35 (1.2)	32 (2.1)	36 (1.6)	25 (0.6)	26 (0.6)	33 (1.1)	31 (1.9)	28 (2.7)	22 (0.6)	21 (0.6)
Once or twice a month	7 (0.6)	5 (0.6)	5 (0.6)	8 (0.4)	7 (0.4)	14 (0.8)	14 (1.7)	17 (1.6)	13 (0.4)	14 (0.4)	17 (0.5)	15 (1.5)	19 (1.7)	17 (0.5)	16 (0.4)
A few times a year	3 (0.3)	3 (0.6)	4 (0.7)	8 (0.4)	7 (0.3)	7 (0.5)	10 (1.1)	11 (1.1)	12 (0.4)	11 (0.4)	10 (0.5)	12 (1.5)	12 (1.7)	16 (0.5)	18 (0.6)
Never or hardly ever	9 (0.5)	9 (0.8)	10 (0.8)	14 (0.6)	11 (0.4)	8 (0.6)	12 (1.7)	9 (1.4)	24 (0.7)	22 (0.7)	9 (0.6)	12 (1.4)	16 (2.4)	24 (0.6)	27 (0.6)
Time spent on homework yesterday															
No homework assigned	35 (1.3)	32 (2.1)	26 (1.6)	18 (1.3)	22 (1.6)	22 (0.7)	23 (1.4)	24 (1.2)	23 (1.2)	21 (1.2)	22 (0.9)	23 (1.4)	26 (1.0)	28 (0.8)	27 (0.9)
Didn't do assignment	4 (0.3)	4 (0.4)	4 (0.3)	5 (0.3)	4 (0.4)	4 (0.2)	6 (0.6)	5 (0.4)	7 (0.3)	5 (0.3)	11 (0.3)	11 (0.6)	13 (0.7)	12 (0.4)	11 (0.4)
Less than 1 hour	41 (1.0)	48 (1.7)	53 (1.4)	60 (1.2)	57 (1.3)	36 (0.6)	34 (1.0)	37 (1.4)	43 (1.2)	44 (0.9)	26 (0.4)	27 (0.9)	26 (1.0)	27 (0.5)	26 (0.8)
1 to 2 hours	13 (0.4)	11 (0.7)	12 (0.7)	12 (0.6)	12 (0.6)	29 (0.5)	28 (1.0)	26 (1.0)	21 (0.7)	23 (0.9)	27 (0.5)	26 (1.2)	23 (0.8)	22 (0.5)	23 (0.6)
More than 2 hours	6 (0.2)	4 (0.4)	5 (0.5)	5 (0.3)	5 (0.3)	9 (0.3)	9 (0.7)	8 (0.8)	6 (0.4)	7 (0.5)	13 (0.5)	13 (0.9)	12 (0.9)	10 (0.5)	13 (0.7)
TV/video watched on school day															
None	3 (0.2)	2 (0.2)	4 (0.8)	4 (0.3)	6 (0.3)	2 (0.2)	3 (0.3)	4 (0.6)	5 (0.3)	6 (0.3)	5 (0.3)	6 (0.8)	6 (0.3)	6 (0.3)	10 (0.3)
1 hour or less	14 (0.3)	23 (1.0)	24 (0.9)	24 (0.6)	27 (0.7)	12 (0.4)	20 (1.0)	22 (0.8)	25 (0.7)	29 (0.6)	25 (0.5)	31 (0.9)	34 (0.9)	33 (0.6)	34 (0.6)
2 hours	16 (0.4)	23 (0.7)	21 (0.9)	18 (0.5)	18 (0.5)	23 (0.4)	27 (0.8)	29 (0.9)	25 (0.5)	27 (0.5)	26 (0.3)	26 (0.8)	26 (0.7)	27 (0.6)	25 (0.5)
3 hours	15 (0.3)	16 (0.5)	14 (0.6)	12 (0.4)	12 (0.4)	23 (0.4)	22 (0.7)	20 (0.9)	18 (0.5)	15 (0.5)	20 (0.3)	18 (0.8)	17 (0.7)	16 (0.4)	16 (0.3)
4 hours	12 (0.2)	11 (0.5)	9 (0.4)	9 (0.4)	8 (0.4)	17 (0.4)	12 (0.7)	11 (0.6)	12 (0.4)	8 (0.3)	12 (0.3)	9 (0.6)	8 (0.5)	8 (0.4)	8 (0.3)
5 hours	9 (0.3)	6 (0.4)	6 (0.4)	6 (0.3)	6 (0.3)	10 (0.3)	7 (0.4)	5 (0.3)	5 (0.2)	4 (0.2)	6 (0.2)	5 (0.5)	4 (0.6)	4 (0.2)	5 (0.2)
6 hours or more	30 (0.7)	20 (0.8)	22 (1.2)	26 (0.8)	23 (0.8)	13 (0.4)	10 (0.9)	9 (0.6)	13 (0.4)	10 (0.5)	6 (0.2)	5 (0.4)	5 (0.6)	4 (0.4)	5 (0.3)

†Not applicable.
‡Reporting standards not met (too few cases for a reliable estimate).
¹Scale ranges from 0 to 500. Students scoring 150 (or higher) are able to follow brief written directions and carry out simple, discrete reading tasks. Students scoring 200 are able to understand, combine ideas, and make inferences based on short uncomplicated passages about specific or sequentially related information. Students scoring 250 are able to search for specific information, interrelate ideas, and make generalizations about literature, science, and social studies materials. Students scoring 300 are able to find, understand, summarize, and explain relatively complicated literary and informational material. For 1984, 1994, and 1999, accommodations were not permitted. For 2008 and later years, includes students tested with accommodations; excludes only those students with disabilities and English language learners who were unable to be tested even with accommodations (2 to 4 percent of all students, depending on age and assessment year). Detail may not sum to totals because of rounding.

NOTE: Includes public and private schools. For 1984, 1994, and 1999, accommodations were not permitted. For 2008 and later

SOURCE: U.S. Department of Education, National Center for Education Statistics, National Assessment of Educational Progress (NAEP), NAEP Trends in Academic Progress, 1996 and 1999; and 2008 and 2012 NAEP Long-Term Trend Reading Assessments, retrieved June 24, 2009, and July 02, 2013, from the Long-Term Trend NAEP Data Explorer (http://nces.ed.gov/nationsreportcard/naepdata/). (This table was prepared July 2013.)

Table 221.40. Average National Assessment of Educational Progress (NAEP) reading scale score of 4th-grade public school students and percentage attaining reading achievement levels, by state: Selected years, 1992 through 2013

[Standard errors appear in parentheses]

State	Average scale score[1]									Percent attaining reading achievement levels, 2013		
	1992	1998	2002	2003	2005	2007	2009	2011	2013	At or above Basic[2]	At or above Proficient[3]	At Advanced[4]
1	2	3	4	5	6	7	8	9	10	11	12	13
United States	215 (1.0)	213 (1.2)	217 (0.5)	216 (0.3)	217 (0.2)	220 (0.3)	220 (0.3)	220 (0.3)	221 (0.3)	67 (0.3)	34 (0.3)	8 (0.2)
Alabama	207 (1.7)	211 (1.9)	207 (1.4)	207 (1.7)	208 (1.2)	216 (1.3)	216 (1.2)	220 (1.3)	219 (1.2)	65 (1.5)	31 (1.4)	6 (0.7)
Alaska..............................	— (†)	— (†)	— (†)	212 (1.6)	211 (1.4)	214 (1.0)	211 (1.2)	208 (1.1)	209 (1.0)	58 (1.2)	27 (1.2)	6 (0.5)
Arizona	209 (1.2)	206 (1.4)	205 (1.5)	209 (1.2)	207 (1.6)	210 (1.2)	210 (1.2)	212 (1.2)	213 (1.4)	60 (1.6)	28 (1.4)	5 (0.6)
Arkansas..........................	211 (1.2)	209 (1.6)	213 (1.4)	214 (1.4)	217 (1.1)	217 (1.2)	216 (1.1)	217 (1.0)	219 (0.9)	66 (1.1)	32 (1.3)	7 (0.7)
California[5,6]	202 (2.0)	202 (2.5)	206 (2.5)	206 (1.2)	207 (0.7)	209 (1.0)	210 (1.5)	211 (1.8)	213 (1.2)	58 (1.4)	27 (1.3)	6 (0.7)
Colorado..........................	217 (1.1)	220 (1.4)	— (†)	224 (1.2)	224 (1.1)	224 (1.1)	226 (1.2)	223 (1.3)	227 (1.0)	74 (1.2)	41 (1.5)	10 (0.9)
Connecticut......................	222 (1.3)	230 (1.6)	229 (1.1)	228 (1.1)	226 (1.0)	227 (1.3)	229 (1.1)	227 (1.3)	230 (0.9)	76 (1.2)	43 (1.2)	12 (0.9)
Delaware[7]	213 (0.6)	207 (1.7)	224 (0.6)	224 (0.7)	226 (0.8)	225 (0.7)	226 (0.5)	225 (0.7)	226 (0.8)	73 (1.1)	38 (1.2)	9 (0.6)
District of Columbia	188 (0.8)	179 (1.2)	191 (0.9)	188 (0.9)	191 (1.0)	197 (0.9)	202 (1.0)	201 (0.8)	206 (0.9)	50 (1.2)	23 (0.9)	7 (0.6)
Florida..............................	208 (1.2)	206 (1.4)	214 (1.4)	218 (1.1)	220 (0.9)	224 (0.8)	226 (1.0)	225 (1.1)	227 (1.1)	75 (1.2)	39 (1.5)	9 (0.8)
Georgia............................	212 (1.5)	209 (1.4)	215 (1.0)	214 (1.3)	214 (1.2)	219 (0.9)	218 (1.1)	221 (1.1)	222 (1.1)	67 (1.3)	34 (1.5)	9 (0.8)
Hawaii..............................	203 (1.7)	200 (1.5)	208 (0.9)	208 (1.4)	210 (1.0)	213 (1.1)	211 (1.0)	214 (1.0)	215 (1.0)	62 (1.3)	30 (1.2)	7 (0.7)
Idaho...............................	219 (0.9)	— (†)	220 (1.1)	218 (1.0)	222 (0.9)	223 (0.8)	221 (0.9)	221 (0.8)	219 (0.9)	68 (1.2)	33 (1.2)	7 (0.6)
Illinois.............................	— (†)	‡ (†)	‡ (†)	222 (1.4)	216 (1.6)	217 (1.2)	219 (1.2)	219 (1.4)	219 (1.1)	64 (1.5)	34 (1.4)	8 (0.8)
Indiana............................	221 (1.3)	— (†)	222 (1.4)	220 (1.0)	218 (1.1)	222 (0.9)	223 (1.1)	221 (0.9)	225 (1.0)	73 (1.2)	38 (1.5)	8 (0.8)
Iowa[5,6]	225 (1.1)	220 (1.6)	223 (1.1)	223 (1.1)	221 (0.9)	225 (1.1)	221 (1.2)	221 (0.8)	224 (1.1)	72 (1.3)	38 (1.4)	9 (0.9)
Kansas[5,6]	— (†)	221 (1.4)	222 (1.4)	220 (1.2)	221 (1.3)	225 (1.1)	224 (1.3)	224 (1.0)	223 (1.3)	71 (1.6)	38 (1.7)	8 (0.9)
Kentucky..........................	213 (1.3)	218 (1.5)	219 (1.1)	219 (1.3)	220 (1.1)	222 (1.1)	226 (1.1)	225 (1.0)	224 (1.2)	71 (1.3)	36 (1.7)	9 (0.8)
Louisiana.........................	204 (1.2)	200 (1.6)	207 (1.7)	205 (1.4)	209 (1.3)	207 (1.6)	207 (1.1)	210 (1.4)	210 (1.3)	56 (1.7)	23 (1.3)	4 (0.6)
Maine...............................	227 (1.1)	225 (1.4)	225 (1.1)	224 (0.9)	225 (0.9)	224 (0.9)	224 (0.9)	222 (0.7)	225 (0.9)	71 (1.0)	37 (1.2)	9 (0.8)
Maryland..........................	211 (1.6)	212 (1.6)	217 (1.5)	219 (1.4)	220 (1.3)	225 (1.1)	226 (1.4)	231 (0.9)	232 (1.3)	77 (1.2)	45 (1.8)	14 (1.3)
Massachusetts[5]	226 (0.9)	223 (1.4)	234 (1.1)	228 (1.2)	231 (0.9)	236 (1.1)	234 (1.1)	237 (1.0)	232 (1.1)	79 (1.1)	47 (1.5)	14 (1.0)
Michigan..........................	216 (1.5)	216 (1.5)	219 (1.1)	219 (1.2)	218 (1.5)	220 (1.4)	218 (1.0)	219 (1.2)	217 (1.4)	64 (1.6)	31 (1.6)	6 (0.8)
Minnesota[5,6]	221 (1.2)	219 (1.7)	225 (1.1)	223 (1.1)	225 (1.3)	225 (1.1)	223 (1.3)	222 (1.2)	227 (1.2)	74 (1.5)	41 (1.4)	10 (0.8)
Mississippi.......................	199 (1.3)	203 (1.3)	203 (1.3)	205 (1.3)	204 (1.4)	208 (1.0)	211 (1.1)	209 (1.2)	209 (0.9)	53 (1.3)	21 (1.0)	3 (0.5)
Missouri...........................	220 (1.2)	216 (1.3)	220 (1.3)	222 (1.2)	221 (0.9)	221 (1.1)	224 (1.1)	220 (0.9)	222 (1.0)	70 (1.3)	35 (1.4)	7 (0.7)
Montana[5,6]	— (†)	225 (1.5)	224 (1.8)	223 (1.2)	225 (1.1)	227 (1.0)	225 (0.8)	225 (0.6)	223 (0.8)	70 (1.1)	35 (1.1)	7 (0.7)
Nebraska[7]	221 (1.1)	— (†)	222 (1.5)	221 (1.0)	221 (1.2)	223 (1.3)	223 (1.0)	223 (1.0)	223 (1.0)	71 (1.1)	37 (1.4)	8 (0.7)
Nevada	— (†)	206 (1.8)	209 (1.2)	207 (1.2)	207 (1.2)	211 (1.2)	211 (1.1)	213 (1.0)	214 (1.1)	61 (1.4)	27 (1.4)	5 (0.6)
New Hampshire[5,7]..............	228 (1.2)	226 (1.7)	— (†)	228 (1.0)	227 (0.9)	229 (0.9)	229 (1.0)	230 (0.8)	232 (0.9)	80 (1.0)	45 (1.5)	11 (0.9)
New Jersey[7]	223 (1.4)	— (†)	— (†)	225 (1.2)	223 (1.3)	231 (1.2)	229 (0.9)	231 (1.2)	229 (1.3)	75 (1.3)	42 (1.7)	12 (1.0)
New Mexico	211 (1.5)	205 (1.4)	208 (1.6)	203 (1.5)	207 (1.3)	212 (1.3)	208 (1.4)	208 (1.0)	206 (1.1)	52 (1.2)	21 (0.9)	4 (0.6)
New York[5,6,7]	215 (1.4)	215 (1.6)	222 (1.5)	222 (1.1)	223 (1.1)	224 (1.0)	224 (1.0)	222 (1.1)	224 (1.2)	70 (1.4)	37 (1.5)	9 (0.8)
North Carolina	212 (1.1)	213 (1.6)	222 (1.0)	221 (1.0)	217 (1.0)	218 (0.9)	219 (1.1)	221 (1.2)	222 (1.1)	69 (1.2)	35 (1.2)	8 (0.7)
North Dakota[6]	226 (1.1)	— (†)	224 (1.0)	222 (0.9)	225 (0.7)	226 (0.9)	226 (0.8)	226 (0.5)	224 (0.5)	73 (0.9)	34 (0.9)	6 (0.5)
Ohio	217 (1.3)	— (†)	222 (1.3)	222 (1.2)	223 (1.4)	226 (1.1)	225 (1.1)	224 (1.0)	224 (1.2)	71 (1.3)	37 (1.6)	9 (0.9)
Oklahoma.........................	220 (0.9)	219 (1.2)	213 (1.2)	214 (1.2)	214 (1.1)	217 (1.1)	217 (1.1)	215 (1.1)	217 (1.1)	65 (1.3)	30 (1.3)	5 (0.6)
Oregon	— (†)	212 (1.8)	220 (1.4)	218 (1.3)	217 (1.4)	215 (1.4)	218 (1.2)	216 (1.1)	219 (1.3)	66 (1.4)	33 (1.6)	9 (1.0)
Pennsylvania....................	221 (1.3)	— (†)	221 (1.2)	219 (1.2)	223 (1.3)	226 (1.0)	224 (1.4)	227 (1.2)	226 (1.3)	73 (1.4)	40 (1.6)	10 (1.0)
Rhode Island	217 (1.8)	218 (1.4)	220 (1.2)	216 (1.3)	216 (1.2)	219 (1.0)	223 (1.1)	222 (0.8)	223 (0.9)	70 (1.2)	38 (1.2)	9 (0.7)
South Carolina	210 (1.3)	209 (1.4)	214 (1.3)	215 (1.3)	213 (1.3)	214 (1.2)	216 (1.1)	215 (1.2)	214 (1.2)	60 (1.4)	28 (1.5)	6 (0.8)
South Dakota....................	— (†)	— (†)	— (†)	222 (1.2)	222 (0.5)	223 (1.0)	222 (0.6)	220 (0.9)	218 (1.0)	66 (1.2)	32 (1.1)	6 (0.5)
Tennessee[6]	212 (1.4)	212 (1.4)	214 (1.2)	212 (1.6)	214 (1.4)	216 (1.2)	217 (1.2)	215 (1.1)	220 (1.4)	67 (1.5)	34 (1.6)	8 (0.9)
Texas...............................	213 (1.6)	214 (1.9)	217 (1.7)	215 (1.0)	219 (0.8)	220 (0.9)	219 (1.2)	218 (1.5)	217 (1.1)	63 (1.3)	28 (1.2)	6 (0.7)
Utah................................	220 (1.1)	216 (1.2)	222 (1.0)	219 (1.0)	221 (1.1)	221 (1.2)	219 (1.0)	220 (1.0)	223 (1.1)	71 (1.2)	37 (1.4)	8 (0.7)
Vermont	— (†)	— (†)	227 (1.1)	226 (0.9)	227 (0.9)	228 (0.8)	229 (0.8)	227 (0.6)	228 (0.6)	75 (1.0)	42 (1.1)	12 (0.7)
Virginia............................	221 (1.4)	217 (1.2)	225 (1.3)	223 (1.5)	226 (0.8)	227 (1.1)	227 (1.2)	226 (1.1)	229 (1.3)	74 (1.3)	43 (1.6)	12 (1.2)
Washington[6]	— (†)	218 (1.4)	224 (1.2)	221 (1.1)	224 (1.1)	224 (1.4)	221 (1.2)	221 (1.1)	225 (1.4)	72 (1.3)	40 (1.7)	10 (1.1)
West Virginia....................	216 (1.3)	216 (1.7)	219 (1.2)	219 (1.0)	215 (0.8)	215 (1.1)	215 (1.0)	214 (0.8)	215 (0.8)	62 (1.3)	27 (1.1)	5 (0.6)
Wisconsin[5,6]....................	224 (1.0)	222 (1.1)	‡ (†)	221 (0.8)	221 (1.0)	223 (1.2)	220 (1.1)	221 (0.8)	221 (1.6)	68 (1.8)	35 (1.6)	8 (0.8)
Wyoming	223 (1.1)	218 (1.5)	221 (1.0)	222 (0.8)	223 (0.7)	225 (0.5)	223 (0.7)	224 (0.8)	226 (0.6)	75 (1.0)	37 (0.9)	7 (0.5)
Department of Defense dependents schools[8]	— (†)	220 (0.7)	224 (0.4)	224 (0.5)	226 (0.6)	229 (0.5)	228 (0.5)	229 (0.5)	232 (0.6)	82 (0.9)	43 (1.1)	8 (0.6)

—Not available.
†Not applicable.
‡Reporting standards not met. Participation rates fell below the required standards for reporting.
[1]Scale ranges from 0 to 500.
[2]Basic denotes partial mastery of the knowledge and skills that are fundamental for proficient work at the 4th-grade level.
[3]Proficient represents solid academic performance for 4th graders. Students reaching this level have demonstrated competency over challenging subject matter.
[4]Advanced signifies superior performance.
[5]Did not satisfy one or more of the guidelines for school participation in 1998. Data are subject to appreciable nonresponse bias.
[6]Did not satisfy one or more of the guidelines for school participation in 2002. Data are subject to appreciable nonresponse bias.
[7]Did not satisfy one or more of the guidelines for school participation in 1992. Data are subject to appreciable nonresponse bias.

[8]Prior to 2005, NAEP divided the Department of Defense (DoD) schools into two jurisdictions, domestic and overseas. In 2005, NAEP began combining the DoD domestic and overseas schools into a single jurisdiction. Data shown in this table for years prior to 2005 were recalculated for comparability.
NOTE: With the exception of 1992, includes public school students who were tested with accommodations; excludes only those students with disabilities (SD) and English language learners (ELL) who were unable to be tested even with accommodations. SD and ELL populations, accommodation rates, and exclusion rates vary from state to state. Race categories exclude persons of Hispanic ethnicity.
SOURCE: U.S. Department of Education, National Center for Education Statistics, National Assessment of Educational Progress (NAEP), 1992, 1998, 2002, 2003, 2005, 2007, 2009, 2011, and 2013 Reading Assessments, retrieved November 8, 2013, from the Main NAEP Data Explorer (http://nces.ed.gov/nationsreportcard/naepdata/). (This table was prepared November 2013.)

Table 221.50. Average National Assessment of Educational Progress (NAEP) reading scale score and percentage of 4th-grade public school students, by race/ethnicity and state: 2013

[Standard errors appear in parentheses]

State	Average scale score[1]													Percent of students												
	White		Black		Hispanic		Asian		Pacific Islander		American Indian/ Alaska Native		White		Black		Hispanic		Asian		Pacific Islander		American Indian/ Alaska Native	
1	2		3		4		5		6		7		8		9		10		11		12		13	
United States	231	(0.3)	205	(0.5)	207	(0.5)	237	(1.1)	210	(2.5)	206	(1.5)	51	(0.4)	15	(0.3)	25	(0.4)	5	(0.2)	#	(†)	1	(#)
Alabama	227	(1.3)	202	(1.8)	206	(4.1)	‡	(†)	‡	(†)	‡	(†)	60	(1.6)	30	(1.8)	7	(0.9)	2	(0.2)	#	(†)	1	(0.3)
Alaska	228	(1.1)	203	(4.3)	213	(2.9)	207	(2.9)	197	(5.1)	173	(2.1)	47	(1.0)	4	(0.3)	7	(0.4)	8	(0.5)	3	(0.3)	24	(1.0)
Arizona	228	(1.4)	206	(4.0)	202	(1.7)	219	(8.8)	‡	(†)	186	(3.9)	41	(1.5)	5	(0.4)	45	(1.5)	3	(0.5)	#	(†)	5	(0.6)
Arkansas	226	(1.0)	200	(2.4)	211	(2.8)	‡	(†)	‡	(†)	‡	(†)	64	(1.3)	21	(1.4)	11	(0.9)	2	(0.3)	#	(†)	1	(0.2)
California	232	(1.6)	202	(2.6)	201	(1.5)	229	(2.8)	‡	(†)	‡	(†)	26	(1.7)	6	(0.7)	54	(1.8)	11	(1.3)	1	(0.1)	1	(0.2)
Colorado	237	(1.2)	203	(4.5)	210	(1.6)	230	(5.0)	‡	(†)	‡	(†)	57	(1.1)	5	(0.5)	31	(1.2)	4	(0.4)	#	(†)	1	(0.2)
Connecticut	238	(1.0)	208	(2.6)	209	(2.2)	246	(3.2)	‡	(†)	‡	(†)	61	(1.3)	11	(0.7)	20	(1.1)	5	(0.4)	#	(†)	#	(†)
Delaware	235	(0.9)	213	(1.3)	216	(1.8)	249	(3.6)	‡	(†)	‡	(†)	47	(1.0)	31	(0.8)	15	(0.7)	4	(0.3)	#	(†)	1	(0.2)
District of Columbia	259	(2.3)	197	(1.0)	208	(2.1)	‡	(†)	‡	(†)	‡	(†)	10	(0.3)	73	(0.5)	14	(0.4)	2	(0.2)	#	(†)	#	(†)
Florida	236	(1.4)	212	(1.6)	225	(1.5)	248	(2.9)	‡	(†)	‡	(†)	40	(1.7)	22	(1.3)	31	(1.6)	3	(0.3)	#	(†)	#	(†)
Georgia	233	(1.5)	209	(1.7)	213	(2.0)	245	(3.5)	‡	(†)	‡	(†)	44	(1.4)	34	(1.9)	15	(1.2)	4	(0.4)	#	(†)	#	(†)
Hawaii	231	(1.9)	223	(6.4)	211	(3.2)	218	(1.7)	203	(1.5)	‡	(†)	15	(0.8)	2	(0.3)	6	(0.5)	36	(1.1)	33	(1.1)	1	(0.1)
Idaho	224	(1.0)	‡	(†)	198	(1.9)	‡	(†)	‡	(†)	‡	(†)	78	(0.8)	1	(0.2)	16	(0.7)	1	(0.2)	#	(†)	1	(0.3)
Illinois	231	(1.8)	199	(2.7)	204	(1.6)	242	(3.4)	‡	(†)	‡	(†)	48	(1.6)	17	(1.2)	27	(1.5)	5	(0.6)	#	(†)	#	(†)
Indiana	229	(1.1)	207	(3.0)	215	(2.3)	236	(7.3)	‡	(†)	‡	(†)	74	(1.6)	10	(1.6)	9	(0.9)	2	(0.4)	#	(†)	#	(†)
Iowa	227	(1.3)	200	(3.8)	210	(2.7)	224	(7.3)	‡	(†)	‡	(†)	80	(1.0)	5	(0.5)	8	(0.7)	3	(0.4)	#	(†)	#	(†)
Kansas	230	(1.2)	200	(3.9)	208	(2.1)	228	(5.6)	‡	(†)	‡	(†)	67	(1.4)	7	(0.8)	17	(1.4)	3	(0.4)	#	(†)	1	(0.2)
Kentucky	227	(1.3)	204	(2.3)	220	(3.1)	243	(4.9)	‡	(†)	‡	(†)	80	(1.0)	11	(0.8)	5	(0.7)	2	(0.3)	#	(†)	#	(†)
Louisiana	223	(1.3)	198	(1.5)	212	(3.4)	‡	(†)	‡	(†)	‡	(†)	44	(2.0)	48	(1.8)	4	(0.6)	1	(0.2)	#	(†)	1	(0.3)
Maine	226	(0.9)	192	(5.0)	‡	(†)	‡	(†)	‡	(†)	‡	(†)	92	(0.4)	3	(0.3)	2	(0.2)	2	(0.2)	#	(†)	1	(0.2)
Maryland	244	(1.6)	214	(1.3)	224	(2.7)	255	(3.8)	‡	(†)	‡	(†)	43	(1.9)	34	(1.7)	12	(0.9)	6	(1.0)	#	(†)	#	(†)
Massachusetts	241	(1.2)	209	(3.3)	208	(2.5)	239	(3.3)	‡	(†)	‡	(†)	64	(1.5)	7	(1.0)	18	(1.2)	7	(0.8)	#	(†)	#	(†)
Michigan	224	(1.8)	196	(2.3)	209	(3.1)	228	(7.4)	‡	(†)	‡	(†)	66	(1.9)	18	(2.1)	9	(1.8)	3	(0.7)	#	(†)	1	(0.3)
Minnesota	233	(1.0)	208	(3.2)	207	(3.1)	223	(5.6)	‡	(†)	‡	(†)	72	(1.7)	9	(1.2)	7	(0.7)	7	(1.0)	#	(†)	1	(0.2)
Mississippi	222	(1.0)	197	(1.5)	206	(3.0)	‡	(†)	‡	(†)	‡	(†)	44	(1.3)	52	(1.3)	3	(0.4)	1	(0.2)	#	(†)	#	(†)
Missouri	228	(1.0)	200	(2.0)	219	(4.6)	‡	(†)	‡	(†)	‡	(†)	72	(1.3)	19	(1.1)	5	(0.7)	2	(0.3)	#	(†)	1	(0.1)
Montana	228	(0.8)	‡	(†)	214	(4.2)	‡	(†)	‡	(†)	198	(2.4)	79	(1.0)	1	(0.2)	4	(0.3)	1	(0.2)	#	(†)	13	(0.9)
Nebraska	229	(1.1)	202	(3.1)	207	(2.1)	232	(6.1)	‡	(†)	‡	(†)	70	(1.3)	6	(0.6)	17	(1.0)	2	(0.3)	#	(†)	1	(0.3)
Nevada	226	(1.2)	201	(2.6)	202	(1.5)	227	(3.2)	‡	(†)	‡	(†)	36	(1.5)	10	(0.8)	41	(1.5)	5	(0.5)	1	(0.2)	1	(0.1)
New Hampshire	233	(0.9)	215	(5.0)	209	(4.1)	237	(4.4)	‡	(†)	‡	(†)	89	(0.8)	2	(0.2)	4	(0.5)	4	(0.4)	#	(†)	#	(†)
New Jersey	238	(1.3)	211	(2.2)	212	(2.3)	250	(2.4)	‡	(†)	‡	(†)	53	(1.6)	17	(1.3)	21	(1.7)	8	(1.3)	#	(†)	#	(†)
New Mexico	225	(1.8)	210	(5.8)	201	(1.2)	‡	(†)	‡	(†)	187	(3.4)	24	(1.1)	2	(0.2)	63	(1.0)	1	(0.2)	#	(†)	9	(1.1)
New York	233	(1.3)	211	(2.2)	210	(1.8)	237	(2.4)	‡	(†)	‡	(†)	48	(1.9)	18	(1.5)	23	(1.5)	9	(0.8)	#	(†)	#	(†)
North Carolina	232	(1.2)	210	(1.5)	210	(2.2)	238	(4.1)	‡	(†)	206	(7.3)	49	(1.5)	26	(1.2)	16	(1.1)	3	(0.3)	#	(†)	2	(0.8)
North Dakota	227	(0.5)	211	(4.4)	217	(4.2)	‡	(†)	‡	(†)	201	(2.1)	84	(0.4)	3	(0.2)	2	(0.2)	1	(0.1)	#	(†)	9	(0.3)
Ohio	231	(1.1)	195	(2.8)	214	(2.9)	244	(5.6)	‡	(†)	‡	(†)	71	(1.8)	17	(1.6)	4	(0.6)	2	(0.3)	#	(†)	#	(†)
Oklahoma	223	(1.3)	201	(2.5)	204	(2.0)	228	(5.1)	‡	(†)	217	(2.4)	52	(1.2)	11	(0.8)	14	(0.9)	2	(0.3)	#	(†)	15	(0.8)
Oregon	225	(1.3)	200	(4.0)	199	(2.0)	234	(6.6)	‡	(†)	‡	(†)	64	(1.1)	3	(0.4)	21	(1.1)	4	(0.7)	1	(0.1)	2	(0.4)
Pennsylvania	233	(1.2)	208	(3.0)	208	(3.6)	236	(3.4)	‡	(†)	‡	(†)	69	(1.9)	16	(1.4)	8	(1.1)	4	(0.5)	#	(†)	#	(†)
Rhode Island	233	(0.9)	205	(2.8)	201	(1.8)	224	(4.9)	‡	(†)	‡	(†)	63	(1.2)	9	(0.4)	22	(1.1)	3	(0.3)	#	(†)	1	(0.1)
South Carolina	224	(1.7)	197	(1.8)	211	(3.8)	‡	(†)	‡	(†)	‡	(†)	53	(1.3)	35	(1.4)	7	(0.7)	1	(0.2)	#	(†)	#	(†)
South Dakota	225	(0.8)	202	(6.1)	207	(4.2)	‡	(†)	‡	(†)	191	(2.5)	76	(1.1)	3	(0.3)	4	(0.4)	2	(0.3)	#	(†)	14	(1.2)
Tennessee	227	(1.3)	201	(2.7)	203	(3.6)	240	(5.4)	‡	(†)	‡	(†)	67	(1.7)	21	(1.4)	8	(0.7)	2	(0.3)	#	(†)	#	(†)
Texas	233	(1.6)	209	(2.1)	206	(1.2)	252	(4.5)	‡	(†)	‡	(†)	30	(1.4)	14	(1.0)	50	(1.4)	4	(0.8)	#	(†)	#	(†)
Utah	229	(0.9)	‡	(†)	196	(2.0)	‡	(†)	‡	(†)	‡	(†)	77	(1.3)	1	(0.2)	16	(1.1)	1	(0.2)	1	(0.2)	1	(0.3)
Vermont	229	(0.7)	‡	(†)	‡	(†)	‡	(†)	‡	(†)	‡	(†)	91	(0.4)	2	(0.2)	1	(0.2)	2	(0.2)	#	(†)	#	(†)
Virginia	236	(1.3)	211	(2.2)	211	(3.4)	248	(4.0)	‡	(†)	‡	(†)	54	(1.7)	20	(1.1)	12	(1.0)	9	(1.2)	#	(†)	#	(†)
Washington	232	(1.4)	211	(3.9)	205	(2.6)	243	(3.9)	‡	(†)	‡	(†)	58	(1.1)	4	(0.5)	21	(1.3)	8	(1.0)	1	(0.2)	1	(0.4)
West Virginia	215	(0.8)	203	(3.5)	‡	(†)	‡	(†)	‡	(†)	‡	(†)	92	(0.7)	5	(0.5)	1	(0.2)	1	(0.2)	#	(†)	#	(†)
Wisconsin	228	(1.1)	193	(3.0)	201	(3.5)	223	(3.9)	‡	(†)	211	(6.6)	71	(1.7)	10	(0.9)	12	(1.1)	4	(0.4)	#	(†)	2	(0.7)
Wyoming	229	(0.6)	‡	(†)	215	(1.6)	‡	(†)	‡	(†)	199	(2.7)	79	(0.4)	1	(0.1)	13	(0.3)	1	(0.2)	#	(†)	4	(0.2)
Department of Defense dependents schools.....	236	(0.9)	222	(1.6)	228	(1.5)	235	(2.5)	‡	(†)	‡	(†)	47	(0.5)	15	(0.4)	19	(0.5)	6	(0.3)	1	(0.2)	#	(†)

†Not applicable.
#Rounds to zero.
‡Reporting standards not met (too few cases for a reliable estimate).
[1]Scale ranges from 0 to 500.
NOTE: Includes public school students who were tested with accommodations; excludes only those students with disabilities (SD) and English language learners (ELL) who were unable to be tested even with accommodations. SD and ELL populations, accommodation rates, and exclusion rates vary from state to state. Race/ethnicity based on school records. Race categories exclude persons of Hispanic ethnicity. Detail may not sum to totals because of rounding and because table does not include students classified as "Two or more races."
SOURCE: U.S. Department of Education, National Center for Education Statistics, National Assessment of Educational Progress (NAEP), 2013 Reading Assessment, retrieved November 15, 2013, from the Main NAEP Data Explorer (http://nces.ed.gov/nationsreportcard/naepdata/). (This table was prepared November 2013.)

Table 221.60. Average National Assessment of Educational Progress (NAEP) reading scale score of 8th-grade public school students and percentage attaining reading achievement levels, by locale and state: Selected years, 2003 through 2013

[Standard errors appear in parentheses]

State	Average scale score[1]						Percent attaining reading achievement levels, 2013		Average scale score[1] by school locale, 2013			
	2003	2005	2007	2009	2011	2013	At or above *Basic*[2]	At or above *Proficient*[3]	City	Suburb	Town	Rural
1	2	3	4	5	6	7	8	9	10	11	12	13
United States	**261 (0.2)**	**260 (0.2)**	**261 (0.2)**	**262 (0.3)**	**264 (0.2)**	**266 (0.2)**	**77 (0.3)**	**34 (0.3)**	**260 (0.6)**	**270 (0.4)**	**263 (0.6)**	**268 (0.5)**
Alabama	253 (1.5)	252 (1.4)	252 (1.0)	255 (1.1)	258 (1.5)	257 (1.2)	68 (1.3)	25 (1.5)	250 (3.5)	261 (3.4)	259 (1.8)	259 (1.4)
Alaska	256 (1.1)	259 (0.9)	259 (1.0)	259 (0.9)	261 (0.9)	261 (0.8)	71 (1.1)	31 (1.1)	‡ (†)	‡ (†)	‡ (†)	‡ (†)
Arizona	255 (1.4)	255 (1.0)	255 (1.2)	258 (1.2)	260 (1.2)	260 (1.1)	72 (1.3)	28 (1.5)	259 (1.5)	266 (2.3)	251 (3.4)	261 (2.2)
Arkansas	258 (1.3)	258 (1.1)	258 (1.0)	258 (1.2)	259 (0.9)	262 (1.1)	73 (1.2)	30 (1.5)	265 (1.5)	261 (2.5)	260 (2.0)	261 (2.0)
California[4]	251 (1.3)	250 (0.6)	251 (0.8)	253 (1.2)	255 (1.0)	262 (1.2)	72 (1.2)	29 (1.4)	261 (2.0)	263 (1.9)	254 (3.4)	266 (5.1)
Colorado	268 (1.2)	265 (1.1)	266 (1.0)	266 (0.8)	271 (1.4)	271 (1.1)	81 (1.1)	40 (1.5)	264 (2.5)	274 (2.1)	268 (3.0)	278 (1.9)
Connecticut	267 (1.1)	264 (1.3)	267 (1.6)	272 (0.9)	275 (0.9)	274 (1.0)	83 (1.0)	45 (1.3)	261 (2.7)	278 (1.1)	282 (2.8)	283 (1.9)
Delaware	265 (0.7)	266 (0.6)	265 (0.6)	265 (0.7)	266 (0.6)	266 (0.7)	77 (1.0)	33 (1.0)	263 (2.2)	264 (1.0)	268 (1.7)	269 (1.1)
District of Columbia	239 (0.8)	238 (0.9)	241 (0.7)	242 (0.9)	242 (0.9)	248 (0.9)	57 (1.3)	17 (0.9)	248 (0.9)	‡ (†)	‡ (†)	‡ (†)
Florida	257 (1.3)	256 (1.2)	260 (1.2)	264 (1.2)	262 (1.0)	266 (1.1)	77 (1.2)	33 (1.5)	265 (3.0)	266 (1.3)	263 (2.3)	267 (2.6)
Georgia	258 (1.1)	257 (1.3)	259 (1.0)	260 (1.0)	262 (1.1)	265 (1.2)	75 (1.4)	32 (1.5)	255 (2.6)	270 (1.9)	264 (3.0)	262 (2.1)
Hawaii	251 (0.9)	249 (0.9)	251 (0.8)	255 (0.6)	257 (0.7)	260 (0.8)	71 (1.0)	28 (1.1)	264 (1.5)	261 (1.5)	257 (1.5)	256 (2.0)
Idaho	264 (0.9)	264 (1.1)	265 (0.9)	265 (0.9)	268 (0.7)	270 (0.8)	82 (0.9)	38 (1.2)	273 (2.0)	271 (1.5)	268 (1.5)	269 (1.5)
Illinois	266 (1.0)	264 (1.0)	263 (1.0)	265 (1.2)	266 (0.8)	267 (1.0)	77 (0.9)	36 (1.4)	259 (2.5)	269 (1.5)	268 (1.5)	276 (2.8)
Indiana	265 (1.0)	261 (1.1)	264 (1.1)	266 (1.0)	265 (1.0)	267 (1.2)	79 (1.2)	35 (1.7)	261 (2.5)	269 (2.6)	267 (2.2)	271 (1.6)
Iowa	268 (0.8)	267 (0.9)	267 (0.9)	265 (0.9)	265 (1.0)	269 (0.8)	81 (0.9)	37 (1.3)	264 (2.0)	281 (2.2)	267 (1.7)	270 (1.0)
Kansas[4]	266 (1.5)	267 (1.0)	267 (0.8)	267 (1.1)	267 (1.0)	267 (1.0)	78 (1.2)	36 (1.2)	259 (2.8)	275 (2.2)	262 (1.6)	272 (1.3)
Kentucky	266 (1.3)	264 (1.1)	262 (1.0)	267 (0.9)	269 (0.8)	270 (0.8)	80 (0.9)	38 (1.4)	266 (1.4)	274 (1.9)	269 (1.7)	270 (1.5)
Louisiana	253 (1.6)	253 (1.6)	253 (1.1)	253 (1.6)	255 (1.5)	257 (1.0)	68 (1.4)	24 (1.3)	253 (2.1)	263 (2.6)	254 (2.0)	259 (1.8)
Maine	268 (1.0)	270 (1.0)	270 (0.8)	268 (0.7)	270 (0.8)	269 (0.8)	79 (1.0)	38 (1.3)	267 (2.6)	276 (2.3)	269 (1.7)	268 (1.0)
Maryland	262 (1.4)	261 (1.2)	265 (1.2)	267 (1.1)	271 (1.2)	274 (1.1)	82 (1.2)	42 (1.4)	269 (2.1)	274 (1.4)	‡ (†)	278 (2.4)
Massachusetts	273 (1.0)	274 (1.0)	273 (1.0)	274 (1.2)	275 (1.0)	277 (1.0)	84 (0.9)	48 (1.4)	263 (2.6)	281 (1.1)	‡ (†)	282 (3.7)
Michigan	264 (1.8)	261 (1.2)	260 (1.2)	262 (1.4)	265 (0.9)	266 (1.0)	77 (1.1)	33 (1.5)	257 (2.5)	271 (1.2)	268 (2.5)	266 (2.3)
Minnesota	268 (1.1)	268 (1.2)	268 (0.9)	270 (1.0)	270 (1.0)	271 (1.0)	82 (1.1)	41 (1.5)	267 (2.1)	274 (1.8)	270 (2.2)	272 (1.9)
Mississippi	255 (1.4)	251 (1.3)	250 (1.1)	251 (1.0)	254 (1.2)	253 (1.0)	64 (1.3)	20 (1.3)	249 (4.8)	258 (2.2)	245 (2.1)	257 (1.3)
Missouri	267 (1.0)	265 (1.0)	263 (1.0)	267 (1.0)	267 (1.1)	267 (1.1)	78 (1.3)	36 (1.4)	257 (4.2)	272 (1.8)	263 (2.6)	271 (1.4)
Montana	270 (1.0)	269 (0.7)	271 (0.8)	270 (0.6)	273 (0.6)	272 (0.8)	84 (0.8)	40 (1.2)	273 (1.6)	277 (3.4)	270 (1.3)	272 (1.2)
Nebraska	266 (0.9)	267 (0.9)	267 (0.9)	267 (0.9)	268 (0.7)	269 (0.8)	81 (0.9)	37 (1.3)	271 (1.5)	270 (1.7)	266 (1.8)	270 (1.6)
Nevada	252 (0.8)	253 (0.9)	252 (0.8)	254 (0.9)	258 (0.9)	262 (0.7)	72 (1.0)	30 (1.1)	262 (1.5)	258 (1.2)	263 (2.0)	266 (1.6)
New Hampshire	271 (0.9)	270 (1.2)	270 (0.9)	271 (1.0)	272 (0.7)	274 (0.8)	84 (0.8)	44 (1.3)	260 (2.0)	277 (1.8)	273 (1.5)	278 (1.2)
New Jersey	268 (1.2)	269 (1.2)	270 (1.1)	273 (1.3)	275 (1.2)	276 (1.1)	85 (1.0)	46 (1.4)	266 (4.5)	277 (1.2)	‡ (†)	280 (2.4)
New Mexico	252 (0.9)	251 (1.0)	251 (0.8)	254 (1.2)	256 (0.9)	256 (0.8)	67 (1.0)	22 (1.0)	257 (1.2)	258 (1.9)	257 (1.6)	253 (1.3)
New York	265 (1.3)	265 (1.0)	264 (1.1)	264 (1.2)	266 (1.1)	266 (1.1)	76 (1.0)	35 (1.6)	256 (1.3)	274 (2.2)	274 (5.3)	272 (2.5)
North Carolina	262 (1.0)	258 (0.9)	259 (1.1)	260 (1.2)	263 (0.9)	265 (1.1)	76 (1.1)	33 (1.6)	266 (2.2)	270 (5.4)	258 (2.0)	264 (1.5)
North Dakota	270 (0.8)	270 (0.6)	268 (0.7)	269 (0.6)	269 (0.7)	268 (0.6)	81 (1.0)	34 (0.9)	268 (1.2)	270 (2.0)	268 (1.2)	267 (0.8)
Ohio	267 (1.3)	267 (1.3)	268 (1.2)	269 (1.3)	268 (1.1)	269 (1.0)	79 (1.0)	39 (1.5)	251 (3.7)	274 (1.2)	265 (2.0)	274 (1.6)
Oklahoma	262 (0.9)	260 (1.1)	260 (0.8)	259 (0.9)	260 (1.1)	262 (0.9)	75 (1.1)	29 (1.2)	257 (2.5)	265 (1.8)	261 (1.3)	263 (1.7)
Oregon	264 (1.2)	263 (1.1)	266 (0.9)	265 (1.0)	264 (0.9)	268 (0.9)	79 (1.1)	37 (1.3)	271 (1.5)	269 (2.0)	264 (2.0)	269 (2.0)
Pennsylvania	264 (1.2)	267 (1.3)	268 (1.2)	271 (0.8)	268 (1.3)	272 (1.0)	81 (1.2)	42 (1.4)	246 (2.3)	280 (1.2)	273 (1.9)	275 (2.5)
Rhode Island	261 (0.7)	261 (0.7)	258 (0.9)	260 (0.6)	265 (0.7)	267 (0.6)	77 (0.9)	36 (1.2)	257 (1.3)	268 (1.0)	279 (4.5)	278 (1.3)
South Carolina	258 (1.3)	257 (1.1)	257 (0.9)	257 (1.2)	260 (0.9)	261 (1.0)	73 (1.4)	29 (1.2)	264 (3.6)	262 (1.9)	258 (2.2)	261 (1.2)
South Dakota	270 (0.8)	269 (0.6)	270 (0.7)	270 (0.5)	269 (0.8)	268 (0.8)	81 (0.9)	36 (1.1)	269 (1.3)	‡ (†)	268 (1.3)	268 (1.2)
Tennessee	258 (1.2)	259 (0.9)	259 (1.0)	261 (1.1)	259 (1.0)	265 (1.1)	77 (1.2)	33 (1.5)	256 (3.1)	275 (2.4)	265 (2.6)	267 (1.3)
Texas	259 (1.1)	258 (0.6)	261 (0.9)	260 (1.1)	261 (1.0)	264 (1.1)	76 (1.4)	31 (1.6)	258 (1.9)	266 (2.0)	260 (3.3)	272 (2.2)
Utah	264 (0.8)	262 (0.8)	262 (1.0)	266 (0.8)	267 (0.8)	270 (0.9)	81 (1.0)	39 (1.2)	272 (3.1)	271 (1.0)	265 (2.0)	270 (2.2)
Vermont	271 (0.8)	269 (0.7)	273 (0.8)	272 (0.6)	274 (0.9)	274 (0.7)	84 (0.9)	45 (1.0)	‡ (†)	‡ (†)	‡ (†)	‡ (†)
Virginia	268 (1.1)	268 (1.0)	267 (1.1)	266 (1.1)	267 (1.2)	268 (1.3)	78 (1.3)	36 (1.6)	262 (2.8)	272 (1.9)	260 (3.3)	267 (2.2)
Washington	264 (0.9)	265 (1.3)	265 (0.9)	267 (1.1)	268 (1.0)	272 (1.0)	81 (1.2)	42 (1.5)	270 (2.3)	275 (1.3)	270 (2.7)	270 (2.0)
West Virginia	260 (1.0)	255 (1.2)	255 (1.0)	255 (0.9)	256 (0.9)	257 (0.9)	70 (1.1)	25 (1.1)	260 (3.6)	260 (2.1)	256 (1.7)	257 (1.2)
Wisconsin	266 (1.3)	266 (1.1)	264 (1.0)	266 (1.0)	267 (0.9)	268 (0.9)	78 (0.9)	36 (1.4)	257 (2.0)	273 (2.3)	272 (1.6)	269 (1.6)
Wyoming	267 (0.5)	268 (0.7)	266 (0.7)	268 (1.0)	270 (1.0)	271 (0.6)	84 (0.7)	38 (1.0)	272 (1.1)	‡ (†)	272 (1.0)	268 (1.2)
Department of Defense dependents schools[5]	272 (0.6)	271 (0.7)	273 (1.0)	272 (0.7)	272 (0.7)	277 (0.7)	89 (0.8)	45 (1.2)	266 (2.6)	275 (1.6)	‡ (†)	275 (3.3)

†Not applicable.
‡Reporting standards not met. Either there are too few cases for a reliable estimate or item response rates fell below the required standards for reporting.
[1]Scale ranges from 0 to 500.
[2]*Basic* denotes partial mastery of the knowledge and skills that are fundamental for proficient work at the 8th-grade level.
[3]*Proficient* represents solid academic performance for 8th-graders. Students reaching this level have demonstrated competency over challenging subject matter.
[4]Did not satisfy one or more of the guidelines for school participation in 2003. Data are subject to appreciable nonresponse bias.
[5]Prior to 2005, NAEP divided the Department of Defense (DoD) schools into two jurisdictions, domestic and overseas. In 2005, NAEP began combining the DoD domestic and overseas schools into a single jurisdiction. Data shown in this table for 2003 were recalculated for comparability.
NOTE: Includes public school students who were tested with accommodations; excludes only those students with disabilities (SD) and English language learners (ELL) who were unable to be tested even with accommodations. SD and ELL populations, accommodation rates, and exclusion rates vary from state to state.
SOURCE: U.S. Department of Education, National Center for Education Statistics, National Assessment of Educational Progress (NAEP), 2003, 2005, 2007, 2009, 2011, and 2013 Reading Assessments, retrieved November 8, 2013, from the Main NAEP Data Explorer (http://nces.ed.gov/nationsreportcard/naepdata/). (This table was prepared November 2013.)

Table 221.70. Average National Assessment of Educational Progress (NAEP) reading scale scores of 4th- and 8th-graders in public schools and percentage scoring at or above selected reading achievement levels, by English language learner (ELL) status and state: 2013

[Standard errors appear in parentheses]

| | 4th-graders | | | | | | | 8th-graders | | | | | | |
| | English language learners | | | | Not English language learners | | | English language learners | | | | Not English language learners | | |
State	Percent of all students assessed	Average scale score[1]	Percent At or above Basic[2]	Percent At or above Proficient[3]	Average scale score[1]	Percent At or above Basic[2]	Percent At or above Proficient[3]	Percent of all students assessed	Average scale score[1]	Percent At or above Basic[2]	Percent At or above Proficient[3]	Average scale score[1]	Percent At or above Basic[2]	Percent At or above Proficient[3]
1	2	3	4	5	6	7	8	9	10	11	12	13	14	15
United States	10 (0.3)	187 (0.7)	31 (0.8)	7 (0.4)	225 (0.3)	71 (0.3)	37 (0.4)	5 (0.1)	225 (0.9)	30 (1.4)	3 (0.4)	268 (0.2)	79 (0.3)	36 (0.3)
Alabama	2 (0.5)	‡ (†)	‡ (†)	‡ (†)	219 (1.2)	66 (1.5)	31 (1.5)	1 (0.2)	‡ (†)	‡ (†)	‡ (†)	258 (1.2)	69 (1.3)	25 (1.5)
Alaska	14 (0.9)	154 (3.0)	10 (2.3)	1 (0.6)	218 (1.0)	65 (1.3)	32 (1.3)	11 (0.7)	214 (2.5)	16 (2.9)	1 (†)	267 (0.7)	78 (1.0)	35 (1.2)
Arizona	7 (0.9)	159 (4.4)	8 (2.4)	1 (†)	217 (1.2)	63 (1.5)	30 (1.4)	1 (0.2)	‡ (†)	‡ (†)	‡ (†)	261 (1.1)	73 (1.3)	28 (1.5)
Arkansas	8 (0.8)	202 (2.8)	47 (3.8)	17 (2.6)	220 (1.0)	68 (1.2)	33 (1.4)	6 (0.5)	245 (3.2)	55 (4.7)	12 (3.8)	263 (1.2)	74 (1.2)	31 (1.6)
California	25 (1.4)	182 (1.8)	26 (1.8)	5 (0.8)	223 (1.1)	69 (1.4)	34 (1.5)	12 (0.9)	220 (2.2)	23 (3.5)	2 (1.0)	267 (1.2)	79 (1.1)	33 (1.4)
Colorado	14 (1.1)	192 (2.3)	37 (2.9)	8 (1.6)	232 (1.0)	80 (1.2)	46 (1.7)	8 (0.8)	232 (2.5)	37 (4.4)	3 (1.5)	274 (1.1)	85 (1.0)	43 (1.6)
Connecticut	5 (0.4)	181 (4.0)	25 (5.1)	4 (1.9)	232 (0.9)	79 (1.2)	45 (1.2)	3 (0.6)	222 (5.7)	27 (7.0)	1 (†)	276 (0.9)	85 (0.9)	47 (1.3)
Delaware	2 (0.2)	184 (5.5)	24 (6.7)	4 (†)	227 (0.7)	74 (1.1)	39 (1.2)	1 (0.2)	‡ (†)	‡ (†)	‡ (†)	267 (0.7)	77 (1.0)	34 (1.0)
District of Columbia	6 (0.3)	182 (3.7)	23 (4.8)	5 (2.6)	207 (0.9)	51 (1.2)	24 (0.9)	5 (0.4)	218 (3.9)	25 (5.4)	2 (†)	249 (0.9)	59 (1.3)	18 (0.9)
Florida	10 (0.8)	199 (2.4)	41 (3.7)	10 (1.9)	230 (1.0)	79 (1.1)	42 (1.5)	4 (0.3)	226 (3.3)	30 (4.8)	3 (1.4)	268 (1.1)	79 (1.2)	35 (1.5)
Georgia	3 (0.6)	189 (4.5)	29 (5.9)	8 (3.5)	223 (1.1)	68 (1.4)	35 (1.5)	2 (0.4)	220 (5.1)	21 (6.7)	4 (†)	265 (1.2)	76 (1.4)	32 (1.5)
Hawaii	7 (0.6)	166 (3.5)	14 (2.9)	3 (1.4)	219 (1.0)	65 (1.3)	32 (1.3)	10 (0.4)	224 (2.4)	29 (3.1)	3 (1.2)	264 (0.8)	76 (1.1)	31 (1.2)
Idaho	4 (0.5)	170 (4.2)	17 (4.3)	3 (1.4)	222 (0.9)	70 (1.1)	34 (1.2)	3 (0.4)	222 (3.8)	21 (5.7)	2 (†)	272 (0.9)	84 (0.8)	39 (1.2)
Illinois	8 (0.7)	174 (2.8)	18 (3.1)	3 (1.7)	222 (1.4)	68 (1.6)	36 (1.5)	5 (0.5)	219 (3.8)	23 (4.9)	1 (†)	269 (1.0)	80 (1.0)	38 (1.4)
Indiana	6 (0.8)	203 (3.5)	48 (5.0)	13 (3.1)	227 (1.1)	75 (1.2)	39 (1.6)	3 (0.4)	236 (4.6)	40 (6.0)	6 (2.3)	268 (1.1)	81 (1.3)	36 (1.8)
Iowa	5 (0.8)	195 (5.2)	41 (6.4)	11 (2.8)	225 (1.2)	73 (1.4)	39 (1.5)	2 (0.3)	226 (3.9)	27 (6.9)	2 (†)	270 (0.8)	83 (0.9)	38 (1.3)
Kansas	13 (1.3)	203 (2.5)	49 (3.4)	17 (2.4)	226 (1.2)	75 (1.5)	41 (1.8)	8 (1.3)	245 (2.4)	55 (3.6)	13 (2.3)	269 (1.1)	80 (1.4)	38 (1.4)
Kentucky	2 (0.3)	197 (6.0)	41 (7.9)	11 (5.9)	225 (1.2)	72 (1.4)	37 (1.7)	1 (0.2)	237 (4.5)	43 (8.1)	5 (†)	270 (0.9)	80 (0.9)	38 (1.4)
Louisiana	2 (0.3)	202 (4.7)	47 (7.8)	10 (5.2)	211 (1.3)	57 (1.7)	23 (1.3)	1 (0.3)	‡ (†)	‡ (†)	‡ (†)	258 (1.0)	68 (1.4)	24 (1.3)
Maine	2 (0.3)	190 (6.5)	35 (8.0)	9 (4.9)	226 (0.9)	72 (1.0)	38 (1.3)	2 (0.3)	‡ (†)	‡ (†)	‡ (†)	270 (0.8)	79 (1.0)	39 (1.3)
Maryland	4 (0.6)	207 (5.0)	51 (7.1)	18 (4.9)	233 (1.3)	78 (1.1)	46 (1.9)	1 (0.4)	‡ (†)	‡ (†)	‡ (†)	274 (1.0)	83 (1.1)	43 (1.4)
Massachusetts	10 (0.8)	192 (4.3)	40 (4.3)	12 (2.4)	237 (1.0)	83 (1.1)	51 (1.5)	5 (0.6)	224 (3.0)	28 (4.0)	4 (1.5)	280 (1.0)	87 (0.9)	50 (1.4)
Michigan	8 (1.6)	194 (4.3)	39 (5.8)	9 (2.3)	219 (1.4)	66 (1.4)	32 (1.7)	3 (0.7)	232 (5.3)	41 (6.7)	8 (3.9)	267 (1.1)	78 (1.2)	34 (1.6)
Minnesota	8 (0.9)	188 (2.9)	33 (4.7)	8 (1.9)	230 (1.1)	78 (1.4)	44 (1.4)	5 (0.8)	231 (5.1)	40 (7.7)	6 (2.6)	273 (1.0)	84 (1.0)	42 (1.6)
Mississippi	1 (0.3)	‡ (†)	‡ (†)	‡ (†)	209 (1.0)	54 (1.3)	21 (1.0)	1 (0.2)	‡ (†)	‡ (†)	‡ (†)	253 (1.0)	64 (1.3)	20 (1.3)
Missouri	2 (0.3)	197 (4.0)	37 (9.0)	6 (3.5)	223 (1.0)	70 (1.2)	36 (1.4)	1 (0.3)	‡ (†)	‡ (†)	‡ (†)	267 (1.1)	79 (1.3)	36 (1.4)
Montana	3 (0.5)	174 (4.3)	16 (4.6)	2 (1.6)	225 (0.8)	72 (1.1)	36 (1.1)	2 (0.3)	‡ (†)	‡ (†)	‡ (†)	273 (0.8)	85 (0.8)	41 (1.2)
Nebraska	7 (0.6)	190 (3.9)	34 (4.3)	7 (1.9)	226 (1.0)	74 (1.0)	39 (1.4)	2 (0.3)	‡ (†)	‡ (†)	‡ (†)	270 (0.8)	82 (0.9)	37 (1.3)
Nevada	22 (1.2)	185 (1.6)	30 (2.5)	6 (1.1)	222 (1.1)	71 (1.4)	33 (1.5)	7 (0.4)	217 (2.5)	21 (3.5)	2 (1.4)	265 (0.7)	76 (1.0)	33 (1.1)
New Hampshire	2 (0.4)	196 (5.7)	34 (7.3)	10 (4.6)	233 (0.9)	81 (1.0)	45 (1.5)	2 (0.2)	‡ (†)	‡ (†)	‡ (†)	275 (0.8)	85 (0.8)	44 (1.4)
New Jersey	3 (0.5)	188 (5.8)	33 (6.8)	9 (3.5)	230 (1.2)	76 (1.2)	43 (1.7)	1 (0.2)	‡ (†)	‡ (†)	‡ (†)	277 (1.0)	86 (1.0)	47 (1.4)
New Mexico	18 (1.3)	168 (1.8)	16 (1.8)	3 (1.0)	214 (1.0)	60 (1.3)	25 (1.0)	13 (0.6)	224 (1.7)	29 (2.8)	2 (1.2)	261 (0.8)	73 (1.1)	25 (1.1)
New York	7 (0.5)	182 (2.7)	25 (3.2)	4 (1.4)	227 (1.2)	74 (1.5)	40 (1.6)	6 (0.5)	215 (2.7)	20 (3.4)	1 (0.7)	270 (1.1)	80 (1.0)	37 (1.7)
North Carolina	6 (0.7)	183 (3.4)	23 (3.8)	4 (1.8)	225 (1.0)	72 (1.2)	37 (1.2)	4 (0.3)	232 (3.6)	41 (5.9)	7 (3.0)	266 (1.1)	77 (1.1)	34 (1.7)
North Dakota	2 (0.2)	‡ (†)	‡ (†)	‡ (†)	225 (0.5)	74 (0.9)	34 (0.9)	2 (0.2)	‡ (†)	‡ (†)	‡ (†)	269 (0.6)	82 (1.0)	35 (0.9)
Ohio	3 (0.5)	205 (5.1)	51 (7.1)	19 (5.2)	224 (1.2)	71 (1.3)	38 (1.6)	1 (0.3)	251 (6.4)	60 (9.0)	20 (8.3)	269 (1.0)	79 (1.0)	39 (1.5)
Oklahoma	6 (0.5)	186 (3.4)	30 (4.0)	6 (1.7)	219 (1.1)	68 (1.3)	31 (1.4)	4 (0.5)	229 (3.8)	39 (5.1)	6 (3.6)	263 (0.9)	76 (1.2)	30 (1.2)
Oregon	13 (0.9)	183 (2.7)	29 (2.8)	6 (1.7)	225 (1.3)	71 (1.4)	38 (1.7)	3 (0.4)	218 (4.5)	23 (5.4)	1 (†)	270 (0.9)	81 (1.1)	38 (1.3)
Pennsylvania	2 (0.3)	181 (7.4)	27 (6.9)	5 (2.5)	227 (1.3)	74 (1.4)	41 (1.6)	2 (0.4)	222 (5.2)	26 (5.3)	3 (1.5)	273 (1.0)	83 (1.1)	43 (1.4)
Rhode Island	6 (0.5)	168 (3.5)	17 (3.4)	4 (2.2)	226 (0.9)	73 (1.1)	40 (1.2)	4 (0.3)	216 (3.5)	20 (4.4)	3 (2.0)	269 (0.6)	79 (0.9)	37 (1.2)
South Carolina	6 (0.7)	206 (3.9)	54 (5.2)	18 (4.1)	214 (1.2)	61 (1.4)	29 (1.5)	3 (0.3)	242 (4.3)	54 (6.1)	10 (3.2)	262 (1.0)	73 (1.4)	30 (1.2)
South Dakota	3 (0.5)	160 (6.6)	20 (4.1)	5 (2.5)	220 (0.8)	67 (1.2)	33 (1.1)	2 (0.3)	‡ (†)	‡ (†)	‡ (†)	269 (0.7)	82 (0.9)	36 (1.1)
Tennessee	3 (0.4)	174 (5.4)	19 (4.6)	2 (†)	221 (1.3)	69 (1.5)	35 (1.6)	1 (0.2)	‡ (†)	‡ (†)	‡ (†)	266 (1.1)	77 (1.2)	33 (1.5)
Texas	22 (1.6)	194 (1.4)	36 (2.4)	9 (1.3)	223 (1.2)	70 (1.4)	34 (1.5)	7 (0.7)	227 (2.6)	32 (3.9)	2 (1.3)	267 (1.1)	79 (1.3)	33 (1.7)
Utah	5 (0.6)	159 (3.6)	9 (2.9)	2 (1.3)	226 (1.0)	74 (1.2)	39 (1.4)	3 (0.4)	220 (3.3)	21 (5.1)	3 (1.9)	272 (0.9)	83 (1.0)	40 (1.2)
Vermont	2 (0.2)	‡ (†)	‡ (†)	‡ (†)	229 (0.6)	76 (1.0)	43 (1.1)	1 (0.1)	‡ (†)	‡ (†)	‡ (†)	275 (0.7)	84 (0.9)	45 (1.0)
Virginia	7 (0.8)	186 (3.6)	28 (4.2)	5 (2.0)	232 (1.2)	77 (1.3)	46 (1.6)	5 (0.6)	242 (3.6)	51 (6.8)	7 (2.9)	269 (1.4)	79 (1.3)	38 (1.6)
Washington	9 (0.8)	179 (2.9)	20 (3.1)	3 (1.4)	229 (1.4)	77 (1.3)	43 (1.8)	5 (0.4)	222 (4.7)	26 (6.1)	3 (2.2)	275 (0.9)	84 (1.1)	44 (1.5)
West Virginia	1 (0.3)	‡ (†)	‡ (†)	‡ (†)	215 (0.8)	62 (1.2)	27 (1.0)	# (†)	‡ (†)	‡ (†)	‡ (†)	257 (0.9)	70 (1.1)	25 (1.1)
Wisconsin	8 (0.8)	190 (2.8)	34 (4.4)	9 (2.2)	223 (1.6)	70 (1.7)	37 (1.7)	5 (0.4)	242 (2.9)	51 (4.3)	9 (2.7)	269 (1.0)	79 (0.9)	38 (1.5)
Wyoming	3 (0.2)	196 (3.9)	37 (6.8)	9 (4.4)	227 (0.5)	76 (1.0)	38 (1.0)	2 (0.2)	‡ (†)	‡ (†)	‡ (†)	272 (0.6)	85 (0.8)	38 (1.0)
Department of Defense dependents schools	5 (0.3)	216 (2.5)	63 (4.7)	20 (4.0)	233 (0.6)	83 (0.9)	44 (1.1)	3 (0.3)	244 (3.7)	52 (7.4)	6 (3.8)	278 (0.7)	91 (0.8)	46 (1.2)

†Not applicable.

#Rounds to zero.

‡Reporting standards not met (too few cases for a reliable estimate).

[1]Scale ranges from 0 to 500.

[2]*Basic* denotes partial mastery of the knowledge and skills that are fundamental for proficient work at a given grade.

[3]*Proficient* represents solid academic performance. Students reaching this level have demonstrated competency over challenging subject matter.

NOTE: The results for English language learners are based on students who were assessed and cannot be generalized to the total population of such students. Although testing accommodations were permitted, some English language learners did not have a sufficient level of English proficiency to participate in the 2013 Reading Assessment.
SOURCE: U.S. Department of Education, National Center for Education Statistics, National Assessment of Educational Progress (NAEP), 2013 Reading Assessment, retrieved November 8, 2013, from the Main NAEP Data Explorer (http://nces.ed.gov/nationsreport card/naepdata/). (This table was prepared November 2013.)

Table 221.75. Average National Assessment of Educational Progress (NAEP) reading scale score and standard deviation, by selected student characteristics, percentile, and grade: Selected years, 1992 through 2013

[Standard errors appear in parentheses]

Selected student characteristic, percentile, and grade	1992[1]	1998	2000	2002	2003	2005	2007	2009	2011	2013 Total	2013 Male	2013 Female
1	2	3	4	5	6	7	8	9	10	11	12	13
Average reading scale score[2]												
All students												
4th grade	217 (0.9)	215 (1.1)	213 (1.3)	219 (0.4)	218 (0.3)	219 (0.2)	221 (0.3)	221 (0.3)	221 (0.3)	222 (0.3)	219 (0.3)	225 (0.3)
8th grade	260 (0.9)	263 (0.8)	— (†)	264 (0.4)	263 (0.3)	262 (0.2)	263 (0.2)	264 (0.3)	265 (0.2)	268 (0.3)	263 (0.3)	273 (0.3)
12th grade	292 (0.6)	290 (0.6)	— (†)	287 (0.7)	— (†)	286 (0.6)	— (†)	288 (0.7)	— (†)	288 (0.6)	284 (0.6)	293 (0.7)
Eligibility for free or reduced-price lunch												
4th grade												
Eligible	— (†)	196 (1.7)	193 (1.7)	203 (0.7)	201 (0.3)	203 (0.3)	205 (0.3)	206 (0.3)	207 (0.3)	207 (0.3)	204 (0.4)	211 (0.3)
Not eligible	— (†)	227 (0.9)	226 (1.2)	230 (0.4)	229 (0.3)	230 (0.2)	232 (0.3)	232 (0.3)	235 (0.3)	236 (0.3)	233 (0.4)	239 (0.4)
Unknown	— (†)	223 (2.7)	225 (2.3)	226 (1.6)	230 (0.9)	232 (0.9)	233 (1.3)	236 (1.3)	235 (0.8)	237 (1.4)	233 (1.7)	240 (2.0)
8th grade												
Eligible	— (†)	245 (1.0)	— (†)	249 (0.5)	247 (0.4)	247 (0.3)	247 (0.3)	249 (0.3)	252 (0.3)	254 (0.2)	249 (0.3)	259 (0.3)
Not eligible	— (†)	269 (1.0)	— (†)	272 (0.4)	271 (0.3)	270 (0.2)	271 (0.3)	273 (0.3)	275 (0.3)	278 (0.3)	273 (0.3)	284 (0.3)
Unknown	— (†)	272 (2.0)	— (†)	271 (1.4)	272 (1.0)	275 (1.1)	277 (1.3)	280 (1.3)	283 (0.9)	286 (1.8)	281 (2.3)	291 (1.7)
12th grade												
Eligible	— (†)	270 (1.1)	— (†)	273 (1.4)	— (†)	271 (1.0)	— (†)	273 (0.7)	— (†)	274 (0.7)	269 (0.9)	278 (0.8)
Not eligible	— (†)	293 (0.6)	— (†)	289 (0.9)	— (†)	290 (0.7)	— (†)	294 (0.8)	— (†)	296 (0.6)	291 (0.7)	302 (0.7)
Unknown	— (†)	295 (1.6)	— (†)	294 (1.5)	— (†)	295 (1.9)	— (†)	296 (2.4)	— (†)	302 (2.6)	298 (3.0)	307 (3.1)
Read for fun on own time												
4th grade												
Almost every day	223 (1.2)	219 (1.5)	218 (1.7)	225 (0.5)	225 (0.3)	225 (0.3)	227 (0.3)	228 (0.4)	228 (0.4)	229 (0.4)	226 (0.5)	231 (0.4)
1–2 times a week	218 (1.2)	217 (1.2)	216 (1.2)	220 (0.5)	219 (0.3)	220 (0.3)	223 (0.3)	221 (0.4)	221 (0.4)	223 (0.4)	220 (0.4)	225 (0.4)
1–2 times a month	210 (1.6)	211 (1.9)	212 (1.6)	210 (0.8)	211 (0.5)	213 (0.4)	216 (0.4)	214 (0.4)	214 (0.4)	216 (0.4)	214 (0.5)	219 (0.6)
Never or hardly ever	199 (1.8)	202 (1.9)	201 (1.8)	208 (0.5)	207 (0.4)	208 (0.3)	211 (0.4)	210 (0.3)	210 (0.5)	211 (0.4)	209 (0.5)	213 (0.7)
8th grade												
Almost every day	277 (1.1)	277 (1.0)	— (†)	279 (0.6)	279 (0.4)	279 (0.3)	281 (0.4)	282 (0.4)	284 (0.4)	286 (0.4)	281 (0.6)	289 (0.5)
1–2 times a week	263 (1.0)	267 (1.1)	— (†)	266 (0.5)	265 (0.4)	265 (0.3)	265 (0.3)	267 (0.4)	268 (0.3)	271 (0.4)	267 (0.6)	274 (0.5)
1–2 times a month	258 (1.2)	263 (0.9)	— (†)	264 (0.6)	262 (0.3)	261 (0.3)	261 (0.4)	261 (0.4)	263 (0.3)	266 (0.3)	262 (0.4)	269 (0.4)
Never or hardly ever	246 (1.4)	251 (1.1)	— (†)	255 (0.4)	253 (0.3)	252 (0.3)	253 (0.3)	253 (0.4)	255 (0.3)	257 (0.3)	255 (0.3)	260 (0.4)
12th grade												
Almost every day	304 (0.9)	304 (1.0)	— (†)	304 (1.1)	— (†)	302 (1.2)	— (†)	305 (0.9)	— (†)	306 (0.8)	303 (1.3)	308 (1.0)
1–2 times a week	296 (0.7)	298 (0.9)	— (†)	292 (1.1)	— (†)	292 (1.0)	— (†)	295 (1.0)	— (†)	297 (0.8)	294 (1.1)	299 (1.0)
1–2 times a month	290 (0.9)	289 (0.7)	— (†)	288 (0.9)	— (†)	285 (0.8)	— (†)	288 (0.8)	— (†)	289 (0.6)	285 (0.8)	292 (0.9)
Never or hardly ever	279 (1.0)	275 (1.0)	— (†)	275 (1.0)	— (†)	274 (0.8)	— (†)	275 (0.6)	— (†)	276 (0.7)	273 (0.8)	281 (0.9)
Percentile[3]												
4th grade												
10th	170 (1.9)	163 (2.1)	159 (2.3)	170 (0.9)	169 (0.5)	171 (0.4)	174 (0.4)	175 (0.5)	174 (0.4)	174 (0.6)	169 (0.8)	179 (0.6)
25th	194 (1.1)	191 (1.7)	189 (1.4)	196 (0.5)	195 (0.4)	196 (0.3)	199 (0.3)	199 (0.4)	200 (0.4)	200 (0.3)	197 (0.5)	204 (0.5)
50th	219 (1.3)	217 (1.3)	218 (1.7)	221 (0.5)	221 (0.3)	221 (0.2)	224 (0.3)	223 (0.3)	224 (0.3)	225 (0.3)	222 (0.4)	228 (0.4)
75th	242 (1.1)	242 (0.9)	243 (0.8)	244 (0.5)	244 (0.3)	244 (0.3)	246 (0.3)	245 (0.3)	246 (0.3)	247 (0.3)	245 (0.4)	250 (0.4)
90th	261 (1.4)	262 (0.9)	262 (1.4)	263 (0.4)	264 (0.3)	263 (0.3)	264 (0.3)	264 (0.3)	264 (0.4)	265 (0.4)	263 (0.5)	268 (0.4)
8th grade												
10th	213 (1.2)	216 (1.7)	— (†)	220 (0.5)	217 (0.6)	216 (0.3)	217 (0.4)	219 (0.5)	221 (0.3)	223 (0.4)	218 (0.6)	229 (0.5)
25th	237 (1.1)	241 (0.7)	— (†)	244 (0.5)	242 (0.3)	240 (0.2)	242 (0.3)	243 (0.4)	244 (0.3)	246 (0.2)	242 (0.4)	251 (0.3)
50th	262 (1.1)	266 (0.7)	— (†)	267 (0.5)	266 (0.3)	265 (0.2)	265 (0.2)	267 (0.3)	267 (0.2)	269 (0.3)	265 (0.3)	274 (0.4)
75th	285 (0.8)	288 (1.0)	— (†)	288 (0.4)	288 (0.3)	286 (0.2)	287 (0.2)	288 (0.4)	289 (0.3)	291 (0.3)	286 (0.4)	296 (0.4)
90th	305 (1.3)	306 (0.8)	— (†)	305 (0.5)	306 (0.2)	305 (0.2)	305 (0.2)	305 (0.4)	307 (0.2)	310 (0.4)	304 (0.4)	314 (0.4)
12th grade												
10th	249 (0.8)	240 (0.6)	— (†)	237 (1.5)	— (†)	235 (1.1)	— (†)	238 (0.8)	— (†)	239 (1.0)	232 (1.1)	246 (1.1)
25th	271 (0.8)	267 (0.8)	— (†)	263 (1.3)	— (†)	262 (0.8)	— (†)	264 (0.8)	— (†)	264 (0.8)	259 (0.9)	270 (1.0)
50th	294 (0.8)	293 (0.6)	— (†)	289 (0.7)	— (†)	288 (0.8)	— (†)	291 (0.7)	— (†)	290 (0.7)	286 (0.9)	295 (0.7)
75th	315 (0.5)	317 (0.7)	— (†)	312 (0.6)	— (†)	313 (1.1)	— (†)	315 (0.9)	— (†)	315 (0.7)	311 (0.8)	319 (0.8)
90th	333 (0.7)	336 (0.8)	— (†)	332 (0.9)	— (†)	333 (1.1)	— (†)	335 (0.9)	— (†)	335 (0.6)	331 (0.7)	339 (1.2)
Standard deviation of the reading scale score[4]												
All students												
4th grade	36 (0.6)	39 (0.7)	42 (0.9)	36 (0.3)	37 (0.2)	36 (0.1)	36 (0.2)	35 (0.2)	36 (0.1)	37 (0.2)	38 (0.3)	36 (0.2)
8th grade	36 (0.3)	35 (0.5)	— (†)	34 (0.3)	35 (0.2)	35 (0.1)	35 (0.2)	34 (0.2)	34 (0.1)	34 (0.1)	34 (0.2)	34 (0.2)
12th grade	33 (0.4)	38 (0.4)	— (†)	37 (0.4)	— (†)	38 (0.4)	— (†)	38 (0.3)	— (†)	38 (0.3)	39 (0.4)	36 (0.4)

—Not available.

†Not applicable.

[1]Accommodations were not permitted for this assessment.

[2]Scale ranges from 0 to 500.

[3]The percentile represents a specific point on the percentage distribution of all students ranked by their reading score from low to high. For example, 10 percent of students scored at or below the 10th percentile score, while 90 percent of students scored above it.

[4]The standard deviation provides an indication of how much the test scores varied. The lower the standard deviation, the closer the scores were clustered around the average score. About two-thirds of the student scores can be expected to fall within the range of one standard deviation above and one standard deviation below the average score. For example, the average score for all 4th-graders in 2013 was 222, and the standard deviation was 37. This means that we would expect about two-thirds of the students to have scores between 259 (one standard deviation above the average) and 185 (one standard deviation below). Standard errors also must be taken into account when making comparisons of these ranges.

NOTE: Includes public and private schools. For 1998 and later years, includes students tested with accommodations (1 to 11 percent of all students, depending on grade level and year); excludes only those students with disabilities and English language learners who were unable to be tested even with accommodations (2 to 6 percent of all students). On the student questionnaire, the format of the question about reading for fun on your own time changed slightly beginning with the 2002 assessment year. In 1992 through 2000, reading for fun was one of several activities included in the same question ("How often do you do each of the following?"), and the response options were listed in order from most frequent to least frequent (that is, "Almost every day" was listed first, and "Never or hardly ever" was listed last); starting in 2002, reading for fun was the only activity in the question, and the order of the response options was reversed.

SOURCE: U.S. Department of Education, National Center for Education Statistics, National Assessment of Educational Progress (NAEP), 1992, 1998, 2000, 2002, 2003, 2005, 2007, 2009, 2011, and 2013 Reading Assessments, retrieved March 17, 2015, from the Main NAEP Data Explorer (http://nces.ed.gov/nationsreportcard/naepdata/). (This table was prepared March 2015.)

Table 221.80. Average National Assessment of Educational Progress (NAEP) reading scale scores of 4th- and 8th-grade public school students and percentage attaining reading achievement levels, by race/ethnicity and jurisdiction or specific urban district: 2009, 2011, and 2013

[Standard errors appear in parentheses]

Grade level and jurisdiction or specific urban district	2009 All students	2011 All students	2011 White	2011 Black	2011 Hispanic	2011 Asian	2013 All students	2013 White	2013 Black	2013 Hispanic	2013 Asian	2013 At or above Basic [2]	2013 At or above Proficient [3]
1	2	3	4	5	6	7	8	9	10	11	12	13	14
4th grade													
United States	220 (0.3)	220 (0.3)	230 (0.3)	205 (0.4)	205 (0.5)	236 (1.3)	221 (0.3)	231 (0.3)	205 (0.5)	207 (0.5)	237 (1.1)	67 (0.3)	34 (0.3)
All large cities	210 (0.7)	211 (0.7)	232 (0.9)	202 (0.7)	203 (0.8)	225 (2.5)	212 (0.7)	235 (1.0)	202 (0.8)	204 (0.8)	229 (2.5)	57 (0.8)	26 (0.7)
Selected urban districts													
Albuquerque	— (†)	209 (1.6)	231 (2.5)	‡ (†)	201 (1.7)	‡ (†)	207 (1.5)	232 (2.4)	‡ (†)	199 (1.7)	‡ (†)	54 (1.7)	24 (1.5)
Atlanta	209 (1.5)	212 (1.4)	251 (1.9)	203 (1.6)	215 (3.4)	‡ (†)	214 (1.3)	252 (1.9)	204 (1.4)	208 (3.5)	‡ (†)	57 (1.6)	27 (1.2)
Austin	220 (1.8)	224 (2.3)	249 (3.3)	215 (4.5)	210 (2.6)	‡ (†)	221 (1.6)	250 (2.2)	206 (5.4)	208 (2.1)	‡ (†)	65 (1.7)	36 (1.7)
Baltimore City	202 (1.7)	200 (1.7)	221 (3.3)	198 (1.7)	‡ (†)	‡ (†)	204 (1.6)	233 (5.2)	201 (1.7)	‡ (†)	‡ (†)	45 (2.2)	14 (1.4)
Boston	215 (1.2)	217 (0.8)	241 (2.5)	211 (1.7)	214 (1.1)	226 (3.8)	214 (1.1)	237 (2.2)	205 (1.9)	210 (1.7)	234 (3.3)	61 (1.4)	26 (1.3)
Charlotte	225 (1.6)	224 (1.2)	244 (1.5)	211 (1.9)	212 (2.6)	233 (5.3)	226 (1.6)	245 (1.8)	215 (2.0)	212 (2.9)	238 (4.9)	72 (1.8)	40 (1.9)
Chicago	202 (1.5)	203 (1.3)	229 (2.4)	197 (1.9)	201 (1.5)	228 (4.2)	206 (1.6)	239 (4.1)	198 (2.5)	203 (1.6)	235 (4.7)	51 (1.6)	20 (1.6)
Cleveland	194 (2.0)	193 (0.9)	209 (2.6)	187 (1.1)	196 (3.3)	‡ (†)	190 (1.9)	206 (3.7)	185 (2.2)	191 (4.1)	‡ (†)	33 (2.2)	9 (1.2)
Dallas	— (†)	204 (1.6)	237 (6.9)	204 (2.0)	200 (1.4)	‡ (†)	205 (1.4)	231 (4.9)	201 (2.1)	204 (1.8)	‡ (†)	49 (2.1)	16 (1.5)
Detroit	187 (1.9)	191 (2.0)	‡ (†)	190 (2.5)	199 (5.5)	‡ (†)	190 (2.2)	‡ (†)	188 (2.6)	199 (3.4)	‡ (†)	30 (2.7)	7 (1.3)
District of Columbia	203 (1.2)	201 (1.0)	255 (3.0)	191 (1.3)	204 (3.3)	‡ (†)	206 (1.2)	260 (2.6)	192 (1.4)	211 (2.6)	‡ (†)	49 (1.4)	25 (1.0)
Fresno	197 (1.7)	194 (2.4)	216 (3.9)	191 (4.3)	190 (2.5)	195 (3.0)	196 (1.7)	218 (2.9)	187 (3.0)	192 (1.9)	199 (3.0)	39 (1.9)	13 (1.0)
Hillsborough County (FL)	— (†)	231 (1.7)	242 (1.8)	218 (2.5)	223 (2.1)	‡ (†)	228 (1.3)	237 (1.8)	214 (3.1)	223 (1.6)	247 (4.6)	75 (1.4)	40 (2.0)
Houston	211 (1.7)	213 (1.6)	243 (3.0)	207 (1.7)	209 (1.6)	245 (6.3)	208 (1.3)	238 (3.3)	202 (2.7)	204 (1.3)	245 (4.7)	52 (1.6)	19 (1.3)
Jefferson County (KY)	219 (1.8)	223 (1.3)	230 (1.4)	208 (2.1)	221 (3.9)	256 (5.7)	221 (1.2)	233 (1.7)	203 (1.9)	221 (3.5)	‡ (†)	66 (1.6)	33 (1.6)
Los Angeles	197 (1.1)	201 (1.2)	225 (3.7)	196 (4.2)	196 (1.1)	226 (4.2)	205 (1.6)	237 (3.4)	204 (2.9)	199 (1.3)	222 (4.3)	50 (1.9)	19 (1.7)
Miami-Dade	221 (1.2)	221 (1.5)	240 (3.4)	210 (2.1)	222 (1.8)	‡ (†)	223 (1.5)	239 (2.8)	209 (2.2)	225 (1.7)	‡ (†)	70 (1.7)	35 (2.1)
Milwaukee	196 (2.0)	195 (1.7)	216 (3.9)	187 (2.0)	198 (2.7)	206 (3.3)	199 (1.9)	223 (3.8)	190 (2.3)	200 (2.6)	201 (8.2)	42 (2.1)	15 (1.8)
New York City	217 (1.4)	216 (1.2)	235 (3.3)	209 (1.7)	207 (1.5)	230 (3.6)	216 (1.4)	231 (3.1)	210 (1.8)	208 (1.5)	233 (3.2)	62 (1.6)	28 (1.7)
Philadelphia	195 (1.8)	199 (1.8)	217 (3.3)	195 (1.9)	191 (3.5)	212 (5.2)	200 (1.7)	214 (3.2)	196 (2.0)	193 (3.0)	215 (4.9)	44 (2.2)	14 (1.7)
San Diego	213 (2.1)	215 (1.7)	240 (2.3)	205 (3.0)	201 (2.2)	225 (3.3)	218 (1.6)	240 (2.2)	205 (4.0)	204 (2.4)	229 (3.9)	64 (2.0)	33 (1.8)
8th grade													
United States	262 (0.3)	264 (0.2)	272 (0.3)	248 (0.5)	251 (0.5)	277 (1.1)	266 (0.2)	275 (0.2)	250 (0.4)	255 (0.4)	280 (1.0)	77 (0.3)	34 (0.3)
All large cities	252 (0.5)	255 (0.5)	273 (1.0)	245 (0.8)	249 (0.8)	271 (1.5)	258 (0.8)	276 (1.0)	246 (0.9)	253 (0.7)	273 (2.8)	68 (0.7)	26 (0.9)
Selected urban districts													
Albuquerque	— (†)	254 (1.2)	271 (2.2)	‡ (†)	248 (1.6)	‡ (†)	256 (1.0)	275 (2.6)	‡ (†)	250 (1.1)	‡ (†)	66 (1.5)	23 (1.4)
Atlanta	250 (1.5)	253 (1.0)	287 (3.2)	249 (1.2)	‡ (†)	‡ (†)	255 (1.0)	294 (2.8)	249 (1.2)	254 (4.5)	‡ (†)	63 (1.5)	22 (1.3)
Austin	261 (2.0)	261 (1.1)	285 (1.8)	246 (3.6)	251 (2.2)	‡ (†)	261 (1.4)	286 (2.9)	245 (3.5)	251 (1.6)	‡ (†)	70 (1.5)	31 (2.1)
Baltimore City	245 (1.7)	246 (1.6)	267 (3.7)	242 (1.7)	‡ (†)	‡ (†)	252 (1.5)	275 (5.6)	249 (1.5)	‡ (†)	‡ (†)	61 (2.7)	16 (1.8)
Boston	257 (1.5)	255 (1.2)	281 (4.3)	246 (2.0)	245 (2.3)	280 (3.4)	257 (1.0)	281 (2.8)	247 (1.8)	250 (1.5)	278 (3.5)	66 (1.5)	28 (1.3)
Charlotte	259 (1.0)	265 (0.9)	283 (1.8)	253 (1.6)	256 (2.5)	264 (5.3)	266 (1.2)	286 (2.0)	253 (1.8)	259 (3.1)	‡ (†)	76 (1.3)	36 (1.7)
Chicago	249 (1.6)	253 (1.1)	271 (3.5)	245 (1.9)	255 (1.3)	262 (13.1)	253 (1.0)	279 (2.6)	244 (1.6)	255 (1.6)	278 (4.3)	64 (1.5)	21 (1.3)
Cleveland	242 (1.6)	240 (1.7)	260 (3.1)	234 (2.2)	241 (3.8)	‡ (†)	239 (1.6)	250 (3.2)	235 (1.8)	241 (3.6)	‡ (†)	49 (2.0)	11 (1.5)
Dallas	— (†)	248 (1.0)	276 (4.1)	244 (2.8)	246 (1.1)	‡ (†)	251 (1.3)	‡ (†)	244 (2.4)	253 (1.6)	‡ (†)	63 (2.0)	15 (1.4)
Detroit	232 (2.4)	237 (1.0)	‡ (†)	235 (1.1)	244 (4.2)	‡ (†)	239 (1.6)	‡ (†)	239 (1.6)	242 (4.7)	‡ (†)	46 (2.1)	9 (1.6)
District of Columbia	240 (1.5)	237 (1.2)	290 (3.4)	231 (1.2)	232 (3.8)	‡ (†)	245 (1.3)	301 (4.0)	237 (1.4)	247 (3.6)	‡ (†)	53 (1.8)	18 (1.1)
Fresno	240 (2.4)	238 (1.8)	257 (3.2)	230 (3.5)	234 (2.2)	241 (3.4)	245 (1.4)	265 (3.4)	236 (3.3)	241 (1.6)	247 (3.1)	54 (2.3)	13 (1.5)
Hillsborough County (FL)	— (†)	264 (1.8)	276 (1.5)	247 (2.4)	258 (2.3)	‡ (†)	267 (1.2)	277 (1.6)	252 (2.3)	263 (1.8)	‡ (†)	77 (1.6)	35 (1.6)
Houston	252 (1.2)	252 (0.9)	283 (2.2)	247 (2.4)	249 (1.3)	‡ (†)	252 (1.2)	284 (3.2)	245 (2.2)	250 (1.4)	284 (5.6)	63 (1.7)	19 (1.3)
Jefferson County (KY)	259 (1.0)	260 (1.1)	269 (1.7)	245 (1.7)	‡ (†)	‡ (†)	261 (1.0)	271 (1.6)	243 (1.4)	258 (4.5)	‡ (†)	69 (1.3)	29 (1.5)
Los Angeles	244 (1.1)	246 (1.1)	273 (3.6)	242 (3.3)	241 (1.2)	269 (4.5)	250 (1.4)	276 (3.2)	240 (3.8)	245 (1.1)	272 (3.1)	60 (1.6)	19 (1.5)
Miami-Dade	261 (1.4)	260 (1.4)	275 (2.4)	246 (1.8)	262 (1.5)	‡ (†)	259 (1.0)	278 (2.8)	245 (2.0)	261 (1.1)	‡ (†)	71 (1.3)	27 (1.7)
Milwaukee	241 (2.0)	238 (1.6)	255 (3.0)	232 (2.0)	243 (2.9)	248 (5.5)	242 (1.4)	262 (3.3)	232 (1.7)	253 (2.5)	‡ (†)	51 (2.0)	13 (1.4)
New York City	252 (1.4)	254 (1.8)	271 (3.6)	248 (2.3)	246 (2.4)	273 (3.3)	256 (1.2)	274 (4.0)	253 (2.0)	249 (2.0)	271 (3.1)	67 (1.2)	25 (1.6)
Philadelphia	247 (2.5)	247 (1.5)	264 (3.8)	244 (1.9)	239 (3.0)	258 (4.7)	249 (1.8)	261 (3.1)	244 (2.4)	243 (3.3)	265 (5.4)	58 (2.2)	16 (2.0)
San Diego	254 (2.8)	256 (2.1)	275 (2.6)	238 (4.8)	245 (3.2)	268 (4.2)	260 (1.5)	281 (2.4)	244 (3.7)	247 (2.1)	266 (3.6)	70 (1.8)	29 (2.3)

—Not available.
†Not applicable.
‡Reporting standards not met (too few cases for a reliable estimate).
[1]Scale ranges from 0 to 500.
[2]*Basic* denotes partial mastery of prerequisite knowledge and skills that are fundamental for proficient work at a given grade.
[3]*Proficient* represents solid academic performance. Students reaching this level have demonstrated competency over challenging subject matter.

NOTE: Race categories exclude persons of Hispanic ethnicity. Totals include racial/ethnic groups not shown separately.
SOURCE: U.S. Department of Education, National Center for Education Statistics, National Assessment of Educational Progress (NAEP), 2009, 2011, and 2013 Reading Assessments, retrieved December 30, 2013, from the Main NAEP Data Explorer (http://nces.ed.gov/nationsreportcard/naepdata/). (This table was prepared December 2013.)

Table 221.85. Average National Assessment of Educational Progress (NAEP) reading scale score, by age and selected student characteristics: Selected years, 1971 through 2012

[Standard errors appear in parentheses]

Selected student characteristic	1971	1975	1980	1984	1988	1990	1992	1994	1996	1999	2004[1] Previous format	2004[1] Revised format	2008	2012
1	2	3	4	5	6	7	8	9	10	11	12	13	14	15
9-year-olds														
All students	208 (1.0)	210 (0.7)	215 (1.0)	211 (0.8)	212 (1.1)	209 (1.2)	211 (0.9)	211 (1.2)	212 (1.0)	212 (1.3)	219 (1.1)	216 (1.0)	220 (0.9)	221 (0.8)
Sex														
Male	201 (1.1)	204 (0.8)	210 (1.1)	207 (1.0)	207 (1.4)	204 (1.7)	206 (1.3)	207 (1.3)	207 (1.4)	209 (1.6)	216 (1.4)	212 (1.1)	216 (1.1)	218 (0.9)
Female	214 (1.0)	216 (0.8)	220 (1.1)	214 (0.9)	216 (1.3)	215 (1.2)	215 (0.9)	215 (1.4)	218 (1.1)	215 (1.5)	221 (1.0)	219 (1.1)	224 (0.9)	223 (0.9)
Gap between female and male score	13 (1.5)	12 (1.1)	10 (1.6)	7 (1.3)	9 (1.9)	11 (2.0)	10 (1.6)	7 (1.9)	11 (1.8)	6 (2.2)	5 (1.8)	8 (1.5)	7 (1.4)	5 (1.3)
Race/ethnicity														
White	214 [2] (0.9)	217 (0.7)	221 (0.8)	218 (0.9)	218 (1.4)	217 (1.3)	218 (1.0)	218 (1.3)	220 (1.2)	221 (1.6)	226 (1.1)	224 (0.9)	228 (1.0)	229 (0.8)
Black	170 [2] (1.7)	181 (1.2)	189 (1.8)	186 (1.3)	189 (2.4)	182 (2.9)	185 (2.2)	185 (2.3)	191 (2.6)	186 (2.3)	200 (2.2)	197 (1.8)	204 (1.7)	206 (1.9)
Hispanic	[3] (†)		183 (2.2)	190 (2.3)	187 (3.0)	194 (3.5)	189 (2.3)	192 (3.1)	186 (3.9)	195 (3.4)	193 (2.7)	205 (1.7)	207 (1.5)	208 (1.5)
Gap between White and Black score	44 (1.9)	35 (1.4)	32 (1.9)	32 (1.6)	29 (2.8)	35 (3.2)	33 (2.4)	33 (2.6)	29 (2.8)	35 (2.8)	26 (2.5)	27 (2.1)	24 (2.0)	23 (2.1)
Gap between White and Hispanic score	† (†)		34 (2.4)	31 (2.4)	31 (3.1)	24 (3.8)	28 (2.6)	26 (3.2)	32 (4.1)	25 (3.6)	28 (3.2)	21 (2.1)	21 (1.8)	21 (1.7)
13-year-olds														
All students	255 (0.9)	256 (0.8)	258 (0.9)	257 (0.6)	257 (1.0)	257 (0.8)	260 (1.2)	258 (0.9)	258 (1.0)	259 (1.0)	259 (1.0)	257 (1.0)	260 (0.8)	263 (1.0)
Sex														
Male	250 (1.0)	250 (0.8)	254 (1.1)	253 (0.7)	252 (1.3)	251 (1.1)	254 (1.7)	251 (1.2)	251 (1.2)	254 (1.3)	254 (1.2)	252 (1.1)	256 (1.0)	259 (1.3)
Female	261 (0.9)	262 (0.9)	263 (0.9)	262 (0.7)	263 (1.0)	263 (1.1)	265 (1.2)	266 (1.2)	264 (1.2)	265 (1.2)	264 (1.3)	262 (1.2)	264 (0.9)	267 (0.9)
Gap between female and male score	11 (1.3)	13 (1.2)	8 (1.4)	9 (1.0)	11 (1.7)	13 (1.6)	11 (2.1)	15 (1.7)	13 (1.7)	12 (1.8)	10 (1.8)	10 (1.6)	8 (1.3)	8 (1.6)
Race/ethnicity														
White	261 [2] (0.7)	262 (0.7)	264 (0.7)	263 (0.6)	261 (1.1)	262 (0.9)	266 (1.2)	265 (1.1)	266 (1.0)	267 (1.2)	266 (1.0)	265 (1.0)	268 (1.0)	270 (1.3)
Black	222 [2] (1.2)	226 (1.2)	233 (1.5)	236 (1.2)	243 (2.4)	241 (2.2)	238 (2.3)	234 (2.4)	234 (2.6)	238 (2.4)	244 (2.0)	239 (1.9)	247 (1.6)	247 (1.6)
Hispanic	[3] (†)		232 (3.0)	237 (2.0)	240 (2.0)	240 (3.5)	238 (2.3)	239 (3.5)	235 (1.9)	238 (2.9)	244 (2.9)	242 (1.6)	242 (1.5)	249 (1.3)
Gap between White and Black score	39 (1.4)	36 (1.4)	32 (1.6)	26 (1.3)	18 (2.6)	21 (2.4)	29 (2.7)	31 (2.7)	32 (2.8)	29 (2.7)	22 (2.3)	25 (2.1)	21 (1.9)	23 (2.1)
Gap between White and Hispanic score	† (†)		30 (3.1)	27 (2.1)	23 (2.1)	21 (3.6)	24 (2.5)	27 (3.7)	30 (2.2)	28 (3.1)	23 (3.1)	24 (1.9)	24 (2.4)	26 (1.8)	21 (1.8)
Parents' highest level of education														
Did not finish high school	— (†)	— (†)	239 (1.1)	240 (1.2)	246 (2.1)	241 (1.8)	239 (2.6)	237 (2.4)	239 (2.8)	238 (3.4)	240 (2.7)	238 (2.3)	239 (1.9)	248 (2.0)
Graduated high school	— (†)	— (†)	253 (0.9)	253 (0.8)	253 (1.2)	251 (0.9)	252 (1.7)	251 (1.4)	251 (1.5)	251 (1.8)	251 (1.6)	249 (1.1)	251 (1.1)	248 (1.7)
Some education after high school	— (†)	— (†)	268 (1.0)	266 (1.1)	265 (1.7)	267 (1.7)	265 (2.7)	266 (1.9)	268 (2.3)	269 (2.4)	264 (2.0)	261 (1.4)	265 (1.1)	264 (1.5)
Graduated college	— (†)	— (†)	273 (0.9)	268 (0.9)	265 (1.6)	267 (1.1)	271 (1.5)	269 (1.2)	269 (1.4)	270 (1.2)	270 (1.0)	266 (1.2)	270 (1.2)	273 (1.3)
17-year-olds														
All students	285 (1.2)	286 (0.8)	285 (1.2)	289 (0.8)	290 (1.0)	290 (1.1)	290 (1.1)	288 (1.3)	288 (1.1)	288 (1.3)	285 (1.2)	283 (1.1)	286 (0.9)	287 (0.9)
Sex														
Male	279 (1.2)	280 (1.0)	282 (1.3)	284 (0.8)	286 (1.5)	284 (1.6)	284 (1.6)	282 (2.2)	281 (1.3)	281 (1.6)	278 (1.5)	276 (1.4)	280 (1.1)	283 (1.1)
Female	291 (1.3)	291 (1.0)	289 (1.2)	294 (0.9)	294 (1.5)	296 (1.2)	296 (1.1)	295 (1.5)	295 (1.2)	295 (1.4)	292 (1.3)	289 (1.2)	291 (1.0)	291 (1.0)
Gap between female and male score	12 (1.8)	12 (1.4)	7 (1.8)	10 (1.2)	8 (2.1)	12 (2.0)	11 (1.9)	13 (2.7)	15 (1.8)	13 (2.1)	14 (2.0)	14 (1.8)	11 (1.5)	8 (1.5)
Race/ethnicity														
White	291 [2] (1.0)	293 (0.6)	293 (0.9)	295 (0.9)	295 (1.2)	297 (1.2)	297 (1.4)	296 (1.5)	295 (1.2)	295 (1.4)	293 (1.1)	289 (1.2)	295 (1.0)	295 (1.0)
Black	239 [2] (1.7)	241 (2.0)	243 (1.8)	264 (1.2)	274 (2.4)	267 (2.3)	261 (2.1)	266 (3.9)	266 (2.7)	264 (1.7)	264 (2.7)	262 (1.9)	266 (2.4)	269 (1.6)
Hispanic	[3] (†)		252 (3.6)	261 (2.7)	268 (2.9)	271 (4.3)	275 (3.6)	271 (3.7)	263 (4.9)	265 (4.1)	271 (3.9)	264 (2.9)	267 (2.5)	269 (1.3)	274 (1.5)
Gap between White and Black score	53 (2.0)	52 (2.1)	50 (2.0)	32 (1.5)	20 (2.7)	29 (2.6)	37 (2.5)	30 (4.2)	29 (3.0)	31 (2.3)	29 (2.9)	27 (2.3)	29 (2.6)	26 (1.9)
Gap between White and Hispanic score	† (†)		41 (3.6)	31 (2.9)	27 (3.0)	24 (4.4)	22 (3.8)	26 (3.9)	33 (5.2)	30 (4.2)	24 (4.2)	29 (3.1)	22 (2.8)	26 (1.6)	21 (1.9)
Parents' highest level of education														
Did not finish high school	— (†)	— (†)	262 (1.5)	269 (1.4)	267 (2.0)	270 (2.8)	271 (3.9)	268 (2.7)	267 (3.2)	265 (3.6)	259 (3.4)	259 (2.7)	266 (2.1)	266 (2.1)
Graduated high school	— (†)	— (†)	277 (1.0)	281 (0.8)	282 (1.3)	283 (1.4)	280 (1.6)	276 (1.9)	273 (1.7)	274 (2.1)	274 (1.6)	271 (1.4)	274 (1.4)	270 (1.6)
Some education after high school	— (†)	— (†)	295 (1.2)	298 (0.9)	299 (2.2)	295 (1.9)	293 (1.9)	294 (1.6)	295 (2.2)	295 (1.8)	286 (1.9)	285 (1.5)	288 (1.1)	287 (1.1)
Graduated college	— (†)	— (†)	301 (1.0)	302 (0.9)	300 (1.4)	302 (1.5)	301 (1.7)	300 (1.7)	299 (1.5)	298 (1.3)	298 (1.3)	295 (1.2)	298 (1.1)	300 (1.0)

—Not available.
†Not applicable.
[1]In 2004, two assessments were conducted—one using the same format that was used in previous assessments, and one using a revised assessment format that provides accommodations for students with disabilities and for English language learners. The 2004 data in column 12 are for the format that was used in previous assessment years, while the 2004 data in column 13 are for the revised format. In subsequent years, only the revised format was used.
[2]Data for 1971 include persons of Hispanic ethnicity.
[3]Test scores of Hispanics were not tabulated separately.
NOTE: Scale ranges from 0 to 500. Students scoring 150 (or higher) are able to follow brief written directions and carry out simple, discrete reading tasks. Students scoring 200 are able to understand, combine ideas, and make inferences based on short uncomplicated passages about specific or sequentially related information. Students scoring 250 are able to search for specific information, interrelate ideas, and make generalizations about literature, science, and social studies materials. Students scoring 300 are able to find, understand, summarize, and explain relatively complicated literary and informational material. Includes public and private schools. For assessment years prior to 2004, accommodations were not permitted. For 2004 (revised format) and later years, includes students tested with accommodations; excludes only those students with disabilities and English language learners who were unable to be tested even with accommodations (2 to 5 percent of all students, depending on age and assessment year). Race categories exclude persons of Hispanic ethnicity, except where noted. Totals include other racial/ethnic groups not shown separately.
SOURCE: U.S. Department of Education, National Center for Education Statistics, National Assessment of Educational Progress (NAEP), NAEP 2012 Trends in Academic Progress; and 2012 NAEP Long-Term Trend Reading Assessment, retrieved June 27, 2013, from Long-Term Trend NAEP Data Explorer (http://nces.ed.gov/nationsreportcard/naepdata/). (This table was prepared June 2013.)

Table 221.90. Percentage of students at or above selected National Assessment of Educational Progress (NAEP) reading score levels, by age, sex, and race/ethnicity: Selected years, 1971 through 2012

[Standard errors appear in parentheses]

Age, sex, race/ethnicity, and score level	1971	1975	1980	1984	1988	1990	1992	1994	1996	1999	2004	2008	2012
1	2	3	4	5	6	7	8	9	10	11	12	13	14
9-year-olds													
Total													
Level 150[1]	91 (0.5)	93 (0.4)	95 (0.4)	92 (0.4)	93 (0.7)	90 (0.9)	92 (0.4)	92 (0.7)	93 (0.6)	93 (0.7)	94 (0.5)	96 (0.4)	96 (0.4)
Level 200[2]	59 (1.0)	62 (0.8)	68 (1.0)	62 (0.8)	63 (1.3)	59 (1.3)	62 (1.1)	63 (1.4)	64 (1.3)	64 (1.4)	69 (1.0)	73 (0.9)	74 (0.9)
Level 250[3]	16 (0.6)	15 (0.6)	18 (0.8)	17 (0.7)	17 (1.1)	18 (1.0)	16 (0.8)	17 (1.2)	17 (0.8)	16 (1.0)	19 (0.7)	21 (0.8)	22 (0.7)
Male													
Level 150[1]	88 (0.7)	91 (0.5)	93 (0.5)	90 (0.5)	90 (0.9)	88 (1.4)	90 (0.8)	90 (1.0)	92 (0.8)	91 (1.1)	92 (0.6)	94 (0.6)	94 (0.6)
Level 200[2]	53 (1.2)	56 (1.0)	63 (1.1)	58 (1.0)	58 (1.8)	54 (1.9)	57 (1.6)	59 (1.5)	58 (2.0)	61 (1.8)	64 (1.3)	70 (1.2)	71 (1.0)
Level 250[3]	12 (0.6)	12 (0.6)	15 (0.9)	16 (0.8)	16 (1.4)	16 (1.2)	14 (1.0)	15 (1.2)	14 (1.3)	15 (1.3)	17 (0.8)	19 (1.0)	21 (0.8)
Female													
Level 150[1]	93 (0.5)	95 (0.3)	96 (0.4)	94 (0.4)	95 (1.0)	92 (1.1)	94 (0.8)	94 (0.8)	95 (0.6)	95 (0.8)	96 (0.5)	97 (0.4)	97 (0.4)
Level 200[2]	65 (1.1)	68 (0.8)	73 (1.0)	65 (1.0)	67 (1.4)	64 (1.2)	67 (1.2)	67 (1.9)	70 (1.6)	67 (1.6)	73 (1.2)	77 (1.1)	77 (1.1)
Level 250[3]	19 (0.8)	18 (0.8)	21 (1.0)	18 (0.8)	19 (1.2)	21 (1.2)	18 (1.1)	18 (1.5)	19 (1.3)	17 (1.3)	20 (1.0)	22 (1.0)	23 (0.9)
White													
Level 150[1]	94 [5] (0.4)	96 (0.3)	97 (0.2)	95 (0.3)	95 (0.7)	94 (0.9)	96 (0.5)	96 (0.5)	96 (0.6)	97 (0.4)	97 (0.4)	98 (0.4)	98 (0.4)
Level 200[2]	65 [5] (1.0)	69 (0.8)	74 (0.7)	69 (0.9)	68 (1.6)	66 (1.4)	69 (1.2)	70 (1.5)	71 (1.5)	73 (1.6)	77 (1.0)	81 (1.0)	82 (0.8)
Level 250[3]	18 [5] (0.7)	17 (0.7)	21 (0.9)	21 (0.8)	20 (1.5)	23 (1.2)	20 (1.0)	20 (1.5)	20 (1.1)	20 (1.4)	24 (0.8)	27 (1.1)	28 (0.8)
Black													
Level 150[1]	70 [5] (1.7)	81 (1.1)	85 (1.4)	81 (1.2)	83 (2.4)	77 (2.7)	80 (2.2)	79 (2.4)	84 (1.9)	82 (2.5)	88 (1.7)	91 (1.1)	94 (1.0)
Level 200[2]	22 [5] (1.5)	32 (1.5)	41 (1.9)	37 (1.5)	39 (2.9)	34 (3.4)	37 (2.2)	38 (2.8)	42 (3.2)	36 (3.0)	50 (2.3)	58 (2.3)	61 (2.1)
Level 250[3]	2 [5] (0.5)	2 (0.3)	4 (0.6)	5 (0.6)	6 (1.2)	5 (1.5)	5 (0.8)	4 (1.5)	6 (1.1)	4 (1.1)	7 (0.8)	9 (0.9)	10 (1.1)
Hispanic													
Level 150[1]	[6] (†)	81 (2.5)	84 (1.8)	82 (3.0)	86 (3.5)	84 (1.8)	83 (2.6)	80 (4.6)	86 (2.4)	87 (3.3)	89 (1.3)	93 (0.8)	92 (1.1)
Level 200[2]	[6] (†)	35 (3.0)	42 (2.6)	40 (2.7)	46 (3.3)	41 (2.7)	43 (3.5)	37 (4.6)	48 (3.8)	44 (3.4)	53 (1.7)	62 (1.7)	63 (1.8)
Level 250[3]	[6] (†)	3 (0.5)	5 (1.4)	4 (0.7)	9 (2.3)	6 (2.0)	7 (2.3)	6 (1.6)	7 (3.2)	6 (1.7)	7 (0.8)	10 (1.2)	11 (1.0)
13-year-olds													
Total													
Level 200[2]	93 (0.5)	93 (0.4)	95 (0.4)	94 (0.3)	95 (0.6)	94 (0.6)	93 (0.7)	92 (0.6)	92 (0.7)	93 (0.7)	92 (0.6)	94 (0.4)	94 (0.4)
Level 250[3]	58 (1.1)	59 (1.0)	61 (1.1)	59 (0.9)	59 (1.3)	59 (1.0)	62 (1.4)	60 (1.2)	60 (1.3)	61 (1.5)	59 (1.1)	63 (0.8)	66 (1.3)
Level 300[4]	10 (0.5)	10 (0.5)	11 (0.5)	11 (0.4)	11 (0.8)	11 (0.6)	15 (0.9)	14 (0.8)	14 (1.0)	15 (1.1)	12 (0.8)	13 (0.5)	15 (1.0)
Male													
Level 200[2]	91 (0.7)	91 (0.6)	93 (0.6)	92 (0.4)	93 (1.0)	91 (0.9)	90 (1.1)	89 (1.1)	89 (1.2)	91 (0.9)	89 (0.8)	92 (0.6)	93 (0.7)
Level 250[3]	52 (1.2)	52 (1.1)	56 (1.2)	54 (0.9)	52 (1.9)	52 (1.5)	55 (2.0)	53 (1.9)	53 (1.6)	55 (1.9)	55 (1.3)	59 (1.2)	62 (1.6)
Level 300[4]	7 (0.5)	7 (0.4)	9 (0.7)	9 (0.5)	9 (0.9)	8 (0.8)	13 (1.1)	10 (0.7)	10 (1.0)	11 (1.1)	11 (0.9)	11 (0.7)	13 (1.1)
Female													
Level 200[2]	95 (0.4)	95 (0.4)	96 (0.4)	96 (0.3)	97 (0.6)	96 (0.6)	95 (0.7)	95 (0.6)	95 (0.6)	96 (0.7)	95 (0.6)	96 (0.5)	96 (0.4)
Level 250[3]	64 (1.1)	65 (1.2)	65 (1.1)	64 (0.8)	65 (1.4)	65 (1.5)	68 (1.4)	68 (1.7)	66 (1.6)	66 (1.9)	65 (1.3)	66 (1.0)	69 (1.4)
Level 300[4]	12 (0.6)	13 (0.7)	13 (0.6)	13 (0.6)	13 (0.9)	14 (0.9)	18 (1.1)	18 (1.1)	17 (1.3)	18 (1.7)	14 (1.0)	16 (0.9)	17 (1.1)
White													
Level 200[2]	96 [5] (0.3)	96 (0.2)	97 (0.2)	96 (0.2)	96 (0.6)	96 (0.6)	96 (0.6)	95 (0.7)	95 (0.5)	96 (0.6)	95 (0.5)	96 (0.4)	96 (0.6)
Level 250[3]	64 [5] (0.9)	65 (0.9)	68 (0.8)	65 (0.8)	64 (1.5)	65 (1.2)	68 (1.4)	68 (1.3)	69 (1.4)	69 (1.7)	68 (1.1)	72 (1.2)	74 (1.8)
Level 300[4]	11 [5] (0.5)	12 (0.5)	14 (0.6)	13 (0.6)	12 (0.9)	13 (0.9)	18 (1.1)	17 (1.0)	17 (1.3)	18 (1.4)	16 (0.9)	18 (0.8)	19 (1.0)
Black													
Level 200[2]	74 [5] (1.7)	77 (1.3)	84 (1.7)	85 (1.2)	91 (2.2)	88 (2.3)	82 (2.7)	81 (2.3)	82 (3.2)	85 (2.3)	86 (1.5)	91 (1.1)	90 (1.3)
Level 250[3]	21 [5] (1.2)	25 (1.6)	30 (2.0)	35 (1.3)	40 (2.3)	42 (3.5)	38 (2.7)	36 (3.5)	34 (3.9)	38 (2.7)	40 (2.3)	48 (2.3)	48 (2.5)
Level 300[4]	1 [5] (0.2)	2 (0.5)	2 (0.5)	3 (0.6)	5 (1.2)	5 (0.8)	6 (1.4)	4 (1.2)	3 (0.9)	5 (1.4)	4 (0.7)	6 (0.8)	6 (0.9)
Hispanic													
Level 200[2]	[6] (†)	81 (2.3)	87 (2.4)	86 (1.7)	87 (2.6)	86 (2.4)	83 (3.5)	82 (2.7)	85 (3.2)	89 (2.8)	85 (1.9)	87 (1.3)	91 (1.2)
Level 250[3]	[6] (†)	32 (3.6)	35 (2.6)	39 (2.3)	38 (4.4)	37 (2.9)	41 (5.1)	34 (3.9)	38 (3.7)	43 (3.8)	44 (2.3)	44 (1.8)	51 (1.7)
Level 300[4]	[6] (†)	2 (1.0)	2 (0.6)	4 (1.0)	4 (1.9)	4 (1.2)	6 (1.9)	4 (1.8)	5 (1.7)	6 (1.8)	5 (1.2)	5 (0.8)	6 (0.5)
17-year-olds													
Total													
Level 250[3]	79 (0.9)	80 (0.7)	81 (0.9)	83 (0.6)	86 (0.8)	84 (1.0)	83 (0.8)	81 (1.0)	82 (0.8)	82 (1.0)	79 (0.9)	80 (0.6)	82 (0.6)
Level 300[4]	39 (1.0)	39 (0.8)	38 (1.1)	40 (1.0)	41 (1.5)	41 (1.0)	43 (1.1)	41 (1.2)	39 (1.4)	40 (1.4)	36 (1.2)	39 (0.8)	39 (0.9)
Male													
Level 250[3]	74 (1.0)	76 (0.8)	78 (1.0)	80 (0.7)	83 (1.4)	80 (1.4)	78 (1.2)	76 (1.5)	77 (1.2)	77 (1.5)	73 (1.2)	76 (0.8)	79 (0.8)
Level 300[4]	34 (1.1)	34 (1.0)	35 (1.3)	36 (1.0)	37 (2.3)	36 (1.5)	38 (1.6)	36 (1.9)	34 (1.9)	34 (1.7)	32 (1.2)	35 (0.9)	36 (1.2)
Female													
Level 250[3]	83 (1.0)	84 (0.9)	84 (1.0)	87 (0.6)	88 (1.1)	89 (1.0)	87 (1.1)	86 (1.2)	87 (1.0)	87 (1.0)	84 (0.9)	84 (0.8)	85 (0.7)
Level 300[4]	44 (1.2)	44 (0.9)	41 (1.2)	45 (1.1)	45 (2.0)	44 (2.0)	47 (1.3)	48 (1.5)	46 (1.5)	45 (1.7)	41 (1.6)	43 (1.0)	42 (1.1)
White													
Level 250[3]	84 [5] (0.7)	86 (0.6)	87 (0.6)	88 (0.5)	89 (0.9)	88 (1.1)	88 (0.9)	86 (1.1)	87 (0.8)	87 (1.3)	83 (0.9)	87 (0.6)	87 (0.6)
Level 300[4]	43 [5] (0.9)	44 (0.8)	43 (1.1)	47 (1.1)	45 (1.6)	48 (1.2)	50 (1.4)	48 (1.4)	46 (1.5)	46 (1.5)	42 (1.3)	47 (1.0)	47 (1.3)
Black													
Level 250[3]	40 [5] (1.6)	43 (1.6)	44 (2.0)	65 (1.5)	76 (2.4)	69 (2.8)	61 (2.3)	66 (4.1)	68 (4.0)	66 (2.5)	64 (2.2)	67 (2.4)	70 (1.4)
Level 300[4]	8 [5] (0.9)	8 (0.7)	7 (0.8)	16 (1.0)	25 (3.1)	20 (1.8)	17 (2.5)	22 (3.7)	18 (2.2)	17 (1.7)	16 (1.8)	21 (1.5)	22 (1.5)
Hispanic													
Level 250[3]	[6] (†)	53 (4.1)	62 (3.1)	68 (2.4)	71 (4.8)	75 (4.7)	69 (4.0)	63 (4.4)	65 (4.2)	68 (4.3)	67 (2.4)	70 (1.5)	74 (1.3)
Level 300[4]	[6] (†)	13 (2.7)	17 (2.1)	21 (3.0)	23 (3.7)	27 (3.3)	27 (3.2)	20 (3.0)	20 (4.8)	24 (3.8)	23 (2.1)	22 (1.0)	26 (1.3)

†Not applicable.

[1]Students scoring 150 (or higher) are able to follow brief written directions and carry out simple, discrete reading tasks.

[2]Students scoring 200 (or higher) are able to understand, combine ideas, and make inferences based on short uncomplicated passages about specific or sequentially related information.

[3]Students scoring 250 (or higher) are able to search for specific information, interrelate ideas, and make generalizations about literature, science, and social studies materials.

[4]Students scoring 300 (or higher) are able to find, understand, summarize, and explain relatively complicated literary and informational material.

[5]Data for 1971 include persons of Hispanic ethnicity.

[6]Test scores of Hispanics were not tabulated separately.

NOTE: The NAEP reading scores have been evaluated at certain performance levels, as outlined in footnotes 1 through 4. Scale ranges from 0 to 500. Includes public and private schools. For assessment years prior to 2004, accommodations were not permitted. For 2004 and later years, includes students tested with accommodations; excludes only those students with disabilities and English language learners who were unable to be tested even with accommodations (2 to 5 percent of all students, depending on age and assessment year). Race categories exclude persons of Hispanic ethnicity, except where noted. Totals include other racial/ethnic groups not shown separately.

SOURCE: U.S. Department of Education, National Center for Education Statistics, National Assessment of Educational Progress (NAEP), NAEP 1999 Trends in Academic Progress; and 2004, 2008, and 2012 Long-Term Trend Reading Assessments, retrieved May 12, 2009, and July 15, 2013, from the Long-Term Trend NAEP Data Explorer (http://nces.ed.gov/nations reportcard/naepdata/). (This table was prepared July 2013.)

Table 222.10. Average National Assessment of Educational Progress (NAEP) mathematics scale score, by sex, race/ethnicity, and grade: Selected years, 1990 through 2013

[Standard errors appear in parentheses]

		Sex			Race/ethnicity										
		Average mathematics scale score		Gap between female and male score	Average mathematics scale score									Gap between White and Black score	Gap between White and Hispanic score
								Asian/Pacific Islander			American Indian/ Alaska Native	Two or more races[1]		
Grade and year	All students	Male	Female		White	Black	Hispanic	Total	Asian[1]	Pacific Islander[1]				
1	2	3	4	5	6	7	8	9	10	11	12	13	14	15
Grade 4														
1990[2]	213 (0.9)	214 (1.2)	213 (1.1)	-1 (1.7)	220 (1.0)	188 (1.8)	200 (2.2)	225 (4.1)	— (†)	— (†)	‡ (†)	— (†)	32 (2.0)	20 (2.4)
1992[2]	220 (0.7)	221 (0.8)	219 (1.0)	-2 (1.2)	227 (0.8)	193 (1.4)	202 (1.5)	231 (2.1)	— (†)	— (†)	‡ (†)	— (†)	35 (1.6)	25 (1.7)
1996	224 (1.0)	224 (1.1)	223 (1.1)	# (†)	232 (1.0)	198 (1.6)	207 (1.9)	229 (4.2)	— (†)	— (†)	217 (5.6)	— (†)	34 (1.8)	25 (2.1)
2000	226 (0.9)	227 (1.0)	224 (0.9)	-3 (1.4)	234 (0.8)	203 (1.2)	208 (1.5)	‡ (†)	— (†)	— (†)	208 (3.5)	— (†)	31 (1.5)	27 (1.7)
2003	235 (0.2)	236 (0.3)	233 (0.2)	-3 (0.3)	243 (0.2)	216 (0.4)	222 (0.4)	246 (1.1)	— (†)	— (†)	223 (1.0)	— (†)	27 (0.4)	22 (0.5)
2005	238 (0.1)	239 (0.2)	237 (0.2)	-3 (0.2)	246 (0.1)	220 (0.3)	226 (0.3)	251 (0.7)	— (†)	— (†)	226 (0.9)	— (†)	26 (0.3)	20 (0.3)
2007	240 (0.2)	241 (0.2)	239 (0.2)	-2 (0.2)	248 (0.2)	222 (0.3)	227 (0.3)	253 (0.8)	— (†)	— (†)	228 (0.7)	— (†)	26 (0.4)	21 (0.4)
2009	240 (0.2)	241 (0.3)	239 (0.3)	-2 (0.4)	248 (0.2)	222 (0.3)	227 (0.4)	255 (1.0)	— (†)	— (†)	225 (0.9)	— (†)	26 (0.4)	21 (0.5)
2011	241 (0.2)	241 (0.2)	240 (0.2)	-1 (0.3)	249 (0.2)	224 (0.4)	229 (0.3)	256 (1.0)	257 (1.0)	236 (2.1)	225 (0.9)	245 (0.6)	25 (0.4)	20 (0.4)
2013	242 (0.2)	242 (0.3)	241 (0.2)	-1 (0.4)	250 (0.2)	224 (0.3)	231 (0.4)	258 (0.8)	259 (0.8)	236 (2.0)	227 (1.1)	245 (0.7)	26 (0.4)	19 (0.5)
Grade 8														
1990[2]	263 (1.3)	263 (1.6)	262 (1.3)	-1 (2.1)	270 (1.3)	237 (2.7)	246 (4.3)	275 (5.0)	— (†)	— (†)	‡ (†)	— (†)	33 (3.0)	24 (4.5)
1992[2]	268 (0.9)	268 (1.1)	269 (1.0)	1 (1.5)	277 (1.0)	237 (1.3)	249 (1.2)	290 (5.9)	— (†)	— (†)	‡ (†)	— (†)	40 (1.7)	28 (1.5)
1996	270 (0.9)	271 (1.1)	269 (1.1)	-2 (1.3)	281 (1.1)	240 (1.9)	251 (1.7)	‡ (†)	— (†)	— (†)	— (†)	— (†)	41 (2.2)	30 (2.0)
2000	273 (0.8)	274 (0.9)	272 (0.9)	-2 (1.3)	284 (0.8)	244 (1.2)	253 (1.3)	288 (3.5)	— (†)	— (†)	259 (7.5)	— (†)	40 (1.5)	31 (1.6)
2003	278 (0.3)	278 (0.3)	277 (0.3)	-2 (0.4)	288 (0.3)	252 (0.5)	259 (0.6)	291 (1.3)	— (†)	— (†)	263 (1.8)	— (†)	35 (0.6)	29 (0.7)
2005	279 (0.2)	280 (0.2)	278 (0.2)	-2 (0.3)	289 (0.2)	255 (0.4)	262 (0.4)	295 (0.9)	— (†)	— (†)	264 (0.9)	— (†)	34 (0.4)	27 (0.5)
2007	281 (0.3)	282 (0.3)	280 (0.3)	-2 (0.4)	291 (0.3)	260 (0.4)	265 (0.4)	297 (0.9)	— (†)	— (†)	264 (1.2)	— (†)	32 (0.5)	26 (0.5)
2009	283 (0.3)	284 (0.3)	282 (0.4)	-2 (0.5)	293 (0.3)	261 (0.3)	266 (0.6)	301 (1.2)	— (†)	— (†)	266 (1.1)	— (†)	32 (0.5)	26 (0.6)
2011	284 (0.2)	284 (0.3)	283 (0.2)	-1 (0.4)	293 (0.2)	262 (0.5)	270 (0.5)	303 (1.0)	305 (1.1)	269 (2.4)	265 (0.9)	288 (1.3)	31 (0.5)	23 (0.5)
2013	285 (0.3)	285 (0.3)	284 (0.3)	-1 (0.4)	294 (0.3)	263 (0.4)	272 (0.5)	306 (1.1)	309 (1.1)	275 (2.3)	269 (1.2)	288 (1.2)	31 (0.5)	22 (0.5)
Grade 12														
1990[2]	[3] (†)	[3] (†)	[3] (†)	[3] (†)	[3] (†)	[3] (†)	[3] (†)	[3] (†)	[3] (†)	[3] (†)	[3] (†)	[3] (†)	[3] (†)	[3] (†)
1992[2]	[3] (†)	[3] (†)	[3] (†)	[3] (†)	[3] (†)	[3] (†)	[3] (†)	[3] (†)	[3] (†)	[3] (†)	[3] (†)	[3] (†)	[3] (†)	[3] (†)
1996	[3] (†)	[3] (†)	[3] (†)	[3] (†)	[3] (†)	[3] (†)	[3] (†)	[3] (†)	[3] (†)	[3] (†)	[3] (†)	[3] (†)	[3] (†)	[3] (†)
2000	[3] (†)	[3] (†)	[3] (†)	[3] (†)	[3] (†)	[3] (†)	[3] (†)	[3] (†)	[3] (†)	[3] (†)	[3] (†)	[3] (†)	[3] (†)	[3] (†)
2003	— (†)	— (†)	— (†)	(†)	(†)	(†)	(†)	(†)	(†)	(†)	(†)	(†)	(†)	(†)
2005	150 (0.6)	151 (0.7)	149 (0.7)	-3 (1.0)	157 (0.6)	127 (1.1)	133 (1.3)	163 (2.0)	— (†)	— (†)	134 (4.1)	— (†)	31 (1.2)	24 (1.4)
2007	— (†)	— (†)	— (†)	— (†)	— (†)	— (†)	— (†)	— (†)	— (†)	— (†)	— (†)	— (†)	— (†)	— (†)
2009	153 (0.7)	155 (0.9)	152 (0.7)	-3 (1.1)	161 (0.6)	131 (0.8)	138 (0.8)	175 (2.7)	— (†)	— (†)	144 (2.8)	— (†)	30 (1.0)	23 (1.0)
2011	— (†)	— (†)	— (†)	— (†)	— (†)	— (†)	— (†)	— (†)	— (†)	— (†)	— (†)	— (†)	— (†)	— (†)
2013	153 (0.5)	155 (0.6)	152 (0.6)	-3 (0.9)	162 (0.6)	132 (0.8)	141 (0.8)	172 (1.3)	174 (1.3)	151 (2.8)	142 (3.2)	155 (1.7)	30 (1.0)	21 (1.0)

—Not available.
†Not applicable.
#Rounds to zero.
‡Reporting standards not met (too few cases for a reliable estimate).
[1]Prior to 2011, separate data for Asians, Pacific Islanders, and those of Two or more races were not collected.
[2]Accommodations were not permitted for this assessment.
[3]Because of major changes to the framework and content of the grade 12 assessment, scores from 2005 and later assessment years cannot be compared with scores from earlier assessment years. Therefore, this table does not include scores from the earlier grade 12 assessment years (1990, 1992, 1996, and 2000). For data pertaining to scale score comparisons between earlier years, see the *Digest of Education Statistics 2009*, table 138 (http://nces.ed.gov/programs/digest/d09/tables/dt09_138.asp).

NOTE: For the grade 4 and grade 8 assessments, scale ranges from 0 to 500. For the grade 12 assessment, scale ranges from 0 to 300. Includes public and private schools. For 1996 and later years, includes students tested with accommodations (1 to 12 percent of all students, depending on grade level and year); excludes only those students with disabilities and English language learners who were unable to be tested even with accommodations (1 to 4 percent of all students). Race categories exclude persons of Hispanic ethnicity.
SOURCE: U.S. Department of Education, National Center for Education Statistics, National Assessment of Educational Progress (NAEP), 1990, 1992, 1996, 2000, 2003, 2005, 2007, 2009, 2011, and 2013 Mathematics Assessments, retrieved June 16, 2014, from the Main NAEP Data Explorer (http://nces.ed.gov/nationsreportcard/naepdata/). (This table was prepared September 2014.)

Table 222.12. Average National Assessment of Educational Progress (NAEP) mathematics scale score and percentage of students attaining selected NAEP mathematics achievement levels, by selected school and student characteristics and grade: Selected years, 1990 through 2013

[Standard errors appear in parentheses]

Grade and year	Percent of students in school eligible for free or reduced-price lunch					English language learner (ELL) status			Disability status[1]			Percent of all students attaining mathematics achievement levels		
	Average mathematics scale score[2]				Gap between low-poverty and high-poverty score	Average mathematics scale score[2]		Gap between non-ELL and ELL score	Average mathematics scale score[2]		Gap between non-SD and SD score	Below Basic[3]	At or above Basic[3]	At or above Proficient[4]
	0–25 percent eligible (low poverty)	26–50 percent eligible	51–75 percent eligible	76–100 percent eligible (high poverty)		ELL	Non-ELL		Identified as student with disability (SD)	Not identified as SD				
1	2	3	4	5	6	7	8	9	10	11	12	13	14	15
Grade 4														
1990[5]	— (†)	— (†)	— (†)	— (†)	— (†)	‡ (†)	‡ (†)	‡ (†)	‡ (†)	‡ (†)	‡ (†)	50 (1.4)	50 (1.4)	13 (1.2)
1992[5]	— (†)	— (†)	— (†)	— (†)	— (†)	‡ (†)	‡ (†)	‡ (†)	‡ (†)	‡ (†)	‡ (†)	41 (1.0)	59 (1.0)	18 (1.0)
1996	— (†)	— (†)	— (†)	— (†)	— (†)	201 (3.6)	225 (0.9)	24 (3.7)	204 (2.9)	225 (1.1)	22 (3.1)	37 (1.3)	63 (1.3)	21 (1.1)
2000	239 (1.2)	227 (1.2)	216 (1.5)	205 (1.2)	34 (1.7)	199 (2.0)	227 (0.8)	28 (2.1)	198 (2.2)	228 (0.9)	30 (2.4)	35 (1.3)	65 (1.3)	24 (1.0)
2003	247 (0.3)	237 (0.3)	229 (0.4)	216 (0.5)	31 (0.6)	214 (0.6)	237 (0.2)	23 (0.6)	214 (0.4)	237 (0.2)	23 (0.4)	23 (0.3)	77 (0.3)	32 (0.3)
2005	250 (0.3)	240 (0.3)	232 (0.3)	220 (0.3)	30 (0.4)	216 (0.5)	240 (0.1)	24 (0.5)	219 (0.4)	240 (0.2)	22 (0.4)	20 (0.2)	80 (0.2)	36 (0.2)
2007	252 (0.3)	242 (0.3)	234 (0.3)	222 (0.4)	30 (0.5)	217 (0.5)	242 (0.2)	25 (0.5)	220 (0.4)	242 (0.2)	22 (0.4)	18 (0.2)	82 (0.2)	39 (0.3)
2009	254 (0.4)	242 (0.4)	234 (0.4)	223 (0.4)	31 (0.6)	218 (0.6)	242 (0.2)	24 (0.7)	221 (0.5)	242 (0.2)	21 (0.5)	18 (0.3)	82 (0.3)	39 (0.3)
2011	255 (0.4)	245 (0.4)	237 (0.3)	226 (0.3)	29 (0.6)	219 (0.5)	243 (0.2)	24 (0.5)	218 (0.4)	244 (0.2)	26 (0.5)	18 (0.2)	82 (0.2)	40 (0.3)
2013	257 (0.4)	246 (0.4)	238 (0.5)	226 (0.5)	31 (0.6)	219 (0.6)	244 (0.2)	25 (0.6)	218 (0.5)	245 (0.2)	26 (0.5)	17 (0.2)	83 (0.2)	42 (0.3)
Grade 8														
1990[5]	— (†)	— (†)	— (†)	— (†)	— (†)	‡ (†)	‡ (†)	‡ (†)	‡ (†)	‡ (†)	‡ (†)	48 (1.4)	52 (1.4)	15 (1.1)
1992[5]	— (†)	— (†)	— (†)	— (†)	— (†)	‡ (†)	‡ (†)	‡ (†)	‡ (†)	‡ (†)	‡ (†)	42 (1.1)	58 (1.1)	21 (1.0)
1996	— (†)	— (†)	— (†)	— (†)	— (†)	226 (3.2)	272 (1.0)	46 (3.4)	231 (2.7)	273 (0.9)	42 (2.9)	39 (1.0)	61 (1.0)	23 (1.0)
2000	287 (1.1)	270 (1.4)	260 (1.8)	246 (2.2)	41 (2.4)	234 (2.7)	274 (0.8)	40 (2.8)	230 (2.1)	276 (0.8)	47 (2.3)	37 (0.9)	63 (0.9)	26 (0.8)
2003	291 (0.4)	278 (0.4)	266 (0.7)	251 (0.8)	40 (0.8)	242 (1.0)	279 (0.3)	38 (1.0)	242 (0.6)	282 (0.3)	39 (0.6)	32 (0.3)	68 (0.3)	29 (0.3)
2005	293 (0.4)	280 (0.3)	268 (0.4)	254 (0.6)	38 (0.7)	244 (0.8)	281 (0.2)	37 (0.8)	245 (0.5)	283 (0.2)	38 (0.5)	31 (0.2)	69 (0.2)	30 (0.2)
2007	296 (0.4)	282 (0.4)	271 (0.6)	259 (0.7)	37 (0.8)	246 (0.8)	283 (0.2)	38 (0.8)	246 (0.6)	285 (0.3)	38 (0.7)	29 (0.3)	71 (0.3)	32 (0.3)
2009	298 (0.5)	284 (0.5)	274 (0.7)	260 (0.7)	38 (0.8)	243 (0.9)	285 (0.3)	42 (0.9)	249 (0.5)	287 (0.3)	38 (0.6)	27 (0.3)	73 (0.3)	34 (0.3)
2011	300 (0.5)	287 (0.5)	276 (0.7)	264 (0.7)	36 (0.9)	244 (1.0)	286 (0.2)	42 (1.0)	250 (0.6)	288 (0.2)	38 (0.7)	27 (0.2)	73 (0.2)	35 (0.2)
2013	301 (0.5)	289 (0.5)	277 (0.4)	265 (0.6)	36 (0.8)	246 (0.8)	287 (0.3)	41 (0.8)	249 (0.5)	289 (0.3)	40 (0.6)	26 (0.3)	74 (0.3)	35 (0.3)
Grade 12														
1990[5]	[6] (†)	[6] (†)	[6] (†)	[6] (†)	[6] (†)	[6] (†)	[6] (†)	[6] (†)	[6] (†)	[6] (†)	[6] (†)	[6] (†)	[6] (†)	[6] (†)
1992[5]	[6] (†)	[6] (†)	[6] (†)	[6] (†)	[6] (†)	[6] (†)	[6] (†)	[6] (†)	[6] (†)	[6] (†)	[6] (†)	[6] (†)	[6] (†)	[6] (†)
1996	[6] (†)	[6] (†)	[6] (†)	[6] (†)	[6] (†)	[6] (†)	[6] (†)	[6] (†)	[6] (†)	[6] (†)	[6] (†)	[6] (†)	[6] (†)	[6] (†)
2000	[6] (†)	[6] (†)	[6] (†)	[6] (†)	[6] (†)	[6] (†)	[6] (†)	[6] (†)	[6] (†)	[6] (†)	[6] (†)	[6] (†)	[6] (†)	[6] (†)
2003	— (†)	— (†)	— (†)	— (†)	— (†)	— (†)	— (†)	— (†)	— (†)	— (†)	— (†)	— (†)	— (†)	— (†)
2005	158 (1.0)	147 (1.0)	136 (1.3)	122 (2.7)	36 (2.8)	120 (2.5)	151 (0.6)	31 (2.5)	114 (1.8)	153 (0.6)	39 (1.9)	39 (0.8)	61 (0.8)	23 (0.7)
2007	— (†)	— (†)	— (†)	— (†)	— (†)	— (†)	— (†)	— (†)	— (†)	— (†)	— (†)	— (†)	— (†)	— (†)
2009	166 (1.0)	150 (0.7)	140 (1.2)	130 (1.7)	36 (2.1)	117 (1.7)	154 (0.7)	38 (1.9)	120 (1.2)	156 (0.7)	36 (1.4)	36 (0.8)	64 (0.8)	26 (0.8)
2011	— (†)	— (†)	— (†)	— (†)	— (†)	— (†)	— (†)	— (†)	— (†)	— (†)	— (†)	— (†)	— (†)	— (†)
2013	169 (1.0)	155 (0.6)	143 (1.0)	134 (1.2)	35 (1.6)	109 (1.7)	155 (0.5)	46 (1.8)	119 (1.0)	157 (0.5)	38 (1.2)	35 (0.7)	65 (0.7)	26 (0.6)

—Not available.
†Not applicable.
[1]The student with disability (SD) variable used in this table includes students who have a 504 plan, even if they do not have an Individualized Education Plan (IEP).
[2]For the grade 4 and grade 8 assessments, scale ranges from 0 to 500. For the grade 12 assessment, scale ranges from 0 to 300.
[3]Basic denotes partial mastery of the knowledge and skills that are fundamental for proficient work at a given grade.
[4]Proficient represents solid academic performance. Students reaching this level have demonstrated competency over challenging subject matter.
[5]Accommodations were not permitted for this assessment.
[6]Because of major changes to the framework and content of the grade 12 assessment, results from 2005 and later assessment years cannot be compared with results from earlier assessment years. Therefore, this table does not include results from the earlier grade 12 assessment years (1990, 1992, 1996, and 2000). For data pertaining to comparisons between earlier years, see the *Digest of Education Statistics 2009*, table 138 (http://nces.ed.gov/programs/digest/d09/tables/dt09_138.asp).
NOTE: Includes public and private schools. For 1996 and later years, includes students tested with accommodations (1 to 12 percent of all students, depending on grade level and year); excludes only those students with disabilities and English language learners who were unable to be tested even with accommodations (1 to 4 percent of all students).
SOURCE: U.S. Department of Education, National Center for Education Statistics, National Assessment of Educational Progress (NAEP), 1990, 1992, 1996, 2000, 2003, 2005, 2007, 2009, 2011, and 2013 Mathematics Assessments, retrieved June 16, 2014, from the Main NAEP Data Explorer (http://nces.ed.gov/nationsreportcard/naepdata/). (This table was prepared September 2014.)

Table 222.20. Percentage of students at or above selected National Assessment of Educational Progress (NAEP) mathematics achievement levels, by grade and selected student characteristics: Selected years, 1996 through 2013

[Standard errors appear in parentheses]

Grade and selected student characteristic	1996		2000		2003		2005		2007		2009		2011		2013	
	At or above Basic[1]	At or above Proficient[2]	At or above Basic[1]	At or above Proficient[2]	At or above Basic[1]	At or above Proficient[2]	At or above Basic[1]	At or above Proficient[2]	At or above Basic[1]	At or above Proficient[2]	At or above Basic[1]	At or above Proficient[2]	At or above Basic[1]	At or above Proficient[2]	At or above Basic[1]	At or above Proficient[2]
1	2	3	4	5	6	7	8	9	10	11	12	13	14	15	16	17
4th grade, all students	63 (1.3)	21 (1.1)	65 (1.3)	24 (1.0)	77 (0.3)	32 (0.3)	80 (0.2)	36 (0.2)	82 (0.2)	39 (0.3)	82 (0.3)	39 (0.3)	82 (0.2)	40 (0.3)	83 (0.2)	42 (0.3)
Sex																
Male	63 (1.5)	22 (1.2)	67 (1.4)	26 (1.2)	78 (0.4)	35 (0.4)	81 (0.2)	38 (0.2)	82 (0.2)	41 (0.3)	82 (0.3)	41 (0.4)	83 (0.3)	42 (0.4)	82 (0.3)	43 (0.4)
Female	63 (1.4)	20 (1.4)	64 (1.5)	22 (1.1)	76 (0.3)	30 (0.3)	80 (0.2)	34 (0.2)	82 (0.2)	37 (0.4)	82 (0.3)	37 (0.3)	82 (0.3)	39 (0.3)	83 (0.2)	41 (0.4)
Race/ethnicity																
White	76 (1.2)	27 (1.3)	78 (1.4)	31 (1.2)	87 (0.2)	43 (0.3)	90 (0.2)	47 (0.2)	91 (0.2)	51 (0.4)	91 (0.2)	51 (0.4)	91 (0.2)	52 (0.4)	91 (0.2)	54 (0.4)
Black	27 (2.0)	3 (0.6)	36 (1.9)	5 (0.8)	54 (0.6)	10 (0.6)	60 (0.5)	13 (0.3)	64 (0.6)	15 (0.4)	64 (0.6)	16 (0.5)	66 (0.5)	17 (0.5)	66 (0.7)	18 (0.5)
Hispanic	40 (2.7)	7 (1.4)	42 (2.6)	7 (1.0)	62 (0.7)	16 (0.5)	68 (0.5)	19 (0.3)	70 (0.5)	22 (0.4)	71 (0.7)	22 (0.7)	72 (0.6)	24 (0.6)	73 (0.7)	26 (0.7)
Asian/Pacific Islander	67 (5.7)	27 (5.0)	‡	‡	87 (0.8)	48 (1.9)	90 (0.5)	55 (1.1)	91 (0.7)	58 (1.3)	92 (0.6)	60 (1.5)	91 (0.6)	62 (1.6)	91 (0.6)	64 (1.2)
Asian	—	—	—	—	—	—	—	—	—	—	—	—	93 (0.6)	63 (1.3)	92 (0.6)	66 (1.2)
Pacific Islander	—	—	—	—	—	—	—	—	—	—	—	—	77 (2.7)	24 (4.7)	77 (3.1)	33 (3.2)
American Indian/Alaska Native	57 (7.5)	‡	40 (6.1)	8 (4.5)	64 (1.7)	17 (1.2)	68 (1.5)	21 (1.2)	70 (1.2)	25 (1.1)	66 (1.6)	21 (1.1)	66 (1.2)	22 (1.2)	68 (1.7)	23 (1.4)
Two or more races	—	—	—	—	—	—	—	—	—	—	—	—	87 (0.7)	45 (1.7)	85 (1.0)	46 (1.4)
Eligibility for free or reduced-price lunch																
Eligible	40 (1.8)	8 (0.9)	43 (1.5)	8 (0.8)	62 (0.5)	15 (0.4)	67 (0.3)	19 (0.2)	70 (0.4)	22 (0.3)	70 (0.4)	22 (0.3)	72 (0.3)	24 (0.3)	73 (0.4)	25 (0.4)
Not eligible	76 (1.2)	27 (1.2)	78 (1.6)	32 (1.6)	88 (0.3)	45 (0.3)	90 (0.3)	49 (0.3)	91 (0.2)	53 (0.4)	91 (0.3)	54 (0.3)	92 (0.2)	57 (0.3)	93 (0.2)	59 (0.4)
Unknown	72 (3.0)	28 (4.1)	80 (2.2)	36 (2.2)	84 (0.9)	41 (1.2)	87 (0.7)	45 (1.2)	90 (0.9)	48 (1.5)	88 (1.3)	47 (1.7)	90 (0.8)	52 (1.4)	90 (1.0)	52 (2.2)
8th grade, all students	61 (1.0)	23 (1.0)	63 (0.9)	26 (0.8)	68 (0.3)	29 (0.3)	69 (0.2)	30 (0.2)	71 (0.3)	32 (0.3)	73 (0.3)	34 (0.3)	73 (0.2)	35 (0.2)	74 (0.3)	35 (0.3)
Sex																
Male	62 (1.2)	25 (1.2)	64 (1.1)	27 (1.0)	69 (0.4)	30 (0.4)	70 (0.3)	31 (0.3)	72 (0.3)	34 (0.4)	73 (0.3)	36 (0.4)	73 (0.4)	36 (0.3)	74 (0.3)	36 (0.4)
Female	60 (1.2)	22 (1.2)	63 (1.1)	24 (0.9)	67 (0.4)	27 (0.4)	69 (0.3)	28 (0.3)	71 (0.3)	30 (0.3)	72 (0.4)	32 (0.4)	73 (0.3)	34 (0.3)	74 (0.4)	35 (0.4)
Race/ethnicity																
White	73 (1.3)	30 (1.3)	76 (0.9)	34 (1.0)	80 (0.3)	37 (0.4)	80 (0.2)	39 (0.3)	82 (0.3)	42 (0.3)	83 (0.3)	44 (0.4)	84 (0.3)	44 (0.3)	84 (0.2)	45 (0.2)
Black	25 (1.8)	4 (0.8)	31 (1.5)	5 (0.6)	39 (0.8)	7 (0.5)	42 (0.5)	9 (0.3)	47 (0.7)	11 (0.3)	50 (0.6)	12 (0.5)	51 (0.6)	13 (0.5)	52 (0.7)	14 (0.5)
Hispanic	39 (2.0)	8 (1.1)	41 (1.9)	8 (1.0)	48 (0.8)	12 (0.5)	52 (0.6)	13 (0.4)	55 (0.7)	15 (0.5)	57 (0.8)	17 (0.6)	61 (0.7)	20 (0.5)	62 (0.7)	21 (0.5)
Asian/Pacific Islander	‡	‡	75 (2.8)	41 (4.4)	78 (1.1)	43 (1.3)	81 (0.8)	47 (1.2)	83 (0.8)	50 (1.1)	85 (1.0)	54 (1.8)	86 (1.0)	55 (1.2)	87 (0.8)	60 (1.3)
Asian	—	—	—	—	—	—	—	—	—	—	—	—	88 (0.9)	58 (1.9)	89 (0.8)	63 (1.3)
Pacific Islander	—	—	—	—	—	—	—	—	—	—	—	—	59 (4.7)	22 (3.5)	67 (3.5)	24 (2.9)
American Indian/Alaska Native	‡	‡	47 (10.4)	‡	52 (2.7)	15 (1.7)	53 (1.3)	14 (1.2)	53 (1.8)	16 (1.2)	56 (1.5)	18 (1.3)	55 (1.1)	17 (1.2)	59 (1.7)	21 (1.5)
Two or more races	—	—	—	—	—	—	—	—	—	—	—	—	78 (1.1)	39 (1.7)	76 (1.2)	38 (1.4)
Eligibility for free or reduced-price lunch																
Eligible	38 (2.1)	8 (1.2)	41 (1.3)	9 (0.8)	48 (0.5)	12 (0.4)	51 (0.4)	13 (0.3)	55 (0.5)	15 (0.3)	57 (0.5)	17 (0.3)	59 (0.4)	17 (0.4)	60 (0.4)	19 (0.4)
Not eligible	69 (1.5)	28 (1.3)	74 (1.1)	34 (1.3)	79 (0.3)	37 (0.4)	79 (0.2)	39 (0.3)	81 (0.3)	42 (0.4)	83 (0.3)	45 (0.4)	84 (0.2)	47 (0.4)	86 (0.3)	49 (0.3)
Unknown	70 (2.6)	30 (2.6)	67 (2.0)	29 (1.5)	75 (1.1)	36 (1.2)	79 (1.1)	40 (1.4)	81 (1.7)	43 (1.7)	83 (1.3)	48 (1.9)	85 (0.9)	48 (1.5)	84 (1.3)	50 (1.3)
12th grade, all students	[3]	[3]	[3]	[3]	—	—	61 (0.8)	23 (0.7)	—	—	64 (0.8)	26 (0.8)	—	(†)	65 (0.7)	26 (0.6)
Sex																
Male	[3]	[3]	[3]	[3]	—	—	62 (0.9)	25 (1.0)	—	—	65 (0.9)	28 (1.0)	—	(†)	66 (0.8)	28 (0.8)
Female	[3]	[3]	[3]	[3]	—	—	60 (1.0)	21 (0.8)	—	—	63 (0.8)	24 (0.8)	—	(†)	64 (0.9)	24 (0.7)
Race/ethnicity																
White	[3]	[3]	[3]	[3]	—	—	70 (0.8)	29 (0.8)	—	—	75 (0.7)	33 (0.8)	—	(†)	75 (0.8)	33 (0.8)
Black	[3]	[3]	[3]	[3]	—	—	30 (1.7)	6 (0.8)	—	—	37 (1.2)	6 (0.6)	—	(†)	38 (1.5)	7 (0.6)
Hispanic	[3]	[3]	[3]	[3]	—	—	40 (2.1)	8 (1.0)	—	—	45 (1.1)	11 (0.6)	—	(†)	50 (1.3)	12 (0.7)
Asian/Pacific Islander	[3]	[3]	[3]	[3]	—	—	73 (2.6)	36 (3.0)	—	—	84 (1.9)	52 (3.4)	—	(†)	81 (1.4)	47 (2.0)
Asian	[3]	[3]	[3]	[3]	—	—	—	—	—	—	—	—	—	(†)	83 (1.5)	49 (2.0)
Pacific Islander	[3]	[3]	[3]	[3]	—	—	—	—	—	—	—	—	—	(†)	65 (7.3)	16 (6.0)
American Indian/Alaska Native	[3]	[3]	[3]	[3]	—	—	42 (8.6)	‡	—	—	56 (5.4)	12 (3.3)	—	(†)	54 (5.8)	12 (4.0)
Two or more races	[3]	[3]	[3]	[3]	—	—	—	—	—	—	—	—	—	(†)	67 (3.0)	26 (2.7)

—Not available.
†Not applicable.
[1] Basic denotes partial mastery of the knowledge and skills that are fundamental for proficient work.
[2] Proficient represents solid academic performance. Students reaching this level have demonstrated competency over challenging subject matter.
[3] Because of major changes to the framework and content of the grade 12 assessment, results from 2005 and later assessment years cannot be compared with results from earlier assessment years. Therefore, this table excludes grade 12 results from 1996 and 2000.

NOTE: Includes public and private schools. Includes students tested with accommodations (1 to 13 percent of all students, depending on grade level and year); excludes only those students with disabilities and English language learners who were unable to be tested even with accommodations (1 to 6 percent of all students). Race categories exclude persons of Hispanic ethnicity. Prior to 2011, separate data for Asians, Pacific Islanders, and those of two or more races were not collected.
SOURCE: U.S. Department of Education, National Center for Education Statistics, National Assessment of Educational Progress (NAEP), 1996, 2000, 2003, 2005, 2007, 2009, 2011, and 2013 Mathematics Assessments, retrieved June 9, 2014, from the Main NAEP Data Explorer (http://nces.ed.gov/nationsreportcard/naepdata/). (This table was prepared June 2014.)

Table 222.30. Average National Assessment of Educational Progress (NAEP) mathematics scale score of 8th-graders with various attitudes toward mathematics and percentage reporting these attitudes, by selected student characteristics: 2013

[Standard errors appear in parentheses]

Student characteristic	Math work is engaging and interesting				Math work is challenging				Math work is too easy			
	Never or hardly ever	Sometimes	Often	Always/ almost always	Never or hardly ever	Sometimes	Often	Always/ almost always	Never or hardly ever	Sometimes	Often	Always/ almost always
1	2	3	4	5	6	7	8	9	10	11	12	13

Average scale score[1]

Student characteristic	2	3	4	5	6	7	8	9	10	11	12	13
All students	280 (0.4)	284 (0.4)	289 (0.3)	287 (0.6)	295 (0.6)	286 (0.3)	284 (0.3)	275 (0.5)	285 (0.5)	283 (0.3)	287 (0.3)	290 (0.7)
Sex												
Male	281 (0.5)	285 (0.4)	290 (0.4)	287 (0.8)	297 (0.9)	287 (0.4)	284 (0.4)	274 (0.7)	284 (0.7)	284 (0.4)	289 (0.5)	292 (0.9)
Female	279 (0.5)	284 (0.4)	289 (0.4)	288 (0.7)	293 (0.7)	285 (0.3)	284 (0.5)	277 (0.7)	286 (0.6)	283 (0.4)	286 (0.5)	288 (1.0)
Race/ethnicity												
White	286 (0.4)	294 (0.4)	300 (0.4)	300 (0.7)	303 (0.5)	295 (0.3)	294 (0.4)	286 (0.7)	292 (0.5)	293 (0.3)	297 (0.4)	299 (0.8)
Black	260 (0.8)	263 (0.6)	267 (0.8)	266 (1.0)	273 (1.4)	265 (0.5)	263 (0.7)	255 (0.9)	264 (1.0)	262 (0.5)	266 (0.7)	269 (1.4)
Hispanic	268 (0.9)	271 (0.7)	275 (0.6)	275 (1.2)	279 (1.6)	273 (0.5)	271 (0.8)	264 (0.9)	272 (1.4)	270 (0.6)	275 (0.7)	277 (1.7)
Asian	303 (2.0)	306 (1.8)	314 (1.4)	311 (2.1)	324 (1.8)	310 (1.2)	303 (1.9)	296 (3.6)	311 (2.7)	307 (1.6)	310 (1.6)	316 (2.2)
Pacific Islander	269 (4.7)	278 (4.1)	273 (5.4)	277 (4.6)	289 (7.0)	278 (3.0)	271 (4.4)	265 (3.6)	277 (7.5)	274 (2.7)	275 (5.3)	283 (5.7)
American Indian/ Alaska Native	270 (2.8)	269 (2.2)	272 (2.2)	271 (3.9)	281 (4.0)	270 (2.2)	271 (2.4)	262 (3.7)	268 (2.9)	268 (1.8)	277 (2.6)	276 (5.3)
Two or more races	281 (1.9)	285 (1.3)	290 (2.2)	302 (5.4)	299 (3.1)	290 (1.7)	285 (1.5)	277 (3.6)	286 (2.5)	285 (1.3)	293 (3.0)	299 (2.8)
Eligibility for free or reduced-price lunch												
Eligible	267 (0.5)	270 (0.4)	274 (0.4)	272 (0.6)	280 (0.9)	272 (0.3)	269 (0.4)	260 (0.6)	268 (0.7)	269 (0.3)	274 (0.4)	277 (0.9)
Not eligible	289 (0.5)	297 (0.4)	303 (0.4)	303 (0.6)	306 (0.6)	298 (0.4)	296 (0.4)	289 (0.8)	296 (0.5)	296 (0.4)	300 (0.5)	304 (1.0)
Unknown	284 (1.8)	297 (2.4)	306 (2.6)	305 (4.1)	308 (3.7)	299 (2.5)	295 (2.4)	292 (3.8)	296 (3.3)	297 (2.2)	304 (2.6)	302 (5.2)
Highest education level of either parent[2]												
Did not finish high school	263 (1.2)	266 (0.8)	270 (1.0)	271 (1.6)	276 (1.9)	269 (0.8)	266 (1.1)	257 (1.4)	263 (1.4)	266 (0.7)	271 (1.0)	275 (2.1)
Graduated high school	268 (0.8)	271 (0.6)	273 (0.7)	272 (1.2)	280 (1.1)	272 (0.6)	270 (0.7)	261 (1.0)	269 (0.9)	269 (0.5)	274 (0.7)	277 (1.4)
Some education after high school	281 (0.7)	286 (0.5)	289 (0.7)	288 (1.2)	295 (1.1)	286 (0.5)	283 (0.7)	278 (1.0)	282 (0.9)	284 (0.5)	288 (0.9)	295 (1.4)
Graduated college	289 (0.6)	296 (0.5)	301 (0.4)	299 (0.7)	305 (0.7)	297 (0.4)	295 (0.4)	287 (0.7)	296 (0.5)	295 (0.4)	298 (0.5)	301 (0.9)

Percent of students

Student characteristic	2	3	4	5	6	7	8	9	10	11	12	13
All students	22 (0.2)	35 (0.2)	28 (0.2)	15 (0.2)	12 (0.2)	45 (0.3)	32 (0.2)	11 (0.1)	17 (0.2)	55 (0.2)	21 (0.2)	7 (0.1)
Sex												
Male	21 (0.3)	33 (0.3)	29 (0.3)	16 (0.3)	12 (0.2)	45 (0.3)	33 (0.3)	10 (0.2)	15 (0.2)	54 (0.3)	23 (0.2)	8 (0.1)
Female	22 (0.3)	37 (0.2)	27 (0.3)	14 (0.2)	11 (0.2)	45 (0.4)	32 (0.3)	12 (0.2)	20 (0.3)	55 (0.3)	19 (0.2)	6 (0.1)
Race/ethnicity												
White	25 (0.3)	36 (0.3)	27 (0.2)	12 (0.2)	12 (0.2)	45 (0.5)	32 (0.3)	11 (0.3)	20 (0.3)	54 (0.3)	19 (0.2)	6 (0.1)
Black	18 (0.5)	33 (0.4)	27 (0.4)	21 (0.5)	11 (0.3)	44 (0.5)	32 (0.5)	14 (0.4)	15 (0.4)	54 (0.5)	22 (0.5)	8 (0.3)
Hispanic	19 (0.5)	36 (0.5)	30 (0.5)	16 (0.4)	10 (0.4)	46 (0.6)	33 (0.5)	11 (0.3)	13 (0.4)	56 (0.5)	23 (0.4)	8 (0.2)
Asian	14 (0.9)	37 (1.0)	31 (0.9)	18 (0.8)	14 (0.8)	50 (1.2)	28 (1.1)	8 (0.4)	9 (0.8)	52 (1.2)	27 (0.9)	12 (0.7)
Pacific Islander	15 (1.9)	36 (2.7)	28 (3.1)	21 (2.4)	11 (2.5)	46 (3.0)	33 (2.9)	11 (1.7)	9 (1.5)	57 (3.2)	28 (3.1)	7 (1.9)
American Indian/ Alaska Native	20 (1.4)	36 (1.5)	28 (1.4)	16 (1.3)	11 (1.3)	44 (1.7)	32 (1.6)	13 (1.0)	16 (1.2)	57 (1.8)	21 (1.2)	7 (1.0)
Two or more races	22 (1.0)	37 (1.3)	28 (1.3)	14 (1.1)	13 (0.9)	44 (1.5)	32 (1.2)	12 (0.8)	18 (0.9)	52 (1.1)	22 (0.9)	8 (0.7)
Eligibility for free or reduced-price lunch												
Eligible	20 (0.3)	35 (0.3)	28 (0.3)	16 (0.3)	11 (0.2)	45 (0.3)	32 (0.3)	12 (0.2)	14 (0.2)	55 (0.3)	23 (0.3)	8 (0.2)
Not eligible	23 (0.3)	36 (0.2)	28 (0.3)	13 (0.2)	12 (0.2)	45 (0.3)	32 (0.3)	10 (0.2)	16 (0.3)	54 (0.3)	20 (0.2)	7 (0.1)
Unknown	22 (1.3)	33 (1.1)	28 (1.3)	16 (1.1)	11 (0.8)	45 (1.5)	33 (1.2)	11 (0.8)	23 (1.2)	56 (1.3)	16 (0.7)	5 (0.5)
Highest education level of either parent[2]												
Did not finish high school	22 (0.7)	35 (0.6)	28 (0.6)	15 (0.6)	10 (0.6)	45 (1.0)	33 (0.8)	12 (0.5)	14 (0.5)	57 (0.7)	22 (0.7)	8 (0.5)
Graduated high school	22 (0.6)	36 (0.6)	27 (0.5)	15 (0.5)	10 (0.5)	45 (0.4)	32 (0.5)	12 (0.4)	16 (0.4)	55 (0.6)	22 (0.5)	7 (0.3)
Some education after high school	23 (0.6)	35 (0.5)	28 (0.5)	14 (0.4)	12 (0.4)	45 (0.5)	33 (0.5)	10 (0.3)	17 (0.4)	55 (0.6)	21 (0.4)	7 (0.3)
Graduated college	22 (0.2)	35 (0.2)	29 (0.3)	15 (0.3)	13 (0.2)	44 (0.3)	32 (0.3)	11 (0.2)	19 (0.3)	53 (0.3)	20 (0.2)	7 (0.1)

[1]Scale ranges from 0 to 500.
[2]Based on student reports. The category of students whose parents have an unknown level of education is not shown, although data for these students is included in table totals.
NOTE: Includes public and private schools. Includes students tested with accommodations (12 percent of all 8th-grade students); excludes only those students with disabilities and English language learners who were unable to be tested even with accommodations (1 percent of all 8th-grade students). Race categories exclude persons of Hispanic ethnicity. Detail may not sum to totals because of rounding.

SOURCE: U.S. Department of Education, National Center for Education Statistics, National Assessment of Educational Progress (NAEP), 2011 Mathematics Assessment, retrieved October, 23, 2014, from the Main NAEP Data Explorer (http://nces.ed.gov/nationsreportcard/naepdata/). (This table was prepared October 2014.)

Table 222.35. Average National Assessment of Educational Progress (NAEP) mathematics scale score of 12th-graders with various attitudes toward mathematics and percentage reporting these attitudes, by selected student characteristics: 2013

[Standard errors appear in parentheses]

Average scale score[1]

Student characteristic	Math work is engaging and interesting — Never or hardly ever (2)	Sometimes (3)	Often (4)	Always/almost always (5)	Math work is challenging — Never or hardly ever (6)	Sometimes (7)	Often (8)	Always/almost always (9)	Math work is too easy — Never or hardly ever (10)	Sometimes (11)	Often (12)	Always/almost always (13)
All students	145 (0.6)	155 (0.6)	165 (0.8)	166 (1.0)	158 (1.4)	157 (0.7)	158 (0.6)	154 (1.0)	156 (0.7)	156 (0.6)	158 (1.0)	162 (1.1)
Sex												
Male	146 (0.9)	158 (0.8)	167 (1.1)	169 (1.3)	161 (1.8)	160 (0.9)	158 (0.8)	155 (1.2)	157 (1.1)	157 (0.8)	163 (1.2)	165 (1.5)
Female	145 (0.8)	153 (0.8)	163 (1.0)	164 (1.4)	154 (1.8)	153 (0.9)	157 (0.9)	154 (1.3)	156 (0.8)	154 (0.8)	152 (1.2)	157 (1.8)
Race/ethnicity												
White	152 (0.8)	164 (0.7)	175 (1.1)	179 (1.4)	165 (1.5)	165 (0.8)	166 (0.8)	163 (1.2)	163 (0.9)	165 (0.8)	168 (1.1)	169 (1.4)
Black	127 (1.3)	133 (1.3)	139 (1.4)	135 (2.4)	136 (2.4)	134 (1.3)	134 (1.3)	129 (1.6)	133 (1.7)	132 (1.1)	134 (1.9)	136 (2.6)
Hispanic	135 (1.3)	142 (1.0)	147 (1.3)	154 (1.7)	141 (3.5)	144 (0.9)	144 (1.1)	141 (1.5)	144 (1.4)	142 (0.9)	144 (1.6)	150 (2.7)
Asian	167 (2.9)	173 (2.3)	182 (2.3)	187 (3.1)	188 (4.0)	179 (2.0)	174 (2.2)	176 (3.3)	181 (2.2)	174 (2.3)	176 (2.7)	185 (3.6)
Pacific Islander	‡ (†)	‡ (†)	‡ (†)	‡ (†)	‡ (†)	‡ (†)	‡ (†)	‡ (†)	‡ (†)	‡ (†)	‡ (†)	‡ (†)
American Indian/Alaska Native	137 (7.7)	149 (4.3)	140 (5.8)	‡ (†)	‡ (†)	140 (7.3)	145 (5.2)	‡ (†)	145 (3.8)	141 (4.8)	‡ (†)	‡ (†)
Two or more races	145 (3.9)	156 (2.4)	168 (5.3)	‡ (†)	‡ (†)	159 (3.8)	158 (3.3)	153 (3.7)	158 (3.7)	153 (3.1)	160 (6.2)	‡ (†)
Eligibility for free or reduced-price lunch												
Eligible	133 (0.9)	139 (0.8)	146 (1.2)	148 (1.9)	143 (1.8)	142 (0.9)	141 (1.0)	137 (1.3)	139 (1.2)	139 (1.0)	143 (1.4)	149 (1.8)
Not eligible	151 (0.8)	164 (0.7)	175 (0.9)	177 (1.2)	166 (1.6)	165 (0.7)	166 (0.7)	163 (1.2)	163 (0.8)	165 (0.7)	167 (1.1)	169 (1.5)
Unknown	155 (2.8)	165 (2.3)	175 (3.6)	183 (3.9)	174 (4.8)	169 (3.1)	166 (2.8)	165 (2.9)	166 (2.6)	167 (2.9)	169 (4.3)	‡ (†)
Highest education level of either parent[2]												
Did not finish high school	131 (2.0)	136 (1.4)	144 (1.8)	148 (3.2)	137 (4.3)	139 (1.6)	140 (1.7)	136 (1.5)	136 (1.6)	138 (1.5)	141 (2.0)	148 (3.9)
Graduated high school	134 (1.2)	141 (1.1)	147 (1.4)	152 (2.4)	147 (2.9)	142 (1.1)	142 (1.2)	137 (1.8)	140 (1.5)	141 (0.9)	142 (2.1)	150 (2.9)
Some education after high school	141 (1.1)	153 (1.0)	161 (1.4)	162 (1.9)	156 (2.5)	152 (1.2)	153 (1.0)	152 (1.3)	151 (1.0)	152 (0.9)	155 (1.5)	159 (2.0)
Graduated college	155 (0.9)	167 (0.8)	177 (1.0)	178 (1.4)	169 (1.7)	168 (0.8)	169 (0.8)	166 (1.2)	167 (0.9)	167 (0.8)	171 (1.2)	171 (1.5)

Percent of students

Student characteristic	Math work is engaging and interesting — Never or hardly ever (2)	Sometimes (3)	Often (4)	Always/almost always (5)	Math work is challenging — Never or hardly ever (6)	Sometimes (7)	Often (8)	Always/almost always (9)	Math work is too easy — Never or hardly ever (10)	Sometimes (11)	Often (12)	Always/almost always (13)
All students	26 (0.5)	36 (0.5)	27 (0.5)	11 (0.4)	7 (0.2)	35 (0.5)	37 (0.5)	21 (0.4)	32 (0.5)	47 (0.5)	15 (0.3)	6 (0.3)
Sex												
Male	25 (0.6)	35 (0.7)	28 (0.7)	12 (0.5)	8 (0.4)	36 (0.7)	37 (0.7)	18 (0.5)	27 (0.6)	48 (0.7)	18 (0.4)	7 (0.4)
Female	27 (0.7)	37 (0.7)	25 (0.5)	11 (0.4)	6 (0.3)	34 (0.7)	36 (0.6)	23 (0.6)	36 (0.8)	47 (0.7)	13 (0.4)	4 (0.3)
Race/ethnicity												
White	28 (0.6)	35 (0.6)	27 (0.6)	10 (0.4)	8 (0.4)	35 (0.6)	37 (0.7)	21 (0.5)	34 (0.7)	45 (0.7)	14 (0.4)	6 (0.3)
Black	27 (1.0)	37 (1.0)	24 (1.0)	13 (0.9)	8 (0.5)	37 (1.3)	34 (1.0)	22 (1.2)	32 (0.8)	48 (1.2)	14 (0.8)	6 (0.5)
Hispanic	24 (0.9)	35 (1.0)	28 (0.8)	13 (0.7)	6 (0.3)	35 (1.0)	39 (1.0)	20 (0.8)	25 (0.8)	52 (1.0)	18 (0.8)	8 (0.5)
Asian	13 (1.1)	37 (1.5)	32 (1.6)	17 (1.4)	7 (1.1)	36 (1.8)	36 (1.7)	21 (1.6)	24 (1.7)	49 (2.1)	20 (1.7)	8 (1.1)
Pacific Islander	20 (5.5)	42 (7.2)	18 (4.6)	20 (6.7)	7 (3.9)	32 (7.0)	31 (7.1)	31 (5.8)	36 (7.7)	41 (6.5)	19 (6.1)	4 (2.5)
American Indian/Alaska Native	27 (4.9)	40 (5.1)	22 (4.8)	11 (3.0)	10 (3.1)	30 (6.9)	38 (5.8)	22 (4.0)	30 (6.0)	50 (6.0)	11 (4.2)	10 (3.6)
Two or more races	28 (2.6)	40 (3.3)	22 (2.7)	10 (1.7)	6 (1.3)	36 (3.3)	37 (3.2)	21 (2.7)	35 (3.3)	46 (3.0)	13 (2.2)	6 (1.6)
Eligibility for free or reduced-price lunch												
Eligible	25 (0.6)	35 (0.7)	27 (0.8)	12 (0.6)	7 (0.4)	36 (0.8)	36 (0.8)	21 (0.6)	27 (0.6)	50 (0.9)	17 (0.5)	6 (0.5)
Not eligible	27 (0.7)	36 (0.6)	26 (0.6)	11 (0.4)	7 (0.3)	35 (0.7)	37 (0.8)	21 (0.6)	34 (0.7)	46 (0.6)	15 (0.4)	6 (0.3)
Unknown	25 (2.0)	37 (1.5)	28 (1.8)	10 (1.3)	6 (0.9)	33 (1.9)	40 (1.6)	21 (1.6)	38 (2.1)	44 (1.9)	14 (1.6)	4 (0.8)
Highest education level of either parent[2]												
Did not finish high school	25 (1.3)	35 (1.0)	26 (1.1)	14 (0.9)	7 (0.7)	38 (1.5)	35 (1.4)	20 (1.2)	24 (1.3)	49 (1.4)	20 (1.0)	7 (0.8)
Graduated high school	29 (1.1)	36 (1.0)	26 (0.9)	10 (0.6)	8 (0.5)	36 (1.1)	37 (1.1)	19 (0.7)	29 (1.0)	49 (1.1)	15 (0.8)	6 (0.5)
Some education after high school	27 (0.9)	38 (1.0)	25 (0.9)	9 (0.5)	8 (0.5)	35 (0.9)	36 (0.9)	21 (0.8)	32 (0.8)	47 (0.8)	15 (0.6)	5 (0.4)
Graduated college	25 (0.7)	35 (0.6)	28 (0.6)	12 (0.5)	7 (0.3)	35 (0.7)	37 (0.8)	21 (0.6)	34 (0.7)	46 (0.7)	14 (0.4)	6 (0.3)

†Not applicable.

‡Reporting standards not met (too few cases for a reliable estimate).

[1]Scale ranges from 0 to 300.

[2]Based on student reports. The category of students whose parents have an unknown level of education is not shown, although data for these students is included in table totals.

NOTE: Includes public and private schools. Includes students tested with accommodations (9 percent of all 12th-grade students); excludes only those students with disabilities and English language learners who were unable to be tested even with accommodations (2 percent of all 12th-grade students). Race categories exclude persons of Hispanic ethnicity. Detail may not sum to totals because of rounding.

SOURCE: U.S. Department of Education, National Center for Education Statistics, National Assessment of Educational Progress (NAEP), 2013 Mathematics Assessment, retrieved October 20, 2014, from the Main NAEP Data Explorer (http://nces.ed.gov/nationsreportcard/naepdata/). (This table was prepared October 2014.)

Table 222.40. Average National Assessment of Educational Progress (NAEP) mathematics scale score of high school graduates at grade 12, by highest mathematics course taken in high school and selected student and school characteristics: 2009

[Standard errors appear in parentheses]

Selected student or school characteristic	Algebra I or below[1]		Geometry		Algebra II/ trigonometry		Analysis/ precalculus		Statistics/ probability		Advanced mathematics, other[2]		Calculus	
1	2		3		4		5		6		7		8	
Total[3]	114	(1.1)	127	(1.0)	143	(0.6)	166	(0.9)	164	(1.8)	154	(1.3)	193	(1.2)
Sex														
Male	117	(1.7)	128	(1.2)	145	(0.8)	169	(1.0)	165	(2.2)	156	(1.5)	197	(1.4)
Female	111	(1.6)	126	(1.1)	142	(0.8)	163	(1.0)	162	(2.0)	153	(1.4)	190	(1.2)
Race/ethnicity														
White	117	(1.6)	133	(1.3)	150	(0.8)	172	(0.9)	169	(1.5)	160	(1.3)	194	(1.1)
Black	104	(2.8)	114	(1.8)	129	(0.9)	147	(1.6)	139	(4.0)	138	(2.1)	170	(2.7)
Hispanic	109	(2.2)	122	(1.0)	136	(0.8)	155	(1.6)	154	(3.2)	142	(2.3)	179	(2.5)
Asian/Pacific Islander	‡	(†)	129	(3.9)	149	(4.1)	170	(2.3)	176	(4.1)	164	(2.9)	203	(1.8)
American Indian/Alaska Native	‡	(†)	‡	(†)	143	(3.8)	‡	(†)	‡	(†)	‡	(†)	‡	(†)
Student with disabilities (SD) status														
SD[4]	103	(1.7)	114	(2.5)	126	(2.1)	166	(5.0)	136	(6.3)	134	(3.5)	197	(3.7)
Non-SD	122	(1.2)	129	(0.9)	144	(0.6)	166	(0.9)	164	(1.7)	156	(1.3)	193	(1.2)
English language learner (ELL) status														
ELL	104	(4.5)	113	(2.8)	121	(2.1)	144	(6.1)	‡	(†)	129	(4.8)	‡	(†)
Non-ELL	114	(1.2)	128	(1.0)	144	(0.6)	166	(0.9)	164	(1.8)	155	(1.3)	193	(1.2)
School type														
Traditional public	114	(1.2)	127	(1.0)	143	(0.7)	166	(0.9)	164	(1.8)	155	(1.4)	193	(1.3)
Public charter	‡	(†)	‡	(†)	137	(10.3)	141	(6.8)	132	(1.6)	‡	(†)	‡	(†)
Private	‡	(†)	123	(3.3)	146	(3.3)	169	(2.7)	168	(3.9)	146	(4.0)	193	(3.3)
Percentage of students eligible for free or reduced-price lunch														
0–25 percent	116	(3.0)	134	(2.0)	151	(1.3)	173	(1.5)	173	(1.5)	162	(1.9)	199	(1.6)
26–50 percent	115	(1.5)	127	(1.4)	144	(1.0)	165	(1.1)	162	(2.9)	154	(1.7)	189	(1.0)
51–75 percent	111	(3.0)	123	(1.8)	136	(1.1)	156	(1.3)	149	(3.6)	146	(3.7)	179	(2.8)
76–100 percent	107	(5.4)	115	(3.1)	126	(2.0)	144	(3.7)	137	(4.1)	131	(2.6)	163	(3.9)
School locale														
City	110	(2.6)	125	(1.7)	140	(1.8)	163	(2.1)	163	(3.3)	151	(3.0)	195	(2.3)
Suburban	112	(2.3)	127	(1.9)	144	(1.0)	169	(1.4)	167	(2.4)	157	(2.0)	195	(2.0)
Town	114	(2.5)	129	(1.9)	144	(1.6)	166	(1.6)	164	(3.1)	152	(3.8)	191	(2.1)
Rural	117	(2.0)	129	(1.4)	145	(1.3)	165	(1.9)	157	(4.9)	155	(2.1)	187	(2.0)

†Not applicable.
‡Reporting standards not met (too few cases for a reliable estimate).
[1]Includes basic math, general math, applied math, prealgebra, and algebra I.
[2]Includes courses such as actuarial sciences, pure mathematics, discrete math, and advanced functions and modeling.
[3]Includes other racial/ethnic groups not shown separately, as well as students for whom information on race/ethnicity or sex was missing.
[4]SD estimates include both students with an Individualized Education Plan (IEP) and students with a plan under Section 504 of the Rehabilitation Act (a "504 plan"). IEPs are only for students who require specialized instruction, whereas 504 plans apply to students who require accommodations but may not require specialized instruction.

NOTE: Scale ranges from 0 to 300. Includes students tested with accommodations (6 percent of all 12th-graders); excludes only those students with disabilities and English language learners who were unable to be tested even with accommodations (3 percent of all 12th-graders). For a transcript to be included in the analyses, it had to meet three requirements: (1) the graduate received either a standard or honors diploma, (2) the graduate's transcript contained 16 or more Carnegie credits, and (3) the graduate's transcript contained more than 0 Carnegie credits in English courses. Race categories exclude persons of Hispanic ethnicity.
SOURCE: U.S. Department of Education, National Center for Education Statistics, National Assessment of Educational Progress (NAEP), 2009 Mathematics Assessment; and 2009 High School Transcript Study (HSTS). (This table was prepared September 2012.)

Table 222.50. Average National Assessment of Educational Progress (NAEP) mathematics scale score of 4th-grade public school students and percentage attaining mathematics achievement levels, by state: Selected years, 1992 through 2013

[Standard errors appear in parentheses]

State	Average scale score[1]																Percent attaining mathematics achievement levels, 2013					
	1992		2000		2003		2005		2007		2009		2011		2013		At or above *Basic*[2]		At or above *Proficient*[3]		At *Advanced*[4]	
1	2		3		4		5		6		7		8		9		10		11		12	
United States	**219**	**(0.8)**	**224**	**(1.0)**	**234**	**(0.2)**	**237**	**(0.2)**	**239**	**(0.2)**	**239**	**(0.2)**	**240**	**(0.2)**	**241**	**(0.2)**	**82**	**(0.2)**	**41**	**(0.3)**	**8**	**(0.2)**
Alabama	208	(1.6)	217	(1.2)	223	(1.2)	225	(0.9)	229	(1.3)	228	(1.1)	231	(1.0)	233	(1.0)	75	(1.4)	30	(1.6)	3	(0.5)
Alaska	—	(†)	—	(†)	233	(0.8)	236	(1.0)	237	(1.0)	237	(0.9)	236	(0.9)	236	(0.8)	77	(1.1)	37	(1.1)	6	(0.6)
Arizona	215	(1.1)	219	(1.3)	229	(1.1)	230	(1.1)	232	(1.0)	230	(1.1)	235	(1.1)	240	(1.2)	82	(1.1)	40	(1.8)	7	(1.0)
Arkansas	210	(0.9)	216	(1.1)	229	(0.9)	236	(0.9)	238	(1.1)	238	(0.9)	238	(0.8)	240	(0.9)	83	(1.0)	39	(1.4)	5	(0.6)
California[5]	208	(1.6)	213	(1.6)	227	(0.9)	230	(0.6)	230	(0.7)	232	(1.2)	234	(1.4)	234	(1.2)	74	(1.5)	33	(1.7)	5	(0.7)
Colorado	221	(1.0)	—	(†)	235	(1.0)	239	(1.1)	240	(1.0)	243	(1.0)	244	(0.9)	247	(0.8)	87	(1.0)	50	(1.3)	11	(0.9)
Connecticut	227	(1.1)	234	(1.1)	241	(0.8)	242	(0.8)	243	(1.1)	245	(1.0)	242	(1.3)	243	(0.9)	83	(1.1)	45	(1.3)	9	(0.9)
Delaware	218	(0.8)	—	(†)	236	(0.5)	240	(0.5)	242	(0.4)	239	(0.5)	240	(0.6)	243	(0.7)	86	(0.9)	42	(1.1)	7	(0.6)
District of Columbia	193	(0.5)	192	(1.1)	205	(0.7)	211	(0.8)	214	(0.8)	219	(0.7)	222	(0.7)	229	(0.7)	66	(1.3)	28	(1.0)	6	(0.7)
Florida	214	(1.5)	—	(†)	234	(1.1)	239	(0.7)	242	(0.8)	242	(1.0)	240	(0.8)	242	(0.8)	84	(0.9)	41	(1.3)	6	(0.7)
Georgia	216	(1.2)	219	(1.1)	230	(1.0)	234	(1.0)	235	(0.8)	236	(0.9)	238	(0.7)	240	(1.0)	81	(1.2)	39	(1.5)	7	(0.7)
Hawaii	214	(1.3)	216	(1.0)	227	(1.0)	230	(0.8)	234	(0.8)	236	(1.1)	239	(0.7)	243	(0.8)	83	(0.8)	46	(1.3)	9	(0.7)
Idaho[5]	222	(1.0)	224	(1.4)	235	(0.7)	242	(0.7)	241	(0.7)	241	(0.8)	240	(0.6)	241	(0.9)	83	(1.0)	40	(1.5)	6	(0.8)
Illinois[5]	—	(†)	223	(1.9)	233	(1.1)	233	(1.0)	237	(1.1)	238	(1.0)	239	(1.1)	239	(1.2)	79	(1.0)	39	(1.7)	8	(1.0)
Indiana[5]	221	(1.0)	233	(1.1)	238	(0.9)	240	(0.9)	245	(0.8)	243	(0.9)	244	(1.0)	249	(0.9)	90	(0.8)	52	(1.5)	10	(1.0)
Iowa[5]	230	(1.0)	231	(1.2)	238	(0.7)	240	(0.7)	243	(0.8)	243	(0.8)	243	(0.8)	246	(0.9)	87	(0.9)	48	(1.6)	9	(0.9)
Kansas[5]	—	(†)	232	(1.6)	242	(1.0)	246	(1.0)	248	(0.9)	245	(1.0)	246	(0.9)	246	(0.8)	89	(0.9)	48	(1.4)	8	(0.7)
Kentucky	215	(1.0)	219	(1.4)	229	(1.1)	232	(0.9)	235	(0.9)	239	(1.1)	241	(0.8)	241	(0.9)	84	(0.9)	41	(1.4)	6	(0.7)
Louisiana	204	(1.5)	218	(1.4)	226	(1.0)	230	(0.9)	230	(1.0)	229	(1.0)	231	(1.0)	231	(1.2)	75	(1.4)	26	(1.8)	3	(0.6)
Maine[5]	232	(1.0)	230	(1.0)	238	(0.7)	241	(0.8)	242	(0.8)	244	(0.8)	244	(0.7)	246	(0.7)	88	(0.8)	47	(1.4)	9	(0.7)
Maryland	217	(1.3)	222	(1.2)	233	(1.3)	238	(1.0)	240	(0.9)	244	(0.9)	247	(0.9)	245	(1.3)	82	(1.1)	47	(1.7)	13	(1.5)
Massachusetts	227	(1.2)	233	(1.2)	242	(0.8)	247	(0.8)	252	(0.8)	252	(0.9)	253	(0.8)	253	(1.0)	90	(0.8)	58	(1.5)	16	(1.1)
Michigan[5]	220	(1.7)	229	(1.6)	236	(0.9)	238	(1.2)	238	(1.3)	236	(1.0)	236	(1.1)	237	(1.1)	77	(1.2)	37	(1.7)	7	(0.8)
Minnesota[5]	228	(0.9)	234	(1.3)	242	(0.9)	246	(1.0)	247	(1.0)	249	(1.1)	249	(0.9)	253	(1.1)	90	(1.0)	59	(1.7)	16	(1.1)
Mississippi	202	(1.1)	211	(1.1)	223	(1.0)	227	(0.9)	228	(1.0)	227	(1.0)	230	(0.9)	231	(0.7)	74	(1.2)	26	(1.2)	2	(0.4)
Missouri	222	(1.2)	228	(1.2)	235	(0.9)	235	(0.9)	239	(0.9)	241	(1.2)	240	(0.9)	240	(0.8)	83	(1.1)	39	(1.3)	5	(0.7)
Montana[5]	—	(†)	228	(1.7)	236	(0.8)	241	(0.8)	244	(0.8)	244	(0.7)	244	(0.6)	244	(0.6)	86	(0.9)	45	(1.2)	7	(0.6)
Nebraska	225	(1.2)	225	(1.8)	236	(0.8)	238	(0.9)	238	(1.1)	239	(1.0)	240	(1.0)	243	(1.0)	84	(1.1)	45	(1.5)	8	(0.7)
Nevada	—	(†)	220	(1.0)	228	(0.8)	230	(0.8)	232	(0.9)	235	(0.9)	237	(0.8)	236	(0.8)	80	(1.1)	34	(1.2)	4	(0.5)
New Hampshire	230	(1.2)	—	(†)	243	(0.9)	246	(0.9)	249	(0.8)	251	(0.8)	252	(0.6)	253	(0.8)	93	(0.8)	59	(1.2)	12	(0.8)
New Jersey	227	(1.5)	—	(†)	239	(1.1)	244	(1.1)	249	(1.1)	247	(1.0)	248	(0.9)	247	(1.1)	87	(0.9)	49	(1.7)	10	(1.1)
New Mexico	213	(1.4)	213	(1.5)	223	(1.1)	224	(0.8)	228	(0.9)	230	(1.0)	233	(0.8)	233	(0.7)	74	(1.0)	31	(1.0)	4	(0.4)
New York[5]	218	(1.2)	225	(1.4)	236	(0.9)	238	(0.9)	243	(0.8)	241	(0.7)	238	(0.8)	240	(1.0)	82	(1.2)	40	(1.5)	7	(0.6)
North Carolina	213	(1.1)	230	(1.1)	242	(0.8)	241	(0.9)	242	(0.8)	244	(0.8)	245	(0.7)	245	(0.9)	87	(0.9)	45	(1.4)	8	(0.8)
North Dakota	229	(0.8)	230	(1.2)	238	(0.7)	243	(0.5)	245	(0.5)	245	(0.6)	245	(0.4)	246	(0.5)	89	(0.6)	48	(1.0)	7	(0.6)
Ohio[5]	219	(1.2)	230	(1.5)	238	(1.0)	242	(1.0)	245	(1.0)	244	(1.1)	244	(0.8)	246	(1.1)	86	(0.9)	48	(1.7)	10	(1.0)
Oklahoma	220	(1.0)	224	(1.0)	229	(1.0)	234	(1.0)	237	(0.8)	237	(0.9)	237	(0.8)	239	(0.7)	83	(1.0)	36	(1.3)	5	(0.6)
Oregon[5]	—	(†)	224	(1.8)	236	(0.9)	238	(0.8)	236	(1.0)	238	(0.9)	237	(0.9)	240	(1.3)	81	(1.2)	40	(2.0)	8	(0.9)
Pennsylvania	224	(1.3)	—	(†)	236	(1.1)	241	(1.2)	244	(0.8)	244	(1.1)	246	(1.1)	244	(1.0)	85	(1.0)	44	(1.7)	8	(0.8)
Rhode Island	215	(1.5)	224	(1.1)	230	(1.0)	233	(0.9)	236	(0.9)	239	(0.8)	242	(0.7)	241	(0.8)	83	(1.0)	42	(1.2)	7	(0.6)
South Carolina	212	(1.1)	220	(1.4)	236	(0.9)	238	(0.9)	237	(0.8)	236	(0.9)	237	(1.0)	237	(1.0)	79	(1.3)	35	(1.5)	5	(0.7)
South Dakota	—	(†)	—	(†)	237	(0.7)	242	(0.5)	241	(0.7)	242	(0.5)	241	(0.6)	241	(0.5)	84	(1.0)	40	(1.1)	5	(0.6)
Tennessee	211	(1.4)	220	(1.4)	228	(1.0)	232	(1.2)	233	(0.9)	232	(1.1)	233	(0.9)	240	(0.9)	80	(1.2)	40	(1.4)	7	(0.9)
Texas	218	(1.2)	231	(1.1)	237	(0.9)	242	(0.6)	242	(0.7)	240	(0.7)	241	(1.1)	242	(0.9)	84	(1.0)	41	(1.5)	7	(0.9)
Utah	224	(1.0)	227	(1.3)	235	(0.8)	239	(0.8)	239	(0.9)	240	(1.0)	243	(0.8)	243	(0.9)	83	(1.0)	44	(1.4)	8	(0.9)
Vermont[5]	—	(†)	232	(1.6)	242	(0.8)	244	(0.5)	246	(0.5)	248	(0.4)	247	(0.5)	248	(0.6)	87	(0.7)	52	(1.1)	11	(0.7)
Virginia	221	(1.3)	230	(1.0)	239	(1.1)	241	(0.9)	244	(0.9)	243	(1.0)	245	(0.8)	246	(1.1)	88	(0.9)	47	(1.7)	9	(1.2)
Washington	—	(†)	—	(†)	238	(1.0)	242	(0.9)	243	(1.0)	242	(0.8)	243	(0.9)	246	(1.1)	86	(0.8)	48	(1.6)	10	(1.2)
West Virginia	215	(1.1)	223	(1.3)	231	(0.8)	231	(0.7)	236	(0.9)	233	(0.8)	235	(0.7)	237	(0.8)	81	(1.0)	35	(1.2)	4	(0.5)
Wisconsin[5]	229	(1.1)	—	(†)	237	(0.9)	241	(0.9)	244	(0.9)	244	(0.9)	245	(0.8)	245	(1.0)	85	(1.1)	47	(1.6)	9	(0.8)
Wyoming	225	(0.9)	229	(1.1)	241	(0.6)	243	(0.6)	244	(0.5)	242	(0.6)	244	(0.4)	247	(0.4)	90	(0.7)	48	(0.9)	7	(0.5)
Department of Defense dependents schools[6]	—	(†)	227	(0.6)	237	(0.4)	239	(0.5)	240	(0.4)	240	(0.5)	241	(0.4)	245	(0.4)	89	(0.6)	45	(0.8)	6	(0.6)

—Not available.
†Not applicable.
[1]Scale ranges from 0 to 500.
[2]*Basic* denotes partial mastery of the knowledge and skills that are fundamental for proficient work at the 4th-grade level.
[3]*Proficient* represents solid academic performance for 4th-graders. Students reaching this level have demonstrated competency over challenging subject matter.
[4]*Advanced* signifies superior performance.
[5]Did not meet one or more of the guidelines for school participation in 2000. Data are subject to appreciable nonresponse bias.
[6]Prior to 2005, NAEP divided the Department of Defense (DoD) schools into two jurisdictions, domestic and overseas. In 2005, NAEP began combining the DoD domestic and overseas schools into a single jurisdiction. Data shown in this table for years prior to 2005 were recalculated for comparability.
NOTE: With the exception of 1992, includes public school students who were tested with accommodations; excludes only those students with disabilities (SD) and English language learners (ELL) who were unable to be tested even with accommodations. SD and ELL populations, accommodation rates, and exclusion rates vary from state to state. Detail may not sum to totals because of rounding.
SOURCE: U.S. Department of Education, National Center for Education Statistics, National Assessment of Educational Progress (NAEP), 1992, 2000, 2003, 2005, 2007, 2009, 2011, and 2013 Mathematics Assessments, retrieved November 21, 2013, from the Main NAEP Data Explorer (http://nces.ed.gov/nationsreportcard/naepdata/). (This table was prepared November 2013.)

Table 222.60. Average National Assessment of Educational Progress (NAEP) mathematics scale score of 8th-grade public school students and percentage attaining mathematics achievement levels, by state: Selected years, 1990 through 2013

[Standard errors appear in parentheses]

| State | Average scale score[1] | | | | | | | | | | | | | | | | | | Percent attaining mathematics achievement levels, 2013 | | |
| | 1990[2] | | 1996[3] | | 2000 | | 2003 | | 2005 | | 2007 | | 2009 | | 2011 | | 2013 | | At or above Basic[4] | At or above Proficient[5] | At Advanced[6] |
1	2		3		4		5		6		7		8		9		10		11	12	13
United States	262	(1.4)	271	(1.2)	272	(0.9)	276	(0.3)	278	(0.2)	280	(0.3)	282	(0.3)	283	(0.2)	284	(0.2)	73 (0.3)	34 (0.3)	8 (0.2)
Alabama	253	(1.1)	257	(2.1)	264	(1.8)	262	(1.5)	262	(1.5)	266	(1.5)	269	(1.2)	269	(1.4)	269	(1.3)	60 (1.5)	20 (1.6)	3 (0.6)
Alaska	—	(†)	278	(1.8)	—	(†)	279	(0.9)	279	(0.8)	283	(1.1)	283	(1.0)	283	(0.8)	282	(0.9)	72 (1.1)	33 (1.1)	7 (0.7)
Arizona[7]	260	(1.3)	268	(1.6)	269	(1.8)	271	(1.2)	274	(1.1)	276	(1.2)	277	(1.4)	279	(1.2)	280	(1.2)	69 (1.3)	31 (1.3)	7 (0.9)
Arkansas	256	(0.9)	262	(1.5)	257	(1.5)	266	(1.2)	272	(1.2)	274	(1.1)	276	(1.1)	279	(1.0)	278	(1.1)	69 (1.4)	28 (1.3)	5 (0.6)
California[7]	256	(1.3)	263	(1.9)	260	(2.1)	267	(1.2)	269	(0.7)	270	(0.8)	270	(1.3)	273	(1.2)	276	(1.2)	65 (1.3)	28 (1.3)	6 (0.7)
Colorado	267	(0.9)	276	(1.1)	—	(†)	283	(1.1)	281	(1.2)	286	(0.9)	287	(1.4)	292	(1.1)	290	(1.2)	77 (1.3)	42 (1.5)	12 (0.9)
Connecticut	270	(1.0)	280	(1.1)	281	(1.3)	284	(1.2)	281	(1.4)	282	(1.5)	289	(1.0)	287	(1.1)	285	(1.1)	74 (1.3)	37 (1.2)	10 (0.8)
Delaware	261	(0.9)	267	(0.9)	—	(†)	277	(0.7)	281	(0.6)	283	(0.6)	284	(0.5)	283	(0.7)	282	(0.7)	71 (1.0)	33 (1.1)	8 (0.6)
District of Columbia	231	(0.9)	233	(1.3)	235	(1.1)	243	(0.8)	245	(0.9)	248	(0.9)	254	(0.9)	260	(0.7)	265	(0.9)	54 (1.3)	19 (1.0)	4 (0.5)
Florida	255	(1.2)	264	(1.8)	—	(†)	271	(1.5)	274	(1.1)	277	(1.3)	279	(1.1)	278	(0.8)	281	(0.8)	70 (1.1)	31 (1.1)	7 (0.6)
Georgia	259	(1.3)	262	(1.6)	265	(1.2)	270	(1.2)	272	(1.1)	275	(1.0)	278	(0.9)	278	(1.0)	279	(1.2)	68 (1.4)	29 (1.3)	7 (0.8)
Hawaii	251	(0.8)	262	(1.0)	262	(1.4)	266	(0.8)	266	(0.7)	269	(0.8)	274	(0.7)	278	(0.7)	281	(0.8)	72 (1.0)	32 (1.1)	7 (0.6)
Idaho[7]	271	(0.8)	—	(†)	277	(1.0)	280	(0.9)	281	(0.9)	284	(0.9)	287	(0.8)	287	(0.8)	286	(0.7)	78 (0.9)	36 (1.1)	7 (0.8)
Illinois[7]	261	(1.7)	—	(†)	275	(1.7)	277	(1.2)	278	(1.1)	280	(1.1)	282	(1.2)	283	(1.1)	285	(1.0)	74 (1.0)	36 (1.2)	9 (0.9)
Indiana[7]	267	(1.2)	276	(1.4)	281	(1.4)	281	(1.1)	282	(1.0)	285	(1.1)	287	(0.9)	285	(1.0)	288	(1.1)	77 (1.1)	38 (1.4)	10 (0.9)
Iowa	278	(1.1)	284	(1.3)	—	(†)	284	(0.8)	284	(0.9)	285	(0.9)	284	(1.0)	285	(0.9)	285	(0.9)	76 (0.9)	36 (1.3)	7 (0.6)
Kansas[7]	—	(†)	—	(†)	283	(1.7)	284	(1.3)	284	(1.0)	290	(1.1)	289	(1.0)	290	(0.9)	290	(1.0)	79 (1.2)	40 (1.2)	10 (0.8)
Kentucky	257	(1.2)	267	(1.1)	270	(1.3)	274	(1.2)	274	(1.2)	279	(1.1)	279	(1.1)	282	(0.9)	281	(0.9)	71 (1.2)	30 (1.2)	6 (0.6)
Louisiana	246	(1.2)	252	(1.6)	259	(1.5)	266	(1.5)	268	(1.4)	272	(1.1)	272	(1.6)	273	(1.2)	273	(0.9)	64 (1.2)	21 (1.0)	3 (0.4)
Maine[7]	—	(†)	284	(1.3)	281	(1.1)	282	(0.9)	281	(0.9)	286	(0.8)	286	(0.7)	289	(0.8)	289	(0.7)	78 (1.0)	40 (1.2)	10 (0.7)
Maryland	261	(1.4)	270	(2.1)	272	(1.7)	278	(1.0)	278	(1.1)	286	(1.2)	288	(1.1)	288	(1.2)	287	(1.1)	74 (1.1)	37 (1.1)	12 (0.9)
Massachusetts	—	(†)	278	(1.7)	279	(1.5)	287	(0.9)	292	(0.9)	298	(1.3)	299	(1.3)	299	(0.8)	301	(1.1)	86 (0.7)	55 (1.2)	18 (1.2)
Michigan[7]	264	(1.2)	277	(1.8)	277	(1.9)	276	(2.0)	277	(1.5)	277	(1.4)	278	(1.6)	280	(1.4)	280	(1.3)	70 (1.6)	30 (1.5)	7 (0.7)
Minnesota	275	(0.9)	284	(1.3)	287	(1.4)	291	(1.1)	290	(1.2)	292	(1.0)	294	(1.0)	295	(1.0)	295	(1.0)	83 (1.0)	47 (1.2)	14 (1.0)
Mississippi	—	(†)	250	(1.2)	254	(1.1)	261	(1.1)	263	(1.2)	265	(0.8)	265	(1.2)	269	(1.4)	271	(0.9)	61 (1.3)	21 (1.2)	3 (0.4)
Missouri	—	(†)	273	(1.4)	271	(1.5)	279	(1.1)	276	(1.3)	281	(1.0)	286	(1.0)	282	(1.1)	283	(1.0)	74 (1.3)	33 (1.3)	7 (0.7)
Montana[7]	280	(0.9)	283	(1.3)	285	(1.4)	286	(0.8)	286	(0.7)	287	(0.7)	292	(0.9)	293	(0.6)	289	(0.9)	80 (1.1)	40 (1.3)	9 (0.7)
Nebraska	276	(1.0)	283	(1.0)	280	(1.2)	282	(0.9)	284	(1.0)	284	(1.0)	284	(1.1)	283	(0.8)	285	(0.9)	76 (1.1)	36 (1.2)	7 (0.7)
Nevada	—	(†)	—	(†)	265	(0.8)	268	(0.8)	270	(0.8)	271	(0.8)	274	(0.7)	278	(0.8)	278	(0.7)	68 (1.1)	28 (1.0)	6 (0.5)
New Hampshire	273	(0.9)	—	(†)	—	(†)	286	(0.8)	285	(0.8)	288	(0.7)	292	(0.9)	292	(0.7)	296	(0.8)	84 (0.8)	47 (1.1)	13 (1.0)
New Jersey	270	(1.1)	—	(†)	—	(†)	281	(1.1)	284	(1.4)	289	(1.2)	293	(1.4)	294	(1.2)	296	(1.1)	82 (1.0)	49 (1.4)	16 (0.9)
New Mexico	256	(0.7)	262	(1.2)	259	(1.3)	263	(1.0)	263	(0.9)	268	(0.9)	270	(1.1)	274	(0.8)	273	(0.7)	63 (1.1)	23 (1.0)	4 (0.4)
New York[7]	261	(1.4)	270	(1.7)	271	(2.2)	280	(1.1)	280	(0.9)	280	(1.2)	283	(1.2)	280	(0.9)	282	(0.9)	72 (1.2)	32 (1.2)	8 (0.7)
North Carolina	250	(1.1)	268	(1.4)	276	(1.3)	281	(1.0)	282	(0.9)	284	(1.1)	284	(1.3)	286	(1.0)	286	(1.1)	75 (1.2)	36 (1.5)	9 (0.8)
North Dakota	281	(1.2)	284	(0.9)	282	(1.1)	287	(0.8)	287	(0.6)	292	(0.7)	293	(0.7)	292	(0.6)	291	(0.5)	82 (0.7)	41 (1.0)	8 (0.6)
Ohio	264	(1.0)	—	(†)	281	(1.6)	282	(1.3)	283	(1.1)	285	(1.2)	286	(1.0)	289	(1.0)	290	(1.1)	79 (1.1)	40 (1.5)	11 (0.9)
Oklahoma	263	(1.3)	—	(†)	270	(1.3)	272	(1.1)	271	(1.0)	275	(0.9)	276	(1.0)	279	(1.0)	276	(1.0)	68 (1.4)	25 (1.1)	4 (0.5)
Oregon[7]	271	(1.0)	276	(1.5)	280	(1.5)	281	(1.3)	282	(1.0)	284	(1.1)	285	(1.0)	283	(1.0)	284	(1.1)	73 (1.0)	34 (1.6)	8 (0.8)
Pennsylvania	266	(1.6)	—	(†)	—	(†)	279	(1.1)	281	(1.5)	286	(1.1)	288	(1.3)	286	(1.2)	290	(1.0)	78 (1.1)	42 (1.5)	10 (0.8)
Rhode Island	260	(0.6)	269	(0.9)	269	(1.3)	272	(0.7)	272	(0.8)	275	(0.7)	278	(0.8)	283	(0.5)	284	(0.6)	74 (0.9)	36 (0.8)	8 (0.6)
South Carolina	—	(†)	261	(1.5)	265	(1.5)	277	(1.3)	281	(0.9)	282	(1.0)	280	(1.3)	281	(1.1)	280	(1.1)	69 (1.4)	31 (1.2)	8 (0.7)
South Dakota	—	(†)	—	(†)	—	(†)	285	(0.8)	287	(0.6)	288	(0.8)	291	(0.5)	291	(0.5)	287	(0.7)	79 (0.9)	38 (1.0)	7 (0.6)
Tennessee	—	(†)	263	(1.4)	262	(1.6)	268	(1.8)	271	(1.1)	274	(1.1)	275	(1.4)	274	(1.2)	278	(1.3)	69 (1.3)	28 (1.4)	5 (0.6)
Texas	258	(1.4)	270	(1.4)	273	(1.6)	277	(1.1)	281	(0.6)	286	(1.0)	287	(1.3)	290	(0.9)	288	(1.0)	80 (1.1)	38 (1.4)	8 (0.8)
Utah	—	(†)	277	(1.0)	274	(1.2)	281	(1.0)	279	(0.7)	281	(0.9)	284	(1.0)	283	(0.8)	284	(0.9)	75 (1.1)	36 (1.1)	8 (0.8)
Vermont[7]	—	(†)	279	(1.0)	281	(1.5)	286	(0.8)	287	(0.8)	291	(0.7)	293	(0.6)	294	(0.7)	295	(0.7)	84 (0.9)	47 (1.0)	14 (0.8)
Virginia	264	(1.5)	270	(1.6)	275	(1.3)	282	(1.3)	284	(1.1)	288	(1.1)	286	(1.1)	289	(1.1)	288	(1.2)	77 (1.2)	38 (1.5)	10 (1.2)
Washington	—	(†)	276	(1.3)	—	(†)	281	(0.9)	285	(1.0)	285	(1.0)	289	(1.0)	288	(1.0)	290	(1.0)	79 (1.0)	42 (1.4)	12 (0.9)
West Virginia	256	(1.0)	265	(1.0)	266	(1.2)	271	(1.2)	269	(1.0)	270	(1.0)	270	(1.0)	273	(0.7)	274	(0.9)	65 (1.2)	24 (1.1)	3 (0.5)
Wisconsin	274	(1.3)	283	(1.5)	—	(†)	284	(1.3)	285	(1.2)	286	(1.1)	288	(0.9)	289	(1.0)	289	(0.9)	78 (0.9)	40 (1.2)	11 (0.7)
Wyoming	272	(0.7)	275	(0.9)	276	(1.0)	284	(0.7)	282	(0.8)	287	(0.7)	286	(0.6)	288	(0.6)	288	(0.5)	81 (0.8)	38 (1.1)	7 (0.5)
Department of Defense dependents schools[8]	—	(†)	274	(0.9)	277	(1.1)	285	(0.7)	284	(0.7)	285	(0.8)	287	(0.9)	288	(0.8)	290	(0.8)	83 (0.9)	40 (1.2)	8 (0.7)

—Not available.
†Not applicable.
[1]Scale ranges from 0 to 500.
[2]Accommodations were not permitted for this assessment.
[3]The 1996 data in this table do not include students who were tested with accommodations. Data for students tested with accommodations are not available at the state level for 1996.
[4]Basic denotes partial mastery of the knowledge and skills that are fundamental for proficient work at the 8th-grade level.
[5]Proficient represents solid academic performance for 8th-graders. Students reaching this level have demonstrated competency over challenging subject matter.
[6]Advanced signifies superior performance.
[7]Did not meet one or more of the guidelines for school participation in 2000. Data are subject to appreciable nonresponse bias.

[8]Prior to 2005, NAEP divided the Department of Defense (DoD) schools into two jurisdictions, domestic and overseas. In 2005, NAEP began combining the DoD domestic and overseas schools into a single jurisdiction. Data shown in this table for years prior to 2005 were recalculated for comparability.
NOTE: For 2000 and later years, includes public school students who were tested with accommodations; excludes only those students with disabilities (SD) and English language learners (ELL) who were unable to be tested even with accommodations. SD and ELL populations, accommodation rates, and exclusion rates vary from state to state. Detail may not sum to totals because of rounding.
SOURCE: U.S. Department of Education, National Center for Education Statistics, National Assessment of Educational Progress (NAEP), 1990, 1996, 2000, 2003, 2005, 2007, 2009, 2011, and 2013 Mathematics Assessments, retrieved November 7, 2013, from the Main NAEP Data Explorer (http://nces.ed.gov/nationsreportcard/naepdata/). (This table was prepared November 2013.)

Table 222.70. Average National Assessment of Educational Progress (NAEP) mathematics scale score of 8th-grade public school students, by race/ethnicity, highest level of parental education, and state: 2013

[Standard errors appear in parentheses]

State	Race/ethnicity[1]													Highest level of education attained by parents[2]							
	White		Black		Hispanic		Asian		Pacific Islander		American Indian/ Alaska Native		Did not finish high school		Graduated high school		Some education after high school		Graduated college	
1	2		3		4		5		6		7		8		9		10		11	
United States	293	(0.3)	263	(0.4)	271	(0.4)	308	(1.1)	274	(2.3)	270	(1.3)	267	(0.5)	270	(0.4)	285	(0.4)	295	(0.3)
Alabama	280	(1.6)	250	(1.4)	257	(3.5)	‡	(†)	‡	(†)	‡	(†)	252	(2.7)	253	(2.0)	274	(1.6)	279	(2.0)
Alaska	294	(1.0)	270	(3.9)	277	(2.4)	278	(2.5)	257	(4.7)	262	(2.3)	‡	(†)	‡	(†)	‡	(†)	‡	(†)
Arizona	294	(1.6)	266	(4.0)	269	(1.3)	306	(4.3)	‡	(†)	259	(3.4)	267	(2.3)	266	(1.9)	281	(1.5)	288	(1.4)
Arkansas	286	(1.2)	255	(1.7)	274	(2.4)	‡	(†)	‡	(†)	‡	(†)	267	(2.4)	266	(1.9)	281	(1.5)	288	(1.4)
California	291	(1.6)	258	(3.0)	263	(1.1)	307	(2.8)	‡	(†)	‡	(†)	260	(1.7)	266	(1.8)	279	(2.1)	292	(1.7)
Colorado	300	(1.3)	260	(3.8)	273	(1.8)	308	(5.4)	‡	(†)	‡	(†)	265	(3.4)	271	(2.3)	293	(1.8)	302	(1.3)
Connecticut	297	(1.0)	260	(2.6)	258	(2.3)	308	(3.6)	‡	(†)	‡	(†)	260	(4.3)	267	(2.0)	280	(2.2)	296	(1.2)
Delaware	293	(0.9)	264	(1.1)	276	(2.0)	312	(4.8)	‡	(†)	‡	(†)	268	(3.7)	271	(1.7)	282	(1.8)	292	(1.1)
District of Columbia	317	(3.5)	261	(1.0)	265	(2.7)	‡	(†)	‡	(†)	‡	(†)	257	(3.6)	253	(2.1)	271	(2.1)	277	(1.7)
Florida	291	(1.2)	264	(1.7)	274	(1.0)	310	(4.7)	‡	(†)	‡	(†)	266	(2.3)	269	(1.5)	286	(1.3)	290	(1.0)
Georgia	292	(1.4)	262	(1.4)	276	(2.8)	310	(6.6)	‡	(†)	‡	(†)	267	(2.4)	267	(1.6)	281	(1.8)	289	(1.5)
Hawaii	290	(2.3)	‡	(†)	280	(3.1)	291	(1.3)	267	(1.3)	‡	(†)	273	(4.0)	270	(1.4)	287	(1.7)	291	(1.2)
Idaho	291	(0.8)	‡	(†)	268	(1.6)	‡	(†)	‡	(†)	‡	(†)	268	(2.2)	270	(2.0)	288	(1.8)	296	(1.1)
Illinois	296	(1.3)	260	(1.3)	272	(1.4)	313	(6.2)	‡	(†)	‡	(†)	267	(2.3)	272	(2.0)	285	(1.8)	297	(1.2)
Indiana	293	(1.1)	265	(2.4)	278	(2.4)	‡	(†)	‡	(†)	‡	(†)	272	(2.9)	276	(1.9)	290	(1.7)	298	(1.5)
Iowa	289	(1.0)	255	(3.1)	265	(2.6)	301	(4.7)	‡	(†)	‡	(†)	261	(4.2)	272	(1.9)	287	(1.8)	294	(1.0)
Kansas	295	(1.1)	268	(3.2)	276	(3.0)	302	(7.1)	‡	(†)	‡	(†)	268	(3.3)	277	(2.0)	287	(1.9)	300	(1.2)
Kentucky	283	(1.0)	260	(1.6)	269	(3.0)	313	(7.1)	‡	(†)	‡	(†)	262	(2.5)	270	(1.4)	281	(1.7)	291	(1.2)
Louisiana	285	(0.8)	259	(1.1)	277	(3.7)	†	(†)	‡	(†)	‡	(†)	266	(2.7)	265	(1.5)	279	(1.4)	279	(1.3)
Maine	290	(0.8)	262	(4.9)	‡	(†)	‡	(†)	‡	(†)	‡	(†)	270	(3.5)	275	(1.9)	285	(1.8)	298	(0.9)
Maryland	299	(1.6)	268	(1.4)	280	(2.3)	319	(4.1)	‡	(†)	‡	(†)	269	(2.7)	272	(1.7)	288	(1.8)	297	(1.4)
Massachusetts	307	(1.0)	277	(1.8)	277	(2.1)	324	(3.5)	‡	(†)	‡	(†)	274	(2.4)	283	(2.2)	298	(1.6)	311	(1.2)
Michigan	287	(1.2)	251	(2.2)	261	(2.6)	310	(7.7)	‡	(†)	‡	(†)	260	(3.9)	264	(2.2)	279	(1.9)	291	(1.6)
Minnesota	301	(1.1)	260	(3.5)	273	(3.1)	291	(3.1)	‡	(†)	‡	(†)	269	(4.5)	274	(2.3)	293	(2.3)	305	(1.2)
Mississippi	285	(1.1)	255	(1.1)	279	(3.7)	‡	(†)	‡	(†)	‡	(†)	265	(2.3)	259	(1.5)	278	(2.2)	279	(1.3)
Missouri	288	(0.9)	260	(3.1)	276	(2.9)	‡	(†)	‡	(†)	‡	(†)	265	(2.7)	269	(1.7)	289	(1.8)	292	(1.3)
Montana	293	(0.9)	‡	(†)	282	(4.0)	‡	(†)	‡	(†)	263	(2.2)	268	(2.5)	279	(1.6)	290	(1.8)	297	(1.1)
Nebraska	292	(0.9)	250	(4.2)	267	(1.7)	302	(4.9)	‡	(†)	‡	(†)	267	(2.7)	272	(1.9)	287	(1.8)	295	(1.0)
Nevada	289	(1.4)	263	(2.2)	268	(1.1)	300	(2.8)	‡	(†)	‡	(†)	265	(2.1)	271	(1.5)	288	(1.4)	289	(1.2)
New Hampshire	297	(0.8)	‡	(†)	270	(3.7)	313	(6.4)	‡	(†)	‡	(†)	274	(3.2)	282	(1.6)	293	(1.6)	304	(1.0)
New Jersey	303	(1.3)	274	(2.6)	283	(2.3)	323	(3.1)	‡	(†)	‡	(†)	279	(3.5)	277	(2.1)	292	(1.9)	306	(1.2)
New Mexico	289	(1.2)	258	(5.0)	268	(0.8)	‡	(†)	‡	(†)	260	(2.3)	264	(1.8)	262	(1.4)	277	(1.3)	285	(1.3)
New York	294	(1.1)	262	(1.9)	265	(1.8)	305	(2.4)	‡	(†)	‡	(†)	265	(2.7)	268	(1.9)	282	(1.8)	292	(1.1)
North Carolina	296	(1.5)	268	(1.6)	279	(2.0)	301	(6.4)	‡	(†)	‡	(†)	272	(2.7)	273	(1.8)	289	(1.8)	296	(1.3)
North Dakota	294	(0.6)	272	(4.1)	‡	(†)	‡	(†)	‡	(†)	265	(2.4)	270	(3.2)	274	(1.8)	290	(1.4)	297	(0.6)
Ohio	294	(1.1)	267	(1.8)	277	(3.9)	312	(5.8)	‡	(†)	‡	(†)	267	(3.3)	276	(1.8)	290	(1.6)	300	(1.2)
Oklahoma	281	(1.2)	256	(3.1)	265	(3.0)	299	(4.3)	‡	(†)	275	(1.9)	261	(2.7)	265	(1.9)	281	(1.6)	284	(1.2)
Oregon	290	(1.1)	‡	(†)	266	(1.8)	306	(5.6)	‡	(†)	‡	(†)	266	(2.3)	270	(1.7)	286	(1.8)	297	(1.6)
Pennsylvania	297	(1.0)	262	(2.1)	264	(2.4)	307	(4.4)	‡	(†)	‡	(†)	269	(3.3)	276	(1.5)	290	(1.6)	299	(1.4)
Rhode Island	294	(0.7)	263	(2.8)	263	(1.6)	285	(4.9)	‡	(†)	‡	(†)	264	(2.5)	269	(1.9)	284	(1.9)	297	(0.9)
South Carolina	292	(1.2)	261	(1.7)	272	(3.8)	‡	(†)	‡	(†)	‡	(†)	267	(2.9)	266	(1.8)	282	(1.8)	290	(1.4)
South Dakota	294	(0.7)	254	(5.5)	274	(3.8)	‡	(†)	‡	(†)	260	(1.7)	265	(3.0)	272	(1.9)	288	(1.9)	297	(0.8)
Tennessee	284	(1.2)	257	(2.8)	270	(3.3)	‡	(†)	‡	(†)	‡	(†)	261	(2.4)	268	(1.9)	282	(1.7)	287	(1.5)
Texas	300	(1.5)	273	(2.0)	281	(1.1)	321	(3.7)	‡	(†)	‡	(†)	277	(1.5)	278	(1.5)	289	(1.7)	299	(1.3)
Utah	291	(0.9)	‡	(†)	258	(1.9)	‡	(†)	‡	(†)	‡	(†)	258	(3.1)	264	(2.1)	284	(1.7)	297	(0.8)
Vermont	296	(0.6)	258	(5.4)	‡	(†)	‡	(†)	‡	(†)	‡	(†)	270	(3.3)	281	(1.4)	295	(1.7)	306	(0.9)
Virginia	296	(1.2)	267	(1.8)	279	(2.1)	311	(3.5)	‡	(†)	‡	(†)	269	(2.7)	271	(1.6)	284	(2.0)	300	(1.6)
Washington	296	(1.2)	269	(4.7)	273	(1.6)	310	(3.5)	‡	(†)	‡	(†)	270	(2.2)	275	(2.1)	290	(1.7)	303	(1.3)
West Virginia	275	(0.9)	264	(2.9)	‡	(†)	‡	(†)	‡	(†)	‡	(†)	259	(2.5)	265	(1.4)	279	(1.5)	284	(1.3)
Wisconsin	296	(0.8)	252	(2.3)	273	(2.2)	290	(3.4)	‡	(†)	‡	(†)	265	(3.1)	274	(1.7)	288	(1.5)	298	(1.0)
Wyoming	290	(0.6)	‡	(†)	278	(1.7)	‡	(†)	‡	(†)	269	(3.4)	272	(2.6)	275	(1.3)	291	(1.3)	296	(0.8)
Department of Defense dependents schools	296	(1.1)	276	(1.8)	283	(1.7)	301	(2.4)	‡	(†)	‡	(†)	‡	(†)	278	(2.0)	288	(1.7)	295	(0.8)

†Not applicable.
‡Reporting standards not met. Either there are too few cases for a reliable estimate or item response rates fell below the required standards for reporting.
[1]Data for students of two or more races are not separately shown.
[2]Excludes students who responded "I don't know" to the question about educational level of parents.
NOTE: Scale ranges from 0 to 500. Includes public school students who were tested with accommodations; excludes only those students with disabilities (SD) and English language learners (ELL) who were unable to be tested even with accommodations. SD and ELL populations, accommodation rates, and exclusion rates vary from state to state. Detail may not sum to totals because of rounding.
SOURCE: U.S. Department of Education, National Center for Education Statistics, National Assessment of Educational Progress (NAEP), 2013 Mathematics Assessment, retrieved November 11, 2013, from the Main NAEP Data Explorer (http://nces.ed.gov/nationsreportcard/naepdata/). (This table was prepared November 2013.)

Table 222.80. Average National Assessment of Educational Progress (NAEP) mathematics scale scores of 4th- and 8th-grade public school students and percentage attaining achievement levels, by race/ethnicity and jurisdiction or specific urban district: 2009, 2011, and 2013

[Standard errors appear in parentheses]

Grade level and jurisdiction or specific urban district	2009 All students	2011 All students	2011 White	2011 Black	2011 Hispanic	2011 Asian	2013 All students	2013 White	2013 Black	2013 Hispanic	2013 Asian	2013 At or above Basic[2]	2013 At or above Proficient[3]
1	2	3	4	5	6	7	8	9	10	11	12	13	14
4th grade													
United States	239 (0.2)	240 (0.2)	249 (0.2)	224 (0.4)	229 (0.3)	257 (1.1)	241 (0.2)	250 (0.2)	224 (0.3)	230 (0.4)	260 (0.8)	82 (0.2)	41 (0.3)
All large cities	231 (0.5)	233 (0.6)	251 (0.8)	222 (0.5)	228 (0.6)	249 (2.1)	235 (0.7)	254 (0.9)	223 (0.6)	229 (0.8)	258 (2.1)	75 (0.7)	33 (0.8)
Selected urban districts													
Albuquerque	— (†)	235 (1.3)	254 (1.9)	‡ (†)	229 (1.3)	‡ (†)	235 (1.0)	253 (2.0)	‡ (†)	229 (1.2)	‡ (†)	75 (1.5)	34 (1.8)
Atlanta	225 (0.8)	228 (0.7)	269 (1.4)	219 (0.8)	230 (2.8)	‡ (†)	233 (0.7)	269 (1.4)	222 (0.9)	233 (2.7)	‡ (†)	72 (1.2)	31 (1.0)
Austin	240 (1.0)	245 (1.1)	266 (1.5)	232 (2.7)	237 (1.5)	‡ (†)	245 (0.9)	264 (1.7)	228 (3.4)	237 (1.2)	‡ (†)	85 (1.2)	46 (1.6)
Baltimore City	222 (1.0)	226 (1.1)	244 (2.6)	223 (1.2)	‡ (†)	‡ (†)	223 (1.2)	250 (4.0)	220 (1.2)	227 (3.9)	‡ (†)	62 (1.9)	19 (1.5)
Boston	236 (0.7)	237 (0.6)	255 (1.8)	230 (1.1)	234 (1.2)	259 (2.5)	237 (0.8)	255 (1.6)	228 (1.4)	233 (1.1)	259 (2.2)	80 (1.3)	34 (1.4)
Charlotte	245 (1.3)	247 (1.1)	264 (1.4)	232 (1.4)	240 (1.6)	259 (3.7)	247 (1.6)	264 (2.0)	235 (2.2)	242 (2.0)	255 (4.1)	87 (1.4)	50 (2.4)
Chicago	222 (1.2)	224 (0.9)	246 (2.5)	217 (1.9)	223 (1.3)	246 (3.2)	231 (1.3)	261 (2.8)	221 (2.1)	230 (1.2)	256 (5.8)	70 (1.6)	28 (1.5)
Cleveland	213 (1.0)	216 (0.7)	232 (2.0)	211 (0.9)	218 (1.8)	‡ (†)	216 (0.9)	233 (2.2)	210 (1.1)	221 (2.6)	‡ (†)	54 (1.7)	13 (1.1)
Dallas	— (†)	233 (1.3)	258 (3.5)	225 (2.0)	234 (1.2)	‡ (†)	234 (1.0)	‡ (†)	226 (1.7)	235 (1.1)	‡ (†)	78 (1.7)	30 (1.8)
Detroit	200 (1.7)	203 (1.4)	‡ (†)	201 (1.5)	215 (2.4)	‡ (†)	204 (1.6)	‡ (†)	201 (1.6)	214 (2.9)	‡ (†)	35 (2.5)	4 (1.0)
District of Columbia	220 (0.8)	222 (1.0)	272 (1.8)	212 (1.2)	223 (2.6)	‡ (†)	229 (0.8)	277 (2.2)	218 (1.0)	226 (2.3)	‡ (†)	64 (1.4)	30 (1.1)
Fresno	219 (1.4)	218 (0.9)	238 (2.2)	214 (2.3)	214 (1.0)	222 (2.0)	220 (1.2)	241 (2.2)	211 (2.5)	217 (1.5)	221 (2.7)	59 (2.2)	15 (1.2)
Hillsborough County (FL)	— (†)	243 (1.1)	253 (1.7)	228 (1.9)	239 (1.2)	‡ (†)	243 (0.9)	254 (1.4)	227 (1.9)	238 (1.3)	263 (3.2)	85 (1.3)	43 (1.6)
Houston	236 (1.2)	237 (0.8)	259 (2.1)	229 (1.4)	236 (0.9)	265 (3.4)	236 (1.1)	261 (1.9)	227 (2.3)	235 (1.0)	‡ (†)	80 (1.5)	32 (1.7)
Jefferson County (KY)	233 (1.6)	235 (0.9)	243 (1.2)	221 (1.3)	238 (3.1)	256 (4.3)	234 (1.0)	245 (1.2)	220 (1.4)	224 (3.0)	‡ (†)	75 (1.4)	33 (1.4)
Los Angeles	222 (1.2)	223 (0.8)	243 (1.6)	215 (3.0)	220 (0.8)	251 (2.6)	228 (1.3)	254 (3.4)	223 (2.3)	224 (0.9)	252 (2.4)	69 (1.5)	25 (2.0)
Miami-Dade	236 (1.3)	236 (1.0)	255 (2.0)	225 (1.5)	237 (1.0)	‡ (†)	237 (1.1)	251 (2.2)	227 (1.9)	238 (1.2)	‡ (†)	81 (1.3)	34 (1.8)
Milwaukee	220 (1.5)	220 (1.0)	239 (1.9)	211 (1.4)	221 (1.8)	230 (3.2)	221 (1.6)	246 (2.8)	209 (1.8)	227 (2.2)	234 (7.5)	61 (2.3)	18 (1.6)
New York City	237 (1.0)	234 (1.2)	248 (3.2)	226 (1.1)	227 (1.7)	252 (2.0)	236 (1.1)	251 (2.7)	225 (1.5)	228 (1.5)	257 (2.6)	77 (1.4)	34 (1.5)
Philadelphia	222 (1.4)	225 (1.2)	243 (3.0)	220 (0.9)	223 (2.4)	251 (2.8)	223 (1.5)	237 (3.3)	218 (1.3)	217 (2.2)	246 (3.9)	62 (2.2)	19 (1.9)
San Diego	236 (1.6)	239 (1.3)	258 (2.1)	222 (2.7)	229 (1.4)	248 (2.5)	241 (1.2)	260 (1.9)	228 (3.1)	228 (1.6)	253 (2.8)	81 (1.5)	42 (1.6)
8th grade													
United States	282 (0.3)	283 (0.2)	293 (0.2)	262 (0.5)	269 (0.5)	305 (1.1)	284 (0.2)	293 (0.3)	263 (0.4)	271 (0.4)	308 (1.1)	73 (0.3)	34 (0.3)
All large cities	271 (0.7)	274 (0.7)	295 (1.1)	261 (0.9)	267 (1.0)	298 (2.3)	276 (0.8)	295 (1.2)	261 (0.8)	269 (0.8)	301 (2.2)	65 (0.9)	27 (0.9)
Selected urban districts													
Albuquerque	— (†)	275 (1.0)	291 (2.3)	‡ (†)	269 (1.2)	‡ (†)	274 (1.2)	295 (2.6)	‡ (†)	267 (1.5)	‡ (†)	62 (1.6)	26 (1.6)
Atlanta	259 (1.6)	266 (1.3)	309 (2.8)	262 (1.4)	264 (3.5)	‡ (†)	267 (1.2)	311 (3.0)	261 (1.3)	262 (3.7)	‡ (†)	54 (1.6)	17 (1.1)
Austin	287 (0.9)	287 (1.2)	313 (1.8)	265 (5.3)	276 (1.7)	‡ (†)	285 (1.0)	312 (1.9)	267 (2.5)	273 (1.3)	‡ (†)	73 (1.3)	35 (1.5)
Baltimore City	257 (1.9)	261 (1.3)	280 (4.0)	259 (1.5)	‡ (†)	‡ (†)	260 (2.0)	286 (6.0)	257 (2.0)	‡ (†)	‡ (†)	46 (2.3)	13 (1.6)
Boston	279 (1.3)	282 (0.9)	305 (3.1)	272 (1.6)	271 (1.6)	319 (3.6)	283 (1.2)	309 (2.4)	271 (1.8)	275 (1.8)	318 (3.7)	70 (1.6)	36 (1.2)
Charlotte	283 (0.9)	285 (0.8)	311 (1.3)	268 (1.2)	272 (2.6)	304 (6.4)	289 (1.2)	313 (1.9)	271 (1.8)	279 (3.4)	314 (6.1)	75 (1.4)	40 (1.6)
Chicago	264 (1.4)	270 (1.0)	296 (4.3)	260 (1.4)	271 (1.4)	296 (3.3)	269 (1.0)	294 (2.4)	259 (1.5)	270 (1.4)	306 (5.4)	57 (1.6)	20 (1.1)
Cleveland	256 (1.0)	256 (2.1)	277 (3.4)	249 (2.1)	258 (4.4)	‡ (†)	253 (1.3)	265 (2.9)	249 (1.5)	252 (3.4)	‡ (†)	39 (1.7)	9 (0.9)
Dallas	— (†)	274 (0.9)	306 (4.5)	264 (2.2)	276 (1.1)	‡ (†)	275 (1.0)	304 (4.7)	263 (2.0)	277 (1.1)	‡ (†)	67 (1.4)	23 (1.4)
Detroit	238 (2.7)	246 (1.2)	‡ (†)	244 (1.4)	258 (2.8)	‡ (†)	240 (1.7)	‡ (†)	239 (1.7)	243 (4.0)	‡ (†)	24 (2.1)	3 (0.7)
District of Columbia	251 (1.3)	255 (0.9)	322 (3.0)	249 (1.2)	253 (2.8)	‡ (†)	260 (1.3)	315 (4.1)	253 (1.4)	262 (3.6)	‡ (†)	47 (1.8)	17 (1.2)
Fresno	258 (1.2)	256 (0.9)	281 (2.6)	243 (2.6)	251 (1.2)	265 (2.9)	260 (1.4)	279 (3.0)	247 (4.0)	256 (1.6)	270 (2.8)	48 (2.2)	12 (1.1)
Hillsborough County (FL)	— (†)	282 (1.5)	293 (2.1)	263 (1.9)	274 (2.4)	‡ (†)	284 (1.1)	296 (1.8)	264 (2.5)	278 (1.9)	‡ (†)	73 (1.3)	34 (1.7)
Houston	277 (1.2)	279 (1.0)	309 (3.0)	271 (1.9)	278 (1.1)	310 (5.2)	280 (1.1)	312 (3.3)	271 (1.7)	279 (1.2)	314 (7.2)	72 (1.4)	28 (1.4)
Jefferson County (KY)	271 (0.9)	274 (1.0)	285 (1.5)	257 (1.4)	270 (4.5)	‡ (†)	273 (1.0)	285 (1.5)	257 (1.7)	265 (3.7)	‡ (†)	61 (1.3)	25 (1.3)
Los Angeles	258 (1.0)	261 (1.3)	291 (4.6)	246 (3.9)	255 (1.3)	297 (3.9)	264 (1.5)	293 (3.2)	256 (3.4)	258 (1.3)	298 (3.3)	54 (1.8)	18 (1.5)
Miami-Dade	273 (1.1)	272 (1.1)	288 (3.1)	256 (2.2)	274 (1.0)	‡ (†)	274 (1.5)	295 (3.4)	259 (2.9)	275 (1.3)	‡ (†)	63 (1.8)	24 (1.5)
Milwaukee	251 (1.5)	254 (1.7)	274 (4.2)	246 (1.8)	259 (3.3)	271 (5.6)	257 (1.4)	282 (3.5)	247 (1.8)	266 (2.2)	‡ (†)	44 (2.1)	11 (1.3)
New York City	273 (1.5)	272 (1.6)	292 (3.2)	262 (2.1)	261 (1.6)	304 (3.2)	274 (1.1)	301 (3.8)	263 (1.9)	263 (1.7)	304 (3.1)	61 (1.3)	25 (1.4)
Philadelphia	265 (2.0)	265 (2.0)	281 (3.9)	260 (2.3)	256 (3.1)	295 (5.4)	266 (1.7)	287 (2.8)	258 (2.2)	261 (4.1)	297 (4.9)	54 (2.0)	19 (1.5)
San Diego	280 (2.0)	278 (1.7)	302 (2.3)	256 (4.0)	263 (2.6)	293 (3.3)	277 (1.4)	300 (2.3)	260 (4.5)	260 (2.2)	294 (2.9)	65 (1.7)	31 (1.6)

—Not available.
†Not applicable.
‡Reporting standards not met (too few cases for a reliable estimate).
[1]Scale ranges from 0 to 500.
[2]Basic denotes partial mastery of the knowledge and skills that are fundamental for proficient work at a given grade.
[3]Proficient represents solid academic performance. Students reaching this level have demonstrated competency over challenging subject matter.

NOTE: Race categories exclude persons of Hispanic ethnicity. Totals include racial/ethnic groups not shown separately.
SOURCE: U.S. Department of Education, National Center for Education Statistics, National Assessment of Educational Progress (NAEP), 2009, 2011, and 2013 Mathematics Assessments, retrieved December 30, 2013, from the Main NAEP Data Explorer (http://nces.ed.gov/nationsreportcard/naepdata/). (This table was prepared December 2013.)

Table 222.85. Average National Assessment of Educational Progress (NAEP) mathematics scale score, by age and selected student characteristics: Selected years, 1973 through 2012

[Standard errors appear in parentheses]

Selected student characteristic	1973	1978	1982	1986	1990	1992	1994	1996	1999	2004[1] Previous format	2004[1] Revised format	2008	2012
1	2	3	4	5	6	7	8	9	10	11	12	13	14
9-year-olds													
All students	219 (0.8)	219 (0.8)	219 (1.1)	222 (1.0)	230 (0.8)	230 (0.8)	231 (0.8)	231 (0.8)	232 (0.8)	241 (0.9)	239 (0.9)	243 (0.8)	244 (1.0)
Sex													
Male	218 (0.7)	217 (0.7)	217 (1.2)	222 (1.1)	229 (0.9)	231 (1.0)	232 (1.0)	233 (1.2)	233 (1.0)	243 (1.1)	239 (1.0)	242 (0.9)	244 (1.2)
Female	220 (1.1)	220 (1.0)	221 (1.2)	222 (1.2)	230 (1.1)	228 (1.0)	230 (0.9)	229 (0.7)	231 (0.9)	240 (1.1)	240 (1.0)	243 (1.0)	244 (1.0)
Gap between female and male score	2 (1.3)	3 (1.3)	4 (1.7)	# (†)	1 (1.4)	-2 (1.4)	-2 (1.4)	-4 (1.4)	-2 (1.3)	-3 (1.5)	1 (1.4)	1 (1.3)	# (†)
Race/ethnicity													
White	225 (1.0)	224 (0.9)	224 (1.1)	227 (1.1)	235 (0.8)	235 (0.8)	237 (1.0)	237 (1.0)	239 (0.9)	247 (0.9)	245 (0.8)	250 (0.8)	252 (1.1)
Black	190 (1.8)	192 (1.1)	195 (1.6)	202 (1.6)	208 (2.2)	208 (2.0)	212 (1.6)	212 (1.4)	211 (1.6)	224 (2.1)	221 (2.1)	224 (1.9)	226 (1.8)
Hispanic	202 (2.4)	203 (2.2)	204 (1.3)	205 (2.1)	214 (2.1)	212 (2.3)	210 (2.3)	215 (1.7)	213 (1.9)	230 (2.0)	229 (2.0)	234 (1.2)	234 (0.9)
Gap between White and Black score	35 (2.1)	32 (1.5)	29 (2.0)	25 (2.0)	27 (2.4)	27 (2.2)	25 (1.8)	25 (1.8)	28 (1.8)	23 (2.2)	24 (2.2)	26 (2.1)	25 (2.1)
Gap between White and Hispanic score	23 (2.6)	21 (2.4)	20 (1.7)	21 (2.3)	21 (2.3)	23 (2.5)	27 (2.5)	22 (2.0)	26 (2.1)	18 (2.2)	16 (2.1)	16 (1.4)	17 (1.5)
13-year-olds													
All students	266 (1.1)	264 (1.1)	269 (1.1)	269 (1.2)	270 (0.9)	273 (0.9)	274 (1.0)	274 (0.8)	276 (0.8)	281 (1.0)	279 (1.0)	281 (0.9)	285 (1.1)
Sex													
Male	265 (1.3)	264 (1.3)	269 (1.4)	270 (1.1)	271 (1.2)	274 (1.1)	276 (1.3)	276 (0.9)	277 (0.9)	283 (1.2)	279 (1.0)	284 (1.0)	286 (1.3)
Female	267 (1.1)	265 (1.1)	268 (1.1)	268 (1.5)	270 (0.9)	272 (1.0)	273 (1.0)	272 (1.0)	274 (1.1)	279 (1.0)	278 (1.2)	279 (1.0)	284 (1.1)
Gap between female and male score	2 (1.7)	1 (1.7)	-1 (1.7)	-2 (1.9)	-2 (1.5)	-2 (1.5)	-3 (1.6)	-4 (1.4)	-3 (1.4)	-3 (1.6)	-1 (1.6)	-4 (1.4)	-2 (1.7)
Race/ethnicity													
White	274 (0.9)	272 (0.8)	274 (1.0)	274 (1.3)	276 (1.1)	279 (0.9)	281 (0.9)	281 (0.9)	283 (0.8)	288 (0.9)	287 (0.9)	290 (1.2)	293 (1.1)
Black	228 (1.9)	230 (1.9)	240 (1.6)	249 (2.3)	249 (2.3)	250 (1.9)	252 (3.5)	252 (1.3)	251 (2.6)	262 (1.6)	257 (1.8)	262 (1.2)	264 (1.9)
Hispanic	239 (2.2)	238 (2.0)	252 (1.7)	254 (2.9)	255 (1.8)	259 (1.8)	256 (1.9)	256 (1.6)	259 (1.7)	265 (2.0)	264 (1.5)	268 (1.2)	271 (1.4)
Gap between White and Black score	46 (2.1)	42 (2.1)	34 (1.9)	24 (2.6)	27 (2.6)	29 (2.1)	29 (3.7)	29 (1.6)	32 (2.7)	27 (1.8)	30 (2.1)	28 (1.7)	28 (2.2)
Gap between White and Hispanic score	35 (2.4)	34 (2.1)	22 (1.9)	19 (3.2)	22 (2.1)	20 (2.0)	25 (2.1)	25 (1.9)	24 (1.9)	23 (2.2)	23 (1.8)	23 (1.7)	21 (1.8)
Parents' highest level of education													
Did not finish high school	— (†)	245 (1.2)	251 (1.4)	252 (2.3)	253 (1.8)	256 (1.0)	255 (2.1)	254 (2.4)	256 (2.8)	262 (2.2)	263 (1.9)	268 (1.3)	266 (2.5)
Graduated high school	— (†)	263 (1.0)	263 (0.8)	263 (1.2)	263 (1.2)	263 (1.2)	266 (1.1)	267 (1.1)	264 (1.1)	271 (1.7)	270 (1.3)	272 (1.1)	270 (1.1)
Some education after high school	— (†)	273 (1.2)	275 (0.9)	274 (0.8)	277 (1.0)	278 (1.0)	277 (1.6)	277 (1.4)	279 (0.9)	283 (1.0)	282 (1.4)	285 (1.1)	286 (1.4)
Graduated college	— (†)	284 (1.2)	282 (1.5)	280 (1.4)	280 (1.0)	283 (1.0)	285 (1.2)	283 (1.2)	286 (1.0)	292 (1.0)	289 (1.1)	291 (1.0)	296 (1.3)
17-year-olds													
All students	304 (1.1)	300 (1.0)	298 (0.9)	302 (0.9)	305 (0.9)	307 (0.9)	306 (1.0)	307 (1.2)	308 (1.0)	307 (0.8)	305 (0.7)	306 (0.6)	306 (0.8)
Sex													
Male	309 (1.2)	304 (1.0)	301 (1.0)	305 (1.2)	306 (1.1)	309 (1.1)	309 (1.4)	310 (1.3)	310 (1.4)	308 (1.0)	307 (0.9)	309 (0.7)	308 (1.0)
Female	301 (1.1)	297 (1.0)	296 (1.0)	299 (1.0)	303 (1.1)	305 (1.1)	304 (1.1)	305 (1.4)	307 (1.0)	305 (0.9)	304 (0.8)	303 (0.8)	304 (0.8)
Gap between female and male score	-8 (1.6)	-7 (1.4)	-6 (1.4)	-5 (1.5)	-3 (1.5)	-4 (1.5)	-4 (1.8)	-5 (1.9)	-3 (1.7)	-3 (1.4)	-3 (1.2)	-5 (1.1)	-4 (1.3)
Race/ethnicity													
White	310 (1.1)	306 (0.9)	304 (0.9)	308 (1.0)	309 (1.0)	312 (0.8)	312 (1.1)	313 (1.4)	315 (1.1)	313 (0.7)	311 (0.7)	314 (0.7)	314 (1.0)
Black	270 (1.3)	268 (1.3)	272 (1.2)	279 (2.1)	289 (2.8)	286 (2.2)	286 (1.8)	286 (1.7)	283 (1.5)	285 (1.6)	284 (1.4)	287 (1.2)	288 (1.3)
Hispanic	277 (2.2)	276 (2.3)	277 (1.8)	283 (2.9)	284 (2.9)	292 (2.6)	291 (3.7)	292 (2.1)	293 (2.5)	289 (1.8)	292 (1.2)	293 (1.1)	294 (1.1)
Gap between White and Black score	40 (1.7)	38 (1.6)	32 (1.5)	29 (2.3)	21 (3.0)	26 (2.4)	27 (2.1)	27 (2.2)	31 (1.9)	28 (1.8)	27 (1.6)	26 (1.4)	26 (1.6)
Gap between White and Hispanic score	33 (2.5)	30 (2.4)	27 (2.0)	24 (3.0)	26 (3.1)	20 (2.8)	22 (3.9)	21 (2.5)	22 (2.7)	24 (1.9)	19 (1.4)	21 (1.3)	19 (1.5)
Parents' highest level of education													
Did not finish high school	— (†)	280 (1.2)	279 (1.0)	279 (2.3)	285 (2.2)	285 (2.3)	284 (2.4)	281 (2.4)	289 (1.8)	287 (2.4)	287 (1.2)	292 (1.3)	290 (1.4)
Graduated high school	— (†)	294 (0.8)	293 (0.8)	293 (1.0)	294 (0.9)	298 (1.7)	295 (1.1)	297 (2.4)	299 (1.6)	295 (1.1)	294 (0.9)	296 (1.2)	291 (1.1)
Some education after high school	— (†)	305 (0.9)	304 (0.9)	305 (1.2)	308 (1.0)	308 (1.1)	305 (1.3)	307 (1.5)	308 (1.6)	306 (1.1)	305 (0.9)	306 (0.8)	306 (0.9)
Graduated college	— (†)	317 (1.0)	312 (1.0)	314 (1.4)	316 (1.3)	316 (1.0)	318 (1.4)	317 (1.3)	317 (1.2)	317 (0.9)	315 (0.9)	316 (0.7)	317 (0.8)

—Not available.
†Not applicable.
#Rounds to zero.
[1]In 2004, two assessments were conducted—one using the same format that was used in previous assessments, and one using a revised assessment format that provides accommodations for students with disabilities and for English language learners. The 2004 data in column 11 are for the format that was used in previous assessment years, while the 2004 data in column 12 are for the revised format. In subsequent years, only the revised format was used.
NOTE: Scale ranges from 0 to 500. Students scoring 150 (or higher) know some basic addition and subtraction facts. Students scoring 200 have a considerable understanding of two-digit numbers and know some basic multiplication and division facts. Students scoring 250 have an initial understanding of the four basic operations and are developing an ability to analyze simple logical relations. Students scoring 300 can perform reasoning and problem solving involving fractions, decimals, percents, elementary geometry, and simple algebra. Students scoring 350 can perform reasoning and problem solving involving geometry, algebra, and beginning statistics and probability. Includes public and private schools. For assessment years prior to 2004, accommodations were not permitted. For 2004 (revised format) and later years, includes students tested with accommodations; excludes only those students with disabilities and English language learners who were unable to be tested even with accommodations (1 to 4 percent of all students, depending on age and assessment year). Race categories exclude persons of Hispanic ethnicity. Totals include other racial/ethnic groups not shown separately.
SOURCE: U.S. Department of Education, National Center for Education Statistics, National Assessment of Educational Progress (NAEP), *NAEP 2012 Trends in Academic Progress*; and 2012 NAEP Long-Term Trend Mathematics Assessment, retrieved August 29, 2013, from Long-Term Trend NAEP Data Explorer (http://nces.ed.gov/nationsreportcard/naepdata/). (This table was prepared August 2013.)

Table 222.90. Percentage of students at or above selected National Assessment of Educational Progress (NAEP) mathematics score levels, by age, sex, and race/ethnicity: Selected years, 1978 through 2012

[Standard errors appear in parentheses]

Sex, race/ ethnicity, and year	9-year-olds Level 150[1]		9-year-olds Level 200[2]		9-year-olds Level 250[3]		13-year-olds Level 200[2]		13-year-olds Level 250[3]		13-year-olds Level 300[4]		17-year-olds Level 250[3]		17-year-olds Level 300[4]		17-year-olds Level 350[5]	
1	2		3		4		5		6		7		8		9		10	
Total																		
1978	96.7	(0.25)	70.4	(0.92)	19.6	(0.73)	94.6	(0.46)	64.9	(1.18)	18.0	(0.73)	92.0	(0.50)	51.5	(1.14)	7.3	(0.44)
1982	97.1	(0.35)	71.4	(1.18)	18.8	(0.96)	97.7	(0.37)	71.4	(1.18)	17.4	(0.95)	93.0	(0.50)	48.5	(1.28)	5.5	(0.43)
1986	97.9	(0.29)	74.1	(1.24)	20.7	(0.88)	98.6	(0.25)	73.3	(1.59)	15.8	(1.01)	95.6	(0.48)	51.7	(1.43)	6.5	(0.52)
1990	99.1	(0.21)	81.5	(0.96)	27.7	(0.86)	98.5	(0.21)	74.7	(1.03)	17.3	(0.99)	96.0	(0.52)	56.1	(1.43)	7.2	(0.63)
1996	99.1	(0.18)	81.5	(0.76)	29.7	(1.02)	98.8	(0.20)	78.6	(0.87)	20.6	(1.24)	96.8	(0.42)	60.1	(1.72)	7.4	(0.77)
1999	98.9	(0.17)	82.5	(0.84)	30.9	(1.07)	98.7	(0.25)	78.8	(1.02)	23.2	(0.95)	96.8	(0.45)	60.7	(1.63)	8.4	(0.83)
2004	98.7	(0.19)	87.0	(0.77)	40.9	(0.89)	98.1	(0.19)	81.1	(0.98)	27.8	(1.09)	95.8	(0.40)	58.3	(1.12)	6.1	(0.47)
2008	99.0	(0.18)	89.1	(0.69)	44.5	(1.01)	98.2	(0.19)	83.4	(0.63)	30.0	(1.08)	96.0	(0.37)	59.4	(0.87)	6.2	(0.40)
2012	98.7	(0.21)	88.7	(0.69)	46.7	(1.28)	98.5	(0.21)	84.7	(0.71)	34.0	(1.38)	95.7	(0.31)	59.7	(1.22)	7.0	(0.51)
Male																		
1978	96.2	(0.48)	68.9	(0.98)	19.2	(0.64)	93.9	(0.49)	63.9	(1.32)	18.4	(0.85)	93.0	(0.52)	55.1	(1.21)	9.5	(0.57)
1982	96.5	(0.55)	68.8	(1.29)	18.1	(1.06)	97.5	(0.55)	71.3	(1.44)	18.9	(1.18)	93.9	(0.58)	51.9	(1.51)	6.9	(0.70)
1986	98.0	(0.51)	74.0	(1.45)	20.9	(1.10)	98.5	(0.32)	73.8	(1.76)	17.6	(1.12)	96.1	(0.63)	54.6	(1.78)	8.4	(0.91)
1990	99.0	(0.26)	80.6	(1.05)	27.5	(0.96)	98.2	(0.34)	75.1	(1.75)	19.0	(1.24)	95.8	(0.77)	57.6	(1.42)	8.8	(0.76)
1996	99.1	(0.20)	82.5	(1.10)	32.7	(1.74)	98.7	(0.25)	79.8	(1.43)	23.0	(1.64)	97.0	(0.66)	62.7	(1.77)	9.5	(1.32)
1999	98.8	(0.28)	82.6	(0.92)	32.4	(1.25)	98.5	(0.27)	79.3	(1.12)	25.4	(1.19)	96.5	(0.81)	63.1	(2.12)	9.8	(1.09)
2004	98.3	(0.27)	86.1	(0.89)	40.7	(1.03)	97.7	(0.29)	80.5	(1.08)	29.9	(1.27)	95.6	(0.45)	60.8	(1.31)	7.3	(0.68)
2008	99.0	(0.27)	88.4	(0.87)	44.4	(1.18)	98.2	(0.28)	84.3	(0.75)	33.4	(1.29)	96.2	(0.47)	62.9	(0.96)	7.6	(0.61)
2012	98.6	(0.24)	88.0	(0.79)	47.0	(1.47)	98.2	(0.27)	84.7	(0.84)	35.7	(1.55)	95.5	(0.43)	61.5	(1.33)	9.0	(0.75)
Female																		
1978	97.2	(0.27)	72.0	(1.05)	19.9	(1.00)	95.2	(0.49)	65.9	(1.17)	17.5	(0.75)	91.0	(0.57)	48.2	(1.29)	5.2	(0.66)
1982	97.6	(0.33)	74.0	(1.30)	19.6	(1.11)	98.0	(0.27)	71.4	(1.29)	15.9	(1.00)	92.1	(0.56)	45.3	(1.37)	4.1	(0.42)
1986	97.8	(0.38)	74.3	(1.32)	20.6	(1.28)	98.6	(0.31)	72.7	(1.95)	14.1	(1.31)	95.1	(0.65)	48.9	(1.73)	4.7	(0.59)
1990	99.1	(0.26)	82.3	(1.26)	27.9	(1.31)	98.9	(0.18)	74.4	(1.32)	15.7	(1.00)	96.2	(0.84)	54.7	(1.84)	5.6	(0.79)
1996	99.1	(0.36)	80.7	(0.93)	26.7	(1.07)	98.8	(0.27)	77.4	(1.09)	18.4	(1.48)	96.7	(0.57)	57.6	(2.21)	5.3	(0.80)
1999	99.0	(0.19)	82.5	(1.15)	29.4	(1.36)	99.0	(0.40)	78.4	(1.22)	21.0	(1.38)	97.2	(0.40)	58.5	(1.89)	7.1	(1.06)
2004	99.0	(0.22)	87.8	(0.96)	41.1	(1.13)	98.4	(0.25)	81.7	(1.10)	25.7	(1.24)	95.9	(0.58)	55.9	(1.18)	4.9	(0.48)
2008	99.0	(0.21)	89.9	(0.78)	44.6	(1.18)	98.2	(0.25)	82.5	(0.86)	26.7	(1.13)	95.7	(0.43)	55.8	(1.25)	4.6	(0.34)
2012	98.8	(0.29)	89.4	(0.80)	46.5	(1.34)	98.8	(0.23)	84.7	(0.91)	32.2	(1.42)	96.0	(0.37)	57.9	(1.45)	5.1	(0.60)
White																		
1978	98.3	(0.19)	76.3	(1.00)	22.9	(0.87)	97.6	(0.27)	72.9	(0.85)	21.4	(0.73)	95.6	(0.30)	57.6	(1.14)	8.5	(0.48)
1982	98.5	(0.25)	76.8	(1.22)	21.8	(1.13)	99.1	(0.14)	78.3	(0.94)	20.5	(1.00)	96.2	(0.33)	54.7	(1.41)	6.4	(0.54)
1986	98.8	(0.24)	79.6	(1.33)	24.6	(1.03)	99.3	(0.27)	78.9	(1.69)	18.6	(1.17)	98.0	(0.36)	59.1	(1.69)	7.9	(0.68)
1990	99.6	(0.16)	86.9	(0.86)	32.7	(1.04)	99.4	(0.14)	82.0	(1.01)	21.0	(1.23)	97.6	(0.28)	63.2	(1.59)	8.3	(0.73)
1996	99.6	(0.15)	86.6	(0.80)	35.7	(1.38)	99.6	(0.16)	86.4	(1.02)	25.4	(1.50)	98.7	(0.37)	68.7	(2.18)	9.2	(1.02)
1999	99.6	(0.12)	88.6	(0.78)	37.1	(1.35)	99.4	(0.29)	86.7	(0.92)	29.0	(1.26)	98.7	(0.40)	69.9	(1.96)	10.4	(1.07)
2004	99.2	(0.18)	91.9	(0.61)	47.2	(0.97)	99.1	(0.16)	89.3	(0.82)	35.1	(1.21)	97.5	(0.28)	66.8	(1.08)	7.6	(0.63)
2008	99.6	(0.12)	94.0	(0.52)	52.9	(1.29)	98.9	(0.17)	90.4	(0.83)	39.2	(1.60)	98.2	(0.26)	70.5	(1.09)	8.1	(0.55)
2012	99.4	(0.18)	93.2	(0.58)	55.9	(1.54)	99.2	(0.15)	91.6	(0.57)	41.4	(1.65)	97.9	(0.33)	70.3	(1.56)	9.1	(0.71)
Black																		
1978	88.4	(1.01)	42.0	(1.44)	4.1	(0.64)	79.7	(1.48)	28.7	(2.06)	2.3	(0.48)	70.7	(1.73)	16.8	(1.57)	0.5	(—)
1982	90.2	(0.97)	46.1	(2.35)	4.4	(0.81)	90.2	(1.60)	37.9	(2.51)	2.9	(0.96)	76.4	(1.47)	17.1	(1.51)	0.5	(—)
1986	93.9	(1.37)	53.4	(2.47)	5.6	(0.92)	95.4	(0.95)	49.0	(3.70)	4.0	(1.42)	85.6	(2.53)	20.8	(2.83)	0.2	(—)
1990	96.9	(0.88)	60.0	(2.76)	9.4	(1.72)	95.4	(1.10)	48.7	(3.56)	3.9	(1.61)	92.4	(2.20)	32.8	(4.49)	2.0	(1.04)
1996	97.3	(0.84)	65.3	(2.38)	10.0	(1.24)	96.2	(1.27)	53.7	(2.56)	4.8	(1.08)	90.6	(1.33)	31.2	(2.51)	0.9	(—)
1999	96.4	(0.64)	63.3	(2.11)	12.3	(1.48)	96.5	(1.06)	50.8	(4.01)	4.4	(1.37)	88.6	(1.95)	26.6	(2.70)	1.0	(—)
2004	97.1	(0.65)	74.3	(2.61)	22.0	(1.72)	95.3	(0.78)	61.5	(2.47)	9.7	(1.35)	89.1	(1.63)	29.4	(2.07)	0.4	(—)
2008	96.9	(0.86)	75.6	(2.31)	24.6	(1.67)	96.6	(0.68)	67.6	(1.69)	10.2	(1.17)	90.6	(1.42)	31.8	(1.60)	0.8	(0.23)
2012	97.5	(0.66)	77.2	(1.56)	26.3	(2.01)	96.7	(0.66)	67.3	(2.10)	14.2	(1.61)	89.8	(1.03)	33.8	(2.04)	1.1	(0.32)
Hispanic																		
1978	93.0	(1.20)	54.2	(2.80)	9.2	(2.49)	86.4	(0.94)	36.0	(2.92)	4.0	(0.95)	78.3	(2.29)	23.4	(2.67)	1.4	(0.58)
1982	94.3	(1.19)	55.7	(2.26)	7.8	(1.74)	95.9	(0.95)	52.2	(2.48)	6.3	(0.97)	81.4	(1.86)	21.6	(2.16)	0.7	(0.36)
1986	96.4	(1.29)	57.6	(2.95)	7.3	(2.81)	96.9	(1.43)	56.0	(5.01)	5.5	(1.15)	89.3	(2.52)	26.5	(4.48)	1.1	(—)
1990	98.0	(0.76)	68.4	(3.03)	11.3	(3.49)	96.8	(1.06)	56.7	(3.32)	6.4	(1.70)	85.8	(4.18)	30.1	(3.09)	1.9	(0.78)
1996	98.1	(0.73)	67.1	(2.14)	13.8	(2.26)	96.2	(0.78)	58.3	(2.28)	6.7	(1.17)	92.2	(2.24)	40.1	(3.47)	1.8	(—)
1999	98.1	(0.71)	67.5	(2.47)	10.5	(1.63)	97.2	(0.60)	62.9	(2.50)	8.2	(1.37)	93.6	(2.21)	37.7	(4.15)	3.1	(1.12)
2004	98.0	(0.46)	80.5	(2.03)	30.2	(2.17)	96.4	(0.66)	68.5	(1.86)	13.7	(1.44)	92.3	(1.05)	38.1	(2.12)	1.9	(0.60)
2008	98.9	(0.28)	85.1	(1.25)	33.5	(1.46)	97.0	(0.44)	73.3	(1.71)	14.4	(1.09)	92.2	(1.10)	41.1	(1.69)	1.5	(0.41)
2012	98.3	(0.40)	84.7	(1.00)	34.6	(1.22)	97.3	(0.54)	76.4	(1.94)	18.5	(1.45)	92.9	(0.59)	43.3	(1.91)	2.4	(0.44)

—Not available.
[1] Students scoring 150 (or higher) know some basic addition and subtraction facts.
[2] Students scoring 200 (or higher) have a considerable understanding of two-digit numbers and know some basic multiplication and division facts.
[3] Students scoring 250 (or higher) have an initial understanding of the four basic operations and are developing an ability to analyze simple logical relations.
[4] Students scoring 300 (or higher) can perform reasoning and problem solving involving fractions, decimals, percents, elementary geometry, and simple algebra.
[5] Students scoring 350 (or above) can perform reasoning and problem solving involving geometry, algebra, and beginning statistics and probability.
NOTE: The NAEP mathematics scores have been evaluated at certain performance levels, as outlined in footnotes 1 through 5. Scale ranges from 0 to 500. Includes public and private schools. For assessment years prior to 2004, accommodations were not permitted. For 2004 and later years, includes students tested with accommodations; excludes only those students with disabilities and English language learners who were unable to be tested even with accommodations (1 to 4 percent of all students, depending on age and assessment year). Race categories exclude persons of Hispanic ethnicity. Totals include other racial/ethnic groups not shown separately.
SOURCE: U.S. Department of Education, National Center for Education Statistics, National Assessment of Educational Progress (NAEP), *NAEP Trends in Academic Progress*, 1996 and 1999; and 2004, 2008, and 2012 Long-Term Trend Mathematics Assessments, retrieved May 4, 2009, and July 20, 2013, from the Long-Term Trend NAEP Data Explorer (http://nces.ed.gov/nationsreportcard/naepdata/). (This table was prepared July 2013.)

Table 222.95. National Assessment of Educational Progress (NAEP) mathematics performance of 17-year-olds, by highest mathematics course taken, sex, and race/ethnicity: Selected years, 1978 through 2012
[Standard errors appear in parentheses]

Year, sex, and race/ethnicity	Percent of students		Average scale score by highest mathematics course taken													Percent of students at or above score levels							
			All students		Prealgebra or general mathematics		Algebra I		Geometry		Algebra II		Precalculus or calculus		200		250		300		350	
1	2		3		4		5		6		7		8		9		10		11		12	
1978																						
All students	100	(†)	300	(1.0)	267	(0.8)	286	(0.7)	307	(0.7)	321	(0.7)	334	(1.4)	100	(†)	92	(0.5)	52	(1.1)	7	(0.4)
Sex																						
Male..........................	49	(0.5)	304	(1.0)	269	(1.0)	289	(0.9)	310	(1.0)	325	(0.8)	337	(2.0)	100	(†)	93	(0.5)	55	(1.2)	10	(0.6)
Female......................	51	(0.5)	297	(1.0)	264	(0.9)	284	(1.0)	304	(0.8)	318	(0.9)	329	(1.8)	100	(†)	91	(0.6)	48	(1.3)	5	(0.7)
Race/ethnicity																						
White........................	83	(1.3)	306	(0.9)	272	(0.6)	291	(0.6)	310	(0.6)	325	(0.6)	338	(1.1)	100	(†)	96	(0.3)	58	(1.1)	8	(0.5)
Black........................	12	(1.1)	268	(1.3)	247	(1.6)	264	(1.5)	281	(1.9)	292	(1.4)	297	(6.5)	99	(0.3)	71	(1.7)	17	(1.6)	#	(†)
Hispanic...................	4	(0.5)	276	(2.3)	256	(2.3)	273	(2.8)	294	(4.4)	303	(2.9)	‡	(†)	99	(0.4)	78	(2.3)	23	(2.7)	1	(0.6)
Other[1].....................	1	(0.1)	313	(3.3)	‡	(†)	‡	(†)	‡	(†)	323	(2.9)	‡	(†)	100	(†)	94	(2.6)	65	(4.9)	15	(3.2)
1990																						
All students	100	(†)	305	(0.9)	273	(1.1)	288	(1.2)	299	(1.5)	319	(1.0)	344	(2.7)	100	(†)	96	(0.5)	56	(1.4)	7	(0.6)
Sex																						
Male..........................	49	(0.9)	306	(1.1)	274	(1.7)	291	(1.6)	302	(1.6)	323	(1.2)	347	(2.4)	100	(†)	96	(0.8)	58	(1.4)	9	(0.8)
Female......................	51	(0.9)	303	(1.1)	271	(1.8)	285	(1.8)	296	(1.8)	316	(1.1)	340	(4.0)	100	(†)	96	(0.8)	55	(1.8)	6	(0.8)
Race/ethnicity																						
White........................	73	(0.5)	309	(1.0)	277	(1.1)	292	(1.6)	304	(1.3)	323	(0.9)	347	(2.8)	100	(†)	98	(0.3)	63	(1.6)	8	(0.7)
Black........................	16	(0.3)	289	(2.8)	264	(2.2)	278	(4.0)	285	(3.5)	302	(3.2)	‡	(†)	100	(†)	92	(2.2)	33	(4.5)	2	(1.0)
Hispanic...................	7	(0.4)	284	(2.9)	‡	(†)	‡	(†)	‡	(†)	306	(3.3)	‡	(†)	100	(†)	86	(4.2)	30	(3.1)	2	(0.8)
Other[1].....................	4	(0.5)	312	(5.2)	‡	(†)	‡	(†)	‡	(†)	321	(3.8)	‡	(†)	100	(†)	98	(‡)	62	(7.0)	16	(4.3)
1996																						
All students	100	(†)	307	(1.2)	269	(1.9)	283	(1.3)	298	(1.3)	316	(1.3)	339	(1.7)	100	(†)	97	(0.4)	60	(1.7)	7	(0.8)
Sex																						
Male..........................	50	(1.2)	310	(1.3)	272	(2.5)	286	(1.5)	302	(1.7)	320	(1.7)	342	(2.3)	100	(†)	97	(0.7)	63	(1.8)	9	(1.3)
Female......................	50	(1.2)	305	(1.4)	265	(2.2)	278	(2.2)	294	(1.5)	313	(1.4)	335	(2.2)	100	(†)	97	(0.6)	58	(2.2)	5	(0.8)
Race/ethnicity																						
White........................	71	(0.6)	313	(1.4)	273	(2.3)	287	(2.0)	304	(1.6)	320	(1.4)	342	(1.9)	100	(†)	99	(0.4)	69	(2.2)	9	(1.0)
Black........................	15	(0.3)	286	(1.7)	‡	(†)	272	(2.4)	280	(3.0)	299	(2.2)	‡	(†)	100	(†)	91	(1.3)	31	(2.5)	1	(—)
Hispanic...................	9	(0.7)	292	(2.1)	‡	(†)	‡	(†)	‡	(†)	306	(2.8)	‡	(†)	100	(†)	92	(2.2)	40	(3.5)	2	(—)
Other[1].....................	4	(0.7)	312	(5.7)	‡	(†)	‡	(†)	‡	(†)	‡	(†)	‡	(†)	100	(†)	97	(1.2)	64	(7.2)	14	(5.0)
1999																						
All students	100	(†)	308	(1.0)	278	(2.8)	285	(1.7)	298	(1.2)	315	(0.8)	341	(1.4)	100	(†)	97	(0.5)	61	(1.6)	8	(0.8)
Sex																						
Male..........................	48	(1.0)	310	(1.4)	281	(3.2)	288	(2.6)	301	(1.8)	317	(1.3)	343	(1.9)	100	(†)	96	(0.8)	63	(2.1)	10	(1.1)
Female......................	52	(1.0)	307	(1.0)	274	(3.2)	282	(2.5)	295	(1.3)	314	(1.1)	340	(2.0)	100	(†)	97	(0.4)	58	(1.9)	7	(1.1)
Race/ethnicity																						
White........................	72	(0.5)	315	(1.1)	282	(3.4)	290	(2.2)	303	(1.5)	320	(0.9)	343	(1.5)	100	(†)	99	(0.4)	70	(2.0)	10	(1.1)
Black........................	15	(0.4)	283	(1.5)	‡	(†)	267	(2.9)	281	(2.5)	293	(1.4)	‡	(†)	100	(†)	89	(2.0)	27	(2.7)	1	(—)
Hispanic...................	10	(0.5)	293	(2.5)	‡	(†)	‡	(†)	‡	(†)	308	(3.0)	‡	(†)	100	(†)	94	(2.2)	38	(4.1)	3	(1.1)
Other[1].....................	4	(0.2)	320	(4.0)	‡	(†)	‡	(†)	‡	(†)	320	(4.4)	‡	(†)	100	(†)	100	(†)	76	(6.3)	14	(4.1)
2008																						
All students	100	(†)	306	(0.6)	270	(1.9)	280	(1.1)	295	(0.8)	307	(0.7)	333	(0.8)	—	(†)	96	(0.4)	59	(0.9)	6	(0.4)
Sex															—	(†)						
Male..........................	50	(0.5)	309	(0.7)	273	(2.9)	283	(1.5)	300	(0.8)	310	(0.8)	336	(1.1)	—	(†)	96	(0.5)	63	(1.0)	8	(0.6)
Female......................	50	(0.5)	303	(0.8)	267	(2.8)	276	(1.6)	289	(1.0)	303	(0.8)	331	(0.9)	—	(†)	96	(0.4)	56	(1.3)	5	(0.3)
Race/ethnicity															—	(†)						
White........................	59	(1.5)	314	(0.7)	275	(2.3)	287	(1.3)	301	(0.9)	314	(0.8)	337	(0.8)	—	(†)	98	(0.3)	71	(1.1)	8	(0.5)
Black........................	14	(1.4)	287	(1.2)	‡	(†)	266	(2.6)	282	(1.6)	291	(1.5)	312	(2.6)	—	(†)	91	(1.4)	32	(1.6)	1	(0.2)
Hispanic...................	19	(1.2)	293	(1.1)	261	(3.2)	274	(2.3)	289	(1.3)	296	(1.2)	320	(1.9)	—	(†)	92	(1.1)	41	(1.7)	1	(0.4)
Other[1].....................	7	(0.5)	316	(1.8)	‡	(†)	‡	(†)	297	(2.8)	311	(1.9)	340	(2.2)	—	(†)	98	(0.7)	71	(2.2)	13	(1.8)
2012																						
All students	100	(†)	306	(0.8)	263	(3.6)	272	(1.5)	290	(1.3)	305	(1.0)	334	(0.8)	—	(†)	96	(0.3)	60	(1.2)	7	(0.5)
Sex																						
Male..........................	49	(0.5)	308	(1.0)	266	(4.4)	276	(1.7)	293	(1.6)	308	(1.1)	337	(1.2)	—	(†)	95	(0.4)	62	(1.3)	9	(0.8)
Female......................	51	(0.5)	304	(0.8)	‡	(†)	267	(2.0)	287	(1.3)	302	(1.1)	331	(1.0)	—	(†)	96	(0.4)	58	(1.4)	5	(0.6)
Race/ethnicity																						
White........................	56	(1.6)	314	(1.0)	268	(5.2)	278	(2.1)	298	(1.8)	311	(1.2)	337	(0.8)	—	(†)	98	(0.3)	70	(1.6)	9	(0.7)
Black........................	13	(1.2)	288	(1.3)	‡	(†)	260	(2.7)	280	(1.6)	290	(1.0)	317	(2.5)	—	(†)	90	(1.0)	34	(2.0)	1	(0.3)
Hispanic...................	22	(1.5)	294	(1.1)	‡	(†)	269	(2.5)	284	(1.4)	296	(1.0)	324	(2.0)	—	(†)	93	(0.6)	43	(1.9)	2	(0.4)
Other[1].....................	8	(0.8)	318	(2.4)	‡	(†)	‡	(†)	293	(3.7)	308	(2.4)	338	(2.1)	—	(†)	98	(0.8)	73	(3.0)	14	(2.3)

—Not available.
†Not applicable.
#Rounds to zero.
‡Reporting standards not met (too few cases for a reliable estimate).
[1]Includes Asians/Pacific Islanders and American Indians/Alaska Natives.
NOTE: Scale ranges from 0 to 500. Students scoring 200 (or higher) have a considerable understanding of two-digit numbers and know some basic multiplication and division facts. Students scoring 250 have an initial understanding of the four basic operations and are developing an ability to analyze simple logical relations. Students scoring 300 can perform reasoning and problem solving involving fractions, decimals, percents, elementary geometry, and simple algebra. Students scoring 350 can perform reasoning and problem solving involving geometry, alge-

bra, and beginning statistics and probability. Includes public and private schools. For assessment years prior to 2004, accommodations were not permitted. For 2004 and later years, includes students tested with accommodations; excludes only those students with disabilities and English language learners who were unable to be tested even with accommodations (1 to 4 percent of all students, depending on age and assessment year). Race categories exclude persons of Hispanic ethnicity. Detail may not sum to totals because of rounding.
SOURCE: U.S. Department of Education, National Center for Education Statistics, National Assessment of Educational Progress (NAEP), *NAEP Trends in Academic Progress*, 1996 and 1999; and 2004, 2008, and 2012 Long-Term Trend Mathematics Assessments, retrieved June 4, 2009, and August 12, 2013, from the Long-Term Trend NAEP Data Explorer (http://nces.ed.gov/nationsreportcard/naepdata/). (This table was prepared August 2013.)

Table 223.10. Average National Assessment of Educational Progress (NAEP) science scale score, standard deviation, and percentage of students attaining science achievement levels, by grade level, selected student and school characteristics, and percentile: 2009 and 2011

[Standard errors appear in parentheses]

Selected characteristic, percentile, and achievement level	Grade 4 — 2009 Total, all students	Grade 4 — 2009 Male	Grade 4 — 2009 Female	Grade 8 — 2009 Total, all students	Grade 8 — 2009 Male	Grade 8 — 2009 Female	Grade 8 — 2011 Total, all students	Grade 8 — 2011 Male	Grade 8 — 2011 Female	Grade 12 — 2009 Total, all students	Grade 12 — 2009 Male	Grade 12 — 2009 Female
1	2	3	4	5	6	7	8	9	10	11	12	13
Average science scale score[1]												
All students	150 (0.3)	151 (0.3)	149 (0.3)	150 (0.3)	152 (0.4)	148 (0.3)	152 (0.3)	154 (0.3)	149 (0.3)	150 (0.8)	153 (0.9)	147 (0.9)
Race/ethnicity												
White	163 (0.2)	164 (0.3)	162 (0.3)	162 (0.2)	164 (0.3)	160 (0.3)	163 (0.2)	166 (0.3)	161 (0.3)	159 (0.7)	162 (0.9)	156 (0.8)
Black	127 (0.4)	126 (0.6)	128 (0.5)	126 (0.4)	125 (0.6)	126 (0.5)	129 (0.5)	130 (0.7)	128 (0.6)	125 (1.2)	127 (1.6)	123 (1.5)
Hispanic	131 (0.5)	132 (0.7)	130 (0.6)	132 (0.6)	134 (0.8)	130 (0.7)	137 (0.5)	140 (0.8)	134 (0.8)	134 (1.3)	138 (2.3)	130 (1.5)
Asian/Pacific Islander	160 (1.2)	159 (1.4)	160 (1.4)	160 (1.0)	162 (1.3)	158 (1.3)	159 (1.3)	161 (1.6)	157 (1.7)	164 (3.7)	161 (2.9)	166 (3.8)
American Indian/Alaska Native	135 (1.3)	135 (1.5)	135 (1.8)	137 (1.4)	141 (1.8)	133 (2.0)	141 (1.4)	143 (2.1)	139 (1.5)	144 (3.7)	‡ (†)	‡ (†)
Highest education level of either parent												
Did not finish high school	— (†)	— (†)	— (†)	131 (0.6)	135 (1.0)	128 (0.7)	132 (0.7)	136 (1.2)	130 (1.0)	131 (1.4)	136 (1.9)	128 (1.8)
Graduated high school	— (†)	— (†)	— (†)	139 (0.4)	141 (0.6)	137 (0.5)	140 (0.4)	143 (0.7)	138 (0.6)	138 (1.2)	140 (1.5)	136 (1.4)
Some education after high school	— (†)	— (†)	— (†)	152 (0.4)	154 (0.5)	150 (0.4)	153 (0.4)	156 (0.7)	151 (0.6)	147 (0.9)	150 (1.3)	144 (1.1)
Graduated college	— (†)	— (†)	— (†)	161 (0.4)	162 (0.5)	159 (0.3)	162 (0.3)	164 (0.4)	160 (0.4)	161 (0.7)	163 (0.9)	159 (1.0)
Eligibility for free or reduced-price lunch												
Eligible	134 (0.3)	134 (0.4)	133 (0.3)	133 (0.4)	135 (0.5)	131 (0.4)	137 (0.3)	139 (0.4)	135 (0.4)	132 (1.0)	135 (1.1)	130 (1.1)
Not eligible	163 (0.3)	164 (0.3)	163 (0.3)	161 (0.3)	163 (0.4)	159 (0.4)	164 (0.3)	166 (0.4)	161 (0.4)	157 (0.9)	159 (1.1)	154 (1.0)
Unknown	162 (1.3)	163 (1.7)	161 (1.3)	164 (1.2)	167 (1.4)	161 (1.2)	164 (1.6)	168 (2.2)	159 (2.2)	156 (2.7)	156 (3.6)	156 (3.0)
School type												
Public	149 (0.3)	149 (0.3)	148 (0.3)	149 (0.3)	151 (0.4)	147 (0.3)	151 (0.2)	153 (0.3)	148 (0.4)	— (—)	— (—)	— (—)
Private	163 (0.9)	165 (1.2)	162 (1.0)	164 (0.9)	167 (1.4)	161 (1.0)	163 (1.4)	168 (1.9)	158 (1.9)	— (—)	— (—)	— (—)
School locale[2]												
City	142 (0.6)	142 (0.6)	142 (0.7)	144 (0.6)	144 (0.7)	141 (0.7)	144 (0.6)	146 (0.8)	142 (0.7)	146 (1.8)	148 (1.6)	144 (2.2)
Suburban	154 (0.4)	154 (0.6)	153 (0.4)	155 (0.5)	155 (0.6)	152 (0.5)	155 (0.7)	158 (0.5)	153 (0.6)	154 (1.4)	157 (1.8)	150 (1.5)
Town	150 (0.6)	151 (0.8)	149 (0.6)	152 (1.0)	152 (1.1)	147 (0.9)	153 (0.7)	155 (0.9)	150 (0.8)	150 (1.2)	153 (1.5)	146 (1.6)
Rural	155 (0.5)	156 (0.7)	154 (0.5)	156 (0.4)	156 (0.5)	152 (0.5)	156 (0.5)	159 (0.6)	153 (0.6)	150 (1.2)	153 (1.5)	146 (1.4)
Percentile[2]												
10th	104 (0.6)	104 (0.6)	104 (0.5)	103 (0.6)	103 (0.7)	103 (0.6)	106 (0.5)	107 (0.9)	105 (0.7)	104 (1.2)	106 (1.8)	103 (1.1)
25th	128 (0.4)	128 (0.5)	128 (0.4)	128 (0.4)	130 (0.5)	127 (0.5)	131 (0.4)	133 (0.5)	129 (0.6)	126 (0.8)	128 (1.0)	125 (1.5)
50th	153 (0.3)	154 (0.4)	152 (0.4)	153 (0.3)	156 (0.4)	151 (0.3)	155 (0.3)	158 (0.5)	152 (0.4)	151 (1.1)	154 (1.4)	148 (1.1)
75th	175 (0.3)	176 (0.3)	174 (0.4)	175 (0.2)	178 (0.4)	172 (0.2)	176 (0.4)	179 (0.5)	173 (0.4)	174 (1.1)	178 (1.2)	171 (1.1)
90th	192 (0.3)	194 (0.4)	191 (0.5)	192 (0.3)	195 (0.2)	188 (0.1)	193 (0.4)	196 (0.4)	189 (0.5)	194 (1.0)	198 (0.9)	190 (1.4)
Standard deviation of the science scale score[3]												
All students	35 (0.2)	36 (0.2)	34 (0.2)	35 (0.2)	36 (0.2)	34 (0.2)	34 (0.2)	35 (0.2)	33 (0.3)	35 (0.4)	36 (0.5)	34 (0.5)
Percent of students attaining science achievement levels												
Achievement level												
Below Basic[4]	28 (0.3)	27 (0.4)	28 (0.3)	37 (0.4)	35 (0.5)	38 (0.4)	35 (0.3)	32 (0.4)	37 (0.5)	40 (1.0)	37 (1.1)	42 (1.3)
At or above Basic	72 (0.3)	73 (0.4)	72 (0.3)	63 (0.4)	65 (0.5)	62 (0.4)	65 (0.3)	68 (0.4)	63 (0.5)	60 (1.0)	63 (1.1)	58 (1.3)
At or above Proficient[5]	34 (0.3)	35 (0.3)	32 (0.3)	30 (0.3)	34 (0.4)	27 (0.3)	32 (0.4)	35 (0.5)	28 (0.5)	21 (0.8)	24 (1.0)	18 (0.8)
At Advanced[6]	1 (0.1)	1 (0.1)	1 (0.1)	2 (0.1)	2 (0.1)	2 (0.1)	2 (0.1)	2 (0.1)	1 (0.1)	1 (0.2)	2 (0.3)	1 (0.2)

—Not available.
†Not applicable.
‡Reporting standards not met (too few cases for a reliable estimate).
[1]Scale ranges from 0 to 300 for all three grades, but scores cannot be compared across grades. For example, the average score of 163 for White 4th-graders does not denote higher performance than the score of 159 for White 12th-graders.
[2]The percentile represents a specific point on the percentage distribution of all students ranked by their science score from low to high. For example, 10 percent of students scored at or below the 10th percentile score, while 90 percent of students scored above it.
[3]The standard deviation provides an indication of how much the test scores varied. The lower the standard deviation, the closer the scores were clustered around the average score. About two-thirds of the student scores can be expected to fall within the range of one standard deviation above and one standard deviation below the average score. For example, the average score for all 4th-graders was 150, and the standard deviation was 35. This means that we would expect about two-thirds of the students to have scores between 185 (one standard deviation above the average) and 115 (one standard deviation below). Standard errors also must be taken into account when making comparisons of these ranges. For a discussion of standard errors, see Appendix A: Guide to Sources.
[4]Basic denotes partial mastery of the knowledge and skills that are fundamental for proficient work.
[5]Proficient represents solid academic performance. Students reaching this level have demonstrated competency over challenging subject matter.
[6]Advanced signifies superior performance.
NOTE: In 2011, only 8th-grade students were assessed in science. Includes students tested with accommodations (7 to 11 percent of all students, depending on grade level and year); excludes only those students with disabilities and English language learners who were unable to be tested even with accommodations (2 to 3 percent of all students). Race categories exclude persons of Hispanic ethnicity.
SOURCE: U.S. Department of Education, National Center for Education Statistics, National Assessment of Educational Progress (NAEP), 2011 Science Assessment, retrieved August 1, 2012, from the Main NAEP Data Explorer (http://nces.ed.gov/nationsreportcard/naepdata/). (This table was prepared August 2012.)

Table 223.20. Average National Assessment of Educational Progress (NAEP) science scale scores of 8th-grade public school students, by race/ethnicity and state: 2009 and 2011

[Standard errors appear in parentheses]

State	2009											2011										
	Total, all students		White		Black		Hispanic		Asian/Pacific Islander			Total, all students		White		Black		Hispanic		Asian/Pacific Islander	
1	2		3		4		5		6			7		8		9		10		11	
United States	149	(0.3)	161	(0.2)	125	(0.4)	131	(0.6)	159	(1.0)		151	(0.2)	163	(0.2)	128	(0.5)	136	(0.5)	159	(1.2)
Alabama	139	(1.1)	152	(1.1)	115	(1.8)	129	(3.5)	‡	(†)		140	(1.4)	152	(1.3)	118	(1.4)	136	(3.6)	‡	(†)
Alaska	—	(†)	—	(†)	—	(†)	—	(†)	—	(†)		153	(0.7)	166	(0.9)	133	(3.2)	147	(2.7)	145	(2.2)
Arizona	141	(1.3)	157	(1.3)	126	(3.2)	127	(1.5)	159	(5.5)		144	(1.3)	158	(1.3)	128	(2.9)	132	(1.6)	‡	(†)
Arkansas	144	(1.3)	154	(0.9)	111	(2.1)	134	(3.0)	‡	(†)		148	(1.1)	158	(1.0)	119	(2.1)	138	(2.1)	‡	(†)
California	137	(1.4)	157	(2.0)	122	(2.8)	122	(1.3)	154	(2.2)		140	(1.3)	159	(1.6)	124	(3.4)	128	(1.4)	157	(2.8)
Colorado	156	(1.0)	166	(1.0)	135	(3.7)	137	(1.6)	161	(3.7)		161	(1.3)	171	(1.4)	149	(3.7)	141	(1.8)	162	(4.5)
Connecticut	155	(0.9)	164	(0.8)	126	(2.3)	128	(1.8)	169	(3.5)		155	(1.1)	165	(1.0)	128	(2.3)	129	(2.5)	170	(4.2)
Delaware	148	(0.6)	159	(0.9)	133	(1.0)	141	(2.2)	160	(4.3)		150	(0.6)	161	(0.8)	134	(1.3)	139	(2.0)	168	(3.3)
District of Columbia	—	(†)	—	(†)	—	(†)	—	(†)	—	(†)		112	(1.0)	174	(3.3)	107	(1.1)	116	(2.6)	‡	(†)
Florida	146	(1.0)	158	(1.4)	126	(1.4)	139	(1.2)	163	(4.1)		148	(1.1)	161	(1.1)	127	(2.0)	144	(1.5)	161	(4.5)
Georgia	147	(1.0)	161	(1.2)	129	(1.3)	137	(2.2)	172	(2.7)		151	(1.4)	166	(1.6)	133	(1.8)	143	(3.1)	168	(3.9)
Hawaii	139	(0.7)	153	(1.5)	133	(5.0)	148	(4.3)	136	(1.0)		142	(0.7)	157	(1.8)	‡	(†)	144	(3.3)	139	(0.9)
Idaho	158	(0.9)	162	(0.9)	‡	(†)	137	(1.4)	‡	(†)		159	(0.7)	163	(0.7)	‡	(†)	139	(1.8)	‡	(†)
Illinois	148	(1.4)	162	(1.2)	118	(1.5)	131	(1.5)	167	(3.2)		147	(1.0)	161	(1.1)	120	(1.9)	135	(1.2)	163	(4.4)
Indiana	152	(1.2)	159	(1.0)	126	(3.9)	135	(3.5)	‡	(†)		153	(0.9)	160	(1.0)	125	(2.7)	136	(3.7)	‡	(†)
Iowa	156	(0.9)	160	(0.8)	127	(3.5)	133	(3.2)	‡	(†)		157	(0.8)	161	(0.8)	128	(3.7)	143	(3.1)	‡	(†)
Kansas	—	(†)	—	(†)	—	(†)	—	(†)	—	(†)		156	(0.8)	163	(0.8)	129	(3.2)	134	(2.1)	156	(5.2)
Kentucky	156	(0.8)	159	(0.9)	137	(1.8)	145	(3.5)	‡	(†)		157	(0.8)	160	(0.9)	135	(1.7)	149	(3.0)	‡	(†)
Louisiana	139	(1.7)	155	(1.5)	120	(1.9)	‡	(†)	‡	(†)		143	(1.7)	156	(1.6)	125	(2.1)	142	(5.2)	‡	(†)
Maine	158	(0.8)	159	(0.8)	126	(4.5)	‡	(†)	‡	(†)		160	(0.5)	160	(0.6)	‡	(†)	‡	(†)	‡	(†)
Maryland	148	(1.1)	164	(1.2)	127	(1.5)	136	(2.8)	169	(2.5)		152	(1.2)	167	(1.2)	131	(1.8)	142	(2.2)	164	(4.3)
Massachusetts	160	(1.1)	167	(1.1)	132	(2.6)	131	(2.7)	168	(4.1)		161	(1.1)	169	(1.1)	133	(4.3)	130	(2.6)	170	(4.1)
Michigan	153	(1.4)	162	(1.0)	121	(2.1)	139	(3.4)	‡	(†)		157	(1.0)	165	(0.8)	124	(2.8)	146	(3.3)	166	(6.9)
Minnesota	159	(1.0)	166	(0.9)	128	(2.8)	132	(3.7)	141	(3.0)		161	(1.0)	168	(1.0)	129	(2.5)	137	(4.0)	149	(3.9)
Mississippi	132	(1.2)	150	(1.2)	114	(1.1)	‡	(†)	‡	(†)		137	(1.3)	156	(1.1)	119	(1.4)	‡	(†)	‡	(†)
Missouri	156	(1.1)	161	(0.9)	129	(2.5)	150	(3.8)	167	(4.7)		156	(1.1)	162	(0.8)	130	(3.5)	‡	(†)	‡	(†)
Montana	162	(0.7)	166	(0.7)	‡	(†)	155	(3.3)	‡	(†)		163	(0.7)	167	(0.7)	‡	(†)	‡	(†)	‡	(†)
Nebraska	—	(†)	—	(†)	—	(†)	—	(†)	—	(†)		157	(0.7)	164	(0.7)	126	(3.5)	135	(1.9)	‡	(†)
Nevada	141	(0.7)	153	(0.9)	127	(2.4)	129	(1.0)	148	(2.4)		144	(0.8)	157	(1.3)	123	(3.3)	133	(1.1)	154	(2.6)
New Hampshire	160	(0.8)	161	(0.8)	‡	(†)	131	(4.2)	‡	(†)		162	(0.7)	164	(0.6)	‡	(†)	137	(4.3)	‡	(†)
New Jersey	155	(1.5)	165	(1.0)	127	(3.3)	138	(2.7)	174	(2.6)		155	(1.2)	166	(1.2)	131	(2.5)	134	(1.9)	173	(2.8)
New Mexico	143	(1.4)	163	(1.4)	‡	(†)	135	(1.4)	‡	(†)		145	(0.8)	161	(1.4)	‡	(†)	139	(0.8)	‡	(†)
New York	149	(1.2)	164	(1.0)	123	(1.8)	125	(1.7)	161	(2.3)		149	(1.0)	163	(1.3)	130	(2.2)	129	(1.7)	154	(2.6)
North Carolina	144	(1.3)	158	(1.3)	121	(1.6)	132	(2.3)	165	(7.1)		148	(1.1)	160	(1.1)	125	(1.8)	138	(2.4)	160	(6.5)
North Dakota	162	(0.5)	166	(0.6)	‡	(†)	‡	(†)	‡	(†)		164	(0.7)	168	(0.8)	‡	(†)	‡	(†)	‡	(†)
Ohio	158	(1.0)	164	(0.9)	126	(2.1)	140	(4.6)	‡	(†)		158	(1.0)	165	(1.0)	132	(2.6)	151	(5.3)	‡	(†)
Oklahoma	146	(0.9)	155	(1.0)	124	(2.6)	127	(2.6)	‡	(†)		148	(1.1)	156	(1.0)	126	(3.6)	135	(2.8)	‡	(†)
Oregon	154	(1.0)	160	(1.1)	135	(4.1)	130	(1.8)	160	(3.5)		155	(0.9)	162	(1.0)	‡	(†)	135	(1.4)	159	(4.3)
Pennsylvania	154	(1.1)	162	(0.9)	123	(2.0)	121	(4.4)	159	(4.1)		151	(1.3)	163	(0.9)	120	(2.3)	118	(4.8)	163	(4.9)
Rhode Island	146	(0.6)	155	(0.8)	125	(2.6)	119	(1.9)	146	(5.3)		149	(0.7)	161	(0.7)	122	(3.4)	120	(1.9)	151	(4.6)
South Carolina	143	(1.6)	158	(1.1)	124	(1.7)	129	(4.2)	‡	(†)		149	(1.0)	163	(1.0)	128	(1.6)	139	(3.0)	‡	(†)
South Dakota	161	(0.6)	165	(0.6)	141	(5.5)	135	(4.1)	‡	(†)		162	(0.5)	166	(0.6)	‡	(†)	151	(4.1)	‡	(†)
Tennessee	148	(1.2)	157	(0.9)	122	(2.0)	139	(3.8)	‡	(†)		150	(1.0)	160	(0.9)	121	(1.6)	137	(3.1)	‡	(†)
Texas	150	(1.2)	167	(1.4)	133	(2.5)	141	(1.5)	170	(3.6)		153	(1.0)	167	(1.2)	137	(2.3)	146	(1.3)	172	(4.3)
Utah	158	(1.0)	164	(1.1)	‡	(†)	129	(1.7)	147	(3.9)		161	(0.8)	167	(0.8)	‡	(†)	137	(2.0)	153	(4.7)
Vermont	—	(†)	—	(†)	—	(†)	—	(†)	—	(†)		163	(0.8)	164	(0.9)	‡	(†)	‡	(†)	‡	(†)
Virginia	156	(1.1)	166	(1.1)	135	(2.0)	144	(2.2)	168	(3.1)		160	(1.0)	169	(1.3)	138	(1.7)	145	(2.8)	172	(2.4)
Washington	155	(1.0)	161	(1.1)	135	(3.7)	132	(2.3)	157	(3.0)		156	(0.9)	163	(1.0)	133	(3.1)	141	(2.5)	156	(2.8)
West Virginia	145	(0.8)	146	(0.8)	127	(2.8)	‡	(†)	‡	(†)		149	(1.0)	150	(1.0)	136	(2.7)	‡	(†)	‡	(†)
Wisconsin	157	(0.9)	165	(0.8)	120	(1.5)	134	(3.9)	152	(3.5)		159	(1.0)	166	(0.9)	121	(3.1)	140	(4.8)	149	(4.7)
Wyoming	158	(0.7)	162	(0.7)	‡	(†)	137	(1.8)	‡	(†)		160	(0.5)	164	(0.6)	‡	(†)	143	(2.0)	‡	(†)
Department of Defense dependents schools	162	(0.7)	170	(1.0)	144	(1.4)	155	(2.0)	160	(2.3)		161	(0.8)	169	(1.1)	143	(2.2)	158	(2.5)	155	(3.2)

—Not available.
†Not applicable.
‡Reporting standards not met (too few cases for a reliable estimate).
NOTE: Scale ranges from 0 to 300. Includes students tested with accommodations (10 percent of all students in 2009 and 9 percent of all students in 2011); excludes only those students with disabilities and English language learners who were unable to be tested even with accommodations (2 percent of all students in both years). Race categories exclude persons of Hispanic ethnicity. Totals include other racial/ethnic groups not shown separately.
SOURCE: U.S. Department of Education, National Center for Education Statistics, National Assessment of Educational Progress (NAEP), 2009 and 2011 Science Assessment, retrieved August 12, 2012, from the Main NAEP Data Explorer (http://nces.ed.gov/nationsreportcard/naepdata/). (This table was prepared August 2012.)

Table 223.25. Average National Assessment of Educational Progress (NAEP) science scale scores of 8th-graders with various attitudes toward science and percentage reporting these attitudes, by selected student characteristics: 2011

[Standard errors appear in parentheses]

Average scale score[1]

Student characteristic	Take science only because it will help in future				Like science				Take science only because required			
	Strongly disagree	Disagree	Agree	Strongly agree	Strongly disagree	Disagree	Agree	Strongly agree	Strongly disagree	Disagree	Agree	Strongly agree
	2	3	4	5	6	7	8	9	10	11	12	13
All students	154 (0.5)	161 (0.4)	150 (0.3)	143 (0.5)	136 (0.6)	144 (0.5)	155 (0.3)	166 (0.5)	164 (0.5)	160 (0.4)	146 (0.3)	138 (0.5)
Sex												
Male	156 (0.7)	163 (0.4)	153 (0.4)	145 (0.7)	136 (0.9)	146 (0.7)	157 (0.4)	168 (0.7)	166 (0.6)	162 (0.5)	148 (0.5)	140 (0.7)
Female	152 (0.9)	158 (0.5)	148 (0.5)	141 (0.6)	136 (0.8)	144 (0.6)	153 (0.5)	162 (0.7)	161 (0.7)	158 (0.6)	144 (0.5)	137 (0.6)
Race/ethnicity												
White	164 (0.6)	169 (0.4)	161 (0.3)	158 (0.6)	148 (0.6)	156 (0.5)	165 (0.3)	175 (0.5)	174 (0.5)	170 (0.4)	157 (0.4)	150 (0.6)
Black	132 (1.3)	137 (1.3)	130 (0.8)	123 (0.9)	120 (1.1)	124 (0.8)	131 (0.6)	141 (1.2)	139 (1.6)	137 (0.7)	126 (0.7)	121 (0.8)
Hispanic	140 (1.6)	145 (1.0)	135 (0.7)	132 (1.0)	124 (1.3)	129 (1.1)	140 (0.6)	151 (1.3)	149 (1.1)	144 (0.9)	132 (0.9)	129 (0.9)
Asian	165 (2.8)	170 (1.9)	159 (2.1)	156 (2.0)	140 (3.3)	151 (2.2)	162 (1.7)	177 (2.1)	176 (2.4)	167 (2.1)	155 (2.0)	144 (2.3)
Pacific Islander	143 (6.5)	146 (3.9)	139 (2.2)	137 (5.1)	117 (5.3)	130 (3.4)	147 (3.1)	153 (3.6)	150 (4.8)	150 (3.4)	134 (3.8)	126 (3.4)
American Indian/Alaska Native	140 (4.4)	151 (2.2)	141 (1.9)	134 (2.2)	126 (3.2)	138 (2.3)	146 (2.2)	150 (3.1)	149 (3.3)	150 (2.0)	140 (2.7)	132 (3.2)
Two or more races	158 (5.0)	161 (1.8)	153 (1.6)	155 (4.2)	139 (4.6)	147 (2.3)	159 (1.2)	170 (3.6)	167 (3.9)	163 (1.7)	152 (2.2)	139 (2.6)
Eligibility for free or reduced-price lunch												
Eligible	140 (0.7)	146 (0.5)	136 (0.4)	130 (0.6)	125 (0.7)	131 (0.7)	140 (0.4)	149 (0.6)	147 (0.5)	145 (0.5)	133 (0.5)	128 (0.6)
Not eligible	165 (0.7)	170 (0.4)	162 (0.4)	158 (0.6)	147 (0.6)	156 (0.6)	166 (0.4)	176 (0.5)	175 (0.6)	170 (0.5)	158 (0.5)	150 (0.5)
Unknown	168 (3.9)	170 (2.3)	161 (2.4)	154 (3.7)	147 (5.4)	156 (2.6)	166 (1.9)	177 (3.4)	174 (3.1)	170 (2.5)	157 (2.4)	147 (5.1)
Parents' highest level of education												
Did not finish high school	134 (1.9)	142 (1.3)	130 (1.4)	128 (1.5)	125 (1.8)	126 (1.6)	136 (0.9)	144 (1.8)	140 (1.6)	140 (1.3)	128 (1.2)	129 (1.5)
Graduated high school	143 (1.4)	148 (0.9)	139 (0.6)	132 (1.1)	129 (1.0)	135 (0.8)	143 (0.6)	153 (1.0)	151 (1.2)	148 (0.7)	136 (0.7)	132 (0.7)
Some education after high school	156 (1.3)	160 (0.8)	152 (0.6)	145 (0.9)	140 (1.3)	146 (0.9)	156 (0.5)	165 (1.0)	164 (0.9)	160 (0.8)	149 (0.7)	141 (0.9)
Graduated college	165 (0.8)	170 (0.4)	161 (0.4)	153 (0.7)	145 (0.9)	155 (0.9)	164 (0.4)	174 (0.5)	173 (0.6)	169 (0.4)	156 (0.5)	146 (0.8)

Percent of students

Student characteristic	Take science only because it will help in future				Like science				Take science only because required			
	Strongly disagree	Disagree	Agree	Strongly agree	Strongly disagree	Disagree	Agree	Strongly agree	Strongly disagree	Disagree	Agree	Strongly agree
	2	3	4	5	6	7	8	9	10	11	12	13
All students	12 (0.2)	32 (0.3)	39 (0.3)	18 (0.2)	12 (0.2)	19 (0.3)	50 (0.3)	19 (0.3)	18 (0.2)	34 (0.3)	30 (0.2)	17 (0.2)
Sex												
Male	14 (0.3)	33 (0.4)	36 (0.4)	16 (0.3)	11 (0.2)	16 (0.3)	51 (0.4)	22 (0.4)	21 (0.3)	35 (0.4)	27 (0.3)	17 (0.2)
Female	10 (0.2)	30 (0.4)	41 (0.4)	19 (0.3)	12 (0.3)	23 (0.4)	49 (0.4)	16 (0.3)	15 (0.2)	34 (0.4)	33 (0.4)	18 (0.3)
Race/ethnicity												
White	13 (0.2)	36 (0.4)	37 (0.4)	13 (0.2)	10 (0.2)	19 (0.3)	50 (0.4)	20 (0.3)	20 (0.2)	37 (0.4)	28 (0.3)	16 (0.2)
Black	12 (0.5)	22 (0.7)	37 (0.7)	29 (0.6)	16 (0.5)	20 (0.6)	46 (0.6)	19 (0.6)	17 (0.7)	28 (0.6)	30 (0.7)	25 (0.5)
Hispanic	11 (0.4)	27 (0.6)	42 (0.6)	20 (0.6)	13 (0.5)	21 (0.7)	50 (0.6)	16 (0.5)	15 (0.5)	33 (0.6)	35 (0.6)	18 (0.5)
Asian	9 (0.8)	26 (1.4)	42 (1.7)	22 (1.1)	8 (0.8)	16 (0.8)	57 (1.4)	19 (1.1)	19 (0.9)	37 (1.4)	30 (1.4)	14 (0.8)
Pacific Islander	11 (2.5)	26 (3.3)	39 (3.7)	23 (3.3)	15 (2.9)	21 (3.1)	50 (4.3)	15 (2.6)	14 (2.9)	37 (3.9)	30 (2.8)	18 (2.9)
American Indian/Alaska Native	10 (1.2)	27 (1.8)	44 (2.0)	18 (1.1)	14 (1.3)	19 (1.2)	52 (1.6)	15 (1.3)	14 (1.3)	29 (1.5)	37 (1.7)	19 (1.5)
Two or more races	13 (1.4)	33 (2.0)	36 (1.9)	18 (1.7)	14 (1.8)	18 (1.0)	47 (2.0)	21 (1.8)	20 (2.4)	34 (1.9)	28 (1.7)	19 (1.5)
Eligibility for free or reduced-price lunch												
Eligible	12 (0.2)	27 (0.3)	40 (0.3)	21 (0.3)	14 (0.3)	20 (0.3)	49 (0.3)	17 (0.3)	16 (0.3)	31 (0.3)	32 (0.3)	21 (0.3)
Not eligible	12 (0.2)	35 (0.3)	38 (0.3)	15 (0.3)	10 (0.2)	18 (0.3)	51 (0.4)	20 (0.3)	20 (0.3)	37 (0.4)	28 (0.3)	15 (0.2)
Unknown	12 (1.9)	38 (2.9)	35 (2.7)	15 (1.6)	10 (1.2)	20 (2.1)	48 (2.5)	22 (2.1)	22 (2.1)	36 (2.5)	30 (2.4)	12 (1.4)
Parents' highest level of education												
Did not finish high school	12 (0.6)	27 (1.1)	40 (1.0)	20 (0.9)	16 (0.7)	23 (0.9)	45 (1.1)	15 (0.7)	14 (0.6)	29 (0.9)	34 (1.0)	23 (0.9)
Graduated high school	12 (0.4)	31 (0.6)	39 (0.6)	18 (0.5)	13 (0.4)	21 (0.4)	50 (0.6)	16 (0.6)	15 (0.5)	32 (0.6)	32 (0.6)	20 (0.4)
Some education after high school	12 (0.3)	31 (0.5)	39 (0.5)	17 (0.4)	12 (0.4)	20 (0.5)	50 (0.6)	18 (0.5)	18 (0.4)	35 (0.6)	29 (0.5)	18 (0.5)
Graduated college	12 (0.3)	33 (0.4)	38 (0.4)	17 (0.3)	10 (0.3)	18 (0.4)	51 (0.5)	22 (0.3)	21 (0.3)	37 (0.5)	28 (0.4)	15 (0.3)

[1]Scale ranges from 0 to 300.
NOTE: Includes public and private schools. Includes students tested with accommodations (11 percent of all 8th-graders); excludes only those students with disabilities and English language learners who were unable to be tested even with accommodations (2 percent of all 8th-graders). Detail may not sum to totals because of rounding. Race categories exclude persons of Hispanic ethnicity.

SOURCE: U.S. Department of Education, National Center for Education Statistics, National Assessment of Educational Progress (NAEP), 2011 Science Assessment, retrieved November 22, 2013, from the Main NAEP Data Explorer (http://nces.ed.gov/nationsreportcard/naepdata/). (This table was prepared November 2013.)

Table 223.30. Average National Assessment of Educational Progress (NAEP) science scale scores of 12th-graders with various educational goals and attitudes toward science, and percentage reporting these goals and attitudes, by selected student characteristics: 2009

[Standard errors appear in parentheses]

Student characteristic	Educational goals[1]				Like science				Take science only because required			
	Graduate high school	Some education after high school	Graduate college	Go to graduate school	Strongly disagree	Disagree	Agree	Strongly agree	Strongly disagree	Disagree	Agree	Strongly agree
	2	3	4	5	6	7	8	9	10	11	12	13
1	(1.9)	(1.3)	(0.6)	(1.0)	(1.3)	(0.9)	(0.9)	(1.1)	(1.1)	(0.9)	(0.9)	(1.0)
Average scale score[2]												
All students	114	131	148	171	132	141	153	172	169	159	142	134
Sex												
Male	121 (2.6)	134 (1.8)	152 (0.8)	177 (1.3)	130 (1.7)	141 (1.4)	155 (1.2)	175 (1.3)	172 (1.4)	162 (1.2)	143 (1.2)	134 (1.3)
Female	103 (2.6)	127 (1.9)	143 (0.8)	166 (1.2)	133 (1.8)	141 (1.1)	150 (0.9)	169 (1.8)	165 (1.8)	156 (0.9)	140 (1.2)	134 (1.4)
Race/ethnicity												
White	127 (2.1)	140 (1.6)	156 (0.7)	178 (1.0)	140 (1.6)	150 (1.1)	161 (0.9)	180 (1.0)	176 (1.1)	167 (0.8)	151 (1.0)	143 (1.4)
Black	89 (3.6)	107 (3.2)	124 (1.1)	144 (1.8)	113 (2.0)	120 (2.0)	128 (1.5)	142 (2.4)	140 (2.6)	135 (2.3)	121 (1.6)	115 (1.7)
Hispanic	106 (3.7)	122 (2.7)	136 (1.2)	154 (2.3)	123 (2.6)	127 (1.5)	135 (1.8)	157 (2.4)	152 (2.9)	143 (1.7)	128 (1.6)	125 (2.3)
Asian/Pacific Islander	‡ (†)	‡ (†)	154 (2.9)	181 (3.4)	141 (5.2)	149 (3.8)	166 (2.9)	188 (4.5)	181 (4.2)	171 (3.3)	154 (3.2)	141 (4.5)
American Indian/Alaska Native	‡ (†)	‡ (†)	‡ (†)	‡ (†)	‡ (†)	‡ (†)	‡ (†)	‡ (†)	‡ (†)	‡ (†)	‡ (†)	‡ (†)
Eligibility for free or reduced-price lunch												
Eligible	105 (2.9)	120 (2.0)	134 (0.8)	151 (2.0)	120 (1.8)	125 (1.4)	135 (1.1)	152 (2.0)	147 (2.7)	142 (1.4)	127 (1.1)	121 (1.6)
Not eligible	122 (2.0)	138 (1.8)	153 (0.8)	176 (1.0)	137 (1.5)	148 (1.1)	159 (1.1)	179 (1.3)	175 (1.2)	165 (1.0)	148 (1.1)	140 (1.4)
Unknown	‡ (†)	‡ (†)	151 (2.4)	169 (3.5)	139 (3.1)	146 (3.6)	158 (2.9)	177 (3.8)	175 (3.6)	164 (3.3)	149 (2.6)	138 (3.3)
Parents' highest level of education												
Did not finish high school	112 (3.7)	124 (2.8)	134 (1.5)	145 (3.1)	119 (2.7)	125 (2.5)	134 (2.0)	153 (3.5)	147 (3.1)	138 (2.5)	127 (2.3)	121 (2.2)
Graduated high school	109 (2.8)	129 (2.7)	141 (1.3)	158 (2.1)	124 (2.2)	132 (1.5)	141 (1.3)	158 (2.7)	149 (2.7)	149 (1.6)	133 (1.8)	126 (1.9)
Some education after high school	126 (4.0)	135 (2.2)	146 (0.9)	162 (2.1)	133 (1.5)	138 (1.2)	149 (1.2)	168 (1.7)	164 (2.3)	156 (1.3)	140 (1.1)	133 (1.7)
Graduated college	120 (3.9)	140 (2.4)	155 (0.8)	177 (0.9)	141 (1.7)	151 (1.3)	163 (1.0)	181 (1.3)	180 (1.3)	168 (1.0)	152 (1.0)	143 (1.2)
Percent of students												
All students	5 (0.3)	7 (0.3)	59 (0.7)	26 (0.8)	14 (0.4)	21 (0.4)	48 (0.5)	16 (0.3)	15 (0.4)	34 (0.5)	31 (0.4)	19 (0.4)
Sex												
Male	6 (0.4)	9 (0.4)	59 (0.8)	22 (0.8)	12 (0.5)	18 (0.5)	52 (0.7)	18 (0.5)	17 (0.5)	37 (0.6)	29 (0.7)	17 (0.5)
Female	4 (0.3)	6 (0.4)	58 (0.9)	31 (1.0)	16 (0.5)	25 (0.6)	45 (0.7)	14 (0.5)	14 (0.6)	31 (0.7)	33 (0.6)	21 (0.6)
Race/ethnicity												
White	4 (0.3)	7 (0.3)	60 (0.7)	26 (0.8)	13 (0.5)	21 (0.5)	49 (0.7)	17 (0.5)	17 (0.5)	36 (0.6)	29 (0.6)	18 (0.5)
Black	6 (0.8)	6 (0.6)	60 (1.3)	25 (1.4)	20 (1.0)	23 (0.9)	43 (1.3)	14 (0.9)	11 (0.8)	28 (1.2)	33 (1.2)	28 (1.1)
Hispanic	7 (0.7)	12 (0.8)	59 (1.4)	18 (1.1)	13 (0.7)	24 (0.9)	49 (1.1)	14 (0.9)	12 (1.1)	31 (1.1)	38 (1.0)	19 (0.9)
Asian/Pacific Islander	3 (0.8)	2 (0.5)	42 (2.6)	50 (2.8)	9 (1.0)	18 (1.7)	55 (1.5)	18 (1.6)	19 (1.6)	40 (1.3)	28 (1.9)	13 (1.1)
American Indian/Alaska Native	‡ (†)	‡ (†)	‡ (†)	‡ (†)	‡ (†)	‡ (†)	‡ (†)	‡ (†)	‡ (†)	‡ (†)	‡ (†)	‡ (†)
Eligibility for free or reduced-price lunch												
Eligible	8 (0.5)	10 (0.6)	60 (1.2)	18 (1.1)	16 (0.7)	23 (0.9)	47 (1.0)	14 (0.6)	13 (0.7)	30 (0.8)	34 (0.7)	22 (0.8)
Not eligible	4 (0.3)	7 (0.4)	59 (0.8)	29 (0.9)	13 (0.4)	21 (0.5)	49 (0.6)	17 (0.4)	16 (0.5)	35 (0.6)	30 (0.6)	18 (0.5)
Unknown	2 (0.7)	4 (1.0)	56 (2.4)	35 (2.7)	13 (1.2)	21 (1.3)	48 (1.9)	18 (1.6)	16 (1.6)	36 (2.3)	29 (1.8)	19 (1.6)
Parents' highest level of education												
Did not finish high school	11 (1.1)	13 (1.0)	53 (2.2)	16 (1.8)	19 (1.4)	22 (1.4)	47 (1.7)	13 (1.2)	13 (1.2)	30 (1.6)	35 (1.7)	23 (1.3)
Graduated high school	10 (0.6)	12 (0.8)	62 (1.4)	13 (1.0)	16 (0.8)	25 (1.0)	46 (1.2)	12 (0.7)	12 (0.7)	31 (1.3)	35 (1.1)	22 (1.1)
Some education after high school	4 (0.4)	9 (0.5)	65 (1.0)	20 (1.1)	15 (0.8)	22 (1.0)	48 (1.2)	15 (0.8)	14 (0.9)	33 (1.0)	32 (0.9)	21 (0.8)
Graduated college	2 (0.2)	4 (0.3)	56 (0.8)	37 (0.9)	12 (0.6)	19 (0.6)	50 (0.7)	19 (0.5)	18 (0.4)	37 (0.7)	28 (0.6)	17 (0.6)

†Not applicable.
‡Reporting standards not met (too few cases for a reliable estimate).
[1]The educational goals columns exclude the 1 percent of students who reported that they would not finish high school and the 2 percent who reported that they did not know how much education they would complete.
[2]Scale ranges from 0 to 300.

NOTE: Includes students tested with accommodations (7 percent of all 12th-graders); excludes only those students with disabilities and English language learners who were unable to be tested even with accommodations (3 percent of all 12th-graders). Race categories exclude persons of Hispanic ethnicity.
SOURCE: U.S. Department of Education, National Center for Education Statistics, National Assessment of Educational Progress (NAEP), 2009 Science Assessment, retrieved May 26, 2011, from the Main NAEP Data Explorer (http://nces.ed.gov/nationsreportcard/naepdata/). (This table was prepared May 2011.)

Table 224.10. Average National Assessment of Educational Progress (NAEP) arts scale score of 8th-graders, percentage distribution by frequency of instruction, and percentage participating in selected activities, by subject and selected characteristics: 2008

[Standard errors appear in parentheses]

Selected characteristic	Average score			Percentage distribution of students by school-reported frequency of instruction								Percent of students reporting participation in musical activities in school		
	Music[1]	Visual arts[2]		Music				Visual arts						
	responding scale score (0 to 300)	Responding scale score (0 to 300)	Creating task score (0 to 100)	Subject not offered	Less than once a week	Once or twice a week	At least 3 or 4 times a week	Subject not offered	Less than once a week	Once or twice a week	At least 3 or 4 times a week	Play in band	Play in orchestra	Sing in chorus or choir
1	2	3	4	5	6	7	8	9	10	11	12	13	14	15
All students	150 (1.2)	150 (1.2)	52 (0.6)	8 (2.0)	8 (2.0)	27 (3.1)	57 (3.2)	14 (2.4)	10 (2.5)	30 (3.5)	47 (3.9)	16 (0.9)	5 (0.5)	17 (1.2)
Sex														
Male	145 (1.3)	145 (1.4)	49 (0.7)	9 (2.1)	8 (2.1)	27 (3.1)	56 (3.2)	14 (2.6)	10 (2.5)	30 (3.6)	46 (4.1)	18 (1.0)	3 (0.5)	9 (1.2)
Female	155 (1.4)	155 (1.2)	54 (0.7)	8 (2.0)	7 (1.9)	28 (3.2)	57 (3.2)	13 (2.3)	10 (2.5)	29 (3.3)	48 (3.8)	14 (1.0)	6 (0.6)	26 (1.8)
Race/ethnicity														
White	161 (1.3)	160 (1.2)	55 (0.5)	6 (2.5)	8 (2.5)	29 (4.0)	57 (3.6)	11 (2.6)	11 (3.4)	34 (4.4)	44 (4.6)	19 (1.2)	5 (0.6)	19 (1.6)
Black	130 (2.0)	129 (2.4)	43 (1.5)	10 (2.9)	8 (4.5)	26 (5.5)	56 (7.0)	18 (4.9)	10 (4.9)	24 (4.5)	49 (5.7)	13 (1.2)	4 (1.0)	21 (1.9)
Hispanic	129 (1.9)	134 (1.9)	46 (1.1)	14 (4.3)	6 (2.3)	21 (4.1)	59 (4.5)	17 (4.5)	5 (2.0)	23 (4.7)	56 (6.0)	8 (1.2)	3 (0.6)	10 (1.6)
Asian/Pacific Islander	159 (4.7)	156 (4.2)	54 (2.0)	7 (4.1)	8 (3.4)	25 (6.6)	60 (8.7)	5 (2.5)	11 (4.6)	29 (6.0)	54 (8.4)	21 (3.5)	6 (2.1)	16 (2.9)
Free or reduced-price lunch eligibility														
Eligible	132 (1.3)	132 (1.4)	46 (1.0)	10 (2.1)	6 (2.1)	26 (3.4)	58 (3.9)	18 (3.4)	9 (3.2)	26 (3.7)	47 (4.7)	12 (1.2)	3 (0.6)	15 (1.4)
Not eligible	161 (1.4)	161 (1.2)	55 (0.6)	8 (2.6)	8 (2.6)	26 (4.0)	59 (4.0)	10 (2.4)	10 (3.2)	30 (4.1)	50 (4.6)	19 (1.0)	5 (0.6)	19 (1.6)
Unknown	156 (5.6)	156 (5.9)	57 (2.6)	4 (†)	19 (8.7)	54 (11.5)	23 (10.5)	16 (10.3)	13 (8.4)	47 (13.6)	24 (10.6)	14 (6.3)	5 (2.3)	13 (2.0)
Control of school														
Public	149 (1.3)	149 (1.2)	51 (0.7)	8 (2.1)	7 (2.1)	24 (3.2)	61 (3.5)	13 (2.4)	10 (2.7)	26 (3.5)	51 (4.2)	17 (0.9)	5 (0.5)	18 (1.3)
Private	163 (2.8)	159 (5.2)	60 (1.3)	10 (6.0)	15 (6.9)	71 (8.8)	3 (†)	17 (8.2)	10 (6.1)	70 (10.2)	3 (0.9)	9 (1.9)	1 (0.4)	13 (2.1)
School location														
City	142 (2.0)	144 (2.1)	49 (1.2)	13 (4.0)	10 (3.8)	24 (5.7)	52 (5.6)	12 (2.6)	9 (3.5)	24 (4.9)	55 (5.4)	14 (1.0)	4 (0.6)	13 (1.3)
Suburban	155 (1.9)	155 (1.8)	54 (0.7)	3 (2.2)	7 (3.5)	32 (5.6)	57 (6.3)	10 (3.1)	10 (4.6)	33 (6.4)	46 (6.1)	14 (1.5)	6 (1.0)	16 (1.6)
Town	156 (3.5)	149 (2.8)	50 (1.2)	4 (1.0)	# (†)	18 (9.0)	78 (9.0)	16 (8.4)	# (†)	23 (9.2)	60 (10.5)	23 (3.0)	4 (1.3)	23 (3.4)
Rural	150 (2.6)	151 (3.0)	52 (1.5)	13 (5.0)	8 (4.8)	29 (5.7)	50 (7.7)	20 (7.3)	17 (6.8)	35 (7.8)	28 (6.7)	18 (2.5)	3 (1.0)	21 (3.4)
Region														
Northeast	154 (3.1)	160 (2.3)	52 (0.9)	10 (5.3)	13 (5.8)	40 (9.0)	37 (8.6)	5 (3.3)	5 (†)	50 (6.2)	39 (9.3)	16 (2.7)	6 (0.9)	17 (2.6)
Midwest	158 (2.9)	155 (2.3)	53 (1.3)	12 (6.6)	# (†)	25 (7.2)	63 (5.8)	9 (2.0)	15 (7.7)	26 (6.7)	50 (7.3)	22 (2.1)	6 (1.3)	24 (3.1)
South	147 (1.9)	147 (2.2)	51 (1.0)	6 (1.8)	10 (4.0)	25 (3.9)	59 (5.7)	19 (5.3)	9 (3.8)	26 (5.0)	46 (6.4)	16 (1.2)	4 (0.6)	16 (2.0)
West	144 (2.0)	143 (2.1)	51 (1.1)	8 (3.7)	8 (3.5)	24 (6.9)	60 (5.4)	15 (4.9)	9 (4.0)	25 (9.0)	51 (8.2)	9 (1.2)	3 (0.6)	12 (1.7)
Frequency of instruction														
Subject not offered	139 (6.3)	138 (4.2)	— (—)	†	†	†	†	†	†	†	†	†	†	†
Less than once a week	149 (6.4)	154 (5.3)	— (—)	†	†	†	†	†	†	†	†	†	†	†
Once or twice a week	152 (2.8)	154 (2.6)	— (—)	†	†	†	†	†	†	†	†	†	†	†
At least 3 or 4 times a week	149 (1.8)	149 (1.8)	— (—)	†	†	†	†	†	†	†	†	†	†	†

—Not available.
†Not applicable.
#Rounds to zero.
[1] Students were asked to analyze and describe aspects of music they heard, critique instrumental and vocal performances, and demonstrate their knowledge of standard musical notation and music's role in society.
[2] The visual arts assessment measured students' ability to respond to and create visual arts. Responding questions asked students to analyze and describe works of art and design, while creating questions required students to create works of art and design of their own.

NOTE: Excludes students unable to be tested due to limited proficiency in English or due to a disability (if the accommodations provided were not sufficient to enable the test to properly reflect the students' music or visual arts proficiency). Detail may not sum to totals because of rounding. Race categories exclude persons of Hispanic ethnicity. Totals include other racial/ethnic groups not shown separately.
SOURCE: U.S. Department of Education, National Center for Education Statistics, National Assessment of Educational Progress (NAEP), 2008 Arts Assessment, retrieved June 30, 2009, from the Main NAEP Data Explorer (http://nces.ed.gov/nationsreportcard/naepdata/). (This table was prepared June 2009.)

Table 224.20. Average National Assessment of Educational Progress (NAEP) civics scale score and percentage of students attaining civics achievement levels, by grade level, selected student characteristics, and percentile: 1998, 2006, 2010, and 2014

[Standard errors appear in parentheses]

Selected student characteristic	4th-graders			8th-graders				12th-graders		
	1998	2006	2010	1998	2006	2010	2014	1998	2006	2010
1	2	3	4	5	6	7	8	9	10	11
	Average civics scale score[1]									
All students	150 (0.7)	154 (1.0)	157 (0.8)	150 (0.7)	150 (0.8)	151 (0.8)	154 (1.1)	150 (0.8)	151 (0.9)	148 (0.8)
Sex										
Male	149 (1.0)	153 (1.1)	153 (1.0)	148 (0.9)	149 (1.0)	150 (0.9)	154 (1.2)	148 (1.1)	150 (1.1)	148 (0.9)
Female	151 (0.9)	155 (1.1)	160 (0.8)	152 (0.8)	151 (0.8)	152 (0.8)	154 (1.1)	152 (0.8)	152 (1.0)	148 (0.9)
Race/ethnicity										
White	158 (0.9)	164 (0.9)	167 (0.8)	158 (0.9)	161 (0.8)	160 (0.8)	164 (1.0)	157 (1.0)	158 (1.0)	156 (0.9)
Black	130 (1.1)	140 (1.5)	143 (1.2)	131 (1.2)	133 (1.5)	135 (1.6)	137 (2.1)	130 (1.6)	131 (1.4)	127 (1.6)
Hispanic	123 (2.2)	138 (1.3)	140 (1.6)	127 (1.3)	131 (1.1)	137 (1.1)	141 (1.4)	132 (1.1)	134 (1.1)	137 (1.4)
Asian/Pacific Islander	147 (4.0)	154 (3.8)	164 (2.0)	151 (8.9)	154 (3.2)	158 (2.5)	165 (3.1)	149 (5.2)	155 (3.1)	153 (2.6)
Asian[2]	— (†)	— (†)	— (†)	— (†)	— (†)	— (†)	166 (3.1)	— (†)	— (†)	— (†)
Pacific Islander[2]	— (†)	— (†)	— (†)	— (†)	— (†)	— (†)	‡ (†)	— (†)	— (†)	— (†)
American Indian/Alaska Native	‡ (†)	124 (7.6)	143 (7.0)	‡ (†)	127 (7.3)	136 (12.6)	‡ (†)	‡ (†)	131 (3.5)	134 (14.6)
Two or more races[2]	— (†)	— (†)	— (†)	— (†)	— (†)	— (†)	160 (2.8)	— (†)	— (†)	— (†)
Parents' highest level of education[3]										
Did not finish high school	— (†)	— (†)	— (†)	123 (3.2)	129 (1.6)	134 (1.3)	134 (1.5)	124 (2.1)	126 (1.8)	128 (1.4)
Graduated high school	— (†)	— (†)	— (†)	144 (1.2)	140 (1.3)	139 (1.1)	140 (1.7)	140 (1.2)	138 (1.0)	137 (1.2)
Some education after high school	— (†)	— (†)	— (†)	143 (1.0)	153 (1.0)	155 (1.1)	155 (1.1)	145 (1.1)	150 (0.9)	147 (1.1)
Graduated college	— (†)	— (†)	— (†)	160 (0.8)	162 (0.9)	162 (0.8)	164 (1.0)	160 (0.9)	162 (1.1)	158 (0.9)
Eligibility for free or reduced-price lunch										
Eligible	132 (0.9)	139 (1.1)	143 (0.9)	131 (1.1)	132 (1.0)	136 (0.9)	139 (1.2)	130 (1.4)	133 (1.0)	132 (1.0)
Not eligible	160 (1.1)	166 (0.8)	169 (0.8)	157 (1.0)	160 (0.8)	163 (0.7)	166 (1.1)	153 (1.0)	156 (1.0)	155 (0.9)
Unknown	154 (2.2)	167 (2.1)	171 (2.7)	156 (2.2)	171 (2.4)	166 (2.3)	166 (2.1)	153 (1.3)	160 (2.4)	159 (3.3)
Percentile[4]										
10th	102 (1.6)	111 (1.9)	115 (1.6)	103 (1.6)	102 (1.6)	106 (1.9)	110 (1.8)	103 (1.2)	104 (1.2)	101 (1.8)
25th	128 (0.9)	134 (1.2)	138 (1.0)	128 (1.1)	128 (1.5)	131 (1.1)	133 (1.7)	128 (1.4)	128 (1.2)	126 (1.4)
50th	153 (1.3)	156 (1.1)	159 (1.2)	153 (0.7)	154 (1.1)	155 (0.9)	157 (1.2)	153 (0.8)	154 (1.1)	152 (1.0)
75th	175 (0.8)	176 (0.9)	179 (1.2)	175 (1.0)	175 (1.0)	175 (0.8)	177 (1.4)	175 (0.8)	176 (1.0)	173 (0.8)
90th	192 (0.7)	192 (1.1)	194 (1.0)	192 (0.7)	191 (0.6)	191 (0.5)	193 (1.0)	192 (0.7)	194 (0.9)	190 (1.3)
	Standard deviation of the civics scale score[5]									
All students	35 (0.5)	31 (0.5)	31 (0.5)	35 (0.4)	35 (0.5)	34 (0.4)	33 (0.5)	35 (0.4)	35 (0.4)	35 (0.4)
	Percent of students achieving civics achievement levels									
Achievement level										
Below *Basic*	31 (1.0)	27 (1.2)	23 (1.0)	30 (0.9)	30 (1.1)	28 (1.0)	26 (1.3)	35 (0.9)	34 (1.1)	36 (1.0)
At or above *Basic*[6]	69 (1.0)	73 (1.2)	77 (1.0)	70 (0.9)	70 (1.1)	72 (1.0)	74 (1.3)	65 (0.9)	66 (1.1)	64 (1.0)
At or above *Basic* by sex										
Male	68 (1.2)	72 (1.3)	73 (1.3)	67 (1.1)	68 (1.3)	70 (1.1)	74 (1.4)	62 (1.2)	64 (1.5)	63 (1.0)
Female	70 (1.0)	75 (1.4)	81 (1.0)	73 (1.2)	72 (1.2)	74 (1.1)	75 (1.4)	68 (1.2)	67 (1.2)	64 (1.3)
At or above *Basic* by sex by race/ethnicity										
White	78 (1.3)	85 (1.0)	87 (0.9)	78 (1.1)	82 (0.9)	82 (1.0)	86 (1.0)	73 (1.1)	74 (1.2)	73 (1.0)
Black	45 (1.7)	57 (2.3)	62 (2.2)	49 (1.7)	50 (2.0)	53 (2.3)	55 (3.4)	41 (2.0)	42 (1.9)	38 (1.9)
Hispanic	40 (2.8)	55 (2.0)	58 (2.3)	44 (2.3)	50 (2.2)	56 (1.4)	61 (1.7)	45 (1.9)	46 (1.7)	50 (1.8)
Asian/Pacific Islander	66 (5.5)	75 (4.5)	82 (2.3)	69 (9.5)	73 (4.0)	78 (2.5)	83 (2.8)	63 (4.8)	68 (3.7)	70 (3.1)
Asian[2]	— (†)	— (†)	— (†)	— (†)	— (†)	— (†)	84 (2.8)	— (†)	— (†)	— (†)
Pacific Islander[2]	— (†)	— (†)	— (†)	— (†)	— (†)	— (†)	‡ (†)	‡ (†)	— (†)	— (†)
American Indian/Alaska Native	‡ (†)	38 (11.3)	63 (10.9)	‡ (†)	46 (9.5)	56 (18.0)	‡ (†)	‡ (†)	42 (8.0)	47 (17.3)
Two or more races[2]	— (†)	— (†)	— (†)	— (†)	— (†)	— (†)	80 (3.4)	— (†)	— (†)	— (†)
At or above *Proficient*[7]	23 (0.9)	24 (1.0)	27 (0.9)	22 (0.8)	22 (0.8)	22 (0.8)	23 (1.1)	26 (0.9)	27 (1.0)	24 (0.9)
At *Advanced*[8]	2 (0.3)	1 (0.2)	2 (0.2)	2 (0.2)	2 (0.2)	1 (0.1)	2 (0.3)	4 (0.4)	5 (0.4)	4 (0.3)

—Not available.

†Not applicable.

‡Reporting standards not met (too few cases for a reliable estimate).

[1]Scale ranges from 0 to 300 for all three grades, but scores cannot be compared across grades. For example, the average score of 167 for White 4th-graders in 2010 does not denote higher performance than the score of 160 for White 8th-graders in 2010.

[2]In civics assessments prior to 2014, separate data for Asians, Pacific Islanders, and students of Two or more races were not collected.

[3]These data are based on students' responses to questions about their parents' education level. Because the wording of the questions was different in 1998 than in the later assessment years, data from 1998 are not directly comparable to data from 2006, 2010, and 2014. For all assessment years, data for students whose parents have an unknown level of education are included in table totals, but not shown separately.

[4]The percentile represents a specific point on the percentage distribution of all students ranked by their civics score from low to high. For example, 10 percent of students scored at or below the 10th percentile score, while 90 percent of students scored above it.

[5]The standard deviation provides an indication of how much the test scores varied. The lower the standard deviation, the closer the scores were clustered around the average score. About two-thirds of the student scores can be expected to fall within the range of one standard deviation above and one standard deviation below the average score. For exam-

ple, the average score for all 8th-graders in 2014 was 154, and the standard deviation was 33. This means that about two-thirds of the students would be expected to have scores between 187 (one standard deviation above the average) and 121 (one standard deviation below). Standard errors also must be taken into account when making comparisons of these ranges.

[6]*Basic* denotes partial mastery of the knowledge and skills that are fundamental for proficient work.

[7]*Proficient* represents solid academic performance. Students reaching this level have demonstrated competency over challenging subject matter.

[8]*Advanced* signifies superior performance.

NOTE: In 2014, only 8th-grade students were assessed in civics. Includes public and private schools. Includes students tested with accommodations (1 to 13 percent of all students, depending on grade level and year); excludes only those students with disabilities and English language learners who were unable to be tested even with accommodations (1 to 5 percent of all students). Race categories exclude persons of Hispanic ethnicity. Detail may not sum to totals because of rounding.

SOURCE: U.S. Department of Education, National Center for Education Statistics, National Assessment of Educational Progress (NAEP), 1998, 2006, 2010, and 2014 Civics Assessments, retrieved April 30, 2015, from the Main NAEP Data Explorer (http://nces.ed.gov/nationsreportcard/naepdata/). (This table was prepared April 2015.)

Table 224.30. Average National Assessment of Educational Progress (NAEP) economics scale score of 12th-graders, percentage attaining economics achievement levels, and percentage with different levels of economics coursework, by selected characteristics: 2006 and 2012

[Standard errors appear in parentheses]

Selected characteristic	Average scale score[1]		At or above Basic[2]		At or above Proficient[3]		At Advanced[4]		No economics courses		Combined course		Consumer economics/ business		General economics		Advanced economics[5]	
1	2		3		4		5		6		7		8		9		10	
2006																		
All students	150	(0.9)	79	(0.8)	42	(1.1)	3	(0.3)	13	(0.9)	12	(0.7)	11	(0.7)	49	(1.4)	16	(0.7)
Sex																		
Male	152	(1.0)	79	(0.8)	45	(1.3)	4	(0.5)	13	(1.0)	10	(0.6)	10	(0.7)	50	(1.4)	16	(0.8)
Female	148	(0.9)	79	(0.9)	38	(1.3)	2	(0.3)	12	(0.9)	13	(0.9)	11	(0.8)	48	(1.6)	15	(0.8)
Race/ethnicity																		
White	158	(0.8)	87	(0.7)	51	(1.2)	4	(0.4)	15	(1.1)	12	(0.8)	11	(0.8)	49	(1.6)	13	(0.9)
Black	127	(1.2)	57	(1.9)	16	(1.3)	#	(†)	8	(0.8)	11	(0.9)	11	(1.2)	49	(1.7)	21	(1.1)
Hispanic	133	(1.2)	64	(1.6)	21	(1.2)	#	(†)	8	(1.7)	13	(1.1)	7	(0.9)	55	(2.6)	18	(1.2)
Asian/Pacific Islander	153	(3.5)	80	(4.0)	44	(4.5)	4	(1.4)	13	(1.8)	10	(1.8)	10	(1.4)	45	(4.1)	22	(1.9)
American Indian/Alaska Native	137	(4.1)	72	(5.6)	26	(4.8)	2	(†)	11	(3.9)	18	(2.7)	17	(3.2)	41	(4.9)	13	(3.1)
Parents' highest level of education																		
Not high school graduate	129	(1.4)	59	(2.1)	17	(1.7)	#	(†)	10	(1.7)	13	(1.4)	10	(1.4)	53	(3.2)	14	(1.3)
Graduated high school	138	(1.2)	69	(1.5)	27	(1.4)	1	(0.3)	11	(1.2)	12	(1.0)	12	(1.0)	52	(1.7)	13	(0.9)
Some college	150	(0.8)	82	(1.1)	39	(1.4)	1	(0.4)	11	(1.0)	13	(0.9)	12	(1.0)	51	(1.9)	14	(1.0)
Graduated college	160	(0.9)	87	(0.8)	54	(1.3)	5	(0.6)	14	(1.0)	11	(0.8)	10	(0.7)	47	(1.5)	17	(1.0)
Free or reduced-price lunch eligibility																		
Eligible	132	(0.9)	62	(1.1)	20	(1.1)	1	(0.2)	9	(0.7)	13	(1.1)	10	(0.9)	50	(1.6)	18	(0.8)
Not eligible	155	(0.9)	84	(0.8)	48	(1.2)	4	(0.4)	13	(1.1)	12	(0.8)	12	(0.9)	48	(1.6)	16	(0.9)
Unknown	157	(1.9)	86	(1.7)	50	(2.8)	4	(1.1)	16	(3.0)	12	(1.6)	7	(1.1)	54	(3.1)	11	(1.4)
Region																		
Northeast	153	(2.0)	81	(1.7)	46	(2.6)	4	(0.9)	26	(2.6)	7	(1.1)	11	(1.3)	43	(3.2)	13	(1.4)
Midwest	153	(1.5)	83	(1.4)	45	(2.0)	3	(0.6)	12	(2.2)	12	(2.2)	15	(1.5)	51	(2.6)	10	(1.0)
South	147	(1.4)	77	(1.4)	37	(1.7)	2	(0.5)	6	(1.1)	14	(1.2)	9	(1.3)	49	(2.0)	22	(1.5)
West	‡	(†)	‡	(†)	‡	(†)	‡	(†)	‡	(†)	‡	(†)	‡	(†)	‡	(†)	‡	(†)
2012																		
All students	152	(0.8)	82	(0.8)	42	(1.1)	3	(0.3)	9	(1.0)	9	(0.8)	10	(1.2)	54	(2.0)	18	(0.9)
Sex																		
Male	155	(0.9)	83	(1.0)	47	(1.3)	4	(0.4)	8	(0.9)	9	(0.8)	10	(1.2)	54	(2.0)	18	(1.0)
Female	149	(0.9)	80	(1.0)	37	(1.3)	2	(0.2)	10	(1.2)	9	(0.9)	10	(1.3)	53	(2.2)	18	(1.1)
Race/ethnicity																		
White	160	(1.0)	89	(0.9)	53	(1.6)	4	(0.4)	10	(1.4)	9	(1.0)	11	(1.6)	54	(2.4)	15	(1.1)
Black	131	(1.4)	61	(2.1)	16	(1.3)	1	(0.2)	6	(1.2)	8	(1.1)	9	(1.2)	54	(2.9)	23	(1.4)
Hispanic	138	(1.4)	71	(2.0)	25	(1.4)	1	(0.3)	5	(1.1)	9	(1.0)	7	(1.2)	57	(2.9)	21	(2.0)
Asian	160	(1.9)	86	(1.9)	53	(2.4)	6	(1.3)	10	(1.5)	9	(1.2)	7	(1.2)	45	(2.7)	29	(2.6)
Pacific Islander	‡	(†)	‡	(†)	‡	(†)	‡	(†)	‡	(†)	‡	(†)	‡	(†)	‡	(†)	‡	(†)
American Indian/Alaska Native	136	(4.7)	72	(7.8)	20	(5.6)	2	(†)	4	(2.7)	7	(2.9)	19	(9.9)	54	(8.0)	16	(4.6)
Two or more races	154	(3.4)	87	(3.0)	42	(5.2)	3	(1.8)	10	(2.9)	6	(1.4)	7	(1.8)	57	(4.5)	20	(2.8)
Parents' highest level of education																		
Not high school graduate	134	(1.5)	66	(2.1)	21	(1.9)	#	(†)	4	(0.7)	10	(1.3)	10	(1.4)	59	(2.4)	17	(1.5)
Graduated high school	139	(1.1)	71	(1.7)	27	(1.6)	1	(0.2)	7	(1.2)	9	(1.1)	11	(1.2)	56	(2.3)	16	(1.0)
Some college	150	(0.8)	84	(1.0)	38	(1.2)	1	(0.3)	8	(1.2)	9	(0.9)	10	(1.5)	56	(2.3)	16	(1.6)
Graduated college	161	(0.9)	89	(1.0)	55	(1.4)	5	(0.5)	10	(1.4)	9	(1.0)	10	(1.3)	51	(2.3)	20	(1.2)
Free or reduced-price lunch eligibility																		
Eligible	138	(0.9)	70	(1.3)	25	(1.1)	#	(†)	7	(0.9)	9	(0.7)	10	(1.2)	57	(2.1)	18	(1.3)
Not eligible	159	(0.9)	88	(0.8)	52	(1.4)	4	(0.4)	10	(1.3)	9	(1.1)	11	(1.4)	51	(2.3)	19	(1.1)
Unknown	164	(3.3)	90	(2.3)	59	(4.2)	5	(1.4)	13	(4.7)	8	(1.8)	6	(1.6)	58	(5.0)	15	(1.9)
School location																		
City	147	(1.8)	77	(1.9)	37	(2.3)	3	(0.5)	8	(1.5)	9	(1.3)	8	(1.4)	54	(3.3)	22	(1.8)
Suburb	156	(0.9)	85	(1.0)	48	(1.1)	4	(0.4)	12	(1.8)	10	(1.1)	11	(1.6)	50	(2.1)	17	(1.5)
Town	149	(2.7)	81	(2.4)	39	(3.8)	2	(0.6)	9	(2.8)	8	(1.2)	10	(2.4)	57	(3.5)	16	(3.8)
Rural	152	(1.5)	83	(1.5)	42	(2.5)	2	(0.6)	5	(1.2)	9	(1.4)	12	(2.8)	57	(4.0)	17	(2.1)
Region																		
Northeast	154	(1.7)	84	(1.8)	46	(2.0)	3	(0.7)	27	(4.0)	9	(1.9)	11	(1.4)	39	(5.5)	14	(2.2)
Midwest	157	(1.6)	86	(1.1)	50	(2.2)	4	(0.7)	5	(1.2)	9	(2.3)	18	(3.4)	57	(4.3)	11	(1.0)
South	149	(1.8)	79	(1.7)	38	(2.7)	2	(0.5)	3	(1.5)	8	(1.2)	5	(0.9)	55	(3.6)	29	(2.0)
West	148	(1.1)	79	(1.4)	40	(1.5)	2	(0.3)	7	(1.2)	11	(1.1)	9	(3.1)	60	(3.0)	13	(1.0)

†Not applicable.
#Rounds to zero.
‡Reporting standards not met. Either there are too few cases for a reliable estimate or item response rates fell below the required standards for reporting.
[1]Scale ranges from 0 to 300.
[2]Basic denotes partial mastery of the knowledge and skills that are fundamental for proficient work at a given grade.
[3]Proficient represents solid academic performance. Students reaching this level have demonstrated competency over challenging subject matter.
[4]Advanced signifies superior performance for a given grade.

[5]Advanced economics includes Advanced Placement, International Baccalaureate, and honors courses.
NOTE: Includes public and private schools. Includes students tested with accommodations; excludes only those students with disabilities and English language learners who were unable to be tested even with accommodations (3 percent of all students in both assessment years). Detail may not sum to totals because of rounding. Race categories exclude persons of Hispanic ethnicity. Totals include other racial/ethnic groups not shown separately.
SOURCE: U.S. Department of Education, National Center for Education Statistics, National Assessment of Educational Progress (NAEP), 2006 and 2012 Economics Assessment, retrieved May 08, 2013, from the NAEP Data Explorer (http://nces.ed.gov/nationsreportcard/naepdata/). (This table was prepared May 2013.)

Table 224.40. Average National Assessment of Educational Progress (NAEP) geography scale score, standard deviation, and percentage of students attaining geography achievement levels, by grade level, selected student characteristics, and percentile: Selected years, 1994 through 2014

[Standard errors appear in parentheses]

Selected student characteristic	4th-graders 1994[1]		2001		2010		8th-graders 1994[1]		2001		2010		2014		12th-graders 1994[1]		2001		2010	
1	2		3		4		5		6		7		8		9		10		11	
Average geography scale score[2]																				
All students	206	(1.2)	208	(0.9)	213	(0.8)	260	(0.7)	260	(1.0)	261	(0.7)	261	(1.0)	285	(0.7)	284	(0.8)	282	(0.6)
Sex																				
Male	208	(1.4)	210	(1.0)	215	(0.9)	262	(0.9)	262	(1.2)	263	(0.8)	263	(1.1)	288	(0.8)	287	(1.0)	285	(0.6)
Female	203	(1.4)	206	(1.3)	211	(0.9)	258	(0.8)	258	(1.0)	259	(0.8)	260	(1.0)	281	(0.9)	281	(0.8)	280	(0.8)
Race/ethnicity																				
White	218	(1.5)	219	(1.1)	224	(0.9)	269	(0.8)	269	(1.4)	272	(0.6)	273	(1.0)	290	(0.8)	291	(0.8)	290	(0.5)
Black	166	(2.4)	180	(1.8)	192	(1.3)	229	(1.7)	233	(1.6)	241	(1.1)	240	(1.1)	258	(1.4)	258	(1.5)	261	(1.2)
Hispanic	177	(3.3)	185	(2.5)	197	(1.2)	238	(2.0)	237	(2.0)	244	(1.0)	248	(1.1)	269	(1.7)	268	(1.6)	270	(1.2)
Asian/Pacific Islander	211	(4.0)	214	(3.5)	224	(3.3)	262	(5.3)	264	(2.7)	268	(2.7)	275	(2.5)	283	(3.1)	284	(5.0)	285	(1.7)
Asian[3]	—	(†)	—	(†)	—	(†)	—	(†)	—	(†)	—	(†)	275	(2.6)	—	(†)	—	(†)	—	(†)
Pacific Islander[3]	—	(†)	—	(†)	—	(†)	—	(†)	—	(†)	—	(†)	‡	(†)	—	(†)	—	(†)	—	(†)
American Indian/Alaska Native	‡	(†)	‡	(†)	201	(3.5)	251	(5.5)	261	(5.3)	250	(3.9)	‡	(†)	‡	(†)	‡	(†)	277	(2.5)
Two or more races[3]	—	(†)	—	(†)	—	(†)	—	(†)	—	(†)	—	(†)	264	(2.5)	—	(†)	—	(†)	—	(†)
Parents' highest level of education[4]																				
Did not finish high school	—	(†)	—	(†)	—	(†)	238	(1.7)	236	(1.8)	243	(1.3)	243	(1.2)	263	(1.2)	266	(1.7)	263	(1.2)
Graduated high school	—	(†)	—	(†)	—	(†)	250	(1.2)	251	(1.2)	251	(1.1)	250	(1.3)	274	(1.1)	275	(0.9)	274	(0.8)
Some education after high school	—	(†)	—	(†)	—	(†)	265	(1.0)	264	(1.1)	262	(1.0)	261	(0.9)	286	(1.0)	284	(0.9)	280	(0.7)
Graduated college	—	(†)	—	(†)	—	(†)	272	(1.0)	273	(1.0)	272	(0.7)	272	(1.2)	294	(0.9)	293	(1.0)	291	(0.7)
Eligibility for free or reduced-price lunch																				
Eligible	—	(†)	185	(1.4)	197	(0.7)	—	(†)	239	(1.3)	246	(0.9)	248	(1.0)	—	(†)	268	(1.7)	269	(0.8)
Not eligible	—	(†)	221	(1.1)	227	(0.8)	—	(†)	269	(1.2)	272	(0.7)	274	(1.2)	—	(†)	287	(1.0)	288	(0.5)
Unknown	—	(†)	219	(2.8)	227	(3.7)	—	(†)	265	(2.3)	276	(2.6)	277	(3.0)	—	(†)	288	(1.6)	289	(2.2)
Percentile[5]																				
10th	146	(1.9)	159	(2.6)	169	(1.8)	213	(1.3)	213	(1.2)	220	(1.2)	220	(1.2)	244	(0.9)	246	(1.1)	247	(0.8)
25th	179	(1.5)	184	(1.4)	192	(1.2)	237	(1.0)	238	(1.3)	241	(0.7)	242	(1.3)	265	(1.1)	266	(1.2)	265	(0.8)
50th	211	(1.1)	211	(1.0)	216	(1.1)	263	(1.2)	264	(1.2)	263	(0.9)	263	(1.0)	287	(0.9)	286	(0.9)	284	(0.7)
75th	237	(1.3)	235	(1.4)	236	(0.7)	285	(0.9)	285	(1.1)	284	(0.9)	283	(0.9)	306	(1.0)	304	(0.9)	301	(0.7)
90th	257	(2.0)	254	(1.3)	253	(0.9)	302	(1.9)	302	(1.1)	300	(0.7)	300	(1.3)	321	(1.0)	319	(1.3)	315	(0.7)
Standard deviation of the geography scale score[6]																				
All students	44	(0.8)	37	(0.8)	33	(0.4)	35	(0.4)	35	(0.5)	31	(0.3)	31	(0.5)	30	(0.4)	28	(0.4)	26	(0.3)
Percent of students achieving geography achievement levels																				
Achievement level																				
Below *Basic*[7]	30	(1.1)	27	(1.0)	21	(0.9)	29	(1.0)	28	(1.2)	26	(0.9)	25	(1.1)	30	(0.9)	29	(1.0)	30	(0.9)
At or above *Basic*[7]	70	(1.1)	73	(1.0)	79	(0.9)	71	(1.0)	72	(1.2)	74	(0.9)	75	(1.1)	70	(0.9)	71	(1.0)	70	(0.9)
At or above *Basic* by sex																				
Male	71	(1.3)	74	(0.9)	80	(1.0)	72	(1.3)	73	(1.5)	75	(1.0)	76	(1.1)	73	(1.1)	74	(1.3)	73	(1.0)
Female	68	(1.4)	71	(1.5)	78	(1.1)	69	(1.1)	71	(1.1)	73	(1.1)	74	(1.2)	67	(1.2)	68	(1.2)	66	(1.2)
At or above *Basic* by race/ethnicity																				
White	81	(1.3)	84	(1.1)	89	(1.0)	81	(0.9)	82	(1.5)	86	(0.7)	88	(0.9)	78	(0.9)	81	(0.9)	81	(0.8)
Black	33	(2.4)	43	(2.5)	57	(2.1)	34	(3.0)	39	(2.4)	49	(1.7)	48	(2.1)	33	(2.3)	33	(2.0)	36	(1.8)
Hispanic	44	(3.1)	50	(3.1)	64	(1.7)	49	(3.8)	45	(2.5)	55	(1.5)	61	(1.7)	48	(3.0)	48	(2.9)	52	(2.0)
Asian/Pacific Islander	72	(4.4)	77	(4.2)	87	(3.2)	72	(6.7)	77	(3.6)	80	(3.3)	87	(2.0)	67	(3.8)	70	(6.2)	73	(2.7)
Asian[3]	—	(†)	—	(†)	—	(†)	—	(†)	—	(†)	—	(†)	87	(2.0)	—	(†)	—	(†)	—	(†)
Pacific Islander[3]	—	(†)	—	(†)	—	(†)	—	(†)	—	(†)	—	(†)	‡	(†)	—	(†)	—	(†)	—	(†)
American Indian/Alaska Native	‡	(†)	‡	(†)	68	(6.4)	62	(7.7)	74	(4.8)	62	(7.2)	‡	(†)	‡	(†)	‡	(†)	62	(5.1)
Two or more races[3]	—	(†)	—	(†)	—	(†)	—	(†)	—	(†)	—	(†)	79	(3.5)	—	(†)	—	(†)	—	(†)
At or above *Proficient*[8]	22	(1.2)	20	(0.9)	21	(0.8)	28	(1.0)	29	(1.3)	27	(0.8)	27	(1.2)	27	(1.2)	24	(1.2)	20	(0.8)
At *Advanced*[9]	3	(0.4)	2	(0.3)	2	(0.2)	4	(0.4)	4	(0.5)	3	(0.2)	3	(0.4)	2	(0.5)	1	(0.3)	1	(0.1)

—Not available.
†Not applicable.
‡Reporting standards not met (too few cases for a reliable estimate).
[1]Accommodations were not permitted for this assessment.
[2]Scale ranges from 0 to 500.
[3]In geography assessments prior to 2014, separate data for Asians, Pacific Islanders, and students of Two or more races were not collected.
[4]Based on student reports. Data for students whose parents have an unknown level of education are included in table totals, but not shown separately.
[5]The percentile represents a specific point on the percentage distribution of all students ranked by their geography score from low to high. For example, 10 percent of students scored at or below the 10th percentile score, while 90 percent of students scored above it.
[6]The standard deviation provides an indication of how much the test scores varied. The lower the standard deviation, the closer the scores were clustered around the average score. About two-thirds of the student scores can be expected to fall within the range of one standard deviation above and one standard deviation below the average score. For example, the average score for all 8th-graders in 2014 was 261, and the standard deviation was 31. This means that about two-thirds of the students would be expected to have scores between 292 (one

standard deviation above the average) and 230 (one standard deviation below). Standard errors also must be taken into account when making comparisons of these ranges.
[7]*Basic* denotes partial mastery of the knowledge and skills that are fundamental for proficient work.
[8]*Proficient* represents solid academic performance. Students reaching this level have demonstrated competency over challenging subject matter.
[9]*Advanced* signifies superior performance.
NOTE: In 2014, only 8th-grade students were assessed in geography. Includes public and private schools. For 2001 and later years, includes students tested with accommodations (3 to 13 percent of all students, depending on grade level and year); excludes only those students with disabilities and English language learners who were unable to be tested even with accommodations (1 to 4 percent of all students). Race categories exclude persons of Hispanic ethnicity. Detail may not sum to totals because of rounding.
SOURCE: U.S. Department of Education, National Center for Education Statistics, National Assessment of Educational Progress (NAEP), 1994, 2001, 2010, and 2014 Geography Assessments, retrieved April 30, 2015, from the Main NAEP Data Explorer (http://nces.ed.gov/nationsreportcard/naepdata/). (This table was prepared April 2015.)

Table 224.50. Average National Assessment of Educational Progress (NAEP) U.S. history scale score, standard deviation, and percentage of students attaining achievement levels, by grade level, selected student characteristics, and percentile: Selected years, 1994 through 2014

[Standard errors appear in parentheses]

Selected student characteristic	4th-graders				8th-graders					12th-graders			
	1994[1]	2001	2006	2010	1994[1]	2001	2006	2010	2014	1994[1]	2001	2006	2010
1	2	3	4	5	6	7	8	9	10	11	12	13	14
Average U.S. history scale score[2]													
All students	205 (1.0)	208 (0.9)	211 (1.1)	214 (0.8)	259 (0.6)	260 (0.8)	263 (0.8)	266 (0.8)	267 (1.0)	286 (0.8)	287 (0.9)	290 (0.7)	288 (0.8)
Sex													
Male	203 (1.5)	207 (1.1)	211 (1.2)	215 (1.0)	259 (0.8)	261 (0.9)	264 (0.9)	268 (0.8)	270 (1.1)	288 (0.8)	288 (1.1)	292 (0.9)	290 (0.8)
Female	206 (1.1)	209 (1.2)	211 (1.1)	213 (0.9)	259 (0.7)	260 (0.9)	261 (0.8)	263 (0.8)	265 (0.9)	285 (0.9)	286 (0.9)	288 (0.8)	286 (1.0)
Race/ethnicity													
White	214 (1.3)	217 (1.3)	223 (1.1)	224 (1.1)	266 (0.8)	268 (0.9)	273 (0.6)	274 (0.7)	277 (0.9)	292 (0.8)	292 (1.0)	297 (0.8)	296 (0.7)
Black	176 (1.6)	186 (2.0)	191 (1.9)	198 (1.9)	238 (1.6)	240 (1.9)	244 (1.2)	250 (1.1)	251 (1.3)	265 (1.5)	267 (1.4)	270 (1.3)	268 (1.5)
Hispanic	175 (2.6)	184 (2.6)	194 (1.9)	198 (1.2)	243 (1.4)	240 (2.0)	248 (1.2)	252 (1.0)	257 (0.9)	267 (1.7)	271 (1.9)	275 (1.0)	275 (1.3)
Asian/Pacific Islander	204 (3.6)	216 (3.7)	214 (5.1)	221 (2.4)	261 (5.0)	264 (2.8)	270 (3.0)	275 (1.8)	279 (2.5)	283 (3.5)	294 (6.0)	296 (2.6)	293 (2.5)
Asian[3]	— (†)	— (†)	— (†)	— (†)	— (†)	— (†)	— (†)	— (†)	280 (2.5)	— (†)	— (†)	— (†)	— (†)
Pacific Islander[3]	— (†)	— (†)	— (†)	— (†)	— (†)	— (†)	— (†)	— (†)	276 (1.9)	— (†)	— (†)	— (†)	— (†)
American Indian/Alaska Native	‡ (†)	‡ (†)	190 (5.9)	193 (6.2)	245 (3.4)	255 (4.4)	244 (6.3)	259 (5.0)	‡ (†)	272 (3.0)	283 (4.2)	278 (4.1)	278 (4.2)
Two or more races[3]	— (†)	— (†)	— (†)	— (†)	— (†)	— (†)	— (†)	— (†)	276 (1.9)	— (†)	— (†)	— (†)	— (†)
Parents' highest level of education[4]													
Did not finish high school	— (†)	— (†)	— (†)	— (†)	241 (1.3)	241 (2.8)	244 (1.2)	249 (0.9)	250 (1.3)	263 (1.4)	266 (1.6)	268 (1.3)	268 (1.7)
Graduated high school	— (†)	— (†)	— (†)	— (†)	251 (0.8)	251 (1.0)	252 (1.3)	255 (0.9)	255 (1.1)	276 (1.1)	274 (1.1)	278 (1.0)	277 (1.0)
Some education after high school	— (†)	— (†)	— (†)	— (†)	264 (0.8)	264 (1.0)	265 (0.9)	267 (0.9)	269 (0.8)	287 (1.2)	286 (0.8)	290 (0.8)	286 (0.8)
Graduated college	— (†)	— (†)	— (†)	— (†)	270 (0.8)	273 (0.9)	274 (0.8)	276 (0.8)	277 (1.1)	296 (0.9)	298 (1.2)	300 (0.8)	298 (0.8)
Eligibility for free or reduced-price lunch													
Eligible	— (†)	188 (1.4)	195 (1.1)	199 (0.9)	— (†)	242 (1.3)	247 (1.1)	253 (0.7)	254 (0.9)	— (†)	269 (1.4)	273 (1.0)	273 (1.0)
Not eligible	— (†)	219 (1.4)	224 (1.0)	227 (0.8)	— (†)	267 (1.0)	273 (0.7)	275 (0.8)	279 (1.0)	— (†)	289 (1.2)	295 (0.8)	294 (0.7)
Unknown	— (†)	217 (2.8)	227 (3.9)	225 (6.1)	— (†)	266 (2.0)	281 (2.7)	278 (2.0)	281 (2.5)	— (†)	294 (2.1)	300 (2.4)	300 (2.5)
Percentile[5]													
10th	147 (2.1)	157 (1.4)	165 (2.3)	169 (1.4)	217 (1.1)	216 (1.3)	221 (1.4)	227 (1.2)	229 (1.1)	243 (1.2)	244 (1.2)	249 (1.3)	246 (1.3)
25th	180 (1.5)	184 (1.4)	189 (1.3)	192 (1.6)	239 (0.9)	239 (0.9)	243 (0.9)	246 (0.9)	248 (1.0)	265 (1.2)	266 (1.1)	270 (1.0)	267 (1.3)
50th	210 (0.9)	211 (1.1)	213 (1.0)	216 (0.6)	261 (1.1)	262 (1.1)	265 (0.7)	267 (0.9)	269 (1.0)	288 (0.8)	288 (1.1)	291 (0.9)	290 (0.7)
75th	234 (1.2)	234 (1.0)	235 (1.1)	238 (0.9)	282 (0.7)	284 (1.0)	285 (0.7)	286 (0.7)	288 (1.0)	309 (0.9)	309 (1.0)	312 (0.7)	311 (0.6)
90th	253 (1.4)	254 (1.4)	254 (1.0)	256 (1.4)	299 (0.6)	302 (0.7)	302 (1.0)	302 (1.1)	303 (1.0)	326 (1.0)	326 (1.5)	329 (0.9)	328 (1.0)
Standard deviation of the U.S. history scale score[6]													
All students	41 (0.7)	38 (0.7)	34 (0.5)	34 (0.7)	32 (0.3)	33 (0.4)	32 (0.4)	29 (0.3)	29 (0.4)	32 (0.4)	32 (0.6)	31 (0.3)	32 (0.4)
Percent of students achieving U.S. history achievement levels													
Achievement level													
Below Basic[7]	36 (1.1)	34 (1.2)	30 (1.3)	27 (0.8)	39 (0.9)	38 (1.0)	35 (1.0)	31 (1.0)	29 (1.3)	57 (1.1)	57 (1.2)	53 (1.1)	55 (1.0)
At or above Basic[7]	64 (1.1)	66 (1.2)	70 (1.3)	73 (0.8)	61 (0.9)	62 (1.0)	65 (1.0)	69 (1.0)	71 (1.3)	43 (1.1)	43 (1.2)	47 (1.1)	45 (1.0)
At or above Basic by sex													
Male	62 (1.6)	65 (1.3)	69 (1.5)	73 (1.0)	61 (1.0)	62 (1.1)	67 (1.3)	71 (1.1)	74 (1.5)	45 (1.2)	45 (1.6)	50 (1.2)	49 (1.1)
Female	65 (1.4)	67 (1.4)	70 (1.2)	73 (1.0)	61 (1.3)	61 (1.2)	64 (1.0)	67 (1.2)	69 (1.4)	40 (1.4)	40 (1.2)	44 (1.2)	41 (1.4)
At or above Basic by race/ethnicity													
White	73 (1.3)	76 (1.5)	84 (1.2)	83 (1.0)	70 (1.1)	71 (1.1)	79 (0.8)	80 (0.9)	84 (1.2)	50 (1.2)	49 (1.3)	56 (1.3)	55 (1.2)
Black	35 (1.5)	41 (2.3)	46 (2.5)	54 (2.6)	32 (2.4)	35 (2.1)	40 (1.7)	48 (2.1)	47 (2.5)	17 (1.5)	19 (1.5)	20 (1.6)	20 (1.2)
Hispanic	36 (3.2)	40 (2.8)	49 (2.7)	56 (1.6)	41 (2.2)	36 (2.6)	46 (2.2)	52 (1.7)	59 (1.5)	22 (2.4)	24 (2.3)	27 (1.4)	28 (1.4)
Asian/Pacific Islander	62 (4.3)	74 (4.5)	71 (4.8)	82 (3.1)	60 (6.9)	65 (3.0)	75 (4.4)	78 (2.1)	82 (2.6)	40 (4.7)	51 (6.7)	54 (3.5)	50 (3.2)
Asian[3]	— (†)	— (†)	— (†)	— (†)	— (†)	— (†)	— (†)	— (†)	84 (2.6)	— (†)	— (†)	— (†)	— (†)
Pacific Islander[3]	— (†)	— (†)	— (†)	— (†)	— (†)	— (†)	— (†)	— (†)	81 (2.5)	— (†)	— (†)	— (†)	— (†)
American Indian/Alaska Native	‡ (†)	‡ (†)	41 (7.7)	49 (5.4)	42 (6.2)	57 (6.5)	43 (6.1)	61 (6.3)	‡ (†)	21 (6.3)	37 (7.8)	32 (7.3)	29 (5.9)
Two or more races[3]	— (†)	— (†)	— (†)	— (†)	— (†)	— (†)	— (†)	— (†)	— (†)	— (†)	— (†)	— (†)	— (†)
At or above Proficient[8]	17 (1.0)	18 (0.9)	18 (1.0)	20 (0.7)	14 (0.6)	16 (0.7)	17 (0.8)	17 (0.8)	18 (0.9)	11 (0.7)	11 (0.9)	13 (0.7)	12 (0.5)
At Advanced[9]	2 (0.3)	2 (0.3)	2 (0.3)	2 (0.3)	1 (0.1)	1 (0.2)	1 (0.1)	1 (0.1)	1 (0.2)	1 (0.2)	1 (0.3)	1 (0.2)	1 (0.1)

—Not available.
†Not applicable.
‡Reporting standards not met (too few cases for a reliable estimate).
[1]Accommodations were not permitted for this assessment.
[2]Scale ranges from 0 to 500.
[3]In U.S. history assessments prior to 2014, separate data for Asians, Pacific Islanders, and students of Two or more races were not collected.
[4]Based on student reports. Data for students whose parents have an unknown level of education are included in table totals, but not shown separately.
[5]The percentile represents a specific point on the percentage distribution of all students ranked by their U.S. history score from low to high. For example, 10 percent of students scored at or below the 10th percentile score, while 90 percent of students scored above it.
[6]The standard deviation provides an indication of how much the test scores varied. The lower the standard deviation, the closer the scores were clustered around the average score. About two-thirds of the student scores can be expected to fall within the range of one standard deviation above and one standard deviation below the average score. For example, the average score for all 8th-graders in 2014 was 267, and the standard deviation was 29. This means that about two-thirds of the students would be expected to have scores between 296 (one standard deviation above the average) and 238 (one standard deviation below). Standard errors also must be taken into account when making comparisons of these ranges.
[7]Basic denotes partial mastery of the knowledge and skills that are fundamental for proficient work.
[8]Proficient represents solid academic performance. Students reaching this level have demonstrated competency over challenging subject matter.
[9]Advanced signifies superior performance.
NOTE: In 2014, only 8th-grade students were assessed in U.S. history. Includes public and private schools. For 2001 and later years, includes students tested with accommodations (3 to 13 percent of all students, depending on grade level and year); excludes only those students with disabilities and English language learners who were unable to be tested even with accommodations (1 to 3 percent of all students). Race categories exclude persons of Hispanic ethnicity. Detail may not sum to totals because of rounding.
SOURCE: U.S. Department of Education, National Center for Education Statistics, National Assessment of Educational Progress (NAEP), 1994, 2001, 2006, 2010, and 2014 U.S. History Assessments, retrieved April 30, 2015, from the Main NAEP Data Explorer (http://nces.ed.gov/nationsreportcard/naepdata/). (This table was prepared April 2015.)

Table 224.60. Average National Assessment of Educational Progress (NAEP) writing scale score of 8th- and 12th-graders, standard deviation, and percentage of students attaining writing achievement levels, by selected student and school characteristics and percentile: 2011

[Standard errors appear in parentheses]

Selected student or school characteristic	8th-graders Total, all students	Eligible	Not eligible	Unknown	12th-graders Total, all students	Eligible	Not eligible	Unknown
1	2	3	4	5	6	7	8	9
Average writing scale score[1]								
All students	150 (0.7)	134 (0.6)	161 (0.8)	163 (2.2)	150 (0.5)	133 (0.7)	157 (0.6)	167 (1.7)
Sex								
Male	140 (0.7)	125 (0.7)	151 (0.9)	154 (2.6)	143 (0.6)	126 (0.8)	150 (0.6)	162 (1.9)
Female	160 (0.7)	144 (0.6)	171 (0.8)	171 (2.5)	157 (0.6)	140 (0.7)	165 (0.6)	173 (1.9)
Race/ethnicity								
White	158 (0.8)	142 (0.8)	163 (0.9)	166 (2.3)	159 (0.7)	144 (1.0)	161 (0.7)	172 (1.6)
Black	132 (1.1)	127 (1.1)	145 (1.4)	140 (4.6)	130 (1.0)	124 (1.1)	140 (1.2)	148 (3.6)
Hispanic	136 (0.7)	130 (0.8)	150 (1.0)	150 (5.4)	134 (0.7)	128 (0.8)	142 (1.0)	149 (3.6)
Asian/Pacific Islander	163 (2.4)	146 (2.8)	171 (2.4)	175 (4.0)	158 (1.6)	146 (2.3)	163 (2.0)	162 (4.9)
Asian	165 (2.0)	148 (2.7)	172 (2.2)	175 (4.0)	158 (1.5)	146 (2.5)	164 (1.7)	162 (5.0)
Native Hawaiian/Pacific Islander	141 (6.3)	‡ (†)	‡ (†)	‡ (†)	144 (6.0)	‡ (†)	‡ (†)	‡ (†)
American Indian/Alaska Native	145 (4.0)	139 (4.3)	‡ (†)	‡ (†)	145 (3.5)	135 (4.4)	153 (4.4)	‡ (†)
Two or more races	155 (1.9)	141 (2.3)	165 (2.5)	‡ (†)	158 (2.3)	137 (4.2)	163 (2.8)	‡ (†)
Parents' highest level of education								
Did not finish high school	133 (1.0)	131 (1.0)	142 (2.0)	‡ (†)	129 (0.9)	127 (1.0)	135 (1.6)	‡ (†)
Graduated high school	138 (0.8)	131 (0.8)	149 (1.3)	146 (4.4)	138 (0.7)	131 (1.0)	145 (0.9)	153 (3.5)
Some education after high school	150 (0.9)	143 (0.9)	158 (1.2)	155 (3.8)	149 (0.5)	140 (0.9)	155 (0.6)	158 (2.2)
Graduated college	160 (0.8)	141 (0.8)	166 (0.9)	167 (2.3)	160 (0.7)	139 (1.1)	164 (0.7)	173 (1.5)
Student's attitude and experience								
Agreed or strongly agreed that "Writing is one of my favorite activities"	157 (0.8)	141 (0.8)	170 (0.9)	172 (2.5)	157 (0.6)	139 (0.8)	165 (0.6)	175 (2.0)
Uses a computer for writing school assignments once or twice a week	157 (0.9)	140 (0.7)	168 (1.2)	169 (2.9)	154 (0.6)	136 (0.8)	161 (0.7)	167 (1.4)
School locale								
City	144 (1.2)	130 (1.0)	160 (1.4)	164 (4.3)	146 (1.0)	131 (0.8)	156 (1.2)	168 (2.5)
Suburban	155 (1.3)	137 (1.0)	165 (1.3)	164 (4.4)	154 (0.9)	135 (1.1)	160 (0.9)	167 (2.1)
Town	148 (1.1)	137 (1.3)	156 (1.3)	157 (3.8)	149 (2.0)	134 (3.1)	156 (1.8)	‡ (†)
Rural	150 (1.4)	137 (1.5)	158 (1.3)	158 (5.3)	149 (1.1)	135 (1.5)	154 (1.0)	164 (5.4)
Percentile[2]								
10th	104 (1.0)	92 (1.1)	119 (1.1)	121 (3.8)	104 (0.9)	90 (0.9)	114 (1.1)	126 (4.6)
25th	127 (0.8)	113 (0.6)	140 (1.0)	142 (2.6)	127 (0.7)	111 (0.9)	136 (0.8)	149 (2.3)
50th	151 (0.8)	135 (0.6)	163 (0.9)	163 (2.6)	152 (0.7)	135 (1.1)	159 (0.8)	170 (2.2)
75th	175 (0.7)	157 (0.8)	184 (1.1)	185 (2.6)	175 (0.6)	156 (0.6)	180 (0.5)	189 (1.7)
90th	194 (0.9)	176 (0.9)	201 (1.4)	203 (3.5)	194 (0.7)	176 (0.8)	198 (0.8)	205 (3.2)
Standard deviation of the writing scale score[3]								
All students	35 (0.3)	33 (0.3)	32 (0.3)	32 (1.1)	35 (0.3)	33 (0.3)	33 (0.3)	31 (0.9)
Percent of students attaining writing achievement levels								
Achievement level								
Below *Basic*[4]	20 (0.6)	32 (0.8)	10 (0.6)	10 (1.6)	21 (0.6)	36 (0.9)	14 (0.5)	9 (1.3)
At or above *Basic*	80 (0.6)	68 (0.8)	90 (0.6)	90 (1.6)	79 (0.6)	64 (0.9)	86 (0.5)	91 (1.3)
At or above *Basic* by race/ethnicity								
White	87 (0.6)	76 (1.1)	91 (0.6)	94 (1.6)	87 (0.6)	76 (1.2)	88 (0.6)	95 (1.1)
Black	65 (1.7)	59 (1.7)	79 (2.1)	74 (6.4)	61 (1.5)	54 (1.7)	71 (1.9)	82 (3.9)
Hispanic	69 (0.9)	63 (1.1)	82 (1.2)	80 (5.4)	65 (0.9)	59 (1.1)	74 (1.4)	79 (4.7)
Asian/Pacific Islander	88 (2.3)	76 (3.4)	93 (1.8)	96 (2.1)	85 (1.4)	78 (2.7)	89 (1.4)	83 (4.4)
Asian	89 (1.9)	79 (3.0)	94 (1.7)	95 (2.2)	85 (1.4)	78 (2.9)	89 (1.3)	83 (4.4)
Native Hawaiian/Pacific Islander	70 (7.3)	‡ (†)	‡ (†)	‡ (†)	78 (5.0)	‡ (†)	‡ (†)	‡ (†)
American Indian/Alaska Native	78 (4.7)	74 (6.6)	‡ (†)	‡ (†)	76 (4.3)	66 (7.2)	84 (5.0)	‡ (†)
Two or more races	87 (1.7)	79 (3.9)	92 (1.9)	‡ (†)	86 (2.7)	70 (7.1)	90 (3.1)	‡ (†)
At or above *Proficient*[5]	27 (0.7)	12 (0.4)	37 (1.0)	39 (2.9)	27 (0.6)	12 (0.5)	33 (0.7)	46 (2.3)
At *Advanced*[6]	3 (0.2)	1 (0.1)	5 (0.4)	5 (1.2)	3 (0.2)	1 (0.1)	4 (0.3)	7 (1.2)

†Not applicable.

‡Reporting standards not met (too few cases for a reliable estimate).

[1]Scale ranges from 0 to 300.

[2]The percentile represents a specific point on the percentage distribution of all students ranked by their writing score from low to high. For example, 10 percent of students scored at or below the 10th percentile score, while 90 percent of students scored above it.

[3]The standard deviation provides an indication of how much the test scores varied. The lower the standard deviation, the closer the scores were clustered around the average score. About two-thirds of the student scores can be expected to fall within the range of one standard deviation above and one standard deviation below the average score. For example, the average score for all 12th-graders was 150 and the standard deviation was 35. This means that we would expect about two-thirds of the students to have scores between 185 (one standard deviation above the average) and 115 (one standard deviation below). Standard errors also must be taken into account when making comparisons of these ranges.

[4]*Basic* denotes partial mastery of the knowledge and skills that are fundamental for proficient work.

[5]*Proficient* represents solid academic performance. Students reaching this level have demonstrated competency over challenging subject matter.

[6]*Advanced* signifies superior performance.

NOTE: Writing scores from 2011 cannot be compared with writing scores from earlier assessment years. The 2011 writing assessment was developed under a new framework and is NAEP's first computer-based writing assessment. Includes public and private schools. Includes students tested with accommodations (8 percent of all 8th-graders and 7 percent of all 12th-graders); excludes only those students with disabilities and English language learners who were unable to be tested even with accommodations (2 percent of all students at both grades). Race categories exclude persons of Hispanic ethnicity. Detail may not sum to totals because of rounding.

SOURCE: U.S. Department of Education, National Center for Education Statistics, National Assessment of Educational Progress (NAEP), 2011 Writing Assessment, retrieved October 1, 2012, from the Main NAEP Data Explorer (http://nces.ed.gov/nationsreportcard/naepdata/). (This table was prepared October 2012.)

Table 225.10. Average number of Carnegie units earned by public high school graduates in various subject fields, by sex and race/ethnicity: Selected years, 1982 through 2009

[Standard errors appear in parentheses]

Graduation year, sex, and race/ethnicity	Total	English	History/ social studies	Mathematics	Science Total	Biology	Chemistry	Physics	Other science[4]	Foreign languages	Arts	Career/ technical (occupational) education[1]	Labor market, family, and consumer education[2]	Personal use[3]
1	2	3	4	5	6	7	8	9	10	11	12	13	14	15
1982 graduates	**21.58 (0.090)**	**3.93 (0.022)**	**3.16 (0.028)**	**2.63 (0.022)**	**2.20 (0.025)**	**0.94 (0.014)**	**0.34 (0.010)**	**0.17 (0.008)**	**0.73 (0.016)**	**0.99 (0.029)**	**1.47 (0.035)**	**— (†)**	**— (†)**	**2.58 (0.048)**
Sex														
Male	21.40 (0.108)	3.88 (0.026)	3.16 (0.034)	2.71 (0.030)	2.27 (0.031)	0.91 (0.016)	0.36 (0.014)	0.23 (0.012)	0.76 (0.018)	0.80 (0.030)	1.29 (0.044)	— (††)	— (††)	2.69 (0.056)
Female	21.75 (0.101)	3.98 (0.026)	3.15 (0.029)	2.57 (0.024)	2.13 (0.029)	0.97 (0.017)	0.33 (0.013)	0.12 (0.008)	0.71 (0.017)	1.17 (0.036)	1.63 (0.044)	— (††)	— (††)	2.48 (0.049)
Race/ethnicity														
White	21.69 (0.107)	3.90 (0.025)	3.19 (0.032)	2.68 (0.026)	2.27 (0.029)	0.97 (0.015)	0.38 (0.013)	0.20 (0.010)	0.73 (0.017)	1.06 (0.033)	1.53 (0.042)	— (††)	— (††)	2.52 (0.052)
Black	21.15 (0.169)	4.08 (0.050)	3.08 (0.054)	2.61 (0.043)	2.06 (0.049)	0.90 (0.033)	0.26 (0.023)	0.09 (0.011)	0.81 (0.033)	0.72 (0.067)	1.26 (0.063)	— (††)	— (††)	2.60 (0.094)
Hispanic	21.23 (0.122)	3.94 (0.037)	3.00 (0.037)	2.33 (0.040)	1.80 (0.038)	0.81 (0.025)	0.16 (0.012)	0.07 (0.007)	0.75 (0.026)	0.77 (0.042)	1.29 (0.054)	— (††)	— (††)	2.87 (0.081)
Asian/Pacific Islander	22.46 (0.216)	4.01 (0.091)	3.16 (0.094)	3.15 (0.095)	2.64 (0.125)	1.11 (0.048)	0.61 (0.046)	0.42 (0.048)	0.51 (0.061)	1.79 (0.105)	1.31 (0.124)	— (††)	— (††)	3.05 (0.146)
American Indian/ Alaska Native	21.45 (0.330)	3.98 (0.114)	3.25 (0.207)	2.35 (0.129)	2.04 (0.090)	0.84 (0.124)	0.42 (0.087)	0.12 ! (0.039)	0.67 (0.087)	0.48 (0.117)	1.72 (0.338)	— (†)	— (†)	2.84 (0.128)
1987 graduates	**23.00 (0.157)**	**4.12 (0.022)**	**3.32 (0.037)**	**3.01 (0.029)**	**2.55 (0.046)**	**1.10 (0.020)**	**0.47 (0.015)**	**0.21 (0.011)**	**0.76 (0.033)**	**1.35 (0.049)**	**1.44 (0.044)**	**— (†)**	**— (†)**	**2.67 (0.073)**
Sex														
Male	22.88 (0.162)	4.08 (0.021)	3.29 (0.037)	3.05 (0.029)	2.59 (0.049)	1.05 (0.021)	0.47 (0.016)	0.26 (0.013)	0.79 (0.032)	1.16 (0.051)	1.24 (0.046)	— (††)	— (††)	2.83 (0.081)
Female	23.12 (0.156)	4.15 (0.026)	3.35 (0.041)	2.96 (0.030)	2.52 (0.048)	1.14 (0.022)	0.47 (0.017)	0.17 (0.012)	0.74 (0.035)	1.53 (0.051)	1.63 (0.050)	— (††)	— (††)	2.51 (0.069)
Race/ethnicity														
White	23.11 (0.189)	4.08 (0.028)	3.29 (0.045)	3.01 (0.034)	2.61 (0.058)	1.12 (0.025)	0.50 (0.020)	0.23 (0.012)	0.75 (0.040)	1.38 (0.055)	1.50 (0.055)	— (††)	— (††)	2.60 (0.082)
Black	22.40 (0.251)	4.22 (0.038)	3.34 (0.073)	2.99 (0.060)	2.33 (0.060)	1.01 (0.036)	0.31 (0.021)	0.10 (0.012)	0.90 (0.051)	1.08 (0.094)	1.20 (0.064)	— (††)	— (††)	2.73 (0.120)
Hispanic	22.84 (0.162)	4.30 (0.055)	3.22 (0.061)	2.81 (0.058)	2.24 (0.045)	1.07 (0.028)	0.29 (0.015)	0.10 (0.013)	0.78 (0.028)	1.25 (0.071)	1.34 (0.056)	— (††)	— (††)	3.19 (0.096)
Asian/Pacific Islander	24.47 (0.332)	4.37 (0.076)	3.65 (0.163)	3.71 (0.094)	3.14 (0.116)	1.17 (0.027)	0.87 (0.069)	0.50 (0.045)	0.59 (0.048)	2.07 (0.105)	1.18 (0.077)	— (††)	— (††)	3.23 (0.185)
American Indian/ Alaska Native	23.23 (0.153)	4.22 (0.033)	3.18 (0.044)	2.98 (0.152)	2.44 (0.104)	1.22 (0.073)	0.32 (0.035)	0.09 ! (0.027)	0.81 (0.041)	0.75 (0.138)	1.68 (0.112)	— (†)	— (†)	3.06 (0.050)
1990 graduates	**23.53 (0.127)**	**4.19 (0.034)**	**3.47 (0.040)**	**3.15 (0.028)**	**2.75 (0.028)**	**1.14 (0.019)**	**0.53 (0.014)**	**0.23 (0.010)**	**0.85 (0.026)**	**1.54 (0.041)**	**1.55 (0.045)**	**— (†)**	**— (†)**	**2.68 (0.073)**
Sex														
Male	23.35 (0.130)	4.13 (0.035)	3.45 (0.041)	3.16 (0.028)	2.78 (0.033)	1.11 (0.021)	0.52 (0.017)	0.28 (0.012)	0.88 (0.027)	1.33 (0.040)	1.31 (0.047)	— (††)	— (††)	2.87 (0.077)
Female	23.69 (0.132)	4.25 (0.036)	3.50 (0.041)	3.14 (0.033)	2.73 (0.027)	1.17 (0.019)	0.53 (0.014)	0.19 (0.010)	0.83 (0.027)	1.72 (0.045)	1.76 (0.050)	— (††)	— (††)	2.51 (0.072)
Race/ethnicity														
White	23.54 (0.133)	4.12 (0.036)	3.46 (0.045)	3.13 (0.032)	2.80 (0.033)	1.15 (0.020)	0.55 (0.016)	0.25 (0.011)	0.84 (0.022)	1.58 (0.049)	1.61 (0.056)	— (††)	— (††)	2.61 (0.076)
Black	23.40 (0.255)	4.34 (0.044)	3.49 (0.071)	3.20 (0.064)	2.68 (0.061)	1.11 (0.042)	0.42 (0.024)	0.16 (0.020)	0.98 (0.068)	1.20 (0.075)	1.34 (0.052)	— (††)	— (††)	2.74 (0.124)
Hispanic	23.83 (0.210)	4.51 (0.075)	3.42 (0.051)	3.13 (0.058)	2.50 (0.046)	1.10 (0.034)	0.42 (0.034)	0.14 (0.016)	0.83 (0.041)	1.57 (0.060)	1.48 (0.072)	— (††)	— (††)	2.93 (0.086)
Asian/Pacific Islander	24.07 (0.236)	4.50 (0.117)	3.70 (0.126)	3.52 (0.060)	2.97 (0.114)	1.12 (0.085)	0.74 (0.057)	0.42 (0.047)	0.68 (0.080)	2.06 (0.150)	1.29 (0.084)	— (††)	— (††)	2.96 (0.221)
American Indian/ Alaska Native	22.64 (0.267)	4.08 (0.092)	3.34 (0.083)	3.04 (0.152)	2.48 (0.175)	1.09 (0.090)	0.42 (0.072)	0.15 (0.039)	0.83 (0.090)	1.15 (0.188)	1.11 (0.126)	— (†)	— (†)	2.81 (0.148)
1994 graduates	**24.17 (0.144)**	**4.29 (0.028)**	**3.55 (0.041)**	**3.33 (0.021)**	**3.04 (0.028)**	**1.26 (0.018)**	**0.62 (0.013)**	**0.28 (0.011)**	**0.88 (0.024)**	**1.71 (0.033)**	**1.66 (0.041)**	**— (†)**	**— (†)**	**2.63 (0.077)**
Sex														
Male	23.79 (0.146)	4.26 (0.028)	3.51 (0.041)	3.32 (0.022)	3.03 (0.030)	1.20 (0.020)	0.59 (0.015)	0.32 (0.014)	0.91 (0.026)	1.49 (0.034)	1.43 (0.038)	— (††)	— (††)	2.83 (0.081)
Female	24.11 (0.147)	4.32 (0.030)	3.59 (0.041)	3.34 (0.023)	3.06 (0.028)	1.31 (0.018)	0.64 (0.014)	0.24 (0.010)	0.86 (0.024)	1.93 (0.034)	1.87 (0.051)	— (††)	— (††)	2.44 (0.078)
Race/ethnicity														
White	24.08 (0.183)	4.23 (0.035)	3.56 (0.049)	3.36 (0.023)	3.13 (0.032)	1.29 (0.022)	0.65 (0.014)	0.30 (0.014)	0.89 (0.030)	1.74 (0.039)	1.74 (0.049)	— (††)	— (††)	2.61 (0.096)
Black	23.28 (0.132)	4.36 (0.034)	3.51 (0.050)	3.23 (0.030)	2.80 (0.042)	1.21 (0.036)	0.49 (0.028)	0.17 (0.013)	0.92 (0.051)	1.35 (0.052)	1.36 (0.066)	— (††)	— (††)	2.69 (0.101)
Hispanic	23.71 (0.131)	4.61 (0.075)	3.45 (0.046)	3.28 (0.041)	2.69 (0.046)	1.19 (0.027)	0.49 (0.047)	0.17 (0.021)	0.83 (0.058)	1.73 (0.062)	1.51 (0.072)	— (††)	— (††)	2.93 (0.086)
Asian/Pacific Islander	23.84 (0.256)	4.60 (0.091)	3.66 (0.097)	3.66 (0.082)	3.35 (0.131)	1.22 (0.042)	0.81 (0.062)	0.48 (0.058)	0.80 (0.034)	2.09 (0.085)	1.32 (0.121)	— (††)	— (††)	2.78 (0.123)
American Indian/ Alaska Native	23.40 (0.541)	4.27 (0.113)	3.57 (0.201)	3.11 (0.038)	2.82 (0.073)	1.28 (0.069)	0.50 (0.065)	0.13 (0.039)	0.91 (0.057)	1.30 (0.150)	2.01 (0.351)	— (†)	— (†)	3.12 (0.355)
1998 graduates	**25.14 (0.162)**	**4.25 (0.037)**	**3.74 (0.038)**	**3.40 (0.024)**	**3.12 (0.026)**	**1.26 (0.021)**	**0.66 (0.015)**	**0.31 (0.015)**	**0.89 (0.024)**	**1.85 (0.039)**	**1.90 (0.079)**	**— (†)**	**— (†)**	**2.89 (0.076)**
Sex														
Male	24.64 (0.162)	4.19 (0.038)	3.68 (0.040)	3.37 (0.024)	3.09 (0.028)	1.20 (0.021)	0.62 (0.014)	0.33 (0.018)	0.93 (0.026)	1.62 (0.040)	1.61 (0.072)	— (††)	— (††)	3.12 (0.079)
Female	25.04 (0.166)	4.31 (0.039)	3.80 (0.036)	3.42 (0.025)	3.17 (0.029)	1.32 (0.023)	0.70 (0.018)	0.28 (0.015)	0.87 (0.023)	2.06 (0.041)	2.15 (0.094)	— (††)	— (††)	2.67 (0.080)
Race/ethnicity														
White	24.87 (0.178)	4.19 (0.049)	3.77 (0.046)	3.40 (0.028)	3.18 (0.028)	1.28 (0.025)	0.69 (0.017)	0.33 (0.019)	0.87 (0.027)	1.90 (0.049)	2.00 (0.078)	— (††)	— (††)	2.80 (0.088)
Black	24.37 (0.250)	4.28 (0.045)	3.69 (0.050)	3.42 (0.042)	3.03 (0.064)	1.24 (0.038)	0.58 (0.025)	0.22 (0.022)	0.97 (0.045)	1.58 (0.062)	1.57 (0.152)	— (††)	— (††)	2.94 (0.080)
Hispanic	24.69 (0.218)	4.51 (0.055)	3.60 (0.051)	3.28 (0.041)	2.81 (0.054)	1.13 (0.026)	0.50 (0.036)	0.20 (0.020)	0.97 (0.042)	1.78 (0.055)	1.78 (0.113)	— (††)	— (††)	3.36 (0.121)
Asian/Pacific Islander	24.67 (0.195)	4.37 (0.068)	3.92 (0.086)	3.62 (0.029)	3.43 (0.079)	1.26 (0.027)	0.83 (0.037)	0.51 (0.036)	0.81 (0.041)	2.29 (0.129)	1.52 (0.056)	— (††)	— (††)	2.95 (0.208)
American Indian/ Alaska Native	23.81 (0.350)	4.18 (0.082)	3.67 (0.093)	3.10 (0.081)	2.68 (0.081)	1.07 (0.056)	0.49 (0.038)	0.15 (0.024)	0.98 (0.070)	1.45 (0.132)	1.94 (0.146)	— (†)	— (†)	3.40 (0.212)

See notes at end of table.

Table 225.10. Average number of Carnegie units earned by public high school graduates in various subject fields, by sex and race/ethnicity: Selected years, 1982 through 2009—Continued
[Standard errors appear in parentheses]

Graduation year, sex, and race/ethnicity	Total	English	History/ social studies	Mathematics	Science					Foreign languages	Arts	Career/ technical (occupational) education[1]	Labor market, family, and consumer education[2]	Personal use[3]
					Total	Biology	Chemistry	Physics	Other science[4]					
1	2	3	4	5	6	7	8	9	10	11	12	13	14	15
2000 graduates	26.15 (0.204)	4.26 (0.037)	3.89 (0.036)	3.62 (0.029)	3.20 (0.038)	1.28 (0.028)	0.71 (0.020)	0.37 (0.018)	0.84 (0.030)	2.01 (0.045)	2.03 (0.054)	2.86 (0.105)	1.35 (0.044)	3.49 (0.071)
Sex														
Male	26.01 (0.210)	4.18 (0.036)	3.83 (0.036)	3.60 (0.032)	3.15 (0.039)	1.20 (0.030)	0.67 (0.020)	0.42 (0.020)	0.87 (0.029)	1.77 (0.045)	1.75 (0.051)	3.24 (0.133)	1.35 (0.049)	3.76 (0.079)
Female	26.26 (0.204)	4.34 (0.040)	3.95 (0.038)	3.64 (0.028)	3.24 (0.041)	1.36 (0.030)	0.74 (0.022)	0.33 (0.018)	0.81 (0.031)	2.25 (0.050)	2.29 (0.065)	2.48 (0.086)	1.34 (0.047)	3.22 (0.068)
Race/ethnicity														
White	26.31 (0.256)	4.26 (0.037)	3.93 (0.042)	3.63 (0.032)	3.24 (0.038)	1.30 (0.034)	0.72 (0.024)	0.39 (0.021)	0.83 (0.033)	1.98 (0.054)	2.11 (0.068)	2.97 (0.136)	1.37 (0.055)	3.37 (0.080)
Black	25.85 (0.233)	4.36 (0.078)	3.81 (0.068)	3.57 (0.046)	3.12 (0.059)	1.25 (0.041)	0.66 (0.030)	0.30 (0.027)	0.91 (0.043)	1.71 (0.070)	1.94 (0.134)	2.74 (0.143)	1.54 (0.075)	3.60 (0.134)
Hispanic	25.59 (0.358)	4.29 (0.125)	3.84 (0.076)	3.48 (0.069)	2.86 (0.112)	1.18 (0.068)	0.58 (0.055)	0.25 (0.026)	0.84 (0.044)	2.22 (0.063)	1.76 (0.062)	2.64 (0.152)	1.20 (0.082)	3.95 (0.173)
Asian/Pacific Islander	26.23 (0.332)	4.12 (0.060)	3.80 (0.055)	4.01 (0.108)	3.70 (0.162)	1.35 (0.066)	0.97 (0.050)	0.67 (0.042)	0.71 (0.086)	2.90 (0.089)	1.78 (0.085)	1.99 (0.149)	0.81 (0.050)	3.52 (0.221)
American Indian/ Alaska Native	25.24 (0.342)	4.08 (0.069)	3.82 (0.102)	3.35 (0.117)	2.88 (0.086)	1.25 (0.080)	0.45 (0.045)	0.19 (0.042)	0.98 (0.038)	1.41 (0.105)	1.99 (0.220)	3.23 (0.380)	1.60 (0.151)	3.60 (0.365)
2005 graduates	26.88 (0.102)	4.33 (0.022)	4.08 (0.027)	3.80 (0.018)	3.35 (0.019)	1.28 (0.016)	0.75 (0.011)	0.37 (0.012)	0.95 (0.019)	2.07 (0.022)	2.06 (0.035)	2.64 (0.045)	1.38 (0.030)	3.83 (0.047)
Sex														
Male	26.70 (0.107)	4.26 (0.024)	4.01 (0.030)	3.78 (0.021)	3.29 (0.023)	1.19 (0.016)	0.71 (0.012)	0.41 (0.014)	0.98 (0.019)	1.87 (0.025)	1.71 (0.035)	3.01 (0.050)	1.36 (0.032)	4.17 (0.055)
Female	27.05 (0.104)	4.39 (0.022)	4.16 (0.028)	3.83 (0.018)	3.41 (0.019)	1.37 (0.017)	0.79 (0.012)	0.33 (0.012)	0.92 (0.020)	2.25 (0.023)	2.38 (0.045)	2.29 (0.049)	1.41 (0.033)	3.52 (0.050)
Race/ethnicity														
White	27.06 (0.127)	4.30 (0.030)	4.12 (0.030)	3.80 (0.022)	3.44 (0.021)	1.31 (0.018)	0.77 (0.014)	0.39 (0.012)	0.96 (0.021)	2.03 (0.025)	2.17 (0.043)	2.75 (0.059)	1.39 (0.036)	3.64 (0.059)
Black	26.76 (0.151)	4.50 (0.028)	4.10 (0.054)	3.86 (0.036)	3.22 (0.035)	1.27 (0.025)	0.69 (0.017)	0.28 (0.025)	0.99 (0.037)	1.77 (0.041)	1.77 (0.055)	2.58 (0.074)	1.56 (0.065)	4.32 (0.096)
Hispanic	26.18 (0.147)	4.33 (0.026)	3.88 (0.052)	3.64 (0.034)	2.93 (0.036)	1.11 (0.021)	0.64 (0.022)	0.25 (0.017)	0.94 (0.031)	2.39 (0.047)	1.78 (0.055)	2.41 (0.086)	1.30 (0.046)	4.44 (0.100)
Asian/Pacific Islander	26.58 (0.183)	4.28 (0.043)	4.02 (0.048)	4.08 (0.051)	3.65 (0.057)	1.31 (0.035)	0.98 (0.028)	0.59 (0.036)	0.77 (0.061)	2.70 (0.066)	1.80 (0.076)	1.94 (0.116)	0.98 (0.052)	3.53 (0.122)
American Indian/ Alaska Native	26.66 (0.454)	4.42 (0.136)	4.15 (0.151)	3.60 (0.175)	3.00 (0.075)	1.27 (0.061)	0.52 (0.053)	0.17 (0.036)	1.04 (0.063)	1.55 (0.125)	2.45 (0.179)	2.45 (0.208)	1.70 (0.184)	4.24 (0.294)
2009 graduates	27.15 (0.100)	4.37 (0.013)	4.19 (0.027)	3.91 (0.017)	3.47 (0.022)	1.35 (0.014)	0.78 (0.011)	0.42 (0.013)	0.92 (0.017)	2.21 (0.027)	2.12 (0.036)	2.47 (0.059)	1.11 (0.030)	3.86 (0.059)
Sex														
Male	26.98 (0.111)	4.30 (0.015)	4.13 (0.028)	3.88 (0.018)	3.46 (0.027)	1.27 (0.014)	0.74 (0.012)	0.48 (0.017)	0.96 (0.017)	2.01 (0.028)	1.76 (0.034)	2.77 (0.068)	1.13 (0.036)	4.18 (0.070)
Female	27.31 (0.095)	4.42 (0.014)	4.25 (0.027)	3.93 (0.018)	3.49 (0.020)	1.43 (0.015)	0.82 (0.011)	0.37 (0.012)	0.88 (0.019)	2.40 (0.028)	2.46 (0.046)	2.19 (0.055)	1.10 (0.028)	3.57 (0.060)
Race/ethnicity														
White	27.30 (0.151)	4.32 (0.016)	4.23 (0.037)	3.91 (0.021)	3.55 (0.026)	1.37 (0.015)	0.80 (0.013)	0.44 (0.016)	0.94 (0.022)	2.19 (0.032)	2.26 (0.042)	2.55 (0.071)	1.16 (0.040)	3.70 (0.075)
Black	27.42 (0.141)	4.56 (0.039)	4.26 (0.036)	4.02 (0.035)	3.31 (0.027)	1.33 (0.025)	0.68 (0.022)	0.30 (0.019)	1.00 (0.024)	1.87 (0.044)	1.87 (0.067)	2.72 (0.127)	1.21 (0.052)	4.29 (0.102)
Hispanic	26.47 (0.194)	4.43 (0.024)	4.04 (0.040)	3.70 (0.029)	3.13 (0.028)	1.24 (0.019)	0.70 (0.015)	0.32 (0.015)	0.87 (0.024)	2.34 (0.034)	1.85 (0.046)	2.31 (0.101)	1.04 (0.040)	4.26 (0.095)
Asian/Pacific Islander	26.94 (0.190)	4.19 (0.039)	4.13 (0.083)	4.16 (0.052)	4.06 (0.091)	1.56 (0.077)	1.08 (0.035)	0.75 (0.033)	0.68 (0.063)	2.98 (0.090)	1.99 (0.065)	1.63 (0.074)	0.62 (0.054)	3.47 (0.100)
American Indian/ Alaska Native	26.17 (0.409)	4.39 (0.085)	4.11 (0.083)	3.76 (0.125)	3.20 (0.070)	1.38 (0.062)	0.50 (0.051)	0.24 (0.046)	1.09 (0.066)	1.56 (0.097)	2.19 (0.157)	2.35 (0.188)	1.20 (0.117)	4.54 (0.370)

—Not available.
†Not applicable.
‡Interpret data with caution. The coefficient of variation (CV) for this estimate is between 30 and 50 percent.
[1]Includes occupational education in agriculture; business and marketing; communications and design; computer and information sciences; construction and architecture; engineering technologies; health sciences; manufacturing; repair and transportation; and personal, public, and legal services. Does not include general labor market preparation courses and family and consumer sciences education courses.
[2]Includes general labor market preparation courses and family and consumer sciences education courses.
[3]Includes general skills, personal health and physical education, religion, military sciences, special education, and other courses not included in other academic subject fields. Some personal-use courses are also included in the Career/technical (occupational) education column and the Labor market, family, and consumer education column.

[4]Includes all science credits earned outside of biology, chemistry, and physics.
NOTE: The Carnegie unit is a standard of measurement that represents one credit for the completion of a 1-year course. Data differ slightly from figures appearing in other NCES reports because of differences in taxonomies and case exclusion criteria. Race categories exclude persons of Hispanic ethnicity. Totals include other racial/ethnic groups not separately shown. Detail may not sum to totals because of rounding.
SOURCE: U.S. Department of Education, National Center for Education Statistics, High School and Beyond Longitudinal Study of 1980 Sophomores (HS&B-So:80/82), "High School Transcript Study"; and 1987, 1990, 1994, 1998, 2000, 2005, and 2009 High School Transcript Study (HSTS). (This table was prepared September 2011.)

Table 225.20. Average number of Carnegie units earned by public high school graduates in career/technical education courses in various occupational fields, by sex and race/ethnicity, and percentage distribution of students, by units earned: Selected years, 2000 through 2009

[Standard errors appear in parentheses]

Graduation year, sex, and race/ethnicity	Total, all occupational education courses[1]	Agriculture	Business and marketing	Communications and design	Computer and information sciences	Construction and architecture	Engineering technologies	Health sciences	Manufacturing	Repair and transportation	Personal, public, and legal services
1	2	3	4	5	6	7	8	9	10	11	12
2000 graduates											
Average units earned, all students[2]	2.86 (0.105)	0.25 (0.029)	0.82 (0.041)	0.30 (0.016)	0.27 (0.021)	0.14 (0.018)	0.20 (0.020)	0.15 (0.019)	0.24 (0.021)	0.18 (0.015)	0.32 (0.018)
Units earned, by sex											
Male	3.24 (0.133)	0.34 (0.041)	0.71 (0.043)	0.28 (0.018)	0.33 (0.026)	0.25 (0.035)	0.34 (0.034)	0.07 (0.013)	0.40 (0.035)	0.33 (0.028)	0.18 (0.015)
Female	2.48 (0.086)	0.16 (0.022)	0.91 (0.042)	0.32 (0.017)	0.21 (0.020)	0.02 (0.003)	0.06 (0.008)	0.22 (0.026)	0.10 (0.011)	0.03 (0.004)	0.46 (0.027)
Units earned, by race/ethnicity											
White	2.97 (0.136)	0.31 (0.038)	0.79 (0.049)	0.31 (0.019)	0.26 (0.023)	0.16 (0.027)	0.22 (0.025)	0.13 (0.019)	0.27 (0.027)	0.20 (0.021)	0.31 (0.020)
Black	2.74 (0.143)	0.11 (0.027)	0.98 (0.068)	0.29 (0.026)	0.24 (0.024)	0.08 (0.017)	0.15 (0.029)	0.17 (0.022)	0.17 (0.023)	0.11 (0.016)	0.44 (0.050)
Hispanic	2.64 (0.152)	0.13 (0.020)	0.86 (0.083)	0.29 (0.024)	0.26 (0.021)	0.09 (0.018)	0.14 (0.019)	0.24 ! (0.100)	0.17 (0.027)	0.15 (0.017)	0.31 (0.029)
Asian/Pacific Islander	1.99 (0.149)	0.06 (0.014)	0.54 (0.065)	0.25 (0.035)	0.45 (0.098)	0.02 ! (0.007)	0.17 (0.033)	0.15 (0.037)	0.12 (0.030)	0.07 (0.018)	0.16 (0.022)
American Indian/Alaska Native	3.23 (0.380)	0.37 ! (0.131)	0.80 (0.088)	0.24 (0.050)	0.32 (0.072)	0.08 ! (0.029)	0.20 ! (0.067)	0.11 (0.030)	0.49 ! (0.160)	‡ (†)	0.41 (0.121)
Percentage distribution of students, by units earned											
0 units	11.1 (0.79)	88.3 (0.86)	49.0 (1.83)	74.5 (1.29)	75.7 (1.61)	93.1 (0.51)	85.8 (1.10)	89.4 (1.28)	83.6 (0.98)	90.7 (0.61)	74.5 (1.34)
More than 0, but less than 1	7.9 (0.57)	2.3 (0.37)	12.1 (1.18)	8.9 (0.72)	8.7 (1.22)	1.8 (0.26)	3.4 (0.44)	5.6 (1.22)	5.4 (0.53)	2.7 (0.43)	11.8 (1.01)
At least 1, but less than 2	22.1 (0.77)	4.5 (0.37)	22.7 (0.91)	12.1 (0.72)	11.9 (0.94)	3.0 (0.33)	7.5 (0.67)	2.3 (0.32)	7.0 (0.61)	3.5 (0.38)	8.6 (0.64)
At least 2, but less than 3	17.0 (0.56)	1.7 (0.18)	8.1 (0.50)	3.0 (0.25)	2.5 (0.39)	0.7 (0.11)	2.1 (0.23)	0.8 (0.13)	2.1 (0.27)	0.9 (0.11)	2.5 (0.29)
3 or more units	41.8 (1.53)	3.3 (0.44)	8.1 (0.63)	1.6 (0.20)	1.1 (0.20)	1.4 (0.21)	1.3 (0.18)	1.9 (0.39)	1.9 (0.26)	2.1 (0.21)	2.6 (0.22)
4 or more units	28.9 (1.48)	2.1 (0.37)	4.0 (0.47)	0.8 (0.13)	0.6 (0.15)	1.0 (0.20)	0.6 (0.13)	1.1 ! (0.37)	1.2 (0.20)	1.4 (0.18)	1.5 (0.19)
2005 graduates											
Average units earned, all students[2]	2.64 (0.045)	0.23 (0.013)	0.64 (0.020)	0.36 (0.012)	0.24 (0.011)	0.12 (0.007)	0.15 (0.008)	0.16 (0.010)	0.21 (0.011)	0.18 (0.011)	0.35 (0.013)
Units earned, by sex											
Male	3.01 (0.050)	0.32 (0.020)	0.62 (0.022)	0.34 (0.014)	0.33 (0.015)	0.21 (0.014)	0.26 (0.014)	0.07 (0.007)	0.33 (0.019)	0.33 (0.019)	0.20 (0.011)
Female	2.29 (0.049)	0.15 (0.011)	0.66 (0.023)	0.38 (0.014)	0.15 (0.010)	0.03 (0.003)	0.05 (0.005)	0.25 (0.016)	0.10 (0.008)	0.03 (0.005)	0.49 (0.018)
Units earned, by race/ethnicity											
White	2.75 (0.059)	0.28 (0.017)	0.63 (0.024)	0.39 (0.015)	0.24 (0.013)	0.13 (0.010)	0.17 (0.010)	0.15 (0.012)	0.25 (0.015)	0.19 (0.014)	0.33 (0.015)
Black	2.58 (0.074)	0.10 (0.018)	0.80 (0.041)	0.28 (0.019)	0.23 (0.021)	0.11 (0.012)	0.11 (0.015)	0.25 (0.023)	0.11 (0.013)	0.13 (0.023)	0.45 (0.030)
Hispanic	2.41 (0.086)	0.14 (0.019)	0.63 (0.033)	0.30 (0.016)	0.21 (0.015)	0.10 (0.014)	0.12 (0.019)	0.16 (0.019)	0.17 (0.022)	0.19 (0.020)	0.39 (0.030)
Asian/Pacific Islander	1.94 (0.116)	0.06 ! (0.019)	0.49 (0.045)	0.32 (0.040)	0.36 (0.032)	0.04 (0.010)	0.13 (0.021)	0.10 (0.022)	0.13 (0.024)	0.09 (0.018)	0.21 (0.020)
American Indian/Alaska Native	2.45 (0.208)	0.46 (0.127)	0.46 (0.080)	0.33 (0.056)	0.24 ! (0.076)	0.09 ! (0.038)	0.02 ! (0.009)	0.10 (0.029)	0.24 (0.055)	0.21 ! (0.069)	0.31 (0.057)
Percentage distribution of students, by units earned											
0 units	13.0 (0.45)	88.4 (0.54)	55.8 (1.05)	69.8 (0.79)	80.5 (0.91)	93.3 (0.33)	88.2 (0.53)	90.4 (0.67)	83.6 (0.82)	91.2 (0.38)	74.9 (0.85)
More than 0, but less than 1	8.2 (0.35)	2.0 (0.20)	11.5 (0.62)	10.6 (0.50)	6.3 (0.36)	1.6 (0.17)	3.7 (0.34)	3.3 (0.52)	6.2 (0.48)	2.6 (0.26)	9.7 (0.61)
At least 1, but less than 2	22.0 (0.41)	4.8 (0.28)	20.7 (0.65)	14.2 (0.59)	9.5 (0.62)	2.9 (0.20)	5.7 (0.28)	2.9 (0.21)	6.4 (0.35)	2.8 (0.17)	9.6 (0.47)
At least 2, but less than 3	17.3 (0.34)	1.8 (0.12)	6.5 (0.29)	3.4 (0.16)	2.3 (0.19)	0.9 (0.11)	1.4 (0.12)	1.1 (0.11)	2.0 (0.18)	1.1 (0.12)	2.7 (0.20)
3 or more units	39.5 (0.76)	3.0 (0.21)	5.4 (0.32)	2.1 (0.17)	1.4 (0.12)	1.2 (0.12)	1.0 (0.13)	2.2 (0.19)	1.8 (0.16)	2.3 (0.20)	3.0 (0.20)
4 or more units	26.5 (0.67)	1.9 (0.16)	2.7 (0.20)	0.9 (0.09)	0.6 (0.09)	0.8 (0.09)	0.5 (0.08)	1.1 (0.13)	0.8 (0.11)	1.5 (0.16)	1.7 (0.15)
2009 graduates											
Average units earned, all students[2]	2.47 (0.059)	0.20 (0.013)	0.51 (0.017)	0.36 (0.011)	0.23 (0.010)	0.11 (0.009)	0.14 (0.008)	0.20 (0.015)	0.17 (0.010)	0.17 (0.015)	0.37 (0.020)
Units earned, by sex											
Male	2.77 (0.068)	0.27 (0.020)	0.52 (0.020)	0.35 (0.012)	0.31 (0.013)	0.20 (0.015)	0.24 (0.013)	0.09 (0.010)	0.26 (0.017)	0.32 (0.027)	0.22 (0.013)
Female	2.19 (0.055)	0.14 (0.009)	0.50 (0.018)	0.38 (0.013)	0.16 (0.009)	0.03 (0.004)	0.05 (0.005)	0.31 (0.021)	0.09 (0.007)	0.03 (0.005)	0.51 (0.028)
Units earned, by race/ethnicity											
White	2.55 (0.071)	0.27 (0.020)	0.50 (0.022)	0.38 (0.013)	0.22 (0.011)	0.13 (0.011)	0.16 (0.010)	0.16 (0.013)	0.20 (0.014)	0.17 (0.012)	0.35 (0.020)
Black	2.72 (0.127)	0.09 (0.010)	0.69 (0.035)	0.34 (0.026)	0.26 (0.026)	0.10 (0.021)	0.10 (0.015)	0.31 (0.044)	0.12 (0.015)	0.19 ! (0.056)	0.52 (0.037)
Hispanic	2.31 (0.101)	0.14 (0.018)	0.43 (0.027)	0.34 (0.015)	0.23 (0.025)	0.08 (0.011)	0.10 (0.009)	0.24 (0.031)	0.13 (0.013)	0.20 (0.026)	0.43 (0.044)
Asian/Pacific Islander	1.63 (0.074)	0.03 (0.009)	0.42 (0.054)	0.26 (0.026)	0.27 (0.024)	0.04 (0.009)	0.13 (0.034)	0.20 (0.048)	0.08 (0.012)	0.07 (0.015)	0.14 (0.020)
American Indian/Alaska Native	2.35 (0.188)	0.17 ! (0.069)	0.43 (0.065)	0.44 (0.065)	0.24 ! (0.079)	‡ (†)	0.07 ! (0.028)	0.12 ! (0.050)	0.30 (0.071)	0.19 ! (0.068)	0.26 (0.057)

See notes at end of table.

Table 225.20. Average number of Carnegie units earned by public high school graduates in career/technical education courses in various occupational fields, by sex and race/ethnicity, and percentage distribution of students, by units earned: Selected years, 2000 through 2009—Continued

[Standard errors appear in parentheses]

Graduation year, sex, and race/ethnicity	Total, all occupational education courses[1]		Agriculture		Business and marketing		Communications and design		Computer and information sciences		Construction and architecture		Engineering technologies		Health sciences		Manufacturing		Repair and transportation		Personal, public, and legal services	
1	2		3		4		5		6		7		8		9		10		11		12	
Percentage distribution of students, by units earned																						
0 units	15.0	(0.61)	89.3	(0.58)	63.4	(1.04)	70.2	(0.91)	78.5	(0.89)	93.3	(0.43)	88.8	(0.62)	89.6	(0.64)	87.1	(0.52)	92.0	(0.43)	74.6	(0.73)
More than 0, but less than 1	8.7	(0.33)	2.1	(0.26)	10.1	(0.51)	10.2	(0.55)	8.3	(0.64)	1.7	(0.18)	2.8	(0.24)	2.3	(0.28)	4.5	(0.30)	2.0	(0.21)	9.2	(0.40)
At least 1, but less than 2	23.0	(0.59)	4.3	(0.32)	17.0	(0.60)	13.8	(0.53)	10.1	(0.50)	2.9	(0.23)	6.1	(0.51)	4.1	(0.44)	5.6	(0.31)	2.8	(0.20)	10.2	(0.45)
At least 2, but less than 3	17.0	(0.33)	1.7	(0.15)	5.4	(0.35)	3.6	(0.20)	2.1	(0.16)	1.0	(0.17)	1.3	(0.12)	1.4	(0.13)	1.6	(0.12)	1.1	(0.10)	2.9	(0.22)
3 or more units	36.2	(1.02)	2.7	(0.24)	4.1	(0.23)	2.2	(0.13)	1.1	(0.14)	1.1	(0.11)	0.9	(0.09)	2.6	(0.25)	1.3	(0.15)	2.1	(0.24)	3.2	(0.24)
4 or more units	23.8	(0.89)	1.6	(0.15)	1.8	(0.16)	1.0	(0.07)	0.4	(0.07)	0.7	(0.08)	0.4	(0.05)	1.7	(0.19)	0.6	(0.09)	1.5	(0.21)	1.9	(0.19)

†Not applicable.
!Interpret data with caution. The coefficient of variation (CV) for this estimate is between 30 and 50 percent.
‡Reporting standards not met. The coefficient of variation (CV) for this estimate is 50 percent or greater.
[1]Includes Carnegie units earned in all occupational education courses. This table does not include general labor market preparation courses and family and consumer sciences education courses.
[2]Total includes other racial/ethnic groups not separately shown.

NOTE: The Carnegie unit is a standard of measurement that represents one credit for the completion of a 1-year course. Data may differ from figures appearing in other NCES reports because of differences in course taxonomies and/or inclusion criteria. The analysis was restricted to graduates who attained either a standard or honors diploma and whose transcripts reflected a total of 16 or more Carnegie credits, with credits in English making up some part of the total. Race categories exclude persons of Hispanic ethnicity. Totals include other racial/ethnic groups not separately shown. Detail may not sum to totals because of rounding. SOURCE: U.S. Department of Education, National Center for Education Statistics, 2000, 2005, and 2009 High School Transcript Study (HSTS). (This table was prepared September 2011.)

Table 225.30. Percentage of public and private high school graduates taking selected mathematics and science courses in high school, by sex and race/ethnicity: Selected years, 1982 through 2009

[Standard errors appear in parentheses]

Course (Carnegie units)	1982	1990	1994	1998	2000	2005	2009 Total	Sex Male	Sex Female	Race/ethnicity White	Race/ethnicity Black	Race/ethnicity Hispanic	Race/ethnicity Asian/Pacific Islander	Race/ethnicity American Indian/Alaska Native
1	2	3	4	5	6	7	8	9	10	11	12	13	14	15
Mathematics[1]														
Any mathematics (≥1.0)........	98.5 (0.21)	99.6 (0.07)	99.5 (0.07)	99.9 (0.05)	99.8 (0.05)	99.9 (0.02)	100.0 (†)	100.0 (†)	100.0 (†)	100.0 (†)	100.0 (†)	100.0 (†)	100.0 (†)	100.0 (†)
Algebra I (≥1.0)[2]........	55.2 (1.01)	64.5 (1.55)	66.9 (1.33)	63.4 (1.44)	66.5 (1.75)	68.4 (0.99)	68.9 (0.94)	68.5 (0.98)	69.3 (1.01)	67.0 (1.09)	77.2 (1.26)	75.4 (1.60)	53.3 (3.52)	74.8 (5.85)
Geometry (≥1.0)........	47.1 (0.99)	64.1 (1.33)	70.6 (1.25)	75.3 (1.06)	78.3 (1.08)	83.8 (0.63)	88.3 (0.53)	86.6 (0.75)	89.9 (0.54)	88.8 (0.73)	88.4 (1.07)	87.0 (0.96)	86.1 (1.47)	81.6 (4.09)
Algebra II (≥0.5)[3]........	39.9 (0.93)	48.8 (1.39)	61.5 (1.38)	61.7 (1.77)	67.6 (1.43)	70.3 (1.01)	75.5 (0.92)	73.5 (1.09)	77.6 (0.91)	77.1 (1.09)	70.5 (1.68)	71.1 (1.83)	82.8 (2.57)	66.3 (4.12)
Trigonometry (≥0.5)........	8.1 (0.54)	18.2 (1.28)	11.8 (1.16)	8.9 (1.06)	7.9 (1.33)	8.4 (0.88)	6.1 (0.77)	5.8 (0.78)	6.4 (0.81)	7.1 (1.01)	3.2 (0.55)	3.6 (0.69)	8.5 (1.96)	6.5 (1.84)
Analysis/precalculus (≥0.5)........	6.2 (0.46)	13.4 (0.95)	17.4 (0.87)	23.2 (1.44)	26.6 (1.40)	29.4 (0.98)	35.3 (0.84)	33.8 (1.02)	36.6 (0.89)	37.9 (0.98)	22.7 (1.29)	26.5 (1.36)	60.5 (2.88)	18.5 (2.98)
Statistics/probability (≥0.5)........	1.0 (0.16)	1.0 (0.21)	2.0 (0.33)	3.7 (0.54)	5.7 (0.85)	7.7 (0.53)	10.8 (0.49)	10.7 (0.51)	10.9 (0.58)	11.6 (0.64)	7.9 (1.04)	7.5 (0.77)	17.6 (1.69)	5.9 ! (2.07)
Calculus (≥1.0)........	5.0 (0.43)	6.5 (0.46)	9.4 (0.56)	11.0 (0.85)	11.6 (0.72)	13.6 (0.53)	15.9 (0.66)	16.1 (0.75)	15.7 (0.69)	17.5 (0.69)	6.1 (0.59)	8.6 (0.64)	42.2 (3.11)	6.3 (1.60)
AP/honors calculus (≥1.0)[4]........	1.6 (0.26)	4.2 (0.44)	7.0 (0.54)	6.8 (0.49)	7.8 (0.58)	9.2 (0.44)	11.0 (0.55)	11.3 (0.65)	10.7 (0.54)	11.5 (0.52)	4.0 (0.37)	6.3 (0.46)	34.8 (2.77)	4.9 (1.44)
Science[1]														
Any science (≥1.0)........	96.4 (0.39)	99.4 (0.13)	99.5 (0.09)	99.5 (0.10)	99.4 (0.12)	99.7 (0.05)	99.9 (0.02)	99.8 (0.04)	99.9 (0.02)	99.9 (0.03)	99.9 (0.04)	99.8 (0.06)	100.0 (†)	100.0 (†)
Biology (≥1.0)........	77.4 (0.87)	91.3 (0.98)	93.7 (0.98)	92.9 (0.68)	91.1 (1.01)	92.5 (0.60)	95.6 (0.40)	94.9 (0.45)	96.2 (0.43)	95.6 (0.51)	96.3 (0.56)	94.8 (0.67)	95.8 (0.95)	94.5 (1.64)
AP/honors biology (≥1.0)[4]........	10.0 (0.64)	5.0 (0.76)	12.0 (0.93)	16.3 (1.32)	16.3 (1.45)	16.0 (0.83)	22.4 (0.78)	19.7 (0.76)	25.0 (0.89)	24.2 (0.88)	14.1 (0.80)	16.1 (0.88)	39.7 (3.58)	15.4 (3.38)
Chemistry (≥1.0)........	32.1 (0.84)	49.2 (1.22)	56.1 (1.01)	60.5 (1.29)	61.8 (1.48)	66.4 (0.94)	70.4 (0.75)	67.4 (0.95)	73.4 (0.76)	71.5 (0.87)	65.3 (1.80)	65.7 (1.41)	84.8 (1.72)	44.5 (4.78)
AP/honors chemistry (≥1.0)[4]........	3.0 (0.33)	3.5 (0.47)	3.9 (0.53)	4.8 (0.50)	5.7 (0.84)	7.6 (0.53)	5.9 (0.43)	6.1 (0.52)	5.8 (0.39)	6.5 (0.47)	2.5 (0.46)	2.6 (0.35)	17.0 (2.36)	3.4 ! (1.39)
Physics (≥1.0)........	15.0 (0.62)	21.3 (0.84)	24.8 (0.86)	28.8 (1.49)	31.3 (1.16)	32.9 (0.91)	36.1 (1.01)	39.2 (1.29)	33.0 (0.92)	37.6 (1.24)	26.9 (1.72)	28.6 (1.33)	61.1 (2.35)	19.8 (3.89)
AP/honors physics (≥1.0)[4]........	1.2 (0.17)	2.0 (0.38)	2.7 (0.34)	3.0 (0.37)	3.9 (0.60)	5.3 (0.33)	5.7 (0.46)	7.7 (0.63)	3.7 (0.38)	6.1 (0.54)	2.5 (0.39)	3.4 (0.39)	15.1 (2.51)	‡ (†)
Engineering (≥1.0)........	1.2 (0.21)	0.1 (0.04)	4.5 (0.80)	6.7 (1.76)	4.1 (0.98)	4.8 (0.56)	8.2 (0.93)	9.0 (1.02)	7.4 (0.93)	8.2 (1.18)	10.1 (1.75)	7.1 (1.06)	6.4 (1.17)	9.0 ! (3.15)
Astronomy (≥0.5)........	1.2 (0.24)	1.2 (0.31)	1.7 (0.50)	1.9 (0.46)	2.8 (0.59)	2.8 (0.37)	3.3 (0.40)	3.9 (0.51)	2.7 (0.33)	4.0 (0.57)	1.8 (0.38)	2.0 (0.36)	1.9 (0.43)	5.3 ! (2.51)
Geology/earth science (≥0.5)........	13.6 (1.04)	25.3 (2.47)	23.1 (2.44)	20.9 (2.35)	18.5 (1.92)	24.7 (1.43)	27.7 (1.70)	28.9 (1.88)	26.5 (1.66)	28.2 (2.04)	30.1 (2.57)	27.1 (2.15)	19.1 (2.38)	26.0 (5.25)
Biology and chemistry (≥2.0)[5]........	29.3 (0.83)	47.8 (1.23)	53.8 (1.18)	59.1 (1.22)	59.2 (1.50)	64.3 (0.97)	68.3 (0.77)	65.0 (0.91)	71.4 (0.84)	68.9 (0.93)	64.3 (1.74)	64.2 (1.45)	82.7 (1.93)	43.9 (4.77)
Biology, chemistry, and physics (≥3.0)[5]........	11.2 (0.51)	18.7 (0.71)	21.4 (0.83)	25.6 (1.34)	25.0 (1.10)	27.4 (0.89)	30.1 (0.87)	31.9 (1.08)	28.3 (0.85)	31.4 (1.04)	21.9 (1.48)	22.7 (1.19)	54.4 (2.77)	13.6 (2.87)

†Not applicable.
!Interpret data with caution. The coefficient of variation (CV) for this estimate is between 30 and 50 percent.
‡Reporting standards not met. The coefficient of variation (CV) for this estimate is 50 percent or greater.
[1]For each course category, percentages include only students who earned at least the number of credits shown in parentheses.
[2]Excludes prealgebra.
[3]Includes courses where trigonometry or geometry has been combined with algebra II.
[4]For 2000 and later years, includes International Baccalaureate (IB) courses in addition to Advanced Placement (AP) and honors courses.
[5]Percentages include only students who earned at least one credit in each of the indicated courses.

NOTE: For a transcript to be included in the analyses, it had to meet three requirements: (1) the student graduated with either a standard or honors diploma, (2) the student's transcript contained 16 or more Carnegie units, and (3) the student's transcript contained more than 0 Carnegie units in English courses. The Carnegie unit is a standard of measurement that represents one credit for the completion of a 1-year course (0.5 = one semester; 1.0 = one academic year). Data differ slightly from figures appearing in other National Center for Education Statistics reports because of differences in taxonomies and case exclusion criteria. Race categories exclude persons of Hispanic ethnicity. Totals include other racial/ethnic groups not separately shown. Some data have been revised from previously published figures.
SOURCE: U.S. Department of Education, National Center for Education Statistics, High School and Beyond Longitudinal Study of 1980 Sophomores (HS&B-So:80/82), "High School Transcript Study"; and 1990, 1994, 1998, 2000, 2005, and 2009 High School Transcript Study (HSTS). (This table was prepared October 2012.)

Table 225.40. Percentage of public and private high school graduates taking selected mathematics and science courses in high school, by selected student and school characteristics: Selected years, 1990 through 2009

[Standard errors appear in parentheses]

Year and student or school characteristic	Mathematics						Science				
	Algebra I[1][2]	Geometry[1]	Algebra II/ trigonometry[3]	Analysis/ precalculus[3]	Statistics/ probability[3]	Calculus[1]	Biology[1]	Chemistry[1]	Physics[1]	Biology and chemistry[4]	Biology, chemistry, and physics[5]
1	2	3	4	5	6	7	8	9	10	11	12
1990											
Total[6]	64.5 (1.55)	64.1 (1.33)	53.6 (1.32)	13.4 (0.95)	1.0 (0.21)	6.5 (0.46)	91.3 (0.98)	49.2 (1.22)	21.3 (0.84)	47.8 (1.23)	18.7 (0.71)
Sex											
Male	62.0 (1.57)	63.0 (1.57)	51.8 (1.44)	14.1 (1.14)	1.2 (0.27)	7.6 (0.64)	90.0 (1.09)	48.1 (1.40)	25.1 (0.95)	46.6 (1.40)	21.8 (0.82)
Female	66.7 (1.69)	65.0 (1.31)	55.2 (1.45)	12.8 (0.94)	0.8 (0.20)	5.6 (0.37)	92.5 (0.94)	50.2 (1.29)	17.7 (0.87)	48.9 (1.30)	16.0 (0.76)
Race/ethnicity											
White	64.6 (1.83)	66.4 (1.43)	56.9 (1.53)	14.9 (1.04)	1.0 (0.22)	6.9 (0.53)	91.5 (1.06)	51.8 (1.33)	22.8 (0.91)	50.5 (1.35)	20.5 (0.82)
Black	65.1 (2.42)	56.3 (2.58)	43.9 (2.77)	6.2 (0.96)	1.1 ! (0.44)	2.8 (0.55)	91.3 (2.19)	40.3 (2.19)	14.5 (1.85)	39.5 (2.24)	12.0 (1.23)
Hispanic	64.8 (2.75)	54.1 (2.89)	39.9 (2.80)	7.1 (0.82)	‡ (†)	3.8 (0.67)	90.2 (1.40)	38.3 (2.90)	12.7 (1.33)	36.4 (2.70)	10.0 (1.21)
Asian/Pacific Islander	63.5 (3.01)	71.5 (2.90)	69.3 (5.51)	25.2 (6.54)	‡ (†)	18.4 (3.23)	90.2 (2.73)	63.5 (4.01)	38.0 (3.36)	60.0 (3.45)	33.4 (2.56)
American Indian/Alaska Native	61.7 (8.40)	55.7 (2.85)	53.9 (4.80)	‡ (†)	‡ (†)	‡ (†)	90.5 (4.37)	35.5 (4.50)	‡ (†)	34.2 (4.46)	‡ (†)
Student with disabilities (SD) status											
SD[7]	20.6 (3.09)	11.8 (2.42)	8.3 (2.04)	‡ (†)	‡ (†)	‡ (†)	65.0 (4.73)	7.7 (1.53)	‡ (†)	‡ (†)	‡ (†)
Non-SD	65.4 (1.59)	65.1 (1.32)	54.5 (1.35)	13.6 (0.97)	1.0 (0.21)	6.7 (0.47)	91.8 (0.92)	50.0 (1.24)	21.6 (0.84)	48.6 (1.23)	19.1 (0.71)
English language learner (ELL) status											
ELL	57.7 (5.79)	42.2 (6.30)	37.1 (6.64)	‡ (†)	‡ (†)	‡ (†)	70.5 (4.66)	‡ (†)	‡ (†)	‡ (†)	‡ (†)
Non-ELL	64.5 (1.56)	64.2 (1.34)	53.7 (1.34)	13.4 (0.95)	1.0 (0.21)	6.6 (0.47)	91.4 (0.98)	49.3 (1.23)	21.3 (0.84)	48.0 (1.23)	18.8 (0.71)
School type											
Traditional public	62.9 (1.66)	61.9 (1.41)	51.4 (1.32)	12.2 (1.11)	0.8 (0.20)	6.2 (0.48)	90.7 (1.08)	47.4 (1.32)	20.2 (0.86)	46.0 (1.33)	17.8 (0.71)
Public charter	— (†)	— (†)	— (†)	— (†)	— (†)	— (†)	— (†)	— (†)	— (†)	— (†)	— (†)
Private	79.9 (2.22)	85.5 (1.98)	75.5 (3.55)	25.3 (3.44)	2.6 ! (1.03)	9.7 (1.33)	97.2 (0.55)	66.7 (2.71)	31.4 (2.30)	65.2 (2.67)	28.2 (2.07)
Percentage of students eligible for free or reduced-price lunch											
0–25 percent	64.9 (2.16)	67.4 (1.67)	57.8 (2.05)	15.3 (1.38)	1.1 (0.31)	7.5 (0.70)	92.4 (1.09)	54.0 (1.60)	22.8 (1.27)	52.8 (1.59)	21.0 (1.12)
26–50 percent	60.6 (3.97)	45.4 (2.90)	44.6 (2.74)	5.5 (1.43)	# (†)	3.8 (0.89)	88.8 (4.60)	36.5 (3.08)	15.3 (2.08)	35.5 (3.33)	12.8 (1.71)
51–75 percent	74.2 (7.31)	56.0 (14.72)	40.1 (5.12)	5.6 (1.54)	# (†)	‡ (†)	93.6 (2.87)	33.5 (4.28)	12.7 (3.12)	33.0 (4.42)	11.7 (2.83)
76–100 percent	96.0 (4.01)	89.4 (0.92)	78.7 (2.96)	‡ (†)	‡ (†)	# (†)	99.0 (0.99)	‡ (†)	‡ (†)	‡ (†)	‡ (†)
2000											
Total[6]	66.5 (1.75)	78.3 (1.08)	68.3 (1.45)	26.6 (1.40)	5.7 (0.85)	11.6 (0.72)	91.1 (1.01)	61.8 (1.48)	31.3 (1.16)	59.2 (1.50)	25.0 (1.10)
Sex											
Male	65.0 (1.72)	74.8 (1.31)	65.2 (1.46)	25.3 (1.39)	5.8 (0.97)	12.1 (0.79)	88.9 (1.32)	57.7 (1.42)	34.1 (1.29)	54.3 (1.49)	26.3 (1.23)
Female	68.0 (1.87)	81.4 (1.01)	71.1 (1.69)	27.8 (1.61)	5.6 (0.85)	11.1 (0.77)	93.2 (0.82)	65.5 (1.75)	28.9 (1.22)	63.6 (1.76)	23.9 (1.14)
Race/ethnicity											
White	65.1 (2.08)	79.2 (1.21)	69.6 (1.57)	28.1 (1.74)	6.1 (1.00)	12.5 (0.77)	91.7 (1.15)	62.9 (1.66)	32.3 (1.34)	60.1 (1.72)	25.6 (1.20)
Black	70.1 (3.20)	77.8 (1.93)	64.7 (2.32)	16.1 (1.52)	3.7 ! (1.24)	4.6 (0.55)	92.4 (1.09)	59.5 (2.38)	25.1 (1.97)	57.8 (2.31)	20.0 (1.76)
Hispanic	73.2 (2.43)	72.6 (3.30)	60.0 (5.06)	19.3 (2.95)	2.3 (0.52)	5.6 (0.86)	87.8 (2.69)	52.0 (4.13)	23.1 (2.32)	50.3 (4.30)	17.7 (2.19)
Asian/Pacific Islander	58.1 (3.28)	81.3 (2.03)	81.3 (2.00)	48.7 (2.79)	11.4 (2.44)	30.4 (5.02)	87.8 (3.20)	75.1 (2.89)	53.8 (2.80)	70.6 (3.03)	47.0 (2.70)
American Indian/Alaska Native	68.7 (5.80)	65.0 (6.18)	60.3 (5.51)	‡ (†)	‡ (†)	‡ (†)	88.4 (2.88)	43.6 (4.03)	‡ (†)	39.4 (3.81)	‡ (†)
Student with disabilities (SD) status											
SD[7]	45.2 (2.96)	36.1 (2.90)	22.9 (2.88)	6.7 ! (2.23)	‡ (†)	‡ (†)	72.0 (2.71)	21.2 (2.88)	13.6 (2.63)	19.9 (2.84)	7.9 ! (2.45)
Non-SD	67.3 (1.77)	79.9 (1.08)	70.1 (1.46)	27.4 (1.43)	5.9 (0.87)	11.9 (0.74)	91.9 (1.02)	63.4 (1.47)	32.0 (1.18)	60.7 (1.51)	25.7 (1.11)
English language learner (ELL) status											
ELL	62.3 (5.71)	57.8 (4.11)	45.8 (4.82)	15.0 (2.20)	‡ (†)	‡ (†)	73.4 (7.02)	34.9 (4.50)	20.8 (4.16)	31.3 (4.97)	11.2 (2.53)
Non-ELL	66.5 (1.75)	78.5 (1.07)	68.6 (1.44)	26.7 (1.41)	5.7 (0.86)	11.6 (0.73)	91.3 (0.98)	62.1 (1.47)	31.4 (1.18)	59.5 (1.50)	25.2 (1.11)
School type											
Traditional public	65.3 (1.76)	77.0 (1.20)	67.1 (1.57)	24.1 (1.43)	5.5 (0.85)	10.9 (0.71)	90.5 (1.11)	59.5 (1.42)	30.0 (1.22)	56.8 (1.44)	23.5 (1.10)
Public charter	— (†)	— (†)	— (†)	— (†)	— (†)	— (†)	— (†)	— (†)	— (†)	— (†)	— (†)
Private	79.1 (3.29)	92.3 (2.52)	81.9 (6.49)	53.8 (5.88)	7.8 ! (3.33)	18.2 (3.99)	98.2 (0.53)	86.6 (3.88)	45.1 (7.62)	85.4 (3.87)	41.5 (7.38)
Percentage of students eligible for free or reduced-price lunch											
0–25 percent	66.8 (2.64)	80.3 (1.47)	68.1 (2.36)	29.6 (2.41)	6.5 (1.53)	13.4 (1.32)	91.4 (1.53)	65.2 (2.51)	34.5 (2.05)	61.9 (2.59)	28.6 (1.83)
26–50 percent	64.8 (3.65)	72.5 (2.90)	67.2 (1.86)	19.1 (2.12)	3.5 (1.00)	8.8 (1.09)	93.4 (1.49)	56.0 (2.10)	26.3 (2.50)	55.0 (2.15)	19.1 (1.19)
51–75 percent	72.7 (3.97)	77.5 (3.48)	66.7 (5.53)	18.0 (2.97)	3.4 ! (1.62)	4.8 (1.11)	90.8 (3.02)	58.9 (3.11)	22.5 (1.75)	57.4 (3.47)	17.5 (1.85)
76–100 percent	81.7 (3.87)	83.1 (5.61)	68.1 (9.69)	23.9 (4.40)	‡ (†)	5.4 (1.05)	91.4 (5.08)	60.8 (9.48)	35.0 (6.03)	59.5 (9.38)	26.1 (5.80)

See notes at end of table.

Table 225.40. Percentage of public and private high school graduates taking selected mathematics and science courses in high school, by selected student and school characteristics: Selected years, 1990 through 2009—Continued

[Standard errors appear in parentheses]

Year and student or school characteristic	Mathematics						Science				
	Algebra II[1,2]	Geometry[1]	Algebra II/ trigonometry[3]	Analysis/ precalculus[3]	Statistics/ probability[3]	Calculus[1]	Biology[1]	Chemistry[1]	Physics[1]	Biology and chemistry[4]	Biology, chemistry, and physics[5]
1	2	3	4	5	6	7	8	9	10	11	12
2005											
Total[6]	68.4 (0.99)	83.8 (0.63)	71.3 (0.97)	29.4 (0.98)	7.7 (0.53)	13.6 (0.53)	92.5 (0.60)	66.4 (0.94)	32.9 (0.91)	64.3 (0.97)	27.4 (0.89)
Sex											
Male	66.8 (1.04)	81.9 (0.70)	68.0 (1.09)	28.0 (1.02)	7.7 (0.57)	14.0 (0.62)	91.0 (0.68)	62.7 (1.08)	34.9 (0.90)	60.3 (1.08)	28.2 (0.86)
Female	69.8 (1.06)	85.6 (0.66)	74.4 (0.98)	30.8 (1.05)	7.8 (0.55)	13.2 (0.58)	93.9 (0.58)	70.0 (0.99)	31.0 (1.09)	68.0 (1.03)	26.5 (1.10)
Race/ethnicity											
White	66.8 (1.17)	83.9 (0.79)	72.4 (1.17)	32.0 (1.18)	8.5 (0.65)	15.3 (0.61)	92.8 (0.67)	67.4 (1.06)	34.8 (0.87)	65.3 (1.10)	29.0 (0.85)
Black	75.4 (1.60)	85.0 (1.04)	69.3 (1.63)	17.9 (1.61)	5.8 (0.83)	5.5 (0.53)	93.7 (0.60)	63.6 (1.61)	25.8 (2.31)	62.0 (1.60)	21.3 (2.25)
Hispanic	70.2 (1.79)	81.0 (1.16)	63.1 (1.55)	20.4 (1.42)	3.4 (0.48)	6.4 (0.63)	89.2 (1.22)	59.3 (2.00)	23.4 (1.66)	57.2 (2.28)	18.8 (1.63)
Asian/Pacific Islander	65.4 (2.71)	87.1 (1.29)	79.5 (2.94)	48.8 (2.84)	12.9 (1.21)	30.0 (1.63)	92.4 (1.83)	79.7 (1.60)	50.3 (2.35)	75.5 (2.16)	42.9 (2.49)
American Indian/Alaska Native	70.1 (4.82)	73.8 (3.36)	67.2 (3.54)	15.8 (3.07)	‡ (†)	‡ (†)	91.5 (1.92)	48.9 (4.70)	18.1 (3.82)	47.6 (4.69)	‡ (†)
Student with disabilities (SD) status											
SD[7]	49.5 (2.05)	47.8 (1.83)	27.9 (1.67)	6.0 (0.71)	2.2 (0.46)	2.0 (0.54)	71.6 (1.58)	26.6 (1.88)	13.2 (1.27)	24.8 (1.75)	6.6 (0.74)
Non-SD	69.9 (1.04)	87.0 (0.68)	75.2 (0.98)	31.6 (1.07)	8.3 (0.56)	14.7 (0.56)	94.4 (0.57)	69.9 (0.92)	34.5 (0.94)	67.8 (0.96)	29.0 (0.93)
English language learner (ELL) status											
ELL	63.7 (2.75)	70.1 (2.10)	48.0 (2.97)	13.8 (1.85)	3.9 (0.88)	6.1 (1.79)	81.4 (1.96)	46.1 (2.61)	20.2 (2.40)	43.0 (2.85)	13.8 (2.02)
Non-ELL	68.4 (1.00)	84.3 (0.67)	72.0 (1.00)	30.0 (1.02)	7.9 (0.54)	13.8 (0.54)	92.9 (0.62)	67.0 (0.97)	33.2 (0.93)	64.9 (1.01)	27.6 (0.91)
School type											
Traditional public	67.6 (1.09)	83.0 (0.71)	69.3 (1.07)	27.6 (0.92)	7.7 (0.55)	12.5 (0.53)	92.1 (0.59)	64.2 (0.87)	30.6 (0.94)	62.0 (0.85)	24.8 (0.86)
Public charter	84.5 (5.72)	78.1 (7.06)	69.3 (11.47)	‡ (†)	‡ (†)	‡ (†)	91.6 (2.47)	72.2 (11.52)	36.7 ! (13.63)	67.0 (10.91)	33.9 ! (13.67)
Private	74.4 (3.27)	91.2 (1.41)	89.6 (1.88)	45.3 (3.93)	8.3 (1.84)	23.9 (2.45)	96.1 (2.31)	86.8 (2.79)	53.8 (2.46)	85.1 (3.10)	49.9 (2.72)
Percentage of students eligible for free or reduced-price lunch											
0–25 percent	65.4 (1.85)	82.2 (1.41)	70.9 (1.73)	34.0 (1.64)	10.2 (0.97)	15.7 (0.92)	92.8 (1.01)	68.4 (1.34)	35.3 (1.40)	65.9 (1.39)	28.7 (1.32)
26–50 percent	69.5 (1.93)	84.2 (1.04)	69.8 (1.37)	23.4 (1.30)	6.7 (0.93)	10.8 (0.58)	93.0 (0.97)	61.0 (1.60)	26.9 (1.44)	59.1 (1.72)	21.8 (1.42)
51–75 percent	74.3 (2.78)	82.2 (1.99)	66.3 (2.80)	19.2 (2.26)	3.3 (0.91)	6.9 (0.86)	86.7 (2.05)	57.0 (2.80)	20.9 (2.38)	54.1 (2.90)	16.1 (2.06)
76–100 percent	75.1 (3.73)	88.2 (1.61)	69.4 (3.05)	18.2 (2.90)	2.8 ! (0.87)	4.9 (0.90)	90.2 (3.04)	67.6 (3.04)	21.2 (3.16)	64.1 (3.60)	17.8 (2.80)
2009											
Total[6]	68.9 (0.94)	88.3 (0.53)	75.8 (0.92)	35.3 (0.84)	10.8 (0.49)	15.9 (0.66)	95.6 (0.40)	70.4 (0.75)	36.1 (1.01)	68.3 (0.77)	30.1 (0.87)
Sex											
Male	68.5 (0.98)	86.6 (0.75)	73.8 (1.09)	33.8 (1.02)	10.7 (0.51)	16.1 (0.75)	94.9 (0.45)	67.4 (0.95)	39.2 (1.29)	65.0 (0.91)	31.9 (1.08)
Female	69.3 (1.01)	89.9 (0.54)	77.8 (0.91)	36.6 (0.89)	10.9 (0.58)	15.7 (0.69)	96.2 (0.43)	73.4 (0.76)	33.0 (0.92)	71.4 (0.84)	28.3 (0.85)
Race/ethnicity											
White	67.0 (1.09)	88.8 (0.73)	77.4 (1.08)	37.9 (0.98)	11.6 (0.64)	17.5 (0.69)	95.6 (0.51)	71.5 (0.87)	37.6 (1.24)	68.9 (0.93)	31.4 (1.04)
Black	77.2 (1.26)	88.4 (1.07)	70.6 (1.69)	22.7 (1.29)	7.9 (1.04)	6.1 (0.59)	96.3 (0.56)	65.3 (1.80)	26.9 (1.72)	64.3 (1.74)	21.9 (1.48)
Hispanic	75.4 (1.60)	87.0 (0.96)	71.4 (1.81)	26.5 (1.36)	7.5 (0.77)	8.6 (0.64)	94.8 (0.67)	65.7 (1.41)	28.6 (1.33)	64.2 (1.45)	22.7 (1.19)
Asian/Pacific Islander	53.3 (3.52)	86.1 (1.47)	83.0 (2.59)	60.5 (2.88)	17.6 (1.69)	42.2 (3.11)	95.8 (0.95)	84.8 (1.72)	61.1 (2.35)	82.7 (1.93)	54.4 (2.77)
American Indian/Alaska Native	74.8 (5.85)	81.6 (4.09)	66.6 (4.12)	18.5 (2.98)	‡ (†)	‡ (†)	94.5 (1.64)	44.5 (4.78)	19.8 (3.89)	43.9 (4.77)	13.6 (2.87)
Student with disabilities (SD) status											
SD[7]	56.0 (1.63)	61.1 (1.82)	39.5 (1.67)	9.7 (1.26)	3.9 (0.57)	3.0 (0.55)	82.4 (1.30)	35.4 (1.69)	19.3 (1.67)	33.8 (1.51)	12.0 (1.51)
Non-SD	70.1 (0.97)	90.7 (0.53)	79.1 (0.93)	37.6 (0.90)	11.4 (0.53)	17.1 (0.71)	96.8 (0.41)	73.6 (0.75)	37.6 (1.06)	71.4 (0.79)	31.7 (0.94)
English language learner (ELL) status											
ELL	73.3 (2.33)	76.2 (1.99)	58.1 (2.54)	19.4 (2.36)	4.4 (1.03)	4.7 (0.87)	86.9 (2.12)	47.4 (2.99)	23.2 (2.41)	43.8 (3.03)	15.4 (2.02)
Non-ELL	68.8 (0.95)	88.5 (0.54)	76.2 (0.93)	35.6 (0.86)	10.9 (0.50)	16.2 (0.67)	95.7 (0.41)	70.9 (0.77)	36.3 (1.02)	68.7 (0.79)	30.3 (0.89)
School type											
Traditional public	68.2 (0.99)	88.1 (0.53)	74.9 (0.96)	34.0 (0.97)	10.7 (0.51)	15.4 (0.73)	95.3 (0.44)	68.9 (0.75)	34.6 (1.03)	66.9 (0.78)	28.8 (0.83)
Public charter	79.0 (4.21)	86.9 (3.57)	77.8 (6.64)	34.1 (9.95)	‡ (†)	‡ (†)	94.0 (1.92)	56.8 (11.13)	40.0 (7.36)	55.7 (10.77)	23.2 ! (7.52)
Private	74.7 (2.95)	90.0 (3.98)	84.6 (4.01)	47.5 (3.76)	12.5 (1.86)	23.3 (2.05)	98.6 (0.28)	87.4 (1.87)	49.5 (3.73)	83.3 (2.67)	43.9 (3.77)
Percentage of students eligible for free or reduced-price lunch											
0–25 percent	61.3 (1.72)	89.7 (0.82)	80.1 (1.75)	43.1 (1.88)	14.8 (1.03)	22.6 (1.37)	96.4 (1.03)	76.3 (1.58)	46.5 (2.02)	74.9 (1.70)	40.4 (2.07)
26–50 percent	70.9 (1.82)	88.4 (0.87)	74.7 (1.38)	29.7 (1.44)	8.6 (0.80)	11.8 (0.76)	94.5 (0.98)	64.0 (1.52)	27.6 (1.79)	61.6 (1.59)	22.2 (1.54)
51–75 percent	75.8 (1.85)	87.4 (1.45)	69.3 (3.35)	25.4 (1.52)	7.5 (1.14)	9.8 (1.05)	95.6 (0.72)	65.6 (2.03)	29.4 (2.56)	64.2 (1.97)	22.7 (2.12)
76–100 percent	80.1 (3.75)	88.8 (2.26)	70.7 (4.02)	25.5 (2.80)	5.1 (1.08)	7.5 (1.34)	95.6 (1.42)	69.4 (3.68)	26.6 (3.07)	68.2 (3.69)	22.8 (2.97)

See notes at end of table.

Table 225.40. Percentage of public and private high school graduates taking selected mathematics and science courses in high school, by selected student and school characteristics: Selected years, 1990 through 2009—Continued

[Standard errors appear in parentheses]

Year and student or school characteristic	Mathematics						Science				
	Algebra I[1,2]	Geometry[1]	Algebra II/ trigonometry[3]	Analysis/ precalculus[3]	Statistics/ probability[3]	Calculus[1]	Biology[1]	Chemistry[1]	Physics[1]	Biology and chemistry[4]	Biology, chemistry, and physics[5]
1	2	3	4	5	6	7	8	9	10	11	12
School locale											
City	72.5 (1.85)	89.1 (0.91)	74.9 (2.06)	36.7 (1.98)	10.6 (0.91)	15.5 (1.42)	96.4 (0.53)	74.0 (1.59)	38.8 (1.99)	70.8 (1.97)	31.6 (1.97)
Suburban	62.8 (1.62)	89.4 (1.27)	78.7 (1.79)	39.0 (1.71)	13.1 (0.97)	19.5 (1.12)	97.1 (0.30)	76.7 (1.14)	43.8 (1.42)	75.4 (1.04)	38.6 (1.21)
Town	76.9 (2.25)	86.4 (1.08)	71.4 (3.00)	30.1 (2.40)	8.4 (1.25)	10.7 (1.02)	92.2 (2.23)	62.3 (1.84)	24.0 (2.45)	60.4 (1.87)	18.9 (1.94)
Rural	70.2 (2.19)	86.3 (0.95)	74.5 (1.38)	30.0 (1.35)	8.6 (1.12)	13.5 (0.87)	93.7 (1.66)	59.6 (1.82)	26.0 (1.95)	57.2 (1.77)	19.7 (1.41)

—Not available.
†Not applicable.
#Rounds to zero.
!Interpret data with caution. The coefficient of variation (CV) for this estimate is between 30 and 50 percent.
‡Reporting standards not met (too few cases for a reliable estimate).
[1]Percentages are for students who earned at least one Carnegie credit.
[2]Excludes prealgebra.
[3]Percentages are for students who earned at least one-half of a Carnegie credit in a course that includes a focus on at least one of the listed content areas.
[4]Percentages are for students who earned at least one Carnegie credit each in biology and chemistry.
[5]Percentages are for students who earned at least one Carnegie credit each in biology, chemistry, and physics.

[6]Includes other racial/ethnic groups not shown separately, as well as students for whom information on race/ethnicity or sex was missing.
[7]SD data include both students with an Individualized Education Plan (IEP) and students with a plan under Section 504 of the Rehabilitation Act (a "504 plan"). IEPs are only for students who require specialized instruction, whereas 504 plans apply to students who require accommodations but may not require specialized instruction.
NOTE: For a transcript to be included in the analyses, it had to meet three requirements: (1) the graduate received either a standard or honors diploma, (2) the graduate's transcript contained 16 or more Carnegie credits, and (3) the graduate's transcript contained more than 0 Carnegie credits in English courses. Race categories exclude persons of Hispanic ethnicity.
SOURCE: U.S. Department of Education, National Center for Education Statistics, 1990, 2000, 2005, and 2009 High School Transcript Study (HSTS). (This table was prepared September 2012.)

Table 225.50. Percentage of public and private high school graduates earning minimum credits in selected combinations of academic courses, by sex and race/ethnicity: Selected years, 1982 through 2009

[Standard errors appear in parentheses]

Year of graduation and course combination taken[1]	All students[2]		Sex				Race/ethnicity								
			Male		Female		White		Black		Hispanic		Asian/Pacific Islander		American Indian/ Alaska Native	
1	2		3		4		5		6		7		8		9	
1982 graduates																
4 Eng, 3 SS, 3 Sci, 3 Math, and 2 FL[3]..	9.5	(0.57)	9.1	(0.70)	9.9	(0.71)	10.9	(0.69)	5.2	(1.02)	3.9	(0.57)	17.0	(2.49)	‡	(†)
4 Eng, 3 SS, 3 Sci, 3 Math...................	14.3	(0.66)	15.2	(0.86)	13.4	(0.79)	15.9	(0.79)	11.0	(1.39)	6.7	(0.79)	21.1	(2.65)	8.1 !	(3.02)
4 Eng, 3 SS, 2 Sci, 2 Math...................	31.5	(1.07)	31.7	(1.26)	31.3	(1.22)	32.4	(1.21)	30.8	(2.32)	25.6	(1.76)	32.0	(3.40)	23.6	(5.39)
1987 graduates																
4 Eng, 3 SS, 3 Sci, 3 Math, and 2 FL[3]..	18.1	(0.91)	18.0	(1.13)	18.3	(1.01)	19.0	(1.10)	12.7	(1.15)	10.8	(1.70)	35.7	(4.49)	4.9	(1.40)
4 Eng, 3 SS, 3 Sci, 3 Math...................	24.8	(1.03)	25.9	(1.27)	23.7	(1.07)	26.1	(1.21)	19.6	(1.99)	14.5	(1.69)	39.8	(4.51)	24.3	(3.69)
4 Eng, 3 SS, 2 Sci, 2 Math...................	48.1	(1.74)	48.0	(2.22)	48.4	(1.56)	48.1	(2.15)	48.3	(2.63)	43.9	(1.92)	57.9	(4.82)	61.8	(5.56)
1990 graduates																
4 Eng, 3 SS, 3 Sci, 3 Math, and 2 FL[3]..	29.9	(1.26)	28.8	(1.38)	31.0	(1.36)	31.7	(1.46)	22.9	(2.27)	25.4	(2.41)	42.6	(2.95)	9.9 !	(3.70)
4 Eng, 3 SS, 3 Sci, 3 Math...................	38.2	(1.50)	38.5	(1.69)	37.9	(1.54)	39.2	(1.63)	39.0	(3.57)	29.8	(2.51)	47.4	(3.04)	19.2	(4.70)
4 Eng, 3 SS, 2 Sci, 2 Math...................	65.5	(1.96)	64.3	(2.09)	66.4	(1.98)	64.9	(2.28)	71.3	(3.00)	63.7	(3.01)	69.1	(3.90)	46.3	(6.39)
1994 graduates																
4 Eng, 3 SS, 3 Sci, 3 Math, and 2 FL[3]..	39.0	(1.12)	35.0	(1.11)	42.7	(1.33)	41.6	(1.32)	29.6	(1.52)	35.6	(2.94)	50.1	(2.39)	22.5	(4.31)
4 Eng, 3 SS, 3 Sci, 3 Math...................	49.3	(1.45)	47.0	(1.45)	51.5	(1.58)	52.4	(1.67)	43.7	(2.39)	40.3	(3.25)	54.9	(2.46)	46.0	(3.30)
4 Eng, 3 SS, 2 Sci, 2 Math...................	73.9	(1.50)	71.2	(1.63)	76.4	(1.46)	75.1	(1.69)	74.5	(2.32)	74.7	(2.61)	72.3	(3.62)	76.3	(3.60)
1998 graduates																
4 Eng, 3 SS, 3 Sci, 3 Math, and 2 FL[3]..	44.2	(1.92)	40.5	(2.19)	48.2	(2.05)	46.2	(2.16)	40.0	(3.41)	32.0	(2.94)	57.8	(4.51)	28.3	(4.53)
4 Eng, 3 SS, 3 Sci, 3 Math...................	55.0	(2.44)	52.9	(2.64)	57.8	(2.48)	56.8	(2.69)	55.6	(4.39)	40.0	(3.28)	66.1	(5.69)	40.0	(4.73)
4 Eng, 3 SS, 2 Sci, 2 Math...................	74.5	(2.18)	72.8	(2.34)	77.0	(2.14)	74.7	(2.64)	76.0	(3.21)	70.1	(2.57)	79.5	(4.76)	76.4	(5.21)
2000 graduates																
4 Eng, 3 SS, 3 Sci, 3 Math, and 2 FL[3]..	47.8	(1.53)	41.5	(1.68)	53.4	(1.65)	48.9	(1.60)	45.6	(2.27)	40.3	(5.47)	58.2	(3.48)	26.8	(3.63)
4 Eng, 3 SS, 3 Sci, 3 Math...................	58.6	(1.64)	54.4	(1.70)	62.3	(1.75)	59.2	(1.74)	64.1	(2.51)	48.3	(5.74)	62.7	(3.44)	42.5	(5.84)
4 Eng, 3 SS, 2 Sci, 2 Math...................	78.2	(1.60)	74.9	(1.88)	81.2	(1.43)	78.3	(1.85)	82.5	(2.26)	75.4	(3.16)	75.0	(3.27)	72.6	(4.48)
2005 graduates																
4 Eng, 3 SS, 3 Sci, 3 Math, and 2 FL[3]..	54.7	(0.96)	49.0	(1.14)	60.1	(0.94)	55.5	(1.19)	54.3	(1.87)	46.3	(2.08)	66.7	(2.10)	38.1	(3.37)
4 Eng, 3 SS, 3 Sci, 3 Math...................	67.4	(1.02)	63.5	(1.22)	71.0	(0.94)	68.5	(1.29)	72.3	(1.76)	53.5	(2.20)	72.2	(2.05)	60.9	(3.40)
4 Eng, 3 SS, 2 Sci, 2 Math...................	83.0	(1.02)	80.3	(1.19)	85.4	(0.94)	82.1	(1.34)	89.7	(0.91)	79.6	(1.38)	85.0	(1.68)	81.0	(3.10)
2009 graduates																
4 Eng, 3 SS, 3 Sci, 3 Math, and 2 FL[3]..	61.8	(0.84)	57.4	(1.06)	66.0	(0.82)	62.4	(0.94)	58.4	(1.71)	58.4	(1.65)	73.1	(2.28)	43.0	(3.44)
4 Eng, 3 SS, 3 Sci, 3 Math...................	74.3	(0.81)	72.1	(0.96)	76.4	(0.77)	75.0	(1.04)	78.1	(1.20)	67.2	(1.49)	76.9	(2.08)	64.7	(4.23)
4 Eng, 3 SS, 2 Sci, 2 Math...................	87.7	(0.74)	86.2	(0.82)	89.1	(0.73)	86.8	(0.97)	92.0	(0.63)	88.0	(0.87)	86.1	(1.52)	86.6	(2.99)

†Not applicable.
!Interpret data with caution. The coefficient of variation (CV) for this estimate is between 30 and 50 percent.
‡Reporting standards not met. The coefficient of variation (CV) for this estimate is 50 percent or greater.
[1]Eng = English; SS = social studies; Sci = science; and FL = foreign language.
[2]Totals include other racial/ethnic groups not separately shown.
[3]In 1983, the National Commission on Excellence in Education recommended that all college-bound high school students take these courses plus 0.5 credits of computer science as a minimum.

NOTE: Data differ slightly from figures appearing in other NCES reports because of differences in taxonomies and case exclusion criteria. Race categories exclude persons of Hispanic ethnicity.
SOURCE: U.S. Department of Education, National Center for Education Statistics, High School and Beyond Longitudinal Study of 1980 Sophomores (HS&B-So:80/82), "High School Transcript Study"; and 1987, 1990, 1994, 1998, 2000, 2005, and 2009 High School Transcript Study (HSTS). (This table was prepared October 2011.)

Table 225.60. Number and percentage of public high school graduates taking dual credit, Advanced Placement (AP), and International Baccalaureate (IB) courses in high school and average credits earned, by selected student and school characteristics: 2000, 2005, and 2009

[Standard errors appear in parentheses]

Year and student or school characteristic	Number of graduates who earned credits in dual credit, AP, or IB courses — Total	Dual credit courses[1]	AP courses	IB courses	Percentage of graduates who earned credits in dual credit, AP, or IB courses — Total	Dual credit courses[1]	AP courses	IB courses	Average total credits[2] in dual credit, AP, and IB courses per graduate taking such courses
1	2	3	4	5	6	7	8	9	10
2000, all public high school graduates	747,000 (42,700)	— (†)	728,000 (39,200)	35,000 ! (15,100)	27.6 (1.59)	— (†)	26.9 (1.48)	1.3 ! (0.56)	0.60 (0.048)
Sex									
Male	325,000 (20,800)	—	317,000 (19,700)	16,000 ! (7,200)	24.7 (1.60)	—	24.1 (1.51)	1.2 ! (0.55)	0.55 (0.049)
Female	422,000 (23,700)	—	410,000 (21,300)	19,000 ! (8,100)	30.4 (1.70)	—	29.5 (1.55)	1.4 ! (0.58)	0.66 (0.050)
Race/ethnicity									
White	513,000 (31,200)	—	499,000 (27,000)	‡ (†)	27.7 (1.70)	—	26.9 (1.50)	1.4 ! (0.69)	0.61 (0.050)
Black	69,000 (7,300)	—	68,000 (7,400)	2,000 ! (1,000)	19.0 (2.08)	—	18.7 (2.09)	0.5 ! (0.26)	0.36 (0.048)
Hispanic	96,000 (13,500)	—	96,000 (13,500)	1,000 ! (600)	28.9 (3.89)	—	28.7 (3.89)	0.4 ! (0.17)	0.51 (0.074)
Asian/Pacific Islander	62,000 (6,700)	—	60,000 (6,400)	‡ (†)	50.6 (3.32)	—	48.6 (3.29)	4.6 ! (2.28)	1.61 (0.216)
American Indian/Alaska Native	4,000 (1,000)	—	4,000 (1,000)	‡ (†)	17.4 (3.02)	—	17.4 (3.02)	‡ (†)	0.21 (0.036)
School enrollment size									
Less than 500	47,000 (11,100)	—	47,000 (11,100)	‡ (†)	13.2 (3.35)	—	13.1 (3.35)	‡ (†)	0.19 ! (0.060)
500 to 1,499	313,000 (36,100)	—	308,000 (35,700)	‡ (†)	26.5 (2.17)	—	26.1 (2.15)	‡ (†)	0.53 (0.062)
1,500 or more	386,000 (44,500)	—	373,000 (43,200)	‡ (†)	33.0 (2.22)	—	31.8 (2.24)	2.3 ! (1.16)	0.80 (0.081)
Region									
Northeast	102,000 (12,900)	—	102,000 (12,700)	‡ (†)	23.6 (3.43)	—	23.5 (3.39)	‡ (†)	0.42 (0.070)
Midwest	164,000 (24,200)	—	152,000 (18,000)	‡ (†)	23.8 (3.55)	—	22.0 (2.73)	‡ (†)	0.49 (0.107)
South	296,000 (34,400)	—	294,000 (34,300)	‡ (†)	29.8 (2.60)	—	29.6 (2.60)	‡ (†)	0.73 (0.085)
West	184,000 (15,700)	—	180,000 (15,400)	‡ (†)	31.2 (2.33)	—	30.5 (2.28)	‡ (†)	0.65 (0.055)
Percent of students eligible for free or reduced-price lunch									
0 to 25 percent	386,000 (36,700)	—	374,000 (36,100)	‡ (†)	28.4 (1.89)	—	27.6 (1.84)	‡ (†)	0.65 (0.066)
26 to 50 percent	140,000 (23,500)	—	139,000 (23,300)	‡ (†)	24.5 (2.88)	—	24.2 (2.88)	‡ (†)	0.49 (0.065)
More than 50 percent	93,000 (21,700)	—	93,000 (21,700)	‡ (†)	26.5 (4.51)	—	26.4 (4.51)	‡ (†)	0.50 (0.086)
School did not participate or data missing	128,000 (23,700)	—	122,000 (22,400)	‡ (†)	29.7 (4.41)	—	28.4 (4.20)	‡ (†)	0.70 (0.154)
2005, all public high school graduates	842,000 (23,800)	216,000 (14,900)	695,000 (20,700)	44,000 (12,600)	34.9 (0.79)	8.9 (0.60)	28.8 (0.68)	1.8 (0.53)	1.04 (0.043)
Sex									
Male	367,000 (12,100)	98,000 (7,600)	294,000 (10,200)	21,000 ! (6,400)	31.2 (0.83)	8.4 (0.63)	25.0 (0.70)	1.8 ! (0.55)	0.94 (0.046)
Female	475,000 (14,100)	117,000 (8,000)	401,000 (12,500)	22,000 (6,500)	38.3 (0.89)	9.5 (0.64)	32.3 (0.78)	1.8 (0.53)	1.13 (0.045)
Race/ethnicity									
White	603,000 (20,900)	165,000 (12,500)	490,000 (18,700)	30,000 ! (9,900)	36.7 (0.95)	10.0 (0.73)	29.8 (0.86)	1.8 ! (0.60)	1.08 (0.047)
Black	72,000 (4,700)	16,000 (2,600)	60,000 (4,300)	5,000 (1,100)	21.8 (1.09)	4.7 (0.80)	18.3 (0.97)	1.4 (0.34)	0.55 (0.044)
Hispanic	100,000 (6,400)	23,000 (3,300)	84,000 (5,800)	4,000 ! (1,300)	33.8 (1.43)	7.7 (1.10)	28.5 (1.29)	1.3 ! (0.45)	0.93 (0.073)
Asian/Pacific Islander	56,000 (5,100)	10,000 (1,400)	51,000 (4,800)	4,000 ! (2,000)	52.0 (2.37)	9.2 (1.25)	47.2 (2.25)	3.9 ! (1.79)	2.12 (0.174)
American Indian/Alaska Native	5,000 (900)	1,000 ! (400)	4,000 (800)	‡ (†)	22.3 (3.83)	5.6 ! (2.00)	17.4 (3.45)	‡ (†)	0.51 (0.131)
Combined Black and Hispanic enrollment in school									
Less than 5 percent	231,000 (19,200)	60,000 (9,500)	189,000 (17,100)	‡ (†)	31.4 (1.62)	8.2 (1.20)	25.7 (1.49)	‡ (†)	0.77 (0.061)
5 to 50 percent	452,000 (23,400)	126,000 (12,400)	363,000 (18,800)	31,000 ! (11,100)	38.1 (1.29)	10.6 (1.04)	30.6 (0.91)	2.6 ! (0.94)	1.22 (0.075)
More than 50 percent	152,000 (11,400)	24,000 (4,800)	138,000 (10,600)	10,000 ! (3,200)	31.8 (1.30)	5.1 (0.94)	28.9 (1.23)	2.1 ! (0.68)	0.96 (0.069)
School enrollment size									
Less than 500	65,000 (8,900)	36,000 (7,300)	41,000 (6,200)	‡ (†)	25.6 (2.73)	14.1 (2.66)	16.2 (1.89)	‡ (†)	0.83 (0.230)
500 to 1,499	309,000 (21,200)	78,000 (9,200)	252,000 (17,500)	19,000 ! (8,000)	33.6 (1.30)	8.5 (0.93)	27.4 (1.13)	2.1 ! (0.83)	1.00 (0.077)
1,500 or more	384,000 (25,200)	81,000 (12,100)	331,000 (21,600)	21,000 ! (9,400)	38.7 (1.38)	8.2 (1.14)	33.4 (1.14)	2.1 ! (0.95)	1.16 (0.061)
Region									
Northeast	128,000 (9,600)	13,000 ! (4,900)	119,000 (8,300)	‡ (†)	26.6 (1.70)	2.7 ! (1.01)	24.6 (1.43)	‡ (†)	0.80 (0.079)
Midwest	196,000 (10,500)	53,000 (7,100)	158,000 (10,700)	‡ (†)	34.7 (1.62)	9.4 (1.32)	27.9 (1.59)	‡ (†)	0.87 (0.062)
South	300,000 (15,500)	92,000 (12,200)	241,000 (10,300)	24,000 ! (8,300)	36.7 (1.42)	11.3 (1.38)	29.5 (0.94)	2.9 ! (1.01)	1.20 (0.100)
West	218,000 (15,100)	57,000 (10,300)	178,000 (10,500)	17,000 ! (8,000)	39.8 (1.98)	10.4 (1.72)	32.4 (1.43)	3.1 ! (1.45)	1.17 (0.089)

See notes at end of table.

Table 225.60. Number and percentage of public high school graduates taking dual credit, Advanced Placement (AP), and International Baccalaureate (IB) courses in high school and average credits earned, by selected student and school characteristics: 2000, 2005, and 2009—Continued

[Standard errors appear in parentheses]

Year and student or school characteristic	Number of graduates who earned credits in dual credit, AP, or IB courses				Percentage of graduates who earned credits in dual credit, AP, or IB courses				Average total credits[2] in dual credit, AP, and IB courses per graduate taking such courses
	Total	Dual credit courses[1]	AP courses	IB courses	Total	Dual credit courses[1]	AP courses	IB courses	
	2	3	4	5	6	7	8	9	10
Percent of students eligible for free or reduced-price lunch									
0 to 25 percent	410,000 (26,700)	102,000 (14,800)	344,000 (23,200)	22,000! (10,500)	39.3 (1.36)	9.8 (1.32)	32.9 (1.27)	2.1! (1.00)	1.24 (0.083)
26 to 50 percent	223,000 (19,400)	67,000 (10,700)	174,000 (13,900)	13,000! (4,300)	32.0 (1.55)	9.6 (1.31)	24.9 (1.16)	1.9! (0.62)	0.91 (0.058)
More than 50 percent	103,000 (10,100)	22,000 (4,900)	89,000 (8,700)	6,000! (2,500)	28.3 (1.83)	5.9 (1.32)	24.5 (1.46)	1.6! (0.69)	0.77 (0.066)
School did not participate or data missing	105,000 (13,900)	25,000 (5,500)	88,000 (12,300)	‡ (†)	34.4 (2.39)	8.2 (1.72)	28.8 (2.04)	‡ (†)	0.94 (0.092)
2009, all public high school graduates	1,104,000 (36,400)	249,000 (20,700)	968,000 (33,900)	50,000 (10,500)	41.4 (1.00)	9.3 (0.76)	36.3 (0.94)	1.9 (0.40)	1.39 (0.051)
Sex									
Male	477,000 (17,900)	110,000 (10,800)	413,000 (16,200)	21,000 (4,900)	36.8 (1.05)	8.5 (0.80)	31.9 (0.98)	1.7 (0.38)	1.24 (0.057)
Female	628,000 (20,100)	139,000 (10,700)	554,000 (19,100)	29,000 (5,800)	45.8 (1.07)	10.1 (0.78)	40.4 (1.01)	2.1 (0.43)	1.53 (0.049)
Race/ethnicity									
White	702,000 (25,700)	160,000 (16,300)	617,000 (23,700)	29,000 (7,100)	42.5 (1.04)	9.7 (1.00)	37.3 (0.95)	1.8 (0.43)	1.41 (0.049)
Black	106,000 (6,600)	25,000 (3,700)	86,000 (5,100)	7,000 (1,700)	27.3 (1.50)	6.4 (0.99)	22.2 (1.00)	1.7 (0.44)	0.75 (0.054)
Hispanic	170,000 (9,300)	46,000 (5,900)	144,000 (7,800)	7,000 (2,000)	39.8 (1.45)	10.8 (1.18)	33.8 (1.30)	1.6 (0.47)	1.17 (0.059)
Asian/Pacific Islander	115,000 (14,800)	15,000 (2,300)	111,000 (14,800)	7,000 (1,900)	69.1 (2.36)	9.2 (1.46)	66.3 (2.56)	4.1! (1.23)	3.25 (0.263)
American Indian/Alaska Native	4,000 (900)	1,000! (400)	3,000 (900)	‡ (†)	25.0 (3.97)	7.0! (2.20)	20.3 (3.74)	‡ (†)	0.79 (0.187)
Combined Black and Hispanic enrollment in school									
Less than 5 percent	239,000 (28,100)	45,000 (13,300)	209,000 (25,500)	‡ (†)	35.9 (2.27)	6.8 (1.92)	31.5 (2.13)	‡ (†)	1.01 (0.102)
5 to 50 percent	601,000 (38,100)	132,000 (15,000)	533,000 (35,200)	32,000 (8,400)	45.4 (1.36)	10.0 (0.96)	40.3 (1.34)	2.5 (0.62)	1.64 (0.092)
More than 50 percent	265,000 (17,900)	72,000 (10,800)	225,000 (15,900)	13,000 (3,600)	39.0 (1.55)	10.6 (1.47)	33.1 (1.34)	1.9 (0.52)	1.26 (0.063)
School enrollment size									
Less than 500	93,000 (12,500)	46,000 (9,400)	61,000 (9,000)	‡ (†)	28.2 (3.13)	13.9 (2.77)	18.3 (2.19)	‡ (†)	0.90 (0.199)
500 to 1,499	355,000 (28,300)	71,000 (11,500)	314,000 (27,900)	6,000! (2,100)	36.8 (1.50)	7.4 (1.11)	32.5 (1.73)	0.7! (0.21)	1.13! (0.100)
1,500 or more	551,000 (32,800)	111,000 (16,200)	500,000 (30,600)	35,000 (8,600)	47.6 (1.24)	9.6 (1.40)	43.1 (1.14)	3.0 (0.70)	1.71 (0.066)
School locale									
City	354,000 (27,500)	81,000 (10,200)	311,000 (24,300)	28,000 (8,100)	48.1 (2.03)	11.0 (1.26)	42.3 (1.78)	3.8 (1.05)	1.72 (0.105)
Suburb	434,000 (26,300)	81,000 (14,800)	396,000 (25,300)	13,000 (3,200)	44.4 (1.52)	8.3 (1.51)	40.6 (1.51)	1.4 (0.33)	1.60 (0.102)
Town	120,000 (14,800)	31,000 (6,900)	101,000 (13,700)	‡ (†)	35.8 (2.05)	9.4 (1.88)	30.3 (2.06)	‡ (†)	0.99 (0.073)
Rural	197,000 (17,100)	56,000 (8,000)	159,000 (16,700)	‡ (†)	31.7 (2.02)	9.0 (1.47)	25.7 (1.77)	‡ (†)	0.89 (0.064)
Region									
Northeast	220,000 (17,600)	46,000 (13,500)	198,000 (15,900)	5,000! (1,800)	40.9 (2.54)	8.5 (2.52)	37.0 (2.20)	0.9! (0.34)	1.28! (0.120)
Midwest	224,000 (13,500)	40,000 (8,000)	194,000 (12,500)	‡ (†)	35.4 (2.00)	6.4 (1.30)	30.6 (1.86)	‡ (†)	0.98 (0.078)
South	385,000 (17,100)	128,000 (12,400)	320,000 (16,800)	16,000 (4,500)	43.8 (1.24)	14.5 (1.37)	36.4 (1.30)	1.9 (0.53)	1.64 (0.084)
West	275,000 (25,800)	35,000 (7,200)	255,000 (25,200)	17,000! (5,800)	44.7 (2.34)	5.7 (1.14)	41.4 (2.41)	2.8! (0.92)	1.54! (0.165)
Percent of students eligible for free or reduced-price lunch									
0 to 25 percent	481,000 (39,800)	91,000 (16,000)	442,000 (37,100)	14,000! (6,400)	48.8 (1.83)	9.3 (1.56)	44.9 (1.72)	1.5! (0.63)	1.75! (0.108)
26 to 50 percent	311,000 (24,700)	77,000 (11,900)	261,000 (21,600)	18,000! (5,700)	37.1 (1.41)	9.2 (1.25)	31.3 (1.40)	2.1! (0.69)	1.17! (0.058)
More than 50 percent	193,000 (16,100)	51,000 (8,400)	160,000 (12,900)	16,000! (5,900)	34.4 (1.92)	9.1 (1.33)	28.6 (1.64)	2.8! (1.02)	1.05! (0.083)
School did not participate or data missing	120,000 (17,500)	30,000 (7,600)	104,000 (16,000)	‡ (†)	42.1 (2.84)	10.4 (2.50)	36.5 (2.42)	‡ (†)	1.44 (0.214)

—Not available.
†Not applicable.
!Interpret data with caution. The coefficient of variation (CV) for this estimate is between 30 and 50 percent.
‡Reporting standards not met. Either there are too few cases for a reliable estimate or the coefficient of variation (CV) is 50 percent or greater.
[1]Dual credit courses are those in which high school students can earn both high school and postsecondary credits for the same course. For 2009, includes some courses for which college credits were conditional upon the student meeting additional requirements. For example, one school offered a consumer economics course for which the student earned college credits only if the student later attended that college and took an advanced consumer economics course there. If the student did not attend that college and take the advanced course, then no college credits would be earned for the course (only high school credits would be earned). In 2009, such conditional college credit courses made up an unweighted 15 percent of the dual credit courses in the sample.

[2]Credits are shown in Carnegie units. The Carnegie unit is a standard unit of measurement that represents one credit for the completion of a 1-year course.
NOTE: For a transcript to be included in the analyses, it had to meet three requirements: (1) the graduate graduated with either a standard or honors diploma, (2) the graduate's transcript contained 16 or more Carnegie credits, and (3) the graduate's transcript contained more than 0 Carnegie credits in English courses. Race categories exclude persons of Hispanic ethnicity. Totals include other racial/ethnic groups not separately shown. Percentages are based on unrounded numbers. Each student is counted only once in each column, regardless of the number of courses taken. Students are counted only once in the total columns even if they earned credits in more than one category—e.g., a student may take both AP courses and dual credit courses, or a single course may fall into both the AP and the dual credit categories. Detail may not sum to totals because of rounding.
SOURCE: U.S. Department of Education, National Center for Education Statistics, 2000, 2005, and 2009 High School Transcript Study (HSTS). (This table was prepared November 2012.)

Table 225.70. Number and percentage of high school graduates who took foreign language courses in high school and average number of credits earned, by language and number of credits: 2000, 2005, and 2009

[Standard errors appear in parentheses]

Language and number of credits	2000						2005						2009					
	Number of graduates (in thousands)		Percent of graduates		Average credits[1]		Number of graduates (in thousands)		Percent of graduates		Average credits[1]		Number of graduates (in thousands)		Percent of graduates		Average credits[1]	
1	2		3		4		5		6		7		8		9		10	
All foreign languages Any credit..........	2,487	(33.8)	84.0	(0.92)	2.5	(0.03)	2,295	(51.1)	85.7	(0.49)	2.5	(0.02)	2,599	(52.7)	88.5	(0.45)	2.6	(0.02)
Spanish																		
Any credit.....................	1,780	(31.9)	60.1	(0.90)	2.2	(0.03)	1,705	(42.2)	63.7	(0.66)	2.2	(0.02)	2,032	(45.0)	69.2	(0.70)	2.3	(0.02)
2 or more credits.......	1,369	(32.2)	46.2	(1.04)	2.6	(0.03)	1,344	(35.9)	50.2	(0.67)	2.6	(0.01)	1,638	(39.2)	55.8	(0.73)	2.6	(0.02)
3 or more credits.......	554	(26.3)	18.7	(0.90)	3.4	(0.03)	531	(20.1)	19.8	(0.57)	3.4	(0.01)	721	(30.2)	24.5	(0.78)	3.4	(0.02)
French																		
Any credit.....................	528	(21.5)	17.8	(0.73)	2.3	(0.05)	414	(14.1)	15.5	(0.49)	2.3	(0.03)	411	(16.1)	14.0	(0.47)	2.4	(0.04)
2 or more credits.......	398	(17.8)	13.4	(0.61)	2.7	(0.04)	309	(11.1)	11.5	(0.38)	2.7	(0.03)	314	(14.1)	10.7	(0.42)	2.8	(0.03)
3 or more credits.......	190	(12.1)	6.4	(0.42)	3.5	(0.04)	143	(7.2)	5.4	(0.25)	3.5	(0.03)	167	(10.6)	5.7	(0.32)	3.5	(0.03)
German																		
Any credit.....................	142	(17.2)	4.8	(0.57)	2.3	(0.08)	139	(10.0)	5.2	(0.36)	2.3	(0.04)	122	(8.6)	4.2	(0.29)	2.3	(0.06)
2 or more credits.......	104	(14.6)	3.5	(0.49)	2.8	(0.07)	102	(8.2)	3.8	(0.29)	2.8	(0.04)	91	(7.8)	3.1	(0.27)	2.8	(0.05)
3 or more credits.......	55	(8.6)	1.8	(0.29)	3.5	(0.06)	53	(4.7)	2.0	(0.17)	3.5	(0.04)	46	(5.3)	1.6	(0.18)	3.5	(0.03)
Latin																		
Any credit.....................	120	(15.3)	4.0	(0.52)	2.1	(0.08)	106	(10.4)	4.0	(0.36)	2.1	(0.05)	108	(10.6)	3.7	(0.35)	2.2	(0.07)
Italian																		
Any credit.....................	29	(5.5)	1.0	(0.19)	2.2	(0.20)	29	(5.3)	1.1	(0.20)	2.4	(0.16)	36	(7.0)	1.2	(0.23)	2.3	(0.18)
Japanese																		
Any credit.....................	36	(7.3)	1.2	(0.25)	2.3	(0.15)	30	(4.4)	1.1	(0.16)	2.1	(0.12)	28	(4.3)	1.0	(0.15)	2.5	(0.12)
Chinese																		
Any credit.....................	12	(3.1)	0.4	(0.10)	2.4	(0.20)	8	(2.1)	0.3	(0.08)	2.1	(0.23)	20	(4.1)	0.7	(0.14)	1.9	(0.13)
Arabic																		
Any credit.....................	‡	(†)	‡	(†)	‡	(†)	‡	(†)	‡	(†)	‡	(†)	‡	(†)	‡	(†)	2.8	(0.36)
Russian																		
Any credit.....................	10	(2.7)	0.3	(0.09)	1.9	(0.24)	5	(1.3)	0.2	(0.05)	1.5	(0.17)	3 !	(1.3)	0.1 !	(0.04)	2.4	(0.14)
Other foreign languages																		
Any credit.....................	106	(12.0)	3.6	(0.40)	2.5	(0.17)	89	(5.9)	3.3	(0.23)	2.8	(0.10)	105	(10.6)	3.6	(0.37)	2.5	(0.18)
AP/IB/honors foreign languages Any credit.....................	183	(23.9)	6.2	(0.81)	1.2	(0.04)	157	(10.3)	5.9	(0.38)	1.2	(0.02)	233	(15.9)	7.9	(0.52)	1.2	(0.02)

†Not applicable.

!Interpret data with caution. The coefficient of variation (CV) for this estimate is between 30 and 50 percent.

‡Reporting standards not met. Either there are too few cases for a reliable estimate or the coefficient of variation (CV) is 50 percent or greater.

[1]Average credits earned are shown only for those graduates who earned any credit in the specified language while in high school. For these students, however, credits earned include both courses taken in high school and courses taken prior to entering high school. Credits are shown in Carnegie units. The Carnegie unit is a standard unit of measurement that represents one credit for the completion of a 1-year course.

NOTE: For a transcript to be included in the analyses, it had to meet three requirements: (1) the graduate received either a standard or honors diploma, (2) the graduate's transcript contained 16 or more Carnegie credits, and (3) the graduate's transcript contained more than 0 Carnegie credits in English courses.

SOURCE: U.S. Department of Education, National Center for Education Statistics, 2000, 2005, and 2009 High School Transcript Study (HSTS). (This table was prepared April 2014.)

Table 225.80. Percentage distribution of elementary and secondary school children, by average grades and selected child and school characteristics: 2003, 2007, and 2012

[Standard errors appear in parentheses]

Selected child or school characteristic	Distribution of children, by parental reports of average grades in all subjects											
	2003				2007				2012			
	Mostly A's	Mostly B's	Mostly C's	Mostly D's or F's	Mostly A's	Mostly B's	Mostly C's	Mostly D's or F's	Mostly A's	Mostly B's	Mostly C's	Mostly D's or F's
1	2	3	4	5	6	7	8	9	10	11	12	13
All students	43.6 (0.62)	37.0 (0.58)	15.9 (0.52)	3.6 (0.24)	47.2 (0.75)	35.0 (0.80)	14.1 (0.72)	3.8 (0.36)	49.2 (0.53)	35.6 (0.57)	12.8 (0.37)	2.5 (0.21)
Sex of child												
Male	36.4 (0.72)	38.6 (0.86)	19.8 (0.74)	5.2 (0.40)	40.3 (1.01)	37.1 (1.17)	17.0 (1.25)	5.7 (0.64)	42.9 (0.74)	37.7 (0.78)	16.1 (0.58)	3.3 (0.34)
Female	51.0 (0.84)	35.3 (0.76)	11.9 (0.61)	1.9 (0.24)	54.7 (0.99)	32.7 (0.97)	11.0 (0.62)	1.7 (0.24)	55.9 (0.82)	33.3 (0.80)	9.3 (0.51)	1.5 (0.22)
Race/ethnicity of child												
White	47.8 (0.86)	35.2 (0.75)	14.0 (0.63)	3.1 (0.25)	53.9 (0.97)	32.2 (0.91)	11.7 (0.68)	2.1 (0.27)	53.6 (0.74)	33.5 (0.77)	10.8 (0.48)	2.1 (0.22)
Black	34.5 (1.75)	39.5 (1.65)	20.9 (1.33)	5.0 (0.82)	28.3 (2.04)	40.5 (2.75)	24.9 (2.89)	6.3 (1.41)	37.0 (1.88)	39.7 (1.97)	19.9 (1.19)	3.4 (0.75)
Hispanic	34.9 (1.14)	42.3 (1.24)	18.6 (1.03)	4.2 (0.48)	40.8 (1.68)	35.2 (1.66)	14.1 (1.24)	6.0 (1.15)	43.2 (1.09)	39.9 (1.05)	14.3 (0.83)	2.6 (0.41)
Asian/Pacific Islander	62.0 (3.47)	25.5 (2.76)	11.3 (3.06)	‡ (†)	68.7 (4.52)	25.7 (4.29)	3.5 (1.03)	‡ (†)	60.6 (2.70)	32.9 (2.79)	5.8 (0.97)	0.7 ! (0.27)
Asian	— (†)	— (†)	— (†)	— (†)	74.5 (3.67)	20.7 (3.60)	3.2 ! (1.10)	‡ (†)	63.2 (2.82)	31.8 (2.86)	4.6 (0.98)	0.4 ! (0.20)
Pacific Islander	— (†)	— (†)	— (†)	— (†)	‡ (†)	‡ (†)	‡ (†)	‡ (†)	23.7 ! (7.70)	43.4 (10.65)	27.5 ! (8.38)	‡ (†)
American Indian/Alaska Native	29.5 (6.53)	53.3 (6.42)	12.1 ! (4.90)	5.1 ! (2.54)	39.7 (9.13)	29.2 (8.22)	19.9 ! (6.67)	‡ (†)	54.6 (8.07)	28.2 (6.56)	16.3 ! (5.26)	‡ (†)
Other	41.4 (4.34)	36.2 (3.91)	18.8 (2.81)	3.5 ! (1.38)	43.4 (3.98)	39.0 (4.33)	11.3 (2.39)	6.4 (1.73)	56.0 (2.82)	27.6 (2.61)	11.3 (1.71)	5.1 ! (2.33)
Highest education level of parents												
Less than high school	27.8 (2.17)	41.6 (2.05)	22.7 (2.27)	7.8 (1.46)	26.8 (3.18)	41.9 (4.27)	22.0 (2.55)	9.3 (2.02)	39.5 (2.25)	39.7 (2.02)	16.8 (1.73)	4.0 (0.93)
High school/GED	32.1 (1.20)	41.4 (1.23)	21.7 (1.12)	4.8 (0.57)	32.9 (1.70)	39.8 (1.64)	21.9 (2.02)	5.4 (0.82)	37.7 (1.51)	40.8 (1.62)	17.6 (1.31)	4.0 (0.71)
Vocational/technical or some college	39.8 (1.34)	38.3 (1.36)	17.2 (0.95)	4.7 (0.58)	40.7 (1.65)	38.6 (2.03)	16.6 (1.43)	4.0 (0.78)	43.5 (1.07)	38.1 (1.05)	15.6 (0.87)	2.8 (0.32)
Associate's degree	46.7 (2.13)	34.5 (1.94)	16.4 (1.51)	2.4 (0.57)	40.3 (2.27)	38.4 (2.00)	15.7 (1.76)	5.5 ! (2.10)	47.0 (1.82)	34.9 (1.78)	15.4 (0.87)	2.7 (0.52)
Bachelor's degree/some graduate school	53.0 (1.26)	34.2 (1.29)	11.1 (0.85)	1.7 (0.28)	58.9 (1.62)	32.2 (1.52)	7.3 (0.85)	1.6 (0.38)	60.1 (1.05)	31.4 (1.02)	7.5 (0.53)	1.0 (0.19)
Graduate/professional degree	61.9 (1.71)	30.5 (1.75)	6.7 (0.67)	0.9 (0.24)	68.2 (1.59)	24.1 (1.37)	6.6 (1.33)	1.2 ! (0.38)	68.1 (1.04)	27.3 (1.04)	4.2 (0.36)	0.5 (0.10)
Family income (in current dollars)												
$20,000 or less	33.1 (1.53)	38.9 (1.56)	22.0 (1.30)	6.0 (0.85)	29.0 (2.20)	39.4 (2.61)	24.7 (2.83)	6.8 (1.14)	37.2 (1.35)	40.2 (1.19)	18.3 (1.04)	4.4 (0.59)
$20,001 to $50,000	37.8 (1.20)	40.0 (1.19)	17.7 (0.85)	4.5 (0.42)	37.6 (1.47)	37.9 (1.65)	18.0 (1.39)	6.4 (0.91)	41.3 (1.22)	38.9 (1.19)	16.7 (0.90)	3.1 (0.44)
$50,001 to $75,000	48.0 (1.29)	35.0 (1.22)	14.0 (0.81)	3.0 (0.45)	53.0 (1.50)	33.8 (1.42)	11.0 (0.97)	2.2 (0.42)	49.3 (1.45)	35.8 (1.37)	12.9 (1.07)	1.9 (0.32)
$75,001 to $100,000	51.8 (1.66)	33.7 (1.45)	13.3 (1.23)	1.3 (0.32)	55.7 (1.74)	33.3 (1.84)	9.7 (1.00)	1.4 (0.33)	53.7 (1.64)	33.5 (1.42)	10.6 (1.03)	2.3 (0.50)
Over $100,000	55.8 (1.74)	33.9 (1.72)	9.1 (1.09)	1.2 (0.24)	61.6 (1.44)	30.2 (1.31)	7.0 (0.88)	1.2 (0.36)	61.8 (1.15)	30.4 (1.19)	6.6 (0.61)	1.1 ! (0.41)
Poverty status[1]												
Poor	33.1 (1.61)	39.4 (1.65)	21.9 (1.39)	5.6 (0.91)	30.4 (2.07)	39.0 (2.52)	23.3 (2.38)	7.2 (1.09)	39.1 (1.39)	38.9 (1.33)	17.8 (1.06)	4.2 (0.54)
Near-poor	34.8 (1.39)	42.0 (1.26)	18.2 (1.08)	5.0 (0.59)	38.4 (1.85)	36.5 (1.85)	18.6 (1.84)	6.5 (1.18)	40.1 (1.19)	40.3 (1.07)	17.0 (0.93)	2.7 (0.45)
Nonpoor	49.9 (0.83)	34.5 (0.76)	13.2 (0.54)	2.4 (0.23)	55.1 (0.89)	33.2 (0.91)	9.8 (0.56)	1.8 (0.21)	56.0 (0.75)	32.7 (0.75)	9.5 (0.45)	1.8 (0.25)
Control of school and enrollment level of child												
Public school	41.8 (0.64)	37.5 (0.62)	16.8 (0.57)	3.8 (0.26)	45.5 (0.80)	35.5 (0.84)	14.9 (0.77)	4.1 (0.39)	47.9 (0.55)	36.0 (0.60)	13.5 (0.39)	2.6 (0.23)
Elementary (kindergarten to grade 8)	46.1 (0.80)	35.9 (0.84)	14.6 (0.74)	3.4 (0.32)	50.0 (0.99)	33.1 (1.00)	13.4 (1.12)	3.5 (0.43)	52.9 (0.69)	34.2 (0.73)	11.0 (0.49)	1.8 (0.22)
Secondary (grades 9 to 12)	34.6 (0.96)	40.2 (0.97)	20.6 (0.94)	4.6 (0.46)	38.6 (1.36)	39.1 (1.27)	17.2 (1.08)	5.2 (0.71)	37.5 (0.83)	39.7 (1.03)	18.4 (0.84)	4.4 (0.54)
Private school	57.6 (1.72)	33.0 (1.68)	8.1 (0.91)	1.3 ! (0.45)	60.6 (2.79)	30.8 (2.85)	7.8 (1.73)	0.9 ! (0.35)	63.4 (1.63)	30.8 (1.51)	5.4 (0.68)	0.4 ! (0.20)
Elementary (kindergarten to grade 8)	61.6 (2.39)	30.3 (2.28)	7.3 (1.03)	0.8 ! (0.28)	66.1 (3.73)	26.6 (4.05)	6.6 (1.66)	‡ (†)	67.8 (1.95)	28.2 (1.91)	3.5 (0.61)	‡ (†)
Secondary (grades 9 to 12)	48.8 (3.22)	38.9 (2.94)	10.0 (1.77)	‡ (†)	51.2 (3.91)	37.8 (3.43)	9.8 ! (3.87)	‡ (†)	52.8 (2.70)	37.2 (2.58)	9.9 (1.60)	‡ (†)

—Not available.
†Not applicable.
‡Reporting standards not met. Either there are too few cases for a reliable estimate or the coefficient of variation (CV) is 50 percent or greater.
!Interpret data with caution. The coefficient of variation (CV) for this estimate is between 30 and 50 percent.

[1]Poor children are those whose family incomes were below the Census Bureau's poverty threshold in the year prior to data collection; near-poor children are those whose family incomes ranged from the poverty threshold to 199 percent of the poverty threshold; and nonpoor children are those whose family incomes were at or above 200 percent of the poverty threshold. The poverty threshold is a dollar amount that varies depending on a family's size and composition and is updated annually to account for inflation. In 2011, for example, the poverty threshold for a family of four with two children was $22,811. Survey respondents are asked to select the range within which their income falls, rather than giving the exact amount of their income; therefore, the measure of poverty status is an approximation.

NOTE: While National Household Education Surveys Program (NHES) administrations prior to 2012 were administered via telephone with an interviewer, NHES:2012 used self-administered paper-and-pencil questionnaires that were mailed to respondents. Measurable differences in estimates between 2012 and prior years could reflect actual changes in the population, or the changes could be due to the mode change from telephone to mail. Includes children enrolled in kindergarten through grade 12. Excludes children whose programs have no classes with lettered grades. Race categories exclude persons of Hispanic ethnicity. Detail may not sum to totals because of rounding. Some data have been revised from previously published figures.
SOURCE: U.S. Department of Education, National Center for Education Statistics, Parent and Family Involvement in Education Survey of the National Household Education Surveys Program (PFI-NHES:2003, 2007, and 2012). (This table was prepared September 2014.)

Table 226.10. SAT mean scores of college-bound seniors, by race/ethnicity: Selected years, 1986–87 through 2013–14

Race/ethnicity	1986–87	1990–91	1996–97	2000–01	2002–03	2003–04	2004–05	2005–06	2006–07	2007–08	2008–09	2009–10	2010–11	2011–12	2012–13	2013–14	Score change			
																	1990–91 to 2003–04	2003–04 to 2013–14	2008–09 to 2013–14	2012–13 to 2013–14
1	2	3	4	5	6	7	8	9	10	11	12	13	14	15	16	17	18	19	20	21
SAT—Critical reading																				
All students	507	499	505	506	507	508	508	503	502	502	501	501	497	496	496	497	9	-11	-4	1
White	524	518	526	529	529	528	532	527	527	528	528	528	528	527	527	529	10	1	1	2
Black	428	427	434	433	431	430	433	434	433	430	429	429	428	428	431	431	3	1	2	0
Mexican American	457	454	451	451	448	451	453	454	455	454	453	454	451	448	449	450	-3	-1	-3	1
Puerto Rican	436	436	454	457	456	457	460	459	459	456	452	454	452	452	456	456	21	-1	4	0
Other Hispanic	464	458	466	460	457	461	463	458	459	455	455	454	451	447	450	451	3	-10	-4	1
Asian/Pacific Islander	479	485	496	501	508	507	511	510	514	513	516	519	517	518	521	523	22	16	7	2
American Indian/Alaska Native	471	470	475	481	480	483	489	487	487	485	486	485	484	482	480	483	13	0	-3	3
Other	480	486	512	503	501	494	495	494	497	496	494	494	493	491	492	493	8	-1	-1	1
SAT—Mathematics																				
All students	501	500	511	514	519	518	520	518	515	515	515	516	514	514	514	513	18	-5	-2	-1
White	514	513	526	531	534	531	536	536	534	537	536	536	535	536	534	534	18	3	-2	0
Black	411	419	423	426	426	427	431	429	429	426	426	428	427	428	429	429	8	2	3	0
Mexican American	455	459	458	458	457	458	463	465	466	463	463	467	466	465	464	461	-1	3	-2	-3
Puerto Rican	432	439	447	451	453	452	457	456	454	453	450	452	452	452	453	450	13	-2	0	-3
Other Hispanic	462	462	468	465	464	465	469	463	463	461	461	462	462	461	461	459	3	-6	-2	-2
Asian/Pacific Islander	541	548	560	566	575	577	580	578	578	581	587	591	595	595	597	598	29	21	11	1
American Indian/Alaska Native	463	468	475	479	482	488	493	494	494	491	493	492	488	489	486	484	20	-4	-9	-2
Other	482	492	514	512	513	508	513	513	512	512	514	514	517	516	519	520	16	12	6	1
SAT—Writing																				
All students	†	†	†	†	†	†	†	497	494	494	493	492	489	488	488	487	†	†	-6	-1
White	†	†	†	†	†	†	†	519	518	518	517	516	516	515	515	513	†	†	-4	-2
Black	†	†	†	†	†	†	†	428	425	424	421	420	417	417	418	418	†	†	-3	0
Mexican American	†	†	†	†	†	†	†	452	450	447	446	448	445	443	442	443	†	†	-3	1
Puerto Rican	†	†	†	†	†	†	†	448	447	445	443	443	442	442	445	443	†	†	0	-2
Other Hispanic	†	†	†	†	†	†	†	450	450	448	443	447	444	442	443	443	†	†	-5	0
Asian/Pacific Islander	†	†	†	†	†	†	†	512	513	516	520	526	528	528	527	530	†	†	10	3
American Indian/Alaska Native	†	†	†	†	†	†	†	474	473	470	469	467	465	462	461	461	†	†	-8	0
Other	†	†	†	†	†	†	†	493	493	494	493	492	492	491	490	491	†	†	-2	1

†Not applicable.
NOTE: Data for 2009–10 and earlier years are for seniors who took the SAT any time during their high school years through March of their senior year. Data for 2010–11 onwards are for seniors who took the SAT any time during their high school years through June of their senior year. If a student took a test more than once, the most recent score was used. The SAT was formerly known

as the Scholastic Assessment Test and the Scholastic Aptitude Test. Possible scores on each part of the SAT range from 200 to 800. The writing section was introduced in March 2005. The critical reading section was formerly known as the verbal section.
SOURCE: College Entrance Examination Board, *College-Bound Seniors: Total Group Profile [National] Report,* selected years, 1986–87 through 2013–14, retrieved November 5, 2014, from http://media.collegeboard.com/digitalServices/pdf/sat/TotalGroup-2014.pdf. (This table was prepared November 2014.)

Table 226.20. SAT mean scores of college-bound seniors, by sex: 1966–67 through 2013–14

School year	SAT[1]									Scholastic Aptitude Test (old scale)					
	Critical reading score			Mathematics score			Writing score[2]			Verbal score			Mathematics score		
	Total	Male	Female	Total	Male	Female	Total	Male	Female	Total	Male	Female	Total	Male	Female
1	2	3	4	5	6	7	8	9	10	11	12	13	14	15	16
1966–67	543	540	545	516	535	495	†	†	†	466	463	468	492	514	467
1967–68	543	541	543	516	533	497	†	†	†	466	464	466	492	512	470
1968–69	540	536	543	517	534	498	†	†	†	463	459	466	493	513	470
1969–70	537	536	538	512	531	493	†	†	†	460	459	461	488	509	465
1970–71	532	531	534	513	529	494	†	†	†	455	454	457	488	507	466
1971–72	530	531	529	509	527	489	†	†	†	453	454	452	484	505	461
1972–73	523	523	521	506	525	489	†	†	†	445	446	443	481	502	460
1973–74	521	524	520	505	524	488	†	†	†	444	447	442	480	501	459
1974–75	512	515	509	498	518	479	†	†	†	434	437	431	472	495	449
1975–76	509	511	508	497	520	475	†	†	†	431	433	430	472	497	446
1976–77	507	509	505	496	520	474	†	†	†	429	431	427	470	497	445
1977–78	507	511	503	494	517	474	†	†	†	429	433	425	468	494	444
1978–79	505	509	501	493	516	473	†	†	†	427	431	423	467	493	443
1979–80	502	506	498	492	515	473	†	†	†	424	428	420	466	491	443
1980–81	502	508	496	492	516	473	†	†	†	424	430	418	466	492	443
1981–82	504	509	499	493	516	473	†	†	†	426	431	421	467	493	443
1982–83	503	508	498	494	516	474	†	†	†	425	430	420	468	493	445
1983–84	504	511	498	497	518	478	†	†	†	426	433	420	471	495	449
1984–85	509	514	503	500	522	480	†	†	†	431	437	425	475	499	452
1985–86	509	515	504	500	523	479	†	†	†	431	437	426	475	501	451
1986–87	507	512	502	501	523	481	†	†	†	430	435	425	476	500	453
1987–88	505	512	499	501	521	483	†	†	†	428	435	422	476	498	455
1988–89	504	510	498	502	523	482	†	†	†	427	434	421	476	500	454
1989–90	500	505	496	501	521	483	†	†	†	424	429	419	476	499	455
1990–91	499	503	495	500	520	482	†	†	†	422	426	418	474	497	453
1991–92	500	504	496	501	521	484	†	†	†	423	428	419	476	499	456
1992–93	500	504	497	503	524	484	†	†	†	424	428	420	478	502	457
1993–94	499	501	497	504	523	487	†	†	†	423	425	421	479	501	460
1994–95	504	505	502	506	525	490	†	†	†	428	429	426	482	503	463
1995–96	505	507	503	508	527	492	†	†	†	—	—	—	—	—	—
1996–97	505	507	503	511	530	494	†	†	†	—	—	—	—	—	—
1997–98	505	509	502	512	531	496	†	†	†	—	—	—	—	—	—
1998–99	505	509	502	511	531	495	†	†	†	—	—	—	—	—	—
1999–2000	505	507	504	514	533	498	†	†	†	†	†	†	†	†	†
2000–01	506	509	502	514	533	498	†	†	†	†	†	†	†	†	†
2001–02	504	507	502	516	534	500	†	†	†	†	†	†	†	†	†
2002–03	507	512	503	519	537	503	†	†	†	†	†	†	†	†	†
2003–04	508	512	504	518	537	501	†	†	†	†	†	†	†	†	†
2004–05	508	513	505	520	538	504	†	†	†	†	†	†	†	†	†
2005–06	503	505	502	518	536	502	497	491	502	†	†	†	†	†	†
2006–07	502	504	502	515	533	499	494	489	500	†	†	†	†	†	†
2007–08	502	504	500	515	533	500	494	488	501	†	†	†	†	†	†
2008–09	501	503	498	515	534	499	493	486	499	†	†	†	†	†	†
2009–10	501	503	498	516	534	500	492	486	498	†	†	†	†	†	†
2010–11	497	500	495	514	531	500	489	482	496	†	†	†	†	†	†
2011–12	496	498	493	514	532	499	488	481	494	†	†	†	†	†	†
2012–13	496	499	494	514	531	499	488	482	493	†	†	†	†	†	†
2013–14	497	499	495	513	530	499	487	481	492	†	†	†	†	†	†

—Not available.
†Not applicable.
[1]Data for 1966–67 to 1985–86 were converted to the recentered scale by using a formula applied to the original mean and standard deviation. For 1986–87 to 1994–95, individual student scores were converted to the recentered scale and then the mean was recomputed. For 1995–96 to 1998–99, nearly all students received scores on the recentered scale; any score on the original scale was converted to the recentered scale prior to recomputing the mean. From 1999–2000 on, all scores have been reported on the recentered scale.
[2]Writing data are based on students who took the SAT writing section, which was introduced in March 2005.
NOTE: Data for 1966–67 through 1970–71 are estimates derived from the test scores of all participants. Data for 1971–72 through 2009–10 are for seniors who took the SAT any time

during their high school years through March of their senior year. Data for 2010–11 onwards are for seniors who took the SAT any time during their high school years through June of their senior year. If a student took a test more than once, the most recent score was used. The SAT was formerly known as the Scholastic Assessment Test and the Scholastic Aptitude Test. Possible scores on each part of the SAT range from 200 to 800. The critical reading section was formerly known as the verbal section.
SOURCE: College Entrance Examination Board, *College-Bound Seniors: Total Group Profile [National] Report*, 1966–67 through 2013–14, retrieved November 5, 2014, from http://media.collegeboard.com/digitalServices/pdf/sat/TotalGroup-2014.pdf. (This table was prepared November 2014.)

Table 226.30. SAT mean scores and percentage distribution of college-bound seniors, by selected student characteristics: Selected years, 1995–96 through 2013–14

Selected student characteristic	1995–96 Critical reading score[1]	1995–96 Mathematics score	1995–96 Percentage distribution	2000–01 Critical reading score[1]	2000–01 Mathematics score	2000–01 Percentage distribution	2005–06 Critical reading score[1]	2005–06 Mathematics score	2005–06 Writing score[2]	2005–06 Percentage distribution	2010–11 Critical reading score[1]	2010–11 Mathematics score	2010–11 Writing score[2]	2010–11 Percentage distribution	2013–14 Critical reading score[1]	2013–14 Mathematics score	2013–14 Writing score[2]	2013–14 Percentage distribution
1	2	3	4	5	6	7	8	9	10	11	12	13	14	15	16	17	18	19
All students	**505**	**508**	**100**	**506**	**514**	**100**	**503**	**518**	**497**	**100**	**497**	**514**	**489**	**100**	**497**	**513**	**487**	**100**
High school rank																		
Top decile	591	606	22	588	607	24	580	604	577	31	575	606	572	35	575	606	569	35
Second decile	530	539	22	526	540	23	516	537	511	25	510	535	503	27	511	534	500	27
Second quintile	494	496	28	490	497	26	484	498	476	20	482	498	470	18	483	497	469	18
Bottom three quintiles[3]	—	—	—	—	—	—	443	449	435	23	438	448	426	20	439	445	424	20
Third quintile	455	448	24	454	452	22	—	—	—	—	—	—	—	—	—	—	—	—
Fourth quintile	429	418	4	423	417	4	—	—	—	—	—	—	—	—	—	—	—	—
Fifth quintile	411	401	1	407	401	1	—	—	—	—	—	—	—	—	—	—	—	—
High school grade point average																		
A+ (97–100)	617	632	6	609	626	7	602	621	599	7	596	620	595	6	595	619	591	6
A (93–96)	573	583	14	566	581	17	563	582	559	17	560	583	556	19	559	580	552	19
A- (90–92)	545	554	15	540	552	17	534	552	529	17	528	548	521	19	524	543	515	20
B (80–89)	486	485	49	482	486	47	479	489	471	47	469	480	458	45	465	474	452	43
C (70–79)	432	426	15	428	425	12	426	428	414	12	416	421	401	10	410	413	395	9
D, E, or F (below 70)	414	408	#	403	404	#	406	413	389	#	409	425	398	#	385	401	372	#
High school type																		
Public	502	506	83	502	510	83	500	514	492	83	494	506	483	84	492	501	478	84
Private, religiously affiliated	525	510	12	530	523	12	531	529	528	12	531	533	528	10	533	537	527	9
Private, independent	547	556	5	549	567	5	544	573	550	5	541	579	550	6	535	580	542	7
Intended college major[4]																		
Agriculture, agriculture operations, and related sciences	491	484	2	487	484	1	481	485	469	1	475	484	461	1	471	475	455	1
Architecture and related services	492	519	3	493	521	2	488	528	485	2	490	534	485	2	486	526	478	2
Area, ethnic, cultural and gender studies	†	†	†	†	†	†	†	†	†	†	545	513	531	#	530	505	515	#
Arts: visual/performing	520	497	6	518	501	8	516	502	507	8	508	497	499	8	505	493	491	7
Biological and biomedical sciences	546	545	6	545	549	5	540	554	532	5	540	557	533	6	538	551	529	7
Business and management, marketing, and related support services	483	500	13	489	511	14	486	511	481	14	488	522	484	11	493	522	486	12
Communication, journalism, and related programs	527	497	4	527	506	4	522	504	520	4	519	502	516	3	516	498	510	3
Computer and information sciences and support services	497	522	3	501	533	7	503	534	482	7	511	539	500	2	525	554	500	3
Construction trades	487	477	8	483	481	9	480	484	478	#	422	451	399	#	427	447	402	#
Education	525	497	8	523	502	9	519	498	506	9	480	487	476	6	482	482	474	4
Engineering	†	569	†	†	572	†	597	577	584	8	528	584	513	8	528	579	513	10
Engineering technologies/technicians	458	452	1	459	458	1	462	466	506	#	464	511	447	2	475	526	460	1
English language and literature/letters	605	545	1	606	549	†	572	541	584	1	584	529	570	1	577	522	560	1
Family and consumer sciences/human sciences[5]	556	534	#	557	540	#	542	549	532	#	456	461	452	#	449	450	443	#
Foreign languages, literatures, and linguistics	576	553	1	554	539	1	485	532	550	1	567	542	557	1	557	533	543	1
General/interdisciplinary	500	505	19	494	502	15	485	498	483	18	†	†	†	†	†	†	†	†
Health professions and related clinical services	†	†	†	†	†	†	485	509	542	19	487	502	484	19	485	495	479	19
History	554	512	1	574	504	1	579	624	537	1	542	510	511	1	539	506	505	1
Legal professions and studies	552	628	†	549	625	1	539	521	†	#	512	507	500	3	519	510	504	2
Liberal arts and sciences, general studies, and humanities	†	†	†	†	†	†	510	541	487	1	552	532	541	1	548	530	536	1
Library science and administration	554	512	#	574	504	#	579	509	542	#	564	505	516	#	562	507	518	#
Mathematics and statistics	552	628	1	549	625	1	539	624	537	1	518	603	519	1	535	613	533	1
Mechanic and repair technologies/technician	†	†	†	†	†	†	†	†	†	†	421	451	400	#	417	442	395	#
Military technologies and applied sciences	†	†	†	†	†	†	510	521	487	†	467	471	433	#	483	489	455	#
Multi/interdisciplinary studies	503	505	†	507	511	†	510	521	487	†	582	580	570	#	585	589	574	1

See notes at end of table.

Table 226.30. SAT mean scores and percentage distribution of college-bound seniors, by selected student characteristics: Selected years, 1995–96 through 2013–14—Continued

Selected student characteristic	1995–96			2000–01			2005–06				2010–11				2013–14			
	Critical reading score[1]	Mathematics score	Percentage distribution	Critical reading score[1]	Mathematics score	Percentage distribution	Critical reading score[1]	Mathematics score	Writing score[2]	Percentage distribution	Critical reading score[1]	Mathematics score	Writing score[2]	Percentage distribution	Critical reading score[1]	Mathematics score	Writing score[2]	Percentage distribution
1	2	3	4	5	6	7	8	9	10	11	12	13	14	15	16	17	18	19
Natural resources and conservation	†	†	†	†	†	†	†	†	†	†	525	524	506	1	522	518	499	#
Parks, recreation, leisure, and fitness studies	†	†	†	†	†	†	†	†	†	†	444	468	435	1	435	458	426	1
Personal and culinary services	†	†	†	†	†	†	†	†	†	†	457	456	440	#	445	442	427	#
Philosophy and religious studies	560	536	#	561	539	1	557	537	535	1	557	535	530	#	545	525	520	#
Physical sciences	575	595	1	568	588	1	557	589	542	1	553	582	537	1	558	585	540	2
Precision production	†	†	†	†	†	†	†	†	†	†	436	468	422	#	456	459	417	#
Psychology	†	†	†	†	†	†	†	†	†	†	505	494	497	5	503	489	492	5
Public administration and social services	458	448	3	461	455	2	462	461	454	2	467	459	462	2	463	453	456	2
Security and protective services	†	†	†	†	†	†	†	†	†	†	445	454	432	2	445	449	432	3
Social sciences and history	532	509	11	531	512	10	539	519	525	9	†	†	†	†	†	†	†	†
Social sciences	†	†	†	†	†	†	†	†	†	†	573	558	559	2	565	550	548	2
Technical and vocational	435	441	1	444	451	1	437	454	421	1	465	462	446	#	459	458	440	#
Theology and religious vocations	†	†	†	†	†	†	†	†	†	†	539	522	513	#	533	515	510	#
Transportation and materials moving	†	†	†	†	†	†	†	†	†	†	453	496	443	#	451	488	440	#
Other	†	†	†	†	†	†	†	†	†	†	†	†	†	†	†	†	†	†
Undecided	500	507	7	515	524	7	512	530	502	7	530	545	522	8	533	545	522	7
Degree-level goal																		
Certificate program	434	439	1	443	455	1	443	462	435	1	445	464	434	1	438	456	427	1
Associate's degree	422	415	2	419	416	2	416	420	409	2	412	416	400	1	409	410	395	1
Bachelor's degree	476	476	23	478	483	23	477	487	469	25	478	490	467	30	482	491	467	30
Master's degree	514	518	29	516	526	29	512	525	505	31	506	524	499	30	510	527	501	30
Doctor's or related degree	548	552	24	547	554	24	539	553	532	21	534	550	527	21	537	550	528	22
Other	430	438	1	438	449	1	439	456	436	1	425	451	423	1	406	436	405	1
Undecided	502	503	20	511	517	19	515	528	508	19	509	522	499	16	506	520	495	15
Family income																		
Less than $20,000	—	—	—	—	—	—	—	—	—	—	434	460	429	13	436	459	429	13
$20,000, but less than $40,000	—	—	—	—	—	—	—	—	—	—	464	480	454	16	467	481	455	16
$40,000, but less than $60,000	—	—	—	—	—	—	—	—	—	—	487	499	475	15	489	500	474	14
$60,000, but less than $80,000	—	—	—	—	—	—	—	—	—	—	502	512	489	14	504	512	487	13
$80,000, but less than $100,000	—	—	—	—	—	—	—	—	—	—	515	527	503	12	516	526	501	11
$100,000, but less than $120,000	—	—	—	—	—	—	—	—	—	—	526	539	515	10	527	539	513	10
$120,000, but less than $140,000	—	—	—	—	—	—	—	—	—	—	530	544	520	5	531	542	518	5
$140,000, but less than $160,000	—	—	—	—	—	—	—	—	—	—	538	552	529	4	539	552	527	4
$160,000, but less than $200,000	—	—	—	—	—	—	—	—	—	—	543	557	536	5	544	558	534	5
More than $200,000	—	—	—	—	—	—	—	—	—	—	568	586	567	7	569	588	565	8
Highest level of parental education																		
No high school diploma	414	439	4	411	438	4	418	445	418	4	421	449	418	6	421	447	418	7
High school diploma	475	474	35	472	476	32	467	478	460	32	463	476	452	31	462	473	450	29
Associate's degree	489	487	8	489	491	9	484	493	474	9	480	489	466	8	480	485	463	8
Bachelor's degree	525	529	28	525	533	28	522	536	514	29	522	538	514	31	523	539	512	32
Graduate degree	556	558	25	559	567	25	558	571	552	26	559	574	554	25	560	575	551	25

—Not available.
†Not applicable.
#Rounds to zero.
[1]Prior to 2006, the critical reading section was known as the verbal section.
[2]Writing data are based on students who took the SAT writing section, which was introduced in March 2005.
[3]Beginning in 2005–06, the College Board has reported third, fourth, and fifth quintiles as the bottom three quintiles instead of reporting them separately as in previous years.
[4]Data may not be comparable over time because of additions to the list of majors and changes in subspecialties within majors.
[5]Prior to 2006–07, family and consumer sciences/human sciences was called home economics.

NOTE: Prior to 2010–11, data are for seniors who took the SAT any time during their high school years through March of their senior year. Data for 2010–11 onwards are for seniors who took the SAT any time during their high school years through June of their senior year. If a student took a test more than once, the most recent score was used. The SAT was formerly known as the Scholastic Assessment Test and the Scholastic Aptitude Test. Possible scores on each part of the SAT range from 200 to 800. Detail may not sum to totals because of rounding.

SOURCE: College Entrance Examination Board, College-Bound Seniors: Total Group Profile [National] Report, selected years, 1995–96 through 2013–14, retrieved November 5, 2014, from https://secure-media.collegeboard.org/digitalServices/pdf/sat/TotalGroup-2014.pdf. (This table was prepared November 2014.)

Table 226.40. Mean SAT scores of college-bound seniors and percentage of graduates taking SAT, by state: Selected years, 1995–96 through 2013–14

State	1995–96		2000–01		2005–06			2010–11			2012–13			2013–14			Percent of graduates taking SAT, 2012–13[1]	Percent of graduates taking SAT, 2013–14[1]
	Critical reading	Mathematics	Critical reading	Mathematics	Critical reading	Mathematics	Writing[2]	Critical reading	Mathematics	Writing[2]	Critical reading	Mathematics	Writing[2]	Critical reading	Mathematics	Writing[2]		
1	2	3	4	5	6	7	8	9	10	11	12	13	14	15	16	17	18	19
United States	505	508	506	514	503	518	497	497	514	489	496	514	488	497	513	487	49	50
Alabama	565	558	559	554	565	561	565	546	541	536	544	534	530	547	538	532	7	7
Alaska	521	513	514	510	517	517	493	515	511	487	508	505	482	507	503	475	52	54
Arizona	525	521	523	525	521	528	507	517	523	499	521	528	502	522	525	500	35	36
Arkansas	566	550	562	550	574	568	567	568	570	554	572	570	555	573	571	554	4	4
California	495	511	498	517	501	518	501	499	515	499	498	512	495	498	510	496	57	60
Colorado	536	538	539	542	558	564	548	570	573	556	578	581	562	582	586	567	14	14
Connecticut	507	504	509	510	512	516	511	509	513	513	508	512	512	507	510	508	85	88
Delaware[3]	508	495	501	499	495	500	484	489	490	476	451	457	443	456	459	444	100	100
District of Columbia[3]	489	473	482	474	487	472	482	469	457	459	473	466	461	440	438	431	91	100
Florida	498	496	498	499	496	497	480	487	489	471	492	490	475	491	485	472	67	72
Georgia	484	477	491	489	494	496	487	485	487	473	490	487	475	488	485	472	75	77
Hawaii	485	510	486	515	482	509	472	479	500	469	481	504	468	484	504	472	64	63
Idaho[3]	543	536	543	542	543	545	525	542	539	517	454	459	451	458	456	450	99	100
Illinois	564	575	576	589	591	609	586	599	617	591	600	617	590	599	616	587	5	5
Indiana	494	494	499	501	498	509	486	493	501	475	493	500	477	497	500	477	70	71
Iowa	590	600	593	603	602	613	591	596	606	575	592	601	570	605	611	578	3	3
Kansas	579	571	577	580	582	590	566	580	591	563	589	595	568	591	596	566	6	5
Kentucky	549	544	550	550	562	562	555	576	572	563	585	584	572	589	585	572	5	5
Louisiana	559	550	564	562	570	571	571	555	550	546	556	553	546	561	556	550	5	5
Maine[4]	504	498	506	500	501	501	491	469	469	453	462	467	451	467	471	449	95	96
Maryland	507	504	508	510	503	509	499	499	502	491	497	500	486	492	495	481	73	79
Massachusetts	507	504	511	515	513	524	510	513	527	509	515	529	509	516	531	509	83	84
Michigan	557	565	561	572	568	583	555	583	604	573	590	610	582	593	610	581	4	4
Minnesota	582	593	580	589	591	600	574	593	608	577	595	608	577	598	610	578	6	6
Mississippi	569	557	566	551	556	541	562	564	543	553	568	547	558	583	566	565	3	3
Missouri	570	569	577	577	587	591	582	592	593	579	596	595	582	595	597	579	4	4
Montana	546	547	539	539	538	545	524	539	537	516	539	540	516	555	552	530	25	18
Nebraska	567	568	562	568	576	583	566	585	591	569	584	583	567	589	587	569	4	4
Nevada	508	507	509	515	498	508	481	494	496	470	492	494	468	495	494	469	48	54
New Hampshire	520	514	520	516	520	524	509	523	525	511	524	528	515	524	530	512	70	70
New Jersey	498	505	499	513	496	515	496	495	516	497	499	522	500	501	523	502	78	79
New Mexico	554	548	551	542	557	549	543	548	541	529	550	545	531	548	543	526	12	12
New York	497	499	495	505	493	510	483	485	499	476	485	501	477	488	502	478	76	76
North Carolina	490	486	493	499	495	513	485	493	508	474	495	506	478	499	507	477	62	64
North Dakota	596	599	592	599	610	617	588	586	612	561	609	609	581	612	620	584	2	2
Ohio	536	535	534	539	535	544	521	539	545	522	548	556	531	555	562	535	17	15
Oklahoma	566	557	567	561	576	574	563	571	565	547	571	569	549	576	571	550	5	5
Oregon	523	521	526	526	523	529	503	520	521	499	520	520	499	523	522	499	49	48
Pennsylvania	498	492	500	499	493	500	483	493	501	479	494	504	482	497	504	480	71	71
Rhode Island	501	491	501	499	495	502	490	495	493	489	491	490	487	497	496	487	72	73
South Carolina	480	474	486	488	487	498	480	482	490	464	484	487	465	488	490	465	64	65
South Dakota	574	566	577	582	590	604	578	584	591	562	592	601	567	604	609	579	3	3
Tennessee	563	552	562	553	573	569	572	575	568	567	574	569	566	578	570	566	8	8
Texas	495	500	493	499	491	506	487	479	502	465	477	499	461	476	495	461	59	62
Utah	583	575	575	570	560	557	550	563	559	545	569	566	549	571	568	551	6	5
Vermont	506	500	511	506	513	519	502	515	518	505	516	519	505	522	525	507	61	63
Virginia	507	496	510	501	512	513	500	512	509	495	516	514	498	518	515	497	71	73
Washington	519	519	527	527	527	532	511	523	529	508	515	523	499	510	518	491	60	63
West Virginia	526	506	527	512	519	510	515	514	501	497	514	501	498	517	505	500	15	15
Wisconsin	577	586	584	596	588	600	577	590	602	575	591	604	576	596	608	578	4	4
Wyoming	544	544	547	545	548	555	537	572	569	551	581	588	588	590	599	573	4	3

[1] Participation rate is based on the projection of high school graduates by the Western Interstate Commission for Higher Education (WICHE), and the number of seniors who took the SAT in each state.
[2] Writing data are based on students who took the SAT writing section, which was introduced in March 2005.
[3] The SAT tests are administered to all public high school juniors in Delaware (as of spring 2011), the District of Columbia (as of spring 2013), and Idaho (as of spring 2012).
[4] Beginning with the spring SAT administration in 2006, all Maine high school juniors, including all students in their third year of high school, are required to take SAT tests in critical reading, writing, and mathematics.

NOTE: Data for 2005–06 and earlier years are for seniors who took the SAT any time during their high school years through March of their senior year. Data for 2010–11 onwards are for seniors who took the SAT any time during their high school years through June of their senior year. If a student took a test more than once, the most recent score was used. The SAT was formerly known as the Scholastic Assessment Test and the Scholastic Aptitude Test. Possible scores on each part of the SAT range from 200 to 800. The critical reading section was formerly known as the verbal section.
SOURCE: College Entrance Examination Board, College-Bound Seniors Tables and Related Items, selected years, selected years, 1995–96 through 2013–14, November 5, 2014, from http://research.collegeboard.org/programs/sat/data/cb-seniors-2014 and https://www.collegeboard.org/program-results/overview. (This table was prepared November 2014.)

Table 226.50. ACT score averages and standard deviations, by sex and race/ethnicity, and percentage of ACT test takers, by selected composite score ranges and planned fields of postsecondary study: Selected years, 1995 through 2014

Score type and test-taker characteristic	1995	2000	2005	2006	2007	2008	2009	2010	2011	2012	2013	2014
1	2	3	4	5	6	7	8	9	10	11	12	13
Total test takers												
Number (in thousands)	945	1,065	1,186	1,206	1,301	1,422	1,480	1,569	1,623	1,666	1,799	1,846
Percent of graduates	37.5	37.6	38.2	38.6	40.6	42.9	44.2	45.6	47.1	48.3	52.8	54.8
						Average test score[1]						
Composite score, total	20.8	21.0	20.9	21.1	21.2	21.1	21.1	21.0	21.1	21.1	20.9	21.0
Sex												
Male	21.0	21.2	21.1	21.2	21.2	21.2	21.3	21.2	21.2	21.2	20.9	21.1
Female	20.7	20.9	20.9	21.0	21.0	21.0	20.9	20.9	21.0	21.0	20.9	20.9
Race/ethnicity												
White	—	22.7	21.9	22.0	22.1	22.1	22.2	22.3	22.4	22.4	22.2	22.3
Black	—	17.8	17.0	17.1	17.0	16.9	16.9	16.9	17.0	17.0	16.9	17.0
Hispanic	—	—	18.6	18.6	18.7	18.7	18.7	18.6	18.7	18.9	18.8	18.8
Asian/Pacific Islander	—	22.4	22.1	22.3	22.6	22.9	23.2	23.4				
Asian	—	—	—	—	—	—	—	—	23.6	23.6	23.5	23.5
Pacific Islander	—	—	—	—	—	—	—	—	19.5	19.8	19.5	18.6
American Indian/Alaska	—	20.4	18.7	18.8	18.9	19.0	18.9	19.0	18.6	18.4	18.0	18.0
Two or more races	—	—	—	—	—	—	—	—	21.1	21.4	21.1	21.2
Subject-area scores												
English	20.2	20.5	20.4	20.6	20.7	20.6	20.6	20.5	20.6	20.5	20.2	20.3
Male	19.8	20.0	20.0	20.1	20.2	20.1	20.2	20.1	20.2	20.2	19.8	20.0
Female	20.6	20.9	20.8	21.0	21.0	21.0	20.9	20.8	20.9	20.9	20.6	20.7
Mathematics	20.2	20.7	20.7	20.8	21.0	21.0	21.0	21.0	21.1	21.1	20.9	20.9
Male	20.9	21.4	21.3	21.5	21.6	21.6	21.6	21.6	21.6	21.7	21.4	21.4
Female	19.7	20.2	20.2	20.3	20.4	20.4	20.4	20.5	20.6	20.6	20.5	20.5
Reading	21.3	21.4	21.3	21.4	21.5	21.4	21.4	21.3	21.3	21.3	21.1	21.3
Male	21.1	21.2	21.0	21.1	21.2	21.2	21.3	21.1	21.1	21.2	20.9	21.1
Female	21.4	21.5	21.5	21.6	21.6	21.5	21.4	21.4	21.4	21.4	21.4	21.5
Science reasoning	21.0	21.0	20.9	20.9	21.0	20.8	20.9	20.9	20.9	20.9	20.7	20.8
Male	21.6	21.6	21.4	21.4	21.4	21.3	21.4	21.4	21.4	21.4	21.2	21.2
Female	20.5	20.6	20.5	20.5	20.5	20.4	20.4	20.5	20.5	20.5	20.4	20.5
						Standard deviation[2]						
Composite score, total	—	4.7	—	4.8	5.0	5.0	5.1	5.2	5.2	5.3	5.4	5.4
Sex												
Male	—	4.9	5.0	—	—	—	—	—	—	—	—	—
Female	—	4.6	4.7	—	—	—	—	—	—	—	—	—
Subject-area scores												
English	—	5.5	—	5.9	6.0	6.1	6.3	6.4	6.5	6.5	6.5	6.6
Male	—	5.6	6.0	—	—	—	—	—	—	—	—	—
Female	—	5.5	5.9	—	—	—	—	—	—	—	—	—
Mathematics	—	5.0	—	5.0	5.1	5.2	5.3	5.3	5.3	5.3	5.3	5.3
Male	—	5.2	5.3	—	—	—	—	—	—	—	—	—
Female	—	4.8	4.8	—	—	—	—	—	—	—	—	—
Reading	—	6.1	—	6.0	6.1	6.1	6.2	6.2	6.2	6.2	6.3	6.3
Male	—	6.1	6.1	—	—	—	—	—	—	—	—	—
Female	—	6.0	6.0	—	—	—	—	—	—	—	—	—
Science reasoning	—	4.5	—	4.6	4.9	4.9	5.0	5.1	5.1	5.2	5.3	5.5
Male	—	4.8	4.9	—	—	—	—	—	—	—	—	—
Female	—	4.3	4.3	—	—	—	—	—	—	—	—	—
						Percent of ACT test takers						
Composite score												
28 or above	—	10	10	11	11	12	12	12	13	13	13	13
17 or below	—	25	26	25	25	26	27	28	28	28	30	30
Planned major field of study												
Business[3]	13	11	9	9	8	11	12	11	10	9	9	9
Education[4]	8	9	6	6	5	6	7	7	6	6	5	5
Engineering[5]	8	8	6	6	5	7	8	8	8	8	9	9
Health sciences and technologies	—	17	16	15	14	17	19	20	19	19	19	19
Social sciences[6]	9	9	7	6	5	6	7	7	8	9	8	8

—Not available.

[1]Minimum score is 1 and maximum score is 36.
[2]Standard deviations not available for racial/ethnic groups.
[3]For years prior to 2011, includes business and management, business and office, and marketing and distribution.
[4]For years prior to 2011, includes education and teacher education.
[5]Includes engineering and engineering-related technologies.
[6]Includes social sciences and philosophy, religion, and theology. For 2011 and later years, also includes law.

NOTE: Data are for high school graduates who took the ACT during their sophomore, junior, or senior year. If a student took a test more than once, the most recent score was used. Race categories exclude persons of Hispanic ethnicity. Some data have been revised from previously published figures.
SOURCE: ACT, *High School Profile Report*, selected years, 1995 through 2014. U.S. Department of Education, National Center for Education Statistics, Common Core of Data (CCD), "State Nonfiscal Survey of Public Elementary/Secondary Education," 1995–96 through 2005–06; "State Dropout and Completion Data File," 2005–06 through 2011–12; Private School Universe Survey (PSS), 1995 through 2011; and National High School Graduates Projection Model, 1972–73 through 2023–24. (This table was prepared March 2015.)

Table 227.10. Percentage of 9th-grade students participating in various school-sponsored and non-school-sponsored activities, by sex and race/ethnicity: 2009

[Standard errors appear in parentheses]

Sex and race/ethnicity	School-sponsored activities					Non-school-sponsored activities					
	Math-related[1]	Science-related[1]	At least one of the math- or science-related activities[1]	Music, dance, art, or theater	Organized sports	Religious youth group or instruction	Scouting or other group or club activity	Academic instruction[2]	Math or science camp	Another camp	At least one of the non-school-sponsored activities
1	2	3	4	5	6	7	8	9	10	11	12
Total	9.8 (0.39)	6.4 (0.36)	13.4 (0.50)	34.6 (0.91)	54.9 (0.81)	51.4 (0.93)	22.8 (0.64)	17.7 (0.62)	4.1 (0.31)	23.8 (0.76)	85.7 (0.60)
Sex											
Male	8.9 (0.44)	6.3 (0.59)	12.6 (0.69)	27.9 (0.93)	59.8 (0.93)	49.5 (1.10)	21.6 (0.87)	17.5 (0.80)	4.1 (0.51)	23.2 (0.92)	86.1 (0.79)
Female	10.7 (0.55)	6.5 (0.45)	14.2 (0.67)	41.3 (1.20)	50.0 (1.10)	53.4 (1.12)	24.1 (0.88)	17.9 (0.80)	4.0 (0.40)	24.4 (0.91)	85.4 (0.75)
Race/ethnicity											
White	8.3 (0.35)	6.4 (0.43)	12.2 (0.46)	36.8 (0.78)	60.5 (0.87)	56.7 (1.04)	24.0 (0.83)	13.2 (0.65)	2.7 (0.26)	30.6 (0.92)	89.7 (0.47)
Black	12.5 (1.54)	5.4 (0.77)	15.3 (1.71)	33.8 (2.90)	49.1 (2.39)	52.3 (2.31)	26.3 (2.02)	32.8 (2.55)	7.4 (1.24)	14.8 (1.79)	84.9 (1.72)
Hispanic	10.5 (0.92)	5.5 (0.72)	13.4 (1.07)	27.5 (1.47)	46.9 (2.46)	39.1 (2.36)	16.6 (1.27)	18.6 (1.20)	3.6 (0.77)	14.5 (1.66)	76.9 (2.28)
Asian	17.3 (2.25)	13.0 (1.93)	22.3 (2.48)	44.4 (3.43)	38.5 (2.87)	38.8 (3.31)	25.8 (2.28)	31.1 (3.49)	15.0 (2.06)	16.2 (2.14)	82.1 (2.76)
Native Hawaiian/Pacific Islander	‡ (†)	‡ (†)	‡ (†)	20.0 ! (6.56)	‡ (†)	‡ (†)	‡ (†)	‡ (†)	‡ (†)	‡ (†)	‡ (†)
American Indian/Alaska Native	9.1 ! (2.95)	‡ (†)	12.8 ! (3.87)	‡ (†)	48.8 ! (6.60)	42.3 (6.00)	31.6 (6.00)	16.8 (4.36)	‡ (†)	19.1 ! (8.31)	78.9 (5.22)
Two or more races	10.5 (1.19)	7.6 (1.02)	14.2 (1.41)	36.4 (2.49)	55.8 (2.46)	53.6 (2.47)	24.9 (2.13)	15.4 (1.57)	3.4 (0.81)	21.2 (1.60)	86.8 (1.53)
Race/ethnicity by sex											
Male											
White	7.6 (0.45)	6.1 (0.61)	11.5 (0.73)	29.1 (0.95)	63.3 (1.06)	54.5 (1.19)	23.2 (1.12)	14.2 (0.93)	2.8 (0.36)	29.6 (1.22)	89.0 (0.61)
Black	12.2 (1.74)	5.8 (1.10)	15.4 (1.92)	27.4 (2.88)	58.2 (3.15)	49.0 (3.03)	21.0 (2.85)	31.1 (3.11)	7.5 (2.01)	14.6 (2.46)	87.3 (1.95)
Hispanic	9.2 (1.22)	5.5 (1.15)	12.1 (1.50)	22.4 (2.04)	54.4 (2.86)	37.1 (2.92)	15.3 (1.69)	16.9 (1.83)	2.9 ! (0.88)	13.1 (2.11)	78.4 (2.70)
Asian	18.4 (2.96)	11.5 (2.38)	22.8 (3.23)	36.9 (4.02)	42.9 (3.89)	32.8 (5.50)	26.1 (3.78)	31.0 (4.54)	18.4 (3.34)	20.3 (3.47)	78.9 (3.87)
Native Hawaiian/Pacific Islander	‡ (†)	‡ (†)	‡ (†)	‡ (†)	‡ (†)	‡ (†)	‡ (†)	‡ (†)	‡ (†)	‡ (†)	‡ (†)
American Indian/Alaska Native	10.9 ! (4.96)	‡ (†)	‡ (†)	18.8 ! (9.40)	49.9 ! (9.31)	38.2 (9.74)	31.3 (8.35)	‡ (†)	‡ (†)	‡ (†)	78.4 (6.67)
Two or more races	8.3 (1.37)	9.0 (1.85)	13.4 (2.04)	29.9 (2.96)	59.2 (3.78)	56.9 (3.48)	26.2 (2.99)	16.0 (2.30)	3.4 ! (1.22)	20.4 (2.28)	88.6 (1.82)
Female											
White	9.0 (0.56)	6.7 (0.61)	13.0 (0.71)	44.9 (1.16)	57.5 (1.13)	59.0 (1.17)	24.8 (1.04)	12.1 (0.76)	2.7 (0.34)	31.7 (1.08)	90.4 (0.62)
Black	12.8 (2.14)	5.0 (1.09)	15.2 (2.38)	39.0 (4.64)	41.8 (3.87)	55.0 (3.33)	30.5 (2.59)	34.2 (3.75)	7.3 (1.53)	14.9 (2.58)	83.0 (2.66)
Hispanic	11.9 (1.16)	5.5 (0.76)	14.6 (1.28)	32.9 (2.06)	39.0 (3.27)	41.1 (2.95)	17.9 (1.83)	20.3 (1.85)	4.4 (1.12)	16.0 (2.15)	75.4 (2.71)
Asian	16.1 (2.49)	14.6 (2.92)	21.8 (3.16)	51.8 (4.88)	34.2 (3.19)	44.8 (3.24)	25.6 (3.53)	31.2 (3.72)	11.7 (3.07)	12.2 (2.55)	85.3 (3.16)
Native Hawaiian/Pacific Islander	‡ (†)	‡ (†)	‡ (†)	‡ (†)	‡ (†)	‡ (†)	‡ (†)	‡ (†)	‡ (†)	‡ (†)	‡ (†)
American Indian/Alaska Native	‡ (†)	‡ (†)	‡ (†)	21.4 ! (8.36)	47.4 ! (9.63)	47.0 (11.74)	32.0 (8.98)	‡ (†)	‡ (†)	‡ (†)	79.5 (8.44)
Two or more races	12.7 (1.71)	6.3 (1.00)	15.0 (1.73)	42.4 (3.39)	52.5 (4.18)	50.4 (3.62)	23.7 (2.95)	14.8 (2.05)	3.4 ! (1.19)	22.0 (2.24)	85.1 (2.47)

†Not applicable.
!Interpret data with caution. The coefficient of variation (CV) for this estimate is between 30 and 50 percent.
‡Reporting standards not met. Either there are too few cases for a reliable estimate or the coefficient of variation (CV) is 50 percent or greater.
[1]Students could indicate that they participated in clubs, competitions, camps, study groups, or tutoring programs.
[2]Academic instruction outside of school such as from a Saturday academy, learning center, personal tutor, or summer school program.

NOTE: Data on school-sponsored activities are based on student responses and are weighted by W1STUDENT. Student reports about school-sponsored activities refer to the period "since the beginning of the last school year," which for most of these students was 8th grade, or the fall of 2008. Data on non-school-sponsored activities are based on parent responses and are weighted by W1PARENT. Parent reports about non-school-sponsored activities refer to the last 12 months. Race categories exclude persons of Hispanic ethnicity.
SOURCE: U.S. Department of Education, National Center for Education Statistics, High School Longitudinal Study of 2009, Base-Year Public-Use Data File. (This table was prepared September 2012.)

Table 227.20. Percentage of high school seniors who say they engage in various activities, by selected student and school characteristics: 1992 and 2004

[Standard errors appear in parentheses]

Activity	Total	Sex		Race/ethnicity					Socioeconomic status[1]			Control of school attended		
		Male	Female	White	Black	Hispanic	Asian/ Pacific Islander	American Indian/Alaska Native	Low	Middle	High	Public	Catholic	Other private
1	2	3	4	5	6	7	8	9	10	11	12	13	14	15
1992														
At least once a week														
Use personal computer[2]	23.6 (0.52)	28.1 (0.76)	19.3 (0.64)	23.9 (0.58)	23.3 (1.71)	20.7 (1.49)	26.6 (1.90)	22.0 (3.88)	18.7 (1.10)	23.4 (0.73)	27.6 (0.91)	23.3 (0.50)	26.0 (2.58)	29.0 (3.04)
Work on hobbies	40.9 (0.62)	44.4 (0.85)	37.6 (0.86)	42.2 (0.71)	34.5 (1.99)	39.7 (1.71)	37.7 (2.16)	51.8 (4.20)	36.3 (1.29)	41.1 (0.84)	43.6 (1.14)	40.6 (0.59)	42.4 (2.69)	41.1 (2.60)
Perform community service	11.3 (0.48)	10.7 (0.80)	11.9 (0.52)	11.1 (0.60)	12.1 (1.26)	11.1 (1.03)	13.8 (1.58)	8.0! (2.56)	7.6 (0.61)	9.6 (0.46)	16.9 (1.22)	9.6 (0.37)	23.6 (2.50)	22.9 (2.63)
Driving or riding around	73.2 (0.59)	74.4 (0.84)	72.1 (0.75)	75.7 (0.64)	67.8 (2.15)	66.0 (1.82)	66.5 (2.05)	67.6 (4.40)	69.6 (1.26)	75.3 (0.75)	72.4 (1.13)	74.0 (0.55)	76.1 (2.41)	68.7 (2.91)
Visiting with friends at a local hangout	88.0 (0.45)	88.2 (0.62)	87.9 (0.62)	90.6 (0.41)	79.8 (2.02)	82.1 (1.27)	85.7 (1.46)	73.0 (4.89)	80.6 (1.05)	88.0 (0.66)	93.2 (0.57)	88.2 (0.39)	93.3 (1.23)	95.1 (0.78)
Talk on phone with friends	80.5 (0.56)	72.6 (0.88)	88.3 (0.64)	81.7 (0.62)	81.3 (2.01)	71.8 (1.60)	77.2 (1.82)	73.7 (6.12)	72.8 (1.13)	81.6 (0.71)	83.7 (1.10)	80.4 (0.54)	86.8 (1.84)	77.9 (2.77)
Take music, art, or dance class	10.2 (0.35)	7.9 (0.44)	12.4 (0.52)	10.0 (0.40)	9.6 (1.11)	9.9 (1.27)	14.1 (1.21)	10.7! (3.40)	7.2 (0.67)	8.9 (0.43)	14.2 (0.75)	9.7 (0.35)	12.4 (1.55)	14.9 (1.49)
Take sports lessons	7.3 (0.38)	9.7 (0.62)	5.0 (0.45)	7.0 (0.46)	7.5 (0.80)	8.0 (1.14)	9.3 (1.06)	10.0! (4.07)	5.5 (0.61)	6.6 (0.40)	9.5 (0.96)	6.5 (0.29)	9.2 (1.60)	7.3 (1.13)
Play nonschool sports	26.2 (0.62)	38.7 (0.91)	14.0 (0.50)	27.1 (0.73)	22.6 (1.79)	23.4 (1.55)	28.1 (2.13)	27.3 (4.25)	20.4 (1.01)	24.5 (0.73)	32.9 (1.29)	25.6 (0.59)	35.1 (2.71)	28.0 (3.00)
Reading 3 or more hours per week (not for school)	33.7 (0.56)	30.9 (0.78)	36.4 (0.78)	34.5 (0.64)	28.6 (1.81)	32.8 (1.75)	35.3 (2.03)	34.4 (3.90)	29.7 (1.10)	33.4 (0.77)	36.7 (1.01)	33.2 (0.59)	32.4 (2.35)	38.8 (2.51)
Plays video/computer games 3 or more hours per day on weekdays	2.0 (0.16)	3.2 (0.29)	0.8 (0.12)	1.8 (0.18)	3.3 (0.64)	2.1 (0.43)	2.7! (0.88)	2.5! (1.19)	3.4 (0.40)	2.1 (0.23)	1.1 (0.19)	2.1 (0.18)	1.6! (0.50)	0.6! (0.26)
Watches television 3 or more hours per day on weekdays	27.0 (0.62)	27.7 (0.88)	26.4 (0.77)	23.6 (0.67)	49.2 (2.29)	26.6 (1.54)	25.0 (2.20)	36.4 (4.85)	34.1 (1.24)	29.3 (0.89)	18.1 (1.03)	26.4 (0.56)	26.1 (2.29)	15.5 (2.34)
2004														
At least once a week														
Use personal computer at home	79.3 (0.52)	79.6 (0.65)	79.0 (0.69)	84.7 (0.54)	62.8 (1.34)	71.4 (1.32)	89.5 (1.06)	68.8 (2.31)	61.9 (1.07)	79.8 (0.63)	92.3 (0.53)	78.2 (0.56)	93.2 (0.69)	89.6 (1.90)
Work on hobbies	46.5 (0.56)	49.6 (0.80)	43.3 (0.71)	46.8 (0.68)	44.3 (1.46)	44.8 (1.39)	49.3 (1.75)	58.4 (2.40)	42.2 (1.07)	46.6 (0.76)	49.6 (0.93)	46.3 (0.60)	47.2 (1.41)	48.6 (1.90)
Perform community service	18.7 (0.45)	15.1 (0.54)	22.3 (0.63)	17.9 (0.52)	21.1 (1.22)	17.5 (1.11)	27.4 (1.36)	11.6 (2.05)	15.7 (0.74)	17.4 (0.64)	23.5 (0.81)	18.3 (0.48)	23.8 (1.29)	22.1 (1.81)
Driving or riding around	65.7 (0.61)	67.5 (0.78)	64.0 (0.79)	70.0 (0.70)	63.9 (1.28)	54.0 (1.28)	58.3 (1.93)	77.0 (3.70)	59.0 (1.17)	67.2 (0.82)	68.4 (0.93)	65.7 (0.66)	68.8 (1.36)	62.8 (2.24)
Visiting with friends at a local hangout	86.1 (0.41)	88.4 (0.46)	83.9 (0.63)	90.7 (0.40)	79.9 (1.03)	77.7 (1.16)	79.0 (1.37)	82.6 (2.52)	76.6 (0.94)	87.7 (0.51)	90.9 (0.56)	85.7 (0.44)	92.2 (0.65)	89.2 (1.05)
Talk on phone with friends	72.1 (0.48)	65.2 (0.71)	78.9 (0.58)	80.5 (0.61)	80.5 (0.98)	66.6 (1.24)	64.7 (1.75)	73.1 (2.68)	66.0 (0.95)	73.5 (0.66)	74.2 (0.82)	71.8 (0.52)	77.5 (1.30)	72.7 (1.53)
Take music, art, or language class	17.7 (0.46)	13.8 (0.52)	21.7 (0.66)	17.5 (0.61)	18.7 (0.96)	15.2 (1.02)	21.2 (1.42)	17.8 (1.30)	13.6 (0.95)	17.0 (0.61)	22.4 (0.71)	17.4 (0.49)	19.6 (1.22)	22.6 (1.75)
Take sports lessons	13.2 (0.41)	15.8 (0.61)	10.7 (0.48)	12.5 (0.47)	15.7 (1.09)	13.5 (1.07)	12.9 (1.31)	12.1 (0.43)	10.8 (0.70)	12.6 (0.57)	16.4 (0.71)	12.9 (0.44)	18.8 (0.92)	14.4 (1.07)
Play nonschool sports	27.4 (0.53)	39.2 (0.77)	15.7 (0.62)	26.8 (0.70)	28.3 (1.14)	27.5 (1.27)	30.7 (1.57)	38.7 (1.61)	24.3 (0.91)	27.3 (0.73)	30.0 (1.06)	27.3 (0.57)	31.2 (1.47)	24.8 (1.74)
Reading 3 or more hours per week (not for school)	32.0 (0.51)	29.5 (0.70)	34.5 (0.71)	31.5 (0.66)	32.7 (1.24)	32.8 (1.28)	30.5 (1.43)	34.4 (3.73)	30.3 (0.99)	30.8 (0.72)	35.6 (0.89)	32.0 (0.55)	29.6 (1.47)	34.9 (1.74)
Plays video/computer games 3 or more hours per day on weekdays	5.9 (0.27)	10.4 (0.48)	1.5 (0.18)	5.1 (0.31)	7.8 (0.78)	6.6 (0.66)	6.1 (0.81)	8.9 (1.17)	7.2 (0.54)	6.3 (0.40)	4.2 (0.35)	6.1 (0.29)	3.8 (0.50)	3.5 (0.59)
Watches television/DVDs 3 or more hours per day on weekdays	28.1 (0.54)	29.3 (0.76)	26.9 (0.69)	21.9 (0.61)	51.7 (1.37)	33.0 (1.06)	24.6 (1.72)	29.9 (3.81)	35.6 (1.00)	29.3 (0.76)	20.0 (0.75)	28.8 (0.58)	24.3 (1.60)	15.8 (1.43)
Hours of homework per week														
Less than 1 hour	13.3 (0.44)	17.3 (0.67)	9.4 (0.48)	14.0 (0.56)	15.1 (0.93)	10.7 (0.83)	6.5 (1.09)	14.9 (1.38)	15.6 (0.78)	14.8 (0.62)	8.7 (0.55)	14.0 (0.47)	5.5 (0.70)	5.4 (1.19)
1 to 3 hours	28.7 (0.52)	30.2 (0.72)	27.3 (0.75)	27.3 (0.64)	32.6 (1.18)	33.9 (1.27)	16.6 (1.52)	29.6 (2.75)	32.7 (0.97)	30.3 (0.71)	22.8 (0.89)	29.7 (0.56)	19.5 (1.32)	16.9 (1.57)
4 to 6 hours	25.0 (0.49)	24.5 (0.68)	25.5 (0.66)	25.8 (0.64)	24.7 (1.18)	23.0 (1.20)	26.7 (1.59)	21.4 (1.19)	24.2 (0.94)	25.1 (0.67)	25.6 (0.89)	25.0 (0.53)	27.3 (1.23)	24.0 (1.48)
7 to 12 hours	21.7 (0.51)	19.8 (0.68)	23.6 (0.68)	22.4 (0.65)	18.0 (0.98)	21.7 (1.26)	27.3 (1.46)	26.9 (3.86)	18.2 (0.81)	20.5 (0.66)	26.8 (0.90)	20.9 (0.55)	29.1 (1.13)	32.2 (1.87)
More than 12 hours	11.2 (0.39)	8.2 (0.43)	14.2 (0.61)	10.5 (0.47)	9.6 (0.85)	10.7 (0.99)	22.8 (1.66)	7.2! (2.20)	9.3 (0.76)	9.3 (0.46)	16.1 (0.73)	10.4 (0.40)	18.6 (1.52)	21.5 (2.83)

! Interpret data with caution. The coefficient of variation (CV) for this estimate is between 30 and 50 percent.

[1] Socioeconomic status (SES) was measured by a composite score on parental education and occupations, and family income. The "low" SES group is the lowest quartile; the "middle" SES group is the middle two quartiles; and the "high" SES group is the upper quartile.

[2] Question does not specify where computer is used.

NOTE: Race categories exclude persons of Hispanic ethnicity. Total includes other racial/ethnic groups not separately shown.
SOURCE: U.S. Department of Education, National Center for Education Statistics, National Education Longitudinal Study of 1988 (NELS:88/92), "Second Follow-up Student Survey, 1992"; and Education Longitudinal Study of 2002 (ELS:2002/04), "First Follow-up, 2004." (This table was prepared December 2009.)

Table 227.30. Percentage of high school seniors who participate in various school-sponsored extracurricular activities, by selected student characteristics: 1992 and 2004

[Standard errors appear in parentheses]

Selected student characteristic	Academic clubs		Sports				Cheerleading and drill team[2]	Hobby clubs (photography, chess, etc.)		Music (band, orchestra, chorus, or choir)		Vocational clubs (Future Farmers of America, Skills USA, etc.)	
			Any sport		Interscholastic[1]	Intramural[1]							
	1992	2004	1992	2004	2004	2004	1992	1992	2004	1992	2004	1992	2004
1	2	3	4	5	6	7	8	9	10	11	12	13	14
All seniors	25.0 (0.58)	21.3 (0.49)	42.7 (0.67)	44.4 (0.56)	38.8 (0.56)	19.2 (0.47)	7.6 (0.34)	7.7 (0.32)	11.7 (0.38)	19.8 (0.51)	21.0 (0.55)	17.6 (0.58)	15.6 (0.55)
Sex													
Male	22.7 (0.80)	17.8 (0.58)	55.5 (0.92)	50.6 (0.80)	44.5 (0.79)	24.2 (0.71)	2.0 (0.24)	8.1 (0.44)	11.9 (0.51)	15.1 (0.62)	16.3 (0.66)	14.7 (0.68)	14.8 (0.68)
Female	27.1 (0.76)	24.7 (0.73)	30.1 (0.80)	38.2 (0.76)	33.2 (0.74)	14.3 (0.57)	13.0 (0.60)	7.4 (0.44)	11.6 (0.48)	24.3 (0.75)	25.5 (0.73)	20.4 (0.75)	16.3 (0.69)
Race/ethnicity													
White	24.3 (4.66)	22.6 (0.62)	41.4 (5.81)	46.9 (0.70)	42.1 (0.69)	18.8 (0.58)	13.3 ! (4.87)	10.1 ! (5.01)	11.4 (0.51)	15.4 (3.65)	22.0 (0.68)	12.2 (2.98)	16.8 (0.74)
Black	21.2 (1.64)	16.5 (0.90)	41.6 (2.29)	45.4 (1.21)	37.5 (1.15)	24.4 (1.05)	10.0 (1.73)	6.9 (0.94)	9.1 (0.75)	24.6 (1.57)	24.0 (1.21)	23.1 (1.82)	17.5 (1.17)
Hispanic	26.1 (0.72)	18.3 (1.15)	44.0 (0.79)	35.3 (1.25)	29.5 (1.25)	16.9 (1.02)	7.6 (0.35)	7.4 (0.37)	11.8 (0.87)	20.0 (0.62)	14.3 (0.97)	17.8 (0.71)	11.8 (1.04)
Asian/Pacific Islander	22.0 (1.55)	34.7 (1.90)	36.2 (1.84)	40.6 (1.81)	33.4 (1.71)	18.0 (1.48)	7.6 (1.15)	8.1 (1.05)	20.3 (1.50)	19.1 (1.68)	19.0 (1.57)	17.6 (1.59)	9.2 (0.78)
American Indian/Alaska Native	31.9 (2.31)	19.7 (2.88)	43.9 (2.25)	45.8 (1.42)	40.8 (2.29)	20.7 (0.34)	5.3 (0.97)	11.2 (1.51)	6.3 (0.37)	18.6 (2.01)	15.9 (2.10)	10.4 (1.53)	22.6 (2.23)
Test performance quartile[3]													
Lowest test quartile	17.0 (1.40)	13.4 (0.74)	40.5 (1.46)	34.5 (1.09)	28.0 (1.02)	20.4 (1.00)	7.6 (0.70)	7.9 (0.64)	8.4 (0.63)	18.7 (1.06)	17.7 (0.90)	25.0 (1.38)	17.8 (0.94)
Second test quartile	20.6 (1.10)	16.1 (0.86)	37.5 (1.22)	42.4 (1.06)	36.1 (1.04)	21.3 (0.85)	7.0 (0.86)	7.0 (0.66)	9.7 (0.63)	17.2 (0.88)	17.7 (0.86)	23.2 (1.19)	17.9 (0.92)
Third test quartile	24.1 (1.02)	20.9 (0.86)	44.0 (1.14)	46.5 (1.05)	41.3 (1.04)	19.2 (0.76)	8.3 (0.62)	7.1 (0.58)	11.2 (0.65)	19.7 (0.94)	20.6 (0.90)	16.6 (0.81)	15.5 (0.82)
Highest test quartile	36.1 (1.10)	31.8 (0.91)	48.3 (1.17)	52.7 (0.98)	48.0 (0.96)	17.1 (0.82)	7.8 (0.54)	8.7 (0.59)	16.7 (0.78)	24.1 (0.94)	26.3 (0.92)	11.9 (0.78)	12.5 (0.75)
Socioeconomic status[4]													
Low	18.3 (0.94)	16.4 (0.89)	32.3 (1.23)	33.1 (1.05)	26.4 (1.01)	16.5 (0.79)	6.7 (0.96)	6.6 (0.62)	8.0 (0.61)	17.6 (0.96)	16.6 (0.75)	24.4 (1.25)	17.3 (0.94)
Middle	24.1 (0.78)	19.6 (0.65)	41.3 (0.84)	43.7 (0.77)	38.5 (0.75)	19.6 (0.62)	8.0 (0.43)	7.0 (0.41)	11.2 (0.48)	19.6 (0.71)	20.7 (0.68)	19.6 (0.79)	16.8 (0.71)
High	30.9 (1.12)	28.3 (0.89)	52.2 (1.21)	54.6 (0.95)	49.3 (0.99)	20.7 (0.86)	7.8 (0.53)	9.3 (0.59)	15.7 (0.77)	22.0 (0.96)	24.9 (0.98)	9.9 (0.59)	12.1 (0.70)
Region													
Northeast	23.3 (1.06)	21.1 (0.93)	48.0 (1.41)	47.6 (1.27)	41.8 (1.42)	21.7 (1.19)	6.9 (0.67)	9.2 (0.79)	14.0 (0.99)	20.8 (1.07)	20.4 (1.19)	8.4 (0.91)	9.9 (1.03)
Midwest	25.2 (1.17)	20.1 (1.00)	45.6 (1.29)	48.3 (1.13)	41.9 (1.06)	20.9 (1.02)	8.3 (0.61)	6.5 (0.54)	9.8 (0.78)	23.8 (1.07)	25.6 (1.22)	18.0 (1.30)	16.3 (1.40)
South	28.4 (1.14)	23.5 (0.83)	38.6 (1.17)	42.1 (0.93)	36.7 (0.90)	17.6 (0.74)	8.4 (0.70)	6.8 (0.60)	10.5 (0.55)	17.8 (0.82)	20.1 (0.86)	27.4 (1.14)	21.4 (0.94)
West	21.3 (1.08)	19.5 (1.17)	40.7 (1.41)	40.9 (1.22)	36.2 (1.19)	17.7 (0.97)	6.3 (0.62)	9.4 (0.72)	13.9 (0.92)	17.6 (1.12)	17.6 (1.19)	10.2 (0.84)	10.8 (0.94)
Senior's school sector													
Public	24.9 (0.61)	20.5 (0.52)	41.4 (0.69)	42.9 (0.60)	37.5 (0.59)	18.5 (0.49)	7.7 (0.36)	7.4 (0.33)	11.1 (0.41)	19.8 (0.53)	20.6 (0.58)	19.0 (0.62)	16.6 (0.60)
Catholic	27.7 (2.50)	29.5 (1.61)	54.5 (2.98)	60.8 (1.64)	53.1 (1.46)	28.1 (1.96)	7.8 (1.39)	10.4 (1.60)	18.8 (1.22)	14.2 (1.96)	19.2 (1.53)	2.7 (0.61)	4.2 (0.66)
Other private	21.6 (2.80)	29.3 (2.40)	58.3 (3.06)	60.5 (2.72)	51.7 (2.98)	25.8 (2.82)	5.7 (1.49)	11.4 (2.32)	18.1 (1.76)	29.9 (2.67)	31.6 (3.51)	2.2 ! (0.76)	4.0 (0.81)

! Interpret data with caution. The coefficient of variation (CV) for this estimate is between 30 and 50 percent.

[1] Interscholastic refers to competition between teams from different schools. Intramural refers to competition between teams or students within the same school. Data on these categories are available only for 2004.

[2] These data were not collected in 2004.

[3] Composite test performance quartile on mathematics, reading, science, and social studies in 1990 (for 1992 seniors) and composite test performance quartile on mathematics, reading, and science in 2002 (for 2004 seniors).

[4] Socioeconomic status (SES) was measured by a composite score on parental education and occupations, and family income.

NOTE: Race categories exclude persons of Hispanic ethnicity.

SOURCE: U.S. Department of Education, National Center for Education Statistics, National Education Longitudinal Study of 1988 (NELS:88/92), "Second Follow-up, 1992"; and Education Longitudinal Study of 2002 (ELS:2002/04), "First Follow-up, 2004." (This table was prepared December 2009.)

Table 227.40. Percentage of elementary and secondary school students who do homework, average time spent, percentage whose parents check that homework is done, and percentage whose parents help with homework, by frequency and selected characteristics: 2007 and 2012

[Standard errors appear in parentheses]

Year and selected characteristic	Percent of students who do homework outside of school	Students who do homework outside of school: Average hours spent per week doing homework	Percentage distribution by how frequently they do homework: Less than once per week	1 to 2 days per week	3 to 4 days per week	5 or more days per week	Percent whose parents check that homework is done[2]	No help given	Percentage distribution by how frequently their parents help with homework: Less than once per week	1 to 2 days per week	3 to 4 days per week	5 or more days per week
1	2	3	4	5	6	7	8	9	10	11	12	13
2007												
All students	94.4 (0.30)	5.4 (0.06)	3.1 (0.34)	13.1 (0.47)	43.6 (0.62)	40.2 (0.60)	85.4 (0.46)	10.2 (0.41)	20.3 (0.51)	31.7 (0.64)	25.3 (0.59)	12.4 (0.41)
All elementary school students (kindergarten through grade 8)	95.0 (0.37)	4.7 (0.07)	2.1 (0.23)	12.3 (0.56)	46.2 (0.73)	39.4 (0.68)	95.0 (0.34)	4.3 (0.34)	13.1 (0.52)	32.6 (0.77)	32.9 (0.76)	17.0 (0.56)
Sex												
Male	94.6 (0.51)	4.6 (0.09)	2.1 (0.31)	12.4 (0.71)	47.9 (1.19)	37.6 (1.09)	95.3 (0.47)	4.3 (0.39)	12.9 (0.63)	32.3 (1.02)	32.7 (1.28)	17.8 (0.85)
Female	95.4 (0.53)	4.9 (0.10)	2.1 (0.31)	12.2 (0.96)	44.4 (1.13)	41.3 (1.08)	94.6 (0.48)	4.3 (0.56)	13.4 (0.76)	32.9 (1.17)	33.2 (1.17)	16.1 (0.79)
Race/ethnicity												
White	94.7 (0.48)	4.4 (0.07)	2.7 (0.36)	13.7 (0.74)	48.3 (1.05)	35.3 (0.99)	94.0 (0.42)	3.8 (0.37)	15.7 (0.74)	34.9 (0.94)	31.3 (0.92)	14.3 (0.63)
Black	95.5 (1.07)	5.6 (0.27)	1.3 ! (0.53)	7.0 (1.19)	44.4 (3.40)	47.2 (3.11)	98.1 (0.63)	3.5 (1.03)	7.4 (1.14)	25.2 (2.22)	38.3 (3.36)	25.5 (2.38)
Hispanic	94.8 (0.85)	4.7 (0.11)	1.3 (0.33)	13.5 (1.39)	40.7 (1.94)	44.4 (1.74)	96.1 (0.70)	7.1 (0.95)	10.3 (0.91)	30.1 (1.79)	34.0 (1.78)	18.6 (1.52)
Asian/Pacific Islander	95.9 (2.14)	5.7 (0.36)	‡ (†)	4.7 (1.35)	54.3 (4.35)	40.1 (4.73)	89.4 (3.22)	3.7 ! (1.35)	15.4 (4.07)	34.7 (4.39)	29.3 (4.03)	17.0 (2.54)
Asian	97.7 (0.97)	5.7 (0.39)	‡ (†)	5.1 ! (1.53)	54.8 (4.31)	39.1 (4.48)	88.5 (3.44)	3.1 ! (1.36)	12.8 (2.84)	37.5 (4.52)	30.7 (4.22)	15.9 (2.56)
Pacific Islander	‡ (†)	‡ (†)	‡ (†)	‡ (†)	‡ (†)	‡ (†)	‡ (†)	‡ (†)	‡ (†)	‡ (†)	‡ (†)	‡ (†)
American Indian/Alaska Native	‡ (†)	‡ (†)	‡ (†)	‡ (†)	‡ (†)	‡ (†)	‡ (†)	‡ (†)	‡ (†)	‡ (†)	‡ (†)	‡ (†)
Other	96.7 (1.24)	4.8 (0.25)	1.2 ! (0.56)	8.5 (1.73)	57.1 (3.81)	33.1 (3.69)	95.1 (1.81)	‡ (†)	12.3 (2.30)	35.5 (3.99)	33.8 (3.81)	16.1 (2.71)
School control												
Public	95.1 (0.38)	4.7 (0.08)	2.0 (0.25)	12.4 (0.62)	46.1 (0.76)	39.4 (0.73)	95.4 (0.36)	4.4 (0.38)	13.1 (0.55)	32.4 (0.86)	32.9 (0.81)	17.2 (0.64)
Private	94.0 (1.01)	4.8 (0.19)	2.7 (0.63)	11.4 (1.96)	46.7 (2.64)	39.2 (2.46)	91.5 (1.19)	3.6 (0.85)	13.6 (1.48)	34.3 (2.10)	33.5 (2.36)	15.2 (1.68)
Poverty status[3]												
Poor	94.2 (0.99)	4.7 (0.20)	2.9 (0.72)	16.3 (2.18)	39.0 (2.53)	41.7 (2.21)	97.9 (0.55)	6.1 (1.01)	8.8 (1.29)	28.5 (2.44)	35.2 (2.41)	21.3 (1.90)
Near-poor	93.1 (1.03)	4.7 (0.16)	2.2 (0.49)	13.4 (1.37)	47.0 (1.89)	37.5 (1.91)	95.8 (1.05)	5.2 (0.92)	11.5 (1.13)	31.8 (1.79)	33.3 (1.63)	18.2 (1.60)
Nonpoor	95.9 (0.38)	4.8 (0.08)	1.8 (0.24)	10.7 (0.59)	48.3 (0.94)	39.2 (0.89)	93.7 (0.48)	3.5 (0.32)	15.1 (0.68)	34.2 (0.85)	32.1 (0.79)	15.2 (0.59)
Locale												
City	95.2 (0.65)	5.1 (0.13)	1.5 (0.31)	9.1 (0.91)	43.4 (1.58)	46.0 (1.43)	95.4 (0.54)	4.8 (0.67)	11.3 (1.02)	29.1 (1.39)	36.0 (1.41)	18.7 (1.15)
Suburb	95.4 (0.51)	4.9 (0.11)	1.9 (0.37)	9.3 (0.71)	46.1 (1.24)	42.7 (1.19)	93.5 (0.67)	4.4 (0.55)	14.5 (0.85)	33.1 (1.05)	30.8 (1.14)	17.1 (0.91)
Town	93.0 (1.50)	4.1 (0.14)	2.7 (0.79)	18.8 (1.98)	46.4 (2.29)	32.2 (2.08)	96.0 (1.04)	3.2 (0.80)	14.2 (1.62)	35.7 (2.68)	31.1 (2.31)	15.7 (1.62)
Rural	95.0 (0.85)	4.2 (0.15)	3.2 (0.69)	19.5 (1.79)	50.6 (1.90)	26.8 (1.63)	96.3 (0.72)	4.1 (0.94)	13.1 (1.30)	35.5 (2.29)	32.8 (2.23)	14.6 (1.37)
All secondary school students (grades 9 through 12)	93.0 (0.55)	6.8 (0.11)	5.4 (0.85)	14.8 (0.96)	38.0 (1.15)	41.9 (1.18)	64.6 (1.21)	23.1 (1.08)	35.9 (1.26)	29.7 (1.19)	8.8 (0.81)	2.5 (0.34)
Sex												
Male	91.2 (0.80)	6.0 (0.19)	7.4 (1.53)	18.3 (1.59)	38.2 (1.78)	36.0 (1.64)	67.8 (1.88)	24.1 (1.56)	36.9 (1.97)	29.1 (1.84)	8.2 (1.11)	1.8 (0.41)
Female	94.9 (0.79)	7.5 (0.16)	3.3 (0.72)	11.2 (1.10)	37.7 (1.79)	47.9 (1.85)	61.4 (1.78)	22.0 (1.32)	35.0 (1.44)	30.4 (1.35)	9.3 (1.11)	3.3 (0.60)
Race/ethnicity												
White	94.5 (0.52)	6.8 (0.13)	4.2 (0.58)	12.9 (0.91)	38.6 (1.51)	44.3 (1.42)	57.2 (1.54)	22.5 (1.28)	41.1 (1.36)	27.7 (1.43)	6.3 (0.66)	2.3 (0.42)
Black	91.8 (1.98)	6.3 (0.38)	‡ (†)	20.1 (3.86)	41.0 (4.72)	29.7 (3.43)	83.1 (2.84)	19.5 (2.97)	26.5 (4.77)	34.4 (4.03)	16.7 (4.45)	2.9 ! (1.13)
Hispanic	90.7 (2.11)	6.4 (0.34)	5.9 (1.29)	17.7 (3.55)	36.6 (2.93)	39.9 (3.03)	75.6 (2.71)	26.2 (2.94)	25.8 (2.38)	33.8 (3.49)	11.0 (1.76)	3.3 ! (1.00)
Asian/Pacific Islander	94.2 (4.66)	10.9 (1.22)	‡ (†)	12.2 ! (4.84)	22.3 (6.26)	63.6 (7.16)	65.0 (7.41)	27.1 (7.15)	34.0 (6.73)	27.0 (6.87)	9.2 ! (3.24)	‡ (†)
Asian	93.6 (5.45)	10.3 (1.37)	‡ (†)	13.8 ! (5.51)	18.5 ! (6.12)	67.7 (7.18)	59.0 (7.69)	26.4 (7.58)	36.1 (7.55)	26.8 (7.61)	7.6 ! (3.11)	‡ (†)
Pacific Islander	‡ (†)	‡ (†)	# (†)	‡ (†)	‡ (†)	‡ (†)	‡ (†)	‡ (†)	‡ (†)	‡ (†)	‡ (†)	‡ (†)
American Indian/Alaska Native	‡ (†)	‡ (†)	‡ (†)	‡ (†)	‡ (†)	‡ (†)	‡ (†)	‡ (†)	‡ (†)	‡ (†)	‡ (†)	‡ (†)
Other	86.7 (4.90)	7.2 (0.72)	‡ (†)	9.9 (2.55)	34.1 (4.90)	50.2 (5.29)	64.4 (6.36)	27.2 (6.80)	35.6 (5.57)	27.8 (5.30)	7.9 ! (2.41)	‡ (†)
School control												
Public	92.3 (0.60)	6.5 (0.11)	5.9 (0.96)	15.9 (1.06)	39.7 (1.26)	38.5 (1.17)	66.1 (1.24)	22.8 (1.16)	35.4 (1.29)	30.0 (1.26)	9.1 (0.87)	2.7 (0.37)
Private	98.5 (0.54)	9.3 (0.39)	0.8 ! (0.35)	5.9 (1.34)	24.0 (2.72)	69.4 (2.89)	53.1 (3.98)	25.0 (2.64)	40.1 (3.68)	27.5 (4.07)	6.1 (1.36)	1.4 ! (0.61)
Poverty status[3]												
Poor	89.5 (2.21)	5.5 (0.32)	‡ (†)	19.2 (3.62)	38.7 (4.32)	33.7 (3.69)	81.0 (3.03)	24.2 (3.80)	24.0 (4.21)	36.1 (3.76)	14.0 (3.21)	1.7 ! (0.63)
Near-poor	89.5 (1.86)	6.4 (0.35)	6.6 (1.58)	20.5 (3.32)	44.2 (3.43)	28.7 (3.10)	70.8 (3.38)	22.9 (2.90)	32.4 (2.97)	28.7 (3.42)	13.0 (2.22)	3.0 ! (1.02)
Nonpoor	94.9 (0.57)	7.2 (0.13)	4.3 (0.54)	12.1 (0.74)	36.1 (1.41)	47.5 (1.34)	58.9 (1.28)	22.8 (1.11)	39.9 (1.29)	28.4 (1.17)	6.3 (0.68)	2.6 (0.45)

See notes at end of table.

Table 227.40. Percentage of elementary and secondary school students who do homework, average time spent, percentage whose parents check that homework is done, and percentage whose parents help with homework, by frequency and selected characteristics: 2007 and 2012—Continued

[Standard errors appear in parentheses]

Year and selected characteristic	Percent of students who do homework outside of school	Average hours spent per week doing homework	Less than once per week	1 to 2 days per week	3 to 4 days per week	5 or more days per week	Percent whose parents[1] check that homework is done[2]	No help given	Less than once per week	1 to 2 days per week	3 to 4 days per week	5 or more days per week
	2	3	4	5	6	7	8	9	10	11	12	13
Coursework												
Enrolled in AP classes	96.9 (0.59)	8.5 (0.22)	2.4 (0.70)	7.5 (0.93)	31.9 (1.81)	58.2 (1.97)	56.3 (2.06)	27.4 (1.90)	36.3 (1.69)	28.3 (1.74)	6.0 (0.99)	1.9 (0.43)
Not enrolled in AP classes	90.6 (0.81)	5.7 (0.13)	7.3 (1.31)	19.5 (1.40)	41.9 (1.56)	31.2 (1.42)	70.1 (1.46)	20.2 (1.14)	35.7 (1.70)	30.7 (1.59)	10.5 (1.23)	2.9 (0.51)
Locale												
City	92.8 (1.01)	6.8 (0.22)	6.3! (2.46)	14.1 (1.90)	35.9 (2.32)	43.7 (2.53)	71.5 (1.89)	22.6 (1.88)	33.4 (2.64)	29.3 (2.00)	12.0 (1.80)	2.7 (0.55)
Suburb	93.6 (0.95)	7.5 (0.17)	4.8 (0.86)	11.4 (1.27)	36.5 (1.71)	47.4 (2.07)	58.9 (2.00)	23.6 (1.74)	39.1 (1.79)	27.8 (1.68)	7.5 (1.01)	2.0 (0.47)
Town	89.7 (2.16)	6.4 (0.27)	5.4 (1.48)	13.2 (1.74)	45.9 (3.46)	35.5 (3.17)	64.8 (3.12)	24.3 (2.81)	34.4 (2.96)	27.9 (3.41)	9.3 (1.80)	4.2! (1.54)
Rural	93.9 (1.23)	5.6 (0.29)	5.1 (1.20)	22.7 (2.76)	39.6 (3.04)	32.6 (2.79)	65.5 (2.94)	22.1 (2.69)	34.4 (2.71)	34.8 (3.43)	6.2 (1.53)	2.5! (0.88)
2012												
All students	96.0 (0.27)	5.2 (0.05)	5.3 (0.22)	15.3 (0.46)	43.5 (0.58)	35.9 (0.59)	96.6 (0.18)	8.5 (0.24)	22.0 (0.43)	26.5 (0.43)	26.5 (0.52)	16.6 (0.41)
All elementary school students (kindergarten through grade 8)	96.3 (0.29)	4.7 (0.06)	4.1 (0.27)	12.8 (0.50)	46.7 (0.74)	36.3 (0.68)	99.0 (0.12)	3.0 (0.24)	14.5 (0.40)	27.0 (0.54)	33.7 (0.64)	21.9 (0.57)
Sex												
Male	96.2 (0.37)	4.5 (0.09)	4.7 (0.41)	13.5 (0.64)	46.7 (0.91)	35.1 (0.90)	99.1 (0.18)	3.3 (0.35)	14.7 (0.60)	26.0 (0.73)	34.5 (0.88)	21.5 (0.83)
Female	96.5 (0.46)	4.8 (0.09)	3.4 (0.37)	12.1 (0.69)	46.8 (1.21)	37.7 (1.04)	98.9 (0.15)	2.7 (0.31)	14.3 (0.59)	28.0 (0.90)	32.7 (1.03)	22.3 (0.88)
Race/ethnicity												
White	95.4 (0.54)	4.4 (0.07)	5.3 (0.40)	14.3 (0.69)	47.4 (0.95)	33.0 (0.91)	98.8 (0.16)	2.5 (0.27)	17.7 (0.61)	27.5 (0.68)	33.4 (0.92)	18.9 (0.82)
Black	96.2 (0.83)	5.5 (0.19)	3.5 (0.86)	14.0 (1.63)	47.9 (2.16)	34.7 (1.75)	99.1 (0.37)	3.7 (0.92)	9.8 (1.62)	24.3 (1.80)	37.0 (2.40)	25.1 (1.80)
Hispanic	98.1 (0.40)	4.7 (0.12)	3.0 (0.57)	10.0 (0.82)	44.7 (1.65)	42.3 (1.53)	99.6 (0.13)	3.8 (0.46)	11.0 (0.96)	28.1 (1.25)	32.7 (1.58)	24.4 (1.34)
Asian	97.3 (0.85)	5.6 (0.27)	1.0! (0.39)	11.1 (2.03)	39.1 (3.03)	48.7 (3.11)	98.4 (0.64)	4.1 (0.91)	14.0 (1.64)	25.7 (2.60)	26.9 (2.49)	29.3 (3.15)
Pacific Islander	97.0 (0.93)	5.7 (0.29)	1.1! (0.42)	11.6 (1.98)	37.2 (2.71)	50.1 (2.96)	98.2 (0.70)	3.9 (0.99)	14.9 (1.73)	27.4 (2.55)	26.5 (2.54)	27.3 (3.10)
American Indian/Alaska Native	97.9 (2.15)	4.5 (0.41)	‡ (†)	8.1! (3.18)	71.2 (7.78)	14.5! (4.82)	100.0 (†)	‡ (†)	9.3! (3.95)	18.8! (6.52)	48.0 (11.41)	23.2! (10.28)
Other	96.9 (0.79)	4.6 (0.25)	2.3! (0.73)	11.2 (1.97)	51.7 (2.94)	34.7 (2.48)	99.1 (0.42)	1.8! (0.58)	14.3 (2.12)	26.8 (2.95)	35.9 (2.76)	21.2 (2.40)
School control												
Public	96.7 (0.30)	4.7 (0.06)	4.1 (0.26)	13.3 (0.54)	47.0 (0.78)	35.7 (0.72)	99.1 (0.12)	3.0 (0.25)	14.5 (0.45)	27.4 (0.57)	33.5 (0.69)	21.6 (0.60)
Private	92.5 (1.23)	4.8 (0.15)	4.0 (1.15)	8.5 (1.19)	43.9 (1.77)	43.5 (1.95)	98.7 (0.49)	3.0 (0.78)	14.2 (1.41)	23.0 (1.83)	35.5 (1.88)	24.3 (1.70)
Poverty status[3]												
Poor	94.9 (1.00)	4.7 (0.16)	4.2 (0.64)	13.7 (1.15)	42.2 (1.87)	39.9 (1.68)	99.2 (0.33)	4.7 (0.74)	10.0 (0.87)	24.9 (1.50)	31.9 (1.83)	28.5 (1.49)
Near-poor	95.4 (0.71)	4.6 (0.14)	4.4 (0.56)	14.6 (1.10)	46.9 (1.51)	34.1 (1.44)	99.1 (0.26)	3.6 (0.57)	12.5 (1.12)	27.2 (1.58)	35.3 (1.61)	21.4 (1.38)
Nonpoor	97.2 (0.30)	4.7 (0.07)	3.9 (0.36)	11.9 (0.60)	48.3 (1.00)	35.9 (0.88)	99.0 (0.14)	2.2 (0.25)	16.8 (0.56)	27.7 (0.68)	33.7 (0.79)	19.7 (0.72)
Locale												
City	96.0 (0.49)	5.0 (0.12)	3.3 (0.51)	11.4 (0.90)	43.7 (1.47)	41.5 (1.39)	98.9 (0.21)	4.0 (0.60)	12.3 (0.77)	26.8 (1.21)	32.0 (1.17)	24.9 (1.21)
Suburb	96.8 (0.64)	4.8 (0.08)	2.9 (0.34)	11.0 (0.84)	46.2 (1.25)	39.9 (1.19)	99.1 (0.18)	2.7 (0.26)	15.6 (0.84)	27.2 (0.93)	32.6 (1.22)	21.9 (0.92)
Town	97.1 (0.65)	4.2 (0.21)	6.2 (1.25)	15.5 (1.52)	49.9 (2.66)	28.3 (2.44)	99.2 (0.36)	2.0 (0.53)	13.7 (1.95)	25.4 (2.12)	35.8 (2.64)	23.1 (2.25)
Rural	95.6 (0.62)	4.3 (0.14)	6.1 (0.73)	16.5 (1.15)	50.2 (1.31)	27.2 (1.35)	99.0 (0.22)	2.7 (0.48)	15.9 (1.03)	27.5 (1.34)	36.6 (1.35)	17.2 (1.08)
All secondary school students (grades 9 through 12)	95.1 (0.58)	6.6 (0.10)	8.4 (0.48)	21.8 (0.92)	35.0 (0.91)	34.9 (0.97)	90.4 (0.55)	22.7 (0.70)	41.5 (1.00)	25.3 (0.84)	7.8 (0.63)	2.8 (0.28)
Sex												
Male	93.4 (1.02)	5.7 (0.15)	10.8 (0.73)	24.7 (1.28)	35.2 (1.24)	29.3 (1.19)	92.5 (0.59)	22.4 (0.92)	41.7 (1.25)	23.9 (1.01)	8.7 (1.07)	3.3 (0.41)
Female	97.0 (0.42)	7.5 (0.15)	5.8 (0.64)	18.7 (1.15)	34.7 (1.19)	40.7 (1.42)	88.2 (0.92)	23.0 (1.13)	41.3 (1.59)	26.6 (1.43)	6.8 (0.62)	2.2 (0.42)
Race/ethnicity												
White	94.9 (1.01)	6.5 (0.10)	8.6 (0.59)	21.2 (0.88)	34.6 (1.04)	35.6 (1.22)	89.0 (0.85)	20.1 (0.85)	48.1 (1.21)	24.2 (1.07)	5.8 (0.49)	1.8 (0.32)
Black	94.5 (0.94)	6.3 (0.24)	7.7 (1.28)	27.2 (2.52)	34.4 (2.51)	30.7 (2.31)	95.2 (0.93)	20.5 (2.12)	32.0 (3.05)	28.7 (2.51)	12.1 (2.23)	6.7 (1.23)
Hispanic	95.3 (0.86)	6.1 (0.22)	8.9 (1.32)	22.3 (2.29)	36.4 (2.72)	32.4 (2.10)	91.7 (1.27)	27.9 (2.10)	27.6 (1.80)	27.6 (1.54)	7.6 (1.54)	3.2 (0.59)
Asian/Pacific Islander	98.4 (0.59)	10.5 (0.76)	5.5 (1.78)	10.0! (3.24)	30.6 (3.66)	53.9 (3.64)	87.3 (3.15)	38.4 (3.90)	33.4 (3.72)	14.8 (2.49)	11.5 (2.25)	‡ (†)
Asian	98.6 (0.61)	10.9 (0.82)	5.0! (1.85)	10.4! (3.58)	31.0 (3.96)	53.7 (3.83)	87.0 (3.44)	40.8 (4.08)	34.7 (3.97)	14.4 (2.52)	9.2 (1.78)	‡ (†)
Pacific Islander	‡ (†)	‡ (†)	‡ (†)	‡ (†)	‡ (†)	‡ (†)	‡ (†)	‡ (†)	‡ (†)	‡ (†)	‡ (†)	‡ (†)
American Indian/Alaska Native	99.7 (0.33)	‡ (†)	‡ (†)	‡ (†)	‡ (†)	‡ (†)	‡ (†)	‡ (†)	‡ (†)	‡ (†)	15.9! (6.95)	‡ (†)
Other	93.9 (2.11)	6.6 (0.63)	6.8 (1.84)	24.6 (6.65)	37.7 (5.27)	31.0 (4.48)	90.2 (3.09)	17.5 (3.71)	38.7 (4.64)	27.0 (4.28)	‡ (†)	‡ (†)

See notes at end of table.

Table 227.40. Percentage of elementary and secondary school students who do homework, average time spent, percentage whose parents check that homework is done, and percentage whose parents help with homework, by frequency and selected characteristics: 2007 and 2012—Continued

[Standard errors appear in parentheses]

Year and selected characteristic	Percent of students who do homework outside of school	Average hours spent per week doing homework	Students who do homework outside of school										
			Percentage distribution by how frequently they do homework				Percent whose parents[1] check that homework is done[2]	Percentage distribution by how frequently their parents[1] help with homework				
			Less than once per week	1 to 2 days per week	3 to 4 days per week	5 or more days per week		No help given	Less than once per week	1 to 2 days per week	3 to 4 days per week	5 or more days per week
1	2	3	4	5	6	7	8	9	10	11	12	13
School control												
Public	94.9 (0.63)	6.3 (0.11)	8.9 (0.52)	22.9 (1.00)	35.8 (0.95)	32.4 (1.04)	90.8 (0.56)	22.7 (0.77)	41.0 (1.07)	25.6 (0.91)	7.9 (0.67)	2.8 (0.31)
Private	97.5 (0.88)	9.4 (0.28)	1.9 ! (0.69)	8.7 (1.32)	25.4 (2.07)	64.0 (2.52)	85.8 (1.87)	22.4 (2.41)	47.4 (2.70)	21.5 (1.94)	6.5 (1.37)	2.2 ! (0.76)
Poverty status[3]												
Poor	90.8 (1.20)	5.5 (0.26)	14.3 (1.36)	24.1 (2.02)	33.8 (1.96)	27.8 (2.37)	90.1 (1.87)	28.2 (2.12)	28.8 (2.12)	27.7 (2.18)	11.3 (1.36)	4.1 (0.91)
Near-poor	94.9 (0.73)	5.8 (0.23)	9.6 (1.05)	26.9 (2.04)	36.6 (2.14)	26.8 (1.58)	90.7 (1.32)	25.8 (2.19)	35.4 (2.36)	27.5 (2.24)	7.1 (1.33)	4.2 (0.84)
Nonpoor	96.3 (0.83)	7.1 (0.12)	6.4 (0.55)	19.2 (0.88)	34.6 (1.12)	39.8 (1.15)	90.4 (0.56)	20.1 (0.82)	47.1 (1.27)	23.8 (0.97)	7.1 (0.86)	1.9 (0.26)
Coursework												
Enrolled in AP classes	98.7 (0.32)	8.3 (0.16)	4.6 (0.50)	13.6 (0.93)	34.3 (1.35)	47.5 (1.30)	88.1 (0.81)	26.5 (1.23)	45.2 (1.44)	21.6 (1.08)	4.6 (0.60)	2.2 (0.39)
Not enrolled in AP classes	92.9 (0.95)	5.4 (0.14)	11.0 (0.79)	27.6 (1.27)	35.5 (1.12)	25.9 (1.18)	92.2 (0.73)	19.9 (1.05)	39.0 (1.34)	28.0 (1.21)	9.9 (0.98)	3.2 (0.39)
Locale												
City	95.1 (0.66)	7.1 (0.21)	7.3 (0.78)	20.0 (1.54)	33.7 (1.85)	39.0 (1.61)	92.8 (0.78)	24.4 (1.49)	37.8 (1.96)	25.4 (1.51)	9.1 (1.23)	3.2 (0.57)
Suburb	96.4 (0.43)	7.0 (0.16)	5.8 (0.66)	19.9 (1.62)	34.9 (1.31)	39.4 (1.42)	89.7 (1.05)	23.4 (1.25)	41.4 (1.48)	24.0 (1.33)	8.1 (1.24)	3.0 (0.51)
Town	94.9 (1.13)	5.1 (0.21)	14.1 (2.02)	26.9 (2.75)	36.5 (2.99)	22.5 (2.89)	89.0 (2.16)	19.7 (2.21)	41.3 (3.45)	28.8 (2.72)	7.3 (1.56)	2.9 ! (0.98)
Rural	93.1 (2.06)	5.8 (0.20)	11.7 (1.13)	25.1 (1.89)	35.9 (1.92)	27.3 (1.55)	89.3 (1.09)	20.5 (1.41)	46.2 (2.07)	25.9 (1.77)	5.7 (0.70)	1.8 (0.49)

†Not applicable.
#Rounds to zero.
!Interpret data with caution. The coefficient of variation (CV) for this estimate is between 30 and 50 percent.
‡Reporting standards not met. Either there are too few cases for a reliable estimate or the coefficient of variation (CV) is 50 percent or greater.
[1]Refers to one or more parent or other household adult.
[2]The wording of the questionnaire item changed from 2007 to 2012. In 2007, parents responded "yes" or "no" to an item asking whether they check that homework is done. In 2012, parents responded to a multiple-choice question asking how often they check that homework is done, and the 2012 estimates include all parents who "rarely," "sometimes," or "always" check. Therefore, the 2007 and 2012 estimates are not comparable.
[3]Poor children are those whose family incomes were below the Census Bureau's poverty threshold in the year prior to data collection; near-poor children are those whose family incomes ranged from the poverty threshold to 199 percent of the poverty threshold; and nonpoor children are those whose family incomes were at or above 200 percent of the poverty threshold. The poverty

threshold is a dollar amount that varies depending on a family's size and composition and is updated annually to account for inflation. In 2011, for example, the poverty threshold for a family of four with two children was $22,811. Survey respondents are asked to select the range within which their income falls, rather than giving the exact amount of their income; therefore, the measure of poverty status is an approximation.
NOTE: While National Household Education Surveys Program (NHES) administrations prior to 2012 were administered via telephone with an interviewer, NHES:2012 used self-administered paper-and-pencil questionnaires that were mailed to respondents. Measurable differences in estimates between 2012 and prior years could reflect actual changes in the population, or the changes could be due to the mode change from telephone to mail. Includes children enrolled in kindergarten through grade 12 and ungraded students. Excludes homeschooled students. Data based on responses of the parent most knowledgeable about the student's education. Race categories exclude persons of Hispanic ethnicity. Detail may not sum to totals because of rounding.
SOURCE: U.S. Department of Education, National Center for Education Statistics, Parent and Family Involvement in Education Survey of the National Household Education Surveys Program (PFI-NHES:2007 and 2012). (This table was prepared May 2015.)

Table 227.50. Average National Assessment of Educational Progress (NAEP) reading and mathematics scale scores of 4th-, 8th-, and 12th-graders and percentage absent from school, by selected characteristics and number of days absent in the last month: 2013

[Standard errors appear in parentheses]

Grade level and days absent from school in the last month	All students	Sex		Race/ethnicity							Eligibility for free or reduced-price lunch (public schools only)			Control of school		
		Male	Female	White	Black	Hispanic	Asian	Pacific Islander	American Indian/Alaska Native	Two or more races	Eligible	Not eligible	Unknown	Public	Catholic	Other private
1	2	3	4	5	6	7	8	9	10	11	12	13	14	15	16	17
							Average mathematics scale score[1]									
4th-graders																
0 days	246 (0.3)	246 (0.3)	245 (0.3)	253 (0.3)	229 (0.4)	235 (0.5)	264 (1.0)	245 (2.5)	231 (2.0)	251 (1.0)	234 (0.3)	257 (0.3)	253 (1.4)	245 (0.3)	249 (1.4)	‡ (†)
1–2 days	241 (0.3)	242 (0.4)	240 (0.3)	250 (0.3)	223 (0.6)	230 (0.6)	253 (1.2)	233 (3.1)	229 (2.2)	241 (1.4)	230 (0.4)	253 (0.4)	249 (1.7)	240 (0.3)	246 (1.9)	‡ (†)
3–4 days	235 (0.3)	235 (0.5)	235 (0.4)	244 (0.4)	219 (0.7)	225 (0.6)	249 (2.7)	227 (5.5)	225 (1.9)	238 (1.6)	226 (0.4)	248 (0.5)	242 (2.0)	235 (0.5)	237 (3.0)	‡ (†)
5–10 days	235 (0.6)	236 (0.8)	235 (0.7)	244 (0.6)	218 (1.2)	224 (1.3)	253 (2.9)	232 (4.0)	223 (3.3)	238 (2.5)	225 (0.7)	249 (0.9)	241 (3.5)	235 (0.5)	241 (4.7)	‡ (†)
More than 10 days	218 (0.8)	219 (1.0)	218 (1.3)	229 (1.0)	208 (1.3)	209 (1.7)	239 (5.4)	219 (3.5)	210 (3.4)	224 (4.8)	212 (0.9)	233 (1.3)	225 (4.6)	218 (0.8)	‡ (†)	‡ (†)
8th-graders																
0 days	290 (0.4)	291 (0.5)	290 (0.4)	299 (0.4)	269 (0.6)	277 (0.7)	313 (1.1)	281 (4.4)	277 (2.5)	296 (2.0)	275 (0.4)	301 (0.4)	302 (2.5)	289 (0.3)	298 (1.8)	‡ (†)
1–2 days	285 (0.3)	285 (0.4)	285 (0.4)	295 (0.3)	263 (0.7)	272 (0.6)	306 (1.7)	277 (2.9)	271 (2.0)	288 (1.5)	271 (0.4)	297 (0.4)	296 (2.5)	284 (0.3)	294 (1.9)	‡ (†)
3–4 days	275 (0.4)	275 (0.6)	274 (0.5)	286 (0.5)	254 (0.9)	263 (0.9)	292 (3.2)	266 (5.1)	265 (2.9)	278 (2.4)	262 (0.5)	288 (0.6)	292 (2.4)	274 (0.4)	290 (2.9)	‡ (†)
5–10 days	271 (0.7)	271 (1.0)	271 (1.0)	281 (0.9)	252 (1.5)	261 (1.4)	299 (4.9)	271 (11.2)	257 (3.8)	269 (4.2)	260 (0.8)	285 (1.1)	284 (4.7)	270 (0.7)	‡ (†)	‡ (†)
More than 10 days	254 (1.4)	252 (1.7)	255 (2.1)	265 (1.9)	237 (2.4)	243 (2.6)	264 (13.2)	‡ (†)	249 (5.3)	267 (6.9)	245 (1.5)	269 (2.2)	265 (11.8)	254 (1.2)	‡ (†)	‡ (†)
12th-graders																
0 days	157 (0.6)	159 (0.7)	156 (0.8)	165 (0.7)	135 (1.2)	146 (0.9)	176 (1.8)	‡ (†)	156 (5.5)	159 (3.3)	143 (0.9)	165 (0.7)	166 (2.6)	— (†)	— (†)	— (†)
1–2 days	155 (0.7)	157 (0.8)	154 (0.8)	163 (0.7)	134 (1.3)	141 (1.1)	174 (2.0)	‡ (†)	146 (6.6)	157 (2.5)	140 (0.9)	163 (0.7)	164 (2.5)	— (†)	— (†)	— (†)
3–4 days	147 (0.9)	149 (1.1)	146 (1.1)	157 (1.0)	126 (1.5)	133 (1.3)	167 (3.3)	‡ (†)	131 (6.7)	150 (4.1)	134 (1.1)	156 (1.0)	156 (3.1)	— (†)	— (†)	— (†)
5–10 days	144 (1.4)	145 (2.0)	143 (2.0)	150 (1.7)	125 (2.4)	133 (2.5)	172 (6.3)	‡ (†)	‡ (†)	‡ (†)	131 (1.8)	152 (1.8)	163 (6.1)	— (†)	— (†)	— (†)
More than 10 days	135 (2.2)	133 (2.9)	137 (2.9)	139 (3.2)	113 (3.5)	126 (3.8)	‡ (†)	‡ (†)	249 (5.3)	‡ (†)	124 (3.2)	142 (2.4)	‡ (†)	— (†)	— (†)	— (†)
							Average reading scale score[2]									
4th-graders																
0 days	225 (0.3)	222 (0.4)	229 (0.4)	235 (0.4)	210 (0.6)	211 (0.6)	240 (1.1)	219 (4.0)	212 (2.3)	230 (1.4)	211 (0.3)	238 (0.4)	238 (1.7)	224 (0.3)	238 (1.7)	‡ (†)
1–2 days	222 (0.3)	218 (0.5)	225 (0.4)	232 (0.4)	204 (0.7)	206 (0.7)	235 (1.8)	213 (4.3)	207 (2.1)	228 (1.5)	207 (0.5)	236 (0.4)	237 (2.0)	221 (0.3)	233 (1.8)	‡ (†)
3–4 days	217 (0.5)	214 (0.7)	220 (0.7)	228 (0.5)	202 (0.9)	204 (1.0)	229 (2.8)	200 (5.5)	204 (2.7)	219 (3.6)	205 (0.5)	233 (0.7)	231 (2.6)	216 (0.5)	227 (3.4)	‡ (†)
5–10 days	216 (0.8)	212 (1.0)	219 (1.1)	226 (0.8)	199 (1.6)	201 (2.0)	225 (4.7)	204 (6.5)	198 (4.0)	222 (4.4)	202 (1.0)	231 (0.9)	235 (3.7)	214 (0.7)	234 (4.0)	‡ (†)
More than 10 days	193 (1.2)	187 (1.7)	201 (1.4)	205 (1.5)	183 (2.0)	182 (2.6)	204 (8.4)	180 (9.3)	186 (6.9)	201 (5.8)	184 (1.4)	212 (2.2)	214 (8.5)	192 (1.2)	‡ (†)	‡ (†)
8th-graders																
0 days	271 (0.3)	266 (0.4)	277 (0.4)	279 (0.3)	255 (0.6)	259 (0.7)	284 (1.0)	264 (4.2)	253 (1.8)	277 (1.5)	257 (0.3)	281 (0.4)	288 (2.0)	270 (0.3)	287 (1.7)	‡ (†)
1–2 days	269 (0.3)	264 (0.4)	273 (0.4)	277 (0.3)	251 (0.6)	256 (0.6)	280 (1.9)	261 (5.5)	254 (1.9)	270 (1.3)	255 (0.3)	279 (0.3)	287 (2.1)	267 (0.3)	286 (1.8)	‡ (†)
3–4 days	260 (0.4)	255 (0.7)	266 (0.5)	270 (0.6)	243 (0.9)	248 (0.9)	275 (2.4)	250 (6.2)	253 (2.3)	267 (2.2)	249 (0.5)	273 (0.6)	281 (3.2)	259 (0.4)	283 (2.7)	‡ (†)
5–10 days	258 (0.7)	252 (1.0)	263 (0.9)	267 (0.9)	240 (1.4)	248 (1.6)	274 (5.8)	250 (5.6)	241 (3.7)	260 (3.4)	247 (0.7)	269 (1.1)	281 (3.8)	256 (0.7)	‡ (†)	‡ (†)
More than 10 days	242 (1.4)	237 (1.9)	249 (2.1)	252 (1.8)	230 (2.6)	233 (2.5)	248 (11.2)	‡ (†)	231 (5.4)	256 (4.7)	235 (1.6)	254 (2.1)	‡ (†)	240 (1.5)	‡ (†)	‡ (†)
12th-graders																
0 days	292 (0.7)	287 (0.8)	297 (0.8)	301 (0.8)	271 (1.4)	280 (1.1)	298 (2.4)	‡ (†)	266 (6.5)	300 (4.8)	276 (1.1)	299 (0.8)	305 (2.9)	— (†)	— (†)	— (†)
1–2 days	290 (0.6)	286 (0.8)	295 (0.7)	299 (0.8)	269 (1.2)	276 (1.1)	300 (2.3)	‡ (†)	288 (4.4)	289 (4.4)	275 (0.7)	298 (0.7)	302 (2.6)	— (†)	— (†)	— (†)
3–4 days	286 (0.8)	281 (1.1)	290 (1.1)	295 (1.0)	264 (1.7)	273 (1.7)	291 (4.8)	‡ (†)	270 (9.3)	285 (4.3)	272 (1.3)	294 (1.1)	301 (3.3)	— (†)	— (†)	— (†)
5–10 days	278 (1.4)	283 (1.6)	285 (2.1)	285 (1.8)	265 (4.2)	266 (2.7)	‡ (†)	‡ (†)	‡ (†)	‡ (†)	270 (2.2)	284 (1.8)	288 (7.8)	— (†)	— (†)	— (†)
More than 10 days	259 (3.0)	251 (3.6)	269 (3.9)	266 (4.6)	239 (4.4)	247 (4.3)	‡ (†)	‡ (†)	‡ (†)	‡ (†)	252 (3.3)	261 (4.1)	‡ (†)	— (†)	— (†)	— (†)

See notes at end of table.

Table 227.50. Average National Assessment of Educational Progress (NAEP) reading and mathematics scale scores of 4th-, 8th-, and 12th-graders and percentage absent from school, by selected characteristics and number of days absent in the last month: 2013—Continued

[Standard errors appear in parentheses]

Grade level and days absent from school in the last month	All students	Sex		Race/ethnicity							Eligibility for free or reduced-price lunch (public schools only)			Control of school		
		Male	Female	White	Black	Hispanic	Asian	Pacific Islander	American Indian/Alaska Native	Two or more races	Eligible	Not eligible	Unknown	Public	Catholic	Other private
1	2	3	4	5	6	7	8	9	10	11	12	13	14	15	16	17

Percent of students absent[3]

Grade level and days absent	All students	Male	Female	White	Black	Hispanic	Asian	Pacific Islander	Am. Indian/Alaska Native	Two or more races	Eligible	Not eligible	Unknown	Public	Catholic	Other private
4th-graders																
0 days	51 (0.2)	53 (0.3)	48 (0.3)	50 (0.3)	50 (0.5)	50 (0.5)	67 (0.7)	47 (3.2)	40 (1.5)	49 (1.1)	47 (0.3)	54 (0.3)	55 (1.5)	50 (0.2)	54 (1.5)	‡
1–2 days	30 (0.2)	29 (0.3)	31 (0.2)	32 (0.3)	29 (0.4)	29 (0.4)	21 (0.8)	26 (2.5)	32 (1.6)	30 (1.0)	30 (0.2)	30 (0.3)	28 (1.1)	30 (0.2)	30 (1.3)	‡
3–4 days	12 (0.1)	11 (0.2)	13 (0.2)	12 (0.2)	13 (0.3)	13 (0.3)	8 (0.4)	17 (2.7)	16 (0.8)	13 (0.7)	14 (0.2)	11 (0.2)	10 (1.0)	12 (0.1)	10 (0.7)	‡
5–10 days	5 (0.1)	5 (0.1)	5 (0.1)	5 (0.1)	5 (0.2)	5 (0.2)	3 (0.3)	8 (1.4)	8 (0.7)	5 (0.5)	6 (0.1)	5 (0.1)	5 (0.6)	5 (0.1)	5 (0.6)	‡
More than 10 days	2 (0.1)	3 (0.1)	2 (0.1)	2 (0.1)	3 (0.2)	3 (0.1)	2 (0.3)	3 (0.4)	4 (0.6)	3 (0.3)	3 (0.1)	2 (0.1)	1 (0.3)	2 (0.1)	1 (0.2)	‡
8th-graders																
0 days	44 (0.2)	47 (0.3)	42 (0.3)	43 (0.3)	46 (0.5)	44 (0.6)	65 (1.0)	35 (2.8)	36 (1.5)	42 (1.2)	41 (0.3)	46 (0.3)	51 (1.2)	44 (0.2)	50 (1.5)	‡
1–2 days	36 (0.2)	35 (0.3)	38 (0.3)	39 (0.2)	33 (0.5)	36 (0.5)	26 (0.8)	44 (3.6)	37 (1.7)	36 (1.0)	36 (0.3)	37 (0.3)	34 (0.8)	37 (0.2)	37 (1.2)	‡
3–4 days	13 (0.1)	12 (0.2)	14 (0.2)	13 (0.2)	14 (0.3)	13 (0.4)	6 (0.5)	13 (1.9)	18 (1.2)	15 (0.8)	15 (0.2)	11 (0.2)	10 (0.8)	13 (0.1)	9 (0.8)	‡
5–10 days	5 (0.1)	5 (0.1)	5 (0.1)	5 (0.1)	5 (0.2)	5 (0.2)	2 (0.3)	5 (1.3)	6 (0.5)	6 (0.6)	6 (0.1)	4 (0.1)	4 (0.4)	5 (0.1)	3 (0.4)	‡
More than 10 days	1 (#)	2 (0.1)	1 (0.1)	1 (#)	2 (0.1)	2 (0.1)	1 (0.2)	2 (0.5)	3 (0.4)	2 (0.3)	2 (0.1)	1 (#)	1 (0.3)	1 (#)	1 (0.2)	‡
12th-graders																
0 days	36 (0.4)	40 (0.6)	32 (0.6)	35 (0.6)	41 (1.1)	35 (0.8)	50 (1.7)	44 (6.8)	24 (4.5)	34 (3.3)	34 (0.6)	37 (0.6)	39 (1.7)	—	—	—
1–2 days	40 (0.4)	38 (0.6)	42 (0.5)	42 (0.5)	36 (0.9)	40 (0.7)	34 (1.5)	36 (6.7)	42 (4.2)	40 (3.0)	39 (0.6)	40 (0.5)	42 (1.5)	—	—	—
3–4 days	16 (0.3)	14 (0.3)	17 (0.4)	16 (0.4)	16 (0.7)	16 (0.6)	11 (1.3)	15 (4.8)	21 (4.0)	17 (2.6)	17 (0.4)	16 (0.4)	12 (0.9)	—	—	—
5–10 days	6 (0.2)	5 (0.2)	6 (0.3)	6 (0.2)	6 (0.6)	6 (0.5)	4 (0.7)	5 (2.8)	11 (3.5)	6 (1.4)	7 (0.4)	5 (0.3)	5 (0.6)	—	—	—
More than 10 days	2 (0.1)	2 (0.2)	2 (0.2)	2 (0.2)	2 (0.2)	2 (0.3)	1 (0.3)	# (†)	3 (0.9)	3 (1.6)	2 (0.2)	2 (0.1)	3 (1.0)	—	—	—

—Not available.
†Not applicable.
#Rounds to zero.
‡Reporting standards not met (too few cases for a reliable estimate).
[1]For grades 4 and 8, mathematics scale ranges from 0 to 500. For grade 12, mathematics scale ranges from 0 to 300.
[2]Reading scale ranges from 0 to 500.
[3]Absenteeism percentages based on 2013 Reading Assessment.

NOTE: Includes public and private schools except where otherwise noted. Includes students tested with accommodations (11 to 13 percent of all students, depending on assessment, grade level, and year); excludes only those students with disabilities and English language learners who were unable to be tested even with accommodations (1 to 3 percent of all students). Race categories exclude persons of Hispanic ethnicity. Detail may not sum to totals because of rounding.
SOURCE: U.S. Department of Education, National Center for Education Statistics, National Assessment of Educational Progress (NAEP), 2013 Mathematics and Reading Assessments, retrieved December 16, 2014, from the Main NAEP Data Explorer (http://nces.ed.gov/nationsreportcard/naepdata/). (This table was prepared December 2014.)

Table 228.10. School-associated violent deaths of all persons, homicides and suicides of youth ages 5–18 at school, and total homicides and suicides of youth ages 5–18, by type of violent death: 1992–93 to 2011–12

Year	School-associated violent deaths[1] of all persons (includes students, staff, and other nonstudents)					Homicides of youth ages 5–18		Suicides of youth ages 5–18	
	Total	Homicides	Suicides	Legal interventions	Unintentional firearm-related deaths	Homicides at school[2]	Total homicides	Suicides at school[2]	Total suicides[3]
1	2	3	4	5	6	7	8	9	10
1992–93	57	47	10	0	0	34	2,721	6	1,680
1993–94	48	38	10	0	0	29	2,932	7	1,723
1994–95	48	39	8	0	1	28	2,696	7	1,767
1995–96	53	46	6	1	0	32	2,545	6	1,725
1996–97	48	45	2	1	0	28	2,221	1	1,633
1997–98	57	47	9	1	0	34	2,100	6	1,626
1998–99	47	38	6	2	1	33	1,777	4	1,597
1999–2000	37[4]	26[4]	11[4]	0[4]	0[4]	14[4]	1,567	8[4]	1,415
2000–01	34[4]	26[4]	7[4]	1[4]	0[4]	14[4]	1,509	6[4]	1,493
2001–02	36[4]	27[4]	8[4]	1[4]	0[4]	16[4]	1,498	5[4]	1,400
2002–03	36[4]	25[4]	11[4]	0[4]	0[4]	18[4]	1,553	10[4]	1,331
2003–04	45[4]	37[4]	7[4]	1[4]	0[4]	23[4]	1,474	5[4]	1,285
2004–05	52[4]	40[4]	10[4]	2[4]	0[4]	22[4]	1,554	8[4]	1,471
2005–06	44[4]	37[4]	6[4]	1[4]	0[4]	21[4]	1,697	3[4]	1,408
2006–07	63[4]	48[4]	13[4]	2[4]	0[4]	32[4]	1,801	9[4]	1,296
2007–08	48[4]	39[4]	7[4]	2[4]	0[4]	21[4]	1,744	5[4]	1,231
2008–09	44[4]	29[4]	15[4]	0[4]	0[4]	18[4]	1,605	7[4]	1,344
2009–10	35[4]	27[4]	5[4]	3[4]	0[4]	19[4]	1,410	2[4]	1,467
2010–11	32[4]	26[4]	6[4]	0[4]	0[4]	11[4]	1,339	3[4]	1,456
2011–12	45[4]	26[4]	14[4]	5[4]	0[4]	15[4]	1,199	5[4]	1,568

[1]A school-associated violent death is defined as "a homicide, suicide, or legal intervention (involving a law enforcement officer), in which the fatal injury occurred on the campus of a functioning elementary or secondary school in the United States," while the victim was on the way to or from regular sessions at school, or while the victim was attending or traveling to or from an official school-sponsored event.
[2]"At school" includes on school property, on the way to or from regular sessions at school, and while attending or traveling to or from a school-sponsored event.
[3]Total youth suicides are reported for calendar years 1992 through 2011 (instead of school years 1992–93 through 2011–12).
[4]Data from 1999–2000 onward are subject to change until interviews with school and law enforcement officials have been completed. The details learned during the interviews can occasionally change the classification of a case.

NOTE: Unless otherwise noted, data are reported for the school year, defined as July 1 through June 30. Some data have been revised from previously published figures.
SOURCE: Centers for Disease Control and Prevention (CDC), 1992–2012 School-Associated Violent Deaths Surveillance Study (SAVD) (partially funded by the U.S. Department of Education, Office of Safe and Healthy Students), previously unpublished tabulation (February 2015); CDC, National Center for Injury Prevention and Control, Web-based Injury Statistics Query and Reporting System Fatal (WISQARS™ Fatal), 1999–2010, retrieved September 2014 from http://www.cdc.gov/injury/wisqars/index.html; and Federal Bureau of Investigation and Bureau of Justice Statistics, Supplementary Homicide Reports (SHR), preliminary data (June 2014). (This table was prepared February 2015.)

Table 228.20. Number of nonfatal victimizations against students ages 12–18 and rate of victimization per 1,000 students, by type of victimization, location, and year: 1992 through 2013

[Standard errors appear in parentheses]

Location and year	Number of nonfatal victimizations						Rate of victimization per 1,000 students						
	Total	Theft	Violent				Total	Theft	Violent			
			All violent		Serious violent[1]				All violent		Serious violent[1]	
1	2	3	4		5		6	7	8		9	
At school[2]												
1992	4,281,200 (225,600)	2,679,400 (147,660)	1,601,800 (121,630)		197,600 (35,430)		181.5 (7.99)	113.6 (5.64)	67.9 (4.77)		8.4 (1.48)	
1993	4,692,800 (321,220)	2,477,100 (121,200)	2,215,700 (194,520)		535,500 (76,050)		193.5 (11.02)	102.1 (4.61)	91.4 (7.23)		22.1 (3.02)	
1994	4,721,000 (271,730)	2,474,100 (121,260)	2,246,900 (165,530)		459,100 (58,110)		187.7 (9.04)	98.4 (4.46)	89.3 (5.95)		18.3 (2.24)	
1995	4,400,700 (267,610)	2,468,400 (120,690)	1,932,200 (152,670)		294,500 (42,890)		172.2 (8.82)	96.6 (4.37)	75.6 (5.44)		11.5 (1.64)	
1996	4,130,400 (281,640)	2,205,200 (107,650)	1,925,300 (166,690)		371,900 (54,150)		158.4 (9.17)	84.5 (3.88)	73.8 (5.81)		14.3 (2.01)	
1997	3,610,900 (282,430)	1,975,000 (111,830)	1,635,900 (164,530)		376,200 (60,990)		136.6 (9.25)	74.7 (3.95)	61.9 (5.74)		14.2 (2.24)	
1998	3,247,300 (254,250)	1,635,100 (104,210)	1,612,200 (155,840)		314,500 (49,770)		121.3 (8.27)	61.1 (3.69)	60.2 (5.34)		11.7 (1.80)	
1999	3,152,400 (258,560)	1,752,400 (104,970)	1,400,000 (148,230)		281,100 (50,060)		117.0 (8.43)	65.1 (3.69)	52.0 (5.11)		10.4 (1.81)	
2000	2,301,000 (211,140)	1,331,500 (95,940)	969,500 (115,680)		214,200 (40,980)		84.9 (7.00)	49.1 (3.34)	35.8 (4.02)		7.9 (1.48)	
2001	2,521,300 (202,890)	1,348,500 (93,240)	1,172,700 (120,560)		259,400 (44,110)		92.3 (6.67)	49.4 (3.23)	42.9 (4.14)		9.5 (1.58)	
2002	2,082,600 (212,520)	1,088,800 (77,110)	993,800 (126,210)		173,500 (37,300)		75.4 (6.96)	39.4 (2.69)	36.0 (4.29)		6.3 (1.32)	
2003	2,308,800 (210,380)	1,270,500 (88,550)	1,038,300 (121,490)		188,400 (38,240)		87.4 (7.16)	48.1 (3.18)	39.3 (4.32)		7.1 (1.42)	
2004	1,762,200 (154,390)	1,065,400 (75,160)	696,800 (83,090)		107,300 (25,110)		67.2 (5.40)	40.6 (2.76)	26.6 (3.03)		4.1 (0.95)	
2005	1,678,600 (169,040)	875,900 (70,140)	802,600 (102,360)		140,300 (32,400)		63.2 (5.85)	33.0 (2.56)	30.2 (3.66)		5.3 (1.20)	
2006[3]	1,799,900 (170,490)	859,000 (68,730)	940,900 (109,880)		249,900 (45,670)		67.5 (5.86)	32.2 (2.52)	35.3 (3.90)		9.4 (1.68)	
2007	1,801,200 (188,450)	896,700 (66,230)	904,400 (114,320)		116,100 (25,430)		67.8 (6.40)	33.7 (2.41)	34.0 (4.02)		4.4 (0.94)	
2008	1,435,500 (161,330)	648,000 (61,170)	787,500 (108,480)		128,700 (34,370)		54.3 (5.67)	24.5 (2.26)	29.8 (3.91)		4.9 (1.28)	
2009	1,322,800 (168,370)	594,500 (54,480)	728,300 (111,550)		233,700 (51,610)		51.0 (6.00)	22.9 (2.05)	28.1 (4.08)		9.0 (1.94)	
2010	892,000 (124,260)	469,800 (45,300)	422,300 (73,310)		155,000 (36,500)		34.9 (4.55)	18.4 (1.75)	16.5 (2.75)		6.1 (1.40)	
2011	1,246,200 (139,940)	647,700 (61,500)	598,600 (84,090)		89,500 (23,360)		49.3 (5.11)	25.6 (2.36)	23.7 (3.16)		3.5 (0.91)	
2012	1,364,900 (133,810)	615,600 (51,440)	749,200 (90,250)		89,000 (23,850)		52.4 (4.78)	23.6 (1.93)	28.8 (3.31)		3.4 (0.91)	
2013	1,420,900 (176,390)	454,900 (43,390)	966,000 (134,140)		125,500 (32,110)		55.0 (6.24)	17.6 (1.65)	37.4 (4.84)		4.9 (1.22)	
Away from school												
1992	4,084,100 (218,910)	1,857,600 (118,610)	2,226,500 (149,210)		1,025,100 (92,600)		173.1 (7.81)	78.7 (4.66)	94.4 (5.70)		43.5 (3.72)	
1993	3,835,900 (280,790)	1,731,100 (96,250)	2,104,800 (187,960)		1,004,300 (114,870)		158.2 (9.90)	71.4 (3.75)	86.8 (7.01)		41.4 (4.47)	
1994	4,147,100 (249,260)	1,713,900 (96,250)	2,433,200 (174,580)		1,074,900 (101,370)		164.9 (8.44)	68.1 (3.61)	96.7 (6.24)		42.7 (3.80)	
1995	3,626,600 (234,640)	1,604,800 (92,000)	2,021,800 (157,470)		829,700 (85,830)		141.9 (7.91)	62.8 (3.41)	79.1 (5.59)		32.5 (3.19)	
1996	3,483,200 (250,620)	1,572,700 (87,830)	1,910,600 (165,810)		870,000 (96,510)		133.5 (8.32)	60.3 (3.22)	73.3 (5.79)		33.4 (3.50)	
1997	3,717,600 (288,080)	1,710,700 (101,810)	2,006,900 (189,180)		853,300 (105,660)		140.7 (9.41)	64.7 (3.62)	75.9 (6.51)		32.3 (3.79)	
1998	3,047,800 (243,270)	1,408,000 (94,900)	1,639,800 (157,700)		684,900 (85,520)		113.8 (7.96)	52.6 (3.38)	61.3 (5.40)		25.6 (3.04)	
1999	2,713,800 (233,350)	1,129,200 (79,770)	1,584,500 (161,350)		675,400 (90,150)		100.8 (7.71)	41.9 (2.85)	58.8 (5.53)		25.1 (3.20)	
2000	2,303,600 (211,310)	1,228,800 (90,770)	1,074,800 (124,280)		402,100 (62,950)		85.0 (7.01)	45.3 (3.17)	39.6 (4.30)		14.8 (2.24)	
2001	1,780,300 (160,090)	961,400 (74,230)	819,000 (94,590)		314,800 (50,070)		65.2 (5.39)	35.2 (2.60)	30.0 (3.30)		11.5 (1.79)	
2002	1,619,500 (178,050)	820,100 (64,530)	799,400 (108,260)		341,200 (59,590)		58.6 (5.92)	29.7 (2.27)	28.9 (3.71)		12.4 (2.09)	
2003	1,824,100 (179,240)	780,900 (64,210)	1,043,200 (121,880)		412,800 (64,660)		69.1 (6.19)	29.6 (2.34)	39.5 (4.33)		15.6 (2.37)	
2004	1,371,600 (130,480)	718,000 (59,070)	653,700 (79,660)		272,500 (45,080)		52.3 (4.63)	27.4 (2.19)	24.9 (2.91)		10.4 (1.68)	
2005	1,429,000 (151,460)	637,700 (57,740)	791,300 (101,380)		257,100 (47,950)		53.8 (5.29)	24.0 (2.12)	29.8 (3.63)		9.7 (1.77)	
2006[3]	1,413,100 (144,660)	714,200 (61,900)	698,900 (89,980)		263,600 (47,280)		53.0 (5.04)	26.8 (2.27)	26.2 (3.22)		9.9 (1.73)	
2007	1,371,700 (154,740)	614,300 (52,740)	757,400 (100,440)		337,700 (55,630)		51.6 (5.34)	23.1 (1.94)	28.5 (3.55)		12.7 (2.01)	
2008	1,132,600 (137,840)	498,500 (52,350)	634,100 (94,160)		258,600 (52,980)		42.8 (4.90)	18.9 (1.94)	24.0 (3.42)		9.8 (1.96)	
2009	857,200 (124,770)	484,200 (48,320)	372,900 (70,660)		176,800 (42,890)		33.1 (4.54)	18.7 (1.83)	14.4 (2.63)		6.8 (1.62)	
2010	689,900 (103,620)	378,800 (40,200)	311,200 (59,190)		167,300 (38,460)		27.0 (3.83)	14.8 (1.55)	12.2 (2.24)		6.5 (1.47)	
2011	966,100 (117,200)	541,900 (55,160)	424,300 (66,550)		137,600 (31,000)		38.2 (4.33)	21.4 (2.13)	16.8 (2.52)		5.4 (1.20)	
2012	991,200 (108,370)	470,800 (44,070)	520,400 (71,280)		169,900 (35,430)		38.0 (3.93)	18.1 (1.66)	20.0 (2.64)		6.5 (1.33)	
2013	778,500 (115,110)	403,000 (40,470)	375,500 (68,800)		151,200 (36,490)		30.1 (4.19)	15.6 (1.54)	14.5 (2.56)		5.8 (1.38)	

[1] Serious violent victimization is also included in all violent victimization.
[2] "At school" includes inside the school building, on school property, or on the way to and from school.
[3] Due to methodological differences, use caution when comparing 2006 estimates to other years.
NOTE: "Serious violent victimization" includes the crimes of rape, sexual assault, robbery, and aggravated assault. "All violent victimization" includes serious violent crimes as well as simple assault. "Theft" includes attempted and completed thefts, with the exception of motor vehicle thefts. Theft does not include pickpocketing, and all attempted and completed thefts, with the exception of motor vehicle thefts. Theft does not include robbery, which involves the threat or use of force and is classified as a violent crime. "Total victimization" includes theft

and violent crimes. Data in this table are from the National Crime Victimization Survey (NCVS); due to differences in time coverage and administration between the NCVS and the School Crime Supplement (SCS) to the NCVS, data in this table cannot be compared with data in tables that are based on the SCS. Detail may not sum to totals because of rounding. Some data have been revised from previously published figures.
SOURCE: U.S. Department of Justice, Bureau of Justice Statistics, National Crime Victimization Survey (NCVS), 1992 through 2013. (This table was prepared August 2014).

Table 228.25. Number of nonfatal victimizations against students ages 12–18 and rate of victimization per 1,000 students, by type of victimization, location, and selected student characteristics: 2013

[Standard errors appear in parentheses]

Location and student characteristic	Number of nonfatal victimizations		Violent		Rate of victimization per 1,000 students		Violent	
	Total	Theft	All violent	Serious violent[1]	Total	Theft	All violent	Serious violent[1]
1	2	3	4	5	6	7	8	9
At school[2]								
Total..........	1,420,900 (176,390)	454,900 (115,110)	966,000 (134,140)	125,500 (32,110)	55.0 (6.24)	17.6 (1.65)	37.4 (4.84)	4.9 (1.22)
Sex								
Male..........	824,500 (119,880)	247,900 (30,710)	576,600 (93,080)	84,300 (24,480)	62.1 (8.14)	18.7 (2.27)	43.5 (6.46)	6.4 ! (1.80)
Female..........	596,400 (95,330)	207,000 (27,750)	389,400 (70,570)	41,200 ! (15,150)	47.4 (6.93)	16.4 (2.17)	30.9 (5.24)	3.3 ! (1.19)
Age								
12–14..........	834,900 (120,960)	194,900 (26,830)	640,000 (100,210)	92,500 (26,070)	67.3 (8.73)	15.7 (2.13)	51.6 (7.36)	7.5 ! (2.05)
15–18..........	586,000 (94,160)	260,100 (31,550)	326,000 (62,290)	33,000 ! (13,100)	43.5 (6.44)	19.3 (2.30)	24.2 (4.37)	2.5 ! (0.96)
Race/ethnicity[3]								
White..........	822,200 (119,650)	199,600 (27,190)	622,500 (98,270)	71,600 ! (21,910)	58.5 (7.71)	14.2 (1.91)	44.3 (6.44)	5.1 ! (1.53)
Black..........	161,900 (38,280)	107,900 (19,350)	54,000 (18,140)	15,500 ! (8,110)	40.7 (8.87)	27.1 (4.75)	13.6 (4.39)	3.9 ! (2.01)
Hispanic..........	367,500 (67,760)	111,200 (19,670)	256,300 (52,650)	28,800 ! (11,990)	63.4 (10.48)	19.2 (3.33)	44.2 (8.33)	5.0 ! (2.03)
Other..........	69,400 (21,460)	36,200 (10,750)	33,100 ! (13,140)	9,500 ! (5,930)	33.9 (9.78)	17.7 (5.17)	16.2 ! (6.16)	4.6 ! (2.85)
Urbanicity[4]								
Urban..........	432,000 (75,920)	192,100 (26,610)	239,900 (50,270)	38,800 ! (14,580)	57.0 (9.05)	25.3 (3.42)	31.6 (6.19)	5.1 ! (1.88)
Suburban..........	860,700 (123,600)	240,700 (30,200)	620,100 (97,900)	76,600 (22,940)	60.4 (7.83)	16.9 (2.08)	43.5 (6.33)	5.4 (1.57)
Rural..........	128,200 (32,580)	22,200 ! (8,290)	106,100 (28,620)	10,100 ! (6,150)	31.9 (7.57)	5.5 ! (2.05)	26.4 (6.70)	2.5 ! (1.51)
Household income								
Less than $15,000	327,500 (62,500)	21,100 ! (8,080)	306,400 (59,650)	50,400 ! (17,320)	161.6 (24.97)	10.4 ! (3.95)	151.2 (24.08)	24.9 ! (8.08)
$15,000–29,999..........	154,200 (37,010)	52,400 (13,080)	101,900 (27,840)	23,900 ! (10,620)	49.6 (10.85)	16.8 (4.14)	32.8 (8.35)	7.7 (3.33)
$30,000–49,999..........	223,500 (47,860)	72,500 (15,580)	151,000 (36,470)	22,600 ! (10,250)	48.4 (9.46)	15.7 (3.32)	32.7 (7.36)	4.9 ! (2.18)
$50,000–74,999..........	167,300 (39,140)	46,700 (12,300)	120,600 (31,250)	9,900 ! (6,090)	50.5 (10.76)	14.1 (3.67)	36.4 (8.76)	3.0 ! (1.82)
$75,000 or more..........	348,800 (65,320)	200,900 (27,290)	147,900 (35,940)	10,200 ! (6,190)	47.5 (8.13)	27.4 (3.62)	20.2 (4.65)	1.4 ! (0.84)
Not reported..........	199,500 (44,220)	61,300 (14,240)	138,200 (34,300)	8,600 ! (5,580)	36.5 (7.50)	11.2 (2.58)	25.3 (5.92)	1.6 ! (1.01)
Away from school								
Total......	778,500 (115,110)	403,000 (40,470)	375,500 (68,800)	151,200 (36,490)	30.1 (4.19)	15.6 (1.54)	14.5 (2.56)	5.8 (1.38)
Sex								
Male..........	383,200 (69,790)	211,100 (28,060)	172,100 (39,910)	79,200 (23,450)	28.9 (4.93)	15.9 (2.08)	13.0 (2.89)	6.0 (1.73)
Female..........	395,300 (71,320)	191,800 (26,590)	203,400 (44,820)	72,000 (22,000)	31.4 (5.29)	15.2 (2.08)	16.2 (3.41)	5.7 (1.71)
Age								
12–14..........	346,700 (65,050)	171,800 (25,010)	174,900 (40,370)	69,000 (21,370)	28.0 (4.93)	13.9 (1.99)	14.1 (3.13)	5.6 (1.69)
15–18..........	431,800 (75,900)	231,200 (29,520)	200,600 (44,390)	82,200 (24,060)	32.1 (5.27)	17.2 (2.15)	14.9 (3.16)	6.1 (1.75)
Race/ethnicity[3]								
White..........	400,300 (71,960)	204,000 (27,530)	196,200 (43,710)	84,500 (24,520)	28.5 (4.81)	14.5 (1.93)	14.0 (2.99)	6.0 (1.71)
Black..........	193,600 (43,810)	91,200 (17,650)	102,400 (27,940)	31,500 ! (12,700)	48.7 (9.94)	23.0 (4.35)	25.8 (6.62)	7.9 ! (3.11)
Hispanic..........	150,300 (36,340)	94,100 (17,960)	56,100 (18,620)	35,200 ! (13,660)	25.9 (5.90)	16.2 (3.05)	9.7 (3.11)	6.1 ! (2.31)
Other..........	34,300 (13,440)	13,600 ! (6,420)	20,700 ! (9,690)	‡ (†)	16.8 (6.29)	6.6 ! (3.12)	10.1 ! (4.60)	— (†)
Urbanicity[4]								
Urban..........	265,400 (53,940)	151,300 (23,300)	114,100 (30,080)	64,700 (20,480)	35.0 (6.61)	20.0 (3.01)	15.1 (3.80)	8.5 (2.62)
Suburban..........	413,800 (73,660)	208,600 (27,870)	205,200 (45,090)	62,600 (20,030)	29.0 (4.85)	14.6 (1.92)	14.4 (3.04)	4.4 (1.38)
Rural..........	99,300 (27,360)	43,100 (11,790)	56,200 (18,630)	23,800 ! (10,610)	24.7 (6.43)	10.7 (2.90)	14.0 (4.46)	5.9 ! (2.58)
Household income								
Less than $15,000	170,100 (39,600)	67,800 (15,030)	102,300 (27,920)	35,500 ! (13,750)	83.9 (17.13)	33.5 (7.21)	50.5 (12.56)	17.5 ! (6.50)
$15,000–29,999..........	123,300 (31,720)	51,300 (12,930)	72,000 (22,000)	35,400 ! (13,720)	39.7 (9.42)	16.5 (4.10)	23.2 (6.70)	11.4 ! (4.27)
$30,000–49,999..........	131,000 (33,070)	77,000 (16,100)	54,000 (18,130)	19,100 ! (9,200)	28.4 (6.72)	16.7 (3.43)	11.7 (3.79)	4.1 ! (1.96)
$50,000–74,999..........	56,100 (18,600)	25,900 ! (9,000)	30,200 ! (12,350)	13,000 (7,210)	16.9 (5.38)	7.8 ! (2.70)	11.7 (3.63)	3.9 ! (2.14)
$75,000 or more..........	151,100 (36,480)	98,100 (18,370)	53,000 (17,910)	23,700 ! (10,570)	20.6 (4.72)	13.4 (2.47)	7.2 (2.38)	3.2 ! (1.42)
Not reported..........	146,900 (35,780)	82,800 (16,740)	64,100 (20,360)	24,400 ! (10,770)	26.9 (6.16)	15.2 (3.02)	11.7 (3.60)	4.5 ! (1.94)

—Not available.
†Not applicable.
‡Reporting standards not met. There are too few cases for a reliable estimate.
!Interpret data with caution. Estimate based on 10 or fewer sample cases, or the coefficient of variation is greater than 50 percent.
[1]"Serious violent victimization" is also included in all violent victimization.
[2]"At school" includes inside the school building, on school property, or on the way to and from school.
[3]Race categories exclude persons of Hispanic ethnicity. "Other" includes Asians, Pacific Islanders, American Indians/Alaska Natives, and persons of Two or more races.
[4]Refers to the Standard Metropolitan Statistical Area (MSA) status of the respondent's household as defined in 2000 by the U.S. Census Bureau. Categories include "central city of an MSA (Urban)," "in MSA but not in central city (Suburban)," and "not MSA (Rural)."

NOTE: "Serious violent victimization" includes the crimes of rape, sexual assault, robbery, and aggravated assault. "All violent victimization" includes serious violent crimes as well as simple assault. "Theft" includes attempted and completed purse-snatching, completed pickpocketing, and all attempted and completed thefts, with the exception of motor vehicle thefts. Theft does not include robbery, which involves the threat or use of force and is classified as a violent crime. "Total victimization" includes theft and violent crimes. Data in this table are from the National Crime Victimization Survey (NCVS) and are reported in accordance with Bureau of Justice Statistics standards. Due to differences in time coverage and administration between the NCVS and the School Crime Supplement (SCS) to the NCVS, data in this table cannot be compared with data in tables that are based on the SCS. Detail may not sum to totals because of rounding and missing data on student characteristics. The population size for students ages 12–18 was 25,866,300 in 2013.
SOURCE: U.S. Department of Justice, Bureau of Justice Statistics, National Crime Victimization Survey (NCVS), 2013. (This table was prepared August 2014.)

Table 228.30. Percentage of students ages 12–18 who reported criminal victimization at school during the previous 6 months, by type of victimization and selected student and school characteristics: Selected years, 1995 through 2013

[Standard errors appear in parentheses]

Type of victimization and student or school characteristic	1995	1999	2001	2003	2005	2007	2009	2011	2013
1	2	3	4	5	6	7	8	9	10
Total	9.5 (0.35)	7.6 (0.35)	5.5 (0.31)	5.1 (0.24)	4.3 (0.31)	4.3 (0.30)	3.9 (0.28)	3.5 (0.28)	3.0 (0.25)
Sex									
Male	10.0 (0.46)	7.8 (0.46)	6.1 (0.41)	5.4 (0.33)	4.6 (0.42)	4.5 (0.43)	4.6 (0.40)	3.7 (0.35)	3.2 (0.40)
Female	9.0 (0.47)	7.3 (0.46)	4.9 (0.39)	4.8 (0.36)	3.9 (0.38)	4.0 (0.39)	3.2 (0.35)	3.4 (0.38)	2.8 (0.34)
Race/ethnicity[1]									
White	9.8 (0.37)	7.5 (0.44)	5.8 (0.39)	5.4 (0.31)	4.7 (0.35)	4.3 (0.38)	3.9 (0.37)	3.6 (0.35)	3.0 (0.32)
Black	10.2 (1.04)	9.9 (0.85)	6.1 (0.78)	5.3 (0.80)	3.8 (0.80)	4.3 (0.83)	4.4 (0.74)	4.6 (0.89)	3.2 (0.71)
Hispanic	7.6 (0.90)	5.7 (0.77)	4.6 (0.64)	3.9 (0.50)	3.9 (0.70)	3.6 (0.54)	3.9 (0.75)	2.9 (0.47)	3.2 (0.46)
Asian	— (†)	— (†)	— (†)	— (†)	1.5! (0.68)	3.6! (1.38)	‡ (†)	2.5! (1.23)	2.6! (1.08)
Other	8.8 (1.54)	6.4 (1.28)	3.1 (0.91)	5.0 (1.08)	4.3! (2.00)	8.1 (2.01)	‡ (†)	3.7! (1.37)	2.2! (1.08)
Grade									
6th	9.6 (0.97)	8.0 (1.24)	5.9 (0.90)	3.8 (0.77)	4.6 (0.83)	4.1 (0.87)	3.7 (0.91)	3.8 (0.85)	4.1 (0.92)
7th	11.2 (0.81)	8.2 (0.81)	5.8 (0.66)	6.3 (0.74)	5.4 (0.71)	4.7 (0.69)	3.4 (0.70)	3.1 (0.61)	2.5 (0.51)
8th	10.5 (0.78)	7.6 (0.84)	4.3 (0.61)	5.2 (0.65)	3.6 (0.63)	4.4 (0.63)	3.8 (0.78)	3.8 (0.67)	2.3 (0.52)
9th	11.9 (0.88)	8.9 (0.79)	7.9 (0.81)	6.3 (0.70)	4.7 (0.69)	5.3 (0.75)	5.3 (0.85)	5.1 (0.83)	4.1 (0.76)
10th	9.1 (0.76)	8.0 (0.82)	6.5 (0.77)	4.8 (0.63)	4.3 (0.71)	4.4 (0.67)	4.2 (0.79)	3.0 (0.58)	3.3 (0.57)
11th	7.3 (0.74)	7.2 (0.88)	4.8 (0.62)	5.1 (0.68)	3.6 (0.51)	4.0 (0.75)	4.7 (0.88)	3.1 (0.65)	3.3 (0.65)
12th	6.1 (0.74)	4.8 (0.81)	2.9 (0.52)	3.6 (0.71)	3.8 (0.85)	2.7 (0.70)	2.0 (0.52)	2.9 (0.68)	2.0! (0.67)
Urbanicity[2]									
Urban	9.3 (0.64)	8.4 (0.69)	5.9 (0.58)	6.1 (0.58)	5.3 (0.65)	4.5 (0.58)	4.2 (0.56)	4.3 (0.56)	3.3 (0.47)
Suburban	10.3 (0.49)	7.6 (0.43)	5.7 (0.40)	4.8 (0.33)	4.2 (0.34)	4.1 (0.38)	4.0 (0.36)	3.3 (0.34)	3.2 (0.35)
Rural	8.3 (0.79)	6.4 (0.96)	4.7 (0.93)	4.7 (0.75)	2.8 (0.69)	4.4 (0.55)	3.1 (0.66)	2.8 (0.57)	2.0 (0.58)
Sector									
Public	9.8 (0.38)	7.9 (0.37)	5.7 (0.34)	5.2 (0.26)	4.4 (0.32)	4.6 (0.32)	4.1 (0.30)	3.7 (0.29)	3.1 (0.27)
Private	6.6 (0.90)	4.5 (0.80)	3.4 (0.72)	4.9 (0.79)	2.7 (0.77)	1.1! (0.50)	1.8! (0.76)	1.9! (0.68)	2.8! (0.89)
Theft	7.1 (0.29)	5.7 (0.32)	4.2 (0.24)	4.0 (0.21)	3.1 (0.27)	3.0 (0.23)	2.8 (0.23)	2.6 (0.23)	1.9 (0.20)
Sex									
Male	7.1 (0.38)	5.7 (0.41)	4.5 (0.34)	4.0 (0.27)	3.1 (0.34)	3.0 (0.34)	3.4 (0.36)	2.6 (0.29)	2.0 (0.30)
Female	7.1 (0.41)	5.7 (0.43)	3.8 (0.33)	4.1 (0.32)	3.2 (0.36)	3.0 (0.33)	2.1 (0.28)	2.6 (0.33)	1.8 (0.28)
Race/ethnicity[1]									
White	7.4 (0.32)	5.8 (0.43)	4.2 (0.30)	4.3 (0.28)	3.4 (0.32)	3.1 (0.29)	2.9 (0.31)	2.5 (0.28)	1.6 (0.22)
Black	7.1 (0.85)	7.4 (0.77)	5.0 (0.68)	4.0 (0.66)	2.7 (0.65)	3.0 (0.70)	2.5 (0.61)	3.7 (0.78)	2.7 (0.67)
Hispanic	5.8 (0.78)	3.9 (0.61)	3.7 (0.69)	3.0 (0.41)	3.1 (0.64)	2.2 (0.47)	3.0 (0.63)	2.0 (0.41)	1.8 (0.39)
Asian	— (†)	— (†)	— (†)	— (†)	‡ (†)	3.2! (1.32)	‡ (†)	2.5! (1.23)	2.6! (1.08)
Other	6.5 (1.40)	4.4 (0.98)	2.9 (0.87)	4.4 (1.04)	‡ (†)	4.5! (1.57)	‡ (†)	2.8! (1.21)	‡ (†)
Grade									
6th	5.4 (0.66)	5.2 (0.97)	4.0 (0.70)	2.2 (0.63)	2.8 (0.75)	2.7 (0.77)	1.3! (0.52)	2.7 (0.70)	1.4! (0.57)
7th	8.1 (0.71)	6.0 (0.73)	3.4 (0.51)	4.8 (0.67)	2.9 (0.50)	2.7 (0.54)	2.1 (0.57)	1.9 (0.44)	1.4 (0.38)
8th	7.9 (0.72)	5.9 (0.81)	3.3 (0.50)	4.1 (0.56)	2.4 (0.53)	2.5 (0.54)	2.0 (0.55)	2.0 (0.48)	1.0! (0.33)
9th	9.1 (0.77)	6.5 (0.71)	6.2 (0.76)	5.3 (0.62)	3.7 (0.61)	4.6 (0.70)	4.9 (0.80)	4.4 (0.78)	2.7 (0.58)
10th	7.7 (0.72)	6.5 (0.73)	5.7 (0.72)	3.7 (0.59)	3.8 (0.66)	3.6 (0.63)	3.5 (0.72)	2.1 (0.50)	2.6 (0.48)
11th	5.5 (0.66)	5.5 (0.67)	3.8 (0.57)	4.1 (0.64)	2.8 (0.45)	2.6 (0.61)	3.3 (0.74)	2.7 (0.58)	2.3 (0.50)
12th	4.6 (0.67)	4.0 (0.71)	2.3 (0.45)	3.1 (0.68)	3.5 (0.85)	1.9 (0.55)	1.5 (0.44)	2.4 (0.62)	1.6! (0.62)
Urbanicity[2]									
Urban	6.6 (0.51)	6.9 (0.59)	4.5 (0.52)	4.5 (0.47)	3.6 (0.51)	2.8 (0.48)	2.9 (0.45)	3.0 (0.45)	2.4 (0.44)
Suburban	7.6 (0.40)	5.4 (0.36)	4.3 (0.32)	3.8 (0.27)	3.2 (0.31)	3.0 (0.31)	2.8 (0.32)	2.5 (0.30)	1.9 (0.27)
Rural	6.8 (0.66)	5.0 (0.95)	3.4 (0.65)	3.9 (0.66)	2.2! (0.68)	3.2 (0.46)	2.3 (0.59)	2.0 (0.47)	0.8 (0.24)
Sector									
Public	7.3 (0.32)	5.9 (0.34)	4.4 (0.26)	4.0 (0.22)	3.3 (0.28)	3.2 (0.25)	2.9 (0.25)	2.7 (0.24)	1.9 (0.21)
Private	5.2 (0.74)	4.3 (0.78)	2.5 (0.67)	4.0 (0.77)	1.3! (0.48)	1.1! (0.50)	‡ (†)	1.2! (0.52)	2.0! (0.76)
Violent	3.0 (0.21)	2.3 (0.18)	1.8 (0.19)	1.3 (0.15)	1.2 (0.15)	1.6 (0.18)	1.4 (0.17)	1.1 (0.15)	1.2 (0.15)
Sex									
Male	3.5 (0.27)	2.5 (0.26)	2.1 (0.26)	1.8 (0.24)	1.6 (0.25)	1.7 (0.26)	1.6 (0.25)	1.2 (0.21)	1.3 (0.23)
Female	2.4 (0.25)	2.0 (0.22)	1.5 (0.24)	0.9 (0.16)	0.8 (0.15)	1.4 (0.23)	1.1 (0.21)	0.9 (0.17)	1.1 (0.23)
Race/ethnicity[1]									
White	3.0 (0.23)	2.1 (0.22)	2.0 (0.24)	1.4 (0.18)	1.3 (0.20)	1.5 (0.22)	1.2 (0.21)	1.2 (0.17)	1.5 (0.24)
Black	3.4 (0.61)	3.5 (0.55)	1.3! (0.40)	1.6 (0.41)	1.3! (0.46)	1.6! (0.50)	2.3 (0.62)	1.1! (0.42)	‡ (†)
Hispanic	2.7 (0.43)	1.9 (0.38)	1.5 (0.41)	1.1 (0.28)	0.9 (0.24)	1.4 (0.42)	1.3! (0.40)	1.0 (0.28)	1.5 (0.26)
Asian	— (†)	— (†)	— (†)	— (†)	‡ (†)	‡ (†)	# (†)	# (†)	‡ (†)
Other	2.5! (0.87)	2.2! (0.81)	‡ (†)	‡ (†)	‡ (†)	4.5! (1.50)	‡ (†)	‡ (†)	‡ (†)
Grade									
6th	5.1 (0.73)	3.8 (0.76)	2.6 (0.66)	1.9 (0.53)	1.9 (0.55)	1.5! (0.54)	2.6! (0.83)	1.3! (0.49)	2.7 (0.73)
7th	3.8 (0.54)	2.6 (0.43)	2.6 (0.47)	1.7 (0.43)	2.6 (0.53)	2.4 (0.50)	1.2! (0.42)	1.2! (0.41)	1.2! (0.38)
8th	3.1 (0.44)	2.4 (0.44)	1.3 (0.34)	1.5 (0.35)	1.4 (0.39)	2.1 (0.47)	2.0 (0.60)	2.1 (0.50)	1.4 (0.42)
9th	3.4 (0.50)	3.2 (0.47)	2.4 (0.46)	1.5 (0.31)	1.0 (0.29)	1.2! (0.37)	0.9! (0.37)	1.1! (0.35)	1.4! (0.44)
10th	2.1 (0.36)	1.7 (0.39)	1.2 (0.31)	1.4 (0.36)	0.5! (0.24)	1.2! (0.39)	1.0 (0.37)	0.9! (0.34)	1.0! (0.35)
11th	1.9 (0.40)	1.8! (0.58)	1.6 (0.39)	1.0! (0.33)	0.7! (0.31)	1.5! (0.46)	1.5! (0.51)	‡ (†)	1.0! (0.43)
12th	1.9 (0.41)	0.8! (0.31)	0.9! (0.31)	0.5! (0.26)	‡ (†)	0.8! (0.35)	‡ (†)	‡ (†)	‡ (†)
Urbanicity[2]									
Urban	3.3 (0.40)	2.3 (0.38)	1.7 (0.29)	1.8 (0.32)	1.8 (0.34)	2.0 (0.35)	1.8 (0.41)	1.4 (0.31)	0.9 (0.21)
Suburban	3.5 (0.30)	2.4 (0.26)	1.7 (0.20)	1.2 (0.19)	1.1 (0.18)	1.3 (0.23)	1.3 (0.23)	0.9 (0.16)	1.4 (0.21)
Rural	1.8 (0.31)	1.9 (0.50)	2.0! (0.64)	0.9! (0.31)	0.6! (0.26)	1.7 (0.36)	0.8! (0.32)	1.0! (0.31)	1.1! (0.46)
Sector									
Public	3.1 (0.22)	2.5 (0.20)	1.9 (0.20)	1.4 (0.15)	1.2 (0.15)	1.7 (0.20)	1.4 (0.19)	1.1 (0.15)	1.2 (0.16)
Private	1.7 (0.45)	‡ (†)	1.0! (0.32)	0.9! (0.39)	1.4! (0.60)	‡ (†)	‡ (†)	‡ (†)	‡ (†)

See notes at end of table.

Table 228.30. Percentage of students ages 12–18 who reported criminal victimization at school during the previous 6 months, by type of victimization and selected student and school characteristics: Selected years, 1995 through 2013—Continued

[Standard errors appear in parentheses]

Type of victimization and student or school characteristic	1995		1999		2001		2003		2005		2007		2009		2011		2013	
1	2		3		4		5		6		7		8		9		10	
Serious violent[3]	0.7	(0.09)	0.5	(0.09)	0.4	(0.08)	0.2	(0.06)	0.3	(0.07)	0.4	(0.08)	0.3	(0.09)	0.1 !	(0.05)	0.2 !	(0.07)
Sex																		
Male	0.9	(0.14)	0.6	(0.12)	0.5	(0.11)	0.3 !	(0.10)	0.3 !	(0.10)	0.5 !	(0.14)	0.6	(0.16)	0.2 !	(0.08)	0.2 !	(0.10)
Female	0.4	(0.10)	0.5	(0.12)	0.4 !	(0.12)	‡	(†)	0.3	(0.07)	0.2 !	(0.08)	‡	(†)	‡	(†)	0.2 !	(0.10)
Race/ethnicity[1]																		
White	0.6	(0.09)	0.4	(0.09)	0.4	(0.08)	0.2 !	(0.06)	0.3 !	(0.09)	0.2 !	(0.08)	0.3 !	(0.10)	0.2 !	(0.07)	0.2 !	(0.09)
Black	1.0 !	(0.31)	1.2	(0.33)	0.5 !	(0.25)	‡	(†)	‡	(†)	‡	(†)	‡	(†)	‡	(†)	‡	(†)
Hispanic	0.9 !	(0.30)	0.6 !	(0.22)	0.8 !	(0.33)	0.4 !	(0.18)	0.4 !	(0.16)	0.8 !	(0.32)	‡	(†)	‡	(†)	0.4 !	(0.17)
Asian	—	(†)	—	(†)	—	(†)	—	(†)	‡	(†)	‡	(†)	#	(†)	#	(†)	‡	(†)
Other	‡	(†)	#	(†)	#	(†)	‡	(†)	‡	(†)	‡	(†)	‡	(†)	#	(†)	‡	(†)
Grade																		
6th	1.5	(0.42)	1.3 !	(0.40)	‡	(†)	#	(†)	‡	(†)	‡	(†)	‡	(†)	‡	(†)	0.8 !	(0.42)
7th	0.9	(0.24)	0.9 !	(0.27)	0.6 !	(0.24)	‡	(†)	‡	(†)	0.4 !	(0.20)	‡	(†)	0.5 !	(0.23)	‡	(†)
8th	0.8 !	(0.23)	0.5 !	(0.22)	0.3 !	(0.14)	0.3 !	(0.15)	‡	(†)	‡	(†)	‡	(†)	#	(†)	‡	(†)
9th	0.7	(0.21)	0.6 !	(0.18)	0.8 !	(0.31)	0.6 !	(0.21)	‡	(†)	‡	(†)	‡	(†)	‡	(†)	‡	(†)
10th	0.4 !	(0.17)	‡	(†)	0.4 !	(0.18)	#	(†)	‡	(†)	‡	(†)	‡	(†)	#	(†)	‡	(†)
11th	0.4 !	(0.16)	‡	(†)	‡	(†)	‡	(†)	‡	(†)	0.6 !	(0.27)	‡	(†)	#	(†)	‡	(†)
12th	‡	(†)	‡	(†)	‡	(†)	#	(†)	‡	(†)	‡	(†)	‡	(†)	‡	(†)	‡	(†)
Urbanicity[2]																		
Urban	1.3	(0.24)	0.7	(0.19)	0.5	(0.15)	0.4 !	(0.14)	0.4 !	(0.17)	0.7 !	(0.23)	0.6 !	(0.22)	‡	(†)	0.3 !	(0.16)
Suburban	0.6	(0.12)	0.5	(0.11)	0.4	(0.09)	0.1 !	(0.05)	0.3 !	(0.08)	0.2 !	(0.09)	0.3 !	(0.11)	‡	(†)	0.2 !	(0.08)
Rural	0.3 !	(0.10)	0.4 !	(0.18)	0.5 !	(0.24)	‡	(†)	‡	(†)	‡	(†)	‡	(†)	‡	(†)	‡	(†)
Sector																		
Public	0.7	(0.10)	0.6	(0.10)	0.5	(0.09)	0.2	(0.06)	0.3	(0.06)	0.4	(0.09)	0.4	(0.10)	0.1 !	(0.06)	0.2 !	(0.08)
Private	‡	(†)	#	(†)	#	(†)	#	(†)	‡	(†)	‡	(†)	‡	(†)	#	(†)	‡	(†)

—Not available.
†Not applicable.
#Rounds to zero.
!Interpret data with caution. The coefficient of variation (CV) for this estimate is between 30 and 50 percent.
‡Reporting standards not met. Either there are too few cases for a reliable estimate or the coefficient of variation (CV) is 50 percent or greater.
[1]Race categories exclude persons of Hispanic ethnicity. "Other" includes American Indians/Alaska Natives, Asians (prior to 2005), Pacific Islanders, and, from 2003 onward, persons of Two or more races. Due to changes in racial/ethnic categories, comparisons of race/ethnicity across years should be made with caution.
[2]Refers to the Standard Metropolitan Statistical Area (MSA) status of the respondent's household as defined in 2000 by the U.S. Census Bureau. Categories include "central city of an MSA (Urban)," "in MSA but not in central city (Suburban)," and "not MSA (Rural)."

[3]Serious violent victimization is also included in violent victimization.
NOTE: "Total victimization" includes theft and violent victimization. A single student could report more than one type of victimization. In the total victimization section, students who reported both theft and violent victimization are counted only once. "Theft" includes attempted and completed purse-snatching, completed pickpocketing, and all attempted and completed thefts, with the exception of motor vehicle thefts. Theft does not include robbery, which involves the threat or use of force and is classified as a violent crime. "Serious violent victimization" includes the crimes of rape, sexual assault, robbery, and aggravated assault. "Violent victimization" includes the serious violent crimes as well as simple assault. "At school" includes the school building, on school property, on a school bus, and, from 2001 onward, going to and from school.
SOURCE: U.S. Department of Justice, Bureau of Justice Statistics, School Crime Supplement (SCS) to the National Crime Victimization Survey, selected years, 1995 through 2013. (This table was prepared August 2014.)

Table 228.40. Percentage of students in grades 9–12 who reported being threatened or injured with a weapon on school property during the previous 12 months, by selected student characteristics and number of times threatened or injured: Selected years, 1993 through 2013

[Standard errors appear in parentheses]

Number of times and year	Total	Sex		Race/ethnicity¹							Grade			
		Male	Female	White	Black	Hispanic	Asian²	Pacific Islander²	American Indian/ Alaska Native²	Two or more races²	9th grade	10th grade	11th grade	12th grade
1	2	3	4	5	6	7	8	9	10	11	12	13	14	15
At least once														
1993	7.3 (0.44)	9.2 (0.64)	5.4 (0.40)	6.3 (0.58)	11.2 (0.95)	8.6 (0.83)	(†)	—	11.7 (2.50)	—	9.4 (0.92)	7.3 (0.59)	7.3 (0.64)	5.5 (0.62)
1995	8.4 (0.52)	10.9 (0.57)	5.8 (0.68)	7.0 (0.53)	11.0 (1.61)	12.4 (1.44)	(†)	—	11.4! (4.22)	—	9.6 (0.96)	9.6 (1.03)	7.7 (0.64)	6.7 (0.57)
1997	7.4 (0.45)	10.2 (0.71)	4.0 (0.32)	6.2 (0.56)	9.9 (0.91)	9.0 (0.63)	(†)	(†)	12.5! (5.15)	(†)	10.1 (1.02)	7.9 (1.14)	5.9 (0.70)	5.8 (0.80)
1999	7.7 (0.42)	9.5 (0.80)	5.8 (0.64)	6.6 (0.35)	7.6 (0.85)	9.8 (1.09)	7.7 (1.05)	15.6 (4.46)	13.2! (5.45)	9.3 (1.22)	10.5 (0.95)	8.2 (0.92)	6.1 (0.46)	5.1 (0.79)
2001	8.9 (0.55)	11.5 (0.66)	6.5 (0.52)	8.5 (0.66)	9.3 (0.71)	8.9 (1.05)	11.3 (2.73)	24.8 (7.16)	15.2! (4.57)	10.3 (2.33)	12.7 (0.89)	9.1 (0.75)	6.9 (0.65)	5.3 (0.52)
2003	9.2 (0.75)	11.6 (0.96)	6.5 (0.61)	7.8 (0.77)	10.9 (0.80)	9.4 (1.23)	11.5 (2.66)	16.3 (4.31)	22.1 (4.79)	18.7 (3.11)	12.1 (1.25)	9.2 (1.02)	7.3 (0.69)	6.3 (0.92)
2005	7.9 (0.35)	9.7 (0.42)	6.1 (0.41)	7.2 (0.46)	8.1 (0.69)	9.8 (0.86)	4.6 (1.10)	14.5! (4.93)	9.8 (2.67)	10.7 (2.33)	10.5 (0.63)	8.8 (0.72)	5.5 (0.43)	5.8 (0.52)
2007	7.8 (0.44)	10.2 (0.59)	5.4 (0.41)	6.9 (0.52)	9.7 (0.86)	8.7 (0.60)	7.6! (2.29)	8.1! (2.45)	5.9 (1.24)	13.3 (2.25)	9.2 (0.69)	8.4 (0.51)	6.8 (0.57)	6.3 (0.64)
2009	7.7 (0.37)	9.6 (0.59)	5.5 (0.37)	6.4 (0.43)	9.4 (0.80)	9.1 (0.61)	5.5 (0.91)	12.5 (3.11)	16.5 (2.68)	9.2 (1.50)	8.7 (0.53)	8.4 (0.72)	7.9 (0.60)	5.2 (0.53)
2011	7.4 (0.31)	9.5 (0.39)	5.2 (0.37)	6.1 (0.35)	8.9 (0.64)	9.2 (0.81)	7.0 (0.99)	11.3 (3.23)	8.2 (1.52)	9.9 (1.35)	8.3 (0.63)	7.7 (0.58)	7.3 (0.61)	5.9 (0.45)
2013	6.9 (0.38)	7.7 (0.54)	6.1 (0.40)	5.8 (0.32)	8.4 (0.82)	8.5 (0.73)	5.3 (1.41)	8.7! (2.71)	18.5 (5.24)	7.7 (2.11)	8.5 (0.75)	7.0 (0.67)	6.8 (0.60)	4.9 (0.61)
Number of times, 2013														
0 times	93.1 (0.38)	92.3 (0.54)	93.9 (0.40)	94.2 (0.32)	91.6 (0.82)	91.5 (0.73)	94.7 (1.41)	91.3 (2.71)	81.5 (5.24)	92.3 (2.11)	91.5 (0.75)	93.0 (0.67)	93.2 (0.60)	95.1 (0.61)
1 time	3.0 (0.22)	3.0 (0.25)	3.0 (0.33)	2.7 (0.27)	3.3 (0.51)	3.3 (0.51)	1.7! (0.51)	2.0 (0.59)	9.6! (3.14)	3.1! (0.96)	3.5 (0.50)	3.0 (0.52)	3.4 (0.39)	2.0 (0.27)
2 or 3 times	1.7 (0.14)	1.7 (0.21)	1.6 (0.20)	1.6 (0.17)	1.8 (0.35)	1.6 (0.29)	‡ (†)	‡ (†)	‡ (†)	2.2! (0.67)	2.5 (0.37)	1.7 (0.26)	1.3 (0.24)	1.1 (0.21)
4 to 11 times	1.3 (0.14)	1.7 (0.21)	0.9 (0.18)	0.8 (0.12)	1.7 (0.36)	2.3 (0.34)	‡ (†)	‡ (†)	4.9! (2.34)	1.5! (0.63)	1.5 (0.22)	1.4 (0.30)	1.3 (0.28)	1.0 (0.21)
12 or more times	0.9 (0.11)	1.3 (0.19)	0.6 (0.08)	0.7 (0.17)	1.2 (0.23)	1.2 (0.25)	‡ (†)	‡ (†)	‡ (†)	‡ (†)	1.0 (0.20)	0.9 (0.20)	0.9 (0.22)	0.9 (0.25)

—Not available.
†Not applicable.
!Interpret data with caution. The coefficient of variation (CV) for this estimate is between 30 and 50 percent.
‡Reporting standards not met. Either there are too few cases for a reliable estimate or the coefficient of variation (CV) is 50 percent or greater.
¹Race categories exclude persons of Hispanic ethnicity.

²Before 1999, Asian students and Pacific Islander students were not categorized separately, and students could not be classified as Two or more races. Because the response categories changed in 1999, caution should be used in comparing data on race from 1993, 1995, and 1997 with data from later years.
NOTE: Survey respondents were asked about being threatened or injured "with a weapon such as a gun, knife, or club on school property." "On school property" was not defined for respondents. Detail may not sum to totals because of rounding.
SOURCE: Centers for Disease Control and Prevention, Division of Adolescent and School Health, Youth Risk Behavior Surveillance System (YRBSS), 1993 through 2013. (This table was prepared June 2014.)

Table 228.50. Percentage of public school students in grades 9–12 who reported being threatened or injured with a weapon on school property at least one time during the previous 12 months, by state: Selected years, 2003 through 2013

[Standard errors appear in parentheses]

State	2003		2005		2007		2009		2011		2013	
1	2		3		4		5		6		7	
United States[1]	9.2	(0.75)	7.9	(0.35)	7.8	(0.44)	7.7	(0.37)	7.4	(0.31)	6.9	(0.38)
Alabama	7.2	(0.91)	10.6	(0.86)	—	(†)	10.4	(1.56)	7.6	(1.20)	9.9	(1.17)
Alaska	8.1	(1.01)	—	(†)	7.7	(0.88)	7.3	(0.90)	5.6	(0.70)	—	(†)
Arizona	9.7	(1.10)	10.7	(0.55)	11.2	(0.79)	9.3	(0.92)	10.4	(0.74)	9.1	(1.32)
Arkansas	—	(†)	9.6	(1.06)	9.1	(1.03)	11.9	(1.38)	6.3	(0.85)	10.9	(1.14)
California	—	(†)	—	(†)	—	(†)	—	(†)	—	(†)	—	(†)
Colorado	—	(†)	7.6	(0.75)	—	(†)	8.0	(0.74)	6.7	(0.80)	—	(†)
Connecticut	—	(†)	9.1	(0.91)	7.7	(0.59)	7.0	(0.62)	6.8	(0.71)	7.1	(0.74)
Delaware	7.7	(0.60)	6.2	(0.63)	5.6	(0.50)	7.8	(0.63)	6.4	(0.62)	5.6	(0.46)
District of Columbia	12.7	(1.42)	12.1	(0.78)	11.3	(0.98)	—	(†)	8.7	(0.92)	—	(†)
Florida	8.4	(0.44)	7.9	(0.45)	8.6	(0.57)	8.2	(0.39)	7.2	(0.31)	7.1	(0.37)
Georgia	8.2	(0.75)	8.3	(2.08)	8.1	(0.81)	8.2	(0.83)	11.7	(2.08)	7.2	(0.81)
Hawaii	—	(†)	6.8	(0.87)	6.4	(1.10)	7.7	(1.03)	6.3	(0.62)	—	(†)
Idaho	9.4	(0.82)	8.3	(0.59)	10.2	(1.07)	7.9	(0.62)	7.3	(0.99)	5.8	(0.59)
Illinois	—	(†)	—	(†)	7.8	(0.69)	8.8	(0.86)	7.6	(0.48)	8.5	(0.82)
Indiana	6.7	(0.91)	8.8	(0.96)	9.6	(0.68)	6.5	(0.66)	6.8	(1.14)	—	(†)
Iowa	—	(†)	7.8	(1.02)	7.1	(0.86)	—	(†)	6.3	(0.85)	—	(†)
Kansas	—	(†)	7.4	(0.82)	8.6	(1.12)	6.2	(0.62)	5.6	(0.68)	5.3	(0.65)
Kentucky	5.2	(0.72)	8.0	(0.75)	8.3	(0.53)	7.9	(1.00)	7.4	(0.98)	5.4	(0.57)
Louisiana	—	(†)	—	(†)	—	(†)	9.5	(1.29)	8.7	(1.18)	10.5	(0.99)
Maine	8.5	(0.78)	7.1	(0.68)	6.8	(0.84)	7.7	(0.32)	6.8	(0.26)	5.3	(0.29)
Maryland	—	(†)	11.7	(1.30)	9.6	(0.86)	9.1	(0.75)	8.4	(0.67)	9.4	(0.22)
Massachusetts	6.3	(0.54)	5.4	(0.44)	5.3	(0.47)	7.0	(0.58)	6.8	(0.67)	4.4	(0.38)
Michigan	9.7	(0.57)	8.6	(0.81)	8.1	(0.77)	9.4	(0.63)	6.8	(0.50)	6.7	(0.52)
Minnesota	—	(†)	—	(†)	—	(†)	—	(†)	—	(†)	—	(†)
Mississippi	6.6	(0.82)	—	(†)	8.3	(0.59)	8.0	(0.69)	7.5	(0.63)	8.8	(0.78)
Missouri	7.5	(0.93)	9.1	(1.19)	9.3	(1.03)	7.8	(0.76)	—	(†)	—	(†)
Montana	7.1	(0.46)	8.0	(0.64)	7.0	(0.51)	7.4	(0.99)	7.5	(0.53)	6.3	(0.40)
Nebraska	8.8	(0.80)	9.7	(0.68)	—	(†)	—	(†)	6.4	(0.54)	6.4	(0.57)
Nevada	6.0	(0.65)	8.1	(0.96)	7.8	(0.70)	10.7	(0.84)	—	(†)	6.4	(0.80)
New Hampshire	7.5	(0.98)	8.6	(0.91)	7.3	(0.69)	—	(†)	—	(†)	—	(†)
New Jersey	—	(†)	8.0	(1.07)	—	(†)	6.6	(0.75)	5.7	(0.51)	6.2	(0.81)
New Mexico	—	(†)	10.4	(0.96)	10.1	(0.68)	—	(†)	—	(†)	—	(†)
New York	7.2	(0.44)	7.2	(0.47)	7.3	(0.57)	7.5	(0.55)	7.3	(0.60)	7.3	(0.61)
North Carolina	7.2	(0.74)	7.9	(0.92)	6.6	(0.62)	6.8	(0.61)	9.1	(0.95)	6.9	(0.45)
North Dakota	5.9	(0.89)	6.6	(0.58)	5.2	(0.59)	—	(†)	—	(†)	—	(†)
Ohio[2]	7.7	(1.30)	8.2	(0.67)	8.3	(0.77)	—	(†)	—	(†)	—	(†)
Oklahoma	7.4	(1.10)	6.0	(0.65)	7.0	(0.72)	5.8	(0.66)	5.7	(0.88)	4.6	(0.53)
Oregon	—	(†)	—	(†)	—	(†)	—	(†)	—	(†)	—	(†)
Pennsylvania	—	(†)	—	(†)	—	(†)	5.6	(0.73)	—	(†)	—	(†)
Rhode Island	8.2	(0.84)	8.7	(0.87)	8.3	(0.42)	6.5	(0.65)	—	(†)	6.4	(0.51)
South Carolina	—	(†)	10.1	(0.93)	9.8	(0.85)	8.8	(1.48)	9.2	(0.92)	6.5	(0.83)
South Dakota[2]	6.5	(0.71)	8.1	(1.04)	5.9	(0.87)	6.8	(0.87)	6.1	(0.77)	5.0	(0.69)
Tennessee	8.4	(1.17)	7.4	(0.79)	7.3	(0.76)	7.0	(0.71)	5.8	(0.52)	9.3	(0.73)
Texas	—	(†)	9.3	(0.84)	8.7	(0.52)	7.2	(0.52)	6.8	(0.40)	7.1	(0.62)
Utah	7.3	(1.44)	9.8	(1.32)	11.4	(1.92)	7.7	(0.88)	7.0	(0.98)	5.5	(0.59)
Vermont	7.3	(0.20)	6.3	(0.46)	6.2	(0.56)	6.0	(0.30)	5.5	(0.37)	6.4	(0.43)
Virginia	—	(†)	—	(†)	—	(†)	—	(†)	7.0	(0.86)	6.1	(0.43)
Washington	—	(†)	—	(†)	—	(†)	—	(†)	—	(†)	—	(†)
West Virginia	8.5	(1.26)	8.0	(0.78)	9.7	(0.77)	9.2	(0.77)	6.6	(0.93)	5.6	(0.51)
Wisconsin	5.5	(0.70)	7.6	(0.73)	5.6	(0.66)	6.7	(0.75)	5.1	(0.48)	4.3	(0.64)
Wyoming	9.7	(1.00)	7.8	(0.67)	8.3	(0.67)	9.4	(0.58)	7.3	(0.58)	6.8	(0.47)

—Not available.

†Not applicable.

[1]Data for the U.S. total include both public and private schools and were collected through a national survey representing the entire country.

[2]Data include both public and private schools.

NOTE: Survey respondents were asked about being threatened or injured "with a weapon such as a gun, knife, or club on school property." "On school property" was not defined for respondents. State-level data include public schools only, with the exception of data for Ohio and South Dakota. Data for the U.S. total, Ohio, and South Dakota include both public and private schools. For specific states, a given year's data may be unavailable (1) because the state did not participate in the survey that year; (2) because the state omitted this particular survey item from the state-level questionnaire; or (3) because the state had an overall response rate of less than 60 percent (the overall response rate is the school response rate multiplied by the student response rate).

SOURCE: Centers for Disease Control and Prevention, Division of Adolescent and School Health, Youth Risk Behavior Surveillance System (YRBSS), 2003 through 2013. (This table was prepared June 2014.)

Table 228.70. Number and percentage of public and private school teachers who reported that they were threatened with injury or physically attacked by a student from school during the previous 12 months, by selected teacher and school characteristics: Selected years, 1993–94 through 2011–12

[Standard errors appear in parentheses]

Year	Total	Sex		Race/ethnicity				Instructional level[1]		Control of school	
		Male	Female	White	Black	Hispanic	Other[2]	Elementary	Secondary	Public[3]	Private
1	2	3	4	5	6	7	8	9	10	11	12
Number of teachers											
Threatened with injury											
1993–94	342,700 (7,140)	115,900 (3,870)	226,800 (5,570)	295,700 (6,320)	23,900 (1,380)	15,900 (1,850)	7,300 (680)	135,200 (4,520)	207,500 (5,380)	326,800 (7,040)	15,900 (1,130)
1999–2000	304,900 (7,090)	95,100 (3,610)	209,800 (5,490)	252,500 (5,670)	28,300 (2,150)	17,200 (1,980)	7,000 (850)	148,100 (5,560)	156,900 (4,360)	287,400 (7,060)	17,500 (1,700)
2003–04	252,800 (8,750)	78,400 (3,930)	174,400 (7,260)	198,900 (6,980)	32,500 (3,050)	12,400 (1,810)	9,000 (1,250)	113,600 (7,240)	139,200 (5,280)	242,100 (7,840)	10,700 (1,780)
2007–08	289,900 (10,660)	88,300 (5,970)	201,600 (8,140)	234,700 (8,850)	28,700 (3,080)	17,900 (3,230)	8,600 (1,630)	130,000 (7,720)	160,000 (7,220)	276,600 (10,570)	13,300 (1,460)
2011–12	352,900 (17,080)	84,500 (5,220)	268,400 (15,450)	279,900 (13,300)	34,200 (4,380)	27,100 (4,660)	11,800 (2,200)	189,800 (13,430)	163,200 (7,520)	338,400 (17,290)	14,500 (1,450)
Physically attacked											
1993–94	121,100 (3,950)	30,800 (1,770)	90,300 (3,900)	104,300 (4,020)	7,700 (860)	6,200 (1,290)	2,800 (450)	77,300 (3,240)	43,800 (1,980)	112,400 (3,730)	8,700 (860)
1999–2000	134,800 (4,820)	30,600 (1,990)	104,200 (4,390)	111,700 (3,810)	11,600 (1,540)	8,800 (1,660)	2,600 (460)	102,200 (4,360)	32,600 (2,270)	125,000 (4,630)	9,800 (1,070)
2003–04	129,200 (7,810)	23,600 (2,610)	105,700 (6,460)	102,200 (5,920)	15,100 (2,300)	7,000 (1,860)	5,000 (1,110)	89,800 (6,680)	39,400 (3,410)	121,400 (7,180)	7,800 (1,450)
2007–08	156,000 (8,090)	34,900 (4,760)	121,100 (6,120)	132,300 (6,860)	12,300 (2,350)	8,200 (2,040)	3,200 ! (1,250)	114,700 (7,220)	41,300 (3,220)	146,400 (8,200)	9,600 (1,170)
2011–12	209,800 (11,880)	32,500 (3,330)	177,300 (11,310)	171,300 (10,950)	18,800 (3,580)	11,800 (2,890)	7,900 (1,990)	160,700 (10,210)	49,100 (4,310)	197,400 (11,730)	12,400 (1,490)
Percent of teachers											
Threatened with injury											
1993–94	11.7 (0.23)	14.7 (0.40)	10.5 (0.25)	11.5 (0.24)	11.9 (0.61)	13.1 (1.32)	13.4 (1.08)	8.7 (0.30)	15.0 (0.28)	12.8 (0.26)	4.2 (0.29)
1999–2000	8.8 (0.20)	11.0 (0.38)	8.1 (0.20)	8.6 (0.19)	11.6 (0.84)	9.1 (1.01)	8.3 (0.98)	8.0 (0.29)	9.9 (0.26)	9.6 (0.22)	3.9 (0.35)
2003–04	6.8 (0.24)	8.5 (0.39)	6.2 (0.27)	6.4 (0.24)	11.8 (0.96)	5.5 (0.82)	8.7 (1.25)	5.7 (0.37)	8.0 (0.27)	7.4 (0.24)	2.3 (0.40)
2007–08	7.4 (0.26)	9.3 (0.59)	6.8 (0.27)	7.2 (0.26)	11.1 (0.93)	6.7 (1.19)	7.6 (1.36)	6.6 (0.38)	8.4 (0.36)	8.1 (0.30)	2.7 (0.30)
2011–12	9.2 (0.42)	9.2 (0.49)	9.2 (0.50)	8.8 (0.40)	13.8 (1.72)	9.4 (1.54)	9.1 (1.54)	9.6 (0.67)	8.7 (0.34)	10.0 (0.48)	3.1 (0.32)
Physically attacked											
1993–94	4.1 (0.13)	3.9 (0.21)	4.2 (0.18)	4.1 (0.16)	3.9 (0.40)	5.2 (0.99)	5.2 (0.76)	5.0 (0.20)	3.2 (0.14)	4.4 (0.14)	2.3 (0.23)
1999–2000	3.9 (0.14)	3.5 (0.22)	4.0 (0.17)	3.8 (0.13)	4.8 (0.59)	4.6 (0.83)	3.1 (0.54)	5.5 (0.23)	2.1 (0.14)	4.2 (0.15)	2.2 (0.22)
2003–04	3.5 (0.21)	2.6 (0.27)	3.8 (0.24)	3.3 (0.20)	5.5 (0.78)	3.1 (0.85)	4.8 (1.10)	4.5 (0.35)	2.3 (0.19)	3.7 (0.22)	1.7 (0.32)
2007–08	4.0 (0.21)	3.7 (0.49)	4.1 (0.21)	4.1 (0.22)	4.7 (0.89)	3.1 (0.73)	2.8 ! (0.97)	5.8 (0.38)	2.2 (0.16)	4.3 (0.24)	2.0 (0.24)
2011–12	5.4 (0.30)	3.5 (0.35)	6.0 (0.37)	5.4 (0.33)	7.6 (1.41)	4.1 (0.96)	6.1 (1.43)	8.2 (0.50)	2.6 (0.21)	5.8 (0.33)	2.7 (0.33)

!Interpret data with caution. The coefficient of variation (CV) for this estimate is between 30 and 50 percent.
[1]Teachers were classified as elementary or secondary on the basis of the grades they taught, rather than on the level of the school in which they taught. In general, elementary teachers include those teaching prekindergarten through grade 5 and those teaching multiple grades, with a preponderance of grades taught being kindergarten through grade 6. In general, secondary teachers include those teaching any of grades 7 through 12 and those teaching multiple grades, with a preponderance of grades taught being grades 7 through 12 and usually with no grade taught being lower than grade 5.
[2]Includes American Indians/Alaska Natives, Asians, and Pacific Islanders; for 2003–04 and later years, also includes persons of two or more races.

[3]Includes traditional public and public charter schools.
NOTE: Teachers who taught only prekindergarten students are excluded. Instructional level divides teachers into elementary or secondary based on a combination of the grades taught, main teaching assignment, and the structure of the teachers' class(es). Race categories exclude persons of Hispanic ethnicity. Detail may not sum to totals because of rounding. Some data have been revised from previously published figures.
SOURCE: U.S. Department of Education, National Center for Education Statistics, Schools and Staffing Survey (SASS), "Public School Teacher Data File" and "Private School Teacher Data File," 1993–94, 1999–2000, 2003–04, 2007–08, and 2011–12; and "Charter School Teacher Data File," 1999–2000. (This table was prepared October 2013.)

Table 228.80. Percentage of public school teachers who reported that they were threatened with injury or physically attacked by a student from school during the previous 12 months, by state: Selected years, 1993–94 through 2011–12

[Standard errors appear in parentheses]

State	Threatened with injury						Physically attacked					
	1993–94	1999–2000	2003–04	2007–08	2011–12		1993–94	1999–2000	2003–04	2007–08	2011–12	
1	2	3	4	5	6		7	8	9	10	11	
United States............	12.8 (0.26)	9.6 (0.22)	7.4 (0.24)	8.1 (0.30)	10.0 (0.48)		4.4 (0.14)	4.2 (0.15)	3.7 (0.22)	4.3 (0.24)	5.8 (0.33)	
Alabama......................	13.3 (1.29)	8.8 (0.99)	6.1 (0.88)	6.8 (1.41)	7.6 (1.92)		3.2 (0.84)	3.8 (0.57)	2.7 (0.75)	3.2 ! (1.12)	3.1 ! (0.94)	
Alaska.........................	13.7 (0.92)	10.9 (0.80)	8.9 (1.25)	7.8 (1.24)	12.3 (2.82)		6.5 (0.48)	5.2 (0.51)	6.0 (0.94)	6.7 (1.50)	5.1 ! (1.78)	
Arizona.......................	13.0 (1.07)	9.5 (1.16)	6.8 (0.98)	6.4 (1.04)	9.1 (2.08)		3.6 (0.67)	4.5 (0.95)	2.6 (0.58)	4.9 (1.29)	4.7 ! (1.43)	
Arkansas....................	13.8 (1.38)	10.1 (1.18)	4.8 (0.81)	5.9 (1.18)	7.8 (1.48)		3.0 (0.67)	2.5 (0.59)	2.7 (0.72)	4.1 (1.07)	5.2 ! (1.80)	
California	7.4 (0.91)	5.8 (0.70)	6.0 (1.00)	8.5 (1.31)	7.7 (1.17)		2.9 (0.61)	2.5 (0.46)	2.0 (0.53)	3.6 (0.78)	4.4 (0.95)	
Colorado.....................	13.1 (1.29)	6.6 (0.97)	3.8 (0.82)	6.8 (1.64)	7.3 (1.69)		4.9 (0.82)	3.1 (0.60)	1.5 ! (0.45)	4.7 (1.33)	3.6 ! (1.26)	
Connecticut.................	11.8 (0.86)	9.1 (0.88)	6.9 (1.28)	7.2 (1.39)	7.5 ! (3.03)		3.5 (0.46)	4.1 (0.55)	2.8 (0.70)	3.3 ! (1.04)	6.2 ! (2.91)	
Delaware.....................	18.7 (1.56)	11.4 (1.37)	7.7 (1.35)	11.7 (1.93)	15.8 (3.49)		7.2 (1.10)	5.3 (0.92)	3.2 ! (1.00)	5.4 (1.46)	9.8 (2.80)	
District of Columbia	24.0 (1.80)	22.3 (1.30)	17.3 (2.63)	16.9 (3.06)	‡ (†)		8.3 (1.34)	9.1 (0.83)	5.2 (1.24)	7.3 (2.00)	‡ (†)	
Florida........................	20.1 (1.65)	12.2 (1.07)	11.2 (1.26)	11.4 (2.11)	‡ (†)		4.9 (0.78)	6.7 (0.91)	6.5 (1.58)	4.0 (1.04)	‡ (†)	
Georgia.......................	14.0 (1.29)	9.5 (1.42)	6.4 (1.21)	5.8 (1.18)	9.5 ! (2.98)		3.4 (0.66)	3.6 (0.84)	4.6 (1.30)	4.0 (1.04)	6.3 ! (2.60)	
Hawaii.........................	9.9 (1.48)	9.4 (0.99)	9.0 (1.33)	8.0 (1.84)	‡ (†)		2.9 (0.57)	3.2 (0.57)	5.7 (1.18)	4.5 (1.30)	‡ (†)	
Idaho..........................	9.7 (1.02)	7.8 (0.44)	5.4 (0.98)	5.9 (1.24)	6.7 (1.42)		4.2 (0.76)	4.3 (0.39)	2.5 ! (0.75)	2.9 ! (0.87)	3.6 ! (1.34)	
Illinois........................	10.9 (0.76)	8.2 (0.89)	7.9 (1.60)	8.1 (1.42)	7.3 (1.41)		4.5 (0.50)	2.7 (0.39)	2.3 ! (0.77)	3.9 (0.90)	4.1 (1.11)	
Indiana........................	13.8 (1.28)	7.6 (1.12)	7.2 (1.18)	10.2 (1.78)	11.2 (2.87)		3.0 (0.66)	3.0 (0.75)	4.1 ! (1.28)	4.7 (0.93)	6.4 (1.88)	
Iowa...........................	9.4 (1.19)	10.7 (0.93)	4.9 (1.13)	7.2 (1.32)	11.7 (2.43)		4.3 (0.88)	3.9 (0.73)	2.4 (0.64)	3.4 (0.93)	7.6 (2.11)	
Kansas.......................	10.9 (0.91)	6.0 (0.78)	3.9 (0.81)	5.7 (1.07)	7.2 (1.66)		3.8 (0.61)	2.9 (0.55)	3.3 (0.79)	5.0 (1.36)	5.5 ! (1.77)	
Kentucky.....................	14.0 (1.33)	12.6 (1.22)	7.8 (1.46)	9.8 (1.86)	10.6 (1.48)		3.8 (0.72)	4.5 (0.62)	2.7 (0.79)	5.8 (1.60)	7.0 (1.25)	
Louisiana....................	17.0 (1.17)	13.4 (2.31)	9.8 (1.42)	10.3 (2.35)	18.3 (2.95)		6.6 (0.82)	5.0 (1.31)	2.7 (0.69)	4.0 ! (1.40)	7.2 ! (2.27)	
Maine.........................	9.0 (1.11)	11.7 (1.13)	5.2 (1.09)	9.5 (1.49)	9.1 (1.98)		2.4 (0.62)	6.3 (0.96)	3.3 ! (1.00)	5.2 (1.37)	5.2 (1.55)	
Maryland.....................	19.8 (2.15)	10.7 (1.31)	13.5 (2.24)	12.6 (2.47)	‡ (†)		8.6 (1.34)	4.6 (0.93)	6.5 (1.40)	8.4 (1.57)	‡ (†)	
Massachusetts.............	10.8 (0.83)	11.3 (1.48)	6.4 (1.23)	9.7 (1.98)	6.2 (1.69)		4.7 (0.64)	4.3 (0.67)	3.8 (0.75)	4.1 (0.93)	5.3 (1.51)	
Michigan.....................	10.7 (1.54)	8.0 (0.93)	9.2 (1.55)	6.0 (1.15)	11.8 (1.62)		6.4 (1.13)	3.8 (0.91)	5.4 (1.04)	3.5 ! (1.32)	9.0 (2.00)	
Minnesota...................	9.6 (1.13)	9.5 (1.11)	8.1 (1.17)	7.3 (1.16)	11.4 (1.49)		4.5 (0.85)	4.4 (1.04)	3.6 (0.68)	6.5 (1.38)	6.5 (1.27)	
Mississippi..................	13.4 (1.48)	11.1 (0.99)	5.5 (0.92)	10.7 (1.59)	7.7 (1.42)		4.1 (0.78)	3.7 (0.58)	0.9 ! (0.34)	2.9 (0.83)	3.1 ! (1.14)	
Missouri......................	12.6 (1.11)	11.3 (1.73)	8.3 (1.27)	8.7 (1.17)	12.3 (2.25)		3.2 (0.73)	5.6 (1.41)	5.5 (1.43)	5.3 (1.15)	7.5 (1.73)	
Montana......................	7.7 (0.58)	8.3 (0.97)	6.0 (0.78)	6.3 (1.25)	7.6 (2.24)		2.7 (0.48)	2.7 (0.38)	1.9 (0.47)	4.0 (0.81)	4.2 ! (1.37)	
Nebraska	10.4 (0.61)	9.9 (0.70)	7.5 (1.12)	7.2 (1.27)	8.0 (1.46)		3.6 (0.64)	3.8 (0.57)	4.1 (0.89)	4.2 (1.11)	5.8 (1.36)	
Nevada.......................	13.2 (1.22)	11.6 (1.34)	7.3 (1.89)	9.2 (2.21)	9.1 (2.65)		4.5 (0.86)	8.1 (1.07)	4.1 ! (1.28)	3.7 ! (1.41)	4.7 ! (2.25)	
New Hampshire	11.1 (1.30)	8.8 (1.43)	5.8 (1.37)	6.5 (1.47)	5.6 ! (2.11)		3.0 (0.70)	4.2 (1.09)	2.8 ! (0.91)	2.2 ! (0.91)	‡ (†)	
New Jersey...................	7.9 (0.87)	7.5 (0.80)	4.3 (1.20)	4.6 (1.26)	6.9 (1.08)		2.4 (0.45)	3.4 (0.78)	2.0 ! (0.67)	2.2 ! (0.82)	3.6 (0.97)	
New Mexico..................	12.8 (1.27)	10.2 (1.75)	7.8 (1.25)	12.8 (1.85)	10.0 (2.76)		4.4 (0.72)	6.8 (1.77)	5.9 (0.97)	4.5 (1.33)	9.9 ! (3.17)	
New York.....................	16.2 (1.32)	11.5 (1.06)	10.4 (1.62)	10.5 (1.85)	11.9 (1.86)		6.7 (0.97)	5.2 (0.79)	6.5 (1.12)	6.4 (1.56)	7.0 (1.48)	
North Carolina	17.1 (1.32)	12.8 (1.63)	8.7 (1.44)	9.6 (1.71)	13.4 (2.79)		6.0 (0.95)	5.5 (1.23)	4.4 (0.95)	5.9 ! (1.84)	6.3 (1.58)	
North Dakota	5.5 (0.62)	5.7 (0.57)	5.0 (0.95)	2.5 (0.70)	6.1 (1.48)		2.9 (0.66)	2.1 (0.37)	2.1 (0.49)	1.6 ! (0.50)	3.3 ! (1.06)	
Ohio..........................	15.2 (1.48)	9.6 (1.35)	6.2 (1.14)	8.7 (1.59)	9.9 (1.20)		3.6 (0.69)	2.9 (0.83)	2.5 ! (0.83)	2.2 ! (0.70)	3.9 (0.88)	
Oklahoma....................	11.0 (1.21)	8.5 (1.17)	6.0 (0.79)	7.4 (0.87)	9.6 (2.12)		4.1 (0.81)	4.5 (1.12)	3.0 (0.53)	3.2 (0.63)	6.2 (1.66)	
Oregon.......................	11.5 (1.00)	6.9 (1.33)	5.5 (1.11)	6.3 (1.30)	5.3 (1.56)		3.4 (0.64)	3.0 (0.60)	1.4 ! (0.55)	3.9 ! (1.18)	3.4 ! (1.27)	
Pennsylvania................	11.0 (1.75)	9.5 (1.28)	9.5 (1.29)	4.6 (1.04)	10.1 (1.54)		3.6 (1.02)	4.5 (0.97)	5.0 (0.82)	3.8 (0.90)	4.4 (0.99)	
Rhode Island	13.4 (1.78)	10.2 (0.64)	4.6 ! (1.39)	8.6 (2.13)	‡ (†)		4.2 (0.91)	4.8 (0.59)	2.4 ! (0.92)	‡ (†)	‡ (†)	
South Carolina...............	15.2 (1.62)	11.5 (1.10)	8.5 (1.30)	8.5 (1.46)	13.1 (2.70)		3.8 (0.92)	5.3 (0.94)	3.1 (0.82)	2.9 ! (1.18)	‡ (†)	
South Dakota	6.5 (0.83)	7.7 (0.91)	4.7 (1.23)	6.9 (1.88)	10.0 (2.28)		2.6 (0.46)	3.9 (0.50)	2.9 (0.79)	4.3 (0.88)	5.2 ! (1.66)	
Tennessee	12.4 (1.45)	13.3 (1.65)	6.5 (1.24)	7.7 (1.26)	9.4 (2.11)		3.5 (0.91)	2.6 (0.67)	3.7 (1.02)	4.1 (1.11)	3.2 ! (1.04)	
Texas	12.6 (1.15)	8.9 (0.89)	7.6 (1.13)	7.6 (1.31)	10.0 (1.81)		4.2 (0.65)	4.8 (0.75)	3.9 (0.92)	4.2 (1.18)	5.7 (1.30)	
Utah..........................	11.1 (0.87)	8.0 (1.15)	5.2 (0.82)	5.7 (1.18)	7.2 (1.96)		7.2 (0.72)	2.6 (0.58)	4.1 (0.90)	3.8 ! (1.26)	5.4 (1.53)	
Vermont......................	12.4 (1.28)	9.9 (1.46)	4.9 (1.18)	7.6 (1.82)	8.7 (1.86)		8.6 (1.38)	5.3 (0.94)	1.8 ! (0.90)	4.2 (1.22)	5.3 (1.29)	
Virginia.......................	14.9 (1.37)	12.1 (1.19)	6.5 (1.11)	8.1 (1.38)	9.9 (1.58)		6.9 (1.23)	4.9 (0.76)	2.9 ! (0.88)	6.0 (1.32)	6.5 (1.68)	
Washington..................	13.0 (1.33)	10.0 (0.98)	6.7 (1.29)	7.0 (1.34)	7.4 (1.36)		4.9 (0.74)	5.0 (0.61)	4.1 (0.85)	4.4 (1.28)	6.8 (1.80)	
West Virginia................	11.7 (0.86)	10.0 (1.19)	7.4 (1.13)	8.1 (1.67)	9.4 (2.08)		3.4 (0.67)	3.4 (0.67)	3.4 (0.82)	4.0 (1.07)	4.3 ! (1.72)	
Wisconsin...................	13.7 (1.82)	10.1 (0.99)	4.7 (0.99)	8.8 (1.51)	13.7 (2.37)		3.9 (0.77)	4.4 (0.79)	2.5 (0.71)	6.5 (1.29)	11.3 (2.56)	
Wyoming.....................	9.0 (0.79)	6.7 (0.96)	3.8 ! (1.31)	5.1 (1.00)	10.9 (3.10)		2.7 (0.49)	2.6 (0.47)	2.5 ! (1.04)	3.0 (0.86)	‡ (†)	

†Not applicable.
!Interpret data with caution. The coefficient of variation (CV) for this estimate is between 30 and 50 percent.
‡Reporting standards not met. Data may be suppressed because the response rate is under 50 percent, there are too few cases for a reliable estimate, or the coefficient of variation (CV) is 50 percent or greater.

NOTE: Teachers who taught only prekindergarten students are excluded. Includes traditional public and public charter schools. Detail may not sum to totals because of rounding. Some data have been revised from previously published figures.
SOURCE: U.S. Department of Education, National Center for Education Statistics, Schools and Staffing Survey (SASS), "Public School Teacher Data File," 1993–94, 1999–2000, 2003–04, 2007–08, and 2011–12; and "Charter School Teacher Data File," 1999–2000. (This table was prepared October 2013.)

Table 229.10. Percentage of public schools recording incidents of crime at school and reporting incidents to police, number of incidents, and rate per 1,000 students, by type of crime: Selected years, 1999–2000 through 2009–10

[Standard errors appear in parentheses]

Type of crime recorded or reported to police	Percent of schools				2009–10		
	1999–2000	2003–04	2005–06	2007–08	Percent of schools	Number of incidents	Rate per 1,000 students
	2	3	4	5	6	7	8
Recorded incidents							
Total	86.4 (1.23)	88.5 (0.85)	85.7 (1.07)	85.5 (0.87)	85.0 (1.07)	1,876,900 (50,900)	39.6 (1.04)
Violent incidents	71.4 (1.37)	81.4 (1.05)	77.7 (1.11)	75.5 (1.09)	73.8 (1.09)	1,183,700 (44,390)	25.0 (0.91)
Serious violent incidents	19.7 (0.98)	18.3 (0.99)	17.1 (0.91)	17.2 (1.06)	16.4 (0.94)	52,500 (5,510)	1.1 (0.12)
Rape or attempted rape	0.7 (0.10)	0.8 (0.17)	0.3 (0.07)	0.8 (0.17)	0.5 (0.10)	600 (120)	# (†)
Sexual battery other than rape	2.5 (0.33)	3.0 (0.32)	2.8 (0.24)	2.5 (0.33)	2.3 (0.34)	3,600 (640)	0.1 (0.01)
Physical attack or fight with a weapon	5.2 (0.60)	4.0 (0.46)	3.0 (0.38)	3.0 (0.33)	3.9 (0.48)	14,300 (3,560)	0.3 (0.08)
Threat of physical attack with a weapon	11.1 (0.70)	8.6 (0.71)	8.8 (0.66)	9.3 (0.77)	7.7 (0.72)	19,200 (2,910)	0.4 (0.06)
Robbery with a weapon	0.5! (0.15)	0.6 (0.15)	0.4 (0.12)	0.4! (0.14)	0.2 (0.05)	400! (160)	# (†)
Robbery without a weapon	5.3 (0.56)	6.3 (0.60)	6.4 (0.59)	5.2 (0.56)	4.4 (0.49)	14,300 (1,930)	0.3 (0.04)
Physical attack or fight without a weapon	63.7 (1.52)	76.7 (1.21)	74.3 (1.20)	72.7 (1.07)	70.5 (1.11)	725,300 (27,810)	15.3 (0.58)
Threat of physical attack without a weapon	52.2 (1.47)	53.0 (1.34)	52.2 (1.27)	47.8 (1.19)	46.4 (1.33)	405,900 (22,990)	8.6 (0.47)
Theft[1]	45.6 (1.37)	46.0 (1.29)	46.0 (1.07)	47.3 (1.29)	44.1 (1.31)	258,500 (8,570)	5.5 (0.18)
Other incidents[2]	72.7 (1.30)	64.0 (1.27)	68.2 (1.07)	67.4 (1.13)	68.1 (1.12)	434,700 (11,100)	9.2 (0.23)
Possession of a firearm/explosive device	5.5 (0.44)	6.1 (0.49)	7.2 (0.60)	4.7 (0.38)	4.7 (0.52)	5,000 (550)	0.1 (0.01)
Possession of a knife or sharp object	42.6 (1.28)	— (†)	42.8 (1.23)	40.6 (1.10)	39.7 (1.06)	72,300 (2,560)	1.5 (0.05)
Distribution of illegal drugs[3]	12.3 (0.50)	12.9 (0.55)	— (†)	— (†)	— (†)	— (†)	— (†)
Possession or use of alcohol or illegal drugs[3]	26.6 (0.72)	29.3 (0.87)	— (†)	— (†)	— (†)	— (†)	— (†)
Distribution, possession, or use of illegal drugs[4]	— (†)	— (†)	25.9 (0.68)	23.2 (0.68)	24.6 (0.57)	115,900 (4,690)	2.4 (0.10)
Inappropriate distribution, possession, or use of prescription drugs[5]	— (†)	— (†)	— (†)	— (†)	12.1 (0.47)	29,300 (1,880)	0.6 (0.04)
Distribution, possession, or use of alcohol[4]	— (†)	— (†)	16.2 (0.68)	14.9 (0.57)	14.1 (0.50)	40,700 (1,790)	0.9 (0.04)
Sexual harassment	36.3 (1.26)	— (†)	— (†)	— (†)	— (†)	— (†)	— (†)
Vandalism	51.4 (1.61)	51.4 (1.17)	50.5 (1.17)	49.3 (1.16)	45.8 (1.12)	171,500 (7,260)	3.6 (0.15)
Reported incidents to police							
Total	62.5 (1.37)	65.2 (1.35)	60.9 (1.15)	62.0 (1.24)	60.0 (1.58)	689,100 (19,240)	14.6 (0.41)
Violent incidents	36.0 (1.26)	43.6 (1.15)	37.7 (1.09)	37.8 (1.16)	39.9 (1.13)	303,900 (13,310)	6.4 (0.28)
Serious violent incidents	14.8 (0.82)	13.3 (0.88)	12.6 (0.70)	12.6 (0.86)	10.4 (0.62)	23,500 (2,320)	0.5 (0.05)
Rape or attempted rape	0.6 (0.10)	0.8 (0.17)	0.3 (0.07)	0.8 (0.17)	0.5 (0.10)	500 (120)	# (†)
Sexual battery other than rape	2.3 (0.34)	2.6 (0.28)	2.6 (0.26)	2.1 (0.29)	1.4 (0.20)	2,200 (360)	# (†)
Physical attack or fight with a weapon	3.9 (0.50)	2.8 (0.38)	2.2 (0.27)	2.1 (0.27)	2.2 (0.32)	4,400 (1,140)	0.1 (0.02)
Threat of physical attack with a weapon	8.5 (0.59)	6.0 (0.55)	5.9 (0.49)	5.7 (0.59)	4.5 (0.43)	7,400 (960)	0.2 (0.02)
Robbery with a weapon	0.3! (0.09)	0.6 (0.15)	0.4 (0.12)	0.4! (0.14)	0.2 (0.05)	400! (160)	# (†)
Robbery without a weapon	3.4 (0.41)	4.2 (0.51)	4.9 (0.48)	4.1 (0.42)	3.5 (0.40)	8,500 (1,190)	0.2 (0.03)
Physical attack or fight without a weapon	25.8 (0.91)	35.6 (0.98)	29.2 (1.00)	28.2 (0.90)	34.3 (0.90)	194,200 (11,810)	4.1 (0.25)
Threat of physical attack without a weapon	18.9 (0.94)	21.0 (0.82)	19.7 (0.69)	19.5 (0.76)	15.2 (0.79)	86,200 (4,940)	1.8 (0.11)
Theft[1]	28.5 (1.04)	30.5 (1.17)	27.9 (0.97)	31.0 (1.12)	25.4 (1.01)	122,800 (4,180)	2.6 (0.09)
Other incidents[2]	52.0 (1.14)	50.0 (1.18)	50.6 (1.00)	48.7 (1.17)	46.3 (1.23)	262,400 (8,260)	5.5 (0.17)
Possession of a firearm/explosive device	4.5 (0.41)	4.9 (0.44)	5.5 (0.51)	3.6 (0.32)	3.1 (0.39)	3,400 (470)	0.1 (0.01)
Possession of a knife or sharp object	23.0 (0.84)	— (†)	25.0 (1.00)	23.3 (0.69)	20.0 (0.88)	37,400 (2,020)	0.8 (0.04)
Distribution of illegal drugs[3]	11.4 (0.48)	12.4 (0.57)	— (†)	— (†)	— (†)	— (†)	— (†)
Possession or use of alcohol or illegal drugs[3]	22.2 (0.67)	26.0 (0.76)	— (†)	— (†)	— (†)	— (†)	— (†)
Distribution, possession, or use of illegal drugs[4]	— (†)	— (†)	22.8 (0.62)	20.7 (0.60)	21.4 (0.57)	94,200 (3,520)	2.0 (0.07)
Inappropriate distribution, possession, or use of prescription drugs[5]	— (†)	— (†)	— (†)	— (†)	9.6 (0.42)	24,900 (1,860)	0.5 (0.04)
Distribution, possession, or use of alcohol[4]	— (†)	— (†)	11.6 (0.61)	10.6 (0.55)	10.0 (0.41)	28,000 (1,460)	0.6 (0.03)
Sexual harassment	14.7 (0.78)	— (†)	— (†)	— (†)	— (†)	— (†)	— (†)
Vandalism	32.7 (1.10)	34.3 (1.06)	31.9 (1.02)	30.8 (1.18)	26.8 (1.09)	74,500 (4,310)	1.6 (0.09)

—Not available.
†Not applicable.
#Rounds to zero.
!Interpret data with caution. The coefficient of variation (CV) for this estimate is between 30 and 50 percent.
[1]Theft/larceny (taking things worth over $10 without personal confrontation) was defined for respondents as "the unlawful taking of another person's property without personal confrontation, threat, violence, or bodily harm." This includes pocket picking, stealing a purse or backpack (if left unattended or no force was used to take it from owner), theft from a building, theft from a motor vehicle or motor vehicle parts or accessories, theft of a bicycle, theft from a vending machine, and all other types of thefts.
[2]Caution should be used when making direct comparisons of "Other incidents" between years because the survey questions about alcohol and drugs changed, as outlined in footnotes 3, 4, and 5.
[3]The survey items "Distribution of illegal drugs" and "Possession or use of alcohol or illegal drugs" appear only on the 1999–2000 and 2003–04 questionnaires. Different alcohol- and drug-related survey items were used on the questionnaires for later years.

[4]The survey items "Distribution, possession, or use of illegal drugs" and "Distribution, possession, or use of alcohol" appear only on the questionnaires for 2005–06 and later years.
[5]The 2009–10 questionnaire was the first to include the survey item "Inappropriate distribution, possession, or use of prescription drugs."
NOTE: Responses were provided by the principal or the person most knowledgeable about crime and safety issues at the school. "At school" was defined to include activities that happen in school buildings, on school grounds, on school buses, and at places that hold school-sponsored events or activities. Respondents were instructed to include incidents that occurred before, during, and after normal school hours or when school activities or events were in session. Detail may not sum to totals because of rounding and because schools that recorded or reported more than one type of crime incident were counted only once in the total percentage of schools recording or reporting incidents.
SOURCE: U.S. Department of Education, National Center for Education Statistics, 1999–2000, 2003–04, 2005–06, 2007–08, and 2009–10 School Survey on Crime and Safety (SSOCS), 2000, 2004, 2006, 2008, and 2010. (This table was prepared September 2013.)

Table 229.20. Number and percentage of public schools recording at least one crime incident that occurred at school, and number and rate of incidents, by school characteristics and type of incident: 1999–2000 and 2009–10

[Standard errors appear in parentheses]

Type of incident	All public schools, 1999–2000	All public schools	Instruction level of school — Primary	Middle	High	Locale — City	Suburban	Town	Rural	Free/reduced-price lunch — 0 to 20	21 to 50	51 or more
1	2	3	4	5	6	7	8	9	10	11	12	13
Number of public schools (in thousands)												
All schools	82 (#)	83 (0.5)	49 (0.3)	15 (0.1)	12 (0.1)	22 (0.2)	24 (0.2)	12 (0.1)	25 (0.3)	14 (0.7)	26 (1.2)	43 (1.1)
Schools with incident	71 (1.0)	70 (1.0)	38 (0.9)	15 (0.1)	12 (0.1)	19 (0.4)	20 (0.6)	11 (0.3)	21 (0.5)	10 (0.7)	23 (1.1)	38 (1.2)
Percent of schools with incident	86.4 (1.23)	85.0 (1.07)	77.9 (1.69)	96.2 (0.66)	98.3 (0.49)	86.9 (1.71)	84.3 (2.07)	89.4 (2.63)	82.1 (2.04)	73.0 (3.28)	85.8 (1.78)	88.4 (1.30)
Violent incidents	71.4 (1.37)	73.8 (1.07)	64.4 (1.63)	90.5 (1.10)	90.9 (1.21)	74.9 (2.12)	73.5 (2.21)	80.3 (3.14)	70.2 (1.91)	61.7 (3.40)	74.6 (2.04)	77.2 (1.66)
Serious violent incidents	19.7 (0.98)	16.4 (0.94)	13.0 (1.42)	18.9 (1.46)	27.6 (1.35)	21.7 (2.12)	15.5 (1.80)	15.6 (2.33)	13.2 (1.51)	10.5 (1.41)	15.4 (1.65)	18.9 (1.50)
Rape or attempted rape	0.7 (0.10)	0.5 (0.10)	— (†)	1.3! (0.42)	2.0 (0.41)	0.7! (0.26)	0.6! (0.25)	0.6! (0.28)	0.3! (0.13)	0.4! (0.20)	0.6 (0.17)	0.5 (0.15)
Sexual battery other than rape	2.5 (0.33)	2.3 (0.34)	1.0! (0.38)	3.2 (0.56)	5.1 (0.73)	3.2 (0.76)	1.6 (0.32)	2.7! (0.82)	1.9! (0.68)	1.4 (0.33)	2.7 (0.72)	2.3 (0.44)
Physical attack or fight with weapon	5.2 (0.60)	3.9 (0.48)	3.0 (0.68)	3.9 (0.75)	7.1 (1.02)	5.5 (1.18)	4.6 (1.00)	4.1! (1.28)	1.8 (0.48)	2.3! (0.77)	3.6 (0.69)	4.6 (0.73)
Threat of attack with weapon	11.1 (0.70)	7.7 (0.72)	6.8 (1.11)	10.3 (1.04)	10.0 (0.99)	10.2 (1.69)	7.7 (1.15)	6.3 (1.57)	6.2 (1.13)	4.7 (1.06)	5.9 (0.72)	9.7 (1.32)
Robbery with weapon	0.5! (0.15)	0.2 (0.05)	— (†)	0.5! (0.20)	1.0 (0.30)	0.6! (0.19)	0.2! (0.10)	‡ (†)	‡ (†)	‡ (†)	0.2! (0.09)	0.3! (0.09)
Robbery without weapon	5.3 (0.56)	4.4 (0.49)	2.7 (0.66)	5.5 (0.74)	10.6 (0.87)	6.5 (0.84)	3.4 (0.55)	3.0 (1.05)	4.3 (0.97)	3.4 (0.74)	4.5 (0.86)	4.7 (0.74)
Physical attack or fight without weapon	63.7 (1.52)	70.5 (1.11)	60.3 (1.65)	88.8 (1.13)	88.4 (1.36)	71.7 (2.02)	69.9 (2.11)	76.8 (2.93)	67.2 (2.26)	57.9 (3.19)	70.4 (2.30)	74.6 (1.63)
Threat of attack without weapon	52.2 (1.47)	46.4 (1.33)	38.0 (1.94)	61.5 (1.73)	61.9 (1.58)	48.6 (2.43)	46.3 (2.44)	56.2 (3.86)	40.0 (2.15)	34.7 (2.84)	47.7 (2.21)	49.4 (1.97)
Theft/larceny[1]	45.6 (1.37)	44.1 (1.31)	25.7 (1.82)	65.2 (1.48)	82.6 (1.35)	47.6 (2.70)	43.1 (1.97)	46.2 (3.22)	41.1 (2.51)	38.0 (2.26)	48.8 (2.50)	43.1 (1.98)
Other incidents[2]	— (†)	68.1 (1.12)	57.3 (1.72)	81.9 (1.25)	92.2 (1.10)	73.5 (2.39)	66.1 (2.23)	74.1 (2.97)	62.6 (2.62)	54.8 (3.31)	67.3 (2.10)	72.9 (1.79)
Possession of firearm/explosive device	5.5 (0.44)	4.7 (0.52)	3.5 (0.81)	5.8 (0.79)	9.4 (1.20)	6.0 (0.99)	4.9 (0.89)	3.8! (1.37)	3.8 (1.01)	3.1 (0.64)	3.3 (0.58)	6.0 (0.93)
Possession of knife or sharp object	42.6 (1.28)	39.7 (1.06)	33.5 (1.51)	51.5 (1.94)	55.2 (1.51)	41.1 (2.36)	38.7 (1.75)	49.8 (3.16)	34.7 (2.13)	26.7 (2.20)	38.0 (1.96)	44.8 (1.72)
Distribution, possession, or use of illegal drugs	— (†)	24.6 (0.57)	3.5 (0.69)	44.7 (1.17)	77.2 (1.51)	27.8 (1.22)	22.4 (0.83)	25.5 (1.42)	23.4 (1.17)	20.3 (1.39)	27.9 (1.67)	23.8 (0.96)
Inappropriate distribution, possession, or use of prescription drugs	— (†)	12.1 (0.47)	1.5! (0.48)	18.8 (1.13)	43.0 (1.64)	10.3 (0.92)	12.1 (0.79)	12.3 (1.12)	13.5 (1.18)	13.1 (1.20)	15.2 (0.98)	9.8 (0.76)
Distribution, possession, or use of alcohol	— (†)	14.1 (0.50)	2.1 (0.52)	19.7 (1.31)	51.6 (1.60)	14.9 (1.14)	15.5 (0.92)	12.8 (1.17)	12.7 (1.03)	14.7 (1.01)	16.5 (1.21)	12.5 (0.76)
Vandalism	51.4 (1.61)	45.8 (1.12)	37.9 (1.69)	55.5 (1.38)	62.5 (1.86)	56.9 (2.11)	47.2 (2.44)	44.7 (3.54)	35.7 (2.25)	38.5 (2.96)	47.0 (2.27)	47.5 (1.92)
Number of incidents (in thousands)	2,259 (117.0)	1,877 (50.9)	626 (39.6)	548 (23.6)	590 (18.2)	642 (32.5)	585 (37.5)	255 (23.1)	395 (19.5)	211 (15.1)	560 (25.6)	1,106 (51.1)
Violent incidents	1,466 (103.7)	1,184 (44.4)	482 (37.3)	375 (19.3)	264 (12.9)	396 (27.4)	371 (33.0)	166 (21.2)	250 (15.9)	110 (10.6)	322 (20.5)	752 (43.2)
Serious violent incidents	61 (7.0)	52 (5.5)	22 (3.8)	14 (2.4)	14 (1.7)	17 (2.8)	16 (3.1)	6 (1.4)	13 (2.9)	6 (1.4)	13 (2.0)	33 (5.4)
Rape or attempted rape	1 (0.1)	1 (0.1)	— (†)	# (†)	# (†)	# (†)	# (†)	# (†)	# (†)	# (†)	# (†)	# (†)
Sexual battery other than rape	4 (1.1)	4 (0.6)	1! (0.4)	1 (0.2)	1 (0.2)	1 (0.4)	1 (0.2)	# (†)	1! (0.4)	# (†)	1! (0.5)	2 (0.4)
Physical attack or fight with weapon	12 (2.5)	14 (3.6)	8! (2.9)	2! (0.7)	3 (0.7)	3! (1.0)	5! (2.1)	3! (1.0)	‡ (†)	1! (0.3)	3 (0.9)	10! (3.6)
Threat of attack with weapon	21 (1.9)	19 (2.9)	8 (1.9)	8 (1.9)	3 (0.6)	7 (1.8)	7 (1.5)	2! (1.1)	3 (0.9)	2! (0.7)	5 (1.3)	12 (2.7)
Robbery with weapon	‡ (†)	# (†)	— (†)	# (†)	# (†)	# (†)	# (†)	# (†)	— (†)	# (†)	# (†)	# (†)
Robbery without weapon	20 (3.2)	14 (1.9)	6! (1.9)	3 (0.6)	6 (0.8)	6 (0.9)	3 (0.7)	1! (0.3)	5! (1.6)	3! (0.9)	5 (1.2)	8 (1.4)
Physical attack or fight without weapon	807 (59.6)	725 (27.8)	295 (24.0)	239 (12.7)	157 (10.6)	249 (19.7)	232 (17.9)	93 (15.1)	152 (10.7)	68 (5.9)	194 (14.3)	464 (27.5)
Threat of attack without weapon	599 (52.7)	406 (23.0)	165 (21.6)	123 (8.8)	94 (5.4)	130 (10.7)	123 (17.0)	67 (9.4)	86 (7.1)	36 (4.6)	115 (11.7)	255 (20.8)
Theft/larceny[1]	218 (9.2)	259 (8.6)	42 (5.7)	69 (4.8)	125 (5.1)	85 (7.0)	81 (4.0)	33 (3.3)	59 (4.6)	41 (3.3)	96 (5.7)	121 (8.4)
Other incidents[2]	— (†)	435 (11.1)	102 (6.4)	104 (4.4)	200 (7.7)	160 (9.2)	133 (6.4)	55 (4.0)	86 (4.5)	60 (4.1)	142 (7.2)	233 (11.7)
Possession of firearm/explosive device	9 (2.2)	5 (0.6)	2 (0.4)	1 (0.3)	2 (0.2)	2 (0.3)	2 (0.3)	1! (0.2)	1 (0.3)	1 (0.1)	1 (0.2)	3 (0.5)
Possession of knife or sharp object	86 (4.0)	72 (2.6)	29 (1.7)	18 (0.9)	21 (1.5)	21 (1.3)	22 (1.9)	12 (0.9)	17 (1.3)	7 (0.6)	22 (1.3)	44 (4.0)
Distribution, possession, or use of illegal drugs	— (†)	116 (4.7)	3 (0.8)	25 (1.6)	79 (3.6)	44 (4.0)	36 (2.0)	15 (1.5)	20 (1.5)	17 (1.4)	42 (2.6)	56 (4.4)
Inappropriate distribution, possession, or use of prescription drugs	— (†)	29 (1.9)	1! (0.3)	6 (0.6)	19 (1.5)	7 (0.9)	10 (1.2)	5! (0.9)	8 (0.9)	5 (0.6)	13 (1.5)	11 (1.1)
Distribution, possession, or use of alcohol	— (†)	41 (1.8)	1 (0.3)	7 (0.6)	29 (1.5)	14 (1.3)	14 (1.1)	5 (0.8)	8 (0.9)	9 (0.9)	16 (1.3)	15 (1.3)
Vandalism	211 (13.6)	172 (7.3)	66 (5.8)	46 (3.1)	49 (4.5)	72 (5.7)	49 (3.6)	18 (1.8)	32 (3.5)	21 (2.6)	47 (2.6)	103 (6.9)

See notes at end of table.

Table 229.20. Number and percentage of public schools recording at least one crime incident that occurred at school, and number and rate of incidents, by school characteristics and type of incident: 1999–2000 and 2009–10—Continued

[Standard errors appear in parentheses]

Type of incident	All public schools, 1999–2000	All public schools (2009–10)	Instruction level of school			Locale				Percent of students eligible for free or reduced-price lunch		
			Primary	Middle	High	City	Suburban	Town	Rural	0 to 20	21 to 50	51 or more
1	2	3	4	5	6	7	8	9	10	11	12	13
Number of incidents per 100,000 students.	4,849 (252.4)	3,965 (103.7)	2,766 (172.3)	5,840 (249.6)	4,773 (149.9)	4,672 (250.7)	3,527 (210.5)	4,320 (350.6)	3,554 (184.8)	2,220 (131.3)	3,613 (149.4)	4,950 (200.9)
Violent incidents	3,147 (223.8)	2,500 (90.9)	2,131 (163.6)	3,997 (203.9)	2,141 (105.3)	2,885 (210.8)	2,236 (192.4)	2,820 (335.6)	2,250 (149.0)	1,153 (93.1)	2,081 (127.4)	3,364 (177.9)
Serious violent incidents	130 (15.2)	111 (11.5)	97 (16.8)	145 (25.2)	110 (13.7)	126 (21.3)	98 (18.4)	107 (23.2)	113 (26.4)	62 (14.3)	86 (13.2)	149 (24.4)
Rape or attempted rape	1 (0.2)	1 (0.3)	— (†)	3 ! (1.0)	1 (0.6)	1 ! (0.5)	1 (0.5)	2 ! (0.9)	1 ! (0.3)	1 ! (0.4)	1 ! (0.3)	2 (0.5)
Sexual battery other than rape	9 (2.4)	8 (1.3)	4 ! (2.0)	10 (2.4)	11 (1.8)	11 (2.7)	4 (1.2)	8 (2.5)	8 ! (3.5)	3 (0.8)	8 (2.9)	9 (1.8)
Physical attack or fight with weapon	26 (5.4)	30 (7.5)	34 ! (13.0)	19 ! (7.4)	23 (5.5)	22 ! (7.5)	32 ! (12.7)	43 ! (16.7)	‡ (†)	9 ! (3.1)	21 (6.1)	46 ! (16.0)
Threat of attack with weapon	45 (4.1)	41 (6.1)	34 (8.4)	81 (20.4)	26 (4.8)	49 (13.2)	40 (9.2)	38 ! (17.9)	31 (7.6)	22 ! (7.7)	30 (8.3)	56 (12.3)
Robbery with weapon	‡ (†)	1 ! (0.3)	— (†)	‡ (†)	‡ (†)	2 ! (1.2)	# (†)	# (†)	‡ (†)	# (†)	# (†)	2 ! (0.7)
Robbery without weapon	43 (6.8)	30 (4.1)	25 ! (8.2)	31 (6.2)	45 (6.5)	40 (6.6)	19 (4.3)	15 ! (4.6)	43 ! (14.3)	28 ! (9.6)	25 (7.6)	35 (6.3)
Physical attack or fight without weapon	1,732 (128.8)	1,532 (57.9)	1,305 (106.9)	2,545 (132.7)	1,271 (85.0)	1,814 (148.1)	1,398 (104.3)	1,571 (242.2)	1,364 (100.3)	713 (49.9)	1,251 (89.8)	2,076 (117.2)
Threat of attack without weapon	1,285 (113.2)	857 (47.4)	730 (94.0)	1,307 (94.3)	760 (45.4)	945 (81.4)	741 (100.8)	1,142 (154.3)	773 (64.6)	378 (44.0)	744 (73.4)	1,139 (86.5)
Theft/larceny[1]	468 (20.2)	546 (18.5)	185 (24.8)	736 (50.7)	1,012 (43.5)	622 (53.0)	488 (21.6)	565 (52.2)	528 (40.7)	436 (34.0)	619 (37.3)	542 (36.2)
Other incidents[2]	— (†)	918 (23.2)	450 (27.9)	1,108 (47.1)	1,620 (60.8)	1,166 (62.6)	803 (32.2)	935 (65.7)	776 (42.2)	631 (41.1)	914 (37.1)	1,044 (46.9)
Possession of firearm/explosive device	18 (4.8)	11 (1.2)	8 (1.9)	15 (2.8)	13 (1.9)	13 (2.2)	10 (1.8)	10 ! (3.5)	9 (2.4)	6 (1.1)	7 (1.2)	15 (2.3)
Possession of knife or sharp object	184 (8.7)	153 (5.2)	126 (7.3)	193 (9.8)	175 (12.5)	156 (9.7)	131 (10.9)	208 (15.1)	151 (10.1)	72 (5.4)	140 (6.6)	196 (11.2)
Distribution, possession, or use of illegal drugs	— (†)	245 (9.8)	14 (3.4)	262 (17.4)	637 (28.9)	321 (27.1)	220 (10.4)	250 (25.6)	184 (13.5)	183 (13.8)	273 (15.8)	251 (18.4)
Inappropriate distribution, possession, or use of prescription drugs	— (†)	62 (4.0)	4 ! (1.3)	68 (6.5)	157 (12.4)	48 (6.4)	60 (7.2)	84 (15.3)	70 (8.3)	55 (6.2)	83 (9.3)	50 (4.8)
Distribution, possession, or use of alcohol	— (†)	86 (3.9)	5 (1.3)	77 (6.9)	238 (13.7)	100 (9.9)	85 (6.2)	82 (14.2)	72 (8.0)	95 (10.6)	105 (8.6)	69 (5.7)
Vandalism	453 (28.6)	362 (15.3)	293 (25.6)	492 (32.4)	400 (35.4)	527 (40.4)	297 (20.5)	301 (30.3)	289 (32.3)	221 (27.0)	305 (18.2)	462 (29.6)

—Not available.
†Not applicable.
#Rounds to zero.
!Interpret data with caution. The coefficient of variation (CV) for this estimate is 30 percent or greater.
‡Reporting standards not met. The coefficient of variation (CV) for this estimate is 50 percent or greater.
[1]Theft/larceny (taking things worth over $10 without personal confrontation) includes pocket picking, stealing a purse or back-pack (if left unattended or if no force was used to take it from owner), theft from a building, theft from a motor vehicle or of motor vehicle parts or accessories, theft of bicycles, theft from vending machines, and all other types of thefts.
[2]This table shows only the "Other incidents" that were included on the 2009–10 questionnaire. In 1999–2000, most of the "Other incidents" differed from those shown in this table.

NOTE: "At school" was defined to include activities that happen in school buildings, on school grounds, on school buses, and at places holding school-sponsored events or activities. Includes incidents that occurred before, during, or after normal school hours or when school activities or events were in session. Primary schools are defined as schools in which the lowest grade is not higher than grade 3 and the highest grade is not higher than grade 8. Middle schools are defined as schools in which the lowest grade is not lower than grade 4 and the highest grade is not higher than grade 9. High schools are defined as schools in which the lowest grade is not lower than grade 9 and the highest grade is not higher than grade 12. All public schools also includes schools with other combinations of grades (including K–12 schools), which are not shown separately. Detail may not sum to totals because of rounding.
SOURCE: U.S. Department of Education, National Center for Education Statistics, 1999–2000 and 2009–10 School Survey on Crime and Safety (SSOCS), 2000 and 2010. (This table was prepared August 2011.)

Table 229.30. Percentage of public schools recording incidents of crime at school, number of incidents, and rate per 1,000 students, by type of crime and selected school characteristics: 2009–10

[Standard errors appear in parentheses]

School characteristic	Total number of schools	Violent incidents						Theft[3]			Other incidents[4]		
		All violent[1]			Serious violent[2]								
		Percent of schools	Number of incidents	Rate per 1,000 students	Percent of schools	Number of incidents	Rate per 1,000 students	Percent of schools	Number of incidents	Rate per 1,000 students	Percent of schools	Number of incidents	Rate per 1,000 students
1	2	3	4	5	6	7	8	9	10	11	12	13	14
Total[5]	82,800 (460)	73.8 (1.07)	1,183,700 (44,390)	25.0 (0.91)	16.4 (0.94)	52,500 (5,510)	1.1 (0.12)	44.1 (1.31)	258,500 (8,570)	5.5 (0.18)	68.1 (1.12)	434,700 (11,100)	9.2 (0.23)
School level[5]													
Primary	48,900 (340)	64.4 (1.63)	482,100 (37,320)	21.3 (1.64)	13.0 (1.42)	21,900 (3,780)	1.0 (0.17)	25.7 (1.82)	41,700 (5,680)	1.8 (0.25)	57.3 (1.72)	101,900 (6,420)	4.5 (0.28)
Middle	15,300 (100)	90.5 (1.10)	375,200 (19,310)	40.0 (2.04)	18.9 (1.46)	13,600 (2,360)	1.5 (0.25)	65.2 (1.48)	69,000 (4,760)	7.4 (0.51)	81.9 (1.25)	104,000 (4,400)	11.1 (0.47)
High school	12,200 (70)	90.9 (1.21)	264,400 (12,910)	21.4 (1.05)	27.6 (1.35)	13,500 (1,690)	1.1 (0.14)	82.6 (1.35)	125,000 (5,090)	10.1 (0.43)	92.2 (1.10)	200,000 (7,680)	16.2 (0.61)
Combined	6,400 (200)	73.7 (5.33)	62,000 (7,570)	20.8 (2.21)	15.5 (3.72)	‡ (†)	‡ (†)	60.5 (5.79)	22,700 (2,940)	7.6 (1.00)	72.5 (4.65)	28,800 (3,670)	9.7 (1.22)
Enrollment size													
Less than 300	18,900 (400)	62.8 (3.25)	111,300 (17,230)	27.2 (4.08)	10.4 (2.11)	6,100 ! (2,100)	1.5 ! (0.51)	30.7 (3.35)	21,400 (3,230)	5.2 (0.73)	55.3 (2.97)	36,600 (3,280)	8.9 (0.87)
300–499	25,200 (180)	71.3 (2.34)	274,400 (25,110)	26.5 (2.44)	15.7 (2.14)	14,200 (3,560)	1.4 (0.35)	36.4 (2.52)	40,900 (6,320)	3.9 (0.62)	63.3 (2.47)	71,100 (5,340)	6.9 (0.53)
500–999	29,800 (100)	76.4 (1.75)	487,900 (35,630)	25.0 (1.78)	15.9 (1.42)	16,400 (2,420)	0.8 (0.12)	46.7 (1.74)	81,800 (5,460)	4.2 (0.29)	72.5 (1.80)	134,600 (6,650)	6.9 (0.34)
1,000 or more	8,900 (60)	95.4 (1.22)	310,100 (16,110)	23.2 (1.19)	32.8 (1.61)	15,700 (2,080)	1.2 (0.15)	84.9 (1.80)	114,500 (4,400)	8.6 (0.36)	94.3 (1.32)	192,500 (8,590)	14.4 (0.67)
Locale													
City	21,500 (190)	74.9 (2.12)	396,300 (27,430)	28.8 (2.11)	21.7 (2.12)	17,400 (2,830)	1.3 (0.21)	47.6 (2.70)	85,400 (7,030)	6.2 (0.53)	73.5 (2.39)	160,200 (9,170)	11.7 (0.63)
Suburban	23,800 (240)	73.5 (2.21)	371,000 (33,010)	22.4 (1.92)	15.5 (1.80)	16,200 (3,070)	1.0 (0.18)	43.1 (1.97)	81,000 (3,980)	4.9 (0.22)	66.1 (2.23)	133,200 (6,380)	8.0 (0.32)
Town	12,100 (110)	80.3 (3.14)	166,300 (21,190)	28.2 (3.36)	15.6 (2.33)	6,300 (1,390)	1.1 (0.23)	46.2 (3.22)	33,400 (3,310)	5.7 (0.52)	74.1 (2.97)	55,100 (3,990)	9.3 (0.66)
Rural	25,300 (300)	70.2 (1.91)	250,100 (15,910)	22.5 (1.49)	13.2 (1.51)	12,600 (2,920)	1.1 (0.26)	41.1 (2.51)	58,700 (4,560)	5.3 (0.41)	62.6 (2.62)	86,200 (4,490)	7.8 (0.42)
Percent combined enrollment of Black, Hispanic, Asian/Pacific Islander, and American Indian/Alaska Native students													
Less than 5 percent	11,700 (980)	69.6 (3.33)	108,500 (20,940)	23.3 (3.62)	12.6 (2.52)	5,400 ! (2,090)	1.2 ! (0.44)	40.8 (3.33)	22,700 (2,450)	4.9 (0.42)	59.0 (3.65)	34,200 (3,820)	7.4 (0.56)
5 percent to less than 20 percent	20,900 (1,080)	67.9 (2.82)	192,800 (15,450)	17.2 (1.19)	9.9 (1.29)	6,500 (1,490)	0.6 (0.13)	38.3 (2.37)	53,300 (4,310)	4.8 (0.36)	61.2 (2.19)	79,800 (5,010)	7.1 (0.37)
20 percent to less than 50 percent	20,000 (650)	75.9 (2.14)	293,600 (20,960)	23.1 (1.76)	18.6 (1.58)	15,100 (3,000)	1.2 (0.23)	46.2 (2.45)	74,400 (5,450)	5.8 (0.42)	69.7 (2.23)	113,000 (5,600)	8.9 (0.42)
50 percent or more	30,100 (1,270)	78.2 (1.75)	588,800 (43,670)	31.4 (1.96)	21.1 (1.82)	25,400 (4,360)	1.4 (0.23)	48.0 (2.35)	108,100 (8,080)	5.8 (0.41)	75.5 (2.33)	207,700 (10,130)	11.1 (0.52)
Percent of students eligible for free or reduced-price lunch													
0–25	17,100 (690)	62.6 (3.07)	141,700 (11,440)	11.9 (0.82)	10.5 (1.22)	6,700 (1,400)	0.6 (0.11)	40.3 (2.20)	56,900 (3,680)	4.8 (0.29)	56.2 (3.03)	80,600 (5,190)	6.8 (0.38)
26–50	22,700 (1,050)	76.0 (2.13)	290,500 (20,440)	22.1 (1.48)	16.2 (1.89)	12,500 (1,970)	1.0 (0.16)	48.8 (2.90)	80,400 (5,420)	6.1 (0.43)	68.2 (2.49)	120,900 (7,020)	9.2 (0.45)
51–75	23,800 (1,020)	73.8 (2.49)	334,400 (24,050)	27.3 (1.82)	15.8 (1.67)	13,100 (2,840)	1.1 (0.24)	41.2 (2.53)	75,400 (6,580)	6.2 (0.52)	73.5 (2.12)	128,100 (8,700)	10.5 (0.66)
76–100	19,100 (940)	81.4 (2.49)	417,200 (42,360)	41.3 (3.73)	22.9 (2.60)	20,100 (4,550)	2.0 (0.45)	45.5 (2.73)	45,800 (4,420)	4.5 (0.40)	72.1 (2.82)	105,100 (7,720)	10.4 (0.71)
Student/teacher ratio[6]													
Less than 12	12,300 (960)	69.7 (3.05)	118,000 (14,700)	28.1 (3.10)	13.2 (2.24)	5,200 (1,210)	1.2 (0.28)	45.2 (3.81)	24,500 (2,290)	5.8 (0.58)	66.2 (3.54)	41,700 (4,250)	10.0 (0.90)
12–16	32,600 (960)	75.3 (1.89)	470,600 (34,260)	27.0 (1.76)	16.0 (1.44)	19,600 (3,670)	1.1 (0.21)	43.5 (2.11)	90,200 (6,070)	5.2 (0.33)	67.7 (2.15)	145,300 (9,220)	8.3 (0.48)
More than 16	37,900 (1,000)	73.9 (1.35)	595,000 (41,560)	23.2 (1.47)	17.9 (1.35)	27,600 (4,380)	1.1 (0.16)	44.2 (1.90)	143,800 (6,680)	5.6 (0.27)	69.2 (1.56)	247,700 (9,810)	9.6 (0.36)

†Not applicable.
!Interpret data with caution. The coefficient of variation (CV) for this estimate is between 30 and 50 percent.
‡Reporting standards not met. Either there are too few cases for a reliable estimate or the coefficient of variation (CV) is 50 percent or greater.
[1]All violent incidents include serious violent incidents (see footnote 2) as well as physical attack or fight without a weapon and threat of physical attack without a weapon.
[2]Serious violent incidents include rape, sexual battery other than rape, physical attack or fight with a weapon, threat of physical attack with a weapon, and robbery with or without a weapon.
[3]Theft/larceny (taking things worth over $10 without personal confrontation) was defined for respondents as "the unlawful taking of another person's property without personal confrontation, threat, violence, or bodily harm." This includes pocket picking, stealing a purse or backpack (if left unattended or no force was used to take it from owner), theft from a building, theft from a motor vehicle or motor vehicle parts or accessories, theft of a bicycle, theft from a vending machine, and all other types of thefts.
[4]"Other incidents" include possession of a firearm or explosive device; possession of a knife or sharp object; distribution, possession, or use of illegal drugs or alcohol; inappropriate distribution, possession, or use of prescription drugs; and vandalism.

[5]Primary schools are defined as schools in which the lowest grade is not higher than grade 3 and the highest grade is not higher than grade 8. Middle schools are defined as schools in which the lowest grade is not lower than grade 4 and the highest grade is not higher than grade 9. High schools are defined as schools in which the lowest grade is not lower than grade 9 and the highest grade is not higher than grade 12. Combined schools include all other combinations of grades, including K–12 schools.
[6]Student/teacher ratio was calculated by dividing the total number of students enrolled in the school by the total number of full-time-equivalent (FTE) teachers. Information regarding the total number of FTE teachers was obtained from the Common Core of Data (CCD), the sampling frame for SSOCS.
NOTE: Responses were provided by the principal or the person most knowledgeable about crime and safety issues at the school. "At school" was defined to include activities that happen in school buildings, on school grounds, on school buses, and at places that hold school-sponsored events or activities. Respondents were instructed to include incidents that occurred before, during, or after normal school hours or when school activities or events were in session. Detail may not sum to totals because of rounding.
SOURCE: U.S. Department of Education, National Center for Education Statistics, 2009–10 School Survey on Crime and Safety (SSOCS), 2010. (This table was prepared September 2013.)

Table 229.40. Percentage of public schools reporting incidents of crime at school to the police, number of incidents, and rate per 1,000 students, by type of crime and selected school characteristics: 2009–10

[Standard errors appear in parentheses]

School characteristic	Total number of schools		All violent incidents[1]				Serious violent incidents[2]			Theft[3]			Other incidents[4]		
			Percent of schools	Number of incidents	Rate per 1,000 students	Percent of schools	Number of incidents	Rate per 1,000 students	Percent of schools	Number of incidents	Rate per 1,000 students	Percent of schools	Number of incidents	Rate per 1,000 students
1	2		3	4	5	6	7	8	9	10	11	12	13	14
Total	82,800	(460)	39.9 (1.13)	303,900 (13,310)	6.4 (0.28)	10.4 (0.62)	23,500 (2,320)	0.5 (0.05)	25.4 (1.01)	122,800 (4,180)	2.6 (0.09)	46.3 (1.23)	262,400 (8,260)	5.5 (0.17)
School level[5]														
Primary	48,900	(340)	21.1 (1.60)	35,300 (5,400)	1.6 (0.23)	5.5 (0.84)	6,100 (1,450)	0.3 (0.06)	9.3 (1.18)	9,500 (1,950)	0.4 (0.09)	30.3 (1.78)	40,100 (3,810)	1.8 (0.17)
Middle	15,300	(100)	65.9 (1.53)	100,100 (6,140)	10.7 (0.64)	15.5 (1.25)	6,300 (850)	0.7 (0.09)	41.1 (1.81)	27,100 (2,110)	2.9 (0.23)	65.4 (1.32)	60,300 (2,600)	6.4 (0.29)
High school	12,200	(70)	76.6 (1.61)	146,200 (10,520)	11.8 (0.84)	24.9 (1.16)	10,200 (1,120)	0.8 (0.09)	64.1 (1.59)	73,800 (3,370)	6.0 (0.31)	83.6 (1.32)	146,200 (5,850)	11.8 (0.50)
Combined	6,400	(200)	51.0 (5.72)	22,300 (3,820)	7.5 (1.20)	8.4 (2.41)	1,000 ! (400)	0.3 ! (0.13)	36.9 (5.41)	12,500 (2,420)	4.2 (0.84)	52.0 (4.86)	15,900 (2,350)	5.3 (0.82)
Enrollment size														
Less than 300	18,900	(400)	22.6 (2.54)	14,800 (2,740)	3.6 (0.67)	4.7 ! (1.44)	1,400 (380)	0.3 (0.09)	14.6 (2.73)	7,800 (2,210)	1.9 (0.53)	30.1 (2.59)	16,000 (2,590)	3.9 (0.66)
300–499	25,200	(180)	31.4 (2.29)	36,800 (4,240)	3.6 (0.42)	7.1 (1.32)	3,700 (860)	0.4 (0.08)	17.1 (1.91)	12,800 (1,780)	1.2 (0.17)	40.2 (2.58)	33,100 (2,720)	3.2 (0.27)
500–999	29,800	(100)	45.6 (1.79)	93,400 (6,070)	4.8 (0.31)	10.6 (1.04)	7,900 (1,440)	0.4 (0.07)	26.4 (1.40)	31,000 (2,410)	1.6 (0.12)	48.9 (2.08)	74,300 (4,010)	3.8 (0.20)
1,000 or more	8,900	(60)	81.1 (1.67)	159,000 (12,100)	11.9 (0.90)	31.1 (1.67)	10,600 (1,100)	0.8 (0.08)	68.4 (1.70)	71,200 (3,640)	5.3 (0.29)	89.0 (1.72)	139,000 (5,870)	10.4 (0.46)
Locale														
City	21,500	(190)	42.5 (2.01)	94,100 (4,900)	6.8 (0.35)	14.0 (1.45)	9,200 (1,460)	0.7 (0.11)	23.7 (1.65)	37,000 (3,420)	2.7 (0.24)	50.6 (1.85)	91,000 (4,370)	6.6 (0.31)
Suburban	23,800	(240)	39.9 (1.80)	107,600 (12,150)	6.5 (0.72)	10.0 (1.11)	7,300 (1,280)	0.4 (0.08)	26.3 (1.46)	39,900 (2,430)	2.4 (0.14)	47.5 (2.11)	85,700 (5,410)	5.2 (0.28)
Town	12,100	(110)	43.1 (3.06)	39,100 (3,510)	6.6 (0.56)	9.9 (1.91)	2,100 (350)	0.4 (0.06)	26.9 (2.33)	16,400 (1,720)	2.8 (0.27)	48.1 (3.27)	35,900 (3,090)	6.1 (0.52)
Rural	25,300	(300)	36.0 (1.93)	63,200 (5,590)	5.7 (0.52)	8.1 (1.22)	4,900 (1,110)	0.4 (0.10)	25.3 (2.00)	29,500 (2,930)	2.7 (0.27)	40.8 (1.89)	49,800 (2,620)	4.5 (0.26)
Percent combined enrollment of Black, Hispanic, Asian/Pacific Islander, and American Indian/Alaska Native students														
Less than 5 percent	11,700	(980)	36.5 (3.00)	20,000 (2,360)	4.3 (0.42)	7.1 (1.64)	1,400 (400)	0.3 (0.09)	23.5 (2.54)	10,200 (1,490)	2.2 (0.32)	38.5 (3.20)	20,200 (2,820)	4.3 (0.49)
5 percent to less than 20 percent	20,900	(1,080)	35.8 (1.72)	48,800 (3,620)	4.4 (0.32)	6.5 (0.80)	3,200 (450)	0.3 (0.04)	24.8 (1.66)	30,100 (2,970)	2.7 (0.26)	40.1 (2.31)	53,200 (3,810)	4.7 (0.32)
20 percent to less than 50 percent	20,000	(660)	41.7 (2.20)	75,000 (5,870)	5.9 (0.50)	10.3 (1.16)	5,000 (710)	0.4 (0.06)	26.8 (1.71)	34,900 (2,900)	2.7 (0.29)	46.3 (2.29)	65,500 (4,240)	5.1 (0.33)
50 percent or more	30,100	(1,270)	42.8 (2.36)	160,200 (13,150)	8.5 (0.67)	14.5 (1.27)	14,100 (2,310)	0.7 (0.12)	25.7 (1.78)	47,500 (3,470)	2.5 (0.19)	53.7 (2.25)	123,500 (6,250)	6.6 (0.34)
Percent of students eligible for free or reduced-price lunch														
0–25	17,100	(690)	33.8 (1.98)	42,200 (3,270)	3.6 (0.25)	7.4 (0.76)	3,600 (560)	0.3 (0.04)	26.8 (1.72)	30,500 (2,420)	2.6 (0.20)	40.6 (2.55)	54,200 (3,980)	4.6 (0.31)
26–50	22,700	(1,050)	42.7 (1.92)	76,100 (4,170)	5.8 (0.33)	10.7 (1.31)	5,000 (670)	0.4 (0.05)	31.2 (1.83)	43,300 (3,740)	3.3 (0.29)	48.0 (2.92)	76,900 (5,010)	5.9 (0.36)
51–75	23,800	(1,020)	40.3 (2.50)	87,200 (6,600)	7.1 (0.51)	8.8 (1.01)	5,400 (1,160)	0.4 (0.09)	22.9 (1.95)	31,200 (3,220)	2.6 (0.25)	47.5 (2.55)	72,300 (5,400)	5.9 (0.40)
76–100	19,100	(940)	41.4 (2.91)	98,400 (13,140)	9.8 (1.28)	14.7 (1.92)	9,500 (2,230)	0.9 (0.22)	20.3 (1.88)	17,800 (2,030)	1.8 (0.19)	48.0 (2.76)	59,000 (4,970)	5.8 (0.49)
Student/teacher ratio[6]														
Less than 12	12,300	(960)	36.8 (3.46)	29,000 (3,330)	6.9 (0.74)	8.7 (1.85)	2,200 (450)	0.5 (0.11)	24.8 (3.36)	11,400 (1,470)	2.7 (0.38)	46.4 (3.51)	22,100 (2,730)	5.3 (0.65)
12–16	32,600	(960)	41.5 (1.96)	128,500 (13,490)	7.4 (0.75)	10.0 (1.10)	7,900 (900)	0.5 (0.05)	25.8 (1.43)	42,100 (3,230)	2.4 (0.18)	45.6 (1.77)	88,900 (6,080)	5.1 (0.33)
More than 16	37,900	(1,000)	39.4 (1.76)	146,400 (8,760)	5.7 (0.33)	11.3 (0.83)	13,400 (2,210)	0.5 (0.08)	25.3 (1.55)	69,300 (3,600)	2.7 (0.15)	46.9 (1.67)	151,500 (6,510)	5.9 (0.26)

! Interpret data with caution. The coefficient of variation (CV) for this estimate is between 30 and 50 percent.

[1] All violent incidents include serious violent incidents (see footnote 2) as well as physical attack or fight without a weapon and threat of physical attack without a weapon.

[2] Serious violent incidents include rape, sexual battery other than rape, physical attack or fight with a weapon, threat of physical attack with a weapon, and robbery with or without a weapon.

[3] Theft/larceny (taking things worth over $10 without personal confrontation) was defined for respondents as "the unlawful taking of another person's property without personal confrontation, threat, violence, or bodily harm." This includes pocket picking, stealing a purse or backpack (if left unattended or no force was used to take it from owner), theft from a building, theft from a motor vehicle or motor vehicle parts or accessories, theft of a bicycle, theft from a vending machine, and all other types of thefts.

[4] "Other incidents" include possession of a firearm or explosive device; possession of a knife or sharp object; distribution, possession, or use of illegal drugs or alcohol; inappropriate distribution, possession, or use of prescription drugs; and vandalism.

[5] Primary schools are defined as schools in which the lowest grade is not higher than grade 3 and the highest grade is not lower than grade 4 and the highest grade is

not higher than grade 9. High schools are defined as schools in which the lowest grade is not lower than grade 9 and the highest grade is not higher than grade 12. Combined schools include all other combinations of grades, including K–12 schools.

[6] Student/teacher ratio was calculated by dividing the total number of students enrolled in the school by the total number of full-time-equivalent (FTE) teachers. Information regarding the total number of FTE teachers was obtained from the Common Core of Data (CCD), the sampling frame for SSOCS.

NOTE: Responses were provided by the principal or the person most knowledgeable about crime and safety issues at the school. "At school" was defined to include activities that happen in school buildings, on school grounds, on school buses, and at places that hold school-sponsored events or activities. Respondents were instructed to include incidents that occurred before, during, or after normal school hours or when school activities or events were in session. Detail may not sum to totals because of rounding.

SOURCE: U.S. Department of Education, National Center for Education Statistics, 2009–10 School Survey on Crime and Safety (SSOCS), 2010. (This table was prepared September 2013.)

Table 229.50. Percentage distribution of public schools, by number of violent incidents of crime at school recorded and reported to the police and selected school characteristics: 2009–10

[Standard errors appear in parentheses]

School characteristic	Number of violent incidents recorded							Number of violent incidents reported to the police						
	None	1–2 incidents	3–5 incidents	6–9 incidents	10–14 incidents	15–19 incidents	20 or more incidents	None	1–2 incidents	3–5 incidents	6–9 incidents	10–14 incidents	15–19 incidents	20 or more incidents
1	2	3	4	5	6	7	8	9	10	11	12	13	14	15
Total............................	26.2 (1.07)	7.6 (0.64)	14.5 (0.82)	14.5 (0.94)	11.1 (0.67)	6.6 (0.54)	19.4 (0.79)	60.1 (1.13)	17.9 (1.08)	7.8 (0.54)	4.3 (0.39)	3.1 (0.26)	1.7 (0.23)	5.0 (0.27)
School level[1]														
Primary..........................	35.6 (1.63)	7.6 (1.09)	15.6 (1.40)	15.9 (1.46)	9.0 (1.03)	4.7 (0.75)	11.4 (1.11)	73.9 (1.60)	16.9 (1.63)	1.9! (0.58)	1.3 (0.38)	‡ (†)	‡ (†)	0.7! (0.25)
Middle...........................	9.5 (1.10)	6.0 (0.86)	12.2 (1.18)	13.7 (1.09)	15.6 (1.03)	8.8 (0.96)	34.3 (1.36)	34.1 (1.53)	22.1 (1.44)	17.1 (1.20)	8.8 (1.09)	5.9 (0.59)	3.1 (0.58)	9.0 (0.70)
High school....................	9.1 (1.21)	8.4 (1.01)	12.1 (1.30)	10.6 (1.07)	14.0 (1.26)	11.0 (1.17)	34.8 (1.47)	23.4 (1.61)	17.8 (1.39)	15.6 (1.14)	9.4 (1.04)	9.8 (0.81)	5.7 (0.83)	18.3 (1.05)
Combined.......................	26.3 (5.33)	10.3! (3.69)	15.4 (3.74)	13.6 (3.50)	11.0! (3.51)	7.6! (3.19)	15.8 (3.49)	49.0 (5.72)	16.2 (4.12)	16.6 (3.20)	7.2! (2.68)	6.9! (2.75)	‡ (†)	2.5! (1.22)
Enrollment size														
Less than 300................	37.2 (3.25)	12.7 (2.05)	19.9 (2.84)	12.4 (2.17)	7.7 (1.72)	2.9! (1.00)	7.3 (1.72)	77.4 (2.54)	13.7 (2.18)	4.8 (1.06)	1.8! (0.72)	2.0! (0.94)	‡ (†)	‡ (†)
300–499.........................	28.7 (2.34)	8.2 (1.55)	13.2 (1.83)	15.9 (2.03)	11.5 (1.35)	6.4 (1.11)	16.0 (1.80)	68.6 (2.29)	18.2 (2.09)	7.2 (1.09)	2.7 (0.63)	1.2! (0.41)	0.9! (0.36)	1.2! (0.38)
500–999.........................	23.6 (1.75)	5.2 (1.01)	15.1 (1.52)	15.6 (1.39)	12.7 (1.16)	8.1 (0.88)	19.8 (1.21)	54.4 (1.79)	22.8 (1.47)	9.4 (0.79)	5.3 (0.73)	2.8 (0.34)	1.4 (0.37)	3.8 (0.44)
1,000 or more................	4.6 (1.22)	3.6 (0.91)	4.2 (0.81)	11.3 (1.76)	12.3 (1.34)	10.3 (1.07)	53.7 (2.49)	18.9 (1.67)	9.7 (1.05)	10.7 (1.12)	11.2 (1.36)	12.1 (1.28)	8.1 (1.15)	29.5 (1.92)
Locale														
City...............................	25.1 (2.12)	4.5 (1.11)	13.4 (2.08)	14.4 (1.65)	10.5 (1.39)	7.2 (1.27)	25.0 (1.84)	57.5 (2.01)	19.3 (1.65)	6.2 (0.81)	4.5 (0.74)	3.4 (0.54)	2.1 (0.54)	7.1 (0.61)
Suburban.......................	26.5 (2.21)	6.3 (1.10)	15.5 (1.61)	14.1 (1.60)	11.8 (1.42)	6.5 (1.00)	19.3 (1.43)	60.1 (1.80)	17.1 (1.63)	8.7 (1.14)	4.0 (0.56)	2.7 (0.37)	1.3 (0.23)	6.1 (0.61)
Town.............................	19.7 (3.14)	8.1 (1.92)	14.8 (2.51)	16.5 (2.87)	12.2 (1.77)	8.0 (1.68)	20.8 (2.50)	56.9 (3.06)	17.9 (2.47)	10.4 (1.48)	4.7 (1.03)	3.9 (0.64)	2.4! (0.76)	4.0 (0.70)
Rural.............................	29.8 (1.91)	11.4 (1.58)	14.2 (1.55)	14.1 (1.38)	10.5 (1.57)	5.8 (1.07)	14.2 (1.47)	64.0 (1.93)	17.6 (1.93)	7.2 (0.87)	4.3 (0.83)	2.9 (0.74)	1.4 (0.39)	2.6 (0.42)
Percent combined enrollment of Black, Hispanic, Asian/Pacific Islander, and American Indian/Alaska Native students														
Less than 5 percent.........	30.4 (3.33)	15.1 (2.68)	12.1 (2.01)	13.8 (2.08)	11.7 (2.26)	4.5! (1.53)	12.4 (2.47)	63.5 (3.00)	18.8 (2.45)	10.5 (1.68)	3.2! (1.08)	1.7! (0.52)	0.9! (0.42)	1.5 (0.35)
5 percent to less than 20 percent....	32.1 (2.82)	7.0 (1.44)	16.5 (1.91)	14.3 (1.81)	9.3 (1.20)	7.3 (1.28)	13.5 (1.38)	64.2 (1.72)	16.3 (1.42)	8.2 (1.09)	4.5 (0.79)	2.8 (0.36)	1.4 (0.42)	2.5 (0.34)
20 percent to less than 50 percent....	24.1 (2.14)	8.4 (1.33)	14.7 (2.07)	15.1 (1.87)	9.5 (1.26)	6.6 (1.06)	21.6 (1.83)	58.3 (2.20)	19.8 (1.98)	7.2 (0.72)	3.8 (0.62)	3.8 (0.62)	1.9 (0.34)	5.3 (0.57)
50 percent or more..........	21.8 (1.75)	4.7 (1.04)	13.8 (1.59)	14.6 (1.55)	13.2 (1.31)	7.0 (1.05)	24.9 (1.65)	57.2 (2.36)	17.4 (1.99)	6.9 (0.87)	5.0 (0.59)	3.5 (0.64)	2.0 (0.46)	7.9 (0.70)
Percent of students eligible for free or reduced-price lunch														
0–25..............................	37.4 (3.07)	7.4 (1.32)	14.9 (2.01)	13.1 (1.64)	10.0 (1.43)	5.1 (0.96)	12.1 (1.38)	66.2 (1.98)	14.4 (1.52)	7.9 (0.53)	3.4 (0.53)	3.8 (0.54)	1.4 (0.32)	3.0 (0.36)
26–50............................	24.0 (2.13)	9.0 (1.60)	16.2 (1.99)	14.3 (1.88)	10.9 (1.37)	6.7 (1.06)	18.9 (1.88)	57.3 (1.92)	19.6 (1.88)	9.7 (1.18)	4.0 (0.55)	2.9 (0.41)	1.8 (0.32)	4.7 (0.46)
51–75............................	26.2 (2.49)	7.9 (1.40)	13.2 (1.58)	14.2 (1.87)	10.0 (1.20)	7.5 (1.17)	21.0 (1.69)	59.7 (2.50)	18.0 (2.04)	7.1 (0.97)	4.9 (0.81)	3.3 (0.70)	2.1 (0.51)	5.1 (0.60)
76–100..........................	18.6 (2.49)	5.9 (1.50)	13.5 (2.18)	16.5 (2.21)	13.8 (2.01)	6.9 (1.28)	24.7 (2.30)	58.6 (2.91)	19.0 (3.03)	6.5 (1.12)	4.9 (0.82)	2.7 (0.52)	1.4! (0.51)	6.9 (0.91)
Student/teacher ratio[2]														
Less than 12...................	30.3 (3.05)	11.1 (2.42)	15.7 (2.01)	16.7 (2.54)	8.1 (2.03)	5.9 (1.64)	12.3 (2.14)	63.2 (3.46)	19.4 (2.97)	6.5 (1.13)	3.9! (1.25)	2.4! (0.96)	1.7! (0.61)	2.8 (0.54)
12–16............................	24.7 (1.89)	7.9 (1.14)	15.2 (1.49)	14.0 (1.31)	12.0 (1.13)	6.1 (0.79)	20.0 (1.33)	58.5 (1.96)	18.2 (1.33)	9.2 (0.92)	4.6 (0.63)	3.2 (0.37)	1.9 (0.44)	4.4 (0.43)
More than 16..................	26.1 (1.35)	6.3 (0.96)	13.4 (1.28)	14.3 (1.44)	11.3 (1.10)	7.3 (0.81)	21.3 (1.29)	60.6 (1.76)	17.2 (1.56)	7.1 (0.79)	4.2 (0.54)	3.4 (0.47)	1.5 (0.22)	6.1 (0.52)

†Not applicable.
!Interpret data with caution. The coefficient of variation (CV) for this estimate is between 30 and 50 percent.
‡Reporting standards not met. Either there are too few cases for a reliable estimate or the coefficient of variation (CV) is 50 percent or greater.
[1]Primary schools are defined as schools in which the lowest grade is not higher than grade 3 and the highest grade is not higher than grade 8. Middle schools are defined as schools in which the lowest grade is not lower than grade 4 and the highest grade is not higher than grade 9. High schools are defined as schools in which the lowest grade is not lower than grade 9 and the highest grade is not higher than grade 12. Combined schools include all other combinations of grades, including K–12 schools.
[2]Student/teacher ratio was calculated by dividing the total number of students enrolled in the school by the total number of full-time-equivalent (FTE) teachers. Information regarding the total number of FTE teachers was obtained from the Common Core of

Data (CCD), the sampling frame for SSOCS.
NOTE: Violent incidents include rape, sexual battery other than rape, physical attack or fight with or without a weapon, threat of physical attack with or without a weapon, and robbery with or without a weapon. Responses were provided by the principal or the person most knowledgeable about crime and safety issues at the school. "At school" was defined to include activities that happen in school buildings, on school grounds, on school buses, and at places that hold school-sponsored events or activities. Respondents were instructed to include incidents that occurred before, during, or after normal school hours or when school activities or events were in session. Detail may not sum to totals because of rounding.
SOURCE: U.S. Department of Education, National Center for Education Statistics, 2009–10 School Survey on Crime and Safety (SSOCS), 2010. (This table was prepared September 2013.)

Table 229.60. Percentage distribution of public schools, by number of serious violent incidents of crime at school recorded and reported to the police and selected school characteristics: 2009–10

[Standard errors appear in parentheses]

School characteristic	Number of serious violent incidents recorded						Number of serious violent incidents reported to the police					
	None	1 incident	2 incidents	3–5 incidents	6–9 incidents	10 or more incidents	None	1 incident	2 incidents	3–5 incidents	6–9 incidents	10 or more incidents
1	2	3	4	5	6	7	8	9	10	11	12	13
Total	83.6 (0.94)	7.9 (0.70)	3.0 (0.38)	2.8 (0.40)	1.2 (0.27)	1.5 (0.31)	89.6 (0.62)	5.9 (0.57)	1.9 (0.26)	1.6 (0.23)	0.5 (0.07)	0.6 (0.16)
School level[1]												
Primary	87.0 (1.42)	6.8 (1.06)	1.8 ! (0.55)	2.2 (0.62)	1.3 ! (0.44)	0.9 ! (0.30)	94.5 (0.84)	3.8 (0.75)	0.7 ! (0.29)	0.6 ! (0.25)	# (t)	‡ (t)
Middle	81.1 (1.46)	8.6 (0.97)	4.5 (0.89)	2.9 (0.65)	1.0 ! (0.29)	1.9 (0.41)	84.5 (1.25)	8.3 (0.94)	4.0 (0.62)	1.7 (0.48)	0.8 ! (0.27)	0.6 ! (0.22)
High school	72.4 (1.35)	11.2 (1.01)	5.2 (0.66)	6.4 (0.83)	2.0 (0.43)	2.9 (0.56)	75.1 (1.16)	10.8 (1.04)	4.5 (0.72)	5.9 (0.83)	2.1 (0.42)	1.6 (0.43)
Combined	84.5 (3.72)	8.6 ! (2.89)	3.9 ! (1.85)	‡ (t)	# (t)	‡ (t)	91.6 (2.41)	6.3 ! (2.27)	‡ (t)	‡ (t)	# (t)	‡ (t)
Enrollment size												
Less than 300	89.6 (2.11)	5.7 (1.60)	‡ (t)	1.8 ! (0.90)	‡ (t)	‡ (t)	95.3 (1.44)	3.9 ! (1.45)	‡ (t)	0.6 ! (0.28)	‡ (t)	# (t)
300–499	84.3 (2.14)	8.4 (1.69)	3.2 (0.96)	1.9 ! (0.73)	1.4 ! (0.60)	‡ (t)	92.9 (1.32)	4.7 (1.14)	1.4 ! (0.55)	0.7 ! (0.35)	‡ (t)	# (t)
500–999	84.1 (1.42)	7.8 (1.13)	2.9 (0.58)	2.8 (0.57)	1.1 ! (0.39)	1.4 ! (0.43)	89.4 (1.04)	6.3 (0.93)	2.1 (0.40)	1.3 (0.38)	0.3 ! (0.11)	0.6 ! (0.30)
1,000 or more	67.2 (1.61)	11.7 (1.02)	6.3 (0.70)	7.5 (1.05)	2.2 (0.49)	5.2 (1.01)	68.9 (1.67)	11.9 (1.11)	6.2 (0.83)	7.3 (1.02)	2.4 (0.41)	3.2 (0.87)
Locale												
City	78.3 (2.12)	10.4 (1.43)	4.0 (0.80)	4.5 (0.93)	1.1 ! (0.41)	1.7 (0.45)	86.0 (1.45)	7.5 (1.11)	2.7 (0.59)	2.2 (0.41)	0.6 (0.14)	0.9 ! (0.30)
Suburban	84.5 (1.80)	6.5 (0.92)	3.4 (0.96)	2.7 (0.73)	1.0 ! (0.43)	2.0 ! (0.76)	90.0 (1.11)	4.7 (0.63)	2.3 (0.57)	1.5 (0.38)	0.7 (0.16)	0.8 ! (0.34)
Town	84.4 (2.33)	9.3 (2.05)	1.3 (0.39)	1.1 (0.33)	3.0 ! (1.20)	0.9 ! (0.36)	90.1 (1.91)	7.0 (1.85)	1.4 ! (0.41)	1.0 ! (0.31)	‡ (t)	‡ (t)
Rural	86.8 (1.51)	6.4 (1.30)	2.5 (0.57)	2.3 ! (0.69)	‡ (t)	1.3 ! (0.48)	91.9 (1.22)	5.0 (1.19)	1.1 (0.28)	1.5 (0.44)	‡ (t)	‡ (t)
Percent combined enrollment of Black, Hispanic, Asian/Pacific Islander, and American Indian/Alaska Native students												
Less than 5 percent	87.4 (2.52)	6.7 (1.64)	1.0 ! (0.47)	2.9 ! (1.33)	# (t)	‡ (t)	92.9 (1.64)	5.5 (1.45)	‡ (t)	‡ (t)	‡ (t)	# (t)
5 percent to less than 20 percent	90.1 (1.29)	5.0 (0.84)	2.3 (0.59)	1.0 ! (0.31)	‡ (t)	0.4 ! (0.14)	93.5 (0.80)	3.6 (0.66)	1.6 ! (0.49)	0.7 (0.21)	0.3 ! (0.13)	0.2 ! (0.11)
20 percent to less than 50 percent	81.4 (1.58)	9.5 (1.48)	2.3 (0.43)	3.5 (0.99)	1.1 ! (0.49)	2.2 (0.64)	89.7 (1.16)	6.3 (1.12)	2.0 (0.45)	1.2 (0.32)	0.3 ! (0.12)	0.5 ! (0.26)
50 percent or more	78.9 (1.82)	9.3 (1.35)	4.6 (0.82)	3.6 (0.55)	1.9 (0.53)	1.6 (0.48)	85.5 (1.27)	7.3 (0.93)	2.6 (0.54)	2.7 (0.48)	0.8 (0.20)	1.1 ! (0.40)
Percent of students eligible for free or reduced-price lunch												
0–25	89.5 (1.22)	5.2 (0.93)	2.0 (0.47)	1.3 (0.39)	0.4 ! (0.16)	1.5 ! (0.47)	92.6 (0.76)	4.1 (0.55)	1.2 (0.30)	1.3 (0.36)	0.5 ! (0.20)	0.4 ! (0.14)
26–50	83.8 (1.89)	8.1 (1.43)	3.2 (0.69)	2.6 ! (0.82)	‡ (t)	1.0 (0.24)	89.3 (1.31)	6.5 (1.28)	2.5 (0.50)	1.1 (0.25)	0.5 (0.14)	‡ (t)
51–75	84.2 (1.67)	7.7 (1.24)	2.7 (0.78)	3.2 (0.67)	1.2 ! (0.51)	1.0 ! (0.44)	91.2 (1.01)	4.8 (0.90)	1.7 (0.45)	1.6 (0.41)	0.2 ! (0.09)	‡ (t)
76–100	77.1 (2.60)	10.3 (1.90)	3.9 (0.89)	3.9 (0.97)	2.1 ! (0.74)	2.7 ! (1.13)	85.3 (1.92)	7.9 (1.55)	2.1 (0.58)	2.7 (0.67)	0.7 ! (0.26)	1.4 ! (0.57)
Student/teacher ratio[2]												
Less than 12	86.8 (2.24)	7.8 (1.94)	1.4 ! (0.55)	1.7 (0.65)	‡ (t)	1.5 ! (0.56)	91.3 (1.85)	5.5 (1.61)	1.7 ! (0.72)	0.8 ! (0.32)	‡ (t)	‡ (t)
12–16	84.0 (1.44)	8.0 (1.13)	2.7 (0.56)	2.6 (0.54)	1.2 ! (0.50)	1.5 ! (0.45)	90.0 (1.10)	6.0 (1.04)	1.5 (0.25)	1.8 (0.38)	0.3 ! (0.12)	0.5 ! (0.16)
More than 16	82.1 (1.35)	7.8 (0.89)	3.8 (0.72)	3.4 (0.62)	1.1 ! (0.39)	1.8 (0.45)	88.7 (0.83)	5.9 (0.64)	2.3 (0.50)	1.8 (0.37)	0.6 (0.11)	0.8 ! (0.32)

†Not applicable.
#Rounds to zero.
!Interpret data with caution. The coefficient of variation (CV) for this estimate is between 30 and 50 percent.
‡Reporting standards not met. Either there are too few cases for a reliable estimate or the coefficient of variation (CV) is 50 percent or greater.
[1]Primary schools are defined as schools in which the lowest grade is not higher than grade 3 and the highest grade is not higher than grade 8. Middle schools are defined as schools in which the lowest grade is not lower than grade 4 and the highest grade is not higher than grade 9. High schools are defined as schools in which the lowest grade is not lower than grade 9 and the highest grade is not higher than grade 12. Combined schools include all other combinations of grades, including K–12 schools.
[2]Student/teacher ratio was calculated by dividing the total number of students enrolled in the school by the total number of full-time-equivalent (FTE) teachers. Information regarding the total number of FTE teachers was obtained from the Common Core of Data (CCD), the sampling frame for SSOCS.
NOTE: Serious violent incidents include rape, sexual battery other than rape, physical attack or fight with a weapon, threat of physical attack with a weapon, and robbery with or without a weapon. Responses were provided by the principal or the person most knowledgeable about crime and safety issues at the school. "At school" was defined to include activities that happen in school buildings, on school grounds, on school buses, and at places that hold school-sponsored events or activities. Respondents were instructed to include incidents that occurred before, during, or after normal school hours or when school activities or events were in session. Detail may not sum to totals because of rounding.
SOURCE: U.S. Department of Education, National Center for Education Statistics, 2009–10 School Survey on Crime and Safety (SSOCS), 2010. (This table prepared September 2013.)

Table 230.10. Percentage of public schools reporting selected discipline problems that occurred at school, by frequency and selected school characteristics: Selected years, 1999–2000 through 2009–10

[Standard errors appear in parentheses]

Year and school characteristic	Happens at least once a week[1]							Happens at all[2]	
	Student racial/ethnic tensions[3]	Student bullying	Student sexual harassment of other students	Student harassment of other students based on sexual orientation or gender identity	Student verbal abuse of teachers	Widespread disorder in classrooms	Student acts of disrespect for teachers other than verbal abuse	Gang activities	Cult or extremist group activities
1	2	3	4	5	6	7	8	9	10
All schools									
1999–2000	3.4 (0.41)	29.3 (1.21)	— (†)	—	12.5 (0.69)	3.1 (0.44)	— (†)	18.7 (0.85)	6.7 (0.46)
2003–04	2.1 (0.28)	26.8 (1.09)	4.0 (0.40)	—	10.7 (0.80)	2.8 (0.39)	—	16.7 (0.78)	3.4 (0.35)
2005–06	2.8 (0.31)	24.5 (1.14)	3.5 (0.40)	—	9.5 (0.61)	2.3 (0.24)	—	16.9 (0.76)	3.7 (0.41)
2007–08	3.7 (0.49)	25.3 (1.11)	3.0 (0.39)	—	6.0 (0.48)	4.0 (0.45)	10.5 (0.71)	19.8 (0.88)	2.6 (0.36)
2009–10									
All schools	2.8 (0.39)	23.1 (1.12)	3.2 (0.55)	2.5 (0.41)	4.8 (0.49)	2.5 (0.37)	8.6 (0.67)	16.4 (0.84)	1.7 (0.31)
School level[4]									
Primary	2.1 (0.62)	19.6 (1.75)	1.8! (0.70)	0.8! (0.35)	3.4 (0.67)	1.9! (0.60)	6.1 (0.92)	7.5 (1.11)	1.4! (0.48)
Middle	5.4 (0.81)	38.6 (1.60)	6.1 (0.89)	6.2 (0.92)	6.8 (0.83)	4.1 (0.67)	13.7 (1.15)	29.2 (1.48)	1.4 (0.36)
High school	3.3 (0.56)	19.8 (1.41)	3.2 (0.58)	3.1 (0.55)	8.6 (1.00)	4.4 (0.80)	14.3 (1.27)	38.4 (1.50)	3.9 (0.48)
Combined	‡ (†)	18.6 (4.38)	7.5! (2.92)	6.0! (2.74)	‡ (†)	# (†)	4.4! (2.05)	11.1 (2.89)	‡ (†)
Enrollment size									
Less than 300	‡ (†)	16.5 (2.48)	4.5! (1.38)	4.3! (1.33)	‡ (†)	‡ (†)	3.3! (1.09)	6.5 (1.34)	‡ (†)
300–499	2.5 (0.72)	24.0 (2.19)	2.4! (0.75)	1.0 (0.28)	5.2 (1.03)	2.4! (0.70)	9.5 (1.57)	11.9 (1.49)	‡ (†)
500–999	3.0 (0.54)	25.3 (1.55)	2.5 (0.55)	2.4 (0.48)	4.3 (0.64)	2.6 (0.60)	8.3 (1.00)	16.4 (1.24)	1.3! (0.44)
1,000 or more	5.5 (1.10)	27.0 (2.12)	4.7 (1.01)	3.8 (0.82)	11.2 (1.37)	4.3 (0.96)	18.2 (1.64)	49.8 (1.72)	5.6 (0.95)
Locale									
City	5.3 (1.14)	27.0 (2.08)	3.6! (1.16)	2.9! (1.06)	9.1 (1.38)	4.5 (0.85)	11.7 (1.46)	28.3 (2.10)	2.5 (0.72)
Suburban	2.7 (0.61)	19.9 (1.96)	2.6 (0.69)	2.0 (0.42)	4.7 (0.92)	3.0 (0.77)	8.1 (1.10)	14.6 (1.16)	1.2 (0.41)
Town	1.0! (0.36)	26.2 (2.71)	2.9! (0.99)	2.0 (0.56)	3.3! (1.24)	0.6! (0.26)	11.6 (2.16)	13.9 (1.56)	1.7! (0.75)
Rural	1.6! (0.63)	21.2 (2.11)	3.6 (1.01)	2.9 (0.69)	1.9! (0.58)	1.3! (0.62)	5.0 (0.93)	9.1 (1.13)	1.6! (0.70)
Percent combined enrollment of Black, Hispanic, Asian/Pacific Islander, and American Indian/Alaska Native students									
Less than 5 percent	‡ (†)	22.0 (3.36)	4.5! (1.91)	2.7! (1.19)	‡ (†)	‡ (†)	3.6! (1.18)	1.5 (0.39)	0.4! (0.19)
5 percent to less than 20 percent	1.5 (0.33)	21.3 (1.66)	1.8! (0.58)	1.9 (0.46)	1.8! (0.48)	0.5! (0.16)	6.1 (1.22)	5.8 (0.80)	1.8! (0.75)
20 percent to less than 50 percent	3.2 (0.96)	22.3 (1.70)	2.6 (0.45)	2.6 (0.47)	4.5 (1.08)	1.1! (0.48)	9.6 (1.12)	16.9 (1.40)	1.4 (0.23)
50 percent or more	4.3 (0.95)	25.2 (2.35)	4.1 (1.25)	2.9! (0.87)	8.5 (1.17)	5.7 (0.94)	11.7 (1.22)	29.1 (1.88)	2.4 (0.64)
Percent of students eligible for free or reduced-price lunch									
0–25	1.9 (0.40)	19.7 (1.99)	2.6 (0.74)	2.1 (0.55)	1.5 (0.28)	0.7! (0.21)	3.6 (0.60)	7.9 (0.91)	1.4 (0.39)
26–50	2.6! (0.85)	21.9 (1.58)	3.2 (0.80)	3.0 (0.67)	2.3 (0.52)	1.3! (0.43)	6.9 (0.91)	13.2 (1.33)	1.9! (0.68)
51–75	2.4! (0.83)	24.1 (2.24)	3.2! (0.98)	2.7! (0.86)	5.6 (0.95)	1.0! (0.37)	10.7 (1.42)	17.4 (1.46)	1.3! (0.57)
76–100	4.3 (1.16)	26.1 (3.07)	3.9! (1.47)	2.1! (0.87)	9.6 (1.64)	7.5 (1.38)	12.5 (1.49)	26.5 (2.19)	2.3! (0.87)
Student/teacher ratio[5]									
Less than 12	1.6! (0.69)	19.6 (2.85)	4.2! (1.46)	3.6! (1.38)	4.3 (1.23)	2.5! (0.82)	7.0 (1.42)	12.3 (1.77)	2.1! (0.70)
12–16	3.1 (0.81)	21.8 (1.73)	2.4 (0.66)	2.0 (0.52)	4.8 (0.73)	3.0 (0.74)	9.0 (1.27)	16.0 (1.54)	2.0 (0.40)
More than 16	2.9 (0.61)	25.3 (1.57)	3.6 (0.87)	2.5 (0.60)	4.9 (0.83)	2.1 (0.54)	8.8 (0.91)	18.1 (1.08)	‡ (†)
Prevalence of violent incidents[6]									
No violent incidents	‡ (†)	7.6 (1.53)	‡ (†)	‡ (†)	‡ (†)	‡ (†)	0.8! (0.39)	1.7! (0.67)	‡ (†)
Any violent incidents	3.5 (0.50)	28.5 (1.36)	4.1 (0.68)	3.2 (0.52)	6.4 (0.63)	3.0 (0.46)	11.4 (0.87)	21.6 (1.04)	2.1 (0.39)

—Not available.
†Not applicable.
#Rounds to zero.
!Interpret data with caution. The coefficient of variation (CV) for this estimate is between 30 and 50 percent.
‡Reporting standards not met. Either there are too few cases for a reliable estimate or the coefficient of variation (CV) is 50 percent or greater.
[1]Includes schools that reported the activity happens either at least once a week or daily.
[2]Includes schools that reported the activity happens at all at their school during the school year. In the 1999–2000 survey administration, the questionnaire specified "undesirable" gang activities and "undesirable" cult or extremist group activities.
[3]Prior to the 2007–08 survey administration, the questionnaire wording was "student racial tensions."
[4]Primary schools are defined as schools in which the lowest grade is not higher than grade 3 and the highest grade is not higher than grade 8. Middle schools are defined as schools in which the lowest grade is not lower than grade 4 and the highest grade is not higher than grade 9. High schools are defined as schools in which the lowest grade is not lower than grade 9 and the highest grade is not higher than grade 12. Combined schools include all other combinations of grades, including K–12 schools.

[5]Student/teacher ratio was calculated by dividing the total number of students enrolled in the school by the total number of full-time-equivalent (FTE) teachers. Information regarding the total number of FTE teachers was obtained from the Common Core of Data (CCD), the sampling frame for SSOCS.
[6]"Violent incidents" include rape or attempted rape, sexual battery other than rape, physical attack or fight with or without a weapon, threat of physical attack or fight with or without a weapon, and robbery with or without a weapon.
NOTE: Responses were provided by the principal or the person most knowledgeable about crime and safety issues at the school. "At school" was defined for respondents to include activities that happen in school buildings, on school grounds, on school buses, and at places that hold school-sponsored events or activities. Respondents were instructed to respond only for those times that were during normal school hours or when school activities or events were in session, unless the survey specified otherwise.
SOURCE: U.S. Department of Education, National Center for Education Statistics, 1999–2000, 2003–04, 2005–06, 2007–08, and 2009–10 School Survey on Crime and Safety (SSOCS), 2000, 2004, 2006, 2008, and 2010. (This table was prepared September 2013.)

Table 230.20. Percentage of students ages 12–18 who reported that gangs were present at school during the school year, by selected student and school characteristics and urbanicity: Selected years, 2001 through 2013

Year and urbanicity	Total	Sex		Race/ethnicity[1]					Grade							Control of school	
		Male	Female	White	Black	Hispanic	Asian	Other	6th grade	7th grade	8th grade	9th grade	10th grade	11th grade	12th grade	Public	Private
1	2	3	4	5	6	7	8	9	10	11	12	13	14	15	16	17	18
2001																	
Total..........	20.1 (0.71)	21.4 (0.86)	18.8 (0.90)	15.5 (0.72)	28.6 (1.90)	32.0 (1.82)	—	21.4 (2.18)	11.2 (1.28)	15.7 (1.09)	17.3 (1.22)	24.3 (1.27)	23.6 (1.48)	24.2 (1.56)	21.1 (1.54)	21.6 (0.77)	4.9 (1.05)
Urban..........	28.9 (1.23)	31.9 (1.62)	25.9 (1.52)	20.5 (1.28)	32.4 (2.79)	40.3 (2.45)	—	27.0 (4.41)	14.9 (2.45)	23.7 (2.54)	24.0 (2.66)	35.3 (2.77)	33.1 (3.08)	34.2 (3.21)	34.1 (3.21)	31.9 (1.35)	5.0 (1.38)
Suburban..........	18.3 (0.72)	18.9 (0.92)	17.5 (1.08)	15.4 (0.75)	25.4 (2.79)	27.1 (2.25)	—	20.0 (2.95)	9.0 (1.52)	13.7 (1.16)	16.6 (1.50)	20.8 (1.48)	22.3 (1.58)	22.7 (1.71)	18.6 (1.81)	19.5 (0.80)	4.3 ! (1.45)
Rural..........	13.3 (1.71)	14.0 (2.08)	12.5 (1.84)	12.1 (1.70)	22.5 (5.78)	16.8 ! (7.49)	—	‡ (†)	11.0 (2.78)	8.9 (1.87)	10.1 (2.24)	18.9 (3.03)	14.4 (3.05)	15.8 (3.85)	11.5 ! (4.51)	13.7 (1.80)	‡ (†)
2003																	
Total..........	20.9 (0.70)	22.3 (0.95)	19.5 (0.79)	14.2 (0.59)	29.5 (2.14)	37.2 (1.76)	—	22.0 (2.54)	10.9 (1.28)	16.3 (1.14)	17.9 (1.29)	26.1 (1.44)	26.3 (1.37)	23.4 (1.64)	22.2 (1.50)	22.5 (0.78)	3.9 (0.82)
Urban..........	30.9 (1.33)	32.1 (1.71)	29.7 (1.84)	19.8 (1.71)	32.8 (2.43)	42.6 (2.17)	—	30.6 (4.09)	21.6 (3.42)	25.5 (2.32)	25.2 (2.63)	38.2 (3.25)	35.3 (2.82)	34.6 (2.81)	34.8 (2.75)	33.7 (1.50)	6.0 (1.62)
Suburban..........	18.4 (0.84)	20.5 (1.07)	16.3 (0.92)	13.8 (0.67)	28.3 (3.93)	34.6 (2.14)	—	18.2 (2.96)	7.5 (1.25)	13.2 (1.28)	16.2 (1.65)	24.3 (1.58)	24.1 (1.72)	20.4 (2.34)	19.3 (1.91)	19.9 (0.91)	2.4 ! (0.78)
Rural..........	12.3 (1.81)	12.2 (2.00)	12.4 (2.34)	10.7 (1.42)	21.8 ! (7.17)	12.7 ! (4.11)	—	‡ (†)	‡ (†)	9.4 (2.56)	10.9 ! (3.26)	13.8 (3.00)	18.0 (3.50)	15.0 (3.30)	13.3 (3.60)	12.8 (2.02)	‡ (†)
2005																	
Total..........	24.2 (0.93)	25.3 (1.07)	22.9 (1.09)	16.8 (0.83)	37.6 (2.41)	38.9 (2.69)	20.2 (2.59)	27.7 (4.62)	12.1 (1.41)	17.3 (1.21)	19.1 (1.79)	28.3 (1.59)	32.6 (1.89)	28.0 (1.89)	27.9 (2.16)	25.8 (1.01)	4.2 (0.94)
Urban..........	36.2 (2.00)	37.4 (2.31)	35.0 (2.42)	23.7 (1.87)	41.8 (2.93)	48.8 (4.44)	25.0 (5.16)	33.9 (8.68)	19.9 (3.11)	24.2 (2.64)	30.5 (3.81)	40.3 (3.70)	50.6 (3.82)	44.3 (3.89)	39.5 (3.73)	39.1 (2.12)	7.7 (2.26)
Suburban..........	20.8 (0.93)	22.4 (1.14)	19.1 (1.15)	16.0 (0.87)	36.2 (4.41)	32.1 (2.52)	18.1 (2.87)	29.0 (6.12)	8.9 (1.52)	14.9 (1.46)	14.6 (2.01)	24.8 (1.92)	27.9 (2.37)	25.5 (2.21)	25.1 (2.60)	22.3 (1.01)	3.0 ! (1.02)
Rural..........	16.4 (2.53)	16.1 (3.20)	16.7 (2.79)	14.1 (2.46)	24.4 (6.75)	26.2 (6.51)	19.0 ! (9.22)	‡ (†)	8.3 (3.29)	15.2 (3.46)	14.7 (4.22)	21.0 (4.00)	22.0 (3.61)	13.3 ! (4.36)	15.8 ! (5.82)	17.2 (2.67)	‡ (†)
2007[2]																	
Total..........	23.2 (0.80)	25.1 (1.07)	21.3 (0.87)	16.0 (0.70)	37.6 (2.26)	36.1 (2.04)	17.4 (2.72)	26.4 (3.63)	15.3 (1.99)	17.4 (1.28)	20.6 (1.68)	28.0 (1.51)	28.1 (1.73)	25.9 (1.61)	24.4 (1.69)	24.9 (0.87)	5.2 (1.14)
Urban..........	32.3 (1.49)	35.3 (2.01)	29.2 (1.62)	23.4 (1.98)	39.7 (3.07)	40.4 (2.90)	18.4 (4.30)	31.9 (6.10)	17.8 (3.45)	24.1 (2.96)	25.9 (2.90)	41.1 (3.40)	38.6 (3.36)	34.7 (3.05)	38.4 (4.01)	35.6 (1.61)	7.3 (2.07)
Suburban..........	21.0 (0.97)	23.1 (1.36)	18.9 (1.19)	15.9 (0.92)	35.5 (3.16)	33.3 (2.66)	16.3 (3.63)	29.0 (5.14)	14.0 (2.40)	15.4 (1.67)	19.6 (2.23)	23.1 (1.78)	26.6 (2.01)	23.6 (2.22)	22.4 (2.26)	18.1 (1.05)	2.8 ! (1.09)
Rural..........	15.5 (2.78)	14.9 (2.69)	16.1 (3.18)	10.9 (1.59)	36.8 (10.42)	27.5 ! (10.34)	‡	14.3 ! (6.01)	15.6 ! (6.21)	13.1 (2.79)	14.7 (4.26)	21.7 (4.43)	15.2 (3.39)	18.7 (3.98)	7.6 ! (2.90)	15.6 (2.91)	11.8 ! (5.84)
2009[2]																	
Total..........	20.4 (0.85)	20.9 (1.12)	19.9 (1.03)	14.1 (0.79)	31.4 (2.62)	33.0 (2.20)	17.2 (3.21)	15.3 (4.07)	11.0 (1.76)	14.8 (1.70)	15.9 (1.60)	24.9 (2.01)	27.7 (1.75)	22.6 (1.53)	21.9 (2.02)	22.0 (0.89)	2.3 ! (0.82)
Urban..........	30.7 (1.86)	32.8 (2.35)	28.6 (2.29)	19.4 (1.99)	40.0 (3.76)	38.9 (3.31)	18.9 (4.63)	23.2 ! (9.05)	14.5 (4.13)	21.0 (3.37)	24.4 (3.24)	34.2 (4.01)	44.8 (3.41)	34.9 (4.08)	36.0 (4.32)	33.7 (1.94)	4.1 ! (1.83)
Suburban..........	16.6 (0.80)	17.2 (1.24)	16.0 (1.17)	11.3 (0.91)	20.2 (2.75)	28.3 (2.64)	14.5 (3.95)	14.8 (6.41)	9.7 (1.90)	11.2 (1.89)	11.8 (1.73)	22.4 (2.10)	21.0 (2.07)	19.4 (1.88)	17.6 (2.26)	18.1 (0.85)	‡ (†)
Rural..........	16.0 (3.08)	13.7 (3.37)	18.1 (3.18)	11.8 (2.09)	35.4 (9.77)	27.3 ! (10.84)	‡	14.3 ! (6.41)	8.3 ! (3.11)	16.5 (4.19)	14.2 ! (4.41)	21.7 (4.43)	15.2 (5.02)	13.4 (3.50)	7.6 ! (5.37)	15.6 (3.18)	11.8 ! (†)
2011[2]																	
Total..........	17.5 (0.71)	17.5 (0.95)	17.5 (0.88)	11.1 (0.67)	32.7 (2.23)	26.4 (1.55)	9.9 (2.24)	9.9 (2.12)	8.2 (1.20)	10.2 (1.08)	11.3 (1.02)	21.7 (1.47)	23.0 (1.63)	23.2 (1.74)	21.3 (1.82)	18.9 (0.77)	1.9 ! (0.69)
Urban..........	22.8 (1.34)	23.0 (1.90)	22.6 (1.53)	13.9 (1.60)	31.6 (2.75)	31.0 (2.34)	7.6 ! (2.29)	12.3 (3.41)	5.4 ! (1.98)	11.7 (2.02)	16.2 (2.29)	27.5 (3.12)	31.1 (3.13)	28.1 (3.17)	32.9 (3.88)	25.7 (1.47)	‡ (†)
Suburban..........	16.1 (0.97)	16.5 (1.24)	15.6 (1.18)	11.3 (0.89)	33.5 (4.08)	23.2 (1.95)	12.0 ! (3.69)	10.4 ! (3.54)	8.6 (1.79)	9.3 (1.37)	9.0 (1.22)	18.9 (1.79)	21.5 (2.10)	23.7 (2.46)	18.5 (2.27)	17.1 (1.01)	2.9 ! (1.20)
Rural..........	12.1 (2.42)	10.2 (2.23)	14.1 (3.18)	7.7 (1.31)	34.5 (6.62)	22.1 ! (10.47)	‡	10.1 (2.64)	11.1 (2.97)	10.1 (2.64)	9.6 ! (2.89)	19.3 (4.99)	13.9 (4.02)	10.6 (3.69)	9.2 ! (3.04)	12.5 (2.49)	‡ (†)
2013[3]																	
Total..........	12.4 (0.62)	12.9 (0.85)	12.0 (0.73)	7.5 (0.63)	18.6 (1.72)	20.1 (1.34)	9.4 (1.85)	14.3 (2.68)	5.0 (1.15)	7.7 (0.96)	7.8 (0.96)	13.9 (1.43)	17.7 (1.46)	17.1 (1.65)	14.6 (1.58)	13.3 (0.67)	2.3 ! (0.94)
Urban..........	18.3 (1.23)	18.6 (1.61)	18.0 (1.38)	14.3 (1.73)	20.6 (2.36)	22.6 (2.15)	10.4 (2.61)	17.9 (5.59)	9.6 (2.75)	12.0 (2.44)	13.2 (2.30)	19.6 (2.53)	24.8 (2.86)	26.7 (3.21)	18.2 (3.07)	19.9 (1.35)	4.6 ! (2.08)
Suburban..........	10.8 (0.76)	11.7 (1.09)	9.8 (0.92)	6.5 (0.76)	17.3 (3.02)	19.3 (1.69)	8.2 ! (2.59)	13.0 (3.29)	3.0 ! (1.25)	6.6 (1.14)	6.3 (1.19)	12.2 (1.95)	15.4 (1.91)	15.1 (2.00)	14.1 (2.06)	11.7 (0.82)	‡ (†)
Rural..........	6.8 (1.44)	5.7 (1.38)	7.9 (1.92)	4.1 (1.20)	16.1 (4.49)	9.4 ! (4.52)	‡	11.9 ! (5.43)	‡ (†)	4.2 ! (1.88)	‡ (†)	8.0 ! (3.19)	11.3 (3.37)	8.1 ! (3.32)	9.0 ! (3.56)	6.8 (1.47)	‡ (†)

—Not available.
†Not applicable.
‡Reporting standards not met. Either there are too few cases for a reliable estimate or the coefficient of variation (CV) is 50 percent or greater.
[1]Race categories exclude persons of Hispanic ethnicity. "Other" includes American Indians/Alaska Natives, Asians (prior to 2005), Pacific Islanders, and, from 2003 onward, persons of Two or more races. Due to changes in racial/ethnic categories, comparisons of race/ethnicity across years should be made with caution.

!Interpret data with caution. The coefficient of variation (CV) for this estimate is between 30 and 50 percent.

[2]Starting in 2007, the reference period was the school year, whereas in prior survey years the reference period was the previous 6 months. Cognitive testing showed that estimates from 2007 onward are comparable to previous years.
NOTE: Urbanicity refers to the Standard Metropolitan Statistical Area (MSA) status of the respondent's household as defined in 2000 by the U.S. Census Bureau. Categories include "central city of an MSA (Urban)," "in MSA but not in central city (Suburban)," and "not MSA (Rural)." All gangs, whether or not they are involved in violent or illegal activity, are included. "At school" includes in the school building, on school property, on a school bus, and going to and from school.
SOURCE: U.S. Department of Justice, Bureau of Justice Statistics, School Crime Supplement (SCS) to the National Crime Victimization Survey, selected years, 2001 through 2013. (This table was prepared August 2014.)

Table 230.30. Percentage of students ages 12–18 who reported being the target of hate-related words and seeing hate-related graffiti at school during the school year, by selected student and school characteristics: Selected years, 1999 through 2013

[Standard errors appear in parentheses]

Student or school characteristic	1999	2001	2003	2005	2007¹	2009¹	2011¹	2013¹
1	2	3	4	5	6	7	8	9
Hate-related words								
Total	— (†)	12.3 (0.46)	11.7 (0.47)	11.2 (0.50)	9.7 (0.43)	8.7 (0.52)	9.1 (0.48)	6.6 (0.40)
Sex								
Male	— (†)	12.8 (0.65)	12.0 (0.61)	11.7 (0.68)	9.9 (0.61)	8.5 (0.62)	9.0 (0.60)	6.6 (0.51)
Female	— (†)	11.7 (0.52)	11.3 (0.64)	10.7 (0.64)	9.6 (0.57)	8.9 (0.72)	9.1 (0.68)	6.7 (0.53)
Race/ethnicity²								
White	— (†)	12.1 (0.58)	10.9 (0.56)	10.3 (0.60)	8.9 (0.50)	7.2 (0.59)	8.3 (0.59)	5.3 (0.43)
Black	— (†)	13.9 (1.08)	14.2 (1.35)	15.1 (1.48)	11.4 (1.35)	11.1 (1.35)	10.7 (1.30)	7.8 (1.20)
Hispanic	— (†)	11.0 (1.15)	11.4 (0.96)	10.5 (1.15)	10.6 (1.18)	11.2 (1.13)	9.8 (0.98)	7.4 (0.84)
Asian	— (†)	— (†)	— (†)	10.9 (2.56)	11.1 (1.97)	10.7 (2.81)	9.0 (2.00)	10.3 (2.19)
Other	— (†)	13.6 (2.05)	14.1 (2.03)	14.2 (3.27)	10.6 (2.71)	10.0 (2.37)	10.4 (2.61)	11.2 (2.47)
Grade								
6th	— (†)	12.1 (1.26)	11.9 (1.31)	11.1 (1.58)	12.1 (1.54)	8.3 (1.39)	9.0 (1.43)	6.7 (1.33)
7th	— (†)	14.1 (1.13)	12.5 (1.04)	13.1 (1.16)	10.7 (1.02)	9.6 (1.22)	9.9 (1.02)	7.5 (0.89)
8th	— (†)	13.0 (1.07)	12.8 (0.92)	11.2 (1.04)	11.0 (1.19)	10.9 (1.22)	8.4 (0.94)	7.4 (1.01)
9th	— (†)	12.1 (1.00)	13.5 (1.23)	12.8 (1.12)	10.9 (1.08)	8.0 (1.09)	10.2 (1.10)	6.6 (0.94)
10th	— (†)	13.1 (0.95)	11.6 (1.12)	10.9 (1.04)	9.0 (0.99)	9.7 (1.18)	9.6 (1.14)	6.4 (0.97)
11th	— (†)	12.7 (1.13)	8.3 (0.97)	9.0 (1.17)	8.6 (1.01)	8.4 (1.14)	8.7 (1.01)	7.5 (1.01)
12th	— (†)	7.9 (0.87)	10.8 (1.25)	9.7 (1.35)	6.0 (0.98)	5.8 (0.96)	7.5 (1.01)	4.1 (0.78)
Urbanicity³								
Urban	— (†)	11.9 (0.73)	13.2 (0.83)	12.2 (0.86)	9.7 (0.83)	9.9 (0.93)	8.0 (0.77)	7.2 (0.76)
Suburban	— (†)	12.4 (0.63)	10.7 (0.58)	9.4 (0.52)	9.3 (0.62)	8.3 (0.64)	9.8 (0.71)	6.6 (0.50)
Rural	— (†)	12.4 (1.11)	12.2 (1.35)	15.5 (1.74)	11.0 (1.07)	8.1 (1.37)	8.5 (1.00)	5.7 (0.80)
Control of school								
Public	— (†)	12.7 (0.51)	11.9 (0.49)	11.6 (0.53)	10.1 (0.46)	8.9 (0.54)	9.3 (0.50)	6.6 (0.41)
Private	— (†)	8.2 (1.13)	9.7 (1.11)	6.8 (1.18)	6.1 (1.25)	6.6 (1.62)	6.9 (1.29)	6.7 (1.41)
Hate-related graffiti								
Total	36.3 (0.94)	35.5 (0.75)	36.3 (0.84)	38.4 (0.83)	34.9 (0.89)	29.2 (0.96)	28.4 (0.88)	24.6 (0.88)
Sex								
Male	33.8 (1.06)	34.9 (0.89)	35.0 (0.97)	37.7 (1.10)	34.4 (1.12)	29.0 (1.26)	28.6 (1.11)	24.1 (1.11)
Female	38.9 (1.14)	36.1 (0.92)	37.6 (1.06)	39.1 (0.93)	35.4 (1.12)	29.3 (1.09)	28.1 (1.07)	25.1 (1.05)
Race/ethnicity²								
White	36.4 (1.20)	36.2 (0.95)	35.2 (0.86)	38.5 (0.96)	35.5 (1.05)	28.3 (1.10)	28.2 (1.19)	23.7 (1.20)
Black	37.6 (1.71)	33.6 (1.52)	38.1 (1.95)	38.0 (2.29)	33.7 (2.37)	29.0 (2.44)	28.1 (1.90)	26.3 (2.10)
Hispanic	35.6 (1.46)	35.1 (1.87)	40.3 (2.24)	38.0 (1.78)	34.8 (1.76)	32.2 (1.61)	29.1 (1.33)	25.6 (1.52)
Asian	— (†)	— (†)	— (†)	34.5 (3.76)	28.2 (3.01)	31.2 (3.59)	29.9 (4.56)	20.8 (3.22)
Other	32.2 (2.53)	32.1 (2.82)	31.4 (2.83)	46.9 (4.68)	38.7 (3.44)	25.8 (4.20)	25.9 (3.79)	28.4 (3.52)
Grade								
6th	30.3 (1.82)	34.9 (1.88)	35.7 (1.83)	34.0 (2.24)	35.5 (2.30)	28.1 (2.26)	25.9 (2.13)	21.9 (1.77)
7th	34.9 (1.43)	34.9 (1.36)	37.2 (1.41)	37.0 (1.63)	32.3 (1.52)	27.9 (1.88)	26.0 (1.70)	21.7 (1.49)
8th	35.6 (1.51)	36.7 (1.40)	34.2 (1.53)	35.7 (1.61)	33.5 (1.81)	30.8 (1.80)	25.9 (1.55)	24.0 (1.80)
9th	39.2 (1.55)	35.7 (1.55)	37.0 (1.48)	41.6 (1.64)	34.5 (1.77)	28.1 (1.83)	28.7 (1.69)	27.2 (1.74)
10th	38.9 (1.77)	36.2 (1.49)	40.7 (1.67)	40.7 (1.83)	36.4 (1.69)	31.0 (2.03)	33.3 (1.78)	26.0 (1.58)
11th	37.0 (1.74)	36.1 (1.76)	36.6 (1.74)	40.2 (1.70)	35.3 (1.81)	27.4 (2.01)	32.1 (1.70)	25.8 (2.03)
12th	35.6 (2.04)	33.0 (1.79)	32.2 (1.78)	37.8 (2.34)	37.7 (2.03)	30.4 (2.00)	25.7 (1.51)	24.2 (1.91)
Urbanicity³								
Urban	37.0 (1.18)	35.7 (1.21)	38.6 (1.27)	40.9 (1.43)	34.4 (1.36)	31.1 (1.56)	27.5 (1.49)	27.5 (1.48)
Suburban	37.3 (1.12)	36.0 (0.87)	35.9 (1.16)	38.0 (1.02)	34.2 (1.03)	28.6 (1.15)	29.9 (1.08)	23.7 (1.11)
Rural	32.7 (2.60)	33.8 (2.56)	33.9 (1.97)	35.8 (2.40)	37.8 (3.06)	27.7 (2.43)	24.9 (2.25)	21.6 (2.71)
Control of school								
Public	38.0 (0.97)	37.3 (0.80)	37.9 (0.90)	40.0 (0.87)	36.4 (0.93)	30.7 (1.01)	29.7 (0.95)	25.6 (0.94)
Private	20.7 (1.85)	16.8 (1.34)	19.5 (1.75)	18.6 (1.97)	18.5 (2.07)	11.8 (1.93)	13.4 (1.56)	12.6 (1.74)

—Not available.
†Not applicable.
¹Starting in 2007, the reference period was the school year, whereas in prior survey years the reference period was the previous 6 months. Cognitive testing showed that estimates from 2007 onward are comparable to previous years.
²Race categories exclude persons of Hispanic ethnicity. "Other" includes American Indians/Alaska Natives, Asians (prior to 2005), Pacific Islanders, and, from 2003 onward, persons of Two or more races. Due to changes in racial/ethnic categories, comparisons of race/ethnicity across years should be made with caution.
³Refers to the Standard Metropolitan Statistical Area (MSA) status of the respondent's household as defined in 2000 by the U.S. Census Bureau. Categories include "central city of an MSA (Urban)," "in MSA but not in central city (Suburban)," and "not MSA (Rural)."
NOTE: "At school" includes in the school building, on school property, on a school bus, and, from 2001 onward, going to and from school. "Hate-related" refers to derogatory terms used by others in reference to students' personal characteristics.
SOURCE: U.S. Department of Justice, Bureau of Justice Statistics, School Crime Supplement (SCS) to the National Crime Victimization Survey, selected years, 1999 through 2013. (This table was prepared August 2014.)

Table 230.35. Percentage of students ages 12–18 who reported being the target of hate-related words at school, by type of hate-related word and selected student and school characteristics: 2013

[Standard errors appear in parentheses]

Student or school characteristic	Total[1]		Hate-related words related to student's characteristic											
			Race		Ethnicity		Religion		Disability		Gender		Sexual orientation	
1	2		3		4		5		6		7		8	
Total.........................	6.6	(0.40)	3.3	(0.31)	1.9	(0.21)	1.2	(0.15)	0.8	(0.14)	1.0	(0.14)	1.1	(0.13)
Sex														
Male.........................	6.6	(0.51)	3.5	(0.41)	1.9	(0.27)	1.0	(0.19)	0.7	(0.16)	0.3	(0.09)	0.9	(0.16)
Female.......................	6.7	(0.53)	3.1	(0.40)	1.9	(0.30)	1.4	(0.22)	0.9	(0.21)	1.7	(0.29)	1.3	(0.22)
Race/ethnicity[2]														
White........................	5.3	(0.43)	1.6	(0.25)	0.8	(0.18)	1.2	(0.22)	1.2	(0.22)	1.1	(0.20)	1.3	(0.22)
Black........................	7.8	(1.20)	5.8	(1.03)	1.9	(0.48)	1.0 !	(0.39)	‡	(†)	1.0 !	(0.41)	1.1 !	(0.43)
Hispanic.....................	7.4	(0.84)	3.9	(0.64)	3.7	(0.62)	1.0	(0.27)	‡	(†)	0.9	(0.25)	0.8 !	(0.27)
Asian........................	10.3	(2.19)	8.5	(2.05)	7.1	(2.00)	2.1 !	(0.87)	‡	(†)	‡	(†)	‡	(†)
Other........................	11.2	(2.47)	8.3	(2.10)	‡	(†)	‡	(†)	‡	(†)	‡	(†)	‡	(†)
Grade														
6th..........................	6.7	(1.33)	3.5	(0.98)	1.9 !	(0.67)	1.1 !	(0.52)	‡	(†)	‡	(†)	‡	(†)
7th..........................	7.5	(0.89)	3.6	(0.64)	2.0	(0.46)	0.8 !	(0.32)	1.1 !	(0.35)	1.1 !	(0.36)	0.9 !	(0.35)
8th..........................	7.4	(1.01)	3.3	(0.72)	1.8 !	(0.54)	1.7	(0.48)	1.0 !	(0.33)	1.4	(0.40)	1.4 !	(0.43)
9th..........................	6.6	(0.94)	3.0	(0.68)	2.0	(0.58)	2.1	(0.56)	0.9 !	(0.36)	0.9 !	(0.33)	0.8 !	(0.31)
10th.........................	6.4	(0.97)	3.9	(0.76)	2.0	(0.50)	1.2 !	(0.39)	0.9 !	(0.32)	0.7 !	(0.28)	0.8 !	(0.32)
11th.........................	7.5	(1.01)	3.9	(0.74)	1.9	(0.53)	1.1 !	(0.40)	‡	(†)	1.4 !	(0.45)	2.3	(0.48)
12th.........................	4.1	(0.78)	1.8	(0.55)	1.9	(0.53)	‡	(†)	‡	(†)	0.6 !	(0.32)	0.8 !	(0.36)
Urbanicity[3]														
Urban........................	7.2	(0.76)	4.2	(0.65)	2.2	(0.37)	0.9	(0.21)	0.6 !	(0.23)	0.8	(0.23)	1.2	(0.25)
Suburban.....................	6.6	(0.50)	3.1	(0.39)	1.9	(0.29)	1.3	(0.21)	0.8	(0.19)	1.0	(0.18)	0.9	(0.18)
Rural........................	5.7	(0.80)	2.3	(0.56)	1.5 !	(0.49)	1.5 !	(0.45)	1.2 !	(0.44)	1.4 !	(0.46)	1.4	(0.39)
Control of school														
Public.......................	6.6	(0.41)	3.3	(0.30)	1.9	(0.21)	1.2	(0.15)	0.8	(0.14)	1.0	(0.15)	1.1	(0.13)
Private......................	6.7	(1.41)	3.7	(1.08)	1.9 !	(0.79)	‡	(†)	‡	(†)	1.2 !	(0.55)	‡	(†)

†Not applicable.

!Interpret data with caution. The coefficient of variation (CV) for this estimate is between 30 and 50 percent.

‡Reporting standards not met. Either there are too few cases for a reliable estimate or the coefficient of variation (CV) is 50 percent or greater.

[1]Students who indicated that they had been called a hate-related word were asked to choose the specific characteristics that the hate-related word or words targeted. Students were allowed to choose more than one characteristic. If a student chose more than one characteristic, he or she is counted only once in the total percentage of students who reported being called a hate-related word; therefore, the total is less than the sum of the students' individual characteristics.

[2]Race categories exclude persons of Hispanic ethnicity. "Other" includes American Indians/ Alaska Natives, Pacific Islanders, and persons of Two or more races.

[3]Refers to the Standard Metropolitan Statistical Area (MSA) status of the respondent's household as defined in 2000 by the U.S. Census Bureau. Categories include "central city of an MSA (Urban)," "in MSA but not in central city (Suburban)," "and not MSA (Rural)."

NOTE: "At school" includes in the school building, on school property, on a school bus, or going to and from school. "Hate-related" refers to derogatory terms used by others in reference to students' personal characteristics. Detail may not sum to totals because of rounding and because students may have reported being targets of hate-related words related to more than one student characteristic.

SOURCE: U.S. Department of Justice, Bureau of Justice Statistics, School Crime Supplement (SCS) to the National Crime Victimization Survey, 2013. (This table was prepared August 2014.)

Table 230.40. Percentage of students ages 12–18 who reported being bullied at school or cyber-bullied anywhere during the school year, by type of bullying at school, reports of injury, and selected student and school characteristics: 2013

[Standard errors appear in parentheses]

Student or school characteristic	Bullied at school or cyber-bullied anywhere			Type of bullying at school							Of students who were pushed, shoved, tripped, or spit on, percent reporting injury[1]
	Total bullied at school or cyber-bullied anywhere[2]	Total cyber-bullied anywhere[3]	Total bullied at school[4]	Made fun of, called names, or insulted	Subject of rumors	Threatened with harm	Tried to make do things did not want to do	Excluded from activities on purpose	Property destroyed on purpose	Pushed, shoved, tripped, or spit on	
1	2	3	4	5	6	7	8	9	10	11	12
Total........................	23.1 (0.67)	6.9 (0.42)	21.5 (0.66)	13.6 (0.51)	13.2 (0.50)	3.9 (0.27)	2.2 (0.21)	4.5 (0.30)	1.6 (0.20)	6.0 (0.39)	20.8 (2.48)
Sex											
Male....................	21.1 (0.84)	5.2 (0.43)	19.5 (0.81)	12.6 (0.70)	9.6 (0.60)	4.1 (0.38)	2.4 (0.30)	3.5 (0.34)	1.8 (0.28)	7.4 (0.59)	20.6 (3.21)
Female..................	25.2 (0.99)	8.6 (0.63)	23.7 (0.98)	14.7 (0.75)	17.0 (0.80)	3.7 (0.37)	1.9 (0.27)	5.5 (0.47)	1.3 (0.25)	4.6 (0.42)	21.1 (3.63)
Race/ethnicity[5]											
White...................	25.3 (0.94)	7.6 (0.57)	23.7 (0.93)	15.6 (0.74)	14.6 (0.76)	4.4 (0.40)	2.0 (0.28)	5.4 (0.46)	1.5 (0.24)	6.1 (0.49)	22.3 (3.39)
Black...................	21.2 (1.85)	4.5 (0.94)	20.3 (1.81)	10.5 (1.22)	12.7 (1.40)	3.2 (0.68)	2.7 (0.59)	2.7 (0.71)	2.0 (0.54)	6.0 (0.97)	15.6 ! (6.04)
Hispanic................	20.5 (1.32)	5.8 (0.78)	19.2 (1.30)	12.1 (1.13)	11.5 (1.02)	4.0 (0.58)	1.6 (0.32)	3.5 (0.53)	1.4 (0.38)	6.3 (0.79)	18.3 (4.15)
Asian...................	11.8 (2.02)	5.8 (1.67)	9.2 (1.67)	7.5 (1.63)	3.7 (0.95)	‡ (†)	3.8 ! (1.32)	2.2 ! (0.71)	1.6 ! (0.78)	2.0 ! (0.85)	‡ (†)
Other....................	29.7 (3.83)	13.4 (2.43)	25.2 (3.60)	16.5 (2.99)	17.3 (3.05)	4.3 ! (1.56)	4.0 ! (1.38)	6.5 (1.85)	2.1 ! (1.00)	8.5 (1.90)	‡ (†)
Grade											
6th......................	29.9 (2.31)	5.9 (1.20)	27.8 (2.31)	21.3 (2.15)	16.1 (1.61)	5.9 (1.13)	3.4 (0.88)	6.5 (1.20)	3.1 (0.77)	11.0 (1.46)	26.8 (6.90)
7th......................	27.3 (1.65)	7.0 (0.91)	26.4 (1.65)	17.9 (1.35)	15.5 (1.35)	6.1 (0.88)	3.0 (0.52)	6.3 (0.86)	2.2 (0.52)	11.6 (1.12)	24.0 (4.11)
8th......................	22.7 (1.43)	6.4 (0.86)	21.7 (1.42)	14.5 (1.23)	12.7 (1.11)	3.9 (0.68)	2.3 (0.54)	5.2 (0.80)	1.5 ! (0.45)	6.5 (0.85)	20.8 (5.92)
9th......................	24.4 (1.46)	6.7 (0.97)	23.0 (1.42)	13.7 (1.16)	13.8 (1.22)	3.6 (0.61)	2.6 (0.58)	4.3 (0.70)	1.2 ! (0.40)	4.9 (0.83)	18.2 ! (7.32)
10th.....................	21.4 (1.52)	8.6 (1.16)	19.5 (1.48)	12.9 (1.21)	12.9 (1.28)	4.3 (0.73)	1.7 (0.47)	4.6 (0.72)	1.3 (0.37)	3.7 (0.68)	21.2 ! (7.78)
11th.....................	22.4 (1.50)	6.8 (0.87)	20.0 (1.50)	11.2 (1.20)	12.5 (1.31)	3.0 (0.60)	1.5 (0.45)	2.4 (0.61)	1.6 ! (0.50)	3.4 (0.72)	‡ (†)
12th.....................	15.4 (1.45)	5.9 (0.93)	14.1 (1.51)	6.4 (1.04)	9.7 (1.15)	1.0 ! (0.43)	1.3 ! (0.48)	2.5 (0.67)	0.7 ! (0.31)	3.0 (0.71)	‡ (†)
Urbanicity[6]											
Urban....................	22.6 (1.10)	7.1 (0.73)	20.7 (1.10)	12.8 (0.80)	12.7 (0.87)	3.9 (0.47)	2.7 (0.45)	4.1 (0.51)	1.4 (0.27)	5.6 (0.60)	20.9 (4.99)
Suburban.................	23.5 (0.93)	7.0 (0.61)	22.0 (0.90)	14.2 (0.69)	13.4 (0.71)	3.9 (0.39)	2.0 (0.28)	4.7 (0.43)	1.3 (0.24)	6.4 (0.52)	21.8 (3.31)
Rural....................	22.7 (1.87)	5.9 (1.02)	21.4 (1.86)	13.2 (1.49)	13.3 (1.45)	4.1 (0.67)	1.7 (0.42)	4.2 (0.73)	2.8 (0.66)	5.8 (0.88)	16.7 ! (5.31)
Control of school											
Public...................	23.0 (0.69)	6.9 (0.45)	21.5 (0.67)	13.5 (0.53)	13.2 (0.52)	3.9 (0.28)	2.2 (0.22)	4.3 (0.31)	1.6 (0.19)	6.1 (0.41)	20.3 (2.57)
Private..................	23.8 (2.79)	6.4 (1.44)	22.4 (2.71)	15.3 (2.01)	13.4 (2.20)	3.9 (1.14)	2.7 ! (0.82)	6.7 (1.31)	1.3 ! (0.60)	5.2 (1.24)	‡ (†)

†Not applicable.
!Interpret data with caution. The coefficient of variation (CV) for this estimate is between 30 and 50 percent.
‡Reporting standards not met. Either there are too few cases for a reliable estimate or the coefficient of variation (CV) is 50 percent or greater.
[1]Only students who reported that they were pushed, shoved, tripped, or spit on were asked if they suffered injuries as a result of the incident.
[2]Students who reported that they were both bullied at school and cyber-bullied anywhere were counted only once in the total for students bullied at school or cyber-bullied anywhere.
[3]Students who reported being cyber-bullied are those who responded that another student had done one or more of the following: posted hurtful information about them on the Internet; purposely shared private information about them on the Internet; threatened or insulted them through instant messaging; threatened or insulted them through text messaging; threatened or insulted them through e-

mail; threatened or insulted them while gaming; or excluded them online. Students who reported more than one of these types of cyber-bullying were counted only once in the total for students cyber-bullied anywhere.
[4]Students who reported experiencing more than one type of bullying at school were counted only once in the total for students bullied at school.
[5]Race categories exclude persons of Hispanic ethnicity. "Other" includes American Indians/Alaska Natives, Pacific Islanders, and persons of Two or more races.
[6]Refers to the Standard Metropolitan Statistical Area (MSA) status of the respondent's household as defined in 2000 by the U.S. Census Bureau. Categories include "central city of an MSA (Urban)," "in MSA but not in central city (Suburban)," and "not MSA (Rural)."
NOTE: "At school" includes the school building, on school property, on a school bus, or going to and from school. Bullying types do not sum to totals because students could have experienced more than one type of bullying.
SOURCE: U.S. Department of Justice, Bureau of Justice Statistics, School Crime Supplement (SCS) to the National Crime Victimization Survey, 2013. (This table was prepared August 2014.)

Table 230.45. Percentage of students ages 12–18 who reported being bullied at school during the school year, by type of bullying and selected student and school characteristics: Selected years, 2005 through 2013

[Standard errors appear in parentheses]

Year and student or school characteristic	Total bullied at school		Made fun of, called names, or insulted		Subject of rumors		Threatened with harm		Tried to make do things did not want to do		Excluded from activities on purpose		Property destroyed on purpose		Pushed, shoved, tripped, or spit on	
1	2		3		4		5		6		7		8		9	
2005																
Total	28.1	(0.70)	18.7	(0.58)	14.7	(0.53)	4.8	(0.31)	3.5	(0.27)	4.6	(0.30)	3.4	(0.29)	9.0	(0.45)
Sex																
Male	27.1	(0.90)	18.5	(0.73)	11.0	(0.64)	5.2	(0.51)	3.9	(0.39)	4.1	(0.40)	3.5	(0.41)	10.9	(0.70)
Female	29.2	(0.84)	19.0	(0.79)	18.5	(0.74)	4.4	(0.37)	3.1	(0.32)	5.2	(0.40)	3.3	(0.35)	7.1	(0.50)
Race/ethnicity[1]																
White	30.0	(0.84)	20.1	(0.72)	15.8	(0.66)	5.1	(0.47)	3.6	(0.35)	5.3	(0.36)	3.4	(0.35)	9.7	(0.62)
Black	28.5	(2.21)	18.5	(1.72)	14.2	(1.36)	4.9	(0.76)	4.7	(1.00)	4.5	(0.91)	4.6	(0.89)	8.9	(1.14)
Hispanic	22.3	(1.28)	14.7	(1.11)	12.4	(1.00)	4.6	(0.64)	2.6	(0.55)	3.0	(0.53)	2.7	(0.49)	7.6	(0.94)
Asian	—	(†)	—	(†)	—	(†)	—	(†)	—	(†)	—	(†)	—	(†)	—	(†)
Other	24.6	(2.06)	16.3	(1.82)	11.6	(1.71)	2.1	(0.59)	2.1 !	(0.74)	2.5 !	(0.79)	2.5 !	(0.77)	6.8	(1.19)
Grade																
6th	36.6	(1.99)	26.3	(2.05)	16.4	(1.60)	6.4	(1.18)	4.4	(0.92)	7.4	(1.19)	3.9	(0.91)	15.1	(1.75)
7th	35.0	(1.72)	25.2	(1.57)	18.9	(1.27)	6.3	(0.80)	4.7	(0.83)	7.1	(0.85)	4.6	(0.79)	15.4	(1.25)
8th	30.4	(1.50)	20.4	(1.30)	14.3	(1.10)	4.3	(0.64)	3.8	(0.71)	5.4	(0.68)	4.5	(0.75)	11.3	(1.23)
9th	28.1	(1.57)	18.9	(1.33)	13.8	(1.23)	5.3	(0.67)	3.2	(0.58)	3.8	(0.63)	2.7	(0.53)	8.2	(0.91)
10th	24.9	(1.43)	15.5	(1.14)	13.6	(1.19)	4.9	(0.82)	3.6	(0.64)	3.6	(0.63)	2.9	(0.64)	6.8	(0.78)
11th	23.0	(1.58)	14.7	(1.32)	13.4	(1.29)	3.2	(0.61)	2.8	(0.59)	3.3	(0.61)	2.6	(0.56)	4.2	(0.69)
12th	19.9	(1.75)	11.3	(1.52)	12.5	(1.54)	3.5	(0.71)	1.8	(0.51)	2.2 !	(0.72)	2.4	(0.63)	2.9	(0.66)
Urbanicity[2]																
Urban	26.0	(1.29)	17.7	(0.95)	13.3	(1.07)	5.5	(0.49)	4.1	(0.53)	4.9	(0.63)	3.9	(0.58)	8.5	(0.73)
Suburban	28.9	(0.81)	18.9	(0.75)	14.6	(0.64)	4.4	(0.42)	3.1	(0.33)	4.5	(0.37)	3.0	(0.32)	9.0	(0.56)
Rural	29.0	(1.96)	19.8	(1.76)	17.2	(1.32)	5.0	(1.10)	3.7	(0.74)	4.5	(0.88)	3.8	(0.87)	9.9	(1.23)
Control of school[3]																
Public	28.6	(0.74)	19.0	(0.61)	14.9	(0.55)	5.1	(0.33)	3.5	(0.27)	4.5	(0.30)	3.5	(0.31)	9.3	(0.48)
Private	22.7	(2.09)	15.3	(1.67)	12.4	(1.66)	0.9 !	(0.40)	3.0 !	(0.90)	6.2	(1.06)	2.0 !	(0.70)	5.5	(1.03)
2007																
Total	31.7	(0.74)	21.0	(0.62)	18.1	(0.61)	5.8	(0.35)	4.1	(0.27)	5.2	(0.30)	4.2	(0.28)	11.0	(0.42)
Sex																
Male	30.3	(0.96)	20.3	(0.83)	13.5	(0.73)	6.0	(0.50)	4.8	(0.43)	4.6	(0.40)	4.0	(0.35)	12.2	(0.58)
Female	33.2	(0.99)	21.7	(0.89)	22.8	(0.91)	5.6	(0.45)	3.4	(0.32)	5.8	(0.43)	4.4	(0.41)	9.7	(0.59)
Race/ethnicity[1]																
White	34.1	(0.97)	23.5	(0.84)	20.3	(0.84)	6.3	(0.47)	4.8	(0.36)	6.1	(0.44)	4.2	(0.35)	11.5	(0.56)
Black	30.4	(2.18)	19.5	(1.71)	15.7	(1.51)	5.8	(0.89)	3.2	(0.69)	3.7	(0.72)	5.6	(0.96)	11.3	(1.42)
Hispanic	27.3	(1.53)	16.1	(1.25)	14.4	(1.27)	4.9	(0.75)	3.0	(0.71)	4.0	(0.60)	3.6	(0.67)	9.9	(1.05)
Asian	18.1	(2.60)	10.6	(2.19)	8.2	(1.93)	‡	(†)	‡	(†)	‡	(†)	1.8 !	(0.89)	3.8 !	(1.25)
Other	34.1	(3.03)	20.1	(3.12)	20.8	(2.98)	7.7	(2.01)	3.1 !	(1.23)	7.7	(2.08)	3.4 !	(1.30)	14.4	(2.73)
Grade																
6th	42.7	(2.23)	31.2	(2.00)	21.3	(1.84)	7.0	(1.13)	5.4	(0.98)	7.4	(1.20)	5.2	(0.98)	17.6	(1.56)
7th	35.6	(1.78)	27.6	(1.58)	20.2	(1.33)	7.4	(0.92)	4.1	(0.64)	7.7	(0.92)	6.0	(0.81)	15.8	(1.28)
8th	36.9	(1.84)	25.1	(1.65)	19.7	(1.41)	6.9	(0.84)	3.6	(0.64)	5.4	(0.77)	4.6	(0.79)	14.2	(1.23)
9th	30.6	(1.72)	20.3	(1.39)	18.1	(1.45)	4.6	(0.77)	5.1	(0.67)	4.5	(0.69)	3.5	(0.63)	11.4	(1.13)
10th	27.7	(1.44)	17.7	(1.22)	15.0	(1.13)	5.8	(0.81)	4.6	(0.68)	4.6	(0.74)	3.4	(0.59)	8.6	(0.89)
11th	28.5	(1.48)	15.3	(1.25)	18.7	(1.40)	4.9	(0.80)	4.2	(0.73)	3.9	(0.68)	4.4	(0.78)	6.5	(0.92)
12th	23.0	(1.60)	12.1	(1.36)	14.1	(1.38)	4.3	(0.83)	2.1	(0.53)	3.5	(0.75)	2.4	(0.61)	4.1	(0.81)
Urbanicity[2]																
Urban	30.7	(1.36)	20.0	(1.09)	15.5	(1.02)	5.2	(0.54)	3.6	(0.46)	4.9	(0.57)	4.2	(0.59)	9.2	(0.76)
Suburban	31.2	(1.07)	21.1	(0.84)	17.4	(0.87)	5.7	(0.48)	4.1	(0.37)	5.0	(0.42)	4.0	(0.38)	11.2	(0.60)
Rural	35.2	(1.73)	22.1	(1.43)	24.1	(1.42)	7.0	(0.78)	5.1	(0.69)	6.3	(0.79)	4.9	(0.63)	13.1	(0.98)
Control of school[3]																
Public	32.0	(0.76)	21.1	(0.65)	18.3	(0.64)	6.2	(0.38)	4.2	(0.28)	5.2	(0.32)	4.1	(0.28)	11.4	(0.45)
Private	29.1	(2.10)	20.1	(1.79)	16.0	(1.76)	1.3 !	(0.50)	3.6	(0.92)	5.9	(1.11)	5.0	(1.11)	6.5	(1.14)
2009																
Total	28.0	(0.83)	18.8	(0.65)	16.5	(0.66)	5.7	(0.34)	3.6	(0.28)	4.7	(0.34)	3.3	(0.28)	9.0	(0.48)
Sex																
Male	26.6	(1.04)	18.4	(0.89)	12.8	(0.79)	5.6	(0.50)	4.0	(0.43)	3.8	(0.39)	3.4	(0.40)	10.1	(0.65)
Female	29.5	(1.08)	19.2	(0.95)	20.3	(0.92)	5.8	(0.50)	3.2	(0.37)	5.7	(0.52)	3.2	(0.39)	7.9	(0.64)
Race/ethnicity[1]																
White	29.3	(1.03)	20.5	(0.89)	17.4	(0.86)	5.4	(0.40)	3.7	(0.38)	5.2	(0.44)	3.3	(0.32)	9.1	(0.61)
Black	29.1	(2.29)	18.4	(1.78)	17.7	(1.60)	7.8	(1.20)	4.8	(0.92)	4.6	(0.97)	4.6	(0.99)	9.9	(1.55)
Hispanic	25.5	(1.71)	15.8	(1.34)	14.8	(1.44)	5.8	(0.87)	2.7	(0.59)	3.6	(0.68)	2.6	(0.55)	9.1	(0.97)
Asian	17.3	(3.01)	9.6	(2.38)	8.1	(2.11)	‡	(†)	‡	(†)	3.4 !	(1.41)	‡	(†)	5.5 !	(1.75)
Other	26.7	(4.61)	17.4	(3.83)	12.9	(3.21)	9.7 !	(3.01)	4.5 !	(1.97)	4.5 !	(1.85)	3.8 !	(1.67)	7.1 !	(2.39)
Grade																
6th	39.4	(2.60)	30.6	(2.32)	21.4	(2.20)	9.3	(1.34)	4.2 !	(1.27)	6.6	(1.31)	4.0	(1.00)	14.5	(1.89)
7th	33.1	(1.87)	23.6	(1.76)	17.3	(1.58)	5.7	(1.00)	4.6	(0.82)	5.6	(0.95)	4.6	(0.85)	13.1	(1.34)
8th	31.7	(1.85)	22.8	(1.64)	18.1	(1.50)	6.8	(0.94)	5.4	(0.91)	6.9	(1.04)	6.1	(0.92)	12.8	(1.29)
9th	28.0	(1.90)	19.2	(1.66)	16.6	(1.53)	7.1	(1.00)	4.0	(0.74)	4.5	(0.78)	2.9	(0.71)	9.7	(1.24)
10th	26.6	(1.71)	15.0	(1.41)	17.0	(1.32)	5.8	(0.91)	3.1	(0.63)	4.0	(0.76)	2.9	(0.63)	7.3	(1.03)
11th	21.1	(1.69)	13.9	(1.42)	13.9	(1.42)	4.8	(0.84)	2.5	(0.63)	3.6	(0.76)	1.5 !	(0.49)	4.4	(0.84)
12th	20.4	(1.63)	11.1	(1.20)	13.1	(1.32)	2.0	(0.57)	1.7 !	(0.52)	2.6	(0.64)	1.3 !	(0.46)	3.0	(0.65)
Urbanicity[2]																
Urban	27.4	(1.25)	17.0	(1.00)	16.5	(1.01)	6.6	(0.67)	4.2	(0.59)	4.0	(0.57)	4.2	(0.63)	9.0	(0.98)
Suburban	27.5	(1.06)	19.3	(0.87)	15.5	(0.97)	5.2	(0.44)	3.2	(0.33)	5.0	(0.46)	2.9	(0.34)	8.9	(0.56)
Rural	30.7	(1.99)	20.2	(1.60)	19.9	(1.56)	6.1	(0.79)	4.1	(0.80)	5.2	(0.85)	3.3	(0.64)	9.5	(1.27)
Control of school[3]																
Public	28.8	(0.88)	19.3	(0.68)	16.9	(0.69)	5.9	(0.37)	3.8	(0.30)	4.7	(0.36)	3.4	(0.29)	9.4	(0.52)
Private	18.9	(2.16)	13.3	(1.87)	11.6	(1.75)	4.4	(1.12)	1.9 !	(0.76)	4.9	(1.16)	1.8 !	(0.68)	4.5	(1.14)

See notes at end of table.

Table 230.45. Percentage of students ages 12–18 who reported being bullied at school during the school year, by type of bullying and selected student and school characteristics: Selected years, 2005 through 2013—Continued

[Standard errors appear in parentheses]

Year and student or school characteristic	Total bullied at school	Type of bullying at school						
		Made fun of, called names, or insulted	Subject of rumors	Threatened with harm	Tried to make do things did not want to do	Excluded from activities on purpose	Property destroyed on purpose	Pushed, shoved, tripped, or spit on
1	2	3	4	5	6	7	8	9
2011								
Total	27.8 (0.76)	17.6 (0.62)	18.3 (0.61)	5.0 (0.30)	3.3 (0.26)	5.6 (0.34)	2.8 (0.23)	7.9 (0.38)
Sex								
Male	24.5 (0.91)	16.2 (0.73)	13.2 (0.66)	5.0 (0.44)	3.6 (0.34)	4.8 (0.41)	3.3 (0.34)	8.9 (0.57)
Female	31.4 (0.99)	19.1 (0.84)	23.8 (0.93)	5.1 (0.41)	3.0 (0.36)	6.4 (0.49)	2.3 (0.30)	6.8 (0.49)
Race/ethnicity[1]								
White	31.5 (1.07)	20.6 (0.89)	20.3 (0.81)	5.8 (0.44)	3.3 (0.35)	7.1 (0.51)	3.1 (0.33)	8.6 (0.55)
Black	27.2 (1.97)	16.4 (1.45)	18.6 (1.79)	5.5 (0.83)	4.3 (0.79)	4.7 (0.90)	3.3 (0.72)	9.3 (1.00)
Hispanic	21.9 (1.07)	12.7 (0.93)	15.1 (0.87)	3.3 (0.53)	2.9 (0.46)	2.8 (0.52)	2.4 (0.52)	6.2 (0.75)
Asian	14.9 (2.70)	9.0 (2.04)	7.7 (2.03)	‡ (†)	2.7 ! (1.10)	2.9 ! (1.13)	‡ (†)	2.1 ! (0.95)
Other	23.7 (3.38)	15.0 (2.47)	17.0 (2.94)	6.5 (1.73)	‡ (†)	5.0 ! (1.62)	‡ (†)	7.2 (1.81)
Grade								
6th	37.0 (2.17)	27.0 (2.03)	23.1 (1.90)	4.9 (0.94)	3.9 (0.85)	6.6 (1.19)	3.7 (0.87)	12.7 (1.56)
7th	30.3 (1.64)	22.4 (1.35)	18.3 (1.31)	6.9 (0.89)	4.5 (0.72)	7.8 (0.95)	4.0 (0.68)	12.6 (1.16)
8th	30.7 (1.68)	20.7 (1.51)	19.0 (1.40)	5.3 (0.75)	2.9 (0.56)	6.4 (0.80)	4.0 (0.73)	10.8 (1.07)
9th	26.5 (1.66)	16.4 (1.28)	16.3 (1.38)	5.4 (0.73)	3.3 (0.64)	4.1 (0.87)	2.5 (0.60)	7.3 (0.85)
10th	28.0 (1.56)	16.9 (1.26)	19.6 (1.24)	5.1 (0.75)	3.9 (0.65)	5.3 (0.71)	2.2 (0.48)	6.7 (0.82)
11th	23.8 (1.72)	12.7 (1.17)	17.1 (1.48)	4.0 (0.68)	2.4 (0.60)	4.7 (0.71)	1.8 (0.50)	3.9 (0.73)
12th	22.0 (1.34)	10.6 (1.12)	16.7 (1.23)	3.5 (0.65)	2.3 (0.55)	4.3 (0.75)	1.9 (0.51)	2.7 (0.59)
Urbanicity[2]								
Urban	24.8 (1.28)	15.9 (1.07)	16.1 (1.05)	4.4 (0.49)	3.1 (0.38)	4.6 (0.50)	2.5 (0.38)	7.6 (0.66)
Suburban	29.0 (1.07)	18.4 (0.85)	18.7 (0.86)	5.0 (0.47)	3.2 (0.33)	6.0 (0.46)	3.0 (0.35)	8.2 (0.56)
Rural	29.7 (1.82)	18.4 (1.33)	21.4 (1.47)	6.3 (0.69)	3.9 (0.80)	5.8 (0.89)	3.0 (0.54)	7.3 (0.78)
Control of school[3]								
Public	28.4 (0.82)	17.9 (0.66)	18.8 (0.65)	5.3 (0.33)	3.3 (0.28)	5.5 (0.37)	2.9 (0.24)	8.1 (0.42)
Private	21.5 (1.91)	13.9 (1.68)	12.6 (1.59)	1.6 ! (0.62)	2.9 (0.76)	5.6 (1.07)	2.1 ! (0.71)	4.7 (1.03)
2013								
Total	21.5 (0.66)	13.6 (0.51)	13.2 (0.50)	3.9 (0.27)	2.2 (0.21)	4.5 (0.30)	1.6 (0.20)	6.0 (0.39)
Sex								
Male	19.5 (0.81)	12.6 (0.70)	9.6 (0.60)	4.1 (0.38)	2.4 (0.30)	3.5 (0.34)	1.8 (0.28)	7.4 (0.59)
Female	23.7 (0.98)	14.7 (0.75)	17.0 (0.80)	3.7 (0.37)	1.9 (0.27)	5.5 (0.47)	1.3 (0.25)	4.6 (0.42)
Race/ethnicity[1]								
White	23.7 (0.93)	15.6 (0.74)	14.6 (0.76)	4.4 (0.40)	2.0 (0.28)	5.4 (0.46)	1.5 (0.24)	6.1 (0.49)
Black	20.3 (1.81)	10.5 (1.22)	12.7 (1.40)	3.2 (0.68)	2.7 (0.59)	2.7 (0.71)	2.0 (0.54)	6.0 (0.97)
Hispanic	19.2 (1.30)	12.1 (1.13)	11.5 (1.02)	4.0 (0.58)	1.6 (0.32)	3.5 (0.53)	1.4 (0.38)	6.3 (0.79)
Asian	9.2 (1.67)	7.5 (1.63)	3.7 (0.95)	‡ (†)	3.8 ! (1.32)	2.2 ! (0.71)	1.6 ! (0.78)	2.0 ! (0.85)
Other	25.2 (3.60)	16.5 (2.99)	17.3 (3.05)	4.3 ! (1.56)	4.0 ! (1.38)	6.5 (1.85)	2.1 ! (1.00)	8.5 (1.90)
Grade								
6th	27.8 (2.31)	21.3 (2.15)	16.1 (1.61)	5.9 (1.13)	3.4 (0.88)	6.5 (1.20)	3.1 (0.77)	11.0 (1.46)
7th	26.4 (1.65)	17.9 (1.35)	15.5 (1.35)	6.1 (0.88)	3.0 (0.52)	6.3 (0.86)	2.2 (0.52)	11.6 (1.12)
8th	21.7 (1.42)	14.5 (1.23)	12.7 (1.11)	3.9 (0.68)	2.3 (0.54)	5.2 (0.80)	1.5 ! (0.45)	6.5 (0.85)
9th	23.0 (1.42)	13.7 (1.16)	13.8 (1.22)	3.6 (0.61)	2.6 (0.58)	4.3 (0.70)	1.2 ! (0.40)	4.9 (0.83)
10th	19.5 (1.48)	12.9 (1.21)	12.9 (1.28)	4.3 (0.73)	1.7 (0.47)	4.6 (0.72)	1.3 (0.37)	3.7 (0.68)
11th	20.0 (1.50)	11.2 (1.20)	12.5 (1.31)	3.0 (0.60)	1.5 (0.45)	2.4 (0.61)	1.6 ! (0.50)	3.4 (0.72)
12th	14.1 (1.51)	6.4 (1.04)	9.7 (1.15)	1.0 ! (0.43)	1.3 ! (0.48)	2.5 (0.67)	0.7 ! (0.31)	3.0 (0.71)
Urbanicity[2]								
Urban	20.7 (1.10)	12.8 (0.80)	12.7 (0.87)	3.9 (0.47)	2.7 (0.45)	4.1 (0.51)	1.4 (0.27)	5.6 (0.60)
Suburban	22.0 (0.90)	14.2 (0.69)	13.4 (0.71)	3.9 (0.39)	2.0 (0.28)	4.7 (0.43)	1.3 (0.24)	6.4 (0.52)
Rural	21.4 (1.86)	13.2 (1.49)	13.3 (1.45)	4.1 (0.67)	1.7 (0.42)	4.2 (0.73)	2.8 (0.66)	5.8 (0.88)
Control of school[3]								
Public	21.5 (0.67)	13.5 (0.53)	13.2 (0.52)	3.9 (0.28)	2.2 (0.22)	4.3 (0.31)	1.6 (0.19)	6.1 (0.41)
Private	22.4 (2.71)	15.3 (2.01)	13.4 (2.20)	3.9 (1.14)	2.7 ! (0.82)	6.7 (1.31)	1.3 ! (0.60)	5.2 (1.24)

—Not available.
†Not applicable.
!Interpret data with caution. The coefficient of variation (CV) for this estimate is between 30 and 50 percent.
‡Reporting standards not met. Either there are too few cases for a reliable estimate or the coefficient of variation (CV) is 50 percent or greater.
[1]Race categories exclude persons of Hispanic ethnicity. "Other" includes American Indians/Alaska Natives, Pacific Islanders, and persons of Two or more races.
[2]Refers to the Standard Metropolitan Statistical Area (MSA) status of the respondent's household as defined in 2000 by the U.S. Census Bureau. Categories include "central city of an MSA (Urban)," "in MSA but not in central city (Suburban)," and "not MSA (Rural)." These data by metropolitan status were based on the location of households and differ from those published in Student Reports of Bullying and Cyber-Bullying: Results from the 2011 School

Crime Supplement to the National Crime Victimization Survey, which were based on the urban-centric measure of the location of the school that the child attended.
[3]Control of school as reported by the respondent. These data differ from those based on a matching of the respondent-reported school name to the Common Core of Data's Public Elementary/Secondary School Universe Survey or the Private School Survey, as reported in Student Reports of Bullying and Cyber-Bullying: Results from the 2011 School Crime Supplement to the National Crime Victimization Survey.
NOTE: "At school" includes the school building, on school property, on a school bus, or going to and from school. Bullying types do not sum to totals because students could have experienced more than one type of bullying.
SOURCE: U.S. Department of Justice, Bureau of Justice Statistics, School Crime Supplement (SCS) to the National Crime Victimization Survey, selected years, 2005 through 2013. (This table was prepared August 2014.)

Table 230.50. Percentage of students ages 12–18 who reported being bullied at school during the school year and, among bullied students, percentage who reported being bullied in various locations, by selected student and school characteristics: 2013

[Standard errors appear in parentheses]

Student or school characteristic	Total	Among students who were bullied, percent by location[1]						
		Inside classroom	In hallway or stairwell	In bathroom or locker room	Cafeteria	Somewhere else in school building	Outside on school grounds	On school bus
1	2	3	4	5	6	7	8	9
Total..	21.5 (0.66)	33.6 (1.54)	45.6 (1.73)	9.1 (0.84)	18.9 (1.17)	0.8 ! (0.30)	22.9 (1.44)	7.8 (0.86)
Sex								
Male...............................	19.5 (0.81)	31.1 (2.13)	45.8 (2.37)	11.6 (1.46)	17.9 (1.76)	‡ (†)	22.3 (1.85)	8.9 (1.41)
Female............................	23.7 (0.98)	35.8 (2.03)	45.3 (2.37)	7.0 (1.01)	19.7 (1.69)	1.2 ! (0.54)	23.4 (1.92)	6.9 (1.12)
Race/ethnicity[2]								
White..............................	23.7 (0.93)	33.9 (2.08)	46.9 (2.09)	11.0 (1.24)	19.8 (1.53)	0.8 ! (0.34)	22.9 (1.89)	9.6 (1.18)
Black..............................	20.3 (1.81)	28.7 (4.03)	39.5 (4.27)	5.1 ! (2.00)	19.2 (3.36)	‡ (†)	18.7 (3.10)	6.4 ! (2.15)
Hispanic.........................	19.2 (1.30)	35.6 (3.02)	44.8 (3.47)	7.1 (1.66)	15.5 (2.45)	‡ (†)	26.4 (3.08)	2.3 ! (1.00)
Asian..............................	9.2 (1.67)	‡ (†)	‡ (†)	‡ (†)	‡ (†)	‡ (†)	‡ (†)	‡ (†)
Other..............................	25.2 (3.60)	31.9 (5.92)	48.3 (7.19)	‡ (†)	14.3 ! (5.14)	‡ (†)	25.1 (5.03)	17.0 ! (5.47)
Grade								
6th.................................	27.8 (2.31)	34.9 (4.23)	40.9 (4.91)	7.3 ! (2.57)	11.6 (2.98)	‡ (†)	36.4 (4.37)	17.1 (3.61)
7th.................................	26.4 (1.65)	32.4 (2.88)	43.6 (3.35)	12.9 (2.25)	20.8 (2.63)	‡ (†)	26.8 (3.03)	10.2 (1.92)
8th.................................	21.7 (1.42)	38.0 (4.12)	41.2 (4.00)	7.7 (2.06)	18.0 (2.97)	‡ (†)	26.1 (3.53)	8.7 (2.40)
9th.................................	23.0 (1.42)	29.9 (3.44)	42.0 (3.61)	9.5 (2.01)	23.9 (3.22)	‡ (†)	19.0 (2.76)	5.7 ! (1.80)
10th...............................	19.5 (1.48)	40.1 (4.32)	52.6 (4.63)	9.0 (2.24)	19.2 (3.15)	‡ (†)	20.0 (3.79)	7.9 (2.17)
11th...............................	20.0 (1.50)	29.5 (3.66)	52.2 (4.05)	8.2 (2.43)	18.8 (3.35)	‡ (†)	16.6 (3.52)	‡ (†)
12th...............................	14.1 (1.51)	30.1 (5.29)	47.4 (5.92)	6.2 ! (2.47)	14.9 (4.18)	‡ (†)	14.1 (3.80)	‡ (†)
Urbanicity[3]								
Urban.............................	20.7 (1.10)	34.3 (3.05)	42.2 (3.07)	7.9 (1.59)	21.5 (2.35)	‡ (†)	26.2 (2.86)	4.8 (1.29)
Suburban	22.0 (0.90)	32.9 (2.01)	48.3 (2.18)	9.5 (1.12)	18.0 (1.61)	‡ (†)	22.3 (1.89)	9.0 (1.25)
Rural..............................	21.4 (1.86)	35.1 (4.17)	41.9 (3.93)	10.2 (2.07)	17.0 (2.79)	‡ (†)	18.7 (3.57)	9.2 (1.84)
Control of school								
Public.............................	21.5 (0.67)	33.3 (1.61)	46.1 (1.80)	9.3 (0.90)	18.7 (1.22)	0.8 ! (0.33)	22.3 (1.47)	8.2 (0.91)
Private............................	22.4 (2.71)	36.7 (5.32)	39.2 (5.26)	6.7 ! (2.64)	20.5 (4.47)	‡ (†)	30.1 (5.17)	‡ (†)

†Not applicable.
!Interpret data with caution. The coefficient of variation (CV) for this estimate is between 30 and 50 percent.
‡Reporting standards not met. Either there are too few cases for a reliable estimate or the coefficient of variation (CV) is 50 percent or greater.
[1]Includes only students who indicated the location of bullying. Excludes students who indicated that they were bullied but did not answer the question about where the bullying occurred.
[2]Race categories exclude persons of Hispanic ethnicity. "Other" includes American Indians/Alaska Natives, Pacific Islanders, and persons of Two or more races.

[3]Refers to the Standard Metropolitan Statistical Area (MSA) status of the respondent's household as defined in 2000 by the U.S. Census Bureau. Categories include "central city of an MSA (Urban)," "in MSA but not in central city (Suburban)," and "not MSA (Rural)."
NOTE: "At school" includes the school building, on school property, on a school bus, or going to and from school. Location totals may sum to more than 100 percent because students could have been bullied in more than one location.
SOURCE: U.S. Department of Justice, Bureau of Justice Statistics, School Crime Supplement (SCS) to the National Crime Victimization Survey, 2013. (This table was prepared August 2014.)

Table 230.55. Percentage of students ages 12–18 who reported being cyber-bullied anywhere during the school year, by type of cyber-bullying and selected student and school characteristics: 2013

[Standard errors appear in parentheses]

Student or school characteristic	Total cyber-bullying[1]		Type of cyber-bullying												
			Hurtful information on Internet		Private information purposely shared on Internet		Subject of harassing instant messages		Subject of harassing text messages		Subject of harassing e-mails		Subject of harassment while gaming		Excluded online	
1	2		3		4		5		6		7		8		9	
Total	6.9	(0.42)	2.8	(0.24)	0.9	(0.15)	2.1	(0.22)	3.2	(0.28)	0.9	(0.15)	1.5	(0.18)	0.9	(0.13)
Sex																
Male	5.2	(0.43)	1.2	(0.22)	0.4	(0.12)	1.0	(0.19)	1.6	(0.25)	0.2 !	(0.09)	2.5	(0.31)	0.9	(0.18)
Female	8.6	(0.63)	4.5	(0.42)	1.5	(0.27)	3.4	(0.39)	4.9	(0.51)	1.7	(0.30)	0.4 !	(0.14)	0.9	(0.18)
Race/ethnicity[2]																
White	7.6	(0.57)	2.9	(0.35)	1.0	(0.22)	2.2	(0.27)	3.8	(0.42)	0.8	(0.19)	1.8	(0.26)	1.0	(0.18)
Black	4.5	(0.94)	2.2	(0.63)	‡	(†)	1.8 !	(0.57)	1.9	(0.49)	0.8 !	(0.35)	‡	(†)	‡	(†)
Hispanic	5.8	(0.78)	2.6	(0.52)	1.0 !	(0.34)	1.9	(0.41)	2.6	(0.52)	0.8 !	(0.28)	0.9 !	(0.30)	1.0	(0.29)
Asian	5.8	(1.67)	1.8 !	(0.85)	‡	(†)	‡	(†)	‡	(†)	‡	(†)	3.1 !	(1.20)	‡	(†)
Other	13.4	(2.43)	6.9	(1.86)	1.9 !	(0.96)	4.9 !	(1.63)	6.2	(1.69)	4.7 !	(1.62)	3.2 !	(1.30)	‡	(†)
Grade																
6th	5.9	(1.20)	1.4 !	(0.58)	‡	(†)	1.2 !	(0.54)	2.3 !	(0.78)	‡	(†)	1.5 !	(0.61)	‡	(†)
7th	7.0	(0.91)	2.1	(0.53)	1.1 !	(0.36)	2.3	(0.51)	3.8	(0.74)	1.0 !	(0.35)	1.8	(0.44)	0.8 !	(0.30)
8th	6.4	(0.86)	3.1	(0.59)	0.9 !	(0.26)	2.3	(0.55)	3.2	(0.64)	1.5 !	(0.48)	1.7	(0.50)	1.5 !	(0.46)
9th	6.7	(0.97)	2.0	(0.49)	‡	(†)	2.9	(0.58)	2.8	(0.62)	‡	(†)	1.6	(0.48)	1.4 !	(0.43)
10th	8.6	(1.16)	4.1	(0.84)	1.2 !	(0.41)	2.8	(0.61)	4.5	(0.81)	1.4 !	(0.41)	1.0 !	(0.35)	1.0 !	(0.34)
11th	6.8	(0.87)	3.9	(0.71)	1.3 !	(0.41)	1.1 !	(0.43)	2.7	(0.55)	‡	(†)	1.3	(0.39)	‡	(†)
12th	5.9	(0.93)	2.6	(0.67)	‡	(†)	1.9	(0.55)	2.3	(0.59)	1.1 !	(0.40)	1.4 !	(0.51)	‡	(†)
Urbanicity[3]																
Urban	7.1	(0.73)	3.4	(0.50)	1.1	(0.32)	2.4	(0.45)	3.1	(0.50)	1.4	(0.34)	1.5	(0.25)	1.2	(0.33)
Suburban	7.0	(0.61)	2.7	(0.35)	0.9	(0.20)	2.0	(0.27)	3.3	(0.40)	0.8	(0.18)	1.6	(0.27)	0.9	(0.17)
Rural	5.9	(1.02)	2.2	(0.43)	0.8 !	(0.29)	2.0 !	(0.62)	2.9	(0.72)	0.7 !	(0.31)	1.0 !	(0.48)	‡	(†)
Control of school																
Public	6.9	(0.45)	2.9	(0.26)	0.9	(0.16)	2.2	(0.23)	3.2	(0.30)	0.9	(0.16)	1.5	(0.19)	0.9	(0.14)
Private	6.4	(1.44)	2.0 !	(0.76)	1.2 !	(0.54)	‡	(†)	2.9 !	(0.98)	‡	(†)	‡	(†)	‡	(†)

†Not applicable.

!Interpret data with caution. The coefficient of variation (CV) for this estimate is between 30 and 50 percent.

‡Reporting standards not met. Either there are too few cases for a reliable estimate or the coefficient of variation (CV) is 50 percent or greater.

[1]Students who reported experiencing more than one type of cyber-bullying were counted only once in the total for students cyber-bullied.

[2]Race categories exclude persons of Hispanic ethnicity. "Other" includes American Indians/Alaska Natives, Pacific Islanders, and persons of Two or more races.

[3]Refers to the Standard Metropolitan Statistical Area (MSA) status of the respondent's household as defined in 2000 by the U.S. Census Bureau. Categories include "central city of an MSA (Urban)," "in MSA but not in central city (Suburban)," and "not MSA (Rural)."

NOTE: Detail may not sum to totals because of rounding and because students could have experienced more than one type of cyber-bullying.

SOURCE: U.S. Department of Justice, Bureau of Justice Statistics, School Crime Supplement (SCS) to the National Crime Victimization Survey, 2013. (This table was prepared August 2014.)

Table 230.60. Among students ages 12–18 who reported being bullied at school or cyber-bullied anywhere during the school year, percentage reporting various frequencies of bullying and the notification of an adult at school, by selected student and school characteristics: 2013

[Standard errors appear in parentheses]

Student or school characteristic	Among students who reported being bullied at school					Among students who reported being cyber-bullied anywhere[1]				
	Once or twice in the school year	Frequency of bullying			Adult at school was notified[2]	Once or twice in the school year	Frequency of cyber-bullying			Adult at school was notified[2]
		Once or twice a month	Once or twice a week	Almost every day			Once or twice a month	Once or twice a week	Almost every day	
1	2	3	4	5	6	7	8	9	10	11
Total	67.3 (1.53)	19.4 (1.32)	7.6 (0.78)	5.7 (0.71)	38.9 (1.45)	73.2 (2.72)	15.0 (2.08)	7.9 (1.46)	3.8 (1.05)	23.3 (2.55)
Sex										
Male	68.0 (2.19)	19.2 (1.98)	7.4 (1.09)	5.5 (1.01)	38.5 (2.01)	75.2 (3.80)	9.3 (2.62)	8.1 (2.24)	7.4! (2.23)	10.5 (2.53)
Female	66.6 (2.13)	19.6 (1.89)	7.8 (1.11)	6.0 (0.94)	39.3 (2.20)	71.9 (3.40)	18.8 (2.90)	7.9 (1.82)	‡ (†)	31.6 (3.54)
Race/ethnicity[3]										
White	64.6 (2.04)	20.6 (1.70)	9.1 (1.20)	5.7 (0.87)	40.5 (2.04)	76.9 (3.27)	15.2 (2.80)	4.6! (1.53)	3.3! (1.23)	24.4 (3.08)
Black	70.2 (3.93)	18.0 (3.40)	5.6! (2.07)	6.2! (2.13)	40.0 (3.44)	68.2 (7.99)	18.9! (6.71)	‡ (†)	‡ (†)	24.5! (10.44)
Hispanic	73.8 (3.24)	17.9 (2.88)	4.4 (1.30)	4.0! (1.26)	37.5 (3.15)	73.5 (6.28)	8.9! (3.78)	12.5! (4.48)	‡ (†)	23.7 (4.92)
Asian	‡ (†)	‡ (†)	‡ (†)	‡ (†)	‡ (†)	‡ (†)	‡ (†)	‡ (†)	‡ (†)	‡ (†)
Other	66.9 (7.42)	15.2! (5.49)	‡ (†)	12.8! (5.30)	36.8 (6.34)	‡ (†)	‡ (†)	‡ (†)	‡ (†)	‡ (†)
Grade										
6th	62.4 (4.19)	22.7 (3.64)	6.5! (2.00)	8.4! (3.10)	58.3 (4.71)	‡ (†)	‡ (†)	‡ (†)	‡ (†)	‡ (†)
7th	63.8 (2.92)	17.3 (2.60)	11.4 (2.18)	7.5 (1.69)	52.3 (3.53)	65.5 (6.74)	24.9 (6.48)	‡ (†)	‡ (†)	28.0 (5.87)
8th	64.0 (3.74)	19.1 (3.05)	7.9 (2.12)	9.1 (2.30)	38.1 (3.82)	70.5 (6.04)	17.1! (5.69)	8.6! (3.16)	‡ (†)	30.4 (6.05)
9th	67.4 (3.49)	24.7 (3.48)	3.7! (1.41)	4.2! (1.59)	35.2 (3.89)	79.6 (5.43)	7.7! (3.68)	9.2! (3.89)	‡ (†)	12.4! (4.90)
10th	65.6 (4.11)	21.5 (3.56)	7.8 (2.29)	5.0! (1.79)	34.6 (3.84)	73.8 (5.76)	16.7! (5.09)	6.7! (3.30)	‡ (†)	23.9 (5.47)
11th	75.8 (3.60)	12.9 (2.83)	8.2 (2.09)	3.2! (1.41)	25.8 (3.37)	71.4 (7.36)	14.2! (5.62)	12.3! (5.36)	‡ (†)	26.7 (6.87)
12th	75.2 (5.35)	17.4 (4.42)	6.1! (2.63)	‡ (†)	22.4 (4.32)	74.6 (7.15)	13.3! (5.46)	‡ (†)	‡ (†)	21.0! (6.70)
Urbanicity[4]										
Urban	71.8 (2.86)	14.9 (2.21)	7.0 (1.36)	6.3 (1.46)	36.6 (2.64)	68.4 (4.76)	15.1 (3.76)	11.9 (3.17)	4.6! (1.99)	21.7 (4.81)
Suburban	67.0 (1.94)	20.6 (1.64)	7.1 (1.09)	5.2 (0.85)	40.7 (2.01)	77.9 (3.29)	13.2 (2.67)	5.0! (1.59)	3.9! (1.48)	24.1 (3.25)
Rural	59.7 (4.96)	23.4 (3.83)	10.2 (2.51)	6.6 (1.66)	36.9 (4.03)	65.2 (8.87)	22.2 (5.79)	10.8! (4.91)	‡ (†)	24.1 (5.37)
Control of school										
Public	67.2 (1.63)	19.7 (1.40)	7.4 (0.81)	5.7 (0.74)	38.9 (1.48)	72.0 (2.78)	16.1 (2.20)	7.8 (1.48)	4.1 (1.13)	22.5 (2.61)
Private	67.9 (5.01)	16.7 (3.74)	9.6! (2.96)	5.8! (2.09)	39.5 (5.50)	‡ (†)	‡ (†)	‡ (†)	‡ (†)	‡ (†)
Total indicating adult at school notified,[2] by frequency of bullying	36.9 (1.86)	38.3 (3.29)	55.0 (5.81)	50.0 (6.95)	†	20.2 (2.57)	21.6 (6.11)	‡ (†)	‡ (†)	†
Males indicating adult notified	39.4 (2.55)	31.8 (4.54)	45.9 (9.12)	‡ (†)	†	8.6! (2.75)	‡ (†)	‡ (†)	‡ (†)	†
Females indicating adult notified	34.7 (2.64)	43.8 (4.83)	62.5 (7.39)	43.7 (8.65)	†	28.2 (4.02)	28.6 (7.67)	‡ (†)	‡ (†)	†

†Not applicable.
!Interpret data with caution. The coefficient of variation (CV) for this estimate is between 30 and 50 percent.
‡Reporting standards not met. Either there are too few cases for a reliable estimate or the coefficient of variation (CV) is 50 percent or greater.
[1]Students who reported being cyber-bullied are those who responded that another student had done one or more of the following: posted hurtful information about them on the Internet; purposely shared private information about them on the Internet; threatened or insulted them through instant messaging; threatened or insulted them through text messaging; threatened or insulted them through e-mail; threatened or insulted them while gaming; or excluded them online.
[2]Teacher or other adult at school notified.

[3]Race categories exclude persons of Hispanic ethnicity. "Other" includes American Indians/Alaska Natives, Pacific Islanders, and persons of Two or more races.
[4]Refers to the Standard Metropolitan Statistical Area (MSA) status of the respondent's household as defined in 2000 by the U.S. Census Bureau. Categories include "central city of an MSA (Urban)," "in MSA but not in central city (Suburban)," and "not MSA (Rural)."
NOTE: "At school" includes the school building, on school property, on a school bus, or going to and from school. Detail may not sum to totals because of rounding.
SOURCE: U.S. Department of Justice, Bureau of Justice Statistics, School Crime Supplement (SCS) to the National Crime Victimization Survey, 2013. (This table was prepared September 2014.)

Table 230.62. Percentage of public school students in grades 9–12 who reported having been bullied on school property or electronically bullied during the previous 12 months, by state: Selected years, 2009 through 2013

[Standard errors appear in parentheses]

State	Bullied on school property[1]						Electronically bullied[2]					
	2009		2011		2013		2009		2011		2013	
1	2		3		4		5		6		7	
United States[3]	19.9	(0.58)	20.1	(0.68)	19.6	(0.55)	—	(†)	16.2	(0.45)	14.8	(0.54)
Alabama	19.3	(1.45)	14.1	(1.22)	20.8	(1.28)	—	(†)	12.3	(1.64)	13.5	(0.95)
Alaska	20.7	(1.29)	23.0	(1.32)	20.7	(1.35)	—	(†)	15.3	(1.04)	14.7	(1.10)
Arizona	—	(†)	—	(†)	—	(†)	—	(†)	—	(†)	—	(†)
Arkansas	—	(†)	21.9	(1.74)	25.0	(1.51)	—	(†)	16.7	(1.48)	17.6	(1.05)
California	—	(†)	—	(†)	—	(†)	—	(†)	—	(†)	—	(†)
Colorado	18.8	(1.60)	19.3	(1.33)	—	(†)	—	(†)	14.4	(1.09)	—	(†)
Connecticut	—	(†)	21.6	(1.09)	21.9	(0.96)	—	(†)	16.3	(0.81)	17.5	(1.23)
Delaware	15.9	(1.11)	16.5	(1.03)	18.5	(0.96)	—	(†)	—	(†)	13.4	(0.78)
District of Columbia	—	(†)	—	(†)	—	(†)	—	(†)	—	(†)	—	(†)
Florida	13.4	(0.51)	14.0	(0.54)	15.7	(0.50)	—	(†)	12.4	(0.53)	12.3	(0.54)
Georgia	—	(†)	19.1	(1.66)	19.5	(1.36)	—	(†)	13.6	(1.09)	13.9	(0.93)
Hawaii	—	(†)	20.3	(1.29)	18.7	(1.00)	—	(†)	14.9	(0.80)	15.6	(0.98)
Idaho	22.3	(1.03)	22.8	(1.76)	25.4	(1.12)	—	(†)	17.0	(1.18)	18.8	(1.18)
Illinois	19.6	(1.46)	19.3	(1.31)	22.2	(1.00)	—	(†)	16.0	(1.38)	16.9	(0.77)
Indiana	22.8	(1.69)	25.0	(1.38)	—	(†)	—	(†)	18.7	(1.15)	—	(†)
Iowa	—	(†)	22.5	(1.47)	—	(†)	—	(†)	16.8	(0.97)	—	(†)
Kansas	18.5	(1.21)	20.5	(1.31)	22.1	(1.57)	—	(†)	15.5	(0.88)	16.9	(0.97)
Kentucky	20.8	(1.30)	18.9	(1.24)	21.4	(1.41)	—	(†)	17.4	(1.14)	13.2	(1.06)
Louisiana	15.9	(1.88)	19.2	(1.40)	24.2	(1.64)	—	(†)	18.0	(1.53)	16.9	(1.91)
Maine	22.4	(0.49)	22.4	(0.43)	24.2	(0.66)	—	(†)	19.7	(0.55)	20.6	(0.61)
Maryland	20.9	(0.96)	21.2	(1.28)	19.6	(0.25)	—	(†)	14.2	(0.78)	14.0	(0.22)
Massachusetts	19.4	(0.89)	18.1	(1.04)	16.6	(0.98)	—	(†)	—	(†)	13.8	(0.79)
Michigan	24.0	(1.77)	22.7	(1.40)	25.3	(1.47)	—	(†)	18.0	(0.91)	18.8	(1.20)
Minnesota	—	(†)	—	(†)	—	(†)	—	(†)	—	(†)	—	(†)
Mississippi	16.0	(1.04)	15.6	(1.32)	19.2	(0.93)	—	(†)	12.5	(0.93)	11.9	(0.74)
Missouri	22.8	(1.74)	—	(†)	25.2	(1.72)	—	(†)	—	(†)	—	(†)
Montana	23.1	(1.32)	26.0	(1.06)	26.3	(0.68)	—	(†)	19.2	(0.92)	18.1	(0.62)
Nebraska	—	(†)	22.9	(0.85)	20.8	(1.10)	—	(†)	15.8	(0.81)	15.7	(0.91)
Nevada	—	(†)	—	(†)	19.7	(1.09)	—	(†)	—	(†)	15.0	(1.28)
New Hampshire	22.1	(1.53)	25.3	(1.21)	22.8	(1.05)	—	(†)	21.6	(1.27)	18.1	(1.02)
New Jersey	20.7	(1.44)	20.0	(1.57)	21.3	(1.12)	—	(†)	15.6	(1.65)	14.8	(1.25)
New Mexico	19.5	(0.80)	18.7	(0.72)	18.2	(0.95)	—	(†)	13.2	(0.66)	13.1	(0.67)
New York	18.2	(1.01)	17.7	(0.66)	19.7	(1.43)	—	(†)	16.2	(0.68)	15.3	(0.89)
North Carolina	16.6	(1.00)	20.5	(1.34)	19.2	(0.94)	—	(†)	15.7	(0.83)	12.5	(1.11)
North Dakota	21.1	(1.29)	24.9	(1.24)	25.4	(1.28)	—	(†)	17.4	(1.15)	17.1	(0.82)
Ohio[4]	—	(†)	22.7	(1.83)	20.8	(1.40)	—	(†)	14.7	(1.08)	15.1	(1.31)
Oklahoma	17.5	(1.25)	16.7	(1.27)	18.6	(1.08)	—	(†)	15.6	(1.21)	14.3	(1.33)
Oregon	—	(†)	—	(†)	—	(†)	—	(†)	—	(†)	—	(†)
Pennsylvania	19.2	(1.18)	—	(†)	—	(†)	—	(†)	—	(†)	—	(†)
Rhode Island	16.3	(0.85)	19.1	(1.74)	18.1	(1.00)	—	(†)	15.3	(1.14)	14.3	(1.11)
South Carolina	15.1	(1.53)	18.3	(1.36)	20.2	(1.33)	—	(†)	15.6	(1.44)	13.8	(1.00)
South Dakota[4]	—	(†)	26.7	(1.25)	24.3	(2.05)	—	(†)	19.6	(0.94)	17.8	(1.05)
Tennessee	17.3	(1.24)	17.5	(0.88)	21.1	(1.22)	—	(†)	13.9	(0.69)	15.5	(0.94)
Texas	18.7	(1.06)	16.5	(0.73)	19.1	(1.06)	—	(†)	13.0	(0.66)	13.8	(1.04)
Utah	18.8	(1.05)	21.7	(0.97)	21.8	(0.99)	—	(†)	16.6	(1.12)	16.9	(0.87)
Vermont	—	(†)	—	(†)	—	(†)	—	(†)	15.2	(0.54)	18.0	(0.32)
Virginia	—	(†)	20.3	(1.37)	21.9	(0.87)	—	(†)	14.8	(1.49)	14.5	(0.61)
Washington	—	(†)	—	(†)	—	(†)	—	(†)	—	(†)	—	(†)
West Virginia	23.5	(1.33)	18.6	(1.71)	22.1	(1.72)	—	(†)	15.5	(1.18)	17.2	(0.89)
Wisconsin	22.5	(1.28)	24.0	(1.35)	22.7	(1.23)	—	(†)	16.6	(0.74)	17.6	(0.86)
Wyoming	24.4	(0.93)	25.0	(0.98)	23.3	(0.82)	—	(†)	18.7	(0.80)	16.1	(0.71)

—Not available.
†Not applicable.
[1]Bullying was defined for respondents as "when one or more students tease, threaten, spread rumors about, hit, shove, or hurt another student over and over again." "On school property" was not defined for survey respondents.
[2]Survey respondents were asked about being electronically bullied ("being bullied through e-mail, chat rooms, instant messaging, websites, or texting"). Data on electronic bullying were not collected in 2009.
[3]Data for the U.S. total include both public and private schools and were collected through a national survey representing the entire country.
[4]Data include both public and private schools.

NOTE: State-level data include public schools only, with the exception of data for Ohio and South Dakota. Data for the U.S. total, Ohio, and South Dakota include both public and private schools. For specific states, a given year's data may be unavailable (1) because the state did not participate in the survey that year; (2) because the state omitted this particular survey item from the state-level questionnaire; or (3) because the state had an overall response rate of less than 60 percent (the overall response rate is the school response rate multiplied by the student response rate).
SOURCE: Centers for Disease Control and Prevention, Division of Adolescent and School Health, Youth Risk Behavior Surveillance System (YRBSS), 2009 through 2013. (This table was prepared September 2014.)

Table 230.65. Percentage of public schools reporting selected types of cyber-bullying problems occurring at school or away from school at least once a week, by selected school characteristics: 2009–10

[Standard errors appear in parentheses]

School characteristic	Cyber-bullying among students		School environment is affected by cyber-bullying		Staff resources are used to deal with cyber-bullying	
1	2		3		4	
All public schools	**7.9**	**(0.49)**	**4.4**	**(0.34)**	**3.8**	**(0.39)**
School level[1]						
Primary	1.5	(0.43)	0.9 !	(0.38)	0.9 !	(0.34)
Middle	18.6	(1.48)	9.8	(1.07)	8.5	(1.01)
High school	17.6	(1.11)	9.9	(0.85)	8.6	(0.81)
Combined	12.6	(3.34)	7.4 !	(2.64)	‡	(†)
Enrollment size						
Less than 300	4.8	(1.21)	3.2 !	(1.05)	2.9 !	(0.89)
300–499...............................	4.6	(0.74)	2.8	(0.57)	2.7	(0.64)
500–999...............................	9.3	(0.63)	4.6	(0.57)	3.7	(0.58)
1,000 or more	19.2	(1.42)	10.7	(1.26)	9.4	(0.96)
Locale						
City.......................................	5.7	(0.62)	3.8	(0.57)	3.6	(0.70)
Suburban	8.5	(0.85)	4.0	(0.48)	3.7	(0.46)
Town.....................................	9.6	(1.45)	5.8	(1.15)	4.1	(1.06)
Rural.....................................	8.4	(1.07)	4.5	(0.89)	4.0	(0.82)
Percent combined enrollment of Black, Hispanic, Asian/Pacific Islander, and American Indian/Alaska Native students						
Less than 5 percent	12.8	(2.05)	7.7	(1.66)	4.7	(1.32)
5 percent to less than 20 percent	10.1	(0.90)	5.1	(0.59)	4.7	(0.72)
20 percent to less than 50 percent	6.7	(0.77)	3.6	(0.67)	3.9	(0.74)
50 percent or more	5.3	(0.60)	3.1	(0.41)	2.8	(0.54)
Percent of students eligible for free or reduced-price lunch						
0–25......................................	10.8	(1.08)	5.0	(0.62)	4.9	(0.72)
26–50....................................	9.7	(1.14)	4.3	(0.55)	3.4	(0.48)
51–75....................................	6.8	(0.83)	4.9	(0.78)	4.1	(0.78)
76–100..................................	4.5	(0.96)	3.3	(0.91)	3.0	(0.73)
Student/teacher ratio[2]						
Less than 12	6.8	(1.36)	4.1	(1.20)	3.5	(1.02)
12–16....................................	7.4	(0.71)	4.0	(0.48)	3.8	(0.66)
More than 16........................	8.7	(0.75)	4.8	(0.60)	3.9	(0.56)
Prevalence of violent incidents[3]						
No violent incidents..............	2.4 !	(0.90)	‡	(†)	‡	(†)
Any violent incidents	9.9	(0.53)	5.6	(0.40)	5.1	(0.53)

†Not applicable.

!Interpret data with caution. The coefficient of variation (CV) for this estimate is between 30 and 50 percent.

‡Reporting standards not met. Either there are too few cases for a reliable estimate or the coefficient of variation (CV) is 50 percent or greater.

[1]Primary schools are defined as schools in which the lowest grade is not higher than grade 3 and the highest grade is not higher than grade 8. Middle schools are defined as schools in which the lowest grade is not lower than grade 4 and the highest grade is not higher than grade 9. High schools are defined as schools in which the lowest grade is not lower than grade 9 and the highest grade is not higher than grade 12. Combined schools include all other combinations of grades, including K–12 schools.

[2]Student/teacher ratio was calculated by dividing the total number of students enrolled in the school by the total number of full-time-equivalent (FTE) teachers. Information regarding the total number of FTE teachers was obtained from the Common Core of Data (CCD), the sampling frame for SSOCS.

[3]"Violent incidents" include rape or attempted rape, sexual battery other than rape, physical attack or fight with or without a weapon, threat of physical attack or fight with or without a weapon, and robbery with or without a weapon. "At school" was defined for respondents to include activities that happen in school buildings, on school grounds, on school buses, and at places that hold school-sponsored events or activities. Respondents were instructed to respond only for those times that were during normal school hours or when school activities and events were in session. NOTE: Includes schools reporting that cyber-bullying happens either "daily" or "at least once a week." "Cyber-bullying" was defined for respondents as occurring "when willful and repeated harm is inflicted through the use of computers, cell phones, or other electronic devices." Responses were provided by the principal or the person most knowledgeable about crime and safety issues at the school. Respondents were instructed to include cyber-bullying "problems that can occur anywhere (both at your school and away from school)."

SOURCE: U.S. Department of Education, National Center for Education Statistics, 2009–10 School Survey on Crime and Safety (SSOCS), 2010. (This table was prepared September 2013.)

Table 230.70. Percentage of students ages 12–18 who reported being afraid of attack or harm, by location and selected student and school characteristics: Selected years, 1995 through 2013

[Standard errors appear in parentheses]

Student or school characteristic	1995	1999	2001	2003	2005	2007[1]	2009[1]	2011[1]	2013[1]
1	2	3	4	5	6	7	8	9	10
At school									
Total	11.8 (0.39)	7.3 (0.37)	6.4 (0.31)	6.1 (0.31)	6.4 (0.39)	5.3 (0.33)	4.2 (0.33)	3.7 (0.28)	3.5 (0.33)
Sex									
Male	10.8 (0.51)	6.5 (0.44)	6.4 (0.38)	5.3 (0.34)	6.1 (0.56)	4.6 (0.42)	3.7 (0.38)	3.7 (0.41)	3.1 (0.38)
Female	12.8 (0.58)	8.2 (0.53)	6.4 (0.43)	6.9 (0.48)	6.7 (0.47)	6.0 (0.45)	4.8 (0.51)	3.8 (0.36)	4.0 (0.48)
Race/ethnicity[2]									
White	8.1 (0.36)	5.0 (0.32)	4.9 (0.35)	4.1 (0.35)	4.6 (0.39)	4.2 (0.37)	3.3 (0.35)	3.0 (0.31)	2.6 (0.33)
Black	20.3 (1.31)	13.5 (1.27)	8.9 (0.87)	10.7 (1.22)	9.2 (1.19)	8.6 (1.18)	7.0 (1.12)	4.9 (1.03)	4.6 (0.85)
Hispanic	20.9 (1.27)	11.7 (1.20)	10.6 (1.07)	9.5 (0.65)	10.3 (1.16)	7.1 (0.88)	4.9 (0.89)	4.8 (0.59)	4.9 (0.78)
Asian	— (†)	— (†)	— (†)	— (†)	6.2 ! (2.09)	2.3 ! (1.05)	5.9 ! (2.25)	4.2 ! (1.52)	3.1 ! (1.09)
Other	13.5 (1.58)	6.7 (1.09)	6.4 (1.11)	5.0 (1.31)	5.7 (1.63)	3.3 ! (1.09)	‡ (†)	4.1 ! (1.31)	3.8 ! (1.44)
Grade									
6th	14.3 (1.13)	10.9 (1.37)	10.6 (1.26)	10.0 (1.35)	9.5 (1.14)	9.9 (1.33)	6.4 (1.20)	5.6 (1.08)	4.7 (1.01)
7th	15.3 (1.02)	9.5 (0.79)	9.2 (0.95)	8.2 (0.86)	9.1 (1.04)	6.7 (0.86)	6.2 (1.06)	4.5 (0.69)	4.3 (0.69)
8th	13.0 (0.84)	8.1 (0.74)	7.6 (0.69)	6.3 (0.68)	7.1 (0.95)	4.6 (0.71)	3.5 (0.75)	4.6 (0.71)	3.3 (0.78)
9th	11.6 (0.82)	7.1 (0.74)	5.5 (0.63)	6.3 (0.61)	5.9 (0.71)	5.5 (0.87)	4.6 (0.75)	4.2 (0.66)	3.4 (0.71)
10th	11.0 (0.82)	7.1 (0.77)	5.0 (0.71)	4.4 (0.67)	5.5 (0.89)	5.2 (0.87)	4.6 (0.79)	3.9 (0.63)	4.4 (0.75)
11th	8.9 (0.80)	4.8 (0.68)	4.8 (0.65)	4.7 (0.66)	4.6 (0.73)	3.1 (0.63)	3.3 (0.74)	1.8 (0.48)	2.6 (0.55)
12th	7.8 (0.94)	4.8 (0.88)	2.9 (0.55)	3.7 (0.53)	3.3 (0.69)	3.1 (0.65)	1.9 ! (0.57)	2.2 (0.57)	2.0 (0.56)
Urbanicity[3]									
Urban	18.4 (0.84)	11.6 (0.81)	9.7 (0.59)	9.5 (0.68)	10.5 (0.92)	7.1 (0.81)	6.9 (0.84)	5.2 (0.60)	4.5 (0.60)
Suburban	9.8 (0.49)	6.2 (0.42)	4.8 (0.33)	4.8 (0.30)	4.7 (0.41)	4.4 (0.41)	3.0 (0.33)	3.1 (0.39)	3.0 (0.38)
Rural	8.6 (0.80)	4.8 (0.70)	6.0 (0.97)	4.7 (0.93)	5.1 (0.97)	4.9 (0.59)	3.9 (0.63)	3.0 (0.63)	3.3 (0.62)
Control of school									
Public	12.2 (0.43)	7.7 (0.38)	6.6 (0.33)	6.4 (0.34)	6.6 (0.42)	5.5 (0.34)	4.4 (0.35)	3.9 (0.30)	3.5 (0.35)
Private	7.3 (1.01)	3.6 (0.81)	4.6 (0.92)	3.0 (0.73)	3.8 (0.82)	2.5 ! (0.89)	1.9 ! (0.74)	1.5 ! (0.64)	2.6 ! (0.83)
Away from school									
Total	— (†)	5.7 (0.32)	4.6 (0.28)	5.4 (0.29)	5.2 (0.33)	3.5 (0.29)	3.3 (0.32)	2.4 (0.23)	2.7 (0.35)
Sex									
Male	— (†)	4.1 (0.34)	3.7 (0.31)	4.0 (0.30)	4.6 (0.42)	2.4 (0.31)	2.5 (0.34)	2.0 (0.27)	2.4 (0.40)
Female	— (†)	7.4 (0.49)	5.6 (0.42)	6.8 (0.48)	5.8 (0.48)	4.5 (0.40)	4.1 (0.51)	2.7 (0.30)	3.0 (0.44)
Race/ethnicity[2]									
White	— (†)	4.3 (0.32)	3.7 (0.29)	3.8 (0.31)	4.2 (0.40)	2.5 (0.28)	2.2 (0.28)	1.6 (0.24)	1.6 (0.30)
Black	— (†)	8.7 (1.00)	6.3 (0.87)	10.0 (1.13)	7.3 (0.96)	4.9 (0.73)	5.7 (1.10)	3.5 (0.86)	3.6 (0.78)
Hispanic	— (†)	8.9 (1.03)	6.5 (0.75)	7.4 (0.80)	6.2 (0.84)	5.9 (0.80)	3.9 (0.70)	3.3 (0.50)	4.5 (0.86)
Asian	— (†)	— (†)	— (†)	— (†)	7.4 ! (2.89)	‡ (†)	7.1 ! (2.50)	3.2 ! (1.15)	2.9 ! (1.03)
Other	— (†)	5.4 (1.04)	6.6 (1.32)	3.9 (1.02)	3.1 ! (1.28)	‡ (†)	4.0 ! (1.79)	2.5 ! (1.05)	3.2 ! (1.42)
Grade									
6th	— (†)	7.8 (1.11)	6.3 (1.15)	6.8 (1.01)	5.6 (0.99)	5.9 (1.20)	3.3 (0.89)	3.0 (0.86)	3.9 (0.88)
7th	— (†)	6.1 (0.72)	5.5 (0.80)	6.7 (0.80)	7.5 (0.89)	3.0 (0.55)	4.0 (0.78)	2.7 (0.58)	2.2 (0.54)
8th	— (†)	5.5 (0.66)	4.4 (0.61)	5.3 (0.71)	5.0 (0.72)	3.6 (0.65)	3.3 (0.72)	2.1 (0.43)	2.4 ! (0.80)
9th	— (†)	4.6 (0.63)	4.5 (0.62)	4.3 (0.55)	3.8 (0.61)	4.0 (0.75)	2.6 (0.62)	3.5 (0.65)	2.8 (0.59)
10th	— (†)	4.8 (0.63)	4.2 (0.63)	5.3 (0.67)	4.7 (0.66)	3.0 (0.60)	5.5 (0.96)	1.7 (0.46)	4.4 (0.83)
11th	— (†)	5.9 (0.72)	4.7 (0.62)	4.7 (0.69)	4.2 (0.74)	2.3 (0.56)	2.2 (0.56)	2.9 (0.70)	2.2 (0.47)
12th	— (†)	6.1 (0.86)	3.3 (0.62)	4.9 (0.72)	5.4 (0.98)	3.2 (0.61)	2.1 (0.63)	1.0 ! (0.37)	1.3 ! (0.46)
Urbanicity[3]									
Urban	— (†)	9.1 (0.82)	7.4 (0.68)	8.1 (0.60)	6.7 (0.61)	5.3 (0.67)	5.8 (0.87)	3.4 (0.42)	4.0 (0.54)
Suburban	— (†)	5.0 (0.31)	3.8 (0.33)	4.4 (0.34)	4.6 (0.43)	2.7 (0.36)	2.5 (0.33)	2.2 (0.30)	2.2 (0.42)
Rural	— (†)	3.0 (0.71)	3.0 (0.59)	4.0 (0.69)	4.7 (0.98)	2.8 (0.54)	1.9 (0.48)	1.0 ! (0.35)	1.7 (0.49)
Control of school									
Public	— (†)	5.8 (0.32)	4.6 (0.30)	5.4 (0.31)	5.2 (0.34)	3.6 (0.30)	3.5 (0.33)	2.4 (0.23)	2.7 (0.36)
Private	— (†)	5.0 (0.92)	5.1 (1.08)	4.7 (0.89)	4.9 (1.41)	2.1 ! (0.72)	1.8 ! (0.71)	1.6 ! (0.68)	2.0 ! (0.70)

—Not available.
†Not applicable.
!Interpret data with caution. The coefficient of variation (CV) for this estimate is between 30 and 50 percent.
‡Reporting standards not met. Either there are too few cases for a reliable estimate or the coefficient of variation (CV) is 50 percent or greater.
[1]Starting in 2007, the reference period was the school year, whereas in prior survey years the reference period was the previous 6 months. Cognitive testing showed that estimates from 2007 onward are comparable to previous years.
[2]Race categories exclude persons of Hispanic ethnicity. "Other" includes American Indians/Alaska Natives, Asians (prior to 2005), Pacific Islanders, and, from 2003 onward, persons of Two or more races. Due to changes in racial/ethnic categories, comparisons of race/ethnicity across years should be made with caution.

[3]Refers to the Standard Metropolitan Statistical Area (MSA) status of the respondent's household as defined in 2000 by the U.S. Census Bureau. Categories include "central city of an MSA (Urban)," "in MSA but not in central city (Suburban)," and "not MSA (Rural)."
NOTE: "At school" includes the school building, on school property, on a school bus, and, from 2001 onward, going to and from school. Students were asked if they "never," "almost never," "sometimes," or "most of the time" feared that someone would attack or harm them at school or away from school. Students responding "sometimes" or "most of the time" were considered fearful. For the 2001 survey only, the wording was changed from "attack or harm" to "attack or threaten to attack."
SOURCE: U.S. Department of Justice, Bureau of Justice Statistics, School Crime Supplement (SCS) to the National Crime Victimization Survey, selected years, 1995 through 2013. (This table was prepared September 2014.)

Table 230.80. Percentage of students ages 12–18 who reported avoiding one or more places in school or avoiding school activities or classes because of fear of attack or harm, by selected student and school characteristics: Selected years, 1995 through 2013

[Standard errors appear in parentheses]

Type of avoidance and student or school characteristic	1995		1999		2001		2003		2005		2007[1]		2009[1]		2011[1]		2013[1]	
1	2		3		4		5		6		7		8		9		10	
Total, any avoidance	—	(†)	6.9	(0.34)	6.1	(0.32)	5.0	(0.30)	5.5	(0.32)	7.2	(0.36)	5.0	(0.35)	5.5	(0.34)	4.7	(0.31)
Avoided one or more places in school																		
Total	8.7	(0.29)	4.6	(0.29)	4.7	(0.27)	4.0	(0.27)	4.5	(0.28)	5.8	(0.31)	4.0	(0.32)	4.7	(0.30)	3.7	(0.27)
Entrance to the school	2.1	(0.15)	1.1	(0.14)	1.2	(0.11)	1.2	(0.11)	1.0	(0.14)	1.5	(0.15)	0.9	(0.15)	0.9	(0.13)	0.8	(0.14)
Hallways or stairs in school	4.2	(0.21)	2.1	(0.17)	2.1	(0.18)	1.7	(0.17)	2.1	(0.21)	2.6	(0.21)	2.2	(0.23)	2.5	(0.21)	1.7	(0.18)
Parts of the school cafeteria	2.5	(0.18)	1.3	(0.15)	1.4	(0.16)	1.2	(0.13)	1.8	(0.16)	1.9	(0.19)	1.1	(0.17)	1.8	(0.18)	1.4	(0.19)
Any school restrooms	4.4	(0.22)	2.1	(0.19)	2.2	(0.19)	2.0	(0.16)	2.1	(0.20)	2.6	(0.24)	1.4	(0.19)	1.7	(0.19)	1.3	(0.16)
Other places inside the school building	2.5	(0.18)	1.4	(0.17)	1.4	(0.14)	1.2	(0.14)	1.4	(0.18)	1.5	(0.17)	1.0	(0.16)	1.1	(0.15)	0.8	(0.13)
Sex																		
Male	8.8	(0.43)	4.6	(0.35)	4.7	(0.40)	3.9	(0.34)	4.9	(0.46)	6.1	(0.47)	3.9	(0.45)	3.9	(0.42)	3.4	(0.34)
Female	8.5	(0.46)	4.6	(0.39)	4.6	(0.35)	4.1	(0.37)	4.1	(0.40)	5.5	(0.41)	4.0	(0.42)	5.5	(0.40)	3.9	(0.43)
Race/ethnicity[2]																		
White	7.1	(0.32)	3.8	(0.27)	3.9	(0.30)	3.0	(0.27)	3.6	(0.30)	5.3	(0.36)	3.3	(0.38)	4.4	(0.38)	3.0	(0.34)
Black	12.1	(1.01)	6.7	(0.90)	6.6	(0.75)	5.1	(0.79)	7.2	(0.98)	8.3	(1.02)	6.1	(1.04)	4.5	(0.80)	3.3	(0.79)
Hispanic	12.9	(0.97)	6.2	(0.73)	5.5	(0.71)	6.3	(0.70)	6.0	(0.80)	6.8	(0.82)	4.8	(0.86)	6.0	(0.68)	4.9	(0.63)
Asian	—	(†)	—	(†)	—	(†)	—	(†)	2.5 !	(0.87)	‡	(†)	3.7 !	(1.53)	2.7 !	(1.06)	3.8 !	(1.26)
Other	11.1	(1.61)	5.4	(0.99)	6.2	(1.16)	4.4	(1.02)	4.3 !	(1.86)	3.5 !	(1.22)	‡	(†)	3.3 !	(1.04)	5.9	(1.72)
Grade																		
6th	11.6	(0.99)	5.9	(0.92)	6.8	(0.93)	5.6	(0.94)	7.9	(1.27)	7.8	(1.20)	7.1	(1.13)	6.9	(0.99)	4.4	(0.92)
7th	11.8	(0.89)	6.1	(0.72)	6.2	(0.79)	5.7	(0.73)	5.8	(0.93)	7.5	(0.86)	5.5	(0.86)	5.1	(0.76)	4.6	(0.72)
8th	8.8	(0.77)	5.5	(0.70)	5.2	(0.62)	4.7	(0.63)	4.5	(0.67)	5.9	(0.84)	4.8	(0.93)	5.2	(0.75)	2.7	(0.62)
9th	9.5	(0.71)	5.3	(0.63)	5.0	(0.61)	5.1	(0.62)	5.2	(0.78)	6.7	(0.81)	4.5	(0.89)	3.7	(0.67)	5.1	(0.78)
10th	7.8	(0.75)	4.7	(0.61)	4.2	(0.64)	3.1	(0.54)	4.2	(0.65)	5.5	(0.80)	4.2	(0.88)	5.4	(0.72)	4.0	(0.72)
11th	6.9	(0.64)	2.5	(0.46)	2.8	(0.43)	2.5	(0.53)	3.3	(0.58)	4.2	(0.70)	1.2 !	(0.44)	3.6	(0.65)	2.5	(0.61)
12th	4.1	(0.74)	2.4	(0.51)	3.0	(0.64)	1.2 !	(0.41)	1.3 !	(0.41)	3.2	(0.71)	1.6 !	(0.50)	3.7	(0.71)	2.3	(0.62)
Urbanicity[3]																		
Urban	11.7	(0.73)	5.8	(0.48)	6.0	(0.52)	5.7	(0.59)	6.3	(0.67)	6.1	(0.65)	5.5	(0.69)	5.3	(0.61)	4.3	(0.54)
Suburban	7.9	(0.40)	4.7	(0.38)	4.3	(0.38)	3.5	(0.30)	3.8	(0.36)	5.2	(0.38)	3.1	(0.38)	4.6	(0.36)	3.3	(0.33)
Rural	7.0	(0.65)	3.0	(0.56)	3.9	(0.70)	2.8	(0.53)	4.2	(0.74)	6.9	(0.69)	4.3	(0.80)	3.5	(0.54)	3.5	(0.68)
School control																		
Public	9.3	(0.33)	5.0	(0.31)	4.9	(0.29)	4.2	(0.29)	4.8	(0.30)	6.2	(0.35)	4.2	(0.34)	4.9	(0.32)	3.9	(0.29)
Private	2.2	(0.47)	1.6	(0.45)	2.0 !	(0.69)	1.5 !	(0.49)	1.4 !	(0.55)	1.4 !	(0.54)	1.8 !	(0.73)	2.1 !	(0.70)	1.0 !	(0.49)
Avoided school activities or classes																		
Total	—	(†)	3.2	(0.22)	2.3	(0.18)	1.9	(0.18)	2.1	(0.23)	2.6	(0.23)	2.1	(0.25)	2.0	(0.20)	2.0	(0.21)
Any activities[4]	1.7	(0.15)	0.8	(0.10)	1.1	(0.12)	1.0	(0.11)	1.0	(0.16)	1.8	(0.20)	1.3	(0.20)	1.2	(0.16)	1.0	(0.13)
Any classes	—	(†)	0.6	(0.09)	0.6	(0.09)	0.6	(0.10)	0.7	(0.13)	0.7	(0.12)	0.6	(0.13)	0.7	(0.10)	0.5	(0.10)
Stayed home from school	—	(†)	2.3	(0.19)	1.1	(0.13)	0.8	(0.11)	0.7	(0.11)	0.8	(0.13)	0.6	(0.14)	0.8	(0.12)	0.9	(0.13)

—Not available.
†Not applicable.
!Interpret data with caution. The coefficient of variation (CV) for this estimate is between 30 and 50 percent.
‡Reporting standards not met. Either there are too few cases for a reliable estimate or the coefficient of variation (CV) is 50 percent or greater.
[1]Starting in 2007, the reference period was the school year, whereas in prior survey years the reference period was the previous 6 months. Cognitive testing showed that estimates from 2007 onward are comparable to previous years.
[2]Race categories exclude persons of Hispanic ethnicity. "Other" includes American Indians/Alaska Natives, Asians (prior to 2005), Pacific Islanders, and, from 2003 onward, persons of Two or more races. Due to changes in racial/ethnic categories, comparisons of race/ethnicity across years should be made with caution.

[3]Refers to the Standard Metropolitan Statistical Area (MSA) status of the respondent's household as defined in 2000 by the U.S. Census Bureau. Categories include "central city of an MSA (Urban)," "in MSA but not in central city (Suburban)," and "not MSA (Rural)."
[4]Before 2007, students were asked whether they avoided "any extracurricular activities." Starting in 2007, the survey wording was changed to "any activities."
NOTE: Students were asked whether they avoided places or activities because they thought that someone might attack or harm them. For the 2001 survey only, the wording was changed from "attack or harm" to "attack or threaten to attack." Detail may not sum to totals because of rounding and because students reporting more than one type of avoidance were counted only once in the totals.
SOURCE: U.S. Department of Justice, Bureau of Justice Statistics, School Crime Supplement (SCS) to the National Crime Victimization Survey, selected years, 1995 through 2013. (This table was prepared September 2014.)

Table 230.90. Percentage of public and private school teachers who agreed that student misbehavior and student tardiness and class cutting interfered with their teaching, by selected teacher and school characteristics: Selected years, 1987–88 through 2011–12

[Standard errors appear in parentheses]

Teacher or school characteristic	Student misbehavior interfered with teaching							Student tardiness and class cutting interfered with teaching						
	1987–88	1990–91	1993–94	1999–2000	2003–04	2007–08	2011–12	1987–88	1990–91	1993–94	1999–2000	2003–04	2007–08	2011–12
1	2	3	4	5	6	7	8	9	10	11	12	13	14	15
Total	40.2 (0.33)	33.8 (0.31)	41.3 (0.34)	38.6 (0.39)	35.1 (0.58)	34.1 (0.50)	38.5 (0.61)	32.6 (0.28)	—	25.4 (0.28)	29.3 (0.30)	31.3 (0.44)	31.5 (0.60)	35.3 (0.46)
Years of teaching experience														
3 or fewer	42.1 (0.95)	35.5 (0.75)	44.8 (0.98)	41.5 (0.79)	39.2 (2.15)	37.3 (1.00)	43.2 (1.21)	34.6 (0.89)	(†)	27.8 (0.71)	32.3 (0.73)	34.0 (1.20)	34.3 (1.01)	38.5 (1.28)
4 to 9	40.1 (0.65)	33.6 (0.69)	41.9 (0.61)	40.5 (0.66)	36.2 (0.75)	35.1 (1.02)	39.8 (1.05)	31.4 (0.50)	(†)	25.5 (0.59)	30.1 (0.55)	32.0 (0.70)	32.6 (1.01)	36.0 (0.96)
10 to 19	39.5 (0.41)	33.0 (0.52)	40.7 (0.57)	36.4 (0.65)	34.0 (0.83)	33.6 (0.83)	38.0 (0.92)	31.7 (0.35)	(†)	24.3 (0.48)	26.7 (0.55)	30.7 (0.75)	30.9 (1.04)	35.3 (0.93)
20 or more	40.7 (0.73)	34.1 (0.70)	40.1 (0.53)	37.6 (0.57)	32.8 (0.68)	31.5 (0.82)	35.4 (0.97)	34.3 (0.61)	(†)	25.5 (0.35)	29.3 (0.51)	29.7 (0.67)	29.1 (0.90)	33.0 (0.95)
School level[1]														
Elementary	39.2 (0.53)	34.1 (0.45)	40.9 (0.54)	39.1 (0.57)	33.8 (0.74)	32.6 (0.73)	38.6 (0.92)	22.6 (0.35)	(†)	17.2 (0.41)	24.2 (0.42)	26.5 (0.57)	25.6 (0.76)	31.0 (0.71)
Secondary	43.2 (0.43)	34.9 (0.43)	43.7 (0.35)	39.5 (0.42)	40.0 (0.60)	38.8 (0.74)	40.5 (0.80)	49.9 (0.45)	(†)	43.0 (0.37)	41.5 (0.46)	43.8 (0.65)	45.4 (0.81)	45.3 (0.69)
School control														
Public[2]	42.3 (0.36)	35.7 (0.34)	44.1 (0.40)	40.8 (0.42)	37.2 (0.52)	36.0 (0.57)	40.7 (0.65)	34.7 (0.29)	(†)	27.9 (0.32)	31.5 (0.35)	33.4 (0.45)	33.4 (0.64)	37.6 (0.51)
Private	24.2 (0.95)	20.0 (0.63)	22.4 (0.43)	24.1 (0.61)	20.7 (2.47)	20.6 (0.72)	22.0 (1.05)	17.2 (0.73)	(†)	8.6 (0.42)	15.0 (0.43)	16.9 (1.11)	17.9 (0.72)	18.8 (1.06)
School enrollment														
Under 200	31.9 (0.89)	25.0 (0.82)	31.1 (0.72)	32.5 (0.93)	29.4 (2.44)	29.9 (1.10)	33.9 (1.27)	24.5 (0.94)	(†)	14.7 (0.51)	21.7 (0.71)	24.9 (1.52)	26.1 (0.91)	29.4 (1.03)
200 to 499	36.6 (0.52)	30.6 (0.60)	36.9 (0.72)	36.4 (0.57)	30.7 (0.91)	32.9 (0.87)	37.3 (0.87)	23.9 (0.37)	(†)	16.9 (0.52)	25.0 (0.60)	26.2 (0.73)	27.4 (0.94)	32.1 (0.92)
500 to 749	41.2 (0.63)	34.9 (0.64)	41.9 (0.74)	40.0 (0.82)	34.0 (0.94)	34.4 (1.28)	37.4 (1.38)	29.0 (0.66)	(†)	21.2 (0.67)	27.1 (0.63)	28.2 (0.83)	28.4 (1.25)	32.5 (1.02)
750 to 999	44.6 (1.10)	39.3 (1.03)	47.6 (0.85)	39.8 (1.32)	37.2 (1.45)	32.4 (1.34)	41.9 (1.82)	35.6 (1.05)	(†)	30.2 (1.19)	27.7 (1.00)	31.0 (1.15)	29.6 (1.24)	36.7 (1.87)
1,000 or more	47.0 (0.75)	38.8 (0.76)	48.0 (0.69)	41.9 (0.65)	43.7 (0.85)	37.9 (1.01)	40.9 (0.97)	54.2 (0.72)	(†)	46.8 (0.70)	41.7 (0.77)	44.9 (0.97)	43.1 (1.13)	44.2 (0.92)
Locale[3]														
City	—	—	(†)	(†)	41.8 (1.14)	39.9 (1.08)	(‡)	—	(†)	(†)	—	37.3 (0.89)	38.5 (0.95)	(‡)
Suburban	—	—	(†)	(†)	32.3 (0.77)	31.7 (0.78)	(‡)	—	(†)	(†)	—	28.5 (0.74)	28.8 (0.86)	(‡)
Town	—	—	(†)	(†)	34.7 (1.32)	34.7 (1.32)	(‡)	—	(†)	(†)	—	31.7 (1.12)	34.0 (1.68)	(‡)
Rural	—	—	(†)	(†)	31.1 (1.31)	30.8 (0.97)	(‡)	—	(†)	(†)	—	27.9 (0.88)	26.4 (0.92)	(‡)

—Not available.
†Not applicable.
‡Reporting standards not met. Data may be suppressed because the response rate is under 50 percent, there are too few cases for a reliable estimate, or the coefficient of variation (CV) is 50 percent or greater.
[1]Elementary schools are those with any of grades kindergarten through grade 6 and none of grades 9 through 12. Secondary schools have any of grades 7 through 12 and none of grades kindergarten through grade 6. Combined elementary/secondary schools are included in totals but are not shown separately.
[2]Includes traditional public and public charter schools.

[3]Substantial improvements in geocoding technology and changes in the Office of Management and Budget's definition of metropolitan and nonmetropolitan areas allow for more precision in describing an area as of 2003–04. Comparisons with earlier years are not possible.
NOTE: Teachers who taught only prekindergarten students are excluded. Includes both teachers who "strongly" agreed and those who "somewhat" agreed that student misbehavior or student tardiness and class cutting interfered with their teaching. Some data have been revised from previously published figures.
SOURCE: U.S. Department of Education, National Center for Education Statistics, Schools and Staffing Survey (SASS), "Public School Teacher Data File" and "Private School Teacher Data File," 1987–88, 1990–91, 1993–94, 1999–2000, 2003–04, 2007–08, and 2011–12; and "Charter School Teacher Data File," 1999–2000. (This table was prepared October 2013.)

Table 230.92. Percentage of public and private school teachers who agreed that other teachers and the principal enforced school rules, by selected teacher and school characteristics: Selected years, 1987–88 through 2011–12

[Standard errors appear in parentheses]

Teacher or school characteristic	Other teachers enforced school rules[1]							Principal enforced school rules[2]						
	1987–88	1990–91	1993–94	1999–2000	2003–04	2007–08	2011–12	1987–88	1990–91	1993–94	1999–2000	2003–04	2007–08	2011–12
1	2	3	4	5	6	7	8	9	10	11	12	13	14	15
Total	65.1 (0.30)	73.4 (0.34)	63.8 (0.36)	64.4 (0.35)	72.4 (0.41)	71.8 (0.47)	68.8 (0.48)	83.7 (0.22)	87.4 (0.26)	81.8 (0.31)	83.0 (0.28)	87.8 (0.30)	88.5 (0.34)	84.4 (0.41)
Years of teaching experience														
3 or fewer	68.6 (0.93)	76.1 (0.88)	68.8 (0.92)	69.4 (0.71)	76.6 (0.91)	73.6 (1.07)	70.2 (1.27)	85.0 (0.52)	88.4 (0.49)	85.1 (0.59)	84.5 (0.52)	88.6 (0.66)	89.9 (0.68)	86.6 (1.15)
4 to 9	65.3 (0.71)	72.7 (0.69)	63.0 (0.78)	61.6 (0.62)	70.6 (0.70)	69.5 (0.88)	66.6 (0.88)	84.1 (0.45)	87.4 (0.55)	80.7 (0.63)	82.7 (0.49)	86.9 (0.57)	88.2 (0.61)	84.6 (0.72)
10 to 19	64.3 (0.49)	72.9 (0.48)	63.1 (0.55)	64.6 (0.65)	71.4 (0.76)	71.0 (0.73)	68.3 (0.86)	83.9 (0.35)	87.5 (0.43)	82.4 (0.41)	83.1 (0.49)	87.8 (0.53)	87.2 (0.62)	82.3 (0.74)
20 or more	64.9 (0.58)	73.5 (0.57)	63.1 (0.58)	63.6 (0.59)	72.5 (0.64)	73.8 (0.80)	71.1 (0.84)	82.8 (0.56)	86.9 (0.41)	80.6 (0.38)	82.4 (0.41)	88.3 (0.43)	89.4 (0.55)	85.9 (0.79)
School level[3]														
Elementary	74.2 (0.41)	80.5 (0.52)	72.2 (0.48)	72.2 (0.49)	79.5 (0.54)	79.4 (0.61)	75.6 (0.71)	85.1 (0.36)	88.0 (0.41)	82.8 (0.45)	84.2 (0.41)	88.3 (0.45)	89.5 (0.44)	85.0 (0.60)
Secondary	49.9 (0.60)	60.2 (0.43)	47.0 (0.34)	47.2 (0.46)	55.7 (0.55)	56.1 (0.64)	54.4 (0.69)	81.5 (0.37)	85.8 (0.37)	79.0 (0.31)	80.0 (0.39)	86.2 (0.41)	86.3 (0.48)	82.5 (0.56)
School control														
Public[4]	63.8 (0.31)	71.9 (0.36)	61.8 (0.42)	62.6 (0.39)	71.1 (0.46)	70.6 (0.55)	67.6 (0.51)	83.1 (0.22)	86.7 (0.29)	80.8 (0.35)	82.2 (0.33)	87.2 (0.34)	88.0 (0.37)	83.7 (0.43)
Private	75.4 (0.98)	84.3 (0.61)	77.6 (0.50)	75.9 (0.51)	81.0 (1.52)	80.1 (0.81)	77.4 (1.49)	88.6 (0.57)	92.0 (0.42)	88.4 (0.41)	88.3 (0.39)	92.2 (0.75)	92.2 (0.57)	89.4 (0.98)
School enrollment														
Under 200	76.1 (0.90)	83.7 (0.60)	76.5 (0.84)	75.4 (0.81)	84.0 (1.54)	81.0 (0.85)	78.7 (0.91)	86.6 (0.54)	89.3 (0.54)	85.2 (0.61)	87.1 (0.48)	90.9 (0.86)	90.8 (0.60)	88.7 (0.84)
200 to 499	72.6 (0.42)	79.4 (0.55)	71.2 (0.65)	71.6 (0.58)	78.9 (0.62)	78.6 (0.71)	74.2 (1.00)	84.6 (0.38)	88.1 (0.42)	83.5 (0.47)	84.2 (0.46)	89.3 (0.48)	89.4 (0.60)	84.7 (0.87)
500 to 749	66.6 (0.74)	75.8 (0.74)	66.8 (0.81)	67.7 (0.66)	75.8 (0.68)	74.1 (1.04)	72.2 (1.06)	84.4 (0.55)	88.5 (0.53)	82.3 (0.76)	83.5 (0.55)	87.7 (0.66)	88.6 (0.68)	85.2 (0.75)
750 to 999	59.8 (1.00)	68.5 (1.01)	58.6 (1.10)	63.0 (0.97)	69.4 (1.32)	71.7 (1.50)	66.0 (1.33)	83.0 (0.80)	85.7 (0.81)	79.6 (0.87)	82.5 (0.83)	86.0 (1.14)	88.4 (0.89)	82.7 (1.30)
1,000 or more	48.1 (0.89)	57.5 (0.67)	45.8 (0.77)	47.3 (0.75)	56.3 (0.88)	57.1 (1.17)	55.4 (1.04)	80.7 (0.62)	84.9 (0.66)	78.0 (0.58)	79.4 (0.57)	85.8 (0.63)	86.5 (0.73)	82.3 (0.81)
Locale[5]														
City	(†)	(†)	—	—	69.6 (0.86)	69.4 (0.98)	‡	(†)	(†)	—	—	85.5 (0.60)	86.5 (0.72)	‡
Suburban	(†)	(†)	—	—	73.5 (0.70)	72.6 (0.76)	‡	(†)	(†)	—	—	89.1 (0.47)	89.7 (0.53)	‡
Town	(†)	(†)	—	—	72.4 (1.03)	71.7 (1.32)	‡	(†)	(†)	—	—	88.9 (0.71)	87.5 (1.26)	‡
Rural	(†)	(†)	—	—	74.3 (0.74)	73.6 (0.81)	‡	(†)	(†)	—	—	88.5 (0.61)	89.5 (0.58)	‡

—Not available.
†Not applicable.
‡Reporting standards not met. Data may be suppressed because the response rate is under 50 percent, there are too few cases for a reliable estimate, or the coefficient of variation (CV) is 50 percent or greater.
[1]Respondents were asked whether "rules for student behavior are consistently enforced by teachers in this school, even for students not in their classes."
[2]Respondents were asked whether their "principal enforces school rules for student conduct and backs me up when I need it."
[3]Elementary schools are those with any of grades kindergarten through grade 6 and none of grades 7 through 12. Secondary schools have any of grades 7 through 12 and none of grades kindergarten through grade 6. Combined elementary/secondary schools are included in totals but are not shown separately.

[4]Includes traditional public and public charter schools.
[5]Substantial improvements in geocoding technology and changes in the Office of Management and Budget's definition of metropolitan and nonmetropolitan areas allow for more precision in describing an area as of 2003–04. Comparisons with earlier years are not possible.
NOTE: Teachers who taught only prekindergarten students are excluded. Includes both teachers who "strongly" agreed and those who "somewhat" agreed that rules were enforced by other teachers and the principal. Some data have been revised from previously published figures.
SOURCE: U.S. Department of Education, National Center for Education Statistics, Schools and Staffing Survey (SASS), "Public School Teacher Data File," 1987–88, 1990–91, 1993–94, 1999–2000, 2003–04, 2007–08, and 2011–12; and "Charter School Teacher Data File," 1999–2000. (This table was prepared October 2013.)

Table 230.95. Percentage of public school teachers who agreed that student misbehavior and student tardiness and class cutting interfered with their teaching and that other teachers and the principal enforced school rules, by state: 2011–12

[Standard errors appear in parentheses]

State	Interfered with teaching				Enforced school rules			
	Student misbehavior		Student tardiness and class cutting		Other teachers[1]		Principal[2]	
1	2		3		4		5	
United States	40.7	(0.65)	37.6	(0.51)	67.6	(0.51)	83.7	(0.43)
Alabama	40.9	(3.36)	38.6	(2.82)	71.8	(2.84)	86.8	(2.26)
Alaska	35.8	(5.73)	56.8	(6.73)	72.2	(4.41)	83.2	(5.16)
Arizona	41.3	(2.56)	44.5	(2.67)	67.9	(2.72)	83.4	(2.06)
Arkansas	39.5	(3.56)	38.5	(3.80)	74.0	(2.60)	90.0	(2.16)
California	38.9	(2.47)	39.7	(2.36)	69.7	(1.83)	83.0	(1.63)
Colorado	45.5	(3.54)	47.6	(4.02)	61.7	(3.39)	80.6	(3.28)
Connecticut	37.2	(2.35)	28.6	(3.81)	61.7	(3.91)	80.7	(2.98)
Delaware	46.7	(4.47)	35.2	(4.58)	68.7	(3.58)	82.9	(3.32)
District of Columbia	‡	(†)	‡	(†)	‡	(†)	‡	(†)
Florida	‡	(†)	‡	(†)	‡	(†)	‡	(†)
Georgia	38.2	(3.56)	32.1	(3.36)	71.9	(2.64)	85.5	(2.29)
Hawaii	‡	(†)	‡	(†)	‡	(†)	‡	(†)
Idaho	34.6	(3.54)	36.1	(3.08)	74.7	(2.48)	87.9	(2.18)
Illinois	40.0	(2.96)	33.9	(3.07)	66.0	(3.18)	83.6	(2.31)
Indiana	38.8	(3.33)	41.0	(2.95)	68.4	(2.47)	81.8	(2.99)
Iowa	37.9	(3.12)	34.6	(3.18)	68.5	(2.77)	81.8	(2.40)
Kansas	32.0	(3.57)	24.9	(2.34)	70.9	(3.29)	91.8	(1.61)
Kentucky	42.8	(3.06)	32.8	(2.92)	67.4	(2.80)	86.9	(2.47)
Louisiana	55.1	(3.92)	36.1	(3.60)	62.5	(3.19)	82.1	(3.89)
Maine	39.1	(3.00)	39.2	(3.02)	62.9	(2.90)	83.2	(3.06)
Maryland	‡	(†)	‡	(†)	‡	(†)	‡	(†)
Massachusetts	37.2	(3.07)	32.0	(2.74)	66.6	(3.04)	83.1	(2.80)
Michigan	46.6	(2.87)	40.9	(2.63)	67.6	(2.12)	84.4	(2.08)
Minnesota	43.7	(2.49)	37.3	(2.50)	68.7	(1.88)	84.5	(1.84)
Mississippi	37.4	(3.30)	35.6	(3.40)	72.4	(2.96)	84.5	(2.51)
Missouri	33.2	(2.10)	33.6	(2.87)	68.9	(2.17)	86.6	(1.76)
Montana	41.3	(3.43)	45.3	(4.08)	66.5	(3.65)	83.1	(2.97)
Nebraska	38.2	(3.01)	33.6	(2.81)	70.9	(2.73)	86.7	(1.66)
Nevada	45.5	(3.77)	42.3	(4.86)	65.5	(3.42)	79.3	(3.22)
New Hampshire	38.3	(4.36)	30.9	(3.11)	62.0	(3.93)	83.2	(2.66)
New Jersey	35.9	(2.36)	29.9	(2.29)	66.8	(2.06)	84.4	(1.70)
New Mexico	39.0	(4.55)	54.5	(5.87)	64.2	(3.80)	78.7	(4.23)
New York	40.3	(2.91)	45.3	(3.06)	65.9	(2.47)	80.7	(2.46)
North Carolina	41.9	(3.13)	37.0	(2.94)	69.0	(2.58)	84.0	(2.34)
North Dakota	34.6	(3.26)	33.5	(3.52)	70.4	(2.77)	86.7	(2.45)
Ohio	41.8	(1.95)	38.8	(1.96)	66.4	(1.73)	84.7	(1.55)
Oklahoma	40.1	(2.74)	40.8	(2.87)	72.5	(2.47)	86.5	(2.12)
Oregon	33.1	(3.24)	35.6	(3.73)	77.3	(2.90)	88.1	(1.77)
Pennsylvania	40.0	(2.64)	33.4	(2.55)	65.2	(2.18)	82.5	(1.88)
Rhode Island	‡	(†)	‡	(†)	‡	(†)	‡	(†)
South Carolina	40.9	(3.22)	33.7	(3.40)	71.8	(3.23)	86.8	(2.15)
South Dakota	40.1	(3.10)	37.2	(3.92)	73.2	(2.91)	84.8	(2.53)
Tennessee	41.5	(3.56)	40.0	(3.56)	71.4	(3.14)	88.7	(2.14)
Texas	45.6	(2.29)	35.1	(2.13)	65.8	(2.56)	81.8	(1.99)
Utah	39.7	(3.67)	45.1	(4.30)	75.8	(3.56)	89.9	(2.27)
Vermont	39.9	(2.61)	36.2	(2.62)	59.2	(2.59)	80.5	(2.28)
Virginia	40.8	(3.46)	35.6	(3.06)	64.9	(2.87)	82.5	(2.52)
Washington	39.2	(2.89)	39.5	(3.16)	73.1	(2.60)	85.6	(2.18)
West Virginia	43.9	(3.87)	42.4	(4.09)	73.4	(2.90)	90.4	(2.58)
Wisconsin	42.7	(2.70)	34.2	(3.07)	69.5	(2.87)	85.8	(1.70)
Wyoming	30.7	(4.76)	40.0	(4.78)	73.9	(3.55)	89.1	(3.41)

†Not applicable.
‡Reporting standards not met. Data may be suppressed because the response rate is under 50 percent, there are too few cases for a reliable estimate, or the coefficient of variation (CV) is 50 percent or greater.
[1]Respondents were asked whether "rules for student behavior are consistently enforced by teachers in this school, even for students not in their classes."
[2]Respondents were asked whether their "principal enforces school rules for student conduct and backs me up when I need it."
NOTE: Teachers who taught only prekindergarten students are excluded. Includes traditional public and public charter school teachers. Includes both teachers who "strongly" agreed and those who "somewhat" agreed.
SOURCE: U.S. Department of Education, National Center for Education Statistics, Schools and Staffing Survey (SASS), "Public School Teacher Data File," 2011–12. (This table was prepared July 2013.)

Table 231.10. Percentage of students in grades 9–12 who reported having been in a physical fight at least one time during the previous 12 months, by location and selected student characteristics: Selected years, 1993 through 2013

[Standard errors appear in parentheses]

Location and student characteristic	1993	1995	1997	1999	2001	2003	2005	2007	2009	2011	2013
	2	3	4	5	6	7	8	9	10	11	12
Anywhere (including on school property)[1]											
Total	41.8 (0.99)	38.7 (1.14)	36.6 (1.01)	35.7 (1.17)	33.2 (0.71)	33.0 (0.99)	35.9 (0.77)	35.5 (0.77)	31.5 (0.70)	32.8 (0.65)	24.7 (0.74)
Sex											
Male	51.2 (1.05)	46.1 (1.09)	45.5 (1.07)	44.0 (1.27)	43.1 (0.84)	40.5 (1.32)	43.4 (1.01)	44.4 (0.89)	39.3 (1.20)	40.7 (0.74)	30.2 (1.10)
Female	31.7 (1.19)	30.6 (1.49)	26.0 (1.26)	27.3 (1.70)	23.9 (0.95)	25.1 (0.85)	28.1 (0.94)	26.5 (0.99)	22.9 (0.74)	24.4 (0.92)	19.2 (0.72)
Race/ethnicity[2]											
White	40.3 (1.13)	36.0 (1.06)	33.7 (1.29)	33.1 (1.45)	32.2 (0.95)	30.5 (1.11)	33.1 (0.88)	31.7 (0.96)	27.8 (0.88)	29.4 (0.74)	20.9 (0.70)
Black	49.5 (1.82)	41.6 (1.99)	43.0 (1.92)	41.4 (3.12)	36.5 (1.60)	39.7 (1.23)	43.1 (1.74)	44.7 (1.33)	41.1 (1.71)	39.1 (1.52)	34.7 (1.67)
Hispanic	43.2 (1.58)	47.9 (2.69)	40.7 (1.68)	39.9 (1.65)	35.8 (0.91)	36.1 (0.98)	41.0 (1.64)	40.4 (1.25)	36.2 (0.95)	36.8 (1.44)	28.4 (1.15)
Asian[3]	—	(†)	—	22.7 (2.71)	22.3 (2.73)	25.9 (2.99)	21.6 (2.43)	24.3 (3.50)	18.9 (1.72)	18.4 (1.87)	16.1 (1.87)
Pacific Islander[3]	—	(†)	(†)	50.7 (3.42)	51.7 (6.25)	30.0 (5.21)	34.4 (5.58)	42.6 (7.74)	32.6 (3.50)	43.0 (5.14)	22.0 (4.95)
American Indian/Alaska Native	49.8 (4.79)	47.2 (6.44)	54.7 (5.75)	48.7 (6.78)	49.2 (6.58)	46.6 (6.53)	44.2 (3.40)	36.0 (1.49)	42.4 (5.23)	42.4 (2.12)	32.1 (7.39)
Two or more races[3]	—	(†)	—	40.2 (2.76)	39.6 (2.85)	38.2 (3.64)	46.9 (4.16)	47.8 (3.30)	34.2 (3.51)	45.0 (2.60)	28.5 (2.31)
Grade											
9th	50.4 (1.54)	47.3 (2.22)	44.8 (1.98)	41.1 (1.96)	39.5 (1.27)	38.6 (1.38)	43.5 (1.15)	40.9 (1.16)	37.0 (1.21)	37.7 (1.11)	28.3 (1.17)
10th	42.2 (1.45)	40.4 (1.49)	40.2 (1.91)	37.7 (2.11)	34.7 (1.37)	33.5 (1.20)	36.6 (1.09)	36.2 (1.34)	33.5 (1.19)	35.3 (1.35)	26.4 (1.42)
11th	40.5 (1.52)	36.9 (1.48)	34.2 (1.72)	31.3 (1.55)	29.1 (1.10)	30.9 (1.38)	31.6 (1.44)	34.8 (1.36)	28.6 (0.93)	29.7 (1.14)	24.0 (1.04)
12th	34.8 (1.56)	31.0 (1.71)	28.8 (1.36)	30.4 (1.91)	26.5 (1.01)	26.5 (1.08)	29.1 (1.26)	28.0 (1.42)	24.9 (0.99)	26.9 (0.95)	18.8 (1.19)
Urbanicity[4]											
Urban	—	(†)	38.2 (2.00)	37.0 (2.66)	36.8 (1.53)	35.5 (2.17)	—	(†)	(†)	(†)	(†)
Suburban	—	(†)	36.7 (1.59)	35.0 (1.56)	31.3 (0.80)	33.1 (1.23)	—	(†)	(†)	(†)	(†)
Rural	—	(†)	32.9 (2.91)	36.6 (2.14)	33.8 (2.58)	29.7 (1.61)	—	(†)	(†)	(†)	(†)
On school property[5]											
Total	16.2 (0.59)	15.5 (0.79)	14.8 (0.64)	14.2 (0.62)	12.5 (0.49)	12.8 (0.76)	13.6 (0.56)	12.4 (0.48)	11.1 (0.54)	12.0 (0.39)	8.1 (0.35)
Sex											
Male	23.5 (0.71)	21.0 (0.90)	20.0 (1.04)	18.5 (0.66)	18.0 (0.74)	17.1 (0.92)	18.2 (0.93)	16.3 (0.60)	15.1 (1.05)	16.0 (0.58)	10.7 (0.55)
Female	8.6 (0.73)	9.5 (1.03)	8.6 (0.78)	9.8 (0.95)	7.2 (0.47)	8.0 (0.70)	8.8 (0.52)	8.5 (0.62)	6.7 (0.42)	7.8 (0.43)	5.6 (0.38)
Race/ethnicity[2]											
White	15.0 (0.68)	12.9 (0.62)	13.3 (0.84)	12.3 (0.86)	11.2 (0.60)	10.0 (0.73)	11.6 (0.66)	10.2 (0.56)	8.6 (0.58)	9.9 (0.51)	6.4 (0.45)
Black	22.0 (1.39)	20.3 (1.25)	20.7 (1.20)	18.7 (1.51)	16.8 (1.26)	17.1 (1.30)	16.9 (1.39)	17.6 (1.10)	17.4 (0.99)	16.4 (0.89)	12.8 (0.84)
Hispanic	17.9 (1.75)	21.1 (1.68)	19.0 (1.50)	15.7 (0.91)	14.1 (0.89)	16.7 (1.14)	18.3 (1.62)	15.5 (0.81)	13.5 (0.82)	14.4 (0.79)	9.4 (0.44)
Asian[3]	—	(†)	—	10.4 (0.95)	10.8 (1.92)	13.1 (2.26)	5.9 (1.53)	8.5 (1.99)	7.7 (1.09)	6.2 (1.06)	5.5 (1.39)
Pacific Islander[3]	—	(†)	—	25.3 (4.60)	29.1 (7.63)	22.2 (4.82)	24.5 (5.60)	9.6 ! (1.99)	14.8 (2.37)	20.9 (4.41)	7.1 ! (2.58)
American Indian/Alaska Native	18.6 (2.74)	31.4 (5.58)	18.9 (5.55)	16.2 ! (5.23)	18.2 (4.41)	24.2 (5.03)	22.0 (3.16)	15.0 (1.12)	20.7 (3.73)	12.0 (1.77)	10.7 (3.13)
Two or more races[3]	—	(†)	—	16.9 (2.40)	14.7 (1.97)	20.2 (3.83)	15.8 (2.61)	19.6 (2.39)	12.4 (2.19)	16.6 (1.41)	10.0 (1.04)
Grade											
9th	23.1 (1.55)	21.6 (1.79)	21.3 (1.29)	18.6 (1.02)	17.3 (0.77)	18.0 (1.24)	18.9 (0.93)	17.0 (0.67)	14.9 (0.98)	16.2 (0.77)	10.9 (0.78)
10th	17.2 (1.07)	16.5 (1.57)	17.0 (1.67)	17.2 (1.23)	13.5 (0.88)	12.8 (0.89)	14.4 (1.08)	11.7 (0.86)	12.1 (0.83)	12.8 (0.86)	8.3 (0.61)
11th	13.8 (1.27)	13.6 (1.00)	12.5 (0.87)	10.8 (1.01)	9.4 (0.71)	10.4 (0.89)	10.4 (0.75)	11.0 (0.73)	9.5 (0.63)	9.2 (0.55)	7.5 (0.53)
12th	11.4 (0.66)	10.6 (0.73)	9.5 (0.73)	8.1 (1.00)	7.5 (0.56)	7.3 (0.70)	8.5 (0.70)	8.6 (0.62)	6.6 (0.59)	8.8 (0.69)	4.9 (0.63)
Urbanicity[4]											
Urban	—	(†)	15.8 (1.50)	14.4 (1.08)	14.8 (0.90)	14.8 (1.31)	—	(†)	(†)	(†)	(†)
Suburban	—	(†)	14.2 (0.95)	13.7 (0.86)	11.0 (0.75)	12.8 (1.23)	—	(†)	(†)	(†)	(†)
Rural	—	(†)	14.7 (2.09)	16.3 (2.33)	13.8 (1.10)	10.0 (1.36)	—	(†)	(†)	(†)	(†)

—Not available.
†Not applicable.
!Interpret data with caution. The coefficient of variation (CV) for this estimate is between 30 and 50 percent.
[1]The term "anywhere" is not used in the Youth Risk Behavior Survey (YRBS) questionnaire; students were simply asked how many times in the past 12 months they had been in a physical fight.
[2]Race categories exclude persons of Hispanic ethnicity.

[3]Before 1999, Asian students and Pacific Islander students were not categorized separately, and students could not be classified as Two or more races. Because the response categories changed in 1999, caution should be used in comparing data on race from 1993, 1995, and 1997 with data from later years.
[4]Refers to the Standard Metropolitan Statistical Area (MSA) status of the respondent's household as defined in 2000 by the U.S. Census Bureau. Categories include "central city of an MSA (Urban)," "in MSA but not in central city (Suburban)," and "not MSA (Rural)."
[5]In the question asking students about physical fights at school, "on school property" was not defined for survey respondents.
SOURCE: Centers for Disease Control and Prevention, Division of Adolescent and School Health, Youth Risk Behavior Surveillance System (YRBSS), 1993 through 2013. (This table was prepared June 2014.)

Table 231.20. Percentage distribution of students in grades 9–12, by number of times they reported having been in a physical fight anywhere or on school property during the previous 12 months and selected student characteristics: 2013

[Standard errors appear in parentheses]

Student characteristic	Anywhere (including on school property)[1]								On school property[2]							
	0 times		1 to 3 times		4 to 11 times		12 or more times		0 times		1 to 3 times		4 to 11 times		12 or more times	
1	2		3		4		5		6		7		8		9	
Total................................	75.3	(0.74)	18.8	(0.59)	4.0	(0.26)	1.9	(0.18)	91.9	(0.35)	7.1	(0.34)	0.6	(0.08)	0.5	(0.07)
Sex																
Male................................	69.8	(1.10)	22.1	(0.82)	5.4	(0.43)	2.7	(0.30)	89.3	(0.55)	9.1	(0.48)	0.8	(0.15)	0.7	(0.12)
Female.............................	80.8	(0.72)	15.6	(0.64)	2.6	(0.21)	1.0	(0.17)	94.4	(0.38)	5.1	(0.38)	0.3 !	(0.09)	0.3	(0.07)
Race/ethnicity[3]																
White................................	79.1	(0.70)	16.5	(0.61)	3.2	(0.30)	1.2	(0.18)	93.6	(0.45)	5.7	(0.44)	0.4	(0.11)	0.3	(0.08)
Black................................	65.3	(1.67)	26.3	(1.49)	5.9	(0.66)	2.5	(0.31)	87.2	(0.84)	11.1	(0.90)	1.2	(0.30)	0.5	(0.13)
Hispanic...........................	71.6	(1.15)	20.4	(1.30)	5.2	(0.55)	2.8	(0.44)	90.6	(0.44)	7.9	(0.41)	0.7	(0.17)	0.7	(0.14)
Asian................................	83.9	(1.87)	10.4	(1.55)	2.1 !	(0.80)	3.7 !	(1.28)	94.5	(1.39)	3.1 !	(0.94)	‡	(†)	‡	(†)
Pacific Islander................	78.0	(4.95)	19.9	(3.98)	‡	(†)	‡	(†)	92.9	(2.58)	7.1 !	(2.58)	‡	(†)	‡	(†)
American Indian/Alaska Native.....................	67.9	(7.39)	23.0	(5.74)	‡	(†)	‡	(†)	89.3	(3.13)	9.1 !	(3.14)	‡	(†)	‡	(†)
Two or more races	71.5	(2.31)	22.3	(2.03)	3.7	(0.83)	2.6 !	(0.81)	90.0	(1.04)	9.1	(1.03)	‡	(†)	‡	(†)
Grade																
9th...................................	71.7	(1.17)	20.8	(1.02)	5.1	(0.38)	2.4	(0.35)	89.1	(0.78)	9.5	(0.77)	0.9	(0.24)	0.5	(0.12)
10th..................................	73.6	(1.42)	20.8	(1.21)	3.8	(0.46)	1.8	(0.31)	91.7	(0.61)	7.4	(0.59)	0.4	(0.10)	0.5	(0.14)
11th..................................	76.0	(1.04)	18.7	(0.82)	3.4	(0.46)	1.9	(0.31)	92.5	(0.53)	6.4	(0.52)	0.4 !	(0.15)	0.6	(0.17)
12th..................................	81.2	(1.19)	14.5	(0.91)	3.1	(0.45)	1.1	(0.19)	95.1	(0.63)	4.1	(0.54)	0.5 !	(0.14)	0.4	(0.10)

†Not applicable.
!Interpret data with caution. The coefficient of variation (CV) for this estimate is between 30 and 50 percent.
‡Reporting standards not met. Either there are too few cases for a reliable estimate or the coefficient of variation (CV) is 50 percent or greater.
[1]The term "anywhere" is not used in the Youth Risk Behavior Survey (YRBS) questionnaire; students were simply asked how many times in the past 12 months they had been in a physical fight.

[2]In the question asking students about physical fights at school, "on school property" was not defined for respondents.
[3]Race categories exclude persons of Hispanic ethnicity.
NOTE: Detail may not sum to totals because of rounding.
SOURCE: Centers for Disease Control and Prevention, Division of Adolescent and School Health, Youth Risk Behavior Surveillance System (YRBSS), 2013. (This table was prepared June 2014.)

Table 231.30. Percentage of public school students in grades 9–12 who reported having been in a physical fight at least one time during the previous 12 months, by location and state: Selected years, 2003 through 2013

[Standard errors appear in parentheses]

State	Anywhere (including on school property)[1]						On school property[2]					
	2003	2005	2007	2009	2011	2013	2003	2005	2007	2009	2011	2013
1	2	3	4	5	6	7	8	9	10	11	12	13
United States[3]	33.0 (0.99)	35.9 (0.77)	35.5 (0.77)	31.5 (0.70)	32.8 (0.65)	24.7 (0.74)	12.8 (0.76)	13.6 (0.56)	12.4 (0.48)	11.1 (0.54)	12.0 (0.39)	8.1 (0.35)
Alabama	30.0 (1.78)	31.7 (1.84)	— (†)	31.7 (2.44)	28.4 (1.79)	29.2 (2.32)	12.9 (1.21)	14.6 (1.29)	— (†)	13.1 (1.41)	11.8 (1.30)	10.9 (0.93)
Alaska	27.1 (1.55)	— (†)	29.2 (1.77)	27.8 (1.52)	23.7 (1.17)	22.7 (1.64)	8.6 (0.92)	— (†)	10.4 (1.17)	9.8 (1.04)	7.7 (0.90)	10.9 (†)
Arizona	32.4 (1.79)	32.4 (1.43)	31.3 (1.54)	35.9 (1.83)	27.7 (1.41)	23.9 (1.48)	11.4 (0.86)	11.7 (0.87)	11.3 (0.72)	12.0 (0.82)	10.8 (0.78)	8.8 (0.94)
Arkansas	— (†)	32.1 (1.67)	32.8 (1.79)	34.7 (2.08)	29.1 (1.76)	27.0 (1.30)	— (†)	13.9 (1.33)	13.0 (1.03)	14.8 (1.30)	11.0 (1.36)	11.4 (0.89)
California	— (†)	— (†)	— (†)	— (†)	— (†)	— (†)	— (†)	— (†)	— (†)	— (†)	— (†)	— (†)
Colorado	— (†)	32.2 (1.54)	— (†)	32.0 (1.51)	24.9 (1.69)	— (†)	— (†)	12.1 (0.89)	— (†)	10.7 (0.83)	— (†)	— (†)
Connecticut	— (†)	32.7 (1.45)	31.4 (1.39)	28.3 (1.26)	25.1 (1.53)	22.4 (1.23)	— (†)	10.5 (0.72)	10.5 (0.83)	9.6 (0.79)	8.7 (0.84)	— (†)
Delaware	34.9 (1.15)	30.3 (1.38)	33.0 (1.31)	30.4 (1.22)	28.0 (1.59)	25.1 (1.24)	11.4 (0.70)	9.8 (0.82)	10.5 (0.72)	8.6 (0.72)	8.8 (1.02)	9.3 (0.82)
District of Columbia	38.0 (1.61)	36.3 (1.26)	43.0 (1.45)	— (†)	37.9 (1.71)	— (†)	15.2 (1.07)	16.4 (0.88)	19.8 (1.21)	— (†)	15.8 (1.55)	— (†)
Florida	32.1 (0.74)	30.0 (0.94)	32.3 (1.24)	29.8 (0.83)	28.0 (0.72)	22.0 (0.77)	13.3 (0.65)	11.5 (0.77)	12.5 (0.84)	10.5 (0.47)	10.2 (0.44)	8.1 (0.52)
Georgia	31.4 (1.20)	33.8 (1.40)	34.0 (1.26)	32.3 (1.76)	33.1 (1.65)	21.4 (1.24)	11.1 (0.74)	12.1 (1.01)	13.1 (1.07)	11.7 (1.21)	11.9 (1.07)	10.3 (1.37)
Hawaii	— (†)	27.0 (1.37)	28.6 (2.20)	29.5 (1.92)	22.3 (1.11)	16.7 (0.87)	— (†)	10.0 (1.01)	7.0 (0.78)	10.2 (0.99)	8.2 (0.75)	— (†)
Idaho	28.3 (2.00)	32.3 (1.38)	30.0 (1.39)	29.0 (1.08)	26.4 (1.45)	21.6 (1.18)	11.7 (1.20)	12.1 (1.14)	12.3 (0.98)	10.2 (0.79)	9.4 (0.81)	7.3 (0.75)
Illinois	— (†)	— (†)	33.9 (1.91)	33.0 (1.38)	29.5 (1.41)	24.6 (1.67)	— (†)	— (†)	11.3 (1.11)	11.5 (0.82)	9.8 (0.69)	8.2 (0.66)
Indiana	30.6 (2.01)	29.3 (1.51)	29.5 (1.35)	29.1 (1.51)	29.0 (1.34)	— (†)	10.9 (1.14)	11.2 (0.98)	11.5 (0.92)	9.5 (1.18)	8.9 (0.80)	— (†)
Iowa	— (†)	28.3 (1.61)	24.0 (1.39)	— (†)	24.4 (1.87)	— (†)	— (†)	11.3 (1.12)	9.1 (0.96)	— (†)	9.6 (0.89)	— (†)
Kansas	— (†)	27.9 (1.51)	30.3 (1.62)	27.8 (1.37)	22.4 (1.40)	20.4 (1.21)	— (†)	10.1 (0.92)	10.6 (1.04)	9.0 (0.81)	7.8 (0.84)	7.2 (0.72)
Kentucky	26.4 (1.66)	29.6 (1.17)	27.0 (0.98)	28.7 (1.66)	28.7 (1.65)	21.2 (1.20)	10.1 (1.05)	12.7 (0.81)	10.6 (0.65)	9.5 (0.93)	11.4 (0.93)	6.0 (0.94)
Louisiana	— (†)	— (†)	— (†)	36.1 (1.60)	36.0 (2.72)	30.8 (2.59)	— (†)	— (†)	— (†)	13.7 (1.28)	15.8 (2.17)	12.0 (1.68)
Maine	26.5 (1.39)	28.2 (1.11)	26.5 (1.93)	22.8 (0.55)	19.5 (0.46)	17.0 (0.40)	9.1 (1.01)	10.0 (1.03)	10.1 (1.09)	9.1 (0.33)	7.9 (0.27)	5.7 (0.29)
Maryland	— (†)	36.6 (1.83)	35.7 (2.62)	32.5 (2.23)	29.1 (1.80)	— (†)	— (†)	14.9 (1.33)	12.4 (1.69)	11.2 (1.30)	11.1 (1.24)	14.3 (0.32)
Massachusetts	30.7 (1.05)	28.6 (1.33)	27.5 (1.34)	29.2 (1.24)	25.4 (0.92)	20.3 (0.91)	10.2 (0.67)	10.2 (0.67)	9.1 (0.81)	8.7 (0.68)	7.1 (0.65)	4.6 (0.49)
Michigan	30.8 (1.51)	30.1 (2.02)	30.7 (1.89)	31.6 (1.72)	27.4 (1.32)	21.6 (0.88)	12.2 (1.02)	11.4 (1.11)	11.4 (0.89)	11.3 (1.02)	9.1 (0.68)	6.9 (0.55)
Minnesota	— (†)	— (†)	— (†)	— (†)	— (†)	— (†)	— (†)	— (†)	— (†)	— (†)	— (†)	— (†)
Mississippi	30.6 (1.66)	— (†)	30.6 (1.43)	34.1 (1.73)	29.3 (1.72)	31.0 (1.84)	10.2 (1.26)	— (†)	11.9 (0.96)	12.6 (1.02)	12.3 (1.06)	13.6 (1.40)
Missouri	28.2 (2.07)	29.8 (2.12)	30.9 (2.18)	28.7 (1.34)	— (†)	— (†)	9.8 (0.95)	10.2 (1.31)	10.7 (1.21)	9.0 (0.97)	— (†)	— (†)
Montana	28.6 (1.16)	30.5 (1.19)	32.8 (1.08)	31.7 (2.25)	25.4 (0.73)	22.8 (0.90)	10.3 (0.68)	10.9 (0.67)	12.0 (0.75)	10.8 (1.33)	9.1 (0.51)	7.3 (0.37)
Nebraska	29.6 (1.14)	28.5 (1.02)	— (†)	— (†)	26.7 (1.09)	20.1 (1.22)	10.6 (0.81)	9.3 (0.60)	— (†)	— (†)	7.4 (0.68)	5.7 (0.70)
Nevada	35.0 (1.56)	34.5 (1.78)	31.6 (1.53)	35.0 (1.45)	— (†)	23.6 (1.93)	12.6 (1.01)	14.2 (1.32)	11.3 (1.10)	10.0 (0.82)	— (†)	6.8 (1.12)
New Hampshire	30.5 (1.84)	26.4 (1.84)	27.0 (1.40)	25.9 (1.59)	23.8 (1.27)	— (†)	11.6 (1.20)	10.7 (1.06)	11.3 (0.70)	9.1 (0.87)	9.9 (0.89)	6.9 (0.81)
New Jersey	— (†)	30.7 (2.18)	— (†)	27.5 (1.46)	23.9 (1.56)	21.8 (1.34)	— (†)	10.1 (1.31)	— (†)	— (†)	— (†)	— (†)
New Mexico	— (†)	36.7 (1.47)	37.1 (1.06)	37.3 (1.07)	31.5 (1.02)	27.2 (1.27)	— (†)	15.6 (1.19)	16.9 (0.70)	15.0 (0.85)	11.3 (0.78)	9.7 (0.61)
New York	32.1 (0.82)	32.1 (1.07)	31.7 (1.08)	29.6 (1.23)	27.0 (1.25)	22.8 (1.10)	14.6 (0.73)	12.5 (0.74)	12.2 (0.91)	11.4 (0.91)	— (†)	9.7 (0.94)
North Carolina	30.9 (1.41)	29.9 (1.41)	30.1 (1.54)	28.6 (0.96)	27.6 (1.37)	24.1 (1.49)	10.7 (1.00)	11.6 (0.85)	10.4 (0.84)	9.4 (0.43)	10.6 (1.01)	7.6 (0.94)
North Dakota	27.2 (1.60)	— (†)	— (†)	— (†)	— (†)	— (†)	8.6 (0.96)	10.7 (1.13)	9.6 (0.79)	7.4 (0.78)	8.2 (0.73)	8.8 (0.75)
Ohio[4]	31.5 (2.83)	30.2 (1.95)	30.4 (1.57)	— (†)	31.2 (1.58)	19.8 (1.49)	11.3 (1.67)	10.2 (1.17)	9.4 (0.82)	— (†)	8.8 (0.68)	6.2 (0.88)
Oklahoma	28.4 (2.61)	31.1 (1.63)	29.2 (1.37)	30.8 (2.10)	28.5 (1.96)	25.1 (1.79)	11.4 (1.15)	12.1 (1.13)	10.6 (0.81)	12.8 (1.43)	9.4 (1.25)	7.2 (1.05)
Oregon	— (†)	— (†)	— (†)	— (†)	— (†)	— (†)	— (†)	— (†)	— (†)	— (†)	— (†)	— (†)
Pennsylvania	— (†)	— (†)	— (†)	29.6 (1.76)	— (†)	— (†)	— (†)	— (†)	— (†)	9.9 (1.01)	— (†)	— (†)
Rhode Island	27.6 (1.59)	28.4 (1.34)	26.3 (1.61)	25.1 (0.83)	23.5 (0.81)	18.8 (1.12)	11.4 (1.18)	11.2 (0.80)	9.6 (0.93)	9.1 (0.73)	7.8 (0.52)	6.4 (0.52)
South Carolina	— (†)	31.3 (1.68)	29.1 (1.37)	36.4 (2.06)	32.6 (2.04)	26.7 (1.42)	— (†)	12.7 (1.18)	10.8 (0.86)	12.1 (1.43)	12.2 (1.48)	9.6 (1.17)
South Dakota[4]	27.0 (2.72)	26.5 (2.86)	29.8 (2.00)	27.1 (1.36)	24.5 (2.22)	24.2 (2.04)	9.0 (1.12)	8.4 (1.56)	9.3 (1.32)	8.3 (0.52)	8.2 (0.92)	6.6 (0.52)
Tennessee	28.3 (1.94)	30.9 (1.66)	31.8 (1.55)	32.3 (1.31)	30.8 (1.24)	25.7 (1.69)	12.2 (1.33)	10.9 (1.00)	12.4 (1.13)	11.3 (0.96)	10.5 (0.83)	10.4 (1.02)
Texas	— (†)	34.2 (1.57)	34.9 (1.17)	33.3 (1.05)	34.1 (0.92)	25.4 (1.33)	— (†)	14.5 (0.94)	13.9 (0.90)	13.2 (0.67)	12.5 (0.65)	9.1 (0.79)
Utah	28.7 (2.74)	25.9 (1.84)	30.1 (2.01)	28.2 (1.61)	23.9 (1.88)	21.3 (1.16)	11.9 (1.80)	10.4 (1.57)	11.6 (1.36)	10.6 (0.84)	8.1 (1.18)	6.9 (0.65)
Vermont	26.9 (0.92)	24.3 (1.36)	26.0 (1.44)	25.6 (0.71)	23.1 (1.42)	— (†)	12.2 (0.71)	12.2 (0.98)	11.5 (0.88)	11.0 (0.36)	8.8 (0.72)	9.4 (0.50)
Virginia	— (†)	— (†)	— (†)	— (†)	24.9 (1.71)	23.5 (0.90)	— (†)	— (†)	— (†)	— (†)	7.9 (0.93)	— (†)
Washington	— (†)	— (†)	— (†)	— (†)	— (†)	— (†)	— (†)	— (†)	— (†)	— (†)	— (†)	— (†)
West Virginia	26.5 (1.62)	29.1 (1.88)	29.9 (2.39)	31.7 (1.96)	25.7 (1.66)	25.2 (1.84)	10.3 (1.39)	12.1 (1.41)	12.9 (1.70)	11.3 (1.07)	10.3 (1.02)	9.1 (1.08)
Wisconsin	31.4 (1.68)	32.6 (1.51)	31.2 (1.46)	25.8 (1.52)	25.3 (1.72)	22.4 (1.46)	11.6 (0.92)	12.2 (1.03)	11.4 (0.97)	9.6 (0.87)	9.1 (0.95)	6.8 (0.69)
Wyoming	31.2 (1.23)	30.4 (1.08)	27.9 (1.12)	30.9 (1.17)	26.5 (1.08)	24.3 (1.11)	12.7 (0.93)	12.2 (0.72)	11.6 (0.83)	12.6 (0.73)	11.3 (0.65)	8.9 (0.60)

—Not available.
†Not applicable.
[1]The term "anywhere" is not used in the Youth Risk Behavior Survey (YRBS) questionnaire; students were simply asked how many times in the past 12 months they had been in a physical fight.
[2]In the question asking students about physical fights at school, "on school property" was not defined for survey respondents.
[3]Data for the U.S. total include both public and private schools and were collected through a national survey representing the entire country.
[4]Data include both public and private schools.

NOTE: State-level data include public schools only, with the exception of data for Ohio and South Dakota. Data for the U.S. total, Ohio, and South Dakota include both public and private schools. For specific states, a given year's data may be unavailable (1) because the state did not participate in the survey that year; (2) because the state omitted this particular survey item from the state-level questionnaire; or (3) because the state had an overall response rate of less than 60 percent (the overall response rate is the school response rate multiplied by the student response rate).
SOURCE: Centers for Disease Control and Prevention, Division of Adolescent and School Health, Youth Risk Behavior Surveillance System (YRBSS), 2003 through 2013. (This table was prepared June 2014.)

Table 231.40. Percentage of students in grades 9–12 who reported carrying a weapon at least 1 day during the previous 30 days, by location and selected student characteristics: Selected years, 1993 through 2013

[Standard errors appear in parentheses]

Location and student characteristic	1993	1995	1997	1999	2001	2003	2005	2007	2009	2011	2013
1	2	3	4	5	6	7	8	9	10	11	12
Anywhere (including on school property)[1]											
Total	22.1 (1.18)	20.0 (0.66)	18.3 (0.91)	17.3 (0.97)	17.4 (0.99)	17.1 (0.90)	18.5 (0.80)	18.0 (0.87)	17.5 (0.73)	16.6 (0.65)	17.9 (0.73)
Sex											
Male	34.3 (1.68)	31.1 (1.03)	27.7 (1.57)	28.6 (1.71)	29.3 (1.67)	26.9 (1.31)	29.8 (1.35)	28.5 (1.41)	27.1 (1.45)	25.9 (1.07)	28.1 (1.31)
Female	9.2 (0.85)	8.3 (0.72)	7.0 (0.54)	6.0 (0.56)	6.2 (0.41)	6.7 (0.60)	7.1 (0.43)	7.5 (0.66)	7.1 (0.38)	6.8 (0.41)	7.9 (0.56)
Race/ethnicity[2]											
White	20.6 (1.43)	18.9 (0.93)	17.0 (1.29)	16.4 (1.36)	17.9 (1.30)	16.7 (0.95)	18.7 (1.13)	18.2 (1.28)	18.6 (1.16)	17.0 (1.05)	20.8 (0.90)
Black	28.5 (1.24)	21.8 (2.03)	21.7 (1.99)	17.2 (2.68)	15.2 (1.23)	17.3 (1.77)	16.4 (0.81)	17.2 (1.05)	14.4 (1.33)	14.2 (0.85)	12.5 (0.96)
Hispanic	24.4 (1.35)	24.7 (1.87)	23.3 (1.44)	18.7 (1.35)	16.5 (0.78)	16.5 (1.31)	19.0 (1.10)	18.5 (1.21)	17.2 (0.94)	16.2 (0.82)	15.5 (0.95)
Asian[3]	— (†)	— (†)	— (†)	13.0 (2.01)	10.6 (2.10)	11.6 (2.67)	7.0 (1.70)	7.8 (1.41)	8.4 (1.28)	9.1 (1.57)	8.7 (1.79)
Pacific Islander[3]	— (†)	— (†)	— (†)	25.3 (5.02)	17.4 (4.35)	16.3! (6.37)	20.0! (6.52)	25.5 (4.35)	20.3 (3.40)	20.7 (5.00)	12.6! (3.98)
American Indian/Alaska Native[3]	34.2 (8.08)	32.0 (5.69)	26.2 (3.65)	21.8 (5.68)	31.2 (5.52)	29.3 (4.58)	25.6 (3.79)	20.6 (3.02)	20.7 (3.40)	27.6 (2.41)	17.8 (4.01)
Two or more races[3]	— (†)	— (†)	— (†)	22.2 (3.34)	25.2 (3.41)	29.8 (5.03)	26.7 (3.11)	19.0 (2.46)	17.9 (1.61)	23.7 (2.58)	18.8 (2.09)
Grade											
9th	25.5 (1.42)	22.6 (1.24)	22.6 (1.34)	17.6 (1.58)	19.8 (1.44)	18.0 (1.81)	19.9 (1.21)	20.1 (1.41)	18.0 (0.87)	17.3 (1.07)	17.5 (0.99)
10th	21.4 (1.11)	21.1 (0.94)	17.4 (1.33)	18.7 (1.31)	16.7 (1.11)	15.9 (1.14)	19.4 (1.19)	18.8 (1.21)	18.4 (1.51)	16.6 (0.89)	17.8 (1.09)
11th	21.5 (1.66)	20.3 (1.40)	18.2 (1.69)	16.1 (1.31)	16.8 (1.26)	18.2 (1.21)	17.1 (1.13)	16.7 (1.08)	16.2 (0.93)	16.2 (0.84)	17.9 (1.43)
12th	19.9 (1.46)	16.1 (0.93)	15.4 (1.65)	15.9 (1.44)	15.1 (1.28)	15.5 (1.06)	16.9 (0.95)	15.5 (1.28)	16.6 (0.85)	15.8 (0.90)	18.3 (1.17)
Urbanicity[4]											
Urban	— (†)	— (†)	18.7 (1.34)	15.8 (0.85)	15.3 (0.99)	17.0 (1.32)	— (†)	— (†)	— (†)	— (†)	— (†)
Suburban	— (†)	— (†)	16.8 (1.02)	17.0 (1.34)	17.4 (1.39)	16.5 (1.36)	— (†)	— (†)	— (†)	— (†)	— (†)
Rural	— (†)	— (†)	22.3 (2.12)	22.3 (2.19)	23.0 (1.86)	18.9 (1.91)	— (†)	— (†)	— (†)	— (†)	— (†)
On school property[5]											
Total	11.8 (0.73)	9.8 (0.45)	8.5 (0.79)	6.9 (0.60)	6.4 (0.52)	6.1 (0.57)	6.5 (0.46)	5.9 (0.37)	5.6 (0.32)	5.4 (0.35)	5.2 (0.44)
Sex											
Male	17.9 (0.96)	14.3 (0.76)	12.5 (1.50)	11.0 (1.07)	10.2 (0.88)	8.9 (0.74)	10.2 (0.83)	9.0 (0.65)	8.0 (0.52)	8.2 (0.59)	7.6 (0.70)
Female	5.1 (0.65)	4.9 (0.53)	3.7 (0.37)	2.8 (0.38)	2.9 (0.27)	3.1 (0.50)	2.6 (0.30)	2.7 (0.33)	2.9 (0.24)	2.3 (0.19)	3.0 (0.40)
Race/ethnicity[2]											
White	10.9 (0.86)	9.0 (0.65)	7.8 (1.16)	6.4 (0.87)	6.1 (0.62)	5.5 (0.57)	6.1 (0.66)	5.3 (0.55)	5.6 (0.44)	5.1 (0.40)	5.7 (0.65)
Black	15.0 (0.85)	10.3 (1.13)	9.2 (0.98)	5.0 (0.50)	6.3 (0.92)	6.9 (0.96)	5.1 (0.66)	6.0 (0.46)	5.3 (0.74)	4.6 (0.67)	3.9 (0.42)
Hispanic	13.3 (1.09)	14.1 (1.63)	10.4 (0.99)	7.9 (0.73)	6.4 (0.53)	6.0 (0.56)	8.2 (0.91)	7.3 (0.82)	5.8 (0.58)	5.8 (0.70)	4.7 (0.61)
Asian[3]	— (†)	— (†)	— (†)	6.5 (1.44)	7.2 (2.05)	6.6! (2.44)	2.8! (1.24)	4.1 (1.01)	3.6 (0.84)	4.3! (1.66)	3.8 (1.13)
Pacific Islander[3]	— (†)	— (†)	— (†)	9.3 (2.66)	10.0! (3.05)	4.9! (2.05)	15.4! (6.10)	9.5! (3.40)	9.8 (2.33)	10.9! (3.73)	4.0! (1.95)
American Indian/Alaska Native[3]	17.6! (5.70)	13.0! (4.35)	15.9 (3.68)	11.6! (5.13)	16.4 (4.02)	12.9 (3.40)	7.2 (1.60)	7.7 (2.08)	4.2! (1.50)	7.5 (1.62)	7.0! (3.22)
Two or more races[3]	— (†)	— (†)	— (†)	11.4 (2.76)	13.2 (3.61)	13.3! (4.10)	11.9 (2.99)	5.0 (1.11)	5.8 (1.35)	7.5 (1.87)	6.3 (1.58)
Grade											
9th	12.6 (0.73)	10.7 (0.76)	10.2 (0.90)	7.2 (1.07)	6.7 (0.66)	5.3 (1.13)	6.4 (0.75)	6.0 (0.59)	4.9 (0.46)	4.8 (0.50)	4.8 (0.69)
10th	11.5 (0.97)	10.4 (0.78)	7.7 (0.99)	6.6 (0.83)	6.7 (0.60)	6.0 (0.53)	6.9 (0.70)	5.8 (0.61)	6.1 (0.57)	6.1 (0.72)	4.8 (0.58)
11th	11.9 (1.41)	10.2 (0.94)	9.4 (1.33)	7.0 (0.60)	6.1 (0.74)	6.6 (0.80)	5.9 (0.71)	5.5 (0.68)	5.2 (0.44)	4.7 (0.44)	5.9 (1.19)
12th	10.8 (0.83)	7.6 (0.68)	7.0 (0.91)	6.2 (0.78)	6.1 (0.71)	6.4 (0.64)	6.7 (0.64)	6.0 (0.58)	6.0 (0.57)	5.6 (0.51)	5.3 (0.88)
Urbanicity[4]											
Urban	— (†)	— (†)	7.0 (0.67)	7.2 (1.09)	6.0 (0.67)	5.6 (0.81)	— (†)	— (†)	— (†)	— (†)	— (†)
Suburban	— (†)	— (†)	8.7 (0.68)	6.2 (0.74)	6.3 (0.68)	6.4 (1.01)	— (†)	— (†)	— (†)	— (†)	— (†)
Rural	— (†)	— (†)	11.2 (2.19)	9.6 (1.61)	8.3 (1.48)	6.3 (0.67)	— (†)	— (†)	— (†)	— (†)	— (†)

—Not available.
†Not applicable.
‡Interpret data with caution. The coefficient of variation (CV) for this estimate is between 30 and 50 percent.
[1]The term "anywhere" is not used in the Youth Risk Behavior Survey (YRBS) questionnaire; students were simply asked how many days they carried a weapon during the past 30 days.
[2]Race categories exclude persons of Hispanic ethnicity.
[3]Before 1999, Asian students and Pacific Islander students were not categorized separately, and students could not be classified as Two or more races. Because the response categories changed in 1999, caution should be used in comparing data on race from 1993, 1995, and 1997 with data from later years.

[4]Refers to the Standard Metropolitan Statistical Area (MSA) status of the respondent's household as defined in 2000 by the U.S. Census Bureau. Categories include "central city of an MSA (Urban)," "in MSA but not in central city (Suburban)," and "not MSA (Rural)."
[5]In the question asking students about carrying "a weapon at school, "on school property," was not defined for survey respondents.
NOTE: Respondents were asked about carrying "a weapon such as a gun, knife, or club."
SOURCE: Centers for Disease Control and Prevention, Division of Adolescent and School Health, Youth Risk Behavior Surveillance System (YRBSS), 1993 through 2013. (This table was prepared June 2014.)

Table 231.50. Percentage distribution of students in grades 9–12, by number of days they reported carrying a weapon anywhere or on school property during the previous 30 days and selected student characteristics: 2013

[Standard errors appear in parentheses]

Student characteristic	Anywhere (including on school property)[1]								On school property[2]							
	0 days		1 day		2 to 5 days		6 or more days		0 days		1 day		2 to 5 days		6 or more days	
1	2		3		4		5		6		7		8		9	
Total............................	82.1	(0.73)	3.4	(0.19)	5.5	(0.22)	9.0	(0.67)	94.8	(0.44)	1.4	(0.14)	1.2	(0.13)	2.6	(0.42)
Sex																
Male................................	71.9	(1.31)	5.0	(0.31)	8.9	(0.45)	14.2	(1.23)	92.4	(0.70)	2.0	(0.23)	1.9	(0.23)	3.7	(0.64)
Female..............................	92.1	(0.56)	1.8	(0.20)	2.2	(0.19)	3.8	(0.39)	97.0	(0.40)	0.8	(0.15)	0.5	(0.14)	1.6	(0.33)
Race/ethnicity[3]																
White................................	79.2	(0.90)	3.4	(0.31)	6.1	(0.30)	11.3	(0.97)	94.3	(0.65)	1.3	(0.19)	1.1	(0.15)	3.3	(0.67)
Black.................................	87.5	(0.96)	2.8	(0.42)	4.2	(0.63)	5.5	(0.57)	96.1	(0.42)	1.6	(0.29)	1.4	(0.31)	0.9	(0.18)
Hispanic............................	84.5	(0.95)	4.0	(0.37)	5.1	(0.46)	6.4	(0.59)	95.3	(0.61)	1.5	(0.33)	1.3	(0.28)	1.9	(0.29)
Asian................................	91.3	(1.79)	1.5 !	(0.55)	2.5 !	(0.76)	4.7 !	(1.49)	96.2	(1.13)	0.8 !	(0.41)	‡	(†)	2.4 !	(1.01)
Pacific Islander..................	87.4	(3.98)	‡	(†)	6.8	(1.95)	4.5 !	(1.99)	96.0	(1.95)	‡	(†)	‡	(†)	‡	(†)
American Indian/Alaska Native....	82.2	(4.01)	‡	(†)	‡	(†)	9.9	(2.12)	93.0	(3.22)	‡	(†)	‡	(†)	2.7 !	(1.31)
Two or more races	81.2	(2.09)	5.3	(1.26)	6.8	(1.14)	6.6	(1.08)	93.7	(1.58)	2.4 !	(0.93)	‡	(†)	2.6	(0.69)
Grade																
9th....................................	82.5	(0.99)	4.0	(0.37)	5.7	(0.69)	7.8	(0.69)	95.2	(0.69)	1.6	(0.28)	1.1	(0.28)	2.1	(0.38)
10th..................................	82.2	(1.09)	3.8	(0.42)	5.9	(0.72)	8.0	(0.64)	95.2	(0.58)	1.7	(0.26)	1.0	(0.21)	2.1	(0.44)
11th..................................	82.1	(1.43)	2.8	(0.34)	5.5	(0.49)	9.6	(1.29)	94.1	(1.19)	1.3	(0.34)	1.4	(0.25)	3.3 !	(1.10)
12th..................................	81.7	(1.17)	2.9	(0.37)	4.9	(0.60)	10.5	(0.86)	94.7	(0.88)	0.9	(0.18)	1.4	(0.37)	3.1	(0.60)

†Not applicable.
!Interpret data with caution. The coefficient of variation (CV) for this estimate is between 30 and 50 percent.
‡Reporting standards not met. Either there are too few cases for a reliable estimate or the coefficient of variation (CV) is 50 percent or greater.
[1]The term "anywhere" is not used in the Youth Risk Behavior Survey (YRBS) questionnaire; students were simply asked how many days they carried a weapon during the past 30 days.

[2]In the question asking students about carrying a weapon at school, "on school property" was not defined for survey respondents.
[3]Race categories exclude persons of Hispanic ethnicity.
NOTE: Respondents were asked about carrying "a weapon such as a gun, knife, or club." Detail may not sum to totals because of rounding.
SOURCE: Centers for Disease Control and Prevention, Division of Adolescent and School Health, Youth Risk Behavior Surveillance System (YRBSS), 2013. (This table was prepared June 2014.)

Table 231.60. Percentage of public school students in grades 9–12 who reported carrying a weapon at least 1 day during the previous 30 days, by location and state: Selected years, 2003 through 2013

[Standard errors appear in parentheses]

State	Anywhere (including on school property)[1]						On school property[2]					
	2003	2005	2007	2009	2011	2013	2003	2005	2007	2009	2011	2013
1	2	3	4	5	6	7	8	9	10	11	12	13
United States[3]	17.1 (0.90)	18.5 (0.80)	18.0 (0.87)	17.5 (0.73)	16.6 (0.65)	17.9 (0.73)	6.1 (0.57)	6.5 (0.46)	5.9 (0.37)	5.6 (0.32)	5.4 (0.35)	5.2 (0.44)
Alabama	19.9 (1.44)	21.0 (1.72)	— (†)	22.9 (2.27)	21.5 (1.54)	23.1 (1.55)	7.3 (1.35)	8.4 (1.44)	— (†)	8.7 (1.42)	8.2 (1.02)	5.5 (0.56)
Alaska	18.4 (1.14)	— (†)	24.4 (1.61)	20.0 (1.30)	19.0 (1.19)	19.2 (1.31)	7.1 (0.81)	— (†)	8.4 (1.07)	7.8 (0.83)	5.7 (0.72)	6.1 (0.80)
Arizona	18.4 (0.82)	20.6 (0.84)	20.5 (0.91)	19.9 (1.25)	17.5 (1.17)	17.5 (1.17)	5.8 (0.68)	7.4 (0.53)	7.0 (0.75)	6.5 (0.64)	5.7 (0.59)	4.8 (0.86)
Arkansas	— (†)	25.9 (1.15)	20.7 (1.36)	22.9 (1.82)	21.1 (1.76)	27.1 (1.76)	— (†)	10.5 (1.10)	6.8 (0.85)	8.4 (1.02)	6.5 (0.95)	9.1 (1.10)
California	— (†)	— (†)	— (†)	— (†)	— (†)	— (†)	— (†)	— (†)	— (†)	— (†)	— (†)	— (†)
Colorado	— (†)	17.0 (1.57)	— (†)	16.7 (1.27)	15.5 (1.31)	— (†)	— (†)	5.4 (0.81)	— (†)	5.5 (0.90)	5.5 (0.69)	— (†)
Connecticut	— (†)	16.3 (1.30)	17.2 (1.72)	12.4 (0.89)	— (†)	— (†)	— (†)	6.4 (0.83)	5.5 (1.03)	3.9 (0.45)	6.6 (0.67)	6.6 (0.82)
Delaware	16.0 (0.88)	16.6 (1.04)	17.1 (1.00)	18.5 (0.92)	13.5 (0.88)	14.4 (0.80)	5.0 (0.47)	5.7 (0.54)	5.4 (0.55)	5.1 (0.59)	5.2 (0.57)	3.1 (0.34)
District of Columbia	25.0 (1.40)	17.2 (1.11)	21.3 (1.45)	— (†)	18.9 (1.34)	— (†)	10.6 (0.96)	6.7 (0.60)	7.4 (0.76)	— (†)	5.5 (0.88)	— (†)
Florida	17.2 (0.76)	15.2 (0.68)	18.0 (0.93)	17.3 (0.60)	15.6 (0.76)	15.7 (0.67)	5.3 (0.38)	4.7 (0.41)	5.6 (0.41)	4.7 (0.35)	— (†)	— (†)
Georgia	18.7 (1.17)	22.1 (1.99)	19.5 (0.96)	18.8 (1.11)	22.8 (2.25)	18.5 (1.51)	5.0 (0.52)	7.5 (1.50)	5.3 (0.48)	6.0 (0.90)	8.6 (1.80)	4.2 (0.66)
Hawaii	— (†)	13.3 (1.03)	14.8 (1.56)	15.9 (2.06)	13.9 (0.81)	10.5 (0.87)	— (†)	4.9 (0.72)	3.7 (0.92)	4.7 (0.63)	4.2 (0.45)	— (†)
Idaho	— (†)	23.9 (1.45)	23.6 (1.35)	21.8 (1.15)	22.8 (1.30)	27.1 (1.31)	7.7 (0.90)	— (†)	8.9 (0.96)	6.7 (0.59)	6.3 (0.78)	6.5 (0.92)
Illinois	— (†)	— (†)	14.3 (1.01)	16.0 (1.04)	12.6 (0.91)	15.8 (1.22)	— (†)	— (†)	3.7 (0.67)	4.8 (0.59)	3.9 (0.53)	4.7 (0.57)
Indiana	17.8 (1.93)	19.2 (1.25)	20.9 (0.80)	18.1 (1.58)	17.0 (1.46)	— (†)	6.2 (0.91)	5.8 (0.71)	6.9 (0.64)	5.7 (0.80)	3.7 (0.46)	— (†)
Iowa	— (†)	15.7 (1.49)	12.8 (1.13)	— (†)	15.8 (1.26)	— (†)	— (†)	4.3 (0.70)	4.4 (0.61)	— (†)	4.5 (0.76)	— (†)
Kansas	— (†)	16.2 (1.37)	18.4 (1.19)	16.0 (1.26)	— (†)	16.1 (0.87)	— (†)	4.9 (0.85)	5.7 (0.75)	5.1 (0.65)	5.2 (0.72)	— (†)
Kentucky	18.5 (1.20)	23.1 (1.49)	24.4 (1.08)	21.7 (1.72)	22.8 (1.72)	20.7 (1.35)	7.4 (0.86)	6.8 (0.72)	8.0 (0.59)	6.5 (0.77)	7.4 (1.25)	6.4 (0.73)
Louisiana	— (†)	— (†)	— (†)	19.6 (1.73)	22.2 (0.98)	22.8 (2.78)	— (†)	— (†)	— (†)	5.8 (1.12)	4.2 (1.01)	7.0 (1.37)
Maine	16.5 (1.20)	18.3 (2.00)	15.0 (1.47)	— (†)	— (†)	— (†)	6.6 (0.91)	5.9 (1.03)	4.9 (0.70)	— (†)	8.0 (0.45)	7.1 (0.46)
Maryland	— (†)	19.1 (1.59)	19.3 (1.51)	16.6 (1.19)	15.9 (1.10)	15.8 (0.27)	— (†)	6.9 (0.88)	5.9 (0.81)	4.6 (0.58)	5.3 (0.55)	4.8 (0.13)
Massachusetts	13.5 (0.89)	15.2 (0.88)	14.9 (0.88)	12.8 (1.00)	12.3 (0.95)	11.6 (0.83)	5.0 (0.50)	5.8 (0.59)	5.0 (0.48)	4.4 (0.58)	3.7 (0.46)	3.1 (0.50)
Michigan	15.2 (0.89)	15.8 (1.49)	17.9 (1.30)	16.6 (0.69)	15.7 (0.94)	15.5 (1.06)	5.1 (0.66)	4.7 (0.54)	5.0 (0.66)	5.4 (0.33)	3.5 (0.37)	3.8 (0.35)
Minnesota	— (†)	— (†)	— (†)	— (†)	— (†)	— (†)	— (†)	— (†)	— (†)	— (†)	— (†)	— (†)
Mississippi	20.0 (1.78)	— (†)	17.3 (1.33)	17.2 (1.02)	18.0 (1.39)	19.1 (1.56)	5.2 (0.78)	— (†)	4.8 (0.60)	4.5 (0.48)	4.2 (0.76)	4.1 (0.66)
Missouri	16.8 (1.87)	19.4 (1.79)	18.6 (1.48)	16.0 (1.44)	— (†)	22.2 (1.93)	5.5 (1.04)	7.3 (0.99)	4.6 (0.83)	5.3 (1.02)	— (†)	— (†)
Montana	19.4 (0.88)	21.4 (1.20)	22.1 (0.76)	23.0 (1.07)	23.5 (0.96)	25.7 (0.84)	7.2 (0.56)	10.2 (0.89)	9.7 (0.57)	7.9 (0.67)	9.3 (0.69)	9.9 (0.58)
Nebraska	16.0 (1.06)	17.9 (0.89)	— (†)	— (†)	18.6 (0.90)	— (†)	5.0 (0.53)	4.8 (0.48)	— (†)	— (†)	3.8 (0.45)	— (†)
Nevada	14.9 (1.09)	18.4 (1.32)	14.5 (1.08)	19.1 (1.08)	— (†)	16.0 (1.50)	6.3 (0.67)	6.8 (0.91)	4.7 (0.61)	6.2 (0.62)	— (†)	3.3 (0.64)
New Hampshire	15.1 (1.59)	16.2 (1.26)	18.1 (1.46)	— (†)	14.5 (1.04)	— (†)	5.8 (1.00)	6.5 (0.93)	5.8 (0.61)	8.8 (1.00)	— (†)	— (†)
New Jersey	— (†)	10.5 (0.95)	— (†)	9.6 (0.81)	9.6 (1.17)	10.2 (1.08)	— (†)	3.1 (0.53)	— (†)	3.1 (0.45)	— (†)	2.7 (0.34)
New Mexico	— (†)	24.5 (1.44)	27.5 (1.20)	27.4 (0.90)	22.8 (0.93)	22.2 (0.88)	— (†)	8.0 (0.29)	9.3 (0.66)	8.1 (0.59)	6.5 (0.51)	5.4 (0.42)
New York	13.5 (1.01)	14.3 (0.74)	14.2 (0.76)	13.9 (0.98)	12.6 (0.76)	12.8 (0.82)	5.2 (0.51)	5.2 (0.42)	4.7 (0.41)	4.8 (0.64)	4.2 (0.32)	4.0 (0.38)
North Carolina	19.2 (1.49)	21.5 (1.35)	21.2 (1.19)	19.6 (0.95)	20.8 (1.24)	20.6 (1.34)	6.3 (0.79)	6.4 (0.77)	6.8 (0.94)	4.7 (0.57)	6.1 (0.64)	4.5 (0.67)
North Dakota	— (†)	— (†)	— (†)	— (†)	— (†)	— (†)	5.7 (0.98)	6.0 (0.74)	5.0 (0.57)	5.4 (0.64)	5.7 (0.73)	6.4 (0.75)
Ohio[4]	12.5 (1.40)	15.2 (1.27)	16.6 (1.42)	— (†)	16.4 (1.37)	14.2 (1.61)	3.6 (0.75)	4.4 (0.63)	4.1 (0.51)	— (†)	— (†)	— (†)
Oklahoma	21.8 (1.72)	18.9 (1.38)	22.3 (1.65)	19.0 (1.44)	19.4 (1.86)	19.9 (1.41)	8.0 (1.01)	7.0 (0.77)	9.0 (1.43)	5.6 (0.79)	6.1 (1.14)	6.0 (0.77)
Oregon	— (†)	— (†)	— (†)	— (†)	— (†)	— (†)	— (†)	— (†)	— (†)	— (†)	— (†)	— (†)
Pennsylvania	— (†)	— (†)	— (†)	14.8 (1.28)	— (†)	— (†)	— (†)	— (†)	— (†)	3.3 (0.47)	— (†)	— (†)
Rhode Island	12.3 (1.01)	12.4 (0.90)	12.0 (0.74)	10.4 (0.50)	11.2 (0.82)	— (†)	5.9 (0.85)	4.9 (0.41)	4.9 (0.63)	4.0 (0.33)	4.0 (0.39)	5.0 (0.78)
South Carolina	— (†)	20.5 (1.42)	19.8 (1.69)	20.4 (2.22)	23.4 (1.86)	21.2 (1.25)	— (†)	6.7 (0.82)	4.8 (0.79)	4.6 (0.67)	6.3 (0.89)	3.7 (0.48)
South Dakota[4]	— (†)	— (†)	— (†)	— (†)	— (†)	— (†)	7.1 (0.73)	8.3 (0.72)	6.3 (0.80)	9.2 (0.76)	5.7 (0.52)	6.8 (0.87)
Tennessee	21.3 (2.06)	24.1 (1.58)	22.6 (1.41)	20.5 (1.64)	21.1 (1.34)	19.2 (1.70)	5.4 (0.80)	8.1 (0.92)	5.6 (0.70)	5.1 (0.70)	5.2 (0.80)	5.4 (0.79)
Texas	— (†)	19.3 (0.93)	18.8 (0.71)	18.2 (0.89)	17.6 (0.73)	18.4 (1.33)	— (†)	7.9 (0.63)	6.8 (0.55)	6.4 (0.76)	4.9 (0.45)	5.6 (0.68)
Utah	15.3 (1.80)	17.7 (1.70)	17.1 (1.38)	16.0 (1.40)	16.8 (1.48)	17.2 (1.19)	5.6 (1.24)	7.0 (1.03)	7.5 (1.00)	4.6 (0.63)	5.9 (1.01)	5.0 (0.57)
Vermont	— (†)	— (†)	— (†)	— (†)	— (†)	— (†)	8.3 (0.31)	9.1 (0.90)	9.6 (1.05)	9.0 (0.61)	9.1 (0.73)	10.4 (1.28)
Virginia	— (†)	— (†)	— (†)	— (†)	20.4 (1.26)	15.8 (0.69)	— (†)	— (†)	— (†)	— (†)	5.7 (0.64)	— (†)
Washington	— (†)	— (†)	— (†)	— (†)	— (†)	— (†)	— (†)	— (†)	— (†)	— (†)	— (†)	— (†)
West Virginia	20.7 (1.37)	22.3 (1.32)	21.3 (1.52)	24.4 (1.05)	20.7 (1.64)	24.3 (2.16)	6.6 (1.25)	8.5 (1.00)	6.9 (0.89)	6.5 (0.72)	5.5 (0.75)	5.5 (0.99)
Wisconsin	13.2 (0.81)	15.8 (1.19)	12.7 (0.76)	10.9 (0.81)	10.4 (0.66)	14.4 (1.32)	3.2 (0.43)	3.9 (0.54)	3.6 (0.49)	3.4 (0.50)	3.1 (0.41)	3.2 (0.52)
Wyoming	24.6 (1.49)	28.0 (1.17)	26.8 (1.28)	26.0 (1.04)	27.1 (1.19)	28.8 (0.95)	10.1 (0.91)	10.0 (0.71)	11.4 (0.76)	11.5 (0.81)	10.5 (0.71)	9.9 (0.62)

—Not available.
†Not applicable.
[1]The term "anywhere" is not used in the Youth Risk Behavior Survey (YRBS) questionnaire; students were simply asked how many days they carried a weapon during the past 30 days.
[2]In the question asking students about carrying a weapon at school, "on school property" was not defined for survey respondents.
[3]Data for the U.S. total include both public and private schools and were collected through a national survey representing the entire country.
[4]Data include both public and private schools.
NOTE: Respondents were asked about carrying "a weapon such as a gun, knife, or club." State-level data include public schools only, with the exception of data for Ohio and South Dakota. Data for the U.S. total, Ohio, and South Dakota include both public and private schools. For specific states, a given year's data may be unavailable (1) because the state did not participate in the survey that year; (2) because the state omitted this particular survey item from the state-level questionnaire; or (3) because the state had an overall response rate of less than 60 percent (the overall response rate is the school response rate multiplied by the student response rate).
SOURCE: Centers for Disease Control and Prevention, Division of Adolescent and School Health, Youth Risk Behavior Surveillance System (YRBSS), 2003 through 2013. (This table was prepared June 2014.)

Table 231.65. Number of incidents of students bringing firearms to or possessing firearms at a public school and ratio of incidents per 100,000 students, by state: 2008–09 through 2012–13

State	Number of firearm incidents					Ratio of firearm incidents per 100,000 students				
	2008–09	2009–10	2010–11	2011–12	2012–13	2008–09	2009–10	2010–11	2011–12	2012–13
1	2	3	4	5	6	7	8	9	10	11
United States	1,608	1,749	1,685	1,333	1,556	3.3	3.5	3.4	2.7	3.1
Alabama	23	23	15	5	46	3.1	3.1	2.0	0.7	6.2
Alaska	8	7	3	5	5	6.1	5.3	2.3	3.8	3.8
Arizona	32	18	7	22	18	2.9	1.7	0.7	2.0	1.7
Arkansas	57 [1]	32	45	50	65	11.9 [1]	6.7	9.3	10.3	13.4
California	138	267	220	79	129	2.2	4.3	3.5	1.3	2.0
Colorado	21	23	19	17	23	2.6	2.8	2.3	2.0	2.7
Connecticut	30	29	12	21	19	5.3	5.1	2.1	3.8	3.4
Delaware	4	7	2	1	2	3.2	5.5	1.5	0.8	1.6
District of Columbia	—	2	2	2	0	—	2.9	2.8	2.7	0.0
Florida	60	66	63	51	62	2.3	2.5	2.4	1.9	2.3
Georgia	125	132	154	104	118	7.5	7.9	9.2	6.2	6.9
Hawaii	2	1	2	1	0	1.1	0.6	1.1	0.5	0.0
Idaho	22	12	—	10	5	8.0	4.3	—	3.6	1.8
Illinois	46 [1]	21	5	5	9	2.2 [1]	1.0	0.2	0.2	0.4
Indiana	39	42	28	26	27	3.7	4.0	2.7	2.5	2.6
Iowa	10	5	2	2	3	2.1	1.0	0.4	0.4	0.6
Kansas	21	32	20	9	28	4.5	6.7	4.1	1.9	5.7
Kentucky	20	12	15	23	20	3.0	1.8	2.2	3.4	2.9
Louisiana	60	50	49	43	66	8.8	7.2	7.0	6.1	9.3
Maine	2	2	2	4	2	1.0	1.1	1.1	2.1	1.1
Maryland	16	8	8	10	11	1.9	0.9	0.9	1.2	1.3
Massachusetts	13	11	12	7	10	1.4	1.1	1.3	0.7	1.0
Michigan	35	37	80	60	70	2.1	2.2	5.0	3.8	4.5
Minnesota	19	21	23	10	19	2.3	2.5	2.7	1.2	2.2
Mississippi	21	42	32	32	38	4.3	8.5	6.5	6.5	7.7
Missouri	119	104	120	81	110	13.0	11.3	13.1	8.8	12.0
Montana	18	14	11	9	8	12.7	9.9	7.8	6.3	5.6
Nebraska	7	8	13	10	16	2.4	2.7	4.4	3.3	5.3
Nevada	—	18	14	14	8	—	4.2	3.2	3.2	1.8
New Hampshire	3	2	5	6	4	1.5	1.0	2.6	3.1	2.1
New Jersey	4	5	5	6	5	0.3	0.4	0.4	0.4	0.4
New Mexico	24	18	25	18	13	7.3	5.4	7.4	5.3	3.8
New York	36 [2]	17 [2]	18 [2]	46	28	1.3 [2]	0.6 [2]	0.7 [2]	1.7	1.0
North Carolina	23	23	9	9	11	1.5	1.6	0.6	0.6	0.7
North Dakota	1	2	11	2	5	1.1	2.1	11.4	2.0	4.9
Ohio	88	103	91	76	71	4.8	5.8	5.2	4.4	4.1
Oklahoma	47	37	22	27	39	7.3	5.7	3.3	4.1	5.8
Oregon	18	14	17	19	16	3.1	2.4	3.0	3.3	2.7
Pennsylvania	25	27	24	23	34	1.4	1.5	1.3	1.3	1.9
Rhode Island	2	3	7	1	0	1.4	2.1	4.9	0.7	0.0
South Carolina	31	32	8	26	49	4.3	4.4	1.1	3.6	6.7
South Dakota	9	8	2	10	9	7.1	6.5	1.6	7.8	6.9
Tennessee	85	79	43	82	64	8.7	8.1	4.4	8.2	6.4
Texas	95	103	93	85	100	2.0	2.1	1.9	1.7	2.0
Utah	19	5	76	99 [1]	49	3.4	0.9	13.0	16.5 [1]	8.0
Vermont	4	1	3	1	2	4.3	1.1	3.1	1.1	2.2
Virginia	48	34	30	32	31	3.9	2.7	2.4	2.5	2.4
Washington	44	162	173	26	33	4.2	15.6	16.6	2.5	3.1
West Virginia	7	4	3	14	1	2.5	1.4	1.1	4.9	0.4
Wisconsin	16	19	33	8	37	1.8	2.2	3.8	0.9	4.2
Wyoming	11	5	9	4	18	12.6	5.7	10.1	4.4	19.7

—Not available.

[1]The state reported a total state-level firearm incident count that was less than the sum of its reported district-level counts. The sum of the district-level firearm incident counts is displayed instead of the reported state-level count.

[2]Data for New York City Public Schools were not reported.

NOTE: Separate counts were collected for incidents involving handguns, rifles/shotguns, other firearms, and multiple types of firearms. The counts reported here exclude the "other firearms" category.

SOURCE: U.S. Department of Education, National Center for Education Statistics, EDFacts file 094, Data Group 601, extracted December 9, 2014, from the EDFacts Data Warehouse (internal U.S. Department of Education source); Common Core of Data (CCD), "State Nonfiscal Survey of Public Elementary and Secondary Education," 2008–09 through 2012–13. (This table was prepared December 2014.)

Table 231.70. Percentage of students ages 12–18 who reported having access to a loaded gun, without adult permission, at school or away from school during the school year, by selected student and school characteristics: Selected years, 2007 through 2013

[Standard errors appear in parentheses]

Student or school characteristic	2007		2009		2011		2013	
1	2		3		4		5	
Total	6.7	(0.40)	5.5	(0.47)	4.7	(0.43)	3.7	(0.38)
Sex								
Male	8.4	(0.56)	7.6	(0.72)	5.6	(0.59)	3.9	(0.56)
Female	5.0	(0.47)	3.4	(0.44)	3.6	(0.44)	3.4	(0.35)
Race/ethnicity[1]								
White	7.7	(0.55)	6.4	(0.60)	5.3	(0.50)	4.2	(0.45)
Black	6.2	(0.98)	3.9	(0.92)	4.1	(0.86)	3.4	(0.78)
Hispanic	4.8	(0.79)	4.9	(0.90)	4.1	(0.89)	3.0	(0.71)
Asian	‡	(†)	‡	(†)	‡	(†)	‡	(†)
Other	9.3	(2.30)	5.4 !	(2.40)	‡	(†)	4.7 !	(1.79)
Grade								
6th	2.4	(0.64)	0.8 !	(0.40)	2.0 !	(0.89)	‡	(†)
7th	2.6	(0.56)	3.6	(0.84)	3.0	(0.63)	2.0	(0.50)
8th	3.2	(0.63)	3.2	(0.63)	2.9	(0.60)	2.4	(0.62)
9th	6.8	(0.98)	4.4	(0.80)	4.0	(0.75)	3.3	(0.80)
10th	9.2	(1.13)	7.3	(1.02)	5.3	(0.70)	4.7	(0.80)
11th	9.9	(1.00)	7.6	(1.16)	6.4	(1.06)	5.9	(0.99)
12th	12.3	(1.33)	9.8	(1.44)	8.2	(1.06)	5.8	(0.99)
Urbanicity[2]								
Urban	5.8	(0.67)	4.7	(0.72)	4.1	(0.61)	3.2	(0.54)
Suburban	6.4	(0.59)	5.5	(0.57)	4.9	(0.55)	3.7	(0.46)
Rural	9.1	(1.04)	7.1	(1.39)	4.9	(0.92)	4.6	(0.91)
Control of school								
Public	6.9	(0.44)	5.8	(0.49)	4.8	(0.42)	3.7	(0.40)
Private	4.5	(0.88)	2.3 !	(0.83)	3.2 !	(0.98)	3.6	(1.01)

†Not applicable.
!Interpret data with caution. The coefficient of variation (CV) for this estimate is between 30 and 50 percent.
‡Reporting standards not met. Either there are too few cases for a reliable estimate or the coefficient of variation (CV) is 50 percent or greater.
[1]Race categories exclude persons of Hispanic ethnicity. "Other" includes American Indians/Alaska Natives, Pacific Islanders, and persons reporting that they are of Two or more races.

[2]Refers to the Standard Metropolitan Statistical Area (MSA) status of the respondent's household as defined in 2000 by the U.S. Census Bureau. Categories include "central city of an MSA (Urban)," "in MSA but not in central city (Suburban)," and "not MSA (Rural)."
SOURCE: U.S. Department of Justice, Bureau of Justice Statistics, School Crime Supplement (SCS) to the National Crime Victimization Survey, 2007 through 2013. (This table was prepared October 2014.)

Table 232.10. Percentage of students in grades 9–12 who reported using alcohol at least 1 day during the previous 30 days, by location and selected student characteristics: Selected years, 1993 through 2013

[Standard errors appear in parentheses]

Location and student characteristic	1993	1995	1997	1999	2001	2003	2005	2007	2009	2011	2013
1	2	3	4	5	6	7	8	9	10	11	12
Anywhere (including on school property)[1]											
Total	48.0 (1.06)	51.6 (1.19)	50.8 (1.43)	50.0 (1.30)	47.1 (1.11)	44.9 (1.21)	43.3 (1.38)	44.7 (1.15)	41.8 (0.80)	38.7 (0.75)	34.9 (1.08)
Sex											
Male	50.1 (1.23)	53.2 (1.33)	53.3 (1.22)	52.3 (1.47)	49.2 (1.42)	43.8 (1.31)	43.8 (1.40)	44.7 (1.39)	40.8 (1.11)	39.5 (0.93)	34.4 (1.30)
Female	45.9 (1.32)	49.9 (1.79)	47.8 (1.99)	47.7 (1.45)	45.0 (1.11)	45.8 (1.29)	42.8 (1.56)	44.6 (1.42)	42.9 (0.85)	37.9 (0.91)	35.5 (1.39)
Race/ethnicity[2]											
White	49.9 (1.26)	54.1 (1.77)	54.0 (1.51)	52.5 (1.62)	50.4 (1.12)	47.1 (1.51)	46.4 (1.84)	47.3 (1.67)	44.7 (1.16)	40.3 (0.97)	36.3 (1.63)
Black	42.5 (1.82)	42.0 (2.24)	36.9 (1.46)	39.9 (4.07)	32.7 (2.33)	37.4 (1.67)	31.2 (1.05)	34.5 (1.65)	33.4 (1.45)	30.5 (1.40)	29.6 (1.65)
Hispanic	50.8 (2.82)	54.7 (2.56)	53.9 (1.96)	52.8 (2.41)	49.2 (1.52)	45.6 (1.39)	46.8 (1.39)	47.6 (1.80)	42.9 (1.43)	42.3 (1.38)	37.5 (2.11)
Asian[3]	— (†)	— (†)	— (†)	25.7 (2.24)	28.4 (3.22)	27.5 (3.47)	21.5 (1.98)	25.4 (2.17)	18.3 (1.60)	25.6 (2.90)	21.7 (1.80)
Pacific Islander[3]	— (†)	— (†)	— (†)	60.8 (5.11)	52.3 (8.54)	40.0 (7.04)	38.7 (8.43)	48.8 (6.58)	34.8 (4.36)	38.4 (6.40)	26.8 (5.84)
American Indian/Alaska Native[3]	45.3! (7.18)	51.4 (7.18)	57.6 (3.79)	49.4 (6.43)	51.4 (3.97)	51.9 (5.29)	57.4 (4.13)	34.5 (1.77)	42.8 (5.43)	44.9 (2.26)	33.4 (5.13)
Two or more races[3]	— (†)	— (†)	— (†)	51.1 (3.98)	45.4 (4.11)	47.1 (3.59)	39.0 (3.59)	46.2 (2.89)	44.3 (2.42)	36.9 (3.08)	36.1 (2.87)
Grade[4]											
9th	40.5 (1.79)	45.6 (1.87)	44.2 (3.12)	40.6 (2.17)	41.1 (1.82)	36.2 (1.43)	36.2 (1.23)	35.7 (1.15)	31.5 (1.28)	29.8 (1.35)	24.4 (1.13)
10th	44.0 (2.00)	49.5 (2.38)	47.2 (2.19)	49.7 (1.89)	45.2 (1.29)	43.5 (1.66)	42.0 (1.95)	41.8 (1.68)	40.6 (1.42)	35.7 (1.37)	30.9 (1.84)
11th	49.7 (1.73)	53.7 (1.51)	53.2 (1.49)	50.9 (1.98)	49.3 (1.70)	47.0 (2.08)	46.0 (1.98)	49.0 (1.83)	45.7 (2.05)	42.7 (1.28)	39.2 (1.52)
12th	56.4 (1.35)	56.5 (1.64)	57.3 (2.50)	61.7 (2.25)	55.2 (1.53)	55.9 (1.65)	50.8 (2.12)	54.9 (2.09)	51.7 (1.37)	48.4 (1.29)	46.8 (1.85)
Urbanicity[4]											
Urban	— (†)	— (†)	48.9 (2.07)	46.5 (2.75)	45.2 (1.97)	41.5 (1.48)	— (†)	— (†)	— (†)	— (†)	— (†)
Suburban	— (†)	— (†)	50.5 (2.11)	51.4 (1.32)	47.6 (1.26)	46.5 (2.10)	— (†)	— (†)	— (†)	— (†)	— (†)
Rural	— (†)	— (†)	55.4 (5.36)	52.2 (4.51)	50.2 (1.91)	45.3 (2.35)	— (†)	— (†)	— (†)	— (†)	— (†)
On school property[5]											
Total	5.2 (0.39)	6.3 (0.45)	5.6 (0.34)	4.9 (0.39)	4.9 (0.28)	5.2 (0.46)	4.3 (0.30)	4.1 (0.32)	4.5 (0.29)	5.1 (0.33)	— (†)
Sex											
Male	6.2 (0.39)	7.2 (0.50)	7.2 (0.66)	6.1 (0.54)	6.1 (0.43)	6.0 (0.61)	5.3 (0.39)	4.6 (0.35)	5.3 (0.41)	5.4 (0.43)	— (†)
Female	4.2 (0.54)	5.3 (0.70)	3.6 (0.37)	3.6 (0.39)	3.8 (0.39)	4.2 (0.41)	3.3 (0.32)	3.6 (0.37)	3.6 (0.34)	4.7 (0.35)	— (†)
Race/ethnicity[2]											
White	4.6 (0.44)	5.6 (0.62)	4.8 (0.42)	4.8 (0.55)	4.2 (0.26)	3.9 (0.45)	3.8 (0.38)	3.2 (0.35)	3.3 (0.27)	4.0 (0.38)	— (†)
Black	6.9 (0.98)	7.6 (0.87)	5.6 (0.72)	4.3 (0.52)	5.3 (0.65)	5.8 (0.80)	3.2 (0.45)	3.4 (0.63)	5.4 (0.59)	5.1 (0.50)	— (†)
Hispanic	6.8 (0.84)	9.6 (1.73)	8.2 (0.96)	7.0 (0.88)	7.0 (0.71)	7.6 (1.08)	7.7 (1.04)	7.5 (0.86)	6.9 (0.70)	7.3 (0.68)	— (†)
Asian[3]	— (†)	— (†)	— (†)	2.0 (0.42)	6.8 (1.42)	5.6 (1.55)	1.3! (0.62)	4.4 (1.17)	2.9 (0.65)	3.5! (1.21)	— (†)
Pacific Islander[3]	— (†)	— (†)	— (†)	6.7 (1.59)	12.4 (3.50)	8.5! (3.29)	‡ (†)	‡ (†)	10.0 (2.34)	8.3! (3.61)	— (†)
American Indian/Alaska Native[3]	6.7! (3.06)	8.1! (3.30)	8.6! (4.15)	‡ (†)	8.2 (1.69)	7.1! (2.61)	6.2! (2.05)	5.0 (0.89)	4.3! (1.58)	20.9 (4.15)	— (†)
Two or more races[3]	— (†)	— (†)	— (†)	5.2 (1.09)	7.0! (2.36)	13.3 (2.93)	3.5 (1.02)	5.4 (1.25)	6.7 (1.37)	5.8 (1.32)	— (†)
Grade[4]											
9th	5.2 (0.38)	7.5 (0.90)	5.9 (0.83)	4.4 (0.60)	5.3 (0.47)	5.1 (0.69)	3.7 (0.48)	3.4 (0.43)	4.4 (0.37)	5.4 (0.56)	— (†)
10th	4.7 (0.43)	5.9 (0.88)	4.6 (0.71)	5.0 (0.67)	5.1 (0.45)	5.6 (0.60)	4.5 (0.45)	4.1 (0.50)	4.8 (0.46)	4.4 (0.51)	— (†)
11th	5.2 (0.80)	5.7 (0.86)	6.0 (0.86)	4.7 (0.57)	4.7 (0.45)	5.0 (0.57)	4.0 (0.47)	4.2 (0.54)	4.6 (0.44)	5.2 (0.56)	— (†)
12th	5.5 (0.64)	6.2 (0.58)	5.9 (0.66)	5.0 (0.89)	4.3 (0.44)	4.5 (0.68)	4.8 (0.57)	4.8 (0.55)	4.1 (0.44)	5.1 (0.48)	— (†)
Urbanicity[4]											
Urban	— (†)	— (†)	6.4 (0.85)	5.0 (0.60)	5.4 (0.61)	6.1 (0.94)	— (†)	— (†)	— (†)	— (†)	— (†)
Suburban	— (†)	— (†)	5.2 (0.43)	4.6 (0.61)	4.9 (0.37)	4.8 (0.54)	— (†)	— (†)	— (†)	— (†)	— (†)
Rural	— (†)	— (†)	5.3 (0.55)	5.6 (0.67)	4.0 (0.83)	4.7 (0.49)	— (†)	— (†)	— (†)	— (†)	— (†)

—Not available.
†Not applicable.
!Interpret data with caution. The coefficient of variation (CV) for this estimate is between 30 and 50 percent.
‡Reporting standards not met. The coefficient of variation (CV) for this estimate is 50 percent or greater.
[1]The term "anywhere" is not used in the Youth Risk Behavior Survey (YRBS) questionnaire; students were simply asked how many days during the previous 30 days they had at least one drink of alcohol.
[2]Race categories exclude persons of Hispanic ethnicity.
[3]Before 1999, Asian students and Pacific Islander students were not categorized separately, and students could not be classified as Two or more races. Because the response categories changed in 1999, caution should be used in comparing data on race from 1993, 1995, and 1997 with data from later years.

[4]Refers to the Standard Metropolitan Statistical Area (MSA) status of the respondent's household as defined in 2000 by the U.S. Census Bureau. Categories include "central city of an MSA (Urban)," "in MSA but not in central city (Suburban)," and "not MSA (Rural)."
[5]In the question about drinking alcohol at school, "on school property" was not defined for survey respondents. Data on alcohol use at school were not collected in 2013.
SOURCE: Centers for Disease Control and Prevention, Division of Adolescent and School Health, Youth Risk Behavior Surveillance System (YRBSS), 1993 through 2013. (This table was prepared June 2014.)

Table 232.20. Percentage distribution of students in grades 9–12, by number of days they reported using alcohol anywhere or on school property during the previous 30 days and selected student characteristics: Selected years, 2009 through 2013

[Standard errors appear in parentheses]

Year and student characteristic	Anywhere (including on school property)[1]								On school property[2]							
	0 days		1 or 2 days		3 to 29 days		All 30 days		0 days		1 or 2 days		3 to 29 days		All 30 days	
1	2		3		4		5		6		7		8		9	
2009																
Total	58.2	(0.80)	20.5	(0.40)	20.5	(0.73)	0.8	(0.09)	95.5	(0.29)	2.8	(0.21)	1.3	(0.14)	0.4	(0.07)
Sex																
Male	59.2	(1.11)	17.9	(0.59)	21.7	(0.90)	1.3	(0.19)	94.7	(0.41)	3.0	(0.27)	1.7	(0.20)	0.6	(0.14)
Female	57.1	(0.85)	23.4	(0.73)	19.2	(0.74)	0.3	(0.05)	96.4	(0.34)	2.6	(0.26)	0.9	(0.16)	0.1 !	(0.03)
Race/ethnicity[3]																
White	55.3	(1.16)	20.9	(0.50)	23.2	(1.10)	0.6	(0.10)	96.7	(0.27)	2.0	(0.20)	1.0	(0.14)	0.2	(0.06)
Black	66.6	(1.45)	18.5	(0.80)	14.0	(1.04)	0.9	(0.25)	94.6	(0.59)	3.0	(0.36)	1.8	(0.32)	0.5 !	(0.22)
Hispanic	57.1	(1.43)	21.9	(0.82)	19.6	(1.12)	1.3	(0.22)	93.1	(0.70)	4.4	(0.46)	1.9	(0.37)	0.6	(0.16)
Asian	81.7	(1.60)	11.5	(1.90)	5.9	(1.22)	0.9 !	(0.44)	97.1	(0.65)	1.4 !	(0.47)	0.9 !	(0.43)	‡	(†)
Pacific Islander	65.2	(4.36)	12.4	(2.86)	22.0	(3.42)	‡	(†)	90.0	(2.34)	5.9	(1.68)	3.8 !	(1.56)	‡	(†)
American Indian/Alaska Native	57.2	(5.43)	17.0 !	(5.28)	24.7	(5.33)	‡	(†)	95.7	(1.58)	3.5 !	(1.45)	‡	(†)	#	(†)
Two or more races	55.7	(2.42)	26.8	(2.58)	16.1	(1.90)	1.4 !	(0.56)	93.3	(1.37)	4.7	(0.98)	1.6 !	(0.64)	‡	(†)
Grade																
9th	68.5	(1.28)	17.9	(1.00)	12.9	(0.64)	0.7	(0.16)	95.6	(0.37)	3.0	(0.28)	1.0	(0.17)	0.4 !	(0.13)
10th	59.4	(1.42)	19.5	(0.79)	20.3	(1.27)	0.8	(0.21)	95.2	(0.46)	2.9	(0.35)	1.5	(0.25)	0.4 !	(0.15)
11th	54.3	(2.05)	21.7	(1.41)	23.2	(1.36)	0.8	(0.13)	95.4	(0.44)	2.9	(0.40)	1.4	(0.24)	0.3	(0.09)
12th	48.3	(1.37)	23.6	(0.95)	27.3	(1.55)	0.8	(0.19)	95.9	(0.44)	2.3	(0.29)	1.5	(0.25)	0.3 !	(0.12)
2011																
Total	61.3	(0.75)	19.4	(0.62)	18.3	(0.47)	0.9	(0.11)	94.9	(0.33)	3.3	(0.23)	1.3	(0.15)	0.5	(0.07)
Sex																
Male	60.5	(0.93)	18.5	(0.68)	19.5	(0.65)	1.5	(0.19)	94.6	(0.43)	3.1	(0.26)	1.5	(0.21)	0.8	(0.14)
Female	62.1	(0.91)	20.5	(0.74)	17.1	(0.63)	0.3	(0.08)	95.3	(0.35)	3.4	(0.29)	1.1	(0.16)	0.1 !	(0.04)
Race/ethnicity[3]																
White	59.7	(0.97)	19.5	(0.83)	20.1	(0.62)	0.7	(0.13)	96.0	(0.38)	2.8	(0.29)	0.9	(0.12)	0.3	(0.06)
Black	69.5	(1.40)	17.5	(1.06)	12.1	(0.97)	0.9	(0.21)	94.9	(0.50)	3.2	(0.41)	1.4	(0.28)	0.5 !	(0.18)
Hispanic	57.7	(1.38)	21.5	(0.75)	19.4	(0.94)	1.4	(0.25)	92.7	(0.68)	4.3	(0.31)	2.2	(0.45)	0.7	(0.17)
Asian	74.4	(2.90)	16.7	(2.86)	7.3	(1.42)	1.6 !	(0.73)	96.5	(1.21)	2.2 !	(0.96)	‡	(†)	‡	(†)
Pacific Islander	61.6	(6.40)	15.6	(3.98)	21.9	(4.87)	‡	(†)	91.7	(3.61)	3.6 !	(1.62)	‡	(†)	‡	(†)
American Indian/Alaska Native	55.1	(2.26)	23.8	(2.23)	20.1	(1.51)	‡	(†)	79.1	(4.15)	15.0	(3.14)	5.3	(0.96)	‡	(†)
Two or more races	63.1	(3.08)	19.6	(2.94)	15.0	(1.88)	2.3 !	(0.96)	94.2	(1.32)	3.3	(0.86)	‡	(†)	1.6 !	(0.74)
Grade																
9th	70.2	(1.35)	17.8	(0.99)	11.2	(0.95)	0.7	(0.18)	94.6	(0.56)	3.7	(0.41)	1.4	(0.31)	0.4	(0.09)
10th	64.3	(1.37)	19.2	(1.11)	15.8	(0.66)	0.6	(0.15)	95.6	(0.51)	2.8	(0.40)	1.2	(0.24)	0.4	(0.11)
11th	57.3	(1.28)	21.1	(0.87)	20.6	(1.31)	1.1	(0.21)	94.8	(0.56)	3.2	(0.39)	1.3	(0.26)	0.7	(0.16)
12th	51.6	(1.29)	20.1	(0.93)	27.1	(1.25)	1.1	(0.24)	94.9	(0.48)	3.5	(0.38)	1.3	(0.26)	0.3 !	(0.10)
2013[4]																
Total	65.1	(1.08)	17.3	(0.56)	16.9	(0.78)	0.8	(0.12)	—	(†)	—	(†)	—	(†)	—	(†)
Sex																
Male	65.6	(1.30)	15.7	(0.75)	17.4	(0.90)	1.2	(0.19)	—	(†)	—	(†)	—	(†)	—	(†)
Female	64.5	(1.39)	18.8	(0.98)	16.3	(0.88)	0.3	(0.09)	—	(†)	—	(†)	—	(†)	—	(†)
Race/ethnicity[3]																
White	63.7	(1.63)	17.6	(0.87)	18.0	(1.11)	0.6	(0.13)	—	(†)	—	(†)	—	(†)	—	(†)
Black	70.4	(1.65)	15.5	(0.90)	13.6	(1.46)	0.6	(0.16)	—	(†)	—	(†)	—	(†)	—	(†)
Hispanic	62.5	(2.11)	18.0	(1.30)	18.3	(1.27)	1.2	(0.35)	—	(†)	—	(†)	—	(†)	—	(†)
Asian	78.3	(1.80)	14.8	(2.26)	6.3	(1.27)	‡	(†)	—	(†)	—	(†)	—	(†)	—	(†)
Pacific Islander	73.2	(5.84)	18.2	(4.71)	7.5	(2.24)	‡	(†)	—	(†)	—	(†)	—	(†)	—	(†)
American Indian/Alaska Native	66.6	(5.13)	14.8	(4.41)	17.4 !	(5.62)	‡	(†)	—	(†)	—	(†)	—	(†)	—	(†)
Two or more races	63.9	(2.87)	18.7	(1.71)	16.4	(2.12)	1.0 !	(0.42)	—	(†)	—	(†)	—	(†)	—	(†)
Grade																
9th	75.6	(1.13)	13.6	(0.89)	10.0	(0.85)	0.7	(0.22)	—	(†)	—	(†)	—	(†)	—	(†)
10th	69.1	(1.84)	15.9	(1.17)	14.5	(1.22)	0.6	(0.16)	—	(†)	—	(†)	—	(†)	—	(†)
11th	60.8	(1.52)	18.6	(1.01)	19.7	(1.26)	0.9	(0.23)	—	(†)	—	(†)	—	(†)	—	(†)
12th	53.2	(1.85)	21.5	(0.93)	24.6	(1.31)	0.7	(0.17)	—	(†)	—	(†)	—	(†)	—	(†)

—Not available.
†Not applicable.
#Rounds to zero.
!Interpret data with caution. The coefficient of variation (CV) for this estimate is between 30 and 50 percent.
‡Reporting standards not met. Either there are too few cases for a reliable estimate or the coefficient of variation (CV) is 50 percent or greater.
[1]The term "anywhere" is not used in the Youth Risk Behavior Survey (YRBS) questionnaire; students were simply asked how many days during the previous 30 days they had at least one drink of alcohol.

[2]In the question about drinking alcohol at school, "on school property" was not defined for survey respondents.
[3]Race categories exclude persons of Hispanic ethnicity.
[4]Data on alcohol use at school were not collected in 2013.
NOTE: Detail may not sum to totals because of rounding.
SOURCE: Centers for Disease Control and Prevention, Division of Adolescent and School Health, Youth Risk Behavior Surveillance System (YRBSS), 2009 through 2013. (This table was prepared September 2014.)

Table 232.30. Percentage of public school students in grades 9–12 who reported using alcohol at least 1 day during the previous 30 days, by location and state: Selected years, 2003 through 2013

[Standard errors appear in parentheses]

State	Anywhere (including on school property)[1]						On school property[2]					
	2003	2005	2007	2009	2011	2013	2003	2005	2007	2009	2011	2013
1	2	3	4	5	6	7	8	9	10	11	12	13
United States[3]	44.9 (1.21)	43.3 (1.38)	44.7 (1.15)	41.8 (0.80)	38.7 (0.75)	34.9 (1.08)	5.2 (0.46)	4.3 (0.30)	4.1 (0.32)	4.5 (0.29)	5.1 (0.33)	— (†)
Alabama	40.2 (2.04)	39.4 (2.55)	— (†)	39.5 (2.22)	35.6 (1.99)	35.0 (2.45)	4.1 (0.82)	4.5 (0.59)	— (†)	5.4 (0.76)	5.7 (1.08)	— (†)
Alaska	38.7 (2.05)	— (†)	39.7 (2.11)	33.2 (1.66)	28.6 (1.95)	22.5 (1.69)	4.9 (0.81)	— (†)	4.1 (0.58)	3.0 (0.48)	3.4 (0.52)	— (†)
Arizona	51.8 (1.93)	47.1 (1.73)	45.6 (1.73)	44.5 (1.67)	43.8 (1.47)	36.0 (2.25)	7.1 (0.67)	7.5 (0.88)	6.0 (0.54)	5.9 (0.61)	6.2 (0.55)	— (†)
Arkansas	— (†)	43.1 (1.99)	42.2 (1.75)	39.7 (1.91)	33.9 (1.81)	36.3 (1.97)	— (†)	5.2 (0.62)	5.1 (0.65)	6.1 (0.89)	4.2 (0.68)	— (†)
California	— (†)	— (†)	— (†)	— (†)	— (†)	— (†)	— (†)	— (†)	— (†)	— (†)	— (†)	— (†)
Colorado	— (†)	47.4 (4.42)	— (†)	40.8 (2.44)	36.4 (2.29)	— (†)	— (†)	5.9 (1.08)	— (†)	4.1 (0.61)	5.3 (0.87)	— (†)
Connecticut	— (†)	45.3 (2.16)	46.0 (2.13)	43.5 (2.22)	41.5 (1.90)	36.7 (2.02)	— (†)	6.6 (0.71)	5.6 (0.99)	5.0 (0.47)	4.6 (0.61)	— (†)
Delaware	45.4 (1.30)	43.1 (1.16)	45.2 (1.40)	43.7 (1.65)	40.4 (1.55)	36.3 (1.34)	4.8 (0.44)	5.5 (0.66)	4.5 (0.48)	5.0 (0.73)	5.0 (0.50)	— (†)
District of Columbia	33.8 (1.72)	23.1 (1.40)	32.6 (1.47)	— (†)	32.8 (1.89)	— (†)	4.9 (0.64)	4.6 (0.55)	6.1 (0.92)	— (†)	6.8 (0.91)	— (†)
Florida	42.7 (1.10)	39.7 (1.43)	42.3 (1.30)	40.5 (1.03)	37.0 (0.98)	34.9 (0.87)	5.1 (0.36)	4.5 (0.30)	5.3 (0.31)	4.9 (0.26)	5.1 (0.29)	— (†)
Georgia	37.7 (1.41)	39.9 (2.12)	37.7 (1.52)	34.3 (1.65)	34.6 (1.93)	27.9 (2.04)	3.7 (0.55)	4.3 (0.67)	4.4 (0.58)	4.2 (0.48)	5.4 (0.80)	— (†)
Hawaii	— (†)	34.8 (2.05)	29.1 (2.93)	37.8 (3.02)	29.1 (1.64)	25.2 (1.75)	— (†)	8.8 (0.93)	6.0 (0.93)	7.9 (1.31)	5.0 (0.42)	— (†)
Idaho	34.8 (2.44)	39.8 (2.62)	42.5 (2.73)	34.2 (1.97)	36.2 (2.28)	28.3 (2.23)	3.8 (0.56)	4.3 (0.69)	6.2 (0.81)	3.5 (0.53)	4.1 (0.50)	— (†)
Illinois	— (†)	— (†)	43.7 (2.72)	39.8 (1.91)	37.8 (1.87)	36.6 (2.41)	— (†)	— (†)	5.5 (0.75)	4.4 (0.64)	3.3 (0.40)	— (†)
Indiana	44.9 (1.57)	41.4 (2.12)	43.9 (2.24)	38.5 (2.13)	33.5 (1.65)	— (†)	3.9 (0.57)	3.4 (0.64)	4.1 (0.47)	3.5 (0.52)	2.0 (0.36)	— (†)
Iowa	— (†)	43.8 (2.56)	41.0 (2.36)	— (†)	37.1 (2.58)	— (†)	— (†)	4.6 (0.89)	3.4 (0.78)	— (†)	2.3 (0.41)	— (†)
Kansas	— (†)	43.9 (1.74)	42.4 (1.69)	38.7 (1.93)	32.6 (1.53)	27.6 (1.02)	— (†)	5.1 (0.74)	4.8 (0.66)	3.2 (0.55)	2.9 (0.45)	— (†)
Kentucky	45.1 (1.87)	37.4 (1.77)	40.6 (1.25)	37.8 (1.30)	34.6 (1.56)	30.4 (1.37)	4.8 (0.69)	3.5 (0.37)	4.7 (0.47)	5.2 (0.87)	4.1 (0.53)	— (†)
Louisiana	— (†)	— (†)	— (†)	47.5 (2.80)	44.4 (2.00)	38.6 (2.75)	— (†)	— (†)	— (†)	5.6 (1.33)	6.0 (1.36)	— (†)
Maine	42.2 (1.78)	43.0 (2.15)	39.3 (2.29)	32.2 (0.66)	28.7 (0.69)	26.6 (0.90)	3.7 (0.48)	3.9 (0.44)	5.6 (0.89)	4.0 (0.23)	3.1 (0.21)	— (†)
Maryland	— (†)	39.8 (2.17)	42.9 (3.13)	37.0 (1.44)	34.8 (1.98)	31.2 (0.45)	— (†)	3.2 (0.42)	6.2 (1.10)	4.8 (0.67)	5.4 (0.63)	— (†)
Massachusetts	45.7 (1.19)	47.8 (1.36)	46.2 (1.57)	43.6 (1.28)	40.1 (1.54)	35.6 (1.14)	5.3 (0.50)	4.2 (0.32)	4.7 (0.45)	3.8 (0.48)	3.6 (0.44)	— (†)
Michigan	44.0 (1.40)	38.1 (1.73)	42.8 (1.70)	37.0 (1.28)	30.6 (1.64)	28.3 (1.81)	4.6 (0.33)	3.6 (0.46)	3.6 (0.51)	3.7 (0.40)	2.7 (0.37)	— (†)
Minnesota	— (†)	— (†)	— (†)	— (†)	— (†)	— (†)	— (†)	— (†)	— (†)	— (†)	— (†)	— (†)
Mississippi	41.8 (1.74)	— (†)	40.6 (1.57)	39.2 (1.43)	36.2 (2.07)	32.9 (2.09)	4.9 (0.70)	— (†)	5.1 (0.71)	4.3 (0.45)	4.6 (0.67)	— (†)
Missouri	49.2 (2.16)	40.8 (2.04)	44.4 (2.35)	39.3 (2.71)	— (†)	35.6 (1.33)	2.6 (0.58)	3.3 (0.57)	3.4 (0.74)	3.0 (0.55)	— (†)	— (†)
Montana	49.5 (1.68)	48.6 (1.50)	46.5 (1.39)	42.8 (1.81)	38.3 (1.08)	37.1 (1.20)	6.7 (0.70)	6.4 (0.73)	5.7 (0.47)	5.1 (0.69)	3.5 (0.35)	— (†)
Nebraska	46.5 (1.29)	42.9 (1.27)	— (†)	— (†)	26.6 (1.24)	22.1 (1.46)	4.6 (0.61)	3.6 (0.42)	— (†)	— (†)	3.0 (0.41)	— (†)
Nevada	43.4 (1.51)	41.4 (1.73)	37.0 (1.52)	38.6 (1.66)	— (†)	34.0 (2.11)	7.4 (0.74)	6.8 (0.92)	4.4 (0.58)	4.4 (0.52)	— (†)	— (†)
New Hampshire	47.1 (2.70)	44.0 (2.31)	44.8 (1.83)	39.3 (2.18)	38.4 (1.83)	32.9 (1.71)	4.0 (0.79)	— (†)	5.1 (0.73)	4.3 (0.68)	5.6 (0.70)	— (†)
New Jersey	— (†)	46.5 (2.65)	— (†)	45.2 (2.21)	42.9 (2.46)	39.3 (1.92)	— (†)	3.7 (0.42)	— (†)	— (†)	— (†)	— (†)
New Mexico	— (†)	42.3 (1.93)	43.2 (1.07)	40.5 (1.41)	36.9 (1.40)	28.9 (1.25)	— (†)	7.6 (0.87)	8.7 (1.35)	8.0 (0.90)	6.4 (0.54)	— (†)
New York	44.2 (1.53)	43.4 (1.47)	43.7 (1.41)	41.4 (1.38)	38.4 (1.96)	32.5 (1.36)	5.2 (0.39)	4.1 (0.45)	5.1 (0.58)	— (†)	— (†)	— (†)
North Carolina	39.4 (2.68)	42.3 (2.16)	37.7 (1.36)	35.0 (2.43)	34.3 (1.41)	32.2 (1.27)	3.6 (0.47)	5.4 (0.74)	4.7 (0.65)	4.1 (0.57)	5.5 (0.77)	— (†)
North Dakota	54.2 (1.74)	49.0 (1.89)	46.1 (1.82)	43.3 (1.79)	38.8 (1.67)	35.3 (1.59)	5.1 (0.79)	3.6 (0.52)	4.4 (0.65)	4.2 (0.53)	3.1 (0.51)	— (†)
Ohio[4]	42.2 (2.40)	42.4 (1.96)	45.7 (1.70)	— (†)	38.0 (2.94)	29.5 (2.21)	3.9 (0.69)	3.2 (0.59)	3.2 (0.50)	— (†)	— (†)	— (†)
Oklahoma	47.8 (1.41)	40.5 (1.62)	43.1 (1.88)	39.0 (1.97)	38.3 (1.75)	33.4 (1.91)	3.2 (0.64)	3.8 (0.49)	5.0 (0.59)	3.9 (0.55)	2.6 (0.65)	— (†)
Oregon	— (†)	— (†)	— (†)	— (†)	— (†)	— (†)	— (†)	— (†)	— (†)	— (†)	— (†)	— (†)
Pennsylvania	— (†)	— (†)	— (†)	38.4 (2.10)	— (†)	— (†)	— (†)	— (†)	— (†)	2.8 (0.50)	— (†)	— (†)
Rhode Island	44.5 (1.92)	42.7 (1.15)	42.9 (1.76)	34.0 (2.01)	34.0 (1.25)	30.9 (1.78)	4.6 (0.73)	5.3 (0.66)	4.8 (0.54)	3.2 (0.50)	— (†)	— (†)
South Carolina	— (†)	43.2 (1.64)	36.8 (2.31)	35.2 (2.80)	39.7 (1.72)	28.9 (1.34)	— (†)	6.0 (0.96)	4.7 (0.73)	3.6 (0.79)	5.9 (0.90)	— (†)
South Dakota[4]	50.2 (2.58)	46.6 (2.12)	44.5 (1.80)	40.1 (1.54)	39.3 (2.14)	30.8 (1.45)	5.4 (1.13)	4.0 (0.70)	3.6 (0.92)	— (†)	— (†)	— (†)
Tennessee	41.1 (2.04)	41.8 (1.90)	36.7 (1.90)	33.5 (1.71)	33.3 (1.39)	28.4 (1.35)	4.2 (0.48)	3.7 (0.66)	4.1 (0.54)	3.0 (0.38)	3.2 (0.34)	— (†)
Texas	— (†)	47.3 (1.93)	48.3 (1.64)	44.8 (1.25)	39.7 (1.15)	36.1 (1.75)	— (†)	5.7 (0.56)	4.9 (0.57)	4.7 (0.36)	3.9 (0.35)	— (†)
Utah	21.3 (2.19)	15.8 (1.92)	17.0 (1.88)	18.2 (2.72)	15.1 (1.54)	11.0 (0.90)	3.8 (0.74)	2.1 (0.39)	4.7 ! (1.69)	2.7 (0.45)	2.7 (0.54)	— (†)
Vermont	43.5 (1.48)	41.8 (1.53)	42.6 (1.04)	39.0 (1.57)	35.3 (1.10)	— (†)	5.3 (0.60)	4.8 (0.54)	4.6 (0.40)	3.3 (0.28)	3.3 (0.50)	— (†)
Virginia	— (†)	— (†)	— (†)	— (†)	30.5 (2.49)	27.3 (1.22)	— (†)	— (†)	— (†)	— (†)	3.3 (0.59)	— (†)
Washington	— (†)	— (†)	— (†)	— (†)	— (†)	— (†)	— (†)	— (†)	— (†)	— (†)	— (†)	— (†)
West Virginia	44.4 (1.81)	41.5 (1.41)	43.5 (1.45)	40.4 (1.10)	34.3 (2.40)	37.1 (2.04)	4.1 (0.84)	6.4 (1.08)	5.5 (0.89)	5.7 (0.61)	4.2 (0.67)	— (†)
Wisconsin	47.3 (1.63)	49.2 (1.51)	48.9 (1.56)	41.3 (1.83)	39.2 (1.35)	32.7 (1.21)	— (†)	— (†)	— (†)	— (†)	— (†)	— (†)
Wyoming	49.0 (2.16)	45.4 (1.47)	42.4 (1.22)	41.7 (1.36)	36.1 (1.34)	34.4 (1.14)	6.2 (0.75)	6.2 (0.56)	6.9 (0.63)	6.4 (0.50)	5.1 (0.48)	— (†)

—Not available.
†Not applicable.
!Interpret data with caution. The coefficient of variation (CV) for this estimate is between 30 and 50 percent.
[1]The term "anywhere" is not used in the Youth Risk Behavior Survey (YRBS) questionnaire; students were simply asked how many days during the previous 30 days they had at least one drink of alcohol.
[2]In the question about drinking alcohol at school, "on school property" was not defined for survey respondents. Data on alcohol use at school were not collected in 2013.
[3]Data for the U.S. total include both public and private schools and were collected through a national survey representing the entire country.

[4]Data include both public and private schools.
NOTE: State-level data include public schools only, with the exception of data for Ohio and South Dakota. Data for the U.S. total, Ohio, and South Dakota include both public and private schools. For specific states, a given year's data may be unavailable (1) because the state did not participate in the survey that year; (2) because the state omitted this particular survey item from the state-level questionnaire; or (3) because the state had an overall response rate of less than 60 percent (the overall response rate is the school response rate multiplied by the student response rate).
SOURCE: Centers for Disease Control and Prevention, Division of Adolescent and School Health, Youth Risk Behavior Surveillance System (YRBSS), 2003 through 2013. (This table was prepared June 2014.)

Table 232.40. Percentage of students in grades 9–12 who reported using marijuana at least one time during the previous 30 days, by location and selected student characteristics: Selected years, 1993 through 2013

[Standard errors appear in parentheses]

Location and student characteristic	1993	1995	1997	1999	2001	2003	2005	2007	2009	2011	2013
1	2	3	4	5	6	7	8	9	10	11	12
Anywhere (including on school property)[1]											
Total	17.7 (1.22)	25.3 (1.03)	26.2 (1.11)	26.7 (1.30)	23.9 (0.77)	22.4 (1.09)	20.2 (0.84)	19.7 (0.97)	20.8 (0.70)	23.1 (0.80)	23.4 (1.08)
Sex											
Male	20.6 (1.61)	28.4 (1.08)	30.2 (1.46)	30.8 (1.92)	27.9 (0.81)	25.1 (1.25)	22.1 (0.98)	22.4 (1.02)	23.4 (0.80)	25.9 (1.01)	25.0 (1.14)
Female	14.6 (1.02)	22.0 (1.44)	21.4 (1.04)	22.6 (0.96)	20.0 (0.87)	19.3 (0.96)	18.2 (0.99)	17.0 (1.13)	17.9 (0.87)	20.1 (0.95)	21.9 (1.28)
Race/ethnicity[2]											
White	17.3 (1.41)	24.5 (1.49)	25.0 (1.56)	26.4 (1.59)	24.4 (1.04)	21.7 (1.20)	20.3 (1.11)	19.9 (1.28)	20.7 (0.93)	21.7 (1.09)	20.4 (1.36)
Black	18.6 (1.84)	28.6 (2.62)	28.2 (1.67)	26.4 (3.49)	21.8 (2.12)	23.9 (1.58)	20.4 (1.11)	21.5 (1.64)	22.2 (1.44)	25.1 (1.35)	28.9 (1.30)
Hispanic	19.4 (1.33)	27.8 (2.92)	28.6 (2.06)	28.2 (2.29)	24.6 (0.81)	23.8 (1.16)	23.0 (1.22)	18.5 (1.41)	21.6 (1.04)	24.4 (1.27)	27.6 (1.50)
Asian[3]	—	—	—	13.5 (2.04)	10.9 (2.12)	9.5 (2.21)	6.7 (1.64)	9.4 (1.63)	7.5 (1.40)	13.6 (3.75)	16.4 (2.99)
Pacific Islander[3]	—	—	—	33.8 (4.11)	21.9 (4.07)	28.1 (6.47)	12.4 ! (3.87)	28.7 (6.14)	24.8 (5.50)	31.1 (7.08)	23.4 ! (7.35)
American Indian/Alaska Native	17.4 (4.77)	28.0 (5.72)	44.2 (4.31)	36.2 (6.55)	36.4 (5.48)	32.8 (5.29)	30.3 (4.36)	27.4 (3.50)	31.6 (5.26)	47.4 (3.20)	35.5 (6.37)
Two or more races[3]	—	—	—	29.1 (4.00)	31.8 (3.22)	28.3 (5.57)	16.9 (2.43)	20.5 (2.73)	21.7 (2.33)	26.8 (2.10)	28.8 (2.55)
Grade											
9th	13.2 (1.10)	20.9 (1.83)	23.6 (1.95)	21.7 (1.84)	19.4 (1.25)	18.5 (1.52)	17.4 (1.16)	14.7 (1.02)	15.5 (0.97)	18.0 (1.11)	17.7 (1.13)
10th	16.5 (1.79)	25.5 (1.89)	25.0 (1.29)	27.8 (2.21)	24.8 (1.12)	22.0 (1.47)	20.2 (1.27)	19.3 (1.12)	21.1 (1.11)	21.6 (1.15)	23.5 (1.89)
11th	18.4 (1.77)	27.6 (1.35)	29.3 (1.81)	26.7 (2.47)	25.8 (1.33)	24.1 (1.56)	21.0 (1.24)	21.4 (1.49)	23.2 (1.52)	25.5 (1.44)	25.5 (1.37)
12th	22.0 (1.40)	26.2 (2.35)	26.6 (2.09)	31.5 (2.81)	26.9 (1.77)	25.8 (1.19)	22.8 (1.23)	25.1 (1.96)	24.6 (1.49)	28.0 (1.08)	27.7 (1.58)
Urbanicity[4]											
Urban	—	—	26.8 (1.50)	27.5 (2.32)	25.6 (1.23)	23.4 (1.65)	(†)	(†)	(†)	(†)	(†)
Suburban	—	—	27.0 (1.05)	26.1 (1.60)	22.5 (0.96)	22.8 (1.90)	(†)	(†)	(†)	(†)	(†)
Rural	—	—	21.9 (3.23)	28.0 (4.36)	26.2 (2.49)	19.9 (2.80)	(†)	(†)	(†)	(†)	(†)
On school property[5]											
Total	5.6 (0.65)	8.8 (0.59)	7.0 (0.52)	7.2 (0.73)	5.4 (0.37)	5.8 (0.68)	4.5 (0.32)	4.5 (0.46)	4.6 (0.35)	5.9 (0.39)	(†)
Sex											
Male	7.8 (0.83)	11.9 (0.85)	9.0 (0.68)	10.1 (1.30)	8.0 (0.54)	7.6 (0.88)	6.0 (0.44)	5.9 (0.61)	6.3 (0.54)	7.5 (0.56)	(†)
Female	3.3 (0.48)	5.5 (0.72)	4.6 (0.56)	4.4 (0.40)	2.9 (0.28)	3.7 (0.48)	3.0 (0.31)	3.0 (0.39)	2.8 (0.32)	4.1 (0.32)	(†)
Race/ethnicity[2]											
White	5.0 (0.72)	7.1 (0.62)	5.8 (0.69)	6.5 (0.84)	4.8 (0.45)	4.5 (0.66)	3.8 (0.41)	4.0 (0.63)	3.8 (0.38)	4.5 (0.42)	(†)
Black	7.3 (1.23)	12.3 (1.88)	9.1 (1.07)	7.2 (1.10)	6.1 (0.60)	6.6 (0.89)	4.9 (0.65)	5.0 (0.73)	5.6 (0.64)	6.7 (0.77)	(†)
Hispanic	7.5 (1.10)	12.9 (2.20)	10.4 (1.03)	10.7 (1.21)	7.4 (0.58)	8.2 (0.72)	7.7 (0.76)	5.4 (0.80)	6.5 (0.76)	7.7 (0.54)	(†)
Asian[3]	—	—	—	4.3 (0.71)	4.7 ! (1.56)	4.3 ! (1.38)	‡ (†)	2.7 ! (1.06)	2.0 (0.54)	4.5 (1.34)	(†)
Pacific Islander[3]	—	—	—	11.0 (3.21)	6.4 ! (2.46)	9.1 ! (3.17)	‡ (†)	13.4 ! (5.38)	9.0 (2.40)	12.5 ! (4.94)	(†)
American Indian/Alaska Native	‡ (†)	10.1 ! (3.39)	16.2 ! (5.56)	‡ (†)	21.5 ! (6.55)	11.4 ! (4.42)	9.2 (1.85)	8.2 (2.30)	2.9 ! (1.25)	20.9 (4.05)	(†)
Two or more races[3]	—	—	—	7.8 (1.81)	5.2 (1.24)	11.4 ! (5.49)	3.6 (0.91)	3.6 ! (1.08)	5.4 (1.34)	8.1 (1.79)	(†)
Grade											
9th	4.4 (0.40)	8.7 (1.38)	8.1 (0.90)	6.6 (0.97)	5.5 (0.62)	6.6 (1.03)	5.0 (0.59)	4.0 (0.52)	4.3 (0.38)	5.4 (0.65)	(†)
10th	6.5 (0.94)	9.8 (0.87)	6.4 (0.73)	7.6 (1.14)	5.8 (0.51)	5.2 (0.70)	4.6 (0.54)	4.8 (0.60)	4.6 (0.50)	6.2 (0.63)	(†)
11th	6.5 (1.07)	8.6 (0.62)	7.9 (1.17)	7.0 (0.72)	5.1 (0.48)	5.6 (0.71)	4.1 (0.49)	4.1 (0.73)	5.0 (0.55)	6.2 (0.70)	(†)
12th	5.1 (0.78)	8.0 (1.15)	5.7 (0.61)	7.3 (1.14)	4.9 (0.71)	5.0 (0.75)	4.1 (0.45)	5.1 (0.73)	4.6 (0.49)	5.4 (0.39)	(†)
Urbanicity[4]											
Urban	—	—	8.0 (1.11)	8.5 (1.03)	6.8 (0.56)	6.8 (1.05)	(†)	(†)	(†)	(†)	(†)
Suburban	—	—	7.0 (0.67)	6.4 (1.03)	4.7 (0.46)	6.0 (1.03)	(†)	(†)	(†)	(†)	(†)
Rural	—	—	4.9 ! (2.02)	8.1 (1.57)	5.3 (0.93)	3.9 (0.64)	(†)	(†)	(†)	(†)	(†)

—Not available.
†Not applicable.
‡Reporting standards not met. The coefficient of variation (CV) for this estimate is 50 percent or greater.
!Interpret data with caution. The coefficient of variation (CV) for this estimate is between 30 and 50 percent.

[1]The term "anywhere" is not used in the Youth Risk Behavior Survey (YRBS) questionnaire; students were simply asked how many times during the previous 30 days they had used marijuana.
[2]Race categories exclude persons of Hispanic ethnicity.
[3]Before 1999, Asian students and Pacific Islander students were not categorized separately, and students could not be classified as Two or more races. Because the response categories changed in 1999, caution should be used in comparing data on race from 1993, 1995, and 1997 with data from later years.
[4]Refers to the Standard Metropolitan Statistical Area (MSA) status of the respondent's household as defined in 2000 by the U.S. Census Bureau. Categories include "central city of an MSA (Urban)," "in MSA but not in central city (Suburban)," and "not MSA (Rural)."
[5]In the question about using marijuana at school, "on school property" was not defined for survey respondents. Data on marijuana use at school were not collected in 2013.

SOURCE: Centers for Disease Control and Prevention, Division of Adolescent and School Health, Youth Risk Behavior Surveillance System (YRBSS), 1993 through 2013. (This table was prepared June 2014.)

Table 232.50. Percentage distribution of students in grades 9–12, by number of times they reported using marijuana anywhere or on school property during the previous 30 days and selected student characteristics: Selected years, 2009 through 2013

[Standard errors appear in parentheses]

Year and student characteristic	Anywhere (including on school property)[1]								On school property[2]							
	0 times		1 or 2 times		3 to 39 times		40 or more times		0 times		1 or 2 times		3 to 39 times		40 or more times	
1	2		3		4		5		6		7		8		9	
2009																
Total	79.2	(0.70)	7.2	(0.30)	9.7	(0.37)	3.8	(0.27)	95.4	(0.35)	2.1	(0.16)	1.8	(0.18)	0.7	(0.10)
Sex																
Male	76.6	(0.80)	6.8	(0.38)	10.8	(0.48)	5.8	(0.46)	93.7	(0.54)	2.6	(0.24)	2.6	(0.27)	1.1	(0.18)
Female	82.1	(0.87)	7.7	(0.39)	8.5	(0.56)	1.7	(0.20)	97.2	(0.32)	1.7	(0.19)	1.0	(0.21)	0.2	(0.06)
Race/ethnicity[3]																
White	79.3	(0.93)	7.4	(0.43)	9.6	(0.49)	3.7	(0.38)	96.2	(0.38)	1.9	(0.21)	1.4	(0.18)	0.5	(0.10)
Black	77.8	(1.44)	6.7	(0.62)	10.9	(0.90)	4.6	(0.68)	94.4	(0.64)	2.2	(0.31)	2.8	(0.44)	0.6 !	(0.24)
Hispanic	78.4	(1.04)	8.2	(0.57)	9.8	(0.71)	3.6	(0.37)	93.5	(0.76)	3.2	(0.43)	2.3	(0.39)	1.0	(0.22)
Asian	92.5	(1.40)	3.0	(0.69)	3.3	(0.85)	1.2 !	(0.55)	98.0	(0.54)	‡	(†)	1.1 !	(0.50)	‡	(†)
Pacific Islander	75.2	(5.50)	5.0 !	(1.61)	13.0	(2.95)	6.8 !	(2.56)	91.0	(2.40)	4.4 !	(1.59)	3.7 !	(1.58)	‡	(†)
American Indian/Alaska Native	68.4	(5.26)	6.7 !	(2.47)	19.6	(3.43)	5.3 !	(2.11)	97.1	(1.25)	‡	(†)	‡	(†)	#	(†)
Two or more races	78.3	(2.33)	7.8	(1.40)	9.8	(1.51)	4.1 !	(1.27)	94.6	(1.34)	1.4 !	(0.51)	2.2 !	(0.90)	1.8 !	(0.66)
Grade																
9th	84.5	(0.97)	5.8	(0.55)	7.6	(0.55)	2.1	(0.29)	95.7	(0.38)	2.3	(0.22)	1.4	(0.21)	0.6	(0.15)
10th	78.9	(1.11)	7.9	(0.59)	9.6	(0.64)	3.6	(0.44)	95.4	(0.50)	1.9	(0.28)	2.1	(0.35)	0.6	(0.12)
11th	76.8	(1.52)	7.9	(0.66)	11.2	(0.89)	4.1	(0.42)	95.0	(0.55)	2.5	(0.37)	2.0	(0.31)	0.5	(0.12)
12th	75.4	(1.49)	7.7	(0.60)	10.9	(0.86)	6.0	(0.64)	95.4	(0.49)	1.9	(0.30)	1.9	(0.27)	0.8	(0.23)
2011																
Total	76.9	(0.80)	7.4	(0.30)	10.9	(0.42)	4.8	(0.30)	94.1	(0.39)	2.8	(0.22)	2.3	(0.21)	0.7	(0.09)
Sex																
Male	74.1	(1.01)	7.1	(0.40)	11.8	(0.57)	7.0	(0.47)	92.5	(0.56)	3.1	(0.28)	3.2	(0.31)	1.2	(0.17)
Female	79.9	(0.95)	7.7	(0.48)	9.9	(0.56)	2.4	(0.26)	95.9	(0.32)	2.5	(0.21)	1.4	(0.19)	0.2	(0.04)
Race/ethnicity[3]																
White	78.3	(1.09)	6.9	(0.42)	10.2	(0.59)	4.6	(0.44)	95.5	(0.42)	2.2	(0.26)	1.9	(0.23)	0.4	(0.09)
Black	74.9	(1.35)	7.9	(0.69)	12.5	(0.81)	4.7	(0.63)	93.3	(0.77)	3.2	(0.43)	2.8	(0.52)	0.7	(0.18)
Hispanic	75.6	(1.27)	8.3	(0.59)	11.5	(0.67)	4.7	(0.46)	92.3	(0.54)	3.6	(0.26)	3.1	(0.40)	1.0	(0.21)
Asian	86.4	(3.75)	‡	(†)	5.5	(0.96)	3.2 !	(1.34)	95.5	(1.34)	2.4 !	(1.15)	‡	(†)	1.5 !	(0.70)
Pacific Islander	68.9	(7.08)	11.3	(3.34)	13.2 !	(5.20)	6.6 !	(2.27)	87.5	(4.94)	5.6 !	(2.24)	‡	(†)	‡	(†)
American Indian/Alaska Native	52.6	(3.20)	10.5	(2.82)	23.6	(2.57)	13.2	(1.81)	79.1	(4.05)	8.6	(2.18)	9.8	(1.79)	2.5	(0.67)
Two or more races	73.2	(2.10)	7.2	(1.20)	12.9	(1.44)	6.7	(1.33)	91.9	(1.79)	3.7	(0.98)	2.4 !	(0.86)	2.0 !	(0.69)
Grade																
9th	82.0	(1.11)	6.2	(0.47)	8.2	(0.63)	3.6	(0.42)	94.6	(0.65)	2.7	(0.41)	2.2	(0.33)	0.5	(0.11)
10th	78.4	(1.15)	7.4	(0.60)	10.0	(0.65)	4.3	(0.50)	93.8	(0.63)	3.2	(0.38)	2.3	(0.40)	0.7	(0.16)
11th	74.5	(1.44)	8.0	(0.59)	12.9	(0.82)	4.5	(0.50)	93.8	(0.70)	3.2	(0.47)	2.3	(0.35)	0.7	(0.16)
12th	72.0	(1.08)	8.3	(0.59)	13.0	(0.69)	6.7	(0.53)	94.6	(0.39)	2.2	(0.30)	2.4	(0.30)	0.8	(0.18)
2013[4]																
Total	76.6	(1.08)	7.1	(0.42)	11.3	(0.68)	5.0	(0.39)	—	(†)	—	(†)	—	(†)	—	(†)
Sex																
Male	75.0	(1.14)	6.5	(0.42)	12.0	(0.72)	6.5	(0.53)	—	(†)	—	(†)	—	(†)	—	(†)
Female	78.1	(1.28)	7.8	(0.59)	10.7	(0.77)	3.4	(0.36)	—	(†)	—	(†)	—	(†)	—	(†)
Race/ethnicity[3]																
White	79.6	(1.36)	6.3	(0.63)	9.7	(0.75)	4.4	(0.42)	—	(†)	—	(†)	—	(†)	—	(†)
Black	71.1	(1.30)	8.2	(0.52)	14.3	(0.90)	6.3	(0.71)	—	(†)	—	(†)	—	(†)	—	(†)
Hispanic	72.4	(1.50)	8.6	(0.52)	13.4	(1.22)	5.6	(0.70)	—	(†)	—	(†)	—	(†)	—	(†)
Asian	83.6	(2.99)	4.1	(1.02)	7.6	(1.32)	4.7 !	(2.03)	—	(†)	—	(†)	—	(†)	—	(†)
Pacific Islander	76.6	(7.35)	4.9 !	(2.31)	17.1 !	(5.82)	‡	(†)	—	(†)	—	(†)	—	(†)	—	(†)
American Indian/Alaska Native	64.5	(6.37)	8.8 !	(2.70)	18.9	(4.54)	7.9 !	(2.77)	—	(†)	—	(†)	—	(†)	—	(†)
Two or more races	71.2	(2.55)	9.7	(1.36)	12.4	(1.45)	6.7	(1.29)	—	(†)	—	(†)	—	(†)	—	(†)
Grade																
9th	82.3	(1.13)	6.3	(0.59)	8.6	(0.70)	2.8	(0.38)	—	(†)	—	(†)	—	(†)	—	(†)
10th	76.5	(1.89)	7.2	(0.65)	11.3	(1.35)	5.0	(0.81)	—	(†)	—	(†)	—	(†)	—	(†)
11th	74.5	(1.37)	7.6	(0.68)	12.0	(0.85)	6.0	(0.56)	—	(†)	—	(†)	—	(†)	—	(†)
12th	72.3	(1.58)	7.6	(0.68)	13.8	(1.00)	6.4	(0.63)	—	(†)	—	(†)	—	(†)	—	(†)

—Not available.
†Not applicable.
#Rounds to zero.
!Interpret data with caution. The coefficient of variation (CV) for this estimate is between 30 and 50 percent.
‡Reporting standards not met. Either there are too few cases for a reliable estimate or the coefficient of variation (CV) is 50 percent or greater.
[1]The term "anywhere" is not used in the Youth Risk Behavior Survey (YRBS) questionnaire; students were simply asked how many times during the previous 30 days they had used marijuana.

[2]In the question about using marijuana at school, "on school property" was not defined for survey respondents.
[3]Race categories exclude persons of Hispanic ethnicity.
[4]Data on marijuana use at school were not collected in 2013.
NOTE: Detail may not sum to totals because of rounding.
SOURCE: Centers for Disease Control and Prevention, Division of Adolescent and School Health, Youth Risk Behavior Surveillance System (YRBSS), 2009 through 2013. (This table was prepared September 2014.)

Table 232.60. Percentage of public school students in grades 9–12 who reported using marijuana at least one time during the previous 30 days, by location and state: Selected years, 2003 through 2013

[Standard errors appear in parentheses]

State	Anywhere (including on school property)[1]						On school property[2]					
	2003	2005	2007	2009	2011	2013	2003	2005	2007	2009	2011	2013
1	2	3	4	5	6	7	8	9	10	11	12	13
United States[3]	22.4 (1.09)	20.2 (0.84)	19.7 (0.97)	20.8 (0.70)	23.1 (0.80)	23.4 (1.08)	5.8 (0.68)	4.5 (0.32)	4.5 (0.46)	4.6 (0.35)	5.9 (0.39)	— (†)
Alabama	17.7 (1.38)	18.5 (1.49)	— (†)	16.2 (1.28)	20.8 (1.62)	19.2 (1.46)	2.6 (0.54)	3.5 (0.80)	— (†)	4.6 (0.81)	4.0 (0.68)	— (†)
Alaska	23.9 (1.29)	— (†)	20.5 (1.47)	22.7 (1.65)	21.2 (1.68)	19.7 (1.35)	6.5 (0.80)	— (†)	5.9 (0.70)	5.9 (0.69)	4.3 (0.59)	— (†)
Arizona	25.6 (1.08)	20.0 (1.08)	22.0 (1.38)	23.7 (1.90)	22.9 (1.59)	23.5 (1.75)	6.5 (0.52)	5.1 (0.63)	6.1 (0.68)	6.4 (0.74)	5.6 (0.75)	— (†)
Arkansas	— (†)	18.9 (1.70)	16.4 (1.08)	17.8 (1.24)	16.8 (1.72)	19.0 (0.98)	— (†)	4.1 (0.61)	2.8 (0.50)	4.5 (1.02)	3.9 (0.78)	— (†)
California	— (†)	— (†)	— (†)	— (†)	— (†)	— (†)	— (†)	— (†)	— (†)	— (†)	— (†)	— (†)
Colorado	— (†)	22.7 (2.99)	— (†)	24.8 (2.22)	22.0 (1.16)	— (†)	— (†)	6.0 (0.88)	— (†)	6.1 (0.89)	6.0 (0.77)	— (†)
Connecticut	— (†)	23.1 (1.37)	23.2 (1.35)	21.8 (1.52)	24.2 (1.44)	26.1 (1.44)	— (†)	5.1 (0.49)	5.9 (0.77)	6.2 (0.76)	5.2 (0.68)	— (†)
Delaware	27.3 (1.13)	22.8 (1.12)	25.1 (1.03)	25.8 (1.30)	27.6 (1.37)	25.6 (1.17)	6.0 (0.54)	5.6 (0.57)	5.4 (0.53)	5.6 (0.71)	6.1 (0.65)	— (†)
District of Columbia	23.5 (1.23)	14.5 (1.08)	20.8 (1.33)	— (†)	26.1 (1.29)	— (†)	7.5 (0.88)	4.8 (0.62)	5.8 (0.66)	— (†)	7.9 (0.91)	— (†)
Florida	21.4 (0.89)	16.8 (0.86)	18.9 (0.88)	21.4 (0.72)	22.5 (0.86)	22.0 (0.81)	4.9 (0.41)	4.0 (0.31)	4.7 (0.40)	5.2 (0.39)	6.3 (0.39)	— (†)
Georgia	19.5 (0.94)	18.9 (1.59)	19.6 (0.96)	18.3 (1.02)	21.2 (1.23)	20.3 (1.64)	3.2 (0.45)	3.3 (0.58)	3.6 (0.58)	3.4 (0.62)	5.6 (0.70)	— (†)
Hawaii	— (†)	17.2 (1.73)	15.7 (1.78)	22.1 (2.03)	22.0 (1.32)	18.9 (1.54)	— (†)	7.2 (1.14)	5.7 (0.85)	8.3 (1.86)	7.6 (0.67)	— (†)
Idaho	14.7 (1.56)	17.1 (1.32)	17.9 (1.73)	13.7 (1.07)	18.8 (1.76)	15.3 (1.10)	2.7 (0.55)	3.9 (0.61)	4.7 (0.80)	3.0 (0.44)	4.9 (0.73)	— (†)
Illinois	— (†)	— (†)	20.3 (1.38)	21.0 (1.53)	23.1 (1.59)	24.0 (1.70)	— (†)	— (†)	4.2 (0.76)	5.0 (0.77)	4.7 (0.50)	— (†)
Indiana	22.1 (1.19)	18.9 (1.38)	18.9 (1.19)	20.9 (1.83)	20.0 (1.13)	— (†)	3.8 (0.67)	3.4 (0.57)	4.1 (0.45)	4.4 (0.62)	3.3 (0.66)	— (†)
Iowa	— (†)	15.6 (1.74)	11.5 (1.53)	— (†)	14.6 (1.99)	— (†)	— (†)	2.7 (0.64)	2.5 (0.66)	— (†)	3.4 (0.88)	— (†)
Kansas	— (†)	15.6 (1.46)	15.3 (0.93)	14.7 (1.19)	16.8 (0.87)	14.3 (1.19)	— (†)	3.2 (0.51)	3.8 (0.53)	2.7 (0.35)	2.9 (0.53)	— (†)
Kentucky	21.1 (1.09)	15.8 (1.19)	16.4 (1.07)	16.1 (1.15)	19.2 (1.47)	17.7 (1.50)	4.3 (0.55)	3.2 (0.45)	3.9 (0.44)	3.6 (0.89)	4.1 (0.59)	— (†)
Louisiana	— (†)	— (†)	— (†)	16.3 (1.29)	16.8 (1.02)	17.5 (1.38)	— (†)	— (†)	— (†)	— (†)	— (†)	— (†)
Maine	26.4 (1.69)	22.2 (2.13)	22.0 (1.55)	20.5 (0.57)	21.2 (0.72)	21.3 (0.89)	6.3 (0.76)	4.6 (0.72)	5.2 (0.65)	— (†)	— (†)	— (†)
Maryland	— (†)	18.5 (2.25)	19.4 (1.91)	21.9 (1.57)	23.2 (1.51)	19.8 (0.36)	— (†)	3.7 (0.82)	4.7 (1.13)	5.0 (0.65)	5.7 (0.70)	— (†)
Massachusetts	27.7 (1.39)	26.2 (1.22)	24.6 (1.43)	27.1 (1.24)	27.9 (1.31)	24.8 (0.92)	6.3 (0.44)	5.3 (0.54)	4.8 (0.44)	5.9 (0.79)	6.3 (0.51)	— (†)
Michigan	24.0 (1.96)	18.8 (1.29)	18.0 (1.10)	20.7 (0.91)	18.6 (1.15)	18.2 (0.73)	7.0 (1.20)	3.7 (0.50)	4.0 (0.57)	4.8 (0.59)	3.3 (0.44)	— (†)
Minnesota	— (†)	— (†)	— (†)	— (†)	— (†)	— (†)	— (†)	— (†)	— (†)	— (†)	— (†)	— (†)
Mississippi	20.6 (1.57)	— (†)	16.7 (1.02)	17.7 (1.21)	17.5 (1.18)	17.7 (1.28)	4.4 (0.90)	— (†)	2.7 (0.35)	2.5 (0.46)	3.2 (0.58)	— (†)
Missouri	21.8 (1.37)	18.1 (2.23)	19.0 (1.23)	20.6 (2.02)	— (†)	20.5 (1.69)	3.0 (0.58)	4.0 (0.82)	3.6 (0.63)	3.4 (0.48)	— (†)	— (†)
Montana	23.1 (1.45)	22.3 (1.43)	21.0 (1.44)	23.1 (1.58)	21.2 (1.50)	21.0 (1.18)	6.4 (0.70)	6.1 (0.70)	5.0 (0.49)	5.8 (0.67)	5.5 (0.59)	— (†)
Nebraska	18.3 (1.23)	17.5 (1.05)	— (†)	— (†)	12.7 (1.06)	11.7 (1.10)	3.9 (0.51)	3.1 (0.41)	— (†)	— (†)	2.7 (0.43)	— (†)
Nevada	22.3 (1.31)	17.3 (1.34)	15.5 (1.07)	20.0 (1.36)	— (†)	18.7 (1.57)	5.3 (0.69)	5.7 (0.81)	3.6 (0.55)	4.9 (0.53)	— (†)	— (†)
New Hampshire	30.6 (2.51)	25.9 (1.69)	22.9 (1.39)	25.6 (1.86)	28.4 (1.82)	24.4 (1.36)	6.6 (0.86)	— (†)	4.7 (0.64)	6.8 (0.78)	7.3 (0.87)	— (†)
New Jersey	— (†)	19.9 (2.18)	— (†)	20.3 (1.53)	21.1 (1.33)	21.0 (1.20)	— (†)	3.4 (0.67)	— (†)	— (†)	— (†)	— (†)
New Mexico	— (†)	26.2 (2.00)	25.0 (2.07)	28.0 (1.52)	27.6 (1.58)	27.8 (1.70)	— (†)	8.4 (0.98)	7.9 (0.86)	9.7 (1.06)	9.7 (0.84)	— (†)
New York	20.7 (1.05)	18.3 (1.13)	18.6 (0.78)	20.9 (1.32)	20.6 (1.07)	21.4 (1.04)	4.5 (0.41)	3.6 (0.41)	4.1 (0.44)	— (†)	— (†)	— (†)
North Carolina	24.3 (1.99)	21.4 (1.61)	19.1 (1.27)	19.8 (1.67)	24.2 (1.25)	23.2 (1.83)	3.5 (0.71)	4.1 (0.65)	4.3 (0.54)	4.0 (0.63)	5.2 (0.91)	— (†)
North Dakota	20.6 (1.58)	15.5 (1.62)	14.8 (1.18)	16.9 (1.55)	15.3 (1.52)	15.9 (1.26)	6.3 (0.98)	4.0 (0.71)	2.7 (0.43)	3.8 (0.59)	3.4 (0.45)	— (†)
Ohio[4]	21.4 (2.33)	20.9 (1.79)	17.7 (1.50)	— (†)	23.6 (1.95)	20.7 (2.30)	4.2 (0.96)	4.3 (0.62)	3.7 (0.67)	— (†)	— (†)	— (†)
Oklahoma	22.0 (2.20)	18.7 (1.12)	15.9 (1.37)	17.2 (2.04)	19.1 (1.90)	16.3 (1.57)	4.3 (0.70)	3.0 (0.38)	2.6 (0.40)	2.9 (0.70)	2.4 (0.58)	— (†)
Oregon	— (†)	— (†)	— (†)	— (†)	— (†)	— (†)	— (†)	— (†)	— (†)	— (†)	— (†)	— (†)
Pennsylvania	— (†)	— (†)	— (†)	19.3 (1.43)	— (†)	— (†)	— (†)	— (†)	— (†)	3.5 (0.58)	— (†)	— (†)
Rhode Island	27.6 (1.11)	25.0 (1.16)	23.2 (1.85)	26.3 (1.33)	26.3 (1.35)	23.9 (1.92)	7.4 (0.70)	7.2 (0.65)	6.5 (0.93)	5.1 (0.60)	— (†)	— (†)
South Carolina	— (†)	19.0 (1.24)	18.6 (1.44)	20.4 (1.56)	24.1 (1.99)	19.7 (1.22)	— (†)	4.6 (0.64)	3.3 (0.52)	3.7 (0.63)	5.2 (0.75)	— (†)
South Dakota[4]	21.5 (3.35)	16.8 (1.87)	17.7 (3.72)	15.2 (1.36)	17.8 (3.57)	16.1 (3.01)	4.5 ! (1.50)	2.9 (0.73)	5.0 ! (2.41)	2.9 (0.49)	— (†)	— (†)
Tennessee	23.6 (2.10)	19.5 (1.38)	19.4 (1.29)	20.1 (1.31)	20.6 (0.96)	21.4 (1.70)	4.1 (0.86)	3.5 (0.67)	4.1 (0.60)	3.8 (0.65)	3.6 (0.40)	— (†)
Texas	— (†)	21.7 (0.99)	19.3 (1.01)	19.5 (0.71)	20.8 (1.30)	20.5 (1.26)	— (†)	3.8 (0.52)	3.6 (0.30)	4.6 (0.51)	4.8 (0.47)	— (†)
Utah	11.4 (1.28)	7.6 (1.18)	8.7 (2.00)	10.0 (1.53)	9.6 (1.26)	7.6 (0.79)	3.7 (0.59)	1.7 (0.42)	3.8 ! (1.24)	2.5 (0.48)	4.0 (0.72)	— (†)
Vermont	28.2 (1.58)	25.3 (1.59)	24.1 (0.88)	24.6 (1.14)	24.4 (1.43)	25.7 (0.83)	8.0 (0.44)	7.0 (0.80)	6.3 (0.63)	6.3 (0.57)	6.0 (0.84)	— (†)
Virginia	— (†)	— (†)	— (†)	— (†)	18.0 (1.79)	17.9 (0.85)	— (†)	— (†)	— (†)	— (†)	3.5 (0.70)	— (†)
Washington	— (†)	— (†)	— (†)	— (†)	— (†)	— (†)	— (†)	— (†)	— (†)	— (†)	— (†)	— (†)
West Virginia	23.1 (2.13)	19.6 (1.70)	23.5 (1.05)	20.3 (1.73)	19.7 (1.61)	18.9 (1.39)	4.5 (0.72)	4.9 (0.85)	5.8 (0.97)	3.9 (0.37)	3.0 (0.45)	— (†)
Wisconsin	21.8 (1.18)	15.9 (1.07)	20.3 (1.30)	18.9 (1.64)	21.6 (1.78)	17.3 (1.12)	— (†)	— (†)	— (†)	— (†)	— (†)	— (†)
Wyoming	20.4 (1.56)	17.8 (1.05)	14.4 (0.79)	16.9 (0.91)	18.5 (1.23)	17.8 (0.81)	5.1 (0.66)	4.0 (0.43)	4.7 (0.52)	5.3 (0.45)	4.7 (0.44)	— (†)

—Not available.
†Not applicable.
!Interpret data with caution. The coefficient of variation (CV) for this estimate is between 30 and 50 percent.
[1]The term "anywhere" is not used in the Youth Risk Behavior Survey (YRBS) questionnaire; students were simply asked how many times during the previous 30 days they had used marijuana.
[2]In the question about using marijuana at school, "on school property" was not defined for survey respondents. Data on marijuana use at school were not collected in 2013.
[3]Data for the U.S. total include both public and private schools and were collected through a national survey representing the entire country.

[4]Data include both public and private schools.
NOTE: State-level data include public schools only, with the exception of data for Ohio and South Dakota. Data for the U.S. total, Ohio, and South Dakota include both public and private schools. For specific states, a given year's data may be unavailable (1) because the state did not participate in the survey that year; (2) because the state omitted this particular survey item from the state-level questionnaire; or (3) because the state had an overall response rate of less than 60 percent (the overall response rate is the school response rate multiplied by the student response rate).
SOURCE: Centers for Disease Control and Prevention, Division of Adolescent and School Health, Youth Risk Behavior Surveillance System (YRBSS), 2003 through 2013. (This table was prepared June 2014.)

Table 232.70. Percentage of students in grades 9–12 who reported that illegal drugs were made available to them on school property during the previous 12 months, by selected student characteristics: Selected years, 1993 through 2013

[Standard errors appear in parentheses]

Student characteristic	1993	1995	1997	1999	2001	2003	2005	2007	2009	2011	2013
1	2	3	4	5	6	7	8	9	10	11	12
Total	24.0 (1.33)	32.1 (1.55)	31.7 (0.90)	30.2 (1.23)	28.5 (1.01)	28.7 (1.95)	25.4 (1.05)	22.3 (1.04)	22.7 (1.04)	25.6 (0.99)	22.1 (0.96)
Sex											
Male	28.5 (1.50)	38.8 (1.73)	37.4 (1.19)	34.7 (1.69)	34.6 (1.20)	31.9 (2.07)	28.8 (1.23)	25.7 (1.15)	25.9 (1.36)	29.2 (1.10)	24.5 (1.21)
Female	19.1 (1.31)	24.8 (1.43)	24.7 (1.22)	25.7 (1.26)	22.7 (1.03)	25.0 (1.92)	21.8 (1.03)	18.7 (1.16)	19.3 (1.01)	21.7 (1.17)	19.7 (0.89)
Race/ethnicity[1]											
White	24.1 (1.69)	31.7 (2.24)	31.0 (1.36)	28.8 (1.50)	28.3 (1.31)	27.5 (2.68)	23.6 (1.32)	20.8 (1.23)	19.8 (1.13)	22.7 (0.96)	20.4 (1.11)
Black	17.5 (1.49)	28.5 (1.98)	25.4 (1.69)	25.3 (2.03)	21.9 (1.72)	23.1 (1.42)	23.9 (2.22)	19.2 (1.36)	22.2 (1.42)	22.8 (1.82)	18.6 (1.11)
Hispanic	34.1 (1.58)	40.7 (2.45)	41.1 (2.04)	36.9 (2.10)	34.2 (1.17)	36.5 (1.91)	33.5 (1.18)	29.1 (1.94)	31.2 (1.53)	33.2 (1.70)	27.4 (1.42)
Asian[2]	— (†)	— (†)	— (†)	25.7 (2.65)	25.7 (2.92)	22.5 (3.71)	15.9 (2.68)	21.0 (2.78)	18.3 (2.03)	23.3 (2.46)	22.6 (2.57)
Pacific Islander[2]	— (†)	— (†)	— (†)	46.9 (4.33)	50.2 (5.73)	34.7 (6.19)	41.3 (5.75)	38.5 (5.45)	27.6 (5.10)	38.9 (5.01)	27.7 (3.68)
American Indian/Alaska Native[2]	20.9 (4.55)	22.8 (4.78)	30.1 (4.54)	30.6 (5.90)	34.5 (5.15)	31.3 (5.64)	24.4 (3.57)	25.1 (2.04)	34.0 (4.81)	40.5 (2.80)	25.5 (4.10)
Two or more races[2]	— (†)	— (†)	— (†)	36.0 (2.72)	34.5 (3.22)	36.6 (3.99)	31.6 (3.13)	24.6 (3.55)	26.9 (2.62)	33.3 (2.79)	26.4 (2.67)
Grade											
9th	21.8 (1.24)	31.1 (1.69)	31.4 (2.33)	27.6 (2.51)	29.0 (1.59)	29.5 (2.39)	24.0 (1.21)	21.2 (1.23)	22.0 (1.32)	23.7 (1.22)	22.4 (1.15)
10th	23.7 (1.86)	35.0 (1.54)	33.4 (1.71)	32.1 (1.94)	29.0 (1.39)	29.2 (2.02)	27.5 (1.68)	25.3 (1.29)	23.7 (1.11)	27.8 (1.21)	23.2 (1.54)
11th	27.5 (1.61)	32.8 (1.88)	33.2 (1.42)	31.1 (2.16)	28.7 (1.39)	29.9 (2.33)	24.9 (1.03)	22.8 (1.42)	24.3 (1.44)	27.0 (1.51)	23.2 (1.32)
12th	23.0 (1.82)	29.1 (2.63)	29.0 (1.80)	30.5 (1.11)	26.9 (1.30)	24.9 (2.24)	24.9 (1.40)	19.6 (1.26)	20.6 (1.21)	23.8 (1.13)	18.8 (1.11)
Urbanicity[3]											
Urban	— (†)	— (†)	31.2 (1.11)	30.3 (1.50)	32.0 (1.36)	31.1 (2.12)	— (†)	— (†)	— (†)	— (†)	— (†)
Suburban	— (†)	— (†)	34.2 (0.94)	29.7 (1.87)	26.6 (1.34)	28.4 (2.16)	— (†)	— (†)	— (†)	— (†)	— (†)
Rural	— (†)	— (†)	22.7 (1.91)	32.1 (5.76)	28.2 (3.10)	26.2 (5.08)	— (†)	— (†)	— (†)	— (†)	— (†)

—Not available.
†Not applicable.
[1]Race categories exclude persons of Hispanic ethnicity.
[2]Before 1999, Asian students and Pacific Islander students were not categorized separately, and students were not given the option of choosing two or more races. Because the response categories changed in 1999, caution should be used in comparing data on race from 1993, 1995, and 1997 with data from later years.

[3]Refers to the Standard Metropolitan Statistical Area (MSA) status of the respondent's household as defined in 2000 by the U.S. Census Bureau. Categories include "central city of an MSA (Urban)," "in MSA but not in central city (Suburban)," and "not MSA (Rural)."
NOTE: "On school property" was not defined for survey respondents.
SOURCE: Centers for Disease Control and Prevention, Division of Adolescent and School Health, Youth Risk Behavior Surveillance System (YRBSS), 1993 through 2013. (This table was prepared June 2014.)

Table 232.80. Percentage of public school students in grades 9–12 who reported that illegal drugs were made available to them on school property during the previous 12 months, by state: Selected years, 2003 through 2013

[Standard errors appear in parentheses]

State	2003		2005		2007		2009		2011		2013	
1	2		3		4		5		6		7	
United States[1]	28.7	(1.95)	25.4	(1.05)	22.3	(1.04)	22.7	(1.04)	25.6	(0.99)	22.1	(0.96)
Alabama	26.0	(1.78)	26.2	(1.90)	—	(†)	27.6	(1.30)	20.3	(1.32)	25.3	(1.11)
Alaska	28.4	(1.24)	—	(†)	25.1	(1.36)	24.8	(1.25)	23.2	(0.98)	—	(†)
Arizona	28.6	(1.23)	38.7	(1.18)	37.1	(1.45)	34.6	(1.43)	34.6	(1.55)	31.3	(1.46)
Arkansas	—	(†)	29.2	(1.35)	28.1	(1.28)	31.4	(1.56)	26.1	(1.30)	27.4	(1.28)
California	—	(†)	—	(†)	—	(†)	—	(†)	—	(†)	—	(†)
Colorado	—	(†)	21.2	(1.81)	—	(†)	22.7	(1.52)	17.2	(1.28)	—	(†)
Connecticut	—	(†)	31.5	(0.90)	30.5	(1.52)	28.9	(1.25)	27.8	(1.43)	27.1	(0.85)
Delaware	27.9	(0.90)	26.1	(1.05)	22.9	(0.99)	20.9	(0.87)	23.1	(1.20)	19.1	(0.83)
District of Columbia	30.2	(1.46)	20.3	(1.18)	25.7	(1.20)	—	(†)	22.6	(1.53)	—	(†)
Florida	25.7	(0.81)	23.2	(0.85)	19.0	(0.80)	21.8	(0.72)	22.9	(0.84)	20.0	(0.64)
Georgia	33.3	(1.00)	30.7	(1.25)	32.0	(1.23)	32.9	(1.22)	32.1	(1.34)	26.5	(1.32)
Hawaii	—	(†)	32.7	(1.74)	36.2	(2.46)	36.1	(1.51)	31.7	(1.48)	31.2	(0.99)
Idaho	19.6	(1.26)	24.8	(1.52)	25.1	(1.63)	22.7	(1.39)	24.4	(1.56)	22.1	(1.31)
Illinois	—	(†)	—	(†)	21.2	(1.18)	27.5	(1.97)	27.3	(1.46)	27.2	(1.06)
Indiana	28.3	(1.55)	28.9	(1.33)	20.5	(1.02)	25.5	(1.24)	28.3	(1.33)	—	(†)
Iowa	—	(†)	15.5	(1.37)	10.1	(1.08)	—	(†)	11.9	(1.16)	—	(†)
Kansas	—	(†)	16.7	(1.27)	15.0	(1.24)	15.1	(0.78)	24.9	(1.19)	19.4	(1.06)
Kentucky	30.4	(1.51)	19.8	(1.23)	27.0	(1.11)	25.6	(1.49)	24.4	(1.40)	20.6	(1.15)
Louisiana	—	(†)	—	(†)	—	(†)	22.8	(1.66)	25.1	(1.82)	—	(†)
Maine	32.6	(1.73)	33.5	(1.89)	29.1	(1.67)	21.2	(0.51)	21.7	(0.80)	18.4	(0.87)
Maryland	—	(†)	28.9	(2.04)	27.4	(1.46)	29.3	(1.35)	30.4	(1.99)	29.1	(0.37)
Massachusetts	31.9	(1.08)	29.9	(1.09)	27.3	(1.06)	26.1	(1.34)	27.1	(1.04)	23.0	(0.90)
Michigan	31.3	(1.50)	28.8	(1.37)	29.1	(1.07)	29.5	(0.90)	25.4	(0.90)	23.8	(0.94)
Minnesota	—	(†)	—	(†)	—	(†)	—	(†)	—	(†)	—	(†)
Mississippi	22.3	(1.31)	—	(†)	15.6	(1.53)	18.0	(1.07)	15.9	(0.89)	12.1	(1.00)
Missouri	21.6	(2.09)	18.2	(1.92)	17.8	(1.49)	17.3	(1.32)	—	(†)	—	(†)
Montana	26.9	(1.23)	25.3	(1.09)	24.9	(0.83)	20.7	(1.10)	25.2	(0.93)	22.8	(0.71)
Nebraska	23.3	(1.04)	22.0	(0.82)	—	(†)	—	(†)	20.3	(1.01)	19.2	(1.15)
Nevada	34.5	(1.30)	32.6	(1.53)	28.8	(1.39)	35.6	(1.30)	—	(†)	31.2	(1.90)
New Hampshire	28.2	(1.87)	26.9	(1.40)	22.5	(1.25)	22.1	(1.44)	23.2	(1.44)	20.1	(1.03)
New Jersey	—	(†)	32.6	(1.32)	—	(†)	32.2	(1.38)	27.3	(1.41)	30.7	(1.70)
New Mexico	—	(†)	33.5	(1.37)	31.3	(1.39)	30.9	(1.54)	34.5	(1.24)	32.8	(1.04)
New York	23.0	(0.97)	23.7	(0.76)	26.6	(1.09)	24.0	(1.05)	—	(†)	—	(†)
North Carolina	31.9	(1.74)	27.4	(1.66)	28.5	(1.37)	30.2	(1.51)	29.8	(1.87)	23.6	(1.61)
North Dakota	21.3	(1.07)	19.6	(1.10)	18.7	(1.05)	19.5	(1.16)	20.8	(1.03)	14.1	(0.79)
Ohio[2]	31.1	(1.68)	30.9	(1.88)	26.7	(1.26)	—	(†)	24.3	(1.70)	19.9	(1.41)
Oklahoma	22.2	(1.23)	18.4	(1.49)	19.1	(1.12)	16.8	(1.50)	17.2	(1.36)	14.0	(1.07)
Oregon	—	(†)	—	(†)	—	(†)	—	(†)	—	(†)	—	(†)
Pennsylvania	—	(†)	—	(†)	—	(†)	16.1	(1.07)	—	(†)	—	(†)
Rhode Island	26.0	(1.26)	24.1	(1.11)	25.3	(1.33)	25.2	(1.52)	22.4	(0.95)	22.6	(1.16)
South Carolina	—	(†)	29.1	(1.45)	26.6	(1.58)	27.6	(1.74)	29.3	(1.83)	24.5	(1.43)
South Dakota[2]	22.1	(1.25)	20.9	(2.30)	21.1	(1.98)	17.7	(0.64)	16.0	(1.81)	15.4	(1.70)
Tennessee	24.3	(2.25)	26.6	(1.21)	21.6	(1.35)	18.8	(1.06)	16.6	(0.88)	24.8	(1.57)
Texas	—	(†)	30.7	(1.73)	26.5	(0.83)	25.9	(1.25)	29.4	(1.34)	26.4	(1.24)
Utah	24.7	(2.04)	20.6	(1.36)	23.2	(1.83)	19.7	(1.52)	21.4	(1.55)	20.0	(1.57)
Vermont	29.4	(1.67)	23.1	(1.59)	22.0	(0.99)	21.1	(1.21)	17.6	(1.51)	—	(†)
Virginia	—	(†)	—	(†)	—	(†)	—	(†)	24.0	(1.67)	—	(†)
Washington	—	(†)	—	(†)	—	(†)	—	(†)	—	(†)	—	(†)
West Virginia	26.5	(2.06)	24.8	(1.36)	28.6	(2.76)	28.0	(1.27)	17.3	(1.04)	17.1	(1.16)
Wisconsin	26.3	(1.18)	21.7	(1.18)	22.7	(1.34)	20.5	(1.03)	20.9	(1.29)	18.3	(1.01)
Wyoming	18.1	(0.99)	22.7	(0.97)	24.7	(1.08)	23.7	(0.93)	25.2	(0.97)	20.2	(0.74)

— Not available.
†Not applicable.
[1]Data for the U.S. total include both public and private schools and were collected through a national survey representing the entire country.
[2]Data include both public and private schools.
NOTE: "On school property" was not defined for survey respondents. State-level data include public schools only, with the exception of data for Ohio and South Dakota. Data for the U.S. total, Ohio, and South Dakota include both public and private schools. For specific states, a given year's data may be unavailable (1) because the state did not participate in the survey that year; (2) because the state omitted this particular survey item from the state-level questionnaire; or (3) because the state had an overall response rate of less than 60 percent (the overall response rate is the school response rate multiplied by the student response rate).
SOURCE: Centers for Disease Control and Prevention, Division of Adolescent and School Health, Youth Risk Behavior Surveillance System (YRBSS), 2003 through 2013. (This table was prepared June 2014.)

Table 232.90. Percentage of high school seniors reporting use of alcohol and illicit drugs, by frequency of use and substance used: Selected years, 1975 through 2013

[Standard errors appear in parentheses]

Frequency of use and substance used	Class of 1975	Class of 1980	Class of 1985	Class of 1990	Class of 1995	Class of 2000	Class of 2005	Class of 2007	Class of 2008	Class of 2009	Class of 2010	Class of 2011	Class of 2012	Class of 2013
1	2	3	4	5	6	7	8	9	10	11	12	13	14	15
Ever used														
Alcohol[1]	90.4 (0.69)	93.2 (0.46)	92.2 (0.48)	89.5 (0.57)	80.7 (0.73)	80.3 (0.80)	75.1 (0.81)	72.2 (0.83)	71.9 (0.85)	72.3 (0.85)	71.0 (0.84)	70.0 (0.88)	69.4 (0.90)	68.2 (0.95)
Any illicit drug	55.2 (1.68)	65.4 (1.23)	60.6 (1.26)	47.9 (1.33)	48.4 (1.32)	54.0 (1.44)	50.4 (1.35)	46.8 (1.33)	47.4 (1.35)	46.7 (1.36)	48.2 (1.33)	49.9 (1.38)	49.1 (1.40)	50.4 (1.46)
Marijuana only	19.0 (1.32)	26.7 (1.15)	20.9 (1.05)	18.5 (1.03)	20.3 (1.06)	25.0 (1.25)	23.0 (1.14)	21.3 (1.09)	22.5 (1.13)	22.7 (1.15)	23.5 (1.13)	25.0 (1.19)	25.0 (1.21)	25.7 (1.27)
Any illicit drug other than marijuana[2]	36.2 (1.33)	38.7 (1.04)	39.7 (1.04)	29.4 (0.99)	28.1 (0.97)	29.0 (1.08)	27.4 (0.99)	25.5 (0.95)	24.9 (0.96)	24.0 (0.96)	24.7 (0.94)	24.9 (0.98)	24.1 (0.98)	24.7 (1.03)
Selected drugs														
Cocaine	9.0 (0.73)	15.7 (0.72)	17.3 (0.74)	9.4 (0.59)	6.0 (0.48)	8.6 (0.62)	8.0 (0.56)	7.8 (0.54)	7.2 (0.53)	6.0 (0.49)	5.5 (0.46)	5.2 (0.47)	4.9 (0.46)	4.5 (0.46)
Heroin	2.2 (0.21)	1.1 (0.12)	1.2 (0.12)	1.3 (0.13)	1.6 (0.14)	2.4 (0.19)	1.5 (0.14)	1.5 (0.14)	1.3 (0.13)	1.2 (0.13)	1.6 (0.14)	1.4 (0.14)	1.1 (0.13)	1.0 (0.13)
LSD	11.3 (0.81)	9.3 (0.57)	7.5 (0.52)	8.7 (0.57)	11.7 (0.64)	11.1 (0.69)	3.5 (0.38)	3.4 (0.37)	4.0 (0.40)	3.1 (0.36)	4.0 (0.40)	4.0 (0.41)	3.8 (0.41)	3.9 (0.43)
Marijuana/hashish	47.3 (1.68)	60.3 (1.27)	54.2 (1.83)	40.7 (1.30)	41.7 (1.30)	48.8 (1.45)	44.8 (1.34)	41.8 (1.31)	42.6 (1.34)	42.0 (1.35)	43.8 (1.32)	45.5 (1.37)	45.2 (1.39)	45.5 (1.45)
PCP	— (†)	9.6 (0.33)	4.9 (0.24)	2.8 (0.19)	2.7 (0.18)	3.4 (0.23)	2.4 (0.18)	2.1 (0.17)	1.8 (0.16)	1.7 (0.15)	1.8 (0.15)	2.3 (0.18)	1.6 (0.15)	1.3 (0.14)
Used during past 12 months														
Alcohol[1]	84.8 (0.84)	87.9 (0.59)	85.6 (0.63)	80.6 (0.73)	73.7 (0.81)	73.2 (0.89)	68.6 (0.87)	66.4 (0.88)	65.5 (0.90)	66.2 (0.90)	65.2 (0.88)	63.5 (0.92)	63.5 (0.94)	62.0 (0.99)
Any illicit drug	45.0 (1.64)	53.1 (1.26)	46.3 (1.26)	32.5 (1.21)	39.0 (1.26)	40.9 (1.39)	38.4 (1.28)	35.9 (1.25)	36.6 (1.27)	36.5 (1.29)	38.3 (1.26)	40.0 (1.32)	39.7 (1.34)	40.3 (1.40)
Marijuana only	18.8 (1.29)	22.7 (1.06)	18.9 (0.99)	14.6 (0.91)	19.6 (1.02)	20.5 (1.14)	18.8 (1.03)	17.4 (0.99)	18.3 (1.02)	19.5 (1.06)	21.0 (1.06)	22.4 (1.12)	22.7 (1.14)	23.0 (1.20)
Any illicit drug other than marijuana[2]	26.2 (1.15)	30.4 (0.92)	27.4 (0.89)	17.9 (0.79)	19.4 (0.81)	20.4 (0.90)	19.7 (0.83)	18.5 (0.80)	18.3 (0.81)	17.0 (0.79)	17.3 (0.78)	17.6 (0.81)	17.0 (0.81)	17.3 (0.85)
Selected drugs														
Cocaine	5.6 (0.52)	12.3 (0.58)	13.1 (0.59)	5.3 (0.40)	4.0 (0.35)	5.0 (0.43)	5.1 (0.40)	5.2 (0.40)	4.4 (0.38)	3.4 (0.34)	2.9 (0.30)	2.9 (0.31)	2.7 (0.31)	2.6 (0.31)
Heroin	1.0 (0.13)	0.5 (0.07)	0.6 (0.07)	0.5 (0.07)	1.1 (0.10)	1.5 (0.13)	0.8 (0.09)	0.9 (0.09)	0.7 (0.08)	0.7 (0.09)	0.9 (0.09)	0.8 (0.09)	0.6 (0.08)	0.6 (0.08)
LSD	7.2 (0.59)	6.5 (0.43)	4.4 (0.36)	5.4 (0.41)	8.4 (0.49)	6.6 (0.49)	1.8 (0.24)	2.1 (0.26)	2.7 (0.30)	1.9 (0.25)	2.6 (0.29)	2.7 (0.30)	2.4 (0.29)	2.2 (0.29)
Marijuana/hashish	40.0 (1.61)	48.8 (1.27)	40.6 (1.24)	27.0 (1.15)	34.7 (1.23)	36.5 (1.36)	33.6 (1.24)	31.7 (1.21)	32.4 (1.24)	32.8 (1.25)	34.8 (1.24)	36.4 (1.29)	36.4 (1.31)	36.4 (1.37)
PCP	— (†)	4.4 (0.20)	2.9 (0.16)	1.2 (0.11)	1.8 (0.13)	2.3 (0.16)	1.3 (0.11)	0.9 (0.09)	1.1 (0.11)	1.0 (0.10)	1.0 (0.10)	1.3 (0.12)	0.9 (0.10)	0.7 (0.09)
Used during past 30 days														
Alcohol[1]	68.2 (1.10)	72.0 (0.81)	65.9 (0.85)	57.1 (0.92)	51.3 (0.92)	50.0 (1.01)	47.0 (0.94)	44.4 (0.92)	43.1 (0.93)	43.5 (0.95)	41.2 (0.91)	40.0 (0.94)	41.5 (0.96)	39.2 (0.99)
Any illicit drug	30.7 (1.35)	37.2 (1.09)	29.7 (1.03)	17.2 (0.87)	23.8 (0.98)	24.9 (1.09)	23.1 (0.99)	21.9 (0.96)	22.3 (0.98)	23.3 (1.01)	23.8 (0.99)	25.2 (1.04)	25.2 (1.06)	25.5 (1.11)
Marijuana only	15.3 (1.06)	18.8 (0.88)	14.8 (0.80)	9.2 (0.67)	13.8 (0.79)	14.5 (0.89)	12.8 (0.78)	12.4 (0.76)	13.0 (0.79)	14.7 (0.84)	15.2 (0.83)	16.3 (0.89)	16.8 (0.91)	17.1 (0.95)
Any illicit drug other than marijuana[2]	15.4 (0.80)	18.4 (0.66)	14.9 (0.60)	8.0 (0.47)	10.0 (0.52)	10.4 (0.58)	10.3 (0.54)	9.5 (0.51)	9.3 (0.52)	8.6 (0.50)	8.6 (0.49)	8.9 (0.51)	8.4 (0.51)	8.4 (0.53)
Selected drugs														
Cocaine	1.9 (0.25)	5.2 (0.31)	6.7 (0.35)	1.9 (0.20)	1.8 (0.19)	2.1 (0.23)	2.3 (0.22)	2.0 (0.20)	1.9 (0.20)	1.3 (0.17)	1.3 (0.16)	1.1 (0.16)	1.1 (0.16)	1.1 (0.17)
Heroin	0.4 (0.08)	0.2 (0.04)	0.3 (0.05)	0.2 (0.04)	0.6 (0.08)	0.7 (0.09)	0.5 (0.07)	0.4 (0.06)	0.4 (0.06)	0.4 (0.06)	0.4 (0.06)	0.4 (0.07)	0.3 (0.06)	0.3 (0.06)
LSD	2.3 (0.28)	2.3 (0.21)	1.6 (0.18)	1.9 (0.20)	4.0 (0.28)	1.6 (0.20)	0.7 (0.12)	0.6 (0.11)	1.1 (0.15)	0.5 (0.11)	0.8 (0.13)	0.8 (0.13)	0.8 (0.14)	0.8 (0.14)
Marijuana/hashish	27.1 (1.30)	33.7 (1.07)	25.7 (0.98)	14.0 (0.80)	21.2 (0.94)	21.6 (1.04)	19.8 (0.94)	18.8 (0.90)	19.4 (0.93)	20.6 (0.96)	21.4 (0.95)	22.6 (1.00)	22.9 (1.02)	22.7 (1.06)
PCP	— (†)	1.4 (0.11)	1.6 (0.12)	0.4 (0.06)	0.6 (0.08)	0.9 (0.10)	0.7 (0.08)	0.5 (0.07)	0.6 (0.08)	0.5 (0.07)	0.8 (0.09)	0.8 (0.09)	0.5 (0.07)	0.4 (0.07)

—Not available.
†Not applicable.
[1]Survey question changed in 1993; later data are not comparable to figures for earlier years.
[2]Other illicit drugs include any use of LSD or other hallucinogens, crack or other cocaine, or heroin, or any use of other narcotics, amphetamines, barbiturates, or tranquilizers not under a doctor's orders.

NOTE: Detail may not sum to totals because of rounding. Standard errors were calculated from formulas to perform trend analysis over an interval greater than 1 year (for example, a comparison between 1975 and 1990). A revised questionnaire was used in 1982 and later years to reduce the inappropriate reporting of nonprescription stimulants. This slightly reduced the positive responses for some types of drug abuse.
SOURCE: University of Michigan, Institute for Social Research, Monitoring the Future, selected years, 1975 through 2013, retrieved November 21, 2014, from http://monitoringthefuture.org/data/13data.html. (This table was prepared November 2014.)

Table 232.95. Percentage of 12- to 17-year-olds reporting use of illicit drugs, alcohol, and cigarettes during the past 30 days and the past year, by substance used, sex, and race/ethnicity: Selected years, 1985 through 2013

[Standard errors appear in parentheses]

Year, sex, and race/ethnicity	Percent reporting use during past 30 days					Percent reporting use during past year				
	Illicit drugs			Alcohol	Cigarettes	Illicit drugs			Alcohol	Cigarettes
	Any[1]	Marijuana	Cocaine			Any[1]	Marijuana	Cocaine		
1	2	3	4	5	6	7	8	9	10	11
1985	13.2 (—)	10.2 (—)	1.5 (—)	41.2 (—)	29.4 (—)	20.7 (—)	16.7 (—)	3.4 (—)	52.7 (—)	29.9 (—)
1990	7.1 (—)	4.4 (—)	0.6 (—)	32.5 (—)	22.4 (—)	14.1 (—)	9.6 (—)	1.9 (—)	41.8 (—)	26.2 (—)
1995	10.9 (—)	8.2 (—)	0.8 (—)	21.1 (—)	20.2 (—)	18.0 (—)	14.2 (—)	1.7 (—)	35.1 (—)	26.6 (—)
1996	9.0 (—)	7.1 (—)	0.6 (—)	18.8 (—)	18.3 (—)	16.7 (—)	13.0 (—)	1.4 (—)	32.7 (—)	24.2 (—)
1997	11.4 (—)	9.4 (—)	1.0 (—)	20.5 (—)	19.9 (—)	18.8 (—)	15.8 (—)	2.2 (—)	34.0 (—)	26.4 (—)
1998	9.9 (—)	8.3 (—)	0.8 (—)	19.1 (—)	18.2 (—)	16.4 (—)	14.1 (—)	1.7 (—)	31.8 (—)	23.8 (—)
1999	9.8 (0.23)	7.2 (0.20)	0.5 (0.06)	16.5 (0.30)	14.9 (0.31)	19.8 (0.32)	14.2 (0.29)	1.6 (0.10)	34.1 (0.41)	23.4 (0.37)
2000	9.7 (0.24)	7.2 (0.21)	0.6 (0.07)	16.4 (0.29)	13.4 (0.28)	18.6 (0.31)	13.4 (0.27)	1.7 (0.12)	33.0 (0.39)	20.8 (0.34)
2001	10.8 (0.26)	8.0 (0.24)	0.4 (0.06)	17.3 (0.33)	13.0 (0.28)	20.8 (0.36)	15.2 (0.32)	1.5 (0.10)	33.9 (0.39)	20.0 (0.35)
2002	11.6 (0.29)	8.2 (0.24)	0.6 (0.07)	17.6 (0.32)	13.0 (0.30)	22.2 (0.38)	15.8 (0.32)	2.1 (0.13)	34.6 (0.42)	20.3 (0.35)
2003	11.2 (0.27)	7.9 (0.24)	0.6 (0.06)	17.7 (0.33)	12.2 (0.29)	21.8 (0.36)	15.0 (0.31)	1.8 (0.11)	34.3 (0.42)	19.0 (0.36)
2004	10.6 (0.27)	7.6 (0.23)	0.5 (0.06)	17.6 (0.32)	11.9 (0.30)	21.0 (0.34)	14.5 (0.31)	1.6 (0.11)	33.9 (0.41)	18.4 (0.35)
2005	9.9 (0.25)	6.8 (0.22)	0.6 (0.06)	16.5 (0.32)	10.8 (0.28)	19.9 (0.35)	13.3 (0.30)	1.7 (0.11)	33.3 (0.41)	17.3 (0.36)
2006	9.8 (0.27)	6.7 (0.21)	0.4 (0.05)	16.6 (0.32)	10.4 (0.26)	19.6 (0.37)	13.2 (0.31)	1.6 (0.11)	32.9 (0.42)	17.0 (0.35)
2007	9.5 (0.27)	6.7 (0.22)	0.4 (0.05)	15.9 (0.34)	9.8 (0.26)	18.7 (0.35)	12.5 (0.30)	1.5 (0.11)	31.8 (0.42)	15.7 (0.34)
2008	9.3 (0.24)	6.7 (0.22)	0.4 (0.05)	14.6 (0.31)	9.1 (0.24)	19.0 (0.35)	13.0 (0.29)	1.2 (0.10)	30.8 (0.40)	15.0 (0.31)
2009	10.0 (0.27)	7.3 (0.24)	0.3 (0.05)	14.7 (0.32)	8.9 (0.26)	19.5 (0.36)	13.6 (0.31)	1.0 (0.09)	30.3 (0.42)	15.0 (0.33)
2010	10.1 (0.29)	7.4 (0.25)	0.2 (0.05)	13.6 (0.33)	8.4 (0.26)	19.5 (0.38)	14.0 (0.34)	1.0 (0.09)	28.7 (0.43)	14.2 (0.34)
2011	10.1 (0.27)	7.9 (0.24)	0.3 (0.05)	13.3 (0.31)	7.8 (0.24)	19.0 (0.37)	14.2 (0.33)	0.9 (0.08)	27.8 (0.43)	13.2 (0.31)
2012	9.5 (0.25)	7.2 (0.22)	0.1 ! (0.03)	12.9 (0.31)	6.6 (0.22)	17.9 (0.33)	13.5 (0.30)	0.7 (0.08)	26.3 (0.42)	11.8 (0.29)
Sex										
Male	9.6 (0.37)	7.5 (0.32)	0.1 ! (0.03)	12.6 (0.43)	6.8 (0.32)	17.8 (0.47)	14.1 (0.45)	0.7 (0.11)	25.5 (0.55)	12.3 (0.42)
Female	9.5 (0.38)	7.0 (0.32)	‡ (†)	13.2 (0.44)	6.3 (0.28)	18.0 (0.50)	12.8 (0.44)	0.8 (0.11)	27.1 (0.57)	11.3 (0.38)
Race/ethnicity										
White	9.6 (0.33)	7.5 (0.29)	0.1 ! (0.04)	14.6 (0.42)	8.2 (0.31)	18.1 (0.44)	14.0 (0.40)	0.8 (0.10)	28.7 (0.53)	13.9 (0.39)
Black	10.2 (0.69)	7.5 (0.63)	‡ (†)	9.3 (0.72)	4.1 (0.46)	19.1 (0.89)	13.5 (0.81)	0.3 ! (0.13)	20.8 (0.99)	7.2 (0.59)
Hispanic	9.7 (0.67)	6.7 (0.51)	‡ (†)	12.8 (0.68)	4.8 (0.43)	18.5 (0.82)	13.7 (0.72)	0.9 (0.19)	27.2 (0.98)	10.8 (0.69)
Asian	2.6 (0.71)	1.8 ! (0.62)	‡ (†)	4.9 (1.12)	1.7 ! (0.61)	6.1 (1.02)	3.8 (0.85)	‡ (†)	9.6 (1.44)	3.0 (0.77)
Pacific Islander	‡ (†)	‡ (†)	‡ (†)	‡ (†)	‡ (†)	‡ (†)	‡ (†)	‡ (†)	‡ (†)	‡ (†)
American Indian/Alaska Native	12.1 (2.65)	8.5 (1.81)	‡ (†)	10.0 (2.29)	11.8 (2.86)	22.2 (3.32)	15.2 (2.50)	‡ (†)	20.7 (3.41)	19.9 (3.52)
Two or more races	14.7 (1.67)	11.9 (1.55)	‡ (†)	11.7 (1.45)	7.5 (1.16)	23.3 (1.95)	18.2 (1.78)	‡ (†)	28.3 (2.20)	15.1 (1.72)
2013	8.8 (0.25)	7.1 (0.23)	0.2 (0.04)	11.6 (0.29)	5.6 (0.20)	17.2 (0.35)	13.4 (0.31)	0.5 (0.06)	24.6 (0.40)	10.3 (0.27)
Sex										
Male	9.6 (0.36)	7.9 (0.33)	0.2 (0.05)	11.2 (0.41)	5.7 (0.28)	17.8 (0.51)	14.1 (0.45)	0.6 (0.09)	23.5 (0.56)	10.3 (0.37)
Female	8.0 (0.34)	6.2 (0.30)	0.2 ! (0.06)	11.9 (0.43)	5.5 (0.30)	16.6 (0.50)	12.8 (0.44)	0.5 (0.09)	25.8 (0.58)	10.3 (0.40)
Race/ethnicity										
White	8.8 (0.32)	7.1 (0.29)	0.2 (0.05)	12.9 (0.40)	7.2 (0.31)	17.0 (0.43)	13.5 (0.40)	0.6 (0.09)	27.1 (0.52)	12.2 (0.38)
Black	10.5 (0.73)	7.4 (0.59)	‡ (†)	9.7 (0.71)	3.2 (0.39)	20.1 (0.90)	14.7 (0.83)	‡ (†)	21.6 (0.97)	6.4 (0.57)
Hispanic	8.7 (0.58)	7.2 (0.52)	0.3 (0.08)	10.7 (0.66)	3.7 (0.37)	17.2 (0.83)	13.5 (0.76)	0.6 (0.13)	23.2 (0.91)	9.0 (0.60)
Asian	3.8 (0.91)	3.6 (0.90)	‡ (†)	8.0 (1.48)	2.5 (0.71)	9.1 (1.37)	7.1 (1.26)	‡ (†)	15.8 (2.25)	5.1 (1.12)
Pacific Islander	‡ (†)	‡ (†)	‡ (†)	8.2 ! (2.90)	3.6 ! (1.48)	‡ (†)	‡ (†)	‡ (†)	‡ (†)	6.0 ! (2.52)
American Indian/Alaska Native	9.1 (2.58)	9.1 (2.58)	‡ (†)	9.3 (2.39)	7.5 (1.95)	27.8 (4.94)	20.1 (3.52)	‡ (†)	20.3 (3.90)	16.1 (3.13)
Two or more races	10.3 (1.25)	8.6 (1.15)	‡ (†)	9.0 (1.10)	7.0 (1.18)	19.0 (1.73)	15.5 (1.59)	‡ (†)	21.8 (1.79)	10.3 (1.36)

—Not available.
†Not applicable.
!Interpret data with caution. The coefficient of variation (CV) for this estimate is between 30 and 50 percent.
‡Reporting standards not met (too few cases for a reliable estimate).
[1]Includes other illegal drug use not shown separately—specifically, the use of heroin, hallucinogens, and inhalants, as well as the nonmedical use of prescription-type pain relievers, tranquilizers, stimulants, and sedatives.
NOTE: Marijuana includes hashish usage. Data for 1999 and later years were gathered using Computer Assisted Interviewing (CAI) and may not be directly comparable to previous years. Because of survey improvements in 2002, the 2002 data constitute a new baseline for tracking trends. Valid trend comparisons can be made for 1985 through 1998, 1999 through 2001, and 2002 through 2013. Race categories exclude persons of Hispanic ethnicity.
SOURCE: U.S. Department of Health and Human Services, Substance Abuse and Mental Health Services Administration, National Household Survey on Drug Abuse: Main Findings, selected years, 1985 through 2001, and National Survey on Drug Use and Health, 2002 through 2013. Retrieved February 20, 2015, from http://www.icpsr.umich.edu/icpsrweb/SAMHDA/series/00064. (This table was prepared March 2015.)

Table 233.10. Number and percentage of public schools that took a serious disciplinary action in response to specific offenses, number of serious actions taken, and percentage distribution of actions, by type of offense, school level, and type of action: Selected years, 1999–2000 through 2009–10

[Standard errors appear in parentheses]

Year, school level, and type of serious disciplinary action	Total	Physical attacks or fights	Insubordination	Distribution, possession, or use of alcohol	Distribution, possession, or use of illegal drugs	Use or possession of a firearm or explosive device	Use or possession of a weapon other than a firearm or explosive device[1]
1	2	3	4	5	6	7	8
Number of schools taking at least one action							
2009–10	32,300 (940)	24,000 (770)	— (†)	7,600 (320)	16,100 (400)	2,500 (340)	11,200 (650)
Percent of schools taking at least one action							
1999–2000[2]	(†)	35.4 (1.02)	18.3 (0.79)	— (†)	— (†)	— (†)	— (†)
2003–04	45.7 (1.15)	32.0 (0.94)	21.6 (0.85)	9.2 (0.50)	21.2 (0.58)	3.9 (0.40)	16.8 (0.84)
2005–06	48.0 (1.18)	31.5 (1.02)	21.2 (0.85)	10.2 (0.47)	20.8 (0.61)	4.5 (0.35)	19.3 (0.91)
2007–08	46.4 (1.16)	31.5 (0.89)	21.4 (0.95)	9.8 (0.48)	19.3 (0.53)	2.8 (0.26)	15.3 (0.77)
2009–10[3]	39.1 (1.14)	29.0 (0.94)	— (†)	9.2 (0.39)	19.5 (0.48)	3.0 (0.41)	13.5 (0.78)
Primary school[4]	18.1 (1.51)	13.2 (1.26)	— (†)	1.0 ! (0.33)	2.0 (0.47)	1.7 ! (0.57)	6.4 (0.93)
Middle school[4]	67.0 (1.68)	49.7 (1.87)	— (†)	13.6 (1.17)	36.9 (1.19)	4.1 (0.65)	25.1 (1.70)
High school[4]	82.7 (1.57)	62.6 (1.63)	— (†)	36.1 (1.47)	66.1 (1.39)	7.3 (1.05)	28.9 (1.39)
Combined school[4]	49.2 (5.31)	35.6 (4.26)	— (†)	9.9 (2.54)	22.7 (3.57)	‡ (†)	10.9 (2.72)
Number of actions taken							
1999–2000[2]	(†)	332,500 (27,420)	253,500 (27,720)	— (†)	— (†)	— (†)	— (†)
2003–04	655,700 (29,160)	273,500 (14,450)	220,400 (16,990)	25,500 (1,600)	91,100 (3,410)	9,900 ! (4,300)	35,400 (1,470)
2005–06	830,700 (45,710)	323,900 (16,690)	309,000 (33,840)	30,100 (1,880)	106,800 (4,950)	14,300 (2,690)	46,600 (2,040)
2007–08	767,900 (44,010)	271,800 (15,180)	327,100 (38,470)	28,400 (1,470)	98,700 (5,780)	5,200 (910)	36,800 (2,630)
2009–10[3]	433,800 (22,880)	265,100 (22,170)	— (†)	28,700 (1,920)	105,400 (4,070)	5,800 (1,360)	28,800 (1,580)
Percentage distribution of actions, 2009–10							
	100.0 (†)	100.0 (†)	— (†)	100.0 (†)	100.0 (†)	100.0 (†)	100.0 (†)
Out-of-school suspensions lasting 5 days or more	73.9 (1.79)	81.2 (2.18)	— (†)	74.3 (2.23)	59.6 (1.70)	55.5 (9.64)	62.2 (2.44)
Removal with no services for remainder of school year	6.1 (0.86)	5.0 (1.22)	— (†)	4.0 (0.92)	8.0 (0.94)	22.2 (4.96)	8.8 (1.31)
Transfer to specialized schools	20.0 (1.36)	13.9 (1.57)	— (†)	21.7 (2.27)	32.4 (1.57)	22.3 ! (7.91)	29.0 (2.32)

—Not available.
†Not applicable.
!Interpret data with caution. The coefficient of variation (CV) for this estimate is between 30 and 50 percent.
‡Reporting standards not met. Either there are too few cases for a reliable estimate or the coefficient of variation (CV) is 50 percent or greater.
[1]Prior to 2005–06, the questionnaire wording was simply "a weapon other than a firearm" (instead of "a weapon other than a firearm or explosive device").
[2]In the 1999–2000 questionnaire, only two items are the same as in questionnaires for later years—the item on physical attacks or fights and the item on insubordination. There are no comparable 1999–2000 data for serious disciplinary actions taken in response to the other specific offenses listed in this table, nor for total actions taken in response to all the listed offenses.
[3]Totals for 2009–10 are not comparable to totals for other years, because the 2009–10 questionnaire did not include an item on insubordination.
[4]Primary schools are defined as schools in which the lowest grade is not higher than grade 3 and the highest grade is not higher than grade 8. Middle schools are defined as schools in which the lowest grade is not lower than grade 4 and the highest grade is not higher than grade 9. High schools are defined as schools in which the lowest grade is not lower than grade 9 and the highest grade is not higher than grade 12. Combined schools include all other combinations of grades, including K–12 schools.
NOTE: Serious disciplinary actions include out-of-school suspensions lasting 5 or more days, but less than the remainder of the school year; removals with no continuing services for at least the remainder of the school year; and transfers to specialized schools for disciplinary reasons. Responses were provided by the principal or the person most knowledgeable about crime and safety issues at the school. Respondents were instructed to respond only for those times that were during normal school hours or when school activities or events were in session, unless the survey specified otherwise. Detail may not sum to totals because of rounding and because schools that reported serious disciplinary actions in response to more than one type of offense were counted only once in the total number or percentage of schools.
SOURCE: U.S. Department of Education, National Center for Education Statistics, 1999–2000, 2003–04, 2005–06, 2007–08, and 2009–10 School Survey on Crime and Safety (SSOCS), 2000, 2004, 2006, 2008, and 2010. (This table was prepared September 2013.)

Table 233.30. Number of students suspended and expelled from public elementary and secondary schools, by sex, race/ethnicity, and state: 2006

[Standard errors appear in parentheses]

		Sex		Race/ethnicity				
State	Total	Male	Female	White	Black	Hispanic	Asian/Pacific Islander	American Indian/ Alaska Native
1	2	3	4	5	6	7	8	9
Students suspended[1]								
United States	3,328,750 (20,038)	2,272,290 (13,667)	1,056,470 (6,842)	1,302,410 (9,493)	1,244,820 (11,267)	670,700 (6,889)	63,220 (836)	47,610 (2,861)
Alabama	75,090 (727)	50,580 (485)	24,510 (256)	25,730 (380)	47,810 (690)	960 (11)	260 (#)	330 (26)
Alaska	8,060 (427)	5,660 (306)	2,390 (124)	3,470 (72)	620 (5)	380 (10)	460 (33)	3,120 (402)
Arizona	56,000 (1,117)	40,900 (800)	15,110 (347)	19,130 (291)	5,960 (118)	25,010 (387)	660 (9)	5,250 (973)
Arkansas	34,920 (1,191)	24,870 (910)	10,050 (318)	16,340 (757)	16,310 (819)	1,870 (121)	260 (23)	150 (19)
California	474,590 (11,349)	340,090 (8,199)	134,500 (3,481)	115,320 (3,178)	84,860 (4,117)	242,110 (6,179)	24,690 (770)	7,600 (1,531)
Colorado	47,650 (463)	33,580 (353)	14,070 (142)	22,380 (339)	6,030 (12)	17,600 (185)	850 (7)	790 (72)
Connecticut	36,370 (2,749)	24,240 (1,770)	12,130 (999)	14,430 (1,304)	12,700 (1,536)	8,620 (890)	510 (43)	100 (17)
Delaware[3]	12,150 (†)	7,890 (†)	4,260 (†)	3,890 (†)	7,110 (†)	1,020 (†)	110 (†)	0 (†)
District of Columbia[3]	210 (†)	120 (†)	80 (†)	10 (†)	190 (†)	10 (†)	0 (†)	20 (†)
Florida	291,820 (3,692)	192,470 (2,270)	99,350 (1,454)	105,550 (1,744)	129,630 (2,599)	54,170 (534)	1,890 (18)	580 (49)
Georgia	143,560 (2,598)	95,080 (1,757)	48,470 (877)	37,670 (1,334)	96,980 (1,684)	7,800 (297)	1,010 (22)	90 (4)
Hawaii[3]	9,770 (†)	6,640 (†)	3,120 (†)	1,290 (†)	290 (†)	310 (†)	7,810 (†)	70 (†)
Idaho	9,100 (434)	6,980 (326)	2,120 (115)	6,850 (385)	90 (5)	1,750 (85)	70 (3)	350 ! (109)
Illinois	130,650 (2,807)	86,950 (1,987)	43,700 (892)	41,270 (1,742)	63,590 (1,940)	24,340 (637)	1,330 (40)	130 (10)
Indiana	77,460 (2,737)	53,300 (1,860)	24,170 (945)	49,720 (2,094)	22,420 (1,266)	4,850 (557)	310 (30)	160 (17)
Iowa	14,190 (440)	9,860 (294)	4,330 (167)	10,000 (397)	2,960 (64)	930 (37)	160 (16)	140 (6)
Kansas	24,300 (701)	17,160 (531)	7,140 (197)	13,680 (621)	5,920 (67)	3,950 (71)	350 (8)	400 (32)
Kentucky	43,420 (2,319)	29,840 (1,636)	13,580 (734)	32,800 (1,780)	9,870 (1,002)	620 (46)	90 (11)	40 (9)
Louisiana	67,780 (2,535)	44,370 (1,636)	23,410 (911)	23,370 (1,721)	43,040 (1,536)	730 (21)	230 (12)	410 (107)
Maine	8,540 (440)	6,340 (345)	2,200 (114)	7,880 (421)	420 (16)	110 (22)	80 (4)	50 (8)
Maryland[3]	60,550 (2,490)	38,780 (1,580)	21,770 (944)	22,600 (1,627)	26,450 (†)	9,220 (1,231)	1,000 (†)	290 (†)
Massachusetts	49,930 (5,404)	32,960 (3,547)	16,970 (2,039)	28,040 (2,916)	7,650 (311)	12,780 (528)	1,230 (136)	230 (27)
Michigan	131,750 (674)	89,450 (476)	42,310 (234)	71,480 (541)	52,580 (4,227)	5,650 (189)	980 (17)	1,060 (133)
Minnesota	30,780 (1,756)	21,360 (721)	9,420 (1,023)	15,760 (189)	9,910 (189)	2,440 (34)	1,130 (18)	1,540 (194)
Mississippi	51,940 (1,385)	34,420 (1,154)	17,520 (623)	13,050 (565)	38,250 (1,495)	380 (34)	120 (13)	130 (35)
Missouri	67,820 (2,020)	47,010 (1,408)	20,810 (643)	32,790 (1,174)	32,560 (1,551)	1,780 (63)	450 (13)	240 (15)
Montana	6,500 (232)	4,600 (163)	1,900 (78)	4,490 (177)	70 (3)	120 (6)	40 (2)	1,780 (157)
Nebraska	10,600 (185)	7,240 (142)	3,360 (49)	5,620 (121)	2,820 (5)	1,770 (71)	100 (2)	280 (25)
Nevada[3]	31,620 (†)	20,690 (†)	10,930 (†)	9,700 (†)	7,360 (†)	12,850 (†)	1,270 (†)	440 (†)
New Hampshire	10,170 (498)	6,770 (399)	3,400 (111)	9,080 (489)	310 (8)	670 (7)	80 (6)	30 (2)
New Jersey	79,030 (3,559)	53,730 (2,347)	25,300 (1,260)	28,260 (2,252)	30,520 (1,609)	18,700 (1,170)	1,490 (104)	70 (12)
New Mexico	17,140 (572)	11,560 (387)	5,570 (196)	3,970 (171)	590 (15)	9,510 (497)	110 (3)	2,960 (79)
New York	106,670 (3,845)	72,970 (2,437)	33,700 (1,456)	49,950 (1,918)	38,640 (2,377)	16,040 (857)	1,360 (88)	680 (124)
North Carolina	149,780 (6,774)	101,920 (4,535)	47,860 (2,350)	50,630 (2,234)	85,000 (4,561)	9,250 (392)	790 (43)	4,100 (1,947)
North Dakota	2,140 (153)	1,460 (100)	670	1,260 (71)	100 (2)	50 (3)	20 (1)	720 (135)
Ohio	109,370 (4,049)	73,860 (2,696)	35,500 (1,442)	62,880 (2,712)	43,030 (2,880)	2,810 (357)	570 (56)	90 (10)
Oklahoma	31,160 (966)	21,830 (706)	9,330 (286)	14,940 (627)	8,210 (403)	3,150 (78)	200 (7)	4,660 (233)
Oregon	27,470 (1,028)	20,140 (732)	7,330 (322)	19,520 (773)	1,620 (44)	4,870 (339)	590 (21)	880 (73)
Pennsylvania	114,040 (6,402)	74,950 (4,013)	39,090 (2,435)	53,090 (2,856)	52,730 (4,090)	6,950 (568)	1,190 (202)	90 (16)
Rhode Island	12,250 (1,071)	8,040 (776)	4,210 (309)	6,920 (847)	1,930 (200)	2,950 (143)	340 (30)	120 (24)
South Carolina	83,830 (2,289)	54,320 (1,547)	29,520 (828)	25,750 (1,067)	55,540 (1,753)	2,120 (302)	240 (21)	180 ! (77)
South Dakota	3,100 (161)	2,180 (112)	910 (52)	1,850 (87)	170 (3)	110 (1)	40 (2)	930 (138)
Tennessee	73,380 (2,200)	49,860 (1,562)	23,520 (666)	39,350 (1,655)	31,280 (924)	2,290 (64)	400 (6)	70 (7)
Texas	253,530 (2,298)	173,460 (1,671)	80,070 (693)	46,910 (824)	82,270 (1,276)	121,480 (1,411)	2,410 (16)	460 (12)
Utah	16,350 (119)	11,740 (97)	4,610 (50)	10,020 (98)	540 (2)	4,640 (20)	660 (5)	490 (4)
Vermont	3,430 (136)	2,420 (99)	1,010 (44)	3,260 (129)	100 (8)	30 (4)	30 (3)	20 (2)
Virginia	91,810 (2,805)	61,580 (1,867)	30,230 (991)	35,200 (1,080)	49,590 (2,284)	5,490 (165)	1,370 (38)	170 (13)
Washington	59,920 (1,326)	44,470 (1,011)	15,450 (335)	36,360 (1,082)	7,060 (37)	10,280 (390)	3,180 (33)	3,040 (370)
West Virginia	30,750 (2,986)	21,430 (2,033)	9,330 (962)	27,270 (2,482)	3,090 (548)	310 (73)	50 (11)	30 (8)
Wisconsin	43,680 (1,126)	28,210 (721)	15,460 (449)	18,480 (724)	18,010 (399)	4,650 (65)	660 (16)	1,880 ! (751)
Wyoming	2,680 (400)	1,970 (288)	710 (119)	2,200 (346)	40 (5)	250 (43)	20 (3)	160 (46)

See notes at end of table.

Table 233.30. Number of students suspended and expelled from public elementary and secondary schools, by sex, race/ethnicity, and state: 2006—Continued

[Standard errors appear in parentheses]

State	Students expelled[2] Total	Sex — Male	Sex — Female	Race/ethnicity — White	Black	Hispanic	Asian/Pacific Islander	American Indian/ Alaska Native
1	10	11	12	13	14	15	16	17
United States	102,080 (1,329)	76,360 (976)	25,720 (398)	38,030 (612)	38,640 (935)	22,140 (388)	1,720 (44)	1,550 (69)
Alabama	1,300 (21)	900 (21)	400 (5)	390 (8)	870 (19)	40 (#)	# (†)	# (†)
Alaska	180 (4)	140 (2)	50 (4)	100 (3)	30 (†)	10 (†)	10 (†)	40 (2)
Arizona	660 (41)	530 (36)	130 (6)	260 (32)	60 (3)	300 (16)	10 (†)	40 (5)
Arkansas	500 (43)	360 (29)	130 (19)	310 (32)	150 (15)	30 ! (9)	10 (2)	40 (†)
California	19,460 (608)	15,600 (477)	3,870 (152)	5,350 (230)	3,010 (128)	9,960 (360)	860 (40)	280 (37)
Colorado	2,210 (62)	1,760 (43)	450 (25)	1,000 (32)	260 (2)	860 (47)	30 (1)	60 (12)
Connecticut	1,330 (135)	970 (87)	360 (56)	470 (54)	490 (80)	340 (53)	20 (4)	# (†)
Delaware[3]	230 (†)	170 (†)	60 (†)	100 (†)	110 (†)	10 (†)	# (†)	0 (†)
District of Columbia[3]	130 (71)	70 (†)	60 (†)	# (†)	120 (33)	10 (†)	# (†)	0 (†)
Florida	1,120 (†)	860 (60)	270 (12)	530 (39)	420 (†)	160 (9)	# (†)	10 (†)
Georgia	3,660 (170)	2,740 (131)	930 (46)	1,390 (93)	2,100 (92)	150 (15)	20 (2)	# (†)
Hawaii[3]	0 (†)	0 (†)	0 (†)	0 (†)	0 (†)	0 (†)	0 (†)	0 (†)
Idaho[3]	230 (11)	190 (9)	40 (9)	140 (†)	# (†)	70 (6)	# (†)	20 (4)
Illinois	2,760 (132)	2,040 (80)	730 (60)	890 (116)	1,390 (31)	460 (14)	20 (4)	# (†)
Indiana	6,620 (395)	4,560 (272)	2,060 (137)	4,510 (309)	1,610 (119)	460 (45)	30 (6)	20 (4)
Iowa	200 (39)	160 (31)	40 (8)	160 (34)	20 (3)	20 ! (6)	# (†)	# (†)
Kansas	850 (63)	630 (35)	220 (30)	430 (58)	280 (†)	110 (6)	20 (2)	10 ! (6)
Kentucky	540 (110)	370 (72)	170 (45)	400 (67)	‡ (157)	# (†)	# (†)	# (†)
Louisiana	5,800 (212)	4,120 (159)	1,680 (56)	1,500 (113)	4,180 (†)	70 ! (3)	20 (4)	20 ! (4)
Maine	160 (21)	130 (14)	40 (10)	160 (21)	# (†)	# (†)	# (†)	# (†)
Maryland[3]	1,560 (†)	1,190 (†)	360 (†)	340 (†)	1,010 (†)	200 (†)	20 (†)	# (†)
Massachusetts	530 (35)	410 (27)	120 (12)	200 (27)	180 (8)	140 (7)	10 (2)	# (†)
Michigan	2,140 (149)	1,610 (113)	530 (46)	1,030 (77)	950 (108)	110 (15)	30 (5)	20 ! (6)
Minnesota	250 (16)	200 (15)	50 (5)	150 (12)	50 (†)	20 (3)	10 (1)	20 ! (7)
Mississippi	1,490 (73)	1,090 (64)	400 (15)	290 (47)	1,190 (45)	10 (†)	# (†)	# (†)
Missouri	280 (36)	220 (26)	60 (15)	210 (35)	60 (4)	10 (†)	# (†)	# (†)
Montana	100 (10)	90 (9)	20 (3)	60 (8)	# (†)	# (†)	# (†)	40 (7)
Nebraska	650 (11)	480 (9)	170 (2)	290 (†)	210 (†)	110 (4)	10 (†)	30 (4)
Nevada[3]	1,520 (†)	1,190 (†)	340 (†)	490 (†)	410 (†)	530 (†)	70 (†)	20 (4)
New Hampshire	120 (38)	80 (22)	40 (17)	100 (36)	10 (2)	# (†)	# (†)	# (†)
New Jersey	270 (118)	250 (118)	20 (5)	100 (49)	70 (23)	80 ! (39)	10 (†)	# (†)
New Mexico	240 (16)	200 (14)	50 (3)	40 (3)	10 (†)	110 (10)	10 (†)	80 (10)
New York	890 (180)	700 (143)	190 (41)	580 (144)	240 (75)	60 ! (11)	10 (3)	‡ (†)
North Carolina	1,970 (830)	1,480 (572)	‡ (†)	300 (52)	1,580 (821)	60 (†)	10 (3)	30 ! (8)
North Dakota	20 (6)	20 (4)	# (†)	10 (2)	# (†)	# (†)	# (†)	10 ! (5)
Ohio	8,150 (319)	5,450 (223)	2,700 (115)	2,810 (214)	4,970 (194)	340 (27)	30 (4)	10 (1)
Oklahoma	2,200 (73)	1,550 (55)	650 (23)	1,070 (47)	640 (22)	130 (7)	20 (4)	330 (22)
Oregon	1,890 (140)	1,490 (124)	400 (24)	1,320 (105)	110 (17)	360 (12)	50 (8)	60 (9)
Pennsylvania	2,750 (122)	1,890 (93)	860 (40)	1,110 (88)	1,440 (61)	160 (11)	30 (6)	# (†)
Rhode Island	# (†)	# (†)	# (†)	# (†)	# (†)	# (†)	10 (†)	# (†)
South Carolina	5,130 (271)	3,730 (201)	1,400 (81)	1,390 (97)	3,650 (224)	70 (10)	20 (4)	10 (3)
South Dakota	120 (52)	90 (39)	30 (13)	‡ (†)	# (†)	10 (3)	# (†)	80 ! (29)
Tennessee	3,200 (77)	2,440 (60)	760 (21)	1,350 (70)	1,700 (9)	120 (2)	30 (3)	10 (†)
Texas	11,990 (232)	9,010 (190)	2,980 (50)	2,630 (115)	3,760 (90)	5,450 (91)	120 (†)	30 (1)
Utah	250 (5)	190 (5)	60 (†)	160 (5)	20 (†)	40 (1)	10 (†)	10 (†)
Vermont	40 ! (16)	40 (14)	10 (2)	40 (16)	# (†)	# (†)	# (†)	# (†)
Virginia	1,150 (174)	980 (163)	170 (18)	580 (162)	440 (45)	90 (5)	40 (2)	# (†)
Washington	3,470 (130)	2,770 (104)	700 (35)	2,140 (101)	280 (5)	720 (40)	140 (†)	190 ! (34)
West Virginia	210 (34)	140 (22)	60 (14)	190 (30)	10 (10)	# (†)	# (†)	# (†)
Wisconsin	1,470 (65)	1,030 (50)	440 (26)	830 (60)	430 (5)	140 (12)	20 (2)	40 ! (13)
Wyoming	100 (16)	90 (12)	10 ! (4)	90 (16)	# (†)	10 (#)	# (†)	# (†)

†Not applicable.
#Rounds to zero.
!Interpret data with caution. The coefficient of variation (CV) for this estimate is between 30 and 50 percent.
‡Reporting standards not met. The coefficient of variation (CV) for this estimate is 50 percent or greater.
[1]A student is counted only once, even if suspended more than once during the same school year.
[2]A student is counted only once, even if expelled more than once during the same school year.
[3]Data are based on universe counts of schools and school districts; therefore, these figures do not have standard errors.

NOTE: Suspension is excluding a student from school for disciplinary reasons for 1 school day or longer. Expulsion is the exclusion of a student from school for disciplinary reasons that results in the student's removal from school attendance rolls or that meets the criteria for expulsion as defined by the appropriate state or local school authority. Race categories exclude persons of Hispanic ethnicity. Detail may not sum to totals because of rounding.
SOURCE: U.S. Department of Education, Office for Civil Rights, Civil Rights Data Collection: 2006. (This table was prepared July 2008.)

Table 233.40. Percentage of students suspended and expelled from public elementary and secondary schools, by sex, race/ethnicity, and state: 2006

[Standard errors appear in parentheses]

State	Percent suspended[1] Total	Sex Male	Sex Female	Race/ethnicity White	Black	Hispanic	Asian/Pacific Islander	American Indian/Alaska Native	Percent expelled[2] Total	Sex Male	Sex Female	Race/ethnicity White	Black	Hispanic	Asian/Pacific Islander	American Indian/Alaska Native
	2	3	4	5	6	7	8	9	10	11	12	13	14	15	16	17
United States	6.9	9.1	4.5	4.8	15.0	6.8	2.7	7.9	0.21	0.31	0.11	0.14	0.47	0.22	0.07	0.26
Alabama	10.1	13.3	6.8	4.5	18.3	4.3	3.2	4.8	0.24	0.33	0.16	0.03	0.33	0.16	0.13	0.01
Alaska	5.9	8.0	3.6	4.6	10.0	5.9	4.6	8.2	0.20	0.45	0.13	0.04	0.45	0.16	0.10	0.08
Arizona	5.9	8.0	3.3	4.6	11.8	6.4	2.6	10.0	0.11	0.12	0.08	0.06	0.12	0.08	0.03	0.03
Arkansas	7.3	10.2	4.3	5.0	15.9	4.9	3.5	4.7	0.15	0.14	0.10	0.10	0.14	0.09	0.11	0.46
California	7.5	10.5	4.4	6.0	17.1	7.9	3.3	12.2	0.48	0.61	0.28	0.13	0.61	0.32	0.11	0.68
Colorado	6.0	8.3	3.7	4.5	13.2	8.1	3.2	8.7	0.43	0.56	0.20	0.07	0.56	0.40	0.12	0.60
Connecticut	6.8	8.9	4.7	4.0	17.2	11.4	2.4	5.2	0.36	0.66	0.13	0.16	0.66	0.45	0.10	0.15
Delaware[3]	10.9	13.8	7.9	6.4	20.1	9.2	3.3	5.5	0.30	0.32	0.17	—	0.32	—	0.10	—
District of Columbia[3]	0.4	0.4	0.3	0.2	0.4	0.2	0.0	0.0	0.25	0.25	0.03	—	0.25	0.17	0.01	0.06
Florida	10.5	13.4	7.3	7.9	19.3	7.7	2.9	7.2	0.06	0.06	0.04	—	0.06	0.02	0.01	0.06
Georgia	8.8	11.4	6.1	4.8	15.0	5.4	2.1	3.7	0.33	0.32	0.18	—	0.32	0.11	0.04	0.08
Hawaii[3]	5.5	7.2	3.6	4.9	7.0	5.7	5.5	6.0	0.00	0.00	0.00	—	0.00	0.20	0.00	0.00
Idaho	3.6	5.3	1.7	3.3	3.5	5.1	1.6	8.6	0.14	0.32	0.07	—	0.32	0.20	0.03	0.07
Illinois	6.4	8.4	4.4	3.8	14.5	6.0	2.6	2.9	0.20	0.08	0.08	0.011	1.24	0.04	0.03	0.60
Indiana	7.4	9.9	4.7	6.0	17.3	7.4	1.8	6.1	0.86	0.53	0.28	0.09	0.09	0.70	0.17	0.60
Iowa	3.0	4.0	1.9	2.4	11.4	3.2	1.6	5.2	0.07	0.01	0.04	0.009	0.07	0.06	0.01	0.09
Kansas	5.1	6.9	3.1	3.8	14.6	6.6	5.8	5.8	0.25	0.10	0.13	0.017	0.68	0.19	0.12	0.04
Kentucky	6.6	8.7	4.3	5.8	13.3	4.0	1.5	3.8	0.11	0.05	0.07	0.012	—	0.01	0.03	0.12
Louisiana	10.3	13.2	7.3	7.1	14.6	4.7	2.6	6.8	1.23	0.52	0.52	0.039	1.42	0.47	0.47	0.14
Maine	4.6	6.6	2.4	4.5	9.0	5.7	2.9	6.4	0.09	0.04	0.06	0.012	0.09	0.05	0.17	0.09
Maryland[3]	7.1	8.9	5.2	5.8	8.2	12.9	2.2	8.5	0.27	0.27	0.08	0.005	0.31	0.27	0.03	0.09
Massachusetts	5.6	7.1	3.9	4.2	10.3	12.0	2.5	5.0	0.19	0.19	0.10	0.010	0.24	0.15	0.02	0.04
Michigan	8.2	10.8	5.4	6.1	17.8	7.4	2.2	6.8	0.19	0.14	0.09	0.007	0.32	0.23	0.06	0.12
Minnesota	3.7	5.0	2.4	2.4	14.4	5.4	2.5	6.6	0.03	0.01	0.01	0.002	0.08	0.07	0.01	0.14
Mississippi	10.2	13.3	7.0	5.4	14.8	12.1	3.0	12.7	0.42	0.16	0.25	0.020	0.46	0.07	0.08	0.17
Missouri	7.3	9.8	4.6	4.6	20.2	5.4	2.9	7.0	0.05	0.01	0.03	0.003	0.04	0.02	0.01	0.09
Montana	4.5	6.1	2.7	3.7	4.9	3.5	2.3	9.6	0.12	0.02	0.05	0.004	0.92	0.32	0.13	0.04
Nebraska	3.7	4.9	2.4	2.6	12.6	5.0	1.9	6.7	0.23	0.13	0.13	0.004	0.86	0.35	0.22	0.12
Nevada[3]	10.8	14.3	7.0	6.5	15.5	8.5	3.9	6.6	0.55	0.16	0.26	0.007	0.52	0.41	0.03	0.14
New Hampshire	2.2	2.9	1.4	1.5	8.7	3.1	2.2	4.8	0.06	0.04	0.06	0.021	0.28	0.07	0.08	0.17
New Jersey	5.7	7.5	3.7	4.6	12.4	6.9	1.4	3.7	0.03	0.01	0.03	0.006	0.03	0.02	0.03	0.21
New Mexico	5.3	6.9	3.5	3.7	7.0	5.4	2.5	8.3	0.12	0.03	0.04	0.003	0.13	0.06	0.06	0.29
New York	3.8	5.1	2.5	4.8	7.3	2.8	0.7	4.5	0.07	0.04	0.04	0.010	0.04	0.01	0.18	0.47
North Carolina	6.8	8.7	4.8	4.6	20.0	8.7	2.7	6.4	0.14	0.14	0.05	0.007	0.05	0.05	0.06	0.04
North Dakota	2.2	2.9	1.4	1.5	5.0	3.1	2.0	8.0	0.02	0.02	0.01	0.002	0.05	0.07	0.09	0.12
Ohio	6.2	8.2	4.2	4.6	14.6	6.0	2.1	3.7	0.47	0.63	0.20	0.016	1.69	0.72	0.09	0.21
Oklahoma	4.9	6.7	3.0	3.9	12.1	5.3	1.8	4.0	0.34	0.26	0.28	0.014	0.94	0.23	0.16	0.29
Oregon	4.9	7.1	2.7	4.8	8.8	5.5	2.1	7.2	0.52	0.44	0.32	0.026	0.58	0.41	0.18	0.47
Pennsylvania	6.8	8.7	4.8	4.2	18.9	8.7	2.7	3.4	0.16	0.16	0.09	0.007	0.58	0.26	0.06	0.04
Rhode Island	8.4	10.7	5.9	6.7	14.6	12.6	7.2	11.8	0.22	0.10	0.04	0.002	0.52	0.06	0.09	0.19
South Carolina	11.9	15.1	8.6	6.9	19.2	6.5	2.9	9.6	1.03	0.63	0.20	0.016	1.26	0.72	0.19	0.42
South Dakota	2.7	3.7	1.6	1.9	7.1	4.3	3.0	6.8	0.16	0.06	0.28	0.014	0.08	0.23	0.16	0.55
Tennessee	7.2	9.6	4.8	5.5	12.8	5.4	2.7	3.4	0.47	0.44	0.32	0.026	0.70	0.41	0.18	0.29
Texas	5.6	7.4	3.6	4.2	12.7	5.7	1.6	3.1	0.39	0.16	0.16	0.011	0.58	0.26	0.08	0.20
Utah	3.2	4.5	1.9	2.4	7.8	3.1	4.2	6.9	0.07	0.10	0.04	0.001	0.22	0.06	0.09	0.19
Vermont	4.0	5.5	2.4	4.0	5.8	4.1	1.8	5.7	0.08	0.02	0.05	0.020	0.12	0.09	0.06	0.10
Virginia	7.2	9.4	4.9	4.7	13.9	5.6	2.1	4.0	0.15	0.08	0.08	0.022	0.48	0.50	0.16	0.69
Washington	7.2	8.6	3.2	5.3	12.0	6.0	3.7	11.3	0.53	0.31	0.31	0.016	0.58	0.26	0.06	0.20
West Virginia	5.6	7.4	3.6	5.7	21.5	11.2	2.4	8.2	0.14	0.14	0.07	0.011	0.09	0.26	0.06	0.04
Wisconsin	10.2	13.8	6.4	9.7	19.7	7.5	2.1	13.5	0.23	0.10	0.06	0.009	0.47	0.22	0.06	0.30
Wyoming	2.8	4.0	‡	2.7	3.2	3.1	1.7	6.4	0.18	0.11	0.11	0.021	0.23	0.09	0.10	‡

†Not applicable.
#Rounds to zero.
!Interpret data with caution. The coefficient of variation (CV) for this estimate is between 30 and 50 percent.
‡Reporting standards not met. The coefficient of variation (CV) for this estimate is 50 percent or greater.
[1]A student is counted only once, even if suspended more than once during the same school year.
[2]A student is counted only once, even if expelled more than once during the same school year.
[3]Data are based on universe counts of schools and school districts; therefore, these figures do not have standard errors.

NOTE: Suspension is excluding a student from school for disciplinary reasons for 1 school day or longer. Expulsion is the exclusion of a student from school for disciplinary reasons that results in the student's removal from school attendance rolls or that meets the criteria for expulsion as defined by the appropriate state or local school authority. Race categories exclude persons of Hispanic ethnicity.
SOURCE: U.S. Department of Education, Office for Civil Rights, Civil Rights Data Collection: 2006. (This table was prepared May 2008.)

Table 233.50. Percentage of public and private schools with various safety and security measures, by school level: 2003–04, 2007–08, and 2011–12

[Standard errors appear in parentheses]

School control and school safety and security measure	Total[1]			Elementary schools[2]			Secondary schools[3]		
	2003–04	2007–08	2011–12	2003–04	2007–08	2011–12	2003–04	2007–08	2011–12
1	2	3	4	5	6	7	8	9	10
Public schools									
Controlled access during school hours									
Buildings (e.g., locked or monitored doors)	81.5 (0.60)	88.8 (0.63)	88.2 (0.56)	84.7 (0.65)	92.1 (0.71)	90.4 (0.67)	75.0 (1.33)	82.1 (1.42)	83.9 (1.04)
Grounds (e.g., locked or monitored gates)	39.4 (0.83)	44.9 (1.12)	44.1 (0.72)	39.0 (1.03)	45.7 (1.61)	45.4 (0.94)	41.4 (1.38)	43.3 (1.53)	39.6 (1.13)
Student dress, IDs, and school supplies									
Required students to wear uniforms	13.5 (0.53)	16.5 (0.83)	19.3 (0.54)	14.7 (0.67)	17.5 (1.05)	20.3 (0.76)	8.8 (1.11)	12.1 (1.19)	12.2 (0.69)
Enforced a strict dress code	49.3 (0.70)	54.0 (0.99)	49.1 (0.68)	45.2 (0.94)	50.0 (1.38)	44.6 (0.94)	59.7 (1.33)	64.4 (1.87)	58.3 (1.02)
Required students to wear badges or picture IDs	6.1 (0.31)	7.5 (0.53)	7.4 (0.33)	3.5 (0.35)	4.1 (0.57)	4.6 (0.32)	14.1 (0.74)	16.8 (1.15)	14.3 (1.02)
Required clear book bags or banned book bags on school grounds	6.0 (0.31)	6.8 (0.43)	5.7 (0.28)	3.3 (0.32)	4.7 (0.54)	3.2 (0.28)	11.3 (0.74)	10.5 (1.07)	9.3 (0.72)
Metal detectors, dogs, sweeps, and cameras									
Random metal detector checks on students	5.7 (0.32)	5.9 (0.45)	5.0 (0.32)	3.4 (0.33)	3.0 (0.48)	2.6 (0.28)	10.2 (0.64)	11.9 (1.05)	7.9 (0.63)
Students required to pass through metal detectors daily	2.0 (0.21)	2.3 (0.31)	2.7 (0.33)	0.8 ! (0.23)	0.3 ! (0.14)	0.8 (0.16)	3.7 (0.38)	5.2 (1.03)	4.6 (0.65)
Random dog sniffs to check for drugs	23.6 (0.59)	25.0 (0.68)	24.0 (0.40)	10.8 (0.62)	13.2 (0.83)	10.6 (0.39)	56.5 (1.59)	54.6 (1.59)	57.3 (1.28)
Random sweeps[4] for contraband (e.g., drugs or weapons)	12.8 (0.48)	14.8 (0.76)	12.1 (0.44)	5.6 (0.44)	7.6 (0.84)	5.0 (0.39)	28.2 (1.33)	30.5 (1.59)	26.1 (1.16)
Security cameras used to monitor the school	32.5 (0.68)	51.8 (0.94)	64.3 (0.75)	26.3 (0.77)	46.1 (1.29)	57.7 (0.97)	51.1 (1.55)	68.7 (1.77)	81.2 (1.07)
Daily presence of police or security personnel	24.8 (0.59)	27.2 (0.99)	28.1 (0.51)	15.5 (0.62)	16.2 (1.14)	17.1 (0.57)	53.9 (1.61)	58.3 (1.93)	57.6 (1.44)
Private schools									
Controlled access during school hours									
Buildings (e.g., locked or monitored doors)	73.5 (1.02)	81.5 (1.15)	80.1 (1.50)	79.5 (1.19)	84.1 (1.35)	82.0 (2.22)	62.9 (3.65)	76.9 (2.83)	71.5 (3.50)
Grounds (e.g., locked or monitored gates)	40.2 (1.08)	42.4 (1.22)	42.1 (1.43)	44.9 (1.32)	45.6 (1.50)	44.0 (1.99)	32.2 (3.80)	34.7 (3.37)	34.0 (4.67)
Student dress, IDs, and school supplies									
Required students to wear uniforms	55.5 (1.06)	55.4 (1.19)	56.9 (1.77)	60.6 (1.27)	62.2 (1.68)	60.0 (2.21)	44.9 (3.53)	42.8 (3.22)	49.2 (4.55)
Enforced a strict dress code	73.7 (1.00)	76.3 (1.08)	71.3 (1.49)	74.1 (1.32)	75.9 (1.48)	71.2 (2.12)	70.0 (3.78)	75.3 (3.36)	70.8 (3.13)
Required students to wear badges or picture IDs	2.2 (0.30)	2.9 (0.42)	2.7 (0.48)	1.0 (0.27)	1.6 (0.38)	1.4 (0.40)	9.8 (2.10)	6.2 (1.27)	8.2 (1.91)
Required clear book bags or banned book bags on school grounds	2.3 (0.35)	3.2 (0.43)	1.7 (0.33)	1.0 (0.30)	1.7 (0.46)	0.9 ! (0.30)	9.4 (2.59)	7.5 (2.11)	5.2 (1.47)
Metal detectors, dogs, sweeps, and cameras									
Random metal detector checks on students	0.7 (0.20)	1.1 (0.24)	1.2 ! (0.42)	† (†)	† (†)	† (†)	† (†)	† (†)	† (†)
Students required to pass through metal detectors daily	0.8 (0.21)	0.6 ! (0.19)	0.4 ! (0.16)	† (†)	† (†)	† (†)	† (†)	† (†)	† (†)
Random dog sniffs to check for drugs	3.4 (0.35)	3.9 (0.43)	4.1 (0.45)	† (†)	0.4 ! (0.20)	† (†)	15.0 (2.04)	17.0 (2.32)	16.3 (2.36)
Random sweeps[4] for contraband (e.g., drugs or weapons)	7.7 (0.61)	8.8 (0.69)	7.5 (0.93)	2.4 (0.52)	2.1 (0.42)	1.5 ! (0.68)	23.3 (3.75)	26.0 (3.64)	20.4 (2.95)
Security cameras used to monitor the school	19.4 (0.79)	32.9 (1.21)	40.6 (1.51)	19.9 (0.97)	31.4 (1.65)	39.8 (2.18)	24.3 (3.11)	43.1 (3.64)	52.0 (5.46)
Daily presence of police or security personnel	5.9 (0.50)	6.4 (0.54)	7.2 (0.77)	3.1 (0.50)	4.3 (0.61)	3.9 (0.80)	16.2 (2.99)	11.8 (2.46)	19.2 (4.77)

†Not applicable.
!Interpret data with caution. The coefficient of variation (CV) for this estimate is between 30 and 50 percent.
‡Reporting standards not met. Either there are too few cases for a reliable estimate or the coefficient of variation (CV) is 50 percent or greater.
[1]Includes combined elementary/secondary schools not separately shown.
[2]Elementary schools are those with any of grades kindergarten through grade 6 and none of grades 9 through 12.
[3]Secondary schools have any of grades 7 through 12 and none of grades kindergarten through grade 6.
[4]Does not include random dog sniffs.
NOTE: Responses were provided by the principal.
SOURCE: U.S. Department of Education, National Center for Education Statistics, Schools and Staffing Survey (SASS), "Public School Principal Data File" and "Private School Principal Data File," 2003–04, 2007–08, and 2011–12. (This table was prepared August 2013.)

Table 233.60. Percentage of public and private schools with various safety and security measures, by school control and selected characteristics: 2011–12

[Standard errors appear in parentheses]

School control and selected characteristic	Total schools — Number	Total schools — Percentage distribution	Controlled access — School buildings[1]	Controlled access — School grounds[2]	Student dress — School uniforms required	Student dress — Strict dress code enforced	Student dress — Badges or picture IDs required	Student dress — Bookbags must be clear or are banned	Metal detectors — Random metal detector checks	Metal detectors — Daily metal detector checks[3]	Random dog sniffs for drugs	Random sweeps for contraband[4]	Security cameras	Daily presence of police or security
1	2	3	4	5	6	7	8	9	10	11	12	13	14	15
Public total	89,800 (410)	100.0 (†)	88.2 (0.56)	44.1 (0.72)	19.3 (0.54)	49.1 (0.68)	7.4 (0.33)	5.7 (0.28)	5.0 (0.32)	2.7 (0.33)	24.0 (0.40)	12.1 (0.44)	64.3 (0.75)	28.1 (0.51)
School enrollment														
Under 100	6,600 (400)	7.3 (0.44)	80.8 (1.98)	43.2 (3.20)	21.8 (2.54)	44.3 (3.15)	4.8 (1.38)	15.2 (2.11)	14.5 (2.22)	14.1 (2.22)	22.6 (2.46)	28.6 (2.45)	52.5 (3.13)	29.0 (2.92)
100 to 299	16,600 (560)	18.5 (0.60)	85.5 (1.57)	32.7 (1.92)	18.5 (1.66)	43.6 (2.21)	6.0 (1.00)	4.7 (0.68)	4.3 (0.77)	2.8 (0.57)	25.0 (1.36)	12.8 (1.06)	55.6 (2.56)	17.8 (1.54)
300 to 499	27,000 (630)	30.1 (0.68)	89.1 (0.98)	42.5 (1.49)	19.8 (1.08)	43.8 (1.45)	5.4 (0.64)	4.2 (0.43)	3.8 (0.58)	1.6 ! (0.56)	16.7 (0.73)	8.4 (0.66)	64.6 (1.59)	15.1 (0.99)
500 to 999	30,500 (600)	34.0 (0.69)	91.1 (0.81)	48.9 (1.41)	20.0 (1.04)	54.3 (1.15)	7.0 (0.59)	5.0 (0.54)	3.7 (0.45)	1.4 ! (0.43)	22.2 (0.80)	9.5 (0.56)	65.5 (1.19)	30.0 (1.05)
1,000 to 1,499	5,300 (240)	5.9 (0.27)	87.1 (1.63)	52.5 (2.35)	19.0 (2.47)	62.1 (2.24)	15.8 (1.72)	7.6 (1.18)	5.4 (0.94)	1.4 ! (0.49)	48.4 (2.64)	16.2 (1.60)	81.8 (2.40)	70.5 (2.37)
1,500 or more	3,700 (220)	4.2 (0.25)	85.4 (1.87)	57.9 (2.40)	9.9 (1.64)	60.0 (2.67)	24.9 (2.18)	7.8 (1.53)	11.4 (1.50)	2.6 (0.81)	55.1 (2.62)	22.4 (2.58)	87.2 (1.90)	90.4 (1.61)
Percent of students approved for free or reduced-price school lunch														
School does not participate	3,100 (260)	3.4 (0.29)	76.1 (4.70)	40.6 (5.40)	27.6 (4.48)	47.9 (5.64)	11.0 (2.19)	12.5 (3.41)	12.2 (3.48)	10.6 ! (3.56)	21.8 (2.92)	29.3 (5.28)	56.2 (5.44)	30.3 (4.42)
0 to 25 percent	18,600 (560)	20.7 (0.62)	89.0 (1.18)	38.3 (1.61)	6.5 (0.98)	37.8 (1.54)	4.0 (0.55)	3.6 (0.46)	1.9 (0.45)	1.1 ! (0.36)	25.2 (1.19)	9.6 (0.92)	65.2 (1.66)	26.3 (1.39)
26 to 50 percent	23,600 (710)	26.3 (0.77)	86.8 (1.04)	38.2 (1.71)	6.5 (0.68)	42.9 (1.50)	4.9 (0.66)	4.7 (0.57)	2.2 (0.40)	0.6 ! (0.24)	29.3 (1.02)	9.7 (0.66)	64.6 (1.63)	24.1 (0.99)
51 to 75 percent	22,700 (540)	25.2 (0.62)	90.4 (0.93)	43.4 (1.67)	15.8 (1.33)	50.4 (1.37)	8.5 (0.74)	5.4 (0.52)	5.3 (0.65)	2.4 (0.42)	24.8 (1.05)	11.5 (0.81)	66.4 (1.52)	25.8 (1.21)
76 to 100 percent	21,800 (640)	24.3 (0.70)	88.7 (1.10)	56.8 (1.75)	46.6 (1.63)	64.3 (1.61)	11.4 (0.96)	7.9 (0.62)	9.5 (0.88)	5.4 (1.16)	16.9 (1.00)	15.1 (1.10)	62.3 (1.86)	36.2 (1.52)
School locale[5]														
City	23,400 (270)	26.1 (0.28)	88.5 (1.22)	54.9 (1.79)	39.9 (1.67)	56.5 (1.81)	11.8 (0.87)	6.0 (0.55)	8.3 (0.90)	5.2 (1.12)	13.4 (0.65)	11.0 (0.93)	59.2 (1.74)	38.8 (1.53)
Suburban	24,500 (360)	27.3 (0.36)	90.5 (0.90)	46.4 (1.33)	16.1 (0.95)	48.0 (1.57)	7.7 (0.75)	4.3 (0.55)	3.8 (0.55)	1.8 (0.31)	17.8 (0.79)	8.6 (0.62)	66.7 (1.34)	29.3 (1.17)
Town	12,300 (340)	13.7 (0.40)	87.4 (1.32)	36.9 (1.88)	12.1 (1.41)	45.9 (1.83)	4.6 (0.59)	6.5 (0.70)	5.1 (1.01)	1.6 (0.38)	32.4 (1.32)	14.3 (1.13)	67.0 (1.86)	22.5 (1.33)
Rural	29,500 (430)	32.9 (0.43)	86.6 (0.80)	36.8 (1.32)	8.6 (0.66)	45.6 (1.26)	4.9 (0.55)	6.3 (0.54)	3.4 (0.45)	1.8 (0.43)	34.1 (0.83)	15.0 (0.71)	65.3 (1.14)	21.0 (0.79)
School level[5]														
Elementary	61,200 (440)	68.2 (0.38)	90.4 (0.67)	45.4 (0.94)	20.3 (0.76)	44.6 (0.94)	4.6 (0.32)	3.2 (0.28)	2.6 (0.28)	0.8 (0.16)	10.6 (0.39)	5.0 (0.39)	57.7 (0.97)	17.1 (0.57)
Secondary	20,500 (540)	22.8 (0.56)	83.9 (1.04)	39.6 (1.13)	12.2 (0.69)	58.3 (1.02)	14.3 (1.02)	9.3 (0.72)	7.9 (0.63)	4.6 (0.65)	57.3 (1.28)	26.1 (1.16)	81.2 (1.07)	57.6 (1.44)
Combined	8,100 (660)	9.0 (0.74)	83.1 (2.43)	46.1 (2.62)	30.0 (2.51)	60.5 (2.35)	11.2 (1.55)	15.3 (1.96)	16.4 (1.68)	12.3 (2.32)	41.5 (2.58)	30.8 (2.90)	71.9 (2.53)	37.1 (2.25)
Private total	25,700 (610)	100.0 (†)	80.1 (1.50)	42.1 (1.43)	56.9 (1.77)	71.3 (1.49)	2.7 (0.48)	1.7 (0.33)	1.2 ! (0.42)	0.4 ! (0.16)	4.1 (0.45)	7.5 (0.93)	40.6 (1.51)	7.2 (0.77)
School enrollment														
Under 100	12,700 (580)	49.5 (1.32)	72.7 (2.57)	38.2 (2.45)	43.8 (2.66)	59.3 (2.67)	2.2 (0.64)	2.4 (0.61)	1.8 ! (0.83)	‡ (†)	1.6 ! (0.58)	10.2 (1.50)	24.7 (2.23)	3.7 (0.85)
100 to 299	8,400 (300)	32.8 (1.13)	89.2 (1.43)	46.1 (2.15)	69.0 (2.21)	81.2 (1.74)	1.7 ! (0.68)	1.0 ! (0.46)	‡ (†)	‡ (†)	2.7 (0.58)	3.1 (0.75)	50.4 (2.34)	4.7 ! (1.63)
300 to 499	2,800 (190)	10.8 (0.83)	84.2 (2.56)	48.1 (3.84)	71.6 (3.77)	88.7 (2.35)	3.8 ! (1.20)	‡ (†)	‡ (†)	‡ (†)	11.1 (2.49)	10.4 (2.33)	56.7 (3.98)	15.1 (2.74)
500 to 999	1,500 (120)	5.7 (0.51)	83.6 (2.87)	39.4 (3.84)	72.6 (4.36)	86.3 (3.17)	9.0 (2.41)	‡ (†)	‡ (†)	‡ (†)	18.9 (3.26)	5.0 ! (1.92)	80.8 (3.86)	24.2 (3.56)
1,000 or more	300 (60)	1.2 (0.24)	81.6 (7.85)	52.8 (11.06)	55.0 (10.35)	70.6 (9.34)	12.1 ! (4.88)	‡ (†)	‡ (†)	‡ (†)	13.5 ! (6.51)	‡ (†)	92.2 (4.54)	66.4 (9.60)
Percent of students approved for free or reduced-price school lunch														
School does not participate	18,900 (590)	73.6 (1.15)	76.6 (1.81)	41.3 (1.76)	52.3 (2.23)	69.5 (1.94)	2.3 (0.53)	1.1 (0.25)	‡ (†)	‡ (†)	4.4 (0.58)	7.5 (1.01)	36.4 (1.73)	7.7 (0.94)
0 to 25 percent	3,400 (240)	13.2 (0.89)	91.2 (2.67)	36.5 (4.08)	75.1 (3.38)	80.2 (2.71)	2.6 ! (0.83)	‡ (†)	‡ (†)	‡ (†)	3.9 (0.87)	1.5 ! (0.63)	56.1 (3.33)	2.7 ! (0.99)
26 to 100 percent	3,400 (230)	13.2 (0.94)	88.5 (3.55)	51.7 (3.79)	64.4 (3.67)	72.9 (3.69)	5.2 ! (1.91)	4.9 ! (1.52)	6.1 ! (2.85)	2.5 ! (1.13)	2.5 ! (0.80)	13.4 (3.59)	48.8 (3.71)	9.1 (2.32)
School level[5]														
Elementary	14,500 (500)	56.4 (0.90)	82.0 (2.22)	44.0 (1.99)	60.0 (2.21)	71.2 (2.12)	1.4 (0.40)	0.9 ! (0.30)	‡ (†)	‡ (†)	‡ (†)	1.5 ! (0.68)	39.8 (2.18)	3.9 (0.80)
Secondary	2,700 (140)	10.3 (0.57)	71.5 (3.50)	34.0 (4.67)	49.2 (4.55)	70.8 (3.13)	8.2 (1.91)	5.2 (1.47)	‡ (†)	‡ (†)	16.3 (2.36)	20.4 (2.95)	52.0 (5.46)	19.2 (4.77)
Combined	8,600 (210)	33.3 (0.71)	79.6 (2.19)	41.3 (2.49)	53.9 (2.73)	71.7 (2.22)	3.3 (0.97)	2.1 ! (0.70)	3.0 ! (1.20)	‡ (†)	7.1 (1.16)	13.7 (2.14)	38.4 (2.61)	9.1 (1.41)

†Not applicable.
!Interpret data with caution. The coefficient of variation (CV) for this estimate is between 30 and 50 percent.
‡Reporting standards not met. Either there are too few cases for a reliable estimate or the coefficient of variation (CV) is 50 percent or greater.
[1]Access to buildings is controlled during school hours (e.g., by locked or monitored doors).
[2]Access to grounds is controlled during school hours (e.g., by locked or monitored gates).
[3]All students must pass through a metal detector each day.
[4]Examples of contraband include drugs and weapons. The "sweeps" category does not include dog sniffs.
[5]Elementary schools have grade 6 or below, with no grade higher than 8; secondary schools have no grade lower than 7; and combined schools have grades lower than 7 and higher than 8.
NOTE: Responses were provided by the principal. Detail may not sum to totals because of rounding.
SOURCE: U.S. Department of Education, National Center for Education Statistics, Schools and Staffing Survey (SASS), "Public School Principal Data File" and "Private School Principal Data File," 2011–12. (This table was prepared October 2013.)

Table 233.70. Percentage of public schools with one or more full-time or part-time security staff present at least once a week, and percentage of schools with security staff routinely carrying a firearm, by selected school characteristics: 2005–06, 2007–08, and 2009–10

[Standard errors appear in parentheses]

School characteristic	Percent with one or more security guards, security personnel, School Resource Officers (SROs), or sworn law enforcement officers who are not SROs[1]									Percent with security guards, security personnel, or sworn law enforcement officers routinely carrying a firearm[2]		
	Total			Full-time			Part-time only					
	2005–06	2007–08	2009–10	2005–06	2007–08	2009–10	2005–06	2007–08	2009–10	2005–06	2007–08	2009–10
1	2	3	4	5	6	7	8	9	10	11	12	13
All public schools	41.7 (1.28)	46.3 (1.29)	42.8 (1.07)	27.0 (0.88)	30.4 (0.98)	28.7 (0.97)	14.6 (1.06)	15.9 (0.89)	14.1 (0.66)	30.7 (1.10)	34.1 (1.11)	28.0 (0.97)
School level[3]												
Primary school	26.2 (1.87)	33.1 (2.04)	27.7 (1.50)	12.5 (1.32)	17.8 (1.37)	15.7 (1.43)	13.7 (1.59)	15.3 (1.31)	12.1 (0.89)	15.7 (1.55)	20.1 (1.68)	12.5 (1.25)
Middle school	63.7 (1.30)	65.5 (1.59)	66.4 (1.45)	44.5 (1.17)	44.9 (1.55)	45.8 (1.39)	19.2 (1.18)	20.7 (1.17)	20.6 (1.32)	51.8 (1.32)	54.2 (1.92)	51.0 (1.84)
High school	75.2 (1.66)	79.6 (1.47)	76.4 (1.45)	64.0 (1.53)	66.1 (1.48)	62.0 (1.56)	11.2 (1.14)	13.5 (1.42)	14.5 (1.50)	64.0 (1.71)	67.5 (1.51)	63.3 (1.75)
Combined school	43.5 (5.25)	39.9 (5.59)	36.6 (4.89)	26.8 (4.44)	26.2 (4.79)	24.0 (4.49)	16.7 (4.13)	13.6 ! (4.15)	12.7 (3.56)	32.4 (4.50)	32.1 (4.89)	24.6 (4.26)
Enrollment size												
Less than 300	22.7 (2.65)	27.6 (2.55)	25.6 (2.91)	10.8 (1.58)	15.1 (2.09)	15.1 (2.29)	11.9 (2.07)	12.5 (2.07)	10.5 (2.20)	16.2 (2.17)	16.1 (2.39)	13.5 (2.16)
300–499	29.8 (2.29)	36.1 (2.66)	33.5 (2.26)	16.7 (1.93)	19.4 (1.84)	18.0 (1.96)	13.0 (1.64)	16.8 (2.05)	15.5 (1.76)	20.5 (1.83)	26.7 (2.37)	19.8 (1.84)
500–999	50.5 (1.90)	52.7 (1.99)	47.3 (1.60)	31.0 (1.27)	34.0 (1.52)	31.2 (1.34)	19.5 (1.62)	18.8 (1.53)	16.1 (1.08)	36.9 (1.67)	39.5 (1.98)	30.3 (1.42)
1,000 or more	86.9 (1.39)	90.6 (1.59)	90.0 (1.37)	77.3 (1.61)	79.5 (1.65)	79.3 (1.82)	9.7 (1.40)	11.1 (1.83)	10.7 (1.50)	70.3 (1.67)	73.5 (1.62)	74.6 (1.75)
Locale												
City	49.1 (2.57)	57.3 (3.05)	50.9 (2.51)	37.7 (2.04)	45.3 (2.24)	39.7 (2.19)	11.4 (1.59)	12.0 (1.97)	11.2 (1.69)	30.5 (1.73)	33.1 (2.32)	27.6 (1.98)
Suburb	42.7 (1.67)	45.4 (2.08)	45.4 (1.90)	27.1 (1.41)	30.0 (1.64)	31.3 (1.58)	15.6 (1.44)	15.4 (1.59)	14.1 (1.50)	32.2 (1.51)	33.7 (1.94)	29.6 (1.45)
Town	44.4 (3.86)	51.1 (3.50)	39.0 (3.11)	26.3 (2.88)	26.9 (2.32)	21.2 (2.15)	18.1 (2.90)	24.2 (2.75)	17.8 (2.39)	38.1 (3.62)	45.0 (3.54)	31.6 (2.81)
Rural	33.8 (1.87)	36.0 (1.98)	35.2 (2.20)	18.6 (1.39)	20.2 (1.67)	20.5 (1.83)	15.2 (1.87)	15.7 (1.70)	14.7 (1.51)	27.1 (1.84)	30.5 (2.05)	25.3 (1.78)
Percent combined enrollment of Black, Hispanic, Asian/Pacific Islander, and American Indian/Alaska Native students												
Less than 5 percent	28.3 (1.96)	35.6 (3.23)	30.4 (2.69)	12.4 (1.60)	16.9 (2.70)	13.6 (2.41)	16.0 (1.81)	18.7 (2.56)	16.8 (2.51)	22.9 (2.07)	27.1 (2.95)	21.9 (2.25)
5 percent to less than 20 percent	38.9 (2.54)	42.9 (2.19)	36.5 (2.91)	23.9 (1.73)	23.1 (1.63)	19.9 (2.26)	15.0 (1.98)	19.9 (1.93)	16.6 (1.71)	30.2 (2.07)	37.7 (2.29)	27.6 (2.08)
20 percent to less than 50 percent	41.6 (2.32)	44.7 (2.76)	41.9 (1.93)	28.3 (1.94)	29.1 (2.21)	27.8 (1.69)	13.3 (1.75)	15.5 (1.93)	14.1 (1.50)	35.3 (1.97)	38.4 (2.65)	30.5 (1.89)
50 percent or more	51.3 (2.46)	55.4 (2.71)	52.5 (2.04)	37.3 (1.91)	43.8 (2.16)	41.3 (2.09)	14.0 (1.81)	11.6 (1.68)	11.2 (1.33)	31.3 (1.84)	31.8 (2.07)	29.1 (1.53)
Percent of students eligible for free or reduced-price lunch												
0–25 percent	37.9 (2.14)	46.5 (2.33)	39.2 (2.44)	24.9 (1.70)	29.7 (2.01)	27.9 (2.17)	13.0 (1.33)	16.8 (1.52)	11.3 (1.21)	30.3 (1.95)	34.8 (2.12)	27.2 (1.93)
26–50 percent	42.1 (2.08)	40.8 (2.52)	40.0 (1.68)	26.4 (1.63)	24.2 (2.01)	21.5 (1.52)	15.7 (2.01)	16.6 (1.65)	18.5 (1.37)	33.8 (1.78)	35.2 (2.02)	30.3 (1.59)
51–75 percent	39.3 (2.21)	46.1 (2.83)	42.3 (2.60)	25.7 (1.85)	29.7 (2.34)	29.0 (2.04)	13.7 (1.90)	16.4 (2.34)	13.3 (1.45)	31.8 (2.05)	35.8 (2.77)	27.4 (2.07)
76–100 percent	49.8 (2.73)	55.0 (3.68)	49.8 (2.76)	33.0 (2.49)	42.1 (3.17)	37.6 (2.66)	16.8 (2.07)	12.9 (2.17)	12.2 (1.84)	25.6 (2.17)	29.7 (2.68)	26.8 (2.32)

!Interpret data with caution. The coefficient of variation (CV) for this estimate is between 30 and 50 percent.

[1]"Security guards" and "security personnel" do not include law enforcement. School Resource Officers include all career law enforcement officers with arrest authority who have specialized training and are assigned to work in collaboration with school organizations.

[2]The survey item about carrying firearms did not include the term "School Resource Officer" in the question text.

[3]Primary schools are defined as schools in which the lowest grade is not higher than grade 3 and the highest grade is not higher than grade 8. Middle schools are defined as schools in which the lowest grade is not lower than grade 4 and the highest grade is not higher than grade 9. High schools are defined as schools in which the lowest grade is not lower than grade 9 and the highest grade is not higher than grade 12. Combined schools include all other combinations of grades, including K–12 schools.

NOTE: Responses were provided by the principal or the person most knowledgeable about crime and safety issues at the school.

SOURCE: U.S. Department of Education, National Center for Education Statistics, 2005–06, 2007–08, and 2009–10 School Survey on Crime and Safety (SSOCS), 2006, 2008, and 2010. (This table was prepared September 2013.)

Table 233.80. Percentage of students ages 12–18 who reported various security measures at school: Selected years, 1999 through 2013

[Standard errors appear in parentheses]

Security measure	1999		2001		2003		2005		2007		2009		2011		2013	
1	2		3		4		5		6		7		8		9	
Total, at least one of the listed security measures	—	(†)	99.4	(0.09)	99.3	(0.12)	99.6	(0.10)	99.8	(0.06)	99.3	(0.10)	99.6	(0.08)	99.6	(0.07)
Metal detectors	9.0	(0.51)	8.7	(0.61)	10.1	(0.84)	10.7	(0.74)	10.1	(0.51)	10.6	(0.76)	11.2	(0.64)	11.0	(0.72)
Locker checks	53.3	(0.83)	53.5	(0.92)	53.0	(0.91)	53.2	(0.90)	53.6	(0.95)	53.8	(1.17)	53.0	(0.99)	52.0	(1.13)
One or more security cameras to monitor the school	—	(†)	38.5	(1.13)	47.9	(1.16)	57.9	(1.35)	66.0	(0.99)	70.0	(1.05)	76.7	(0.83)	76.7	(1.06)
Security guards and/or assigned police officers	54.1	(1.36)	63.6	(1.25)	69.6	(0.91)	68.3	(1.13)	68.8	(0.98)	68.1	(1.05)	69.8	(1.01)	70.4	(1.04)
Other school staff or other adults supervising the hallway	85.4	(0.54)	88.3	(0.45)	90.6	(0.39)	90.1	(0.42)	90.0	(0.50)	90.6	(0.46)	88.9	(0.46)	90.5	(0.51)
A requirement that students wear badges or picture identification	—	(†)	21.2	(0.99)	22.5	(1.11)	24.9	(1.20)	24.3	(1.00)	23.4	(1.14)	24.8	(1.02)	26.2	(1.02)
A written code of student conduct	—	(†)	95.1	(0.34)	95.3	(0.37)	95.5	(0.36)	95.9	(0.29)	95.6	(0.39)	95.7	(0.30)	95.9	(0.30)
Locked entrance or exit doors during the day	38.1	(0.97)	48.8	(1.12)	52.8	(1.16)	54.3	(1.06)	60.9	(1.07)	64.3	(1.27)	64.5	(1.02)	75.8	(1.10)
A requirement that visitors sign in	87.1	(0.62)	90.2	(0.58)	91.7	(0.48)	93.0	(0.49)	94.3	(0.38)	94.3	(0.52)	94.9	(0.37)	95.8	(0.37)

—Not available.
†Not applicable.
NOTE: "At school" includes the school building, on school property, on a school bus, and, from 2001 onward, going to and from school.

SOURCE: U.S. Department of Justice, Bureau of Justice Statistics, School Crime Supplement (SCS) to the National Crime Victimization Survey, selected years, 1999 through 2013. (This table was prepared September 2014.)

Table 234.10. Age range for compulsory school attendance and special education services, and policies on year-round schools and kindergarten programs, by state: Selected years, 2000 through 2014

State	Compulsory attendance							Compulsory special education services, 2004[1]	Year-round schools, 2008		Kindergarten programs, 2014		
									Has policy on year-round schools	Has districts with year-round schools	School districts required to offer		Attendance required
	2000	2002	2004	2006	2008	2010	2014				Program	Full-day program	
1	2	3	4	5	6	7	8	9	10	11	12	13	14
Alabama	7 to 16	7 to 16	7 to 16[2]	7 to 16	7 to 16	7 to 17	6 to 17[3]	6 to 21		Yes	X	X	
Alaska	7 to 16	7 to 16	7 to 16[2]	7 to 16	7 to 16	7 to 16	7 to 16[2]	3 to 22		Yes			
Arizona	6 to 16[2]	6 to 16[2]	6 to 16[2]	6 to 16[2]	6 to 16[2]	6 to 16[2]	6 to 16[2]	3 to 21	—		X		
Arkansas	5 to 17[2,3]	5 to 17[2,3]	5 to 17[2,3]	5 to 17[2,3]	5 to 17[2,3]	5 to 17[2,3]	5 to 18	5 to 21	X	Yes	X	X	X
California	6 to 18[2]	6 to 18	6 to 18	6 to 18	6 to 18	6 to 18	6 to 18	Birth to 21[4]	X	Yes	X		
Colorado	—	—	7 to 16	7 to 16	6 to 17	6 to 17	6 to 17	3 to 21		Yes	X		
Connecticut	7 to 16	7 to 18[2]	7 to 18[2]	5 to 18[3]	5 to 18[3]	5 to 18[3]	5 to 18[3]	3 to 21		—	X		X
Delaware	5 to 16	5 to 16	5 to 16[2]	5 to 16	5 to 16	5 to 16	5 to 16	Birth to 20		Yes	X		X
District of Columbia	—	5 to 18[5]	5 to 18	5 to 18	5 to 18	5 to 18	5 to 18	Birth to 20		—	X	X	X
Florida	6 to 16[5]	6 to 16[5]	6 to 16[5]	6 to 16[5]	6 to 16[5]	6 to 16[5]	6 to 16	3 to 21	X	Yes	X	X	
Georgia	6 to 16	6 to 16	6 to 16	6 to 16	6 to 16	6 to 16	6 to 16	Birth to 21[6]		Yes	X		
Hawaii	6 to 18	6 to 18	6 to 18	6 to 18	6 to 18	6 to 18	5 to 18	Birth to 19		[7]	X		
Idaho	7 to 16	7 to 16	7 to 16	7 to 16	7 to 16	7 to 16	7 to 16	3 to 21		Yes	X		
Illinois	7 to 16	7 to 16	7 to 17	7 to 17	7 to 17	7 to 17	6 to 17	3 to 21	X	Yes	X		
Indiana	7 to 16	7 to 16	7 to 16	7 to 18[2]	7 to 18[2]	7 to 18[2]	7 to 18	3 to 22		Yes	X		
Iowa	6 to 16[2]	6 to 16[2]	6 to 16	6 to 16	6 to 16	6 to 16	6 to 16[8]	Birth to 21	X	Yes	X		
Kansas	7 to 18[2]	7 to 18[2]	7 to 18[2]	7 to 18[2]	7 to 18[2]	7 to 18[2]	7 to 18	3 to 21[9]		—	X		
Kentucky	6 to 16	6 to 16	6 to 16[2]	6 to 16	6 to 16	6 to 16	6 to 18[10]	Birth to 21		Yes	X		
Louisiana	7 to 17	7 to 17	7 to 17[2]	7 to 17[2]	7 to 18[2]	7 to 18[2]	7 to 18	3 to 21[11]		Yes	X	X	X
Maine	7 to 17	7 to 17	7 to 17[2]	7 to 17[2]	7 to 17[2]	7 to 17[2]	7 to 17	5 to 19[11,12]		—	X		
Maryland	5 to 16	5 to 16	5 to 16	5 to 16	5 to 16	5 to 16[3]	5 to 17	Birth to 21	X	—	X	X	X
Massachusetts	6 to 16	6 to 16	6 to 16	6 to 16[2]	6 to 16[2]	6 to 16[2]	6 to 16	3 to 21[6]	[13]	—	X		
Michigan	6 to 16	6 to 16	6 to 16	6 to 16	6 to 16	6 to 16	6 to 18	Birth to 25	X	Yes	X		
Minnesota	7 to 18[2]	7 to 16	7 to 16	7 to 16[2]	7 to 16[2]	7 to 16[2]	7 to 17	Birth to 21	X	Yes	X		
Mississippi	6 to 17	6 to 17	6 to 16	6 to 16	6 to 17	6 to 17	6 to 17	Birth to 20		—	X	X	
Missouri	7 to 16	7 to 16	7 to 16	7 to 16	7 to 16	7 to 17	7 to 17[2,3]	Birth to 20		Yes[14]	X		
Montana	7 to 16[2]	7 to 16[2]	7 to 16[2]	7 to 16[2]	7 to 16[2]	7 to 16[2]	7 to 16[2]	3 to 18[11]		—	X		
Nebraska	7 to 16	7 to 16	7 to 16	6 to 18	6 to 18	6 to 18	6 to 18	Birth to 20		Yes	X		
Nevada	7 to 17	7 to 17	7 to 17	7 to 17	7 to 18[2]	7 to 18[2]	7 to 18	Birth to 21[4]		Yes	X	[15]	X
New Hampshire	6 to 16	6 to 16	6 to 16	6 to 16	6 to 16	6 to 18	6 to 18	3 to 21		—	X		
New Jersey	6 to 16	6 to 16	6 to 16	6 to 16	6 to 16	6 to 16	6 to 16	5 to 21		—	X	[16]	
New Mexico	5 to 18	5 to 18	5 to 18[2]	5 to 18[2]	5 to 18[2]	5 to 18[2]	5 to 18	3 to 21	X	Yes	X		X
New York	6 to 16[2]	6 to 16	6 to 16	6 to 16[17]	6 to 16[17]	6 to 16[17]	6 to 16[17]	Birth to 20		—	X		
North Carolina	7 to 16	7 to 16	7 to 16	7 to 16	7 to 16	7 to 16	7 to 16	5 to 20	X	Yes	X	X	
North Dakota	7 to 16	7 to 16	7 to 16	7 to 16	7 to 16	7 to 16	7 to 16	3 to 21		No	X		
Ohio	6 to 18	6 to 18	6 to 18	6 to 18	6 to 18	6 to 18	6 to 18	3 to 21	X	—	X		X
Oklahoma	5 to 18	5 to 18	5 to 18	5 to 18	5 to 18	5 to 18	5 to 18	Birth to 21[11]		Yes	X	X	X
Oregon	7 to 18	7 to 18	7 to 18[2]	7 to 18	7 to 18	7 to 18[2]	7 to 18	3 to 20		Yes	X		
Pennsylvania	8 to 17	8 to 17	8 to 17[2]	8 to 17[2]	8 to 17[2]	8 to 17[2]	8 to 17	6 to 21	X[14]	—[14]	X		
Rhode Island	6 to 16	6 to 16	6 to 16	6 to 16	6 to 16	6 to 16	6 to 18[2]	3 to 21		—	X		X
South Carolina	5 to 16	5 to 16	5 to 16	5 to 17[3]	5 to 17[3]	5 to 17[3]	5 to 17	3 to 21[18]		—	X		X
South Dakota	6 to 16	6 to 16	6 to 16	6 to 16	6 to 16	6 to 18[2]	6 to 18[2]	Birth to 21	X	—	X		X[19]
Tennessee	6 to 17	6 to 17	6 to 17	6 to 17[3]	6 to 17[3]	6 to 17[3]	6 to 18	3 to 21[4]	X	Yes	X	X	X
Texas	6 to 18	6 to 18	6 to 18	6 to 18	6 to 18	6 to 18	6 to 18	3 to 21	X	Yes	X		
Utah	6 to 18	6 to 18	6 to 18	6 to 18	6 to 18	6 to 18	6 to 18	3 to 22		Yes	X		
Vermont	7 to 16	6 to 16	6 to 16	6 to 16[2]	6 to 16[2]	6 to 16[2]	6 to 16[2]	3 to 21		—[14]	X		
Virginia	5 to 18	5 to 18	5 to 18	5 to 18[2]	5 to 18[2]	5 to 18[2,3]	5 to 18	2 to 21	X	Yes	X		X
Washington	8 to 17[2]	8 to 17[2]	8 to 16[2]	8 to 18	8 to 18	8 to 18	8 to 18	3 to 21[18]		Yes	X	[20]	
West Virginia	6 to 16	6 to 16	6 to 16	6 to 16	6 to 16	6 to 17	6 to 17	5 to 21[21]	X	Yes	X	X	X
Wisconsin	6 to 18	6 to 18	6 to 18	6 to 18	6 to 18	6 to 18	6 to 18	3 to 21		Yes	X		
Wyoming	6 to 16[2]	6 to 16[2]	7 to 16[2]	7 to 16[2]	7 to 16[2]	7 to 16[2]	7 to 16[2]	3 to 21		—	X	[22]	

—Not available.

X Denotes that the state has a policy. A blank denotes that the state does not have a policy.

[1]Most states have a provision whereby education is provided up to a certain age or completion of secondary school, whichever comes first.

[2]Child may be exempted from compulsory attendance if he/she meets state requirements for early withdrawal with or without meeting conditions for a diploma or equivalency.

[3]Parent/guardian may delay child's entry until a later age per state law/regulation.

[4]Student may continue in the program if 22nd birthday falls before the end of the school year.

[5]Attendance is compulsory until age 18 for Manatee County students, unless they earn a high school diploma prior to reaching their 18th birthday.

[6]Through age 21 or until child graduates with a high school or special education diploma or equivalent.

[7]Some schools operate on a multitrack system; the schools are open year-round, but different cohorts start and end at different times.

[8]Children enrolled in preschool programs (4 years old on or before September 15) are considered to be of compulsory school attendance age.

[9]To be determined by rules and regulations adopted by the state board.

[10]All districts have adopted a policy to raise the upper compulsory school age from 16 to 18. The policy will take effect for most districts in the 2015–16 school year.

[11]Children from birth through age 2 are eligible for additional services.

[12]Must be age 5 before October 15, and not age 20 before start of school year.

[13]Policies about year-round schools are decided locally.

[14]State did not participate in 2008 online survey. Data are from 2006.

[15]In certain school districts in Nevada, the lowest performing schools with the highest numbers of limited English proficient students will start offering full-day kindergarten programs.

[16]The Abbott District is required to offer full-day kindergarten.

[17]Local boards of education can require school attendance until age 17 unless employed. The boards of education of Syracuse, New York City, Rochester, Utica, and Buffalo are authorized to require kindergarten attendance at age 5 unless the parents elect not to enroll their child until the following September or the child is enrolled in nonpublic school or in home instruction.

[18]Student may complete school year if 21st birthday occurs while attending school.

[19]All children must attend kindergarten before age 7.

[20]Full-day kindergarten is being phased in beginning in the 2012–13 school year, starting with the highest poverty schools. Statewide implementation will be achieved by 2017–18.

[21]Severely handicapped children may begin receiving services at age 3.

[22]Statute requires one full-day program per district.

NOTE: The Education of the Handicapped Act (EHA) Amendments of 1986 make it mandatory for all states receiving EHA funds to serve all 3- to 18-year-old disabled children.

SOURCE: Council of Chief State School Officers, *Key State Education Policies on PK–12 Education*, 2000, 2002, 2004, and 2008; Education Commission of the States (ECS), ECS StateNotes, *Compulsory School Age Requirements*, retrieved August 9, 2010, from http://www.ecs.org/clearinghouse/86/62/8662.pdf; ECS StateNotes, *Special Education: State Special Education Definitions, Ages Served*, retrieved August 9, 2010, from http://www.ecs.org/clearinghouse/52/29/5229.pdf; ECS StateNotes, *Compulsory School Age Requirements*, retrieved May 19, 2015, from http://www.ecs.org/clearinghouse/01/18/68/11868.pdf; ESC StateNotes, *District Must Offer Kindergarten*, retrieved April 18, 2014, from http://ecs.force.com/mbdata/mbquestRT?rep=Kg1416; ESC StateNotes, *Child Must Attend Kindergarten*, retrieved April 18, 2014, from http://ecs.force.com/mbdata/mbquestRT?rep=Kg1403; and supplemental information retrieved from various state websites. (This table was prepared May 2015.)

Table 234.20. Minimum amount of instructional time per year and policies on textbooks, by state: Selected years, 2000 through 2014

| State | Minimum amount of instructional time per year | | | | | Policies on textbooks, 2014 | | |
| | In days | | | | In hours | Textbook selection level | | Free textbooks provided to students |
	2000	2006	2011	2014	2014	State	Local education agency	
1	2	3	4	5	6	7	8	9
Alabama	175	175	180	180[1]	740 (K–3); 900 (4–12)	X		X
Alaska	180	180	170[2]	180[3]	†		X	X
Arizona	—	180	180[1]	180[1]	356 (K); 712 (1–3); 890 (4–6); 1,000 (7–8); 720[4] (9–12)		X[6]	X[5]
Arkansas	178	178	178[2]	178[3]	†			X
California	175	180	180/175[7]	180/175[7]	600 (K); 840 (1–3); 900 (4–8); 1,080 (9–12)	X[8]	X	X
Colorado	[9]	160	160	160	435/870[6] (K); 968[2] (1–5); 1,056[2] (6–12)		X	X
Connecticut	180	180	180	180	450/900 (K); 900 (1–12)		X	X
Delaware	[9]	†	†	†	1,060 (K–11); 1,032 (12)		X	X
District of Columbia	180[10]	180	178	180	†			
Florida	180	180	180	180	720[11] (K–3); 900[11] (4–12)	X		X
Georgia	180[10]	180	180	180	810 (K–3); 900 (4–5); 990 (6–12)	X		X[14]
Hawaii	184	179	180[12]	180[12]	915 (K–6)[12,13]; 990 (7–12)[12,13]	X		X[14]
Idaho	180	†	†	†	450[3] (K); 810[3] (1–3); 900[3] (4–8); 990[3,15] (9–12)	X		X[17]
Illinois	180[16]	176	176	180[3]	†			
Indiana	180	180	180	180	†		X	X[18]
Iowa	180	180	180	180	1,080	X	X	
Kansas	186	186 (K–11);181 (12)	186 (K–11);181 (12)	186 (K–11);181 (12)	465 (K); 1,116 (1–11); 1,086 (12)	X		X
Kentucky	175	175	175[2]	170[2]	1,062	X	X	X
Louisiana	175	177	177[2]	177[2,15]	1,062		X	
Maine	175	175	175[2]	175[2]	†		X	
Maryland	180	180	180	180	1,080; 1,170 (8–12)		X	X
Massachusetts	180	180	180	180	425 (K); 900 (1–5); 990 (6–12)		X	X
Michigan	180	†	165	175	1,098		X	X[19]
Minnesota	[9]	[9]	†	†	425/850 (K); 935 (1–6); 1,020 (7–12)		X	X
Mississippi	180	180	180	180	†	X		
Missouri	174	174	174/142[20]	174/142[20]	1,044		X	X
Montana	180	90 (K);180 (K–12)	†	†	360/720[3] (K); 720[3] (1–3); 1,080[3,15] (4–12)		X	X
Nebraska	[9]	†	†	†	400 (K); 1,032 (1–8); 1,080 (9–12)		X	X[14]
Nevada	180	180	180	180	450 (K); 945 (1–5); 990[15] (6–12)	X	X	X
New Hampshire	180	180	180	180	†		X	X
New Jersey	180	180	180	180	†	X		X
New Mexico	180	180	180	†	450/990 (K); 990 (1–6); 1,080 (7–12)		X	X
New York	180[10]	180	180	180	†	X		X
North Carolina	180	180	180	185	1,025	X		X[19]
North Dakota	173	173	175[2]	175[2]	951.5 (K–8); 1,038 (9–12)		X	
Ohio	182	182	182[3]	†	455/910[3] (1–6); 1,001[3] (7–12)	X		X
Oklahoma	180	180	180[3]	180	1,083[3]			X
Oregon	[9]	†	†	†	405 (K); 810 (1–3); 900 (4–8); 990[15] (9–12)	X		X
Pennsylvania	180	180	180	180	450 (K); 900 (1–8); 990 (9–12)		X	X[19]
Rhode Island	180	180	180	180	1,080		X	X
South Carolina	180	180	180[2]	180[2]	†		X	X
South Dakota	—	†	†	†	437.5 (K); 875 (1–5); 962.5[15] (6–12)	X		X
Tennessee	180	180	180[2]	180[2]	†	X		X
Texas	187	180	180	180	†	X	(21)	
Utah	180	180	180	180	450 (K); 810 (1); 990 (2–12)	X		

See notes at end of table.

Table 234.20. Minimum amount of instructional time per year and policies on textbooks, by state: Selected years, 2000 through 2014—Continued

State	Minimum amount of instructional time per year					Policies on textbooks, 2014		
	In days				In hours	Textbook selection level		Free textbooks provided to students
	2000	2006	2011	2014	2014	State	Local education agency	
1	2	3	4	5	6	7	8	9
Vermont	175	175	175	175	†		X	X
Virginia	180	180	180	180	540 (K); 990 (1–12)	X		X
Washington	180 [16]	180	180	180	450² (K); 1,000² (1–12)		X	[23]
West Virginia	180	180	180	180	†	X		X
Wisconsin	180	180	180	†	437/1,050² (K); 1,050² (1–6); 1,137² (7–12)		X	
Wyoming	175	175	180	175	450 (K); 900 (Elementary); 1,050 (Middle/Jr. High); 1,100 (Secondary)		X	X

—Not available.
†Not applicable.
X Denotes that the state has a policy. A blank denotes that the state does not have a policy.
[1]Or an equivalent number of hours or minutes of instruction per year.
[2]Does not include time for in-service or staff development or parent-teacher conferences.
[3]Includes time for in-service or staff development or parent-teacher conferences.
[4]Students must enroll in at least 4 subjects that meet at least 720 hours.
[5]Fees permitted at the high school level for nonrequired or supplementary textbooks.
[6]State Department of Education prepares a list of suggestions, but the districts choose.
[7]Through 2014–15, districts are allowed to shorten the 180-day instructional year to 175 days without fiscal penalty.
[8]Statewide textbook adoption is only at the elementary level. Adoption practices have been suspended until the 2015–16 school year.
[9]No statewide policy; varies by district.
[10]1996 data.
[11]For schools on double-session or approved experimental calendar: 630 (K–3); 810 (4–12).
[12]Does not apply to charter and multitrack schools.
[13]For the 2014–15 and 2015–16 school years.
[14]Fees for lost or damaged books permitted.
[15]Instructional time for graduating seniors may be reduced.
[16]1998 data.

[17]Fees permitted, but if 5 percent or more of the voters in a district petition the school board, a majority of the district's voters may decide to furnish free textbooks to students.
[18]Fees permitted for students in grades 9–12, but students who qualify for free or reduced-price lunch are exempted.
[19]Refundable or security deposits permitted.
[20]174 days required for a 5-day week; 142 days required for a 4-day week.
[21]Local districts may select textbooks not on the state recommended list provided the textbooks meet specific criteria and the selection is based on recommendations by the district's curriculum materials review committee.
[22]Starting in the 2015–16 school year, grades 9 through 12 will transition to 1,080 hours and kindergarten will transition to 1,000 hours statewide by the 2017–18 school year.
[23]A district may provide free textbooks to students when, in its judgment, the best interests of the district will be served.
NOTE: Minimum number of instructional days refers to the actual number of days that pupils have contact with a teacher. Some states allow for different types of school calendars by setting instructional time in both days and hours, while others use only days or only hours. For states in which the number of days or hours varies by grade, the relevant grade(s) appear in parentheses.
SOURCE: Council of Chief State School Officers, StateNotes, *Number of Instructional Days/Hours in the School Year* (October 2014 revision), retrieved May 19, 2015, from http://www.ecs.org/clearinghouse/01/15/05/11505.pdf; *Key State Education Policies on PK–12 Education*, 2000 and 2006; Education Commission of the States, *State Textbook Adoption* (September 2013 edition), retrieved May 19, 2015, from http://www.ecs.org/clearinghouse/01/09/23/10923.pdf; and supplemental information retrieved from various state websites. (This table was prepared May 2015.)

Table 234.30. Course credit requirements and exit exam requirements for a standard high school diploma and the use of other high school completion credentials, by state: 2013

State	Course credits (in Carnegie units)						High school exit exams				Other completion credentials	
	Total required credits for standard diploma, all courses	Required credits in selected subject areas					Exit exam required for standard diploma	Characteristics of required exams			Advanced recognition for exceeding standard requirements	Alternative credential for not meeting all standard requirements[2]
		English/ language arts	Social studies	Science	Mathematics	Other credits		Subjects tested[1]	Exam based on standards for 10th grade or higher	Appeals or alternative route to standard diploma if exam failed		
1	2	3	4	5	6	7	8	9	10	11	12	13
Alabama	24.0	4.0	4.0	4.0	4.0	8.0	Yes	EMSH	Yes	Yes	Yes	Yes
Alaska	21.0	4.0	3.0	2.0	2.0	10.0	Yes	EM	Yes	Yes	No	Yes
Arizona	22.0	4.0	3.0	3.0	4.0	8.0	Yes	EM	Yes	Yes	Yes	No
Arkansas	22.0	4.0	3.0	3.0	4.0	8.0	Yes	M	No	Yes	Yes	No
California	13.0	3.0	3.0	2.0	2.0	3.0	Yes	EM	Yes	Yes	Yes	Yes
Colorado	—	—	0.5	—	—	—	No	†	†	†	No	No
Connecticut	20.0	4.0	3.0	2.0	3.0	8.0	No[3]	†	†	†	No	No
Delaware	22.0	4.0	3.0	3.0	4.0	8.0	No	†	†	†	No	Yes
District of Columbia	24.0	4.0	4.0	4.0	4.0	8.0	No	†	†	†	No	Yes
Florida	24.0	4.0	3.0	3.0	4.0	10.0	Yes	EM	Yes	Yes	No	Yes
Georgia	23.0	4.0	3.0	4.0	4.0	8.0	Yes	EMSH	Yes	Yes	No	Yes
Hawaii	24.0	4.0	4.0	3.0	3.0	10.0	No	†	†	†	Yes	Yes
Idaho	23.0	4.5	2.5	3.0	3.0	10.0	Yes	EM	Yes	Yes	No	No
Illinois	16.0	4.0	2.0	2.0	3.0	5.0	No	†	†	†	No	No
Indiana	20.0	4.0	3.0	3.0	3.0	7.0	Yes	EM	Yes	Yes	Yes	Yes
Iowa	14.0	4.0	3.0	3.0	3.0	1.0	No	†	†	†	Yes	No
Kansas	21.0	4.0	3.0	3.0	3.0	8.0	No	†	†	†	No	No
Kentucky	22.0	4.0	3.0	3.0	3.0	9.0	No	†	†	†	Yes	Yes
Louisiana	24.0	4.0	4.0	4.0	4.0	8.0	Yes	EMSH[4]	Yes	Yes	Yes	Yes
Maine	16.0	4.0	2.0	2.0	2.0	6.0	No	†	†	†	No	Yes
Maryland	21.0	4.0	3.0	3.0	3.0	8.0	Yes	EMS	Yes	Yes	Yes	Yes
Massachusetts	—	—	—	—	—	—	Yes	EMS	Yes	Yes	No	No
Michigan	16.0	4.0	3.0	3.0	4.0	2.0	No	†	†	†	No	No
Minnesota	21.5	4.0	3.5	3.0	3.0	8.0	Yes	EM[5]	Yes	Yes	No	No
Mississippi	24.0	4.0	4.0	4.0	4.0	8.0	Yes	EMSH	Yes	Yes	No	Yes
Missouri	24.0	4.0	3.0	3.0	3.0	11.0	No	†	†	†	No	No
Montana	20.0	4.0	2.0	2.0	2.0	10.0	No	†	†	†	No	No
Nebraska	200.0[6]	—	—	—	—	—	No	†	†	†	No	No
Nevada	22.5	4.0	2.0	2.0	3.0	11.5	Yes	EMS	Yes	Yes	Yes	Yes
New Hampshire	20.0	4.0	2.5	2.0	3.0	8.5	No	†	†	†	Yes	Yes
New Jersey	24.0	4.0	3.0	3.0	3.0	11.0	Yes	EM	Yes	Yes	No	No
New Mexico	24.0	4.0	3.5	3.0	4.0	9.5	Yes	EMSH	Yes	Yes	No	Yes
New York	22.0	4.0	4.0	3.0	3.0	8.0	Yes	EMSH	Yes	Yes	Yes	Yes
North Carolina	21.0	4.0	3.0	3.0	4.0	7.0	No	†	†	†	Yes	Yes
North Dakota	22.0	4.0	3.0	3.0	3.0	9.0	No	†	†	†	No	No
Ohio	20.0	4.0	3.0	3.0	3.0	7.0	Yes	EMSH	Yes	Yes	Yes	No
Oklahoma	23.0	4.0	3.0	3.0	3.0	10.0	Yes	EMSH[7]	Yes	Yes	Yes	No
Oregon	24.0	4.0	3.0	3.0	3.0	11.0	No	†	†	†	No	Yes
Pennsylvania	—	—	—	—	—	—	No	†	†	†	No	No
Rhode Island	20.0	4.0	3.0	3.0	4.0	6.0	No[8]	†	†	†	No	No
South Carolina	24.0	4.0	3.0	3.0	4.0	10.0	Yes	EM	Yes	No	Yes	Yes
South Dakota	22.0	4.0	3.0	3.0	3.0	9.0	No	†	†	†	Yes	No
Tennessee	22.0	4.0	3.0	3.0	4.0	8.0	No	†	†	No	Yes	Yes
Texas	26.0	4.0	4.0	4.0	4.0	10.0	Yes	EMSH	Yes	Yes	Yes	Yes
Utah	24.0	4.0	3.0	3.0	3.0	11.0	No	†	†	†	No	Yes
Vermont	20.0	4.0	3.0	3.0	3.0	7.0	No	†	†	†	No	No
Virginia	22.0	4.0	3.0	3.0	3.0	9.0	Yes	EMSH[9]	Yes	Yes	Yes	Yes
Washington	20.0	3.0	2.5	2.0	3.0	9.5	Yes	EM	Yes	Yes	No	No
West Virginia	24.0	4.0	4.0	3.0	4.0	9.0	No	†	†	†	Yes	Yes
Wisconsin	13.0	4.0	3.0	2.0	2.0	2.0	No	†	†	†	No	Yes
Wyoming	13.0	4.0	3.0	3.0	3.0	0.0	No	†	†	†	Yes	No

—Not available.

†Not applicable.

[1]Exit exam subjects tested: E = English (including writing), M = Mathematics, S = Science, and H = History/social studies.

[2]A certificate of attendance is an example of an alternative credential for students who do not meet all requirements for a standard diploma. Depending on an individual state's policies, alternative credentials may be offered to students with disabilities, students who fail exit exams, or other students who do not meet all requirements.

[3]Requirement takes effect for class of 2020.

[4]Students must pass either the science or social studies components of the Graduation Exit Examination (GEE) to receive a standard diploma.

[5]Students can graduate by passing statewide reading and writing assessments and either passing mathematics assessments or meeting other requirements.

[6]Expressed in semester credits instead of Carnegie units.

[7]To receive the standard diploma, students must pass tests in algebra 1, English 2, and two of the following five subjects: algebra 2, biology 1, English 3, geometry, and U.S. history.

[8]Requirement takes effect for class of 2014.

[9]To receive the standard diploma, students must earn at least six verified credits by passing end-of-course assessments. One of those credits may be earned by passing a student-selected test in computer science, technology, career and technical education, or other areas.

NOTE: Local school districts frequently have other graduation requirements in addition to state requirements. The Carnegie unit is a standard of measurement that represents one credit for the completion of a 1-year course.

SOURCE: Editorial Projects in Education Research Center, custom table, retrieved August 27, 2013, from Education Counts database (http://www.edcounts.org/createtable/step1.php). (This table was prepared August 2013.)

Table 234.40. States that use criterion-referenced tests (CRTs) aligned to state standards, by subject area and level: 2006–07

State	Aligned to state standards		Off-the-shelf/ norm-referenced test (NRT)[1]	CRTs,[2] by subject area and level			
	CRT[2]	Augmented or hybrid test[3]		English/ language arts	Mathematics	Science	Social studies/ history
1	2	3	4	5	6	7	8
Alabama	X		X	ES, MS, HS	ES, MS, HS	HS	HS
Alaska	X		X	ES, MS, HS	ES, MS, HS		
Arizona	X	X	X	ES, MS, HS	ES, MS, HS		
Arkansas	X		X	ES, MS, HS	ES, MS, HS	ES, MS	
California	X		X	ES, MS, HS	ES, MS, HS	ES, MS, HS	MS, HS
Colorado	X		X	ES, MS, HS	ES, MS, HS	ES, MS, HS	
Connecticut	X			ES, MS, HS	ES, MS, HS	HS	
Delaware		X		ES, MS, HS	ES, MS, HS	ES, MS, HS	ES, MS, HS
District of Columbia	X			ES, MS, HS	ES, MS, HS		
Florida	X		X	ES, MS, HS	ES, MS, HS	ES, MS, HS	
Georgia	X		X	ES, MS, HS	ES, MS, HS	ES, MS, HS	ES, MS, HS
Hawaii		X		ES, MS, HS	ES, MS, HS		
Idaho	X			ES, MS, HS	ES, MS, HS		
Illinois	X	X		ES, MS, HS	ES, MS, HS	HS	
Indiana	X			ES, MS, HS	ES, MS, HS	ES, MS	
Iowa			X	ES, MS, HS	ES, MS, HS	ES, MS, HS	
Kansas	X			ES, MS, HS	ES, MS, HS		
Kentucky	X		X	ES, MS, HS	ES, MS, HS	ES, MS, HS	ES, MS, HS
Louisiana	X	X		ES, MS, HS	ES, MS, HS	ES, MS, HS	ES, MS, HS
Maine	X		X	ES, MS, HS	ES, MS, HS	ES, MS	
Maryland	X	X		ES, MS, HS	ES, MS, HS	HS	HS
Massachusetts	X			ES, MS, HS	ES, MS, HS	ES, MS, HS	
Michigan	X		X	ES, MS, HS	ES, MS, HS	ES, MS, HS	MS, HS
Minnesota	X			ES, MS, HS	ES, MS, HS		
Mississippi	X		X	ES, MS, HS	ES, MS, HS	ES, MS, HS	HS
Missouri		X		ES, MS, HS	ES, MS, HS		
Montana	X		X	ES, MS, HS	ES, MS, HS		
Nebraska	X			ES, MS, HS			
Nevada	X		X	ES, MS, HS	ES, MS, HS		
New Hampshire	X			ES, MS	ES, MS		
New Jersey	X			ES, MS, HS	ES, MS, HS	ES, MS	
New Mexico	X		X	ES, MS, HS	ES, MS, HS	ES, MS, HS	
New York	X			ES, MS, HS	ES, MS, HS	ES, MS, HS	ES, MS, HS
North Carolina	X			ES, MS, HS	ES, MS, HS	HS	HS
North Dakota	X			ES, MS, HS	ES, MS, HS	ES, MS, HS	
Ohio	X			ES, MS, HS	ES, MS, HS	ES, MS, HS	ES, MS, HS
Oklahoma	X			ES, MS, HS	ES, MS, HS	ES, MS, HS	ES, MS, HS
Oregon	X			ES, MS, HS	ES, MS, HS	MS, HS	
Pennsylvania	X			ES, MS, HS	ES, MS, HS		
Rhode Island	X	X		ES, MS, HS	ES, MS, HS		
South Carolina	X			ES, MS, HS	ES, MS, HS	ES, MS, HS	ES, MS, HS
South Dakota		X	X	ES, MS, HS	ES, MS, HS	ES, MS, HS	
Tennessee	X			ES, MS, HS	ES, MS, HS	ES, MS, HS	ES, MS, HS
Texas	X			ES, MS, HS	ES, MS, HS	ES, MS, HS	MS, HS
Utah	X		X	ES, MS, HS	ES, MS, HS	ES, MS, HS	
Vermont	X			ES, MS	ES, MS		
Virginia	X			ES, MS, HS	ES, MS, HS	ES, MS, HS	ES, MS, HS
Washington	X			ES, MS, HS	ES, MS, HS	ES, MS, HS	
West Virginia	X		X	ES, MS, HS	ES, MS, HS	ES, MS, HS	ES, MS
Wisconsin		X		ES, MS, HS	ES, MS, HS	ES, MS, HS	ES, MS, HS
Wyoming	X			ES, MS, HS	ES, MS, HS		

X State has a test. A blank denotes that the state does not have this type of test.
[1]Off-the-shelf/norm-referenced tests (NRTs) are commercially developed tests that have not been modified to reflect state content standards.
[2]Criterion-referenced tests (CRTs) are custom-developed and explicitly designed to measure state content standards.

[3]Augmented or hybrid tests incorporate elements of both NRTs and CRTs. These tests include NRTs that have been augmented or modified to reflect state standards.
NOTE: ES = elementary school, MS = middle school, and HS = high school.
SOURCE: Quality Counts 2007, Cradle to Career, *Education Week*, 2007. (This table was prepared September 2008.)

Table 234.50. Required testing for initial certification of elementary and secondary school teachers, by type of assessment and state: 2013 and 2014

State	Assessment for certification, 2013				Assessment for certification, 2014			
	Basic skills exam	Subject-matter exam	Knowledge of teaching exam	Assessment of teaching performance	Basic skills exam	Subject-matter exam	Knowledge of teaching exam	Assessment of teaching performance
1	2	3	4	5	6	7	8	9
Alabama	X	X	X	X	X	X	X	X
Alaska	X				X			
Arizona		X	X			X	X	
Arkansas	X	X	X	X	X	X	X	X
California	X	—		X	X	—		X
Colorado		X				X		
Connecticut	X	X	—	—	X	X	—	—
Delaware	X	X			X	X		
District of Columbia	X	X	X		X	X	X	
Florida	X			X	X			X
Georgia	X	X			X	X		
Hawaii	X	X	—		X	X		—
Idaho		X		X		X		X
Illinois	X	X	X		X	X	X	
Indiana	X	X		X	X	X		X
Iowa								
Kansas		X	X			X	X	
Kentucky	X	X	X	X	X	X	X	X
Louisiana	X	X	X	X	X	X	X	X
Maine	—	—	—	—	—	—	—	—
Maryland	X	X	X	X	X	X	X	X
Massachusetts	X	X		X	X	X		X
Michigan	X	X		X	X	X		X
Minnesota	X	X	X		X	X	X	
Mississippi	—	—	—	—	—	—	—	—
Missouri	X	X		X	X	X		X
Montana								
Nebraska	X				X			
Nevada	—	X	—	—	—	X	—	—
New Hampshire	X	X			X	X		
New Jersey	—	—	—	—	—	—	—	—
New Mexico	X	X	X	X	X	X	X	X
New York		X	X			X	X	
North Carolina	—	—	—	—	—	—	—	—
North Dakota	—	X	—	—	—	X	—	—
Ohio		X	X	X		X	X	X
Oklahoma	—	—	—	—	—	—	—	—
Oregon	X	X		X	X	X		X
Pennsylvania	X	X	X	X	X	X	X	X
Rhode Island				X			X	X
South Carolina		X	X			X	X	
South Dakota	X	X	X	X	X	X	X	X
Tennessee	X	X	X		X	X	X	
Texas	X	X	X	X	X	X	X	X
Utah		X		X		X		X
Vermont	X	X			X	X		
Virginia	X	X	X		X	X	X	
Washington	X	X		X	X	X		X
West Virginia	X	X	X	X	X	X	X	X
Wisconsin	X	X			X	X		
Wyoming	—			—	—			—

—Not available.
X Denotes that the state requires testing. A blank denotes that the state does not require testing.

SOURCE: National Association of State Directors of Teacher Education and Certification (NASDTEC), NASDTEC Knowledgebase, retrieved June 16, 2014, from https://www.nasdtec.net/. (This table was prepared November 2014.)

Table 235.10. Revenues for public elementary and secondary schools, by source of funds: Selected years, 1919–20 through 2011–12

	Revenues (in thousands)							Revenues per pupil						
				Local (including intermediate sources below the state level)							Local (including intermediate sources below the state level)			
School year	Total	Federal	State	Total	Property taxes	Other public revenue	Private[1]	Total	Federal	State	Total	Property taxes	Other public revenue	Private[1]
1	2	3	4	5	6	7	8	9	10	11	12	13	14	15

Current dollars

School year	Total	Federal	State	Local Total	Property taxes	Other public revenue	Private[1]	Total	Federal	State	Local Total	Property taxes	Other public revenue	Private[1]
1919–20	$970,121	$2,475	$160,085	$807,561	—	—	—	$45	#	$7	$37	—	—	—
1929–30	2,088,557	7,334	353,670	1,727,553	—	—	—	81	#	14	67	—	—	—
1939–40	2,260,527	39,810	684,354	1,536,363	—	—	—	89	$2	27	60	—	—	—
1949–50	5,437,044	155,848	2,165,689	3,115,507	—	—	—	217	6	86	124	—	—	—
1959–60	14,746,618	651,639	5,768,047	8,326,932	—	—	—	419	19	164	237	—	—	—
1969–70	40,266,922	3,219,557	16,062,776	20,984,589	—	—	—	884	71	353	461	—	—	—
1979–80	96,881,164	9,503,537	45,348,814	42,028,813	—	—	—	2,326	228	1,089	1,009	—	—	—
1989–90	208,547,573	12,700,784	98,238,633	97,608,157	$74,867,627	$17,084,494	$5,656,036	5,144	313	2,423	2,408	$1,847	$421	$140
1990–91	223,340,537	13,776,066	105,324,533	104,239,939	80,373,547	17,951,451	5,914,941	5,419	334	2,555	2,529	1,950	436	144
1991–92	234,581,384	15,493,330	108,783,449	110,304,605	85,874,700	18,213,748	6,216,157	5,579	368	2,587	2,623	2,042	433	148
1992–93	247,626,168	17,261,252	113,403,436	116,961,481	87,143,955	23,116,567	6,700,958	5,783	403	2,648	2,731	2,035	540	156
1993–94	260,159,468	18,341,483	117,474,209	124,343,776	97,762,990	19,661,128	6,919,657	5,986	422	2,703	2,861	2,249	452	159
1994–95	273,149,449	18,582,157	127,729,576	126,837,717	97,978,129	21,560,162	7,299,425	6,192	421	2,896	2,875	2,221	489	165
1995–96	287,702,844	19,104,019	136,670,754	131,928,071	101,785,858	22,522,345	7,619,869	6,416	426	3,048	2,942	2,270	502	170
1996–97	305,065,192	20,081,287	146,435,584	138,548,321	106,545,881	24,288,693	7,713,747	6,688	440	3,211	3,038	2,336	533	169
1997–98	325,925,708	22,201,965	157,645,372	146,078,370	111,184,150	26,676,244	8,217,977	7,066	481	3,418	3,167	2,410	578	178
1998–99	347,377,993	24,521,817	169,298,232	153,557,944	119,483,487	25,348,879	8,725,578	7,464	527	3,638	3,300	2,567	545	187
1999–2000	372,943,802	27,097,866	184,613,352	161,232,584	124,735,516	27,628,923	8,868,145	7,959	578	3,940	3,441	2,662	590	189
2000–01	401,356,120	29,100,183	199,583,097	172,672,840	132,575,925	30,889,273	9,207,643	8,503	616	4,228	3,658	2,809	654	195
2001–02	419,501,976	33,144,633	206,541,793	179,815,551	141,095,685	28,924,825	9,795,041	8,800	695	4,333	3,772	2,960	607	205
2002–03	440,111,653	37,515,909	214,277,407	188,318,337	148,511,786	29,579,240	10,227,310	9,134	779	4,447	3,908	3,082	614	212
2003–04	462,026,099	41,923,435	217,384,191	202,718,474	160,602,055	31,651,489	10,464,930	9,518	864	4,478	4,176	3,309	652	216
2004–05	487,753,525	44,809,532	228,553,579	214,390,414	167,909,883	35,433,486	11,047,044	9,996	918	4,684	4,394	3,441	726	226
2005–06	520,621,788	47,553,778	242,151,076	230,916,934	178,279,408	41,111,066	11,526,460	10,600	968	4,930	4,702	3,630	837	235
2006–07	555,710,762	47,150,608	263,608,741	244,951,413	188,287,298	44,806,422	11,857,694	11,281	957	5,351	4,972	3,822	910	241
2007–08	584,683,686	47,788,467	282,622,523	254,272,697	196,521,569	45,314,965	12,436,163	11,879	971	5,742	5,166	3,993	921	253
2008–09	592,422,033	56,670,261	276,525,603	259,226,169	205,821,844	41,195,313	12,209,012	12,032	1,151	5,616	5,265	4,180	837	248
2009–10	596,390,664	75,997,858	258,863,973	261,528,833	210,837,095	38,771,186	11,920,551	12,089	1,540	5,247	5,301	4,274	786	242
2010–11[2]	604,228,585	75,549,471	266,786,402	261,892,711	211,649,523	38,558,755	11,684,433	12,218	1,528	5,395	5,296	4,280	780	236
2011–12	600,488,586	61,043,194	271,452,810	267,992,581	215,813,214	40,365,948	11,813,419	12,152	1,235	5,493	5,423	4,367	817	239

Constant 2013–14 dollars[3]

School year	Total	Federal	State	Local Total	Property taxes	Other public revenue	Private[1]	Total	Federal	State	Local Total	Property taxes	Other public revenue	Private[1]
1919–20	$11,960,618	$30,514	$1,973,687	$9,956,416	—	—	—	$554	$1	$91	$461	—	—	—
1929–30	28,669,737	100,674	4,854,848	23,714,215	—	—	—	1,117	4	189	924	—	—	—
1939–40	38,006,940	669,338	11,506,256	25,831,347	—	—	—	1,494	26	452	1,016	—	—	—
1949–50	53,942,511	1,546,214	21,486,437	30,909,860	—	—	—	2,148	62	856	1,231	—	—	—
1959–60	117,923,760	5,210,939	46,125,138	66,587,684	—	—	—	3,352	148	1,311	1,893	—	—	—
1969–70	250,466,118	20,026,113	99,912,805	130,527,199	—	—	—	5,499	440	2,193	2,866	—	—	—
1979–80	293,222,980	28,763,645	137,253,867	127,205,468	—	—	—	7,040	691	3,295	3,054	—	—	—
1989–90	385,915,252	23,502,676	181,789,632	180,622,943	$138,541,814	$31,614,690	$10,466,439	9,519	580	4,484	4,455	$3,417	$780	$258
1990–91	391,865,355	24,170,995	184,798,675	182,895,685	141,020,563	31,496,997	10,378,144	9,507	586	4,484	4,437	3,421	764	252
1991–92	398,809,400	26,340,051	184,941,624	187,527,725	145,994,695	30,965,005	10,568,025	9,485	626	4,398	4,460	3,472	736	251
1992–93	408,235,259	28,456,813	186,956,336	192,822,110	143,665,087	38,109,857	11,047,166	9,533	665	4,366	4,503	3,355	890	258
1993–94	418,067,869	29,474,172	188,777,262	199,816,435	157,101,970	31,594,799	11,119,666	9,619	678	4,343	4,597	3,614	727	256
1994–95	426,711,568	29,028,875	199,537,973	198,144,719	153,060,536	33,681,088	11,403,095	9,673	658	4,523	4,492	3,470	764	259
1995–96	437,542,954	29,053,689	207,851,005	200,638,260	154,797,514	34,252,331	11,588,415	9,758	648	4,635	4,474	3,452	764	258
1996–97	451,078,283	29,692,776	216,523,922	204,861,585	157,541,845	35,913,969	11,405,771	9,890	651	4,747	4,491	3,454	787	250
1997–98	473,479,120	32,253,261	229,014,743	212,211,116	161,519,549	38,753,139	11,938,427	10,265	699	4,965	4,601	3,502	840	259
1998–99	496,055,825	35,017,159	241,757,899	219,280,767	170,622,437	36,198,204	12,460,127	10,659	752	5,195	4,712	3,666	778	268

See notes at end of table.

Table 235.10. Revenues for public elementary and secondary schools, by source of funds: Selected years, 1919–20 through 2011–12—Continued

School year	Revenues (in thousands)							Revenues per pupil						
	Total	Federal	State	Local (including intermediate sources below the state level)				Total	Federal	State	Local (including intermediate sources below the state level)			
				Total	Property taxes	Other public revenue	Private[1]	Total	Federal	State	Total	Property taxes	Other public revenue	Private[1]
1	2	3	4	5	6	7	8	9	10	11	12	13	14	15
1999–2000	517,621,112	37,610,030	256,231,014	223,780,068	173,124,573	38,347,101	12,308,394	11,047	803	5,468	4,776	3,695	818	263
2000–01	538,602,803	39,051,205	267,832,008	231,719,591	177,911,240	41,452,087	12,356,264	11,410	827	5,674	4,909	3,769	878	262
2001–02	553,160,082	43,704,890	272,348,359	237,106,832	186,050,377	38,140,604	12,915,852	11,603	917	5,713	4,974	3,903	800	271
2002–03	567,856,847	48,405,139	276,472,781	242,978,926	191,618,273	38,164,802	13,195,851	11,785	1,005	5,738	5,043	3,977	792	274
2003–04	583,369,648	52,933,935	274,476,569	255,959,144	202,781,540	39,984,232	13,213,372	12,018	1,091	5,655	5,273	4,178	823	272
2004–05	597,862,689	54,925,174	280,148,990	262,788,525	205,815,129	43,432,509	13,540,888	12,252	1,126	5,741	5,386	4,218	890	278
2005–06	614,740,387	56,150,604	285,927,423	272,662,360	210,508,962	48,543,171	13,610,227	12,517	1,143	5,822	5,552	4,286	988	277
2006–07	639,631,695	54,271,080	303,417,744	281,942,871	216,721,596	51,572,885	13,648,389	12,984	1,102	6,159	5,723	4,399	1,047	277
2007–08	648,934,762	53,039,956	313,680,001	282,214,804	218,117,386	50,294,641	13,802,777	13,184	1,078	6,373	5,734	4,431	1,022	280
2008–09	648,468,892	62,031,625	302,686,668	283,750,598	225,293,888	45,092,649	13,364,061	13,171	1,260	6,148	5,763	4,576	916	271
2009–10	646,556,988	82,390,535	280,638,717	283,527,735	228,571,984	42,032,485	12,923,267	13,106	1,670	5,689	5,747	4,633	852	262
2010–11[2]	642,159,755	80,292,179	283,534,237	278,333,339	224,936,074	40,979,327	12,417,938	12,985	1,624	5,733	5,628	4,549	829	251
2011–12	620,018,021	63,028,476	280,281,155	276,708,390	222,832,016	41,678,752	12,197,622	12,547	1,275	5,672	5,600	4,509	843	247
Percentage distribution														
1919–20	100.0	0.3	16.5	83.2	—	—	—	100.0	0.3	16.5	83.2	—	—	—
1929–30	100.0	0.4	16.9	82.7	—	—	—	100.0	0.4	16.9	82.7	—	—	—
1939–40	100.0	1.8	30.3	68.0	—	—	—	100.0	1.8	30.3	68.0	—	—	—
1949–50	100.0	2.9	39.8	57.3	—	—	—	100.0	2.9	39.8	57.3	—	—	—
1959–60	100.0	4.4	39.1	56.5	—	—	—	100.0	4.4	39.1	56.5	—	—	—
1969–70	100.0	8.0	39.9	52.1	—	—	—	100.0	8.0	39.9	52.1	—	—	—
1979–80	100.0	9.8	46.8	43.4	—	—	—	100.0	9.8	46.8	43.4	—	—	—
1989–90	100.0	6.1	47.1	46.8	35.9	8.2	2.7	100.0	6.1	47.1	46.8	35.9	8.2	2.7
1990–91	100.0	6.2	47.2	46.7	36.0	8.0	2.6	100.0	6.2	47.2	46.7	36.0	8.0	2.6
1991–92	100.0	6.6	46.4	47.0	36.6	7.8	2.6	100.0	6.6	46.4	47.0	36.6	7.8	2.6
1992–93	100.0	7.0	45.8	47.2	35.2	9.3	2.7	100.0	7.0	45.8	47.2	35.2	9.3	2.7
1993–94	100.0	7.1	45.2	47.8	37.6	7.6	2.7	100.0	7.1	45.2	47.8	37.6	7.6	2.7
1994–95	100.0	6.8	46.8	46.4	35.9	7.9	2.7	100.0	6.8	46.8	46.4	35.9	7.9	2.7
1995–96	100.0	6.6	47.5	45.9	35.4	7.8	2.6	100.0	6.6	47.5	45.9	35.4	7.8	2.6
1996–97	100.0	6.6	48.0	45.4	34.9	8.0	2.5	100.0	6.6	48.0	45.4	34.9	8.0	2.5
1997–98	100.0	6.8	48.4	44.8	34.1	8.2	2.5	100.0	6.8	48.4	44.8	34.1	8.2	2.5
1998–99	100.0	7.1	48.7	44.2	34.4	7.3	2.5	100.0	7.1	48.7	44.2	34.4	7.3	2.5
1999–2000	100.0	7.3	49.5	43.2	33.4	7.4	2.4	100.0	7.3	49.5	43.2	33.4	7.4	2.4
2000–01	100.0	7.3	49.7	43.0	33.0	7.7	2.3	100.0	7.3	49.7	43.0	33.0	7.7	2.3
2001–02	100.0	7.9	49.2	42.9	33.6	6.9	2.3	100.0	7.9	49.2	42.9	33.6	6.9	2.3
2002–03	100.0	8.5	48.7	42.8	33.7	6.7	2.3	100.0	8.5	48.7	42.8	33.7	6.7	2.3
2003–04	100.0	9.1	47.1	43.9	34.8	6.9	2.3	100.0	9.1	47.1	43.9	34.8	6.9	2.3
2004–05	100.0	9.2	46.9	44.0	34.4	7.3	2.3	100.0	9.2	46.9	44.0	34.4	7.3	2.3
2005–06	100.0	9.1	46.5	44.4	34.2	7.9	2.2	100.0	9.1	46.5	44.4	34.2	7.9	2.2
2006–07	100.0	8.5	47.4	44.1	33.9	8.1	2.1	100.0	8.5	47.4	44.1	33.9	8.1	2.1
2007–08	100.0	8.2	48.3	43.5	33.6	7.8	2.1	100.0	8.2	48.3	43.5	33.6	7.8	2.1
2008–09	100.0	9.6	46.7	43.8	34.7	7.0	2.1	100.0	9.6	46.7	43.8	34.7	7.0	2.1
2009–10	100.0	12.7	43.4	43.9	35.4	6.5	2.0	100.0	12.7	43.4	43.9	35.4	6.5	2.0
2010–11[2]	100.0	12.5	44.2	43.3	35.0	6.4	1.9	100.0	12.5	44.2	43.3	35.0	6.4	1.9
2011–12	100.0	10.2	45.2	44.6	35.9	6.7	2.0	100.0	10.2	45.2	44.6	35.9	6.7	2.0

—Not available.
#Rounds to zero.
[1]Includes revenues from gifts, and tuition and fees from patrons.
[2]Data have been revised from previously published figures.
[3]Constant dollars based on the Consumer Price Index, prepared by the Bureau of Labor Statistics, U.S. Department of Labor, adjusted to a school-year basis.

NOTE: Beginning in 1989–90, revenues for state education agencies were excluded and new survey collection procedures were initiated; data may not be entirely comparable with figures for earlier years. Detail may not sum to totals because of rounding.
SOURCE: U.S. Department of Education, National Center for Education Statistics, Biennial Survey of Education in the United States, 1919–20 through 1949–50; Statistics of State School Systems, 1959–60 and 1969–70; Revenues and Expenditures for Public Elementary and Secondary Education, 1979–80; and Common Core of Data (CCD), "National Public Education Financial Survey," 1989–90 through 2011–12. (This table was prepared July 2014.)

Table 235.20. Revenues for public elementary and secondary schools, by source of funds and state or jurisdiction: 2011–12

[In current dollars]

State or jurisdiction	Total (in thousands)	Federal			State		Local (including intermediate sources below the state level)					
		Amount (in thousands)	Per pupil	Percent of total	Amount (in thousands)	Percent of total	Amount (in thousands)[1]	Percent of total	Property taxes		Private[2]	
									Amount (in thousands)	Percent of total	Amount (in thousands)	Percent of total
1	2	3	4	5	6	7	8	9	10	11	12	13
United States	$600,488,586	$61,043,194	$1,235	10.2	$271,452,810	45.2	$267,992,581	44.6	$215,813,214	35.9	$11,813,419	2.0
Alabama	7,099,553	838,285	1,126	11.8	3,934,577	55.4	2,326,690	32.8	1,088,896	15.3	314,693	4.4
Alaska	2,496,679	353,993	2,699	14.2	1,618,975	64.8	523,711	21.0	297,730	11.9	21,069	0.8
Arizona	9,305,199	1,374,629	1,272	14.8	3,804,900	40.9	4,125,669	44.3	3,007,906	32.3	242,635	2.6
Arkansas	5,284,555	698,938	1,447	13.2	2,723,740	51.5	1,861,878	35.2	1,608,527	30.4	148,872	2.8
California	65,808,329	8,260,861	1,329	12.6	37,079,384	56.3	20,468,083	31.1	16,065,320	24.4	427,487	0.6
Colorado	8,698,810	722,810	846	8.3	3,765,940	43.3	4,210,060	48.4	3,394,918	39.0	339,720	3.9
Connecticut	10,274,602	535,208	965	5.2	3,978,525	38.7	5,760,869	56.1	5,607,191	54.6	109,351	1.1
Delaware	1,871,464	235,905	1,829	12.6	1,096,243	58.6	539,316	28.8	464,458	24.8	16,067	0.9
District of Columbia	2,073,564	208,249	2,818	10.0	†	†	1,865,315	90.0	583,315	28.1	11,295	0.5
Florida	23,988,519	3,122,488	1,170	13.0	8,702,310	36.3	12,163,720	50.7	10,191,658	42.5	999,689	4.2
Georgia	17,620,300	1,920,092	1,140	10.9	7,533,980	42.8	8,166,229	46.3	5,576,107	31.6	487,664	2.8
Hawaii	2,535,039	318,728	1,744	12.6	2,161,254	85.3	55,057	2.2	0	0.0	32,842	1.3
Idaho	2,062,254	278,914	997	13.5	1,302,949	63.2	480,391	23.3	399,952	19.4	35,389	1.7
Illinois	29,165,373	2,406,643	1,156	8.3	9,385,630	32.2	17,373,101	59.6	15,347,696	52.6	489,205	1.7
Indiana	11,940,988	1,149,521	1,104	9.6	6,510,737	54.5	4,280,730	35.8	2,886,835	24.2	338,359	2.8
Iowa	6,038,962	526,409	1,062	8.7	2,681,029	44.4	2,831,524	46.9	1,977,465	32.7	141,451	2.3
Kansas	5,796,537	485,235	998	8.4	3,209,527	55.4	2,101,775	36.3	1,584,595	27.3	140,899	2.4
Kentucky	7,086,717	971,266	1,424	13.7	3,841,443	54.2	2,274,008	32.1	1,632,734	23.0	108,175	1.5
Louisiana	8,412,167	1,458,572	2,074	17.3	3,602,717	42.8	3,350,878	39.8	1,404,203	16.7	68,960	0.8
Maine	2,556,186	233,761	1,237	9.1	1,022,269	40.0	1,300,156	50.9	1,231,367	48.2	39,813	1.6
Maryland	13,744,621	859,635	1,006	6.3	5,980,909	43.5	6,904,078	50.2	3,354,919	24.4	128,061	0.9
Massachusetts	15,835,037	1,059,639	1,111	6.7	6,206,699	39.2	8,568,699	54.1	8,060,794	50.9	214,459	1.4
Michigan	18,751,262	2,031,233	1,291	10.8	10,700,372	57.1	6,019,657	32.1	5,061,587	27.0	287,267	1.5
Minnesota	10,989,685	797,917	950	7.3	7,044,954	64.1	3,146,814	28.6	2,013,840	18.3	330,096	3.0
Mississippi	4,441,163	795,121	1,621	17.9	2,195,730	49.4	1,450,312	32.7	1,169,902	26.3	112,490	2.5
Missouri	10,221,689	1,034,047	1,128	10.1	3,275,438	32.0	5,912,203	57.8	4,623,345	45.2	349,994	3.4
Montana	1,622,721	218,297	1,534	13.5	770,180	47.5	634,244	39.1	402,736	24.8	59,287	3.7
Nebraska	3,778,749	358,930	1,245	9.5	1,167,743	30.9	2,252,076	59.6	1,918,000	50.8	161,742	4.3
Nevada	4,137,704	413,861	941	10.0	1,366,314	33.0	2,357,529	57.0	1,133,785	27.4	41,808	1.0
New Hampshire	2,864,747	188,927	985	6.6	1,031,778	36.0	1,644,043	57.4	1,571,664	54.9	48,682	1.7
New Jersey	26,590,517	1,425,761	1,051	5.4	10,507,939	39.5	14,656,818	55.1	13,818,756	52.0	561,254	2.1
New Mexico	3,611,545	540,071	1,602	15.0	2,455,787	68.0	615,688	17.0	493,780	13.7	53,220	1.5
New York	58,645,470	3,956,260	1,463	6.7	23,131,272	39.4	31,557,937	53.8	28,290,435	48.2	351,068	0.6
North Carolina	13,113,012	1,878,905	1,246	14.3	7,877,949	60.1	3,356,157	25.6	2,781,052	21.2	235,542	1.8
North Dakota	1,296,813	170,085	1,742	13.1	653,842	50.4	472,886	36.5	351,001	27.1	54,046	4.2
Ohio	22,886,511	2,186,000	1,256	9.6	10,132,936	44.3	10,567,575	46.2	8,702,819	38.0	676,160	3.0
Oklahoma	5,862,837	794,080	1,192	13.5	2,882,879	49.2	2,185,878	37.3	1,591,425	27.1	260,466	4.4
Oregon	6,172,422	618,981	1,089	10.0	3,038,044	49.2	2,515,397	40.8	2,034,939	33.0	153,561	2.5
Pennsylvania	26,807,485	2,201,593	1,243	8.2	9,594,823	35.8	15,011,068	56.0	11,973,510	44.7	434,758	1.6
Rhode Island	2,278,095	217,363	1,522	9.5	846,435	37.2	1,214,297	53.3	1,181,575	51.9	20,379	0.9
South Carolina	8,041,045	871,480	1,198	10.8	3,670,717	45.6	3,498,848	43.5	2,628,375	32.7	242,015	3.0
South Dakota	1,303,055	215,937	1,687	16.6	400,362	30.7	686,756	52.7	568,577	43.6	38,621	3.0
Tennessee	8,979,871	1,263,157	1,264	14.1	4,059,869	45.2	3,656,845	40.7	1,750,319	19.5	426,483	4.7
Texas	49,533,579	6,311,758	1,262	12.7	20,341,491	41.1	22,880,330	46.2	20,766,669	41.9	972,423	2.0
Utah	4,619,102	461,333	786	10.0	2,418,166	52.4	1,739,603	37.7	1,308,562	28.3	198,911	4.3
Vermont	1,644,282	127,644	1,420	7.8	1,451,850	88.3	64,787	3.9	961	0.1	21,862	1.3
Virginia	14,659,153	1,356,037	1,078	9.3	5,564,497	38.0	7,738,618	52.8	4,648,724	31.7	271,223	1.9
Washington	11,844,779	1,057,047	1,011	8.9	7,001,099	59.1	3,786,633	32.0	3,209,638	27.1	319,128	2.7
West Virginia	3,556,656	433,205	1,531	12.2	2,069,942	58.2	1,053,510	29.6	934,089	26.3	31,316	0.9
Wisconsin	10,879,541	953,230	1,103	8.8	4,806,328	44.2	5,119,983	47.1	4,665,016	42.9	224,611	2.1
Wyoming	1,659,641	145,148	1,620	8.7	850,339	51.2	664,154	40.0	451,537	27.2	18,852	1.1
Other jurisdictions												
American Samoa	99,334	88,536	—	89.1	10,528	10.6	271	0.3	0	0.0	58	0.1
Guam	307,591	74,850	2,396	24.3	0	0.0	232,741	75.7	0	0.0	677	0.2
Northern Marianas	65,214	33,334	3,027	51.1	31,880	48.9	0	0.0	0	0.0	0	0.0
Puerto Rico	3,374,611	1,153,166	2,547	34.2	2,221,384	65.8	62	#	0	0.0	62	#
U.S. Virgin Islands	221,673	37,899	2,412	17.1	0	0.0	183,774	82.9	0	0.0	36	#

—Not available.
†Not applicable.
#Rounds to zero.
[1]Includes other categories of revenue not separately shown.
[2]Includes revenues from gifts, and tuition and fees from patrons.

NOTE: Excludes revenues for state education agencies. Detail may not sum to totals because of rounding.
SOURCE: U.S. Department of Education, National Center for Education Statistics, Common Core of Data (CCD), "National Public Education Financial Survey," 2011–12. (This table was prepared July 2014.)

Table 235.30. Revenues for public elementary and secondary schools, by source of funds and state or jurisdiction: 2010–11

[In current dollars]

State or jurisdiction	Total (in thousands)	Federal Amount (in thousands)	Federal Per pupil	Federal Percent of total	State Amount (in thousands)	State Percent of total	Local Amount (in thousands)[1]	Local Percent of total	Property taxes Amount (in thousands)	Property taxes Percent of total	Private[2] Amount (in thousands)	Private[2] Percent of total
1	2	3	4	5	6	7	8	9	10	11	12	13
United States	$604,228,585	$75,549,471	$1,528	12.5	$266,786,402	44.2	$261,892,711	43.3	$211,649,523	35.0	$11,684,433	1.9
Alabama	7,386,471	1,250,581	1,655	16.9	3,827,907	51.8	2,307,983	31.2	1,070,276	14.5	305,976	4.1
Alaska	2,470,274	424,422	3,213	17.2	1,524,083	61.7	521,768	21.1	297,718	12.1	21,508	0.9
Arizona	9,764,472	1,639,892	1,530	16.8	3,924,369	40.2	4,200,211	43.0	3,094,295	31.7	233,710	2.4
Arkansas	5,273,728	859,309	1,782	16.3	2,703,033	51.3	1,711,386	32.5	1,449,958	27.5	144,113	2.7
California	67,864,062	9,248,710	1,470	13.6	38,411,425	56.6	20,203,927	29.8	16,065,777	23.7	445,791	0.7
Colorado	8,820,783	991,623	1,176	11.2	3,540,865	40.1	4,288,294	48.6	3,470,848	39.3	328,898	3.7
Connecticut	9,989,986	827,618	1,476	8.3	3,422,642	34.3	5,739,726	57.5	5,568,317	55.7	112,250	1.1
Delaware	1,748,658	207,823	1,606	11.9	1,024,557	58.6	516,279	29.5	435,581	24.9	16,655	1.0
District of Columbia	1,925,824	227,198	3,187	11.8	†	†	1,698,626	88.2	553,482	28.7	10,651	0.6
Florida	26,358,355	4,796,329	1,814	18.2	9,069,113	34.4	12,492,913	47.4	10,549,648	40.0	945,427	3.6
Georgia	18,047,879	2,312,872	1,379	12.8	7,526,257	41.7	8,208,751	45.5	5,806,444	32.2	478,313	2.7
Hawaii	2,470,432	347,361	1,934	14.1	2,059,791	83.4	63,280	2.6	0	0.0	33,120	1.3
Idaho	2,183,491	305,826	1,109	14.0	1,382,052	63.3	495,614	22.7	412,701	18.9	33,597	1.5
Illinois	28,895,633	2,900,110	1,387	10.0	9,304,471	32.2	16,691,051	57.8	14,482,300	50.1	494,189	1.7
Indiana	11,761,793	1,046,267	999	8.9	6,534,419	55.6	4,181,108	35.5	2,810,010	23.9	332,819	2.8
Iowa	5,906,171	613,528	1,238	10.4	2,550,546	43.2	2,742,097	46.4	1,913,657	32.4	139,587	2.4
Kansas	5,670,547	662,971	1,371	11.7	2,979,230	52.5	2,028,345	35.8	1,537,068	27.1	139,159	2.5
Kentucky	6,993,349	1,149,658	1,708	16.4	3,622,461	51.8	2,221,230	31.8	1,584,905	22.7	111,343	1.6
Louisiana	8,246,484	1,533,440	2,201	18.6	3,479,231	42.2	3,233,813	39.2	1,339,367	16.2	66,866	0.8
Maine	2,597,927	289,249	1,530	11.1	1,052,058	40.5	1,256,620	48.4	1,191,068	45.8	39,584	1.5
Maryland	13,286,936	1,256,210	1,474	9.5	5,508,344	41.5	6,522,382	49.1	3,173,859	23.9	130,063	1.0
Massachusetts	15,357,042	1,271,995	1,331	8.3	5,797,874	37.8	8,287,173	54.0	7,801,657	50.8	203,619	1.3
Michigan	19,466,487	2,705,858	1,705	13.9	10,717,834	55.1	6,042,795	31.0	5,182,643	26.6	290,290	1.5
Minnesota	10,938,581	905,392	1,080	8.3	6,397,541	58.5	3,635,648	33.2	2,498,019	22.8	321,762	2.9
Mississippi	4,483,191	1,006,453	2,052	22.4	2,071,471	46.2	1,405,267	31.3	1,132,742	25.3	113,009	2.5
Missouri	10,169,473	1,381,908	1,504	13.6	3,008,369	29.6	5,779,196	56.8	4,563,463	44.9	347,661	3.4
Montana	1,654,729	298,964	2,110	18.1	723,125	43.7	632,641	38.2	402,720	24.3	58,652	3.5
Nebraska	3,997,538	642,407	2,247	16.1	1,186,279	29.7	2,168,852	54.3	1,844,669	46.1	156,193	3.9
Nevada	4,212,793	463,653	1,061	11.0	1,388,359	33.0	2,360,780	56.0	1,209,583	28.7	42,173	1.0
New Hampshire	2,844,769	205,572	1,056	7.2	1,041,561	36.6	1,597,636	56.2	1,521,271	53.5	48,241	1.7
New Jersey	25,217,564	1,336,982	953	5.3	9,403,391	37.3	14,477,191	57.4	13,665,700	54.2	559,163	2.2
New Mexico	3,744,076	721,936	2,135	19.3	2,423,599	64.7	598,541	16.0	480,053	12.8	49,301	1.3
New York	57,538,128	5,368,090	1,963	9.3	23,097,859	40.1	29,072,179	50.5	26,342,464	45.8	348,905	0.6
North Carolina	13,228,999	2,139,214	1,435	16.2	7,688,360	58.1	3,401,425	25.7	2,737,195	20.7	245,351	1.9
North Dakota	1,258,921	186,727	1,939	14.8	629,843	50.0	442,351	35.1	331,542	26.3	50,814	4.0
Ohio	22,973,368	2,702,863	1,541	11.8	9,921,997	43.2	10,348,507	45.0	8,514,889	37.1	681,257	3.0
Oklahoma	5,874,001	994,189	1,507	16.9	2,754,252	46.9	2,125,560	36.2	1,529,148	26.0	247,868	4.2
Oregon	6,120,056	864,118	1,514	14.1	2,792,707	45.6	2,463,231	40.2	1,986,832	32.5	150,580	2.5
Pennsylvania	27,174,139	3,318,881	1,851	12.2	9,378,294	34.5	14,476,964	53.3	11,633,093	42.8	427,746	1.6
Rhode Island	2,278,564	250,194	1,740	11.0	830,217	36.4	1,198,154	52.6	1,166,220	51.2	19,890	0.9
South Carolina	7,873,340	1,085,533	1,496	13.8	3,414,705	43.4	3,373,102	42.8	2,577,353	32.7	240,757	3.1
South Dakota	1,307,520	265,922	2,108	20.3	380,410	29.1	661,188	50.6	552,136	42.2	37,121	2.8
Tennessee	8,915,335	1,312,271	1,329	14.7	3,995,291	44.8	3,607,773	40.5	1,754,306	19.7	437,131	4.9
Texas	50,874,695	7,968,095	1,614	15.7	20,430,187	40.2	22,476,413	44.2	20,382,782	40.1	967,193	1.9
Utah	4,597,983	577,903	1,005	12.6	2,340,850	50.9	1,679,229	36.5	1,263,423	27.5	193,309	4.2
Vermont	1,641,955	175,721	1,814	10.7	1,340,743	81.7	125,491	7.6	1,276	0.1	21,928	1.3
Virginia	14,444,511	1,427,295	1,141	9.9	5,349,193	37.0	7,668,024	53.1	4,654,033	32.2	271,692	1.9
Washington	11,801,402	1,365,968	1,309	11.6	6,757,950	57.3	3,677,484	31.2	3,058,791	25.9	317,048	2.7
West Virginia	3,499,055	513,739	1,816	14.7	1,951,616	55.8	1,033,700	29.5	922,889	26.4	28,531	0.8
Wisconsin	11,429,211	1,045,227	1,208	9.1	5,246,795	45.9	5,137,189	44.9	4,714,226	41.2	225,258	2.0
Wyoming	1,647,905	155,403	1,757	9.4	878,878	53.3	613,623	37.2	417,124	25.3	18,376	1.1
Other jurisdictions												
American Samoa	82,921	72,007	—	86.8	10,689	12.9	225	0.3	0	0.0	37	#
Guam	333,235	142,766	4,515	42.8	0	0.0	190,469	57.2	0	0.0	793	0.2
Northern Marianas	87,377	57,619	5,189	65.9	29,758	34.1	0	0.0	0	0.0	0	0.0
Puerto Rico	3,711,167	1,382,157	2,918	37.2	2,328,968	62.8	43	#	0	0.0	42	#
U.S. Virgin Islands	243,250	44,858	2,895	18.4	0	0.0	198,392	81.6	0	0.0	48	#

—Not available.
†Not applicable.
#Rounds to zero.
[1]Includes other categories of revenue not separately shown.
[2]Includes revenues from gifts, and tuition and fees from patrons.

NOTE: Excludes revenues for state education agencies. Some data have been revised from previously published figures. Detail may not sum to totals because of rounding.
SOURCE: U.S. Department of Education, National Center for Education Statistics, Common Core of Data (CCD), "National Public Education Financial Survey," 2010–11. (This table was prepared July 2014.)

Table 235.40. Public elementary and secondary revenues and expenditures, by locale, source of revenue, and purpose of expenditure: 2011–12

Source of revenue and purpose of expenditure	Total	City, large[1]	City, midsize[2]	City, small[3]	Suburban, large[4]	Suburban, midsize[5]	Suburban, small[6]	Town, fringe[7]	Town, distant[8]	Town, remote[9]	Rural, fringe[10]	Rural, distant[11]	Rural, remote[12]
1	2	3	4	5	6	7	8	9	10	11	12	13	14
Revenue amounts (in millions of current dollars)													
Total revenue	$615,165	$107,327	$41,754	$46,187	$202,556	$18,560	$10,651	$9,167	$32,752	$21,241	$73,059	$36,833	$14,861
Federal	60,717	14,109	5,262	4,976	14,981	1,554	935	705	3,476	2,555	6,637	3,602	1,892
Title I	15,098	4,788	1,397	1,236	3,160	299	185	150	830	648	1,184	784	437
Child Nutrition Act	13,186	2,696	1,111	1,077	3,360	353	208	175	829	552	1,582	893	349
Children with disabilities (IDEA)..	11,481	1,905	879	1,039	3,766	362	219	152	631	424	1,318	571	209
Impact aid	1,164	138	84	46	198	22	8	22	46	82	118	114	284
Bilingual education	357	99	37	38	107	8	6	6	13	7	27	6	3
Indian education	103	12	3	5	7	1	2	1	7	15	12	11	28
Math, science, and professional development	1,660	386	157	152	337	47	28	21	104	93	166	107	61
Safe and drug-free schools	132	20	12	10	22	1	3	2	13	9	19	13	8
Vocational and technical education	549	117	45	45	145	12	9	4	33	31	69	27	12
Other and unclassified	16,987	3,948	1,537	1,328	3,880	448	268	172	970	695	2,142	1,075	501
State	272,380	46,258	19,508	21,657	79,580	8,511	4,896	4,381	16,214	10,480	34,434	19,273	7,137
Special education programs	16,891	3,378	1,171	1,366	5,974	532	281	249	821	503	1,557	773	285
Compensatory and basic skills ..	4,989	958	400	453	1,797	197	95	67	200	119	372	228	100
Bilingual education	720	63	27	40	459	43	4	2	19	9	45	8	3
Gifted and talented	503	19	30	10	328	26	2	1	13	5	51	12	5
Vocational education	824	38	47	56	240	31	16	8	71	58	160	68	31
Other	248,453	41,802	17,833	19,732	70,782	7,683	4,498	4,054	15,090	9,786	32,249	18,183	6,713
Local[13]	282,068	46,960	16,984	19,553	107,995	8,495	4,819	4,081	13,062	8,206	31,987	13,958	5,832
Property tax[14]	172,685	22,036	9,830	11,906	71,238	4,778	3,188	2,741	8,680	5,729	19,685	8,893	3,982
Parent government contribution[14]..	47,390	15,046	2,891	2,574	17,668	1,829	577	372	619	153	4,120	1,253	289
Private (fees from individuals).....	14,305	1,273	842	949	5,145	507	249	252	817	510	2,283	1,021	381
Other[13]	47,689	8,606	3,421	4,124	13,945	1,382	805	716	2,945	1,814	5,899	2,792	1,180
Percentage distribution of revenue													
Total revenue	100.0	100.0	100.0	100.0	100.0	100.0	100.0	100.0	100.0	100.0	100.0	100.0	100.0
Federal	9.9	13.1	12.6	10.8	7.4	8.4	8.8	7.7	10.6	12.0	9.1	9.8	12.7
State	44.3	43.1	46.7	46.9	39.3	45.9	46.0	47.8	49.5	49.3	47.1	52.3	48.0
Local	45.9	43.8	40.7	42.3	53.3	45.8	45.2	44.5	39.9	38.6	43.8	37.9	39.2
Expenditure amounts (in millions of current dollars)													
Total expenditures	$616,305	$110,078	$42,114	$46,494	$200,984	$18,584	$10,516	$9,073	$32,698	$21,421	$72,813	$36,523	$14,764
Current expenditures for schools	520,402	89,668	35,334	39,156	171,435	15,814	8,978	7,687	27,890	18,149	61,891	31,629	12,574
Instruction	315,772	55,727	21,018	23,544	104,933	9,605	5,392	4,662	16,712	10,879	37,186	18,772	7,307
Support services, students	29,589	4,251	2,223	2,469	10,681	924	533	444	1,520	1,028	3,477	1,488	534
Support services, instructional staff	24,012	4,199	1,946	2,075	7,740	722	403	297	1,279	787	2,763	1,285	488
Administration	38,976	5,996	2,609	2,835	12,505	1,163	679	609	2,233	1,535	4,801	2,771	1,225
Operation and maintenance	49,234	8,661	3,246	3,621	16,213	1,523	857	716	2,612	1,760	5,730	2,979	1,311
Transportation	23,373	3,653	1,383	1,435	7,722	664	406	372	1,259	727	3,188	1,864	698
Food service	20,834	3,514	1,494	1,577	5,872	604	356	308	1,303	874	2,758	1,550	624
Other	18,611	3,668	1,416	1,600	5,767	609	352	279	972	560	1,989	919	385
Other current expenditures	21,897	3,598	1,536	1,654	6,270	679	383	321	1,338	903	2,915	1,603	671
Interest on school debt	18,104	3,772	1,140	1,218	5,872	533	327	271	814	471	2,590	874	220
Capital outlay	50,783	10,192	3,922	3,891	15,016	1,438	847	774	2,746	2,168	5,740	2,740	1,303
Percentage distribution of current expenditures for schools													
All current expenditures for schools....	100.0	100.0	100.0	100.0	100.0	100.0	100.0	100.0	100.0	100.0	100.0	100.0	100.0
Instruction	60.7	62.1	59.5	60.1	61.2	60.7	60.1	60.6	59.9	59.9	60.1	59.4	58.1
Support services	10.3	9.4	11.8	11.6	10.7	10.4	10.4	9.6	10.0	10.0	10.1	8.8	8.1
Administration	7.5	6.7	7.4	7.2	7.3	7.4	7.6	7.9	8.0	8.5	7.8	8.8	9.7
Operation and maintenance	9.5	9.7	9.2	9.2	9.5	9.6	9.5	9.3	9.4	9.7	9.3	9.4	10.4
Transportation	4.5	4.1	3.9	3.7	4.5	4.2	4.5	4.8	4.5	4.0	5.2	5.9	5.6
Food service and other	7.6	8.0	8.2	8.1	6.8	7.7	7.9	7.6	8.2	7.9	7.7	7.8	8.0
Per student amounts (in current dollars)													
Current expenditure per student	$10,541	$11,520	$9,963	$10,525	$10,984	$10,266	$9,864	$10,083	$9,870	$9,662	$9,498	$9,965	$11,375
Instruction expenditure per student.	6,396	7,159	5,926	6,328	6,723	6,235	5,923	6,115	5,914	5,791	5,707	5,915	6,610

[1]Located inside an urbanized area and inside a principal city with a population of at least 250,000.

[2]Located inside an urbanized area and inside a principal city with a population of at least 100,000, but less than 250,000.

[3]Located inside an urbanized area and inside a principal city with a population less than 100,000.

[4]Located inside an urbanized area and outside a principal city with a population of 250,000 or more.

[5]Located inside an urbanized area and outside a principal city with a population of at least 100,000, but less than 250,000.

[6]Located inside an urbanized area and outside a principal city with a population less than 100,000.

[7]Located inside an urban cluster that is 10 miles or less from an urbanized area.

[8]Located inside an urban cluster that is more than 10 but less than or equal to 35 miles from an urbanized area.

[9]Located inside an urban cluster that is more than 35 miles from an urbanized area.

[10]Located outside any urbanized area or urban cluster, but 5 miles or less from an urbanized area or 2.5 miles or less from an urban cluster.

[11]Located outside any urbanized area or urban cluster and more than 5 miles but less than or equal to 25 miles from an urbanized area, or more than 2.5 miles but less than or equal to 10 miles from an urban cluster.

[12]Located outside any urbanized area or urban cluster, more than 25 miles from an urbanized area, and more than 10 miles from an urban cluster.

[13]Includes tuition and fee revenues from other in-state school systems, which are excluded from state data reported through the "National Public Education Financial Survey."

[14]Property tax and parent government contributions are determined on the basis of independence or dependence of the local school system and are mutually exclusive.

NOTE: Total includes data for some school districts not identified by locale. Detail may not sum to totals because of rounding.

SOURCE: U.S. Department of Education, National Center for Education Statistics, Common Core of Data (CCD), "Local Education Agency (School District) Finance Survey (F33)," 2011–12. (This table was prepared March 2015.)

Table 236.10. Summary of expenditures for public elementary and secondary education and other related programs, by purpose: Selected years, 1919–20 through 2011–12

School year	Total expenditures	Current expenditures for public elementary and secondary education							Current expenditures for other programs[1]	Capital outlay[2]	Interest on school debt
		Total	Administration	Instruction	Plant operation	Plant maintenance	Fixed charges	Other school services[3]			
1	2	3	4	5	6	7	8	9	10	11	12
Amounts in thousands of current dollars											
1919–20	$1,036,151	$861,120	$36,752	$632,556	$115,707	$30,432	$9,286	$36,387	$3,277	$153,543	$18,212
1929–30	2,316,790	1,843,552	78,680	1,317,727	216,072	78,810	50,270	101,993	9,825	370,878	92,536
1939–40	2,344,049	1,941,799	91,571	1,403,285	194,365	73,321	50,116	129,141	13,367	257,974	130,909
1949–50	5,837,643	4,687,274	220,050	3,112,340	427,587	214,164	261,469	451,663	35,614	1,014,176	100,578
1959–60	15,613,254	12,329,388	528,408	8,350,738	1,085,036	422,586	909,323	1,033,297	132,566	2,661,786	489,514
1969–70	40,683,429	34,217,773	1,606,646	23,270,158	2,537,257	974,941	3,266,920	2,561,856	635,803	4,659,072	1,170,782
1979–80	95,961,561	86,984,142	4,263,757	53,257,937	9,744,785	(4)	11,793,934	7,923,729	597,585	6,506,167	1,873,666
1989–90	212,769,564	188,229,359	16,346,991 [5]	113,550,405 [5]	20,261,415 [5]	(4)	—	38,070,548 [5]	2,982,543	17,781,342	3,776,321
1999–2000	381,838,155	323,888,508	25,079,298 [5]	199,968,138 [5]	31,190,295 [5]	(4)	—	67,650,776 [5]	5,457,015	43,357,186	9,135,445
2001–02	435,364,404	368,378,006	28,309,047 [5]	226,668,386 [5]	34,829,109 [5]	(4)	—	78,571,464 [5]	6,530,554	49,960,542	10,495,301
2002–03	454,906,912	387,593,617	29,751,958 [5]	237,731,734 [5]	36,830,517 [5]	(4)	—	83,279,408 [5]	6,873,762	48,940,374	11,499,160
2003–04	474,241,531	403,390,369	30,864,875 [5]	247,444,620 [5]	38,720,429 [5]	(4)	—	86,360,444 [5]	6,927,551	50,842,973	13,080,638
2004–05	499,568,736	425,047,565	32,666,223 [5]	260,046,266 [5]	40,926,881 [5]	(4)	—	91,408,195 [5]	7,691,468	53,528,382	13,301,322
2005–06	528,268,772	449,131,342	34,197,083 [5]	273,760,798 [5]	44,313,835 [5]	(4)	—	96,859,626 [5]	7,415,575	57,375,299	14,346,556
2006–07	562,194,807	476,814,206	36,213,814 [5]	290,678,482 [5]	46,828,916 [5]	(4)	—	103,092,995 [5]	7,804,253	62,863,465	14,712,882
2007–08	597,313,726	506,884,219	38,203,341 [5]	308,238,664 [5]	49,362,661 [5]	(4)	—	111,079,554 [5]	8,307,720	66,426,299	15,695,488
2008–09	610,326,007	518,922,842	38,811,325 [5]	316,075,710 [5]	50,559,027 [5]	(4)	—	113,476,779 [5]	8,463,793	65,890,367	17,049,004
2009–10	607,018,292	524,715,242	38,972,700 [5]	321,213,401 [5]	50,023,919 [5]	(4)	—	114,505,223 [5]	8,355,761	56,714,992	17,232,297
2010–11[6]	604,355,852	527,291,339	39,154,833 [5]	322,536,983 [5]	50,214,709 [5]	(4)	—	115,384,813 [5]	8,161,474	50,968,815	17,934,224
2011–12	601,766,981	527,096,473	39,490,207 [5]	320,952,573 [5]	49,833,706 [5]	(4)	—	116,819,988 [5]	8,195,907	48,773,386	17,701,216
Amounts in thousands of constant 2013–14 dollars[7]											
1919–20	$12,774,701	$10,616,745	$453,115	$7,798,780	$1,426,551	$375,196	$114,487	$448,615	$40,402	$1,893,031	$224,536
1929–30	31,802,704	25,306,540	1,080,045	18,088,511	2,966,032	1,081,829	690,059	1,400,064	134,868	5,091,063	1,270,247
1939–40	39,411,221	32,648,068	1,539,612	23,593,865	3,267,919	1,232,769	842,616	2,171,288	224,744	4,337,397	2,201,014
1949–50	57,916,971	46,503,812	2,183,181	30,878,439	4,242,216	2,124,784	2,594,111	4,481,081	353,337	10,061,938	997,864
1959–60	124,853,958	98,593,982	4,225,502	66,778,052	8,676,669	3,379,279	7,271,551	8,262,930	1,060,086	21,285,410	3,914,479
1969–70	253,056,852	212,839,561	9,993,572	144,743,771	15,782,108	6,064,275	20,320,718	15,935,117	3,954,787	28,980,106	7,282,435
1979–80	290,439,686	263,268,403	12,904,795	161,191,818	29,493,813	(4)	35,695,819	23,982,158	1,808,666	19,691,729	5,670,885
1989–90	393,728,005	348,316,594	30,249,948 [5]	210,123,918 [5]	37,493,551 [5]	(4)	—	70,449,178 [5]	5,519,167	32,904,200	6,988,045
1999–2000	529,965,880	449,535,638	34,808,392 [5]	277,542,433 [5]	43,290,048 [5]	(4)	—	93,894,763 [5]	7,573,973	60,176,882	12,679,389
2001–02	574,076,461	485,747,433	37,328,632 [5]	298,887,514 [5]	45,926,059 [5]	(4)	—	103,605,227 [5]	8,611,263	65,878,540	13,839,224
2002–03	586,946,523	500,095,118	38,387,653 [5]	306,734,875 [5]	47,520,807 [5]	(4)	—	107,451,783 [5]	8,868,914	63,145,628	14,836,863
2003–04	598,793,261	509,334,207	38,971,027 [5]	312,431,875 [5]	48,889,712 [5]	(4)	—	109,041,593 [5]	8,746,958	64,196,043	16,516,052
2004–05	612,345,156	521,001,013	40,040,543 [5]	318,751,074 [5]	50,166,024 [5]	(4)	—	112,043,372 [5]	9,427,798	65,612,283	16,304,062
2005–06	623,769,801	530,325,817	40,379,271 [5]	323,251,587 [5]	52,324,940 [5]	(4)	—	114,370,019 [5]	8,756,171	67,747,670	16,940,142
2006–07	647,094,931	548,820,537	41,682,661 [5]	334,575,435 [5]	53,900,807 [5]	(4)	—	118,661,634 [5]	8,982,817	72,356,822	16,934,756
2007–08	662,952,721	562,585,887	42,401,518 [5]	342,111,108 [5]	54,787,139 [5]	(4)	—	123,286,121 [5]	9,220,658	73,725,906	17,420,270
2008–09	668,066,694	568,016,214	42,483,121 [5]	345,978,464 [5]	55,342,230 [5]	(4)	—	124,212,398 [5]	9,264,522	72,124,011	18,661,948
2009–10	658,075,801	568,852,477	42,250,949 [5]	348,232,763 [5]	54,231,758 [5]	(4)	—	124,137,007 [5]	9,058,619	61,485,661	18,681,818
2010–11[6]	642,295,011	560,392,681	41,612,824 [5]	342,784,627 [5]	53,366,998 [5]	(4)	—	122,628,232 [5]	8,673,820	54,168,443	19,060,067
2011–12	621,337,994	544,239,008	40,774,530 [5]	331,390,777 [5]	51,454,426 [5]	(4)	—	120,619,275 [5]	8,462,459	50,359,622	18,276,905
Percentage distribution											
1919–20	100.0	83.1	3.5	61.0	11.2	2.9	0.9	3.5	0.3	14.8	1.8
1929–30	100.0	79.6	3.4	56.9	9.3	3.4	2.2	4.4	0.4	16.0	4.0
1939–40	100.0	82.8	3.9	59.9	8.3	3.1	2.1	5.5	0.6	11.0	5.6
1949–50	100.0	80.3	3.8	53.3	7.3	3.7	4.5	7.7	0.6	17.4	1.7
1959–60	100.0	79.0	3.4	53.5	6.9	2.7	5.8	6.6	0.8	17.0	3.1
1969–70	100.0	84.1	3.9	57.2	6.2	2.4	8.0	6.3	1.6	11.5	2.9
1979–80	100.0	90.6	4.4	55.5	10.2	(4)	12.3	8.3	0.6	6.8	2.0
1989–90	100.0	88.5	7.7 [5]	53.4 [5]	9.5 [5]	(4)	—	17.9 [5]	1.4	8.4	1.8
1999–2000	100.0	84.8	6.6 [5]	52.4 [5]	8.2 [5]	(4)	—	17.7 [5]	1.4	11.4	2.4
2001–02	100.0	84.6	6.5 [5]	52.1 [5]	8.0 [5]	(4)	—	18.0 [5]	1.5	11.5	2.4
2002–03	100.0	85.2	6.5 [5]	52.3 [5]	8.1 [5]	(4)	—	18.3 [5]	1.5	10.8	2.5
2003–04	100.0	85.1	6.5 [5]	52.2 [5]	8.2 [5]	(4)	—	18.2 [5]	1.5	10.7	2.8
2004–05	100.0	85.1	6.5 [5]	52.1 [5]	8.2 [5]	(4)	—	18.3 [5]	1.5	10.7	2.7
2005–06	100.0	85.0	6.5 [5]	51.8 [5]	8.4 [5]	(4)	—	18.3 [5]	1.4	10.9	2.7
2006–07	100.0	84.8	6.4 [5]	51.7 [5]	8.3 [5]	(4)	—	18.3 [5]	1.4	11.2	2.6
2007–08	100.0	84.9	6.4 [5]	51.6 [5]	8.3 [5]	(4)	—	18.6 [5]	1.4	11.1	2.6
2008–09	100.0	85.0	6.4 [5]	51.8 [5]	8.3 [5]	(4)	—	18.6 [5]	1.4	10.8	2.8
2009–10	100.0	86.4	6.4 [5]	52.9 [5]	8.2 [5]	(4)	—	18.9 [5]	1.4	9.3	2.8
2010–11[6]	100.0	87.2	6.5 [5]	53.4 [5]	8.3 [5]	(4)	—	19.1 [5]	1.4	8.4	3.0
2011–12	100.0	87.6	6.6 [5]	53.3 [5]	8.3 [5]	(4)	—	19.4 [5]	1.4	8.1	2.9

—Not available.

[1]Includes expenditures for summer schools, adult education, community colleges, and community services.

[2]Prior to 1969–70, excludes capital outlay by state and local school housing authorities.

[3]Prior to 1959–60, items included under "other school services" were listed under "auxiliary services," a more comprehensive classification that also included community services.

[4]Plant operation also includes plant maintenance.

[5]Data not comparable to figures prior to 1989–90.

[6]Data have been revised from previously published figures.

[7]Constant dollars based on the Consumer Price Index, prepared by the Bureau of Labor Statistics, U.S. Department of Labor, adjusted to a school-year basis.

NOTE: Beginning in 1959–60, includes Alaska and Hawaii. Beginning in 1989–90, state administration expenditures were excluded from both "total" and "current" expenditures. Beginning in 1989–90, extensive changes were made in the data collection procedures. Detail may not sum to totals because of rounding.
SOURCE: U.S. Department of Education, National Center for Education Statistics, *Biennial Survey of Education in the United States*, 1919–20 through 1949–50; *Statistics of State School Systems*, 1959–60 and 1969–70; *Revenues and Expenditures for Public Elementary and Secondary Education*, 1979–80; and Common Core of Data (CCD), "National Public Education Financial Survey," 1989–90 through 2011–12. (This table was prepared July 2014.)

Table 236.15. Current expenditures and current expenditures per pupil in public elementary and secondary schools: 1989–90 through 2024–25

| | Current expenditures in unadjusted dollars[1] | | | Current expenditures in constant 2013–14 dollars[2] | | | | | |
| | | | | Total current expenditures | | Per pupil in fall enrollment | | Per pupil in average daily attendance (ADA) | |
School year	Total, in billions	Per pupil in fall enrollment	Per pupil in average daily attendance (ADA)	In billions	Annual percentage change	Per pupil enrolled	Annual percentage change	Per pupil in ADA	Annual percentage change
1	2	3	4	5	6	7	8	9	10
1989–90	$188.2	$4,643	$4,980	$343.0	3.8	$8,459	2.9	$9,073	2.3
1990–91	202.0	4,902	5,258	349.0	1.8	8,468	0.1	9,083	0.1
1991–92	211.2	5,023	5,421	353.6	1.3	8,409	-0.7	9,075	-0.1
1992–93	220.9	5,160	5,584	358.7	1.4	8,375	-0.4	9,064	-0.1
1993–94	231.5	5,327	5,767	366.4	2.1	8,429	0.6	9,126	0.7
1994–95	243.9	5,529	5,989	375.1	2.4	8,504	0.9	9,212	0.9
1995–96	255.1	5,689	6,147	382.0	1.8	8,519	0.2	9,205	-0.1
1996–97	270.2	5,923	6,393	393.3	3.0	8,624	1.2	9,307	1.1
1997–98	285.5	6,189	6,676	408.4	3.8	8,853	2.7	9,549	2.6
1998–99	302.9	6,508	7,013	425.9	4.3	9,151	3.4	9,861	3.3
1999–2000	323.9	6,912	7,394	442.6	3.9	9,446	3.2	10,104	2.5
2000–01	348.4	7,380	7,904	460.3	4.0	9,751	3.2	10,443	3.4
2001–02	368.4	7,727	8,259	478.3	3.9	10,033	2.9	10,723	2.7
2002–03	387.6	8,044	8,610	492.4	3.0	10,219	1.9	10,938	2.0
2003–04	403.4	8,310	8,900	501.5	1.8	10,332	1.1	11,064	1.2
2004–05	425.0	8,711	9,316	513.0	2.3	10,513	1.8	11,243	1.6
2005–06	449.1	9,145	9,778	522.2	1.8	10,632	1.1	11,368	1.1
2006–07	476.8	9,679	10,336	540.4	3.5	10,969	3.2	11,714	3.0
2007–08	506.9	10,298	10,982	553.9	2.5	11,254	2.6	12,001	2.5
2008–09	518.9	10,540	11,239	559.3	1.0	11,359	0.9	12,113	0.9
2009–10	524.7	10,636	11,427	568.9	0.1	11,531	-0.1	12,388	0.7
2010–11	527.3	10,663	11,433	560.4	-1.5	11,332	-1.7	12,151	-1.9
2011–12	527.1	10,667	11,363	544.2	-2.9	11,014	-2.8	11,732	-3.4
2012–13[3]	514.5	10,412	11,060	522.5	-4.0	10,574	0.7	11,232	1.1
2013–14[3]	529.9	10,610	11,352	529.9	1.4	10,610	0.9	11,352	0.9
2014–15[3]	542.4	10,851	11,610	539.2	1.8	10,787	2.0	11,541	2.0
2015–16[3]	559.5	11,169	11,950	548.3	1.7	10,946	1.8	11,711	1.8
2016–17[3]	584.8	11,643	12,457	560.0	2.1	11,150	2.0	11,929	2.0
2017–18[3]	615.3	12,164	13,015	575.2	2.7	11,370	2.0	12,166	2.0
2018–19[3]	644.0	12,660	13,546	587.3	2.1	11,545	1.5	12,353	1.5
2019–20[3]	674.9	13,185	14,108	600.7	2.3	11,737	1.3	12,558	1.3
2020–21[3]	706.4	13,705	14,663	613.7	2.2	11,906	1.0	12,739	1.0
2021–22[3]	736.8	14,193	15,186	626.0	2.0	12,059	1.0	12,902	1.0
2022–23[3]	768.0	14,696	15,723	638.2	2.0	12,212	1.1	13,066	1.1
2023–24[3]	800.2	15,213	16,277	650.5	1.9	12,366	0.7	13,231	0.7
2024–25[3]	824.9	15,589	16,679	659.4	1.4	12,460	#	13,332	#

#Rounds to zero.
[1]Unadjusted (or "current") dollars have not been adjusted to compensate for inflation.
[2]Constant dollars based on the Consumer Price Index, prepared by the Bureau of Labor Statistics, U.S. Department of Labor, adjusted to a school-year basis.
[3]Projected.
NOTE: Current expenditures include instruction, support services, food services, and enterprise operations. Some data have been revised from previously published figures.

SOURCE: U.S. Department of Education, National Center for Education Statistics, Common Core of Data (CCD), "National Public Education Financial Survey," 1989–90 through 2011–12; National Elementary and Secondary Enrollment Projection Model, 1972 through 2024; and Public Elementary and Secondary Education Current Expenditure Projection Model, 1973–74 through 2024–25. (This table was prepared August 2015.)

Table 236.20. Total expenditures for public elementary and secondary education and other related programs, by function and subfunction: Selected years, 1990–91 through 2011–12

Function and subfunction	Expenditures (in thousands of current dollars)								Percentage distribution of current expenditures for public schools							
	1990–91	2000–01	2005–06	2007–08	2008–09	2009–10	2010–11[1]	2011–12	1990–91	2000–01	2005–06	2007–08	2008–09	2009–10	2010–11[1]	2011–12
1	2	3	4	5	6	7	8	9	10	11	12	13	14	15	16	17
Total expenditures...........	$229,429,715	$410,811,185	$528,268,772	$597,313,726	$610,326,007	$607,018,292	$604,355,852	$601,766,981	†	†	†	†	†	†	†	†
Current expenditures for public schools...........	202,037,752	348,360,841	449,131,342	506,884,219	518,922,842	524,715,242	527,291,339	527,096,473	100.00	100.00	100.00	100.00	100.00	100.00	100.00	100.00
Salaries...........	132,730,931[2]	224,305,806	273,142,308	304,021,671	312,552,150	314,037,286	311,541,792	308,472,126	65.70	64.39	60.82	59.98	60.23	59.85	59.08	58.52
Employee benefits...........	33,954,456[2]	57,976,490	87,888,909	103,012,045	105,667,462	108,475,595	111,750,200	114,316,626	16.81	16.64	19.57	20.32	20.36	20.67	21.19	21.69
Purchased services...........	16,380,643[2]	31,778,754	43,195,665	49,206,425	50,715,562	51,969,406	53,498,786	54,398,157	8.11	9.12	9.62	9.71	9.77	9.90	10.15	10.32
Tuition...........	1,192,505[2]	2,458,366	3,828,079	4,574,030	4,492,060	4,749,301	4,988,203	5,038,715	0.59	0.71	0.85	0.90	0.87	0.91	0.95	0.96
Supplies...........	14,805,956[2]	28,262,078	36,637,037	41,362,823	40,629,203	40,334,985	40,417,163	40,026,564	7.33	8.11	8.16	8.16	7.83	7.69	7.67	7.59
Other...........	2,973,261[2]	3,579,347	4,439,345	4,707,226	4,866,404	5,148,668	5,095,195	4,844,286	1.47	1.03	0.99	0.93	0.94	0.98	0.97	0.92
Instruction...........	122,223,362	214,333,003	273,760,798	308,238,664	316,075,710	321,213,401	322,536,983	320,952,573	60.50	61.53	60.95	60.81	60.91	61.22	61.17	60.89
Salaries...........	90,742,284	154,512,089	186,905,065	206,688,984	212,963,123	214,435,825	212,998,609	210,664,931	44.91	44.35	41.61	40.78	41.04	40.87	40.39	39.97
Employee benefits...........	22,347,524	39,522,678	59,032,817	69,275,522	71,029,220	73,051,571	75,248,811	76,946,902	11.06	11.35	13.14	13.67	13.69	13.92	14.27	14.60
Purchased services...........	2,722,639	6,430,708	10,083,561	12,246,282	12,782,555	13,843,875	14,694,620	14,540,794	1.35	1.85	2.25	2.42	2.46	2.64	2.79	2.76
Tuition...........	1,192,505	2,458,366	3,828,079	4,574,030	4,492,060	4,749,301	4,988,203	5,038,715	0.59	0.71	0.85	0.90	0.87	0.91	0.95	0.96
Supplies...........	4,584,754	10,377,554	12,731,138	14,145,041	13,421,846	13,689,672	13,135,284	12,436,951	2.27	2.98	2.83	2.79	2.59	2.61	2.49	2.36
Textbooks...........	—		2,537,532	2,720,526	2,934,846	2,547,273	2,324,846	2,181,673	—		0.56	0.54	0.57	0.49	0.44	0.41
Other...........	633,656	1,031,608	1,180,138	1,308,805	1,386,906	1,443,155	1,471,457	1,324,280	0.31	0.30	0.26	0.26	0.27	0.28	0.28	0.25
Student support[3]...........	8,926,010	17,292,756	23,336,224	27,492,686	28,533,413	29,134,124	29,368,646	29,352,547	4.42	4.96	5.20	5.42	5.50	5.55	5.57	5.57
Salaries...........	6,565,965	12,354,464	15,833,312	18,327,236	19,109,617	19,397,151	19,367,865	19,084,613	3.25	3.55	3.53	3.62	3.68	3.70	3.67	3.62
Employee benefits...........	1,660,082	3,036,037	4,859,310	5,914,825	6,145,103	6,337,026	6,533,691	6,812,839	0.82	0.87	1.08	1.17	1.18	1.21	1.24	1.29
Purchased services...........	455,996	1,328,600	1,958,934	2,382,679	2,414,847	2,490,533	2,583,714	2,709,926	0.23	0.38	0.44	0.47	0.47	0.47	0.49	0.51
Supplies...........	191,482	421,838	497,201	537,295	525,459	544,965	521,729	538,311	0.09	0.12	0.11	0.11	0.10	0.10	0.10	0.10
Other...........	52,485	151,817	187,468	330,652	338,387	364,449	361,647	206,858	0.03	0.04	0.04	0.07	0.07	0.07	0.07	0.04
Instructional staff services[4]...........	8,467,142	15,926,856	21,923,223	25,364,532	25,018,199	25,108,146	24,893,140	24,444,321	4.19	4.57	4.88	5.00	4.82	4.79	4.72	4.64
Salaries...........	5,560,129	9,790,767	13,005,332	15,212,248	14,962,194	14,827,754	14,490,521	14,209,414	2.75	2.81	2.90	3.00	2.88	2.83	2.75	2.70
Employee benefits...........	1,408,217	2,356,440	3,898,171	4,686,748	4,746,650	4,835,699	4,933,118	4,946,058	0.70	0.68	0.87	0.92	0.91	0.92	0.94	0.94
Purchased services...........	622,487	2,003,598	2,944,703	3,300,159	3,256,725	3,379,483	3,438,979	3,384,374	0.31	0.58	0.66	0.65	0.63	0.64	0.65	0.64
Supplies...........	776,863	1,566,954	1,867,878	1,957,097	1,834,852	1,838,108	1,810,950	1,686,729	0.38	0.45	0.42	0.39	0.35	0.35	0.34	0.32
Other...........	99,445	209,097	207,139	208,280	217,778	227,101	219,573	217,746	0.05	0.06	0.05	0.04	0.04	0.04	0.04	0.04
General administration...........	5,791,253	7,108,291	8,920,041	9,866,659	10,202,846	10,421,207	10,494,526	10,567,572	2.87	2.04	1.99	1.95	1.97	1.99	1.99	2.00
Salaries...........	2,603,562	3,351,554	3,860,883	4,294,513	4,420,788	4,452,059	4,401,697	4,376,827	1.29	0.96	0.86	0.85	0.85	0.85	0.83	0.83
Employee benefits...........	777,381	1,000,698	1,479,556	1,682,009	1,747,378	1,801,413	1,856,221	1,920,231	0.38	0.29	0.33	0.33	0.34	0.35	0.35	0.36
Purchased services...........	1,482,427	2,099,032	2,735,714	2,975,038	3,174,832	3,145,503	3,236,857	3,304,851	0.73	0.60	0.61	0.59	0.61	0.60	0.61	0.63
Supplies...........	172,898	206,137	225,230	241,979	230,822	233,729	228,417	241,994	0.09	0.06	0.05	0.05	0.04	0.04	0.04	0.05
Other...........	754,985	450,870	618,657	673,120	629,025	788,501	771,334	723,668	0.37	0.13	0.14	0.13	0.12	0.15	0.15	0.14
School administration...........	11,695,344	19,580,890	25,277,042	28,336,682	28,608,480	28,551,493	28,660,307	28,922,635	5.79	5.62	5.63	5.59	5.51	5.44	5.44	5.49
Salaries...........	8,935,903	14,817,213	18,181,910	20,180,936	20,521,736	20,351,317	20,191,545	20,198,248	4.42	4.25	4.05	3.98	3.95	3.88	3.83	3.83
Employee benefits...........	2,257,783	3,689,689	5,622,342	6,554,820	6,600,069	6,722,417	6,972,708	7,167,104	1.12	1.06	1.25	1.29	1.27	1.28	1.32	1.36
Purchased services...........	247,750	611,638	862,664	973,499	934,243	931,494	931,765	976,085	0.12	0.18	0.19	0.19	0.18	0.18	0.18	0.19
Supplies...........	189,711	369,257	474,816	484,491	430,083	419,531	426,864	425,140	0.09	0.11	0.11	0.10	0.08	0.08	0.08	0.08
Other...........	64,197	93,093	135,311	142,936	122,349	126,734	137,426	156,059	0.03	0.03	0.03	0.03	0.02	0.02	0.03	0.03
Operation and maintenance...........	21,290,655	34,034,158	44,313,835	49,362,661	50,559,027	50,023,919	50,214,709	49,833,706	10.54	9.77	9.87	9.74	9.74	9.53	9.52	9.45
Salaries...........	8,849,903	13,461,242	16,021,701	17,656,583	18,045,474	17,956,826	17,604,634	17,433,706	4.38	3.86	3.57	3.48	3.48	3.42	3.34	3.31
Employee benefits...........	2,633,075	3,778,520	5,840,665	6,701,757	6,881,875	7,040,412	7,195,927	7,327,835	1.30	1.08	1.30	1.32	1.33	1.34	1.36	1.39
Purchased services...........	5,721,125	9,642,217	11,913,734	13,051,419	13,150,025	13,095,871	13,351,922	13,436,116	2.83	2.77	2.65	2.57	2.53	2.50	2.53	2.55
Supplies...........	3,761,738	6,871,845	10,147,971	11,508,237	12,043,690	11,483,968	11,638,187	11,242,772	1.86	1.97	2.26	2.27	2.32	2.19	2.21	2.13
Other...........	325,157	280,334	389,764	444,665	437,964	446,842	424,039	393,107	0.16	0.08	0.09	0.09	0.08	0.09	0.08	0.07

See notes at end of table.

Table 236.20. Total expenditures for public elementary and secondary education and other related programs, by function and subfunction: Selected years, 1990–91 through 2011–12—Continued

Function and subfunction	Expenditures (in thousands of current dollars)								Percentage distribution of current expenditures for public schools							
	1990–91	2000–01	2005–06	2007–08	2008–09	2009–10	2010–11[1]	2011–12	1990–91	2000–01	2005–06	2007–08	2008–09	2009–10	2010–11[1]	2011–12
1	2	3	4	5	6	7	8	9	10	11	12	13	14	15	16	17
Student transportation	8,678,954	14,052,654	18,850,234	21,536,978	21,679,876	21,819,304	22,370,807	22,907,082	4.30	4.03	4.20	4.25	4.18	4.16	4.24	4.35
Salaries	3,285,127	5,406,092	6,701,455	7,507,100	7,591,289	7,633,213	7,527,611	7,480,832	1.63	1.55	1.49	1.48	1.46	1.45	1.43	1.42
Employee benefits	892,985	1,592,127	2,535,296	2,867,686	2,933,989	3,048,962	3,124,937	3,168,678	0.44	0.46	0.56	0.57	0.57	0.58	0.59	0.60
Purchased services	3,345,232	5,767,462	7,547,730	8,556,631	9,001,837	8,982,432	9,153,621	9,470,230	1.66	1.66	1.68	1.69	1.73	1.71	1.74	1.80
Supplies	961,447	1,159,350	1,867,495	2,427,117	1,983,454	1,967,717	2,370,182	2,565,380	0.48	0.33	0.42	0.48	0.38	0.38	0.45	0.49
Other	194,163	127,623	198,259	178,444	169,307	186,979	194,456	221,961	0.10	0.04	0.04	0.04	0.03	0.04	0.04	0.04
Other support services[5]	5,587,837	11,439,134	14,463,815	16,310,815	17,187,109	17,189,474	17,246,807	17,830,629	2.77	3.28	3.22	3.22	3.31	3.28	3.27	3.38
Salaries	2,900,394	5,521,381	6,577,129	7,517,159	8,091,102	8,162,557	8,139,084	8,162,351	1.44	1.58	1.46	1.48	1.56	1.56	1.54	1.55
Employee benefits	980,859	1,594,540	2,483,366	2,982,979	3,148,252	3,136,979	3,295,052	3,395,915	0.49	0.46	0.55	0.59	0.61	0.60	0.62	0.64
Purchased services	798,922	2,783,176	3,455,292	3,778,311	3,928,346	3,915,823	3,876,650	4,221,441	0.40	0.80	0.77	0.75	0.76	0.75	0.74	0.80
Supplies	294,527	626,889	793,997	988,542	884,381	852,467	876,293	912,741	0.15	0.18	0.18	0.20	0.17	0.16	0.17	0.17
Other	613,135	913,148	1,154,031	1,043,824	1,135,027	1,121,648	1,059,728	1,138,181	0.30	0.26	0.26	0.21	0.22	0.21	0.20	0.22
Food services	8,430,490	13,816,635	17,263,582	19,190,249	19,794,945	19,996,995	20,394,768	21,194,414	4.17	3.97	3.84	3.79	3.81	3.81	3.87	4.02
Salaries	—	4,966,092	5,841,522	6,332,680	6,505,821	6,483,443	6,482,085	6,559,747	†	1.43	1.30	1.25	1.25	1.24	1.23	1.24
Employee benefits	—	1,381,923	2,061,344	2,264,203	2,343,119	2,409,983	2,492,673	2,529,156	†	0.40	0.46	0.45	0.45	0.46	0.47	0.48
Purchased services	—	923,091	1,464,511	1,699,764	1,815,966	1,926,821	2,058,018	2,177,107	†	0.26	0.33	0.34	0.35	0.37	0.39	0.41
Supplies	—	6,420,201	7,727,182	8,727,170	8,908,841	8,943,177	9,118,886	9,681,540	†	1.84	1.72	1.72	1.72	1.70	1.73	1.84
Other	—	125,327	169,023	166,431	221,198	233,573	243,105	246,864	†	0.04	0.04	0.03	0.04	0.04	0.05	0.05
Enterprise operations[6]	946,705	776,463	1,022,549	1,184,293	1,263,238	1,257,180	1,110,646	1,090,995	0.47	0.22	0.23	0.23	0.24	0.24	0.21	0.21
Salaries	—	124,913	213,999	304,233	341,007	337,140	338,141	301,285	†	0.04	0.05	0.06	0.07	0.06	0.06	0.06
Employee benefits	—	23,837	76,042	81,496	91,807	91,133	97,063	101,907	†	0.01	0.02	0.02	0.02	0.02	0.02	0.02
Purchased services	—	189,230	228,823	242,643	256,186	257,570	172,641	177,234	†	0.05	0.05	0.05	0.05	0.05	0.03	0.03
Supplies	—	242,052	304,129	345,854	365,775	361,651	290,372	295,006	†	0.07	0.07	0.07	0.07	0.07	0.06	0.06
Other	—	196,430	199,556	210,068	208,463	209,686	212,430	215,563	†	0.06	0.04	0.04	0.04	0.04	0.04	0.04
Current expenditures for other programs	3,295,717	6,063,700	7,415,575	8,307,720	8,463,793	8,355,761	8,161,474	8,195,907	†	†	†	†	†	†	†	†
Community services	964,370	2,426,189	3,015,207	3,289,736	3,364,620	3,398,025	3,269,802	3,209,272	†	†	†	†	†	†	†	†
Private school programs	527,609	1,026,695	1,389,204	1,564,201	1,541,922	1,423,681	1,427,539	1,441,688	†	†	†	†	†	†	†	†
Adult education	1,365,523	1,838,265	2,001,459	2,148,351	2,187,628	2,084,477	2,013,156	1,937,819	†	†	†	†	†	†	†	†
Community colleges	5,356	351	0	32,694	33,303	33,274	34,045	30,598	†	†	†	†	†	†	†	†
Other	432,858	772,200	1,009,704	1,272,738	1,336,321	1,416,305	1,416,931	1,576,530	†	†	†	†	†	†	†	†
Capital outlay[7]	19,771,478	46,220,704	57,375,299	66,426,299	65,890,367	56,714,992	50,968,815	48,773,386	†	†	†	†	†	†	†	†
Public schools	19,655,496	46,078,494	57,281,425	66,331,738	65,799,088	56,621,337	50,888,951	48,696,985	†	†	†	†	†	†	†	†
Other current expenditures	115,982	142,210	93,874	94,561	91,279	93,655	79,864	76,401	†	†	†	†	†	†	†	†
Interest on school debt	4,324,768	10,165,940	14,346,556	15,695,488	17,049,004	17,232,297	17,934,224	17,701,216	†	†	†	†	†	†	†	†

—Not available.
†Not applicable.
[1]Data have been revised from previously published figures.
[2]Includes estimated data for subfunctions of food services and enterprise operations.
[3]Includes expenditures for guidance, health, attendance, and speech pathology services.
[4]Includes expenditures for curriculum development, staff training, libraries, and media and computer centers.
[5]Includes business support services concerned with paying, transporting, exchanging, and maintaining goods and services for local education agencies; central support services, including planning, research, evaluation, information, staff, and data processing services; and other support services.

[6]Includes expenditures for operations funded by sales of products or services (e.g., school bookstore or computer time). Includes very small amounts for direct program support made by state education agencies for local school districts.
[7]Includes expenditures for property and for buildings and alterations completed by school district staff or contractors.
NOTE: Excludes expenditures for state education agencies. Detail may not sum to totals because of rounding.

SOURCE: U.S. Department of Education, National Center for Education Statistics, Common Core of Data (CCD), "National Public Education Financial Survey," 1990–91 through 2011–12. (This table was prepared July 2014.)

Table 236.25. Current expenditures for public elementary and secondary education, by state or jurisdiction: Selected years, 1969–70 through 2011–12
[In thousands of current dollars]

State or jurisdiction	1969–70	1979–80	1989–90	1999–2000	2000–01	2001–02	2002–03	2003–04	2004–05	2005–06	2006–07	2007–08	2008–09	2009–10	2010–11[1]	2011–12
1	2	3	4	5	6	7	8	9	10	11	12	13	14	15	16	17
United States	$34,217,773	$86,984,142	$188,229,359	$323,888,508	$348,360,841	$368,378,006	$387,593,617	$403,390,369	$425,047,565	$449,131,342	$476,814,206	$506,884,219	$518,922,842	$524,715,242	$527,291,339	$527,096,473
Alabama	422,730	1,146,713	2,275,233	4,176,082	4,354,794	4,444,390	4,657,643	4,812,479	5,164,406	5,699,076	6,245,031	6,832,439	6,683,843	6,670,517	6,592,925	6,386,517
Alaska	81,374	377,947	828,051	1,183,499	1,229,036	1,284,854	1,326,226	1,354,846	1,442,269	1,529,645	1,634,316	1,918,375	2,007,319	2,084,019	2,201,270	2,292,205
Arizona	281,941	949,753	2,258,660	4,288,739	4,846,105	5,395,814	5,892,227	6,071,785	6,579,957	7,130,341	7,815,720	8,403,221	8,726,755	8,482,552	8,340,211	7,974,545
Arkansas	235,083	666,949	1,404,545	2,380,331	2,505,179	2,822,877	2,923,401	3,109,644	3,546,999	3,808,011	3,997,701	4,156,368	4,240,839	4,459,910	4,578,136	4,606,995
California	3,881,595	9,172,158	21,485,782	38,129,479	42,908,787	46,265,544	47,983,402	49,215,866	50,918,654	53,436,103	57,352,599	61,570,555	60,080,929	58,248,662	57,526,835	57,975,189
Colorado	369,218	1,243,049	2,451,833	4,401,010	4,758,173	5,151,003	5,551,506	5,666,191	5,994,440	6,368,289	6,579,053	7,338,766	7,187,267	7,429,302	7,409,462	7,341,585
Connecticut	588,710	1,227,892	3,444,520	5,402,836	5,693,207	6,031,062	6,302,988	6,600,767	7,080,396	7,517,025	7,855,459	8,336,789	8,708,294	8,853,337	9,094,036	9,344,999
Delaware	108,747	269,108	520,953	937,630	1,027,224	1,072,875	1,127,745	1,201,631	1,299,349	1,405,465	1,437,707	1,489,594	1,518,786	1,549,812	1,613,304	1,751,143
District of Columbia	141,138	298,448	639,983	780,192	830,299	912,432	902,318	1,011,536	1,067,500	1,057,166	1,130,006	1,282,437	1,352,905	1,451,870	1,482,202	1,466,888
Florida	961,273	2,766,468	8,228,531	13,885,988	15,023,514	15,535,864	16,355,123	17,578,884	19,042,877	20,897,327	22,887,024	24,224,114	23,328,028	23,349,314	23,870,090	22,732,752
Georgia	599,371	1,608,028	4,505,962	9,158,624	10,011,343	10,853,496	11,630,576	11,788,616	12,528,856	13,739,263	14,828,715	16,030,039	15,976,945	15,730,409	15,527,907	15,623,633
Hawaii	141,324	351,889	700,012	1,213,695	1,215,968	1,348,381	1,489,092	1,566,792	1,648,086	1,805,521	2,045,198	2,122,779	2,225,438	2,136,144	2,141,561	2,187,480
Idaho	103,107	313,927	627,794	1,302,817	1,403,190	1,481,803	1,511,862	1,555,006	1,618,215	1,694,827	1,777,491	1,891,505	1,957,740	1,961,867	1,881,746	1,854,556
Illinois	1,896,067	4,579,355	8,125,493	14,462,773	15,634,490	16,480,787	17,271,301	18,081,827	18,658,428	19,244,960	20,326,591	21,874,484	23,495,271	24,695,773	24,554,467	25,012,915
Indiana	809,105	1,851,292	4,074,578	7,110,930	7,548,487	7,704,547	8,088,684	8,524,980	9,108,931	9,241,986	9,497,077	9,281,709	9,680,895	9,921,243	9,687,949	9,978,491
Iowa	527,086	1,186,659	2,004,742	3,264,336	3,430,885	3,565,796	3,652,022	3,669,797	3,808,200	4,039,389	4,231,932	4,499,236	4,731,463	4,794,308	4,855,871	4,971,944
Kansas	362,593	830,133	1,848,302	2,971,814	3,264,698	3,450,923	3,510,675	3,658,421	3,718,153	4,039,417	4,339,477	4,633,517	4,806,603	4,731,676	4,741,372	4,871,381
Kentucky	353,265	1,054,459	2,134,011	3,837,794	4,047,392	4,268,608	4,401,627	4,553,382	4,812,591	5,213,620	5,424,621	5,822,550	5,886,890	6,091,814	6,211,453	6,360,799
Louisiana	503,217	1,303,902	2,838,283	4,391,189	4,485,878	4,802,565	5,056,583	5,290,964	5,554,766	5,554,278	6,040,368	6,814,455	7,276,651	7,393,452	7,522,098	7,544,782
Maine	155,907	385,492	1,048,195	1,604,438	1,704,422	1,812,798	1,909,268	1,969,497	2,056,266	2,119,408	2,258,764	2,308,071	2,350,447	2,370,085	2,377,878	2,330,842
Maryland	721,794	1,783,056	3,894,644	6,545,135	7,044,881	7,480,723	7,933,055	8,198,454	8,682,586	9,381,613	10,210,303	11,211,176	11,591,965	11,883,677	11,885,333	11,846,681
Massachusetts	907,341	2,638,734	4,760,390	8,564,039	9,272,387	9,957,292	10,281,820	10,799,765	11,357,857	11,747,010	12,383,447	13,182,987	13,937,097	13,356,373	13,962,366	14,151,659
Michigan	1,799,945	4,642,847	8,025,621	13,994,294	14,243,597	14,975,150	15,983,044	16,205,111	16,353,591	16,681,981	17,013,259	17,053,521	17,217,584	17,227,515	16,786,444	16,485,178
Minnesota	781,243	1,786,768	3,474,398	6,140,442	6,531,198	6,586,559	6,867,403	7,084,005	7,310,284	7,686,638	8,060,410	8,426,264	9,182,281	8,927,288	8,944,867	9,053,021
Mississippi	262,760	756,018	1,472,710	2,510,376	2,576,457	2,642,116	2,853,531	3,059,569	3,243,888	3,550,261	3,692,358	3,898,401	3,967,232	3,990,876	3,887,981	3,972,787
Missouri	642,030	1,504,988	3,288,738	5,655,531	6,076,169	6,491,885	6,793,957	6,832,454	7,115,207	7,592,485	7,957,705	8,526,641	8,827,224	8,923,448	8,691,887	8,719,925
Montana	127,176	358,118	641,345	994,770	1,041,760	1,073,005	1,124,291	1,160,838	1,193,182	1,254,360	1,320,112	1,392,449	1,436,062	1,498,252	1,518,818	1,504,531
Nebraska	231,612	581,615	1,233,431	1,926,500	2,067,290	2,206,946	2,304,223	2,413,404	2,512,914	2,672,629	2,825,608	2,970,323	3,053,575	3,213,646	3,345,530	3,356,734
Nevada	87,273	281,901	712,898	1,875,467	1,978,480	2,169,000	2,251,044	2,470,581	2,722,264	2,959,728	3,311,471	3,515,004	3,606,035	3,592,994	3,676,997	3,574,233
New Hampshire	101,370	295,400	821,671	1,418,503	1,518,792	1,641,378	1,781,594	1,900,240	2,021,144	2,139,113	2,246,692	2,399,330	2,490,623	2,576,956	2,637,911	2,643,256
New Jersey	1,343,564	3,638,533	8,119,336	13,327,645	14,773,650	15,822,609	17,185,966	18,416,695	19,669,576	20,869,993	22,448,262	24,357,079	23,446,911	24,261,392	23,639,281	24,391,278
New Mexico	183,736	515,451	1,020,148	1,880,274	2,022,093	2,204,165	2,281,608	2,446,115	2,554,638	2,729,707	2,904,474	3,057,061	3,186,252	3,217,328	3,127,463	3,039,423
New York	4,111,839	8,760,500	18,090,978	28,433,240	30,884,292	32,218,975	34,546,965	36,205,111	38,866,853	41,149,457	43,679,908	46,443,426	48,635,363	50,251,461	51,574,134	52,460,494
North Carolina	676,193	1,880,862	4,342,826	7,713,293	8,201,901	8,543,290	8,766,968	8,994,620	9,835,550	10,476,056	11,248,336	11,482,912	12,598,382	12,200,362	12,322,555	12,303,426
North Dakota	97,895	228,483	459,391	638,946	668,814	711,437	716,007	749,697	832,157	857,774	838,221	886,317	928,528	1,000,095	1,049,772	1,098,090
Ohio	1,639,805	3,836,576	7,994,379	12,974,575	13,893,495	14,774,065	15,868,494	16,662,985	17,167,866	17,829,599	18,251,361	18,892,374	19,387,318	19,801,670	19,988,921	19,701,810
Oklahoma	339,105	1,055,844	1,905,332	3,382,581	3,750,542	3,875,547	3,804,570	3,853,308	4,161,024	4,406,002	4,750,536	4,932,913	5,082,062	5,192,124	5,036,031	5,170,978
Oregon	403,844	1,126,812	2,297,944	3,896,287	4,112,069	4,214,512	4,150,747	4,199,485	4,458,028	4,773,751	5,039,632	5,409,630	5,529,831	5,401,667	5,430,888	5,389,273
Pennsylvania	1,912,644	4,584,320	9,496,788	14,120,112	14,895,316	15,550,975	16,344,459	17,680,332	18,711,100	19,531,006	20,404,304	21,157,430	21,831,816	22,733,518	23,485,203	23,190,198
Rhode Island	145,443	362,046	801,908	1,393,143	1,465,703	1,553,455	1,647,587	1,765,585	1,825,900	1,934,429	2,039,633	2,134,609	2,139,317	2,136,582	2,149,366	2,167,450
South Carolina	367,689	997,984	2,322,618	4,087,355	4,492,161	4,744,809	4,888,250	5,017,833	5,312,739	5,696,629	6,023,043	6,453,817	6,626,763	6,566,165	6,465,486	6,600,733
South Dakota	109,375	238,332	447,074	737,998	796,133	819,296	851,429	887,328	916,563	948,671	977,006	1,037,875	1,080,054	1,115,861	1,126,503	1,100,100
Tennessee	473,226	1,319,303	2,790,808	4,931,734	5,170,379	5,501,029	5,674,773	6,056,657	6,446,691	6,681,445	6,975,099	7,540,306	7,768,063	7,894,661	8,225,374	8,351,056
Texas	1,518,181	4,997,689	12,763,954	25,098,703	26,546,557	28,191,128	30,399,603	30,974,890	31,919,107	33,851,773	36,105,784	39,033,235	40,688,181	42,621,886	42,864,291	41,067,619
Utah	179,981	518,251	1,130,135	2,102,655	2,250,339	2,374,702	2,366,897	2,475,550	2,627,022	2,778,236	2,987,810	3,444,936	3,638,775	3,635,085	3,704,133	3,779,760

See notes at end of table.

Table 236.25. Current expenditures for public elementary and secondary education, by state or jurisdiction: Selected years, 1969–70 through 2011–12—Continued

[In thousands of current dollars]

State or jurisdiction	1969–70	1979–80	1989–90	1999–2000	2000–01	2001–02	2002–03	2003–04	2004–05	2005–06	2006–07	2007–08	2008–09	2009–10	2010–11[1]	2011–12
1	2	3	4	5	6	7	8	9	10	11	12	13	14	15	16	17
Vermont	78,921	189,811	546,901	870,198	934,031	992,149	1,045,213	1,111,029	1,177,478	1,237,442	1,300,149	1,356,165	1,413,329	1,432,683	1,424,507	1,497,093
Virginia	704,677	1,881,519	4,621,071	7,757,598	8,335,805	8,718,554	9,208,329	9,798,239	10,705,162	11,470,735	12,465,858	13,125,666	13,505,290	13,193,633	12,968,457	13,403,576
Washington	699,984	1,825,782	3,550,819	6,399,885	6,782,136	7,103,817	7,359,566	7,549,235	7,870,979	8,239,716	8,752,007	9,331,539	9,940,325	9,832,913	10,040,312	10,054,077
West Virginia	249,404	678,386	1,316,637	2,086,937	2,157,568	2,219,013	2,349,833	2,415,043	2,527,767	2,651,491	2,742,344	2,841,962	2,998,657	3,328,177	3,388,294	3,275,246
Wisconsin	777,288	1,908,523	3,929,920	6,852,178	7,249,081	7,592,176	7,994,755	8,131,276	8,435,359	8,745,195	9,029,660	9,366,134	9,696,228	9,966,244	10,333,016	9,704,932
Wyoming	69,584	226,067	509,084	683,918	704,695	761,830	791,732	814,092	863,423	965,350	1,124,564	1,191,736	1,268,407	1,334,655	1,398,444	1,432,216
Other jurisdictions																
American Samoa	—	—	21,838	42,395	40,642	46,192	47,566	55,519	58,163	58,539	57,093	63,105	65,436	70,305	75,355	80,105
Guam	16,652	—	101,130	—	—	—	—	182,506	—	210,119	219,881	229,243	235,711	235,639	266,952	290,575
Northern Marianas	—	—	20,476	49,832	49,151	46,508	50,843	47,681	58,400	57,694	55,048	51,241	62,787	62,210	84,657	68,775
Puerto Rico	—	—	1,045,407	2,086,414	2,257,837	2,152,724	2,541,385	2,425,372	2,865,945	3,082,295	3,268,200	3,433,229	3,502,757	3,464,044	3,519,547	3,351,423
U.S. Virgin Islands	—	—	128,065	135,174	125,252	107,343	125,405	128,250	137,793	146,872	157,446	196,533	201,326	220,234	204,932	183,333

—Not available.
[1]Data have been revised from previously published figures.
NOTE: Current expenditures include instruction, support services, food services, and enterprise operations. Beginning in 1989–90, expenditures for state administration are excluded. Data are not adjusted for changes in the purchasing power of the dollar due to inflation. Detail may not sum to totals because of rounding.

SOURCE: U.S. Department of Education, National Center for Education Statistics, *Statistics of State School Systems, 1969–70*; *Revenues and Expenditures for Public Elementary and Secondary Education, 1979–80*; and Common Core of Data (CCD), "National Public Education Financial Survey," 1989–90 through 2011–12. (This table was prepared July 2014.)

Table 236.30. Total expenditures for public elementary and secondary education and other related programs, by function and state or jurisdiction: 2011–12

[In thousands of current dollars]

State or jurisdiction	Total	Elementary/ secondary current expenditures, total	Instruction	Total	Student support[4]	Instructional staff[6]	General administration	School administration	Operation and maintenance	Student transportation	Other support services	Food services	Enterprise operations[3]	Current expenditures for other programs[1]	Capital outlay[2]	Interest on school debt
1	2	3	4	5	6	7	8	9	10	11	12	13	14	15	16	17
United States	$601,766,981	$527,096,473	$320,952,573	$183,858,490	$29,352,547	$24,444,321	$10,567,572	$28,922,635	$49,833,706	$22,907,082	$17,830,629	$21,194,414	$1,090,995	$8,195,907	$48,773,386	$17,701,216
Alabama	7,229,299	6,386,517	3,698,119	2,245,315	388,382	288,628	145,490	393,961	581,679	329,498	137,677	443,083	0	118,530	582,173	142,079
Alaska	2,486,951	2,292,205	1,265,045	955,644	192,256	150,609	33,379	138,799	284,072	69,594	86,933	62,573	8,943	11,357	145,341	38,048
Arizona	9,179,262	7,974,545	4,359,402	3,208,746	574,404	409,196	134,033	416,046	1,001,891	354,236	318,941	404,875	1,522	55,948	922,249	226,521
Arkansas	5,393,330	4,606,995	2,606,990	1,792,433	236,339	385,799	113,873	232,152	450,651	179,815	133,804	262,041	5,531	30,470	625,078	130,787
California	67,993,295	57,975,189	34,834,633	20,615,172	3,069,455	3,451,830	557,468	3,831,331	5,775,903	1,406,656	2,522,529	2,377,552	147,832	849,005	6,693,286	2,415,815
Colorado	8,548,413	7,341,585	4,226,136	2,816,136	360,503	405,398	124,477	498,026	702,106	220,549	505,126	262,291	36,486	66,505	706,236	434,087
Connecticut	10,305,777	9,344,999	5,909,965	3,132,730	592,808	278,470	188,712	540,966	841,833	472,697	217,243	225,988	76,316	145,794	680,346	134,638
Delaware	1,978,562	1,751,143	1,116,490	575,915	74,118	31,668	25,377	91,724	182,906	87,655	82,466	58,738	0	43,176	160,864	23,380
District of Columbia	1,880,466	1,466,888	835,297	570,575	52,176	55,291	77,610	128,732	128,651	95,733	32,381	57,844	3,172	29,242	350,947	33,390
Florida	25,827,411	22,732,752	13,863,360	7,778,213	988,122	1,444,964	200,665	1,262,173	2,366,281	943,642	572,365	1,091,180	0	531,446	1,837,262	725,950
Georgia	17,465,095	15,623,633	9,661,561	5,069,710	721,257	804,370	205,132	938,987	1,162,751	702,706	534,508	847,025	45,336	28,718	1,566,185	246,559
Hawaii	2,431,422	2,187,480	1,253,486	809,606	205,572	77,727	10,622	133,574	251,251	75,894	54,965	124,388	0	18,339	124,096	101,508
Idaho	2,052,295	1,854,556	1,118,508	635,933	103,651	73,963	42,845	104,940	171,375	92,810	46,349	99,904	210	4,818	135,343	57,578
Illinois	28,197,052	25,012,915	15,062,473	9,173,619	1,670,799	1,004,347	1,035,931	1,270,844	2,163,144	1,177,291	851,264	776,822	0	147,857	2,169,707	866,573
Indiana	11,412,416	9,978,491	5,869,436	3,660,416	477,217	379,746	252,792	584,868	1,110,673	605,250	249,869	448,640	0	143,578	943,637	346,710
Iowa	6,021,744	4,971,944	3,056,382	1,684,655	277,615	238,874	126,418	286,572	423,592	185,378	146,216	226,252	4,645	32,354	905,980	111,467
Kansas	5,759,773	4,871,381	2,960,225	1,680,456	288,453	203,500	144,033	280,207	456,009	191,668	116,586	230,700	0	4,325	682,546	201,522
Kentucky	7,394,709	6,360,799	3,683,142	2,282,369	291,664	347,964	142,037	361,259	581,667	395,751	162,027	379,094	16,194	82,974	770,827	180,110
Louisiana	8,457,692	7,544,782	4,296,513	2,835,500	454,281	398,623	185,249	453,378	683,208	443,255	217,505	412,389	380	49,166	744,610	119,135
Maine	2,536,202	2,330,842	1,393,423	857,340	152,289	117,581	72,257	126,668	240,166	119,519	28,859	79,839	240	27,586	121,421	56,354
Maryland	13,204,777	11,846,681	7,362,229	4,167,836	536,147	640,551	106,627	848,596	1,008,194	635,115	392,606	316,617	0	23,329	1,166,856	167,911
Massachusetts	15,572,302	14,151,659	9,156,777	4,611,079	1,000,934	648,571	196,699	576,269	1,238,278	604,424	345,904	383,803	0	57,753	1,117,722	245,167
Michigan	19,056,799	16,485,178	9,569,531	6,313,528	1,258,620	812,118	339,716	897,935	1,473,648	702,868	828,624	602,119	0	311,414	1,376,616	883,591
Minnesota	10,938,012	9,053,021	5,996,623	2,694,668	241,917	389,865	280,590	360,455	641,585	512,952	267,305	396,582	25,148	425,508	1,069,044	390,439
Mississippi	4,341,018	3,972,787	2,266,650	1,459,137	193,147	205,228	126,294	230,737	417,379	195,478	90,874	246,687	314	29,067	270,440	68,724
Missouri	10,173,456	8,719,925	5,197,338	3,106,738	407,036	377,844	281,381	505,252	871,532	456,838	206,856	415,850	0	202,882	894,459	356,189
Montana	1,654,625	1,504,531	895,081	542,398	93,009	57,111	46,197	82,345	152,916	74,246	36,574	64,452	2,599	12,147	120,771	17,177
Nebraska	3,795,271	3,356,734	2,141,943	979,090	129,717	106,943	106,059	165,390	289,952	106,080	74,950	145,628	90,072	5,123	348,343	85,071
Nevada	4,164,339	3,574,233	2,094,490	1,343,876	191,677	179,804	53,452	267,375	379,003	146,186	126,380	135,504	363	22,486	327,173	240,447
New Hampshire	2,856,080	2,643,256	1,703,049	868,500	196,953	79,849	88,636	144,574	217,501	113,241	27,745	71,707	0	7,357	159,998	45,469
New Jersey	26,131,462	24,391,278	14,621,161	8,962,705	2,417,153	757,081	494,351	1,152,284	2,383,511	1,216,595	541,731	546,146	261,266	145,630	912,022	682,532
New Mexico	3,559,706	3,039,423	1,737,115	1,157,045	312,821	85,241	67,783	181,676	316,282	100,818	92,424	143,476	1,788	4,191	516,030	62
New York	58,096,880	52,460,494	36,402,730	14,954,302	1,760,925	1,318,950	999,411	2,019,007	4,555,669	2,784,794	1,515,546	1,103,462	0	2,324,980	2,097,414	1,213,993
North Carolina	13,060,157	10,983,426	7,670,507	3,945,148	579,241	485,298	190,431	769,521	1,044,027	545,327	381,302	687,771	34,268	64,190	683,545	8,996
North Dakota	1,280,669	1,098,090	641,580	364,739	47,135	39,380	49,409	55,404	99,354	47,199	26,859	57,503		8,589	160,058	13,932
Ohio	23,186,166	19,701,810	11,213,502	7,818,594	1,252,066	1,287,265	599,478	1,121,867	1,722,344	952,381	883,193	668,572	1,143	419,786	2,467,639	596,930
Oklahoma	5,748,976	5,170,978	2,876,209	1,917,119	352,443	213,457	165,841	275,679	577,120	179,111	159,468	326,066	51,583	26,452	496,205	55,341
Oregon	6,178,860	5,389,273	3,130,150	2,056,269	382,606	200,455	72,074	342,400	444,810	256,779	157,145	200,953	1,901	25,275	448,212	316,100
Pennsylvania	26,596,835	23,190,198	14,158,464	8,125,146	1,228,638	795,160	717,818	1,065,797	2,250,183	1,188,792	878,759	800,030	106,557	554,665	1,822,156	1,029,815
Rhode Island	2,317,880	2,167,450	1,343,508	767,921	223,902	76,246	30,517	105,644	171,275	83,893	76,444	55,197	824	68,570	36,926	44,943
South Carolina	7,956,070	6,600,733	3,743,777	2,484,294	492,122	398,350	71,022	399,056	631,459	271,360	220,925	354,171	18,491	66,542	889,986	398,809
South Dakota	1,302,875	1,100,100	646,885	385,880	60,231	44,018	36,716	53,656	111,350	41,049	38,859	60,524	6,811	2,894	172,738	27,142
Tennessee	9,295,241	8,351,056	5,192,746	2,713,045	359,656	522,641	175,728	477,465	714,723	313,078	149,754	445,264	0	75,695	664,129	204,361
Texas	49,991,336	41,067,619	24,251,087	14,453,152	1,996,385	2,055,843	618,148	2,330,464	4,547,753	1,185,258	1,719,301	2,363,381	0	340,085	5,536,572	3,047,060
Utah	4,790,073	3,779,760	2,406,489	1,143,856	147,162	153,201	44,775	234,966	343,867	120,566	99,319	212,909	16,506	111,616	746,262	152,435

See notes at end of table.

Table 236.30. Total expenditures for public elementary and secondary education and other related programs, by function and state or jurisdiction: 2011–12—Continued

[In thousands of current dollars]

State or jurisdiction	Total expenditures													Current expenditures for other programs[1]	Capital outlay[2]	Interest on school debt
	Total	Elementary/ secondary current expenditures, total	Current expenditures for elementary and secondary programs													
			Instruction	Support services												
				Total	Student support[4]	Instructional staff[4]	General administration	School administration[5]	Operation and maintenance	Student transportation	Other support services	Food services	Enterprise operations[3]			
1	2	3	4	5	6	7	8	9	10	11	12	13	14	15	16	17
Vermont..............	1,568,294	1,497,093	938,085	516,635	114,891	63,152	30,641	97,006	125,004	49,290	36,651	41,333	1,040	12,479	46,009	12,713
Virginia..............	14,730,695	13,403,576	8,123,189	4,744,409	652,507	888,941	207,325	775,363	1,282,360	726,330	211,583	533,759	2,218	75,794	1,078,786	172,540
Washington..............	12,052,898	10,054,077	5,863,499	3,723,294	870,086	381,806	187,088	582,827	904,239	414,602	382,645	346,975	120,310	35,983	1,545,989	416,850
West Virginia..............	3,409,105	3,275,246	1,919,623	1,170,981	155,961	135,590	64,988	174,123	339,632	243,898	56,789	184,643	0	47,168	69,611	17,079
Wisconsin..............	10,609,035	9,704,932	5,830,090	3,506,067	462,397	458,211	270,244	477,135	887,149	419,844	531,086	368,643	133	258,100	450,303	195,700
Wyoming..............	1,655,911	1,432,216	847,393	540,500	83,700	87,601	29,735	77,161	137,797	69,092	55,413	43,469	854	8,968	213,240	1,487
Other jurisdictions																
American Samoa..........	95,015	80,105	35,110	26,735	37	9,009	3,987	4,587	6,529	1,134	1,451	18,260	0	1,888	13,022	0
Guam..............	307,068	290,575	142,979	136,193	26,092	4,855	1,749	16,840	46,928	5,626	34,102	11,403	0	0	13,369	3,124
Northern Marianas......	71,875	68,775	29,685	29,802	6,600	5,517	2,514	5,415	4,578	3,048	2,131	9,288	0	1,913	1,186	0
Puerto Rico..............	3,500,379	3,351,423	1,478,763	1,397,250	225,707	169,227	56,082	156,295	310,868	133,786	345,285	475,410	0	87,694	61,262	0
U.S. Virgin Islands..........	185,853	183,333	95,711	76,567	14,395	5,162	7,245	9,332	13,000	7,038	20,396	10,700	356	2,434	86	0

[1]Includes expenditures for adult education, community colleges, private school programs funded by local and state education agencies, and community services.
[2]Includes expenditures for property and for buildings and alterations completed by school district staff or contractors.
[3]Includes expenditures for operations funded by sales of products or services (e.g., school bookstore or computer time). Also includes small amounts for direct program support made by state education agencies for local school districts.

[4]Includes expenditures for guidance, health, attendance, and speech pathology services.
[5]Includes expenditures for curriculum development, staff training, libraries, and media and computer centers.
NOTE: Excludes expenditures for state education agencies. Detail may not sum to totals because of rounding.
SOURCE: U.S. Department of Education, National Center for Education Statistics, Common Core of Data (CCD), "National Public Education Financial Survey," 2011–12. (This table was prepared July 2014.)

Table 236.40. Total expenditures for public elementary and secondary education and other related programs, by function and state or jurisdiction: 2010–11

[In thousands of current dollars]

State or jurisdiction	Total expenditures														Capital outlay[2]	Interest on school debt
		Total expenditures for elementary and secondary programs														
		Elementary/ secondary current expenditures, total	Current expenditures for elementary and secondary programs											Current expenditures for other programs[1]		
			Instruction	Support services												
				Total	Student support[4]	Instructional staff[5]	General administration[5]	School administration	Operation and maintenance	Student transportation	Other support services	Food services	Enterprise operations[3]			
	2	3	4	5	6	7	8	9	10	11	12	13	14	15	16	17
United States	$604,355,852	$527,291,339	$322,536,983	$183,248,941	$29,368,646	$24,893,140	$10,494,526	$28,660,307	$50,214,709	$22,370,807	$17,246,807	$20,394,768	$1,110,646	$8,161,474	$50,968,815	$17,934,224
Alabama	7,410,192	6,592,925	3,846,419	2,301,718	382,417	297,721	158,287	407,947	594,180	330,019	131,147	444,788	0	116,732	565,985	134,550
Alaska	2,430,593	2,201,270	1,218,685	913,896	180,052	154,044	30,576	133,786	269,143	64,056	82,239	60,491	8,198	8,633	181,341	39,349
Arizona	9,888,798	8,340,211	4,506,883	3,394,014	1,087,247	195,308	126,897	392,530	937,481	323,522	331,029	393,701	45,613	46,586	864,847	637,155
Arkansas	5,392,058	4,578,136	2,615,474	1,702,516	233,099	392,196	112,986	231,473	435,105	172,141	125,517	254,728	5,418	30,556	657,234	126,132
California	67,570,728	57,526,835	34,679,610	20,417,014	3,004,968	3,499,992	555,828	3,811,666	5,695,223	1,386,604	2,462,742	2,287,136	143,075	938,345	6,763,699	2,341,849
Colorado	8,743,162	7,409,462	4,250,693	2,868,302	361,218	420,592	159,259	495,909	695,046	217,522	518,757	254,581	35,885	58,479	835,266	439,936
Connecticut	9,944,121	9,094,036	5,768,873	3,031,013	555,702	281,253	178,833	515,530	842,535	449,853	207,308	219,101	75,049	145,124	563,519	141,441
Delaware	1,855,007	1,613,304	1,018,491	536,283	75,881	21,042	22,133	88,755	160,882	94,237	73,355	58,529		28,277	189,766	23,660
District of Columbia	2,063,029	1,482,202	754,464	670,690	86,134	114,951	61,731	110,235	165,485	100,107	32,047	54,224	2,824	37,802	391,652	151,373
Florida	27,433,536	23,870,090	14,566,298	8,237,108	1,066,264	1,541,508	253,657	1,343,045	2,471,262	959,102	602,272	1,066,684	0	570,458	2,217,064	775,923
Georgia	17,178,095	15,527,907	9,668,819	5,009,451	733,717	777,196	234,176	932,355	1,156,798	658,161	517,049	806,569	43,067	26,993	1,367,894	255,301
Hawaii	2,342,924	2,141,561	1,242,693	782,875	201,020	71,439	10,796	137,151	251,208	66,436	44,825	115,993	0	17,627	85,475	98,261
Idaho	2,107,272	1,881,746	1,148,131	637,447	106,724	75,237	42,676	105,642	171,558	91,532	44,077	95,780	389	4,151	160,083	61,292
Illinois	27,621,033	24,554,467	14,690,696	9,118,001	1,658,199	1,059,076	999,732	1,249,947	2,211,843	1,152,373	786,830	745,770	0	151,196	2,093,497	821,873
Indiana	11,037,564	9,687,949	5,702,356	3,555,487	456,293	367,778	251,190	558,236	1,097,726	582,621	241,642	430,106	0	139,215	871,863	358,537
Iowa	5,859,335	4,855,871	2,994,346	1,640,916	273,995	231,275	125,472	274,596	412,748	177,495	145,336	215,791	4,817	30,310	871,157	101,997
Kansas	5,824,926	4,741,372	2,873,575	1,651,762	275,382	202,415	139,658	271,235	443,398	191,568	128,107	216,035		4,295	869,746	209,512
Kentucky	7,200,059	6,211,453	3,641,680	2,197,751	279,805	337,676	137,247	345,210	576,020	376,894	144,898	356,658	15,365	83,981	747,269	157,355
Louisiana	8,502,295	7,522,098	4,380,197	2,743,272	369,620	410,213	177,276	437,419	700,509	435,310	212,926	398,537	92	45,343	812,767	122,086
Maine	2,630,548	2,377,878	1,442,329	859,075	155,421	124,072	76,259	127,845	232,893	114,101	28,484	76,393	80	28,301	172,590	51,778
Maryland	13,101,339	11,885,333	7,424,153	4,149,496	528,145	668,989	92,610	833,866	1,070,409	612,124	343,352	311,684	0	28,220	1,022,082	165,704
Massachusetts	15,069,052	13,962,366	9,065,657	4,533,618	976,118	626,630	187,359	568,925	1,272,280	574,858	327,449	363,090	0	56,033	799,311	251,343
Michigan	19,444,952	16,786,444	9,672,947	6,535,509	1,269,121	889,719	343,162	914,817	1,572,870	706,467	839,353	577,989	0	332,187	1,434,833	891,488
Minnesota	10,816,918	8,944,867	5,888,594	2,649,197	236,405	377,320	269,575	357,613	646,876	498,338	263,070	381,430	25,646	417,151	1,052,205	402,695
Mississippi	4,268,801	3,887,981	2,247,757	1,399,692	187,586	197,923	115,358	224,147	400,360	186,606	87,713	240,263	269	28,526	281,036	71,258
Missouri	10,072,167	8,691,887	5,208,082	3,090,488	406,335	389,078	274,499	496,717	871,391	444,318	208,149	393,317		198,591	854,963	326,725
Montana	1,653,315	1,518,818	909,036	543,485	93,752	57,707	43,611	81,039	158,869	72,215	36,291	62,689	3,607	11,231	107,204	16,062
Nebraska	3,761,444	3,345,530	2,184,356	940,164	119,389	105,806	102,689	161,343	282,492	100,850	67,594	135,441	85,569	2,629	331,914	81,372
Nevada	4,244,029	3,676,997	2,190,166	1,364,559	187,908	194,601	45,813	261,636	386,890	152,658	135,054	122,068	204	25,308	297,155	244,570
New Hampshire	2,896,807	2,637,911	1,712,141	855,470	190,003	81,626	85,942	140,018	217,962	111,866	28,052	70,300		7,823	206,275	44,799
New Jersey	25,308,865	23,639,281	14,209,004	8,659,183	2,290,750	732,617	483,063	1,117,966	2,345,908	1,169,718	519,162	510,851	260,243	146,882	855,532	667,171
New Mexico	3,641,735	3,127,463	1,793,031	1,191,752	325,026	88,261	70,665	187,111	322,521	103,320	94,849	140,845	1,836	3,862	510,320	90
New York	57,415,382	51,574,134	35,991,699	14,551,108	1,708,186	1,330,057	984,651	1,965,568	4,561,313	2,686,597	1,314,738	1,031,327	0	2,165,740	2,513,775	1,161,734
North Carolina	13,277,669	12,322,555	7,702,399	3,955,217	581,125	451,273	198,490	767,107	1,057,753	526,541	372,928	664,939	0	67,080	878,592	9,442
North Dakota	1,198,926	1,049,772	607,522	356,906	47,023	35,583	48,894	51,693	102,037	44,942	26,734	54,145	31,199	8,143	123,406	17,605
Ohio	23,500,247	19,988,921	11,372,653	7,956,671	1,268,590	1,335,790	598,776	1,130,956	1,782,173	949,390	890,996	658,520	1,077	436,310	2,535,352	539,664
Oklahoma	5,618,816	5,036,031	2,862,054	1,829,693	341,623	205,512	165,478	266,368	531,204	165,215	154,292	295,573	48,711	13,899	508,086	60,800
Oregon	6,201,702	5,430,888	3,165,170	2,067,274	387,583	219,223	71,446	340,070	447,946	249,061	351,945	195,412	3,032	25,737	461,338	283,739
Pennsylvania	27,393,554	23,485,203	14,382,313	8,213,549	1,215,179	866,873	692,759	1,028,872	2,327,779	1,188,411	893,677	786,566	102,775	569,951	2,271,818	1,066,582
Rhode Island	2,316,164	2,149,366	1,324,326	771,429	225,594	78,607	29,670	102,131	176,137	82,675	76,616	52,553	1,057	69,475	47,874	49,449
South Carolina	7,948,911	6,465,486	3,688,634	2,423,037	474,538	396,370	71,970	389,412	629,655	259,730	201,362	335,226	18,589	65,127	1,010,952	407,345
South Dakota	1,347,213	1,126,503	666,180	396,459	62,504	46,946	37,112	55,538	115,533	40,275	38,550	57,729	6,135	2,947	190,229	27,535
Tennessee	9,141,803	8,225,374	5,172,814	2,647,827	342,363	512,100	169,585	465,391	718,289	293,094	147,006	404,732	0	84,493	641,341	190,595
Texas	52,711,794	42,864,291	25,719,093	14,811,471	2,081,440	2,224,154	626,347	2,377,519	4,675,412	1,211,190	1,615,409	2,333,728	0	337,583	6,556,136	2,953,783
Utah	4,642,830	3,704,133	2,382,888	1,104,285	143,615	147,035	42,186	225,694	335,661	115,410	94,685	200,910	16,050	103,832	701,431	133,434

See notes at end of table.

Table 236.40. Total expenditures for public elementary and secondary education and other related programs, by function and state or jurisdiction: 2010-11—Continued

[In thousands of current dollars]

State or jurisdiction	Total	Elementary/ secondary current expenditures, total	Total expenditures — Current expenditures for elementary and secondary programs											Current expenditures for other programs[3]	Capital outlay[2]	Interest on school debt
			Instruction	Support services												
				Total	Student support[4]	Instructional staff[5]	General administration	School administration	Operation and maintenance	Student transportation	Other support services	Food services	Enterprise operations[4]			
1	2	3	4	5	6	7	8	9	10	11	12	13	14	15	16	17
Vermont	1,515,638	1,424,507	876,070	507,645	111,637	63,719	31,782	95,207	122,930	48,791	33,579	40,024	769	13,106	63,945	14,079
Virginia	14,291,767	12,968,457	7,861,182	4,602,565	627,158	862,346	199,556	750,559	1,263,117	695,293	204,535	502,837	1,873	74,580	1,075,075	173,655
Washington	12,025,483	10,040,312	6,067,366	3,516,776	671,779	402,544	192,069	572,454	896,173	408,823	372,934	335,166	121,004	57,362	1,514,773	413,036
West Virginia	3,515,624	3,388,294	2,029,616	1,178,712	153,000	133,942	66,053	180,907	337,813	248,745	58,252	179,966	0	46,185	65,730	15,415
Wisconsin	11,334,293	10,333,016	6,322,480	3,648,765	490,843	504,489	270,163	504,803	928,720	415,340	534,406	361,656	115	240,233	539,007	222,038
Wyoming	1,643,359	1,398,444	826,891	528,345	81,181	91,318	28,523	74,347	135,194	64,292	53,490	42,193	1,015	8,844	234,410	1,660
Other jurisdictions																
American Samoa	84,478	75,355	32,770	22,938	535	7,983	2,089	5,338	4,803	1,014	1,176	19,647	0	2,084	7,039	0
Guam	342,273	266,952	149,292	105,475	27,736	5,319	2,225	16,482	35,068	7,616	11,029	12,186	0	0	72,196	3,124
Northern Marianas	88,121	84,657	36,014	40,089	11,416	4,848	3,141	4,384	8,492	2,089	5,719	8,554	0	2,320	1,145	0
Puerto Rico	3,664,247	3,519,547	1,460,167	1,779,736	235,775	289,143	331,065	144,192	401,622	72,901	305,037	279,644	0	82,528	62,172	0
U.S. Virgin Islands	208,097	204,932	108,061	84,572	15,828	5,922	7,504	11,060	14,151	7,907	22,199	11,596	703	3,071	94	0

[1]Includes expenditures for adult education, community colleges, private school programs funded by local and state education agencies, and community services.

[2]Includes expenditures for property and for buildings and alterations completed by school district staff or contractors.

[3]Includes expenditures for operations funded by sales of products or services (e.g., school bookstore or computer time). Also includes small amounts for direct program support made by state education agencies for local school districts.

[4]Includes expenditures for guidance, health, attendance, and speech pathology services.

[5]Includes expenditures for curriculum development, staff training, libraries, and media and computer centers.

NOTE: Excludes expenditures for state education agencies. Detail may not sum to totals because of rounding. Some data have been revised from previously published figures.

SOURCE: U.S. Department of Education, National Center for Education Statistics, Common Core of Data (CCD), "National Public Education Financial Survey," 2010–11. (This table was prepared July 2014.)

Table 236.50. Expenditures for instruction in public elementary and secondary schools, by subfunction and state or jurisdiction: 2010–11 and 2011–12

[In thousands of current dollars]

| State or jurisdiction | 2010–11[1] | | | | | | 2011–12 | | | | | |
	Total	Salaries	Employee benefits	Purchased services[2]	Supplies	Tuition and other	Total	Salaries	Employee benefits	Purchased services[2]	Supplies	Tuition and other
1	2	3	4	5	6	7	8	9	10	11	12	13
United States	$322,536,983	$212,998,609	$75,248,811	$14,694,620	$13,135,284	$6,459,660	$320,952,573	$210,664,931	$76,946,902	$14,540,794	$12,436,951	$6,362,995
Alabama	3,846,419	2,500,993	983,940	112,088	235,134	14,264	3,698,119	2,442,365	872,821	120,379	246,710	15,844
Alaska	1,218,685	666,919	413,655	61,055	67,196	9,860	1,265,045	673,082	460,009	56,675	65,145	10,136
Arizona	4,506,883	3,256,513	770,957	225,929	99,765	153,720	4,359,402	3,027,601	861,743	269,410	173,792	26,856
Arkansas	2,615,474	1,798,852	492,291	98,070	196,051	30,210	2,606,990	1,791,543	490,983	95,351	198,824	30,288
California	34,679,610	22,874,871	7,843,569	1,741,303	1,461,634	758,232	34,834,633	22,845,108	8,250,199	1,724,400	1,254,825	760,100
Colorado	4,250,693	3,018,418	743,335	112,520	271,478	104,942	4,226,623	2,987,372	762,688	114,592	253,575	108,397
Connecticut	5,768,873	3,601,405	1,448,012	199,225	115,141	405,089	5,909,965	3,597,321	1,602,150	200,190	104,888	405,415
Delaware	1,018,491	643,671	281,665	24,378	54,010	14,767	1,116,490	675,131	334,281	14,835	56,812	35,431
District of Columbia	754,464	451,341	79,700	52,967	18,961	151,496	835,297	565,156	71,658	39,238	17,088	142,158
Florida	14,566,298	8,826,445	2,860,946	2,196,960	582,507	99,440	13,863,360	8,614,099	2,328,432	2,295,047	524,711	101,072
Georgia	9,668,819	6,661,760	2,226,686	224,261	505,759	50,354	9,661,561	6,626,114	2,231,871	235,960	521,023	46,593
Hawaii	1,242,693	829,260	263,734	68,519	64,916	16,264	1,253,486	814,926	284,553	63,248	73,373	17,386
Idaho	1,148,131	801,451	265,057	40,803	39,309	1,511	1,118,508	776,701	261,534	38,478	40,443	1,352
Illinois	14,690,696	9,447,166	3,839,639	678,624	397,632	327,634	15,062,473	9,543,026	4,086,127	723,338	390,371	319,612
Indiana	5,702,356	3,668,624	1,771,180	93,399	159,286	9,867	5,869,436	3,642,956	1,896,207	94,510	225,786	9,977
Iowa	2,994,346	2,111,774	670,350	82,724	99,366	30,132	3,056,382	2,136,793	701,068	80,257	105,506	32,757
Kansas	2,873,575	2,075,510	543,674	90,862	138,936	24,593	2,960,225	2,082,098	632,726	84,449	138,981	21,971
Kentucky	3,641,680	2,580,067	866,875	67,417	116,696	10,625	3,683,142	2,597,859	889,303	68,085	115,498	12,396
Louisiana	4,380,197	2,869,599	1,146,439	102,961	250,343	10,856	4,296,513	2,742,735	1,226,052	99,045	212,088	16,593
Maine	1,442,329	914,977	387,202	31,789	37,564	70,797	1,393,423	905,608	355,106	27,509	34,722	70,478
Maryland	7,424,153	4,708,564	2,025,230	227,255	206,217	256,886	7,362,229	4,632,076	2,070,610	205,132	190,263	264,149
Massachusetts	9,065,657	5,795,955	2,286,049	58,611	268,095	656,947	9,156,777	5,877,769	2,307,285	63,400	223,619	684,704
Michigan	9,672,947	5,711,512	2,916,048	732,872	293,849	18,666	9,569,531	5,565,714	2,945,017	789,381	249,001	20,417
Minnesota	5,888,594	4,026,985	1,258,416	337,946	188,447	76,800	5,936,623	4,058,508	1,294,397	318,001	185,373	80,343
Mississippi	2,247,757	1,569,391	475,160	62,080	126,656	14,469	2,266,650	1,577,427	482,207	64,024	127,490	15,504
Missouri	5,208,082	3,632,510	1,030,137	171,191	343,008	31,236	5,197,338	3,619,733	1,045,107	162,026	339,844	30,628
Montana	909,036	601,939	177,068	60,063	65,466	4,500	895,081	593,487	173,388	58,350	64,519	5,338
Nebraska	2,184,356	1,424,068	481,935	134,206	114,831	29,317	2,141,943	1,407,205	478,046	128,008	99,649	29,035
Nevada	2,190,166	1,439,113	536,624	56,334	155,303	2,791	2,094,490	1,381,696	537,318	59,790	111,032	4,654
New Hampshire	1,712,141	1,045,326	440,816	44,965	42,637	138,398	1,703,049	1,035,563	447,494	45,673	38,356	135,963
New Jersey	14,209,004	9,006,686	3,647,162	470,068	377,576	707,513	14,621,161	9,110,277	3,839,863	512,220	448,775	710,025
New Mexico	1,793,031	1,227,588	387,735	71,269	106,129	310	1,737,115	1,212,444	361,785	66,333	96,389	165
New York	35,991,699	22,144,969	10,225,443	2,139,690	714,985	766,612	36,402,730	22,224,345	10,879,678	1,947,269	629,095	722,344
North Carolina	7,702,399	5,450,501	1,566,742	267,061	418,096	0	7,670,507	5,318,475	1,658,938	263,158	429,912	24
North Dakota	607,522	426,980	131,943	17,890	27,023	3,686	641,580	446,277	142,380	19,344	26,894	6,684
Ohio	11,372,653	7,419,242	2,578,234	578,882	412,847	383,447	11,213,502	7,295,354	2,544,023	588,716	389,687	395,722
Oklahoma	2,862,054	2,017,034	613,229	47,986	174,222	9,583	2,876,209	2,036,896	621,640	53,612	152,807	11,254
Oregon	3,165,170	1,927,067	920,550	120,586	158,327	38,641	3,130,150	1,836,484	996,077	112,237	148,930	36,422
Pennsylvania	14,382,313	9,318,410	3,381,178	810,393	569,513	302,818	14,158,464	9,045,636	3,633,493	719,952	468,636	290,746
Rhode Island	1,324,326	861,668	347,020	10,339	25,252	80,047	1,343,508	860,983	368,579	11,330	19,188	83,428
South Carolina	3,688,634	2,569,308	796,285	128,228	171,226	23,588	3,743,777	2,571,505	821,616	126,537	200,712	23,407
South Dakota	666,180	449,743	130,050	32,994	44,733	8,660	646,885	433,855	129,205	31,170	42,887	9,768
Tennessee	5,172,814	3,467,350	1,132,546	110,668	447,223	15,027	5,192,746	3,483,791	1,144,100	106,230	444,156	14,470
Texas	25,719,093	19,881,407	3,074,615	865,178	1,602,088	295,805	24,251,087	18,848,805	2,844,914	828,320	1,445,811	283,237
Utah	2,382,888	1,503,172	632,253	73,759	165,709	7,994	2,406,489	1,514,906	637,549	79,258	166,169	8,606
Vermont	876,070	566,647	173,695	47,370	22,856	65,501	938,085	569,351	226,734	50,935	20,910	70,155
Virginia	7,861,182	5,573,464	1,732,130	191,019	353,681	10,888	8,123,189	5,651,526	1,903,355	195,852	360,645	11,812
Washington	6,067,366	4,120,582	1,294,236	349,878	249,485	53,185	5,863,499	3,962,433	1,324,490	314,111	211,497	50,968
West Virginia	2,029,616	1,116,785	747,810	38,357	122,536	4,128	1,919,623	1,146,316	613,799	40,563	114,884	4,061
Wisconsin	6,322,480	3,855,317	1,997,077	103,837	211,031	155,218	5,830,090	3,707,668	1,651,212	106,133	193,774	171,303
Wyoming	826,891	539,711	212,491	27,788	44,554	2,346	847,393	550,836	223,093	28,730	41,885	2,849
Other jurisdictions												
American Samoa	32,770	20,734	3,593	1,599	2,670	4,174	35,110	20,798	3,374	1,576	4,751	4,612
Guam	149,292	102,505	40,305	5,134	1,348	0	142,979	101,797	34,873	4,443	1,773	92
Northern Marianas	36,014	27,206	6,469	563	75	1,702	29,685	22,581	4,948	708	696	752
Puerto Rico	1,460,167	1,029,741	238,718	165,297	24,310	2,101	1,478,763	1,017,564	216,619	221,632	21,806	1,143
U.S. Virgin Islands	108,061	75,314	28,392	1,784	2,571	0	95,711	66,584	25,302	1,861	1,964	0

[1]Data have been revised from previously published figures.
[2]Includes purchased professional services of teachers or others who provide instruction for students.
NOTE: Excludes expenditures for state education agencies. Detail may not sum to totals because of rounding.

SOURCE: U.S. Department of Education, National Center for Education Statistics, Common Core of Data (CCD), "National Public Education Financial Survey," 2010–11 and 2011–12. (This table was prepared July 2014.)

Table 236.55. Total and current expenditures per pupil in public elementary and secondary schools: Selected years, 1919–20 through 2011–12

School year	Expenditure per pupil in average daily attendance				Expenditure per pupil in fall enrollment[1]				
	Unadjusted dollars[2]		Constant 2013–14 dollars[3]		Unadjusted dollars[2]		Constant 2013–14 dollars[3]		
	Total expenditure[4]	Current expenditure	Total expenditure[4]	Current expenditure	Total expenditure[4]	Current expenditure	Total expenditure[4]	Current expenditure	Annual percent change in current expenditure
1	2	3	4	5	6	7	8	9	10
1919–20	$64	$53	$788	$657	$48	$40	$590	$492	—
1929–30	108	87	1,489	1,190	90	72	1,233	986	—
1931–32	97	81	1,579	1,321	82	69	1,337	1,119	—
1933–34	76	67	1,353	1,197	65	57	1,149	1,017	—
1935–36	88	74	1,504	1,270	74	63	1,272	1,074	—
1937–38	100	84	1,635	1,376	86	72	1,404	1,181	—
1939–40	106	88	1,778	1,481	92	76	1,541	1,284	—
1941–42	110	98	1,658	1,482	94	84	1,420	1,269	—
1943–44	125	117	1,681	1,578	105	99	1,416	1,329	—
1945–46	146	136	1,879	1,757	124	116	1,601	1,497	—
1947–48	205	181	2,066	1,830	179	158	1,804	1,598	—
1949–50	260	210	2,583	2,087	231	187	2,292	1,852	—
1951–52	314	246	2,811	2,200	275	215	2,462	1,926	—
1953–54	351	265	3,066	2,314	312	236	2,727	2,058	—
1955–56	387	294	3,383	2,572	354	269	3,092	2,351	—
1957–58	447	341	3,681	2,807	408	311	3,357	2,560	—
1959–60	471	375	3,767	3,000	440	350	3,519	2,802	—
1961–62	517	419	4,043	3,275	485	393	3,793	3,073	—
1963–64	559	460	4,256	3,507	520	428	3,962	3,264	—
1965–66	654	538	4,815	3,960	607	499	4,470	3,676	—
1967–68	786	658	5,434	4,548	732	612	5,055	4,231	—
1969–70	955	816	5,940	5,076	879	751	5,469	4,673	—
1970–71	1,049	911	6,207	5,389	970	842	5,739	4,982	6.6
1971–72	1,128	990	6,440	5,651	1,034	908	5,906	5,183	4.0
1972–73	1,211	1,077	6,645	5,911	1,117	993	6,129	5,452	5.2
1973–74	1,364	1,207	6,873	6,084	1,244	1,101	6,267	5,547	1.7
1974–75	1,545	1,365	7,008	6,190	1,423	1,257	6,456	5,703	2.8
1975–76	1,697	1,504	7,191	6,371	1,563	1,385	6,622	5,866	2.9
1976–77	1,816	1,638	7,271	6,556	1,674	1,509	6,700	6,041	3.0
1977–78	2,002	1,823	7,512	6,838	1,842	1,677	6,909	6,289	4.1
1978–79	2,210	2,020	7,580	6,931	2,029	1,855	6,961	6,365	1.2
1979–80	2,491	2,272	7,538	6,876	2,290	2,088	6,930	6,321	-0.7
1980–81	2,742 [5]	2,502	7,438 [5]	6,786	2,529 [5]	2,307	6,861 [5]	6,259	-1.0
1981–82	2,973 [5]	2,726	7,424 [5]	6,805	2,754 [5]	2,525	6,877 [5]	6,304	0.7
1982–83	3,203 [5]	2,955	7,669 [5]	7,075	2,966 [5]	2,736	7,101 [5]	6,551	3.9
1983–84	3,471 [5]	3,173	8,013 [5]	7,326	3,216 [5]	2,940	7,424 [5]	6,786	3.6
1984–85	3,722 [5]	3,470	8,268 [5]	7,710	3,456 [5]	3,222	7,677 [5]	7,158	5.5
1985–86	4,020 [5]	3,756	8,680 [5]	8,109	3,724 [5]	3,479	8,042 [5]	7,513	5.0
1986–87	4,308 [5]	3,970	9,100 [5]	8,387	3,995 [5]	3,682	8,439 [5]	7,777	3.5
1987–88	4,654 [5]	4,240	9,440 [5]	8,600	4,310 [5]	3,927	8,742 [5]	7,965	2.4
1988–89	5,108	4,645	9,903	9,005	4,737	4,307	9,183	8,351	4.8
1989–90	5,547	4,980	10,265	9,215	5,172	4,643	9,570	8,591	2.9
1990–91	5,882	5,258	10,320	9,225	5,484	4,902	9,621	8,601	0.1
1991–92	6,072	5,421	10,323	9,216	5,626	5,023	9,565	8,540	-0.7
1992–93	6,279	5,584	10,352	9,205	5,802	5,160	9,566	8,506	-0.4
1993–94	6,489	5,767	10,428	9,268	5,994	5,327	9,632	8,561	0.6
1994–95	6,723	5,989	10,502	9,356	6,206	5,529	9,695	8,637	0.9
1995–96	6,959	6,147	10,584	9,348	6,441	5,689	9,796	8,652	0.2
1996–97	7,297	6,393	10,790	9,453	6,761	5,923	9,998	8,759	1.2
1997–98	7,701	6,676	11,187	9,698	7,139	6,189	10,372	8,991	2.7
1998–99	8,115	7,013	11,589	10,015	7,531	6,508	10,754	9,294	3.4
1999–2000	8,589	7,394	11,921	10,262	8,030	6,912	11,145	9,594	3.2
2000–01	9,180	7,904	12,319	10,606	8,572	7,380	11,503	9,904	3.2
2001–02	9,611	8,259	12,673	10,890	8,993	7,727	11,858	10,189	2.9
2002–03	9,950	8,610	12,838	11,109	9,296	8,044	11,995	10,379	1.9
2003–04	10,308	8,900	13,015	11,237	9,625	8,310	12,153	10,493	1.1
2004–05	10,779	9,316	13,212	11,419	10,078	8,711	12,354	10,677	1.8
2005–06	11,338	9,778	13,387	11,546	10,603	9,145	12,520	10,798	1.1
2006–07	12,015	10,336	13,830	11,897	11,252	9,679	12,951	11,141	3.2
2007–08	12,759	10,982	14,161	12,189	11,965	10,298	13,280	11,430	2.6
2008–09	13,033	11,239	14,266	12,302	12,222	10,540	13,379	11,537	0.9
2009–10	13,035	11,427	14,132	12,388	12,133	10,636	13,154	11,531	-0.1
2010–11[6]	12,926	11,433	13,737	12,151	12,054	10,663	12,811	11,332	-1.7
2011–12	12,794	11,363	13,210	11,732	12,010	10,667	12,401	11,014	-2.8

—Not available.
[1]Data for 1919–20 to 1953–54 are based on school-year enrollment.
[2]Unadjusted (or "current") dollars have not been adjusted to compensate for inflation.
[3]Constant dollars based on the Consumer Price Index, prepared by the Bureau of Labor Statistics, U.S. Department of Labor, adjusted to a school-year basis.
[4]Excludes "Other current expenditures," such as community services, private school programs, adult education, and other programs not allocable to expenditures per student at public schools.
[5]Estimated.
[6]Revised from previously published figures.

NOTE: Beginning in 1980–81, state administration expenditures are excluded from both "total" and "current" expenditures. Current expenditures include instruction, support services, food services, and enterprise operations. Total expenditures include current expenditures, capital outlay, and interest on debt. Beginning in 1988–89, extensive changes were made in the data collection procedures.
SOURCE: U.S. Department of Education, National Center for Education Statistics, *Biennial Survey of Education in the United States*, 1919–20 through 1955–56; *Statistics of State School Systems*, 1957–58 through 1969–70; *Revenues and Expenditures for Public Elementary and Secondary Education*, 1970–71 through 1986–87; and Common Core of Data (CCD), "National Public Education Financial Survey," 1987–88 through 2011–12. (This table was prepared July 2014.)

Table 236.60. Total and current expenditures per pupil in fall enrollment in public elementary and secondary schools, by function and subfunction: Selected years, 1990–91 through 2011–12

Function and subfunction	Expenditures per pupil in current dollars									Expenditures per pupil in constant 2013–14 dollars[1]								
	1990–91	1999–2000	2000–01	2005–06	2007–08	2008–09	2009–10	2010–11[2]	2011–12	1990–91	1999–2000	2000–01	2005–06	2007–08	2008–09	2009–10	2010–11[2]	2011–12
1	2	3	4	5	6	7	8	9	10	11	12	13	14	15	16	17	18	19
Total expenditures	$5,484	$8,030	$8,572	$10,603	$11,965	$12,222	$12,133	$12,054	$12,010	$9,621	$11,145	$11,503	$12,520	$13,280	$13,379	$13,154	$12,811	$12,401
Current expenditures for public schools	4,902	6,912	7,380	9,145	10,298	10,540	10,636	10,663	10,667	8,601	9,594	9,904	10,798	11,430	11,537	11,531	11,332	11,014
Salaries	3,220[3]	4,485	4,752	5,561	6,177	6,348	6,366	6,300	6,242	5,650[3]	6,225	6,377	6,567	6,855	6,949	6,901	6,695	6,446
Employee benefits	824[3]	1,138	1,228	1,790	2,093	2,146	2,199	2,260	2,313	1,445[3]	1,580	1,648	2,113	2,323	2,349	2,384	2,402	2,389
Purchased services	397[3]	620	673	880	1,000	1,030	1,053	1,082	1,101	697[3]	861	903	1,039	1,110	1,128	1,142	1,150	1,137
Tuition	29[3]	48	52	78	93	91	96	101	102	51[3]	66	70	92	103	100	104	107	105
Supplies	359[3]	553	599	746	840	825	818	817	810	630[3]	767	803	881	933	903	886	869	836
Other	72[3]	69	76	90	96	99	104	103	98	127[3]	95	102	107	106	108	113	109	101
Instruction	2,965	4,268	4,541	5,574	6,262	6,420	6,511	6,522	6,495	5,203	5,923	6,093	6,582	6,951	7,027	7,059	6,932	6,706
Salaries	2,202	3,096	3,273	3,806	4,199	4,325	4,347	4,307	4,263	3,863	4,297	4,393	4,494	4,661	4,735	4,712	4,578	4,402
Employee benefits	542	773	837	1,202	1,407	1,443	1,481	1,522	1,557	951	1,072	1,124	1,419	1,562	1,579	1,605	1,617	1,608
Purchased services	66	125	136	205	249	260	281	297	294	116	173	183	242	276	284	304	316	304
Tuition	29	48	52	78	93	91	96	101	102	51	66	70	92	103	100	104	107	105
Supplies	111	208	220	259	287	273	277	266	252	195	289	295	306	319	298	301	282	260
Textbooks	—	—	—	52	55	60	52	47	44	—	—	—	61	61	65	56	50	46
Other	15	19	22	24	27	28	29	30	27	27	26	29	28	30	31	32	32	28
Student support[4]	217	342	366	475	559	580	591	594	594	380	475	492	561	620	634	640	631	613
Salaries	159	245	262	322	372	388	393	392	386	280	341	351	381	413	425	426	416	399
Employee benefits	40	61	64	99	120	125	128	132	138	71	84	86	117	133	137	139	140	142
Purchased services	11	25	28	40	48	49	50	52	55	19	35	38	47	54	54	55	56	57
Supplies	5	8	9	10	11	11	11	11	11	8	12	12	12	12	12	12	11	11
Other	1	3	3	4	7	7	7	7	4	2	4	4	5	7	8	8	8	4
Instructional staff services[5]	205	312	337	446	515	508	509	503	495	360	434	453	527	572	556	552	535	511
Salaries	135	191	207	265	309	304	301	293	288	237	266	278	313	343	333	326	311	297
Employee benefits	34	46	50	79	95	96	98	100	100	60	64	67	94	106	106	106	106	103
Purchased services	15	38	42	60	67	66	69	70	68	26	53	57	71	74	72	74	74	71
Supplies	19	32	33	38	40	37	40	37	34	33	44	45	45	44	41	40	39	35
Other	2	5	4	4	4	4	5	4	4	4	7	6	5	5	8	8	5	5
General administration	141	143	151	182	200	207	211	212	214	247	198	202	214	222	227	229	226	221
Salaries	63	68	71	79	87	90	90	89	89	111	94	95	93	97	98	98	95	91
Employee benefits	19	20	21	30	34	35	37	38	39	33	28	28	36	38	39	40	40	40
Purchased services	36	41	44	56	60	64	64	65	67	63	58	60	66	67	71	69	70	69
Supplies	4	4	4	5	5	5	5	5	5	7	6	9	5	5	6	5	5	5
Other	18	9	10	13	14	13	16	16	15	32	13	13	15	15	14	17	17	15
School administration	284	392	415	515	576	581	579	580	585	498	544	557	608	639	636	627	616	604
Salaries	217	297	314	370	410	417	413	408	409	380	412	421	437	455	456	447	434	422
Employee benefits	55	74	78	114	133	134	136	141	145	96	102	105	135	148	147	148	150	150
Purchased services	6	12	13	18	20	19	19	19	20	11	17	17	21	22	21	20	20	9
Supplies	5	7	8	10	10	9	9	9	9	8	10	10	11	11	10	9	9	9
Other	2	2	2	3	3	2	3	3	3	5	3	3	3	3	3	3	3	3
Operation and maintenance	517	666	721	902	1,003	1,027	1,014	1,015	1,008	906	924	968	1,065	1,113	1,124	1,099	1,079	1,041
Salaries	215	272	285	326	359	367	364	356	353	377	378	383	385	398	401	395	378	364
Employee benefits	64	75	80	119	136	140	143	146	148	112	105	107	140	151	153	155	155	153
Purchased services	139	189	204	243	265	267	265	270	272	244	263	274	286	294	292	288	287	281
Supplies	91	124	146	207	234	245	233	235	228	160	172	195	244	260	268	252	250	235
Other	8	6	6	8	9	9	9	8	8	14	7	9	5	10	10	10	9	9
Student transportation	211	278	298	384	438	440	442	452	464	369	385	400	453	486	482	479	481	479
Salaries	80	108	115	136	153	154	155	152	151	140	150	154	161	169	169	168	162	156
Employee benefits	22	31	34	52	58	60	62	63	64	38	43	45	61	65	65	67	67	66
Purchased services	81	114	122	154	174	183	182	185	192	142	158	164	181	193	200	197	197	198
Supplies	23	22	25	38	49	40	40	48	52	41	31	33	45	55	44	43	51	54
Other	5	2	3	3	3	3	4	4	4	8	2	4	5	4	4	4	4	5

See notes at end of table.

Table 236.60. Total and current expenditures per pupil in fall enrollment in public elementary and secondary schools, by function and subfunction: Selected years, 1990–91 through 2011–12—Continued

Function and subfunction	Expenditures per pupil in current dollars									Expenditures per pupil in constant 2013–14 dollars[1]								
	1990–91	1999–2000	2000–01	2005–06	2007–08	2008–09	2009–10	2010–11[2]	2011–12	1990–91	1999–2000	2000–01	2005–06	2007–08	2008–09	2009–10	2010–11[2]	2011–12
1	2	3	4	5	6	7	8	9	10	11	12	13	14	15	16	17	18	19
Other support services[6]	136	217	242	294	331	349	348	349	361	238	302	325	348	368	382	378	371	373
Salaries	70	105	117	134	153	164	165	165	165	123	146	157	158	170	180	179	175	171
Employee benefits	24	31	34	51	61	64	64	67	69	42	42	45	60	67	70	69	71	71
Purchased services	19	53	59	70	77	80	79	78	85	34	73	79	83	85	87	86	83	88
Supplies	7	12	13	16	20	18	17	18	18	13	17	18	19	22	20	19	19	19
Other	15	17	19	23	21	23	23	21	23	26	23	26	28	24	25	25	23	24
Food services	205	276	293	352	390	402	405	412	429	359	384	393	415	433	440	439	438	443
Salaries	—	98	105	119	129	132	131	131	133	—	136	141	140	143	145	142	139	137
Employee benefits	—	27	29	42	46	48	49	50	51	—	38	39	50	51	52	53	54	53
Purchased services	—	19	20	30	35	37	39	42	44	—	27	26	35	38	40	42	44	45
Supplies	—	129	136	157	177	181	181	184	196	—	179	183	186	197	198	197	196	202
Other	—	3	3	3	3	4	5	5	5	—	4	4	4	4	5	5	5	5
Enterprise operations[7]	23	17	16	21	24	26	25	22	22	40	24	22	25	27	28	28	24	23
Salaries	—	4	3	4	6	7	7	7	6	—	5	4	5	7	8	7	7	6
Employee benefits	—	1	1	2	2	2	2	2	2	—	1	1	2	2	2	2	2	2
Purchased services	—	4	4	5	5	5	5	3	4	—	5	5	6	5	6	6	4	4
Supplies	—	6	5	6	7	7	7	6	6	—	8	7	7	8	8	8	6	6
Other	—	3	4	4	4	4	4	4	4	—	4	6	5	5	5	5	5	6
Capital outlay[8]	477	923	976	1,166	1,348	1,336	1,148	1,029	985	837	1,281	1,310	1,377	1,496	1,463	1,244	1,094	1,018
Interest on school debt	105	195	215	292	319	346	349	363	358	184	271	289	345	354	379	379	385	370

—Not available.
[1]Constant dollars based on the Consumer Price Index, prepared by the Bureau of Labor Statistics, U.S. Department of Labor, adjusted to a school-year basis.
[2]Data have been revised from previously published figures.
[3]Includes estimated data for subfunctions of food services and enterprise operations.
[4]Includes expenditures for guidance, health, attendance, and speech pathology services.
[5]Includes expenditures for curriculum development, staff training, libraries, and media and computer centers.
[6]Includes business support services concerned with paying, transporting, exchanging, and maintaining goods and services for local education agencies; central support services, including planning, research, evaluation, information, staff, and data processing services; and other support services.
[7]Includes expenditures for operations funded by sales of products or services (e.g., school bookstore or computer time).
[8]Includes expenditures for property and for buildings and alterations completed by school district staff or contractors.
NOTE: Excludes expenditures for state education agencies. Detail may not sum to totals because of rounding.
SOURCE: U.S. Department of Education, National Center for Education Statistics, Common Core of Data (CCD), "National Public Education Financial Survey," 1990–91 through 2011–12. (This table was prepared July 2014.)

Table 236.65. Current expenditure per pupil in fall enrollment in public elementary and secondary schools, by state or jurisdiction: Selected years, 1969–70 through 2011–12

State or jurisdiction	1969–70	1979–80	1989–90	1999–2000	2001–02	2002–03	2003–04	2004–05	2005–06	2006–07	2007–08	2008–09	2009–10	2010–11	2011–12
1	2	3	4	5	6	7	8	9	10	11	12	13	14	15	16
United States	$751	$2,088	$4,643	$6,912	$7,727	$8,044	$8,310	$8,711	$9,145	$9,679	$10,298	$10,540	$10,636	$10,663	$10,667
Alabama	512	1,520	3,144	5,638	6,029	6,300	6,581	7,073	7,683	8,398	9,197	8,964	8,907	8,726	8,577
Alaska	1,059	4,267	7,577	8,806	9,564	9,870	10,116	10,847	11,476	12,324	14,641	15,363	15,829	16,663	17,475
Arizona	674	1,865	3,717	5,030	5,851	6,283	5,999	6,307	6,515	7,316	7,727	8,022	7,870	7,782	7,382
Arkansas	511	1,472	3,229	5,277	6,276	6,482	6,842	7,659	8,030	8,391	8,677	8,854	9,281	9,496	9,536
California	833	2,227	4,502	6,314	7,405	7,552	7,673	7,905	8,301	8,952	9,706	9,503	9,300	9,146	9,329
Colorado	686	2,258	4,357	6,215	6,941	7,384	7,478	7,826	8,166	8,286	9,152	8,782	8,926	8,786	8,594
Connecticut	911	2,167	7,463	9,753	10,577	11,057	11,436	12,263	13,072	13,659	14,610	15,353	15,698	16,224	16,855
Delaware	833	2,587	5,326	8,310	9,285	9,693	10,212	10,911	11,621	11,760	12,153	12,109	12,222	12,467	13,580
District of Columbia	947	2,811	7,872	10,107	12,102	11,847	12,959	13,915	13,752	15,511	16,353	19,698	20,910	20,793	19,847
Florida	683	1,834	4,597	5,831	6,213	6,439	6,793	7,215	7,812	8,567	9,084	8,867	8,863	9,030	8,520
Georgia	539	1,491	4,000	6,437	7,380	7,774	7,742	8,065	8,595	9,102	9,718	9,649	9,432	9,259	9,272
Hawaii	792	2,086	4,130	6,530	7,306	8,100	8,533	8,997	9,876	11,316	11,800	12,400	11,855	11,924	11,973
Idaho	573	1,548	2,921	5,315	6,011	6,081	6,168	6,319	6,469	6,648	6,951	7,118	7,100	6,821	6,626
Illinois	816	2,241	4,521	7,133	7,956	8,287	8,606	8,896	9,113	9,596	10,353	11,097	11,739	11,742	12,011
Indiana	661	1,708	4,270	7,192	7,734	8,057	8,431	8,919	8,929	9,080	8,867	9,254	9,479	9,251	9,588
Iowa	798	2,164	4,190	6,564	7,338	7,574	7,626	7,962	8,355	8,791	9,520	9,704	9,748	9,795	10,027
Kansas	699	1,963	4,290	6,294	7,339	7,454	7,776	7,926	8,640	9,243	9,894	10,204	9,972	9,802	10,021
Kentucky	502	1,557	3,384	5,921	6,523	6,661	6,864	7,132	7,668	7,941	8,740	8,786	8,957	9,228	9,327
Louisiana	589	1,629	3,625	5,804	6,567	6,922	7,271	7,669	8,486	8,937	10,006	10,625	10,701	10,799	10,726
Maine	649	1,692	4,903	7,667	8,818	9,344	9,746	10,342	10,841	11,644	11,761	12,183	12,525	12,576	12,335
Maryland	809	2,293	5,573	7,731	8,692	9,153	9,433	10,031	10,909	11,989	13,257	13,737	14,007	13,946	13,871
Massachusetts	791	2,548	5,766	8,816	10,232	10,460	11,015	11,642	12,087	12,784	13,690	14,534	13,956	14,612	14,844
Michigan	841	2,495	5,090	8,110	8,653	8,781	9,094	9,338	9,575	9,876	10,075	10,373	10,447	10,577	10,477
Minnesota	855	2,296	4,698	7,190	7,736	8,109	8,405	8,718	9,159	9,589	10,060	10,983	10,665	10,674	10,781
Mississippi	457	1,568	2,934	5,014	5,354	5,792	6,199	6,548	7,173	7,459	7,890	8,064	8,104	7,926	8,097
Missouri	596	1,724	4,071	6,187	7,136	7,495	7,542	7,858	8,273	8,848	9,532	9,617	9,721	9,461	9,514
Montana	728	2,264	4,240	6,314	7,062	7,496	7,825	8,133	8,626	9,191	9,786	10,120	10,565	10,719	10,569
Nebraska	700	2,025	4,553	6,683	7,741	8,074	8,452	8,794	9,324	10,068	10,565	10,846	11,339	11,704	11,640
Nevada	706	1,908	3,816	5,760	6,079	6,092	6,410	6,804	7,177	7,796	8,187	8,321	8,376	8,411	8,130
New Hampshire	666	1,732	4,786	6,860	7,935	8,579	9,161	9,771	10,396	11,036	11,951	12,583	13,072	13,548	13,774
New Jersey	924	2,825	7,546	10,337	11,793	12,568	13,338	14,117	14,954	16,163	17,620	16,973	17,379	16,855	17,982
New Mexico	665	1,870	3,446	5,825	6,882	7,125	7,572	7,834	8,354	8,849	9,291	9,648	9,621	9,250	9,013
New York	1,194	2,950	7,051	9,846	11,218	11,961	12,638	13,703	14,615	15,546	16,794	17,746	18,167	18,857	19,396
North Carolina	570	1,635	4,018	6,045	6,495	6,562	6,613	7,098	7,396	7,878	7,798	8,463	8,225	8,267	8,160
North Dakota	662	1,941	3,899	5,667	6,709	6,870	7,333	8,279	8,728	8,671	9,324	9,802	10,519	10,898	11,246
Ohio	677	1,894	4,531	7,065	8,069	8,632	9,029	9,330	9,692	9,937	10,340	10,669	11,224	11,395	11,323
Oklahoma	554	1,810	3,293	5,395	6,229	6,092	6,154	6,610	6,941	7,430	7,683	7,878	7,929	7,631	7,763
Oregon	843	2,412	4,864	7,149	7,642	7,491	7,618	8,069	8,645	8,958	9,565	9,611	9,268	9,516	9,485
Pennsylvania	815	2,328	5,737	7,772	8,537	8,997	9,708	10,235	10,723	10,905	11,741	12,299	12,729	13,096	13,091
Rhode Island	807	2,340	5,908	8,904	9,703	10,349	11,078	11,667	12,609	13,453	14,459	14,719	14,723	14,948	15,172
South Carolina	567	1,597	3,769	6,130	7,017	7,040	7,177	7,549	8,120	8,507	9,060	9,228	9,080	8,908	9,077
South Dakota	656	1,781	3,511	5,632	6,424	6,547	7,068	7,464	7,775	8,064	8,535	8,543	9,020	8,931	8,593
Tennessee	531	1,523	3,405	5,383	5,948	6,118	6,466	6,850	7,004	7,129	7,820	7,992	8,117	8,330	8,354
Texas	551	1,740	3,835	6,288	6,771	7,136	7,151	7,246	7,480	7,850	8,350	8,562	8,788	8,685	8,213
Utah	595	1,556	2,577	4,378	4,899	4,838	4,991	5,216	5,464	5,709	5,978	6,612	6,452	6,440	6,441
Vermont	790	1,930	5,770	8,323	9,806	10,454	11,211	11,972	12,805	13,629	14,421	15,096	15,666	14,707	16,651
Virginia	654	1,824	4,690	6,841	7,496	7,822	8,219	8,886	9,452	10,214	10,664	10,928	10,594	10,363	10,656
Washington	853	2,387	4,382	6,376	7,039	7,252	7,391	7,717	7,984	8,524	9,058	9,585	9,497	9,619	9,617
West Virginia	621	1,749	4,020	7,152	7,844	8,319	8,588	9,024	9,440	9,727	10,059	10,606	11,774	11,978	11,579
Wisconsin	793	2,225	5,020	7,806	8,634	9,004	9,240	9,755	9,993	10,372	10,791	11,183	11,507	11,947	11,233
Wyoming	805	2,369	5,239	7,425	8,645	8,985	9,308	10,190	11,437	13,266	13,856	14,628	15,232	15,815	15,988
Other jurisdictions															
American Samoa	—	—	1,781	2,739	2,906	2,976	3,493	3,607	3,561	3,481	—	—	—	—	—
Guam	766	—	3,817	—	—	—	5,781	—	6,781	—	—	—	—	8,443	9,300
Northern Marianas	—	—	3,356	5,120	4,438	4,519	4,241	5,034	4,924	4,707	4,535	5,753	5,676	7,623	6,246
Puerto Rico	—	—	1,605	3,404	3,563	4,260	4,147	4,979	5,470	6,006	6,520	6,955	7,021	7,429	7,403
U.S. Virgin Islands	—	—	6,043	6,478	5,716	6,840	7,239	8,387	8,768	9,669	12,358	12,768	14,215	13,226	11,669

See notes at end of table.

Table 236.65. Current expenditure per pupil in fall enrollment in public elementary and secondary schools, by state or jurisdiction: Selected years, 1969–70 through 2010–11—Continued

State or jurisdiction	Constant 2013–14 dollars[2]														
	1969–70	1979–80	1989–90	1999–2000	2001–02	2002–03	2003–04	2004–05	2005–06	2006–07	2007–08	2008–09	2009–10	2010–11	2011–12
1	17	18	19	20	21	22	23	24	25	26	27	28	29	30	31
United States..............	$4,673	$6,321	$8,591	$9,594	$10,189	$10,379	$10,493	$10,677	$10,798	$11,141	$11,430	$11,537	$11,531	$11,332	$11,014
Alabama..........................	3,182	4,602	5,817	7,825	7,950	8,128	8,310	8,670	9,072	9,666	10,207	9,812	9,656	9,274	8,856
Alaska.............................	6,588	12,915	14,022	12,223	12,611	12,735	12,773	13,295	13,551	14,186	16,250	16,816	17,160	17,709	18,044
Arizona...........................	4,195	5,645	6,879	6,981	7,715	8,107	7,575	7,731	7,693	8,421	8,577	8,781	8,532	8,270	7,622
Arkansas.........................	3,178	4,455	5,975	7,325	8,275	8,364	8,638	9,388	9,482	9,659	9,630	9,692	10,061	10,092	9,846
California........................	5,184	6,739	8,332	8,764	9,765	9,744	9,689	9,689	9,802	10,304	10,773	10,402	10,082	9,721	9,633
Colorado.........................	4,267	6,834	8,062	8,626	9,152	9,527	9,442	9,593	9,643	9,537	10,158	9,612	9,676	9,338	8,874
Connecticut.....................	5,665	6,559	13,810	13,536	13,946	14,267	14,439	15,031	15,435	15,722	16,215	16,806	17,019	17,242	17,403
Delaware.........................	5,184	7,829	9,856	11,533	12,243	12,507	12,894	13,374	13,722	13,536	13,488	13,254	13,251	13,250	14,022
District of Columbia	5,890	8,509	14,567	14,028	15,958	15,285	16,362	17,057	16,238	17,854	18,150	21,562	22,669	22,098	20,492
Florida............................	4,246	5,551	8,507	8,093	8,193	8,308	8,578	8,844	9,224	9,861	10,082	9,705	9,608	9,597	8,797
Georgia..........................	3,351	4,513	7,402	8,934	9,732	10,031	9,776	9,886	10,149	10,477	10,785	10,562	10,226	9,840	9,574
Hawaii.............................	4,926	6,315	7,643	9,063	9,634	10,452	10,774	11,028	11,661	13,025	13,097	13,573	12,852	12,673	12,362
Idaho..............................	3,566	4,686	5,405	7,376	7,926	7,847	7,788	7,746	7,639	7,652	7,715	7,791	7,698	7,250	6,842
Illinois............................	5,074	6,783	8,366	9,900	10,491	10,692	10,867	10,904	10,761	11,045	11,491	12,147	12,726	12,479	12,402
Indiana............................	4,113	5,170	7,902	9,982	10,199	10,396	10,645	10,932	10,543	10,451	9,841	10,129	10,276	9,832	9,899
Iowa................................	4,965	6,550	7,753	9,111	9,676	9,772	9,629	9,759	9,865	10,119	10,566	10,622	10,568	10,409	10,353
Kansas...........................	4,347	5,941	7,938	8,735	9,678	9,618	9,818	9,715	10,202	10,638	10,982	11,169	10,811	10,418	10,347
Kentucky.........................	3,122	4,713	6,261	8,218	8,602	8,595	8,667	8,742	9,055	9,140	9,700	9,617	9,711	9,807	9,630
Louisiana........................	3,666	4,930	6,708	8,056	8,659	8,932	9,180	9,401	10,020	10,287	11,106	11,630	11,601	11,477	11,075
Maine..............................	4,038	5,121	9,073	10,642	11,627	12,056	12,306	12,677	12,801	13,402	13,054	13,335	13,579	13,366	12,736
Maryland.........................	5,033	6,939	10,313	10,730	11,461	11,809	11,911	12,296	12,881	13,800	14,713	15,036	15,185	14,822	14,322
Massachusetts.................	4,918	7,711	10,670	12,236	13,492	13,496	13,908	14,270	14,272	14,715	15,195	15,909	15,130	15,529	15,327
Michigan.........................	5,234	7,553	9,419	11,256	11,410	11,329	11,482	11,446	11,306	11,368	11,182	11,354	11,325	11,241	10,817
Minnesota.......................	5,317	6,950	8,694	9,979	10,201	10,463	10,612	10,686	10,815	11,037	11,166	12,022	11,562	11,344	11,131
Mississippi......................	2,841	4,747	5,429	6,959	7,060	7,474	7,827	8,027	8,470	8,585	8,757	8,827	8,785	8,424	8,361
Missouri..........................	3,707	5,218	7,533	8,587	9,409	9,670	9,523	9,632	9,769	10,184	10,580	10,527	10,538	10,055	9,823
Montana..........................	4,526	6,851	7,846	8,763	9,312	9,671	9,880	9,969	10,185	10,579	10,862	11,078	11,454	11,392	10,913
Nebraska.........................	4,353	6,127	8,425	9,276	10,207	10,417	10,672	10,779	11,009	11,589	11,726	11,872	12,293	12,439	12,018
Nevada	4,390	5,775	7,061	7,994	8,016	7,860	8,094	8,340	8,474	8,973	9,086	9,108	9,081	8,939	8,394
New Hampshire.................	4,143	5,242	8,856	9,521	10,463	11,069	11,568	11,977	12,275	12,703	13,264	13,774	14,171	14,398	14,222
New Jersey......................	5,746	8,551	13,963	14,348	15,551	16,216	16,841	17,304	17,658	18,604	19,556	18,579	18,841	17,913	18,567
New Mexico	4,137	5,661	6,376	8,085	9,075	9,193	9,560	9,602	9,864	10,186	10,312	10,561	10,430	9,830	9,306
New York..........................	7,429	8,930	13,047	13,666	14,792	15,433	15,957	16,797	17,257	17,894	18,640	19,425	19,695	20,041	20,027
North Carolina..................	3,548	4,950	7,436	8,390	8,564	8,467	8,349	8,700	8,733	9,067	8,655	9,264	8,916	8,786	8,425
North Dakota....................	4,120	5,876	7,215	7,865	8,846	8,864	9,259	10,148	10,305	9,980	10,348	10,729	11,404	11,583	11,611
Ohio................................	4,208	5,734	8,384	9,805	10,640	11,138	11,401	11,436	11,444	11,438	11,476	11,678	12,168	12,110	11,691
Oklahoma........................	3,444	5,477	6,094	7,487	8,214	7,860	7,770	8,103	8,196	8,552	8,527	8,623	8,596	8,110	8,015
Oregon............................	5,245	7,301	9,002	9,922	10,077	9,666	9,618	9,890	10,208	10,311	10,616	10,520	10,047	10,113	9,793
Pennsylvania....................	5,071	7,047	10,617	10,787	11,257	11,608	12,258	12,546	12,662	12,552	13,032	13,463	13,799	13,918	13,517
Rhode Island	5,018	7,083	10,933	12,359	12,794	13,353	13,988	14,301	14,888	15,485	16,048	16,112	15,962	15,886	15,666
South Carolina..................	3,528	4,834	6,975	8,508	9,253	9,083	9,061	9,254	9,588	9,792	10,056	10,101	9,844	9,467	9,372
South Dakota...................	4,081	5,390	6,497	7,817	8,470	8,447	8,925	9,149	9,181	9,282	9,473	9,351	9,778	9,492	8,873
Tennessee.......................	3,302	4,610	6,301	7,471	7,843	7,893	8,164	8,397	8,270	8,206	8,679	8,748	8,800	8,853	8,625
Texas..............................	3,428	5,265	7,096	8,727	8,928	9,208	9,029	8,881	8,833	9,035	9,267	9,372	9,527	9,230	8,480
Utah................................	3,702	4,710	4,769	6,077	6,461	6,242	6,302	6,394	6,452	6,571	6,635	7,238	6,995	6,844	6,650
Vermont...........................	4,911	5,842	10,678	11,551	12,930	13,489	14,155	14,675	15,120	15,687	16,006	16,524	16,984	15,630	17,193
Virginia............................	4,071	5,521	8,678	9,495	9,884	10,092	10,378	10,892	11,160	11,757	11,836	11,962	11,486	11,013	11,002
Washington......................	5,307	7,225	8,110	8,850	9,282	9,357	9,333	9,459	9,428	9,811	10,053	10,311	10,492	10,296	9,930
West Virginia....................	3,865	5,292	7,439	9,926	10,343	10,734	10,843	11,061	11,147	11,196	11,164	11,610	12,765	12,730	11,955
Wisconsin........................	4,933	6,734	9,289	10,835	11,385	11,618	11,666	11,957	11,799	11,938	11,977	12,241	12,475	12,697	11,599
Wyoming.........................	5,007	7,170	9,695	10,306	11,399	11,593	11,753	12,490	13,504	15,269	15,379	16,012	16,513	16,807	16,508
Other jurisdictions															
American Samoa	—	—	3,297	3,802	3,831	3,840	4,411	4,421	4,205	4,007	—	—	—	—	—
Guam..............................	4,768	—	7,064	—	—	—	7,299	—	8,007	—	—	—	—	8,973	9,603
Northern Marianas...........	—	—	6,211	7,107	5,852	5,831	5,354	6,170	5,814	5,418	5,033	6,298	6,153	8,102	6,449
Puerto Rico......................	—	—	2,971	4,724	4,698	5,497	5,236	6,103	6,459	6,913	7,237	7,613	7,611	7,896	7,643
U.S. Virgin Islands............	—	—	11,182	8,991	7,537	8,826	9,140	10,281	10,354	11,129	13,716	13,976	15,411	14,056	12,049

—Not available.
[1]Unadjusted (or "current") dollars have not been adjusted to compensate for inflation.
[2]Constant dollars based on the Consumer Price Index (CPI), prepared by the Bureau of Labor Statistics, U.S. Department of Labor, adjusted to a school-year basis. The CPI does not account for differences in inflation rates from state to state.
NOTE: Current expenditures include instruction, support services, food services, and enterprise operations. Expenditures for state administration are excluded in all years except

1969–70 and 1979–80. Beginning in 1989–90, extensive changes were made in the data collection procedures. Some data have been revised from previously published figures.
SOURCE: U.S. Department of Education, National Center for Education Statistics, *Statistics of State School Systems*, 1969–70; *Revenues and Expenditures for Public Elementary and Secondary Schools*, 1979–80; and Common Core of Data (CCD), "National Public Education Financial Survey," 1989–90 through 2011–12. (This table was prepared July 2014.)

Table 236.70. Current expenditure per pupil in average daily attendance in public elementary and secondary schools, by state or jurisdiction: Selected years, 1969–70 through 2011–12

State or jurisdiction	Unadjusted dollars														
	1969–70	1979–80	1989–90	1999–2000	2001–02	2002–03	2003–04	2004–05	2005–06	2006–07	2007–08	2008–09	2009–10	2010–11	2011–12
1	2	3	4	5	6	7	8	9	10	11	12	13	14	15	16
United States	$816	$2,272	$4,980	$7,394	$8,259	$8,610	$8,900	$9,316	$9,778	$10,336	$10,982	$11,239	$11,427	$11,433	$11,363
Alabama	544	1,612	3,327	5,758	6,327	6,642	6,812	7,309	7,980	8,743	9,345	9,385	9,554	9,296	8,927
Alaska........................	1,123	4,728	8,431	9,668	10,419	10,770	11,074	11,851	12,537	13,508	16,002	16,822	17,350	18,352	19,134
Arizona	720	1,971	4,053	5,478	6,470	6,784	6,908	7,218	7,637	8,038	8,630	8,732	8,756	8,646	8,223
Arkansas....................	568	1,574	3,485	5,628	6,676	6,981	7,307	8,243	8,748	9,152	9,460	9,651	10,237	10,332	10,397
California	867	2,268	4,391	6,401	7,439	7,601	7,708	7,989	8,416	9,029	9,673	9,439	9,680	9,540	9,608
Colorado	738	2,421	4,720	6,702	7,284	7,826	8,416	8,558	8,938	9,110	9,977	9,611	9,747	9,709	9,415
Connecticut................	951	2,420	7,837	10,122	11,022	11,302	11,755	12,655	13,461	14,143	15,063	15,840	16,133	16,932	17,472
Delaware....................	900	2,861	5,799	8,809	9,959	10,257	11,049	11,770	12,330	12,612	12,789	12,753	12,928	13,228	14,253
District of Columbia	1,018	3,259	8,955	11,935	14,557	14,735	15,414	15,074	17,877	18,285	20,807	19,766	21,283	21,304	20,399
Florida........................	732	1,889	4,997	6,383	6,679	6,922	7,269	7,731	8,376	9,055	9,711	9,452	9,363	9,394	8,825
Georgia......................	588	1,625	4,275	6,903	7,870	8,308	8,278	8,577	9,164	9,615	10,263	10,178	9,855	9,577	9,492
Hawaii........................	841	2,322	4,448	7,090	7,919	8,770	9,341	9,705	10,747	12,364	12,774	13,397	12,887	12,603	12,735
Idaho.........................	603	1,659	3,078	5,644	6,391	6,454	6,559	6,698	6,861	7,074	7,402	7,567	7,481	7,155	7,041
Illinois........................	909	2,587	5,118	8,084	8,967	9,309	9,710	10,020	10,282	10,816	11,624	12,489	13,083	13,180	13,459
Indiana.......................	728	1,882	4,606	7,652	8,268	8,582	9,033	9,640	9,558	9,727	9,569	9,946	10,160	9,924	10,220
Iowa..........................	844	2,326	4,453	6,925	7,714	7,943	8,017	8,341	8,460	8,789	9,128	10,482	10,524	10,565	10,748
Kansas.......................	771	2,173	4,752	6,962	8,342	8,373	8,804	9,037	9,905	10,280	11,065	11,485	10,859	10,700	10,712
Kentucky	545	1,701	3,745	6,784	7,536	7,728	7,976	8,379	8,975	9,303	9,940	10,054	10,376	10,469	10,700
Louisiana....................	648	1,792	3,903	6,256	7,061	7,492	7,846	8,288	8,568	9,650	10,797	11,410	11,492	11,500	11,352
Maine.........................	692	1,824	5,373	8,247	9,517	10,114	10,504	11,153	11,760	12,628	13,177	13,558	14,090	14,406	14,000
Maryland.....................	918	2,598	6,275	8,273	9,266	9,801	10,140	10,790	11,719	12,836	14,122	14,612	14,937	14,876	14,741
Massachusetts............	859	2,819	6,237	9,375	10,808	11,161	11,583	12,208	12,629	13,263	14,373	15,249	14,632	15,334	15,607
Michigan	904	2,640	5,546	8,886	9,428	9,847	10,049	10,328	10,598	10,932	11,155	11,493	11,661	11,661	11,462
Minnesota	904	2,387	4,971	7,499	8,050	8,440	8,934	9,273	9,761	10,185	10,663	11,602	11,366	11,368	11,424
Mississippi	501	1,664	3,094	5,356	5,719	6,186	6,601	6,994	7,699	7,988	8,448	8,610	8,670	8,436	8,623
Missouri.....................	709	1,936	4,507	6,764	7,700	8,002	8,022	8,360	8,834	9,266	10,007	10,341	10,468	10,348	10,370
Montana.....................	782	2,476	4,736	6,990	7,861	8,391	8,771	9,108	9,653	10,244	10,541	10,881	11,463	11,599	11,290
Nebraska....................	736	2,150	4,736	7,360	8,238	8,550	9,270	9,638	10,170	10,711	11,217	11,457	11,920	12,324	12,263
Nevada.......................	769	2,088	4,117	6,148	6,477	6,496	6,780	7,198	7,720	8,372	8,891	8,865	8,869	9,035	8,677
New Hampshire	723	1,916	5,304	7,082	8,230	8,900	9,391	10,043	10,698	11,347	12,280	12,912	13,424	13,964	14,215
New Jersey.................	1,016	3,191	8,139	10,903	12,197	13,093	13,776	14,666	15,362	16,650	18,174	17,466	18,060	17,654	18,197
New Mexico	707	2,034	3,515	5,835	6,886	7,126	7,653	7,933	8,426	8,876	9,377	9,727	9,716	9,356	9,066
New York....................	1,327	3,462	8,062	10,957	12,343	13,211	13,926	15,054	16,095	17,182	18,423	19,373	19,965	20,517	20,881
North Carolina	612	1,754	4,290	6,505	6,970	7,057	7,114	7,628	7,940	8,373	8,415	9,167	8,930	8,943	8,828
North Dakota	690	1,920	4,189	6,078	7,112	7,315	7,791	8,776	9,239	9,203	9,637	10,113	10,976	11,356	11,643
Ohio..........................	730	2,075	5,045	7,816	8,928	9,427	9,799	9,984	10,306	10,792	11,374	11,905	12,307	12,484	12,271
Oklahoma...................	604	1,926	3,508	5,770	6,672	6,540	6,599	7,086	7,449	7,968	8,270	8,423	8,511	8,165	8,281
Oregon.......................	925	2,692	5,474	8,129	8,725	8,514	8,640	8,799	9,294	9,762	10,487	10,673	10,476	10,497	10,386
Pennsylvania..............	882	2,535	6,228	8,380	9,196	9,648	10,393	11,014	11,530	11,995	12,493	12,989	13,678	14,072	13,973
Rhode Island	891	2,601	6,368	9,646	10,552	11,377	12,279	12,685	13,917	14,674	15,843	16,211	16,243	16,346	16,498
South Carolina............	613	1,752	4,082	6,545	7,549	7,759	7,893	8,302	8,795	9,226	9,823	10,007	9,887	9,735	9,796
South Dakota..............	690	1,908	3,731	6,037	6,890	7,192	7,607	7,960	8,273	8,506	9,047	9,457	9,683	9,431	9,095
Tennessee	566	1,635	3,664	5,837	6,476	6,674	7,047	7,426	7,580	7,843	8,459	8,676	8,810	9,146	9,241
Texas........................	624	1,916	4,150	6,771	7,302	7,714	7,711	7,814	8,085	8,484	9,029	9,260	9,528	9,418	8,862
Utah..........................	626	1,657	2,764	4,692	5,294	5,247	5,427	5,654	5,809	6,116	6,841	7,081	6,877	6,851	6,787
Vermont.....................	807	1,997	6,227	8,799	10,229	10,903	11,675	12,579	13,377	14,219	15,089	16,073	16,586	16,661	17,575
Virginia......................	708	1,970	4,672	6,491	7,928	8,300	8,761	9,441	10,046	10,913	11,410	11,696	11,383	11,123	11,385
Washington.................	915	2,568	4,702	6,914	7,626	7,882	8,051	8,362	8,702	9,233	9,846	10,423	10,242	10,402	10,427
West Virginia...............	670	1,920	4,360	7,637	8,451	9,025	9,076	9,321	9,756	10,080	10,605	11,122	12,378	12,505	11,982
Wisconsin...................	883	2,477	5,524	8,299	9,237	9,538	9,834	10,141	10,484	10,813	11,370	11,773	12,194	12,515	11,750
Wyoming.....................	856	2,527	5,577	7,944	9,321	9,906	10,351	11,087	12,415	14,219	14,936	15,658	16,535	17,126	17,228
Other jurisdictions															
American Samoa...........	—	—	1,908	2,807	2,983	3,121	3,671	3,801	3,842	3,909	4,309	4,468	4,881	4,877	5,154
Guam.......................	820	—	4,234	—	—	—	6,449	—	7,095	7,450	8,084	8,264	8,393	9,280	10,112
Northern Marianas.........	—	—	3,007	5,720	4,934	5,221	4,746	5,669	5,307	5,356	5,162	6,397	6,284	8,495	7,068
Puerto Rico	—	—	1,750	3,859	4,013	4,743	4,534	5,304	5,897	6,152	6,937	7,329	7,426	8,560	7,798
U.S. Virgin Islands...........	—	—	6,767	7,238	6,248	7,747	8,077	8,698	9,637	10,548	12,358	12,768	14,215	13,014	11,669

See notes at end of table.

Table 236.70. Current expenditure per pupil in average daily attendance in public elementary and secondary schools, by state or jurisdiction: Selected years, 1969–70 through 2010–11—Continued

State or jurisdiction	Constant 2013–14 dollars[1]														
	1969–70	1979–80	1989–90	1999–2000	2001–02	2002–03	2003–04	2004–05	2005–06	2006–07	2007–08	2008–09	2009–10	2010–11	2011–12
1	17	18	19	20	21	22	23	24	25	26	27	28	29	30	31
United States............	$5,076	$6,876	$9,215	$10,262	$10,890	$11,109	$11,237	$11,419	$11,546	$11,897	$12,189	$12,302	$12,388	$12,151	$11,732
Alabama.........................	3,384	4,878	6,157	7,992	8,343	8,570	8,601	8,959	9,422	10,063	10,372	10,273	10,357	9,880	9,218
Alaska............................	6,983	14,309	15,602	13,419	13,739	13,896	13,983	14,526	14,804	15,548	17,761	18,413	18,809	19,504	19,756
Arizona..........................	4,479	5,965	7,500	7,604	8,531	8,753	8,723	8,847	9,018	9,251	9,579	9,558	9,493	9,188	8,490
Arkansas........................	3,531	4,765	6,449	7,811	8,804	9,007	9,226	10,104	10,330	10,534	10,500	10,564	11,098	10,980	10,735
California........................	5,394	6,863	8,125	8,884	9,809	9,808	9,733	9,792	9,938	10,393	10,736	10,332	10,494	10,139	9,920
Colorado........................	4,590	7,327	8,735	9,302	9,604	10,098	10,626	10,489	10,554	10,486	11,074	10,520	10,567	10,319	9,722
Connecticut....................	5,917	7,325	14,502	14,048	14,533	14,582	14,842	15,512	15,895	16,279	16,719	17,338	17,490	17,995	18,041
Delaware........................	5,599	8,659	10,731	12,226	13,132	13,235	13,951	14,427	14,559	14,517	14,195	13,960	14,016	14,059	14,716
District of Columbia.........	6,334	9,864	16,571	16,565	19,195	19,012	19,462	18,477	21,108	21,047	23,093	23,093	21,636	23,073	22,641	21,062
Florida...........................	4,555	5,718	9,248	8,859	8,807	8,931	9,178	9,476	9,891	10,423	10,779	10,346	10,151	9,984	9,112
Georgia..........................	3,657	4,919	7,910	9,581	10,377	10,719	10,453	10,513	10,820	11,067	11,391	11,141	10,684	10,178	9,800
Hawaii............................	5,228	7,027	8,232	9,841	10,442	11,315	11,794	11,895	12,689	14,231	14,178	14,664	13,970	13,394	13,150
Idaho.............................	3,752	5,022	5,695	7,834	8,427	8,328	8,281	8,210	8,102	8,142	8,216	8,283	8,111	7,604	7,270
Illinois............................	5,657	7,829	9,470	11,220	11,824	12,010	12,260	12,282	12,141	12,450	12,902	13,671	14,184	14,007	13,897
Indiana...........................	4,528	5,697	8,524	10,621	10,902	11,073	11,406	11,816	11,286	11,196	10,621	10,887	11,015	10,547	10,553
Iowa..............................	5,251	7,041	8,240	9,611	10,171	10,249	10,122	10,224	9,989	10,116	10,131	11,473	11,409	11,228	11,098
Kansas...........................	4,796	6,577	8,793	9,663	11,000	10,803	11,117	11,077	11,696	11,832	12,281	12,572	11,772	11,371	11,061
Kentucky........................	3,391	5,149	6,931	9,416	9,937	9,972	10,070	10,270	10,597	10,708	11,032	11,005	11,249	11,126	11,048
Louisiana........................	4,031	5,424	7,223	8,682	9,311	9,666	9,907	10,159	10,117	11,108	11,983	12,489	12,458	12,222	11,721
Maine.............................	4,307	5,519	9,943	11,446	12,549	13,050	13,263	13,670	13,886	14,535	14,625	14,841	15,275	15,310	14,456
Maryland.........................	5,712	7,863	11,613	11,483	12,218	12,646	12,803	13,226	13,837	14,774	15,674	15,994	16,194	15,810	15,220
Massachusetts................	5,343	8,533	11,542	13,012	14,252	14,401	14,625	14,964	14,912	15,266	15,953	16,692	15,863	16,296	16,115
Michigan.........................	5,623	7,991	10,264	12,333	12,432	12,705	12,688	12,659	12,514	12,583	12,381	12,580	12,642	12,286	11,835
Minnesota.......................	5,620	7,224	9,198	10,408	10,615	10,890	11,281	11,366	11,525	11,723	11,835	12,700	12,322	12,082	11,796
Mississippi......................	3,115	5,036	5,725	7,433	7,542	7,982	8,335	8,573	9,091	9,194	9,376	9,424	9,399	8,965	8,904
Missouri.........................	4,407	5,860	8,340	9,388	10,153	10,325	10,128	10,247	10,431	10,665	11,106	11,320	11,348	10,997	10,707
Montana.........................	4,863	7,495	8,765	9,702	10,366	10,827	11,074	11,165	11,398	11,791	11,699	11,910	12,427	12,327	11,657
Nebraska........................	4,581	6,507	8,959	10,215	10,862	11,032	11,704	11,814	12,008	12,329	12,449	12,540	12,923	13,097	12,662
Nevada...........................	4,786	6,320	7,619	8,533	8,541	8,382	8,560	8,823	9,115	9,636	9,868	9,703	9,616	9,602	8,959
New Hampshire...............	4,497	5,799	9,815	9,830	10,853	11,483	11,857	12,311	12,632	13,060	13,630	14,134	14,553	14,840	14,677
New Jersey.....................	6,321	9,659	15,061	15,132	16,084	16,893	17,394	17,977	18,139	19,164	20,171	19,119	19,579	18,763	18,789
New Mexico....................	4,398	6,155	6,504	8,098	9,080	9,194	9,663	9,723	9,949	10,216	10,407	10,647	10,533	9,943	9,361
New York........................	8,253	10,479	14,918	15,207	16,276	17,046	17,583	18,453	19,004	19,776	20,448	21,205	21,645	21,805	21,560
North Carolina.................	3,809	5,310	7,939	9,029	9,191	9,106	8,983	9,350	9,376	9,638	9,340	10,035	9,682	9,504	9,116
North Dakota...................	4,289	5,812	7,752	8,436	9,378	9,439	9,837	10,757	10,909	10,593	10,696	11,070	11,900	12,069	12,022
Ohio..............................	4,541	6,279	9,335	10,849	11,772	12,163	12,372	12,238	12,169	12,422	12,624	13,031	13,342	13,267	12,670
Oklahoma.......................	3,760	5,831	6,491	8,008	8,797	8,438	8,332	8,686	8,796	9,172	9,179	9,220	9,227	8,678	8,551
Oregon...........................	5,752	8,147	10,130	11,282	11,505	10,985	10,909	10,786	10,974	11,236	11,640	11,683	11,357	11,156	10,724
Pennsylvania..................	5,484	7,672	11,525	11,631	12,125	12,448	13,123	13,501	13,615	13,807	13,866	14,218	14,829	14,956	14,428
Rhode Island..................	5,543	7,872	11,783	13,388	13,913	14,680	15,504	15,549	16,433	16,890	17,584	17,745	17,609	17,372	17,034
South Carolina................	3,810	5,303	7,553	9,085	9,955	10,011	9,966	10,176	10,385	10,620	10,903	10,953	10,718	10,346	10,114
South Dakota..................	4,291	5,774	6,904	8,379	9,085	9,280	9,604	9,757	9,768	9,790	10,041	10,351	10,497	10,023	9,391
Tennessee......................	3,521	4,950	6,779	8,102	8,540	8,611	8,897	9,102	8,951	9,028	9,388	9,497	9,551	9,720	9,542
Texas............................	3,882	5,798	7,680	9,398	9,629	9,953	9,737	9,578	9,547	9,765	10,021	10,136	10,330	10,010	9,150
Utah..............................	3,895	5,014	5,114	6,513	6,981	6,770	6,852	6,930	6,860	7,040	7,593	7,751	7,455	7,281	7,008
Vermont.........................	5,021	6,044	11,522	12,213	13,488	14,067	14,742	15,418	15,795	16,366	16,747	17,594	17,981	17,707	18,146
Virginia..........................	4,403	5,962	8,645	9,009	10,454	10,709	11,061	11,572	11,862	12,561	12,664	12,803	12,340	11,821	11,756
Washington.....................	5,693	7,773	8,701	9,596	10,056	10,170	10,166	10,250	10,276	10,628	10,927	11,409	11,103	11,055	10,766
West Virginia..................	4,167	5,812	8,069	10,599	11,143	11,645	11,460	11,425	11,520	11,603	11,770	12,174	13,420	13,290	12,371
Wisconsin.......................	5,490	7,496	10,222	11,518	12,180	12,306	12,417	12,430	12,379	12,446	12,620	12,887	13,220	13,301	12,132
Wyoming........................	5,324	7,647	10,321	11,026	12,291	12,782	13,069	13,590	14,659	16,366	16,578	17,140	17,926	18,202	17,789
Other jurisdictions															
American Samoa.............	—	—	3,530	3,896	3,933	4,026	4,635	4,659	4,536	4,499	4,782	4,891	5,292	5,183	5,322
Guam.............................	5,099	—	7,836	—	—	—	8,142	—	8,377	8,575	8,972	9,046	9,099	9,863	10,441
Northern Marianas..........	—	—	5,565	7,939	6,506	6,736	5,992	6,949	6,267	6,165	5,729	7,002	6,812	9,029	7,297
Puerto Rico....................	—	—	3,238	5,356	5,291	6,119	5,725	6,501	6,964	7,081	7,700	8,023	8,051	9,097	8,051
U.S. Virgin Islands..........	—	—	12,523	10,046	8,238	9,996	10,199	10,662	11,379	12,141	13,716	13,976	15,411	13,831	12,049

—Not available.
[1]Constant dollars based on the Consumer Price Index (CPI), prepared by the Bureau of Labor Statistics, U.S. Department of Labor, adjusted to a school-year basis. The CPI does not account for differences in inflation rates from state to state.
NOTE: Current expenditures include instruction, support services, food services, and enterprise operations. Expenditures for state administration are excluded in all years except 1969–70 and 1979–80. Beginning in 1989–90, extensive changes were made in the data collection procedures. There are discrepancies in average daily attendance reporting practices from state to state. Some data have been revised from previously published figures.
SOURCE: U.S. Department of Education, National Center for Education Statistics, *Statistics of State School Systems*, 1969–70; *Revenues and Expenditures for Public Elementary and Secondary Education*, 1979–80; and Common Core of Data (CCD), "National Public Education Financial Survey," 1989–90 through 2011–12. (This table was prepared July 2014.)

Table 236.75. Total and current expenditures per pupil in fall enrollment in public elementary and secondary education, by function and state or jurisdiction: 2011–12

State or jurisdiction	Total[1]	Current expenditures, capital expenditures, and interest on school debt per pupil													Interest on school debt
		Current expenditures												Capital outlay[2]	
		Total	Instruction	Support services									Food services	Enterprise operations[3]		
				Total	Student support[4]	Instructional staff[5]	General administration	School administration	Operation and maintenance	Student transportation	Other support services				
1	2	3	4	5	6	7	8	9	10	11	12	13	14	15	16
United States	$12,010	$10,667	$6,495	$3,721	$594	$495	$214	$585	$1,008	$464	$361	$429	$22	$985	$358
Alabama	9,549	8,577	4,966	3,015	495	388	195	529	781	443	185	595	0	782	191
Alaska	18,873	17,475	9,645	7,286	1,466	1,148	254	1,058	2,166	531	663	477	68	1,108	290
Arizona	8,444	7,382	4,035	2,970	532	379	124	385	927	328	295	375	1	852	210
Arkansas	11,100	9,536	5,396	3,586	489	799	236	481	933	372	277	542	11	1,293	271
California	10,795	9,329	5,606	3,317	494	555	90	617	929	226	406	383	24	1,077	389
Colorado	9,928	8,594	4,948	3,297	422	475	146	583	822	258	591	307	43	826	508
Connecticut	18,324	16,855	10,659	5,650	1,069	502	340	976	1,518	853	392	408	138	1,226	243
Delaware	15,009	13,580	8,659	4,466	575	246	197	711	1,418	680	640	456	0	1,248	181
District of Columbia	25,038	19,847	11,301	7,720	706	748	1,050	1,742	1,741	1,295	438	783	43	4,740	452
Florida	9,480	8,520	5,196	2,915	370	542	75	473	887	354	215	409	0	688	272
Georgia	10,348	9,272	5,734	3,009	428	477	122	557	690	417	317	503	27	929	146
Hawaii	13,206	11,973	6,861	4,431	1,125	425	58	731	1,375	415	301	681	0	678	556
Idaho	7,316	6,626	3,996	2,272	370	264	153	375	612	332	166	357	1	483	206
Illinois	13,468	12,011	7,233	4,405	802	482	497	610	1,039	565	409	373	0	1,041	416
Indiana	10,825	9,588	5,640	3,517	459	365	243	562	1,067	582	240	431	0	905	333
Iowa	12,078	10,027	6,164	3,397	560	482	255	578	854	374	295	456	9	1,826	225
Kansas	11,840	10,021	6,090	3,457	593	419	296	576	938	394	240	475	0	1,404	415
Kentucky	10,720	9,327	5,401	3,347	428	510	208	530	853	580	238	556	24	1,129	264
Louisiana	11,954	10,726	6,108	4,031	646	567	263	645	971	630	309	586	1	1,059	169
Maine	13,274	12,335	7,374	4,537	806	622	382	670	1,271	632	153	422	1	641	298
Maryland	15,433	13,871	8,620	4,880	628	750	125	994	1,180	744	460	371	0	1,366	197
Massachusetts	16,273	14,844	9,605	4,837	1,050	680	206	604	1,299	634	363	403	0	1,172	257
Michigan	11,911	10,477	6,082	4,012	800	516	216	571	937	447	527	383	0	873	562
Minnesota	12,515	10,781	7,070	3,209	288	464	334	429	764	611	318	472	30	1,269	465
Mississippi	8,788	8,097	4,620	2,974	394	418	257	470	851	398	185	503	1	550	140
Missouri	10,876	9,514	5,670	3,389	444	412	307	551	951	498	226	454	0	974	389
Montana	11,537	10,569	6,288	3,810	653	401	325	578	1,074	522	257	453	18	847	121
Nebraska	13,142	11,640	7,427	3,395	450	371	368	573	1,005	368	260	505	312	1,208	295
Nevada	9,421	8,130	4,764	3,057	436	409	122	608	862	333	287	308	1	744	547
New Hampshire	14,844	13,774	8,875	4,526	1,026	416	462	753	1,133	590	145	374	0	833	237
New Jersey	19,156	17,982	10,779	6,608	1,782	558	364	849	1,757	897	399	403	193	671	503
New Mexico	10,543	9,013	5,151	3,431	928	253	201	539	938	299	274	425	5	1,530	0
New York	20,617	19,396	13,459	5,529	651	488	370	746	1,684	1,030	560	408	0	772	449
North Carolina	8,619	8,160	5,087	2,616	384	289	126	510	692	362	253	456	0	453	6
North Dakota	13,026	11,246	6,570	3,735	483	403	506	567	1,017	483	275	589	351	1,637	143
Ohio	13,066	11,323	6,444	4,493	720	740	345	645	990	547	508	384	1	1,401	343
Oklahoma	8,591	7,763	4,318	2,878	529	320	249	414	857	269	239	490	77	745	83
Oregon	10,830	9,485	5,509	3,619	673	353	127	603	783	452	629	354	3	789	556
Pennsylvania	14,699	13,091	7,993	4,587	694	449	405	602	1,270	671	496	452	60	1,027	581
Rhode Island	15,745	15,172	9,405	5,376	1,567	534	214	740	1,199	587	535	386	6	257	315
South Carolina	10,849	9,077	5,148	3,416	677	548	98	549	868	373	304	487	25	1,223	548
South Dakota	10,155	8,593	5,053	3,014	470	344	287	419	870	321	304	473	53	1,349	212
Tennessee	9,221	8,354	5,194	2,714	360	523	176	478	715	313	150	445	0	663	204
Texas	9,929	8,213	4,850	2,890	399	411	124	466	909	237	344	473	0	1,107	609
Utah	7,969	6,441	4,101	1,949	251	261	76	400	586	205	169	363	28	1,269	260
Vermont	17,303	16,651	10,434	5,746	1,278	702	341	1,079	1,390	548	408	460	12	511	141
Virginia	11,650	10,656	6,458	3,772	519	707	165	616	1,019	577	168	424	2	857	137
Washington	11,494	9,617	5,609	3,561	832	365	179	557	865	397	366	332	115	1,478	399
West Virginia	11,884	11,579	6,786	4,140	551	479	230	616	1,201	862	201	653	0	245	60
Wisconsin	11,979	11,233	6,748	4,058	535	530	313	552	1,027	486	615	427	0	519	227
Wyoming	18,382	15,988	9,460	6,034	934	978	332	861	1,538	771	619	485	10	2,378	17
Other jurisdictions															
American Samoa	—	—	—	—	—	—	—	—	—	—	—	—	—	—	—
Guam	9,828	9,300	4,576	4,359	835	155	56	539	1,502	180	1,092	365	0	428	100
Northern Marianas	6,354	6,246	2,696	2,707	599	501	228	492	416	277	194	844	0	108	0
Puerto Rico	7,536	7,403	3,266	3,086	499	374	124	345	687	296	763	1,050	0	133	0
U.S. Virgin Islands	11,675	11,669	6,092	4,873	916	329	461	594	827	448	1,298	681	23	5	0

—Not available.
[1]Excludes "Other current expenditures," such as community services, private school programs, adult education, and other programs not allocable to expenditures per pupil in public schools.
[2]Includes expenditures for property and for buildings and alterations completed by school district staff or contractors.
[3]Includes expenditures for operations funded by sales of products or services (e.g., school bookstore or computer time).
[4]Includes expenditures for guidance, health, attendance, and speech pathology services.
[5]Includes expenditures for curriculum development, staff training, libraries, and media and computer centers.
NOTE: Excludes expenditures for state education agencies. "0" indicates none or less than $0.50. Detail may not sum to totals because of rounding.
SOURCE: U.S. Department of Education, National Center for Education Statistics, Common Core of Data (CCD), "National Public Education Financial Survey," 2011–12. (This table was prepared July 2014.)

Table 236.80. Total and current expenditures per pupil in fall enrollment in public elementary and secondary education, by function and state or jurisdiction: 2010–11

	Current expenditures, capital expenditures, and interest on school debt per pupil														
			Current expenditures												
				Support services											Interest on school debt[5]
State or jurisdiction	Total[1]	Total	Instruction	Total	Student support[4]	Instructional staff[5]	General administration	School administration	Operation and maintenance	Student transportation	Other support services	Food services	Enterprise operations[3]	Capital outlay[2]	Interest on school debt
1	2	3	4	5	6	7	8	9	10	11	12	13	14	15	16
United States	$12,054	$10,663	$6,522	$3,706	$594	$503	$212	$580	$1,015	$452	$349	$412	$22	$1,029	$363
Alabama	9,653	8,726	5,091	3,046	506	394	209	540	786	437	174	589	0	749	178
Alaska	18,333	16,663	9,225	6,918	1,363	1,166	231	1,013	2,037	485	623	458	62	1,372	298
Arizona	9,183	7,782	4,205	3,167	1,014	182	118	366	875	302	309	367	43	807	594
Arkansas	11,120	9,496	5,425	3,531	483	813	234	480	902	357	260	528	11	1,363	262
California	10,594	9,146	5,514	3,246	478	556	88	606	906	220	392	364	23	1,075	372
Colorado	10,298	8,786	5,040	3,401	428	499	189	588	824	258	615	302	43	990	522
Connecticut	17,480	16,224	10,292	5,407	991	502	319	920	1,503	803	370	391	134	1,004	252
Delaware	14,117	12,467	7,871	4,144	586	163	171	686	1,243	728	567	452	0	1,466	183
District of Columbia	28,403	20,793	10,584	9,409	1,208	1,613	866	1,546	2,321	1,404	450	761	40	5,487	2,124
Florida	10,162	9,030	5,511	3,116	403	583	96	508	935	363	228	404	0	838	294
Georgia	10,227	9,259	5,765	2,987	438	463	140	556	690	392	308	481	26	816	152
Hawaii	12,946	11,924	6,919	4,359	1,119	398	60	764	1,399	370	250	646	0	475	547
Idaho	7,624	6,821	4,162	2,311	387	273	155	383	622	332	160	347	1	580	222
Illinois	13,135	11,742	7,025	4,360	793	506	478	598	1,058	551	376	357	0	1,000	393
Indiana	10,405	9,251	5,445	3,395	436	351	240	533	1,048	556	231	411	0	831	323
Iowa	11,757	9,795	6,040	3,310	553	466	253	554	833	358	293	435	10	1,756	206
Kansas	12,033	9,802	5,941	3,415	569	418	289	561	917	396	265	447	0	1,798	433
Kentucky	10,570	9,228	5,410	3,265	416	502	204	513	856	560	215	530	23	1,109	234
Louisiana	12,141	10,799	6,288	3,938	531	589	255	628	1,006	625	306	572	0	1,167	175
Maine	13,761	12,576	7,628	4,544	822	656	403	676	1,232	603	151	404	0	911	274
Maryland	15,340	13,946	8,712	4,869	620	785	109	978	1,256	718	403	366	0	1,199	194
Massachusetts	15,711	14,612	9,487	4,744	1,022	656	196	595	1,331	602	343	380	0	836	263
Michigan	12,041	10,577	6,095	4,118	800	561	216	576	991	445	529	364	0	902	562
Minnesota	12,406	10,674	7,027	3,161	282	450	322	427	772	595	314	455	31	1,252	481
Mississippi	8,643	7,926	4,582	2,853	382	403	235	457	816	380	179	490	1	572	145
Missouri	10,746	9,461	5,669	3,364	442	424	299	541	948	484	227	428	0	929	356
Montana	11,572	10,719	6,416	3,836	662	407	308	572	1,121	510	256	442	25	739	113
Nebraska	13,150	11,704	7,642	3,289	418	370	359	564	988	353	236	474	299	1,161	285
Nevada	9,650	8,411	5,010	3,121	430	445	105	599	885	349	309	279	0	679	559
New Hampshire	14,836	13,548	8,793	4,394	976	419	441	719	1,119	575	144	361	0	1,058	230
New Jersey	17,940	16,855	10,131	6,174	1,633	522	344	797	1,673	834	370	364	186	609	476
New Mexico	10,759	9,250	5,303	3,525	961	261	209	553	954	306	281	417	5	1,509	0
New York	20,198	18,857	13,160	5,320	625	486	360	719	1,668	982	481	377	0	915	425
North Carolina	8,862	8,267	5,167	2,653	390	303	133	515	710	353	250	446	0	589	6
North Dakota	12,362	10,898	6,307	3,705	488	369	508	537	1,059	467	278	562	324	1,281	183
Ohio	13,130	11,395	6,483	4,536	723	761	341	645	1,016	541	508	375	1	1,427	308
Oklahoma	8,493	7,631	4,337	2,773	518	311	251	404	805	250	234	448	74	770	92
Oregon	10,821	9,516	5,546	3,622	679	384	125	596	785	436	617	342	5	808	497
Pennsylvania	14,956	13,096	8,020	4,580	678	483	386	574	1,298	663	498	439	57	1,265	595
Rhode Island	15,624	14,948	9,210	5,365	1,569	547	206	710	1,225	575	533	365	7	332	344
South Carolina	10,861	8,908	5,082	3,338	654	546	99	537	867	358	277	462	26	1,392	561
South Dakota	10,658	8,931	5,282	3,143	496	372	294	440	916	319	306	458	49	1,508	218
Tennessee	9,171	8,330	5,239	2,682	347	519	172	471	727	297	149	410	0	648	193
Texas	10,611	8,685	5,211	3,001	422	451	127	482	947	245	327	473	0	1,328	598
Utah	7,889	6,440	4,143	1,920	250	256	73	392	584	201	165	349	28	1,217	232
Vermont	15,511	14,707	9,045	5,241	1,153	658	328	983	1,269	504	347	413	8	659	145
Virginia	11,360	10,363	6,282	3,678	501	689	159	600	1,009	556	163	402	1	859	139
Washington	11,465	9,619	5,813	3,369	644	386	184	548	859	392	357	321	116	1,451	396
West Virginia	12,263	11,978	7,175	4,167	541	473	234	640	1,194	879	206	636	0	231	54
Wisconsin	12,824	11,947	7,310	4,219	568	583	312	584	1,074	480	618	418	0	620	257
Wyoming	18,474	15,815	9,351	5,975	918	1,033	323	841	1,529	727	605	477	11	2,640	19
Other jurisdictions															
American Samoa	—	—	—	—	—	—	—	—	—	—	—	—	—	—	—
Guam	10,825	8,443	4,722	3,336	877	168	70	521	1,109	241	349	385	0	2,283	99
Northern Marianas	7,726	7,623	3,243	3,610	1,028	437	283	395	765	188	515	770	0	103	0
Puerto Rico	7,561	7,429	3,082	3,757	498	610	699	304	848	154	644	590	0	131	0
U.S. Virgin Islands	13,232	13,226	6,974	5,458	1,021	382	484	714	913	510	1,433	748	45	6	0

—Not available.

[1]Excludes "Other current expenditures," such as community services, private school programs, adult education, and other programs not allocable to expenditures per pupil in public schools.

[2]Includes expenditures for property and for buildings and alterations completed by school district staff or contractors.

[3]Includes expenditures for operations funded by sales of products or services (e.g., school bookstore or computer time).

[4]Includes expenditures for guidance, health, attendance, and speech pathology services.

[5]Includes expenditures for curriculum development, staff training, libraries, and media and computer centers.

NOTE: Excludes expenditures for state education agencies. "0" indicates none or less than $0.50. Some data have been revised from previously published figures. Detail may not sum to totals because of rounding.

SOURCE: U.S. Department of Education, National Center for Education Statistics, Common Core of Data (CCD), "National Public Education Financial Survey," 2010–11. (This table was prepared July 2014.)

Table 236.90. Students transported at public expense and current expenditures for transportation: Selected years, 1929–30 through 2011–12

School year	Average daily attendance, all students	Students transported at public expense		Expenditures for transportation (in unadjusted dollars)[1]		Expenditures for transportation (in constant 2013–14 dollars)[2]	
		Number	Percent of total	Total[3] (in thousands)	Average per student transported	Total[3] (in thousands)	Average per student transported
1	2	3	4	5	6	7	8
1929–30	21,265,000	1,902,826	8.9	$54,823	$29	$752,558	$395
1931–32	22,245,000	2,419,173	10.9	58,078	24	946,546	391
1933–34	22,458,000	2,794,724	12.4	53,908	19	956,543	342
1935–36	22,299,000	3,250,658	14.6	62,653	19	1,071,265	330
1937–38	22,298,000	3,769,242	16.9	75,637	20	1,240,637	329
1939–40	22,042,000	4,144,161	18.8	83,283	20	1,400,263	338
1941–42	21,031,000	4,503,081	21.4	92,922	21	1,400,302	311
1943–44	19,603,000	4,512,412	23.0	107,754	24	1,453,000	322
1945–46	19,849,000	5,056,966	25.5	129,756	26	1,671,322	330
1947–48	20,910,000	5,854,041	28.0	176,265	30	1,777,523	304
1949–50	22,284,000	6,947,384	31.2	214,504	31	2,128,157	306
1951–52	23,257,000	7,697,130	33.1	268,827	35	2,403,272	312
1953–54	25,643,871	8,411,719	32.8	307,437	37	2,686,198	319
1955–56	27,740,149	9,695,819	35.0	353,972	37	3,093,828	319
1957–58	29,722,275	10,861,689	36.5	416,491	38	3,426,753	315
1959–60	32,477,440	12,225,142	37.6	486,338	40	3,889,082	318
1961–62	34,682,340	13,222,667	38.1	576,361	44	4,505,464	341
1963–64	37,405,058	14,475,778	38.7	673,845	47	5,133,606	355
1965–66	39,154,497	15,536,567	39.7	787,358	51	5,797,993	373
1967–68	40,827,965	17,130,873	42.0	981,006	57	6,777,907	396
1969–70	41,934,376	18,198,577	43.4	1,218,557	67	7,579,602	416
1971–72	42,254,272	19,474,355	46.1	1,507,830	77	8,609,691	442
1973–74	41,438,054	21,347,039	51.5	1,858,141	87	9,364,074	439
1975–76	41,269,720	21,772,483	52.8	2,377,313	109	10,072,266	463
1977–78	40,079,590	21,800,000 [4]	54.4	2,731,041	125 [4]	10,245,426	470 [4]
1979–80	38,288,911	21,713,515	56.7	3,833,145	177	11,601,494	534
1980–81	37,703,744	22,272,000 [4]	59.1	4,408,000 [4]	198 [4]	11,956,481 [4]	537 [4]
1981–82	37,094,652	22,246,000 [4]	60.0	4,793,000 [4]	215 [4]	11,967,017 [4]	538 [4]
1982–83	36,635,868	22,199,000 [4]	60.6	5,000,000 [4]	225 [4]	11,969,740 [4]	539 [4]
1983–84	36,362,978	22,031,000 [4]	60.6	5,284,000 [4]	240 [4]	12,198,111 [4]	554 [4]
1984–85	36,404,261	22,320,000 [4]	61.3	5,722,000 [4]	256 [4]	12,711,672 [4]	570 [4]
1985–86	36,523,103	22,041,000 [4]	60.3	6,123,000 [4]	278 [4]	13,221,251 [4]	600 [4]
1986–87	36,863,867	22,397,000 [4]	60.8	6,551,000 [4]	292 [4]	13,838,180 [4]	618 [4]
1987–88	37,050,707	22,158,000 [4]	59.8	6,888,000 [4]	311 [4]	13,971,149 [4]	631 [4]
1988–89	37,268,072	22,635,000 [4]	60.7	7,550,000 [4]	334 [4]	14,637,875 [4]	647 [4]
1989–90	37,799,296	22,459,000 [4]	59.4	8,030,990	358 [4]	14,861,269	662 [4]
1990–91	38,426,543	22,000,000 [4]	57.3	8,678,954	394 [4]	15,227,784	692 [4]
1991–92	38,960,783	23,165,000 [4]	59.5	8,769,754	379 [4]	14,909,368	644 [4]
1992–93	39,570,462	23,439,000 [4]	59.2	9,252,300	395 [4]	15,253,296	651 [4]
1993–94	40,146,393	23,858,000 [4]	59.4	9,627,155	404 [4]	15,470,528	648 [4]
1994–95	40,720,763	23,693,000 [4]	58.2	9,889,034	417 [4]	15,448,558	652 [4]
1995–96	41,501,596	24,155,000 [4]	58.2	10,396,426	430 [4]	15,811,045	655 [4]
1996–97	42,262,004	24,090,000 [4]	57.0	10,989,809	456 [4]	16,249,852	675 [4]
1997–98	42,765,774	24,342,000 [4]	56.9	11,465,658	471 [4]	16,656,402	684 [4]
1998–99	43,186,715	24,898,000 [4]		12,224,454	491 [4]	17,456,523	701 [4]
1999–2000	43,806,726	24,951,000 [4]	57.0	13,007,625	521 [4]	18,053,716	724 [4]
2000–01	44,075,930	24,471,000 [4]	55.5	14,052,654	574 [4]	18,858,063	771 [4]
2001–02	44,604,592	24,529,000 [5]	55.0	14,799,365	603 [5]	19,514,612	796 [5]
2002–03	45,017,360	24,621,000 [5]	54.7	15,648,821	636 [5]	20,190,990	820 [5]
2003–04	45,325,731	25,159,000 [5]	55.5	16,348,784	650 [5]	20,642,522	820 [5]
2004–05	45,625,458	25,318,000 [5]	55.5	17,459,659	690 [5]	21,401,134	845 [5]
2005–06	45,931,617	25,252,000 [5]	55.0	18,850,234	746 [5]	22,258,001	881 [5]
2006–07	46,132,663	25,285,000 [5]	54.8	19,979,068	790 [5]	22,996,217	909 [5]
2007–08	46,155,880	25,221,000 [5]	54.6	21,536,978	854 [4]	23,903,683	948 [4]
2008–09	46,173,477	—	—	21,679,876	860 [4]	23,730,928	941 [4]
2009–10	45,919,206	—	—	21,819,304	870 [4]	23,654,668	943 [4]
2010–11	46,118,737	—	—	22,370,807	888 [4]	24,252,562	963 [4]
2011–12	46,388,428	—	—	22,907,082	904 [4]	24,345,101	961 [4]

—Not available.

[1] Unadjusted (or "current") dollars have not been adjusted to compensate for inflation.
[2] Constant dollars based on the Consumer Price Index, prepared by the Bureau of Labor Statistics, U.S. Department of Labor, adjusted to a school-year basis.
[3] Excludes capital outlay for years through 1979–80, and 1989–90 to the latest year. From 1980–81 to 1988–89, total transportation figures include capital outlay.
[4] Estimate based on data appearing in January issues of School Bus Fleet.
[5] Estimate based on data reported by School Transportation News.
NOTE: Some data have been revised from previously published figures.

SOURCE: U.S. Department of Education, National Center for Education Statistics, *Statistics of State School Systems*, 1929–30 through 1975–76; *Revenues and Expenditures for Public Elementary and Secondary Education*, 1977–78 and 1979–80; Common Core of Data (CCD), "National Public Education Financial Survey," 1987–88 through 2011–12; Bobit Publishing Co., *School Bus Fleet*, "School Transportation: 2000–2001 School Year" and "*2010 Fact Book*"; *School Transportation News*, "K–12 Enrollment/Transportation Data," 2001–02 through 2007–08; and unpublished data. (This table was prepared July 2014.)

CHAPTER 3
Postsecondary Education

Postsecondary education includes academic, career and technical, and continuing professional education programs after high school. American colleges and universities and career/technical institutions offer a diverse array of postsecondary educational experiences. For example, a community college normally offers the first 2 years of a standard college curriculum as well as a selection of terminal career and technical education programs. A university typically offers a full undergraduate course of study leading to a bachelor's degree, as well as programs leading to advanced degrees. A specialized career/technical institution offers training programs of varying lengths that are designed to prepare students for specific careers.

This chapter provides an overview of the latest statistics on postsecondary education, including data on various types of postsecondary institutions and programs. However, to maintain comparability over time, most of the data in the *Digest* are for degree-granting institutions, which are defined as postsecondary institutions that grant an associate's or higher degree and whose students are eligible to participate in the Title IV federal financial aid programs.[1] Degree-granting institutions include almost all 2- and 4-year colleges and universities; they exclude institutions offering only career and technical programs of less than 2 years' duration and continuing education programs. The degree-granting institution classification currently used by the National Center for Education Statistics (NCES) includes approximately the same set of institutions as the higher education institution classification that was used by NCES prior to 1996–97.[2] This chapter highlights historical data that enable the reader to observe long-range trends in college education in America.

Other chapters provide related information on postsecondary education. Data on price indexes and on the number of degrees held by the general population are shown in chapter 1. Chapter 4 contains tabulations on federal funding for postsecondary education. Information on employment outcomes for college graduates is shown in chapter 5. Chapter 7 contains data on college libraries. Further information on survey methodologies is presented in Appendix A: Guide to Sources and in the publications cited in the table source notes. See chapter 5 for information on adults' participation in nonpostsecondary education, such as adult secondary education classes (e.g., to prepare for the GED test) or English as a Second Language (ESL) classes.

Enrollment

Enrollment in degree-granting postsecondary institutions increased by 18 percent between 1993 and 2003 (table 303.10 and figure 12). Between 2003 and 2013, enrollment increased 20 percent, from 16.9 million to 20.4 million. Much of the growth between 2003 and 2013 was in full-time enrollment; the number of full-time students rose 22 percent, while the number of part-time students rose 18 percent. During the same period, the number of female students rose 19 percent, while the number of male students rose 22 percent. Although male enrollment increased by a larger percentage during this period, the majority (57 percent) of students in 2013 were female. Enrollment increases can be affected both by population growth and by rising rates of enrollment. Between 2003 and 2013, the number of 18- to 24-year-olds in the population increased from 28.9 million to 31.5 million, an increase of 9 percent (table 101.10), and the percentage of 18- to 24-year-olds enrolled in degree-granting postsecondary institutions rose from 38 percent in 2003 to 40 percent in 2013 (table 302.60). In addition to enrollment in degree-granting institutions, about 472,000 students attended non-degree-granting, Title IV eligible, postsecondary institutions in fall 2013 (table 303.20). These institutions are postsecondary institutions that do not award associate's or higher degrees; they include, for example, institutions that offer only career and technical programs of less than 2 years' duration.

Like enrollment in degree-granting institutions for the United States as a whole, the number of students enrolled in degree-granting institutions located within individual states was generally higher in 2013 than in 2008 (table 304.10 and

---

[1]Title IV programs, which are administered by the U.S. Department of Education, provide financial aid to postsecondary students.

[2]Included in the current degree-granting classification are some institutions (primarily 2-year colleges) that were not previously designated as higher education institutions. Excluded from the current degree-granting classification are a few institutions that were previously designated as higher education institutions even though they did not award an associate's or higher degree. The former higher education classification was defined as including institutions that were accredited by an agency or association that was recognized by the U.S. Department of Education, or recognized directly by the Secretary of Education. The former institutions of higher education offered courses that led to an associate's or higher degree, or were accepted for credit towards a degree.

figure 13). Overall, enrollment in degree-granting institutions was 7 percent higher in 2013 than in 2008. Similarly, enrollment was higher in most states (43) in 2013 than in 2008. However, enrollment changes varied from state to state. The largest increase was in Idaho (36 percent), followed by New Hampshire (29 percent), West Virginia (26 percent), and Utah (22 percent). In 13 states, enrollment was 10 to 20 percent higher in 2013 than in 2008. In 7 states and the District of Columbia, enrollment was lower in 2013 than in 2008.

Between 2003 and 2013, the percentage increase in the number of students enrolled in degree-granting institutions was higher for students under age 25 than for older students; however, the rate of increase is expected to be lower for students under age 25 than for older students in the coming years (table 303.40 and figure 14). The enrollment of students under age 25 increased by 22 percent from 2003 to 2013, while the enrollment of those age 25 and over increased by 19 percent. From 2013 to 2024, however, NCES projects the increase for students under age 25 to be 13 percent, compared with 14 percent for students age 25 and over.

Enrollment trends have differed at the undergraduate and postbaccalaureate levels. Undergraduate enrollment increased 47 percent between 1970 and 1983, when it reached 10.8 million (table 303.70). Undergraduate enrollment dipped to 10.6 million in 1984 and 1985, but then increased each year from 1985 to 1992, rising 18 percent before stabilizing between 1992 and 1998. Between 2003 and 2013, undergraduate enrollment rose 21 percent overall, from 14.5 million to 17.5 million; however, undergraduate enrollment in 2013 was lower than in 2010 (18.1 million). Postbaccalaureate enrollment increased 34 percent between 1970 and 1984, with most of this increase occurring in the early 1970s (table 303.80). Postbaccalaureate enrollment increased from 1985 to 2013, rising a total of 76 percent. During the last decade of this period, between 2003 and 2013, postbaccalaureate enrollment rose 19 percent, from 2.4 million to 2.9 million.

Since 1988, the number of females in postbaccalaureate programs has exceeded the number of males. Between 2003 and 2013, the number of full-time male postbaccalaureate students increased by 24 percent, compared with a 34 percent increase in the number of full-time female postbaccalaureate students. Among part-time postbaccalaureate students, the number of males increased by 6 percent and the number of females increased by 10 percent.

Eleven percent of undergraduates in both 2007–08 and 2011–12 reported having a disability (table 311.10). In 2011–12, the percentage of undergraduates who reported having a disability was 11 percent for both males and females. However, there were some differences in the percentages of undergraduates with disabilities by characteristics such as veteran status, age, dependency status, and race/ethnicity. For example, 21 percent of undergraduates who were veterans reported having a disability, compared with 11 percent of undergraduates who were not veterans. The percentage of undergraduates having a disability was higher among those age 30 and over (16 percent) than among 15- to

23-year-olds (9 percent) and 24- to 29-year-olds (11 percent). Among dependent undergraduates, 9 percent reported having a disability, which was lower than the percentages for independent undergraduates who were married (13 percent) or unmarried (14 percent). Compared to undergraduates of other racial/ethnic groups, a lower percentage of Asian undergraduates (8 percent) had a disability. The percentage of postbaccalaureate students who reported having a disability in 2011–12 (5 percent) was lower than the percentage for undergraduates (11 percent).

The percentage of American college students who are Hispanic, Asian/Pacific Islander, Black, and American Indian/Alaska Native has been increasing (table 306.10). From 1976 to 2013, the percentage of Hispanic students rose from 4 percent to 16 percent, the percentage of Asian/Pacific Islander students rose from 2 percent to 6 percent, the percentage of Black students rose from 10 percent to 15 percent, and the percentage of American Indian/Alaska Native students rose from 0.7 to 0.8 percent. During the same period, the percentage of White students fell from 84 percent to 59 percent.

Of 20.4 million students enrolled in fall 2013, some 14 percent took at least one distance education course as part of their program that included a mix of in-person and distance education courses (table 311.15). In addition, about 13 percent of students took their college program exclusively through distance education courses. The remaining 73 percent of students took no distance education courses. About 9 percent of students at public institutions took their coursework exclusively through distance education courses, in comparison to 13 percent of students at private nonprofit institutions and 52 percent of students at private for-profit institutions.

Despite the sizable numbers of small degree-granting colleges, most students attend larger colleges and universities. In fall 2013, some 44 percent of institutions had fewer than 1,000 students; however, these campuses enrolled 4 percent of all college students (table 317.40). While 12 percent of campuses enrolled 10,000 or more students, they accounted for 60 percent of total college enrollment.

In 2013, the five postsecondary institutions with the highest enrollment were University of Phoenix, Online Campus, with 212,000 students; Ivy Tech Community College, with 98,800 students; Liberty University, with 77,300 students; Miami Dade College, with 66,300 students; and Lone Star College System, with 64,100 students (table 312.10).

Faculty, Staff, and Salaries

Approximately 3.9 million people were employed in degree-granting postsecondary institutions in fall 2013, including 1.5 million faculty, 0.4 million graduate assistants, and 2.0 million other staff (table 314.20). Out of the 1.5 million faculty in 2013, 0.8 million were full-time and 0.8 million were part-time faculty. From 2003 to 2013, the proportion of staff who were faculty rose from 37 percent to 40 percent. The proportion of other staff not engaged in teaching decreased from 54 percent in 2003 to 51 percent in 2013. The proportion of graduate assistants was 9 percent in both 2003 and 2013.

The full-time-equivalent (FTE) student/FTE staff ratio at degree-granting institutions was 5.2 in both 2003 and 2013 (table 314.10 and figure 15). The FTE student/FTE faculty ratio was lower in 2013 (14.8) than in 2003 (15.6).

Colleges and universities differ in their practices of employing part-time and full-time staff. In fall 2013, some 47 percent of the employees at public 2-year colleges were employed full time, compared with 68 percent at public 4-year colleges and universities, 69 percent at private nonprofit 4-year colleges and universities, and 60 percent at private non-profit 2-year colleges (table 314.30). A higher percentage of the faculty at public 4-year colleges and universities were employed full time (67 percent) than at private nonprofit 4-year colleges and universities (57 percent), private for-profit 4-year colleges and universities (15 percent), private non-profit 2-year colleges (43 percent), private for-profit 2-year colleges (42 percent), or public 2-year colleges (30 percent). In general, the number of full-time staff has been growing at a slower rate than the number of part-time staff (table 314.20). Between 2003 and 2013, the number of full-time staff increased by 19 percent, compared to an increase of 29 percent in the number of part-time staff. Most of the increase in part-time staff was due to the increase in the number of part-time faculty (38 percent) and graduate assistants (23 percent) during this time period.

In fall 2013, some 7 percent of college and university faculty were Black (based on a faculty count that excludes persons whose race/ethnicity was unknown), 7 percent were Asian, 5 percent were Hispanic, 1 percent were American Indian/Alaska Native, 1 percent were of Two or more races, and less than 0.5 percent were Pacific Islander (table 314.40). About 79 percent of all faculty with known race/ethnicity were White; 41 percent were White males and 38 percent were White females. Staff who were Black, Hispanic, Asian, Pacific Islander, American Indian/Alaska Native, or of Two or more races made up 25 percent of graduate assistants and 29 percent of other staff in nonfaculty positions in 2013. The proportion of total staff made up of Blacks, Hispanics, Asians, Pacific Islanders, American Indians/Alaska Natives, and persons of Two or more races was similar at public 4-year colleges (26 percent), private nonprofit 4-year colleges (24 percent), public 2-year colleges (25 percent), and private nonprofit 2-year colleges (26 percent), but the proportion was higher at private for-profit 4-year colleges (31 percent) and at private for-profit 2-year colleges (38 percent).

On average, full-time faculty and instructional staff spent 58 percent of their time teaching in 2003 (table 315.30). Research and scholarship accounted for 20 percent of their time, and 22 percent was spent on other activities (administration, professional growth, etc.).

Faculty salaries generally lost purchasing power during the 1970s. In constant 2013–14 dollars, average salaries for faculty on 9-month contracts declined by 16 percent during the period from 1970–71 ($75,200) to 1980–81 ($63,200) (table 316.10). During the 1980s, average salaries rose and recouped most of the losses. Between 1990–91 and 2013–14, there was

a further increase in average faculty salaries, resulting in an average salary in 2013–14 ($78,600) that was about 5 percent higher than the average salary in 1970–71. The average salary for males was higher than the average salary for females in all years for which data are available. The average salary for males in 2013–14 ($85,500) was slightly higher than in 2003–04 ($85,200 in constant 2013–14 dollars). For females, the average salary in 2013–14 ($70,400) also was slightly higher than the salary in 2003–04 ($69,900). In 2013–14, average salaries were about 22 percent higher for males than for females ($85,500 versus $70,400).

The percentage of faculty with tenure has declined. Of those faculty at institutions with tenure systems, 48 percent of full-time faculty had tenure in 2013–14, compared with 56 percent in 1993–94 (table 316.80). Also, the percentage of institutions with tenure systems decreased between 1993–94 (63 percent) and 2013–14 (49 percent). Part of this change was due to the expansion in the number of for-profit institutions (table 317.10), relatively few of which have tenure systems (1.2 percent in 2013–14) (table 316.80). At institutions with tenure systems, there were differences between males and females in the percentage of full-time instructional faculty having tenure. Fifty-seven percent of males had tenure in 2013–14, compared with 43 percent of females. In 2013–14, about 53 percent of full-time instructional faculty had tenure at public institutions with tenure systems, compared with 46 percent at private nonprofit institutions with tenure systems and 20 percent at private for-profit institutions with tenure systems.

Degrees

During the 2013–14 academic year, 4,724 accredited institutions offered degrees at the associate's degree level or above (table 317.10). These included 1,625 public institutions, 1,675 private nonprofit institutions, and 1,424 private for-profit institutions. Of the 4,724 institutions, 3,039 were 4-year institutions that awarded degrees at the bachelor's or higher level, and 1,685 were 2-year institutions that offered associate's degrees as their highest award. Institutions awarding various degrees in 2012–13 numbered 3,029 for associate's degrees, 2,578 for bachelor's degrees, 1,930 for master's degrees, and 915 for doctor's degrees (table 318.60).

Growing numbers of people are completing college degrees. Between 2002–03 and 2012–13, the number of associate's, bachelor's, master's, and doctor's degrees that were conferred rose (table 318.10). The doctor's degree total includes most degrees formerly classified as first-professional, such as M.D. (medical), D.D.S. (dental), and J.D. (law) degrees. During this period, the number of associate's degrees increased by 59 percent, the number of bachelor's degrees increased by 36 percent, the number of master's degrees increased by 45 percent, and the number of doctor's degrees increased by 44 percent. Since the mid-1980s, more females than males have earned associate's, bachelor's, and master's degrees. Beginning in 2005–06, the number of females earning doctor's degrees has exceeded the number of males. Also, the number of associate's, master's, and doctor's degrees awarded to females has increased at a faster rate than the number awarded to males. Between 2002–03 and 2012–13, the number of associate's degrees awarded to females increased by 62 percent, while the number awarded to males increased by 53 percent. The number of females earning master's degrees rose 48 percent during this period, while the number of males earning master's degrees rose 40 percent. The number of females earning doctor's degrees increased 53 percent, while the number of males earning doctor's degrees increased 36 percent. Between 2002–03 and 2012–13, the number of bachelor's degrees awarded to males increased 37 percent and the number awarded to females increased by 36 percent. In addition to degrees awarded at the associate's and higher levels, 966,000 certificates were awarded by postsecondary institutions participating in federal Title IV financial aid programs in 2012–13 (table 320.20).

Of the 1,840,000 bachelor's degrees conferred in 2012–13, the greatest numbers of degrees were conferred in the fields of business (361,000), health professions and related programs (181,000), social sciences and history (178,000), psychology (114,000), education (105,000), and biological and biomedical sciences (100,000) (table 322.10). At the master's degree level, the greatest numbers of degrees were conferred in the fields of business (189,000) and education (165,000) (table 323.10). At the doctor's degree level, the greatest numbers of degrees were conferred in the fields of health professions and related programs (64,200), legal professions and studies (47,200), education (10,600), engineering (9,400), biological and biomedical sciences (7,900), psychology (6,300), and physical sciences and science technologies (5,500) (table 324.10).

In recent years, the numbers of bachelor's degrees conferred have followed patterns that differed significantly by field of study. While the number of degrees conferred increased by 36 percent overall between 2002–03 and 2012–13, there was substantial variation among the different fields of study, as well as shifts in the patterns of change during this time period (table 322.10 and figure 16). For example, the number of degrees conferred in computer and information sciences decreased 33 percent between 2002–03 and 2007–08, but then increased 32 percent between 2007–08 and 2012–13. In contrast, the number of bachelor's degrees conferred in the combined fields of engineering and engineering technologies increased 8 percent between 2002–03 and 2007–08, and then increased a further 23 percent between 2007–08 and 2012–13. In a number of other major fields, the number of bachelor's degrees also increased by somewhat higher percentages in the second half of the 10-year period than in the first half. For example, the number of degrees conferred in physical sciences and science technologies increased by 23 percent between 2002–03 and 2007–08 and then by 26 percent between 2007–08 and 2012–13. The number of degrees conferred in health professions and related programs increased by 56 percent between 2002–03 and 2007–08 and then by 62 percent between 2007–08 and 2012–13. Also, the number of degrees conferred in public administration and social

services increased by 18 percent between 2002–03 and 2007–08 and then by 36 percent between 2007–08 and 2012–13. Other fields with sizable numbers of degrees (over 5,000 in 2012–13) that showed increases of 30 percent or more between 2007–08 and 2012–13 included homeland security, law enforcement, and firefighting (50 percent); parks, recreation, leisure, and fitness studies (43 percent); multi/interdisciplinary studies (39 percent); agriculture and natural resources (39 percent); and mathematics and statistics (35 percent).

Among first-time students who were seeking a bachelor's degree or its equivalent and attending a 4-year institution full time in 2007, 39 percent completed a bachelor's degree or its equivalent at that institution within 4 years, while 55 percent did so within 5 years, and 59 percent did so within 6 years (table 326.10). These graduation rates were calculated as the total number of completers within the specified time to degree attainment divided by the cohort of students who first enrolled at that institution in 2007. Graduation rates were higher at private nonprofit institutions than at public or private for-profit institutions. For example, the 6-year graduation rate for the 2007 cohort at private nonprofit institutions was 65 percent, compared with 58 percent at public institutions and 32 percent at private for-profit institutions. Graduation rates also varied by race/ethnicity. At 4-year institutions overall, the 6-year graduation rate for Asians in the 2007 cohort was 71 percent, compared with 68 percent for students of Two or more races, 63 percent for Whites, 53 percent for Hispanics, 50 percent for Pacific Islanders, 41 percent for Blacks, and 41 percent for American Indians/Alaska Natives.

Finances and Financial Aid

For the 2013–14 academic year, annual current dollar prices for undergraduate tuition, fees, room, and board were estimated to be $15,640 at public institutions, $40,614 at private nonprofit institutions, and $23,135 at private for-profit institutions (table 330.10). Between 2003–04 and 2013–14, prices for undergraduate tuition, fees, room, and board at public institutions rose 34 percent, and prices at private nonprofit institutions rose 25 percent, after adjustment for inflation. The price for undergraduate tuition, fees, room, and board at private for-profit institutions decreased 16 percent between 2003–04 and 2013–14, after adjustment for inflation.

In 2011–12, about 84 percent of full-time undergraduate students received financial aid (grants, loans, work-study, or aid of multiple types) (table 331.10). About 73 percent of full-time undergraduates received federal financial aid in 2011–12, and 57 percent received aid from nonfederal sources. (Some students receive aid from both federal and nonfederal sources.) Section 484(r) of the Higher Education Act of 1965, as amended, suspends a student's eligibility for Title IV federal financial aid if the student is convicted of certain drug-related offenses that were committed while the student was receiving Title IV aid. For 2013–14, less than 0.01 percent of postsecondary students had their eligibility to receive aid suspended due to a conviction (table C).

Table C. Suspension of eligibility for Title IV federal student financial aid due to a drug-related conviction or failure to report conviction status on aid application form: 2007–08 through 2013–14

Award year	No suspension of eligibility	Suspension of eligibility		
		For part of award year	For full award year	
			Due to conviction	Due to failure to report
2007–08				
Number..........	14,610,371	361	2,832	2,433
Percent.........	99.96	#	0.02	0.02
2008–09				
Number..........	16,410,285	398	1,064	724
Percent.........	99.99	#	0.01	#
2009–10				
Number..........	19,487,370	666	1,751	879
Percent.........	99.98	#	0.01	#
2010–11				
Number..........	21,114,404	606	1,284	406
Percent.........	99.99	#	0.01	#
2011–12				
Number..........	21,947,204	404	968	732
Percent.........	99.99	#	#	#
2012–13				
Number..........	21,803,176	322	778	432
Percent.........	99.99	#	#	#
2013–14				
Number..........	21,192,389	257	572	535
Percent.........	99.99	#	#	#

#Rounds to zero.
NOTE: It is not possible to determine whether a student who lost eligibility due to a drug conviction otherwise would have received Title IV aid, since there are other reasons why an applicant may not receive aid. Detail may not sum to totals because of rounding.
SOURCE: U.S. Department of Education, Federal Student Aid, Free Application for Federal Student Aid (FAFSA), unpublished data.

In 2012–13, total revenue was $328 billion at public institutions, $202 billion at private nonprofit institutions, and $25 billion at private for-profit institutions (tables 333.10, 333.40, and 333.55 and figures 17, 18, and 19). The category of student tuition and fees typically accounts for a significant percentage of total revenue and was the largest single revenue source at both private nonprofit and for-profit institutions in 2012–13 (32 and 91 percent, respectively). Tuition and fees accounted for 21 percent of revenue at public institutions in 2012–13. Public institutions typically report Pell grants as revenue from federal grants, while private institutions report Pell grants as revenue from tuition and fees; this difference in reporting contributes to the smaller percentage of revenue reported as tuition and fees at public institutions compared to private institutions. At public institutions, the share of revenue from tuition and fees in 2012–13 (21 per-

cent) was higher than the share from state appropriations (18 percent), while the share from state appropriations in 2007–08 (25 percent) was higher than that from tuition and fees (18 percent) (table 333.10). In 2012–13, tuition and fees constituted the largest revenue category at private nonprofit 2- and 4-year institutions, private for-profit 2- and 4-year institutions, and public 4-year institutions (tables 333.10, 333.40, and 333.55). At public 2-year institutions, tuition and fees constituted the fourth largest revenue category.

In 2012–13, average total expenditures per full-time-equivalent (FTE) student at public degree-granting colleges were $28,900 in current dollars (table 334.10). The 2012–13 total expenditures per FTE student were 1 percent lower than in 2008–09, after adjustment for inflation. In 2012–13, public 4-year colleges had average total expenditures per FTE student of $38,100 in current dollars, compared with $13,400 at public 2-year colleges. At private nonprofit colleges, total expenditures per FTE student in 2012–13 were about the same as in 2008–09, after adjustment for inflation (table 334.30). In 2012–13, total expenditures per FTE student at private nonprofit institutions averaged $49,600 in current dollars at 4-year colleges and $17,900 at 2-year colleges (table 334.40). The expenditures per FTE student at private for-profit institutions were $15,500 in current dollars in 2012–13 (table 334.60), reflecting an increase of 12 percent since 2008–09, after adjustment for inflation (table 334.50). In 2012–13, total expenditures per FTE student at private for-profit institutions averaged $15,200 in current dollars at 4-year colleges and $16,800 at 2-year colleges (table 334.60), reflecting a difference in expenditures per FTE student between 4-year and 2-year for-profit colleges that was relatively small compared to the differences between 4-year and 2-year public and private nonprofit colleges.

At the end of fiscal year 2013, the market value of the endowment funds of colleges and universities was $467 billion, reflecting an increase of 10 percent compared to the beginning of the fiscal year, when the total was $425 billion (table 333.90). At the end of fiscal year 2013, the 120 colleges with the largest endowments accounted for $345 billion, or about three-fourths of the national total. The five colleges with the largest endowments in 2013 were Harvard University ($33 billion), Yale University ($21 billion), the University of Texas System ($20 billion), Princeton University ($19 billion), and Stanford University ($19 billion).

Figure 12. Enrollment, degrees conferred, and expenditures in degree-granting postsecondary institutions: 1960–61 through 2013–14

Fall enrollment, in millions

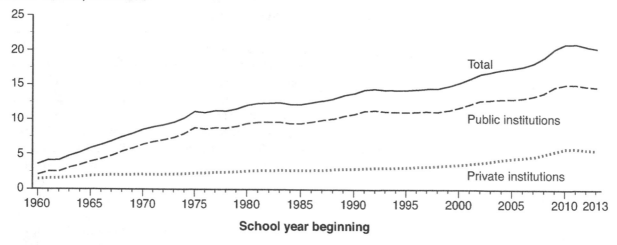

Degrees, in millions

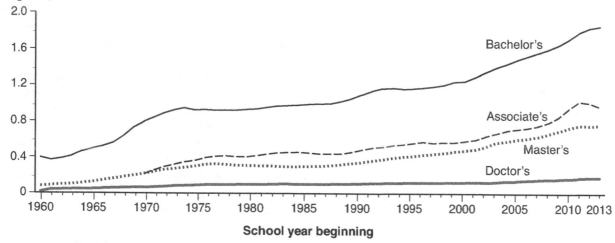

Total expenditures, in billions of constant 2013–14 dollars

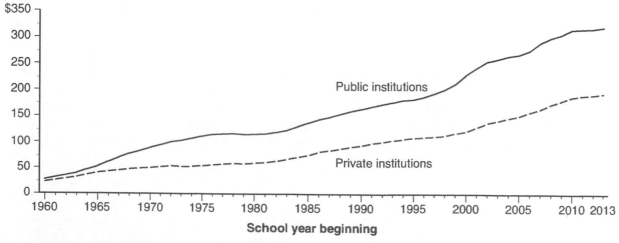

NOTE: Expenditure data for school year 2013 (2013–14) are estimated. Degree data for school year 2013 are projected. Doctor's degrees include Ph.D., Ed.D., and comparable degrees at the doctoral level, as well as such degrees as M.D., D.D.S., and law degrees that were formerly classified as first-professional degrees.
SOURCE: U.S. Department of Education, National Center for Education Statistics, *Opening Fall Enrollment in Higher Education*, 1960 through 1965; *Financial Statistics of Higher Education*, 1959–60 through 1964–65; *Earned Degrees Conferred*, 1959–60 through 1964–65; Degrees Conferred Projection Model, 1980–81 through 2024–25; Higher Education General Information Survey (HEGIS), "Fall Enrollment in Institutions of Higher Education," "Degrees and Other Formal Awards Conferred," and "Financial Statistics of Institutions of Higher Education" surveys, 1965–66 through 1985–86; Integrated Postsecondary Education Data System (IPEDS), "Fall Enrollment Survey" (IPEDS-EF:86–99), "Completions Survey" (IPEDS-C:87–99), and "Finance Survey" (IPEDS-F:FY87–99); IPEDS Fall 2000 through Fall 2013, Completions component; and IPEDS Spring 2001 through Spring 2014, Enrollment and Finance components.

Figure 13. Percentage change in total enrollment in degree-granting postsecondary institutions, by state: Fall 2008 to fall 2013

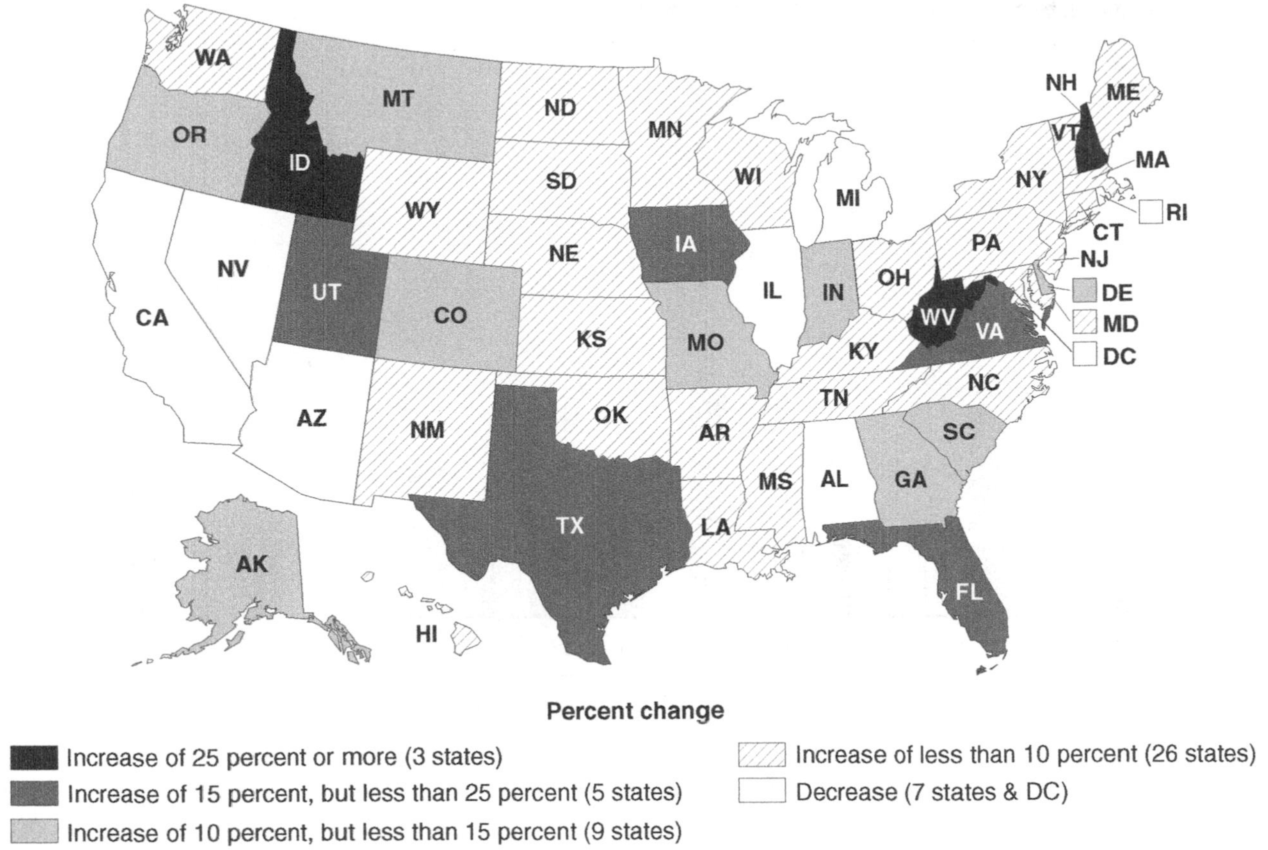

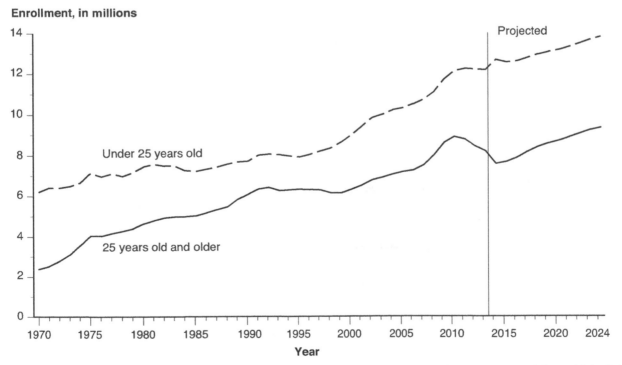

Percent change

- ■ Increase of 25 percent or more (3 states)
- ■ Increase of 15 percent, but less than 25 percent (5 states)
- ■ Increase of 10 percent, but less than 15 percent (9 states)
- ▨ Increase of less than 10 percent (26 states)
- □ Decrease (7 states & DC)

SOURCE: U.S. Department of Education, National Center for Education Statistics, Integrated Postsecondary Education Data System (IPEDS), Spring 2009 and Spring 2014, Enrollment component.

Figure 14. Enrollment in degree-granting postsecondary institutions, by age: Fall 1970 through fall 2024

Enrollment, in millions

SOURCE: U.S. Department of Education, National Center for Education Statistics, Higher Education General Information Survey (HEGIS), "Fall Enrollment in Colleges and Universities" surveys, 1970 through 1985; Integrated Postsecondary Education Data System (IPEDS), "Fall Enrollment Survey" (IPEDS-EF:86–99); IPEDS Spring 2001 through Spring 2014, Enrollment component; and Enrollment in Degree-Granting Institutions Projection Model, 1980 through 2024. U.S. Department of Commerce, Census Bureau, Current Population Survey (CPS), October, selected years, 1970 through 2013.

Figure 15. Ratio of full-time-equivalent (FTE) students to total FTE staff and to FTE faculty in degree-granting postsecondary institutions, by control of institution: 1993, 2003, and 2013

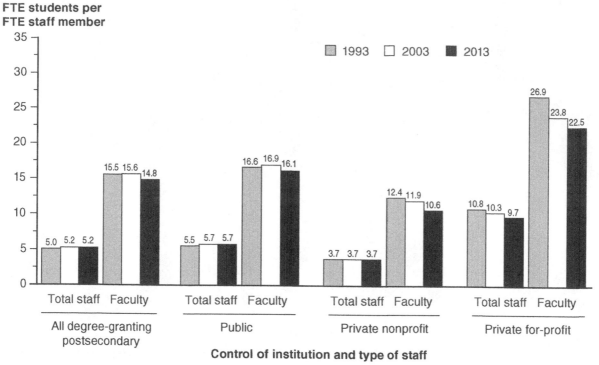

SOURCE: U.S. Department of Education, National Center for Education Statistics, Integrated Postsecondary Education Data System (IPEDS), "Fall Enrollment Survey" (IPEDS-EF:93) and "Fall Staff Survey" (IPEDS-S:93); IPEDS Spring 2003 and 2013, Enrollment component; and IPEDS Winter 2003–04 and Spring 2014, Human Resources component, Fall Staff section.

Figure 16. Bachelor's degrees conferred by postsecondary institutions in selected fields of study: 2002–03, 2007–08, and 2012–13

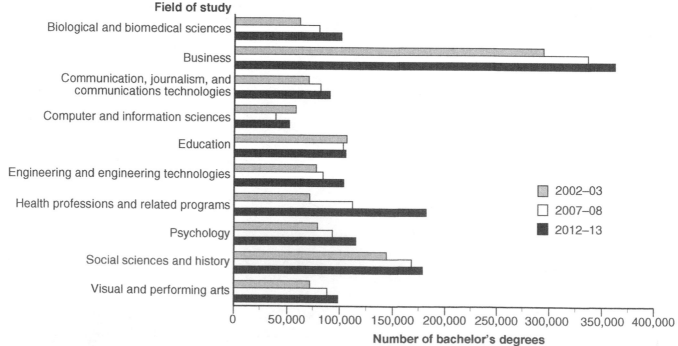

SOURCE: U.S. Department of Education, National Center for Education Statistics, Integrated Postsecondary Education Data System (IPEDS), Fall 2003, Fall 2008, and Fall 2013, Completions component.

Figure 17. **Percentage distribution of total revenues of public degree-granting postsecondary institutions, by source of funds: 2012–13**

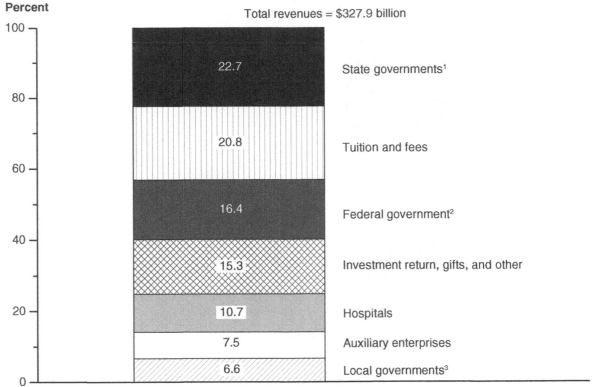

Total revenues = $327.9 billion

22.7	State governments[1]
20.8	Tuition and fees
16.4	Federal government[2]
15.3	Investment return, gifts, and other
10.7	Hospitals
7.5	Auxiliary enterprises
6.6	Local governments[3]

Source of funds

[1]Revenues from state governments include operating grants and contracts, nonoperating revenue appropriations, nonoperating grants, and capital appropriations.
[2]Revenues from the federal government include operating grants and contracts, funds for independent operations, nonoperating revenue appropriations, and nonoperating grants.
[3]Revenues from local governments include operating grants and contracts, private grants and contracts, nonoperating revenue appropriations, and nonoperating grants.
NOTE: Detail may not sum to totals because of rounding.
SOURCE: U.S. Department of Education, National Center for Education Statistics, Integrated Postsecondary Education Data System (IPEDS), Spring 2014, Finance component.

Figure 18. Percentage distribution of total revenues of private nonprofit degree-granting postsecondary institutions, by source of funds: 2012–13

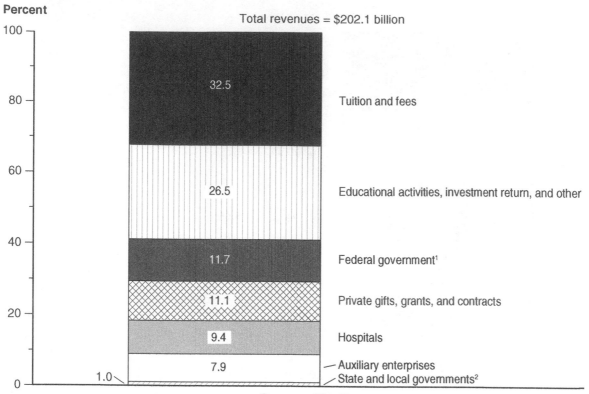

Percent

Total revenues = $202.1 billion

- 32.5 — Tuition and fees
- 26.5 — Educational activities, investment return, and other
- 11.7 — Federal government[1]
- 11.1 — Private gifts, grants, and contracts
- 9.4 — Hospitals
- 7.9 — Auxiliary enterprises
- 1.0 — State and local governments[2]

Source of funds

[1]Includes appropriations, grants, contracts, and independent operations.
[2]Includes appropriations, grants, and contracts.
SOURCE: U.S. Department of Education, National Center for Education Statistics, Integrated Postsecondary Education Data System (IPEDS), Spring 2014, Finance component.

Figure 19. **Percentage distribution of total revenues of private for-profit degree-granting postsecondary institutions, by source of funds: 2012–13**

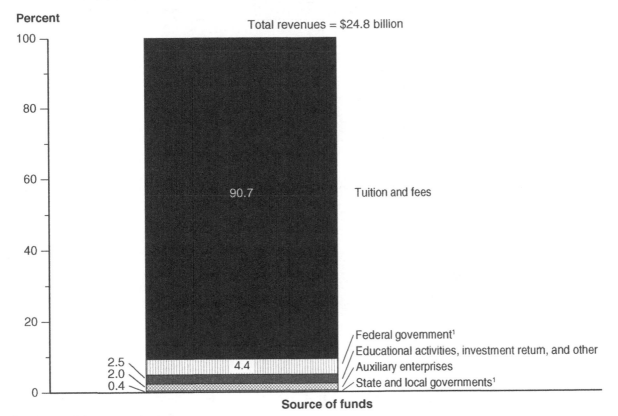

[1]Includes appropriations, grants, and contracts.
NOTE: Detail may not sum to totals because of rounding.
SOURCE: U.S. Department of Education, National Center for Education Statistics, Integrated Postsecondary Education Data System (IPEDS), Spring 2014, Finance component.

Table 301.10. Enrollment, staff, and degrees/certificates conferred in degree-granting and non-degree-granting postsecondary institutions, by control and level of institution, sex of student, type of staff, and level of degree: Fall 2013 and 2012–13

Level of institution, sex of student, type of staff, and level of degree	Total[1]	Degree-granting institutions					Non-degree-granting institutions				
		Total	Public	Private			Total	Public	Private		
				Total	Nonprofit	For-profit			Total	Nonprofit	For-profit
1	2	3	4	5	6	7	8	9	10	11	12
Enrollment, fall 2013											
Total	20,847,787	20,375,789	14,745,558	5,630,231	3,974,004	1,656,227	471,998	109,854	362,144	19,458	342,686
4-year institutions	13,407,463	13,407,050	8,120,417	5,286,633	3,941,806	1,344,827	413	44	369	369	0
Males	5,862,964	5,862,870	3,683,546	2,179,324	1,681,047	498,277	94	18	76	76	0
Females	7,544,499	7,544,180	4,436,871	3,107,309	2,260,759	846,550	319	26	293	293	0
2-year institutions	7,097,068	6,968,739	6,625,141	343,598	32,198	311,400	128,329	52,378	75,951	9,301	66,650
Males	3,057,641	2,997,916	2,885,293	112,623	11,856	100,767	59,725	28,955	30,770	2,557	28,213
Females	4,039,427	3,970,823	3,739,848	230,975	20,342	210,633	68,604	23,423	45,181	6,744	38,437
Less-than-2-year institutions	343,256	†	†	†	†	†	343,256	57,432	285,824	9,788	276,036
Males	94,463	†	†	†	†	†	94,463	26,520	67,943	3,703	64,240
Females	248,793	†	†	†	†	†	248,793	30,912	217,881	6,085	211,796
Staff, fall 2013											
Total	3,969,396	3,896,149	2,527,329	1,368,820	1,157,030	211,790	73,247	22,521	50,726	4,394	46,332
Faculty (instruction/research/ public service)	1,580,932	1,544,060	967,703	576,357	448,724	127,633	36,872	11,481	25,391	2,015	23,376
Instruction	1,473,325	1,436,453	898,685	537,768	410,337	127,431	36,872	11,481	25,391	2,015	23,376
Research	81,665	81,665	51,479	30,186	30,074	112	†	†	†	†	†
Public service	25,942	25,942	17,539	8,403	8,313	90	†	†	†	†	†
Graduate assistants	359,546	359,546	283,516	76,030	75,579	451	†	†	†	†	†
Librarians, curators, and archivists	44,885	44,656	24,737	19,919	18,320	1,599	229	79	150	42	108
Student and academic affairs and other education services	165,061	158,521	105,628	52,893	39,809	13,084	6,540	2,834	3,706	438	3,268
Management	259,580	252,560	139,800	112,760	96,319	16,441	7,020	1,305	5,715	468	5,247
Business and financial operations	196,014	193,016	127,099	65,917	58,707	7,210	2,998	458	2,540	137	2,403
Computer, engineering, and science	232,396	231,768	158,631	73,137	70,410	2,727	628	340	288	25	263
Community, social service, legal, arts, design, entertainment, sports, and media	167,907	167,415	101,069	66,346	58,449	7,897	492	317	175	42	133
Healthcare practitioners and technicians	122,682	121,948	81,206	40,742	40,489	253	734	450	284	130	154
Service occupations	244,608	241,142	160,511	80,631	78,346	2,285	3,466	1,636	1,830	491	1,339
Sales and related occupations	17,801	15,390	5,003	10,387	4,526	5,861	2,411	32	2,379	37	2,342
Office and administrative support	481,889	471,266	302,746	168,520	142,961	25,559	10,623	2,901	7,722	526	7,196
Natural resources, construction, and maintenance	76,415	75,404	55,482	19,922	19,395	527	1,011	509	502	33	469
Production, transportation, and material moving	19,680	19,457	14,198	5,259	4,996	263	223	179	44	10	34
Degrees/certificates conferred, 2012–13											
Total	4,740,113	4,423,917	2,850,116	1,573,801	1,017,541	556,260	316,196	64,213	251,983	13,017	238,966
Less-than-1-year and 1- to less-than-4-year certificates	966,084	650,003	480,668	169,335	17,665	151,670	316,081	64,213	251,868	13,017	238,851
4-year institutions	93,880	93,823	52,485	41,338	10,900	30,438	57	0	57	57	0
Males	37,141	37,131	24,619	12,512	4,369	8,143	10	0	10	10	0
Females	56,739	56,692	27,866	28,826	6,531	22,295	47	0	47	47	0
2-year institutions	629,139	556,180	428,183	127,997	6,765	121,232	72,959	29,869	43,090	4,294	38,796
Males	270,954	239,775	200,660	39,115	2,160	36,955	31,179	14,230	16,949	1,272	15,677
Females	358,185	316,405	227,523	88,882	4,605	84,277	41,780	15,639	26,141	3,022	23,119
Less-than-2-year institutions	243,065	†	†	†	†	†	243,065	34,344	208,721	8,666	200,055
Males	67,251	†	†	†	†	†	67,251	13,970	53,281	3,889	49,392
Females	175,814	†	†	†	†	†	175,814	20,374	155,440	4,777	150,663
Associate's degrees	1,007,076	1,006,961	772,588	234,373	55,617	178,756	115	0	115	0	115
4-year institutions	298,527	298,527	133,774	164,753	49,032	115,721	0	0	0	0	0
Males	113,520	113,520	53,185	60,335	17,669	42,666	0	0	0	0	0
Females	185,007	185,007	80,589	104,418	31,363	73,055	0	0	0	0	0
2-year institutions	708,547	708,434	638,814	69,620	6,585	63,035	113	0	113	0	113
Males	275,351	275,326	249,752	25,574	2,462	23,112	25	0	25	0	25
Females	433,196	433,108	389,062	44,046	4,123	39,923	88	0	88	0	88
Less-than-2-year institutions	2	†	†	†	†	†	2	0	2	0	2
Males	1	†	†	†	†	†	1	0	1	0	1
Females	1	†	†	†	†	†	1	0	1	0	1
Bachelor's degrees	1,840,164	1,840,164	1,163,620	676,544	535,736	140,808	0	0	0	0	0
Males	787,231	787,231	510,331	276,900	220,837	56,063	0	0	0	0	0
Females	1,052,933	1,052,933	653,289	399,644	314,899	84,745	0	0	0	0	0
Master's degrees	751,751	751,751	346,813	404,938	326,984	77,954	0	0	0	0	0
Males	301,575	301,575	141,705	159,870	132,571	27,299	0	0	0	0	0
Females	450,176	450,176	205,108	245,068	194,413	50,655	0	0	0	0	0
Doctor's degrees	175,038	175,038	86,427	88,611	81,539	7,072	0	0	0	0	0
Males	85,104	85,104	42,581	42,523	39,698	2,825	0	0	0	0	0
Females	89,934	89,934	43,846	46,088	41,841	4,247	0	0	0	0	0

†Not applicable.
[1]Includes both degree-granting and non-degree-granting institutions.
NOTE: Data are for postsecondary institutions participating in Title IV federal financial aid programs. Degree-granting institutions grant degrees at the associate's or higher level, while non-degree-granting institutions grant only awards below that level. The non-degree-granting classification includes some institutions transitioning to higher level program offer- ings, though still classified at a lower level; therefore, a small number of associate's degrees are shown as awarded by non-degree-granting institutions.
SOURCE: U.S. Department of Education, National Center for Education Statistics, Integrated Postsecondary Education Data System (IPEDS), Spring 2014, Human Resources component and Enrollment component; and Fall 2013, Completions component. (This table was prepared April 2014.)

Table 301.20. Historical summary of faculty, enrollment, degrees conferred, and finances in degree-granting postsecondary institutions: Selected years, 1869–70 through 2012–13

Selected characteristic	1869–70	1879–80	1889–90	1899–1900	1909–10	1919–20	1929–30	1939–40	1949–50	1959–60	1969–70	1979–80	1989–90	1999–2000	2009–10	2012–13
1	2	3	4	5	6	7	8	9	10	11	12	13	14	15	16	17
Total institutions[1]	563	811	998	977	951	1,041	1,409	1,708	1,851	2,004	2,525	3,152	3,535	4,084	4,495	4,726
Total faculty[2]	5,553[3]	11,522[3]	15,809	23,868	36,480	48,615	82,386	146,929	246,722	380,554	450,000[4]	675,000[4]	824,220[5]	1,027,830[5]	1,439,074[5]	—
Males	4,887[3]	7,328[3]	12,704[3]	19,151	29,132	35,807	60,017	106,328	186,189	296,773	346,000[4]	479,000[4]	534,254[5]	602,469[5]	761,002[5]	—
Females	666[3]	4,194[3]	3,105[3]	4,717	7,348	12,808	22,369	40,601	60,533	83,781	104,000[4]	196,000[4]	299,966[5]	425,361[5]	678,072[5]	—
Total fall enrollment[6]	52,286	115,817	156,756	237,592	355,213	597,880	1,100,737	1,494,203	2,444,900	3,639,847	8,004,660	11,569,899	13,538,560	14,791,224	20,313,594	20,642,819
Males	41,160[3]	77,972[3]	100,453[3]	152,254	214,648[3]	314,938	619,935	893,250	1,721,572	2,332,617	4,746,201	5,682,877	6,190,015	6,490,646	8,732,953	8,919,087
Females	11,126[3]	37,845[3]	56,303[3]	85,338	140,565[3]	282,942	480,802	600,953	723,328	1,307,230	3,258,459	5,887,022	7,348,545	8,300,578	11,580,641	11,723,732
Degrees conferred																
Associate's, total	—	—	—	—	—	—	—	—	—	—	206,023	400,910	455,102	564,933	848,856	1,006,961
Males	—	—	—	—	—	—	—	—	—	—	117,432	183,737	191,195	224,721	322,747	388,846
Females	—	—	—	—	—	—	—	—	—	—	88,591	217,173	263,907	340,212	526,109	618,115
Bachelor's, total[7]	9,371	12,896	15,539	27,410	37,199	48,622	122,484	186,500	432,058	392,440	792,316	929,417	1,051,344	1,237,875	1,649,919	1,840,164
Males	7,993	10,411	12,857	22,173	28,762	31,980	73,615	109,546	328,841	254,063	451,097	473,611	491,696	530,367	706,660	787,231
Females	1,378	2,485	2,682	5,237	8,437	16,642	48,869	76,954	103,217	138,377	341,219	455,806	559,648	707,508	943,259	1,052,933
Master's, total[8]	0	879	1,015	1,583	2,113	4,279	14,969	26,731	58,183	74,435	213,589	305,196	330,152	463,185	693,313	751,751
Males	0	868	821	1,280	1,555	2,985	8,925	16,508	41,220	50,898	130,799	156,882	158,052	196,129	275,317	301,575
Females	0	11	194	303	558	1,294	6,044	10,223	16,963	23,537	82,790	148,314	172,100	267,056	417,996	450,176
Doctor's, total[9]	1	54	149	382	443	615	2,299	3,290	6,420	9,829	59,486	95,631	103,508	118,736	158,590	175,038
Males	1	51	147	359	399	522	1,946	2,861	5,804	8,801	53,792	69,526	63,963	64,930	76,610	85,104
Females	0	3	2	23	44	93	353	429	616	1,028	5,694	26,105	39,545	53,806	81,980	89,934
Finances									*In thousands of current dollars*							
Current-fund revenue	—	—	$21,464	$35,084	$76,683	$199,922	$554,511	$715,211	$2,374,645	$5,785,537	$21,515,242	$58,519,982	$139,635,477	$236,784,000	$446,484,000	$489,939,000
Educational and general income[10]	—	—	—	—	57,917	172,929	483,065	571,288	1,833,846	4,688,352	16,486,177	—	—	—	—	—
Expenditures[10]	—	—	—	—	—	—	507,142	674,688	2,245,661	5,601,376	21,043,113	56,913,588	134,655,571	—	—	—
Value of physical property	—	—	95,426	253,599	457,594	747,333	2,065,049	2,753,780[11]	4,799,964	13,548,548	42,093,580	83,733,387	164,635,000	—	—	—
Market value of endowment funds	—	—	78,788[12]	194,998[12]	323,661[12]	569,071[12]	1,372,068[12]	1,686,283[12]	2,601,223[12]	5,322,080[12]	11,206,632	20,743,045	67,978,726	—	355,790,614	466,659,158
Finances									*In thousands of constant 2013–14 dollars[13]*							
Current-fund revenue	—	—	—	—	—	—	$7,611,803	$12,025,064	$23,559,551	$46,265,000	$133,827,938	$177,118,057	$258,394,089	$328,640,000	$484,040,000	$506,733,000
Educational and general income[10]	—	—	—	—	—	—	6,631,060	9,605,242	18,194,115	37,491,179	102,546,421	—	—	—	—	—
Expenditures[10]	—	—	—	—	—	—	6,961,566	11,343,738	22,279,862	44,792,226	130,891,227	172,256,104	249,178,822	—	—	—
Value of physical property	—	—	—	—	—	—	28,347,041	46,300,155[11]	47,621,853	108,343,196	261,828,196	253,429,585	304,655,463	—	—	—
Market value of endowment funds	—	—	—	—	—	—	18,834,453[12]	28,351,998[12]	25,807,498[12]	42,558,889[12]	69,706,883	62,781,424	125,793,970	—	385,718,492	473,948,942

—Not available.
[1]Prior to 1979–80, excludes branch campuses.
[2]Total number of different individuals (not reduced to full-time equivalent). Beginning in 1959–60, data are for the first term of the academic year.
[3]Estimated.
[4]Estimated number of senior instructional staff based on actual enrollment data for the designated year and enrollment/staff ratios for the prior staff survey. Excludes graduate assistants.
[5]Because of revised survey procedures, data may not be directly comparable with figures prior to 1989–90. Excludes graduate assistants.
[6]Data for 1869–70 to 1939–40 are for resident degree-credit students who enrolled at any time during the academic year. From 1869–70 to 1959–60, bachelor's degrees include degrees formerly classified as first-professional, such as M.D., D.D.S., and law degrees.
[7]Figures for years prior to 1939–70 are not precisely comparable with later data.
[8]Includes Ph.D., Ed.D., and comparable degrees at the doctoral level. Includes most degrees formerly classified as first-professional, such as M.D., D.D.S., and law degrees.
[9]Data for 1929–30 and 1933–40 include current-fund expenditures and additions to plant value. Includes most degrees formerly classified as first-professional, such as M.D., D.D.S., and law degrees.
[10]Data for 1929–30 and 1933–40 include current-fund expenditures and additions to plant value. Data for 1949–50 through 1989–90 include total expenditures for private institutions and current-fund expenditures for public institutions. Data for 1929–30 and 1933–40 include current-fund expenditures only. Data for 1999–2000 include total expenditures for private institutions and current-fund expenditures for public institutions. Data for later years are for total expenditures.

[11]Includes unexpended plant funds.
[12]Book value. Includes other nonexpendable funds.
[13]Constant dollars based on the Consumer Price Index, prepared by the Bureau of Labor Statistics, U.S. Department of Labor, adjusted to a school-year basis.
NOTE: Data through 1989–90 are for institutions of higher education, while later data are for degree-granting institutions. Degree-granting institutions grant associate's or higher degrees and participate in Title IV federal financial aid programs. The degree-granting classification is very similar to the earlier higher education classification, but it includes more 2-year colleges and excludes a few higher education institutions that did not grant degrees. Detail may not sum to totals because of rounding.
SOURCE: U.S. Department of Education, National Center for Education Statistics, *Biennial Survey of Education in the United States; Education Directory, Colleges and Universities; Faculty and Other Professional Staff in Institutions of Higher Education; Fall Enrollment in Colleges and Universities; Earned Degrees Conferred; Financial Statistics of Institutions of Higher Education;* Higher Education General Information Survey (HEGIS), "Fall Enrollment in Institutions of Higher Education;" Integrated Postsecondary Education Data System (IPEDS), "Fall Enrollment Survey" (IPEDS-EF:89–99), "Fall Staff Survey" (IPEDS-S:89–99), "Completions Survey" (IPEDS-C:90–00), and "Institutional Characteristics Survey" (IPEDS-IC:89–99); IPEDS Winter 2009–10, Human Resources component, Fall Staff section; IPEDS Spring 2010 and Spring 2013, Enrollment component; IPEDS Fall 2010 and Fall 2013, Completions component; and IPEDS Spring 2010 and Spring 2014, Finance component. (This table was prepared April 2015.)

Table 302.10. Recent high school completers and their enrollment in 2-year and 4-year colleges, by sex: 1960 through 2013

[Standard errors appear in parentheses]

Year	Number of high school completers[1] (in thousands)			Percent of recent high school completers[1] enrolled in college[2]								
	Total	Males	Females	Total			Males			Females		
				Total	2-year	4-year	Total	2-year	4-year	Total	2-year	4-year
1	2	3	4	5	6	7	8	9	10	11	12	13
1960	1,679 (43.8)	756 (31.8)	923 (29.6)	45.1 (2.13)	— (†)	— (†)	54.0 (3.18)	— (†)	— (†)	37.9 (2.80)	— (†)	— (†)
1961	1,763 (46.0)	790 (33.2)	973 (31.3)	48.0 (2.09)	— (†)	— (†)	56.3 (3.10)	— (†)	— (†)	41.3 (2.77)	— (†)	— (†)
1962	1,838 (43.6)	872 (31.5)	966 (30.0)	49.0 (2.05)	— (†)	— (†)	55.0 (2.96)	— (†)	— (†)	43.5 (2.80)	— (†)	— (†)
1963	1,741 (44.2)	794 (32.1)	947 (30.0)	45.0 (2.09)	— (†)	— (†)	52.3 (3.11)	— (†)	— (†)	39.0 (2.78)	— (†)	— (†)
1964	2,145 (43.0)	997 (31.9)	1,148 (28.5)	48.3 (1.89)	— (†)	— (†)	57.2 (2.75)	— (†)	— (†)	40.7 (2.54)	— (†)	— (†)
1965	2,659 (47.7)	1,254 (35.1)	1,405 (32.0)	50.9 (1.70)	— (†)	— (†)	57.3 (2.45)	— (†)	— (†)	45.3 (2.33)	— (†)	— (†)
1966	2,612 (45.0)	1,207 (33.8)	1,405 (29.0)	50.1 (1.72)	— (†)	— (†)	58.7 (2.49)	— (†)	— (†)	42.7 (2.32)	— (†)	— (†)
1967	2,525 (37.9)	1,142 (28.4)	1,383 (24.3)	51.9 (1.42)	— (†)	— (†)	57.6 (2.09)	— (†)	— (†)	47.2 (1.92)	— (†)	— (†)
1968	2,606 (37.3)	1,184 (28.2)	1,422 (23.8)	55.4 (1.39)	— (†)	— (†)	63.2 (2.00)	— (†)	— (†)	48.9 (1.89)	— (†)	— (†)
1969	2,842 (36.0)	1,352 (26.8)	1,490 (23.7)	53.3 (1.34)	— (†)	— (†)	60.1 (1.90)	— (†)	— (†)	47.2 (1.85)	— (†)	— (†)
1970	2,758 (37.4)	1,343 (26.1)	1,415 (26.8)	51.7 (1.36)	— (†)	— (†)	55.2 (1.94)	— (†)	— (†)	48.5 (1.90)	— (†)	— (†)
1971	2,875 (38.0)	1,371 (26.6)	1,504 (27.1)	53.5 (1.33)	— (†)	— (†)	57.6 (1.90)	— (†)	— (†)	49.8 (1.84)	— (†)	— (†)
1972	2,964 (37.8)	1,423 (27.0)	1,542 (26.4)	49.2 (1.31)	— (†)	— (†)	52.7 (1.89)	— (†)	— (†)	46.0 (1.81)	— (†)	— (†)
1973	3,058 (37.1)	1,460 (27.6)	1,599 (24.6)	46.6 (1.29)	14.9 (0.92)	31.6 (1.20)	50.0 (1.87)	14.6 (1.32)	35.4 (1.79)	43.4 (1.77)	15.2 (1.28)	28.2 (1.61)
1974	3,101 (38.6)	1,491 (27.8)	1,611 (26.8)	47.6 (1.28)	15.2 (0.92)	32.4 (1.20)	49.4 (1.85)	16.6 (1.37)	32.8 (1.74)	45.9 (1.77)	13.9 (1.23)	32.0 (1.66)
1975	3,185 (38.6)	1,513 (27.3)	1,672 (27.2)	50.7 (1.26)	18.2 (0.98)	32.6 (1.19)	52.6 (1.83)	19.0 (1.44)	33.6 (1.73)	49.0 (1.75)	17.4 (1.32)	31.6 (1.62)
1976	2,986 (39.8)	1,451 (28.9)	1,535 (27.3)	48.8 (1.31)	15.6 (0.95)	33.3 (1.23)	47.2 (1.87)	14.5 (1.32)	32.7 (1.76)	50.3 (1.82)	16.6 (1.35)	33.8 (1.72)
1977	3,141 (40.7)	1,483 (29.7)	1,659 (27.7)	50.6 (1.29)	17.5 (0.98)	33.1 (1.21)	52.1 (1.87)	17.2 (1.41)	35.0 (1.79)	49.3 (1.77)	17.8 (1.36)	31.5 (1.65)
1978	3,163 (39.7)	1,485 (29.3)	1,677 (26.7)	50.1 (1.28)	17.0 (0.96)	33.1 (1.21)	51.1 (1.87)	15.6 (1.36)	35.5 (1.79)	49.3 (1.76)	18.3 (1.36)	31.0 (1.63)
1979	3,160 (40.0)	1,475 (29.2)	1,685 (27.2)	49.3 (1.28)	17.5 (0.98)	31.8 (1.20)	50.4 (1.88)	16.9 (1.41)	33.5 (1.78)	48.4 (1.76)	18.1 (1.35)	30.3 (1.62)
1980	3,088 (39.4)	1,498 (28.4)	1,589 (27.3)	49.3 (1.30)	19.4 (1.03)	29.9 (1.19)	46.7 (1.86)	17.1 (1.40)	29.7 (1.70)	51.8 (1.81)	21.6 (1.49)	30.2 (1.66)
1981	3,056 (42.2)	1,491 (30.4)	1,565 (29.1)	53.9 (1.30)	20.5 (1.05)	33.5 (1.23)	54.8 (1.86)	20.9 (1.52)	33.9 (1.77)	53.1 (1.82)	20.1 (1.46)	33.0 (1.72)
1982	3,100 (40.4)	1,509 (29.0)	1,592 (28.2)	50.6 (1.36)	19.1 (1.07)	31.5 (1.26)	49.1 (1.95)	17.5 (1.48)	31.6 (1.81)	52.0 (1.90)	20.6 (1.54)	31.4 (1.76)
1983	2,963 (41.6)	1,389 (30.4)	1,573 (28.2)	52.7 (1.39)	19.2 (1.10)	33.5 (1.31)	51.9 (2.03)	20.2 (1.63)	31.7 (1.89)	53.4 (1.91)	18.4 (1.48)	35.1 (1.82)
1984	3,012 (36.5)	1,429 (28.7)	1,584 (21.9)	55.2 (1.37)	19.4 (1.09)	35.8 (1.32)	56.0 (1.99)	17.7 (1.53)	38.4 (1.95)	54.5 (1.90)	21.0 (1.55)	33.5 (1.80)
1985	2,668 (40.1)	1,287 (28.7)	1,381 (27.9)	57.7 (1.45)	19.6 (1.16)	38.1 (1.43)	58.6 (2.08)	19.9 (1.69)	38.8 (2.06)	56.8 (2.02)	19.3 (1.61)	37.5 (1.97)
1986	2,786 (38.6)	1,332 (28.5)	1,454 (26.0)	53.8 (1.43)	19.2 (1.13)	34.5 (1.37)	55.8 (2.06)	21.3 (1.70)	34.5 (1.97)	51.9 (1.99)	17.3 (1.50)	34.6 (1.89)
1987	2,647 (40.9)	1,278 (29.8)	1,369 (28.0)	56.8 (1.46)	18.9 (1.15)	37.9 (1.43)	58.3 (2.09)	17.3 (1.60)	41.0 (2.09)	55.3 (2.04)	20.3 (1.65)	35.0 (1.95)
1988	2,673 (47.0)	1,334 (34.1)	1,339 (32.3)	58.9 (1.57)	21.9 (1.32)	37.1 (1.54)	57.1 (2.24)	21.3 (1.85)	35.8 (2.17)	60.7 (2.20)	22.4 (1.88)	38.3 (2.19)
1989	2,450 (46.5)	1,204 (32.9)	1,246 (32.8)	59.6 (1.64)	20.7 (1.35)	38.9 (1.63)	57.6 (2.35)	18.3 (1.84)	39.3 (2.32)	61.6 (2.27)	23.1 (1.97)	38.5 (2.28)
1990	2,362 (43.0)	1,173 (30.6)	1,189 (30.2)	60.1 (1.60)	20.1 (1.31)	40.0 (1.60)	58.0 (2.29)	19.6 (1.85)	38.4 (2.26)	62.2 (2.24)	20.6 (1.87)	41.6 (2.28)
1991	2,276 (41.0)	1,140 (29.0)	1,136 (29.0)	62.5 (1.62)	24.9 (1.44)	37.7 (1.62)	57.9 (2.33)	22.9 (1.98)	35.0 (2.25)	67.1 (2.22)	26.8 (2.09)	40.3 (2.32)
1992	2,397 (40.4)	1,216 (29.1)	1,180 (28.1)	61.9 (1.58)	23.0 (1.37)	38.9 (1.59)	60.0 (2.24)	22.1 (1.89)	37.8 (2.21)	63.8 (2.23)	23.9 (1.98)	40.0 (2.27)
1993	2,342 (41.4)	1,120 (30.6)	1,223 (27.7)	62.6 (1.59)	22.8 (1.38)	39.8 (1.61)	59.9 (2.33)	22.9 (2.00)	37.0 (2.30)	65.2 (2.17)	22.8 (1.91)	42.4 (2.25)
1994	2,517 (38.1)	1,244 (27.9)	1,273 (25.9)	61.9 (1.43)	21.0 (1.20)	40.9 (1.45)	60.6 (2.05)	23.0 (1.76)	37.5 (2.03)	63.2 (1.99)	19.1 (1.63)	44.1 (2.05)
1995	2,599 (40.9)	1,238 (29.9)	1,361 (27.7)	61.9 (1.41)	21.5 (1.19)	40.4 (1.42)	62.6 (2.03)	25.3 (1.82)	37.4 (2.03)	61.3 (1.95)	18.1 (1.54)	43.2 (1.98)
1996	2,660 (40.5)	1,297 (29.5)	1,363 (27.7)	65.0 (1.42)	23.1 (1.26)	41.9 (1.47)	60.1 (2.09)	21.5 (1.76)	38.5 (2.08)	69.7 (1.92)	24.6 (1.80)	45.1 (2.07)
1997	2,769 (41.8)	1,354 (31.0)	1,415 (27.9)	67.0 (1.38)	22.8 (1.23)	44.3 (1.45)	63.6 (2.01)	21.4 (1.71)	42.2 (2.07)	70.3 (1.87)	24.1 (1.75)	46.2 (2.04)
1998	2,810 (43.9)	1,452 (31.0)	1,358 (31.0)	65.6 (1.38)	24.4 (1.25)	41.3 (1.43)	62.4 (1.96)	24.4 (1.74)	38.0 (1.96)	69.1 (1.93)	24.3 (1.79)	44.8 (2.08)
1999	2,897 (41.5)	1,474 (29.9)	1,423 (28.8)	62.9 (1.38)	21.0 (1.17)	41.9 (1.41)	61.4 (1.95)	21.0 (1.63)	40.5 (1.97)	64.4 (1.95)	21.1 (1.67)	43.3 (2.02)
2000	2,756 (45.3)	1,251 (33.6)	1,505 (29.7)	63.3 (1.41)	21.4 (1.20)	41.9 (1.45)	59.9 (2.13)	23.1 (1.83)	36.8 (2.10)	66.2 (1.88)	20.0 (1.59)	46.2 (1.98)
2001	2,549 (46.5)	1,277 (33.7)	1,273 (32.0)	61.8 (1.48)	19.6 (1.21)	42.1 (1.51)	60.1 (2.11)	18.6 (1.68)	41.4 (2.12)	63.5 (2.08)	20.6 (1.75)	42.8 (2.13)
2002	2,796 (42.7)	1,412 (31.3)	1,384 (29.0)	65.2 (1.31)	21.6 (1.14)	43.6 (1.37)	62.1 (1.88)	20.4 (1.57)	41.7 (1.92)	68.4 (1.82)	22.8 (1.65)	45.6 (1.95)
2003	2,677 (42.2)	1,306 (29.9)	1,372 (29.7)	63.9 (1.35)	21.5 (1.16)	42.5 (1.39)	61.2 (1.97)	21.9 (1.67)	39.3 (1.97)	66.5 (1.86)	21.0 (1.61)	45.5 (1.96)
2004	2,752 (40.0)	1,327 (29.1)	1,425 (27.3)	66.7 (1.31)	22.4 (1.16)	44.2 (1.38)	61.4 (1.95)	21.8 (1.65)	39.6 (1.96)	71.5 (1.74)	23.1 (1.63)	48.5 (1.93)
2005	2,675 (40.8)	1,262 (31.5)	1,414 (24.9)	68.6 (1.31)	24.0 (1.21)	44.6 (1.40)	66.5 (1.94)	24.7 (1.77)	41.8 (2.03)	70.4 (1.77)	23.4 (1.64)	47.0 (1.94)
2006	2,692 (44.6)	1,328 (32.7)	1,363 (30.1)	66.0 (1.33)	24.7 (1.21)	41.3 (1.39)	65.8 (1.90)	24.9 (1.73)	40.9 (1.97)	66.1 (1.87)	24.5 (1.70)	41.7 (1.95)
2007	2,955 (42.6)	1,511 (30.0)	1,444 (30.3)	67.2 (1.26)	24.1 (1.15)	43.1 (1.33)	66.1 (1.78)	22.7 (1.57)	43.4 (1.86)	68.3 (1.79)	25.5 (1.67)	42.8 (1.90)
2008	3,151 (42.8)	1,640 (29.6)	1,511 (30.9)	68.6 (1.21)	27.7 (1.16)	40.9 (1.28)	65.9 (1.71)	24.9 (1.56)	41.0 (1.77)	71.6 (1.69)	30.6 (1.73)	40.9 (1.85)
2009	2,937 (45.0)	1,407 (32.8)	1,531 (30.6)	70.1 (1.23)	27.7 (1.21)	42.4 (1.33)	66.0 (1.84)	25.1 (1.69)	40.9 (1.91)	73.8 (1.64)	30.1 (1.71)	43.8 (1.85)
2010[3]	3,160 (91.8)	1,679 (64.6)	1,482 (58.4)	68.1 (1.49)	26.7 (1.52)	41.4 (1.61)	62.8 (1.88)	28.5 (2.03)	34.3 (1.97)	74.0 (2.31)	24.6 (2.32)	49.5 (2.59)
2011[3]	3,079 (88.3)	1,611 (60.6)	1,468 (58.4)	68.2 (1.45)	25.9 (1.49)	42.3 (1.44)	64.7 (2.16)	24.7 (1.79)	40.0 (2.10)	72.2 (1.98)	27.3 (2.17)	44.9 (2.37)
2012[3]	3,203 (96.2)	1,622 (70.1)	1,581 (54.0)	66.2 (1.59)	28.8 (1.57)	37.5 (1.60)	61.3 (2.17)	26.9 (2.20)	34.4 (2.15)	71.3 (2.11)	30.7 (2.09)	40.6 (2.21)
2013[3]	2,977 (84.4)	1,524 (62.9)	1,453 (57.0)	65.9 (1.58)	23.8 (1.44)	42.1 (1.76)	63.5 (2.20)	24.5 (2.14)	39.0 (2.48)	68.4 (2.17)	23.0 (2.15)	45.3 (2.21)

—Not available.
†Not applicable.
[1]Individuals ages 16 to 24 who graduated from high school or completed a GED during the calendar year.
[2]Enrollment in college as of October of each year for individuals ages 16 to 24 who completed high school during the calendar year.
[3]Beginning in 2010, standard errors were computed using replicate weights, which produced more precise values than the generalized variance function methodology used in prior years.

NOTE: Data are based on sample surveys of the civilian population. High school completion data in this table differ from figures appearing in other tables because of varying survey procedures and coverage. High school completers include GED recipients. Detail may not sum to totals because of rounding.
SOURCE: American College Testing Program, unpublished tabulations, derived from statistics collected by the Census Bureau, 1960 through 1969. U.S. Department of Commerce, Census Bureau, Current Population Survey (CPS), October, 1970 through 2013. (This table was prepared July 2014.)

Table 302.20. Percentage of recent high school completers enrolled in 2- and 4-year colleges, by race/ethnicity: 1960 through 2013
[Standard errors appear in parentheses]

	Percent of recent high school completers[1] enrolled in college[2] (annual data)					3-year moving averages[3]							
						Percent of recent high school completers[1] enrolled in college[2]					Difference between percent enrolled		
Year	Total	White	Black	Hispanic	Asian	Total	White	Black	Hispanic	Asian	White-Black	White-Hispanic	White-Asian
1	2	3	4	5	6	7	8	9	10	11	12	13	14
1960[4]	45.1 (2.13)	45.8 (2.21)	— (†)	— (†)	— (†)	46.6 (1.49)	47.7 (1.56)	— (†)	— (†)	— (†)	— (†)	— (†)	— (†)
1961[4]	48.0 (2.09)	49.5 (2.19)	— (†)	— (†)	— (†)	47.4 (1.21)	48.7 (1.26)	— (†)	— (†)	— (†)	— (†)	— (†)	— (†)
1962[4]	49.0 (2.05)	50.6 (2.15)	— (†)	— (†)	— (†)	47.4 (1.20)	48.6 (1.25)	— (†)	— (†)	— (†)	— (†)	— (†)	— (†)
1963[4]	45.0 (2.09)	45.6 (2.17)	— (†)	— (†)	— (†)	47.5 (1.16)	48.5 (1.21)	— (†)	— (†)	— (†)	— (†)	— (†)	— (†)
1964[4]	48.3 (1.89)	49.2 (1.98)	— (†)	— (†)	— (†)	48.5 (1.08)	49.2 (1.13)	— (†)	— (†)	— (†)	— (†)	— (†)	— (†)
1965[4]	50.9 (1.70)	51.7 (1.78)	— (†)	— (†)	— (†)	49.9 (1.02)	51.0 (1.07)	— (†)	— (†)	— (†)	— (†)	— (†)	— (†)
1966[4]	50.1 (1.72)	51.7 (1.79)	— (†)	— (†)	— (†)	51.0 (0.99)	52.1 (1.04)	— (†)	— (†)	— (†)	— (†)	— (†)	— (†)
1967[4]	51.9 (1.42)	53.0 (1.50)	— (†)	— (†)	— (†)	52.5 (0.81)	53.8 (0.85)	— (†)	— (†)	— (†)	— (†)	— (†)	— (†)
1968[4]	55.4 (1.39)	56.6 (1.47)	— (†)	— (†)	— (†)	53.6 (0.80)	55.0 (0.84)	— (†)	— (†)	— (†)	— (†)	— (†)	— (†)
1969[4]	53.3 (1.34)	55.2 (1.41)	— (†)	— (†)	— (†)	53.5 (0.79)	54.6 (0.83)	— (†)	— (†)	— (†)	— (†)	— (†)	— (†)
1970[4]	51.7 (1.36)	52.0 (1.44)	— (†)	— (†)	— (†)	52.9 (0.77)	53.8 (0.82)	— (†)	— (†)	— (†)	— (†)	— (†)	— (†)
1971[4]	53.5 (1.33)	54.0 (1.40)	— (†)	— (†)	— (†)	51.5 (0.77)	51.9 (0.82)	— (†)	— (†)	— (†)	— (†)	— (†)	— (†)
1972	49.2 (1.31)	49.7 (1.42)	44.6 (4.62)	45.0 (9.74)	— (†)	49.7 (0.76)	50.5 (0.81)	38.4 (3.18)	49.9 (6.64)	— (†)	12.1 (3.28)	‡ (†)	— (†)
1973	46.6 (1.29)	47.8 (1.40)	32.5 (4.30)	54.1 (9.01)	— (†)	47.8 (0.75)	48.2 (0.81)	41.4 (2.62)	48.8 (5.33)	— (†)	6.8 ! (2.74)	‡ (†)	— (†)
1974	47.6 (1.28)	47.2 (1.39)	47.2 (4.58)	46.9 (8.94)	— (†)	48.3 (0.74)	48.7 (0.80)	40.5 (2.63)	53.1 (5.09)	— (†)	8.3 ! (2.75)	‡ (†)	— (†)
1975	50.7 (1.26)	51.1 (1.37)	41.7 (3.97)	58.0 (8.44)	— (†)	49.1 (0.74)	49.1 (0.81)	44.5 (2.29)	52.7 (4.88)	— (†)	‡ (†)	‡ (†)	— (†)
1976	48.8 (1.31)	48.8 (1.43)	44.4 (4.08)	52.7 (7.97)	— (†)	50.1 (0.74)	50.3 (0.81)	45.3 (2.30)	53.6 (4.68)	— (†)	5.0 ! (2.44)	‡ (†)	— (†)
1977	50.6 (1.29)	50.8 (1.41)	49.5 (4.65)	50.8 (7.96)	— (†)	49.9 (0.75)	50.1 (0.82)	46.8 (2.70)	48.8 (4.72)	— (†)	‡ (†)	‡ (†)	— (†)
1978	50.1 (1.28)	50.5 (1.41)	46.4 (4.51)	42.0 (8.44)	— (†)	50.0 (0.74)	50.4 (0.81)	47.5 (2.67)	46.1 (4.69)	— (†)	‡ (†)	‡ (†)	— (†)
1979	49.3 (1.28)	49.9 (1.41)	46.7 (4.69)	45.0 (7.92)	— (†)	49.6 (0.74)	50.1 (0.82)	45.2 (2.62)	46.3 (4.83)	— (†)	‡ (†)	‡ (†)	— (†)
1980	49.3 (1.30)	49.8 (1.43)	42.7 (4.44)	52.3 (8.70)	— (†)	50.8 (0.75)	51.5 (0.82)	44.0 (2.61)	49.6 (4.78)	— (†)	7.5 ! (2.74)	‡ (†)	— (†)
1981	53.9 (1.30)	54.9 (1.44)	42.7 (4.44)	52.1 (8.19)	— (†)	51.3 (0.75)	52.4 (0.83)	40.3 (2.50)	48.7 (4.68)	— (†)	12.2 (2.64)	‡ (†)	— (†)
1982	50.6 (1.36)	52.7 (1.52)	35.8 (4.33)	43.2 (7.96)	— (†)	52.4 (0.79)	54.2 (0.84)	38.8 (2.57)	49.4 (4.94)	— (†)	15.4 (2.70)	‡ (†)	— (†)
1983	52.7 (1.39)	55.0 (1.55)	38.2 (4.34)	54.2 (8.96)	— (†)	52.8 (0.79)	55.5 (0.89)	38.0 (2.47)	46.7 (4.72)	— (†)	17.5 (2.62)	‡ (†)	— (†)
1984	55.2 (1.37)	59.0 (1.54)	39.8 (4.15)	44.3 (7.67)	— (†)	55.1 (0.81)	57.9 (0.91)	39.9 (2.54)	49.3 (4.89)	— (†)	18.0 (2.70)	‡ (†)	— (†)
1985	57.7 (1.45)	60.1 (1.62)	42.2 (4.78)	51.0 (9.76)	— (†)	55.5 (0.82)	58.6 (0.92)	39.5 (2.55)	46.1 (5.18)	— (†)	19.1 (2.71)	12.5 ! (5.27)	— (†)
1986	53.8 (1.43)	56.8 (1.62)	36.9 (4.38)	44.0 (8.85)	— (†)	56.1 (0.84)	58.5 (0.94)	43.5 (2.71)	42.3 (5.20)	— (†)	15.0 (2.87)	16.2 ! (5.28)	— (†)
1987	56.8 (1.46)	58.6 (1.65)	52.2 (4.82)	33.5 (8.25)	— (†)	56.5 (0.83)	58.8 (0.95)	44.2 (2.65)	45.0 (5.04)	— (†)	14.6 (2.82)	13.8 ! (5.13)	— (†)
1988	58.9 (1.57)	61.1 (1.79)	44.4 (4.91)	57.1 (10.14)	— (†)	58.4 (0.92)	60.1 (0.96)	49.7 (2.98)	48.5 (5.99)	— (†)	10.4 ! (3.13)	‡ (†)	— (†)
1989	59.6 (1.64)	60.7 (1.85)	53.4 (5.27)	55.1 (10.51)	— (†)	59.5 (0.94)	61.6 (1.06)	48.0 (2.98)	52.7 (6.33)	— (†)	13.6 (3.16)	‡ (†)	— (†)
1990	60.1 (1.60)	63.0 (1.80)	46.8 (5.08)	42.7 (10.82)	— (†)	60.7 (0.92)	63.0 (1.08)	48.9 (2.97)	52.5 (5.70)	— (†)	14.0 (3.16)	‡ (†)	— (†)
1991	62.5 (1.62)	65.4 (1.82)	46.4 (5.25)	57.2 (9.58)	— (†)	61.5 (0.92)	64.2 (1.05)	47.2 (2.93)	52.6 (5.52)	— (†)	17.0 (3.11)	11.7 ! (5.62)	— (†)
1992	61.9 (1.58)	64.3 (1.84)	48.2 (4.92)	55.0 (8.50)	— (†)	62.3 (0.92)	64.2 (1.06)	50.0 (2.98)	58.2 (5.04)	— (†)	14.2 (3.16)	‡ (†)	— (†)
1993	62.6 (1.59)	62.9 (1.85)	55.6 (5.28)	62.2 (8.22)	— (†)	62.1 (0.91)	63.9 (1.04)	51.3 (2.97)	55.7 (4.97)	— (†)	12.6 (3.14)	‡ (†)	— (†)
1994	61.9 (1.43)	64.5 (1.61)	50.8 (4.42)	49.1 (6.28)	— (†)	62.1 (0.83)	64.0 (1.03)	52.4 (2.52)	55.0 (3.23)	— (†)	11.5 (2.72)	8.9 ! (3.39)	— (†)
1995	61.9 (1.41)	64.3 (1.64)	51.2 (4.20)	53.7 (4.92)	— (†)	63.0 (0.81)	65.4 (0.93)	52.9 (2.40)	51.6 (3.18)	— (†)	12.5 (2.57)	13.8 (3.31)	— (†)
1996	65.0 (1.42)	67.4 (1.67)	56.0 (4.03)	50.8 (5.79)	— (†)	64.7 (0.82)	66.6 (0.93)	55.4 (2.41)	57.6 (2.96)	— (†)	11.3 (2.58)	9.0 ! (3.10)	— (†)
1997	67.0 (1.38)	68.2 (1.64)	58.5 (4.12)	65.6 (4.53)	— (†)	65.9 (0.80)	68.1 (0.95)	58.8 (2.35)	55.3 (2.93)	— (†)	9.3 (2.53)	12.8 (3.08)	— (†)
1998	65.6 (1.38)	68.5 (1.61)	61.9 (4.05)	47.4 (4.92)	— (†)	65.2 (0.80)	67.7 (0.94)	59.8 (2.31)	51.9 (2.79)	— (†)	7.9 ! (2.50)	15.7 (2.94)	— (†)
1999	62.9 (1.38)	66.3 (1.64)	58.9 (3.86)	42.3 (4.76)	— (†)	64.0 (0.80)	66.8 (0.94)	58.6 (2.31)	47.4 (2.84)	— (†)	8.3 ! (2.50)	19.5 (2.99)	— (†)
2000	63.3 (1.41)	65.7 (1.66)	54.9 (4.11)	52.9 (5.03)	— (†)	62.7 (0.82)	65.4 (0.97)	56.4 (2.33)	48.6 (2.96)	— (†)	9.1 (2.53)	16.9 (3.11)	— (†)
2001	61.8 (1.48)	64.3 (1.72)	55.0 (4.17)	51.7 (5.63)	— (†)	63.5 (0.82)	66.3 (0.97)	56.4 (2.39)	52.8 (2.93)	— (†)	10.0 (2.58)	13.5 (3.09)	— (†)
2002	65.2 (1.31)	69.1 (1.55)	59.4 (3.90)	53.6 (4.46)	— (†)	63.7 (0.78)	66.5 (0.97)	57.3 (2.33)	54.8 (2.75)	— (†)	9.3 (2.52)	11.7 (2.92)	— (†)
2003[5]	63.9 (1.35)	66.2 (1.61)	57.5 (4.25)	58.6 (4.61)	84.1 (5.10)	65.3 (0.77)	68.0 (0.91)	59.9 (2.29)	57.7 (2.66)	80.0 (3.99)	8.1 ! (2.46)	10.3 (2.81)	-11.9 ! (4.10)
2004[5]	66.7 (1.31)	68.8 (1.57)	62.5 (3.77)	61.8 (4.76)	75.6 (6.13)	66.4 (0.77)	69.4 (0.91)	58.8 (2.34)	57.7 (2.60)	81.6 (3.37)	10.6 (2.51)	11.7 (2.75)	-12.2 (3.49)
2005[5]	68.6 (1.31)	73.2 (1.52)	55.7 (4.15)	54.0 (4.18)	86.7 (5.99)	67.1 (0.76)	70.2 (0.90)	58.2 (2.35)	57.5 (2.52)	80.9 (3.64)	12.0 (2.52)	12.6 (2.67)	-10.7 ! (3.75)
2006[5]	66.0 (1.33)	68.5 (1.60)	55.5 (4.33)	57.9 (4.18)	82.3 (5.32)	67.2 (0.75)	70.4 (0.89)	55.6 (2.35)	58.5 (2.43)	85.1 (3.64)	14.7 (2.53)	11.9 (2.59)	-14.7 (3.74)
2007[5]	67.2 (1.26)	69.5 (1.49)	55.7 (3.78)	64.0 (4.22)	88.8 (6.26)	67.3 (0.73)	70.0 (0.87)	55.7 (2.27)	62.0 (2.33)	85.8 (3.45)	14.3 (2.43)	8.0 ! (2.48)	-15.8 (3.56)
2008[5]	68.6 (1.21)	71.7 (1.44)	55.7 (3.78)	63.9 (3.72)	88.4 (5.08)	68.6 (0.71)	70.8 (0.86)	60.3 (2.15)	62.3 (2.25)	90.1 (3.01)	10.5 (2.31)	8.6 (2.41)	-19.2 (3.13)
2009[5]	70.1 (1.23)	71.3 (1.53)	69.5 (3.51)	59.3 (3.80)	92.1 (3.90)	68.9 (0.70)	71.2 (0.86)	62.4 (2.09)	60.9 (2.14)	88.1 (2.85)	8.8 (2.26)	10.3 (2.31)	-16.9 (2.98)
2010[5,6]	68.1 (1.49)	70.5 (1.68)	62.0 (4.81)	59.7 (4.18)	84.7 (5.27)	68.8 (0.71)	70.1 (0.90)	66.1 (2.01)	62.3 (2.01)	87.4 (2.78)	‡ (†)	7.8 (2.21)	-17.3 (2.92)
2011[5,6]	68.2 (1.45)	68.3 (1.86)	67.1 (4.01)	66.6 (3.50)	86.1 (4.25)	67.5 (0.89)	68.2 (1.03)	62.1 (2.86)	66.1 (2.17)	83.9 (2.79)	6.1 ! (3.04)	‡ (†)	-15.7 (2.97)
2012[5,6]	66.2 (1.59)	65.7 (1.94)	56.4 (4.84)	70.3 (3.22)	81.5 (5.15)	66.8 (0.94)	67.6 (1.12)	60.5 (2.64)	65.9 (1.99)	82.3 (3.59)	7.1 ! (2.87)	‡ (†)	-14.7 (3.76)
2013[5,6]	65.9 (1.58)	68.8 (1.90)	56.7 (5.59)	59.8 (3.62)	80.1 (6.52)	66.1 (1.07)	67.2 (1.35)	56.5 (3.51)	65.6 (2.39)	80.8 (4.32)	10.7 ! (3.76)	‡ (†)	-13.6 ! (4.53)

—Not available.
†Not applicable.
!Interpret data with caution. The coefficient of variation (CV) for this estimate is between 30 and 50 percent.
‡Reporting standards not met. The coefficient of variation (CV) for this estimate is 50 percent or greater.
[1]Individuals ages 16 to 24 who graduated from high school or completed a GED during the calendar year.
[2]Enrollment in college as of October of each year for individuals ages 16 to 24 who completed high school during the calendar year.
[3]A 3-year moving average is a weighted average of the year indicated, the year immediately preceding, and the year immediately following. For the first and final years of available data, a 2-year moving average is used: The moving average for 1960 reflects an average of 1960 and 1961; for Black and Hispanic data, the moving average for 1972 reflects an average of 1972 and 1973; for Asian data, the moving average for 2003 reflects an average of 2003 and 2004; and the moving average for 2013 reflects an average of 2012 and 2013. Moving averages are used to produce more stable estimates.
[4]Prior to 1972, White data include persons of Hispanic ethnicity.
[5]White, Black, and Asian data exclude persons identifying themselves as two or more races.
[6]Beginning in 2010, standard errors were computed using replicate weights, which produced more precise values than the generalized variance function methodology used in prior years.
NOTE: Race categories exclude persons of Hispanic ethnicity except where otherwise noted. Total includes persons of other racial/ethnic groups not separately shown.
SOURCE: American College Testing Program, unpublished tabulations, derived from statistics collected by the Census Bureau, 1960 through 1969. U.S. Department of Commerce, Census Bureau, Current Population Survey (CPS), October, 1970 through 2013. (This table was prepared July 2014.)

Table 302.30. Percentage of recent high school completers enrolled in 2-year and 4-year colleges, by income level: 1975 through 2013
[Standard errors appear in parentheses]

Year	Percent of recent high school completers[1] enrolled in college[2] (annual data)				3-year moving averages[3]						
	Total	Low income	Middle income	High income	Percent of recent high school completers[1] enrolled in college[2]				Difference between percent enrolled	
					Total	Low income	Middle income	High income	High-low income	High-middle income
1	2	3	4	5	6	7	8	9	10	11
1975	50.7 (1.26)	31.2 (3.59)	46.2 (1.69)	64.5 (2.09)	49.1 (0.74)	34.7 (2.74)	43.5 (1.22)	63.7 (1.47)	29.0 (3.11)	20.2 (1.91)
1976	48.8 (1.31)	39.1 (4.20)	40.5 (1.76)	63.0 (2.06)	50.1 (0.74)	32.3 (2.17)	43.8 (1.00)	64.6 (1.18)	32.3 (2.47)	20.8 (1.55)
1977	50.6 (1.29)	27.7 (3.54)	44.2 (1.76)	66.3 (2.01)	49.9 (0.75)	32.4 (2.22)	43.1 (1.02)	64.4 (1.18)	32.1 (2.51)	21.4 (1.56)
1978	50.1 (1.28)	31.4 (3.74)	44.3 (1.74)	64.0 (2.05)	50.0 (0.74)	29.8 (2.13)	43.9 (1.01)	64.5 (1.17)	34.6 (2.43)	20.5 (1.55)
1979	49.3 (1.28)	30.5 (3.78)	43.2 (1.74)	63.2 (2.04)	49.6 (0.74)	31.6 (2.11)	43.4 (1.01)	64.1 (1.19)	32.6 (2.42)	20.8 (1.56)
1980	49.3 (1.30)	32.5 (3.47)	42.5 (1.78)	65.2 (2.08)	50.8 (0.75)	32.2 (2.14)	45.0 (1.02)	65.3 (1.20)	33.0 (2.45)	20.2 (1.57)
1981	53.9 (1.30)	33.6 (3.90)	49.2 (1.75)	67.6 (2.09)	51.3 (0.75)	32.9 (2.11)	44.5 (1.01)	67.9 (1.19)	34.9 (2.42)	23.4 (1.57)
1982	50.6 (1.36)	32.8 (3.81)	41.7 (1.81)	70.9 (2.13)	52.4 (0.79)	33.6 (2.29)	45.4 (1.06)	69.6 (1.25)	36.0 (2.61)	24.2 (1.64)
1983	52.7 (1.39)	34.6 (4.02)	45.2 (1.88)	70.3 (2.17)	52.8 (0.79)	34.0 (2.20)	45.1 (1.08)	71.7 (1.23)	37.8 (2.52)	26.7 (1.63)
1984	55.2 (1.37)	34.5 (3.62)	48.4 (1.89)	74.0 (2.09)	55.1 (0.81)	36.3 (2.26)	48.0 (1.11)	72.9 (1.24)	36.6 (2.58)	24.9 (1.66)
1985	57.7 (1.45)	40.2 (4.14)	50.6 (2.02)	74.6 (2.16)	55.5 (0.82)	35.9 (2.18)	49.1 (1.13)	73.2 (1.26)	37.3 (2.51)	24.1 (1.69)
1986	53.8 (1.43)	33.9 (3.59)	48.5 (1.97)	71.0 (2.28)	56.1 (0.84)	36.8 (2.23)	49.6 (1.17)	73.2 (1.27)	36.4 (2.57)	23.5 (1.72)
1987	56.8 (1.46)	36.9 (3.88)	50.0 (2.07)	73.8 (2.16)	56.5 (0.83)	37.6 (2.21)	51.1 (1.16)	72.6 (1.30)	35.0 (2.57)	21.5 (1.74)
1988	58.9 (1.57)	42.5 (4.39)	54.7 (2.14)	72.8 (2.52)	58.4 (0.92)	42.4 (2.54)	53.4 (1.28)	72.5 (1.44)	30.2 (2.92)	19.1 (1.93)
1989	59.6 (1.64)	48.1 (4.56)	55.4 (2.28)	70.7 (2.61)	59.5 (0.94)	45.6 (2.66)	54.9 (1.28)	73.2 (1.50)	27.6 (3.06)	18.4 (1.97)
1990	60.1 (1.60)	46.7 (4.76)	54.4 (2.14)	76.6 (2.54)	60.7 (0.92)	44.8 (2.63)	56.0 (1.27)	75.0 (1.44)	30.2 (3.00)	19.0 (1.92)
1991	62.5 (1.62)	39.5 (4.50)	58.4 (2.25)	78.2 (2.39)	61.5 (0.92)	42.2 (2.62)	56.5 (1.26)	78.0 (1.40)	35.8 (2.97)	21.4 (1.88)
1992	61.9 (1.58)	40.9 (4.37)	57.0 (2.18)	79.0 (2.35)	62.3 (0.92)	43.6 (2.60)	57.4 (1.26)	78.8 (1.38)	35.3 (2.94)	21.4 (1.87)
1993	62.6 (1.59)	50.4 (4.56)	56.9 (2.15)	79.3 (2.46)	62.1 (0.91)	44.7 (2.55)	57.3 (1.23)	78.7 (1.39)	34.0 (2.90)	21.5 (1.86)
1994	61.9 (1.43)	43.3 (3.96)	57.8 (1.94)	77.9 (2.22)	62.1 (0.83)	42.0 (2.27)	57.0 (1.14)	80.4 (1.22)	38.4 (2.57)	23.4 (1.67)
1995	61.9 (1.41)	34.2 (3.56)	56.0 (2.00)	83.5 (1.86)	63.0 (0.81)	42.1 (2.16)	58.9 (1.12)	79.9 (1.20)	37.8 (2.47)	21.0 (1.64)
1996	65.0 (1.42)	48.6 (3.78)	62.7 (1.95)	78.0 (2.27)	64.7 (0.82)	47.1 (2.18)	59.9 (1.16)	81.3 (1.19)	34.3 (2.49)	21.4 (1.66)
1997	67.0 (1.38)	57.0 (3.66)	60.7 (1.97)	82.2 (1.98)	65.9 (0.80)	50.6 (2.14)	62.7 (1.12)	79.3 (1.24)	28.7 (2.47)	16.6 (1.67)
1998	65.6 (1.38)	46.4 (3.62)	64.7 (1.89)	77.5 (2.21)	65.2 (0.80)	50.3 (2.14)	61.9 (1.10)	78.4 (1.24)	28.1 (2.47)	16.6 (1.66)
1999	62.9 (1.38)	47.6 (3.77)	60.2 (1.87)	75.4 (2.26)	64.0 (0.80)	47.9 (2.13)	61.5 (1.10)	76.6 (1.29)	28.7 (2.49)	15.1 (1.70)
2000	63.3 (1.41)	49.7 (3.67)	59.5 (1.97)	76.9 (2.22)	62.7 (0.82)	47.1 (2.17)	58.8 (1.14)	77.4 (1.29)	30.3 (2.52)	18.6 (1.72)
2001	61.8 (1.48)	43.8 (3.81)	56.4 (2.07)	80.0 (2.19)	63.5 (0.82)	49.9 (2.19)	59.1 (1.14)	78.3 (1.28)	28.4 (2.53)	19.3 (1.71)
2002	65.2 (1.31)	56.3 (3.64)	60.9 (1.78)	78.2 (2.12)	63.7 (0.78)	50.9 (2.14)	58.4 (1.08)	79.5 (1.20)	28.6 (2.45)	21.0 (1.61)
2003	63.9 (1.35)	52.8 (3.83)	57.6 (1.87)	80.1 (2.02)	65.3 (0.77)	52.5 (2.20)	60.6 (1.05)	79.5 (1.18)	27.0 (2.49)	18.9 (1.58)
2004	66.7 (1.31)	47.8 (3.95)	63.3 (1.79)	80.1 (1.98)	66.4 (0.77)	51.4 (2.24)	62.0 (1.05)	80.5 (1.15)	29.0 (2.52)	18.5 (1.56)
2005	68.6 (1.31)	53.5 (3.86)	65.1 (1.81)	81.2 (1.98)	67.1 (0.76)	50.8 (2.26)	63.3 (1.04)	80.7 (1.15)	29.9 (2.53)	17.4 (1.55)
2006	66.0 (1.33)	50.9 (3.92)	61.4 (1.82)	80.7 (2.01)	67.2 (0.75)	54.5 (2.18)	63.3 (1.03)	80.0 (1.15)	25.5 (2.47)	16.7 (1.55)
2007	67.2 (1.26)	58.4 (3.57)	63.3 (1.73)	78.2 (2.01)	67.3 (0.73)	55.3 (2.11)	63.5 (0.99)	80.2 (1.14)	24.9 (2.40)	16.8 (1.51)
2008	68.6 (1.21)	55.9 (3.50)	65.2 (1.62)	81.9 (1.90)	68.6 (0.71)	56.1 (2.08)	65.1 (0.96)	81.4 (1.11)	25.3 (2.36)	16.2 (1.47)
2009	70.1 (1.23)	53.9 (3.75)	66.7 (1.66)	84.2 (1.84)	68.9 (0.70)	53.3 (2.02)	66.2 (0.94)	82.8 (1.10)	29.5 (2.30)	16.6 (1.44)
2010[4]	68.1 (1.49)	50.7 (3.88)	66.7 (2.03)	82.2 (2.34)	68.8 (0.71)	52.6 (1.97)	66.5 (0.94)	83.0 (1.12)	30.4 (2.27)	16.4 (1.46)
2011[4]	68.2 (1.45)	53.5 (4.25)	66.2 (1.94)	82.4 (2.46)	67.5 (0.89)	51.6 (2.47)	65.9 (1.11)	81.7 (1.42)	30.1 (2.85)	15.9 (1.81)
2012[4]	66.2 (1.59)	50.9 (4.39)	64.7 (2.10)	80.7 (2.54)	66.8 (0.94)	50.3 (2.63)	64.9 (1.26)	80.4 (1.59)	30.1 (3.07)	15.5 (2.03)
2013[4]	65.9 (1.58)	45.5 (4.31)	63.8 (2.32)	78.5 (2.68)	66.1 (1.07)	48.8 (3.27)	64.2 (1.52)	79.5 (1.87)	30.8 (3.77)	15.3 (2.41)

[1] Individuals ages 16 to 24 who graduated from high school or completed a GED during the calendar year.
[2] Enrollment in college as of October of each year for individuals ages 16 to 24 who completed high school during the calendar year.
[3] A 3-year moving average is a weighted average of the year indicated, the year immediately preceding, and the year immediately following. For 1975 and 2013, a 2-year moving average is used: The moving average for income groups in 1975 reflects an average of 1975 and 1976, and the moving average for 2013 reflects an average of 2012 and 2013. Moving averages are used to produce more stable estimates.
[4] Beginning in 2010, standard errors were computed using replicate weights, which produced more precise values than the generalized variance function methodology used in prior years.
NOTE: Low income refers to the bottom 20 percent of all family incomes, high income refers to the top 20 percent of all family incomes, and middle income refers to the 60 percent in between.
SOURCE: U.S. Department of Commerce, Census Bureau, Current Population Survey (CPS), October, 1975 through 2013. (This table was prepared July 2014.)

Table 302.40. Number of high schools with 12th-graders and percentage of high school graduates attending 4-year colleges, by selected high school characteristics: Selected years, 1998–99 through 2011–12

[Standard errors appear in parentheses]

Selected high school characteristic	Number of high schools with 12th-graders				Graduation rate of 12th-graders in 2010–11[1]	Percent of graduates attending 4-year colleges			
	1998–99	2002–03	2006–07	2010–11		1998–99 graduates attending in 1999–2000	2002–03 graduates attending in 2003–04	2006–07 graduates attending in 2007–08	2010–11 graduates attending in 2011–12
1	2	3	4	5	6	7	8	9	10
Public high schools	20,000 (230)	22,500 (400)	24,100 (540)	23,300 (330)	88.7 (0.90)	35.4 (0.43)	35.0 (0.61)	39.5 (0.91)	39.4 (0.59)
Percent of students who are Black, Hispanic, Asian, Pacific Islander, American Indian/Alaska Native, or two or more races									
Less than 5 percent	6,400 (170)	6,100 (220)	5,200 (270)	3,600 (140)	94.7 (1.19)	41.3 (0.67)	42.6 (0.96)	46.8 (1.54)	43.9 (1.40)
5 to 19 percent	4,800 (180)	5,200 (270)	5,400 (320)	5,700 (310)	92.4 (2.55)	36.6 (0.88)	38.0 (1.77)	48.4 (2.06)	44.9 (1.02)
20 to 49 percent	4,000 (170)	4,700 (180)	6,200 (440)	5,900 (270)	91.2 (1.14)	32.5 (0.92)	34.1 (1.77)	35.0 (1.89)	39.6 (1.31)
50 percent or more	4,800 (150)	6,500 (280)	7,300 (430)	8,100 (320)	81.7 (1.58)	28.7 (0.89)	25.8 (1.43)	30.8 (2.00)	33.0 (1.17)
Percent of students approved for free or reduced-price lunch									
School does not participate	2,400 (130)	2,400 (230)	2,800 (320)	1,900 (250)	72.8 (7.11)	30.0 (1.75)	23.2 (2.26)	25.4 (4.12)	27.6 (5.24)
0 to 25 percent	8,600 (180)	6,800 (230)	6,700 (360)	5,100 (220)	93.3 (1.02)	42.6 (0.67)	46.9 (0.78)	52.1 (1.63)	50.7 (1.42)
26 to 50 percent	4,800 (160)	6,700 (220)	7,300 (350)	6,800 (230)	92.8 (0.91)	33.4 (0.81)	36.7 (1.08)	41.5 (1.44)	42.5 (1.00)
51 to 75 percent	2,300 (140)	4,000 (270)	4,100 (290)	5,100 (260)	90.3 (1.06)	29.1 (1.57)	27.3 (1.58)	33.2 (1.91)	35.8 (1.35)
76 to 100 percent	2,000 (100)	2,600 (260)	3,300 (360)	4,300 (230)	82.3 (1.93)	22.2 (1.35)	20.7 (2.79)	26.0 (2.93)	29.1 (1.66)
School locale									
City	— (†)	4,500 (240)	4,800 (300)	5,100 (220)	81.3 (3.11)	— (†)	32.5 (1.61)	36.1 (2.73)	38.6 (1.53)
Suburb	— (†)	4,800 (200)	5,400 (360)	4,800 (160)	86.1 (1.50)	— (†)	40.3 (1.11)	41.2 (2.35)	42.2 (1.42)
Town	— (†)	3,700 (200)	3,900 (310)	3,300 (260)	89.9 (2.21)	— (†)	31.1 (1.65)	35.2 (2.28)	35.3 (1.76)
Rural	— (†)	9,500 (390)	10,000 (460)	10,100 (260)	93.4 (0.67)	— (†)	35.2 (1.28)	41.9 (1.47)	39.8 (0.88)
Private high schools	7,600 (240)	8,200 (260)	8,900 (280)	8,900 (310)	92.4 (1.34)	55.6 (1.74)	56.2 (1.77)	66.5 (1.57)	64.3 (2.10)
Percent of students who are Black, Hispanic, Asian, Pacific Islander, American Indian/Alaska Native, or two or more races									
Less than 5 percent	2,700 (150)	2,500 (180)	2,100 (160)	1,600 (190)	96.1 (1.72)	53.3 (2.85)	54.4 (3.31)	68.2 (3.81)	58.0 (6.31)
5 to 19 percent	2,500 (130)	2,900 (170)	3,500 (200)	3,100 (230)	95.1 (1.90)	63.6 (2.37)	64.2 (2.71)	70.3 (2.24)	67.9 (3.40)
20 to 49 percent	1,400 (100)	1,700 (140)	2,000 (190)	2,200 (200)	90.4 (2.33)	55.3 (3.29)	56.7 (3.70)	58.7 (3.39)	69.4 (3.89)
50 percent or more	1,000 (110)	1,100 (140)	1,400 (130)	1,900 (190)	87.1 (3.49)	41.6 (5.34)	38.3 (4.52)	65.3 (3.37)	57.6 (5.18)
Percent of students approved for free or reduced-price lunch									
School does not participate	6,700 (230)	7,100 (250)	7,300 (280)	7,400 (280)	93.3 (1.27)	57.0 (1.74)	56.2 (2.00)	68.3 (1.77)	66.5 (2.29)
0 to 25 percent	700 (70)	600 (80)	700 (100)	600 (80)	96.8 (2.45)	53.8 (5.69)	66.2 (4.35)	73.2 (4.64)	74.6 (5.23)
26 to 100 percent	‡ (†)	400 (80)	1,000 (130)	900 (140)	83.0 (5.65)	‡	38.9 (6.70)	46.7 (6.86)	37.8 (8.06)
School locale									
City	— (†)	— (†)	3,100 (170)	‡ (†)	‡ (†)	— (†)	— (†)	71.8 (2.62)	‡ (†)
Suburb	— (†)	— (†)	2,800 (180)	‡ (†)	‡ (†)	— (†)	— (†)	67.0 (2.99)	‡ (†)
Town	— (†)	— (†)	1,000 (150)	‡ (†)	‡ (†)	— (†)	— (†)	63.8 (5.02)	‡ (†)
Rural	— (†)	— (†)	2,000 (190)	‡ (†)	‡ (†)	— (†)	— (†)	58.9 (3.54)	‡ (†)

—Not available.
†Not applicable.
‡Reporting standards not met. Data may be suppressed because the response rate is under 50 percent, there are too few cases for a reliable estimate, or the coefficient of variation (CV) is 50 percent or greater.
[1]The 12th-grade graduation rate is the number of students who graduated from grade 12 with a diploma during the 2010–11 school year divided by 12th-grade enrollment in October 2010.

NOTE: Data are based on a sample survey and may not be strictly comparable with data reported elsewhere. Includes all schools, including combined schools, with students enrolled in the 12th grade. Some data have been revised from previously published figures. Detail may not sum to totals because of rounding.
SOURCE: U.S. Department of Education, National Center for Education Statistics, Schools and Staffing Survey (SASS), "Public School Teacher Data File" and "Private School Teacher Data File," 1999–2000, 2003–04, 2007–08, and 2011–12; and "Charter School Teacher Data File," 1999–2000. (This table was prepared April 2014.)

Table 302.50. Estimated rate of 2009–10 high school graduates attending degree-granting institutions, by state: 2010

State	Number of graduates from high schools located in the state			Number of fall 2010 first-time freshmen graduating from high school in the previous 12 months		Estimated rate of high school graduates going to college	
	Total[1]	Public 2009–10	Private, 2008–09	State residents enrolled in institutions in any state[2]	State residents enrolled in institutions in their home state[3]	In any state	In their home state
1	2	3	4	5	6	7	8
United States	3,436,835	3,128,022	308,813	2,158,258 [4]	1,765,406	62.8	51.4
Alabama	48,443	43,166	5,277	31,160	28,165	64.3	58.1
Alaska	8,434	8,245	189	3,915	2,390	46.4	28.3
Arizona	63,900	61,145	2,755	37,006	33,090	57.9	51.8
Arkansas	29,606	28,276	1,330	19,348	17,624	65.4	59.5
California	440,240	404,987	35,253	271,669	243,382	61.7	55.3
Colorado	52,159	49,321	2,838	31,902	24,171	61.2	46.3
Connecticut	40,728	34,495	6,233	32,068	17,724	78.7	43.5
Delaware	9,980	8,133	1,847	4,718	2,745	47.3	27.5
District of Columbia[5]	4,941	3,602	1,339	2,503	517	50.7	10.5
Florida	174,352	156,130	18,222	109,789	97,733	63.0	56.1
Georgia	99,883	91,561	8,322	67,659	57,253	67.7	57.3
Hawaii	13,657	10,998	2,659	8,683	5,862	63.6	42.9
Idaho	18,340	17,793	547	8,273	5,589	45.1	30.5
Illinois	154,142	139,035	15,107	90,456	64,307	58.7	41.7
Indiana	69,783	64,551	5,232	45,900	40,350	65.8	57.8
Iowa	36,711	34,462	2,249	24,442	21,209	66.6	57.8
Kansas	33,809	31,642	2,167	21,889	18,627	64.7	55.1
Kentucky	46,601	42,664	3,937	29,320	26,191	62.9	56.2
Louisiana	44,709	36,573	8,136	28,912	26,094	64.7	58.4
Maine	16,431	14,069	2,362	9,234	6,072	56.2	37.0
Maryland	68,306	59,078	9,228	43,730	28,253	64.0	41.4
Massachusetts	75,092	64,462	10,630	54,966	36,917	73.2	49.2
Michigan	119,201	110,682	8,519	73,740	65,840	61.9	55.2
Minnesota	63,908	59,667	4,241	45,340	32,751	70.9	51.2
Mississippi	28,836	25,478	3,358	22,726	21,098	78.8	73.2
Missouri	71,037	63,994	7,043	43,633	36,803	61.4	51.8
Montana	10,443	10,075	368	6,320	5,020	60.5	48.1
Nebraska	21,374	19,370	2,004	14,858	12,442	69.5	58.2
Nevada	21,780	20,956	824	11,280	8,511	51.8	39.1
New Hampshire	17,497	15,034	2,463	11,256	6,388	64.3	36.5
New Jersey	110,573	96,225	14,348	75,893	44,738	68.6	40.5
New Mexico	19,983	18,595	1,388	14,461	12,542	72.4	62.8
New York	215,105	183,826	31,279	148,101	119,445	68.9	55.5
North Carolina	94,431	88,704	5,727	60,395	53,995	64.0	57.2
North Dakota	7,604	7,155	449	5,125	3,841	67.4	50.5
Ohio	136,740	123,437	13,303	84,068	71,583	61.5	52.3
Oklahoma	40,034	38,503	1,531	24,100	21,735	60.2	54.3
Oregon	37,810	34,671	3,139	18,072	13,960	47.8	36.9
Pennsylvania	149,845	131,182	18,663	91,298	75,702	60.9	50.5
Rhode Island	11,726	9,908	1,818	7,667	4,907	65.4	41.8
South Carolina	43,511	40,438	3,073	29,709	26,706	68.3	61.4
South Dakota	8,680	8,162	518	6,232	4,774	71.8	55.0
Tennessee	68,627	62,408	6,219	42,515	36,038	62.0	52.5
Texas	293,797	280,894	12,903	164,980	145,781	56.2	49.6
Utah	32,751	31,481	1,270	17,442	15,970	53.3	48.8
Vermont	8,366	7,199	1,167	4,478	2,228	53.5	26.6
Virginia	88,022	81,511	6,511	56,202	45,599	63.9	51.8
Washington	70,497	66,046	4,451	34,030	25,881	48.3	36.7
West Virginia	18,390	17,651	739	10,885	9,696	59.2	52.7
Wisconsin	70,294	64,687	5,607	42,241	34,196	60.1	48.6
Wyoming	5,730	5,695	35	3,459	2,699	60.4	47.1

[1]Total includes public high school graduates for 2009–10 and private high school graduates for 2008–09. Data on private high school graduates are not available for 2009–10.
[2]All U.S. resident students living in a particular state when admitted to an institution in any state. Students may be enrolled in any state.
[3]Students who attend institutions in their home state. Total includes 272 students attending U.S. Service Academies in their home state, not shown separately.
[4]U.S. total includes some U.S. residents whose home state is unknown.
[5]A percentage of the private high school graduates are not residents of the District of Columbia.

NOTE: Degree-granting institutions grant associate's or higher degrees and participate in Title IV federal financial aid programs. Detail may not sum to totals because of rounding. Some data have been revised from previously published figures.
SOURCE: U.S. Department of Education, National Center for Education Statistics, Common Core of Data (CCD), "NCES Common Core of Data State Dropout and Completion Data File," 2009–10; Private School Universe Survey (PSS), 2009–10; and Integrated Postsecondary Education Data System (IPEDS), Spring 2011, Enrollment component. (This table was prepared April 2012.)

Table 302.60. Percentage of 18- to 24-year-olds enrolled in degree-granting institutions, by level of institution and sex and race/ethnicity of student: 1967 through 2013

[Standard errors appear in parentheses]

Year	Total, all students	Level of institution		Sex		Race/ethnicity							Race/ethnicity by sex					
													White		Black		Hispanic	
		2-year	4-year	Male	Female	White	Black	Hispanic	Asian	Pacific Islander	American Indian/ Alaska Native	Two or more races	Male	Female	Male	Female	Male	Female
1	2	3	4	5	6	7	8	9	10	11	12	13	14	15	16	17	18	19
1967[1]	25.5 (0.44)	— (†)	— (†)	33.1 (0.71)	19.2 (0.54)	26.9 (0.48)	13.0 (1.16)	— (†)	— (†)	— (†)	— (†)	— (†)	— (†)	— (†)	— (†)	— (†)	— (†)	— (†)
1968[1]	26.1 (0.44)	— (†)	— (†)	34.1 (0.70)	19.5 (0.53)	27.5 (0.48)	14.5 (1.18)	— (†)	— (†)	— (†)	— (†)	— (†)	— (†)	— (†)	— (†)	— (†)	— (†)	— (†)
1969[1]	27.3 (0.44)	— (†)	— (†)	35.2 (0.69)	20.9 (0.54)	28.7 (0.47)	16.0 (1.20)	— (†)	— (†)	— (†)	— (†)	— (†)	— (†)	— (†)	— (†)	— (†)	— (†)	— (†)
1970[1]	25.7 (0.42)	— (†)	— (†)	32.1 (0.65)	20.3 (0.52)	27.1 (0.45)	15.5 (1.15)	— (†)	— (†)	— (†)	— (†)	— (†)	— (†)	— (†)	— (†)	— (†)	— (†)	— (†)
1971[1]	26.2 (0.41)	— (†)	— (†)	32.5 (0.63)	20.8 (0.52)	27.2 (0.44)	18.2 (1.19)	— (†)	— (†)	— (†)	— (†)	— (†)	— (†)	— (†)	— (†)	— (†)	— (†)	— (†)
1972	25.5 (0.37)	— (†)	— (†)	30.2 (0.56)	21.2 (0.47)	27.2 (0.41)	18.3 (1.18)	13.4 (1.83)	— (†)	— (†)	— (†)	— (†)	32.3 (0.63)	22.5 (0.54)	21.1 (1.83)	15.9 (1.51)	15.1 (2.85)	12.0 (2.37)
1973	24.0 (0.35)	6.9 (0.21)	17.1 (0.31)	27.7 (0.54)	20.5 (0.46)	25.5 (0.40)	15.9 (1.09)	16.1 (2.02)	— (†)	— (†)	— (†)	— (†)	29.6 (0.60)	21.8 (0.53)	18.7 (1.71)	13.5 (1.38)	16.7 (2.94)	15.5 (2.77)
1974	24.6 (0.35)	7.6 (0.22)	17.0 (0.31)	27.7 (0.53)	21.7 (0.47)	25.8 (0.40)	17.6 (1.14)	18.0 (1.95)	— (†)	— (†)	— (†)	— (†)	28.9 (0.60)	22.9 (0.53)	19.8 (1.77)	15.9 (1.47)	19.7 (2.92)	16.5 (2.60)
1975	26.3 (0.36)	9.0 (0.23)	17.3 (0.31)	29.0 (0.53)	23.7 (0.48)	27.4 (0.40)	20.4 (1.18)	20.4 (2.09)	— (†)	— (†)	— (†)	— (†)	30.7 (0.59)	24.3 (0.54)	19.9 (1.74)	20.8 (1.61)	21.4 (3.10)	19.5 (2.81)
1976	26.7 (0.35)	6.4 (0.20)	20.2 (0.32)	28.2 (0.52)	25.2 (0.48)	27.6 (0.40)	22.5 (1.20)	20.0 (2.00)	— (†)	— (†)	— (†)	— (†)	29.3 (0.58)	26.1 (0.55)	22.0 (1.77)	22.9 (1.64)	21.3 (3.05)	18.8 (2.64)
1977	26.1 (0.38)	6.8 (0.22)	19.4 (0.35)	28.1 (0.56)	24.3 (0.52)	27.2 (0.43)	21.1 (1.18)	17.2 (1.87)	— (†)	— (†)	— (†)	— (†)	29.4 (0.64)	25.1 (0.59)	20.3 (1.73)	21.9 (1.61)	18.3 (2.80)	16.3 (2.50)
1978	25.3 (0.38)	6.6 (0.22)	18.7 (0.34)	27.1 (0.55)	23.6 (0.51)	26.5 (0.43)	20.1 (1.15)	15.2 (1.74)	— (†)	— (†)	— (†)	— (†)	28.4 (0.63)	24.6 (0.59)	19.7 (1.70)	20.4 (1.56)	16.1 (2.61)	14.3 (2.33)
1979	25.0 (0.37)	6.3 (0.21)	18.7 (0.34)	25.9 (0.54)	24.2 (0.52)	26.3 (0.43)	19.8 (1.13)	16.7 (1.77)	— (†)	— (†)	— (†)	— (†)	27.1 (0.61)	25.5 (0.59)	19.1 (1.67)	20.3 (1.54)	18.3 (2.65)	15.2 (2.35)
1980	25.7 (0.38)	7.1 (0.22)	18.6 (0.33)	26.4 (0.54)	25.0 (0.52)	27.3 (0.43)	19.4 (1.12)	16.1 (1.64)	— (†)	— (†)	— (†)	— (†)	28.4 (0.63)	26.3 (0.60)	17.5 (1.60)	20.9 (1.55)	15.9 (2.33)	16.2 (2.32)
1981	26.1 (0.37)	7.5 (0.22)	18.6 (0.33)	27.1 (0.54)	25.2 (0.51)	27.7 (0.43)	19.9 (1.09)	16.6 (1.63)	— (†)	— (†)	— (†)	— (†)	28.7 (0.62)	26.6 (0.60)	18.9 (1.58)	20.7 (1.51)	16.6 (2.35)	16.7 (2.27)
1982	26.6 (0.39)	7.7 (0.24)	18.9 (0.35)	27.2 (0.57)	26.0 (0.55)	28.1 (0.46)	19.9 (1.14)	16.8 (1.77)	— (†)	— (†)	— (†)	— (†)	28.9 (0.66)	27.4 (0.64)	18.7 (1.64)	21.0 (1.59)	14.9 (2.45)	18.6 (2.52)
1983	26.2 (0.39)	7.4 (0.23)	18.8 (0.35)	27.3 (0.57)	25.1 (0.54)	27.9 (0.46)	19.2 (1.12)	17.3 (1.77)	— (†)	— (†)	— (†)	— (†)	29.4 (0.66)	26.5 (0.64)	18.1 (1.60)	20.1 (1.56)	15.6 (2.46)	18.8 (2.54)
1984	27.1 (0.40)	7.3 (0.24)	19.8 (0.36)	28.6 (0.58)	25.6 (0.55)	28.9 (0.47)	20.3 (1.15)	17.9 (1.80)	— (†)	— (†)	— (†)	— (†)	30.8 (0.68)	27.1 (0.65)	20.3 (1.67)	20.3 (1.57)	16.1 (2.51)	19.6 (2.57)
1985	27.8 (0.41)	7.4 (0.24)	20.4 (0.37)	28.4 (0.60)	27.2 (0.57)	30.0 (0.49)	19.6 (1.16)	16.9 (1.84)	— (†)	— (†)	— (†)	— (†)	30.9 (0.70)	29.2 (0.67)	20.2 (1.72)	19.1 (1.56)	14.9 (2.46)	18.9 (2.75)
1986	27.9 (0.42)	7.6 (0.25)	20.3 (0.37)	28.2 (0.60)	27.6 (0.58)	29.7 (0.50)	21.9 (1.21)	17.6 (1.76)	— (†)	— (†)	— (†)	— (†)	30.6 (0.72)	28.8 (0.68)	20.0 (1.72)	23.4 (1.69)	16.7 (2.36)	18.7 (2.64)
1987	29.6 (0.43)	8.1 (0.26)	21.5 (0.39)	30.6 (0.62)	28.7 (0.59)	31.9 (0.51)	22.8 (1.25)	17.5 (1.73)	— (†)	— (†)	— (†)	— (†)	33.0 (0.74)	30.8 (0.71)	22.6 (1.83)	22.9 (1.70)	18.5 (2.46)	16.5 (2.43)
1988	30.3 (0.47)	8.8 (0.29)	21.5 (0.42)	30.2 (0.68)	30.4 (0.66)	33.2 (0.57)	21.2 (1.33)	17.0 (2.00)	— (†)	— (†)	— (†)	— (†)	33.4 (0.82)	33.0 (0.79)	18.5 (1.87)	23.5 (1.88)	16.5 (2.74)	17.6 (2.93)
1989	30.9 (0.48)	8.0 (0.28)	22.9 (0.44)	30.2 (0.68)	31.6 (0.67)	34.2 (0.58)	23.4 (1.38)	16.1 (1.90)	46.1 (3.92)	— (†)	15.7 ! (5.33)	— (†)	34.1 (0.83)	34.4 (0.81)	19.7 (1.89)	26.7 (1.97)	14.6 (2.55)	17.6 (2.81)
1990	32.0 (0.47)	8.7 (0.28)	23.3 (0.43)	32.3 (0.68)	31.8 (0.66)	35.1 (0.57)	25.4 (1.37)	15.8 (1.67)	56.9 (3.56)	— (†)	15.8 ! (5.08)	— (†)	35.5 (0.82)	34.7 (0.80)	26.0 (2.03)	24.8 (1.86)	15.3 (2.31)	16.4 (2.42)
1991	33.3 (0.48)	9.7 (0.30)	23.6 (0.43)	32.8 (0.68)	33.6 (0.67)	36.8 (0.58)	23.5 (1.34)	17.9 (1.72)	57.1 (3.19)	— (†)	15.9 ! (5.45)	— (†)	36.5 (0.83)	37.0 (0.82)	23.2 (1.95)	23.8 (1.84)	14.0 (2.15)	22.2 (2.70)
1992	34.4 (0.49)	9.9 (0.31)	24.4 (0.44)	32.7 (0.68)	36.0 (0.69)	37.3 (0.59)	25.2 (1.37)	21.3 (1.87)	58.4 (3.28)	— (†)	18.5 ! (6.18)	— (†)	36.2 (0.83)	38.3 (0.83)	21.3 (1.87)	28.8 (1.96)	17.8 (2.47)	24.7 (2.80)
1993	34.0 (0.49)	9.8 (0.30)	24.2 (0.44)	33.6 (0.69)	34.4 (0.68)	36.8 (0.59)	24.5 (1.35)	21.7 (1.88)	61.2 (3.27)	— (†)	18.9 (5.66)	— (†)	36.5 (0.84)	37.1 (0.83)	22.9 (1.92)	26.0 (1.90)	19.7 (2.59)	23.7 (2.71)
1994	34.6 (0.42)	9.1 (0.26)	25.5 (0.39)	33.1 (0.59)	36.0 (0.60)	38.1 (0.53)	27.7 (1.17)	18.8 (1.10)	62.7 (2.81)	— (†)	29.4 (5.64)	— (†)	37.0 (0.74)	39.2 (0.74)	25.6 (1.66)	29.5 (1.64)	16.5 (1.43)	21.5 (1.71)
1995	34.3 (0.44)	8.9 (0.27)	25.4 (0.41)	33.1 (0.63)	35.5 (0.63)	37.9 (0.55)	27.5 (1.18)	20.7 (1.13)	54.6 (3.10)	— (†)	27.6 (6.14)	— (†)	37.0 (0.78)	38.8 (0.78)	26.0 (1.71)	28.7 (1.62)	18.7 (1.49)	23.0 (1.71)
1996	35.5 (0.47)	9.5 (0.29)	26.1 (0.43)	34.1 (0.66)	37.0 (0.67)	39.5 (0.59)	27.4 (1.23)	20.1 (1.18)	53.9 (2.47)	— (†)	30.3 (5.25)	— (†)	38.3 (0.83)	40.6 (0.84)	25.7 (1.77)	28.8 (1.70)	16.5 (1.52)	24.0 (1.81)
1997	36.8 (0.47)	9.9 (0.29)	27.0 (0.43)	35.0 (0.66)	38.7 (0.67)	40.6 (0.59)	29.8 (1.25)	22.4 (1.21)	55.1 (2.60)	— (†)	27.1 (4.63)	— (†)	39.3 (0.82)	41.8 (0.84)	25.4 (1.75)	33.7 (1.77)	19.2 (1.56)	26.1 (1.88)
1998	36.5 (0.46)	10.2 (0.29)	26.3 (0.42)	34.5 (0.65)	38.6 (0.66)	40.6 (0.59)	29.8 (1.24)	20.4 (1.11)	60.4 (2.49)	— (†)	20.3 (4.91)	— (†)	39.4 (0.82)	41.9 (0.84)	26.1 (1.76)	32.9 (1.73)	16.4 (1.41)	24.9 (1.73)
1999	35.6 (0.46)	9.1 (0.27)	26.5 (0.42)	34.1 (0.64)	37.0 (0.65)	39.4 (0.58)	30.4 (1.24)	18.7 (1.08)	55.7 (2.42)	— (†)	19.5 (4.71)	— (†)	38.3 (0.81)	40.6 (0.82)	28.9 (1.81)	31.6 (1.70)	15.8 (1.41)	21.9 (1.65)
2000	35.5 (0.45)	9.4 (0.28)	26.0 (0.41)	32.6 (0.62)	38.4 (0.65)	38.7 (0.57)	30.5 (1.21)	21.7 (1.12)	55.9 (2.42)	— (†)	15.9 (4.30)	— (†)	36.2 (0.79)	41.3 (0.81)	25.1 (1.67)	35.2 (1.72)	18.5 (1.45)	25.4 (1.72)
2001	36.3 (0.45)	9.8 (0.28)	26.6 (0.41)	33.6 (0.63)	39.0 (0.64)	39.5 (0.57)	31.4 (1.22)	21.7 (1.10)	61.3 (2.35)	— (†)	23.3 (4.29)	— (†)	37.2 (0.79)	41.9 (0.82)	26.7 (1.70)	35.5 (1.71)	17.4 (1.42)	26.1 (1.67)
2002	36.7 (0.43)	9.7 (0.26)	27.0 (0.39)	33.7 (0.59)	39.7 (0.61)	40.9 (0.55)	31.9 (1.18)	19.9 (0.94)	60.9 (2.10)	— (†)	23.6 (3.96)	— (†)	38.9 (0.77)	42.8 (0.78)	26.3 (1.63)	36.9 (1.68)	16.2 (1.17)	24.4 (1.51)
2003[2]	37.8 (0.43)	10.2 (0.27)	27.7 (0.39)	34.3 (0.59)	41.3 (0.61)	41.6 (0.55)	32.3 (1.20)	23.5 (1.02)	61.2 (2.27)	43.3 (9.97)	17.7 (4.45)	41.6 (3.58)	38.5 (0.77)	44.5 (0.78)	28.2 (1.68)	36.0 (1.69)	18.3 (1.27)	29.4 (1.60)
2004[2]	38.0 (0.42)	9.4 (0.25)	28.6 (0.39)	34.7 (0.59)	41.2 (0.61)	41.7 (0.55)	31.8 (1.18)	24.7 (1.02)	60.6 (2.24)	55.8 (8.99)	24.4 (4.52)	36.8 (3.44)	38.4 (0.76)	45.0 (0.78)	26.5 (1.63)	36.6 (1.67)	21.7 (1.33)	28.2 (1.56)
2005[2]	38.9 (0.43)	9.6 (0.26)	29.2 (0.40)	35.3 (0.59)	42.5 (0.61)	42.8 (0.55)	33.1 (1.18)	24.8 (1.02)	61.0 (2.26)	50.6 (10.95)	27.8 (4.88)	41.8 (3.48)	39.4 (0.76)	46.1 (0.79)	28.2 (1.64)	37.6 (1.69)	20.7 (1.31)	29.5 (1.58)
2006[2]	37.3 (0.42)	9.6 (0.25)	27.8 (0.39)	34.1 (0.58)	40.6 (0.60)	41.0 (0.54)	32.6 (1.16)	23.6 (0.99)	58.3 (2.28)	39.1 (8.36)	26.2 (5.18)	38.5 (3.51)	37.9 (0.75)	44.1 (0.78)	28.1 (1.60)	36.9 (1.65)	20.0 (1.29)	27.6 (1.52)
2007[2]	38.8 (0.42)	10.9 (0.27)	27.9 (0.39)	35.5 (0.58)	42.1 (0.60)	42.6 (0.54)	33.1 (1.15)	26.6 (1.02)	57.2 (2.28)	37.1 (9.07)	24.7 (4.63)	39.2 (3.48)	39.6 (0.76)	45.7 (0.78)	32.2 (1.63)	34.0 (1.61)	20.7 (1.29)	33.0 (1.57)
2008[2]	39.6 (0.42)	11.8 (0.28)	27.8 (0.38)	37.0 (0.58)	42.3 (0.60)	44.2 (0.54)	32.1 (1.13)	25.8 (1.01)	59.3 (2.32)	27.3 ! (8.92)	21.9 (4.22)	45.7 (3.55)	41.7 (0.76)	46.9 (0.78)	29.7 (1.61)	34.2 (1.59)	23.0 (1.35)	28.9 (1.50)
2009[2]	41.3 (0.42)	11.7 (0.27)	29.6 (0.39)	38.4 (0.59)	44.2 (0.60)	45.0 (0.55)	37.7 (1.17)	27.5 (1.01)	65.2 (2.17)	33.4 (7.45)	29.8 (5.10)	39.3 (3.32)	42.3 (0.76)	47.7 (0.78)	33.2 (1.64)	41.9 (1.64)	24.2 (1.35)	31.0 (1.50)
2010[2,3]	41.2 (0.57)	12.9 (0.36)	28.2 (0.53)	38.3 (0.78)	44.1 (0.84)	43.3 (0.81)	38.4 (1.66)	31.9 (1.15)	63.6 (2.70)	36.0 (8.36)	41.4 (6.60)	38.3 (4.38)	40.6 (1.00)	46.1 (1.17)	35.2 (2.13)	41.4 (2.16)	27.9 (1.57)	36.1 (1.60)
2011[2,3]	42.0 (0.59)	12.0 (0.35)	30.0 (0.58)	39.1 (0.80)	44.9 (0.80)	44.7 (0.77)	37.1 (1.53)	34.8 (1.20)	60.1 (2.45)	37.8 (7.93)	23.5 (5.30)	38.8 (3.60)	42.4 (0.96)	47.1 (1.08)	34.0 (2.29)	39.9 (1.90)	31.0 (1.63)	39.4 (1.58)
2012[2,3]	41.0 (0.62)	12.7 (0.38)	28.3 (0.58)	37.6 (0.79)	44.5 (0.86)	42.1 (0.83)	36.4 (1.62)	37.5 (1.18)	59.8 (2.61)	50.3 (9.60)	27.8 (4.43)	39.4 (3.64)	38.3 (1.06)	46.0 (1.08)	33.9 (2.04)	38.7 (2.33)	33.5 (1.58)	41.7 (1.73)
2013[2,3]	39.9 (0.63)	11.6 (0.36)	28.3 (0.57)	36.6 (0.85)	43.3 (0.80)	41.6 (0.90)	34.2 (1.58)	33.8 (1.24)	62.3 (2.62)	32.9 (8.26)	31.8 (5.58)	44.7 (3.99)	38.1 (1.11)	45.3 (1.11)	30.6 (2.13)	37.6 (2.18)	29.1 (1.72)	38.8 (1.58)

—Not available.
†Not applicable.
!Interpret data with caution. The coefficient of variation (CV) for this estimate is between 30 and 50 percent.
[1]Prior to 1972, White and Black data include persons of Hispanic ethnicity.
[2]After 2002, data for individual race categories exclude persons identifying themselves as two or more races.
[3]Beginning in 2010, standard errors were computed using replicate weights, which produced more precise values than the generalized variance function methodology used in prior years.
NOTE: Data are based on sample surveys of the civilian noninstitutional population. Totals include other racial/ethnic groups not separately shown. Race categories exclude persons of Hispanic ethnicity except where otherwise noted.
SOURCE: U.S. Department of Commerce, Census Bureau, Current Population Survey (CPS), October, 1967 through 2013. (This table was prepared July 2014.)

Table 303.10. Total fall enrollment in degree-granting postsecondary institutions, by attendance status, sex of student, and control of institution: Selected years, 1947 through 2024

Year	Total enrollment	Attendance status			Sex of student			Control of institution			
		Full-time	Part-time	Percent part-time	Male	Female	Percent female	Public	Private		
									Total	Nonprofit	For-profit
1	2	3	4	5	6	7	8	9	10	11	12
1947[1]	2,338,226	—	—	—	1,659,249	678,977	29.0	1,152,377	1,185,849	—	—
1948[1]	2,403,396	—	—	—	1,709,367	694,029	28.9	1,185,588	1,217,808	—	—
1949[1]	2,444,900	—	—	—	1,721,572	723,328	29.6	1,207,151	1,237,749	—	—
1950[1]	2,281,298	—	—	—	1,560,392	720,906	31.6	1,139,699	1,141,599	—	—
1951[1]	2,101,962	—	—	—	1,390,740	711,222	33.8	1,037,938	1,064,024	—	—
1952[1]	2,134,242	—	—	—	1,380,357	753,885	35.3	1,101,240	1,033,002	—	—
1953[1]	2,231,054	—	—	—	1,422,598	808,456	36.2	1,185,876	1,045,178	—	—
1954[1]	2,446,693	—	—	—	1,563,382	883,311	36.1	1,353,531	1,093,162	—	—
1955[1]	2,653,034	—	—	—	1,733,184	919,850	34.7	1,476,282	1,176,752	—	—
1956[1]	2,918,212	—	—	—	1,911,458	1,006,754	34.5	1,656,402	1,261,810	—	—
1957	3,323,783				2,170,765	1,153,018	34.7	1,972,673	1,351,110	—	—
1959	3,639,847	2,421,016	1,218,831 [2]	33.5	2,332,617	1,307,230	35.9	2,180,982	1,458,865	—	—
1961	4,145,065	2,785,133	1,359,932 [2]	32.8	2,585,821	1,559,244	37.6	2,561,447	1,583,618	—	—
1963	4,779,609	3,183,833	1,595,776 [2]	33.4	2,961,540	1,818,069	38.0	3,081,279	1,698,330	—	—
1964	5,280,020	3,573,238	1,706,782 [2]	32.3	3,248,713	2,031,307	38.5	3,467,708	1,812,312	—	—
1965	5,920,864	4,095,728	1,825,136 [2]	30.8	3,630,020	2,290,844	38.7	3,969,596	1,951,268	—	—
1966	6,389,872	4,438,606	1,951,266 [2]	30.5	3,856,216	2,533,656	39.7	4,348,917	2,040,955	—	—
1967	6,911,748	4,793,128	2,118,620 [2]	30.7	4,132,800	2,778,948	40.2	4,816,028	2,095,720	2,074,041	21,679
1968	7,513,091	5,210,155	2,302,936	30.7	4,477,649	3,035,442	40.4	5,430,652	2,082,439	2,061,211	21,228
1969	8,004,660	5,498,883	2,505,777	31.3	4,746,201	3,258,459	40.7	5,896,868	2,107,792	2,087,653	20,139
1970	8,580,887	5,816,290	2,764,597	32.2	5,043,642	3,537,245	41.2	6,428,134	2,152,753	2,134,420	18,333
1971	8,948,644	6,077,232	2,871,412	32.1	5,207,004	3,741,640	41.8	6,804,309	2,144,335	2,121,913	22,422
1972	9,214,860	6,072,389	3,142,471	34.1	5,238,757	3,976,103	43.1	7,070,635	2,144,225	2,123,245	20,980
1973	9,602,123	6,189,493	3,412,630	35.5	5,371,052	4,231,071	44.1	7,419,516	2,182,607	2,148,784	33,823
1974	10,223,729	6,370,273	3,853,456	37.7	5,622,429	4,601,300	45.0	7,988,500	2,235,229	2,200,963	34,266
1975	11,184,859	6,841,334	4,343,525	38.8	6,148,997	5,035,862	45.0	8,834,508	2,350,351	2,311,448	38,903
1976	11,012,137	6,717,058	4,295,079	39.0	5,810,828	5,201,309	47.2	8,653,477	2,358,660	2,314,298	44,362
1977	11,285,787	6,792,925	4,492,862	39.8	5,789,016	5,496,771	48.7	8,846,993	2,438,794	2,386,652	52,142
1978	11,260,092	6,667,657	4,592,435	40.8	5,640,998	5,619,094	49.9	8,785,893	2,474,199	2,408,331	65,868
1979	11,569,899	6,794,039	4,775,860	41.3	5,682,877	5,887,022	50.9	9,036,822	2,533,077	2,461,773	71,304
1980	12,096,895	7,097,958	4,998,937	41.3	5,874,374	6,222,521	51.4	9,457,394	2,639,501	2,527,787	111,714 [3]
1981	12,371,672	7,181,250	5,190,422	42.0	5,975,056	6,396,616	51.7	9,647,032	2,724,640	2,572,405	152,235 [3]
1982	12,425,780	7,220,618	5,205,162	41.9	6,031,384	6,394,396	51.5	9,696,087	2,729,693	2,552,739	176,954 [3]
1983	12,464,661	7,261,050	5,203,611	41.7	6,023,725	6,440,936	51.7	9,682,734	2,781,927	2,589,187	192,740
1984	12,241,940	7,098,388	5,143,552	42.0	5,863,574	6,378,366	52.1	9,477,370	2,764,570	2,574,419	190,151
1985	12,247,055	7,075,221	5,171,834	42.2	5,818,450	6,428,605	52.5	9,479,273	2,767,782	2,571,791	195,991
1986	12,503,511	7,119,550	5,383,961	43.1	5,884,515	6,618,996	52.9	9,713,893	2,789,618	2,572,479	217,139 [4]
1987	12,766,642	7,231,085	5,535,557	43.4	5,932,056	6,834,586	53.5	9,973,254	2,793,388	2,602,350	191,038 [4]
1988	13,055,337	7,436,768	5,618,569	43.0	6,001,896	7,053,441	54.0	10,161,388	2,893,949	2,673,567	220,382
1989	13,538,560	7,660,950	5,877,610	43.4	6,190,015	7,348,545	54.3	10,577,963	2,960,597	2,731,174	229,423
1990	13,818,637	7,820,985	5,997,652	43.4	6,283,909	7,534,728	54.5	10,844,717	2,973,920	2,760,227	213,693
1991	14,358,953	8,115,329	6,243,624	43.5	6,501,844	7,857,109	54.7	11,309,563	3,049,390	2,819,041	230,349
1992	14,487,359	8,162,118	6,325,241	43.7	6,523,989	7,963,370	55.0	11,384,567	3,102,792	2,872,523	230,269
1993	14,304,803	8,127,618	6,177,185	43.2	6,427,450	7,877,353	55.1	11,189,088	3,115,715	2,888,897	226,818
1994	14,278,790	8,137,776	6,141,014	43.0	6,371,898	7,906,892	55.4	11,133,680	3,145,110	2,910,107	235,003
1995	14,261,781	8,128,802	6,132,979	43.0	6,342,539	7,919,242	55.5	11,092,374	3,169,407	2,929,044	240,363
1996	14,367,520	8,302,953	6,064,567	42.2	6,352,825	8,014,695	55.8	11,120,499	3,247,021	2,942,556	304,465
1997	14,502,334	8,438,062	6,064,272	41.8	6,396,028	8,106,306	55.9	11,196,119	3,306,215	2,977,614	328,601
1998	14,506,967	8,563,338	5,943,629	41.0	6,369,265	8,137,702	56.1	11,137,769	3,369,198	3,004,925	364,273
1999	14,849,691	8,803,139	6,046,552	40.7	6,515,164	8,334,527	56.1	11,375,739	3,473,952	3,055,029	418,923
2000	15,312,289	9,009,600	6,302,689	41.2	6,721,769	8,590,520	56.1	11,752,786	3,559,503	3,109,419	450,084
2001	15,927,987	9,447,502	6,480,485	40.7	6,960,815	8,967,172	56.3	12,233,156	3,694,831	3,167,330	527,501
2002	16,611,711	9,946,359	6,665,352	40.1	7,202,116	9,409,595	56.6	12,751,993	3,859,718	3,265,476	594,242
2003	16,911,481	10,326,133	6,585,348	38.9	7,260,264	9,651,217	57.1	12,858,698	4,052,783	3,341,048	711,735
2004	17,272,044	10,610,177	6,661,867	38.6	7,387,262	9,884,782	57.2	12,980,112	4,291,932	3,411,685	880,247
2005	17,487,475	10,797,011	6,690,464	38.3	7,455,925	10,031,550	57.4	13,021,834	4,465,641	3,454,692	1,010,949
2006	17,758,870	10,957,305	6,801,565	38.3	7,574,815	10,184,055	57.3	13,180,133	4,578,737	3,512,866	1,065,871
2007	18,248,128	11,269,892	6,978,236	38.2	7,815,914	10,432,214	57.2	13,490,780	4,757,348	3,571,150	1,186,198
2008	19,102,814	11,747,743	7,355,071	38.5	8,188,895	10,913,919	57.1	13,972,153	5,130,661	3,661,519	1,469,142
2009	20,313,594	12,605,355	7,708,239	37.9	8,732,953	11,580,641	57.0	14,810,768	5,502,826	3,767,672	1,735,154
2010	21,019,438	13,087,182	7,932,256	37.7	9,045,759	11,973,679	57.0	15,142,171	5,877,267	3,854,482	2,022,785
2011	21,010,590	13,002,531	8,008,059	38.1	9,034,256	11,976,334	57.0	15,116,303	5,894,287	3,926,819	1,967,468
2012	20,642,819	12,737,013	7,905,806	38.3	8,919,087	11,723,732	56.8	14,880,343	5,762,476	3,953,578	1,808,898
2013	20,375,789	12,597,112	7,778,677	38.2	8,860,786	11,515,003	56.5	14,745,558	5,630,231	3,974,004	1,656,227
2014[5]	20,255,000	12,664,000	7,590,000	38.2	8,726,000	11,528,000	57.0	14,660,000	5,595,000	—	—

See notes at end of table.

Table 303.10. Total fall enrollment in degree-granting postsecondary institutions, by attendance status, sex of student, and control of institution: Selected years, 1947 through 2024—Continued

Year	Total enrollment	Attendance status			Sex of student			Control of institution			
		Full-time	Part-time	Percent part-time	Male	Female	Percent female	Public	Private		
									Total	Nonprofit	For-profit
1	2	3	4	5	6	7	8	9	10	11	12
2015[5]	20,234,000	12,615,000	7,619,000	38.3	8,717,000	11,516,000	57.3	14,646,000	5,588,000	—	—
2016[5]	20,486,000	12,783,000	7,703,000	38.5	8,783,000	11,702,000	57.6	14,820,000	5,666,000	—	—
2017[5]	20,925,000	13,064,000	7,860,000	38.6	8,941,000	11,984,000	57.9	15,129,000	5,796,000	—	—
2018[5]	21,330,000	13,305,000	8,025,000	38.7	9,105,000	12,225,000	58.1	15,421,000	5,909,000	—	—
2019[5]	21,630,000	13,467,000	8,162,000	38.8	9,217,000	12,412,000	58.2	15,639,000	5,991,000	—	—
2020[5]	21,859,000	13,595,000	8,264,000	38.9	9,297,000	12,561,000	58.4	15,802,000	6,057,000	—	—
2021[5]	22,168,000	13,774,000	8,394,000	39.0	9,423,000	12,745,000	58.5	16,022,000	6,146,000	—	—
2022[5]	22,511,000	13,972,000	8,538,000	39.0	9,567,000	12,943,000	58.7	16,267,000	6,243,000	—	—
2023[5]	22,881,000	14,202,000	8,679,000	39.1	9,719,000	13,162,000	58.8	16,531,000	6,350,000	—	—
2024[5]	23,135,000	14,352,000	8,783,000	39.1	9,830,000	13,304,000	58.8	16,716,000	6,419,000	—	—

—Not available.
[1]Degree-credit enrollment only.
[2]Includes part-time resident students and all extension students (students attending courses at sites separate from the primary reporting campus). In later years, part-time student enrollment was collected as a distinct category.
[3]Large increases are due to the addition of schools accredited by the Accrediting Commission of Career Schools and Colleges of Technology.
[4]Because of imputation techniques, data are not consistent with figures for other years.
[5]Projected.
NOTE: Data through 1995 are for institutions of higher education, while later data are for degree-granting institutions. Degree-granting institutions grant associate's or higher degrees and partici-

pate in Title IV federal financial aid programs. The degree-granting classification is very similar to the earlier higher education classification, but it includes more 2-year colleges and excludes a few higher education institutions that did not grant degrees. Some data have been revised from previously published figures.
SOURCE: U.S. Department of Education, National Center for Education Statistics, *Biennial Survey of Education in the United States; Opening Fall Enrollment in Higher Education*, 1963 through 1965; Higher Education General Information Survey (HEGIS), "Fall Enrollment in Colleges and Universities" surveys, 1966 through 1985; Integrated Postsecondary Education Data System (IPEDS), "Fall Enrollment Survey" (IPEDS-EF:86–99); IPEDS Spring 2001 through Spring 2014, Enrollment component; and Enrollment in Degree-Granting Institutions Projection Model, 1980 through 2024. (This table was prepared March 2015.)

Table 303.20. Total fall enrollment in all postsecondary institutions participating in Title IV programs and annual percentage change in enrollment, by degree-granting status and control of institution: 1995 through 2013

Year	All Title IV institutions[1]				Degree-granting institutions[2]					Non-degree-granting institutions[3]			
			Private				Private					Private	
	Total	Public	Nonprofit	For-profit	Total	Public	Total	Nonprofit	For-profit	Total	Public	Nonprofit	For-profit
1	2	3	4	5	6	7	8	9	10	11	12	13	14
						Enrollment							
1995	14,836,338	11,312,491	2,977,794	546,053	14,261,781	11,092,374	3,169,407	2,929,044	240,363	574,557	220,117	48,750	305,690
1996	14,809,897	11,312,775	2,976,850	520,272	14,367,520	11,120,499	3,247,021	2,942,556	304,465	442,377	192,276	34,294	215,807
1997	14,900,416	11,370,755	3,012,106	517,555	14,502,334	11,196,119	3,306,215	2,977,614	328,601	398,082	174,636	34,492	188,954
1998	14,923,839	11,330,811	3,040,251	552,777	14,506,967	11,137,769	3,369,198	3,004,925	364,273	416,872	193,042	35,326	188,504
1999	15,262,888	11,556,731	3,088,233	617,924	14,849,691	11,375,739	3,473,952	3,055,029	418,923	413,197	180,992	33,204	199,001
2000	15,701,409	11,891,450	3,137,108	672,851	15,312,289	11,752,786	3,559,503	3,109,419	450,084	389,120	138,664	27,689	222,767
2001	16,334,134	12,370,079	3,198,354	765,701	15,927,987	12,233,156	3,694,831	3,167,330	527,501	406,147	136,923	31,024	238,200
2002	17,035,027	12,883,071	3,299,094	852,862	16,611,711	12,751,993	3,859,718	3,265,476	594,242	423,316	131,078	33,618	258,620
2003	17,330,775	12,965,502	3,372,647	992,626	16,911,481	12,858,698	4,052,783	3,341,048	711,735	419,294	106,804	31,599	280,891
2004	17,710,798	13,081,358	3,440,559	1,188,881	17,272,044	12,980,112	4,291,932	3,411,685	880,247	438,754	101,246	28,874	308,634
2005	17,921,804	13,115,177	3,484,013	1,322,614	17,487,475	13,021,834	4,465,641	3,454,692	1,010,949	434,329	93,343	29,321	311,665
2006	18,205,474	13,281,664	3,543,455	1,380,355	17,758,870	13,180,133	4,578,737	3,512,866	1,065,871	446,604	101,531	30,589	314,484
2007	18,671,084	13,595,849	3,595,207	1,480,028	18,248,128	13,490,780	4,757,348	3,571,150	1,186,198	422,956	105,069	24,057	293,830
2008	19,574,395	14,092,109	3,684,723	1,797,563	19,102,814	13,972,153	5,130,661	3,661,519	1,469,142	471,581	119,956	23,204	328,421
2009	20,853,423	14,936,402	3,793,751	2,123,270	20,313,594	14,810,768	5,502,826	3,767,672	1,735,154	539,829	125,634	26,079	388,116
2010	21,591,742	15,279,455	3,881,630	2,430,657	21,019,438	15,142,171	5,877,267	3,854,482	2,022,785	572,304	137,284	27,148	407,872
2011	21,573,798	15,251,185	3,954,173	2,368,440	21,010,590	15,116,303	5,894,287	3,926,819	1,967,468	563,208	134,882	27,354	400,972
2012	21,147,055	14,996,482	3,975,542	2,175,031	20,642,819	14,880,343	5,762,476	3,953,578	1,808,898	504,236	116,139	21,964	366,133
2013	20,847,787	14,855,412	3,993,462	1,998,913	20,375,789	14,745,558	5,630,231	3,974,004	1,656,227	471,998	109,854	19,458	342,686
						Annual percentage change							
1995 to 1996	-0.2	#	#	-4.7	0.7	0.3	2.4	0.5	26.7	-23.0	-12.6	-29.7	-29.4
1996 to 1997	0.6	0.5	1.2	-0.5	0.9	0.7	1.8	1.2	7.9	-10.0	-9.2	0.6	-12.4
1997 to 1998	0.2	-0.4	0.9	6.8	#	-0.5	1.9	0.9	10.9	4.7	10.5	2.4	-0.2
1998 to 1999	2.3	2.0	1.6	11.8	2.4	2.1	3.1	1.7	15.0	-0.9	-6.2	-6.0	5.6
1999 to 2000	2.9	2.9	1.6	8.9	3.1	3.3	2.5	1.8	7.4	-5.8	-23.4	-16.6	11.9
2000 to 2001	4.0	4.0	2.0	13.8	4.0	4.1	3.8	1.9	17.2	4.4	-1.3	12.0	6.9
2001 to 2002	4.3	4.1	3.1	11.4	4.3	4.2	4.5	3.1	12.7	4.2	-4.3	8.4	8.6
2002 to 2003	1.7	0.6	2.2	16.4	1.8	0.8	5.0	2.3	19.8	-1.0	-18.5	-6.0	8.6
2003 to 2004	2.2	0.9	2.0	19.8	2.1	0.9	5.9	2.1	23.7	4.6	-5.2	-8.6	9.9
2004 to 2005	1.2	0.3	1.3	11.2	1.2	0.3	4.0	1.3	14.8	-1.0	-7.8	1.5	1.0
2005 to 2006	1.6	1.3	1.7	4.4	1.6	1.2	2.5	1.7	5.4	2.8	8.8	4.3	0.9
2006 to 2007	2.6	2.4	1.5	7.2	2.8	2.4	3.9	1.7	11.3	-5.3	3.5	-21.4	-6.6
2007 to 2008	4.8	3.7	2.5	21.5	4.7	3.6	7.8	2.5	23.9	11.5	14.2	-3.5	11.8
2008 to 2009	6.5	6.0	3.0	18.1	6.3	6.0	7.3	2.9	18.1	14.5	4.7	12.4	18.2
2009 to 2010	3.5	2.3	2.3	14.5	3.5	2.2	6.8	2.3	16.6	6.0	9.3	4.1	5.1
2010 to 2011	-0.1	-0.2	1.9	-2.6	#	-0.2	0.3	1.9	-2.7	-1.6	-1.7	0.8	-1.7
2011 to 2012	-2.0	-1.7	0.5	-8.2	-1.8	-1.6	-2.2	0.7	-8.1	-10.5	-13.9	-19.7	-8.7
2012 to 2013	-1.4	-0.9	0.5	-8.1	-1.3	-0.9	-2.3	0.5	-8.4	-6.4	-5.4	-11.4	-6.4

#Rounds to zero.
[1]Includes degree-granting and non-degree-granting institutions.
[2]Data for 1995 are for institutions of higher education, while later data are for degree-granting institutions. Degree-granting institutions grant associate's or higher degrees and participate in Title IV federal financial aid programs. The degree-granting classification is very similar to the earlier higher education classification, but it includes more 2-year colleges and excludes a few higher education institutions that did not grant degrees.

[3]Data are for institutions that did not offer accredited 4-year or 2-year programs, but were participating in Title IV federal financial aid programs. Includes some institutions transitioning to higher level offerings, though still classified at a lower level.
NOTE: Some data have been revised from previously published figures.
SOURCE: U.S. Department of Education, National Center for Education Statistics, Integrated Postsecondary Education Data System (IPEDS), "Fall Enrollment Survey" (IPEDS-EF:95–99); and IPEDS Spring 2001 through Spring 2014, Enrollment component. (This table was prepared March 2015.)

Table 303.25. Total fall enrollment in degree-granting postsecondary institutions, by control and level of institution: 1970 through 2013

	All institutions			Public institutions			Private institutions								
							All private institutions			Nonprofit			For-profit		
Year	Total	4-year	2-year	Total	4-year	2-year	Total	4-year	2-year	Total	4-year	2-year	Total	4-year	2-year
1	2	3	4	5	6	7	8	9	10	11	12	13	14	15	16
1970	8,580,887	6,261,502	2,319,385	6,428,134	4,232,722	2,195,412	2,152,753	2,028,780	123,973	2,134,420	2,021,121	113,299	18,333	7,659	10,674
1971	8,948,644	6,369,355	2,579,289	6,804,309	4,346,990	2,457,319	2,144,335	2,022,365	121,970	2,121,913	2,011,682	110,231	22,422	10,683	11,739
1972	9,214,860	6,458,674	2,756,186	7,070,635	4,429,696	2,640,939	2,144,225	2,028,978	115,247	2,123,245	2,019,380	103,865	20,980	9,598	11,382
1973	9,602,123	6,590,023	3,012,100	7,419,516	4,529,895	2,889,621	2,182,607	2,060,128	122,479	2,148,784	2,045,804	102,980	33,823	14,324	19,499
1974	10,223,729	6,819,735	3,403,994	7,988,500	4,703,018	3,285,482	2,235,229	2,116,717	118,512	2,200,963	2,098,599	102,364	34,266	18,118	16,148
1975	11,184,859	7,214,740	3,970,119	8,834,508	4,998,142	3,836,366	2,350,351	2,216,598	133,753	2,311,448	2,198,451	112,997	38,903	18,147	20,756
1976	11,012,137	7,128,816	3,883,321	8,653,477	4,901,691	3,751,786	2,358,660	2,227,125	131,535	2,314,298	2,206,457	107,841	44,362	20,668	23,694
1977	11,285,787	7,242,845	4,042,942	8,846,993	4,945,224	3,901,769	2,438,794	2,297,621	141,173	2,386,652	2,277,072	109,580	52,142	20,549	31,593
1978	11,260,092	7,231,625	4,028,467	8,785,893	4,912,203	3,873,690	2,474,199	2,319,422	154,777	2,408,331	2,299,132	109,199	65,868	20,290	45,578
1979	11,569,899	7,353,233	4,216,666	9,036,822	4,980,012	4,056,810	2,533,077	2,373,221	159,856	2,461,773	2,351,364	110,409	71,304	21,857	49,447
1980	12,096,895	7,570,608	4,526,287	9,457,394	5,128,612	4,328,782	2,639,501	2,441,996	197,505[1]	2,527,787	2,413,693	114,094	111,714	28,303	83,411[1]
1981	12,371,672	7,655,461	4,716,211	9,647,032	5,166,324	4,480,708	2,724,640	2,489,137	235,503[1]	2,572,405	2,453,239	119,166	152,235	35,898	116,337[1]
1982	12,425,780	7,654,074	4,771,706	9,696,087	5,176,434	4,519,653	2,729,693	2,477,640	252,053[1]	2,552,739	2,437,763	114,976	176,954	39,877	137,077[1]
1983	12,464,661	7,741,195	4,723,466	9,682,734	5,223,404	4,459,330	2,781,927	2,517,791	264,136	2,589,187	2,472,894	116,293	192,740	44,897	147,843
1984	12,241,940	7,711,167	4,530,773	9,477,370	5,198,273	4,279,097	2,764,570	2,512,894	251,676	2,574,419	2,466,172	108,247	190,151	46,722	143,429
1985	12,247,055	7,715,978	4,531,077	9,479,273	5,209,540	4,269,733	2,767,782	2,506,438	261,344	2,571,791	2,463,000	108,791	195,991	43,438	152,553
1986	12,503,511	7,823,963	4,679,548	9,713,893	5,300,202	4,413,691	2,789,618	2,523,761	265,857[2]	2,572,479	2,470,981	101,498	217,139	52,780	164,359[2]
1987	12,766,642	7,990,420	4,776,222	9,973,254	5,432,200	4,541,054	2,793,388	2,558,220	235,168[2]	2,602,350	2,512,248	90,102	191,038	45,972	145,066[2]
1988	13,055,337	8,180,182	4,875,155	10,161,388	5,545,901	4,615,487	2,893,949	2,634,281	259,668	—	—	—	—	—	—
1989	13,538,560	8,387,671	5,150,889	10,577,963	5,694,303	4,883,660	2,960,597	2,693,368	267,229	—	—	—	—	—	—
1990	13,818,637	8,578,554	5,240,083	10,844,717	5,848,242	4,996,475	2,973,920	2,730,312	243,608	2,760,227	2,671,069	89,158	213,693	59,243	154,450
1991	14,358,953	8,707,053	5,651,900	11,309,563	5,904,748	5,404,815	3,049,390	2,802,305	247,085	2,819,041	2,729,752	89,289	230,349	72,553	157,796
1992	14,487,359	8,764,969	5,722,390	11,384,567	5,900,012	5,484,555	3,102,792	2,864,957	237,835	2,872,523	2,789,235	83,288	230,269	75,722	154,547
1993	14,304,803	8,738,936	5,565,867	11,189,088	5,851,760	5,337,328	3,115,715	2,887,176	228,539	2,888,897	2,802,540	86,357	226,818	84,636	142,182
1994	14,278,790	8,749,080	5,529,710	11,133,680	5,825,213	5,308,467	3,145,110	2,923,894	221,243	2,910,107	2,824,500	85,607	235,003	99,367	135,636
1995	14,261,781	8,769,252	5,492,529	11,092,374	5,814,545	5,277,829	3,169,407	2,954,707	214,700	2,929,044	2,853,890	75,154	240,363	100,817	139,546
1996	14,367,520	8,804,193	5,563,327	11,120,499	5,806,036	5,314,463	3,247,021	2,998,157	248,864	2,942,556	2,867,181	75,375	304,465	130,976	173,489
1997	14,502,334	8,896,765	5,605,569	11,196,119	5,835,433	5,360,686	3,306,215	3,061,332	244,883	2,977,614	2,905,820	71,794	328,601	155,512	173,089
1998	14,506,967	9,017,653	5,489,314	11,137,769	5,891,806	5,245,963	3,369,198	3,125,847	243,351	3,004,925	2,939,055	65,870	364,273	186,792	177,481
1999	14,849,691	9,196,160	5,653,531	11,375,739	5,977,678	5,398,061	3,473,952	3,218,482	255,470	3,055,061	2,991,728	63,301	418,923	226,754	192,169
2000	15,312,289	9,363,858	5,948,431	11,752,786	6,055,398	5,697,388	3,559,503	3,308,460	251,043	3,109,419	3,050,575	58,844	450,084	257,885	192,199
2001	15,927,987	9,677,408	6,250,579	12,233,156	6,236,455	5,996,701	3,694,831	3,440,953	253,878	3,167,330	3,119,781	47,549	527,501	321,172	206,329
2002	16,611,711	10,082,332	6,529,379	12,751,993	6,481,613	6,270,380	3,859,718	3,600,719	258,999	3,265,476	3,218,389	47,087	594,242	382,330	211,912
2003	16,911,481	10,417,247	6,494,234	12,858,698	6,649,441	6,209,257	4,052,783	3,767,806	284,977	3,341,048	3,297,180	43,868	711,735	470,626	241,109
2004	17,272,044	10,726,181	6,545,863	12,980,112	6,736,536	6,243,576	4,291,932	3,989,645	302,287	3,411,685	3,369,435	42,250	880,247	620,210	260,037
2005	17,487,475	10,999,420	6,488,055	13,021,834	6,837,605	6,184,229	4,465,641	4,161,815	303,826	3,454,692	3,411,170	43,522	1,010,949	750,645	260,304
2006	17,758,870	11,240,330	6,518,540	13,180,133	6,955,013	6,225,120	4,578,737	4,285,317	293,420	3,512,866	3,473,710	39,156	1,065,871	811,607	254,264
2007	18,248,128	11,630,198	6,617,930	13,490,780	7,166,661	6,324,119	4,757,348	4,463,537	293,811	3,571,150	3,537,664	33,486	1,186,198	925,873	260,325
2008	19,102,814	12,131,436	6,971,378	13,972,153	7,331,809	6,640,344	5,130,661	4,799,627	331,034	3,661,519	3,626,168	35,351	1,469,142	1,173,459	295,683
2009	20,313,594	12,791,012	7,522,582	14,810,768	7,709,198	7,101,570	5,502,826	5,081,814	421,012	3,767,672	3,732,900	34,772	1,735,154	1,348,914	386,240
2010	21,019,438	13,335,841	7,683,597	15,142,171	7,924,108	7,218,063	5,877,267	5,411,733	465,534	3,854,482	3,821,799	32,683	2,022,785	1,589,934	432,851
2011	21,010,590	13,499,440	7,511,150	15,116,303	8,048,145	7,068,158	5,894,287	5,451,295	442,992	3,926,819	3,886,964	39,855	1,967,468	1,564,331	403,137
2012	20,642,819	13,478,846	7,163,973	14,880,343	8,092,683	6,787,660	5,762,476	5,386,163	376,313	3,953,578	3,915,972	37,606	1,808,898	1,470,191	338,707
2013	20,375,789	13,407,050	6,968,739	14,745,558	8,120,417	6,625,141	5,630,231	5,286,633	343,598	3,974,004	3,941,806	32,198	1,656,222	1,344,827	311,400

—Not available.
[1]Large increases are due to the addition of schools accredited by the Accrediting Commission of Career Schools and Colleges of Technology.
[2]Because of imputation techniques, data are not consistent with figures for other years.
NOTE: Data through 1995 are for institutions of higher education, while later data are for degree-granting institutions. Degree-granting institutions grant associate's or higher degrees and participate in Title IV federal financial aid programs. The degree-granting classification is very similar to the earlier higher education classification, but it includes more 2-year colleges and

excludes a few higher education institutions that did not grant degrees. Some data have been revised from previously published figures.
SOURCE: U.S. Department of Education, National Center for Education Statistics, Higher Education General Information Survey (HEGIS), "Fall Enrollment in Institutions of Higher Education" surveys, 1970 through 1985; Integrated Postsecondary Education Data System (IPEDS), "Fall Enrollment Survey" (IPEDS-EF:86–99); and IPEDS Spring 2001 through Spring 2014, Enrollment component. (This table was prepared October 2014.)

Table 303.30. Total fall enrollment in degree-granting postsecondary institutions, by level and control of institution, attendance status, and sex of student: Selected years, 1970 through 2024

Level and control of institution, attendance status, and sex of student	Actual													
	1970	1975	1980[1]	1985	1990	1995	2000	2005	2008	2009	2010	2011	2012	2013
1	2	3	4	5	6	7	8	9	10	11	12	13	14	15
Total	8,580,887	11,184,859	12,096,895	12,247,055	13,818,637	14,261,781	15,312,289	17,487,475	19,102,814	20,313,594	21,019,438	21,010,590	20,642,819	20,375,789
Full-time	5,816,290	6,841,334	7,097,958	7,075,221	7,820,985	8,128,802	9,009,600	10,797,011	11,747,743	12,605,355	13,087,182	13,002,531	12,737,013	12,597,112
Males	3,504,095	3,926,753	3,689,244	3,607,720	3,807,752	3,807,392	4,111,093	4,803,388	5,234,357	5,632,097	5,838,383	5,792,818	5,709,792	5,682,166
Females	2,312,195	2,914,581	3,408,714	3,467,501	4,013,233	4,321,410	4,898,507	5,993,623	6,513,386	6,973,258	7,248,799	7,209,713	7,027,221	6,914,946
Part-time	2,764,597	4,343,525	4,998,937	5,171,834	5,997,652	6,132,979	6,302,689	6,690,464	7,355,071	7,708,239	7,932,256	8,008,059	7,905,806	7,778,677
Males	1,539,547	2,222,244	2,185,130	2,210,730	2,476,157	2,535,147	2,610,676	2,652,537	2,954,538	3,100,856	3,207,376	3,241,438	3,209,295	3,178,620
Females	1,225,050	2,121,281	2,813,807	2,961,104	3,521,495	3,597,832	3,692,013	4,037,927	4,400,533	4,607,383	4,724,880	4,766,621	4,696,511	4,600,057
4-year	6,261,502	7,214,740	7,570,608	7,715,978	8,578,554	8,769,252	9,363,858	10,999,420	12,131,436	12,791,013	13,335,841	13,499,440	13,478,846	13,407,050
Full-time	4,587,379	5,080,256	5,344,163	5,384,614	5,937,023	6,151,755	6,792,551	8,150,209	8,915,546	9,361,404	9,721,803	9,832,324	9,794,436	9,764,196
Males	2,732,796	2,891,192	2,809,528	2,781,412	2,926,360	2,929,177	3,115,252	3,649,622	3,984,494	4,185,726	4,355,153	4,401,635	4,403,960	4,403,914
Females	1,854,583	2,189,064	2,534,635	2,603,202	3,010,663	3,222,578	3,677,299	4,500,587	4,931,052	5,175,678	5,366,650	5,430,689	5,390,476	5,360,282
Part-time	1,674,123	2,134,484	2,226,445	2,331,364	2,641,531	2,617,497	2,571,307	2,849,211	3,215,890	3,429,609	3,614,038	3,667,116	3,684,410	3,642,854
Males	936,189	1,092,461	1,017,813	1,034,804	1,124,780	1,084,753	1,047,917	1,125,935	1,268,517	1,349,890	1,424,721	1,456,818	1,470,423	1,458,956
Females	737,934	1,042,023	1,208,632	1,296,560	1,516,751	1,532,744	1,523,390	1,723,276	1,947,373	2,079,719	2,189,317	2,210,298	2,213,987	2,183,898
Public 4-year	4,232,722	4,998,142	5,128,612	5,209,540	5,848,242	5,814,545	6,055,398	6,837,605	7,331,809	7,709,198	7,924,108	8,048,145	8,092,683	8,120,417
Full-time	3,086,491	3,469,821	3,592,193	3,623,341	4,033,654	4,084,711	4,371,218	5,021,745	5,378,123	5,649,722	5,811,214	5,890,689	5,910,198	5,934,852
Males	1,813,584	1,947,823	1,873,397	1,863,689	1,982,369	1,951,140	2,008,618	2,295,456	2,488,168	2,626,174	2,707,307	2,743,773	2,756,941	2,772,506
Females	1,272,907	1,521,998	1,718,796	1,759,652	2,051,285	2,133,571	2,362,600	2,726,289	2,889,955	3,023,548	3,103,907	3,146,916	3,153,257	3,162,346
Part-time	1,146,231	1,528,321	1,536,419	1,586,199	1,814,588	1,729,834	1,684,180	1,815,860	1,953,686	2,059,476	2,112,894	2,157,456	2,182,485	2,185,565
Males	609,422	760,469	685,051	693,115	764,248	720,402	683,100	724,375	788,594	833,155	860,968	885,045	901,197	911,040
Females	536,809	767,852	851,368	893,084	1,050,340	1,009,432	1,001,080	1,091,485	1,165,092	1,226,321	1,251,926	1,272,411	1,281,288	1,274,525
Private 4-year	2,028,780	2,216,598	2,441,996	2,506,438	2,730,312	2,954,707	3,308,460	4,161,815	4,799,627	5,081,815	5,411,733	5,451,295	5,386,163	5,286,633
Full-time	1,500,888	1,610,435	1,751,970	1,761,273	1,903,369	2,067,044	2,421,333	3,128,464	3,537,423	3,711,682	3,910,589	3,941,635	3,884,238	3,829,344
Males	919,212	943,369	936,131	917,723	943,991	978,037	1,106,634	1,354,166	1,496,326	1,559,552	1,647,846	1,657,862	1,647,019	1,631,408
Females	581,676	667,066	815,839	843,550	959,378	1,089,007	1,314,699	1,774,298	2,041,097	2,152,130	2,262,743	2,283,773	2,237,219	2,197,936
Part-time	527,892	606,163	690,026	745,165	826,943	887,663	887,127	1,033,351	1,262,204	1,370,133	1,501,144	1,509,660	1,501,925	1,457,289
Males	326,767	331,992	332,762	341,689	360,532	364,351	364,817	401,560	479,923	516,735	563,753	571,773	569,226	547,916
Females	201,125	274,171	357,264	403,476	466,411	523,312	522,310	631,791	782,281	853,398	937,391	937,887	932,699	909,373
Nonprofit 4-year	2,021,121	2,198,451	2,413,693	2,463,000	2,671,069	2,853,890	3,050,575	3,411,170	3,626,168	3,732,900	3,821,799	3,886,964	3,915,972	3,941,806
Full-time	1,494,625	1,596,074	1,733,014	1,727,707	1,859,124	1,989,457	2,226,028	2,534,793	2,698,819	2,787,321	2,864,640	2,905,674	2,928,938	2,961,998
Males	914,020	930,842	921,253	894,080	915,100	931,956	996,113	1,109,075	1,184,895	1,223,333	1,259,638	1,275,590	1,290,080	1,303,567
Females	580,605	665,232	811,761	833,627	944,024	1,057,501	1,229,915	1,425,718	1,513,924	1,563,988	1,605,002	1,630,084	1,638,858	1,658,431
Part-time	526,496	602,377	680,679	735,293	811,945	864,433	824,547	876,377	927,349	945,579	957,159	981,290	987,034	979,808
Males	325,693	329,662	327,986	336,168	352,106	351,874	332,814	339,572	357,974	363,789	366,735	375,713	377,740	377,480
Females	200,803	272,715	352,693	399,125	459,839	512,559	491,733	536,805	569,375	581,790	590,424	605,577	609,294	602,328
For-profit 4-year	7,659	18,147	28,303	43,438	59,243	100,817	257,885	750,645	1,173,459	1,348,915	1,589,934	1,564,331	1,470,191	1,344,827
2-year	2,319,385	3,970,119	4,526,287	4,531,077	5,240,083	5,492,529	5,948,431	6,488,055	6,971,378	7,522,581	7,683,597	7,511,150	7,163,973	6,968,739
Full-time	1,228,911	1,761,078	1,753,795	1,690,607	1,883,962	1,977,047	2,217,049	2,646,802	2,832,197	3,243,951	3,365,379	3,170,207	2,942,577	2,832,916
Males	771,299	1,035,561	879,716	826,308	881,392	878,215	995,841	1,153,766	1,249,863	1,446,371	1,483,230	1,391,183	1,305,832	1,278,252
Females	457,612	725,517	874,079	864,299	1,002,570	1,098,832	1,221,208	1,493,036	1,582,334	1,797,580	1,882,149	1,779,024	1,636,745	1,554,664
Part-time	1,090,474	2,209,041	2,772,492	2,840,470	3,356,121	3,515,482	3,731,382	3,841,253	4,139,181	4,278,630	4,318,218	4,340,943	4,221,396	4,135,823
Males	603,358	1,129,783	1,167,317	1,175,926	1,351,377	1,450,394	1,562,759	1,526,602	1,686,021	1,750,966	1,782,655	1,784,620	1,738,872	1,719,664
Females	487,116	1,079,258	1,605,175	1,664,544	2,004,744	2,065,088	2,168,623	2,314,651	2,453,160	2,527,664	2,535,563	2,556,323	2,482,524	2,416,159
Public 2-year	2,195,412	3,836,366	4,328,782	4,269,733	4,996,475	5,277,829	5,697,388	6,184,229	6,640,344	7,101,569	7,218,063	7,068,158	6,787,660	6,625,141
Full-time	1,129,165	1,662,621	1,595,493	1,496,905	1,716,843	1,840,590	2,000,008	2,387,016	2,548,488	2,875,291	2,950,024	2,781,419	2,615,620	2,529,957
Males	720,440	988,701	811,871	742,673	810,664	818,605	891,282	1,055,029	1,152,037	1,315,200	1,340,820	1,260,759	1,197,173	1,176,699
Females	408,725	673,920	783,622	754,232	906,179	1,021,985	1,108,726	1,331,987	1,396,451	1,560,091	1,609,204	1,520,660	1,418,447	1,353,258
Part-time	1,066,247	2,173,745	2,733,289	2,772,828	3,279,632	3,437,239	3,697,380	3,797,213	4,091,856	4,226,278	4,268,039	4,286,739	4,172,040	4,095,184
Males	589,439	1,107,680	1,152,268	1,138,011	1,317,730	1,417,488	1,549,407	1,514,363	1,671,716	1,735,300	1,769,737	1,770,197	1,725,988	1,708,594
Females	476,808	1,066,065	1,581,021	1,634,817	1,961,902	2,019,751	2,147,973	2,282,850	2,420,140	2,490,978	2,498,302	2,516,542	2,446,052	2,386,590
Private 2-year	123,973	133,753	197,505	261,344	243,608	214,700	251,043	303,826	331,034	421,012	465,534	442,992	376,313	343,598
Full-time	99,746	98,457	158,302	193,702	167,119	136,457	217,041	259,786	283,709	368,660	415,355	388,788	326,957	302,959
Males	50,859	46,860	67,845	83,635	70,728	59,610	104,559	98,737	97,826	131,171	142,410	130,424	108,659	101,553
Females	48,887	51,597	90,457	110,067	96,391	76,847	112,482	161,049	185,883	237,489	272,945	258,364	218,298	201,406
Part-time	24,227	35,296	39,203	67,642	76,489	78,243	34,002	44,040	47,325	52,352	50,179	54,204	49,356	40,639
Males	13,919	22,103	15,049	37,915	33,647	32,906	13,352	12,239	14,305	15,666	12,918	14,423	12,884	11,070
Females	10,308	13,193	24,154	29,727	42,842	45,337	20,650	31,801	33,020	36,686	37,261	39,781	36,472	29,569
Nonprofit 2-year	113,299	112,997	114,094	108,791	89,158	75,154	58,844	43,522	35,351	34,772	32,683	39,855	37,606	32,198
Full-time	91,514	82,158	83,009	76,547	62,003	54,033	46,670	28,939	23,270	23,488	23,127	30,584	29,320	24,055
Males	46,030	40,548	34,968	30,878	25,946	23,265	21,950	12,086	9,244	9,578	9,944	11,298	10,459	9,470
Females	45,484	41,610	48,041	45,669	36,057	30,768	24,720	16,853	14,026	13,910	13,183	19,286	18,861	14,585
Part-time	21,785	30,839	31,085	32,244	27,155	21,121	12,174	14,583	12,081	11,284	9,556	9,271	8,286	8,143
Males	12,097	18,929	11,445	10,786	7,970	6,080	4,499	3,566	2,867	2,721	2,585	2,540	2,465	2,386
Females	9,688	11,910	19,640	21,458	19,185	15,041	7,675	11,017	9,214	8,563	6,971	6,731	5,821	5,757
For-profit 2-year	10,674	20,756	83,411	152,553	154,450	139,546	192,199	260,304	295,683	386,240	432,851	403,137	338,707	311,400

See notes at end of table.

Table 303.30. Total fall enrollment in degree-granting postsecondary institutions, by level and control of institution, attendance status, and sex of student: Selected years, 1970 through 2024—Continued

Level and control of institution, attendance status, and sex of student	Projected										
	2014	2015	2016	2017	2018	2019	2020	2021	2022	2023	2024
1	16	17	18	19	20	21	22	23	24	25	26
Total	**20,255,000**	**20,234,000**	**20,486,000**	**20,925,000**	**21,330,000**	**21,630,000**	**21,859,000**	**22,168,000**	**22,511,000**	**22,881,000**	**23,135,000**
Full-time	12,664,000	12,615,000	12,783,000	13,064,000	13,305,000	13,467,000	13,595,000	13,774,000	13,972,000	14,202,000	14,352,000
Males	5,654,000	5,671,000	5,721,000	5,811,000	5,903,000	5,972,000	6,021,000	6,089,000	6,167,000	6,254,000	6,316,000
Females	7,010,000	6,943,000	7,062,000	7,253,000	7,402,000	7,495,000	7,574,000	7,685,000	7,805,000	7,948,000	8,035,000
Part-time	7,590,000	7,619,000	7,703,000	7,861,000	8,025,000	8,163,000	8,264,000	8,394,000	8,539,000	8,679,000	8,783,000
Males	3,072,000	3,046,000	3,063,000	3,130,000	3,202,000	3,245,000	3,277,000	3,333,000	3,400,000	3,465,000	3,514,000
Females	4,519,000	4,573,000	4,640,000	4,731,000	4,823,000	4,918,000	4,987,000	5,061,000	5,139,000	5,214,000	5,269,000
4-year	**13,246,000**	**13,222,000**	**13,395,000**	**13,690,000**	**13,952,000**	**14,142,000**	**14,297,000**	**14,505,000**	**14,728,000**	**14,975,000**	**15,140,000**
Full-time	9,739,000	9,699,000	9,826,000	10,039,000	10,219,000	10,341,000	10,443,000	10,581,000	10,729,000	10,903,000	11,016,000
Males	4,358,000	4,371,000	4,409,000	4,478,000	4,546,000	4,599,000	4,638,000	4,692,000	4,751,000	4,816,000	4,863,000
Females	5,381,000	5,328,000	5,417,000	5,561,000	5,673,000	5,742,000	5,804,000	5,889,000	5,979,000	6,087,000	6,153,000
Part-time	3,506,000	3,523,000	3,569,000	3,651,000	3,733,000	3,801,000	3,855,000	3,924,000	3,999,000	4,072,000	4,123,000
Males	1,412,000	1,403,000	1,415,000	1,450,000	1,487,000	1,510,000	1,527,000	1,557,000	1,593,000	1,626,000	1,651,000
Females	2,094,000	2,120,000	2,154,000	2,201,000	2,246,000	2,292,000	2,328,000	2,366,000	2,407,000	2,445,000	2,472,000
Public 4-year	8,008,000	7,991,000	8,091,000	8,265,000	8,421,000	8,535,000	8,627,000	8,750,000	8,883,000	9,030,000	9,130,000
Full-time	5,911,000	5,884,000	5,958,000	6,083,000	6,191,000	6,265,000	6,325,000	6,408,000	6,496,000	6,600,000	6,669,000
Males	2,734,000	2,741,000	2,763,000	2,805,000	2,847,000	2,879,000	2,904,000	2,937,000	2,973,000	3,013,000	3,043,000
Females	3,177,000	3,144,000	3,195,000	3,279,000	3,344,000	3,385,000	3,422,000	3,472,000	3,524,000	3,587,000	3,626,000
Part-time	2,097,000	2,107,000	2,133,000	2,181,000	2,230,000	2,270,000	2,302,000	2,342,000	2,387,000	2,430,000	2,461,000
Males	877,000	872,000	878,000	900,000	922,000	936,000	947,000	965,000	987,000	1,007,000	1,023,000
Females	1,220,000	1,235,000	1,255,000	1,281,000	1,307,000	1,334,000	1,355,000	1,377,000	1,400,000	1,423,000	1,438,000
Private 4-year	5,237,000	5,231,000	5,304,000	5,425,000	5,531,000	5,608,000	5,671,000	5,754,000	5,845,000	5,945,000	6,010,000
Full-time	3,828,000	3,814,000	3,868,000	3,956,000	4,028,000	4,077,000	4,117,000	4,173,000	4,233,000	4,303,000	4,347,000
Males	1,624,000	1,630,000	1,646,000	1,673,000	1,699,000	1,719,000	1,735,000	1,755,000	1,778,000	1,803,000	1,820,000
Females	2,205,000	2,184,000	2,222,000	2,282,000	2,329,000	2,357,000	2,383,000	2,418,000	2,455,000	2,500,000	2,527,000
Part-time	1,409,000	1,417,000	1,436,000	1,470,000	1,503,000	1,531,000	1,553,000	1,581,000	1,612,000	1,642,000	1,663,000
Males	535,000	532,000	537,000	550,000	564,000	573,000	580,000	592,000	606,000	619,000	628,000
Females	874,000	885,000	900,000	919,000	939,000	958,000	973,000	989,000	1,006,000	1,023,000	1,034,000
Nonprofit 4-year	—	—	—	—	—	—	—	—	—	—	—
Full-time	—	—	—	—	—	—	—	—	—	—	—
Males	—	—	—	—	—	—	—	—	—	—	—
Females	—	—	—	—	—	—	—	—	—	—	—
Part-time	—	—	—	—	—	—	—	—	—	—	—
Males	—	—	—	—	—	—	—	—	—	—	—
Females	—	—	—	—	—	—	—	—	—	—	—
For-profit 4-year	—	—	—	—	—	—	—	—	—	—	—
2-year	**7,009,000**	**7,011,000**	**7,090,000**	**7,235,000**	**7,378,000**	**7,487,000**	**7,562,000**	**7,664,000**	**7,782,000**	**7,907,000**	**7,996,000**
Full-time	2,925,000	2,916,000	2,957,000	3,026,000	3,085,000	3,126,000	3,153,000	3,193,000	3,243,000	3,299,000	3,335,000
Males	1,296,000	1,300,000	1,311,000	1,333,000	1,356,000	1,374,000	1,383,000	1,398,000	1,416,000	1,438,000	1,453,000
Females	1,629,000	1,616,000	1,645,000	1,692,000	1,729,000	1,752,000	1,770,000	1,796,000	1,826,000	1,862,000	1,882,000
Part-time	4,084,000	4,096,000	4,134,000	4,210,000	4,292,000	4,362,000	4,409,000	4,470,000	4,540,000	4,607,000	4,660,000
Males	1,660,000	1,643,000	1,648,000	1,680,000	1,716,000	1,736,000	1,749,000	1,776,000	1,808,000	1,839,000	1,863,000
Females	2,425,000	2,453,000	2,485,000	2,530,000	2,577,000	2,626,000	2,660,000	2,694,000	2,732,000	2,769,000	2,797,000
Public 2-year	6,651,000	6,655,000	6,729,000	6,865,000	7,000,000	7,104,000	7,175,000	7,272,000	7,384,000	7,502,000	7,586,000
Full-time	2,611,000	2,603,000	2,639,000	2,700,000	2,754,000	2,790,000	2,813,000	2,850,000	2,894,000	2,944,000	2,976,000
Males	1,193,000	1,197,000	1,207,000	1,227,000	1,249,000	1,264,000	1,273,000	1,287,000	1,304,000	1,323,000	1,338,000
Females	1,418,000	1,406,000	1,432,000	1,473,000	1,505,000	1,525,000	1,540,000	1,563,000	1,590,000	1,620,000	1,638,000
Part-time	4,040,000	4,052,000	4,089,000	4,165,000	4,246,000	4,315,000	4,362,000	4,422,000	4,491,000	4,558,000	4,610,000
Males	1,648,000	1,631,000	1,637,000	1,668,000	1,704,000	1,724,000	1,737,000	1,764,000	1,795,000	1,826,000	1,850,000
Females	2,392,000	2,420,000	2,452,000	2,496,000	2,543,000	2,591,000	2,624,000	2,658,000	2,695,000	2,732,000	2,760,000
Private 2-year	358,000	357,000	362,000	371,000	378,000	383,000	387,000	392,000	398,000	405,000	410,000
Full-time	314,000	313,000	317,000	325,000	332,000	336,000	339,000	344,000	349,000	355,000	359,000
Males	103,000	103,000	104,000	106,000	108,000	109,000	110,000	111,000	113,000	114,000	115,000
Females	211,000	209,000	213,000	219,000	224,000	227,000	229,000	233,000	237,000	241,000	244,000
Part-time	44,000	44,000	45,000	45,000	46,000	47,000	48,000	48,000	49,000	50,000	50,000
Males	11,000	11,000	11,000	12,000	12,000	12,000	12,000	12,000	12,000	13,000	13,000
Females	32,000	33,000	33,000	34,000	34,000	35,000	36,000	36,000	37,000	37,000	37,000
Nonprofit 2-year	—	—	—	—	—	—	—	—	—	—	—
Full-time	—	—	—	—	—	—	—	—	—	—	—
Males	—	—	—	—	—	—	—	—	—	—	—
Females	—	—	—	—	—	—	—	—	—	—	—
Part-time	—	—	—	—	—	—	—	—	—	—	—
Males	—	—	—	—	—	—	—	—	—	—	—
Females	—	—	—	—	—	—	—	—	—	—	—
For-profit 2-year	—	—	—	—	—	—	—	—	—	—	—

—Not available.

[1]Large increase in private 2-year institutions in 1980 is due to the addition of schools accredited by the Accrediting Commission of Career Schools and Colleges of Technology. NOTE: Data through 1995 are for institutions of higher education, while later data are for degree-granting institutions. Degree-granting institutions grant associate's or higher degrees and participate in Title IV federal financial aid programs. The degree-granting classification is very similar to the earlier higher education classification, but it includes more 2-year colleges and excludes a few higher education institutions that did not grant degrees. Some data have been revised from previously published figures.

SOURCE: U.S. Department of Education, National Center for Education Statistics, Higher Education General Information Survey (HEGIS), "Fall Enrollment in Colleges and Universities" surveys, 1970 through 1985; Integrated Postsecondary Education Data System (IPEDS), "Fall Enrollment Survey" (IPEDS-EF:90–99); IPEDS Spring 2001 through Spring 2014, Enrollment component; and Enrollment in Degree-Granting Institutions Projection Model, 1980 through 2024. (This table was prepared March 2015.)

Table 303.40. Total fall enrollment in degree-granting postsecondary institutions, by attendance status, sex, and age: Selected years, 1970 through 2024

[In thousands]

Attendance status, sex, and age	1970	1980	1990	2000	2003	2004	2005	2006	2007	2008	2009	2010	2011	2012	2013	Projected 2014	Projected 2015	Projected 2019	Projected 2024
1	2	3	4	5	6	7	8	9	10	11	12	13	14	15	16	17	18	19	20
All students	8,581	12,097	13,819	15,312	16,911	17,272	17,487	17,759	18,248	19,103	20,314	21,019	21,011	20,643	20,376	20,255	20,234	21,630	23,135
14 to 17 years old	263	257	153	131	169	166	187	184	200	195	215	202	221	242	270	254	259	278	311
18 and 19 years old	2,579	2,852	2,777	3,258	3,355	3,367	3,444	3,561	3,690	3,813	4,009	4,057	3,956	3,782	3,710	3,879	3,850	4,132	4,313
20 and 21 years old	1,885	2,395	2,593	3,005	3,391	3,516	3,563	3,573	3,570	3,649	3,916	4,103	4,269	4,235	4,248	4,472	4,414	4,526	4,747
22 to 24 years old	1,469	1,947	2,202	2,600	3,086	3,166	3,114	3,185	3,280	3,443	3,571	3,759	3,793	3,950	3,949	4,075	4,035	4,121	4,429
25 to 29 years old	1,091	1,843	2,083	2,044	2,311	2,418	2,469	2,506	2,651	2,840	3,082	3,254	3,272	3,154	3,031	2,995	3,071	3,467	3,525
30 to 34 years old	527	1,227	1,384	1,333	1,418	1,440	1,438	1,472	1,519	1,609	1,735	1,805	1,788	1,683	1,629	1,494	1,508	1,685	1,931
35 years old and over	767	1,577	2,627	2,942	3,181	3,199	3,272	3,277	3,339	3,554	3,785	3,840	3,712	3,595	3,538	3,086	3,097	3,421	3,879
Males	5,044	5,874	6,284	6,722	7,260	7,387	7,456	7,575	7,816	8,189	8,733	9,046	9,034	8,919	8,861	8,726	8,717	9,217	9,831
14 to 17 years old	125	106	66	58	67	62	68	69	88	93	103	94	104	119	130	118	119	124	136
18 and 19 years old	1,355	1,368	1,298	1,464	1,474	1,475	1,523	1,604	1,669	1,704	1,795	1,820	1,782	1,707	1,682	1,696	1,688	1,792	1,860
20 and 21 years old	1,064	1,219	1,259	1,411	1,541	1,608	1,658	1,628	1,634	1,695	1,866	1,948	1,985	1,960	1,956	2,025	1,997	2,022	2,108
22 to 24 years old	1,004	1,075	1,129	1,222	1,411	1,437	1,410	1,445	1,480	1,555	1,599	1,723	1,769	1,864	1,879	1,931	1,917	1,918	2,029
25 to 29 years old	796	983	1,024	908	1,007	1,039	1,057	1,040	1,148	1,222	1,378	1,410	1,404	1,353	1,327	1,282	1,316	1,489	1,524
30 to 34 years old	333	564	605	581	602	619	591	628	638	691	707	731	700	661	638	587	593	667	777
35 years old and over	366	559	902	1,077	1,158	1,147	1,149	1,160	1,159	1,228	1,285	1,320	1,290	1,255	1,249	1,087	1,088	1,205	1,397
Females	3,537	6,223	7,535	8,591	9,651	9,885	10,032	10,184	10,432	10,914	11,581	11,974	11,976	11,724	11,515	11,529	11,516	12,412	13,305
14 to 17 years old	137	151	87	73	102	104	119	115	112	102	113	108	116	123	140	137	140	154	175
18 and 19 years old	1,224	1,484	1,479	1,794	1,880	1,892	1,920	1,956	2,021	2,109	2,214	2,237	2,173	2,075	2,028	2,182	2,162	2,340	2,453
20 and 21 years old	821	1,177	1,334	1,593	1,851	1,908	1,905	1,945	1,936	1,954	2,050	2,155	2,284	2,276	2,293	2,447	2,417	2,504	2,639
22 to 24 years old	464	871	1,073	1,378	1,675	1,729	1,704	1,740	1,800	1,888	1,972	2,036	2,024	2,087	2,070	2,144	2,118	2,203	2,400
25 to 29 years old	296	859	1,059	1,136	1,304	1,379	1,413	1,466	1,502	1,618	1,704	1,844	1,868	1,801	1,704	1,713	1,755	1,978	2,002
30 to 34 years old	194	663	779	752	816	821	847	844	881	918	1,028	1,074	1,088	1,022	991	907	916	1,018	1,154
35 years old and over	401	1,018	1,725	1,865	2,023	2,052	2,123	2,117	2,180	2,326	2,500	2,520	2,422	2,340	2,289	1,999	2,009	2,215	2,482
Full-time	5,816	7,098	7,821	9,010	10,326	10,610	10,797	10,957	11,270	11,748	12,605	13,087	13,003	12,737	12,597	12,664	12,615	13,467	14,352
14 to 17 years old	246	231	134	121	146	138	152	148	169	168	179	170	185	207	226	214	218	235	263
18 and 19 years old	2,374	2,544	2,471	2,823	2,934	2,960	3,026	3,120	3,244	3,359	3,481	3,496	3,351	3,227	3,151	3,171	3,147	3,393	3,553
20 and 21 years old	1,649	2,007	2,137	2,452	2,841	2,926	2,976	2,972	2,985	3,043	3,241	3,364	3,427	3,386	3,362	3,443	3,391	3,496	3,680
22 to 24 years old	904	1,181	1,405	1,714	2,083	2,143	2,122	2,127	2,205	2,347	2,511	2,585	2,580	2,603	2,630	2,688	2,651	2,729	2,946
25 to 29 years old	426	641	791	886	1,086	1,132	1,174	1,225	1,299	1,369	1,506	1,605	1,600	1,555	1,515	1,487	1,531	1,745	1,784
30 to 34 years old	113	272	383	418	489	517	547	571	556	571	657	745	763	711	701	688	697	784	900
35 years old and over	104	221	500	596	747	795	800	794	812	890	1,030	1,122	1,096	1,047	1,012	974	979	1,085	1,225
Males	3,504	3,689	3,808	4,111	4,638	4,739	4,803	4,879	5,029	5,234	5,632	5,838	5,793	5,710	5,682	5,654	5,671	5,972	6,316
14 to 17 years old	121	95	55	51	58	49	53	52	74	73	77	71	85	102	110	98	100	104	114
18 and 19 years old	1,261	1,219	1,171	1,252	1,291	1,297	1,339	1,404	1,465	1,516	1,570	1,574	1,510	1,462	1,435	1,412	1,411	1,502	1,560
20 and 21 years old	955	1,046	1,035	1,156	1,305	1,360	1,398	1,372	1,366	1,407	1,536	1,586	1,586	1,537	1,520	1,536	1,518	1,542	1,608
22 to 24 years old	686	717	768	834	995	1,001	982	992	1,043	1,105	1,169	1,215	1,217	1,254	1,267	1,294	1,289	1,294	1,371
25 to 29 years old	346	391	433	410	503	498	506	533	578	597	661	715	727	728	733	720	747	849	871
30 to 34 years old	77	142	171	186	209	231	225	235	231	249	279	301	299	278	274	268	275	310	363
35 years old and over	58	80	174	222	277	302	300	291	273	287	341	376	369	349	344	326	332	370	430
Females	2,312	3,409	4,013	4,899	5,688	5,871	5,994	6,078	6,240	6,513	6,973	7,249	7,210	7,027	6,915	7,010	6,943	7,495	8,035
14 to 17 years old	125	136	78	70	88	89	98	95	95	95	102	99	100	105	117	116	119	131	149
18 and 19 years old	1,113	1,325	1,300	1,571	1,643	1,662	1,687	1,716	1,779	1,843	1,911	1,922	1,842	1,765	1,716	1,759	1,736	1,891	1,993
20 and 21 years old	693	961	1,101	1,296	1,536	1,566	1,578	1,601	1,619	1,636	1,705	1,778	1,840	1,849	1,842	1,907	1,873	1,954	2,071
22 to 24 years old	218	464	638	880	1,088	1,142	1,140	1,135	1,163	1,242	1,343	1,370	1,364	1,349	1,363	1,394	1,363	1,434	1,575
25 to 29 years old	80	250	358	476	583	634	668	692	721	772	845	891	873	827	782	767	784	896	914
30 to 34 years old	37	130	212	232	280	286	322	336	324	322	378	444	464	433	427	420	422	473	537
35 years old and over	46	141	326	374	471	493	500	503	539	603	690	746	727	698	667	648	647	715	795
Part-time	2,765	4,999	5,998	6,303	6,585	6,662	6,690	6,802	6,978	7,355	7,708	7,932	8,008	7,906	7,779	7,590	7,619	8,163	8,783
14 to 17 years old	16	26	19	10	23	28	36	36	31	27	36	32	36	35	44	40	40	43	48
18 and 19 years old	205	308	306	435	421	407	417	440	446	453	528	561	604	555	559	708	702	739	759
20 and 21 years old	236	388	456	553	551	590	586	601	585	606	675	738	842	849	886	1,029	1,023	1,030	1,067
22 to 24 years old	564	765	796	886	1,003	1,023	992	1,058	1,074	1,096	1,059	1,174	1,212	1,347	1,319	1,387	1,383	1,393	1,483
25 to 29 years old	665	1,202	1,291	1,158	1,224	1,286	1,296	1,282	1,352	1,471	1,576	1,648	1,672	1,599	1,516	1,508	1,540	1,722	1,741
30 to 34 years old	414	954	1,001	915	929	923	891	901	963	1,037	1,079	1,060	1,025	972	928	806	812	901	1,031
35 years old and over	663	1,356	2,127	2,345	2,434	2,404	2,472	2,483	2,527	2,664	2,754	2,718	2,616	2,548	2,527	2,113	2,119	2,335	2,654
Males	1,540	2,185	2,476	2,611	2,622	2,648	2,653	2,696	2,786	2,955	3,101	3,207	3,241	3,209	3,179	3,072	3,046	3,245	3,514
14 to 17 years old	4	12	11	7	9	13	15	17	14	20	25	23	20	17	21	19	19	20	22
18 and 19 years old	94	149	127	212	183	178	184	200	204	188	226	245	273	246	247	284	276	290	300
20 and 21 years old	108	172	224	255	236	248	260	257	269	289	330	362	398	423	436	489	479	481	499
22 to 24 years old	318	359	361	388	416	436	428	452	438	450	430	508	552	609	613	637	628	623	659
25 to 29 years old	450	592	591	498	504	540	551	507	570	625	718	695	677	625	594	562	569	640	653
30 to 34 years old	257	422	435	395	392	388	365	393	406	442	428	430	401	383	364	319	318	356	414
35 years old and over	309	479	728	855	882	845	850	869	886	941	944	944	921	906	905	762	757	835	967
Females	1,225	2,814	3,521	3,692	3,963	4,014	4,038	4,106	4,192	4,401	4,607	4,725	4,767	4,697	4,600	4,519	4,573	4,918	5,269
14 to 17 years old	12	14	9	3	14	15	21	20	17	7	11	9	16	18	23	21	21	23	26
18 and 19 years old	112	159	179	223	238	230	233	240	242	265	303	316	332	310	312	424	426	449	460
20 and 21 years old	128	216	233	298	315	342	327	344	317	318	345	377	444	427	450	540	544	549	568
22 to 24 years old	246	407	435	497	587	588	564	605	637	646	629	666	660	738	706	750	755	769	824
25 to 29 years old	216	609	700	660	721	746	745	774	781	846	859	953	995	974	922	946	971	1,083	1,088
30 to 34 years old	158	532	567	520	537	535	526	508	557	595	651	630	624	589	564	487	493	545	617
35 years old and over	354	876	1,399	1,491	1,552	1,560	1,623	1,614	1,640	1,723	1,810	1,774	1,695	1,642	1,622	1,351	1,362	1,500	1,687

NOTE: Distributions by age are estimates based on samples of the civilian noninstitutional population from the U.S. Census Bureau's Current Population Survey. Data through 1995 are for institutions of higher education, while later data are for degree-granting institutions. Degree-granting institutions grant associate's or higher degrees and participate in Title IV federal financial aid programs. The degree-granting classification is very similar to the earlier higher education classification, but it includes more 2-year colleges and excludes a few higher education institutions that did not grant degrees. Some data have been revised from previously published figures. Detail may not sum to totals because of rounding.

SOURCE: U.S. Department of Education, National Center for Education Statistics, Higher Education General Information Survey (HEGIS), "Fall Enrollment in Colleges and Universities" surveys, 1970 and 1980; Integrated Postsecondary Education Data System (IPEDS), "Fall Enrollment Survey" (IPEDS-EF:90–99); IPEDS Spring 2001 through Spring 2014, Enrollment component; and Enrollment in Degree-Granting Institutions Projection Model, 1980 through 2024. U.S. Department of Commerce, Census Bureau, Current Population Survey (CPS), October, selected years, 1970 through 2013. (This table was prepared May 2015.)

Table 303.45. Total fall enrollment in degree-granting postsecondary institutions, by level of enrollment, sex, attendance status, and age of student: 2009, 2011, and 2013

Attendance status and age of student	Fall 2009 All levels Total	Fall 2011 All levels Total	Males	Females	Fall 2013 All levels Total	Males	Females	Undergraduate Total	Males	Females	Postbaccalaureate Total	Males	Females
1	2	3	4	5	6	7	8	9	10	11	12	13	14
All students	20,313,594	21,010,590	9,034,256	11,976,334	20,375,789	8,860,786	11,515,003	17,474,835	7,659,626	9,815,209	2,900,954	1,201,160	1,699,794
Under 18	758,719	796,322	330,026	466,296	879,127	363,634	515,493	878,960	363,571	515,389	167	63	104
18 and 19	4,291,786	4,291,189	1,935,116	2,356,073	4,265,853	1,920,939	2,344,914	4,264,764	1,920,536	2,344,228	1,089	403	686
20 and 21	3,995,409	4,161,496	1,874,220	2,287,276	4,085,724	1,852,000	2,233,724	4,051,605	1,839,026	2,212,579	34,119	12,974	21,145
22 to 24	3,300,898	3,434,603	1,574,540	1,860,063	3,430,650	1,580,020	1,850,630	2,812,445	1,331,251	1,481,194	618,205	248,769	369,436
25 to 29	2,934,931	3,045,652	1,329,306	1,716,346	2,857,056	1,259,180	1,597,876	1,949,698	859,923	1,089,775	907,358	399,257	508,101
30 to 34	1,614,852	1,759,975	726,923	1,033,052	1,642,431	695,841	946,590	1,166,637	482,591	684,046	475,794	213,250	262,544
35 to 39	1,113,548	1,125,125	427,973	697,152	1,034,148	403,714	630,434	756,185	288,377	467,808	277,963	115,337	162,626
40 to 49	1,432,883	1,503,908	526,491	977,417	1,346,655	483,480	863,175	988,078	351,076	637,002	358,577	132,404	226,173
50 to 64	728,033	760,089	253,539	506,550	717,300	252,559	464,741	518,914	186,574	332,340	198,386	65,985	132,401
65 and over	69,679	65,122	27,123	37,999	66,161	28,065	38,096	55,195	23,056	32,139	10,966	5,009	5,957
Age unknown	72,856	67,109	28,999	38,110	50,684	21,354	29,330	32,354	13,645	18,709	18,330	7,709	10,621
Full-time	12,605,355	13,002,531	5,792,818	7,209,713	12,597,112	5,682,166	6,914,946	10,938,494	4,949,572	5,988,922	1,658,618	732,594	926,024
Under 18	176,567	181,159	72,371	108,788	185,718	74,583	111,135	185,631	74,555	111,076	87	28	59
18 and 19	3,630,783	3,571,443	1,597,775	1,973,668	3,548,294	1,585,220	1,963,074	3,547,315	1,584,855	1,962,460	979	365	614
20 and 21	3,240,417	3,311,201	1,495,119	1,816,082	3,244,414	1,472,318	1,772,096	3,213,421	1,460,365	1,753,056	30,993	11,953	19,040
22 to 24	2,183,499	2,257,755	1,072,259	1,185,496	2,239,397	1,066,976	1,172,421	1,743,151	861,461	881,690	496,246	205,515	290,731
25 to 29	1,513,822	1,607,135	745,669	861,466	1,499,143	705,540	793,603	923,550	434,039	489,511	575,593	271,501	304,092
30 to 34	705,835	793,229	342,108	451,121	725,416	325,394	400,022	491,630	212,248	279,382	233,786	113,146	120,640
35 to 39	433,345	459,050	176,259	282,791	409,512	164,713	244,799	295,425	114,157	181,268	114,087	50,556	63,531
40 to 49	485,700	550,606	195,769	354,837	484,308	182,654	301,654	355,343	132,126	223,217	128,965	50,528	78,437
50 to 64	201,201	232,693	79,027	153,666	226,606	89,774	136,832	162,457	67,040	95,417	64,149	22,734	41,415
65 and over	6,502	8,387	3,586	4,801	9,133	4,082	5,051	5,931	2,599	3,332	3,202	1,483	1,719
Age unknown	27,684	29,873	12,876	16,997	25,171	10,912	14,259	14,640	6,127	8,513	10,531	4,785	5,746
Part-time	7,708,239	8,008,059	3,241,438	4,766,621	7,778,677	3,178,620	4,600,057	6,536,341	2,710,054	3,826,287	1,242,336	468,566	773,770
Under 18	582,152	615,163	257,655	357,508	693,409	289,051	404,358	693,329	289,016	404,313	80	35	45
18 and 19	661,003	719,746	337,341	382,405	717,559	335,719	381,840	717,449	335,681	381,768	110	38	72
20 and 21	754,992	850,295	379,101	471,194	841,310	379,682	461,628	838,184	378,661	459,523	3,126	1,021	2,105
22 to 24	1,117,399	1,176,848	502,281	674,567	1,191,253	513,044	678,209	1,069,294	469,790	599,504	121,959	43,254	78,705
25 to 29	1,421,109	1,438,517	583,637	854,880	1,357,913	553,640	804,273	1,026,148	425,884	600,264	331,765	127,756	204,009
30 to 34	909,017	966,746	384,815	581,931	917,015	370,447	546,568	675,007	270,343	404,664	242,008	100,104	141,904
35 to 39	680,203	666,075	251,714	414,361	624,636	239,001	385,635	460,760	174,220	286,540	163,876	64,781	99,095
40 to 49	947,183	953,302	330,722	622,580	862,347	300,826	561,521	632,735	218,950	413,785	229,612	81,876	147,736
50 to 64	526,832	527,396	174,512	352,884	490,694	162,785	327,909	356,457	119,534	236,923	134,237	43,251	90,986
65 and over	63,177	56,735	23,537	33,198	57,028	23,983	33,045	49,264	20,457	28,807	7,764	3,526	4,238
Age unknown	45,172	37,236	16,123	21,113	25,513	10,442	15,071	17,714	7,518	10,196	7,799	2,924	4,875
					Percentage distribution								
All students	100.0	100.0	100.0	100.0	100.0	100.0	100.0	100.0	100.0	100.0	100.0	100.0	100.0
Under 18	3.7	3.8	3.7	3.9	4.3	4.1	4.5	5.0	4.7	5.3	#	#	#
18 and 19	21.1	20.4	21.4	19.7	20.9	21.7	20.4	24.4	25.1	23.9	#	#	#
20 and 21	19.7	19.8	20.7	19.1	20.1	20.9	19.4	23.2	24.0	22.5	1.2	1.1	1.2
22 to 24	16.2	16.3	17.4	15.5	16.8	17.8	16.1	16.1	17.4	15.1	21.3	20.7	21.7
25 to 29	14.4	14.5	14.7	14.3	14.0	14.2	13.9	11.2	11.2	11.1	31.3	33.2	29.9
30 to 34	7.9	8.4	8.0	8.6	8.1	7.9	8.2	6.7	6.3	7.0	16.4	17.8	15.4
35 to 39	5.5	5.4	4.7	5.8	5.1	4.6	5.5	4.3	3.8	4.8	9.6	9.6	9.6
40 to 49	7.1	7.2	5.8	8.2	6.6	5.5	7.5	5.7	4.6	6.5	12.4	11.0	13.3
50 to 64	3.6	3.6	2.8	4.2	3.5	2.9	4.0	3.0	2.4	3.4	6.8	5.5	7.8
65 and over	0.3	0.3	0.3	0.3	0.3	0.3	0.3	0.3	0.3	0.3	0.4	0.4	0.4
Age unknown	0.4	0.3	0.3	0.3	0.2	0.2	0.3	0.2	0.2	0.2	0.6	0.6	0.6
Full-time	100.0	100.0	100.0	100.0	100.0	100.0	100.0	100.0	100.0	100.0	100.0	100.0	100.0
Under 18	1.4	1.4	1.2	1.5	1.5	1.3	1.6	1.7	1.5	1.9	0.1	#	0.1
18 and 19	28.8	27.5	27.6	27.4	28.2	27.9	28.4	32.4	32.0	32.8	1.9	#	0.1
20 and 21	25.7	25.5	25.8	25.2	25.8	25.9	25.6	29.4	29.5	29.3	1.9	1.6	2.1
22 to 24	17.3	17.4	18.5	16.4	17.8	18.8	17.0	15.9	17.4	14.7	29.9	28.1	31.4
25 to 29	12.0	12.4	12.9	11.9	11.9	12.4	11.5	8.4	8.8	8.2	34.7	37.1	32.8
30 to 34	5.6	6.1	5.9	6.3	5.8	5.7	5.8	4.5	4.3	4.7	14.1	15.4	13.0
35 to 39	3.4	3.5	3.0	3.9	3.3	2.9	3.5	2.7	2.3	3.0	6.9	6.9	6.9
40 to 49	3.9	4.2	3.4	4.9	3.8	3.2	4.4	3.2	2.7	3.7	7.8	6.9	8.5
50 to 64	1.6	1.8	1.4	2.1	1.8	1.6	2.0	1.5	1.4	1.6	3.9	3.1	4.5
65 and over	0.1	0.1	0.1	0.1	0.1	0.1	0.1	0.1	0.1	0.1	0.2	0.2	0.2
Age unknown	0.2	0.2	0.2	0.2	0.2	0.2	0.2	0.1	0.1	0.1	0.6	0.7	0.6
Part-time	100.0	100.0	100.0	100.0	100.0	100.0	100.0	100.0	100.0	100.0	100.0	100.0	100.0
Under 18	7.6	7.7	7.9	7.5	8.9	9.1	8.8	10.6	10.7	10.6	#	#	#
18 and 19	8.6	9.0	10.4	8.0	9.2	10.6	8.3	11.0	12.4	10.0	#	#	#
20 and 21	9.8	10.6	11.7	9.9	10.8	11.9	10.0	12.8	14.0	12.0	0.3	0.2	0.3
22 to 24	14.5	14.7	15.5	14.2	15.3	16.1	14.7	16.4	17.3	15.7	9.8	9.2	10.2
25 to 29	18.4	18.0	18.0	17.9	17.5	17.4	17.5	15.7	15.7	15.7	26.7	27.3	26.4
30 to 34	11.8	12.1	11.9	12.2	11.8	11.7	11.9	10.3	10.0	10.6	19.5	21.4	18.3
35 to 39	8.8	8.3	7.8	8.7	8.0	7.5	8.4	7.0	6.4	7.5	13.2	13.8	12.8
40 to 49	12.3	11.9	10.2	13.1	11.1	9.5	12.2	9.7	8.1	10.8	18.5	17.5	19.1
50 to 64	6.8	6.6	5.4	7.4	6.3	5.1	7.1	5.5	4.4	6.2	10.8	9.2	11.8
65 and over	0.8	0.7	0.7	0.7	0.7	0.8	0.7	0.8	0.8	0.8	0.6	0.8	0.5
Age unknown	0.6	0.5	0.5	0.4	0.3	0.3	0.3	0.3	0.3	0.3	0.6	0.6	0.6

#Rounds to zero.
NOTE: Degree-granting institutions grant associate's or higher degrees and participate in Title IV federal financial aid programs. Detail may not sum to totals because of rounding. Some data have been revised from previously published figures.

SOURCE: U.S. Department of Education, National Center for Education Statistics, Integrated Postsecondary Education Data System (IPEDS), Spring 2010, 2012, and 2014, Enrollment component. (This table was prepared November 2014.)

Table 303.50. Total fall enrollment in degree-granting postsecondary institutions, by level of enrollment, control and level of institution, attendance status, and age of student: 2013

Attendance status and age of student	Undergraduate										Postbaccalaureate			
	Total	Public			Private, nonprofit			Private, for-profit			Total	Public	Private, nonprofit	Private, for-profit
		Total	4-year	2-year	Total	4-year	2-year	Total	4-year	2-year				
1	2	3	4	5	6	7	8	9	10	11	12	13	14	15
All students	17,474,835	13,347,002	6,721,861	6,625,141	2,757,447	2,725,249	32,198	1,370,386	1,058,986	311,400	2,900,954	1,398,556	1,216,557	285,841
Under 18	878,960	784,803	242,293	542,510	87,570	86,484	1,086	6,587	5,324	1,263	167	48	83	36
18 and 19	4,264,764	3,349,245	1,896,915	1,452,330	826,654	820,296	6,358	88,865	54,440	34,425	1,089	461	608	20
20 and 21	4,051,605	3,087,024	1,947,466	1,139,558	826,717	821,161	5,556	137,864	88,292	49,572	34,119	17,077	16,460	582
22 to 24	2,812,445	2,240,127	1,284,653	955,474	369,438	364,227	5,211	202,880	144,567	58,313	618,205	338,529	265,056	14,620
25 to 29	1,949,698	1,458,960	595,850	863,110	198,958	194,108	4,850	291,780	229,218	62,562	907,358	465,212	390,187	51,959
30 to 34	1,166,637	815,017	285,188	529,829	132,642	129,704	2,938	218,978	182,140	36,838	475,794	230,680	192,088	53,026
35 to 39	756,185	512,097	165,362	346,735	95,749	93,694	2,055	148,339	124,662	23,677	277,963	123,327	109,698	44,938
40 to 49	988,078	664,808	197,606	467,202	136,255	133,669	2,586	187,015	158,318	28,697	358,577	141,825	143,168	73,584
50 to 64	518,914	371,772	93,356	278,416	65,567	64,252	1,315	81,575	67,903	13,672	198,386	72,180	81,789	44,417
65 and over	55,195	48,830	8,861	39,969	3,805	3,721	84	2,560	2,097	463	10,966	4,063	4,678	2,225
Age unknown	32,354	14,319	4,311	10,008	14,092	13,933	159	3,943	2,025	1,918	18,330	5,154	12,742	434
Full-time	10,938,494	7,685,669	5,155,712	2,529,957	2,261,723	2,237,668	24,055	991,102	712,198	278,904	1,658,618	779,140	724,330	155,148
Under 18	185,631	144,552	68,114	76,438	36,463	36,234	229	4,616	3,466	1,150	87	20	44	23
18 and 19	3,547,315	2,664,561	1,768,650	895,911	804,479	798,645	5,834	78,275	45,455	32,820	979	429	540	10
20 and 21	3,213,421	2,304,294	1,759,408	544,886	796,874	792,100	4,774	112,253	66,580	45,673	30,993	15,478	15,140	375
22 to 24	1,743,151	1,286,138	958,567	327,571	303,865	299,925	3,940	153,148	100,753	52,395	496,246	270,991	215,711	9,544
25 to 29	923,550	593,123	325,284	267,839	119,627	116,184	3,443	210,800	155,170	55,630	575,593	286,545	259,401	29,647
30 to 34	491,630	272,350	124,514	147,836	66,912	64,925	1,987	152,368	120,141	32,227	233,786	106,195	99,125	28,466
35 to 39	295,425	151,244	61,252	89,992	44,044	42,691	1,353	100,137	79,591	20,546	114,087	43,225	46,799	24,063
40 to 49	355,343	174,691	62,740	111,951	57,405	55,833	1,572	123,247	98,467	24,780	128,965	36,942	52,829	39,194
50 to 64	162,457	86,358	24,229	62,129	24,143	23,365	778	51,956	40,191	11,765	64,149	14,532	27,111	22,506
65 and over	5,931	3,407	891	2,516	986	929	57	1,538	1,159	379	3,202	578	1,549	1,075
Age unknown	14,640	4,951	2,063	2,888	6,925	6,837	88	2,764	1,225	1,539	10,531	4,205	6,081	245
Part-time	6,536,341	5,661,333	1,566,149	4,095,184	495,724	487,581	8,143	379,284	346,788	32,496	1,242,336	619,416	492,227	130,693
Under 18	693,329	640,251	174,179	466,072	51,107	50,250	857	1,971	1,858	113	80	28	39	13
18 and 19	717,449	684,684	128,265	556,419	22,175	21,651	524	10,590	8,985	1,605	110	32	68	10
20 and 21	838,184	782,730	188,058	594,672	29,843	29,061	782	25,611	21,712	3,899	3,126	1,599	1,320	207
22 to 24	1,069,294	953,989	326,086	627,903	65,573	64,302	1,271	49,732	43,814	5,918	121,959	67,538	49,345	5,076
25 to 29	1,026,148	865,837	270,566	595,271	79,331	77,924	1,407	80,980	74,048	6,932	331,765	178,667	130,786	22,312
30 to 34	675,007	542,667	160,674	381,993	65,730	64,779	951	66,610	61,999	4,611	242,008	124,485	92,963	24,560
35 to 39	460,760	360,853	104,110	256,743	51,705	51,003	702	48,202	45,071	3,131	163,876	80,102	62,899	20,875
40 to 49	632,735	490,117	134,866	355,251	78,850	77,836	1,014	63,768	59,851	3,917	229,612	104,883	90,339	34,390
50 to 64	356,457	285,414	69,127	216,287	41,424	40,887	537	29,619	27,712	1,907	134,237	57,648	54,678	21,911
65 and over	49,264	45,423	7,970	37,453	2,819	2,792	27	1,022	938	84	7,764	3,485	3,129	1,150
Age unknown	17,714	9,368	2,248	7,120	7,167	7,096	71	1,179	800	379	7,799	949	6,661	189
	Percentage distribution													
All students	100.0	100.0	100.0	100.0	100.0	100.0	100.0	100.0	100.0	100.0	100.0	100.0	100.0	100.0
Under 18	5.0	5.9	3.6	8.2	3.2	3.2	3.4	0.5	0.5	0.4	#	#	#	#
18 and 19	24.4	25.1	28.2	21.9	30.0	30.1	19.7	6.5	5.1	11.1	#	#	#	#
20 and 21	23.2	23.1	29.0	17.2	30.0	30.1	17.3	10.1	8.3	15.9	1.2	1.2	1.4	0.2
22 to 24	16.1	16.8	19.1	14.4	13.4	13.4	16.2	14.8	13.7	18.7	21.3	24.2	21.8	5.1
25 to 29	11.2	10.9	8.9	13.0	7.2	7.1	15.1	21.3	21.6	20.1	31.3	33.3	32.1	18.2
30 to 34	6.7	6.1	4.2	8.0	4.8	4.8	9.1	16.0	17.2	11.8	16.4	16.5	15.8	18.6
35 to 39	4.3	3.8	2.5	5.2	3.5	3.4	6.4	10.8	11.8	7.6	9.6	8.8	9.0	15.7
40 to 49	5.7	5.0	2.9	7.1	4.9	4.9	8.0	13.6	14.9	9.2	12.4	10.1	11.8	25.7
50 to 64	3.0	2.8	1.4	4.2	2.4	2.4	4.1	6.0	6.4	4.4	6.8	5.2	6.7	15.5
65 and over	0.3	0.4	0.1	0.6	0.1	0.1	0.3	0.2	0.2	0.1	0.4	0.3	0.4	0.8
Age unknown	0.2	0.1	0.1	0.2	0.5	0.5	0.5	0.3	0.2	0.6	0.6	0.4	1.0	0.2
Full-time	100.0	100.0	100.0	100.0	100.0	100.0	100.0	100.0	100.0	100.0	100.0	100.0	100.0	100.0
Under 18	1.7	1.9	1.3	3.0	1.6	1.6	1.0	0.5	0.5	0.4	#	#	#	#
18 and 19	32.4	34.7	34.3	35.4	35.6	35.7	24.3	7.9	6.4	11.8	0.1	0.1	0.1	#
20 and 21	29.4	30.0	34.1	21.5	35.2	35.4	19.8	11.3	9.3	16.4	1.9	2.0	2.1	0.2
22 to 24	15.9	16.7	18.6	12.9	13.4	13.4	16.4	15.5	14.1	18.8	29.9	34.8	29.8	6.2
25 to 29	8.4	7.7	6.3	10.6	5.3	5.2	14.3	21.3	21.8	19.9	34.7	36.8	35.8	19.1
30 to 34	4.5	3.5	2.4	5.8	3.0	2.9	8.3	15.4	16.9	11.6	14.1	13.6	13.7	18.3
35 to 39	2.7	2.0	1.2	3.6	1.9	1.9	5.6	10.1	11.2	7.4	6.9	5.5	6.5	15.5
40 to 49	3.2	2.3	1.2	4.4	2.5	2.5	6.5	12.4	13.8	8.9	7.8	4.7	7.3	25.3
50 to 64	1.5	1.1	0.5	2.5	1.1	1.0	3.2	5.2	5.6	4.2	3.9	1.9	3.7	14.5
65 and over	0.1	#	#	0.1	#	#	0.2	0.2	0.2	0.1	0.2	0.1	0.2	0.7
Age unknown	0.1	0.1	#	0.1	0.3	0.3	0.4	0.3	0.2	0.6	0.6	0.5	0.8	0.2
Part-time	100.0	100.0	100.0	100.0	100.0	100.0	100.0	100.0	100.0	100.0	100.0	100.0	100.0	100.0
Under 18	10.6	11.3	11.1	11.4	10.3	10.3	10.5	0.5	0.5	0.3	#	#	#	#
18 and 19	11.0	12.1	8.2	13.6	4.5	4.4	6.4	2.8	2.6	4.9	#	#	#	#
20 and 21	12.8	13.8	12.0	14.5	6.0	6.0	9.6	6.8	6.3	12.0	0.3	0.3	0.3	0.2
22 to 24	16.4	16.9	20.8	15.3	13.2	13.2	15.6	13.1	12.6	18.2	9.8	10.9	10.0	3.9
25 to 29	15.7	15.3	17.3	14.5	16.0	16.0	17.3	21.4	21.4	21.3	26.7	28.8	26.6	17.1
30 to 34	10.3	9.6	10.3	9.3	13.3	13.3	11.7	17.6	17.9	14.2	19.5	20.1	18.9	18.8
35 to 39	7.0	6.4	6.6	6.3	10.4	10.5	8.6	12.7	13.0	9.6	13.2	12.9	12.8	16.0
40 to 49	9.7	8.7	8.6	8.7	15.9	16.0	12.5	16.8	17.3	12.1	18.5	16.9	18.4	26.3
50 to 64	5.5	5.0	4.4	5.3	8.4	8.4	6.6	7.8	8.0	5.9	10.8	9.3	11.1	16.8
65 and over	0.8	0.8	0.5	0.9	0.6	0.6	0.3	0.3	0.3	0.3	0.6	0.6	0.6	0.9
Age unknown	0.3	0.2	0.1	0.2	1.4	1.5	0.9	0.3	0.2	1.2	0.6	0.2	1.4	0.1

#Rounds to zero.
NOTE: Degree-granting institutions grant associate's or higher degrees and participate in Title IV federal financial aid programs. Detail may not sum to totals because of rounding.

SOURCE: U.S. Department of Education, National Center for Education Statistics, Integrated Postsecondary Education Data System (IPEDS), Spring 2014, Enrollment component. (This table was prepared November 2014.)

Table 303.55. Total fall enrollment in degree-granting postsecondary institutions, by control and level of institution, attendance status, and age of student: 2013

Attendance status and age of student	All institutions			Public institutions			Private (nonprofit and for-profit) institutions						
								Nonprofit institutions			For-profit institutions		
	Total	4-year	2-year	Total	4-year	2-year	Total	Total	4-year	2-year	Total	4-year	2-year
1	2	3	4	5	6	7	8	9	10	11	12	13	14
All students	20,375,789	13,407,050	6,968,739	14,745,558	8,120,417	6,625,141	5,630,231	3,974,004	3,941,806	32,198	1,656,227	1,344,827	311,400
Under 18	879,127	334,268	544,859	784,851	242,341	542,510	94,276	87,653	86,567	1,086	6,623	5,360	1,263
18 and 19	4,265,853	2,772,740	1,493,113	3,349,706	1,897,376	1,452,330	916,147	827,262	820,904	6,358	88,885	54,460	34,425
20 and 21	4,085,724	2,891,038	1,194,686	3,104,101	1,964,543	1,139,558	981,623	843,177	837,621	5,556	138,446	88,874	49,572
22 to 24	3,430,650	2,411,652	1,018,998	2,578,656	1,623,182	955,474	851,994	634,494	629,283	5,211	217,500	159,187	58,313
25 to 29	2,857,056	1,926,534	930,522	1,924,172	1,061,062	863,110	932,884	589,145	584,295	4,850	343,739	281,177	62,562
30 to 34	1,642,431	1,072,826	569,605	1,045,697	515,868	529,829	596,734	324,730	321,792	2,938	272,004	235,166	36,838
35 to 39	1,034,148	661,681	372,467	635,424	288,689	346,735	398,724	205,447	203,392	2,055	193,277	169,600	23,677
40 to 49	1,346,655	848,170	498,485	806,633	339,431	467,202	540,022	279,423	276,837	2,586	260,599	231,902	28,697
50 to 64	717,300	423,897	293,403	443,952	165,536	278,416	273,348	147,356	146,041	1,315	125,992	112,320	13,672
65 and over	66,161	25,645	40,516	52,893	12,924	39,969	13,268	8,483	8,399	84	4,785	4,322	463
Age unknown	50,684	38,599	12,085	19,473	9,465	10,008	31,211	26,834	26,675	159	4,377	2,459	1,918
Full-time	12,597,112	9,764,196	2,832,916	8,464,809	5,934,852	2,529,957	4,132,303	2,986,053	2,961,998	24,055	1,146,250	867,346	278,904
Under 18	185,718	107,901	77,817	144,572	68,134	76,438	41,146	36,507	36,278	229	4,639	3,489	1,150
18 and 19	3,548,294	2,613,729	934,565	2,664,990	1,769,079	895,911	883,304	805,019	799,185	5,834	78,285	45,465	32,820
20 and 21	3,244,414	2,649,081	595,333	2,319,772	1,774,886	544,886	924,642	812,014	807,240	4,774	112,628	66,955	45,673
22 to 24	2,239,397	1,855,491	383,906	1,557,129	1,229,558	327,571	682,268	519,576	515,636	3,940	162,692	110,297	52,395
25 to 29	1,499,143	1,172,231	326,912	879,668	611,829	267,839	619,475	379,028	375,585	3,443	240,447	184,817	55,630
30 to 34	725,416	543,366	182,050	378,545	230,709	147,836	346,871	166,037	164,050	1,987	180,834	148,607	32,227
35 to 39	409,512	297,621	111,891	194,469	104,477	89,992	215,043	90,843	89,490	1,353	124,200	103,654	20,546
40 to 49	484,308	346,005	138,303	211,633	99,682	111,951	272,675	110,234	108,662	1,572	162,441	137,661	24,780
50 to 64	226,606	151,934	74,672	100,890	38,761	62,129	125,716	51,254	50,476	778	74,462	62,697	11,765
65 and over	9,133	6,181	2,952	3,985	1,469	2,516	5,148	2,535	2,478	57	2,613	2,234	379
Age unknown	25,171	20,656	4,515	9,156	6,268	2,888	16,015	13,006	12,918	88	3,009	1,470	1,539
Part-time	7,778,677	3,642,854	4,135,823	6,280,749	2,185,565	4,095,184	1,497,928	987,951	979,808	8,143	509,977	477,481	32,496
Under 18	693,409	226,367	467,042	640,279	174,207	466,072	53,130	51,146	50,289	857	1,984	1,871	113
18 and 19	717,559	159,011	558,548	684,716	128,297	556,419	32,843	22,243	21,719	524	10,600	8,995	1,605
20 and 21	841,310	241,957	599,353	784,329	189,657	594,672	56,981	31,163	30,381	782	25,818	21,919	3,899
22 to 24	1,191,253	556,161	635,092	1,021,527	393,624	627,903	169,726	114,918	113,647	1,271	54,808	48,890	5,918
25 to 29	1,357,913	754,303	603,610	1,044,504	449,233	595,271	313,409	210,117	208,710	1,407	103,292	96,360	6,932
30 to 34	917,015	529,460	387,555	667,152	285,159	381,993	249,863	158,693	157,742	951	91,170	86,559	4,611
35 to 39	624,636	364,060	260,576	440,955	184,212	256,743	183,681	114,604	113,902	702	69,077	65,946	3,131
40 to 49	862,347	502,165	360,182	595,000	239,749	355,251	267,347	169,189	168,175	1,014	98,158	94,241	3,917
50 to 64	490,694	271,963	218,731	343,062	126,775	216,287	147,632	96,102	95,565	537	51,530	49,623	1,907
65 and over	57,028	19,464	37,564	48,908	11,455	37,453	8,120	5,948	5,921	27	2,172	2,088	84
Age unknown	25,513	17,943	7,570	10,317	3,197	7,120	15,196	13,828	13,757	71	1,368	989	379
	Percentage distribution												
All students	100.0	100.0	100.0	100.0	100.0	100.0	100.0	100.0	100.0	100.0	100.0	100.0	100.0
Under 18	4.3	2.5	7.8	5.3	3.0	8.2	1.7	2.2	2.2	3.4	0.4	0.4	0.4
18 and 19	20.9	20.7	21.4	22.7	23.4	21.9	16.3	20.8	20.8	19.7	5.4	4.0	11.1
20 and 21	20.1	21.6	17.1	21.1	24.2	17.2	17.4	21.2	21.2	17.3	8.4	6.6	15.9
22 to 24	16.8	18.0	14.6	17.5	20.0	14.4	15.1	16.0	16.0	16.2	13.1	11.8	18.7
25 to 29	14.0	14.4	13.4	13.0	13.1	13.0	16.6	14.8	14.8	15.1	20.8	20.9	20.1
30 to 34	8.1	8.0	8.2	7.1	6.4	8.0	10.6	8.2	8.2	9.1	16.4	17.5	11.8
35 to 39	5.1	4.9	5.3	4.3	3.6	5.2	7.1	5.2	5.2	6.4	11.7	12.6	7.6
40 to 49	6.6	6.3	7.2	5.5	4.2	7.1	9.6	7.0	7.0	8.0	15.7	17.2	9.2
50 to 64	3.5	3.2	4.2	3.0	2.0	4.2	4.9	3.7	3.7	4.1	7.6	8.4	4.4
65 and over	0.3	0.2	0.6	0.4	0.2	0.6	0.2	0.2	0.2	0.3	0.3	0.3	0.1
Age unknown	0.2	0.3	0.2	0.1	0.1	0.2	0.6	0.7	0.7	0.5	0.3	0.2	0.6
Full-time	100.0	100.0	100.0	100.0	100.0	100.0	100.0	100.0	100.0	100.0	100.0	100.0	100.0
Under 18	1.5	1.1	2.7	1.7	1.1	3.0	1.0	1.2	1.2	1.0	0.4	0.4	0.4
18 and 19	28.2	26.8	33.0	31.5	29.8	35.4	21.4	27.0	27.0	24.3	6.8	5.2	11.8
20 and 21	25.8	27.1	21.0	27.4	29.9	21.5	22.4	27.2	27.3	19.8	9.8	7.7	16.4
22 to 24	17.8	19.0	13.6	18.4	20.7	12.9	16.5	17.4	17.4	16.4	14.2	12.7	18.8
25 to 29	11.9	12.0	11.5	10.4	10.3	10.6	15.0	12.7	12.7	14.3	21.0	21.3	19.9
30 to 34	5.8	5.6	6.4	4.5	3.9	5.8	8.4	5.6	5.5	8.3	15.8	17.1	11.6
35 to 39	3.3	3.0	3.9	2.3	1.8	3.6	5.2	3.0	3.0	5.6	10.8	12.0	7.4
40 to 49	3.8	3.5	4.9	2.5	1.7	4.4	6.6	3.7	3.7	6.5	14.2	15.9	8.9
50 to 64	1.8	1.6	2.6	1.2	0.7	2.5	3.0	1.7	1.7	3.2	6.5	7.2	4.2
65 and over	0.1	0.1	0.1	#	#	0.1	0.1	0.1	0.1	0.2	0.2	0.3	0.1
Age unknown	0.2	0.2	0.2	0.1	0.1	0.1	0.4	0.4	0.4	0.4	0.3	0.2	0.6
Part-time	100.0	100.0	100.0	100.0	100.0	100.0	100.0	100.0	100.0	100.0	100.0	100.0	100.0
Under 18	8.9	6.2	11.3	10.2	8.0	11.4	3.5	5.2	5.1	10.5	0.4	0.4	0.3
18 and 19	9.2	4.4	13.5	10.9	5.9	13.6	2.2	2.3	2.2	6.4	2.1	1.9	4.9
20 and 21	10.8	6.6	14.5	12.5	8.7	14.5	3.8	3.2	3.1	9.6	5.1	4.6	12.0
22 to 24	15.3	15.3	15.4	16.3	18.0	15.3	11.3	11.6	11.6	15.6	10.7	10.2	18.2
25 to 29	17.5	20.7	14.6	16.6	20.6	14.5	20.9	21.3	21.3	17.3	20.3	20.2	21.3
30 to 34	11.8	14.5	9.4	10.6	13.0	9.3	16.7	16.1	16.1	11.7	17.9	18.1	14.2
35 to 39	8.0	10.0	6.3	7.0	8.4	6.3	12.3	11.6	11.6	8.6	13.5	13.8	9.6
40 to 49	11.1	13.8	8.7	9.5	11.0	8.7	17.8	17.1	17.2	12.5	19.2	19.7	12.1
50 to 64	6.3	7.5	5.3	5.5	5.8	5.3	9.9	9.7	9.8	6.6	10.1	10.4	5.9
65 and over	0.7	0.5	0.9	0.8	0.5	0.9	0.5	0.6	0.6	0.3	0.4	0.4	0.3
Age unknown	0.3	0.5	0.2	0.2	0.1	0.2	1.0	1.4	1.4	0.9	0.3	0.2	1.2

#Rounds to zero.
NOTE: Degree-granting institutions grant associate's or higher degrees and participate in Title IV federal financial aid programs. Detail may not sum to totals because of rounding.

SOURCE: U.S. Department of Education, National Center for Education Statistics, Integrated Postsecondary Education Data System (IPEDS), Spring 2014, Enrollment component. (This table was prepared November 2014.)

Table 303.60. Total fall enrollment in degree-granting postsecondary institutions, by level of enrollment, sex of student, and other selected characteristics: 2013

Level and control of institution and attendance status of student	Total			Undergraduate			Postbaccalaureate		
	Total	Males	Females	Total	Males	Females	Total	Males	Females
1	2	3	4	5	6	7	8	9	10
Total	20,375,789	8,860,786	11,515,003	17,474,835	7,659,626	9,815,209	2,900,954	1,201,160	1,699,794
Full-time	12,597,112	5,682,166	6,914,946	10,938,494	4,949,572	5,988,922	1,658,618	732,594	926,024
Part-time	7,778,677	3,178,620	4,600,057	6,536,341	2,710,054	3,826,287	1,242,336	468,566	773,770
4-year	13,407,050	5,862,870	7,544,180	10,506,096	4,661,710	5,844,386	2,900,954	1,201,160	1,699,794
Full-time	9,764,196	4,403,914	5,360,282	8,105,578	3,671,320	4,434,258	1,658,618	732,594	926,024
Part-time	3,642,854	1,458,956	2,183,898	2,400,518	990,390	1,410,128	1,242,336	468,566	773,770
2-year	6,968,739	2,997,916	3,970,823	6,968,739	2,997,916	3,970,823	†	†	†
Full-time	2,832,916	1,278,252	1,554,664	2,832,916	1,278,252	1,554,664	†	†	†
Part-time	4,135,823	1,719,664	2,416,159	4,135,823	1,719,664	2,416,159	†	†	†
Public	14,745,558	6,568,839	8,176,719	13,347,002	5,970,158	7,376,844	1,398,556	598,681	799,875
Full-time	8,464,809	3,949,205	4,515,604	7,685,669	3,590,522	4,095,147	779,140	358,683	420,457
Part-time	6,280,749	2,619,634	3,661,115	5,661,333	2,379,636	3,281,697	619,416	239,998	379,418
Public 4-year	8,120,417	3,683,546	4,436,871	6,721,861	3,084,865	3,636,996	1,398,556	598,681	799,875
Full-time	5,934,852	2,772,506	3,162,346	5,155,712	2,413,823	2,741,889	779,140	358,683	420,457
Part-time	2,185,565	911,040	1,274,525	1,566,149	671,042	895,107	619,416	239,998	379,418
Public 2-year	6,625,141	2,885,293	3,739,848	6,625,141	2,885,293	3,739,848	†	†	†
Full-time	2,529,957	1,176,699	1,353,258	2,529,957	1,176,699	1,353,258	†	†	†
Part-time	4,095,184	1,708,594	2,386,590	4,095,184	1,708,594	2,386,590	†	†	†
Private	5,630,231	2,291,947	3,338,284	4,127,833	1,689,468	2,438,365	1,502,398	602,479	899,919
Full-time	4,132,303	1,732,961	2,399,342	3,252,825	1,359,050	1,893,775	879,478	373,911	505,567
Part-time	1,497,928	558,986	938,942	875,008	330,418	544,590	622,920	228,568	394,352
Private 4-year	5,286,633	2,179,324	3,107,309	3,784,235	1,576,845	2,207,390	1,502,398	602,479	899,919
Full-time	3,829,344	1,631,408	2,197,936	2,949,866	1,257,497	1,692,369	879,478	373,911	505,567
Part-time	1,457,289	547,916	909,373	834,369	319,348	515,021	622,920	228,568	394,352
Private 2-year	343,598	112,623	230,975	343,598	112,623	230,975	†	†	†
Full-time	302,959	101,553	201,406	302,959	101,553	201,406	†	†	†
Part-time	40,639	11,070	29,569	40,639	11,070	29,569	†	†	†
Nonprofit	3,974,004	1,692,903	2,281,101	2,757,447	1,181,564	1,575,883	1,216,557	511,339	705,218
Full-time	2,986,053	1,313,037	1,673,016	2,261,723	990,472	1,271,251	724,330	322,565	401,765
Part-time	987,951	379,866	608,085	495,724	191,092	304,632	492,227	188,774	303,453
Nonprofit 4-year	3,941,806	1,681,047	2,260,759	2,725,249	1,169,708	1,555,541	1,216,557	511,339	705,218
Full-time	2,961,998	1,303,567	1,658,431	2,237,668	981,002	1,256,666	724,330	322,565	401,765
Part-time	979,808	377,480	602,328	487,581	188,706	298,875	492,227	188,774	303,453
Nonprofit 2-year	32,198	11,856	20,342	32,198	11,856	20,342	†	†	†
Full-time	24,055	9,470	14,585	24,055	9,470	14,585	†	†	†
Part-time	8,143	2,386	5,757	8,143	2,386	5,757	†	†	†
For-profit	1,656,227	599,044	1,057,183	1,370,386	507,904	862,482	285,841	91,140	194,701
Full-time	1,146,250	419,924	726,326	991,102	368,578	622,524	155,148	51,346	103,802
Part-time	509,977	179,120	330,857	379,284	139,326	239,958	130,693	39,794	90,899
For-profit 4-year	1,344,827	498,277	846,550	1,058,986	407,137	651,849	285,841	91,140	194,701
Full-time	867,346	327,841	539,505	712,198	276,495	435,703	155,148	51,346	103,802
Part-time	477,481	170,436	307,045	346,788	130,642	216,146	130,693	39,794	90,899
For-profit 2-year	311,400	100,767	210,633	311,400	100,767	210,633	†	†	†
Full-time	278,904	92,083	186,821	278,904	92,083	186,821	†	†	†
Part-time	32,496	8,684	23,812	32,496	8,684	23,812	†	†	†

†Not applicable.
NOTE: Degree-granting institutions grant associate's or higher degrees and participate in Title IV federal financial aid programs.

SOURCE: U.S. Department of Education, National Center for Education Statistics, Integrated Postsecondary Education Data System (IPEDS), Spring 2014, Enrollment component. (This table was prepared October 2014.)

Table 303.65. Total fall enrollment in degree-granting postsecondary institutions, by level of enrollment, sex of student, and other selected characteristics: 2012

Level and control of institution and attendance status of student	Total			Undergraduate			Postbaccalaureate		
	Total	Males	Females	Total	Males	Females	Total	Males	Females
1	2	3	4	5	6	7	8	9	10
Total.........................	20,642,819	8,919,087	11,723,732	17,732,431	7,713,901	10,018,530	2,910,388	1,205,186	1,705,202
Full-time.............................	12,737,013	5,709,792	7,027,221	11,097,779	4,984,696	6,113,083	1,639,234	725,096	914,138
Part-time.............................	7,905,806	3,209,295	4,696,511	6,634,652	2,729,205	3,905,447	1,271,154	480,090	791,064
4-year.........................	13,478,846	5,874,383	7,604,463	10,568,458	4,669,197	5,899,261	2,910,388	1,205,186	1,705,202
Full-time.............................	9,794,436	4,403,960	5,390,476	8,155,202	3,678,864	4,476,338	1,639,234	725,096	914,138
Part-time.............................	3,684,410	1,470,423	2,213,987	2,413,256	990,333	1,422,923	1,271,154	480,090	791,064
2-year.........................	7,163,973	3,044,704	4,119,269	7,163,973	3,044,704	4,119,269	†	†	†
Full-time.............................	2,942,577	1,305,832	1,636,745	2,942,577	1,305,832	1,636,745	†	†	†
Part-time.............................	4,221,396	1,738,872	2,482,524	4,221,396	1,738,872	2,482,524	†	†	†
Public.........................	14,880,343	6,581,299	8,299,044	13,473,743	5,983,450	7,490,293	1,406,600	597,849	808,751
Full-time.............................	8,525,818	3,954,114	4,571,704	7,752,356	3,599,518	4,152,838	773,462	354,596	418,866
Part-time.............................	6,354,525	2,627,185	3,727,340	5,721,387	2,383,932	3,337,455	633,138	243,253	389,885
Public 4-year...........	8,092,683	3,658,138	4,434,545	6,686,083	3,060,289	3,625,794	1,406,600	597,849	808,751
Full-time.............................	5,910,198	2,756,941	3,153,257	5,136,736	2,402,345	2,734,391	773,462	354,596	418,866
Part-time.............................	2,182,485	901,197	1,281,288	1,549,347	657,944	891,403	633,138	243,253	389,885
Public 2-year...........	6,787,660	2,923,161	3,864,499	6,787,660	2,923,161	3,864,499	†	†	†
Full-time......................	2,615,620	1,197,173	1,418,447	2,615,620	1,197,173	1,418,447	†	†	†
Part-time......................	4,172,040	1,725,988	2,446,052	4,172,040	1,725,988	2,446,052	†	†	†
Private.........................	5,762,476	2,337,788	3,424,688	4,258,688	1,730,451	2,528,237	1,503,788	607,337	896,451
Full-time.............................	4,211,195	1,755,678	2,455,517	3,345,423	1,385,178	1,960,245	865,772	370,500	495,272
Part-time.............................	1,551,281	582,110	969,171	913,265	345,273	567,992	638,016	236,837	401,179
Private 4-year..................	5,386,163	2,216,245	3,169,918	3,882,375	1,608,908	2,273,467	1,503,788	607,337	896,451
Full-time.............................	3,884,238	1,647,019	2,237,219	3,018,466	1,276,519	1,741,947	865,772	370,500	495,272
Part-time.............................	1,501,925	569,226	932,699	863,909	332,389	531,520	638,016	236,837	401,179
Private 2-year..................	376,313	121,543	254,770	376,313	121,543	254,770	†	†	†
Full-time.............................	326,957	108,659	218,298	326,957	108,659	218,298	†	†	†
Part-time.............................	49,356	12,884	36,472	49,356	12,884	36,472	†	†	†
Nonprofit.........................	3,953,578	1,680,744	2,272,834	2,745,075	1,170,305	1,574,770	1,208,503	510,439	698,064
Full-time.............................	2,958,258	1,300,539	1,657,719	2,249,980	982,298	1,267,682	708,278	318,241	390,037
Part-time.............................	995,320	380,205	615,115	495,095	188,007	307,088	500,225	192,198	308,027
Nonprofit 4-year...........	3,915,972	1,667,820	2,248,152	2,707,469	1,157,381	1,550,088	1,208,503	510,439	698,064
Full-time......................	2,928,938	1,290,080	1,638,858	2,220,660	971,839	1,248,821	708,278	318,241	390,037
Part-time......................	987,034	377,740	609,294	486,809	185,542	301,267	500,225	192,198	308,027
Nonprofit 2-year...........	37,606	12,924	24,682	37,606	12,924	24,682	†	†	†
Full-time	29,320	10,459	18,861	29,320	10,459	18,861	†	†	†
Part-time	8,286	2,465	5,821	8,286	2,465	5,821	†	†	†
For-profit.........................	1,808,898	657,044	1,151,854	1,513,613	560,146	953,467	295,285	96,898	198,387
Full-time.............................	1,252,937	455,139	797,798	1,095,443	402,880	692,563	157,494	52,259	105,235
Part-time.............................	555,961	201,905	354,056	418,170	157,266	260,904	137,791	44,639	93,152
For-profit 4-year...........	1,470,191	548,425	921,766	1,174,906	451,527	723,379	295,285	96,898	198,387
Full-time	955,300	356,939	598,361	797,806	304,680	493,126	157,494	52,259	105,235
Part-time	514,891	191,486	323,405	377,100	146,847	230,253	137,791	44,639	93,152
For-profit 2-year...........	338,707	108,619	230,088	338,707	108,619	230,088	†	†	†
Full-time	297,637	98,200	199,437	297,637	98,200	199,437	†	†	†
Part-time	41,070	10,419	30,651	41,070	10,419	30,651	†	†	†

†Not applicable.
NOTE: Degree-granting institutions grant associate's or higher degrees and participate in Title IV federal financial aid programs.

SOURCE: U.S. Department of Education, National Center for Education Statistics, Integrated Postsecondary Education Data System (IPEDS), Spring 2013, Enrollment component. (This table was prepared October 2013.)

Table 303.70. Total undergraduate fall enrollment in degree-granting postsecondary institutions, by attendance status, sex of student, and control and level of institution: Selected years, 1970 through 2024

Level and year	Total	Full-time	Part-time	Males	Females	Males		Females		Public	Private		
						Full-time	Part-time	Full-time	Part-time		Total	Nonprofit	For-profit
1	2	3	4	5	6	7	8	9	10	11	12	13	14
Total, all levels													
1970	7,368,644	5,280,064	2,088,580	4,249,702	3,118,942	3,096,371	1,153,331	2,183,693	935,249	5,620,255	1,748,389	1,730,133	18,256
1975	9,679,455	6,168,396	3,511,059	5,257,005	4,422,450	3,459,328	1,797,677	2,709,068	1,713,382	7,826,032	1,853,423	1,814,844	38,579
1980	10,475,055	6,361,744	4,113,311	5,000,177	5,474,878	3,226,857	1,773,320	3,134,887	2,339,991	8,441,955	2,033,100	1,926,703	106,397
1981	10,754,522	6,449,068	4,305,454	5,108,271	5,646,251	3,260,473	1,847,798	3,188,595	2,457,656	8,648,363	2,106,159	1,958,848	147,311
1982	10,825,062	6,483,805	4,341,257	5,170,494	5,654,568	3,299,436	1,871,058	3,184,369	2,470,199	8,713,073	2,111,989	1,939,389	172,600
1983	10,845,995	6,514,034	4,331,961	5,158,300	5,687,695	3,304,247	1,854,053	3,209,787	2,477,908	8,697,118	2,148,877	1,961,076	187,801
1984	10,618,071	6,347,653	4,270,418	5,006,813	5,611,258	3,194,930	1,811,883	3,152,723	2,458,535	8,493,491	2,124,580	1,940,310	184,270
1985	10,596,674	6,319,592	4,277,082	4,962,080	5,634,594	3,156,446	1,805,634	3,163,146	2,471,448	8,477,125	2,119,549	1,928,996	190,553
1986	10,797,975	6,352,073	4,445,902	5,017,505	5,780,470	3,146,330	1,871,175	3,205,743	2,574,727	8,660,716	2,137,259	1,928,294	208,965
1987	11,046,235	6,462,549	4,583,686	5,068,457	5,977,778	3,163,676	1,904,781	3,298,873	2,678,905	8,918,589	2,127,646	1,939,942	187,704
1988	11,316,548	6,642,428	4,674,120	5,137,644	6,178,904	3,206,442	1,931,202	3,435,986	2,742,918	9,103,146	2,213,402	—	—
1989	11,742,531	6,840,696	4,901,835	5,310,990	6,431,541	3,278,647	2,032,343	3,562,049	2,869,492	9,487,742	2,254,789	—	—
1990	11,959,106	6,976,030	4,983,076	5,379,759	6,579,347	3,336,535	2,043,224	3,639,495	2,939,852	9,709,596	2,249,510	2,043,407	206,103
1991	12,439,287	7,221,412	5,217,875	5,571,003	6,868,284	3,435,526	2,135,477	3,785,886	3,082,398	10,147,957	2,291,330	2,072,354	218,976
1992	12,537,700	7,244,442	5,293,258	5,582,936	6,954,764	3,424,739	2,158,197	3,819,703	3,135,061	10,216,297	2,321,403	2,101,721	219,682
1993	12,323,959	7,179,482	5,144,477	5,483,682	6,840,277	3,381,997	2,101,685	3,797,485	3,042,792	10,011,787	2,312,172	2,099,197	212,975
1994	12,262,608	7,168,706	5,093,902	5,422,113	6,840,495	3,341,591	2,080,522	3,827,115	3,013,380	9,945,128	2,317,480	2,100,465	217,015
1995	12,231,719	7,145,268	5,086,451	5,401,130	6,830,589	3,296,610	2,104,520	3,848,658	2,981,931	9,903,626	2,328,093	2,104,693	223,400
1996	12,326,948	7,298,839	5,028,109	5,420,672	6,906,276	3,339,108	2,081,564	3,959,731	2,946,545	9,935,283	2,391,665	2,112,318	279,347
1997	12,450,587	7,418,598	5,031,989	5,468,532	6,982,055	3,379,597	2,088,935	4,039,001	2,943,054	10,007,479	2,443,108	2,139,824	303,284
1998	12,436,937	7,538,711	4,898,226	5,446,133	6,990,804	3,428,161	2,017,972	4,110,550	2,880,254	9,950,212	2,486,725	2,152,655	334,070
1999	12,739,445	7,753,548	4,985,897	5,584,234	7,155,211	3,524,586	2,059,648	4,228,962	2,926,249	10,174,228	2,565,217	2,185,290	379,927
2000	13,155,393	7,922,926	5,232,467	5,778,268	7,377,125	3,588,246	2,190,022	4,334,680	3,042,445	10,539,322	2,616,071	2,213,180	402,891
2001	13,715,610	8,327,640	5,387,970	6,004,431	7,711,179	3,768,630	2,235,801	4,559,010	3,152,169	10,985,871	2,729,739	2,257,718	472,021
2002	14,257,077	8,734,252	5,522,825	6,192,390	8,064,687	3,934,168	2,258,222	4,800,084	3,264,603	11,432,855	2,824,222	2,306,091	518,131
2003	14,480,364	9,045,253	5,435,111	6,227,372	8,252,992	4,048,682	2,178,690	4,996,571	3,256,421	11,523,103	2,957,261	2,346,673	610,588
2004	14,780,630	9,284,336	5,496,294	6,340,048	8,440,582	4,140,628	2,199,420	5,143,708	3,296,874	11,650,580	3,130,050	2,389,366	740,684
2005	14,963,964	9,446,430	5,517,534	6,408,871	8,555,093	4,200,863	2,208,008	5,245,567	3,309,526	11,697,730	3,266,234	2,418,368	847,866
2006	15,184,302	9,571,079	5,613,223	6,513,756	8,670,546	4,264,606	2,249,150	5,306,473	3,364,073	11,847,426	3,336,876	2,448,240	888,636
2007	15,603,771	9,840,978	5,762,793	6,727,600	8,876,171	4,396,868	2,330,732	5,444,110	3,432,061	12,137,583	3,466,188	2,470,327	995,861
2008	16,365,738	10,254,930	6,110,808	7,066,623	9,299,115	4,577,431	2,489,192	5,677,499	3,621,616	12,591,217	3,774,521	2,536,532	1,237,989
2009	17,464,179	11,038,275	6,425,904	7,563,176	9,901,003	4,942,120	2,621,056	6,096,155	3,804,848	13,386,375	4,077,804	2,595,171	1,482,633
2010	18,082,427	11,457,040	6,625,387	7,836,282	10,246,145	5,118,975	2,717,307	6,338,065	3,908,080	13,703,000	4,379,427	2,652,993	1,726,434
2011	18,077,303	11,365,175	6,712,128	7,822,992	10,254,311	5,070,553	2,752,439	6,294,622	3,959,689	13,694,899	4,382,404	2,718,923	1,663,481
2012	17,732,431	11,097,779	6,634,652	7,713,901	10,018,530	4,984,696	2,729,205	6,113,083	3,905,447	13,473,743	4,258,688	2,745,075	1,513,613
2013	17,474,835	10,938,494	6,536,341	7,659,626	9,815,209	4,949,572	2,710,054	5,988,922	3,826,287	13,347,002	4,127,833	2,757,447	1,370,386
2014[1]	17,322,000	10,966,000	6,356,000	7,466,000	9,855,000	4,874,000	2,592,000	6,092,000	3,763,000	13,245,000	4,077,000	—	—
2015[1]	17,280,000	10,904,000	6,376,000	7,446,000	9,834,000	4,878,000	2,568,000	6,026,000	3,808,000	13,221,000	4,059,000	—	—
2016[1]	17,472,000	11,033,000	6,439,000	7,490,000	9,982,000	4,911,000	2,579,000	6,122,000	3,859,000	13,366,000	4,106,000	—	—
2017[1]	17,823,000	11,261,000	6,562,000	7,612,000	10,210,000	4,981,000	2,631,000	6,280,000	3,931,000	13,633,000	4,189,000	—	—
2018[1]	18,156,000	11,463,000	6,693,000	7,745,000	10,412,000	5,055,000	2,689,000	6,407,000	4,004,000	13,890,000	4,266,000	—	—
2019[1]	18,404,000	11,601,000	6,804,000	7,836,000	10,569,000	5,113,000	2,723,000	6,488,000	4,081,000	14,083,000	4,321,000	—	—
2020[1]	18,591,000	11,708,000	6,883,000	7,898,000	10,692,000	5,152,000	2,747,000	6,556,000	4,136,000	14,225,000	4,365,000	—	—
2021[1]	18,843,000	11,857,000	6,986,000	7,998,000	10,845,000	5,207,000	2,791,000	6,650,000	4,194,000	14,418,000	4,425,000	—	—
2022[1]	19,119,000	12,019,000	7,100,000	8,113,000	11,006,000	5,269,000	2,844,000	6,750,000	4,256,000	14,631,000	4,488,000	—	—
2023[1]	19,423,000	12,211,000	7,211,000	8,236,000	11,187,000	5,340,000	2,895,000	6,871,000	4,316,000	14,863,000	4,560,000	—	—
2024[1]	19,640,000	12,345,000	7,295,000	8,330,000	11,310,000	5,395,000	2,935,000	6,949,000	4,361,000	15,029,000	4,611,000	—	—
2-year institutions[2]													
1970	2,318,956	1,228,909	1,090,047	1,374,426	944,530	771,298	603,128	457,611	486,919	2,194,983	123,973	113,299	10,674
1975	3,965,726	1,761,009	2,204,717	2,163,604	1,802,122	1,035,531	1,128,073	725,478	1,076,644	3,831,973	133,753	112,997	20,756
1980	4,525,097	1,753,637	2,771,460	2,046,642	2,478,455	879,619	1,167,023	874,018	1,604,437	4,327,592	197,505	114,094	83,411
1981	4,715,403	1,795,858	2,919,545	2,124,136	2,591,267	897,657	1,226,479	898,201	1,693,066	4,479,900	235,503	119,166	116,337
1982	4,770,712	1,839,704	2,931,008	2,169,802	2,600,910	930,606	1,239,196	909,098	1,691,812	4,518,659	252,053	114,976	137,077
1983	4,723,466	1,826,801	2,896,665	2,131,109	2,592,357	914,704	1,216,405	912,097	1,680,260	4,459,330	264,136	116,293	147,843
1984	4,530,337	1,703,786	2,826,551	2,016,463	2,513,874	841,347	1,175,116	862,439	1,651,435	4,278,661	251,676	108,247	143,429
1985	4,531,077	1,690,607	2,840,470	2,002,234	2,528,843	826,308	1,175,926	864,299	1,664,544	4,269,733	261,344	108,791	152,553
1986	4,679,548	1,696,261	2,983,287	2,060,932	2,618,616	824,551	1,236,381	871,710	1,746,906	4,413,691	265,857	101,498	164,359
1987	4,776,222	1,708,669	3,067,553	2,072,823	2,703,399	820,167	1,252,656	888,502	1,814,897	4,541,054	235,168	90,102	145,066
1988	4,875,155	1,743,592	3,131,563	2,089,689	2,785,466	818,593	1,271,096	924,999	1,860,467	4,615,487	259,668	—	—
1989	5,150,889	1,855,701	3,295,188	2,216,800	2,934,089	869,688	1,347,112	986,013	1,948,076	4,883,660	267,229	—	—
1990	5,240,083	1,883,962	3,356,121	2,232,769	3,007,314	881,392	1,351,377	1,002,570	2,004,744	4,996,475	243,608	89,158	154,450
1991	5,651,900	2,074,530	3,577,370	2,401,910	3,249,990	961,397	1,440,513	1,113,133	2,136,857	5,404,815	247,085	89,289	157,796
1992	5,722,349	2,080,005	3,642,344	2,413,266	3,309,083	951,816	1,461,450	1,128,189	2,180,894	5,484,514	237,835	83,288	154,547
1993	5,565,561	2,043,319	3,522,242	2,345,396	3,220,165	928,216	1,417,180	1,115,103	2,105,062	5,337,022	228,539	86,357	142,182
1994	5,529,609	2,031,713	3,497,896	2,323,161	3,206,448	911,589	1,411,572	1,120,124	2,086,324	5,308,366	221,243	85,607	135,636
1995	5,492,098	1,977,046	3,515,052	2,328,500	3,163,598	878,215	1,450,285	1,098,831	2,064,767	5,277,398	214,700	75,154	139,546
1996	5,562,780	2,072,215	3,490,565	2,358,792	3,203,988	916,452	1,442,340	1,155,763	2,048,225	5,314,038	248,742	75,253	173,489
1997	5,605,569	2,095,171	3,510,398	2,389,711	3,215,858	931,394	1,458,317	1,163,777	2,052,081	5,360,686	244,883	71,794	173,089
1998	5,489,314	2,085,906	3,403,408	2,333,334	3,155,980	936,421	1,396,913	1,149,485	2,006,495	5,245,963	243,351	65,870	177,481
1999	5,653,256	2,167,242	3,486,014	2,413,322	3,239,934	979,203	1,434,119	1,188,039	2,051,895	5,397,786	255,470	63,301	192,169
2000	5,948,104	2,217,044	3,731,060	2,558,520	3,389,584	995,839	1,562,681	1,221,205	2,168,379	5,697,061	251,043	58,844	192,199
2001	6,250,529	2,374,490	3,876,039	2,675,193	3,575,336	1,066,281	1,608,912	1,308,209	2,267,127	5,996,651	253,878	47,549	206,329
2002	6,529,198	2,556,032	3,973,166	2,753,405	3,775,793	1,135,669	1,617,736	1,420,363	2,355,430	6,270,199	258,999	47,087	211,912
2003	6,493,862	2,650,337	3,843,525	2,689,928	3,803,934	1,162,555	1,527,373	1,487,782	2,316,152	6,208,885	284,977	43,868	241,109
2004	6,545,570	2,683,489	3,862,081	2,697,507	3,848,063	1,166,554	1,530,953	1,516,935	2,331,128	6,243,344	302,226	42,250	259,976

See notes at end of table.

Table 303.70. Total undergraduate fall enrollment in degree-granting postsecondary institutions, by attendance status, sex of student, and control and level of institution: Selected years, 1970 through 2024—Continued

Level and year	Total	Full-time	Part-time	Males	Females	Males Full-time	Males Part-time	Females Full-time	Females Part-time	Public	Private Total	Private Nonprofit	Private For-profit
1	2	3	4	5	6	7	8	9	10	11	12	13	14
2005	6,487,826	2,646,763	3,841,063	2,680,299	3,807,527	1,153,759	1,526,540	1,493,004	2,314,523	6,184,000	303,826	43,522	260,304
2006	6,518,291	2,643,222	3,875,069	2,704,654	3,813,637	1,159,800	1,544,854	1,483,422	2,330,215	6,224,871	293,420	39,156	254,264
2007	6,617,621	2,692,491	3,925,130	2,770,457	3,847,164	1,190,067	1,580,390	1,502,424	2,344,740	6,323,810	293,811	33,486	260,325
2008	6,971,105	2,832,110	4,138,995	2,935,793	4,035,312	1,249,832	1,685,961	1,582,278	2,453,034	6,640,071	331,034	35,351	295,683
2009	7,522,581	3,243,952	4,278,629	3,197,338	4,325,243	1,446,372	1,750,966	1,797,580	2,527,663	7,101,569	421,012	34,772	386,240
2010	7,683,597	3,365,379	4,318,218	3,265,885	4,417,712	1,483,230	1,782,655	1,882,149	2,535,563	7,218,063	465,534	32,683	432,851
2011	7,511,150	3,170,207	4,340,943	3,175,803	4,335,347	1,391,183	1,784,620	1,779,024	2,556,323	7,068,158	442,992	39,855	403,137
2012	7,163,973	2,942,577	4,221,396	3,044,704	4,119,269	1,305,832	1,738,872	1,636,745	2,482,524	6,787,660	376,313	37,606	338,707
2013	6,968,739	2,832,916	4,135,823	2,997,916	3,970,823	1,278,252	1,719,664	1,554,664	2,416,159	6,625,141	343,598	32,198	311,400
2014[1]	7,009,000	2,925,000	4,084,000	2,956,000	4,053,000	1,296,000	1,660,000	1,629,000	2,425,000	6,651,000	358,000	—	—
2015[1]	7,011,000	2,916,000	4,096,000	2,943,000	4,069,000	1,300,000	1,643,000	1,616,000	2,453,000	6,655,000	357,000	—	—
2016[1]	7,090,000	2,957,000	4,134,000	2,960,000	4,131,000	1,311,000	1,648,000	1,645,000	2,485,000	6,729,000	362,000	—	—
2017[1]	7,235,000	3,026,000	4,210,000	3,013,000	4,222,000	1,333,000	1,680,000	1,692,000	2,530,000	6,865,000	371,000	—	—
2018[1]	7,378,000	3,085,000	4,292,000	3,072,000	4,306,000	1,356,000	1,716,000	1,729,000	2,577,000	7,000,000	378,000	—	—
2019[1]	7,487,000	3,126,000	4,362,000	3,109,000	4,378,000	1,374,000	1,736,000	1,752,000	2,626,000	7,104,000	383,000	—	—
2020[1]	7,562,000	3,153,000	4,409,000	3,132,000	4,429,000	1,383,000	1,749,000	1,770,000	2,660,000	7,175,000	387,000	—	—
2021[1]	7,664,000	3,193,000	4,470,000	3,174,000	4,490,000	1,398,000	1,776,000	1,796,000	2,694,000	7,272,000	392,000	—	—
2022[1]	7,782,000	3,243,000	4,540,000	3,224,000	4,558,000	1,416,000	1,808,000	1,826,000	2,732,000	7,384,000	398,000	—	—
2023[1]	7,907,000	3,299,000	4,607,000	3,276,000	4,630,000	1,438,000	1,839,000	1,862,000	2,769,000	7,502,000	405,000	—	—
2024[1]	7,996,000	3,335,000	4,660,000	3,316,000	4,679,000	1,453,000	1,863,000	1,882,000	2,797,000	7,586,000	410,000	—	—
4-year institutions													
1970	5,049,688	4,051,155	998,533	2,875,276	2,174,412	2,325,073	550,203	1,726,082	448,330	3,425,272	1,624,416	1,616,834	7,582
1975	5,713,729	4,407,387	1,306,342	3,093,401	2,620,328	2,423,797	669,604	1,983,590	636,738	3,994,059	1,719,670	1,701,847	17,823
1980	5,949,958	4,608,107	1,341,851	2,953,535	2,996,423	2,347,238	606,297	2,260,869	735,554	4,114,363	1,835,595	1,812,609	22,986
1981	6,039,119	4,653,210	1,385,909	2,984,135	3,054,984	2,362,816	621,319	2,290,394	764,590	4,168,463	1,870,656	1,839,682	30,974
1982	6,054,350	4,644,101	1,410,249	3,000,692	3,053,658	2,368,830	631,862	2,275,271	778,387	4,194,414	1,859,936	1,824,413	35,523
1983	6,122,529	4,687,233	1,435,296	3,027,191	3,095,338	2,389,543	637,648	2,297,690	797,648	4,237,788	1,884,741	1,844,783	39,958
1984	6,087,734	4,643,867	1,443,867	2,990,350	3,097,384	2,353,583	636,767	2,290,284	807,100	4,214,830	1,872,904	1,832,063	40,841
1985	6,065,597	4,628,985	1,436,612	2,959,846	3,105,751	2,330,138	629,708	2,298,847	806,904	4,207,392	1,858,205	1,820,205	38,000
1986	6,118,427	4,655,812	1,462,615	2,956,573	3,161,854	2,321,779	634,794	2,334,033	827,821	4,247,025	1,871,402	1,826,796	44,606
1987	6,270,013	4,753,880	1,516,133	2,995,634	3,274,379	2,343,509	652,125	2,410,371	864,008	4,377,535	1,892,478	1,849,840	42,638
1988	6,441,393	4,898,836	1,542,557	3,047,955	3,393,438	2,387,849	660,106	2,510,987	882,451	4,487,659	1,953,734	—	—
1989	6,591,642	4,984,995	1,606,647	3,094,190	3,497,452	2,408,959	685,231	2,576,036	921,416	4,604,082	1,987,560		
1990	6,719,023	5,092,068	1,626,955	3,146,990	3,572,033	2,455,143	691,847	2,636,925	935,108	4,713,121	2,005,902	1,954,249	51,653
1991	6,787,387	5,146,882	1,640,505	3,169,093	3,618,294	2,474,129	694,964	2,672,753	945,541	4,743,142	2,044,245	1,983,065	61,180
1992	6,815,351	5,164,437	1,650,914	3,169,670	3,645,681	2,472,923	696,747	2,691,514	954,167	4,731,783	2,083,568	2,018,433	65,135
1993	6,758,398	5,136,163	1,622,235	3,138,286	3,620,112	2,453,781	684,505	2,682,382	937,730	4,674,765	2,083,633	2,012,840	70,793
1994	6,732,999	5,136,993	1,596,006	3,098,952	3,634,047	2,430,002	668,950	2,706,991	927,056	4,636,762	2,096,237	2,014,858	81,379
1995	6,739,621	5,168,222	1,571,399	3,072,630	3,666,991	2,418,395	654,235	2,749,827	917,164	4,626,228	2,113,393	2,029,539	83,854
1996	6,764,168	5,226,624	1,537,544	3,061,880	3,702,288	2,422,656	639,224	2,803,968	898,320	4,621,245	2,142,923	2,037,065	105,858
1997	6,845,018	5,323,427	1,521,591	3,078,821	3,766,197	2,448,203	630,618	2,875,224	890,973	4,646,793	2,198,225	2,068,030	130,195
1998	6,947,623	5,452,805	1,494,818	3,112,799	3,834,824	2,491,740	621,059	2,961,065	873,759	4,704,249	2,243,374	2,086,785	156,589
1999	7,086,189	5,586,306	1,499,883	3,170,912	3,915,277	2,545,383	625,529	3,040,923	874,354	4,776,442	2,309,747	2,121,989	187,758
2000	7,207,289	5,705,882	1,501,407	3,219,748	3,987,541	2,592,407	627,341	3,113,475	874,066	4,842,261	2,365,028	2,154,336	210,692
2001	7,465,081	5,953,150	1,511,931	3,329,238	4,135,843	2,702,349	626,889	3,250,801	885,042	4,989,220	2,475,861	2,210,169	265,692
2002	7,727,879	6,178,220	1,549,659	3,438,985	4,288,894	2,798,499	640,486	3,379,721	909,173	5,162,656	2,565,223	2,259,004	306,219
2003	7,986,502	6,394,916	1,591,586	3,537,444	4,449,058	2,886,127	651,317	3,508,789	940,269	5,314,218	2,672,284	2,302,805	369,479
2004	8,235,060	6,600,847	1,634,213	3,642,541	4,592,519	2,974,074	668,467	3,626,773	965,746	5,407,236	2,827,824	2,347,116	480,708
2005	8,476,138	6,799,667	1,676,471	3,728,572	4,747,566	3,047,104	681,468	3,752,563	995,003	5,513,730	2,962,408	2,374,846	587,562
2006	8,666,011	6,927,857	1,738,154	3,809,102	4,856,909	3,104,806	704,296	3,823,051	1,033,858	5,622,555	3,043,456	2,409,084	634,372
2007	8,986,150	7,148,487	1,837,663	3,957,143	5,029,007	3,206,801	750,342	3,941,686	1,087,321	5,813,773	3,172,377	2,436,841	735,536
2008	9,394,633	7,422,820	1,971,813	4,130,830	5,263,803	3,327,599	803,231	4,095,221	1,168,582	5,951,146	3,443,487	2,501,181	942,306
2009	9,941,598	7,794,323	2,147,275	4,365,838	5,575,760	3,495,748	870,090	4,298,575	1,277,185	6,284,806	3,656,792	2,560,399	1,096,393
2010	10,398,830	8,091,661	2,307,169	4,570,397	5,828,433	3,635,745	934,652	4,455,916	1,372,517	6,484,937	3,913,893	2,620,310	1,293,583
2011	10,566,153	8,194,968	2,371,185	4,647,189	5,918,964	3,679,370	967,819	4,515,598	1,403,366	6,626,741	3,939,412	2,679,068	1,260,344
2012	10,568,458	8,155,202	2,413,256	4,669,197	5,899,261	3,678,864	990,333	4,476,338	1,422,923	6,686,083	3,882,375	2,707,469	1,174,906
2013	10,506,096	8,105,578	2,400,518	4,661,710	5,844,386	3,671,320	990,390	4,434,258	1,410,128	6,721,861	3,784,235	2,725,249	1,058,986
2014[1]	10,312,000	8,041,000	2,271,000	4,510,000	5,802,000	3,578,000	933,000	4,463,000	1,339,000	6,594,000	3,719,000	—	—
2015[1]	10,269,000	7,989,000	2,280,000	4,503,000	5,765,000	3,578,000	925,000	4,411,000	1,355,000	6,566,000	3,702,000	—	—
2016[1]	10,381,000	8,077,000	2,305,000	4,531,000	5,851,000	3,600,000	931,000	4,477,000	1,374,000	6,638,000	3,744,000	—	—
2017[1]	10,587,000	8,235,000	2,352,000	4,599,000	5,988,000	3,647,000	952,000	4,588,000	1,401,000	6,768,000	3,819,000	—	—
2018[1]	10,778,000	8,377,000	2,401,000	4,673,000	6,105,000	3,699,000	974,000	4,678,000	1,427,000	6,890,000	3,888,000	—	—
2019[1]	10,917,000	8,475,000	2,442,000	4,726,000	6,191,000	3,739,000	987,000	4,736,000	1,455,000	6,979,000	3,938,000	—	—
2020[1]	11,029,000	8,555,000	2,474,000	4,766,000	6,263,000	3,769,000	997,000	4,786,000	1,477,000	7,050,000	3,979,000	—	—
2021[1]	11,179,000	8,664,000	2,515,000	4,824,000	6,355,000	3,809,000	1,015,000	4,855,000	1,500,000	7,146,000	4,033,000	—	—
2022[1]	11,337,000	8,776,000	2,561,000	4,889,000	6,448,000	3,853,000	1,036,000	4,924,000	1,524,000	7,247,000	4,090,000	—	—
2023[1]	11,516,000	8,912,000	2,604,000	4,959,000	6,557,000	3,903,000	1,057,000	5,009,000	1,547,000	7,361,000	4,155,000	—	—
2024[1]	11,645,000	9,009,000	2,635,000	5,014,000	6,631,000	3,942,000	1,072,000	5,067,000	1,564,000	7,443,000	4,201,000	—	—

—Not available.

[1]Projected.

[2]Beginning in 1980, 2-year institutions include schools accredited by the Accrediting Commission of Career Schools and Colleges of Technology.

NOTE: Data include unclassified undergraduate students. Data through 1995 are for institutions of higher education, while later data are for degree-granting institutions. Degree-granting institutions grant associate's or higher degrees and participate in Title IV federal financial aid programs. The degree-granting classification is very similar to the earlier higher education classification, but it includes more 2-year colleges and excludes a few higher education institutions that did not grant degrees. Some data have been revised from previously published figures.

SOURCE: U.S. Department of Education, National Center for Education Statistics, Higher Education General Information Survey (HEGIS), "Fall Enrollment in Colleges and Universities" surveys, 1970 through 1985; Integrated Postsecondary Education Data System (IPEDS), "Fall Enrollment Survey" (IPEDS-EF:86–99); IPEDS Spring 2001 through Spring 2014, Enrollment component; and Enrollment in Degree-Granting Institutions Projection Model, 1980 through 2024. (This table was prepared March 2015.)

Table 303.80. Total postbaccalaureate fall enrollment in degree-granting postsecondary institutions, by attendance status, sex of student, and control of institution: 1967 through 2024

Year	Total	Full-time	Part-time	Males	Females	Males Full-time	Males Part-time	Females Full-time	Females Part-time	Public	Private Total	Private Nonprofit	Private For-profit
1	2	3	4	5	6	7	8	9	10	11	12	13	14
1967	896,065	448,238	447,827	630,701	265,364	354,628	276,073	93,610	171,754	522,623	373,442	373,336	106
1968	1,037,377	469,747	567,630	696,649	340,728	358,686	337,963	111,061	229,667	648,657	388,720	388,681	39
1969	1,120,175	506,833	613,342	738,673	381,502	383,630	355,043	123,203	258,299	738,551	381,624	381,558	66
1970	1,212,243	536,226	676,017	793,940	418,303	407,724	386,216	128,502	289,801	807,879	404,364	404,287	77
1971	1,204,390	564,236	640,154	789,131	415,259	428,167	360,964	136,069	279,190	796,516	407,874	407,804	70
1972	1,272,421	583,299	689,122	810,164	462,257	436,533	373,631	146,766	315,491	848,031	424,390	424,278	112
1973	1,342,452	610,935	731,517	833,453	508,999	444,219	389,234	166,716	342,283	897,104	445,348	445,205	143
1974	1,425,001	643,927	781,074	856,847	568,154	454,706	402,141	189,221	378,933	956,770	468,231	467,950	281
1975	1,505,404	672,938	832,466	891,992	613,412	467,425	424,567	205,513	407,899	1,008,476	496,928	496,604	324
1976	1,577,546	683,825	893,721	904,551	672,995	459,286	445,265	224,539	448,456	1,033,115	544,431	541,064	3,367
1977	1,569,084	698,902	870,182	891,819	677,265	462,038	429,781	236,864	440,401	1,004,013	565,071	561,384	3,687
1978	1,575,693	704,831	870,862	879,931	695,762	458,865	421,066	245,966	449,796	998,608	577,085	573,563	3,522
1979	1,571,922	714,624	857,298	862,754	709,168	456,197	406,557	258,427	450,741	989,991	581,931	578,425	3,506
1980	1,621,840	736,214	885,626	874,197	747,643	462,387	411,810	273,827	473,816	1,015,439	606,401	601,084	5,317
1981	1,617,150	732,182	884,968	866,785	750,365	452,364	414,421	279,818	470,547	998,669	618,481	613,557	4,924
1982	1,600,718	736,813	863,905	860,890	739,828	453,519	407,371	283,294	456,534	983,014	617,704	613,350	4,354
1983	1,618,666	747,016	871,650	865,425	753,241	455,540	409,885	291,476	461,765	985,616	633,050	628,111	4,939
1984	1,623,869	750,735	873,134	856,761	767,108	452,579	404,182	298,156	468,952	983,879	639,990	634,109	5,881
1985	1,650,381	755,629	894,752	856,370	794,011	451,274	405,096	304,355	489,656	1,002,148	648,233	642,795	5,438
1986	1,705,536	767,477	938,059	867,010	838,526	452,717	414,293	314,760	523,766	1,053,177	652,359	644,185	8,174
1987	1,720,407	768,536	951,871	863,599	856,808	447,212	416,387	321,324	535,484	1,054,665	665,742	662,408	3,334
1988	1,738,789	794,340	944,449	864,252	874,537	455,337	408,915	339,003	535,534	1,058,242	680,547	—	—
1989	1,796,029	820,254	975,775	879,025	917,004	461,596	417,429	358,658	558,346	1,090,221	705,808	—	—
1990	1,859,531	844,955	1,014,576	904,150	955,381	471,217	432,933	373,738	581,643	1,135,121	724,410	716,820	7,590
1991	1,919,666	893,917	1,025,749	930,841	988,825	493,849	436,992	400,068	588,757	1,161,606	758,060	746,687	11,373
1992	1,949,659	917,676	1,031,983	941,053	1,008,606	502,166	438,887	415,510	593,096	1,168,270	781,389	770,802	10,587
1993	1,980,844	948,136	1,032,708	943,768	1,037,076	508,574	435,194	439,562	597,514	1,177,301	803,543	789,700	13,843
1994	2,016,182	969,070	1,047,112	949,785	1,066,397	513,592	436,193	455,478	610,919	1,188,552	827,630	809,642	17,988
1995	2,030,062	983,534	1,046,528	941,409	1,088,653	510,782	430,627	472,752	615,901	1,188,748	841,314	824,351	16,963
1996	2,040,572	1,004,114	1,036,458	932,153	1,108,419	512,100	420,053	492,014	616,405	1,185,216	855,356	830,238	25,118
1997	2,051,747	1,019,464	1,032,283	927,496	1,124,251	510,845	416,651	508,619	615,632	1,188,640	863,107	837,790	25,317
1998	2,070,030	1,024,627	1,045,403	923,132	1,146,898	505,492	417,640	519,135	627,763	1,187,557	882,473	852,270	30,203
1999	2,110,246	1,049,591	1,060,655	930,930	1,179,316	508,930	422,000	540,661	638,655	1,201,511	908,735	869,739	38,996
2000	2,156,896	1,086,674	1,070,222	943,501	1,213,395	522,847	420,654	563,827	649,568	1,213,464	943,432	896,239	47,193
2001	2,212,377	1,119,862	1,092,515	956,384	1,255,993	531,260	425,124	588,602	667,391	1,247,285	965,092	909,612	55,480
2002	2,354,634	1,212,107	1,142,527	1,009,726	1,344,908	566,930	442,796	645,177	699,731	1,319,138	1,035,496	959,385	76,111
2003	2,431,117	1,280,880	1,150,237	1,032,892	1,398,225	589,190	443,702	691,690	706,535	1,335,595	1,095,522	994,375	101,147
2004	2,491,414	1,325,841	1,165,573	1,047,214	1,444,200	598,727	448,487	727,114	717,086	1,329,532	1,161,882	1,022,319	139,563
2005	2,523,511	1,350,581	1,172,930	1,047,054	1,476,457	602,525	444,529	748,056	728,401	1,324,104	1,199,407	1,036,324	163,083
2006	2,574,568	1,386,226	1,188,342	1,061,059	1,513,509	614,709	446,350	771,517	741,992	1,332,707	1,241,861	1,064,626	177,235
2007	2,644,357	1,428,914	1,215,443	1,088,314	1,556,043	632,576	455,738	796,338	759,705	1,353,197	1,291,160	1,100,823	190,337
2008	2,737,076	1,492,813	1,244,263	1,122,272	1,614,804	656,926	465,346	835,887	778,917	1,380,936	1,356,140	1,124,987	231,153
2009	2,849,415	1,567,080	1,282,335	1,169,777	1,679,638	689,977	479,800	877,103	802,535	1,424,393	1,425,022	1,172,501	252,521
2010	2,937,011	1,630,142	1,306,869	1,209,477	1,727,534	719,408	490,069	910,734	816,800	1,439,171	1,497,840	1,201,489	296,351
2011	2,933,287	1,637,356	1,295,931	1,211,264	1,722,023	722,265	488,999	915,091	806,932	1,421,404	1,511,883	1,207,896	303,987
2012	2,910,388	1,639,234	1,271,154	1,205,186	1,705,202	725,096	480,090	914,138	791,064	1,406,600	1,503,788	1,208,503	295,285
2013	2,900,954	1,658,618	1,242,336	1,201,160	1,699,794	732,594	468,566	926,024	773,770	1,398,556	1,502,398	1,216,557	285,841
2014[1]	2,933,000	1,698,000	1,234,000	1,260,000	1,673,000	780,000	479,000	918,000	755,000	1,415,000	1,518,000	—	—
2015[1]	2,953,000	1,710,000	1,243,000	1,271,000	1,682,000	793,000	478,000	917,000	765,000	1,425,000	1,529,000	—	—
2016[1]	3,013,000	1,749,000	1,264,000	1,293,000	1,720,000	809,000	484,000	940,000	780,000	1,454,000	1,560,000	—	—
2017[1]	3,102,000	1,804,000	1,298,000	1,329,000	1,773,000	830,000	498,000	973,000	800,000	1,496,000	1,606,000	—	—
2018[1]	3,173,000	1,842,000	1,331,000	1,360,000	1,813,000	847,000	513,000	995,000	818,000	1,531,000	1,643,000	—	—
2019[1]	3,225,000	1,866,000	1,359,000	1,382,000	1,843,000	859,000	522,000	1,007,000	836,000	1,556,000	1,670,000	—	—
2020[1]	3,268,000	1,888,000	1,381,000	1,399,000	1,869,000	869,000	530,000	1,018,000	851,000	1,577,000	1,692,000	—	—
2021[1]	3,325,000	1,917,000	1,408,000	1,424,000	1,901,000	882,000	542,000	1,035,000	866,000	1,604,000	1,721,000	—	—
2022[1]	3,391,000	1,953,000	1,438,000	1,454,000	1,937,000	898,000	556,000	1,055,000	882,000	1,636,000	1,755,000	—	—
2023[1]	3,458,000	1,991,000	1,467,000	1,483,000	1,975,000	913,000	569,000	1,078,000	898,000	1,669,000	1,790,000	—	—
2024[1]	3,495,000	2,007,000	1,488,000	1,500,000	1,994,000	921,000	579,000	1,086,000	908,000	1,686,000	1,809,000	—	—

—Not available.
[1]Projected.
NOTE: Data include unclassified graduate students. Data through 1995 are for institutions of higher education, while later data are for degree-granting institutions. Degree-granting institutions grant associate's or higher degrees and participate in Title IV federal financial aid programs. The degree-granting classification is very similar to the earlier higher education classification, but it includes more 2-year colleges and excludes a few higher education institutions that did not grant degrees. Some data have been revised from previously published figures.

SOURCE: U.S. Department of Education, National Center for Education Statistics, Higher Education General Information Survey (HEGIS), "Fall Enrollment in Colleges and Universities" surveys, 1967 through 1985; Integrated Postsecondary Education Data System (IPEDS), "Fall Enrollment Survey" (IPEDS-EF:86–99); IPEDS Spring 2001 through Spring 2014, Enrollment component; and Enrollment in Degree-Granting Institutions Projection Model, 1980 through 2024. (This table was prepared March 2015.)

Table 303.90. Fall enrollment and number of degree-granting postsecondary institutions, by control and religious affiliation of institution: Selected years, 1980 through 2013

Control and religious affiliation of institution	Total enrollment						Enrollment, fall 2013					Number of institutions[1]				
								Full-time		Part-time						
	Fall 1980	Fall 1990	Fall 2000	Fall 2010	Fall 2011	Fall 2012	Total	Males	Females	Males	Females	Fall 1980	Fall 1990	Fall 2000	Fall 2010	Fall 2013
1	2	3	4	5	6	7	8	9	10	11	12	13	14	15	16	17
All institutions	12,096,895	13,818,637	15,312,289	21,019,438	21,010,590	20,642,819	20,375,789	5,682,166	6,914,946	3,178,620	4,600,057	3,226	3,501	4,056	4,589	4,716
Public institutions	9,457,394	10,844,717	11,752,786	15,142,171	15,116,303	14,880,343	14,745,558	3,949,205	4,515,604	2,619,634	3,661,115	1,493	1,548	1,676	1,652	1,625
Federal	50,989	50,669	16,917	21,610	21,304	20,691	19,802	13,278	5,077	468	979	12	17	12	14	14
State	(²)	7,181,380	9,548,090	12,364,881	12,351,143	12,195,526	12,120,534	3,447,896	3,963,904	1,956,501	2,752,233	(²)	978	1,355	1,331	1,313
Local	(²)	3,508,941	2,078,090	2,542,044	2,528,020	2,453,053	2,398,360	434,304	484,696	626,154	853,206	(²)	523	277	261	257
Other public	9,406,405	103,727	109,689	213,636	215,836	211,073	206,862	53,727	61,927	36,511	54,697	1,481	30	32	46	41
Private institutions	2,639,501	2,973,920	3,559,503	5,877,267	5,894,287	5,762,476	5,630,231	1,732,961	2,399,342	558,986	938,942	1,733	1,953	2,380	2,937	3,091
Independent nonprofit	1,521,614	1,474,818	1,577,242	1,994,900	2,054,955	2,064,076	2,089,266	714,810	864,027	204,095	306,334	795	709	729	736	791
For-profit	111,714	213,693	450,084	2,022,785	1,967,468	1,808,898	1,656,227	419,924	726,326	179,120	330,857	164	322	724	1,310	1,416
Religiously affiliated[3]	1,006,173	1,285,409	1,532,177	1,859,582	1,871,864	1,889,502	1,884,738	598,227	808,989	175,771	301,751	774	922	927	891	884
Advent Christian Church	143	—	—	1,536	1,537	1,459	1,541	844	648	25	24	1	1	1	3	3
African Methodist Episcopal Zion Church	1,091	88	34	2,674	2,355	2,674	2,700	1,080	1,419	74	127	3	1	1	5	6
African Methodist Episcopal	4,541	3,220	5,980	15,120	15,027	14,229	13,990	4,187	5,400	1,445	2,958	6	5	6	18	18
American Baptist	6,131	10,800	15,410	1,340	1,415	1,315	1,341	615	653	36	37	11	15	17	1	1
American Evangelical Lutheran Church	—	—	743	—	—	—	—	—	—	—	—	—	—	—	—	—
American Lutheran and Lutheran Church in America	3,092	—	1,460	—	—	—	—	—	—	—	—	3	—	1	—	—
American Lutheran	21,608	8,307	14,272	15,806	15,449	15,320	15,953	5,355	6,758	1,699	2,141	13	11	14	16	14
Assemblies of God Church	7,814	99,510	107,610	174,538	172,940	112,351	111,586	36,180	47,466	11,285	16,655	10	69	68	69	71
Baptist	38,231	958	2,088	8,506	7,766	7,979	8,070	2,080	2,959	1,460	1,571	33	3	3	3	3
Brethren Church	3,925	2,239	2,797	6,455	6,536	6,688	6,530	2,074	2,895	673	888	3	1	1	4	4
Brethren in Christ Church	1,301	2,519	5,278	52,839	54,401	54,915	47,253	14,302	21,189	4,681	7,081	1	4	4	18	17
Christian and Missionary Alliance Church	1,705	30,397	35,984	10,074	10,488	10,700	10,536	4,201	4,214	1,085	1,036	3	18	18	18	19
Christian Church (Disciples of Christ)	14,913	2,263	7,277	4,817	4,514	4,048	4,191	2,193	1,849	76	73	12	8	18	18	3
Christian Churches and Churches of Christ	1,342	2,174	1,502	5,625	5,647	5,697	5,770	2,644	2,791	182	153	7	4	1	3	3
Christian Methodist Episcopal	2,486	4,488	5,999	16,731	17,093	17,821	17,977	5,422	8,132	1,888	2,535	4	2	3	3	8
Christian Reformed Church	5,408	2,557	—	—	—	—	—	—	—	—	—	3	2	—	—	—
Church of Christ (Scientist)	2,773	249	—	—	—	—	—	—	—	—	—	6	8	—	—	—
Church of God of Prophecy	—	—	—	—	—	—	—	—	—	—	—	9	—	—	—	—
Church of God	6,082	5,627	—	—	—	—	—	—	—	—	—	1	9	—	—	—
Church of New Jerusalem	170	—	—	—	—	—	—	—	—	—	—	—	—	—	—	—
Church of the Brethren	8,482	4,463	4,187	6,154	6,028	6,261	6,245	2,468	3,187	223	367	6	5	4	5	6
Church of the Nazarene	11,716	10,779	16,661	21,144	20,866	21,401	21,597	6,216	9,991	1,958	3,432	10	9	12	9	10
Churches of Christ	9,343	14,611	30,140	35,538	36,472	35,871	35,281	11,535	15,338	3,221	5,187	9	19	19	17	17
Cumberland Presbyterian	594	746	1,112	4,652	5,744	6,500	6,926	2,317	3,146	604	859	2	2	2	2	2
Episcopal Church, Reformed	67	—	—	—	—	1,204	1,238	69	398	91	680	1	—	—	—	1
Evangelical Christian	—	—	—	—	—	74,372	77,338	15,335	21,018	16,060	24,925	—	1	1	1	1
Evangelical Congregational Church	80	88	148	153	125	123	113	13	18	54	28	1	1	1	1	1
Evangelical Covenant Church of America	1,401	1,035	2,387	3,233	3,220	3,141	3,189	772	1,247	371	799	1	1	1	2	2
Evangelical Free Church of America	833	2,355	4,022	2,926	2,833	2,651	2,472	790	557	680	445	2	2	3	2	2
Evangelical Lutheran Church	743	49,210	49,085	56,162	55,889	52,122	51,796	20,529	25,946	2,066	3,255	3	33	34	33	31
Free Methodist	5,543	5,902	7,323	12,270	12,412	12,254	12,372	3,463	6,099	771	2,039	5	3	4	5	5
Free Will Baptist Church	1,132	1,177	2,378	528	534	568	570	241	180	88	61	4	3	4	3	3
Friends United Meeting	1,109	—	—	—	—	—	—	—	—	—	—	1	1	—	—	—
Friends	5,157	5,844	10,898	13,876	13,570	12,921	12,555	4,537	5,403	1,046	1,569	5	6	8	7	7
General Conference Mennonite Church	820	1,243	1,059	—	—	—	—	—	—	—	—	2	2	1	—	—
Greek Orthodox	204	148	132	220	222	209	208	148	52	6	2	1	2	1	1	1
Interdenominational	1,254	11,103	9,788	33,778	38,136	39,376	39,277	12,937	16,195	4,749	5,396	4	17	14	31	32
Jewish	5,738	12,217	14,182	12,755	14,720	15,120	15,390	9,866	3,380	713	1,431	24	63	62	36	35
Latter-Day Saints	39,172	42,274	44,680	53,514	57,150	63,027	63,733	23,085	22,319	8,120	10,209	4	4	4	4	4
Lutheran Church—Missouri Synod	11,727	13,827	18,866	28,255	29,288	30,332	34,105	8,265	14,157	3,681	8,002	15	14	13	12	12

See notes at end of table.

Table 303.90. Fall enrollment and number of degree-granting postsecondary institutions, by control and religious affiliation of institution: Selected years, 1980 through 2013—Continued

Control and religious affiliation of institution	Total enrollment						Enrollment, fall 2013					Number of institutions[1]				
								Full-time		Part-time						
	Fall 1980	Fall 1990	Fall 2000	Fall 2010	Fall 2011	Fall 2012	Total	Males	Females	Males	Females	Fall 1980	Fall 1990	Fall 2000	Fall 2010	Fall 2013
1	2	3	4	5	6	7	8	9	10	11	12	13	14	15	16	17
Lutheran Church in America	23,877	5,796	4,322	8,240	8,111	8,193	8,732	3,508	4,392	255	577	20	5	2	3	3
Mennonite Brethren Church	1,344	1,864	2,390	4,136	4,302	4,121	4,129	1,100	1,888	343	798	3	3	3	3	2
Mennonite Church	4,008	2,859	3,553	4,263	4,366	4,236	4,265	1,462	1,917	310	576	6	5	5	6	6
Missionary Church Inc.	487	699	1,647	2,152	2,074	1,963	1,804	477	856	157	314	1	1	1	1	1
Moravian Church	2,434	2,511	2,939	3,095	3,132	3,075	3,024	633	1,659	146	586	2	2	2	2	2
Multiple Protestant denominations	5,526	211	4,690	5,350	5,400	5,274	5,126	1,235	1,478	1,462	951	8	1	7	6	6
North American Baptist	155	211	124	120	141	148	143	30	24	51	38	1	1	1	1	1
Original Free Will Baptist	—	—	—	3,855	3,825	3,714	3,414	547	839	593	1,435	—	—	1	1	1
Pentecostal Holiness Church	767	566	976	1,272	1,504	1,524	1,653	647	655	137	214	3	3	2	3	2
Presbyterian	—	—	—	—	—	—	2,882	941	1,460	164	317	—	—	—	—	2
Presbyterian U.S.A.	47,144	77,700	78,950	85,719	86,696	86,699	83,648	30,805	40,742	3,917	8,184	57	70	64	58	57
Presbyterian Church in America	—	1,877	4,499	2,071	1,792	1,803	1,775	672	687	286	130	1	1	5	2	2
Protestant Episcopal	5,396	4,559	5,479	5,006	4,604	4,202	3,935	1,822	1,842	117	154	12	9	12	11	8
Protestant, other	4,072	38,136	30,116	13,450	14,688	16,167	16,884	5,054	5,918	2,706	3,206	11	44	34	23	24
Reformed Church in America	2,713	5,525	6,002	6,555	6,501	6,502	6,453	2,560	3,365	229	299	4	4	5	5	5
Reformed Presbyterian Church	2,014	1,556	2,355	2,982	2,866	2,700	2,748	1,233	1,217	160	138	4	2	2	3	3
Reorganized Latter-Day Saints Church	4,274	4,793	3,390	—	—	—	—	—	—	—	—	2	1	2	3	3
Roman Catholic	422,842	530,585	636,336	751,091	749,609	746,942	740,576	220,340	324,091	65,165	130,980	229	239	239	237	233
Russian Orthodox	47	38	106	60	53	55	81	58	10	11	2	1	1	1	1	1
Seventh-Day Adventists	19,168	15,771	19,223	25,430	25,751	26,343	25,590	8,179	11,284	2,176	3,951	11	11	13	14	13
Southern Baptist	85,281	49,493	54,275	49,936	51,832	52,610	55,363	16,146	21,185	7,454	10,578	54	29	32	22	23
Undenominational	—	6,758	23,573	27,748	29,653	29,966	32,391	8,708	12,094	4,947	6,642	—	14	16	16	18
Unitarian Universalist	87	82	132	166	190	227	174	24	54	31	65	2	2	2	2	2
United Brethren Church	545	601	938	1,260	1,260	1,204	1,124	413	577	62	72	1	1	1	1	1
United Church of Christ	14,169	20,175	23,709	20,537	17,627	17,473	16,850	5,350	6,555	1,775	3,170	16	18	18	17	14
United Methodist	127,099	148,851	171,109	206,744	206,268	204,506	203,116	74,062	94,938	12,562	21,554	91	96	100	96	94
Wesleyan Church	3,583	5,311	11,128	20,670	20,577	20,160	19,733	5,933	11,118	955	1,727	5	4	4	6	6
Wisconsin Evangelical Lutheran Synod	808	931	1,660	1,677	1,799	1,889	2,002	823	898	142	139	1	3	2	2	2
Other religiously affiliated	462	5,743	2,534	4,778	4,866	5,340	5,280	1,702	2,242	347	989	1	9	4	11	10

—Not available.
[1]Counts of institutions in this table may be lower than reported in other tables, because counts in this table include only institutions reporting separate enrollment data.
[2]Included under "Other public."
[3]Religious affiliation as reported by institution.
NOTE: Data for 1980 and 1990 are for institutions of higher education, while later data are for institutions of higher education. Degree-granting institutions grant associate's or higher degrees and participate in Title IV federal financial aid programs. The degree-granting classification is very similar to the earlier higher education classification, but it includes more 2-year colleges and excludes a few higher education institutions that did not grant degrees. Some data have been revised from previously published figures.

SOURCE: U.S. Department of Education, National Center for Education Statistics, Higher Education General Information Survey (HEGIS), "Fall Enrollment in Institutions of Higher Education" and "Institutional Characteristics" surveys, 1980; Integrated Postsecondary Education Data System (IPEDS), "Fall Enrollment Survey" (IPEDS-EF:90) and "Institutional Characteristics Survey" (IPEDS-IC:90); and IPEDS Spring 2001 through Spring 2014, Enrollment component. (This table was prepared June 2015.)

Table 304.10. Total fall enrollment in degree-granting postsecondary institutions, by state or jurisdiction: Selected years, 1970 through 2013

State or jurisdiction	Fall 1970	Fall 1980	Fall 1990	Fall 2000	Fall 2008	Fall 2009	Fall 2010	Fall 2011	Fall 2012	Fall 2013	Percent change, 2008 to 2013
1	2	3	4	5	6	7	8	9	10	11	12
United States	8,580,887	12,096,895	13,818,637	15,312,289	19,102,814	20,313,594	21,019,438	21,010,590	20,642,819	20,375,789	6.7
Alabama	103,936	164,306	218,589	233,962	310,941	311,641	327,606	320,349	310,311	305,712	-1.7
Alaska	9,471	21,296	29,833	27,953	30,717	32,406	34,799	34,932	32,797	34,890	13.6
Arizona	109,619	202,716	264,148	342,490	704,245	738,753	793,871	796,974	736,379	694,123	-1.4
Arkansas	52,039	77,607	90,425	115,172	158,374	168,081	175,848	179,345	176,458	172,224	8.7
California	1,257,245	1,790,993	1,808,740	2,256,708	2,652,241	2,732,147	2,714,699	2,691,852	2,621,460	2,636,921	-0.6
Colorado	123,395	162,916	227,131	263,872	325,232	345,034	369,450	365,939	362,935	358,723	10.3
Connecticut	124,700	159,632	168,604	161,243	184,178	191,790	199,384	201,638	201,658	200,966	9.1
Delaware	25,260	32,939	42,004	43,897	53,088	54,735	55,258	56,547	58,128	59,615	12.3
District of Columbia	77,158	86,675	79,551	72,689	126,110	136,792	91,992	90,245	90,150	89,257	-29.2
Florida	235,525	411,891	588,086	707,684	972,699	1,051,917	1,124,778	1,149,160	1,154,929	1,125,810	15.7
Georgia	126,511	184,159	251,786	346,204	476,581	531,510	568,916	565,414	545,358	533,424	11.9
Hawaii	36,562	47,181	56,436	60,182	70,104	74,668	78,073	79,006	78,456	76,434	9.0
Idaho	34,567	43,018	51,881	65,594	80,456	84,349	85,201	90,142	108,008	109,318	35.9
Illinois	452,146	644,245	729,246	743,918	859,242	893,207	906,845	892,452	867,110	842,888	-1.9
Indiana	192,668	247,253	284,832	314,334	401,956	441,031	459,493	457,506	447,262	444,364	10.6
Iowa	108,902	140,449	170,515	188,974	286,891	351,036	381,867	372,146	361,183	339,738	18.4
Kansas	102,485	136,605	163,733	179,968	198,991	210,819	214,849	216,662	213,786	215,855	8.5
Kentucky	98,591	143,066	177,852	188,341	257,583	277,876	291,104	293,766	282,125	273,073	6.0
Louisiana	120,728	160,058	186,840	223,800	236,375	251,468	263,676	265,740	258,825	251,887	6.6
Maine	34,134	43,264	57,186	58,473	67,796	70,183	72,406	72,297	72,810	70,849	4.5
Maryland	149,607	225,526	259,700	273,745	338,914	358,775	377,967	380,097	374,496	363,771	7.3
Massachusetts	303,809	418,415	417,833	421,142	477,056	497,234	507,753	508,546	516,331	514,008	7.7
Michigan	392,726	520,131	569,803	567,631	652,799	685,628	697,765	685,420	663,825	643,592	-1.4
Minnesota	160,788	206,691	253,789	293,445	411,055	442,109	465,449	457,737	451,661	441,491	7.4
Mississippi	73,967	102,364	122,883	137,389	160,441	173,136	179,995	180,576	176,665	173,634	8.2
Missouri	183,930	234,421	289,899	321,348	396,409	424,541	444,750	456,994	441,371	438,222	10.5
Montana	30,062	35,177	35,876	42,240	47,840	51,588	53,282	54,042	53,254	52,777	10.3
Nebraska	66,915	89,488	112,831	112,117	130,458	139,594	144,692	142,875	139,578	137,943	5.7
Nevada	13,669	40,455	61,728	87,893	120,490	124,896	129,360	121,013	118,300	116,738	-3.1
New Hampshire	29,400	46,794	59,510	61,718	71,739	74,234	75,539	77,436	82,678	92,440	28.9
New Jersey	216,121	321,610	324,286	335,945	410,160	431,978	444,092	443,750	439,965	436,939	6.5
New Mexico	44,461	58,283	85,500	110,739	142,413	153,055	162,552	159,058	156,424	153,455	7.8
New York	806,479	992,237	1,048,286	1,043,395	1,234,858	1,290,046	1,305,151	1,318,076	1,309,986	1,304,230	5.6
North Carolina	171,925	287,537	352,138	404,652	528,977	567,841	585,792	585,013	578,031	575,198	8.7
North Dakota	31,495	34,069	37,878	40,248	51,327	54,456	56,903	56,482	55,169	55,063	7.3
Ohio	376,267	489,145	557,690	549,553	653,585	712,192	745,115	735,034	709,818	697,647	6.7
Oklahoma	110,155	160,295	173,221	178,016	206,757	220,377	230,560	230,176	228,464	220,897	6.8
Oregon	122,177	157,458	165,741	183,065	220,474	243,271	251,708	259,064	254,695	251,106	13.9
Pennsylvania	411,044	507,716	604,060	609,521	740,288	778,054	804,640	787,960	777,242	765,582	3.4
Rhode Island	45,898	66,869	78,273	75,450	83,893	84,673	85,110	84,647	83,952	83,460	-0.5
South Carolina	69,518	132,476	159,302	185,931	230,695	246,525	257,064	260,002	259,617	257,844	11.8
South Dakota	30,639	32,761	34,208	43,221	50,444	53,342	58,360	55,899	56,058	55,129	9.3
Tennessee	135,103	204,581	226,238	263,910	307,610	332,555	351,762	350,186	343,641	338,197	9.9
Texas	442,225	701,391	901,437	1,033,973	1,327,148	1,447,028	1,535,864	1,564,208	1,540,298	1,541,378	16.1
Utah	81,687	93,987	121,303	163,776	217,224	236,204	255,653	264,394	267,309	264,255	21.7
Vermont	22,209	30,628	36,398	35,489	42,946	44,975	45,572	45,143	44,703	43,534	1.4
Virginia	151,915	280,504	353,442	381,893	500,796	544,665	577,922	589,145	588,696	583,755	16.6
Washington	183,544	303,603	263,384	320,840	362,535	382,613	388,116	372,839	365,514	363,377	0.2
West Virginia	63,153	81,973	84,790	87,888	125,333	142,492	152,431	162,347	162,179	157,954	26.0
Wisconsin	202,058	269,086	299,774	307,179	352,875	373,307	384,181	376,535	369,732	364,021	3.2
Wyoming	15,220	21,147	31,326	30,004	35,936	37,019	38,298	38,092	37,812	37,084	3.2
U.S. Service Academies[1]	17,079	49,808	48,692	13,475	15,539	15,748	15,925	15,692	15,227	14,997	-3.5
Other jurisdictions	67,237	137,749	164,618	194,633	236,167	243,447	264,240	267,159	259,943	254,543	7.8
American Samoa	0	976	1,219	297	1,806	2,189	2,193	2,091	1,795	1,488	-17.6
Federated States of Micronesia	0	224	975	1,576	2,457	3,401	2,699	2,915	2,744	2,446	-0.4
Guam	2,719	3,217	4,741	5,215	5,351	5,755	6,188	6,360	5,924	6,518	21.8
Marshall Islands	0	0	0	328	689	847	869	989	1,123	1,000	45.1
Northern Marianas	0	0	661	1,078	791	989	1,137	1,046	1,178	1,109	40.2
Palau	0	0	491	581	502	651	694	742	680	646	28.7
Puerto Rico	63,073	131,184	154,065	183,290	222,178	227,013	247,727	250,402	244,076	239,015	7.6
U.S. Virgin Islands	1,445	2,148	2,466	2,268	2,393	2,602	2,733	2,614	2,423	2,321	-3.0

[1]Data for 2000 and later years reflect a substantial reduction in the number of Department of Defense institutions included in the IPEDS survey.
NOTE: Data through 1990 are for institutions of higher education, while later data are for degree-granting institutions. Degree-granting institutions grant associate's or higher degrees and participate in Title IV federal financial aid programs. The degree-granting classification is very similar to the earlier higher education classification, but it includes more 2-year colleges and excludes a few higher education institutions that did not grant degrees. Some data have been revised from previously published figures.
SOURCE: U.S. Department of Education, National Center for Education Statistics, Higher Education General Information Survey (HEGIS), "Fall Enrollment in Colleges and Universities" surveys, 1970 and 1980; Integrated Postsecondary Education Data System (IPEDS), "Fall Enrollment Survey" (IPEDS-EF:90); and IPEDS Spring 2001 through Spring 2014, Enrollment component. (This table was prepared October 2014.)

Table 304.15. Total fall enrollment in public degree-granting postsecondary institutions, by state or jurisdiction: Selected years, 1970 through 2013

State or jurisdiction	Fall 1970	Fall 1980	Fall 1990	Fall 2000	Fall 2008	Fall 2009	Fall 2010	Fall 2011	Fall 2012	Fall 2013	Percent change, 2008 to 2013
1	2	3	4	5	6	7	8	9	10	11	12
United States	6,428,134	9,457,394	10,844,717	11,752,786	13,972,153	14,810,768	15,142,171	15,116,303	14,880,343	14,745,558	5.5
Alabama	87,884	143,674	195,939	207,435	245,040	260,277	267,083	260,523	251,045	248,284	1.3
Alaska	8,563	20,561	27,792	26,559	29,167	30,493	32,303	32,158	30,595	31,600	8.3
Arizona	107,315	194,034	248,213	284,522	331,310	350,435	366,976	366,116	359,229	354,462	7.0
Arkansas	43,599	66,068	78,645	101,775	140,706	149,474	155,780	158,824	157,224	153,690	9.2
California	1,123,529	1,599,838	1,594,710	1,927,771	2,239,487	2,289,427	2,223,163	2,181,675	2,129,152	2,148,147	-4.1
Colorado	108,562	145,598	200,653	217,897	235,265	255,438	269,433	269,298	272,444	271,223	15.3
Connecticut	73,391	97,788	109,556	101,027	118,694	123,211	127,194	126,487	124,952	123,093	3.7
Delaware	21,151	28,325	34,252	34,194	38,952	39,989	39,935	40,729	41,113	40,992	5.2
District of Columbia	12,194	13,900	11,990	5,499	5,584	5,253	5,840	5,312	5,476	5,347	-4.2
Florida	189,450	334,349	489,081	556,912	709,593	759,479	790,027	803,200	804,693	795,860	12.2
Georgia	101,900	140,158	196,413	271,755	376,468	418,037	436,047	428,708	422,189	413,706	9.9
Hawaii	32,963	43,269	45,728	44,579	53,526	57,945	60,090	60,330	60,295	58,941	10.1
Idaho	27,072	34,491	41,315	53,751	61,190	63,261	64,204	65,753	78,781	75,910	24.1
Illinois	315,634	491,274	551,333	534,155	560,411	588,741	585,515	577,043	557,137	546,483	-2.5
Indiana	136,739	189,224	223,953	240,023	296,950	325,072	337,705	339,946	333,769	335,923	13.1
Iowa	68,390	97,454	117,834	135,008	157,019	171,283	177,781	178,491	173,558	168,644	7.4
Kansas	88,215	121,987	149,117	159,976	172,640	182,736	185,623	186,475	183,976	184,075	6.6
Kentucky	77,240	114,884	147,095	151,973	208,970	221,508	229,725	233,427	224,092	218,472	4.5
Louisiana	101,127	136,703	158,290	189,213	203,098	215,511	224,811	225,210	220,971	215,653	6.2
Maine	25,405	31,878	41,500	40,662	48,191	49,668	50,903	50,253	50,270	49,602	2.9
Maryland	118,988	195,051	220,783	223,797	280,603	298,185	309,779	314,383	310,503	301,565	7.5
Massachusetts	116,127	183,765	186,035	183,248	205,820	218,999	224,542	227,006	228,178	228,255	10.9
Michigan	339,625	454,147	487,359	467,861	528,040	553,022	562,448	554,704	540,242	527,740	-0.1
Minnesota	130,567	162,379	199,211	218,617	256,633	270,336	276,176	274,192	272,290	266,440	3.8
Mississippi	64,968	90,661	109,038	125,355	144,224	155,517	161,493	161,842	157,995	154,916	7.4
Missouri	132,540	165,179	200,093	201,509	228,737	245,568	256,030	260,585	257,430	254,650	11.3
Montana	27,287	31,178	31,865	37,387	43,565	46,653	48,231	48,912	48,333	47,851	9.8
Nebraska	51,454	73,509	94,614	88,531	99,593	104,149	107,979	106,794	104,166	101,893	2.3
Nevada	13,576	40,280	61,242	83,120	108,559	112,397	113,103	105,048	103,619	102,538	-5.5
New Hampshire	15,979	24,119	32,163	35,870	42,192	43,507	44,077	43,325	43,289	42,711	1.2
New Jersey	145,373	247,028	261,601	266,921	328,838	348,934	358,256	359,458	356,456	352,822	7.3
New Mexico	40,795	55,077	83,403	101,450	132,983	143,987	150,844	148,018	146,792	144,381	8.6
New York	449,437	563,251	616,884	583,417	675,892	712,467	723,500	731,914	722,274	720,934	6.7
North Carolina	123,761	228,154	285,405	329,422	434,976	469,590	475,064	470,989	465,684	460,100	5.8
North Dakota	30,192	31,709	34,690	36,014	44,268	46,727	48,904	49,578	48,929	48,751	10.1
Ohio	281,099	381,765	427,613	411,161	475,521	522,033	547,551	542,733	524,338	520,039	9.4
Oklahoma	91,438	137,188	151,073	153,699	178,253	189,953	197,641	197,373	195,111	187,078	5.0
Oregon	108,483	140,102	144,427	154,756	181,515	201,246	208,001	215,469	212,310	208,317	14.8
Pennsylvania	232,982	292,499	343,478	339,229	404,976	425,979	432,923	428,335	425,890	419,849	3.7
Rhode Island	25,527	35,052	42,350	38,458	42,601	43,409	43,224	43,254	43,204	42,786	0.4
South Carolina	47,101	107,683	131,134	155,519	187,253	200,204	205,080	208,302	209,023	207,717	10.9
South Dakota	23,936	24,328	26,596	34,857	39,743	41,674	44,569	43,729	44,185	44,272	11.4
Tennessee	98,897	156,835	175,049	202,530	214,140	231,741	242,486	241,917	235,010	229,302	7.1
Texas	365,522	613,552	802,314	896,534	1,163,132	1,258,841	1,334,110	1,366,829	1,347,860	1,349,609	16.0
Utah	49,588	59,598	86,108	123,046	158,037	170,921	179,061	179,208	171,001	168,311	6.5
Vermont	12,536	17,984	20,910	20,021	25,552	27,028	27,524	27,132	26,501	25,852	1.2
Virginia	123,279	246,500	291,286	313,780	383,121	401,093	409,004	413,761	409,753	405,915	5.9
Washington	162,718	276,028	227,632	273,928	312,071	328,391	330,853	317,066	311,497	310,192	-0.6
West Virginia	51,363	71,228	74,108	76,136	88,695	94,533	96,104	95,634	93,017	90,782	2.4
Wisconsin	170,374	235,179	253,529	249,737	280,394	295,090	301,259	296,795	293,416	289,339	3.2
Wyoming	15,220	21,121	30,623	28,715	34,426	35,608	36,292	36,368	35,859	35,547	3.3
U.S. Service Academies[1]	17,079	49,808	48,692	13,475	15,539	15,748	15,925	15,692	15,227	14,997	-3.5
Other jurisdictions	46,680	60,692	66,244	84,464	82,424	87,030	83,719	78,928	78,369	78,136	-5.2
American Samoa	0	976	1,219	297	1,806	2,189	2,193	2,091	1,795	1,488	-17.6
Federated States of Micronesia	0	224	975	1,576	2,457	3,401	2,699	2,915	2,744	2,446	-0.4
Guam	2,719	3,217	4,741	5,215	5,202	5,661	6,103	6,274	5,847	6,439	23.8
Marshall Islands	0	0	0	328	689	847	869	989	1,123	1,000	45.1
Northern Marianas	0	0	661	1,078	791	989	1,137	1,046	1,178	1,109	40.2
Palau	0	0	491	581	502	651	694	742	680	646	28.7
Puerto Rico	42,516	54,127	55,691	73,121	68,584	70,690	67,291	62,257	62,579	62,687	-8.6
U.S. Virgin Islands	1,445	2,148	2,466	2,268	2,393	2,602	2,733	2,614	2,423	2,321	-3.0

[1]Data for 2000 and later years reflect a substantial reduction in the number of Department of Defense institutions included in the IPEDS survey.

NOTE: Data through 1990 are for institutions of higher education, while later data are for degree-granting institutions. Degree-granting institutions grant associate's or higher degrees and participate in Title IV federal financial aid programs. The degree-granting classification is very similar to the earlier higher education classification, but it includes more 2-year colleges and excludes a few higher education institutions that did not grant degrees. Some data have been revised from previously published figures.

SOURCE: U.S. Department of Education, National Center for Education Statistics, Higher Education General Information Survey (HEGIS), "Fall Enrollment in Colleges and Universities" surveys, 1970 and 1980; Integrated Postsecondary Education Data System (IPEDS), "Fall Enrollment Survey" (IPEDS-EF:90); and IPEDS Spring 2001 through Spring 2014, Enrollment component. (This table was prepared October 2014.)

Table 304.20. Total fall enrollment in private degree-granting postsecondary institutions, by state or jurisdiction: Selected years, 1970 through 2013

State or jurisdiction	Fall 1970	Fall 1980	Fall 1990	Fall 2000	Fall 2008	Fall 2009	Fall 2010	Fall 2011	Fall 2012	Fall 2013	Percent change, 2008 to 2013
1	2	3	4	5	6	7	8	9	10	11	12
United States	2,152,753	2,639,501	2,973,920	3,559,503	5,130,661	5,502,826	5,877,267	5,894,287	5,762,476	5,630,231	9.7
Alabama	16,052	20,632	22,650	26,527	65,901	51,364	60,523	59,826	59,266	57,428	-12.9
Alaska	908	735	2,041	1,394	1,550	1,913	2,496	2,774	2,202	3,290	112.3
Arizona	2,304	8,682	15,935	57,968	372,935	388,318	426,895	430,858	377,150	339,661	-8.9
Arkansas	8,440	11,539	11,780	13,397	17,668	18,607	20,068	20,521	19,234	18,534	4.9
California	133,716	191,155	214,030	328,937	412,754	442,720	491,536	510,177	492,308	488,774	18.4
Colorado	14,833	17,318	26,478	45,975	89,967	89,596	100,017	96,641	90,491	87,500	-2.7
Connecticut	51,309	61,844	59,048	60,216	65,484	68,579	72,190	75,151	76,706	77,873	18.9
Delaware	4,109	4,614	7,752	9,703	14,136	14,746	15,323	15,818	17,015	18,623	31.7
District of Columbia	64,964	72,775	67,561	67,190	120,526	131,539	86,152	84,933	84,674	83,910	-30.4
Florida	46,075	77,542	99,005	150,772	263,106	292,438	334,751	345,960	350,236	329,950	25.4
Georgia	24,611	44,001	55,373	74,449	100,113	113,473	132,869	136,706	123,169	119,718	19.6
Hawaii	3,599	3,912	10,708	15,603	16,578	16,723	17,983	18,676	18,161	17,493	5.5
Idaho	7,495	8,527	10,566	11,843	19,266	21,088	20,997	24,389	29,227	33,408	73.4
Illinois	136,512	152,971	177,913	209,763	298,831	304,466	321,330	315,409	309,973	296,405	-0.8
Indiana	55,929	58,029	60,879	74,311	105,006	115,959	121,788	117,560	113,493	108,441	3.3
Iowa	40,512	42,995	52,681	53,966	129,872	179,753	204,086	193,655	187,625	171,094	31.7
Kansas	14,270	14,618	14,616	19,992	26,351	28,083	29,226	30,187	29,810	31,780	20.6
Kentucky	21,351	28,182	30,757	36,368	48,613	56,368	61,379	60,339	58,033	54,601	12.3
Louisiana	19,601	23,355	28,550	34,587	33,277	35,957	38,865	40,530	37,854	36,234	8.9
Maine	8,729	11,386	15,686	17,811	19,605	20,515	21,503	22,044	22,540	21,247	8.4
Maryland	30,619	30,475	38,917	49,948	58,311	60,590	68,188	65,714	63,993	62,206	6.7
Massachusetts	187,682	234,650	231,798	237,894	271,236	278,235	283,211	281,540	288,153	285,753	5.4
Michigan	53,101	65,984	82,444	99,770	124,759	132,606	135,317	130,716	123,583	115,852	-7.1
Minnesota	30,221	44,312	54,578	74,828	154,422	171,773	189,273	183,545	179,371	175,051	13.4
Mississippi	8,999	11,703	13,845	12,034	16,217	17,619	18,502	18,734	18,670	18,718	15.4
Missouri	51,390	69,242	89,806	119,839	167,672	178,973	188,720	196,409	183,941	183,572	9.5
Montana	2,775	3,999	4,011	4,853	4,275	4,935	5,051	5,130	4,921	4,926	15.2
Nebraska	15,461	15,979	18,217	23,586	30,865	35,445	36,713	36,081	35,412	36,050	16.8
Nevada	93	175	486	4,773	11,931	12,499	16,257	15,965	14,681	14,200	19.0
New Hampshire	13,421	22,675	27,347	25,848	29,547	30,727	31,462	34,111	39,389	49,729	68.3
New Jersey	70,748	74,582	62,685	69,024	81,322	83,044	85,836	84,292	83,509	84,117	3.4
New Mexico	3,666	3,206	2,097	9,289	9,430	9,068	11,708	11,040	9,632	9,074	-3.8
New York	357,042	428,986	431,402	459,978	558,966	577,579	581,651	586,162	587,712	583,296	4.4
North Carolina	48,164	59,383	66,733	75,230	94,001	98,251	110,728	114,024	112,347	115,098	22.4
North Dakota	1,303	2,360	3,188	4,234	7,059	7,729	7,999	6,904	6,240	6,312	-10.6
Ohio	95,168	107,380	130,077	138,392	178,064	190,159	197,564	192,301	185,480	177,608	-0.3
Oklahoma	18,717	23,107	22,148	24,317	28,504	30,424	32,919	32,803	33,353	33,819	18.6
Oregon	13,694	17,356	21,314	28,309	38,959	42,025	43,707	43,595	42,385	42,789	9.8
Pennsylvania	178,062	215,217	260,582	270,292	335,312	352,075	371,717	359,625	351,352	345,733	3.1
Rhode Island	20,371	31,817	35,923	36,992	41,292	41,264	41,886	41,393	40,748	40,674	-1.5
South Carolina	22,417	24,793	28,168	30,412	43,442	46,321	51,984	51,700	50,594	50,127	15.4
South Dakota	6,703	8,433	7,612	8,364	10,701	11,668	13,791	12,170	11,873	10,857	1.5
Tennessee	36,206	47,746	51,189	61,380	93,470	100,814	109,276	108,269	108,631	108,895	16.5
Texas	76,703	87,839	99,123	137,439	164,016	188,187	201,754	197,379	192,438	191,769	16.9
Utah	32,099	34,389	35,195	40,730	59,187	65,283	76,592	85,186	96,308	95,944	62.1
Vermont	9,673	12,644	15,488	15,468	17,394	17,947	18,048	18,011	18,202	17,682	1.7
Virginia	28,636	34,004	62,156	68,113	117,675	143,572	168,918	175,384	178,943	177,840	51.1
Washington	20,826	27,575	35,752	46,912	50,464	54,222	57,263	55,773	54,017	53,185	5.4
West Virginia	11,790	10,745	10,682	11,752	36,638	47,959	56,327	66,713	69,162	67,172	83.3
Wisconsin	31,684	33,907	46,245	57,442	72,481	78,217	82,922	79,740	76,316	74,682	3.0
Wyoming	0	26	703	1,289	1,510	1,411	2,006	1,724	1,953	1,537	1.8
Other jurisdictions	20,557	77,057	98,374	110,169	153,743	156,417	180,521	188,231	181,574	176,407	14.7
American Samoa	0	0	0	0	0	0	0	0	0	0	†
Federated States of Micronesia	0	0	0	0	0	0	0	0	0	0	†
Guam	0	0	0	0	149	94	85	86	77	79	-47.0
Marshall Islands	0	0	0	0	0	0	0	0	0	0	†
Northern Marianas	0	0	0	0	0	0	0	0	0	0	†
Palau	0	0	0	0	0	0	0	0	0	0	†
Puerto Rico	20,557	77,057	98,374	110,169	153,594	156,323	180,436	188,145	181,497	176,328	14.8
U.S. Virgin Islands	0	0	0	0	0	0	0	0	0	0	†

†Not applicable.
NOTE: Data through 1990 are for institutions of higher education, while later data are for degree-granting institutions. Degree-granting institutions grant associate's or higher degrees and participate in Title IV federal financial aid programs. The degree-granting classification is very similar to the earlier higher education classification, but it includes more 2-year colleges and excludes a few higher education institutions that did not grant degrees. Some data have been revised from previously published figures.

SOURCE: U.S. Department of Education, National Center for Education Statistics, Higher Education General Information Survey (HEGIS), "Fall Enrollment in Colleges and Universities" surveys, 1970 and 1980; Integrated Postsecondary Education Data System (IPEDS), "Fall Enrollment Survey" (IPEDS-EF:90); and IPEDS Spring 2001 through Spring 2014, Enrollment component. (This table was prepared October 2014.)

Table 304.30. Total fall enrollment in degree-granting postsecondary institutions, by attendance status, sex, and state or jurisdiction: 2012 and 2013

State or jurisdiction	Fall 2012					Fall 2013					Percent change in total, 2012 to 2013
	Total	Full-time		Part-time		Total	Full-time		Part-time		
		Males	Females	Males	Females		Males	Females	Males	Females	
1	2	3	4	5	6	7	8	9	10	11	12
United States	20,642,819	5,709,792	7,027,221	3,209,295	4,696,511	20,375,789	5,682,166	6,914,946	3,178,620	4,600,057	-1.3
Alabama	310,311	90,166	117,546	41,347	61,252	305,712	90,022	116,634	40,092	58,964	-1.5
Alaska	32,797	6,903	8,590	6,319	10,985	34,890	7,090	9,311	7,190	11,299	6.4
Arizona	736,379	189,906	312,036	90,374	144,063	694,123	179,273	280,864	89,686	144,300	-5.7
Arkansas	176,458	48,732	64,126	23,991	39,609	172,224	48,312	62,455	23,371	38,086	-2.4
California	2,621,460	643,499	767,810	552,645	657,506	2,636,921	658,149	783,689	549,589	645,494	0.6
Colorado	362,935	96,877	112,802	64,992	88,264	358,723	97,207	110,187	63,491	87,838	-1.2
Connecticut	201,658	57,725	69,247	27,619	47,067	200,966	58,225	69,394	27,432	45,915	-0.3
Delaware	58,128	16,066	21,225	7,613	13,224	59,615	16,025	21,171	8,263	14,156	2.6
District of Columbia	90,150	26,516	36,262	10,630	16,742	89,257	26,553	36,646	10,058	16,000	-1.0
Florida	1,154,929	289,914	378,372	191,569	295,074	1,125,810	285,310	369,326	188,032	283,142	-2.5
Georgia	545,358	152,101	208,500	67,696	117,061	533,424	151,280	202,518	66,863	112,763	-2.2
Hawaii	78,456	19,490	25,199	13,913	19,854	76,434	19,192	25,493	13,314	18,435	-2.6
Idaho	108,008	30,739	35,113	16,971	25,185	109,318	29,299	33,350	18,606	28,063	1.2
Illinois	867,110	227,236	266,645	148,020	225,209	842,888	225,063	260,136	142,705	214,984	-2.8
Indiana	447,262	133,079	160,786	62,940	90,457	444,364	131,401	155,023	66,047	91,893	-0.6
Iowa	361,183	100,278	145,603	41,747	73,555	339,738	93,824	130,782	41,146	73,986	-5.9
Kansas	213,786	60,888	67,483	34,658	50,757	215,855	61,637	67,826	35,551	50,841	1.0
Kentucky	282,125	74,587	100,132	45,150	62,256	273,073	74,015	97,800	42,072	59,186	-3.2
Louisiana	258,825	72,570	100,621	32,283	53,351	251,887	71,515	99,225	31,272	49,875	-2.7
Maine	72,810	20,401	25,248	9,805	17,356	70,849	20,489	24,644	9,241	16,475	-2.7
Maryland	374,496	89,744	107,029	70,872	106,851	363,771	88,953	104,820	68,778	101,220	-2.9
Massachusetts	516,331	162,118	193,131	61,486	99,596	514,008	161,041	192,013	61,751	99,203	-0.4
Michigan	663,825	179,840	207,038	112,648	164,299	643,592	176,077	200,368	109,899	157,248	-3.0
Minnesota	451,661	110,594	141,701	71,213	128,153	441,491	107,181	138,939	69,361	126,010	-2.3
Mississippi	176,665	54,869	80,688	14,145	26,963	173,634	54,536	78,688	14,030	26,380	-1.7
Missouri	441,371	121,509	148,853	69,223	101,786	438,222	123,191	148,389	67,546	99,096	-0.7
Montana	53,254	18,976	19,808	5,671	8,799	52,777	18,898	19,213	5,637	9,029	-0.9
Nebraska	139,578	41,450	48,031	20,921	29,176	137,943	42,041	48,809	19,382	27,711	-1.2
Nevada	118,300	27,068	33,356	24,999	32,877	116,738	27,231	33,413	24,380	31,714	-1.3
New Hampshire	82,678	25,317	30,563	9,939	16,859	92,440	26,839	33,198	12,136	20,267	11.8
New Jersey	439,965	131,690	144,883	68,052	95,340	436,939	131,970	144,931	66,932	93,106	-0.7
New Mexico	156,424	36,365	45,782	30,625	43,652	153,455	35,597	44,413	30,544	42,901	-1.9
New York	1,309,986	411,826	499,646	154,560	243,954	1,304,230	412,687	498,437	155,437	237,669	-0.4
North Carolina	578,031	159,799	212,823	76,001	129,408	575,198	160,139	210,027	77,201	127,831	-0.5
North Dakota	55,169	19,615	19,025	7,364	9,165	55,063	19,367	18,442	7,636	9,618	-0.2
Ohio	709,818	210,520	247,915	96,385	154,998	697,647	206,392	239,811	97,694	153,750	-1.7
Oklahoma	228,464	66,449	78,857	34,412	48,746	220,897	65,027	76,578	31,804	47,488	-3.3
Oregon	254,695	72,887	84,896	42,191	54,721	251,106	72,684	84,379	41,058	52,985	-1.4
Pennsylvania	777,242	258,272	296,753	83,360	138,857	765,582	256,235	292,466	82,455	134,426	-1.5
Rhode Island	83,952	28,211	33,864	8,256	13,621	83,460	28,045	33,612	8,379	13,424	-0.6
South Carolina	259,617	76,606	101,081	28,338	53,592	257,844	77,600	99,597	28,075	52,572	-0.7
South Dakota	56,058	16,578	17,585	7,667	14,228	55,129	16,595	17,384	7,601	13,549	-1.7
Tennessee	343,641	106,090	135,801	38,069	63,681	338,197	104,647	133,296	37,748	62,506	-1.6
Texas	1,540,298	376,249	452,397	289,986	421,666	1,541,378	378,901	448,538	293,708	420,231	0.1
Utah	267,309	87,394	93,358	42,011	44,546	264,255	86,006	91,907	41,809	44,533	-1.1
Vermont	44,703	16,654	16,928	3,695	7,426	43,534	16,033	16,415	3,885	7,201	-2.6
Virginia	588,696	158,832	194,281	94,933	140,650	583,755	159,354	194,623	92,646	137,132	-0.8
Washington	365,514	115,203	134,609	49,003	66,699	363,377	115,712	134,861	47,934	64,870	-0.6
West Virginia	162,179	38,488	44,270	43,340	36,081	157,954	38,040	43,252	40,833	35,829	-2.6
Wisconsin	369,732	109,774	125,483	52,520	81,955	364,021	108,999	124,492	51,003	79,527	-1.5
Wyoming	37,812	10,968	10,402	7,105	9,337	37,084	10,375	10,083	7,294	9,332	-1.9
U.S. Service Academies	15,227	12,164	3,038	23	2	14,997	11,892	3,078	23	4	-1.5
Other jurisdictions	259,943	88,041	122,014	19,818	30,070	254,543	86,584	118,101	20,101	29,757	-2.1
American Samoa	1,795	207	355	463	770	1,488	285	450	291	462	-17.1
Federated States of Micronesia	2,744	786	996	465	497	2,446	778	852	405	411	-10.9
Guam	5,924	1,539	2,179	939	1,267	6,518	1,583	2,288	1,201	1,446	10.0
Marshall Islands	1,123	394	380	192	157	1,000	333	340	180	147	-11.0
Northern Marianas	1,178	413	596	71	98	1,109	352	562	77	118	-5.9
Palau	680	203	220	94	163	646	200	217	102	127	-5.0
Puerto Rico	244,076	84,029	116,287	17,354	26,406	239,015	82,604	112,445	17,591	26,375	-2.1
U.S. Virgin Islands	2,423	470	1,001	240	712	2,321	449	947	254	671	-4.2

NOTE: Degree-granting institutions grant associate's or higher degrees and participate in Title IV federal financial aid programs.

SOURCE: U.S. Department of Education, National Center for Education Statistics, Integrated Postsecondary Education Data System (IPEDS), Spring 2013 and Spring 2014, Enrollment component. (This table was prepared October 2014.)

Table 304.35. Total fall enrollment in public degree-granting postsecondary institutions, by attendance status, sex, and state or jurisdiction: 2012 and 2013

State or jurisdiction		Fall 2012				Fall 2013					Percent change in total, 2012 to 2013
			Full-time		Part-time			Full-time		Part-time		
	Total	Males	Females	Males	Females	Total	Males	Females	Males	Females	
1	2	3	4	5	6	7	8	9	10	11	12
United States	14,880,343	3,954,114	4,571,704	2,627,185	3,727,340	14,745,558	3,949,205	4,515,604	2,619,634	3,661,115	-0.9
Alabama	251,045	71,945	93,788	32,510	52,802	248,284	71,809	92,545	32,295	51,635	-1.1
Alaska	30,595	6,258	7,291	6,230	10,816	31,600	6,260	7,222	7,068	11,050	3.3
Arizona	359,229	86,638	93,387	75,039	104,165	354,462	88,061	92,556	73,416	100,429	-1.3
Arkansas	157,224	41,840	55,557	22,657	37,170	153,690	41,480	54,014	22,050	36,146	-2.2
California	2,129,152	477,812	549,712	505,652	595,976	2,148,147	494,156	563,299	505,112	585,580	0.9
Colorado	272,444	73,746	76,955	52,816	68,927	271,223	74,225	76,612	52,217	68,169	-0.4
Connecticut	124,952	33,661	37,289	20,812	33,190	123,093	33,460	37,022	20,680	31,931	-1.5
Delaware	41,113	12,579	16,690	4,429	7,415	40,992	12,775	16,875	4,346	6,996	-0.3
District of Columbia	5,476	1,012	1,368	1,094	2,002	5,347	1,003	1,391	988	1,965	-2.4
Florida	804,693	185,061	230,703	155,165	233,764	795,860	183,850	226,339	155,416	230,255	-1.1
Georgia	422,189	116,805	148,785	58,145	98,454	413,706	116,515	144,667	57,758	94,766	-2.0
Hawaii	60,295	14,296	17,574	11,486	16,939	58,941	14,018	17,588	11,261	16,074	-2.2
Idaho	78,781	22,044	23,382	13,319	20,036	75,910	21,044	22,306	12,839	19,721	-3.6
Illinois	557,137	138,611	152,096	110,132	156,298	546,483	137,551	147,809	109,238	151,885	-1.9
Indiana	333,769	94,954	108,383	54,542	75,890	335,923	93,707	104,803	58,278	79,135	0.6
Iowa	173,558	53,368	55,170	28,264	36,756	168,644	52,089	52,774	28,027	35,754	-2.8
Kansas	183,976	52,523	56,452	30,723	44,278	184,075	52,481	56,199	31,469	43,926	0.1
Kentucky	224,092	58,865	74,487	39,582	51,158	218,472	58,768	73,416	37,186	49,102	-2.5
Louisiana	220,971	61,516	81,310	29,932	48,213	215,653	60,722	80,581	29,118	45,232	-2.4
Maine	50,270	13,583	14,935	8,390	13,362	49,602	13,520	14,497	8,073	13,512	-1.3
Maryland	310,503	71,637	84,012	62,083	92,771	301,565	71,090	82,010	60,690	87,775	-2.9
Massachusetts	228,178	60,775	67,748	37,560	62,095	228,255	61,064	67,564	38,029	61,598	#
Michigan	540,242	148,522	166,376	93,249	132,095	527,740	145,866	162,494	91,646	127,734	-2.3
Minnesota	272,290	76,149	79,119	48,443	68,579	266,440	73,921	77,286	47,326	67,907	-2.1
Mississippi	157,995	50,031	72,399	12,580	22,985	154,916	49,661	70,748	12,295	22,212	-1.9
Missouri	257,430	72,697	86,575	38,311	59,847	254,650	73,112	85,376	38,054	58,108	-1.1
Montana	48,333	17,161	17,340	5,451	8,381	47,851	17,094	16,850	5,414	8,493	-1.0
Nebraska	104,166	30,865	32,943	17,278	23,080	101,893	30,443	32,406	16,620	22,424	-2.2
Nevada	103,619	21,765	26,031	24,010	31,813	102,538	21,833	26,314	23,573	30,818	-1.0
New Hampshire	43,289	13,607	15,744	5,401	8,537	42,711	13,378	15,414	5,423	8,496	-1.3
New Jersey	356,456	101,921	113,758	58,813	81,964	352,822	101,666	112,725	58,319	80,112	-1.0
New Mexico	146,792	33,402	40,576	30,195	42,619	144,381	32,928	39,677	30,070	41,706	-1.6
New York	722,274	220,235	254,888	98,896	148,255	720,934	221,114	254,482	99,059	146,279	-0.2
North Carolina	465,684	121,607	160,989	68,844	114,244	460,100	120,316	157,466	69,489	112,829	-1.2
North Dakota	48,929	17,914	16,164	6,769	8,082	48,751	17,728	15,710	6,989	8,324	-0.4
Ohio	524,338	151,224	170,151	79,080	123,883	520,039	148,566	164,349	82,222	124,902	-0.8
Oklahoma	195,111	53,377	63,932	32,156	45,646	187,078	51,692	61,309	29,573	44,504	-4.1
Oregon	212,310	59,575	64,246	38,945	49,544	208,317	59,241	62,772	37,941	48,363	-1.9
Pennsylvania	425,890	140,662	150,364	52,245	82,619	419,849	139,030	148,130	52,231	80,458	-1.4
Rhode Island	43,204	11,002	14,375	6,329	11,498	42,786	10,816	14,107	6,606	11,257	-1.0
South Carolina	209,023	60,447	76,327	25,224	47,025	207,717	61,336	75,293	25,067	46,021	-0.6
South Dakota	44,185	14,241	13,869	5,763	10,312	44,272	14,460	14,008	5,904	9,900	0.2
Tennessee	235,010	68,366	84,263	30,773	51,608	229,302	66,912	81,621	30,771	49,998	-2.4
Texas	1,347,860	312,322	367,538	271,188	396,812	1,349,609	313,562	363,104	276,100	396,843	0.1
Utah	171,001	47,487	44,362	38,302	40,850	168,311	45,721	42,782	38,474	41,334	-1.6
Vermont	26,501	8,253	9,391	2,775	6,082	25,852	7,995	9,151	2,803	5,903	-2.4
Virginia	409,753	111,553	130,367	69,603	98,230	405,915	112,506	130,503	67,608	95,298	-0.9
Washington	311,497	97,742	109,129	44,455	60,171	310,192	98,583	109,261	43,527	58,821	-0.4
West Virginia	93,017	32,482	36,557	8,989	14,989	90,782	31,737	35,381	8,838	14,826	-2.4
Wisconsin	293,416	88,627	93,587	45,428	65,774	289,339	87,500	91,745	44,821	65,273	-1.4
Wyoming	35,859	9,185	10,232	7,105	9,337	35,547	8,948	9,973	7,294	9,332	-0.9
U.S. Service Academies	15,227	12,164	3,038	23	2	14,997	11,892	3,078	23	4	-1.5
Other jurisdictions	78,369	28,016	37,607	5,295	7,451	78,136	28,083	37,217	5,490	7,346	-0.3
American Samoa	1,795	207	355	463	770	1,488	285	450	291	462	-17.1
Federated States of Micronesia	2,744	786	996	465	497	2,446	778	852	405	411	-10.9
Guam	5,847	1,512	2,154	925	1,256	6,439	1,551	2,263	1,187	1,438	10.1
Marshall Islands	1,123	394	380	192	157	1,000	333	340	180	147	-11.0
Northern Marianas	1,178	413	596	71	98	1,109	352	562	77	118	-5.9
Palau	680	203	220	94	163	646	200	217	102	127	-5.0
Puerto Rico	62,579	24,031	31,905	2,845	3,798	62,687	24,135	31,586	2,994	3,972	0.2
U.S. Virgin Islands	2,423	470	1,001	240	712	2,321	449	947	254	671	-4.2

#Rounds to zero.
NOTE: Degree-granting institutions grant associate's or higher degrees and participate in Title IV federal financial aid programs.

SOURCE: U.S. Department of Education, National Center for Education Statistics, Integrated Postsecondary Education Data System (IPEDS), Spring 2013 and Spring 2014, Enrollment component. (This table was prepared October 2014.)

Table 304.40. Total fall enrollment in private degree-granting postsecondary institutions, by attendance status, sex, and state or jurisdiction: 2012 and 2013

State or jurisdiction	Fall 2012					Fall 2013					Percent change in total, 2012 to 2013
		Full-time		Part-time			Full-time		Part-time		
	Total	Males	Females	Males	Females	Total	Males	Females	Males	Females	
1	2	3	4	5	6	7	8	9	10	11	12
United States	5,762,476	1,755,678	2,455,517	582,110	969,171	5,630,231	1,732,961	2,399,342	558,986	938,942	-2.3
Alabama	59,266	18,221	23,758	8,837	8,450	57,428	18,213	24,089	7,797	7,329	-3.1
Alaska	2,202	645	1,299	89	169	3,290	830	2,089	122	249	49.4
Arizona	377,150	103,268	218,649	15,335	39,898	339,661	91,212	188,308	16,270	43,871	-9.9
Arkansas	19,234	6,892	8,569	1,334	2,439	18,534	6,832	8,441	1,321	1,940	-3.6
California	492,308	165,687	218,098	46,993	61,530	488,774	163,993	220,390	44,477	59,914	-0.7
Colorado	90,491	23,131	35,847	12,176	19,337	87,500	22,982	33,575	11,274	19,669	-3.3
Connecticut	76,706	24,064	31,958	6,807	13,877	77,873	24,765	32,372	6,752	13,984	1.5
Delaware	17,015	3,487	4,535	3,184	5,809	18,623	3,250	4,296	3,917	7,160	9.5
District of Columbia	84,674	25,504	34,894	9,536	14,740	83,910	25,550	35,255	9,070	14,035	-0.9
Florida	350,236	104,853	147,669	36,404	61,310	329,950	101,460	142,987	32,616	52,887	-5.8
Georgia	123,169	35,296	59,715	9,551	18,607	119,718	34,765	57,851	9,105	17,997	-2.8
Hawaii	18,161	5,194	7,625	2,427	2,915	17,493	5,174	7,905	2,053	2,361	-3.7
Idaho	29,227	8,695	11,731	3,652	5,149	33,408	8,255	11,044	5,767	8,342	14.3
Illinois	309,973	88,625	114,549	37,888	68,911	296,405	87,512	112,327	33,467	63,099	-4.4
Indiana	113,493	38,125	52,403	8,398	14,567	108,441	37,694	50,220	7,769	12,758	-4.5
Iowa	187,625	46,910	90,433	13,483	36,799	171,094	41,735	78,008	13,119	38,232	-8.8
Kansas	29,810	8,365	11,031	3,935	6,479	31,780	9,156	11,627	4,082	6,915	6.6
Kentucky	58,033	15,722	25,645	5,568	11,098	54,601	15,247	24,384	4,886	10,084	-5.9
Louisiana	37,854	11,054	19,311	2,351	5,138	36,234	10,793	18,644	2,154	4,643	-4.3
Maine	22,540	6,818	10,313	1,415	3,994	21,247	6,969	10,147	1,168	2,963	-5.7
Maryland	63,993	18,107	23,017	8,789	14,080	62,206	17,863	22,810	8,088	13,445	-2.8
Massachusetts	288,153	101,343	125,383	23,926	37,501	285,753	99,977	124,449	23,722	37,605	-0.8
Michigan	123,583	31,318	40,662	19,399	32,204	115,852	30,211	37,874	18,253	29,514	-6.3
Minnesota	179,371	34,445	62,582	22,770	59,574	175,051	33,260	61,653	22,035	58,103	-2.4
Mississippi	18,670	4,838	8,289	1,565	3,978	18,718	4,875	7,940	1,735	4,168	0.3
Missouri	183,941	48,812	62,278	30,912	41,939	183,572	50,079	63,013	29,492	40,988	-0.2
Montana	4,921	1,815	2,468	220	418	4,926	1,804	2,363	223	536	0.1
Nebraska	35,412	10,585	15,088	3,643	6,096	36,050	11,598	16,403	2,762	5,287	1.8
Nevada	14,681	5,303	7,325	989	1,064	14,200	5,398	7,099	807	896	-3.3
New Hampshire	39,389	11,710	14,819	4,538	8,322	49,729	13,461	17,784	6,713	11,771	26.3
New Jersey	83,509	29,769	31,125	9,239	13,376	84,117	30,304	32,206	8,613	12,994	0.7
New Mexico	9,632	2,963	5,206	430	1,033	9,074	2,669	4,736	474	1,195	-5.8
New York	587,712	191,591	244,758	55,664	95,699	583,296	191,573	243,955	56,378	91,390	-0.8
North Carolina	112,347	38,192	51,834	7,157	15,164	115,098	39,823	52,561	7,712	15,002	2.4
North Dakota	6,240	1,701	2,861	595	1,083	6,312	1,639	2,732	647	1,294	1.2
Ohio	185,480	59,296	77,764	17,305	31,115	177,608	57,826	75,462	15,472	28,848	-4.2
Oklahoma	33,353	13,072	14,925	2,256	3,100	33,819	13,335	15,269	2,231	2,984	1.4
Oregon	42,385	13,312	20,650	3,246	5,177	42,789	13,443	21,607	3,117	4,622	1.0
Pennsylvania	351,352	117,610	146,389	31,115	56,238	345,733	117,205	144,336	30,224	53,968	-1.6
Rhode Island	40,748	17,209	19,489	1,927	2,123	40,674	17,229	19,505	1,773	2,167	-0.2
South Carolina	50,594	16,159	24,754	3,114	6,567	50,127	16,264	24,304	3,008	6,551	-0.9
South Dakota	11,873	2,337	3,716	1,904	3,916	10,857	2,135	3,376	1,697	3,649	-8.6
Tennessee	108,631	37,724	51,538	7,296	12,073	108,895	37,735	51,675	6,977	12,508	0.2
Texas	192,438	63,927	84,859	18,798	24,854	191,769	65,339	85,434	17,608	23,388	-0.3
Utah	96,308	39,907	48,996	3,709	3,696	95,944	40,285	49,125	3,335	3,199	-0.4
Vermont	18,202	8,401	7,537	920	1,344	17,682	8,038	7,264	1,082	1,298	-2.9
Virginia	178,943	47,279	63,914	25,330	42,420	177,840	46,848	64,120	25,038	41,834	-0.6
Washington	54,017	17,461	25,480	4,548	6,528	53,185	17,129	25,600	4,407	6,049	-1.5
West Virginia	69,162	6,006	7,713	34,351	21,092	67,172	6,303	7,871	31,995	21,003	-2.9
Wisconsin	76,316	21,147	31,896	7,092	16,181	74,682	21,499	32,747	6,182	14,254	-2.1
Wyoming	1,953	1,783	170	0	0	1,537	1,427	110	0	0	-21.3
Other jurisdictions	181,574	60,025	84,407	14,523	22,619	176,407	58,501	80,884	14,611	22,411	-2.8
American Samoa	0	0	0	0	0	0	0	0	0	0	†
Federated States of Micronesia	0	0	0	0	0	0	0	0	0	0	†
Guam	77	27	25	14	11	79	32	25	14	8	2.6
Marshall Islands	0	0	0	0	0	0	0	0	0	0	†
Northern Marianas	0	0	0	0	0	0	0	0	0	0	†
Palau	0	0	0	0	0	0	0	0	0	0	†
Puerto Rico	181,497	59,998	84,382	14,509	22,608	176,328	58,469	80,859	14,597	22,403	-2.8
U.S. Virgin Islands	0	0	0	0	0	0	0	0	0	0	†

†Not applicable.
NOTE: Degree-granting institutions grant associate's or higher degrees and participate in Title IV federal financial aid programs.

SOURCE: U.S. Department of Education, National Center for Education Statistics, Integrated Postsecondary Education Data System (IPEDS), Spring 2013 and Spring 2014, Enrollment component. (This table was prepared October 2014.)

Table 304.45. Total fall enrollment in private nonprofit degree-granting postsecondary institutions, by attendance status, sex, and state or jurisdiction: 2012 and 2013

State or jurisdiction	Fall 2012					Fall 2013					Percent change in total, 2012 to 2013
	Total	Full-time		Part-time		Total	Full-time		Part-time		
		Males	Females	Males	Females		Males	Females	Males	Females	
1	2	3	4	5	6	7	8	9	10	11	12
United States	3,953,578	1,300,539	1,657,719	380,205	615,115	3,974,004	1,313,037	1,673,016	379,866	608,085	0.5
Alabama	26,109	9,721	12,634	1,392	2,362	25,146	9,292	12,303	1,357	2,194	-3.7
Alaska	715	178	279	89	169	764	159	234	122	249	6.9
Arizona	9,101	4,058	2,806	1,095	1,142	9,582	4,275	3,232	986	1,089	5.3
Arkansas	17,152	6,249	7,417	1,210	2,276	16,919	6,299	7,597	1,231	1,792	-1.4
California	297,254	99,153	132,475	26,817	38,809	307,826	101,094	137,146	28,268	41,318	3.6
Colorado	33,519	8,340	12,265	5,071	7,843	35,112	8,799	12,999	5,278	8,036	4.8
Connecticut	67,765	22,732	29,198	4,905	10,930	68,717	23,358	29,950	4,625	10,784	1.4
Delaware	16,628	3,449	4,492	3,081	5,606	18,245	3,227	4,266	3,815	6,937	9.7
District of Columbia	79,000	25,051	34,327	8,016	11,606	78,908	24,976	34,506	7,784	11,642	-0.1
Florida	179,932	57,107	69,764	23,391	29,670	180,614	58,492	71,253	22,322	28,547	0.4
Georgia	73,233	23,795	35,988	5,038	8,412	73,394	23,901	36,018	5,067	8,408	0.2
Hawaii	14,292	3,967	6,088	2,056	2,181	13,087	3,717	5,928	1,700	1,742	-8.4
Idaho	26,749	7,936	10,197	3,577	5,039	31,763	7,806	10,016	5,710	8,231	18.7
Illinois	227,827	74,821	94,707	21,580	36,719	224,127	75,260	94,730	20,358	33,779	-1.6
Indiana	88,915	32,333	41,064	5,639	9,879	88,789	32,351	40,965	5,644	9,829	-0.1
Iowa	56,207	20,459	24,888	3,542	7,318	56,283	20,364	25,104	3,541	7,274	0.1
Kansas	25,871	7,494	9,340	3,574	5,463	26,693	7,620	9,361	3,735	5,977	3.2
Kentucky	40,223	11,895	17,382	3,657	7,289	39,830	12,005	17,231	3,438	7,156	-1.0
Louisiana	28,881	8,893	14,060	2,022	3,906	28,065	8,722	13,974	1,836	3,533	-2.8
Maine	21,121	6,630	9,771	1,281	3,439	19,766	6,723	9,552	1,025	2,466	-6.4
Maryland	54,917	15,469	20,701	7,286	11,461	53,928	15,507	20,580	6,748	11,093	-1.8
Massachusetts	281,119	99,115	122,819	23,104	36,081	280,130	98,097	122,525	23,062	36,446	-0.4
Michigan	114,798	28,481	37,204	18,243	30,870	108,188	27,279	34,898	17,371	28,640	-5.8
Minnesota	71,446	22,776	31,723	6,067	10,880	71,258	22,303	31,289	6,403	11,263	-0.3
Mississippi	16,053	4,502	6,771	1,422	3,358	16,046	4,516	6,467	1,575	3,488	#
Missouri	154,225	39,664	49,835	26,514	38,212	152,218	39,420	49,242	26,074	37,482	-1.3
Montana	4,921	1,815	2,468	220	418	4,926	1,804	2,363	223	536	0.1
Nebraska	32,781	9,927	13,882	3,388	5,584	33,400	10,981	15,184	2,511	4,724	1.9
Nevada	3,421	1,428	1,503	148	342	3,546	1,490	1,592	126	338	3.7
New Hampshire	35,681	10,613	13,360	4,173	7,535	46,681	12,491	16,617	6,426	11,147	30.8
New Jersey	74,391	27,721	27,187	7,958	11,525	73,483	28,048	27,001	7,462	10,972	-1.2
New Mexico	1,334	396	449	114	375	1,503	380	467	172	484	12.7
New York	535,676	176,687	218,206	52,157	88,626	532,881	177,267	217,982	53,205	84,427	-0.5
North Carolina	94,055	34,440	45,024	4,901	9,690	96,336	36,092	45,521	5,465	9,258	2.4
North Dakota	5,240	1,629	2,571	401	639	5,348	1,511	2,334	504	999	2.1
Ohio	146,271	50,636	59,015	13,496	23,124	143,121	50,131	58,175	12,495	22,320	-2.2
Oklahoma	23,988	9,230	10,084	1,956	2,718	25,117	9,782	10,813	1,974	2,548	4.7
Oregon	33,370	10,860	16,360	2,463	3,687	35,308	11,275	18,053	2,487	3,493	5.8
Pennsylvania	296,691	102,225	127,655	23,073	43,738	294,772	102,786	126,974	22,621	42,391	-0.6
Rhode Island	40,748	17,209	19,489	1,927	2,123	40,674	17,229	19,505	1,773	2,167	-0.2
South Carolina	34,601	12,124	17,494	1,853	3,130	34,195	12,310	17,124	1,739	3,022	-1.2
South Dakota	7,273	2,011	3,037	869	1,356	7,153	1,897	2,885	824	1,547	-1.6
Tennessee	82,816	29,444	39,836	5,231	8,305	83,909	29,558	40,303	5,337	8,711	1.3
Texas	136,125	46,504	56,600	14,097	18,924	136,053	47,735	57,232	13,389	17,697	-0.1
Utah	81,270	34,722	41,291	2,819	2,438	87,957	37,556	45,337	2,750	2,314	8.2
Vermont	17,685	8,195	7,382	836	1,272	17,220	7,847	7,108	1,018	1,247	-2.6
Virginia	128,309	32,626	45,452	19,166	31,065	130,794	32,830	46,630	19,564	31,770	1.9
Washington	43,162	13,840	20,360	3,449	5,513	43,222	13,799	20,762	3,407	5,254	0.1
West Virginia	7,680	3,300	3,581	292	507	8,505	3,655	3,887	300	663	10.7
Wisconsin	63,037	18,689	27,238	5,549	11,561	62,427	18,995	27,752	5,019	10,661	-1.0
Wyoming	0	0	0	0	0	75	26	49	0	0	†
Other jurisdictions	138,660	43,601	63,631	12,331	19,097	134,587	42,658	61,234	12,223	18,472	-2.9
American Samoa	0	0	0	0	0	0	0	0	0	0	†
Federated States of Micronesia	0	0	0	0	0	0	0	0	0	0	†
Guam	77	27	25	14	11	79	32	25	14	8	2.6
Marshall Islands	0	0	0	0	0	0	0	0	0	0	†
Northern Marianas	0	0	0	0	0	0	0	0	0	0	†
Palau	0	0	0	0	0	0	0	0	0	0	†
Puerto Rico	138,583	43,574	63,606	12,317	19,086	134,508	42,626	61,209	12,209	18,464	-2.9
U.S. Virgin Islands	0	0	0	0	0	0	0	0	0	0	†

†Not applicable.
#Rounds to zero.
NOTE: Degree-granting institutions grant associate's or higher degrees and participate in Title IV federal financial aid programs.

SOURCE: U.S. Department of Education, National Center for Education Statistics, Integrated Postsecondary Education Data System (IPEDS), Spring 2013 and Spring 2014, Enrollment component. (This table was prepared October 2014.)

Table 304.50. Total fall enrollment in private for-profit degree-granting postsecondary institutions, by attendance status, sex, and state or jurisdiction: 2012 and 2013

State or jurisdiction	Fall 2012					Fall 2013					Percent change in total, 2012 to 2013
	Total	Full-time		Part-time		Total	Full-time		Part-time		
		Males	Females	Males	Females		Males	Females	Males	Females	
1	2	3	4	5	6	7	8	9	10	11	12
United States	1,808,898	455,139	797,798	201,905	354,056	1,656,227	419,924	726,326	179,120	330,857	-8.4
Alabama	33,157	8,500	11,124	7,445	6,088	32,282	8,921	11,786	6,440	5,135	-2.6
Alaska	1,487	467	1,020	0	0	2,526	671	1,855	0	0	69.9
Arizona	368,049	99,210	215,843	14,240	38,756	330,079	86,937	185,076	15,284	42,782	-10.3
Arkansas	2,082	643	1,152	124	163	1,615	533	844	90	148	-22.4
California	195,054	66,534	85,623	20,176	22,721	180,948	62,899	83,244	16,209	18,596	-7.2
Colorado	56,972	14,791	23,582	7,105	11,494	52,388	14,183	20,576	5,996	11,633	-8.0
Connecticut	8,941	1,332	2,760	1,902	2,947	9,156	1,407	2,422	2,127	3,200	2.4
Delaware	387	38	43	103	203	378	23	30	102	223	-2.3
District of Columbia	5,674	453	567	1,520	3,134	5,002	574	749	1,286	2,393	-11.8
Florida	170,304	47,746	77,905	13,013	31,640	149,336	42,968	71,734	10,294	24,340	-12.3
Georgia	49,936	11,501	23,727	4,513	10,195	46,324	10,864	21,833	4,038	9,589	-7.2
Hawaii	3,869	1,227	1,537	371	734	4,406	1,457	1,977	353	619	13.9
Idaho	2,478	759	1,534	75	110	1,645	449	1,028	57	111	-33.6
Illinois	82,146	13,804	19,842	16,308	32,192	72,278	12,252	17,597	13,109	29,320	-12.0
Indiana	24,578	5,792	11,339	2,759	4,688	19,652	5,343	9,255	2,125	2,929	-20.0
Iowa	131,418	26,451	65,545	9,941	29,481	114,811	21,371	52,904	9,578	30,958	-12.6
Kansas	3,939	871	1,691	361	1,016	5,087	1,536	2,266	347	938	29.1
Kentucky	17,810	3,827	8,263	1,911	3,809	14,771	3,242	7,153	1,448	2,928	-17.1
Louisiana	8,973	2,161	5,251	329	1,232	8,169	2,071	4,670	318	1,110	-9.0
Maine	1,419	188	542	134	555	1,481	246	595	143	497	4.4
Maryland	9,076	2,638	2,316	1,503	2,619	8,278	2,356	2,230	1,340	2,352	-8.8
Massachusetts	7,034	2,228	2,564	822	1,420	5,623	1,880	1,924	660	1,159	-20.1
Michigan	8,785	2,837	3,458	1,156	1,334	7,664	2,932	2,976	882	874	-12.8
Minnesota	107,925	11,669	30,859	16,703	48,694	103,793	10,957	30,364	15,632	46,840	-3.8
Mississippi	2,617	336	1,518	143	620	2,672	359	1,473	160	680	2.1
Missouri	29,716	9,148	12,443	4,398	3,727	31,354	10,659	13,771	3,418	3,506	5.5
Montana	0	0	0	0	0	0	0	0	0	0	†
Nebraska	2,631	658	1,206	255	512	2,650	617	1,219	251	563	0.7
Nevada	11,260	3,875	5,822	841	722	10,654	3,908	5,507	681	558	-5.4
New Hampshire	3,708	1,097	1,459	365	787	3,048	970	1,167	287	624	-17.8
New Jersey	9,118	2,048	3,938	1,281	1,851	10,634	2,256	5,205	1,151	2,022	16.6
New Mexico	8,298	2,567	4,757	316	658	7,571	2,289	4,269	302	711	-8.8
New York	52,036	14,904	26,552	3,507	7,073	50,415	14,306	25,973	3,173	6,963	-3.1
North Carolina	18,292	3,752	6,810	2,256	5,474	18,762	3,731	7,040	2,247	5,744	2.6
North Dakota	1,000	72	290	194	444	964	128	398	143	295	-3.6
Ohio	39,209	8,660	18,749	3,809	7,991	34,487	7,695	17,287	2,977	6,528	-12.0
Oklahoma	9,365	3,842	4,841	300	382	8,702	3,553	4,456	257	436	-7.1
Oregon	9,015	2,452	4,290	783	1,490	7,481	2,168	3,554	630	1,129	-17.0
Pennsylvania	54,661	15,385	18,734	8,042	12,500	50,961	14,419	17,362	7,603	11,577	-6.8
Rhode Island	0	0	0	0	0	0	0	0	0	0	†
South Carolina	15,993	4,035	7,260	1,261	3,437	15,932	3,954	7,180	1,269	3,529	-0.4
South Dakota	4,600	326	679	1,035	2,560	3,704	238	491	873	2,102	-19.5
Tennessee	25,815	8,280	11,702	2,065	3,768	24,986	8,177	11,372	1,640	3,797	-3.2
Texas	56,313	17,423	28,259	4,701	5,930	55,716	17,604	28,202	4,219	5,691	-1.1
Utah	15,038	5,185	7,705	890	1,258	7,987	2,729	3,788	585	885	-46.9
Vermont	517	206	155	84	72	462	191	156	64	51	-10.6
Virginia	50,634	14,653	18,462	6,164	11,355	47,046	14,018	17,490	5,474	10,064	-7.1
Washington	10,855	3,621	5,120	1,099	1,015	9,963	3,330	4,838	1,000	795	-8.2
West Virginia	61,482	2,706	4,132	34,059	20,585	58,667	2,648	3,984	31,695	20,340	-4.6
Wisconsin	13,279	2,458	4,658	1,543	4,620	12,255	2,504	4,995	1,163	3,593	-7.7
Wyoming	1,953	1,783	170	0	0	1,462	1,401	61	0	0	-25.1
Other jurisdictions	42,914	16,424	20,776	2,192	3,522	41,820	15,843	19,650	2,388	3,939	-2.5
American Samoa	0	0	0	0	0	0	0	0	0	0	†
Federated States of Micronesia	0	0	0	0	0	0	0	0	0	0	†
Guam	0	0	0	0	0	0	0	0	0	0	†
Marshall Islands	0	0	0	0	0	0	0	0	0	0	†
Northern Marianas	0	0	0	0	0	0	0	0	0	0	†
Palau	0	0	0	0	0	0	0	0	0	0	†
Puerto Rico	42,914	16,424	20,776	2,192	3,522	41,820	15,843	19,650	2,388	3,939	-2.5
U.S. Virgin Islands	0	0	0	0	0	0	0	0	0	0	†

†Not applicable.
NOTE: Degree-granting institutions grant associate's or higher degrees and participate in Title IV federal financial aid programs.

SOURCE: U.S. Department of Education, National Center for Education Statistics, Integrated Postsecondary Education Data System (IPEDS), Spring 2013 and Spring 2014, Enrollment component. (This table was prepared October 2014.)

Table 304.60. Total fall enrollment in degree-granting postsecondary institutions, by control and level of institution and state or jurisdiction: 2012 and 2013

State or jurisdiction	Fall 2012						Fall 2013					
	Public 4-year	Public 2-year	Private 4-year		Private 2-year		Public 4-year	Public 2-year	Private 4-year		Private 2-year	
			Nonprofit	For-profit	Nonprofit	For-profit			Nonprofit	For-profit	Nonprofit	For-profit
1	2	3	4	5	6	7	8	9	10	11	12	13
United States	8,092,683	6,787,660	3,915,972	1,470,191	37,606	338,707	8,120,417	6,625,141	3,941,806	1,344,827	32,198	311,400
Alabama	164,770	86,275	25,591	30,012	518	3,145	163,660	84,624	24,674	29,338	472	2,944
Alaska	29,837	758	715	1,259	0	228	29,525	2,075	711	2,191	53	335
Arizona	141,562	217,667	9,101	357,200	0	10,849	145,409	209,053	9,582	320,062	0	10,017
Arkansas	97,380	59,844	16,833	1,897	319	185	97,705	55,985	16,360	1,531	559	84
California	669,831	1,459,321	295,589	126,964	1,665	68,090	685,096	1,463,051	306,233	117,411	1,593	63,537
Colorado	174,650	97,794	33,274	46,900	245	10,072	177,678	93,545	35,105	42,742	7	9,646
Connecticut................	66,724	58,228	67,765	8,669	0	272	66,116	56,977	68,717	9,094	0	62
Delaware....................	26,180	14,933	16,417	387	211	0	26,502	14,490	18,049	378	196	0
District of Columbia	5,476	0	79,000	5,674	0	0	5,347	0	78,908	4,822	0	180
Florida.......................	732,643	72,050	178,302	126,147	1,630	44,157	743,237	52,623	178,825	115,425	1,789	33,911
Georgia......................	274,522	147,667	72,729	41,588	504	8,348	273,434	140,272	72,904	37,830	490	8,494
Hawaii	30,962	29,333	14,292	2,158	0	1,711	30,486	28,455	13,087	2,302	0	2,104
Idaho.........................	53,141	25,640	26,749	1,970	0	508	51,635	24,275	31,763	1,093	0	552
Illinois.......................	198,407	358,730	227,109	74,136	718	8,010	194,913	351,570	223,384	66,458	743	5,820
Indiana	233,497	100,272	88,476	18,873	439	5,705	237,145	98,778	88,365	15,221	424	4,431
Iowa..........................	73,150	100,408	56,004	131,134	203	284	74,862	93,782	56,283	114,208	0	603
Kansas.......................	100,745	83,231	23,591	2,390	2,280	1,549	100,524	83,551	26,248	3,292	445	1,795
Kentucky	126,510	97,582	40,223	14,497	0	3,313	126,535	91,937	39,830	12,133	0	2,638
Louisiana	142,929	78,042	27,827	3,541	1,054	5,432	139,717	75,936	27,121	3,222	944	4,947
Maine.........................	32,002	18,268	20,836	962	285	457	31,383	18,219	19,458	1,017	308	464
Maryland.....................	165,489	145,014	54,917	6,392	0	2,684	162,722	138,843	53,928	5,593	0	2,685
Massachusetts.............	122,884	105,294	280,160	5,170	959	1,864	123,892	104,363	279,066	4,219	1,064	1,404
Michigan	302,129	238,113	114,718	7,152	80	1,633	305,454	222,286	108,188	6,116	0	1,548
Minnesota	137,156	135,134	71,359	106,074	87	1,851	136,044	130,396	71,198	102,465	60	1,328
Mississippi	80,435	77,560	16,053	564	0	2,053	79,708	75,208	16,046	343	0	2,329
Missouri.....................	148,382	109,048	153,018	22,751	1,207	6,965	149,285	105,365	151,006	25,449	1,212	5,905
Montana	39,091	9,242	4,514	0	407	0	39,145	8,706	4,476	0	450	0
Nebraska	58,786	45,380	32,620	2,022	161	609	59,389	42,504	33,234	2,148	166	502
Nevada	92,016	11,603	3,421	6,495	0	4,765	91,334	11,204	3,546	5,771	0	4,883
New Hampshire	28,642	14,647	35,397	3,708	284	0	28,056	14,655	46,463	3,048	218	0
New Jersey..................	183,668	172,788	74,391	6,215	0	2,903	185,242	167,580	73,483	6,639	0	3,995
New Mexico.................	65,673	81,119	1,334	6,622	0	1,676	64,647	79,734	1,503	5,994	0	1,577
New York.....................	393,208	329,066	531,501	31,685	4,175	20,351	393,331	327,603	528,920	31,567	3,961	18,848
North Carolina	221,010	244,674	93,349	14,790	706	3,502	220,121	239,979	95,658	14,894	678	3,868
North Dakota	42,061	6,868	5,240	1,000	0	0	41,729	7,022	5,348	964	0	0
Ohio..........................	334,866	189,472	144,251	22,970	2,020	16,239	334,980	185,059	142,035	20,151	1,086	14,336
Oklahoma	126,358	68,753	23,988	4,891	0	4,474	124,596	62,482	25,117	4,632	0	4,070
Oregon.......................	103,463	108,847	33,370	5,452	0	3,563	105,140	103,177	35,308	4,529	0	2,952
Pennsylvania...............	281,541	144,349	288,180	23,346	8,511	31,315	280,546	139,303	286,084	21,782	8,688	29,179
Rhode Island	25,320	17,884	40,748	0	0	0	25,087	17,699	40,674	0	0	0
South Carolina	107,063	101,960	33,651	11,939	950	4,054	107,733	99,984	33,377	11,472	818	4,460
South Dakota...............	37,838	6,347	6,979	4,600	294	0	37,819	6,453	6,900	3,704	253	0
Tennessee	142,708	92,302	81,307	15,752	1,509	10,063	139,579	89,723	83,270	14,644	639	10,342
Texas	646,849	701,011	132,490	30,468	3,635	25,845	654,008	695,601	133,708	29,081	2,345	26,635
Utah..........................	141,004	29,997	79,079	13,143	2,191	1,895	136,308	32,003	85,921	6,839	2,036	1,148
Vermont	20,190	6,311	17,685	517	0	0	19,652	6,200	17,220	462	0	0
Virginia......................	215,326	194,427	127,983	41,745	326	8,889	215,370	190,545	130,345	39,029	449	8,017
Washington..................	172,186	139,311	43,129	6,538	33	4,317	179,895	130,297	43,170	5,793	52	4,170
West Virginia................	71,856	21,161	7,680	59,185	0	2,297	70,303	20,479	8,505	56,250	0	2,417
Wisconsin	182,437	110,979	63,037	12,502	0	777	180,618	108,721	62,427	11,479	0	776
Wyoming.....................	12,903	22,956	0	145	0	1,808	12,778	22,769	75	0	0	1,462
U.S. Service Academies........	15,227	0	†	†	†	†	14,997	0	†	†	†	†
Other jurisdictions.......	68,501	9,868	137,856	11,836	804	31,078	68,531	9,605	134,587	13,923	0	27,897
American Samoa..................	1,795	0	0	0	0	0	1,488	0	0	0	0	0
Federated States of Micronesia	0	2,744	0	0	0	0	0	2,446	0	0	0	0
Guam.........................	3,702	2,145	77	0	0	0	3,836	2,603	79	0	0	0
Marshall Islands...................	0	1,123	0	0	0	0	0	1,000	0	0	0	0
Northern Marianas	1,178	0	0	0	0	0	1,109	0	0	0	0	0
Palau.........................	0	680	0	0	0	0	0	646	0	0	0	0
Puerto Rico..................	59,403	3,176	137,779	11,836	804	31,078	59,777	2,910	134,508	13,923	0	27,897
U.S. Virgin Islands................	2,423	0	0	0	0	0	2,321	0	0	0	0	0

†Not applicable.
NOTE: Degree-granting institutions grant associate's or higher degrees and participate in Title IV federal financial aid programs.

SOURCE: U.S. Department of Education, National Center for Education Statistics, Integrated Postsecondary Education Data System (IPEDS), Spring 2013 and Spring 2014, Enrollment component. (This table was prepared October 2014.)

Table 304.70. Total fall enrollment in degree-granting postsecondary institutions, by level of enrollment and state or jurisdiction: Selected years, 2000 through 2013

State or jurisdiction	Undergraduate						Postbaccalaureate					
	Fall 2000	Fall 2009	Fall 2010	Fall 2011	Fall 2012	Fall 2013	Fall 2000	Fall 2009	Fall 2010	Fall 2011	Fall 2012	Fall 2013
1	2	3	4	5	6	7	8	9	10	11	12	13
United States	13,155,393	17,464,179	18,082,427	18,077,303	17,732,431	17,474,835	2,156,896	2,849,415	2,937,011	2,933,287	2,910,388	2,900,954
Alabama	201,389	267,787	282,128	274,837	265,917	261,188	32,573	43,854	45,478	45,512	44,394	44,524
Alaska	26,222	29,605	31,925	32,104	30,018	32,097	1,731	2,801	2,874	2,828	2,779	2,793
Arizona	299,529	627,151	672,083	675,028	621,610	580,602	42,961	111,602	121,788	121,946	114,769	113,521
Arkansas	104,580	150,885	156,970	159,973	157,504	153,640	10,592	17,196	18,878	19,372	18,954	18,584
California	2,012,213	2,462,013	2,444,496	2,424,395	2,359,659	2,371,922	244,495	270,134	270,203	267,457	261,801	264,999
Colorado	220,059	289,979	312,099	308,249	305,234	300,452	43,813	55,055	57,351	57,690	57,701	58,271
Connecticut	127,715	156,219	163,291	165,707	166,812	166,181	33,528	35,571	36,093	35,931	34,846	34,785
Delaware	37,930	45,166	45,848	46,973	47,816	48,226	5,967	9,569	9,410	9,574	10,312	11,389
District of Columbia	40,703	83,494	50,330	48,491	47,699	47,187	31,986	53,298	41,662	41,754	42,451	42,070
Florida	623,071	925,980	993,545	1,017,088	1,023,813	997,958	84,613	125,937	131,233	132,072	131,116	127,852
Georgia	296,980	465,156	499,187	495,192	476,813	464,779	49,224	66,354	69,729	70,222	68,545	68,645
Hawaii	51,783	65,022	68,244	69,595	69,272	67,683	8,399	9,646	9,829	9,411	9,184	8,751
Idaho	58,644	76,583	76,998	82,297	99,901	101,162	6,950	7,766	8,203	7,845	8,107	8,156
Illinois	623,018	739,755	748,921	735,155	713,711	694,009	120,900	153,452	157,924	157,297	153,399	148,789
Indiana	273,198	386,516	404,033	401,854	392,625	389,805	41,136	54,515	55,460	55,652	54,637	54,559
Iowa	165,360	315,405	339,036	328,242	315,418	293,677	23,614	35,631	42,831	43,904	45,765	46,061
Kansas	156,385	183,791	188,326	190,125	187,868	189,780	23,583	27,028	26,523	26,537	25,918	26,075
Kentucky	164,183	245,360	256,447	257,828	245,942	237,737	24,158	32,516	34,657	35,938	36,183	35,336
Louisiana	191,517	219,359	230,370	233,374	227,269	221,120	32,283	32,109	33,306	32,366	31,556	30,767
Maine	50,728	62,013	63,599	62,924	63,084	62,062	7,745	8,170	8,807	9,373	9,726	8,787
Maryland	221,952	289,395	305,358	307,345	302,485	294,381	51,793	69,380	72,609	72,752	72,011	69,390
Massachusetts	320,012	369,095	377,241	376,515	381,832	380,870	101,130	128,139	130,512	132,031	134,499	133,138
Michigan	480,618	593,309	605,990	594,842	575,510	557,770	87,013	92,319	91,775	90,578	88,315	85,822
Minnesota	254,632	331,221	346,864	340,621	335,747	326,325	38,813	110,888	118,585	117,116	115,914	115,166
Mississippi	123,299	153,914	159,262	159,627	155,386	152,076	14,090	19,222	20,733	20,949	21,279	21,558
Missouri	266,802	346,816	367,032	378,421	363,308	359,630	54,546	77,725	77,718	78,573	78,063	78,592
Montana	38,481	47,061	48,446	49,143	48,424	47,903	3,759	4,527	4,836	4,899	4,830	4,874
Nebraska	96,759	117,008	121,430	119,310	115,721	113,432	15,358	22,586	23,262	23,565	23,857	24,511
Nevada	79,053	112,823	116,743	108,998	106,854	105,501	8,840	12,073	12,617	12,015	11,446	11,237
New Hampshire	51,990	61,181	62,442	63,412	66,770	72,706	9,728	13,053	13,097	14,024	15,908	19,734
New Jersey	284,785	368,379	380,060	380,081	376,901	374,073	51,160	63,599	64,032	63,669	63,064	62,866
New Mexico	96,377	138,666	147,976	144,287	141,773	138,898	14,362	14,389	14,576	14,771	14,651	14,557
New York	839,423	1,044,927	1,059,332	1,075,580	1,071,051	1,065,771	203,972	245,119	245,819	242,496	238,935	238,459
North Carolina	358,912	502,013	516,254	515,436	508,270	503,532	45,740	65,828	69,538	69,577	69,761	71,666
North Dakota	36,899	48,000	50,003	49,340	48,123	47,592	3,349	6,456	6,900	7,142	7,046	7,471
Ohio	469,999	619,852	650,546	641,780	618,887	606,625	79,554	92,340	94,569	93,254	90,931	91,022
Oklahoma	157,021	195,073	204,217	203,708	202,064	194,723	20,995	25,304	26,343	26,468	26,400	26,174
Oregon	160,805	214,355	221,825	229,389	225,194	219,454	22,260	28,916	29,883	29,675	29,501	31,652
Pennsylvania	506,948	642,799	664,384	651,257	640,348	630,320	102,573	135,255	140,256	136,703	136,894	135,262
Rhode Island	65,067	73,805	73,974	73,952	73,338	73,256	10,383	10,868	11,136	10,695	10,614	10,204
South Carolina	161,699	221,487	231,375	234,149	233,835	232,089	24,232	25,038	25,689	25,853	25,782	25,755
South Dakota	37,497	46,898	50,605	49,205	49,259	48,190	5,724	6,444	7,755	6,694	6,799	6,939
Tennessee	230,376	286,896	302,248	301,406	295,289	290,530	33,534	45,659	49,514	48,780	48,352	47,667
Texas	905,649	1,282,284	1,360,528	1,386,966	1,362,852	1,364,096	128,324	164,744	175,336	177,242	177,446	177,282
Utah	149,954	213,976	231,721	239,189	239,025	234,683	13,822	22,228	23,932	25,205	28,284	29,572
Vermont	30,809	37,944	38,608	38,182	37,798	37,111	4,680	7,031	6,964	6,961	6,905	6,423
Virginia	325,395	460,305	486,820	495,078	492,552	487,858	56,498	84,360	91,102	94,067	96,144	95,897
Washington	290,292	346,477	351,863	336,893	329,617	327,655	30,548	36,136	36,253	35,946	35,897	35,722
West Virginia	76,556	120,073	128,335	137,314	136,155	132,914	11,332	22,419	24,096	25,033	26,024	25,040
Wisconsin	271,839	330,848	341,698	335,447	329,773	324,121	35,340	42,459	42,483	41,088	39,959	39,900
Wyoming	26,811	34,330	35,466	35,330	35,103	34,423	3,193	2,689	2,832	2,762	2,709	2,661
U.S. Service Academies	13,475	15,730	15,905	15,669	15,202	14,970	0	18	20	23	25	27
Other jurisdictions	174,410	213,281	234,281	237,048	231,363	226,152	20,223	30,166	29,959	30,111	28,580	28,391
American Samoa	297	2,189	2,193	2,091	1,795	1,488	0	0	0	0	0	0
Federated States of Micronesia	1,576	3,401	2,699	2,915	2,744	2,446	0	0	0	0	0	0
Guam	4,746	5,484	5,857	6,009	5,631	6,210	469	271	331	351	293	308
Marshall Islands	328	847	869	989	1,123	1,000	0	0	0	0	0	0
Northern Marianas	1,078	989	1,137	1,046	1,178	1,109	0	0	0	0	0	0
Palau	581	651	694	742	680	646	0	0	0	0	0	0
Puerto Rico	163,690	197,289	218,312	220,857	215,972	211,110	19,600	29,724	29,415	29,545	28,104	27,905
U.S. Virgin Islands	2,114	2,431	2,520	2,399	2,240	2,143	154	171	213	215	183	178

NOTE: Degree-granting institutions grant associate's or higher degrees and participate in Title IV federal financial aid programs. Some data have been revised from previously published figures.

SOURCE: U.S. Department of Education, National Center for Education Statistics, Integrated Postsecondary Education Data System (IPEDS), Spring 2001 through Spring 2014, Enrollment component. (This table was prepared October 2014.)

Table 304.80. Total fall enrollment in degree-granting postsecondary institutions, by control, level of enrollment, level of institution, and state or jurisdiction: 2013

State or jurisdiction	Public				Private							
	Undergraduate			Post-baccalaureate	Undergraduate					Postbaccalaureate		
	Total	4-year	2-year		Total	Nonprofit 4-year	For-profit 4-year	Nonprofit 2-year	For-profit 2-year	Total	Nonprofit 4-year	For-profit 4-year
1	2	3	4	5	6	7	8	9	10	11	12	13
United States	13,347,002	6,721,861	6,625,141	1,398,556	4,127,833	2,725,249	1,058,986	32,198	311,400	1,502,398	1,216,557	285,841
Alabama	213,669	129,045	84,624	34,615	47,519	20,808	23,295	472	2,944	9,909	3,866	6,043
Alaska	29,089	27,014	2,075	2,511	3,008	429	2,191	53	335	282	282	0
Arizona	326,431	117,378	209,053	28,031	254,171	4,193	239,961	0	10,017	85,490	5,389	80,101
Arkansas	137,645	81,660	55,985	16,045	15,995	14,021	1,331	559	84	2,539	2,339	200
California	2,043,487	580,436	1,463,051	104,660	328,435	168,155	95,150	1,593	63,537	160,339	138,078	22,261
Colorado	236,661	143,116	93,545	34,562	63,791	21,833	32,305	7	9,646	23,709	13,272	10,437
Connecticut	109,851	52,874	56,977	13,242	56,330	47,885	8,383	0	62	21,543	20,832	711
Delaware	36,869	22,379	14,490	4,123	11,357	10,875	286	196	0	7,266	7,174	92
District of Columbia	4,712	4,712	0	635	42,475	39,273	3,022	0	180	41,435	39,635	1,800
Florida	730,678	678,055	52,623	65,182	267,280	125,440	106,140	1,789	33,911	62,670	53,385	9,285
Georgia	373,957	233,685	140,272	39,749	90,822	51,860	29,978	490	8,494	28,896	21,044	7,852
Hawaii	52,848	24,393	28,455	6,093	14,835	11,124	1,607	0	2,104	2,658	1,963	695
Idaho	68,563	44,288	24,275	7,347	32,599	30,978	1,069	0	552	809	785	24
Illinois	496,801	145,231	351,570	49,682	197,298	136,856	53,879	743	5,820	99,107	86,528	12,579
Indiana	297,602	198,824	98,778	38,321	92,203	72,511	14,837	424	4,431	16,238	15,854	384
Iowa	153,795	60,013	93,782	14,849	139,882	44,563	94,716	0	603	31,212	11,720	19,492
Kansas	163,070	79,519	83,551	21,005	26,710	21,179	3,291	445	1,795	5,070	5,069	1
Kentucky	195,144	103,207	91,937	23,328	42,593	29,321	10,634	0	2,638	12,008	10,509	1,499
Louisiana	193,160	117,224	75,936	22,493	27,960	19,122	2,947	944	4,947	8,274	7,999	275
Maine	45,528	27,309	18,219	4,074	16,534	14,774	988	308	464	4,713	4,684	29
Maryland	258,014	119,171	138,843	43,551	36,367	29,304	4,378	0	2,685	25,839	24,624	1,215
Massachusetts	201,424	97,061	104,363	26,831	179,446	172,993	3,985	1,064	1,404	106,307	106,073	234
Michigan	461,824	239,538	222,286	65,916	95,946	88,854	5,544	0	1,548	19,906	19,334	572
Minnesota	242,062	111,666	130,396	24,378	84,263	50,384	32,491	60	1,328	90,788	20,814	69,974
Mississippi	138,512	63,304	75,208	16,404	13,564	11,013	222	0	2,329	5,154	5,033	121
Missouri	227,673	122,308	105,365	26,977	131,957	101,568	23,272	1,212	5,905	51,615	49,438	2,177
Montana	43,148	34,442	8,706	4,703	4,755	4,305	0	450	0	171	171	0
Nebraska	88,133	45,629	42,504	13,760	25,299	22,586	2,045	166	502	10,751	10,648	103
Nevada	94,688	83,484	11,204	7,850	10,813	798	5,132	0	4,883	3,387	2,748	639
New Hampshire	38,591	23,936	14,655	4,120	34,115	30,981	2,916	218	0	15,614	15,482	132
New Jersey	315,183	147,603	167,580	37,639	58,890	48,731	6,164	0	3,995	25,227	24,752	475
New Mexico	131,149	51,415	79,734	13,232	7,749	657	5,515	0	1,577	1,325	846	479
New York	652,024	324,421	327,603	68,910	413,747	362,167	28,771	3,961	18,848	169,549	166,753	2,796
North Carolina	415,307	175,328	239,979	44,793	88,225	72,369	11,310	678	3,868	26,873	23,289	3,584
North Dakota	42,188	35,166	7,022	6,563	5,404	4,440	964	0	0	908	908	0
Ohio	459,095	274,036	185,059	60,944	147,530	113,021	19,087	1,086	14,336	30,078	29,014	1,064
Oklahoma	165,890	103,408	62,482	21,188	28,833	20,259	4,504	0	4,070	4,986	4,858	128
Oregon	190,555	87,378	103,177	17,762	28,899	21,628	4,319	0	2,952	13,890	13,680	210
Pennsylvania	373,376	234,073	139,303	46,473	256,944	198,395	20,682	8,688	29,179	88,789	87,689	1,100
Rhode Island	38,558	20,859	17,699	4,228	34,698	34,698	0	0	0	5,976	5,976	0
South Carolina	188,088	88,104	99,984	19,629	44,001	29,600	9,123	818	4,460	6,126	3,777	2,349
South Dakota	38,604	32,151	6,453	5,668	9,586	6,043	3,290	253	0	1,271	857	414
Tennessee	204,850	115,127	89,723	24,452	85,680	62,058	12,641	639	10,342	23,215	21,212	2,003
Texas	1,211,302	515,701	695,601	138,307	152,794	97,516	26,298	2,345	26,635	38,975	36,192	2,783
Utah	155,720	123,717	32,003	12,591	78,963	70,280	5,499	2,036	1,148	16,981	15,641	1,340
Vermont	23,624	17,424	6,200	2,228	13,487	13,025	462	0	0	4,195	4,195	0
Virginia	358,480	167,935	190,545	47,435	129,378	87,264	33,648	449	8,017	48,462	43,081	5,381
Washington	287,233	156,936	130,297	22,959	40,422	31,058	5,142	52	4,170	12,763	12,112	651
West Virginia	78,675	58,196	20,479	12,107	54,239	7,240	44,582	0	2,417	12,933	1,265	11,668
Wisconsin	265,616	156,895	108,721	23,723	58,505	46,739	10,990	0	776	16,177	15,688	489
Wyoming	32,886	10,117	22,769	2,661	1,537	75	0	0	1,462	0	0	0
U.S. Service Academies	14,970	14,970	0	27	†	†	†	†	†	†	†	†
Other jurisdictions	71,584	61,979	9,605	6,552	154,568	113,585	13,086	0	27,897	21,839	21,002	837
American Samoa	1,488	1,488	0	0	0	0	0	0	0	0	0	0
Federated States of Micronesia	2,446	0	2,446	0	0	0	0	0	0	0	0	0
Guam	6,135	3,532	2,603	304	75	75	0	0	0	4	4	0
Marshall Islands	1,000	0	1,000	0	0	0	0	0	0	0	0	0
Northern Marianas	1,109	1,109	0	0	0	0	0	0	0	0	0	0
Palau	646	0	646	0	0	0	0	0	0	0	0	0
Puerto Rico	56,617	53,707	2,910	6,070	154,493	113,510	13,086	0	27,897	21,835	20,998	837
U.S. Virgin Islands	2,143	2,143	0	178	0	0	0	0	0	0	0	0

†Not applicable.
NOTE: Degree-granting institutions grant associate's or higher degrees and participate in Title IV federal financial aid programs.

SOURCE: U.S. Department of Education, National Center for Education Statistics, Integrated Postsecondary Education Data System (IPEDS), Spring 2014, Enrollment component. (This table was prepared October 2014.)

Table 305.10. Total fall enrollment of first-time degree/certificate-seeking students in degree-granting postsecondary institutions, by attendance status, sex of student, and level and control of institution: 1955 through 2024

Year	Total	Full-time	Part-time	Males Total	Males Full-time	Males Part-time	Females Total	Females Full-time	Females Part-time	4-year Public	4-year Private	2-year Public	2-year Private
1	2	3	4	5	6	7	8	9	10	11	12	13	14
1955[1]	670,013	—	—	415,604	—	—	254,409	—	—	283,084[2]	246,960[2]	117,288[2]	22,681[2]
1956[1]	717,504	—	—	442,903	—	—	274,601	—	—	292,743[2]	261,951[2]	137,406[2]	25,404[2]
1957[1]	723,879	—	—	441,969	—	—	281,910	—	—	293,544[2]	262,695[2]	140,522[2]	27,118[2]
1958[1]	775,308	—	—	465,422	—	—	309,886	—	—	328,242[2]	272,117[2]	146,379[2]	28,570[2]
1959[1]	821,520	—	—	487,890	—	—	333,630	—	—	348,150[2]	291,691[2]	153,393[2]	28,286[2]
1960[1]	923,069	—	—	539,512	—	—	383,557	—	—	395,884[2]	313,209[2]	181,860[2]	32,116[2]
1961[1]	1,018,361	—	—	591,913	—	—	426,448	—	—	438,135[2]	336,449[2]	210,101[2]	33,676[2]
1962[1]	1,030,554	—	—	598,099	—	—	432,455	—	—	445,191[2]	324,923[2]	224,537[2]	35,903[2]
1963[1]	1,046,424	—	—	604,282	—	—	442,142	—	—	—	—	—	—
1964[1]	1,224,840	—	—	701,524	—	—	523,316	—	—	539,251[2]	363,348[2]	275,413[2]	46,828[2]
1965[1]	1,441,822	—	—	829,215	—	—	612,607	—	—	642,233[2]	398,792[2]	347,788[2]	53,009[2]
1966	1,554,337	—	—	889,516	—	—	664,821	—	—	626,472[2]	382,889[2]	478,459[2]	66,517[2]
1967	1,640,936	1,335,512	305,424	931,127	761,299	169,828	709,809	574,213	135,596	644,525	368,300	561,488	66,623
1968	1,892,849	1,470,653	422,196	1,082,367	847,005	235,362	810,482	623,648	186,834	724,377	378,052	718,562	71,858
1969	1,967,104	1,525,290	441,814	1,118,269	876,280	241,989	848,835	649,010	199,825	699,167	391,508	814,132	62,297
1970	2,063,397	1,587,072	476,325	1,151,960	896,281	255,679	911,437	690,791	220,646	717,449	395,886	890,703	59,359
1971	2,119,018	1,606,036	512,982	1,170,518	895,715	274,803	948,500	710,321	238,179	704,052	384,695	971,295	58,976
1972	2,152,778	1,574,197	578,581	1,157,501	858,254	299,247	995,277	715,943	279,334	680,337	380,982	1,036,616	54,843
1973	2,226,041	1,607,269	618,772	1,182,173	867,314	314,859	1,043,868	739,955	303,913	698,777	378,994	1,089,182	59,088
1974	2,365,761	1,673,333	692,428	1,243,790	896,077	347,713	1,121,971	777,256	344,715	745,637	386,391	1,175,759	57,974
1975	2,515,155	1,763,296	751,859	1,327,935	942,198	385,737	1,187,220	821,098	366,122	771,725	395,440	1,283,523	64,467
1976	2,347,014	1,662,333	684,681	1,170,326	854,597	315,729	1,176,688	807,736	368,952	717,373	413,961	1,152,944	62,736
1977	2,394,426	1,680,916	713,510	1,155,856	839,848	316,008	1,238,570	841,068	397,502	737,497	404,631	1,185,648	66,650
1978	2,389,627	1,650,848	738,779	1,141,777	817,294	324,483	1,247,850	833,554	414,296	736,703	406,669	1,173,544	72,711
1979	2,502,896	1,706,732	796,164	1,179,846	840,315	339,531	1,323,050	866,417	456,633	760,119	415,126	1,253,854	73,797
1980	2,587,644	1,749,928	837,716	1,218,961	862,458	356,503	1,368,683	887,470	481,213	765,395	417,937	1,313,591	90,721[3]
1981	2,595,421	1,737,714	857,707	1,217,680	851,833	365,847	1,377,741	885,881	491,860	754,007	419,257	1,318,436	103,721[3]
1982	2,505,466	1,688,620	816,846	1,199,237	837,223	362,014	1,306,229	851,397	454,832	730,775	404,252	1,254,193	116,246[3]
1983	2,443,703	1,678,071	765,632	1,159,049	824,609	334,440	1,284,654	853,462	431,192	728,244	403,882	1,189,869	121,708
1984	2,356,898	1,613,185	743,713	1,112,303	786,099	326,204	1,244,595	827,086	417,509	713,790	402,959	1,130,311	109,838
1985	2,292,222	1,602,038	690,184	1,075,736	774,858	300,878	1,216,486	827,180	389,306	717,199	398,556	1,060,275	116,192
1986	2,219,208	1,589,451	629,757	1,046,527	768,856	277,671	1,172,681	820,595	352,086	719,974	391,673	990,973	116,588
1987	2,246,359	1,626,719	619,640	1,046,615	779,226	267,389	1,199,744	847,493	352,251	757,833	405,113	979,820	103,593
1988	2,378,803	1,698,927	679,876	1,100,026	807,319	292,707	1,278,777	891,608	387,169	783,358	425,907	1,048,914	120,624
1989	2,341,035	1,656,594	684,441	1,094,750	791,295	303,455	1,246,285	865,299	380,986	762,217	413,836	1,048,529	116,453
1990	2,256,624	1,617,118	639,506	1,045,191	771,372	273,819	1,211,433	845,746	365,687	727,264	400,120	1,041,097	88,143
1991	2,277,920	1,652,983	624,937	1,068,433	798,043	270,390	1,209,487	854,940	354,547	717,697	392,904	1,070,048	97,271
1992	2,184,113	1,603,737	580,376	1,013,058	760,290	252,768	1,171,055	843,447	327,608	697,393	408,306	993,074	85,340
1993	2,160,710	1,608,274	552,436	1,007,647	762,240	245,407	1,153,063	846,034	307,029	702,273	410,688	973,545	74,204
1994	2,133,205	1,603,106	530,099	984,558	751,081	233,477	1,148,647	852,025	296,622	709,042	405,917	952,468	65,778
1995	2,168,831	1,646,812	522,019	1,001,052	767,185	233,867	1,167,779	879,627	288,152	731,836	419,025	954,595	63,375
1996	2,274,319	1,739,852	534,467	1,046,662	805,982	240,680	1,227,657	933,870	293,787	741,164	427,442	989,536	116,177
1997	2,219,255	1,733,512	485,743	1,026,058	806,054	220,004	1,193,197	927,458	265,739	755,362	442,397	923,954	97,542
1998	2,212,593	1,775,412	437,181	1,022,656	825,577	197,079	1,189,937	949,835	240,102	792,772	460,948	858,417	100,456
1999	2,357,590	1,849,741	507,849	1,094,539	865,545	228,994	1,263,051	984,196	278,855	819,503	474,223	955,499	108,365
2000	2,427,551	1,918,093	509,458	1,123,948	894,432	229,516	1,303,603	1,023,661	279,942	842,228	498,532	952,175	134,616
2001	2,497,078	1,989,179	507,899	1,152,837	926,393	226,444	1,344,241	1,062,786	281,455	866,619	508,030	988,726	133,703
2002	2,570,611	2,053,065	517,546	1,170,609	945,938	224,671	1,400,002	1,107,127	292,875	886,297	517,621	1,037,267	129,426
2003	2,591,754	2,102,394	489,360	1,175,856	965,075	210,781	1,415,898	1,137,319	278,579	918,602	537,726	1,004,428	130,998
2004	2,630,243	2,147,546	482,697	1,190,268	981,591	208,677	1,439,975	1,165,955	274,020	925,249	562,485	1,009,082	133,427
2005	2,657,338	2,189,884	467,454	1,200,055	995,610	204,445	1,457,283	1,194,274	263,009	953,903	606,712	977,224	119,499
2006	2,707,213	2,219,853	487,360	1,228,665	1,015,585	213,080	1,478,548	1,204,268	274,280	990,262	598,412	1,013,080	105,459
2007	2,776,168	2,293,855	482,313	1,267,030	1,052,600	214,430	1,509,138	1,241,255	267,883	1,023,543	633,296	1,016,262	103,067
2008	3,024,723	2,427,740	596,983	1,389,302	1,115,500	273,802	1,635,421	1,312,240	323,181	1,053,838	673,581	1,186,576	110,728
2009	3,156,882	2,534,440	622,442	1,464,424	1,177,119	287,305	1,692,458	1,357,321	335,137	1,090,980	658,808	1,275,974	131,120
2010	3,156,727	2,533,636	623,091	1,461,016	1,171,090	289,926	1,695,711	1,362,546	333,165	1,110,601	674,573	1,238,491	133,062
2011	3,091,496	2,479,155	612,341	1,424,140	1,140,843	283,297	1,667,356	1,338,312	329,044	1,131,091	656,864	1,195,083	108,458
2012	2,990,280	2,406,038	584,242	1,385,096	1,114,025	271,071	1,605,184	1,292,013	313,171	1,127,832	642,686	1,133,486	86,276
2013	2,986,596	2,415,925	570,671	1,384,314	1,117,375	266,939	1,602,282	1,298,550	303,732	1,143,870	633,041	1,128,054	81,631
2014[4]	2,958,000	—	—	1,349,000	—	—	1,609,000	—	—	—	—	—	—
2015[4]	2,950,000	—	—	1,345,000	—	—	1,605,000	—	—	—	—	—	—
2016[4]	2,983,000	—	—	1,353,000	—	—	1,629,000	—	—	—	—	—	—
2017[4]	3,042,000	—	—	1,375,000	—	—	1,667,000	—	—	—	—	—	—
2018[4]	3,099,000	—	—	1,399,000	—	—	1,700,000	—	—	—	—	—	—
2019[4]	3,141,000	—	—	1,415,000	—	—	1,725,000	—	—	—	—	—	—
2020[4]	3,172,000	—	—	1,427,000	—	—	1,745,000	—	—	—	—	—	—
2021[4]	3,215,000	—	—	1,445,000	—	—	1,770,000	—	—	—	—	—	—
2022[4]	3,262,000	—	—	1,466,000	—	—	1,797,000	—	—	—	—	—	—
2023[4]	3,314,000	—	—	1,488,000	—	—	1,826,000	—	—	—	—	—	—
2024[4]	3,351,000	—	—	1,505,000	—	—	1,846,000	—	—	—	—	—	—

—Not available.

[1]Excludes first-time degree/certificate-seeking students in occupational programs not creditable towards a bachelor's degree.

[2]Data for 2-year branches of 4-year college systems are aggregated with the 4-year institutions.

[3]Large increases are due to the addition of schools accredited by the Accrediting Commission of Career Schools and Colleges of Technology.

[4]Projected.

NOTE: Data through 1995 are for institutions of higher education, while later data are for degree-granting institutions. Degree-granting institutions grant associate's or higher degrees and participate in Title IV federal financial aid programs. The degree-granting classification is very similar to the earlier higher education classification, but it includes more 2-year colleges and excludes a few higher education institutions that did not grant degrees. Alaska and Hawaii are included in all years. Some data have been revised from previously published figures.

SOURCE: U.S. Department of Education, National Center for Education Statistics, *Biennial Survey of Education in the United States; Opening Fall Enrollment in Higher Education*, 1963 through 1965; Higher Education General Information Survey (HEGIS), "Fall Enrollment in Colleges and Universities" surveys, 1966 through 1985; Integrated Postsecondary Education Data System (IPEDS), "Fall Enrollment Survey" (IPEDS-EF:86–99); IPEDS Spring 2001 through Spring 2014, Enrollment component; and First-Time Freshmen Projection Model, 1980 through 2024. (This table was prepared March 2015.)

Table 305.20. Total fall enrollment of first-time degree/certificate-seeking students in degree-granting postsecondary institutions, by attendance status, sex of student, control of institution, and state or jurisdiction: Selected years, 2000 through 2013

State or jurisdiction	Total, fall 2000	Total, fall 2009	Total, fall 2010	Total, fall 2011	Total, fall 2012	Fall 2013 Total	Full-time Total	Full-time Males	Full-time Females	Part-time Total	Part-time Males	Part-time Females	Public	Private
1	2	3	4	5	6	7	8	9	10	11	12	13	14	15
United States	2,427,551	3,156,882	3,156,727	3,091,496	2,990,280	2,986,596	2,415,925	1,117,375	1,298,550	570,671	266,939	303,732	2,271,924	714,672
Alabama	43,411	52,934	52,990	50,921	51,975	51,563	45,440	19,985	25,455	6,123	2,678	3,445	42,777	8,786
Alaska	2,432	3,769	5,400	4,891	4,474	4,791	3,768	1,554	2,214	1,023	475	548	3,571	1,220
Arizona	46,646	75,570	76,832	89,062	79,100	74,559	56,418	24,466	31,952	18,141	8,352	9,789	52,605	21,954
Arkansas	22,695	28,391	29,321	29,366	28,830	27,967	25,293	11,499	13,794	2,674	1,227	1,447	24,353	3,614
California	246,128	426,304	402,832	392,410	373,490	395,033	257,531	118,734	138,797	137,502	70,367	67,135	342,775	52,258
Colorado	43,201	54,538	54,594	51,130	47,226	45,129	35,723	17,528	18,195	9,406	4,314	5,092	36,634	8,495
Connecticut	24,212	31,282	32,719	32,307	32,193	32,204	27,030	12,396	14,634	5,174	2,264	2,910	20,004	12,200
Delaware	7,636	9,253	8,947	10,290	9,655	9,549	8,344	3,607	4,737	1,205	515	690	7,990	1,559
District of Columbia	9,150	15,683	10,747	9,822	9,546	9,606	8,851	3,464	5,387	755	267	488	562	9,044
Florida	109,931	166,169	176,040	173,010	165,420	163,741	128,348	56,177	72,171	35,393	15,968	19,425	119,603	44,138
Georgia	67,616	97,250	100,140	91,912	88,437	89,407	71,789	32,044	39,745	17,618	7,611	10,007	72,294	17,113
Hawaii	8,931	10,360	10,740	10,407	10,271	10,123	7,790	3,229	4,561	2,333	1,114	1,219	8,277	1,846
Idaho	10,669	13,015	12,668	13,032	14,232	13,292	11,178	4,915	6,263	2,114	952	1,162	9,787	3,505
Illinois	107,592	113,768	114,467	109,223	104,815	102,217	85,901	41,549	44,352	16,316	7,839	8,477	69,791	32,426
Indiana	59,320	78,914	82,406	74,455	72,021	70,008	58,860	27,618	31,242	11,148	5,235	5,913	51,856	18,152
Iowa	39,564	49,986	47,257	44,514	43,637	43,309	34,659	17,379	17,280	8,650	2,723	5,927	28,381	14,928
Kansas	31,424	32,796	33,544	32,773	32,737	32,171	28,174	13,959	14,215	3,997	1,820	2,177	27,152	5,019
Kentucky	34,140	42,671	43,735	40,676	40,401	39,805	34,739	15,369	19,370	5,066	2,264	2,802	32,127	7,678
Louisiana	45,383	41,192	43,144	44,737	42,183	40,977	35,703	15,332	20,371	5,274	2,541	2,733	35,280	5,697
Maine	9,231	11,598	12,203	12,364	12,433	11,748	10,398	5,036	5,362	1,350	585	765	7,817	3,931
Maryland	35,552	50,210	51,104	49,625	48,002	47,459	35,170	16,679	18,491	12,289	5,392	6,897	40,181	7,278
Massachusetts	66,044	78,015	76,857	76,263	76,090	76,628	67,192	30,904	36,288	9,436	4,052	5,384	37,490	39,138
Michigan	84,998	101,628	101,063	99,576	95,351	91,459	72,822	34,614	38,208	18,637	8,674	9,963	75,557	15,902
Minnesota	63,893	57,682	55,723	51,496	49,875	47,957	40,498	19,955	20,543	7,459	3,384	4,075	35,777	12,180
Mississippi	30,356	35,301	37,034	35,624	34,534	34,885	31,004	13,538	17,466	3,881	1,524	2,357	32,247	2,638
Missouri	48,639	63,067	64,381	63,964	61,459	60,906	53,000	24,426	28,574	7,906	3,870	4,036	42,312	18,594
Montana	7,771	9,191	9,959	9,286	8,918	8,924	7,663	3,989	3,674	1,261	572	689	7,996	928
Nebraska	19,027	18,901	19,284	18,143	18,201	18,789	16,807	8,093	8,714	1,982	875	1,107	15,032	3,757
Nevada	10,490	19,948	18,572	16,659	15,890	16,388	11,335	4,986	6,349	5,053	2,525	2,528	14,620	1,768
New Hampshire	13,143	13,208	13,613	13,439	13,761	14,009	11,996	5,540	6,456	2,013	859	1,154	8,552	5,457
New Jersey	52,233	69,387	71,296	67,420	65,607	67,906	58,356	28,218	30,138	9,550	4,609	4,941	57,328	10,578
New Mexico	15,261	21,387	22,353	20,924	20,094	19,581	16,083	7,392	8,691	3,498	1,715	1,783	18,414	1,167
New York	168,181	200,104	197,849	196,562	191,958	190,713	181,433	85,659	95,774	9,280	4,458	4,822	114,688	76,025
North Carolina	69,343	96,129	92,627	91,893	94,267	94,285	73,552	33,083	40,469	20,733	9,141	11,592	74,207	20,078
North Dakota	8,929	9,025	9,073	9,053	9,034	8,833	8,425	4,607	3,818	408	176	232	7,801	1,032
Ohio	98,823	121,126	123,063	113,892	110,404	107,152	92,319	43,517	48,802	14,833	6,931	7,902	78,386	28,766
Oklahoma	35,094	38,066	39,107	38,221	36,821	36,724	30,301	14,364	15,937	6,423	2,799	3,624	30,632	6,092
Oregon	26,946	37,613	35,442	33,663	32,765	31,638	24,493	11,413	13,080	7,145	3,285	3,860	26,137	5,501
Pennsylvania	125,578	143,935	144,184	138,814	132,337	131,399	115,243	54,415	60,828	16,156	6,996	9,160	75,508	55,891
Rhode Island	13,789	15,800	15,698	15,829	15,454	15,494	13,689	6,124	7,565	1,805	821	984	7,508	7,986
South Carolina	32,353	47,611	47,535	48,443	48,307	47,965	40,716	18,491	22,225	7,249	3,084	4,165	37,981	9,984
South Dakota	8,597	9,627	10,074	9,561	9,301	9,253	8,279	4,268	4,011	974	388	586	7,718	1,535
Tennessee	43,327	58,647	59,279	58,720	54,594	54,610	48,225	21,263	26,962	6,385	2,644	3,741	37,302	17,308
Texas	181,813	221,453	228,503	228,066	231,755	238,255	173,805	79,006	94,799	64,450	30,525	33,925	203,984	34,271
Utah	24,953	33,028	35,126	32,712	30,184	27,283	22,634	8,849	13,785	4,649	2,285	2,364	20,228	7,055
Vermont	6,810	8,043	8,242	7,830	7,881	7,671	6,967	3,570	3,397	704	247	457	4,627	3,044
Virginia	52,661	86,396	83,166	83,000	82,270	83,288	68,130	31,161	36,969	15,158	6,774	8,384	64,215	19,073
Washington	36,287	43,177	41,124	41,529	40,961	41,942	37,635	17,373	20,262	4,307	2,041	2,266	33,901	8,041
West Virginia	15,659	22,021	23,020	26,127	25,018	24,828	17,787	8,408	9,379	7,041	3,473	3,568	15,534	9,294
Wisconsin	53,662	60,891	61,249	57,993	56,570	54,162	45,914	22,147	23,767	8,248	3,481	4,767	43,851	10,311
Wyoming	4,209	6,454	6,042	5,851	5,759	5,075	4,579	2,382	2,197	496	228	268	4,638	437
U.S. Service Academies	3,818	4,368	4,359	4,016	3,782	3,936	3,936	3,101	835	0	0	0	3,936	†
Other jurisdictions	39,609	45,083	52,222	54,788	51,926	50,425	47,874	21,757	26,117	2,551	1,133	1,418	15,261	35,164
American Samoa	297	586	657	737	545	438	264	126	138	174	68	106	438	0
Federated States of Micronesia	786	924	653	742	700	481	338	172	166	143	77	66	481	0
Guam	770	874	1,043	1,063	961	792	602	231	371	190	86	104	775	17
Marshall Islands	199	254	240	372	349	260	235	117	118	25	13	12	260	0
Northern Marianas	333	306	360	287	322	284	256	110	146	28	12	16	284	0
Palau	147	87	114	125	236	216	182	93	89	34	22	12	216	0
Puerto Rico	36,773	41,572	48,672	51,009	48,414	47,609	45,696	20,804	24,892	1,913	836	1,077	12,462	35,147
U.S. Virgin Islands	304	480	483	453	399	345	301	104	197	44	19	25	345	0

†Not applicable.
NOTE: Degree-granting institutions grant associate's or higher degrees and participate in Title IV federal financial aid programs. Some data have been revised from previously published figures.

SOURCE: U.S. Department of Education, National Center for Education Statistics, Integrated Postsecondary Education Data System (IPEDS), Spring 2001 through Spring 2014, Enrollment component. (This table was prepared March 2015.)

Table 305.30. Number and percentage of degree-granting postsecondary institutions with first-year undergraduates using various selection criteria for admission, by control and level of institution: Selected years, 2000–01 through 2013–14

Selection criteria	All institutions			Public institutions			Private institutions			Nonprofit			For-profit		
	Total	4-year	2-year	Total	4-year	2-year	Total	4-year	2-year	Total	4-year	2-year	Total	4-year	2-year
1	2	3	4	5	6	7	8	9	10	11	12	13	14	15	16
Number of institutions with first-year undergraduates															
2000–01	3,717	2,034	1,683	1,647	580	1,067	2,070	1,454	616	1,383	1,247	136	687	207	480
2005–06	3,880	2,198	1,682	1,638	588	1,050	2,242	1,610	632	1,351	1,240	111	891	370	521
2010–11	4,208	2,487	1,721	1,614	637	977	2,594	1,850	744	1,320	1,238	82	1,274	612	662
2013–14	4,294	2,634	1,660	1,584	651	933	2,710	1,983	727	1,365	1,282	83	1,345	701	644
Percent of institutions															
Open admissions															
2000–01	40.2	12.9	73.2	63.8	12.1	91.9	21.4	13.3	40.7	14.0	11.7	34.6	36.5	22.7	42.5
2005–06	44.7	18.3	79.3	66.1	13.6	95.4	29.2	20.1	52.4	15.3	13.1	40.5	50.2	43.5	54.9
2010–11	47.2	22.5	83.0	65.6	17.6	96.9	35.8	24.2	64.7	15.5	13.0	52.4	56.9	46.9	66.2
2013–14	52.5	28.8	90.1	65.0	18.1	97.6	45.2	32.3	80.5	17.0	14.6	54.2	73.8	64.6	83.9
Some admission requirements[1]															
2000–01	58.4	85.8	25.1	35.4	87.4	7.1	76.6	85.2	56.3	84.5	86.8	63.2	60.7	75.4	54.4
2005–06	53.4	80.5	18.0	33.6	86.1	4.3	67.9	78.5	40.8	84.2	86.5	57.7	43.2	51.6	37.2
2010–11	50.1	75.6	13.2	34.4	82.4	3.1	59.9	73.3	26.6	84.2	86.7	47.6	34.7	46.2	24.0
2013–14	46.7	70.7	8.7	35.0	81.9	2.4	53.6	67.1	16.8	81.8	84.9	32.5	25.0	34.4	14.8
Secondary grades															
2000–01	34.6	58.7	5.5	23.9	63.4	2.4	43.0	56.7	10.7	60.1	64.1	23.5	8.7	12.6	7.1
2005–06	34.1	57.1	4.2	25.9	68.4	2.2	40.1	53.0	7.4	62.8	66.2	25.2	5.7	8.6	3.6
2010–11	33.3	54.2	3.2	27.8	67.8	1.7	36.7	49.5	5.1	66.1	68.7	26.8	6.4	10.6	2.4
2013–14	33.5	52.8	2.9	29.4	69.3	1.6	35.9	47.4	4.5	65.9	68.8	21.7	5.4	8.3	2.3
Secondary class rank															
2000–01	13.7	24.3	1.0	10.9	30.3	0.3	16.0	21.9	2.3	23.2	25.1	5.9	1.6	2.4	1.3
2005–06	11.3	19.4	0.7	10.4	28.7	0.2	11.9	16.0	1.6	19.3	20.5	6.3	0.7	0.8	0.6
2010–11	8.4	13.9	0.4	9.2	22.9	0.3	7.8	10.8	0.5	15.0	15.8	3.7	0.4	0.7	0.2
2013–14	7.7	12.4	0.3	8.5	20.6	0.1	7.3	9.7	0.6	12.2	12.9	2.4	2.2	4.0	0.3
Secondary school record															
2000–01	45.8	70.3	16.2	29.4	72.9	5.8	58.7	69.2	34.1	73.2	75.5	52.2	29.5	30.9	29.0
2005–06	48.5	73.3	15.9	30.8	78.2	4.2	61.4	71.6	35.4	77.6	79.7	55.0	36.7	44.3	31.3
2010–11	45.9	70.1	10.8	33.0	78.8	3.1	53.9	67.1	21.0	77.1	79.4	42.7	29.8	42.3	18.3
2013–14	43.3	65.6	8.0	33.5	78.3	2.1	49.1	61.4	15.5	74.3	77.2	28.9	23.5	32.4	13.8
College preparatory program															
2000–01	15.5	27.3	1.2	16.2	44.0	1.1	14.9	20.7	1.3	22.1	24.1	4.4	0.4	0.5	0.4
2005–06	15.2	26.4	0.6	17.4	47.1	0.8	13.6	18.8	0.3	22.4	24.3	1.8	0.2	0.5	0.0
2010–11	14.7	24.4	0.6	18.3	45.4	0.7	12.4	17.1	0.5	24.0	25.4	2.4	0.3	0.3	0.3
2013–14	14.1	22.7	0.5	18.7	44.4	0.8	11.5	15.6	0.1	22.8	24.2	1.2	0.0	0.0	0.0
Recommendations															
2000–01	20.4	34.4	3.5	2.7	7.4	0.2	34.4	45.1	9.3	46.6	49.2	22.8	10.0	20.8	5.4
2005–06	19.2	31.9	2.5	2.9	7.7	0.2	31.1	40.8	6.3	49.1	51.5	23.4	3.7	5.1	2.7
2010–11	18.1	29.2	2.1	3.3	8.3	0.1	27.3	36.3	4.7	51.6	53.3	25.6	2.0	2.0	2.1
2013–14	17.8	28.0	1.5	4.5	10.6	0.2	25.5	33.7	3.2	49.1	51.2	15.7	1.6	1.7	1.6
Demonstration of competencies[2]															
2000–01	8.0	12.1	3.0	2.2	5.0	0.7	12.7	15.0	7.1	12.1	12.7	7.4	13.7	29.0	7.1
2005–06	7.0	9.8	3.3	2.3	6.1	0.2	10.3	11.1	8.4	10.2	10.3	9.0	10.5	13.8	8.3
2010–11	5.8	8.0	2.5	1.8	4.6	0.0	8.2	9.2	5.8	8.9	8.8	9.8	7.6	10.1	5.3
2013–14	4.0	5.5	1.5	1.5	3.4	0.1	5.5	6.3	3.3	8.1	8.1	7.2	2.8	2.9	2.8
Test scores[3]															
2000–01	47.2	72.5	16.7	33.2	83.4	5.8	58.5	68.2	35.6	70.3	73.4	41.9	34.6	36.7	33.8
2005–06	36.5	62.5	2.6	31.1	82.3	2.4	40.5	55.2	3.0	65.7	70.5	12.6	2.2	4.1	1.0
2010–11	31.3	51.6	1.9	30.4	73.9	1.9	31.8	43.9	1.7	61.7	64.9	13.4	0.9	1.6	0.3
2013–14	30.4	48.7	1.3	32.1	75.9	1.5	29.4	39.8	1.0	57.7	61.0	7.2	0.7	1.1	0.2
TOEFL[4]															
2000–01	43.4	71.2	9.9	30.2	77.4	4.6	54.0	68.7	19.2	66.2	70.1	30.9	29.3	60.4	15.8
2005–06	41.5	67.9	7.1	31.0	79.3	3.9	49.3	63.8	12.3	67.0	70.6	27.0	22.4	41.1	9.2
2010–11	38.7	61.9	5.1	29.9	71.6	2.7	44.1	58.6	8.2	66.3	69.1	24.4	21.2	37.4	6.2
2013–14	36.6	57.8	3.1	30.1	70.8	1.7	40.4	53.5	4.8	63.8	67.1	13.3	16.7	28.7	3.7
No admission requirements, only recommendations for admission															
2000–01	1.4	1.2	1.7	0.8	0.5	0.9	1.9	1.5	2.9	1.5	1.4	2.2	2.8	1.9	3.1
2005–06	1.8	1.1	2.7	0.3	0.3	0.3	2.9	1.4	6.8	0.5	0.4	1.8	6.6	4.9	7.9
2010–11	2.6	1.8	3.8	0.0	0.0	0.0	4.3	2.5	8.7	0.3	0.3	0.0	8.4	6.9	9.8
2013–14	0.8	0.5	1.2	0.0	0.0	0.0	1.2	0.7	2.8	1.2	0.5	13.3	1.2	1.0	1.4

[1]Many institutions have more than one admission requirement.
[2]Formal demonstration of competencies (e.g., portfolios, certificates of mastery, assessment instruments).
[3]Includes SAT, ACT, or other admission tests.
[4]Test of English as a Foreign Language.
NOTE: Degree-granting institutions grant associate's or higher degrees and participate in Title IV federal financial aid programs. Excludes institutions not enrolling any first-time degree/certificate-seeking undergraduates. Detail may not sum to totals because of rounding. Some data have been revised from previously published figures.
SOURCE: U.S. Department of Education, National Center for Education Statistics, Integrated Postsecondary Education Data System (IPEDS), Fall 2000 through Fall 2013, Institutional Characteristics component. (This table was prepared October 2014.)

Table 305.40. Acceptance rates; number of applications, admissions, and enrollees; and enrollees' SAT and ACT scores for degree-granting postsecondary institutions with first-year undergraduates, by control and level of institution: 2013–14

Acceptance rates, applications, admissions, enrollees, and SAT and ACT scores	All institutions			Public institutions			Private institutions								
							Total			Nonprofit			For-profit		
	Total	4-year	2-year	Total	4-year	2-year	Total	4-year	2-year	Total	4-year	2-year	Total	4-year	2-year
	2	3	4	5	6	7	8	9	10	11	12	13	14	15	16
Number of institutions reporting application data[1]	4,272	2,616	1,656	1,583	650	933	2,689	1,966	723	1,356	1,273	83	1,333	693	640
Percentage distribution of institutions by their acceptance of applications	100.0	100.0	100.0	100.0	100.0	100.0	100.0	100.0	100.0	100.0	100.0	100.0	100.0	100.0	100.0
No application criteria	52.8	29.0	90.3	65.0	18.2	97.6	45.6	32.6	80.9	17.1	14.7	54.2	74.5	65.4	84.4
90 percent or more accepted	7.2	9.3	3.7	3.0	6.5	0.6	9.6	10.3	7.7	9.5	9.8	4.8	9.7	11.1	8.1
75.0 to 89.9 percent accepted	11.2	16.8	2.4	10.4	24.9	0.3	11.6	14.1	5.0	16.3	16.2	18.1	6.9	10.2	3.3
50.0 to 74.9 percent accepted	20.3	31.8	2.2	15.5	36.5	0.3	23.2	30.2	4.0	38.5	40.5	7.2	7.6	11.3	3.6
25.0 to 49.9 percent accepted	7.0	10.7	1.1	5.4	12.5	0.5	8.0	10.2	1.9	14.5	14.6	12.0	1.4	2.0	0.6
10.0 to 24.9 percent accepted	1.2	1.9	0.1	0.5	1.2	0.0	1.6	2.1	0.3	3.2	3.2	2.4	0.0	0.0	0.0
Less than 10 percent accepted	0.4	0.5	0.1	0.1	0.3	0.0	0.5	0.6	0.1	1.0	0.9	1.2	0.0	0.0	0.0
Number of applications (in thousands)	9,199	9,113	86	5,025	4,975	50	4,174	4,139	36	4,065	4,051	14	110	88	22
Percentage distribution of applications by institutions' acceptance of applications	100.0	100.0	100.0	100.0	100.0	100.0	100.0	100.0	100.0	100.0	100.0	100.0	100.0	100.0	100.0
No application criteria	†	†	†	†	†	†	†	†	†	†	†	†	†	†	†
90 percent or more accepted	3.9	3.7	33.3	4.5	4.2	35.0	3.3	3.1	30.9	2.6	2.6	2.3	27.3	21.9	48.8
75.0 to 89.9 percent accepted	16.7	16.7	16.5	19.5	19.6	10.4	13.4	13.3	25.0	13.1	13.0	25.8	25.6	25.9	24.5
50.0 to 74.9 percent accepted	43.0	43.1	30.1	46.2	46.3	35.7	39.2	39.3	22.4	39.1	39.2	20.6	40.3	44.5	23.5
25.0 to 49.9 percent accepted	25.3	25.4	18.4	25.2	25.3	18.9	25.4	25.4	17.6	25.9	25.8	40.6	6.7	7.6	3.2
10.0 to 24.9 percent accepted	7.7	7.8	1.7	3.9	3.9	0.0	12.4	12.4	4.0	12.7	12.7	10.5	0.0	0.0	0.0
Less than 10 percent accepted	3.3	3.3	#	0.7	0.7	0.0	6.4	6.5	0.1	6.6	6.6	0.2	0.0	0.0	0.0
Number of admissions (in thousands)	5,129	5,067	62	3,003	2,968	36	2,126	2,099	27	2,043	2,036	8	82	64	19
Percentage distribution of admissions by institutions acceptance of applications	100.0	100.0	100.0	100.0	100.0	100.0	100.0	100.0	100.0	100.0	100.0	100.0	100.0	100.0	100.0
No application criteria	†	†	†	†	†	†	†	†	†	†	†	†	†	†	†
90 percent or more accepted	6.7	6.2	45.4	7.1	6.6	49.0	6.1	5.7	40.7	4.9	4.9	4.0	35.0	28.8	55.8
75.0 to 89.9 percent accepted	24.3	24.3	19.5	26.5	26.7	12.6	21.1	21.0	28.8	20.8	20.8	38.5	28.1	29.1	24.9
50.0 to 74.9 percent accepted	48.3	48.6	24.3	48.2	48.4	27.5	48.4	48.8	20.1	49.0	49.1	25.5	33.3	37.9	17.9
25.0 to 49.9 percent accepted	17.8	17.9	10.4	16.8	16.9	11.0	19.2	19.4	9.6	19.9	19.8	29.3	3.6	4.2	1.5
10.0 to 24.9 percent accepted	2.5	2.5	0.3	1.3	1.4	0.0	4.2	4.2	0.8	4.3	4.3	2.8	0.0	0.0	0.0
Less than 10 percent accepted	0.4	0.5	#	0.1	0.1	0.0	0.9	1.0	#	1.0	1.0	#	0.0	0.0	0.0
Number of enrollees (in thousands)	1,543	1,507	36	1,008	986	22	535	521	14	495	491	4	40	30	10
Percentage distribution of enrollees by institutions acceptance of applications	100.0	100.0	100.0	100.0	100.0	100.0	100.0	100.0	100.0	100.0	100.0	100.0	100.0	100.0	100.0
No application criteria	†	†	†	†	†	†	†	†	†	†	†	†	†	†	†
90 percent or more accepted	7.9	7.0	45.7	7.4	6.6	46.0	8.8	7.8	45.3	6.7	6.7	6.8	34.9	26.6	59.0
75.0 to 89.9 percent accepted	24.5	24.6	19.8	27.5	27.8	14.4	19.0	18.7	28.2	18.1	17.9	43.4	29.2	31.5	22.8
50.0 to 74.9 percent accepted	46.4	46.9	24.6	48.3	48.7	29.3	42.8	43.5	17.4	43.7	43.9	19.6	31.2	36.2	16.6
25.0 to 49.9 percent accepted	16.8	17.0	9.5	15.2	15.3	10.3	19.9	20.2	8.2	21.1	21.1	26.6	4.7	5.7	1.6
10.0 to 24.9 percent accepted	3.4	3.4	0.4	1.4	1.4	0.0	7.1	7.3	1.0	7.7	7.8	3.6	0.0	0.0	0.0
Less than 10 percent accepted	1.0	1.0	#	0.2	0.2	0.0	2.4	2.5	#	2.6	2.6	#	0.0	0.0	0.0
SAT scores of enrollees															
Critical reading, 25th percentile[2]	468	469	389	458	459	397	474	475	380	475	475	380	441	441	‡
Critical reading, 75th percentile[2]	577	578	515	564	565	512	585	585	520	585	586	520	545	545	‡
Mathematics, 25th percentile[2]	477	479	398	473	474	402	480	481	393	481	482	393	437	437	‡
Mathematics, 75th percentile[2]	586	587	522	580	581	521	589	590	523	590	591	523	548	548	‡
ACT scores of enrollees															
Composite, 25th percentile[2]	20.4	20.5	15.2	19.8	19.9	16.1	20.8	20.8	13.3	20.8	20.9	13.3	19.0	19.0	‡
Composite, 75th percentile[2]	25.4	25.5	19.9	24.6	24.8	20.6	25.9	25.9	18.4	25.9	26.0	18.4	24.6	24.6	‡
English, 25th percentile[2]	19.4	19.5	14.4	18.7	18.9	15.5	19.8	19.9	12.1	19.9	19.9	12.1	18.9	18.9	‡
English, 75th percentile[2]	25.6	25.7	19.6	24.8	24.9	20.8	26.1	26.2	17.0	26.1	26.2	17.0	‡	‡	‡
Mathematics, 25th percentile[2]	19.5	19.6	14.8	19.1	19.2	16.0	19.7	19.8	12.1	19.8	19.8	12.1	18.3	18.3	‡
Mathematics, 75th percentile[2]	25.2	25.3	19.6	24.8	24.9	20.4	25.5	25.6	18.0	25.5	25.6	18.0	25.0	25.0	‡

†Not applicable.
#Rounds to zero.
‡Reporting standards not met (too few cases).
[1]The total on this table differs slightly from other counts of institutions with first-year undergraduates because approximately 0.5 percent of these institutions did not report application information.
[2]Data are only for institutions that require test scores for admission. Relatively few 2-year institutions require test scores for admission. The SAT Critical reading and Mathematics scales range from 200 to 800. The ACT Composite, English, and Mathematics scales range from 1 to 36.

NOTE: Degree-granting institutions grant associate's or higher degrees and participate in Title IV federal financial aid programs. Excludes institutions not enrolling any first-time degree/certificate-seeking undergraduates. Detail may not sum to totals because of rounding.
SOURCE: U.S. Department of Education, National Center for Education Statistics, Integrated Postsecondary Education Data System (IPEDS), Fall 2013, Institutional Characteristics component. (This table was prepared November 2014.)

Table 306.10. Total fall enrollment in degree-granting postsecondary institutions, by level of enrollment, sex, attendance status, and race/ethnicity of student: Selected years, 1976 through 2013

Level of enrollment, sex, attendance status, and race/ethnicity of student	Fall enrollment (in thousands)											Percentage distribution of U.S. residents										
	1976	1980	1990	2000	2005	2008	2009	2010	2011	2012	2013	1976	1980	1990	2000	2005	2008	2009	2010	2011	2012	2013
1	2	3	4	5	6	7	8	9	10	11	12	13	14	15	16	17	18	19	20	21	22	23
All students, total	10,985.6	12,086.8	13,818.6	15,312.3	17,487.5	19,102.8	20,313.6	21,019.4	21,010.6	20,642.8	20,375.8	100.0	100.0	100.0	100.0	100.0	100.0	100.0	100.0	100.0	100.0	100.0
White	9,076.1	9,833.0	10,722.5	10,462.1	11,495.4	12,088.8	12,668.9	12,720.8	12,401.9	11,981.1	11,590.7	84.3	83.5	79.9	70.8	68.0	65.5	64.5	62.6	61.2	60.3	59.3
Total, selected races/ethnicities	1,690.8	1,948.8	2,704.7	4,321.5	5,407.2	6,353.5	6,962.5	7,591.0	7,868.2	7,878.8	7,944.8	15.7	16.5	20.1	29.2	32.0	34.5	35.5	37.4	38.8	39.7	40.7
Black	1,033.0	1,106.8	1,247.0	1,730.3	2,214.6	2,584.5	2,883.9	3,039.0	3,079.1	2,962.1	2,872.1	9.6	9.4	9.3	11.7	13.1	14.0	14.7	15.0	15.2	14.9	14.7
Hispanic	383.8	471.7	782.4	1,461.8	1,882.0	2,272.9	2,537.4	2,748.8	2,893.0	2,979.4	3,091.0	3.6	4.0	5.8	9.9	11.1	12.3	12.9	13.5	14.3	15.0	15.8
Asian/Pacific Islander	197.9	286.4	572.4	978.2	1,134.4	1,302.8	1,335.3	1,281.6	1,277.0	1,259.2	1,259.6	1.8	2.4	4.3	6.6	6.7	7.1	6.8	6.3	6.3	6.3	6.4
Asian	—	—	—	—	—	—	—	1,217.6	1,211.0	1,195.6	1,198.5	—	—	—	—	—	—	—	6.0	6.0	6.0	6.1
Pacific Islander	—	—	—	—	—	—	—	64.0	66.0	63.6	61.1	—	—	—	—	—	—	—	0.3	0.3	0.3	0.3
American Indian/Alaska Native	76.1	83.9	102.8	151.2	176.3	193.3	205.9	196.2	186.2	172.9	162.6	0.7	0.7	0.8	1.0	1.0	1.0	1.0	1.0	0.9	0.9	0.8
Two or more races	—	—	—	—	—	—	—	325.4	432.7	505.1	559.4	—	—	—	—	—	—	—	1.6	2.1	2.5	2.9
Nonresident alien	218.7	305.0	391.5	528.7	584.8	660.6	682.2	707.7	740.5	782.9	840.3	†	†	†	†	†	†	†	†	†	†	†
Male	5,794.4	5,868.1	6,283.9	6,721.8	7,455.9	8,188.9	8,733.0	9,045.8	9,034.3	8,919.1	8,860.8	100.0	100.0	100.0	100.0	100.0	100.0	100.0	100.0	100.0	100.0	100.0
White	4,813.7	4,772.9	4,861.0	4,634.6	5,007.2	5,302.9	5,572.8	5,605.8	5,457.6	5,285.0	5,133.1	85.3	84.4	80.5	72.1	70.1	67.7	66.6	64.7	63.2	62.2	61.1
Total, selected races/ethnicities	826.6	884.4	1,176.6	1,789.8	2,139.2	2,532.8	2,794.6	3,060.4	3,177.6	3,209.4	3,267.6	14.7	15.6	19.5	27.9	29.9	32.3	33.4	35.3	36.8	37.8	38.9
Black	469.9	463.7	484.7	635.3	774.1	911.8	1,028.1	1,089.0	1,107.5	1,079.4	1,065.0	8.3	8.2	8.0	9.9	10.8	11.6	12.3	12.6	12.8	12.7	12.7
Hispanic	209.7	231.6	353.9	627.1	774.6	946.7	1,063.0	1,157.6	1,215.8	1,254.3	1,306.5	3.7	4.1	5.9	9.8	10.8	12.1	12.7	13.4	14.1	14.8	15.6
Asian/Pacific Islander	108.4	151.3	294.9	465.9	522.0	597.4	620.7	600.6	600.7	593.7	594.3	1.9	2.7	4.9	7.3	7.3	7.6	7.4	6.9	7.0	7.0	7.1
Asian	—	—	—	—	—	—	—	572.1	571.6	565.3	567.0	—	—	—	—	—	—	—	6.6	6.6	6.7	6.7
Pacific Islander	—	—	—	—	—	—	—	28.5	29.1	28.5	27.3	—	—	—	—	—	—	—	0.3	0.3	0.3	0.3
American Indian/Alaska Native	38.5	37.8	43.1	61.4	68.4	76.9	82.8	78.7	73.8	68.6	64.8	0.7	0.7	0.7	1.0	1.0	1.0	1.0	0.9	0.9	0.8	0.8
Two or more races	—	—	—	—	—	—	—	134.4	179.8	213.3	236.9	—	—	—	—	—	—	—	1.6	2.1	2.5	2.8
Nonresident alien	154.1	210.8	246.3	297.3	309.5	353.3	365.6	379.6	399.1	424.7	460.1	†	†	†	†	†	†	†	†	†	†	†
Female	5,191.2	6,218.7	7,534.7	8,590.5	10,031.6	10,913.9	11,580.6	11,973.7	11,976.3	11,723.7	11,515.0	100.0	100.0	100.0	100.0	100.0	100.0	100.0	100.0	100.0	100.0	100.0
White	4,262.4	5,060.1	5,861.5	5,827.5	6,488.2	6,785.9	7,096.1	7,115.0	6,944.6	6,696.1	6,457.6	83.1	82.6	79.3	69.7	66.5	64.0	63.0	61.1	59.7	58.9	58.0
Total, selected races/ethnicities	864.2	1,064.4	1,528.1	2,531.7	3,268.0	3,820.7	4,167.9	4,530.7	4,690.4	4,669.4	4,677.2	16.9	17.4	20.7	30.3	33.5	36.0	37.0	38.9	40.3	41.1	42.0
Black	563.1	643.0	762.3	1,095.0	1,440.4	1,672.7	1,855.8	1,949.9	1,971.6	1,882.7	1,807.1	10.8	10.5	10.3	13.1	14.8	15.8	16.5	16.7	16.9	16.6	16.2
Hispanic	174.1	240.1	428.5	834.7	1,107.3	1,326.1	1,474.4	1,591.2	1,677.2	1,725.1	1,784.6	3.4	3.9	5.2	10.0	11.4	12.5	13.1	13.7	14.4	15.2	16.0
Asian/Pacific Islander	89.4	135.2	277.5	512.3	612.4	705.4	714.6	681.0	676.3	665.5	665.3	1.7	2.2	3.8	6.1	6.3	6.7	6.3	5.8	5.8	5.9	6.0
Asian	—	—	—	—	—	—	—	645.5	639.4	630.3	631.5	—	—	—	—	—	—	—	5.5	5.5	5.5	5.7
Pacific Islander	—	—	—	—	—	—	—	35.5	36.9	35.1	33.8	—	—	—	—	—	—	—	0.3	0.3	0.3	0.3
American Indian/Alaska Native	37.6	46.1	59.7	89.8	107.9	116.4	123.1	117.5	112.4	104.3	97.8	0.7	0.8	0.8	1.1	1.1	1.1	1.1	1.0	1.0	0.9	0.9
Two or more races	—	—	—	—	—	—	—	191.0	252.9	291.8	322.5	—	—	—	—	—	—	—	1.6	2.2	2.6	2.9
Nonresident alien	64.6	94.2	145.2	231.4	275.3	307.3	316.6	328.1	341.4	358.2	380.2	†	†	†	†	†	†	†	†	†	†	†
Full-time	6,703.6	7,088.9	7,821.0	9,009.6	10,797.0	11,747.7	12,605.4	13,087.0	13,002.5	12,737.0	12,597.1	100.0	100.0	100.0	100.0	100.0	100.0	100.0	100.0	100.0	100.0	100.0
White	5,512.6	5,717.0	6,016.5	6,231.1	7,220.5	7,593.5	8,016.2	8,053.5	7,781.2	7,485.6	7,239.2	84.2	83.4	79.9	72.5	69.8	67.6	66.4	64.3	62.7	61.9	60.8
Total, selected races/ethnicities	1,030.9	1,137.5	1,514.9	2,368.5	3,117.1	3,631.9	4,049.6	4,468.5	4,623.1	4,610.0	4,662.5	15.8	16.6	20.1	27.5	30.2	32.4	33.6	35.7	37.3	38.1	39.2
Black	659.9	685.6	718.3	982.6	1,321.7	1,530.7	1,727.6	1,811.3	1,807.1	1,715.1	1,701.0	10.1	10.0	9.5	11.4	12.8	13.6	14.3	14.5	14.6	14.2	14.3
Hispanic	211.1	247.0	394.7	710.3	979.7	1,177.2	1,350.9	1,501.0	1,593.3	1,632.4	1,700.3	3.2	3.6	5.2	8.3	9.5	10.5	11.2	12.0	12.8	13.5	14.3
Asian/Pacific Islander	117.7	162.0	347.4	591.2	710.1	808.9	845.9	820.8	822.1	815.4	821.3	1.8	2.4	4.6	6.9	6.9	7.2	7.0	6.6	6.6	6.7	6.9
Asian	—	—	—	—	—	—	—	785.5	782.9	778.5	785.6	—	—	—	—	—	—	—	6.3	6.3	6.4	6.6
Pacific Islander	—	—	—	—	—	—	—	35.3	39.2	36.9	35.7	—	—	—	—	—	—	—	0.3	0.3	0.3	0.3
American Indian/Alaska Native	43.0	43.0	54.4	84.4	105.6	115.1	123.2	118.2	110.8	102.1	94.5	0.7	0.6	0.7	1.0	1.0	1.0	1.0	0.9	0.9	0.8	0.8
Two or more races	—	—	—	—	—	—	—	217.2	289.6	340.0	377.2	—	—	—	—	—	—	—	1.7	2.3	2.8	3.2
Nonresident alien	160.0	234.4	289.6	410.0	459.4	522.3	539.6	565.2	598.2	641.4	695.3	†	†	†	†	†	†	†	†	†	†	†
Part-time	4,282.1	4,997.9	5,997.7	6,302.7	6,690.5	7,355.1	7,708.2	7,932.3	8,008.1	7,905.8	7,778.7	100.0	100.0	100.0	100.0	100.0	100.0	100.0	100.0	100.0	100.0	100.0
White	3,563.5	4,116.0	4,706.0	4,231.0	4,274.9	4,495.3	4,652.7	4,667.3	4,620.6	4,495.5	4,351.5	84.4	83.5	79.8	68.4	65.1	62.3	61.5	59.9	58.7	57.9	57.0
Total, selected races/ethnicities	659.9	811.3	1,189.8	1,953.0	2,290.1	2,721.5	2,912.9	3,122.5	3,245.2	3,268.8	3,282.2	15.6	16.5	20.2	31.6	34.9	37.7	38.5	40.1	41.3	42.1	43.0
Black	373.1	421.2	528.7	747.7	892.9	1,053.8	1,156.3	1,227.7	1,272.0	1,247.0	1,171.1	8.8	8.5	9.0	12.1	13.6	14.6	15.3	15.8	16.2	16.1	15.3
Hispanic	172.7	224.8	387.7	751.5	902.2	1,095.7	1,186.5	1,247.7	1,299.7	1,347.0	1,390.8	4.1	4.6	6.6	12.2	13.7	15.2	15.7	16.0	16.5	17.3	18.2
Asian/Pacific Islander	80.2	124.4	225.1	387.1	424.3	493.9	489.4	460.8	454.9	443.8	438.3	1.9	2.5	3.8	6.3	6.5	6.8	6.5	5.9	5.8	5.7	5.7
Asian	—	—	—	—	—	—	—	432.1	428.1	417.1	413.0	—	—	—	—	—	—	—	5.5	5.5	5.4	5.4
Pacific Islander	—	—	—	—	—	—	—	28.7	26.8	26.7	25.3	—	—	—	—	—	—	—	0.3	0.3	0.3	0.3
American Indian/Alaska Native	33.1	40.9	48.4	66.8	70.7	78.2	82.7	78.0	75.4	70.8	68.1	0.8	0.8	0.8	1.1	1.1	1.1	1.1	1.0	1.0	0.9	0.9
Two or more races	—	—	—	—	—	—	—	108.2	143.2	165.0	182.1	—	—	—	—	—	—	—	1.4	1.8	2.1	2.4
Nonresident alien	58.7	70.6	101.8	118.7	125.5	138.3	142.6	142.5	142.3	141.5	145.0	†	†	†	†	†	†	†	†	†	†	†

See notes at end of table.

Table 306.10. Total fall enrollment in degree-granting postsecondary institutions, by level of enrollment, sex, attendance status, and race/ethnicity of student: Selected years, 1976 through 2013—Continued

Columns 2–12: Fall enrollment (in thousands). Columns 13–23: Percentage distribution of U.S. residents.

Level of enrollment, sex, attendance status, and race/ethnicity of student	1976	1980	1990	2000	2005	2008	2009	2010	2011	2012	2013	1976	1980	1990	2000	2005	2008	2009	2010	2011	2012	2013
1	2	3	4	5	6	7	8	9	10	11	12	13	14	15	16	17	18	19	20	21	22	23
Undergraduate, total	9,419.0	10,469.1	11,959.1	13,155.4	14,964.0	16,365.7	17,464.2	18,082.4	18,077.3	17,732.4	17,474.8	100.0	100.0	100.0	100.0	100.0	100.0	100.0	100.0	100.0	100.0	100.0
White	7,740.5	8,480.7	9,272.6	8,983.5	9,828.6	10,339.2	10,859.4	10,895.9	10,618.6	10,247.4	9,899.2	83.4	82.7	79.0	69.8	67.1	64.6	63.6	61.6	60.1	59.3	58.3
Total, selected races/ethnicities	1,535.3	1,778.5	2,467.7	3,884.0	4,820.7	5,666.2	6,228.3	6,788.1	7,036.1	7,034.6	7,092.3	16.6	17.3	21.0	30.2	32.9	35.4	36.4	38.4	39.9	40.7	41.7
Black	943.4	1,018.8	1,147.2	1,548.9	1,955.4	2,269.3	2,545.9	2,677.1	2,708.3	2,592.8	2,504.8	10.2	9.9	9.8	12.0	13.3	14.2	14.9	15.1	15.3	15.0	14.7
Hispanic	352.9	433.1	724.6	1,351.0	1,733.6	2,103.5	2,354.4	2,551.0	2,687.9	2,766.1	2,870.2	3.8	4.2	6.2	10.5	11.8	13.1	13.8	14.4	15.2	16.0	16.9
Asian/Pacific Islander	169.3	248.7	500.5	845.5	971.4	1,117.9	1,140.3	—	—	—	—	1.8	2.4	4.3	6.6	6.6	7.0	6.7	—	—	—	—
Asian	—	—	—	—	—	—	—	1,029.8	1,020.2	1,006.5	1,010.1	—	—	—	—	—	—	—	5.8	5.8	5.8	5.9
Pacific Islander	—	—	—	—	—	—	—	57.5	59.4	56.7	54.2	—	—	—	—	—	—	—	0.3	0.3	0.3	0.3
American Indian/Alaska Native	69.7	77.9	95.5	138.5	160.4	175.6	187.6	179.1	170.2	157.5	147.8	0.8	0.8	0.8	1.1	1.1	1.1	1.1	1.0	1.0	0.9	0.9
Two or more races	—	—	—	—	—	—	—	293.7	390.2	455.0	505.2	—	—	—	—	—	—	—	1.7	2.2	2.6	3.0
Nonresident alien	143.2	209.9	218.7	288.0	314.7	360.3	376.5	398.4	422.6	450.5	483.4	†	†	†	†	†	†	†	†	†	†	†
Male	4,896.8	4,997.4	5,379.8	5,778.3	6,408.9	7,066.6	7,563.2	7,836.3	7,823.0	7,713.9	7,659.6	100.0	100.0	100.0	100.0	100.0	100.0	100.0	100.0	100.0	100.0	100.0
White	4,052.2	4,054.6	4,184.4	4,010.1	4,330.4	4,598.6	4,840.7	4,861.0	4,725.5	4,571.9	4,439.6	84.4	83.5	79.6	71.3	69.2	66.8	65.6	63.7	62.1	61.1	60.0
Total, selected races/ethnicities	748.2	802.7	1,069.3	1,618.0	1,926.6	2,290.3	2,534.2	2,773.8	2,879.8	2,904.9	2,961.6	15.6	16.5	20.0	28.7	30.8	33.2	34.4	36.3	37.9	38.9	40.0
Black	430.7	428.2	448.0	577.0	697.5	821.3	930.4	982.9	998.6	969.7	955.4	9.0	8.8	8.5	10.3	11.1	11.9	12.6	12.9	13.1	13.0	12.9
Hispanic	191.7	211.2	326.9	582.6	718.5	884.0	994.5	1,082.9	1,137.8	1,173.0	1,222.9	4.0	4.3	6.2	10.4	11.5	12.8	13.5	14.2	15.0	15.7	16.5
Asian/Pacific Islander	91.1	128.5	254.5	401.9	448.1	514.6	533.4	—	—	—	—	1.9	2.6	4.8	7.1	7.2	7.5	7.2	—	—	—	—
Asian	—	—	—	—	—	—	—	487.4	485.5	479.9	482.9	—	—	—	—	—	—	—	6.4	6.4	6.4	6.5
Pacific Islander	—	—	—	—	—	—	—	26.0	26.5	25.6	24.5	—	—	—	—	—	—	—	0.3	0.3	0.3	0.3
American Indian/Alaska Native	34.8	34.8	39.9	56.4	62.5	70.3	75.9	72.3	67.9	62.9	59.5	0.7	0.7	0.8	1.0	1.0	1.0	1.0	0.9	0.9	0.8	0.8
Two or more races	—	—	—	—	—	—	—	122.3	163.6	193.8	216.3	—	—	—	—	—	—	—	1.6	2.2	2.6	2.9
Nonresident alien	96.4	139.8	126.1	150.2	151.8	177.7	188.3	201.5	217.7	237.1	258.4	†	†	†	†	†	†	†	†	†	†	†
Female	4,522.1	5,471.7	6,579.3	7,377.1	8,555.1	9,299.1	9,901.0	10,246.1	10,254.3	10,018.5	9,815.2	100.0	100.0	100.0	100.0	100.0	100.0	100.0	100.0	100.0	100.0	100.0
White	3,688.3	4,425.8	5,088.2	4,973.3	5,498.2	5,740.6	6,018.6	6,035.0	5,893.1	5,675.5	5,459.6	82.4	81.9	78.4	68.7	65.5	63.0	62.0	60.1	58.6	57.9	56.9
Total, selected races/ethnicities	787.1	975.8	1,398.5	2,266.0	2,894.0	3,375.9	3,694.1	4,014.0	4,156.4	4,129.7	4,130.6	17.6	18.1	21.6	31.3	34.5	37.0	38.0	39.9	41.4	42.1	43.1
Black	512.7	590.6	699.2	971.9	1,257.8	1,448.0	1,615.5	1,694.2	1,709.7	1,623.1	1,549.4	11.5	10.9	10.8	13.4	15.0	15.9	16.6	16.9	17.0	16.6	16.2
Hispanic	161.2	221.8	397.6	768.4	1,015.0	1,219.5	1,359.9	1,468.1	1,550.1	1,593.0	1,647.2	3.6	4.1	6.1	10.6	12.1	13.4	14.0	14.6	15.4	16.2	17.2
Asian/Pacific Islander	78.2	120.2	246.0	443.6	523.2	603.2	607.0	—	—	—	—	1.7	2.2	3.8	6.1	6.2	6.6	6.2	—	—	—	—
Asian	—	—	—	—	—	—	—	542.4	534.7	526.6	527.3	—	—	—	—	—	—	—	5.4	5.3	5.4	5.5
Pacific Islander	—	—	—	—	—	—	—	31.5	32.9	31.1	29.7	—	—	—	—	—	—	—	0.3	0.3	0.3	0.3
American Indian/Alaska Native	34.9	43.1	55.5	82.1	98.0	105.2	111.7	106.8	102.3	94.6	88.2	0.8	0.8	0.9	1.1	1.2	1.2	1.2	1.1	1.0	1.0	0.9
Two or more races	—	—	—	—	—	—	—	171.3	226.7	261.3	288.8	—	—	—	—	—	—	—	1.7	2.3	2.7	3.0
Nonresident alien	46.8	70.1	92.6	137.8	162.9	182.6	188.3	196.9	204.9	213.3	225.0	†	†	†	†	†	†	†	†	†	†	†
Postbaccalaureate, total	1,566.6	1,617.7	1,859.5	2,156.9	2,523.5	2,737.1	2,849.4	2,937.0	2,933.3	2,910.4	2,901.0	100.0	100.0	100.0	100.0	100.0	100.0	100.0	100.0	100.0	100.0	100.0
White	1,335.6	1,352.4	1,449.8	1,478.6	1,666.8	1,749.6	1,809.5	1,824.9	1,783.3	1,733.8	1,691.5	89.6	88.8	86.0	77.2	74.0	71.8	71.1	69.4	68.2	67.3	66.5
Total, selected races/ethnicities	155.5	170.3	237.0	437.5	586.6	687.2	734.2	802.8	832.1	844.2	852.5	10.4	11.2	14.0	22.8	26.0	28.2	28.9	30.6	31.8	32.7	33.5
Black	89.7	87.9	99.8	181.4	259.2	315.2	338.0	361.9	370.9	369.3	367.3	6.0	5.8	5.9	9.5	11.5	12.9	13.3	13.8	14.2	14.3	14.4
Hispanic	30.9	38.6	57.9	110.8	148.4	169.4	183.0	197.8	205.1	213.4	221.0	2.1	2.5	3.4	5.8	6.6	7.0	7.2	7.5	7.8	8.3	8.7
Asian/Pacific Islander	28.6	37.7	72.0	132.7	163.0	184.9	194.9	—	—	—	—	1.9	2.5	4.3	6.9	7.2	7.6	7.7	—	—	—	—
Asian	—	—	—	—	—	—	—	187.8	190.8	189.1	188.4	—	—	—	—	—	—	—	7.1	7.3	7.3	7.4
Pacific Islander	—	—	—	—	—	—	—	6.5	6.7	6.9	6.8	—	—	—	—	—	—	—	0.2	0.3	0.3	0.3
American Indian/Alaska Native	6.4	6.0	7.3	12.6	15.9	17.7	18.3	17.1	16.1	15.4	14.8	0.4	0.4	0.4	0.7	0.7	0.7	0.7	0.7	0.6	0.6	0.6
Two or more races	—	—	—	—	—	—	—	31.7	42.5	50.1	54.2	—	—	—	—	—	—	—	1.2	1.6	1.9	2.1
Nonresident alien	75.5	95.1	172.7	240.7	270.1	300.3	305.7	309.3	317.9	332.4	356.9	†	†	†	†	†	†	†	†	†	†	†
Male	897.6	870.7	904.2	943.5	1,047.1	1,122.3	1,169.8	1,209.5	1,211.3	1,205.2	1,201.2	100.0	100.0	100.0	100.0	100.0	100.0	100.0	100.0	100.0	100.0	100.0
White	761.6	718.1	676.6	624.5	676.8	704.3	732.0	744.9	731.8	713.1	693.5	90.7	89.8	86.3	78.4	76.1	74.4	73.8	72.2	71.1	70.1	69.4
Total, selected races/ethnicities	78.4	81.7	107.4	171.9	212.5	242.5	260.4	286.5	298.1	304.5	306.0	9.3	10.2	13.7	21.6	23.9	25.6	26.2	27.8	28.9	29.9	30.6
Black	39.2	35.5	36.7	58.3	76.6	90.5	97.7	106.1	109.3	109.7	109.6	4.7	4.4	4.7	7.3	8.6	9.6	9.8	10.3	10.6	10.8	11.0
Hispanic	18.1	20.4	27.0	44.5	56.1	62.7	68.6	74.7	78.0	81.3	83.6	2.2	2.5	3.4	5.6	6.3	6.6	6.9	7.2	7.6	8.0	8.4
Asian/Pacific Islander	17.4	22.8	40.4	64.0	73.9	82.7	87.3	—	—	—	—	2.1	2.8	5.2	8.0	8.3	8.7	8.8	—	—	—	—
Asian	—	—	—	—	—	—	—	84.7	86.1	85.4	84.2	—	—	—	—	—	—	—	8.2	8.4	8.4	8.4
Pacific Islander	—	—	—	—	—	—	—	2.5	2.6	2.8	2.7	—	—	—	—	—	—	—	0.2	0.3	0.3	0.3
American Indian/Alaska Native	3.7	3.0	3.2	5.0	5.9	6.5	6.8	6.4	5.9	5.7	5.3	0.4	0.4	0.4	0.6	0.7	0.7	0.7	0.6	0.6	0.6	0.5
Two or more races	—	—	—	—	—	—	—	12.0	16.2	19.6	20.6	—	—	—	—	—	—	—	1.2	1.6	1.9	2.1
Nonresident alien	57.7	71.0	120.2	147.1	157.7	175.5	177.4	178.2	181.4	187.5	201.7	†	†	†	†	†	†	†	†	†	†	†

See notes at end of table.

Table 306.10. Total fall enrollment in degree-granting postsecondary institutions, by level of enrollment, sex, attendance status, and race/ethnicity of student: Selected years, 1976 through 2013—Continued

Level of enrollment, sex, attendance status, and race/ethnicity of student	Fall enrollment (in thousands)											Percentage distribution of U.S. residents										
	1976	1980	1990	2000	2005	2008	2009	2010	2011	2012	2013	1976	1980	1990	2000	2005	2008	2009	2010	2011	2012	2013
1	2	3	4	5	6	7	8	9	10	11	12	13	14	15	16	17	18	19	20	21	22	23
Female	669.1	747.0	955.4	1,213.4	1,476.5	1,614.8	1,679.6	1,727.5	1,722.0	1,705.2	1,699.8	100.0	100.0	100.0	100.0	100.0	100.0	100.0	100.0	100.0	100.0	100.0
White	574.1	634.3	773.2	854.1	990.0	1,045.3	1,077.5	1,080.0	1,051.5	1,020.6	998.0	88.1	87.7	85.6	76.3	72.6	70.2	69.5	67.7	66.3	65.4	64.6
Total, selected races/ethnicities	77.2	88.6	129.6	265.7	374.0	444.8	473.8	516.4	534.0	539.7	546.5	11.9	12.3	14.4	23.7	27.4	29.8	30.5	32.3	33.7	34.6	35.4
Black	50.5	52.4	63.1	123.1	182.6	224.7	240.3	255.8	261.7	259.6	257.7	7.7	7.2	7.0	11.0	13.4	15.1	15.5	16.0	16.5	16.6	16.7
Hispanic	12.8	18.3	30.9	66.3	92.3	106.7	114.5	123.1	127.1	132.1	137.4	2.0	2.5	3.4	5.9	6.8	7.2	7.4	7.7	8.0	8.5	8.9
Asian/Pacific Islander	11.2	15.0	31.5	68.7	89.1	102.2	107.6	107.0	108.7	107.8	108.4	1.7	2.1	3.5	6.1	6.5	6.9	6.9	6.7	6.9	6.9	7.0
Asian	—	—	—	—	—	—	—	103.1	104.7	103.7	104.2	—	—	—	—	—	—	—	6.5	6.6	6.6	6.7
Pacific Islander	—	—	—	—	—	—	—	3.9	4.0	4.1	4.1	—	—	—	—	—	—	—	0.2	0.3	0.3	0.3
American Indian/Alaska Native	2.7	3.0	4.1	7.6	10.0	11.2	11.5	10.7	10.2	9.8	9.5	0.4	0.4	0.5	0.7	0.7	0.8	0.7	0.7	0.6	0.6	0.6
Two or more races	—	—	—	—	—	—	—	19.7	26.3	30.5	33.6	—	—	—	—	—	—	—	1.2	1.7	2.0	2.2
Nonresident alien	17.8	24.1	52.5	93.6	112.4	124.8	128.3	131.1	136.5	144.9	155.2	†	†	†	†	†	†	†	†	†	†	†

—Not available.
†Not applicable.
NOTE: Race categories exclude persons of Hispanic ethnicity. Because of underreporting and nonreporting of racial/ethnic data, some figures are slightly lower than corresponding data in other tables. Data through 1990 are for institutions of higher education, while later data are for degree-granting institutions. Degree-granting institutions grant associate's or higher degrees and participate in Title IV federal financial aid programs. The degree-granting classification is very similar to the earlier higher educa-

tion classification, but it includes more 2-year colleges and excludes a few higher education institutions that did not grant degrees. Some data have been revised from previously published figures. Detail may not sum to totals because of rounding.
SOURCE: U.S. Department of Education, National Center for Education Statistics, Higher Education General Information Survey (HEGIS), "Fall Enrollment in Colleges and Universities" surveys, 1976 and 1980; Integrated Postsecondary Education Data System (IPEDS), "Fall Enrollment Survey" (IPEDS-EF:90); and IPEDS Spring 2001 through Spring 2014, Enrollment component. (This table was prepared November 2014.)

Table 306.20. Total fall enrollment in degree-granting postsecondary institutions, by level and control of institution and race/ethnicity of student: Selected years, 1976 through 2013

Level and control of institution and race/ethnicity of student	Fall enrollment (in thousands)											Percentage distribution of U.S. residents										
	1976	1980	1990	2000	2005	2008	2009	2010	2011	2012	2013	1976	1980	1990	2000	2005	2008	2009	2010	2011	2012	2013
1	2	3	4	5	6	7	8	9	10	11	12	13	14	15	16	17	18	19	20	21	22	23
All students, total	10,985.6	12,086.8	13,818.6	15,312.3	17,487.5	19,102.8	20,313.6	21,019.4	21,010.6	20,642.8	20,375.8	100.0	100.0	100.0	100.0	100.0	100.0	100.0	100.0	100.0	100.0	100.0
White	9,076.1	9,833.0	10,722.5	10,462.1	11,495.4	12,088.8	12,668.9	12,720.8	12,401.9	11,981.1	11,590.7	84.3	83.5	79.9	70.8	68.0	65.5	64.5	62.6	61.2	60.3	59.3
Total, selected races/ethnicities	1,690.8	1,948.8	2,704.7	4,321.5	5,407.2	6,353.5	6,962.5	7,591.0	7,868.2	7,878.8	7,944.8	15.7	16.5	20.1	29.2	32.0	34.5	35.5	37.4	38.8	39.7	40.7
Black	1,033.0	1,106.8	1,247.0	1,730.3	2,214.6	2,584.5	2,883.9	3,039.0	3,079.2	2,962.1	2,872.1	9.6	9.4	9.3	11.7	13.1	14.0	14.7	15.0	15.2	14.9	14.7
Hispanic	383.8	471.7	782.4	1,461.8	1,882.0	2,272.9	2,537.4	2,748.8	2,893.0	2,979.4	3,091.1	3.6	4.0	5.8	9.9	11.1	12.3	12.9	13.5	14.3	15.0	15.8
Asian/Pacific Islander	197.9	286.4	572.4	978.2	1,134.4	1,302.8	1,335.3	1,281.6	1,277.0	1,259.2	1,259.6	1.8	2.4	4.3	6.6	6.7	7.1	6.8	6.3	6.3	6.3	6.4
Asian	—	—	—	—	—	—	—	1,217.6	1,211.0	1,195.6	1,198.5	—	—	—	—	—	—	—	6.0	6.0	6.0	6.1
Pacific Islander	—	—	—	—	—	—	—	64.0	66.0	63.6	61.1	—	—	—	—	—	—	—	0.3	0.3	0.3	0.3
American Indian/Alaska Native	76.1	83.9	102.8	151.2	176.3	193.3	205.9	196.2	186.2	172.9	162.6	0.7	0.7	0.8	1.0	1.0	1.0	1.0	1.0	0.9	0.9	0.8
Two or more races	—	—	—	—	—	—	—	325.4	432.7	505.1	559.4	—	—	—	—	—	—	—	1.6	2.1	2.5	2.9
Nonresident alien	218.7	305.0	391.5	528.7	584.8	660.6	682.2	707.7	740.5	782.9	840.3	†	†	†	†	†	†	†	†	†	†	†
Public	8,641.0	9,456.4	10,844.7	11,752.8	13,021.8	13,972.2	14,810.8	15,142.2	15,116.3	14,880.3	14,745.6	100.0	100.0	100.0	100.0	100.0	100.0	100.0	100.0	100.0	100.0	100.0
White	7,094.5	7,656.1	8,385.4	7,963.4	8,518.2	8,817.7	9,232.4	9,182.1	8,938.2	8,634.3	8,364.1	83.5	82.7	79.2	69.8	67.3	65.1	64.2	62.5	61.0	60.0	58.9
Total, selected races/ethnicities	1,401.0	1,596.2	2,199.2	3,446.3	4,130.8	4,727.5	5,137.5	5,507.1	5,706.0	5,747.5	5,847.0	16.5	17.3	20.8	30.2	32.7	34.9	35.8	37.5	39.0	40.0	41.1
Black	831.2	876.1	976.4	1,319.2	1,580.4	1,759.2	1,936.7	1,988.8	2,014.0	1,937.0	1,886.8	9.8	9.5	9.2	11.6	12.5	13.0	13.5	13.5	13.8	13.5	13.3
Hispanic	336.8	406.2	671.4	1,229.3	1,525.6	1,832.4	2,020.4	2,163.8	2,277.6	2,365.9	2,477.5	4.0	4.4	6.3	10.8	12.1	13.5	14.1	14.7	15.6	16.5	17.4
Asian/Pacific Islander	165.7	239.7	461.0	770.5	881.9	982.9	1,018.7	968.7	958.5	942.5	944.8	2.0	2.6	4.4	6.8	7.0	7.3	7.1	6.6	6.5	6.6	6.6
Asian	—	—	—	—	—	—	—	924.8	915.5	901.1	905.6	—	—	—	—	—	—	—	6.3	6.3	6.3	6.4
Pacific Islander	—	—	—	—	—	—	—	43.9	43.0	41.4	39.2	—	—	—	—	—	—	—	0.3	0.3	0.3	0.3
American Indian/Alaska Native	67.5	74.2	90.4	127.3	143.0	153.0	161.7	150.8	142.5	131.7	124.6	0.8	0.8	0.9	1.1	1.1	1.1	1.1	1.0	1.0	0.9	0.9
Two or more races	—	—	—	—	—	—	—	235.0	313.4	370.4	413.4	—	—	—	—	—	—	—	1.6	2.1	2.6	2.9
Nonresident alien	145.3	204.2	260.0	343.1	372.8	427.0	440.9	453.0	472.0	498.6	534.4	†	†	†	†	†	†	†	†	†	†	†
Private	2,344.6	2,630.4	2,973.9	3,559.5	4,465.6	5,130.7	5,502.8	5,877.3	5,894.3	5,762.5	5,630.2	100.0	100.0	100.0	100.0	100.0	100.0	100.0	100.0	100.0	100.0	100.0
White	1,981.6	2,176.9	2,337.0	2,498.7	2,977.3	3,271.1	3,436.5	3,538.7	3,463.6	3,346.9	3,226.6	87.3	86.1	82.2	74.1	70.0	66.8	65.3	62.9	61.6	61.1	60.6
Total, selected races/ethnicities	289.6	352.7	505.5	875.2	1,276.4	1,625.9	1,825.0	2,083.9	2,162.2	2,131.3	2,097.8	12.7	13.9	17.8	25.9	30.0	33.2	34.7	37.1	38.4	38.9	39.4
Black	201.8	230.7	270.6	411.1	634.2	825.3	947.2	1,050.2	1,065.2	1,025.1	985.3	8.9	9.1	9.5	12.2	14.9	16.9	18.0	18.7	18.9	18.7	18.5
Hispanic	47.0	65.6	111.0	232.5	356.4	440.5	517.1	585.0	615.4	613.6	613.6	2.1	2.6	3.9	6.9	8.4	9.0	9.8	10.4	10.9	11.2	11.5
Asian/Pacific Islander	32.2	46.7	111.5	207.7	252.4	319.9	316.5	312.8	318.6	316.7	314.8	1.4	1.8	3.9	6.2	5.9	6.5	6.0	5.6	5.7	5.8	5.9
Asian	—	—	—	—	—	—	—	292.7	295.5	294.5	293.0	—	—	—	—	—	—	—	5.2	5.3	5.4	5.5
Pacific Islander	—	—	—	—	—	—	—	20.1	23.0	22.2	21.9	—	—	—	—	—	—	—	0.4	0.4	0.4	0.4
American Indian/Alaska Native	8.6	9.7	12.4	23.9	33.3	40.3	44.3	45.5	43.7	41.2	37.9	0.4	0.4	0.4	0.7	0.8	0.8	0.8	0.8	0.8	0.8	0.7
Two or more races	—	—	—	—	—	—	—	90.4	119.3	134.7	146.0	—	—	—	—	—	—	—	1.6	2.1	2.5	2.7
Nonresident alien	73.4	100.8	131.4	185.6	212.0	233.6	241.3	254.7	268.5	284.3	305.9	†	†	†	†	†	†	†	†	†	†	†
4-year, total	7,106.5	7,565.4	8,578.6	9,363.9	10,999.4	12,131.4	12,791.0	13,335.8	13,499.4	13,478.8	13,407.1	100.0	100.0	100.0	100.0	100.0	100.0	100.0	100.0	100.0	100.0	100.0
White	5,999.0	6,274.5	6,768.1	6,658.0	7,496.9	7,987.1	8,296.8	8,399.5	8,309.6	8,144.2	7,954.6	86.6	85.7	82.0	74.6	71.4	69.0	68.0	66.0	64.6	63.7	62.8
Total, selected races/ethnicities	931.0	1,049.9	1,486.1	2,266.1	3,009.5	3,588.4	3,912.2	4,328.0	4,545.2	4,645.4	4,704.2	13.4	14.3	18.0	25.4	28.6	31.0	32.0	34.0	35.4	36.3	37.2
Black	603.7	634.3	722.8	995.4	1,313.4	1,565.0	1,730.9	1,840.0	1,879.7	1,845.7	1,799.1	8.7	8.7	8.8	11.2	12.5	13.5	14.2	14.5	14.6	14.4	14.2
Hispanic	173.6	216.6	358.2	617.9	900.5	1,092.2	1,226.3	1,355.9	1,453.5	1,533.3	1,599.9	2.5	3.0	4.3	6.9	8.6	9.4	10.0	10.7	11.3	12.0	12.6
Asian/Pacific Islander	118.7	162.1	357.2	576.3	700.0	823.4	839.3	818.5	831.9	835.4	843.9	1.7	2.2	4.3	6.5	6.7	7.1	6.9	6.4	6.5	6.5	6.7
Asian	—	—	—	—	—	—	—	782.5	793.2	796.7	806.2	—	—	—	—	—	—	—	6.1	6.2	6.2	6.4
Pacific Islander	—	—	—	—	—	—	—	36.0	38.7	38.8	37.7	—	—	—	—	—	—	—	0.3	0.3	0.3	0.3
American Indian/Alaska Native	35.0	36.9	47.9	76.5	95.6	107.8	115.7	109.0	105.1	98.0	91.6	0.5	0.5	0.6	0.9	0.9	0.9	0.9	0.9	0.8	0.8	0.7
Two or more races	—	—	—	—	—	—	—	204.6	275.0	333.0	369.8	—	—	—	—	—	—	—	1.6	2.1	2.6	2.9
Nonresident alien	176.5	240.9	324.3	439.7	493.1	555.9	582.1	608.3	644.6	689.2	748.3	†	†	†	†	†	†	†	†	†	†	†
Public	4,892.9	5,127.6	5,848.2	6,055.4	6,837.6	7,331.8	7,709.2	7,924.1	8,048.1	8,092.7	8,120.4	100.0	100.0	100.0	100.0	100.0	100.0	100.0	100.0	100.0	100.0	100.0
White	4,120.2	4,243.0	4,605.6	4,311.2	4,678.1	4,879.2	5,057.0	5,069.6	5,028.3	4,952.2	4,866.8	86.1	85.1	81.5	74.4	71.4	69.6	68.7	67.0	65.6	64.4	63.4
Total, selected races/ethnicities	666.7	740.8	1,046.2	1,486.4	1,876.9	2,128.2	2,308.3	2,496.8	2,640.2	2,733.1	2,808.8	13.9	14.9	18.5	25.6	28.6	30.4	31.3	33.0	34.4	35.6	36.6
Black	421.8	438.2	495.1	627.8	754.0	827.3	896.7	912.6	931.8	922.6	908.9	8.8	8.8	8.8	10.8	11.5	11.8	12.2	12.1	12.2	12.0	11.8
Hispanic	129.3	156.4	262.5	420.0	595.6	709.9	794.9	869.5	945.5	1,007.8	1,063.6	2.7	3.1	4.6	7.2	9.1	10.1	10.8	11.5	12.3	13.1	13.9
Asian/Pacific Islander	87.5	117.2	250.6	381.3	460.1	518.3	540.1	522.8	531.4	535.1	544.7	1.8	2.4	4.4	6.6	7.0	7.4	7.3	6.9	6.9	7.0	7.1
Asian	—	—	—	—	—	—	—	504.7	512.3	516.1	526.2	—	—	—	—	—	—	—	6.7	6.7	6.7	6.9
Pacific Islander	—	—	—	—	—	—	—	18.1	19.0	19.0	18.6	—	—	—	—	—	—	—	0.2	0.2	0.2	0.2
American Indian/Alaska Native	28.2	29.0	38.0	57.2	67.2	72.6	76.6	69.5	66.2	61.3	58.1	0.6	0.6	0.7	1.0	1.0	1.0	1.0	0.9	0.9	0.8	0.8
Two or more races	—	—	—	—	—	—	—	122.4	165.4	206.3	233.4	—	—	—	—	—	—	—	1.6	2.2	2.7	3.0
Nonresident alien	106.0	143.8	196.4	257.8	282.6	324.4	343.9	357.8	379.6	407.3	444.9	†	†	†	†	†	†	†	†	†	†	†

See notes at end of table.

Table 306.20. Total fall enrollment in degree-granting postsecondary institutions, by level and control of institution and race/ethnicity of student: Selected years, 1976 through 2013—Continued

Level and control of institution and race/ethnicity of student	Fall enrollment (in thousands)											Percentage distribution of U.S. residents										
	1976	1980	1990	2000	2005	2008	2009	2010	2011	2012	2013	1976	1980	1990	2000	2005	2008	2009	2010	2011	2012	2013
1	2	3	4	5	6	7	8	9	10	11	12	13	14	15	16	17	18	19	20	21	22	23
Private	2,213.6	2,437.8	2,730.3	3,308.5	4,161.8	4,799.6	5,081.8	5,411.7	5,451.3	5,386.2	5,286.6	100.0	100.0	100.0	100.0	100.0	100.0	100.0	100.0	100.0	100.0	100.0
White	1,878.8	2,031.5	2,162.5	2,346.9	2,818.8	3,107.9	3,239.8	3,330.0	3,281.2	3,191.9	3,087.8	87.7	86.8	83.1	75.1	71.3	68.0	66.9	64.5	63.3	62.5	62.0
Total, selected races/ethnicities	264.3	309.2	439.8	779.7	1,132.5	1,460.2	1,603.9	1,831.0	1,905.0	1,912.3	1,895.4	12.3	13.2	16.9	24.9	28.7	32.0	33.1	35.5	36.7	37.5	38.0
Black	182.0	196.1	227.7	367.6	559.4	737.6	834.2	927.4	947.9	923.1	890.1	8.5	8.4	8.7	11.8	14.2	16.1	17.2	18.0	18.3	18.1	17.9
Hispanic	44.3	60.2	95.7	197.9	304.9	382.3	431.3	486.3	508.0	525.5	536.3	2.1	2.6	3.7	6.3	7.7	8.4	8.9	9.4	9.8	10.3	10.8
Asian/Pacific Islander	31.2	44.9	106.6	195.0	239.8	305.1	299.3	295.7	300.6	300.3	299.1	1.5	1.9	4.1	6.2	6.1	6.7	6.2	5.7	5.8	5.9	6.0
Asian	—	—	—	—	—	—	—	277.8	280.8	280.6	280.0	—	—	—	—	—	—	—	5.4	5.4	5.5	5.6
Pacific Islander	—	—	—	—	—	—	—	17.9	19.7	19.8	19.1	—	—	—	—	—	—	—	0.3	0.4	0.4	0.4
American Indian/Alaska Native	6.8	7.9	9.9	19.3	28.4	35.2	39.1	39.6	38.9	36.7	33.5	0.3	0.3	0.4	0.6	0.7	0.8	0.8	0.8	0.8	0.7	0.7
Two or more races	—	—	—	—	—	—	—	82.2	109.6	126.7	136.4	—	—	—	—	—	—	—	1.6	2.1	2.5	2.7
Nonresident alien	70.5	97.1	127.9	181.9	210.4	231.5	238.1	250.6	265.1	281.9	303.4	†	†	†	†	†	†	†	†	†	†	†
2-year, total	3,879.1	4,521.4	5,240.1	5,948.4	6,488.1	6,971.4	7,522.6	7,683.6	7,511.2	7,164.0	6,968.7	100.0	100.0	100.0	100.0	100.0	100.0	100.0	100.0	100.0	100.0	100.0
White	3,077.1	3,558.5	3,954.3	3,804.1	3,998.6	4,101.6	4,372.1	4,321.3	4,092.3	3,837.0	3,636.1	80.2	79.8	76.4	64.9	62.5	59.7	58.9	57.0	55.2	54.3	52.9
Total, selected races/ethnicities	759.8	898.9	1,218.6	2,055.4	2,397.7	2,765.0	3,050.3	3,263.0	3,323.0	3,233.3	3,240.6	19.8	20.2	23.6	35.1	37.5	40.3	41.1	43.0	44.8	45.7	47.1
Black	429.3	472.5	524.3	734.9	901.1	1,019.5	1,153.0	1,198.9	1,199.5	1,116.4	1,073.1	11.2	10.6	10.1	12.5	14.1	14.8	15.5	15.8	16.2	15.8	15.6
Hispanic	210.2	255.1	424.2	843.9	981.5	1,180.7	1,311.1	1,393.0	1,439.5	1,446.1	1,491.2	5.5	5.7	8.2	14.4	15.3	17.2	17.7	18.4	19.4	20.5	21.7
Asian/Pacific Islander	79.2	124.3	215.2	401.9	434.4	479.4	496.0	463.1	445.1	423.7	415.7	2.1	2.8	4.2	6.9	6.8	7.0	6.7	6.1	6.0	6.0	6.0
Asian	—	—	—	—	—	—	—	435.1	417.8	398.9	392.3	—	—	—	—	—	—	—	5.7	5.6	5.6	5.7
Pacific Islander	—	—	—	—	—	—	—	28.0	27.3	24.8	23.4	—	—	—	—	—	—	—	0.4	0.4	0.4	0.3
American Indian/Alaska Native	41.2	47.0	54.9	74.7	80.7	85.5	90.2	87.2	81.1	74.9	71.0	1.1	1.1	1.1	1.3	1.3	1.2	1.2	1.1	1.1	1.1	1.0
Two or more races	—	—	—	—	—	—	—	120.8	157.7	172.1	189.6	—	—	—	—	—	—	—	1.6	2.1	2.4	2.8
Nonresident alien	42.2	64.1	67.1	89.0	91.8	104.7	100.1	99.3	95.9	93.6	92.0	†	†	†	†	†	†	†	†	†	†	†
Public	3,748.1	4,328.8	4,996.5	5,697.4	6,184.2	6,640.3	7,101.6	7,218.1	7,068.2	6,787.7	6,625.1	100.0	100.0	100.0	100.0	100.0	100.0	100.0	100.0	100.0	100.0	100.0
White	2,974.3	3,413.1	3,779.8	3,652.0	3,840.1	3,938.5	4,175.4	4,112.5	3,909.9	3,682.0	3,497.4	80.2	80.2	76.6	65.1	63.0	60.2	59.6	57.7	56.1	55.0	53.5
Total, selected races/ethnicities	734.5	855.4	1,153.0	1,959.9	2,253.9	2,599.3	2,829.2	3,010.3	3,065.8	3,014.4	3,038.2	19.8	20.0	23.4	34.9	37.0	39.8	40.4	42.3	45.0	45.0	46.5
Black	409.5	437.9	481.4	691.4	826.3	931.9	1,040.0	1,076.1	1,082.2	1,014.4	977.9	11.0	10.3	9.8	12.3	13.6	14.3	14.8	15.1	15.5	15.1	15.0
Hispanic	207.5	249.8	408.9	809.2	930.0	1,122.5	1,225.4	1,294.3	1,332.1	1,358.1	1,413.9	5.6	5.9	8.3	14.4	15.3	17.2	17.5	18.2	19.1	20.3	21.6
Asian/Pacific Islander	78.2	122.5	210.3	389.2	421.8	464.5	478.7	445.9	427.1	407.4	400.0	2.1	2.9	4.3	6.9	6.9	7.1	6.8	6.3	6.1	6.1	6.1
Asian	—	—	—	—	—	—	—	420.2	403.1	385.0	379.4	—	—	—	—	—	—	—	5.9	5.8	5.7	5.8
Pacific Islander	—	—	—	—	—	—	—	25.7	24.0	22.4	20.6	—	—	—	—	—	—	—	0.4	0.3	0.3	0.3
American Indian/Alaska Native	39.3	45.2	52.4	70.1	75.7	80.4	85.1	81.3	76.3	70.4	66.5	1.1	1.1	1.1	1.2	1.2	1.2	1.2	1.1	1.1	1.1	1.0
Two or more races	—	—	—	—	—	—	—	112.7	148.0	164.1	180.0	—	—	—	—	—	—	—	1.6	2.1	2.5	2.8
Nonresident alien	39.2	60.3	63.6	85.2	90.2	102.6	96.9	95.2	92.5	91.2	89.6	†	†	†	†	†	†	†	†	†	†	†
Private	131.0	192.6	243.6	251.0	303.8	331.0	421.0	465.5	443.0	376.3	343.6	100.0	100.0	100.0	100.0	100.0	100.0	100.0	100.0	100.0	100.0	100.0
White	102.8	145.4	174.5	151.8	158.4	163.2	196.7	208.8	182.4	154.9	138.7	80.3	77.0	72.7	61.4	52.4	49.6	47.1	45.2	41.5	41.4	40.7
Total, selected races/ethnicities	25.3	43.5	65.6	95.5	143.8	165.7	221.2	252.7	257.2	219.0	202.4	19.7	23.0	27.3	38.6	47.6	50.4	52.9	54.8	58.5	58.6	59.3
Black	19.8	34.6	42.9	43.5	74.8	87.7	113.0	122.8	117.3	102.1	95.2	15.5	18.3	17.9	17.6	24.7	26.7	27.0	26.6	26.7	27.3	27.9
Hispanic	2.6	5.3	15.3	34.7	51.4	58.2	85.7	98.7	107.4	88.0	77.3	2.1	2.8	6.4	14.0	17.0	17.7	20.5	21.4	24.4	23.5	22.7
Asian/Pacific Islander	0.9	1.8	4.9	12.7	12.6	14.8	17.3	17.2	18.0	16.3	15.7	0.7	1.0	2.0	5.1	4.2	4.5	4.1	3.7	4.1	4.4	4.6
Asian	—	—	—	—	—	—	—	14.9	14.7	13.9	12.9	—	—	—	—	—	—	—	3.2	3.3	3.7	3.8
Pacific Islander	—	—	—	—	—	—	—	2.2	3.3	2.4	2.8	—	—	—	—	—	—	—	0.5	0.7	0.6	0.8
American Indian/Alaska Native	1.8	1.8	2.5	4.5	5.0	5.0	5.1	5.9	4.8	4.5	4.5	1.4	1.0	1.1	1.8	1.6	1.5	1.2	1.3	1.1	1.2	1.3
Two or more races	—	—	—	—	—	—	—	8.1	9.7	8.0	9.7	—	—	—	—	—	—	—	1.8	2.2	2.1	2.8
Nonresident alien	3.0	3.7	3.5	3.8	1.6	2.1	3.2	4.1	3.4	2.4	2.5	†	†	†	†	†	†	†	†	†	†	†

—Not available.
†Not applicable.
NOTE: Race categories exclude persons of Hispanic ethnicity. Because of underreporting and nonreporting of racial/ethnic data, some figures are slightly lower than corresponding data in other tables. Data through 1990 are for institutions of higher education, while later data are for degree-granting institutions. Degree-granting institutions grant associate's or higher degrees and participate in Title IV federal financial aid programs. The degree-granting classification is very similar to the earlier higher educa- tion classification, but it includes more 2-year colleges and excludes a few higher education institutions that did not grant degrees. Some data have been revised from previously published figures. Detail may not sum to totals because of rounding.
SOURCE: U.S. Department of Education, National Center for Education Statistics, Higher Education General Information Survey (HEGIS), "Fall Enrollment in Colleges and Universities" surveys, 1976 and 1980; Integrated Postsecondary Education Data System (IPEDS), "Fall Enrollment Survey" (IPEDS-EF:90); and IPEDS Spring 2001 through Spring 2014, Enrollment component. (This table was prepared November 2014.)

Table 306.30. Fall enrollment of U.S. residents in degree-granting postsecondary institutions, by race/ethnicity: Selected years, 1976 through 2024

	Enrollment (in thousands)									Percentage distribution								
					Asian/Pacific Islander			American Indian/ Alaska Native	Two or more races					Asian/Pacific Islander			American Indian/ Alaska Native	Two or more races
Year	Total	White	Black	Hispanic	Total	Asian	Pacific Islander			Total	White	Black	Hispanic	Total	Asian	Pacific Islander		
1	2	3	4	5	6	7	8	9	10	11	12	13	14	15	16	17	18	19
1976	10,767	9,076	1,033	384	198	—	—	76	—	100.0	84.3	9.6	3.6	1.8	—	—	0.7	—
1980	11,782	9,833	1,107	472	286	—	—	84	—	100.0	83.5	9.4	4.0	2.4	—	—	0.7	—
1990	13,427	10,722	1,247	782	572	—	—	103	—	100.0	79.9	9.3	5.8	4.3	—	—	0.8	—
1994	13,823	10,427	1,449	1,046	774	—	—	127	—	100.0	75.4	10.5	7.6	5.6	—	—	0.9	—
1995	13,807	10,311	1,474	1,094	797	—	—	131	—	100.0	74.7	10.7	7.9	5.8	—	—	1.0	—
1996	13,901	10,264	1,506	1,166	828	—	—	138	—	100.0	73.8	10.8	8.4	6.0	—	—	1.0	—
1997	14,037	10,266	1,551	1,218	859	—	—	142	—	100.0	73.1	11.0	8.7	6.1	—	—	1.0	—
1998	14,063	10,179	1,583	1,257	900	—	—	144	—	100.0	72.4	11.3	8.9	6.4	—	—	1.0	—
1999	14,361	10,329	1,649	1,324	914	—	—	146	—	100.0	71.9	11.5	9.2	6.4	—	—	1.0	—
2000	14,784	10,462	1,730	1,462	978	—	—	151	—	100.0	70.8	11.7	9.9	6.6	—	—	1.0	—
2001	15,363	10,775	1,850	1,561	1,019	—	—	158	—	100.0	70.1	12.0	10.2	6.6	—	—	1.0	—
2002	16,021	11,140	1,979	1,662	1,074	—	—	166	—	100.0	69.5	12.4	10.4	6.7	—	—	1.0	—
2003	16,314	11,281	2,068	1,716	1,076	—	—	173	—	100.0	69.1	12.7	10.5	6.6	—	—	1.1	—
2004	16,682	11,423	2,165	1,810	1,109	—	—	176	—	100.0	68.5	13.0	10.8	6.6	—	—	1.1	—
2005	16,903	11,495	2,215	1,882	1,134	—	—	176	—	100.0	68.0	13.1	11.1	6.7	—	—	1.0	—
2006	17,163	11,572	2,280	1,964	1,165	—	—	181	—	100.0	67.4	13.3	11.4	6.8	—	—	1.1	—
2007	17,624	11,756	2,383	2,076	1,218	—	—	190	—	100.0	66.7	13.5	11.8	6.9	—	—	1.1	—
2008	18,442	12,089	2,584	2,273	1,303	—	—	193	—	100.0	65.5	14.0	12.3	7.1	—	—	1.0	—
2009	19,631	12,669	2,884	2,537	1,335	—	—	206	325	100.0	64.5	14.7	12.9	6.8	—	—	1.0	—
2010	20,312	12,721	3,039	2,749	1,282	1,218	64	196	325	100.0	62.6	15.0	13.5	6.3	6.0	0.3	1.0	1.6
2011	20,270	12,402	3,079	2,893	1,277	1,211	66	186	433	100.0	61.2	15.2	14.3	6.3	6.0	0.3	0.9	2.1
2012	19,860	11,981	2,962	2,979	1,259	1,196	64	173	505	100.0	60.3	14.9	15.0	6.3	6.0	0.3	0.9	2.5
2013	19,535	11,591	2,872	3,091	1,260	1,199	61	163	559	100.0	59.3	14.7	15.8	6.4	6.1	0.3	0.8	2.9
2014[1]	19,426	11,582	2,966	2,951	1,214	—	—	156	556	100.0	59.6	15.3	15.2	6.3	—	—	0.8	2.9
2015[1]	19,399	11,460	3,016	3,013	1,200	—	—	154	555	100.0	59.1	15.5	15.5	6.2	—	—	0.8	2.9
2016[1]	19,632	11,509	3,100	3,098	1,208	—	—	154	562	100.0	58.6	15.8	15.8	6.2	—	—	0.8	2.9
2017[1]	20,045	11,674	3,204	3,208	1,230	—	—	155	574	100.0	58.2	16.0	16.0	6.1	—	—	0.8	2.9
2018[1]	20,421	11,835	3,286	3,306	1,252	—	—	157	585	100.0	58.0	16.1	16.2	6.1	—	—	0.8	2.9
2019[1]	20,696	11,935	3,349	3,390	1,272	—	—	158	593	100.0	57.7	16.2	16.4	6.1	—	—	0.8	2.9
2020[1]	20,902	11,982	3,407	3,468	1,287	—	—	159	598	100.0	57.3	16.3	16.6	6.2	—	—	0.8	2.9
2021[1]	21,184	12,074	3,477	3,556	1,311	—	—	160	607	100.0	57.0	16.4	16.8	6.2	—	—	0.8	2.9
2022[1]	21,496	12,184	3,546	3,651	1,339	—	—	161	615	100.0	56.7	16.5	17.0	6.2	—	—	0.7	2.9
2023[1]	21,836	12,298	3,626	3,758	1,366	—	—	162	625	100.0	56.3	16.6	17.2	6.3	—	—	0.7	2.9
2024[1]	22,064	12,346	3,683	3,851	1,389	—	—	162	632	100.0	56.0	16.7	17.5	6.3	—	—	0.7	2.9

—Not available.

[1]Projected.

NOTE: Race categories exclude persons of Hispanic ethnicity. Prior to 2010, institutions were not required to report separate data on Asians, Pacific Islanders, and students of Two or more races. Detail may not sum to totals because of rounding. Some data have been revised from previously published figures. Some data have been revised from previously published figures.

SOURCE: U.S. Department of Education, National Center for Education Statistics, Higher Education General Information Survey (HEGIS), "Fall Enrollment in Colleges and Universities" surveys, 1976 and 1980; Integrated Postsecondary Education Data System (IPEDS), "Fall Enrollment Survey" (IPEDS-EF:90–99); IPEDS Spring 2001 through Spring 2014, Enrollment component; and Enrollment in Degree-Granting Institutions by Race/Ethnicity Projection Model, 1980 through 2024. (This table was prepared March 2015.)

Table 306.40. Fall enrollment of males and females and specific racial/ethnic groups in degree-granting postsecondary institutions, by control and level of institution and percentage of U.S. resident enrollment in the same racial/ethnic group: 2013

		Public institutions								Nonprofit institutions								For-profit institutions		
Sex, racial/ethnic group, and percentage of U.S. resident enrollment	Total, all institutions	Total	4-year						2-year	Total	4-year						2-year	Total	4-year	2-year
			Research university, very high[1]	Research university, high[2]	Doctoral/research[3]	Master's[4]	Baccalaureate[5]	Special focus[6]			Research university, very high[1]	Research university, high[2]	Doctoral/research[3]	Master's[4]	Baccalaureate[5]	Special focus[6]				
1	2	3	4	5	6	7	8	9	10	11	12	13	14	15	16	17	18	19	20	21
All institutions																				
Total enrollment	20,375,789	14,745,558	2,363,477	1,478,612	416,284	2,655,967	1,115,474	90,603	6,625,141	3,974,004	557,026	310,887	322,508	1,566,964	810,477	373,944	32,198	1,656,227	1,344,827	311,400
Sex																				
Male	8,860,786	6,568,839	1,168,376	695,263	173,659	1,119,156	492,318	34,774	2,885,293	1,692,903	274,830	144,299	130,476	611,309	340,766	179,367	11,856	599,044	498,277	100,767
Female	11,515,003	8,176,719	1,195,101	783,349	242,625	1,536,811	623,156	55,829	3,739,848	2,281,101	282,196	166,588	192,032	955,655	469,711	194,577	20,342	1,057,183	846,550	210,633
Race/ethnicity																				
White	11,590,717	8,364,146	1,428,602	927,266	244,641	1,594,482	619,767	52,003	3,497,385	2,475,173	279,614	187,369	180,612	1,034,423	543,866	233,758	15,531	751,398	628,203	123,195
Black	2,872,126	1,886,791	148,717	147,203	95,666	340,453	169,167	7,722	977,863	488,747	32,400	30,089	39,423	211,631	124,679	41,558	8,967	496,588	410,352	86,236
Hispanic	3,091,112	2,477,489	234,598	184,106	39,179	380,456	218,347	6,925	1,413,878	354,386	46,530	27,606	42,132	148,078	59,290	26,552	4,198	259,237	186,089	73,148
Asian	1,198,545	905,582	236,360	73,773	10,520	151,617	43,442	10,466	379,404	239,549	75,818	20,926	24,363	62,374	22,596	32,130	1,342	53,414	41,819	11,595
Pacific Islander	61,053	39,171	4,762	2,699	416	5,840	4,746	101	20,607	9,953	566	778	816	4,370	1,927	1,377	119	11,929	9,267	2,662
American Indian/Alaska Native	162,563	124,615	10,140	10,575	1,622	19,267	9,047	7,468	66,496	21,726	1,421	875	1,499	8,243	4,449	4,468	771	16,222	12,514	3,708
Two or more races	559,362	413,354	75,703	41,301	9,768	74,831	29,736	2,064	179,951	101,284	17,779	7,960	8,534	35,922	21,963	8,570	556	44,724	35,627	9,097
Nonresident alien	840,311	534,410	224,595	91,689	14,472	89,021	21,222	3,854	89,557	283,186	102,898	35,284	25,129	61,923	31,707	25,531	714	22,715	20,956	1,759
White enrollment, by percentage White																				
Less than 10.0 percent	39,671	32,906	0	2,701	2,132	4,640	6,860	152	16,421	2,579	0	300	10	670	1,143	286	170	4,186	2,142	2,044
10.0 to 24.9 percent	248,263	206,250	8,089	5,905	4,661	25,687	20,260	0	141,648	7,738	0	0	587	2,948	1,993	1,508	702	34,275	21,671	12,604
25.0 to 49.9 percent	1,529,350	1,122,978	118,794	82,230	11,578	163,321	52,602	3,996	690,457	152,282	15,857	10,628	24,278	64,800	21,896	11,643	3,180	254,090	218,802	35,288
50.0 to 74.9 percent	4,697,053	3,167,873	534,489	319,612	123,682	535,158	267,214	27,180	1,360,538	1,141,481	241,529	97,128	98,811	442,714	134,784	122,696	3,819	387,699	341,954	45,745
75.0 to 89.9 percent	4,404,086	3,316,812	742,011	477,532	100,726	741,438	210,819	20,675	1,023,611	1,027,855	22,228	79,313	56,926	486,496	316,913	59,959	6,020	59,419	37,917	21,502
90.0 percent or more	672,294	517,327	25,219	39,286	1,862	124,238	62,012	0	264,710	143,238	0	0	0	36,795	67,137	37,666	1,640	11,729	5,717	6,012
Black enrollment, by percentage Black																				
Less than 10.0 percent	522,611	388,854	86,237	36,331	7,364	78,278	19,476	2,889	158,279	122,866	28,439	13,593	7,687	40,156	23,007	9,729	255	10,891	6,253	4,638
10.0 to 24.9 percent	901,865	681,200	50,807	90,733	33,112	109,485	63,539	4,316	329,208	157,706	3,961	1,115	17,705	90,807	27,518	14,881	1,719	62,959	48,567	14,392
25.0 to 49.9 percent	912,026	501,884	11,673	11,900	9,104	62,302	56,967	120	349,818	112,499	0	6,544	10,694	66,774	17,451	7,995	3,041	297,643	267,246	30,397
50.0 to 74.9 percent	238,964	129,607	0	0	6,194	16,364	6,314	397	100,338	25,263	0	0	0	6,617	10,646	5,351	2,649	84,094	60,052	24,042
75.0 to 89.9 percent	145,003	97,229	0	0	26,907	31,023	12,622	0	26,677	13,206	0	0	0	5,973	4,666	1,591	976	34,568	24,611	9,957
90.0 percent or more	151,657	88,017	0	8,239	12,985	43,001	10,249	0	13,543	57,207	0	8,837	3,337	1,304	41,391	2,011	327	6,433	3,623	2,810
Hispanic enrollment, by percentage Hispanic																				
Less than 10.0 percent	537,196	362,269	78,137	40,583	14,676	72,161	21,464	2,567	132,681	129,903	22,517	7,860	5,540	53,855	27,139	12,239	753	45,024	40,600	4,424
10.0 to 24.9 percent	790,632	573,258	114,932	63,540	11,881	67,107	47,833	3,536	264,429	138,704	20,223	13,160	24,201	52,797	17,013	10,401	909	78,670	66,889	11,781
25.0 to 49.9 percent	985,689	840,524	41,529	9,396	4,811	157,031	71,261	822	555,674	67,894	3,790	6,586	10,455	29,929	12,551	2,960	1,623	77,271	49,494	27,777
50.0 to 74.9 percent	590,827	538,788	0	52,227	7,811	47,951	47,023	0	383,776	13,836	0	0	1,936	10,714	175	581	430	38,203	16,471	21,732
75.0 to 89.9 percent	90,860	74,830	0	18,360	0	0	0	0	56,470	2,327	0	0	0	783	932	129	483	13,703	8,228	5,475
90.0 percent or more	95,908	87,820	0	0	0	36,206	30,766	0	20,848	1,722	0	0	0	0	1,480	242	0	6,366	4,407	1,959
Asian enrollment, by percentage Asian																				
Less than 10.0 percent	509,986	377,080	80,483	37,489	10,520	54,988	24,289	1,623	167,688	98,248	5,005	13,292	10,378	44,068	17,275	7,863	367	34,658	29,396	5,262
10.0 to 24.9 percent	465,148	342,282	80,420	32,116	0	61,553	15,594	6,500	146,099	110,269	59,962	6,522	11,822	15,371	4,193	11,976	423	12,597	8,573	4,024
25.0 to 49.9 percent	221,700	186,220	75,457	4,168	0	35,076	3,559	2,343	65,617	29,971	10,851	1,112	2,163	2,899	1,128	11,266	552	5,509	3,200	2,309
50.0 to 74.9 percent	1,200	0	0	0	0	0	0	0	0	756	0	0	0	0	0	756	0	444	444	0
75.0 to 89.9 percent	15	0	0	0	0	0	0	0	0	15	0	0	0	0	0	15	0	0	0	0
90.0 percent or more	496	0	0	0	0	0	0	0	0	290	0	0	0	36	0	254	0	206	206	0

See notes at end of table.

Table 306.40. Fall enrollment of males and females and specific racial/ethnic groups in degree-granting postsecondary institutions, by control and level of institution and percentage of U.S. resident enrollment in the same racial/ethnic group: 2013—Continued

Sex, racial/ethnic group, and percentage of U.S. resident enrollment	Total, all institutions	Public institutions Total	Research university, very high[1]	Research university, high[2]	Doctoral/ research[3]	Master's[4]	Baccalau- reate[5]	Special focus[6]	2-year	Nonprofit institutions Total	Research university, very high[1]	Research university, high[2]	Doctoral/ research[3]	Master's[4]	Baccalau- reate[5]	Special focus[6]	2-year	For-profit institutions Total	4-year	2-year
1	2	3	4	5	6	7	8	9	10	11	12	13	14	15	16	17	18	19	20	21
Pacific Islander enrollment, by percentage Pacific Islander																				
Less than 10.0 percent	57,115	37,486	4,762	2,699	416	5,840	3,789	101	19,879	8,794	566	778	816	3,859	1,524	1,132	119	10,835	8,616	2,219
10.0 to 24.9 percent	3,351	1,685	0	0	0	0	957	0	728	904	0	0	0	511	210	183	0	762	319	443
25.0 to 49.9 percent	587	0	0	0	0	0	0	0	0	255	0	0	0	0	193	62	0	332	332	0
50.0 to 74.9 percent	0	0	0	0	0	0	0	0	0	0	0	0	0	0	0	0	0	0	0	0
75.0 to 89.9 percent	0	0	0	0	0	0	0	0	0	0	0	0	0	0	0	0	0	0	0	0
90.0 percent or more	0	0	0	0	0	0	0	0	0	0	0	0	0	0	0	0	0	0	0	0
American Indian/Alaska Native enrollment, by percentage American Indian/Alaska Native																				
Less than 10.0 percent	123,137	90,808	10,140	8,916	1,622	14,406	6,291	448	48,985	17,804	1,421	875	1,499	8,140	4,044	1,713	112	14,525	11,910	2,615
10.0 to 24.9 percent	15,709	13,950	0	1,659	0	4,861	2,756	0	4,674	250	0	0	0	103	83	64	0	1,509	604	905
25.0 to 49.9 percent	7,205	6,739	0	0	0	0	0	0	6,739	278	0	0	0	0	278	0	0	188	0	188
50.0 to 74.9 percent	1,940	737	0	0	0	0	0	0	737	1,203	0	0	0	0	44	1,159	0	0	0	0
75.0 to 89.9 percent	4,729	3,671	0	0	0	0	0	515	3,156	1,058	0	0	0	0	0	968	90	0	0	0
90.0 percent or more	9,843	8,710	0	0	0	0	0	6,505	2,205	1,133	0	0	0	0	0	564	569	0	0	0
Two or more races enrollment, by percentage two or more races																				
Less than 10.0 percent	528,765	393,286	71,216	41,301	9,768	73,432	25,984	2,064	169,521	97,614	17,779	7,960	8,534	34,352	21,008	7,460	521	37,865	30,513	7,352
10.0 to 24.9 percent	18,600	8,658	4,487	0	0	1,399	897	0	1,875	3,643	0	0	0	1,570	955	1,083	35	6,299	5,114	1,185
25.0 to 49.9 percent	11,997	11,410	0	0	0	0	2,855	0	8,555	27	0	0	0	0	0	27	0	560	0	560
50.0 to 74.9 percent	0	0	0	0	0	0	0	0	0	0	0	0	0	0	0	0	0	0	0	0
75.0 to 89.9 percent	0	0	0	0	0	0	0	0	0	0	0	0	0	0	0	0	0	0	0	0
90.0 percent or more	0	0	0	0	0	0	0	0	0	0	0	0	0	0	0	0	0	0	0	0
Nonresident alien enrollment, by percentage nonresident alien[7]																				
Less than 10.0 percent	478,373	375,044	99,126	78,244	14,472	80,485	19,094	2,489	81,134	90,308	2,272	8,049	11,960	38,428	22,625	6,846	128	13,021	12,503	518
10.0 to 24.9 percent	303,729	155,020	125,469	13,445	0	4,784	2,128	771	8,423	146,386	84,814	20,039	7,191	19,754	7,141	6,921	526	2,323	1,713	610
25.0 to 49.9 percent	52,875	4,346	0	0	0	3,752	0	594	0	41,554	15,812	7,196	5,978	2,442	1,725	8,341	60	6,975	6,683	292
50.0 to 74.9 percent	3,432	0	0	0	0	0	0	0	0	3,036	0	0	0	679	216	2,141	0	396	57	339
75.0 to 89.9 percent	1,185	0	0	0	0	0	0	0	0	1,185	0	0	0	620	0	565	0	0	0	0
90.0 percent or more	717	0	0	0	0	0	0	0	0	717	0	0	0	0	0	717	0	0	0	0

[1]Research universities with a very high level of research activity.

[2]Research universities with a high level of research activity.

[3]Institutions that award at least 20 doctor's degrees per year, but did not have high levels of research activity.

[4]Institutions that award at least 50 master's degrees per year.

[5]Institutions that primarily emphasize undergraduate education. Also includes institutions classified as 4-year under the IPEDS system, which had been classified as 2-year in the Carnegie system because they primarily award associate's degrees.

[6]Four-year institutions that award degrees primarily in single fields of study, such as medicine, business, fine arts, theology, and engineering.

[7]Nonresident alien enrollment percentages based on total enrollment in the institution, rather than on the U.S. resident enrollment.

NOTE: Relative levels of research activity for research universities were determined by an analysis of research and development expenditures, science and engineering research staffing, and doctoral degrees conferred, by field. Further information on the research index ranking may be obtained from http://classifications.carnegiefoundation.org/resources/. Degree-granting institutions grant associate's or higher degrees and participate in Title IV federal financial aid programs. Race categories exclude persons of Hispanic ethnicity.

SOURCE: U.S. Department of Education, National Center for Education Statistics, Integrated Postsecondary Education Data System (IPEDS), Spring 2014, Enrollment component. (This table was prepared December 2014.)

Table 306.50. Total fall enrollment in degree-granting postsecondary institutions, by control and level of institution, level of enrollment, and race/ethnicity of student: 2013

Level of enrollment and race/ethnicity of student	Total, all institutions	Public — Total	Public 4-year — Total	Research university, very high[1]	Research university, high[2]	Doctoral/research university[3]	Master's[4]	Baccalaureate[5]	Special focus[6]	Public 2-year	Nonprofit — Total	Nonprofit 4-year — Total	Research university, very high[1]	Research university, high[2]	Doctoral/research university[3]	Master's[4]	Baccalaureate[5]	Special focus[6]	Nonprofit 2-year	For-profit — Total	For-profit 4-year	For-profit 2-year
1	2	3	4	5	6	7	8	9	10	11	12	13	14	15	16	17	18	19	20	21	22	23
Fall enrollment																						
All students, total	20,375,789	14,745,558	8,120,417	2,363,477	1,478,612	416,284	2,655,967	1,115,474	90,603	6,625,141	3,974,004	3,941,806	557,026	310,887	322,508	1,566,964	810,477	373,944	32,198	1,656,227	1,344,827	311,400
White	11,590,717	8,364,146	4,866,761	1,428,602	927,266	244,641	1,594,482	619,767	52,003	3,497,385	2,475,173	2,459,642	279,614	187,369	180,612	1,034,423	543,866	233,758	15,531	751,398	628,203	123,195
Black	2,872,126	1,886,791	908,928	148,717	147,203	95,666	340,453	169,167	7,722	977,863	488,747	479,780	32,400	30,089	39,423	211,631	124,679	41,558	8,967	496,588	410,352	86,236
Hispanic	3,091,112	2,477,489	1,063,611	234,598	184,106	39,179	380,456	218,347	6,925	1,413,878	354,386	350,188	46,530	27,606	42,132	148,106	59,290	26,552	4,198	259,237	186,089	73,148
Asian	1,198,545	905,582	526,178	236,360	73,773	10,520	151,617	43,442	10,466	379,404	239,549	238,207	75,818	20,926	24,363	62,374	22,596	32,130	1,342	53,414	41,819	11,595
Pacific Islander	61,053	39,171	18,564	4,762	2,689	416	5,840	4,746	101	20,607	9,953	9,834	566	778	816	4,370	1,927	1,377	119	11,929	9,267	2,662
American Indian/Alaska Native	162,563	124,615	58,119	10,140	10,575	1,622	19,267	9,047	7,468	66,496	21,726	20,955	1,421	875	1,499	8,243	4,449	4,468	771	16,222	12,514	3,708
Two or more races	559,962	413,354	233,403	75,703	41,301	9,768	74,831	29,736	2,064	179,951	100,728	100,172	17,779	7,960	8,534	35,922	21,963	8,570	556	44,724	35,627	9,097
Nonresident alien	840,311	534,410	444,853	224,595	91,689	14,472	89,021	21,222	3,854	89,557	283,186	282,472	102,898	35,284	25,129	61,923	31,707	25,531	714	22,715	20,956	1,759
Undergraduate	17,474,835	13,347,002	6,721,861	1,782,454	1,175,173	335,829	2,289,498	1,106,290	32,617	6,625,141	2,757,447	2,725,249	271,659	191,449	199,786	1,111,847	760,039	190,469	32,198	1,370,386	1,058,986	311,400
White	9,899,168	7,522,236	4,024,851	1,091,635	738,885	198,244	1,365,163	613,472	17,452	3,497,385	1,755,481	1,739,950	140,177	124,335	110,720	737,824	507,863	119,031	15,531	621,451	498,256	123,195
Black	2,504,814	1,758,975	781,112	116,931	123,506	79,191	290,640	168,029	2,815	977,863	350,822	341,855	16,643	16,007	23,493	143,840	117,895	23,977	8,967	395,017	308,781	86,236
Hispanic	2,870,150	2,369,192	955,314	198,609	160,635	32,936	343,080	217,789	2,265	1,413,878	266,438	262,240	28,525	16,881	29,384	115,244	56,535	15,670	4,198	234,520	161,372	73,148
Asian	1,010,138	820,653	441,249	194,586	60,059	8,010	133,971	42,962	1,661	379,404	147,827	146,485	43,839	13,751	15,668	40,942	20,819	11,466	1,342	41,658	30,063	11,595
Pacific Islander	54,221	37,137	16,530	3,840	2,282	353	5,295	4,704	56	20,607	7,062	6,943	209	399	508	3,212	1,846	780	119	10,022	7,360	2,662
American Indian/Alaska Native	147,766	117,277	50,781	7,610	8,927	1,301	16,810	8,993	7,140	66,496	15,909	15,138	760	618	851	5,914	4,079	3,697	771	13,609	10,101	3,708
Two or more races	505,174	387,393	207,442	64,184	36,066	8,487	68,340	29,504	861	179,951	78,202	77,646	11,768	5,813	6,305	28,617	21,294	4,405	556	39,023	29,926	9,097
Nonresident alien	483,404	334,139	244,582	105,059	44,813	7,307	66,199	20,837	367	89,557	134,379	133,665	29,737	13,655	12,857	36,254	29,709	11,453	714	14,886	13,127	1,759
Postbaccalaureate	2,900,954	1,398,556	1,398,556	581,023	303,439	80,455	366,469	9,184	57,986	†	1,216,557	1,216,557	285,367	119,438	122,722	455,117	50,438	183,475	†	285,841	285,841	†
White	1,691,549	841,910	841,910	336,967	188,381	46,397	229,319	6,295	34,551	†	719,692	719,692	139,437	63,034	69,882	296,599	36,003	114,727	†	129,947	129,947	†
Black	367,312	127,816	127,816	31,786	23,697	16,475	49,813	1,138	4,907	†	137,925	137,925	15,757	14,082	15,930	67,791	6,784	17,581	†	101,571	101,571	†
Hispanic	220,962	108,297	108,297	35,989	23,471	6,243	37,376	558	4,660	†	87,948	87,948	18,004	10,725	12,748	32,834	2,755	10,882	†	24,717	24,717	†
Asian	188,407	84,929	84,929	41,774	13,714	2,510	17,646	480	8,805	†	91,722	91,722	31,979	7,175	8,695	21,432	1,777	20,664	†	11,756	11,756	†
Pacific Islander	6,832	2,034	2,034	922	417	63	545	42	45	†	2,891	2,891	357	389	308	1,158	82	597	†	1,907	1,907	†
American Indian/Alaska Native	14,797	7,338	7,338	2,530	1,648	321	2,457	54	328	†	5,046	5,046	661	257	648	2,329	370	781	†	2,413	2,413	†
Two or more races	54,188	25,961	25,961	11,519	5,235	1,281	6,491	232	1,203	†	22,526	22,526	6,011	2,147	2,229	7,305	669	4,165	†	5,701	5,701	†
Nonresident alien	356,907	200,271	200,271	119,536	46,876	7,165	22,822	385	3,487	†	148,807	148,807	73,161	21,629	12,272	25,689	1,998	14,078	†	7,829	7,829	†
Percentage distribution of U.S. residents																						
U.S. residents, total	100.0	100.0	100.0	100.0	100.0	100.0	100.0	100.0	100.0	100.0	100.0	100.0	100.0	100.0	100.0	100.0	100.0	100.0	100.0	100.0	100.0	100.0
White	59.3	58.9	63.4	66.8	66.9	60.9	62.1	56.6	59.9	53.5	67.1	67.2	61.6	68.0	60.7	68.7	69.8	67.1	49.3	46.0	47.5	39.8
Black	14.7	13.3	11.8	7.0	10.6	23.8	13.3	15.5	8.9	15.0	13.2	13.1	7.1	10.9	13.3	14.1	16.0	11.9	28.5	30.4	31.0	27.9
Hispanic	15.8	17.4	13.9	11.0	13.3	9.8	14.8	20.0	8.0	21.6	9.6	9.6	10.2	10.0	14.2	9.8	7.6	7.6	13.3	15.9	14.1	23.6
Asian	6.1	6.4	6.9	11.1	5.3	2.6	5.9	4.0	12.1	5.8	6.5	6.5	16.7	7.6	8.2	4.1	2.9	9.2	4.3	3.3	3.2	3.7
Pacific Islander	0.3	0.3	0.2	0.2	0.2	0.1	0.2	0.4	0.1	0.3	0.3	0.3	0.1	0.3	0.3	0.3	0.2	0.4	0.4	0.7	0.7	0.9
American Indian/Alaska Native	0.8	0.9	0.8	0.5	0.8	0.4	0.8	0.8	8.6	1.0	0.6	0.6	0.3	0.3	0.5	0.5	0.6	1.3	2.4	1.0	0.9	1.2
Two or more races	2.9	2.9	3.0	3.5	3.0	2.4	2.9	2.7	2.4	2.8	2.7	2.8	3.9	2.9	2.9	2.4	2.8	2.5	1.8	2.7	2.7	2.9
Undergraduate	100.0	100.0	100.0	100.0	100.0	100.0	100.0	100.0	100.0	100.0	100.0	100.0	100.0	100.0	100.0	100.0	100.0	100.0	100.0	100.0	100.0	100.0
White	58.3	57.8	62.1	65.1	65.4	60.3	61.4	56.5	54.1	53.5	66.9	67.1	57.9	69.9	59.2	68.6	69.5	66.5	49.3	45.8	47.6	39.8
Black	14.7	13.5	12.1	7.0	10.9	24.1	13.1	15.5	8.7	15.0	13.4	13.2	6.9	9.0	12.6	13.4	16.1	13.4	28.5	29.1	29.5	27.9
Hispanic	16.9	18.2	14.7	11.8	14.2	10.0	15.4	20.1	7.0	21.6	10.2	10.1	11.8	9.5	15.7	10.7	7.7	8.8	13.3	17.3	15.4	23.6
Asian	5.9	6.3	6.8	11.6	5.3	2.4	6.0	4.0	5.2	5.8	5.7	5.7	18.1	7.7	8.4	3.8	2.9	6.4	4.3	3.1	2.9	3.7
Pacific Islander	0.3	0.3	0.2	0.2	0.2	0.1	0.2	0.4	0.2	0.3	0.3	0.3	0.1	0.2	0.3	0.3	0.3	0.4	0.4	0.7	0.7	0.9
American Indian/Alaska Native	0.9	0.9	0.8	0.5	0.8	0.4	0.8	0.8	22.1	1.0	0.6	0.6	0.3	0.3	0.5	0.5	0.6	2.1	2.4	1.0	1.0	1.2
Two or more races	3.0	3.0	3.2	3.8	3.2	2.6	3.1	2.7	2.7	2.8	3.0	3.0	4.9	3.3	3.4	2.7	2.9	2.5	1.8	2.9	2.9	2.9

See notes at end of table.

Table 306.50. Total fall enrollment in degree-granting postsecondary institutions, by control and level of institution, level of enrollment, and race/ethnicity of student: 2013—Continued

Level of enrollment and race/ethnicity of student	Total, all institutions	Public institutions									Nonprofit institutions									For-profit institutions		
		Total	4-year							2-year	Total	4-year							2-year	Total	4-year	2-year
			Total	Research university, very high[1]	Research university, high[2]	Doctoral/ research university[3]	Master's[4]	Bacca-laureate[5]	Special focus[6]			Total	Research university, very high	Research university, high[1]	Doctoral/ research university[3]	Master's[4]	Bacca-laureate[5]	Special focus[6]				
1	2	3	4	5	6	7	8	9	10	11	12	13	14	15	16	17	18	19	20	21	22	23
Postbaccalaureate	100.0	100.0	100.0	100.0	100.0	100.0	100.0	100.0	100.0	†	100.0	100.0	100.0	100.0	100.0	100.0	100.0	100.0	†	100.0	100.0	†
White	66.5	70.3	70.3	73.0	73.4	63.3	66.7	71.5	63.4	†	67.4	67.4	65.7	64.4	63.3	69.1	74.3	67.7	†	46.7	46.7	†
Black	14.4	10.7	10.7	6.9	9.2	22.5	14.5	12.9	9.0	†	12.9	12.9	7.4	14.4	14.4	15.8	14.0	10.4	†	36.5	36.5	†
Hispanic	8.7	9.0	9.0	7.8	9.1	8.5	10.9	6.3	8.6	†	8.2	8.2	8.5	11.0	11.5	7.6	5.7	6.4	†	8.9	8.9	†
Asian	7.4	7.1	7.1	9.1	5.3	3.4	5.1	5.5	16.2	†	8.6	8.6	15.1	7.3	7.9	5.0	3.7	12.2	†	4.2	4.2	†
Pacific Islander	0.3	0.2	0.2	0.2	0.2	0.1	0.2	0.5	0.1	†	0.3	0.3	0.2	0.4	0.3	0.3	0.2	0.4	†	0.7	0.7	†
American Indian/Alaska Native	0.6	0.6	0.6	0.5	0.6	0.4	0.7	0.6	0.6	†	0.5	0.5	0.3	0.3	0.6	0.5	0.8	0.5	†	0.9	0.9	†
Two or more races	2.1	2.2	2.2	2.5	2.0	1.7	1.9	2.6	2.2	†	2.1	2.1	2.8	2.2	2.0	1.7	1.4	2.5	†	2.1	2.1	†

†Not applicable.

[1]Research universities with a very high level of research activity.

[2]Research universities with a high level of research activity.

[3]Research universities that award at least 20 doctor's degrees per year, but did not have high levels of research activity.

[4]Institutions that award at least 50 master's degrees per year.

[5]Institutions that primarily emphasize undergraduate education. Also includes institutions classified as 4-year under the IPEDS system, which had been classified as 2-year in the Carnegie system because they primarily award associate's degrees.

[6]Four-year institutions that award degrees primarily in single fields of study, such as medicine, business, fine arts, theology, and engineering.

NOTE: Relative levels of research activity for research universities were determined by an analysis of research and development expenditures, science and engineering research staffing, and doctoral degrees conferred, by field. Further information on the research index ranking may be obtained from http://classifications.carnegiefoundation.org/resources/. Includes imputed Carnegie system classifications for institutions with missing data. Degree-granting institutions grant associate's or higher degrees and participate in Title IV federal financial aid programs. Race categories exclude persons of Hispanic ethnicity.
SOURCE: U.S. Department of Education, National Center for Education Statistics, Integrated Postsecondary Education Data System (IPEDS), Spring 2014, Enrollment component. (This table was prepared December 2014.)

Table 306.60. Fall enrollment in degree-granting postsecondary institutions, by race/ethnicity of student and state or jurisdiction: 2013

State or jurisdiction	Number									Percentage distribution of U.S. residents							
	Total	White	Black	Hispanic	Asian	Pacific Islander	American Indian/ Alaska Native	Two or more races	Non-resident alien	Total	White	Black	Hispanic	Asian	Pacific Islander	American Indian/ Alaska Native	Two or more races
1	2	3	4	5	6	7	8	9	10	11	12	13	14	15	16	17	18
United States	20,375,789	11,590,717	2,872,126	3,091,112	1,198,545	61,053	162,563	559,362	840,311	100.0	59.3	14.7	15.8	6.1	0.3	0.8	2.9
Alabama	305,712	188,416	89,628	8,590	5,254	302	2,156	4,592	6,774	100.0	63.0	30.0	2.9	1.8	0.1	0.7	1.5
Alaska	34,890	21,558	1,101	2,909	1,606	386	4,073	2,607	650	100.0	63.0	3.2	8.5	4.7	1.1	11.9	7.6
Arizona	694,123	370,754	105,803	137,451	22,562	3,753	16,796	18,394	18,610	100.0	54.9	15.7	20.3	3.3	0.6	2.5	2.7
Arkansas	172,224	119,496	30,646	8,166	2,671	151	1,481	4,528	5,085	100.0	71.5	18.3	4.9	1.6	0.1	0.9	2.7
California	2,636,921	850,885	184,644	950,748	402,851	15,289	11,715	109,434	111,355	100.0	33.7	7.3	37.6	16.0	0.6	0.5	4.3
Colorado	358,723	238,774	26,769	53,350	11,918	993	3,723	12,924	10,272	100.0	68.5	7.7	15.3	3.4	0.3	1.1	3.7
Connecticut	200,966	125,847	25,098	26,463	9,565	253	572	4,405	8,763	100.0	65.5	13.1	13.8	5.0	0.1	0.3	2.3
Delaware	59,615	35,249	12,924	3,528	1,985	92	268	1,211	4,358	100.0	63.8	23.4	6.4	3.6	0.2	0.5	2.2
District of Columbia	89,257	41,537	23,780	6,395	5,768	161	423	2,128	9,065	100.0	51.8	29.7	8.0	7.2	0.2	0.5	2.7
Florida	1,125,810	529,550	222,019	267,958	35,010	2,660	4,076	27,819	36,718	100.0	48.6	20.4	24.6	3.2	0.2	0.4	2.6
Georgia	533,424	269,511	179,172	29,862	23,447	772	1,689	11,474	17,497	100.0	52.2	34.7	5.8	4.5	0.1	0.3	2.2
Hawaii	76,434	14,240	1,701	7,388	23,632	6,315	218	18,434	4,506	100.0	19.8	2.4	10.3	32.9	8.8	0.3	25.6
Idaho	109,318	86,957	1,375	9,631	1,588	686	1,038	3,480	4,563	100.0	83.0	1.3	9.2	1.5	0.7	1.0	3.3
Illinois	842,888	482,340	124,133	130,009	49,721	1,682	2,414	17,658	34,931	100.0	59.7	15.4	16.1	6.2	0.2	0.3	2.2
Indiana	444,364	328,486	46,611	22,379	10,312	324	1,270	10,723	24,259	100.0	78.2	11.1	5.3	2.5	0.1	0.3	2.6
Iowa	339,738	239,186	51,102	21,952	7,081	1,057	2,320	5,687	11,353	100.0	72.8	15.6	6.7	2.2	0.3	0.7	1.7
Kansas	215,855	154,576	16,376	17,233	5,630	343	2,910	5,779	13,008	100.0	76.2	8.1	8.5	2.8	0.2	1.4	2.8
Kentucky	273,073	222,236	26,984	6,904	3,822	274	750	5,697	6,406	100.0	83.3	10.1	2.6	1.4	0.1	0.3	2.1
Louisiana	251,887	142,224	79,051	11,073	5,770	238	1,504	5,014	7,013	100.0	58.1	32.3	4.5	2.4	0.1	0.6	2.0
Maine	70,849	61,829	2,107	1,703	1,460	72	786	1,432	1,460	100.0	89.1	3.0	2.5	2.1	0.1	1.1	2.1
Maryland	363,771	179,642	104,169	25,714	24,574	718	1,066	10,930	16,958	100.0	51.8	30.0	7.4	7.1	0.2	0.3	3.2
Massachusetts	514,008	319,668	44,594	50,921	37,881	571	1,233	12,974	46,166	100.0	68.3	9.5	10.9	8.1	0.1	0.3	2.8
Michigan	643,592	456,483	89,734	24,463	22,558	788	4,277	15,273	30,016	100.0	74.4	14.6	4.0	3.7	0.1	0.7	2.5
Minnesota	441,491	307,924	61,656	19,842	20,719	640	3,571	13,244	13,895	100.0	72.0	14.4	4.6	4.8	0.1	0.8	3.1
Mississippi	173,634	95,947	67,336	3,087	1,970	161	762	1,955	2,416	100.0	56.0	39.3	1.8	1.2	0.1	0.4	1.1
Missouri	438,222	316,187	63,402	17,536	11,919	666	2,349	9,696	16,467	100.0	75.0	15.0	4.2	2.8	0.2	0.6	2.3
Montana	52,777	43,053	447	1,706	684	90	3,827	1,354	1,616	100.0	84.2	0.9	3.3	1.3	0.2	7.5	2.6
Nebraska	137,943	108,201	8,109	9,752	3,526	232	1,051	2,546	4,526	100.0	81.1	6.1	7.3	2.6	0.2	0.8	1.9
Nevada	116,738	58,394	9,621	26,006	11,829	1,698	1,055	5,924	2,211	100.0	51.0	8.4	22.7	10.3	1.5	0.9	5.2
New Hampshire	92,440	74,834	6,026	3,927	2,705	71	648	1,229	3,000	100.0	83.7	6.7	4.4	3.0	0.1	0.7	1.4
New Jersey	436,939	224,149	65,092	82,514	36,930	1,488	1,275	7,873	17,618	100.0	53.5	15.5	19.7	8.8	0.4	0.3	1.9
New Mexico	153,455	54,482	4,775	69,005	2,543	365	14,810	2,895	4,580	100.0	36.6	3.2	46.4	1.7	0.2	9.9	1.9
New York	1,304,230	679,868	181,225	202,955	114,350	3,055	4,677	23,443	94,657	100.0	56.2	15.0	16.8	9.5	0.3	0.4	1.9
North Carolina	575,198	345,486	144,720	32,275	16,337	860	6,922	12,154	16,444	100.0	61.8	25.9	5.8	2.9	0.2	1.2	2.2
North Dakota	55,063	44,656	1,669	1,408	635	72	2,532	1,101	2,990	100.0	85.8	3.2	2.7	1.2	0.1	4.9	2.1
Ohio	697,647	521,361	90,098	22,286	15,803	579	2,223	15,743	29,554	100.0	78.0	13.5	3.3	2.4	0.1	0.3	2.4
Oklahoma	220,897	136,576	21,346	14,697	5,760	382	18,635	13,057	10,444	100.0	64.9	10.1	7.0	2.7	0.2	8.9	6.2
Oregon	251,106	177,275	7,988	25,140	13,231	1,624	3,412	10,783	11,653	100.0	74.0	3.3	10.5	5.5	0.7	1.4	4.5
Pennsylvania	765,582	537,542	88,874	45,748	35,936	902	1,769	16,329	38,482	100.0	73.9	12.2	6.3	4.9	0.1	0.2	2.2
Rhode Island	83,460	57,089	5,739	9,513	3,595	58	312	2,369	4,785	100.0	72.6	7.3	12.1	4.6	0.1	0.4	3.0

See notes at end of table.

Table 306.60. Fall enrollment in degree-granting postsecondary institutions, by race/ethnicity of student and state or jurisdiction: 2013—Continued

State or jurisdiction	Number									Percentage distribution of U.S. residents							
	Total	White	Black	Hispanic	Asian	Pacific Islander	American Indian/ Alaska Native	Two or more races	Non-resident alien	Total	White	Black	Hispanic	Asian	Pacific Islander	American Indian/ Alaska Native	Two or more races
1	2	3	4	5	6	7	8	9	10	11	12	13	14	15	16	17	18
South Carolina	257,844	161,193	72,091	9,076	3,810	318	1,046	5,588	4,722	100.0	63.7	28.5	3.6	1.5	0.1	0.4	2.2
South Dakota	55,129	45,115	1,934	1,513	580	104	3,269	1,186	1,428	100.0	84.0	3.6	2.8	1.1	0.2	6.1	2.2
Tennessee	338,197	233,888	69,060	11,114	6,974	372	1,020	7,794	7,975	100.0	70.8	20.9	3.4	2.1	0.1	0.3	2.4
Texas	1,541,378	625,597	209,449	524,825	82,516	2,606	6,546	30,717	59,122	100.0	42.2	14.1	35.4	5.6	0.2	0.4	2.1
Utah	264,255	205,590	9,223	23,498	7,226	1,971	2,478	6,296	7,973	100.0	80.2	3.6	9.2	2.8	0.8	1.0	2.5
Vermont	43,534	36,823	1,126	1,815	1,048	64	264	1,135	1,259	100.0	87.1	2.7	4.3	2.5	0.2	0.6	2.7
Virginia	583,755	342,637	129,638	39,210	33,127	1,530	2,281	18,808	16,524	100.0	60.4	22.9	6.9	5.8	0.3	0.4	3.3
Washington	363,377	230,461	16,515	36,557	32,293	2,088	4,338	20,907	20,218	100.0	67.2	4.8	10.7	9.4	0.6	1.3	6.1
West Virginia	157,954	118,909	19,928	7,992	2,522	593	758	3,707	3,545	100.0	77.0	12.9	5.2	1.6	0.4	0.5	2.4
Wisconsin	364,021	286,583	24,024	18,945	12,162	393	3,269	7,454	11,191	100.0	81.2	6.8	5.4	3.4	0.1	0.9	2.1
Wyoming	37,084	31,042	525	2,830	337	107	614	611	1,018	100.0	86.1	1.5	7.8	0.9	0.3	1.7	1.7
U.S. Service Academies	14,997	10,411	969	1,550	812	84	92	867	212	100.0	70.4	6.6	10.5	5.5	0.6	0.6	5.9
Other jurisdictions	**254,543**	**1,485**	**2,154**	**237,042**	**3,181**	**9,497**	**114**	**545**	**525**	**100.0**	**0.6**	**0.8**	**93.3**	**1.3**	**3.7**	**#**	**0.2**
American Samoa	1,488	3	0	0	16	1,367	0	0	102	100.0	0.2	0.0	0.0	1.2	98.6	0.0	0.0
Federated States of Micronesia	2,446	2	2	0	6	2,436	0	0	0	100.0	0.1	0.1	0.0	0.2	99.6	0.0	0.0
Guam	6,518	219	46	42	2,682	3,466	10	0	53	100.0	3.4	0.7	0.6	41.5	53.6	0.2	0.0
Marshall Islands	1,000	3	0	0	7	983	7	0	0	100.0	0.3	0.0	0.0	0.7	98.3	0.7	0.0
Northern Marianas	1,109	15	1	5	333	587	1	73	94	100.0	1.5	0.1	0.5	32.8	57.8	0.1	7.2
Palau	646	0	0	0	0	642	0	0	0	100.0	0.0	0.0	0.0	0.6	99.4	0.0	0.0
Puerto Rico	239,015	1,083	237	236,841	125	13	96	472	148	100.0	0.5	0.1	99.2	0.1	#	#	0.2
U.S. Virgin Islands	2,321	160	1,868	154	8	3	0	0	128	100.0	7.3	85.2	7.0	0.4	0.1	0.0	0.0

#Rounds to zero.
NOTE: Race categories exclude persons of Hispanic ethnicity. Degree-granting institutions grant associate's or higher degrees and participate in Title IV federal financial aid programs. Detail may not sum to totals because of rounding.

SOURCE: U.S. Department of Education, National Center for Education Statistics, Integrated Postsecondary Education Data System (IPEDS), Spring 2014, Enrollment component. (This table was prepared November 2014.)

Table 306.70. Fall enrollment in degree-granting postsecondary institutions, by race/ethnicity of student and state or jurisdiction: 2012

State or jurisdiction	Number									Percentage distribution of U.S. residents							
	Total	White	Black	Hispanic	Asian	Pacific Islander	American Indian/ Alaska Native	Two or more races	Non-resident alien	Total	White	Black	Hispanic	Asian	Pacific Islander	American Indian/ Alaska Native	Two or more races
1	2	3	4	5	6	7	8	9	10	11	12	13	14	15	16	17	18
United States	20,642,819	11,981,143	2,962,140	2,979,443	1,195,578	63,609	172,923	505,092	782,891	100.0	60.3	14.9	15.0	6.0	0.3	0.9	2.5
Alabama	310,311	191,653	92,602	8,216	5,130	282	2,341	3,600	6,487	100.0	63.1	30.5	2.7	1.7	0.1	0.8	1.2
Alaska	32,797	20,584	1,109	2,486	1,559	261	3,677	2,406	715	100.0	64.2	3.5	7.7	4.9	0.8	11.5	7.5
Arizona	736,379	403,607	115,300	135,585	22,630	4,007	19,185	18,296	17,769	100.0	56.2	16.0	18.9	3.1	0.6	2.7	2.5
Arkansas	176,458	122,860	32,690	7,571	2,736	179	1,558	3,979	4,885	100.0	71.6	19.1	4.4	1.6	0.1	0.9	2.3
California	2,621,460	890,525	187,692	905,947	408,668	16,198	12,866	99,622	99,942	100.0	35.3	7.4	35.9	16.2	0.6	0.5	4.0
Colorado	362,935	244,458	27,669	53,267	12,027	933	3,886	11,599	9,096	100.0	69.1	7.8	15.1	3.4	0.3	1.1	3.3
Connecticut	201,658	128,581	25,222	25,370	9,349	261	586	4,054	8,235	100.0	66.5	13.0	13.1	4.8	0.1	0.3	2.1
Delaware	58,128	35,573	12,692	3,306	2,164	71	189	1,205	2,928	100.0	64.4	23.0	6.0	3.9	0.1	0.3	2.2
District of Columbia	90,150	43,022	24,175	6,322	5,927	174	422	1,924	8,184	100.0	52.5	29.5	7.7	7.2	0.2	0.5	2.3
Florida	1,154,929	554,691	231,049	267,272	36,003	2,480	4,720	26,424	32,290	100.0	49.4	20.6	23.8	3.2	0.2	0.4	2.4
Georgia	545,358	278,142	186,086	28,715	22,881	808	1,734	10,654	16,338	100.0	52.6	35.2	5.4	4.3	0.2	0.3	2.0
Hawaii	78,456	15,103	1,760	7,602	24,506	6,935	268	17,524	4,758	100.0	20.5	2.4	10.3	33.3	9.4	0.4	23.8
Idaho	108,008	88,425	1,284	9,628	1,752	769	1,263	1,577	3,310	100.0	84.5	1.2	9.2	1.7	0.7	1.2	1.5
Illinois	867,110	507,070	131,989	125,718	49,493	2,089	2,577	15,717	32,457	100.0	60.8	15.8	15.1	5.9	0.3	0.3	1.9
Indiana	447,262	335,390	47,903	21,446	9,801	320	1,394	8,534	22,474	100.0	79.0	11.3	5.0	2.3	0.1	0.3	2.0
Iowa	361,183	255,717	55,447	22,327	7,180	1,108	2,793	5,510	11,101	100.0	73.0	15.8	6.4	2.1	0.3	0.8	1.6
Kansas	213,786	155,205	16,204	15,680	5,305	327	2,920	5,181	12,964	100.0	77.3	8.1	7.8	2.6	0.2	1.5	2.6
Kentucky	282,125	231,271	28,387	6,643	3,860	307	827	5,046	5,775	100.0	83.7	10.3	2.4	1.4	0.1	0.3	1.8
Louisiana	258,825	147,305	82,190	10,948	5,860	226	1,498	4,139	6,659	100.0	58.4	32.6	4.3	2.3	0.1	0.6	1.6
Maine	72,810	64,222	2,017	1,553	1,390	206	799	1,275	1,348	100.0	89.9	2.8	2.2	1.9	0.3	1.1	1.8
Maryland	374,496	188,836	108,182	24,378	24,308	736	1,169	9,519	17,368	100.0	52.9	30.3	6.8	6.8	0.2	0.3	2.7
Massachusetts	516,331	328,247	44,292	48,408	37,499	526	1,315	12,913	43,131	100.0	69.4	9.4	10.2	7.9	0.1	0.3	2.7
Michigan	663,825	472,796	97,815	23,589	22,306	882	4,749	13,584	28,104	100.0	74.4	15.4	3.7	3.5	0.1	0.7	2.1
Minnesota	451,661	319,361	63,035	18,865	19,926	635	3,883	12,714	13,242	100.0	72.8	14.4	4.3	4.5	0.1	0.9	2.9
Mississippi	176,665	97,562	69,674	2,852	1,898	138	738	1,452	2,351	100.0	56.0	40.0	1.6	1.1	0.1	0.4	0.8
Missouri	441,371	322,252	62,942	17,139	11,617	740	2,466	8,973	15,242	100.0	75.6	14.8	4.0	2.7	0.2	0.6	2.1
Montana	53,254	43,460	409	1,622	662	100	4,352	1,170	1,479	100.0	83.9	0.8	3.1	1.3	0.2	8.4	2.3
Nebraska	139,578	111,323	8,169	8,922	3,447	254	1,161	1,930	4,372	100.0	82.3	6.0	6.6	2.5	0.2	0.9	1.4
Nevada	118,300	61,132	10,054	24,640	11,672	1,812	1,191	5,474	2,325	100.0	52.7	8.7	21.2	10.1	1.6	1.0	4.7
New Hampshire	82,678	67,886	3,333	4,250	2,719	71	474	1,181	2,764	100.0	84.9	4.2	5.3	3.4	0.1	0.6	1.5
New Jersey	439,965	231,485	64,331	79,793	36,732	1,759	1,656	7,242	16,967	100.0	54.7	15.2	18.9	8.7	0.4	0.4	1.7
New Mexico	156,424	57,146	4,801	69,861	2,572	404	14,469	2,775	4,396	100.0	37.6	3.2	46.0	1.7	0.3	9.5	1.8
New York	1,309,986	702,587	183,052	193,540	113,494	2,781	4,729	20,925	88,878	100.0	57.5	15.0	15.8	9.3	0.2	0.4	1.7
North Carolina	578,031	350,950	148,251	29,019	15,549	726	6,902	9,908	16,726	100.0	62.5	26.4	5.2	2.8	0.1	1.2	1.8
North Dakota	55,169	45,094	1,548	1,293	653	76	2,573	951	2,981	100.0	86.4	3.0	2.5	1.3	0.1	4.9	1.8
Ohio	709,818	532,862	97,005	21,692	15,314	541	2,518	12,890	26,996	100.0	78.0	14.2	3.2	2.2	0.1	0.4	1.9
Oklahoma	228,464	144,188	23,236	13,794	5,653	364	19,801	12,082	9,346	100.0	65.8	10.6	6.3	2.6	0.2	9.0	5.5
Oregon	254,695	184,925	7,930	23,422	13,293	1,731	3,666	9,467	10,261	100.0	75.7	3.2	9.6	5.4	0.7	1.5	3.9
Pennsylvania	777,242	557,555	90,828	42,313	34,757	984	2,038	14,069	34,698	100.0	75.1	12.2	5.7	4.7	0.1	0.3	1.9
Rhode Island	83,952	59,026	5,788	8,855	3,553	60	325	1,732	4,613	100.0	74.4	7.3	11.2	4.5	0.1	0.4	2.2

See notes at end of table.

Table 306.70. Fall enrollment in degree-granting postsecondary institutions, by race/ethnicity of student and state or jurisdiction: 2012—Continued

| State or jurisdiction | Number | | | | | | | | | Percentage distribution of U.S. residents | | | | | | | |
	Total	White	Black	Hispanic	Asian	Pacific Islander	American Indian/Alaska Native	Two or more races	Non-resident alien	Total	White	Black	Hispanic	Asian	Pacific Islander	American Indian/Alaska Native	Two or more races
1	2	3	4	5	6	7	8	9	10	11	12	13	14	15	16	17	18
South Carolina	259,617	162,624	73,900	8,332	3,979	348	1,073	4,726	4,635	100.0	63.8	29.0	3.3	1.6	0.1	0.4	1.9
South Dakota	56,058	46,144	1,854	1,350	532	94	3,509	1,176	1,399	100.0	84.4	3.4	2.5	1.0	0.2	6.4	2.2
Tennessee	343,641	239,307	70,334	10,776	6,726	290	1,115	7,487	7,506	100.0	71.2	20.9	3.2	2.0	0.1	0.3	2.2
Texas	1,540,298	644,116	211,637	510,328	80,136	2,523	6,786	28,101	56,571	100.0	43.4	14.3	34.4	5.4	0.2	0.5	1.9
Utah	267,309	210,953	9,134	21,578	6,836	2,006	2,419	6,255	8,128	100.0	81.4	3.5	8.3	2.6	0.8	0.9	2.4
Vermont	44,703	38,187	1,212	1,832	1,072	40	232	1,121	1,007	100.0	87.4	2.8	4.2	2.5	0.1	0.5	2.6
Virginia	588,696	348,379	133,460	37,478	32,734	1,581	2,420	16,369	16,275	100.0	60.9	23.3	6.5	5.7	0.3	0.4	2.9
Washington	365,514	238,192	17,101	33,879	32,010	2,159	4,902	18,753	18,518	100.0	68.6	4.9	9.8	9.2	0.6	1.4	5.4
West Virginia	162,179	123,383	19,869	8,079	2,607	743	781	3,491	3,226	100.0	77.6	12.5	5.1	1.6	0.5	0.5	2.2
Wisconsin	369,732	295,035	24,023	17,712	11,989	408	3,284	7,014	10,267	100.0	82.1	6.7	4.9	3.3	0.1	0.9	2.0
Wyoming	37,812	31,992	561	2,669	341	78	637	539	995	100.0	86.9	1.5	7.2	0.9	0.2	1.7	1.5
U.S. Service Academies	15,227	10,754	913	1,581	762	78	87	843	209	100.0	71.6	6.1	10.5	5.1	0.5	0.6	5.6
Other jurisdictions	259,943	1,022	2,291	242,670	2,922	9,956	114	353	615	100.0	0.4	0.9	93.6	1.1	3.8	#	0.1
American Samoa	1,795	0	0	0	16	1,639	0	0	138	100.0	0.1	0.0	0.0	1.0	98.9	0.0	0.0
Federated States of Micronesia	2,744	4	0	0	2	2,738	0	0	0	100.0	0.1	0.0	0.0	0.1	99.8	0.0	0.0
Guam	5,924	200	26	36	2,434	3,159	7	6	56	100.0	3.4	0.4	0.6	41.5	53.8	0.1	0.1
Marshall Islands	1,123	0	0	0	0	1,109	0	0	14	100.0	0.0	0.0	0.0	0.0	100.0	0.0	0.0
Northern Marianas	1,178	15	3	2	319	625	1	68	145	100.0	1.5	0.3	0.2	30.9	60.5	0.1	6.6
Palau	680	1	1	0	6	672	0	0	0	100.0	0.1	0.1	0.0	0.9	98.8	0.0	0.0
Puerto Rico	244,076	663	265	242,486	139	14	105	279	125	100.0	0.3	0.1	99.4	0.1	#	#	0.1
U.S. Virgin Islands	2,423	137	1,996	146	6	0	1	0	137	100.0	6.0	87.3	6.4	0.3	0.0	#	0.0

#Rounds to zero.
NOTE: Race categories exclude persons of Hispanic ethnicity. Degree-granting institutions grant associate's or higher degrees and participate in Title IV federal financial aid programs. Detail may not sum to totals because of rounding.

SOURCE: U.S. Department of Education, National Center for Education Statistics, Integrated Postsecondary Education Data System (IPEDS), Spring 2013, Enrollment component. (This table was prepared November 2013.)

Table 307.10. Full-time-equivalent fall enrollment in degree-granting postsecondary institutions, by control and level of institution: 1967 through 2024

Year	All institutions			Public institutions			Private institutions						
	Total	4-year	2-year	Total	4-year	2-year	Total	4-year			2-year		
								Total	Nonprofit	For-profit	Total	Nonprofit	For-profit
1	2	3	4	5	6	7	8	9	10	11	12	13	14
1967	5,499,360	4,448,302	1,051,058	3,777,701	2,850,432	927,269	1,721,659	1,597,870	—	—	123,789	—	—
1968	5,977,768	4,729,522	1,248,246	4,248,639	3,128,057	1,120,582	1,729,129	1,601,465	—	—	127,664	—	—
1969	6,333,357	4,899,034	1,434,323	4,577,353	3,259,323	1,318,030	1,756,004	1,639,711	—	—	116,293	—	—
1970	6,737,819	5,145,422	1,592,397	4,953,144	3,468,569	1,484,575	1,784,675	1,676,853	—	—	107,822	—	—
1971	7,148,558	5,357,647	1,790,911	5,344,402	3,660,626	1,683,776	1,804,156	1,697,021	—	—	107,135	—	—
1972	7,253,757	5,406,833	1,846,924	5,452,854	3,706,238	1,746,616	1,800,903	1,700,595	—	—	100,308	—	—
1973	7,453,463	5,439,230	2,014,233	5,629,563	3,721,037	1,908,526	1,823,900	1,718,193	—	—	105,707	—	—
1974	7,805,452	5,606,247	2,199,205	5,944,799	3,847,543	2,097,256	1,860,653	1,758,704	—	—	101,949	—	—
1975	8,479,698	5,900,408	2,579,290	6,522,319	4,056,502	2,465,817	1,957,379	1,843,906	—	—	113,473	—	—
1976	8,312,502	5,848,001	2,464,501	6,349,903	3,998,450	2,351,453	1,962,599	1,849,551	—	—	113,048	—	—
1977	8,415,339	5,935,076	2,480,263	6,396,476	4,039,071	2,357,405	2,018,863	1,896,005	—	—	122,858	—	—
1978	8,348,482	5,932,357	2,416,125	6,279,199	3,996,126	2,283,073	2,069,283	1,936,231	—	—	133,052	—	—
1979	8,487,317	6,016,072	2,471,245	6,392,617	4,059,304	2,333,313	2,094,700	1,956,768	—	—	137,932	—	—
1980	8,819,013	6,161,372	2,657,641	6,642,294	4,158,267	2,484,027	2,176,719	2,003,105	—	—	173,614 [1]	—	—
1981	9,014,521	6,249,847	2,764,674	6,781,300	4,208,506	2,572,794	2,233,221	2,041,341	—	—	191,880 [1]	—	—
1982	9,091,648	6,248,923	2,842,725	6,850,589	4,220,648	2,629,941	2,241,059	2,028,275	—	—	212,784 [1]	—	—
1983	9,166,398	6,325,222	2,841,176	6,881,479	4,265,807	2,615,672	2,284,919	2,059,415	—	—	225,504	—	—
1984	8,951,695	6,292,711	2,658,984	6,684,664	4,237,895	2,446,769	2,267,031	2,054,816	—	—	212,215	—	—
1985	8,943,433	6,294,339	2,649,094	6,667,781	4,239,622	2,428,159	2,275,652	2,054,717	—	—	220,935	—	—
1986	9,064,165	6,360,325	2,703,842	6,778,045	4,295,494	2,482,551	2,286,122	2,064,831	—	—	221,291 [2]	—	—
1987	9,229,736	6,486,504	2,743,230	6,937,690	4,395,728	2,541,961	2,292,045	2,090,776	—	—	201,269 [2]	—	—
1988	9,464,271	6,664,146	2,800,125	7,096,905	4,505,774	2,591,131	2,367,366	2,158,372	—	—	208,994	—	—
1989	9,780,881	6,813,602	2,967,279	7,371,590	4,619,828	2,751,762	2,409,291	2,193,774	—	—	215,517	—	—
1990	9,983,436	6,968,008	3,015,428	7,557,982	4,740,049	2,817,933	2,425,454	2,227,959	2,177,668	50,291	197,495	72,785	124,710
1991	10,360,606	7,081,454	3,279,152	7,862,845	4,795,704	3,067,141	2,497,761	2,285,750	2,223,463	62,287	212,011	72,545	139,466
1992	10,436,776	7,129,379	3,307,397	7,911,701	4,797,884	3,113,817	2,525,075	2,331,495	2,267,373	64,122	193,580	66,647	126,933
1993	10,351,415	7,120,921	3,230,494	7,812,394	4,765,983	3,046,411	2,539,021	2,354,938	2,282,643	72,295	184,083	70,469	113,614
1994	10,348,072	7,137,341	3,210,731	7,784,396	4,749,524	3,034,872	2,563,676	2,387,817	2,301,063	86,754	175,859	69,578	106,281
1995	10,334,956	7,172,844	3,162,112	7,751,815	4,757,223	2,994,592	2,583,141	2,415,621	2,328,730	86,891	167,520	62,416	105,104
1996	10,481,886	7,234,541	3,247,345	7,794,895	4,767,117	3,027,778	2,686,991	2,467,424	2,353,561	113,863	219,567	63,954	155,613
1997	10,615,028	7,338,794	3,276,234	7,869,764	4,813,849	3,055,915	2,745,264	2,524,945	2,389,627	135,318	220,319	61,761	158,558
1998	10,698,775	7,467,828	3,230,947	7,880,135	4,868,857	3,011,278	2,818,640	2,598,971	2,436,188	162,783	219,669	56,834	162,835
1999	10,974,519	7,634,247	3,340,272	8,059,240	4,949,851	3,109,389	2,915,279	2,684,396	2,488,140	196,256	230,883	53,956	176,927
2000	11,267,025	7,795,139	3,471,886	8,266,932	5,025,588	3,241,344	3,000,093	2,769,551	2,549,676	219,875	230,542	51,503	179,039
2001	11,765,945	8,087,980	3,677,965	8,639,154	5,194,035	3,445,119	3,126,791	2,893,945	2,612,833	281,112	232,846	41,037	191,809
2002	12,331,319	8,439,064	3,892,255	9,061,411	5,406,283	3,655,128	3,269,908	3,032,781	2,699,702	333,079	237,127	40,110	197,017
2003	12,687,597	8,744,188	3,943,409	9,240,724	5,557,680	3,683,044	3,446,873	3,186,508	2,776,850	409,658	260,365	36,815	223,550
2004	13,000,994	9,018,024	3,982,970	9,348,081	5,640,650	3,707,431	3,652,913	3,377,374	2,837,251	540,123	275,539	34,202	241,337
2005	13,200,790	9,261,634	3,939,156	9,390,216	5,728,327	3,661,889	3,810,574	3,533,307	2,878,354	654,953	277,267	34,729	242,538
2006	13,403,097	9,456,166	3,946,931	9,503,558	5,824,768	3,678,790	3,899,539	3,631,398	2,936,172	695,226	268,141	31,203	236,938
2007	13,782,702	9,769,560	4,013,142	9,739,709	5,994,230	3,745,479	4,042,993	3,775,330	2,993,729	781,601	267,663	26,134	241,529
2008	14,394,238	10,169,454	4,224,784	10,061,812	6,139,525	3,922,287	4,332,426	4,029,929	3,060,308	969,621	302,497	28,065	274,432
2009	15,379,473	10,695,816	4,683,657	10,746,637	6,452,414	4,294,223	4,632,836	4,243,402	3,153,294	1,090,108	389,434	27,964	361,470
2010	15,947,474	11,129,239	4,818,235	11,018,756	6,635,799	4,382,957	4,928,718	4,493,440	3,235,149	1,258,291	435,278	26,920	408,358
2011	15,892,792	11,261,845	4,630,947	10,954,754	6,734,116	4,220,638	4,938,038	4,527,729	3,285,711	1,242,018	410,309	34,267	376,042
2012	15,594,638	11,231,758	4,362,880	10,780,749	6,764,423	4,016,326	4,813,889	4,467,335	3,311,250	1,156,085	346,554	32,609	313,945
2013	15,409,944	11,185,987	4,223,957	10,695,774	6,790,901	3,904,873	4,714,170	4,395,086	3,341,575	1,053,511	319,084	27,290	291,794
2014[3]	15,407,000	11,108,000	4,299,000	10,699,000	6,732,000	3,967,000	4,707,000	4,376,000	—	—	331,000	—	—
2015[3]	15,367,000	11,074,000	4,293,000	10,672,000	6,709,000	3,963,000	4,695,000	4,365,000	—	—	330,000	—	—
2016[3]	15,566,000	11,219,000	4,347,000	10,805,000	6,793,000	4,012,000	4,761,000	4,426,000	—	—	335,000	—	—
2017[3]	15,905,000	11,464,000	4,441,000	11,035,000	6,937,000	4,098,000	4,870,000	4,527,000	—	—	343,000	—	—
2018[3]	16,205,000	11,676,000	4,529,000	11,243,000	7,064,000	4,179,000	4,962,000	4,612,000	—	—	350,000	—	—
2019[3]	16,417,000	11,825,000	4,593,000	11,391,000	7,153,000	4,238,000	5,027,000	4,672,000	—	—	355,000	—	—
2020[3]	16,582,000	11,947,000	4,635,000	11,503,000	7,226,000	4,277,000	5,079,000	4,721,000	—	—	358,000	—	—
2021[3]	16,809,000	12,112,000	4,697,000	11,658,000	7,324,000	4,334,000	5,150,000	4,788,000	—	—	363,000	—	—
2022[3]	17,059,000	12,290,000	4,769,000	11,831,000	7,430,000	4,401,000	5,228,000	4,860,000	—	—	369,000	—	—
2023[3]	17,341,000	12,492,000	4,849,000	12,024,000	7,551,000	4,474,000	5,316,000	4,941,000	—	—	375,000	—	—
2024[3]	17,528,000	12,625,000	4,903,000	12,155,000	7,632,000	4,524,000	5,373,000	4,993,000	—	—	379,000	—	—

—Not available.
[1]Large increases are due to the addition of schools accredited by the Accrediting Commission of Career Schools and Colleges of Technology.
[2]Because of imputation techniques, data are not consistent with figures for other years.
[3]Projected.
NOTE: Full-time-equivalent enrollment is the full-time enrollment, plus the full-time equivalent of the part-time students. Data through 1995 are for institutions of higher education, while later data are for degree-granting institutions. Degree-granting institutions grant associate's or higher degrees and participate in Title IV federal financial aid programs. The degree-granting classification is very similar to the earlier higher education classification, but it includes more 2-year colleges and excludes a few higher education institutions that did not grant degrees. Some data have been revised from previously published figures.
SOURCE: U.S. Department of Education, National Center for Education Statistics, Higher Education General Information Survey (HEGIS), "Fall Enrollment in Colleges and Universities" surveys, 1967 through 1985; Integrated Postsecondary Education Data System (IPEDS), "Fall Enrollment Survey" (IPEDS-EF:86-99); IPEDS Spring 2001 through Spring 2014, Enrollment component; and Enrollment in Degree-Granting Institutions Projection Model, 1980 through 2024. (This table was prepared March 2015.)

Table 307.20. Full-time-equivalent fall enrollment in degree-granting postsecondary institutions, by control and level of institution and state or jurisdiction: 2000, 2010, and 2013

	Public						Private nonprofit 4-year		Private for-profit			
	4-year			2-year					4-year		2-year	
State or jurisdiction	2000	2010	2013	2000	2010	2013	2010	2013	2010	2013	2010	2013
1	2	3	4	5	6	7	8	9	10	11	12	13
United States	5,025,588	6,635,799	6,790,901	3,241,344	4,382,957	3,904,873	3,235,149	3,341,575	1,258,291	1,053,511	408,358	291,794
Alabama	111,322	140,235	137,813	48,545	68,677	56,915	22,982	22,506	23,570	22,551	3,138	2,699
Alaska	16,335	20,618	19,646	473	357	966	529	486	1,764	2,191	0	335
Arizona	87,301	120,269	129,116	85,778	122,717	111,280	7,487	8,309	369,895	284,666	15,622	9,866
Arkansas	57,897	77,384	80,350	21,519	41,223	36,205	14,559	14,550	2,450	1,385	683	84
California	476,027	582,256	630,833	707,558	858,417	797,733	245,393	263,513	102,012	99,909	78,898	59,860
Colorado	109,844	134,234	143,330	41,322	59,409	50,855	25,447	26,957	49,704	32,261	11,486	9,397
Connecticut	46,826	58,329	56,974	20,934	34,116	31,912	57,013	59,273	3,757	5,863	257	54
Delaware	20,427	23,125	24,738	6,939	9,365	8,876	10,550	11,471	218	180	0	0
District of Columbia	3,364	3,964	3,576	0	0	0	65,755	66,937	3,789	2,572	0	180
Florida	190,472	484,181	529,888	173,433	78,027	32,818	132,201	147,802	100,670	95,300	39,981	32,975
Georgia	136,069	224,448	233,262	66,571	118,307	83,004	63,327	64,658	37,344	30,245	9,268	7,764
Hawaii	17,015	24,136	24,425	14,996	17,786	16,914	11,244	10,989	1,670	1,988	1,459	1,826
Idaho	34,125	40,828	40,549	6,807	9,847	14,809	16,641	23,296	1,951	1,025	777	518
Illinois	164,592	178,192	170,063	186,533	228,507	204,809	190,040	190,184	58,243	41,197	9,379	5,217
Indiana	155,982	194,407	192,944	28,131	66,664	55,889	79,106	79,006	18,546	12,261	9,168	4,321
Iowa	61,763	64,706	67,921	44,717	71,021	58,856	50,088	49,666	107,172	89,535	533	603
Kansas	74,307	84,156	84,805	39,457	53,257	50,529	17,882	20,361	1,420	2,512	1,989	1,795
Kentucky	86,080	105,252	107,173	32,239	65,402	55,711	31,858	33,339	13,585	9,786	5,478	2,323
Louisiana	126,372	124,062	119,308	27,130	52,670	48,908	23,509	23,840	3,939	2,904	6,608	4,402
Maine	24,678	25,966	24,501	4,797	11,555	11,430	16,928	17,425	0	690	1,303	403
Maryland	94,929	125,536	127,367	57,367	85,789	78,419	42,957	42,943	5,403	3,439	4,143	2,589
Massachusetts	78,452	97,474	101,415	47,972	65,041	62,350	238,759	242,936	4,181	3,280	2,108	1,238
Michigan	223,981	257,896	261,171	101,794	155,150	124,574	91,255	80,109	8,772	5,089	1,098	1,506
Minnesota	95,345	114,954	111,835	65,167	89,858	80,258	62,150	60,377	71,988	64,183	2,200	1,247
Mississippi	56,107	67,989	70,856	47,245	70,356	61,810	13,601	12,943	289	190	2,470	1,975
Missouri	99,187	120,933	124,607	46,793	74,399	68,366	113,252	112,575	17,435	21,377	10,713	5,767
Montana	28,278	32,375	33,184	3,900	7,715	5,979	4,073	4,057	0	0	0	0
Nebraska	44,374	50,013	50,743	20,812	30,680	25,864	27,836	28,845	2,151	1,660	1,037	495
Nevada	27,631	68,001	63,663	20,468	6,571	5,691	3,028	3,260	6,841	5,209	5,151	4,692
New Hampshire	21,064	26,150	25,322	5,442	9,172	8,343	22,449	35,775	3,898	2,495	0	0
New Jersey	111,449	144,174	150,288	79,367	125,787	113,605	63,113	62,165	5,993	5,223	1,891	3,485
New Mexico	39,779	52,191	52,352	29,541	49,580	45,435	1,012	1,099	6,612	5,440	3,316	1,515
New York	269,664	328,542	329,530	168,911	242,030	233,933	440,038	445,688	27,670	27,152	21,686	17,111
North Carolina	140,203	193,970	193,772	96,999	158,480	147,228	83,931	86,655	10,987	10,572	2,694	3,319
North Dakota	24,728	35,435	34,752	6,515	4,572	4,453	4,832	4,427	1,154	698	0	0
Ohio	215,993	292,493	281,989	92,749	131,274	105,318	123,493	120,912	13,682	16,204	29,858	12,515
Oklahoma	79,786	102,471	102,073	34,997	44,842	37,849	20,213	22,355	5,434	4,230	4,539	4,051
Oregon	59,588	82,751	87,576	46,099	69,825	65,103	28,591	31,633	5,530	3,631	3,791	2,781
Pennsylvania	211,132	257,017	253,907	58,759	93,216	79,923	248,139	247,603	17,802	12,318	38,769	27,002
Rhode Island	17,967	21,720	21,641	8,650	10,107	9,568	39,093	38,266	0	0	0	0
South Carolina	74,309	93,512	98,260	41,804	66,813	62,973	31,078	30,480	11,326	9,281	2,621	3,728
South Dakota	23,881	29,247	29,163	4,193	5,746	5,430	7,133	5,586	2,831	1,895	0	0
Tennessee	99,636	125,069	120,957	53,146	64,802	56,298	69,240	74,789	15,154	11,857	12,371	9,820
Texas	358,523	506,279	533,655	268,057	403,005	379,769	110,416	114,823	24,705	24,284	39,172	25,404
Utah	71,982	100,176	102,402	16,454	26,302	16,506	56,824	83,209	11,881	6,134	1,393	957
Vermont	13,581	18,461	17,541	1,845	3,114	2,724	15,710	15,833	615	392	0	0
Virginia	147,370	185,096	191,266	72,913	113,060	108,248	87,912	98,979	37,169	30,261	9,380	7,321
Washington	83,899	143,012	153,039	114,754	109,154	91,951	37,741	37,846	7,050	4,749	5,098	4,121
West Virginia	58,171	64,650	62,148	3,969	15,609	13,637	11,487	7,916	18,867	24,660	2,819	2,295
Wisconsin	130,661	160,463	157,314	56,195	68,908	61,108	53,254	52,822	11,045	8,587	2,134	776
Wyoming	9,665	11,089	10,918	10,588	14,676	13,741	0	75	127	0	1,879	1,462
U.S. Service Academies	13,475	15,912	14,980	0	0	0	†	†	†	†	†	†
Other jurisdictions	66,376	65,847	62,810	7,200	8,758	7,400	113,458	115,861	9,417	11,089	30,467	26,896
American Samoa	0	0	1,039	214	1,275	0	0	0	0	0	0	0
Federated States of Micronesia	0	0	0	1,308	2,243	1,904	0	0	0	0	0	0
Guam	2,802	3,074	3,206	777	1,424	1,552	73	66	0	0	0	0
Marshall Islands	0	0	0	166	739	783	0	0	0	0	0	0
Northern Marianas	0	1,031	993	707	0	0	0	0	0	0	0	0
Palau	0	0	0	450	541	494	0	0	0	0	0	0
Puerto Rico	61,987	59,658	55,808	3,578	2,536	2,667	113,385	115,795	9,417	11,089	30,467	26,896
U.S. Virgin Islands	1,587	2,084	1,764	0	0	0	0	0	0	0	0	0

†Not applicable.
NOTE: Full-time-equivalent enrollment is the full-time enrollment, plus the full-time equivalent of the part-time students. Degree-granting institutions grant associate's or higher degrees and participate in Title IV federal financial aid programs. Some data have been revised from previously published figures.

SOURCE: U.S. Department of Education, National Center for Education Statistics, Integrated Postsecondary Education Data System (IPEDS), Spring 2001, 2011, and 2014, Enrollment component. (This table was prepared November 2014.)

Table 307.30. Full-time-equivalent fall enrollment in degree-granting postsecondary institutions, by control of institution and state or jurisdiction: 2000, 2010, and 2013

State or jurisdiction	Total			Public			Private nonprofit			Private for-profit		
	2000	2010	2013	2000	2010	2013	2000	2010	2013	2000	2010	2013
1	2	3	4	5	6	7	8	9	10	11	12	13
United States	11,267,025	15,947,474	15,409,944	8,266,932	11,018,756	10,695,774	2,601,179	3,262,069	3,368,865	398,914	1,666,649	1,345,305
Alabama	184,031	258,602	242,956	159,867	208,912	194,728	20,605	22,982	22,978	3,559	26,708	25,250
Alaska	17,787	23,268	23,675	16,808	20,975	20,612	672	529	537	307	1,764	2,526
Arizona	225,396	635,990	543,237	173,079	242,986	240,396	8,079	7,487	8,309	44,238	385,517	294,532
Arkansas	91,886	136,299	133,092	79,416	118,607	116,555	11,713	14,559	15,068	757	3,133	1,469
California	1,468,486	1,868,187	1,853,430	1,183,585	1,440,673	1,428,566	214,444	246,604	265,095	70,457	180,910	159,769
Colorado	188,117	280,408	262,807	151,166	193,643	194,185	20,991	25,575	26,964	15,960	61,190	41,658
Connecticut	117,954	153,746	154,076	67,760	92,445	88,886	48,648	57,287	59,273	1,546	4,014	5,917
Delaware	34,057	43,470	45,453	27,366	32,490	33,614	6,691	10,762	11,659	0	218	180
District of Columbia	59,560	73,508	73,265	3,364	3,964	3,576	54,177	65,755	66,937	2,019	3,789	2,752
Florida	486,818	835,295	840,462	363,905	562,208	562,706	90,530	132,436	149,481	32,383	140,651	128,275
Georgia	268,707	453,209	419,419	202,640	342,755	316,266	57,444	63,842	65,144	8,623	46,612	38,009
Hawaii	45,329	56,295	56,142	32,011	41,922	41,339	11,521	11,244	10,989	1,797	3,129	3,814
Idaho	52,353	70,044	80,197	40,932	50,675	55,358	10,751	16,641	23,296	670	2,728	1,543
Illinois	520,087	665,347	612,146	351,125	406,699	374,872	150,578	191,026	190,860	18,384	67,622	46,414
Indiana	250,998	368,373	344,761	184,113	261,071	248,833	60,387	79,588	79,346	6,498	27,714	16,582
Iowa	152,505	293,680	266,581	106,480	135,727	126,777	43,735	50,248	49,666	2,290	107,705	90,138
Kansas	129,839	160,434	160,405	113,764	137,413	135,334	15,605	19,612	20,764	470	3,409	4,307
Kentucky	149,395	221,575	208,332	118,319	170,654	162,884	23,859	31,858	33,339	7,217	19,063	12,109
Louisiana	183,661	210,788	200,306	153,502	176,732	168,216	25,646	23,509	24,784	4,513	10,547	7,306
Maine	43,384	55,950	54,657	29,475	37,521	35,931	13,020	17,126	17,633	889	1,303	1,093
Maryland	188,887	263,828	254,757	152,296	211,325	205,786	34,445	42,957	42,943	2,146	9,546	6,028
Massachusetts	327,984	408,300	411,845	126,424	162,515	163,765	199,745	239,496	243,562	1,815	6,289	4,518
Michigan	402,019	514,171	472,449	325,775	413,046	385,745	73,144	91,255	80,109	3,100	9,870	6,595
Minnesota	223,232	341,248	317,946	160,512	204,827	192,093	52,974	62,248	60,423	9,746	74,188	65,430
Mississippi	113,804	154,705	147,774	103,352	138,345	132,666	10,073	13,601	12,943	379	2,759	2,165
Missouri	237,161	337,846	333,470	145,980	195,332	192,973	82,425	114,366	113,353	8,756	28,148	27,144
Montana	36,005	44,605	43,629	32,178	40,090	39,163	3,827	4,515	4,466	0	0	0
Nebraska	85,993	111,869	107,730	65,186	80,693	76,607	18,956	27,988	28,968	1,851	3,188	2,155
Nevada	52,577	89,592	82,515	48,099	74,572	69,354	455	3,028	3,260	4,023	11,992	9,901
New Hampshire	48,230	61,919	72,090	26,506	35,322	33,665	18,732	22,699	35,930	2,992	3,898	2,495
New Jersey	245,447	340,958	334,766	190,816	269,961	263,893	48,751	63,113	62,165	5,880	7,884	8,708
New Mexico	77,415	112,711	105,841	69,320	101,771	97,787	3,274	1,012	1,099	4,821	9,928	6,955
New York	826,078	1,063,531	1,056,400	438,575	570,572	563,463	355,832	443,603	448,674	31,671	49,356	44,263
North Carolina	305,805	450,726	442,222	237,202	352,450	341,000	68,127	84,595	87,331	476	13,681	13,891
North Dakota	35,230	46,556	44,330	31,243	40,007	39,205	3,876	5,395	4,427	111	1,154	698
Ohio	426,080	591,980	537,874	308,742	423,767	387,307	105,004	124,673	121,848	12,334	43,540	28,719
Oklahoma	136,833	177,499	170,558	114,783	147,313	139,922	18,827	20,213	22,355	3,223	9,973	8,281
Oregon	130,705	190,488	190,724	105,687	152,576	152,679	22,079	28,591	31,633	2,939	9,321	6,412
Pennsylvania	499,729	661,592	628,061	269,891	350,233	333,830	201,136	254,788	254,911	28,702	56,571	39,320
Rhode Island	59,639	70,920	69,475	26,617	31,827	31,209	32,813	39,093	38,266	209	0	0
South Carolina	143,343	206,261	205,528	116,113	160,325	161,233	26,504	31,989	31,286	726	13,947	13,009
South Dakota	34,876	45,155	42,195	28,074	34,993	34,593	4,751	7,331	5,707	2,051	2,831	1,895
Tennessee	209,100	286,834	274,250	152,782	189,871	177,255	50,967	69,438	75,318	5,351	27,525	21,677
Texas	741,012	1,085,155	1,080,113	626,580	909,284	913,424	98,445	111,994	117,001	15,987	63,877	49,688
Utah	125,622	198,079	210,866	88,436	126,478	118,908	32,727	58,327	84,867	4,459	13,274	7,091
Vermont	29,099	38,387	36,490	15,426	21,575	20,265	13,336	16,197	15,833	337	615	392
Virginia	277,270	432,617	436,450	220,283	298,156	299,514	44,825	87,912	99,354	12,162	46,549	37,582
Washington	236,609	302,113	291,758	198,653	252,166	244,990	32,726	37,799	37,898	5,230	12,148	8,870
West Virginia	72,962	113,432	110,656	62,140	80,259	75,785	8,891	11,487	7,916	1,931	21,686	26,955
Wisconsin	232,912	296,246	280,607	186,856	229,371	218,422	44,416	53,696	52,822	1,640	13,179	9,363
Wyoming	21,542	27,771	26,196	20,253	25,765	24,659	0	0	75	1,289	2,006	1,462
U.S. Service Academies	13,475	15,912	14,980	13,475	15,912	14,980	†	†	†	†	†	†
Other jurisdictions	166,039	232,204	224,056	73,576	74,605	70,210	81,642	117,715	115,861	10,821	39,884	37,985
American Samoa	214	1,275	1,039	214	1,275	1,039	0	0	0	0	0	0
Federated States of Micronesia	1,308	2,243	1,904	1,308	2,243	1,904	0	0	0	0	0	0
Guam	3,579	4,571	4,824	3,579	4,498	4,758	0	73	66	0	0	0
Marshall Islands	166	739	783	166	739	783	0	0	0	0	0	0
Northern Marianas	707	1,031	993	707	1,031	993	0	0	0	0	0	0
Palau	450	541	494	450	541	494	0	0	0	0	0	0
Puerto Rico	158,028	219,720	212,255	65,565	62,194	58,475	81,642	117,642	115,795	10,821	39,884	37,985
U.S. Virgin Islands	1,587	2,084	1,764	1,587	2,084	1,764	0	0	0	0	0	0

†Not applicable.
NOTE: Full-time-equivalent enrollment is the full-time enrollment, plus the full-time equivalent of the part-time students. Degree-granting institutions grant associate's or higher degrees and participate in Title IV federal financial aid programs. Some data have been revised from previously published figures.

SOURCE: U.S. Department of Education, National Center for Education Statistics, Integrated Postsecondary Education Data System (IPEDS), Spring 2001, 2011, and 2014, Enrollment component. (This table was prepared November 2014.)

Table 308.10. Total 12-month enrollment in degree-granting postsecondary institutions, by control and level of institution and state or jurisdiction: 2011–12 and 2012–13

State or jurisdiction	2011–12							2012–13						
	Total	Public 4-year	Public 2-year	Private 4-year Nonprofit	Private 4-year For-profit	Private 2-year Nonprofit	Private 2-year For-profit	Total	Public 4-year	Public 2-year	Private 4-year Nonprofit	Private 4-year For-profit	Private 2-year Nonprofit	Private 2-year For-profit
1	2	3	4	5	6	7	8	9	10	11	12	13	14	15
United States	28,172,198	9,727,985	10,528,606	4,736,935	2,509,900	57,802	610,970	27,523,190	9,677,077	10,128,642	4,807,440	2,311,768	47,807	550,456
Alabama	423,697	196,566	134,767	30,034	56,005	1,126	5,199	409,372	192,373	125,477	29,309	55,664	945	5,604
Alaska	60,103	50,420	3,125	969	5,128	0	461	56,900	48,540	3,812	1,001	2,983	56	508
Arizona	1,161,102	156,435	374,569	11,522	598,773	0	19,803	1,074,586	160,382	352,226	12,086	533,490	0	16,402
Arkansas	230,899	115,684	90,944	19,822	3,520	627	302	225,342	115,715	86,944	18,959	2,765	710	249
California	3,580,417	713,254	2,199,798	349,121	190,819	2,602	124,823	3,451,001	712,174	2,082,862	360,393	182,479	2,548	110,545
Colorado	524,887	216,595	162,544	41,941	85,464	418	17,925	504,450	216,149	153,144	43,078	73,985	131	17,963
Connecticut	254,715	79,384	81,663	78,762	14,343	0	563	256,040	77,314	82,416	79,687	16,344	0	279
Delaware	70,454	28,057	20,912	20,508	714	263	0	72,787	28,197	20,364	23,329	659	238	0
District of Columbia	106,523	7,216	0	88,572	10,735	0	0	107,907	7,277	0	90,009	10,144	0	477
Florida	1,612,394	988,432	105,628	247,765	193,991	2,323	74,255	1,579,186	998,241	77,144	244,544	196,085	2,220	60,952
Georgia	730,684	327,961	223,573	82,345	80,454	591	15,760	710,578	326,970	218,850	83,119	66,556	561	14,522
Hawaii	101,481	36,801	40,254	18,643	2,766	0	3,017	100,042	36,729	39,645	17,586	2,943	0	3,139
Idaho	142,195	67,914	35,900	33,939	3,629	0	813	151,014	68,335	35,223	44,597	2,100	0	759
Illinois	1,350,322	231,761	709,319	276,377	116,826	1,327	14,712	1,314,363	225,384	687,396	274,560	113,534	1,104	12,385
Indiana	609,700	277,945	175,313	106,896	40,229	630	8,687	606,092	275,912	180,464	107,232	33,616	531	8,337
Iowa	557,823	82,466	148,981	71,036	254,492	236	612	529,741	84,594	145,389	69,685	228,822	0	1,251
Kansas	298,578	119,555	136,155	32,727	3,808	3,521	2,812	308,407	118,754	141,720	38,206	5,517	488	3,722
Kentucky	374,000	157,597	145,802	46,577	26,357	0	6,594	357,814	146,461	136,143	47,153	22,519	0	5,538
Louisiana	338,468	169,434	118,826	32,595	6,000	2,340	9,273	328,551	165,735	113,908	31,927	5,721	1,985	9,275
Maine	94,341	40,412	26,531	24,910	1,363	338	787	94,708	39,646	25,649	26,852	1,434	355	772
Maryland	496,859	206,298	206,316	67,386	11,920	0	4,939	486,734	205,683	200,812	65,746	10,029	0	4,464
Massachusetts	644,103	153,575	146,318	329,037	6,457	1,453	3,241	646,996	157,184	146,481	333,374	5,966	1,282	2,709
Michigan	889,359	350,216	366,518	155,522	13,090	61	3,952	863,352	352,632	346,521	148,958	11,238	0	4,003
Minnesota	614,033	165,865	193,118	85,975	165,851	136	3,088	604,899	164,666	190,779	84,712	162,109	114	2,519
Mississippi	233,236	93,372	114,041	20,598	1,012	0	4,213	225,199	92,676	106,355	20,542	743	0	4,883
Missouri	609,945	174,338	161,180	205,839	52,240	1,609	14,739	587,254	175,326	154,295	203,141	41,929	1,502	11,061
Montana	68,163	47,315	14,835	5,364	0	649	0	66,874	46,648	14,429	5,188	0	609	0
Nebraska	202,876	68,897	86,459	42,465	3,441	265	1,349	200,724	68,773	85,245	41,856	3,517	271	1,062
Nevada	165,857	126,539	16,617	4,100	10,581	0	8,020	159,029	121,603	16,722	3,757	9,351	0	7,596
New Hampshire	101,835	34,489	22,638	39,206	5,054	448	0	113,187	34,124	22,231	51,869	4,555	408	0
New Jersey	566,181	209,777	256,689	85,727	9,632	0	4,356	549,933	202,230	249,637	83,090	8,733	0	6,243
New Mexico	216,076	78,244	122,960	1,528	10,400	0	2,944	212,172	78,507	120,342	1,695	9,152	0	2,476
New York	1,674,438	483,588	471,510	625,430	49,653	6,229	38,028	1,660,411	479,477	466,869	625,127	49,473	6,255	33,210
North Carolina	751,635	253,249	359,336	106,403	24,418	791	7,438	748,797	252,618	353,984	109,908	24,281	782	7,224
North Dakota	70,816	51,457	9,779	7,664	1,916	0	0	69,180	51,110	9,435	7,025	1,610	0	0
Ohio	966,766	414,062	299,171	175,399	42,535	3,384	32,215	918,258	400,007	279,273	174,411	36,436	2,019	26,112
Oklahoma	300,108	153,575	103,064	28,199	7,954	0	7,316	295,124	151,633	99,854	29,043	7,885	0	6,709
Oregon	377,098	131,500	189,869	39,863	9,183	0	6,683	369,740	131,871	182,545	41,805	7,990	0	5,529
Pennsylvania	996,327	326,798	219,873	337,476	45,304	12,313	54,563	966,585	319,211	212,655	334,885	38,136	12,371	49,327
Rhode Island	100,938	29,888	24,616	46,434	0	0	0	99,627	29,655	24,252	45,720	0	0	0
South Carolina	335,091	123,023	143,839	42,056	18,465	1,050	6,658	333,106	123,322	141,342	41,953	17,557	866	8,066
South Dakota	73,936	49,115	7,838	8,611	7,876	496	0	73,881	49,336	8,064	9,244	6,711	526	0
Tennessee	435,377	166,829	131,704	91,584	25,468	2,834	16,958	431,373	163,915	127,151	96,629	24,214	993	18,471
Texas	2,119,327	759,099	1,102,140	153,845	49,890	6,647	47,706	2,096,856	766,405	1,078,570	157,787	45,780	4,387	43,927
Utah	350,906	185,635	48,876	89,916	20,629	2,574	3,276	356,805	179,494	47,599	112,971	11,749	2,901	2,091
Vermont	60,059	24,693	11,009	23,672	685	0	0	59,583	24,347	10,429	24,142	665	0	0
Virginia	798,893	257,162	290,976	159,120	75,212	428	15,995	785,129	253,359	281,976	168,495	66,161	595	14,543
Washington	525,030	222,991	234,613	49,538	10,010	93	7,785	506,467	228,878	212,018	49,088	9,196	54	7,233
West Virginia	242,223	86,491	30,836	8,260	112,395	0	4,241	246,148	84,684	29,216	9,545	118,516	0	4,187
Wisconsin	492,758	213,300	168,253	85,657	23,004	0	2,544	483,032	212,697	165,928	82,322	20,726	0	1,359
Wyoming	53,384	14,707	36,143	0	209	0	2,325	52,524	14,794	34,857	100	0	0	2,773
U.S. Service Academies ..	15,782	15,782	0	†	†	†	†	15,330	15,330	0	†	†	†	†
Other jurisdictions .	317,210	75,532	14,469	166,691	15,451	1,431	43,636	308,189	75,172	14,076	160,290	17,194	0	41,457
American Samoa	2,621	2,621	0	0	0	0	0	2,464	2,464	0	0	0	0	0
Federated States of Micronesia	5,457	0	5,457	0	0	0	0	5,082	0	5,082	0	0	0	0
Guam	8,005	4,427	3,481	97	0	0	0	8,345	4,785	3,481	79	0	0	0
Marshall Islands	1,310	0	1,310	0	0	0	0	1,411	0	1,411	0	0	0	0
Northern Marianas	1,332	1,332	0	0	0	0	0	1,445	1,445	0	0	0	0	0
Palau	981	0	981	0	0	0	0	897	0	897	0	0	0	0
Puerto Rico	294,259	63,907	3,240	166,594	15,451	1,431	43,636	285,388	63,321	3,205	160,211	17,194	0	41,457
U.S. Virgin Islands	3,245	3,245	0	0	0	0	0	3,157	3,157	0	0	0	0	0

†Not applicable.
NOTE: Includes students who enrolled at any point during a 12-month period ending during the summer of the academic year indicated. Degree-granting institutions grant associate's or higher degrees and participate in Title IV federal financial aid programs. Some data have been revised from previously published figures.

SOURCE: U.S. Department of Education, National Center for Education Statistics, Integrated Postsecondary Education Data System (IPEDS), Fall 2012 and Fall 2013, 12-Month Enrollment component. (This table was prepared April 2015.)

Table 308.20. Total 12-month enrollment in degree-granting postsecondary institutions, by control of institution and state or jurisdiction: Selected years, 2004–05 through 2012–13

State or jurisdiction	Total					Public			Private nonprofit			Private for-profit		
	2004–05	2009–10	2010–11	2011–12	2012–13	2004–05	2010–11	2012–13	2004–05	2010–11	2012–13	2004–05	2010–11	2012–13
1	2	3	4	5	6	7	8	9	10	11	12	13	14	15
United States	23,798,595	27,996,768	28,561,503	28,172,198	27,523,190	18,058,078	20,516,945	19,805,719	4,222,755	4,761,799	4,855,247	1,517,762	3,282,759	2,862,224
Alabama	349,783	420,768	431,219	423,697	409,372	310,878	341,757	317,850	28,847	30,152	30,254	10,058	59,310	61,268
Alaska	53,786	57,086	58,668	60,103	56,900	51,689	53,841	52,352	1,253	998	1,057	844	3,829	3,491
Arizona	821,240	1,207,074	1,238,668	1,161,102	1,074,586	499,192	544,922	512,608	13,162	11,438	12,086	308,886	682,308	549,892
Arkansas	182,497	222,868	228,659	230,899	225,342	164,751	204,632	202,659	15,260	19,536	19,669	2,486	4,491	3,014
California	3,341,107	3,835,943	3,748,013	3,580,417	3,451,001	2,843,929	3,070,257	2,795,036	327,661	344,961	362,941	169,517	332,795	293,024
Colorado	428,215	502,569	519,811	524,887	504,450	333,100	364,905	369,293	40,144	41,959	43,209	54,971	112,947	91,948
Connecticut	219,327	244,048	251,521	254,715	256,040	144,681	162,795	159,730	71,235	78,212	79,687	3,411	10,514	16,623
Delaware	63,817	69,293	70,098	70,454	72,787	47,148	48,991	48,561	16,669	20,408	23,567	0	699	659
District of Columbia	129,349	114,243	114,264	106,523	107,907	10,095	12,786	7,277	81,718	89,433	90,009	37,536	12,045	10,621
Florida	1,232,578	1,514,986	1,585,959	1,612,394	1,579,186	912,150	1,080,517	1,075,385	191,789	251,966	246,764	128,639	253,476	257,037
Georgia	569,805	742,005	776,316	730,684	710,578	466,589	584,787	545,820	70,449	82,614	83,680	32,767	108,915	81,078
Hawaii	92,643	99,350	101,719	101,481	100,042	67,835	76,929	76,374	20,749	19,182	17,586	4,059	5,608	6,082
Idaho	108,415	120,890	126,866	142,195	151,014	84,627	92,865	103,558	20,802	28,421	44,597	2,986	5,580	2,859
Illinois	1,293,156	1,380,669	1,374,177	1,350,322	1,314,363	933,506	948,489	912,780	257,053	280,649	275,664	102,597	145,039	125,919
Indiana	488,374	606,235	621,156	609,700	606,092	363,817	455,107	456,376	103,295	107,813	107,763	21,262	58,236	41,953
Iowa	309,318	539,626	573,112	557,823	529,741	200,039	236,600	229,983	72,538	78,103	69,685	36,741	258,409	230,073
Kansas	276,293	298,004	302,966	298,578	308,407	241,778	259,654	260,474	32,480	36,532	38,694	2,035	6,780	9,239
Kentucky	303,785	362,208	374,660	374,000	357,814	248,402	293,292	282,604	33,565	44,135	47,153	21,818	37,233	28,057
Louisiana	323,630	337,290	338,898	338,468	328,551	276,599	288,958	279,643	34,050	34,127	33,912	12,981	15,813	14,996
Maine	88,644	90,608	92,858	94,341	94,708	64,380	66,013	65,295	22,474	24,233	27,207	1,790	2,612	2,206
Maryland	412,867	483,474	490,738	496,859	486,734	340,538	404,916	406,495	64,377	66,660	65,746	7,952	19,162	14,493
Massachusetts	565,872	632,424	640,116	644,103	646,996	266,316	301,999	303,665	293,677	327,569	334,656	5,879	10,548	8,675
Michigan	844,731	908,369	911,818	889,359	863,352	690,014	734,343	699,153	141,670	159,624	148,958	13,047	17,851	15,241
Minnesota	469,986	609,768	625,540	614,033	604,899	318,448	361,582	355,445	83,577	88,876	84,826	67,961	175,082	164,628
Mississippi	206,917	228,648	235,071	233,236	225,199	187,594	209,115	199,031	17,299	20,162	20,542	2,024	5,794	5,626
Missouri	504,860	585,165	615,010	609,945	587,254	289,162	336,606	329,621	187,886	209,055	204,643	27,812	69,349	52,990
Montana	60,259	67,990	68,083	68,163	66,874	53,889	61,911	61,077	6,370	6,172	5,797	0	0	0
Nebraska	178,595	205,786	205,496	202,876	200,724	140,544	156,586	154,018	34,369	43,617	42,127	3,682	5,293	4,579
Nevada	153,540	177,178	178,375	165,857	159,029	136,158	154,792	138,325	1,087	4,332	3,757	16,295	19,251	16,947
New Hampshire	92,067	96,660	98,788	101,835	113,187	52,671	58,196	56,355	31,809	34,560	52,277	7,587	6,032	4,555
New Jersey	484,892	557,071	569,225	566,181	549,933	395,088	467,558	451,867	80,936	87,569	83,090	8,868	14,098	14,976
New Mexico	190,031	213,148	220,705	216,076	212,172	175,425	204,209	198,849	5,007	1,386	1,695	9,599	15,110	11,628
New York	1,457,951	1,629,966	1,657,093	1,674,438	1,660,411	820,849	950,505	946,346	560,583	622,623	631,382	76,519	83,965	82,683
North Carolina	637,309	744,508	757,889	751,635	748,797	537,735	620,890	606,602	94,361	106,129	110,690	5,213	30,870	31,505
North Dakota	62,743	67,369	70,185	70,816	69,180	54,671	59,830	60,545	7,090	7,667	7,025	982	2,688	1,610
Ohio	809,712	953,511	992,062	966,766	918,258	601,853	726,472	679,280	167,235	179,987	176,430	40,624	85,603	62,548
Oklahoma	276,437	290,226	299,365	300,108	295,124	238,444	257,400	251,487	27,920	26,726	29,043	10,073	15,239	14,594
Oregon	296,574	363,314	374,342	377,098	369,740	251,800	320,026	314,416	31,580	39,258	41,805	13,194	15,058	13,519
Pennsylvania	868,185	1,009,956	1,019,990	996,327	966,585	493,773	548,169	531,866	307,862	351,503	347,256	66,550	120,318	87,463
Rhode Island	99,103	102,211	101,610	100,938	99,627	52,263	54,535	53,907	45,906	47,075	45,720	934	0	0
South Carolina	268,590	323,886	331,280	335,091	333,106	221,632	262,422	264,664	43,450	43,306	42,819	3,508	25,552	25,623
South Dakota	63,989	70,067	74,210	73,936	73,881	48,570	56,861	57,400	9,858	9,783	9,770	5,561	7,566	6,711
Tennessee	353,167	426,013	438,901	435,377	431,373	254,104	299,545	291,066	72,505	92,761	97,622	26,558	46,595	42,685
Texas	1,695,267	2,010,641	2,107,654	2,119,327	2,096,856	1,492,623	1,843,574	1,844,975	148,812	160,405	162,174	53,832	103,675	89,707
Utah	278,798	319,218	340,784	350,906	356,805	213,428	236,332	227,093	50,268	80,445	115,872	15,102	24,007	13,840
Vermont	51,313	60,651	59,997	60,059	59,583	31,099	36,594	34,776	19,771	22,623	24,142	443	780	665
Virginia	583,958	755,566	783,117	798,893	785,129	462,958	541,978	535,335	80,805	141,580	169,090	40,195	99,559	80,704
Washington	520,108	560,655	554,551	525,030	506,467	451,410	483,491	440,896	52,896	50,395	49,142	15,802	20,665	16,429
West Virginia	126,082	210,512	231,331	242,223	246,148	104,704	119,247	113,900	15,416	16,749	9,545	5,962	95,335	122,703
Wisconsin	444,120	496,779	507,252	492,758	483,032	353,215	390,899	378,625	83,180	88,330	82,322	7,725	28,023	22,085
Wyoming	48,651	53,147	53,987	53,384	52,524	45,756	50,935	49,651	0	0	100	2,895	3,052	2,773
U.S. Service Academies ..	16,159	17,128	17,330	15,782	15,330	16,159	17,330	15,330	†	†	†	†	†	†
Other jurisdictions .	258,744	312,646	316,672	317,210	308,189	95,808	94,233	89,248	136,708	163,515	160,290	26,228	58,924	58,651
American Samoa	2,299	2,900	2,744	2,621	2,464	2,299	2,744	2,464	0	0	0	0	0	0
Federated States of Micronesia	3,570	4,805	5,097	5,457	5,082	3,570	5,097	5,082	0	0	0	0	0	0
Guam	7,125	7,621	8,105	8,005	8,345	6,936	8,001	8,266	189	104	79	0	0	0
Marshall Islands	466	1,164	1,176	1,310	1,411	466	1,176	1,411	0	0	0	0	0	0
Northern Marianas	1,590	1,134	1,388	1,332	1,445	1,590	1,388	1,445	0	0	0	0	0	0
Palau	987	990	922	981	897	987	922	897	0	0	0	0	0	0
Puerto Rico	239,442	290,649	293,820	294,259	285,388	76,695	71,485	66,526	136,519	163,411	160,211	26,228	58,924	58,651
U.S. Virgin Islands	3,265	3,383	3,420	3,245	3,157	3,265	3,420	3,157	0	0	0	0	0	0

†Not applicable.
NOTE: Includes students who enrolled at any point during a 12-month period ending during the summer of the academic year indicated. Degree-granting institutions grant associate's or higher degrees and participate in Title IV federal financial aid programs. Some data have been revised from previously published figures.

SOURCE: U.S. Department of Education, National Center for Education Statistics, Integrated Postsecondary Education Data System (IPEDS), Fall 2005 through Fall 2013, 12-Month Enrollment component. (This table was prepared April 2015.)

Table 309.10. Residence and migration of all first-time degree/certificate-seeking undergraduates in degree-granting postsecondary institutions, by state or jurisdiction: Fall 2012

State or jurisdiction	Total first-time enrollment in institutions located in the state	State residents enrolled in institutions		Ratio of in-state students		Migration of students		
		In any state[1]	In their home state	To first-time enrollment (col. 4/col. 2)	To residents enrolled in any state (col. 4/col. 3)	Out of state (col. 3 - col. 4)	Into state[2] (col. 2 - col. 4)	Net (col. 8 - col. 7)
1	2	3	4	5	6	7	8	9
United States	2,994,187	2,906,877	2,388,509	0.80	0.82	518,368	605,678	87,310
Alabama	52,065	43,277	37,148	0.71	0.86	6,129	14,917	8,788
Alaska	4,474	5,410	3,565	0.80	0.66	1,845	909	-936
Arizona	79,099	54,988	49,529	0.63	0.90	5,459	29,570	24,111
Arkansas............................	28,830	26,515	23,137	0.80	0.87	3,378	5,693	2,315
California	373,541	373,229	334,678	0.90	0.90	38,551	38,863	312
Colorado	47,335	46,257	36,784	0.78	0.80	9,473	10,551	1,078
Connecticut........................	32,193	37,765	22,229	0.69	0.59	15,536	9,964	-5,572
Delaware............................	9,655	8,237	5,812	0.60	0.71	2,425	3,843	1,418
District of Columbia	9,546	3,660	822	0.09	0.22	2,838	8,724	5,886
Florida................................	165,165	155,583	137,864	0.83	0.89	17,719	27,301	9,582
Georgia..............................	88,463	94,119	75,575	0.85	0.80	18,544	12,888	-5,656
Hawaii................................	10,271	11,790	8,223	0.80	0.70	3,567	2,048	-1,519
Idaho.................................	14,238	13,177	9,758	0.69	0.74	3,419	4,480	1,061
Illinois...............................	105,472	121,719	88,603	0.84	0.73	33,116	16,869	-16,247
Indiana..............................	71,921	63,821	55,592	0.77	0.87	8,229	16,329	8,100
Iowa...................................	43,608	30,293	26,443	0.61	0.87	3,850	17,165	13,315
Kansas...............................	33,166	29,783	25,656	0.77	0.86	4,127	7,510	3,383
Kentucky............................	41,506	38,621	33,457	0.81	0.87	5,164	8,049	2,885
Louisiana...........................	42,204	41,105	36,328	0.86	0.88	4,777	5,876	1,099
Maine.................................	12,433	11,722	8,368	0.67	0.71	3,354	4,065	711
Maryland............................	48,002	56,758	38,418	0.80	0.68	18,340	9,584	-8,756
Massachusetts....................	76,146	66,893	47,486	0.62	0.71	19,407	28,660	9,253
Michigan	95,588	94,859	84,217	0.88	0.89	10,642	11,371	729
Minnesota..........................	49,875	53,822	39,387	0.79	0.73	14,435	10,488	-3,947
Mississippi.........................	34,313	33,460	28,283	0.82	0.85	5,177	6,030	853
Missouri.............................	60,989	56,430	47,080	0.77	0.83	9,350	13,909	4,559
Montana.............................	8,918	8,167	6,403	0.72	0.78	1,764	2,515	751
Nebraska	18,174	17,681	14,396	0.79	0.81	3,285	3,778	493
Nevada...............................	15,908	18,205	14,224	0.89	0.78	3,981	1,684	-2,297
New Hampshire	13,764	12,572	7,029	0.51	0.56	5,543	6,735	1,192
New Jersey.........................	66,910	96,113	61,207	0.91	0.64	34,906	5,703	-29,203
New Mexico........................	20,094	19,876	16,903	0.84	0.85	2,973	3,191	218
New York............................	192,170	186,109	153,315	0.80	0.82	32,794	38,855	6,061
North Carolina....................	94,541	90,079	78,487	0.83	0.87	11,592	16,054	4,462
North Dakota	9,066	6,075	4,446	0.49	0.73	1,629	4,620	2,991
Ohio...................................	110,651	107,451	90,724	0.82	0.84	16,727	19,927	3,200
Oklahoma...........................	36,815	31,863	28,106	0.76	0.88	3,757	8,709	4,952
Oregon...............................	32,574	28,925	23,870	0.73	0.83	5,055	8,704	3,649
Pennsylvania......................	132,469	116,395	96,155	0.73	0.83	20,240	36,314	16,074
Rhode Island	15,454	9,801	6,772	0.44	0.69	3,029	8,682	5,653
South Carolina....................	48,307	43,058	37,572	0.78	0.87	5,486	10,735	5,249
South Dakota......................	9,316	7,834	6,090	0.65	0.78	1,744	3,226	1,482
Tennessee	54,394	53,995	44,730	0.82	0.83	9,265	9,664	399
Texas	231,816	240,300	213,635	0.92	0.89	26,665	18,181	-8,484
Utah...................................	30,456	22,952	20,845	0.68	0.91	2,107	9,611	7,504
Vermont..............................	7,889	5,117	2,696	0.34	0.53	2,421	5,193	2,772
Virginia..............................	82,243	75,060	61,570	0.75	0.82	13,490	20,673	7,183
Washington.........................	40,976	44,637	33,911	0.83	0.76	10,726	7,065	-3,661
West Virginia......................	25,076	13,956	12,172	0.49	0.87	1,784	12,904	11,120
Wisconsin...........................	56,567	54,479	44,948	0.79	0.83	9,531	11,619	2,088
Wyoming............................	5,759	4,613	3,590	0.62	0.78	1,023	2,169	1,146
U.S. Service Academies	3,782	†	271 [3]	0.07	†	-271	3,511	3,782
State unknown[4].................	†	18,271	†	†	†	18,271	†	-18,271
Other jurisdictions	51,838	53,153	51,274	0.99	0.96	1,879	564	-1,315
American Samoa................	545	645	545	1.00	0.84	100	0	-100
Federated States of Micronesia	700	809	700	1.00	0.87	109	0	-109
Guam.................................	846	951	750	0.89	0.79	201	96	-105
Marshall Islands.................	349	353	336	0.96	0.95	17	13	-4
Northern Marianas	322	387	318	0.99	0.82	69	4	-65
Palau.................................	236	193	176	0.75	0.91	17	60	43
Puerto Rico........................	48,441	49,044	48,070	0.99	0.98	974	371	-603
U.S. Virgin Islands	399	771	379	0.95	0.49	392	20	-372
Foreign countries...............	†	74,628	†	†	†	74,628	†	-74,628
Residence unknown	†	11,367	†	†	†	11,367	†	-11,367

†Not applicable.
[1]Students residing in a particular state when admitted to an institution anywhere—either in their home state or another state.
[2]Includes students coming to U.S. colleges from foreign countries and other jurisdictions.
[3]Students whose residence is in the same state as the service academy.
[4]Institution unable to determine student's home state.

NOTE: Includes all first-time postsecondary students enrolled at reporting institutions. Degree-granting institutions grant associate's or higher degrees and participate in Title IV federal financial aid programs. Some data have been revised from previously published figures. SOURCE: U.S. Department of Education, National Center for Education Statistics, Integrated Postsecondary Education Data System (IPEDS), Spring 2013, Enrollment component. (This table was prepared April 2015.)

Table 309.20. Residence and migration of all first-time degree/certificate-seeking undergraduates in degree-granting postsecondary institutions who graduated from high school in the previous 12 months, by state or jurisdiction: Fall 2012

State or jurisdiction	Total first-time enrollment in institutions located in the state	State residents enrolled in institutions		Ratio of in-state students		Migration of students		
		In any state[1]	In their home state	To first-time enrollment (col. 4/col. 2)	To residents enrolled in any state (col. 4/col. 3)	Out of state (col. 3 - col. 4)	Into state[2] (col. 2 - col. 4)	Net (col. 8 - col. 7)
1	2	3	4	5	6	7	8	9
United States	2,176,005	2,132,264	1,729,792	0.79	0.81	402,472	446,213	43,741
Alabama	37,018	29,728	26,567	0.72	0.89	3,161	10,451	7,290
Alaska	2,909	3,732	2,413	0.83	0.65	1,319	496	-823
Arizona	41,144	35,181	31,132	0.76	0.88	4,049	10,012	5,963
Arkansas	23,356	20,185	18,244	0.78	0.90	1,941	5,112	3,171
California	251,290	263,843	231,215	0.92	0.88	32,628	20,075	-12,553
Colorado	30,287	31,139	23,268	0.77	0.75	7,871	7,019	-852
Connecticut	26,044	31,662	17,396	0.67	0.55	14,266	8,648	-5,618
Delaware	8,110	6,500	4,632	0.57	0.71	1,868	3,478	1,610
District of Columbia	8,284	2,463	450	0.05	0.18	2,013	7,834	5,821
Florida	107,672	107,716	94,985	0.88	0.88	12,731	12,687	-44
Georgia	64,943	66,494	55,399	0.85	0.83	11,095	9,544	-1,551
Hawaii	7,578	9,040	6,091	0.80	0.67	2,949	1,487	-1,462
Idaho	9,776	8,782	6,179	0.63	0.70	2,603	3,597	994
Illinois	76,003	92,394	63,610	0.84	0.69	28,784	12,393	-16,391
Indiana	51,403	44,612	38,812	0.76	0.87	5,800	12,591	6,791
Iowa	30,959	23,488	20,340	0.66	0.87	3,148	10,619	7,471
Kansas	24,876	22,239	19,058	0.77	0.86	3,181	5,818	2,637
Kentucky	33,300	29,830	26,624	0.80	0.89	3,206	6,676	3,470
Louisiana	31,144	28,831	26,024	0.84	0.90	2,807	5,120	2,313
Maine	8,515	8,681	5,829	0.68	0.67	2,852	2,686	-166
Maryland	33,372	41,033	25,773	0.77	0.63	15,260	7,599	-7,661
Massachusetts	62,344	53,836	36,132	0.58	0.67	17,704	26,212	8,508
Michigan	72,446	70,843	63,296	0.87	0.89	7,547	9,150	1,603
Minnesota	38,710	43,264	30,237	0.78	0.70	13,027	8,473	-4,554
Mississippi	26,761	23,436	21,752	0.81	0.93	1,684	5,009	3,325
Missouri	46,091	42,762	35,648	0.77	0.83	7,114	10,443	3,329
Montana	6,763	5,907	4,598	0.68	0.78	1,309	2,165	856
Nebraska	15,045	14,750	11,969	0.80	0.81	2,781	3,076	295
Nevada	10,752	12,288	9,310	0.87	0.76	2,978	1,442	-1,536
New Hampshire	11,260	10,418	5,618	0.50	0.54	4,800	5,642	842
New Jersey	45,585	72,631	41,204	0.90	0.57	31,427	4,381	-27,046
New Mexico	15,117	14,831	12,903	0.85	0.87	1,928	2,214	286
New York	151,667	146,458	117,960	0.78	0.81	28,498	33,707	5,209
North Carolina	69,346	62,531	55,578	0.80	0.89	6,953	13,768	6,815
North Dakota	7,425	4,751	3,527	0.48	0.74	1,224	3,898	2,674
Ohio	85,065	81,428	69,039	0.81	0.85	12,389	16,026	3,637
Oklahoma	27,100	22,667	20,207	0.75	0.89	2,460	6,893	4,433
Oregon	20,285	17,509	13,343	0.66	0.76	4,166	6,942	2,776
Pennsylvania	101,404	87,075	70,625	0.70	0.81	16,450	30,779	14,329
Rhode Island	13,110	7,715	5,056	0.39	0.66	2,659	8,054	5,395
South Carolina	35,530	29,023	26,154	0.74	0.90	2,869	9,376	6,507
South Dakota	7,136	5,825	4,443	0.62	0.76	1,382	2,693	1,311
Tennessee	42,187	41,027	34,318	0.81	0.84	6,709	7,869	1,160
Texas	166,896	176,871	156,566	0.94	0.89	20,305	10,330	-9,975
Utah	22,087	16,650	15,101	0.68	0.91	1,549	6,986	5,437
Vermont	6,939	4,142	2,040	0.29	0.49	2,102	4,899	2,797
Virginia	62,748	58,035	47,582	0.76	0.82	10,453	15,166	4,713
Washington	32,069	34,168	25,854	0.81	0.76	8,314	6,215	-2,099
West Virginia	14,869	10,241	9,110	0.61	0.89	1,131	5,759	4,628
Wisconsin	44,345	41,715	33,972	0.77	0.81	7,743	10,373	2,630
Wyoming	4,015	3,170	2,426	0.60	0.77	744	1,589	845
U.S. Service Academies	2,925	†	183 [3]	0.06	†	-183	2,742	2,925
State unknown[4]	†	8,724	†	†	†	8,724	†	-8,724
Other jurisdictions	35,574	36,835	35,372	0.99	0.96	1,463	202	-1,261
American Samoa	405	488	405	1.00	0.83	83	0	-83
Federated States of Micronesia	0	73	0	†	†	73	0	-73
Guam	639	738	581	0.91	0.79	157	58	-99
Marshall Islands	0	10	0	†	†	10	0	-10
Northern Marianas	243	290	240	0.99	0.83	50	3	-47
Palau	184	164	150	0.82	0.91	14	34	20
Puerto Rico	33,806	34,530	33,710	1.00	0.98	820	96	-724
U.S. Virgin Islands	297	542	286	0.96	0.53	256	11	-245
Foreign countries	†	42,480	†	†	†	42,480	†	-42,480
Residence unknown	†	†	†	†	†	†	†	†

†Not applicable.
[1]Students residing in a particular state when admitted to an institution anywhere—either in their home state or another state.
[2]Includes students coming to U.S. colleges from foreign countries and other jurisdictions.
[3]Students whose residence is in the same state as the service academy.
[4]Institution unable to determine student's home state.

NOTE: Includes all first-time postsecondary students who graduated from high school in the previous 12 months and were enrolled at reporting institutions. Degree-granting institutions grant associate's or higher degrees and participate in Title IV federal financial aid programs. Some data have been revised from previously published figures.
SOURCE: U.S. Department of Education, National Center for Education Statistics, Integrated Postsecondary Education Data System (IPEDS), Spring 2013, Enrollment component. (This table was prepared April 2015.)

Table 309.30. Residence and migration of all first-time degree/certificate-seeking undergraduates in 4-year degree-granting postsecondary institutions who graduated from high school in the previous 12 months, by state or jurisdiction: Fall 2012

| State or jurisdiction | Total first-time enrollment in institutions located in the state | State residents enrolled in institutions | | Ratio of in-state students | | Migration of students | | |
| | | In any state[1] | In their home state | To first-time enrollment (col. 4/col. 2) | To residents enrolled in any state (col. 4/col. 3) | Out of state (col. 3 - col. 4) | Into state[2] (col. 2 - col. 4) | Net (col. 8 - col. 7) |
1	2	3	4	5	6	7	8	9
United States	1,500,130	1,459,931	1,082,835	0.72	0.74	377,096	417,295	40,199
Alabama......................	23,727	17,368	14,684	0.62	0.85	2,684	9,043	6,359
Alaska.........................	2,847	3,540	2,353	0.83	0.66	1,187	494	-693
Arizona.......................	23,520	18,044	14,323	0.61	0.79	3,721	9,197	5,476
Arkansas....................	16,875	13,562	11,943	0.71	0.88	1,619	4,932	3,313
California	124,879	139,943	108,238	0.87	0.77	31,705	16,641	-15,064
Colorado.....................	23,787	24,467	17,179	0.72	0.70	7,288	6,608	-680
Connecticut................	18,775	24,243	10,174	0.54	0.42	14,069	8,601	-5,468
Delaware....................	6,075	4,504	2,727	0.45	0.61	1,777	3,348	1,571
District of Columbia	8,284	2,183	450	0.05	0.21	1,733	7,834	6,101
Florida........................	97,321	96,992	85,067	0.87	0.88	11,925	12,254	329
Georgia......................	50,398	52,062	41,749	0.83	0.80	10,313	8,649	-1,664
Hawaii........................	4,274	5,669	2,900	0.68	0.51	2,769	1,374	-1,395
Idaho..........................	7,731	6,460	4,318	0.56	0.67	2,142	3,413	1,271
Illinois........................	48,729	64,672	36,735	0.75	0.57	27,937	11,994	-15,943
Indiana.......................	42,875	35,781	30,492	0.71	0.85	5,289	12,383	7,094
Iowa...........................	19,575	13,178	10,311	0.53	0.78	2,867	9,264	6,397
Kansas.......................	14,534	13,470	10,481	0.72	0.78	2,989	4,053	1,064
Kentucky....................	23,497	20,184	17,235	0.73	0.85	2,949	6,262	3,313
Louisiana...................	23,625	20,983	18,634	0.79	0.89	2,349	4,991	2,642
Maine.........................	6,634	6,855	4,054	0.61	0.59	2,801	2,580	-221
Maryland....................	18,385	26,518	11,714	0.64	0.44	14,804	6,671	-8,133
Massachusetts...........	50,944	42,690	25,218	0.50	0.59	17,472	25,726	8,254
Michigan....................	50,009	48,227	41,132	0.82	0.85	7,095	8,877	1,782
Minnesota..................	25,729	30,754	18,394	0.71	0.60	12,360	7,335	-5,025
Mississippi.................	10,768	7,930	6,408	0.60	0.81	1,522	4,360	2,838
Missouri.....................	30,847	26,899	20,707	0.67	0.77	6,192	10,140	3,948
Montana.....................	5,803	4,711	3,702	0.64	0.79	1,009	2,101	1,092
Nebraska....................	10,697	10,182	7,944	0.74	0.78	2,238	2,753	515
Nevada	9,482	10,738	8,081	0.85	0.75	2,657	1,401	-1,256
New Hampshire	8,655	7,499	3,077	0.36	0.41	4,422	5,578	1,156
New Jersey.................	26,299	52,987	22,096	0.84	0.42	30,891	4,203	-26,688
New Mexico................	7,896	7,993	6,342	0.80	0.79	1,651	1,554	-97
New York....................	106,756	101,900	73,942	0.69	0.73	27,958	32,814	4,856
North Carolina	46,835	40,243	33,772	0.72	0.84	6,471	13,063	6,592
North Dakota	6,483	3,722	2,893	0.45	0.78	829	3,590	2,761
Ohio...........................	69,379	65,666	53,861	0.78	0.82	11,805	15,518	3,713
Oklahoma...................	19,243	15,139	13,172	0.68	0.87	1,967	6,071	4,104
Oregon.......................	14,782	12,470	8,539	0.58	0.68	3,931	6,243	2,312
Pennsylvania..............	81,803	67,686	51,961	0.64	0.77	15,725	29,842	14,117
Rhode Island	10,860	5,428	2,875	0.26	0.53	2,553	7,985	5,432
South Carolina...........	23,275	16,966	14,365	0.62	0.85	2,601	8,910	6,309
South Dakota	6,111	4,744	3,571	0.58	0.75	1,173	2,540	1,367
Tennessee	29,685	28,688	22,475	0.76	0.78	6,213	7,210	997
Texas	93,616	104,945	85,548	0.91	0.82	19,397	8,068	-11,329
Utah...........................	20,482	15,119	13,830	0.68	0.91	1,289	6,652	5,363
Vermont......................	6,504	3,633	1,627	0.25	0.45	2,006	4,877	2,871
Virginia.......................	42,725	38,710	28,730	0.67	0.74	9,980	13,995	4,015
Washington................	24,698	26,538	18,681	0.76	0.70	7,857	6,017	-1,840
West Virginia..............	12,855	8,213	7,249	0.56	0.88	964	5,606	4,642
Wisconsin..................	36,138	33,019	25,951	0.72	0.79	7,068	10,187	3,119
Wyoming....................	1,499	1,411	748	0.50	0.53	663	751	88
U.S. Service Academies.....	2,925	†	183 [3]	0.06	†	-183	2,742	2,925
State unknown[4]..................	†	4,403	†	†	†	4,403	†	-4,403
Other jurisdictions	30,142	31,290	29,982	0.99	0.96	1,308	160	-1,148
American Samoa...............	405	463	405	1.00	0.87	58	0	-58
Federated States of Micronesia	†	34	†	†	†	34	0	-34
Guam..........................	528	622	473	0.90	0.76	149	55	-94
Marshall Islands................	†	6	†	†	†	6	0	-6
Northern Marianas	243	285	240	0.99	0.84	45	3	-42
Palau..........................	†	12	†	†	†	12	0	-12
Puerto Rico......................	28,669	29,347	28,578	1.00	0.97	769	91	-678
U.S. Virgin Islands	297	521	286	0.96	0.55	235	11	-224
Foreign countries...............	†	39,051	†	†	†	39,051	†	-39,051
Residence unknown	†	0	†	†	†	0	†	0

†Not applicable.
[1]Students residing in a particular state when admitted to an institution anywhere—either in their home state or another state.
[2]Includes students coming to U.S. colleges from foreign countries and other jurisdictions.
[3]Students whose residence is in the same state as the service academy.
[4]Institution unable to determine student's home state.

NOTE: Includes all first-time postsecondary students who graduated from high school in the previous 12 months and were enrolled at reporting institutions. Degree-granting institutions grant associate's or higher degrees and participate in Title IV federal financial aid programs. Some data have been revised from previously published figures.
SOURCE: U.S. Department of Education, National Center for Education Statistics, Integrated Postsecondary Education Data System (IPEDS), Spring 2013, Enrollment component. (This table was prepared April 2015.)

Table 310.10. Number of U.S. students studying abroad and percentage distribution, by sex, race/ethnicity, and other selected characteristics: Selected years, 2000–01 through 2012–13

Sex, race/ethnicity, and other selected characteristics	2000–01	2002–03	2003–04	2004–05	2005–06	2006–07	2007–08	2008–09	2009–10	2010–11	2011–12	2012–13	From 2002–03 to 2012–13
1	2	3	4	5	6	7	8	9	10	11	12	13	14
													Percent change in number of students
Total number of students..	154,168	174,629	191,231	205,983	223,534	241,791	262,416	260,327	270,604	273,996	283,332	289,408	65.7
Percentage distribution of students													Percentage-point change in student distribution
Sex..........................	100.0	100.0	100.0	100.0	100.0	100.0	100.0	100.0	100.0	100.0	100.0	100.0	†
Male..........................	35.0	35.3	34.4	34.5	34.5	34.9	34.9	35.8	36.5	35.6	35.2	34.7	-0.6
Female........................	65.0	64.7	65.6	65.5	65.5	65.1	65.1	64.2	63.5	64.4	64.8	65.3	0.6
Race/ethnicity	100.0	100.0	100.0	100.0	100.0	100.0	100.0	100.0	100.0	100.0	100.0	100.0	†
White..........................	84.3	83.2	83.7	83.0	83.0	81.9	81.8	80.5	78.7	77.8	76.4	76.3	-6.9
Black..........................	3.5	3.4	3.4	3.5	3.5	3.8	4.0	4.2	4.7	4.8	5.3	5.3	1.9
Hispanic......................	5.4	5.1	5.0	5.6	5.4	6.0	5.9	6.0	6.4	6.9	7.6	7.6	2.5
Asian/Pacific Islander.....	5.4	6.0	6.1	6.3	6.3	6.7	6.6	7.3	7.9	7.9	7.7	7.3	1.3
American Indian/ Alaska Native..........	0.5	0.5	0.5	0.4	0.6	0.5	0.5	0.5	0.5	0.5	0.5	0.5	#
Two or more races	0.9	1.8	1.3	1.2	1.2	1.2	1.2	1.6	1.9	2.1	2.5	3.0	1.2
Academic level..................	100.0	100.0	100.0	100.0	100.0	100.0	100.0	100.0	100.0	100.0	100.0	100.0	†
Freshman	3.1	2.9	3.0	3.1	3.7	3.3	3.5	3.4	3.5	3.3	3.3	3.8	0.9
Sophomore	14.0	11.8	12.0	12.2	12.8	12.9	13.1	13.9	13.2	12.6	13.0	13.7	1.9
Junior.........................	38.9	38.0	34.7	35.8	34.2	36.6	35.9	36.8	35.8	35.8	36.0	34.7	-3.3
Senior........................	20.0	20.2	19.3	19.6	19.8	21.3	21.3	21.6	21.8	23.4	24.4	24.7	4.5
Associate's students	0.9	2.1	1.6	2.7	2.7	2.7	2.2	1.1	0.1	0.2	1.1	1.1	-1.0
Bachelor's unspecified ...	13.5	15.3	16.3	15.2	14.9	12.5	13.4	11.3	11.0	10.3	8.4	8.4	-6.9
Master's level or higher ..	8.3	9.1	8.6	8.9	10.0	10.5	10.5	11.8	14.0	13.5	13.5	13.5	4.4
Other academic level	1.1	0.7	4.2	2.5	1.9	#	0.1	#	1.0	0.9	0.3	0.1	-0.6
Host region	100.0	100.0	100.0	100.0	100.0	100.0	100.0	100.0	100.0	100.0	100.0	100.0	†
Sub-Saharan Africa[1]	2.5	2.5	2.5	2.9	3.1	3.5	3.6	4.2	4.2	4.3	4.5	4.6	2.1
Asia[2]...........................	6.0	5.6	6.9	8.0	9.3	10.3	11.1	11.4	12.0	11.7	12.4	12.4	6.8
Europe[3].......................	63.3	63.1	61.0	60.3	58.3	57.4	56.3	54.5	53.5	54.6	53.3	53.3	-9.8
Latin America[4]	14.5	15.3	15.2	14.4	15.2	15.0	15.3	15.4	15.0	14.6	15.8	15.7	0.4
Middle East and North Africa[1,3]	1.6	0.7	1.0	1.5	1.8	1.8	2.2	2.5	3.1	2.6	2.5	2.2	1.5
North America[4,5]	0.7	0.7	0.6	0.5	0.5	0.6	0.4	0.5	0.7	0.5	0.6	0.5	-0.2
Oceania	6.0	7.3	7.4	6.7	6.3	5.7	5.3	5.5	5.0	4.8	4.5	4.0	-3.3
Multiple destinations	5.6	5.1	5.5	5.6	5.5	5.6	5.7	6.0	6.5	6.8	6.4	7.3	2.2
Duration of stay................	100.0	100.0	100.0	100.0	100.0	100.0	100.0	100.0	100.0	100.0	100.0	100.0	†
Summer term................	33.7	32.7	37.0	37.2	37.2	38.7	38.1	35.8	37.8	37.7	37.1	37.8	5.1
One semester	38.5	40.3	38.1	37.5	36.9	36.3	35.5	37.3	35.8	34.5	35.0	33.6	-6.7
8 weeks or less during academic year.........	7.4	9.4	8.9	8.0	9.5	9.8	11.0	11.7	11.9	13.3	14.4	15.3	5.9
January term.................	7.0	5.6	5.7	6.0	5.4	6.8	7.2	7.0	6.9	7.1	7.0	7.1	1.5
Academic year	7.3	6.7	6.0	6.0	5.3	4.3	4.1	4.1	3.8	3.7	3.2	3.1	-3.6
One quarter	4.1	3.8	3.3	3.3	3.3	3.4	3.4	3.3	3.1	3.0	2.5	2.4	-1.4
Two quarters	0.6	0.4	0.5	1.3	0.9	0.5	0.6	0.5	0.4	0.5	0.4	0.3	-0.1
Calendar year	0.6	0.5	0.2	0.2	0.2	0.1	0.1	0.1	0.1	0.1	0.1	0.1	-0.4
Other...........................	0.8	0.6	0.3	0.5	1.3	0.1	#	0.2	0.1	0.1	0.3	0.3	-0.3

†Not applicable.
#Rounds to zero.
[1]North Africa was combined with the Middle East to create the "Middle East and North Africa" category as of 2011–12, and the former "Africa" category was replaced by "Sub-Saharan Africa" (which excludes North Africa). Data for years prior to 2011–12 have been revised for comparability.
[2]Asia excludes the Middle Eastern countries (Bahrain, Iran, Iraq, Israel, Jordan, Kuwait, Lebanon, Oman, the Palestinian Authority, Qatar, Saudi Arabia, Syria, the United Arab Emirates, and Yemen).

[3]Cyprus and Turkey were classified as being in the Middle East prior to 2004–05, but in Europe for 2004–05 and later years. Data for years prior to 2004–05 have been revised for comparability.
[4]Mexico and Central America are included in Latin America, not in North America.
[5]Includes Antarctica from 2002–03 onward.
NOTE: Detail may not sum to totals because of rounding.
SOURCE: Institute of International Education, *Open Doors: Report on International Educational Exchange*, 2014. (This table was prepared November 2014.)

Table 310.20. Foreign students enrolled in institutions of higher education in the United States, by continent, region, and selected countries of origin: Selected years, 1980–81 through 2013–14

Continent, region, and selected countries of origin	1980–81 Number	1980–81 Percent	1985–86 Number	1985–86 Percent	1990–91 Number	1990–91 Percent	1995–96 Number	1995–96 Percent	2000–01 Number	2000–01 Percent	2005–06 Number	2005–06 Percent	2010–11 Number	2010–11 Percent	2011–12 Number	2011–12 Percent	2012–13 Number	2012–13 Percent	2013–14 Number	2013–14 Percent
1	2	3	4	5	6	7	8	9	10	11	12	13	14	15	16	17	18	19	20	21
Total	311,880	100.0	343,780	100.0	407,272	100.0	453,787	100.0	547,873	100.0	564,766	100.0	723,277	100.0	764,495	100.0	819,644	100.0	886,052	100.0
Sub-Saharan Africa[1]	30,870	9.9	28,210	8.2	19,262	4.7	17,422	3.8	29,033	5.3	32,538	5.8	31,470	4.4	30,046	3.9	30,585	3.7	31,113	3.5
East Africa	6,260	2.0	6,730	2.0	7,592	1.9	7,596	1.7	13,516	2.5	13,635	2.4	8,863	1.2	7,827	1.0	7,761	0.9	7,549	0.9
Kenya	1,990	0.6	1,720	0.5	2,357	0.6	2,934	0.6	6,229	1.1	6,559	1.2	4,666	0.6	3,898	0.5	3,516	0.4	3,201	0.4
Central Africa	1,130	0.4	1,540	0.4	1,647	0.4	1,346	0.3	1,859	0.3	2,825	0.5	2,831	0.4	2,778	0.4	2,861	0.3	2,883	0.3
Southern Africa	1,480	0.5	2,360	0.7	2,835	0.7	2,657	0.6	3,304	0.6	2,232	0.4	5,330	0.7	5,196	0.7	5,511	0.7	5,683	0.6
West Africa[1]	22,000	7.1	17,580	5.1	7,178	1.8	5,818	1.3	10,346	1.9	13,846	2.5	14,446	2.0	14,245	1.9	14,452	1.8	14,998	1.7
Nigeria	17,350	5.6	13,710	4.0	3,714	0.9	2,093	0.5	3,820	0.7	6,192	1.1	7,148	1.0	7,028	0.9	7,316	0.9	7,921	0.9
Asia[2]	94,640	30.3	156,830	45.6	229,825	56.4	259,893	57.3	302,058	55.1	327,785	58.0	461,903	63.9	489,970	64.1	525,849	64.2	568,510	64.2
East Asia	51,650	16.6	80,720	23.5	146,017	35.9	166,717	36.7	189,371	34.6	197,576	35.0	286,925	39.7	319,515	41.8	357,596	43.6	393,205	44.4
China	2,770	0.9	13,980	4.1	39,597	9.7	39,613	8.7	59,939	10.9	62,582	11.1	157,558	21.8	194,029	25.4	235,597	28.7	274,439	31.0
Hong Kong	9,660	3.1	10,710	3.1	12,018	3.0	12,625	2.8	7,627	1.4	7,849	1.4	8,136	1.1	8,032	1.1	8,026	1.0	8,104	0.9
Japan	13,500	4.3	13,360	3.9	36,611	9.0	45,531	10.0	46,497	8.5	38,712	6.9	21,290	2.9	19,966	2.6	19,568	2.4	19,334	2.2
South Korea	6,150	2.0	18,660	5.4	23,362	5.7	36,231	8.0	45,685	8.3	59,022	10.5	73,351	10.1	72,295	9.5	70,627	8.6	68,047	7.7
Taiwan	19,460	6.2	23,770	6.9	33,531	8.2	32,702	7.2	28,566	5.2	27,876	4.9	24,818	3.4	23,250	3.0	21,897	2.7	21,266	2.4
South and Central Asia[2]	14,540	4.7	25,800	7.5	42,367	10.4	45,402	10.0	71,771	13.1	94,965	16.8	128,958	17.8	124,392	16.3	121,100	14.8	127,301	14.4
India	9,250	3.0	16,070	4.7	28,857	7.1	31,743	7.0	54,664	10.0	76,503	13.5	103,895	14.4	100,270	13.1	96,754	11.8	102,673	11.6
Nepal	250	0.1	390	0.1	670	0.2	1,219	0.3	2,618	0.5	6,061	1.1	10,301	1.4	9,621	1.3	8,920	1.1	8,155	0.9
Pakistan	2,990	1.0	5,440	1.6	7,725	1.9	6,427	1.4	6,948	1.3	5,759	1.0	5,045	0.7	4,600	0.6	4,772	0.6	4,935	0.6
Southeast Asia	28,450	9.1	50,310	14.6	41,441	10.2	47,774	10.5	40,916	7.5	35,244	6.2	46,020	6.4	46,063	6.0	47,152	5.8	48,004	5.4
Indonesia	6,010	1.9	8,210	2.4	9,524	2.3	12,820	2.8	11,625	2.1	7,575	1.3	6,942	1.0	6,743	0.9	7,670	0.9	7,920	0.9
Malaysia	5,810	1.9	23,020	6.7	13,606	3.3	14,015	3.1	7,795	1.4	5,515	1.0	6,735	0.9	6,743	0.9	6,791	0.8	6,822	0.8
Philippines	3,390	1.1	3,920	1.1	4,495	1.1	4,273	0.9	3,139	0.6	3,798	0.7	3,604	0.5	3,194	0.4	3,215	0.4	3,112	0.4
Singapore	1,320	0.4	3,930	1.1	4,098	1.0	4,098	0.9	4,166	0.8	3,909	0.7	4,316	0.6	4,505	0.6	4,558	0.6	4,592	0.5
Thailand	6,550	2.1	6,940	2.0	7,092	1.7	12,165	2.7	11,187	2.0	8,765	1.6	8,236	1.1	7,626	1.0	7,314	0.9	7,341	0.8
Vietnam	6,490	2.1	3,270	1.0	1,396	0.3	922	0.2	2,022	0.4	4,597	0.8	14,888	2.1	15,572	2.0	16,098	2.0	16,579	1.9
Europe[2]	28,650	9.2	38,910	11.3	55,422	13.6	76,855	16.9	93,784	17.1	84,697	15.0	84,296	11.7	85,423	11.2	85,823	10.5	86,885	9.8
Cyprus[2]	720	0.2	2,140	0.6	1,710	0.4	1,819	0.4	2,217	0.4	1,111	0.2	470	0.1	438	0.1	425	0.1	419	#
France	2,570	0.8	3,680	1.1	5,633	1.4	5,710	1.3	7,273	1.3	6,640	1.2	8,098	1.1	8,232	1.1	8,297	1.0	8,302	0.9
Germany[3]	3,310	1.1	4,730	1.4	7,003	1.7	9,017	2.0	10,128	1.8	8,829	1.6	9,458	1.3	9,347	1.2	9,819	1.2	10,160	1.1
Greece	3,750	1.2	4,440	1.3	4,304	1.1	4,809	1.1	4,156	0.8	2,088	0.4	1,874	0.3	1,922	0.3	2,046	0.2	2,170	0.2
Spain	3,950	1.3	1,740	0.5	4,357	1.1	3,365	0.7	2,768	0.5	3,455	0.6	4,330	0.6	4,924	0.6	5,033	0.6	5,350	0.6
Turkey[2]	2,600	0.8	2,460	0.7	4,078	1.0	7,678	1.7	10,983	2.0	11,622	2.1	12,184	1.7	11,973	1.6	11,278	1.4	10,821	1.2
United Kingdom	4,440	1.4	5,940	1.7	7,298	1.8	7,799	1.7	8,139	1.5	8,274	1.5	8,947	1.2	9,186	1.2	9,467	1.2	10,191	1.2
Latin America	49,810	16.0	45,480	13.2	47,318	11.6	47,253	10.4	63,634	11.6	64,769	11.5	64,169	8.9	64,416	8.4	66,864	8.2	72,318	8.2
Caribbean	10,650	3.4	11,100	3.2	12,349	3.0	10,737	2.4	14,423	2.6	13,855	2.5	11,644	1.6	11,376	1.5	11,100	1.4	10,879	1.2
Central America	12,970	4.2	12,740	3.7	15,949	3.9	14,220	3.1	16,764	3.1	15,709	2.8	20,361	2.8	20,432	2.7	21,072	2.6	22,276	2.5
Mexico	6,730	2.2	5,460	1.6	6,739	1.7	8,687	1.9	10,670	1.9	13,931	2.5	13,713	1.9	13,893	1.8	14,199	1.7	14,779	1.7
South America	26,190	8.4	21,640	6.3	19,019	4.7	22,296	4.9	32,447	5.9	31,205	5.5	32,164	4.4	32,602	4.3	34,692	4.2	39,163	4.4
Brazil	2,870	0.9	2,840	0.8	3,898	1.0	5,497	1.2	8,846	1.6	7,009	1.2	8,777	1.2	9,029	1.2	10,868	1.3	13,286	1.5
Colombia	6,770	2.2	4,010	1.2	3,584	0.9	3,462	0.8	6,765	1.2	6,835	1.2	6,456	0.9	6,295	0.8	6,543	0.8	7,083	0.8
Venezuela	11,750	3.8	7,040	2.0	2,894	0.7	4,456	1.0	5,217	1.0	4,792	0.8	5,491	0.8	6,281	0.8	6,158	0.8	7,022	0.8
Middle East and North Africa[1]	88,700	28.4	54,100	15.7	32,177	7.9	24,488	5.4	28,842	5.3	21,576	3.8	47,963	6.6	62,120	8.1	77,049	9.4	92,618	10.5
Middle East[2]	81,390	26.1	48,120	14.0	27,636	6.8	21,066	4.6	23,658	4.3	17,806	3.2	42,543	5.9	56,664	7.4	71,170	8.7	86,372	9.7
Iran	47,550	15.2	14,210	4.1	6,267	1.5	2,628	0.6	1,844	0.3	2,420	0.4	5,626	0.8	6,982	0.9	8,744	1.1	10,194	1.2
Israel	2,550	0.8	2,600	0.8	2,977	0.7	2,637	0.6	2,187	0.4	1,733	0.3	2,701	0.4	2,490	0.3	2,430	0.3	2,457	0.3
Jordan	2,770	0.9	3,810	1.1	4,321	1.1	2,222	0.5	2,005	0.4	2,187	0.4	2,002	0.3	2,062	0.3	2,109	0.3	2,148	0.2
Kuwait	6,140	2.0	6,590	1.9	1,624	0.4	1,554	0.3	1,950	0.4	1,703	0.3	2,998	0.4	3,722	0.5	5,115	0.6	7,288	0.8
Lebanon	6,770	2.2	7,090	2.1	3,899	1.0	4,191	0.9	2,005	0.4	1,950	0.3	1,462	0.2	1,350	0.2	1,266	0.2	1,367	0.2
Saudi Arabia	10,440	3.3	6,900	2.0	4,031	1.0	3,422	0.8	5,273	1.0	3,448	0.6	22,704	3.1	34,139	4.5	44,566	5.4	53,919	6.1
North Africa[1]	7,310	2.3	5,980	1.7	4,541	1.1	3,422	0.8	5,184	0.9	3,770	0.7	5,420	0.7	5,456	0.7	5,879	0.7	6,246	0.7
North America[4]	14,790	4.7	16,030	4.7	18,949	4.7	23,644	5.2	25,888	4.7	28,699	5.1	27,941	3.9	26,821	3.5	27,357	3.3	28,304	3.2
Canada	14,320	4.6	15,410	4.5	18,350	4.5	23,005	5.1	25,279	4.6	28,202	5.0	27,546	3.8	26,821	3.5	27,357	3.3	28,304	3.2
Oceania	4,180	1.3	4,030	1.2	4,230	1.0	4,202	0.9	4,624	0.8	4,702	0.8	5,610	0.8	5,697	0.7	6,104	0.7	6,292	0.7
Australia	1,530	0.5	1,530	0.4	1,906	0.5	2,244	0.5	2,645	0.5	2,806	0.5	3,777	0.5	3,848	0.5	4,121	0.5	4,377	0.5
Unidentified[5]	240	0.1	190	0.1	89	#	30	#	10	#	#	#	10	#	8	#	13	#	12	#

#Rounds to zero.
[1]"North Africa" was combined with the Middle East to create the "Middle East and North Africa" category as of 2012–13, and the former "Africa" category was replaced by "Sub-Saharan Africa" (which excludes North Africa). Data for years prior to 2012–13 have been revised for comparability.
[2]Cyprus and Turkey were classified as being in the Middle East prior to 2004–05, but in Europe for 2004–05 and later years. Data for years prior to 2004–05 have been revised for comparability.
[3]Data for 1980–81 and 1985–86 are for West Germany (Federal Republic of Germany before unification).
[4]Excludes Mexico and Central America, which are included in Latin America.
[5]Place of origin unknown or undeclared.

NOTE: Includes foreign students enrolled in American Samoa, Guam, Puerto Rico, and the U.S. Virgin Islands. Totals and subtotals include other countries not shown separately. Region totals may not sum to continent totals, because some continent totals include students who are not classified by country or region. Data are for "nonimmigrants" (i.e., students who have not migrated to the United States). Detail may not sum to totals because of rounding.
SOURCE: Institute of International Education, Open Doors: Report on International Educational Exchange, selected years, 1981 through 2014. (This table was prepared November 2014.)

Table 311.10. Number and percentage distribution of students enrolled in postsecondary institutions, by level, disability status, and selected student characteristics: 2007–08 and 2011–12

[Standard errors appear in parentheses]

Selected student characteristic	Undergraduate						Postbaccalaureate, 2011–12		
	2007–08			2011–12					
	All students	Students with disabilities[1]	Nondisabled students	All students	Students with disabilities[1]	Nondisabled students	All students	Students with disabilities[1]	Nondisabled students
1	2	3	4	5	6	7	8	9	10
Number of students (in thousands)	20,511 (—)	2,243 (—)	18,268 (—)	23,055 (—)	2,563 (—)	20,493 (—)	3,682 (—)	195 (—)	3,487 (—)
Percentage distribution of students									
Total	100.0 (†)	10.9 (0.19)	89.1 (0.19)	100.0 (†)	11.1 (0.17)	88.9 (0.17)	100.0 (†)	5.3 (0.36)	94.7 (0.36)
Sex									
Male	100.0 (†)	10.9 (0.26)	89.1 (0.26)	100.0 (†)	11.3 (0.27)	88.7 (0.27)	100.0 (†)	4.8 (0.40)	95.2 (0.40)
Female	100.0 (†)	11.0 (0.23)	89.0 (0.23)	100.0 (†)	11.0 (0.23)	89.0 (0.23)	100.0 (†)	5.6 (0.50)	94.4 (0.50)
Race/ethnicity of student									
White	100.0 (†)	11.7 (0.23)	88.3 (0.23)	100.0 (†)	11.1 (0.24)	88.9 (0.24)	100.0 (†)	5.0 (0.39)	95.0 (0.39)
Black	100.0 (†)	9.9 (0.44)	90.1 (0.44)	100.0 (†)	12.2 (0.38)	87.8 (0.38)	100.0 (†)	6.9 (1.19)	93.1 (1.19)
Hispanic	100.0 (†)	9.4 (0.42)	90.6 (0.42)	100.0 (†)	10.4 (0.41)	89.7 (0.41)	100.0 (†)	6.4 (1.40)	93.7 (1.40)
Asian	100.0 (†)	8.0 (0.66)	92.0 (0.66)	100.0 (†)	8.0 (0.64)	92.0 (0.64)	100.0 (†)	4.3 (0.86)	95.7 (0.86)
Pacific Islander	100.0 (†)	7.6 (1.25)	92.4 (1.25)	100.0 (†)	14.9 (2.97)	85.1 (2.97)	‡ (†)	‡ (†)	‡ (†)
American Indian/Alaska Native	100.0 (†)	10.0 (1.42)	90.0 (1.42)	100.0 (†)	14.4 (2.32)	85.6 (2.32)	‡ (†)	‡ (†)	‡ (†)
Two or more races	100.0 (†)	13.5 (1.11)	86.5 (1.11)	100.0 (†)	13.6 (0.98)	86.4 (0.98)	100.0 (†)	6.4 (1.84)	93.6 (1.84)
Other	100.0 (†)	11.3 (2.63)	88.7 (2.63)	— (†)	— (†)	— (†)	— (†)	— (†)	— (†)
Age									
15 to 23	100.0 (†)	9.8 (0.19)	90.2 (0.19)	100.0 (†)	9.0 (0.22)	91.0 (0.22)	100.0 (†)	3.9 (0.70)	96.1 (0.70)
24 to 29	100.0 (†)	12.8 (0.48)	87.2 (0.48)	100.0 (†)	11.3 (0.38)	88.7 (0.38)	100.0 (†)	4.6 (0.50)	95.4 (0.50)
30 or older	100.0 (†)	12.4 (0.39)	87.7 (0.39)	100.0 (†)	15.7 (0.44)	84.3 (0.44)	100.0 (†)	6.2 (0.57)	93.8 (0.57)
Attendance status									
Full-time, full-year	100.0 (†)	9.5 (0.19)	90.5 (0.19)	100.0 (†)	9.5 (0.22)	90.5 (0.22)	100.0 (†)	5.4 (0.47)	94.6 (0.47)
Part-time or part-year	100.0 (†)	11.7 (0.27)	88.3 (0.27)	100.0 (†)	12.1 (0.24)	87.9 (0.24)	100.0 (†)	5.3 (0.45)	94.7 (0.45)
Student housing status									
On-campus	100.0 (†)	8.6 (0.34)	91.4 (0.34)	100.0 (†)	8.6 (0.37)	91.4 (0.37)	— (†)	— (†)	— (†)
Off-campus	100.0 (†)	11.4 (0.25)	88.6 (0.25)	100.0 (†)	11.8 (0.27)	88.2 (0.27)	— (†)	— (†)	— (†)
With parents or relatives	100.0 (†)	11.2 (0.33)	88.8 (0.33)	100.0 (†)	11.3 (0.30)	88.7 (0.30)	— (†)	— (†)	— (†)
Attended more than one institution	100.0 (†)	10.8 (0.43)	89.3 (0.43)	100.0 (†)	10.0 (0.42)	90.0 (0.42)	— (†)	— (†)	— (†)
Dependency status									
Dependent	100.0 (†)	9.6 (0.19)	90.4 (0.19)	100.0 (†)	8.6 (0.21)	91.4 (0.21)	— (†)	— (†)	— (†)
Independent, unmarried	100.0 (†)	14.1 (0.51)	85.9 (0.51)	100.0 (†)	14.3 (0.44)	85.7 (0.44)	100.0 (†)	5.6 (0.47)	94.4 (0.47)
Independent, married	100.0 (†)	12.0 (0.80)	88.0 (0.80)	100.0 (†)	13.3 (0.74)	86.7 (0.74)	100.0 (†)	4.2 (0.85)	95.8 (0.85)
Independent with dependents	100.0 (†)	11.5 (0.34)	88.5 (0.34)	100.0 (†)	13.1 (0.39)	86.9 (0.39)	100.0 (†)	5.3 (0.58)	94.7 (0.58)
Veteran status									
Veteran	100.0 (†)	15.0 (1.10)	85.0 (1.10)	100.0 (†)	20.6 (1.35)	79.4 (1.35)	100.0 (†)	7.9 (1.70)	92.1 (1.70)
Not veteran	100.0 (†)	10.8 (0.18)	89.2 (0.18)	100.0 (†)	10.8 (0.17)	89.3 (0.17)	100.0 (†)	5.2 (0.36)	94.8 (0.36)
Field of study									
Business/management	100.0 (†)	10.0 (0.43)	90.0 (0.43)	100.0 (†)	10.0 (0.42)	90.0 (0.42)	100.0 (†)	5.9 (1.60)	94.2 (1.60)
Education	100.0 (†)	10.0 (0.56)	90.0 (0.56)	100.0 (†)	10.1 (0.75)	89.9 (0.75)	100.0 (†)	5.6 (0.88)	94.4 (0.88)
Engineering/computer science/mathematics	100.0 (†)	10.6 (0.76)	89.4 (0.76)	100.0 (†)	10.6 (0.63)	89.4 (0.63)	100.0 (†)	4.8 (1.04)	95.2 (1.04)
Health	100.0 (†)	11.2 (0.45)	88.8 (0.45)	100.0 (†)	10.8 (0.38)	89.2 (0.38)	100.0 (†)	4.6 (0.68)	95.4 (0.68)
Humanities	100.0 (†)	12.2 (0.41)	87.8 (0.41)	100.0 (†)	12.2 (0.49)	87.8 (0.49)	100.0 (†)	5.9 (1.12)	94.1 (1.12)
Law	— (†)	— (†)	— (†)	— (†)	— (†)	— (†)	100.0 (†)	7.7 (1.17)	92.3 (1.17)
Life/physical sciences	100.0 (†)	9.8 (0.55)	90.2 (0.55)	100.0 (†)	9.2 (0.54)	90.8 (0.54)	100.0 (†)	3.8 (0.67)	96.2 (0.67)
Social/behavioral sciences	100.0 (†)	10.8 (0.65)	89.2 (0.65)	100.0 (†)	11.8 (0.76)	88.2 (0.76)	100.0 (†)	5.8 (0.79)	94.2 (0.79)
Vocational/technical	100.0 (†)	11.2 (0.99)	88.8 (0.99)	100.0 (†)	14.5 (1.09)	85.5 (1.09)	— (†)	— (†)	— (†)
Undeclared	100.0 (†)	11.1 (0.56)	88.9 (0.56)	100.0 (†)	11.8 (0.91)	88.2 (0.91)	100.0 (†)	4.2 ! (1.72)	95.8 (1.72)
Other	100.0 (†)	11.2 (0.45)	88.8 (0.45)	100.0 (†)	11.8 (0.44)	88.2 (0.44)	100.0 (†)	4.8 (0.80)	95.2 (0.80)

—Not available.
†Not applicable.
!Interpret data with caution. The coefficient of variation (CV) for this estimate is between 30 and 50 percent.
‡Reporting standards not met. Either there are too few cases for a reliable estimate or the coefficient of variation (CV) is 50 percent or greater.
[1]Students with disabilities are those who reported that they had one or more of the following conditions: a specific learning disability, a visual handicap, hard of hearing, deafness, a speech disability, an orthopedic handicap, or a health impairment.

NOTE: Data are based on a sample survey of students who enrolled at any time during the school year. Data exclude Puerto Rico. Detail may not sum to totals because of rounding. Race categories exclude persons of Hispanic ethnicity. Some data have been revised from previously published figures.
SOURCE: U.S. Department of Education, National Center for Education Statistics, 2007–08 and 2011–12 National Postsecondary Student Aid Study (NPSAS:08 and NPSAS:12). (This table was prepared August 2014.)

Table 311.15. Number and percentage of students enrolled in degree-granting postsecondary institutions, by distance education participation, location of student, level of enrollment, and control and level of institution: Fall 2012 and fall 2013

Year, level of enrollment, and control and level of institution	Total	Number of students									Percent of students									
		No distance education courses	Taking any distance education course(s)								Total	No distance education courses	Taking any distance education course(s)							
			Total, any distance education course(s)	At least one, but not all, of student's courses	Exclusively distance education courses by location of student								Total, any distance education course(s)	At least one, but not all, of student's courses	Exclusively distance education courses by location of student					
					Total	Same state	Different state	State not known	Outside of the United States	Location unknown					Total	Same state	Different state	State not known	Outside of the United States	Location unknown
1	2	3	4	5	6	7	8	9	10	11	12	13	14	15	16	17	18	19	20	21
Fall 2012																				
All students, total	20,642,819	15,198,118	5,444,701	2,806,048	2,638,653	1,336,873	1,176,009	36,779	33,561	55,431	**100.0**	**73.6**	**26.4**	**13.6**	**12.8**	**6.5**	**5.7**	**0.2**	**0.2**	**0.3**
Public	14,880,343	11,227,331	3,653,012	2,405,021	1,247,991	1,031,658	145,655	23,173	13,277	34,228	100.0	75.5	24.5	16.2	8.4	6.9	1.0	0.2	0.1	0.2
Private																				
Nonprofit	3,953,578	3,226,385	727,193	259,696	467,497	183,450	253,173	9,050	7,378	14,446	100.0	81.6	18.4	6.6	11.8	4.6	6.4	0.2	0.2	0.4
For-profit	1,808,898	744,402	1,064,496	141,331	923,165	121,765	777,181	4,556	12,906	6,757	100.0	41.2	58.8	7.8	51.0	6.7	43.0	0.3	0.7	0.4
Fall 2013																				
All students, total	20,375,789	14,853,595	5,522,194	2,862,991	2,659,203	1,388,195	1,119,577	30,244	35,767	85,420	**100.0**	**72.9**	**27.1**	**14.1**	**13.1**	**6.8**	**5.5**	**0.1**	**0.2**	**0.4**
4-year	13,407,050	9,790,774	3,616,276	1,638,507	1,977,769	778,853	1,074,387	12,905	31,867	79,757	100.0	73.0	27.0	12.2	14.8	5.8	8.0	0.1	0.2	0.6
2-year	6,968,739	5,062,821	1,905,918	1,224,484	681,434	609,342	45,190	17,339	3,900	5,663	100.0	72.7	27.3	17.6	9.8	8.7	0.6	0.2	0.1	0.1
Public	14,745,558	11,001,316	3,744,242	2,462,362	1,281,880	1,065,214	159,637	24,401	12,718	19,910	100.0	74.6	25.4	16.7	8.7	7.2	1.1	0.2	0.1	0.1
4-year	8,120,417	6,244,659	1,875,758	1,255,372	620,386	462,008	128,232	7,062	8,834	14,250	100.0	76.9	23.1	15.5	7.6	5.7	1.6	0.1	0.1	0.2
2-year	6,625,141	4,756,657	1,868,484	1,206,990	661,494	603,206	31,405	17,339	3,884	5,660	100.0	71.8	28.2	18.2	10.0	9.1	0.5	0.3	0.1	0.1
Private																				
Nonprofit	3,974,004	3,178,594	795,410	275,020	520,390	205,897	289,967	2,349	9,435	12,742	100.0	80.0	20.0	6.9	13.1	5.2	7.3	0.1	0.2	0.3
4-year	3,941,806	3,148,416	793,390	273,802	519,588	205,493	289,569	2,349	9,435	12,742	100.0	79.9	20.1	6.9	13.2	5.2	7.3	0.1	0.2	0.3
2-year	32,198	30,178	2,020	1,218	802	404	398	0	0	0	100.0	93.7	6.3	3.8	2.5	1.3	1.2	0.0	0.0	0.0
For-profit	1,656,227	673,685	982,542	125,609	856,933	117,084	669,973	3,494	13,614	52,768	100.0	40.7	59.3	7.6	51.7	7.1	40.5	0.2	0.8	3.2
4-year	1,344,827	397,699	947,128	109,333	837,795	111,352	656,596	3,494	13,598	52,765	100.0	29.6	70.4	8.1	62.3	8.3	48.8	0.3	1.0	3.9
2-year	311,400	275,986	35,414	16,276	19,138	5,732	13,387	0	16	3	100.0	88.6	11.4	5.2	6.1	1.8	4.3	0.0	#	#
Undergraduate																				
Total	17,474,835	12,847,210	4,627,625	2,645,183	1,982,442	1,114,983	757,448	26,211	21,105	62,695	**100.0**	**73.5**	**26.5**	**15.1**	**11.3**	**6.4**	**4.3**	**0.1**	**0.1**	**0.4**
4-year	10,506,096	7,784,389	2,721,707	1,420,699	1,301,008	505,641	712,258	8,872	17,205	57,032	100.0	74.1	25.9	13.5	12.4	4.8	6.8	0.1	0.2	0.5
2-year	6,968,739	5,062,821	1,905,918	1,224,484	681,434	609,342	45,190	17,339	3,900	5,663	100.0	72.7	27.3	17.6	9.8	8.7	0.6	0.2	0.1	0.1
Public	13,347,002	9,949,253	3,397,749	2,337,560	1,060,189	916,864	96,899	22,988	8,958	14,480	100.0	74.5	25.5	17.5	7.9	6.9	0.7	0.2	0.1	0.1
4-year	6,721,861	5,192,596	1,529,265	1,130,570	398,695	313,658	65,494	5,649	5,074	8,820	100.0	77.2	22.8	16.8	5.9	4.7	1.0	0.1	0.1	0.1
2-year	6,625,141	4,756,657	1,868,484	1,206,990	661,494	603,206	31,405	17,339	3,884	5,660	100.0	71.8	28.2	18.2	10.0	9.1	0.5	0.3	0.1	0.1
Private																				
Nonprofit	2,757,447	2,271,597	485,850	194,886	290,964	108,191	169,663	758	4,655	7,697	100.0	82.4	17.6	7.1	10.6	3.9	6.2	#	0.2	0.3
4-year	2,725,249	2,241,419	483,830	193,668	290,162	107,787	169,265	758	4,655	7,697	100.0	82.2	17.8	7.1	10.6	4.0	6.2	#	0.2	0.3
2-year	32,198	30,178	2,020	1,218	802	404	398	0	0	0	100.0	93.7	6.3	3.8	2.5	1.3	1.2	0.0	0.0	0.0
For-profit	1,370,386	626,360	744,026	112,737	631,289	89,928	490,886	2,465	7,492	40,518	100.0	45.7	54.3	8.2	46.1	6.6	35.8	0.2	0.5	3.0
4-year	1,058,986	350,374	708,612	96,461	612,151	84,196	477,499	2,465	7,476	40,515	100.0	33.1	66.9	9.1	57.8	8.0	45.1	0.2	0.7	3.8
2-year	311,400	275,986	35,414	16,276	19,138	5,732	13,387	0	16	3	100.0	88.6	11.4	5.2	6.1	1.8	4.3	0.0	#	#
Postbaccalaureate																				
Total	2,900,954	2,006,385	894,569	217,808	676,761	273,212	362,129	4,033	14,662	22,725	**100.0**	**69.2**	**30.8**	**7.5**	**23.3**	**9.4**	**12.5**	**0.1**	**0.5**	**0.8**
Public	1,398,556	1,052,063	346,493	124,802	221,691	148,350	62,738	1,413	3,760	5,430	100.0	75.2	24.8	8.9	15.9	10.6	4.5	0.1	0.3	0.4
Private																				
Nonprofit	1,216,557	906,997	309,560	80,134	229,426	97,706	120,304	1,591	4,780	5,045	100.0	74.6	25.4	6.6	18.9	8.0	9.9	0.1	0.4	0.4
For-profit	285,841	47,325	238,516	12,872	225,644	27,156	179,087	1,029	6,122	12,250	100.0	16.6	83.4	4.5	78.9	9.5	62.7	0.4	2.1	4.3

#Rounds to zero.
NOTE: Degree-granting institutions grant associate's or higher degrees and participate in Title IV federal financial aid programs.

SOURCE: U.S. Department of Education, National Center for Education Statistics, Integrated Postsecondary Education Data System (IPEDS), Spring 2013 and Spring 2014, Enrollment component. (This table was prepared December 2014.)

Table 311.20. Number and percentage of undergraduate students taking night, weekend, or online classes, by selected characteristics: 2011–12

[Standard errors appear in parentheses]

Selected characteristic	Total taking any night, weekend, or online classes[1]		Percent of students taking night, weekend, or online classes							Percent of students whose entire degree program is online[2]
	Number of students (in thousands)	Percent of students	Night classes		Weekend classes		Online classes		
			Any night classes	Exclusively night classes	Any weekend classes	Exclusively weekend classes	Any online classes	Exclusively online classes	
1	2	3	4	5	6	7	8	9	10
Total	11,917	51.7 (0.33)	32.4 (0.29)	5.2 (0.14)	7.0 (0.17)	0.3 (0.03)	32.0 (0.33)	8.4 (0.20)	6.5 (0.18)
Sex									
Male	4,865	49.0 (0.46)	32.0 (0.40)	5.1 (0.18)	6.7 (0.22)	0.3 (0.05)	28.5 (0.45)	6.5 (0.25)	4.9 (0.24)
Female	7,052	53.7 (0.40)	32.7 (0.39)	5.3 (0.19)	7.2 (0.22)	0.3 (0.04)	34.5 (0.39)	9.8 (0.24)	7.7 (0.21)
Race/ethnicity									
White	7,019	52.6 (0.45)	32.5 (0.39)	4.9 (0.18)	6.3 (0.20)	0.2 (0.04)	33.5 (0.41)	9.0 (0.24)	6.8 (0.21)
Black	1,930	52.0 (0.68)	30.8 (0.59)	6.0 (0.28)	7.8 (0.41)	0.5 (0.10)	32.7 (0.70)	10.7 (0.57)	9.1 (0.56)
Hispanic	1,863	50.4 (0.64)	33.9 (0.61)	6.3 (0.40)	8.3 (0.36)	0.4 (0.08)	27.9 (0.57)	5.5 (0.29)	4.3 (0.24)
Asian	588	45.5 (1.22)	31.0 (1.18)	3.3 (0.41)	7.4 (0.62)	‡ (†)	26.0 (1.06)	4.2 (0.45)	2.9 (0.35)
Pacific Islander	64	54.4 (3.80)	45.8 (3.84)	4.6 ! (1.46)	11.2 (2.40)	# (†)	29.9 (3.18)	3.5 ! (1.33)	3.1 ! (1.29)
American Indian/Alaska Native	107	51.2 (2.75)	31.8 (2.44)	6.6 (1.56)	6.7 (1.38)	‡ (†)	32.6 (2.56)	9.1 (1.60)	7.0 (1.43)
Two or more races	346	50.5 (1.63)	31.9 (1.48)	4.9 (0.83)	7.4 (0.76)	0.3 ! (0.15)	30.6 (1.48)	8.3 (0.93)	5.5 (0.69)
Age									
15 through 23	5,884	45.4 (0.38)	29.8 (0.32)	3.0 (0.11)	5.2 (0.17)	0.2 (0.02)	26.5 (0.36)	4.5 (0.16)	3.2 (0.13)
24 through 29	2,474	58.2 (0.71)	36.6 (0.70)	7.7 (0.40)	9.0 (0.38)	0.3 (0.06)	36.5 (0.67)	10.4 (0.43)	8.0 (0.41)
30 or older	3,559	60.9 (0.63)	35.3 (0.69)	8.5 (0.34)	9.5 (0.34)	0.6 (0.10)	40.9 (0.64)	15.6 (0.51)	13.0 (0.50)
Attendance status									
Exclusively full-time	5,579	48.0 (0.43)	30.3 (0.35)	3.9 (0.16)	6.0 (0.20)	0.2 (0.03)	28.8 (0.41)	7.6 (0.22)	6.5 (0.20)
Exclusively part-time	4,136	56.6 (0.62)	34.8 (0.57)	8.3 (0.32)	8.3 (0.31)	0.5 (0.09)	35.3 (0.62)	10.7 (0.42)	7.4 (0.38)
Mixed full-time and part-time	2,203	53.5 (0.60)	34.3 (0.54)	3.3 (0.19)	7.3 (0.33)	0.2 (0.04)	35.0 (0.62)	6.4 (0.31)	5.0 (0.28)
Had job during academic year[3]									
Yes	8,219	57.2 (0.40)	35.9 (0.35)	6.1 (0.19)	7.9 (0.21)	0.3 (0.04)	36.2 (0.42)	9.8 (0.26)	7.6 (0.24)
No	3,699	42.5 (0.45)	26.7 (0.38)	3.9 (0.19)	5.5 (0.24)	0.2 (0.04)	24.9 (0.42)	6.1 (0.25)	4.8 (0.20)
Dependency status									
Dependent	4,994	44.5 (0.39)	29.5 (0.34)	2.6 (0.11)	4.9 (0.18)	0.1 (0.02)	25.5 (0.36)	3.9 (0.16)	2.7 (0.12)
Independent, no dependents, not married[4]	2,331	55.1 (0.71)	35.5 (0.69)	7.5 (0.42)	8.2 (0.34)	0.3 (0.07)	33.6 (0.63)	8.9 (0.38)	6.7 (0.33)
Independent, no dependents, married	736	58.8 (1.27)	36.5 (1.28)	7.8 (0.76)	8.3 (0.70)	0.5 ! (0.17)	37.4 (1.22)	11.7 (0.75)	10.1 (0.72)
Independent, with dependents, not married[4]	2,040	58.2 (0.72)	34.3 (0.79)	8.2 (0.41)	9.4 (0.39)	0.5 (0.10)	38.2 (0.67)	12.7 (0.48)	10.7 (0.45)
Independent, with dependents, married	1,817	64.0 (0.84)	35.2 (0.84)	7.7 (0.50)	9.8 (0.50)	0.6 (0.15)	44.9 (0.92)	18.8 (0.77)	14.7 (0.75)
Control of institution									
Public	8,796	52.0 (0.38)	33.0 (0.32)	4.3 (0.15)	6.6 (0.19)	0.3 (0.04)	33.2 (0.39)	6.3 (0.21)	4.0 (0.16)
Private nonprofit	1,291	42.9 (0.91)	30.6 (0.90)	3.8 (0.38)	5.2 (0.41)	0.2 ! (0.07)	21.0 (0.85)	5.8 (0.61)	4.5 (0.57)
Private for-profit	1,830	58.7 (0.74)	31.2 (0.71)	11.7 (0.48)	10.9 (0.50)	0.6 (0.09)	35.5 (0.83)	22.2 (0.79)	21.6 (0.82)

†Not applicable.
#Rounds to zero.
!Interpret data with caution. The coefficient of variation (CV) for this estimate is between 30 and 50 percent.
‡Reporting standards not met. Either there are too few cases for a reliable estimate or the coefficient of variation (CV) is 50 percent or greater.
[1]Students who reported taking more than one type of class (e.g., night classes and online classes) are counted only once in the total.
[2]Excludes students not in a degree or certificate program.

[3]Excludes work-study/assistantships.
[4]Includes separated.
NOTE: Night classes start after 6:00 p.m. on Monday through Thursday nights; weekend classes start after 6:00 p.m. on Friday or take place any time on Saturday or Sunday; and online classes are taught only online. Detail may not sum to totals because of rounding. Race categories exclude persons of Hispanic ethnicity.
SOURCE: U.S. Department of Education, National Center for Education Statistics, 2011–12 National Postsecondary Student Aid Study (NPSAS:12). (This table was prepared March 2014.)

Table 311.22. Number and percentage of undergraduate students taking distance education or online classes and degree programs, by selected characteristics: Selected years, 2003–04 through 2011–12

[Standard errors appear in parentheses]

| | Percent of undergraduate students taking distance education classes | | | | | | 2011–12 | | | | | |
| | 2003–04 | | | 2007–08 | | | Number of undergraduate students (in thousands) | | Percent of undergraduate students taking online classes | | | |
Selected characteristic	Total, any distance education classes	Entire degree program through distance education[1]	Total, any distance education classes	Entire degree program through distance education[1]		Total, all students	Number taking any online classes	Total, any online classes		Exclusively online classes	Entire degree program is online[1]
1	2	3	4	5		6	7	8		9	10
Total......	15.6 (0.29)	4.9 (0.17)	20.6 (0.23)	3.8 (0.16)		23,055	7,368	32.0 (0.33)		8.4 (0.20)	6.5 (0.18)
Sex											
Male......	13.6 (0.31)	4.3 (0.19)	18.8 (0.31)	3.4 (0.16)		9,921	2,831	28.5 (0.45)		6.5 (0.25)	4.9 (0.24)
Female......	17.0 (0.40)	5.4 (0.23)	21.9 (0.28)	4.2 (0.22)		13,135	4,537	34.5 (0.39)		9.8 (0.24)	7.7 (0.21)
Race/ethnicity											
White......	16.2 (0.33)	5.0 (0.19)	21.9 (0.29)	3.9 (0.19)		13,345	4,472	33.5 (0.41)		9.0 (0.24)	6.8 (0.21)
Black......	14.9 (0.59)	4.9 (0.37)	19.9 (0.66)	5.1 (0.48)		3,709	1,214	32.7 (0.70)		10.7 (0.57)	9.1 (0.56)
Hispanic......	13.4 (0.54)	4.1 (0.27)	16.5 (0.53)	2.7 (0.23)		3,696	1,032	27.9 (0.57)		5.5 (0.29)	4.3 (0.24)
Asian......	14.0 (0.92)	5.2 (0.58)	18.1 (0.86)	2.9 (0.40)		1,292	336	26.0 (1.06)		4.2 (0.45)	2.9 (0.35)
Pacific Islander......	19.1 (2.37)	6.9 (1.69)	17.0 (1.89)	1.2 ! (0.53)		119	35	29.9 (3.18)		3.5 ! (1.33)	3.1 ! (1.29)
American Indian/Alaska Native	15.5 (1.85)	6.2 (1.41)	21.9 (2.41)	1.8 ! (0.55)		209	68	32.6 (2.56)		9.1 (1.60)	7.0 (1.43)
Two or more races......	16.5 (1.33)	5.1 (1.16)	20.4 (1.08)	3.6 (0.86)		686	210	30.6 (1.48)		8.3 (0.93)	5.5 (0.69)
Age											
15 through 23......	11.7 (0.26)	3.1 (0.13)	15.2 (0.22)	1.4 (0.09)		12,956	3,429	26.5 (0.36)		4.5 (0.16)	3.2 (0.13)
24 through 29......	18.4 (0.46)	6.7 (0.41)	25.7 (0.56)	5.6 (0.45)		4,253	1,551	36.5 (0.67)		10.4 (0.43)	8.0 (0.41)
30 or older......	22.4 (0.65)	8.3 (0.42)	30.0 (0.55)	9.0 (0.40)		5,846	2,388	40.9 (0.64)		15.6 (0.51)	13.0 (0.50)
Attendance status											
Exclusively full-time......	12.7 (0.32)	3.8 (0.20)	16.7 (0.33)	3.2 (0.29)		11,632	3,346	28.8 (0.41)		7.6 (0.22)	6.5 (0.20)
Exclusively part-time......	18.7 (0.46)	6.9 (0.32)	24.8 (0.39)	5.2 (0.22)		7,308	2,583	35.3 (0.62)		10.7 (0.42)	7.4 (0.38)
Mixed full-time and part-time......	17.4 (0.53)	4.7 (0.23)	22.5 (0.42)	2.9 (0.20)		4,116	1,440	35.0 (0.62)		6.4 (0.31)	5.0 (0.28)
Undergraduate field of study											
Business/management......	18.7 (0.58)	7.0 (0.43)	24.2 (0.55)	6.4 (0.45)		3,487	1,371	39.3 (0.75)		13.1 (0.48)	11.4 (0.45)
Computer/information science......	19.5 (0.96)	7.2 (0.71)	26.9 (1.53)	8.4 (1.17)		942	385	40.8 (1.37)		11.6 (0.90)	9.8 (0.81)
Education......	17.1 (0.89)	4.6 (0.45)	22.8 (0.81)	3.2 (0.33)		1,175	397	33.8 (1.17)		8.4 (0.71)	6.4 (0.59)
Engineering......	12.1 (0.83)	3.3 (0.40)	16.1 (0.77)	2.3 (0.36)		1,087	252	23.2 (0.93)		3.8 (0.54)	2.3 (0.48)
Health......	17.4 (0.48)	5.6 (0.30)	21.9 (0.60)	4.2 (0.33)		4,271	1,420	33.3 (0.67)		8.5 (0.48)	6.7 (0.43)
Humanities......	14.0 (0.53)	3.9 (0.26)	19.7 (0.53)	2.6 (0.22)		3,817	1,175	30.8 (0.65)		5.8 (0.41)	4.1 (0.33)
Life sciences......	11.0 (0.81)	2.7 (0.39)	15.8 (0.68)	1.8 (0.21)		1,448	386	26.7 (0.92)		4.5 (0.44)	3.3 (0.37)
Mathematics......	12.8 (2.48)	3.8 ! (1.42)	15.1 (2.51)	‡ (†)		111	23	20.4 (3.02)		4.1 ! (1.32)	2.2 ! (1.05)
Physical sciences......	9.8 (2.02)	0.9 ! (0.41)	12.8 (1.56)	0.3 ! (0.16)		207	46	22.1 (1.93)		1.5 ! (0.51)	1.2 ! (0.46)
Social/behavioral sciences......	12.5 (0.63)	3.4 (0.33)	17.1 (0.68)	2.3 (0.31)		1,568	499	31.8 (0.93)		8.9 (0.59)	7.0 (0.48)
Vocational/technical......	13.1 (0.96)	4.2 (0.60)	18.5 (1.26)	3.3 (0.50)		718	160	22.3 (1.54)		4.1 (0.77)	2.8 (0.59)
Undeclared/no major......	15.0 (0.61)	4.6 (0.34)	20.5 (0.56)	3.1 (0.45)		1,232	340	27.6 (1.16)		12.0 (0.96)	5.2 (0.81)
Other......	14.4 (0.68)	4.3 (0.29)	19.0 (0.69)	3.9 (0.38)		2,992	913	30.5 (0.83)		8.6 (0.53)	6.9 (0.50)
Had job during academic year[2]											
Yes......	16.8 (0.34)	5.5 (0.22)	22.2 (0.25)	4.2 (0.16)		14,363	5,204	36.2 (0.42)		9.8 (0.26)	7.6 (0.24)
No	11.9 (0.32)	3.3 (0.17)	15.8 (0.37)	2.8 (0.25)		8,693	2,163	24.9 (0.42)		6.1 (0.25)	4.8 (0.20)
Dependency status											
Dependent......	11.1 (0.24)	2.9 (0.13)	14.4 (0.24)	1.0 (0.08)		11,231	2,865	25.5 (0.36)		3.9 (0.17)	2.7 (0.12)
Independent, no dependents, not married[3]......	15.6 (0.50)	5.1 (0.37)	23.6 (0.56)	4.8 (0.30)		4,233	1,421	33.6 (0.64)		8.9 (0.38)	6.7 (0.33)
Independent, no dependents, married....	19.6 (0.78)	6.9 (0.52)	28.6 (0.96)	7.2 (0.84)		1,250	468	37.4 (1.22)		11.7 (0.75)	10.1 (0.72)
Independent, with dependents, not married[3]......	20.5 (0.70)	6.9 (0.49)	25.3 (0.61)	7.4 (0.52)		3,504	1,340	38.2 (0.67)		12.7 (0.48)	10.7 (0.45)
Independent, with dependents, married..	25.1 (0.79)	9.7 (0.53)	32.9 (0.71)	9.4 (0.51)		2,837	1,273	44.9 (0.92)		18.8 (0.77)	14.7 (0.75)
Control and level of institution											
Public......	16.2 (0.35)	4.7 (0.18)	21.5 (0.25)	2.7 (0.11)		16,926	5,627	33.2 (0.39)		6.3 (0.21)	4.0 (0.16)
4-year......	13.5 (0.54)	3.8 (0.23)	18.4 (0.41)	2.2 (0.19)		7,214	2,356	32.7 (0.51)		5.7 (0.27)	4.3 (0.24)
2-year......	18.2 (0.43)	5.4 (0.25)	23.9 (0.33)	3.1 (0.16)		9,624	3,262	33.9 (0.54)		6.8 (0.31)	3.8 (0.24)
Less-than-2-year......	11.8 (1.19)	3.0 (0.66)	8.1 (1.66)	1.9 ! (0.73)		87	10	11.3 (2.24)		7.7 ! (2.32)	‡ (†)
Private nonprofit......	12.3 (0.79)	4.1 (0.46)	14.3 (0.43)	2.9 (0.23)		3,010	633	21.0 (0.85)		5.8 (0.61)	4.5 (0.57)
4-year......	12.3 (0.83)	4.1 (0.48)	14.2 (0.44)	2.8 (0.23)		2,923	622	21.3 (0.87)		5.9 (0.63)	4.6 (0.59)
2-year......	11.2 (2.20)	3.1 ! (1.11)	19.4 (2.30)	5.9 (1.02)		79	10	12.7 (3.26)		‡ (†)	0.5 ! (0.22)
Less-than-2-year......	17.2 (2.63)	8.1 (1.35)	15.6 ! (4.69)	2.7 (0.66)		7	1	13.6 ! (5.68)		# (†)	# (†)
Private for-profit......	15.3 (1.08)	8.6 (1.06)	21.7 (1.18)	12.8 (1.24)		3,120	1,108	35.5 (0.83)		22.2 (0.79)	21.6 (0.82)
4-year......	26.3 (2.25)	15.6 (2.26)	29.1 (1.95)	19.1 (1.92)		1,943	1,030	53.0 (1.26)		34.1 (1.25)	33.3 (1.30)
2-year......	12.1 (1.64)	6.3 (1.25)	17.6 (1.49)	8.0 (1.34)		707	60	8.4 (1.28)		3.8 (1.09)	2.9 ! (1.01)
Less-than-2-year......	5.4 (0.26)	1.9 (0.13)	6.2 (0.40)	1.8 (0.28)		470	18	3.9 (0.77)		1.0 ! (0.34)	‡ (†)

†Not applicable.
#Rounds to zero.
!Interpret data with caution. The coefficient of variation (CV) for this estimate is between 30 and 50 percent.
‡Reporting standards not met. Either there are too few cases for a reliable estimate or the coefficient of variation (CV) is 50 percent or greater.
[1]Excludes students not in a degree or certificate program.
[2]Excludes work-study/assistantships.
[3]Includes separated.
NOTE: In 2011–12, students were asked whether they took classes that were "taught only online" and, if so, whether their entire degree program was online. In 2003–04 and 2007–08, students were asked about distance education, which was defined in 2007–08 as "primarily delivered using live, interactive audio or videoconferencing, pre-recorded instructional videos, webcasts, CD-ROM, or DVD, or computer-based systems delivered over the Internet." The 2003–04 definition was very similar, with only minor differences in wording. In both years, distance education did not include correspondence courses. Data exclude Puerto Rico. Detail may not sum to totals because of rounding. Race categories exclude persons of Hispanic ethnicity.
SOURCE: U.S. Department of Education, National Center for Education Statistics, 2003–04, 2007–08, and 2011–12 National Postsecondary Student Aid Study (NPSAS:04, NPSAS:08, and NPSAS:12). (This table was prepared October 2014.)

Table 311.30. Number and percentage of graduate students taking night, weekend, or online classes, by selected characteristics: 2011–12

[Standard errors appear in parentheses]

Selected characteristic	Total taking any night, weekend, or online classes[1]		Percent of students taking night, weekend, or online classes						
	Number of students (in thousands)	Percent of students	Night classes		Weekend classes		Online classes	
			Any night classes	Exclusively night classes	Any weekend classes	Exclusively weekend classes	Any online classes	Exclusively online classes
1	2	3	4	5	6	7	8	9
Total	**2,309**	**62.7** (0.75)	**33.6** (0.70)	**9.4** (0.43)	**11.8** (0.49)	**2.0** (0.24)	**36.0** (0.74)	**20.1** (0.64)
Sex								
Male	849	58.0 (1.29)	33.4 (1.20)	9.6 (0.73)	10.9 (0.86)	1.6 (0.31)	31.5 (1.17)	17.8 (1.03)
Female	1,460	65.8 (0.94)	33.8 (0.85)	9.3 (0.52)	12.4 (0.68)	2.3 (0.34)	39.0 (0.97)	21.7 (0.84)
Race/ethnicity								
White	1,483	63.4 (0.92)	33.6 (0.82)	9.1 (0.56)	11.4 (0.61)	1.8 (0.26)	36.9 (0.98)	20.2 (0.92)
Black	319	73.6 (1.66)	33.7 (1.94)	10.8 (1.23)	10.8 (1.06)	2.2 (0.54)	48.8 (2.12)	33.0 (1.75)
Hispanic	221	68.6 (2.24)	38.8 (2.56)	14.3 (2.05)	14.2 (1.77)	3.8 ! (1.27)	34.6 (2.73)	19.3 (2.51)
Asian	211	44.5 (1.92)	30.4 (1.99)	7.0 (1.16)	12.3 (1.61)	2.0 ! (0.70)	19.4 (1.67)	7.5 (1.28)
Pacific Islander	14	70.8 (11.38)	29.9 ! (12.43)	‡ (†)	18.9 ! (8.14)	‡ (†)	44.2 (11.10)	20.3 ! (9.95)
American Indian/Alaska Native	12	75.0 (10.31)	28.7 ! (10.01)	16.6 ! (7.55)	‡ (†)	‡ (†)	55.1 (12.39)	42.5 ! (15.09)
Two or more races	48	63.5 (4.17)	36.6 (4.48)	5.4 ! (2.02)	15.8 ! (4.78)	‡ (†)	40.4 (4.24)	20.9 (3.82)
Age								
15 through 23	196	46.8 (1.94)	36.3 (1.93)	8.4 (1.11)	8.1 (1.18)	0.7 ! (0.33)	19.5 (1.45)	4.5 (0.74)
24 through 29	852	57.4 (1.20)	33.4 (1.07)	8.7 (0.58)	10.6 (0.68)	1.6 (0.32)	30.8 (1.05)	15.8 (0.95)
30 or older	1,261	70.8 (0.95)	33.3 (1.09)	10.3 (0.65)	13.6 (0.82)	2.7 (0.40)	44.3 (1.21)	27.4 (1.07)
Attendance status								
Exclusively full-time	910	53.1 (1.11)	27.5 (0.96)	6.0 (0.51)	8.9 (0.58)	1.3 (0.30)	31.7 (1.16)	18.4 (1.04)
Exclusively part-time	1,013	72.6 (1.08)	39.0 (1.24)	13.5 (0.89)	14.4 (0.91)	2.8 (0.43)	41.0 (1.21)	22.7 (1.19)
Mixed full-time and part-time	386	67.3 (1.75)	39.2 (1.60)	9.9 (1.19)	14.1 (1.28)	2.1 (0.41)	36.9 (1.98)	19.1 (1.69)
Had job during academic year[2]								
Yes	1,837	73.7 (0.87)	37.8 (0.86)	11.4 (0.57)	13.6 (0.65)	2.7 (0.32)	43.7 (0.91)	26.3 (0.79)
No	472	39.7 (1.22)	25.0 (1.11)	5.2 (0.50)	7.9 (0.73)	0.7 ! (0.24)	19.9 (1.12)	7.2 (0.82)
Dependency status								
Dependent	—	— (†)	† (†)	† (†)	— (†)	† (†)	— (†)	— (†)
Independent, no dependents, not married[3]	1,025	55.5 (1.03)	34.0 (0.98)	8.5 (0.52)	11.1 (0.64)	1.5 (0.31)	28.1 (0.88)	13.2 (0.74)
Independent, no dependents, married	345	62.6 (1.89)	32.7 (1.68)	9.2 (1.21)	11.3 (1.37)	2.1 ! (0.67)	36.1 (1.75)	21.0 (1.63)
Independent, with dependents, not married[3]	284	79.3 (1.71)	35.1 (2.57)	10.2 (1.55)	14.9 (1.68)	3.7 (1.02)	52.0 (2.49)	33.4 (2.48)
Independent, with dependents, married	654	70.8 (1.52)	33.0 (1.42)	11.0 (0.96)	12.3 (1.13)	2.4 (0.49)	45.6 (1.60)	28.3 (1.55)
Control of institution								
Public	1,002	57.4 (0.95)	34.3 (0.97)	7.6 (0.51)	9.9 (0.63)	2.0 (0.29)	32.8 (0.93)	14.1 (0.72)
Private nonprofit	924	61.8 (1.14)	38.1 (1.17)	12.8 (0.84)	15.2 (0.88)	2.3 (0.42)	28.5 (1.16)	13.8 (1.08)
Private for-profit	382	86.7 (2.12)	16.1 (1.70)	5.0 (0.79)	8.0 (1.08)	1.1 ! (0.37)	74.1 (2.09)	65.3 (2.58)

—Not available.
†Not applicable.
!Interpret data with caution. The coefficient of variation (CV) for this estimate is between 30 and 50 percent.
‡Reporting standards not met. The coefficient of variation (CV) for this estimate is 50 percent or greater.
[1]Students who reported taking more than one type of class (e.g., night classes and online classes) are counted only once in the total.
[2]Excludes work-study/assistantships.
[3]Includes separated.
NOTE: Night classes start after 6:00 p.m. on Monday through Thursday nights; weekend classes start after 6:00 p.m. on Friday or take place any time on Saturday or Sunday; and online classes are taught only online. Detail may not sum to totals because of rounding. Race categories exclude persons of Hispanic ethnicity.
SOURCE: U.S. Department of Education, National Center for Education Statistics, 2011–12 National Postsecondary Student Aid Study (NPSAS:12). (This table was prepared March 2014.)

Table 311.32. Number and percentage of graduate students taking distance education or online classes and degree programs, by selected characteristics: Selected years, 2003–04 through 2011–12

[Standard errors appear in parentheses]

Selected characteristic	Percent of graduate students taking distance education classes				2011–12				
	2003–04		2007–08		Number of graduate students (in thousands)		Percent of graduate students taking online classes		
	Total, any distance education classes	Entire degree program through distance education[1]	Total, any distance education classes	Entire degree program through distance education[1]	Total, all graduate students	Number taking any online classes	Total, any online classes	Exclusively online classes	Entire degree program is online[1]
1	2	3	4	5	6	7	8	9	10
Total	16.5 (0.76)	6.1 (0.58)	22.8 (0.76)	9.5 (0.68)	3,682	1,326	36.0 (0.74)	20.1 (0.64)	18.2 (0.63)
Sex									
Male	15.4 (1.17)	4.9 (0.74)	20.6 (1.17)	7.8 (1.07)	1,463	461	31.5 (1.17)	17.8 (1.03)	15.9 (1.06)
Female	17.3 (1.00)	7.0 (0.74)	24.2 (0.99)	10.6 (0.77)	2,219	865	39.0 (0.97)	21.7 (0.84)	19.8 (0.78)
Race/ethnicity									
White	17.7 (0.88)	6.7 (0.74)	23.6 (0.99)	9.6 (0.95)	2,341	864	36.9 (0.98)	20.2 (0.92)	18.2 (0.88)
Black	19.2 (2.44)	7.5 (1.72)	25.8 (2.94)	11.5 (2.11)	434	212	48.8 (2.12)	33.0 (1.75)	31.4 (1.66)
Hispanic	13.1 (1.81)	5.0 (1.26)	23.7 (3.09)	9.4 ! (2.85)	321	111	34.6 (2.73)	19.3 (2.51)	17.9 (2.53)
Asian	9.4 (1.40)	3.0 ! (1.01)	12.8 (1.10)	4.5 (0.68)	474	92	19.4 (1.67)	7.5 (1.28)	6.0 (1.13)
Pacific Islander	‡ (†)	‡ (†)	31.1 ! (9.43)	13.5 ! (6.20)	20	9	44.2 (11.10)	20.3 ! (9.95)	‡ (†)
American Indian/Alaska Native	8.7 ! (3.54)	‡ (†)	16.7 ! (6.78)	‡ (†)	16	‡	55.1 (12.39)	42.5 ! (15.09)	43.4 ! (15.26)
Two or more races	17.1 (4.46)	4.8 ! (2.33)	27.7 ! (8.38)	21.3 ! (9.56)	75	30	40.4 (4.24)	20.9 (3.82)	18.4 (3.84)
Age									
15 through 23	11.1 (1.73)	3.7 (0.77)	16.6 (2.64)	1.6 (0.40)	419	82	19.5 (1.45)	4.5 (0.74)	4.3 (0.76)
24 through 29	13.6 (0.82)	3.6 (0.43)	16.1 (0.79)	5.7 (0.54)	1,483	456	30.8 (1.05)	15.8 (0.95)	14.4 (0.91)
30 or older	20.2 (1.21)	9.0 (1.06)	29.5 (1.39)	14.5 (1.31)	1,781	788	44.3 (1.21)	27.4 (1.07)	24.9 (1.01)
Attendance status									
Exclusively full-time	12.0 (1.00)	3.4 (0.72)	16.4 (1.35)	6.5 (1.24)	1,713	543	31.7 (1.16)	18.4 (1.04)	17.4 (0.98)
Exclusively part-time	20.0 (1.01)	8.8 (0.97)	28.1 (1.17)	13.3 (1.07)	1,396	572	41.0 (1.21)	22.7 (1.19)	19.5 (1.21)
Mixed full-time and part-time	15.6 (1.89)	4.1 (0.71)	23.6 (2.15)	6.8 (0.95)	573	212	36.9 (1.98)	19.1 (1.69)	17.9 (1.66)
Graduate field of study									
Business/management	22.6 (2.30)	10.3 (1.98)	27.6 (2.90)	13.9 (2.68)	615	246	40.0 (2.09)	26.8 (2.00)	25.1 (1.82)
Education	20.7 (1.74)	8.2 (1.29)	28.3 (1.67)	9.9 (1.36)	775	379	48.9 (1.65)	26.1 (1.56)	23.7 (1.47)
Health	12.6 (1.23)	3.9 (0.79)	22.0 (1.59)	8.9 (1.33)	679	248	36.5 (1.42)	18.9 (1.04)	16.5 (1.00)
Humanities	12.9 (2.43)	2.9 ! (0.87)	15.7 (1.72)	3.1 (0.65)	290	81	28.1 (3.13)	14.1 (2.87)	12.1 (2.88)
Law	5.6 (1.15)	‡ (†)	6.1 (0.87)	1.7 ! (0.54)	146	15	10.3 (1.46)	2.9 (0.72)	2.5 (0.65)
Life and physical sciences	— (†)	— (†)	— (†)	— (†)	208	29	13.9 (1.49)	7.3 (1.36)	5.3 (1.21)
Life sciences	12.4 (2.51)	6.9 ! (2.14)	14.0 (2.15)	4.3 (1.14)	—	—	— (†)	— (†)	— (†)
Mathematics, engineering, and computer science	12.0 (2.03)	4.6 ! (1.48)	19.7 (3.06)	9.4 ! (2.96)	315	80	25.5 (1.78)	14.6 (1.44)	13.3 (1.42)
Social/behavioral sciences	8.5 (1.42)	3.4 ! (1.11)	21.3 (3.66)	12.7 (3.68)	223	82	36.6 (2.22)	22.6 (1.84)	21.7 (1.89)
Other[2]	19.0 (1.56)	4.6 (1.08)	22.2 (1.49)	9.4 (1.49)	430	166	38.6 (2.03)	20.5 (2.19)	19.2 (2.29)
Had job during academic year[3]									
Yes	19.6 (0.97)	7.7 (0.78)	27.2 (0.89)	11.9 (0.79)	2,494	1,090	43.7 (0.91)	26.3 (0.79)	24.1 (0.79)
No	9.0 (0.81)	2.7 (0.41)	10.0 (1.36)	2.8 ! (1.27)	1,188	236	19.9 (1.12)	7.2 (0.82)	6.2 (0.78)
Dependency status									
Dependent	— (†)	— (†)	— (†)	— (†)	—	—	— (†)	— (†)	— (†)
Independent, no dependents, not married[4]	12.1 (0.75)	3.7 (0.39)	16.6 (0.90)	5.2 (0.59)	1,848	520	28.1 (0.88)	13.2 (0.74)	11.8 (0.67)
Independent, no dependents, married	15.5 (1.22)	5.0 (0.77)	22.3 (1.67)	10.1 (1.56)	551	199	36.1 (1.75)	21.0 (1.63)	19.5 (1.64)
Independent, with dependents, not married[4]	21.3 (3.18)	9.4 (2.21)	26.8 (3.23)	10.8 (1.86)	359	187	52.0 (2.49)	33.4 (2.48)	32.5 (2.54)
Independent, with dependents, married	24.2 (1.72)	10.8 (1.46)	34.2 (1.76)	17.5 (2.14)	923	421	45.6 (1.60)	28.3 (1.55)	25.1 (1.52)
Control of institution									
Public	15.2 (0.68)	4.8 (0.39)	23.1 (0.99)	8.9 (0.95)	1,745	573	32.8 (0.93)	14.1 (0.72)	11.8 (0.69)
Private nonprofit	16.3 (1.25)	6.7 (1.03)	18.5 (0.74)	6.0 (0.41)	1,496	426	28.5 (1.16)	13.8 (1.08)	12.3 (1.03)
Private for-profit	35.3 (8.12)	18.6 ! (6.64)	41.6 (5.47)	29.9 (5.89)	440	327	74.1 (2.09)	65.3 (2.58)	62.5 (2.49)

—Not available.
†Not applicable.
!Interpret data with caution. The coefficient of variation (CV) for this estimate is between 30 and 50 percent.
‡Reporting standards not met. Either there are too few cases for a reliable estimate or the coefficient of variation (CV) is 50 percent or greater.
[1]Excludes students not in a degree or certificate program.
[2]Includes students who are not in a degree program or have not declared a major. For 2003–04 and 2007–08, includes physical sciences.
[3]Excludes work-study/assistantships.
[4]Includes separated.

NOTE: In 2011–12, students were asked whether they took classes that were "taught only online" and, if so, whether their entire degree program was online. In 2003–04 and 2007–08, students were asked about distance education, which was defined in 2007–08 as "primarily delivered using live, interactive audio or videoconferencing, pre-recorded instructional videos, webcasts, CD-ROM, or DVD, or computer-based systems delivered over the Internet." The 2003–04 definition was very similar, with only minor differences in wording. In both years, distance education did not include correspondence courses. Data exclude Puerto Rico. Detail may not sum to totals because of rounding. Race categories exclude persons of Hispanic ethnicity.
SOURCE: U.S. Department of Education, National Center for Education Statistics, 2003–04, 2007–08, and 2011–12 National Postsecondary Student Aid Study (NPSAS:04, NPSAS:08, and NPSAS:12) (This table was prepared October 2014.)

Table 311.33. Selected statistics for degree-granting postsecondary institutions that primarily offer online programs, by control of institution and selected characteristics: 2013

Selected characteristic	All institutions	Primarily online institutions[1]					Other institutions[1]			
		Total	Percent of all institutions	Public	Nonprofit	For-profit	Total	Public	Nonprofit	For-profit
1	2	3	4	5	6	7	8	9	10	11
Number of institutions, fall 2013	4,716	61	1.3	4	14	43	4,655	1,621	1,661	1,373
Fall 2013 enrollment										
Total enrollment	20,375,789	778,619	3.8	39,490	100,424	638,705	19,597,170	14,706,068	3,873,580	1,017,522
Full-time	12,597,112	480,269	3.8	5,075	52,929	422,265	12,116,843	8,459,734	2,933,124	723,985
Males	5,682,166	155,592	2.7	2,235	20,755	132,602	5,526,574	3,946,970	1,292,282	287,322
Females	6,914,946	324,677	4.7	2,840	32,174	289,663	6,590,269	4,512,764	1,640,842	436,663
Part-time	7,778,677	298,350	3.8	34,415	47,495	216,440	7,480,327	6,246,334	940,456	293,537
Males	3,178,620	118,952	3.7	17,612	20,109	81,231	3,059,668	2,602,022	359,757	97,889
Females	4,600,057	179,398	3.9	16,803	27,386	135,209	4,420,659	3,644,312	580,699	195,648
Undergraduate	17,474,835	573,888	3.3	32,143	82,694	459,051	16,900,947	13,314,859	2,674,753	911,335
Full-time	10,938,494	353,921	3.2	4,314	40,252	309,355	10,584,573	7,681,355	2,221,471	681,747
Part-time	6,536,341	219,967	3.4	27,829	42,442	149,696	6,316,374	5,633,504	453,282	229,588
Postbaccalaureate	2,900,954	204,731	7.1	7,347	17,730	179,654	2,696,223	1,391,209	1,198,827	106,187
Full-time	1,658,618	126,348	7.6	761	12,677	112,910	1,532,270	778,379	711,653	42,238
Part-time	1,242,336	78,383	6.3	6,586	5,053	66,744	1,163,953	612,830	487,174	63,949
White	11,590,717	422,826	3.6	27,549	68,776	326,501	11,167,891	8,336,597	2,406,397	424,897
Black	2,872,126	229,118	8.0	4,960	16,197	207,961	2,643,008	1,881,831	472,550	288,627
Hispanic	3,091,112	70,839	2.3	3,666	7,832	59,341	3,020,273	2,473,823	346,554	199,896
Asian	1,198,545	16,916	1.4	1,486	3,305	12,125	1,181,629	904,096	236,244	41,289
Pacific Islander	61,053	5,271	8.6	207	539	4,525	55,782	38,964	9,414	7,404
American Indian/Alaska Native	162,563	7,292	4.5	239	711	6,342	155,271	124,376	21,015	9,880
Two or more races	559,362	19,257	3.4	750	2,649	15,858	540,105	412,604	98,635	28,866
Nonresident alien	840,311	7,100	0.8	633	415	6,052	833,211	533,777	282,771	16,663
4-year institutions	13,407,050	777,916	5.8	39,490	100,424	638,002	12,629,134	8,080,927	3,841,382	706,825
Full-time	9,764,196	479,868	4.9	5,075	52,929	421,864	9,284,328	5,929,777	2,909,069	445,482
Part-time	3,642,854	298,048	8.2	34,415	47,495	216,138	3,344,806	2,151,150	932,313	261,343
2-year institutions	6,968,739	703	#	0	0	703	6,968,036	6,625,141	32,198	310,697
Full-time	2,832,916	401	#	0	0	401	2,832,515	2,529,957	24,055	278,503
Part-time	4,135,823	302	#	0	0	302	4,135,521	4,095,184	8,143	32,194
Earned degrees conferred, 2012–13										
Associate's	1,006,961	47,040	4.7	901	2,391	43,748	959,921	771,687	53,226	135,008
Males	388,846	15,223	3.9	588	969	13,666	373,623	302,349	19,162	52,112
Females	618,115	31,817	5.1	313	1,422	30,082	586,298	469,338	34,064	82,896
Bachelor's	1,840,164	83,981	4.6	4,213	8,965	70,803	1,756,183	1,159,407	526,771	70,005
Males	787,231	31,539	4.0	2,002	3,781	25,756	755,692	508,329	217,056	30,307
Females	1,052,933	52,442	5.0	2,211	5,184	45,047	1,000,491	651,078	309,715	39,698
Master's	751,751	52,735	7.0	1,217	4,517	47,001	699,016	345,596	322,467	30,953
Males	301,575	18,010	6.0	603	1,598	15,809	283,565	141,102	130,973	11,490
Females	450,176	34,725	7.7	614	2,919	31,192	415,451	204,494	191,494	19,463
Doctor's[2]	175,038	3,064	1.8	0	71	2,993	171,974	86,427	81,468	4,079
Males	85,104	1,112	1.3	0	18	1,094	83,992	42,581	39,680	1,731
Females	89,934	1,952	2.2	0	53	1,899	87,982	43,846	41,788	2,348
First-time students' rates of graduation from and retention at first institution attended										
Among full-time bachelor's degree-seekers starting at 4-year institutions in 2007, percent earning bachelor's degree										
Within 4 years after start	39.4	8.0	†	‡	29.0	7.3	39.5	33.5	52.8	23.8
Within 5 years after start	55.1	12.8	†	‡	31.8	12.1	55.2	52.3	63.2	29.0
Within 6 years after start	59.4	14.8	†	‡	33.6	14.1	59.5	57.7	65.3	33.3
Among full-time degree/certificate-seekers starting at 2-year institutions in 2010, percent completing credential within 150 percent of normal time	29.4	14.7	†	‡	‡	14.7	29.4	19.5	53.6	62.8
Among degree-seekers starting in 2012, percent returning in 2013										
Full-time entrants	72.9	38.4	†	‡	69.9	38.0	73.0	71.4	80.3	64.4
Part-time entrants	43.1	43.2	†	‡	56.5	26.2	43.3	43.1	43.3	40.4	39.7

†Not applicable.
#Rounds to zero.
‡Reporting standards not met (too few cases for a reliable estimate).
[1]Primarily online institutions have more than 90 percent of their students attending classes exclusively online. Other institutions may have some online offerings, but they are not primarily online.
[2]Includes Ph.D., Ed.D., and comparable degrees at the doctoral level. Includes most degrees formerly classified as first-professional, such as M.D., D.D.S., and law degrees.

NOTE: Degree-granting institutions grant associate's or higher degrees and participate in Title IV federal financial aid programs.
SOURCE: U.S. Department of Education, National Center for Education Statistics, Integrated Postsecondary Education Data System (IPEDS), Spring 2014, Enrollment component; IPEDS, Fall 2013, Completions component; and IPEDS, Spring 2014, Graduation Rates component. (This table was prepared June 2015.)

Table 311.40. Percentage of first-year undergraduate students who reported taking remedial education courses, by selected student and institution characteristics: 2003–04, 2007–08, and 2011–12

[Standard errors appear in parentheses]

Selected student or institution characteristic	2003–04 first-year undergraduates[1]								2007–08 first-year undergraduates[1]		
	Percent who took any remedial courses		Percent who took specific remedial courses in 2003–04						Percent who took any remedial courses		
	Ever	In 2003–04	English		Mathematics		Reading		Writing	Ever	In 2007–08
1	2	3	4		5		6		7	8	9
Total	34.8 (0.36)	19.2 (0.30)	5.7 (0.21)		14.6 (0.26)		5.6 (0.17)		6.9 (0.18)	36.2 (0.38)	20.0 (0.35)
Sex											
Male	33.0 (0.53)	18.4 (0.46)	5.6 (0.29)		13.9 (0.41)		5.2 (0.22)		6.6 (0.27)	33.0 (0.53)	19.3 (0.51)
Female	36.2 (0.54)	19.8 (0.39)	5.8 (0.23)		15.1 (0.34)		5.8 (0.24)		7.1 (0.26)	38.7 (0.51)	20.6 (0.46)
Race/ethnicity of student											
White	31.7 (0.42)	17.8 (0.35)	4.9 (0.21)		13.5 (0.32)		4.4 (0.18)		6.4 (0.22)	31.3 (0.46)	17.7 (0.41)
Black	41.2 (1.00)	22.4 (0.76)	7.5 (0.52)		17.1 (0.66)		7.8 (0.49)		6.9 (0.44)	45.1 (0.99)	24.4 (0.86)
Hispanic	38.5 (0.91)	21.5 (0.72)	6.6 (0.52)		17.0 (0.66)		7.1 (0.48)		8.3 (0.47)	43.7 (1.12)	23.3 (0.84)
Asian	39.6 (1.72)	17.6 (1.56)	8.2 (1.09)		10.9 (1.19)		7.0 (0.83)		8.4 (0.93)	38.9 (2.05)	20.0 (1.90)
Pacific Islander	40.8 (5.11)	22.4 (4.55)	10.2 ! (4.18)		19.8 (4.64)		10.1 ! (4.07)		11.3 ! (4.00)	39.9 (4.63)	19.1 (3.90)
American Indian/Alaska Native	44.8 (4.34)	23.7 (3.10)	3.4 (1.0)		17.3 (2.80)		8.4 (2.28)		8.1 (2.35)	47.9 (4.66)	29.7 (3.88)
Two or more races	33.9 (2.02)	20.9 (1.80)	4.7 (0.90)		14.8 (1.48)		4.9 (0.98)		6.5 (1.12)	32.3 (2.29)	20.4 (2.06)
Other	31.1 (2.78)	17.3 (2.34)	5.0 (1.35)		14.3 (2.12)		6.1 (1.30)		6.9 (1.63)	35.2 (6.00)	21.7 (5.11)
Age											
15 to 23	33.7 (0.41)	21.5 (0.39)	6.6 (0.28)		16.1 (0.35)		6.4 (0.22)		8.2 (0.22)	34.5 (0.46)	22.0 (0.43)
24 to 29	35.0 (0.99)	16.0 (0.78)	4.3 (0.41)		12.8 (0.65)		4.0 (0.40)		5.0 (0.55)	39.7 (0.98)	19.5 (0.86)
30 or older	37.6 (0.87)	15.6 (0.52)	4.5 (0.35)		12.1 (0.51)		4.4 (0.32)		4.7 (0.31)	38.1 (0.84)	15.2 (0.68)
Attendance status											
Exclusively full-time	31.4 (0.45)	19.1 (0.37)	5.7 (0.22)		14.1 (0.35)		5.6 (0.23)		7.5 (0.24)	31.4 (0.52)	19.4 (0.46)
Exclusively part-time	37.5 (0.65)	17.9 (0.51)	5.3 (0.31)		14.0 (0.47)		5.0 (0.28)		5.6 (0.28)	39.8 (0.71)	19.0 (0.59)
Mixed full- and part-time	41.1 (0.97)	23.7 (0.85)	7.1 (0.56)		18.7 (0.81)		7.1 (0.48)		8.3 (0.45)	42.6 (0.98)	26.3 (0.93)
Student housing status											
On-campus	24.5 (0.70)	16.8 (0.56)	4.8 (0.31)		11.3 (0.49)		4.8 (0.31)		8.2 (0.40)	23.2 (0.84)	17.1 (0.76)
Off-campus	35.9 (0.58)	17.0 (0.40)	5.1 (0.30)		13.4 (0.35)		4.6 (0.22)		5.5 (0.28)	37.2 (0.57)	17.8 (0.49)
With parents or relatives	37.9 (0.59)	24.5 (0.61)	7.1 (0.36)		18.5 (0.53)		7.7 (0.35)		8.7 (0.37)	39.6 (0.78)	25.2 (0.66)
Attended more than one institution	36.5 (1.18)	18.3 (0.98)	6.4 (0.59)		14.5 (0.98)		5.0 (0.48)		6.2 (0.48)	36.1 (1.11)	20.2 (0.97)
Dependency status											
Dependent	33.4 (0.45)	22.1 (0.41)	6.6 (0.27)		16.4 (0.36)		6.5 (0.24)		8.6 (0.23)	34.4 (0.51)	22.8 (0.46)
Independent	36.4 (0.61)	16.1 (0.39)	4.8 (0.27)		12.7 (0.37)		4.5 (0.23)		5.0 (0.26)	38.1 (0.59)	17.1 (0.51)
Veteran status											
Veteran	35.9 (2.33)	13.2 (1.52)	1.9 (0.51)		9.9 (1.40)		3.2 (0.68)		4.3 (0.84)	35.8 (2.36)	17.1 (2.08)
Not veteran	34.8 (0.38)	19.4 (0.31)	5.8 (0.22)		14.8 (0.27)		5.7 (0.18)		7.0 (0.18)	36.2 (0.38)	20.1 (0.36)
Field of study											
Business/management	36.4 (1.00)	19.6 (0.97)	5.5 (0.41)		14.7 (1.01)		6.0 (0.44)		7.3 (0.61)	37.0 (1.13)	21.7 (1.06)
Computer science	33.7 (1.59)	19.2 (1.39)	4.7 (0.67)		14.7 (1.27)		5.3 (0.82)		5.6 (0.73)	34.7 (2.28)	19.8 (1.77)
Education	41.5 (1.61)	23.1 (1.14)	6.3 (0.74)		17.6 (1.03)		6.4 (0.72)		8.8 (0.86)	40.3 (1.90)	23.0 (1.48)
Engineering	30.9 (1.79)	16.6 (1.41)	5.6 (0.77)		12.9 (1.26)		4.8 (0.77)		6.8 (0.91)	33.0 (1.81)	19.0 (1.57)
Health	37.0 (0.83)	19.7 (0.68)	6.1 (0.48)		15.5 (0.63)		5.7 (0.43)		6.2 (0.50)	38.6 (2.49)	18.9 (4.49)
Humanities	34.0 (1.29)	18.8 (0.94)	5.6 (0.46)		14.2 (0.87)		5.0 (0.52)		7.3 (0.52)	31.2 (1.94)	20.5 (1.77)
Life sciences	31.2 (1.81)	19.7 (1.72)	5.7 (1.29)		14.6 (1.47)		5.4 (1.21)		7.9 (1.20)	31.2 (6.21)	20.5 ! (8.64)
Mathematics	23.0 (5.55)	11.0 ! (4.43)	‡ (†)		9.3 ! (4.26)		‡ (†)		‡ (†)	41.1 (6.31)	15.6 ! (5.20)
Physical sciences	24.0 (4.39)	12.9 (3.49)	7.5 ! (2.85)		5.3 ! (2.13)		6.4 ! (3.05)		‡ (†)	24.5 (4.31)	15.7 (3.92)
Social/behavioral sciences	33.2 (2.08)	19.4 (1.57)	5.5 (0.90)		14.5 (1.39)		6.5 (1.01)		8.7 (1.05)	35.0 (2.16)	23.4 (1.94)
Vocational/technical	38.5 (2.11)	18.3 (1.60)	5.0 (0.86)		14.5 (1.40)		5.6 (1.0)		4.7 (0.61)	31.1 (1.93)	15.7 (1.78)
Undeclared	33.6 (0.67)	19.2 (0.59)	6.0 (0.38)		14.5 (0.49)		5.2 (0.33)		7.2 (0.38)	35.8 (1.29)	20.0 (1.14)
Other	33.3 (1.49)	18.0 (1.06)	5.3 (0.67)		13.6 (0.94)		6.2 (0.57)		5.9 (0.56)	34.6 (1.23)	18.5 (0.97)
Type of institution											
Public less-than-2-year	30.6 (1.85)	10.9 (1.09)	4.8 (0.80)		9.3 (1.05)		4.0 (0.86)		3.9 (0.90)	31.9 (1.99)	9.0 (0.89)
Public 2-year	41.4 (0.59)	23.0 (0.47)	6.9 (0.33)		18.3 (0.42)		7.1 (0.28)		7.2 (0.27)	41.8 (0.54)	23.7 (0.48)
Public 4-year nondoctorate	34.2 (1.77)	21.4 (1.12)	5.3 (0.61)		16.3 (1.05)		5.2 (0.56)		8.5 (0.63)	38.9 (1.24)	25.4 (1.14)
Public 4-year doctorate	25.7 (1.11)	16.3 (0.64)	4.4 (0.34)		11.7 (0.60)		3.9 (0.39)		8.1 (0.42)	25.0 (1.03)	17.8 (0.86)
Private nonprofit less-than-4-year	31.3 (2.06)	12.9 (1.89)	4.5 (1.03)		10.2 (1.49)		2.8 (0.82)		5.0 (1.27)	30.3 (3.75)	10.2 (2.81)
Private nonprofit 4-year nondoctorate	26.0 (1.16)	14.7 (0.78)	5.3 (0.68)		9.5 (0.58)		4.0 (0.41)		6.7 (0.76)	25.5 (1.74)	16.6 (1.46)
Private nonprofit 4-year doctorate	18.3 (1.67)	11.6 (1.39)	2.4 (0.54)		7.4 (1.37)		2.9 (0.57)		6.3 (0.91)	22.1 (1.70)	12.6 (1.38)
Private for-profit less-than-2-year	24.1 (0.50)	7.8 (0.23)	3.1 (0.18)		4.6 (0.16)		2.2 (0.19)		3.5 (0.22)	26.5 (1.02)	5.5 (0.51)
Private for-profit 2 years or more	25.4 (1.63)	11.7 (1.04)	4.1 (0.51)		7.5 (0.75)		3.3 (0.45)		4.9 (0.71)	28.8 (1.46)	11.3 (1.20)

See notes at end of table.

Table 311.40. Percentage of first-year undergraduate students who reported taking remedial education courses, by selected student and institution characteristics: 2003–04, 2007–08, and 2011–12—Continued
[Standard errors appear in parentheses]

Selected student or institution characteristic	2011–12 first-year undergraduates[1]												
	Total number of students (in thousands)	Students who took any remedial courses				Percent who took specific remedial courses in 2011–12						
		Percent who ever took		Number who took in 2011–12 (in thousands)	Percent who took in 2011–12		English		Mathematics		Reading		Writing
1	10	11		12	13		14		15		16		17
Total..............................	9,437	32.6	(0.42)	1,864	19.7	(0.36)	10.0 (0.25)		16.2 (0.34)		7.4 (0.23)		7.5 (0.25)
Sex												
Male..........................	4,079	30.8	(0.61)	811	19.9	(0.55)	10.4 (0.37)		16.0 (0.49)		7.2 (0.32)		7.6 (0.36)
Female.......................	5,359	34.0	(0.52)	1,053	19.7	(0.46)	9.7 (0.35)		16.3 (0.43)		7.5 (0.29)		7.4 (0.26)
Race/ethnicity of student												
White........................	4,997	29.4	(0.51)	885	17.7	(0.47)	8.1 (0.33)		14.7 (0.43)		5.8 (0.29)		6.3 (0.29)
Black........................	1,871	37.6	(0.89)	416	22.2	(0.75)	12.8 (0.54)		18.2 (0.72)		10.1 (0.53)		9.2 (0.55)
Hispanic....................	1,728	35.8	(0.99)	388	22.4	(0.81)	11.5 (0.56)		18.7 (0.76)		8.4 (0.46)		8.5 (0.48)
Asian........................	410	37.6	(2.25)	94	23.0	(1.75)	14.6 (1.53)		15.2 (1.19)		11.1 (1.57)		11.5 (1.52)
Pacific Islander..........	46	33.4	(5.16)	7	15.2	(3.50)	9.6 ! (3.15)		11.9 (3.11)		4.2 (1.25)		5.5 ! (1.65)
American Indian/Alaska Native..........	106	34.9	(4.11)	21	19.8	(2.79)	10.2 (2.03)		17.4 (2.79)		9.0 (2.03)		7.1 (1.71)
Two or more races	280	29.8	(2.02)	53	19.0	(1.68)	9.8 (1.56)		15.4 (1.58)		5.5 (1.01)		5.7 (0.91)
Other........................	—	—	(†)	—	—	(†)	— (†)		— (†)		— (†)		— (†)
Age												
15 to 23.....................	5,549	31.0	(0.49)	1,169	21.1	(0.38)	10.6 (0.30)		17.3 (0.36)		7.6 (0.24)		7.7 (0.28)
24 to 29.....................	1,618	34.4	(1.12)	278	17.2	(0.91)	8.3 (0.61)		14.2 (0.86)		6.4 (0.55)		6.4 (0.52)
30 or older..................	2,270	35.4	(0.94)	417	18.4	(0.82)	9.7 (0.53)		14.9 (0.73)		7.6 (0.57)		7.7 (0.56)
Attendance status												
Exclusively full-time.....	4,774	28.1	(0.48)	840	17.6	(0.41)	9.1 (0.28)		14.2 (0.41)		6.6 (0.27)		6.7 (0.26)
Exclusively part-time....	3,280	37.4	(0.81)	699	21.3	(0.78)	10.3 (0.50)		17.7 (0.71)		7.7 (0.43)		7.9 (0.50)
Mixed full- and part-time	1,383	37.0	(0.95)	324	23.4	(0.74)	12.2 (0.57)		19.5 (0.71)		9.3 (0.53)		9.1 (0.50)
Student housing status												
On-campus	1,055	17.9	(0.78)	148	14.1	(0.67)	6.5 (0.48)		10.9 (0.58)		3.9 (0.37)		5.0 (0.46)
Off-campus	4,326	34.0	(0.65)	846	19.6	(0.63)	9.7 (0.41)		15.9 (0.58)		7.8 (0.41)		7.8 (0.43)
With parents or relatives ...	3,462	35.3	(0.78)	768	22.2	(0.61)	11.6 (0.43)		18.5 (0.56)		8.2 (0.37)		8.1 (0.42)
Attended more than one institution	594	32.7	(1.09)	101	17.0	(0.95)	8.9 (0.77)		14.1 (0.86)		5.7 (0.56)		6.3 (0.62)
Dependency status												
Dependent	4,543	31.2	(0.53)	1,001	22.0	(0.42)	11.0 (0.34)		17.9 (0.41)		8.0 (0.27)		8.1 (0.31)
Independent.................	4,894	33.9	(0.57)	863	17.6	(0.52)	9.0 (0.34)		14.5 (0.50)		6.8 (0.34)		6.9 (0.30)
Veteran status												
Veteran......................	310	31.4	(2.21)	54	17.4	(1.74)	8.5 (1.22)		15.9 (1.67)		3.3 (0.68)		5.2 (0.97)
Not veteran	9,127	32.7	(0.42)	1,809	19.8	(0.37)	10.1 (0.26)		16.2 (0.35)		7.5 (0.24)		7.6 (0.25)
Field of study												
Business/management	1,203	32.7	(1.11)	238	19.8	(0.85)	10.5 (0.72)		15.3 (0.75)		8.7 (0.66)		8.2 (0.60)
Computer science..........	402	29.3	(1.69)	70	17.4	(1.40)	8.9 (1.14)		14.0 (1.29)		6.2 (1.02)		6.8 (1.16)
Education....................	387	36.0	(1.84)	84	21.6	(1.53)	10.6 (1.08)		16.4 (1.23)		7.9 (1.03)		7.2 (0.90)
Engineering.................	409	33.1	(1.88)	86	20.9	(1.63)	11.0 (1.22)		15.4 (1.33)		7.9 (1.23)		9.1 (1.22)
Health	2,023	34.6	(0.74)	381	18.8	(0.70)	9.1 (0.55)		16.7 (0.67)		6.7 (0.45)		6.7 (0.39)
Humanities..................	1,776	36.6	(1.03)	424	23.9	(0.91)	11.7 (0.60)		19.6 (0.80)		8.9 (0.62)		8.9 (0.60)
Life sciences	416	26.7	(1.71)	75	17.9	(1.11)	9.0 (0.92)		14.2 (1.01)		6.4 (0.89)		7.1 (0.82)
Mathematics	24	14.3 !	(4.57)	‡	8.4 !	(2.81)	4.6 ! (2.26)		7.6 ! (2.67)		‡ (†)		6.2 ! (2.51)
Physical sciences..........	58	29.2	(4.72)	14	24.7	(4.59)	17.2 (4.25)		20.8 (4.24)		8.9 ! (3.16)		13.6 (3.98)
Social/behavioral sciences...............	392	27.7	(1.87)	78	19.8	(1.38)	9.1 (0.87)		16.6 (1.37)		6.0 (0.88)		7.6 (0.79)
Vocational/technical.......	431	26.9	(1.94)	68	15.7	(1.59)	7.6 (1.12)		13.0 (1.56)		5.9 (0.85)		5.7 (1.02)
Undeclared	299	31.8	(2.10)	66	22.0	(1.86)	10.7 (1.53)		17.4 (1.68)		7.9 (1.41)		6.6 (1.13)
Other........................	1,350	29.3	(0.94)	225	16.7	(0.77)	9.4 (0.64)		13.9 (0.70)		6.4 (0.52)		6.7 (0.56)
Type of institution												
Public less-than-2-year	58	30.2	(6.13)	7	12.2 !	(3.86)	8.5 ! (4.11)		10.5 ! (3.34)		6.5 ! (3.19)		1.6 ! (0.75)
Public 2-year...............	5,038	40.3	(0.67)	1,289	25.6	(0.64)	13.2 (0.43)		21.0 (0.60)		10.3 (0.38)		9.7 (0.41)
Public 4-year nondoctorate	817	37.8	(2.12)	198	24.3	(1.30)	10.2 (0.79)		20.4 (1.25)		6.9 (0.78)		7.9 (0.88)
Public 4-year doctorate	893	21.9	(0.84)	139	15.6	(0.80)	6.8 (0.47)		12.8 (0.71)		3.5 (0.33)		4.5 (0.45)
Private nonprofit less-than-4-year......	58	22.3	(4.25)	6	9.4 !	(3.42)	5.9 (1.73)		8.1 ! (2.86)		‡ (†)		3.5 ! (1.64)
Private nonprofit 4-year nondoctorate .	375	24.4	(1.66)	58	15.3	(1.23)	7.8 (1.04)		10.9 (1.06)		4.9 (0.77)		7.0 (0.97)
Private nonprofit 4-year doctorate......	356	14.6	(1.85)	34	9.6	(1.24)	4.0 (0.65)		7.3 (1.26)		3.4 ! (1.03)		4.2 (0.70)
Private for-profit less-than-2-year.......	402	16.7	(0.74)	15	3.8	(0.56)	2.2 (0.39)		3.4 (0.57)		1.9 (0.46)		1.7 (0.39)
Private for-profit 2 years or more	1,439	20.9	(0.74)	118	8.2	(0.37)	5.2 (0.34)		6.6 (0.36)		3.2 (0.24)		4.3 (0.29)

—Not available.
†Not applicable.
!Interpret data with caution. The coefficient of variation (CV) for this estimate is between 30 and 50 percent.
‡Reporting standards not met. The coefficient of variation (CV) is 50 percent or greater.
[1]Student status was determined by accumulation of credits. Students attending postsecondary education part time, or not completing the credit accumulation requirements for second-year status, could be considered first-year students for more than one year.

NOTE: Data are based on a sample survey of students who enrolled at any time during the school year. Percentages of students who took remedial courses are based on student reports. Data exclude Puerto Rico. Detail may not sum to totals because of survey item nonresponse and rounding. Race categories exclude persons of Hispanic ethnicity. Some data have been revised from previously published figures.
SOURCE: U.S. Department of Education, National Center for Education Statistics, 2003–04, 2007–08, and 2011–12 National Postsecondary Student Aid Study (NPSAS:04, NPSAS:08, and NPSAS:12). (This table was prepared August 2014.)

Table 311.50. Percentage of degree-granting postsecondary institutions with first-year undergraduates offering remedial services, by control and level of institution: 1989–90 through 2013–14

	Public and private			Public			Private								
							Total			Nonprofit			For-profit		
Year	Total	4-year	2-year	Total	4-year	2-year	Total	4-year	2-year	Total	4-year	2-year	Total	4-year	2-year
1	2	3	4	5	6	7	8	9	10	11	12	13	14	15	16
1989–90	76.6	69.6	87.2	92.4	82.9	98.2	64.1	64.5	63.0	65.0	64.2	71.8	59.5	71.7	57.0
1990–91	77.7	70.6	88.4	93.0	83.5	98.9	65.6	65.6	65.5	65.6	64.9	71.3	65.6	81.3	62.0
1991–92	78.6	71.4	89.2	93.9	84.5	99.6	66.3	66.4	65.8	66.2	65.8	69.9	66.6	79.2	63.2
1992–93	78.5	71.5	88.8	93.5	84.5	98.8	66.4	66.5	65.8	66.7	66.2	71.5	64.6	73.7	62.0
1993–94	79.0	72.2	89.5	93.5	84.6	98.7	67.4	67.5	67.0	67.7	67.0	73.5	65.6	76.3	62.1
1994–95	79.8	73.6	89.1	93.7	85.3	98.6	68.6	69.2	66.6	69.3	68.7	74.0	65.2	76.0	60.8
1995–96	79.5	73.0	89.4	93.7	85.4	98.6	68.0	68.4	66.3	68.9	68.3	73.3	63.5	69.2	60.5
1996–97	80.0	73.1	91.0	94.0	85.1	99.2	68.6	68.6	68.4	69.2	68.3	77.3	65.2	72.7	60.8
1997–98	76.7	72.5	82.2	93.8	85.2	98.7	64.2	67.8	55.1	69.0	68.3	75.4	51.7	63.9	47.5
1998–99	76.1	72.0	81.5	93.6	84.2	99.0	63.6	67.7	52.8	68.6	68.3	71.6	51.1	63.4	46.2
1999–2000	76.1	71.6	82.2	93.5	83.6	99.2	63.9	67.4	54.4	69.2	68.5	76.7	51.5	60.1	47.7
2000–01	75.1	71.4	80.4	93.1	81.7	99.7	62.8	67.9	48.8	67.6	67.0	73.6	52.7	72.9	41.8
2001–02	73.3	69.0	79.5	92.3	79.9	99.4	60.2	65.3	45.0	66.1	65.5	72.6	48.0	64.5	37.3
2002–03	72.5	67.6	79.5	91.7	78.4	99.4	59.0	63.9	44.8	65.4	64.7	74.0	45.6	59.6	37.2
2003–04	72.1	67.1	79.7	91.3	77.3	99.5	59.0	63.7	44.8	65.0	64.0	77.1	47.4	62.0	37.3
2004–05	72.6	67.4	80.3	90.6	75.6	99.6	60.4	64.7	47.4	63.1	62.5	71.4	55.4	73.7	42.2
2005–06	72.2	66.9	80.2	90.2	75.2	99.3	60.4	64.2	48.8	62.2	61.3	74.3	57.2	75.0	43.4
2006–07	72.8	67.5	80.9	90.4	75.6	99.5	61.4	64.9	50.6	62.2	61.3	74.8	60.1	77.0	45.8
2007–08	72.4	67.2	80.9	89.7	74.1	99.5	61.6	64.9	51.0	61.4	60.6	73.9	61.8	78.4	47.2
2008–09	72.6	67.9	80.2	89.9	74.5	99.6	62.1	65.8	50.5	61.4	60.8	70.7	63.1	80.4	47.2
2009–10	72.7	68.3	79.7	89.8	75.3	99.6	62.5	66.1	52.1	61.2	60.6	72.9	64.3	81.2	49.4
2010–11	72.0	69.1	76.7	89.6	75.5	99.4	62.1	67.2	47.3	61.2	60.6	71.3	63.2	82.7	44.1
2011–12	70.4	67.1	75.9	89.6	75.7	99.5	60.0	64.6	46.3	60.2	60.3	59.0	59.8	73.8	44.4
2012–13	70.7	67.8	75.8	89.3	75.5	99.5	60.9	65.5	46.9	60.3	60.5	56.7	61.6	75.4	45.4
2013–14	70.0	66.4	76.4	89.0	74.8	99.5	60.0	64.0	47.7	59.9	59.9	60.2	60.1	72.4	46.0
Change in percentage points															
1993–94 to 2003–04	-6.9	-5.1	-9.8	-2.1	-7.3	0.8	-8.3	-3.8	-22.1	-2.7	-3.0	3.6	-18.2	-14.3	-24.8
2003–04 to 2013–14	-2.2	-0.6	-3.3	-2.4	-2.5	-0.1	1.0	0.3	2.8	-5.0	-4.1	-16.9	12.7	10.4	8.8

NOTE: Remedial services are instructional activities designed for students deficient in the general competencies necessary for a regular postsecondary curriculum and educational setting. Data through 1995–96 are for institutions of higher education, while later data are for degree-granting institutions. Degree-granting institutions grant associate's or higher degrees and participate in Title IV federal financial aid programs. Excludes institutions not enrolling any first-time degree/certificate-seeking undergraduates. Some data have been revised from previously published figures.

SOURCE: U.S. Department of Education, National Center for Education Statistics, Integrated Postsecondary Education Data System (IPEDS), "Institutional Characteristics Survey" (IPEDS-IC:89–99); and Fall 2000 through Fall 2013, Institutional Characteristics component. (This table was prepared October 2014.)

Table 311.60. Enrollment in postsecondary education, by level of enrollment, level of institution, student age, and major field of study: 2011–12

[Standard errors appear in parentheses]

Major field of study[1]	All students — Total (in thousands)	All students — Percentage distribution, by age — Under 25	25 to 35	Over 35	Undergraduate — 2-year and less-than-2-year institutions[2] — Total (in thousands)	Percentage distribution, by age — Under 25	25 to 35	Over 35	4-year institutions — Total (in thousands)	Percentage distribution, by age — Under 25	25 to 35	Over 35	Postbaccalaureate — Total (in thousands)
1	2	3	4	5	6	7	8	9	10	11	12	13	14
Total	23,055	60.5 (0.31)	23.9 (0.25)	15.5 (0.28)	11,990	55.3 (0.42)	26.9 (0.38)	17.8 (0.33)	11,065	66.2 (0.46)	20.8 (0.34)	13.1 (0.39)	3,682
Agriculture and related sciences	132	68.0 (3.71)	15.0 (2.48)	17.0 (3.37)	60	51.5 (5.55)	18.7 (3.94)	29.8 (5.62)	72	81.7 (3.83)	12.0 (3.00)	6.3 ! (3.05)	12
Anthropology	55	78.8 (4.20)	20.5 (4.12)	‡ (†)	11	67.2 (10.91)	32.8 ! (10.91)	# (†)	45	81.5 (4.65)	17.6 (4.50)	‡ (†)	12
Architecture and related services	88	73.2 (3.97)	19.4 (3.47)	7.4 ! (2.47)	32	58.9 (7.86)	24.5 ! (7.86)	16.6 ! (5.88)	56	81.2 (3.42)	16.6 (3.36)	‡ (†)	27
Area, ethnic, and gender studies	40	74.6 (4.86)	14.2 (3.78)	11.2 ! (3.80)	10	66.8 (10.87)	22.1 ! (9.91)	‡ (†)	30	77.2 (5.43)	11.6 ! (5.43)	11.2 ! (4.75)	8
Biological and biomedical sciences	719	86.2 (0.98)	11.8 (0.90)	2.0 (0.49)	223	79.1 (2.05)	17.4 (1.93)	3.5 ! (1.18)	496	89.4 (1.14)	9.3 (1.04)	1.3 ! (0.48)	100
Business, management, and marketing	3,487	54.3 (0.68)	26.7 (0.59)	19.0 (0.60)	1,399	53.7 (1.04)	27.4 (1.00)	18.9 (1.09)	2,089	54.7 (0.99)	26.3 (0.87)	19.0 (0.77)	615
Communication and journalism	425	83.8 (1.38)	11.5 (1.13)	4.7 (0.86)	96	77.9 (3.26)	14.0 (2.35)	8.0 (2.32)	329	85.5 (1.46)	10.8 (1.23)	3.7 (0.82)	32
Communications technologies/technicians	99	63.2 (3.88)	24.0 (3.49)	12.9 (2.32)	53	59.6 (4.72)	25.0 (4.44)	15.4 (3.81)	46	67.3 (6.18)	22.8 (5.43)	10.0 (2.79)	‡
Computer and information sciences	942	47.5 (1.39)	32.3 (1.30)	20.2 (1.14)	467	47.0 (2.19)	30.7 (1.85)	22.3 (1.75)	475	48.0 (1.69)	33.9 (1.84)	18.1 (1.42)	104
Construction trades	86	53.9 (3.63)	25.3 (3.22)	20.7 (3.98)	78	52.5 (3.91)	25.9 (3.55)	21.6 (4.25)	8	66.7 (10.97)	20.1 ! (6.75)	‡ (†)	‡
Criminology	39	73.5 (4.96)	14.9 (3.82)	11.6 ! (4.15)	10	66.2 (10.90)	‡ (†)	‡ (†)	29	76.1 (4.99)	16.1 (4.44)	7.8 ! (3.50)	‡
Economics	118	86.0 (3.23)	13.2 (3.19)	‡ (†)	14	67.0 (12.45)	30.6 ! (12.52)	‡ (†)	104	88.6 (3.28)	10.9 (3.23)	‡ (†)	18
Education	1,175	65.4 (1.12)	19.2 (0.84)	15.4 (1.03)	495	57.1 (1.79)	23.7 (1.49)	19.2 (1.77)	679	71.5 (1.39)	15.9 (0.90)	12.6 (1.14)	775
Engineering	697	79.5 (1.21)	15.9 (1.16)	4.6 (0.70)	238	67.2 (2.36)	23.6 (2.48)	9.2 (1.72)	459	85.9 (1.18)	11.9 (1.15)	2.2 (0.47)	176
Engineering technologies/technicians	390	50.3 (2.14)	29.5 (1.91)	20.2 (1.83)	254	44.5 (2.58)	30.5 (2.63)	25.0 (2.44)	136	61.3 (3.80)	27.6 (2.83)	11.1 (2.46)	11
English language and literature/letters	282	77.2 (2.18)	12.5 (1.46)	10.3 (1.57)	82	65.4 (5.02)	14.0 (2.91)	20.6 (4.17)	201	82.1 (2.16)	11.9 (1.87)	6.1 (1.33)	55
Family and consumer/human sciences	225	60.8 (2.69)	17.9 (2.20)	21.3 (2.29)	117	55.9 (4.11)	19.1 (3.37)	25.1 (3.63)	108	66.1 (4.12)	16.6 (2.64)	17.3 (3.08)	11
Foreign languages and literatures	96	71.5 (3.80)	20.7 (3.28)	7.8 (2.02)	27	60.4 (7.53)	23.4 (6.66)	16.2 ! (5.00)	69	76.0 (4.11)	19.6 (3.88)	4.5 ! (2.04)	26
Geography	17	59.4 (10.54)	24.6 ! (7.87)	‡ (†)	‡	‡ (†)	‡ (†)	‡ (†)	‡	‡ (†)	‡ (†)	‡ (†)	‡
Health professions and related sciences	4,271	48.5 (0.73)	30.8 (0.70)	20.7 (0.62)	2,790	45.6 (0.88)	33.5 (0.80)	20.9 (0.75)	1,482	54.0 (1.10)	25.7 (1.04)	20.3 (0.97)	679
History	206	77.7 (2.83)	16.4 (2.24)	5.9 (1.59)	43	78.5 (5.39)	17.3 ! (5.28)	‡ (†)	163	77.5 (3.35)	16.2 (2.61)	6.3 (1.86)	26
International relations and affairs	40	86.4 (5.51)	13.6 ! (5.51)	# (†)	‡	‡ (†)	‡ (†)	‡ (†)	33	87.2 (5.48)	12.8 ! (5.48)	# (†)	15
Legal professions and studies	177	45.7 (3.46)	30.5 (2.44)	23.8 (2.75)	96	45.7 (5.02)	27.1 (3.40)	27.1 (4.04)	80	45.6 (4.17)	34.6 (3.91)	19.8 (3.22)	146
Liberal arts, sciences and humanities	2,341	62.6 (0.89)	23.7 (0.75)	13.7 (0.68)	1,857	63.0 (0.93)	24.0 (0.86)	13.0 (0.76)	484	61.0 (2.43)	22.6 (1.63)	16.4 (1.79)	17
Library science	‡	‡ (†)	‡ (†)	‡ (†)	‡	‡ (†)	‡ (†)	‡ (†)	‡	‡ (†)	‡ (†)	‡ (†)	21
Mathematics and statistics	111	86.2 (2.28)	10.8 (2.22)	3.0 ! (1.13)	28	70.9 (6.04)	25.1 (6.26)	‡ (†)	82	91.5 (2.17)	5.8 (1.84)	2.6 ! (1.22)	25
Mechanic and repair technologies	376	54.7 (2.43)	27.8 (1.93)	17.5 (1.72)	341	54.0 (2.43)	29.1 (1.94)	17.0 (1.80)	35	62.3 (8.37)	15.0 ! (5.50)	22.7 (6.78)	‡
Military technologies	‡	‡ (†)	‡ (†)	‡ (†)	13	‡ (†)	‡ (†)	‡ (†)	‡	‡ (†)	‡ (†)	‡ (†)	‡
Multi/interdisciplinary studies	283	61.4 (2.35)	24.7 (2.04)	13.9 (1.91)	117	60.7 (3.66)	26.1 (3.46)	13.3 (2.89)	166	61.9 (2.99)	23.8 (2.44)	14.3 (2.63)	36
Natural resources and conservation	121	79.3 (3.13)	11.7 (1.92)	9.0 (2.52)	39	79.1 (5.64)	11.6 (3.02)	9.3 ! (4.51)	82	79.4 (3.42)	11.7 (2.28)	8.8 ! (2.81)	22
Parks, recreation, and fitness studies	253	85.8 (1.65)	10.1 (1.50)	4.1 (1.22)	67	74.9 (3.95)	17.2 (3.73)	7.9 ! (3.17)	186	89.7 (1.71)	7.6 (1.36)	2.7 ! (1.28)	17
Personal and culinary services	562	57.2 (2.01)	27.3 (1.44)	15.5 (1.53)	500	57.3 (2.16)	27.1 (1.40)	15.5 (1.59)	63	56.6 (5.75)	28.3 (5.93)	15.0 (4.41)	‡
Philosophy and religious studies	64	71.6 (6.19)	22.4 (5.96)	6.1 ! (2.67)	13	82.3 (10.84)	‡ (†)	‡ (†)	51	68.9 (6.93)	26.7 (6.92)	‡ (†)	20
Physical sciences	207	80.4 (2.65)	13.3 (1.90)	6.4 (1.75)	67	69.8 (5.11)	19.0 (3.14)	11.2 ! (4.37)	140	85.5 (2.97)	10.5 (2.38)	4.0 ! (1.62)	61
Political science and government	175	87.7 (2.11)	9.6 (1.79)	2.7 ! (1.01)	35	74.2 (8.12)	20.9 ! (7.21)	‡ (†)	140	91.2 (1.67)	6.7 (1.38)	2.1 ! (0.96)	17
Precision production	103	50.9 (4.64)	24.7 (4.13)	24.4 (3.88)	99	50.4 (4.75)	25.4 (4.26)	24.2 (3.84)	‡	‡ (†)	‡ (†)	‡ (†)	‡
Psychology	794	69.0 (1.49)	20.3 (1.24)	10.7 (0.92)	210	66.6 (2.95)	23.1 (2.53)	10.3 (1.88)	584	69.9 (1.60)	19.3 (1.39)	10.8 (1.08)	150
Public administration and social services	305	46.0 (2.14)	29.5 (2.23)	24.4 (2.08)	131	45.2 (3.54)	27.2 (3.13)	27.5 (3.34)	174	46.7 (2.76)	31.2 (3.14)	22.1 (2.48)	124
Science technologies/technicians	41	49.2 (6.78)	28.2 (6.33)	22.5 (5.67)	32	43.7 (7.27)	29.3 (7.59)	27.1 (7.12)	‡	‡ (†)	‡ (†)	‡ (†)	‡
Security and protective services	970	59.5 (1.76)	26.9 (1.13)	13.7 (1.37)	476	66.5 (1.76)	25.6 (1.61)	7.9 (0.93)	494	52.6 (2.70)	28.1 (1.53)	19.2 (2.36)	43

See notes at end of table.

Table 311.60. Enrollment in postsecondary education, by level of enrollment, level of institution, student age, and major field of study: 2011–12—Continued

[Standard errors appear in parentheses]

Major field of study[1]	All students				Undergraduate								Post-baccalaureate
					2-year and less-than-2-year institutions[2]				4-year institutions				
	Total (in thousands)	Percentage distribution, by age			Total (in thousands)	Percentage distribution, by age			Total (in thousands)	Percentage distribution, by age			Total (in thousands)
		Under 25	25 to 35	Over 35		Under 25	25 to 35	Over 35		Under 25	25 to 35	Over 35	
1	2	3	4	5	6	7	8	9	10	11	12	13	14
Social sciences, other...........	87	47.4 (4.78)	27.6 (4.39)	25.1 (4.58)	42	50.5 (6.73)	31.3 (6.59)	18.1 (4.77)	45	44.4 (8.26)	24.1 (5.33)	31.5 (8.37)	8
Sociology...........	149	68.0 (3.15)	21.5 (2.56)	10.5 (2.16)	40	57.2 (7.22)	24.4 (5.75)	18.4 ! (5.65)	109	72.0 (3.46)	20.4 (2.98)	7.6 (2.02)	9
Theology and religious vocations	50	60.5 (14.01)	14.7 (4.26)	24.8 ! (11.18)	‡	‡ (†)	‡ (†)	‡ (†)	46	59.3 (15.13)	14.1 ! (4.45)	26.6 ! (12.09)	63
Transportation and materials moving...........	72	40.8 (6.18)	39.4 (6.63)	19.8 (4.76)	43	25.5 (5.06)	45.6 (6.33)	28.9 (7.16)	30	62.9 (12.40)	30.4 ! (12.38)	‡ (†)	‡
Visual and performing arts	944	75.2 (1.70)	16.2 (1.14)	8.6 (1.02)	341	65.3 (2.30)	20.2 (1.89)	14.5 (1.80)	604	80.7 (2.39)	13.9 (1.51)	5.4 (1.20)	76
Undecided	465	76.8 (1.68)	15.4 (1.43)	7.8 (1.10)	278	70.6 (2.35)	18.0 (1.99)	11.4 (1.68)	187	86.0 (2.07)	11.7 (1.83)	2.3 ! (1.02)	†

†Not applicable.
#Rounds to zero.
!Interpret data with caution. The coefficient of variation (CV) for this estimate is between 30 and 50 percent.
‡Reporting standards not met. Either there are too few cases for a reliable estimate or the coefficient of variation (CV) is 50 percent or greater.
[1]For undergraduate students, the field of study categories include students who had decided on, but not yet declared, a major as well as students who had decided on, but not yet declared, an intended major. The "Undecided" category consists of undergraduate students who had neither declared nor decided on a major.

[2]Also includes students attending more than one institution.
NOTE: Because of different survey editing and processing procedures, enrollment data in this table may differ from those appearing in other tables. Includes students who enrolled at any time during the 2011–12 academic year. Data exclude Puerto Rico. Data have been revised from previously published figures. Detail may not sum to totals because of rounding.
SOURCE: U.S. Department of Education, National Center for Education Statistics, 2011–12 National Postsecondary Student Aid Study (NPSAS:12). (This table was prepared March 2014.)

Table 311.70. Course enrollments in languages other than English compared with total enrollment at degree-granting postsecondary institutions, by enrollment level, institution level, and language: Selected years, 1965 through 2009

Enrollment level, institution level, and language	1965	1970	1974	1980	1986	1990	1995	2002	2006[1]	2009	Percent change				
											1965 to 1974	1974 to 1986	1986 to 1995	1986 to 2006	2006 to 2009
1	2	3	4	5	6	7	8	9	10	11	12	13	14	15	16
Number of language course enrollments															
All levels, institutions, and languages	1,059,258	1,153,747	946,389	924,352	1,003,548	1,185,555	1,138,772	1,397,253	1,577,810	1,682,627	-10.7	6.0	13.5	57.2	6.6
Undergraduate	—	—	904,498	892,290	970,382	1,149,713	1,100,095	1,360,538	1,536,840	1,644,390	†	7.3	13.4	58.4	7.0
2-year institutions	—	—	154,466	—	162,881	228,420	236,702	350,297	366,282	417,448	†	5.4	45.3	124.9	14.0
4-year institutions	—	—	750,277	—	807,084	920,092	863,393	1,010,297	1,170,558	1,226,481	†	7.6	7.0	45.0	4.8
Graduate	—	—	41,892	32,062	33,269	35,628	38,677	36,715	40,970	38,237	†	-20.6	16.3	23.1	-6.7
American Sign Language	—	—	—	—	—	1,602	4,304	60,781	78,829	91,763	†	†	†	†	16.4
Arabic	911	—	2,034	3,471	3,417	3,683	4,444	10,584	23,974	35,083	123.3	68.0	30.1	601.6	46.3
Chinese	3,359	—	10,576	11,366	16,892	19,427	26,471	34,153	51,582	60,976	214.9	59.7	56.7	205.4	18.2
French	371,735	358,617	253,208	248,307	275,235	273,143	205,351	201,979	206,426	216,419	-31.9	8.7	-25.4	-25.0	4.8
German	213,909	201,928	152,119	127,015	121,065	133,594	96,263	91,100	94,264	96,349	-28.9	-20.4	-20.5	-22.1	2.2
Greek, Ancient[2]	19,495	16,643	24,283	22,132	17,806	16,414	16,272	20,376	22,849	20,695	24.6	-26.7	-8.6	28.3	-9.4
Hebrew[3]	8,093	—	22,371	19,290	15,669	12,966	13,127	22,802	23,752	22,052	176.4	-30.0	-16.2	51.6	-7.2
Italian	22,950	34,236	33,048	34,796	40,904	49,843	43,760	63,899	78,368	80,752	44.0	23.8	7.0	91.6	3.0
Japanese	3,505	—	9,604	11,516	23,457	45,830	44,723	52,238	66,605	73,434	174.0	144.2	90.7	183.9	10.3
Korean	82	—	87	365	875	2,375	3,343	5,211	7,145	8,511	6.1	905.7	282.1	716.6	19.1
Latin	38,038	28,452	25,167	25,019	25,038	28,178	25,897	29,841	32,191	32,606	-33.8	-0.5	3.4	28.6	1.3
Portuguese	3,040	—	5,072	4,894	5,071	6,118	6,531	8,385	10,267	11,371	66.8	#	28.8	102.5	10.8
Russian	33,818	36,369	32,522	23,987	33,945	44,476	24,729	23,921	24,845	26,883	-3.8	4.4	-27.1	-26.8	8.2
Spanish	310,015	386,709	361,911	378,960	411,499	534,182	606,286	746,267	822,985	864,986	16.7	13.7	47.3	100.0	5.1
Other languages	30,308	90,793	14,387	13,234	12,675	13,724	17,271	25,716	33,728	40,747	-52.5	-11.9	36.3	166.1	20.8
Total enrollment at degree-granting institutions															
All levels	5,920,864	8,580,887	10,223,729	12,096,895	12,503,511	13,818,637	14,261,781	16,611,711	17,758,870	20,427,711	72.7	22.3	14.1	42.0	15.0
Undergraduate	—	7,368,644	8,798,728	10,475,055	10,797,975	11,959,106	12,231,719	14,257,077	15,184,302	17,565,320	†	22.7	13.3	40.6	15.7
2-year institutions	—	2,318,956	3,402,732	4,525,097	4,679,548	5,240,083	5,492,098	6,529,198	6,518,291	7,521,405	†	37.5	17.4	39.3	15.4
4-year institutions	—	5,049,688	5,395,996	5,949,958	6,118,427	6,719,023	6,739,621	7,727,879	8,666,011	10,043,915	†	13.4	10.2	41.6	15.9
Graduate	—	1,212,243	1,425,001	1,621,840	1,705,536	1,859,531	2,030,062	2,354,634	2,574,568	2,862,391	†	19.7	19.0	51.0	11.2
Number of language course enrollments per 100 students enrolled											Change in percentage points				
All levels	17.9	13.4	9.3	7.6	8.0	8.6	8.0	8.4	8.9	8.2	-8.6	-1.2	#	0.9	-0.6
Undergraduate	—	—	10.3	8.5	9.0	9.6	9.0	9.5	10.1	9.4	†	-1.3	#	1.1	-0.8
2-year institutions	—	—	4.5	0.0	3.5	4.4	4.3	5.4	5.6	5.6	†	-1.1	0.8	2.1	-0.1
4-year institutions	—	—	13.9	0.0	13.2	13.7	12.8	13.1	13.5	12.2	†	-0.7	-0.4	0.3	-1.3
Graduate	—	—	2.9	2.0	2.0	1.9	1.9	1.6	1.6	1.3	†	-1.0	#	-0.4	-0.3

—Not available.
†Not applicable.
#Rounds to zero.

[1]In 2006, a few 2-year institutions reported a total of 226 graduate course enrollments (86 in Spanish and 140 in American Sign Language). In this table, these 226 enrollments are shown as undergraduate enrollments in 2-year institutions; these enrollments are not included under graduate enrollments.

[2]The apparent drop in Ancient Greek from 2006 to 2009 may be attributed to changes in reporting. Some premodern Greek language categories, such as Koine Greek and Old Testament Greek, were reported for the first time in 2009. In previous surveys, these languages may have been reported under the category "Ancient Greek."

[3]For 1990 and later years, includes only "Modern Hebrew" and "Biblical Hebrew"; other reported categories of Hebrew courses are excluded.

NOTE: The number of course enrollments is not the same as the number of students studying a given language. A single student majoring in a language may be enrolled in more than one class in that language. Unless otherwise noted, enrollments do not include those in classical, religious, or regional dialects of the language. Data through 1995 are for institutions of higher education, while later data are for degree-granting institutions. Degree-granting institutions grant associate's or higher degrees and participate in Title IV federal financial aid programs. The degree-granting classification is very similar to the earlier higher education classification, but it includes more 2-year colleges and excludes a few higher education institutions that did not grant degrees. (See Appendix A: Guide to Sources for details.)

SOURCE: The Modern Language Association of America, Enrollments in Languages Other Than English in United States Institutions of Higher Education, Fall 2009, Table 2c; and MLA historical enrollment data, 1958–70, 1971–86, 1990–98, and 2002–09, retrieved July 21, 2011, from http://www.mla.org/about_search_flsurvey. U.S. Department of Education, National Center for Education Statistics, Opening Fall Enrollment in Higher Education, 1965; Higher Education General Information Survey (HEGIS), "Fall Enrollment in Institutions of Higher Education" surveys, 1970 through 1980; Integrated Postsecondary Education Data System (IPEDS), "Fall Enrollment Survey" (IPEDS-EF:86–95); and IPEDS Spring 2003 through Spring 2010, Enrollment component. (This table was prepared July 2011.)

Table 311.80. Number and percentage distribution of course enrollments in languages other than English at degree-granting postsecondary institutions, by language and enrollment level: 2002, 2006, and 2009

Enrollment and year	Total, all languages	American Sign Language	Arabic	Chinese	French	German	Greek, Ancient[1]	Hebrew[2]	Italian	Japanese	Korean	Latin	Portuguese	Russian	Spanish	Other languages
1	2	3	4	5	6	7	8	9	10	11	12	13	14	15	16	17
All levels																
Number of enrollments																
2002	1,397,253	60,781	10,584	34,153	201,979	91,100	20,376	22,802	53,899	52,238	5,211	29,841	8,385	23,921	746,267	25,716
2006	1,577,810	78,829	23,974	51,582	206,426	94,264	22,849	23,752	78,368	66,605	7,145	32,191	10,267	24,845	822,985	33,728
2009	1,682,627	91,763	35,083	60,976	216,419	96,349	20,695	22,052	80,752	73,434	8,511	32,606	11,371	26,883	864,986	40,747
Percent change in enrollments, 2006 to 2009	6.6	16.4	46.3	18.2	4.8	2.2	-9.4	-7.2	3.0	10.3	19.1	1.3	10.8	8.2	5.1	20.8
Percentage distribution of enrollments																
2002	100.0	4.4	0.8	2.4	14.5	6.5	1.5	1.6	4.6	3.7	0.4	2.1	0.6	1.7	53.4	1.8
2006	100.0	5.0	1.5	3.3	13.1	6.0	1.4	1.5	5.0	4.2	0.5	2.0	0.7	1.6	52.2	2.1
2009	100.0	5.5	2.1	3.6	12.9	5.7	1.2	1.3	4.8	4.4	0.5	1.9	0.7	1.6	51.4	2.4
Undergraduate level																
Number of enrollments																
2002	1,360,538	60,660	10,053	33,219	197,374	88,297	14,343	17,251	62,852	51,308	5,100	28,796	7,898	23,151	736,317	23,919
2006[3]	1,536,840	78,083	23,034	50,455	201,663	91,192	16,426	17,474	77,350	65,746	6,908	31,170	9,809	24,096	812,120	31,314
2009	1,644,390	90,937	34,301	59,967	212,178	93,749	15,858	16,606	79,977	72,717	8,163	31,582	10,933	26,287	852,781	38,354
Introductory courses[4]	1,370,250	83,450	29,650	47,676	172,573	76,317	12,812	11,202	72,403	59,892	6,010	27,273	8,112	19,850	711,032	31,998
Advanced courses[4]	274,140	7,487	4,651	12,291	39,605	17,432	3,046	5,404	7,574	12,825	2,153	4,309	2,821	6,437	141,749	6,356
Percent change in enrollments, 2006 to 2009	7.0	16.5	48.9	18.9	5.2	2.8	-3.5	-5.0	3.4	10.6	18.2	1.3	11.5	9.1	5.0	22.5
Percentage distribution of enrollments																
2002	100.0	4.5	0.7	2.4	14.5	6.5	1.1	1.3	4.6	3.8	0.4	2.1	0.6	1.7	54.1	1.8
2006	100.0	5.1	1.5	3.3	13.1	5.9	1.1	1.1	5.0	4.3	0.4	2.0	0.6	1.6	52.8	2.0
2009	100.0	5.5	2.1	3.6	12.9	5.7	1.0	1.0	4.9	4.4	0.5	1.9	0.7	1.6	51.9	2.3
Graduate level																
Number of enrollments																
2002	36,715	121	531	934	4,605	2,803	6,033	5,551	1,047	930	111	1,045	487	770	9,950	1,797
2006[3]	40,970	746	940	1,127	4,763	3,072	6,423	6,278	1,018	859	237	1,021	458	749	10,865	2,414
2009	38,237	826	782	1,009	4,241	2,600	4,837	5,446	775	717	348	1,024	438	596	12,205	2,393
Percent change in enrollments, 2006 to 2009	-6.7	10.7	-16.8	-10.5	-11.0	-15.4	-24.7	-13.3	-23.9	-16.5	46.8	0.3	-4.4	-20.4	12.3	-0.9
Percentage distribution of enrollments																
2002	100.0	0.3	1.4	2.5	12.5	7.6	16.4	15.1	2.9	2.5	0.3	2.8	1.3	2.1	27.1	4.9
2006	100.0	1.8	2.3	2.8	11.6	7.5	15.7	15.3	2.5	2.1	0.6	2.5	1.1	1.8	26.5	5.9
2009	100.0	2.2	2.0	2.6	11.1	6.8	12.7	14.2	2.0	1.9	0.9	2.7	1.1	1.6	31.9	6.3

[1]The apparent drop in Ancient Greek from 2006 to 2009 may be attributed to changes in reporting. Some premodern Greek language categories, such as Koine Greek and Old Testament Greek, were reported for the first time in 2009. In previous surveys, these languages may have been reported under the category "Ancient Greek."
[2]Includes only "Modern Hebrew" and "Biblical Hebrew"; other reported categories of Hebrew courses are excluded.
[3]In 2006, a few 2-year institutions reported a total of 226 graduate course enrollments (86 in Spanish and 140 in American Sign Language). In this table, these 226 enrollments are shown as undergraduate enrollments; these enrollments are not included under graduate enrollments.

[4]Introductory courses are first- and second-year courses. Advanced courses are third- and fourth-year courses.
NOTE: This table shows course enrollments, not the number of students studying a given language. A single student majoring in a language may be enrolled in more than one class in that language. Unless otherwise indicated, totals for specific languages do not include classical, religious, or regional dialects. Degree-granting institutions grant associate's or higher degrees and participate in Title IV federal financial aid programs.
SOURCE: The Modern Language Association of America, MLA historical enrollment data, 2002–09, retrieved July 21, 2011, from http://www.mla.org/about_flsurvey_search_flsurvey. (This table was prepared July 2011.)

Table 311.90. Graduate enrollment in programs in engineering, physical and biological sciences, mathematical and computer sciences, social sciences, and research-based health fields in degree-granting postsecondary institutions, by discipline: Fall 2007 through fall 2013

Discipline	2007	2008	2009	2010	2011	2012	2013
1	2	3	4	5	6	7	8
Total, all surveyed disciplines	619,499	631,489	631,645	632,652	626,820	627,243	633,010
Engineering	131,676	137,856	144,677	149,241	146,501	148,385	153,049
Aerospace	4,616	4,902	5,266	5,540	5,691	5,069	5,181
Agricultural	1,126	1,233	1,303	1,457	1,656	1,552	1,642
Architecture	4,601	5,905	6,804	6,795	3,111	2,363	2,176
Biomedical	6,904	7,339	7,904	8,497	9,175	9,157	9,198
Chemical	7,584	7,892	8,188	8,668	8,828	9,222	9,698
Civil	16,071	16,931	18,638	19,559	19,596	19,922	20,110
Electrical	40,588	41,164	41,218	41,336	41,580	42,347	45,562
Engineering science	1,806	2,099	2,168	2,071	2,101	2,227	2,142
Industrial/manufacturing	14,474	15,692	15,825	15,205	14,494	14,469	14,363
Mechanical	18,347	19,585	21,243	22,509	21,883	23,088	24,087
Metallurgical/materials	5,314	5,539	5,863	6,274	6,649	6,985	7,144
Mining	222	290	312	419	500	356	357
Nuclear	1,180	1,201	1,243	1,459	1,499	1,513	1,459
Petroleum	1,014	1,009	1,190	1,295	1,301	1,525	1,609
Other engineering	7,829	7,075	7,512	8,157	8,437	8,590	8,321
Physical sciences	36,824	37,319	38,149	38,973	39,694	39,928	40,019
Astronomy	1,232	1,275	1,409	1,331	1,345	1,278	1,250
Chemistry	21,298	21,574	22,094	22,436	22,802	23,117	22,949
Physics	13,816	13,862	14,060	14,507	14,829	14,940	15,239
Other physical sciences	478	608	586	699	718	593	581
Earth, atmospheric, and ocean sciences	14,100	14,389	14,839	15,655	15,820	16,069	15,816
Atmospheric sciences	1,178	1,400	1,355	1,455	1,513	1,546	1,534
Geosciences	7,020	7,089	7,539	8,251	8,361	8,659	8,754
Oceanography	2,615	2,634	2,633	2,556	2,680	2,642	2,682
Other earth, atmospheric, and ocean sciences	3,287	3,266	3,312	3,393	3,266	3,222	2,846
Family and consumer science/human science	2,780	3,549	3,794	4,191	4,509	4,110	4,014
Mathematical sciences	20,975	21,400	22,226	23,136	23,801	24,575	24,804
Mathematics and applied mathematics	16,528	16,449	17,204	17,589	18,157	18,577	18,323
Statistics	4,447	4,951	5,022	5,547	5,644	5,998	6,481
Multidisciplinary/interdisciplinary studies	4,484	5,559	6,557	7,944	6,537	6,038	5,892
Neuroscience	1,584	2,012	2,356	2,798	4,117	4,547	4,795
Communication	7,303	8,444	9,418	9,825	11,029	11,010	11,114
Computer sciences	48,246	49,553	51,161	51,546	51,234	51,789	56,339
Life sciences	188,760	189,033	174,464	166,704	157,431	158,506	155,788
Agricultural sciences	13,528	14,153	15,200	15,656	16,129	16,234	16,429
Biological sciences	71,932	72,666	73,304	74,928	75,423	76,447	76,649
Anatomy	867	764	833	849	762	700	527
Biochemistry	5,853	5,473	5,271	5,308	5,183	5,245	4,970
Biology	15,898	16,514	16,840	17,210	16,911	16,321	16,004
Biometry/epidemiology	5,694	5,971	5,739	6,398	6,786	7,800	8,478
Biophysics	1,193	1,084	1,042	1,072	1,016	976	952
Botany	1,821	1,803	1,831	1,863	1,915	1,852	1,878
Cell biology	6,839	7,096	7,153	7,047	6,905	6,799	6,543
Ecology	2,026	2,026	1,746	1,828	1,713	1,667	1,437
Entomology/parasitology	1,078	1,079	1,079	1,116	1,119	1,187	1,278
Genetics	2,120	2,120	2,242	2,333	2,403	2,342	2,315
Microbiology, immunology, and virology	5,212	5,054	4,968	4,896	5,031	4,950	4,961
Nutrition	4,890	5,177	5,330	5,548	5,345	5,336	5,387
Pathology	1,580	1,618	1,450	1,376	1,313	1,196	1,112
Pharmacology	3,013	3,005	3,163	3,101	3,053	3,088	2,979
Physiology	2,738	2,863	2,866	2,879	3,000	3,046	3,224
Zoology	1,108	925	875	896	1,060	1,083	1,188
Other biosciences	10,002	10,094	10,876	11,208	11,908	12,859	13,416
Health fields[1]	103,300	102,214	85,960	76,120	65,879	65,825	62,710
Clinical medicine fields	22,751	23,939	24,125	25,699	26,634	26,798	26,362
Other health fields[2]	80,549	78,275	61,835	50,421	39,245	39,027	36,348
Psychology[2]	59,617	58,991	56,184	53,419	54,486	54,117	54,102
Social sciences	103,150	103,384	107,820	109,220	111,661	108,169	107,278
Agricultural economics	1,989	2,132	2,222	2,180	2,095	2,045	1,916
Economics (except agricultural)	12,597	12,971	13,993	14,317	14,920	14,959	14,819
Geography	4,660	4,745	4,810	5,059	5,188	5,016	4,891
Linguistics	2,879	3,095	3,170	3,132	3,219	3,256	3,509
Political science	41,349	40,871	43,919	45,045	49,660	48,855	48,411
Sociology and anthropology	18,453	18,988	18,666	18,740	18,365	17,404	17,360
Other social sciences	21,223	20,582	21,040	20,747	18,214	16,634	16,372

[1]Excludes enrollments in practitioner-oriented programs, which have the primary purpose of providing the knowledge and skills required for credentials or licensure to practice in a medical or other health field.
[2]For 2008 and later years, enrollment declines in psychology and in other health fields such as nursing may be due to more rigorous follow-up with institutions to exclude enrollments in practitioner-oriented graduate degree programs. Examples of excluded programs are those leading to DNP, PsyD, and DPT degrees.

NOTE: The survey on which this table is based includes all institutions in the United States and its territories (Guam and Puerto Rico) that grant research-based master's degrees or doctorates in science, engineering, and selected health fields.
SOURCE: National Science Foundation, National Center for Science and Engineering Statistics, NSF-NIH Survey of Graduate Students and Postdoctorates in Science and Engineering, 2007 through 2013. (This table was prepared April 2015.)

Table 312.10.   Enrollment of the 120 largest degree-granting college and university campuses, by selected characteristics and institution: Fall 2013

Institution	State	Rank[1]	Control[2]	Level	Total enroll-ment	Institution	State	Rank[1]	Control[2]	Level	Total enroll-ment
1	2	3	4	5	6	1	2	3	4	5	6
University of Phoenix, Online Campus	AZ	1	PrivFp	4-year	212,044	University of Texas at Arlington	TX	61	Public	4-year	33,329
Ivy Tech Community College	IN	2	Public	2-year	98,778	University of California, Davis	CA	62	Public	4-year	33,307
Liberty University	VA	3	PrivNp	4-year	77,338	Texas Tech University	TX	63	Public	4-year	33,111
Miami Dade College	FL	4	Public	4-year	66,298	Iowa State University	IA	64	Public	4-year	32,955
Lone Star College System	TX	5	Public	2-year	64,072	Boston University	MA	65	PrivNp	4-year	32,411
University of Central Florida	FL	6	Public	4-year	59,589	Portland Community College	OR	66	Public	2-year	32,411
Ashford University	IA	7	PrivFp	4-year	58,104	Georgia State University	GA	67	Public	4-year	32,165
Houston Community College	TX	8	Public	2-year	57,978	University of Utah	UT	68	Public	4-year	32,077
Ohio State University, Main Campus	OH	9	Public	4-year	57,466	University of Colorado, Boulder	CO	69	Public	4-year	32,017
Texas A&M University, College Station	TX	10	Public	4-year	55,697	Salt Lake Community College	UT	70	Public	2-year	32,003
Grand Canyon University	AZ	11	PrivFp	4-year	55,497	University of South Carolina, Columbia	SC	71	Public	4-year	31,964
American Public University System	WV	12	PrivFp	4-year	55,422	San Diego State University	CA	72	Public	4-year	31,899
Kaplan University, Davenport Campus	IA	13	PrivFp	4-year	52,407	Saint Petersburg College	FL	73	Public	4-year	31,820
University of Texas at Austin	TX	14	Public	4-year	52,059	San Jose State University	CA	74	Public	4-year	31,278
Northern Virginia Community College	VA	15	Public	2-year	51,803	South Texas College	TX	75	Public	4-year	31,232
University of Minnesota, Twin Cities	MN	16	Public	4-year	51,526	Virginia Polytechnic Institute and State University	VA	76	Public	4-year	31,205
Walden University	MN	17	PrivFp	4-year	51,016	Colorado State University, Fort Collins	CO	77	Public	4-year	31,186
Tarrant County College District	TX	18	Public	2-year	50,771	Brigham Young University, Provo	UT	78	PrivNp	4-year	31,123
University of Florida	FL	19	Public	4-year	49,878	Virginia Commonwealth University	VA	79	Public	4-year	30,974
Michigan State University	MI	20	Public	4-year	49,317	Florida Atlantic University	FL	80	Public	4-year	30,759
Arizona State University, Tempe[3]	AZ	21	Public	4-year	48,702	Utah Valley University	UT	81	Public	4-year	30,564
Rutgers University, New Brunswick	NJ	22	Public	4-year	48,036	Indiana University-Purdue University, Indianapolis	IN	82	Public	4-year	30,488
Florida International University	FL	23	Public	4-year	47,663	Louisiana State U. and Agricultural & Mechanical	LA	83	Public	4-year	30,478
Indiana University, Bloomington	IN	24	Public	4-year	46,817	El Paso Community College	TX	84	Public	2-year	30,468
Western Governors University	UT	25	PrivNp	4-year	46,733	Pima Community College	AZ	85	Public	2-year	30,082
Pennsylvania State University, Main Campus	PA	26	Public	4-year	46,615	University of Tennessee, Knoxville	TN	86	Public	4-year	30,030
University of Illinois at Urbana-Champaign	IL	27	Public	4-year	44,942	Santa Monica College	CA	87	Public	2-year	29,999
New York University	NY	28	PrivNp	4-year	44,599	San Francisco State University	CA	88	Public	4-year	29,905
Broward College	FL	29	Public	4-year	43,883	University at Buffalo	NY	89	Public	4-year	29,850
University of Washington, Seattle Campus	WA	30	Public	4-year	43,762	Palm Beach State College	FL	90	Public	4-year	29,763
University of Michigan, Ann Arbor	MI	31	Public	4-year	43,710	University of Iowa	IA	91	Public	4-year	29,748
University of Wisconsin, Madison	WI	32	Public	4-year	42,677	American River College	CA	92	Public	2-year	29,701
Valencia College	FL	33	Public	4-year	42,180	Everest University, South Orlando	FL	93	PrivFp	4-year	29,693
Austin Community College District	TX	34	Public	2-year	41,627	University of California, San Diego	CA	94	Public	4-year	29,517
University of South Florida, Main Campus	FL	35	Public	4-year	41,428	West Virginia University	WV	95	Public	4-year	29,466
University of Southern California	CA	36	PrivNp	4-year	41,368	University of North Carolina at Chapel Hill	NC	96	Public	4-year	29,127
Florida State University	FL	37	Public	4-year	40,909	Tidewater Community College	VA	97	Public	2-year	28,999
University of California, Los Angeles	CA	38	Public	4-year	40,795	Kent State University at Kent	OH	98	Public	4-year	28,998
University of Arizona	AZ	39	Public	4-year	40,621	University of California, Irvine	CA	99	Public	4-year	28,895
Excelsior College	NY	40	PrivNp	4-year	39,897	Central New Mexico Community College	NM	100	Public	2-year	28,891
Purdue University, Main Campus	IN	41	Public	4-year	39,794	California State University, Sacramento	CA	101	Public	4-year	28,811
University of Maryland University College	MD	42	Public	4-year	39,557	Ohio University, Main Campus	OH	102	Public	4-year	28,786
University of Houston	TX	43	Public	4-year	39,540	University of Pittsburgh, Pittsburgh Campus	PA	103	Public	4-year	28,649
California State University, Fullerton	CA	44	Public	4-year	38,325	College of DuPage	IL	104	Public	2-year	28,627
University of North Texas	TX	45	Public	4-year	38,315	University of Texas at San Antonio	TX	105	Public	4-year	28,623
California State University, Northridge	CA	46	Public	4-year	38,310	Santa Ana College	CA	106	Public	2-year	28,598
University of Maryland, College Park	MD	47	Public	4-year	37,272	University of New Mexico, Main Campus	NM	107	Public	4-year	28,592
Temple University	PA	48	Public	4-year	37,270	University of Massachusetts, Amherst	MA	108	Public	4-year	28,518
East Los Angeles College	CA	49	Public	2-year	36,606	Mount San Antonio College	CA	109	Public	2-year	28,481
University of California, Berkeley	CA	50	Public	4-year	36,198	University of Kentucky	KY	110	Public	4-year	28,435
California State University, Long Beach	CA	51	Public	4-year	35,586	Southern New Hampshire University	NH	111	PrivNp	4-year	28,389
Texas State University	TX	52	Public	4-year	35,546	San Jacinto Community College	TX	112	Public	2-year	28,385
University of Alabama	AL	53	Public	4-year	34,752	Harvard University	MA	113	PrivNp	4-year	28,297
University of Missouri, Columbia	MO	54	Public	4-year	34,616	Portland State University	OR	114	Public	4-year	28,260
University of Georgia	GA	55	Public	4-year	34,536	Florida State College at Jacksonville	FL	115	Public	4-year	28,134
University of Cincinnati, Main Campus	OH	56	Public	4-year	34,379	University of Illinois at Chicago	IL	116	Public	4-year	28,038
College of Southern Nevada	NV	57	Public	4-year	34,177	Collin County Community College District	TX	117	Public	2-year	27,972
North Carolina State University at Raleigh	NC	58	Public	4-year	34,009	Cuyahoga Community College District	OH	118	Public	2-year	27,910
Capella University	MN	59	PrivFp	4-year	34,007	Oregon State University	OR	119	Public	4-year	27,902
George Mason University	VA	60	Public	4-year	33,917	Wayne State University	MI	120	Public	4-year	27,897

[1]College and university campuses ranked by fall 2013 enrollment data.
[2] "PrivNp" stands for private nonprofit. "PrivFp" stands for private for-profit.
[3]Data for Arizona State University exclude enrollments for the following four branch campuses, which are now reported separately: Downtown Phoenix, Skysong, West, and Polytechnic.

NOTE: Degree-granting institutions grant associate's or higher degrees and participate in Title IV federal financial aid programs. Includes online and distance education courses.
SOURCE: U.S. Department of Education, National Center for Education Statistics, Integrated Postsecondary Education Data System (IPEDS), Spring 2014, Enrollment component. (This table was prepared April 2015.)

Table 312.20. Selected statistics for degree-granting postsecondary institutions enrolling more than 15,000 students in 2013, by selected institution and student characteristics: Selected years, 1990 through 2012–13

Line number	Institution	State	Con-trol[1]	Level	Total fall enrollment					Fall enrollment, 2013		
											Sex	
					Fall 1990	Fall 2000	Fall 2010	Fall 2011	Fall 2012	Total	Male	Female
1	2	3	4	5	6	7	8	9	10	11	12	13
i	United States, all institutions[6]	†	†	†	13,818,637	15,312,289	21,019,438	21,010,590	20,642,819	20,375,789	8,860,786	11,515,003
ii	Colleges with enrollment over 15,000	†	†	†	6,161,439	6,595,007	9,162,379	9,282,162	9,319,317	9,255,496	4,194,812	5,060,684
1	Auburn University	AL	Public	4-year	21,537	21,860	25,078	25,469	25,134	24,864	12,628	12,236
2	Columbia Southern University	AL	PrivFp	4-year	†	†	17,695	19,122	19,933	20,185	12,248	7,937
3	Troy University	AL	Public	4-year	5,024	12,541	28,322	26,172	22,554	20,573	7,506	13,067
4	University of Alabama	AL	Public	4-year	19,794	19,277	30,127	31,647	33,503	34,752	15,763	18,989
5	University of Alabama at Birmingham	AL	Public	4-year	15,356	14,951	17,543	17,575	17,999	18,568	7,309	11,259
6	University of South Alabama	AL	Public	4-year	11,584	11,673	14,776	14,769	14,636	15,065	5,806	9,259
7	University of Alaska, Anchorage	AK	Public	4-year	17,490	14,794	18,154	18,128	17,497	17,363	7,086	10,277
8	Arizona State University, Tempe[7]	AZ	Public	4-year	42,936	44,126	70,440	72,254	73,378	48,702	27,532	21,170
9	Glendale Community College	AZ	Public	2-year	18,512	20,091	21,373	21,376	21,361	20,872	9,673	11,199
10	Grand Canyon University	AZ	PrivFp	4-year	1,813	3,615	37,440	40,487	48,650	55,497	13,704	41,793
11	Mesa Community College	AZ	Public	2-year	19,818	22,821	26,408	25,695	25,024	23,678	11,519	12,159
12	Northern Arizona University	AZ	Public	4-year	16,992	19,964	25,197	25,359	25,991	26,594	10,799	15,795
13	Pima Community College	AZ	Public	2-year	28,766	28,078	36,823	36,969	32,988	30,082	14,119	15,963
14	Rio Salado College	AZ	Public	2-year	10,480	11,275	25,266	25,109	24,342	21,472	8,163	13,309
15	University of Arizona	AZ	Public	4-year	35,729	34,488	39,086	39,236	40,223	40,621	19,520	21,101
16	University of Phoenix, Online Campus	AZ	PrivFp	4-year	†	14,783	307,965	307,871	256,402	212,044	64,930	147,114
17	University of Arkansas	AR	Public	4-year	14,732	15,346	21,405	23,199	24,537	25,341	12,601	12,740
18	Academy of Art University	CA	PrivFp	4-year	1,767	5,995	17,695	18,093	17,871	16,001	6,787	9,214
19	American River College	CA	Public	2-year	18,716	28,420	33,440	31,750	31,088	29,701	13,643	16,058
20	Bakersfield College	CA	Public	2-year	10,776	14,466	19,569	17,619	17,344	17,770	7,796	9,974
21	California Polytechnic State U., San Luis Obispo	CA	Public	4-year	17,751	16,877	18,360	18,762	18,679	19,703	10,772	8,931
22	California State Polytechnic University, Pomona	CA	Public	4-year	19,468	18,424	20,747	21,107	22,156	22,501	12,584	9,917
23	California State University, Chico	CA	Public	4-year	16,633	15,912	15,989	15,920	16,470	16,356	7,685	8,671
24	California State University, Fresno	CA	Public	4-year	19,960	19,056	20,932	21,981	22,565	23,060	9,682	13,378
25	California State University, Fullerton	CA	Public	4-year	25,592	28,381	35,590	36,156	37,677	38,325	16,854	21,471
26	California State University, Long Beach	CA	Public	4-year	33,987	30,918	33,416	34,870	36,279	35,586	15,204	20,382
27	California State University, Los Angeles	CA	Public	4-year	21,597	19,593	20,142	21,284	21,755	23,258	9,471	13,787
28	California State University, Northridge	CA	Public	4-year	31,167	29,066	35,272	36,911	36,164	38,310	17,020	21,290
29	California State University, Sacramento	CA	Public	4-year	26,336	25,714	27,033	28,016	28,539	28,811	12,272	16,539
30	California State University, San Bernardino	CA	Public	4-year	11,923	14,909	16,400	17,250	18,234	18,398	7,030	11,368
31	Cerritos College	CA	Public	2-year	15,886	24,536	22,142	21,335	20,719	21,404	9,717	11,687
32	Chaffey College	CA	Public	2-year	10,985	15,220	19,469	18,597	17,804	19,211	8,135	11,076
33	City College of San Francisco	CA	Public	2-year	24,408	39,386	32,966	34,558	30,106	26,706	12,917	13,789
34	College of the Canyons	CA	Public	2-year	4,815	10,528	23,332	17,216	15,177	18,508	9,658	8,850
35	Cypress College	CA	Public	2-year	11,917	21,361	16,153	15,426	15,144	15,881	7,164	8,717
36	De Anza College	CA	Public	2-year	21,948	22,770	23,630	24,187	23,833	23,261	12,003	11,258
37	Diablo Valley College	CA	Public	2-year	20,255	21,581	20,703	20,310	20,329	20,286	9,755	10,531
38	East Los Angeles College	CA	Public	2-year	12,447	27,199	35,100	37,057	37,055	36,606	19,253	17,353
39	El Camino Community College District	CA	Public	2-year	25,789	24,067	24,756	24,463	23,405	23,996	11,672	12,324
40	Fresno City College	CA	Public	2-year	14,710	19,351	23,902	20,135	21,630	21,344	9,930	11,414
41	Fullerton College	CA	Public	2-year	17,548	19,993	22,562	18,827	19,624	24,301	11,864	12,437
42	Glendale Community College	CA	Public	2-year	12,072	15,596	16,876	16,518	15,978	15,744	7,124	8,620
43	Grossmont College	CA	Public	2-year	15,357	16,309	19,659	19,509	17,758	18,618	8,259	10,359
44	Long Beach City College	CA	Public	2-year	18,378	20,926	26,517	25,782	24,839	24,020	10,893	13,127
45	Los Angeles City College	CA	Public	2-year	14,479	15,174	20,430	21,028	20,385	19,635	8,680	10,955
46	Los Angeles Pierce College	CA	Public	2-year	16,970	16,111	21,368	20,506	19,938	20,080	9,407	10,673
47	Los Angeles Valley College	CA	Public	2-year	16,457	17,393	20,667	18,789	18,640	18,762	8,086	10,676
48	Modesto Junior College	CA	Public	2-year	11,300	15,158	18,492	17,609	16,985	17,084	7,383	9,701
49	Mount San Antonio College	CA	Public	2-year	20,563	28,329	29,064	28,780	28,036	28,481	13,874	14,607
50	National University	CA	PrivNp	4-year	8,836	16,848	16,249	16,671	17,898	18,207	7,236	10,971
51	Orange Coast College	CA	Public	2-year	22,365	23,315	24,239	22,654	21,088	21,886	11,344	10,542
52	Palomar College	CA	Public	2-year	16,707	21,062	26,231	25,427	24,626	24,665	13,773	10,892
53	Pasadena City College	CA	Public	2-year	19,581	22,948	27,023	26,057	22,859	25,268	12,172	13,096
54	Rio Hondo College	CA	Public	2-year	12,048	19,506	21,782	17,862	17,643	16,548	8,911	7,637
55	Riverside City College	CA	Public	2-year	15,683	22,107	20,585	18,395	17,218	18,165	8,017	10,148
56	Sacramento City College	CA	Public	2-year	14,474	20,878	25,039	24,106	24,381	23,509	10,309	13,200
57	Saddleback College	CA	Public	2-year	14,527	18,563	24,793	22,578	21,728	20,871	9,593	11,278
58	San Diego City College	CA	Public	2-year	13,737	27,165	18,549	17,728	16,797	16,310	7,722	8,588
59	San Diego Mesa College	CA	Public	2-year	23,410	21,233	25,972	25,504	24,943	24,251	11,692	12,559
60	San Diego State University	CA	Public	4-year	35,493	31,609	29,187	30,541	30,843	31,899	14,160	17,739
61	San Francisco State University	CA	Public	4-year	29,343	26,826	29,718	29,541	30,500	29,905	12,709	17,196
62	San Joaquin Delta College	CA	Public	2-year	14,792	16,973	18,610	19,495	17,002	17,629	7,543	10,086
63	San Jose State University	CA	Public	4-year	30,334	26,698	29,076	30,236	30,448	31,278	15,413	15,865
64	Santa Ana College	CA	Public	2-year	20,532	27,571	31,377	30,289	32,354	28,598	18,484	10,114
65	Santa Barbara City College	CA	Public	2-year	11,031	13,834	18,827	19,672	19,265	19,331	8,964	10,367
66	Santa Monica College	CA	Public	2-year	18,108	27,868	31,118	29,971	30,254	29,999	14,306	15,693
67	Santa Rosa Junior College	CA	Public	2-year	20,475	27,200	24,879	24,199	22,823	22,094	10,069	12,025
68	Sierra College	CA	Public	2-year	11,637	17,517	19,986	18,831	18,247	18,374	8,482	9,892
69	Southwestern College	CA	Public	2-year	13,010	17,994	19,476	20,409	18,362	19,591	9,232	10,359
70	Stanford University	CA	PrivNp	4-year	14,724	18,549	19,535	19,945	18,519	18,346	10,382	7,964
71	University of California, Berkeley	CA	Public	4-year	30,634	31,277	35,833	36,137	35,893	36,198	18,099	18,099
72	University of California, Davis	CA	Public	4-year	23,890	26,094	31,392	31,732	32,354	33,307	14,894	18,413
73	University of California, Irvine	CA	Public	4-year	16,808	20,211	26,994	27,189	27,479	28,895	13,832	15,063
74	University of California, Los Angeles	CA	Public	4-year	36,420	36,890	38,157	39,271	39,945	40,795	19,349	21,446
75	University of California, Riverside	CA	Public	4-year	8,708	13,015	20,692	20,900	20,947	21,207	10,529	10,678

See notes at end of table.

Table 312.20. Selected statistics for degree-granting postsecondary institutions enrolling more than 15,000 students in 2013, by selected institution and student characteristics: Selected years, 1990 through 2012–13—Continued

Fall enrollment, 2013					Full-time-equivalent enrollment		Earned degrees/certificates conferred, 2012–13					Total expenditures and deductions, 2012–13 (in thousands)[2]	Line number
Attendance status		Percent minority[3]	Student level										
Full-time	Part-time		Under-graduate	Postbacca-laureate	Fall 2012	Fall 2013	Certificates[4]	Associate's	Bachelor's	Master's	Doctor's[5]		
14	15	16	17	18	19	20	21	22	23	24	25	26	27
12,597,112	7,778,677	40.7	17,474,835	2,900,954	15,594,638	15,409,944	650,003	1,006,961	1,840,164	751,751	175,038	$498,938,564	i
5,795,626	3,459,870	43.6	7,704,976	1,550,520	7,109,742	7,058,586	148,783	331,977	952,640	397,054	94,561	256,600,258	ii
21,093	3,771	13.4	19,799	5,065	22,628	22,532	0	0	4,278	1,086	483	810,035	1
12,365	7,820	39.9	14,853	5,332	14,469	15,437	142	1,922	3,173	1,592	6	57,838	2
10,334	10,239	48.8	16,316	4,257	15,474	14,337	0	494	2,821	1,507	9	248,987	3
29,498	5,254	19.1	29,440	5,312	30,583	31,519	0	0	5,000	1,659	493	841,359	4
11,961	6,607	33.2	11,502	7,066	14,274	14,482	20	0	2,195	1,540	542	2,258,234	5
12,028	3,037	30.3	11,307	3,758	12,718	13,233	181	0	1,801	713	168	624,433	6
7,904	9,459	35.8	16,380	983	11,870	11,689	190	843	1,064	312	2	295,006	7
42,498	6,204	35.8	38,730	9,972	64,635	44,899	742	0	9,278	2,795	723	1,714,157	8
7,224	13,648	49.5	20,872	0	12,044	11,806	1,852	1,518	0	0	0	112,683	9
8,023	47,474	50.4	35,205	20,292	22,466	26,455	0	0	5,371	5,356	29	397,205	10
7,550	16,128	42.6	23,678	0	13,783	12,965	2,158	2,095	0	0	0	139,613	11
20,533	6,061	32.7	22,160	4,434	22,495	22,875	448	0	4,427	1,423	100	457,631	12
10,776	19,306	54.8	30,082	0	18,975	17,258	2,946	2,630	0	0	0	196,586	13
3,054	18,418	35.7	21,472	0	10,630	9,238	4,478	571	0	0	0	109,676	14
35,388	5,233	39.5	31,670	8,951	36,848	37,417	0	0	6,494	1,663	854	1,698,968	15
212,044	0	45.8	170,144	41,900	256,402	212,044	450	25,820	31,776	14,147	439	1,804,687	16
20,379	4,962	18.7	21,009	4,332	21,433	22,276	0	0	3,347	1,121	333	704,740	17
9,038	6,963	50.0	10,508	5,493	13,096	11,750	0	264	1,159	1,066	0	297,670	18
7,560	22,141	50.4	29,701	0	15,373	14,994	4,383	2,337	0	0	0	159,945	19
5,615	12,155	75.2	17,770	0	9,370	9,696	1,017	803	0	0	0	118,034	20
18,775	928	36.1	18,739	964	18,126	19,139	0	0	3,300	535	0	358,599	21
18,995	3,506	75.4	20,952	1,549	19,891	20,370	0	0	4,177	475	0	283,997	22
14,960	1,396	39.9	15,290	1,066	15,477	15,510	0	0	3,495	348	0	235,276	23
19,511	3,549	70.5	20,295	2,765	20,408	20,908	0	0	3,702	831	49	287,985	24
29,023	9,302	70.1	33,116	5,209	32,048	32,656	0	0	7,472	1,566	26	479,428	25
28,440	7,146	74.6	30,593	4,993	31,556	31,225	0	0	6,831	1,696	20	436,611	26
18,104	5,154	88.7	19,589	3,669	18,750	20,106	0	0	3,599	1,152	9	273,410	27
30,423	7,887	67.9	33,771	4,539	31,133	33,509	0	0	6,885	1,838	13	472,240	28
22,735	6,076	62.9	26,094	2,717	24,820	25,142	0	0	5,514	983	34	358,135	29
15,213	3,185	78.5	16,191	2,207	16,257	16,445	0	0	3,129	663	6	260,465	30
6,958	14,446	90.1	21,404	0	11,369	11,808	734	1,194	0	0	0	155,742	31
5,664	13,547	80.3	19,211	0	9,566	10,212	773	1,602	0	0	0	142,997	32
9,198	17,508	74.9	26,706	0	16,336	15,076	2,012	1,884	0	0	0	332,377	33
6,446	12,062	61.0	18,508	0	8,997	10,496	549	847	0	0	0	125,998	34
5,079	10,802	76.6	15,881	0	8,035	8,706	725	818	0	0	0	108,954	35
10,774	12,487	75.1	23,261	0	14,887	14,966	602	1,458	0	0	0	157,579	36
7,690	12,596	55.8	20,286	0	11,788	11,919	1,200	1,065	0	0	0	112,554	37
7,090	29,516	90.1	36,606	0	16,994	17,000	2,258	1,615	0	0	0	163,959	38
7,866	16,130	85.4	23,996	0	12,548	13,281	592	2,012	0	0	0	201,194	39
7,815	13,529	76.3	21,344	0	12,057	12,357	366	1,224	0	0	0	139,557	40
8,440	15,861	74.8	24,301	0	9,308	13,765	157	1,387	0	0	0	163,431	41
7,164	8,580	48.8	15,744	0	10,368	10,045	292	411	0	0	0	137,561	42
6,654	11,964	55.6	18,618	0	10,009	10,671	861	1,245	0	0	0	86,951	43
9,530	14,490	84.3	24,020	0	14,587	14,395	2,822	843	0	0	0	197,311	44
4,462	15,173	80.4	19,635	0	10,407	9,556	480	494	0	0	0	113,595	45
4,489	15,591	69.3	20,080	0	10,372	9,723	603	1,046	0	0	0	111,945	46
4,526	14,236	68.1	18,762	0	9,267	9,306	732	685	0	0	0	105,282	47
6,241	10,843	60.2	17,084	0	9,535	9,881	616	1,191	0	0	0	90,413	48
10,499	17,982	87.0	28,481	0	16,553	16,536	836	1,962	0	0	0	233,268	49
8,877	9,330	53.3	10,074	8,133	12,857	12,511	58	112	1,611	3,101	107	204,459	50
8,497	13,389	63.1	21,886	0	12,333	12,992	478	1,641	0	0	0	146,489	51
8,252	16,413	54.1	24,665	0	13,650	13,762	1,694	1,614	0	0	0	172,418	52
9,463	15,805	86.3	25,268	0	13,050	14,769	610	1,646	0	0	0	179,528	53
4,389	12,159	92.8	16,548	0	9,130	8,471	287	868	0	0	0	105,756	54
4,863	13,302	77.3	18,165	0	8,506	9,329	939	1,525	0	0	0	132,842	55
6,144	17,365	71.4	23,509	0	12,190	11,974	532	1,476	0	0	0	125,156	56
6,334	14,537	42.1	20,871	0	11,628	11,215	1,833	1,088	0	0	0	124,762	57
3,828	12,482	75.0	16,310	0	8,112	8,019	343	626	0	0	0	103,852	58
6,409	17,842	64.6	24,251	0	12,445	12,399	332	989	0	0	0	102,671	59
26,859	5,040	57.4	27,099	4,800	27,714	28,810	0	0	5,881	1,777	107	474,173	60
24,422	5,483	70.2	26,156	3,749	27,135	26,574	0	0	6,344	1,361	57	463,583	61
7,062	10,567	75.6	17,629	0	9,977	10,610	502	2,441	0	0	0	152,737	62
24,196	7,082	72.4	25,862	5,416	26,164	26,967	0	0	5,209	2,352	0	402,848	63
3,435	25,163	69.1	28,598	0	14,211	11,883	1,463	1,683	0	0	0	107,014	64
8,516	10,815	51.2	19,331	0	11,744	12,147	1,146	1,695	0	0	0	149,505	65
10,720	19,279	70.6	29,999	0	17,201	17,193	1,373	1,207	0	0	0	233,701	66
6,712	15,382	43.2	22,094	0	12,373	11,876	3,040	1,952	0	0	0	152,445	67
6,951	11,423	38.6	18,374	0	10,738	10,786	480	2,132	0	0	0	118,927	68
7,672	11,919	74.5	19,591	0	9,799	11,674	227	867	0	0	0	133,284	69
15,585	2,761	46.8	7,274	11,072	16,640	16,643	0	0	1,660	2,310	1,052	3,972,849	70
34,675	1,523	60.0	25,951	10,247	34,971	35,256	0	0	7,775	2,199	1,304	2,400,079	71
31,986	1,321	61.0	26,533	6,774	31,585	32,493	0	0	7,015	1,055	1,009	3,576,494	72
28,046	849	74.9	23,530	5,365	26,966	28,370	0	0	5,963	1,255	622	2,271,185	73
39,794	1,001	61.7	28,674	12,121	39,334	40,181	0	0	7,329	2,978	1,393	5,514,581	74
20,653	554	81.1	18,621	2,586	20,587	20,871	0	0	4,402	435	255	678,403	75

See notes at end of table.

Table 312.20. Selected statistics for degree-granting postsecondary institutions enrolling more than 15,000 students in 2013, by selected institution and student characteristics: Selected years, 1990 through 2012–13—Continued

Line number	Institution	State	Control[1]	Level	Fall 1990	Fall 2000	Fall 2010	Fall 2011	Fall 2012	Total	Male	Female
						Total fall enrollment				Fall enrollment, 2013	Sex	
1	2	3	4	5	6	7	8	9	10	11	12	13
76	University of California, San Diego	CA	Public	4-year	17,790	20,197	29,176	28,593	28,294	29,517	15,752	13,765
77	University of California, Santa Barbara	CA	Public	4-year	18,385	19,962	22,218	21,685	21,927	22,225	10,848	11,377
78	University of California, Santa Cruz	CA	Public	4-year	10,054	12,144	17,187	17,454	17,404	17,203	8,160	9,043
79	University of Southern California	CA	PrivNp	4-year	28,374	29,194	36,896	38,010	39,958	41,368	19,897	21,471
80	Colorado State University, Fort Collins	CO	Public	4-year	26,828	26,807	30,155	30,467	30,659	31,186	15,194	15,992
81	Colorado Technical University, Online	CO	PrivFp	4-year	†	†	29,588	24,617	22,608	20,826	7,588	13,238
82	Front Range Community College	CO	Public	2-year	9,706	12,962	20,092	20,568	20,527	19,619	8,537	11,082
83	Metropolitan State University of Denver	CO	Public	4-year	17,400	17,688	23,948	23,789	23,381	22,752	10,441	12,311
84	University of Colorado, Boulder	CO	Public	4-year	28,600	29,352	32,697	32,558	31,945	32,017	17,671	14,346
85	University of Colorado, Denver	CO	Public	4-year	11,512	13,737	24,108	22,495	22,396	22,206	9,657	12,549
86	University of Connecticut	CT	Public	4-year	25,497	19,393	25,498	25,868	25,483	25,911	12,957	12,954
87	University of Delaware	DE	Public	4-year	20,818	19,072	21,177	21,489	21,856	22,166	9,778	12,388
88	George Washington University	DC	PrivNp	4-year	19,103	20,527	25,135	25,260	25,653	25,264	11,115	14,149
89	Georgetown University	DC	PrivNp	4-year	11,525	12,427	16,937	17,130	17,357	17,849	8,264	9,585
90	Broward College	FL	Public	4-year	24,365	27,389	40,375	42,198	42,309	43,883	18,035	25,848
91	Eastern Florida State College	FL	Public	4-year	14,319	13,265	18,096	17,917	17,202	16,711	7,042	9,669
92	Edison State College	FL	Public	4-year	8,919	8,919	16,951	17,107	15,731	15,423	6,163	9,260
93	Everest University, South Orlando	FL	PrivFp	4-year	†	938	15,189	25,537	33,852	29,693	6,911	22,782
94	Florida Atlantic University	FL	Public	4-year	12,767	21,046	28,270	29,246	29,994	30,759	13,178	17,581
95	Florida International University	FL	Public	4-year	22,466	31,945	42,197	44,616	46,171	47,663	21,064	26,599
96	Florida State College at Jacksonville	FL	Public	4-year	20,974	20,838	28,642	30,863	30,053	28,134	11,532	16,602
97	Florida State University	FL	Public	4-year	28,170	33,971	40,416	41,087	40,695	40,909	18,407	22,502
98	Full Sail University	FL	PrivFp	4-year	†	1,910	15,695	20,160	23,497	20,949	15,170	5,779
99	Hillsborough Community College	FL	Public	2-year	19,134	18,497	27,955	28,329	27,754	26,590	11,565	15,025
100	Indian River State College	FL	Public	4-year	12,774	13,186	17,511	17,528	17,816	17,248	6,977	10,271
101	Keiser University, Fort Lauderdale	FL	PrivNp	4-year	104	3,086	16,968	17,042	16,713	17,129	5,432	11,697
102	Miami Dade College	FL	Public	4-year	50,078	46,834	61,674	63,736	66,701	66,298	27,724	38,574
103	Nova Southeastern University	FL	PrivNp	4-year	9,562	18,587	28,741	28,457	26,808	25,670	7,844	17,826
104	Palm Beach State College	FL	Public	4-year	18,392	17,326	29,534	29,354	29,974	29,763	12,887	16,876
105	Saint Leo University	FL	PrivNp	4-year	5,308	8,720	15,565	15,564	15,986	16,275	6,773	9,502
106	Saint Petersburg College	FL	Public	4-year	20,012	19,900	31,793	33,128	32,612	31,820	12,600	19,220
107	Santa Fe College	FL	Public	4-year	11,053	12,464	15,745	15,493	15,362	15,113	6,738	8,375
108	Seminole State College of Florida	FL	Public	4-year	7,799	9,042	18,028	18,514	19,450	18,427	8,003	10,424
109	University of Central Florida	FL	Public	4-year	21,541	33,713	56,106	58,465	59,601	59,589	26,844	32,745
110	University of Florida	FL	Public	4-year	35,477	45,114	49,827	49,589	49,913	49,878	23,028	26,850
111	University of Miami	FL	PrivNp	4-year	13,841	13,963	15,657	16,068	16,172	16,935	8,268	8,667
112	University of North Florida	FL	Public	4-year	8,021	12,550	16,153	16,198	16,201	16,083	7,093	8,990
113	University of South Florida, Main Campus	FL	Public	4-year	32,326	35,561	40,431	39,566	41,116	41,428	17,988	23,440
114	Valencia College	FL	Public	4-year	18,438	27,565	41,583	42,631	42,915	42,180	18,843	23,337
115	Georgia Institute of Technology, Main Campus	GA	Public	4-year	12,241	14,805	20,720	20,941	21,557	21,471	14,846	6,625
116	Georgia Perimeter College	GA	Public	2-year	13,944	13,708	25,113	26,996	23,619	21,123	8,647	12,476
117	Georgia Southern University	GA	Public	4-year	12,249	14,184	19,691	20,212	20,574	20,517	9,860	10,657
118	Georgia State University	GA	Public	4-year	23,336	23,625	31,533	32,022	32,087	32,165	13,372	18,793
119	Kennesaw State University	GA	Public	4-year	10,018	13,360	23,452	24,175	24,604	24,629	10,204	14,425
120	University of Georgia	GA	Public	4-year	28,395	31,288	34,677	34,816	34,519	34,536	14,773	19,763
121	University of North Georgia	GA	Public	4-year	†	†	†	†	†	15,455	6,775	8,680
122	University of Hawaii at Manoa	HI	Public	4-year	18,799	17,263	20,337	20,429	20,426	20,006	8,849	11,157
123	Boise State University	ID	Public	4-year	13,367	16,287	19,992	19,664	22,344	21,981	9,973	12,008
124	Brigham Young University, Idaho	ID	PrivNp	4-year	7,795	8,949	14,933	18,110	23,261	27,692	11,780	15,912
125	College of DuPage	IL	Public	2-year	29,185	28,862	26,722	26,209	26,156	28,627	13,325	15,302
126	College of Lake County	IL	Public	2-year	13,526	14,441	18,091	17,389	17,577	17,685	7,934	9,751
127	DePaul University	IL	PrivNp	4-year	15,711	20,548	25,145	25,398	24,966	24,414	11,397	13,017
128	DeVry University, Illinois	IL	PrivFp	4-year	3,303	4,095	40,859	27,921	24,246	26,851	12,381	14,470
129	Illinois State University	IL	Public	4-year	22,662	20,755	21,134	21,310	20,706	20,272	8,878	11,394
130	Joliet Junior College	IL	Public	2-year	9,645	11,334	15,676	15,322	15,589	16,869	7,791	9,078
131	Loyola University Chicago	IL	PrivNp	4-year	14,780	12,605	15,951	16,040	15,720	15,957	5,771	10,186
132	Moraine Valley Community College	IL	Public	2-year	13,601	12,972	17,387	18,169	16,650	16,106	7,668	8,438
133	Northern Illinois University	IL	Public	4-year	24,509	23,248	23,850	22,990	21,869	21,138	10,262	10,876
134	Northwestern University	IL	PrivNp	4-year	17,041	16,952	20,481	20,959	21,215	21,592	11,489	10,103
135	Southern Illinois University, Carbondale	IL	Public	4-year	24,078	22,552	20,037	19,817	18,847	17,964	9,644	8,320
136	University of Chicago	IL	PrivNp	4-year	10,867	12,531	15,152	14,979	15,245	15,048	8,722	6,326
137	University of Illinois at Chicago	IL	Public	4-year	24,959	24,942	27,850	28,091	27,875	28,038	12,860	15,178
138	University of Illinois at Urbana-Champaign	IL	Public	4-year	38,163	38,465	43,862	44,407	44,520	44,942	24,798	20,144
139	Ball State University	IN	Public	4-year	20,343	19,004	22,083	22,147	21,053	20,503	8,210	12,293
140	Indiana University, Bloomington	IN	Public	4-year	35,451	37,076	42,464	42,731	42,133	46,817	23,141	23,676
141	Indiana University-Purdue University, Indianapolis	IN	Public	4-year	27,517	27,525	30,566	30,530	30,451	30,488	13,273	17,215
142	Ivy Tech Community College	IN	Public	2-year	4,871	6,748	20,847	21,046	100,272	98,778	40,884	57,894
143	Purdue University, Main Campus	IN	Public	4-year	37,588	39,667	41,063	40,849	40,393	39,794	23,234	16,560
144	Vincennes University	IN	Public	4-year	9,162	9,169	16,595	16,822	17,530	18,383	10,203	8,180
145	Ashford University	IA	PrivFp	4-year	311	616	63,096	74,596	77,734	58,104	16,414	41,690
146	Des Moines Area Community College	IA	Public	2-year	10,553	10,998	24,658	25,425	23,685	20,167	9,304	10,863

See notes at end of table.

Table 312.20. Selected statistics for degree-granting postsecondary institutions enrolling more than 15,000 students in 2013, by selected institution and student characteristics: Selected years, 1990 through 2012–13—Continued

Fall enrollment, 2013					Full-time-equivalent enrollment		Earned degrees/certificates conferred, 2012–13					Total expenditures and deductions, 2012–13 (in thousands)[2]	Line number
Attendance status			Student level										
Full-time	Part-time	Percent minority[3]	Under-graduate	Postbacca-laureate	Fall 2012	Fall 2013	Certificates[4]	Associate's	Bachelor's	Master's	Doctor's[5]		
14	15	16	17	18	19	20	21	22	23	24	25	26	27
28,606	911	67.4	23,805	5,712	27,715	28,963	0	0	6,344	1,198	684	3,519,031	76
21,771	454	54.0	19,362	2,863	21,666	21,947	0	0	5,222	584	387	898,421	77
16,755	448	59.8	15,695	1,508	17,118	16,932	0	0	4,038	271	160	640,006	78
35,895	5,473	53.8	18,445	22,923	36,793	37,993	0	0	4,740	6,332	1,554	3,273,784	79
23,371	7,815	18.5	23,548	7,638	26,030	26,329	0	0	4,736	1,578	370	871,096	80
12,777	8,049	50.0	18,061	2,765	17,916	15,938	0	2,288	2,594	1,174	0	270,932	81
6,120	13,499	24.3	19,619	0	11,299	10,652	1,771	1,673	0	0	0	107,763	82
13,508	9,244	35.6	22,289	463	17,539	17,232	0	0	2,962	112	0	164,548	83
26,242	5,775	21.0	26,096	5,921	28,309	28,421	0	0	5,752	1,281	557	1,140,271	84
11,800	10,406	32.3	13,010	9,196	15,807	15,783	0	0	2,153	2,008	669	1,466,865	85
22,482	3,429	26.9	18,032	7,879	23,250	23,756	0	26	5,122	1,557	720	1,908,404	86
19,685	2,481	20.6	18,487	3,679	20,391	20,651	0	256	3,741	720	229	843,382	87
17,109	8,155	32.0	10,357	14,907	20,555	20,233	175	192	2,454	4,210	1,071	1,119,772	88
14,407	3,442	30.3	7,636	10,213	15,407	15,726	13	0	1,836	2,965	973	1,117,893	89
13,342	30,541	76.6	43,883	0	24,762	25,667	1,401	6,084	354	0	0	257,811	90
5,929	10,782	28.7	16,711	0	10,721	10,280	1,119	2,836	0	0	0	107,889	91
5,040	10,383	41.7	15,423	0	9,385	9,230	250	2,300	343	0	0	92,264	92
15,437	14,256	61.0	29,460	233	24,428	21,036	236	2,422	348	48	0	163,839	93
17,779	12,980	50.3	25,790	4,969	22,453	22,888	0	297	5,124	1,415	103	453,926	94
31,932	15,731	86.7	39,142	8,521	36,376	38,174	0	89	7,746	3,014	407	780,422	95
9,217	18,917	44.2	28,134	0	17,862	16,851	2,325	4,964	533	0	0	205,902	96
34,882	6,027	30.4	32,528	8,381	36,994	37,213	0	133	7,938	2,316	736	987,280	97
20,949	0	54.5	18,880	2,069	23,497	20,949	279	185	2,635	1,024	0	345,351	98
11,532	15,058	56.0	26,590	0	17,354	16,588	1,957	3,727	0	0	0	187,067	99
5,940	11,308	38.4	17,248	0	10,823	10,503	1,166	2,682	429	0	0	123,920	100
12,264	4,865	59.1	16,039	1,090	13,385	14,166	4	3,842	636	191	7	324,690	101
26,579	39,719	92.7	66,298	0	42,550	42,607	3,068	10,425	829	0	0	442,417	102
13,390	12,280	61.5	5,156	20,514	18,730	18,100	1	1	1,538	3,708	1,729	578,845	103
9,460	20,303	57.6	29,763	0	18,166	17,653	1,699	4,598	217	0	0	160,941	104
12,228	4,047	53.8	12,640	3,635	13,485	13,817	38	962	2,824	1,216	0	145,586	105
9,118	22,702	30.9	31,820	0	18,843	18,279	708	4,077	1,141	0	0	200,871	106
6,059	9,054	36.6	15,113	0	9,882	9,713	517	2,688	90	0	0	107,094	107
6,885	11,542	46.9	18,427	0	12,358	11,543	3,202	2,788	46	0	0	115,526	108
39,966	19,623	40.7	51,333	8,256	48,072	47,696	0	439	12,320	2,285	280	807,308	109
42,490	7,388	36.6	33,168	16,710	45,520	45,282	0	840	8,244	3,929	1,964	2,366,749	110
15,597	1,338	45.7	11,380	5,555	15,446	16,116	5	0	2,451	912	874	2,518,542	111
10,829	5,254	28.4	14,263	1,820	13,072	12,904	0	318	3,221	542	40	240,423	112
29,437	11,991	40.2	31,100	10,328	33,825	34,082	0	153	7,617	2,545	448	1,158,477	113
16,523	25,657	62.2	42,180	0	27,457	26,877	4,209	7,117	10	0	0	239,062	114
18,743	2,728	36.6	14,558	6,913	19,880	19,782	0	0	3,122	1,961	488	1,338,734	115
8,140	12,983	65.6	21,123	0	14,357	12,499	12	2,014	0	0	0	150,967	116
16,767	3,750	34.8	17,904	2,613	18,217	18,213	0	0	2,912	762	63	319,618	117
23,677	8,488	61.5	24,868	7,297	26,674	27,017	26	0	4,608	2,308	450	617,657	118
17,690	6,939	33.5	22,621	2,008	20,489	20,440	26	0	3,491	709	16	320,814	119
31,364	3,172	24.8	26,278	8,258	32,409	32,575	0	0	6,872	1,662	901	1,243,595	120
10,205	5,250	18.6	14,851	604	†	12,306	31	918	1,212	142	29	157,006	121
14,803	5,203	76.9	14,499	5,507	17,028	16,787	0	0	3,202	1,049	421	967,771	122
13,264	8,717	17.1	19,026	2,955	16,971	16,692	22	168	2,716	691	11	329,780	123
14,376	13,316	15.9	27,692	0	18,388	19,607	0	1,945	3,297	0	0	216,818	124
9,908	18,719	41.6	28,627	0	15,177	16,193	1,668	1,921	0	0	0	186,615	125
4,764	12,921	51.5	17,685	0	9,186	9,102	4,123	1,785	0	0	0	144,938	126
18,706	5,708	38.0	16,420	7,994	21,311	20,917	2	0	3,802	2,797	318	524,143	127
7,571	19,280	45.2	20,366	6,485	13,396	15,088	0	1,135	2,595	2,876	0	99,845	128
17,864	2,408	18.8	17,749	2,523	19,223	18,779	0	0	4,438	722	51	529,530	129
5,849	11,020	38.3	16,869	0	9,228	9,549	486	1,484	0	0	0	135,092	130
13,463	2,494	32.7	10,168	5,789	14,232	14,425	5	0	2,220	1,617	585	478,366	131
6,764	9,342	37.2	16,106	0	10,229	9,900	779	1,798	0	0	0	120,341	132
16,053	5,085	35.0	15,814	5,324	18,664	17,975	0	0	3,848	1,339	297	611,776	133
17,190	4,402	36.0	9,283	12,309	18,736	18,880	243	0	2,193	3,274	1,009	1,899,301	134
14,478	3,486	31.0	13,306	4,658	16,503	15,802	0	89	3,863	998	354	775,425	135
12,848	2,200	36.2	5,703	9,345	13,685	13,690	0	0	1,278	2,717	710	3,240,518	136
23,239	4,799	53.2	16,671	11,367	24,862	25,028	0	0	3,809	2,170	974	2,566,405	137
41,118	3,824	34.9	32,695	12,247	42,133	42,551	3	0	7,645	3,222	1,159	2,379,757	138
16,588	3,915	13.0	16,300	4,203	18,713	18,053	0	49	3,217	1,604	68	428,787	139
37,467	9,350	17.7	36,862	9,955	39,084	41,092	182	20	7,300	2,607	771	1,352,296	140
21,097	9,391	23.4	22,409	8,079	24,179	24,730	481	160	3,783	1,567	755	1,150,123	141
34,212	64,566	24.0	98,778	0	58,682	55,889	7,730	9,265	0	0	0	640,018	142
34,871	4,923	17.9	30,446	9,348	37,382	36,726	368	93	7,058	1,545	926	1,618,365	143
6,049	12,334	19.2	18,383	0	10,772	11,026	158	1,684	132	0	0	121,042	144
58,078	26	52.0	50,895	7,209	77,707	58,088	0	2,065	12,722	4,548	0	529,040	145
7,735	12,432	18.9	20,167	0	13,554	11,909	1,041	2,109	0	0	0	145,814	146

See notes at end of table.

Table 312.20. Selected statistics for degree-granting postsecondary institutions enrolling more than 15,000 students in 2013, by selected institution and student characteristics: Selected years, 1990 through 2012–13—Continued

Line number	Institution	State	Con-trol[1]	Level	Total fall enrollment					Fall enrollment, 2013		
					Fall 1990	Fall 2000	Fall 2010	Fall 2011	Fall 2012	Total	Sex	
											Male	Female
1	2	3	4	5	6	7	8	9	10	11	12	13
147	Iowa State University	IA	Public	4-year	25,737	26,845	28,682	29,611	30,748	32,955	18,466	14,489
148	Kaplan University, Davenport Campus	IA	PrivFp	4-year	641	376	77,966	56,606	48,865	52,407	12,838	39,569
149	Kirkwood Community College	IA	Public	2-year	8,623	11,645	18,456	17,625	16,659	15,076	7,500	7,576
150	University of Iowa	IA	Public	4-year	28,785	28,311	29,518	29,810	30,129	29,748	14,372	15,376
151	Johnson County Community College	KS	Public	2-year	13,740	16,383	20,865	21,020	20,421	19,672	9,157	10,515
152	Kansas State University	KS	Public	4-year	21,137	21,929	23,588	23,863	24,378	24,581	12,459	12,122
153	University of Kansas	KS	Public	4-year	26,434	25,920	28,697	27,939	27,135	26,968	13,137	13,831
154	Eastern Kentucky University	KY	Public	4-year	15,290	13,285	16,567	16,062	15,968	16,111	6,949	9,162
155	Northern Kentucky University	KY	Public	4-year	11,254	12,080	15,716	15,724	15,634	15,263	6,713	8,550
156	University of Kentucky	KY	Public	4-year	22,538	23,114	27,108	27,226	28,034	28,435	13,569	14,866
157	University of Louisville	KY	Public	4-year	22,979	19,771	21,234	21,152	21,239	21,444	10,338	11,106
158	Western Kentucky University	KY	Public	4-year	15,170	15,481	20,897	21,036	21,110	20,448	8,559	11,889
159	Delgado Community College	LA	Public	2-year	11,614	12,784	18,767	20,436	18,096	18,698	6,379	12,319
160	Louisiana State U. and Agricultural & Mechanical	LA	Public	4-year	26,112	31,527	29,451	29,718	30,225	30,478	14,793	15,685
161	University of Louisiana at Lafayette	LA	Public	4-year	15,764	15,742	16,763	16,885	16,688	16,646	7,435	9,211
162	Anne Arundel Community College	MD	Public	2-year	12,148	11,761	17,665	17,957	17,650	16,463	6,679	9,784
163	Community College of Baltimore County	MD	Public	2-year	†	18,168	26,425	26,271	25,188	23,981	9,502	14,479
164	Johns Hopkins University	MD	PrivNp	4-year	13,363	17,774	20,977	20,996	20,871	20,918	10,230	10,688
165	Montgomery College	MD	Public	2-year	14,361	20,923	26,015	26,996	27,453	26,155	12,288	13,867
166	Towson University	MD	Public	4-year	15,035	16,729	21,840	21,464	21,960	22,499	8,572	13,927
167	University of Maryland, College Park	MD	Public	4-year	34,829	33,189	37,641	37,631	37,248	37,272	19,712	17,560
168	University of Maryland, University College	MD	Public	4-year	14,476	18,276	39,577	42,713	42,268	39,557	19,544	20,013
169	Boston University	MA	PrivNp	4-year	27,996	28,318	32,179	32,439	32,603	32,411	13,628	18,783
170	Harvard University	MA	PrivNp	4-year	22,851	24,279	27,594	27,392	28,147	28,297	14,478	13,819
171	Northeastern University	MA	PrivNp	4-year	30,510	23,897	29,519	26,959	27,694	20,053	10,092	9,961
172	University of Massachusetts, Amherst	MA	Public	4-year	26,025	24,416	27,569	28,084	28,236	28,518	14,467	14,051
173	University of Massachusetts, Boston	MA	Public	4-year	13,723	13,346	15,454	15,741	15,874	16,277	6,664	9,613
174	University of Massachusetts, Lowell	MA	Public	4-year	14,259	12,189	14,702	15,431	16,294	16,932	10,017	6,915
175	Central Michigan University	MI	Public	4-year	18,286	26,845	28,292	28,194	27,626	26,841	11,501	15,340
176	Eastern Michigan University	MI	Public	4-year	25,011	23,561	23,565	23,419	23,518	23,447	9,557	13,890
177	Grand Rapids Community College	MI	Public	2-year	12,054	13,400	17,870	17,575	17,448	16,590	7,963	8,627
178	Grand Valley State University	MI	Public	4-year	11,725	18,569	24,541	24,662	24,654	24,477	9,981	14,496
179	Lansing Community College	MI	Public	2-year	22,343	16,011	21,969	20,603	19,082	17,562	7,970	9,592
180	Macomb Community College	MI	Public	2-year	31,538	22,001	24,468	23,969	23,729	23,446	11,039	12,407
181	Michigan State University	MI	Public	4-year	44,307	43,366	46,985	47,825	48,783	49,317	23,884	25,433
182	Oakland Community College	MI	Public	2-year	28,069	23,188	28,925	29,158	27,296	26,405	11,338	15,067
183	Oakland University	MI	Public	4-year	12,400	15,235	19,053	19,379	19,740	20,169	8,232	11,937
184	University of Michigan, Ann Arbor	MI	Public	4-year	36,391	38,103	41,924	42,716	43,426	43,710	22,830	20,880
185	Wayne County Community College District	MI	Public	2-year	11,986	9,008	21,198	20,440	18,176	18,119	6,067	12,052
186	Wayne State University	MI	Public	4-year	33,872	30,408	31,505	30,765	28,938	27,897	12,133	15,764
187	Western Michigan University	MI	Public	4-year	26,989	28,657	25,045	25,086	24,598	24,294	11,741	12,553
188	Capella University	MN	PrivFp	4-year	†	36	39,457	36,375	35,754	34,007	8,527	25,480
189	Minnesota State University, Mankato	MN	Public	4-year	16,575	12,842	15,435	15,709	15,441	15,426	7,210	8,216
190	Saint Cloud State University	MN	Public	4-year	17,075	15,181	18,650	17,604	16,922	16,765	7,949	8,816
191	University of Minnesota, Twin Cities	MN	Public	4-year	57,168	45,481	51,721	52,557	51,853	51,526	25,050	26,476
192	Walden University	MN	PrivFp	4-year	422	1,544	47,456	48,982	50,209	51,016	11,696	39,320
193	Mississippi State University	MS	Public	4-year	14,391	16,561	19,644	20,424	20,365	20,161	10,406	9,755
194	University of Mississippi	MS	Public	4-year	11,288	12,118	17,085	18,224	18,794	19,431	8,767	10,664
195	University of Southern Mississippi	MS	Public	4-year	13,490	14,509	15,778	16,604	16,468	15,249	5,595	9,654
196	Columbia College	MO	PrivNp	4-year	4,214	7,948	16,962	18,091	17,830	16,946	6,867	10,079
197	Metropolitan Community College, Kansas City	MO	Public	2-year	9,625	8,117	6,539	6,209	20,141	19,234	8,328	10,906
198	Missouri State University, Springfield	MO	Public	4-year	19,480	17,703	20,383	20,276	20,629	21,271	9,020	12,251
199	Saint Louis Community College	MO	Public	2-year	32,347	6,749	8,716	29,200	26,603	24,005	9,780	14,225
200	Saint Louis University	MO	PrivNp	4-year	12,891	13,847	17,709	17,859	17,640	17,343	7,192	10,151
201	University of Missouri, Columbia	MO	Public	4-year	25,058	23,309	32,341	33,762	34,704	34,616	16,321	18,295
202	University of Missouri, Kansas City	MO	Public	4-year	11,263	12,762	15,259	15,473	15,990	15,718	6,839	8,879
203	University of Missouri, Saint Louis	MO	Public	4-year	15,393	15,397	16,791	16,809	16,705	16,809	6,806	10,003
204	Webster University	MO	PrivNp	4-year	8,745	13,783	19,342	19,224	18,456	17,904	7,577	10,327
205	Metropolitan Community College Area	NE	Public	2-year	8,516	11,534	18,523	18,518	17,376	15,752	7,107	8,645
206	University of Nebraska, Lincoln	NE	Public	4-year	24,453	22,268	24,610	24,593	24,207	24,445	12,892	11,553
207	University of Nebraska, Omaha	NE	Public	4-year	15,804	13,479	14,665	14,712	14,786	15,227	7,211	8,016
208	College of Southern Nevada	NV	Public	4-year	14,161	29,905	42,747	37,717	35,678	34,177	15,467	18,710
209	University of Nevada, Las Vegas	NV	Public	4-year	17,937	22,041	28,203	27,364	27,389	27,848	12,360	15,488
210	University of Nevada, Reno	NV	Public	4-year	11,487	13,149	17,680	18,004	18,227	18,776	8,929	9,847
211	Southern New Hampshire University	NH	PrivNp	4-year	6,403	4,584	8,034	11,851	17,454	28,389	11,456	16,933
212	Bergen Community College	NJ	Public	2-year	12,119	11,993	17,197	17,271	17,015	15,882	8,252	7,630
213	Montclair State University	NJ	Public	4-year	13,067	13,502	18,402	18,498	18,382	19,464	7,152	12,312
214	Rutgers University, New Brunswick	NJ	Public	4-year	33,016	35,236	38,912	39,950	40,434	48,036	22,267	25,769
215	Thomas Edison State College	NJ	Public	4-year	7,813	8,137	18,736	20,251	20,606	20,877	10,816	10,061

See notes at end of table.

Table 312.20. Selected statistics for degree-granting postsecondary institutions enrolling more than 15,000 students in 2013, by selected institution and student characteristics: Selected years, 1990 through 2012–13—Continued

Fall enrollment, 2013					Full-time-equivalent enrollment		Earned degrees/certificates conferred, 2012–13					Total expenditures and deductions, 2012–13 (in thousands)[2]	Line number
Attendance status		Percent minority[3]	Student level										
Full-time	Part-time		Under-graduate	Postbacca-laureate	Fall 2012	Fall 2013	Certificates[4]	Associate's	Bachelor's	Master's	Doctor's[5]		
14	15	16	17	18	19	20	21	22	23	24	25	26	27
29,398	3,557	13.2	27,659	5,296	28,600	30,747	0	0	5,047	783	491	1,051,387	147
12,935	39,472	47.1	40,349	12,058	25,671	28,382	44	3,097	5,601	2,586	163	575,656	148
6,960	8,116	17.9	15,076	0	10,938	9,685	465	2,107	0	0	0	139,522	149
24,295	5,453	16.5	21,974	7,774	26,680	26,369	40	0	4,565	1,415	1,045	2,637,132	150
6,331	13,341	22.2	19,672	0	11,325	10,810	1,333	1,724	0	0	0	181,523	151
20,549	4,032	15.7	20,169	4,412	21,845	22,094	0	49	3,561	988	263	727,325	152
23,034	3,934	19.5	19,217	7,751	24,619	24,542	8	0	4,265	1,547	870	1,164,769	153
11,651	4,460	11.3	13,891	2,220	13,496	13,386	50	208	2,357	773	9	271,844	154
10,597	4,666	12.2	12,794	2,469	12,626	12,413	15	98	2,109	491	162	224,749	155
25,658	2,777	16.8	21,441	6,994	26,214	26,727	6	0	4,022	1,299	864	2,363,103	156
16,364	5,080	21.4	15,954	5,490	18,130	18,349	24	28	2,731	1,320	513	881,002	157
14,315	6,133	17.0	17,509	2,939	17,229	16,706	67	267	2,623	992	14	324,913	158
7,906	10,792	64.0	18,698	0	11,394	11,529	1,686	1,242	0	0	0	134,082	159
27,172	3,306	22.6	24,923	5,555	28,356	28,456	0	0	4,529	1,167	605	1,031,139	160
13,221	3,425	28.1	15,053	1,593	14,712	14,575	0	0	2,346	424	52	258,267	161
4,940	11,523	32.8	16,463	0	9,312	8,809	608	1,581	0	0	0	147,842	162
7,983	15,998	53.0	23,981	0	14,018	13,354	606	2,086	0	0	0	209,070	163
13,256	7,662	36.8	6,117	14,801	16,091	16,186	0	0	1,691	4,439	662	4,698,581	164
9,240	16,915	70.1	26,155	0	15,785	14,919	359	2,318	0	0	0	282,858	165
17,786	4,713	29.7	18,779	3,720	18,917	19,582	0	0	4,147	1,161	31	344,430	166
32,199	5,073	40.4	26,658	10,614	34,159	34,123	70	0	7,214	2,686	726	1,606,590	167
6,131	33,426	55.2	26,740	12,817	20,313	19,093	560	472	4,159	3,918	80	362,534	168
25,797	6,614	33.3	18,165	14,246	28,577	28,341	0	0	4,071	4,197	1,175	1,648,031	169
20,370	7,927	38.8	10,534	17,763	23,394	23,434	0	9	1,803	4,041	1,464	4,248,371	170
17,957	2,096	29.8	13,223	6,830	22,367	18,758	0	22	3,915	3,449	781	881,890	171
22,808	5,710	22.1	22,134	6,384	24,729	24,941	239	73	5,363	1,338	334	956,149	172
9,999	6,278	43.8	12,366	3,911	12,067	12,421	35	0	2,275	1,017	37	332,389	173
10,322	6,610	26.4	12,734	4,198	12,330	12,868	124	48	2,031	745	102	317,690	174
19,653	7,188	20.3	20,534	6,307	23,047	22,364	0	0	3,913	1,863	97	423,246	175
14,493	8,954	30.3	19,189	4,258	17,849	17,968	0	0	3,108	1,299	28	342,310	176
5,669	10,921	26.3	16,590	0	10,019	9,336	170	1,726	0	0	0	140,951	177
19,853	4,624	14.7	21,235	3,242	21,646	21,633	21	0	4,487	986	51	401,527	178
6,587	10,975	22.3	17,562	0	11,175	10,272	1,790	1,871	0	0	0	137,027	179
7,508	15,938	21.2	23,446	0	13,031	12,859	713	2,768	0	0	0	152,429	180
43,276	6,041	19.7	37,985	11,332	44,946	45,593	122	0	7,909	2,042	993	2,060,044	181
8,058	18,347	37.2	26,405	0	14,918	14,218	477	2,969	0	0	0	196,634	182
13,863	6,306	18.8	16,594	3,575	15,822	16,325	0	0	2,827	822	106	280,795	183
41,152	2,558	28.4	28,283	15,427	41,895	42,117	0	0	6,741	4,281	1,647	5,942,420	184
3,862	14,257	81.4	18,119	0	8,695	8,649	855	2,389	0	0	0	146,984	185
18,096	9,801	37.1	18,602	9,295	22,444	21,908	2	0	2,657	1,956	777	843,600	186
17,042	7,252	21.2	19,198	5,096	20,178	19,804	0	0	3,887	1,402	114	557,918	187
2,108	31,899	53.8	7,947	26,060	15,018	14,367	0	0	899	4,706	889	366,699	188
12,097	3,329	14.6	13,467	1,959	13,408	13,386	37	45	2,381	539	9	202,988	189
10,447	6,318	15.8	15,134	1,631	13,387	12,953	13	159	2,387	543	14	197,053	190
38,767	12,759	20.2	34,449	17,077	43,823	43,612	178	0	7,559	3,228	1,826	2,823,887	191
29,437	21,579	53.4	8,205	42,811	38,174	37,761	1	0	1,412	7,104	805	452,133	192
16,951	3,210	25.9	16,399	3,762	18,281	18,168	0	0	3,215	811	208	582,135	193
17,612	1,819	22.4	16,677	2,754	17,664	18,314	0	0	2,863	661	361	446,242	194
12,317	2,932	35.6	12,475	2,774	14,224	13,445	12	0	2,503	697	169	317,187	195
9,572	7,374	38.4	15,998	948	13,286	12,461	46	1,583	2,719	262	0	88,398	196
7,734	11,500	34.9	19,234	0	11,901	11,595	617	1,922	0	0	0	0	197
15,407	5,864	12.2	18,027	3,244	17,308	17,705	37	0	2,995	1,001	47	275,532	198
9,968	14,037	45.6	24,005	0	16,103	14,681	456	2,011	0	0	0	207,854	199
10,521	6,822	21.9	12,567	4,776	13,438	13,186	0	0	1,786	870	629	668,243	200
30,318	4,298	16.2	26,928	7,688	31,970	31,943	0	0	5,692	1,515	743	1,946,568	201
9,917	5,801	30.0	10,227	5,491	12,200	12,158	0	0	1,759	954	568	363,171	202
6,988	9,821	24.3	13,569	3,240	10,860	10,855	2	0	1,974	871	101	211,780	203
5,783	12,121	52.4	3,528	14,376	10,671	10,424	81	0	947	5,433	6	205,066	204
5,976	9,776	29.1	15,752	0	10,229	9,258	486	1,571	0	0	0	114,618	205
20,880	3,565	12.8	19,376	5,069	21,948	22,223	0	6	3,716	859	464	896,410	206
10,374	4,853	21.3	12,335	2,892	11,811	12,248	0	0	2,205	717	21	215,618	207
8,903	25,274	58.6	34,177	0	20,177	19,102	235	2,495	11	0	0	190,524	208
18,795	9,053	55.5	23,007	4,751	21,782	22,345	1	0	3,857	1,010	360	509,874	209
14,208	4,568	32.4	15,694	3,082	15,470	15,976	0	0	2,759	665	188	549,000	210
13,179	15,210	23.7	18,083	10,306	11,852	19,084	28	209	1,355	1,154	6	175,282	211
8,885	6,997	53.8	15,882	0	12,153	11,234	63	2,222	0	0	0	129,688	212
14,702	4,762	44.0	15,431	4,033	15,398	16,511	140	0	3,201	983	18	350,266	213
40,321	7,715	49.6	33,901	14,135	37,242	43,201	0	0	6,924	2,054	638	2,038,797	214
138	20,739	33.7	19,596	1,281	8,355	8,453	8	705	2,506	180	0	62,558	215

See notes at end of table.

Table 312.20.   Selected statistics for degree-granting postsecondary institutions enrolling more than 15,000 students in 2013, by selected institution and student characteristics: Selected years, 1990 through 2012–13—Continued

Line number	Institution	State	Con-trol[1]	Level	Total fall enrollment					Fall enrollment, 2013		
										Total	Sex	
					Fall 1990	Fall 2000	Fall 2010	Fall 2011	Fall 2012		Male	Female
1	2	3	4	5	6	7	8	9	10	11	12	13
216	Central New Mexico Community College	NM	Public	2-year	9,739	17,265	29,948	29,180	28,323	28,891	12,835	16,056
217	New Mexico State University, Main Campus	NM	Public	4-year	14,812	14,958	18,600	18,024	17,651	16,765	7,690	9,075
218	University of New Mexico, Main Campus	NM	Public	4-year	23,950	23,670	28,688	28,977	29,033	28,592	12,685	15,907
219	CUNY Bernard M. Baruch College	NY	Public	4-year	15,849	15,698	17,063	18,055	17,373	17,505	8,906	8,599
220	CUNY Borough of Manhattan Community College	NY	Public	2-year	14,819	15,875	22,534	24,463	24,537	24,186	10,333	13,853
221	CUNY Brooklyn College	NY	Public	4-year	16,605	15,039	16,912	16,835	16,524	17,004	6,697	10,307
222	CUNY City College	NY	Public	4-year	14,085	11,055	15,416	16,005	16,023	15,331	7,221	8,110
223	CUNY Hunter College	NY	Public	4-year	19,639	20,011	22,407	22,822	23,005	23,019	7,396	15,623
224	CUNY John Jay College of Criminal Justice	NY	Public	4-year	8,665	10,612	15,206	14,788	14,996	15,010	6,437	8,573
225	CUNY Kingsborough Community College	NY	Public	2-year	13,809	14,801	18,606	19,261	18,934	18,634	8,404	10,230
226	CUNY LaGuardia Community College	NY	Public	2-year	9,167	11,778	17,569	18,623	19,287	19,564	8,363	11,201
227	CUNY New York City College of Technology	NY	Public	4-year	10,908	11,028	15,366	15,961	16,207	16,860	9,373	7,487
228	CUNY Queens College	NY	Public	4-year	18,072	15,061	20,906	20,993	20,100	18,974	7,720	11,254
229	CUNY Queensborough Community College	NY	Public	2-year	12,184	10,598	15,316	16,837	15,711	16,291	7,495	8,796
230	Columbia University in the City of New York	NY	PrivNp	4-year	18,242	19,639	25,208	26,050	26,471	26,957	13,303	13,654
231	Cornell University	NY	PrivNp	4-year	11,533	12,043	20,939	21,131	21,424	21,593	11,074	10,519
232	Excelsior College	NY	PrivNp	4-year	13,303	18,067	32,029	35,608	39,728	39,897	17,374	22,523
233	Fordham University	NY	PrivNp	4-year	13,158	13,650	15,158	15,189	15,170	15,097	6,412	8,685
234	Monroe Community College	NY	Public	2-year	13,545	15,315	18,995	17,699	17,296	16,458	7,637	8,821
235	Nassau Community College	NY	Public	2-year	21,537	19,621	23,767	23,550	23,340	23,318	11,640	11,678
236	New York University	NY	PrivNp	4-year	32,813	37,150	43,797	43,911	44,516	44,599	18,619	25,980
237	Rochester Institute of Technology	NY	PrivNp	4-year	12,391	14,106	15,792	16,166	16,357	16,583	11,235	5,348
238	Saint John's University, New York	NY	PrivNp	4-year	19,105	18,621	21,354	21,067	21,087	20,729	9,055	11,674
239	State University of New York at Albany	NY	Public	4-year	17,400	16,751	17,615	17,114	17,312	17,338	8,400	8,938
240	State University of New York at Binghamton	NY	Public	4-year	12,202	12,473	14,895	14,746	15,308	16,077	8,474	7,603
241	Stony Brook University	NY	Public	4-year	17,624	19,924	24,363	23,920	23,946	24,143	12,210	11,933
242	Suffolk County Community College	NY	Public	2-year	†	†	26,719	26,787	26,219	26,711	12,423	14,288
243	Syracuse University	NY	PrivNp	4-year	21,900	18,186	20,407	20,829	21,029	21,267	9,789	11,478
244	University at Buffalo	NY	Public	4-year	27,638	24,830	29,117	28,849	28,952	29,850	15,804	14,046
245	Appalachian State University	NC	Public	4-year	11,931	13,227	17,222	17,344	17,589	17,838	8,050	9,788
246	Central Piedmont Community College	NC	Public	2-year	16,311	14,908	19,921	19,840	19,498	20,198	8,790	11,408
247	Duke University	NC	PrivNp	4-year	11,293	12,192	15,016	15,427	15,386	15,467	7,712	7,755
248	East Carolina University	NC	Public	4-year	17,564	18,750	27,783	27,386	26,947	26,887	10,684	16,203
249	North Carolina State University at Raleigh	NC	Public	4-year	27,199	28,619	34,376	34,767	34,340	34,009	18,913	15,096
250	University of North Carolina at Chapel Hill	NC	Public	4-year	23,878	24,892	29,390	29,137	29,278	29,127	12,442	16,685
251	University of North Carolina at Charlotte	NC	Public	4-year	14,699	17,241	25,063	25,277	26,232	26,571	13,153	13,418
252	University of North Carolina at Greensboro	NC	Public	4-year	12,882	13,125	18,771	18,627	18,516	18,074	6,149	11,925
253	Wake Technical Community College	NC	Public	2-year	6,129	9,654	17,071	19,158	20,440	19,160	8,630	10,530
254	University of North Dakota	ND	Public	4-year	11,659	11,031	14,194	14,697	15,250	15,143	8,018	7,125
255	Bowling Green State University, Main Campus	OH	Public	4-year	18,657	18,096	17,706	17,577	17,286	16,958	7,298	9,660
256	Cleveland State University	OH	Public	4-year	19,214	15,294	17,386	17,229	17,278	17,497	7,811	9,686
257	Columbus State Community College	OH	Public	2-year	13,290	18,094	30,513	30,921	25,863	25,249	11,523	13,726
258	Cuyahoga Community College District	OH	Public	2-year	23,157	19,518	31,250	30,853	29,701	27,910	10,936	16,974
259	Kent State University at Kent	OH	Public	4-year	24,434	21,924	26,589	27,855	28,602	28,998	11,682	17,316
260	Miami University, Oxford	OH	Public	4-year	15,835	16,757	17,472	17,395	17,683	17,901	8,239	9,662
261	Ohio State University, Main Campus	OH	Public	4-year	54,087	47,952	56,064	56,867	56,387	57,466	29,421	28,045
262	Ohio University, Main Campus	OH	Public	4-year	18,505	19,920	25,108	26,201	27,402	28,786	11,887	16,899
263	Sinclair Community College	OH	Public	2-year	16,367	19,026	21,993	21,106	19,537	19,176	8,280	10,896
264	Stark State College	OH	Public	2-year	3,996	4,507	14,826	15,536	15,655	15,450	6,173	9,277
265	University of Akron, Main Campus	OH	Public	4-year	28,801	21,363	27,076	27,470	26,581	24,932	12,640	12,292
266	University of Cincinnati, Main Campus	OH	Public	4-year	31,013	27,327	32,283	33,329	33,347	34,379	16,079	18,300
267	University of Toledo	OH	Public	4-year	24,691	19,491	23,085	22,610	21,453	20,743	10,322	10,421
268	Wright State University, Main Campus	OH	Public	4-year	16,393	13,964	18,447	18,304	16,780	16,656	8,001	8,655
269	Oklahoma State University, Main Campus	OK	Public	4-year	19,827	18,676	23,667	24,390	25,708	26,073	13,446	12,627
270	Tulsa Community College	OK	Public	2-year	17,955	16,270	20,577	20,154	19,557	18,640	7,370	11,270
271	University of Central Oklahoma	OK	Public	4-year	14,232	14,099	17,101	17,239	17,211	17,220	7,171	10,049
272	University of Oklahoma, Norman Campus	OK	Public	4-year	20,774	24,205	26,476	27,138	27,507	27,292	13,814	13,478
273	Oregon State University	OR	Public	4-year	16,361	16,758	23,753	24,962	26,363	27,902	14,912	12,990
274	Portland Community College	OR	Public	2-year	21,888	24,209	32,013	34,632	33,767	32,411	15,117	17,294
275	Portland State University	OR	Public	4-year	16,921	18,889	28,035	28,584	28,287	28,260	13,191	15,069
276	University of Oregon	OR	Public	4-year	18,840	17,801	23,342	24,396	24,518	24,473	11,657	12,816
277	Community College of Allegheny County	PA	Public	2-year	20,553	15,556	20,706	20,430	19,567	18,229	7,812	10,417
278	Community College of Philadelphia	PA	Public	2-year	15,151	15,953	19,503	19,751	18,920	19,063	7,222	11,841
279	Drexel University	PA	PrivNp	4-year	11,926	13,128	23,637	24,860	25,500	26,132	12,625	13,507
280	Harrisburg Area Community College, Harrisburg	PA	Public	2-year	8,355	7,572	23,210	22,595	21,945	20,780	7,745	13,035
281	Pennsylvania State University, Main Campus	PA	Public	4-year	38,864	40,571	45,233	45,628	45,783	46,615	25,090	21,525
282	Temple University	PA	Public	4-year	29,714	28,355	37,367	36,855	36,744	37,270	17,917	19,353
283	University of Pennsylvania	PA	PrivNp	4-year	21,868	21,853	25,007	24,832	24,725	24,630	11,698	12,932
284	University of Pittsburgh, Pittsburgh Campus	PA	Public	4-year	28,120	26,329	28,823	28,766	28,769	28,649	13,873	14,776
285	West Chester University of Pennsylvania	PA	Public	4-year	12,076	12,272	14,490	15,100	15,411	15,845	6,209	9,636
286	Community College of Rhode Island	RI	Public	2-year	16,620	15,583	17,775	17,893	17,884	17,699	7,223	10,476
287	University of Rhode Island	RI	Public	4-year	16,047	14,362	16,294	16,317	16,451	16,387	7,455	8,932

See notes at end of table.

Table 312.20. Selected statistics for degree-granting postsecondary institutions enrolling more than 15,000 students in 2013, by selected institution and student characteristics: Selected years, 1990 through 2012–13—Continued

Fall enrollment, 2013					Full-time-equivalent enrollment		Earned degrees/certificates conferred, 2012–13					Total expenditures and deductions, 2012–13 (in thousands)[2]	Line number
Attendance status			Student level										
Full-time	Part-time	Percent minority[3]	Under-graduate	Postbacca-laureate	Fall 2012	Fall 2013	Certificates[4]	Associate's	Bachelor's	Master's	Doctor's[5]		
14	15	16	17	18	19	20	21	22	23	24	25	26	27
9,546	19,345	65.5	28,891	0	15,703	16,041	6,242	3,368	0	0	0	169,554	216
13,006	3,759	63.4	13,582	3,183	15,049	14,461	0	25	2,599	810	132	457,691	217
20,668	7,924	57.6	22,416	6,176	23,930	23,757	0	0	3,493	1,231	487	1,808,841	218
11,222	6,283	63.8	14,082	3,423	13,557	13,648	0	0	3,042	1,437	0	250,637	219
15,889	8,297	89.8	24,186	0	18,966	18,675	0	2,928	0	0	0	254,368	220
10,061	6,943	58.6	13,596	3,408	12,372	12,742	1	0	2,379	1,100	0	253,296	221
9,721	5,610	78.5	12,501	2,830	12,322	11,885	0	0	2,026	1,029	9	383,114	222
13,087	9,932	58.8	16,689	6,330	17,036	16,886	10	0	2,876	2,211	0	346,444	223
10,764	4,246	74.4	13,217	1,793	12,349	12,418	34	104	2,323	525	0	267,553	224
10,734	7,900	68.1	18,634	0	13,569	13,386	4	2,386	0	0	0	174,013	225
10,455	9,109	87.2	19,564	0	13,129	13,513	82	2,217	0	0	0	197,912	226
10,318	6,542	86.5	16,860	0	12,516	12,958	21	1,077	954	0	0	191,845	227
11,249	7,725	59.3	15,351	3,623	14,952	14,235	0	0	3,207	1,185	0	278,507	228
9,626	6,665	80.6	16,291	0	11,508	11,864	17	1,951	0	0	0	148,609	229
22,731	4,226	44.4	7,970	18,987	23,774	24,352	0	0	2,121	6,958	1,382	3,460,017	230
21,528	65	44.4	14,393	7,200	21,376	21,553	0	0	3,578	2,289	771	1,779,141	231
0	39,897	38.5	37,440	2,457	15,585	15,648	41	1,725	2,686	232	0	77,470	232
12,015	3,082	34.0	8,345	6,752	13,194	13,200	0	0	1,924	2,256	607	522,306	233
10,260	6,198	35.8	16,458	0	12,818	12,341	183	2,620	0	0	0	158,907	234
14,209	9,109	54.8	23,318	0	17,508	17,267	135	3,175	0	0	0	228,029	235
35,096	9,503	43.6	22,615	21,984	38,626	38,740	37	96	5,333	6,965	1,494	3,953,776	236
14,119	2,464	22.7	13,880	2,703	15,100	15,080	58	177	2,484	959	18	503,795	237
13,719	7,010	52.4	15,773	4,956	16,713	16,450	87	19	2,252	1,203	632	462,693	238
14,398	2,940	36.3	12,822	4,516	15,387	15,494	0	0	3,069	1,149	154	879,012	239
14,383	1,694	34.5	12,997	3,080	14,227	15,014	0	0	2,915	828	143	422,420	240
20,044	4,099	47.2	15,992	8,151	21,355	21,573	40	0	3,799	1,801	553	2,049,447	241
14,831	11,880	33.9	26,711	0	18,662	18,820	87	3,398	0	0	0	254,951	242
19,092	2,175	32.4	15,097	6,170	19,660	19,930	1	6	3,146	1,909	403	808,871	243
24,816	5,034	32.0	19,831	10,019	25,886	26,709	18	0	4,395	2,039	992	986,466	244
16,021	1,817	11.3	16,025	1,813	16,397	16,716	0	0	3,404	774	16	355,322	245
7,140	13,058	53.1	20,198	0	11,276	11,524	622	1,790	0	0	0	172,145	246
14,894	573	36.7	6,646	8,821	15,100	15,113	0	0	1,801	1,998	1,100	4,670,261	247
20,971	5,916	26.3	21,508	5,379	23,170	23,237	0	0	4,336	1,575	157	795,306	248
26,770	7,239	21.0	24,536	9,473	29,849	29,517	0	129	5,446	2,327	560	1,294,690	249
24,390	4,737	29.0	18,370	10,757	26,267	26,137	4	0	4,627	2,043	1,203	2,629,497	250
20,436	6,135	33.8	21,503	5,068	22,394	22,789	0	0	4,194	1,227	133	488,701	251
13,858	4,216	38.2	14,753	3,321	15,970	15,479	0	0	3,038	909	134	375,345	252
5,986	13,174	41.2	19,160	0	11,938	10,409	1,041	1,730	0	0	0	145,100	253
11,160	3,983	11.8	11,724	3,419	12,877	12,699	99	0	1,736	646	258	428,628	254
14,764	2,194	17.7	14,477	2,481	15,922	15,603	0	0	2,801	781	84	356,451	255
10,825	6,672	30.2	12,133	5,364	13,060	13,369	0	0	2,117	1,426	222	304,587	256
8,817	16,432	32.8	25,249	0	14,670	14,334	2,446	2,220	0	0	0	205,134	257
9,526	18,384	40.7	27,910	0	17,004	15,698	511	2,482	0	0	0	303,990	258
21,737	7,261	16.2	22,968	6,030	24,355	24,549	85	0	4,738	1,478	156	540,645	259
16,038	1,863	12.8	15,462	2,439	16,443	16,731	47	215	3,734	668	49	471,952	260
50,012	7,454	19.8	44,201	13,265	51,846	52,883	0	0	9,301	2,759	1,661	4,829,106	261
19,449	9,337	12.3	23,504	5,282	22,603	23,108	224	140	6,070	1,252	273	588,392	262
6,774	12,402	23.8	19,176	0	11,628	10,938	1,519	1,841	0	0	0	166,545	263
4,469	10,981	26.2	15,450	0	8,363	8,156	465	1,035	0	0	0	103,954	264
18,340	6,592	21.3	20,477	4,455	22,284	20,917	198	651	2,993	1,118	276	506,735	265
25,873	8,506	17.8	23,706	10,673	28,347	29,091	367	90	4,607	2,643	745	1,002,588	266
16,179	4,564	24.1	16,153	4,590	18,506	17,960	0	70	2,855	1,038	561	850,812	267
12,900	3,756	22.4	12,796	3,860	14,509	14,377	0	0	2,369	1,124	177	408,786	268
19,959	6,114	24.3	20,660	5,413	21,924	22,290	0	0	3,652	1,099	327	798,058	269
6,367	12,273	37.4	18,640	0	11,212	10,488	376	2,421	0	0	0	144,107	270
11,644	5,576	33.2	15,218	2,002	13,889	13,838	2	94	2,329	598	0	184,619	271
20,627	6,665	31.8	20,985	6,307	23,653	23,182	0	0	4,062	1,712	392	837,851	272
21,958	5,944	23.8	23,157	4,745	23,162	24,304	0	0	4,157	746	353	878,283	273
13,580	18,831	31.5	32,411	0	20,824	19,902	1,071	4,217	0	0	0	300,533	274
17,308	10,952	29.6	22,927	5,333	21,535	21,615	0	0	4,321	1,675	78	485,955	275
21,920	2,553	24.3	20,797	3,676	22,938	22,923	0	0	4,622	949	318	782,223	276
6,317	11,912	26.8	18,229	0	11,391	10,316	786	1,886	0	0	0	133,698	277
5,075	13,988	74.0	19,063	0	9,740	9,771	248	1,764	0	0	0	168,876	278
18,909	7,223	32.4	16,616	9,516	20,902	21,697	169	26	2,986	2,446	682	891,847	279
6,506	14,274	27.1	20,780	0	11,939	11,298	344	1,955	0	0	0	184,503	280
44,639	1,976	19.6	40,085	6,530	44,502	45,406	146	26	10,573	1,291	800	4,336,481	281
31,436	5,834	34.1	28,068	9,202	33,267	33,686	123	2	5,914	1,433	1,191	2,604,504	282
21,344	3,286	39.3	11,525	13,105	22,695	22,613	0	1	2,848	3,767	1,207	5,896,431	283
25,069	3,580	19.6	18,615	10,034	26,388	26,411	982	0	4,345	2,315	1,086	1,876,905	284
13,250	2,595	18.6	13,711	2,134	13,851	14,241	6	0	2,760	713	0	233,676	285
5,459	12,240	36.6	17,699	0	9,895	9,568	269	1,832	0	0	0	116,707	286
13,662	2,725	21.0	13,354	3,033	14,806	14,711	0	0	2,873	589	220	462,408	287

See notes at end of table.

Table 312.20. Selected statistics for degree-granting postsecondary institutions enrolling more than 15,000 students in 2013, by selected institution and student characteristics: Selected years, 1990 through 2012–13—Continued

Line number	Institution	State	Control[1]	Level	Total fall enrollment					Fall enrollment, 2013		
										Total	Sex	
					Fall 1990	Fall 2000	Fall 2010	Fall 2011	Fall 2012		Male	Female
1	2	3	4	5	6	7	8	9	10	11	12	13
288	Clemson University	SC	Public	4-year	15,714	17,465	19,453	19,914	20,768	21,303	11,574	9,729
289	Trident Technical College	SC	Public	2-year	6,939	10,246	15,790	16,781	17,224	17,489	6,921	10,568
290	University of South Carolina, Columbia	SC	Public	4-year	25,613	23,728	29,599	30,721	31,288	31,964	14,338	17,626
291	Middle Tennessee State University	TN	Public	4-year	14,865	19,121	26,430	26,442	25,394	23,881	10,906	12,975
292	University of Memphis	TN	Public	4-year	20,681	19,986	22,420	22,725	22,139	21,480	8,575	12,905
293	University of Tennessee, Knoxville	TN	Public	4-year	26,055	25,890	30,300	30,194	29,833	30,030	14,871	15,159
294	Austin Community College District	TX	Public	2-year	24,251	25,735	44,100	45,100	43,315	41,627	18,510	23,117
295	Baylor University	TX	PrivNp	4-year	12,014	13,719	14,900	15,029	15,364	15,616	6,806	8,810
296	Blinn College	TX	Public	2-year	6,849	11,588	17,755	18,106	17,839	18,561	9,012	9,549
297	Central Texas College	TX	Public	2-year	4,815	14,636	26,055	26,995	22,443	21,647	11,508	10,139
298	Collin County Community College District	TX	Public	2-year	9,059	12,996	27,069	27,593	27,424	27,972	12,393	15,579
299	El Paso Community College	TX	Public	2-year	17,081	18,001	29,909	30,723	32,127	30,468	13,068	17,400
300	Houston Community College	TX	Public	2-year	36,437	40,929	60,303	63,015	58,476	57,978	24,574	33,404
301	Lone Star College System	TX	Public	2-year	15,653	24,554	54,412	63,029	60,428	64,072	25,797	38,275
302	Northwest Vista College	TX	Public	2-year	†	3,893	15,921	16,067	15,992	15,965	7,125	8,840
303	Richland College	TX	Public	2-year	12,567	12,537	19,201	20,000	19,552	19,287	8,675	10,612
304	Sam Houston State University	TX	Public	4-year	12,753	12,358	17,291	17,527	18,461	19,210	7,667	11,543
305	San Antonio College	TX	Public	2-year	20,083	19,253	25,269	25,567	23,134	23,004	9,366	13,638
306	San Jacinto Community College	TX	Public	2-year	9,424	10,507	28,549	29,392	28,721	28,385	12,368	16,017
307	South Texas College	TX	Public	4-year	†	11,319	27,692	29,604	30,824	31,232	13,554	17,678
308	Tarrant County College District	TX	Public	2-year	28,161	26,868	49,108	50,062	50,439	50,771	21,162	29,609
309	Texas A & M University, College Station	TX	Public	4-year	41,171	44,026	49,129	50,230	50,627	55,697	29,610	26,087
310	Texas State University	TX	Public	4-year	20,940	22,423	32,572	34,087	34,225	35,546	15,478	20,068
311	Texas Tech University	TX	Public	4-year	25,363	24,558	31,637	32,327	32,467	33,111	18,057	15,054
312	Texas Woman's University	TX	Public	4-year	9,850	8,404	14,180	14,718	15,168	15,058	1,673	13,385
313	University of Houston	TX	Public	4-year	33,115	32,123	38,752	39,820	40,747	39,540	19,854	19,686
314	University of North Texas	TX	Public	4-year	27,160	27,054	36,305	37,818	37,950	38,315	17,621	20,694
315	University of Texas at Arlington	TX	Public	4-year	24,782	20,424	32,975	33,439	33,239	33,329	14,687	18,642
316	University of Texas at Austin	TX	Public	4-year	49,617	49,996	51,195	51,112	52,186	52,059	25,651	26,408
317	University of Texas at Dallas	TX	Public	4-year	8,558	10,945	17,128	18,864	19,727	21,193	11,955	9,238
318	University of Texas at El Paso	TX	Public	4-year	16,524	15,224	22,106	22,640	22,749	23,003	10,608	12,395
319	University of Texas at San Antonio	TX	Public	4-year	15,489	18,830	30,258	30,968	30,474	28,623	14,723	13,900
320	University of Texas, Pan American	TX	Public	4-year	12,337	12,759	18,744	19,034	19,302	20,053	8,825	11,228
321	Brigham Young University, Provo	UT	PrivNp	4-year	31,662	32,554	33,841	34,101	34,409	31,123	16,979	14,144
322	Salt Lake Community College	UT	Public	2-year	13,344	21,596	34,654	33,420	29,997	32,003	15,452	16,551
323	University of Utah	UT	Public	4-year	24,922	24,948	30,819	31,660	32,388	32,077	17,754	14,323
324	Utah State University	UT	Public	4-year	15,155	21,490	16,472	26,757	28,786	27,812	12,724	15,088
325	Utah Valley University	UT	Public	4-year	7,879	20,946	32,670	33,395	31,562	30,564	16,984	13,580
326	Weber State University	UT	Public	4-year	13,449	16,050	24,048	25,301	26,532	25,155	11,824	13,331
327	Western Governors University	UT	PrivNp	4-year	†	205	22,497	30,970	41,369	46,733	18,984	27,749
328	George Mason University	VA	Public	4-year	20,308	23,408	32,562	33,320	32,961	33,917	15,601	18,316
329	James Madison University	VA	Public	4-year	11,251	15,326	19,434	19,722	19,927	20,181	8,063	12,118
330	Liberty University	VA	PrivNp	4-year	18,533	6,192	56,625	64,096	74,372	77,338	31,395	45,943
331	Northern Virginia Community College	VA	Public	2-year	35,194	37,073	48,996	50,044	51,864	51,803	25,260	26,543
332	Old Dominion University	VA	Public	4-year	16,729	18,969	24,466	24,753	24,670	24,828	11,199	13,629
333	Tidewater Community College	VA	Public	2-year	17,726	20,184	31,308	32,101	30,134	28,999	11,837	17,162
334	University of Virginia, Main Campus	VA	Public	4-year	21,110	22,411	24,391	24,297	23,907	23,464	10,754	12,710
335	Virginia Commonwealth University	VA	Public	4-year	21,764	24,066	32,027	31,627	31,445	30,974	13,091	17,883
336	Virginia Polytechnic Institute and State University	VA	Public	4-year	25,568	27,869	31,006	30,936	31,087	31,205	18,094	13,111
337	University of Washington, Seattle Campus	WA	Public	4-year	33,854	36,139	42,451	42,444	43,485	43,762	20,941	22,821
338	Washington State University	WA	Public	4-year	18,412	20,492	26,287	27,329	27,679	27,642	13,607	14,035
339	American Public University System	WV	PrivFp	4-year	†	†	39,296	50,838	58,115	55,422	33,356	22,066
340	West Virginia University	WV	Public	4-year	20,854	21,987	29,306	29,617	29,707	29,466	15,321	14,145
341	Madison Area Technical College	WI	Public	4-year	12,410	14,474	17,463	16,405	16,139	15,402	6,925	8,477
342	Milwaukee Area Technical College	WI	Public	2-year	21,600	14,296	19,827	19,480	18,118	17,961	7,813	10,148
343	University of Wisconsin, Madison	WI	Public	4-year	43,209	40,658	42,180	41,946	42,269	42,677	20,958	21,719
344	University of Wisconsin, Milwaukee	WI	Public	4-year	26,020	23,578	30,470	29,350	28,712	27,416	13,062	14,354

†Not applicable.
[1]"PrivNp" stands for private nonprofit. "PrivFp" stands for private for-profit.
[2]Includes private and some public institutions reporting total expenses and deductions under Financial Accounting Standards Board (FASB) reporting standards and public institutions reporting total expenses and deductions under Governmental Accounting Standards Board (GASB) 34/35 reporting standards.

[3]Combined enrollment of Black, Hispanic, Asian/Pacific Islander, American Indian/Alaska Native, and Two or more races students who are U.S. citizens or resident aliens as a percentage of total enrollment, excluding nonresident aliens.

Table 312.20. Selected statistics for degree-granting postsecondary institutions enrolling more than 15,000 students in 2013, by selected institution and student characteristics: Selected years, 1990 through 2012–13—Continued

Fall enrollment, 2013					Full-time-equivalent enrollment		Earned degrees/certificates conferred, 2012–13					Total expenditures and deductions, 2012–13 (in thousands)[2]	Line number
Attendance status			Student level										
Full-time	Part-time	Percent minority[3]	Under-graduate	Postbacca-laureate	Fall 2012	Fall 2013	Certificates[4]	Associate's	Bachelor's	Master's	Doctor's[5]		
14	15	16	17	18	19	20	21	22	23	24	25	26	27
18,963	2,340	13.8	16,931	4,372	19,303	19,847	0	0	3,720	1,152	187	722,395	288
7,521	9,968	42.2	17,489	0	10,803	10,868	1,921	1,648	0	0	0	135,336	289
28,022	3,942	21.1	24,180	7,784	28,443	29,517	13	4	4,622	1,735	748	879,401	290
18,280	5,601	30.2	21,162	2,719	21,722	20,464	0	0	4,159	882	23	348,054	291
14,385	7,095	45.6	17,223	4,257	17,708	17,156	0	0	2,887	1,047	259	421,114	292
26,283	3,747	16.7	21,182	8,848	27,614	27,696	0	0	4,445	1,826	1,112	1,642,770	293
9,476	32,151	48.8	41,627	0	21,122	20,270	704	1,792	0	0	0	296,875	294
15,016	600	31.9	13,292	2,324	14,975	15,248	0	0	2,709	741	318	500,159	295
9,503	9,058	34.6	18,561	0	12,320	12,544	359	830	0	0	0	92,756	296
3,754	17,893	54.7	21,647	0	11,117	9,761	622	3,137	0	0	0	125,670	297
9,529	18,443	43.3	27,972	0	15,635	15,721	361	1,900	0	0	0	148,880	298
9,792	20,676	91.7	30,468	0	17,711	16,734	776	3,404	0	0	0	172,504	299
17,728	40,250	83.0	57,978	0	31,905	31,241	1,525	4,410	0	0	0	408,122	300
19,815	44,257	62.7	64,072	0	33,329	34,674	1,873	4,373	0	0	0	392,911	301
3,902	12,063	72.4	15,965	0	7,983	7,952	161	1,208	0	0	0	66,041	302
4,613	14,674	70.0	19,287	0	9,823	9,540	227	1,551	0	0	0	85,446	303
14,132	5,078	41.1	16,255	2,955	15,567	16,090	0	0	3,256	865	55	280,854	304
5,672	17,332	70.5	23,004	0	11,644	11,491	452	2,034	0	0	0	146,650	305
7,656	20,729	68.0	28,385	0	15,372	14,615	1,939	2,696	0	0	0	206,790	306
10,349	20,883	97.2	31,232	0	18,697	18,776	1,610	2,231	122	0	0	156,285	307
17,420	33,351	55.0	50,771	0	28,536	28,617	1,849	4,059	0	0	0	357,737	308
48,780	6,917	30.6	44,072	11,625	46,707	51,467	0	0	9,538	2,238	824	2,147,278	309
28,185	7,361	43.7	31,005	4,541	29,643	31,071	0	0	5,715	1,444	93	514,962	310
28,287	4,824	32.7	27,044	6,067	29,425	30,145	0	0	5,207	1,418	522	720,883	311
8,428	6,630	52.4	9,515	5,543	10,962	10,943	8	0	1,926	1,652	175	181,855	312
28,486	11,054	65.7	31,706	7,834	33,749	32,855	0	0	5,730	2,052	796	896,879	313
27,282	11,033	44.1	31,243	7,072	31,336	31,570	0	0	6,365	1,893	212	587,823	314
19,318	14,011	55.5	25,690	7,639	24,761	24,793	0	0	6,244	2,984	149	529,326	315
47,741	4,318	46.0	39,979	12,080	49,628	49,432	794	0	9,154	3,058	1,351	2,566,677	316
16,006	5,187	52.8	13,049	8,144	16,375	17,983	0	0	2,761	2,548	184	525,472	317
14,241	8,762	90.2	19,696	3,307	17,514	17,692	0	0	3,194	1,110	124	435,098	318
21,943	6,680	68.4	24,342	4,281	26,011	24,540	0	0	4,384	1,298	92	510,388	319
14,138	5,915	96.2	17,230	2,823	15,736	16,450	0	0	2,734	744	25	261,242	320
27,114	4,009	12.6	27,765	3,358	31,938	28,674	0	0	6,619	1,102	246	949,595	321
8,674	23,329	26.0	32,003	0	16,141	16,506	564	3,485	0	0	0	205,712	322
23,084	8,993	20.2	24,492	7,585	26,870	26,637	0	0	5,139	1,921	726	3,239,336	323
16,436	11,376	12.2	24,385	3,427	21,404	20,932	71	851	3,557	895	109	579,382	324
15,755	14,809	16.2	30,370	194	22,718	21,723	35	1,768	2,739	69	0	267,470	325
11,155	14,000	24.0	24,498	657	17,901	16,789	68	1,995	2,360	301	0	207,579	326
46,733	0	24.7	35,493	11,240	41,369	46,733	0	0	5,184	2,936	0	232,423	327
21,421	12,496	42.3	21,990	11,927	25,061	26,138	0	0	4,920	2,980	510	739,217	328
18,626	1,555	16.8	18,431	1,750	18,980	19,226	1	0	4,047	741	24	436,327	329
36,353	40,985	34.0	47,464	29,874	49,930	52,244	79	817	6,657	6,283	308	469,507	330
19,700	32,103	57.9	51,803	0	30,172	30,478	2,083	5,636	0	0	0	303,400	331
16,957	7,871	41.6	19,819	5,009	19,859	20,002	0	0	3,938	1,197	188	389,108	332
11,500	17,499	51.3	28,999	0	17,999	17,375	1,284	3,075	0	0	0	184,180	333
21,086	2,378	28.3	16,087	7,377	22,079	21,988	0	0	3,738	1,635	908	2,450,366	334
24,803	6,171	41.2	23,356	7,618	27,445	27,186	30	0	4,659	1,652	758	903,749	335
28,425	2,780	22.4	24,034	7,171	29,305	29,453	0	56	5,604	1,469	572	1,174,903	336
38,327	5,435	41.5	29,756	14,006	39,594	40,406	0	0	7,651	3,438	1,329	4,198,130	337
23,604	4,038	27.8	23,070	4,572	25,059	25,180	144	0	5,275	800	457	937,714	338
3,786	51,636	40.9	43,964	11,458	25,071	23,953	304	1,341	4,020	3,323	0	271,242	339
25,796	3,670	12.9	22,757	6,709	27,346	27,196	0	0	4,078	1,607	582	968,320	340
5,160	10,242	23.0	15,340	62	9,728	9,291	2,531	1,380	0	0	0	203,687	341
5,731	12,230	53.8	17,961	0	9,916	9,837	1,134	1,381	0	0	0	266,697	342
38,428	4,249	16.9	30,728	11,949	39,655	40,056	0	0	6,661	2,156	1,440	2,401,367	343
21,548	5,868	24.8	22,648	4,768	24,867	23,826	0	0	3,984	1,471	178	529,188	344

[4]Includes less-than-1-year awards and 1- to less-than-4-year awards (excluding associate's degrees) conferred by degree-granting institutions.
[5]Includes Ph.D., Ed.D., and comparable degrees at the doctoral level, as well as such degrees as M.D., D.D.S., and law degrees that were formerly classified as first-professional degrees.
[6]Data for total enrollment in 1990 are for institutions of higher education, rather than degree-granting institutions.
[7]Beginning with enrollment data for fall 2013, and degree and finance data for 2012–13, totals for Arizona State University exclude data for the following four branch campuses, which are now reported separately: Downtown Phoenix, Skysong, West, and Polytechnic.

NOTE: Degree-granting institutions grant associate's or higher degrees and participate in Title IV federal financial aid programs. Includes online and distance education courses.
SOURCE: U.S. Department of Education, National Center for Education Statistics, Integrated Postsecondary Education Data System (IPEDS), "Fall Enrollment Survey" (IPEDS-EF:90); Spring 2001 through Spring 2014, Enrollment and Finance components; and Fall 2013, Completions component. (This table was prepared April 2015.)

Table 312.30. Enrollment and degrees conferred in degree-granting women's colleges, by selected characteristics and institution: Fall 2013 and 2012–13

Institution[1]	State	Enrollment, fall 2013							Degrees awarded to females, 2012–13			
		Total	Females	Percent female	Males, full-time	Females, full-time	Males, part-time	Females, part-time	Associate's	Bachelor's	Master's	Doctor's
1	2	3	4	5	6	7	8	9	10	11	12	13
Total..........................	†	75,058	70,447	93.9	2,060	52,140	2,551	18,307	727	12,459	5,762	232
Judson College......................	AL	347	331	95.4	1	261	15	70	20	38	†	†
Mills College......................	CA	1,595	1,469	92.1	115	1,309	11	160	†	241	217	8
Mount Saint Mary's College...	CA	3,274	2,965	90.6	184	2,324	125	641	159	424	168	29
Scripps College	CA	1,009	998	98.9	8	988	3	10	†	209	†	†
University of Saint Joseph	CT	2,640	2,369	89.7	97	1,123	174	1,246	†	259	573	0
Trinity Washington University....	DC	2,506	2,309	92.1	43	1,258	154	1,051	9	209	228	†
Agnes Scott College.............	GA	915	905	98.9	8	889	2	16	†	175	†	†
Brenau University	GA	2,854	2,426	85.0	172	1,356	256	1,070	9	377	331	†
Spelman College	GA	2,129	2,129	100.0	0	2,061	0	68	†	484	†	†
Wesleyan College................	GA	700	668	95.4	6	511	26	157	†	87	35	†
Lexington College..................	IL	55	55	100.0	0	45	0	10	1	9	†	†
Saint Mary-of-the-Woods College	IN	887	847	95.5	20	528	20	319	5	158	93	†
Saint Mary's College.............	IN	1,479	1,479	100.0	0	1,469	0	10	†	373	†	†
Midway College..................	KY	1,351	1,070	79.2	160	585	121	485	87	191	55	†
Notre Dame of Maryland University......................	MD	2,877	2,510	87.2	99	789	268	1,721	†	360	358	56
Bay Path College.................	MA	2,357	2,252	95.5	64	1,524	41	728	55	399	276	†
Mount Holyoke College..........	MA	2,251	2,239	99.5	8	2,180	4	59	†	612	6	†
Simmons College	MA	4,655	4,271	91.8	90	2,245	294	2,026	†	447	965	62
Smith College	MA	3,033	2,965	97.8	50	2,887	18	78	†	698	159	10
Wellesley College	MA	2,474	2,424	98.0	0	2,344	50	80	†	604	†	†
College of Saint Benedict........	MN	2,051	2,051	100.0	0	2,015	0	36	†	504	†	†
Saint Catherine University	MN	5,017	4,744	94.6	133	3,121	140	1,623	224	534	429	40
Cottey College	MO	277	277	100.0	0	275	0	2	98	14	†	†
Stephens College	MO	854	819	95.9	22	651	13	168	0	162	100	†
College of Saint Mary	NE	970	938	96.7	12	765	20	173	57	143	120	1
College of Saint Elizabeth........	NJ	1,552	1,374	88.5	53	644	125	730	†	262	162	14
Barnard College..................	NY	2,489	2,489	100.0	0	2,463	0	26	†	623	†	†
College of New Rochelle	NY	3,966	3,547	89.4	300	2,565	119	982	†	716	234	†
Bennett College	NC	680	680	100.0	0	609	0	71	†	125	†	†
Meredith College	NC	1,872	1,833	97.9	12	1,590	27	243	†	424	82	†
Salem College.....................	NC	1,187	1,120	94.4	25	820	42	300	†	182	26	†
Ursuline College	OH	1,357	1,226	90.3	44	582	87	644	†	229	195	2
Bryn Mawr College	PA	1,738	1,655	95.2	75	1,588	8	67	†	327	116	10
Cedar Crest College.............	PA	1,486	1,377	92.7	40	641	69	736	†	313	70	†
Moore College of Art and Design	PA	484	479	99.0	4	436	1	43	†	113	16	†
Columbia College.................	SC	1,169	1,103	94.4	33	834	33	269	†	225	131	†
Converse College	SC	1,333	1,194	89.6	15	760	124	434	†	158	156	†
Hollins University	VA	750	712	94.9	14	602	24	110	†	159	93	†
Mary Baldwin College...........	VA	1,711	1,582	92.5	57	1,092	72	490	†	261	96	†
Sweet Briar College..............	VA	710	694	97.7	12	675	4	19	†	97	9	†
Alverno College....................	WI	2,536	2,463	97.1	47	1,703	26	760	3	341	102	†
Mount Mary University...........	WI	1,481	1,409	95.1	37	1,033	35	376	†	193	161	0

†Not applicable.
[1]Data are for colleges and universities identified by the Women's College Coalition as women's colleges in 2015. Excludes women's colleges whose IPEDS data are reported together with a coed institution or coordinate men's college. The following institutions were excluded for this reason: the Colorado Women's College of the University of Denver; Douglass Residential College of Rutgers University; and Russell Sage College of the Sage Colleges.

NOTE: The institutions in this table are all 4-year private nonprofit institutions. Degree-granting institutions grant associate's or higher degrees and participate in Title IV federal financial aid programs.
SOURCE: U.S. Department of Education, National Center for Education Statistics, Integrated Postsecondary Education Data System (IPEDS), Spring 2014, Enrollment component; and Fall 2013, Completions component. (This table was prepared May 2015.)

Table 312.40. Enrollment and degrees conferred in degree-granting postsecondary institutions that serve large proportions of Hispanic undergraduate students, by institution level and control, percentage Hispanic, degree level, and other selected characteristics: Fall 2013 and 2012–13

State and institution	Level and control[1]	Total, all enrollment[2,3]	Enrollment, fall 2013 U.S. citizens and permanent residents only Total[3]	Hispanic[3]	Percent Hispanic[4]	Hispanic undergraduate	Hispanic postbaccalaureate	Degrees awarded to Hispanics, 2012–13 Associate's	Bachelor's	Master's	Doctor's[5]
1	2	3	4	5	6	7	8	9	10	11	12
Total, 50 states and District of Columbia..........	†	4,343,755	4,213,775	1,818,633	43.2	1,745,615	73,018	101,648	75,783	17,804	1,817
Total, 50 states, District of Columbia, and Puerto Rico	†	4,580,350	4,450,223	2,053,191	46.1	1,955,079	98,112	108,866	95,248	22,531	2,770
Alaska											
Charter College, Anchorage	5	2,191	2,191	730	33.3	730	†	137	3	†	†
Arizona											
Argosy University, Phoenix	5	743	743	137	18.4	60	77	0	7	17	7
Arizona College, Glendale	6	937	937	371	39.6	371	†	36	†	†	†
Arizona College, Mesa	5	162	162	61	37.7	61	†	0	0	†	†
Arizona State University, Downtown Phoenix	1	10,400	10,193	2,610	25.6	2,326	284	†	454	125	3
Arizona State University, West	1	3,661	3,596	941	26.2	880	61	†	200	26	5
Arizona Western College	2	8,000	7,450	5,264	70.7	5,264	†	340	†	†	†
Art Institute of Phoenix	5	1,045	1,045	488	46.7	488	†	12	30	†	†
Art Institute of Tucson	5	426	425	230	54.1	230	†	16	14	†	†
Brookline College, Phoenix	5	844	825	225	27.3	225	0	32	12	†	†
Brookline College, Tempe	6	223	222	80	36.0	80	†	10	†	†	†
Brookline College, Tucson	5	420	415	218	52.5	218	†	47	4	†	†
Brown Mackie College, Phoenix	5	637	637	204	32.0	204	†	38	1	†	†
Brown Mackie College, Tucson	5	684	684	288	42.1	288	†	94	5	†	†
Bryman School of Arizona	6	594	594	238	40.1	238	†	23	†	†	†
Carrington College, Mesa	6	691	691	234	33.9	234	†	9	†	†	†
Carrington College, Phoenix............................	5	676	676	375	55.5	375	†	2	1	†	†
Carrington College, Phoenix Westside	6	513	513	144	28.1	144	†	54	†	†	†
Carrington College, Tucson	6	440	440	278	63.2	278	†	6	†	†	†
Central Arizona College..................................	2	6,445	6,427	1,979	30.8	1,979	†	130	†	†	†
Cochise College	2	4,453	4,426	1,904	43.0	1,904	†	430	†	†	†
College America, Phoenix...............................	3	451	451	166	36.8	166	†	42	4	†	†
DeVry University, Arizona	5	1,565	1,546	372	24.1	319	53	7	70	18	†
Estrella Mountain Community College	2	8,832	8,801	4,265	48.5	4,265	†	269	†	†	†
Everest College, Mesa...................................	5	367	367	106	28.9	106	†	8	1	†	†
Fortis College, Phoenix	6	271	271	102	37.6	102	†	2	†	†	†
GateWay Community College............................	2	6,440	6,291	2,176	34.6	2,176	†	121	†	†	†
Glendale Community College............................	2	20,872	20,530	6,759	32.9	6,759	†	351	†	†	†
ITT Technical Institute, Phoenix West...............	5	262	262	119	45.4	119	†	16	0	†	†
ITT Technical Institute, Tucson........................	5	409	409	159	38.9	159	†	47	18	†	†
Kaplan College, Phoenix	6	93	93	35	37.6	35	†	18	†	†	†
Phoenix College	2	12,676	12,617	5,839	46.3	5,839	†	412	†	†	†
Pima Community College	2	30,082	29,843	12,338	41.3	12,338	†	878	†	†	†
Pima Medical Institute, East Valley..................	6	511	511	146	28.6	146	†	2	†	†	†
Pima Medical Institute, Mesa..........................	6	1,146	1,146	340	29.7	340	†	43	†	†	†
Pima Medical Institute, Tucson	5	1,726	1,722	685	39.8	685	†	79	15	†	†
Refrigeration School Inc.................................	6	621	620	178	28.7	178	†	8	†	†	†
South Mountain Community College	2	4,718	4,695	2,274	48.4	2,274	†	250	†	†	†
Southwest University of Visual Arts, Tucson......	5	221	221	66	29.9	66	†	†	15	0	†
University of Arizona......................................	1	40,621	37,257	8,871	23.8	7,801	1,070	†	1,163	172	53
University of Phoenix, Phoenix........................	5	4,480	4,361	1,144	26.2	893	251	0	105	71	†
University of Phoenix, Southern Arizona	5	1,849	1,794	857	47.8	734	123	†	74	38	†
Arkansas											
Bryan University	6	84	84	27	32.1	27	†	13	†	†	†
California											
Academy of Couture Art..................................	5	21	16	4	25.0	4	†	0	1	†	†
Advanced College...	6	227	227	159	70.0	159	†	9	†	†	†
Allan Hancock College....................................	2	10,885	10,863	5,547	51.1	5,547	†	428	†	†	†
Alliant International University	3	4,201	3,981	1,224	30.7	630	594	†	10	75	56
American Career College, Anaheim	6	1,565	1,565	769	49.1	769	†	60	†	†	†
American Career College, Los Angeles	6	1,770	1,770	1,141	64.5	1,141	†	26	†	†	†
American Career College, Ontario	6	1,634	1,634	948	58.0	948	†	49	†	†	†
Angeles College	5	145	145	39	26.9	39	†	†	†	†	†
Antelope Valley College..................................	2	14,262	14,245	6,421	45.1	6,421	†	345	†	†	†
Antioch University, Los Angeles......................	3	986	963	221	22.9	132	89	†	6	32	†
Antioch University, Santa Barbara	3	375	369	106	28.7	43	63	†	17	27	4
Argosy University, Inland Empire......................	5	704	704	280	39.8	175	105	0	11	21	4
Argosy University, Los Angeles	5	620	620	207	33.4	132	75	0	7	17	2
Argosy University, Orange County	5	673	673	214	31.8	119	95	0	12	18	10
Argosy University, San Diego	5	487	487	125	25.7	82	43	0	6	21	3
Art Institute of California, Argosy U., Hollywood.......	5	1,906	1,906	942	49.4	942	†	53	66	†	†
Art Institute of California, Argosy U., Inland Empire	5	2,307	2,307	1,315	57.0	1,315	†	139	77	†	†
Art Institute of California, Argosy U., Los Angeles...........	5	1,808	1,808	1,301	72.0	1,301	†	68	94	†	†
Art Institute of California, Argosy U., Orange County	5	1,761	1,761	1,020	57.9	1,020	†	58	54	†	†

See notes at end of table.

Table 312.40. Enrollment and degrees conferred in degree-granting postsecondary institutions that serve large proportions of Hispanic undergraduate students, by institution level and control, percentage Hispanic, degree level, and other selected characteristics: Fall 2013 and 2012–13—Continued

| | | | Enrollment, fall 2013 | | | | | Degrees awarded to Hispanics, 2012–13 | | | |
| | | | U.S. citizens and permanent residents only | | | | | | | | |
State and institution	Level and control[1]	Total, all enrollment[2,3]	Total[3]	Hispanic[3]	Percent Hispanic[4]	Hispanic under-graduate	Hispanic postbacca-laureate	Associate's	Bachelor's	Master's	Doctor's[5]
1	2	3	4	5	6	7	8	9	10	11	12
Art Institute of California, Argosy U., Sacramento	5	1,185	1,184	474	40.0	474	†	21	22	†	†
Art Institute of California, Argosy U., San Diego	5	1,869	1,864	1,620	86.9	1,620	†	79	88	†	†
Art Institute of California, Argosy U., San Francisco	5	1,317	1,317	726	55.1	725	†	23	49	0	†
Art Institute of California, Argosy U., Silicon Valley	5	570	570	257	45.1	257	†	25	12	†	†
Ashdown College of Health Sciences	6	41	41	11	26.8	11	†	11	†	†	†
Azusa Pacific Online University	3	726	726	241	33.2	241	†	1	0	†	†
Bakersfield College	2	17,770	17,740	11,061	62.4	11,061	†	415	†	†	†
Barstow Community College	2	3,211	3,209	1,237	38.5	1,237	†	76	†	†	†
Berkeley City College	2	6,471	6,198	1,608	25.9	1,608	†	21	†	†	†
Bethesda University of California	3	353	174	78	44.8	77	1	†	11	0	†
Brandman University	3	7,746	7,739	1,923	24.8	1,132	791	16	289	216	1
Bristol University	5	82	82	21	25.6	20	1	2	0	0	†
Cabrillo College	2	13,666	13,602	5,229	38.4	5,229	†	415	†	†	†
California Baptist University	3	7,144	7,001	2,236	31.9	1,844	392	†	195	100	†
California Christian College	3	30	29	7	24.1	7	†	1	1	†	†
California College San Diego	3	762	762	214	28.1	214	†	117	26	†	†
California College San Diego, National City	3	203	203	104	51.2	104	†	10	0	†	†
California College San Diego, San Marcos	3	269	269	116	43.1	116	†	3	0	†	†
California Lutheran University	3	4,282	3,776	1,021	27.0	758	263	†	154	94	3
California State Polytechnic University, Pomona	1	22,501	21,451	8,621	40.2	8,137	484	†	1,262	79	†
California State University, Bakersfield	1	8,371	8,162	4,493	55.0	4,077	416	†	596	120	†
California State University, Channel Islands	1	5,140	5,132	2,254	43.9	2,206	48	†	372	19	†
California State University, Chico	1	16,356	15,693	3,951	25.2	3,792	159	†	479	37	†
California State University, Dominguez Hills	1	14,670	14,316	7,765	54.2	6,978	787	†	1,098	187	†
California State University, East Bay	1	14,526	13,247	3,667	27.7	3,319	348	†	461	96	0
California State University, Fresno	1	23,060	22,165	9,990	45.1	9,027	963	†	1,284	228	12
California State University, Fullerton	1	38,325	36,123	14,172	39.2	12,920	1,252	†	2,219	249	6
California State University, Long Beach	1	35,586	33,313	13,069	39.2	11,715	1,354	†	1,850	386	1
California State University, Los Angeles	1	23,258	21,841	13,708	62.8	12,220	1,488	†	1,552	356	2
California State University, Monterey Bay	1	5,732	5,584	2,402	43.0	2,273	129	†	373	35	†
California State University, Northridge	1	38,310	35,310	15,528	44.0	14,372	1,156	†	1,910	285	1
California State University, Sacramento	1	28,811	28,171	7,632	27.1	7,119	513	†	983	137	9
California State University, San Bernardino	1	18,398	17,243	10,260	59.5	9,381	879	†	1,360	156	4
California State University, San Marcos	1	11,300	11,043	4,363	39.5	4,218	145	†	482	35	†
California State University, Stanislaus	1	8,917	8,727	4,204	48.2	3,714	490	†	532	79	1
Cambridge Junior College, Yuba City	6	167	167	66	39.5	66	†	3	†	†	†
Canada College	2	6,620	6,558	3,327	50.7	3,327	†	171	†	†	†
Career Networks Institute	6	561	561	247	44.0	247	†	0	†	†	†
Carrington College California, Pleasant Hill	6	589	587	169	28.8	169	†	17	†	†	†
Carrington College California, Pomona	6	301	300	185	61.7	185	†	19	†	†	†
Carrington College California, San Jose	6	693	689	311	45.1	311	†	64	†	†	†
Carrington College California, San Leandro	6	521	520	215	41.3	215	†	28	†	†	†
Carrington College California, Stockton	6	465	465	197	42.4	197	†	27	†	†	†
Casa Loma College, Van Nuys	4	606	606	270	44.6	270	†	10	†	†	†
CBD College	4	230	230	89	38.7	89	†	4	†	†	†
Cerritos College	2	21,404	21,215	14,732	69.4	14,732	†	610	†	†	†
Cerro Coso Community College	2	4,523	4,515	1,524	33.8	1,524	†	38	†	†	†
Chabot College	2	13,142	13,073	4,718	36.1	4,718	†	199	†	†	†
Chaffey College	2	19,211	19,030	11,567	60.8	11,567	†	765	†	†	†
Charles R. Drew University of Medicine and Science	3	515	511	74	14.5	18	56	4	1	9	†
Charter College, Canyon Country	6	1,317	1,317	666	50.6	666	†	†	†	†	†
Citrus College	2	12,920	12,503	7,770	62.1	7,770	†	690	†	†	†
College of San Mateo	2	9,377	9,180	2,881	31.4	2,881	†	158	†	†	†
College of the Canyons	2	18,508	18,398	7,954	43.2	7,954	†	256	†	†	†
College of the Desert	2	9,259	9,066	6,196	68.3	6,196	†	361	†	†	†
College of the Sequoias	2	10,720	10,701	6,504	60.8	6,504	†	485	†	†	†
Community Christian College	4	60	59	28	47.5	28	†	4	†	†	†
Concorde Career College, Garden Grove	6	898	898	269	30.0	269	†	30	†	†	†
Concorde Career College, North Hollywood	6	925	925	503	54.4	503	†	29	†	†	†
Concorde Career College, San Bernardino	6	753	753	242	32.1	242	†	34	†	†	†
Concorde Career College, San Diego	6	895	895	276	30.8	276	†	21	†	†	†
Contra Costa College	2	6,865	6,723	2,596	38.6	2,596	†	171	†	†	†
Crafton Hills College	2	5,697	5,689	2,438	42.9	2,438	†	145	†	†	†
Cuesta College	2	9,256	9,220	2,657	28.8	2,657	†	128	†	†	†
Cuyamaca College	2	8,859	8,810	2,834	32.2	2,834	†	147	†	†	†
Cypress College	2	15,881	15,718	7,066	45.0	7,066	†	277	†	†	†
De Anza College	2	23,261	21,209	5,812	27.4	5,812	†	335	†	†	†
DeVry University, California	5	9,156	8,859	3,280	37.0	2,923	357	83	384	117	†
Dominican University of California	3	2,147	2,093	505	24.1	429	76	†	53	16	†
East Los Angeles College	2	36,606	35,887	25,866	72.1	25,866	†	1,141	†	†	†

See notes at end of table.

Table 312.40. Enrollment and degrees conferred in degree-granting postsecondary institutions that serve large proportions of Hispanic undergraduate students, by institution level and control, percentage Hispanic, degree level, and other selected characteristics: Fall 2013 and 2012–13—Continued

State and institution	Level and control[1]	Total, all enrollment[2,3]	Enrollment, fall 2013					Degrees awarded to Hispanics, 2012–13			
			U.S. citizens and permanent residents only								
			Total[3]	Hispanic[3]	Percent Hispanic[4]	Hispanic under-graduate	Hispanic postbacca-laureate	Associate's	Bachelor's	Master's	Doctor's[5]
1	2	3	4	5	6	7	8	9	10	11	12
El Camino College, Compton Center	2	7,693	7,677	3,784	49.3	3,784	†	137	†	†	†
El Camino Community College District	2	23,996	23,419	11,572	49.4	11,572	†	775	†	†	†
Empire College School of Business	6	419	419	159	37.9	159	†	32	†	†	†
Everest College, Anaheim	6	574	574	375	65.3	375	†	37	†	†	†
Everest College, City of Industry	6	1,029	1,028	835	81.2	835	†	9	†	†	†
Everest College, Los Angeles, Wilshire	6	232	232	124	53.4	124	†	6	†	†	†
Everest College, Ontario Metro	5	962	962	610	63.4	610	†	167	39	†	†
Everest College, Reseda	6	696	696	459	65.9	459	†	11	†	†	†
Everest College, San Bernardino	6	747	747	413	55.3	413	†	38	†	†	†
Everest College, West Los Angeles	6	422	422	218	51.7	218	†	32	†	†	†
Evergreen Valley College	2	9,211	9,180	3,903	42.5	3,903	†	202	†	†	†
Fashion Institute of Design & Merchandising, Los Angeles	5	3,459	3,014	858	28.5	858	†	418	33	†	†
Fashion Institute of Design & Merchandising, Orange County	6	214	206	65	31.6	65	†	†	†	†	†
Fashion Institute of Design & Merchandising, San Diego	6	169	163	63	38.7	63	†	10	†	†	†
Foothill College	2	14,814	13,612	3,421	25.1	3,421	†	122	†	†	†
Four-D College	6	641	641	233	36.3	233	†	†	†	†	†
Fremont College	5	344	344	203	59.0	203	†	78	6	†	†
Fresno City College	2	21,344	21,337	10,867	50.9	10,867	†	452	†	†	†
Fresno Pacific University	3	3,393	3,339	1,363	40.8	1,108	255	0	305	56	†
Fullerton College	2	24,301	24,021	12,709	52.9	12,709	†	632	†	†	†
Gavilan College	2	5,834	5,830	3,190	54.7	3,190	†	218	†	†	†
Glendale Community College	2	15,744	15,122	4,921	32.5	4,921	†	98	†	†	†
Golden West College	2	12,717	12,526	3,942	31.5	3,942	†	205	†	†	†
Grossmont College	2	18,618	18,045	5,887	32.6	5,887	†	273	†	†	†
Hartnell College	2	9,439	9,434	7,012	74.3	7,012	†	411	†	†	†
Heald College, Concord	6	1,503	1,503	443	29.5	443	†	117	†	†	†
Heald College, Fresno	6	1,791	1,791	1,144	63.9	1,144	†	190	†	†	†
Heald College, Hayward	6	1,249	1,249	504	40.4	504	†	230	†	†	†
Heald College, Modesto	6	1,091	1,091	550	50.4	550	†	97	†	†	†
Heald College, Salinas	6	1,076	1,068	680	63.7	680	†	233	†	†	†
Heald College, San Francisco	6	1,074	1,074	341	31.8	341	†	115	†	†	†
Heald College, San Jose	6	1,671	1,671	846	50.6	846	†	217	†	†	†
Heald College, Stockton	6	1,418	1,418	632	44.6	632	†	91	†	†	†
Holy Names University	3	1,343	1,311	347	26.5	263	84	†	36	16	†
Humboldt State University	1	8,293	8,206	2,302	28.1	2,232	70	†	235	11	†
Humphreys College, Stockton and Modesto	3	990	990	437	44.1	363	74	33	38	1	5
Imperial Valley College	2	7,701	7,696	7,443	96.7	7,443	†	639	†	†	†
Institute of Technology Inc.	6	1,989	1,989	739	37.2	739	†	166	†	†	†
InterCoast Colleges, Fairfield	6	118	118	32	27.1	32	†	†	†	†	†
InterCoast Colleges, Orange	6	134	134	53	39.6	53	†	22	†	†	†
Irvine Valley College	2	13,362	12,667	3,242	25.6	3,242	†	129	†	†	†
ITT Technical Institute, Clovis	5	439	439	223	50.8	223	†	81	19	†	†
ITT Technical Institute, Concord	5	258	258	65	25.2	65	†	33	3	†	†
ITT Technical Institute, Corona	5	479	479	202	42.2	202	†	64	0	†	†
ITT Technical Institute, Culver City	5	319	319	172	53.9	172	†	45	0	†	†
ITT Technical Institute, Lathrop	5	492	492	204	41.5	204	†	56	24	†	†
ITT Technical Institute, National City	5	1,209	1,209	397	32.8	397	†	145	26	†	†
ITT Technical Institute, Oakland	5	169	169	50	29.6	50	†	5	0	†	†
ITT Technical Institute, Orange	5	823	823	414	50.3	414	†	159	62	†	†
ITT Technical Institute, Oxnard	5	312	312	144	46.2	144	†	77	26	†	†
ITT Technical Institute, San Bernardino	5	730	730	349	47.8	349	†	150	57	†	†
ITT Technical Institute, San Dimas	5	534	534	313	58.6	313	†	78	40	†	†
ITT Technical Institute, Sylmar	5	557	557	303	54.4	303	†	120	42	†	†
ITT Technical Institute, Torrance	5	457	457	224	49.0	224	†	89	50	†	†
ITT Technical Institute, West Covina	5	148	148	104	70.3	104	†	105	4	†	†
Kaplan College, Bakersfield	6	512	511	402	78.7	402	†	36	†	†	†
Kaplan College, Chula Vista	6	299	299	225	75.3	225	†	28	†	†	†
Kaplan College, Fresno	6	312	312	224	71.8	224	†	36	†	†	†
Kaplan College, Modesto	6	490	490	271	55.3	271	†	21	†	†	†
Kaplan College, North Hollywood	6	792	791	400	50.6	400	†	0	†	†	†
Kaplan College, Palm Springs	6	362	362	250	69.1	250	†	20	†	†	†
Kaplan College, Riverside	6	234	234	148	63.2	148	†	12	†	†	†
Kaplan College, Sacramento	6	547	546	171	31.3	171	†	5	†	†	†
Kaplan College, San Diego	6	1,354	1,354	414	30.6	414	†	35	†	†	†
Kaplan College, Vista	6	896	896	378	42.2	378	†	10	†	†	†
La Sierra University	3	2,440	2,055	935	45.5	876	59	†	61	15	2
Las Positas College	2	8,631	8,497	2,401	28.3	2,401	†	111	†	†	†
Loma Linda University	3	4,693	4,259	796	18.7	366	430	28	71	76	44
Long Beach City College	2	24,020	23,864	12,624	52.9	12,624	†	310	†	†	†
Los Angeles City College	2	19,635	19,201	10,043	52.3	10,043	†	219	†	†	†

See notes at end of table.

Table 312.40. Enrollment and degrees conferred in degree-granting postsecondary institutions that serve large proportions of Hispanic undergraduate students, by institution level and control, percentage Hispanic, degree level, and other selected characteristics: Fall 2013 and 2012–13—Continued

State and institution	Level and control[1]	Total, all enrollment[2,3]	Enrollment, fall 2013 — U.S. citizens and permanent residents only — Total[3]	Hispanic[3]	Percent Hispanic[4]	Hispanic undergraduate	Hispanic postbaccalaureate	Degrees awarded to Hispanics, 2012–13 — Associate's	Bachelor's	Master's	Doctor's[5]
1	2	3	4	5	6	7	8	9	10	11	12
Los Angeles Co. College of Nursing and Allied Health....	2	185	185	71	38.4	71	†	35	†	†	†
Los Angeles Film School................	5	2,218	2,166	622	28.7	622	†	193	0	†	†
Los Angeles Harbor College................	2	10,098	10,043	5,928	59.0	5,928	†	280	†	†	†
Los Angeles Mission College	2	8,990	8,889	6,944	78.1	6,944	†	503	†	†	†
Los Angeles Music Academy................	6	148	107	31	29.0	31	†	3	†	†	†
Los Angeles Pierce College	2	20,080	19,921	9,495	47.7	9,495	†	351	†	†	†
Los Angeles Southwest College................	2	7,864	7,847	2,985	38.0	2,985	†	83	†	†	†
Los Angeles Trade Technical College................	2	13,879	13,795	8,442	61.2	8,442	†	194	†	†	†
Los Angeles Valley College	2	18,762	18,669	9,623	51.5	9,623	†	289	†	†	†
Los Medanos College................	2	8,525	8,489	3,161	37.2	3,161	†	242	†	†	†
Marymount California University................	3	1,037	892	402	45.1	401	1	27	12	†	†
Mayfield College	6	329	329	203	61.7	203	†	†	†	†	†
Mendocino College................	2	3,729	3,729	915	24.5	915	†	77	†	†	†
Menlo College................	3	745	650	174	26.8	174	†	†	23	†	†
Merced College	2	10,205	10,142	5,777	57.0	5,777	†	356	†	†	†
Merritt College	2	5,887	5,823	1,554	26.7	1,554	†	61	†	†	†
MiraCosta College................	2	14,537	14,391	4,756	33.0	4,756	†	319	†	†	†
Modesto Junior College	2	17,084	17,079	7,592	44.5	7,592	†	397	†	†	†
Monterey Peninsula College	2	9,519	9,478	3,079	32.5	3,079	†	122	†	†	†
Moorpark College................	2	14,206	14,134	4,214	29.8	4,214	†	258	†	†	†
Moreno Valley College................	2	8,420	8,407	4,794	57.0	4,794	†	286	†	†	†
Mount Saint Mary's College................	3	3,274	3,252	1,852	56.9	1,593	259	81	186	68	1
Mount San Antonio College................	2	28,481	28,030	16,989	60.6	16,989	†	1,002	†	†	†
Mount San Jacinto Community College District................	2	14,170	14,170	6,219	43.9	6,219	†	579	†	†	†
Mount Sierra College	5	538	533	290	54.4	290	†	†	11	†	†
Napa Valley College	2	6,308	6,299	2,462	39.1	2,462	†	168	†	†	†
National Career College	6	43	43	21	48.8	21	†	0	†	†	†
National Hispanic University................	5	813	809	469	58.0	265	204	1	33	7	†
National University................	3	18,207	17,725	4,552	25.7	2,671	1,881	28	320	615	†
Newschool of Architecture and Design................	5	514	442	174	39.4	144	30	†	9	7	†
Norco College................	2	9,648	9,612	5,312	55.3	5,312	†	330	†	†	†
Notre Dame de Namur University................	3	2,030	1,934	614	31.7	461	153	†	60	24	†
Orange Coast College	2	21,886	21,115	7,279	34.5	7,279	†	387	†	†	†
Oxnard College................	2	6,939	6,934	4,923	71.0	4,923	†	418	†	†	†
Pacific College................	5	277	277	152	54.9	152	†	6	0	†	†
Pacific Oaks College................	3	1,072	1,066	511	47.9	235	276	†	60	56	†
Pacific Union College................	3	1,647	1,621	486	30.0	486	0	31	33	0	†
Palo Alto University................	3	948	931	144	15.5	52	92	†	10	9	7
Palo Verde College	2	3,253	3,251	1,101	33.9	1,101	†	50	†	†	†
Palomar College	2	24,665	24,424	9,301	38.1	9,301	†	522	†	†	†
Pasadena City College	2	25,268	24,226	11,984	49.5	11,984	†	543	†	†	†
Pima Medical Institute, Chula Vista................	6	927	927	448	48.3	448	†	56	†	†	†
Pinnacle College................	6	147	147	48	32.7	48	†	0	†	†	†
Platt College, Los Angeles	5	608	608	425	69.9	425	†	162	20	†	†
Platt College, Ontario	5	467	466	268	57.5	268	†	156	26	†	†
Platt College, Riverside	5	334	334	209	62.6	209	†	19	0	†	†
Platt College, San Diego	5	370	365	102	27.9	102	†	23	19	†	†
Porterville College	2	3,810	3,806	2,709	71.2	2,709	†	176	†	†	†
Reedley College	2	13,807	13,806	7,904	57.3	7,904	†	346	†	†	†
Rio Hondo College	2	16,548	16,528	13,361	80.8	13,361	†	636	†	†	†
Riverside City College	2	18,165	17,875	10,162	56.9	10,162	†	626	†	†	†
Sacramento City College................	2	23,509	23,358	6,676	28.6	6,676	†	349	†	†	†
Saddleback College................	2	20,871	20,454	5,058	24.7	5,058	†	205	†	†	†
Sage College	6	447	447	143	32.0	143	†	8	†	†	†
Saint Mary's College of California................	3	4,257	4,181	1,021	24.4	798	223	1	144	35	0
San Bernardino Valley College................	2	12,329	12,300	7,816	63.5	7,816	†	453	†	†	†
San Diego City College	2	16,310	16,157	7,763	48.0	7,763	†	252	†	†	†
San Diego Mesa College	2	24,251	23,833	8,081	33.9	8,081	†	229	†	†	†
San Diego State University................	1	31,899	30,001	9,396	31.3	8,377	1,019	†	1,580	256	15
San Diego State University, Imperial Valley................	1	883	879	831	94.5	697	134	†	193	12	†
San Francisco State University................	1	29,905	27,538	7,236	26.3	6,668	568	†	1,163	188	4
San Joaquin Delta College	2	17,629	17,593	7,288	41.4	7,288	†	908	†	†	†
San Joaquin Valley College, Bakersfield	6	642	621	390	62.8	390	†	212	†	†	†
San Joaquin Valley College, Fresno................	6	686	676	429	63.5	429	†	219	†	†	†
San Joaquin Valley College, Fresno Aviation	6	87	84	28	33.3	28	†	10	†	†	†
San Joaquin Valley College, Hesperia................	6	578	572	312	54.5	312	†	187	†	†	†
San Joaquin Valley College, Lancaster	6	167	165	83	50.3	83	†	0	†	†	†
San Joaquin Valley College, Modesto	6	318	305	157	51.5	157	†	74	†	†	†
San Joaquin Valley College, Ontario	6	698	682	437	64.1	437	†	212	†	†	†
San Joaquin Valley College, Temecula................	6	393	370	153	41.4	153	†	62	†	†	†

See notes at end of table.

Table 312.40. Enrollment and degrees conferred in degree-granting postsecondary institutions that serve large proportions of Hispanic undergraduate students, by institution level and control, percentage Hispanic, degree level, and other selected characteristics: Fall 2013 and 2012–13—Continued

| | | | Enrollment, fall 2013 | | | | | Degrees awarded to Hispanics, 2012–13 | | | |
| | | | U.S. citizens and permanent residents only | | | | | | | | |
State and institution	Level and control[1]	Total, all enrollment[2,3]	Total[3]	Hispanic[3]	Percent Hispanic[4]	Hispanic undergraduate	Hispanic postbacca-laureate	Associate's	Bachelor's	Master's	Doctor's[5]
1	2	3	4	5	6	7	8	9	10	11	12
San Joaquin Valley College, Visalia	6	1,616	1,574	696	44.2	696	†	298	†	†	†
San Jose City College	2	9,446	9,412	3,914	41.6	3,914	†	216	†	†	†
San Jose State University	1	31,278	28,585	7,186	25.1	6,391	795	†	1,105	304	†
Santa Ana College	2	28,598	28,390	15,801	55.7	15,801	†	989	†	†	†
Santa Barbara Business College, Bakersfield	5	543	542	412	76.0	412	†	153	0	†	†
Santa Barbara Business College, Santa Maria	5	188	188	142	75.5	142	†	43	0	†	†
Santa Barbara Business College, Ventura	5	349	341	202	59.2	201	1	65	1	0	†
Santa Barbara City College	2	19,331	17,855	6,573	36.8	6,573	†	497	†	†	†
Santa Monica College	2	29,999	26,746	11,389	42.6	11,389	†	362	†	†	†
Santa Rosa Junior College	2	22,094	22,058	6,608	30.0	6,608	†	416	†	†	†
Santiago Canyon College	2	10,939	10,900	5,175	47.5	5,175	†	417	†	†	†
Sierra College	2	18,374	18,212	4,575	25.1	4,575	†	377	†	†	†
Skyline College	2	10,067	9,952	2,959	29.7	2,959	†	162	†	†	†
Solano Community College	2	9,583	9,553	2,447	25.6	2,447	†	249	†	†	†
Sonoma State University	1	9,120	8,968	2,232	24.9	2,144	88	†	237	25	†
South Coast College	6	374	372	132	35.5	132	†	8	†	†	†
Southern California Institute of Architecture	3	493	279	63	22.6	44	19	†	13	7	†
Southern California Institute of Technology	5	496	496	245	49.4	245	†	0	18	†	†
Southwestern College	2	19,591	19,547	10,471	53.6	10,471	†	479	†	†	†
Stanbridge College	5	963	963	312	32.4	312	†	23	0	0	†
Taft College	2	5,444	5,440	2,774	51.0	2,774	†	166	†	†	†
United Education Institute, Huntington Park	6	2,732	2,729	1,917	70.2	1,917	†	24	†	†	†
United States University	5	282	275	155	56.4	94	61	†	33	9	†
University of Antelope Valley	5	804	804	369	45.9	363	6	49	12	1	†
University of California, Merced	1	6,195	5,927	2,646	44.6	2,598	48	†	274	2	3
University of California, Riverside	1	21,207	19,818	7,098	35.8	6,785	313	†	1,319	57	13
University of California, Santa Barbara	1	22,225	20,859	5,235	25.1	4,968	267	†	1,190	51	29
University of California, Santa Cruz	1	17,203	16,801	5,025	29.9	4,839	186	†	797	36	14
University of La Verne	3	8,796	7,898	3,912	49.5	2,724	1,188	0	478	272	38
University of Phoenix, Bay Area Campus	5	1,655	1,616	420	26.0	364	56	†	25	13	†
University of Phoenix, Central Valley	5	2,725	2,674	1,283	48.0	1,141	142	†	101	41	†
University of Phoenix, Sacramento Valley Campus	5	3,421	3,342	801	24.0	684	117	†	64	27	†
University of Phoenix, San Diego	5	6,122	6,034	2,527	41.9	2,270	257	0	194	55	†
University of Phoenix, Southern California	5	9,954	9,744	4,285	44.0	3,760	525	†	443	117	†
University of Redlands	3	5,147	5,083	1,516	29.8	1,033	483	†	130	114	1
University of the West	3	362	146	48	32.9	39	9	†	2	1	0
Vanguard University of Southern California	3	2,415	2,398	818	34.1	760	58	0	103	13	†
Ventura College	2	12,908	12,881	7,169	55.7	7,169	†	531	†	†	†
Victor Valley College	2	11,504	11,498	5,436	47.3	5,436	†	404	†	†	†
West Coast Ultrasound Institute	6	796	796	309	38.8	309	†	0	†	†	†
West Hills College, Coalinga	2	3,055	2,997	1,843	61.5	1,843	†	130	†	†	†
West Hills College, Lemoore	2	4,102	4,088	2,264	55.4	2,264	†	145	†	†	†
West Los Angeles College	2	10,767	10,637	4,567	42.9	4,567	†	128	†	†	†
West Valley College	2	9,636	9,566	2,299	24.0	2,299	†	136	†	†	†
Westwood College, Anaheim	5	772	772	267	34.6	267	†	11	157	†	†
Westwood College, Inland Empire	5	979	974	439	45.1	439	†	12	154	†	†
Westwood College, Los Angeles	5	672	672	228	33.9	228	0	16	144	8	†
Westwood College, South Bay	5	571	571	184	32.2	184	†	6	84	†	†
Whittier College	3	2,339	2,259	905	40.1	705	200	†	125	23	30
Woodbury University	3	1,607	1,317	441	33.5	397	44	†	72	39	†
Woodland Community College	2	2,641	2,640	1,309	49.6	1,309	†	69	†	†	†
Wyotech, Fremont	6	1,199	1,198	435	36.3	435	†	9	†	†	†
Wyotech, Long Beach	6	1,400	1,400	836	59.7	836	†	19	†	†	†
Yuba College	2	6,874	6,873	2,057	29.9	2,057	†	125	†	†	†
Colorado											
Academy of Natural Therapy Inc.	6	69	69	27	39.1	27	†	1	†	†	†
Adams State University	1	3,211	3,211	862	26.8	727	135	33	92	35	†
Aims Community College	2	4,955	4,947	1,548	31.3	1,548	†	128	†	†	†
Anthem College, Denver	6	207	207	52	25.1	52	†	19	†	†	†
Art Institute of Colorado	5	1,794	1,794	457	25.5	457	†	24	37	†	†
CollegeAmerica, Denver	3	497	497	165	33.2	165	†	33	5	†	†
CollegeAmerica, Fort Collins	3	159	159	44	27.7	44	†	10	3	†	†
CollegeAmerica, Colorado Springs South	3	31	31	9	29.0	9	†	0	0	†	†
Colorado Heights University	3	375	192	99	51.6	98	1	†	5	0	†
Colorado State University, Pueblo	1	7,089	6,964	1,724	24.8	1,625	99	†	196	19	†
Community College of Denver	2	10,432	9,904	3,140	31.7	3,140	†	121	†	†	†
Everest College, Aurora	6	383	383	135	35.2	135	†	12	†	†	†
Everest College, Thornton	6	371	371	167	45.0	167	†	17	†	†	†
Heritage College, Denver	6	466	466	168	36.1	168	†	111	†	†	†

See notes at end of table.

Table 312.40. Enrollment and degrees conferred in degree-granting postsecondary institutions that serve large proportions of Hispanic undergraduate students, by institution level and control, percentage Hispanic, degree level, and other selected characteristics: Fall 2013 and 2012–13—Continued

State and institution	Level and control[1]	Total, all enrollment[2,3]	Total[3]	Hispanic[3]	Percent Hispanic[4]	Hispanic under-graduate	Hispanic postbacca-laureate	Associate's	Bachelor's	Master's	Doctor's[5]
1	2	3	4	5	6	7	8	9	10	11	12
Institute of Business and Medical Careers	6	258	258	84	32.6	84	†	32	†	†	†
Intellitec College, Grand Junction	6	536	536	172	32.1	172	†	61	†	†	†
ITT Technical Institute, Westminster	5	218	218	58	26.6	58	†	26	6	†	†
Lamar Community College	2	902	867	242	27.9	242	†	16	†	†	†
Lincoln College of Technology, Denver	6	1,262	1,262	390	30.9	390	†	44	†	†	†
Otero Junior College	2	1,449	1,404	440	31.3	440	†	59	†	†	†
Pima Medical Institute, Denver	6	951	951	381	40.1	381	†	17	†	†	†
Pima Medical Institute, South Denver	6	211	211	92	43.6	92	†	0	†	†	†
Pueblo Community College	2	6,718	6,692	2,011	30.1	2,011	†	213	†	†	†
Trinidad State Junior College	2	1,791	1,768	743	42.0	743	†	81	†	†	†
Connecticut											
Capital Community College	2	4,168	4,164	1,272	30.5	1,272	†	117	†	†	†
Housatonic Community College	2	5,813	5,795	1,600	27.6	1,600	†	132	†	†	†
Norwalk Community College	2	6,556	6,414	2,220	34.6	2,220	†	140	†	†	†
Sanford-Brown College, Farmington	6	62	62	18	29.0	18	†	18	†	†	†
Florida											
Acupuncture and Massage College	5	173	167	94	56.3	19	75	†	16	16	†
Adventist University of Health Sciences	3	2,293	2,282	518	22.7	497	21	56	44	1	†
Ai Miami International University of Art and Design	5	3,208	3,204	2,740	85.5	2,699	41	84	278	16	†
American Institute	5	269	269	122	45.4	122	†	19	0	†	†
American InterContinental University, South Florida	5	164	164	53	32.3	51	2	6	46	18	†
American Medical Academy	6	343	343	278	81.0	278	†	21	†	†	†
Anthem College, Orlando	6	491	491	248	50.5	248	†	11	†	†	†
Art Institute of Fort Lauderdale	5	1,924	1,922	898	46.7	898	†	119	112	†	†
Atlantic Institute of Oriental Medicine	3	142	142	49	34.5	11	38	†	6	6	†
Barry University	3	9,030	8,517	2,684	31.5	1,389	1,295	†	297	253	40
Broward College	1	43,883	42,699	15,380	36.0	15,380	†	1,935	80	†	†
Brown Mackie College, Miami	5	953	953	274	28.8	274	†	74	10	†	†
Carlos Albizu University, Miami	3	991	948	783	82.6	250	533	†	94	139	19
CBT College, Cutler Bay	6	174	174	99	56.9	99	†	36	†	†	†
Chamberlain College of Nursing, Florida	5	649	633	195	30.8	195	†	†	5	†	†
City College, Altamonte Springs	4	425	425	133	31.3	133	†	19	†	†	†
City College, Hollywood	4	126	126	40	31.7	40	†	0	†	†	†
City College, Miami	3	283	283	175	61.8	175	†	70	9	†	†
College of Business and Technology, Flagler	6	323	323	322	99.7	322	†	50	†	†	†
College of Business and Technology, Hialeah	6	178	178	176	98.9	176	†	60	†	†	†
College of Business and Technology, Kendall	5	127	125	109	87.2	109	†	34	0	†	†
College of Business and Technology, Miami Gardens	5	54	54	46	85.2	46	†	3	0	†	†
Concorde Career Institute, Tampa	6	454	454	126	27.8	126	†	7	†	†	†
Dade Medical College, Hollywood	6	303	303	85	28.1	85	†	22	†	†	†
Dade Medical College, Homestead	6	309	309	230	74.4	230	†	76	†	†	†
Dade Medical College, Miami	5	1,083	1,083	950	87.7	950	†	200	0	†	†
Dade Medical College, Miami Lakes	6	607	607	397	65.4	397	†	129	†	†	†
DeVry University, Florida	5	3,252	3,143	1,064	33.9	806	258	24	162	99	†
Digital Media Arts College	5	300	300	79	26.3	75	4	†	2	1	†
Edison State College	1	15,423	15,192	3,920	25.8	3,920	†	479	50	†	†
Everest Institute, Kendall	6	461	461	322	69.8	322	†	37	†	†	†
Everest Institute, North Miami	6	768	768	233	30.3	233	†	8	†	†	†
Everest University, Tampa	5	770	770	254	33.0	249	5	43	11	4	†
Florida Career College, Miami	5	5,818	5,818	1,923	33.1	1,923	†	181	29	†	†
Florida College of Natural Health, Miami	6	201	198	137	69.2	137	†	32	†	†	†
Florida College of Natural Health, Pompano Beach	6	262	262	88	33.6	88	†	13	†	†	†
Florida International University	1	47,663	44,283	30,223	68.2	26,578	3,645	55	5,007	1,333	128
Florida National University, Main Campus	5	2,448	2,322	2,182	94.0	2,157	25	399	91	5	†
Florida Technical College	5	4,330	4,328	2,399	55.4	2,399	†	153	0	†	†
Fortis College, Cutler Bay	5	203	203	106	52.2	106	†	0	†	†	†
Fortis College, Miami	6	88	88	84	95.5	84	†	74	†	†	†
Fortis Institute, Miami	6	130	130	103	79.2	103	†	12	†	†	†
Heritage Institute, Fort Myers	6	614	614	165	26.9	165	†	97	†	†	†
Hillsborough Community College	2	26,590	25,876	7,608	29.4	7,608	†	829	†	†	†
Hodges University	3	2,078	2,078	713	34.3	661	52	81	69	17	†
Institute of Technical Arts	6	263	263	96	36.5	96	†	†	†	†	†
International Academy of Design and Technology, Orlando	5	348	348	121	34.8	121	†	9	52	†	†
ITT Technical Institute, Fort Lauderdale	5	531	531	140	26.4	140	†	56	14	†	†
ITT Technical Institute, Miami	5	417	417	301	72.2	301	†	125	57	†	†
ITT Technical Institute, Orlando	5	377	377	131	34.7	131	†	15	0	†	†
ITT Technical Institute, Tampa	5	463	463	120	25.9	120	†	37	6	†	†
Johnson & Wales University, North Miami	3	1,952	1,710	544	31.8	544	†	64	52	†	†
Jose Maria Vargas University	5	159	155	155	100.0	151	4	0	0	5	†

See notes at end of table.

Table 312.40. Enrollment and degrees conferred in degree-granting postsecondary institutions that serve large proportions of Hispanic undergraduate students, by institution level and control, percentage Hispanic, degree level, and other selected characteristics: Fall 2013 and 2012–13—Continued

State and institution	Level and control[1]	Total, all enrollment[2,3]	Enrollment, fall 2013 U.S. citizens and permanent residents only					Degrees awarded to Hispanics, 2012–13			
			Total[3]	Hispanic[3]	Percent Hispanic[4]	Hispanic under-graduate	Hispanic postbacca-laureate	Associate's	Bachelor's	Master's	Doctor's[5]
1	2	3	4	5	6	7	8	9	10	11	12
Keiser University, Fort Lauderdale	3	17,129	17,050	5,265	30.9	5,033	232	953	192	47	1
Le Cordon Bleu College of Culinary Arts, Miami	6	721	721	311	43.1	311	†	258	†	†	†
Lincoln Technical Institute, Fern Park	6	231	231	64	27.7	64	†	0	†	†	†
Management Resources Institute	6	822	819	729	89.0	729	†	55	†	†	†
Medvance Institute, West Palm	6	365	365	97	26.6	97	†	10	†	†	†
Miami Dade College	1	66,298	62,610	45,853	73.2	45,853	†	7,074	495	†	†
Millennia Atlantic University	5	112	55	47	85.5	28	19	1	4	14	†
Northwood University, Florida	3	646	454	117	25.8	117	0	0	18	2	†
Nova Southeastern University	3	25,670	24,747	6,586	26.6	1,693	4,893	0	482	818	299
Palm Beach State College	1	29,763	29,297	7,951	27.1	7,951	†	1,044	41	†	†
Polytechnic University of Puerto Rico, Miami	3	120	120	119	99.2	62	57	†	14	25	†
Polytechnic University of Puerto Rico, Orlando	3	125	125	123	98.4	80	43	†	19	14	†
Professional Hands Institute	6	38	38	38	100.0	38	†	†	†	†	†
Professional Training Centers	5	801	801	766	95.6	766	†	160	0	†	†
Remington College, Tampa	3	189	189	59	31.2	59	†	4	1	†	†
SABER College	4	544	544	483	88.8	483	†	132	†	†	†
Saint John Vianney College Seminary	3	94	78	31	39.7	28	3	†	7	†	†
Saint Thomas University	3	2,315	1,996	1,036	51.9	472	564	†	123	77	96
Sanford-Brown Institute, Orlando	6	107	106	44	41.5	44	†	25	†	†	†
South Florida State College	1	2,699	2,669	794	29.7	794	†	81	0	†	†
South University, Tampa	5	983	983	240	24.4	183	57	10	18	14	†
Southeastern College, Greenacres	6	1,157	1,157	326	28.2	326	†	80	†	†	†
Southern Technical College	6	1,502	1,502	408	27.2	408	†	140	†	†	†
Strayer University, Florida	5	2,973	2,945	747	25.4	522	225	17	47	32	†
Trinity International University, Florida	3	347	346	158	45.7	126	32	†	12	9	†
University of Miami	3	16,935	14,305	3,790	26.5	2,637	1,153	†	621	235	131
University of Phoenix, Central Florida	5	1,560	1,524	392	25.7	342	50	†	43	19	†
University of Phoenix, South Florida	5	1,364	1,251	503	40.2	405	98	†	60	26	†
University of Southernmost Florida	5	103	103	74	71.8	71	3	4	†	†	†
Valencia College	1	42,180	41,545	14,678	35.3	14,678	†	2,017	2	†	†
Georgia											
Interactive College of Technology, Gainesville	6	39	39	23	59.0	23	†	0	†	†	†
Illinois											
City Colleges of Chicago, Harold Washington College	2	9,036	9,002	3,489	38.8	3,489	†	222	†	†	†
City Colleges of Chicago, Harry S Truman College	2	11,800	11,797	4,936	41.8	4,936	†	134	†	†	†
City Colleges of Chicago, Richard J. Daley College	2	9,384	9,383	6,724	71.7	6,724	†	229	†	†	†
City Colleges of Chicago, Wilbur Wright College	2	12,640	12,623	7,172	56.8	7,172	†	381	†	†	†
College of Lake County	2	17,685	17,685	6,114	34.6	6,114	†	256	†	†	†
Coyne College	6	590	590	173	29.3	173	†	25	†	†	†
Dominican University	3	3,470	3,386	1,035	30.6	833	202	†	109	59	0
Elgin Community College	2	11,285	11,237	4,318	38.4	4,318	†	243	†	†	†
Fox College	6	387	387	145	37.5	145	†	71	†	†	†
Illinois Institute of Art, Chicago	5	2,322	2,286	1,033	45.2	1,033	†	26	51	†	†
Illinois Institute of Art, Schaumburg	5	1,066	1,051	330	31.4	330	†	2	28	†	†
ITT Technical Institute, Arlington Heights	5	248	248	72	29.0	72	†	28	9	†	†
ITT Technical Institute, Oak Brook	5	336	336	114	33.9	114	†	36	13	†	†
Lexington College	3	55	54	16	29.6	16	†	1	6	†	†
Lincoln College of Technology, Melrose Park	6	617	617	302	48.9	302	†	123	†	†	†
Morton College	2	4,886	4,886	4,179	85.5	4,179	†	303	†	†	†
National Louis University	3	4,814	4,800	746	15.5	383	363	†	81	121	5
Northeastern Illinois University	1	10,821	10,364	3,489	33.7	3,202	287	†	404	67	†
Northwestern College, Chicago	6	430	430	118	27.4	118	†	35	†	†	†
Northwestern College, Southwestern	6	756	756	179	23.7	179	†	61	†	†	†
Robert Morris University, Illinois	3	3,233	3,173	831	26.2	762	69	174	175	50	†
Saint Augustine College	3	1,607	1,570	1,480	94.3	1,480	†	277	24	†	†
Saint Xavier University	3	4,252	4,235	832	19.6	712	120	†	87	30	†
Triton College	2	11,225	11,225	4,790	42.7	4,790	†	272	†	†	†
University of Illinois at Chicago	1	28,038	25,670	5,287	20.6	4,208	1,079	†	725	146	79
Waubonsee Community College	2	10,721	10,721	3,723	34.7	3,723	†	232	†	†	†
Indiana											
Calumet College of Saint Joseph	3	1,140	1,139	338	29.7	311	27	8	59	11	†
Kaplan College, Hammond	6	366	365	92	25.2	92	†	4	†	†	†
Kansas											
Dodge City Community College	2	1,785	1,776	629	35.4	629	†	52	†	†	†
Donnelly College	3	474	446	201	45.1	201	†	18	4	†	†
Garden City Community College	2	1,997	1,990	796	40.0	796	†	77	†	†	†
Northwest Kansas Technical College	2	626	621	141	22.7	141	†	15	†	†	†
Seward County Community College and Area Technical School	2	1,857	1,838	902	49.1	902	†	70	†	†	†

See notes at end of table.

Table 312.40. Enrollment and degrees conferred in degree-granting postsecondary institutions that serve large proportions of Hispanic undergraduate students, by institution level and control, percentage Hispanic, degree level, and other selected characteristics: Fall 2013 and 2012–13—Continued

State and institution	Level and control[1]	Total, all enrollment[2,3]	Enrollment, fall 2013 — U.S. citizens and permanent residents only — Total[3]	Hispanic[3]	Percent Hispanic[4]	Hispanic undergraduate	Hispanic postbacca-laureate	Degrees awarded to Hispanics, 2012–13 — Associate's	Bachelor's	Master's	Doctor's[5]
1	2	3	4	5	6	7	8	9	10	11	12
Louisiana											
Saint Joseph Seminary College	3	133	133	42	31.6	42	†	†	7	†	†
Massachusetts											
Benjamin Franklin Institute of Technology	3	482	472	119	25.2	119	†	11	0	†	†
Cambridge College	3	3,114	2,976	591	19.9	299	292	†	68	103	0
New England Institute of Art	5	779	776	274	35.3	274	†	5	34	†	†
Northern Essex Community College	2	7,352	7,300	2,649	36.3	2,649	†	148	†	†	†
Pine Manor College	3	346	254	58	22.8	55	3	0	11	0	†
Salter College, Chicopee	6	70	70	29	41.4	29	†	19	†	†	†
Salter College, West Boylston	6	699	699	212	30.3	212	†	21	†	†	†
Springfield Technical Community College	2	6,792	6,743	1,753	26.0	1,753	†	148	†	†	†
Urban College of Boston	4	762	762	430	56.4	430	†	25	†	†	†
Nevada											
Art Institute of Las Vegas	5	1,097	1,089	720	66.1	720	†	26	23	†	†
College of Southern Nevada	1	34,177	33,767	9,610	28.5	9,610	†	551	1	†	†
Everest College, Henderson	6	915	915	314	34.3	314	†	40	†	†	†
Kaplan College, Las Vegas	6	994	991	278	28.1	278	†	23	†	†	†
Pima Medical Institute, Las Vegas	6	1,018	1,018	315	30.9	315	†	8	†	†	†
University of Phoenix, Las Vegas	5	2,180	2,159	514	23.8	437	77	†	31	18	†
New Jersey											
Bergen Community College	2	15,882	14,736	4,879	33.1	4,879	†	560	†	†	†
Berkeley College, Woodland Park	5	3,671	3,644	1,650	45.3	1,650	†	97	197	†	†
Cumberland County College	2	3,919	3,915	1,070	27.3	1,070	†	98	†	†	†
DeVry University, New Jersey	5	1,725	1,684	464	27.6	412	52	28	40	6	†
Eastern International College, Belleville	6	216	216	93	43.1	93	†	15	†	†	†
Eastern International College, Jersey City	6	222	222	114	51.4	114	†	11	†	†	†
Eastwick College, Hackensack	6	324	324	168	51.9	168	†	†	†	†	†
Essex County College	2	12,175	11,220	3,216	28.7	3,216	†	337	†	†	†
Fairleigh Dickinson University, Metropolitan	3	8,546	7,808	2,220	28.4	1,896	324	38	189	57	0
Felician College	3	1,933	1,891	463	24.5	409	54	2	54	5	0
Hudson County Community College	2	9,036	9,001	5,487	61.0	5,487	†	460	†	†	†
Kean University	1	14,404	14,209	3,559	25.0	3,179	380	†	545	80	0
Middlesex County College	2	12,602	12,339	3,842	31.1	3,842	†	266	†	†	†
Montclair State University	1	19,464	18,931	4,555	24.1	3,947	608	†	656	111	1
New Jersey City University	1	8,442	8,337	2,961	35.5	2,450	511	†	397	87	0
Passaic County Community College	2	9,129	9,068	5,054	55.7	5,054	†	296	†	†	†
Pillar College	3	418	418	132	31.6	132	†	0	12	†	†
Rutgers University, Newark	1	11,212	10,450	2,111	20.2	1,754	357	†	368	61	39
Saint Peter's University	3	3,194	3,131	874	27.9	736	138	4	111	42	†
Union County College	2	11,969	11,607	4,502	38.8	4,502	†	206	†	†	†
University of Phoenix, Jersey City	5	455	436	147	33.7	147	†	†	5	†	†
William Paterson University of New Jersey	1	11,414	11,304	2,777	24.6	2,566	211	†	413	40	0
New Mexico											
Anamarc College, Santa Teresa	5	96	96	92	95.8	92	†	27	0	†	†
Brookline College, Albuquerque	5	272	271	205	75.6	205	†	37	5	†	†
Brown Mackie College, Albuquerque	5	780	780	356	45.6	356	†	90	0	†	†
Carrington College, Albuquerque	6	647	647	341	52.7	341	†	54	†	†	†
Central New Mexico Community College	2	28,891	27,995	13,899	49.6	13,899	†	1,445	†	†	†
Clovis Community College	2	3,596	3,596	1,087	30.2	1,087	†	122	†	†	†
Eastern New Mexico University, Main Campus	1	5,847	5,686	2,065	36.3	1,694	371	5	192	33	†
Eastern New Mexico University, Roswell	2	3,883	3,818	1,854	48.6	1,854	†	138	†	†	†
Eastern New Mexico University, Ruidoso	2	895	893	291	32.6	291	†	6	†	†	†
ITT Technical Institute, Albuquerque	5	476	476	206	43.3	206	†	77	24	†	†
Luna Community College	2	1,657	1,657	1,243	75.0	1,243	†	91	†	†	†
Mesalands Community College	2	697	689	309	44.8	309	†	33	†	†	†
National American University, Albuquerque	5	397	397	149	37.5	149	†	17	12	†	†
National American University, Albuquerque West	5	346	346	134	38.7	134	†	15	11	†	†
New Mexico Highlands University	1	3,690	3,457	2,009	58.1	1,366	643	0	229	163	†
New Mexico Institute of Mining and Technology	1	2,134	2,019	487	24.1	418	69	1	50	19	0
New Mexico Junior College	2	2,320	2,310	1,205	52.2	1,205	†	96	†	†	†
New Mexico State University, Alamogordo	2	2,458	2,409	903	37.5	903	†	83	†	†	†
New Mexico State University, Carlsbad	2	1,861	1,842	984	53.4	984	†	53	†	†	†
New Mexico State University, Dona Ana	2	8,837	8,558	6,394	74.7	6,394	†	720	†	†	†
New Mexico State University, Grants	2	970	959	449	46.8	449	†	43	†	†	†
New Mexico State University, Main Campus	1	16,765	15,629	8,496	54.4	7,315	1,181	15	1,193	249	22
Northern New Mexico College	1	1,681	1,679	1,170	69.7	1,159	11	66	52	†	†
Pima Medical Institute, Albuquerque	6	930	930	504	54.2	504	†	33	†	†	†
Santa Fe Community College	2	6,265	6,255	3,072	49.1	3,072	†	174	†	†	†
Santa Fe University of Art and Design	5	826	634	177	27.9	177	†	†	7	1	†

See notes at end of table.

Table 312.40. Enrollment and degrees conferred in degree-granting postsecondary institutions that serve large proportions of Hispanic undergraduate students, by institution level and control, percentage Hispanic, degree level, and other selected characteristics: Fall 2013 and 2012–13—Continued

State and institution	Level and control[1]	Total, all enrollment[2,3]	Total[3]	Hispanic[3]	Percent Hispanic[4]	Hispanic under-graduate	Hispanic postbacca-laureate	Associate's	Bachelor's	Master's	Doctor's[5]
1	2	3	4	5	6	7	8	9	10	11	12
Southwest University of Visual Arts, Albuquerque	5	224	224	105	46.9	105	†	†	6	†	†
University of New Mexico, Los Alamos	2	744	741	332	44.8	332	†	34	†	†	†
University of New Mexico, Main Campus	1	28,592	27,529	11,740	42.6	10,011	1,729	†	1,286	326	104
University of New Mexico, Taos	2	1,802	1,796	1,204	67.0	1,204	†	24	†	†	†
University of New Mexico, Valencia County	2	2,245	2,230	1,438	64.5	1,438	†	134	†	†	†
University of Phoenix, Albuquerque	5	2,462	2,415	1,836	76.0	1,593	243	†	278	92	†
University of the Southwest	3	923	919	230	25.0	156	74	†	17	9	†
Western New Mexico University	1	3,560	3,507	1,922	54.8	1,691	231	66	92	37	†
New York											
Art Institute of New York City	6	1,158	1,158	727	62.8	727	†	130	†	†	†
ASA College	6	4,706	4,129	2,019	48.9	2,019	†	576	†	†	†
Berkeley College, New York	5	4,596	3,778	1,346	35.6	1,346	†	81	215	†	†
Boricua College	3	1,118	1,118	932	83.4	875	57	143	132	20	†
Cochran School of Nursing	4	79	79	21	26.6	21	†	8	†	†	†
College of Mount Saint Vincent	3	1,938	1,876	663	35.3	591	72	0	100	13	†
College of Westchester	5	1,197	1,197	527	44.0	527	†	89	31	†	†
Concordia College, New York	3	953	817	213	26.1	204	9	1	30	0	†
CUNY, Borough of Manhattan Community College	2	24,186	22,605	10,299	45.6	10,299	†	972	†	†	†
CUNY, Bronx Community College	2	11,368	11,106	7,221	65.0	7,221	†	830	†	†	†
CUNY, City College	1	15,331	13,999	4,843	34.6	4,165	678	†	656	170	1
CUNY, Hostos Community College	2	7,006	6,677	4,467	66.9	4,467	†	466	†	†	†
CUNY, Hunter College	1	23,019	21,707	5,164	23.8	4,115	1,049	†	562	288	0
CUNY, John Jay College of Criminal Justice	1	15,010	14,577	6,082	41.7	5,683	399	43	824	87	†
CUNY, LaGuardia Community College	2	19,564	18,079	8,675	48.0	8,675	†	790	†	†	†
CUNY, Lehman College	1	12,085	11,560	6,021	52.1	5,263	758	†	773	184	†
CUNY, New York City College of Technology	1	16,860	16,087	5,175	32.2	5,175	†	324	214	†	†
CUNY, Queens College	1	18,974	18,080	4,831	26.7	4,091	740	†	529	136	†
CUNY, Queensborough Community College	2	16,291	15,365	5,128	33.4	5,128	†	462	†	†	†
DeVry College of New York	5	2,127	1,941	662	34.1	540	122	12	50	32	†
Dominican College of Blauvelt	3	1,998	1,998	596	29.8	549	47	1	58	4	0
Globe Institute of Technology	5	557	523	169	32.3	169	†	17	3	†	†
Mandl School, The College of Allied Health	6	782	782	406	51.9	406	†	132	†	†	†
Manhattanville College	3	2,750	2,534	557	22.0	427	130	†	57	18	0
Mercy College	3	11,648	11,576	3,566	30.8	2,839	727	9	306	191	4
Mildred Elley, New York	6	617	617	185	30.0	185	†	11	†	†	†
Monroe College	5	7,215	6,627	2,985	45.0	2,894	91	598	377	43	†
Nyack College	3	3,082	2,922	823	28.2	514	309	1	74	56	0
Pacific College of Oriental Medicine, New York	5	602	576	73	12.7	40	33	9	0	2	†
Plaza College	5	726	726	227	31.3	227	†	64	19	†	†
Professional Business College	4	884	884	241	27.3	241	†	61	†	†	†
Saint Francis College	3	2,819	2,665	677	25.4	665	12	0	80	2	†
Stella and Charles Guttman Community College	2	493	476	265	55.7	265	†	0	†	†	†
SUNY, Westchester Community College	2	13,781	13,611	4,238	31.1	4,238	†	358	†	†	†
Swedish Institute College of Health Sciences	6	848	846	251	29.7	251	†	34	†	0	†
Technical Career Institutes	6	3,020	3,001	1,210	40.3	1,210	†	370	†	†	†
Vaughn College of Aeronautics and Technology	3	1,741	1,707	644	37.7	641	3	79	46	0	†
Wood Tobe-Coburn School	6	476	476	253	53.2	253	†	127	†	†	†
Ohio											
Union Institute & University	3	1,660	1,660	351	21.1	331	20	†	99	6	1
Oregon											
Mount Angel Seminary	3	170	138	42	30.4	24	18	†	2	6	†
Pennsylvania											
Berks Technical Institute	6	976	976	430	44.1	430	†	82	†	†	†
Consolidated School of Business, Lancaster	6	112	112	53	47.3	53	†	12	†	†	†
Lincoln Technical Institute, Allentown	6	568	568	149	26.2	149	†	17	†	†	†
Pace Institute	6	65	65	43	66.2	43	†	34	†	†	†
Reading Area Community College	2	4,538	4,538	1,304	28.7	1,304	†	72	†	†	†
Tennessee											
Mid-South Christian College	3	29	25	11	44.0	11	†	0	0	†	†
Texas											
Allied Health Careers	6	177	177	90	50.8	90	†	19	†	†	†
Alvin Community College	2	5,118	5,118	1,549	30.3	1,549	†	160	†	†	†
Amarillo College	2	10,873	10,873	3,933	36.2	3,933	†	312	†	†	†
Anamarc College, El Paso Central	6	347	347	299	86.2	299	†	47	†	†	†
Anamarc College, El Paso East	6	269	269	228	84.8	228	†	4	†	†	†
Angelo State University	1	6,536	6,374	1,850	29.0	1,668	182	37	205	48	1
Anthem College, Irving	6	288	288	125	43.4	125	†	4	†	†	†
Art Institute of Austin	5	1,413	1,413	776	54.9	776	†	13	73	†	†
Art Institute of Houston	5	2,338	2,338	1,001	42.8	1,001	†	61	92	†	†

See notes at end of table.

Table 312.40. Enrollment and degrees conferred in degree-granting postsecondary institutions that serve large proportions of Hispanic undergraduate students, by institution level and control, percentage Hispanic, degree level, and other selected characteristics: Fall 2013 and 2012–13—Continued

State and institution	Level and control[1]	Total, all enrollment[2,3]	Enrollment, fall 2013 U.S. citizens and permanent residents only					Degrees awarded to Hispanics, 2012–13			
			Total[3]	Hispanic[3]	Percent Hispanic[4]	Hispanic under-graduate	Hispanic postbacca-laureate	Associate's	Bachelor's	Master's	Doctor's[5]
1	2	3	4	5	6	7	8	9	10	11	12
Art Institute of San Antonio	5	1,115	1,115	607	54.4	607	†	17	11	†	†
Austin Community College District	2	41,627	40,372	12,925	32.0	12,925	†	428	†	†	†
Baptist Health System School of Health Professions	5	444	444	189	42.6	189	†	78	†	†	†
Baptist University of the Americas	3	189	150	129	86.0	129	†	3	17	†	†
Brazosport College	1	4,127	4,127	1,443	35.0	1,443	†	132	3	†	†
Brookhaven College	2	12,319	12,278	4,475	36.4	4,475	†	208	†	†	†
Brown Mackie College, Dallas	5	308	308	85	27.6	85	†	0	0	†	†
Brown Mackie College, San Antonio	5	785	785	432	55.0	432	†	30	0	†	†
Capitol City Careers	6	10	10	5	50.0	5	†	4	†	†	†
Career Point College	5	1,208	1,208	452	37.4	452	†	82	†	†	†
Center for Advanced Legal Studies	5	182	182	46	25.3	37	9	15	†	†	†
Cisco College	2	3,617	3,545	905	25.5	905	†	69	†	†	†
Coastal Bend College	2	3,533	3,533	2,392	67.7	2,392	†	193	†	†	†
College of Biblical Studies, Houston	3	498	498	150	30.1	150	†	11	10	†	†
College of Health Care Professions, Austin	6	223	223	108	48.4	108	†	4	†	†	†
College of Health Care Professions, Dallas	6	134	134	59	44.0	59	†	0	†	†	†
College of Health Care Professions, Fort Worth	6	208	208	71	34.1	71	†	0	†	†	†
College of Health Care Professions, Northwest	6	810	810	341	42.1	341	†	4	†	†	†
College of the Mainland	2	4,188	4,188	1,145	27.3	1,145	†	99	†	†	†
Concorde Career Institute, San Antonio	6	681	681	401	58.9	401	†	16	†	†	†
Culinary Institute Inc.	6	374	374	134	35.8	134	†	30	†	†	†
Del Mar College	2	10,502	10,488	6,727	64.1	6,727	†	528	†	†	†
DeVry University, Texas	5	3,382	3,262	816	25.0	705	111	36	136	54	†
Eastfield College	2	14,529	14,510	5,847	40.3	5,847	†	238	†	†	†
El Centro College	2	10,771	10,745	4,448	41.4	4,448	†	214	†	†	†
El Paso Community College	2	30,468	29,834	26,218	87.9	26,218	†	2,876	†	†	†
Everest College, Arlington	6	643	643	213	33.1	213	†	22	†	†	†
Everest College, Dallas	6	1,071	1,071	354	33.1	354	†	51	†	†	†
Everest College, Fort Worth	6	505	505	180	35.6	180	†	13	†	†	†
Everest College, Fort Worth, South	6	535	535	221	41.3	221	†	2	†	†	†
Galen College of Nursing, San Antonio	6	1,119	1,119	537	48.0	537	†	60	†	†	†
Galveston College	2	2,131	2,117	659	31.1	659	†	72	†	†	†
Hallmark College	3	735	734	378	51.5	376	2	127	11	†	†
Houston Baptist University	3	2,910	2,802	703	25.1	583	120	†	102	26	†
Houston Community College	2	57,978	52,642	18,702	35.5	18,702	†	1,228	†	†	†
Howard College	2	4,130	4,114	1,859	45.2	1,859	†	110	†	†	†
Interactive Learning Systems, North Houston	6	25	25	12	48.0	12	†	0	†	†	†
Interactive Learning Systems, Pasadena	6	30	30	27	90.0	27	†	0	†	†	†
International Academy of Design and Technology, San Antonio	5	356	356	196	55.1	196	†	25	42	†	†
International Business College, El Paso, Cromo	6	196	196	175	89.3	175	†	5	†	†	†
International Business College, El Paso, North Zarogosa Road	6	195	195	163	83.6	163	†	50	†	†	†
ITT Technical Institute, Austin	5	432	432	145	33.6	145	†	57	11	†	†
ITT Technical Institute, Houston North	5	650	650	197	30.3	197	†	105	10	†	†
ITT Technical Institute, Houston West	5	609	609	218	35.8	218	†	103	15	†	†
ITT Technical Institute, San Antonio	5	585	585	319	54.5	319	†	95	19	†	†
ITT Technical Institute, San Antonio East	5	170	170	74	43.5	74	†	0	0	†	†
ITT Technical Institute, Waco	5	231	231	59	25.5	59	†	12	0	†	†
ITT Technical Institute, Webster	5	303	303	100	33.0	100	†	36	8	†	†
Jacksonville College, Main Campus	4	524	517	193	37.3	193	†	3	†	†	†
Kaplan College, Arlington	6	422	422	180	42.7	180	†	18	†	†	†
Kaplan College, Brownsville	6	461	461	454	98.5	454	†	15	†	†	†
Kaplan College, Corpus Christi	6	370	370	299	80.8	299	†	24	†	†	†
Kaplan College, Dallas	6	357	357	150	42.0	150	†	13	†	†	†
Kaplan College, El Paso	6	681	681	590	86.6	590	†	55	†	†	†
Kaplan College, Fort Worth	6	282	282	118	41.8	118	†	3	†	†	†
Kaplan College, Laredo	6	329	329	324	98.5	324	†	5	†	†	†
Kaplan College, Lubbock	6	267	267	171	64.0	171	†	7	†	†	†
Kaplan College, McAllen	6	540	540	534	98.9	534	†	63	†	†	†
Kaplan College, San Antonio	6	625	625	503	80.5	503	†	19	†	†	†
Kaplan College, San Antonio, San Pedro	6	645	645	418	64.8	418	†	36	†	†	†
Laredo Community College	2	8,726	8,717	8,527	97.8	8,527	†	746	†	†	†
Lee College	2	5,911	5,840	2,291	39.2	2,291	†	224	†	†	†
Lincoln College of Technology, Grand Prairie	6	867	867	372	42.9	372	†	5	†	†	†
Lone Star College System	2	64,072	64,072	22,540	35.2	22,540	†	1,157	†	†	†
McLennan Community College	2	8,555	8,544	2,096	24.5	2,096	†	185	†	†	†
Midland College	1	5,233	5,220	2,271	43.5	2,271	†	156	11	†	†
Mountain View College	2	8,797	8,784	4,977	56.7	4,977	†	351	†	†	†
North American University	3	378	207	49	23.7	49	0	†	0	†	†

See notes at end of table.

Table 312.40. Enrollment and degrees conferred in degree-granting postsecondary institutions that serve large proportions of Hispanic undergraduate students, by institution level and control, percentage Hispanic, degree level, and other selected characteristics: Fall 2013 and 2012–13—Continued

State and institution	Level and control[1]	Total, all enrollment[2,3]	Enrollment, fall 2013					Degrees awarded to Hispanics, 2012–13			
			U.S. citizens and permanent residents only								
			Total[3]	Hispanic[3]	Percent Hispanic[4]	Hispanic undergraduate	Hispanic postbaccalaureate	Associate's	Bachelor's	Master's	Doctor's[5]
1	2	3	4	5	6	7	8	9	10	11	12
North Lake College	2	11,365	11,313	4,184	37.0	4,184	†	273	†	†	†
Northwest Vista College	2	15,965	15,932	9,507	59.7	9,507	†	619	†	†	†
Northwood University, Texas	3	713	682	214	31.4	202	12	1	33	3	†
Odessa College	2	5,059	5,003	3,047	60.9	3,047	†	215	†	†	†
Our Lady of the Lake University, San Antonio	3	2,927	2,908	1,936	66.6	1,194	742	†	208	168	16
Palo Alto College	2	8,427	8,420	5,952	70.7	5,952	†	569	†	†	†
Pima Medical Institute, Houston	6	898	898	429	47.8	429	†	14	†	†	†
Quest College	6	355	352	168	47.7	168	†	†	†	†	†
Remington College, Dallas	3	904	904	414	45.8	414	†	52	0	†	†
Remington College, Fort Worth	4	408	408	144	35.3	144	†	6	†	†	†
Remington College, Houston	4	354	354	129	36.4	129	†	17	†	†	†
Remington College, Houston Southeast	4	252	252	104	41.3	104	†	3	†	†	†
Remington College, North Houston	4	474	473	231	48.8	231	†	15	†	†	†
Richland College	2	19,287	19,127	5,893	30.8	5,893	†	356	†	†	†
Saint Edward's University	3	4,861	4,499	1,709	38.0	1,535	174	†	293	65	†
Saint Mary's University	3	3,868	3,567	2,273	63.7	1,785	488	†	340	103	80
Saint Philip's College	2	10,238	10,197	5,382	52.8	5,382	†	393	†	†	†
San Antonio College	2	23,004	22,899	13,197	57.6	13,197	†	1,051	†	†	†
San Jacinto Community College	2	28,385	27,877	13,856	49.7	13,856	†	1,042	†	†	†
Sanford-Brown College, Austin	6	17	17	5	29.4	5	†	0	†	†	†
Sanford-Brown College, Houston	6	756	748	206	27.5	206	†	19	†	†	†
Sanford-Brown College, Houston North Loop	6	81	81	23	28.4	23	†	5	†	†	†
Sanford-Brown College, San Antonio	6	274	274	100	36.5	100	†	16	†	†	†
Schreiner University	3	1,136	1,131	325	28.7	307	18	0	60	9	†
South Plains College	2	9,559	9,488	3,667	38.6	3,667	†	190	†	†	†
South Texas College	1	31,232	31,228	29,935	95.9	29,935	†	2,052	114	†	†
South University, Art Institute of Dallas	5	1,423	1,421	750	52.8	748	2	32	51	1	†
South University, Art Institute of Fort Worth	5	346	346	107	30.9	107	†	2	2	†	†
South University, Austin	5	156	156	34	21.8	34	0	0	0	0	†
Southwest Collegiate Institute for the Deaf	2	149	130	63	48.5	63	†	2	†	†	†
Southwest Institute of Technology	6	10	10	5	50.0	5	†	6	†	†	†
Southwest Texas Junior College	2	5,410	5,410	4,525	83.6	4,525	†	495	†	†	†
Southwest University at El Paso	5	1,296	1,296	1,212	93.5	1,212	†	200	0	†	†
Southwestern Adventist University	3	808	745	335	45.0	331	4	1	35	4	†
Sul Ross State University	1	2,842	2,827	1,773	62.7	1,274	499	0	226	95	†
Tarrant County College District	2	50,771	50,389	13,957	27.7	13,957	†	879	†	†	†
Texas A & M International University	1	7,431	7,208	6,938	96.3	6,238	700	†	739	197	0
Texas A & M University, Corpus Christi	1	10,913	10,398	4,811	46.3	4,274	537	†	592	147	7
Texas A & M University, Kingsville	1	12,229	11,346	7,811	68.8	6,482	1,329	†	1,187	286	13
Texas Lutheran University	3	1,341	1,339	421	31.4	420	1	†	55	3	†
Texas School of Business, Friendswood	6	262	262	92	35.1	92	†	7	†	†	†
Texas School of Business, North	6	436	436	180	41.3	180	†	12	†	†	†
Texas State Technical College, Harlingen	2	5,332	5,328	4,878	91.6	4,878	†	359	†	†	†
Texas State Technical College, West Texas	2	1,281	1,280	356	27.8	356	†	42	†	†	†
Texas State University	1	35,546	35,172	10,929	31.1	9,947	982	†	1,428	276	12
Texas Wesleyan University	3	2,397	1,967	447	22.7	365	82	†	80	21	17
University of Houston	1	39,540	35,807	10,275	28.7	9,429	846	†	1,496	229	80
University of Houston, Clear Lake	1	8,164	7,155	2,133	29.8	1,625	508	†	351	132	4
University of Houston, Downtown	1	13,757	13,055	5,468	41.9	5,392	76	†	855	13	†
University of Houston, Victoria	1	4,491	4,314	1,147	26.6	903	244	†	152	74	†
University of Phoenix, Austin Campus	5	756	745	193	25.9	180	13	†	6	0	†
University of Phoenix, Houston Campus	5	1,841	1,810	429	23.7	399	30	†	41	10	†
University of Phoenix, McAllen	5	139	138	121	87.7	111	10	†	0	†	†
University of Phoenix, San Antonio	5	1,048	1,037	433	41.8	355	78	†	45	19	†
University of Saint Thomas	3	3,525	3,142	1,158	36.9	600	558	†	113	225	1
University of Texas at Arlington	1	33,329	30,241	7,444	24.6	6,583	861	†	1,156	307	4
University of Texas at Brownsville	1	12,285	11,752	10,935	93.0	10,139	796	757	928	186	4
University of Texas at El Paso	1	23,003	21,541	18,360	85.2	16,318	2,042	†	2,552	641	62
University of Texas at San Antonio	1	28,623	26,845	13,508	50.3	11,935	1,573	†	2,059	444	15
University of Texas Health Science Center at San Antonio	1	3,148	3,005	822	27.4	282	540	†	186	73	88
University of Texas of the Permian Basin	1	5,131	5,073	2,152	42.4	1,835	317	†	229	51	†
University of Texas, Pan American	1	20,053	19,530	18,333	93.9	15,925	2,408	†	2,446	604	12
University of the Incarnate Word	3	8,685	8,281	4,962	59.9	4,094	868	2	706	174	38
Vet Tech Institute of Houston	6	196	196	64	32.7	64	†	41	†	†	†
Victoria College	2	4,419	4,417	1,850	41.9	1,850	†	86	†	†	†
Virginia College, Austin	6	642	641	282	44.0	282	†	38	†	†	†
Vista College	6	2,746	2,745	1,419	51.7	1,419	†	93	†	†	†
Wayland Baptist University	3	6,222	6,172	1,569	25.4	1,236	333	38	310	120	†
Western Technical College, Diana Drive	6	651	621	465	74.9	465	†	74	†	†	†
Western Technical College, Plaza Circle	6	815	815	646	79.3	646	†	117	†	†	†

See notes at end of table.

Table 312.40. Enrollment and degrees conferred in degree-granting postsecondary institutions that serve large proportions of Hispanic undergraduate students, by institution level and control, percentage Hispanic, degree level, and other selected characteristics: Fall 2013 and 2012–13—Continued

State and institution	Level and control[1]	Total, all enrollment[2,3]	Enrollment, fall 2013 U.S. citizens and permanent residents only Total[3]	Hispanic[3]	Percent Hispanic[4]	Hispanic undergraduate	Hispanic postbaccalaureate	Degrees awarded to Hispanics, 2012–13 Associate's	Bachelor's	Master's	Doctor's[5]
1	2	3	4	5	6	7	8	9	10	11	12
Western Texas College	2	2,044	1,992	587	29.5	587	†	65	†	†	†
Wharton County Junior College	2	7,386	7,381	2,579	34.9	2,579	†	209	†	†	†
Utah											
Art Institute of Salt Lake City	5	466	460	175	38.0	175	†	16	8	†	†
Everest College, Salt Lake City	5	404	404	108	26.7	108	†	11	1	†	†
Vista College, Online	6	207	207	57	27.5	57	†	10	†	†	†
Virginia											
Art Institute of Washington	5	1,499	1,471	571	38.8	571	†	24	26	†	†
Art Institute of Washington, Dulles	5	244	243	67	27.6	67	†	1	2	†	†
Bethel College	3	54	52	11	21.2	11	†	0	0	†	†
Columbia College	6	310	179	56	31.3	56	†	0	†	†	†
Everest College, McLean	6	237	237	73	30.8	73	†	12	†	†	†
ITT Technical Institute, Chantilly	5	573	573	154	26.9	154	†	55	12	†	†
Medtech Institute	6	1,373	1,372	600	43.7	600	†	1	†	†	†
Washington											
Art Institute of Seattle	5	1,573	1,548	475	30.7	475	†	15	30	†	†
Big Bend Community College	2	1,991	1,985	652	32.8	652	†	99	†	†	†
Columbia Basin College	1	6,480	6,473	1,925	29.7	1,925	†	223	9	†	†
Heritage University	3	1,128	1,123	591	52.6	517	74	7	66	35	†
Wenatchee Valley College	2	3,619	3,611	1,126	31.2	1,126	†	133	†	†	†
Yakima Valley Community College	2	4,105	4,100	1,891	46.1	1,891	†	266	†	†	†
Puerto Rico											
American University of Puerto Rico, Bayamon	3	968	968	968	100.0	858	110	24	159	36	†
American University of Puerto Rico, Manati	3	1,082	1,082	1,082	100.0	1,008	74	29	117	22	†
Atenas College	3	1,269	1,269	1,269	100.0	1,269	†	170	54	†	†
Atlantic University College	3	1,429	1,429	1,429	100.0	1,365	64	17	179	36	†
Bayamon Central University	3	2,065	2,065	2,055	99.5	1,647	408	12	175	127	†
Caribbean University, Bayamon	3	1,876	1,876	1,876	100.0	1,578	298	27	153	65	†
Caribbean University, Carolina	3	827	827	827	100.0	704	123	41	46	40	†
Caribbean University, Ponce	3	1,529	1,529	1,529	100.0	1,161	368	21	120	106	†
Caribbean University, Vega Baja	3	604	604	604	100.0	489	115	36	44	43	†
Carlos Albizu University, San Juan	3	919	919	917	99.8	141	776	†	47	155	83
Centro de Estudios Multidisciplinarios, Bayamon	3	631	631	631	100.0	631	†	178	25	†	†
Centro de Estudios Multidisciplinarios, Humacao	3	743	724	724	100.0	724	†	216	43	†	†
Centro de Estudios Multidisciplinarios, San Juan	3	987	987	987	100.0	987	†	365	120	†	†
Colegio de Cinematografía, Artes y Television	6	867	867	867	100.0	867	†	76	†	†	†
Colegio Universitario de San Juan	1	1,387	1,387	1,387	100.0	1,387	†	154	151	†	†
Columbia Centro Universitario, Caguas	5	1,823	1,823	1,823	100.0	1,680	143	254	190	77	†
Columbia Centro Universitario, Yauco	5	402	402	402	100.0	402	†	71	44	†	†
Dewey University, Hato Rey	3	2,565	2,565	2,565	100.0	2,470	95	266	203	†	†
EDIC College	6	752	752	752	100.0	752	†	132	†	†	†
EDP University of Puerto Rico Inc., San Juan	3	1,348	1,348	1,348	100.0	1,275	73	114	73	15	†
EDP University of Puerto Rico Inc., San Sebastian	3	1,195	1,195	1,195	100.0	1,195	†	182	62	†	†
Escuela de Artes Plasticas de Puerto Rico	1	529	528	527	99.8	527	†	†	77	†	†
Huertas College	6	1,255	1,255	1,255	100.0	1,255	†	351	†	†	†
Humacao Community College	3	705	705	705	100.0	705	†	112	21	†	†
ICPR Junior College, Arecibo	6	542	542	542	100.0	542	†	18	†	†	†
ICPR Junior College, General Institutional	6	789	789	789	100.0	789	†	16	†	†	†
ICPR Junior College, Manatí	6	613	613	613	100.0	613	†	†	†	†	†
ICPR Junior College, Mayaguez	6	596	596	596	100.0	596	†	56	†	†	†
Instituto de Banca y Comercio Inc.	6	16,339	16,339	16,339	100.0	16,339	†	50	†	†	†
Instituto Tecnologico de Puerto Rico, Recinto de Guayama	2	861	861	861	100.0	861	†	188	†	†	†
Instituto Tecnologico de Puerto Rico, Recinto de Manati	2	755	755	755	100.0	755	†	211	†	†	†
Instituto Tecnologico de Puerto Rico, Recinto de Ponce	2	644	644	644	100.0	644	†	131	†	†	†
Instituto Tecnologico de Puerto Rico, Recinto de San Juan	2	650	650	650	100.0	650	†	141	†	†	†
Inter American University of Puerto Rico, Aguadilla	3	4,595	4,595	4,588	99.8	4,275	313	115	351	67	†
Inter American University of Puerto Rico, Arecibo	3	4,799	4,799	4,791	99.8	4,305	486	128	441	101	†
Inter American University of Puerto Rico, Barranquitas	3	2,073	2,073	2,068	99.8	2,011	57	115	218	26	†
Inter American University of Puerto Rico, Bayamon	3	4,857	4,857	4,830	99.4	4,688	142	33	477	25	†
Inter American University of Puerto Rico, Fajardo	3	2,259	2,259	2,256	99.9	2,176	80	18	193	6	†
Inter American University of Puerto Rico, Guayama	3	2,169	2,169	2,163	99.7	2,087	76	80	195	10	†
Inter American University of Puerto Rico, Metro	3	9,853	9,853	9,743	98.9	7,037	2,706	84	1,056	524	43
Inter American University of Puerto Rico, Ponce	3	5,821	5,821	5,809	99.8	5,405	404	166	505	51	†
Inter American University of Puerto Rico, San German	3	5,177	5,177	5,153	99.5	4,375	778	53	462	116	19
Mech-Tech College	6	3,262	3,262	3,262	100.0	3,262	†	257	†	†	†
National University College, Arecibo	5	1,650	1,650	1,650	100.0	1,650	†	224	153	†	†
National University College, Bayamon	5	5,213	5,213	5,213	100.0	4,998	215	289	227	5	†
National University College, Caguas	5	920	920	920	100.0	920	†	0	0	†	†
National University College, Ponce	5	1,118	1,118	1,118	100.0	1,118	†	82	151	†	†

See notes at end of table.

Table 312.40. Enrollment and degrees conferred in degree-granting postsecondary institutions that serve large proportions of Hispanic undergraduate students, by institution level and control, percentage Hispanic, degree level, and other selected characteristics: Fall 2013 and 2012–13—Continued

State and institution	Level and control[1]	Total, all enrollment[2,3]	Enrollment, fall 2013					Degrees awarded to Hispanics, 2012–13			
			U.S. citizens and permanent residents only								
			Total[3]	Hispanic[3]	Percent Hispanic[4]	Hispanic under-graduate	Hispanic postbacca-laureate	Associate's	Bachelor's	Master's	Doctor's[5]
1	2	3	4	5	6	7	8	9	10	11	12
National University College, Rio Grande	5	1,869	1,869	1,869	100.0	1,869	†	101	148	†	†
Ponce Paramedical College Inc.	6	2,882	2,882	2,882	100.0	2,882	†	334	†	†	†
Pontifical Catholic University of Puerto Rico, Arecibo	3	986	986	980	99.4	652	328	8	59	55	†
Pontifical Catholic University of Puerto Rico, Mayaguez	3	1,501	1,500	1,499	99.9	1,385	114	7	128	16	†
Pontifical Catholic University of Puerto Rico, Ponce	3	8,341	8,296	8,292	100.0	5,993	2,299	20	608	172	296
Puerto Rico Conservatory of Music	1	492	476	470	98.7	425	45	†	53	11	†
San Juan Bautista School of Medicine	3	295	295	139	47.1	27	112	†	1	1	38
Universal Technology College of Puerto Rico	3	1,260	1,260	1,260	100.0	1,260	†	138	†	†	†
Universidad Adventista de las Antillas	3	1,403	1,360	1,336	98.2	1,226	110	8	154	15	†
Universidad Central Del Caribe	3	467	467	451	96.6	144	307	15	15	5	63
Universidad Del Este	3	13,420	13,420	13,420	100.0	12,287	1,133	376	1,197	228	†
Universidad del Sagrado Corazon	3	5,892	5,892	5,892	100.0	5,159	733	56	783	141	†
Universidad Del Turabo	3	17,287	17,287	17,287	100.0	14,556	2,731	238	1,375	796	42
Universidad Metropolitana	3	13,631	13,631	13,631	100.0	11,503	2,128	203	1,233	674	10
Universidad Pentecostal Mizpa	3	412	412	412	100.0	375	37	13	23	0	†
Universidad Politecnica de Puerto Rico, Hato Rey	3	4,646	4,646	4,638	99.8	3,855	783	†	493	222	†
Universidad Teologica del Caribe	3	202	202	202	100.0	202	†	†	20	†	†
University of Phoenix, Puerto Rico	5	928	918	897	97.7	437	460	†	127	160	†
University of Puerto Rico, Aguadilla	1	2,973	2,973	2,941	98.9	2,941	†	5	336	†	†
University of Puerto Rico, Arecibo	1	3,759	3,759	3,759	100.0	3,759	†	39	519	†	†
University of Puerto Rico, Bayamon	1	5,075	5,075	5,075	100.0	5,075	†	28	529	†	†
University of Puerto Rico, Carolina	1	3,994	3,994	3,876	97.0	3,876	†	64	477	†	†
University of Puerto Rico, Cayey	1	3,816	3,816	3,816	100.0	3,816	†	†	547	†	†
University of Puerto Rico, Humacao	1	3,495	3,493	3,419	97.9	3,419	†	73	511	†	†
University of Puerto Rico, Mayaguez	1	11,838	11,838	11,838	100.0	10,944	894	†	1,696	128	13
University of Puerto Rico, Medical Sciences	1	2,253	2,253	2,220	98.5	489	1,731	43	158	249	176
University of Puerto Rico, Ponce	1	3,120	3,120	3,120	100.0	3,120	†	67	353	†	†
University of Puerto Rico, Rio Piedras	1	15,487	15,477	15,199	98.2	11,954	3,245	†	1,331	201	170
University of Puerto Rico, Utuado	1	1,559	1,559	661	42.4	661	†	79	59	†	†

†Not applicable.

[1] 1 = 4-year public; 2 = 2-year public; 3 = 4-year private nonprofit; 4 = 2-year private nonprofit; 5 = 4-year private for-profit; and 6 = 2-year private for-profit.

[2] Includes nonresident alien students as well as U.S. citizens and permanent residents.

[3] Includes graduate as well as undergraduate students.

[4] Hispanic headcount enrollment (U.S. citizens and permanent residents only) as a percentage of total headcount enrollment of U.S. citizens and permanent residents.

[5] Includes Ph.D., Ed.D., and comparable degrees at the doctoral level, as well as such degrees as M.D., D.D.S., and law degrees that were formerly classified as first-professional degrees.

NOTE: Degree-granting institutions grant associate's or higher degrees and participate in Title IV federal financial aid programs. This table includes institutions that serve large proportions of Hispanic undergraduate students, defined as institutions with a full-time-equivalent undergraduate enrollment of Hispanic students at 25 percent or more of full-time-equivalent undergraduate enrollment of U.S. citizens. Data for Hispanics include only persons who were U.S. citizens or permanent residents.

SOURCE: U.S. Department of Education, National Center for Education Statistics, Integrated Postsecondary Education Data System (IPEDS), Spring 2014, Enrollment component; and Fall 2013, Completions component. (This table was prepared May 2015.)

Table 312.50. Fall enrollment and degrees conferred in degree-granting tribally controlled postsecondary institutions, by state and institution: Selected years, fall 2000 through fall 2013, and 2011–12 and 2012–13

		Total fall enrollment							2013				Degrees to American Indians/ Alaska Natives			
													Associate's		Bachelor's	
State and institution	Level and control[1]	2000	2005	2008	2009	2010	2011	2012	Total	Total American Indian/ Alaska Native	Percent American Indian/ Alaska Native	Under-graduate American Indian/ Alaska Native	2011–12	2012–13	2011–12	2012–13
1	2	3	4	5	6	7	8	9	10	11	12	13	14	15	16	17
Tribally controlled institutions[2]	†	13,680	17,167	17,014	19,686	21,179	19,126	18,881	18,274	14,393	78.8	14,287	1,360	1,240	253	284
Alaska																
Ilisagvik College	2	322	278	251	226	288	226	231	257	152	59.1	152	9	10	†	†
Arizona																
Diné College	1	1,712	1,825	1,527	1,935	2,033	2,021	1,970	1,466	1,452	99.0	1,452	145	115	7	8
Tohono O'odham Community College	2	—	270	163	254	207	295	214	243	213	87.7	213	3	3	†	†
Kansas																
Haskell Indian Nations University	1	918	918	997	1,059	958	826	846	742	742	100.0	742	110	96	75	102
Michigan																
Bay Mills Community College	2	360	406	501	608	607	575	536	531	300	56.5	300	16	25	†	†
Keweenaw Bay Ojibwa Community College	2	—	—	—	—	—	80	86	106	79	74.5	79	4	6	†	†
Saginaw Chippewa Tribal College	2	—	123	133	134	153	133	127	117	94	80.3	94	8	12	†	†
Minnesota																
Fond du Lac Tribal and Community College	2	999	1,981	2,206	2,305	2,339	2,319	2,307	2,272	170	7.5	170	28	23	†	†
Leech Lake Tribal College	2	240	189	228	233	235	206	338	348	311	89.4	311	19	24	†	†
White Earth Tribal and Community College	4	—	61	106	113	117	88	87	60	46	76.7	46	9	8	†	†
Montana																
Aaniiih Nakoda College	2	295	175	168	236	214	169	221	139	123	88.5	123	24	18	†	†
Blackfeet Community College	4	299	485	492	533	473	464	407	450	435	96.7	435	57	55	†	†
Chief Dull Knife College	2	461	554	443	472	433	374	361	201	189	94.0	189	17	19	†	†
Fort Peck Community College	2	400	408	436	427	452	513	438	405	340	84.0	340	24	15	†	†
Little Big Horn College	2	320	259	337	415	380	366	325	329	315	95.7	315	46	50	†	†
Salish Kootenai College	3	1,042	1,142	993	1,204	1,158	1,112	906	840	617	73.5	617	62	53	27	35
Stone Child College	2	38	344	236	303	332	410	501	404	369	91.3	369	22	29	†	†
Nebraska																
Little Priest Tribal College	4	141	109	116	141	148	172	144	144	134	93.1	134	9	15	†	†
Nebraska Indian Community College	2	170	107	92	129	177	163	150	199	195	98.0	195	8	9	†	†
New Mexico																
Institute of American Indian and Alaska Native Culture[2]	1	139	113	249	350	313	374	392	422	339	80.3	322	4	8	33	31
Navajo Technical College	1	841	333	571	751	1,019	1,173	1,777	1,956	1,932	98.8	1,932	45	56	0	1
Southwestern Indian Polytechnic Institute	2	304	614	470	635	531	480	488	530	530	100.0	530	78	62	†	†
North Dakota																
Candeska Cikana Community College	2	9	198	201	250	220	219	247	254	242	95.3	242	22	27	†	†
Fort Berthold Community College	1	50	241	162	323	215	199	205	203	176	86.7	176	22	24	5	8
Sitting Bull College	1	22	287	296	335	314	313	277	279	262	93.9	262	23	30	19	14
Turtle Mountain Community College	3	686	615	951	1,058	969	588	532	602	564	93.7	564	144	90	7	8
United Tribes Technical College	3	204	885	375	476	600	651	505	505	447	88.5	447	73	54	6	3
Oklahoma																
College of the Muscogee Nation	2	—	—	—	—	—	—	—	191	190	99.5	190	†	16	†	†
South Dakota																
Oglala Lakota College[2]	1	1,174	1,302	1,531	1,804	1,830	1,685	1,583	1,551	1,478	95.3	1,446	113	83	42	28
Sinte Gleska University[2]	3	900	1,123	1,012	936	2,473	835	728	689	521	75.6	464	47	41	22	35
Sisseton-Wahpeton College	2	250	290	227	237	261	264	175	194	175	90.2	175	18	21	†	†
Washington																
Northwest Indian College	1	524	495	554	609	626	701	699	681	639	93.8	639	61	77	8	9
Wisconsin																
College of the Menominee Nation	3	371	532	512	634	615	699	721	661	416	62.9	416	67	32	2	2
Lac Courte Oreilles Ojibwa Community College	2	489	505	478	561	489	433	357	303	206	68.0	206	23	34	†	†

—Not available.
†Not applicable.
[1]1 = public, 4-year; 2 = public, 2-year; 3 = private nonprofit, 4-year; and 4 = private nonprofit, 2-year.
[2]"Total American Indian/Alaska Native" enrollment (column 11) includes graduate students and therefore does not equal "Undergraduate American Indian/Alaska Native" enrollment (column 13).
NOTE: This table only includes institutions that were in operation during the 2013–14 academic year. They are all members of the American Indian Higher Education Consortium and, with few exceptions, are tribally controlled and located on reservations. Degree-granting institutions grant associate's or higher degrees and participate in Title IV federal financial aid programs. Totals include persons of other racial/ethnic groups not separately identified. Some data have been revised from previously published figures.
SOURCE: U.S. Department of Education, National Center for Education Statistics, Integrated Postsecondary Education Data System (IPEDS), Spring 2001 through Spring 2014, Enrollment component; and Fall 2012 and Fall 2013, Completions component. (This table was prepared May 2015.)

Table 313.10. Fall enrollment, degrees conferred, and expenditures in degree-granting historically Black colleges and universities, by institution: 2012, 2013, and 2012–13

Institution	State	Level and control[1]	Total enrollment, fall 2012	Enrollment, fall 2013 Total	Black enrollment	Full-time-equivalent enrollment, fall 2013	Associate's	Bachelor's	Master's	Doctor's[2]	Total expenditures, 2012–13 (in thousands)
1	2	3	4	5	6	7	8	9	10	11	12
Total[3]	†	†	312,438	303,167	241,476	263,090	4,421	33,736	7,945	2,421	$7,663,851
Alabama A&M University[4]	AL	1	4,853	5,020	4,669	4,660	†	604	213	8	141,835
Alabama State University	AL	1	5,816	6,075	5,610	5,525	†	600	147	48	152,500
Bishop State Community College	AL	2	3,791	3,896	2,416	2,750	217	†	†	†	36,426
Concordia College, Alabama	AL	3	611	600	568	565	39	42	†	†	12,305
Gadsden State Community College	AL	2	5,882	5,797	1,230	4,062	541	†	†	†	56,325
H. Councill Trenholm State Technical College	AL	2	1,445	1,351	777	926	154	†	†	†	18,753
J. F. Drake State Community and Technical College	AL	2	1,248	1,383	751	886	62	†	†	†	13,863
Lawson State Community College, Birmingham Campus	AL	2	3,419	3,028	2,465	2,204	281	†	†	†	36,576
Miles College	AL	3	1,691	1,666	1,615	1,612	†	187	†	†	27,950
Oakwood University	AL	3	2,019	1,903	1,651	1,846	2	358	14	†	47,598
Selma University	AL	3	643	611	596	530	0	26	9	†	2,575
Shelton State Community College, C. A. Fredd campus	AL	2	5,104	5,068	1,837	3,341	323	†	†	†	45,229
Stillman College	AL	3	1,019	863	798	830	†	137	†	†	21,180
Talladega College	AL	3	1,203	932	843	882	†	78	†	†	15,523
Tuskegee University[4]	AL	3	3,117	3,118	2,969	3,018	†	344	59	49	148,051
Arkansas Baptist College	AR	3	1,082	1,027	946	930	59	64	†	†	15,081
Philander Smith College	AR	3	666	556	496	536	†	126	†	†	17,076
Shorter College	AR	4	52	330	327	289	1	†	†	†	1,150
University of Arkansas at Pine Bluff[4]	AR	1	2,828	2,615	2,406	2,441	0	394	35	0	70,408
Delaware State University[4]	DE	1	4,324	4,336	3,054	4,087	†	535	120	19	122,591
Howard University	DC	3	10,002	10,297	8,837	9,577	†	1,225	377	509	834,428
University of the District of Columbia[4]	DC	1	5,110	5,011	3,823	3,330	300	372	82	†	141,338
Bethune-Cookman University	FL	3	3,543	3,787	3,434	3,716	†	451	24	†	69,378
Edward Waters College	FL	3	925	862	804	852	†	92	†	†	22,046
Florida A&M University[4]	FL	1	12,057	10,743	9,725	10,049	102	1,482	274	400	278,497
Florida Memorial University	FL	3	1,579	1,560	1,304	1,480	†	205	24	†	39,086
Albany State University	GA	1	4,275	4,260	3,888	3,637	†	519	143	†	71,538
Clark Atlanta University	GA	3	3,419	3,458	3,337	3,203	†	479	184	37	87,217
Fort Valley State University[4]	GA	1	3,568	3,180	3,062	2,882	†	488	61	†	78,566
Interdenominational Theological Center	GA	3	827	562	546	332	†	†	70	7	10,716
Morehouse College	GA	3	2,374	2,170	2,115	2,070	†	422	†	†	90,353
Morehouse School of Medicine	GA	3	360	372	269	368	†	†	27	59	151,952
Paine College	GA	3	837	924	859	872	†	91	†	†	19,589
Savannah State University	GA	1	4,582	4,772	4,192	4,441	0	407	57	†	92,093
Spelman College	GA	3	2,145	2,129	2,022	2,088	†	484	†	†	87,624
Kentucky State University[4]	KY	1	2,524	2,533	1,624	2,144	45	206	50	†	71,207
Dillard University	LA	3	1,307	1,183	1,106	1,150	†	147	†	†	47,585
Grambling State University	LA	1	5,277	5,071	4,595	4,607	15	725	226	6	102,017
Southern University and A&M College[4]	LA	1	6,397	6,777	6,304	6,095	†	854	314	27	136,818
Southern University at New Orleans	LA	1	2,820	2,292	2,184	1,910	24	327	184	†	39,993
Southern University at Shreveport	LA	2	2,937	3,018	2,698	2,422	264	†	†	†	33,834
Xavier University of Louisiana	LA	3	3,178	3,121	2,253	3,012	†	326	44	145	102,799
Bowie State University	MD	1	5,421	5,561	4,804	4,583	†	739	267	10	90,396
Coppin State College	MD	1	3,612	3,383	2,880	2,773	†	409	72	0	76,875
Morgan State University	MD	1	7,952	7,546	6,277	6,655	†	976	267	33	203,404
University of Maryland, Eastern Shore[4]	MD	1	4,454	4,220	2,870	3,840	†	514	50	101	110,947
Alcorn State University[4]	MS	1	3,950	3,848	3,573	3,272	13	352	136	†	86,696
Coahoma Community College	MS	2	2,305	2,073	1,969	1,928	245	†	†	†	36,831
Hinds Community College, Utica Campus	MS	2	767	717	682	675	82	0	0	0	—
Jackson State University	MS	1	8,819	9,134	8,239	7,603	†	946	446	74	188,373
Mississippi Valley State University	MS	1	2,479	2,203	2,097	1,903	†	366	89	†	55,869
Rust College	MS	3	934	922	890	881	16	130	†	†	16,665
Tougaloo College	MS	3	972	878	858	860	7	135	†	†	24,461

See notes at end of table.

Table 313.10. Fall enrollment, degrees conferred, and expenditures in degree-granting historically Black colleges and universities, by institution: 2012, 2013, and 2012–13—Continued

Institution	State	Level and control[1]	Total enrollment, fall 2012	Enrollment, fall 2013		Full-time-equivalent enrollment, fall 2013	Degrees conferred, 2012–13				Total expenditures, 2012–13 (in thousands)
				Total	Black enrollment		Associate's	Bachelor's	Master's	Doctor's[2]	
1	2	3	4	5	6	7	8	9	10	11	12
Harris-Stowe State University	MO	1	1,484	1,298	1,102	1,111	†	162	†	†	27,340
Lincoln University[4]	MO	1	3,205	3,043	1,125	2,366	75	309	73	†	52,731
Bennett College for Women	NC	3	707	680	645	637	†	125	†	†	20,658
Elizabeth City State University	NC	1	2,878	2,421	1,948	2,259	†	445	37	†	82,036
Fayetteville State University	NC	1	6,060	6,179	4,273	5,056	†	937	179	7	112,839
Johnson C. Smith University	NC	3	1,669	1,387	1,184	1,348	†	252	†	†	47,272
Livingstone College	NC	3	1,111	1,175	1,149	1,168	0	136	†	†	25,436
North Carolina A&T State University[4]	NC	1	10,636	10,561	8,874	9,652	†	1,313	456	29	259,470
North Carolina Central University	NC	1	8,604	8,093	6,490	7,146	†	1,010	449	167	190,167
Saint Augustine's College	NC	3	1,442	1,299	1,262	1,278	†	228	†	†	37,336
Shaw University	NC	3	2,183	2,062	1,957	1,948	6	278	33	†	43,794
Winston-Salem State University	NC	1	5,689	5,399	3,893	4,924	†	1,398	157	0	146,205
Central State University	OH	1	2,152	2,068	1,989	1,931	†	258	1	†	63,459
Wilberforce University	OH	3	518	479	453	471	†	103	5	†	12,569
Langston University[4]	OK	1	2,518	2,533	2,057	2,218	20	276	115	14	60,905
Cheyney University of Pennsylvania	PA	1	1,284	1,212	1,089	1,158	†	157	21	†	47,486
Lincoln University of Pennsylvania	PA	1	2,101	1,963	1,799	1,809	†	297	155	†	54,894
Allen University	SC	3	672	651	648	641	†	81	†	†	17,420
Benedict College	SC	3	2,917	2,512	2,485	2,486	†	377	†	†	62,928
Claflin College	SC	3	1,946	1,884	1,711	1,837	†	311	25	†	43,525
Clinton Junior College	SC	3	139	185	185	183	33	0	†	†	3,445
Denmark Technical College	SC	2	2,003	1,838	1,789	1,557	107	†	†	†	19,516
Morris College	SC	3	874	824	801	820	†	133	†	†	19,860
South Carolina State University[4]	SC	1	3,807	3,463	3,260	3,142	†	546	125	24	111,026
Voorhees College	SC	3	648	536	524	524	†	131	†	†	16,863
Fisk University	TN	3	620	646	607	626	†	72	13	†	24,567
Lane College	TN	3	1,512	1,554	1,552	1,542	†	281	†	†	25,025
Le Moyne-Owen College	TN	3	1,078	1,023	1,015	936	†	125	†	†	16,781
Meharry Medical College	TN	3	782	801	658	801	†	†	54	146	130,749
Tennessee State University[4]	TN	1	8,740	8,883	6,194	7,273	128	943	397	66	178,458
Huston-Tillotson University	TX	3	918	973	714	892	†	121	†	†	18,856
Jarvis Christian College	TX	3	603	609	538	585	†	42	†	†	16,017
Paul Quinn College	TX	3	192	243	211	227	†	16	†	†	7,503
Prairie View A&M University[4]	TX	1	8,336	8,283	7,013	7,376	†	1,006	426	18	182,836
Saint Philip's College	TX	2	10,313	10,238	1,054	4,612	837	†	†	†	74,821
Southwestern Christian College	TX	3	206	172	149	163	30	3	†	†	5,923
Texas College	TX	3	845	971	836	947	38	102	†	†	11,421
Texas Southern University	TX	1	9,646	8,703	6,952	7,615	†	774	368	320	211,925
Wiley College	TX	3	1,401	1,392	1,183	1,352	2	142	†	†	24,827
Hampton University	VA	3	4,765	4,622	4,037	4,312	5	668	194	80	163,762
Norfolk State University	VA	1	7,100	6,728	5,840	5,941	118	854	247	5	153,367
Virginia State University[4]	VA	1	6,208	5,763	5,402	5,391	8	920	138	6	143,479
Virginia Union University	VA	3	1,751	1,749	1,669	1,719	†	160	140	4	31,594
Virginia University of Lynchburg	VA	3	540	582	573	426	59	15	3	3	7,143
Bluefield State College	WV	1	1,935	1,747	181	1,564	98	249	†	†	23,079
West Virginia State University[4]	WV	1	2,644	2,677	394	2,226	†	397	13	†	48,582
University of the Virgin Islands[4]	VI	1	2,423	2,321	1,868	1,764	65	211	56	†	81,772

—Not available.
†Not applicable.
[1]1 = public, 4-year; 2 = public, 2-year; 3 = private nonprofit, 4-year; and 4 = private nonprofit, 2-year.
[2]Includes Ph.D., Ed.D., and comparable degrees at the doctoral level, as well as such degrees as M.D., D.D.S., and law degrees that were formerly classified as first-professional degrees.
[3]Total fall 2012 enrollment includes enrollment at St. Paul's College in Virginia. This institution closed in 2013 and therefore does not appear in this table.
[4]Land-grant institution.

NOTE: Degree-granting institutions grant associate's or higher degrees and participate in Title IV federal financial aid programs. Excludes historically Black colleges and universities that are not participating in Title IV programs. Historically Black colleges and universities are degree-granting institutions established prior to 1964 with the principal mission of educating Black Americans. Federal regulations, 20 U.S. Code, Section 1061 (2), allow for certain exceptions to the founding date. Totals include persons of other racial/ethnic groups not separately identified. Detail may not sum to totals because of rounding.
SOURCE: U.S. Department of Education, National Center for Education Statistics, Integrated Postsecondary Education Data System (IPEDS), Fall 2013, Completions component; Spring 2013 and Spring 2014, Enrollment component; and Spring 2014, Finance component. (This table was prepared May 2015.)

Table 313.20. Fall enrollment in degree-granting historically Black colleges and universities, by sex of student and level and control of institution: Selected years, 1976 through 2013

Year	Total enrollment	Males	Females	4-year	2-year	Public Total	Public 4-year	Public 2-year	Private Total	Private 4-year	Private 2-year
1	2	3	4	5	6	7	8	9	10	11	12
						All students					
1976	222,613	104,669	117,944	206,676	15,937	156,836	143,528	13,308	65,777	63,148	2,629
1980	233,557	106,387	127,170	218,009	15,548	168,217	155,085	13,132	65,340	62,924	2,416
1982	228,371	104,897	123,474	212,017	16,354	165,871	151,472	14,399	62,500	60,545	1,955
1984	227,519	102,823	124,696	212,844	14,675	164,116	151,289	12,827	63,403	61,555	1,848
1986	223,275	97,523	125,752	207,231	16,044	162,048	147,631	14,417	61,227	59,600	1,627
1988	239,755	100,561	139,194	223,250	16,505	173,672	158,606	15,066	66,083	64,644	1,439
1990	257,152	105,157	151,995	240,497	16,655	187,046	171,969	15,077	70,106	68,528	1,578
1991	269,335	110,442	158,893	252,093	17,242	197,847	182,204	15,643	71,488	69,889	1,599
1992	279,541	114,622	164,919	261,089	18,452	204,966	188,143	16,823	74,575	72,946	1,629
1993	282,856	116,397	166,459	262,430	20,426	208,197	189,032	19,165	74,659	73,398	1,261
1994	280,071	114,006	166,065	259,997	20,074	206,520	187,735	18,785	73,551	72,262	1,289
1995	278,725	112,637	166,088	259,409	19,316	204,726	186,278	18,448	73,999	73,131	868
1996	273,018	109,498	163,520	253,654	19,364	200,569	182,063	18,506	72,449	71,591	858
1997	269,167	106,865	162,302	248,860	20,307	194,674	175,297	19,377	74,493	73,563	930
1998	273,472	108,752	164,720	248,931	24,541	198,603	174,776	23,827	74,869	74,155	714
1999	274,321	108,301	166,020	249,156	25,165	199,826	175,364	24,462	74,495	73,792	703
2000	275,680	108,164	167,516	250,710	24,970	199,725	175,404	24,321	75,955	75,306	649
2001	289,985	112,874	177,111	260,547	29,438	210,083	181,346	28,737	79,902	79,201	701
2002	299,041	115,466	183,575	269,020	30,021	218,433	189,183	29,250	80,608	79,837	771
2003	306,727	117,795	188,932	274,326	32,401	228,096	196,077	32,019	78,631	78,249	382
2004	308,939	118,129	190,810	276,136	32,803	231,179	198,810	32,369	77,760	77,326	434
2005	311,768	120,023	191,745	272,666	39,102	235,875	197,200	38,675	75,893	75,466	427
2006	308,774	118,865	189,909	272,770	36,004	234,505	198,676	35,829	74,269	74,094	175
2007	306,515	118,640	187,875	270,915	35,600	233,807	198,300	35,507	72,708	72,615	93
2008	313,491	121,873	191,618	274,568	38,923	235,824	197,025	38,799	77,667	77,543	124
2009	322,860	125,728	197,132	280,133	42,727	246,595	204,016	42,579	76,265	76,117	148
2010	326,614	127,437	199,177	283,099	43,515	249,146	205,774	43,372	77,468	77,325	143
2011	323,648	126,160	197,488	281,150	42,498	246,685	204,363	42,322	76,963	76,787	176
2012	312,438	121,722	190,716	273,033	39,405	237,782	198,568	39,214	74,656	74,465	191
2013	303,167	119,291	183,876	264,430	38,737	230,325	191,918	38,407	72,842	72,512	330
						Black students					
1976	190,305	84,492	105,813	179,848	10,457	129,770	121,851	7,919	60,535	57,997	2,538
1980	190,989	81,818	109,171	181,237	9,752	131,661	124,236	7,425	59,328	57,001	2,327
1982	182,639	78,874	103,765	171,942	10,697	126,368	117,562	8,806	56,271	54,380	1,891
1984	180,803	76,819	103,984	171,401	9,402	124,445	116,845	7,600	56,358	54,556	1,802
1986	178,628	74,276	104,352	167,971	10,657	123,555	114,502	9,053	55,073	53,469	1,604
1988	194,151	78,268	115,883	183,402	10,749	133,786	124,438	9,348	60,365	58,964	1,401
1990	208,682	82,897	125,785	198,237	10,445	144,204	134,924	9,280	64,478	63,313	1,165
1991	218,366	87,380	130,986	207,449	10,917	152,864	143,411	9,453	65,502	64,038	1,464
1992	228,963	91,949	137,014	217,614	11,349	159,585	149,754	9,831	69,378	67,860	1,518
1993	231,198	93,110	138,088	219,431	11,767	161,444	150,867	10,577	69,754	68,564	1,190
1994	230,162	91,908	138,254	218,565	11,597	161,098	150,682	10,416	69,064	67,883	1,181
1995	229,418	91,132	138,286	218,379	11,039	159,925	149,661	10,264	69,493	68,718	775
1996	224,201	88,306	135,895	213,309	10,892	156,851	146,753	10,098	67,350	66,556	794
1997	222,331	86,641	135,690	210,741	11,590	153,039	142,326	10,713	69,292	68,415	877
1998	223,745	87,163	136,582	211,822	11,923	154,244	142,985	11,259	69,501	68,837	664
1999	226,592	87,987	138,605	213,779	12,813	156,292	144,166	12,126	70,300	69,613	687
2000	227,239	87,319	139,920	215,172	12,067	156,706	145,277	11,429	70,533	69,895	638
2001	238,638	90,718	147,920	224,417	14,221	164,354	150,831	13,523	74,284	73,586	698
2002	247,292	93,538	153,754	231,834	15,458	172,203	157,507	14,696	75,089	74,327	762
2003	253,257	95,703	157,554	236,753	16,504	180,104	163,977	16,127	73,153	72,776	377
2004	257,545	96,750	160,795	241,030	16,515	184,708	168,619	16,089	72,837	72,411	426
2005	256,584	96,891	159,693	238,030	18,554	186,047	167,916	18,131	70,537	70,114	423
2006	255,150	96,508	158,642	238,446	16,704	185,894	169,365	16,529	69,256	69,081	175
2007	253,415	96,313	157,102	236,885	16,530	185,344	168,906	16,438	68,071	67,979	92
2008	258,403	98,634	159,769	240,133	18,270	186,446	168,299	18,147	71,957	71,834	123
2009	264,092	100,590	163,502	243,956	20,136	194,088	174,099	19,989	70,004	69,857	147
2010	265,908	101,605	164,303	245,158	20,750	193,840	173,233	20,607	72,068	71,925	143
2011	263,435	100,526	162,909	242,881	20,554	192,042	171,664	20,378	71,393	71,217	176
2012	251,530	96,084	155,446	232,900	18,630	183,019	164,579	18,440	68,511	68,321	190
2013	241,476	92,454	149,022	223,481	17,995	175,287	157,619	17,668	66,189	65,862	327

NOTE: Historically Black colleges and universities are degree-granting institutions established prior to 1964 with the principal mission of educating Black Americans. Federal regulations, 20 U.S. Code, Section 1061 (2), allow for certain exceptions to the founding date. Data through 1995 are for institutions of higher education, while later data are for degree-granting institutions. Degree-granting institutions grant associate's or higher degrees and participate in Title IV federal financial aid programs. The degree-granting classification is very similar to the earlier higher education classification, but it includes more 2-year colleges and excludes a few higher education institutions that did not grant degrees. Some data have been revised from previously published figures.
SOURCE: U.S. Department of Education, National Center for Education Statistics, Higher Education General Information Survey (HEGIS), "Fall Enrollment in Colleges and Universities," 1976 through 1985 surveys; Integrated Postsecondary Education Data System (IPEDS), "Fall Enrollment Survey" (IPEDS-EF:86-99); and IPEDS Spring 2001 through Spring 2014, Enrollment component. (This table was prepared May 2015.)

Table 313.30. Selected statistics on degree-granting historically Black colleges and universities, by control and level of institution: Selected years, 1990 through 2013

Selected statistics	Total	Public Total	Public 4-year	Public 2-year	Private Total	Private 4-year	Private 2-year
1	2	3	4	5	6	7	8
Number of institutions, fall 2013	100	51	40	11	49	48	1
Fall enrollment							
Total enrollment, fall 1990	257,152	187,046	171,969	15,077	70,106	68,528	1,578
Males	105,157	76,541	70,220	6,321	28,616	28,054	562
Males, Black	82,897	57,255	54,041	3,214	25,642	25,198	444
Females	151,995	110,505	101,749	8,756	41,490	40,474	1,016
Females, Black	125,785	86,949	80,883	6,066	38,836	38,115	721
Total enrollment, fall 2000	275,680	199,725	175,404	24,321	75,955	75,306	649
Males	108,164	78,186	68,322	9,864	29,978	29,771	207
Males, Black	87,319	60,029	56,017	4,012	27,290	27,085	205
Females	167,516	121,539	107,082	14,457	45,977	45,535	442
Females, Black	139,920	96,677	89,260	7,417	43,243	42,810	433
Total enrollment, fall 2010	326,614	249,146	205,774	43,372	77,468	77,325	143
Males	127,437	95,883	78,528	17,355	31,554	31,482	72
Males, Black	101,605	72,629	65,512	7,117	28,976	28,904	72
Females	199,177	153,263	127,246	26,017	45,914	45,843	71
Females, Black	164,303	121,211	107,721	13,490	43,092	43,021	71
Total enrollment, fall 2013	303,167	230,325	191,918	38,407	72,842	72,512	330
Males	119,291	89,299	73,351	15,948	29,992	29,902	90
Males, Black	92,454	65,644	59,058	6,586	26,810	26,722	88
Females	183,876	141,026	118,567	22,459	42,850	42,610	240
Females, Black	149,022	109,643	98,561	11,082	39,379	39,140	239
Full-time enrollment, fall 2013	239,273	172,118	153,347	18,771	67,155	66,893	262
Males	96,578	68,957	60,660	8,297	27,621	27,546	75
Females	142,695	103,161	92,687	10,474	39,534	39,347	187
Part-time enrollment, fall 2013	63,894	58,207	38,571	19,636	5,687	5,619	68
Males	22,713	20,342	12,691	7,651	2,371	2,356	15
Females	41,181	37,865	25,880	11,985	3,316	3,263	53
Earned degrees conferred, 2012–13							
Associate's	4,421	4,124	1,011	3,113	297	296	1
Males	1,531	1,397	226	1,171	134	133	1
Males, Black	637	517	117	400	120	119	1
Females	2,890	2,727	785	1,942	163	163	0
Females, Black	1,534	1,381	392	989	153	153	0
Bachelor's	33,736	24,277	24,277	†	9,459	9,459	†
Males	12,137	8,790	8,790	†	3,347	3,347	†
Males, Black	10,007	6,960	6,960	†	3,047	3,047	†
Females	21,599	15,487	15,487	†	6,112	6,112	†
Females, Black	18,266	12,592	12,592	†	5,674	5,674	†
Master's	7,945	6,646	6,646	†	1,299	1,299	†
Males	2,357	1,904	1,904	†	453	453	†
Males, Black	1,672	1,277	1,277	†	395	395	†
Females	5,588	4,742	4,742	†	846	846	†
Females, Black	4,117	3,414	3,414	†	703	703	†
Doctor's[1]	2,421	1,382	1,382	†	1,039	1,039	†
Males	951	545	545	†	406	406	†
Males, Black	532	250	250	†	282	282	†
Females	1,470	837	837	†	633	633	†
Females, Black	969	507	507	†	462	462	†
Financial statistics, 2012–13[2]	In thousands of current dollars						
Total revenue	$8,106,461	$5,009,690	$4,617,938	$391,752	$3,096,770	$3,095,497	$1,273
Student tuition and fees	1,842,023	971,241	924,197	47,044	870,782	870,160	622
Federal government[3]	2,157,981	1,321,738	1,146,482	175,256	836,243	835,930	313
State governments	1,817,609	1,748,993	1,625,060	123,934	68,615	68,615	0
Local governments	112,018	93,217	64,420	28,797	18,801	18,801	0
Private gifts and grants[4]	304,709	86,449	85,427	1,022	218,260	217,969	291
Investment return (gain or loss)	458,710	42,680	42,245	436	416,029	416,029	0
Auxiliary (essentially self-supporting) enterprises	856,514	522,422	515,435	6,987	334,092	334,092	0
Hospitals and other sources	556,897	222,949	214,672	8,277	333,948	333,902	47
Total expenditures	7,663,851	4,916,190	4,544,016	372,174	2,747,661	2,746,510	1,150
Instruction	2,072,205	1,342,309	1,219,133	123,176	729,897	729,495	401
Research	451,922	279,717	279,176	541	172,206	172,206	0
Academic support	568,281	383,315	358,847	24,468	184,966	184,753	212
Institutional support	1,235,840	635,071	581,386	53,685	600,769	600,436	334
Auxiliary (essentially self-supporting) enterprises	830,759	529,457	520,004	9,453	301,302	301,302	0
Other expenditures	2,504,843	1,746,322	1,585,470	160,851	758,521	758,319	203

†Not applicable.
[1]Includes Ph.D., Ed.D., and comparable degrees at the doctoral level, as well as such degrees as M.D., D.D.S., and law degrees that were formerly classified as first-professional degrees.
[2]Totals (column 2) of public and private institutions together are approximate because public and private nonprofit institutions fill out different survey forms with different accounting concepts.
[3]Includes independent operations.
[4]Includes contributions from affiliated entities.
NOTE: Degree-granting institutions grant associate's or higher degrees and participate in Title IV federal financial aid programs. Historically Black colleges and universities are degree-granting institutions established prior to 1964 with the principal mission of educating Black Americans. Federal regulations, 20 U.S. Code, Section 1061 (2), allow for certain exceptions to the founding date. Federal, state, and local governments revenue includes appropriations, grants, and contracts. Totals include persons of other racial/ethnic groups not separately identified. Detail may not sum to totals because of rounding. Some data have been revised from previously published figures.
SOURCE: U.S. Department of Education, National Center for Education Statistics, Integrated Postsecondary Education Data System (IPEDS), "Fall Enrollment Survey" (IPEDS–EF:90); IPEDS Spring 2001, Spring 2011, and Spring 2014, Enrollment component; IPEDS Spring 2014, Finance component; and IPEDS Fall 2013, Completions component. (This table was prepared May 2015.)

Table 314.10. Total and full-time-equivalent (FTE) staff and FTE student/FTE staff ratios in postsecondary institutions participating in Title IV programs, by degree-granting status, control of institution, and primary occupation: Fall 1993, fall 2003, and fall 2013

Degree-granting status, control of institution, and primary occupation	Fall 1993				Fall 2003				Fall 2013			
	Total		Full-time-equivalent (FTE)		Total		Full-time-equivalent (FTE)		Total		Full-time-equivalent (FTE)	
	Number	Percent	Total	FTE students per FTE staff	Number	Percent	Total	FTE students per FTE staff	Number	Percent	Total	FTE students per FTE staff
1	2	3	4	5	6	7	8	9	10	11	12	13
All postsecondary institutions	2,727,504	100.0	2,152,184	5.2	3,237,089	100.0	2,491,009	5.2	3,969,396	100.0	3,006,389	5.3
Faculty (instruction/research/public service)	973,289	35.7	707,820	15.7	1,198,420	37.0	828,883	15.8	1,580,932	39.8	1,067,966	14.8
Graduate assistants	203,049	7.4	67,683	164.6	292,094	9.0	97,365	134.1	359,546	9.1	119,849	132.0
Other staff	1,551,166	56.9	1,376,681	8.1	1,746,575	54.0	1,564,761	8.3	2,028,918	51.1	1,818,574	8.7
Degree-granting institutions[1]												
Total	2,602,612	100.0	2,056,544	5.0	3,187,907	100.0	2,451,397	5.2	3,896,149	100.0	2,949,362	5.2
Faculty (instruction/research/public service)	915,474	35.2	668,962	15.5	1,173,593	36.8	811,259	15.6	1,544,060	39.6	1,042,281	14.8
Graduate assistants	202,819	7.8	67,606	153.1	292,061	9.2	97,354	130.3	359,546	9.2	119,849	128.6
Other staff	1,484,319	57.0	1,319,976	7.8	1,722,253	54.0	1,542,784	8.2	1,992,543	51.1	1,787,232	8.6
Public	1,812,513	100.0	1,408,451	5.5	2,163,336	100.0	1,633,890	5.7	2,527,329	100.0	1,890,401	5.7
Faculty (instruction/research/public service)	650,434	35.9	471,977	16.6	791,766	36.6	547,294	16.9	967,703	38.3	664,056	16.1
Graduate assistants	173,678	9.6	57,893	134.9	239,923	11.1	79,974	115.5	283,516	11.2	94,505	113.2
Other staff	988,401	54.5	878,582	8.9	1,131,647	52.3	1,006,622	9.2	1,276,110	50.5	1,131,839	9.4
Private, nonprofit	766,723	100.0	630,876	3.7	934,992	100.0	755,743	3.7	1,157,030	100.0	920,570	3.7
Faculty (instruction/research/public service)	254,130	33.1	190,083	12.4	330,097	35.3	237,397	11.9	448,724	38.8	318,456	10.6
Graduate assistants	28,065	3.7	9,355	251.5	52,026	5.6	17,342	162.2	75,579	6.5	25,193	133.7
Other staff	484,528	63.2	431,438	5.5	552,869	59.1	501,004	5.6	632,727	54.7	576,921	5.8
Private, for-profit	23,376	100.0	17,217	10.8	89,579	100.0	61,764	10.3	211,790	100.0	138,391	9.7
Faculty (instruction/research/public service)	10,910	46.7	6,903	26.9	51,730	57.7	26,568	23.8	127,633	60.3	59,768	22.5
Graduate assistants	1,076	4.6	359	518.3	112	0.1	37	16,960.9	451	0.2	150	8,948.8
Other staff	11,390	48.7	9,956	18.7	37,737	42.1	35,159	18.0	83,706	39.5	78,472	17.1
Non-degree-granting institutions[2]												
Total	124,892	100.0	95,640	8.3	49,182	100.0	39,612	9.3	73,247	100.0	57,027	7.1
Faculty (instruction/research/public service)	57,815	46.3	38,858	20.3	24,827	50.5	17,624	20.9	36,872	50.3	25,685	15.8
Graduate assistants	230	0.2	77	10,293.8	33	0.1	11	33,429.2	0	0.0	0	†
Other staff	66,847	53.5	56,705	13.9	24,322	49.5	21,977	16.7	36,375	49.7	31,342	13.0
Public	31,554	100.0	24,231	9.5	25,276	100.0	19,665	4.1	22,521	100.0	16,156	4.8
Faculty (instruction/research/public service)	18,142	57.5	12,878	17.9	12,749	50.4	8,358	9.5	11,481	51.0	7,160	10.8
Graduate assistants	22	0.1	7	31,442.6	0	0.0	0	†	0	0.0	0	†
Other staff	13,390	42.4	11,346	20.3	12,527	49.6	11,307	7.1	11,040	49.0	8,996	8.6
Private, nonprofit	34,348	100.0	25,897	5.0	4,091	100.0	3,274	8.8	4,394	100.0	3,401	5.3
Faculty (instruction/research/public service)	12,485	36.3	7,810	16.5	2,021	49.4	1,500	19.3	2,015	45.9	1,440	12.6
Graduate assistants	189	0.6	63	2,049.5	0	0.0	0	†	0	0.0	0	†
Other staff	21,674	63.1	18,023	7.2	2,070	50.6	1,774	16.3	2,379	54.1	1,961	9.2
Private, for-profit	58,990	100.0	45,512	9.4	19,815	100.0	16,672	15.5	46,332	100.0	37,470	8.3
Faculty (instruction/research/public service)	27,188	46.1	18,170	23.6	10,057	50.8	7,766	33.4	23,376	50.5	17,085	18.2
Graduate assistants	19	#	6	67,814.4	33	0.2	11	23,546.0	0	0.0	0	†
Other staff	31,783	53.9	27,336	15.7	9,725	49.1	8,896	29.1	22,956	49.5	20,385	15.2

†Not applicable.
#Rounds to zero.
[1]Data for 1993 are for institutions of higher education, while later data are for degree-granting institutions. Degree-granting institutions grant associate's or higher degrees and participate in Title IV federal financial aid programs. The degree-granting classification is very similar to the earlier higher education classification, but it includes more 2-year colleges and excludes a few higher education institutions that did not grant degrees.
[2]Data are for institutions that did not offer accredited 4-year or 2-year degree programs, but were participating in Title IV federal financial aid programs. Includes some institutions transitioning to higher level program offerings, though still classified at a lower level.

NOTE: Full-time-equivalent staff is the full-time staff, plus the full-time equivalent of the part-time staff. Data for 2013 include institutions with fewer than 15 full-time employees; these institutions did not report staff data prior to 2007. By definition, all graduate assistants are part time. Detail may not sum to totals because of rounding.
SOURCE: U.S. Department of Education, National Center for Education Statistics, Integrated Postsecondary Education Data System (IPEDS), "Fall Enrollment Survey" (IPEDS-EF:93) and "Fall Staff Survey" (IPEDS-S:93); IPEDS Spring 2003 and 2013, Enrollment component; and IPEDS Winter 2003–04 and Spring 2014, Human Resources component, Fall Staff section. (This table was prepared May 2015.)

Table 314.20. Employees in degree-granting postsecondary institutions, by sex, employment status, control and level of institution, and primary occupation: Selected years, fall 1991 through fall 2013

Sex, employment status, control and level of institution, and primary occupation	1991	1993	1995	1997	1999	2001	2003	2005	2007	2009	2011	2013	Percent change, 2003 to 2013
1	2	3	4	5	6	7	8	9	10	11	12	13	14
All institutions	2,545,235	2,602,612	2,662,075	2,752,504	2,883,175	3,083,353	3,187,907	3,379,087	3,561,428	3,723,419	3,840,980	3,896,149	22.2
Executive/administrative/managerial	144,755	143,675	147,445	151,363	159,888	152,038	184,913	196,324	217,518	230,579	238,718	(¹)	†
Faculty (instruction/research/public service)	826,252	915,474	931,706	989,813	1,027,830	1,113,183	1,173,593	1,290,426	1,371,390	1,439,144	1,523,615	1,544,060	31.6
Graduate assistants	197,751	202,819	215,909	222,724	239,738	261,136	292,061	317,141	328,979	342,393	355,916	359,546	23.1
Other	1,376,477	1,340,644	1,367,015	1,388,604	1,455,719	1,556,996	1,537,340	1,575,196	1,643,541	1,711,303	1,722,731	1,992,543	†
Males	1,227,591	1,256,037	1,274,676	1,315,311	1,365,812	1,451,773	1,496,867	1,581,498	1,650,350	1,709,636	1,754,713	1,772,768	18.4
Executive/administrative/managerial	85,423	82,748	82,127	81,931	83,883	79,348	91,604	95,223	102,258	106,892	109,374	(¹)	†
Faculty (instruction/research/public service)	525,599	561,123	562,893	587,420	602,469	644,514	663,723	714,453	743,812	761,035	789,197	791,310	19.2
Graduate assistants	119,125	120,384	123,962	125,873	132,607	142,120	156,881	167,529	173,121	180,941	188,468	189,556	20.8
Other	497,444	491,782	505,694	520,087	546,853	585,791	584,659	604,293	631,159	660,768	667,674	791,902	†
Females	1,317,644	1,346,575	1,387,399	1,437,193	1,517,363	1,631,580	1,691,040	1,797,589	1,911,078	2,013,783	2,086,267	2,123,381	25.6
Executive/administrative/managerial	59,332	60,927	65,318	69,432	76,005	72,690	93,309	101,101	115,260	123,687	129,344	(¹)	†
Faculty (instruction/research/public service)	300,653	354,351	368,813	402,393	425,361	468,669	509,870	575,973	627,578	678,109	734,418	752,750	47.6
Graduate assistants	78,626	82,435	91,947	96,851	107,131	119,016	135,180	149,612	155,858	161,452	167,448	169,990	25.8
Other	879,033	848,862	861,321	868,517	908,866	971,205	952,681	970,903	1,012,382	1,050,535	1,055,057	1,200,641	26.0
Full-time	1,812,912	1,783,510	1,801,371	1,828,507	1,918,676	2,043,208	2,083,142	2,179,864	2,281,223	2,381,702	2,435,533	2,475,968	18.9
Executive/administrative/managerial	139,116	137,834	140,990	144,529	153,722	146,523	178,691	190,078	210,257	222,282	231,602	(¹)	†
Faculty (instruction/research/public service)	535,623	545,706	550,822	568,719	590,937	617,868	630,092	675,624	703,463	728,977	761,619	791,391	25.6
Other	1,138,173	1,099,970	1,109,559	1,115,259	1,174,017	1,278,817	1,274,359	1,314,162	1,367,503	1,430,443	1,442,312	1,684,577	†
Part-time	732,323	819,102	860,704	923,997	964,499	1,040,145	1,104,765	1,199,223	1,280,205	1,341,717	1,405,447	1,420,181	28.6
Executive/administrative/managerial	5,639	5,841	6,455	6,834	6,166	5,515	6,222	6,246	7,261	8,297	7,116	(¹)	†
Faculty (instruction/research/public service)	290,629	369,768	380,884	421,094	436,893	495,315	543,501	614,802	667,927	710,167	761,996	752,669	38.5
Graduate assistants	197,751	202,819	215,909	222,724	239,738	261,136	292,061	317,141	328,979	342,393	355,916	359,546	23.1
Other	238,304	240,674	257,456	273,345	281,702	278,179	262,981	261,034	276,038	280,860	280,419	307,966	†
Public 4-year	1,341,914	1,333,533	1,383,476	1,418,661	1,470,842	1,558,576	1,569,870	1,656,709	1,741,699	1,803,724	1,843,204	1,884,520	20.0
Executive/administrative/managerial	63,674	59,678	60,590	61,984	64,336	60,245	70,397	74,241	81,364	84,355	84,911	(¹)	†
Faculty (instruction/research/public service)	358,376	374,021	384,399	404,109	417,086	438,459	450,123	486,691	518,221	539,901	575,534	599,985	33.3
Graduate assistants	144,344	170,916	178,342	182,481	196,393	218,260	239,600	257,578	266,429	275,872	285,905	283,503	18.3
Other	775,520	728,918	760,145	770,087	793,027	841,612	809,750	838,199	875,685	903,596	896,854	1,001,032	†
Private 4-year	734,509	762,034	770,004	786,634	857,820	912,924	988,895	1,073,764	1,157,226	1,229,784	1,297,486	1,318,756	33.4
Executive/administrative/managerial	57,148	59,230	62,314	62,580	69,626	65,739	84,306	90,415	103,183	111,616	118,268	(¹)	†
Faculty (instruction/research/public service)	232,893	251,948	262,660	278,541	296,737	325,713	364,166	430,305	472,628	498,582	540,093	550,167	51.1
Graduate assistants	23,989	28,880	33,853	36,064	38,597	41,611	52,101	59,147	62,550	66,521	70,011	76,003	45.9
Other	420,479	421,976	411,177	409,449	452,860	479,861	488,322	493,897	518,865	553,065	569,114	692,586	†
Public 2-year	441,414	478,980	482,454	512,086	517,967	578,394	593,466	610,978	620,784	638,352	641,616	642,809	8.3
Executive/administrative/managerial	20,772	21,531	21,806	22,822	21,459	22,566	25,872	26,770	27,363	27,827	27,562	(¹)	†
Faculty (instruction/research/public service)	222,532	276,413	272,434	290,451	296,239	332,665	341,643	354,497	358,925	373,778	377,696	367,718	7.6
Graduate assistants	29,216	2,762	3,401	3,561	4,170	1,215	323	374	0	0	0	13	-96.0
Other	168,894	178,274	184,813	195,252	196,099	221,948	225,628	229,337	234,496	236,747	236,358	275,078	†
Private 2-year	27,398	28,065	26,141	35,123	36,546	33,459	35,676	37,636	41,719	51,559	58,674	50,064	40.3
Executive/administrative/managerial	3,161	3,236	2,735	3,977	4,467	3,488	4,338	4,898	5,608	6,781	7,977	(¹)	†
Faculty (instruction/research/public service)	12,451	13,092	12,213	16,712	17,768	16,346	17,661	18,933	21,616	26,883	30,292	26,190	48.3
Graduate assistants	202	261	313	618	578	50	37	42	0	0	0	27	-27.0
Other	11,584	11,476	10,880	13,816	13,733	13,575	13,640	13,763	14,495	17,895	20,405	23,847	†

†Not applicable.
¹Included in other. Primary occupations were reclassified as of fall 2013; only the faculty and graduate assistant categories are comparable with data from earlier years.
NOTE: Data through 1995 are for institutions of higher education, while later data are for degree-granting institutions. Degree-granting institutions grant associate's or higher degrees and participate in Title IV federal financial aid programs. The degree-granting classification is very similar to the earlier higher education classification, but it includes more 2-year colleges and excludes a few higher education institutions that did not grant degrees. Beginning in 2007, includes institutions with fewer than 15 full-time employees; these institutions did not report staff data prior to 2007. By definition, all graduate assistants are part time.
SOURCE: U.S. Department of Education, National Center for Education Statistics, Integrated Postsecondary Education Data System (IPEDS), "Fall Staff Survey" (IPEDS-S:91–99); IPEDS Winter 2001–02 through Winter 2011–12, Human Resources component, Fall Staff section; and IPEDS Spring 2014, Human Resources component, Fall Staff section. (This table was prepared April 2015.)

Table 314.30. Employees in degree-granting postsecondary institutions, by employment status, sex, control and level of institution, and primary occupation: Fall 2013

Control and level of institution and primary occupation	Full-time and part-time					Full-time				Part-time		
	Total		Males	Females		Total		Males	Females	Total	Males	Females
	Number	Percentage distribution		Number	Percent of all employees	Number	Percent of all employees					
1	2	3	4	5	6	7	8	9	10	11	12	13
All institutions	**3,896,149**	**100.0**	**1,772,768**	**2,123,381**	**54.5**	**2,475,968**	**63.5**	**1,113,454**	**1,362,514**	**1,420,181**	**659,314**	**760,867**
Faculty (instruction/research/public service)	1,544,060	39.6	791,310	752,750	48.8	791,391	51.3	436,456	354,935	752,669	354,854	397,815
Instruction	1,436,453	36.9	730,405	706,048	49.2	705,820	49.1	386,463	319,357	730,633	343,942	386,691
Research	81,665	2.1	48,415	33,250	40.7	67,965	83.2	41,090	26,875	13,700	7,325	6,375
Public service	25,942	0.7	12,490	13,452	51.9	17,606	67.9	8,903	8,703	8,336	3,587	4,749
Graduate assistants	359,546	9.2	189,556	169,990	47.3	†	†	†	†	359,546	189,556	169,990
Librarians, curators, and archivists	44,656	1.1	13,022	31,634	70.8	37,654	84.3	11,341	26,313	7,002	1,681	5,321
Student and academic affairs and other education services	158,521	4.1	52,227	106,294	67.1	100,001	63.1	30,309	69,692	58,520	21,918	36,602
Management	252,560	6.5	113,817	138,743	54.9	244,791	96.9	110,819	133,972	7,769	2,998	4,771
Business and financial operations	193,016	5.0	52,014	141,002	73.1	178,496	92.5	48,097	130,399	14,520	3,917	10,603
Computer, engineering, and science	231,768	5.9	140,188	91,580	39.5	210,172	90.7	130,392	79,780	21,596	9,796	11,800
Community, social service, legal, arts, design, entertainment, sports, and media	167,415	4.3	74,664	92,751	55.4	135,092	80.7	59,415	75,677	32,323	15,249	17,074
Healthcare practitioners and technicians	121,948	3.1	35,394	86,554	71.0	98,061	80.4	29,314	68,747	23,887	6,080	17,807
Service occupations	241,142	6.2	140,650	100,492	41.7	200,358	83.1	118,381	81,977	40,784	22,269	18,515
Sales and related occupations	15,390	0.4	5,368	10,022	65.1	12,493	81.2	4,608	7,885	2,897	760	2,137
Office and administrative support	471,266	12.1	79,292	391,974	83.2	380,624	80.8	54,973	325,651	90,642	24,319	66,323
Natural resources, construction, and maintenance	75,404	1.9	69,201	6,203	8.2	70,691	93.7	65,765	4,926	4,713	3,436	1,277
Production, transportation, and material moving	19,457	0.5	16,065	3,392	17.4	16,144	83.0	13,584	2,560	3,313	2,481	832
Public 4-year	**1,884,520**	**100.0**	**880,954**	**1,003,566**	**53.3**	**1,272,306**	**67.5**	**589,927**	**682,379**	**612,214**	**291,027**	**321,187**
Faculty (instruction/research/public service)	599,985	31.8	324,809	275,176	45.9	400,724	66.8	229,762	170,962	199,261	95,047	104,214
Instruction	534,252	28.3	288,087	246,165	46.1	347,541	65.1	199,298	148,243	186,711	88,789	97,922
Research	51,398	2.7	29,939	21,459	41.8	42,126	82.0	25,102	17,024	9,272	4,837	4,435
Public service	14,335	0.8	6,783	7,552	52.7	11,057	77.1	5,362	5,695	3,278	1,421	1,857
Graduate assistants	283,503	15.0	149,226	134,277	47.4	†	†	†	†	283,503	149,226	134,277
Librarians, curators, and archivists	19,022	1.0	5,735	13,287	69.9	17,302	91.0	5,319	11,983	1,720	416	1,304
Student and academic affairs and other education services	58,234	3.1	19,391	38,843	66.7	40,657	69.8	12,609	28,048	17,577	6,782	10,795
Management	107,444	5.7	50,253	57,191	53.2	103,775	96.6	48,779	54,996	3,669	1,474	2,195
Business and financial operations	109,151	5.8	28,869	80,282	73.6	100,676	92.2	26,680	73,996	8,475	2,189	6,286
Computer, engineering, and science	142,048	7.5	85,748	56,300	39.6	128,619	90.5	79,952	48,667	13,429	5,796	7,633
Community, social service, legal, arts, design, entertainment, sports, and media	77,532	4.1	32,937	44,595	57.5	66,978	86.4	28,730	38,248	10,554	4,207	6,347
Healthcare practitioners and technicians	79,441	4.2	24,338	55,103	69.4	65,455	82.4	20,863	44,592	13,986	3,475	10,511
Service occupations	125,409	6.7	68,345	57,064	45.5	108,011	86.1	59,632	48,379	17,398	8,713	8,685
Sales and related occupations	2,882	0.2	910	1,972	68.4	2,230	77.4	745	1,485	652	165	487
Office and administrative support	218,603	11.6	34,913	183,690	84.0	180,662	82.6	24,334	156,328	37,941	10,579	27,362
Natural resources, construction, and maintenance	48,294	2.6	44,688	3,606	7.5	45,900	95.0	42,927	2,973	2,394	1,761	633
Production, transportation, and material moving	12,972	0.7	10,792	2,180	16.8	11,317	87.2	9,595	1,722	1,655	1,197	458
Public 2-year	**642,809**	**100.0**	**271,973**	**370,836**	**57.7**	**299,631**	**46.6**	**120,779**	**178,852**	**343,178**	**151,194**	**191,984**
Faculty (instruction/research/public service)	367,718	57.2	167,383	200,335	54.5	111,509	30.3	50,114	61,395	256,209	117,269	138,940
Instruction	364,433	56.7	166,133	198,300	54.4	111,149	30.5	49,983	61,166	253,284	116,150	137,134
Research	81	#	38	43	53.1	65	80.2	31	34	16	7	9
Public service	3,204	0.5	1,212	1,992	62.2	295	9.2	100	195	2,909	1,112	1,797
Graduate assistants	13	#	6	7	53.8	†	†	†	†	13	6	7
Librarians, curators, and archivists	5,715	0.9	1,261	4,454	77.9	3,902	68.3	898	3,004	1,813	363	1,450
Student and academic affairs and other education services	47,394	7.4	16,399	30,995	65.4	20,212	42.6	6,102	14,110	27,182	10,297	16,885
Management	32,356	5.0	13,591	18,765	58.0	31,171	96.3	13,110	18,061	1,185	481	704
Business and financial operations	17,948	2.8	4,962	12,986	72.4	15,207	84.7	4,021	11,186	2,741	941	1,800
Computer, engineering, and science	16,583	2.6	11,113	5,470	33.0	13,805	83.2	9,455	4,350	2,778	1,658	1,120
Community, social service, legal, arts, design, entertainment, sports, and media	23,537	3.7	8,849	14,688	62.4	15,920	67.6	5,601	10,319	7,617	3,248	4,369
Healthcare practitioners and technicians	1,765	0.3	559	1,206	68.3	772	43.7	290	482	993	269	724
Service occupations	35,102	5.5	24,553	10,549	30.1	24,839	70.8	18,000	6,839	10,263	6,553	3,710
Sales and related occupations	2,121	0.3	568	1,553	73.2	1,107	52.2	312	795	1,014	256	758
Office and administrative support	84,143	13.1	15,369	68,774	81.7	54,321	64.6	6,680	47,641	29,822	8,689	21,133
Natural resources, construction, and maintenance	7,188	1.1	6,378	810	11.3	6,050	84.2	5,535	515	1,138	843	295
Production, transportation, and material moving	1,226	0.2	982	244	19.9	816	66.6	661	155	410	321	89

See notes at end of table.

Table 314.30. Employees in degree-granting postsecondary institutions, by employment status, sex, control and level of institution, and primary occupation: Fall 2013—Continued

Control and level of institution and primary occupation	Full-time and part-time					Full-time				Part-time		
	Total		Males	Females		Total		Males	Females	Total	Males	Females
	Number	Percentage distribution		Number	Percent of all employees	Number	Percent of all employees					
1	2	3	4	5	6	7	8	9	10	11	12	13
Private nonprofit 4-year	1,151,200	100.0	529,335	621,865	54.0	798,839	69.4	361,425	437,414	352,361	167,910	184,451
Faculty (instruction/research/public service)	445,729	38.7	240,584	205,145	46.0	252,036	56.5	144,217	107,819	193,693	96,367	97,326
Instruction	407,355	35.4	217,734	189,621	46.5	220,109	54.0	124,863	95,246	187,246	92,871	94,375
Research	30,065	2.6	18,388	11,677	38.8	25,698	85.5	15,923	9,775	4,367	2,465	1,902
Public service	8,309	0.7	4,462	3,847	46.3	6,229	75.0	3,431	2,798	2,080	1,031	1,049
Graduate assistants	75,572	6.6	40,153	35,419	46.9	†	†	†	†	75,572	40,153	35,419
Librarians, curators, and archivists	18,206	1.6	5,596	12,610	69.3	15,242	83.7	4,823	10,419	2,964	773	2,191
Student and academic affairs and other education services	39,444	3.4	12,315	27,129	68.8	27,996	71.0	8,151	19,845	11,448	4,164	7,284
Management	95,758	8.3	42,531	53,227	55.6	93,043	97.2	41,564	51,479	2,715	967	1,748
Business and financial operations	58,504	5.1	15,991	42,513	72.7	55,542	94.9	15,286	40,256	2,962	705	2,257
Computer, engineering, and science	70,296	6.1	41,070	29,226	41.6	65,035	92.5	38,818	26,217	5,261	2,252	3,009
Community, social service, legal, arts, design, entertainment, sports, and media	58,225	5.1	29,608	28,617	49.1	44,759	76.9	22,148	22,611	13,466	7,460	6,006
Healthcare practitioners and technicians	40,466	3.5	10,414	30,052	74.3	31,737	78.4	8,132	23,605	8,729	2,282	6,447
Service occupations	78,046	6.8	46,001	32,045	41.1	65,754	84.3	39,504	26,250	12,292	6,497	5,795
Sales and related occupations	4,414	0.4	1,540	2,874	65.1	3,443	78.0	1,264	2,179	971	276	695
Office and administrative support	142,242	12.4	21,838	120,404	84.6	122,142	85.9	17,440	104,702	20,100	4,398	15,702
Natural resources, construction, and maintenance	19,313	1.7	17,621	1,692	8.8	18,272	94.6	16,886	1,386	1,041	735	306
Production, transportation, and material moving	4,985	0.4	4,073	912	18.3	3,838	77.0	3,192	646	1,147	881	266
Private nonprofit 2-year	5,830	100.0	2,268	3,562	61.1	3,501	60.1	1,358	2,143	2,329	910	1,419
Faculty (instruction/research/public service)	2,995	51.4	1,170	1,825	60.9	1,286	42.9	497	789	1,709	673	1,036
Instruction	2,982	51.1	1,162	1,820	61.0	1,280	42.9	493	787	1,702	669	1,033
Research	9	0.2	6	3	33.3	4	44.4	3	1	5	3	2
Public service	4	0.1	2	2	50.0	2	50.0	1	1	2	1	1
Graduate assistants	7	0.1	5	2	28.6	†	†	†	†	7	5	2
Librarians, curators, and archivists	114	2.0	21	93	81.6	69	60.5	13	56	45	8	37
Student and academic affairs and other education services	365	6.3	129	236	64.7	281	77.0	105	176	84	24	60
Management	561	9.6	250	311	55.4	539	96.1	244	295	22	6	16
Business and financial operations	203	3.5	54	149	73.4	169	83.3	48	121	34	6	28
Computer, engineering, and science	114	2.0	92	22	19.3	98	86.0	79	19	16	13	3
Community, social service, legal, arts, design, entertainment, sports, and media	224	3.8	124	100	44.6	155	69.2	72	83	69	52	17
Healthcare practitioners and technicians	23	0.4	3	20	87.0	17	73.9	3	14	6	0	6
Service occupations	300	5.1	201	99	33.0	167	55.7	124	43	133	77	56
Sales and related occupations	112	1.9	39	73	65.2	100	89.3	36	64	12	3	9
Office and administrative support	719	12.3	106	613	85.3	546	75.9	78	468	173	28	145
Natural resources, construction, and maintenance	82	1.4	65	17	20.7	69	84.1	55	14	13	10	3
Production, transportation, and material moving	11	0.2	9	2	18.2	5	45.5	4	1	6	5	1
Private for-profit 4-year	167,556	100.0	72,104	95,452	57.0	73,630	43.9	30,000	43,630	93,926	42,104	51,822
Faculty (instruction/research/public service)	104,438	62.3	48,073	56,365	54.0	16,178	15.5	7,867	8,311	88,260	40,206	48,054
Instruction	104,319	62.3	48,027	56,292	54.0	16,146	15.5	7,852	8,294	88,173	40,175	47,998
Research	55	#	23	32	58.2	27	49.1	13	14	28	10	18
Public service	64	#	23	41	64.1	5	7.8	2	3	59	21	38
Graduate assistants	431	0.3	159	272	63.1	†	†	†	†	431	159	272
Librarians, curators, and archivists	1,150	0.7	297	853	74.2	849	73.8	224	625	301	73	228
Student and academic affairs and other education services	10,372	6.2	3,210	7,162	69.1	8,489	81.8	2,697	5,792	1,883	513	1,370
Management	11,717	7.0	5,263	6,454	55.1	11,601	99.0	5,223	6,378	116	40	76
Business and financial operations	4,765	2.8	1,516	3,249	68.2	4,584	96.2	1,476	3,108	181	40	141
Computer, engineering, and science	2,344	1.4	1,840	504	21.5	2,264	96.6	1,785	479	80	55	25
Community, social service, legal, arts, design, entertainment, sports, and media	7,265	4.3	2,945	4,320	59.5	6,727	92.6	2,686	4,041	538	259	279
Healthcare practitioners and technicians	137	0.1	44	93	67.9	68	49.6	24	44	69	20	49
Service occupations	1,574	0.9	1,088	486	30.9	1,124	71.4	800	324	450	288	162
Sales and related occupations	3,330	2.0	1,412	1,918	57.6	3,259	97.9	1,397	1,862	71	15	56
Office and administrative support	19,519	11.6	5,830	13,689	70.1	18,100	92.7	5,492	12,608	1,419	338	1,081
Natural resources, construction, and maintenance	270	0.2	235	35	13.0	227	84.1	204	23	43	31	12
Production, transportation, and material moving	244	0.1	192	52	21.3	160	65.6	125	35	84	67	17

See notes at end of table.

Table 314.30. Employees in degree-granting postsecondary institutions, by employment status, sex, control and level of institution, and primary occupation: Fall 2013—Continued

Control and level of institution and primary occupation	Full-time and part-time					Full-time				Part-time		
	Total			Females		Total						
	Number	Percentage distribution	Males	Number	Percent of all employees	Number	Percent of all employees	Males	Females	Total	Males	Females
1	2	3	4	5	6	7	8	9	10	11	12	13
Private for-profit 2-year	**44,234**	**99.9**	**16,134**	**28,100**	**63.5**	**28,061**	**63.4**	**9,965**	**18,096**	**16,173**	**6,169**	**10,004**
Faculty (instruction/research/public service)	23,195	52.4	9,291	13,904	59.9	9,658	41.6	3,999	5,659	13,537	5,292	8,245
Instruction	23,112	52.2	9,262	13,850	59.9	9,595	41.5	3,974	5,621	13,517	5,288	8,229
Research	57	0.1	21	36	63.2	45	78.9	18	27	12	3	9
Public service	26	0.1	8	18	69.2	18	69.2	7	11	8	1	7
Graduate assistants	20	#	7	13	65.0	†	†	†	†	20	7	13
Librarians, curators, and archivists	449	1.0	112	337	75.1	290	64.6	64	226	159	48	111
Student and academic affairs and other education services	2,712	6.1	783	1,929	71.1	2,366	87.2	645	1,721	346	138	208
Management	4,724	10.7	1,929	2,795	59.2	4,662	98.7	1,899	2,763	62	30	32
Business and financial operations	2,445	5.5	622	1,823	74.6	2,318	94.8	586	1,732	127	36	91
Computer, engineering, and science	383	0.9	325	58	15.1	351	91.6	303	48	32	22	10
Community, social service, legal, arts, design, entertainment, sports, and media	632	1.4	201	431	68.2	553	87.5	178	375	79	23	56
Healthcare practitioners and technicians	116	0.3	36	80	69.0	12	10.3	2	10	104	34	70
Service occupations	711	1.6	462	249	35.0	463	65.1	321	142	248	141	107
Sales and related occupations	2,531	5.7	899	1,632	64.5	2,354	93.0	854	1,500	177	45	132
Office and administrative support	6,040	13.7	1,236	4,804	79.5	4,853	80.3	949	3,904	1,187	287	900
Natural resources, construction, and maintenance	257	0.6	214	43	16.7	173	67.3	158	15	84	56	28
Production, transportation, and material moving	19	#	17	2	10.5	8	42.1	7	1	11	10	1

†Not applicable.
#Rounds to zero.
NOTE: Degree-granting institutions grant associate's or higher degrees and participate in Title IV federal financial aid programs. Includes institutions with fewer than 15 full-time employees; these institutions did not report staff data prior to 2007. By definition, all graduate assistants are part time. Detail may not sum to totals because of rounding.
SOURCE: U.S. Department of Education, National Center for Education Statistics, Integrated Postsecondary Education Data System (IPEDS), Spring 2014, Human Resources component, Fall Staff section. (This table was prepared February 2015.)

Table 314.40. Employees in degree-granting postsecondary institutions, by race/ethnicity, sex, employment status, control and level of institution, and primary occupation: Fall 2013

Sex, employment status, control and level of institution, and primary occupation	Total	White	Minority								Race/ethnicity unknown	Nonresident alien[2]
			Total	Percent[1]	Black	Hispanic	Asian	Pacific Islander	American Indian/Alaska Native	Two or more races		
1	2	3	4	5	6	7	8	9	10	11	12	13
All institutions	**3,896,149**	**2,649,526**	**920,001**	**25.8**	**376,747**	**251,155**	**225,220**	**8,856**	**20,968**	**37,055**	**150,926**	**175,696**
Faculty (instruction/research/public service)	1,544,060	1,124,667	296,364	20.9	104,733	67,711	101,873	3,794	7,373	10,880	73,404	49,625
Instruction	1,436,453	1,065,654	273,989	20.5	101,032	63,941	88,164	3,669	6,979	10,204	69,002	27,808
Research	81,665	40,049	16,555	29.2	1,742	2,482	11,516	96	210	509	3,679	21,382
Public service	25,942	18,964	5,820	23.5	1,959	1,288	2,193	29	184	167	723	435
Graduate assistants	359,546	178,321	60,257	25.3	14,311	16,174	23,227	889	1,003	4,653	21,182	99,786
Librarians, curators, and archivists	44,656	35,028	8,302	19.2	3,287	2,138	2,052	76	259	490	1,018	308
Student and academic affairs and other education services	158,521	108,344	41,809	27.8	20,001	12,263	5,856	449	1,311	1,929	6,645	1,723
Management	252,560	196,075	50,015	20.3	24,659	13,064	8,841	322	1,298	1,831	5,309	1,161
Business and financial operations	193,016	135,301	51,615	27.6	21,538	14,863	11,853	404	1,082	1,875	4,875	1,225
Computer, engineering, and science	231,768	156,450	57,365	26.8	14,533	13,779	25,485	385	1,055	2,128	6,288	11,665
Community, social service, legal, arts, design, entertainment, sports, and media	167,415	121,281	39,223	24.4	18,819	11,743	5,259	486	985	1,931	5,849	1,062
Healthcare practitioners and technicians	121,948	78,631	34,463	30.5	12,356	7,359	13,358	176	459	755	4,796	4,058
Service occupations	241,142	131,190	100,712	43.4	55,925	32,714	7,925	579	1,859	1,710	7,231	2,009
Sales and related occupations	15,390	9,669	5,096	34.5	2,727	1,502	443	55	77	292	591	34
Office and administrative support	471,266	305,929	151,338	33.1	72,615	49,446	17,097	1,043	3,275	7,862	11,341	2,658
Natural resources, construction, and maintenance	75,404	55,593	17,703	24.2	8,243	6,522	1,425	170	758	585	1,841	267
Production, transportation, and material moving	19,457	13,047	5,739	30.5	3,000	1,877	526	28	174	134	556	115
Males	**1,772,768**	**1,211,505**	**383,096**	**24.0**	**140,010**	**106,402**	**109,067**	**3,605**	**8,994**	**15,018**	**72,273**	**105,894**
Faculty (instruction/research/public service)	791,310	580,507	143,296	19.8	41,650	33,833	57,609	1,722	3,496	4,986	36,517	30,990
Instruction	730,405	548,254	131,546	19.4	40,227	32,000	49,652	1,668	3,331	4,668	34,155	16,450
Research	48,415	22,988	9,112	28.4	726	1,228	6,789	37	92	240	2,029	14,286
Public service	12,490	9,265	2,638	22.2	697	605	1,168	17	73	78	333	254
Graduate assistants	189,556	89,556	27,973	23.8	5,687	7,495	12,030	153	470	2,138	11,008	61,019
Librarians, curators, and archivists	13,022	10,365	2,208	17.6	727	741	518	18	59	145	340	109
Student and academic affairs and other education services	52,227	35,629	13,285	27.2	5,944	4,070	2,076	134	444	617	2,528	785
Management	113,817	90,723	19,864	18.0	9,092	5,423	3,927	147	557	718	2,610	620
Business and financial operations	52,014	37,401	12,546	25.1	4,773	3,954	2,927	123	272	497	1,629	438
Computer, engineering, and science	140,188	98,156	31,268	24.2	7,723	8,158	13,152	264	639	1,332	3,752	7,012
Community, social service, legal, arts, design, entertainment, sports, and media	74,664	55,221	16,013	22.5	8,432	4,453	1,775	204	397	752	2,925	505
Healthcare practitioners and technicians	35,394	21,321	10,225	32.4	2,838	2,207	4,751	59	136	234	1,664	2,184
Service occupations	140,650	80,391	54,962	40.6	30,391	17,817	4,298	340	1,110	1,006	4,307	990
Sales and related occupations	5,368	3,349	1,784	34.8	977	507	161	26	25	88	226	9
Office and administrative support	79,292	46,419	29,317	38.7	12,377	10,148	4,116	235	572	1,869	2,623	933
Natural resources, construction, and maintenance	69,201	51,604	15,694	23.3	7,068	5,989	1,266	157	678	536	1,688	215
Production, transportation, and material moving	16,065	10,863	4,661	30.0	2,331	1,607	461	23	139	100	456	85
Females	**2,123,381**	**1,438,021**	**536,905**	**27.2**	**236,737**	**144,753**	**116,153**	**5,251**	**11,974**	**22,037**	**78,653**	**69,802**
Faculty (instruction/research/public service)	752,750	544,160	153,068	22.0	63,083	33,878	44,264	2,072	3,877	5,894	36,887	18,635
Instruction	706,048	517,400	142,443	21.6	60,805	31,941	38,512	2,001	3,648	5,536	34,847	11,358
Research	33,250	17,061	7,443	30.4	1,016	1,254	4,727	59	118	269	1,650	7,096
Public service	13,452	9,699	3,182	24.7	1,262	683	1,025	12	111	89	390	181
Graduate assistants	169,990	88,765	32,284	26.7	8,624	8,679	11,197	736	533	2,515	10,174	38,767
Librarians, curators, and archivists	31,634	24,663	6,094	19.8	2,560	1,397	1,534	58	200	345	678	199
Student and academic affairs and other education services	106,294	72,715	28,524	28.2	14,057	8,193	3,780	315	867	1,312	4,117	938
Management	138,743	105,352	30,151	22.3	15,567	7,641	4,914	175	741	1,113	2,699	541
Business and financial operations	141,002	97,900	39,069	28.5	16,765	10,909	8,926	281	810	1,378	3,246	787
Computer, engineering, and science	91,580	58,294	26,097	30.9	6,810	5,621	12,333	121	416	796	2,536	4,653
Community, social service, legal, arts, design, entertainment, sports, and media	92,751	66,060	23,210	26.0	10,387	7,290	3,484	282	588	1,179	2,924	557
Healthcare practitioners and technicians	86,554	57,310	24,238	29.7	9,518	5,152	8,607	117	323	521	3,132	1,874
Service occupations	100,492	50,799	45,750	47.4	25,534	14,897	3,627	239	749	704	2,924	1,019
Sales and related occupations	10,022	6,320	3,312	34.4	1,750	995	282	29	52	204	365	25
Office and administrative support	391,974	259,510	122,021	32.0	60,238	39,298	12,981	808	2,703	5,993	8,718	1,725
Natural resources, construction, and maintenance	6,203	3,989	2,009	33.5	1,175	533	159	13	80	49	153	52
Production, transportation, and material moving	3,392	2,184	1,078	33.0	669	270	65	5	35	34	100	30
Full-time	**2,475,968**	**1,717,224**	**636,780**	**27.1**	**263,604**	**174,118**	**156,531**	**4,743**	**14,289**	**23,495**	**62,289**	**59,675**
Faculty (instruction/research/public service)	791,391	575,491	157,480	21.5	43,188	33,217	71,038	1,208	3,538	5,291	20,013	38,407
Instruction	705,820	529,771	139,297	20.8	40,562	30,305	59,254	1,110	3,290	4,776	16,840	19,912
Research	67,965	32,727	14,190	30.2	1,480	2,032	10,050	78	155	395	2,916	18,132
Public service	17,606	12,993	3,993	23.5	1,146	880	1,734	20	93	120	257	363
Graduate assistants	†	†	†	†	†	†	†	†	†	†	†	†
Librarians, curators, and archivists	37,654	29,657	6,999	19.1	2,744	1,802	1,771	58	218	406	734	264
Student and academic affairs and other education services	100,001	68,939	27,060	28.2	13,322	7,542	3,693	349	963	1,191	2,992	1,010
Management	244,791	189,870	48,756	20.4	24,087	12,761	8,537	318	1,271	1,782	5,090	1,075
Business and financial operations	178,496	124,500	48,591	28.1	20,427	13,930	11,096	367	1,016	1,755	4,310	1,095
Computer, engineering, and science	210,172	142,332	51,825	26.7	13,160	12,199	23,276	356	922	1,912	5,507	10,508
Community, social service, legal, arts, design, entertainment, sports, and media	135,092	97,345	32,891	25.3	15,776	9,819	4,443	407	833	1,613	4,012	844
Healthcare practitioners and technicians	98,061	62,054	28,873	31.8	10,549	6,357	10,824	144	373	626	3,969	3,165
Service occupations	200,358	107,057	86,450	44.7	48,039	28,166	6,881	482	1,511	1,371	5,214	1,637
Sales and related occupations	12,493	7,596	4,431	36.8	2,411	1,294	373	52	59	242	449	17
Office and administrative support	380,624	249,299	121,888	32.8	59,690	39,126	12,825	821	2,744	6,682	8,078	1,359
Natural resources, construction, and maintenance	70,691	52,351	16,595	24.1	7,699	6,208	1,313	155	697	523	1,543	202
Production, transportation, and material moving	16,144	10,733	4,941	31.5	2,512	1,697	461	26	144	101	378	92

See notes at end of table.

Table 314.40. Employees in degree-granting postsecondary institutions, by race/ethnicity, sex, employment status, control and level of institution, and primary occupation: Fall 2013—Continued

Sex, employment status, control and level of institution, and primary occupation	Total	White	Minority Total	Percent[1]	Black	Hispanic	Asian	Pacific Islander	American Indian/ Alaska Native	Two or more races	Race/ ethnicity unknown	Nonresident alien[2]
1	2	3	4	5	6	7	8	9	10	11	12	13
Part-time	1,420,181	932,302	283,221	23.3	113,143	77,037	68,689	4,113	6,679	13,560	88,637	116,021
Faculty (instruction/research/public service)	752,669	549,176	138,884	20.2	61,545	34,494	30,835	2,586	3,835	5,589	53,391	11,218
Instruction	730,633	535,883	134,692	20.1	60,470	33,636	28,910	2,559	3,689	5,428	52,162	7,896
Research	13,700	7,322	2,365	24.4	262	450	1,466	18	55	114	763	3,250
Public service	8,336	5,971	1,827	23.4	813	408	459	9	91	47	466	72
Graduate assistants	359,546	178,321	60,257	25.3	14,311	16,174	23,227	889	1,003	4,653	21,182	99,786
Librarians, curators, and archivists	7,002	5,371	1,303	19.5	543	336	281	18	41	84	284	44
Student and academic affairs and other education services	58,520	39,405	14,749	27.2	6,679	4,721	2,163	100	348	738	3,653	713
Management	7,769	6,205	1,259	16.9	572	303	304	4	27	49	219	86
Business and financial operations	14,520	10,801	3,024	21.9	1,111	933	757	37	66	120	565	130
Computer, engineering, and science	21,596	14,118	5,540	28.2	1,373	1,580	2,209	29	133	216	781	1,157
Community, social service, legal, arts, design, entertainment, sports, and media	32,323	23,936	6,332	20.9	3,043	1,924	816	79	152	318	1,837	218
Healthcare practitioners and technicians	23,887	16,577	5,590	25.2	1,807	1,002	2,534	32	86	129	827	893
Service occupations	40,784	24,133	14,262	37.1	7,886	4,548	1,044	97	348	339	2,017	372
Sales and related occupations	2,897	2,073	665	24.3	316	208	70	3	18	50	142	17
Office and administrative support	90,642	56,630	29,450	34.2	12,925	10,320	4,272	222	531	1,180	3,263	1,299
Natural resources, construction, and maintenance	4,713	3,242	1,108	25.5	544	314	112	15	61	62	298	65
Production, transportation, and material moving	3,313	2,314	798	25.6	488	180	65	2	30	33	178	23
Public 4-year	1,884,520	1,247,594	448,472	26.4	170,584	122,093	125,593	3,585	10,577	16,040	64,994	123,460
Faculty (instruction/research/public service)	599,985	429,681	117,182	21.4	31,200	26,056	52,130	1,045	3,000	3,751	23,419	29,703
Instruction	534,252	392,099	104,458	21.0	29,308	23,869	44,243	954	2,692	3,392	20,725	16,970
Research	51,398	26,369	10,243	28.0	1,032	1,602	7,080	74	164	291	2,338	12,448
Public service	14,335	11,213	2,481	18.1	860	585	807	17	144	68	356	285
Graduate assistants	283,503	143,376	46,977	24.7	11,430	13,080	17,243	799	852	3,573	14,934	78,216
Librarians, curators, and archivists	19,022	14,735	3,736	20.2	1,478	1,016	858	19	138	227	425	126
Student and academic affairs and other education services	58,234	40,034	15,045	27.3	7,201	4,391	2,150	166	555	582	2,249	906
Management	107,444	83,003	21,889	20.9	10,924	5,513	4,074	98	570	710	1,969	583
Business and financial operations	109,151	76,368	29,632	28.0	11,714	8,647	7,465	204	665	937	2,435	716
Computer, engineering, and science	142,048	97,614	33,386	25.5	7,878	7,916	15,517	182	665	1,228	3,385	7,663
Community, social service, legal, arts, design, entertainment, sports, and media	77,532	54,809	19,616	26.4	9,032	6,182	2,857	237	475	833	2,520	587
Healthcare practitioners and technicians	79,441	50,707	22,889	31.1	7,632	4,650	9,684	109	338	476	3,376	2,469
Service occupations	125,409	66,097	54,401	45.1	30,773	16,718	4,766	258	1,053	833	3,875	1,036
Sales and related occupations	2,882	2,000	802	28.6	407	217	92	4	16	66	66	14
Office and administrative support	218,603	144,248	68,441	32.2	34,177	22,487	7,462	328	1,627	2,360	4,696	1,218
Natural resources, construction, and maintenance	48,294	36,161	10,718	22.9	4,929	3,854	928	126	493	388	1,269	146
Production, transportation, and material moving	12,972	8,761	3,758	30.0	1,809	1,366	367	10	130	76	376	77
Public 2-year	642,809	463,814	152,426	24.7	68,869	48,656	22,421	2,346	5,066	5,068	22,450	4,119
Faculty (instruction/research/public service)	367,718	281,058	68,158	19.5	29,417	19,572	12,850	1,523	2,382	2,414	16,023	2,479
Instruction	364,433	278,860	67,264	19.4	28,812	19,405	12,789	1,522	2,343	2,393	15,853	2,456
Research	81	50	29	36.7	6	8	5	0	9	1	2	0
Public service	3,204	2,148	865	28.7	599	159	56	1	30	20	168	23
Graduate assistants	13	10	2	16.7	2	0	0	0	0	0	0	1
Librarians, curators, and archivists	5,715	4,354	1,209	21.7	530	348	215	12	54	50	129	23
Student and academic affairs and other education services	47,394	31,587	13,833	30.5	6,446	4,655	1,678	131	442	481	1,786	188
Management	32,356	24,554	7,185	22.6	3,905	1,981	759	47	288	205	528	89
Business and financial operations	17,948	12,107	5,430	31.0	2,544	1,699	761	66	181	179	318	93
Computer, engineering, and science	16,583	11,724	4,456	27.5	1,496	1,505	1,068	59	152	176	281	122
Community, social service, legal, arts, design, entertainment, sports, and media	23,537	15,942	6,925	30.3	3,591	2,117	634	94	244	245	610	60
Healthcare practitioners and technicians	1,765	1,346	305	18.5	158	65	43	1	20	18	107	7
Service occupations	35,102	20,003	13,846	40.9	7,182	4,989	964	113	345	253	932	321
Sales and related occupations	2,121	1,576	486	23.6	196	183	55	5	21	26	54	5
Office and administrative support	84,143	53,597	28,282	34.5	12,325	10,729	3,225	275	789	939	1,573	691
Natural resources, construction, and maintenance	7,188	5,108	1,947	27.6	899	679	144	15	137	73	93	40
Production, transportation, and material moving	1,226	848	362	29.9	178	134	25	5	11	9	16	0
Private nonprofit 4-year	1,151,200	801,995	253,606	24.0	103,130	63,472	68,285	2,136	3,904	12,679	48,224	47,375
Faculty (instruction/research/public service)	445,729	330,013	75,152	18.5	23,464	14,897	31,523	854	1,241	3,173	23,627	16,937
Instruction	407,355	310,904	66,485	17.6	22,301	13,495	25,787	821	1,201	2,880	22,090	7,876
Research	30,065	13,552	6,241	31.5	690	864	4,419	22	32	214	1,338	8,934
Public service	8,309	5,557	2,426	30.4	473	538	1,317	11	8	79	199	127
Graduate assistants	75,572	34,588	13,180	27.6	2,830	3,075	5,973	82	149	1,071	6,240	21,564
Librarians, curators, and archivists	18,206	14,693	2,960	16.8	1,132	641	909	38	59	181	397	156
Student and academic affairs and other education services	39,444	28,588	8,738	23.4	4,207	2,064	1,531	97	252	587	1,511	607
Management	95,758	76,652	16,680	17.9	7,848	4,275	3,412	130	310	705	1,968	458
Business and financial operations	58,504	42,338	14,145	25.0	6,332	3,711	3,209	101	206	586	1,615	406
Computer, engineering, and science	70,296	45,290	18,690	29.2	4,926	4,091	8,651	131	207	684	2,450	3,866
Community, social service, legal, arts, design, entertainment, sports, and media	58,225	45,762	10,025	18.0	5,075	2,587	1,497	100	202	564	2,046	392
Healthcare practitioners and technicians	40,466	26,367	11,213	29.8	4,541	2,632	3,616	65	100	259	1,306	1,580
Service occupations	78,046	43,825	31,265	41.6	17,467	10,452	2,112	203	443	588	2,309	647
Sales and related occupations	4,414	3,135	1,116	26.3	504	392	121	19	18	62	153	10
Office and administrative support	142,242	93,492	44,133	32.1	21,489	12,462	5,284	277	565	4,056	3,983	634
Natural resources, construction, and maintenance	19,313	13,986	4,784	25.5	2,328	1,853	335	29	120	119	462	81
Production, transportation, and material moving	4,985	3,266	1,525	31.8	987	340	112	10	32	44	157	37

See notes at end of table.

Table 314.40. Employees in degree-granting postsecondary institutions, by race/ethnicity, sex, employment status, control and level of institution, and primary occupation: Fall 2013—Continued

Sex, employment status, control and level of institution, and primary occupation	Total	White	Minority								Race/ ethnicity unknown	Nonresident alien[2]
			Total	Percent[1]	Black	Hispanic	Asian	Pacific Islander	American Indian/ Alaska Native	Two or more races		
1	2	3	4	5	6	7	8	9	10	11	12	13
Private nonprofit 2-year	**5,830**	**4,111**	**1,456**	**26.2**	**750**	**286**	**163**	**15**	**169**	**73**	**253**	**10**
Faculty (instruction/research/public service)	2,995	2,112	668	24.0	372	97	80	12	52	55	212	3
Instruction	2,982	2,107	660	23.9	371	97	80	12	45	55	212	3
Research	9	3	6	66.7	1	0	0	0	5	0	0	0
Public service	4	2	2	50.0	0	0	0	0	2	0	0	0
Graduate assistants	7	6	0	0.0	0	0	0	0	0	0	0	1
Librarians, curators, and archivists	114	92	20	17.9	5	5	5	0	4	1	0	2
Student and academic affairs and other education services	365	239	120	33.4	62	32	14	1	8	3	5	1
Management	561	437	115	20.8	53	25	9	0	26	2	8	1
Business and financial operations	203	156	46	22.8	19	10	6	0	11	0	1	0
Computer, engineering, and science	114	86	27	23.9	11	6	5	0	5	0	1	0
Community, social service, legal, arts, design, entertainment, sports, and media	224	154	59	27.7	26	12	3	0	16	2	10	1
Healthcare practitioners and technicians	23	20	3	13.0	2	0	1	0	0	0	0	0
Service occupations	300	197	102	34.1	55	29	5	1	12	0	1	0
Sales and related occupations	112	65	47	42.0	19	16	9	0	1	2	0	0
Office and administrative support	719	492	213	30.2	107	46	25	1	27	7	14	0
Natural resources, construction, and maintenance	82	47	35	42.7	19	7	1	0	7	1	0	0
Production, transportation, and material moving	11	8	1	11.1	0	1	0	0	0	0	1	1
Private for-profit 4-year	**167,556**	**106,322**	**48,433**	**31.3**	**25,679**	**11,724**	**7,040**	**503**	**1,068**	**2,419**	**12,197**	**604**
Faculty (instruction/research/public service)	104,438	67,599	27,787	29.1	16,158	5,295	4,357	224	600	1,153	8,632	420
Instruction	104,319	67,528	27,740	29.1	16,135	5,291	4,340	224	600	1,150	8,631	420
Research	55	45	9	16.7	1	1	4	0	0	3	1	0
Public service	64	26	38	59.4	22	3	13	0	0	0	0	0
Graduate assistants	431	333	86	20.5	44	14	11	7	2	8	8	4
Librarians, curators, and archivists	1,150	833	258	23.6	86	87	51	5	3	26	58	1
Student and academic affairs and other education services	10,372	6,406	3,016	32.0	1,644	688	380	35	36	233	940	10
Management	11,717	8,366	2,802	25.1	1,277	832	430	25	85	153	522	27
Business and financial operations	4,765	3,071	1,349	30.5	477	415	332	21	13	91	342	3
Computer, engineering, and science	2,344	1,501	672	30.9	192	201	214	9	24	32	161	10
Community, social service, legal, arts, design, entertainment, sports, and media	7,265	4,381	2,330	34.7	984	734	244	51	47	270	532	22
Healthcare practitioners and technicians	137	102	26	20.3	7	4	11	1	1	2	7	2
Service occupations	1,574	670	821	55.1	338	391	56	3	4	29	83	0
Sales and related occupations	3,330	1,626	1,543	48.7	927	394	105	18	15	84	160	1
Office and administrative support	19,519	11,140	7,532	40.3	3,486	2,555	822	101	236	332	743	104
Natural resources, construction, and maintenance	270	141	126	47.2	37	79	7	0	1	2	3	0
Production, transportation, and material moving	244	153	85	35.7	22	35	20	3	1	4	6	0
Private for-profit 2-year	**44,234**	**25,690**	**15,608**	**37.8**	**7,735**	**4,924**	**1,718**	**271**	**184**	**776**	**2,808**	**128**
Faculty (instruction/research/public service)	23,195	14,204	7,417	34.3	4,122	1,794	933	136	98	334	1,491	83
Instruction	23,112	14,156	7,382	34.3	4,105	1,784	925	136	98	334	1,491	83
Research	57	30	27	47.4	12	7	8	0	0	0	0	0
Public service	26	18	8	30.8	5	3	0	0	0	0	0	0
Graduate assistants	20	8	12	60.0	5	5	0	1	0	1	0	0
Librarians, curators, and archivists	449	321	119	27.0	56	41	14	2	1	5	9	0
Student and academic affairs and other education services	2,712	1,490	1,057	41.5	441	433	103	19	18	43	154	11
Management	4,724	3,063	1,344	30.5	652	438	157	22	19	56	314	3
Business and financial operations	2,445	1,261	1,013	44.5	452	381	80	12	6	82	164	7
Computer, engineering, and science	383	235	134	36.3	30	60	30	4	2	8	10	4
Community, social service, legal, arts, design, entertainment, sports, and media	632	233	268	53.5	111	111	24	4	1	17	131	0
Healthcare practitioners and technicians	116	89	27	23.3	16	8	3	0	0	0	0	0
Service occupations	711	398	277	41.0	110	135	22	1	2	7	31	5
Sales and related occupations	2,531	1,267	1,102	46.5	674	300	61	9	6	52	158	4
Office and administrative support	6,040	2,960	2,737	48.0	1,031	1,167	279	61	31	168	332	11
Natural resources, construction, and maintenance	257	150	93	38.3	31	50	10	0	0	2	14	0
Production, transportation, and material moving	19	11	8	42.1	4	1	2	0	0	1	0	0

†Not applicable.
[1]Combined total of staff who were Black, Hispanic, Asian, Pacific Islander, American Indian/ Alaska Native, and of Two or more races as a percentage of total staff, excluding race/ethnicity unknown and nonresident alien.
[2]Race/ethnicity not collected.
NOTE: Degree-granting institutions grant associate's or higher degrees and participate in Title IV federal financial aid programs. Includes institutions with fewer than 15 full-time employees; these

institutions did not report staff data prior to 2007. By definition, all graduate assistants are part time. Race categories exclude persons of Hispanic ethnicity.
SOURCE: U.S. Department of Education, National Center for Education Statistics, Integrated Postsecondary Education Data System (IPEDS), Spring 2014, Human Resources component, Fall Staff section. (This table was prepared March 2015.)

Table 314.50. Ratios of full-time-equivalent (FTE) students to FTE staff and FTE faculty in public degree-granting postsecondary institutions, by level of institution and state or jurisdiction: Fall 2013

State or jurisdiction	Full-time-equivalent (FTE) staff			FTE faculty			FTE faculty as a percent of FTE staff		FTE students per FTE staff			FTE students per FTE faculty		
	Total	4-year	2-year	Total	4-year	2-year	4-year	2-year	Total	4-year	2-year	Total	4-year	2-year
1	2	3	4	5	6	7	8	9	10	11	12	13	14	15
United States	1,890,401	1,476,377	414,024	664,056	467,144	196,912	31.6	47.6	5.7	4.6	9.4	16.1	14.5	19.8
Alabama	38,441	32,156	6,285	12,146	9,284	2,862	28.9	45.5	5.1	4.3	9.1	16.0	14.8	19.9
Alaska	5,524	5,268	256	2,504	2,409	94	45.7	36.8	3.7	3.7	3.8	8.2	8.2	10.2
Arizona	36,797	25,409	11,388	12,479	7,185	5,294	28.3	46.5	6.5	5.1	9.8	19.3	18.0	21.0
Arkansas	22,322	17,506	4,815	7,024	4,987	2,037	28.5	42.3	5.2	4.6	7.5	16.6	16.1	17.8
California	186,622	130,122	56,499	71,822	40,984	30,837	31.5	54.6	7.7	4.8	14.1	19.9	15.4	25.9
Colorado	38,368	33,103	5,265	15,920	13,386	2,534	40.4	48.1	5.1	4.3	9.7	12.2	10.7	20.1
Connecticut	16,949	13,726	3,223	6,122	4,303	1,819	31.3	56.4	5.2	4.2	9.9	14.5	13.2	17.5
Delaware	6,808	5,489	1,319	2,070	1,411	659	25.7	50.0	4.9	4.5	6.7	16.2	17.5	13.5
District of Columbia	922	922	0	456	456	0	49.5	†	3.9	3.9	†	7.8	7.8	†
Florida	78,778	75,417	3,361	26,395	25,025	1,370	33.2	40.8	7.1	7.0	9.8	21.3	21.2	24.0
Georgia	58,807	48,005	10,802	18,102	13,167	4,936	27.4	45.7	5.4	4.9	7.7	17.5	17.7	16.8
Hawaii	8,346	6,541	1,805	3,149	2,269	879	34.7	48.7	5.0	3.7	9.4	13.1	10.8	19.2
Idaho	9,271	7,180	2,090	3,333	2,428	905	33.8	43.3	6.0	5.6	7.1	16.6	16.7	16.4
Illinois	70,449	48,874	21,575	20,898	11,728	9,170	24.0	42.5	5.3	3.5	9.5	17.9	14.5	22.3
Indiana	45,934	40,441	5,493	15,637	12,824	2,813	31.7	51.2	5.4	4.8	10.2	15.9	15.0	19.9
Iowa	25,466	18,185	7,281	8,938	5,482	3,456	30.1	47.5	5.0	3.7	8.1	14.2	12.4	17.0
Kansas	26,243	19,210	7,033	9,489	6,499	2,991	33.8	42.5	5.2	4.4	7.2	14.3	13.0	16.9
Kentucky	33,510	27,154	6,356	10,692	7,631	3,061	28.1	48.2	4.9	3.9	8.8	15.2	14.0	18.2
Louisiana	26,102	22,128	3,974	9,430	7,336	2,094	33.2	52.7	6.4	5.4	12.3	17.8	16.3	23.4
Maine	6,717	5,395	1,321	2,472	1,631	841	30.2	63.7	5.3	4.5	8.7	14.5	15.0	13.6
Maryland	43,483	31,043	12,440	17,173	11,529	5,645	37.1	45.4	4.7	4.1	6.3	12.0	11.0	13.9
Massachusetts	30,567	22,410	8,157	11,338	7,812	3,526	34.9	43.2	5.4	4.5	7.6	14.4	13.0	17.7
Michigan	71,768	59,269	12,499	27,347	21,237	6,110	35.8	48.9	5.4	4.4	10.0	14.1	12.3	20.4
Minnesota	32,878	25,603	7,275	12,240	8,561	3,679	33.4	50.6	5.8	4.4	11.0	15.7	13.1	21.8
Mississippi	29,148	22,176	6,972	7,976	4,823	3,153	21.7	45.2	4.6	3.2	8.9	16.6	14.7	19.6
Missouri	37,874	29,642	8,232	11,243	7,690	3,553	25.9	43.2	5.1	4.2	8.3	17.2	16.2	19.2
Montana	7,482	6,453	1,029	2,662	2,242	419	34.8	40.7	5.2	5.1	5.8	14.7	14.8	14.3
Nebraska	17,454	13,936	3,518	5,929	4,163	1,766	29.9	50.2	4.4	3.6	7.4	12.9	12.2	14.6
Nevada	9,674	9,090	584	3,544	3,260	284	35.9	48.7	7.2	7.0	9.8	19.6	19.5	20.0
New Hampshire	6,181	4,701	1,480	2,384	1,512	872	32.2	59.0	5.4	5.4	5.6	14.1	16.7	9.6
New Jersey	45,134	34,046	11,087	16,301	11,058	5,243	32.5	47.3	5.8	4.4	10.2	16.2	13.6	21.7
New Mexico	20,014	14,463	5,551	6,775	4,458	2,317	30.8	41.7	4.9	3.6	8.2	14.4	11.7	19.6
New York	78,002	54,420	23,583	31,494	20,848	10,646	38.3	45.1	7.2	6.1	9.9	17.9	15.8	22.0
North Carolina	71,499	48,573	22,926	25,579	14,235	11,344	29.3	49.5	4.8	4.0	6.4	13.3	13.6	13.0
North Dakota	8,019	7,186	833	2,688	2,359	329	32.8	39.5	4.9	4.8	5.3	14.6	14.7	13.5
Ohio	78,505	66,060	12,445	23,424	17,583	5,842	26.6	46.9	4.9	4.3	8.5	16.5	16.0	18.0
Oklahoma	29,087	24,476	4,611	9,083	7,257	1,826	29.6	39.6	4.8	4.2	8.2	15.4	14.1	20.7
Oregon	28,997	21,256	7,740	10,664	7,204	3,460	33.9	44.7	5.3	4.1	8.4	14.3	12.2	18.8
Pennsylvania	64,436	54,705	9,731	25,320	20,264	5,056	37.0	52.0	5.2	4.6	8.2	13.2	12.5	15.8
Rhode Island	4,703	3,742	960	1,868	1,345	523	35.9	54.5	6.6	5.8	10.0	16.7	16.1	18.3
South Carolina	28,938	22,116	6,822	10,671	7,367	3,304	33.3	48.4	5.6	4.4	9.2	15.1	13.3	19.1
South Dakota	5,975	5,247	728	2,338	1,921	417	36.6	57.3	5.8	5.6	7.5	14.8	15.2	13.0
Tennessee	32,040	26,137	5,903	10,766	7,914	2,851	30.3	48.3	5.5	4.6	9.5	16.5	15.3	19.7
Texas	174,401	131,147	43,254	53,946	34,654	19,293	26.4	44.6	5.2	4.1	8.8	16.9	15.4	19.7
Utah	22,594	20,786	1,808	8,646	7,925	722	38.1	39.9	5.3	4.9	9.1	13.8	12.9	22.9
Vermont	5,309	4,925	385	2,061	1,844	217	37.4	56.3	3.8	3.6	7.1	9.8	9.5	12.6
Virginia	55,575	45,112	10,463	20,424	15,255	5,169	33.8	49.4	5.4	4.2	10.3	14.7	12.5	20.9
Washington	43,958	34,403	9,555	16,419	12,308	4,111	35.8	43.0	5.6	4.4	9.6	14.9	12.4	22.4
West Virginia	13,232	11,827	1,405	5,330	4,501	830	38.1	59.0	5.7	5.3	9.7	14.2	13.8	16.4
Wisconsin	41,801	32,392	9,409	16,060	11,457	4,602	35.4	48.9	5.2	4.9	6.5	13.6	13.7	13.3
Wyoming	5,689	3,194	2,495	2,213	1,063	1,151	33.3	46.1	4.3	3.4	5.5	11.1	10.3	11.9
U.S. Service Academies	3,609	3,609	0	1,071	1,071	0	29.7	†	4.2	4.2	†	14.0	14.0	†
Other jurisdictions	15,904	14,633	1,270	5,709	5,217	492	35.7	38.7	4.4	4.3	5.8	12.3	12.0	15.1
American Samoa	304	304	0	81	81	0	26.6	†	3.4	3.4	†	12.8	12.8	†
Federated States of Micronesia	384	0	384	105	0	105	†	27.3	5.0	†	5.0	18.1	†	18.1
Guam	898	655	243	279	213	66	32.5	27.2	5.3	4.9	6.4	17.1	15.1	23.5
Marshall Islands	148	0	148	48	0	48	†	32.4	5.3	†	5.3	16.3	†	16.3
Northern Marianas	185	185	0	60	60	0	32.4	†	5.4	5.4	†	16.6	16.6	†
Palau	192	0	192	53	0	53	†	27.4	2.6	†	2.6	9.4	†	9.4
Puerto Rico	13,213	12,910	303	4,865	4,645	220	36.0	72.6	4.4	4.3	8.8	12.0	12.0	12.1
U.S. Virgin Islands	580	580	0	219	219	0	37.7	†	3.0	3.0	†	8.1	8.1	†

†Not applicable.
NOTE: Full-time-equivalent staff is the full-time staff, plus the full-time equivalent of the part-time staff. Degree-granting institutions grant associate's or higher degrees and participate in Title IV federal financial aid programs. Data are for all degree-granting institutions, including those with fewer than 15 employees. Detail may not sum to totals because of rounding.

SOURCE: U.S. Department of Education, National Center for Education Statistics, Integrated Postsecondary Education Data System (IPEDS), Spring 2014, Human Resources component, Fall Staff section; and Spring 2014, Enrollment component. (This table was prepared May 2015.)

Table 314.60. Ratios of full-time-equivalent (FTE) students to FTE staff and FTE faculty in private degree-granting postsecondary institutions, by level of institution and state or jurisdiction: Fall 2013

State or jurisdiction	Full-time-equivalent (FTE) staff				FTE faculty				FTE faculty as a percent of FTE staff		FTE students per FTE staff		FTE students per FTE faculty	
	All private	Nonprofit 4-year	Nonprofit 2-year	For-profit	All private	Nonprofit 4-year	Nonprofit 2-year	For-profit	Nonprofit 4-year	For-profit	Nonprofit 4-year	For-profit	Nonprofit 4-year	For-profit
1	2	3	4	5	6	7	8	9	10	11	12	13	14	15
United States	1,058,961	916,293	4,277	138,391	378,224	316,600	1,856	59,768	34.6	43.2	3.6	9.7	10.6	22.5
Alabama	6,497	4,563	56	1,879	2,519	1,715	24	781	37.6	41.6	4.9	13.4	13.1	32.3
Alaska	500	166	26	308	200	76	5	119	45.6	38.6	2.9	8.2	6.4	21.2
Arizona	21,690	1,699	0	19,991	9,164	597	0	8,567	35.1	42.9	4.9	14.7	13.9	34.4
Arkansas	3,255	3,012	66	177	1,140	1,016	17	107	33.7	60.4	4.8	8.3	14.3	13.8
California	90,669	72,779	230	17,659	32,806	25,220	83	7,503	34.7	42.5	3.6	9.0	10.4	21.3
Colorado	9,858	5,607	4	4,247	3,909	2,084	1	1,825	37.2	43.0	4.8	9.8	12.9	22.8
Connecticut	25,010	24,146	0	864	8,614	8,283	0	331	34.3	38.3	2.5	6.8	7.2	17.9
Delaware	1,452	1,397	33	22	714	691	13	10	49.5	44.8	8.2	8.1	16.6	18.0
District of Columbia	21,076	20,456	0	621	7,205	6,775	0	429	33.1	69.2	3.3	4.4	9.9	6.4
Florida	46,629	32,914	204	13,511	16,305	10,467	98	5,739	31.8	42.5	4.5	9.5	14.1	22.4
Georgia	25,391	21,439	84	3,868	9,883	8,089	31	1,763	37.7	45.6	3.0	9.8	8.0	21.6
Hawaii	1,995	1,641	0	354	890	712	0	179	43.4	50.4	6.7	10.8	15.4	21.3
Idaho	2,411	2,207	0	204	1,158	1,052	0	107	47.7	52.3	10.6	7.6	22.2	14.5
Illinois	63,588	56,407	82	7,099	22,284	19,548	34	2,703	34.7	38.1	3.4	6.5	9.7	17.2
Indiana	20,809	18,196	71	2,541	7,119	6,223	25	872	34.2	34.3	4.3	6.5	12.7	19.0
Iowa	17,070	10,385	0	6,685	6,827	4,005	0	2,822	38.6	42.2	4.8	13.5	12.4	31.9
Kansas	4,804	4,072	116	617	1,916	1,631	42	243	40.1	39.4	5.0	7.0	12.5	17.7
Kentucky	8,176	6,301	0	1,875	3,348	2,480	0	868	39.4	46.3	5.3	6.5	13.4	14.0
Louisiana	8,418	7,431	122	865	3,103	2,614	56	433	35.2	50.1	3.2	8.4	9.1	16.9
Maine	4,747	4,588	43	116	1,562	1,499	26	37	32.7	31.5	3.8	9.4	11.6	29.8
Maryland	23,964	23,344	0	620	6,990	6,751	0	240	28.9	38.7	1.8	9.7	6.4	25.2
Massachusetts	82,173	81,534	86	553	28,658	28,349	58	251	34.8	45.3	3.0	8.2	8.6	18.0
Michigan	13,949	12,986	0	963	5,817	5,372	0	444	41.4	46.1	6.2	6.8	14.9	14.8
Minnesota	18,130	12,405	28	5,697	7,690	5,046	9	2,635	40.7	46.3	4.9	11.5	12.0	24.8
Mississippi	2,655	2,300	0	355	1,067	896	0	171	39.0	48.1	5.6	6.1	14.4	12.7
Missouri	33,347	30,810	126	2,411	11,859	10,905	69	885	35.4	36.7	3.7	11.3	10.3	30.7
Montana	970	865	105	0	357	333	24	0	38.5	†	4.7	†	12.2	†
Nebraska	5,323	4,980	49	294	1,995	1,855	19	121	37.2	41.0	5.8	7.3	15.5	17.9
Nevada	1,542	652	0	889	748	315	0	433	48.3	48.7	5.0	11.1	10.3	22.9
New Hampshire	8,499	8,089	38	372	2,556	2,378	26	152	29.4	40.9	4.4	6.7	15.0	16.4
New Jersey	16,153	14,839	0	1,314	5,237	4,610	0	627	31.1	47.7	4.2	6.6	13.5	13.9
New Mexico	1,045	276	0	769	494	88	0	406	31.8	52.9	4.0	9.0	12.5	17.1
New York	146,158	139,714	545	5,899	51,751	48,833	292	2,626	35.0	44.5	3.2	7.5	9.1	16.9
North Carolina	37,442	35,566	128	1,748	12,009	11,244	37	728	31.6	41.7	2.4	7.9	7.7	19.1
North Dakota	1,305	1,236	0	69	434	410	0	25	33.1	35.8	3.6	10.1	10.8	28.3
Ohio	31,177	27,047	137	3,993	12,066	10,135	42	1,889	37.5	47.3	4.5	7.2	11.9	15.2
Oklahoma	5,766	4,676	0	1,090	2,153	1,651	0	502	35.3	46.1	4.8	7.6	13.5	16.5
Oregon	7,233	6,396	0	837	3,012	2,625	0	387	41.0	46.3	4.9	7.7	12.0	16.6
Pennsylvania	77,719	71,282	1,273	5,164	27,174	24,184	551	2,440	33.9	47.2	3.5	7.6	10.2	16.1
Rhode Island	9,985	9,985	0	0	3,127	3,127	0	0	31.3	†	3.8	†	12.2	†
South Carolina	8,483	6,104	123	2,256	2,989	2,187	36	766	35.8	34.0	5.0	5.8	13.9	17.0
South Dakota	1,914	1,278	30	607	717	516	14	187	40.4	30.8	4.4	3.1	10.8	10.2
Tennessee	38,349	35,905	72	2,372	9,714	8,577	32	1,105	23.9	46.6	2.1	9.1	8.7	19.6
Texas	36,531	30,527	246	5,757	13,264	10,755	120	2,388	35.2	41.5	3.8	8.6	10.7	20.8
Utah	8,898	7,916	66	916	3,723	3,256	16	451	41.1	49.2	10.5	7.7	25.6	15.7
Vermont	4,043	3,933	0	110	1,387	1,364	0	23	34.7	21.1	4.0	3.6	11.6	16.8
Virginia	22,521	17,624	80	4,817	8,782	6,542	51	2,189	37.1	45.4	5.6	7.8	15.1	17.2
Washington	9,052	8,002	9	1,041	3,779	3,353	5	421	41.9	40.4	4.7	8.5	11.3	21.1
West Virginia	4,135	1,759	0	2,375	1,712	583	0	1,129	33.1	47.5	4.5	11.3	13.6	23.9
Wisconsin	16,261	14,842	0	1,418	6,223	5,578	0	644	37.6	45.4	3.6	6.6	9.5	14.5
Wyoming	194	14	0	180	73	5	0	68	37.2	37.7	5.2	8.1	14.1	21.6
Other jurisdictions	14,737	11,721	0	3,016	6,099	4,848	0	1,251	41.4	41.5	9.9	12.6	23.9	30.4
American Samoa	0	0	0	0	0	0	0	0	†	†	†	†	†	†
Federated States of Micronesia	0	0	0	0	0	0	0	0	†	†	†	†	†	†
Guam	10	10	0	0	6	6	0	0	56.7	†	6.6	†	11.6	†
Marshall Islands	0	0	0	0	0	0	0	0	†	†	†	†	†	†
Northern Marianas	0	0	0	0	0	0	0	0	†	†	†	†	†	†
Palau	0	0	0	0	0	0	0	0	†	†	†	†	†	†
Puerto Rico	14,727	11,711	0	3,016	6,093	4,842	0	1,251	41.3	41.5	9.9	12.6	23.9	30.4
U.S. Virgin Islands	0	0	0	0	0	0	0	0	†	†	†	†	†	†

†Not applicable.

NOTE: Full-time-equivalent staff is the full-time staff, plus the full-time equivalent of the part-time staff. Degree-granting institutions grant associate's or higher degrees and participate in Title IV federal financial aid programs. Data are for all degree-granting institutions, including those with fewer than 15 employees. Detail may not sum to totals because of rounding.

SOURCE: U.S. Department of Education, National Center for Education Statistics, Integrated Postsecondary Education Data System (IPEDS), Spring 2014, Human Resources component, Fall Staff section; and Spring 2014, Enrollment component. (This table was prepared May 2015.)

Table 315.10. Number of faculty in degree-granting postsecondary institutions, by employment status, sex, control, and level of institution: Selected years, fall 1970 through fall 2013

Year	Total	Employment status			Sex			Control				Level	
		Full-time	Part-time	Percent full-time	Males	Females	Percent female	Public	Private			4-year	2-year
									Total	Nonprofit	For-profit		
1	2	3	4	5	6	7	8	9	10	11	12	13	14
1970	474,000	369,000	104,000	77.8	—	—	—	314,000	160,000	—	—	382,000	92,000
1971[1]	492,000	379,000	113,000	77.0	—	—	—	333,000	159,000	—	—	387,000	105,000
1972	500,000	380,000	120,000	76.0	—	—	—	343,000	157,000	—	—	384,000	116,000
1973[1]	527,000	389,000	138,000	73.8	—	—	—	365,000	162,000	—	—	401,000	126,000
1974[1]	567,000	406,000	161,000	71.6	—	—	—	397,000	170,000	—	—	427,000	140,000
1975[1]	628,000	440,000	188,000	70.1	—	—	—	443,000	185,000	—	—	467,000	161,000
1976	633,000	434,000	199,000	68.6	—	—	—	449,000	184,000	—	—	467,000	166,000
1977	678,000	448,000	230,000	66.1	—	—	—	492,000	186,000	—	—	485,000	193,000
1979[1]	675,000	445,000	230,000	65.9	—	—	—	488,000	187,000	—	—	494,000	182,000
1980[1]	686,000	450,000	236,000	65.6	—	—	—	495,000	191,000	—	—	494,000	192,000
1981	705,000	461,000	244,000	65.4	—	—	—	509,000	196,000	—	—	493,000	212,000
1982[1]	710,000	462,000	248,000	65.1	—	—	—	506,000	204,000	—	—	493,000	217,000
1983	724,000	471,000	254,000	65.1	—	—	—	512,000	212,000	—	—	504,000	220,000
1984[1]	717,000	462,000	255,000	64.4	—	—	—	505,000	212,000	—	—	504,000	213,000
1985[1]	715,000	459,000	256,000	64.2	—	—	—	503,000	212,000	—	—	504,000	211,000
1986[1]	722,000	459,000	263,000	63.6	—	—	—	510,000	212,000	—	—	506,000	216,000
1987[2]	793,070	523,420	269,650	66.0	529,413	263,657	33.2	552,749	240,321	—	—	547,505	245,565
1989[2]	824,220	524,426	299,794	63.6	534,254	289,966	35.2	577,298	246,922	—	—	583,700	240,520
1991[2]	826,252	535,623	290,629	64.8	525,599	300,653	36.4	580,908	245,344	236,066	9,278	591,269	234,983
1993[2]	915,474	545,706	369,768	59.6	561,123	354,351	38.7	650,434	265,040	254,130	10,910	625,969	289,505
1995[2]	931,706	550,822	380,884	59.1	562,893	368,813	39.6	656,833	274,873	260,900	13,973	647,059	284,647
1997[2]	989,813	568,719	421,094	57.5	587,420	402,393	40.7	694,560	295,253	271,257	23,996	682,650	307,163
1999[2]	1,027,830	590,937	436,893	57.5	602,469	425,361	41.4	713,325	314,505	284,652	29,853	713,823	314,007
2001[2]	1,113,183	617,868	495,315	55.5	644,514	468,669	42.1	771,124	342,059	306,487	35,572	764,172	349,011
2003[2]	1,173,593	630,092	543,501	53.7	663,723	509,870	43.4	791,766	381,827	330,097	51,730	814,289	359,304
2005[2]	1,290,426	675,624	614,802	52.4	714,453	575,973	44.6	841,188	449,238	361,523	87,715	916,996	373,430
2007[2]	1,371,390	703,463	667,927	51.3	743,812	627,578	45.8	877,146	494,244	385,875	108,369	990,849	380,541
2009[2]	1,439,074	729,152	709,922	50.7	761,002	678,072	47.1	913,788	525,286	408,382	116,904	1,038,349	400,725
2011[2]	1,524,469	762,114	762,355	50.0	789,567	734,902	48.2	954,159	570,310	432,630	137,680	1,115,642	408,827
2013[2]	1,544,060	791,391	752,669	51.3	791,310	752,750	48.8	967,703	576,357	448,724	127,633	1,150,152	393,908

—Not available.

[1]Estimated on the basis of enrollment. For methodological details on estimates, see National Center for Education Statistics, *Projections of Education Statistics to 2000.*

[2]Because of revised survey methods, data are not directly comparable with figures for years prior to 1987.

NOTE: Includes faculty members with the title of professor, associate professor, assistant professor, instructor, lecturer, assisting professor, adjunct professor, or interim professor (or the equivalent). Excluded are graduate students with titles such as graduate or teaching fellow who assist senior faculty. Data through 1995 are for institutions of higher education, while later data are for degree-granting institutions. Degree-granting institutions grant associate's or higher degrees and participate in Title IV federal financial aid programs. The degree-granting classification is very similar to the earlier higher education classification, but it includes more 2-year colleges and excludes a few higher education institutions that did not grant degrees. Beginning in 2007, includes institutions with fewer than 15 full-time employees; these institutions did not report staff data prior to 2007. Detail may not sum to totals because of rounding.

SOURCE: U.S. Department of Education, National Center for Education Statistics, Higher Education General Information Survey (HEGIS), *Employees in Institutions of Higher Education,* 1970 and 1972, and "Staff Survey" 1976; *Projections of Education Statistics to 2000;* Integrated Postsecondary Education Data System (IPEDS), "Fall Staff Survey" (IPEDS-S:87–99); IPEDS Winter 2001–02 through Winter 2011–12, Human Resources component, Fall Staff section; IPEDS Spring 2014, Human Resources component, Fall Staff section; and U.S. Equal Employment Opportunity Commission, Higher Education Staff Information Survey (EEO-6), 1977, 1981, and 1983. (This table was prepared March 2015.)

Table 315.20. Full-time faculty in degree-granting postsecondary institutions, by race/ethnicity, sex, and academic rank: Fall 2009, fall 2011, and fall 2013

Year, sex, and academic rank	Total	White	Black, Hispanic, Asian, Pacific Islander, American Indian/Alaska Native, and Two or more races									Race/ethnicity unknown	Non-resident-alien[2]
			Total	Percent[1]	Black	Hispanic	Asian/Pacific Islander			American Indian/Alaska Native	Two or more races		
							Total	Asian	Pacific Islander				
1	2	3	4	5	6	7	8	9	10	11	12	13	14
2009													
Total	729,152	551,230	130,903	19.2	39,706	28,022	59,480	—	—	3,458	—	16,059	31,197
Professors	177,566	149,553	24,633	14.1	6,086	4,683	13,281	—	—	580	—	1,923	1,460
Associate professors	148,959	117,241	26,779	18.6	8,162	5,382	12,626	—	—	601	—	2,387	2,560
Assistant professors	171,622	117,794	37,199	24.0	10,974	6,783	18,634	—	—	717	—	4,616	12,104
Instructors	104,554	78,346	20,951	21.1	7,807	6,575	5,546	—	—	1,002	—	3,399	1,879
Lecturers	33,372	24,925	5,851	19.0	1,813	1,583	2,319	—	—	139	—	882	1,711
Other faculty	93,079	63,371	15,490	19.7	4,864	3,016	7,074	—	—	419	—	2,852	11,483
2011													
Total	762,114	564,218	147,495	20.7	41,662	31,335	66,842	65,469	1,373	3,534	4,122	16,999	33,402
Professors	181,509	150,364	27,559	15.5	6,517	5,180	14,617	14,425	192	589	656	2,202	1,384
Associate professors	155,201	119,415	30,605	20.4	8,695	6,144	14,364	14,129	235	597	805	2,477	2,704
Assistant professors	174,052	118,022	39,986	25.3	10,994	7,428	19,820	19,445	375	701	1,043	4,926	11,118
Instructors	109,042	80,690	23,162	22.3	8,602	6,907	5,807	5,448	359	981	865	3,262	1,928
Lecturers	34,473	25,821	6,261	19.5	1,688	1,773	2,455	2,420	35	135	210	848	1,543
Other faculty	107,837	69,906	19,922	22.2	5,166	3,903	9,779	9,602	177	531	543	3,284	14,725
Males	427,214	316,133	79,707	20.1	18,636	16,341	40,989	40,368	621	1,752	1,989	9,600	21,774
Professors	128,649	106,069	19,812	15.7	3,984	3,499	11,550	11,420	130	362	417	1,643	1,125
Associate professors	89,742	68,493	17,820	20.6	4,373	3,437	9,260	9,142	118	313	437	1,574	1,855
Assistant professors	88,173	58,538	19,877	25.3	4,458	3,692	10,970	10,820	150	303	454	2,694	7,064
Instructors	48,124	35,864	9,750	21.4	3,138	3,133	2,668	2,525	143	463	348	1,486	1,024
Lecturers	15,690	11,721	2,740	18.9	751	753	1,110	1,090	20	47	79	410	819
Other faculty	56,836	35,448	9,708	21.5	1,932	1,827	5,431	5,371	60	264	254	1,793	9,887
Females	334,900	248,085	67,788	21.5	23,026	14,994	25,853	25,101	752	1,782	2,133	7,399	11,628
Professors	52,860	44,295	7,747	14.9	2,533	1,681	3,067	3,005	62	227	239	559	259
Associate professors	65,459	50,922	12,785	20.1	4,322	2,707	5,104	4,987	117	284	368	903	849
Assistant professors	85,879	59,484	20,109	25.3	6,536	3,736	8,850	8,625	225	398	589	2,232	4,054
Instructors	60,918	44,826	13,412	23.0	5,464	3,774	3,139	2,923	216	518	517	1,776	904
Lecturers	18,783	14,100	3,521	20.0	937	1,020	1,345	1,330	15	88	131	438	724
Other faculty	51,001	34,458	10,214	22.9	3,234	2,076	4,348	4,231	117	267	289	1,491	4,838
2013[3]													
Total	791,391	575,491	157,480	21.5	43,188	33,217	72,246	71,038	1,208	3,538	5,291	20,013	38,407
Professors	181,530	148,577	29,111	16.4	6,665	5,604	15,417	15,247	170	573	852	2,323	1,519
Associate professors	155,095	116,817	32,580	21.8	8,812	6,381	15,809	15,626	183	591	987	2,859	2,839
Assistant professors	166,045	112,262	38,011	25.3	10,542	7,130	18,402	18,070	332	683	1,254	5,695	10,077
Instructors	99,304	73,859	20,684	21.9	7,448	6,340	5,236	4,950	286	879	781	3,180	1,581
Lecturers	36,728	27,453	6,591	19.4	1,728	2,015	2,436	2,403	33	117	295	1,151	1,533
Other faculty	152,689	96,523	30,503	24.0	7,993	5,747	14,946	14,742	204	695	1,122	4,805	20,858
Males	436,456	316,912	83,905	20.9	18,905	17,198	43,519	42,928	591	1,736	2,547	10,813	24,826
Professors	125,836	102,520	20,450	16.6	4,018	3,669	11,882	11,772	110	350	531	1,664	1,202
Associate professors	87,420	65,320	18,552	22.1	4,321	3,533	9,897	9,810	87	287	514	1,727	1,821
Assistant professors	82,331	54,700	18,387	25.2	4,169	3,506	9,887	9,725	162	304	521	2,957	6,287
Instructors	42,877	32,014	8,665	21.3	2,714	2,888	2,304	2,179	125	430	329	1,349	849
Lecturers	16,588	12,464	2,756	18.1	760	834	992	983	9	39	131	580	788
Other faculty	81,404	49,894	15,095	23.2	2,923	2,768	8,557	8,459	98	326	521	2,536	13,879
Females	354,935	258,579	73,575	22.2	24,283	16,019	28,727	28,110	617	1,802	2,744	9,200	13,581
Professors	55,694	46,057	8,661	15.8	2,647	1,935	3,535	3,475	60	223	321	659	317
Associate professors	67,675	51,497	14,028	21.4	4,491	2,848	5,912	5,816	96	304	473	1,132	1,018
Assistant professors	83,714	57,562	19,624	25.4	6,373	3,624	8,515	8,345	170	379	733	2,738	3,790
Instructors	56,427	41,845	12,019	22.3	4,734	3,452	2,932	2,771	161	449	452	1,831	732
Lecturers	20,140	14,989	3,835	20.4	968	1,181	1,444	1,420	24	78	164	571	745
Other faculty	71,285	46,629	15,408	24.8	5,070	2,979	6,389	6,283	106	369	601	2,269	6,979

—Not available.
[1]Combined total of faculty who were Black, Hispanic, Asian, Pacific Islander, American Indian/Alaska Native, and of Two or more races as a percentage of total faculty, excluding race/ethnicity unknown and nonresident alien.
[2]Race/ethnicity not collected.
[3]Only instructional faculty were classified by academic rank. Primarily research and primarily public service faculty, as well as faculty without ranks, appear under "other faculty."
NOTE: Degree-granting institutions grant associate's or higher degrees and participate in Title IV federal financial aid programs. Includes institutions with fewer than 15 full-time employees; these institutions did not report staff data prior to 2007. Race categories exclude persons of Hispanic ethnicity. Some data have been revised from previously published figures.
SOURCE: U.S. Department of Education, National Center for Education Statistics, Integrated Postsecondary Education Data System (IPEDS), Winter 2009–10 and Winter 2011–12, Human Resources component, Fall Staff section; and IPEDS Spring 2014, Human Resources component, Fall Staff section. (This table was prepared March 2015.)

Table 315.30. Percentage distribution of full-time faculty and instructional staff in degree-granting postsecondary institutions, by level and control of institution, selected instruction activities, and number of classes taught for credit: Fall 2003

[Standard errors appear in parentheses]

Instruction activity and number of classes	All institutions	Research Public	Research Private	Doctoral Public	Doctoral Private	Comprehensive Public	Comprehensive Private	Private liberal arts	Public 2-year	Other
1	2	3	4	5	6	7	8	9	10	11
Number of full-time faculty and instructional staff (in thousands)	681.8 (0.05)	162.1 (0.85)	63.5 (1.58)	51.3 (0.76)	21.7 (0.79)	107.3 (2.98)	41.4 (1.59)	49.6 (1.80)	114.6 (1.09)	70.2 (3.36)
Percentage distribution	100.0 (†)	23.8 (0.12)	9.3 (0.23)	7.5 (0.11)	3.2 (0.12)	15.7 (0.44)	6.1 (0.23)	7.3 (0.26)	16.8 (0.16)	10.3 (0.49)
Average hours worked per week	53.3 (0.13)	55.6 (0.21)	55.8 (0.42)	54.0 (0.38)	52.4 (0.59)	53.2 (0.31)	51.8 (0.53)	54.0 (0.39)	49.2 (0.34)	53.1 (0.49)
Paid activities within institution	45.4 (0.12)	48.8 (0.19)	47.8 (0.36)	45.9 (0.31)	44.7 (0.47)	44.4 (0.27)	42.9 (0.55)	45.6 (0.39)	40.9 (0.27)	45.1 (0.59)
Unpaid activities within institution	3.8 (0.04)	3.1 (0.08)	3.3 (0.15)	3.9 (0.14)	3.8 (0.20)	4.4 (0.13)	4.4 (0.15)	4.4 (0.11)	4.2 (0.12)	3.6 (0.22)
Paid activities outside institution	2.2 (0.05)	1.8 (0.08)	2.7 (0.21)	2.1 (0.13)	2.3 (0.25)	2.3 (0.12)	2.2 (0.17)	2.0 (0.13)	2.3 (0.12)	2.8 (0.24)
Unpaid activities outside institution	1.9 (0.03)	1.9 (0.05)	2.0 (0.09)	2.1 (0.11)	1.7 (0.11)	2.1 (0.09)	2.3 (0.12)	2.0 (0.14)	1.7 (0.08)	1.6 (0.10)
Work time distribution (percent)	100.0 (†)	100.0 (†)	100.0 (†)	100.0 (2.08)	100.0 (†)	100.0 (†)	100.0 (†)	100.0 (†)	100.0 (†)	100.0 (†)
Teaching	58.2 (0.27)	43.5 (0.43)	43.1 (0.76)	55.5 (0.72)	55.0 (1.15)	64.7 (0.70)	67.5 (0.78)	65.9 (0.80)	78.4 (0.65)	55.0 (1.61)
Research/scholarship	20.0 (0.44)	33.2 (0.42)	34.0 (0.84)	22.3 (0.72)	24.6 (0.34)	15.0 (0.49)	11.2 (0.57)	12.7 (0.67)	3.7 (0.26)	18.7 (0.97)
Other activities (administration, professional growth, etc.)	21.7 (0.17)	23.2 (0.45)	22.8 (0.67)	22.2 (0.64)	20.4 (1.21)	20.4 (0.66)	21.3 (0.75)	21.3 (0.73)	17.9 (0.54)	26.3 (1.27)
Faculty/staff distribution by instruction activity (percent)										
Distribution by hours taught per week	100.0 (†)	100.0 (†)	100.0 (†)	100.0 (†)	100.0 (†)	100.0 (†)	100.0 (†)	100.0 (†)	100.0 (†)	100.0 (†)
Less than 4.0	30.3 (0.44)	48.9 (0.83)	52.2 (1.31)	30.0 (1.70)	26.5 (1.74)	16.3 (1.08)	14.9 (1.06)	15.5 (1.15)	14.5 (0.86)	36.0 (2.35)
4.0 to 5.9	5.8 (0.21)	8.4 (0.50)	8.8 (0.77)	6.0 (0.58)	8.4 (1.37)	4.1 (0.53)	4.1 (0.57)	4.1 (0.57)	2.5 (0.33)	6.7 (0.99)
6.0 to 7.9	13.8 (0.37)	20.0 (0.80)	15.2 (1.20)	22.2 (1.14)	22.0 (1.77)	12.0 (0.78)	11.0 (1.43)	13.3 (1.48)	4.4 (0.60)	9.0 (0.88)
8.0 to 9.9	12.5 (0.30)	9.0 (0.49)	9.3 (0.87)	16.9 (1.20)	19.3 (1.76)	21.5 (0.93)	18.7 (1.78)	19.5 (1.83)	5.7 (0.61)	7.2 (0.98)
10.0 to 14.9	18.2 (0.39)	7.9 (0.55)	8.8 (0.88)	15.1 (1.13)	15.0 (1.53)	31.5 (1.24)	32.7 (2.15)	33.5 (1.93)	14.7 (0.90)	19.6 (1.95)
15.0 or more	19.4 (0.40)	5.8 (0.43)	5.7 (0.67)	9.7 (0.92)	8.7 (1.34)	14.6 (0.93)	18.5 (1.92)	14.1 (1.39)	58.2 (1.47)	21.5 (1.73)
Distribution by number of students taught	100.0 (†)	100.0 (†)	100.0 (†)	100.0 (†)	100.0 (†)	100.0 (†)	100.0 (†)	100.0 (†)	100.0 (†)	100.0 (†)
Less than 25	30.6 (0.46)	46.0 (0.84)	51.5 (1.56)	29.7 (1.53)	31.9 (1.88)	16.5 (1.25)	16.5 (1.23)	20.8 (1.44)	15.9 (0.94)	36.8 (1.96)
25 to 49	17.0 (0.34)	17.0 (0.83)	16.9 (1.06)	17.1 (0.99)	18.8 (1.74)	17.9 (0.96)	22.7 (1.57)	25.4 (1.62)	12.0 (0.77)	13.4 (1.41)
50 to 74	16.2 (0.33)	11.9 (0.69)	10.0 (0.99)	16.3 (1.29)	20.9 (1.64)	18.7 (0.77)	26.5 (1.32)	24.4 (1.40)	16.2 (0.86)	14.4 (1.07)
75 to 99	13.0 (0.30)	7.6 (0.51)	6.2 (0.57)	13.9 (0.91)	11.2 (0.95)	17.5 (0.86)	17.6 (1.15)	15.8 (1.09)	18.1 (0.78)	11.5 (1.03)
100 to 149	14.2 (0.39)	7.6 (0.54)	7.0 (0.78)	13.2 (0.87)	9.9 (1.21)	19.4 (1.22)	13.1 (1.61)	10.6 (0.96)	25.7 (0.98)	14.9 (1.58)
150 or more	9.0 (0.27)	9.8 (0.59)	8.4 (0.73)	9.8 (0.87)	7.4 (1.04)	9.7 (0.85)	3.6 (0.72)	3.0 (0.62)	12.1 (0.86)	8.9 (0.63)
Distribution by student classroom contact hours per week[1]	100.0 (†)	100.0 (†)	100.0 (†)	100.0 (†)	100.0 (†)	100.0 (†)	100.0 (†)	100.0 (†)	100.0 (†)	100.0 (†)
Less than 50	24.2 (0.40)	38.3 (0.83)	42.7 (1.33)	23.2 (1.52)	22.0 (1.53)	11.9 (1.04)	12.6 (1.02)	12.2 (1.05)	11.9 (0.77)	30.8 (1.87)
50 to 99	5.3 (0.23)	7.7 (0.56)	7.0 (0.82)	6.4 (0.68)	7.0 (1.20)	4.3 (0.52)	2.7 (0.55)	4.9 (0.48)	2.5 (0.39)	5.2 (0.88)
100 to 199	7.1 (0.20)	9.4 (0.54)	10.7 (0.87)	8.0 (0.88)	8.6 (1.38)	6.2 (0.62)	4.5 (0.66)	7.2 (1.02)	3.4 (0.43)	6.1 (0.99)
200 to 349	9.0 (0.28)	10.9 (0.52)	10.4 (0.83)	10.4 (0.88)	12.8 (1.74)	8.6 (0.71)	10.9 (1.38)	11.9 (1.27)	3.6 (0.54)	6.8 (0.79)
350 to 499	7.7 (0.24)	8.0 (0.44)	8.1 (0.83)	10.6 (1.03)	11.5 (1.03)	7.9 (0.91)	10.2 (0.79)	12.4 (0.93)	3.5 (0.40)	4.6 (0.70)
500 or more	46.8 (0.44)	25.6 (0.74)	21.2 (1.21)	41.4 (1.36)	38.0 (1.81)	61.1 (1.46)	59.1 (1.75)	51.4 (2.13)	75.0 (1.16)	46.6 (2.30)
Distribution by total classroom credit hours	100.0 (†)	100.0 (†)	100.0 (†)	100.0 (†)	100.0 (†)	100.0 (†)	100.0 (†)	100.0 (†)	100.0 (†)	100.0 (†)
Less than 4.0	31.8 (0.54)	48.9 (0.82)	52.1 (1.55)	30.1 (1.46)	29.0 (1.75)	18.0 (1.03)	17.5 (1.44)	23.7 (2.18)	15.4 (0.84)	38.1 (2.23)
4.0 to 5.9	6.6 (0.22)	9.4 (0.54)	10.2 (0.63)	6.8 (0.67)	10.5 (1.53)	3.5 (0.35)	4.5 (0.61)	5.6 (0.67)	3.7 (0.44)	7.0 (0.83)
6.0 to 7.9	15.0 (0.37)	21.6 (0.66)	14.0 (1.04)	25.1 (1.29)	21.3 (1.71)	14.2 (0.94)	12.2 (1.04)	11.4 (1.15)	6.6 (0.72)	10.1 (1.07)
8.0 to 9.9	14.8 (0.33)	10.4 (0.60)	10.7 (0.84)	19.9 (1.28)	20.8 (1.47)	25.3 (1.15)	23.4 (1.73)	19.1 (1.16)	8.1 (0.60)	10.0 (1.19)
10.0 to 14.9	20.2 (0.38)	7.7 (0.51)	9.7 (0.99)	14.8 (1.17)	13.2 (1.40)	32.0 (1.20)	35.4 (1.94)	32.5 (2.20)	24.3 (1.28)	22.3 (1.38)
15.0 or more	11.6 (0.31)	1.9 (0.24)	3.2 (0.52)	3.3 (0.64)	5.2 (0.99)	7.0 (0.88)	6.9 (0.71)	7.7 (1.28)	41.8 (1.50)	12.5 (1.17)

See notes at end of table.

Table 315.30. Percentage distribution of full-time faculty and instructional staff in degree-granting postsecondary institutions, by level and control of institution, selected instruction activities, and number of classes taught for credit: Fall 2003—Continued

[Standard errors appear in parentheses]

Instruction activity and number of classes	All institutions	Research		Doctoral		Comprehensive		Private liberal arts	Public 2-year	Other
		Public	Private	Public	Private	Public	Private			
1	2	3	4	5	6	7	8	9	10	11
Faculty/staff distribution by number of classes taught for credit (percent)										
Faculty/staff with undergraduate classes only, by total for-credit courses	100.0 (†)	100.0 (†)	100.0 (†)	100.0 (†)	100.0 (†)	100.0 (†)	100.0 (†)	100.0 (†)	100.0 (†)	100.0 (†)
1	11.0 (0.43)	24.2 (2.40)	20.2 (2.97)	14.1 (2.91)	10.0 (2.52)	10.5 (1.31)	9.3 (1.13)	9.9 (0.98)	8.7 (0.75)	11.2 (2.17)
2	17.4 (0.62)	38.0 (2.80)	31.2 (3.96)	24.2 (3.05)	38.6 (5.05)	14.6 (1.51)	18.5 (2.14)	22.7 (2.32)	10.7 (0.77)	13.7 (2.29)
3	23.7 (0.65)	22.6 (2.21)	30.8 (3.42)	31.1 (2.98)	37.3 (3.60)	28.6 (1.89)	30.3 (2.48)	34.3 (2.57)	16.0 (0.96)	17.3 (2.77)
4	21.9 (0.73)	10.8 (1.43)	11.7 (2.99)	20.4 (1.92)	10.9 (2.75)	33.3 (1.87)	30.7 (2.77)	21.1 (2.22)	16.9 (1.00)	28.4 (2.48)
5 or more	26.1 (0.70)	4.4 (0.86)	6.1 (1.74)	10.1 (1.97)	3.2 ! (1.15)	13.0 (1.56)	11.2 (1.53)	12.0 (1.44)	47.6 (1.49)	29.4 (2.14)
Faculty/staff with graduate classes only, by total for-credit courses	100.0 (†)	100.0 (†)	100.0 (†)	100.0 (†)	100.0 (†)	100.0 (†)	100.0 (†)	100.0 (†)	‡	100.0 (†)
1	40.1 (1.21)	50.4 (2.17)	48.0 (3.69)	34.3 (3.04)	25.9 (4.02)	23.6 (3.86)	13.0 (3.72)	15.8 ! (6.35)	‡	37.8 (3.15)
2	31.0 (1.07)	26.3 (1.81)	27.9 (2.93)	39.1 (3.32)	50.7 (4.02)	33.6 (5.32)	28.7 (4.00)	31.6 ! (12.42)	‡	32.9 (2.93)
3	16.7 (0.88)	14.3 (1.38)	13.3 (2.60)	16.3 (2.76)	14.1 (3.52)	29.6 (4.35)	36.3 (4.99)	22.7 ! (9.79)	‡	13.4 (2.48)
4	7.1 (0.80)	4.5 (1.24)	7.4 (2.07)	7.4 (2.04)	3.7 ! (1.44)	10.1 ! (3.39)	16.5 (3.92)	16.7 ! (8.04)	‡	7.2 ! (2.21)
5 or more	5.1 (0.52)	4.4 (0.69)	3.4 ! (1.33)	‡ (†)	5.7 ! (2.80)	3.1 ! (1.52)	5.5 ! (2.85)	‡ (†)	‡	8.7 (1.94)
Faculty/staff with both undergraduate and graduate classes, by total for-credit courses	100.0 (†)	100.0 (†)	100.0 (†)	100.0 (†)	100.0 (†)	100.0 (†)	100.0 (†)	100.0 (†)	‡	100.0 (†)
1	23.3 (0.68)	32.5 (1.37)	38.4 (1.89)	21.1 (2.17)	20.2 (2.37)	9.0 (1.04)	10.3 (2.14)	9.4 (2.00)	‡	24.8 (3.18)
2	33.4 (0.83)	44.3 (1.36)	42.8 (2.33)	37.1 (2.15)	37.8 (2.58)	19.6 (1.30)	19.0 (2.78)	18.3 (2.62)	‡	18.7 (3.00)
3	24.3 (0.70)	15.5 (0.99)	12.4 (1.37)	26.5 (1.75)	32.0 (3.01)	38.1 (1.91)	34.8 (2.85)	29.5 (3.77)	‡	21.2 (3.06)
4	12.2 (0.54)	4.5 (0.64)	3.7 (1.06)	10.1 (1.37)	6.6 ! (2.02)	23.4 (1.69)	24.4 (3.39)	27.5 (3.74)	‡	16.6 (3.55)
5 or more	6.7 (0.43)	3.1 (0.45)	2.8 (0.78)	5.2 (0.75)	‡ (†)	9.9 (1.01)	11.4 (2.07)	15.2 (3.65)	‡	18.6 (2.88)

†Not applicable.
!Interpret data with caution. The coefficient of variation (CV) for this estimate is between 30 and 50 percent.
‡Reporting standards not met. Either there are too few cases for a reliable estimate or the coefficient of variation (CV) is 50 percent or greater.
¹Distribution by student classroom contact hours per week is based on the number of contact hours that faculty and instructional staff spend each week with students during classroom instruction multiplied by the number of students taught.

NOTE: Degree-granting institutions grant associate's or higher degrees and participate in Title IV federal financial aid programs. Totals may differ from figures reported in other tables because of varying survey methodologies. Detail may not sum to totals because of rounding.
SOURCE: U.S. Department of Education, National Center for Education Statistics, 2004 National Study of Postsecondary Faculty (NSOPF:04). (This table was prepared December 2008.)

Table 315.40. Percentage distribution of part-time faculty and instructional staff in degree-granting postsecondary institutions, by level and control of institution, selected instruction activities, and number of classes taught for credit: Fall 2003

[Standard errors appear in parentheses]

Instruction activity and number of classes	All institutions	Research		Doctoral		Comprehensive		Private liberal arts	Public 2-year	Other
		Public	Private	Public	Private	Public	Private			
1	2	3	4	5	6	7	8	9	10	11
Number of part-time faculty and instructional staff (in thousands)	530.0 (0.02)	39.7 (0.78)	23.2 (0.96)	20.8 (0.82)	15.4 (0.83)	60.3 (2.49)	53.5 (2.17)	28.4 (2.19)	230.1 (2.00)	58.7 (3.38)
Percentage distribution	100.0 (†)	7.5 (0.15)	4.4 (0.18)	3.9 (0.15)	2.9 (0.16)	11.4 (0.47)	10.1 (0.41)	5.4 (0.41)	43.4 (0.38)	11.1 (0.64)
Average hours worked per week	39.9 (0.30)	41.1 (0.85)	42.6 (1.24)	43.5 (1.37)	42.1 (1.29)	38.8 (1.01)	42.7 (1.14)	39.6 (1.23)	38.0 (0.45)	41.8 (1.18)
Paid activities within institution	13.7 (0.13)	19.0 (0.61)	14.0 (0.65)	16.4 (0.76)	13.5 (0.97)	14.9 (0.48)	12.1 (0.56)	13.5 (0.73)	12.5 (0.19)	14.2 (0.46)
Unpaid activities within institution	1.7 (0.06)	1.8 (0.25)	2.5 (0.25)	2.3 (0.28)	2.8 (0.37)	2.3 (0.19)	2.7 (0.12)	2.6 (0.17)	2.1 (0.08)	2.5 (0.17)
Paid activities outside institution	22.1 (0.28)	18.3 (0.98)	23.9 (1.34)	23.3 (1.55)	24.1 (1.40)	19.9 (1.00)	26.6 (1.38)	21.9 (0.98)	21.6 (0.41)	23.3 (1.06)
Unpaid activities outside institution	2.3 (0.06)	2.0 (0.25)	2.2 (0.25)	1.6 (0.28)	1.7 (0.37)	1.8 (0.19)	1.3 (0.12)	1.6 (0.17)	1.7 (0.08)	1.8 (0.17)
Work time distribution (percent)	100.0 (†)	100.0 (†)	100.0 (†)	100.0 (†)	100.0 (†)	100.0 (†)	100.0 (†)	100.0 (†)	100.0 (†)	100.0 (†)
Teaching	88.3 (0.32)	74.1 (1.79)	80.6 (1.89)	84.9 (1.71)	87.2 (1.87)	90.8 (0.83)	90.4 (0.70)	90.2 (1.20)	91.3 (0.43)	85.4 (1.19)
Research/scholarship	3.9 (0.80)	13.3 (1.62)	7.0 (0.97)	7.4 (1.35)	5.2 (1.42)	3.2 (0.46)	2.4 (0.49)	2.6 (0.54)	2.1 (0.21)	4.4 (0.61)
Other activities (administration, professional growth, etc.)	7.8 (0.20)	12.6 (1.04)	12.4 (1.75)	7.6 (1.03)	7.6 (1.22)	6.0 (0.63)	7.2 (0.81)	7.2 (0.92)	6.6 (0.40)	10.3 (0.93)
Faculty/staff distribution by instruction activity (percent)										
Distribution by hours taught per week	100.0 (†)	100.0 (†)	100.0 (†)	100.0 (†)	100.0 (†)	100.0 (†)	100.0 (†)	100.0 (†)	100.0 (†)	100.0 (†)
Less than 4.0	45.3 (0.80)	58.1 (2.25)	62.4 (3.87)	53.3 (2.71)	48.0 (2.67)	45.5 (1.68)	39.8 (2.34)	44.8 (2.96)	41.3 (1.30)	46.5 (2.46)
4.0 to 5.9	12.2 (0.48)	9.3 (1.25)	12.9 (2.46)	12.5 (1.49)	15.0 (1.57)	9.7 (1.25)	17.7 (2.07)	13.2 (1.73)	11.7 (0.71)	12.6 (1.62)
6.0 to 7.9	14.3 (0.57)	12.5 (1.50)	10.1 (1.69)	14.5 (1.76)	14.3 (2.01)	19.4 (1.68)	12.9 (2.14)	13.8 (1.98)	14.5 (1.04)	13.0 (1.72)
8.0 to 9.9	10.4 (0.47)	8.9 (1.22)	5.6 (1.46)	8.3 (1.82)	7.8 (1.58)	10.8 (1.11)	11.7 (1.93)	10.7 (1.54)	11.3 (0.73)	9.5 (1.45)
10.0 to 14.9	9.4 (0.47)	7.5 (1.27)	3.0 ! (1.16)	5.5 (1.29)	7.3 (2.03)	8.0 (1.27)	7.7 (1.29)	8.3 (1.55)	11.7 (0.99)	9.8 (1.27)
15.0 or more	8.3 (0.43)	3.6 (0.90)	6.0 ! (1.94)	5.9 (1.50)	7.6 (1.26)	6.5 (1.05)	10.3 (1.61)	9.1 (2.38)	9.5 (0.67)	8.5 (1.19)
Distribution by number of students taught	100.0 (†)	100.0 (†)	100.0 (†)	100.0 (†)	100.0 (†)	100.0 (†)	100.0 (†)	100.0 (†)	100.0 (†)	100.0 (†)
Less than 25	52.0 (0.82)	55.6 (2.16)	68.9 (3.98)	44.6 (2.68)	56.9 (3.29)	41.6 (2.07)	57.9 (2.45)	60.5 (2.34)	49.7 (1.37)	54.0 (3.15)
25 to 49	24.9 (0.58)	17.4 (1.54)	16.9 (2.13)	27.4 (2.51)	20.7 (2.48)	24.5 (2.10)	29.4 (1.90)	24.1 (1.76)	26.7 (0.97)	22.6 (2.74)
50 to 74	12.1 (0.54)	11.6 (1.23)	3.7 ! (1.15)	12.5 (1.71)	9.8 (2.48)	17.5 (1.52)	8.5 (0.77)	10.0 (1.65)	12.9 (0.95)	11.7 (1.55)
75 to 99	5.8 (0.30)	5.4 (0.89)	4.1 ! (1.57)	7.6 (1.52)	6.8 (1.62)	6.7 (1.22)	2.0 (0.44)	3.7 (0.97)	6.2 (0.48)	7.5 (1.18)
100 to 149	3.4 (0.23)	4.8 (1.07)	2.0 ! (0.72)	4.2 ! (1.46)	2.9 ! (0.89)	7.2 (1.14)	1.8 ! (0.55)	‡ (†)	3.2 (0.41)	2.4 ! (0.76)
150 or more	1.9 (0.19)	5.2 (0.96)	4.5 (1.35)	3.7 (0.94)	2.8 ! (1.12)	2.6 (0.59)	‡ (†)	‡ (†)	1.2 (0.35)	1.7 (0.44)
Distribution by student classroom contact hours per week[1]	100.0 (†)	100.0 (†)	100.0 (†)	100.0 (†)	100.0 (†)	100.0 (†)	100.0 (†)	100.0 (†)	100.0 (†)	100.0 (†)
Less than 50	33.9 (0.80)	41.6 (2.52)	53.4 (3.89)	27.7 (2.98)	40.2 (2.67)	25.4 (1.88)	36.0 (2.52)	38.2 (2.66)	31.3 (1.34)	36.7 (3.40)
50 to 99	17.0 (0.54)	13.1 (1.46)	17.5 (2.13)	23.0 (3.38)	17.0 (2.30)	18.9 (1.40)	19.5 (1.53)	17.4 (1.97)	16.6 (0.96)	14.5 (1.65)
100 to 199	13.2 (0.49)	13.3 (1.51)	8.5 (1.44)	14.2 (2.34)	7.5 (1.56)	14.8 (1.72)	13.3 (1.65)	14.1 (2.01)	13.4 (0.82)	13.5 (2.19)
200 to 349	11.2 (0.46)	10.8 (1.29)	5.6 (1.42)	10.9 (1.97)	12.3 (1.88)	10.3 (1.80)	13.5 (0.93)	10.1 (1.26)	11.4 (0.66)	12.1 (1.62)
350 to 499	7.2 (0.34)	6.1 (0.98)	3.0 ! (0.96)	7.7 (1.74)	8.5 (1.74)	10.2 (1.0)	4.5 (0.64)	5.5 (0.95)	8.0 (0.69)	6.0 (0.93)
500 or more	17.5 (0.58)	15.1 (1.89)	12.1 (2.50)	16.5 (2.29)	14.5 (2.58)	20.3 (1.97)	13.3 (1.53)	14.6 (2.85)	19.3 (0.98)	17.2 (1.87)
Distribution by total classroom credit hours	100.0 (†)	100.0 (†)	100.0 (†)	100.0 (†)	100.0 (†)	100.0 (†)	100.0 (†)	100.0 (†)	100.0 (†)	100.0 (†)
Less than 4.0	53.3 (0.89)	59.8 (2.39)	67.5 (3.65)	62.2 (2.96)	55.4 (2.34)	52.0 (2.05)	51.3 (2.05)	58.9 (2.14)	50.2 (1.43)	52.2 (3.00)
4.0 to 5.9	11.7 (0.52)	12.2 (1.52)	11.8 (2.12)	10.8 (1.63)	10.6 (1.81)	9.3 (1.09)	14.1 (1.77)	10.3 (1.68)	12.2 (0.75)	11.5 (1.68)
6.0 to 7.9	16.9 (0.55)	12.8 (1.61)	10.2 (2.20)	14.9 (1.96)	18.7 (2.12)	23.1 (2.10)	18.1 (1.22)	15.4 (1.81)	16.5 (0.98)	17.5 (1.62)
8.0 to 9.9	9.4 (0.42)	8.2 (0.92)	6.2 (1.22)	8.5 (1.64)	8.3 (2.03)	9.5 (0.99)	9.0 (1.08)	8.3 (1.34)	10.8 (0.81)	7.4 (1.33)
10.0 to 14.9	6.6 (0.35)	5.6 (1.48)	1.8 ! (0.75)	3.6 (0.97)	4.8 (1.22)	3.8 (0.81)	5.2 (0.82)	5.1 ! (1.57)	8.1 (0.62)	9.2 (1.54)
15.0 or more	2.1 (0.21)	1.4 ! (0.58)	2.5 ! (0.91)	‡ (†)	2.2 ! (0.78)	2.2 (0.57)	2.3 (0.64)	2.0 ! (0.80)	2.2 (0.31)	2.2 (0.63)

See notes at end of table.

Table 315.40. Percentage distribution of part-time faculty and instructional staff in degree-granting postsecondary institutions, by level and control of institution, selected instruction activities, and number of classes taught for credit: Fall 2003—Continued

[Standard errors appear in parentheses]

Instruction activity and number of classes	All institutions	Research		Doctoral		Comprehensive		Private liberal arts	Public 2-year	Other
		Public	Private	Public	Private	Public	Private			
1	2	3	4	5	6	7	8	9	10	11
Faculty/staff distribution by number of classes taught for credit (percent)										
Faculty/staff with undergraduate classes only, by total for-credit courses......	100.0 (†)	100.0 (†)	100.0 (†)	100.0 (†)	100.0 (†)	100.0 (†)	100.0 (†)	100.0 (†)	100.0 (†)	100.0 (†)
1	49.2 (0.90)	53.1 (3.85)	62.3 (5.20)	58.8 (4.27)	45.4 (4.58)	48.4 (2.43)	54.1 (2.78)	53.7 (3.42)	47.9 (1.20)	43.2 (3.57)
2	29.7 (0.86)	31.2 (3.04)	28.5 (5.51)	26.9 (3.12)	39.8 (4.33)	33.1 (2.35)	29.2 (2.27)	25.0 (2.20)	29.3 (1.24)	29.7 (2.70)
3	12.5 (0.47)	9.4 (1.83)	6.9 ! (2.33)	11.5 (2.36)	13.1 (3.15)	10.8 (1.26)	9.4 (1.35)	10.2 (1.62)	13.9 (0.84)	13.7 (1.71)
4	5.3 (0.41)	4.6 ! (1.41)	‡ (†)	‡ (†)	‡ (†)	4.0 (1.06)	5.4 (1.08)	5.6 ! (1.95)	5.9 (0.65)	6.9 (1.73)
5 or more	3.3 (0.32)	‡ (†)	‡ (†)	2.6 ! (1.27)	‡ (†)	3.7 (0.95)	1.8 ! (0.77)	5.5 ! (1.69)	3.1 (0.44)	6.5 (1.87)
Faculty/staff with graduate classes only, by total for-credit courses......	100.0 (†)	100.0 (†)	100.0 (†)	100.0 (†)	100.0 (†)	100.0 (†)	100.0 (†)	100.0 (†)	‡ (†)	100.0 (†)
1	72.6 (1.73)	71.7 (5.24)	81.7 (4.89)	81.8 (4.93)	72.2 (5.28)	74.8 (5.62)	62.2 (3.67)	69.9 (6.67)	‡ (†)	75.6 (5.21)
2	16.6 (1.30)	20.6 (4.61)	7.4 ! (3.23)	10.8 ! (4.07)	16.2 (4.50)	12.9 ! (4.45)	23.3 (2.37)	18.8 ! (5.77)	‡ (†)	16.4 (3.91)
3	5.3 (0.93)	‡ (†)	5.7 ! (2.74)	‡ (†)	‡ (†)	‡ (†)	7.6 ! (2.41)	‡ (†)	‡ (†)	‡ (†)
4	3.1 (0.81)	‡ (†)	‡ (†)	‡ (†)	4.0 ! (1.41)	‡ (†)	3.9 ! (1.32)	‡ (†)	‡ (†)	‡ (†)
5 or more	2.4 (0.53)	‡ (†)	‡ (†)	‡ (†)	‡ (†)	‡ (†)	2.9 ! (1.38)	‡ (†)	‡ (†)	3.0 ! (1.45)
Faculty/staff with both undergraduate and graduate classes, by total for-credit courses......	100.0 (†)	100.0 (†)	100.0 (†)	100.0 (†)	100.0 (†)	100.0 (†)	100.0 (†)	100.0 (†)	‡ (†)	100.0 (†)
1	46.5 (2.05)	51.3 (5.19)	46.4 (10.59)	59.3 (5.24)	63.7 (8.93)	38.0 (6.03)	38.9 (4.23)	44.1 (8.69)	‡ (†)	47.4 (6.18)
2	28.7 (1.96)	29.6 (4.47)	36.3 (8.39)	18.5 ! (6.24)	18.1 ! (5.75)	30.7 (3.91)	32.7 (5.11)	35.1 (9.57)	‡ (†)	23.9 (5.54)
3	13.5 (1.79)	11.3 (3.25)	‡ (†)	16.9 ! (6.27)	‡ (†)	17.8 (4.04)	16.6 (3.72)	12.3 ! (4.69)	‡ (†)	‡ (†)
4	5.9 (1.19)	3.3 ! (1.63)	‡ (†)	‡ (†)	‡ (†)	7.9 ! (3.54)	‡ (†)	5.8 ! (2.25)	‡ (†)	10.0 ! (4.03)
5 or more	5.4 (1.18)	4.4 ! (2.08)	‡ (†)	‡ (†)	‡ (†)	5.7 ! (2.75)	6.4 ! (2.36)	‡ (†)	‡ (†)	9.2 ! (4.56)

†Not applicable.
!Interpret data with caution. The coefficient of variation (CV) for this estimate is between 30 and 50 percent.
‡Reporting standards not met. Either there are too few cases for a reliable estimate or the coefficient of variation (CV) is 50 percent or greater.
¹Distribution by student classroom contact hours per week is based on the number of contact hours that faculty and instructional staff spend each week with students during classroom instruction multiplied by the number of students taught.

NOTE: Degree-granting institutions grant associate's or higher degrees and participate in Title IV federal financial aid programs. Totals may differ from figures reported in other tables because of varying survey methodologies. Detail may not sum to totals because of rounding.
SOURCE: U.S. Department of Education, National Center for Education Statistics, 2004 National Study of Postsecondary Faculty (NSOPF:04). (This table was prepared December 2008.)

Table 315.50. Full-time and part-time faculty and instructional staff in degree-granting postsecondary institutions, by level and control of institution and selected characteristics: Fall 1992, fall 1998, and fall 2003

[Standard errors appear in parentheses]

Selected characteristic	Number (in thousands) 1992	1998	2003	Fall 2003 Total	Research Public	Research Private	Doctoral Public	Doctoral Private	Comprehensive Public	Comprehensive Private	Private liberal arts	Public 2-year	Other
1	2	3	4	5	6	7	8	9	10	11	12	13	14
Full-time faculty and instructional staff													
Number (in thousands)	528.3	560.4	681.8	681.8 (0.05)	162.1 (0.85)	63.5 (1.58)	51.3 (0.76)	21.7 (0.79)	107.3 (2.98)	41.4 (1.59)	49.6 (1.80)	114.6 (1.09)	70.2 (3.36)
Percentage distribution	†	†	†	100.0 (†)	23.8 (0.12)	9.3 (0.23)	7.5 (0.11)	3.2 (0.12)	15.7 (0.44)	6.1 (0.23)	7.3 (0.26)	16.8 (0.16)	10.3 (0.49)
							Percentage distribution of full-time faculty and instructional staff						
Total	528.3	560.4	681.8	100.0 (†)	100.0 (†)	100.0 (†)	100.0 (†)	100.0 (†)	100.0 (†)	100.0 (†)	100.0 (†)	100.0 (†)	100.0 (†)
Sex													
Male	352.7	356.9	420.4	61.7 (0.35)	69.9 (0.62)	68.8 (0.90)	62.8 (1.29)	66.7 (2.04)	58.8 (0.84)	57.6 (2.03)	59.7 (1.14)	50.5 (1.08)	60.3 (1.41)
Female	175.5	203.5	261.4	38.3 (0.35)	30.1 (0.62)	31.2 (0.90)	37.2 (1.29)	33.3 (2.04)	41.2 (0.84)	42.4 (2.03)	40.3 (1.14)	49.5 (1.08)	39.7 (1.41)
Race/ethnicity													
White	456.7	477.0	547.7	80.3 (0.27)	79.0 (0.50)	77.6 (0.73)	81.3 (1.33)	82.7 (1.55)	78.0 (1.12)	85.6 (1.02)	86.0 (0.81)	80.9 (0.84)	79.8 (1.14)
Black	27.4	28.4	38.1	5.6 (0.17)	3.7 (0.26)	4.9 (0.49)	4.1 (0.50)	5.1 (0.79)	8.7 (0.73)	4.8 (0.65)	6.3 (0.69)	6.9 (0.43)	4.7 (0.81)
Hispanic	13.9	18.5	23.8	3.5 (0.10)	2.9 (0.18)	3.5 (0.36)	2.9 (0.37)	2.2 (0.59)	3.6 (0.23)	2.4 (0.36)	2.3 (0.26)	5.8 (0.44)	3.1 (0.44)
Asian/Pacific Islander	27.7	32.5	62.3	9.1 (0.16)	13.2 (0.45)	12.8 (0.63)	10.1 (1.17)	9.3 (1.40)	7.9 (0.34)	5.9 (0.74)	3.8 (0.33)	4.2 (0.44)	11.3 (0.94)
American Indian/Alaska Native	2.6	4.0	10.0	1.5 (0.11)	1.1 (0.17)	1.2 ! (0.40)	1.6 (0.35)	0.7 ! (0.36)	1.8 (0.50)	1.2 ! (0.38)	1.6 (0.31)	2.2 (0.36)	1.0 ! (0.32)
Age													
Under 30	7.6	8.8	11.9	1.7 (0.13)	1.7 (0.24)	1.5 (0.28)	1.8 (0.37)	1.3 ! (0.44)	1.7 (0.29)	2.3 (0.56)	2.1 (0.41)	1.8 (0.36)	1.7 ! (0.68)
30 to 34	35.4	32.2	47.2	6.9 (0.21)	7.5 (0.44)	8.6 (0.89)	7.2 (0.82)	5.9 (0.73)	6.5 (0.74)	7.0 (0.92)	8.9 (0.73)	5.1 (0.52)	6.4 (0.75)
35 to 39	66.8	60.1	77.1	11.3 (0.29)	12.8 (0.58)	14.3 (1.35)	11.8 (0.95)	8.9 (1.45)	10.1 (0.86)	9.6 (0.88)	12.8 (1.22)	9.0 (0.70)	11.1 (1.05)
40 to 44	90.2	81.9	92.6	13.6 (0.31)	15.0 (0.57)	15.0 (0.75)	11.9 (0.83)	11.8 (1.36)	12.1 (0.78)	14.4 (1.15)	12.3 (0.75)	12.7 (0.88)	14.4 (1.38)
45 to 49	97.7	96.8	105.3	15.4 (0.32)	15.9 (0.53)	14.6 (1.24)	16.5 (1.38)	16.0 (1.89)	15.2 (0.75)	13.0 (1.18)	14.3 (1.10)	14.7 (0.70)	18.0 (1.36)
50 to 54	94.9	104.7	114.4	16.8 (0.34)	16.3 (0.66)	14.6 (0.87)	16.1 (1.09)	14.9 (1.34)	16.6 (0.90)	17.1 (1.26)	16.5 (1.0)	19.3 (0.84)	17.1 (1.35)
55 to 59	67.3	90.2	111.6	16.4 (0.37)	13.9 (0.66)	12.0 (0.61)	15.1 (1.01)	16.5 (1.60)	17.3 (0.89)	16.8 (1.24)	15.6 (0.87)	21.9 (1.05)	16.8 (1.46)
60 to 64	44.6	55.0	78.3	11.5 (0.31)	10.7 (0.58)	10.9 (0.74)	13.8 (0.90)	12.8 (1.54)	13.4 (0.72)	12.9 (1.42)	11.8 (1.10)	10.5 (0.68)	9.4 (0.83)
65 or older	23.8	30.6	43.3	6.3 (0.23)	6.0 (0.40)	8.6 (0.64)	5.9 (0.83)	11.8 (1.53)	7.1 (0.67)	6.8 (0.78)	5.7 (0.80)	4.9 (0.67)	5.2 (0.59)
Highest degree													
Less than bachelor's	6.3	6.7	10.0	1.5 (0.12)	0.2 ! (0.09)	‡ (†)	0.2 ! (0.09)	‡ (†)	0.1 ! (0.07)	‡ (†)	0.8 ! (0.26)	6.1 (0.58)	2.4 (0.64)
Bachelor's	20.9	22.5	29.4	4.3 (0.24)	2.0 (0.27)	2.0 (0.41)	2.9 (0.51)	1.6 (0.46)	3.1 (0.63)	2.1 (0.58)	2.1 (0.53)	11.1 (0.97)	6.9 (0.82)
Master's	155.8	156.0	179.8	26.4 (0.39)	12.3 (0.49)	9.9 (0.93)	20.3 (1.19)	12.9 (1.17)	22.7 (1.08)	28.7 (2.10)	27.2 (1.71)	63.3 (1.22)	25.5 (1.68)
First-professional	58.3	51.7	56.1	8.2 (0.30)	11.8 (0.53)	18.4 (1.19)	4.7 (0.49)	9.7 (1.47)	2.0 (0.30)	3.5 (0.89)	0.9 (0.18)	1.6 (0.30)	21.3 (1.99)
Doctoral	283.8	323.5	406.6	59.6 (0.48)	73.7 (0.61)	69.4 (1.45)	71.9 (1.30)	75.4 (2.03)	72.1 (1.34)	65.0 (2.47)	69.1 (1.92)	17.9 (1.13)	43.8 (2.47)
Academic rank													
Professor	160.6	172.2	194.4 (3.67)	28.5 (0.54)	33.8 (0.95)	34.0 (1.15)	27.3 (1.34)	30.3 (2.37)	29.8 (1.23)	24.8 (1.61)	28.5 (1.79)	21.7 (1.89)	22.9 (1.39)
Associate professor	123.7	132.0	149.6 (2.56)	21.9 (0.37)	23.3 (0.63)	22.0 (1.12)	25.9 (1.54)	31.6 (1.73)	23.2 (1.30)	27.0 (1.41)	24.6 (1.27)	12.1 (1.22)	22.3 (1.47)
Assistant professor	124.3	125.0	158.1 (2.81)	23.2 (0.41)	22.5 (0.68)	26.6 (1.38)	23.5 (1.36)	21.6 (1.63)	28.3 (1.08)	31.8 (1.02)	30.3 (1.14)	10.3 (1.12)	25.2 (1.37)
Instructor	73.9	74.9	82.7 (2.85)	12.1 (0.42)	4.3 (0.27)	5.0 (0.79)	9.0 (0.94)	4.5 (0.89)	7.6 (0.81)	6.8 (1.02)	6.6 (0.91)	37.5 (2.13)	13.9 (1.30)
Lecturer	11.9	14.1	21.9 (1.48)	3.2 (0.22)	4.6 (0.34)	4.9 (0.59)	5.4 (0.80)	2.5 (0.40)	5.4 (0.99)	1.9 ! (0.67)	1.0 (0.23)	0.3 (0.09)	0.9 (0.27)
Other	17.1	26.3	56.5 (2.15)	8.3 (0.32)	10.6 (0.64)	7.1 (0.54)	5.4 (0.59)	8.9 (1.23)	5.7 (0.94)	7.3 (1.12)	8.8 (1.11)	8.3 (0.80)	7.9 (0.90)
No rank	16.9	15.8	18.6 (1.28)	2.7 (0.19)	0.8 (0.14)	‡ (†)	‡ (†)	‡ (†)	0.1 ! (0.05)	0.5 (0.10)	‡ (†)	9.8 (0.88)	7.0 (1.14)
Base salary													
Under $10,000	13.8	9.7	4.4 (0.49)	0.7 (0.07)	0.8 (0.19)	0.7 ! (0.31)	0.8 ! (0.25)	‡ (†)	0.5 ! (0.20)	‡ (†)	0.6 ! (0.18)	0.6 (0.15)	0.9 ! (0.35)
$10,000 to 24,999	29.4	19.3	19.0 (1.03)	2.8 (0.15)	2.5 (0.28)	3.0 (0.44)	3.8 (0.55)	1.7 ! (0.74)	3.1 (0.36)	2.9 (0.45)	2.6 (0.58)	2.9 (0.42)	2.4 (0.59)
$25,000 to 39,999	181.8	123.7	79.7 (2.90)	11.7 (0.42)	8.0 (0.49)	5.6 (0.66)	13.0 (0.65)	6.6 (1.03)	12.2 (1.12)	12.8 (1.63)	15.2 (1.38)	18.0 (1.44)	12.5 (1.28)
$40,000 to 54,999	163.8	171.1	192.4 (3.09)	28.2 (0.45)	19.2 (0.78)	15.5 (1.13)	27.4 (1.10)	21.3 (2.12)	34.0 (1.40)	38.8 (1.63)	39.6 (1.64)	37.1 (1.48)	25.7 (1.55)
$55,000 to 69,999	76.7	106.2	147.7 (3.54)	21.7 (0.52)	18.9 (0.58)	16.0 (0.99)	22.3 (1.05)	26.4 (2.02)	24.1 (1.26)	24.9 (1.78)	23.1 (1.34)	24.3 (1.58)	20.9 (1.43)
$70,000 to 84,999	32.1	57.9	94.8 (2.19)	13.9 (0.32)	15.3 (0.64)	15.3 (1.01)	14.7 (1.03)	15.6 (1.52)	14.7 (1.21)	10.5 (1.18)	11.2 (1.46)	12.9 (1.10)	11.2 (1.38)
$85,000 to 99,999	11.1	28.1	50.7 (1.98)	7.4 (0.29)	11.1 (0.54)	11.1 (0.80)	10.1 (0.79)	10.1 (1.32)	8.1 (0.78)	4.0 (1.15)	3.7 (0.56)	3.6 (0.59)	5.7 (0.58)
$100,000 or more	19.6	44.4	93.1 (2.29)	13.7 (0.34)	24.1 (0.76)	24.1 (1.20)	10.2 (0.82)	18.2 (1.63)	3.3 (0.46)	5.8 (0.90)	4.0 (0.57)	0.8 (0.21)	20.4 (2.00)

See notes at end of table.

Table 315.50. Full-time and part-time faculty and instructional staff in degree-granting postsecondary institutions, by level and control of institution and selected characteristics: Fall 1992, fall 1998, and fall 2003—Continued

[Standard errors appear in parentheses]

Selected characteristic	Number (in thousands) 1992	1998	2003	Total	Research Public	Research Private	Doctoral Public	Doctoral Private	Comprehensive Public	Comprehensive Private	Private liberal arts	Public 2-year	Other
1	2	3	4	5	6	7	8	9	10	11	12	13	14
Part-time faculty and instructional staff													
Number (in thousands)	376.7	416.0	530.0	530.0 (0.02)	39.7 (0.78)	23.2 (0.96)	20.8 (0.82)	15.4 (0.83)	60.3 (2.49)	53.5 (2.17)	28.4 (2.19)	230.1 (2.00)	58.7 (3.38)
Percentage distribution	†	†	†	100.0 (†)	7.5 (0.15)	4.4 (0.18)	3.9 (0.15)	2.9 (0.16)	11.4 (0.47)	10.1 (0.41)	5.4 (0.41)	43.4 (0.38)	11.1 (0.64)
				Percentage distribution of part-time faculty and instructional staff									
Total	376.7	416.0	530.0	100.0 (†)	100.0 (†)	100.0 (†)	100.0 (†)	100.0 (†)	100.0 (†)	100.0 (†)	100.0 (†)	100.0 (†)	100.0 (†)
Sex													
Male	208.7	217.0	275.9	52.1 (0.45)	50.4 (1.97)	60.2 (1.92)	50.2 (2.26)	58.4 (3.34)	50.0 (1.59)	53.9 (1.53)	50.3 (1.95)	50.7 (0.57)	55.4 (1.66)
Female	168.0	199.1	254.1	47.9 (0.45)	49.6 (1.97)	39.8 (1.92)	49.8 (2.26)	41.6 (3.34)	50.0 (1.59)	46.1 (1.53)	49.7 (1.95)	49.3 (0.57)	44.6 (1.66)
Race/ethnicity													
White	332.8	364.4	451.6	85.2 (0.38)	82.4 (1.63)	85.8 (1.78)	87.9 (2.19)	88.9 (1.99)	87.2 (1.89)	91.0 (0.85)	86.1 (1.59)	83.7 (0.54)	83.0 (1.84)
Black	18.3	18.9	29.7	5.6 (0.38)	2.7 (0.72)	4.1 (1.14)	2.4! (1.01)	2.8! (0.99)	4.7 (1.20)	2.8 (0.40)	8.1 (1.27)	6.9 (0.25)	7.2 (1.02)
Hispanic	11.2	15.5	18.7	3.5 (0.13)	3.2 (0.56)	3.2 (0.78)	4.1 (0.81)	2.8 (0.66)	3.1 (0.39)	2.4 (0.30)	2.1 (0.48)	4.4 (0.21)	3.0 (0.57)
Asian/Pacific Islander	12.3	13.2	20.3	3.8 (0.22)	9.9 (1.39)	6.4 (1.05)	4.5 (1.14)	4.9! (1.79)	3.3 (0.59)	1.9! (0.61)	2.7 (0.63)	2.9 (0.23)	4.7 (1.02)
American Indian/Alaska Native	2.3	4.0	9.7	1.8 (0.22)	1.8! (0.68)	‡ (†)	‡ (†)	‡ (†)	1.7! (0.61)	1.9 (0.42)	0.9! (0.35)	2.1 (0.38)	2.1! (0.70)
Age													
Under 30	20.5	15.1	22.8	4.3 (0.30)	5.6 (0.94)	3.1 (1.11)	8.9 (1.75)	4.8! (1.58)	5.7 (1.04)	1.8 (0.51)	3.8 (0.72)	4.4 (0.46)	3.1 (0.72)
30 to 34	35.9	37.1	43.4	8.3 (0.38)	10.0 (1.32)	8.8 (1.79)	6.8 (1.20)	6.5 (1.81)	8.1 (1.11)	7.9 (1.16)	8.9 (1.33)	8.2 (0.68)	7.6 (1.11)
35 to 39	58.9	47.2	54.6	10.3 (0.48)	8.7 (1.36)	9.4 (1.48)	8.3 (1.74)	12.5 (2.38)	11.1 (1.55)	10.1 (1.18)	10.8 (1.78)	10.4 (0.74)	10.8 (1.35)
40 to 44	70.0	60.4	61.0	11.5 (0.44)	12.9 (1.78)	11.4 (1.81)	13.2 (2.26)	11.2 (2.26)	11.9 (1.34)	10.1 (1.27)	12.2 (1.37)	11.3 (0.78)	11.3 (1.40)
45 to 49	68.0	72.1	76.5	14.4 (0.48)	15.6 (1.51)	16.0 (1.54)	16.3 (2.42)	7.9 (1.93)	11.3 (1.17)	14.3 (1.24)	14.0 (1.95)	14.6 (0.75)	17.1 (1.84)
50 to 54	45.1	69.8	82.8	15.6 (0.42)	14.5 (1.39)	12.2 (1.49)	16.3 (2.27)	16.5 (2.76)	13.6 (1.50)	18.5 (1.32)	15.0 (1.66)	15.9 (0.72)	15.8 (1.57)
55 to 59	28.8	47.1	77.0	14.5 (0.48)	12.1 (1.53)	14.4 (2.14)	13.5 (1.99)	14.2 (2.99)	14.8 (1.35)	14.2 (1.69)	13.7 (1.69)	15.3 (0.71)	14.1 (1.59)
60 to 64	22.9	28.8	51.6	9.7 (0.50)	8.4 (1.38)	9.6 (1.78)	8.0 (1.86)	12.5 (2.58)	11.2 (1.30)	10.5 (1.38)	9.5 (1.41)	9.7 (0.85)	8.5 (1.25)
65 or older	26.6	38.4	60.3	11.4 (0.46)	12.3 (1.49)	15.1 (1.95)	8.7 (1.61)	13.8 (2.90)	12.2 (1.19)	13.1 (1.93)	12.1 (1.93)	10.1 (0.77)	11.7 (2.06)
Highest degree													
Less than bachelor's	17.2	20.3	41.1	7.8 (0.59)	2.2 (0.59)	‡ (†)	‡ (†)	‡ (†)	2.1 (0.61)	0.7! (0.28)	0.9! (0.38)	14.3 (1.21)	7.6 (1.51)
Bachelor's	62.7	58.8	83.8	15.8 (0.55)	9.9 (1.32)	10.9 (1.94)	13.9 (2.09)	7.6! (1.94)	13.1 (1.84)	7.5 (1.08)	8.6 (1.52)	21.5 (1.17)	15.9 (1.67)
Master's	190.2	225.1	273.1	51.5 (0.80)	35.6 (2.39)	36.6 (3.36)	53.8 (3.16)	41.7 (3.47)	57.8 (2.32)	64.4 (2.33)	61.0 (2.21)	52.1 (1.63)	44.7 (3.32)
First-professional	39.6	36.0	38.5	7.3 (0.39)	16.7 (1.98)	21.3 (2.68)	13.6 (1.52)	4.2 (2.41)	4.8 (0.79)	4.8 (0.90)	7.2 (1.50)	3.3 (0.49)	14.4 (1.83)
Doctor's	58.9	75.8	93.5	17.6 (0.60)	35.6 (2.56)	28.7 (3.88)	24.1 (3.30)	35.0 (2.65)	22.7 (1.83)	22.6 (1.88)	22.2 (2.09)	8.7 (0.66)	17.4 (2.28)
Academic rank													
Professor	32.3	30.2	23.3	4.4 (0.30)	8.1 (1.54)	5.6 (1.18)	4.6! (1.43)	5.7 (1.40)	5.7 (1.01)	2.4 (0.55)	4.4 (0.85)	3.2 (0.52)	6.0 (1.03)
Associate professor	22.5	19.4	14.6	2.8 (0.22)	4.3 (0.94)	6.0 (1.45)	2.6! (1.14)	2.9! (1.03)	2.1! (0.69)	3.1 (0.79)	4.7 (1.11)	1.5 (0.27)	4.8 (1.07)
Assistant professor	24.2	23.1	19.8	3.7 (0.29)	11.0 (1.49)	11.9 (3.02)	3.3 (0.80)	7.0 (1.73)	2.0 (0.49)	3.0 (0.86)	5.1 (1.81)	0.8 (0.20)	8.3 (1.24)
Instructor	215.4	205.4	187.7	35.4 (0.83)	20.8 (1.72)	18.2 (1.92)	28.7 (2.27)	20.1 (3.25)	25.4 (2.41)	21.9 (2.13)	24.5 (2.13)	48.5 (1.54)	35.2 (2.66)
Lecturer	45.3	46.3	40.9	7.7 (0.41)	21.5 (1.67)	18.6 (2.30)	13.2 (2.07)	9.6 (1.72)	15.8 (2.18)	8.6 (2.32)	6.7 (1.72)	2.7 (0.42)	2.7 (0.80)
Other	27.6	75.2	230.9	43.6 (0.85)	33.3 (2.17)	38.2 (2.49)	45.4 (2.50)	53.4 (3.25)	47.7 (3.01)	59.7 (3.84)	52.2 (3.03)	40.5 (1.38)	38.3 (3.23)
No rank	9.3	16.5	12.8	2.4 (0.20)	1.0! (0.30)	‡ (†)	2.3! (0.80)	‡ (†)	1.2! (0.39)	1.2 (0.32)	2.3! (0.70)	2.8 (0.39)	4.6 (1.10)
Base salary													
Under $10,000	280.5	256.2	340.5	64.2 (0.60)	43.7 (2.35)	54.7 (2.80)	65.1 (2.94)	59.3 (3.10)	66.0 (2.44)	71.8 (2.97)	67.5 (2.75)	66.6 (1.02)	63.5 (1.97)
$10,000 to 24,999	68.1	112.4	140.8	26.6 (0.60)	29.3 (2.32)	27.5 (2.55)	24.7 (2.63)	30.3 (3.38)	26.3 (2.05)	21.4 (2.40)	23.4 (2.00)	28.1 (0.97)	24.6 (1.74)
$25,000 to 39,999	15.8	26.3	27.5	5.2 (0.32)	12.2 (1.38)	7.7 (1.18)	5.7 (1.48)	4.8! (1.72)	4.9 (1.09)	4.4 (1.15)	5.3 (1.24)	4.1 (0.46)	4.7 (0.92)
$40,000 to 54,999	5.3	11.8	9.6	1.8 (0.14)	5.8 (1.05)	5.0 (1.00)	1.9! (0.70)	3.0! (1.00)	1.6 (0.44)	0.9! (0.31)	1.1! (0.55)	0.5! (0.15)	4.0 (0.83)
$55,000 to 69,999	2.2	4.2	4.7	0.9 (0.15)	3.0 (0.65)	2.0! (1.00)	‡ (†)	‡ (†)	0.8! (0.31)	0.8! (0.31)	1.6! (0.65)	0.4! (0.14)	0.9! (0.30)
$70,000 to 84,999	1.1	2.4	1.9	0.4 (0.07)	2.2 (0.57)	‡ (†)	‡ (†)	‡ (†)	‡ (†)	‡ (†)	‡ (†)	‡ (†)	‡ (†)
$85,000 to 99,999	0.9	#	1.5	0.3 (0.07)	1.0! (0.46)	‡ (†)	‡ (†)	‡ (†)	‡ (†)	‡ (†)	‡ (†)	‡ (†)	‡ (†)
$100,000 or more	2.7	#	3.5	0.7 (0.10)	2.9 (0.63)	‡ (†)	‡ (†)	‡ (†)	‡ (†)	‡ (†)	‡ (†)	0.1! (0.07)	1.8! (0.56)

—Not available.
†Not applicable.
#Rounds to zero.
!Interpret data with caution. The coefficient of variation (CV) for this estimate is between 30 and 50 percent.
‡Reporting standards not met. Either there are too few cases for a reliable estimate or the coefficient of variation (CV) is 50 percent or greater.

NOTE: Degree-granting institutions grant associate's or higher degrees and participate in Title IV federal financial aid programs. Totals may differ from figures reported in other tables because of varying survey methodologies. Race categories exclude persons of Hispanic ethnicity. Detail may not sum to totals because of rounding.
SOURCE: U.S. Department of Education, National Center for Education Statistics, 1993, 1999, and 2004 National Study of Postsecondary Faculty (NSOPF:93;99;04). (This table was prepared January 2009.)

Table 315.60. Full-time and part-time faculty and instructional staff in degree-granting postsecondary institutions, by race/ethnicity, sex, and selected characteristics: Fall 2003

[Standard errors appear in parentheses]

Selected characteristic	Number (in thousands)	Percent	White Male	White Female	Black Male	Black Female	Hispanic Male	Hispanic Female	Asian/Pacific Islander Male	Asian/Pacific Islander Female	American Indian/Alaska Native Male	American Indian/Alaska Native Female
1	2	3	4	5	6	7	8	9	10	11	12	13
Full-time faculty and instructional staff												
Number (in thousands)	681.8 (0.05)	†	338.4 (2.63)	209.3 (2.45)	19.5 (1.03)	18.5 (0.87)	13.4 (0.60)	10.4 (0.56)	43.2 (1.00)	19.0 (1.03)	5.8 (0.57)	4.2 (0.50)
Percentage distribution	†	100.0	49.6 (0.39)	30.7 (0.36)	2.9 (0.15)	2.7 (0.13)	2.0 (0.09)	1.5 (0.08)	6.3 (0.15)	2.8 (0.15)	0.8 (0.08)	0.6 (0.07)
Type and control												
Public research	162.1 (0.85)	100.0	55.4 (0.67)	23.6 (0.59)	2.1 (0.27)	1.7 (0.19)	1.8 (0.16)	1.1 (0.15)	10.0 (0.47)	3.2 (0.35)	0.6 (0.14)	0.6 (0.11)
Private research	63.5 (1.58)	100.0	54.7 (1.00)	22.9 (0.80)	2.2 (0.30)	2.7 (0.37)	2.1 (0.30)	1.4 (0.31)	8.9 (0.66)	3.9 (0.48)	0.8! (0.39)	‡ (†)
Public doctoral	51.3 (0.76)	100.0	50.2 (1.48)	31.1 (1.22)	2.1 (0.44)	2.0 (0.30)	1.6 (0.20)	1.3 (0.27)	7.9 (1.27)	2.2 (0.56)	1.0! (0.32)	0.6! (0.22)
Private doctoral	21.7 (0.79)	100.0	56.0 (2.39)	26.7 (1.94)	3.0 (0.70)	2.1 (0.42)	1.4! (0.49)	0.8! (0.38)	5.8 (1.06)	3.5 (0.93)	‡ (†)	‡ (†)
Public comprehensive	107.3 (2.98)	100.0	45.9 (1.03)	32.1 (0.98)	4.7 (0.64)	4.0 (0.42)	2.1 (0.20)	1.6 (0.19)	5.3 (0.40)	2.6 (0.28)	0.8 (0.23)	1.0! (0.33)
Private comprehensive	41.4 (1.59)	100.0	48.9 (2.00)	36.7 (1.93)	2.3 (0.53)	2.4 (0.44)	1.6 (0.31)	0.8 (0.22)	4.1 (0.65)	1.9 (0.53)	0.6! (0.26)	‡ (†)
Private liberal arts	49.6 (1.80)	100.0	51.9 (1.20)	34.1 (0.99)	3.5 (0.56)	2.8 (0.36)	1.0 (0.20)	1.3 (0.27)	2.2 (0.28)	1.5 (0.29)	1.0 (0.24)	0.6! (0.18)
Public 2-year	114.6 (1.09)	100.0	40.8 (1.19)	40.1 (0.90)	3.1 (0.29)	3.8 (0.34)	3.0 (0.38)	2.7 (0.34)	2.2 (0.27)	2.1 (0.39)	1.3 (0.30)	0.8 (0.19)
Other	70.2 (3.36)	100.0	48.3 (1.65)	31.5 (1.20)	2.4 (0.59)	2.3 (0.59)	1.7 (0.36)	1.5 (0.29)	7.2 (0.87)	4.1 (0.78)	0.7! (0.34)	0.3! (0.14)
Academic rank												
Professor	194.4 (3.67)	100.0	65.5 (0.74)	20.3 (0.61)	2.6 (0.27)	1.1 (0.21)	1.8 (0.13)	0.8 (0.13)	5.7 (0.42)	1.1 (0.21)	0.8 (0.14)	0.4 (0.12)
Associate professor	149.6 (2.56)	100.0	51.6 (0.98)	28.4 (0.78)	3.1 (0.42)	2.4 (0.26)	1.7 (0.19)	1.3 (0.15)	7.0 (0.52)	2.9 (0.36)	1.0 (0.21)	0.5 (0.11)
Assistant professor	158.1 (2.81)	100.0	41.0 (0.83)	33.6 (0.81)	3.1 (0.37)	3.8 (0.38)	2.3 (0.22)	1.9 (0.15)	8.7 (0.49)	4.3 (0.35)	0.7 (0.16)	0.6 (0.15)
Instructor	82.7 (2.85)	100.0	38.2 (1.23)	41.2 (1.09)	3.2 (0.56)	4.4 (0.57)	2.5 (0.37)	2.3 (0.31)	3.1 (0.44)	3.1 (0.48)	0.9 (0.26)	1.1 (0.31)
Lecturer	21.9 (1.48)	100.0	36.7 (2.59)	43.9 (2.21)	2.9! (0.91)	3.0! (0.91)	1.3! (0.38)	3.8 (0.77)	2.4! (0.89)	4.0 (0.99)	1.3! (0.52)	0.7! (0.30)
Other	56.5 (2.15)	100.0	38.8 (1.51)	39.8 (1.37)	2.5 (0.54)	3.9 (0.56)	1.7 (0.22)	2.2 (0.35)	7.0 (0.98)	2.8 (0.56)	0.8! (0.39)	0.6! (0.18)
No rank	18.6 (1.28)	100.0	40.2 (2.37)	43.0 (2.45)	1.5! (0.52)	2.0! (0.83)	2.3! (0.75)	0.7! (0.24)	4.5 (1.17)	3.8! (1.39)	‡ (†)	‡ (†)
Age												
Under 35	59.1 (1.77)	100.0	39.4 (1.31)	33.4 (1.36)	2.9 (0.53)	4.7 (0.62)	2.5 (0.40)	2.8 (0.41)	8.9 (0.85)	4.2 (0.70)	0.6! (0.25)	0.5! (0.17)
35 to 44	169.8 (2.78)	100.0	43.7 (0.96)	30.2 (0.82)	2.7 (0.31)	3.4 (0.36)	2.8 (0.25)	1.8 (0.18)	9.3 (0.45)	5.0 (0.44)	0.8 (0.17)	0.5 (0.16)
45 to 54	219.7 (3.28)	100.0	47.0 (0.86)	34.4 (0.79)	3.1 (0.28)	2.6 (0.22)	1.8 (0.17)	1.6 (0.18)	5.7 (0.32)	2.2 (0.25)	1.0 (0.16)	0.6 (0.12)
55 to 64	190.0 (3.10)	100.0	57.1 (0.74)	28.7 (0.59)	2.8 (0.26)	1.9 (0.17)	1.4 (0.12)	1.1 (0.13)	4.1 (0.36)	1.4 (0.24)	0.9 (0.17)	0.7 (0.12)
65 to 69	31.8 (1.43)	100.0	67.6 (2.05)	20.2 (1.82)	1.7 (0.50)	2.0! (0.61)	1.6 (0.44)	0.4! (0.19)	4.5 (0.94)	1.1! (0.42)	‡ (†)	‡ (†)
70 or older	11.5 (0.67)	100.0	69.0 (3.16)	15.7 (2.71)	5.4 (1.54)	‡ (†)	‡ (†)	‡ (†)	3.8! (1.40)	‡ (†)	‡ (†)	‡ (†)
Base salary												
Under $10,000	4.4 (0.49)	100.0	39.7 (5.71)	34.2 (5.09)	5.8 (0.92)	‡ (†)	‡ (†)	4.4! (1.96)	7.8! (3.27)	‡ (†)	‡ (†)	‡ (†)
$10,000 to 24,999	19.0 (1.03)	100.0	43.2 (2.61)	34.8 (2.40)	1.3 (0.37)	3.2 (0.89)	2.1 (0.61)	2.4 (0.60)	6.5 (1.23)	4.6 (0.93)	1.1! (0.48)	‡ (†)
$25,000 to 39,999	79.7 (2.90)	100.0	36.0 (1.21)	44.5 (1.25)	2.9 (0.55)	3.7 (0.46)	1.8 (0.29)	2.1 (0.28)	3.8 (0.68)	3.6 (0.48)	0.8 (0.26)	0.9 (0.23)
$40,000 to 54,999	192.4 (3.09)	100.0	42.2 (0.95)	38.2 (0.79)	2.7 (0.27)	3.7 (0.37)	1.9 (0.18)	1.8 (0.14)	5.0 (0.43)	2.6 (0.27)	1.0 (0.15)	0.9 (0.14)
$55,000 to 69,999	147.7 (3.54)	100.0	48.7 (0.88)	31.9 (0.80)	3.1 (0.35)	2.5 (0.28)	2.0 (0.25)	1.6 (0.21)	6.0 (0.43)	2.6 (0.31)	1.0 (0.23)	0.6 (0.15)
$70,000 to 84,999	94.8 (2.19)	100.0	55.8 (1.29)	24.2 (1.14)	2.9 (0.39)	1.7 (0.40)	2.4 (0.34)	1.0 (0.20)	8.1 (0.67)	2.6 (0.41)	0.9 (0.23)	0.5! (0.19)
$85,000 to 99,999	50.7 (1.98)	100.0	61.9 (1.58)	18.5 (1.03)	3.8 (0.69)	1.5 (0.38)	1.5 (0.41)	1.0 (0.28)	8.3 (1.06)	2.5 (0.57)	0.8! (0.24)	‡ (†)
$100,000 or more	93.1 (2.29)	100.0	66.9 (0.99)	13.7 (0.74)	2.4 (0.38)	1.6 (0.33)	2.1 (0.29)	0.8 (0.17)	9.0 (0.80)	2.8 (0.50)	0.6! (0.20)	‡ (†)
Total household income												
Under $10,000	‡ (†)	100.0	‡ (6.54)	‡ (6.12)	‡ (1.13)	1.4! (0.97)	‡ (†)	‡ (†)	‡ (3.74)	‡ (3.59)	‡ (†)	‡ (†)
$10,000 to 24,999	3.0 (0.33)	100.0	42.0 (2.68)	29.3 (2.28)	1.4! (1.56)	3.3! (0.59)	‡ (†)	‡ (†)	9.8! (1.56)	8.7! (0.95)	‡ (†)	‡ (†)
$25,000 to 39,999	20.1 (1.13)	100.0	36.5 (1.66)	39.0 (1.42)	2.9 (0.59)	4.5 (0.59)	1.5 (0.43)	2.5 (0.62)	7.3 (0.80)	3.8 (0.51)	0.4! (0.18)	0.9! (0.29)
$40,000 to 54,999	55.0 (1.76)	100.0	39.8 (1.23)	38.4 (1.21)	4.1 (0.50)	4.2 (0.42)	2.5 (0.35)	1.9 (0.29)	6.2 (0.56)	2.5 (0.37)	1.1 (0.26)	1.2 (0.31)
$55,000 to 69,999	86.2 (1.56)	100.0	43.1 (1.23)	34.2 (1.21)	2.4 (0.40)	4.4 (0.45)	2.1 (0.29)	1.3 (0.17)	5.6 (0.59)	2.1 (0.40)	0.9! (0.30)	1.0 (0.29)
$70,000 to 84,999	75.2 (2.19)	100.0	50.6 (1.20)	31.2 (1.11)	2.8 (0.39)	2.8 (0.58)	1.9 (0.32)	1.6 (0.24)	6.3 (0.81)	2.5 (0.50)	0.6! (0.18)	0.5 (0.17)
$85,000 to 99,999	95.0 (2.16)	100.0	46.7 (1.15)	32.5 (0.83)	2.6 (0.39)	3.0 (0.58)	2.7 (0.32)	1.6 (0.24)	7.0 (0.81)	2.5 (0.50)	0.6! (0.18)	0.5 (0.14)
$100,000 or more	347.3 (3.57)	100.0	50.9 (0.52)	27.5 (0.52)	2.6 (0.18)	1.9 (0.16)	1.7 (0.14)	1.3 (0.11)	6.3 (0.29)	3.0 (0.24)	0.9 (0.11)	0.4 (0.07)

See notes at end of table

Table 315.60. Full-time and part-time faculty and instructional staff in degree-granting postsecondary institutions, by race/ethnicity, sex, and selected characteristics: Fall 2003—Continued

[Standard errors appear in parentheses]

Selected characteristic	Number (in thousands)	Percent	White Male	White Female	Black Male	Black Female	Hispanic Male	Hispanic Female	Asian/Pacific Islander Male	Asian/Pacific Islander Female	American Indian/Alaska Native Male	American Indian/Alaska Native Female
1	2	3	4	5	6	7	8	9	10	11	12	13
Part-time faculty and instructional staff												
Number (in thousands)	530.0 (0.02)	†	235.5 (2.44)	216.1 (2.87)	13.8 (0.91)	15.9 (0.75)	10.2 (0.61)	8.5 (0.56)	10.9 (0.82)	9.4 (0.97)	5.5 (0.78)	4.2 (0.77)
Percentage distribution	‡ (†)	100.0	44.4 (0.46)	40.8 (0.54)	2.6 (0.17)	3.0 (0.14)	1.9 (0.12)	1.6 (0.10)	2.1 (0.15)	1.8 (0.18)	1.0 (0.15)	0.8 (0.15)
Type and control												
Public research	39.7 (0.78)	100.0	41.7 (1.93)	40.7 (2.12)	1.1 (0.37)	1.6! (0.60)	1.5 (0.40)	1.7 (0.43)	4.5 (1.03)	5.4 (0.90)	1.6! (0.67)	‡ (†)
Private research	23.2 (0.96)	100.0	51.1 (2.51)	34.7 (2.29)	2.7! (1.00)	1.4 (0.57)	1.5! (0.62)	‡ (†)	3.6 (1.07)	2.8 (0.77)	‡ (†)	‡ (†)
Public doctoral	20.8 (0.82)	100.0	44.3 (2.27)	43.6 (2.39)	‡ (†)	1.0! (0.47)	1.9! (0.68)	2.2 (0.61)	2.6! (0.86)	1.9! (0.83)	‡ (†)	‡ (†)
Private doctoral	15.4 (0.83)	100.0	51.7 (3.99)	37.3 (3.60)	1.7! (0.77)	1.1! (0.55)	1.6! (0.64)	1.2! (0.36)	3.4! (1.06)	‡ (†)	‡ (†)	‡ (†)
Public comprehensive	60.3 (2.49)	100.0	44.1 (1.34)	44.1 (2.18)	2.3! (0.74)	2.4! (0.79)	1.6 (0.31)	1.5 (0.32)	2.0 (0.38)	1.3! (0.43)	1.0! (0.43)	0.9! (0.32)
Private comprehensive	53.5 (2.17)	100.0	49.1 (1.43)	41.9 (1.56)	1.7 (0.34)	1.1 (0.21)	1.0 (0.19)	1.4 (0.26)	1.1! (0.54)	0.8! (0.35)	1.0! (0.30)	‡ (†)
Private liberal arts	28.4 (2.19)	100.0	44.2 (1.98)	42.0 (2.14)	2.5! (0.85)	5.6 (1.24)	1.1! (0.42)	1.0! (0.35)	1.7! (0.61)	1.1! (0.49)	0.9! (0.35)	0.9! (0.25)
Public 2-year	230.1 (2.00)	100.0	42.8 (0.70)	41.0 (0.67)	2.9 (0.22)	4.0 (0.18)	2.4 (0.20)	2.0 (0.19)	1.5 (0.18)	1.4 (0.19)	1.1 (0.23)	1.0 (0.25)
Other	58.7 (3.38)	100.0	45.7 (1.83)	37.3 (2.14)	4.2 (0.79)	3.0 (0.74)	2.2 (0.53)	0.8 (0.22)	2.4! (0.75)	2.4! (0.92)	1.0! (0.40)	1.1! (0.50)
Academic rank												
Professor	23.3 (1.58)	100.0	59.3 (2.83)	25.0 (2.60)	4.0 (1.17)	2.6! (0.84)	‡ (†)	1.0! (0.41)	3.6 (0.96)	‡ (†)	‡ (†)	‡ (†)
Associate professor	14.6 (1.18)	100.0	43.7 (4.03)	39.5 (3.88)	2.8! (0.84)	‡ (†)	‡ (†)	1.4! (0.49)	6.3! (2.27)	‡ (†)	‡ (†)	‡ (†)
Assistant professor	19.8 (1.53)	100.0	38.8 (3.39)	42.7 (3.37)	2.8! (1.19)	‡ (†)	‡ (†)	1.0! (0.42)	4.8! (1.65)	6.0 (1.62)	‡ (†)	‡ (†)
Instructor	187.7 (4.42)	100.0	41.5 (1.09)	43.9 (1.11)	2.5 (0.30)	3.4 (0.25)	2.2 (0.24)	1.7 (0.22)	1.6 (0.25)	1.6 (0.28)	1.1 (0.26)	0.6 (0.18)
Lecturer	40.9 (2.15)	100.0	41.4 (2.05)	40.1 (1.96)	2.7 (0.63)	2.1! (0.77)	2.1 (0.45)	1.7 (0.42)	3.7 (0.80)	4.2 (0.93)	1.6! (0.56)	‡ (†)
Other	230.9 (4.51)	100.0	46.5 (1.01)	39.9 (1.04)	2.5 (0.29)	3.1 (0.28)	1.8 (0.23)	1.5 (0.17)	1.5 (0.22)	1.3 (0.31)	0.9 (0.22)	1.0! (0.22)
No rank	12.8 (1.07)	100.0	43.8 (3.52)	39.8 (4.63)	‡ (†)	0.9! (0.43)	2.8! (1.31)	3.5! (1.34)	2.0! (0.94)	‡ (†)	‡ (†)	‡ (†)
Age												
Under 35	66.2 (2.30)	100.0	35.3 (1.73)	43.1 (2.04)	3.2 (0.63)	4.3 (0.53)	3.0 (0.49)	3.0 (0.35)	2.4 (0.52)	3.6 (0.93)	1.6! (0.68)	‡ (†)
35 to 44	115.6 (3.03)	100.0	40.7 (1.42)	41.5 (1.41)	2.6 (0.39)	3.0 (0.33)	2.5 (0.30)	2.4 (0.32)	2.6 (0.37)	2.9 (0.45)	0.7! (0.24)	1.2 (0.30)
45 to 54	159.3 (3.22)	100.0	41.7 (1.13)	44.0 (1.17)	2.9 (0.34)	3.2 (0.33)	1.6 (0.24)	1.5 (0.19)	2.1 (0.35)	1.3 (0.26)	0.9 (0.24)	0.8! (0.27)
55 to 64	128.6 (3.31)	100.0	48.2 (1.09)	40.4 (1.06)	2.1 (0.35)	2.8 (0.35)	1.3 (0.30)	0.6 (0.10)	1.6 (0.32)	0.9 (0.23)	1.1! (0.34)	1.0 (0.26)
65 to 69	33.5 (1.81)	100.0	62.8 (3.10)	27.6 (2.83)	2.3! (0.81)	0.9! (0.32)	1.6! (0.54)	1.3! (0.55)	1.3! (0.52)	‡ (†)	1.5! (0.63)	‡ (†)
70 or older	26.8 (1.83)	100.0	58.3 (2.99)	30.7 (3.32)	2.4! (0.79)	1.6! (0.70)	2.5! (0.87)	‡ (†)	2.1! (0.65)	‡ (†)	‡ (†)	‡ (†)
Base salary												
Under $10,000	340.5 (3.17)	100.0	45.4 (0.68)	39.9 (0.77)	2.6 (0.23)	3.5 (0.23)	1.9 (0.17)	1.6 (0.12)	1.6 (0.17)	1.4 (0.26)	1.1 (0.20)	1.0 (0.20)
$10,000 to $24,999	140.8 (3.17)	100.0	41.3 (1.36)	43.6 (1.50)	2.8 (0.38)	2.3 (0.25)	2.1 (0.26)	1.8 (0.24)	2.3 (0.40)	2.4 (0.40)	0.9 (0.25)	0.5! (0.18)
$25,000 to $39,999	27.5 (1.72)	100.0	47.3 (3.06)	38.8 (2.72)	3.3 (0.83)	‡ (†)	1.2! (0.58)	1.6! (0.55)	3.2! (1.02)	1.9! (0.61)	‡ (†)	‡ (†)
$40,000 to $54,999	9.6 (0.74)	100.0	48.2 (4.55)	34.0 (4.33)	‡ (†)	1.4! (0.68)	3.2! (1.19)	‡ (†)	6.2! (2.60)	3.8! (1.70)	‡ (†)	‡ (†)
$55,000 to $69,999	4.7 (0.78)	100.0	45.5 (6.46)	40.4 (6.35)	‡ (†)	‡ (†)	2.2! (1.08)	‡ (†)	‡ (†)	‡ (†)	1.1! (0.34)	1.0! (0.26)
$70,000 to $84,999	1.9 (0.35)	100.0	39.0 (11.51)	43.0 (10.25)	‡ (†)	‡ (†)	‡ (†)	‡ (†)	‡ (†)	‡ (†)	1.5! (0.63)	‡ (†)
$85,000 to $99,999	1.5 (0.39)	100.0	33.4! (13.01)	51.7 (13.73)	‡ (†)	‡ (†)	‡ (†)	‡ (†)	‡ (†)	‡ (†)	‡ (†)	‡ (†)
$100,000 or more	3.5 (0.53)	100.0	47.4 (7.01)	37.1 (5.35)	‡ (†)	‡ (†)	‡ (†)	‡ (†)	10.8! (5.15)	‡ (†)	‡ (†)	‡ (†)
Total household income												
Under $10,000	1.3 (0.37)	100.0	‡ (†)	46.4! (14.12)	‡ (†)	‡ (†)	‡ (†)	‡ (†)	‡ (†)	‡ (†)	‡ (†)	‡ (†)
$10,000 to $24,999	28.5 (1.93)	100.0	36.5 (3.33)	42.5 (3.42)	2.0! (0.71)	4.0 (0.80)	1.7! (0.53)	2.4 (0.55)	1.6! (0.76)	3.5 (1.71)	3.7! (1.34)	2.2! (1.01)
$25,000 to $39,999	47.7 (1.92)	100.0	35.5 (2.27)	46.5 (2.32)	3.9 (0.58)	3.4 (0.66)	2.2 (0.44)	1.8 (0.47)	1.7! (0.55)	2.9 (0.92)	1.1! (0.46)	1.0! (0.43)
$40,000 to $54,999	55.7 (2.52)	100.0	38.1 (2.05)	46.2 (2.35)	3.4 (0.71)	4.1 (0.52)	3.1 (0.67)	2.5 (0.60)	1.1 (0.40)	1.1 (0.35)	0.8! (0.27)	0.5! (0.21)
$55,000 to $69,999	87.2 (2.95)	100.0	41.1 (1.50)	43.0 (1.48)	1.9 (0.38)	4.1 (0.38)	1.7 (0.37)	2.5 (0.35)	2.1 (0.42)	1.6 (0.45)	0.8! (0.27)	1.0! (0.37)
$70,000 to $84,999	58.1 (2.66)	100.0	44.7 (2.15)	41.2 (2.38)	2.3 (0.44)	2.3 (0.57)	2.3 (0.41)	1.3 (0.34)	1.4 (0.41)	2.0 (0.58)	1.1! (0.41)	1.1! (0.37)
$85,000 to $99,999	66.4 (2.39)	100.0	48.6 (1.85)	38.4 (1.81)	2.4 (0.59)	3.1 (0.52)	1.8 (0.37)	1.2 (0.34)	1.9 (0.49)	1.3! (0.41)	0.6! (0.29)	0.7! (0.25)
$100,000 or more	185.1 (3.59)	100.0	34.9 (0.68)	37.0 (0.91)	2.8 (0.32)	2.1 (0.21)	1.5 (0.21)	1.0 (0.17)	2.8 (0.34)	1.6 (0.25)	0.4! (0.22)	0.4! (0.17)

†Not applicable.
!Interpret data with caution. The coefficient of variation (CV) for this estimate is between 30 and 50 percent.
‡Reporting standards not met. Either there are too few cases for a reliable estimate or the coefficient of variation (CV) is 50 percent or greater.
NOTE: Degree-granting institutions grant associate's or higher degrees and participate in Title IV federal financial aid programs. Totals may differ from figures reported in other tables because of varying survey methodologies. Race categories exclude persons of Hispanic ethnicity. Detail may not sum to totals because of rounding.
SOURCE: U.S. Department of Education, National Center for Education Statistics, 2003 National Study of Postsecondary Faculty (NSOPF:04). (This table was prepared January 2009.)

Table 315.70. Full-time and part-time faculty and instructional staff in degree-granting postsecondary institutions, by field and faculty characteristics: Fall 1992, fall 1998, and fall 2003

[Standard errors appear in parentheses]

Selected faculty and instructional staff characteristic	Number (in thousands)			Fall 2003										
	Fall 1992	Fall 1998	Fall 2003	All fields	Agriculture and home economics	Business	Education	Engineering	Fine arts	Health	Humanities[1]	Natural sciences[2]	Social sciences[3]	Other[4]
1	2	3	4	5	6	7	8	9	10	11	12	13	14	15
Full-time faculty and instructional staff														
Number (in thousands)...	528	560	682 (#)	681.8 (0.05)	16.9 (0.80)	43.2 (1.40)	50.9 (1.89)	33.4 (1.32)	43.3 (1.68)	93.9 (2.67)	58.8 (1.82)	127.2 (2.19)	88.7 (2.07)	125.5 (2.36)
Percentage distribution...	†	†	† (†)	100.0 (†)	2.5 (0.12)	6.3 (0.21)	7.5 (0.28)	4.9 (0.19)	6.3 (0.25)	13.8 (0.39)	8.6 (0.27)	18.7 (0.32)	13.0 (0.30)	18.4 (0.35)
				Percentage distribution of full-time faculty and instructional staff										
Total...................	528	560	682 (#)	100.0 (†)	100.0 (†)	100.0 (†)	100.0 (†)	100.0 (†)	100.0 (†)	100.0 (†)	100.0 (†)	100.0 (†)	100.0 (†)	100.0 (†)
Sex														
Male.................	353	357	420	61.7 (0.35)	64.6 (2.88)	68.5 (1.61)	39.3 (1.57)	91.5 (1.06)	61.9 (1.38)	46.7 (1.32)	45.3 (1.47)	74.5 (0.88)	64.3 (1.13)	64.0 (0.94)
Female.............	176	203	261	38.3 (0.35)	35.4 (2.88)	31.5 (1.61)	60.7 (1.57)	8.5 (1.06)	38.1 (1.38)	53.3 (1.32)	54.7 (1.47)	25.5 (0.88)	35.7 (1.13)	36.0 (0.94)
Race/ethnicity														
White................	457	477	548	80.3 (0.27)	87.8 (1.61)	79.5 (1.51)	80.5 (1.26)	70.9 (1.85)	86.4 (1.24)	79.7 (0.84)	80.7 (1.31)	77.8 (0.75)	81.4 (1.09)	82.0 (0.69)
Black.................	27	28	38	5.6 (0.17)	2.3 ! (0.76)	4.5 (0.79)	7.8 (1.01)	5.4 (0.99)	6.0 (0.88)	5.0 (0.50)	5.6 (0.58)	4.1 (0.48)	7.3 (0.72)	6.1 (0.44)
Hispanic............	14	19	24	3.5 (0.10)	2.5 ! (0.76)	2.3 (0.51)	4.7 (0.63)	2.6 (0.47)	3.3 (0.75)	3.0 (0.32)	6.7 (0.53)	2.9 (0.30)	4.0 (0.47)	2.9 (0.33)
Asian/Pacific Islander......	28	33	62	9.1 (0.16)	6.4 (1.34)	12.2 (1.22)	4.8 (0.70)	20.1 (1.64)	2.9 (0.74)	10.7 (0.79)	5.2 (0.94)	14.3 (0.69)	5.9 (0.71)	7.1 (0.49)
American Indian/Alaska Native....	3	4	10	1.5 (0.11)	1.0 ! (0.49)	1.6 (0.37)	2.2 (0.40)	‡ (†)	1.4 (0.38)	1.6 (0.33)	1.8 (0.35)	0.8 (0.17)	1.4 (0.22)	1.8 (0.32)
Age														
Under 30...........	8	9	12	1.7 (0.13)	2.0 ! (0.67)	0.7 ! (0.31)	2.6 (0.78)	1.6 ! (0.48)	1.6 (0.45)	1.1 (0.26)	1.8 (0.33)	1.3 (0.21)	1.8 (0.35)	2.7 (0.41)
30 to 34............	35	32	47	6.9 (0.21)	5.6 (1.27)	4.0 (0.71)	6.8 (0.83)	7.0 (0.99)	6.2 (0.84)	6.3 (0.60)	8.2 (0.74)	6.8 (0.41)	7.6 (0.47)	7.9 (0.52)
35 to 39............	67	60	77	11.3 (0.29)	7.5 (1.19)	11.0 (1.15)	7.6 (0.95)	11.3 (1.18)	10.5 (1.20)	13.1 (0.88)	10.9 (0.88)	12.0 (0.65)	12.7 (0.92)	10.9 (0.74)
40 to 44............	90	82	93	13.6 (0.31)	13.3 (1.63)	11.8 (1.43)	9.9 (1.03)	15.0 (1.21)	12.3 (1.75)	15.0 (0.91)	13.6 (1.15)	15.4 (0.79)	13.7 (0.79)	12.8 (0.69)
45 to 49............	98	97	105	15.4 (0.32)	15.4 (1.84)	17.9 (1.51)	12.7 (1.04)	17.1 (1.70)	18.0 (1.42)	17.3 (0.95)	14.8 (1.24)	15.5 (0.86)	12.9 (0.79)	15.0 (0.66)
50 to 54............	95	105	114	16.8 (0.34)	25.3 (2.31)	19.0 (1.30)	17.6 (1.27)	15.2 (1.61)	18.5 (1.38)	19.9 (1.03)	14.1 (1.04)	14.8 (0.64)	14.2 (0.89)	17.1 (0.93)
55 to 59............	67	90	112	16.4 (0.37)	16.8 (1.83)	18.8 (1.32)	21.9 (1.43)	15.1 (2.32)	16.8 (1.58)	15.4 (0.80)	16.6 (1.07)	13.3 (0.75)	16.2 (0.85)	17.3 (0.73)
60 to 64............	45	55	78	11.5 (0.31)	10.4 (1.61)	10.9 (1.11)	13.7 (1.27)	10.3 (1.33)	11.4 (1.12)	7.8 (0.62)	12.9 (1.07)	12.5 (0.64)	14.0 (0.76)	10.6 (0.61)
65 or older........	24	31	43	6.3 (0.23)	3.7 ! (1.20)	5.9 (0.74)	7.2 (0.74)	7.5 (1.09)	4.7 (0.82)	4.1 (0.51)	7.0 (0.81)	8.5 (0.54)	6.8 (0.59)	5.6 (0.53)
Highest degree														
Less than bachelor's........	6	7	10	1.5 (0.12)	‡ (†)	‡ (†)	1.7 ! (0.74)	2.6 (0.77)	1.4 ! (0.46)	1.7 (0.31)	‡ (†)	‡ (†)	‡ (†)	4.4 (0.54)
Bachelor's.........	21	23	29	4.3 (0.24)	6.4 (1.71)	4.0 (0.80)	4.0 (0.64)	6.5 (1.22)	9.1 (1.10)	5.5 (0.69)	1.1 (0.31)	1.4 (0.23)	1.0 (0.26)	7.9 (0.67)
Master's............	156	156	180	26.4 (0.39)	29.2 (2.18)	31.8 (1.69)	35.5 (1.37)	13.2 (1.64)	53.9 (1.82)	22.9 (1.16)	35.1 (1.42)	14.9 (0.72)	12.5 (0.72)	34.4 (1.24)
First-professional......	58	52	56	8.2 (0.30)	‡ (†)	2.1 (0.45)	1.1 ! (0.35)	‡ (†)	1.1 ! (0.41)	41.1 (1.32)	0.4 ! (0.18)	3.0 (0.35)	0.5 ! (0.19)	8.7 (0.76)
Doctor's.............	284	324	407	59.6 (0.48)	63.0 (2.74)	61.9 (1.73)	57.7 (1.53)	77.1 (2.08)	34.6 (1.96)	28.9 (1.06)	63.2 (1.43)	80.6 (0.67)	86.0 (0.74)	44.6 (1.23)
Academic rank														
Professor..........	161	172	194	28.5 (0.54)	33.0 (2.71)	29.1 (1.66)	21.9 (1.41)	37.6 (1.69)	28.4 (1.85)	20.1 (0.93)	26.2 (1.46)	35.5 (0.87)	35.4 (1.20)	23.5 (1.09)
Associate professor......	124	132	150	21.9 (0.37)	21.0 (2.55)	22.6 (1.32)	17.6 (1.07)	25.3 (1.77)	23.7 (1.64)	23.5 (0.96)	20.0 (1.27)	23.4 (0.93)	22.8 (0.97)	19.9 (1.08)
Assistant professor......	124	125	158	23.2 (0.41)	19.2 (1.79)	23.4 (1.51)	23.8 (1.56)	19.6 (1.67)	23.2 (1.75)	32.2 (1.12)	21.7 (1.30)	21.1 (0.82)	24.8 (1.22)	19.2 (0.73)
Instructor..........	74	75	83	12.1 (0.42)	9.9 (1.60)	13.4 (1.37)	12.6 (1.18)	9.1 (1.39)	9.7 (1.01)	15.3 (0.90)	14.9 (1.17)	7.7 (0.56)	5.7 (0.53)	18.7 (1.02)
Lecturer............	12	14	22	3.2 (0.32)	3.4 ! (1.50)	3.6 (0.68)	3.0 (0.60)	2.0 (0.52)	4.3 (0.64)	1.9 (0.37)	7.9 (0.78)	2.1 (0.25)	2.3 (0.42)	3.6 (0.57)
Other................	17	26	57	8.3 (0.32)	11.8 (2.16)	4.9 (0.64)	18.2 (1.57)	5.4 (0.82)	7.1 (1.03)	5.5 (0.50)	5.7 (0.69)	6.7 (0.48)	6.4 (0.67)	12.4 (0.76)
No rank.............	17	16	19	2.7 (0.19)	‡ (†)	3.0 (0.68)	2.9 ! (1.05)	0.9 ! (0.38)	3.6 ! (1.24)	1.5 (0.27)	3.6 (0.67)	3.5 (0.48)	2.6 (0.47)	2.7 (0.36)

See notes at end of table.

Table 315.70. Full-time and part-time faculty and instructional staff in degree-granting postsecondary institutions, by field and faculty characteristics: Fall 1992, fall 1998, and fall 2003—Continued

[Standard errors appear in parentheses]

Selected faculty and instructional staff characteristic	Number (in thousands) Fall 1992	Fall 1998	Fall 2003	Fall 2003 All fields	Agriculture and home economics	Business	Education	Engineering	Fine arts	Health	Humanities[1]	Natural sciences[2]	Social sciences[3]	Other[4]
1	2	3	4	5	6	7	8	9	10	11	12	13	14	15
Part-time faculty and instructional staff														
Number (in thousands)......	377	416	530 (#)	530.0 (0.02)	7.3 (0.97)	44.9 (2.98)	63.5 (2.57)	14.0 (1.49)	47.8 (3.65)	57.8 (3.06)	58.9 (2.05)	63.7 (2.46)	53.0 (2.39)	119.2 (3.48)
Percentage distribution......	†	†	† (†)	100.0 (†)	1.4 (0.18)	8.5 (0.56)	12.0 (0.48)	2.7 (0.28)	9.0 (0.69)	10.9 (0.58)	11.1 (0.39)	12.0 (0.46)	10.0 (0.45)	22.5 (0.66)
Total......	377	416	530 (#)	100.0 (†)	100.0 (†)	100.0 (†)	100.0 (†)	100.0 (†)	100.0 (†)	100.0 (†)	100.0 (†)	100.0 (†)	100.0 (†)	100.0 (†)
				Percentage distribution of part-time faculty and instructional staff										
Sex														
Male......	209	217	276 (1.6)	52.1 (0.45)	32.0 (6.05)	69.6 (1.89)	29.1 (1.71)	90.8 (2.68)	51.4 (2.26)	34.5 (1.60)	31.6 (1.86)	58.2 (2.22)	60.5 (1.90)	66.2 (1.41)
Female......	168	199	254 (--)	47.9 (0.45)	68.0 (6.05)	30.4 (1.89)	70.9 (1.71)	9.2 (2.68)	48.6 (2.26)	65.5 (1.60)	68.4 (1.86)	41.8 (2.22)	39.5 (1.90)	33.8 (1.41)
Race/ethnicity														
White......	333	364	452 (--)	85.2 (0.38)	91.4 (3.66)	86.8 (1.54)	85.1 (1.34)	85.4 (2.89)	88.7 (1.22)	85.0 (1.14)	83.0 (1.14)	83.4 (1.35)	84.2 (1.62)	85.5 (0.80)
Black......	18	19	30 (--)	5.6 (0.20)	‡ (†)	6.7 (0.96)	6.6 (0.98)	‡ (†)	3.0 (0.70)	5.2 (0.68)	5.0 (0.71)	6.0 (0.66)	5.8 (0.75)	6.5 (0.57)
Hispanic......	11	16	19 (--)	3.5 (0.13)	‡ (†)	2.2! (0.79)	5.1 (0.71)	2.6 (0.64)	2.7 (0.52)	2.2 (0.47)	6.5 (0.81)	2.2 (0.40)	3.7 (0.61)	3.6 (0.39)
Asian/Pacific Islander......	12	13	20 (--)	3.8 (0.22)	‡ (†)	3.0 (0.80)	1.6 (0.43)	8.4 (2.11)	2.9 (0.70)	6.5 (1.17)	4.2 (0.71)	7.1 (0.89)	2.7! (1.04)	2.5 (0.34)
American Indian/Alaska Native......	2	4	10 (--)	1.8 (0.22)	‡ (†)	1.4! (0.54)	1.5 (0.37)	‡ (†)	2.8! (0.84)	1.0! (0.35)	1.3 (0.38)	1.4! (0.60)	3.6 (0.91)	1.9 (0.36)
Age														
Under 30......	20	15	23 (--)	4.3 (0.30)	6.4! (2.51)	2.3! (0.70)	2.7 (0.64)	‡ (†)	4.4 (0.79)	3.7 (0.72)	5.7 (0.95)	7.2 (1.15)	3.5 (0.66)	4.3 (0.60)
30 to 34......	36	37	43 (--)	8.2 (0.38)	7.7! (2.78)	6.7 (1.28)	7.0 (1.03)	‡ (†)	9.4 (1.24)	8.9 (1.01)	10.0 (1.01)	7.6 (1.16)	10.6 (1.17)	7.7 (0.62)
35 to 39......	59	47	55 (--)	10.3 (0.48)	5.5! (1.97)	9.6 (1.49)	8.7 (1.21)	10.7! (3.34)	11.7 (1.38)	9.5 (1.34)	8.7 (1.07)	10.2 (1.16)	9.9 (1.27)	12.6 (1.20)
40 to 44......	70	60	61 (--)	11.5 (0.44)	6.3! (2.79)	10.5 (1.35)	7.9 (0.88)	15.6 (3.25)	12.0 (1.13)	14.9 (1.54)	9.2 (0.91)	10.1 (1.19)	11.2 (1.26)	13.8 (0.96)
45 to 49......	68	72	76 (--)	14.4 (0.48)	17.4! (5.26)	13.1 (1.45)	11.7 (1.12)	11.4! (3.50)	16.4 (1.68)	19.7 (1.56)	14.3 (1.65)	9.5 (1.05)	13.1 (1.24)	16.5 (1.13)
50 to 54......	45	70	83 (--)	15.6 (0.42)	16.4 (4.15)	16.3 (1.42)	17.4 (1.41)	22.3 (3.60)	18.4 (1.76)	15.9 (1.55)	14.1 (1.35)	11.9 (1.34)	11.1 (1.29)	17.1 (1.15)
55 to 59......	29	47	77 (--)	14.5 (0.48)	17.6 (4.45)	17.9 (2.01)	15.5 (1.58)	11.7 (2.89)	14.6 (1.78)	11.5 (1.27)	13.8 (1.46)	15.6 (1.56)	17.5 (1.88)	12.8 (0.82)
60 to 64......	23	29	52 (--)	9.7 (0.50)	18.0 (5.10)	11.5 (1.25)	13.1 (1.26)	6.5! (1.96)	5.7 (1.05)	6.7 (1.13)	12.7 (1.42)	12.8 (1.67)	10.9 (1.29)	6.6 (0.76)
65 or older......	27	38	60 (--)	11.4 (0.46)	4.7! (2.09)	12.2 (1.65)	15.8 (1.26)	17.2 (3.46)	7.4 (1.33)	9.3 (1.22)	11.6 (1.50)	15.0 (1.99)	12.2 (1.48)	8.6 (0.79)
Highest degree														
Less than bachelor's......	17	20	41 (1.6)	7.8 (0.59)	5.5! (2.53)	1.8! (0.79)	3.7 (0.96)	17.1 (4.44)	9.1 (1.42)	17.3 (1.86)	‡ (†)	‡ (†)	0.5! (0.25)	16.2 (1.31)
Bachelor's......	63	59	84 (--)	15.8 (0.55)	26.7 (5.80)	13.9 (1.84)	12.0 (1.25)	17.9 (3.50)	28.2 (2.09)	16.2 (1.61)	12.9 (1.65)	16.1 (1.46)	3.2 (0.82)	19.4 (1.11)
Master's......	190	225	273 (--)	51.5 (0.80)	50.3 (6.09)	66.5 (2.34)	63.0 (1.84)	32.3 (4.61)	54.7 (2.95)	30.2 (1.86)	70.2 (2.33)	49.0 (1.94)	55.5 (1.83)	41.6 (1.56)
First-professional......	40	36	39 (--)	7.3 (0.39)	‡ (†)	6.3 (1.10)	1.9 (0.45)	‡ (†)	0.9! (0.39)	25.2 (2.12)	2.3 (0.55)	4.3 (0.85)	3.1 (0.62)	11.2 (1.00)
Doctor's......	59	76	94 (--)	17.6 (0.60)	15.5 (4.57)	11.5 (1.48)	19.4 (1.61)	31.2 (4.13)	7.1 (1.39)	11.1 (1.28)	13.4 (1.80)	29.7 (1.72)	37.7 (1.90)	11.7 (0.94)
Academic rank														
Professor......	32	30	23 (1.6)	4.4 (0.30)	8.9! (4.03)	4.6 (1.06)	3.4 (0.55)	5.9! (2.27)	3.9 (1.05)	5.4 (0.84)	3.5 (0.75)	4.8 (0.82)	4.7 (1.01)	4.1 (0.63)
Associate professor......	23	19	15 (1.2)	2.8 (0.22)	‡ (†)	2.3! (0.74)	1.9 (0.47)	5.7! (2.24)	3.7 (0.92)	5.4 (0.89)	1.6 (0.35)	3.3 (0.63)	2.9 (0.60)	1.6 (0.30)
Assistant professor......	24	23	20 (1.5)	3.7 (0.29)	‡ (†)	1.5! (0.55)	2.0 (0.50)	‡ (†)	3.6 (0.86)	15.1 (1.64)	1.7! (0.64)	2.8 (0.66)	3.7 (0.89)	1.7 (0.34)
Instructor......	215	205	188 (4.4)	35.4 (0.83)	39.9 (5.70)	29.2 (2.00)	37.0 (2.11)	25.3 (4.10)	33.6 (2.12)	36.5 (2.40)	42.9 (2.29)	32.4 (2.05)	30.4 (1.85)	38.2 (1.54)
Lecturer......	45	46	41 (2.1)	7.7 (0.41)	14.8 (4.39)	7.6 (1.52)	6.8 (0.97)	9.3 (2.49)	9.7 (1.16)	4.7 (0.93)	11.2 (1.10)	7.8 (1.02)	9.5 (1.20)	5.8 (0.67)
Other......	28	75	231 (4.5)	43.6 (0.85)	30.8 (5.98)	51.8 (2.46)	46.6 (1.78)	49.4 (5.02)	42.4 (3.00)	30.5 (1.88)	37.4 (2.23)	45.8 (2.02)	46.0 (2.22)	46.6 (1.47)
No rank......	9	16	13 (1.1)	2.4 (0.20)	‡ (†)	3.0 (0.75)	2.1 (0.59)	‡ (†)	3.2! (1.10)	2.4 (0.68)	1.7 (0.49)	3.1 (0.79)	2.8 (0.71)	2.1 (0.40)

—Not available.
†Not applicable.
#Rounds to zero.
!Interpret data with caution. The coefficient of variation (CV) for this estimate is between 30 and 50 percent.
‡Reporting standards not met. Either there are too few cases for a reliable estimate or the coefficient of variation (CV) is 50 percent or greater.
[1]Excludes history and philosophy.
[2]Excludes computer sciences.
[3]Includes history.
[4]Includes philosophy, law, occupationally specific programs, computer sciences, and other.
NOTE: Degree-granting institutions grant associate's or higher degrees and participate in Title IV federal financial aid programs. Totals may differ from figures reported in other tables because of varying survey methodologies. Race categories exclude persons of Hispanic ethnicity. Detail may not sum to totals because of survey item nonresponse and rounding.
SOURCE: U.S. Department of Education, National Center for Education Statistics, 1993, 1999, and 2004 National Study of Postsecondary Faculty (NSOPF:93;99:04). (This table was prepared January 2009.)

Table 315.80. Full-time and part-time faculty and instructional staff in degree-granting postsecondary institutions, by race/ethnicity, sex, and program area: Fall 1998 and fall 2003

[Standard errors appear in parentheses]

Program area	Number (in thousands)		Percentage distribution, fall 2003										
	Fall 1998	Fall 2003	Total	White		Black		Hispanic		Asian/Pacific Islander		American Indian/Alaska Native	
				Male	Female	Male	Female	Male	Female	Male	Female	Male	Female
1	2	3	4	5	6	7	8	9	10	11	12	13	14
Full-time faculty and instructional staff	560 (4.8)	682 (#)	100.0	49.6 (0.39)	30.7 (0.36)	2.9 (0.15)	2.7 (0.13)	2.0 (0.09)	1.5 (0.08)	6.3 (0.15)	2.8 (0.15)	0.8 (0.08)	0.6 (0.07)
Agriculture and home economics	10 (0.4)	17 (0.8)	100.0	58.9 (3.03)	28.9 (2.72)	‡ (†)	1.8 ! (0.73)	1.2 ! (0.46)	1.3 ! (0.52)	3.6 ! (1.13)	2.8 ! (0.86)	‡ (†)	‡ (†)
Business	39 (1.1)	43 (1.4)	100.0	53.2 (1.49)	26.2 (1.71)	2.5 (0.73)	2.0 (0.44)	1.8 (0.48)	0.5 ! (0.16)	9.7 (1.06)	2.5 (0.46)	1.3 (0.35)	0.4 ! (0.17)
Communications	10 (1.0)	16 (1.4)	100.0	48.1 (3.39)	38.7 (3.30)	2.0 ! (0.73)	3.3 (0.94)	1.9 ! (0.58)	1.5 ! (0.59)	1.9 ! (0.87)	‡ (†)	‡ (†)	‡ (†)
Education	40 (1.4)	51 (1.9)	100.0	32.5 (1.49)	48.0 (1.64)	3.0 (0.60)	4.9 (0.64)	1.5 (0.34)	3.2 (0.52)	1.3 ! (0.43)	3.5 (0.59)	0.9 (0.25)	1.3 (0.34)
Teacher education	14 (0.6)	18 (1.0)	100.0	31.1 (2.31)	54.4 (2.54)	2.1 ! (0.86)	5.2 (1.10)	‡ (†)	3.1 (0.89)	‡ (†)	2.1 ! (0.87)	‡ (†)	‡ (†)
Other education	26 (1.3)	33 (1.5)	100.0	33.3 (2.09)	44.4 (2.46)	3.4 (0.84)	4.7 (0.75)	2.2 (0.51)	3.2 (0.57)	1.9 ! (0.64)	4.2 (0.81)	1.1 ! (0.40)	1.5 ! (0.45)
Engineering	25 (0.9)	33 (1.3)	100.0	65.6 (1.93)	5.3 (0.90)	4.9 (0.84)	‡ (†)	2.2 (0.42)	0.4 ! (0.17)	17.9 (1.61)	2.2 (0.63)	1.2 ! (0.36)	‡ (†)
Fine arts	33 (1.4)	43 (1.7)	100.0	52.8 (1.68)	33.6 (1.36)	4.4 (0.83)	1.6 (0.34)	2.0 (0.59)	1.3 ! (0.44)	1.5 (0.42)	1.4 ! (0.59)	0.7 ! (0.22)	1.0 (0.28)
Health sciences	84 (2.0)	94 (2.7)	100.0	36.2 (1.23)	43.5 (1.15)	1.6 (0.26)	3.4 (0.44)	1.6 (0.25)	1.4 (0.19)	6.6 (0.60)	4.1 (0.57)	1.1 ! (0.37)	‡ (†)
First-professional	40 (1.6)	45 (1.7)	100.0	53.9 (1.58)	20.1 (1.42)	2.2 (0.49)	2.5 (0.58)	2.2 (0.40)	1.3 (0.30)	10.6 (1.08)	5.3 (0.89)	‡ (†)	‡ (†)
Nursing	20 (0.6)	20 (1.2)	100.0	3.5 (0.86)	84.6 (2.21)	‡ (†)	5.3 (1.29)	‡ (†)	0.7 ! (0.27)	‡ (†)	3.4 ! (1.10)	‡ (†)	1.8 ! (0.85)
Other health sciences	24 (1.0)	29 (1.4)	100.0	31.0 (1.98)	52.0 (2.05)	1.5 ! (0.50)	3.6 (0.84)	1.6 (0.44)	1.9 (0.48)	4.8 (1.02)	2.6 (0.71)	‡ (†)	0.7 ! (0.31)
Humanities	81 (1.8)	90 (2.4)	100.0	47.3 (1.40)	35.0 (1.33)	2.4 (0.43)	2.6 (0.39)	2.2 (0.24)	2.9 (0.31)	2.9 (0.48)	2.9 (0.54)	0.9 (0.23)	0.9 (0.25)
English and literature	40 (1.2)	39 (1.5)	100.0	38.8 (1.90)	46.0 (2.10)	2.1 (0.45)	4.5 (0.70)	1.3 (0.27)	1.9 (0.50)	0.8 ! (0.34)	2.7 ! (0.87)	0.5 ! (0.18)	1.4 (0.39)
Foreign languages	15 (0.8)	20 (1.0)	100.0	36.2 (1.86)	36.7 (2.07)	2.7 ! (0.89)	0.9 ! (0.46)	5.1 (0.75)	8.3 (1.07)	4.0 (1.11)	4.5 (1.01)	‡ (†)	‡ (†)
History	14 (0.6)	18 (1.0)	100.0	59.4 (2.90)	23.0 (2.12)	2.7 (0.80)	2.4 ! (0.94)	1.9 ! (0.71)	1.2 ! (0.52)	5.0 (1.49)	3.2 (0.91)	1.0 ! (0.45)	‡ (†)
Philosophy	12 (0.8)	13 (1.0)	100.0	72.3 (3.55)	16.6 (2.33)	2.3 ! (1.11)	‡ (†)	1.0 ! (0.35)	‡ (†)	4.0 ! (1.49)	‡ (†)	‡ (†)	‡ (†)
Law	8 (0.6)	10 (1.0)	100.0	54.5 (3.56)	29.9 (3.63)	3.3 ! (1.10)	‡ (†)	‡ (†)	2.4 ! (1.15)	2.8 ! (1.36)	‡ (†)	‡ (†)	‡ (†)
Natural sciences	111 (2.1)	151 (2.5)	100.0	57.3 (1.12)	20.3 (0.80)	2.5 (0.31)	1.5 (0.22)	2.0 (0.20)	0.9 (0.15)	11.2 (0.65)	3.3 (0.35)	0.6 (0.16)	0.3 ! (0.09)
Biological sciences	40 (1.3)	59 (1.7)	100.0	55.4 (1.69)	21.6 (1.30)	2.2 (0.48)	1.2 (0.28)	1.9 (0.39)	1.2 (0.31)	11.1 (1.13)	4.8 (0.67)	‡ (†)	0.3 ! (0.12)
Physical sciences	27 (0.8)	36 (1.3)	100.0	68.9 (2.03)	12.8 (1.50)	2.6 (0.59)	0.7 ! (0.31)	1.4 (0.29)	0.6 ! (0.19)	9.4 (1.05)	3.0 (0.64)	1.2 ! (0.56)	‡ (†)
Mathematics	26 (1.0)	32 (1.3)	100.0	52.2 (2.15)	22.7 (1.84)	3.8 (0.67)	2.6 (0.67)	2.8 (0.67)	0.7 ! (0.28)	11.7 (1.41)	1.8 ! (0.67)	1.1 ! (0.48)	‡ (†)
Computer sciences	17 (0.9)	24 (1.2)	100.0	51.0 (2.74)	25.1 (2.15)	1.5 ! (0.59)	2.0 (0.58)	2.3 (0.52)	0.9 ! (0.31)	13.5 (1.69)	2.0 ! (0.66)	‡ (†)	‡ (†)
Social sciences	58 (1.3)	70 (1.8)	100.0	52.2 (1.46)	29.0 (1.23)	3.7 (0.45)	4.1 (0.81)	2.6 (0.36)	1.7 (0.35)	3.4 (0.58)	1.9 (0.48)	0.9 (0.25)	0.6 (0.15)
Economics	9 (0.6)	12 (0.7)	100.0	62.3 (3.46)	18.0 (3.09)	3.5 (0.92)	‡ (†)	3.1 ! (1.13)	‡ (†)	8.9 (2.18)	‡ (†)	‡ (†)	‡ (†)
Political science	8 (0.5)	10 (0.7)	100.0	67.1 (3.74)	16.8 (2.59)	2.8 ! (1.19)	‡ (†)	5.1 ! (1.57)	‡ (†)	2.9 ! (1.31)	‡ (†)	‡ (†)	‡ (†)
Psychology	20 (0.7)	25 (1.1)	100.0	46.3 (2.33)	37.8 (2.16)	3.4 (1.01)	5.0 ! (1.99)	1.6 (0.42)	2.7 (0.70)	1.1 ! (0.49)	1.2 ! (0.39)	1.2 ! (0.75)	‡ (†)
Sociology	9 (0.4)	9 (0.6)	100.0	49.9 (3.72)	30.1 (3.42)	3.9 ! (1.69)	8.0 ! (2.43)	3.0 ! (0.97)	‡ (†)	‡ (†)	‡ (†)	‡ (†)	‡ (†)
Other social sciences	13 (0.6)	14 (0.9)	100.0	45.2 (3.59)	30.5 (3.09)	4.8 (1.33)	3.9 ! (1.28)	1.9 ! (0.80)	2.4 (0.71)	4.7 ! (1.50)	3.7 ! (1.22)	1.9 ! (0.75)	1.1 ! (0.54)
Occupationally specific programs	16 (0.8)	27 (1.1)	100.0	60.7 (2.47)	24.2 (2.16)	4.2 (1.16)	1.9 (0.55)	2.5 (0.63)	0.8 ! (0.26)	2.0 ! (0.92)	1.4 ! (0.46)	1.9 ! (0.62)	‡ (†)
All other programs	44 (1.2)	29 (1.4)	100.0	42.0 (2.03)	37.4 (2.00)	4.7 (1.01)	6.0 (1.01)	1.7 (0.44)	1.7 ! (0.53)	3.2 ! (0.99)	2.0 ! (0.64)	0.7 ! (0.31)	0.6 ! (0.28)

See notes at end of table.

Table 315.80. Full-time and part-time faculty and instructional staff in degree-granting postsecondary institutions, by race/ethnicity, sex, and program area: Fall 1998 and fall 2003—Continued

[Standard errors appear in parentheses]

	Number (in thousands)		Percentage distribution, fall 2003										
				White		Black		Hispanic		Asian/Pacific Islander		American Indian/Alaska Native	
Program area	Fall 1998	Fall 2003	Total	Male	Female	Male	Female	Male	Female	Male	Female	Male	Female
1	2	3	4	5	6	7	8	9	10	11	12	13	14
Part-time faculty and instructional staff	416 (5.9)	530 (#)	100.0	44.4 (0.46)	40.8 (0.54)	2.6 (0.17)	3.0 (0.14)	1.9 (0.12)	1.6 (0.10)	2.1 (0.15)	1.8 (0.18)	1.0 (0.15)	0.8 (0.15)
Agriculture and home economics	3 (0.2)	7 (1.0)	100.0	30.8 (6.24)	60.6 (6.30)	‡ (†)	‡ (†)	‡ (†)	‡ (†)	‡ (†)	‡ (†)	‡ (†)	‡ (†)
Business	32 (1.8)	45 (3.0)	100.0	60.6 (1.96)	26.2 (1.73)	4.3 (0.70)	2.3 (0.54)	1.7! (0.77)	‡ (†)	2.0! (0.69)	‡ (†)	‡ (†)	‡ (†)
Communications	10 (1.0)	14 (1.2)	100.0	47.7 (3.71)	39.3 (3.89)	2.1! (0.97)	2.8! (0.95)	‡ (†)	‡ (†)	‡ (†)	‡ (†)	‡ (†)	‡ (†)
Education	34 (1.6)	64 (2.6)	100.0	25.3 (1.65)	59.8 (2.11)	1.4 (0.41)	5.2 (0.90)	1.7 (0.37)	3.4 (0.49)	0.4! (0.19)	1.3! (0.38)	0.3! (0.15)	1.2! (0.36)
Teacher education	13 (1.0)	29 (1.8)	100.0	22.2 (2.41)	63.9 (2.84)	0.9! (0.35)	6.4 (1.17)	1.3! (0.41)	2.2 (0.52)	‡ (†)	‡ (†)	‡ (†)	1.6! (0.69)
Other education	20 (1.2)	34 (1.8)	100.0	27.9 (2.53)	56.4 (2.98)	1.9! (0.66)	4.1 (1.17)	2.0 (0.57)	4.5 (0.77)	‡ (†)	1.6! (0.60)	‡ (†)	0.8! (0.37)
Engineering	9 (0.8)	14 (1.5)	100.0	78.6 (3.70)	6.8! (2.77)	‡ (†)	‡ (†)	1.7 (0.46)	‡ (†)	8.0 (2.13)	‡ (†)	‡ (†)	‡ (†)
Fine arts	38 (1.5)	48 (3.6)	100.0	44.8 (2.06)	43.9 (2.44)	1.7! (0.54)	1.3 (0.34)	1.8 (0.49)	0.9 (0.25)	1.0! (0.36)	1.9! (0.58)	2.1! (0.84)	0.7! (0.30)
Health sciences	49 (2.2)	58 (3.1)	100.0	27.9 (1.65)	57.1 (1.74)	1.2! (0.41)	4.0 (0.52)	0.8! (0.26)	1.4 (0.38)	4.0 (0.87)	2.4 (0.72)	‡ (†)	0.5! (0.23)
First-professional	15 (1.3)	17 (1.2)	100.0	47.2 (3.33)	34.7 (3.64)	‡ (†)	2.1! (0.92)	‡ (†)	‡ (†)	6.4! (2.10)	5.1! (2.41)	‡ (†)	‡ (†)
Nursing	12 (0.8)	13 (1.3)	100.0	‡ (†)	86.3 (2.04)	‡ (†)	8.0 (1.30)	‡ (†)	1.4! (0.56)	‡ (†)	‡ (†)	‡ (†)	‡ (†)
Other health sciences	21 (1.7)	28 (2.0)	100.0	29.4 (2.86)	56.4 (3.07)	‡ (†)	3.2 (0.76)	0.8! (0.32)	1.7! (0.70)	4.3 (1.23)	1.4! (0.56)	‡ (†)	‡ (†)
Humanities	74 (2.1)	80 (2.5)	100.0	35.9 (1.52)	49.2 (1.61)	1.6 (0.35)	2.9 (0.45)	2.3 (0.35)	2.9 (0.44)	0.9! (0.30)	2.7 (0.55)	1.0! (0.33)	0.6! (0.22)
English and literature	43 (1.4)	44 (1.9)	100.0	29.5 (2.31)	58.5 (2.47)	1.2 (0.33)	4.3 (0.78)	1.0! (0.35)	1.3 (0.37)	1.0! (0.41)	1.6 (0.46)	0.8! (0.34)	0.8! (0.29)
Foreign languages	12 (1.2)	15 (1.2)	100.0	16.6 (3.57)	52.0 (3.38)	‡ (†)	2.0! (0.80)	7.2! (1.50)	11.4 (1.97)	‡ (†)	7.9 (2.18)	‡ (†)	‡ (†)
History	11 (0.7)	11 (1.0)	100.0	61.1 (4.58)	28.9 (4.15)	‡ (†)	‡ (†)	2.5! (1.05)	‡ (†)	‡ (†)	‡ (†)	‡ (†)	‡ (†)
Philosophy	9 (0.6)	10 (1.2)	100.0	65.7 (4.20)	26.0 (4.60)	3.5! (1.71)	‡ (†)	‡ (†)	‡ (†)	‡ (†)	‡ (†)	‡ (†)	‡ (†)
Law	11 (0.8)	11 (1.2)	100.0	52.6 (4.43)	32.8 (4.18)	4.4! (1.41)	2.0! (0.82)	2.2! (1.05)	‡ (†)	‡ (†)	‡ (†)	‡ (†)	‡ (†)
Natural sciences	65 (2.2)	90 (2.9)	100.0	50.5 (1.72)	32.4 (1.73)	3.8 (0.44)	2.7 (0.36)	1.9 (0.41)	0.7 (0.16)	4.2 (0.61)	2.3 (0.46)	1.0! (0.34)	0.5! (0.26)
Biological sciences	11 (0.9)	16 (1.0)	100.0	41.7 (3.76)	40.1 (3.78)	2.2! (0.67)	2.1! (0.90)	1.0! (0.39)	1.0! (0.40)	5.6! (2.32)	5.3! (1.63)	‡ (†)	‡ (†)
Physical sciences	11 (0.8)	16 (1.1)	100.0	57.8 (3.30)	28.7 (3.42)	3.9! (1.37)	‡ (†)	0.9! (0.48)	0.9! (0.41)	3.1! (1.06)	2.6! (0.99)	‡ (†)	‡ (†)
Mathematics	24 (1.4)	32 (2.3)	100.0	46.6 (3.20)	36.0 (3.04)	4.4 (0.78)	3.1 (0.83)	1.4! (0.48)	0.5! (0.24)	3.9 (0.85)	1.8! (0.64)	‡ (†)	‡ (†)
Computer sciences	19 (1.2)	26 (1.7)	100.0	56.4 (2.98)	25.3 (2.64)	4.1 (1.03)	3.7 (0.60)	3.0! (0.93)	‡ (†)	4.2 (1.10)	‡ (†)	1.4! (0.63)	‡ (†)
Social sciences	41 (2.4)	42 (2.0)	100.0	49.8 (1.85)	32.9 (2.09)	3.7 (0.68)	3.0 (0.66)	2.5 (0.65)	1.5 (0.31)	‡ (†)	‡ (†)	1.5! (0.65)	2.0! (0.62)
Economics	4 (0.5)	5 (0.8)	100.0	68.6 (7.36)	9.3! (4.08)	7.2! (3.52)	‡ (†)	‡ (†)	‡ (†)	‡ (†)	‡ (†)	‡ (†)	‡ (†)
Political science	4 (0.4)	5 (0.8)	100.0	71.1 (5.32)	11.9! (3.93)	5.7! (2.79)	‡ (†)	‡ (†)	‡ (†)	‡ (†)	‡ (†)	‡ (†)	‡ (†)
Psychology	18 (2.1)	18 (1.2)	100.0	42.2 (3.36)	44.4 (3.12)	2.0! (0.76)	3.0! (0.91)	1.4! (0.64)	1.7! (0.58)	‡ (†)	‡ (†)	‡ (†)	2.2! (0.93)
Sociology	6 (0.5)	7 (0.9)	100.0	44.6 (6.09)	30.7 (6.03)	4.0! (1.61)	4.1! (1.54)	‡ (†)	1.6! (0.76)	‡ (†)	‡ (†)	‡ (†)	‡ (†)
Other social sciences	10 (0.9)	8 (0.8)	100.0	46.2 (4.24)	36.4 (4.19)	‡ (†)	4.5! (1.85)	‡ (†)	1.9! (0.83)	‡ (†)	2.8! (1.29)	‡ (†)	‡ (†)
Occupationally specific programs	17 (1.1)	37 (2.4)	100.0	68.2 (2.51)	18.6 (2.19)	4.5 (1.03)	1.8! (0.63)	4.0 (0.92)	0.6! (0.23)	‡ (†)	‡ (†)	1.1! (0.50)	‡ (†)
All other programs	35 (1.6)	19 (1.2)	100.0	41.8 (3.30)	42.6 (2.95)	2.5! (0.81)	5.5 (1.46)	1.9! (0.58)	2.6! (0.90)	‡ (†)	1.2! (0.63)	‡ (†)	‡ (†)

†Not applicable.
#Rounds to zero.
!Interpret data with caution. The coefficient of variation (CV) for this estimate is between 30 and 50 percent.
‡Reporting standards not met. Either there are too few cases for a reliable estimate or the coefficient of variation (CV) is 50 percent or greater.

NOTE: Degree-granting institutions grant associate's or higher degrees and participate in Title IV federal financial aid programs. Totals may differ from figures reported in other tables because of varying survey methodologies. Race categories exclude persons of Hispanic ethnicity. Detail may not sum to totals because of rounding and nonresponse to program area question.
SOURCE: U.S. Department of Education, National Center for Education Statistics, 1999 and 2004 National Study of Postsecondary Faculty (NSOPF:99:04). (This table was prepared December 2008.)

Table 316.10. Average salary of full-time instructional faculty on 9-month contracts in degree-granting postsecondary institutions, by academic rank, control and level of institution, and sex: Selected years, 1970–71 through 2013–14

Sex and academic year	All faculty	Academic rank						Public institutions			Private institutions		
		Professor	Associate professor	Assistant professor	Instructor	Lecturer	No rank	Total	4-year	2-year	Total	4-year	2-year
1	2	3	4	5	6	7	8	9	10	11	12	13	14
							Current dollars						
Total													
1970–71	$12,710	$17,958	$13,563	$11,176	$9,360	$11,196	$12,333	$12,953	$13,121	$12,644	$11,619	$11,824	$8,664
1975–76	16,659	22,649	17,065	13,986	13,672	12,906	15,196	16,942	17,400	15,820	15,921	16,116	10,901
1980–81	23,302	30,753	23,214	18,901	15,178	17,301	22,334	23,745	24,373	22,177	22,093	22,325	15,065
1982–83	27,196	35,540	26,921	22,056	17,601	20,072	25,557	27,488	28,293	25,567	26,393	26,691	16,595
1984–85	30,447	39,743	29,945	24,668	20,230	22,334	27,683	30,646	31,764	27,864	29,910	30,247	18,510
1985–86	32,392	42,268	31,787	26,277	20,918	23,770	29,088	32,750	34,033	29,590	31,402	31,732	19,436
1987–88	35,897	47,040	35,231	29,110	22,728	25,977	31,532	36,231	37,840	32,209	35,049	35,346	21,867
1989–90	40,133	52,810	39,392	32,689	25,030	28,990	34,559	40,416	42,365	35,516	39,464	39,817	24,601
1990–91	42,165	55,540	41,414	34,434	26,332	30,097	36,395	42,317	44,510	37,055	41,788	42,224	24,088
1991–92	43,851	57,433	42,929	35,745	30,916	30,456	37,783	43,641	45,638	38,959	44,376	44,793	25,673
1992–93	44,714	58,788	43,945	36,625	28,499	30,543	37,771	44,197	46,515	38,935	45,985	46,427	26,105
1993–94	46,364	60,649	45,278	37,630	28,828	32,729	40,584	45,920	48,019	41,040	47,465	47,880	28,435
1994–95	47,811	62,709	46,713	38,756	29,665	33,198	41,227	47,432	49,738	42,101	48,741	49,379	25,613
1995–96	49,309	64,540	47,966	39,696	30,344	34,136	42,996	48,837	51,172	43,295	50,466	50,819	31,915
1996–97	50,829	66,659	49,307	40,687	31,193	34,962	44,200	50,303	52,718	44,584	52,112	52,443	32,628
1997–98	52,335	68,731	50,828	41,830	32,449	35,484	45,268	51,638	54,114	45,919	54,039	54,379	33,592
1998–99	54,097	71,322	52,576	43,348	33,819	36,819	46,250	53,319	55,948	47,285	55,981	56,284	34,821
1999–2000	55,888	74,410	54,524	44,978	34,918	38,194	47,389	55,011	57,950	48,240	58,013	58,323	35,925
2001–02	59,742	80,792	58,724	48,796	46,959	41,798	46,569	58,524	62,013	50,837	62,818	63,088	33,139
2002–03	61,330	83,466	60,471	50,552	48,304	42,622	46,338	60,014	63,486	52,330	64,533	64,814	34,826
2003–04	62,579	85,333	61,746	51,798	49,065	43,648	47,725	60,874	64,340	53,076	66,666	66,932	36,322
2004–05	64,234	88,158	63,558	53,308	49,730	44,514	48,942	62,346	66,053	53,932	68,755	68,995	37,329
2005–06	66,172	91,208	65,714	55,106	50,883	45,896	50,425	64,158	67,951	55,405	71,016	71,263	38,549
2006–07	68,585	94,870	68,153	57,143	53,278	47,478	52,161	66,566	70,460	57,466	73,419	73,636	41,138
2007–08	71,085	98,548	70,826	59,294	55,325	49,392	54,405	68,981	72,857	59,646	76,133	76,341	43,402
2008–09	73,570	102,346	73,439	61,550	56,918	51,188	56,370	71,237	75,245	61,433	79,147	79,410	43,542
2009–10	74,620	103,682	74,125	62,245	57,791	52,185	56,803	72,178	76,147	62,264	80,379	80,597	44,748
2010–11	75,481	104,961	75,107	63,136	58,003	52,584	56,549	72,715	76,857	62,359	81,897	82,098	45,146
2011–12	76,567	107,090	76,177	64,011	58,350	53,359	56,898	73,496	77,843	62,553	83,540	83,701	47,805
2012–13	77,278	108,074	77,029	64,673	57,674	53,072	58,752	73,877	78,012	62,907	84,932	85,096	44,978
2013–14	78,625	109,905	78,593	66,025	58,080	54,238	58,902	75,241	79,711	63,198	86,265	86,467	44,566
Males													
1975–76	17,414	22,902	17,209	14,174	14,430	13,579	15,761	17,661	18,121	16,339	16,784	16,946	11,378
1980–81	24,499	31,082	23,451	19,227	15,545	18,281	23,170	24,873	25,509	22,965	23,493	23,669	16,075
1982–83	28,664	35,956	27,262	22,586	18,160	21,225	26,541	28,851	29,661	26,524	28,159	28,380	17,346
1984–85	32,182	40,269	30,392	25,330	21,159	23,557	28,670	32,240	33,344	28,891	32,028	32,278	19,460
1985–86	34,294	42,833	32,273	27,094	21,693	25,238	30,267	34,528	35,786	30,758	33,656	33,900	20,412
1987–88	38,112	47,735	35,823	30,086	23,645	27,652	32,747	38,314	39,898	33,477	37,603	37,817	22,641
1989–90	42,763	53,650	40,131	33,781	25,933	31,162	35,980	42,959	44,834	37,081	42,312	42,595	25,218
1990–91	45,065	56,549	42,239	35,636	27,388	32,398	38,036	45,084	47,168	38,787	45,019	45,319	25,937
1991–92	46,848	58,494	43,814	36,969	33,359	32,843	39,422	46,483	48,401	40,811	47,733	48,042	26,825
1992–93	47,866	59,972	44,855	37,842	29,583	32,512	39,365	47,175	49,392	40,725	49,518	49,837	27,402
1993–94	49,579	61,857	46,229	38,794	29,815	34,796	42,251	48,956	50,989	42,938	51,076	51,397	30,783
1994–95	51,228	64,046	47,705	39,923	30,528	35,082	43,103	50,629	52,874	44,020	52,653	53,036	29,639
1995–96	52,814	65,949	49,037	40,858	30,940	36,135	44,624	52,163	54,448	45,209	54,364	54,649	33,301
1996–97	54,465	68,214	50,457	41,864	31,738	36,932	45,688	53,737	56,162	46,393	56,185	56,453	34,736
1997–98	56,115	70,468	52,041	43,017	33,070	37,481	46,822	55,191	57,744	47,690	58,293	58,576	36,157
1998–99	58,048	73,260	53,830	44,650	34,741	38,976	47,610	57,038	59,805	48,961	60,392	60,641	38,040
1999–2000	60,084	76,478	55,939	46,414	35,854	40,202	48,788	58,984	62,030	50,033	62,631	62,905	38,636
2001–02	64,320	83,356	60,300	50,518	48,844	44,519	48,049	62,835	66,577	52,360	67,871	68,100	33,395
2002–03	66,126	86,191	62,226	52,441	50,272	45,469	47,412	64,564	68,322	53,962	69,726	69,976	34,291
2003–04	67,485	88,262	63,466	53,649	50,985	46,214	48,973	65,476	69,248	54,623	72,021	72,250	35,604
2004–05	69,337	91,290	65,394	55,215	51,380	46,929	50,102	67,130	71,145	55,398	74,318	74,540	34,970
2005–06	71,569	94,733	67,654	57,099	52,519	48,256	51,811	69,191	73,353	56,858	76,941	77,143	38,215
2006–07	74,167	98,563	70,168	59,150	55,061	49,641	53,665	71,797	76,072	58,971	79,491	79,663	41,196
2007–08	76,935	102,555	72,940	61,368	57,116	51,804	56,196	74,389	78,673	61,166	82,681	82,850	42,995
2008–09	79,706	106,759	75,634	63,726	58,819	53,777	58,341	76,897	81,394	62,870	86,008	86,205	43,871
2009–10	80,881	108,225	76,400	64,451	59,793	54,947	58,647	77,948	82,423	63,697	87,382	87,546	44,500
2010–11	81,873	109,656	77,429	65,391	59,851	55,457	58,392	78,609	83,279	63,745	89,000	89,160	44,542
2011–12	83,150	112,066	78,560	66,303	60,066	56,367	58,807	79,544	84,444	63,918	90,840	90,976	45,250
2012–13	83,979	113,311	79,423	67,085	59,350	55,759	61,086	80,016	84,700	64,282	92,385	92,530	42,906
2013–14	85,528	115,455	81,156	68,534	59,614	56,920	61,279	81,560	86,562	64,564	94,016	94,177	44,234

See notes at end of table.

Table 316.10. Average salary of full-time instructional faculty on 9-month contracts in degree-granting postsecondary institutions, by academic rank, control and level of institution, and sex: Selected years, 1970–71 through 2013–14—Continued

Sex and academic year	All faculty	Academic rank						Public institutions			Private institutions		
		Professor	Associate professor	Assistant professor	Instructor	Lecturer	No rank	Total	4-year	2-year	Total	4-year	2-year
1	2	3	4	5	6	7	8	9	10	11	12	13	14
Females													
1975–76	14,308	20,308	16,364	13,522	12,572	11,901	14,094	14,762	14,758	14,769	13,030	13,231	10,201
1980–81	19,996	27,959	22,295	18,302	14,854	16,168	20,843	20,673	20,608	20,778	18,073	18,326	13,892
1982–83	23,261	32,221	25,738	21,130	17,102	18,830	23,855	23,892	23,876	23,917	21,451	21,785	15,845
1984–85	25,941	35,824	28,517	23,575	19,362	21,004	26,050	26,566	26,813	26,172	24,186	24,560	17,575
1985–86	27,576	38,252	30,300	24,966	20,237	22,273	27,171	28,299	28,680	27,693	25,523	25,889	18,504
1987–88	30,499	42,371	33,528	27,600	21,962	24,370	29,605	31,215	31,820	30,228	28,621	28,946	21,215
1989–90	34,183	47,663	37,469	31,090	24,320	26,995	32,528	34,796	35,704	33,307	32,650	33,010	24,002
1990–91	35,881	49,728	39,329	32,724	25,534	28,111	34,179	36,459	37,573	34,720	34,359	34,898	22,585
1991–92	37,534	51,621	40,766	34,063	28,873	28,550	35,622	37,800	38,634	36,517	36,828	37,309	24,683
1992–93	38,385	52,755	41,861	35,032	27,700	28,922	35,792	38,356	39,470	36,710	38,460	38,987	25,068
1993–94	40,058	54,746	43,178	36,169	28,136	31,048	38,474	40,118	41,031	38,707	39,902	40,378	26,142
1994–95	41,369	56,555	44,626	37,352	29,072	31,677	38,967	41,548	42,663	39,812	40,908	41,815	22,851
1995–96	42,871	58,318	45,803	38,345	29,940	32,584	41,085	42,871	43,986	41,086	42,871	43,236	30,671
1996–97	44,325	60,160	47,101	39,350	30,819	33,415	42,474	44,306	45,402	42,531	44,374	44,726	30,661
1997–98	45,775	61,965	48,597	40,504	32,011	33,918	43,491	45,648	46,709	43,943	46,106	46,466	30,995
1998–99	47,421	64,236	50,347	41,894	33,152	35,115	44,723	47,247	48,355	45,457	47,874	48,204	31,524
1999–2000	48,997	67,079	52,091	43,367	34,228	36,607	45,865	48,714	50,168	46,340	49,737	50,052	32,951
2001–02	52,662	72,542	56,186	46,824	45,262	39,538	45,003	52,123	53,895	49,290	54,149	54,434	32,921
2002–03	54,105	75,028	57,716	48,380	46,573	40,265	45,251	53,435	55,121	50,717	55,881	56,158	35,296
2003–04	55,378	76,652	59,095	49,689	47,404	41,536	46,519	54,408	56,117	51,591	57,921	58,192	36,896
2004–05	56,926	79,160	60,809	51,154	48,351	42,455	47,860	55,780	57,714	52,566	59,919	60,143	39,291
2005–06	58,665	81,514	62,860	52,901	49,533	43,934	49,172	57,462	59,437	54,082	61,830	62,092	38,786
2006–07	61,016	85,090	65,237	54,974	51,832	45,693	50,812	59,781	61,875	56,127	64,246	64,481	41,099
2007–08	63,347	88,301	67,816	57,111	53,889	47,407	52,837	62,129	64,226	58,318	66,528	66,745	43,670
2008–09	65,638	91,522	70,375	59,286	55,424	49,078	54,649	64,231	66,393	60,195	69,300	69,593	43,344
2009–10	66,647	92,830	71,017	59,997	56,239	49,957	55,206	65,139	67,276	61,047	70,507	70,746	44,892
2010–11	67,473	94,041	72,003	60,888	56,566	50,270	54,985	65,632	67,935	61,193	72,091	72,306	45,518
2011–12	68,468	95,845	73,057	61,763	57,013	50,994	55,299	66,368	68,897	61,417	73,629	73,788	49,382
2012–13	69,124	96,563	73,966	62,321	56,361	50,963	56,777	66,703	69,083	61,774	74,987	75,149	46,407
2013–14	70,355	98,064	75,388	63,599	56,884	52,156	56,916	67,944	70,713	62,079	76,173	76,390	44,769
					Constant 2013–14 dollars[1]								
Total													
1970–71	75,175	106,216	80,225	66,104	55,361	66,222	72,949	76,617	77,611	74,787	68,721	69,938	51,246
1975–76	70,579	95,961	72,302	59,257	57,928	54,680	64,383	71,780	73,721	67,025	67,453	68,283	46,184
1980–81	63,206	83,416	62,967	51,268	41,170	46,928	60,580	64,407	66,111	60,154	59,926	60,555	40,863
1982–83	65,106	85,081	64,447	52,801	42,136	48,051	61,182	65,805	67,732	61,206	63,183	63,897	39,728
1984–85	67,639	88,291	66,524	54,801	44,942	49,616	61,499	68,081	70,565	61,901	66,446	67,195	41,121
1985–86	69,943	91,268	68,637	56,739	45,168	51,326	62,809	70,716	73,487	63,893	67,806	68,518	41,968
1987–88	72,811	95,413	71,460	59,045	46,099	52,689	63,958	73,488	76,752	65,331	71,091	71,693	44,354
1989–90	74,266	97,724	72,895	60,491	46,318	53,646	63,950	74,789	78,396	65,722	73,027	73,682	45,524
1990–91	73,982	97,449	72,663	60,417	46,201	52,808	63,858	74,249	78,096	65,015	73,320	74,085	42,264
1991–92	74,551	97,641	72,983	60,771	52,560	51,777	64,235	74,194	77,588	66,234	75,443	76,152	43,647
1992–93	73,715	96,917	72,447	60,379	46,984	50,353	62,269	72,863	76,684	64,188	75,810	76,540	43,037
1993–94	74,506	97,461	72,760	60,470	46,326	52,594	65,217	73,792	77,165	65,949	76,275	76,941	45,694
1994–95	74,691	97,963	72,975	60,544	46,342	51,862	64,404	74,097	77,700	65,770	76,142	77,139	40,012
1995–96	74,991	98,154	72,947	60,371	46,148	51,914	65,389	74,272	77,824	65,844	76,749	77,287	48,537
1996–97	75,158	98,564	72,907	60,161	46,123	51,696	65,356	74,379	77,950	65,923	77,054	77,544	48,245
1997–98	76,028	99,848	73,839	60,767	47,139	51,549	65,762	75,015	78,613	66,708	78,504	78,998	48,799
1998–99	77,250	101,848	75,078	61,901	48,293	52,577	66,046	76,140	79,893	67,522	79,941	80,374	49,724
1999–2000	77,569	103,276	75,675	62,427	48,464	53,011	65,773	76,352	80,430	66,954	80,518	80,948	49,861
2001–02	78,776	106,533	77,434	64,343	61,921	55,116	61,406	77,170	81,771	67,034	82,832	83,189	43,697
2002–03	79,131	107,693	78,023	65,226	62,325	54,994	59,788	77,434	81,913	67,519	83,265	83,627	44,934
2003–04	79,014	107,745	77,962	65,402	61,951	55,111	60,260	76,862	81,238	67,016	84,174	84,510	45,861
2004–05	78,735	108,060	77,906	65,342	60,956	54,563	59,990	76,420	80,964	66,107	84,276	84,571	45,756
2005–06	78,135	107,697	77,594	65,068	60,081	54,193	59,541	75,757	80,235	65,421	83,855	84,147	45,517
2006–07	78,942	109,196	78,445	65,772	61,323	54,648	60,039	76,618	81,100	66,144	84,506	84,756	47,351
2007–08	78,896	109,378	78,609	65,810	61,405	54,819	60,383	76,562	80,863	66,201	84,499	84,730	48,172
2008–09	80,530	112,029	80,387	67,373	62,303	56,031	61,703	77,977	82,363	67,245	86,634	86,922	47,661
2009–10	80,897	112,403	80,360	67,481	62,652	56,575	61,581	78,250	82,552	67,502	87,140	87,376	48,512
2010–11	80,220	111,550	79,822	67,100	61,644	55,885	60,099	77,280	81,681	66,274	87,038	87,252	47,980
2011–12	79,058	110,573	78,655	66,093	60,248	55,095	58,749	75,886	80,375	64,587	86,257	86,423	49,360
2012–13	78,485	109,762	78,232	65,683	58,574	53,901	59,670	75,031	79,230	63,890	86,259	86,426	45,681
2013–14	78,625	109,905	78,593	66,025	58,080	54,238	58,902	75,241	79,711	63,198	86,265	86,467	44,566

See notes at end of table.

Table 316.10. Average salary of full-time instructional faculty on 9-month contracts in degree-granting postsecondary institutions, by academic rank, control and level of institution, and sex: Selected years, 1970–71 through 2013–14—Continued

Sex and academic year	All faculty	Academic rank						Public institutions			Private institutions		
		Professor	Associate professor	Assistant professor	Instructor	Lecturer	No rank	Total	4-year	2-year	Total	4-year	2-year
1	2	3	4	5	6	7	8	9	10	11	12	13	14
Males													
1975–76	73,779	97,031	72,910	60,054	61,137	57,531	66,776	74,828	76,774	69,227	71,112	71,796	48,205
1980–81	66,452	84,308	63,610	52,152	42,165	49,586	62,847	67,467	69,192	62,291	63,724	64,201	43,603
1982–83	68,620	86,077	65,264	54,070	43,474	50,812	63,538	69,068	71,007	63,497	67,411	67,940	41,525
1984–85	71,494	89,459	67,517	56,272	47,006	52,333	63,692	71,623	74,075	64,183	71,152	71,707	43,231
1985–86	74,050	92,488	69,686	58,503	46,841	54,496	65,355	74,556	77,272	66,415	72,673	73,199	44,075
1987–88	77,303	96,821	72,661	61,025	47,959	56,088	66,422	77,714	80,926	67,902	76,271	76,705	45,923
1989–90	79,133	99,279	74,262	62,511	47,988	57,664	66,580	79,495	82,965	68,619	78,299	78,821	46,667
1990–91	79,070	99,219	74,110	62,525	48,055	56,844	66,736	79,103	82,759	68,054	78,989	79,516	45,508
1991–92	79,646	99,444	74,488	62,850	56,713	55,837	67,021	79,025	82,286	69,383	81,150	81,675	45,604
1992–93	78,911	98,869	73,948	62,386	48,771	53,599	64,897	77,772	81,428	67,138	81,635	82,161	45,174
1993–94	79,671	99,402	74,288	62,340	47,912	55,916	67,896	78,670	81,938	69,000	82,078	82,593	49,468
1994–95	80,028	100,053	74,525	62,367	47,691	54,805	67,336	79,092	82,599	68,768	82,254	82,853	46,302
1995–96	80,321	100,297	74,577	62,137	47,054	54,955	67,866	79,330	82,806	68,755	82,677	83,112	50,645
1996–97	80,533	100,863	74,607	61,902	46,929	54,608	67,556	79,457	83,043	68,597	83,077	83,473	51,361
1997–98	81,520	102,370	75,601	62,491	48,042	54,450	68,019	80,177	83,886	69,280	84,684	85,095	52,526
1998–99	82,892	104,616	76,869	63,760	49,610	55,657	67,988	81,450	85,402	69,917	86,240	86,595	54,322
1999–2000	83,392	106,146	77,639	64,419	49,763	55,797	67,714	81,865	86,094	69,443	86,928	87,308	53,624
2001–02	84,814	109,914	79,512	66,613	64,406	58,704	63,358	82,854	87,789	69,043	89,495	89,797	44,035
2002–03	85,320	111,208	80,287	67,662	64,864	58,666	61,174	83,304	88,153	69,625	89,964	90,287	44,244
2003–04	85,208	111,442	80,135	67,738	64,375	58,351	61,835	82,672	87,434	68,969	90,936	91,225	44,955
2004–05	84,990	111,898	80,156	67,680	62,979	57,523	61,412	82,284	87,206	67,904	91,095	91,368	42,864
2005–06	84,507	111,859	79,884	67,421	62,014	56,980	61,177	81,699	86,614	67,137	90,851	91,089	45,124
2006–07	85,367	113,447	80,764	68,083	63,376	57,137	61,770	82,640	87,560	67,877	91,495	91,693	47,418
2007–08	85,390	113,825	80,955	68,112	63,393	57,497	62,371	82,563	87,319	67,887	91,767	91,954	47,720
2008–09	87,246	116,859	82,790	69,755	64,384	58,865	63,860	84,172	89,094	68,818	94,144	94,361	48,021
2009–10	87,685	117,329	82,827	69,873	64,822	59,569	63,580	84,504	89,356	69,055	94,732	94,910	48,243
2010–11	87,013	116,540	82,290	69,495	63,608	58,939	62,058	83,543	88,507	67,747	94,587	94,757	47,338
2011–12	85,855	115,710	81,115	68,460	62,019	58,200	60,719	82,131	87,190	65,997	93,794	93,934	46,722
2012–13	85,291	115,081	80,663	68,133	60,277	56,630	62,040	81,266	86,023	65,287	93,828	93,975	43,576
2013–14	85,528	115,455	81,156	68,534	59,614	56,920	61,279	81,560	86,562	64,564	94,016	94,177	44,234
Females													
1975–76	60,619	86,041	69,331	57,290	53,264	50,420	59,714	62,546	62,529	62,573	55,208	56,056	43,218
1980–81	54,238	75,837	60,474	49,643	40,291	43,855	56,536	56,074	55,898	56,359	49,022	49,708	37,681
1982–83	55,686	77,135	61,615	50,584	40,941	45,078	57,108	57,196	57,158	57,256	51,353	52,152	37,932
1984–85	57,629	79,585	63,352	52,373	43,014	46,661	57,871	59,018	59,566	58,142	53,730	54,561	39,044
1985–86	59,544	82,597	65,426	53,908	43,697	48,094	58,670	61,105	61,928	59,797	55,111	55,902	39,955
1987–88	61,863	85,942	68,006	55,982	44,546	49,430	60,049	63,314	64,542	61,312	58,053	58,712	43,031
1989–90	63,255	88,199	69,336	57,531	45,003	49,955	60,193	64,390	66,071	61,634	60,418	61,085	44,416
1990–91	62,955	87,252	69,006	57,417	44,801	49,323	59,969	63,970	65,925	60,919	60,285	61,231	39,627
1991–92	63,811	87,760	69,306	57,910	49,087	48,537	60,561	64,264	65,681	62,082	62,611	63,428	41,964
1992–93	63,281	86,972	69,011	57,754	45,667	47,681	59,006	63,233	65,070	60,520	63,405	64,273	41,327
1993–94	64,373	87,975	69,385	58,122	45,214	49,893	61,826	64,468	65,935	62,201	64,122	64,886	42,009
1994–95	64,627	88,349	69,715	58,351	45,417	49,485	60,874	64,905	66,647	62,193	63,906	65,323	35,698
1995–96	65,199	88,690	69,658	58,316	45,533	49,554	62,483	65,199	66,894	62,485	65,199	65,754	46,646
1996–97	65,540	88,954	69,645	58,184	45,570	49,409	62,804	65,512	67,133	62,887	65,612	66,133	45,337
1997–98	66,498	90,018	70,598	58,841	46,503	49,273	63,180	66,314	67,855	63,837	66,979	67,503	45,028
1998–99	67,717	91,729	71,896	59,824	47,342	50,144	63,864	67,469	69,050	64,912	68,365	68,836	45,016
1999–2000	68,004	93,101	72,298	60,191	47,506	50,808	63,657	67,612	69,630	64,317	69,032	69,469	45,734
2001–02	69,440	95,654	74,088	61,743	59,683	52,135	59,341	68,730	71,067	64,994	71,402	71,778	43,410
2002–03	69,809	96,805	74,469	62,422	60,091	51,952	58,385	68,945	71,120	65,438	72,101	72,459	45,541
2003–04	69,922	96,783	74,616	62,740	59,854	52,445	58,737	68,697	70,856	65,141	73,133	73,475	46,586
2004–05	69,777	97,030	74,536	62,702	59,266	52,039	58,664	68,372	70,743	64,433	73,446	73,720	48,160
2005–06	69,270	96,250	74,223	62,465	58,488	51,877	58,062	67,850	70,182	63,860	73,008	73,317	45,798
2006–07	70,230	97,940	75,089	63,276	59,659	52,594	58,485	68,809	71,219	64,603	73,948	74,218	47,306
2007–08	70,308	98,005	75,268	63,387	59,811	52,616	58,644	68,956	71,283	64,727	73,839	74,080	48,469
2008–09	71,848	100,180	77,033	64,895	60,667	53,721	59,819	70,308	72,674	65,890	75,856	76,177	47,444
2009–10	72,253	100,639	76,990	65,044	60,970	54,159	59,849	70,619	72,935	66,182	76,438	76,697	48,668
2010–11	71,709	99,945	76,524	64,710	60,117	53,426	58,436	69,752	72,200	65,034	76,616	76,845	48,376
2011–12	70,695	98,962	75,433	63,772	58,868	52,652	57,098	68,526	71,138	63,415	76,024	76,188	50,988
2012–13	70,203	98,071	75,121	63,295	57,241	51,759	57,664	67,745	70,162	62,739	76,158	76,323	47,132
2013–14	70,355	98,064	75,388	63,599	56,884	52,156	56,916	67,944	70,713	62,079	76,173	76,390	44,769

[1]Constant dollars based on the Consumer Price Index, prepared by the Bureau of Labor Statistics, U.S. Department of Labor, adjusted to an academic-year basis.
NOTE: Data through 1995–96 are for institutions of higher education, while later data are for degree-granting institutions. Degree-granting institutions grant associate's or higher degrees and participate in Title IV federal financial aid programs. Data for 1987–88 and later years include imputations for nonrespondent institutions. Some data have been revised from previously published figures.

SOURCE: U.S. Department of Education, National Center for Education Statistics, Higher Education General Information Survey (HEGIS), "Faculty Salaries, Tenure, and Fringe Benefits" surveys, 1970–71 through 1985–86; Integrated Postsecondary Education Data System (IPEDS), "Salaries, Tenure, and Fringe Benefits of Full-Time Instructional Faculty Survey" (IPEDS-SA:87–99); and IPEDS Winter 2001–02 through Winter 2011–12, Spring 2013, and Spring 2014, Human Resources component, Salaries section. (This table was prepared February 2015.)

Table 316.20. Average salary of full-time instructional faculty on 9-month contracts in degree-granting postsecondary institutions, by academic rank, sex, and control and level of institution: Selected years, 1999–2000 through 2013–14

Academic year, control and level of institution	Constant 2013–14 dollars[1] — All faculty, total	All faculty — Total	Males	Females	Professor — Total	Males	Females	Associate professor — Total	Males	Females	Assistant professor	Instructor	Lecturer	No academic rank
1	2	3	4	5	6	7	8	9	10	11	12	13	14	15
1999–2000														
All institutions	$77,569	$55,888	$60,084	$48,997	$74,410	$76,478	$67,079	$54,524	$55,939	$52,091	$44,978	$34,918	$38,194	$47,389
Public	76,352	55,011	58,984	48,714	72,475	74,501	65,568	54,641	55,992	52,305	45,285	35,007	37,403	47,990
4-year	80,430	57,950	62,030	50,168	75,204	76,530	69,619	55,681	56,776	53,599	45,822	33,528	37,261	40,579
Doctoral[2]	86,402	62,253	66,882	52,287	81,182	82,445	74,653	57,744	58,999	55,156	48,190	33,345	38,883	39,350
Master's[3]	73,246	52,773	55,565	48,235	66,588	67,128	64,863	53,048	53,686	51,977	43,396	33,214	34,448	43,052
Other 4-year	66,436	47,867	49,829	44,577	60,360	60,748	59,052	49,567	50,133	48,548	42,306	35,754	36,088	38,330
2-year	66,954	48,240	50,033	46,340	57,806	59,441	55,501	48,056	49,425	46,711	41,984	37,634	40,061	48,233
Nonprofit	80,738	58,172	62,788	49,881	78,512	80,557	70,609	54,300	55,836	51,687	44,423	34,670	40,761	41,415
4-year	81,090	58,425	63,028	50,117	78,604	80,622	70,774	54,388	55,898	51,809	44,502	34,813	40,783	41,761
Doctoral[2]	99,755	71,873	77,214	59,586	95,182	96,768	87,342	62,503	63,951	59,536	52,134	39,721	42,693	45,887
Master's[3]	69,218	49,871	52,642	45,718	62,539	63,603	59,353	50,176	51,470	48,165	41,447	33,991	37,923	44,153
Other 4-year	64,922	46,776	48,847	43,544	60,200	60,757	58,364	46,822	47,135	46,365	38,775	31,574	33,058	35,120
2-year	52,163	37,583	39,933	34,733	39,454	38,431	40,571	36,349	37,342	35,608	31,818	27,696	25,965	40,373
For-profit	41,004	29,543	30,023	28,942	45,505	44,248	49,693	48,469	53,548	43,389	33,043	29,894	—	27,958
2005–06														
All institutions	78,135	66,172	71,569	58,665	91,208	94,733	81,514	65,714	67,654	62,860	55,106	50,883	45,896	50,425
Public	75,757	64,158	69,191	57,462	87,599	91,080	78,412	65,107	67,077	62,231	55,029	52,297	44,628	50,096
4-year	80,235	67,951	73,353	59,437	91,600	93,976	83,946	66,745	68,475	64,013	56,181	40,044	44,598	47,107
Doctoral[2]	86,782	73,495	79,688	62,509	99,872	101,856	91,960	70,008	71,991	66,659	59,471	39,863	45,222	46,201
Master's[3]	71,371	60,444	63,659	56,157	77,752	78,677	75,547	62,029	62,967	60,706	52,419	39,542	43,502	45,640
Other 4-year	65,775	55,705	58,157	52,490	71,469	73,188	68,141	58,817	59,957	57,061	49,749	42,185	43,951	51,863
2-year	65,421	55,405	56,858	54,082	65,740	67,782	63,544	54,870	55,825	54,004	48,425	57,224	45,427	50,513
Nonprofit	84,076	71,203	77,136	61,985	98,253	101,638	88,144	66,877	68,753	64,074	55,278	41,302	49,777	53,231
4-year	84,331	71,419	77,314	62,212	98,378	101,713	88,379	66,981	68,818	64,226	55,367	41,494	49,786	53,907
Doctoral[2]	101,951	86,342	93,646	72,638	119,187	121,728	109,444	76,945	79,224	73,038	65,038	45,862	51,110	55,289
Master's[3]	69,723	59,048	61,984	55,245	74,334	75,769	71,081	59,962	61,026	58,545	49,804	40,446	45,173	57,505
Other 4-year	67,792	57,413	59,743	54,149	74,655	75,548	72,485	57,536	57,613	57,430	47,629	38,145	45,957	44,713
2-year	46,170	39,101	38,817	39,307	47,174	48,786	45,945	42,433	43,628	41,753	35,437	36,264	38,908	39,399
For-profit	50,159	42,480	42,878	42,027	60,111	59,423	61,417	56,621	55,546	58,393	47,598	35,661	—	41,579
2012–13														
All institutions	78,485	77,278	83,979	69,124	108,074	113,311	96,563	77,029	79,423	73,966	64,673	57,674	53,072	58,752
Public	75,031	73,877	80,016	66,703	101,527	106,769	90,506	75,438	77,962	72,215	64,108	59,321	50,705	57,356
4-year	79,230	78,012	84,700	69,083	107,281	111,042	97,735	77,444	79,664	74,406	65,783	47,689	50,857	54,562
Doctoral[2]	85,441	84,126	91,861	72,850	116,777	120,054	106,985	81,252	83,715	77,697	69,811	46,160	52,183	53,799
Master's[3]	69,140	68,077	71,480	64,168	87,376	88,601	85,093	70,535	71,611	69,213	60,270	45,648	47,693	53,637
Other 4-year	61,508	60,562	62,620	58,332	74,871	77,450	70,905	64,945	66,317	63,267	54,785	55,403	46,542	56,307
2-year	63,890	62,907	64,282	61,774	71,707	73,125	70,439	61,119	62,011	60,417	54,045	65,098	44,505	58,380
Nonprofit	86,707	85,374	92,824	75,403	120,169	124,916	108,812	80,023	82,156	77,281	65,661	48,381	59,878	68,800
4-year	86,805	85,470	92,913	75,491	120,216	124,950	108,880	80,042	82,172	77,302	65,697	48,424	59,878	68,899
Doctoral[2]	101,437	99,877	109,525	85,436	143,432	147,794	130,909	90,449	93,378	86,432	74,672	51,572	61,019	74,703
Master's[3]	69,986	68,909	71,870	65,455	86,473	87,764	84,102	69,661	70,753	68,358	58,256	47,207	56,230	62,395
Other 4-year	69,024	67,963	70,420	65,010	89,246	89,746	88,255	68,177	67,971	68,429	56,060	43,603	57,625	53,220
2-year	48,958	48,205	44,085	51,000	48,111	45,368	50,512	43,650	42,635	44,480	43,117	46,565	—	60,621
For-profit	46,441	45,727	48,650	42,675	73,302	75,475	70,604	77,143	82,509	71,975	65,826	39,289	30,873	31,824
2013–14														
All institutions	78,625	78,625	85,528	70,355	109,905	115,455	98,064	78,593	81,156	75,388	66,025	58,080	54,238	58,902
Public	75,241	75,241	81,560	67,944	103,587	109,118	92,281	77,106	79,760	73,783	65,659	59,742	51,923	57,233
4-year	79,711	79,711	86,562	70,713	109,541	113,579	99,646	79,151	81,495	76,009	67,387	48,816	52,055	56,528
Doctoral[2]	85,851	85,851	93,677	74,675	118,814	122,452	108,523	83,032	85,507	79,550	71,429	47,822	53,262	56,347
Master's[3]	68,737	68,737	72,067	64,971	87,794	88,863	85,847	71,355	72,678	69,750	61,117	46,288	48,785	55,818
Other 4-year	61,145	61,145	63,227	58,992	74,333	76,927	70,634	66,053	67,918	63,892	56,116	56,123	47,437	57,110
2-year	63,198	63,198	64,564	62,079	72,737	74,264	71,377	62,258	63,168	61,557	55,423	65,524	48,222	57,498
Nonprofit	86,777	86,777	94,498	76,659	121,995	127,064	110,208	81,478	83,869	78,493	66,690	48,088	60,506	70,174
4-year	86,858	86,858	94,572	76,733	122,042	127,097	110,278	81,494	83,882	78,510	66,719	48,005	60,506	70,411
Doctoral[2]	101,684	101,684	111,792	86,884	146,366	151,239	132,794	92,201	95,342	88,010	75,760	51,412	61,601	74,456
Master's[3]	69,638	69,638	72,555	66,299	86,082	87,087	84,255	70,658	71,961	69,164	59,093	48,322	56,837	69,934
Other 4-year	69,292	69,292	71,765	66,384	90,780	91,178	90,028	69,880	70,079	69,641	57,103	41,388	58,445	56,004
2-year	50,790	50,790	47,259	53,092	51,307	49,960	52,415	59,231	47,530	63,689	41,799	52,227	—	49,582
For-profit	50,723	50,723	52,553	49,176	65,002	65,902	63,875	66,921	68,784	65,184	63,354	42,292	62,743	37,673

—Not available.
[1]Constant dollars based on the Consumer Price Index, prepared by the Bureau of Labor Statistics, U.S. Department of Labor, adjusted to an academic-year basis.
[2]Institutions that awarded 20 or more doctor's degrees during the previous academic year.
[3]Institutions that awarded 20 or more master's degrees, but less than 20 doctor's degrees, during the previous academic year.

NOTE: Degree-granting institutions grant associate's or higher degrees and participate in Title IV federal financial aid programs. Some data have been revised from previously published figures. SOURCE: U.S. Department of Education, National Center for Education Statistics, Integrated Postsecondary Education Data System (IPEDS), "Salaries, Tenure, and Fringe Benefits of Full-Time Instructional Faculty Survey" (IPEDS-SA:99); and IPEDS Winter 2005–06, Spring 2013, and Spring 2014, Human Resources component, Salaries section. (This table was prepared February 2015.)

Table 316.30. Average salary of full-time instructional faculty on 9-month contracts in degree-granting postsecondary institutions, by control and level of institution and state or jurisdiction: 2013–14

[In current dollars]

State or jurisdiction	All institu-tions	Public institutions						Nonprofit institutions						For-profit institutions
		Total	4-year institutions				2-year	Total	4-year institutions				2-year	
			Total	Doctoral[1]	Master's[2]	Other			Total	Doctoral[1]	Master's[2]	Other		
1	2	3	4	5	6	7	8	9	10	11	12	13	14	15
United States	$78,625	$75,241	$79,711	$85,851	$68,737	$61,145	$63,198	$86,777	$86,858	$101,684	$69,638	$69,292	$50,790	$50,723
Alabama	68,313	69,940	75,867	82,746	61,849	69,235	53,485	59,521	59,521	67,352	49,570	52,501	†	46,671
Alaska	75,825	77,107	77,241	79,790	75,604	†	63,167	47,232	46,832	†	46,832	†	53,100	†
Arizona	79,704	80,700	84,601	86,015	72,859	52,000	70,427	60,815	60,815	†	44,027	74,123	39,794	55,089
Arkansas	58,545	58,690	63,998	67,494	56,122	59,024	44,534	57,893	58,059	64,367	58,590	53,222	†	26,072
California	92,595	89,323	95,543	104,868	76,652	74,236	81,984	104,090	104,090	113,411	80,409	91,977	†	48,720
Colorado	75,433	73,887	78,927	83,950	58,625	66,621	49,460	86,028	86,028	88,732	84,169	65,605	†	37,519
Connecticut	96,841	89,490	95,260	106,016	84,040	†	71,797	105,659	105,659	115,867	87,779	82,464	†	60,632
Delaware	93,436	94,561	101,103	107,228	66,484	†	67,071	81,007	81,007	124,890	63,749	†	†	‡
District of Columbia	101,098	82,058	82,058	130,900	77,748	†	†	102,838	102,838	104,016	57,683	†	†	66,982
Florida	73,391	72,214	73,105	82,035	73,464	59,019	51,845	77,691	77,691	90,193	68,091	60,171	†	52,434
Georgia	69,731	68,128	70,315	80,532	59,901	54,144	45,774	74,551	74,566	91,619	63,930	60,166	‡	52,611
Hawaii	80,704	81,530	87,697	89,490	†	71,297	67,597	77,288	77,288	†	75,547	92,747	†	26,173
Idaho	60,003	60,565	63,358	65,636	63,009	50,099	49,944	54,130	54,130	†	52,475	55,648	†	21,256
Illinois	83,057	77,299	80,547	83,623	68,636	†	71,408	91,623	91,623	108,452	69,077	62,098	†	42,079
Indiana	75,527	74,623	79,608	86,037	62,620	54,756	44,771	77,448	77,448	92,602	57,370	67,935	†	26,696
Iowa	71,252	77,111	86,432	86,432	†	†	55,595	62,482	62,482	71,038	55,253	62,382	†	52,587
Kansas	64,913	67,074	73,773	78,241	58,703	65,036	51,277	50,366	50,544	51,820	54,895	44,352	45,549	54,350
Kentucky	63,504	65,155	70,668	80,213	60,996	†	50,638	57,284	57,284	60,391	51,384	61,255	†	63,212
Louisiana	64,609	60,795	65,632	71,748	55,351	46,680	43,171	80,574	80,574	87,988	55,946	52,558	†	22,588
Maine	73,444	68,244	72,598	78,421	†	†	58,292	81,018	81,555	66,502	54,460	92,003	53,872	†
Maryland	78,110	75,111	78,952	82,851	67,271	†	67,659	88,252	88,252	101,246	72,987	68,875	†	53,901
Massachusetts	99,515	83,192	90,012	98,953	76,139	†	62,587	107,415	107,415	121,536	84,011	86,814	†	62,966
Michigan	83,540	86,485	88,240	90,192	73,606	62,652	77,156	65,983	65,983	79,801	60,614	66,742	†	22,231
Minnesota	74,191	73,933	80,996	98,117	70,805	58,729	62,292	74,966	74,966	78,369	65,343	78,628	†	39,273
Mississippi	58,187	58,405	64,236	66,473	54,108	†	50,716	56,141	56,141	63,890	59,498	41,952	†	48,391
Missouri	70,919	66,367	70,124	77,228	60,228	48,114	53,223	79,194	79,194	97,590	60,493	52,078	†	48,961
Montana	67,559	70,426	73,540	80,743	58,159	47,290	47,137	49,711	50,889	†	52,612	50,318	36,377	‡
Nebraska	71,781	73,790	79,367	85,275	62,930	†	54,285	65,147	65,325	83,515	56,184	54,862	48,600	†
Nevada	78,430	78,942	80,302	87,844	†	62,300	63,526	60,778	60,778	†	60,778	†	†	29,060
New Hampshire	87,923	82,736	90,191	99,633	76,648	87,700	60,256	95,523	95,523	127,250	67,712	68,627	†	†
New Jersey	98,143	96,043	104,976	112,869	95,775	†	72,488	104,231	104,231	123,769	79,384	73,436	†	50,244
New Mexico	63,318	63,732	70,792	77,237	58,076	45,795	47,613	†	†	†	†	†	†	41,546
New York	91,351	77,324	80,861	98,441	70,523	63,620	70,245	99,455	99,529	110,395	78,344	83,461	71,247	44,359
North Carolina	71,647	67,344	77,902	83,071	68,288	66,680	48,668	83,536	83,790	105,279	54,895	60,458	40,288	82,317
North Dakota	64,948	67,026	68,787	75,004	59,797	52,753	53,401	51,845	51,845	55,421	†	49,453	†	†
Ohio	72,993	74,880	78,742	81,222	57,129	62,560	60,622	69,266	69,266	78,140	63,377	66,700	†	52,855
Oklahoma	64,838	64,799	68,585	75,042	58,802	50,232	49,418	65,258	65,258	78,413	55,338	36,484	†	19,154
Oregon	71,791	71,201	73,660	77,837	58,233	60,922	66,793	73,870	73,870	76,948	64,037	78,730	†	20,455
Pennsylvania	84,832	81,610	84,946	91,998	81,477	68,810	63,764	88,820	89,147	102,294	71,102	80,143	46,434	39,154
Rhode Island	91,302	72,670	76,642	81,049	68,424	†	60,853	104,135	104,135	126,375	88,606	†	†	†
South Carolina	64,711	66,536	75,472	85,691	67,408	54,527	47,828	58,327	58,450	†	60,949	55,034	51,714	51,829
South Dakota	60,294	61,813	64,768	65,421	66,442	47,352	47,557	53,403	53,403	†	53,478	53,365	†	44,871
Tennessee	69,840	66,808	72,217	74,187	64,007	†	49,373	76,513	76,513	96,160	56,356	54,749	†	41,899
Texas	74,014	72,052	79,175	83,577	65,113	55,910	56,722	83,539	83,658	94,400	66,882	56,440	37,333	38,458
Utah	68,825	69,696	71,728	82,142	62,892	55,327	50,470	61,433	61,522	92,503	53,277	†	56,752	24,780
Vermont	76,077	76,792	76,792	86,208	57,010	56,621	†	75,414	75,414	†	78,937	54,114	†	†
Virginia	72,630	77,966	83,246	87,570	67,820	66,036	60,252	60,530	60,518	60,776	55,606	62,049	63,231	44,359
Washington	71,189	70,358	76,536	85,265	72,073	55,679	56,579	74,194	74,194	80,125	62,286	72,560	†	65,634
West Virginia	62,353	64,027	66,891	74,075	58,823	54,548	47,114	50,069	50,069	53,246	50,177	47,589	†	‡
Wisconsin	71,855	73,431	72,945	83,115	59,835	92,630	74,607	66,136	66,136	74,741	60,782	59,323	†	36,560
Wyoming	70,158	70,181	80,027	80,027	†	†	58,862	‡	‡	†	†	†	‡	†
U.S. Service Academies	101,488	101,488	101,488	†	†	101,488	†	†	†	†	†	†	†	†
Other jurisdictions	44,440	51,872	56,515	51,248	65,393	53,041	32,910	25,996	25,996	33,728	33,767	20,267	†	21,281
American Samoa	25,503	25,503	25,503	†	†	25,503	†	†	†	†	†	†	†	†
Federated States of Micronesia	24,590	24,590	†	†	†	†	24,590	†	†	†	†	†	†	†
Guam	61,982	61,982	65,773	†	65,773	†	53,091	†	†	†	†	†	†	†
Marshall Islands	†	†	†	†	†	†	†	†	†	†	†	†	†	†
Northern Marianas	42,028	42,028	42,028	†	†	42,028	†	†	†	†	†	†	†	†
Palau	†	†	†	†	†	†	†	†	†	†	†	†	†	†
Puerto Rico	41,968	55,047	57,680	51,248	†	59,367	25,059	25,996	25,996	33,728	33,767	20,267	†	21,281
U.S. Virgin Islands	64,918	64,918	64,918	†	64,918	†	†	†	†	†	†	†	†	†

†Not applicable.
‡Reporting standards not met (too few cases).
[1]Institutions that awarded 20 or more doctor's degrees during the previous academic year.
[2]Institutions that awarded 20 or more master's degrees, but less than 20 doctor's degrees, during the previous academic year.

NOTE: Degree-granting institutions grant associate's or higher degrees and participate in Title IV federal financial aid programs. Data include imputations for nonrespondent institutions.
SOURCE: U.S. Department of Education, National Center for Education Statistics, Integrated Postsecondary Education Data System (IPEDS), Spring 2014, Human Resources component, Salaries section. (This table was prepared February 2015.)

Table 316.40. Average salary of full-time instructional faculty on 9-month contracts in degree-granting postsecondary institutions, by control and level of institution and state or jurisdiction: 2012–13

[In current dollars]

State or jurisdiction	All institutions	Public institutions						Nonprofit institutions						For-profit institutions
		Total	4-year institutions				2-year	Total	4-year institutions				2-year	
			Total	Doctoral[1]	Master's[2]	Other			Total	Doctoral[1]	Master's[2]	Other		
1	2	3	4	5	6	7	8	9	10	11	12	13	14	15
United States	$77,278	$73,877	$78,012	$84,126	$68,077	$60,562	$62,907	$85,374	$85,470	$99,877	$68,909	$67,963	$48,205	$45,727
Alabama	67,167	69,104	73,882	79,486	60,981	68,071	54,997	57,154	57,154	64,988	50,274	49,795	†	†
Alaska	74,170	75,138	75,188	77,403	73,788	†	68,859	54,063	54,063	†	54,063	†	†	†
Arizona	78,045	78,555	83,691	84,163	†	50,271	69,360	58,993	58,993	†	43,373	71,773	†	70,486
Arkansas	56,415	56,453	61,203	65,460	51,020	58,651	44,170	56,164	56,189	62,710	56,828	51,126	‡	†
California	91,820	88,786	94,223	106,300	77,447	73,485	82,505	102,998	102,998	112,503	81,362	89,258	†	48,168
Colorado	72,599	71,215	76,693	83,650	59,353	63,659	47,339	82,152	82,152	83,972	82,306	62,503	†	31,893
Connecticut	94,524	85,944	91,336	101,798	81,403	†	69,383	103,640	103,640	112,537	89,205	81,456	†	61,939
Delaware	95,567	96,471	99,985	105,928	65,461	†	78,075	86,505	86,505	121,734	64,385	†	†	†
District of Columbia	100,381	82,067	82,067	129,471	77,810	†	†	101,751	101,751	102,408	69,000	†	†	33,150
Florida	71,807	70,180	71,288	80,114	67,057	58,337	52,915	76,624	76,624	89,041	68,839	57,407	†	72,031
Georgia	69,625	67,874	69,974	77,358	58,527	53,359	45,489	74,959	74,973	91,874	64,862	60,681	‡	†
Hawaii	78,375	79,346	85,115	86,873	†	69,041	66,139	73,141	73,141	†	72,056	83,502	†	†
Idaho	60,762	61,345	64,550	65,087	67,937	49,551	49,198	54,047	54,047	†	51,898	56,036	†	†
Illinois	81,588	75,921	79,400	83,083	66,138	‡	69,859	90,118	90,118	105,912	64,912	61,443	†	39,951
Indiana	73,958	72,891	78,137	84,771	61,204	54,846	43,112	76,110	76,110	90,062	60,768	65,188	†	†
Iowa	71,643	77,617	86,911	90,905	70,469	†	54,966	62,379	62,379	68,849	55,444	63,011	†	56,041
Kansas	63,575	65,981	72,519	77,127	57,633	66,216	51,239	49,104	49,604	†	53,265	43,272	43,524	†
Kentucky	62,183	63,618	68,834	73,634	59,209	†	49,789	56,537	56,537	63,381	51,005	59,274	†	†
Louisiana	62,980	59,473	64,755	70,339	55,305	47,701	42,394	78,817	78,817	84,878	57,692	52,714	†	30,111
Maine	72,351	67,520	71,956	77,728	†	60,201	52,527	79,917	80,151	65,544	55,481	89,659	51,930	†
Maryland	76,229	73,484	77,145	86,128	64,840	†	66,417	86,284	86,284	101,660	65,462	74,397	†	†
Massachusetts	98,280	81,090	87,151	95,702	73,804	†	61,126	106,136	106,198	117,540	85,963	84,507	72,631	65,606
Michigan	81,727	84,386	85,904	88,478	74,620	54,242	77,397	65,540	65,540	79,232	61,847	63,493	†	†
Minnesota	73,369	73,572	80,316	95,717	70,780	59,928	62,913	73,172	73,172	76,028	65,302	74,997	†	49,740
Mississippi	58,089	58,171	62,606	64,803	52,451	†	51,099	57,340	57,340	66,696	58,912	42,475	†	†
Missouri	69,777	65,773	68,967	75,673	59,628	57,484	54,254	76,884	76,884	94,128	59,050	51,415	†	60,512
Montana	57,610	58,933	60,914	63,473	57,195	48,418	44,931	49,055	50,316	†	48,175	51,829	35,678	†
Nebraska	68,267	69,947	74,770	79,581	62,817	†	54,488	63,118	63,274	79,727	54,802	54,105	49,900	†
Nevada	78,888	79,091	80,526	89,020	†	63,724	63,164	62,703	62,703	†	62,703	†	†	†
New Hampshire	86,996	80,729	87,988	96,420	75,569	85,285	52,046	96,075	96,075	129,862	67,416	68,462	†	†
New Jersey	97,292	95,003	103,633	109,927	96,231	†	73,174	102,715	102,715	120,032	77,305	71,835	†	†
New Mexico	63,004	63,004	68,980	74,822	57,939	45,767	48,950	†	†	†	†	†	†	†
New York	89,734	76,415	80,644	98,701	70,054	64,098	68,333	97,658	97,681	109,607	76,704	81,079	77,426	36,394
North Carolina	71,362	67,482	78,149	83,585	68,189	68,477	49,398	81,882	82,121	101,958	56,745	58,840	40,111	87,040
North Dakota	63,228	65,675	67,413	73,864	57,536	52,125	52,128	49,086	49,086	52,188	†	46,726	†	†
Ohio	71,555	73,708	77,345	79,762	54,796	61,699	60,120	69,350	69,393	76,853	62,087	68,987	52,909	15,127
Oklahoma	64,747	64,345	67,698	73,084	60,036	49,493	48,293	66,603	66,603	72,657	56,611	39,580	†	†
Oregon	70,049	69,117	71,093	75,250	55,828	61,552	65,731	73,043	73,043	75,961	63,461	77,315	†	†
Pennsylvania	83,228	79,867	82,817	90,157	78,810	67,254	63,141	86,763	87,190	98,896	70,300	78,854	44,380	53,903
Rhode Island	89,435	72,374	75,990	80,797	67,731	†	61,249	101,310	101,310	123,303	86,115	†	†	†
South Carolina	63,668	65,590	74,226	86,607	65,284	54,533	48,092	57,640	57,777	†	59,777	54,774	49,852	52,308
South Dakota	59,058	60,422	63,240	63,966	64,365	45,440	45,751	52,963	52,963	†	52,736	53,076	†	†
Tennessee	67,851	64,605	70,088	72,142	61,226	†	46,719	74,403	74,403	93,823	55,252	54,249	†	†
Texas	72,007	70,074	76,063	82,088	63,583	56,632	55,647	80,933	81,011	93,833	65,106	55,759	34,305	‡
Utah	68,886	68,303	70,317	79,913	61,961	55,038	49,735	77,000	78,366	90,785	71,995	†	55,787	‡
Vermont	74,293	75,470	75,470	83,693	59,207	56,990	†	73,213	73,213	†	76,805	52,451	†	†
Virginia	70,673	75,582	80,558	87,366	66,648	67,732	58,644	59,719	59,719	60,066	57,810	59,863	†	35,498
Washington	69,245	68,108	73,585	81,826	67,714	55,280	56,170	73,345	73,371	78,860	61,247	70,157	‡	†
West Virginia	61,585	63,344	65,874	73,683	58,059	53,404	48,150	49,801	49,801	53,751	47,342	48,450	†	27,446
Wisconsin	70,431	72,250	71,073	80,487	58,689	90,577	75,483	64,286	64,286	72,291	59,847	57,743	†	55,687
Wyoming	69,566	69,566	78,955	78,955	†	†	58,606	†	†	†	†	†	†	†
U.S. Service Academies	102,568	102,568	102,568	†	†	102,568	†	†	†	†	†	†	†	†
Other jurisdictions	56,727	60,357	63,271	49,191	69,763	52,257	42,182	26,788	26,788	31,402	29,979	17,028	†	14,815
American Samoa	29,767	29,767	29,767	†	†	29,767	†	†	†	†	†	†	†	†
Federated States of Micronesia	24,674	24,674	†	†	†	†	24,674	†	†	†	†	†	†	†
Guam	62,641	62,641	66,229	†	66,229	†	53,606	†	†	†	†	†	†	†
Marshall Islands	58,174	58,174	†	†	†	†	58,174	†	†	†	†	†	†	†
Northern Marianas	43,216	43,216	43,216	†	†	43,216	†	†	†	†	†	†	†	†
Palau	†	†	†	†	†	†	†	†	†	†	†	†	†	†
Puerto Rico	59,357	65,265	65,265	49,191	71,629	56,733	†	26,788	26,788	31,402	29,979	17,028	†	14,815
U.S. Virgin Islands	62,810	62,810	62,810	†	62,810	†	†	†	†	†	†	†	†	†

†Not applicable.
‡Reporting standards not met (too few cases).
[1] Institutions that awarded 20 or more doctor's degrees during the previous academic year.
[2] Institutions that awarded 20 or more master's degrees, but less than 20 doctor's degrees, during the previous academic year.

NOTE: Degree-granting institutions grant associate's or higher degrees and participate in Title IV federal financial aid programs. Data include imputations for nonrespondent institutions. Some data have been revised from previously published figures.
SOURCE: U.S. Department of Education, National Center for Education Statistics, Integrated Postsecondary Education Data System (IPEDS), Spring 2013, Human Resources component, Salaries section. (This table was prepared February 2015.)

Table 316.50. Average salary of full-time instructional faculty on 9-month contracts in 4-year degree-granting postsecondary institutions, by control and classification of institution, academic rank of faculty, and state or jurisdiction: 2013–14

[In current dollars]

State or jurisdiction	Public doctoral[1]			Public master's[2]			Nonprofit doctoral[1]			Nonprofit master's[2]		
	Professor	Associate professor	Assistant professor	Professor	Associate professor	Assistant professor	Professor	Associate professor	Assistant professor	Professor	Associate professor	Assistant professor
1	2	3	4	5	6	7	8	9	10	11	12	13
United States	$118,814	$83,032	$71,429	$87,794	$71,355	$61,117	$146,366	$92,201	$75,760	$86,082	$70,658	$59,093
Alabama	120,171	82,219	67,589	79,379	65,427	56,602	78,054	70,300	64,203	61,765	52,132	45,072
Alaska	109,585	81,809	67,816	103,962	79,374	67,277	†	†	†	56,199	50,257	40,222
Arizona	122,633	84,611	72,855	108,007	87,134	76,232	†	†	†	47,223	46,653	‡
Arkansas	95,715	71,017	64,091	69,597	63,398	52,041	77,736	64,875	58,985	65,071	60,709	51,911
California	134,141	88,510	80,199	91,680	74,486	68,541	151,728	99,315	85,001	96,894	78,738	67,968
Colorado	115,045	86,038	73,725	74,413	60,769	52,950	128,374	88,148	77,542	114,541	77,390	62,009
Connecticut	143,133	96,782	77,513	99,139	79,766	64,916	168,263	90,295	79,538	110,606	88,178	72,678
Delaware	142,243	98,352	83,489	76,891	66,542	62,998	151,213	121,916	‡	74,786	64,894	52,705
District of Columbia	149,350	118,450	‡	101,722	76,412	60,670	147,825	96,840	80,391	54,468	66,144	55,257
Florida	112,847	79,427	71,590	120,486	80,434	63,063	124,248	85,140	72,159	88,398	72,506	59,356
Georgia	110,723	78,950	68,914	78,092	63,902	55,815	130,293	82,692	69,005	71,679	60,826	51,587
Hawaii	114,168	86,568	76,287	†	†	†	†	†	†	94,327	80,634	71,059
Idaho	86,027	68,827	58,098	80,115	66,870	59,134	†	†	†	62,147	52,516	47,246
Illinois	119,266	82,356	71,901	93,463	73,687	64,301	163,620	94,672	83,680	85,792	69,406	58,658
Indiana	120,474	84,291	72,214	86,706	67,833	59,260	133,263	84,648	72,962	68,867	57,919	50,724
Iowa	114,915	83,226	72,263	†	†	†	88,775	68,268	61,216	66,686	57,284	50,868
Kansas	108,316	76,570	65,552	73,860	59,352	57,101	63,306	50,976	44,808	63,249	55,811	51,586
Kentucky	110,940	78,327	68,521	80,596	64,493	56,049	72,804	58,263	52,667	61,525	53,673	44,658
Louisiana	99,791	73,612	64,623	72,201	59,938	52,102	126,491	85,308	71,930	65,293	55,272	53,617
Maine	96,483	75,485	60,954	†	†	†	89,097	75,414	65,492	71,541	55,422	49,110
Maryland	116,268	84,878	74,052	85,468	68,340	62,645	147,555	92,859	81,292	82,680	71,958	68,483
Massachusetts	131,921	97,748	81,821	90,261	72,469	64,116	167,977	103,995	88,668	103,175	85,515	67,167
Michigan	121,637	85,385	72,714	96,096	80,159	64,515	102,047	79,122	64,460	71,147	59,950	55,548
Minnesota	128,943	89,749	78,605	85,401	70,263	60,444	102,463	77,175	63,681	76,875	65,516	55,807
Mississippi	93,702	72,302	64,776	67,144	57,048	52,893	77,906	66,454	56,874	73,530	57,744	55,009
Missouri	102,420	74,228	63,463	75,860	61,505	52,729	141,528	90,323	73,784	75,234	61,703	52,970
Montana	102,559	82,388	68,651	71,408	63,081	53,881	†	†	†	63,134	50,447	44,698
Nebraska	110,123	84,065	75,892	78,652	62,714	53,189	110,286	80,712	67,238	65,001	55,529	52,261
Nevada	117,993	85,485	68,344	†	†	†	†	†	†	71,158	62,136	60,570
New Hampshire	120,488	93,349	75,853	90,873	75,074	61,673	162,307	105,049	75,172	84,701	68,074	57,618
New Jersey	154,555	104,441	85,777	117,025	95,561	79,083	176,455	92,763	83,468	96,747	83,654	66,044
New Mexico	93,376	70,694	60,364	73,321	59,836	52,768	†	†	†	†	†	†
New York	132,813	92,985	76,800	90,917	72,348	61,133	155,954	99,995	81,978	98,919	78,220	66,393
North Carolina	119,400	80,828	73,142	89,708	70,623	62,833	152,906	91,454	75,331	63,271	57,929	52,673
North Dakota	101,274	79,189	66,498	79,501	64,853	54,606	65,271	61,393	51,991	†	†	†
Ohio	111,451	79,939	67,862	72,485	61,546	52,597	110,149	75,491	64,442	76,056	64,893	54,574
Oklahoma	104,634	74,846	65,094	77,639	65,452	55,032	99,854	76,793	66,174	63,432	57,183	51,875
Oregon	108,848	82,268	72,348	74,991	60,356	48,121	100,388	75,228	61,765	77,369	67,970	55,494
Pennsylvania	132,876	91,452	70,953	105,841	85,203	68,453	146,382	93,849	82,008	90,918	72,695	60,779
Rhode Island	103,635	76,302	68,143	77,945	66,653	57,817	164,255	107,299	88,505	115,882	86,336	72,131
South Carolina	120,902	84,999	74,153	86,491	68,839	59,579	†	†	†	77,336	60,096	53,706
South Dakota	86,627	70,225	61,855	85,201	69,448	60,349	†	†	†	63,686	56,612	48,615
Tennessee	101,120	74,866	63,219	81,320	66,080	55,829	137,481	88,220	67,304	67,117	55,140	49,115
Texas	120,822	82,758	72,045	85,125	70,105	61,116	129,752	89,240	78,516	86,936	69,042	55,264
Utah	110,791	78,224	69,806	78,088	64,607	57,553	113,141	81,862	69,538	89,014	54,146	63,610
Vermont	117,128	86,451	71,884	68,028	52,977	42,659	†	†	†	103,611	75,119	64,461
Virginia	123,748	84,864	71,463	85,668	70,030	61,332	112,662	82,173	45,656	68,835	57,620	49,686
Washington	112,652	83,321	76,489	89,320	75,582	70,378	107,583	81,067	65,460	78,222	64,170	58,348
West Virginia	97,562	76,450	63,340	70,361	62,827	53,263	65,843	55,725	51,563	61,847	52,113	46,627
Wisconsin	107,566	77,241	70,892	72,542	61,517	57,957	102,103	76,332	65,774	75,169	63,325	53,957
Wyoming	108,737	75,564	68,879	†	†	†	†	†	†	†	†	†
U.S. Service Academies	†	†	†	†	†	†	†	†	†	†	†	†
Other jurisdictions	‡	58,503	56,735	85,344	68,704	54,465	†	†	40,738	†	†	40,589
American Samoa	†	†	†	†	†	†	†	†	†	†	†	†
Federated States of Micronesia	†	†	†	†	†	†	†	†	†	†	†	†
Guam	†	†	†	88,584	70,126	52,965	†	†	†	†	†	†
Marshall Islands	†	†	†	†	†	†	†	†	†	†	†	†
Northern Marianas	†	†	†	†	†	†	†	†	†	†	†	†
Palau	†	†	†	†	†	†	†	†	†	†	†	†
Puerto Rico	‡	58,503	56,735	†	†	†	†	†	40,738	†	†	40,589
U.S. Virgin Islands	†	†	†	81,981	66,743	55,928	†	†	†	†	†	†

†Not applicable.
‡Reporting standards not met (too few cases).
[1]Institutions that awarded 20 or more doctor's degrees during the previous academic year.
[2]Institutions that awarded 20 or more master's degrees, but less than 20 doctor's degrees, during the previous academic year.

NOTE: Degree-granting institutions grant associate's or higher degrees and participate in Title IV federal financial aid programs. Data include imputations for nonrespondent institutions.
SOURCE: U.S. Department of Education, National Center for Education Statistics, Integrated Postsecondary Education Data System (IPEDS), Spring 2014, Human Resources component, Salaries section. (This table was prepared February 2015.)

Table 316.60. Average salary of full-time instructional faculty on 9-month contracts in 4-year degree-granting postsecondary institutions, by control and classification of institution, academic rank of faculty, and state or jurisdiction: 2012–13

[In current dollars]

State or jurisdiction	Public doctoral[1]			Public master's[2]			Nonprofit doctoral[1]			Nonprofit master's[2]		
	Professor	Associate professor	Assistant professor	Professor	Associate professor	Assistant professor	Professor	Associate professor	Assistant professor	Professor	Associate professor	Assistant professor
1	2	3	4	5	6	7	8	9	10	11	12	13
United States	$116,777	$81,252	$69,811	$87,376	$70,535	$60,270	$143,432	$90,449	$74,672	$86,473	$69,661	$58,256
Alabama	113,876	79,555	65,152	78,498	65,177	54,809	85,763	67,504	55,956	61,825	52,371	46,982
Alaska	107,609	78,560	65,591	100,496	78,320	65,345	†	†	†	67,416	56,317	47,158
Arizona	117,827	81,762	71,824	†	†	†	†	†	†	‡	63,092	‡
Arkansas	92,227	68,906	62,447	66,216	54,414	49,898	75,296	63,921	58,161	63,746	60,041	51,655
California	133,774	88,431	78,816	93,049	75,770	68,504	149,596	98,747	83,434	99,114	79,761	66,519
Colorado	114,987	84,950	71,623	79,407	63,605	55,334	125,997	81,390	72,872	113,777	72,826	60,594
Connecticut	135,885	92,085	74,559	96,902	78,071	63,153	163,142	89,362	77,511	120,062	86,422	71,493
Delaware	141,691	97,167	82,431	79,760	65,550	61,153	152,547	117,386	97,370	74,865	64,322	54,544
District of Columbia	148,833	115,000	85,788	101,864	76,643	59,525	146,717	95,081	78,452	73,179	65,766	69,162
Florida	109,330	78,003	69,303	96,525	71,929	60,429	122,128	82,423	71,548	89,178	71,694	59,848
Georgia	108,683	76,338	67,156	75,350	63,592	54,504	131,154	83,769	68,201	72,687	58,459	52,466
Hawaii	111,111	84,582	73,217	†	†	†	†	†	†	90,156	77,123	68,956
Idaho	85,346	67,037	58,548	98,034	71,093	56,345	†	†	†	60,845	51,396	42,903
Illinois	119,184	81,468	70,911	91,610	71,453	62,470	156,453	92,029	81,183	82,626	68,818	57,946
Indiana	118,452	82,566	70,584	86,434	67,558	58,110	129,388	81,594	70,524	74,419	62,726	52,337
Iowa	123,740	85,673	74,880	87,708	70,247	61,296	90,172	68,178	56,031	68,305	56,964	49,390
Kansas	107,337	75,046	64,075	73,476	59,756	54,934	†	†	†	61,590	53,547	49,329
Kentucky	104,075	73,671	63,072	76,892	61,893	53,387	79,857	63,076	53,694	59,520	52,679	45,367
Louisiana	96,765	70,808	63,377	73,244	60,511	52,610	123,372	83,352	69,293	67,921	54,802	53,057
Maine	95,457	75,159	61,472	†	†	†	87,793	72,645	64,713	74,108	55,882	49,721
Maryland	119,314	85,563	76,759	85,751	68,222	61,561	147,178	95,041	81,940	83,190	66,756	58,856
Massachusetts	126,773	94,514	78,886	86,867	71,290	62,301	161,163	100,343	85,724	117,571	83,475	65,880
Michigan	121,176	83,719	71,537	93,896	77,065	64,611	108,093	76,237	67,060	72,588	60,463	52,492
Minnesota	126,782	86,677	77,293	85,843	70,251	60,420	99,424	74,892	61,725	76,874	66,000	55,031
Mississippi	92,693	70,604	62,139	64,674	55,355	51,855	83,979	67,390	59,091	76,096	57,718	52,345
Missouri	101,285	73,191	61,754	74,695	60,777	51,822	137,708	84,204	71,438	72,618	60,496	51,845
Montana	76,966	62,566	61,201	71,108	62,439	52,095	†	†	†	55,970	46,893	42,122
Nebraska	104,456	76,392	69,826	77,571	62,544	52,070	106,245	77,367	64,393	64,263	55,070	50,345
Nevada	118,121	84,526	69,809	†	†	†	†	†	†	71,919	65,478	62,542
New Hampshire	116,758	90,711	72,862	89,968	74,047	61,127	161,374	106,013	75,887	84,115	72,258	52,169
New Jersey	149,954	101,586	84,216	119,833	95,161	76,241	168,282	93,263	83,238	95,140	81,864	64,604
New Mexico	98,259	72,718	63,623	71,053	58,592	51,520	†	†	†	†	†	†
New York	131,739	92,390	75,936	90,674	72,218	60,865	154,224	97,771	82,215	96,778	77,072	64,916
North Carolina	121,494	81,350	73,287	89,279	71,163	62,284	153,421	92,067	75,803	67,788	59,256	53,097
North Dakota	99,043	77,325	66,195	76,044	62,291	54,048	68,401	65,732	52,144	†	†	†
Ohio	109,531	78,516	66,309	72,621	62,340	52,832	109,255	74,460	63,394	74,679	63,670	53,150
Oklahoma	102,395	73,003	62,858	74,933	63,715	56,170	93,101	71,891	59,144	67,201	58,674	50,917
Oregon	103,964	78,898	71,168	73,054	58,924	46,957	98,183	74,225	62,005	78,993	65,418	54,925
Pennsylvania	129,129	89,431	69,118	103,099	82,086	65,317	141,050	91,529	78,783	90,130	71,641	60,512
Rhode Island	103,140	77,007	66,609	78,664	67,080	57,452	157,248	101,670	85,880	111,848	84,732	70,990
South Carolina	120,635	85,286	75,220	82,838	66,519	58,958	†	†	†	75,474	58,545	52,740
South Dakota	83,811	67,547	60,150	82,906	67,863	56,816	†	†	†	65,321	52,941	50,966
Tennessee	98,308	73,657	61,672	75,801	66,081	52,703	129,076	85,196	71,088	66,015	54,625	48,470
Texas	119,466	82,284	72,376	84,190	67,815	61,122	128,717	88,657	78,612	83,037	67,325	56,135
Utah	110,647	75,337	64,224	76,289	63,666	55,999	110,754	79,869	68,274	85,472	72,374	59,550
Vermont	115,985	85,441	69,453	71,511	55,534	44,908	†	†	†	103,009	74,285	64,838
Virginia	123,183	83,030	70,295	83,891	67,226	60,018	115,063	83,141	47,527	69,947	59,141	52,165
Washington	107,097	79,686	73,280	84,227	70,255	67,632	106,575	79,543	64,920	77,526	62,238	55,615
West Virginia	95,107	76,538	63,023	70,980	59,930	52,065	69,231	56,008	50,989	56,521	49,352	44,214
Wisconsin	103,642	75,096	69,178	71,018	60,191	56,503	98,890	74,478	62,883	73,834	60,703	53,276
Wyoming	106,226	76,016	67,426	†	†	†	†	†	†	†	†	†
U.S. Service Academies	†	†	†	†	†	†	†	†	†	†	†	†
Other jurisdictions	‡	†	50,566	80,156	66,908	57,702	50,061	30,556	23,343	†	†	†
American Samoa	†	†	†	†	†	†	†	†	†	†	†	†
Federated States of Micronesia	†	†	†	†	†	†	†	†	†	†	†	†
Guam	†	†	†	89,134	70,677	55,034	†	†	†	†	†	†
Marshall Islands	†	†	†	†	†	†	†	†	†	†	†	†
Northern Marianas	†	†	†	†	†	†	†	†	†	†	†	†
Palau	†	†	†	†	†	†	†	†	†	†	†	†
Puerto Rico	‡	†	50,566	79,604	65,807	60,216	50,061	30,556	23,343	†	†	†
U.S. Virgin Islands			†	77,944	66,815	53,062	†	†	†	†	†	†

†Not applicable.
‡Reporting standards not met (too few cases).
[1]Institutions that awarded 20 or more doctor's degrees during the previous academic year.
[2]Institutions that awarded 20 or more master's degrees, but less than 20 doctor's degrees, during the previous academic year.

NOTE: Degree-granting institutions grant associate's or higher degrees and participate in Title IV federal financial aid programs. Data include imputations for nonrespondent institutions. Some data have been revised from previously published figures.
SOURCE: U.S. Department of Education, National Center for Education Statistics, Integrated Postsecondary Education Data System (IPEDS), Spring 2013, Human Resources component, Salaries section. (This table was prepared February 2015.)

Table 316.70. Average benefit expenditure for full-time instructional faculty on 9-month contracts in degree-granting postsecondary institutions, by type of benefit and control of institution: Selected years, 1977–78 through 2010–11

Control of institution and year	Average total benefit per full-time faculty member	Retirement plans Total	Vested within 5 years	Vested after 5 years	Medical/ dental plans	Guaranteed disability income protection	Tuition plan for dependents	Housing plan	Social Security taxes	Unemployment compensation taxes	Group life insurance	Worker's compensation taxes	Other insurance	Other benefits
1	2	3	4	5	6	7	8	9	10	11	12	13	14	15
						Current dollars								
Total														
1977–78	$3,203	$1,725	$1,739	$1,691	$521	$96	$1,410	$886	$899	$109	$105	$80	—	$288
1982–83	5,799	2,731	2,741	2,703	1,111	151	1,993	1,639	1,712	146	138	114	—	915
1987–88	7,227	3,677	3,494	4,028	1,682	132	1,585	2,004	2,379	134	178	190	—	716
1989–90	8,241	4,048	3,974	4,192	2,339	147	2,070	2,643	2,764	121	182	49	—	637
1992–93	10,473	4,397	4,391	4,410	3,266	179	2,196	2,574	3,168	143	237	344	—	874
1997–98	12,263	5,289	5,195	5,498	3,535	218	2,765	4,100	3,562	158	195	340	$1,501	1,043
1998–99	12,580	5,256	5,268	5,228	3,726	213	3,012	3,698	3,668	152	190	347	1,267	845
1999–2000	13,227	5,292	5,365	5,125	3,989	237	3,362	4,187	3,793	146	190	343	1,512	1,303
2001–02	14,408	5,541	5,738	5,126	4,792	250	3,487	4,931	4,079	164	231	402	668	1,267
2002–03	15,552	5,781	6,039	5,208	5,396	264	3,308	4,329	4,158	170	211	411	797	1,263
2003–04	16,437	5,895	6,161	5,281	5,919	261	3,506	6,101	4,260	191	215	435	951	1,452
2004–05	17,269	6,211	6,429	5,682	6,314	272	4,072	4,176	4,354	225	199	481	853	1,637
2005–06	18,082	6,402	6,571	6,010	6,863	280	4,511	5,599	4,451	228	210	473	1,095	1,457
2006–07	18,783	6,710	6,851	6,361	7,217	280	5,029	6,914	4,627	176	217	484	1,226	1,564
2007–08	19,756	7,033	7,142	6,767	7,635	282	5,607	7,436	4,773	168	215	509	1,172	1,706
2008–09	20,332	7,222	7,396	6,797	7,900	291	5,596	9,001	4,918	169	213	498	1,156	1,540
2009–10	20,978	7,292	7,472	6,846	8,389	276	6,016	8,729	4,993	180	211	499	1,155	1,561
2010–11	21,744	7,436	7,672	6,883	8,843	281	6,396	9,071	5,042	219	210	502	1,191	1,546
Public														
1977–78	3,252	1,791	1,833	1,724	560	99	430	846	911	99	105	88	—	94
1982–83	5,920	2,846	2,880	2,776	1,189	153	576	1,027	1,741	139	140	115	—	980
1987–88	7,146	3,815	3,602	4,086	1,757	140	404	1,172	2,399	109	180	192	—	611
1989–90	8,361	4,186	4,128	4,259	2,425	154	605	1,767	2,771	97	182	60	—	602
1992–93	10,280	4,467	4,469	4,464	3,352	188	693	1,135	3,122	117	250	318	—	827
1997–98	12,114	5,432	5,302	5,617	3,646	219	830	2,614	3,482	133	187	340	1,643	1,175
1998–99	12,192	5,249	5,230	5,276	3,830	202	828	1,826	3,553	127	183	348	1,252	709
1999–2000	12,756	5,258	5,297	5,200	4,131	237	962	2,283	3,660	121	176	347	1,603	1,272
2001–02	13,919	5,437	5,641	5,158	4,936	254	994	686	3,930	137	233	402	694	1,162
2002–03	15,097	5,703	5,968	5,323	5,565	274	978	2,415	4,005	142	198	402	872	1,274
2003–04	15,916	5,757	6,044	5,330	6,127	262	1,022	4,589	4,073	173	206	425	901	1,334
2004–05	16,769	6,104	6,321	5,760	6,498	274	1,280	3,655	4,161	202	189	479	866	1,725
2005–06	17,594	6,308	6,458	6,078	7,126	279	1,483	4,418	4,237	210	202	446	1,209	1,299
2006–07	18,299	6,620	6,743	6,419	7,446	281	1,609	393	4,409	149	202	494	1,303	1,523
2007–08	19,245	6,994	7,071	6,872	7,858	289	1,815	3,382	4,542	136	197	520	1,209	1,516
2008–09	19,778	7,156	7,292	6,941	8,079	291	1,876	4,635	4,657	138	194	511	1,245	1,475
2009–10	20,435	7,237	7,387	6,998	8,613	276	1,972	4,276	4,717	148	189	509	1,269	1,543
2010–11	21,234	7,360	7,616	6,977	9,053	269	2,317	4,802	4,750	196	192	514	1,253	1,322
Private														
1977–78	3,071	1,509	1,542	905	404	89	2,025	890	873	131	103	60	—	838
1982–83	5,462	2,340	2,404	1,295	886	146	3,403	1,798	1,648	170	134	113	—	212
1987–88	7,438	3,280	3,306	2,906	1,488	120	3,666	2,303	2,337	197	175	184	—	977
1989–90	7,954	3,657	3,718	2,478	2,112	134	4,259	3,032	2,750	188	182	25	—	712
1992–93	10,958	4,206	4,259	2,877	3,039	163	4,523	2,956	3,267	212	207	402	—	957
1997–98	12,629	4,915	5,023	2,531	3,255	216	5,513	4,228	3,735	222	209	339	1,207	897
1998–99	13,519	5,274	5,327	3,879	3,468	231	6,722	3,936	3,915	219	205	345	1,313	1,020
1999–2000	14,366	5,380	5,471	3,354	3,638	237	6,951	4,349	4,074	213	215	335	1,331	1,342
2001–02	15,644	5,818	5,897	4,518	4,416	245	7,159	5,083	4,414	242	225	403	628	1,450
2002–03	16,660	5,981	6,153	2,983	4,964	249	6,943	4,348	4,490	247	236	429	629	1,248
2003–04	17,687	6,245	6,346	4,225	5,395	259	7,481	6,104	4,667	239	231	457	1,057	1,584
2004–05	18,465	6,483	6,603	4,092	5,849	269	7,600	4,455	4,775	284	217	484	821	1,527
2005–06	19,258	6,637	6,756	5,037	6,195	281	8,594	6,001	4,914	275	223	528	860	1,658
2006–07	19,942	6,935	7,027	5,382	6,632	278	9,610	7,750	5,097	248	246	465	1,049	1,619
2007–08	20,984	7,131	7,257	4,843	7,062	272	10,368	7,474	5,275	253	248	487	1,098	1,944
2008–09	21,656	7,385	7,564	4,195	7,442	292	9,941	9,017	5,489	251	251	472	985	1,628
2009–10	22,258	7,426	7,608	3,951	7,824	275	10,805	8,750	5,590	265	250	479	919	1,580
2010–11	22,927	7,626	7,761	4,797	8,323	299	11,330	9,091	5,664	281	244	479	1,059	1,819

See notes at end of table.

Table 316.70. Average benefit expenditure for full-time instructional faculty on 9-month contracts in degree-granting postsecondary institutions, by type of benefit and control of institution: Selected years, 1977–78 through 2010–11—Continued

Control of institution and year	Average total benefit per full-time faculty member	Retirement plans			Medical/ dental plans	Guaranteed disability income protection	Tuition plan for dependents	Housing plan	Social Security taxes	Unemployment compensation taxes	Group life insurance	Worker's compensation taxes	Other insurance	Other benefits
		Total	Vested within 5 years	Vested after 5 years										
1	2	3	4	5	6	7	8	9	10	11	12	13	14	15
Constant 2013–14 dollars[1]														
Total														
1977–78	12,017	6,470	6,525	6,345	1,954	360	5,289	3,326	3,374	407	392	299	—	1,079
1982–83	13,882	6,538	6,562	6,471	2,661	360	4,771	3,923	4,098	350	331	274	—	2,190
1987–88	14,658	7,458	7,087	8,170	3,412	269	3,215	4,065	4,825	272	362	385	—	1,451
1989–90	15,250	7,491	7,354	7,758	4,328	271	3,831	4,892	5,115	225	337	91	—	1,179
1992–93	17,265	7,249	7,240	7,271	5,385	294	3,621	4,243	5,223	236	391	567	—	1,442
1997–98	17,815	7,683	7,547	7,987	5,136	317	4,017	5,956	5,175	229	283	494	2,181	1,515
1998–99	17,964	7,505	7,523	7,465	5,320	304	4,301	5,280	5,237	217	272	496	1,809	1,207
1999–2000	18,358	7,345	7,446	7,113	5,536	329	4,666	5,811	5,265	203	263	477	2,098	1,808
2001–02	18,998	7,306	7,567	6,760	6,318	330	4,598	6,503	5,379	217	304	531	880	1,670
2002–03	20,066	7,459	7,792	6,720	6,963	341	4,268	5,585	5,365	219	272	530	1,028	1,629
2003–04	20,754	7,443	7,778	6,667	7,474	330	4,427	7,704	5,379	241	271	550	1,201	1,833
2004–05	21,167	7,614	7,880	6,965	7,739	334	4,991	5,119	5,337	276	244	589	1,045	2,007
2005–06	21,351	7,559	7,759	7,097	8,104	330	5,326	6,611	5,255	270	247	559	1,293	1,720
2006–07	21,620	7,723	7,885	7,322	8,307	322	5,789	7,958	5,325	203	250	558	1,411	1,800
2007–08	21,927	7,806	7,927	7,511	8,475	313	6,223	8,253	5,298	187	238	565	1,301	1,894
2008–09	22,255	7,905	8,095	7,440	8,647	319	6,126	9,853	5,384	185	234	546	1,266	1,685
2009–10	22,743	7,905	8,100	7,422	9,095	299	6,522	9,463	5,413	195	228	541	1,252	1,692
2010–11	23,109	7,903	8,154	7,315	9,398	299	6,797	9,641	5,359	233	223	534	1,266	1,643
Public														
1977–78	12,199	6,718	6,876	6,467	2,102	373	1,613	3,175	3,418	371	394	331	—	351
1982–83	14,173	6,814	6,895	6,646	2,845	366	1,379	2,459	4,168	332	335	275	—	2,347
1987–88	14,495	7,738	7,307	8,288	3,564	285	820	2,377	4,865	222	365	390	—	1,240
1989–90	15,472	7,746	7,638	7,881	4,488	286	1,120	3,269	5,127	179	337	110	—	1,113
1992–93	16,948	7,365	7,368	7,359	5,526	309	1,142	1,871	5,147	192	413	525	—	1,364
1997–98	17,598	7,891	7,702	8,161	5,296	319	1,205	3,797	5,059	194	272	494	2,386	1,708
1998–99	17,411	7,495	7,469	7,534	5,469	288	1,183	2,607	5,073	181	261	497	1,788	1,013
1999–2000	17,705	7,297	7,352	7,217	5,734	329	1,335	3,168	5,080	168	245	482	2,224	1,766
2001–02	18,353	7,169	7,438	6,801	6,509	335	1,311	905	5,182	181	308	530	915	1,532
2002–03	19,479	7,358	7,701	6,868	7,180	354	1,262	3,116	5,168	183	256	518	1,126	1,643
2003–04	20,096	7,269	7,632	6,729	7,736	331	1,290	5,794	5,143	218	260	537	1,138	1,685
2004–05	20,554	7,481	7,748	7,061	7,965	336	1,569	4,480	5,100	248	232	587	1,061	2,115
2005–06	20,774	7,448	7,625	7,177	8,415	329	1,751	5,216	5,003	248	239	527	1,427	1,534
2006–07	21,063	7,619	7,762	7,388	8,571	324	1,852	453	5,074	172	232	569	1,500	1,753
2007–08	21,359	7,762	7,848	7,627	8,722	321	2,014	3,754	5,041	151	219	577	1,342	1,682
2008–09	21,649	7,833	7,982	7,598	8,843	318	2,054	5,073	5,097	151	212	559	1,363	1,615
2009–10	22,154	7,846	8,008	7,586	9,338	300	2,137	4,636	5,113	161	205	552	1,376	1,673
2010–11	22,567	7,822	8,094	7,415	9,621	286	2,462	5,103	5,049	208	204	546	1,331	1,405
Private														
1977–78	11,523	5,660	5,784	3,396	1,517	334	7,598	3,337	3,273	490	388	225	—	3,143
1982–83	13,076	5,602	5,755	3,101	2,122	349	8,146	4,304	3,945	407	322	270	—	508
1987–88	15,086	6,654	6,707	5,895	3,018	243	7,436	4,672	4,741	400	355	373	—	1,982
1989–90	14,720	6,768	6,880	4,585	3,908	248	7,881	5,611	5,090	349	337	46	—	1,318
1992–93	18,065	6,934	7,021	4,744	5,010	269	7,456	4,873	5,386	349	341	662	—	1,577
1997–98	18,346	7,141	7,298	3,676	4,728	314	8,008	6,143	5,427	323	304	493	1,753	1,303
1998–99	19,305	7,532	7,608	5,539	4,952	329	9,598	5,620	5,590	313	293	492	1,874	1,457
1999–2000	19,939	7,467	7,593	4,655	5,049	329	9,647	6,036	5,655	296	299	465	1,848	1,862
2001–02	20,628	7,671	7,776	5,958	5,823	322	9,440	6,703	5,821	319	297	531	828	1,913
2002–03	21,496	7,717	7,938	3,849	6,405	321	8,959	5,611	5,793	318	305	554	812	1,610
2003–04	22,332	7,885	8,012	5,335	6,811	327	9,446	7,708	5,893	301	292	577	1,335	2,000
2004–05	22,633	7,947	8,094	5,016	7,170	330	9,316	5,461	5,854	348	266	593	1,007	1,871
2005–06	22,740	7,837	7,977	5,947	7,314	332	10,148	7,086	5,803	325	263	623	1,016	1,958
2006–07	22,954	7,982	8,088	6,195	7,634	319	11,062	8,920	5,867	286	283	535	1,207	1,863
2007–08	23,290	7,914	8,055	5,375	7,838	302	11,508	8,296	5,855	281	275	541	1,218	2,158
2008–09	23,704	8,083	8,279	4,591	8,146	320	10,882	9,870	6,009	275	274	517	1,079	1,782
2009–10	24,130	8,051	8,248	4,284	8,482	298	11,714	9,487	6,060	287	271	519	996	1,713
2010–11	24,366	8,105	8,248	5,099	8,845	317	12,042	9,662	6,020	299	259	509	1,126	1,933

—Not available.
[1]Constant dollars based on the Consumer Price Index, prepared by the Bureau of Labor Statistics, U.S. Department of Labor, adjusted to an academic-year basis.
NOTE: Data through 1992–93 are for institutions of higher education, while later data are for degree-granting institutions. Degree-granting institutions grant associate's or higher degrees and participate in Title IV federal financial aid programs.

SOURCE: U.S. Department of Education, National Center for Education Statistics, Higher Education General Information Survey (HEGIS), "Faculty Salaries, Tenure, and Fringe Benefits" surveys, 1977–78 and 1982–83; Integrated Postsecondary Education Data System (IPEDS), "Salaries, Tenure, and Fringe Benefits of Full-Time Instructional Faculty Survey" (IPEDS-SA:87–99); and IPEDS Winter 2001–02 through Winter 2010–11, Human Resources component, Salaries section. (This table was prepared March 2014.)

Table 316.80. Percentage of degree-granting postsecondary institutions with a tenure system and of full-time faculty with tenure at these institutions, by control and level of institution and selected characteristics of faculty: Selected years, 1993–94 through 2013–14

Selected characteristic and academic year	All insti-tutions	Public institutions						Nonprofit institutions						For-profit insti-tutions
		Total	4-year institutions				2-year	Total	4-year institutions				2-year	
			Total	Doctoral[1]	Master's[2]	Other			Total	Doctoral[1]	Master's[2]	Other		
1	2	3	4	5	6	7	8	9	10	11	12	13	14	15
Percent of institutions with a tenure system														
1993–94	62.6	73.6	92.6	100.0	98.3	76.4	62.1	62.0	66.3	90.5	76.5	58.3	26.1	7.8
1999–2000	55.0	72.8	94.6	100.0	95.5	86.3	60.3	59.0	63.4	81.2	72.6	54.9	14.0	4.0
2003–04	52.7	71.3	90.9	100.0	98.0	70.9	59.4	57.9	61.2	86.6	71.6	49.5	14.4	3.6
2005–06	50.9	71.5	90.9	99.5	98.0	71.6	59.4	56.5	59.8	85.1	67.1	49.2	11.5	2.0
2007–08	49.5	70.7	91.0	100.0	98.6	71.6	57.4	57.5	60.2	87.8	66.0	49.0	13.0	1.4
2009–10	47.8	71.2	90.9	99.6	98.5	71.3	57.7	57.1	59.5	80.6	64.4	44.6	12.9	1.5
2011–12	45.3	71.6	90.8	99.6	98.5	70.5	57.8	55.6	58.6	79.5	64.0	42.7	8.0	1.3
2013–14	49.3	74.6	95.8	99.7	97.0	86.9	58.9	59.8	61.9	77.4	61.7	46.6	12.5	1.2
Percent of faculty with tenure at institutions with a tenure system														
All full-time faculty (instruction, research, and public service)														
1993–94	56.2	58.9	56.3	54.5	60.5	51.1	69.9	49.5	49.5	47.6	51.8	50.4	47.9	33.8
1999–2000	53.7	55.9	53.2	50.4	59.1	54.7	67.7	48.2	48.1	43.4	52.3	53.5	59.7	77.4
2003–04	50.4	53.0	50.2	48.9	52.9	51.2	65.2	44.6	44.6	40.1	48.7	51.9	47.7	69.2
2005–06	49.6	51.5	48.7	47.2	52.3	49.1	64.1	45.1	45.1	40.7	49.1	52.5	45.2	69.3
2007–08	48.8	50.5	47.8	46.1	51.9	49.1	63.6	44.7	44.7	40.1	49.8	52.7	41.3	51.3
2009–10	48.7	50.6	47.8	45.7	53.6	51.3	64.1	44.3	44.3	40.4	50.5	54.1	38.5	51.0
2011–12	48.5	50.7	48.0	45.8	54.3	53.4	64.7	43.7	43.7	39.7	50.7	54.3	31.4	31.0
2013–14	48.4	50.6	47.7	45.8	56.3	52.8	67.1	43.8	43.8	40.2	51.5	56.3	31.5	19.8
Full-time instructional faculty in 2013–14														
Total	50.9	53.1	50.4	48.9	56.5	53.8	67.1	46.3	46.3	43.5	51.6	56.3	30.5	19.8
Male	56.8	58.8	57.2	56.2	62.4	56.3	69.6	52.8	52.8	50.4	57.0	62.2	36.7	21.7
Female	43.3	45.9	41.2	38.4	49.7	51.2	65.0	37.6	37.6	33.5	45.2	49.3	26.4	18.3
Professor	90.9	92.2	92.1	91.0	98.0	91.4	92.9	88.4	88.4	86.5	91.8	96.2	79.2	61.3
Male	91.2	92.5	92.4	91.5	98.1	92.1	94.0	88.8	88.8	87.3	91.6	96.3	91.7	64.4
Female	90.0	91.3	91.2	89.5	97.8	90.2	92.0	87.4	87.4	84.2	92.2	96.1	66.7	55.9
Associate professor	77.3	80.9	81.0	78.8	90.5	85.7	79.3	70.4	70.4	64.9	78.3	87.6	42.2	22.9
Male	77.4	81.2	81.3	79.3	90.5	86.1	80.4	70.1	70.1	65.2	78.2	86.0	44.4	20.0
Female	77.0	80.4	80.6	78.0	90.5	85.2	78.4	70.7	70.7	64.6	78.4	89.6	41.7	25.0
Assistant professor	6.8	8.8	5.2	2.5	12.3	25.5	45.2	3.4	3.4	2.3	6.6	4.1	11.1	‡
Male	6.5	8.2	5.0	2.4	12.4	25.1	48.2	3.5	3.5	2.5	6.5	4.1	11.5	‡
Female	7.1	9.3	5.4	2.6	12.2	25.9	43.0	3.3	3.3	2.1	6.6	4.0	10.8	†
Instructor	28.4	34.5	2.1	1.0	1.9	12.4	61.6	0.6	0.5	0.4	0.5	1.8	9.1	66.7
Lecturer	1.6	2.1	1.4	0.8	3.9	3.8	21.8	0.3	0.3	0.1	2.4	†	†	†
No academic rank	31.7	40.3	20.4	1.9	1.8	64.3	68.3	9.6	9.5	1.2	27.9	43.5	37.1	11.7

†Not applicable.
‡Reporting standards not met (too few cases).
[1]Institutions that awarded 20 or more doctor's degrees during the previous academic year.
[2]Institutions that awarded 20 or more master's degrees, but less than 20 doctor's degrees, during the previous academic year.

NOTE: Degree-granting institutions grant associate's or higher degrees and participate in Title IV federal financial aid programs. Data include imputations for nonrespondent institutions. Some data have been revised from previously published figures.
SOURCE: U.S. Department of Education, National Center for Education Statistics, Integrated Postsecondary Education Data System (IPEDS), "Fall Staff Survey" (IPEDS-S:93-99); and IPEDS Winter 2003–04 through Winter 2011–12 and Spring 2014, Human Resources component, Fall Staff section. (This table was prepared February 2015.)

Table 317.10. Degree-granting postsecondary institutions, by control and level of institution: Selected years, 1949–50 through 2013–14

Year	All institutions			Public			Private			Nonprofit			For-profit		
	Total	4-year	2-year	Total	4-year	2-year	Total	4-year, total	2-year, total	Total	4-year	2-year	Total	4-year	2-year
1	2	3	4	5	6	7	8	9	10	11	12	13	14	15	16
Excluding branch campuses															
1949–50	1,851	1,327	524	641	344	297	1,210	983	227	—	—	—	—	—	—
1959–60	2,004	1,422	582	695	367	328	1,309	1,055	254	—	—	—	—	—	—
1969–70	2,525	1,639	886	1,060	426	634	1,465	1,213	252	—	—	—	—	—	—
1970–71	2,556	1,665	891	1,089	435	654	1,467	1,230	237	—	—	—	—	—	—
1971–72	2,606	1,675	931	1,137	440	697	1,469	1,235	234	—	—	—	—	—	—
1972–73	2,665	1,701	964	1,182	449	733	1,483	1,252	231	—	—	—	—	—	—
1973–74	2,720	1,717	1,003	1,200	440	760	1,520	1,277	243	—	—	—	—	—	—
1974–75	2,747	1,744	1,003	1,214	447	767	1,533	1,297	236	—	—	—	—	—	—
1975–76	2,765	1,767	998	1,219	447	772	1,546	1,320	226	—	—	—	—	—	—
1976–77	2,785	1,783	1,002	1,231	452	779	1,554	1,331	223	—	—	—	—	—	—
1977–78	2,826	1,808	1,018	1,241	454	787	1,585	1,354	231	—	—	—	—	—	—
1978–79	2,954	1,843	1,111	1,308	463	845	1,646	1,380	266	—	—	—	—	—	—
1979–80	2,975	1,863	1,112	1,310	464	846	1,665	1,399	266	—	—	—	—	—	—
1980–81	3,056	1,861	1,195	1,334	465	869	1,722	1,396	326 [1]	—	—	—	—	—	—
1981–82	3,083	1,883	1,200	1,340	471	869	1,743	1,412	331 [1]	—	—	—	—	—	—
1982–83	3,111	1,887	1,224	1,336	472	864	1,775	1,415	360 [1]	—	—	—	—	—	—
1983–84	3,117	1,914	1,203	1,325	474	851	1,792	1,440	352	—	—	—	—	—	—
1984–85	3,146	1,911	1,235	1,329	461	868	1,817	1,450	367	—	—	—	—	—	—
1985–86	3,155	1,915	1,240	1,326	461	865	1,829	1,454	375	—	—	—	—	—	—
Including branch campuses															
1974–75	3,004	1,866	1,138	1,433	537	896	1,571	1,329	242	—	—	—	—	—	—
1975–76	3,026	1,898	1,128	1,442	545	897	1,584	1,353	231	—	—	—	—	—	—
1976–77	3,046	1,913	1,133	1,455	550	905	1,591	1,363	228	1,536	1,348	188	55	15	40
1977–78	3,095	1,938	1,157	1,473	552	921	1,622	1,386	236	—	—	—	—	—	—
1978–79	3,134	1,941	1,193	1,474	550	924	1,660	1,391	269	1,564	1,376	188	96	15	81
1979–80	3,152	1,957	1,195	1,475	549	926	1,677	1,408	269	—	—	—	—	—	—
1980–81	3,231	1,957	1,274	1,497	552	945	1,734	1,405	329 [1]	1,569	1,387	182	165	18	147
1981–82	3,253	1,979	1,274	1,498	558	940	1,755	1,421	334 [1]	—	—	—	—	—	—
1982–83	3,280	1,984	1,296	1,493	560	933	1,787	1,424	363 [1]	—	—	—	—	—	—
1983–84	3,284	2,013	1,271	1,481	565	916	1,803	1,448	355	—	—	—	—	—	—
1984–85	3,331	2,025	1,306	1,501	566	935	1,830	1,459	371	1,616	1,430	186	214	29	185
1985–86	3,340	2,029	1,311	1,498	566	932	1,842	1,463	379	—	—	—	—	—	—
1986–87	3,406	2,070	1,336	1,533	573	960	1,873	1,497	376	1,635	1,462	173	238	35	203
1987–88	3,587	2,135	1,452	1,591	599	992	1,996	1,536	460	1,673	1,487	186	323	49	274
1988–89	3,565	2,129	1,436	1,582	598	984	1,983	1,531	452	1,658	1,478	180	325	53	272
1989–90	3,535	2,127	1,408	1,563	595	968	1,972	1,532	440	1,656	1,479	177	316	53	263
1990–91	3,559	2,141	1,418	1,567	595	972	1,992	1,546	446	1,649	1,482	167	343	64	279
1991–92	3,601	2,157	1,444	1,598	599	999	2,003	1,558	445	1,662	1,486	176	341	72	269
1992–93	3,638	2,169	1,469	1,624	600	1,024	2,014	1,569	445	1,672	1,493	179	342	76	266
1993–94	3,632	2,190	1,442	1,625	604	1,021	2,007	1,586	421	1,687	1,506	181	320	80	240
1994–95	3,688	2,215	1,473	1,641	605	1,036	2,047	1,610	437	1,702	1,510	192	345	100	245
1995–96	3,706	2,244	1,462	1,655	608	1,047	2,051	1,636	415	1,706	1,519	187	345	117	228
1996–97	4,009	2,267	1,742	1,702	614	1,088	2,307	1,653	654	1,693	1,509	184	614	144	470
1997–98	4,064	2,309	1,755	1,707	615	1,092	2,357	1,694	663	1,707	1,528	179	650	166	484
1998–99	4,048	2,335	1,713	1,681	612	1,069	2,367	1,723	644	1,695	1,531	164	672	192	480
1999–2000	4,084	2,363	1,721	1,682	614	1,068	2,402	1,749	653	1,681	1,531	150	721	218	503
2000–01	4,182	2,450	1,732	1,698	622	1,076	2,484	1,828	656	1,695	1,551	144	789	277	512
2001–02	4,197	2,487	1,710	1,713	628	1,085	2,484	1,859	625	1,676	1,541	135	808	318	490
2002–03	4,168	2,466	1,702	1,712	631	1,081	2,456	1,835	621	1,665	1,538	127	791	297	494
2003–04	4,236	2,530	1,706	1,720	634	1,086	2,516	1,896	620	1,664	1,546	118	852	350	502
2004–05	4,216	2,533	1,683	1,700	639	1,061	2,516	1,894	622	1,637	1,525	112	879	369	510
2005–06	4,276	2,582	1,694	1,693	640	1,053	2,583	1,942	641	1,647	1,534	113	936	408	528
2006–07	4,314	2,629	1,685	1,688	643	1,045	2,626	1,986	640	1,640	1,533	107	986	453	533
2007–08	4,352	2,675	1,677	1,685	653	1,032	2,667	2,022	645	1,624	1,532	92	1,043	490	553
2008–09	4,409	2,719	1,690	1,676	652	1,024	2,733	2,067	666	1,629	1,537	92	1,104	530	574
2009–10	4,495	2,774	1,721	1,672	672	1,000	2,823	2,102	721	1,624	1,539	85	1,199	563	636
2010–11	4,599	2,870	1,729	1,656	678	978	2,943	2,192	751	1,630	1,543	87	1,313	649	664
2011–12	4,706	2,968	1,738	1,649	682	967	3,057	2,286	771	1,653	1,553	100	1,404	733	671
2012–13	4,706	2,968	1,738	1,649	682	967	3,057	2,286	771	1,653	1,553	100	1,404	733	671
2013–14	4,724	3,039	1,685	1,625	691	934	3,099	2,348	751	1,675	1,587	88	1,424	761	663

—Not available.

[1]Large increases are due to the addition of schools accredited by the Accrediting Commission of Career Schools and Colleges of Technology.

NOTE: Data through 1995–96 are for institutions of higher education, while later data are for degree-granting institutions. Degree-granting institutions grant associate's or higher degrees and participate in Title IV federal financial aid programs. Changes in counts of institutions over time are partly affected by increasing or decreasing numbers of institutions submitting separate data for branch campuses.

SOURCE: U.S. Department of Education, National Center for Education Statistics, *Education Directory, Colleges and Universities*, 1949–50 through 1965–66; Higher Education General Information Survey (HEGIS), "Institutional Characteristics of Colleges and Universities" surveys, 1966–67 through 1985–86; Integrated Postsecondary Education Data System (IPEDS), "Institutional Characteristics Survey" (IPEDS-IC:86–99); and IPEDS Fall 2000 through Fall 2013, Institutional Characteristics component. (This table was prepared December 2014.)

Table 317.20. Degree-granting postsecondary institutions, by control and level of institution and state or jurisdiction: 2013–14

State or jurisdiction	Total	All public institutions	Public 4-year institutions							Public 2-year	All nonprofit institutions	Nonprofit 4-year institutions							Nonprofit 2-year	For-profit institutions		
			Total	Research university, very high[1]	Research university, high[2]	Doctoral/research university[3]	Master's[4]	Baccalaureate[5]	Special focus[6]			Total	Research university, very high[1]	Research university, high[2]	Doctoral/research university[3]	Master's[4]	Baccalaureate[5]	Special focus[6]		Total	4-year	2-year
1	2	3	4	5	6	7	8	9	10	11	12	13	14	15	16	17	18	19	20	21	22	23
United States	4,724	1,625	691	73	73	29	273	197	46	934	1,675	1,587	34	25	48	363	519	598	88	1,424	761	663
Alabama	77	39	14	2	3	0	8	1	0	25	20	19	0	0	0	2	12	5	1	18	11	7
Alaska	11	6	3	0	1	0	2	0	0	3	3	2	0	0	0	1	0	1	1	2	1	1
Arizona	91	28	8	1	1	0	4	0	1	20	13	13	0	0	0	2	3	8	0	50	34	16
Arkansas	52	33	11	1	0	1	6	2	1	22	14	12	0	1	0	1	9	2	2	5	4	1
California	469	149	35	8	1	0	21	3	2	114	146	140	3	1	10	25	23	78	6	174	88	86
Colorado	92	28	14	2	2	1	4	5	0	14	16	15	0	1	0	3	5	6	1	48	26	22
Connecticut	46	21	9	1	0	0	4	4	0	12	19	19	1	0	1	9	5	4	0	6	5	0
Delaware	12	5	2	1	0	0	1	0	0	3	5	4	0	2	1	0	1	2	1	2	2	1
District of Columbia	20	2	2	0	0	0	1	0	1	0	13	13	2	1	3	2	0	6	0	5	4	0
Florida	235	41	36	4	2	2	4	24	0	5	65	61	1	3	0	13	22	21	4	129	69	60
Georgia	136	57	27	3	0	2	9	12	1	30	35	33	1	0	1	4	19	8	2	44	25	19
Hawaii	22	10	4	1	0	0	0	3	0	6	7	7	0	0	0	2	2	3	0	5	3	2
Idaho	19	8	4	0	2	0	1	1	0	4	6	6	0	0	0	1	1	3	0	5	4	1
Illinois	185	60	12	2	2	1	7	0	0	48	83	80	2	2	4	17	18	37	3	42	25	17
Indiana	84	16	15	2	2	1	6	3	1	1	40	39	1	0	0	9	19	10	1	28	19	9
Iowa	66	19	3	2	0	0	1	0	0	16	34	34	0	0	0	6	18	10	0	13	11	2
Kansas	74	33	8	1	2	0	4	0	1	25	25	24	0	0	1	6	12	6	1	16	10	6
Kentucky	79	24	8	2	0	0	5	1	0	16	27	27	0	0	0	6	13	7	0	28	18	10
Louisiana	70	34	17	1	3	0	9	1	3	17	13	10	1	0	0	2	4	3	3	23	9	14
Maine	31	15	8	0	1	0	1	6	0	7	14	12	0	0	0	3	6	3	2	2	1	1
Maryland	62	29	13	1	1	2	7	1	1	16	22	22	1	0	0	6	6	9	0	11	6	5
Massachusetts	125	30	14	1	2	2	7	2	2	16	84	82	5	3	1	16	24	33	2	11	6	5
Michigan	117	46	16	3	2	2	7	2	0	30	51	51	0	0	3	11	23	16	0	20	13	7
Minnesota	118	43	12	1	0	0	8	3	1	31	35	34	0	0	0	6	12	13	1	40	34	6
Mississippi	42	24	9	2	3	0	1	6	0	15	9	9	0	0	0	3	4	2	2	9	2	7
Missouri	136	27	13	1	3	0	6	3	1	14	54	51	1	3	0	6	6	25	3	55	31	24
Montana	22	17	6	1	1	0	1	3	0	11	5	4	0	0	1	0	3	1	1	0	0	0
Nebraska	43	15	7	1	0	1	3	1	1	8	18	16	0	0	0	5	7	4	2	10	6	4
Nevada	26	7	6	0	2	0	0	4	0	1	3	3	0	0	0	1	0	2	0	16	8	8
New Hampshire	27	12	5	0	1	0	2	0	0	7	13	11	1	0	0	5	3	2	2	2	2	0
New Jersey	70	32	13	2	2	0	10	0	0	19	28	28	1	0	1	10	2	13	0	10	4	6
New Mexico	44	28	9	1	1	0	4	1	2	19	3	3	0	0	0	0	3	0	0	13	11	2
New York	304	79	43	4	1	1	21	12	4	36	178	165	6	7	5	39	27	81	13	47	22	25
North Carolina	151	75	16	2	1	3	7	2	1	59	50	49	0	0	0	7	27	13	1	26	17	9
North Dakota	21	14	9	1	1	0	1	4	2	5	6	6	0	0	0	1	1	4	0	0	0	0
Ohio	219	60	35	2	8	0	10	23	0	25	73	68	1	0	2	20	19	25	5	86	31	55
Oklahoma	66	30	17	1	1	0	8	5	2	13	14	14	0	0	1	4	6	3	0	22	11	11
Oregon	65	26	9	2	1	0	3	2	1	17	24	24	0	0	0	5	7	12	0	15	8	7
Pennsylvania	263	62	45	2	1	1	18	21	2	17	119	105	2	3	2	30	35	33	14	82	11	71
Rhode Island	13	3	2	0	1	0	1	0	0	1	10	10	1	0	0	1	1	3	0	0	0	0
South Carolina	78	33	13	1	1	1	5	4	1	20	23	22	0	0	0	5	14	3	1	22	12	10
South Dakota	25	12	7	0	1	0	4	1	2	5	8	7	0	0	0	0	5	2	1	5	5	0
Tennessee	113	22	9	1	1	1	4	0	0	13	50	47	1	1	2	11	16	17	3	41	22	19
Texas	275	107	44	3	6	7	16	4	8	63	65	58	1	2	2	17	14	22	7	103	44	59
Utah	41	8	7	1	1	0	2	3	0	1	11	10	0	1	0	2	3	4	1	22	17	5

See notes at end of table.

Table 317.20. Degree-granting postsecondary institutions, by control and level of institution and state or jurisdiction: 2013–14—Continued

State or jurisdiction	Total	All public institutions, Total	Public 4-year institutions, Total	Research university, very high[1]	Research university, high[2]	Doctoral/research university[3]	Master's[4]	Baccalaureate[5]	Special focus[6]	Public 2-year institutions	All nonprofit institutions, Total	Nonprofit 4-year institutions, Total	Research university, very high[1]	Research university, high[2]	Doctoral/research university[3]	Master's[4]	Baccalaureate[5]	Special focus[6]	Nonprofit 2-year	For-profit institutions, Total	For-profit 4-year	For-profit 2-year
1	2	3	4	5	6	7	8	9	10	11	12	13	14	15	16	17	18	19	20	21	22	23
Vermont	24	6	5	0	1	0	1	3	0	1	17	17	0	0	0	4	11	2	0	1	1	0
Virginia	130	40	16	3	3	0	7	2	1	24	40	38	0	0	1	7	19	11	2	50	29	21
Washington	86	43	18	2	0	0	6	8	2	25	24	23	0	0	0	10	5	8	1	19	11	8
West Virginia	44	23	13	0	1	0	3	8	1	10	9	9	0	0	0	0	7	2	0	12	3	9
Wisconsin	88	31	14	1	1	0	10	2	0	17	30	30	0	0	3	8	10	9	0	27	24	3
Wyoming	10	8	1	0	1	0	0	0	0	7	1	1	0	0	0	0	0	1	0	1	0	1
U.S. Service Academies	5	5	5	0	0	0	0	5	0	0	†	†	†	†	†	†	†	†	†	†	†	†
Other jurisdictions	**90**	**26**	**18**	**0**	**1**	**1**	**1**	**12**	**3**	**8**	**46**	**46**	**0**	**0**	**3**	**12**	**19**	**12**	**0**	**18**	**8**	**10**
American Samoa	1	1	1	0	0	0	0	1	0	0	0	0	0	0	0	0	0	0	0	0	0	0
Federated States of Micronesia	1	1	0	0	0	0	0	0	0	1	0	0	0	0	0	0	0	0	0	0	0	0
Guam	3	2	1	0	0	0	1	0	0	1	1	1	0	0	0	0	0	1	0	0	0	0
Marshall Islands	1	1	0	0	0	0	0	0	0	1	0	0	0	0	0	0	0	0	0	0	0	0
Northern Marianas	1	1	1	0	0	0	0	0	1	0	0	0	0	0	0	0	0	0	0	0	0	0
Palau	1	1	0	0	0	0	0	0	0	1	0	0	0	0	0	0	0	0	0	0	0	0
Puerto Rico	81	18	14	0	1	1	0	9	3	4	45	45	0	0	3	12	19	11	0	18	8	10
U.S. Virgin Islands	1	1	1	0	0	0	0	1	0	0	0	0	0	0	0	0	0	0	0	0	0	0

†Not applicable.
[1]Research universities with a very high level of research activity.
[2]Research universities with a high level of research activity.
[3]Institutions that award at least 20 doctor's degrees per year, but did not have a high level of research activity.
[4]Institutions that award at least 50 master's degrees per year.
[5]Institutions that primarily emphasize undergraduate education.
[6]Four-year institutions that award degrees primarily in single fields of study, such as medicine, business, fine arts, theology, and engineering. Includes some institutions that have 4-year programs, but have not reported sufficient data to identify pro-

gram category. Also includes institutions classified as 4-year under the IPEDS system, which had been classified as 2-year in the Carnegie classification system because they primarily award associate's degrees.
NOTE: Branch campuses are counted as separate institutions. Relative levels of research activity for research universities were determined by an analysis of research and development expenditures, science and engineering research staffing, and doctoral degrees conferred, by field. Further information on the research index ranking may be obtained from http://classifications.carnegiefoundation.org/. Degree-granting institutions grant associate's or higher degrees and participate in Title IV federal financial aid programs.
SOURCE: U.S. Department of Education, National Center for Education Statistics, Integrated Postsecondary Education Data System (IPEDS), Fall 2013, Institutional Characteristics component. (This table was prepared December 2014.)

Table 317.30. Number of non-degree-granting Title IV institutions offering postsecondary education, by control of institution and state or jurisdiction: Selected years, 2000–01 through 2013–14

State or jurisdiction	2000–01, total	2005–06, total	2010–11, total	2011–12 Total	Public	Private Total	Non-profit	For-profit	2012–13 Total	Public	Private Total	Non-profit	For-profit	2013–14 Total	Public	Private Total	Non-profit	For-profit
1	2	3	4	5	6	7	8	9	10	11	12	13	14	15	16	17	18	19
United States	2,297	2,187	2,422	2,528	362	2,166	177	1,989	2,527	358	2,169	168	2,001	2,512	355	2,157	159	1,998
Alabama	10	9	9	12	0	12	1	11	13	0	13	1	12	14	0	14	1	13
Alaska..............................	3	2	3	2	1	1	1	0	2	1	1	1	0	0	0	0	0	0
Arizona...........................	33	34	42	48	2	46	0	46	50	2	48	1	47	47	2	45	0	45
Arkansas..........................	36	32	32	36	2	34	2	32	34	2	32	2	30	33	2	31	2	29
California	230	235	248	262	14	248	22	226	265	12	253	24	229	258	14	244	22	222
Colorado	21	26	33	39	3	36	4	32	40	3	37	3	34	39	3	36	3	33
Connecticut.......................	37	36	59	56	11	45	3	42	50	11	39	3	36	48	11	37	3	34
Delaware...........................	4	6	8	8	0	8	1	7	8	0	8	1	7	8	0	8	1	7
District of Columbia	5	6	5	4	0	4	1	3	4	0	4	1	3	4	0	4	1	3
Florida..............................	124	126	150	153	43	110	4	106	152	42	110	4	106	155	43	112	3	109
Georgia	38	44	46	46	1	45	2	43	45	1	44	1	43	46	1	45	2	43
Hawaii	6	5	5	7	0	7	1	6	6	0	6	0	6	5	0	5	0	5
Idaho................................	11	13	17	19	1	18	0	18	23	1	22	0	22	23	1	22	0	22
Illinois..............................	88	94	108	117	2	115	10	105	116	3	113	10	103	119	2	117	8	109
Indiana	34	28	42	48	4	44	1	43	49	4	45	1	44	48	2	46	1	45
Iowa.................................	27	26	26	28	0	28	2	26	28	0	28	2	26	27	0	27	2	25
Kansas..............................	23	25	22	22	1	21	0	21	25	1	24	0	24	22	1	21	0	21
Kentucky...........................	52	32	30	32	0	32	2	30	32	0	32	2	30	33	0	33	2	31
Louisiana	57	57	47	51	0	51	2	49	52	0	52	2	50	51	0	51	3	48
Maine...............................	11	9	7	8	0	8	0	8	8	0	8	0	8	9	0	9	0	9
Maryland...........................	34	27	32	33	0	33	0	33	31	0	31	0	31	35	0	35	0	35
Massachusetts.....................	60	61	75	73	11	62	3	59	68	11	57	3	54	68	12	56	3	53
Michigan...........................	72	65	89	86	1	85	2	83	83	1	82	2	80	82	1	81	3	78
Minnesota..........................	20	21	26	26	0	26	2	24	27	0	27	2	25	27	0	27	2	25
Mississippi	16	20	20	20	0	20	0	20	20	0	20	0	20	20	0	20	0	20
Missouri............................	69	61	74	80	34	46	3	43	77	30	47	3	44	77	29	48	2	46
Montana............................	10	8	8	9	0	9	0	9	9	0	9	0	9	8	0	8	0	8
Nebraska...........................	12	10	7	7	0	7	1	6	7	0	7	1	6	7	0	7	1	6
Nevada	10	9	18	20	0	20	1	19	23	0	23	1	22	23	0	23	1	22
New Hampshire....................	11	14	14	15	0	15	1	14	15	0	15	1	14	15	0	15	1	14
New Jersey	89	91	87	90	5	85	8	77	94	5	89	8	81	95	5	90	7	83
New Mexico	6	7	7	8	0	8	0	8	8	0	8	0	8	8	0	8	0	8
New York...........................	152	133	151	156	33	123	32	91	155	33	122	30	92	152	33	119	26	93
North Carolina	36	29	42	43	1	42	2	40	44	1	43	2	41	45	1	44	3	41
North Dakota	5	5	8	8	0	8	0	8	8	0	8	0	8	9	0	9	0	9
Ohio.................................	130	119	138	139	53	86	8	78	140	53	87	6	81	138	51	87	6	81
Oklahoma..........................	84	78	83	82	47	35	0	35	78	47	31	0	31	79	49	30	0	30
Oregon..............................	28	27	26	30	0	30	3	27	29	0	29	3	26	30	0	30	3	27
Pennsylvania.......................	167	131	126	127	34	93	22	71	125	34	91	21	70	126	34	92	20	72
Rhode Island	12	10	11	11	0	11	2	9	11	0	11	2	9	11	0	11	2	9
South Carolina	14	21	27	33	1	32	1	31	33	1	32	1	31	33	1	32	1	31
South Dakota......................	5	6	6	6	0	6	3	3	6	0	6	3	3	6	0	6	3	3
Tennessee	54	58	66	72	26	46	1	45	72	26	46	1	45	72	26	46	1	45
Texas	161	169	170	174	0	174	4	170	175	0	175	4	171	174	0	174	4	170
Utah.................................	26	24	34	38	5	33	0	33	40	7	33	0	33	40	7	33	0	33
Vermont............................	3	4	4	4	1	3	0	3	3	0	3	0	3	3	0	3	0	3
Virginia.............................	56	42	33	36	7	29	5	24	40	8	32	4	28	40	6	34	3	31
Washington........................	42	37	37	37	1	36	3	33	38	1	37	3	34	35	1	34	4	30
West Virginia......................	36	31	33	32	17	15	5	10	33	17	16	5	11	34	17	17	5	12
Wisconsin..........................	24	22	30	34	0	34	6	28	32	0	32	3	29	30	0	30	4	26
Wyoming...........................	3	2	1	1	0	1	0	1	1	0	1	0	1	1	0	1	0	1
Other jurisdictions	74	74	68	70	2	68	11	57	72	2	70	13	57	71	2	69	12	57
American Samoa.................	0	0	0	0	0	0	0	0	0	0	0	0	0	0	0	0	0	0
Guam...............................	0	0	0	0	0	0	0	0	0	0	0	0	0	0	0	0	0	0
Northern Marianas	0	0	0	0	0	0	0	0	0	0	0	0	0	0	0	0	0	0
Palau................................	0	0	0	0	0	0	0	0	0	0	0	0	0	0	0	0	0	0
Puerto Rico........................	74	74	68	70	2	68	11	57	72	2	70	13	57	71	2	69	12	57
U.S. Virgin Islands	0	0	0	0	0	0	0	0	0	0	0	0	0	0	0	0	0	0

NOTE: Includes all institutions that participated in Title IV federal financial aid programs but did not grant degrees at the associate's or higher level.

SOURCE: U.S. Department of Education, National Center for Education Statistics, Integrated Postsecondary Education Data System (IPEDS), Fall 2000 through Fall 2013, Institutional Characteristics component. (This table was prepared December 2014.)

Table 317.40. Number of degree-granting postsecondary institutions and enrollment in these institutions, by enrollment size, control, and level of institution: Fall 2013

Control and level of institution	Number of institutions, by enrollment size of institution									
	Total	Under 200	200 to 499	500 to 999	1,000 to 2,499	2,500 to 4,999	5,000 to 9,999	10,000 to 19,999	20,000 to 29,999	30,000 or more
1	2	3	4	5	6	7	8	9	10	11
Total................................	4,716	613	813	643	927	635	501	354	144	86
Research university, very high[1]..............	107	0	0	0	1	0	9	21	35	41
Research university, high[2]	98	0	0	0	1	3	14	42	27	11
Doctoral/research university[3]...................	89	1	1	2	13	12	22	26	9	3
Master's[4].................................	690	0	15	23	140	208	181	89	21	13
Baccalaureate[5]...........................	850	25	87	187	364	130	29	16	5	7
Special-focus institutions[6]......................	1,198	367	376	225	158	52	11	7	2	0
2-year...................................	1,684	220	334	206	250	230	235	153	45	11
Public....................................	1,625	9	34	63	285	354	391	293	124	72
Research university, very high[1].............	73	0	0	0	0	0	2	5	28	38
Research university, high[2].....................	73	0	0	0	0	0	7	33	23	10
Doctoral/research university[3].................	29	0	0	0	1	1	4	16	7	0
Master's[4].................................	273	0	1	0	11	50	114	73	18	6
Baccalaureate[5]...........................	198	0	1	19	61	66	27	14	3	7
Special-focus institutions[6]...................	45	1	8	8	13	13	2	0	0	0
Art, music, or design	2	0	0	1	1	0	0	0	0	0
Business and management	1	0	0	0	0	0	1	0	0	0
Engineering or technology	2	0	0	0	0	2	0	0	0	0
Law....................................	5	1	2	1	1	0	0	0	0	0
Medical or other health	27	0	3	4	8	11	1	0	0	0
Tribal..................................	8	0	3	2	3	0	0	0	0	0
2-year...................................	934	8	24	36	199	224	235	152	45	11
Private nonprofit	1,675	284	253	247	476	244	98	51	15	7
Research university, very high[1].............	34	0	0	0	1	0	7	16	7	3
Research university, high[2].....................	25	0	0	0	1	3	7	9	4	1
Doctoral/research university[3]..................	48	1	1	0	7	11	17	9	2	0
Master's[4].................................	363	0	10	16	107	149	63	14	1	3
Baccalaureate[5]...........................	519	14	44	114	283	62	0	1	1	0
Special-focus institutions[6].....................	598	239	158	103	73	19	4	2	0	0
Art, music, or design	59	13	14	16	12	3	0	1	0	0
Business and management	42	11	12	9	5	3	2	0	0	0
Engineering or technology	13	6	2	2	2	0	0	1	0	0
Law....................................	22	1	6	8	7	0	0	0	0	0
Medical or other health	142	26	38	34	34	9	1	0	0	0
Theological...............................	298	176	80	27	11	3	1	0	0	0
Tribal..................................	5	0	0	5	0	0	0	0	0	0
Other special focus	17	6	6	2	2	1	0	0	0	0
2-year...................................	88	30	40	14	4	0	0	0	0	0
Private for-profit	1,416	320	526	333	166	37	12	10	5	7
Doctoral/research university[3]..............	12	0	0	2	5	0	1	1	0	3
Master's[4].................................	54	0	4	7	22	9	4	2	2	4
Baccalaureate[5]...........................	133	11	42	54	20	2	2	1	1	0
Special-focus institutions[6].....................	555	127	210	114	72	20	5	5	2	0
Art, music, or design	84	9	22	18	29	4	0	2	0	0
Business and management	235	66	76	43	29	13	4	2	2	0
Engineering or technology	151	24	88	34	2	2	1	0	0	0
Law....................................	9	1	1	4	3	0	0	0	0	0
Medical or other health	71	26	21	15	8	0	0	1	0	0
Other special focus	5	1	2	0	1	1	0	0	0	0
2-year...................................	662	182	270	156	47	6	0	1	0	0

See notes at end of table.

Table 317.40. Number of degree-granting postsecondary institutions and enrollment in these institutions, by enrollment size, control, and level of institution: Fall 2013—Continued

Control and level of institution	Enrollment, by enrollment size of institution									
	Total	Under 200	200 to 499	500 to 999	1,000 to 2,499	2,500 to 4,999	5,000 to 9,999	10,000 to 19,999	20,000 to 29,999	30,000 or more
1	12	13	14	15	16	17	18	19	20	21
Total	20,375,789	68,238	272,969	461,346	1,558,054	2,291,815	3,557,147	4,873,152	3,540,996	3,752,072
Research university, very high[1]	2,920,503	0	0	0	2,181	0	63,325	300,593	892,778	1,661,626
Research university, high[2]	1,789,499	0	0	0	2,204	12,167	107,003	617,433	668,066	382,626
Doctoral/research university[3]	1,062,436	113	322	1,466	22,635	44,771	156,959	328,822	210,281	297,067
Master's[4]	4,612,050	0	5,124	17,947	261,257	767,329	1,277,215	1,192,869	486,309	604,000
Baccalaureate[5]	2,070,316	3,485	32,686	138,779	595,971	445,265	199,106	236,836	138,034	280,154
Special-focus institutions[6]	952,246	40,967	123,924	158,145	242,830	176,357	73,814	89,173	47,036	0
2-year	6,968,739	23,673	110,913	145,009	430,976	845,926	1,679,725	2,107,426	1,098,492	526,599
Public	14,745,558	1,422	12,626	50,220	511,990	1,308,177	2,805,706	4,076,416	3,058,895	2,920,106
Research university, very high[1]	2,363,477	0	0	0	0	0	14,112	82,590	723,527	1,543,248
Research university, high[2]	1,478,612	0	0	0	0	0	56,893	495,272	574,944	351,503
Doctoral/research university[3]	416,284	0	0	0	2,229	3,463	30,693	214,761	165,138	0
Master's[4]	2,655,967	0	473	0	22,424	195,501	824,147	978,675	416,145	218,602
Baccalaureate[5]	1,115,474	0	495	15,365	104,702	239,863	185,384	208,862	80,649	280,154
Special-focus institutions[6]	90,603	142	2,758	6,328	23,186	43,437	14,752	0	0	0
Art, music, or design	3,176	0	0	912	2,264	0	0	0	0	0
Business and management	8,468	0	0	0	0	0	8,468	0	0	0
Engineering or technology	6,459	0	0	0	0	6,459	0	0	0	0
Law	2,640	142	719	691	1,088	0	0	0	0	0
Medical or other health	62,560	0	1,135	3,302	14,861	36,978	6,284	0	0	0
Tribal	7,300	0	904	1,423	4,973	0	0	0	0	0
2-year	6,625,141	1,280	8,900	28,527	359,449	825,913	1,679,725	2,096,256	1,098,492	526,599
Private nonprofit	3,974,004	30,529	83,688	182,318	796,755	857,039	669,139	677,470	363,597	313,469
Research university, very high[1]	557,026	0	0	0	2,181	0	49,213	218,003	169,251	118,378
Research university, high[2]	310,887	0	0	0	2,204	12,167	50,110	122,161	93,122	31,123
Doctoral/research university[3]	322,508	113	322	0	13,316	41,308	119,173	103,133	45,143	0
Master's[4]	1,566,964	0	3,318	13,238	202,577	539,327	424,760	191,387	28,389	163,968
Baccalaureate[5]	810,477	1,928	16,765	85,308	461,561	200,094	0	17,129	27,692	0
Special-focus institutions[6]	373,944	25,402	50,310	73,782	108,767	64,143	25,883	25,657	0	0
Art, music, or design	60,940	1,257	5,177	10,977	19,722	12,714	0	11,093	0	0
Business and management	40,351	1,316	4,016	6,247	6,790	9,401	12,581	0	0	0
Engineering or technology	21,015	663	837	1,578	3,373	0	0	14,564	0	0
Law	17,964	194	1,870	6,182	9,718	0	0	0	0	0
Medical or other health	127,582	3,165	12,683	25,278	49,701	30,207	6,548	0	0	0
Theological	93,379	18,347	23,987	18,656	16,628	9,007	6,754	0	0	0
Tribal	3,297	0	0	3,297	0	0	0	0	0	0
Other special focus	9,416	460	1,740	1,567	2,835	2,814	0	0	0	0
2-year	32,198	3,086	12,973	9,990	6,149	0	0	0	0	0
Private for-profit	1,656,227	36,287	176,655	228,808	249,309	126,599	82,302	119,266	118,504	518,497
Doctoral/research university[3]	323,644	0	0	1,466	7,090	0	7,093	10,928	0	297,067
Master's[4]	389,119	0	1,333	4,709	36,256	32,501	28,308	22,807	41,775	221,430
Baccalaureate[5]	144,365	1,557	15,426	38,106	29,708	5,308	13,722	10,845	29,693	0
Special-focus institutions[6]	487,699	15,423	70,856	78,035	110,877	68,777	33,179	63,516	47,036	0
Art, music, or design	108,199	978	7,891	12,211	46,129	14,083	0	26,907	0	0
Business and management	251,657	8,068	24,169	31,526	44,895	45,713	27,361	22,889	47,036	0
Engineering or technology	69,093	3,422	30,422	21,323	2,491	5,617	5,818	0	0	0
Law	7,152	84	431	2,859	3,778	0	0	0	0	0
Medical or other health	45,618	2,695	7,054	10,116	12,033	0	0	13,720	0	0
Other special focus	5,980	176	889	0	1,551	3,364	0	0	0	0
2-year	311,400	19,307	89,040	106,492	65,378	20,013	0	11,170	0	0

[1]Research universities with a very high level of research activity.

[2]Research universities with a high level of research activity.

[3]Institutions that award at least 20 doctor's degrees per year, but did not have a high level of research activity.

[4]Institutions that award at least 50 master's degrees per year.

[5]Institutions that primarily emphasize undergraduate education. Also includes institutions classified as 4-year under the IPEDS system, which had been classified as 2-year in the Carnegie system because they primarily award associate's degrees.

[6]Special-focus 4-year institutions award degrees primarily in single fields of study, such as medicine, business, fine arts, theology, and engineering.

NOTE: Degree-granting institutions grant associate's or higher degrees and participate in Title IV federal financial aid programs. Relative levels of research activity for research universities were determined by an analysis of research and development expenditures, science and engineering research staffing, and doctoral degrees conferred, by field. Further information on the research index ranking may be obtained from http://classifications.carnegiefoundation.org/resources/.
SOURCE: U.S. Department of Education, National Center for Education Statistics, Integrated Postsecondary Education Data System (IPEDS), Spring 2014, Enrollment component. (This table was prepared May 2015.)

Table 317.50. Degree-granting postsecondary institutions that have closed their doors, by control and level of institution: 1969–70 through 2013–14

Year	All institutions			Public			Private								
							Total			Nonprofit			For-profit		
	Total	4-year	2-year	Total	4-year	2-year	Total	4-year	2-year	Total	4-year	2-year	Total	4-year	2-year
1	2	3	4	5	6	7	8	9	10	11	12	13	14	15	16
1969–70	24	10	14	5	1	4	19	9	10	—	—	—	—	—	—
1970–71	35	10	25	11	0	11	24	10	14	—	—	—	—	—	—
1971–72	14	5	9	3	0	3	11	5	6	—	—	—	—	—	—
1972–73	21	12	9	4	0	4	17	12	5	—	—	—	—	—	—
1973–74	20	12	8	1	0	1	19	12	7	—	—	—	—	—	—
1974–75	18	13	5	4	0	4	14	13	1	—	—	—	—	—	—
1975–76	9	7	2	2	1	1	7	6	1	—	—	—	—	—	—
1976–77	9	6	3	0	0	0	9	6	3	—	—	—	—	—	—
1977–78	12	9	3	0	0	0	12	9	3	—	—	—	—	—	—
1978–79	9	4	5	0	0	0	9	4	5	—	—	—	—	—	—
1979–80	6	5	1	0	0	0	6	5	1	—	—	—	—	—	—
1980–81	4	3	1	0	0	0	4	3	1	—	—	—	—	—	—
1981–82	7	6	1	0	0	0	7	6	1	—	—	—	—	—	—
1982–83	7	4	3	0	0	0	7	4	3	—	—	—	—	—	—
1983–84	5	5	0	1	1	0	4	4	0	—	—	—	—	—	—
1984–85	4	4	0	0	0	0	4	4	0	—	—	—	—	—	—
1985–86	12	8	4	1	1	0	11	7	4	—	—	—	—	—	—
1986–87 and 1987–88	26	19	7	1	0	1	25	19	6	—	—	—	—	—	—
1988–89	14	6	8	0	0	0	14	6	8	—	—	—	—	—	—
1989–90	19	8	11	0	0	0	19	8	11	—	—	—	—	—	—
1990–91	18	6	12	0	0	0	18	6	12	0	0	0	0	0	0
1991–92	26	8	18	1	0	1	25	8	17	0	0	0	0	0	0
1992–93	23	6	17	0	0	0	23	6	17	0	0	0	0	0	0
1993–94	38	11	27	1	0	1	37	11	26	0	0	0	0	0	0
1994–95	15	8	7	2	0	2	13	8	5	0	0	0	0	0	0
1995–96	21	8	13	1	1	0	20	7	13	0	0	0	0	0	0
1996–97	36	13	23	2	0	2	34	13	21	0	0	0	0	0	0
1997–98	5	0	5	0	0	0	5	0	5	0	0	0	0	0	0
1998–99	7	1	6	1	0	1	6	1	5	0	0	0	0	0	0
1999–2000	16	3	13	3	0	3	13	3	10	0	0	0	0	0	0
2000–01	14	9	5	0	0	0	14	9	5	8	8	0	6	1	5
2001–02	14	2	12	0	0	0	14	2	12	1	1	0	13	1	12
2002–03	13	7	6	0	0	0	13	7	6	6	6	0	7	1	6
2003–04	12	5	7	0	0	0	12	5	7	8	5	3	4	0	4
2004–05	3	1	2	0	0	0	3	1	2	1	1	0	2	0	2
2005–06	11	6	5	1	1	0	10	5	5	5	4	1	5	1	4
2006–07	13	4	9	0	0	0	13	4	9	6	4	2	7	0	7
2007–08	26	10	16	0	0	0	26	10	16	9	6	3	17	4	13
2008–09	16	6	10	0	0	0	16	6	10	6	5	1	10	1	9
2009–10	17	11	6	0	0	0	17	11	6	9	9	0	8	2	6
2010–11	20	9	11	0	0	0	20	9	11	7	6	1	13	3	10
2011–12	10	5	5	4	0	4	6	5	1	2	2	0	4	3	1
2012–13	21	3	18	1	1	0	20	2	18	4	2	2	16	0	16
2013–14	20	8	12	1	1	0	19	7	12	4	3	1	15	4	11

—Not available.
NOTE: This table indicates the year by which the institution no longer operated (generally it closed at the end of or during the prior year). Data through 1995–96 are for institutions of higher education, while later data are for degree-granting institutions. Degree-granting institutions grant associate's or higher degrees and participate in Title IV federal financial aid programs. The degree-granting classification is very similar to the earlier higher education classification, but it includes more 2-year colleges and excludes a few higher education institutions that did not grant degrees.

SOURCE: U.S. Department of Education, National Center for Education Statistics, *Education Directory, Higher Education*, 1969–70 through 1974–75; *Education Directory, Colleges and Universities*, 1975–76 through 1985–86; *1982–83 Supplement to the Education Directory, Colleges and Universities*; Integrated Postsecondary Education Data System (IPEDS), "Institutional Characteristics Survey" (IPEDS-IC:86–99); and IPEDS Fall 2000 through Fall 2013, Institutional Characteristics component. (This table was prepared June 2015.)

Table 318.10. Degrees conferred by postsecondary institutions, by level of degree and sex of student: Selected years, 1869–70 through 2024–25

Year	Associate's degrees				Bachelor's degrees				Master's degrees				Doctor's degrees[1]			
	Total	Males	Females	Percent female	Total	Males	Females	Percent female	Total	Males	Females	Percent female	Total	Males	Females	Percent female
1	2	3	4	5	6	7	8	9	10	11	12	13	14	15	16	17
1869–70	—	—	—	—	9,371 [2]	7,993 [2]	1,378 [2]	14.7	0	0	0	—	1	1	0	0.0
1879–80	—	—	—	—	12,896 [2]	10,411 [2]	2,485 [2]	19.3	879	868	11	1.3	54	51	3	5.6
1889–90	—	—	—	—	15,539 [2]	12,857 [2]	2,682 [2]	17.3	1,015	821	194	19.1	149	147	2	1.3
1899–1900	—	—	—	—	27,410 [2]	22,173 [2]	5,237 [2]	19.1	1,583	1,280	303	19.1	382	359	23	6.0
1909–10	—	—	—	—	37,199 [2]	28,762 [2]	8,437 [2]	22.7	2,113	1,555	558	26.4	443	399	44	9.9
1919–20	—	—	—	—	48,622 [2]	31,980 [2]	16,642 [2]	34.2	4,279	2,985	1,294	30.2	615	522	93	15.1
1929–30	—	—	—	—	122,484 [2]	73,615 [2]	48,869 [2]	39.9	14,969	8,925	6,044	40.4	2,299	1,946	353	15.4
1939–40	—	—	—	—	186,500 [2]	109,546 [2]	76,954 [2]	41.3	26,731	16,508	10,223	38.2	3,290	2,861	429	13.0
1949–50	—	—	—	—	432,058 [2]	328,841 [2]	103,217 [2]	23.9	58,183	41,220	16,963	29.2	6,420	5,804	616	9.6
1959–60	—	—	—	—	392,440 [2]	254,063 [2]	138,377 [2]	35.3	74,435	50,898	23,537	31.6	9,829	8,801	1,028	10.5
1969–70	206,023	117,432	88,591	43.0	792,316	451,097	341,219	43.1	213,589	130,799	82,790	38.8	59,486	53,792	5,694	9.6
1970–71	252,311	144,144	108,167	42.9	839,730	475,594	364,136	43.4	235,564	143,083	92,481	39.3	64,998	58,137	6,861	10.6
1971–72	292,014	166,227	125,787	43.1	887,273	500,590	386,683	43.6	257,201	155,010	102,191	39.7	71,206	63,353	7,853	11.0
1972–73	316,174	175,413	140,761	44.5	922,362	518,191	404,171	43.8	268,654	159,569	109,085	40.6	79,512	69,959	9,553	12.0
1973–74	343,924	188,591	155,333	45.2	945,776	527,313	418,463	44.2	282,074	162,606	119,468	42.4	82,591	71,131	11,460	13.9
1974–75	360,171	191,017	169,154	47.0	922,933	504,841	418,092	45.3	297,545	166,318	131,227	44.1	84,904	71,025	13,879	16.3
1975–76	391,454	209,996	181,458	46.4	925,746	504,925	420,821	45.5	317,477	172,519	144,958	45.7	91,007	73,888	17,119	18.8
1976–77	406,377	210,842	195,535	48.1	919,549	495,545	424,004	46.1	323,025	173,090	149,935	46.4	91,730	72,209	19,521	21.3
1977–78	412,246	204,718	207,528	50.3	921,204	487,347	433,857	47.1	317,987	166,857	151,130	47.5	92,345	70,283	22,062	23.9
1978–79	402,702	192,091	210,611	52.3	921,390	477,344	444,046	48.2	307,686	159,111	148,575	48.3	94,971	70,452	24,519	25.8
1979–80	400,910	183,737	217,173	54.2	929,417	473,611	455,806	49.0	305,196	156,882	148,314	48.6	95,631	69,526	26,105	27.3
1980–81	416,377	188,638	227,739	54.7	935,140	469,883	465,257	49.8	302,637	152,979	149,658	49.5	98,016	69,567	28,449	29.0
1981–82	434,526	196,944	237,582	54.7	952,998	473,364	479,634	50.3	302,447	151,349	151,098	50.0	97,838	68,630	29,208	29.9
1982–83	449,620	203,991	245,629	54.6	969,510	479,140	490,370	50.6	296,415	150,092	146,323	49.4	99,335	67,757	31,578	31.8
1983–84	452,240	202,704	249,536	55.2	974,309	482,319	491,990	50.5	291,141	149,268	141,873	48.7	100,799	67,769	33,030	32.8
1984–85	454,712	202,932	251,780	55.4	979,477	482,528	496,949	50.7	293,472	149,276	144,196	49.1	100,785	66,269	34,516	34.2
1985–86	446,047	196,166	249,881	56.0	987,823	485,923	501,900	50.8	295,850	149,373	146,477	49.5	100,280	65,215	35,065	35.0
1986–87	436,304	190,839	245,465	56.3	991,264	480,782	510,482	51.5	296,530	147,063	149,467	50.4	98,477	62,790	35,687	36.2
1987–88	435,085	190,047	245,038	56.3	994,829	477,203	517,626	52.0	305,783	150,243	155,540	50.9	99,139	63,019	36,120	36.4
1988–89	436,764	186,316	250,448	57.3	1,018,755	483,346	535,409	52.6	316,626	153,993	162,633	51.4	100,571	63,055	37,516	37.3
1989–90	455,102	191,195	263,907	58.0	1,051,344	491,696	559,648	53.2	330,152	158,052	172,100	52.1	103,508	63,963	39,545	38.2
1990–91	481,720	198,634	283,086	58.8	1,094,538	504,045	590,493	53.9	342,863	160,842	182,021	53.1	105,547	64,242	41,305	39.1
1991–92	504,231	207,481	296,750	58.9	1,136,553	520,811	615,742	54.2	358,089	165,867	192,222	53.7	109,554	66,603	42,951	39.2
1992–93	514,756	211,964	302,792	58.8	1,165,178	532,881	632,297	54.3	375,032	173,354	201,678	53.8	112,072	67,130	44,942	40.1
1993–94	530,632	215,261	315,371	59.4	1,169,275	532,422	636,853	54.5	393,037	180,571	212,466	54.1	112,636	66,773	45,863	40.7
1994–95	539,691	218,352	321,339	59.5	1,160,134	526,131	634,003	54.6	403,609	183,043	220,566	54.6	114,266	67,324	46,942	41.1
1995–96	555,216	219,514	335,702	60.5	1,164,792	522,454	642,338	55.1	412,180	183,481	228,699	55.5	115,507	67,189	48,318	41.8
1996–97	571,226	223,948	347,278	60.8	1,172,879	520,515	652,364	55.6	425,260	185,270	239,990	56.4	118,747	68,387	50,360	42.4
1997–98	558,555	217,613	340,942	61.0	1,184,406	519,956	664,450	56.1	436,037	188,718	247,319	56.7	118,735	67,232	51,503	43.4
1998–99	564,984	220,508	344,476	61.0	1,202,239	519,961	682,278	56.8	446,038	190,230	255,808	57.4	116,700	65,340	51,360	44.0
1999–2000	564,933	224,721	340,212	60.2	1,237,875	530,367	707,508	57.2	463,185	196,129	267,056	57.7	118,736	64,930	53,806	45.3
2000–01	578,865	231,645	347,220	60.0	1,244,171	531,840	712,331	57.3	473,502	197,770	275,732	58.2	119,585	64,171	55,414	46.3
2001–02	595,133	238,109	357,024	60.0	1,291,900	549,816	742,084	57.4	487,313	202,604	284,709	58.4	119,663	62,731	56,932	47.6
2002–03	634,016	253,451	380,565	60.0	1,348,811	573,258	775,553	57.5	518,699	215,172	303,527	58.5	121,579	62,730	58,849	48.4
2003–04	665,301	260,033	405,268	60.9	1,399,542	595,425	804,117	57.5	564,272	233,056	331,216	58.7	126,087	63,981	62,106	49.3
2004–05	696,660	267,536	429,124	61.6	1,439,264	613,000	826,264	57.4	580,151	237,155	342,996	59.1	134,387	67,257	67,130	50.0
2005–06	713,066	270,095	442,971	62.1	1,485,242	630,600	854,642	57.5	599,731	241,656	358,075	59.7	138,056	68,912	69,144	50.1
2006–07	728,114	275,187	452,927	62.2	1,524,092	649,570	874,522	57.4	610,597	242,189	368,408	60.3	144,690	71,308	73,382	50.7
2007–08	750,164	282,521	467,643	62.3	1,563,069	667,928	895,141	57.3	630,666	250,169	380,497	60.3	149,378	73,453	75,925	50.8
2008–09	787,243	298,066	489,177	62.1	1,601,399	685,422	915,977	57.2	662,082	263,515	398,567	60.2	154,564	75,674	78,890	51.0
2009–10	848,856	322,747	526,109	62.0	1,649,919	706,660	943,259	57.2	693,313	275,317	417,996	60.3	158,590	76,610	81,980	51.7
2010–11	943,506	361,408	582,098	61.7	1,716,053	734,159	981,894	57.2	730,922	291,680	439,242	60.1	163,827	79,672	84,155	51.4
2011–12	1,021,718	393,479	628,239	61.5	1,792,163	765,772	1,026,391	57.3	755,967	302,484	453,483	60.0	170,217	82,670	87,547	51.4
2012–13	1,006,961	388,846	618,115	61.4	1,840,164	787,231	1,052,933	57.2	751,751	301,575	450,176	59.9	175,038	85,104	89,934	51.4
2013–14[3]	964,000	379,000	585,000	60.7	1,859,000	794,000	1,065,000	57.3	760,000	305,000	455,000	59.9	178,000	86,000	91,000	51.1
2014–15[3]	949,000	375,000	574,000	60.5	1,852,000	789,000	1,063,000	57.4	778,000	318,000	459,000	59.0	178,000	86,000	91,000	51.1
2015–16[3]	952,000	375,000	577,000	60.6	1,847,000	788,000	1,059,000	57.3	802,000	335,000	467,000	58.2	179,000	87,000	92,000	51.4
2016–17[3]	973,000	380,000	593,000	60.9	1,845,000	775,000	1,069,000	57.9	824,000	344,000	480,000	58.3	182,000	89,000	93,000	51.1
2017–18[3]	991,000	385,000	606,000	61.2	1,847,000	779,000	1,069,000	57.9	851,000	354,000	496,000	58.3	187,000	93,000	94,000	50.3
2018–19[3]	1,016,000	391,000	625,000	61.5	1,871,000	785,000	1,086,000	58.0	877,000	365,000	511,000	58.3	190,000	94,000	96,000	50.5
2019–20[3]	1,041,000	398,000	644,000	61.9	1,903,000	795,000	1,108,000	58.2	899,000	374,000	525,000	58.4	194,000	96,000	98,000	50.5
2020–21[3]	1,062,000	403,000	659,000	62.1	1,933,000	805,000	1,128,000	58.4	920,000	382,000	539,000	58.6	198,000	98,000	100,000	50.5
2021–22[3]	1,082,000	409,000	673,000	62.2	1,956,000	814,000	1,142,000	58.4	943,000	389,000	554,000	58.7	201,000	99,000	102,000	50.7
2022–23[3]	1,103,000	415,000	688,000	62.4	1,977,000	821,000	1,156,000	58.5	969,000	398,000	571,000	58.9	203,000	100,000	103,000	50.7
2023–24[3]	1,126,000	421,000	706,000	62.7	2,004,000	830,000	1,173,000	58.5	996,000	408,000	588,000	59.0	206,000	101,000	105,000	51.0
2024–25[3]	1,150,000	427,000	723,000	62.9	2,029,000	840,000	1,190,000	58.6	1,019,000	416,000	603,000	59.2	209,000	102,000	107,000	51.2

—Not available.

[1]Includes Ph.D., Ed.D., and comparable degrees at the doctoral level. Includes most degrees formerly classified as first-professional, such as M.D., D.D.S., and law degrees.

[2]Includes some degrees classified as master's or doctor's degrees in later years.

[3]Projected.

NOTE: Data through 1994–95 are for institutions of higher education, while later data are for degree-granting institutions. Degree-granting institutions grant associate's or higher degrees and participate in Title IV federal financial aid programs. Some data have been revised from previously published figures. Detail may not sum to totals because of rounding.

SOURCE: U.S. Department of Education, National Center for Education Statistics, *Earned Degrees Conferred*, 1869–70 through 1964–65; Higher Education General Information Survey (HEGIS), "Degrees and Other Formal Awards Conferred" surveys, 1965–66 through 1985–86; Integrated Postsecondary Education Data System (IPEDS), "Completions Survey" (IPEDS-C:87–99); IPEDS Fall 2000 through Fall 2013, Completions component; and Degrees Conferred Projection Model, 1980–81 through 2024–25. (This table was prepared April 2015.)

Table 318.20. Bachelor's, master's, and doctor's degrees conferred by postsecondary institutions, by field of study: Selected years, 1970–71 through 2012–13

Degree and year	Number of degrees conferred								Percentage distribution of degrees conferred							
	Total degrees	Humanities[1]	Social and behavioral sciences[2]	Natural sciences and mathematics[3]	Computer sciences and engineering[4]	Education	Business	Other fields[5]	Total degrees	Humanities[1]	Social and behavioral sciences[2]	Natural sciences and mathematics[3]	Computer sciences and engineering[4]	Education	Business	Other fields[5]
1	2	3	4	5	6	7	8	9	10	11	12	13	14	15	16	17
Bachelor's degrees																
1970–71	839,730	143,549	193,511	81,916	52,570	176,307	115,396	76,481	100.0	17.1	23.0	9.8	6.3	21.0	13.7	9.1
1975–76	925,746	150,736	176,674	91,596	52,328	154,437	143,171	156,804	100.0	16.3	19.1	9.9	5.7	16.7	15.5	16.9
1980–81	935,140	134,139	141,581	78,092	90,476	108,074	200,521	182,257	100.0	14.3	15.1	8.4	9.7	11.6	21.4	19.5
1985–86	987,823	132,891	134,468	76,228	139,459	87,147	236,700	180,930	100.0	13.5	13.6	7.7	14.1	8.8	24.0	18.3
1990–91	1,094,538	172,485	183,762	70,209	104,910	110,807	249,165	203,200	100.0	15.8	16.8	6.4	9.6	10.1	22.8	18.6
1995–96	1,164,792	193,404	199,895	93,443	102,503	105,384	226,623	243,540	100.0	16.6	17.2	8.0	8.8	9.0	19.5	20.9
2000–01	1,244,171	214,107	201,681	89,772	117,011	105,458	263,515	252,627	100.0	17.2	16.2	7.2	9.4	8.5	21.2	20.3
2005–06	1,485,242	261,696	249,619	105,899	128,886	107,238	318,042	313,862	100.0	17.6	16.8	7.1	8.7	7.2	21.4	21.1
2008–09	1,601,399	278,408	262,790	121,026	122,396	101,026	348,056	367,007	100.0	17.4	16.4	7.6	7.6	6.4	21.7	22.9
2009–10	1,649,919	281,056	269,997	125,801	128,328	101,287	358,119	385,331	100.0	17.0	16.4	7.6	7.8	6.1	21.7	23.4
2010–11	1,716,053	288,446	278,075	131,871	136,163	104,008	365,133	412,357	100.0	16.8	16.2	7.7	7.9	6.1	21.3	24.0
2011–12	1,792,163	295,182	287,633	141,355	146,060	105,656	367,235	449,042	100.0	16.5	16.0	7.9	8.1	5.9	20.5	25.1
2012–13	1,840,164	297,337	292,228	148,822	153,946	104,647	360,823	482,361	100.0	16.2	15.9	8.1	8.4	5.7	19.6	26.2
Master's degrees																
1970–71	235,564	34,510	22,256	17,152	18,535	87,666	26,490	28,955	100.0	14.6	9.4	7.3	7.9	37.2	11.2	12.3
1975–76	317,477	37,079	26,120	15,742	19,403	126,061	42,592	50,480	100.0	11.7	8.2	5.0	6.1	39.7	13.4	15.9
1980–81	302,637	35,130	22,168	13,579	21,434	96,713	57,888	55,725	100.0	11.6	7.3	4.5	7.1	32.0	19.1	18.4
1985–86	295,850	34,834	20,409	14,055	30,216	74,816	66,676	54,844	100.0	11.8	6.9	4.8	10.2	25.3	22.5	18.5
1990–91	342,863	35,984	23,582	13,664	34,774	87,352	78,255	69,252	100.0	10.5	6.9	4.0	10.1	25.5	22.8	20.2
1995–96	412,180	40,795	30,164	16,154	39,422	104,936	93,554	87,155	100.0	9.9	7.3	3.9	9.6	25.5	22.7	21.1
2000–01	473,502	40,625	30,330	15,360	44,098	127,829	115,602	99,658	100.0	8.6	6.4	3.2	9.3	27.0	24.4	21.0
2005–06	599,731	49,584	37,139	19,574	50,444	174,620	146,406	121,964	100.0	8.3	6.2	3.3	8.4	29.1	24.4	20.3
2008–09	662,082	53,215	42,656	21,091	55,915	178,538	168,404	142,263	100.0	8.0	6.4	3.2	8.4	27.0	25.4	21.5
2009–10	693,313	54,957	43,997	22,435	57,346	182,165	177,748	154,665	100.0	7.9	6.3	3.2	8.3	26.3	25.6	22.3
2010–11	730,922	57,160	46,147	23,576	62,695	185,127	187,178	169,039	100.0	7.8	6.3	3.2	8.6	25.3	25.6	23.1
2011–12	755,967	59,901	48,943	25,576	66,041	179,047	191,606	184,853	100.0	7.9	6.5	3.4	8.7	23.7	25.3	24.5
2012–13	751,751	60,660	49,431	27,303	68,102	164,624	188,625	193,006	100.0	8.1	6.6	3.6	9.1	21.9	25.1	25.7
Doctor's degrees[6]																
1970–71	64,998	4,402	5,804	9,126	3,816	6,041	774	35,035	100.0	6.8	8.9	14.0	5.9	9.3	1.2	53.9
1975–76	91,007	5,461	7,314	7,591	3,118	7,202	906	59,415	100.0	6.0	8.0	8.3	3.4	7.9	1.0	65.3
1980–81	98,016	4,827	6,698	7,473	2,860	7,279	808	68,071	100.0	4.9	6.8	7.6	2.9	7.4	0.8	69.4
1985–86	100,280	4,648	6,548	7,668	3,800	6,610	923	70,083	100.0	4.6	6.5	7.6	3.8	6.6	0.9	69.9
1990–91	105,547	4,858	6,944	9,378	6,006	6,189	1,185	70,987	100.0	4.6	6.6	8.9	5.7	5.9	1.1	67.3
1995–96	115,507	6,356	7,901	10,997	7,223	6,246	1,366	75,418	100.0	5.5	6.8	9.5	6.3	5.4	1.2	65.3
2000–01	119,585	6,466	9,021	10,190	6,315	6,284	1,180	80,129	100.0	5.4	7.5	8.5	5.3	5.3	1.0	67.0
2005–06	138,056	6,628	8,835	12,097	8,734	7,584	1,711	92,467	100.0	4.8	6.4	8.8	6.3	5.5	1.2	67.0
2008–09	154,564	7,261	9,711	14,271	9,383	9,028	2,123	102,787	100.0	4.7	6.3	9.2	6.1	5.8	1.4	66.5
2009–10	158,590	7,742	9,778	14,333	9,372	9,237	2,249	105,879	100.0	4.9	6.2	9.0	5.9	5.8	1.4	66.8
2010–11	163,827	8,359	10,241	14,574	10,013	9,642	2,286	108,712	100.0	5.1	6.3	8.9	6.1	5.9	1.4	66.4
2011–12	170,217	8,732	10,533	14,974	10,554	10,118	2,538	112,768	100.0	5.1	6.2	8.8	6.2	5.9	1.5	66.2
2012–13	175,038	8,581	10,942	15,280	11,293	10,572	2,836	115,534	100.0	4.9	6.3	8.7	6.5	6.0	1.6	66.0

[1]Includes degrees in Area, ethnic, cultural, gender, and group studies; English language and literature/letters; Foreign languages, literatures, and linguistics; Liberal arts and sciences, general studies, and humanities; Multi/interdisciplinary studies; Philosophy and religious studies; Theology and religious vocations; and Visual and performing arts.
[2]Includes Psychology; Social sciences; and History.
[3]Includes Biological and biomedical sciences; Mathematics and statistics; and Physical sciences and science technologies.
[4]Includes Computer and information sciences; Engineering; and Engineering technologies.
[5]Includes Agriculture and natural resources; Architecture and related services; Communication, journalism, and related programs; Communications technologies; Family and consumer sciences/human sciences; Health professions and related programs; Homeland security, law enforcement, and firefighting; Legal professions and studies; Library science; Military technologies and applied sciences; Parks, recreation, leisure, and fitness studies; Precision production; Public administration and social services; Transportation and materials moving; and Not classified by field of study.
[6]Includes Ph.D., Ed.D., and comparable degrees at the doctoral level. Includes most degrees formerly classified as first-professional, such as M.D., D.D.S., and law degrees.

NOTE: Data are for postsecondary institutions participating in Title IV federal financial aid programs. The new Classification of Instructional Programs was initiated in 2009–10. The figures for earlier years have been reclassified when necessary to make them conform to the new taxonomy. To facilitate trend comparisons, certain aggregations have been made of the degree fields as reported in the Integrated Postsecondary Education Data System (IPEDS): "Agriculture and natural resources" includes Agriculture, agriculture operations, and related sciences and Natural resources and conservation; "Business" includes Business, management, marketing, and related support services and Personal and culinary services; and "Engineering technologies" includes Engineering technologies and engineering-related fields, Construction trades, and Mechanic and repair technologies/technicians. Detail may not sum to totals because of rounding. Some data have been revised from previously published figures.
SOURCE: U.S. Department of Education, National Center for Education Statistics, Higher Education General Information Survey (HEGIS), "Degrees and Other Formal Awards Conferred" surveys, 1970–71 through 1985–86; Integrated Postsecondary Education Data System (IPEDS), "Completions Survey" (IPEDS-C:91–96); and IPEDS Fall 2001 through Fall 2013, Completions component. (This table was prepared August 2014.)

Table 318.30. Bachelor's, master's, and doctor's degrees conferred by postsecondary institutions, by sex of student and discipline division: 2012–13

Discipline division	Bachelor's degrees			Master's degrees			Doctor's degrees[1]		
	Total	Males	Females	Total	Males	Females	Total	Males	Females
1	2	3	4	5	6	7	8	9	10
All fields, total..................	1,840,164	787,231	1,052,933	751,751	301,575	450,176	175,038	85,104	89,934
Agriculture and natural resources..................	33,593	16,618	16,975	6,339	2,917	3,422	1,411	767	644
Agriculture, agriculture operations, and related sciences	17,083	8,144	8,939	2,595	1,199	1,396	817	443	374
Agriculture, general..................	1,736	959	777	287	108	179	22	9	13
Agricultural business and management, general..................	1,047	674	373	67	38	29	0	0	0
Agribusiness/agricultural business operations..................	1,402	942	460	33	17	16	0	0	0
Agricultural economics..................	1,535	1,103	432	411	227	184	151	95	56
Farm/farm and ranch management	114	85	29	8	6	2	0	0	0
Agricultural/farm supplies retailing and wholesaling..................	92	47	45	0	0	0	0	0	0
Agricultural business technology..................	11	4	7	0	0	0	0	0	0
Agricultural business and management, other	35	20	15	4	2	2	0	0	0
Agricultural mechanization, general..................	334	321	13	0	0	0	0	0	0
Agricultural production operations, general..................	76	50	26	20	7	13	0	0	0
Animal/livestock husbandry and production	182	60	122	0	0	0	0	0	0
Aquaculture	49	36	13	32	21	11	14	8	6
Crop production	30	25	5	8	2	6	1	1	0
Horse husbandry/equine science and management	77	3	74	3	0	3	0	0	0
Agroecology and sustainable agriculture..................	48	19	29	11	6	5	2	0	2
Viticulture and enology	107	63	44	12	7	5	0	0	0
Agricultural and food products processing..................	89	36	53	7	4	3	6	2	4
Equestrian/equine studies	333	12	321	0	0	0	0	0	0
Agricultural and domestic animal services, other	0	0	0	0	0	0	0	0	0
Applied horticulture/horticultural operations, general	165	95	70	21	13	8	8	4	4
Ornamental horticulture..................	67	41	26	12	3	9	1	0	1
Landscaping and groundskeeping..................	193	133	60	4	1	3	0	0	0
Plant nursery operations and management..................	5	2	3	0	0	0	0	0	0
Turf and turfgrass management..................	122	118	4	11	10	1	0	0	0
Floriculture/floristry operations and management	6	3	3	0	0	0	0	0	0
Applied horticulture/horticultural business services, other	12	10	2	0	0	0	0	0	0
International agriculture..................	47	17	30	26	10	16	3	0	3
Agricultural and extension education services	47	23	24	55	20	35	3	0	3
Agricultural communication/journalism	333	75	258	17	3	14	0	0	0
Agricultural public services, other..................	94	46	48	0	0	0	0	0	0
Animal sciences, general..................	4,830	1,074	3,756	389	153	236	146	70	76
Agricultural animal breeding	0	0	0	0	0	0	5	4	1
Animal health..................	0	0	0	5	2	3	0	0	0
Animal nutrition	0	0	0	0	0	0	3	3	0
Dairy science	133	60	73	7	2	5	3	1	2
Livestock management..................	16	8	8	1	1	0	3	3	0
Poultry science	138	69	69	18	11	7	15	9	6
Animal sciences, other..................	74	14	60	7	4	3	0	0	0
Food science	1,289	364	925	385	122	263	137	50	87
Food technology and processing..................	5	2	3	11	3	8	1	0	1
Food science and technology, other	3	2	1	31	12	19	4	2	2
Plant sciences, general..................	430	304	126	86	53	33	31	11	20
Agronomy and crop science	552	443	109	203	126	77	87	62	25
Horticultural science	599	355	244	102	43	59	35	25	10
Agricultural and horticultural plant breeding	2	2	0	25	18	7	19	12	7
Plant protection and integrated pest management..................	33	22	11	18	12	6	5	3	2
Range science and management..................	138	87	51	43	24	19	2	1	1
Plant sciences, other..................	41	30	11	50	20	30	28	24	4
Soil science and agronomy, general..................	115	80	35	123	68	55	72	36	36
Soil chemistry and physics	21	13	8	6	1	5	0	0	0
Soil sciences, other..................	36	22	14	11	6	5	3	2	1
Agriculture, agriculture operations, and related sciences, other	240	171	69	25	13	12	10	6	4
Natural resources and conservation..................	16,510	8,474	8,036	3,744	1,718	2,026	594	324	270
Natural resources/conservation, general..................	1,395	773	622	604	252	352	76	40	36
Environmental studies	5,972	2,654	3,318	790	325	465	74	30	44
Environmental science..................	5,187	2,554	2,633	1,078	479	599	160	84	76
Natural resources conservation and research, other..................	27	16	11	39	18	21	6	2	4
Natural resources management and policy	528	303	225	460	217	243	28	16	12
Natural resource economics..................	48	29	19	8	3	5	12	9	3
Water, wetlands, and marine resources management	104	57	47	98	49	49	0	0	0
Land use planning and management/development	47	27	20	39	24	15	6	1	5
Natural resource recreation and tourism	62	46	16	6	1	5	0	0	0
Natural resources law enforcement and protective services	28	24	4	0	0	0	0	0	0
Natural resources management and policy, other..................	192	115	77	29	15	14	2	2	0
Fishing and fisheries sciences and management..................	264	161	103	50	22	28	17	10	7
Forestry, general..................	546	422	124	136	86	50	53	35	18
Forest sciences and biology	175	139	36	129	67	62	78	41	37
Forest management/forest resources management	182	157	25	45	27	18	5	5	0
Urban forestry..................	14	6	8	9	6	3	2	1	1
Wood science and wood products/pulp and paper technology	58	49	9	24	16	8	4	3	1
Forest resources production and management	2	2	0	21	13	8	8	7	1
Forest technology/technician	10	6	4	0	0	0	10	7	3
Forestry, other..................	48	38	10	14	10	4	2	1	1
Wildlife, fish, and wildlands science and management..................	1,386	772	614	151	83	68	45	27	18
Natural resources and conservation, other..................	235	124	111	14	5	9	6	3	3
Architecture and related services..................	9,757	5,581	4,176	8,095	4,261	3,834	247	134	113
Architecture	6,165	3,617	2,548	4,307	2,491	1,816	116	64	52
City/urban, community and regional planning	840	531	309	2,270	1,101	1,169	94	52	42
Environmental design/architecture	748	428	320	127	53	74	26	11	15
Interior architecture..................	510	49	461	168	26	142	0	0	0
Landscape architecture	982	641	341	782	333	449	2	0	2
Architectural history and criticism, general..................	83	36	47	28	6	22	0	0	0
Architectural technology/technician	204	143	61	0	0	0	0	0	0
Architectural and building sciences/technology	48	38	10	58	36	22	4	3	1
Architectural sciences and technology, other..................	0	0	0	15	7	8	4	3	1
Real estate development	0	0	0	226	166	60	0	0	0
Architecture and related services, other..................	177	98	79	114	42	72	5	4	1

See notes at end of table.

Table 318.30. Bachelor's, master's, and doctor's degrees conferred by postsecondary institutions, by sex of student and discipline division: 2012–13—Continued

Discipline division	Bachelor's degrees			Master's degrees			Doctor's degrees[1]		
	Total	Males	Females	Total	Males	Females	Total	Males	Females
1	2	3	4	5	6	7	8	9	10
Area, ethnic, cultural, gender, and group studies	8,851	2,624	6,227	1,897	667	1,230	291	125	166
African studies	89	33	56	50	22	28	2	1	1
American/United States studies/civilization	1,406	528	878	222	70	152	104	49	55
Asian studies/civilization	816	344	472	126	51	75	1	0	1
East Asian studies	462	183	279	167	72	95	11	8	3
Russian, Central European, East European and Eurasian studies	28	12	16	43	21	22	0	0	0
European studies/civilization	148	43	105	31	13	18	0	0	0
Latin American studies	478	151	327	241	81	160	2	1	1
Near and Middle Eastern studies	249	98	151	158	82	76	42	22	20
Pacific Area/Pacific Rim studies	9	6	3	1	0	1	0	0	0
Russian studies	104	50	54	50	27	23	0	0	0
Scandinavian studies	22	7	15	4	3	1	2	1	1
South Asian studies	23	11	12	11	6	5	1	1	0
Southeast Asian studies	3	0	3	20	11	9	0	0	0
Western European studies	4	2	2	60	22	38	4	0	4
Canadian studies	3	2	1	0	0	0	0	0	0
Slavic studies	5	1	4	1	0	1	0	0	0
Ural-Altaic and Central Asian studies	0	0	0	13	10	3	2	0	2
Regional studies (U.S., Canadian, foreign)	42	12	30	27	5	22	8	6	2
Chinese studies	46	21	25	21	10	11	0	0	0
French studies	49	10	39	4	1	3	5	1	4
German studies	67	24	43	14	6	8	3	1	2
Italian studies	39	12	27	14	5	9	2	1	1
Japanese studies	54	25	29	3	1	2	0	0	0
Korean studies	0	0	0	7	5	2	0	0	0
Spanish and Iberian studies	17	5	12	0	0	0	0	0	0
Irish studies	0	0	0	14	7	7	0	0	0
Latin American and Caribbean studies	53	13	40	6	1	5	1	0	1
Area studies, other	812	247	565	44	19	25	2	1	1
Ethnic studies	139	36	103	10	2	8	7	1	6
African-American/Black studies	651	194	457	98	34	64	25	12	13
American Indian/Native American studies	256	93	163	47	17	30	7	2	5
Hispanic-American, Puerto Rican, and Mexican-American/Chicano studies	454	138	316	41	15	26	12	10	2
Asian-American studies	151	61	90	14	1	13	0	0	0
Women's studies	1,446	85	1,361	193	6	187	26	0	26
Gay/lesbian studies	8	2	6	0	0	0	0	0	0
Folklore studies	9	5	4	24	10	14	6	3	3
Disability studies	0	0	0	31	7	24	2	0	2
Ethnic, cultural minority, gender, and group studies, other	709	170	539	87	24	63	15	4	11
Biological and biomedical sciences	100,319	41,511	58,808	13,335	5,816	7,519	7,943	3,692	4,251
Biology/biological sciences, general	66,699	26,535	40,164	3,500	1,461	2,039	1,004	481	523
Biomedical sciences, general	2,541	1,006	1,535	1,273	614	659	426	180	246
Biochemistry	7,011	3,596	3,415	347	168	179	544	276	268
Biophysics	114	80	34	27	19	8	118	84	34
Molecular biology	697	352	345	216	95	121	231	103	128
Molecular biochemistry	369	186	183	57	24	33	88	52	36
Molecular biophysics	0	0	0	1	1	0	10	6	4
Structural biology	0	0	0	2	2	0	14	11	3
Radiation biology/radiobiology	5	0	5	10	9	1	13	9	4
Biochemistry and molecular biology	705	371	334	76	35	41	152	72	80
Biochemistry, biophysics and molecular biology, other	199	122	77	5	3	2	24	13	11
Botany/plant biology	188	88	100	86	49	37	97	43	54
Plant pathology/phytopathology	12	4	8	69	35	34	73	35	38
Plant physiology	0	0	0	1	1	0	10	5	5
Plant molecular biology	0	0	0	3	0	3	9	8	1
Botany/plant biology, other	24	14	10	15	8	7	1	0	1
Cell/cellular biology and histology	376	178	198	25	13	12	141	65	76
Anatomy	391	183	208	128	72	56	49	23	26
Developmental biology and embryology	45	27	18	22	9	13	38	15	23
Cell/cellular and molecular biology	2,218	1,044	1,174	181	72	109	437	212	225
Cell biology and anatomy	7	2	5	8	3	5	48	21	27
Cell/cellular biology and anatomical sciences, other	79	28	51	104	46	58	137	56	81
Microbiology, general	1,732	784	948	147	71	76	200	89	111
Medical microbiology and bacteriology	618	281	337	143	47	96	137	59	78
Virology	0	0	0	0	0	0	16	6	10
Parasitology	0	0	0	0	0	0	1	0	1
Immunology	0	0	0	27	11	16	182	69	113
Microbiology and immunology	114	59	55	46	19	27	93	37	56
Microbiological sciences and immunology, other	118	56	62	39	21	18	75	33	42
Zoology/animal biology	1,663	567	1,096	171	54	117	89	45	44
Entomology	100	39	61	145	72	73	104	51	53
Animal physiology	45	23	22	67	23	44	29	16	13
Animal behavior and ethology	55	10	45	5	0	5	8	4	4
Wildlife biology	361	170	191	10	5	5	1	0	1
Zoology/animal biology, other	22	5	17	18	6	12	0	0	0
Genetics, general	229	81	148	55	19	36	140	64	76
Molecular genetics	175	62	113	17	9	8	82	39	43
Animal genetics	27	6	21	30	16	14	68	27	41
Plant genetics	4	4	0	5	2	3	8	1	7
Human/medical genetics	1	0	1	87	12	75	91	40	51
Genome sciences/genomics	0	0	0	2	1	1	17	12	5
Genetics, other	0	0	0	2	1	1	17	12	5
Physiology, general	1,474	659	815	466	265	201	151	88	63
Molecular physiology	0	0	0	14	8	6	25	12	13
Cell physiology	0	0	0	5	1	4	17	9	8
Endocrinology	0	0	0	4	1	3	7	4	3
Reproductive biology	0	0	0	3	0	3	0	0	0
Cardiovascular science	0	0	0	3	2	1	7	3	4
Exercise physiology	2,046	976	1,070	208	96	112	51	26	25
Vision science/physiological optics	139	45	94	25	10	15	20	11	9
Pathology/experimental pathology	23	6	17	87	33	54	192	86	106
Oncology and cancer biology	0	0	0	36	9	27	105	47	58

See notes at end of table.

Table 318.30. Bachelor's, master's, and doctor's degrees conferred by postsecondary institutions, by sex of student and discipline division: 2012–13—Continued

Discipline division	Bachelor's degrees			Master's degrees			Doctor's degrees[1]		
	Total	Males	Females	Total	Males	Females	Total	Males	Females
1	2	3	4	5	6	7	8	9	10
Physiology, pathology, and related sciences, other	0	0	0	10	6	4	11	4	7
Pharmacology	40	26	14	104	49	55	213	99	114
Molecular pharmacology	0	0	0	10	5	5	58	23	35
Neuropharmacology	0	0	0	10	6	4	0	0	0
Toxicology	104	35	69	52	17	35	87	40	47
Molecular toxicology	0	0	0	0	0	0	4	1	3
Environmental toxicology	39	17	22	43	13	30	20	13	7
Pharmacology and toxicology	64	23	41	62	30	32	47	18	29
Biometry/biometrics	37	19	18	18	15	3	12	8	4
Biostatistics	18	11	7	461	190	271	151	72	79
Bioinformatics	127	91	36	293	194	99	100	70	30
Computational biology	17	7	10	8	5	3	27	19	8
Biomathematics, bioinformatics, and computational biology, other	23	12	11	22	10	12	15	10	5
Biotechnology	738	385	353	1,198	531	667	4	1	3
Ecology	763	344	419	182	68	114	188	76	112
Marine biology and biological oceanography	1,182	397	785	194	68	126	68	34	34
Evolutionary biology	97	34	63	20	7	13	31	14	17
Aquatic biology/limnology	89	50	39	15	9	6	0	0	0
Environmental biology	239	104	135	43	20	23	2	1	1
Population biology	0	0	0	4	2	2	8	2	6
Conservation biology	163	58	105	90	32	58	17	8	9
Systematic biology/biological systematics	0	0	0	1	1	0	8	6	2
Epidemiology	23	8	15	1,056	322	734	273	78	195
Ecology and evolutionary biology	302	125	177	38	14	24	81	42	39
Ecology, evolution, systematics and population biology, other	140	48	92	25	11	14	31	14	17
Molecular medicine	0	0	0	13	6	7	37	14	23
Neuroscience	3,532	1,350	2,182	160	62	98	515	215	300
Neuroanatomy	0	0	0	0	0	0	0	0	0
Neurobiology and anatomy	626	279	347	16	9	7	107	54	53
Neurobiology and behavior	70	27	43	27	11	16	22	9	13
Neurobiology and neurosciences, other	6	1	5	0	0	0	1	0	1
Biological and biomedical sciences, other	1,254	411	843	1,138	551	587	224	99	125
Business, management, marketing, and personal and culinary services	360,823	187,789	173,034	188,625	101,584	87,041	2,836	1,612	1,224
Business, management, marketing, and related support services	359,521	187,199	172,322	188,585	101,577	87,008	2,836	1,612	1,224
Business/commerce, general	25,109	13,333	11,776	11,116	6,656	4,460	372	216	156
Business administration and management, general	135,833	70,546	65,287	111,313	62,514	48,799	1,420	867	553
Purchasing, procurement/acquisitions and contracts management	583	331	252	579	289	290	0	0	0
Logistics, materials, and supply chain management	2,633	1,879	754	664	430	234	1	0	1
Office management and supervision	360	151	209	170	79	91	0	0	0
Operations management and supervision	3,828	2,287	1,541	688	466	222	10	7	3
Nonprofit/public/organizational management	366	133	233	1,964	604	1,360	15	5	10
Customer service management	72	26	46	2	1	1	0	0	0
E-commerce/electronic commerce	192	110	82	141	63	78	0	0	0
Transportation/mobility management	281	226	55	111	84	27	2	2	0
Research and development management	0	0	0	26	10	16	0	0	0
Project management	387	287	100	768	473	295	13	8	5
Retail management	229	44	185	0	0	0	0	0	0
Organizational leadership	2,131	962	1,169	2,078	876	1,202	233	97	136
Business administration, management and operations, other	11,020	5,545	5,475	5,283	2,677	2,606	37	17	20
Accounting	49,362	23,653	25,709	17,587	8,328	9,259	45	25	20
Accounting technology/technician and bookkeeping	198	99	99	0	0	0	0	0	0
Auditing	30	4	26	119	50	69	0	0	0
Accounting and finance	525	286	239	1,603	635	968	0	0	0
Accounting and business/management	2,866	730	2,136	260	140	120	0	0	0
Accounting and related services, other	173	83	90	217	117	100	3	1	2
Administrative assistant and secretarial science, general	60	27	33	0	0	0	0	0	0
Business/office automation/technology/data entry	57	17	40	0	0	0	0	0	0
General office occupations and clerical services	16	6	10	0	0	0	0	0	0
Parts, warehousing, and inventory management operations	0	0	0	6	4	2	0	0	0
Business operations support and secretarial services, other	0	0	0	53	22	31	0	0	0
Business/corporate communications	679	222	457	176	40	136	0	0	0
Business/managerial economics	4,821	3,319	1,502	342	190	152	66	38	28
Entrepreneurship/entrepreneurial studies	2,387	1,590	797	772	508	264	15	12	3
Small business administration/management	62	35	27	20	9	11	0	0	0
Entrepreneurial and small business operations, other	28	15	13	36	22	14	2	1	1
Finance, general	30,885	21,601	9,284	6,155	3,940	2,215	35	24	11
Banking and financial support services	351	223	128	102	56	46	5	5	0
Financial planning and services	222	153	69	278	169	109	3	3	0
International finance	4	1	3	24	14	10	0	0	0
Investments and securities	82	66	16	254	169	85	0	0	0
Public finance	14	12	2	0	0	0	0	0	0
Finance and financial management services, other	181	101	80	186	126	60	0	0	0
Hospitality administration/management, general	7,591	2,388	5,203	468	140	328	32	18	14
Tourism and travel services management	531	139	392	104	34	70	0	0	0
Hotel/motel administration/management	1,941	724	1,217	127	51	76	10	5	5
Restaurant/food services management	804	363	441	2	0	2	0	0	0
Resort management	236	93	143	0	0	0	0	0	0
Meeting and event planning	370	34	336	0	0	0	0	0	0
Casino management	6	5	1	0	0	0	0	0	0
Hotel, motel, and restaurant management	105	36	69	0	0	0	0	0	0
Hospitality administration/management, other	490	200	290	153	59	94	5	3	2
Human resources management/personnel administration, general	6,683	1,844	4,839	4,419	1,126	3,293	37	13	24
Labor and industrial relations	835	436	399	779	262	517	6	3	3
Organizational behavior studies	2,488	1,079	1,409	2,143	743	1,400	215	96	119
Labor studies	41	29	12	25	12	13	3	1	2
Human resources development	585	166	419	1,101	321	780	25	9	16
Human resources management and services, other	339	157	182	1,445	532	913	18	7	11
International business/trade/commerce	5,597	2,758	2,839	2,344	1,376	968	30	18	12
Management information systems, general	7,396	5,506	1,890	3,306	2,320	986	52	41	11
Information resources management	182	140	42	541	407	134	17	13	4
Knowledge management	23	17	6	85	65	20	0	0	0
Management information systems and services, other	200	150	50	168	97	71	10	7	3
Management science, general	2,974	1,741	1,233	1,275	718	557	10	7	3

See notes at end of table.

Table 318.30. Bachelor's, master's, and doctor's degrees conferred by postsecondary institutions, by sex of student and discipline division: 2012–13—Continued

Discipline division	Bachelor's degrees			Master's degrees			Doctor's degrees[1]		
	Total	Males	Females	Total	Males	Females	Total	Males	Females
1	2	3	4	5	6	7	8	9	10
Business statistics	60	43	17	33	22	11	0	0	0
Actuarial science	1,015	601	414	328	202	126	0	0	0
Management sciences and quantitative methods, other	258	146	112	141	94	47	9	4	5
Marketing/marketing management, general	29,392	13,978	15,414	1,718	665	1,053	28	9	19
Marketing research	53	25	28	96	48	48	1	1	0
International marketing	146	26	120	98	29	69	3	2	1
Marketing, other	1,035	482	553	191	63	128	3	2	1
Real estate	538	390	148	697	527	170	1	1	0
Taxation	0	0	0	1,807	920	887	0	0	0
Insurance	755	505	250	84	50	34	4	3	1
Sales, distribution, and marketing operations, general	1,161	599	562	213	80	133	4	1	3
Merchandising and buying operations	15	2	13	18	0	18	0	0	0
Retailing and retail operations	269	45	224	5	0	5	0	0	0
Selling skills and sales operations	311	199	112	0	0	0	0	0	0
General merchandising/sales/related marketing operations, other	105	45	60	9	9	0	0	0	0
Fashion merchandising	2,594	139	2,455	8	2	6	0	0	0
Apparel and accessories marketing operations	905	72	833	15	3	12	0	0	0
Tourism and travel services marketing operations	23	5	18	0	0	0	0	0	0
Tourism promotion operations	41	6	35	0	0	0	0	0	0
Vehicle and vehicle parts and accessories marketing operations	77	61	16	0	0	0	0	0	0
Special products marketing operations	174	64	110	14	5	9	0	0	0
Hospitality and recreation marketing operations	70	53	17	0	0	0	0	0	0
Specialized merchandising/sales/related marketing operations, other	55	22	33	55	22	33	0	0	0
Construction management	2,371	2,162	209	282	206	76	6	5	1
Telecommunications management	6	6	0	0	0	0	0	0	0
Business/management/marketing/related support services, other	2,648	1,415	1,233	1,195	606	589	35	19	16
Personal and culinary services	1,302	590	712	40	7	33	0	0	0
Funeral service and mortuary science, general	138	58	80	0	0	0	0	0	0
Funeral direction/service	35	13	22	0	0	0	0	0	0
Cosmetology/cosmetologist, general	2	0	2	0	0	0	0	0	0
Cooking and related culinary arts, general	0	0	0	0	0	0	0	0	0
Baking and pastry arts/baker/pastry chef	71	5	66	0	0	0	0	0	0
Culinary arts/chef training	334	170	164	0	0	0	0	0	0
Restaurant, culinary, and catering management/manager	654	319	335	0	0	0	0	0	0
Food service, waiter/waitress, and dining room management	0	0	0	0	0	0	0	0	0
Culinary science/culinology	26	5	21	0	0	0	0	0	0
Culinary arts and related services, other	38	17	21	40	7	33	0	0	0
Personal and culinary services, other	4	3	1	0	0	0	0	0	0
Communication and communications technologies	89,806	33,671	56,135	9,334	3,022	6,312	612	246	366
Communication, journalism, and related programs	84,817	30,147	54,670	8,757	2,685	6,072	612	246	366
Communication, general	6,989	2,310	4,679	510	154	356	66	23	43
Speech communication and rhetoric	31,223	11,057	20,166	2,053	615	1,438	257	100	157
Mass communication/media studies	9,271	3,399	5,872	1,001	335	666	130	54	76
Communication and media studies, other	1,831	620	1,211	673	191	482	47	17	30
Journalism	12,069	3,929	8,140	1,658	562	1,096	27	10	17
Broadcast journalism	1,029	482	547	63	22	41	0	0	0
Photojournalism	193	61	132	23	8	15	0	0	0
Journalism, other	745	235	510	212	56	156	0	0	0
Radio and television	5,011	2,714	2,297	189	92	97	10	5	5
Digital communication and media/multimedia	1,949	1,062	887	305	159	146	27	18	9
Radio, television, and digital communication, other	904	470	434	12	9	3	0	0	0
Public relations, advertising, and applied communication	1,128	278	850	13	2	11	0	0	0
Organizational communication, general	1,086	330	756	138	34	104	6	3	3
Public relations/image management	4,222	844	3,378	553	116	437	0	0	0
Advertising	4,621	1,422	3,199	300	103	197	5	1	4
Political communication	69	29	40	0	0	0	0	0	0
Health communication	30	2	28	132	23	109	7	1	6
Sports communication	77	58	19	14	11	3	0	0	0
International and intercultural communication	27	13	14	48	8	40	0	0	0
Technical and scientific communication	15	5	10	15	5	10	1	1	0
Public relations, advertising and applied communication, other	1,016	293	723	188	38	150	0	0	0
Publishing	3	0	3	169	20	149	0	0	0
Communication, journalism, and related programs, other	1,309	534	775	488	122	366	29	13	16
Communications technologies/technicians and support services	4,989	3,524	1,465	577	337	240	0	0	0
Communications technology/technician	129	96	33	46	19	27	0	0	0
Photographic and film/video technology/technician and assistant	84	57	27	0	0	0	0	0	0
Radio and television broadcasting technology/technician	527	328	199	122	47	75	0	0	0
Recording arts technology/technician	1,354	1,184	170	31	29	2	0	0	0
Audiovisual communications technologies/technicians, other	118	91	27	0	0	0	0	0	0
Graphic communications, general	241	92	149	0	0	0	0	0	0
Printing management	61	23	38	5	3	2	0	0	0
Prepress/desktop publishing and digital imaging design	66	31	35	0	0	0	0	0	0
Animation/interactive technology/video graphics/special effects	2,183	1,505	678	342	227	115	0	0	0
Graphic and printing equipment operator, general production	50	26	24	0	0	0	0	0	0
Printing press operator	8	3	5	0	0	0	0	0	0
Graphic communications, other	29	8	21	9	3	6	0	0	0
Communications technologies/technicians and support services, other	139	80	59	22	9	13	0	0	0
Computer and information sciences and support services	50,962	41,874	9,088	22,777	16,538	6,239	1,826	1,473	353
Computer and information sciences, general	11,524	9,706	1,818	4,886	3,756	1,130	604	498	106
Artificial intelligence	0	0	0	81	67	14	23	18	5
Information technology	6,270	4,971	1,299	2,734	1,930	804	62	45	17
Informatics	461	385	76	274	103	171	16	14	2
Computer and information sciences, other	245	188	57	84	61	23	6	3	3
Computer programming/programmer, general	1,425	1,234	191	73	61	12	5	5	0
Computer programming, specific applications	154	144	10	32	26	6	0	0	0
Computer programming, other	90	86	4	0	0	0	0	0	0
Data processing and data processing technology/technician	79	68	11	0	0	0	0	0	0
Information science/studies	5,795	4,534	1,261	4,089	2,637	1,452	152	95	57
Computer systems analysis/analyst	1,485	1,167	318	298	212	86	0	0	0
Computer science	10,985	9,560	1,425	6,472	4,965	1,507	881	745	136
Web page, digital/multimedia and information resources design	1,513	915	598	265	114	151	0	0	0
Data modeling/warehousing and database administration	176	110	66	96	60	36	0	0	0
Computer graphics	1,598	1,054	544	201	119	82	0	0	0

See notes at end of table.

Table 318.30. Bachelor's, master's, and doctor's degrees conferred by postsecondary institutions, by sex of student and discipline division: 2012–13—Continued

Discipline division	Bachelor's degrees			Master's degrees			Doctor's degrees[1]		
	Total	Males	Females	Total	Males	Females	Total	Males	Females
1	2	3	4	5	6	7	8	9	10
Modeling, virtual environments and simulation	211	183	28	50	43	7	0	0	0
Computer software and media applications, other	202	176	26	65	51	14	0	0	0
Computer systems networking and telecommunications	1,727	1,557	170	734	561	173	5	4	1
Network and system administration/administrator	877	792	85	22	19	3	0	0	0
System, networking, and LAN/WAN management/manager	149	130	19	18	14	4	0	0	0
Computer and information systems security/information assurance	4,171	3,552	619	1,504	1,188	316	17	14	3
Web/multimedia management and webmaster	502	335	167	8	7	1	0	0	0
Information technology project management	281	224	57	181	119	62	5	4	1
Computer support specialist	59	45	14	0	0	0	0	0	0
Computer/information tech. services admin. and management, other	525	383	142	193	134	59	0	0	0
Computer and information sciences and support services, other	458	375	83	417	291	126	50	28	22
Education	104,647	21,805	82,842	164,624	37,804	126,820	10,572	3,418	7,154
Education, general	3,434	597	2,837	24,240	5,471	18,769	2,020	587	1,433
Bilingual and multilingual education	272	23	249	309	43	266	9	1	8
Multicultural education	0	0	0	212	60	152	23	6	17
Indian/Native American education	3	3	0	0	0	0	0	0	0
Bilingual, multilingual, and multicultural education, other	0	0	0	6	2	4	0	0	0
Curriculum and instruction	198	44	154	16,490	3,055	13,435	1,256	307	949
Educational leadership and administration, general	2	1	1	18,242	6,510	11,732	3,831	1,400	2,431
Administration of special education	0	0	0	13	3	10	11	2	9
Adult and continuing education administration	5	5	0	943	253	690	53	24	29
Educational, instructional, and curriculum supervision	47	6	41	972	251	721	69	19	50
Higher education/higher education administration	3	1	2	2,578	772	1,806	471	187	284
Community college education	0	0	0	62	19	43	31	13	18
Elementary and middle school administration/principalship	0	0	0	863	355	508	24	11	13
Secondary school administration/principalship	0	0	0	496	204	292	24	8	16
Urban education and leadership	144	31	113	404	110	294	62	22	40
Superintendency and educational system administration	0	0	0	559	202	357	56	19	37
Educational administration and supervision, other	1	0	1	1,497	507	990	312	117	195
Educational/instructional technology	32	19	13	3,891	1,184	2,707	155	54	101
Educational evaluation and research	0	0	0	56	13	43	64	27	37
Educational statistics and research methods	0	0	0	43	18	25	34	16	18
Educational assessment, testing, and measurement	0	0	0	51	10	41	17	5	12
Learning sciences	15	2	13	34	8	26	2	1	1
Educational assessment, evaluation, and research, other	8	2	6	131	36	95	27	12	15
International and comparative education	37	11	26	196	39	157	12	0	12
Social and philosophical foundations of education	20	5	15	517	126	391	98	36	62
Special education and teaching, general	7,610	874	6,736	13,543	2,113	11,430	203	39	164
Education/teaching of individuals with hearing impairments/deafness	103	4	99	183	17	166	4	1	3
Education/teaching of the gifted and talented	0	0	0	310	36	274	0	0	0
Education/teaching of individuals with emotional disturbances	149	19	130	111	25	86	13	2	11
Education/teaching of individuals with mental retardation	159	21	138	151	21	130	6	0	6
Education/teaching of individuals with multiple disabilities	114	10	104	345	44	301	0	0	0
Educ./teach. of individuals with orthopedic/physical health impair.	0	0	0	14	1	13	6	0	6
Education/teaching of individuals with vision impairments/blindness	28	2	26	147	26	121	0	0	0
Educ./teach. of individuals with specific learning disabilities	271	20	251	323	31	292	1	1	0
Education/teaching of individuals with speech/language impairments	260	9	251	273	12	261	0	0	0
Education/teaching of individuals with autism	0	0	0	247	17	230	0	0	0
Education/teaching of individuals who are developmentally delayed	2	0	2	147	31	116	0	0	0
Educ./teach. of individuals in early childhood spec. educ. programs	377	15	362	1,014	116	898	0	0	0
Education/teaching of individuals in elementary special educ. programs	172	13	159	574	64	510	0	0	0
Educ./teach. of individuals in jr. high/middle school special educ. prog.	8	2	6	203	69	134	0	0	0
Education/teaching of individuals in secondary special educ. prog.	16	2	14	248	67	181	0	0	0
Special education and teaching, other	412	41	371	741	113	628	10	3	7
Counselor education/school counseling and guidance services	19	0	19	12,295	2,000	10,295	332	77	255
College student counseling and personnel services	0	0	0	1,009	274	735	29	13	16
Student counseling and personnel services, other	7	3	4	271	40	231	4	0	4
Adult and continuing education and teaching	32	11	21	1,238	298	940	136	46	90
Elementary education and teaching	35,985	3,376	32,609	11,863	1,461	10,402	67	13	54
Junior high/intermediate/middle school education and teaching	3,111	777	2,334	918	268	650	2	0	2
Secondary education and teaching	3,767	1,558	2,209	7,657	2,945	4,712	23	9	14
Teacher education, multiple levels	1,863	328	1,535	3,730	951	2,779	15	5	10
Montessori teacher education	7	0	7	175	13	162	0	0	0
Waldorf/Steiner teacher education	0	0	0	0	0	0	0	0	0
Kindergarten/preschool education and teaching	1,590	72	1,518	306	11	295	4	2	2
Early childhood education and teaching	13,154	487	12,667	3,041	103	2,938	21	0	21
Teacher educ. and prof. dev., specific levels and methods, other	196	35	161	3,602	861	2,741	75	18	57
Agricultural teacher education	590	233	357	260	79	181	31	15	16
Art teacher education	1,415	206	1,209	969	162	807	23	6	17
Business teacher education	321	157	164	131	53	78	0	0	0
Driver and safety teacher education	0	0	0	14	8	6	0	0	0
English/language arts teacher education	2,773	598	2,175	940	234	706	12	2	10
Foreign language teacher education	84	16	68	189	28	161	10	3	7
Health teacher education	1,513	453	1,060	650	142	508	44	9	35
Family and consumer sciences/home economics teacher education	353	7	346	54	1	53	8	1	7
Technology teacher education/industrial arts teacher education	419	322	97	297	145	152	3	2	1
Sales and marketing operations/marketing and dist. teacher educ.	20	9	11	0	0	0	0	0	0
Mathematics teacher education	2,250	754	1,496	1,647	543	1,104	66	24	42
Music teacher education	3,821	1,597	2,224	1,175	442	733	84	41	43
Physical education teaching and coaching	8,830	5,208	3,622	2,142	1,256	886	37	22	15
Reading teacher education	84	7	77	6,940	362	6,578	90	10	80
Science teacher education/general science teacher education	682	274	408	840	285	555	52	18	34
Social science teacher education	585	327	258	137	56	81	0	0	0
Social studies teacher education	1,870	1,107	763	596	307	289	8	4	4
Technical teacher education	249	140	109	198	76	122	54	12	42
Trade and industrial teacher education	720	461	259	242	93	149	9	6	3
Computer teacher education	8	0	8	490	142	348	9	6	3
Biology teacher education	499	176	323	335	98	237	3	1	2
Chemistry teacher education	79	35	44	104	30	74	0	0	0
Drama and dance teacher education	170	32	138	52	9	43	0	0	0
French language teacher education	60	10	50	22	3	19	0	0	0
German language teacher education	18	5	13	1	1	0	0	0	0
Health occupations teacher education	14	0	14	34	10	24	34	5	29

See notes at end of table.

Table 318.30. Bachelor's, master's, and doctor's degrees conferred by postsecondary institutions, by sex of student and discipline division: 2012–13—Continued

Discipline division	Bachelor's degrees			Master's degrees			Doctor's degrees[1]		
	Total	Males	Females	Total	Males	Females	Total	Males	Females
1	2	3	4	5	6	7	8	9	10
History teacher education	700	430	270	95	50	45	0	0	0
Physics teacher education	49	34	15	62	43	19	0	0	0
Spanish language teacher education	433	115	318	165	29	136	0	0	0
Speech teacher education	37	13	24	65	12	53	13	4	9
Geography teacher education	8	7	1	14	5	9	0	0	0
Latin teacher education	7	2	5	14	5	9	0	0	0
School librarian/library media specialist	2	0	2	170	14	156	0	0	0
Psychology teacher education	10	4	6	0	0	0	0	0	0
Earth science teacher education	44	23	21	48	18	30	0	0	0
Environmental education	4	1	3	13	3	10	0	0	0
Teacher educ. and prof. dev., specific subject areas, other	322	100	222	1,937	501	1,436	53	16	37
Teaching English as a second/foreign language/ESL language instructor	267	64	203	3,059	591	2,468	28	10	18
Teaching French as a second or foreign language	0	0	0	0	0	0	0	0	0
Teaching English or French as a second or foreign lang., other	40	12	28	0	0	0	0	0	0
Teacher assistant/aide	0	0	0	3	1	2	0	0	0
Adult literacy tutor/instructor	0	0	0	41	1	40	0	0	0
Education, other	1,664	437	1,227	2,995	687	2,308	289	98	191
Engineering and engineering technologies	102,984	84,633	18,351	45,325	34,494	10,831	9,467	7,305	2,162
Engineering	85,980	69,425	16,555	40,417	30,854	9,563	9,356	7,231	2,125
Engineering, general	2,168	1,692	476	2,029	1,552	477	394	308	86
Pre-engineering	17	11	6	0	0	0	0	0	0
Aerospace, aeronautical and astronautical engineering	3,490	3,011	479	1,266	1,076	190	310	261	49
Agricultural engineering	954	655	299	310	176	134	135	92	43
Architectural engineering	767	575	192	142	101	41	8	5	3
Bioengineering and biomedical engineering	4,838	2,961	1,877	1,931	1,134	797	945	613	332
Ceramic sciences and engineering	79	51	28	15	11	4	10	8	2
Chemical engineering	7,411	5,068	2,343	1,398	904	494	822	565	257
Chemical and biomolecular engineering	118	70	48	51	29	22	13	10	3
Chemical engineering, other	0	0	0	1	1	0	0	0	0
Civil engineering, general	13,043	10,275	2,768	4,966	3,588	1,378	839	630	209
Geotechnical and geoenvironmental engineering	0	0	0	3	2	1	0	0	0
Structural engineering	195	141	54	220	169	51	11	10	1
Transportation and highway engineering	0	0	0	79	48	31	7	5	2
Water resources engineering	10	6	4	59	25	34	11	8	3
Civil engineering, other	14	8	6	26	18	8	0	0	0
Computer engineering, general	4,574	4,122	452	1,769	1,425	344	343	292	51
Computer hardware engineering	0	0	0	77	69	8	0	0	0
Computer software engineering	576	528	48	1,078	794	284	4	4	0
Computer engineering, other	2	2	0	19	18	1	6	6	0
Electrical and electronics engineering	12,764	11,253	1,511	9,180	7,407	1,773	2,081	1,776	305
Laser and optical engineering	6	5	1	32	24	8	22	17	5
Telecommunications engineering	0	0	0	233	178	55	2	1	1
Electrical, electronics and communications engineering, other	65	59	6	40	35	5	13	11	2
Engineering mechanics	92	81	11	87	76	11	63	51	12
Engineering physics/applied physics	457	383	74	78	69	9	70	54	16
Engineering science	438	325	113	294	222	72	121	89	32
Environmental/environmental health engineering	1,181	654	527	825	433	392	159	81	78
Materials engineering	1,114	784	330	868	604	264	600	447	153
Mechanical engineering	21,989	19,345	2,644	5,871	5,055	816	1,321	1,121	200
Metallurgical engineering	107	82	25	38	32	6	19	14	5
Mining and mineral engineering	239	209	30	66	52	14	19	17	2
Naval architecture and marine engineering	412	362	50	43	37	6	7	4	3
Nuclear engineering	593	503	90	351	303	48	120	99	21
Ocean engineering	201	164	37	91	71	20	14	10	4
Petroleum engineering	1,130	975	155	395	325	70	96	80	16
Systems engineering	735	588	147	1,945	1,498	447	118	85	33
Textile sciences and engineering	228	69	159	46	16	30	33	17	16
Polymer/plastics engineering	109	85	24	84	58	26	66	45	21
Construction engineering	407	373	34	118	90	28	1	1	0
Forest engineering	21	20	1	4	3	1	2	2	0
Industrial engineering	3,616	2,566	1,050	2,023	1,428	595	313	225	88
Manufacturing engineering	254	217	37	279	230	49	7	6	1
Operations research	389	264	125	649	437	212	65	49	16
Surveying engineering	43	38	5	6	6	0	0	0	0
Geological/geophysical engineering	159	95	64	142	108	34	16	9	7
Paper science and engineering	20	18	2	4	3	1	6	3	3
Electromechanical engineering	43	37	6	0	0	0	0	0	0
Mechatronics, robotics, and automation engineering	26	23	3	61	52	9	12	12	0
Biochemical engineering	54	34	20	4	1	3	0	0	0
Engineering chemistry	5	3	2	0	0	0	0	0	0
Biological/biosystems engineering	170	109	61	14	9	5	9	5	4
Engineering, other	657	526	131	1,107	852	255	123	83	40
Engineering technologies/construction trades/mechanics and repairers	17,004	15,208	1,796	4,908	3,640	1,268	111	74	37
Engineering technologies and engineering-related fields	16,493	14,742	1,751	4,902	3,636	1,266	111	74	37
Engineering technology, general	1,267	1,121	146	300	227	73	7	5	2
Architectural engineering technology/technician	404	334	70	0	0	0	0	0	0
Civil engineering technology/technician	558	484	74	0	0	0	0	0	0
Electrical/electronic/communications eng. technology/technician	2,115	1,963	152	44	39	5	0	0	0
Laser and optical technology/technician	0	0	0	0	0	0	0	0	0
Telecommunications technology/technician	94	76	18	106	82	24	0	0	0
Electrical/electronic eng. technologies/technicians, other	386	362	24	2	1	1	0	0	0
Biomedical technology/technician	135	105	30	14	8	6	0	0	0
Electromechanical technology/electromechanical eng. technology	95	91	4	2	2	0	1	0	1
Instrumentation technology/technician	28	26	2	0	0	0	0	0	0
Robotics technology/technician	12	12	0	0	0	0	0	0	0
Automation engineer technology/technician	28	26	2	0	0	0	0	0	0
Electromechanical/instrumentation and maintenance technol./tech.	7	7	0	0	0	0	0	0	0
Heating, ventilation, air conditioning and refrig. eng. technol./tech.	4	3	1	0	0	0	0	0	0
Energy management and systems technology/technician	116	107	9	51	39	12	0	0	0
Solar energy technology/technician	58	56	2	13	10	3	0	0	0
Water quality/wastewater treatment manage./recycling technol./tech.	28	15	13	0	0	0	0	0	0
Environmental engineering technology/environmental technology	97	60	37	73	41	32	0	0	0
Hazardous materials management and waste technology/technician	0	0	0	0	0	0	0	0	0

See notes at end of table.

Table 318.30. Bachelor's, master's, and doctor's degrees conferred by postsecondary institutions, by sex of student and discipline division: 2012–13—Continued

Discipline division	Bachelor's degrees			Master's degrees			Doctor's degrees[1]		
	Total	Males	Females	Total	Males	Females	Total	Males	Females
1	2	3	4	5	6	7	8	9	10
Environmental control technologies/technicians, other	10	4	6	51	34	17	0	0	0
Plastics and polymer engineering technology/technician	92	84	8	2	0	2	0	0	0
Industrial technology/technician	1,696	1,536	160	311	220	91	14	11	3
Manufacturing engineering technology/technician	563	529	34	56	42	14	0	0	0
Welding engineering technology/technician	7	7	0	0	0	0	0	0	0
Industrial production technologies/technicians, other	284	238	46	7	7	0	0	0	0
Occupational safety and health technology/technician	1,205	990	215	447	330	117	0	0	0
Quality control technology/technician	14	11	3	100	54	46	0	0	0
Industrial safety technology/technician	67	58	9	23	14	9	0	0	0
Quality control and safety technologies/technicians, other	44	38	6	1	0	1	0	0	0
Aeronautical/aerospace engineering technology/technician	63	58	5	0	0	0	0	0	0
Automotive engineering technology/technician	273	267	6	14	13	1	0	0	0
Mechanical engineering/mechanical technology/technician	1,545	1,469	76	17	13	4	0	0	0
Mechanical engineering related technologies/technicians, other	223	208	15	0	0	0	0	0	0
Mining technology/technician	4	4	0	0	0	0	0	0	0
Petroleum technology/technician	14	13	1	0	0	0	0	0	0
Mining and petroleum technologies/technicians, other	0	0	0	0	0	0	0	0	0
Construction engineering technology/technician	1,842	1,682	160	112	94	18	1	1	0
Surveying technology/surveying	147	136	11	9	7	2	11	8	3
Hydraulics and fluid power technology/technician	2	2	0	0	0	0	0	0	0
Engineering-related technologies, other	0	0	0	0	0	0	0	0	0
Computer engineering technology/technician	471	423	48	0	0	0	0	0	0
Computer technology/computer systems technology	314	283	31	6	4	2	1	1	0
Computer hardware technology/technician	0	0	0	0	0	0	0	0	0
Computer software technology/technician	41	40	1	0	0	0	0	0	0
Computer engineering technologies/technicians, other	17	16	1	0	0	0	0	0	0
Drafting and design technologies/technicians, general	75	63	12	0	0	0	0	0	0
CAD/CADD drafting and/or design technology/technician	93	84	9	11	10	1	0	0	0
Civil drafting and civil engineering CAD/CADD	6	6	0	0	0	0	0	0	0
Mechanical drafting and mechanical drafting CAD/CADD	26	22	4	0	0	0	0	0	0
Drafting/design engineering technologies/technicians, other	7	1	6	0	0	0	0	0	0
Nuclear engineering technology/technician	186	174	12	0	0	0	0	0	0
Engineering/industrial management	750	625	125	2,896	2,194	702	63	42	21
Engineering design	0	0	0	32	21	11	0	0	0
Packaging science	293	204	89	51	28	23	2	1	1
Engineering-related fields, other	14	14	0	4	2	2	9	3	6
Nanotechnology	0	0	0	19	16	3	2	2	0
Engineering tech. and engineering-related fields, other	673	605	68	128	84	44	0	0	0
Construction trades	244	225	19	6	4	2	0	0	0
Construction trades, general	0	0	0	0	0	0	0	0	0
Mason/masonry	1	1	0	0	0	0	0	0	0
Electrician	1	1	0	0	0	0	0	0	0
Building/property maintenance	0	0	0	6	4	2	0	0	0
Building/construction site management/manager	142	131	11	0	0	0	0	0	0
Building construction technology	40	38	2	0	0	0	0	0	0
Building/construction finishing, mgmt., and inspection, other	60	54	6	0	0	0	0	0	0
Construction trades, other	0	0	0	0	0	0	0	0	0
Mechanic and repair technologies/technicians	267	241	26	0	0	0	0	0	0
Communications systems installation and repair technology	2	2	0	0	0	0	0	0	0
Industrial electronics technology/technician	1	0	1	0	0	0	0	0	0
Heating, air conditioning, ventilation and refrig. main. tech.	1	1	0	0	0	0	0	0	0
Heavy equipment maintenance technology/technician	19	19	0	0	0	0	0	0	0
Autobody/collision and repair technology/technician	0	0	0	0	0	0	0	0	0
Automobile/automotive mechanics technology/technician	22	22	0	0	0	0	0	0	0
Diesel mechanics technology/technician	17	17	0	0	0	0	0	0	0
Airframe mechanics and aircraft maintenance technology/technician	44	37	7	0	0	0	0	0	0
Aircraft powerplant technology/technician	57	50	7	0	0	0	0	0	0
Avionics maintenance technology/technician	104	93	11	0	0	0	0	0	0
Vehicle maintenance and repair technologies, other	0	0	0	0	0	0	0	0	0
English language and literature/letters	52,424	16,515	35,909	9,755	3,215	6,540	1,373	553	820
English language and literature, general	42,168	12,891	29,277	5,279	1,720	3,559	1,173	487	686
Writing, general	574	226	348	104	30	74	0	0	0
Creative writing	2,716	960	1,756	3,410	1,191	2,219	9	4	5
Professional, technical, business, and scientific writing	669	221	448	329	101	228	22	7	15
Rhetoric and composition	4,943	1,790	3,153	285	78	207	115	38	77
Rhetoric and composition/writing studies, other	42	9	33	1	1	0	2	1	1
General literature	214	75	139	20	6	14	10	2	8
American literature (United States)	41	13	28	1	0	1	0	0	0
English literature (British and Commonwealth)	338	100	238	155	42	113	8	4	4
Children's and adolescent literature	1	0	1	0	0	0	0	0	0
Literature, other	12	4	8	0	0	0	0	0	0
English language and literature/letters, other	706	226	480	171	46	125	34	10	24
Family and consumer sciences/human sciences	23,934	2,872	21,062	3,253	434	2,819	351	79	272
Work and family studies	3	0	3	0	0	0	0	0	0
Family and consumer sciences/human sciences, general	3,900	397	3,503	565	88	477	46	18	28
Business family and consumer sciences/human sciences	162	46	116	7	5	2	3	0	3
Family and consumer sciences/human sciences communication	27	3	24	0	0	0	0	0	0
Consumer merchandising/retailing management	167	25	142	6	1	5	3	1	2
Family resource management studies, general	763	206	557	84	38	46	9	3	6
Consumer economics	220	97	123	1	0	1	0	0	0
Consumer services and advocacy	1	0	1	0	0	0	0	0	0
Family and consumer economics and related services, other	369	41	328	2	0	2	10	2	8
Foods, nutrition, and wellness studies, general	2,466	474	1,992	605	71	534	33	6	27
Human nutrition	708	116	592	347	57	290	33	12	21
Food service systems administration/management	849	341	508	3	1	2	0	0	0
Foods, nutrition, and related services, other	13	1	12	43	3	40	0	0	0
Housing and human environments, general	206	33	173	32	10	22	8	5	3
Facilities planning and management	59	51	8	4	2	2	0	0	0
Housing and human environments, other	18	0	18	0	0	0	0	0	0
Human development and family studies, general	7,899	630	7,269	650	80	570	107	21	86
Adult development and aging	13	2	11	172	19	153	0	0	0
Family systems	493	51	442	21	7	14	5	1	4

See notes at end of table.

Table 318.30. Bachelor's, master's, and doctor's degrees conferred by postsecondary institutions, by sex of student and discipline division: 2012–13—Continued

Discipline division	Bachelor's degrees			Master's degrees			Doctor's degrees[1]		
	Total	Males	Females	Total	Males	Females	Total	Males	Females
1	2	3	4	5	6	7	8	9	10
Child development	1,619	60	1,559	204	6	198	25	4	21
Family and community services	1,051	126	925	274	21	253	30	2	28
Child care and support services management	205	18	187	48	1	47	0	0	0
Child care provider/assistant	9	1	8	4	0	4	0	0	0
Human development, family studies, and related services, other	490	37	453	49	12	37	17	3	14
Apparel and textiles, general	1,802	83	1,719	63	6	57	15	0	15
Apparel and textile manufacture	67	11	56	0	0	0	0	0	0
Textile science	0	0	0	0	0	0	1	0	1
Apparel and textile marketing management	312	15	297	42	3	39	4	0	4
Apparel and textiles, other	15	1	14	2	0	2	0	0	0
Family and consumer sciences/human sciences, other	28	6	22	25	3	22	2	1	1
Foreign languages, literatures, and linguistics	21,673	6,847	14,826	3,708	1,235	2,473	1,304	531	773
Foreign languages and literatures, general	1,612	475	1,137	233	50	183	19	7	12
Linguistics	2,001	654	1,347	745	280	465	224	95	129
Language interpretation and translation	49	17	32	152	37	115	9	5	4
Comparative literature	920	275	645	165	55	110	196	74	122
Applied linguistics	13	1	12	7	3	4	2	1	1
Linguistic/comparative/related language studies and serv., other	170	37	133	25	6	19	11	1	10
African languages, literatures, and linguistics	9	3	6	2	2	0	4	2	2
East Asian languages, literatures, and linguistics, general	169	70	99	73	33	40	41	21	20
Chinese language and literature	510	226	284	61	10	51	12	4	8
Japanese language and literature	717	334	383	23	6	17	4	2	2
Korean language and literature	43	20	23	14	9	5	0	0	0
East Asian languages, literatures, and linguistics, other	112	55	57	11	3	8	24	15	9
Slavic languages, literatures, and linguistics, general	73	36	37	71	29	42	33	14	19
Russian language and literature	392	188	204	11	3	8	5	2	3
Polish language and literature	8	3	5	0	0	0	0	0	0
Slavic/Baltic/Albanian languages, lit., and linguistics, other	0	0	0	3	1	2	0	0	0
Germanic languages, literatures, and linguistics, general	85	39	46	29	13	16	17	7	10
German language and literature	931	432	499	102	41	61	52	23	29
Scandinavian languages, literatures, and linguistics	8	1	7	5	2	3	5	2	3
Danish language and literature	1	0	1	0	0	0	0	0	0
Dutch/Flemish language and literature	1	1	0	0	0	0	0	0	0
Norwegian language and literature	5	5	0	0	0	0	0	0	0
Swedish language and literature	2	1	1	0	0	0	0	0	0
Germanic languages, literatures, and linguistics, other	1	0	1	0	0	0	0	0	0
Modern Greek language and literature	3	1	2	0	0	0	0	0	0
South Asian languages, literatures, and linguistics, general	4	0	4	1	0	1	3	3	0
Iranian languages, literatures, and linguistics	10	3	7	0	0	0	0	0	0
Romance languages, literatures, and linguistics, general	151	44	107	83	24	59	45	17	28
French language and literature	2,281	558	1,723	332	82	250	115	39	76
Italian language and literature	289	94	195	73	21	52	27	9	18
Portuguese language and literature	55	25	30	11	6	5	6	2	4
Spanish language and literature	8,429	2,265	6,164	928	263	665	205	69	136
Hispanic and Latin American languages, lit., and linguistics, general	95	29	66	16	4	12	20	9	11
Romance languages, literatures, and linguistics, other	88	12	76	64	21	43	54	16	38
American Indian/Native American languages, literatures, and linguistics	0	0	0	6	3	3	1	1	0
Middle/Near Eastern and Semitic languages, lit., and linguistics, general	13	7	6	25	15	10	15	10	5
Arabic language and literature	167	100	67	12	4	8	1	0	1
Hebrew language and literature	63	16	47	31	12	19	9	5	4
Ancient Near Eastern and biblical languages, lit., and linguistics	38	24	14	20	14	6	6	5	1
Middle/Near Eastern and Semitic languages, lit., and ling., other	79	39	40	46	25	21	29	13	16
Classics and classical languages, lit., and linguistics, general	1,205	543	662	198	100	98	90	47	43
Ancient/classical Greek language and literature	31	18	13	1	1	0	0	0	0
Latin language and literature	77	30	47	13	4	9	0	0	0
Classics and classical languages, lit., and linguistics, other	20	11	9	13	10	3	2	1	1
Celtic languages, literatures, and linguistics	4	3	1	2	0	2	0	0	0
Filipino/Tagalog language and literature	3	3	0	0	0	0	0	0	0
Turkish language and literature	2	2	0	0	0	0	0	0	0
Uralic languages, literatures, and linguistics	2	1	1	0	0	0	0	0	0
American sign language (ASL)	145	18	127	22	14	8	0	0	0
Sign language interpretation and translation	302	40	262	17	3	14	0	0	0
American sign language, other	1	0	1	0	0	0	0	0	0
Foreign languages, literatures, and linguistics, other	284	88	196	62	26	36	18	10	8
Health professions and related programs	181,144	28,214	152,930	90,931	16,747	74,184	64,195	26,867	37,328
Health and wellness, general	8,182	2,040	6,142	656	288	368	96	34	62
Chiropractic	0	0	0	0	0	0	2,224	1,366	858
Communication sciences and disorders, general	4,565	242	4,323	1,869	105	1,764	43	5	38
Audiology/audiologist	229	16	213	118	8	110	600	92	508
Speech-language pathology/pathologist	1,232	43	1,189	2,571	121	2,450	21	0	21
Audiology/audiologist and speech-language pathology/pathologist	4,264	193	4,071	2,696	104	2,592	208	32	176
Communication disorders sciences and services, other	63	6	57	119	4	115	11	0	11
Dentistry	0	0	0	0	0	0	5,111	2,651	2,460
Dental clinical sciences, general	0	0	0	237	144	93	9	5	4
Advanced general dentistry	0	0	0	8	7	1	111	59	52
Oral biology and oral maxillofacial pathology	0	0	0	84	37	47	21	12	9
Dental public health and education	0	0	0	10	3	7	0	0	0
Dental materials	0	0	0	6	3	3	0	0	0
Endodontics/endodontology	0	0	0	31	23	8	0	0	0
Oral/maxillofacial surgery	0	0	0	3	3	0	0	0	0
Orthodontics/orthodontology	0	0	0	81	48	33	2	0	2
Pediatric dentistry/pedodontics	0	0	0	16	3	13	2	0	2
Periodontics/periodontology	0	0	0	40	24	16	1	0	1
Prosthodontics/prosthodontology	0	0	0	27	15	12	2	2	0
Advanced/graduate dentistry and oral sciences, other	0	0	0	35	16	19	4	1	3
Dental assisting/assistant	1	0	1	0	0	0	0	0	0
Dental hygiene/hygienist	2,020	75	1,945	71	3	68	0	0	0
Dental laboratory technology/technician	0	0	0	20	4	16	0	0	0
Dental services and allied professions, other	17	1	16	5	2	3	0	0	0
Health/health care administration/management	8,489	1,751	6,738	7,455	2,378	5,077	203	81	122
Hospital and health care facilities administration/management	4,025	465	3,560	784	227	557	4	1	3
Health unit manager/ward supervisor	8	1	7	2	0	2	0	0	0
Medical office management/administration	1	0	1	0	0	0	0	0	0

See notes at end of table.

Table 318.30. Bachelor's, master's, and doctor's degrees conferred by postsecondary institutions, by sex of student and discipline division: 2012–13—Continued

Discipline division	Bachelor's degrees			Master's degrees			Doctor's degrees[1]		
	Total	Males	Females	Total	Males	Females	Total	Males	Females
1	2	3	4	5	6	7	8	9	10
Health information/medical records administration/administrator	1,479	224	1,255	267	75	192	0	0	0
Health information/medical records technology/technician	32	7	25	13	4	9	0	0	0
Medical office assistant/specialist	2	0	2	0	0	0	0	0	0
Medical/health management and clinical assistant/specialist	84	10	74	5	1	4	0	0	0
Medical staff services technology/technician	3	2	1	0	0	0	0	0	0
Long term care administration/management	438	30	408	10	2	8	0	0	0
Clinical research coordinator	15	3	12	121	31	90	0	0	0
Health and medical administrative services, other	557	111	446	311	88	223	7	3	4
Medical/clinical assistant	21	3	18	0	0	0	0	0	0
Occupational therapist assistant	3	0	3	0	0	0	0	0	0
Pharmacy technician/assistant	0	0	0	0	0	0	0	0	0
Physical therapy technician/assistant	7	2	5	0	0	0	0	0	0
Veterinary/animal health technology/technician and vet. assistant	350	36	314	0	0	0	0	0	0
Anesthesiologist assistant	0	0	0	107	47	60	0	0	0
Pathology/pathologist assistant	11	2	9	66	17	49	0	0	0
Respiratory therapy technician/assistant	23	6	17	0	0	0	0	0	0
Radiologist assistant	0	0	0	5	3	2	0	0	0
Allied health and medical assisting services, other	304	81	223	144	30	114	0	0	0
Cardiovascular technology/technologist	55	18	37	1	1	0	0	0	0
Emergency medical technology/technician (EMT paramedic)	250	176	74	15	8	7	0	0	0
Nuclear medical technology/technologist	320	121	199	0	0	0	0	0	0
Perfusion technology/perfusionist	7	4	3	64	39	25	0	0	0
Medical radiologic technology/science radiation therapist	1,275	331	944	58	31	27	0	0	0
Respiratory care therapy/therapist	1,044	338	706	41	15	26	0	0	0
Surgical technology/technologist	2	0	2	12	6	6	0	0	0
Diagnostic medical sonography/sonographer and ultrasound technician	532	78	454	6	1	5	0	0	0
Radiologic technology/science radiographer	1,193	286	907	63	22	41	0	0	0
Physician assistant	565	163	402	5,988	1,495	4,493	12	11	1
Athletic training/trainer	3,362	1,308	2,054	510	207	303	1	1	0
Gene/genetic therapy	10	1	9	0	0	0	3	3	0
Radiation protection/health physics technician	11	4	7	5	4	1	0	0	0
Magnetic resonance imaging (MRI) technology/technician	19	7	12	0	0	0	0	0	0
Allied health diagnostic/intervention/treatment professions, other	228	90	138	28	10	18	107	27	80
Blood bank technology specialist	0	0	0	2	1	1	0	0	0
Cytotechnology/cytotechnologist	53	20	33	11	1	10	0	0	0
Hematology technology/technician	0	0	0	7	2	5	0	0	0
Clinical/medical laboratory technician	113	33	80	0	0	0	0	0	0
Clinical laboratory science/medical technology/technologist	2,668	767	1,901	181	67	114	1	0	1
Histologic technology/histotechnologist	14	4	10	5	2	3	0	0	0
Cytogenetics/genetics/clinical genetics technology/technologist	54	13	41	0	0	0	0	0	0
Clinical/medical laboratory science and allied professions, other	102	29	73	42	13	29	0	0	0
Pre-dentistry studies	15	6	9	0	0	0	0	0	0
Pre-medicine/pre-medical studies	883	407	476	53	19	34	0	0	0
Pre-pharmacy studies	19	6	13	10	4	6	0	0	0
Pre-veterinary studies	286	46	240	0	0	0	0	0	0
Pre-nursing studies	8	0	8	0	0	0	0	0	0
Pre-occupational therapy studies	147	11	136	0	0	0	0	0	0
Pre-optometry studies	2	1	1	0	0	0	0	0	0
Pre-physical therapy studies	208	76	132	0	0	0	0	0	0
Health/medical preparatory programs, other	1,135	327	808	86	31	55	0	0	0
Medicine	0	0	0	0	0	0	17,264	8,976	8,288
Medical scientist	0	0	0	468	210	258	20	13	7
Substance abuse/addiction counseling	431	111	320	491	139	352	0	0	0
Psychiatric/mental health services technician	279	50	229	21	4	17	0	0	0
Clinical/medical social work	162	15	147	376	50	326	3	0	3
Community health services/liaison/counseling	982	165	817	237	36	201	10	3	7
Marriage and family therapy/counseling	0	0	0	3,099	502	2,597	89	25	64
Clinical pastoral counseling/patient counseling	15	4	11	67	33	34	21	6	15
Psychoanalysis and psychotherapy	0	0	0	21	4	17	6	4	2
Mental health counseling/counselor	9	1	8	4,067	705	3,362	15	2	13
Genetic counseling/counselor	0	0	0	130	8	122	0	0	0
Mental and social health services and allied professions, other	556	64	492	134	30	104	9	3	6
Optometry	0	0	0	0	0	0	1,521	557	964
Ophthalmic technician/technologist	3	0	3	0	0	0	0	0	0
Orthoptics/orthoptist	1	0	1	0	0	0	0	0	0
Ophthalmic/optometric support services/allied professions, other	9	5	4	37	19	18	2	1	1
Osteopathic medicine/osteopathy	0	0	0	0	0	0	4,691	2,489	2,202
Pharmacy	1,024	417	607	25	8	17	13,352	5,133	8,219
Pharmacy admin. and pharmacy policy and regulatory affairs	0	0	0	392	146	246	31	14	17
Pharmaceutics and drug design	216	103	113	111	47	64	178	90	88
Medicinal and pharmaceutical chemistry	10	5	5	70	37	33	83	43	40
Natural products chemistry and pharmacognosy	0	0	0	2	1	1	12	6	6
Clinical and industrial drug development	30	9	21	122	39	83	0	0	0
Pharmacoeconomics/pharmaceutical economics	0	0	0	0	0	0	94	40	54
Clinical, hospital, and managed care pharmacy	0	0	0	3	2	1	0	0	0
Industrial and physical pharmacy and cosmetic sciences	0	0	0	18	4	14	0	0	0
Pharmaceutical sciences	451	184	267	158	72	86	116	59	57
Pharmaceutical marketing and management	37	11	26	18	8	10	0	0	0
Pharmacy, pharmaceutical sciences, and administration, other	439	177	262	338	139	199	35	16	19
Podiatric medicine/podiatry	0	0	0	0	0	0	471	296	175
Public health, general	2,114	436	1,678	7,774	1,996	5,778	336	107	229
Environmental health	300	121	179	492	178	314	74	33	41
Health/medical physics	38	23	15	96	70	26	41	27	14
Occupational health and industrial hygiene	145	101	44	72	43	29	3	3	0
Public health education and promotion	2,299	428	1,871	853	103	750	62	11	51
Community health and preventive medicine	1,226	236	990	178	41	137	24	6	18
Maternal and child health	10	0	10	144	6	138	16	0	16
International public health/international health	55	10	45	453	122	331	22	13	9
Health services administration	727	125	602	519	162	357	16	8	8
Behavioral aspects of health	118	33	85	56	9	47	25	7	18
Public health, other	769	205	564	451	88	363	91	24	67
Art therapy/therapist	151	8	143	494	19	475	0	0	0
Dance therapy/therapist	0	0	0	55	2	53	0	0	0

See notes at end of table.

Table 318.30. Bachelor's, master's, and doctor's degrees conferred by postsecondary institutions, by sex of student and discipline division: 2012–13—Continued

Discipline division	Bachelor's degrees			Master's degrees			Doctor's degrees[1]		
	Total	Males	Females	Total	Males	Females	Total	Males	Females
1	2	3	4	5	6	7	8	9	10
Music therapy/therapist	286	37	249	120	20	100	5	1	4
Occupational therapy/therapist	764	70	694	5,351	559	4,792	278	28	250
Orthotist/prosthetist	20	16	4	86	49	37	0	0	0
Physical therapy/therapist	325	96	229	229	88	141	9,815	3,239	6,576
Therapeutic recreation/recreational therapy	530	72	458	34	5	29	0	0	0
Vocational rehabilitation counseling/counselor	311	58	253	1,100	222	878	14	6	8
Kinesiotherapy/kinesiotherapist	45	15	30	7	3	4	0	0	0
Assistive/augmentative technology and rehabilitation engineering	0	0	0	0	0	0	1	0	1
Animal-assisted therapy	6	1	5	5	0	5	0	0	0
Rehabilitation science	485	116	369	128	44	84	43	13	30
Rehabilitation and therapeutic professions, other	617	139	478	268	41	227	35	11	24
Veterinary medicine	0	0	0	0	0	0	2,610	593	2,017
Veterinary sciences/veterinary clinical sciences, general	42	4	38	215	85	130	215	63	152
Veterinary physiology	0	0	0	0	0	0	3	2	1
Veterinary microbiology and immunobiology	34	19	15	6	4	2	6	5	1
Veterinary pathology and pathobiology	0	0	0	2	0	2	11	7	4
Large animal/food animal/equine surgery and medicine	0	0	0	4	3	1	2	0	2
Small/companion animal surgery and medicine	0	0	0	2	1	1	0	0	0
Comparative and laboratory animal medicine	0	0	0	25	5	20	0	0	0
Veterinary preventive medicine epidemiology/public health	0	0	0	11	5	6	0	0	0
Veterinary infectious diseases	0	0	0	0	0	0	6	3	3
Medical illustration/medical illustrator	54	19	35	43	9	34	0	0	0
Medical informatics	66	35	31	368	155	213	55	35	20
Dietetics/dietitian	2,682	313	2,369	421	26	395	1	0	1
Clinical nutrition/nutritionist	131	22	109	201	32	169	2	0	2
Dietetic technician	0	0	0	25	6	19	0	0	0
Dietetics and clinical nutrition services, other	358	51	307	23	4	19	0	0	0
Bioethics/medical ethics	6	1	5	263	108	155	21	12	9
Alternative and complementary medicine and medical systems, general	115	13	102	36	11	25	29	14	15
Acupuncture and oriental medicine	87	27	60	1,386	426	960	65	27	38
Traditional Chinese medicine and Chinese herbology	0	0	0	315	79	236	11	6	5
Naturopathic medicine/naturopathy	0	0	0	0	0	0	273	48	225
Holistic health	55	7	48	27	2	25	0	0	0
Alternative and complementary medicine and medical systems, other	27	1	26	21	1	20	0	0	0
Direct entry midwifery	15	0	15	8	0	8	0	0	0
Massage therapy/therapeutic massage	0	0	0	0	0	0	0	0	0
Asian bodywork therapy	0	0	0	0	0	0	0	0	0
Movement therapy and movement education	48	21	27	23	0	23	7	5	2
Herbalism/herbalist	12	2	10	17	0	17	0	0	0
Energy and biologically based therapies, other	0	0	0	0	0	0	0	0	0
Registered nursing/registered nurse	101,628	12,323	89,305	12,963	1,217	11,746	577	53	524
Nursing administration	567	61	506	4,040	414	3,626	264	25	239
Adult health nurse/nursing	250	42	208	1,099	90	1,009	59	5	54
Nurse anesthetist	0	0	0	1,806	663	1,143	47	10	37
Family practice nurse/nursing	320	51	269	4,679	509	4,170	198	20	178
Maternal/child health and neonatal nurse/nursing	0	0	0	207	5	202	0	0	0
Nurse midwife/nursing midwifery	0	0	0	301	7	294	4	0	4
Nursing science	1,092	142	950	2,046	186	1,860	524	44	480
Pediatric nurse/nursing	0	0	0	280	6	274	3	2	1
Psychiatric/mental health nurse/nursing	0	0	0	292	47	245	10	4	6
Public health/community nurse/nursing	4	0	4	259	28	231	0	0	0
Perioperative/operating room and surgical nurse/nursing	0	0	0	29	3	26	0	0	0
Clinical nurse specialist	67	3	64	246	31	215	40	3	37
Critical care nursing	0	0	0	206	30	176	2	2	0
Occupational and environmental health nursing	0	0	0	33	3	30	5	0	5
Emergency room/trauma nursing	0	0	0	16	4	12	0	0	0
Nursing education	58	9	49	1,553	88	1,465	22	1	21
Nursing practice	765	88	677	358	53	305	1,131	129	1,002
Palliative care nursing	5	0	5	15	0	15	2	0	2
Clinical nurse leader	8	0	8	292	33	259	0	0	0
Geriatric nurse/nursing	0	0	0	172	12	160	1	0	1
Women's health nurse/nursing	0	0	0	145	1	144	0	0	0
Reg. nursing, nursing admin., nursing research and clinical nursing, other	1,155	141	1,014	1,017	98	919	153	6	147
Licensed practical/vocational nurse training	23	4	19	0	0	0	0	0	0
Practical nursing, vocational nursing and nursing assistants, other	49	3	46	41	4	37	0	0	0
Health professions and related clinical sciences, other	4,421	1,124	3,297	846	296	550	108	43	65
Homeland security, law enforcement, firefighting and related prot. services	60,269	31,796	28,473	8,868	4,351	4,517	147	72	75
Corrections	486	212	274	19	4	15	0	0	0
Criminal justice/law enforcement administration	18,849	9,540	9,309	2,813	1,271	1,542	25	9	16
Criminal justice/safety studies	30,698	15,968	14,730	2,938	1,192	1,746	107	57	50
Forensic science and technology	1,011	274	737	605	131	474	0	0	0
Criminal justice/police science	2,795	1,717	1,078	72	31	41	2	1	1
Security and loss prevention services	47	34	13	28	18	10	0	0	0
Juvenile corrections	22	6	16	0	0	0	4	0	4
Criminalistics and criminal science	167	43	124	42	15	27	0	0	0
Securities services administration/management	865	442	423	284	237	47	0	0	0
Corrections administration	82	49	33	25	7	18	0	0	0
Cyber/computer forensics and counterterrorism	85	60	25	62	49	13	0	0	0
Financial forensics and fraud investigation	32	10	22	111	57	54	0	0	0
Law enforcement intelligence analysis	46	32	14	0	0	0	0	0	0
Critical incident response/special police operations	0	0	0	0	0	0	0	0	0
Protective services operations	0	0	0	11	7	4	0	0	0
Corrections and criminal justice, other	1,775	714	1,061	139	71	68	0	0	0
Fire prevention and safety technology/technician	215	200	15	7	5	2	0	0	0
Fire services administration	437	416	21	74	49	25	1	1	0
Fire science/firefighting	696	654	42	3	3	0	0	0	0
Fire/arson investigation and prevention	4	4	0	0	0	0	0	0	0
Fire protection, other	46	42	4	2	1	1	0	0	0
Homeland security	531	436	95	417	320	97	0	0	0
Crisis/emergency/disaster management	448	306	142	386	283	103	7	3	4
Critical infrastructure protection	52	36	16	78	54	24	0	0	0
Homeland security, other	66	49	17	111	77	34	0	0	0
Homeland sec., law enforcement, firefighting and related prot. serv., other	814	552	262	641	469	172	1	1	0

See notes at end of table.

Table 318.30. Bachelor's, master's, and doctor's degrees conferred by postsecondary institutions, by sex of student and discipline division: 2012–13—Continued

Discipline division	Bachelor's degrees			Master's degrees			Doctor's degrees[1]		
	Total	Males	Females	Total	Males	Females	Total	Males	Females
1	2	3	4	5	6	7	8	9	10
Legal professions and studies	4,425	1,308	3,117	7,013	3,329	3,684	47,246	25,321	21,925
Pre-law studies	257	115	142	0	0	0	0	0	0
Legal studies, general	1,776	641	1,135	385	127	258	15	5	10
Law	0	0	0	0	0	0	46,811	25,087	21,724
Advanced legal research/studies, general	97	47	50	1,458	700	758	96	60	36
Programs for foreign lawyers	0	0	0	952	505	447	0	0	0
American/U.S. law/legal studies/jurisprudence	32	15	17	270	108	162	20	9	11
Banking, corporate, finance, and securities law	0	0	0	163	89	74	0	0	0
Comparative law	0	0	0	39	17	22	0	0	0
Energy, environment, and natural resources law	0	0	0	92	42	50	5	1	4
Health law	0	0	0	195	40	155	0	0	0
International law and legal studies	1	1	0	367	136	231	23	10	13
International business, trade, and tax law	0	0	0	188	114	74	0	0	0
Tax law/taxation	0	0	0	619	373	246	42	21	21
Intellectual property law	0	0	0	118	56	62	27	9	18
Legal research and advanced professional studies, other	0	0	0	694	379	315	105	65	40
Legal administrative assistant/secretary	0	0	0	0	0	0	0	0	0
Legal assistant/paralegal	1,918	382	1,536	122	18	104	0	0	0
Court reporting/court reporter	10	0	10	0	0	0	0	0	0
Legal support services, other	0	0	0	9	2	7	0	0	0
Legal professions and studies, other	334	107	227	1,342	623	719	102	54	48
Liberal arts and sciences, general studies and humanities	46,761	16,968	29,793	3,268	1,297	1,971	98	42	56
Liberal arts and sciences/liberal studies	25,909	8,534	17,375	2,113	851	1,262	15	6	9
General studies	14,933	6,100	8,833	184	67	117	2	0	2
Humanities/humanistic studies	2,654	936	1,718	630	251	379	76	35	41
Liberal arts and sciences, general studies and humanities, other	3,265	1,398	1,867	341	128	213	5	1	4
Library science	102	12	90	6,983	1,295	5,688	50	23	27
Library and information science	102	12	90	6,802	1,274	5,528	49	23	26
Library science, other	0	0	0	181	21	160	1	0	1
Mathematics and statistics	20,453	11,602	8,851	6,957	4,178	2,779	1,823	1,292	531
Mathematics, general	16,762	9,371	7,391	2,866	1,823	1,043	1,138	844	294
Topology and foundations	0	0	0	0	0	0	2	2	0
Mathematics, other	258	153	105	48	17	31	11	9	2
Applied mathematics, general	1,537	995	542	969	643	326	217	145	72
Computational mathematics	127	95	32	16	10	6	28	22	6
Computational and applied mathematics	63	37	26	49	38	11	24	22	2
Financial mathematics	69	35	34	547	317	230	0	0	0
Mathematical biology	7	1	6	0	0	0	0	0	0
Applied mathematics, other	149	89	60	122	84	38	14	14	0
Statistics, general	1,043	564	479	2,107	1,106	1,001	361	220	141
Mathematical statistics and probability	134	78	56	113	80	33	15	8	7
Mathematics and statistics	55	31	24	64	27	37	0	0	0
Statistics, other	53	33	20	20	9	11	1	0	1
Mathematics and statistics, other	196	120	76	36	24	12	12	6	6
Military technologies and applied sciences	105	80	25	32	17	15	0	0	0
Intelligence, general	4	3	1	0	0	0	0	0	0
Strategic intelligence	0	0	0	24	13	11	0	0	0
Intelligence, command control and information operations, other	0	0	0	6	4	2	0	0	0
Military applied sciences, other	51	47	4	2	0	2	0	0	0
Military technologies and applied sciences, other	50	30	20	0	0	0	0	0	0
Multi/interdisciplinary studies	47,654	15,330	32,324	7,956	3,001	4,955	730	307	423
Multi/interdisciplinary studies, general	2,708	1,087	1,621	28	8	20	45	11	34
Biological and physical sciences	2,265	921	1,344	410	178	232	64	32	32
Peace studies and conflict resolution	468	168	300	617	221	396	29	12	17
Systems science and theory	221	141	80	261	128	133	13	9	4
Mathematics and computer science	186	145	41	31	21	10	25	19	6
Biopsychology	163	40	123	2	1	1	3	1	2
Gerontology	293	36	257	431	57	374	28	4	24
Historic preservation and conservation	122	28	94	221	41	180	1	0	1
Cultural resource management and policy analysis	1	1	0	29	6	23	0	0	0
Historic preservation and conservation, other	0	0	0	0	0	0	2	0	2
Medieval and renaissance studies	30	13	17	20	11	9	10	4	6
Museology/museum studies	31	10	21	471	47	424	0	0	0
Science, technology and society	620	355	265	143	54	89	15	10	5
Accounting and computer science	4	0	4	13	8	5	0	0	0
Behavioral sciences	5,782	1,086	4,696	74	23	51	22	5	17
Natural sciences	589	210	379	124	41	83	9	4	5
Nutrition sciences	1,893	341	1,552	634	86	548	124	35	89
International/global studies	5,309	2,005	3,304	1,257	746	511	2	0	2
Holocaust and related studies	3	1	2	17	5	12	0	0	0
Ancient studies/civilization	107	44	63	2	2	0	8	5	3
Classical, ancient Mediterranean/Near Eastern studies/archaeology	111	42	69	3	3	0	4	2	2
Intercultural/multicultural and diversity studies	180	59	121	134	42	92	7	5	2
Cognitive science	701	323	378	56	26	30	23	12	11
Cultural studies/critical theory and analysis	99	42	57	31	9	22	0	0	0
Human biology	530	158	372	0	0	0	0	0	0
Dispute resolution	1	1	0	260	94	166	0	0	0
Maritime studies	17	6	11	0	0	0	0	0	0
Computational science	11	9	2	24	18	6	14	13	1
Human computer interaction	10	3	7	134	65	69	3	2	1
Marine sciences	44	17	27	39	14	25	6	3	3
Sustainability studies	170	68	102	276	114	162	4	4	0
Multi/interdisciplinary studies, other	24,985	7,970	17,015	2,214	932	1,282	269	115	154
Parks, recreation, leisure, and fitness studies	42,714	23,228	19,486	7,139	4,038	3,101	295	159	136
Parks, recreation and leisure studies	2,780	1,368	1,412	236	109	127	29	15	14
Parks, recreation and leisure facilities management	2,953	1,546	1,407	429	221	208	19	10	9
Golf course operation and grounds management	9	7	2	0	0	0	0	0	0
Parks, recreation and leisure facilities management, other	12	11	1	2	2	0	0	0	0
Health and physical education/fitness, general	8,858	4,584	4,274	1,054	607	447	23	11	12
Sport and fitness administration/management	7,424	5,491	1,933	3,055	1,900	1,155	12	6	6
Kinesiology and exercise science	19,116	9,338	9,778	2,179	1,117	1,062	182	102	80
Physical fitness technician	44	26	18	0	0	0	0	0	0
Sports studies	260	204	56	102	46	56	0	0	0

See notes at end of table.

Table 318.30. Bachelor's, master's, and doctor's degrees conferred by postsecondary institutions, by sex of student and discipline division: 2012–13—Continued

Discipline division	Bachelor's degrees			Master's degrees			Doctor's degrees[1]		
	Total	Males	Females	Total	Males	Females	Total	Males	Females
1	2	3	4	5	6	7	8	9	10
Health and physical education/fitness, other	1,010	503	507	43	16	27	26	12	14
Outdoor education	75	48	27	31	18	13	0	0	0
Parks, recreation, leisure, and fitness studies, other	173	102	71	8	2	6	4	3	1
Philosophy and religious studies	12,793	8,150	4,643	1,931	1,259	672	796	552	244
Philosophy and religious studies, general	47	23	24	11	7	4	17	11	6
Philosophy	7,262	5,106	2,156	794	622	172	472	351	121
Logic	4	2	2	3	3	0	5	4	1
Ethics	91	27	64	33	16	17	0	0	0
Applied and professional ethics	26	17	9	18	11	7	0	0	0
Philosophy, other	186	108	78	4	3	1	8	6	2
Religion/religious studies	4,046	2,228	1,818	568	305	263	250	152	98
Buddhist studies	0	0	0	0	0	0	1	1	0
Christian studies	483	300	183	245	151	94	0	0	0
Islamic studies	12	8	4	7	3	4	3	2	1
Jewish/Judaic studies	201	63	138	86	28	58	17	10	7
Religion/religious studies, other	125	72	53	36	22	14	3	1	2
Philosophy and religious studies, other	310	196	114	126	88	38	20	14	6
Physical sciences and science technologies	28,050	17,143	10,907	7,011	4,375	2,636	5,514	3,646	1,868
Physical sciences	27,468	16,829	10,639	6,971	4,356	2,615	5,512	3,644	1,868
Physical sciences	390	210	180	58	36	22	26	19	7
Astronomy	190	120	70	98	55	43	99	64	35
Astrophysics	128	89	39	47	29	18	44	28	16
Planetary astronomy and science	5	1	4	16	6	10	21	11	10
Astronomy and astrophysics, other	34	19	15	9	4	5	10	8	2
Atmospheric sciences and meteorology, general	538	359	179	199	124	75	121	67	54
Atmospheric physics and dynamics	0	0	0	1	1	0	1	1	0
Meteorology	199	137	62	26	16	10	12	9	3
Atmospheric sciences and meteorology, other	12	4	8	7	1	6	3	2	1
Chemistry, general	13,193	6,937	6,256	2,265	1,233	1,032	2,515	1,502	1,013
Analytical chemistry	9	0	9	41	23	18	7	5	2
Inorganic chemistry	0	0	0	0	0	0	3	3	0
Organic chemistry	0	0	0	2	1	1	6	3	3
Physical chemistry	4	3	1	1	0	0	7	5	2
Polymer chemistry	5	3	2	32	18	14	30	23	7
Chemical physics	27	22	5	4	3	1	14	10	4
Environmental chemistry	7	4	3	0	0	0	5	2	3
Forensic chemistry	43	9	34	0	0	0	0	0	0
Theoretical chemistry	8	5	3	0	0	0	0	0	0
Chemistry, other	521	261	260	52	29	23	30	17	13
Geology/earth science, general	4,655	2,891	1,764	1,403	792	611	398	218	180
Geochemistry	13	6	7	7	4	3	7	1	6
Geophysics and seismology	145	93	52	122	76	46	53	37	16
Paleontology	0	0	0	2	1	1	0	0	0
Hydrology and water resources science	57	37	20	63	34	29	22	15	7
Geochemistry and petrology	0	0	0	0	0	0	0	0	0
Oceanography, chemical and physical	240	121	119	142	75	67	127	52	75
Geological and earth sciences/geosciences, other	422	237	185	106	54	52	50	27	23
Physics, general	5,777	4,673	1,104	1,751	1,401	350	1,596	1,288	308
Atomic/molecular physics	2	2	0	10	7	3	5	3	2
Elementary particle physics	0	0	0	1	1	0	0	0	0
Nuclear physics	0	0	0	1	1	0	1	1	0
Optics/optical sciences	34	28	6	77	64	13	41	35	6
Condensed matter and materials physics	0	0	0	0	0	0	5	4	1
Acoustics	37	34	3	15	10	5	3	3	0
Theoretical and mathematical physics	13	9	4	0	0	0	0	0	0
Physics, other	219	178	41	117	90	27	89	71	18
Materials science	148	101	47	178	117	61	128	86	42
Materials chemistry	9	6	3	12	11	1	6	5	1
Materials sciences, other	0	0	0	1	1	0	3	3	0
Physical sciences, other	384	230	154	106	38	68	24	16	8
Science technologies/technicians	582	314	268	40	19	21	2	2	0
Science technologies/technicians, general	16	15	1	0	0	0	0	0	0
Biology technician/biotechnology laboratory technician	51	22	29	0	0	0	2	2	0
Nuclear/nuclear power technology/technician	22	22	0	5	4	1	0	0	0
Nuclear and industrial radiologic technologies/technicians, other	2	0	2	0	0	0	0	0	0
Chemical technology/technician	10	5	5	6	3	3	0	0	0
Physical science technologies/technicians, other	0	0	0	0	0	0	0	0	0
Science technologies/technicians, other	481	250	231	29	12	17	0	0	0
Precision production	36	23	13	9	4	5	0	0	0
Tool and die technology/technician	0	0	0	0	0	0	0	0	0
Welding technology/welder	8	7	1	0	0	0	0	0	0
Furniture design and manufacturing	28	16	12	9	4	5	0	0	0
Psychology	114,450	26,816	87,634	27,846	5,730	22,116	6,323	1,624	4,699
Psychology, general	107,210	25,186	82,024	6,320	1,670	4,650	1,776	535	1,241
Cognitive psychology and psycholinguistics	76	27	49	7	0	7	13	5	8
Comparative psychology	0	0	0	5	1	4	0	0	0
Developmental and child psychology	673	55	618	318	36	282	42	5	37
Experimental psychology	759	184	575	165	49	116	97	32	65
Personality psychology	19	1	18	3	1	2	0	0	0
Physiological psychology/psychobiology	1,007	325	682	26	4	22	5	2	3
Social psychology	946	200	746	49	19	30	53	13	40
Psychometrics and quantitative psychology	2	0	2	11	2	9	13	5	8
Psychopharmacology	0	0	0	39	13	26	0	0	0
Research and experimental psychology, other	845	240	605	5	2	3	25	15	10
Clinical psychology	84	20	64	2,790	607	2,183	2,427	540	1,887
Community psychology	471	60	411	222	35	187	35	16	19
Counseling psychology	616	119	497	9,304	1,607	7,697	486	114	372
Industrial and organizational psychology	202	66	136	1,019	367	652	145	61	84
School psychology	0	0	0	1,709	261	1,448	314	60	254
Educational psychology	121	12	109	1,342	256	1,086	456	117	339
Clinical child psychology	0	0	0	12	3	9	48	10	38
Environmental psychology	27	17	10	23	13	10	5	1	4
Geropsychology	0	0	0	0	0	0	0	0	0

See notes at end of table.

Table 318.30. Bachelor's, master's, and doctor's degrees conferred by postsecondary institutions, by sex of student and discipline division: 2012–13—Continued

Discipline division	Bachelor's degrees			Master's degrees			Doctor's degrees[1]		
	Total	Males	Females	Total	Males	Females	Total	Males	Females
1	2	3	4	5	6	7	8	9	10
Health/medical psychology	21	7	14	57	11	46	11	2	9
Family psychology	19	5	14	79	10	69	1	0	1
Forensic psychology	483	115	368	681	96	585	86	16	70
Applied psychology	399	78	321	539	81	458	12	5	7
Applied behavior analysis	83	23	60	229	26	203	30	7	23
Clinical, counseling and applied psychology, other	0	0	0	503	119	384	58	17	41
Psychology, other	387	76	311	2,389	441	1,948	185	46	139
Public administration and social service professions	31,950	5,664	26,286	43,590	10,862	32,728	979	351	628
Human services, general	6,873	870	6,003	1,997	396	1,601	47	13	34
Community organization and advocacy	2,012	423	1,589	630	186	444	9	1	8
Public administration	3,240	1,595	1,645	13,562	5,569	7,993	241	133	108
Public policy analysis, general	1,278	573	705	2,849	1,294	1,555	228	96	132
Education policy analysis	0	0	0	22	3	19	18	5	13
Health policy analysis	69	18	51	77	38	39	1	1	0
International policy analysis	9	1	8	30	22	8	0	0	0
Public policy analysis, other	0	0	0	2	0	2	4	1	3
Social work	18,118	2,103	16,015	23,238	3,074	20,164	359	78	281
Youth services/administration	42	5	37	26	2	24	0	0	0
Social work, other	31	6	25	252	39	213	0	0	0
Public administration and social service professions, other	278	70	208	905	239	666	72	23	49
Social sciences and history	177,778	90,148	87,630	21,585	10,832	10,753	4,619	2,470	2,149
Social sciences	143,587	69,688	73,899	17,483	8,533	8,950	3,616	1,917	1,699
Social sciences, general	9,141	3,383	5,758	593	194	399	31	17	14
Research methodology and quantitative methods	1	0	1	3	1	2	0	0	0
Anthropology	11,143	3,249	7,894	1,121	352	769	571	199	372
Physical and biological anthropology	19	4	15	15	5	10	3	0	3
Cultural anthropology	27	7	20	0	0	0	0	0	0
Anthropology, other	91	17	74	15	5	10	8	1	7
Archeology	234	75	159	44	14	30	13	6	7
Criminology	6,806	3,454	3,352	659	261	398	40	18	22
Demography and population studies	0	0	0	36	17	19	11	7	4
Economics, general	26,832	18,766	8,066	2,838	1,760	1,078	999	653	346
Applied economics	236	139	97	268	179	89	31	18	13
Econometrics and quantitative economics	575	381	194	48	35	13	15	8	7
Development economics and international development	236	76	160	333	121	212	13	10	3
International economics	226	117	109	227	115	112	6	2	4
Economics, other	350	241	109	158	74	84	12	5	7
Geography	4,730	3,072	1,658	851	485	366	260	140	120
Geographic information science and cartography	212	176	36	298	196	102	6	4	2
Geography, other	164	89	75	19	16	3	2	1	1
International relations and affairs	9,676	3,833	5,843	4,681	2,266	2,415	78	45	33
National security policy studies	28	23	5	157	101	56	0	0	0
International relations and national security studies, other	117	65	52	74	42	32	0	0	0
Political science and government, general	37,378	21,014	16,364	2,077	1,214	863	829	495	334
American government and politics (United States)	200	118	82	148	89	59	0	0	0
Political economy	136	74	62	1	1	0	0	0	0
Political science and government, other	753	403	350	106	53	53	1	1	0
Sociology	30,528	9,365	21,163	1,603	523	1,080	615	252	363
Urban studies/affairs	1,130	513	617	457	173	284	45	23	22
Sociology and anthropology	404	111	293	8	4	4	0	0	0
Rural sociology	16	3	13	1	0	1	0	0	0
Social sciences, other	2,198	920	1,278	644	237	407	27	12	15
History	34,191	20,460	13,731	4,102	2,299	1,803	1,003	553	450
History, general	33,434	20,029	13,405	3,489	1,950	1,539	945	523	422
American history (United States)	62	47	15	100	34	66	5	3	2
European history	27	16	11	0	0	0	0	0	0
History and philosophy of science and technology	119	42	77	33	19	14	29	11	18
Public/applied history	26	10	16	171	42	129	5	3	2
Asian history	1	1	0	0	0	0	3	2	1
Military history	78	66	12	155	134	21	0	0	0
History, other	444	249	195	154	120	34	16	11	5
Theology and religious vocations	9,385	6,351	3,034	14,276	9,484	4,792	2,175	1,592	583
Bible/biblical studies	2,828	1,830	998	564	426	138	38	29	9
Missions/missionary studies and missiology	483	174	309	285	156	129	157	134	23
Religious education	817	389	428	500	245	255	49	33	16
Religious/sacred music	284	160	124	120	65	55	0	0	0
Theology/theological studies	1,071	748	323	4,022	2,802	1,220	587	469	118
Divinity/ministry	200	137	63	5,723	3,960	1,763	553	362	191
Pre-theology/pre-ministerial studies	186	159	27	0	0	0	0	0	0
Rabbinical studies	0	0	0	111	84	27	12	12	0
Talmudic studies	1,546	1,546	0	465	461	4	31	31	0
Theological and ministerial studies, other	341	194	147	732	455	277	306	228	78
Pastoral studies/counseling	423	290	133	813	338	475	146	97	49
Youth ministry	571	366	205	62	32	30	0	0	0
Urban ministry	53	19	34	32	16	16	3	3	0
Women's ministry	1	0	1	0	0	0	0	0	0
Lay ministry	106	65	41	57	20	37	0	0	7
Pastoral counseling and specialized ministries, other	124	48	76	169	91	78	25	18	7
Theology and religious vocations, other	351	226	125	621	333	288	268	176	92
Transportation and materials moving	4,526	3,997	529	1,420	1,177	243	1	1	0
Aeronautics/aviation/aerospace science and technology, general	2,528	2,243	285	135	109	26	0	0	0
Airline/commercial/professional pilot and flight crew	597	543	54	986	846	140	0	0	0
Aviation/airway management and operations	816	712	104	253	192	61	1	1	0
Air traffic controller	243	199	44	0	0	0	0	0	0
Flight instructor	18	15	3	0	0	0	0	0	0
Air transportation, other	25	21	4	44	28	16	0	0	0
Marine science/merchant marine officer	298	263	35	0	0	0	0	0	0
Transportation and materials moving, other	1	1	0	2	2	0	0	0	0
Visual and performing arts	97,796	38,061	59,735	17,869	7,612	10,257	1,814	850	964
Visual and performing arts, general	1,741	568	1,173	194	76	118	10	6	4
Digital arts	474	299	175	113	76	37	0	0	0
Crafts/craft design, folk art and artisanry	147	37	110	6	2	4	0	0	0

See notes at end of table.

Table 318.30. Bachelor's, master's, and doctor's degrees conferred by postsecondary institutions, by sex of student and discipline division: 2012–13—Continued

Discipline division	Bachelor's degrees			Master's degrees			Doctor's degrees[1]		
	Total	Males	Females	Total	Males	Females	Total	Males	Females
1	2	3	4	5	6	7	8	9	10
Dance, general	2,128	269	1,859	246	47	199	4	1	3
Ballet	34	3	31	3	1	2	0	0	0
Dance, other	19	2	17	2	0	2	6	0	6
Design and visual communications, general	3,024	1,049	1,975	526	209	317	2	1	1
Commercial and advertising art	1,410	543	867	93	36	57	0	0	0
Industrial and product design	1,531	985	546	198	113	85	0	0	0
Commercial photography	487	146	341	18	10	8	0	0	0
Fashion/apparel design	2,467	198	2,269	213	22	191	1	0	1
Interior design	3,564	328	3,236	448	73	375	0	0	0
Graphic design	6,223	2,526	3,697	317	120	197	0	0	0
Illustration	1,704	575	1,129	125	62	63	0	0	0
Game and interactive media design	1,339	1,096	243	123	78	45	0	0	0
Design and applied arts, other	961	348	613	281	111	170	10	3	7
Drama and dramatics/theatre arts, general	9,264	3,436	5,828	1,150	479	671	100	42	58
Technical theatre/theatre design and technology	598	262	336	155	63	92	0	0	0
Playwriting and screenwriting	161	86	75	185	98	87	0	0	0
Theatre literature, history and criticism	31	6	25	8	2	6	7	1	6
Acting	611	257	354	200	93	107	0	0	0
Directing and theatrical production	77	28	49	72	25	47	0	0	0
Musical theatre	312	132	180	0	0	0	0	0	0
Costume design	8	0	8	5	1	4	0	0	0
Dramatic/theatre arts and stagecraft, other	341	123	218	63	25	38	1	0	1
Film/cinema/video studies	3,225	1,978	1,247	408	212	196	32	14	18
Cinematography and film/video production	4,742	3,190	1,552	901	561	340	10	6	4
Photography	1,888	636	1,252	331	147	184	0	0	0
Documentary production	8	2	6	24	12	12	0	0	0
Film/video and photographic arts, other	957	555	402	187	116	71	0	0	0
Art/art studies, general	13,072	3,902	9,170	789	306	483	6	1	5
Fine/studio arts, general	10,413	3,238	7,175	1,490	631	859	0	0	0
Art history, criticism and conservation	3,311	430	2,881	977	133	844	251	54	197
Drawing	302	95	207	21	11	10	0	0	0
Intermedia/multimedia	440	224	216	28	8	20	0	0	0
Painting	726	227	499	203	80	123	0	0	0
Sculpture	278	108	170	69	31	38	0	0	0
Printmaking	209	63	146	53	16	37	0	0	0
Ceramic arts and ceramics	210	57	153	46	16	30	0	0	0
Fiber, textile and weaving arts	213	9	204	43	2	41	1	1	0
Metal and jewelry arts	103	13	90	40	7	33	0	0	0
Fine arts and art studies, other	1,177	371	806	366	111	255	0	0	0
Music, general	8,066	4,270	3,796	2,021	1,036	985	578	318	260
Music history, literature, and theory	116	60	56	36	15	21	16	8	8
Music performance, general	4,271	2,264	2,007	2,279	1,158	1,121	469	217	252
Music theory and composition	576	422	154	276	197	79	74	52	22
Musicology and ethnomusicology	41	26	15	90	37	53	44	23	21
Conducting	2	1	1	108	77	31	40	32	8
Keyboard instruments	154	62	92	128	43	85	45	15	30
Voice and opera	320	100	220	217	79	138	19	6	13
Jazz/jazz studies	284	249	35	142	122	20	14	10	4
Stringed instruments	180	81	99	203	84	119	15	8	7
Music pedagogy	57	22	35	36	8	28	9	5	4
Music technology	144	121	23	34	29	5	4	3	1
Brass instruments	29	20	9	30	20	10	8	7	1
Woodwind instruments	43	19	24	55	26	29	4	3	1
Percussion instruments	20	18	2	9	7	2	1	1	0
Music, other	749	460	289	273	161	112	13	8	5
Arts, entertainment, and media management, general	216	86	130	186	36	150	0	0	0
Fine and studio arts management	557	194	363	480	79	401	2	0	2
Music management	1,530	959	571	0	0	0	0	0	0
Theatre/theatre arts management	68	22	46	44	14	30	0	0	0
Arts, entertainment, and media management, other	33	11	22	1	0	1	0	0	0
Visual and performing arts, other	410	194	216	501	162	339	18	4	14
Not classified by field of study	0	0	0	0	0	0	0	0	0

[1]Includes Ph.D., Ed.D., and comparable degrees at the doctoral level. Includes most degrees formerly classified as first-professional, such as M.D., D.D.S., and law degrees.
NOTE: Data are for postsecondary institutions participating in Title IV federal financial aid programs. Aggregations by field of study derived from the Classification of Instructional Programs developed by the National Center for Education Statistics.

SOURCE: U.S. Department of Education, National Center for Education Statistics, Integrated Postsecondary Education Data System (IPEDS), Fall 2013, Completions component. (This table was prepared September 2014.)

Table 318.40. Degrees/certificates conferred by postsecondary institutions, by control of institution and level of degree: 1969–70 through 2012–13

Year	Public: Certificates below the associate's	Public: Associate's degrees	Public: Bachelor's degrees	Public: Master's degrees	Public: Doctor's degrees[1]	Private Total: Certificates below the associate's	Private Total: Associate's degrees	Private Total: Bachelor's degrees	Private Total: Master's degrees	Private Total: Doctor's degrees[1]	Nonprofit: Certificates below the associate's	Nonprofit: Associate's degrees	Nonprofit: Bachelor's degrees	Nonprofit: Master's degrees	Nonprofit: Doctor's degrees[1]	For-profit: Certificates below the associate's	For-profit: Associate's degrees	For-profit: Bachelor's degrees	For-profit: Master's degrees	For-profit: Doctor's degrees[1]
1	2	3	4	5	6	7	8	9	10	11	12	13	14	15	16	17	18	19	20	21
1969–70	—	170,966	519,550	134,545	33,725	—	35,057	272,766	79,044	25,761	—	—	—	—	—	—	—	—	—	—
1970–71	—	215,645	557,996	151,603	36,927	—	36,666	281,734	83,961	28,071	—	—	—	—	—	—	—	—	—	—
1971–72	—	255,218	599,615	167,075	40,297	—	36,796	287,658	90,126	30,909	—	—	—	—	—	—	—	—	—	—
1972–73	—	278,132	630,899	174,405	44,229	—	38,042	291,463	94,249	35,283	—	—	—	—	—	—	—	—	—	—
1973–74	—	303,188	651,544	184,632	45,018	—	40,736	294,232	97,442	37,573	—	—	—	—	—	—	—	—	—	—
1974–75	—	318,474	634,785	193,804	45,788	—	41,697	288,148	103,741	39,116	—	—	—	—	—	—	—	—	—	—
1975–76	—	345,006	635,161	206,298	47,517	—	46,448	290,585	111,179	43,490	—	—	—	—	—	—	—	—	—	—
1976–77	—	355,650	630,463	208,901	47,573	—	50,727	289,086	114,124	44,157	—	—	—	—	—	—	—	—	—	—
1977–78	—	358,874	627,903	202,099	47,553	—	53,372	293,301	115,888	44,792	—	—	—	—	—	—	—	—	—	—
1978–79	—	346,808	621,666	192,016	48,602	—	55,894	299,724	115,670	46,369	—	—	—	—	—	—	—	—	—	—
1979–80	—	344,536	624,084	187,499	48,550	—	56,374[2]	305,333	117,697	47,081	—	—	—	—	—	—	—	—	—	—
1980–81	—	352,391	626,452	184,384	50,023	—	63,986[2]	308,688	118,253	47,993	—	—	—	—	—	—	—	—	—	—
1981–82	—	366,732	636,475	182,295	50,500	—	67,794[2]	316,523	120,152	47,338	—	—	—	—	—	—	—	—	—	—
1982–83	—	377,817	646,317	176,246	50,943	—	71,803[2]	323,193	120,169	48,392	—	—	—	—	—	—	—	—	—	—
1983–84	—	379,249	646,013	170,693	50,727	—	72,991	328,236	120,448	50,072	—	—	—	—	—	—	—	—	—	—
1984–85	—	377,625	652,246	170,000	51,489	—	77,087	327,231	123,472	49,296	—	—	—	—	—	—	—	—	—	—
1985–86	—	369,052	658,586	169,903	51,001	—	76,995	329,237	125,947	49,279	—	—	—	—	—	—	—	—	—	—
1986–87	—	358,811	659,260	167,797	51,216	—	77,493	332,004	128,733	47,261	—	—	—	—	—	—	—	—	—	—
1987–88	—	354,180	658,491	173,778	51,641	—	80,905	336,338	132,005	47,498	—	—	—	—	—	—	—	—	—	—
1988–89	—	357,001	675,675	179,109	51,963	—	79,763	343,080	137,517	48,608	—	—	—	—	—	—	—	—	—	—
1989–90	—	375,635	700,015	186,104	53,451	—	79,467	351,329	144,048	50,057	—	42,497	344,569	142,681	49,655	—	36,970	6,760	1,367	402
1990–91	—	398,055	724,062	193,057	55,235	—	83,665	370,476	149,806	50,312	—	45,821	360,634	146,161	49,841	—	37,844	9,842	3,645	471
1991–92	—	420,265	759,475	203,398	55,186	—	83,966	377,078	154,691	53,368	—	45,700	370,718	153,291	52,830	—	38,266	6,360	1,400	538
1992–93	—	430,321	785,112	213,843	57,020	—	84,435	380,066	161,189	55,052	—	47,713	373,346	159,562	54,399	—	36,722	6,720	1,627	653
1993–94	—	444,373	789,148	221,428	58,366	—	86,259	380,127	171,609	54,270	—	48,493	371,561	168,718	53,502	—	37,766	8,566	2,891	768
1994–95	307,358	451,539	776,670	224,152	58,788	313,311	88,152	383,464	179,457	55,478	34,259	48,643	373,454	176,485	54,675	279,052	39,509	10,010	2,972	803
1995–96	326,587	454,291	774,070	227,179	59,398	272,237	100,925	390,722	185,001	56,109	35,560	50,678	379,916	181,142	55,506	236,677	50,247	10,806	3,859	603
1996–97	319,291	455,494	776,677	233,237	61,081	246,571	105,732	396,202	192,023	57,666	32,166	49,168	384,086	186,963	56,864	214,405	56,564	12,116	5,060	802
1997–98	305,910	455,084	784,296	235,922	60,948	251,589	103,471	400,110	200,115	57,787	29,402	47,625	386,455	194,048	57,089	222,187	55,846	13,655	6,067	698
1998–99	304,294	452,616	792,392	238,954	60,028	—	112,368	409,847	207,084	56,672	—	47,757	394,749	198,481	55,663	—	64,611	15,098	8,603	1,009
1999–2000	294,312	448,446	810,855	243,157	60,655	263,217	116,487	427,020	220,028	58,081	28,580	46,337	406,958	209,720	56,972	234,637	70,150	20,062	10,308	1,109
2000–01	309,524	456,487	812,438	246,054	60,820	242,879	122,378	431,733	227,448	58,765	29,336	45,711	408,701	215,815	57,722	213,543	76,667	23,032	11,633	1,043
2001–02	319,291	471,660	841,180	249,820	61,061	264,957	123,473	450,720	237,493	58,602	32,904	45,761	424,322	223,229	57,707	232,053	77,712	26,398	14,264	895
2002–03	355,727	498,279	875,596	265,643	61,611	290,698	135,737	473,215	253,056	59,968	36,926	46,183	442,060	238,069	58,894	253,772	89,554	31,155	14,987	1,074
2003–04	364,053	524,875	905,718	285,138	64,205	323,734	140,426	493,824	279,134	61,882	35,316	45,759	451,518	250,894	60,447	288,418	94,667	42,306	28,240	1,435
2004–05	370,683	547,519	932,443	291,505	67,511	340,190	149,141	506,821	288,646	66,876	35,968	45,344	457,963	253,564	65,278	304,222	103,797	48,858	35,082	1,598
2005–06	371,211	557,134	955,369	293,517	70,036	344,190	155,932	529,873	306,214	68,020	35,888	46,442	467,836	261,090	66,066	308,302	109,490	62,037	45,124	1,954
2006–07	389,640	566,535	975,513	291,971	73,085	339,397	161,579	548,579	318,626	71,605	34,195	43,829	477,805	267,690	69,239	305,202	117,750	70,774	50,936	2,366
2007–08	399,081	578,520	996,435	299,983	75,533	350,802	171,644	566,634	330,683	73,845	34,084	44,788	490,685	275,829	70,679	316,718	126,856	75,949	54,854	3,166
2008–09	428,849	596,391	1,020,521	308,215	77,270	375,771	190,852	580,878	353,867	77,294	31,939	46,930	496,353	290,401	73,583	343,832	143,922	84,525	63,466	3,711
2009–10	472,428	640,265	1,049,179	332,389	78,805	463,291	208,591	600,740	370,924	79,785	35,652	46,673	503,264	300,053	75,172	427,639	161,918	97,476	70,871	4,613
2010–11	519,711	696,884	1,088,722	339,420	82,013	510,766	246,622	627,331	391,502	81,814	36,534	51,967	512,821	313,317	76,595	474,232	194,655	114,510	78,185	5,219
2011–12	525,264	756,484	1,131,885	349,349	84,730	463,797	265,234	660,278	406,618	85,487	32,856	54,347	526,022	325,175	79,498	430,941	210,887	134,256	81,443	5,989
2012–13	544,881	772,588	1,163,620	346,813	86,427	421,203	234,373	676,544	404,938	88,611	30,682	55,617	535,736	326,984	81,539	390,521	178,756	140,808	77,954	7,072

—Not available.

[1] Includes Ph.D., Ed.D., and comparable degrees at the doctoral level. Includes most degrees formerly classified as first-professional, such as M.D., D.D.S., and law degrees.

[2] Part of the increase is due to the addition of schools accredited by the Accrediting Commission of Career Schools and Colleges of Technology.

NOTE: Data through 1990–91 are for institutions of higher education, while later data are for postsecondary institutions that participate in Title IV federal financial aid programs. Data for associate's degrees and programs. Data for associate's degrees and higher awards are for degree-granting institutions. Some data have been revised from previously published figures. SOURCE: U.S. Department of Education, National Center for Education Statistics, Higher Education General Information Survey (HEGIS), "Degrees and Other Formal Awards Conferred" surveys, 1969–70 through 1985–86; Integrated Postsecondary Education Data System (IPEDS), "Completions Survey" (IPEDS-C:87–99); and IPEDS Fall 2000 through Fall 2013, Completions component. (This table was prepared September 2014.)

Table 318.50. Degrees conferred by postsecondary institutions, by control of institution, level of degree, and field of study: 2012–13

Field of study	All institutions				Public institutions				Private nonprofit institutions				Private for-profit institutions			
	Associate's degrees	Bachelor's degrees	Master's degrees	Doctor's degrees[1]	Associate's degrees	Bachelor's degrees	Master's degrees	Doctor's degrees[1]	Associate's degrees	Bachelor's degrees	Master's degrees	Doctor's degrees[1]	Associate's degrees	Bachelor's degrees	Master's degrees	Doctor's degrees[1]
1	2	3	4	5	6	7	8	9	10	11	12	13	14	15	16	17
All fields, total	1,006,961	1,840,164	751,751	175,038	772,588	1,163,620	346,813	86,427	55,617	535,736	326,984	81,539	178,756	140,808	77,954	7,072
Agriculture and natural resources	6,827	33,593	6,339	1,411	6,521	27,925	5,018	1,335	306	5,079	1,213	76	0	589	108	0
Architecture and related services	468	9,757	8,095	247	455	6,869	4,884	177	13	2,824	3,095	70	0	64	116	0
Area, ethnic, cultural, gender, and group studies	271	8,851	1,897	291	265	5,770	1,093	176	6	3,079	804	115	0	2	0	0
Biological and biomedical sciences	4,185	100,319	13,335	7,943	4,057	68,643	7,945	5,282	127	31,487	5,390	2,661	1	189	0	0
Business	133,966	360,823	188,625	2,836	84,433	200,213	66,574	1,049	11,562	108,870	87,499	833	37,971	51,740	34,552	954
Communication, journalism, and related programs	4,299	84,817	8,757	612	3,930	59,640	3,840	486	121	23,799	4,693	126	248	1,378	224	0
Communications technologies	5,026	4,989	577	0	3,277	1,390	69	0	126	1,420	291	0	1,623	2,179	217	0
Computer and information sciences	38,931	50,962	22,777	1,826	21,110	25,822	11,516	1,247	1,688	11,755	8,921	503	16,133	13,385	2,340	76
Construction trades	5,038	244	6	0	4,020	242	6	0	175	1		0	843	0	0	0
Education	18,719	104,647	164,624	10,572	15,395	71,502	80,411	5,709	683	29,074	69,933	3,319	2,641	4,071	14,280	1,544
Engineering	3,735	85,980	40,417	9,356	3,630	66,724	26,569	6,807	28	18,963	13,601	2,549	77	293	247	0
Engineering technologies and engineering-related fields[2]	33,766	16,493	4,902	111	23,208	12,375	2,749	77	1,152	1,845	1,817	34	9,406	2,273	336	39
English language and literature/letters	2,085	52,424	9,755	1,373	1,679	36,548	6,189	1,063	5	15,447	3,368	310	401	429	198	0
Family and consumer sciences	8,994	23,934	3,253	351	8,338	19,601	1,957	270	466	3,926	963	64	190	407	333	17
Foreign languages, literatures, and linguistics	2,130	21,673	3,708	1,304	1,784	15,573	2,594	856	346	6,082	1,114	448	0	18	0	0
Health professions and related programs	214,004	181,144	90,931	64,195	130,472	101,056	39,692	32,231	19,223	56,806	38,591	30,697	64,309	23,282	12,648	1,267
Homeland security, law enforcement, and firefighting	48,425	60,269	8,868	147	30,467	33,701	3,499	98	1,667	12,413	2,971	10	16,291	14,155	2,398	39
Legal professions and studies	11,826	4,425	7,013	47,246	6,470	2,245	1,833	15,662	599	1,306	5,001	29,590	4,757	874	179	1,994
Liberal arts and sciences, general studies, and humanities	344,091	46,761	3,268	98	329,600	32,053	1,480	45	10,877	14,417	1,746	36	3,614	291	42	17
Library science	181	102	6,983	50	181	94	5,765	42	0	0	1,218	8	0	8	0	0
Mathematics and statistics	1,802	20,453	6,957	1,823	1,794	13,838	4,756	1,336	7	6,609	2,201	487	1	6	0	0
Mechanic and repair technologies/technicians	20,444	267	0	0	12,740	193	0	0	1,848	74	0	0	5,856	0	0	0
Military technologies and applied sciences	1,002	105	32	0	984	70	24	0	103	4	8	0	18	31	0	0
Multi/interdisciplinary studies	27,404	47,654	7,956	730	23,676	31,906	4,035	516	334	10,231	3,216	214	3,394	5,517	705	0
Parks, recreation, leisure and fitness studies	3,453	42,714	7,139	295	2,382	31,829	5,009	272	299	10,437	1,947	23	772	448	183	0
Philosophy and religious studies	326	12,793	1,931	796	141	5,702	701	313	185	6,887	1,132	481	0	204	98	2
Physical sciences and science technologies	6,376	28,050	7,011	5,514	6,305	19,652	5,322	3,949	68	8,394	1,689	1,565	3	4	0	0
Precision production	3,344	36	9	0	2,984	6	0	0	103	30	9	0	257	0	0	0
Psychology	6,119	114,450	27,846	6,323	5,641	76,834	8,830	2,517	374	34,108	14,770	2,792	104	3,508	4,246	1,014
Public administration and social service professions	8,781	31,950	43,590	979	6,055	19,721	25,105	551	474	8,923	16,317	291	2,252	3,306	2,168	137
Social sciences and history	15,669	177,778	20,784	4,619	15,523	121,823	11,347	3,091	120	53,623	9,437	1,528	26	2,332	0	0
Social sciences	14,750	143,587	17,483	3,616	14,640	98,342	8,725	2,435	106	43,292	8,347	1,181	4	1,953	411	0
History	919	34,191	4,102	1,003	883	23,481	2,622	656	14	10,331	1,090	347	22	379	390	0
Theology and religious vocations	881	9,385	14,276	2,175	3	1	0	0	857	9,295	14,215	2,167	21	89	61	8
Transportation and materials moving	2,087	4,526	1,420	1	1,544	2,024	102	0	469	2,411	1,258	1	74	91	60	8
Visual and performing arts	22,306	97,796	17,869	1,814	13,524	52,035	7,899	1,270	1,309	36,117	8,556	541	7,473	9,644	1,414	3

[1]Includes Ph.D., Ed.D., and comparable degrees at the doctoral level, as well as such degrees as M.D., D.D.S., and law degrees that were formerly classified as first-professional degrees.
[2]Excludes "Construction trades" and "Mechanic and repair technologies/technicians," which are listed separately.
NOTE: Data are for degree-granting postsecondary institutions, which are institutions that grant associate's or higher degrees and participate in Title IV federal financial aid programs. To facilitate trend comparisons, certain aggregations have been made of the degree fields as reported in the Integrated Postsecondary Education Data System (IPEDS): "Agriculture and natural resources" includes Agriculture, agriculture operations, and related sciences and Natural resources and conservation; and "Business" includes Business management, marketing, and related support services and Personal and culinary services. SOURCE: U.S. Department of Education, National Center for Education Statistics, Integrated Postsecondary Education Data System (IPEDS), Fall 2013, Completions component. (This table was prepared April 2015.)

Table 318.60. Number of postsecondary institutions conferring degrees, by control, level of degree, and field of study: 2012–13

Field of study	All institutions				Public institutions				Private nonprofit institutions				Private for-profit institutions			
	Associate's degrees	Bachelor's degrees	Master's degrees	Doctor's degrees[1]	Associate's degrees	Bachelor's degrees	Master's degrees	Doctor's degrees[1]	Associate's degrees	Bachelor's degrees	Master's degrees	Doctor's degrees[1]	Associate's degrees	Bachelor's degrees	Master's degrees	Doctor's degrees[1]
1	2	3	4	5	6	7	8	9	10	11	12	13	14	15	16	17
All fields, total	**3,029**	**2,578**	**1,930**	**915**	**1,242**	**653**	**532**	**322**	**635**	**1,318**	**1,120**	**537**	**1,152**	**607**	**278**	**56**
Agriculture and natural resources	494	694	235	97	465	321	178	89	29	367	55	8	0	6	2	0
Architecture and related services	74	197	150	34	71	119	100	24	3	74	48	10	0	4	2	0
Area, ethnic, cultural, gender, and group studies	66	489	141	54	63	239	90	36	3	249	51	18	0	1	1	0
Biological and biomedical sciences	281	1,351	493	261	263	521	348	182	17	822	145	79	1	8	0	0
Business	1,971	2,038	1,238	198	1,091	590	424	102	282	941	599	67	598	507	215	29
Communication, journalism, and related programs	310	1,175	337	76	269	455	214	59	29	671	119	17	12	49	4	0
Communications technologies	310	207	18	0	272	52	6	0	10	66	10	0	28	89	2	0
Computer and information sciences	1,518	1,525	492	166	905	517	284	113	94	661	146	50	519	347	62	3
Construction trades	348	13	1	0	311	11	1	0	11	1	0	0	26	1	0	0
Education	729	1,254	1,189	402	623	465	470	227	75	762	637	146	31	27	82	29
Engineering	345	517	319	209	330	283	209	151	9	216	103	58	6	18	7	0
Engineering technologies and engineering-related fields[2]	1,159	391	169	16	850	227	117	11	48	59	50	5	261	105	2	0
English language and literature/letters	175	1,338	482	153	169	515	316	104	4	815	164	49	2	8	2	0
Family and consumer sciences/human sciences	540	340	156	48	509	199	111	36	23	133	43	11	8	8	2	1
Foreign languages, literatures, and linguistics	198	915	223	100	187	414	163	68	11	499	60	32	0	2	0	0
Health professions and related programs	2,005	1,442	1,017	476	1,064	526	392	220	231	693	500	235	710	223	125	21
Homeland security, law enforcement, and firefighting	1,406	1,062	300	24	852	341	161	21	99	386	102	2	455	335	37	1
Legal professions and studies	818	248	140	210	422	69	53	84	51	112	83	118	345	67	4	8
Liberal arts and sciences, general studies, and humanities	1,391	914	186	15	1,085	384	93	6	275	509	91	8	31	21	2	0
Library science	32	8	65	14	32	7	53	12	0	0	12	2	0	1	0	0
Mathematics and statistics	197	1,196	348	176	193	501	266	124	3	694	82	52	1	1	0	0
Mechanic and repair technologies/technicians	713	20	0	0	623	12	0	0	23	8	0	0	67	0	0	0
Military technologies and applied sciences	8	5	3	0	6	2	1	0	0	1	2	0	2	2	0	0
Multi/interdisciplinary studies	390	922	348	114	363	354	194	80	23	524	152	34	4	44	2	0
Parks, recreation, leisure and fitness studies	289	826	275	48	241	339	196	43	18	474	73	5	30	13	6	0
Philosophy and religious studies	58	925	214	117	42	317	95	58	16	606	118	58	0	2	1	1
Physical sciences and science technologies	360	1,100	332	214	343	480	245	149	15	619	87	65	2	1	0	0
Precision production	355	9	2	0	334	3	0	0	10	6	2	0	11	0	0	0
Psychology	223	1,433	677	320	196	523	321	159	23	864	319	136	4	46	37	25
Public administration and social services	355	787	504	117	303	338	298	78	34	408	168	37	18	41	38	2
Social sciences and history	269	1,374	466	195	240	531	316	135	25	822	147	60	4	21	3	0
Social sciences	257	1,279	386	176	231	515	264	123	23	745	120	53	3	19	2	0
History	124	1,238	364	143	117	494	275	99	6	738	87	44	1	6	2	0
Theology and religious vocations	98	412	368	155	2	1	2	0	94	408	367	154	2	3	1	1
Transportation and materials moving	108	80	17	1	90	49	7	0	11	27	8	1	7	4	2	0
Visual and performing arts	887	1,466	455	115	582	496	254	76	62	836	187	38	243	134	14	1

[1]Includes Ph.D., Ed.D., and comparable degrees at the doctoral level, as well as such degrees as M.D., D.D.S., and law degrees that were formerly classified as first-professional degrees.
[2]Excludes "Construction trades" and "Mechanic and repair technologies/technicians," which are listed separately.
NOTE: Data are for degree-granting postsecondary institutions, which are institutions that grant associate's or higher degrees and participate in Title IV federal financial aid programs. To facilitate trend comparisons, certain aggregations have been made of the degree fields as reported in the Integrated Postsecondary Education Data System (IPEDS): "Agriculture and natural resources" includes Agriculture, agriculture operations, and related sciences and Natural resources and conservation; and "Business" includes Business management, marketing, and related support services and Personal and culinary services.
SOURCE: U.S. Department of Education, National Center for Education Statistics, Integrated Postsecondary Education Data System (IPEDS), Fall 2013, Completions component. (This table was prepared April 2015.)

Table 319.10. Degrees conferred by postsecondary institutions, by control of institution, level of degree, and state or jurisdiction: 2012–13

State or jurisdiction	Public				Private nonprofit				Private for-profit			
	Associate's degrees	Bachelor's degrees	Master's degrees	Doctor's degrees[1]	Associate's degrees	Bachelor's degrees	Master's degrees	Doctor's degrees[1]	Associate's degrees	Bachelor's degrees	Master's degrees	Doctor's degrees[1]
1	2	3	4	5	6	7	8	9	10	11	12	13
United States	772,588	1,163,620	346,813	86,427	55,617	535,736	326,984	81,539	178,756	140,808	77,954	7,072
Alabama	9,793	22,746	9,047	1,789	164	3,594	824	502	3,801	3,537	1,799	6
Alaska	1,268	1,757	679	54	9	76	45	0	481	62	0	0
Arizona	17,369	24,843	7,249	1,794	206	860	1,182	702	31,336	40,593	22,147	1,275
Arkansas	8,218	11,638	4,674	918	107	2,545	503	62	173	135	48	0
California	96,126	130,749	29,322	7,117	1,718	36,319	33,832	10,704	22,674	13,460	6,102	945
Colorado	8,728	23,436	7,237	1,798	670	4,083	4,254	619	6,152	4,927	3,516	330
Connecticut	5,547	11,239	3,076	746	908	9,563	6,275	1,218	371	668	219	0
Delaware	1,858	4,276	840	248	199	1,927	1,889	310	15	27	24	0
District of Columbia	300	372	84	81	219	8,556	10,455	3,540	167	371	456	0
Florida	75,543	64,089	17,414	4,447	7,503	22,489	12,535	3,793	17,781	7,726	2,963	788
Georgia	14,393	35,021	10,878	2,333	1,236	9,820	4,887	1,609	3,260	2,813	2,107	468
Hawaii	3,336	4,236	1,095	508	553	1,928	699	0	513	199	184	48
Idaho	3,158	6,313	1,761	389	2,146	3,911	280	9	458	112	8	0
Illinois	33,546	34,403	12,333	3,101	1,416	30,598	25,903	5,317	5,612	10,991	5,018	180
Indiana	12,132	30,873	9,589	2,597	1,698	14,732	4,927	878	5,008	946	147	0
Iowa	12,138	11,961	2,694	1,566	726	10,689	2,249	1,302	5,903	18,797	7,184	163
Kansas	9,462	15,396	4,903	1,355	622	4,146	1,718	119	563	80	4	0
Kentucky	9,712	16,563	6,065	1,578	691	4,625	3,334	282	3,450	684	461	91
Louisiana	5,404	18,643	5,317	1,566	551	3,397	2,167	966	1,195	294	68	0
Maine	2,654	4,251	886	153	168	3,042	1,049	336	345	42	0	0
Maryland	14,741	24,686	10,815	2,281	20	6,495	7,232	762	626	548	397	0
Massachusetts	11,375	18,935	5,839	765	1,405	37,630	29,464	7,524	962	526	137	0
Michigan	28,529	44,493	16,407	4,115	4,505	13,379	4,520	1,938	1,158	692	121	0
Minnesota	17,002	21,436	5,187	1,870	645	11,011	4,788	1,189	4,017	3,879	12,227	1,754
Mississippi	11,410	11,696	3,328	1,065	55	2,370	1,460	196	532	10	16	0
Missouri	12,310	21,186	6,620	1,554	3,066	17,942	13,256	3,128	4,445	1,835	701	0
Montana	2,141	4,925	1,214	395	155	719	66	0	0	0	0	0
Nebraska	5,093	8,449	2,653	821	249	5,565	2,324	674	619	105	31	0
Nevada	4,186	6,975	1,675	548	0	302	304	397	1,187	688	267	0
New Hampshire	1,927	5,366	1,130	65	422	4,025	2,740	436	475	378	8	0
New Jersey	20,491	29,658	7,856	1,447	184	9,846	6,295	888	972	791	116	0
New Mexico	8,137	7,684	2,856	629	0	121	175	0	804	781	208	0
New York	50,257	60,278	18,896	3,068	8,048	68,473	50,460	12,261	9,799	3,855	1,051	3
North Carolina	25,855	36,536	11,452	2,427	1,179	14,356	5,291	2,043	1,541	890	558	354
North Dakota	1,943	5,275	1,257	429	163	648	419	36	280	60	0	0
Ohio	23,169	44,222	14,644	4,423	2,782	21,027	7,907	1,694	7,618	944	443	0
Oklahoma	10,856	15,945	5,020	1,324	175	3,869	1,418	334	1,374	233	59	0
Oregon	12,958	16,583	4,143	999	58	5,043	3,305	961	1,256	459	93	0
Pennsylvania	16,724	46,707	12,011	3,480	3,258	42,690	24,760	6,298	8,812	2,013	364	0
Rhode Island	1,832	4,062	842	228	1,895	7,017	1,812	514	0	0	0	0
South Carolina	9,516	17,220	4,568	1,382	402	5,596	1,064	67	1,710	1,188	488	292
South Dakota	2,115	4,313	1,140	335	194	1,055	222	0	301	273	150	0
Tennessee	9,729	20,893	5,902	1,763	780	11,826	5,522	1,525	2,721	1,047	532	18
Texas	62,317	92,663	35,668	7,823	1,257	20,107	9,809	2,577	5,354	2,344	987	26
Utah	10,383	15,237	3,501	835	1,473	12,728	4,514	246	1,165	632	397	166
Vermont	997	3,572	552	228	197	2,557	2,639	206	86	77	0	0
Virginia	18,623	35,521	11,728	3,379	1,023	14,695	8,827	1,680	6,143	4,533	2,227	134
Washington	28,291	24,649	5,810	1,828	73	7,293	3,502	742	917	747	207	31
West Virginia	3,263	9,082	2,611	905	108	1,185	300	127	2,040	4,090	3,498	0
Wisconsin	12,977	26,939	5,855	1,679	327	9,262	3,582	828	2,224	726	216	0
Wyoming	2,756	2,053	486	199	9	4	0	0	360	0	0	0
U.S. Service Academies	0	3,576	4	0	†	†	†	†	†	†	†	†
Other jurisdictions	2,296	8,036	893	482	3,686	11,672	4,006	989	2,311	1,162	325	0
American Samoa	235	5	0	0	0	0	0	0	0	0	0	0
Federated States of Micronesia	293	0	0	0	0	0	0	0	0	0	0	0
Guam	137	389	113	0	0	6	0	0	0	0	0	0
Marshall Islands	79	0	0	0	0	0	0	0	0	0	0	0
Northern Marianas	133	29	0	0	0	0	0	0	0	0	0	0
Palau	99	0	0	0	0	0	0	0	0	0	0	0
Puerto Rico	1,255	7,402	724	482	3,686	11,666	4,006	989	2,311	1,162	325	0
U.S. Virgin Islands	65	211	56	0	0	0	0	0	0	0	0	0

†Not applicable.
[1]Includes Ph.D., Ed.D., and comparable degrees at the doctoral level. Includes most degrees formerly classified as first-professional, such as M.D., D.D.S., and law degrees.
NOTE: Data are for postsecondary institutions participating in Title IV federal financial aid programs.

SOURCE: U.S. Department of Education, National Center for Education Statistics, Integrated Postsecondary Education Data System (IPEDS), Fall 2013, Completions component. (This table was prepared September 2014.)

Table 319.20. Degrees conferred by postsecondary institutions, by level of degree and state or jurisdiction: 2010–11 through 2012–13

State or jurisdiction	2010–11				2011–12				2012–13			
	Associate's degrees	Bachelor's degrees	Master's degrees	Doctor's degrees[1]	Associate's degrees	Bachelor's degrees	Master's degrees	Doctor's degrees[1]	Associate's degrees	Bachelor's degrees	Master's degrees	Doctor's degrees[1]
1	2	3	4	5	6	7	8	9	10	11	12	13
United States	943,506	1,716,053	730,922	163,827	1,021,718	1,792,163	755,967	170,217	1,006,961	1,840,164	751,751	175,038
Alabama	11,795	27,248	11,888	2,144	14,197	28,277	11,539	2,256	13,758	29,877	11,670	2,297
Alaska	1,523	1,770	693	46	1,706	1,750	703	50	1,758	1,895	724	54
Arizona	58,992	50,940	36,231	2,937	62,994	64,707	36,178	3,533	48,911	66,296	30,578	3,771
Arkansas	10,181	13,259	4,793	813	8,645	14,190	5,320	913	8,498	14,318	5,225	980
California	107,675	169,623	67,467	17,113	114,613	172,419	68,502	17,448	120,518	180,528	69,256	18,766
Colorado	16,145	29,540	14,264	2,170	16,939	31,136	15,406	2,352	15,550	32,446	15,007	2,747
Connecticut	6,079	19,735	9,131	1,808	6,511	20,710	9,457	1,954	6,826	21,470	9,570	1,964
Delaware	1,820	5,877	2,705	546	1,947	5,885	2,680	585	2,072	6,230	2,753	558
District of Columbia	555	8,402	10,078	3,458	463	9,212	10,211	3,567	686	9,299	10,995	3,621
Florida	87,386	86,230	31,766	9,297	103,158	91,225	33,859	9,485	100,827	94,304	32,912	9,028
Georgia	17,949	45,079	17,533	4,005	18,728	45,936	17,674	4,267	18,889	47,654	17,872	4,410
Hawaii	3,766	5,751	2,062	529	4,199	6,016	2,115	533	4,402	6,363	1,978	556
Idaho	3,977	9,171	1,790	321	4,952	9,781	2,041	331	5,762	10,336	2,049	398
Illinois	40,009	71,584	43,018	7,882	41,925	72,541	43,664	8,132	40,574	75,992	43,254	8,598
Indiana	18,603	43,519	14,337	3,386	19,430	45,534	14,230	3,465	18,838	46,551	14,663	3,475
Iowa	19,317	36,266	9,982	3,112	20,515	40,676	12,100	2,957	18,767	41,447	12,127	3,031
Kansas	9,499	18,170	7,144	1,476	10,218	18,999	7,021	1,452	10,647	19,622	6,625	1,474
Kentucky	13,029	21,078	8,350	1,812	14,680	21,531	9,411	1,935	13,853	21,872	9,860	1,951
Louisiana	7,236	21,357	7,017	2,236	7,706	22,015	7,275	2,585	7,150	22,334	7,552	2,532
Maine	3,309	7,347	1,766	367	3,321	7,596	1,902	383	3,167	7,335	1,935	489
Maryland	13,923	29,247	16,975	2,652	15,156	30,863	17,845	2,822	15,387	31,729	18,444	3,043
Massachusetts	12,907	53,749	34,090	7,637	13,645	55,593	35,748	8,146	13,742	57,091	35,440	8,289
Michigan	30,859	56,448	21,252	5,807	33,322	57,815	21,392	5,884	34,192	58,564	21,048	6,053
Minnesota	20,480	33,386	21,823	4,352	21,868	35,428	22,424	4,420	21,664	36,326	22,202	4,813
Mississippi	11,440	13,230	4,726	1,170	12,996	13,516	4,809	1,217	11,997	14,076	4,804	1,261
Missouri	18,545	41,648	20,656	4,656	19,895	43,688	20,979	4,669	19,821	40,963	20,577	4,682
Montana	2,058	5,512	1,201	357	2,364	5,384	1,286	372	2,296	5,644	1,280	395
Nebraska	5,351	13,510	4,684	1,371	5,761	14,248	5,178	1,392	5,961	14,119	5,008	1,495
Nevada	4,997	7,556	2,720	839	5,350	7,639	2,604	950	5,373	7,965	2,246	945
New Hampshire	3,062	9,479	3,666	448	3,119	9,270	3,825	480	2,824	9,769	3,878	501
New Jersey	21,124	37,087	14,427	3,101	21,631	39,804	15,490	3,122	21,647	40,295	14,267	2,335
New Mexico	6,552	8,179	3,266	583	7,709	8,259	3,259	614	8,941	8,586	3,239	629
New York	66,644	127,209	70,264	14,251	69,654	129,429	71,406	14,809	68,104	132,606	70,407	15,332
North Carolina	25,154	48,670	16,226	4,116	27,673	50,737	16,948	4,420	28,575	51,782	17,301	4,824
North Dakota	2,552	5,564	1,572	456	2,523	5,742	1,725	480	2,386	5,983	1,676	465
Ohio	33,477	63,882	22,636	6,033	35,871	66,736	24,148	5,992	33,569	66,193	22,994	6,117
Oklahoma	10,710	19,511	6,356	1,611	11,513	19,846	6,481	1,728	12,405	20,047	6,497	1,658
Oregon	10,945	19,542	7,326	1,849	12,637	21,114	7,541	1,910	14,272	22,085	7,541	1,960
Pennsylvania	29,241	88,205	36,016	9,316	29,875	90,688	36,832	9,384	28,794	91,410	37,135	9,778
Rhode Island	3,461	10,863	2,545	709	3,537	11,013	2,566	745	3,727	11,079	2,654	742
South Carolina	9,771	22,822	5,789	1,606	10,790	22,973	5,972	1,604	11,628	24,004	6,120	1,741
South Dakota	2,601	5,211	1,427	300	2,699	5,392	1,467	353	2,610	5,641	1,512	335
Tennessee	12,478	31,026	11,099	2,989	13,548	32,309	11,929	3,152	13,230	33,766	11,956	3,306
Texas	58,553	107,950	42,203	9,744	67,768	111,312	45,325	10,108	68,928	115,114	46,464	10,426
Utah	12,398	24,461	6,995	1,087	13,280	26,554	7,669	1,184	13,021	28,597	8,412	1,247
Vermont	1,223	6,100	2,377	388	1,196	6,283	2,474	415	1,280	6,206	3,191	434
Virginia	24,193	49,077	20,697	4,923	26,199	52,998	21,516	5,328	25,789	54,749	22,782	5,193
Washington	27,045	31,294	9,830	2,405	28,977	32,376	9,595	2,561	29,281	32,689	9,519	2,601
West Virginia	4,688	13,001	5,884	1,007	4,897	13,284	5,892	986	5,411	14,357	6,409	1,032
Wisconsin	15,012	35,279	9,695	2,418	16,494	36,005	9,856	2,590	15,528	36,927	9,653	2,507
Wyoming	3,217	1,860	482	188	2,924	2,064	489	197	3,125	2,057	486	199
U.S. Service Academies	0	3,549	2	0	0	3,665	9	0	0	3,576	4	0
Other jurisdictions	7,690	18,332	5,871	1,421	9,135	20,358	5,309	1,405	8,293	20,870	5,224	1,471
American Samoa	216	0	0	0	269	2	0	0	235	5	0	0
Federated States of Micronesia	267	0	0	0	262	0	0	0	293	0	0	0
Guam	119	375	134	0	278	408	132	0	137	395	113	0
Marshall Islands	68	0	0	0	71	0	0	0	79	0	0	0
Northern Marianas	105	14	0	0	103	14	0	0	133	29	0	0
Palau	26	0	0	0	85	0	0	0	99	0	0	0
Puerto Rico	6,814	17,714	5,703	1,421	7,994	19,697	5,124	1,405	7,252	20,230	5,055	1,471
U.S. Virgin Islands	75	229	34	0	73	237	53	0	65	211	56	0

[1]Includes Ph.D., Ed.D., and comparable degrees at the doctoral level. Includes most degrees formerly classified as first-professional, such as M.D., D.D.S., and law degrees.
NOTE: Data are for postsecondary institutions participating in Title IV federal financial aid programs. Some data have been revised from previously published figures.

SOURCE: U.S. Department of Education, National Center for Education Statistics, Integrated Postsecondary Education Data System (IPEDS), Fall 2011 through Fall 2013, Completions component. (This table was prepared September 2014.)

Table 319.30. Bachelor's degrees conferred by postsecondary institutions, by field of study and state or jurisdiction: 2012–13

State or jurisdiction	Total	Humanities[1]	Psychology	Social sciences and history	Natural sciences[2]	Computer sciences	Engineering[3]	Education	Business/ management	Health professions and related programs	Other fields[4]
1	2	3	4	5	6	7	8	9	10	11	12
United States	1,840,164	297,337	114,450	177,778	148,822	50,962	102,984	104,647	360,823	181,144	301,217
Alabama	29,877	2,789	1,506	1,692	2,167	594	2,313	2,697	7,178	3,186	5,755
Alaska	1,895	321	132	153	193	31	161	79	362	172	291
Arizona	66,296	8,848	2,359	2,694	2,829	3,663	1,628	3,528	19,218	10,565	10,964
Arkansas	14,318	2,317	740	1,021	1,096	257	641	1,440	2,651	1,695	2,460
California	180,528	36,122	13,695	25,092	17,461	4,338	10,905	2,776	31,021	11,893	27,225
Colorado	32,446	5,175	1,897	3,427	2,854	943	2,092	255	7,235	2,844	5,724
Connecticut	21,470	4,100	1,735	2,965	1,849	241	915	712	3,457	2,182	3,314
Delaware	6,230	743	366	592	321	156	333	509	1,410	680	1,120
District of Columbia	9,299	1,333	552	2,863	564	203	257	53	1,635	657	1,182
Florida	94,304	11,707	6,329	8,358	6,232	2,681	4,567	5,309	22,060	9,879	17,182
Georgia	47,654	6,973	3,018	4,170	4,095	1,605	2,665	4,034	9,799	4,104	7,191
Hawaii	6,363	1,055	415	819	440	134	202	350	1,358	475	1,115
Idaho	10,336	1,539	554	820	857	290	499	1,109	1,566	1,316	1,786
Illinois	75,992	12,248	4,231	6,035	5,634	2,537	3,817	5,274	14,789	9,531	11,896
Indiana	46,551	6,528	1,994	3,256	3,170	1,418	3,674	3,734	9,568	5,716	7,493
Iowa	41,447	3,995	3,121	3,557	1,873	867	1,512	3,774	10,454	4,258	8,036
Kansas	19,622	2,825	717	1,362	1,166	364	1,228	1,704	4,802	2,346	3,108
Kentucky	21,872	3,010	1,188	1,659	1,596	375	1,096	2,217	3,778	2,157	4,796
Louisiana	22,334	3,688	1,211	1,715	1,978	360	1,482	1,743	4,396	2,488	3,273
Maine	7,335	1,245	438	916	781	83	455	557	795	990	1,075
Maryland	31,729	4,126	2,169	4,153	2,950	2,177	1,493	1,493	5,592	2,544	5,032
Massachusetts	57,091	10,070	4,076	7,554	5,369	1,412	3,473	1,496	10,316	4,942	8,383
Michigan	58,564	7,657	3,440	4,352	4,810	1,620	4,546	3,545	11,671	6,509	10,414
Minnesota	36,326	5,632	2,489	3,003	3,699	1,090	1,512	2,419	7,349	3,477	5,656
Mississippi	14,076	1,899	766	879	1,185	146	656	1,912	2,686	1,544	2,403
Missouri	40,963	5,602	2,575	2,595	2,841	1,097	2,203	3,413	9,300	4,359	6,978
Montana	5,644	799	279	539	553	84	516	501	876	461	1,036
Nebraska	14,119	1,369	688	920	940	392	467	1,523	3,607	1,749	2,464
Nevada	7,965	1,022	506	657	539	181	360	506	2,152	820	1,222
New Hampshire	9,769	1,492	764	1,231	690	200	513	489	2,073	720	1,597
New Jersey	40,295	7,688	3,428	4,791	3,637	908	2,121	2,016	7,278	2,436	5,992
New Mexico	8,586	1,617	522	582	639	222	587	878	1,529	653	1,357
New York	132,606	26,534	10,387	15,323	10,903	3,353	6,429	6,945	23,724	10,534	18,474
North Carolina	51,782	6,623	3,609	5,317	4,853	1,224	2,868	3,919	8,644	4,382	10,343
North Dakota	5,983	529	243	240	399	111	502	657	1,218	747	1,337
Ohio	66,193	8,737	3,349	5,155	4,828	1,287	4,453	5,524	12,485	9,497	10,878
Oklahoma	20,047	3,695	878	1,036	1,358	379	1,387	1,678	4,026	1,931	3,679
Oregon	22,085	4,620	1,442	2,999	1,810	439	1,112	679	3,342	1,847	3,795
Pennsylvania	91,410	14,099	5,559	8,703	8,375	2,923	5,793	5,444	16,655	10,330	13,529
Rhode Island	11,079	1,512	549	947	859	290	472	502	2,798	642	2,508
South Carolina	24,004	3,351	1,418	2,321	2,682	464	1,131	1,951	5,514	1,796	3,376
South Dakota	5,641	554	237	461	401	182	424	533	766	1,008	1,075
Tennessee	33,766	6,477	1,839	2,647	2,435	680	1,566	2,615	6,048	3,495	5,964
Texas	115,114	23,716	6,229	8,774	9,641	2,153	7,221	1,929	22,377	11,749	21,325
Utah	28,597	3,417	1,227	2,204	1,846	1,621	1,282	3,212	5,049	4,656	4,083
Vermont	6,206	1,354	382	866	555	197	290	270	804	347	1,141
Virginia	54,749	10,934	4,545	6,489	4,408	2,453	2,984	1,443	10,210	3,972	7,311
Washington	32,689	6,573	2,048	4,481	3,351	1,073	1,802	1,411	5,097	2,141	4,712
West Virginia	14,357	3,075	636	1,139	815	511	669	891	2,357	986	3,278
Wisconsin	36,927	5,355	1,855	3,293	3,668	803	2,197	2,735	7,295	3,474	6,252
Wyoming	2,057	215	94	142	209	23	223	264	233	262	392
U.S. Service Academies	3,576	433	24	819	418	127	1,290	0	220	0	245
Other jurisdictions	20,870	979	1,044	729	1,738	624	1,321	1,933	5,626	3,797	3,079
American Samoa	5	0	0	0	0	0	0	5	0	0	0
Guam	395	40	14	17	16	13	0	72	99	30	94
Northern Marianas	29	0	0	0	0	0	0	29	0	0	0
Puerto Rico	20,230	927	1,003	707	1,688	605	1,321	1,807	5,452	3,752	2,968
U.S. Virgin Islands	211	12	27	5	34	6	0	20	75	15	17

[1]Includes degrees in area, ethnic, cultural, and gender studies; English language and literature/letters; foreign languages, literatures, and linguistics; liberal arts and sciences, general studies and humanities; multi/interdisciplinary studies; philosophy and religious studies; theology and religious vocations; and visual and performing arts.
[2]Includes biological and biomedical sciences; physical sciences; science technologies/technicians; and mathematics and statistics.
[3]Includes engineering; engineering technologies/technicians; mechanic and repair technologies/technicians; and construction trades.
[4]Includes agriculture, agricultural operations, and related sciences; natural resources and conservation; architecture and related services; communication, journalism, and related programs; communications technologies/technicians and support services; family and consumer services/human sciences; legal professions and studies; library science; military technologies and applied sciences; parks, recreation, leisure, and fitness studies; homeland security, law enforcement, and firefighting; public administration and social service professions; transportation and materials moving; and precision production.
NOTE: Data are for postsecondary institutions participating in Title IV federal financial aid programs. This table includes only those jurisdictions with 4-year institutions.
SOURCE: U.S. Department of Education, National Center for Education Statistics, Integrated Postsecondary Education Data System (IPEDS), Fall 2013, Completions component. (This table was prepared September 2014.)

Table 319.40. Master's degrees conferred by postsecondary institutions, by field of study and state or jurisdiction: 2012–13

State or jurisdiction	Total	Humanities[1]	Psychology	Social sciences and history	Natural sciences[2]	Computer sciences	Engineering[3]	Education	Business/ management	Health professions and related programs	Other fields[4]
1	2	3	4	5	6	7	8	9	10	11	12
United States	751,751	60,660	27,846	21,585	27,303	22,777	45,325	164,624	188,625	90,931	102,075
Alabama	11,670	412	378	248	256	146	997	2,541	3,039	1,898	1,755
Alaska	724	47	33	16	32	2	65	293	115	19	102
Arizona	30,578	745	2,293	210	399	500	820	8,185	10,948	4,169	2,309
Arkansas	5,225	243	39	92	157	70	317	2,310	650	673	674
California	69,256	7,997	4,291	1,958	2,489	2,166	6,162	12,358	14,676	7,720	9,439
Colorado	15,007	922	923	518	458	677	1,124	2,439	5,000	1,209	1,737
Connecticut	9,570	942	353	248	555	240	674	2,268	1,991	1,126	1,173
Delaware	2,753	87	18	75	100	34	74	808	968	243	346
District of Columbia	10,995	1,208	156	1,417	671	394	615	755	2,107	966	2,706
Florida	32,912	1,699	1,172	635	1,324	589	2,201	4,328	11,022	4,579	5,363
Georgia	17,872	1,677	280	476	672	584	1,106	3,702	4,929	2,501	1,945
Hawaii	1,978	176	129	73	77	28	73	485	390	178	369
Idaho	2,049	147	11	43	123	26	174	603	249	244	429
Illinois	43,254	3,071	1,672	944	1,546	1,859	1,921	8,635	13,370	4,463	5,773
Indiana	14,663	1,324	264	294	534	329	1,010	3,137	4,086	1,976	1,709
Iowa	12,127	496	377	71	189	413	277	3,299	4,205	1,464	1,336
Kansas	6,625	620	174	131	175	61	455	1,869	1,338	635	1,167
Kentucky	9,860	689	514	180	291	199	348	3,399	1,467	1,338	1,435
Louisiana	7,552	613	183	181	442	116	283	1,576	1,609	1,341	1,208
Maine	1,935	138	20	13	51	6	37	676	302	387	305
Maryland	18,444	1,199	336	963	1,054	1,785	1,123	3,027	5,285	2,042	1,630
Massachusetts	35,440	2,840	927	1,401	1,311	1,009	2,238	7,551	9,141	3,681	5,341
Michigan	21,048	1,304	496	477	965	550	2,155	4,119	5,470	2,192	3,320
Minnesota	22,202	928	1,529	277	342	643	523	5,947	4,097	5,123	2,793
Mississippi	4,804	187	87	87	469	51	132	1,724	924	555	588
Missouri	20,577	1,160	725	560	416	385	936	4,013	7,605	2,447	2,330
Montana	1,280	115	22	49	80	13	54	398	116	187	246
Nebraska	5,008	316	107	341	191	168	127	1,341	1,128	757	532
Nevada	2,246	104	33	76	125	51	92	727	492	286	260
New Hampshire	3,878	181	43	53	69	129	199	913	1,461	496	334
New Jersey	14,267	1,372	461	316	690	701	1,334	3,172	3,229	992	2,000
New Mexico	3,239	306	77	135	161	43	253	899	583	453	329
New York	70,407	7,513	1,968	2,650	2,796	2,423	3,876	16,680	13,548	7,458	11,495
North Carolina	17,301	1,556	202	528	788	614	1,223	3,618	4,093	2,393	2,286
North Dakota	1,676	44	51	30	47	36	96	367	422	315	268
Ohio	22,994	1,854	689	585	1,069	286	1,510	5,081	5,567	3,375	2,978
Oklahoma	6,497	811	280	120	238	151	505	1,250	1,662	750	730
Oregon	7,541	769	294	156	268	79	346	2,765	1,287	780	797
Pennsylvania	37,135	2,888	1,279	847	1,326	1,426	2,642	8,816	7,724	5,391	4,796
Rhode Island	2,654	225	82	125	152	50	132	406	813	206	463
South Carolina	6,120	439	163	121	245	103	376	1,631	1,395	789	858
South Dakota	1,512	103	94	32	76	63	121	360	327	177	159
Tennessee	11,956	944	440	222	302	148	412	3,245	2,725	2,193	1,325
Texas	46,464	3,749	2,045	1,142	2,019	1,704	3,202	9,726	12,628	4,712	5,537
Utah	8,412	330	134	119	215	327	385	2,091	2,743	1,225	843
Vermont	3,191	629	59	647	39	20	162	450	540	106	539
Virginia	22,782	3,357	1,046	556	518	843	1,194	5,183	5,067	1,759	3,259
Washington	9,519	709	454	144	399	311	468	2,044	2,104	1,200	1,686
West Virginia	6,409	814	94	716	99	61	138	1,124	1,283	499	1,581
Wisconsin	9,653	592	344	269	237	159	593	2,192	2,645	1,228	1,394
Wyoming	486	69	5	18	56	6	41	98	60	35	98
U.S. Service Academies	4	0	0	0	0	0	4	0	0	0	0
Other jurisdictions	5,224	210	372	24	137	56	266	1,375	1,446	671	667
American Samoa	0	0	0	0	0	0	0	0	0	0	0
Guam	113	1	7	0	1	0	0	66	7	0	31
Northern Marianas	0	0	0	0	0	0	0	0	0	0	0
Puerto Rico	5,055	209	356	24	136	56	266	1,286	1,433	671	618
U.S. Virgin Islands	56	0	9	0	0	0	0	23	6	0	18

[1]Includes degrees in area, ethnic, cultural, and gender studies; English language and literature/letters; foreign languages, literatures, and linguistics; liberal arts and sciences, general studies and humanities; multi/interdisciplinary studies; philosophy and religious studies; theology and religious vocations; and visual and performing arts.
[2]Includes biological and biomedical sciences; physical sciences; science technologies/technicians; and mathematics and statistics.
[3]Includes engineering; engineering technologies/technicians; mechanic and repair technologies/technicians; and construction trades.
[4]Includes agriculture, agricultural operations, and related sciences; natural resources and conservation; architecture and related services; communication, journalism, and related programs; communications technologies/technicians and support services; family and consumer services/human sciences; legal professions and studies; library science; military technologies and applied sciences; parks, recreation, leisure, and fitness studies; homeland security, law enforcement, and firefighting; public administration and social service professions; transportation and materials moving; and precision production.
NOTE: Data are for postsecondary institutions participating in Title IV federal financial aid programs. This table includes only those jurisdictions with 4-year institutions.
SOURCE: U.S. Department of Education, National Center for Education Statistics, Integrated Postsecondary Education Data System (IPEDS), Fall 2013, Completions component. (This table was prepared September 2014.)

Table 320.10. Certificates below the associate's degree level conferred by postsecondary institutions, by length of curriculum, sex of student, institution level and control, and discipline division: 2012–13

Discipline division	Less-than-1-year certificates								1- to less-than-4-year certificates							
	Sex			Institution level		Institution control			Sex			Institution level		Institution control		
	Total	Males	Females	Non-degree-granting (less-than-2-year)	Degree-granting (2-year and 4-year)	Public	Nonprofit	For-profit	Total	Males	Females	Non-degree-granting (less-than-2-year)	Degree-granting (2-year and 4-year)	Public	Nonprofit	For-profit
1	2	3	4	5	6	7	8	9	10	11	12	13	14	15	16	17
Total	**452,202**	**196,007**	**256,195**	**112,633**	**339,569**	**321,286**	**13,665**	**117,251**	**513,882**	**179,339**	**334,543**	**203,448**	**310,434**	**223,595**	**17,017**	**273,270**
Agriculture and natural resources	3,587	2,449	1,138	72	3,515	3,473	16	98	2,470	1,606	864	159	2,311	2,256	136	78
Agriculture, agriculture operations, and related sciences	2,646	1,661	985	72	2,564	2,564	0	82	2,378	1,539	839	159	2,219	2,166	134	78
Natural resources and conservation	941	788	153	0	941	909	16	16	92	67	25	0	92	90	2	0
Architecture and related services	209	111	98	0	209	165	43	1	135	95	40	0	135	104	31	0
Area, ethnic, cultural, gender, and group studies	448	117	331	0	448	427	21	0	101	32	69	0	101	100	1	0
Biological and biomedical sciences	729	174	555	104	625	630	8	91	124	45	79	61	63	103	6	15
Business, management, marketing, and support services	47,248	15,162	32,086	3,832	43,416	42,284	1,059	3,905	24,621	6,712	17,909	3,490	21,131	20,492	1,271	2,858
Accounting and related services	8,754	2,356	6,398	612	8,142	7,742	100	912	6,123	1,479	4,644	771	5,352	5,105	516	502
Business/commerce, general	2,736	1,186	1,550	11	2,725	2,564	155	17	1,477	736	741	11	1,477	1,387	10	80
Business administration, management, and operations	8,932	3,283	5,649	55	8,877	8,595	206	131	3,906	1,415	2,491	117	3,789	3,594	42	270
Management information systems and services	712	384	328	352	360	295	51	366	362	191	171	135	227	336	0	26
Business operations support and assistant services	12,300	2,924	9,376	1,754	10,546	10,741	47	1,512	8,032	1,153	6,879	1,872	6,160	6,219	424	1,389
Business and management, other	13,814	5,029	8,785	1,048	12,766	12,347	500	967	4,721	1,738	2,983	595	4,126	3,851	279	591
Communication, journalism, and related programs	1,651	881	770	487	1,164	1,137	90	424	1,504	883	621	945	559	368	186	950
Communications technologies	2,261	1,360	901	594	1,667	1,819	39	403	3,321	2,570	751	1,783	1,538	1,414	27	1,880
Computer and information sciences and support services	17,981	12,401	5,580	1,854	16,127	15,515	208	2,258	10,495	8,031	2,464	2,076	8,419	6,884	202	3,409
Construction trades	10,984	10,447	537	2,685	8,299	9,770	747	467	13,308	12,753	555	4,054	9,254	8,301	588	4,419
Education	4,925	670	4,255	62	4,863	4,028	303	594	3,288	321	2,967	477	2,811	2,380	495	413
Engineering	573	470	103	197	376	568	0	5	160	18	142	26	134	136	22	2
Engineering technologies and engineering-related fields[1]	16,472	14,125	2,347	2,093	14,379	14,351	173	1,948	12,760	11,584	1,176	2,365	10,395	7,936	344	4,480
English language and literature/letters	2,317	801	1,516	1,143	1,174	643	659	1,015	361	126	235	97	264	102	117	142
Family and consumer sciences/human sciences	14,497	1,419	13,078	1,015	13,482	14,311	68	118	3,377	305	3,072	219	3,158	3,321	30	26
Foreign languages, literatures, and linguistics	920	192	728	0	920	856	56	8	631	89	542	7	624	600	31	0
Health professions and related programs	171,122	33,147	137,975	49,492	121,630	102,351	5,947	62,824	209,347	29,891	179,456	74,442	134,905	72,622	8,523	128,202
Dental assisting	7,655	722	6,933	2,755	4,900	1,478	249	5,928	15,313	1,445	13,868	4,722	10,591	4,230	49	11,034
Emergency medical technician (EMT paramedic)	15,854	10,294	5,560	1,296	14,558	15,627	54	173	5,477	4,169	1,308	416	5,061	4,763	250	464
Clinical/medical lab science	8,547	1,214	7,333	2,053	6,494	6,153	163	2,231	2,214	421	1,793	738	1,476	752	380	1,082
Medical assisting	18,549	1,794	16,755	7,842	10,707	2,590	2,053	13,906	64,684	6,254	58,430	25,980	38,704	6,626	1,721	56,337
Pharmacy assisting	7,003	1,588	5,415	2,398	4,605	2,198	672	4,133	9,187	2,173	7,014	2,497	6,690	2,072	70	7,045
Other allied health assisting	8,634	2,532	6,102	2,657	5,977	5,034	7	3,593	3,295	392	2,903	1,458	1,837	927	171	2,197
Nursing and patient care assistant	46,663	6,221	40,442	10,537	36,126	39,254	925	6,484	1,245	144	1,101	709	536	397	0	848
Practical nursing	5,878	643	5,235	702	5,176	5,368	45	465	53,082	6,250	46,832	17,771	35,311	35,469	1,672	15,941
Nursing, registered nurse and other	1,689	176	1,513	22	1,667	1,667	10	12	3,586	531	3,055	2,229	1,357	1,133	2,145	308
Health sciences, other	50,650	7,963	42,687	19,252	31,398	22,982	1,767	25,901	51,264	8,112	43,152	17,922	33,342	16,253	2,065	32,946
Homeland security, law enforcement, and firefighting	26,438	19,820	6,618	2,853	23,585	25,451	313	674	6,374	4,351	2,023	230	6,144	5,769	145	460
Criminal justice and corrections	19,222	13,353	5,869	1,181	18,041	18,773	255	194	5,159	3,253	1,906	214	4,945	4,667	37	455
Fire control and safety	6,354	5,886	468	1,441	4,913	6,333	8	13	1,051	987	64	16	1,035	1,051	0	0
Homeland security and related protective services, other	862	581	281	231	631	345	50	467	164	111	53	0	164	51	108	5
Legal professions and studies	1,976	349	1,627	81	1,895	1,368	100	508	3,341	575	2,766	549	2,792	2,584	195	562
Liberal arts and sciences, general studies, and humanities	3,355	1,214	2,141	0	3,355	3,351	4	0	30,821	12,208	18,613	0	30,821	30,749	64	8
Library science	212	27	185	0	212	212	0	0	71	5	66	0	71	68	3	0
Mathematics and statistics	62	52	10	0	62	40	22	0	10	6	4	0	10	7	3	0
Mechanic and repair technologies/technicians	31,741	29,792	1,949	4,161	27,580	28,866	612	2,263	52,407	50,381	2,026	23,074	29,333	21,915	807	29,685
Military technologies and applied sciences	21	16	5	0	21	0	2	19	4	4	0	0	4	4	0	0
Multi/interdisciplinary studies	1,622	803	819	24	1,598	1,265	47	310	1,125	539	586	0	1,125	1,100	25	0
Parks, recreation, leisure, and fitness studies	2,135	921	1,214	475	1,660	1,580	26	529	723	396	327	224	499	362	6	355
Personal and culinary services	38,160	6,227	31,933	27,368	10,792	9,532	282	28,346	105,286	16,222	89,064	82,775	22,511	13,973	1,123	90,190
Philosophy and religious studies	73	38	35	0	73	48	25	0	20	11	9	0	20	2	18	0

See notes at end of table.

Table 320.10. Certificates below the associate's degree level conferred by postsecondary institutions, by length of curriculum, sex of student, institution level and control, and discipline division: 2012–13—Continued

Discipline division	Less-than-1-year certificates								1- to less-than-4-year certificates							
	Sex			Institution level		Institution control				Sex		Institution level		Institution control		
	Total	Males	Females	Non-degree-granting (less-than-2-year)	Degree-granting (2-year and 4-year)	Public	Nonprofit	For-profit	Total	Males	Females	Non-degree-granting (less-than-2-year)	Degree-granting (2-year and 4-year)	Public	Nonprofit	For-profit
	2	3	4	5	6	7	8	9	10	11	12	13	14	15	16	17
Physical sciences and science technologies	855	608	247	166	689	760	9	86	666	495	171	0	666	665	0	1
Physical sciences	62	37	25	0	62	53	9	0	10	8	2	0	10	10	0	0
Science technologies/technicians	793	571	222	166	627	707	0	86	656	487	169	0	656	655	0	1
Precision production	17,721	16,795	926	2,900	14,821	15,872	781	1,068	13,748	13,037	711	4,121	9,627	10,140	723	2,885
Psychology	36	10	26	0	36	35	1	0	70	16	54	0	70	66	4	0
Public administration and social services	1,139	226	913	17	1,122	1,002	91	46	903	156	747	0	903	890	9	4
Social sciences and history	874	492	382	0	874	809	65	0	334	181	153	0	334	317	17	0
Social sciences	841	488	353	0	841	778	63	0	333	180	153	0	333	317	16	0
History	33	4	29	0	33	31	2	0	1	1	0	0	1	0	1	0
Theology and religious vocations	188	77	111	0	188	0	188	0	1,059	482	577	585	474	0	1,059	0
Transportation and materials moving	24,529	22,310	2,219	9,975	14,554	15,436	976	8,117	987	925	62	378	609	650	16	321
Visual and performing arts	5,141	2,304	2,837	983	4,158	3,329	686	1,126	9,930	4,164	5,766	1,311	8,619	7,215	790	1,925
Fine and studio arts	819	318	501	690	129	113	546	160	4,864	1,766	3,098	2	4,862	4,822	41	1
Music and dance	553	411	142	0	553	170	3	380	679	493	186	226	453	158	176	345
Visual and performing arts, other[2]	3,769	1,575	2,194	293	3,476	3,046	137	586	4,387	1,905	2,482	1,083	3,304	2,235	573	1,579

[1] Excludes "Construction trades" and "Mechanic and repair technologies/technicians," which are listed separately.
[2] Includes design and applied arts, drama and theatre arts, film and photographic arts, and all other arts not included under "Fine and studio arts" or "Music and dance."

NOTE: Data are for postsecondary institutions participating in Title IV federal financial aid programs. Degree-granting institutions grant degrees at the associate's or higher level, while non-degree-granting institutions grant only awards below that level.
SOURCE: U.S. Department of Education, National Center for Education Statistics, Integrated Postsecondary Education Data System (IPEDS), Fall 2013, Completions component. (This table was prepared October 2014.)

Table 320.20. Certificates below the associate's degree level conferred by postsecondary institutions, by race/ethnicity and sex of student: 1998–99 through 2012–13

Year and sex	Number of certificates conferred to U.S. citizens and nonresident aliens								Percentage distribution of certificates conferred to U.S. citizens						
	Total	White	Black	Hispanic	Asian/ Pacific Islander	American Indian/ Alaska Native	Two or more races	Non-resident alien	Total	White	Black	Hispanic	Asian/ Pacific Islander	American Indian/ Alaska Native	Two or more races
1	2	3	4	5	6	7	8	9	10	11	12	13	14	15	16
Total															
1998–99	555,883	345,359	92,800	76,833	27,920	7,510	—	5,461	100.0	62.7	16.9	14.0	5.1	1.4	—
1999–2000	558,129	337,546	97,329	81,132	29,361	6,966	—	5,795	100.0	61.1	17.6	14.7	5.3	1.3	—
2000–01	552,503	333,478	99,397	78,528	28,123	6,598	—	6,379	100.0	61.1	18.2	14.4	5.1	1.2	—
2001–02	584,248	352,559	106,647	83,950	27,490	7,430	—	6,172	100.0	61.0	18.4	14.5	4.8	1.3	—
2002–03	646,425	382,289	120,582	95,499	32,981	8,117	—	6,957	100.0	59.8	18.9	14.9	5.2	1.3	—
2003–04	687,787	402,989	129,891	107,216	32,819	8,375	—	6,497	100.0	59.2	19.1	15.7	4.8	1.2	—
2004–05	710,873	415,670	133,601	114,089	32,783	8,150	—	6,580	100.0	59.0	19.0	16.2	4.7	1.2	—
2005–06	715,401	412,077	135,460	118,853	34,110	8,400	—	6,501	100.0	58.1	19.1	16.8	4.8	1.2	—
2006–07	729,037	420,585	139,995	119,501	32,962	8,793	—	7,201	100.0	58.3	19.4	16.6	4.6	1.2	—
2007–08	749,883	430,187	145,181	122,676	35,985	8,596	—	7,258	100.0	57.9	19.5	16.5	4.8	1.2	—
2008–09	804,620	450,562	161,487	138,301	37,941	9,485	—	6,844	100.0	56.5	20.2	17.3	4.8	1.2	—
2009–10	935,719	511,186	191,657	172,015	41,407	12,003		7,451	100.0	55.1	20.6	18.5	4.5	1.3	—
2010–11	1,030,477	557,595	207,693	187,433	44,294	11,204	14,999	7,259	100.0	54.5	20.3	18.3	4.3	1.1	1.5
2011–12	989,061	535,621	190,253	187,014	43,048	10,638	14,140	8,347	100.0	54.6	19.4	19.1	4.4	1.1	1.4
2012–13	966,084	523,334	176,700	186,029	44,357	10,813	17,635	7,216	100.0	54.6	18.4	19.4	4.6	1.1	1.8
Males															
1998–99	219,872	144,735	29,875	27,719	11,742	3,061	—	2,740	100.0	66.7	13.8	12.8	5.4	1.4	—
1999–2000	226,110	143,634	33,792	30,337	13,082	2,862	—	2,403	100.0	64.2	15.1	13.6	5.8	1.3	—
2000–01	223,951	143,144	34,381	28,685	12,072	2,719	—	2,950	100.0	64.8	15.6	13.0	5.5	1.2	—
2001–02	235,275	152,226	36,482	29,749	10,938	3,226	—	2,654	100.0	65.4	15.7	12.8	4.7	1.4	—
2002–03	254,238	161,001	40,080	33,925	12,930	3,506	—	2,796	100.0	64.0	15.9	13.5	5.1	1.4	—
2003–04	257,138	161,684	40,809	36,157	12,713	3,135	—	2,640	100.0	63.5	16.0	14.2	5.0	1.2	—
2004–05	259,261	161,126	41,644	38,297	12,448	3,068	—	2,678	100.0	62.8	16.2	14.9	4.9	1.2	—
2005–06	259,737	158,747	41,863	40,752	12,790	3,219	—	2,366	100.0	61.7	16.3	15.8	5.0	1.3	—
2006–07	269,589	164,939	44,870	40,958	12,622	3,527	—	2,673	100.0	61.8	16.8	15.3	4.7	1.3	—
2007–08	283,266	172,398	48,024	43,085	13,527	3,452	—	2,780	100.0	61.5	17.1	15.4	4.8	1.2	—
2008–09	302,449	179,813	53,879	47,860	14,427	3,856	—	2,614	100.0	60.0	18.0	16.0	4.8	1.3	—
2009–10	355,381	205,404	65,487	60,771	15,940	5,067	—	2,712	100.0	58.2	18.6	17.2	4.5	1.4	—
2010–11	391,676	223,755	71,867	66,514	16,944	4,760	4,884	2,952	100.0	57.6	18.5	17.1	4.4	1.2	1.3
2011–12	374,086	213,833	65,224	65,838	16,180	4,507	4,952	3,552	100.0	57.7	17.6	17.8	4.4	1.2	1.3
2012–13	375,346	215,071	61,529	67,269	17,416	4,438	6,504	3,119	100.0	57.8	16.5	18.1	4.7	1.2	1.7
Females															
1998–99	336,011	200,624	62,925	49,114	16,178	4,449	—	2,721	100.0	60.2	18.9	14.7	4.9	1.3	—
1999–2000	332,019	193,912	63,537	50,795	16,279	4,104	—	3,392	100.0	59.0	19.3	15.5	5.0	1.2	—
2000–01	328,552	190,334	65,016	49,843	16,051	3,879	—	3,429	100.0	58.5	20.0	15.3	4.9	1.2	—
2001–02	348,973	200,333	70,165	54,201	16,552	4,204	—	3,518	100.0	58.0	20.3	15.7	4.8	1.2	—
2002–03	392,187	221,288	80,502	61,574	20,051	4,611	—	4,161	100.0	57.0	20.7	15.9	5.2	1.2	—
2003–04	430,649	241,305	89,082	71,059	20,106	5,240	—	3,857	100.0	56.5	20.9	16.6	4.7	1.2	—
2004–05	451,612	254,544	91,957	75,792	20,335	5,082	—	3,902	100.0	56.9	20.5	16.9	4.5	1.1	—
2005–06	455,664	253,330	93,597	78,101	21,320	5,181	—	4,135	100.0	56.1	20.7	17.3	4.7	1.1	—
2006–07	459,448	255,646	95,125	78,543	20,340	5,266	—	4,528	100.0	56.2	20.9	17.3	4.5	1.2	—
2007–08	466,617	257,789	97,157	79,591	22,458	5,144	—	4,478	100.0	55.8	21.0	17.2	4.9	1.1	—
2008–09	502,171	270,749	107,608	90,441	23,514	5,629	—	4,230	100.0	54.4	21.6	18.2	4.7	1.1	—
2009–10	580,338	305,782	126,170	111,244	25,467	6,936	—	4,739	100.0	53.1	21.9	19.3	4.4	1.2	—
2010–11	638,801	333,840	135,826	120,919	27,350	6,444	10,115	4,307	100.0	52.6	21.4	19.1	4.3	1.0	1.6
2011–12	614,975	321,788	125,029	121,176	26,868	6,131	9,188	4,795	100.0	52.7	20.5	19.9	4.4	1.0	1.5
2012–13	590,738	308,263	115,171	118,760	26,941	6,375	11,131	4,097	100.0	52.5	19.6	20.2	4.6	1.1	1.9

—Not available.
NOTE: Includes less-than-1-year awards and 1- to less-than-4-year awards (excluding associate's degrees) conferred by postsecondary institutions participating in Title IV federal financial aid programs. Race categories exclude persons of Hispanic ethnicity. Reported racial/ethnic distributions of students by level of degree, field of degree, and sex were used to estimate race/ethnicity for students whose race/ethnicity was not reported.

Some data have been revised from previously published figures. Detail may not sum to totals because of rounding.
SOURCE: U.S. Department of Education, National Center for Education Statistics, Integrated Postsecondary Education Data System (IPEDS), "Completions Survey" (IPEDS-C:99); and IPEDS Fall 2000 through Fall 2013, Completions component. (This table was prepared October 2014.)

Table 321.10. Associate's degrees conferred by postsecondary institutions, by sex of student and discipline division: 2002–03 through 2012–13

Discipline division	2002–03	2003–04	2004–05	2005–06	2006–07	2007–08	2008–09	2009–10	2010–11	2011–12	2012–13 Total	2012–13 Males	2012–13 Females
1	2	3	4	5	6	7	8	9	10	11	12	13	14
Total	634,016	665,301	696,660	713,066	728,114	750,164	787,243	848,856	943,506	1,021,718	1,006,961	388,846	618,115
Agriculture and natural resources	6,210	6,283	6,404	6,168	5,838	5,738	5,724	5,852	6,430	7,068	6,827	4,305	2,522
Agriculture, agriculture operations, and related sciences	4,892	4,959	5,137	4,958	4,638	4,554	4,525	4,615	4,925	5,400	5,228	3,134	2,094
Natural resources and conservation	1,318	1,324	1,267	1,210	1,200	1,184	1,199	1,237	1,505	1,668	1,599	1,171	428
Architecture and related services	440	492	583	656	517	568	605	553	569	593	468	305	163
Area, ethnic, cultural, gender, and group studies	120	105	115	124	164	169	174	199	209	194	271	101	170
Biological and biomedical sciences	1,496	1,456	1,709	1,827	2,060	2,200	2,337	2,664	3,276	3,834	4,185	1,337	2,848
Business, management, marketing, and support services	89,627	92,065	96,067	96,933	99,998	104,566	111,524	116,798	121,735	123,014	114,740	41,505	73,235
Accounting and related services	13,229	14,506	13,988	13,620	14,232	15,965	16,707	17,925	20,180	20,270	18,044	4,816	13,228
Business/commerce, general	13,054	13,387	12,050	13,297	12,725	12,473	13,100	14,553	15,083	17,301	17,199	7,222	9,977
Business administration, management, and operations	28,943	31,522	37,258	39,152	43,667	47,911	52,938	46,086	46,253	45,879	49,684	20,564	29,120
Management information systems and services	5,600	4,214	2,812	2,179	2,007	1,237	1,103	1,221	1,244	1,164	1,082	754	328
Business operations support and assistant services	11,524	11,400	11,196	10,044	8,864	7,841	7,550	7,399	8,259	8,977	7,958	746	7,212
Business and management, other	17,277	17,036	18,763	18,641	18,503	19,139	20,126	29,614	30,716	29,423	20,773	7,403	13,370
Communication, journalism, and related programs	2,589	2,444	2,545	2,629	2,609	2,620	2,722	2,841	3,051	3,495	4,299	1,969	2,330
Communications technologies	3,304	3,401	3,516	3,380	3,095	4,237	4,418	4,209	5,004	5,026	3,486	1,540
Computer and information sciences and support services	46,234	41,845	36,173	31,246	27,712	28,296	29,912	32,351	37,689	41,250	38,931	30,638	8,293
Construction trades	3,009	3,560	3,512	3,850	3,895	4,309	4,252	4,684	5,402	5,750	5,038	4,802	236
Education	11,205	12,465	13,329	14,475	13,021	13,108	14,123	17,346	20,460	20,762	18,719	2,203	16,516
Engineering	2,166	2,726	2,430	2,154	2,128	2,279	2,170	2,508	2,825	3,382	3,735	3,221	514
Engineering technologies and engineering-related fields[1]	39,998	36,915	33,548	30,461	29,199	29,334	30,441	31,883	35,519	36,642	33,766	29,610	4,156
English language and literature/letters	896	828	995	1,105	1,249	1,402	1,534	1,658	2,019	2,137	2,085	675	1,410
Family and consumer sciences/human sciences	9,496	9,478	9,707	9,488	9,124	8,613	9,035	9,515	8,532	9,506	8,994	376	8,618
Foreign languages, literatures, and linguistics	1,050	1,047	1,234	1,161	1,207	1,258	1,630	1,683	1,888	1,980	2,130	435	1,695
Health professions and related programs	90,716	106,208	122,520	134,931	145,436	155,816	165,015	177,321	202,920	219,491	214,004	33,637	180,367
Dental assisting	5,498	5,652	5,813	6,085	6,313	6,642	6,574	7,063	7,498	7,790	7,821	398	7,423
Emergency medical technician (EMT paramedic)	1,410	1,617	1,825	1,980	2,008	2,140	2,270	2,413	2,895	3,352	3,525	2,423	1,102
Clinical/medical lab science	1,592	1,786	2,055	2,163	2,306	2,316	2,538	2,621	2,811	3,240	3,379	804	2,575
Medical and other health assisting	11,920	15,543	19,005	22,267	23,491	24,276	25,858	29,776	39,277	46,950	41,917	5,787	36,130
Nursing and patient care assistant	8	4	38	101	158	329	385	1	33	36	35	7	28
Practical nursing	916	1,049	1,388	1,421	1,509	1,417	1,299	1,973	2,069	2,366	2,361	248	2,113
Nursing, registered nurse and other	45,117	51,552	58,007	62,095	66,516	73,277	77,922	81,281	83,023	84,569	86,393	12,476	73,917
Health sciences, other	24,255	29,005	34,389	38,759	43,135	45,419	48,169	52,193	65,314	71,188	68,573	11,494	57,079
Homeland security, law enforcement, and firefighting	18,614	20,573	23,749	26,425	28,208	29,590	33,012	37,154	44,922	51,318	48,425	26,438	21,987
Criminal justice and corrections	15,155	17,040	19,942	22,351	23,917	25,588	28,998	32,648	40,022	45,971	42,762	21,355	21,407
Fire control and safety	2,941	3,012	3,366	3,554	3,811	3,937	3,947	4,307	4,603	4,779	4,898	4,540	358
Homeland security and related protective services, other	518	521	441	520	480	65	67	199	297	568	765	543	222
Legal professions and studies	8,412	9,466	9,885	10,509	10,391	9,465	9,062	9,999	11,619	12,315	11,826	1,696	10,130
Liberal arts and sciences, general studies, and humanities	217,361	227,650	240,131	244,689	250,030	254,012	263,947	284,954	306,674	336,938	344,091	132,575	211,516
Library science	87	114	108	136	84	117	116	112	160	159	181	29	152
Mathematics and statistics	732	801	807	753	827	855	933	1,051	1,644	1,529	1,802	1,243	559
Mechanic and repair technologies/technicians	12,028	12,553	13,619	14,454	15,432	15,297	16,059	16,326	19,969	20,715	20,444	19,392	1,052
Military technologies and applied sciences	85	293	355	610	781	851	721	668	856	986	1,002	773	229
Multi/interdisciplinary studies	14,067	14,794	13,888	14,473	15,838	16,255	15,472	17,279	23,729	27,263	27,404	10,862	16,542
Parks, recreation, leisure, and fitness studies	805	923	966	1,128	1,251	1,344	1,587	2,006	2,366	3,123	3,453	2,156	1,297
Personal and culinary services	12,607	14,239	16,311	17,162	16,103	16,592	16,358	16,467	18,259	20,376	19,226	8,052	11,174
Philosophy and religious studies	379	404	422	367	375	458	193	256	283	308	326	212	114
Physical sciences and science technologies	2,201	2,687	2,825	2,910	3,412	3,395	3,650	4,141	5,078	5,827	6,376	3,790	2,586
Physical sciences	1,152	1,599	1,637	1,741	2,023	1,980	2,196	2,378	3,148	3,652	4,084	2,345	1,739
Science technologies/technicians	1,049	1,088	1,188	1,169	1,389	1,415	1,454	1,763	1,930	2,175	2,292	1,445	847
Precision production	2,287	1,968	2,039	1,977	1,973	1,968	2,127	2,794	3,254	3,320	3,344	3,110	234
Psychology	1,785	1,887	1,942	1,944	2,213	2,412	3,957	6,582	3,866	4,717	6,119	1,496	4,623
Public administration and social services	3,534	3,728	4,027	4,415	4,338	4,192	4,177	4,522	7,472	9,222	8,781	1,237	7,544
Social sciences and history	5,720	6,245	6,533	6,730	7,080	7,812	9,157	10,649	12,772	14,132	15,669	5,770	9,899
Social sciences	5,404	5,875	6,233	6,308	6,673	7,358	8,670	10,108	12,072	13,321	14,750	5,202	9,548
History	316	370	300	422	407	454	487	541	700	811	919	568	351
Theology and religious vocations	425	492	581	570	608	582	676	613	758	839	881	425	456
Transportation and materials moving	1,211	1,217	1,435	1,472	1,674	1,550	1,430	1,444	1,698	2,098	2,087	1,714	373
Visual and performing arts	23,120	23,949	22,650	21,754	20,244	18,890	18,606	19,565	21,394	22,431	22,306	9,271	13,035
Fine and studio arts	1,760	1,450	1,614	1,638	1,753	1,705	2,019	2,277	2,414	2,339	2,541	784	1,757
Music and dance	2,093	2,584	2,333	2,389	2,290	1,317	1,152	1,335	1,356	1,683	1,743	1,114	629
Visual and performing arts, other[2]	19,267	19,915	18,703	17,727	16,201	15,868	15,435	15,953	17,624	18,409	18,022	7,373	10,649
Not classified by field of study	0	0	0	0	0	14	0	0	0	0	0	0	0

[1]Excludes "Construction trades" and "Mechanic and repair technologies/technicians," which are listed separately.
[2]Includes design and applied arts, drama and theatre arts, film and photographic arts, and all other arts not included under "Fine and studio arts" or "Music and dance."
NOTE: Data are for degree-granting postsecondary institutions, which are institutions that grant associate's or higher degrees and participate in Title IV federal financial aid programs. Some data have been revised from previously published figures.

SOURCE: U.S. Department of Education, National Center for Education Statistics, Integrated Postsecondary Education Data System (IPEDS), "Completions Survey" (IPEDS-C:98–99); and IPEDS Fall 2003 through Fall 2013, Completions component. (This table was prepared October 2014.)

Table 321.20. Associate's degrees conferred by postsecondary institutions, by race/ethnicity and sex of student: Selected years, 1976–77 through 2012–13

Year and sex	Number of degrees conferred to U.S. citizens and nonresident aliens								Percentage distribution of degrees conferred to U.S. citizens						
	Total	White	Black	Hispanic	Asian/ Pacific Islander	American Indian/ Alaska Native	Two or more races	Non-resident alien	Total	White	Black	Hispanic	Asian/ Pacific Islander	American Indian/ Alaska Native	Two or more races
1	2	3	4	5	6	7	8	9	10	11	12	13	14	15	16
Total															
1976–77[1]	404,956	342,290	33,159	16,636	7,044	2,498	—	3,329	100.0	85.2	8.3	4.1	1.8	0.6	—
1980–81[2]	410,174	339,167	35,330	17,800	8,650	2,584	—	6,643	100.0	84.0	8.8	4.4	2.1	0.6	—
1990–91	481,720	391,264	38,835	25,540	15,257	3,871	—	6,953	100.0	82.4	8.2	5.4	3.2	0.8	—
1996–97	571,226	429,464	56,306	43,549	25,159	5,984	—	10,764	100.0	76.6	10.0	7.8	4.5	1.1	—
1997–98	558,555	413,561	55,314	45,876	25,196	6,246	—	12,362	100.0	75.7	10.1	8.4	4.6	1.1	—
1998–99	564,984	412,985	58,417	48,845	27,628	6,395	—	10,714	100.0	74.5	10.5	8.8	5.0	1.2	—
1999–2000	564,933	408,822	60,208	51,563	27,778	6,474	—	10,088	100.0	73.7	10.9	9.3	5.0	1.2	—
2000–01	578,865	411,075	63,855	57,288	28,463	6,623	—	11,561	100.0	72.5	11.3	10.1	5.0	1.2	—
2001–02	595,133	417,733	67,343	60,003	30,945	6,832	—	12,277	100.0	71.7	11.6	10.3	5.3	1.2	—
2002–03	634,016	438,261	75,609	66,673	32,629	7,461	—	13,383	100.0	70.6	12.2	10.7	5.3	1.2	—
2003–04	665,301	456,047	81,183	72,270	33,149	8,119	—	14,533	100.0	70.1	12.5	11.1	5.1	1.2	—
2004–05	696,660	475,513	86,402	78,557	33,669	8,435	—	14,084	100.0	69.7	12.7	11.5	4.9	1.2	—
2005–06	713,066	485,297	89,784	80,854	35,201	8,552	—	13,378	100.0	69.4	12.8	11.6	5.0	1.2	—
2006–07	728,114	491,572	91,529	85,410	37,266	8,583	—	13,754	100.0	68.8	12.8	12.0	5.2	1.2	—
2007–08	750,164	501,079	95,702	91,274	38,843	8,849	—	14,417	100.0	68.1	13.0	12.4	5.3	1.2	—
2008–09	787,243	521,834	101,631	98,408	41,364	8,823	—	15,183	100.0	67.6	13.2	12.7	5.4	1.1	—
2009–10	848,856	552,376	113,867	112,403	44,026	10,101	—	16,083	100.0	66.3	13.7	13.5	5.3	1.2	—
2010–11	943,506	604,745	129,044	126,297	45,489	10,180	11,126	16,625	100.0	65.2	13.9	13.6	4.9	1.1	1.2
2011–12	1,021,718	635,755	142,512	151,807	48,861	10,738	14,858	17,187	100.0	63.3	14.2	15.1	4.9	1.1	1.5
2012–13	1,006,961	616,990	135,777	157,966	49,456	10,540	19,402	16,830	100.0	62.3	13.7	16.0	5.0	1.1	2.0
Males															
1976–77[1]	209,672	178,236	15,330	9,105	3,630	1,216	—	2,155	100.0	85.9	7.4	4.4	1.7	0.6	—
1980–81[2]	183,819	151,242	14,290	8,327	4,557	1,108	—	4,295	100.0	84.2	8.0	4.6	2.5	0.6	—
1990–91	198,634	161,858	14,143	10,738	7,164	1,439	—	3,292	100.0	82.9	7.2	5.5	3.7	0.7	—
1996–97	223,948	168,882	19,394	17,990	10,937	2,068	—	4,677	100.0	77.0	8.8	8.2	5.0	0.9	—
1997–98	217,613	161,212	18,686	19,108	10,953	2,252	—	5,402	100.0	76.0	8.8	9.0	5.2	1.1	—
1998–99	220,508	162,339	19,844	19,484	11,688	2,234	—	4,919	100.0	75.3	9.2	9.0	5.4	1.0	—
1999–2000	224,721	164,317	20,968	20,947	12,009	2,222	—	4,258	100.0	74.5	9.5	9.5	5.4	1.0	—
2000–01	231,645	166,322	22,147	23,350	12,339	2,294	—	5,193	100.0	73.4	9.8	10.3	5.4	1.0	—
2001–02	238,109	170,622	22,806	23,963	13,256	2,308	—	5,154	100.0	73.2	9.8	10.3	5.7	1.0	—
2002–03	253,451	179,163	25,591	26,461	14,057	2,618	—	5,561	100.0	72.3	10.3	10.7	5.7	1.1	—
2003–04	260,033	183,819	25,961	27,828	13,907	2,740	—	5,778	100.0	72.3	10.2	10.9	5.5	1.1	—
2004–05	267,536	188,569	27,151	29,658	13,802	2,774	—	5,582	100.0	72.0	10.4	11.3	5.3	1.1	—
2005–06	270,095	190,139	27,619	30,040	14,224	2,774	—	5,299	100.0	71.8	10.4	11.3	5.4	1.0	—
2006–07	275,187	191,565	28,273	31,646	15,510	2,873	—	5,320	100.0	71.0	10.5	11.7	5.7	1.1	—
2007–08	282,521	194,099	30,016	33,817	15,936	3,003	—	5,650	100.0	70.1	10.8	12.2	5.8	1.1	—
2008–09	298,066	202,670	32,004	36,919	17,305	3,075	—	6,093	100.0	69.4	11.0	12.6	5.9	1.1	—
2009–10	322,747	215,977	36,148	42,210	18,268	3,555	—	6,589	100.0	68.3	11.4	13.4	5.8	1.1	—
2010–11	361,408	238,012	41,649	47,911	19,085	3,727	4,197	6,827	100.0	67.1	11.7	13.5	5.4	1.1	1.2
2011–12	393,479	251,964	46,377	57,926	20,537	3,924	5,569	7,182	100.0	65.2	12.0	15.0	5.3	1.0	1.4
2012–13	388,846	243,607	45,408	60,498	21,213	3,636	7,450	7,034	100.0	63.8	11.9	15.8	5.6	1.0	2.0
Females															
1976–77[1]	195,284	164,054	17,829	7,531	3,414	1,282	—	1,174	100.0	84.5	9.2	3.9	1.8	0.7	—
1980–81[2]	226,355	187,925	21,040	9,473	4,093	1,476	—	2,348	100.0	83.9	9.4	4.2	1.8	0.7	—
1990–91	283,086	229,406	24,692	14,802	8,093	2,432	—	3,661	100.0	82.1	8.8	5.3	2.9	0.9	—
1996–97	347,278	260,582	36,912	25,559	14,222	3,916	—	6,087	100.0	76.4	10.8	7.5	4.2	1.1	—
1997–98	340,942	252,349	36,628	26,768	14,243	3,994	—	6,960	100.0	75.6	11.0	8.0	4.3	1.2	—
1998–99	344,476	250,646	38,573	29,361	15,940	4,161	—	5,795	100.0	74.0	11.4	8.7	4.7	1.2	—
1999–2000	340,212	244,505	39,240	30,616	15,769	4,252	—	5,830	100.0	73.1	11.7	9.2	4.7	1.3	—
2000–01	347,220	244,753	41,708	33,938	16,124	4,329	—	6,368	100.0	71.8	12.2	10.0	4.7	1.3	—
2001–02	357,024	247,111	44,537	36,040	17,689	4,524	—	7,123	100.0	70.6	12.7	10.3	5.1	1.3	—
2002–03	380,565	259,098	50,018	40,212	18,572	4,843	—	7,822	100.0	69.5	13.4	10.8	5.0	1.3	—
2003–04	405,268	272,228	55,222	44,442	19,242	5,379	—	8,755	100.0	68.7	13.9	11.2	4.9	1.4	—
2004–05	429,124	286,944	59,251	48,899	19,867	5,661	—	8,502	100.0	68.2	14.1	11.6	4.7	1.3	—
2005–06	442,971	295,158	62,165	50,814	20,977	5,778	—	8,079	100.0	67.9	14.3	11.7	4.8	1.3	—
2006–07	452,927	300,007	63,256	53,764	21,756	5,710	—	8,434	100.0	67.5	14.2	12.1	4.9	1.3	—
2007–08	467,643	306,980	65,686	57,457	22,907	5,846	—	8,767	100.0	66.9	14.3	12.5	5.0	1.3	—
2008–09	489,177	319,164	69,627	61,489	24,059	5,748	—	9,090	100.0	66.5	14.5	12.8	5.0	1.2	—
2009–10	526,109	336,399	77,719	70,193	25,758	6,546	—	9,494	100.0	65.1	15.0	13.6	5.0	1.3	—
2010–11	582,098	366,733	87,395	78,386	26,404	6,453	6,929	9,798	100.0	64.1	15.3	13.7	4.6	1.1	1.2
2011–12	628,239	383,791	96,135	93,881	28,324	6,814	9,289	10,005	100.0	62.1	15.5	15.2	4.6	1.1	1.5
2012–13	618,115	373,383	90,369	97,468	28,243	6,904	11,952	9,796	100.0	61.4	14.9	16.0	4.6	1.1	2.0

—Not available.
[1]Excludes 1,170 males and 251 females whose racial/ethnic group was not available.
[2]Excludes 4,819 males and 1,384 females whose racial/ethnic group was not available.
NOTE: Data through 1990–91 are for institutions of higher education, while later data are for degree-granting postsecondary institutions, which are institutions that grant associate's or higher degrees and participate in Title IV federal financial aid programs. Race categories exclude persons of Hispanic ethnicity. For 1989–90 and later years, reported racial/ethnic distributions of students by level of degree, field of degree, and sex were used to estimate race/eth-

nicity for students whose race/ethnicity was not reported. Detail may not sum to totals because of rounding. Some data have been revised from previously published figures.
SOURCE: U.S. Department of Education, National Center for Education Statistics, Higher Education General Information Survey (HEGIS), "Degrees and Other Formal Awards Conferred" surveys, 1976–77 and 1980–81; Integrated Postsecondary Education Data System (IPEDS), "Completions Survey" (IPEDS-C:90–99); and IPEDS Fall 2000 through Fall 2013, Completions component. (This table was prepared October 2014.)

Table 321.30. Associate's degrees conferred by postsecondary institutions, by race/ethnicity and field of study: 2011–12 and 2012–13

Field of study	2011–12				Asian/Pacific Islander			American Indian/ Alaska Native	Two or more races	Non-resident alien	2012–13				Asian/Pacific Islander			American Indian/ Alaska Native	Two or more races	Non-resident alien
	Total	White	Black	Hispanic	Total	Asian	Pacific Islander				Total	White	Black	Hispanic	Total	Asian	Pacific Islander			
	2	3	4	5	6	7	8	9	10	11	12	13	14	15	16	17	18	19	20	21
All fields, total	1,021,718	635,755	142,512	151,807	48,861	44,969	3,892	10,738	14,858	17,187	1,006,961	616,990	135,777	157,966	49,456	45,599	3,857	10,540	19,402	16,830
Agriculture and natural resources	7,068	6,475	81	259	58	44	14	114	57	24	6,827	6,176	92	301	55	46	9	109	67	27
Architecture and related services	593	291	33	188	52	49	3	1	7	21	468	187	21	192	40	40	0	2	4	22
Area, ethnic, cultural, gender, and group studies	194	37	18	45	13	10	3	72	4	5	271	58	29	66	23	12	11	74	15	6
Biological and biomedical sciences	3,834	1,842	325	938	509	499	10	70	57	93	4,185	1,907	359	1,089	544	522	22	82	94	110
Business	143,390	84,106	24,291	18,949	7,958	7,372	586	1,624	2,182	4,280	133,966	77,727	21,527	18,903	7,888	7,313	575	1,518	2,415	3,988
Communication, journalism, and related programs	3,495	2,105	379	654	156	133	23	27	61	113	4,299	2,483	396	905	229	212	17	26	129	131
Communications technologies	5,004	3,379	586	599	207	195	12	41	124	68	5,026	3,113	671	691	193	167	26	43	221	94
Computer and information sciences	41,250	26,977	6,308	4,532	2,038	1,873	165	392	496	507	38,931	24,504	6,114	4,642	2,077	1,912	165	391	676	527
Construction trades	5,750	4,459	632	387	92	75	17	91	75	14	5,038	3,813	544	435	76	62	14	100	55	15
Education	20,762	13,132	3,094	3,231	375	333	42	485	225	220	18,719	11,427	3,039	3,027	324	290	34	471	236	195
Engineering	3,382	2,122	241	423	305	283	22	26	28	237	3,735	2,313	256	560	326	305	21	44	61	175
Engineering technologies and engineering-related fields[1]	36,642	25,716	4,474	4,287	1,184	1,095	89	383	350	248	33,766	23,211	4,183	4,040	1,149	1,047	102	408	515	260
English language and literature/letters	2,137	1,141	232	512	150	139	11	22	38	42	2,085	1,059	199	563	151	140	11	13	66	34
Family and consumer sciences/human sciences	9,506	4,840	2,094	1,844	422	391	31	99	90	117	8,994	4,569	1,739	1,911	441	409	32	106	114	114
Foreign languages, literatures, and linguistics	1,980	1,215	104	519	56	51	5	6	24	56	2,130	1,275	92	569	79	74	5	17	39	59
Health professions and related programs	219,491	147,857	31,358	23,846	10,008	9,292	716	2,004	2,791	1,627	214,004	143,125	29,611	24,622	9,678	8,956	722	2,055	3,452	1,461
Homeland security, law enforcement, and firefighting	51,318	29,295	8,903	10,571	1,199	978	221	501	660	189	48,425	27,293	8,224	10,308	1,148	958	190	441	822	189
Legal professions and studies	12,315	7,711	2,068	1,849	303	279	24	133	184	67	11,826	7,340	1,885	1,895	286	262	24	160	201	59
Liberal arts and sciences, general studies, and humanities	336,938	204,375	44,452	57,319	15,531	14,257	1,274	3,215	5,437	6,609	344,091	206,704	44,273	59,925	16,129	14,849	1,280	3,137	7,308	6,615
Library science	159	128	1	18	7	6	1	3	1	1	181	132	6	27	12	12	0	1	3	0
Mathematics and statistics	1,529	703	64	420	212	207	5	23	21	86	1,802	808	73	493	294	291	3	14	51	69
Mechanic and repair technologies/technicians	20,715	14,303	2,031	2,861	704	613	91	325	350	141	20,444	14,270	1,841	2,780	658	548	110	313	428	154
Military technologies and applied sciences	986	653	150	101	55	45	10	7	20	0	1,002	687	116	129	41	38	3	8	21	0
Multi/interdisciplinary studies	27,263	15,177	2,386	5,236	3,231	3,076	155	202	443	588	27,404	14,743	2,228	5,876	3,195	3,083	112	194	618	550
Parks, recreation, leisure, and fitness studies	3,123	1,891	403	533	105	91	14	53	58	80	3,453	1,981	424	685	149	137	12	43	87	84
Philosophy and religious studies	308	166	75	50	3	3	0	3	5	6	326	160	69	67	14	12	2	1	13	2
Physical sciences and science technologies	5,827	3,107	670	909	645	621	24	63	100	333	6,376	3,388	700	1,045	676	652	24	74	188	305
Precision production	3,320	2,784	151	220	74	69	5	50	32	9	3,344	2,706	166	275	87	76	11	45	54	11
Psychology	4,717	2,317	446	1,453	280	259	21	94	90	37	6,119	2,840	486	2,044	418	386	32	90	179	62
Public administration and social services	9,222	4,761	2,717	1,322	135	109	26	134	99	54	8,781	4,667	2,415	1,229	147	119	28	135	134	54
Social sciences and history	14,132	6,695	1,390	3,902	1,353	1,202	151	294	329	229	15,669	6,938	1,440	4,672	1,632	1,480	152	209	495	283
Social sciences	13,321	6,166	1,359	3,703	1,328	1,182	146	226	317	222	14,750	6,391	1,406	4,428	1,591	1,440	151	197	456	281
History	811	529	31	199	25	20	5	8	12	7	919	547	34	244	41	40	1	12	39	2
Theology and religious vocations	839	558	189	67	8	5	3	2	7	8	881	566	215	70	15	10	5	3	6	6
Transportation and materials moving	2,098	1,446	134	294	111	97	14	22	20	71	2,087	1,309	177	317	102	93	9	11	68	103
Visual and performing arts	22,431	13,991	2,032	3,469	1,322	1,218	104	217	393	1,007	22,306	13,511	2,167	3,613	1,180	1,086	94	202	567	1,066
Other and not classified	0	0	0	0	0	0	0	0	0	0	0	0	0	0	0	0	0	0	0	0

[1]Excludes "Construction trades" and "Mechanic and repair technologies/technicians," which are listed separately.

NOTE: Data are for degree-granting postsecondary institutions, which are institutions that grant associate's or higher degrees and participate in Title IV federal financial aid programs. Race categories exclude persons of Hispanic ethnicity. Reported racial/ethnic distributions of students by level of degree, field of degree, and sex were used to estimate race/ethnicity for students whose race/ethnicity was not reported. To facilitate trend comparisons, certain aggregations have been made of the degree fields as reported in the Inte-

grated Postsecondary Education Data System (IPEDS): "Agriculture and natural resources" includes Agriculture, agriculture operations, and related sciences and Natural resources and conservation; and "Business" includes Business management, marketing, and related support services and Personal and culinary services. Some data have been revised from previously published figures.

SOURCE: U.S. Department of Education, National Center for Education Statistics, Integrated Postsecondary Education Data System (IPEDS), Fall 2012 and Fall 2013, Completions component. (This table was prepared October 2014.)

Table 321.40. Associate's degrees conferred to males by postsecondary institutions, by race/ethnicity and field of study: 2011–12 and 2012–13

Field of study	2011–12										2012–13									
	Total	White	Black	Hispanic	Asian/Pacific Islander Total	Asian	Pacific Islander	American Indian/Alaska Native	Two or more races	Nonresident alien	Total	White	Black	Hispanic	Asian/Pacific Islander Total	Asian	Pacific Islander	American Indian/Alaska Native	Two or more races	Nonresident alien
1	2	3	4	5	6	7	8	9	10	11	12	13	14	15	16	17	18	19	20	21
All fields, total	393,479	251,964	46,377	57,926	20,537	18,910	1,627	3,924	5,569	7,182	388,846	243,607	45,408	60,498	21,213	19,503	1,710	3,636	7,450	7,034
Agriculture and natural resources	4,607	4,257	52	156	29	19	10	67	32	14	4,305	3,923	69	175	31	27	4	60	36	11
Architecture and related services	332	144	15	123	33	31	2	1	3	13	305	127	15	129	22	22	0	1	2	9
Area, ethnic, cultural, gender, and group studies	62	7	9	15	7	4	3	23	1	0	101	21	11	30	11	6	5	23	5	0
Biological and biomedical sciences	1,281	638	103	284	178	173	5	21	21	36	1,337	613	103	337	191	182	9	27	30	36
Business	52,503	31,275	7,790	7,261	3,195	2,978	217	516	785	1,681	49,557	29,040	7,096	7,194	3,238	3,008	230	465	883	1,641
Communication, journalism, and related programs	1,626	1,026	166	295	68	59	9	19	21	31	1,969	1,207	180	383	108	102	6	18	43	30
Communications technologies	3,433	2,266	460	416	135	123	12	31	83	42	3,486	2,101	507	519	120	101	19	22	160	57
Computer and information sciences	32,339	21,540	4,505	3,666	1,601	1,481	120	278	360	389	30,638	19,641	4,424	3,736	1,652	1,530	122	265	530	390
Construction trades	5,481	4,281	589	361	88	72	16	86	64	12	4,802	3,657	502	416	71	59	12	93	49	14
Education	2,653	1,782	336	365	38	35	3	76	30	26	2,203	1,418	331	289	38	37	1	76	28	23
Engineering	2,931	1,898	207	342	244	227	17	17	25	198	3,221	2,046	222	452	264	246	18	32	56	149
Engineering technologies and engineering-related fields[1]	32,340	22,913	3,823	3,796	1,003	931	72	333	283	189	29,610	20,575	3,555	3,530	985	899	86	327	424	214
English language and literature/letters	708	373	71	175	60	56	4	6	7	16	675	350	54	183	54	52	2	2	26	6
Family and consumer sciences/human sciences	369	189	84	58	23	20	3	3	6	6	376	174	72	81	25	24	1	3	7	14
Foreign languages, literatures, and linguistics	417	216	18	131	27	25	2	1	6	18	435	219	13	141	28	28	0	4	10	20
Health professions and related programs	34,145	21,878	4,077	4,375	2,607	2,399	208	309	501	398	33,637	21,352	3,987	4,548	2,607	2,383	224	275	558	310
Homeland security, law enforcement, and firefighting	27,479	17,716	3,129	5,226	787	678	109	207	317	97	26,438	16,643	3,056	5,235	804	689	115	198	392	110
Legal professions and studies	1,698	940	332	298	61	58	3	28	26	13	1,696	986	282	312	61	59	2	20	25	10
Liberal arts and sciences, general studies, and humanities	129,389	81,200	14,875	20,852	6,508	5,990	518	1,155	2,000	2,799	132,575	81,895	15,213	22,063	6,797	6,255	542	1,067	2,718	2,822
Library science	19	10	0	4	4	3	1	0	1	0	29	22	0	6	1	1	0	0	0	0
Mathematics and statistics	1,050	481	52	289	139	138	1	18	17	54	1,243	570	45	338	197	194	3	9	37	47
Mechanic and repair technologies/technicians	19,710	13,635	1,896	2,731	686	598	88	299	330	133	19,392	13,576	1,728	2,632	625	519	106	285	401	145
Military technologies and applied sciences	770	529	99	81	42	34	8	5	14	0	773	550	73	97	32	29	3	7	14	0
Multi/interdisciplinary studies	10,177	5,870	745	1,830	1,258	1,211	47	72	170	232	10,862	6,037	781	2,158	1,352	1,303	49	55	240	239
Parks, recreation, leisure, and fitness studies	1,999	1,235	272	289	77	65	12	37	35	54	2,156	1,252	285	406	83	77	6	23	49	58
Philosophy and religious studies	181	114	29	30	1	1	0	1	4	2	212	110	32	49	12	10	2	0	8	1
Physical sciences and science technologies	3,407	1,934	275	547	356	343	13	36	55	204	3,790	2,118	313	655	367	354	13	42	121	174
Precision production	3,118	2,631	130	207	72	68	4	40	29	9	3,110	2,531	150	252	82	73	9	36	49	10
Psychology	1,093	536	87	329	98	88	10	17	21	5	1,496	677	128	487	134	128	6	18	38	14
Public administration and social services	1,388	669	456	195	17	14	3	22	16	13	1,237	650	358	163	24	21	3	22	15	5
Social sciences and history	5,139	2,560	432	1,328	508	455	53	78	135	98	5,770	2,676	457	1,581	675	607	68	68	198	115
Social sciences	4,650	2,237	411	1,215	493	444	49	73	128	93	5,202	2,326	443	1,436	648	580	68	61	174	114
History	489	323	21	113	15	11	4	5	7	5	568	350	14	145	27	27	0	7	24	1
Theology and religious vocations	423	280	94	31	7	4	3	1	5	5	425	275	103	31	8	4	4	1	3	4
Transportation and materials moving	1,782	1,256	115	234	91	81	10	19	15	52	1,714	1,124	146	250	76	72	4	8	51	59
Visual and performing arts	9,430	5,685	1,054	1,606	489	448	41	102	151	343	9,271	5,451	1,117	1,640	438	402	36	84	244	297
Other and not classified	0	0	0	0	0	0	0	0	0	0	0	0	0	0	0	0	0	0	0	0

[1]Excludes "Construction trades" and "Mechanic and repair technologies/technicians," which are listed separately.

NOTE: Data are for degree-granting postsecondary institutions, which are institutions that grant associate's or higher degrees and participate in Title IV federal financial aid programs. Reported racial/ethnic distributions of students by level of degree, field of degree, and sex were used to estimate race/ethnicity for students whose race/ethnicity was not reported. To facilitate trend comparisons, certain aggregations have been made of the degree fields as reported in the Integrated Postsecondary Education Data System (IPEDS): "Agriculture and natural resources" includes Agriculture, agriculture operations, and related sciences and Natural resources and conservation; and "Business" includes Business management, marketing, and related support services and Personal and culinary services. Some data have been revised from previously published figures.

SOURCE: U.S. Department of Education, National Center for Education Statistics, Integrated Postsecondary Education Data System (IPEDS), Fall 2012 and Fall 2013, Completions component. (This table was prepared October 2014.)

Table 321.50. Associate's degrees conferred to females by postsecondary institutions, by race/ethnicity and field of study: 2011–12 and 2012–13

Field of study	2011–12										2012–13									
	Total	White	Black	Hispanic	Asian/Pacific Islander			American Indian/ Alaska Native	Two or more races	Non-resident alien	Total	White	Black	Hispanic	Asian/Pacific Islander			American Indian/ Alaska Native	Two or more races	Non-resident alien
					Total	Asian	Pacific Islander								Total	Asian	Pacific Islander			
1	2	3	4	5	6	7	8	9	10	11	12	13	14	15	16	17	18	19	20	21
All fields, total	628,239	383,791	96,135	93,881	28,324	26,059	2,265	6,814	9,289	10,005	618,115	373,383	90,369	97,468	28,243	26,096	2,147	6,904	11,952	9,796
Agriculture and natural resources	2,461	2,218	29	103	29	25	4	47	25	10	2,522	2,253	6	63	24	19	5	49	31	16
Architecture and related services	261	147	18	65	19	18	1	0	4	8	163	60	6	63	18	18	0	1	2	13
Area, ethnic, cultural, gender and group studies	132	30	9	30	6	6	0	49	3	5	170	37	18	36	12	6	6	51	10	6
Biological and biomedical sciences	2,553	1,204	222	654	331	326	5	49	36	57	2,848	1,294	256	752	353	340	13	55	64	74
Business	90,887	52,831	16,501	11,688	4,763	4,394	369	1,108	1,397	2,599	84,409	48,687	14,431	11,709	4,650	4,305	345	1,053	1,532	2,347
Communication, journalism, and related programs	1,869	1,079	213	359	88	74	14	8	40	82	2,330	1,276	216	522	121	110	11	8	86	101
Communications technologies	1,571	1,113	126	183	72	72	0	10	41	26	1,540	1,012	164	172	73	66	7	21	61	37
Computer and information sciences	8,911	5,437	1,803	866	437	392	45	114	136	118	8,293	4,863	1,690	906	425	382	43	126	146	137
Construction trades	269	178	43	26	4	3	1	5	11	2	236	156	42	19	5	3	2	7	6	1
Education	18,109	11,350	2,758	2,866	337	298	39	409	195	194	16,516	10,009	2,708	2,738	286	253	33	395	208	172
Engineering	451	224	34	81	61	56	5	9	3	39	514	267	34	108	62	59	3	12	5	26
Engineering technologies and engineering-related fields[1]	4,302	2,803	651	491	181	164	17	50	67	59	4,156	2,636	628	510	164	148	16	81	91	46
English language and literature/letters	1,429	768	161	337	90	83	7	16	31	26	1,410	709	145	380	97	88	9	11	40	28
Family and consumer sciences/human sciences	9,137	4,651	2,010	1,786	399	371	28	96	84	111	8,618	4,395	1,667	1,830	416	385	31	103	107	100
Foreign languages, literatures, and linguistics	1,563	999	86	388	29	26	3	5	18	38	1,695	1,056	79	428	51	46	5	13	29	39
Health professions and related programs	185,346	125,979	27,281	19,471	7,401	6,893	508	1,695	2,290	1,229	180,367	121,773	25,624	20,074	7,071	6,573	498	1,780	2,894	1,151
Homeland security, law enforcement, and firefighting	23,839	11,579	5,774	5,345	412	300	112	294	343	92	21,987	10,650	5,168	5,073	344	269	75	243	430	79
Legal professions and studies	10,617	6,771	1,736	1,551	242	221	21	105	158	54	10,130	6,354	1,603	1,583	225	203	22	140	176	49
Liberal arts and sciences, general studies, and humanities	207,549	123,175	29,577	36,467	9,023	8,267	756	2,060	3,437	3,810	211,516	124,809	29,060	37,862	9,332	8,594	738	2,070	4,590	3,793
Library science	140	118	1	14	3	3	0	3	0	1	152	110	6	21	11	11	0	1	3	0
Mathematics and statistics	479	222	12	131	73	69	4	5	4	32	559	238	28	155	97	97	0	5	14	22
Mechanic and repair technologies/technicians	1,005	668	135	130	18	15	3	26	20	8	1,052	694	113	148	33	29	4	28	27	9
Military technologies and applied sciences	216	124	51	20	13	11	2	10	6	0	229	137	43	32	9	9	0	1	7	0
Multi/interdisciplinary studies	17,086	9,307	1,641	3,406	1,973	1,865	108	130	273	356	16,542	8,706	1,447	3,718	1,843	1,780	63	139	378	311
Parks, recreation, leisure, and fitness studies	1,124	656	131	244	28	26	2	16	23	26	1,297	729	139	279	66	60	6	20	38	26
Philosophy and religious studies	127	52	46	20	2	2	0	2	1	4	114	50	37	18	2	2	0	1	5	1
Physical sciences and science technologies	2,420	1,173	395	362	289	278	11	27	45	129	2,586	1,270	387	390	309	298	11	32	67	131
Precision production	202	153	21	13	2	1	1	10	3	0	234	175	16	23	5	3	2	9	5	1
Psychology	3,624	1,781	359	1,124	182	171	11	77	69	32	4,623	2,163	358	1,557	284	258	26	72	141	48
Public administration and social services	7,834	4,092	2,261	1,127	118	95	23	112	83	41	7,544	4,017	2,057	1,066	123	98	25	113	119	49
Social sciences and history	8,993	4,135	958	2,574	845	747	98	156	194	131	9,899	4,262	983	3,091	957	873	84	141	297	168
Social sciences	8,671	3,929	948	2,488	835	738	97	153	189	129	9,548	4,065	963	2,992	943	860	83	136	282	167
History	322	206	10	86	10	9	1	3	5	2	351	197	20	99	14	13	1	5	15	1
Theology and religious vocations	416	278	95	36	13	11	2	1	2	3	456	291	112	39	7	6	1	2	3	2
Transportation and materials moving	316	190	19	60	20	16	4	3	5	19	373	185	31	67	26	21	5	3	17	44
Visual and performing arts	13,001	8,306	978	1,863	833	770	63	115	242	664	13,035	8,060	1,050	1,973	742	684	58	118	323	769
Other and not classified	0	0	0	0	0	0	0	0	0	0	0	0	0	0	0	0	0	0	0	0

[1]Excludes "Construction trades" and "Mechanic and repair technologies/technicians," which are listed separately.
NOTE: Data are for degree-granting postsecondary institutions, which are institutions that grant associate's or higher degrees and participate in Title IV federal financial aid programs. Race categories exclude persons of Hispanic ethnicity. Reported racial/ethnic distributions of students by level of degree, field of degree, and sex were used to estimate race/ethnicity for students whose race/ethnicity was not reported. To facilitate trend comparisons, certain aggregations have been made of the degree fields as reported in the Inte-

grated Postsecondary Education Data System (IPEDS): "Agriculture and natural resources" includes Agriculture, agriculture operations, and related sciences and Natural resources and conservation; and "Business" includes Business management, marketing, and related support services and Personal and culinary services. Some data have been revised from previously published figures.
SOURCE: U.S. Department of Education, National Center for Education Statistics, Integrated Postsecondary Education Data System (IPEDS), Fall 2012 and Fall 2013, Completions component. (This table was prepared October 2014.)

Table 322.10. Bachelor's degrees conferred by postsecondary institutions, by field of study: Selected years, 1970–71 through 2012–13

Field of study	1970–71	1975–76	1980–81	1985–86	1990–91	1995–96	2000–01	2002–03	2003–04	2004–05	2005–06	2006–07	2007–08	2008–09	2009–10	2010–11	2011–12	2012–13
1	2	3	4	5	6	7	8	9	10	11	12	13	14	15	16	17	18	19
Total	839,730	925,746	935,140	987,823	1,094,538	1,164,792	1,244,171	1,348,811	1,399,542	1,439,264	1,485,242	1,524,092	1,563,069	1,601,399	1,649,919	1,716,053	1,792,163	1,840,164
Agriculture and natural resources	12,672	19,402	21,886	16,823	13,124	21,425	23,370	23,348	22,835	23,002	23,053	23,133	24,113	24,982	26,343	28,630	30,972	33,593
Architecture and related services	5,570	9,146	9,455	9,119	9,781	8,352	8,480	9,056	8,838	9,237	9,515	9,717	9,805	10,119	10,051	9,831	9,727	9,757
Area, ethnic, cultural, gender, and group studies	2,579	3,577	2,887	3,021	4,776	5,633	6,160	6,634	7,181	7,569	7,879	8,194	8,454	8,772	8,620	8,955	9,228	8,851
Biological and biomedical sciences	35,705	54,154	43,078	38,395	39,482	61,014	60,576	61,294	62,624	65,915	70,607	76,832	79,829	82,828	86,391	89,984	95,850	100,319
Business	115,396	143,171	200,521	236,700	249,165	226,623	263,515	293,391	307,149	311,574	318,042	327,531	335,254	348,056	358,119	365,133	367,235	360,823
Communication, journalism, and related programs	10,324	20,045	29,428	41,666	51,650	47,320	58,013	67,895	70,968	72,715	73,955	74,783	76,382	77,984	81,280	83,231	83,771	84,817
Communications technologies	478	1,237	1,854	1,479	1,397	853	1,178	1,933	2,034	2,523	2,981	3,637	4,666	5,100	4,782	4,858	4,983	4,989
Computer and information sciences	2,388	5,652	15,121	42,337	25,159	24,506	44,142	57,433	59,488	54,111	47,480	42,170	38,476	37,992	39,593	43,066	47,406	50,962
Education	176,307	154,437	108,074	87,147	110,807	105,384	105,458	105,845	106,278	105,451	107,238	105,641	102,582	101,716	101,287	104,008	105,656	104,647
Engineering	45,034	38,733	63,642	77,391	62,448	62,168	58,209	62,567	63,410	64,707	66,841	66,874	68,431	68,911	72,657	76,356	81,371	85,980
Engineering technologies	5,148	7,943	11,713	19,731	17,303	15,829	14,660	14,664	14,669	14,837	14,565	14,980	15,177	15,493	16,078	16,741	17,283	17,004
English language and literature/letters	63,914	41,452	31,922	34,083	51,064	49,928	50,569	53,699	53,984	54,379	55,096	55,122	55,038	55,465	53,229	52,754	53,765	52,424
Family and consumer sciences/human sciences	11,167	17,409	18,370	13,847	13,920	14,353	16,421	17,929	19,172	20,074	20,775	21,400	21,870	21,906	21,832	22,438	23,441	23,934
Foreign languages, literatures, and linguistics	20,988	17,068	11,638	11,550	13,937	14,832	16,128	16,912	17,754	18,386	19,410	20,275	20,977	21,169	21,507	21,705	21,756	21,673
Health professions and related programs	25,223	53,885	63,665	65,309	59,875	86,087	75,933	71,261	73,934	80,685	91,973	101,810	111,478	120,420	129,623	143,463	163,675	181,144
Homeland security, law enforcement, and firefighting	2,045	12,507	13,707	12,704	16,806	24,810	25,211	26,200	28,175	30,723	35,319	39,206	40,235	41,788	43,613	47,600	54,091	60,269
Legal professions and studies	545	531	776	1,223	1,827	2,123	1,991	2,474	2,841	3,161	3,302	3,596	3,771	3,822	3,886	4,429	4,595	4,425
Liberal arts and sciences, general studies, and humanities	7,481	18,855	21,643	21,336	30,526	33,997	37,962	40,480	42,106	43,751	44,898	44,255	46,940	47,095	46,963	46,717	46,961	46,761
Library science	1,013	843	375	155	90	58	52	99	72	76	76	82	68	78	85	96	95	102
Mathematics and statistics	24,801	15,984	11,078	16,122	14,393	12,713	11,171	12,505	13,327	14,351	14,770	14,954	15,192	15,507	16,029	17,182	18,841	20,453
Military technologies and applied sciences	357	952	42	255	183	7	21	6	10	40	33	168	39	55	56	64	86	105
Multi/interdisciplinary studies	6,324	13,709	12,986	13,754	17,774	26,885	26,478	27,449	28,047	28,939	30,583	32,111	34,174	35,376	37,717	42,473	45,717	47,654
Parks, recreation, leisure and fitness studies	1,621	5,182	5,729	4,623	4,315	12,974	17,948	21,432	22,164	22,888	25,490	27,430	29,931	31,683	33,332	35,934	38,998	42,714
Philosophy and religious studies	8,149	8,447	6,776	6,396	7,423	7,541	8,717	10,344	11,152	11,584	11,985	11,969	12,257	12,448	12,503	12,830	12,645	12,793
Physical sciences and science technologies	21,410	21,458	23,936	21,711	16,334	19,716	18,025	18,038	18,131	19,104	20,522	21,291	22,179	22,691	23,381	24,705	26,664	28,050
Precision production	0	0	0	2	2	12	31	42	61	64	55	23	33	29	29	43	37	36
Psychology	38,187	50,278	41,068	40,628	58,655	73,416	73,645	78,650	82,098	85,614	88,134	90,039	92,587	94,273	97,215	100,906	109,099	114,450
Public administration and social services	5,466	15,440	16,707	11,887	14,350	19,849	19,447	19,900	20,552	21,769	21,986	23,147	23,852	23,852	25,421	26,799	29,695	31,950
Social sciences and history	155,324	126,396	100,513	93,840	125,107	126,479	128,036	143,256	150,357	156,892	161,485	164,183	167,363	168,517	172,782	177,169	178,534	177,778
Theology and religious vocations	3,720	5,490	5,808	5,510	4,799	5,292	6,945	7,962	8,126	9,284	8,548	8,696	8,992	8,940	8,719	9,073	9,304	9,385
Transportation and materials moving	0	225	263	1,838	2,622	3,561	3,748	4,631	4,824	4,904	5,349	5,657	5,203	5,189	4,998	4,941	4,876	4,526
Visual and performing arts	30,394	42,138	40,479	37,241	42,186	49,296	61,148	71,482	77,181	80,955	83,297	85,186	87,703	89,143	91,798	93,939	95,806	97,796
Not classified by field of study	0	0	0	0	13,258	1,756	783	0	0	0	0	0	377	0	0	0	0	0

NOTE: Data through 1990–91 are for institutions of higher education, while later data are for postsecondary institutions that participate in Title IV federal financial aid programs. The new Classification of Instructional Programs was initiated in 2009–10. The figures for earlier years have been reclassified when necessary to make them conform to the new taxonomy. To facilitate trend comparisons, certain aggregations have been made of the degree fields as reported in the Integrated Postsecondary Education Data System (IPEDS): "Agriculture and natural resources" includes Agriculture, agriculture operations, and related sciences and Natural resources and conservation; "Business" includes Business, management, marketing, and related support services and Personal and culinary services; and "Engineering technologies" includes Engineering technologies and engineering-related fields, Construction trades, and Mechanic and repair technologies/technicians. Some data have been revised from previously published figures.
SOURCE: U.S. Department of Education, National Center for Education Statistics, Higher Education General Information Survey (HEGIS), "Degrees and Other Formal Awards Conferred" surveys, 1970–71 through 1985–86; Integrated Postsecondary Education Data System (IPEDS), "Completions Survey" (IPEDS:C:91–99); and IPEDS Fall 2000 through Fall 2013, Completions component. (This table was prepared August 2014.)

Table 322.20. Bachelor's degrees conferred by postsecondary institutions, by race/ethnicity and sex of student: Selected years, 1976–77 through 2012–13

	Number of degrees conferred to U.S. citizens and nonresident aliens								Percentage distribution of degrees conferred to U.S. citizens						
Year and sex	Total	White	Black	Hispanic	Asian/ Pacific Islander	American Indian/ Alaska Native	Two or more races	Non-resident alien	Total	White	Black	Hispanic	Asian/ Pacific Islander	American Indian/ Alaska Native	Two or more races
1	2	3	4	5	6	7	8	9	10	11	12	13	14	15	16
Total															
1976–77[1]	917,900	807,688	58,636	18,743	13,793	3,326	—	15,714	100.0	89.5	6.5	2.1	1.5	0.4	—
1980–81[2]	934,800	807,319	60,673	21,832	18,794	3,593	—	22,589	100.0	88.5	6.7	2.4	2.1	0.4	—
1990–91	1,094,538	914,093	66,375	37,342	42,529	4,583	—	29,616	100.0	85.8	6.2	3.5	4.0	0.4	—
1996–97	1,172,879	900,809	94,349	62,509	68,859	7,425	—	38,928	100.0	79.4	8.3	5.5	6.1	0.7	—
1997–98	1,184,406	901,344	98,251	66,005	71,678	7,903	—	39,225	100.0	78.7	8.6	5.8	6.3	0.7	—
1998–99	1,202,239	909,562	101,910	69,735	74,126	8,658	—	38,248	100.0	78.1	8.8	6.0	6.4	0.7	—
1999–2000	1,237,875	929,102	108,018	75,063	77,909	8,717	—	39,066	100.0	77.5	9.0	6.3	6.5	0.7	—
2000–01	1,244,171	927,357	111,307	77,745	78,902	9,049	—	39,811	100.0	77.0	9.2	6.5	6.6	0.8	—
2001–02	1,291,900	958,597	116,623	82,966	83,093	9,165	—	41,456	100.0	76.7	9.3	6.6	6.6	0.7	—
2002–03	1,348,811	994,616	124,253	89,029	87,964	9,875	—	43,074	100.0	76.2	9.5	6.8	6.7	0.8	—
2003–04	1,399,542	1,026,114	131,241	94,644	92,073	10,638	—	44,832	100.0	75.7	9.7	7.0	6.8	0.8	—
2004–05	1,439,264	1,049,141	136,122	101,124	97,209	10,307	—	45,361	100.0	75.3	9.8	7.3	7.0	0.7	—
2005–06	1,485,242	1,075,561	142,420	107,588	102,376	10,940	—	46,357	100.0	74.7	9.9	7.5	7.1	0.8	—
2006–07	1,524,092	1,099,850	146,653	114,936	105,297	11,455	—	45,901	100.0	74.4	9.9	7.8	7.1	0.8	—
2007–08	1,563,069	1,122,675	152,457	123,048	109,058	11,509	—	44,322	100.0	73.9	10.0	8.1	7.2	0.8	—
2008–09	1,601,399	1,144,628	156,603	129,473	112,581	12,221	—	45,893	100.0	73.6	10.1	8.3	7.2	0.8	—
2009–10	1,649,919	1,167,322	164,789	140,426	117,391	12,405	—	47,586	100.0	72.9	10.3	8.8	7.3	0.8	—
2010–11	1,716,053	1,182,690	172,731	154,450	121,118	11,935	20,589	52,540	100.0	71.1	10.4	9.3	7.3	0.7	1.2
2011–12	1,792,163	1,212,417	185,916	169,736	126,177	11,498	27,234	59,185	100.0	70.0	10.7	9.8	7.3	0.7	1.6
2012–13	1,840,164	1,221,576	191,180	186,650	130,144	11,445	34,338	64,831	100.0	68.8	10.8	10.5	7.3	0.6	1.9
Males															
1976–77[1]	494,424	438,161	25,147	10,318	7,638	1,804	—	11,356	100.0	90.7	5.2	2.1	1.6	0.4	—
1980–81[2]	469,625	406,173	24,511	10,810	10,107	1,700	—	16,324	100.0	89.6	5.4	2.4	2.2	0.4	—
1990–91	504,045	421,290	24,800	16,598	21,203	1,938	—	18,216	100.0	86.7	5.1	3.4	4.4	0.4	—
1996–97	520,515	403,366	33,616	26,318	32,521	2,996	—	21,698	100.0	80.9	6.7	5.3	6.5	0.6	—
1997–98	519,956	399,553	34,510	27,677	33,445	3,151	—	21,620	100.0	80.2	6.9	5.6	6.7	0.6	—
1998–99	519,961	398,310	34,856	28,477	34,179	3,407	—	20,732	100.0	79.8	7.0	5.7	6.8	0.7	—
1999–2000	530,367	402,954	37,029	30,304	35,853	3,463	—	20,764	100.0	79.1	7.3	5.9	7.0	0.7	—
2000–01	531,840	401,780	38,103	31,368	35,865	3,700	—	21,024	100.0	78.7	7.5	6.1	7.0	0.7	—
2001–02	549,816	414,892	39,196	32,951	37,660	3,624	—	21,493	100.0	78.5	7.4	6.2	7.1	0.7	—
2002–03	573,258	430,248	41,494	35,101	40,230	3,870	—	22,315	100.0	78.1	7.5	6.4	7.3	0.7	—
2003–04	595,425	445,483	43,851	37,288	41,360	4,244	—	23,199	100.0	77.9	7.7	6.5	7.2	0.7	—
2004–05	613,000	456,592	45,810	39,490	43,711	4,143	—	23,254	100.0	77.4	7.8	6.7	7.4	0.7	—
2005–06	630,600	467,467	48,079	41,814	45,809	4,203	—	23,228	100.0	77.0	7.9	6.9	7.5	0.7	—
2006–07	649,570	480,558	49,685	44,750	47,582	4,505	—	22,490	100.0	76.6	7.9	7.1	7.6	0.7	—
2007–08	667,928	492,137	52,247	47,884	49,485	4,523	—	21,652	100.0	76.1	8.1	7.4	7.7	0.7	—
2008–09	685,422	503,396	53,465	50,596	50,773	4,849	—	22,343	100.0	75.9	8.1	7.6	7.7	0.7	—
2009–10	706,660	513,711	56,136	55,139	53,365	4,879	—	23,430	100.0	75.2	8.2	8.1	7.8	0.7	—
2010–11	734,159	519,992	59,015	60,869	55,321	4,798	8,028	26,136	100.0	73.4	8.3	8.6	7.8	0.7	1.1
2011–12	765,772	532,463	63,736	67,083	57,521	4,476	10,945	29,548	100.0	72.3	8.7	9.1	7.8	0.6	1.5
2012–13	787,231	535,082	67,306	74,043	59,802	4,616	14,032	32,350	100.0	70.9	8.9	9.8	7.9	0.6	1.9
Females															
1976–77[1]	423,476	369,527	33,489	8,425	6,155	1,522	—	4,358	100.0	88.2	8.0	2.0	1.5	0.4	—
1980–81[2]	465,175	401,146	36,162	11,022	8,687	1,893	—	6,265	100.0	87.4	7.9	2.4	1.9	0.4	—
1990–91	590,493	492,803	41,575	20,744	21,326	2,645	—	11,400	100.0	85.1	7.2	3.6	3.7	0.5	—
1996–97	652,364	497,443	60,733	36,191	36,338	4,429	—	17,230	100.0	78.3	9.6	5.7	5.7	0.7	—
1997–98	664,450	501,791	63,741	38,328	38,233	4,752	—	17,605	100.0	77.6	9.9	5.9	5.9	0.7	—
1998–99	682,278	511,252	67,054	41,258	39,947	5,251	—	17,516	100.0	76.9	10.1	6.2	6.0	0.8	—
1999–2000	707,508	526,148	70,989	44,759	42,056	5,254	—	18,302	100.0	76.3	10.3	6.5	6.1	0.8	—
2000–01	712,331	525,577	73,204	46,377	43,037	5,349	—	18,787	100.0	75.8	10.6	6.7	6.2	0.8	—
2001–02	742,084	543,705	77,427	50,015	45,433	5,541	—	19,963	100.0	75.3	10.7	6.9	6.3	0.8	—
2002–03	775,553	564,368	82,759	53,928	47,734	6,005	—	20,759	100.0	74.8	11.0	7.1	6.3	0.8	—
2003–04	804,117	580,631	87,390	57,356	50,713	6,394	—	21,633	100.0	74.2	11.2	7.3	6.5	0.8	—
2004–05	826,264	592,549	90,312	61,634	53,498	6,164	—	22,107	100.0	73.7	11.2	7.7	6.7	0.8	—
2005–06	854,642	608,094	94,341	65,774	56,567	6,737	—	23,129	100.0	73.1	11.3	7.9	6.8	0.8	—
2006–07	874,522	619,292	96,968	70,186	57,715	6,950	—	23,411	100.0	72.8	11.4	8.2	6.8	0.8	—
2007–08	895,141	630,538	100,210	75,164	59,573	6,986	—	22,670	100.0	72.3	11.5	8.6	6.8	0.8	—
2008–09	915,977	641,232	103,138	78,877	61,808	7,372	—	23,550	100.0	71.9	11.6	8.8	6.9	0.8	—
2009–10	943,259	653,611	108,653	85,287	64,026	7,526	—	24,156	100.0	71.1	11.8	9.3	7.0	0.8	—
2010–11	981,894	662,698	113,716	93,581	65,797	7,137	12,561	26,404	100.0	69.4	11.9	9.8	6.9	0.7	1.3
2011–12	1,026,391	679,954	122,180	102,653	68,656	7,022	16,289	29,637	100.0	68.2	12.3	10.3	6.9	0.7	1.6
2012–13	1,052,933	686,494	123,874	112,607	70,342	6,829	20,306	32,481	100.0	67.3	12.1	11.0	6.9	0.7	2.0

—Not available.
[1]Excludes 1,121 males and 528 females whose racial/ethnic group was not available.
[2]Excludes 258 males and 82 females whose racial/ethnic group was not available.
NOTE: Data through 1990–91 are for institutions of higher education, while later data are for postsecondary institutions participating in Title IV federal financial aid programs. Race categories exclude persons of Hispanic ethnicity. For 1989–90 and later years, reported racial/ethnic distributions of students by level of degree, field of degree, and sex were used to esti-mate race/ethnicity for students whose race/ethnicity was not reported. Detail may not sum to totals because of rounding. Some data have been revised from previously published figures.
SOURCE: U.S. Department of Education, National Center for Education Statistics, Higher Education General Information Survey (HEGIS), "Degrees and Other Formal Awards Conferred" surveys, 1976–77 and 1980–81; Integrated Postsecondary Education Data System (IPEDS), "Completions Survey" (IPEDS-C:90–99); and IPEDS Fall 2000 through Fall 2013, Completions component. (This table was prepared September 2014.)

Table 322.30. Bachelor's degrees conferred by postsecondary institutions, by race/ethnicity and field of study: 2011–12 and 2012–13

Field of study	2011–12										2012–13									
	Total	White	Black	Hispanic	Asian/Pacific Islander			American Indian/ Alaska Native	Two or more races	Nonresident alien	Total	White	Black	Hispanic	Asian/Pacific Islander			American Indian/ Alaska Native	Two or more races	Nonresident alien
					Total	Asian	Pacific Islander								Total	Asian	Pacific Islander			
1	2	3	4	5	6	7	8	9	10	11	12	13	14	15	16	17	18	19	20	21
All fields, total	1,792,163	1,212,417	185,916	169,796	126,177	121,550	4,627	11,498	27,234	59,185	1,840,164	1,221,576	191,180	186,650	130,144	125,098	5,046	11,445	34,338	64,831
Agriculture and natural resources	30,972	25,980	944	1,611	1,260	1,206	54	257	454	466	33,593	27,648	960	2,050	1,358	1,283	75	285	649	643
Architecture and related services	9,727	6,420	504	1,174	884	871	13	48	126	571	9,757	6,253	505	1,257	892	871	21	36	160	654
Area, ethnic, cultural, gender, and group studies	9,228	4,499	1,323	1,593	1,088	1,043	45	192	294	239	8,851	4,304	1,148	1,588	1,008	957	51	225	360	218
Biological and biomedical sciences	95,850	59,564	7,234	7,875	16,170	15,909	261	588	1,633	2,786	100,319	61,737	7,642	8,884	16,498	16,245	253	539	2,088	2,931
Business	367,235	233,073	44,397	34,344	28,062	26,977	1,085	2,146	4,364	20,849	360,823	225,365	42,451	35,421	27,074	25,899	1,175	2,079	5,374	23,059
Communication, journalism, and related programs	83,771	59,829	9,211	7,356	3,625	3,429	196	426	1,293	2,031	84,817	59,422	9,116	8,223	3,654	3,452	202	426	1,688	2,288
Communications technologies	4,983	3,247	545	564	268	258	10	25	121	213	4,989	3,167	622	610	242	237	5	22	120	206
Computer and information sciences	47,406	30,214	5,425	4,006	4,416	4,256	160	257	727	2,361	50,962	31,722	6,015	4,502	5,106	4,937	169	292	945	2,380
Construction trades	377	326	10	26	9	9	0	1	2	3	244	186	6	36	5	3	2	1	9	1
Education	105,656	86,047	7,634	6,970	2,149	1,953	196	767	1,055	1,034	104,647	84,173	8,300	7,153	2,121	1,925	196	725	1,249	926
Engineering	81,371	54,224	3,328	6,266	9,731	9,559	172	318	1,163	6,341	85,980	56,120	3,620	7,041	10,590	10,394	196	360	1,475	6,774
Engineering technologies and engineering-related fields[1]	16,656	12,259	1,704	1,176	692	669	23	150	182	493	16,493	11,762	1,684	1,369	728	693	35	167	186	597
English language and literature/letters	53,765	40,162	4,138	4,983	2,511	2,410	101	319	1,111	541	52,424	38,541	4,102	5,313	2,429	2,335	94	280	1,205	554
Family and consumer sciences/human sciences	23,441	16,473	2,941	2,016	1,203	1,167	36	164	312	332	23,934	16,411	3,033	2,267	1,336	1,275	61	141	408	338
Foreign languages, literatures, and linguistics	21,756	14,604	944	3,977	1,261	1,235	26	99	442	429	21,673	14,145	964	4,146	1,278	1,248	30	118	549	473
Health professions and related programs	163,675	114,262	19,823	12,012	12,146	11,571	575	959	2,168	2,305	181,144	124,572	22,060	14,437	13,618	12,970	648	1,101	3,014	2,342
Homeland security, law enforcement, and firefighting	54,091	31,280	11,139	8,497	1,573	1,394	179	443	850	309	60,269	34,528	12,299	9,836	1,757	1,552	205	482	1,003	364
Legal professions and studies	4,595	2,787	822	586	232	223	9	29	71	68	4,425	2,713	759	590	202	194	8	30	87	44
Liberal arts and sciences, general studies, and humanities	46,961	31,142	6,796	5,027	1,737	1,605	132	521	820	918	46,761	30,689	6,619	5,298	1,686	1,547	139	511	1,022	936
Library science	95	89	2	3	1	1	0	0	0	0	102	90	6	4	2	0	2	0	2	0
Mathematics and statistics	18,841	12,735	976	1,308	1,876	1,837	39	59	247	1,640	20,453	13,276	1,022	1,526	2,119	2,080	39	80	351	2,079
Mechanic and repair technologies/technicians	250	171	12	17	12	12	0	5	1	32	267	201	10	14	11	10	1	5	3	23
Military technologies and applied sciences	86	51	25	6	0	0	0	1	1	2	105	61	29	12	6	6	0	1	0	1
Multi/interdisciplinary studies	45,717	30,099	5,053	5,951	2,639	2,532	107	357	708	910	47,654	30,520	5,575	6,473	2,756	2,605	151	359	1,008	963
Parks, recreation, leisure, and fitness studies	38,998	29,172	3,750	3,185	1,497	1,386	111	267	524	603	42,714	31,514	4,146	3,737	1,685	1,569	116	262	774	596
Philosophy and religious studies	12,645	9,467	964	1,052	622	598	24	85	254	201	12,793	9,228	1,027	1,175	750	722	28	76	315	222
Physical sciences and science technologies	26,664	18,982	1,541	1,682	2,741	2,702	39	154	447	1,117	28,050	19,659	1,519	1,981	2,887	2,825	62	156	536	1,312
Precision production	37	30	1	2	2	2	0	0	2	0	36	25	0	2	6	6	0	0	2	2
Psychology	109,099	70,051	13,576	13,338	7,332	7,087	245	755	2,045	2,002	114,450	72,084	14,125	15,172	7,600	7,318	282	705	2,538	2,226
Public administration and social services	29,685	16,963	6,915	3,736	1,013	907	106	287	462	319	31,950	17,849	7,527	4,230	1,118	1,015	103	300	589	337
Social sciences and history	178,534	117,846	17,146	19,551	13,020	12,550	470	1,115	3,463	6,393	177,778	114,139	16,961	21,339	12,886	12,473	413	1,012	4,098	7,343
Social sciences	143,412	89,719	15,427	16,583	11,791	11,382	409	887	2,860	6,145	143,587	87,074	15,303	18,206	11,719	11,357	362	830	3,370	7,085
History	35,122	28,127	1,719	2,968	1,229	1,168	61	228	603	248	34,191	27,065	1,658	3,133	1,167	1,116	51	182	728	258
Theology and religious vocations	9,304	7,751	637	385	233	217	16	42	88	168	9,385	7,672	689	445	250	224	26	41	101	187
Transportation and materials moving	4,876	3,737	343	380	185	163	22	44	53	134	4,526	3,233	314	356	220	192	28	22	260	121
Visual and performing arts	95,806	68,881	6,112	9,082	5,987	5,812	175	618	1,751	3,375	97,796	68,567	6,325	10,163	6,273	6,041	232	606	2,171	3,691
Other and not classified	0	0	0	0	0	0	0	0	0	0	0	0	0	0	0	0	0	0	0	0

[1]Excludes "Construction trades" and "Mechanic and repair technologies/technicians," which are listed separately.
NOTE: Data are for postsecondary institutions participating in Title IV federal financial aid programs. Race categories exclude persons of Hispanic ethnicity. Reported racial/ethnic distributions of students by level of degree, field of degree, and sex were used to estimate race/ethnicity for students whose race/ethnicity was not reported. To facilitate trend comparisons, certain aggregations have been made of the degree fields as reported in the Integrated Postsecondary Education Data System (IPEDS): "Agriculture and natural resources" includes Agriculture, agriculture operations, and related sciences and Natural resources and conservation; and "Business" includes Business management, marketing, and related support services and Personal and culinary services. Some data have been revised from previously published figures.
SOURCE: U.S. Department of Education, National Center for Education Statistics, Integrated Postsecondary Education Data System (IPEDS), Fall 2012 and Fall 2013, Completions component. (This table was prepared September 2014.)

Table 322.40. Bachelor's degrees conferred to males by postsecondary institutions, by race/ethnicity and field of study: 2011–12 and 2012–13

	2011–12										2012–13									
					Asian/Pacific Islander			American Indian/Alaska Native	Two or more races	Non-resident alien					Asian/Pacific Islander			American Indian/Alaska Native	Two or more races	Non-resident alien
Field of study	Total	White	Black	Hispanic	Total	Asian	Pacific Islander				Total	White	Black	Hispanic	Total	Asian	Pacific Islander			
1	2	3	4	5	6	7	8	9	10	11	12	13	14	15	16	17	18	19	20	21
All fields, total	765,772	532,463	63,736	67,083	57,521	55,525	1,996	4,476	10,945	29,548	787,231	535,082	67,306	74,043	59,802	57,563	2,239	4,616	14,032	32,350
Agriculture and natural resources	15,485	13,314	422	715	513	491	22	117	194	210	16,618	14,127	418	864	496	463	33	139	300	274
Architecture and related services	5,566	3,796	280	679	444	440	4	27	69	271	5,581	3,685	284	756	446	432	14	22	82	306
Area, ethnic, cultural, gender, and group studies	2,757	1,394	379	456	315	296	19	60	80	73	2,624	1,293	320	419	329	309	20	84	104	75
Biological and biomedical sciences	39,542	25,271	2,157	3,115	6,978	6,871	107	222	659	1,140	41,511	26,175	2,361	3,571	7,174	7,065	109	222	853	1,155
Business	190,180	128,354	17,587	16,150	14,322	13,781	541	975	2,173	10,619	187,789	124,414	17,290	16,828	13,873	13,307	566	979	2,741	11,664
Communication, journalism, and related programs	29,921	21,904	3,211	2,471	1,175	1,108	67	137	408	615	30,147	21,601	3,320	2,698	1,166	1,092	74	145	532	685
Communications technologies	3,604	2,347	368	445	190	184	6	15	90	149	3,524	2,214	446	469	152	150	2	20	86	137
Computer and information sciences	38,796	25,691	3,768	3,257	3,428	3,313	115	200	577	1,875	41,874	26,958	4,360	3,621	4,077	3,935	142	218	742	1,898
Construction trades	359	313	9	23	9	9	0	1	2	2	225	173	6	30	5	3	2	1	9	1
Education	21,714	17,704	1,773	1,194	440	389	51	173	199	231	21,805	17,461	1,892	1,292	461	415	46	169	296	234
Engineering	65,819	44,780	2,429	4,942	7,490	7,358	132	246	896	5,036	69,425	46,194	2,737	5,565	8,213	8,055	158	277	1,135	5,304
Engineering technologies and engineering-related fields[1]	14,951	11,208	1,376	1,021	624	603	21	132	154	436	14,742	10,668	1,414	1,194	624	594	30	149	166	527
English language and literature/letters	16,976	13,007	1,058	1,614	745	716	29	104	312	136	16,515	12,300	1,089	1,759	768	732	36	99	340	160
Family and consumer sciences/human sciences	2,693	1,746	433	214	188	179	9	15	37	60	2,872	1,809	429	283	199	187	12	17	59	76
Foreign languages, literatures, and linguistics	6,629	4,677	252	1,023	377	365	12	38	138	124	6,847	4,611	295	1,164	426	412	14	43	176	132
Health professions and related programs	24,905	16,411	2,710	2,106	2,664	2,537	127	129	354	531	28,214	18,310	3,104	2,504	3,050	2,900	150	189	502	555
Homeland security, law enforcement, and firefighting	27,957	18,392	4,010	3,882	960	858	102	184	378	151	31,796	20,475	4,784	4,555	1,123	1,013	110	205	467	187
Legal professions and studies	1,389	901	185	163	83	81	2	6	23	28	1,308	844	197	148	67	66	1	10	31	11
Liberal arts and sciences, general studies, and humanities	16,953	11,785	2,326	1,404	626	570	56	185	282	345	16,968	11,601	2,393	1,547	554	502	52	168	354	351
Library science	7	7	0	0	0	0	0	0	0	0	12	11	0	1	0	0	0	0	0	0
Mathematics and statistics	10,722	7,284	508	714	1,104	1,085	19	37	151	924	11,602	7,559	503	840	1,297	1,273	24	51	194	1,158
Mechanic and repair technologies/technicians	235	164	10	17	12	12	0	3	1	28	241	182	10	11	11	10	0	5	1	21
Military technologies and applied sciences	69	42	18	5	0	0	0	1	2	2	80	54	15	10	10	10	0	1	0	1
Multi/interdisciplinary studies	14,597	9,990	1,502	1,534	883	849	34	114	240	334	15,330	10,320	1,628	1,607	939	887	52	138	326	372
Parks, recreation, leisure, and fitness studies	20,834	15,351	2,211	1,764	791	732	59	142	244	331	23,228	16,846	2,489	2,072	923	859	64	138	414	346
Philosophy and religious studies	7,958	6,112	483	664	372	352	20	50	154	123	8,150	5,973	582	756	462	443	19	50	187	140
Physical sciences and science technologies	15,972	11,924	620	963	1,481	1,459	22	85	242	657	17,143	12,514	670	1,200	1,612	1,578	34	71	309	767
Precision production	28	23	2	1	2			0	0	0	23	18	0	3	3			0	0	1
Psychology	25,420	16,666	2,598	2,903	2,110	2,040	70	194	498	451	26,816	16,995	2,904	3,381	2,172	2,091	81	182	610	572
Public administration and social services	5,386	3,158	1,093	645	266	237	29	47	95	82	5,664	3,228	1,161	740	295	277	18	54	110	76
Social sciences and history	90,628	63,667	6,624	8,620	6,391	6,178	213	513	1,579	3,234	90,148	61,910	6,683	9,256	6,272	6,045	227	475	1,837	3,715
Social sciences	69,657	46,457	5,764	6,983	5,711	5,537	174	389	1,256	3,097	69,688	45,353	5,852	7,481	5,625	5,434	191	367	1,437	3,573
History	20,971	17,210	860	1,637	680	641	39	124	323	137	20,460	16,557	831	1,775	647	611	36	108	400	142
Theology and religious vocations	6,251	5,329	345	230	152	142	10	20	54	121	6,351	5,348	363	272	149	128	21	33	50	136
Transportation and materials moving	4,305	3,333	297	323	160	141	19	32	46	114	3,997	2,882	267	301	194	168	26	18	235	100
Visual and performing arts	37,164	26,418	2,692	3,826	2,226	2,147	79	272	615	1,115	38,061	26,329	2,892	4,328	2,270	2,169	101	245	784	1,213
Other and not classified	0	0	0	0	0	0	0	0	0	0	0	0	0	0	0	0	0	0	0	0

[1]Excludes "Construction trades" and "Mechanic and repair technologies/technicians," which are listed separately.

NOTE: Data are for postsecondary institutions participating in Title IV federal financial aid programs. Race categories exclude persons of Hispanic ethnicity. Reported racial/ethnic distributions of students by level of degree, field of degree, and sex were used to estimate race/ethnicity for students whose race/ethnicity was not reported. To facilitate trend comparisons, certain aggregations have been made of the degree fields as reported in the Integrated Postsecondary Education Data System (IPEDS): "Agriculture and natu- ral resources" includes Agriculture, agriculture operations, and related sciences and Natural resources and conservation; and "Business" includes Business management, marketing, and related support services and Personal and culinary services. Some data have been revised from previously published figures.

SOURCE: U.S. Department of Education, National Center for Education Statistics, Integrated Postsecondary Education Data System (IPEDS), Fall 2012 and Fall 2013, Completions component. (This table was prepared September 2014.)

Table 322.50. Bachelor's degrees conferred to females by postsecondary institutions, by race/ethnicity and field of study: 2011–12 and 2012–13

Field of study	2011–12										2012–13									
	Total	White	Black	Hispanic	Asian/Pacific Islander Total	Asian	Pacific Islander	American Indian/Alaska Native	Two or more races	Nonresident alien	Total	White	Black	Hispanic	Asian/Pacific Islander Total	Asian	Pacific Islander	American Indian/Alaska Native	Two or more races	Nonresident alien
1	2	3	4	5	6	7	8	9	10	11	12	13	14	15	16	17	18	19	20	21
All fields, total	1,026,391	679,954	122,180	102,653	68,656	66,025	2,631	7,022	16,289	29,637	1,052,933	686,494	123,874	112,607	70,342	67,535	2,807	6,829	20,306	32,481
Agriculture and natural resources	15,487	12,666	522	896	747	715	32	140	260	256	16,975	13,521	542	1,186	862	820	42	146	349	369
Architecture and related services	4,161	2,624	224	495	440	431	9	21	57	300	4,176	2,568	221	501	446	439	7	14	78	348
Area, ethnic, cultural, gender, and group studies	6,471	3,105	944	1,137	773	747	26	132	214	166	6,227	3,011	828	1,169	679	648	31	141	256	143
Biological and biomedical sciences	56,308	34,293	5,077	4,760	9,192	9,038	154	366	974	1,646	58,808	35,562	5,281	5,313	9,324	9,180	144	317	1,235	1,776
Business	177,055	104,719	26,810	18,194	13,740	13,196	544	1,171	2,191	10,230	173,034	100,951	25,161	18,593	13,201	12,592	609	1,100	2,633	11,395
Communication, journalism, and related programs	53,850	37,925	6,000	4,885	2,450	2,321	129	289	885	1,416	54,670	37,821	5,796	5,525	2,488	2,360	128	281	1,156	1,603
Communications technologies	1,379	900	177	119	78	74	4	10	31	64	1,465	953	176	141	90	87	3	2	34	69
Computer and information sciences	8,610	4,523	1,657	749	988	943	45	57	150	486	9,088	4,764	1,655	881	1,029	1,002	27	74	203	482
Construction trades	18	13	1				0	0	0	1	13	13	0							0
Education	83,942	68,343	5,861	5,776	1,709	1,564	145	594	856	803	82,842	66,712	6,408	5,861	1,660	1,510	150	556	953	692
Engineering	15,552	9,444	899	1,324	2,241	2,201	40	72	267	1,305	16,555	9,926	883	1,476	2,377	2,339	38	83	340	1,470
Engineering technologies and engineering-related fields[1]	1,705	1,051	328	155	68	66	2	18	28	57	1,751	1,094	270	175	104	99	5	18	20	70
English language and literature/letters	36,789	27,155	3,080	3,369	1,766	1,694	72	215	799	405	35,909	26,241	3,013	3,554	1,661	1,603	58	181	865	394
Family and consumer sciences/human sciences	20,748	14,727	2,508	1,802	1,015	988	27	149	275	272	21,062	14,602	2,604	1,984	1,137	1,088	49	124	349	262
Foreign languages, literatures, and linguistics	15,127	9,927	692	2,954	884	870	14	61	304	305	14,826	9,534	669	2,982	852	836	16	75	373	341
Health professions and related programs	138,770	97,851	17,113	9,906	9,482	9,034	448	830	1,814	1,774	152,930	106,262	18,956	11,933	10,568	10,070	498	912	2,512	1,787
Homeland security, law enforcement, and firefighting	26,134	12,888	7,129	4,615	613	536	77	259	472	158	28,473	14,053	7,515	5,281	634	539	95	277	536	177
Legal professions and studies	3,206	1,886	637	423	149	142	7	23	48	40	3,117	1,869	562	442	135	128	7	20	56	33
Liberal arts and sciences, general studies,	30,008	19,357	4,470	3,623	1,111	1,035	76	336	538	573	29,793	19,088	4,226	3,751	1,132	1,045	87	343	668	585
Library science	88	82	2	3	1	1	0	0	0	0	90	79	6	3	0	0	0	0	2	0
Mathematics and statistics	8,119	5,451	468	594	772	752	20	22	96	716	8,851	5,717	519	686	822	807	15	29	157	921
Mechanic and repair technologies/technicians	15	7	2	0	0	0	0	2	0	4	26	19	2	3	1	0	0	0	2	2
Military technologies and applied sciences	17	9	7	1	0	0	0	0	0	0	25	7	14	2	1	1	0	1	0	0
Multi/interdisciplinary studies	31,120	20,109	3,551	4,417	1,756	1,683	73	243	468	576	32,324	20,200	3,947	4,866	1,817	1,718	99	221	682	591
Parks, recreation, leisure, and fitness studies	18,164	13,821	1,539	1,421	706	654	52	125	280	272	19,486	14,668	1,657	1,665	762	710	52	124	360	250
Philosophy and religious studies	4,687	3,355	481	388	250	246	4	35	100	78	4,643	3,255	445	419	288	279	9	26	128	82
Physical sciences and science technologies	10,692	7,058	921	719	1,260	1,243	17	69	205	460	10,907	7,145	849	781	1,275	1,247	28	85	227	545
Precision production	9	7								2	13	7	0	1	3	3	0	0	1	0
Psychology	83,679	53,385	10,978	10,435	5,222	5,047	175	561	1,547	1,551	87,634	55,089	11,221	11,791	5,428	5,227	201	523	1,928	1,654
Public administration and social services	24,309	13,805	5,822	3,091	747	670	77	240	367	237	26,286	14,621	6,366	3,490	823	738	85	246	479	261
Social sciences and history	87,906	54,179	10,522	10,931	6,629	6,372	257	602	1,884	3,159	87,630	52,229	10,278	12,083	6,614	6,428	186	537	2,261	3,628
Social sciences	73,755	43,262	9,663	9,600	6,080	5,845	235	498	1,604	3,048	73,899	41,721	9,451	10,725	6,094	5,923	171	463	1,933	3,512
History	14,151	10,917	859	1,331	549	527	22	104	280	111	13,731	10,508	827	1,358	520	505	15	74	328	116
Theology and religious vocations	3,053	2,422	292	155	81	75	6	22	34	47	3,034	2,324	326	173	101	96	5	22	34	51
Transportation and materials moving	571	404	46	57	25	22	3	12	7	20	529	351	47	55	26	24	2	7	7	21
Visual and performing arts	58,642	42,463	3,420	5,256	3,761	3,665	96	346	1,136	2,260	59,735	42,238	3,433	5,835	4,003	3,872	131	361	1,387	2,478
Other and not classified	0	0	0	0	0	0	0	0	0	0	0	0	0	0	0	0	0	0	0	0

[1]Excludes "Construction trades" and "Mechanic and repair technologies/technicians," which are listed separately.

NOTE: Data are for postsecondary institutions participating in Title IV federal financial aid programs. Race categories exclude persons of Hispanic ethnicity. Reported racial/ethnic distributions of students by level of degree, field of degree, and sex were used to estimate race/ethnicity for students whose race/ethnicity was not reported. To facilitate trend comparisons, certain aggregations have been made of the degree fields as reported in the Integrated Postsecondary Education Data System (IPEDS): "Agriculture and natural resources" includes Agriculture, agriculture operations, and related sciences and Natural resources and conservation; and "Business" includes Business management, marketing, and related support services and Personal and culinary services. Some data have been revised from previously published figures.

SOURCE: U.S. Department of Education, National Center for Education Statistics, Integrated Postsecondary Education Data System (IPEDS), Fall 2012 and Fall 2013, Completions component. (This table was prepared September 2014.)

Table 323.10. Master's degrees conferred by postsecondary institutions, by field of study: Selected years, 1970–71 through 2012–13

Field of study	1970–71	1975–76	1980–81	1985–86	1990–91	1995–96	2000–01	2002–03	2003–04	2004–05	2005–06	2006–07	2007–08	2008–09	2009–10	2010–11	2011–12	2012–13
1	2	3	4	5	6	7	8	9	10	11	12	13	14	15	16	17	18	19
Total	235,564	317,477	302,637	295,850	342,863	412,180	473,502	518,699	564,272	580,151	599,731	610,597	630,666	662,082	693,313	730,922	755,967	751,751
Agriculture and natural resources	2,457	3,340	4,003	3,801	3,295	4,551	4,272	4,492	4,783	4,746	4,640	4,623	4,684	4,878	5,215	5,766	6,390	6,339
Architecture and related services	1,705	3,215	3,153	3,260	3,490	3,993	4,302	4,925	5,424	5,674	5,743	5,951	6,065	6,587	7,280	7,788	8,448	8,095
Area, ethnic, cultural, gender, and group studies	1,032	993	802	915	1,233	1,652	1,555	1,509	1,683	1,755	2,080	1,699	1,778	1,779	1,775	1,913	1,947	1,897
Biological and biomedical sciences	5,625	6,457	5,766	5,064	4,834	6,593	7,017	7,050	7,732	8,284	8,781	8,898	9,689	10,018	10,730	11,324	12,419	13,335
Business	26,490	42,592	57,888	66,676	78,255	93,554	115,602	127,685	139,347	142,617	146,406	150,211	155,637	168,404	177,748	187,178	191,606	188,625
Communication, journalism, and related programs	1,770	2,961	2,896	3,500	4,123	5,080	5,218	6,053	6,535	6,762	7,244	6,773	6,915	7,042	7,630	8,302	9,005	8,757
Communications technologies	86	165	209	308	204	481	427	442	365	433	501	499	631	475	463	502	497	577
Computer and information sciences	1,588	2,603	4,218	8,070	9,324	10,579	16,911	19,509	20,143	18,416	17,055	16,232	17,087	17,907	17,955	19,516	20,925	22,777
Education	87,666	126,061	96,713	74,816	87,352	104,936	127,829	147,883	162,345	167,490	174,620	176,572	175,880	178,538	182,165	185,127	179,047	164,624
Engineering	16,813	16,472	16,893	21,529	24,454	26,789	25,174	28,251	32,554	32,488	30,848	29,299	31,557	34,546	35,133	38,664	40,323	40,417
Engineering technologies	134	328	323	617	996	2,054	2,013	2,332	2,499	2,500	2,541	2,690	2,873	3,462	4,258	4,515	4,793	4,908
English language and literature/letters	10,441	8,599	5,742	5,335	6,784	7,657	6,763	7,428	7,956	8,468	8,845	8,742	9,161	9,262	9,202	9,475	9,938	9,755
Family and consumer sciences/human sciences	1,452	2,179	2,570	2,011	1,541	1,712	1,838	1,607	1,794	1,827	1,983	2,080	2,199	2,453	2,592	2,918	3,155	3,253
Foreign languages, literatures, and linguistics	5,480	4,432	2,934	2,690	3,049	3,443	3,035	3,049	3,124	3,407	3,539	3,443	3,565	3,592	3,756	3,727	3,827	3,708
Health professions and related programs	5,330	12,164	16,176	18,603	21,354	33,920	43,623	42,748	44,939	46,703	51,380	54,531	58,120	62,642	69,112	75,571	84,355	90,931
Homeland security, law enforcement, and firefighting	194	1,197	1,538	1,074	1,108	1,812	2,514	2,956	3,717	3,991	4,277	4,906	5,760	6,125	6,717	7,433	8,420	8,868
Legal professions and studies	955	1,442	1,832	1,924	2,057	2,751	3,829	4,141	4,243	4,170	4,453	4,486	4,815	5,150	5,767	6,475	6,614	7,013
Liberal arts and sciences, general studies, and humanities	885	2,633	2,375	1,586	2,213	2,778	3,193	3,314	3,697	3,680	3,702	3,634	3,797	3,729	3,822	3,997	3,792	3,268
Library science	7,001	8,037	4,859	3,564	4,763	5,099	4,727	5,295	6,015	6,213	6,448	6,767	7,162	7,091	7,448	7,729	7,443	6,983
Mathematics and statistics	5,191	3,857	2,567	3,131	3,549	3,651	3,209	3,620	4,191	4,477	4,730	4,884	4,980	5,211	5,639	5,866	6,246	6,957
Military technologies and applied sciences	2	0	43	83	0	136	0	0	0	0	0	202	0	3	0	0	29	32
Multi/interdisciplinary studies	924	1,283	2,356	2,869	2,079	2,713	3,413	3,721	3,972	4,167	4,391	4,611	5,165	5,225	5,947	6,762	7,746	7,956
Parks, recreation, leisure, and fitness studies	218	571	643	570	483	1,684	2,354	2,978	3,199	3,740	3,992	4,110	4,440	4,825	5,617	6,546	7,047	7,139
Philosophy and religious studies	1,326	1,358	1,231	1,193	1,471	1,363	1,386	1,578	1,578	1,647	1,739	1,716	1,879	1,859	2,045	1,839	2,003	1,931
Physical sciences and science technologies	6,336	5,428	5,246	5,860	5,281	5,910	5,134	5,196	5,714	5,823	6,063	6,012	6,061	5,862	6,066	6,386	6,911	7,011
Precision production	0	0	0	0	0	8	0	3	13	6	9	5	3	10	10	5	11	9
Psychology	5,717	10,167	10,223	9,845	11,349	15,152	16,539	17,161	17,898	18,830	19,770	21,037	21,431	23,415	23,763	25,062	27,052	27,846
Public administration and social services	7,785	15,209	17,803	15,692	17,905	24,229	25,268	25,903	26,250	29,552	30,510	31,131	33,029	33,934	35,740	38,614	41,737	43,590
Social sciences and history	16,539	15,953	11,945	10,564	12,233	15,012	13,791	14,630	16,110	16,952	17,369	17,665	18,495	19,241	20,234	21,085	21,891	21,585
Theology and religious vocations	7,747	8,964	11,061	11,826	10,498	10,909	9,876	10,493	10,818	11,348	11,758	12,436	12,578	12,851	12,848	13,170	13,341	14,276
Transportation and materials moving	0	0	0	454	406	919	756	765	728	802	784	985	982	1,048	1,074	1,390	1,702	1,420
Visual and performing arts	6,675	8,817	8,629	8,420	8,657	10,280	11,404	11,982	12,906	13,183	13,530	13,767	14,164	14,918	15,562	16,277	17,307	17,869
Not classified by field of study	0	0	0	0	8,523	780	528	0	0	0	0	0	84	0	0	0	0	0

NOTE: Data through 1990–91 are for institutions of higher education, while later data are for postsecondary institutions that participate in Title IV federal financial aid programs. The new Classification of Instructional Programs was initiated in 2009–10. The figures for earlier years have been reclassified when necessary to make them conform to the new taxonomy. To facilitate trend comparisons, certain aggregations have been made of the degree fields as reported in the Integrated Postsecondary Education Data System (IPEDS): "Agriculture and natural resources" includes Agriculture, agriculture operations, and related sciences and Natural resources and conservation; "Business" includes Business, management, marketing, and related support services and Personal and culinary services; and "Engineering technologies" includes Engineering technolo-

gies and engineering-related fields, Construction trades, and Mechanic and repair technologies/technicians. Some data have been revised from previously published figures.
SOURCE: U.S. Department of Education, National Center for Education Statistics, Higher Education General Information Survey (HEGIS), "Degrees and Other Formal Awards Conferred" surveys, 1970–71 through 1985–86; Integrated Postsecondary Education Data System (IPEDS), "Completions Survey" (IPEDS-C:91–99); and IPEDS Fall 2000 through Fall 2013, Completions component. (This table was prepared August 2014.)

Table 323.20. Master's degrees conferred by postsecondary institutions, by race/ethnicity and sex of student: Selected years, 1976–77 through 2012–13

Year and sex	Number of degrees conferred to U.S. citizens and nonresident aliens								Percentage distribution of degrees conferred to U.S. citizens						
	Total	White	Black	Hispanic	Asian/Pacific Islander	American Indian/Alaska Native	Two or more races	Non-resident alien	Total	White	Black	Hispanic	Asian/Pacific Islander	American Indian/Alaska Native	Two or more races
1	2	3	4	5	6	7	8	9	10	11	12	13	14	15	16
Total															
1976–77[1]	322,463	271,402	21,252	6,136	5,127	1,018	—	17,528	100.0	89.0	7.0	2.0	1.7	0.3	—
1980–81[2]	301,081	247,475	17,436	6,534	6,348	1,044	—	22,244	100.0	88.8	6.3	2.3	2.3	0.4	—
1990–91	342,863	265,927	17,023	8,981	11,869	1,189	—	37,874	100.0	87.2	5.6	2.9	3.9	0.4	—
1996–97	425,260	309,637	28,875	15,560	19,372	1,954	—	49,862	100.0	82.5	7.7	4.1	5.2	0.5	—
1997–98	436,037	312,752	30,703	16,370	21,415	2,068	—	52,729	100.0	81.6	8.0	4.3	5.6	0.5	—
1998–99	446,038	318,555	33,010	17,781	22,262	2,075	—	52,355	100.0	80.9	8.4	4.5	5.7	0.5	—
1999–2000	463,185	324,990	36,606	19,379	23,523	2,263	—	56,424	100.0	79.9	9.0	4.8	5.8	0.6	—
2000–01	473,502	324,211	38,853	21,661	24,544	2,496	—	61,737	100.0	78.7	9.4	5.3	6.0	0.6	—
2001–02	487,313	331,427	41,006	22,517	25,681	2,632	—	64,050	100.0	78.3	9.7	5.3	6.1	0.6	—
2002–03	518,699	346,003	45,150	25,200	27,492	2,886	—	71,968	100.0	77.5	10.1	5.6	6.2	0.6	—
2003–04	564,272	373,448	51,402	29,806	31,202	3,206	—	75,208	100.0	76.4	10.5	6.1	6.4	0.7	—
2004–05	580,151	383,246	55,330	31,639	33,042	3,310	—	73,584	100.0	75.7	10.9	6.2	6.5	0.7	—
2005–06	599,731	397,439	59,806	32,567	34,289	3,519	—	72,111	100.0	75.3	11.3	6.2	6.5	0.7	—
2006–07	610,597	403,562	63,412	34,967	36,491	3,589	—	68,576	100.0	74.5	11.7	6.5	6.7	0.7	—
2007–08	630,666	413,179	65,914	36,972	37,722	3,777	—	73,102	100.0	74.1	11.8	6.6	6.8	0.7	—
2008–09	662,082	427,713	70,772	39,567	40,510	3,777	—	79,743	100.0	73.4	12.2	6.8	7.0	0.6	—
2009–10	693,313	445,158	76,472	43,603	42,520	3,965	—	81,595	100.0	72.8	12.5	7.1	7.0	0.6	—
2010–11	730,922	462,922	80,742	46,823	43,482	3,946	6,597	86,410	100.0	71.8	12.5	7.3	6.7	0.6	1.0
2011–12	755,967	470,822	86,007	50,994	45,379	3,681	9,823	89,261	100.0	70.6	12.9	7.6	6.8	0.6	1.5
2012–13	751,751	455,892	87,988	52,990	44,912	3,697	11,839	94,433	100.0	69.4	13.4	8.1	6.8	0.6	1.8
Males															
1976–77[1]	172,703	144,042	7,970	3,328	3,128	565	—	13,670	100.0	90.6	5.0	2.1	2.0	0.4	—
1980–81[2]	151,602	120,927	6,418	3,155	3,830	507	—	16,765	100.0	89.7	4.8	2.3	2.8	0.4	—
1990–91	160,842	117,993	6,201	4,017	6,765	495	—	25,371	100.0	87.1	4.6	3.0	5.0	0.4	—
1996–97	185,270	128,946	9,252	6,335	9,488	743	—	30,506	100.0	83.3	6.0	4.1	6.1	0.5	—
1997–98	188,718	128,987	9,978	6,612	10,500	792	—	31,849	100.0	82.2	6.4	4.2	6.7	0.5	—
1998–99	190,230	129,912	10,346	7,044	10,638	794	—	31,496	100.0	81.8	6.5	4.4	6.7	0.5	—
1999–2000	196,129	131,221	11,642	7,738	11,299	845	—	33,384	100.0	80.6	7.2	4.8	6.9	0.5	—
2000–01	197,770	128,516	11,878	8,371	11,561	925	—	36,519	100.0	79.7	7.4	5.2	7.2	0.6	—
2001–02	202,604	131,316	12,119	8,539	11,956	995	—	37,679	100.0	79.6	7.3	5.2	7.2	0.6	—
2002–03	215,172	135,938	13,224	9,389	12,704	1,043	—	42,874	100.0	78.9	7.7	5.4	7.4	0.6	—
2003–04	233,056	146,369	15,027	10,929	14,551	1,137	—	45,043	100.0	77.9	8.0	5.8	7.7	0.6	—
2004–05	237,155	150,076	16,136	11,501	15,238	1,167	—	43,037	100.0	77.3	8.3	5.9	7.8	0.6	—
2005–06	241,656	153,666	17,384	11,739	16,031	1,252	—	41,584	100.0	76.8	8.7	5.9	8.0	0.6	—
2006–07	242,189	154,241	18,333	12,473	16,728	1,275	—	39,139	100.0	76.0	9.0	6.1	8.2	0.6	—
2007–08	250,169	157,596	18,761	13,189	17,476	1,293	—	41,854	100.0	75.7	9.0	6.3	8.4	0.6	—
2008–09	263,515	162,863	20,146	14,314	18,865	1,349	—	45,978	100.0	74.9	9.3	6.6	8.7	0.6	—
2009–10	275,317	170,243	22,121	15,554	19,423	1,419	—	46,557	100.0	74.4	9.7	6.8	8.5	0.6	—
2010–11	291,680	177,786	23,746	17,183	19,918	1,409	2,540	49,098	100.0	73.3	9.8	7.1	8.2	0.6	1.0
2011–12	302,484	183,222	25,284	18,633	20,751	1,298	3,518	49,778	100.0	72.5	10.0	7.4	8.2	0.5	1.4
2012–13	301,575	177,195	26,421	19,446	20,456	1,280	4,511	52,266	100.0	71.1	10.6	7.8	8.2	0.5	1.8
Females															
1976–77[1]	149,760	127,360	13,282	2,808	1,999	453	—	3,858	100.0	87.3	9.1	1.9	1.4	0.3	—
1980–81[2]	149,479	126,548	11,018	3,379	2,518	537	—	5,479	100.0	87.9	7.7	2.3	1.7	0.4	—
1990–91	182,021	147,934	10,822	4,964	5,104	694	—	12,503	100.0	87.3	6.4	2.9	3.0	0.4	—
1996–97	239,990	180,691	19,623	9,225	9,884	1,211	—	19,356	100.0	81.9	8.9	4.2	4.5	0.5	—
1997–98	247,319	183,765	20,725	9,758	10,915	1,276	—	20,880	100.0	81.2	9.2	4.3	4.8	0.6	—
1998–99	255,808	188,643	22,664	10,737	11,624	1,281	—	20,859	100.0	80.3	9.6	4.6	4.9	0.5	—
1999–2000	267,056	193,769	24,964	11,641	12,224	1,418	—	23,040	100.0	79.4	10.2	4.8	5.0	0.6	—
2000–01	275,732	195,695	26,975	13,290	12,983	1,571	—	25,218	100.0	78.1	10.8	5.3	5.2	0.6	—
2001–02	284,709	200,111	28,887	13,978	13,725	1,637	—	26,371	100.0	77.5	11.2	5.4	5.3	0.6	—
2002–03	303,527	210,065	31,926	15,811	14,788	1,843	—	29,094	100.0	76.5	11.6	5.8	5.4	0.7	—
2003–04	331,216	227,079	36,375	18,877	16,651	2,069	—	30,165	100.0	75.4	12.1	6.3	5.5	0.7	—
2004–05	342,996	233,170	39,194	20,138	17,804	2,143	—	30,547	100.0	74.6	12.5	6.4	5.7	0.7	—
2005–06	358,075	243,773	42,422	20,828	18,258	2,267	—	30,527	100.0	74.4	13.0	6.4	5.6	0.7	—
2006–07	368,408	249,321	45,079	22,494	19,763	2,314	—	29,437	100.0	73.6	13.3	6.6	5.8	0.7	—
2007–08	380,497	255,583	47,153	23,783	20,246	2,484	—	31,248	100.0	73.2	13.5	6.8	5.8	0.7	—
2008–09	398,567	264,850	50,626	25,253	21,645	2,428	—	33,765	100.0	72.6	13.9	6.9	5.9	0.7	—
2009–10	417,996	274,915	54,351	28,049	23,097	2,546	—	35,038	100.0	71.8	14.2	7.3	6.0	0.7	—
2010–11	439,242	285,136	56,996	29,640	23,564	2,537	4,057	37,312	100.0	70.9	14.2	7.4	5.9	0.6	1.0
2011–12	453,483	287,600	60,723	32,361	24,628	2,383	6,305	39,483	100.0	69.5	14.7	7.8	5.9	0.6	1.5
2012–13	450,176	278,697	61,567	33,544	24,456	2,417	7,328	42,167	100.0	68.3	15.1	8.2	6.0	0.6	1.8

—Not available.
[1]Excludes 387 males and 175 females whose racial/ethnic group was not available.
[2]Excludes 1,377 males and 179 females whose racial/ethnic group was not available.
NOTE: Data through 1990–91 are for institutions of higher education, while later data are for postsecondary institutions participating in Title IV federal financial aid programs. Race categories exclude persons of Hispanic ethnicity. For 1989–90 and later years, reported racial/ethnic distributions of students by level of degree, field of degree, and sex were used to estimate race/ethnicity for students whose race/ethnicity was not reported. Detail may not sum to totals because of rounding. Some data have been revised from previously published figures.
SOURCE: U.S. Department of Education, National Center for Education Statistics, Higher Education General Information Survey (HEGIS), "Degrees and Other Formal Awards Conferred" surveys, 1976–77 and 1980–81; Integrated Postsecondary Education Data System (IPEDS), "Completions Survey" (IPEDS-C:90–99); and IPEDS Fall 2000 through Fall 2013, Completions component. (This table was prepared September 2014.)

Table 323.30. Master's degrees conferred by postsecondary institutions, by race/ethnicity and field of study: 2011–12 and 2012–13

Field of study	2011–12										2012–13									
	Total	White	Black	Hispanic	Asian/Pacific Islander Total	Asian	Pacific Islander	American Indian/Alaska Native	Two or more races	Nonresident alien	Total	White	Black	Hispanic	Asian/Pacific Islander Total	Asian	Pacific Islander	American Indian/Alaska Native	Two or more races	Nonresident alien
1	2	3	4	5	6	7	8	9	10	11	12	13	14	15	16	17	18	19	20	21
All fields, total	755,967	470,822	86,007	50,994	45,379	43,747	1,632	3,681	9,823	89,261	751,751	455,892	87,988	52,990	44,912	43,110	1,802	3,697	11,839	94,433
Agriculture and natural resources	6,390	4,699	194	255	262	254	8	37	79	864	6,339	4,542	233	256	221	206	15	41	112	934
Architecture and related services	8,448	5,395	361	645	562	552	10	29	105	1,351	8,095	4,955	338	623	521	513	8	21	169	1,468
Area, ethnic, cultural, gender, and group studies	1,947	1,057	181	245	119	104	15	32	60	253	1,897	981	168	228	125	117	8	30	69	296
Biological and biomedical sciences	12,419	6,981	751	665	1,634	1,605	29	55	185	2,148	13,335	7,407	866	740	1,811	1,789	22	41	309	2,161
Business	191,606	105,314	28,196	12,692	16,134	15,605	529	882	2,221	26,167	188,625	100,901	28,363	12,833	14,908	14,336	572	875	2,587	28,158
Communication, journalism, and related programs	9,005	5,444	982	640	388	374	14	35	166	1,350	8,757	5,107	956	665	375	362	13	20	205	1,429
Communications technologies	497	216	35	36	20	20	0	5	2	183	577	230	49	36	44	43	1	0	4	214
Computer and information sciences	20,925	6,962	1,649	730	1,838	1,818	20	59	209	9,478	22,777	7,438	2,032	875	2,012	1,984	28	51	261	10,108
Construction trades	5	1	0	0	0	0	0	0	0	4	6	3	0	0	0	0	0	0	0	3
Education	179,047	133,167	19,790	13,470	5,098	4,726	372	936	2,141	4,445	164,624	120,655	18,671	13,154	4,874	4,466	408	952	2,249	4,069
Engineering	40,323	15,981	1,185	1,734	3,959	3,924	35	82	392	16,990	40,417	15,507	1,192	1,864	3,968	3,934	34	80	496	17,310
Engineering technologies and engineering-related fields[1]	4,788	2,327	377	262	329	319	10	32	51	1,410	4,902	2,342	400	224	401	399	2	23	65	1,447
English language and literature/letters	9,938	7,822	598	591	343	329	14	61	185	338	9,755	7,601	530	595	323	309	14	53	256	397
Family and consumer sciences/human sciences	3,155	2,201	440	167	106	101	5	18	39	184	3,253	2,131	500	207	126	122	4	15	63	211
Foreign languages, literatures, and linguistics	3,827	2,133	101	637	148	137	11	9	59	740	3,708	1,988	78	636	146	141	5	14	57	789
Health professions and related programs	84,355	57,860	9,832	5,116	6,531	6,281	250	466	998	3,552	90,931	61,413	11,376	5,800	6,860	6,538	322	516	1,291	3,675
Homeland security, law enforcement, and firefighting	8,420	5,189	1,864	825	204	185	19	73	106	159	8,868	5,409	1,948	869	245	212	33	73	158	166
Legal professions and studies	6,614	2,081	489	291	217	211	6	35	45	3,456	7,013	2,041	464	317	235	227	8	23	78	3,855
Liberal arts and sciences, general studies, and humanities	3,792	2,668	412	237	151	150	1	28	81	215	3,268	2,264	408	266	93	90	3	28	83	126
Library science	7,443	6,067	326	504	285	271	14	32	110	119	6,983	5,739	284	436	246	238	8	36	148	94
Mathematics and statistics	6,246	2,758	190	230	501	495	6	11	62	2,494	6,957	2,806	220	290	572	571	1	6	86	2,977
Mechanic and repair technologies/technicians	29	23	1	3	0	0	0	0	0	1	32	23	0	0	0	0	0	0	0	3
Military technologies and applied sciences	522	377	46	29	22	19	3	5	4	39	539	380	60	26	25	22	3	6	3	36
Multi/interdisciplinary studies	7,746	5,306	603	561	407	395	12	42	133	694	7,956	5,073	680	649	416	404	12	60	170	908
Parks, recreation, leisure, and fitness studies	7,047	5,208	749	347	166	151	15	34	116	427	7,139	5,214	835	363	164	157	7	26	130	407
Philosophy and religious studies	2,003	1,448	191	103	91	89	2	9	31	130	1,931	1,432	149	125	69	66	3	12	31	113
Physical sciences and science technologies	6,911	4,005	231	238	330	325	5	30	90	1,987	7,011	4,017	202	274	405	395	10	34	135	1,944
Precision production	11	10	0	0	1	1	0	0	0	0	9	7	0	0	1	1	0	0	0	1
Psychology	27,052	18,188	3,802	2,397	1,147	1,085	62	138	507	873	27,846	18,390	3,719	2,749	1,192	1,125	67	169	579	1,048
Public administration and social services	41,737	24,709	8,020	4,191	1,744	1,658	86	298	801	1,974	43,590	24,972	8,681	4,562	1,791	1,687	104	276	954	2,354
Social sciences and history	21,891	13,752	1,489	1,538	1,053	1,025	28	105	402	3,552	21,585	13,055	1,593	1,551	1,000	979	21	96	457	3,833
Social sciences	17,736	10,313	1,342	1,284	973	950	23	77	340	3,407	17,483	9,675	1,461	1,296	928	910	18	68	368	3,687
History	4,155	3,439	147	254	80	75	5	28	62	145	4,102	3,380	132	255	72	69	3	28	89	146
Theology and religious vocations	13,341	9,119	2,007	480	635	612	23	41	139	920	14,276	9,749	2,072	604	717	682	35	46	162	926
Transportation and materials moving	1,702	1,340	124	114	66	61	5	9	8	41	1,420	999	118	113	50	43	7	15	57	68
Visual and performing arts	17,307	11,391	837	1,050	910	884	26	58	299	2,762	17,869	11,501	863	1,083	999	974	25	65	415	2,943
Other and not classified	0	0	0	0	0	0	0	0	0	0	0	0	0	0	0	0	0	0	0	0

[1] Excludes "Construction trades" and "Mechanic and repair technologies/technicians," which are listed separately.

NOTE: Data are for postsecondary institutions participating in Title IV federal financial aid programs. Race categories exclude persons of Hispanic ethnicity. Reported racial/ethnic distributions of students by level of degree, field of degree, and sex were used to estimate race/ethnicity for students whose race/ethnicity was not reported. To facilitate trend comparisons, certain aggregations have been made of the degree fields as reported in the Integrated Postsecondary Education Data System (IPEDS): "Agriculture and natural resources" includes Agriculture, agriculture operations, and related sciences and Natural resources and conservation; and "Business" includes Business management, marketing, and related support services and Personal and culinary services. Some data have been revised from previously published figures.

SOURCE: U.S. Department of Education, National Center for Education Statistics, Integrated Postsecondary Education Data System (IPEDS), Fall 2012 and Fall 2013, Completions component. (This table was prepared September 2014.)

Table 323.40. Master's degrees conferred to males by postsecondary institutions, by race/ethnicity and field of study: 2011–12 and 2012–13

Field of study	2011–12										2012–13									
	Total	White	Black	Hispanic	Asian/Pacific Islander Total	Asian	Pacific Islander	American Indian/ Alaska Native	Two or more races	Non-resident alien	Total	White	Black	Hispanic	Asian/Pacific Islander Total	Asian	Pacific Islander	American Indian/ Alaska Native	Two or more races	Non-resident alien
	2	3	4	5	6	7	8	9	10	11	12	13	14	15	16	17	18	19	20	21
All fields, total	302,484	183,222	25,284	18,633	20,751	20,133	618	1,298	3,518	49,778	301,575	177,195	26,421	19,446	20,456	19,739	717	1,280	4,511	52,266
Agriculture and natural resources	3,026	2,248	80	122	103	97	6	18	41	414	2,917	2,147	95	105	76	70	6	12	48	434
Architecture and related services	4,504	3,054	195	344	225	221	4	15	63	608	4,261	2,760	189	326	229	223	6	12	89	656
Area, ethnic, cultural, gender, and group studies	717	419	47	90	41	37	4	11	17	92	667	379	44	83	38	34	4	8	26	89
Biological and biomedical sciences	5,378	3,128	234	271	707	697	10	18	74	946	5,816	3,384	257	316	797	785	12	19	125	918
Business	103,250	61,358	10,325	6,555	9,107	8,834	273	427	1,108	14,370	101,584	58,655	10,656	6,587	8,475	8,173	302	450	1,359	15,402
Communication, journalism, and related programs	2,759	1,842	233	192	93	90	3	13	41	345	2,685	1,704	239	188	95	91	4	3	66	390
Communications technologies	309	146	18	23	11	11	0	4	1	106	337	156	14	20	29	29	0	0	0	118
Computer and information sciences	15,132	5,506	973	534	1,251	1,239	12	38	154	6,676	16,538	5,855	1,235	678	1,412	1,389	23	35	175	7,148
Construction trades	4	1	0	0	0	0	0	0	0	2	2	0	0	0	0	0	0	0	0	2
Education	41,364	31,283	4,148	2,996	1,132	1,049	83	222	484	1,099	37,804	27,939	4,003	2,991	1,073	961	112	205	553	1,040
Engineering	31,190	13,009	842	1,289	2,913	2,887	26	58	268	12,811	30,854	12,421	872	1,406	2,886	2,861	25	58	380	12,831
Engineering technologies and engineering-related fields[1]	3,518	1,829	228	186	229	220	9	20	32	994	3,636	1,827	267	158	272	270	2	15	47	1,050
English language and literature/letters	3,403	2,777	141	225	81	74	7	23	55	101	3,215	2,556	149	206	92	84	8	15	76	121
Family and consumer sciences/human sciences	412	281	47	29	14	13	1	3	4	34	434	275	62	30	14	14	0	3	8	42
Foreign languages, literatures, and linguistics	1,280	762	39	189	40	33	7	3	23	224	1,235	709	32	190	31	29	2	4	24	245
Health professions and related programs	15,675	9,931	1,549	1,009	1,647	1,594	53	78	204	1,257	16,747	10,484	1,741	1,214	1,694	1,616	78	105	244	1,265
Homeland security, law enforcement, and firefighting	3,954	2,701	639	390	78	70	8	38	36	72	4,351	2,904	741	368	125	109	16	39	78	96
Legal professions and studies	3,209	1,044	165	126	134	131	3	15	13	1,712	3,329	1,032	134	138	107	106	1	7	24	1,887
Liberal arts and sciences, general studies, and humanities	1,490	1,066	131	95	76	76	0	13	25	84	1,297	942	127	105	34	32	2	11	29	49
Library science	1,426	1,159	43	108	60	58	2	5	25	26	1,295	1,064	42	83	51	49	2	4	29	22
Mathematics and statistics	3,695	1,728	111	146	268	264	4	9	40	1,393	4,178	1,767	149	190	342	342	0	4	57	1,669
Mechanic and repair technologies/technicians	0	0	0	0	0	0	0	0	0	0	0	0	0	0	0	0	0	0	0	0
Military technologies and applied sciences	21	17	0	2	0	0	0	0	0	1	17	14	0	0	2	0	1	0	0	1
Multi/interdisciplinary studies	2,988	2,039	210	209	156	148	8	18	40	316	3,001	1,918	238	257	142	136	6	21	61	364
Parks, recreation, leisure, and fitness studies	3,938	2,947	417	198	78	74	4	18	64	216	4,038	2,957	490	211	92	90	2	22	65	201
Philosophy and religious studies	1,253	945	91	58	54	53	1	6	18	81	1,259	966	76	77	44	42	2	9	19	68
Physical sciences and science technologies	4,299	2,520	124	142	194	192	2	16	47	1,256	4,375	2,520	110	186	233	226	7	18	84	1,224
Precision production	9	9	0	0	0	0	0	0	0	0	4	4	0	0	0	0	0	0	0	0
Psychology	5,482	3,823	635	441	277	260	17	25	96	185	5,730	3,916	602	547	258	245	13	26	123	258
Public administration and social services	10,494	6,282	1,595	1,016	466	446	20	78	165	892	10,862	6,390	1,701	1,046	469	439	30	61	203	992
Social sciences and history	10,987	7,222	550	726	476	466	10	47	183	1,783	10,832	6,939	610	739	452	444	8	46	201	1,845
Social sciences	8,745	5,328	496	585	442	433	9	36	142	1,716	8,533	5,020	544	601	419	412	7	33	152	1,764
History	2,242	1,894	54	141	34	33	1	11	41	67	2,299	1,919	66	138	33	32	1	13	49	81
Theology and religious vocations	8,557	6,013	1,013	309	456	438	18	26	69	671	9,484	6,722	1,033	401	502	476	26	30	94	702
Transportation and materials moving	1,441	1,139	97	109	54	49	5	7	7	28	1,177	840	99	85	38	35	3	10	46	59
Visual and performing arts	7,320	4,994	363	504	330	312	18	26	121	982	7,612	5,047	414	515	352	338	14	28	178	1,078
Other and not classified	0	0	0	0	0	0	0	0	0	0	0	0	0	0	0	0	0	0	0	0

[1]Excludes "Construction trades" and "Mechanic and repair technologies/technicians," which are listed separately.

NOTE: Data are for postsecondary institutions participating in Title IV federal financial aid programs. Race categories exclude persons of Hispanic ethnicity. Reported racial/ethnic distributions of students by level of degree, field of degree, and sex were used to estimate race/ethnicity for students whose race/ethnicity was not reported. To facilitate trend comparisons, certain aggregations have been made of the degree fields as reported in the Integrated Postsecondary Education Data System (IPEDS). "Agriculture and natural resources" includes Agriculture, agriculture operations, and related sciences and Natural resources and conservation; and "Business" includes Business management, marketing, and related support services and Personal and culinary services. Some data have been revised from previously published figures.
SOURCE: U.S. Department of Education, National Center for Education Statistics, Integrated Postsecondary Education Data System (IPEDS), Fall 2012 and Fall 2013, Completions component. (This table was prepared August 2014.)

Table 323.50. Master's degrees conferred to females by postsecondary institutions, by race/ethnicity and field of study: 2011–12 and 2012–13

Field of study	2011–12 Total	White	Black	Hispanic	Asian/Pacific Islander Total	Asian	Pacific Islander	American Indian/Alaska Native	Two or more races	Nonresident alien	2012–13 Total	White	Black	Hispanic	Asian/Pacific Islander Total	Asian	Pacific Islander	American Indian/Alaska Native	Two or more races	Nonresident alien
	2	3	4	5	6	7	8	9	10	11	12	13	14	15	16	17	18	19	20	21
All fields, total	453,483	287,600	60,723	32,361	24,628	23,614	1,014	2,383	6,305	39,483	450,176	278,697	61,567	33,544	24,456	23,371	1,085	2,417	7,328	42,167
Agriculture and natural resources	3,364	2,451	114	133	159	157	2	19	38	450	3,422	2,395	138	151	145	136	9	29	64	500
Architecture and related services	3,944	2,341	166	301	337	331	6	14	42	743	3,834	2,195	149	297	292	290	2	9	80	812
Area, ethnic, cultural, gender and group studies	1,230	638	134	155	78	67	11	21	43	161	1,230	602	124	145	87	83	4	22	43	207
Biological and biomedical sciences	7,041	3,853	517	394	927	908	19	37	111	1,202	7,519	4,023	609	424	1,014	1,004	10	22	184	1,243
Business	88,356	43,956	17,871	6,137	7,027	6,771	256	455	1,113	11,797	87,041	42,246	17,707	6,246	6,433	6,163	270	425	1,228	12,756
Communication, journalism, and related programs	6,246	3,602	749	448	295	284	11	22	125	1,005	6,072	3,403	717	477	280	271	9	17	139	1,039
Communications technologies	188	70	17	13	9	9	0	1	1	77	240	74	35	16	15	14	1	0	4	96
Computer and information sciences	5,793	1,456	676	196	587	579	8	21	55	2,802	6,239	1,583	797	197	600	595	5	16	86	2,960
Construction trades	1	1	0	0	0	0	0	0	0	1	2	1	0	0	0	0	0	0	0	1
Education	137,683	101,884	15,642	10,474	3,966	3,677	289	714	1,657	3,346	126,820	92,716	14,668	10,163	3,801	3,505	296	747	1,696	3,029
Engineering	9,133	2,972	343	445	1,046	1,037	9	24	124	4,179	9,563	3,086	320	458	1,082	1,073	9	22	116	4,479
Engineering technologies and engineering-related fields[1]	1,270	498	149	76	100	99	1	12	19	416	1,266	515	133	66	129	129	0	8	18	397
English language and literature/letters	6,535	5,045	457	366	262	255	7	38	130	237	6,540	5,045	381	389	231	225	6	38	180	276
Family and consumer sciences/human sciences	2,743	1,920	393	138	92	88	4	15	35	150	2,819	1,856	438	177	112	108	4	12	55	169
Foreign languages, literatures, and linguistics	2,547	1,371	62	448	108	104	4	6	36	516	2,473	1,279	46	446	115	112	3	10	33	544
Health professions and related programs	68,680	47,929	8,283	4,107	4,884	4,687	197	388	794	2,295	74,184	50,929	9,635	4,586	5,166	4,922	244	411	1,047	2,410
Homeland security, law enforcement, and firefighting	4,466	2,488	1,225	435	126	115	11	35	70	87	4,517	2,505	1,207	501	120	103	17	34	80	70
Legal professions and studies	3,405	1,037	324	165	83	80	3	20	32	1,744	3,684	1,009	330	179	128	121	7	16	54	1,968
Liberal arts and sciences, general studies, and humanities	2,302	1,602	281	142	75	74	1	15	56	131	1,971	1,322	281	161	59	58	1	17	54	77
Library science	6,017	4,908	283	396	225	213	12	27	85	93	5,688	4,675	242	353	195	189	6	32	119	72
Mathematics and statistics	2,551	1,030	79	84	233	231	2	2	22	1,101	2,779	1,039	71	100	230	229	1	2	29	1,308
Mechanic and repair technologies/technicians	0	0	0	0	0	0	0	0	0	0	0	0	0	0	0	0	0	0	0	0
Military technologies and applied sciences	8	6	0	1	0	0	0	0	0	0	15	3	0	3	0	0	0	0	0	0
Multi/interdisciplinary studies	4,758	3,267	393	352	251	247	4	24	93	378	4,955	3,155	442	392	274	268	6	39	109	544
Parks, recreation, leisure, and fitness studies	3,109	2,261	332	149	88	77	11	16	52	211	3,101	2,257	345	152	72	67	5	4	65	206
Philosophy and religious studies	750	503	100	45	37	36	1	3	13	49	672	466	73	48	25	24	1	3	12	45
Physical sciences and science technologies	2,612	1,485	107	96	136	133	3	14	43	731	2,636	1,497	92	88	172	169	3	16	51	720
Precision production	2	2	0	0	1	1	0	1	0	0	5	3	0	0	1	0	1	0	0	1
Psychology	21,570	14,365	3,167	1,956	870	825	45	113	411	688	22,116	14,474	3,117	2,202	934	880	54	143	456	790
Public administration and social services	31,243	18,427	6,425	3,175	1,278	1,212	66	220	636	1,082	32,728	18,582	6,980	3,516	1,322	1,248	74	215	751	1,362
Social sciences and history	10,904	6,530	939	812	577	559	18	58	219	1,769	10,753	6,116	983	812	548	535	13	50	256	1,988
Social sciences	8,991	4,985	846	699	531	517	14	41	198	1,691	8,950	4,655	917	695	509	498	11	35	216	1,923
History	1,913	1,545	93	113	46	42	4	17	21	78	1,803	1,461	66	117	39	37	2	15	40	65
Theology and religious vocations	4,784	3,106	994	171	179	174	5	15	70	249	4,792	3,027	1,039	203	215	206	9	16	68	224
Transportation and materials moving	261	201	27	5	12	12	0	2	1	13	243	159	19	28	12	8	4	5	11	9
Visual and performing arts	9,987	6,397	474	546	580	572	8	32	178	1,780	10,257	6,454	449	568	647	636	11	37	237	1,865
Other and not classified	0	0	0	0	0	0	0	0	0	0	0	0	0	0	0	0	0	0	0	0

[1]Excludes "Construction trades" and "Mechanic and repair technologies/technicians," which are listed separately.

NOTE: Data are for postsecondary institutions participating in Title IV federal financial aid programs. Race categories exclude persons of Hispanic ethnicity. Reported racial/ethnic distributions of students by level of degree, field of degree, and sex were used to estimate race/ethnicity for students whose race/ethnicity was not reported. To facilitate trend comparisons, certain aggregations have been made of the degree fields as reported in the Integrated Postsecondary Education Data System (IPEDS): "Agriculture and natural resources" includes Agriculture, agriculture operations, and related sciences and Natural resources and conservation; and "Business" includes Business management, marketing, and related support services and Personal and culinary services. Some data have been revised from previously published figures.
SOURCE: U.S. Department of Education, National Center for Education Statistics, Integrated Postsecondary Education Data System (IPEDS), Fall 2012 and Fall 2013, Completions component. (This table was prepared September 2014.)

Table 324.10. Doctor's degrees conferred by postsecondary institutions, by field of study: Selected years, 1970–71 through 2012–13

Field of study	1970–71	1975–76	1980–81	1985–86	1990–91	1995–96	2000–01	2002–03	2003–04	2004–05	2005–06	2006–07	2007–08	2008–09	2009–10	2010–11	2011–12	2012–13
1	2	3	4	5	6	7	8	9	10	11	12	13	14	15	16	17	18	19
Total	**64,998**	**91,007**	**98,016**	**100,280**	**105,547**	**115,507**	**119,585**	**121,579**	**126,087**	**134,387**	**138,056**	**144,690**	**149,378**	**154,564**	**158,590**	**163,827**	**170,217**	**175,038**
Agriculture and natural resources	1,086	928	1,067	1,158	1,185	1,259	1,127	1,229	1,185	1,173	1,194	1,272	1,257	1,328	1,149	1,246	1,333	1,411
Architecture and related services	36	82	93	73	135	141	153	152	173	179	201	178	199	212	210	205	255	247
Area, ethnic, cultural, gender, and group studies	143	186	161	156	159	183	216	186	209	189	226	233	270	239	253	278	302	291
Biological and biomedical sciences	3,603	3,347	3,640	3,405	4,152	5,250	5,225	5,268	5,538	5,935	6,162	6,764	7,400	7,499	7,672	7,693	7,935	7,943
Business	774	906	808	923	1,185	1,366	1,180	1,252	1,481	1,498	1,711	2,029	2,084	2,123	2,249	2,286	2,538	2,836
Communication, journalism, and related programs	145	196	171	212	259	338	368	394	418	465	461	479	489	533	570	577	563	612
Communications technologies	0	8	11	6	13	7	2	4	8	3	3	1	7	2	3	1	4	0
Computer and information sciences	128	244	252	344	676	869	768	816	909	1,119	1,416	1,595	1,698	1,580	1,599	1,588	1,698	1,826
Education	6,041	7,202	7,279	6,610	6,189	6,246	6,284	6,832	7,088	7,681	7,584	8,261	8,491	9,028	9,237	9,642	10,118	10,572
Engineering	3,687	2,872	2,598	3,444	5,316	6,304	5,485	5,195	5,801	6,413	7,243	7,867	7,922	7,744	7,706	8,369	8,722	9,356
Engineering technologies	1	2	10	12	14	50	62	57	58	54	75	61	55	59	67	56	134	111
English language and literature/letters	1,554	1,514	1,040	895	1,056	1,395	1,330	1,246	1,207	1,212	1,254	1,178	1,262	1,271	1,334	1,344	1,427	1,373
Family and consumer sciences/human sciences	123	178	247	307	229	375	354	376	329	331	340	337	323	333	296	320	325	351
Foreign languages, literatures, and linguistics	1,084	1,245	931	768	889	1,020	1,078	1,042	1,031	1,027	1,074	1,059	1,078	1,111	1,091	1,158	1,231	1,304
Health professions and related programs	15,988	25,267	29,595	31,922	29,842	32,678	39,019	39,799	41,861	44,201	45,677	48,943	51,675	54,846	57,750	60,221	62,097	64,195
Homeland security, law enforcement, and firefighting	1	9	21	21	28	38	44	72	54	94	80	85	88	97	106	131	117	147
Legal professions and studies	17,441	32,369	36,391	35,898	38,035	39,919	38,190	39,172	40,328	43,521	43,569	43,629	43,880	44,304	44,627	44,853	46,836	47,246
Liberal arts and sciences, general studies, and humanities	32	162	121	90	70	75	102	78	95	109	84	77	76	67	96	95	93	98
Library science	39	71	71	62	56	53	58	62	47	42	44	52	64	35	64	50	60	50
Mathematics and statistics	1,199	856	728	742	978	1,158	997	1,007	1,060	1,176	1,293	1,351	1,360	1,535	1,596	1,586	1,669	1,823
Multi/interdisciplinary studies	101	156	236	352	306	549	512	634	580	626	600	683	660	731	631	660	727	730
Parks, recreation, leisure, and fitness studies	2	15	42	39	28	104	177	199	222	207	194	218	228	285	266	257	288	295
Philosophy and religious studies	555	556	411	480	464	550	600	662	595	586	578	637	635	686	667	804	778	796
Physical sciences and science technologies	4,324	3,388	3,105	3,521	4,248	4,589	3,968	3,939	3,937	4,248	4,642	5,041	4,994	5,237	5,065	5,295	5,370	5,514
Psychology	2,144	3,157	3,576	3,593	3,932	4,141	5,091	4,835	4,827	5,106	4,921	5,153	5,296	5,477	5,540	5,851	5,936	6,323
Public administration and social services	174	292	362	382	430	499	574	599	649	673	704	726	760	812	838	851	890	979
Social sciences and history	3,660	4,157	3,122	2,955	3,012	3,760	3,930	3,850	3,811	3,819	3,914	3,844	4,059	4,234	4,238	4,390	4,597	4,619
Theology and religious vocations	312	1,022	1,273	1,185	1,076	1,517	1,461	1,329	1,304	1,422	1,429	1,573	1,615	1,587	2,071	2,374	2,446	2,175
Transportation and materials moving	0	0	0	3	0	0	0	0	0	0	0	0	0	0	0	0	0	1
Visual and performing arts	621	620	654	722	838	1,067	1,167	1,293	1,282	1,278	1,383	1,364	1,453	1,569	1,599	1,646	1,728	1,814
Not classified by field of study	0	0	0	0	747	7	63	0	0	0	0	0	0	0	0	0	0	0

NOTE: Data through 1990–91 are for institutions of higher education, while later data are for postsecondary institutions that participate in Title IV federal financial aid programs. The new Classification of Instructional Programs was initiated in 2009–10. Includes Ph.D., Ed.D., and comparable degrees at the doctoral level, as well as such degrees as M.D., D.D.S., and law degrees that were formerly classified as first-professional degrees. The figures for earlier years have been reclassified when necessary to make them conform to the new taxonomy. To facilitate trend comparisons, certain aggregations have been made of the degree fields as reported in the Integrated Postsecondary Education Data System (IPEDS): "Agriculture and natural resources" includes Agriculture, agriculture operations, and related sciences and Natural resources and conservation;

"Business" includes Business, management, marketing, and related support services and Personal and culinary services; and "Engineering technologies" includes Engineering technologies and engineering-related fields, Construction trades, and Mechanic and repair technologies/technicians. Some data have been revised from previously published figures. SOURCE: U.S. Department of Education, National Center for Education Statistics, Higher Education General Information Survey (HEGIS), "Degrees and Other Formal Awards Conferred" surveys, 1970–71 through 1985–86; Integrated Postsecondary Education Data System (IPEDS), "Completions Survey" (IPEDS-C:91–99); and IPEDS Fall 2000 through Fall 2013, Completions component. (This table was prepared August 2014.)

Table 324.20. Doctor's degrees conferred by postsecondary institutions, by race/ethnicity and sex of student: Selected years, 1976–77 through 2012–13

	Number of degrees conferred[1] to U.S. citizens and nonresident aliens								Percentage distribution of degrees conferred[1] to U.S. citizens						
Year and sex	Total	White	Black	Hispanic	Asian/ Pacific Islander	American Indian/ Alaska Native	Two or more races	Non-resident alien	Total	White	Black	Hispanic	Asian/ Pacific Islander	American Indian/ Alaska Native	Two or more races
1	2	3	4	5	6	7	8	9	10	11	12	13	14	15	16
Total															
1976–77[2]	91,218	79,932	3,575	1,533	1,674	240	—	4,264	100.0	91.9	4.1	1.8	1.9	0.3	—
1980–81[3]	97,281	84,200	3,893	1,924	2,267	312	—	4,685	100.0	90.9	4.2	2.1	2.4	0.3	—
1990–91	105,547	81,791	4,429	3,210	5,120	356	—	10,641	100.0	86.2	4.7	3.4	5.4	0.4	—
1996–97	118,747	84,244	6,694	4,615	9,730	675	—	12,789	100.0	79.5	6.3	4.4	9.2	0.6	—
1997–98	118,735	83,690	7,018	4,705	9,814	732	—	12,776	100.0	79.0	6.6	4.4	9.3	0.7	—
1998–99	116,700	82,066	7,004	4,959	10,025	774	—	11,872	100.0	78.3	6.7	4.7	9.6	0.7	—
1999–2000	118,736	82,984	7,078	5,042	10,682	708	—	12,242	100.0	77.9	6.6	4.7	10.0	0.7	—
2000–01	119,585	82,321	7,035	5,204	11,587	705	—	12,733	100.0	77.0	6.6	4.9	10.8	0.7	—
2001–02	119,663	81,995	7,570	5,267	11,633	753	—	12,445	100.0	76.5	7.1	4.9	10.8	0.7	—
2002–03	121,579	82,549	7,537	5,503	12,008	759	—	13,223	100.0	76.2	7.0	5.1	11.1	0.7	—
2003–04	126,087	84,695	8,089	5,795	12,371	771	—	14,366	100.0	75.8	7.2	5.2	11.1	0.7	—
2004–05	134,387	89,763	8,527	6,115	13,176	788	—	16,018	100.0	75.8	7.2	5.2	11.1	0.7	—
2005–06	138,056	91,050	8,523	6,202	13,686	929	—	17,666	100.0	75.6	7.1	5.2	11.4	0.8	—
2006–07	144,690	94,248	9,377	6,593	14,924	918	—	18,630	100.0	74.8	7.4	5.2	11.8	0.7	—
2007–08	149,378	97,839	9,463	6,949	15,203	932	—	18,992	100.0	75.0	7.3	5.3	11.7	0.7	—
2008–09	154,564	101,400	10,188	7,497	15,840	978	—	18,661	100.0	74.6	7.5	5.5	11.7	0.7	—
2009–10	158,590	104,419	10,413	8,085	16,560	952	—	18,161	100.0	74.4	7.4	5.8	11.8	0.7	—
2010–11	163,827	105,990	10,934	8,662	17,078	947	1,251	18,965	100.0	73.2	7.5	6.0	11.8	0.7	0.9
2011–12	170,217	109,365	11,794	9,223	17,896	915	1,571	19,453	100.0	72.5	7.8	6.1	11.9	0.6	1.0
2012–13	175,038	110,775	12,084	10,107	18,408	900	2,438	20,326	100.0	71.6	7.8	6.5	11.9	0.6	1.6
Males															
1976–77[2]	71,709	62,977	2,338	1,216	1,311	182	—	3,685	100.0	92.6	3.4	1.8	1.9	0.3	—
1980–81[3]	68,853	59,574	2,206	1,338	1,589	223	—	3,923	100.0	91.8	3.4	2.1	2.4	0.3	—
1990–91	64,242	48,812	1,991	1,835	3,038	196	—	8,370	100.0	87.4	3.6	3.3	5.4	0.4	—
1996–97	68,387	48,113	2,704	2,481	5,334	368	—	9,387	100.0	81.5	4.6	4.2	9.0	0.6	—
1997–98	67,232	47,189	2,808	2,525	5,171	364	—	9,175	100.0	81.3	4.8	4.3	8.9	0.6	—
1998–99	65,340	45,802	2,793	2,533	5,382	402	—	8,428	100.0	80.5	4.9	4.5	9.5	0.7	—
1999–2000	64,930	45,308	2,762	2,602	5,467	333	—	8,458	100.0	80.2	4.9	4.6	9.7	0.6	—
2000–01	64,171	44,131	2,655	2,564	5,759	346	—	8,716	100.0	79.6	4.8	4.6	10.4	0.6	—
2001–02	62,731	43,014	2,821	2,586	5,645	357	—	8,308	100.0	79.0	5.2	4.8	10.4	0.7	—
2002–03	62,730	42,569	2,735	2,671	5,683	358	—	8,714	100.0	78.8	5.1	4.9	10.5	0.7	—
2003–04	63,981	43,014	2,888	2,731	5,620	357	—	9,371	100.0	78.8	5.3	5.0	10.3	0.7	—
2004–05	67,257	44,749	2,904	2,863	5,913	370	—	10,458	100.0	78.8	5.1	5.0	10.4	0.7	—
2005–06	68,912	45,476	2,949	2,850	5,977	429	—	11,231	100.0	78.8	5.1	4.9	10.4	0.7	—
2006–07	71,308	46,228	3,225	3,049	6,597	421	—	11,788	100.0	77.7	5.4	5.1	11.1	0.7	—
2007–08	73,453	48,203	3,296	3,146	6,535	447	—	11,826	100.0	78.2	5.3	5.1	10.6	0.7	—
2008–09	75,674	49,880	3,531	3,388	6,914	460	—	11,501	100.0	77.7	5.5	5.3	10.8	0.7	—
2009–10	76,610	50,707	3,609	3,642	7,184	430	—	11,038	100.0	77.3	5.5	5.6	11.0	0.7	—
2010–11	79,672	51,688	3,838	3,990	7,545	454	557	11,600	100.0	75.9	5.6	5.9	11.1	0.7	0.8
2011–12	82,670	53,488	4,121	4,218	7,792	418	701	11,932	100.0	75.6	5.8	6.0	11.0	0.6	1.0
2012–13	85,104	54,219	4,309	4,473	8,191	400	1,084	12,428	100.0	74.6	5.9	6.2	11.3	0.6	1.5
Females															
1976–77[2]	19,509	16,955	1,237	317	363	58	—	579	100.0	89.6	6.5	1.7	1.9	0.3	—
1980–81[3]	28,428	24,626	1,687	586	678	89	—	762	100.0	89.0	6.1	2.1	2.5	0.3	—
1990–91	41,305	32,979	2,438	1,375	2,082	160	—	2,271	100.0	84.5	6.2	3.5	5.3	0.4	—
1996–97	50,360	36,131	3,990	2,134	4,396	307	—	3,402	100.0	76.9	8.5	4.5	9.4	0.7	—
1997–98	51,503	36,501	4,210	2,180	4,643	368	—	3,601	100.0	76.2	8.8	4.6	9.7	0.8	—
1998–99	51,360	36,264	4,211	2,426	4,643	372	—	3,444	100.0	75.7	8.8	5.1	9.7	0.8	—
1999–2000	53,806	37,676	4,316	2,440	5,215	375	—	3,784	100.0	75.3	8.6	4.9	10.4	0.7	—
2000–01	55,414	38,190	4,380	2,640	5,828	359	—	4,017	100.0	74.3	8.5	5.1	11.3	0.7	—
2001–02	56,932	38,981	4,749	2,681	5,988	396	—	4,137	100.0	73.8	9.0	5.1	11.3	0.8	—
2002–03	58,849	39,980	4,802	2,832	6,325	401	—	4,509	100.0	73.6	8.8	5.2	11.6	0.7	—
2003–04	62,106	41,681	5,201	3,064	6,751	414	—	4,995	100.0	73.0	9.1	5.4	11.8	0.7	—
2004–05	67,130	45,014	5,623	3,252	7,263	418	—	5,560	100.0	73.1	9.1	5.3	11.8	0.7	—
2005–06	69,144	45,574	5,574	3,352	7,709	500	—	6,435	100.0	72.7	8.9	5.3	12.3	0.8	—
2006–07	73,382	48,020	6,152	3,544	8,327	497	—	6,842	100.0	72.2	9.2	5.3	12.5	0.7	—
2007–08	75,925	49,636	6,167	3,803	8,668	485	—	7,166	100.0	72.2	9.0	5.5	12.6	0.7	—
2008–09	78,890	51,520	6,657	4,109	8,926	518	—	7,160	100.0	71.8	9.3	5.7	12.4	0.7	—
2009–10	81,980	53,712	6,804	4,443	9,376	522	—	7,123	100.0	71.8	9.1	5.9	12.5	0.7	—
2010–11	84,155	54,302	7,096	4,672	9,533	493	694	7,365	100.0	70.7	9.2	6.1	12.4	0.6	0.9
2011–12	87,547	55,877	7,673	5,005	10,104	497	870	7,521	100.0	69.8	9.6	6.3	12.6	0.6	1.1
2012–13	89,934	56,556	7,775	5,634	10,217	500	1,354	7,898	100.0	68.9	9.5	6.9	12.5	0.6	1.7

—Not available.
[1]Includes Ph.D., Ed.D., and comparable degrees at the doctoral level, as well as such degrees as M.D., D.D.S., and law degrees that were formerly classified as first-professional degrees.
[2]Excludes 500 males and 12 females whose racial/ethnic group was not available.
[3]Excludes 714 males and 21 females whose racial/ethnic group was not available.
NOTE: Data through 1990–91 are for institutions of higher education, while later data are for postsecondary institutions participating in Title IV federal financial aid programs. Race categories exclude persons of Hispanic ethnicity. For 1989–90 and later years, reported racial/ethnic

distributions of students by level of degree, field of degree, and sex were used to estimate race/ethnicity for students whose race/ethnicity was not reported. Detail may not sum to totals because of rounding. Some data have been revised from previously published figures.
SOURCE: U.S. Department of Education, National Center for Education Statistics, Higher Education General Information Survey (HEGIS), "Degrees and Other Formal Awards Conferred" surveys, 1976–77 and 1980–81; Integrated Postsecondary Education Data System (IPEDS), "Completions Survey" (IPEDS-C:90–99); and IPEDS Fall 2000 through Fall 2013, Completions component. (This table was prepared September 2014.)

Table 324.25. Doctor's degrees conferred by postsecondary institutions, by race/ethnicity and field of study: 2011–12 and 2012–13

Field of study	2011–12										2012–13									
					Asian/Pacific Islander			American Indian/ Alaska Native	Two or more races	Non-resident alien					Asian/Pacific Islander			American Indian/ Alaska Native	Two or more races	Non-resident alien
	Total	White	Black	Hispanic	Total	Asian	Pacific Islander				Total	White	Black	Hispanic	Total	Asian	Pacific Islander			
1	2	3	4	5	6	7	8	9	10	11	12	13	14	15	16	17	18	19	20	21
All fields, total	170,217	109,365	11,794	9,223	17,896	17,562	334	915	1,571	19,453	175,038	110,775	12,084	10,107	18,408	18,022	386	900	2,438	20,326
Agriculture and natural resources	1,333	637	42	47	41	41	0	9	4	553	1,411	707	45	53	39	38	1	4	7	556
Architecture and related services	255	95	12	9	28	27	1	1	5	105	247	97	13	10	30	29	1	0	7	90
Area, ethnic, cultural, gender, and group studies	302	134	42	29	28	28	0	8	4	57	291	148	43	30	21	21	0	11	2	36
Biological and biomedical sciences	7,935	4,304	300	352	747	739	8	35	63	2,134	7,943	4,250	323	409	735	728	7	27	69	2,130
Business	2,538	1,237	403	88	170	167	3	15	12	613	2,836	1,337	489	125	202	198	4	15	20	648
Communication, journalism, and related programs	563	352	33	23	29	27	2	2	8	116	612	372	45	22	25	25	0	4	7	137
Communications technologies	4	4	0	0	0	0	0	0	0	0	0	0	0	0	0	0	0	0	0	0
Computer and information sciences	1,698	597	46	31	146	146	0	2	5	871	1,826	612	62	46	145	145	0	0	3	958
Construction trades	0	0	0	0	0	0	0	0	0	0	0	0	0	0	0	0	0	0	0	0
Education	10,118	6,446	1,937	682	365	350	15	74	73	541	10,572	6,652	1,981	704	429	396	33	82	101	623
Engineering	8,722	2,775	184	198	622	620	2	11	43	4,889	9,356	2,911	191	213	644	636	8	7	63	5,327
Engineering technologies and engineering-related fields[1]	134	74	9	2	5	5	0	2	2	40	111	41	4	4	7	7	0	1	0	54
English language and literature/letters	1,427	1,085	64	71	49	47	2	11	10	137	1,373	1,069	60	60	51	51	0	7	17	109
Family and consumer sciences/human sciences	325	191	41	3	17	16	1	1	2	70	351	182	49	10	20	20	0	2	3	85
Foreign languages, literatures, and linguistics	1,231	657	17	117	60	59	1	2	12	366	1,304	674	16	136	46	45	1	8	12	412
Health professions and related programs	62,097	41,826	3,775	2,942	10,591	10,452	139	344	550	2,069	64,195	42,846	3,738	3,356	11,018	10,871	147	292	861	2,084
Homeland security, law enforcement, and firefighting	117	81	7	7	1	1	0	1	1	19	147	100	19	2	4	4	0	0	0	22
Legal professions and studies	46,836	34,329	3,398	3,561	3,679	3,545	134	330	560	979	47,246	33,921	3,494	3,824	3,670	3,509	161	327	1,013	997
Liberal arts and sciences, general studies, and humanities	93	68	7	2	3	3	0	3	1	9	98	75	7	5	0	0	0	1	0	10
Library science	60	32	0	1	6	6	0	0	1	20	50	28	5	0	1	1	0	0	0	16
Mathematics and statistics	1,669	696	23	43	79	77	2	0	10	818	1,823	716	30	38	112	112	0	0	12	912
Mechanics and repair technologies/technicians	0	0	0	0	0	0	0	0	0	0	0	0	0	0	0	0	0	0	0	0
Military technologies and applied sciences	0	0	0	0	0	0	0	0	0	0	0	0	0	0	0	0	0	0	0	0
Multi/interdisciplinary studies	727	432	67	38	34	32	2	5	6	145	730	433	55	29	41	40	1	5	6	161
Parks, recreation, leisure, and fitness studies	288	187	17	8	8	7	1	0	3	65	295	198	24	5	8	7	1	4	0	56
Philosophy and religious studies	778	541	36	27	33	33	0	2	9	130	796	548	28	29	35	34	1	0	17	139
Physical sciences and science technologies	5,370	2,621	104	155	287	282	5	9	40	2,154	5,514	2,716	120	154	265	265	0	13	48	2,198
Precision production	0	0	0	0	0	0	0	0	0	0	0	0	0	0	0	0	0	0	0	0
Psychology	5,936	4,312	445	394	357	354	3	27	70	331	6,323	4,565	497	435	350	342	8	44	83	349
Public administration and social services	890	496	145	51	44	43	1	0	9	145	979	538	168	36	53	51	2	1	8	175
Social sciences and history	4,597	2,611	214	214	210	207	3	12	39	1,297	4,619	2,675	203	234	212	207	5	25	44	1,226
Social sciences	3,628	1,918	149	172	179	178	1	10	30	1,170	3,616	1,943	159	170	180	176	4	14	39	1,111
History	969	693	65	42	31	29	2	2	9	127	1,003	732	44	64	32	31	1	11	5	115
Theology and religious vocations	2,446	1,468	386	65	155	149	6	7	19	346	2,175	1,262	335	56	122	118	4	15	13	372
Transportation and materials moving	0	0	0	0	0	0	0	0	0	0	0	0	0	0	0	0	0	0	0	0
Visual and performing arts	1,728	1,077	40	63	102	99	3	2	10	434	1,814	1,101	40	82	123	122	1	2	22	444
Other and not classified	0	0	0	0	0	0	0	0	0	0	0	0	0	0	0	0	0	0	0	0

[1]Excludes "Construction trades" and "Mechanic and repair technologies/technicians," which are listed separately.

NOTE: Data are for postsecondary institutions participating in Title IV federal financial aid programs. Race categories exclude persons of Hispanic ethnicity. Reported racial/ethnic distributions of students by level of degree, field of degree, and sex were used to estimate race/ethnicity for students whose race/ethnicity was not reported. To facilitate trend comparisons, certain aggregations have been made of the degree fields as reported in the Integrated Postsecondary Education Data System (IPEDS): "Agricul-

ture and natural resources" includes Agriculture, agriculture operations, and related sciences and Natural resources and conservation; and "Business" includes Business management, marketing, and related support services and Personal and culinary services. Some data have been revised from previously published figures.

SOURCE: U.S. Department of Education, National Center for Education Statistics, Integrated Postsecondary Education Data System (IPEDS), Fall 2012 and Fall 2013, Completions component. (This table was prepared September 2014.)

Table 324.30. Doctor's degrees conferred to males by postsecondary institutions, by race/ethnicity and field of study: 2011–12 and 2012–13

Field of study	2011–12 Total	White	Black	Hispanic	Asian/Pac. Isl. Total	Asian	Pacific Islander	American Indian/Alaska Native	Two or more races	Nonresident alien	2012–13 Total	White	Black	Hispanic	Asian/Pac. Isl. Total	Asian	Pacific Islander	American Indian/Alaska Native	Two or more races	Nonresident alien
(column)	2	3	4	5	6	7	8	9	10	11	12	13	14	15	16	17	18	19	20	21
All fields, total	82,670	53,488	4,121	4,218	7,792	7,631	161	418	701	11,932	85,104	54,219	4,309	4,473	8,191	8,010	181	400	1,084	12,428
Agriculture and natural resources	721	355	15	26	14	14	0	5	4	302	767	385	18	23	24	23	1	1	4	312
Architecture and related services	147	52	6	4	14	14	0	1	4	66	134	52	9	8	11	10	1	0	1	53
Area, ethnic, cultural, gender, and group studies	112	46	19	10	8	8	0	5	1	23	125	66	22	11	6	6	0	4	0	16
Biological and biomedical sciences	3,708	2,039	115	156	287	283	4	16	25	1,070	3,692	2,031	117	177	302	300	2	10	26	1,029
Business	1,461	733	179	51	101	99	2	8	7	382	1,612	788	218	69	115	113	2	9	9	404
Communication, journalism, and related programs	239	153	14	8	7	7	0	1	2	54	246	164	14	5	5	5	0	3	3	52
Communications technologies	3	3	0	0	0	0	0	0	0	0	0	0	0	0	0	0	0	0	0	0
Computer and information sciences	1,332	497	26	24	105	105	0	1	5	674	1,473	496	38	37	111	111	0	0	2	789
Construction trades	0	0	0	0	0	0	0	0	0	0	0	0	0	0	0	0	0	0	0	0
Education	3,262	2,183	513	226	105	101	4	21	25	189	3,418	2,240	535	223	120	110	10	31	38	231
Engineering	6,770	2,139	113	139	436	435	1	9	29	3,905	7,231	2,282	126	144	435	428	7	7	48	4,189
Engineering technologies and engineering-related fields[1]	68	28	3	1	3	3	0	1	2	30	74	29	2	3	4	4	0	1	0	35
English language and literature/letters	548	436	18	26	19	19	0	3	3	43	553	434	18	21	21	21	0	4	6	49
Family and consumer sciences/human sciences	59	32	6	0	2	2	0	0	0	19	79	46	8	2	3	3	0	0	0	20
Foreign languages, literatures, and linguistics	497	272	7	36	19	18	1	0	3	160	531	299	7	45	11	10	1	2	7	160
Health professions and related programs	26,074	17,840	1,227	1,252	4,482	4,420	62	148	234	891	26,867	18,210	1,200	1,365	4,738	4,668	70	122	344	888
Homeland security, law enforcement, and firefighting	63	41	3	7	0	0	0	1	1	10	72	52	6	0	0	0	0	0	0	13
Legal professions and studies	24,764	19,202	1,248	1,767	1,628	1,555	73	172	258	489	25,321	19,212	1,416	1,855	1,720	1,642	78	150	477	491
Liberal arts and sciences, general studies, and humanities	32	21	4	1	0	0	0	0	0	6	42	35	1	2	0	0	0	1	0	3
Library science	24	12	0	1	3	3	0	0	1	7	23	10	2	0	1	1	0	0	0	10
Mathematics and statistics	1,198	522	12	32	55	53	2	0	6	571	1,292	529	23	31	75	75	0	2	9	623
Mechanic and repair technologies/technicians	0	0	0	0	0	0	0	0	0	0	0	0	0	0	0	0	0	0	0	0
Military technologies and applied sciences	0	0	0	0	0	0	0	0	0	0	0	0	0	0	0	0	0	0	0	0
Multi/interdisciplinary studies	297	172	22	16	12	11	1	2	1	72	307	178	17	12	14	14	1	2	1	83
Parks, recreation, leisure, and fitness studies	161	106	9	6	2	2	0	0	3	35	159	96	11	4	5	4	1	2	0	41
Philosophy and religious studies	542	394	18	17	20	20	0	1	6	86	552	387	16	21	20	19	1	0	11	97
Physical sciences and science technologies	3,609	1,797	61	100	148	146	2	6	32	1,465	3,646	1,814	59	93	148	148	0	11	31	1,490
Precision production	0	0	0	0	0	0	0	0	0	0	0	0	0	0	0	0	0	0	0	0
Psychology	1,525	1,157	81	109	70	69	1	1	16	83	1,624	1,221	91	103	76	75	1	12	21	100
Public administration and social services	343	175	55	20	19	18	1	0	9	74	351	195	45	13	17	16	1	0	2	79
Social sciences and history	2,464	1,379	86	97	89	87	2	4	16	793	2,470	1,464	87	107	80	78	2	14	22	696
Social sciences	1,931	996	57	73	75	74	1	4	12	714	1,917	1,047	67	78	61	60	1	7	18	639
History	533	383	29	24	14	13	1	0	4	79	553	417	20	29	19	18	1	7	4	57
Theology and religious vocations	1,857	1,131	241	51	122	117	5	4	14	294	1,592	915	183	48	95	93	2	11	11	329
Transportation and materials moving	4	1	0	0	2	2	0	0	0	1	1	1	0	0	0	0	0	0	0	0
Visual and performing arts	790	571	20	35	22	22	0	0	3	139	850	588	20	51	33	32	1	1	11	146
Other and not classified	0	0	0	0	0	0	0	0	0	0	0	0	0	0	0	0	0	0	0	0

[1]Excludes "Construction trades" and "Mechanic and repair technologies/technicians," which are listed separately.

NOTE: Data are for postsecondary institutions participating in Title IV federal financial aid programs. Race categories exclude persons of Hispanic ethnicity. Reported racial/ethnic distributions of students by level of degree, field of degree, and sex were used to estimate race/ethnicity for students whose race/ethnicity was not reported. To facilitate trend comparisons, certain aggregations have been made of the degree fields as reported in the Integrated Postsecondary Education Data System (IPEDS): "Agriculture and natural resources" includes Agriculture, agriculture operations, and related sciences and Natural resources and conservation; and "Business" includes Business management, marketing, and related support services and Personal and culinary services. Some data have been revised from previously published figures.
SOURCE: U.S. Department of Education, National Center for Education Statistics, Integrated Postsecondary Education Data System (IPEDS), Fall 2012 and Fall 2013, Completions component. (This table was prepared September 2014.)

Table 324.35. Doctor's degrees conferred to females by postsecondary institutions, by race/ethnicity and field of study: 2011–12 and 2012–13

Field of study	2011–12										2012–13									
	Total	White	Black	Hispanic	Asian/Pacific Islander			American Indian/ Alaska Native	Two or more races	Non-resident alien	Total	White	Black	Hispanic	Asian/Pacific Islander			American Indian/ Alaska Native	Two or more races	Non-resident alien
					Total	Asian	Pacific Islander								Total	Asian	Pacific Islander			
1	2	3	4	5	6	7	8	9	10	11	12	13	14	15	16	17	18	19	20	21
All fields, total	87,547	55,877	7,673	5,005	10,104	9,931	173	497	870	7,521	89,934	56,556	7,775	5,634	10,217	10,012	205	500	1,354	7,898
Agriculture and natural resources	612	282	27	21	27	27	0	4	0	251	644	322	27	30	15	15	0	3	3	244
Architecture and related services	108	43	6	5	14	13	1	0	1	39	113	45	4	2	19	19	0	0	6	37
Area, ethnic, cultural, gender, and group studies	190	88	23	19	20	20	0	3	3	34	166	82	21	19	15	15	0	7	2	20
Biological and biomedical sciences	4,227	2,265	185	196	460	456	4	19	38	1,064	4,251	2,219	206	232	433	428	5	17	43	1,101
Business	1,077	504	224	37	69	68	1	7	5	231	1,224	549	271	56	87	85	2	6	11	244
Communication, journalism, and related programs	324	199	19	15	22	20	2	1	6	62	366	208	31	17	20	20	0	1	4	85
Communications technologies	1	1	0	0	0	0	0	0	0	0	0	0	0	0	0	0	0	0	0	0
Computer and information sciences	366	100	20	7	41	41	0	1	0	197	353	116	24	9	34	34	0	0	1	169
Construction trades	0	0	0	0	0	0	0	0	0	0	0	0	0	0	0	0	0	0	0	0
Education	6,856	4,263	1,424	456	260	249	11	53	48	352	7,154	4,412	1,446	481	309	286	23	51	63	392
Engineering	1,952	636	71	59	186	185	1	2	14	984	2,125	629	65	69	209	208	1	2	15	1,138
Engineering technologies and engineering-related fields[1]	66	46	6	1	2	2	0	1	0	10	37	12	2	1	3	3	0	1	0	19
English language and literature/letters	879	649	46	45	30	28	2	8	7	94	820	635	42	39	30	30	0	3	11	60
Family and consumer sciences/human sciences	266	159	35	3	15	14	1	1	2	51	272	136	41	8	17	17	0	2	3	65
Foreign languages, literatures, and linguistics	734	385	10	81	41	41	0	2	9	206	773	375	9	91	35	35	0	6	5	252
Health professions and related programs	36,023	23,986	2,548	1,690	6,109	6,032	77	196	316	1,178	37,328	24,636	2,538	1,991	6,280	6,203	77	170	517	1,196
Homeland security, law enforcement, and firefighting	54	40	4	0	1	1	0	0	0	9	75	48	13	2	3	3	0	0	0	9
Legal professions and studies	22,072	15,127	2,150	1,794	2,051	1,990	61	158	302	490	21,925	14,709	2,078	1,969	1,950	1,867	83	177	536	506
Liberal arts and sciences, general studies, and humanities	61	47	3	1	3	3	0	3	1	3	56	40	6	3	0	0	0	0	0	7
Library science	36	20	0	0	3	3	0	0	0	13	27	18	3	0	0	0	0	0	0	6
Mathematics and statistics	471	174	11	11	24	24	0	0	4	247	531	187	7	7	37	37	0	1	3	289
Mechanic and repair technologies/technicians	0	0	0	0	0	0	0	0	0	0	0	0	0	0	0	0	0	0	0	0
Military technologies and applied sciences	0	0	0	0	0	0	0	0	0	0	0	0	0	0	0	0	0	0	0	0
Multi/interdisciplinary studies	430	260	45	22	22	21	1	3	5	73	423	255	38	17	27	26	1	3	5	78
Parks, recreation, leisure, and fitness studies	127	81	8	2	6	5	1	0	0	30	136	102	13	1	3	3	0	2	0	15
Philosophy and religious studies	236	147	18	10	13	13	0	1	3	44	244	161	12	8	15	15	0	0	6	42
Physical sciences and science technologies	1,761	824	43	55	139	136	3	3	8	689	1,868	902	61	61	117	117	0	2	17	708
Precision production	0	0	0	0	0	0	0	0	0	0	0	0	0	0	0	0	0	0	0	0
Psychology	4,411	3,155	364	285	287	285	2	18	54	248	4,699	3,344	406	332	274	267	7	32	62	249
Public administration and social services	547	321	90	31	25	25	0	0	9	71	628	343	123	23	36	35	1	1	6	96
Social sciences and history	2,133	1,232	128	117	121	120	1	8	23	504	2,149	1,211	116	127	132	129	3	11	22	530
Social sciences	1,697	922	92	99	104	104	0	6	18	456	1,699	896	92	92	119	116	3	7	21	472
History	436	310	36	18	17	16	1	2	5	48	450	315	24	35	13	13	0	4	1	58
Theology and religious vocations	589	337	145	14	33	32	1	3	5	52	583	347	152	8	27	25	2	4	2	43
Transportation and materials moving	0	0	0	0	0	0	0	0	0	0	0	0	0	0	0	0	0	0	0	0
Visual and performing arts	938	506	20	28	80	77	3	2	7	295	964	513	20	31	90	90	0	1	11	298
Other and not classified	0	0	0	0	0	0	0	0	0	0	0	0	0	0	0	0	0	0	0	0

[1]Excludes "Construction trades" and "Mechanic and repair technologies/technicians," which are listed separately.

NOTE: Data are for postsecondary institutions participating in Title IV federal financial aid programs. Race categories exclude persons of Hispanic ethnicity. Reported racial/ethnic distributions of students by level of degree, field of degree, and sex were used to estimate race/ethnicity for students whose race/ethnicity was not reported. To facilitate trend comparisons, certain aggregations have been made of the degree fields as reported in the Integrated Postsecondary Education Data System (IPEDS). "Agriculture and natural resources" includes Agriculture, agriculture operations, and related sciences and Natural resources and conservation; and "Business" includes Business management, marketing, and related support services and Personal and culinary services. Some data have been revised from previously published figures. SOURCE: U.S. Department of Education, National Center for Education Statistics, Integrated Postsecondary Education Data System (IPEDS), Fall 2012 and Fall 2013, Completions component. (This table was prepared August 2014.)

Table 324.40. Number of postsecondary institutions conferring doctor's degrees in dentistry, medicine, and law, and number of such degrees conferred, by sex of student: Selected years, 1949–50 through 2012–13

Year	Dentistry (D.D.S. or D.M.D.) Number of institutions conferring degrees	Number of degrees conferred Total	Males	Females	Medicine (M.D.) Number of institutions conferring degrees	Number of degrees conferred Total	Males	Females	Law (LL.B. or J.D.) Number of institutions conferring degrees	Number of degrees conferred Total	Males	Females
1	2	3	4	5	6	7	8	9	10	11	12	13
1949–50	40	2,579	2,561	18	72	5,612	5,028	584	—	—	—	—
1951–52	41	2,918	2,895	23	72	6,201	5,871	330	—	—	—	—
1953–54	42	3,102	3,063	39	73	6,712	6,377	335	—	—	—	—
1955–56	42	3,009	2,975	34	73	6,810	6,464	346	131	8,262	7,974	288
1957–58	43	3,065	3,031	34	75	6,816	6,469	347	131	9,394	9,122	272
1959–60	45	3,247	3,221	26	79	7,032	6,645	387	134	9,240	9,010	230
1961–62	46	3,183	3,166	17	81	7,138	6,749	389	134	9,364	9,091	273
1963–64	46	3,180	3,168	12	82	7,303	6,878	425	133	10,679	10,372	307
1964–65	46	3,108	3,086	22	81	7,304	6,832	472	137	11,583	11,216	367
1965–66	47	3,178	3,146	32	84	7,673	7,170	503	136	13,246	12,776	470
1967–68	48	3,422	3,375	47	85	7,944	7,318	626	138	16,454	15,805	649
1968–69	—	3,408	3,376	32	—	8,025	7,415	610	—	17,053	16,373	680
1969–70	48	3,718	3,684	34	86	8,314	7,615	699	145	14,916	14,115	801
1970–71	48	3,745	3,703	42	89	8,919	8,110	809	147	17,421	16,181	1,240
1971–72	48	3,862	3,819	43	92	9,253	8,423	830	147	21,764	20,266	1,498
1972–73	51	4,047	3,992	55	97	10,307	9,388	919	152	27,205	25,037	2,168
1973–74	52	4,440	4,355	85	99	11,356	10,093	1,263	151	29,326	25,986	3,340
1974–75	52	4,773	4,627	146	104	12,447	10,818	1,629	154	29,296	24,881	4,415
1975–76	56	5,425	5,187	238	107	13,426	11,252	2,174	166	32,293	26,085	6,208
1976–77	57	5,138	4,764	374	109	13,461	10,891	2,570	169	34,104	26,447	7,657
1977–78	57	5,189	4,623	566	109	14,279	11,210	3,069	169	34,402	25,457	8,945
1978–79	58	5,434	4,794	640	109	14,786	11,381	3,405	175	35,206	25,180	10,026
1979–80	58	5,258	4,558	700	112	14,902	11,416	3,486	179	35,647	24,893	10,754
1980–81	58	5,460	4,672	788	116	15,505	11,672	3,833	176	36,331	24,563	11,768
1981–82	59	5,282	4,467	815	119	15,814	11,867	3,947	180	35,991	23,965	12,026
1982–83	59	5,585	4,631	954	118	15,484	11,350	4,134	177	36,853	23,550	13,303
1983–84	60	5,353	4,302	1,051	119	15,813	11,359	4,454	179	37,012	23,382	13,630
1984–85	59	5,339	4,233	1,106	120	16,041	11,167	4,874	181	37,491	23,070	14,421
1985–86	59	5,046	3,907	1,139	120	15,938	11,022	4,916	181	35,844	21,874	13,970
1986–87	58	4,741	3,603	1,138	121	15,428	10,431	4,997	179	36,056	21,561	14,495
1987–88	57	4,477	3,300	1,177	122	15,358	10,278	5,080	180	35,397	21,067	14,330
1988–89	58	4,265	3,124	1,141	124	15,460	10,310	5,150	182	35,634	21,069	14,565
1989–90	57	4,100	2,834	1,266	124	15,075	9,923	5,152	182	36,485	21,079	15,406
1990–91	55	3,699	2,510	1,189	121	15,043	9,629	5,414	179	37,945	21,643	16,302
1991–92	52	3,593	2,431	1,162	120	15,243	9,796	5,447	177	38,848	22,260	16,588
1992–93	55	3,605	2,383	1,222	122	15,531	9,679	5,852	184	40,302	23,182	17,120
1993–94	53	3,787	2,330	1,457	121	15,368	9,544	5,824	185	40,044	22,826	17,218
1994–95	53	3,897	2,480	1,417	119	15,537	9,507	6,030	183	39,349	22,592	16,757
1995–96	53	3,697	2,374	1,323	119	15,341	9,061	6,280	183	39,828	22,508	17,320
1996–97	52	3,784	2,387	1,397	118	15,571	9,121	6,450	184	40,079	22,548	17,531
1997–98	53	4,032	2,490	1,542	117	15,424	9,006	6,418	185	39,331	21,876	17,455
1998–99	53	4,143	2,673	1,470	118	15,566	8,972	6,594	185	38,297	21,102	17,195
1999–2000	54	4,250	2,547	1,703	118	15,286	8,761	6,525	190	38,152	20,638	17,514
2000–01	54	4,391	2,696	1,695	118	15,403	8,728	6,675	192	37,904	19,981	17,923
2001–02	53	4,239	2,608	1,631	118	15,237	8,469	6,768	192	38,981	20,254	18,727
2002–03	53	4,345	2,654	1,691	118	15,034	8,221	6,813	194	39,067	19,916	19,151
2003–04	53	4,335	2,532	1,803	118	15,442	8,273	7,169	195	40,209	20,332	19,877
2004–05	53	4,454	2,505	1,949	120	15,461	8,151	7,310	198	43,423	22,297	21,126
2005–06	54	4,389	2,435	1,954	119	15,455	7,900	7,555	197	43,440	22,597	20,843
2006–07	55	4,596	2,548	2,048	120	15,730	7,987	7,743	200	43,486	22,777	20,709
2007–08	55	4,795	2,661	2,134	120	15,646	7,935	7,711	201	43,769	23,197	20,572
2008–09	55	4,918	2,637	2,281	120	15,987	8,164	7,823	203	44,045	23,860	20,185
2009–10	55	5,062	2,745	2,317	120	16,356	8,468	7,888	205	44,346	23,384	20,962
2010–11	55	5,071	2,764	2,307	120	16,863	8,701	8,162	206	44,421	23,481	20,940
2011–12	55	5,109	2,748	2,361	120	16,927	8,809	8,118	207	46,445	24,576	21,869
2012–13	55	5,111	2,651	2,460	122	17,264	8,976	8,288	209	46,811	25,087	21,724

—Not available.
NOTE: Data are for postsecondary institutions participating in Title IV federal financial aid programs. Some data have been revised from previously published figures.
SOURCE: U.S. Department of Education, National Center for Education Statistics, *Earned Degrees Conferred*, 1949–50 through 1964–65; Higher Education General Information Survey (HEGIS), "Degrees and Other Formal Awards Conferred" surveys, 1965–66 through 1985–86; Integrated Postsecondary Education Data System (IPEDS), "Completions Survey" (IPEDS-C:87–99); and IPEDS Fall 2000 through Fall 2013, Completions component. (This table was prepared March 2015.)

Table 324.50. Degrees conferred by postsecondary institutions in selected professional fields, by sex of student, control of institution, and field of study: Selected years, 1985–86 through 2012–13

Control of institution and field of study	1985–86	1990–91	1995–96	2000–01	2002–03	2003–04	2004–05	2005–06	2006–07	2007–08	2008–09	2009–10	2010–11			2011–12			2012–13		
													Total	Males	Females	Total	Males	Females	Total	Males	Females
1	2	3	4	5	6	7	8	9	10	11	12	13	14	15	16	17	18	19	20	21	22
Total, all institutions	73,910	71,948	76,734	79,707	80,897	83,041	87,289	87,655	90,064	91,309	92,009	94,128	95,722	48,787	46,935	98,699	50,329	48,370	100,356	51,478	48,878
Dentistry (D.D.S. or D.M.D.)	5,046	3,699	3,697	4,391	4,345	4,335	4,454	4,389	4,596	4,795	4,918	5,062	5,071	2,764	2,307	5,109	2,748	2,361	5,111	2,651	2,460
Medicine (M.D.)	15,938	15,043	15,341	15,403	15,034	15,442	15,461	15,455	15,730	15,646	15,987	16,356	16,863	8,701	8,162	16,927	8,809	8,118	17,264	8,976	8,288
Optometry (O.D.)	1,029	1,115	1,231	1,289	1,281	1,275	1,252	1,198	1,311	1,304	1,338	1,335	1,322	475	847	1,361	476	885	1,521	557	964
Osteopathic medicine (D.O.)	1,547	1,459	1,895	2,450	2,596	2,722	2,762	2,718	2,992	3,232	3,665	3,890	4,141	2,121	2,020	4,336	2,283	2,053	4,691	2,489	2,202
Pharmacy (Pharm.D.)	903	1,244	2,555	6,324	7,474	8,221	8,885	9,292	10,439	10,932	11,291	11,873	12,271	4,692	7,579	12,943	4,971	7,972	13,377	5,141	8,236
Podiatry (Pod.D. or D.P.) or podiatric medicine (D.P.M.)	612	589	650	528	439	382	343	347	331	555	431	491	543	318	225	535	342	193	471	296	175
Veterinary medicine (D.V.M.)	2,270	2,032	2,109	2,248	2,354	2,228	2,354	2,370	2,443	2,504	2,377	2,478	2,564	580	1,984	2,616	588	2,028	2,610	593	2,017
Chiropractic (D.C. or D.C.M.)	3,395	2,640	3,379	3,796	2,718	2,730	2,560	2,564	2,525	2,639	2,512	2,601	2,694	1,666	1,028	2,496	1,538	958	2,224	1,366	858
Law (LL.B. or J.D.)	35,844	37,945	39,828	37,904	39,067	40,209	43,423	43,440	43,486	43,769	44,045	44,346	44,421	23,481	20,940	46,445	24,576	21,869	46,811	25,087	21,724
Theology (M. Div, M.H.L., B.D., or Ord. and M.H.L./Rav., B.D., or Ord.)	7,283	5,695	5,879	5,026	5,360	5,332	5,533	5,666	5,990	5,751	5,367	5,696	5,832	3,989	1,843	5,931	3,998	1,933	6,276	4,322	1,954
Other[1]	43	487	170	348	229	165	262	216	221	182	78	0	0	0	0	0	0	0	0	0	0
Total, public institutions	29,568	29,554	29,882	32,633	33,549	34,499	35,768	36,269	36,855	37,278	37,357	38,132	39,071	19,027	20,044	39,776	19,589	20,187	39,777	19,601	20,176
Dentistry (D.D.S. or D.M.D.)	2,827	2,308	2,198	2,477	2,493	2,498	2,577	2,669	2,769	2,760	2,870	2,984	3,008	1,687	1,321	3,053	1,708	1,345	2,975	1,585	1,390
Medicine (M.D.)	9,991	9,364	9,370	9,408	9,276	9,418	9,536	9,650	9,733	9,646	9,795	10,043	10,577	5,522	5,055	10,626	5,591	5,035	10,654	5,593	5,061
Optometry (O.D.)	441	477	499	497	481	476	477	462	518	492	517	507	515	180	335	508	178	330	520	189	331
Osteopathic medicine (D.O.)	486	493	528	562	571	586	568	585	637	634	679	817	856	429	427	841	442	399	854	441	413
Pharmacy (Pharm.D.)	473	808	1,557	3,876	4,558	4,930	5,352	5,523	5,903	6,218	6,395	6,587	6,888	2,643	4,245	6,919	2,679	4,240	6,897	2,596	4,301
Podiatry (Pod.D. or D.P.) or podiatric medicine (D.P.M.)	0	0	0	84	81	64	64	65	66	73	68	85	87	41	46	204	128	76	105	72	33
Veterinary medicine (D.V.M.)	1,931	1,814	1,889	2,017	2,023	1,912	2,033	2,048	2,116	2,123	1,968	2,048	2,134	485	1,649	2,168	493	1,675	2,184	495	1,689
Chiropractic (D.C. or D.C.M.)	0	0	0	0	0	0	0	0	0	0	0	0	0	0	0	0	0	0	0	0	0
Law (LL.B. or J.D.)	13,419	14,290	13,841	13,712	14,066	14,615	15,161	15,267	15,113	15,332	15,065	15,061	15,006	8,040	6,966	15,457	8,370	7,087	15,588	8,630	6,958
Theology (M. Div, M.H.L., B.D., or Ord. and M.H.L./Rav., B.D., or Ord.)	0	0	0	0	0	0	0	0	0	0	0	0	0	0	0	0	0	0	0	0	0
Other[1]	0	0	0	0	0	0	0	0	0	0	0	0	0	0	0	0	0	0	0	0	0
Total, private institutions	44,342	42,394	46,852	47,074	47,348	48,542	51,521	51,386	53,209	54,031	54,652	55,996	56,651	29,760	26,891	58,923	30,740	28,183	60,579	31,877	28,702
Dentistry (D.D.S. or D.M.D.)	2,219	1,391	1,499	1,914	1,852	1,837	1,877	1,720	1,827	2,035	2,048	2,078	2,063	1,077	986	2,056	1,040	1,016	2,136	1,066	1,070
Medicine (M.D.)	5,947	5,679	5,971	5,995	5,758	6,024	5,925	5,805	5,997	6,000	6,192	6,313	6,286	3,179	3,107	6,301	3,218	3,083	6,610	3,383	3,227
Optometry (O.D.)	588	638	732	792	800	799	775	736	793	812	821	828	807	295	512	853	298	555	1,001	368	633
Osteopathic medicine (D.O.)	1,061	966	1,367	1,888	2,025	2,136	2,194	2,133	2,355	2,598	2,986	3,073	3,285	1,692	1,593	3,495	1,841	1,654	3,837	2,048	1,789
Pharmacy (Pharm.D.)	430	436	998	2,448	2,916	3,291	3,533	3,769	4,536	4,714	4,896	5,286	5,383	2,049	3,334	6,024	2,292	3,732	6,480	2,545	3,935
Podiatry (Pod.D. or D.P.) or podiatric medicine (D.P.M.)	612	589	650	444	358	318	279	282	265	482	363	406	456	277	179	331	214	117	366	224	142
Veterinary medicine (D.V.M.)	339	218	220	231	331	316	321	322	327	381	409	430	430	95	335	448	95	353	426	98	328
Chiropractic (D.C. or D.C.M.)	3,395	2,640	3,379	3,796	2,718	2,730	2,560	2,564	2,525	2,639	2,512	2,601	2,694	1,666	1,028	2,496	1,538	958	2,224	1,366	858
Law (LL.B. or J.D.)	22,425	23,655	25,987	24,192	25,001	25,594	28,262	28,173	28,373	28,437	28,980	29,285	29,415	15,441	13,974	30,988	16,206	14,782	31,223	16,457	14,766
Theology (M. Div, M.H.L., B.D., or Ord. and M.H.L./Rav., B.D., or Ord.)	7,283	5,695	5,879	5,026	5,360	5,332	5,533	5,666	5,990	5,751	5,367	5,696	5,832	3,989	1,843	5,931	3,998	1,933	6,276	4,322	1,954
Other[1]	43	487	170	348	229	165	262	216	221	182	78	0	0	0	0	0	0	0	0	0	0

[1]Includes naturopathic medicine and degrees that were not classified by field by the reporting institution.
NOTE: Data are for postsecondary institutions participating in Title IV federal financial aid programs. Includes degrees that require at least 6 years of college work for completion (including at least 2 years of preprofessional training). Some data have been revised from previously published figures.

SOURCE: U.S. Department of Education, National Center for Education Statistics, Higher Education General Information Survey (HEGIS), "Degrees and Other Formal Awards Conferred," 1985–86; Integrated Postsecondary Education Data System (IPEDS), "Completions Survey" (IPEDS-C:91–99); and IPEDS Fall 2013, Completions component. (This table was prepared March 2015.)

Table 324.55. Degrees conferred by postsecondary institutions in selected professional fields, by race/ethnicity and field of study: 2011–12 and 2012–13

Field of study	2011–12										2012–13									
	Total	White	Black	Hispanic	Asian/Pacific Islander Total	Asian	Pacific Islander	American Indian/Alaska Native	Two or more races	Non-resident alien	Total	White	Black	Hispanic	Asian/Pacific Islander Total	Asian	Pacific Islander	American Indian/Alaska Native	Two or more races	Non-resident alien
	2	3	4	5	6	7	8	9	10	11	12	13	14	15	16	17	18	19	20	21
All fields, total	98,699	68,121	7,103	6,010	13,449	13,147	302	591	1,038	2,387	100,356	68,144	7,202	6,595	13,714	13,431	283	538	1,723	2,440
Dentistry (D.D.S. or D.M.D.)	5,109	3,047	252	276	1,043	1,033	10	33	36	422	5,111	2,983	226	308	1,101	1,091	10	24	39	430
Medicine (M.D.)	16,927	10,676	1,180	957	3,569	3,542	27	106	220	219	17,264	10,887	1,096	1,067	3,632	3,606	26	71	275	236
Optometry (O.D.)	1,361	802	36	41	371	365	6	1	7	103	1,521	872	35	61	437	434	3	5	18	93
Osteopathic medicine (D.O.)	4,336	3,136	132	184	792	770	22	27	31	34	4,691	3,387	116	148	887	876	11	20	105	28
Pharmacy (Pharm.D.)	12,943	7,827	876	526	3,205	3,172	33	62	99	348	13,377	7,924	1,014	576	3,296	3,250	46	44	148	375
Podiatry (Pod.D. or D.P.) or podiatric medicine (D.P.M.)	535	367	41	31	68	68	0	3	4	21	471	289	15	26	106	104	2	13	10	12
Veterinary medicine (D.V.M.)	2,616	2,252	66	140	109	109	0	18	19	12	2,610	2,134	67	273	74	74	0	11	40	11
Chiropractic (D.C. or D.C.M.)	2,496	1,955	128	134	185	175	10	8	25	61	2,224	1,759	75	116	174	163	11	16	26	58
Law (LL.B. or J.D.)	46,445	34,276	3,304	3,513	3,724	3,548	176	314	527	787	46,811	33,816	3,449	3,783	3,611	3,457	154	308	990	854
Theology (M.Div, M.H.L./Rav., B.D., or Ord.)	5,931	3,783	1,088	208	383	365	18	19	70	380	6,276	4,093	1,109	237	396	376	20	26	72	343

NOTE: Data are for postsecondary institutions participating in Title IV federal financial aid programs. Includes degrees that require at least 6 years of college work for completion (including at least 2 years of preprofessional training). Race categories exclude persons of Hispanic ethnicity. Reported racial/ethnic distributions of students by level of degree, field of degree, and sex were used to estimate race/ethnicity for students whose race/ethnicity was not reported. Some data have been revised from previously published figures.
SOURCE: U.S. Department of Education, National Center for Education Statistics, Integrated Postsecondary Education Data System (IPEDS), Fall 2012 and Fall 2013, Completions component. (This table was prepared March 2015.)

Table 324.60. Degrees conferred to males by postsecondary institutions in selected professional fields, by race/ethnicity and field of study: 2011–12 and 2012–13

Field of study	2011–12										2012–13									
	Total	White	Black	Hispanic	Asian/Pacific Islander Total	Asian	Pacific Islander	American Indian/Alaska Native	Two or more races	Non-resident alien	Total	White	Black	Hispanic	Asian/Pacific Islander Total	Asian	Pacific Islander	American Indian/Alaska Native	Two or more races	Non-resident alien
	2	3	4	5	6	7	8	9	10	11	12	13	14	15	16	17	18	19	20	21
All fields, total	50,329	36,623	2,742	2,944	5,991	5,812	179	299	484	1,246	51,478	36,890	2,907	3,106	6,283	6,136	147	259	783	1,250
Dentistry (D.D.S. or D.M.D.)	2,748	1,832	97	123	453	447	6	20	22	201	2,651	1,738	96	127	468	464	4	11	16	195
Medicine (M.D.)	8,809	5,895	416	497	1,752	1,741	11	53	94	102	8,976	6,003	383	510	1,809	1,795	14	36	120	115
Optometry (O.D.)	476	325	7	14	91	88	3	0	4	35	557	362	11	17	127	126	1	2	5	33
Osteopathic medicine (D.O.)	2,283	1,718	44	85	389	377	12	13	20	14	2,489	1,837	44	78	454	449	5	10	49	17
Pharmacy (Pharm.D.)	4,971	3,064	335	203	1,153	1,141	12	24	41	151	5,141	3,094	371	223	1,210	1,186	24	19	63	161
Podiatry (Pod.D. or D.P.) or podiatric medicine (D.P.M.)	342	258	17	14	37	37	0	1	4	11	296	197	5	11	65	63	2	7	3	8
Veterinary medicine (D.V.M.)	588	504	17	36	17	17	0	6	5	3	593	487	17	60	18	18	0	2	6	3
Chiropractic (D.C. or D.C.M.)	1,538	1,230	64	85	110	108	2	6	10	33	1,366	1,101	26	65	119	114	5	11	13	31
Law (LL.B. or J.D.)	24,576	19,153	1,210	1,741	1,673	1,555	118	164	241	394	25,087	19,160	1,380	1,840	1,689	1,614	75	141	465	412
Theology (M.Div, M.H.L./Rav., B.D., or Ord.)	3,998	2,644	535	146	316	301	15	12	43	302	4,322	2,911	574	175	324	307	17	20	43	275

NOTE: Data are for postsecondary institutions participating in Title IV federal financial aid programs. Includes degrees that require at least 6 years of college work for completion (including at least 2 years of preprofessional training). Race categories exclude persons of Hispanic ethnicity. Reported racial/ethnic distributions of students by level of degree, field of degree, and sex were used to estimate race/ethnicity for students whose race/ethnicity was not reported. Some data have been revised from previously published figures.
SOURCE: U.S. Department of Education, National Center for Education Statistics, Integrated Postsecondary Education Data System (IPEDS), Fall 2012 and Fall 2013, Completions component. (This table was prepared March 2015.)

Table 324.70. Degrees conferred to females by postsecondary institutions in selected professional fields, by race/ethnicity and field of study: 2011–12 and 2012–13

Field of study	2011–12										2012–13									
	Total	White	Black	Hispanic	Asian/Pacific Islander			American Indian/Alaska Native	Two or more races	Non-resident alien	Total	White	Black	Hispanic	Asian/Pacific Islander			American Indian/Alaska Native	Two or more races	Non-resident alien
					Total	Asian	Pacific Islander								Total	Asian	Pacific Islander			
1	2	3	4	5	6	7	8	9	10	11	12	13	14	15	16	17	18	19	20	21
All fields, total	**48,370**	**31,498**	**4,361**	**3,066**	**7,458**	**7,335**	**123**	**292**	**554**	**1,141**	**48,878**	**31,254**	**4,295**	**3,489**	**7,431**	**7,295**	**136**	**279**	**940**	**1,190**
Dentistry (D.D.S. or D.M.D.)	2,361	1,215	155	153	590	586	4	13	14	221	2,460	1,245	130	181	633	627	6	13	23	235
Medicine (M.D.)	8,118	4,781	764	460	1,817	1,801	16	53	126	117	8,288	4,884	713	557	1,823	1,811	12	35	155	121
Optometry (O.D.)	885	477	29	27	280	277	3	1	3	68	964	510	24	44	310	308	2	3	13	60
Osteopathic medicine (D.O.)	2,053	1,418	88	99	403	393	10	14	11	20	2,202	1,550	72	70	433	427	6	10	56	11
Pharmacy (Pharm.D.)	7,972	4,763	541	323	2,052	2,031	21	38	58	197	8,236	4,830	643	353	2,086	2,064	22	25	85	214
Podiatry (Pod.D. or D.P.; or podiatric medicine (D.P.M.)	193	109	24	17	31	31	0	2	0	10	175	92	10	15	41	41	0	6	7	4
Veterinary medicine (D.V.M.)	2,028	1,748	49	104	92	92	0	12	14	9	2,017	1,647	50	213	56	56	0	9	34	8
Chiropractic (D.C. or D.C.M.)	958	725	64	49	75	67	8	2	15	28	858	658	49	51	55	49	6	5	13	27
Law (LL.B or J.D.)	21,869	15,123	2,094	1,772	2,051	1,993	58	150	286	393	21,724	14,656	2,069	1,943	1,922	1,843	79	167	525	442
Theology (M.Div, M.H.L./Rav., B.D., or Ord.)	1,933	1,139	553	62	67	64	3	7	27	78	1,954	1,182	535	62	72	69	3	6	29	68

NOTE: Data are for postsecondary institutions participating in Title IV federal financial aid programs. Includes degrees that require at least 6 years of college work for completion (including at least 2 years of preprofessional training). Race categories exclude persons of Hispanic ethnicity. Reported racial/ethnic distributions of students by level of degree, field of degree, and sex were used to estimate race/ethnicity for students whose race/ethnicity was not reported. Some data have been revised from previously published figures.
SOURCE: U.S. Department of Education, National Center for Education Statistics, Integrated Postsecondary Education Data System (IPEDS), Fall 2012 and Fall 2013, Completions component. (This table was prepared March 2015.)

Table 324.80. Statistical profile of persons receiving doctor's degrees, by field of study and selected characteristics: 2010–11 and 2011–12

Selected characteristic	All fields, 2010–11	Field of study, 2011–12								
		All fields	Education	Engineering	Humanities	Life sciences	Physical sciences, mathematics, and computer science[1] Total	Mathematics	Social sciences and psychology	Other fields
1	2	3	4	5	6	7	8	9	10	11
Number of doctor's degrees conferred	49,010	51,008	4,802	8,427	5,503	12,045	8,952	1,702	8,353	2,926
Sex (percent)[2]										
Male	53.5	53.7	31.3	77.5	48.2	44.3	71.4	71.6	41.8	51.1
Female	46.4	46.2	68.7	22.3	51.7	55.6	28.5	28.3	58.2	48.7
Race/ethnicity (percent)[3]										
White	74.1	73.5	70.6	69.8	78.6	72.3	77.3	78.1	73.7	69.7
Black	6.1	6.3	14.5	4.3	4.3	5.5	3.4	2.7	5.8	10.0
Hispanic	6.3	6.5	6.4	5.4	7.6	6.0	4.9	5.5	8.5	6.0
Asian	9.0	9.1	4.5	15.7	4.7	11.5	9.9	8.7	7.0	10.7
American Indian/Alaska Native	0.4	0.3	0.7	0.2	0.3	0.3	0.1	0.0	0.3	0.2
Two or more races	2.3	2.5	2.0	2.1	2.6	2.6	2.4	2.9	2.8	2.0
Other and unknown[4]	1.7	1.8	1.3	2.5	1.9	1.7	2.0	2.1	1.9	1.4
Citizenship (percent)										
U.S. citizen/permanent resident	64.9	64.6	83.8	42.0	79.8	68.4	53.3	49.3	74.0	61.0
Temporary visa holder	29.1	29.0	9.6	51.4	13.4	26.5	40.2	43.8	19.0	29.6
Unknown	6.1	6.5	6.6	6.6	6.8	5.1	6.5	6.9	7.0	9.4
Median age at doctorate (years)	32.0	31.8	39.0	30.2	33.9	31.3	30.1	29.7	32.4	35.1
Percent with bachelor's degree in same field as doctorate	55.0	54.5	25.8	77.6	52.2	50.0	64.1	65.9	52.0	35.8
Median time lapse to doctorate (years)										
Since bachelor's degree completion	9.1	9.0	15.0	7.5	11.0	8.5	7.5	7.2	9.5	11.8
Since starting graduate school	7.7	7.7	11.8	6.7	9.0	6.9	6.7	6.3	7.7	9.1
Postdoctoral plans (percent)[5]										
Definite postdoctoral study[6]	27.4	25.5	4.9	21.4	9.1	40.0	36.8	32.6	25.1	4.8
Fellowship	14.1	13.4	2.3	7.0	7.5	23.0	15.2	18.3	17.6	2.9
Research associateship	12.2	11.1	2.2	14.0	1.3	15.3	20.7	13.6	5.8	1.7
Other[7]	1.1	1.0	0.3	0.4	0.3	1.6	0.8	0.8	1.7	0.2
Definite postdoctoral employment[8]	36.8	38.6	62.3	40.8	47.1	20.9	30.5	35.1	43.3	66.1
Postsecondary educational institution[9]	19.5	19.9	36.4	6.7	39.0	9.8	10.3	19.1	26.3	52.6
Government	3.1	3.0	2.4	3.8	1.0	2.6	2.1	2.0	5.2	2.9
Industry, business	9.6	10.9	3.0	28.5	2.0	5.7	16.8	12.8	6.2	5.8
Nonprofit organization	2.1	2.1	3.6	1.1	2.4	2.1	0.7	‡	3.4	2.9
Other[10] and unknown	2.6	2.7	16.9	0.7	2.7	0.7	0.6	‡	2.2	2.0
Seeking employment or study	31.9	32.1	29.6	34.2	40.5	32.4	30.4	30.4	28.9	26.7
Other/unknown	3.9	3.9	3.2	3.6	3.3	6.7	2.4	1.9	2.7	2.4
Primary work activity after doctorate (percent)[11]										
Research and development	40.2	40.9	11.7	76.0	10.5	44.5	62.3	43.8	37.5	34.6
Teaching	37.1	36.0	43.2	7.7	75.8	28.4	23.3	43.4	37.5	48.5
Management or administration	11.1	11.5	32.5	5.2	6.8	12.1	4.6	3.0	8.8	10.6
Professional services	9.6	9.7	11.3	7.9	5.8	12.9	7.2	7.4	14.7	5.6
Other	1.9	1.9	1.2	3.2	1.1	2.1	2.7	2.4	1.4	0.7
Employment location after doctorate (percent)[12]										
New England	8.6	8.5	4.2	8.1	9.4	10.4	8.8	8.4	8.8	5.5
Middle Atlantic	13.1	12.9	10.5	11.4	16.2	12.5	13.3	14.8	13.9	12.9
East North Central	11.9	11.5	14.9	11.3	12.9	10.4	10.7	13.5	10.7	13.3
West North Central	5.4	5.4	8.0	3.8	5.5	6.2	4.1	4.9	4.9	7.0
South Atlantic	16.9	16.8	21.2	12.7	15.8	18.4	13.4	14.0	19.7	18.3
East South Central	4.1	4.2	9.2	2.1	5.6	4.5	2.7	4.0	3.2	4.9
West South Central	6.9	7.5	9.9	8.2	7.5	7.0	6.5	6.7	6.9	8.5
Mountain	5.1	5.3	7.9	6.1	4.2	4.6	5.5	3.9	4.3	5.5
Pacific and insular	16.5	16.6	8.7	24.6	12.1	16.4	21.2	14.3	13.9	9.8
Foreign	10.8	10.8	4.8	11.2	10.2	8.9	13.2	15.1	13.1	13.6
Region unknown	0.1	0.1	#	0.1	0.1	#	#	0.0	0.1	0.0

#Rounds to zero.
‡Reporting standards not met (too few cases).
[1]Includes mathematics, computer science, physics and astronomy, chemistry, and earth, atmospheric, and marine sciences.
[2]Distribution based on respondents reporting sex data.
[3]Distribution based on U.S. citizens and permanent residents.
[4]Includes Native Hawaiians and other Pacific Islanders.
[5]Percentages are based on only those doctorate recipients who responded to questions about postdoctoral plans.
[6]Percentages are based on only those doctorate recipients who indicated definite postdoctoral plans for study and who indicated the type of study.
[7]Includes respondents who indicated definite postgraduation study plans for traineeship, internship/clinical residency, or other study.
[8]Percentages are based on only those doctorate recipients who indicated definite postdoctoral plans for employment and who indicated the sector of employment.
[9]Includes 2-year, 4-year, and foreign colleges and universities, and medical schools.
[10]Other is mainly composed of elementary and secondary schools.
[11]Percentages are based on only those doctorate recipients who indicated definite postdoctoral plans for employment and who indicated their primary work activity.

[12]Percentages are based on only those doctorate recipients who indicated definite postdoctoral plans and type of plans.
NOTE: The above classification of degrees by field differs somewhat from that in most publications of the National Center for Education Statistics (NCES). One major difference is that history is included under humanities rather than social sciences. Includes Ph.D., Ed.D., and comparable degrees at the doctoral level. Includes only graduates of research programs, which typically require the preparation and defense of a dissertation based on original research, or the planning and execution of an original project demonstrating substantial artistic or scholarly achievement. Excludes nonresearch professional practice doctor's degrees (e.g., M.D., D.D.S., and J.D.) that are conferred upon completion of a program providing the knowledge and skills for the recognition, credential, or license required for professional practice in such fields as health and theology. The number of doctor's degrees in this table differs from that reported in the NCES Integrated Postsecondary Education Data System (IPEDS), which includes both the research and nonresearch degrees. Race categories exclude persons of Hispanic ethnicity. Detail may not sum to totals because of rounding.
SOURCE: Doctorate Recipients From U.S. Universities: 2011 and 2012, Survey of Earned Doctorates, National Science Foundation, National Institutes of Health, U.S. Department of Education, National Endowment for the Humanities, U.S. Department of Agriculture, and the National Aeronautics and Space Administration. (This table was prepared August 2014.)

Table 324.90. Doctor's degrees conferred by the 60 institutions conferring the most doctor's degrees, by rank order: 2003–04 through 2012–13

Institution	Rank order[1]	Total, 2003–04 to 2012–13	2003–04	2004–05	2005–06	2006–07	2007–08	2008–09	2009–10	2010–11	2011–12	2012–13
1	2	3	4	5	6	7	8	9	10	11	12	13
United States, all institutions	†	1,514,834	126,087	134,387	138,056	144,690	149,378	154,564	158,590	163,827	170,217	175,038
Total, 60 institutions conferring most doctorates	†	579,753	50,640	52,807	54,436	57,198	58,428	59,356	59,892	61,405	62,208	63,383
University of Florida	1	19,319	1,658	1,665	1,732	1,957	2,107	2,028	2,127	2,127	1,954	1,964
Nova Southeastern University	2	17,141	1,540	1,629	1,521	1,913	1,772	1,732	1,806	1,699	1,800	1,729
University of Minnesota, Twin Cities	3	15,938	1,307	1,455	1,536	1,667	1,563	1,594	1,618	1,692	1,680	1,826
Ohio State University, Main Campus	4	15,595	1,342	1,432	1,549	1,501	1,611	1,617	1,596	1,658	1,628	1,661
University of Michigan, Ann Arbor	5	15,137	1,365	1,406	1,514	1,496	1,483	1,576	1,534	1,550	1,566	1,647
University of Southern California	6	14,419	1,269	1,361	1,312	1,378	1,523	1,571	1,459	1,474	1,518	1,554
Harvard University	7	14,165	1,333	1,288	1,393	1,476	1,468	1,418	1,401	1,450	1,474	1,464
New York University	8	14,040	1,339	1,385	1,321	1,331	1,413	1,419	1,444	1,413	1,481	1,494
University of Wisconsin, Madison	9	13,776	1,213	1,314	1,261	1,425	1,407	1,430	1,355	1,417	1,514	1,440
University of Texas at Austin	10	13,736	1,299	1,404	1,443	1,358	1,439	1,379	1,382	1,309	1,372	1,351
University of California, Los Angeles	11	13,204	1,251	1,225	1,271	1,307	1,361	1,382	1,358	1,330	1,326	1,393
Columbia University in the City of New York	12	12,646	1,116	1,231	1,300	1,203	1,218	1,281	1,295	1,291	1,329	1,382
University of California, Berkeley	13	12,249	1,169	1,151	1,110	1,280	1,218	1,216	1,245	1,292	1,264	1,304
Temple University	14	11,783	1,141	1,119	1,205	1,194	1,220	1,169	1,144	1,246	1,154	1,191
University of Washington, Seattle Campus	15	11,626	991	1,003	1,124	1,130	1,125	1,176	1,224	1,251	1,273	1,329
University of Pennsylvania	16	11,615	1,032	1,170	1,162	1,136	1,105	1,190	1,212	1,212	1,189	1,207
University of North Carolina at Chapel Hill	17	11,320	1,026	1,069	1,098	1,113	1,204	1,101	1,155	1,172	1,179	1,203
Boston University	18	10,974	876	926	1,062	1,210	1,161	1,179	1,097	1,111	1,177	1,175
University of Illinois at Urbana-Champaign	19	10,558	882	971	998	1,018	1,067	1,081	1,066	1,106	1,210	1,159
University of Pittsburgh, Pittsburgh Campus	20	10,088	980	936	926	996	1,026	1,022	944	1,113	1,059	1,086
George Washington University	21	9,707	875	879	937	949	956	1,011	1,005	974	1,050	1,071
Stanford University	22	9,684	891	904	954	969	944	920	978	1,053	1,019	1,052
University of Tennessee, Knoxville	23	9,525	813	790	873	895	912	994	1,024	1,002	1,110	1,112
University at Buffalo	24	9,338	856	933	905	970	938	964	919	948	913	992
University of Iowa	25	9,309	847	924	887	926	926	937	920	949	948	1,045
Georgetown University	26	9,277	934	890	844	923	926	967	950	936	934	973
University of California, Davis	27	8,872	770	791	812	876	900	894	891	927	1,002	1,009
University of Virginia, Main Campus	28	8,807	851	826	840	852	925	907	861	933	904	908
Northwestern University	29	8,747	761	798	837	878	876	872	891	927	898	1,009
University of Illinois at Chicago	30	8,695	748	789	807	862	873	851	965	914	912	974
Michigan State University	31	8,644	774	774	768	855	770	876	921	951	962	993
University of Georgia	32	8,613	833	818	828	858	832	897	854	889	903	901
Purdue University, Main Campus	33	8,344	662	763	785	837	840	882	845	924	880	926
Thomas M. Cooley Law School	34	8,342	405	524	614	756	845	981	955	1,039	1,080	1,143
University of Maryland, Baltimore	35	8,166	787	750	813	767	775	775	835	875	900	889
University of Arizona	36	7,853	702	696	698	814	778	824	824	813	850	854
University of Houston	37	7,848	697	824	772	778	809	786	757	831	798	796
Duke University	38	7,744	662	615	570	680	682	718	820	887	1,010	1,100
University of Miami	39	7,656	682	685	673	707	703	758	860	803	911	874
Cornell University[2]	40	7,568	678	740	754	752	752	785	779	782	775	771
Wayne State University	41	7,461	701	682	703	688	758	772	717	856	807	777
University of Kansas	42	7,406	557	562	585	789	781	766	819	856	821	870
University of Kentucky	43	7,267	605	670	634	653	717	719	734	783	888	864
Washington University in St. Louis	44	7,266	599	641	678	727	730	760	737	805	783	806
Texas A & M University, College Station	45	7,167	633	651	660	727	723	717	703	739	790	824
Indiana University-Purdue University, Indianapolis	46	7,122	640	655	669	719	720	687	751	755	771	755
University of the Pacific	47	7,093	642	733	684	691	708	681	713	749	732	760
Indiana University, Bloomington	48	7,002	647	683	667	651	695	729	718	693	748	771
Case Western Reserve University	49	6,951	638	636	681	654	718	750	781	730	658	705
University of Chicago	50	6,814	624	638	695	653	704	682	682	711	715	710
Florida State University	51	6,785	479	577	601	631	730	680	683	818	850	736
Yale University	52	6,776	625	625	622	640	671	685	752	686	712	758
Pennsylvania State University, Main Campus	53	6,775	539	571	646	664	643	703	718	736	755	800
University of South Carolina, Columbia	54	6,650	621	636	642	641	639	703	643	703	674	748
Yeshiva University	55	6,628	621	659	627	635	649	657	680	690	684	726
A.T. Still University of Health Sciences	56	6,620	412	477	551	644	694	730	815	810	755	732
University of Connecticut	57	6,524	510	554	629	609	576	687	746	720	773	720
Arizona State University, Tempe	58	6,520	524	478	569	574	656	766	656	746	828	723
Capella University	59	6,489	178	272	499	667	814	700	841	819	810	889
Virginia Commonwealth University	60	6,369	488	554	585	548	649	622	687	730	748	758

†Not applicable.
[1]Institutions are ranked by the total number of doctor's degrees conferred during the 10-year period from July 1, 2003, to June 30, 2013.
[2]Includes degrees conferred by the Endowed and Statutory Colleges.
NOTE: Includes Ph.D., Ed.D., and comparable degrees at the doctoral level, as well as such degrees as M.D., D.D.S., and law degrees that were formerly classified as first-professional degrees. Some data have been revised from previously published figures.
SOURCE: U.S. Department of Education, National Center for Education Statistics, Integrated Postsecondary Education Data System (IPEDS), Fall 2004 through Fall 2013, Completions component. (This table was prepared April 2015.)

Table 325.10. Degrees in agriculture and natural resources conferred by postsecondary institutions, by level of degree and sex of student: 1970–71 through 2012–13

Year	Bachelor's degrees					Master's degrees			Doctor's degrees		
	Total				Females as a percent of total	Total	Males	Females	Total	Males	Females
	Number	Annual percent change	Males	Females							
1	2	3	4	5	6	7	8	9	10	11	12
1970–71	12,672	†	12,136	536	4.2	2,457	2,313	144	1,086	1,055	31
1971–72	13,516	6.7	12,779	737	5.5	2,680	2,490	190	971	945	26
1972–73	14,756	9.2	13,661	1,095	7.4	2,807	2,588	219	1,059	1,031	28
1973–74	16,253	10.1	14,684	1,569	9.7	2,928	2,640	288	930	897	33
1974–75	17,528	7.8	15,061	2,467	14.1	3,067	2,703	364	991	958	33
1975–76	19,402	10.7	15,845	3,557	18.3	3,340	2,862	478	928	867	61
1976–77	21,467	10.6	16,690	4,777	22.3	3,724	3,177	547	893	831	62
1977–78	22,650	5.5	17,069	5,581	24.6	4,023	3,268	755	971	909	62
1978–79	23,134	2.1	16,854	6,280	27.1	3,994	3,187	807	950	877	73
1979–80	22,802	-1.4	16,045	6,757	29.6	3,976	3,082	894	991	879	112
1980–81	21,886	-4.0	15,154	6,732	30.8	4,003	3,061	942	1,067	940	127
1981–82	21,029	-3.9	14,443	6,586	31.3	4,163	3,114	1,049	1,079	925	154
1982–83	20,909	-0.6	14,085	6,824	32.6	4,254	3,129	1,125	1,149	1,004	145
1983–84	19,317	-7.6	13,206	6,111	31.6	4,178	2,989	1,189	1,172	1,001	171
1984–85	18,107	-6.3	12,477	5,630	31.1	3,928	2,846	1,082	1,213	1,036	177
1985–86	16,823	-7.1	11,544	5,279	31.4	3,801	2,701	1,100	1,158	966	192
1986–87	14,991	-10.9	10,314	4,677	31.2	3,522	2,460	1,062	1,049	871	178
1987–88	14,222	-5.1	9,744	4,478	31.5	3,479	2,427	1,052	1,142	926	216
1988–89	13,492	-5.1	9,298	4,194	31.1	3,245	2,231	1,014	1,183	950	233
1989–90	12,900	-4.4	8,822	4,078	31.6	3,382	2,239	1,143	1,295	1,038	257
1990–91	13,124	1.7	8,832	4,292	32.7	3,295	2,160	1,135	1,185	953	232
1991–92	15,113	15.2	9,867	5,246	34.7	3,730	2,409	1,321	1,205	955	250
1992–93	16,769	11.0	11,079	5,690	33.9	3,959	2,474	1,485	1,159	869	290
1993–94	18,056	7.7	11,746	6,310	34.9	4,110	2,512	1,598	1,262	969	293
1994–95	19,832	9.8	12,686	7,146	36.0	4,234	2,541	1,693	1,256	955	301
1995–96	21,425	8.0	13,531	7,894	36.8	4,551	2,642	1,909	1,259	926	333
1996–97	22,597	5.5	13,791	8,806	39.0	4,505	2,601	1,904	1,202	875	327
1997–98	23,276	3.0	13,806	9,470	40.7	4,464	2,545	1,919	1,290	924	366
1998–99	24,179	3.9	14,045	10,134	41.9	4,376	2,360	2,016	1,249	869	380
1999–2000	24,238	0.2	13,843	10,395	42.9	4,360	2,356	2,004	1,168	803	365
2000–01	23,370	-3.6	12,840	10,530	45.1	4,272	2,251	2,021	1,127	741	386
2001–02	23,331	-0.2	12,630	10,701	45.9	4,503	2,340	2,163	1,148	760	388
2002–03	23,348	0.1	12,343	11,005	47.1	4,492	2,232	2,260	1,229	790	439
2003–04	22,835	-2.2	11,889	10,946	47.9	4,783	2,306	2,477	1,185	758	427
2004–05	23,002	0.7	11,987	11,015	47.9	4,746	2,288	2,458	1,173	763	410
2005–06	23,053	0.2	12,063	10,990	47.7	4,640	2,280	2,360	1,194	710	484
2006–07	23,133	0.3	12,309	10,824	46.8	4,623	2,174	2,449	1,272	768	504
2007–08	24,113	4.2	12,634	11,479	47.6	4,684	2,180	2,504	1,257	742	515
2008–09	24,982	3.6	13,096	11,886	47.6	4,878	2,328	2,550	1,328	741	587
2009–10	26,343	5.4	13,524	12,819	48.7	5,215	2,512	2,703	1,149	626	523
2010–11	28,630	8.7	14,678	13,952	48.7	5,766	2,746	3,020	1,246	675	571
2011–12	30,972	8.2	15,485	15,487	50.0	6,390	3,026	3,364	1,333	721	612
2012–13	33,593	8.5	16,618	16,975	50.5	6,339	2,917	3,422	1,411	767	644
Percent change											
2002–03 to 2007–08	3.3	†	2.4	4.3	†	4.3	-2.3	10.8	2.3	-6.1	17.3
2007–08 to 2012–13	39.3	†	31.5	47.9	†	35.3	33.8	36.7	12.3	3.4	25.0

†Not applicable.
NOTE: Data are for postsecondary institutions participating in Title IV federal financial aid programs. Includes degrees in agriculture, agriculture operations, and related sciences and in natural resources and conservation. Some data have been revised from previously published figures.

SOURCE: U.S. Department of Education, National Center for Education Statistics, Higher Education General Information Survey (HEGIS), "Degrees and Other Formal Awards Conferred" surveys, 1970–71 through 1985–86; Integrated Postsecondary Education Data System (IPEDS), "Completions Survey" (IPEDS-C:87–99); and IPEDS Fall 2000 through Fall 2013, Completions component. (This table was prepared August 2014.)

Table 325.15. Degrees in architecture and related services conferred by postsecondary institutions, by level of degree and sex of student: Selected years, 1949–50 through 2012–13

	Bachelor's degrees					Master's degrees			Doctor's degrees		
	Total				Females as a percent of total						
Year	Number	Annual percent change	Males	Females		Total	Males	Females	Total	Males	Females
1	2	3	4	5	6	7	8	9	10	11	12
1949–50	2,563	†	2,441	122	4.8	166	159	7	1	1	0
1959–60	1,801	†	1,744	57	3.2	319	305	14	17	17	0
1967–68	3,057	†	2,931	126	4.1	1,021	953	68	15	15	0
1969–70	4,105	†	3,888	217	5.3	1,427	1,260	167	35	33	2
1970–71	5,570	35.7	4,906	664	11.9	1,705	1,469	236	36	33	3
1971–72	6,440	15.6	5,667	773	12.0	1,899	1,626	273	50	43	7
1972–73	6,962	8.1	6,042	920	13.2	2,307	1,943	364	58	54	4
1973–74	7,822	12.4	6,665	1,157	14.8	2,702	2,208	494	69	65	4
1974–75	8,226	5.2	6,791	1,435	17.4	2,938	2,343	595	69	58	11
1975–76	9,146	11.2	7,396	1,750	19.1	3,215	2,545	670	82	69	13
1976–77	9,222	0.8	7,249	1,973	21.4	3,213	2,489	724	73	62	11
1977–78	9,250	0.3	7,054	2,196	23.7	3,115	2,304	811	73	57	16
1978–79	9,273	0.2	6,876	2,397	25.8	3,113	2,226	887	96	74	22
1979–80	9,132	-1.5	6,596	2,536	27.8	3,139	2,245	894	79	66	13
1980–81	9,455	3.5	6,800	2,655	28.1	3,153	2,234	919	93	73	20
1981–82	9,728	2.9	6,825	2,903	29.8	3,327	2,242	1,085	80	58	22
1982–83	9,823	1.0	6,403	3,420	34.8	3,357	2,224	1,133	97	74	23
1983–84	9,186	-6.5	5,895	3,291	35.8	3,223	2,197	1,026	84	62	22
1984–85	9,325	1.5	6,019	3,306	35.5	3,275	2,148	1,127	89	66	23
1985–86	9,119	-2.2	5,824	3,295	36.1	3,260	2,129	1,131	73	56	17
1986–87	8,950	-1.9	5,617	3,333	37.2	3,163	2,086	1,077	92	66	26
1987–88	8,603	-3.9	5,271	3,332	38.7	3,159	2,042	1,117	98	66	32
1988–89	9,150	6.4	5,545	3,605	39.4	3,383	2,192	1,191	86	63	23
1989–90	9,364	2.3	5,703	3,661	39.1	3,499	2,228	1,271	103	73	30
1990–91	9,781	4.5	5,788	3,993	40.8	3,490	2,244	1,246	135	101	34
1991–92	8,753	-10.5	5,805	2,948	33.7	3,640	2,271	1,369	132	93	39
1992–93	9,167	4.7	5,940	3,227	35.2	3,808	2,376	1,432	148	105	43
1993–94	8,975	-2.1	5,764	3,211	35.8	3,943	2,428	1,515	161	111	50
1994–95	8,756	-2.4	5,741	3,015	34.4	3,923	2,310	1,613	141	95	46
1995–96	8,352	-4.6	5,340	3,012	36.1	3,993	2,361	1,632	141	96	45
1996–97	7,944	-4.9	5,090	2,854	35.9	4,034	2,336	1,698	135	93	42
1997–98	7,652	-3.7	4,966	2,686	35.1	4,347	2,537	1,810	131	80	51
1998–99	8,245	7.7	5,145	3,100	37.6	4,235	2,435	1,800	119	76	43
1999–2000	8,462	2.6	5,193	3,269	38.6	4,268	2,508	1,760	129	85	44
2000–01	8,480	0.2	5,086	3,394	40.0	4,302	2,515	1,787	153	83	70
2001–02	8,808	3.9	5,224	3,584	40.7	4,566	2,606	1,960	183	117	66
2002–03	9,056	2.8	5,331	3,725	41.1	4,925	2,832	2,093	152	83	69
2003–04	8,838	-2.4	5,059	3,779	42.8	5,424	3,049	2,375	173	94	79
2004–05	9,237	4.5	5,222	4,015	43.5	5,674	3,180	2,494	179	110	69
2005–06	9,515	3.0	5,414	4,101	43.1	5,743	3,165	2,578	201	108	93
2006–07	9,717	2.1	5,393	4,324	44.5	5,951	3,304	2,647	178	104	74
2007–08	9,805	0.9	5,579	4,226	43.1	6,065	3,252	2,813	199	103	96
2008–09	10,119	3.2	5,797	4,322	42.7	6,587	3,657	2,930	212	113	99
2009–10	10,051	-0.7	5,694	4,357	43.3	7,280	4,012	3,268	210	116	94
2010–11	9,831	-2.2	5,698	4,133	42.0	7,788	4,265	3,523	205	110	95
2011–12	9,727	-1.1	5,566	4,161	42.8	8,448	4,504	3,944	255	147	108
2012–13	9,757	0.3	5,581	4,176	42.8	8,095	4,261	3,834	247	134	113
Percent change											
2002–03 to 2007–08	8.3	†	4.7	13.4	†	23.1	14.8	34.4	30.9	24.1	39.1
2007–08 to 2012–13	-0.5	†	#	-1.2	†	33.5	31.0	36.3	24.1	30.1	17.7

†Not applicable.
Rounds to zero.
NOTE: Data are for postsecondary institutions participating in Title IV federal financial aid programs. Some data have been revised from previously published figures.
SOURCE: U.S. Department of Education, National Center for Education Statistics, *Earned Degrees Conferred*, 1949–50 and 1959–60; Higher Education General Information Survey (HEGIS), "Degrees and Other Formal Awards Conferred" surveys, 1967–68 through 1985–86; Integrated Postsecondary Education Data System (IPEDS), "Completions Survey" (IPEDS-C:87–99); and IPEDS Fall 2000 through Fall 2013, Completions component. (This table was prepared August 2014.)

Table 325.20. Degrees in the biological and biomedical sciences conferred by postsecondary institutions, by level of degree and sex of student: Selected years, 1951–52 through 2012–13

	Bachelor's degrees					Master's degrees			Doctor's degrees		
	Total				Females as a percent of total	Total	Males	Females	Total	Males	Females
Year	Number	Annual percent change	Males	Females							
1	2	3	4	5	6	7	8	9	10	11	12
1951–52	11,094	†	8,212	2,882	26.0	2,307	1,908	399	764	680	84
1953–54	9,279	†	6,710	2,569	27.7	1,610	1,287	323	1,077	977	100
1955–56	12,423	†	9,515	2,908	23.4	1,759	1,379	380	1,025	908	117
1957–58	14,308	†	11,159	3,149	22.0	1,852	1,448	404	1,125	987	138
1959–60	15,576	†	11,654	3,922	25.2	2,154	1,668	486	1,205	1,086	119
1961–62	16,915	†	12,136	4,779	28.3	2,642	1,982	660	1,338	1,179	159
1963–64	22,723	†	16,321	6,402	28.2	3,296	2,348	948	1,625	1,432	193
1965–66	26,916	†	19,368	7,548	28.0	4,232	3,085	1,147	2,097	1,792	305
1967–68	31,826	†	22,986	8,840	27.8	5,506	3,959	1,547	2,784	2,345	439
1969–70	34,034	†	23,919	10,115	29.7	5,800	3,975	1,825	3,289	2,820	469
1970–71	35,705	4.9	25,319	10,386	29.1	5,625	3,782	1,843	3,603	3,018	585
1971–72	37,269	4.4	26,314	10,955	29.4	5,989	4,056	1,933	3,587	2,981	606
1972–73	42,207	13.2	29,625	12,582	29.8	6,156	4,317	1,839	3,583	2,892	691
1973–74	48,244	14.3	33,217	15,027	31.1	6,408	4,512	1,896	3,358	2,684	674
1974–75	51,609	7.0	34,580	17,029	33.0	6,429	4,554	1,875	3,334	2,612	722
1975–76	54,154	4.9	35,498	18,656	34.4	6,457	4,466	1,991	3,347	2,631	716
1976–77	53,464	-1.3	34,178	19,286	36.1	6,953	4,670	2,283	3,335	2,627	708
1977–78	51,360	-3.9	31,673	19,687	38.3	6,651	4,353	2,298	3,255	2,481	774
1978–79	48,713	-5.2	29,173	19,540	40.1	6,638	4,198	2,440	3,459	2,593	866
1979–80	46,254	-5.0	26,797	19,457	42.1	6,339	4,042	2,297	3,568	2,651	917
1980–81	43,078	-6.9	24,124	18,954	44.0	5,766	3,602	2,164	3,640	2,620	1,020
1981–82	41,501	-3.7	22,722	18,779	45.2	5,679	3,384	2,295	3,662	2,611	1,051
1982–83	39,924	-3.8	21,572	18,352	46.0	5,711	3,298	2,413	3,386	2,306	1,080
1983–84	38,593	-3.3	20,565	18,028	46.7	5,489	3,123	2,366	3,496	2,416	1,080
1984–85	38,354	-0.6	20,071	18,283	47.7	5,109	2,775	2,334	3,465	2,335	1,130
1985–86	38,395	0.1	20,000	18,395	47.9	5,064	2,733	2,331	3,405	2,273	1,132
1986–87	38,074	-0.8	19,684	18,390	48.3	4,995	2,646	2,349	3,469	2,268	1,201
1987–88	36,688	-3.6	18,267	18,421	50.2	4,871	2,530	2,341	3,688	2,389	1,299
1988–89	36,068	-1.7	17,998	18,070	50.1	5,034	2,598	2,436	3,617	2,299	1,318
1989–90	37,304	3.4	18,363	18,941	50.8	4,941	2,509	2,432	3,922	2,478	1,444
1990–91	39,482	5.8	19,418	20,064	50.8	4,834	2,417	2,417	4,152	2,618	1,534
1991–92	42,892	8.6	20,816	22,076	51.5	4,862	2,437	2,425	4,442	2,749	1,693
1992–93	47,009	9.6	22,870	24,139	51.3	5,026	2,540	2,486	4,749	2,866	1,883
1993–94	51,296	9.1	25,071	26,225	51.1	5,462	2,681	2,781	4,891	2,910	1,981
1994–95	55,983	9.1	26,734	29,249	52.2	5,873	2,920	2,953	5,069	3,012	2,057
1995–96	61,014	9.0	28,921	32,093	52.6	6,593	3,212	3,381	5,250	3,062	2,188
1996–97	63,973	4.8	29,562	34,411	53.8	6,986	3,419	3,567	5,313	3,014	2,299
1997–98	65,917	3.0	29,663	36,254	55.0	6,848	3,336	3,512	5,474	3,123	2,351
1998–99	65,310	-0.9	28,507	36,803	56.4	6,966	3,279	3,687	5,250	3,010	2,240
1999–2000	63,630	-2.6	26,579	37,051	58.2	6,850	3,171	3,679	5,463	3,068	2,395
2000–01	60,576	-4.8	24,600	35,976	59.4	7,017	3,075	3,942	5,225	2,923	2,302
2001–02	60,309	-0.4	23,694	36,615	60.7	7,011	3,033	3,978	5,104	2,836	2,268
2002–03	61,294	1.6	23,356	37,938	61.9	7,050	3,015	4,035	5,268	2,866	2,402
2003–04	62,624	2.2	23,691	38,933	62.2	7,732	3,271	4,461	5,538	2,975	2,563
2004–05	65,915	5.3	25,104	40,811	61.9	8,284	3,361	4,923	5,935	3,025	2,910
2005–06	70,607	7.1	27,183	43,424	61.5	8,781	3,709	5,072	6,162	3,138	3,024
2006–07	76,832	8.8	30,600	46,232	60.2	8,898	3,639	5,259	6,764	3,440	3,324
2007–08	79,829	3.9	32,401	47,428	59.4	9,689	4,094	5,595	7,400	3,645	3,755
2008–09	82,828	3.8	33,707	49,121	59.3	10,018	4,250	5,768	7,499	3,549	3,950
2009–10	86,391	4.3	35,866	50,525	58.5	10,730	4,612	6,118	7,672	3,603	4,069
2010–11	89,984	4.2	36,888	53,096	59.0	11,324	4,869	6,455	7,693	3,648	4,045
2011–12	95,850	6.5	39,542	56,308	58.7	12,419	5,378	7,041	7,935	3,708	4,227
2012–13	100,319	4.7	41,511	58,808	58.6	13,335	5,816	7,519	7,943	3,692	4,251
Percent change											
2002–03 to 2007–08	30.2	†	38.7	25.0	†	37.4	35.8	38.7	40.5	27.2	56.3
2007–08 to 2012–13	25.7	†	28.1	24.0	†	37.6	42.1	34.4	7.3	1.3	13.2

†Not applicable.
NOTE: Data are for postsecondary institutions participating in Title IV federal financial aid programs. Some data have been revised from previously published figures.
SOURCE: U.S. Department of Education, National Center for Education Statistics, *Earned Degrees Conferred*, 1951–52 through 1963–64; Higher Education General Information Sur-

vey (HEGIS), "Degrees and Other Formal Awards Conferred" surveys, 1965–66 through 1985–86; Integrated Postsecondary Education Data System (IPEDS), "Completions Survey" (IPEDS-C:87–99); and IPEDS Fall 2000 through Fall 2013, Completions component. (This table was prepared August 2014.)

Table 325.22. Degrees in biology, microbiology, and zoology conferred by postsecondary institutions, by level of degree: 1970–71 through 2012–13

Year	Biology, general[1]			Microbiology[2]			Zoology[3]		
	Bachelor's	Master's	Doctor's	Bachelor's	Master's	Doctor's	Bachelor's	Master's	Doctor's
1	2	3	4	5	6	7	8	9	10
1970–71	26,294	2,665	536	1,475	456	365	5,721	1,027	878
1971–72	27,473	2,943	580	1,548	470	351	5,518	1,040	836
1972–73	31,185	2,959	627	1,940	517	344	5,763	1,042	803
1973–74	36,188	3,186	657	2,311	505	384	6,128	1,091	677
1974–75	38,748	3,109	637	2,767	552	345	6,110	1,039	697
1975–76	40,163	3,177	624	2,927	585	364	6,077	976	645
1976–77	39,530	3,322	608	2,884	659	325	5,574	985	696
1977–78	37,598	3,094	664	2,695	615	353	5,096	958	624
1978–79	35,962	3,093	663	2,670	597	395	4,738	946	669
1979–80	33,523	2,911	718	2,631	596	376	4,301	922	639
1980–81	31,323	2,598	734	2,414	482	370	3,873	881	613
1981–82	29,651	2,579	678	2,377	470	350	3,615	868	625
1982–83	28,022	2,354	521	2,324	499	358	3,407	738	533
1983–84	27,379	2,313	617	2,349	505	388	3,231	700	521
1984–85	27,593	2,130	658	2,207	471	319	3,069	664	508
1985–86	27,618	2,173	574	2,257	392	362	2,894	618	548
1986–87	27,465	2,022	537	2,159	451	380	2,791	623	464
1987–88	26,838	1,981	576	2,061	404	442	2,537	629	492
1988–89	26,229	2,097	527	1,833	449	423	2,549	634	466
1989–90	27,213	1,998	551	1,973	403	441	2,473	548	545
1990–91	29,285	1,956	632	1,788	343	443	2,641	551	516
1991–92	31,909	1,995	657	1,750	372	532	2,811	530	494
1992–93	34,932	2,000	671	1,798	367	621	3,036	559	465
1993–94	38,103	2,178	665	1,872	359	591	3,162	658	503
1994–95	41,658	2,350	729	1,992	326	572	3,149	586	487
1995–96	44,818	2,606	768	2,220	364	606	3,463	677	501
1996–97	46,632	2,742	693	2,530	363	612	3,438	720	474
1997–98	47,054	2,617	809	2,926	401	585	3,653	685	465
1998–99	46,172	2,616	718	2,885	406	544	3,508	606	462
1999–2000	44,982	2,599	727	3,049	383	551	3,226	616	481
2000–01	42,310	2,582	780	2,779	334	553	3,045	560	380
2001–02	42,281	2,424	689	2,622	325	538	2,979	578	413
2002–03	42,699	2,340	680	2,455	297	507	2,488	379	355
2003–04	43,465	2,529	681	2,365	350	599	2,454	367	245
2004–05	45,540	2,564	712	2,318	390	610	2,159	384	268
2005–06	48,855	2,719	776	2,243	372	612	2,140	384	254
2006–07	52,527	2,679	788	2,347	369	667	2,223	416	263
2007–08	54,384	2,935	866	2,458	353	734	2,235	381	281
2008–09	55,859	2,987	896	2,480	291	716	2,140	347	297
2009–10	58,700	3,087	919	2,449	303	767	2,147	360	243
2010–11	61,236	3,283	935	2,466	337	739	2,062	338	230
2011–12	64,616	3,494	964	2,532	395	687	2,174	346	258
2012–13	66,699	3,500	1,004	2,582	402	704	2,246	416	231
Percent change									
2002–03 to 2007–08	27.4	25.4	27.4	0.1	18.9	44.8	-10.2	0.5	-20.8
2007–08 to 2012–13	22.6	19.3	15.9	5.0	13.9	-4.1	0.5	9.2	-17.8

[1]Includes biology/biological sciences, general.
[2]Includes microbiology, general; medical microbiology and bacteriology; virology; parasitology; immunology; and microbiological sciences and immunology, other.
[3]Includes zoology/animal biology; entomology; animal physiology; animal behavior and ethology; wildlife biology; and zoology/animal biology, other.
NOTE: Data are for postsecondary institutions participating in Title IV federal financial aid programs. Some data have been revised from previously published figures.

SOURCE: U.S. Department of Education, National Center for Education Statistics, Higher Education General Information Survey (HEGIS), "Degrees and Other Formal Awards Conferred" surveys, 1970–71 through 1985–86; Integrated Postsecondary Education Data System (IPEDS), "Completions Survey" (IPEDS-C:87–99); and IPEDS Fall 2000 through Fall 2013, Completions component. (This table was prepared August 2014.)

Table 325.25. Degrees in business conferred by postsecondary institutions, by level of degree and sex of student: Selected years, 1955–56 through 2012–13

	Bachelor's degrees					Master's degrees			Doctor's degrees		
	Total				Females as a percent of total						
Year	Number	Annual percent change	Males	Females		Total	Males	Females	Total	Males	Females
1	2	3	4	5	6	7	8	9	10	11	12
1955–56	42,813	†	38,706	4,107	9.6	3,280	3,118	162	129	127	2
1957–58	51,991	†	48,063	3,928	7.6	4,223	4,072	151	110	105	5
1959–60	51,076	†	47,262	3,814	7.5	4,643	4,476	167	135	133	2
1961–62	49,017	†	45,184	3,833	7.8	7,691	7,484	207	226	221	5
1963–64	55,474	†	51,056	4,418	8.0	9,251	9,008	243	275	268	7
1965–66	62,721	†	57,516	5,205	8.3	12,959	12,628	331	387	370	17
1967–68	79,074	†	72,126	6,948	8.8	17,795	17,186	609	441	427	14
1969–70	105,580	†	96,346	9,234	8.7	21,561	20,792	769	620	610	10
1970–71	115,396	9.3	104,936	10,460	9.1	26,490	25,458	1,032	774	753	21
1971–72	121,917	5.7	110,331	11,586	9.5	30,509	29,317	1,192	876	857	19
1972–73	126,717	3.9	113,337	13,380	10.6	31,208	29,689	1,519	917	864	53
1973–74	132,304	4.4	115,363	16,941	12.8	32,691	30,557	2,134	922	873	49
1974–75	133,639	1.0	111,983	21,656	16.2	36,315	33,274	3,041	939	900	39
1975–76	143,171	7.1	114,986	28,185	19.7	42,592	37,654	4,938	906	856	50
1976–77	152,010	6.2	116,394	35,616	23.4	46,505	39,852	6,653	839	785	54
1977–78	160,775	5.8	117,103	43,672	27.2	48,347	40,224	8,123	834	760	74
1978–79	172,392	7.2	119,765	52,627	30.5	50,397	40,766	9,631	852	752	100
1979–80	186,264	8.0	123,639	62,625	33.6	55,008	42,744	12,264	767	650	117
1980–81	200,521	7.7	126,798	73,723	36.8	57,888	43,411	14,477	808	686	122
1981–82	215,190	7.3	130,693	84,497	39.3	61,251	44,230	17,021	826	676	150
1982–83	226,442	5.2	131,451	94,991	41.9	64,741	45,987	18,754	770	638	132
1983–84	229,013	1.1	129,296	99,717	43.5	66,129	46,167	19,962	926	727	199
1984–85	232,282	1.4	127,467	104,815	45.1	66,981	46,199	20,782	827	685	142
1985–86	236,700	1.9	128,415	108,285	45.7	66,676	45,927	20,749	923	720	203
1986–87	240,346	1.5	128,506	111,840	46.5	67,093	44,913	22,180	1,062	808	254
1987–88	242,859	1.0	129,467	113,392	46.7	69,230	45,980	23,250	1,063	810	253
1988–89	246,262	1.4	131,098	115,164	46.8	73,065	48,540	24,525	1,100	800	300
1989–90	248,568	0.9	132,284	116,284	46.8	76,676	50,585	26,091	1,093	818	275
1990–91	249,165	0.2	131,557	117,608	47.2	78,255	50,883	27,372	1,185	876	309
1991–92	256,298	2.9	135,263	121,035	47.2	84,517	54,609	29,908	1,242	953	289
1992–93	256,473	0.1	135,368	121,105	47.2	89,425	57,504	31,921	1,346	969	377
1993–94	246,265	-4.0	128,946	117,319	47.6	93,285	59,223	34,062	1,364	980	384
1994–95	233,895	-5.0	121,663	112,232	48.0	93,540	58,931	34,609	1,391	1,011	380
1995–96	226,623	-3.1	116,545	110,078	48.6	93,554	58,400	35,154	1,366	972	394
1996–97	225,934	-0.3	116,023	109,911	48.6	97,204	59,333	37,871	1,336	947	389
1997–98	232,079	2.7	119,379	112,700	48.6	101,652	62,357	39,295	1,290	885	405
1998–99	239,924	3.4	121,741	118,183	49.3	106,830	64,271	42,559	1,216	848	368
1999–2000	256,070	6.7	128,521	127,549	49.8	111,532	67,078	44,454	1,194	812	382
2000–01	263,515	2.9	132,275	131,240	49.8	115,602	68,471	47,131	1,180	783	397
2001–02	278,217	5.6	138,343	139,874	50.3	119,725	70,463	49,262	1,156	746	410
2002–03	293,391	5.5	145,075	148,316	50.6	127,685	75,239	52,446	1,252	820	432
2003–04	307,149	4.7	152,513	154,636	50.3	139,347	80,858	58,489	1,481	960	521
2004–05	311,574	1.4	155,940	155,634	50.0	142,617	82,151	60,466	1,498	901	597
2005–06	318,042	2.1	159,683	158,359	49.8	146,406	83,550	62,856	1,711	1,049	662
2006–07	327,531	3.0	166,350	161,181	49.2	150,211	84,115	66,096	2,029	1,188	841
2007–08	335,254	2.4	170,978	164,276	49.0	155,637	86,258	69,379	2,084	1,250	834
2008–09	348,056	3.8	177,924	170,132	48.9	168,404	91,991	76,413	2,123	1,302	821
2009–10	358,119	2.9	183,272	174,847	48.8	177,748	96,742	81,006	2,249	1,338	911
2010–11	365,133	2.0	187,116	178,017	48.8	187,178	101,440	85,738	2,286	1,357	929
2011–12	367,235	0.6	190,180	177,055	48.2	191,606	103,250	88,356	2,538	1,461	1,077
2012–13	360,823	-1.7	187,789	173,034	48.0	188,625	101,584	87,041	2,836	1,612	1,224
Percent change											
2002–03 to 2007–08	14.3	†	17.9	10.8	†	21.9	14.6	32.3	66.5	52.4	93.1
2007–08 to 2012–13	7.6	†	9.8	5.3	†	21.2	17.8	25.5	36.1	29.0	46.8

†Not applicable.
NOTE: Data are for postsecondary institutions participating in Title IV federal financial aid programs. Includes degrees in business, management, marketing, and related support services and in personal and culinary services. Some data have been revised from previously published figures.

SOURCE: U.S. Department of Education, National Center for Education Statistics, *Earned Degrees Conferred*, 1955–56 through 1963–64; Higher Education General Information Survey (HEGIS), "Degrees and Other Formal Awards Conferred" surveys, 1965–66 through 1985–86; Integrated Postsecondary Education Data System (IPEDS), "Completions Survey" (IPEDS-C:87–99); and IPEDS Fall 2000 through Fall 2013, Completions component. (This table was prepared August 2014.)

Table 325.30. Degrees in communication, journalism, and related programs and in communications technologies conferred by postsecondary institutions, by level of degree and sex of student: 1970–71 through 2012–13

Year	Bachelor's degrees					Master's degrees			Doctor's degrees		
	Total				Females as a percent of total						
	Number	Annual percent change	Males	Females		Total	Males	Females	Total	Males	Females
1	2	3	4	5	6	7	8	9	10	11	12
1970–71	10,802	†	6,989	3,813	35.3	1,856	1,214	642	145	126	19
1971–72	12,340	14.2	7,964	4,376	35.5	2,200	1,443	757	111	96	15
1972–73	14,317	16.0	9,074	5,243	36.6	2,406	1,546	860	139	114	25
1973–74	17,096	19.4	10,536	6,560	38.4	2,640	1,668	972	175	146	29
1974–75	19,248	12.6	11,455	7,793	40.5	2,794	1,618	1,176	165	119	46
1975–76	21,282	10.6	12,458	8,824	41.5	3,126	1,818	1,308	204	154	50
1976–77	23,214	9.1	12,932	10,282	44.3	3,091	1,719	1,372	171	130	41
1977–78	25,400	9.4	13,480	11,920	46.9	3,296	1,673	1,623	191	138	53
1978–79	26,457	4.2	13,266	13,191	49.9	2,882	1,483	1,399	192	138	54
1979–80	28,616	8.2	13,656	14,960	52.3	3,082	1,527	1,555	193	121	72
1980–81	31,282	9.3	14,179	17,103	54.7	3,105	1,448	1,657	182	107	75
1981–82	34,222	9.4	14,917	19,305	56.4	3,327	1,578	1,749	200	136	64
1982–83	38,647	12.9	16,213	22,434	58.0	3,600	1,660	1,940	208	123	85
1983–84	40,203	4.0	16,662	23,541	58.6	3,620	1,578	2,042	216	129	87
1984–85	42,102	4.7	17,233	24,869	59.1	3,657	1,574	2,083	232	141	91
1985–86	43,145	2.5	17,681	25,464	59.0	3,808	1,603	2,205	218	116	102
1986–87	45,521	5.5	18,201	27,320	60.0	3,881	1,584	2,297	275	158	117
1987–88	46,916	3.1	18,672	28,244	60.2	3,916	1,568	2,348	233	133	100
1988–89	48,889	4.2	19,357	29,532	60.4	4,249	1,734	2,515	248	137	111
1989–90	51,572	5.5	20,374	31,198	60.5	4,353	1,705	2,648	272	145	127
1990–91	53,047	2.9	20,806	32,241	60.8	4,327	1,711	2,616	272	150	122
1991–92	55,144	4.0	21,601	33,543	60.8	4,463	1,692	2,771	255	132	123
1992–93	54,907	-0.4	22,154	32,753	59.7	5,179	1,969	3,210	301	146	155
1993–94	52,033	-5.2	21,484	30,549	58.7	5,388	2,088	3,300	345	174	171
1994–95	48,969	-5.9	20,501	28,468	58.1	5,559	2,086	3,473	321	162	159
1995–96	48,173	-1.6	19,868	28,305	58.8	5,561	2,153	3,408	345	190	155
1996–97	47,894	-0.6	19,771	28,123	58.7	5,552	1,989	3,563	300	155	145
1997–98	50,263	4.9	20,103	30,160	60.0	6,097	2,369	3,728	359	171	188
1998–99	52,397	4.2	20,943	31,454	60.0	5,582	2,001	3,581	348	182	166
1999–2000	57,058	8.9	22,152	34,906	61.2	5,525	2,030	3,495	357	168	189
2000–01	59,191	3.7	22,542	36,649	61.9	5,645	1,964	3,681	370	190	180
2001–02	64,036	8.2	23,692	40,344	63.0	5,980	2,169	3,811	383	168	215
2002–03	69,828	9.0	25,338	44,490	63.7	6,495	2,301	4,194	398	179	219
2003–04	73,002	4.5	25,813	47,189	64.6	6,900	2,329	4,571	426	186	240
2004–05	75,238	3.1	26,926	48,312	64.2	7,195	2,535	4,660	468	195	273
2005–06	76,936	2.3	28,142	48,794	63.4	7,745	2,611	5,134	464	207	257
2006–07	78,420	1.9	29,009	49,411	63.0	7,272	2,485	4,787	480	188	292
2007–08	81,048	3.4	30,384	50,664	62.5	7,546	2,580	4,966	496	209	287
2008–09	83,084	2.5	31,207	51,877	62.4	7,517	2,446	5,071	535	225	310
2009–10	86,062	3.6	32,048	54,014	62.8	8,093	2,656	5,437	573	225	348
2010–11	88,089	2.4	33,018	55,071	62.5	8,804	2,819	5,985	578	207	371
2011–12	88,754	0.8	33,525	55,229	62.2	9,502	3,068	6,434	567	242	325
2012–13	89,806	1.2	33,671	56,135	62.5	9,334	3,022	6,312	612	246	366
Percent change											
2002–03 to 2007–08	16.1	†	19.9	13.9	†	16.2	12.1	18.4	24.6	16.8	31.1
2007–08 to 2012–13	10.8	†	10.8	10.8	†	23.7	17.1	27.1	23.4	17.7	27.5

†Not applicable.
NOTE: Data are for postsecondary institutions participating in Title IV federal financial aid programs. Some data have been revised from previously published figures.
SOURCE: U.S. Department of Education, National Center for Education Statistics, Higher Education General Information Survey (HEGIS), "Degrees and Other Formal Awards Conferred" surveys, 1970–71 through 1985–86; Integrated Postsecondary Education Data System (IPEDS), "Completions Survey" (IPEDS-C:87–99); and IPEDS Fall 2000 through Fall 2013, Completions component. (This table was prepared August 2014.)

Table 325.35. Degrees in computer and information sciences conferred by postsecondary institutions, by level of degree and sex of student: 1970–71 through 2012–13

| | Bachelor's degrees | | | | | Master's degrees | | | Doctor's degrees | | |
| | Total | | | | Females as a percent of total | | | | | | |
Year	Number	Annual percent change	Males	Females		Total	Males	Females	Total	Males	Females
1	2	3	4	5	6	7	8	9	10	11	12
1970–71	2,388	†	2,064	324	13.6	1,588	1,424	164	128	125	3
1971–72	3,402	42.5	2,941	461	13.6	1,977	1,752	225	167	155	12
1972–73	4,304	26.5	3,664	640	14.9	2,113	1,888	225	196	181	15
1973–74	4,756	10.5	3,976	780	16.4	2,276	1,983	293	198	189	9
1974–75	5,033	5.8	4,080	953	18.9	2,299	1,961	338	213	199	14
1975–76	5,652	12.3	4,534	1,118	19.8	2,603	2,226	377	244	221	23
1976–77	6,407	13.4	4,876	1,531	23.9	2,798	2,332	466	216	197	19
1977–78	7,201	12.4	5,349	1,852	25.7	3,038	2,471	567	196	181	15
1978–79	8,719	21.1	6,272	2,447	28.1	3,055	2,480	575	236	206	30
1979–80	11,154	27.9	7,782	3,372	30.2	3,647	2,883	764	240	213	27
1980–81	15,121	35.6	10,202	4,919	32.5	4,218	3,247	971	252	227	25
1981–82	20,267	34.0	13,218	7,049	34.8	4,935	3,625	1,310	251	230	21
1982–83	24,565	21.2	15,641	8,924	36.3	5,321	3,813	1,508	262	228	34
1983–84	32,439	32.1	20,416	12,023	37.1	6,190	4,379	1,811	251	225	26
1984–85	39,121	20.6	24,737	14,384	36.8	7,101	5,064	2,037	248	223	25
1985–86	42,337	8.2	27,208	15,129	35.7	8,070	5,658	2,412	344	299	45
1986–87	39,767	-6.1	25,962	13,805	34.7	8,481	5,985	2,496	374	322	52
1987–88	34,651	-12.9	23,414	11,237	32.4	9,197	6,726	2,471	428	380	48
1988–89	30,560	-11.8	21,143	9,417	30.8	9,414	6,775	2,639	551	466	85
1989–90	27,347	-10.5	19,159	8,188	29.9	9,677	6,960	2,717	627	534	93
1990–91	25,159	-8.0	17,771	7,388	29.4	9,324	6,563	2,761	676	584	92
1991–92	24,821	-1.3	17,685	7,136	28.7	9,655	6,980	2,675	772	669	103
1992–93	24,519	-1.2	17,606	6,913	28.2	10,353	7,557	2,796	805	689	116
1993–94	24,527	#	17,528	6,999	28.5	10,568	7,836	2,732	810	685	125
1994–95	24,737	0.9	17,684	7,053	28.5	10,595	7,805	2,790	887	726	161
1995–96	24,506	-0.9	17,757	6,749	27.5	10,579	7,729	2,850	869	743	126
1996–97	25,422	3.7	18,527	6,895	27.1	10,513	7,526	2,987	857	721	136
1997–98	27,829	9.5	20,372	7,457	26.8	11,765	8,343	3,422	858	718	140
1998–99	30,552	9.8	22,289	8,263	27.0	12,843	8,866	3,977	806	656	150
1999–2000	37,788	23.7	27,185	10,603	28.1	14,990	9,978	5,012	779	648	131
2000–01	44,142	16.8	31,923	12,219	27.7	16,911	11,195	5,716	768	632	136
2001–02	50,365	14.1	36,462	13,903	27.6	17,173	11,447	5,726	752	581	171
2002–03	57,433	14.0	41,950	15,483	27.0	19,509	13,267	6,242	816	648	168
2003–04	59,488	3.6	44,585	14,903	25.1	20,143	13,868	6,275	909	709	200
2004–05	54,111	-9.0	42,125	11,986	22.2	18,416	13,136	5,280	1,119	905	214
2005–06	47,480	-12.3	37,705	9,775	20.6	17,055	12,470	4,585	1,416	1,109	307
2006–07	42,170	-11.2	34,342	7,828	18.6	16,232	11,985	4,247	1,595	1,267	328
2007–08	38,476	-8.8	31,694	6,782	17.6	17,087	12,513	4,574	1,698	1,323	375
2008–09	37,992	-1.3	31,213	6,779	17.8	17,907	13,063	4,844	1,580	1,226	354
2009–10	39,593	4.2	32,414	7,179	18.1	17,955	13,019	4,936	1,599	1,250	349
2010–11	43,066	8.8	35,477	7,589	17.6	19,516	14,010	5,506	1,588	1,267	321
2011–12	47,406	10.1	38,796	8,610	18.2	20,925	15,132	5,793	1,698	1,332	366
2012–13	50,962	7.5	41,874	9,088	17.8	22,777	16,538	6,239	1,826	1,473	353
Percent change											
2002–03 to 2007–08	-33.0	†	-24.4	-56.2	†	-12.4	-5.7	-26.7	108.1	104.2	123.2
2007–08 to 2012–13	32.5	†	32.1	34.0	†	33.3	32.2	36.4	7.5	11.3	-5.9

†Not applicable.
#Rounds to zero.
NOTE: Data are for postsecondary institutions participating in Title IV federal financial aid programs. Some data have been revised from previously published figures.

SOURCE: U.S. Department of Education, National Center for Education Statistics, Higher Education General Information Survey (HEGIS), "Degrees and Other Formal Awards Conferred" surveys, 1970–71 through 1985–86; Integrated Postsecondary Education Data System (IPEDS), "Completions Survey" (IPEDS-C:87–99); and IPEDS Fall 2000 through Fall 2013, Completions component. (This table was prepared August 2014.)

Table 325.40. Degrees in education conferred by postsecondary institutions, by level of degree and sex of student: Selected years, 1949–50 through 2012–13

Year	Bachelor's degrees					Master's degrees			Doctor's degrees		
	Total										
	Number	Annual percent change	Males	Females	Females as a percent of total	Total	Males	Females	Total	Males	Females
1	2	3	4	5	6	7	8	9	10	11	12
1949–50	61,472	†	31,398	30,074	48.9	20,069	12,025	8,044	953	797	156
1959–60	89,002	†	25,556	63,446	71.3	33,433	18,057	15,376	1,591	1,279	312
1967–68	133,965	†	31,926	102,039	76.2	63,399	30,672	32,727	4,078	3,250	828
1969–70	163,964	†	40,420	123,544	75.3	78,020	34,832	43,188	5,588	4,479	1,109
1970–71	176,307	7.5	44,896	131,411	74.5	87,666	38,365	49,301	6,041	4,771	1,270
1971–72	190,880	8.3	49,344	141,536	74.1	96,668	41,141	55,527	6,648	5,104	1,544
1972–73	193,984	1.6	51,300	142,684	73.6	103,777	43,298	60,479	6,857	5,191	1,666
1973–74	184,907	-4.7	48,997	135,910	73.5	110,402	44,112	66,290	6,757	4,974	1,783
1974–75	166,758	-9.8	44,463	122,295	73.3	117,841	44,430	73,411	6,975	4,856	2,119
1975–76	154,437	-7.4	42,004	112,433	72.8	126,061	44,831	81,230	7,202	4,826	2,376
1976–77	143,234	-7.3	39,867	103,367	72.2	124,267	42,308	81,959	7,338	4,832	2,506
1977–78	135,821	-5.2	37,410	98,411	72.5	116,916	37,662	79,254	7,018	4,281	2,737
1978–79	125,873	-7.3	33,743	92,130	73.2	109,866	34,410	75,456	7,170	4,174	2,996
1979–80	118,038	-6.2	30,901	87,137	73.8	101,819	30,300	71,519	7,314	4,100	3,214
1980–81	108,074	-8.4	27,039	81,035	75.0	96,713	27,548	69,165	7,279	3,843	3,436
1981–82	100,932	-6.6	24,380	76,552	75.8	91,601	25,339	66,262	6,999	3,612	3,387
1982–83	97,908	-3.0	23,651	74,257	75.8	83,254	22,824	60,430	7,063	3,550	3,513
1983–84	92,310	-5.7	22,200	70,110	76.0	75,700	21,164	54,536	6,914	3,448	3,466
1984–85	88,078	-4.6	21,254	66,824	75.9	74,667	20,539	54,128	6,614	3,174	3,440
1985–86	87,147	-1.1	20,982	66,165	75.9	74,816	20,302	54,514	6,610	3,088	3,522
1986–87	86,788	-0.4	20,705	66,083	76.1	72,619	18,955	53,664	5,905	2,745	3,160
1987–88	90,928	4.8	20,947	69,981	77.0	75,270	18,777	56,493	5,568	2,530	3,038
1988–89	96,740	6.4	21,643	75,097	77.6	79,793	19,616	60,177	5,884	2,522	3,362
1989–90	105,112	8.7	23,007	82,105	78.1	84,890	20,469	64,421	6,503	2,776	3,727
1990–91	110,807	5.4	23,417	87,390	78.9	87,352	20,448	66,904	6,189	2,614	3,575
1991–92	107,836	-2.7	22,655	85,181	79.0	91,225	20,897	70,328	6,423	2,652	3,771
1992–93	107,578	-0.2	23,199	84,379	78.4	94,497	21,857	72,640	6,581	2,712	3,869
1993–94	107,440	-0.1	24,424	83,016	77.3	97,427	22,656	74,771	6,450	2,555	3,895
1994–95	105,929	-1.4	25,619	80,310	75.8	99,835	23,511	76,324	6,475	2,490	3,985
1995–96	105,384	-0.5	26,214	79,170	75.1	104,936	24,955	79,981	6,246	2,404	3,842
1996–97	105,116	-0.3	26,242	78,874	75.0	108,720	25,518	83,202	6,297	2,367	3,930
1997–98	105,833	0.7	26,285	79,548	75.2	113,374	26,814	86,560	6,261	2,334	3,927
1998–99	107,372	1.5	26,321	81,051	75.5	118,226	28,077	90,149	6,471	2,297	4,174
1999–2000	108,034	0.6	26,103	81,931	75.8	123,045	29,081	93,964	6,409	2,295	4,114
2000–01	105,458	-2.4	24,580	80,878	76.7	127,829	29,997	97,832	6,284	2,237	4,047
2001–02	106,295	0.8	24,049	82,246	77.4	135,189	31,907	103,282	6,549	2,211	4,338
2002–03	105,845	-0.4	22,604	83,241	78.6	147,883	34,033	113,850	6,832	2,314	4,518
2003–04	106,278	0.4	22,802	83,476	78.5	162,345	37,843	124,502	7,088	2,403	4,685
2004–05	105,451	-0.8	22,513	82,938	78.7	167,490	38,863	128,627	7,681	2,557	5,124
2005–06	107,238	1.7	22,448	84,790	79.1	174,620	40,700	133,920	7,584	2,664	4,920
2006–07	105,641	-1.5	22,516	83,125	78.7	176,572	40,164	136,408	8,261	2,681	5,580
2007–08	102,582	-2.9	21,828	80,754	78.7	175,880	40,055	135,825	8,491	2,773	5,718
2008–09	101,716	-0.8	21,163	80,553	79.2	178,538	40,312	138,226	9,028	2,956	6,072
2009–10	101,287	-0.4	20,739	80,548	79.5	182,165	41,284	140,881	9,237	3,023	6,214
2010–11	104,008	2.7	21,206	82,802	79.6	185,127	42,043	143,084	9,642	3,070	6,572
2011–12	105,656	1.6	21,714	83,942	79.4	179,047	41,364	137,683	10,118	3,262	6,856
2012–13	104,647	-1.0	21,805	82,842	79.2	164,624	37,804	126,820	10,572	3,418	7,154
Percent change											
2002–03 to 2007–08	-3.1	†	-3.4	-3.0	†	18.9	17.7	19.3	24.3	19.8	26.6
2007–08 to 2012–13	2.0	†	-0.1	2.6	†	-6.4	-5.6	-6.6	24.5	23.3	25.1

†Not applicable.
NOTE: Data are for postsecondary institutions participating in Title IV federal financial aid programs. Some data have been revised from previously published figures.
SOURCE: U.S. Department of Education, National Center for Education Statistics, *Earned Degrees Conferred*, 1949–50 and 1959–60; Higher Education General Information Survey (HEGIS), "Degrees and Other Formal Awards Conferred" surveys, 1967–68 through 1985–86; Integrated Postsecondary Education Data System (IPEDS), "Completions Survey" (IPEDS-C:87–99); and Fall 2000 through Fall 2013, Completions component. (This table was prepared August 2014.)

Table 325.45. Degrees in engineering and engineering technologies conferred by postsecondary institutions, by level of degree and sex of student: Selected years, 1949–50 through 2012–13

Year	Bachelor's degrees					Master's degrees			Doctor's degrees		
	Total										
	Number	Annual percent change	Males	Females	Females as a percent of total	Total	Males	Females	Total	Males	Females
1	2	3	4	5	6	7	8	9	10	11	12
1949–50	52,246	†	52,071	175	0.3	4,496	4,481	15	417	416	1
1959–60	37,679	†	37,537	142	0.4	7,159	7,133	26	786	783	3
1969–70	44,479	†	44,149	330	0.7	15,593	15,421	172	3,681	3,657	24
1970–71	50,182	12.8	49,775	407	0.8	16,947	16,734	213	3,688	3,663	25
1971–72	51,258	2.1	50,726	532	1.0	17,299	17,009	290	3,708	3,685	23
1972–73	51,384	0.2	50,766	618	1.2	16,988	16,694	294	3,513	3,459	54
1973–74	50,412	-1.9	49,611	801	1.6	15,851	15,470	381	3,374	3,318	56
1974–75	47,131	-6.5	46,105	1,026	2.2	15,837	15,426	411	3,181	3,113	68
1975–76	46,676	-1.0	45,184	1,492	3.2	16,800	16,174	626	2,874	2,805	69
1976–77	49,482	6.0	47,238	2,244	4.5	16,659	15,891	768	2,622	2,547	75
1977–78	56,150	13.5	52,353	3,797	6.8	16,887	15,940	947	2,483	2,424	59
1978–79	62,898	12.0	57,603	5,295	8.4	16,012	14,971	1,041	2,545	2,459	86
1979–80	69,387	10.3	62,877	6,510	9.4	16,765	15,535	1,230	2,546	2,447	99
1980–81	75,355	8.6	67,573	7,782	10.3	17,216	15,761	1,455	2,608	2,499	109
1981–82	80,632	7.0	71,305	9,327	11.6	18,475	16,747	1,728	2,676	2,532	144
1982–83	89,811	11.4	78,673	11,138	12.4	19,949	18,038	1,911	2,871	2,742	129
1983–84	95,295	6.1	82,841	12,454	13.1	21,197	18,916	2,281	3,032	2,864	168
1984–85	97,099	1.9	83,991	13,108	13.5	22,124	19,688	2,436	3,269	3,055	214
1985–86	97,122	#	84,050	13,072	13.5	22,146	19,545	2,601	3,456	3,220	236
1986–87	93,560	-3.7	80,543	13,017	13.9	23,101	20,137	2,964	3,854	3,585	269
1987–88	89,406	-4.4	76,886	12,520	14.0	23,839	20,815	3,024	4,237	3,941	296
1988–89	85,982	-3.8	74,020	11,962	13.9	25,066	21,731	3,335	4,572	4,160	412
1989–90	82,480	-4.1	70,859	11,621	14.1	25,294	21,753	3,541	5,030	4,576	454
1990–91	79,751	-3.3	68,482	11,269	14.1	25,450	21,780	3,670	5,330	4,834	496
1991–92	78,036	-2.2	67,086	10,950	14.0	26,373	22,397	3,976	5,499	4,967	532
1992–93	78,619	0.7	67,214	11,405	14.5	29,103	24,721	4,382	5,870	5,300	570
1993–94	78,580	#	66,867	11,713	14.9	30,102	25,394	4,708	5,954	5,288	666
1994–95	78,483	-0.1	66,157	12,326	15.7	29,949	25,028	4,921	6,108	5,378	730
1995–96	77,997	-0.6	65,362	12,635	16.2	28,843	23,840	5,003	6,354	5,559	795
1996–97	75,659	-3.0	62,994	12,665	16.7	27,016	22,047	4,969	6,166	5,408	758
1997–98	74,557	-1.5	61,880	12,677	17.0	27,244	21,800	5,444	5,966	5,230	736
1998–99	72,796	-2.4	59,859	12,937	17.8	26,689	21,348	5,341	5,413	4,643	770
1999–2000	73,323	0.7	59,668	13,655	18.6	26,648	21,047	5,601	5,367	4,539	828
2000–01	72,869	-0.6	59,489	13,380	18.4	27,187	21,341	5,846	5,547	4,630	917
2001–02	74,588	2.4	60,417	14,171	19.0	26,987	21,212	5,775	5,181	4,285	896
2002–03	77,231	3.5	62,821	14,410	18.7	30,583	24,097	6,486	5,252	4,353	899
2003–04	78,079	1.1	63,401	14,678	18.8	35,053	27,561	7,492	5,859	4,821	1,038
2004–05	79,544	1.9	65,033	14,511	18.2	34,988	27,049	7,939	6,467	5,263	1,204
2005–06	81,406	2.3	66,866	14,540	17.9	33,389	25,568	7,821	7,318	5,848	1,470
2006–07	81,854	0.6	68,081	13,773	16.8	31,989	24,746	7,243	7,928	6,285	1,643
2007–08	83,608	2.1	69,540	14,068	16.8	34,430	26,461	7,969	7,977	6,263	1,714
2008–09	84,404	1.0	70,504	13,900	16.5	38,008	29,458	8,550	7,803	6,123	1,680
2009–10	88,735	5.1	73,838	14,897	16.8	39,391	30,554	8,837	7,773	5,986	1,787
2010–11	93,097	4.9	77,080	16,017	17.2	43,179	33,372	9,807	8,425	6,548	1,877
2011–12	98,654	6.0	81,364	17,290	17.5	45,116	34,712	10,404	8,856	6,838	2,018
2012–13	102,984	4.4	84,633	18,351	17.8	45,325	34,494	10,831	9,467	7,305	2,162
Percent change											
2002–03 to 2007–08	8.3	†	10.7	-2.4	†	12.6	9.8	22.9	51.9	43.9	90.7
2007–08 to 2012–13	23.2	†	21.7	30.4	†	31.6	30.4	35.9	18.7	16.6	26.1

†Not applicable.
#Rounds to zero.
NOTE: Data are for postsecondary institutions participating in Title IV federal financial aid programs. Includes degrees in engineering, engineering-related technologies, mechanic and repair technologies, and construction trades for 1969–70 and later years. Degrees in engineering include degrees in all areas of engineering—for example, chemical, civil, electrical, and mechanical engineering—as well as degrees in general engineering. Some data have been revised from previously published figures.

SOURCE: U.S. Department of Education, National Center for Education Statistics, *Earned Degrees Conferred*, 1949–50 and 1959–60; Higher Education General Information Survey (HEGIS), "Degrees and Other Formal Awards Conferred" surveys, 1969–70 through 1985–86; Integrated Postsecondary Education Data System (IPEDS), "Completions Survey" (IPEDS-C:87–99); and IPEDS Fall 2000 through Fall 2013, Completions component. (This table was prepared August 2014.)

Table 325.47. Degrees in chemical, civil, electrical, and mechanical engineering conferred by postsecondary institutions, by level of degree: 1970–71 through 2012–13

Year	Chemical engineering			Civil engineering			Electrical, electronics, and communications engineering			Mechanical engineering		
	Bachelor's	Master's	Doctor's	Bachelor's	Master's	Doctor's	Bachelor's	Master's	Doctor's	Bachelor's	Master's	Doctor's
1	2	3	4	5	6	7	8	9	10	11	12	13
1970–71	3,579	1,100	406	6,526	2,425	446	12,198	4,282	879	8,858	2,237	438
1971–72	3,625	1,154	394	6,803	2,487	415	12,101	4,206	824	8,530	2,282	411
1972–73	3,578	1,051	397	7,390	2,627	397	12,313	3,895	791	8,523	2,141	370
1973–74	3,399	1,044	400	8,017	2,652	368	11,316	3,499	705	7,677	1,843	385
1974–75	3,070	990	346	7,651	2,769	356	10,161	3,469	701	6,890	1,858	340
1975–76	3,140	1,031	308	7,923	2,999	370	9,791	3,774	649	6,800	1,907	305
1976–77	3,524	1,086	291	8,228	2,964	309	9,936	3,788	566	7,703	1,952	283
1977–78	4,569	1,235	259	9,135	2,685	277	11,133	3,740	503	8,875	1,942	279
1978–79	5,568	1,149	304	9,809	2,646	253	12,338	3,591	586	10,107	1,877	271
1979–80	6,320	1,270	284	10,326	2,683	270	13,821	3,836	525	11,808	2,060	281
1980–81	6,527	1,267	300	10,678	2,891	325	14,938	3,901	535	13,329	2,291	276
1981–82	6,740	1,285	311	10,524	2,995	329	16,455	4,462	526	13,922	2,399	333
1982–83	7,185	1,368	319	9,989	3,074	340	18,049	4,531	550	15,675	2,511	299
1983–84	7,475	1,514	330	9,693	3,146	369	19,943	5,078	585	16,629	2,797	319
1984–85	7,146	1,544	418	9,162	3,172	377	21,691	5,153	660	16,794	3,053	409
1985–86	5,877	1,361	446	8,679	2,926	395	23,742	5,534	722	16,194	3,075	426
1986–87	4,991	1,184	497	8,147	2,901	451	24,547	6,183	724	15,450	3,198	528
1987–88	3,917	1,088	579	7,488	2,836	481	23,597	6,688	860	14,900	3,329	596
1988–89	3,663	1,093	602	7,312	2,903	505	21,908	7,028	998	14,843	3,498	633
1989–90	3,430	1,035	562	7,252	2,812	516	20,711	7,225	1,162	14,336	3,424	742
1990–91	3,444	903	611	7,314	2,927	536	19,320	7,095	1,220	13,977	3,516	757
1991–92	3,754	956	590	8,034	3,113	540	17,958	7,360	1,282	14,067	3,653	851
1992–93	4,459	990	595	8,868	3,610	577	17,281	7,870	1,413	14,464	3,982	871
1993–94	5,163	1,032	604	9,479	3,873	651	15,823	7,791	1,470	15,030	4,099	887
1994–95	5,901	1,085	571	9,927	4,077	625	14,929	7,693	1,543	14,794	4,213	890
1995–96	6,319	1,176	670	10,607	3,905	616	13,900	7,103	1,591	14,177	3,881	940
1996–97	6,564	1,131	650	10,437	3,833	640	13,336	6,393	1,512	13,493	3,608	913
1997–98	6,319	1,128	652	9,926	3,795	610	12,995	6,737	1,458	13,071	3,441	933
1998–99	6,038	1,130	575	9,178	3,656	534	12,606	6,708	1,309	12,753	3,268	788
1999–2000	5,807	1,078	590	8,136	3,433	543	12,930	6,926	1,392	12,807	3,273	776
2000–01	5,611	1,083	610	7,588	3,310	571	13,091	6,815	1,417	12,817	3,371	849
2001–02	5,462	973	605	7,665	3,295	574	13,056	6,587	1,235	13,058	3,391	772
2002–03	5,109	1,065	542	7,836	3,596	599	13,627	7,621	1,256	13,693	3,695	747
2003–04	4,742	1,165	623	7,827	3,790	636	14,123	9,511	1,440	14,050	4,420	787
2004–05	4,397	1,183	773	8,186	3,834	713	14,171	9,054	1,566	14,609	4,637	915
2005–06	4,326	1,116	819	9,090	3,768	750	13,966	8,123	1,860	15,850	4,443	1,096
2006–07	4,492	957	835	9,671	3,482	805	13,089	7,777	2,042	16,601	4,294	1,106
2007–08	4,795	933	853	10,455	3,595	752	12,375	8,631	1,996	17,367	4,497	1,109
2008–09	5,036	994	789	10,785	3,794	763	11,620	9,178	1,812	17,352	4,620	1,142
2009–10	5,740	1,043	830	11,335	4,079	717	11,450	9,052	1,869	18,498	4,818	996
2010–11	6,311	1,283	831	12,557	4,860	751	11,575	9,691	2,037	19,171	5,802	1,106
2011–12	7,027	1,389	823	12,808	5,359	787	12,110	9,696	2,119	20,541	5,840	1,213
2012–13	7,529	1,450	835	13,262	5,353	868	12,835	9,485	2,118	21,989	5,871	1,321
Percent change												
2002–03 to 2007–08	-6.1	-12.4	57.4	33.4	#	25.5	-9.2	13.3	58.9	26.8	21.7	48.5
2007–08 to 2012–13	57.0	55.4	-2.1	26.8	48.9	15.4	3.7	9.9	6.1	26.6	30.6	19.1

Rounds to zero.
NOTE: Data are for postsecondary institutions participating in Title IV federal financial aid programs. From 1970–71 through 1981–82, civil engineering includes construction and transportation engineering. From 1991–92, civil engineering includes geotechnical, structural, transportation, and water resources engineering. Degrees in engineering technologies are not included in this table. Some data have been revised from previously published figures.

SOURCE: U.S. Department of Education, National Center for Education Statistics, Higher Education General Information Survey (HEGIS), "Degrees and Other Formal Awards Conferred" surveys, 1970–71 through 1985–86; Integrated Postsecondary Education Data System (IPEDS), "Completions Survey" (IPEDS-C:87–99); and IPEDS Fall 2000 through Fall 2013, Completions component. (This table was prepared September 2014.)

Table 325.50. Degrees in English language and literature/letters conferred by postsecondary institutions, by level of degree and sex of student: Selected years, 1949–50 through 2012–13

	Bachelor's degrees					Master's degrees			Doctor's degrees		
	Total				Females as a percent of total	Total	Males	Females	Total	Males	Females
Year	Number	Annual percent change	Males	Females							
1	2	3	4	5	6	7	8	9	10	11	12
1949–50	17,240	†	8,221	9,019	52.3	2,259	1,320	939	230	181	49
1959–60	20,128	†	7,580	12,548	62.3	2,931	1,458	1,473	397	314	83
1967–68	47,977	†	15,700	32,277	67.3	7,916	3,434	4,482	977	717	260
1969–70	56,410	†	18,650	37,760	66.9	8,517	3,326	5,191	1,213	837	376
1970–71	63,914	13.3	22,005	41,909	65.6	10,441	4,126	6,315	1,554	1,107	447
1971–72	63,707	-0.3	22,580	41,127	64.6	10,412	4,066	6,346	1,734	1,173	561
1972–73	60,607	-4.9	22,022	38,585	63.7	10,035	3,988	6,047	1,817	1,189	628
1973–74	54,190	-10.6	20,082	34,108	62.9	9,573	3,824	5,749	1,755	1,142	613
1974–75	47,062	-13.2	17,689	29,373	62.4	9,178	3,463	5,715	1,595	974	621
1975–76	41,452	-11.9	15,898	25,554	61.6	8,599	3,290	5,309	1,514	895	619
1976–77	37,343	-9.9	14,135	23,208	62.1	7,824	2,907	4,917	1,373	768	605
1977–78	34,799	-6.8	12,972	21,827	62.7	7,444	2,623	4,821	1,272	698	574
1978–79	33,218	-4.5	12,085	21,133	63.6	6,503	2,307	4,196	1,186	639	547
1979–80	32,187	-3.1	11,237	20,950	65.1	6,026	2,181	3,845	1,196	635	561
1980–81	31,922	-0.8	11,082	20,840	65.3	5,742	2,026	3,716	1,040	497	543
1981–82	33,078	3.6	11,300	21,778	65.8	5,593	1,916	3,677	986	467	519
1982–83	31,327	-5.3	10,699	20,628	65.8	4,866	1,653	3,213	877	419	458
1983–84	32,296	3.1	11,007	21,289	65.9	4,814	1,681	3,133	899	413	486
1984–85	32,686	1.2	11,195	21,491	65.7	4,987	1,723	3,264	915	414	501
1985–86	34,083	4.3	11,657	22,426	65.8	5,335	1,811	3,524	895	390	505
1986–87	35,667	4.6	12,133	23,534	66.0	5,298	1,819	3,479	853	367	486
1987–88	38,106	6.8	12,687	25,419	66.7	5,366	1,796	3,570	858	380	478
1988–89	41,786	9.7	13,729	28,057	67.1	5,716	1,930	3,786	929	405	524
1989–90	46,803	12.0	15,437	31,366	67.0	6,317	2,125	4,192	986	444	542
1990–91	51,064	9.1	16,891	34,173	66.9	6,784	2,203	4,581	1,056	469	587
1991–92	54,250	6.2	18,314	35,936	66.2	7,215	2,441	4,774	1,142	484	658
1992–93	55,289	1.9	19,007	36,282	65.6	7,537	2,570	4,967	1,201	495	706
1993–94	53,150	-3.9	18,214	34,936	65.7	7,611	2,620	4,991	1,205	512	693
1994–95	51,170	-3.7	17,581	33,589	65.6	7,612	2,672	4,940	1,393	589	804
1995–96	49,928	-2.4	17,007	32,921	65.9	7,657	2,727	4,930	1,395	535	860
1996–97	48,641	-2.6	16,325	32,316	66.4	7,487	2,650	4,837	1,431	610	821
1997–98	49,016	0.8	16,280	32,736	66.8	7,587	2,568	5,019	1,489	611	878
1998–99	49,877	1.8	16,332	33,545	67.3	7,326	2,452	4,874	1,412	554	858
1999–2000	50,106	0.5	16,124	33,982	67.8	7,022	2,315	4,707	1,470	611	859
2000–01	50,569	0.9	15,997	34,572	68.4	6,763	2,160	4,603	1,330	533	797
2001–02	52,375	3.6	16,457	35,918	68.6	7,097	2,270	4,827	1,291	532	759
2002–03	53,699	2.5	16,738	36,961	68.8	7,428	2,433	4,995	1,246	492	754
2003–04	53,984	0.5	16,792	37,192	68.9	7,956	2,459	5,497	1,207	479	728
2004–05	54,379	0.7	17,154	37,225	68.5	8,468	2,615	5,853	1,212	494	718
2005–06	55,096	1.3	17,316	37,780	68.6	8,845	2,860	5,985	1,254	510	744
2006–07	55,122	#	17,475	37,647	68.3	8,742	2,867	5,875	1,178	478	700
2007–08	55,038	#	17,681	37,357	67.9	9,161	3,027	6,134	1,262	453	809
2008–09	55,465	0.8	17,973	37,492	67.6	9,262	3,000	6,262	1,271	464	807
2009–10	53,229	-4.0	17,050	36,179	68.0	9,202	3,006	6,196	1,334	523	811
2010–11	52,754	-0.9	16,917	35,837	67.9	9,475	3,137	6,338	1,344	529	815
2011–12	53,765	1.9	16,976	36,789	68.4	9,938	3,403	6,535	1,427	548	879
2012–13	52,424	-2.5	16,515	35,909	68.5	9,755	3,215	6,540	1,373	553	820
Percent change											
2002–03 to 2007–08	2.5	†	5.6	1.1	†	23.3	24.4	22.8	1.3	-7.9	7.3
2007–08 to 2012–13	-4.7	†	-6.6	-3.9	†	6.5	6.2	6.6	8.8	22.1	1.4

†Not applicable.
#Rounds to zero.
NOTE: Data are for postsecondary institutions participating in Title IV federal financial aid programs. Some data have been revised from previously published figures.
SOURCE: U.S. Department of Education, National Center for Education Statistics, *Earned Degrees Conferred*, 1949–50 and 1959–60; Higher Education General Information Survey (HEGIS), "Degrees and Other Formal Awards Conferred" surveys, 1967–68 through 1985–86; Integrated Postsecondary Education Data System (IPEDS), "Completions Survey" (IPEDS-C:87–99); and IPEDS Fall 2000 through Fall 2013, Completions component. (This table was prepared August 2014.)

Table 325.55. Degrees in foreign languages and literatures conferred by postsecondary institutions, by level of degree and sex of student: Selected years, 1959–60 through 2012–13

	Bachelor's degrees					Master's degrees			Doctor's degrees		
	Total										
Year	Number	Annual percent change	Males	Females	Females as a percent of total	Total	Males	Females	Total	Males	Females
1	2	3	4	5	6	7	8	9	10	11	12
1959–60	5,462	†	2,090	3,372	61.7	1,125	590	535	229	166	63
1967–68	19,254	†	5,253	14,001	72.7	4,849	2,068	2,781	707	503	204
1969–70	21,109	†	5,613	15,496	73.4	5,137	1,917	3,220	869	579	290
1970–71	20,988	-0.6	5,508	15,480	73.8	5,480	1,961	3,519	1,084	714	370
1971–72	19,890	-5.2	5,196	14,694	73.9	5,283	1,919	3,364	1,134	742	392
1972–73	20,170	1.4	5,119	15,051	74.6	5,068	1,909	3,159	1,347	829	518
1973–74	20,197	0.1	5,063	15,134	74.9	4,851	1,788	3,063	1,248	703	545
1974–75	19,103	-5.4	4,723	14,380	75.3	4,721	1,672	3,049	1,220	665	555
1975–76	17,068	-10.7	4,270	12,798	75.0	4,432	1,581	2,851	1,245	643	602
1976–77	15,496	-9.2	3,965	11,531	74.4	4,056	1,365	2,691	1,103	574	529
1977–78	14,334	-7.5	3,684	10,650	74.3	3,624	1,194	2,430	1,002	490	512
1978–79	13,211	-7.8	3,391	9,820	74.3	3,248	1,092	2,156	960	471	489
1979–80	12,480	-5.5	3,226	9,254	74.2	3,067	1,026	2,041	857	412	445
1980–81	11,638	-6.7	3,013	8,625	74.1	2,934	1,039	1,895	931	460	471
1981–82	11,175	-4.0	2,919	8,256	73.9	2,892	997	1,895	869	407	462
1982–83	11,170	#	3,048	8,122	72.7	2,706	1,001	1,705	790	362	428
1983–84	10,985	-1.7	3,098	7,887	71.8	2,814	984	1,830	779	353	426
1984–85	11,436	4.1	3,186	8,250	72.1	2,708	932	1,776	761	342	419
1985–86	11,550	1.0	3,374	8,176	70.8	2,690	878	1,812	768	338	430
1986–87	11,706	1.4	3,374	8,332	71.2	2,574	847	1,727	769	332	437
1987–88	11,515	-1.6	3,223	8,292	72.0	2,680	931	1,749	725	330	395
1988–89	12,403	7.7	3,432	8,971	72.3	2,837	955	1,882	727	317	410
1989–90	13,133	5.9	3,625	9,508	72.4	3,018	987	2,031	816	348	468
1990–91	13,937	6.1	4,008	9,929	71.2	3,049	1,018	2,031	889	396	493
1991–92	14,634	5.0	4,225	10,409	71.1	3,229	1,074	2,155	984	434	550
1992–93	15,305	4.6	4,435	10,870	71.0	3,513	1,182	2,331	977	417	560
1993–94	15,242	-0.4	4,573	10,669	70.0	3,612	1,199	2,413	1,033	418	615
1994–95	14,558	-4.5	4,496	10,062	69.1	3,439	1,124	2,315	1,081	479	602
1995–96	14,832	1.9	4,514	10,318	69.6	3,443	1,141	2,302	1,020	446	574
1996–97	14,487	-2.3	4,388	10,099	69.7	3,361	1,104	2,257	1,064	450	614
1997–98	15,279	5.5	4,585	10,694	70.0	3,181	1,033	2,148	1,118	473	645
1998–99	15,835	3.6	4,738	11,097	70.1	3,109	976	2,133	1,049	443	606
1999–2000	15,886	0.3	4,616	11,270	70.9	3,037	944	2,093	1,086	446	640
2000–01	16,128	1.5	4,695	11,433	70.9	3,035	969	2,066	1,078	420	658
2001–02	16,258	0.8	4,685	11,573	71.2	3,075	958	2,117	1,003	418	585
2002–03	16,912	4.0	4,996	11,916	70.5	3,049	874	2,175	1,042	424	618
2003–04	17,754	5.0	5,215	12,539	70.6	3,124	957	2,167	1,031	410	621
2004–05	18,386	3.6	5,370	13,016	70.8	3,407	1,056	2,351	1,027	410	617
2005–06	19,410	5.6	5,842	13,568	69.9	3,539	1,049	2,490	1,074	436	638
2006–07	20,275	4.5	6,173	14,102	69.6	3,443	1,058	2,385	1,059	437	622
2007–08	20,977	3.5	6,254	14,723	70.2	3,565	1,128	2,437	1,078	431	647
2008–09	21,169	0.9	6,305	14,864	70.2	3,592	1,211	2,381	1,111	426	685
2009–10	21,507	1.6	6,607	14,900	69.3	3,756	1,254	2,502	1,091	446	645
2010–11	21,705	0.9	6,719	14,986	69.0	3,727	1,256	2,471	1,158	477	681
2011–12	21,756	0.2	6,629	15,127	69.5	3,827	1,280	2,547	1,231	497	734
2012–13	21,673	-0.4	6,847	14,826	68.4	3,708	1,235	2,473	1,304	531	773
Percent change											
2002–03 to 2007–08	24.0	†	25.2	23.6	†	16.9	29.1	12.0	3.5	1.7	4.7
2007–08 to 2012–13	3.3	†	9.5	0.7	†	4.0	9.5	1.5	21.0	23.2	19.5

†Not applicable.
#Rounds to zero.
NOTE: Data are for postsecondary institutions participating in Title IV federal financial aid programs. Some data have been revised from previously published figures.
SOURCE: U.S. Department of Education, National Center for Education Statistics, *Earned*

Degrees Conferred, 1949–50 and 1959–60; Higher Education General Information Survey (HEGIS), "Degrees and Other Formal Awards Conferred" surveys, 1967–68 through 1985–86; Integrated Postsecondary Education Data System (IPEDS), "Completions Survey" (IPEDS-C:87–99); and IPEDS Fall 2000 through Fall 2013, Completions component. (This table was prepared August 2014.)

Table 325.57. Degrees in French, German, Italian, and Spanish language and literature conferred by postsecondary institutions, by level of degree: Selected years, 1949–50 through 2012–13

Year	French			German			Italian			Spanish		
	Bachelor's	Master's	Doctor's	Bachelor's	Master's	Doctor's	Bachelor's	Master's	Doctor's	Bachelor's	Master's	Doctor's
1	2	3	4	5	6	7	8	9	10	11	12	13
1949–50	1,471	299	53	540	121	40	—	—	—	2,122	373	34
1959–60	1,927	316	58	659	126	21	—	—	—	1,610	261	31
1967–68	7,068	1,301	152	2,368	771	117	—	—	—	6,381	1,188	123
1969–70	7,624	1,409	181	2,652	669	118	242	71	14	7,226	1,372	139
1970–71	7,306	1,437	192	2,601	690	144	201	87	10	7,068	1,456	168
1971–72	6,822	1,421	193	2,477	608	167	287	104	19	6,847	1,421	152
1972–73	6,705	1,277	203	2,520	598	176	313	78	27	7,209	1,298	206
1973–74	6,263	1,195	213	2,425	550	149	292	81	19	7,250	1,217	203
1974–75	5,745	1,077	200	2,289	480	147	329	100	13	6,719	1,228	202
1975–76	4,783	914	190	1,983	471	164	342	85	19	5,984	1,080	176
1976–77	4,228	875	177	1,820	394	126	325	89	16	5,359	930	153
1977–78	3,708	692	155	1,647	357	101	301	58	19	4,832	822	113
1978–79	3,558	576	143	1,524	344	106	236	60	14	4,563	720	118
1979–80	3,285	513	128	1,466	309	94	272	49	9	4,331	685	103
1980–81	3,178	460	115	1,286	294	79	205	65	13	3,870	592	131
1981–82	3,054	485	92	1,327	324	76	208	55	14	3,633	568	140
1982–83	2,871	360	106	1,367	281	68	224	45	18	3,349	506	129
1983–84	2,876	418	86	1,292	241	63	206	41	13	3,254	537	102
1984–85	2,991	385	74	1,411	240	58	190	44	9	3,415	505	115
1985–86	3,015	409	86	1,396	249	73	240	42	10	3,385	521	95
1986–87	3,062	421	85	1,366	234	70	219	53	17	3,450	504	104
1987–88	3,082	437	89	1,350	244	71	224	45	7	3,416	553	93
1988–89	3,297	444	83	1,428	263	59	239	45	17	3,748	552	101
1989–90	3,259	478	115	1,437	253	67	247	38	19	4,176	573	108
1990–91	3,355	480	98	1,543	242	58	253	36	21	4,480	609	125
1991–92	3,371	465	112	1,616	273	85	238	55	18	4,768	647	143
1992–93	3,280	513	98	1,572	317	86	274	50	13	5,233	667	145
1993–94	3,094	479	104	1,580	298	61	264	47	24	5,505	691	160
1994–95	2,764	470	118	1,352	278	83	271	69	31	5,602	709	161
1995–96	2,655	446	113	1,290	305	75	232	44	22	5,995	769	151
1996–97	2,468	414	119	1,214	281	80	234	49	18	6,161	677	175
1997–98	2,530	389	104	1,181	209	94	252	60	25	6,595	781	160
1998–99	2,565	365	115	1,237	242	78	257	41	12	6,992	697	153
1999–2000	2,514	343	129	1,125	184	76	237	48	13	7,031	718	175
2000–01	2,371	376	115	1,143	242	73	286	42	11	7,164	716	185
2001–02	2,396	356	89	1,092	208	64	263	46	15	7,243	792	193
2002–03	2,294	348	75	1,097	188	77	307	54	20	7,619	791	190
2003–04	2,362	361	85	1,031	153	30	279	49	31	7,991	833	199
2004–05	2,394	356	80	1,103	180	56	277	70	12	8,304	919	190
2005–06	2,410	395	84	1,106	172	48	321	94	17	8,690	981	192
2006–07	2,462	364	95	1,055	158	56	280	97	20	9,013	982	195
2007–08	2,432	359	102	1,085	173	51	359	88	25	9,278	990	193
2008–09	2,450	386	86	1,058	163	47	341	76	34	9,333	878	218
2009–10	2,488	391	87	1,028	143	46	336	73	23	9,138	962	199
2010–11	2,490	366	81	1,019	156	43	313	83	28	8,920	955	179
2011–12	2,358	341	96	1,001	130	67	332	72	35	8,714	991	189
2012–13	2,281	332	115	931	102	52	289	73	27	8,429	928	205
Percent change												
2002–03 to 2007–08	6.0	3.2	36.0	-1.1	-8.0	-33.8	16.9	63.0	25.0	21.8	25.2	1.6
2007–08 to 2012–13	-6.2	-7.5	12.7	-14.2	-41.0	2.0	-19.5	-17.0	8.0	-9.2	-6.3	6.2

—Not available.
NOTE: Data are for postsecondary institutions participating in Title IV federal financial aid programs. Some data have been revised from previously published figures.
SOURCE: U.S. Department of Education, National Center for Education Statistics, *Earned Degrees Conferred*, 1949–50 and 1959–60; Higher Education General Information Survey (HEGIS), "Degrees and Other Formal Awards Conferred" surveys, 1967–68 through 1985–86; Integrated Postsecondary Education Data System (IPEDS), "Completions Survey" (IPEDS-C:87–99); and IPEDS Fall 2000 through Fall 2013, Completions component. (This table was prepared August 2014.)

Table 325.59. Degrees in Arabic, Chinese, Korean, and Russian language and literature conferred by postsecondary institutions, by level of degree: 1969–70 through 2012–13

Year	Arabic			Chinese			Korean			Russian		
	Bachelor's	Master's	Doctor's	Bachelor's	Master's	Doctor's	Bachelor's	Master's	Doctor's	Bachelor's	Master's	Doctor's
1	2	3	4	5	6	7	8	9	10	11	12	13
1969–70	—	—	—	81	34	0	—	—	—	768	172	24
1970–71	15	6	4	89	22	8	—	—	—	715	110	14
1971–72	10	4	0	103	20	11	—	—	—	658	150	15
1972–73	12	3	1	98	29	13	—	—	—	622	120	27
1973–74	20	5	1	121	37	5	—	—	—	624	100	27
1974–75	13	11	2	141	26	12	—	—	—	598	106	20
1975–76	10	7	2	150	23	6	—	—	—	531	81	13
1976–77	7	15	1	112	32	6	—	—	—	528	66	19
1977–78	8	3	1	116	23	4	—	—	—	442	50	12
1978–79	4	4	5	91	22	12	—	—	—	465	51	9
1979–80	13	2	5	79	33	7	—	—	—	402	60	6
1980–81	6	7	0	73	20	6	—	—	—	409	68	8
1981–82	15	4	4	68	14	10	—	—	—	324	49	7
1982–83	12	4	1	92	15	7	—	—	—	342	33	5
1983–84	6	2	0	115	14	10	—	—	—	340	39	3
1984–85	9	4	0	97	21	3	—	—	—	432	47	6
1985–86	5	4	0	87	23	11	—	—	—	493	33	3
1986–87	8	1	1	110	16	10	—	—	—	502	54	8
1987–88	9	4	0	103	31	9	—	—	—	472	54	8
1988–89	6	2	1	138	27	8	—	—	—	469	55	6
1989–90	4	0	1	144	33	8	—	—	—	549	52	5
1990–91	9	0	1	150	24	9	—	—	—	593	70	6
1991–92	13	0	0	183	36	14	—	—	—	629	68	7
1992–93	8	3	2	129	54	8	—	—	—	612	68	4
1993–94	8	2	0	112	48	18	—	—	—	611	71	3
1994–95	10	1	1	107	63	16	—	—	—	572	66	3
1995–96	8	3	2	136	42	19	—	—	—	494	58	7
1996–97	9	3	0	152	31	15	—	—	—	455	46	9
1997–98	16	2	1	161	21	13	—	—	—	383	49	9
1998–99	13	3	1	178	20	14	—	—	—	398	29	4
1999–2000	6	4	5	183	18	15	—	—	—	340	33	10
2000–01	7	2	3	183	13	7	—	—	—	335	24	7
2001–02	13	2	2	189	16	12	—	—	—	277	34	5
2002–03	13	3	0	190	12	9	5	0	0	271	16	6
2003–04	13	3	1	186	15	5	9	2	1	301	21	3
2004–05	21	5	0	208	21	8	8	0	0	298	18	0
2005–06	26	4	2	241	20	10	17	4	3	279	28	7
2006–07	68	2	0	261	30	2	13	0	0	311	18	4
2007–08	57	8	1	289	35	5	15	4	1	294	20	1
2008–09	85	14	1	384	45	11	24	2	1	325	21	1
2009–10	121	10	6	456	51	12	27	19	1	356	19	1
2010–11	141	5	1	449	51	8	28	10	3	340	11	3
2011–12	143	8	7	496	46	9	38	8	3	392	17	2
2012–13	167	12	1	510	61	12	43	14	0	392	11	5
Percent change												
2002–03 to 2007–08	338.5	166.7	†	52.1	191.7	-44.4	200.0	†	†	8.5	25.0	-83.3
2007–08 to 2012–13	193.0	50.0	#	76.5	74.3	140.0	186.7	250.0	-100.0	33.3	-45.0	400.0

—Not available.
†Not applicable.
#Rounds to zero.
NOTE: Data are for postsecondary institutions participating in Title IV federal financial aid programs. Some data have been revised from previously published figures.

SOURCE: U.S. Department of Education, National Center for Education Statistics, Higher Education General Information Survey (HEGIS), "Degrees and Other Formal Awards Conferred" surveys, 1969–70 through 1985–86; Integrated Postsecondary Education Data System (IPEDS), "Completions Survey" (IPEDS-C:87–99); and IPEDS Fall 2000 through Fall 2013, Completions component. (This table was prepared August 2014.)

Table 325.60. Degrees in the health professions and related programs conferred by postsecondary institutions, by level of degree and sex of student: 1970–71 through 2012–13

	Bachelor's degrees					Master's degrees			Doctor's degrees		
	Total										
Year	Number	Annual percent change	Males	Females	Females as a percent of total	Total	Males	Females	Total	Males	Females
1	2	3	4	5	6	7	8	9	10	11	12
1970–71	25,223	†	5,785	19,438	77.1	5,330	2,165	3,165	15,988	14,863	1,125
1971–72	28,611	13.4	7,005	21,606	75.5	6,811	2,749	4,062	16,538	15,373	1,165
1972–73	33,562	17.3	7,752	25,810	76.9	7,978	3,189	4,789	18,215	16,870	1,345
1973–74	41,421	23.4	9,347	32,074	77.4	9,232	3,444	5,788	20,094	18,287	1,807
1974–75	49,002	18.3	10,844	38,158	77.9	10,277	3,686	6,591	22,191	19,808	2,383
1975–76	53,885	10.0	11,386	42,499	78.9	12,164	3,837	8,327	25,267	21,980	3,287
1976–77	57,222	6.2	11,896	45,326	79.2	12,627	3,865	8,762	24,972	21,022	3,950
1977–78	59,445	3.9	11,600	47,845	80.5	14,027	3,972	10,055	26,516	21,622	4,894
1978–79	62,095	4.5	11,214	50,881	81.9	15,110	4,155	10,955	27,766	22,194	5,572
1979–80	63,848	2.8	11,330	52,518	82.3	15,374	4,060	11,314	28,190	22,157	6,033
1980–81	63,665	-0.3	10,531	53,134	83.5	16,176	4,024	12,152	29,595	22,792	6,803
1981–82	63,660	#	10,110	53,550	84.1	16,212	3,743	12,469	30,096	22,968	7,128
1982–83	65,642	3.1	10,247	55,395	84.4	16,941	4,138	12,803	30,800	22,920	7,880
1983–84	65,305	-0.5	10,068	55,237	84.6	17,351	4,124	13,227	31,655	22,851	8,804
1984–85	65,331	#	9,741	55,590	85.1	17,442	4,046	13,396	31,493	22,045	9,448
1985–86	65,309	#	9,629	55,680	85.3	18,603	4,355	14,248	31,922	22,069	9,853
1986–87	63,963	-2.1	9,137	54,826	85.7	18,442	3,818	14,624	29,500	19,686	9,814
1987–88	61,614	-3.7	8,955	52,659	85.5	18,774	4,004	14,770	30,060	19,853	10,207
1988–89	59,850	-2.9	8,878	50,972	85.2	19,493	4,197	15,296	30,546	19,893	10,653
1989–90	58,983	-1.4	9,075	49,908	84.6	20,406	4,486	15,920	30,101	19,118	10,983
1990–91	59,875	1.5	9,619	50,256	83.9	21,354	4,423	16,931	29,842	18,492	11,350
1991–92	62,779	4.9	10,330	52,449	83.5	23,671	4,794	18,877	31,479	19,362	12,117
1992–93	68,434	9.0	11,605	56,829	83.0	26,190	5,249	20,941	31,089	18,446	12,643
1993–94	75,890	10.9	13,377	62,513	82.4	28,442	5,813	22,629	30,959	17,988	12,971
1994–95	81,596	7.5	14,812	66,784	81.8	31,770	6,718	25,052	32,124	18,463	13,661
1995–96	86,087	5.5	15,942	70,145	81.5	33,920	7,017	26,903	32,678	18,495	14,183
1996–97	87,997	2.2	16,440	71,557	81.3	36,162	7,536	28,626	34,971	19,619	15,352
1997–98	86,843	-1.3	15,700	71,143	81.9	39,567	8,644	30,923	35,369	19,370	15,999
1998–99	84,989	-2.1	15,191	69,798	82.1	40,628	9,152	31,476	35,939	19,673	16,266
1999–2000	80,863	-4.9	13,342	67,521	83.5	42,593	9,500	33,093	37,829	19,984	17,845
2000–01	75,933	-6.1	12,514	63,419	83.5	43,623	9,711	33,912	39,019	20,260	18,759
2001–02	72,887	-4.0	10,869	62,018	85.1	43,560	9,588	33,972	39,435	19,760	19,675
2002–03	71,261	-2.2	10,096	61,165	85.8	42,748	9,280	33,468	39,799	19,493	20,306
2003–04	73,934	3.8	10,017	63,917	86.5	44,939	9,670	35,269	41,861	19,587	22,274
2004–05	80,685	9.1	10,858	69,827	86.5	46,703	9,816	36,887	44,201	19,697	24,504
2005–06	91,973	14.0	12,914	79,059	86.0	51,380	10,630	40,750	45,677	19,640	26,037
2006–07	101,810	10.7	14,325	87,485	85.9	54,531	10,636	43,895	48,943	20,522	28,421
2007–08	111,478	9.5	16,286	95,192	85.4	58,120	11,010	47,110	51,675	21,616	30,059
2008–09	120,420	8.0	17,776	102,644	85.2	62,642	11,848	50,794	54,846	22,678	32,168
2009–10	129,623	7.6	19,309	110,314	85.1	69,112	12,874	56,238	57,750	23,946	33,804
2010–11	143,463	10.7	21,540	121,923	85.0	75,571	14,034	61,537	60,221	25,386	34,835
2011–12	163,675	14.1	24,905	138,770	84.8	84,355	15,675	68,680	62,097	26,074	36,023
2012–13	181,144	10.7	28,214	152,930	84.4	90,931	16,747	74,184	64,195	26,867	37,328
Percent change											
2002–03 to 2007–08	56.4	†	61.3	55.6	†	36.0	18.6	40.8	29.8	10.9	48.0
2007–08 to 2012–13	62.5	†	73.2	60.7	†	56.5	52.1	57.5	24.2	24.3	24.2

†Not applicable.
#Rounds to zero.
NOTE: Data are for postsecondary institutions participating in Title IV federal financial aid programs. Doctor's degrees include medicine (M.D.), dentistry (D.D.S. and D.M.D), and other medical specialty degrees that were formerly classified as first-professional. Some data have been revised from previously published figures.

SOURCE: U.S. Department of Education, National Center for Education Statistics, Higher Education General Information Survey (HEGIS), "Degrees and Other Formal Awards Conferred" surveys, 1970–71 through 1985–86; Integrated Postsecondary Education Data System (IPEDS), "Completions Survey" (IPEDS-C:87–99); and IPEDS Fall 2000 through Fall 2013, Completions component. (This table was prepared August 2014.)

Table 325.65. Degrees in mathematics and statistics conferred by degree-granting institutions, by level of degree and sex of student: Selected years, 1949–50 through 2012–13

	Bachelor's degrees					Master's degrees			Doctor's degrees		
	Total										
Year	Number	Annual percent change	Males	Females	Females as a percent of total	Total	Males	Females	Total	Males	Females
1	2	3	4	5	6	7	8	9	10	11	12
1949–50	6,382	†	4,942	1,440	22.6	974	784	190	160	151	9
1959–60	11,399	†	8,293	3,106	27.2	1,757	1,422	335	303	285	18
1967–68	23,513	†	14,782	8,731	37.1	5,527	4,199	1,328	947	895	52
1969–70	27,442	†	17,177	10,265	37.4	5,636	3,966	1,670	1,236	1,140	96
1970–71	24,801	-9.6	15,369	9,432	38.0	5,191	3,673	1,518	1,199	1,106	93
1971–72	23,713	-4.4	14,454	9,259	39.0	5,198	3,655	1,543	1,128	1,039	89
1972–73	23,067	-2.7	13,796	9,271	40.2	5,028	3,525	1,503	1,068	966	102
1973–74	21,635	-6.2	12,791	8,844	40.9	4,834	3,337	1,497	1,031	931	100
1974–75	18,181	-16.0	10,586	7,595	41.8	4,327	2,905	1,422	975	865	110
1975–76	15,984	-12.1	9,475	6,509	40.7	3,857	2,547	1,310	856	762	94
1976–77	14,196	-11.2	8,303	5,893	41.5	3,695	2,396	1,299	823	714	109
1977–78	12,569	-11.5	7,398	5,171	41.1	3,373	2,228	1,145	805	681	124
1978–79	11,806	-6.1	6,899	4,907	41.6	3,036	1,985	1,051	730	608	122
1979–80	11,378	-3.6	6,562	4,816	42.3	2,860	1,828	1,032	724	624	100
1980–81	11,078	-2.6	6,342	4,736	42.8	2,567	1,692	875	728	614	114
1981–82	11,599	4.7	6,593	5,006	43.2	2,727	1,821	906	681	587	94
1982–83	12,294	6.0	6,888	5,406	44.0	2,810	1,838	972	697	581	116
1983–84	13,087	6.5	7,290	5,797	44.3	2,723	1,773	950	695	569	126
1984–85	15,009	14.7	8,080	6,929	46.2	2,859	1,858	1,001	699	590	109
1985–86	16,122	7.4	8,623	7,499	46.5	3,131	2,028	1,103	742	618	124
1986–87	16,257	0.8	8,673	7,584	46.7	3,283	1,995	1,288	723	598	125
1987–88	15,712	-3.4	8,408	7,304	46.5	3,413	2,052	1,361	750	625	125
1988–89	15,017	-4.4	8,081	6,936	46.2	3,405	2,061	1,344	866	700	166
1989–90	14,276	-4.9	7,674	6,602	46.2	3,624	2,172	1,452	917	754	163
1990–91	14,393	0.8	7,580	6,813	47.3	3,549	2,096	1,453	978	790	188
1991–92	14,468	0.5	7,668	6,800	47.0	3,558	2,151	1,407	1,048	825	223
1992–93	14,384	-0.6	7,566	6,818	47.4	3,644	2,151	1,493	1,138	867	271
1993–94	14,171	-1.5	7,594	6,577	46.4	3,682	2,237	1,445	1,125	880	245
1994–95	13,494	-4.8	7,154	6,340	47.0	3,820	2,289	1,531	1,181	919	262
1995–96	12,713	-5.8	6,847	5,866	46.1	3,651	2,178	1,473	1,158	919	239
1996–97	12,401	-2.5	6,649	5,752	46.4	3,504	2,055	1,449	1,134	861	273
1997–98	11,795	-4.9	6,247	5,548	47.0	3,409	1,985	1,424	1,215	903	312
1998–99	12,011	1.8	6,206	5,805	48.3	3,304	1,912	1,392	1,107	812	295
1999–2000	11,418	-4.9	5,955	5,463	47.8	3,208	1,749	1,459	1,075	803	272
2000–01	11,171	-2.2	5,791	5,380	48.2	3,209	1,857	1,352	997	715	282
2001–02	11,950	7.0	6,333	5,617	47.0	3,350	1,913	1,437	923	658	265
2002–03	12,505	4.6	6,784	5,721	45.7	3,620	1,996	1,624	1,007	734	273
2003–04	13,327	6.6	7,203	6,124	46.0	4,191	2,302	1,889	1,060	762	298
2004–05	14,351	7.7	7,937	6,414	44.7	4,477	2,525	1,952	1,176	841	335
2005–06	14,770	2.9	8,115	6,655	45.1	4,730	2,712	2,018	1,293	911	382
2006–07	14,954	1.2	8,360	6,594	44.1	4,884	2,859	2,025	1,351	949	402
2007–08	15,192	1.6	8,490	6,702	44.1	4,980	2,860	2,120	1,360	938	422
2008–09	15,507	2.1	8,801	6,706	43.2	5,211	3,064	2,147	1,535	1,059	476
2009–10	16,029	3.4	9,087	6,942	43.3	5,639	3,378	2,261	1,596	1,118	478
2010–11	17,182	7.2	9,782	7,400	43.1	5,866	3,459	2,407	1,586	1,132	454
2011–12	18,841	9.7	10,722	8,119	43.1	6,246	3,695	2,551	1,669	1,198	471
2012–13	20,453	8.6	11,602	8,851	43.3	6,957	4,178	2,779	1,823	1,292	531
Percent change											
2002–03 to 2007–08	21.5	†	25.1	17.1	†	37.6	43.3	30.5	35.1	27.8	54.6
2007–08 to 2012–13	34.6	†	36.7	32.1	†	39.7	46.1	31.1	34.0	37.7	25.8

†Not applicable.
NOTE: Data are for postsecondary institutions participating in Title IV federal financial aid programs. Some data have been revised from previously published figures.
SOURCE: U.S. Department of Education, National Center for Education Statistics, *Earned Degrees Conferred*, 1949–50 and 1959–60; Higher Education General Information Survey (HEGIS), "Degrees and Other Formal Awards Conferred" surveys, 1967–68 through 1985–86; Integrated Postsecondary Education Data System (IPEDS), "Completions Survey" (IPEDS-C:87–99); and IPEDS Fall 2000 through Fall 2013, Completions component. (This table was prepared August 2014.)

Table 325.70. Degrees in the physical sciences and science technologies conferred by postsecondary institutions, by level of degree and sex of student: Selected years, 1959–60 through 2012–13

Year	Bachelor's degrees					Master's degrees			Doctor's degrees		
	Total				Females as a percent of total						
	Number	Annual percent change	Males	Females		Total	Males	Females	Total	Males	Females
1	2	3	4	5	6	7	8	9	10	11	12
1959–60	16,007	†	14,013	1,994	12.5	3,376	3,049	327	1,838	1,776	62
1967–68	19,380	†	16,739	2,641	13.6	5,499	4,869	630	3,593	3,405	188
1969–70	21,439	†	18,522	2,917	13.6	5,908	5,069	839	4,271	4,038	233
1970–71	21,410	-0.1	18,457	2,953	13.8	6,336	5,495	841	4,324	4,082	242
1971–72	20,743	-3.1	17,661	3,082	14.9	6,268	5,390	878	4,075	3,805	270
1972–73	20,692	-0.2	17,622	3,070	14.8	6,230	5,388	842	3,961	3,698	263
1973–74	21,170	2.3	17,669	3,501	16.5	6,019	5,157	862	3,558	3,312	246
1974–75	20,770	-1.9	16,986	3,784	18.2	5,782	4,949	833	3,577	3,284	293
1975–76	21,458	3.3	17,349	4,109	19.1	5,428	4,622	806	3,388	3,097	291
1976–77	22,482	4.8	17,985	4,497	20.0	5,281	4,411	870	3,295	2,981	314
1977–78	22,975	2.2	18,083	4,892	21.3	5,507	4,583	924	3,073	2,763	310
1978–79	23,197	1.0	17,976	5,221	22.5	5,418	4,438	980	3,061	2,717	344
1979–80	23,407	0.9	17,861	5,546	23.7	5,167	4,210	957	3,044	2,669	375
1980–81	23,936	2.3	18,052	5,884	24.6	5,246	4,172	1,074	3,105	2,733	372
1981–82	24,045	0.5	17,861	6,184	25.7	5,446	4,274	1,172	3,246	2,804	442
1982–83	23,374	-2.8	16,988	6,386	27.3	5,250	4,131	1,119	3,214	2,767	447
1983–84	23,645	1.2	17,112	6,533	27.6	5,541	4,249	1,292	3,269	2,789	480
1984–85	23,694	0.2	17,065	6,629	28.0	5,752	4,425	1,327	3,349	2,808	541
1985–86	21,711	-8.4	15,750	5,961	27.5	5,860	4,443	1,417	3,521	2,946	575
1986–87	20,060	-7.6	14,365	5,695	28.4	5,586	4,193	1,393	3,629	3,004	625
1987–88	17,797	-11.3	12,385	5,412	30.4	5,696	4,300	1,396	3,758	3,085	673
1988–89	17,179	-3.5	12,071	5,108	29.7	5,691	4,180	1,511	3,795	3,046	749
1989–90	16,056	-6.5	11,026	5,030	31.3	5,410	3,996	1,414	4,116	3,328	788
1990–91	16,334	1.7	11,170	5,164	31.6	5,281	3,823	1,458	4,248	3,417	831
1991–92	16,970	3.9	11,443	5,527	32.6	5,397	3,935	1,462	4,378	3,433	945
1992–93	17,577	3.6	11,853	5,724	32.6	5,392	3,840	1,552	4,372	3,426	946
1993–94	18,474	5.1	12,271	6,203	33.6	5,718	4,069	1,649	4,652	3,657	995
1994–95	19,247	4.2	12,556	6,691	34.8	5,798	4,058	1,740	4,486	3,443	1,043
1995–96	19,716	2.4	12,634	7,082	35.9	5,910	4,031	1,879	4,589	3,543	1,046
1996–97	19,594	-0.6	12,285	7,309	37.3	5,616	3,799	1,817	4,501	3,479	1,022
1997–98	19,454	-0.7	11,999	7,455	38.3	5,411	3,484	1,927	4,592	3,451	1,141
1998–99	18,448	-5.2	11,119	7,329	39.7	5,241	3,454	1,787	4,229	3,206	1,023
1999–2000	18,427	-0.1	11,019	7,408	40.2	4,888	3,167	1,721	4,017	3,002	1,015
2000–01	18,025	-2.2	10,628	7,397	41.0	5,134	3,276	1,858	3,968	2,914	1,054
2001–02	17,890	-0.7	10,349	7,541	42.2	5,082	3,186	1,896	3,824	2,766	1,058
2002–03	18,038	0.8	10,625	7,413	41.1	5,196	3,284	1,912	3,939	2,854	1,085
2003–04	18,131	0.5	10,577	7,554	41.7	5,714	3,470	2,244	3,937	2,855	1,082
2004–05	19,104	5.4	11,065	8,039	42.1	5,823	3,569	2,254	4,248	3,071	1,177
2005–06	20,522	7.4	11,978	8,544	41.6	6,063	3,666	2,397	4,642	3,258	1,384
2006–07	21,291	3.7	12,604	8,687	40.8	6,012	3,675	2,337	5,041	3,454	1,587
2007–08	22,179	4.2	13,143	9,036	40.7	6,061	3,762	2,299	4,994	3,513	1,481
2008–09	22,691	2.3	13,465	9,226	40.7	5,862	3,576	2,286	5,237	3,554	1,683
2009–10	23,381	3.0	13,866	9,515	40.7	6,066	3,654	2,412	5,065	3,406	1,659
2010–11	24,705	5.7	14,778	9,927	40.2	6,386	3,907	2,479	5,295	3,608	1,687
2011–12	26,664	7.9	15,972	10,692	40.1	6,911	4,299	2,612	5,370	3,609	1,761
2012–13	28,050	5.2	17,143	10,907	38.9	7,011	4,375	2,636	5,514	3,646	1,868
Percent change											
2002–03 to 2007–08	23.0	†	23.7	21.9	†	16.6	14.6	20.2	26.8	23.1	36.5
2007–08 to 2012–13	26.5	†	30.4	20.7	†	15.7	16.3	14.7	10.4	3.8	26.1

†Not applicable.
NOTE: Data are for postsecondary institutions participating in Title IV federal financial aid programs. Some data have been revised from previously published figures.
SOURCE: U.S. Department of Education, National Center for Education Statistics, *Earned Degrees Conferred*, 1959–60; Higher Education General Information Survey (HEGIS), "Degrees and Other Formal Awards Conferred" surveys, 1967–68 through 1985–86; Integrated Postsecondary Education Data System (IPEDS), "Completions Survey" (IPEDS-C:87–99); and IPEDS Fall 2000 through Fall 2013, Completions component. (This table was prepared August 2014.)

Table 325.72. Degrees in chemistry, geology and earth science, and physics conferred by postsecondary institutions, by level of degree: 1970–71 through 2012–13

Year	Chemistry			Geology and earth science[1]			Physics[2]		
	Bachelor's	Master's	Doctor's	Bachelor's	Master's	Doctor's	Bachelor's	Master's	Doctor's
1	2	3	4	5	6	7	8	9	10
1970–71	11,061	2,244	2,093	3,312	1,074	408	5,071	2,188	1,482
1971–72	10,588	2,229	1,943	3,766	1,233	433	4,634	2,033	1,344
1972–73	10,124	2,198	1,827	4,117	1,296	430	4,259	1,747	1,338
1973–74	10,430	2,082	1,755	4,526	1,479	416	3,952	1,655	1,115
1974–75	10,541	1,961	1,773	4,566	1,320	433	3,706	1,574	1,080
1975–76	11,015	1,745	1,578	4,677	1,384	445	3,544	1,451	997
1976–77	11,200	1,717	1,522	5,280	1,446	480	3,420	1,319	945
1977–78	11,304	1,832	1,461	5,648	1,633	419	3,330	1,294	873
1978–79	11,499	1,724	1,475	5,753	1,596	414	3,337	1,319	918
1979–80	11,229	1,671	1,500	5,785	1,623	440	3,396	1,192	830
1980–81	11,331	1,616	1,586	6,332	1,702	404	3,441	1,294	866
1981–82	11,058	1,683	1,682	6,650	1,848	452	3,472	1,284	873
1982–83	10,789	1,582	1,691	6,981	1,784	406	3,793	1,369	873
1983–84	10,698	1,632	1,707	7,524	1,747	408	3,907	1,532	953
1984–85	10,472	1,675	1,735	7,194	1,927	401	4,097	1,523	951
1985–86	10,110	1,712	1,878	5,760	2,036	395	4,180	1,501	1,010
1986–87	9,660	1,695	1,932	3,943	1,835	399	4,318	1,543	1,074
1987–88	9,043	1,671	1,944	3,204	1,722	462	4,100	1,675	1,093
1988–89	8,618	1,742	1,974	2,847	1,609	492	4,352	1,736	1,112
1989–90	8,122	1,643	2,135	2,372	1,399	562	4,155	1,831	1,192
1990–91	8,311	1,637	2,196	2,367	1,336	600	4,236	1,725	1,209
1991–92	8,629	1,746	2,233	2,784	1,245	549	4,098	1,834	1,337
1992–93	8,903	1,822	2,216	3,123	1,195	626	4,063	1,777	1,277
1993–94	9,417	1,968	2,298	3,456	1,221	577	4,001	1,945	1,465
1994–95	9,706	2,062	2,211	4,032	1,280	539	3,823	1,817	1,424
1995–96	10,395	2,214	2,228	4,019	1,288	555	3,679	1,678	1,462
1996–97	10,609	2,203	2,202	4,023	1,258	564	3,376	1,496	1,410
1997–98	10,528	2,108	2,291	3,866	1,227	588	3,441	1,371	1,393
1998–99	10,109	2,019	2,175	3,570	1,196	533	3,200	1,326	1,257
1999–2000	9,989	1,857	2,028	3,516	1,186	492	3,342	1,232	1,208
2000–01	9,466	1,952	2,056	3,495	1,220	472	3,418	1,365	1,169
2001–02	9,084	1,823	1,984	3,449	1,263	494	3,627	1,344	1,096
2002–03	9,013	1,777	2,092	3,381	1,323	466	3,900	1,438	1,089
2003–04	9,016	2,009	2,033	3,312	1,389	463	4,118	1,625	1,119
2004–05	9,664	1,879	2,148	3,276	1,420	476	4,182	1,785	1,254
2005–06	10,606	2,044	2,403	3,322	1,476	505	4,541	1,846	1,341
2006–07	10,994	2,097	2,514	3,319	1,437	640	4,843	1,777	1,442
2007–08	11,568	2,194	2,410	3,561	1,350	577	4,862	1,791	1,507
2008–09	11,852	2,085	2,556	3,809	1,352	614	4,824	1,653	1,580
2009–10	12,107	2,123	2,470	4,093	1,447	613	4,984	1,793	1,571
2010–11	12,656	2,272	2,599	4,611	1,568	567	5,199	1,769	1,670
2011–12	13,473	2,435	2,537	5,111	1,807	612	5,531	1,873	1,752
2012–13	13,817	2,396	2,617	5,532	1,845	657	6,082	1,972	1,740
Percent change									
2002–03 to 2007–08	28.3	23.5	15.2	5.3	2.0	23.8	24.7	24.5	38.4
2007–08 to 2012–13	19.4	9.2	8.6	55.3	36.7	13.9	25.1	10.1	15.5

[1]Includes geology/earth science, general; geochemistry; geophysics; paleontology; hydrology; oceanography; and geological and earth sciences, other.
[2]Includes physics, general; atomic/molecular physics; elementary particle physics; nuclear physics; optics; acoustics; theoretical physics; and physics, other.
NOTE: Data are for postsecondary institutions participating in Title IV federal financial aid programs. Some data have been revised from previously published figures.

SOURCE: U.S. Department of Education, National Center for Education Statistics, Higher Education General Information Survey (HEGIS), "Degrees and Other Formal Awards Conferred" surveys, 1970–71 through 1985–86; Integrated Postsecondary Education Data System (IPEDS), "Completions Survey" (IPEDS-C:87–99); and IPEDS Fall 2000 through Fall 2013, Completions component. (This table was prepared August 2014.)

Table 325.80. Degrees in psychology conferred by postsecondary institutions, by level of degree and sex of student: Selected years, 1949–50 through 2012–13

	Bachelor's degrees					Master's degrees			Doctor's degrees		
	Total				Females as a percent of total	Total	Males	Females	Total	Males	Females
Year	Number	Annual percent change	Males	Females							
1	2	3	4	5	6	7	8	9	10	11	12
1949–50	9,569	†	6,055	3,514	36.7	1,316	948	368	283	241	42
1959–60	8,061	†	4,773	3,288	40.8	1,406	981	425	641	544	97
1967–68	23,819	†	13,792	10,027	42.1	3,479	2,321	1,158	1,268	982	286
1969–70	33,679	†	19,077	14,602	43.4	5,158	2,975	2,183	1,962	1,505	457
1970–71	38,187	13.4	21,227	16,960	44.4	5,717	3,395	2,322	2,144	1,629	515
1971–72	43,433	13.7	23,352	20,081	46.2	6,764	3,934	2,830	2,277	1,694	583
1972–73	47,940	10.4	25,117	22,823	47.6	7,619	4,325	3,294	2,550	1,797	753
1973–74	52,139	8.8	25,868	26,271	50.4	8,796	4,983	3,813	2,872	1,987	885
1974–75	51,245	-1.7	24,284	26,961	52.6	9,394	5,035	4,359	2,913	1,979	934
1975–76	50,278	-1.9	22,898	27,380	54.5	10,167	5,136	5,031	3,157	2,115	1,042
1976–77	47,861	-4.8	20,627	27,234	56.9	10,859	5,293	5,566	3,386	2,127	1,259
1977–78	44,879	-6.2	18,422	26,457	59.0	10,282	4,670	5,612	3,164	1,974	1,190
1978–79	42,697	-4.9	16,540	26,157	61.3	10,132	4,405	5,727	3,228	1,895	1,333
1979–80	42,093	-1.4	15,440	26,653	63.3	9,938	4,096	5,842	3,395	1,921	1,474
1980–81	41,068	-2.4	14,332	26,736	65.1	10,223	4,066	6,157	3,576	2,002	1,574
1981–82	41,212	0.4	13,645	27,567	66.9	9,947	3,823	6,124	3,461	1,856	1,605
1982–83	40,460	-1.8	13,131	27,329	67.5	9,981	3,647	6,334	3,602	1,838	1,764
1983–84	39,955	-1.2	12,812	27,143	67.9	9,525	3,400	6,125	3,535	1,774	1,761
1984–85	39,900	-0.1	12,706	27,194	68.2	9,891	3,452	6,439	3,447	1,739	1,708
1985–86	40,628	1.8	12,605	28,023	69.0	9,845	3,347	6,498	3,593	1,724	1,869
1986–87	43,152	6.2	13,395	29,757	69.0	11,000	3,516	7,484	4,062	1,801	2,261
1987–88	45,371	5.1	13,579	31,792	70.1	10,488	3,256	7,232	3,973	1,783	2,190
1988–89	49,083	8.2	14,265	34,818	70.9	11,329	3,465	7,864	4,143	1,773	2,370
1989–90	53,952	9.9	15,336	38,616	71.6	10,730	3,377	7,353	3,811	1,566	2,245
1990–91	58,655	8.7	16,067	42,588	72.6	11,349	3,329	8,020	3,932	1,520	2,412
1991–92	63,683	8.6	17,062	46,621	73.2	11,659	3,335	8,324	3,814	1,490	2,324
1992–93	66,931	5.1	17,942	48,989	73.2	12,518	3,380	9,138	4,100	1,570	2,530
1993–94	69,419	3.7	18,668	50,751	73.1	13,723	3,763	9,960	4,021	1,497	2,524
1994–95	72,233	4.1	19,570	52,663	72.9	15,378	4,210	11,168	4,252	1,562	2,690
1995–96	73,416	1.6	19,836	53,580	73.0	15,152	4,090	11,062	4,141	1,380	2,761
1996–97	74,308	1.2	19,408	54,900	73.9	15,769	4,155	11,614	4,507	1,495	3,012
1997–98	74,107	-0.3	18,976	55,131	74.4	15,142	3,978	11,164	4,541	1,470	3,071
1998–99	73,747	-0.5	18,376	55,371	75.1	15,560	3,959	11,601	4,678	1,528	3,150
1999–2000	74,194	0.6	17,451	56,743	76.5	15,740	3,821	11,919	4,731	1,529	3,202
2000–01	73,645	-0.7	16,585	57,060	77.5	16,539	3,892	12,647	5,091	1,598	3,493
2001–02	76,775	4.3	17,284	59,491	77.5	16,357	3,814	12,543	4,759	1,503	3,256
2002–03	78,650	2.4	17,514	61,136	77.7	17,161	3,839	13,322	4,835	1,483	3,352
2003–04	82,098	4.4	18,193	63,905	77.8	17,898	3,789	14,109	4,827	1,496	3,331
2004–05	85,614	4.3	19,000	66,614	77.8	18,830	3,900	14,930	5,106	1,466	3,640
2005–06	88,134	2.9	19,865	68,269	77.5	19,770	4,079	15,691	4,921	1,347	3,574
2006–07	90,039	2.2	20,343	69,696	77.4	21,037	4,265	16,772	5,153	1,382	3,771
2007–08	92,587	2.8	21,202	71,385	77.1	21,431	4,356	17,075	5,296	1,440	3,856
2008–09	94,273	1.8	21,490	72,783	77.2	23,415	4,789	18,626	5,477	1,478	3,999
2009–10	97,215	3.1	22,262	74,953	77.1	23,763	4,799	18,964	5,540	1,478	4,062
2010–11	100,906	3.8	23,230	77,676	77.0	25,062	5,127	19,935	5,851	1,481	4,370
2011–12	109,099	8.1	25,420	83,679	76.7	27,052	5,482	21,570	5,936	1,525	4,411
2012–13	114,450	4.9	26,816	87,634	76.6	27,846	5,730	22,116	6,323	1,624	4,699
Percent change											
2002–03 to 2007–08	17.7	†	21.1	16.8	†	24.9	13.5	28.2	9.5	-2.9	15.0
2007–08 to 2012–13	23.6	†	26.5	22.8	†	29.9	31.5	29.5	19.4	12.8	21.9

†Not applicable.
NOTE: Data are for postsecondary institutions participating in Title IV federal financial aid programs. Some data have been revised from previously published figures.
SOURCE: U.S. Department of Education, National Center for Education Statistics, *Earned Degrees Conferred*, 1949–50 and 1959–60; Higher Education General Information Survey (HEGIS), "Degrees and Other Formal Awards Conferred" surveys, 1967–68 through 1985–86; Integrated Postsecondary Education Data System (IPEDS), "Completions Survey" (IPEDS-C:87–99); and IPEDS Fall 2000 through Fall 2013, Completions component. (This table was prepared August 2014.)

Table 325.85. Degrees in public administration and social services conferred by postsecondary institutions, by level of degree and sex of student: 1970–71 through 2012–13

Year	Bachelor's degrees					Master's degrees			Doctor's degrees		
	Total		Males	Females	Females as a percent of total	Total	Males	Females	Total	Males	Females
	Number	Annual percent change									
1	2	3	4	5	6	7	8	9	10	11	12
1970–71	5,466	†	1,726	3,740	68.4	7,785	3,893	3,892	174	132	42
1971–72	7,508	37.4	2,588	4,920	65.5	8,756	4,537	4,219	193	150	43
1972–73	10,690	42.4	3,998	6,692	62.6	10,068	5,271	4,797	198	160	38
1973–74	11,966	11.9	4,266	7,700	64.3	11,415	6,028	5,387	201	154	47
1974–75	13,661	14.2	4,630	9,031	66.1	13,617	7,200	6,417	257	192	65
1975–76	15,440	13.0	5,706	9,734	63.0	15,209	7,969	7,240	292	192	100
1976–77	16,136	4.5	5,544	10,592	65.6	17,026	8,810	8,216	292	197	95
1977–78	16,607	2.9	5,096	11,511	69.3	17,337	8,513	8,824	357	237	120
1978–79	17,328	4.3	4,938	12,390	71.5	17,306	8,051	9,255	315	215	100
1979–80	16,644	-3.9	4,451	12,193	73.3	17,560	7,866	9,694	342	216	126
1980–81	16,707	0.4	4,248	12,459	74.6	17,803	7,460	10,343	362	212	150
1981–82	16,495	-1.3	4,176	12,319	74.7	17,416	6,975	10,441	372	205	167
1982–83	14,414	-12.6	3,343	11,071	76.8	16,046	5,961	10,085	347	184	163
1983–84	12,570	-12.8	2,998	9,572	76.1	15,060	5,634	9,426	420	230	190
1984–85	11,754	-6.5	2,829	8,925	75.9	15,575	5,573	10,002	431	213	218
1985–86	11,887	1.1	2,966	8,921	75.0	15,692	5,594	10,098	382	171	211
1986–87	12,328	3.7	2,993	9,335	75.7	16,432	5,673	10,759	398	216	182
1987–88	12,385	0.5	2,923	9,462	76.4	16,424	5,631	10,793	470	238	232
1988–89	13,162	6.3	3,214	9,948	75.6	17,020	5,615	11,405	428	210	218
1989–90	13,908	5.7	3,334	10,574	76.0	17,399	5,634	11,765	508	235	273
1990–91	14,350	3.2	3,215	11,135	77.6	17,905	5,679	12,226	430	190	240
1991–92	15,987	11.4	3,479	12,508	78.2	19,243	5,769	13,474	432	204	228
1992–93	16,775	4.9	3,801	12,974	77.3	20,634	6,105	14,529	459	215	244
1993–94	17,815	6.2	3,919	13,896	78.0	21,833	6,406	15,427	519	238	281
1994–95	18,586	4.3	3,935	14,651	78.8	23,501	6,870	16,631	556	274	282
1995–96	19,849	6.8	4,205	15,644	78.8	24,229	6,927	17,302	499	220	279
1996–97	20,649	4.0	4,177	16,472	79.8	24,781	6,957	17,824	518	243	275
1997–98	20,408	-1.2	3,881	16,527	81.0	25,144	7,025	18,119	499	223	276
1998–99	20,323	-0.4	3,799	16,524	81.3	25,038	6,621	18,417	534	240	294
1999–2000	20,185	-0.7	3,816	16,369	81.1	25,594	6,808	18,786	537	227	310
2000–01	19,447	-3.7	3,670	15,777	81.1	25,268	6,544	18,724	574	263	311
2001–02	19,392	-0.3	3,706	15,686	80.9	25,448	6,505	18,943	571	250	321
2002–03	19,900	2.6	3,726	16,174	81.3	25,903	6,391	19,512	599	265	334
2003–04	20,552	3.3	3,793	16,759	81.5	28,250	7,001	21,249	649	275	374
2004–05	21,769	5.9	4,209	17,560	80.7	29,552	7,370	22,182	673	272	401
2005–06	21,986	1.0	4,126	17,860	81.2	30,510	7,572	22,938	704	285	419
2006–07	23,147	5.3	4,354	18,793	81.2	31,131	7,758	23,373	726	253	473
2007–08	23,493	1.5	4,202	19,291	82.1	33,029	8,140	24,889	760	269	491
2008–09	23,852	1.5	4,373	19,479	81.7	33,934	8,346	25,588	812	306	506
2009–10	25,421	6.6	4,578	20,843	82.0	35,740	8,868	26,872	838	323	515
2010–11	26,799	5.4	4,913	21,886	81.7	38,614	9,791	28,823	851	327	524
2011–12	29,695	10.8	5,386	24,309	81.9	41,737	10,494	31,243	890	343	547
2012–13	31,950	7.6	5,664	26,286	82.3	43,590	10,862	32,728	979	351	628
Percent change											
2002–03 to 2007–08	18.1	†	12.8	19.3	†	27.5	27.4	27.6	26.9	1.5	47.0
2007–08 to 2012–13	36.0	†	34.8	36.3	†	32.0	33.4	31.5	28.8	30.5	27.9

†Not applicable.
NOTE: Data are for postsecondary institutions participating in Title IV federal financial aid programs. Some data have been revised from previously published figures.
SOURCE: U.S. Department of Education, National Center for Education Statistics, Higher Education General Information Survey (HEGIS), "Degrees and Other Formal Awards Conferred" surveys, 1970–71 through 1985–86; Integrated Postsecondary Education Data System (IPEDS), "Completions Survey" (IPEDS-C:87–99); and IPEDS Fall 2000 through Fall 2013, Completions component. (This table was prepared August 2014.)

Table 325.90. Degrees in the social sciences and history conferred by postsecondary institutions, by level of degree and sex of student: 1970–71 through 2012–13

	Bachelor's degrees					Master's degrees			Doctor's degrees		
	Total										
Year	Number	Annual percent change	Males	Females	Females as a percent of total	Total	Males	Females	Total	Males	Females
1	2	3	4	5	6	7	8	9	10	11	12
1970–71	155,324	†	98,173	57,151	36.8	16,539	11,833	4,706	3,660	3,153	507
1971–72	158,060	1.8	100,895	57,165	36.2	17,445	12,540	4,905	4,081	3,483	598
1972–73	155,970	-1.3	99,735	56,235	36.1	17,477	12,605	4,872	4,234	3,573	661
1973–74	150,320	-3.6	95,650	54,670	36.4	17,293	12,321	4,972	4,124	3,383	741
1974–75	135,190	-10.1	84,826	50,364	37.3	16,977	11,875	5,102	4,212	3,334	878
1975–76	126,396	-6.5	78,691	47,705	37.7	15,953	10,918	5,035	4,157	3,262	895
1976–77	117,040	-7.4	71,128	45,912	39.2	15,533	10,413	5,120	3,802	2,957	845
1977–78	112,952	-3.5	67,217	45,735	40.5	14,718	9,845	4,873	3,594	2,722	872
1978–79	108,059	-4.3	62,852	45,207	41.8	12,963	8,395	4,568	3,371	2,501	870
1979–80	103,662	-4.1	58,511	45,151	43.6	12,176	7,794	4,382	3,230	2,357	873
1980–81	100,513	-3.0	56,131	44,382	44.2	11,945	7,457	4,488	3,122	2,274	848
1981–82	99,705	-0.8	55,196	44,509	44.6	12,002	7,468	4,534	3,061	2,237	824
1982–83	95,228	-4.5	52,771	42,457	44.6	11,205	6,974	4,231	2,931	2,042	889
1983–84	93,323	-2.0	52,154	41,169	44.1	10,577	6,551	4,026	2,911	2,030	881
1984–85	91,570	-1.9	51,226	40,344	44.1	10,503	6,475	4,028	2,851	1,933	918
1985–86	93,840	2.5	52,724	41,116	43.8	10,564	6,419	4,145	2,955	1,970	985
1986–87	96,342	2.7	53,949	42,393	44.0	10,506	6,373	4,133	2,916	2,026	890
1987–88	100,460	4.3	56,377	44,083	43.9	10,412	6,310	4,102	2,781	1,849	932
1988–89	108,151	7.7	60,121	48,030	44.4	11,023	6,599	4,424	2,885	1,949	936
1989–90	118,083	9.2	65,887	52,196	44.2	11,634	6,898	4,736	3,010	2,019	991
1990–91	125,107	5.9	68,701	56,406	45.1	12,233	7,016	5,217	3,012	1,956	1,056
1991–92	133,974	7.1	73,001	60,973	45.5	12,702	7,237	5,465	3,218	2,126	1,092
1992–93	135,703	1.3	73,589	62,114	45.8	13,471	7,671	5,800	3,460	2,203	1,257
1993–94	133,680	-1.5	72,006	61,674	46.1	14,561	8,152	6,409	3,627	2,317	1,310
1994–95	128,154	-4.1	68,139	60,015	46.8	14,845	8,207	6,638	3,725	2,319	1,406
1995–96	126,479	-1.3	65,872	60,607	47.9	15,012	8,093	6,919	3,760	2,339	1,421
1996–97	124,891	-1.3	64,115	60,776	48.7	14,787	7,830	6,957	3,989	2,479	1,510
1997–98	125,040	0.1	63,537	61,503	49.2	14,938	7,960	6,978	4,127	2,445	1,682
1998–99	124,815	-0.2	61,843	62,972	50.5	14,396	7,440	6,956	3,873	2,290	1,583
1999–2000	127,101	1.8	62,062	65,039	51.2	14,066	7,024	7,042	4,095	2,407	1,688
2000–01	128,036	0.7	61,749	66,287	51.8	13,791	6,816	6,975	3,930	2,302	1,628
2001–02	132,874	3.8	64,170	68,704	51.7	14,112	6,941	7,171	3,902	2,219	1,683
2002–03	143,256	7.8	69,517	73,739	51.5	14,630	7,202	7,428	3,850	2,196	1,654
2003–04	150,357	5.0	73,834	76,523	50.9	16,110	7,810	8,300	3,811	2,188	1,623
2004–05	156,892	4.3	77,702	79,190	50.5	16,952	8,256	8,696	3,819	2,184	1,635
2005–06	161,485	2.9	80,799	80,686	50.0	17,369	8,415	8,954	3,914	2,218	1,696
2006–07	164,183	1.7	82,417	81,766	49.8	17,665	8,577	9,088	3,844	2,110	1,734
2007–08	167,363	1.9	84,868	82,495	49.3	18,495	9,349	9,146	4,059	2,194	1,865
2008–09	168,517	0.7	85,202	83,315	49.4	19,241	9,605	9,636	4,234	2,353	1,881
2009–10	172,782	2.5	87,404	85,378	49.4	20,234	9,967	10,267	4,238	2,292	1,946
2010–11	177,169	2.5	89,809	87,360	49.3	21,085	10,578	10,507	4,390	2,331	2,059
2011–12	178,534	0.8	90,628	87,906	49.2	21,891	10,987	10,904	4,597	2,464	2,133
2012–13	177,778	-0.4	90,148	87,630	49.3	21,585	10,832	10,753	4,619	2,470	2,149
Percent change											
2002–03 to 2007–08	16.8	†	22.1	11.9	†	26.4	29.8	23.1	5.4	-0.1	12.8
2007–08 to 2012–13	6.2	†	6.2	6.2	†	16.7	15.9	17.6	13.8	12.6	15.2

†Not applicable.
NOTE: Data are for postsecondary institutions participating in Title IV federal financial aid programs. Some data have been revised from previously published figures.
SOURCE: U.S. Department of Education, National Center for Education Statistics, Higher Education General Information Survey (HEGIS), "Degrees and Other Formal Awards Conferred" surveys, 1970–71 through 1985–86; Integrated Postsecondary Education Data System (IPEDS), "Completions Survey" (IPEDS-C:87–99); and IPEDS Fall 2000 through Fall 2013, Completions component. (This table was prepared August 2014.)

Table 325.92. Degrees in economics, history, political science and government, and sociology conferred by postsecondary institutions, by level of degree: Selected years, 1949–50 through 2012–13

Year	Economics			History			Political science and government			Sociology		
	Bachelor's	Master's	Doctor's	Bachelor's	Master's	Doctor's	Bachelor's	Master's	Doctor's	Bachelor's	Master's	Doctor's
1	2	3	4	5	6	7	8	9	10	11	12	13
1949–50	14,568	921	200	13,542	1,801	275	6,336	710	127	7,870	552	98
1951–52	8,593	695	239	10,187	1,445	317	4,911	525	147	6,648	517	141
1953–54	6,719	609	245	9,363	1,220	355	5,314	534	153	5,692	440	184
1955–56	6,555	581	232	10,510	1,114	259	5,633	509	203	5,878	402	170
1957–58	7,457	669	239	12,840	1,397	297	6,116	665	170	6,568	397	150
1959–60	7,453	708	237	14,737	1,794	342	6,596	722	201	7,147	440	161
1961–62	8,366	853	268	17,340	2,163	343	8,326	839	214	8,120	578	173
1963–64	10,583	1,104	385	23,668	2,705	507	12,126	1,163	263	10,943	646	198
1965–66	11,555	1,522	458	28,612	3,883	599	15,242	1,429	336	15,038	981	244
1967–68	15,193	1,916	600	35,291	4,845	688	20,387	1,937	457	21,710	1,193	367
1969–70	17,197	1,988	794	43,386	5,049	1,038	25,713	2,105	525	30,436	1,813	534
1970–71	15,758	1,995	721	44,663	5,157	991	27,482	2,318	700	33,263	1,808	574
1971–72	15,231	2,224	794	43,695	5,217	1,133	28,135	2,451	758	35,216	1,944	636
1972–73	14,770	2,225	845	40,943	5,030	1,140	30,100	2,398	747	35,436	1,923	583
1973–74	14,285	2,141	788	37,049	4,533	1,114	30,744	2,448	766	35,491	2,196	632
1974–75	14,046	2,127	815	31,470	4,226	1,117	29,126	2,333	680	31,488	2,112	693
1975–76	14,741	2,087	763	28,400	3,658	1,014	28,302	2,191	723	27,634	2,009	729
1976–77	15,296	2,158	758	25,433	3,393	921	26,411	2,222	641	24,713	1,830	714
1977–78	15,661	1,995	706	23,004	3,033	813	26,069	2,069	636	22,750	1,611	599
1978–79	16,409	1,955	712	21,019	2,536	756	25,628	2,037	563	20,285	1,415	612
1979–80	17,863	1,821	677	19,301	2,367	712	25,457	1,938	535	18,881	1,341	583
1980–81	18,753	1,911	727	18,301	2,237	643	24,977	1,875	484	17,272	1,240	610
1981–82	19,876	1,964	677	17,146	2,210	636	25,658	1,954	513	16,042	1,145	558
1982–83	20,517	1,972	734	16,467	2,041	575	25,791	1,829	435	14,105	1,112	522
1983–84	20,719	1,891	729	16,643	1,940	561	25,719	1,769	457	13,145	1,008	520
1984–85	20,711	1,992	749	16,049	1,921	468	25,834	1,500	441	11,968	1,022	480
1985–86	21,602	1,937	789	16,415	1,961	497	26,439	1,704	439	12,271	965	504
1986–87	22,378	1,855	750	16,997	2,021	534	26,817	1,618	435	12,239	950	451
1987–88	22,911	1,847	770	18,207	2,093	517	27,207	1,579	391	13,024	984	452
1988–89	23,454	1,886	827	20,159	2,121	487	30,450	1,598	452	14,435	1,135	451
1989–90	23,923	1,950	806	22,476	2,369	570	33,560	1,580	480	16,035	1,198	432
1990–91	23,488	1,951	802	24,541	2,591	606	35,737	1,772	468	17,550	1,260	465
1991–92	23,423	2,106	866	26,966	2,754	644	37,805	1,908	535	19,568	1,347	501
1992–93	21,321	2,292	879	27,774	2,952	690	37,931	1,943	529	20,896	1,521	536
1993–94	19,496	2,521	869	27,503	3,009	752	36,097	2,147	616	22,368	1,639	530
1994–95	17,673	2,400	910	26,598	3,091	816	33,013	2,019	637	22,886	1,748	546
1995–96	16,674	2,533	916	26,005	2,898	805	30,775	2,024	634	24,071	1,772	527
1996–97	16,539	2,433	968	25,214	2,901	873	28,969	1,909	686	24,672	1,731	591
1997–98	17,074	2,435	928	25,726	2,895	937	28,044	1,957	705	24,806	1,737	596
1998–99	17,577	2,332	819	24,742	2,618	931	27,476	1,667	694	24,979	1,940	521
1999–2000	18,441	2,168	851	25,247	2,573	984	27,635	1,627	693	25,598	1,996	595
2000–01	19,437	2,139	851	25,090	2,365	931	27,792	1,596	688	25,268	1,845	546
2001–02	20,927	2,330	826	26,001	2,420	924	29,354	1,641	625	25,202	1,928	534
2002–03	23,007	2,582	836	27,757	2,521	861	33,205	1,664	671	26,095	1,897	591
2003–04	24,069	2,824	849	29,808	2,522	855	35,581	1,869	618	26,939	2,009	558
2004–05	24,217	3,092	973	31,398	2,893	819	38,107	1,983	636	28,473	1,499	527
2005–06	23,807	2,941	930	33,153	2,992	852	39,409	2,054	649	28,467	1,547	562
2006–07	23,916	2,962	941	34,446	3,144	807	39,899	2,102	614	28,960	1,545	569
2007–08	25,278	3,187	1,025	34,441	3,403	860	40,259	2,156	639	28,815	1,560	585
2008–09	26,301	3,233	1,015	34,713	3,543	918	39,202	2,171	709	28,735	1,580	628
2009–10	27,623	3,358	983	35,191	3,858	888	39,462	2,252	745	28,650	1,428	603
2010–11	28,517	3,731	1,018	35,008	4,003	908	40,133	2,488	722	29,281	1,559	656
2011–12	27,994	3,890	1,130	35,122	4,155	969	39,792	2,510	746	30,136	1,696	626
2012–13	28,455	3,872	1,076	34,191	4,102	1,003	38,467	2,332	830	30,528	1,603	615
Percent change												
2002–03 to 2007–08	9.9	23.4	22.6	24.1	35.0	-0.1	21.2	29.6	-4.8	10.4	-17.8	-1.0
2007–08 to 2012–13	12.6	21.5	5.0	-0.7	20.5	16.6	-4.5	8.2	29.9	5.9	2.8	5.1

NOTE: Data are for postsecondary institutions participating in Title IV federal financial aid programs. Some data have been revised from previously published figures.
SOURCE: U.S. Department of Education, National Center for Education Statistics, *Earned Degrees Conferred*, 1949–50 through 1963–64; Higher Education General Information Survey (HEGIS), "Degrees and Other Formal Awards Conferred" surveys, 1965–66 through 1985–86; Integrated Postsecondary Education Data System (IPEDS), "Completions Survey" (IPEDS-C:87–99); and IPEDS Fall 2000 through Fall 2013, Completions component. (This table was prepared August 2014.)

Table 325.95. Degrees in visual and performing arts conferred by postsecondary institutions, by level of degree and sex of student: 1970–71 through 2012–13

Year	Bachelor's degrees					Master's degrees			Doctor's degrees		
	Total				Females as a percent of total	Total	Males	Females	Total	Males	Females
	Number	Annual percent change	Males	Females							
1	2	3	4	5	6	7	8	9	10	11	12
1970–71	30,394	†	12,256	18,138	59.7	6,675	3,510	3,165	621	483	138
1971–72	33,831	11.3	13,580	20,251	59.9	7,537	4,049	3,488	572	428	144
1972–73	36,017	6.5	14,267	21,750	60.4	7,254	4,005	3,249	616	449	167
1973–74	39,730	10.3	15,821	23,909	60.2	8,001	4,325	3,676	585	440	145
1974–75	40,782	2.6	15,532	25,250	61.9	8,362	4,448	3,914	649	446	203
1975–76	42,138	3.3	16,491	25,647	60.9	8,817	4,507	4,310	620	447	173
1976–77	41,793	-0.8	16,166	25,627	61.3	8,636	4,211	4,425	662	447	215
1977–78	40,951	2.0	15,572	25,379	62.0	9,036	4,327	4,709	708	448	260
1978–79	40,969	#	15,380	25,589	62.5	8,524	3,933	4,591	700	454	246
1979–80	40,892	-0.2	15,065	25,827	63.2	8,708	4,067	4,641	655	413	242
1980–81	40,479	-1.0	14,798	25,681	63.4	8,629	4,056	4,573	654	396	258
1981–82	40,422	-0.1	14,819	25,603	63.3	8,746	3,866	4,880	670	380	290
1982–83	39,804	-1.5	14,695	25,109	63.1	8,763	4,013	4,750	692	404	288
1983–84	40,131	0.8	15,089	25,042	62.4	8,526	3,897	4,629	730	406	324
1984–85	38,285	-4.6	14,518	23,767	62.1	8,720	3,896	4,824	696	407	289
1985–86	37,241	-2.7	14,236	23,005	61.8	8,420	3,775	4,645	722	396	326
1986–87	36,873	-1.0	13,980	22,893	62.1	8,508	3,756	4,752	793	447	346
1987–88	37,150	0.8	14,225	22,925	61.7	7,939	3,442	4,497	727	424	303
1988–89	38,420	3.4	14,698	23,722	61.7	8,267	3,611	4,656	753	446	307
1989–90	39,934	3.9	15,189	24,745	62.0	8,481	3,706	4,775	849	472	377
1990–91	42,186	5.6	15,761	26,425	62.6	8,657	3,830	4,827	838	466	372
1991–92	46,522	10.3	17,616	28,906	62.1	9,353	4,078	5,275	906	504	402
1992–93	47,761	2.7	18,610	29,151	61.0	9,440	4,099	5,341	882	478	404
1993–94	49,053	2.7	19,538	29,515	60.2	9,925	4,229	5,696	1,054	585	469
1994–95	48,690	-0.7	19,781	28,909	59.4	10,277	4,374	5,903	1,080	545	535
1995–96	49,296	1.2	20,126	29,170	59.2	10,280	4,361	5,919	1,067	524	543
1996–97	50,083	1.6	20,729	29,354	58.6	10,627	4,470	6,157	1,060	525	535
1997–98	52,077	4.0	21,483	30,594	58.7	11,145	4,596	6,549	1,163	566	597
1998–99	54,446	4.5	22,270	32,176	59.1	10,762	4,544	6,218	1,117	567	550
1999–2000	58,791	8.0	24,003	34,788	59.2	10,918	4,672	6,246	1,127	537	590
2000–01	61,148	4.0	24,967	36,181	59.2	11,404	4,788	6,616	1,167	568	599
2001–02	66,773	9.2	27,130	39,643	59.4	11,595	4,912	6,683	1,114	490	624
2002–03	71,482	7.1	27,922	43,560	60.9	11,982	4,975	7,007	1,293	613	680
2003–04	77,181	8.0	30,037	47,144	61.1	12,906	5,531	7,375	1,282	572	710
2004–05	80,955	4.9	31,355	49,600	61.3	13,183	5,646	7,537	1,278	594	684
2005–06	83,297	2.9	32,117	51,180	61.4	13,530	5,801	7,729	1,383	639	744
2006–07	85,186	2.3	32,729	52,457	61.6	13,767	5,910	7,857	1,364	625	739
2007–08	87,703	3.0	33,862	53,841	61.4	14,164	5,998	8,166	1,453	675	778
2008–09	89,143	1.6	35,055	54,088	60.7	14,918	6,325	8,593	1,569	726	843
2009–10	91,798	3.0	35,768	56,030	61.0	15,562	6,531	9,031	1,599	700	899
2010–11	93,939	2.3	36,342	57,597	61.3	16,277	6,881	9,396	1,646	770	876
2011–12	95,806	2.0	37,164	58,642	61.2	17,307	7,320	9,987	1,728	790	938
2012–13	97,796	2.1	38,061	59,735	61.1	17,869	7,612	10,257	1,814	850	964
Percent change											
2002–03 to 2007–08	22.7	†	21.3	23.6	†	18.2	20.6	16.5	12.4	10.1	14.4
2007–08 to 2012–13	11.5	†	12.4	10.9	†	26.2	26.9	25.6	24.8	25.9	23.9

†Not applicable.
#Rounds to zero.
NOTE: Data are for postsecondary institutions participating in Title IV federal financial aid programs. Some data have been revised from previously published figures.

SOURCE: U.S. Department of Education, National Center for Education Statistics, Higher Education General Information Survey (HEGIS), "Degrees and Other Formal Awards Conferred" surveys, 1970–71 through 1985–86; Integrated Postsecondary Education Data System (IPEDS), "Completions Survey" (IPEDS-C:87–99); and IPEDS Fall 2000 through Fall 2013, Completions component. (This table was prepared August 2014.)

Table 326.10. Graduation rate from first institution attended for first-time, full-time bachelor's degree-seeking students at 4-year postsecondary institutions, by race/ethnicity, time to completion, sex, control of institution, and acceptance rate: Selected cohort entry years, 1996 through 2007

Time to completion, sex, control of institution, acceptance rate, and cohort entry year	Total	White	Black	Hispanic	Asian/Pacific Islander			American Indian/ Alaska Native	Two or more races	Nonresident alien
					Total	Asian	Pacific Islander			
1	2	3	4	5	6	7	8	9	10	11
Graduating within 4 years after start, males and females										
All 4-year institutions										
1996 starting cohort	33.7	36.3	19.5	22.8	37.5	—	—	18.8	—	41.7
2000 starting cohort	36.1	38.9	21.3	25.9	41.0	—	—	21.0	—	41.9
2002 starting cohort	36.4	39.3	20.4	26.4	42.8	—	—	20.5	—	38.7
2003 starting cohort	37.0	40.2	20.2	26.7	43.9	—	—	20.6	—	39.4
2004 starting cohort	38.0	41.3	20.5	27.9	45.0	—	—	21.8	—	43.7
2005 starting cohort	38.3	41.8	20.2	28.2	45.1	45.5	22.2	21.8	44.1	44.0
2006 starting cohort	39.0	42.6	20.5	29.2	45.8	46.3	24.2	21.9	46.5	44.1
2007 starting cohort	39.4	43.3	20.8	29.8	46.2	46.7	25.8	23.0	49.1	44.6
Public institutions										
1996 starting cohort	26.0	28.3	15.0	15.8	28.5	—	—	14.5	—	30.9
2000 starting cohort	29.0	31.4	17.9	18.9	33.7	—	—	16.4	—	32.7
2002 starting cohort	29.9	32.3	16.9	20.1	35.8	—	—	16.0	—	33.4
2003 starting cohort	30.7	33.5	16.5	20.7	37.5	—	—	17.0	—	33.8
2004 starting cohort	31.4	34.2	16.4	21.5	38.0	—	—	17.2	—	34.4
2005 starting cohort	32.0	35.1	16.8	22.4	38.7	39.1	16.9	17.9	28.7	33.5
2006 starting cohort	32.8	36.0	17.0	23.1	39.8	40.2	18.6	17.9	30.5	33.8
2007 starting cohort	33.5	36.9	17.4	24.0	39.8	40.2	20.9	19.5	35.9	34.4
Nonprofit institutions										
1996 starting cohort	48.6	51.3	29.3	39.9	57.9	—	—	33.7	—	50.4
2000 starting cohort	50.3	53.5	28.2	42.9	58.8	—	—	36.0	—	50.3
2002 starting cohort	51.0	54.0	29.4	44.1	61.0	—	—	36.6	—	54.8
2003 starting cohort	51.6	54.7	29.8	44.0	61.5	—	—	34.4	—	55.3
2004 starting cohort	52.6	55.5	30.6	46.2	62.8	—	—	39.0	—	57.4
2005 starting cohort	52.2	55.4	29.2	45.1	62.3	62.8	34.9	35.2	59.9	57.4
2006 starting cohort	52.9	56.2	29.7	47.4	62.8	63.5	37.2	38.2	61.9	56.8
2007 starting cohort	52.8	56.4	29.7	46.7	63.6	64.2	40.1	37.0	62.6	56.9
For-profit institutions										
1996 starting cohort	21.8	26.3	14.8	20.1	24.6	—	—	16.5	—	33.8
2000 starting cohort	25.7	30.3	22.5	27.4	42.7	—	—	28.0	—	36.5
2002 starting cohort	14.2	17.5	10.0	19.1	29.4	—	—	11.2	—	3.4
2003 starting cohort	14.8	18.2	10.4	19.5	25.5	—	—	8.4	—	4.7
2004 starting cohort	20.6	27.3	13.3	20.7	31.4	—	—	9.4	—	10.6
2005 starting cohort	20.0	27.9	11.0	19.6	31.7	33.8	15.4	15.2	24.7	15.4
2006 starting cohort	22.8	32.6	12.7	23.0	30.1	32.4	9.4	13.0	27.6	22.4
2007 starting cohort	22.5	32.7	11.6	22.7	32.2	36.4	8.2	12.6	27.2	24.4
Graduating within 4 years after start, males										
All 4-year institutions										
1996 starting cohort	28.5	30.6	13.9	19.0	32.2	—	—	15.1	—	38.6
2000 starting cohort	31.1	33.4	15.5	21.8	35.7	—	—	17.1	—	39.3
2002 starting cohort	31.3	33.8	14.7	21.8	37.4	—	—	17.2	—	36.6
2003 starting cohort	32.2	34.8	14.7	22.5	39.0	—	—	17.7	—	37.7
2004 starting cohort	33.0	35.7	15.1	23.3	39.9	—	—	18.9	—	39.7
2005 starting cohort	33.5	36.4	15.0	24.2	39.9	40.2	19.6	18.8	40.2	40.1
2006 starting cohort	34.2	37.1	15.6	24.9	41.1	41.5	21.6	17.6	43.1	39.6
2007 starting cohort	34.5	37.7	15.7	25.4	41.1	41.5	24.0	18.6	44.7	39.3
Public institutions										
1996 starting cohort	20.8	22.6	9.9	12.5	23.4	—	—	10.9	—	28.6
2000 starting cohort	23.6	25.5	11.7	14.5	27.8	—	—	11.9	—	30.2
2002 starting cohort	24.5	26.6	11.0	15.8	30.4	—	—	12.7	—	30.3
2003 starting cohort	25.7	27.9	10.9	16.4	32.5	—	—	14.1	—	30.8
2004 starting cohort	26.2	28.5	11.2	16.9	32.9	—	—	14.5	—	30.1
2005 starting cohort	27.1	29.6	11.7	18.3	33.5	33.8	14.1	15.0	26.4	29.8
2006 starting cohort	27.8	30.3	11.9	18.7	34.8	35.1	15.4	13.7	29.2	29.5
2007 starting cohort	28.3	31.1	12.1	19.5	34.8	35.0	18.8	14.7	33.8	29.4
Nonprofit institutions										
1996 starting cohort	43.6	46.2	22.1	35.0	53.5	—	—	28.9	—	47.0
2000 starting cohort	46.0	48.9	22.3	38.2	56.1	—	—	33.2	—	48.0
2002 starting cohort	46.3	49.1	22.9	38.8	57.6	—	—	32.1	—	50.6
2003 starting cohort	47.0	49.8	23.1	39.9	58.6	—	—	30.7	—	51.3
2004 starting cohort	47.8	50.6	23.2	41.2	59.0	—	—	35.4	—	53.2
2005 starting cohort	47.5	50.5	22.6	40.7	58.8	59.3	29.4	30.8	55.7	52.7
2006 starting cohort	48.2	51.2	23.5	42.4	60.2	60.9	34.6	34.3	58.2	52.2
2007 starting cohort	47.8	51.4	23.0	42.3	60.0	60.5	37.3	32.2	57.8	51.4
For-profit institutions										
1996 starting cohort	22.3	25.5	16.1	23.0	27.7	—	—	25.6	—	33.1
2000 starting cohort	30.1	34.3	23.7	30.9	44.5	—	—	28.7	—	36.7
2002 starting cohort	17.0	20.9	11.8	20.1	33.3	—	—	17.6	—	4.0
2003 starting cohort	17.4	20.9	11.8	20.8	28.1	—	—	11.1	—	6.4
2004 starting cohort	23.5	30.5	15.0	21.6	36.6	—	—	12.1	—	10.7
2005 starting cohort	23.6	31.4	12.0	22.2	32.2	33.2	24.0	20.8	25.2	16.7
2006 starting cohort	27.8	37.3	16.6	26.0	33.7	35.2	17.2	14.7	30.1	23.7
2007 starting cohort	28.4	39.3	15.3	25.7	35.8	38.3	14.1	19.0	25.8	26.9

See notes at end of table.

Table 326.10. Graduation rate from first institution attended for first-time, full-time bachelor's degree-seeking students at 4-year postsecondary institutions, by race/ethnicity, time to completion, sex, control of institution, and acceptance rate: Selected cohort entry years, 1996 through 2007—Continued

Time to completion, sex, control of institution, acceptance rate, and cohort entry year	Total	White	Black	Hispanic	Asian/Pacific Islander Total	Asian	Pacific Islander	American Indian/ Alaska Native	Two or more races	Nonresident alien
1	2	3	4	5	6	7	8	9	10	11
Graduating within 4 years after start, females										
All 4-year institutions										
1996 starting cohort	38.0	41.1	23.2	25.8	42.2	—	—	21.7	—	45.8
2000 starting cohort	40.2	43.5	25.2	29.0	45.7	—	—	24.0	—	45.3
2002 starting cohort	40.5	43.9	24.3	29.9	47.4	—	—	23.0	—	41.0
2003 starting cohort	41.0	44.8	23.9	29.8	48.1	—	—	22.8	—	41.1
2004 starting cohort	42.2	45.9	24.2	31.4	49.4	—	—	24.0	—	48.1
2005 starting cohort	42.2	46.4	23.7	31.3	49.6	50.1	24.2	24.1	47.3	48.4
2006 starting cohort	43.0	47.3	23.7	32.5	50.1	50.6	26.1	25.1	49.0	49.3
2007 starting cohort	43.5	48.0	24.3	33.1	50.7	51.3	27.0	26.3	52.3	50.8
Public institutions										
1996 starting cohort	30.3	33.3	18.3	18.4	33.2	—	—	17.3	—	34.1
2000 starting cohort	33.5	36.3	22.0	22.2	39.1	—	—	19.9	—	36.2
2002 starting cohort	34.3	37.2	20.9	23.4	40.8	—	—	18.5	—	37.0
2003 starting cohort	35.0	38.3	20.2	23.9	42.0	—	—	19.2	—	37.2
2004 starting cohort	35.7	39.2	19.9	24.9	42.6	—	—	19.3	—	39.6
2005 starting cohort	36.2	39.9	20.2	25.5	43.5	43.9	19.0	20.1	30.7	37.7
2006 starting cohort	37.0	41.0	20.4	26.4	44.5	45.0	21.3	21.1	31.5	39.2
2007 starting cohort	37.8	42.0	21.0	27.5	44.6	45.1	22.5	23.1	37.5	40.8
Nonprofit institutions										
1996 starting cohort	52.6	55.5	34.2	43.5	61.6	—	—	37.5	—	54.4
2000 starting cohort	53.7	57.3	32.3	46.2	60.9	—	—	38.1	—	53.2
2002 starting cohort	54.7	57.8	34.0	47.8	63.6	—	—	39.9	—	59.2
2003 starting cohort	55.3	58.6	34.4	46.7	63.7	—	—	37.0	—	59.7
2004 starting cohort	56.4	59.4	35.9	49.6	65.6	—	—	41.5	—	61.9
2005 starting cohort	55.9	59.2	34.1	48.1	64.9	65.5	38.6	38.5	63.1	62.7
2006 starting cohort	56.7	60.2	34.5	50.8	64.9	65.6	39.1	40.7	64.3	61.8
2007 starting cohort	56.7	60.4	34.7	49.8	66.4	67.2	41.8	40.6	65.6	62.8
For-profit institutions										
1996 starting cohort	21.1	27.5	13.7	16.1	20.3	—	—	9.6	—	34.6
2000 starting cohort	20.7	24.5	21.4	23.1	39.3	—	—	27.2	—	36.3
2002 starting cohort	11.6	14.0	8.7	18.1	23.9	—	—	6.0	—	3.1
2003 starting cohort	12.8	15.9	9.5	18.3	22.8	—	—	6.7	—	3.7
2004 starting cohort	17.8	23.8	12.2	19.9	25.0	—	—	7.4	—	10.5
2005 starting cohort	16.9	24.1	10.4	17.3	30.9	34.6	5.9	11.4	24.0	14.4
2006 starting cohort	18.1	26.7	10.2	20.3	26.2	29.3	3.7	11.8	24.1	21.3
2007 starting cohort	17.0	24.5	9.2	19.9	28.8	34.4	5.1	8.1	29.4	22.3
Graduating within 5 years after start, males and females										
All 4-year institutions										
1996 starting cohort	50.2	53.3	33.3	38.9	56.4	—	—	33.3	—	54.3
2000 starting cohort	52.6	55.7	36.0	42.4	60.1	—	—	35.1	—	55.2
2002 starting cohort	52.3	55.7	34.3	42.5	61.0	—	—	33.8	—	50.6
2003 starting cohort	53.2	56.9	34.2	43.0	62.1	—	—	33.7	—	52.1
2004 starting cohort	54.1	57.7	34.5	44.0	62.9	—	—	34.7	—	57.2
2005 starting cohort	54.2	58.0	34.2	44.6	63.2	63.6	40.6	34.7	58.6	58.1
2006 starting cohort	54.9	58.7	34.9	45.8	64.3	64.8	41.7	35.6	61.8	59.0
2007 starting cohort	55.1	59.1	35.5	46.4	64.2	64.7	42.6	36.3	63.9	58.9
Public institutions										
1996 starting cohort	45.9	49.0	30.5	34.1	51.3	—	—	30.0	—	46.5
2000 starting cohort	49.1	51.9	34.6	38.0	56.8	—	—	31.9	—	49.8
2002 starting cohort	49.2	52.2	32.9	38.8	57.7	—	—	30.8	—	50.4
2003 starting cohort	50.3	53.6	32.4	39.5	59.0	—	—	31.6	—	51.4
2004 starting cohort	50.7	54.1	32.2	40.2	59.3	—	—	31.6	—	51.9
2005 starting cohort	51.1	54.7	32.6	41.4	59.9	60.2	39.1	32.5	47.6	51.3
2006 starting cohort	51.9	55.5	33.5	42.1	61.5	61.9	41.3	32.9	50.2	52.0
2007 starting cohort	52.3	56.0	34.1	43.3	61.0	61.4	41.1	34.4	54.9	51.9
Nonprofit institutions										
1996 starting cohort	59.2	61.8	40.2	51.4	68.7	—	—	45.2	—	60.4
2000 starting cohort	60.8	63.8	39.9	55.1	70.0	—	—	46.9	—	60.4
2002 starting cohort	61.3	64.2	40.2	55.7	71.1	—	—	46.7	—	64.7
2003 starting cohort	62.3	65.2	41.2	56.1	72.0	—	—	44.4	—	65.6
2004 starting cohort	63.0	65.8	41.8	57.8	73.1	—	—	47.9	—	67.9
2005 starting cohort	62.6	65.6	40.5	56.6	73.1	73.6	49.4	44.0	71.5	67.9
2006 starting cohort	63.2	66.2	41.2	59.0	73.5	74.2	47.4	48.7	74.2	68.6
2007 starting cohort	63.1	66.3	41.5	58.5	74.2	74.8	53.9	45.9	74.1	68.2
For-profit institutions										
1996 starting cohort	25.4	30.1	17.8	23.1	27.3	—	—	19.8	—	51.6
2000 starting cohort	30.0	34.8	28.0	31.3	45.1	—	—	29.4	—	44.0
2002 starting cohort	17.2	20.7	12.5	22.7	32.0	—	—	12.6	—	6.0
2003 starting cohort	20.2	23.6	15.6	24.4	30.4	—	—	11.4	—	10.0
2004 starting cohort	25.9	32.9	19.1	25.8	36.5	—	—	15.5	—	17.7
2005 starting cohort	25.5	33.3	15.8	26.0	38.2	40.2	23.1	18.9	27.3	24.1
2006 starting cohort	28.0	37.2	17.9	29.8	38.0	40.2	18.7	16.8	30.5	30.3
2007 starting cohort	27.8	37.6	16.7	29.1	38.9	43.1	14.4	16.2	31.0	34.6

See notes at end of table.

Table 326.10. Graduation rate from first institution attended for first-time, full-time bachelor's degree-seeking students at 4-year postsecondary institutions, by race/ethnicity, time to completion, sex, control of institution, and acceptance rate: Selected cohort entry years, 1996 through 2007—Continued

Time to completion, sex, control of institution, acceptance rate, and cohort entry year	Total	White	Black	Hispanic	Asian/Pacific Islander			American Indian/ Alaska Native	Two or more races	Nonresident alien
					Total	Asian	Pacific Islander			
1	2	3	4	5	6	7	8	9	10	11
Graduating within 5 years after start, males										
All 4-year institutions										
1996 starting cohort	46.2	49.2	27.0	34.4	51.8	—	—	31.2	—	51.5
2000 starting cohort	49.0	52.0	29.9	37.8	56.5	—	—	31.6	—	53.0
2002 starting cohort	48.7	52.1	28.2	37.5	57.4	—	—	30.9	—	49.3
2003 starting cohort	49.9	53.5	28.5	38.6	58.6	—	—	31.1	—	50.9
2004 starting cohort	50.6	54.2	28.8	39.3	59.3	—	—	31.9	—	53.5
2005 starting cohort	50.9	54.7	28.8	40.7	59.4	59.7	39.0	33.1	55.6	54.2
2006 starting cohort	51.6	55.2	29.8	41.4	61.0	61.4	39.8	31.7	59.2	54.4
2007 starting cohort	51.6	55.5	29.9	42.2	60.3	60.7	42.1	32.6	60.4	53.9
Public institutions										
1996 starting cohort	41.6	44.6	24.0	29.4	46.4	—	—	27.7	—	44.1
2000 starting cohort	44.8	47.6	27.4	32.6	52.1	—	—	27.7	—	47.2
2002 starting cohort	45.3	48.3	26.0	33.7	53.7	—	—	27.5	—	47.0
2003 starting cohort	46.7	50.0	26.3	34.7	55.1	—	—	28.7	—	48.2
2004 starting cohort	47.0	50.4	26.3	35.2	55.4	—	—	28.6	—	47.2
2005 starting cohort	47.8	51.3	26.9	37.2	56.0	56.3	37.1	31.2	44.9	46.9
2006 starting cohort	48.3	51.8	27.8	37.4	57.7	58.0	38.8	29.0	48.7	46.9
2007 starting cohort	48.6	52.2	28.1	38.6	56.9	57.2	40.7	30.2	53.5	46.8
Nonprofit institutions										
1996 starting cohort	55.8	58.5	34.0	47.4	65.9	—	—	42.9	—	57.7
2000 starting cohort	58.5	61.3	35.1	51.7	69.9	—	—	45.9	—	58.9
2002 starting cohort	58.5	61.5	34.7	51.4	70.0	—	—	44.0	—	61.9
2003 starting cohort	59.3	62.3	35.0	53.2	70.7	—	—	41.5	—	62.2
2004 starting cohort	60.1	62.9	35.6	54.0	71.2	—	—	46.0	—	64.4
2005 starting cohort	59.5	62.5	34.7	53.3	70.6	71.0	45.2	40.4	69.3	63.9
2006 starting cohort	60.1	63.2	35.6	55.4	72.2	72.9	44.7	45.7	72.5	64.4
2007 starting cohort	59.7	63.2	35.0	55.1	71.5	72.0	50.8	42.5	70.9	63.1
For-profit institutions										
1996 starting cohort	25.6	29.2	18.1	25.4	29.9	—	—	30.8	—	51.0
2000 starting cohort	33.6	38.1	27.6	34.4	46.4	—	—	28.7	—	43.1
2002 starting cohort	19.9	24.1	14.3	23.6	35.4	—	—	18.5	—	6.3
2003 starting cohort	22.6	26.3	16.0	24.9	32.0	—	—	16.0	—	10.2
2004 starting cohort	27.8	35.1	19.1	25.9	41.6	—	—	15.0	—	16.8
2005 starting cohort	28.7	36.4	16.4	27.4	38.1	38.7	33.3	23.8	28.5	24.9
2006 starting cohort	32.5	41.5	20.9	32.0	40.8	42.1	25.9	18.2	34.0	32.4
2007 starting cohort	32.7	43.3	19.5	30.7	41.8	44.2	21.1	23.1	27.7	34.8
Graduating within 5 years after start, females										
All 4-year institutions										
1996 starting cohort	53.6	56.8	37.5	42.4	60.5	—	—	34.9	—	57.9
2000 starting cohort	55.6	58.8	40.2	45.9	63.4	—	—	37.8	—	58.0
2002 starting cohort	55.2	58.6	38.4	46.2	64.1	—	—	36.0	—	52.0
2003 starting cohort	55.9	59.7	38.0	46.2	65.1	—	—	35.8	—	53.5
2004 starting cohort	56.9	60.7	38.3	47.6	66.0	—	—	36.8	—	61.4
2005 starting cohort	56.8	60.8	37.8	47.5	66.5	66.9	41.9	35.9	61.2	62.4
2006 starting cohort	57.6	61.7	38.4	49.0	67.3	67.9	43.2	38.5	63.6	64.2
2007 starting cohort	58.1	62.2	39.3	49.7	67.7	68.4	42.9	39.0	66.3	64.9
Public institutions										
1996 starting cohort	49.5	52.7	34.8	37.8	56.0	—	—	31.8	—	50.0
2000 starting cohort	52.7	55.5	39.3	42.1	61.0	—	—	35.1	—	53.5
2002 starting cohort	52.5	55.4	37.6	42.6	61.5	—	—	33.2	—	54.4
2003 starting cohort	53.3	56.8	36.5	43.1	62.6	—	—	33.9	—	55.0
2004 starting cohort	53.8	57.4	36.2	44.0	62.9	—	—	34.0	—	57.6
2005 starting cohort	53.9	57.7	36.3	44.5	63.4	63.7	40.5	33.5	50.0	56.5
2006 starting cohort	54.9	58.7	37.2	45.7	65.1	65.5	43.3	36.0	51.4	58.2
2007 starting cohort	55.5	59.4	38.1	46.8	64.8	65.3	41.4	37.6	56.0	58.4
Nonprofit institutions										
1996 starting cohort	61.8	64.5	44.5	54.3	71.0	—	—	47.0	—	63.7
2000 starting cohort	62.7	65.8	43.2	57.4	70.0	—	—	47.7	—	62.3
2002 starting cohort	63.5	66.4	44.0	58.7	71.9	—	—	48.6	—	67.7
2003 starting cohort	64.6	67.5	45.5	58.0	73.0	—	—	46.5	—	69.3
2004 starting cohort	65.4	68.0	46.3	60.4	74.6	—	—	49.3	—	71.6
2005 starting cohort	65.1	68.0	44.8	58.8	75.0	75.5	52.3	46.7	73.1	72.4
2006 starting cohort	65.7	68.5	45.5	61.5	74.5	75.2	49.3	50.6	75.3	73.2
2007 starting cohort	65.9	68.9	46.4	60.7	76.3	76.9	55.8	48.5	76.2	73.7
For-profit institutions										
1996 starting cohort	25.1	31.4	17.6	20.0	23.7	—	—	11.5	—	52.2
2000 starting cohort	25.9	30.0	28.4	27.5	42.6	—	—	30.4	—	45.1
2002 starting cohort	14.7	17.3	11.2	21.7	27.1	—	—	8.0	—	5.8
2003 starting cohort	18.3	21.4	15.3	23.9	28.8	—	—	8.5	—	9.9
2004 starting cohort	24.2	30.5	19.1	25.6	30.3	—	—	15.8	—	18.3
2005 starting cohort	22.6	29.9	15.5	24.7	38.3	42.3	11.8	15.5	26.0	23.5
2006 starting cohort	23.8	31.8	15.8	27.8	35.1	38.1	13.6	15.8	25.9	28.5
2007 starting cohort	23.2	30.5	14.8	27.6	36.1	42.0	10.9	11.4	35.8	34.4

See notes at end of table.

Table 326.10. Graduation rate from first institution attended for first-time, full-time bachelor's degree-seeking students at 4-year postsecondary institutions, by race/ethnicity, time to completion, sex, control of institution, and acceptance rate: Selected cohort entry years, 1996 through 2007—Continued

Time to completion, sex, control of institution, acceptance rate, and cohort entry year	Total	White	Black	Hispanic	Asian/Pacific Islander Total	Asian	Pacific Islander	American Indian/ Alaska Native	Two or more races	Nonresident alien
1	2	3	4	5	6	7	8	9	10	11
Graduating within 6 years after start, males and females										
All 4-year institutions										
1996 starting cohort	55.4	58.1	38.9	45.7	63.4	—	—	38.0	—	58.0
2000 starting cohort	57.5	60.2	42.1	49.1	66.7	—	—	40.2	—	59.6
2002 starting cohort	57.2	60.2	40.1	48.9	67.1	—	—	38.3	—	55.3
2003 starting cohort	57.8	61.1	39.5	49.1	68.1	—	—	38.7	—	56.1
2004 starting cohort	58.4	61.6	39.6	50.2	68.7	—	—	39.4	—	61.6
2005 starting cohort	58.6	62.0	39.5	51.0	69.2	69.6	48.3	39.3	64.2	62.6
2006 starting cohort	59.2	62.5	40.2	51.9	70.1	70.6	48.5	40.2	66.6	63.6
2007 starting cohort[1]	59.4	62.9	40.8	52.5	70.0	70.5	49.6	40.6	67.8	63.9
Open admissions	34.1	42.1	23.2	29.4	40.3	43.2	22.4	19.7	44.5	40.1
90 percent or more accepted	46.7	49.6	28.4	38.1	48.6	49.1	37.4	25.7	43.8	54.6
75.0 to 89.9 percent accepted	55.2	58.2	36.9	48.1	59.2	59.5	46.7	42.6	55.9	57.1
50.0 to 74.9 percent accepted	61.6	65.1	44.6	53.3	68.2	68.6	52.2	42.6	66.5	61.7
25.0 to 49.9 percent accepted	69.3	74.7	46.1	63.7	79.6	79.8	65.0	55.0	80.0	74.4
Less than 25.0 percent accepted	88.9	89.0	80.5	86.2	94.4	94.4	91.5	78.8	92.5	89.9
Public institutions										
1996 starting cohort	51.7	54.3	36.8	42.1	59.5	—	—	35.3	—	51.3
2000 starting cohort	54.8	57.1	40.8	46.0	64.1	—	—	37.5	—	54.6
2002 starting cohort	54.9	57.4	39.4	46.3	64.7	—	—	35.7	—	55.5
2003 starting cohort	55.8	58.7	38.6	47.0	65.9	—	—	37.2	—	56.4
2004 starting cohort	56.1	59.0	38.5	47.9	66.3	—	—	37.0	—	57.2
2005 starting cohort	56.6	59.6	38.8	48.9	67.0	67.2	49.7	37.8	55.7	57.3
2006 starting cohort	57.2	60.2	39.7	49.5	68.2	68.5	49.1	38.2	57.0	57.7
2007 starting cohort[1]	57.7	60.7	40.3	50.7	68.0	68.3	49.6	39.5	60.4	58.2
Open admissions	32.9	38.2	23.6	25.0	38.9	40.2	21.7	16.6	38.7	40.1
90 percent or more accepted	46.9	49.5	28.8	38.0	49.1	49.4	19.2	25.7	42.6	53.8
75.0 to 89.9 percent accepted	53.7	56.3	36.4	47.4	59.5	59.7	45.9	43.4	45.5	55.7
50.0 to 74.9 percent accepted	61.4	64.9	45.0	52.3	68.0	68.5	48.4	41.0	65.2	60.6
25.0 to 49.9 percent accepted	64.4	69.3	44.0	60.3	76.2	76.2	72.5	56.8	77.5	63.0
Less than 25.0 percent accepted	84.8	83.8	69.3	82.7	92.7	92.8	88.9	66.2	85.1	88.9
Nonprofit institutions										
1996 starting cohort	63.1	65.7	44.6	55.7	73.5	—	—	48.1	—	63.4
2000 starting cohort	64.5	67.0	45.9	59.0	75.2	—	—	50.9	—	64.5
2002 starting cohort	64.6	67.2	44.9	59.5	75.3	—	—	49.8	—	68.3
2003 starting cohort	65.1	67.8	45.0	59.4	76.0	—	—	47.6	—	69.3
2004 starting cohort	65.5	67.9	45.0	60.6	76.2	—	—	50.8	—	71.3
2005 starting cohort	65.2	67.8	43.9	60.4	76.5	77.0	52.6	46.5	75.2	71.0
2006 starting cohort	65.5	68.1	44.5	62.0	76.8	77.5	52.6	51.3	77.5	71.9
2007 starting cohort[1]	65.3	68.3	44.7	60.9	77.0	77.5	58.2	47.9	76.8	71.5
Open admissions	38.2	46.7	24.4	33.2	43.3	42.9	50.0	24.1	59.0	51.7
90 percent or more accepted	48.2	52.5	28.2	40.7	49.5	50.7	44.6	26.7	53.7	56.3
75.0 to 89.9 percent accepted	59.8	63.3	40.2	50.8	58.3	58.9	47.9	39.4	69.3	59.9
50.0 to 74.9 percent accepted	62.4	65.7	44.2	56.7	69.5	69.6	64.3	49.5	68.8	63.3
25.0 to 49.9 percent accepted	76.7	81.0	51.4	72.9	85.6	86.1	59.4	56.0	83.3	80.4
Less than 25.0 percent accepted	90.6	91.1	83.0	87.8	95.3	95.3	95.0	86.6	94.6	90.0
For-profit institutions										
1996 starting cohort	28.0	33.2	19.2	24.6	28.9	—	—	23.1	—	54.0
2000 starting cohort	32.6	38.1	29.7	33.8	47.3	—	—	30.4	—	47.5
2002 starting cohort	22.0	25.5	16.3	27.5	35.5	—	—	17.1	—	12.5
2003 starting cohort	23.5	27.3	18.3	26.8	33.3	—	—	13.9	—	11.8
2004 starting cohort	28.6	35.5	21.4	29.0	38.8	—	—	19.0	—	21.8
2005 starting cohort	29.1	36.2	19.8	30.2	42.3	44.3	27.3	22.3	27.8	28.4
2006 starting cohort	31.5	40.3	21.1	33.7	42.5	44.4	25.2	18.8	32.4	35.5
2007 starting cohort	31.9	39.9	22.4	35.0	43.1	46.9	21.2	19.6	32.5	41.1
Graduating within 6 years after start, males										
All 4-year institutions										
1996 starting cohort	52.0	54.8	32.8	41.3	59.5	—	—	36.2	—	55.4
2000 starting cohort	54.3	57.1	35.6	44.6	62.9	—	—	37.1	—	56.8
2002 starting cohort	54.1	57.3	34.0	44.1	64.0	—	—	35.1	—	53.9
2003 starting cohort	55.1	58.4	34.1	44.9	65.1	—	—	36.7	—	55.0
2004 starting cohort	55.6	58.9	34.3	45.7	65.7	—	—	37.5	—	58.5
2005 starting cohort	56.0	59.4	34.2	47.2	66.3	66.6	48.6	37.9	61.3	59.2
2006 starting cohort	56.5	59.8	35.2	47.7	67.4	67.8	46.5	37.2	64.5	60.1
2007 starting cohort[1]	56.5	60.0	35.3	48.6	66.7	67.1	50.0	37.3	64.8	59.8
Open admissions	34.8	43.0	20.2	30.1	40.0	41.8	23.5	23.7	36.0	40.0
90 percent or more accepted	43.1	46.1	24.6	32.5	44.2	44.3	43.2	21.5	41.0	49.7
75.0 to 89.9 percent accepted	52.1	55.1	32.8	44.6	55.6	55.8	44.9	37.5	50.3	54.2
50.0 to 74.9 percent accepted	58.4	62.0	39.0	49.0	65.2	65.5	52.5	39.3	63.8	57.0
25.0 to 49.9 percent accepted	66.3	71.9	38.8	59.1	76.0	76.1	68.2	48.3	77.1	70.6
Less than 25.0 percent accepted	87.9	88.3	76.7	85.1	93.0	93.1	83.3	79.3	91.1	88.2

See notes at end of table.

Table 326.10. Graduation rate from first institution attended for first-time, full-time bachelor's degree-seeking students at 4-year postsecondary institutions, by race/ethnicity, time to completion, sex, control of institution, and acceptance rate: Selected cohort entry years, 1996 through 2007—Continued

Time to completion, sex, control of institution, acceptance rate, and cohort entry year	Total	White	Black	Hispanic	Asian/Pacific Islander			American Indian/ Alaska Native	Two or more races	Nonresident alien
					Total	Asian	Pacific Islander			
1	2	3	4	5	6	7	8	9	10	11
Public institutions										
1996 starting cohort	48.1	50.8	30.3	37.5	55.2	—	—	33.1	—	48.8
2000 starting cohort	51.3	53.8	34.1	41.1	60.0	—	—	33.6	—	52.1
2002 starting cohort	51.7	54.4	32.9	41.4	61.3	—	—	32.2	—	52.5
2003 starting cohort	52.9	55.9	32.9	42.4	62.7	—	—	35.0	—	53.5
2004 starting cohort	53.2	56.2	32.9	43.1	63.0	—	—	34.9	—	53.1
2005 starting cohort	53.9	57.0	33.3	44.9	64.0	64.2	50.9	36.8	52.7	53.3
2006 starting cohort	54.4	57.4	34.2	45.0	65.1	65.4	47.2	35.2	56.1	53.7
2007 starting cohort[1]	54.6	57.7	34.7	46.3	64.4	64.7	49.5	35.8	59.1	54.1
Open admissions	30.5	35.7	19.6	21.3	37.1	38.9	14.8	19.7	28.1	36.9
90 percent or more accepted	43.7	46.5	26.6	32.3	44.3	44.5	12.5	21.4	44.4	50.8
75.0 to 89.9 percent accepted	50.9	53.6	32.2	43.9	56.0	56.2	43.1	38.2	39.4	53.1
50.0 to 74.9 percent accepted	58.6	62.0	39.3	48.1	65.1	65.4	49.9	38.1	64.5	56.4
25.0 to 49.9 percent accepted	60.1	64.9	36.4	54.9	71.7	71.7	72.2	46.7	78.2	57.3
Less than 25.0 percent accepted	84.0	83.8	65.9	82.0	91.2	91.3	81.3	65.1	85.8	87.5
Nonprofit institutions										
1996 starting cohort	60.4	63.0	38.9	52.1	71.5	—	—	46.7	—	60.9
2000 starting cohort	61.7	64.4	39.3	55.3	73.1	—	—	50.1	—	61.7
2002 starting cohort	61.9	64.8	38.6	55.4	73.8	—	—	46.6	—	65.4
2003 starting cohort	62.5	65.3	38.9	56.7	74.2	—	—	45.4	—	65.8
2004 starting cohort	63.0	65.7	39.3	57.1	74.5	—	—	49.5	—	68.3
2005 starting cohort	62.5	65.3	38.2	57.2	74.6	75.1	49.2	42.8	73.5	67.4
2006 starting cohort	62.9	65.6	39.2	58.7	75.7	76.3	49.2	48.6	76.2	68.8
2007 starting cohort[1]	62.3	65.1	36.4	54.1	73.2	73.8	50.4	40.8	64.5	61.1
Open admissions	36.7	46.1	19.4	31.9	42.3	40.7	70.0	23.2	68.8	49.2
90 percent or more accepted	43.0	47.3	21.8	36.9	47.3	46.8	50.0	23.5	46.2	47.0
75.0 to 89.9 percent accepted	55.8	59.4	35.9	47.1	53.6	53.9	46.9	34.2	66.2	56.4
50.0 to 74.9 percent accepted	58.5	62.0	38.8	52.5	66.2	66.3	61.7	44.9	63.0	58.1
25.0 to 49.9 percent accepted	75.3	79.9	44.3	70.4	84.0	84.3	64.2	50.9	80.4	77.7
Less than 25.0 percent accepted	89.6	90.4	79.7	86.6	94.0	94.0	87.5	88.3	93.7	88.2
For-profit institutions										
1996 starting cohort	28.0	32.3	19.4	26.7	31.7	—	—	30.8	—	53.0
2000 starting cohort	35.5	40.2	29.8	36.2	48.4	—	—	30.3	—	46.3
2002 starting cohort	23.6	27.8	16.6	26.7	38.4	—	—	23.5	—	11.7
2003 starting cohort	25.7	29.3	18.5	26.9	35.0	—	—	18.8	—	12.1
2004 starting cohort	30.3	37.2	21.5	29.0	43.6	—	—	18.6	—	23.7
2005 starting cohort	31.6	38.8	19.5	30.4	42.5	43.3	36.0	27.7	28.5	29.4
2006 starting cohort	35.4	43.9	23.5	35.3	44.0	45.5	27.6	19.6	34.6	37.4
2007 starting cohort	35.7	45.0	23.4	36.0	43.7	45.9	23.9	27.2	28.9	41.4
Graduating within 6 years after start, females										
All 4-year institutions										
1996 starting cohort	58.2	60.9	43.0	49.1	66.8	—	—	39.5	—	61.5
2000 starting cohort	60.2	62.8	46.4	52.4	70.1	—	—	42.7	—	63.1
2002 starting cohort	59.7	62.5	44.2	52.5	69.8	—	—	40.7	—	56.7
2003 starting cohort	60.0	63.3	43.2	52.2	70.7	—	—	40.2	—	57.3
2004 starting cohort	60.7	63.9	43.3	53.5	71.3	—	—	40.9	—	65.0
2005 starting cohort	60.8	64.2	43.0	53.8	71.8	72.2	48.1	40.3	66.7	66.6
2006 starting cohort	61.4	64.9	43.6	54.9	72.6	73.1	50.1	42.4	68.1	67.6
2007 starting cohort[1]	61.9	65.4	44.6	55.5	73.0	73.6	49.3	43.1	69.9	68.7
Open admissions	33.5	41.2	25.5	28.8	40.7	44.6	21.8	16.9	51.0	40.2
90 percent or more accepted	50.1	52.9	31.9	43.0	53.0	54.1	33.8	28.9	45.9	60.8
75.0 to 89.9 percent accepted	57.9	60.8	40.0	50.8	62.6	63.0	47.9	46.5	60.0	61.4
50.0 to 74.9 percent accepted	64.1	67.6	48.2	56.4	70.9	71.4	52.0	45.0	68.3	67.1
25.0 to 49.9 percent accepted	71.7	77.1	50.8	67.0	82.7	83.0	62.9	60.1	82.0	77.9
Less than 25.0 percent accepted	90.0	89.9	83.7	87.2	95.6	95.5	100.0	78.1	93.9	92.1
Public institutions										
1996 starting cohort	54.7	57.4	41.0	45.7	63.5	—	—	37.0	—	54.9
2000 starting cohort	57.7	59.9	45.2	49.7	67.8	—	—	40.5	—	58.1
2002 starting cohort	57.5	59.9	43.7	50.0	67.7	—	—	38.3	—	59.0
2003 starting cohort	58.2	61.0	42.4	50.4	68.8	—	—	38.9	—	59.7
2004 starting cohort	58.6	61.5	42.3	51.5	69.2	—	—	38.5	—	62.3
2005 starting cohort	58.8	61.8	42.4	51.9	69.7	70.0	48.7	38.5	58.4	62.0
2006 starting cohort	59.6	62.7	43.3	52.9	71.1	71.5	50.7	40.5	57.8	62.6
2007 starting cohort[1]	60.3	63.3	44.1	54.1	71.3	71.8	49.7	42.3	61.4	63.4
Open admissions	35.1	40.5	26.6	28.2	41.1	41.7	31.6	14.2	47.4	44.2
90 percent or more accepted	49.9	52.3	30.7	43.0	54.0	54.5	22.2	29.0	41.1	58.2
75.0 to 89.9 percent accepted	56.1	58.7	39.5	50.1	63.0	63.3	47.7	47.4	50.3	59.5
50.0 to 74.9 percent accepted	63.8	67.4	48.4	55.5	70.7	71.3	47.3	43.0	65.7	65.7
25.0 to 49.9 percent accepted	67.9	73.1	48.8	64.2	80.3	80.4	72.7	64.2	77.0	68.4
Less than 25.0 percent accepted	85.9	83.8	73.6	83.7	94.2	94.1	100.0	67.7	83.6	90.6

See notes at end of table.

Table 326.10. Graduation rate from first institution attended for first-time, full-time bachelor's degree-seeking students at 4-year postsecondary institutions, by race/ethnicity, time to completion, sex, control of institution, and acceptance rate: Selected cohort entry years, 1996 through 2007—Continued

Time to completion, sex, control of institution, acceptance rate, and cohort entry year	Total	White	Black	Hispanic	Asian/Pacific Islander			American Indian/ Alaska Native	Two or more races	Nonresident alien
					Total	Asian	Pacific Islander			
1	2	3	4	5	6	7	8	9	10	11
Nonprofit institutions										
1996 starting cohort......................	65.4	67.9	48.4	58.3	75.0	—	—	49.2	—	66.4
2000 starting cohort......................	66.7	69.1	50.4	61.7	76.7	—	—	51.5	—	67.9
2002 starting cohort......................	66.7	69.1	49.4	62.2	76.3	—	—	52.1	—	71.5
2003 starting cohort......................	67.2	69.8	49.2	61.3	77.3	—	—	49.3	—	73.2
2004 starting cohort......................	67.4	69.7	49.2	63.0	77.6	—	—	51.7	—	74.5
2005 starting cohort......................	67.3	69.8	48.1	62.6	77.9	78.4	54.9	49.2	76.5	75.1
2006 starting cohort......................	67.6	70.1	48.5	64.2	77.7	78.4	55.0	52.9	78.3	75.4
2007 starting cohort[1]	67.7	70.4	49.4	62.9	78.7	79.3	58.2	50.5	78.4	76.0
Open admissions......................	39.7	47.3	29.2	34.3	44.2	45.0	30.0	24.7	52.2	56.0
90 percent or more accepted	52.9	57.3	34.1	43.5	51.2	54.0	41.7	29.3	57.1	65.5
75.0 to 89.9 percent accepted.....	62.8	66.0	43.6	53.2	61.7	62.3	48.8	43.1	71.4	64.7
50.0 to 74.9 percent accepted.....	65.5	68.5	48.3	59.4	72.0	72.1	65.8	52.9	72.0	69.1
25.0 to 49.9 percent accepted.....	77.9	81.8	55.8	74.6	86.8	87.5	56.9	59.9	85.0	82.9
Less than 25.0 percent accepted.	91.5	91.8	85.5	88.9	96.3	96.3	100.0	84.7	95.3	92.2
For-profit institutions										
1996 starting cohort......................	27.9	34.5	19.0	21.9	24.9	—	—	17.3	—	55.1
2000 starting cohort......................	29.1	35.1	29.7	30.9	45.2	—	—	30.4	—	48.9
2002 starting cohort......................	20.5	23.1	16.1	28.3	31.3	—	—	12.0	—	13.0
2003 starting cohort......................	21.8	25.6	18.2	26.7	31.6	—	—	10.8	—	11.6
2004 starting cohort......................	26.9	33.6	21.3	28.9	33.1	—	—	19.3	—	20.4
2005 starting cohort......................	26.9	33.3	20.0	30.0	42.1	45.8	17.6	18.7	26.9	27.7
2006 starting cohort......................	28.0	35.8	19.5	32.1	40.8	43.3	23.5	18.2	29.3	33.9
2007 starting cohort......................	28.3	33.7	21.7	34.1	42.6	48.0	19.7	14.3	37.6	40.8

—Not available.
[1]Includes data for institutions not reporting admissions data, which are not separately shown.
NOTE: Data are for 4-year degree-granting postsecondary institutions participating in Title IV federal financial aid programs. Graduation rates refer to students receiving bachelor's degrees from their initial institutions of attendance only. Totals include data for persons whose race/ethnicity was not reported. Race categories exclude persons of Hispanic ethnicity. Some data have been revised from previously published figures.
SOURCE: U.S. Department of Education, National Center for Education Statistics, Integrated Postsecondary Education Data System (IPEDS), Fall 2001 and Spring 2007 through Spring 2014, Graduation Rates component. (This table was prepared November 2014.)

Table 326.20. Graduation rate from first institution attended within 150 percent of normal time for first-time, full-time degree/certificate-seeking students at 2-year postsecondary institutions, by race/ethnicity, sex, and control of institution: Selected cohort entry years, 2000 through 2010

Sex, control of institution, and cohort entry year	Percent graduating with a certificate or associate's degree within 150 percent of normal time									
	Total	White	Black	Hispanic	Asian/Pacific Islander			American Indian/ Alaska Native	Two or more races	Nonresident alien
					Total	Asian	Pacific Islander			
1	2	3	4	5	6	7	8	9	10	11
Males and females										
All 2-year institutions										
2000 starting cohort	30.5	31.5	26.1	30.1	33.3	—	—	29.3	—	25.5
2002 starting cohort	29.3	30.4	24.2	30.7	31.4	—	—	26.3	—	26.7
2003 starting cohort	29.1	29.9	24.2	30.2	31.7	—	—	25.9	—	27.2
2004 starting cohort	27.8	29.0	22.9	26.3	30.2	—	—	26.7	—	32.9
2005 starting cohort	27.5	28.5	22.6	25.7	31.5	—	—	24.9	—	32.2
2006 starting cohort	29.2	29.3	24.4	30.7	33.9	—	—	24.4	—	30.1
2007 starting cohort	29.8	29.4	25.4	33.3	33.1	—	—	25.5	—	30.9
2008 starting cohort	31.2	30.1	27.6	35.1	34.3	35.2	24.1	25.7	33.3	33.7
2009 starting cohort	31.0	30.2	26.4	36.4	35.1	36.0	25.0	25.7	30.5	34.6
2010 starting cohort	29.4	29.4	23.7	33.8	35.4	35.2	37.9	24.0	26.0	36.2
Public institutions										
2000 starting cohort	23.6	25.7	17.8	16.8	25.5	—	—	19.6	—	23.2
2002 starting cohort	21.9	24.5	13.2	16.7	23.8	—	—	18.8	—	25.5
2003 starting cohort	21.5	24.1	12.7	16.3	24.8	—	—	17.9	—	25.8
2004 starting cohort	20.3	22.9	11.5	15.0	24.2	—	—	17.8	—	30.5
2005 starting cohort	20.6	22.9	12.1	15.6	25.8	—	—	18.2	—	29.9
2006 starting cohort	20.4	23.1	12.0	15.5	25.4	—	—	16.9	—	25.0
2007 starting cohort	20.3	22.9	11.8	15.9	25.3	—	—	17.4	—	25.5
2008 starting cohort	20.2	22.8	11.8	15.8	26.2	27.2	15.2	15.4	17.0	30.5
2009 starting cohort	19.8	22.5	11.3	15.9	26.1	27.3	11.9	15.9	18.3	32.6
2010 starting cohort	19.5	22.4	10.8	16.2	26.7	27.5	15.6	15.0	17.4	32.6
Nonprofit institutions										
2000 starting cohort	50.1	49.6	37.5	56.3	61.4	—	—	62.1	—	43.1
2002 starting cohort	49.1	55.1	36.5	46.1	49.5	—	—	20.3	—	45.3
2003 starting cohort	49.0	56.0	35.8	39.4	50.1	—	—	17.9	—	64.2
2004 starting cohort	44.4	48.9	37.3	35.6	36.6	—	—	19.5	—	54.7
2005 starting cohort	48.2	52.3	41.6	47.3	41.6	—	—	14.8	—	51.7
2006 starting cohort	52.8	55.0	46.5	47.5	51.2	—	—	22.6	—	69.3
2007 starting cohort	51.0	56.1	43.6	46.1	51.0	—	—	15.3	—	63.9
2008 starting cohort	56.6	59.7	53.4	62.4	52.9	53.9	‡	25.0	55.8	59.5
2009 starting cohort	62.3	66.0	59.7	68.3	57.9	57.7	‡	30.4	66.5	50.0
2010 starting cohort	53.6	55.9	51.0	62.1	51.7	52.2	‡	18.2	39.5	52.5
For-profit institutions										
2000 starting cohort	59.1	63.1	47.6	60.3	64.4	—	—	60.3	—	55.4
2002 starting cohort	57.1	61.0	49.3	59.7	61.7	—	—	58.1	—	58.9
2003 starting cohort	57.2	61.8	48.4	60.0	55.8	—	—	59.1	—	36.5
2004 starting cohort	58.2	64.3	48.4	59.6	65.4	—	—	59.0	—	71.1
2005 starting cohort	57.7	62.9	47.8	61.4	65.8	—	—	55.8	—	57.7
2006 starting cohort	58.3	62.8	46.9	62.7	72.1	—	—	57.5	—	65.6
2007 starting cohort	60.6	65.0	49.7	65.1	68.8	—	—	59.0	—	67.6
2008 starting cohort	61.7	64.1	52.6	67.9	69.9	70.2	66.2	60.3	57.4	62.0
2009 starting cohort	62.8	65.1	53.0	68.8	70.8	71.6	64.1	60.8	59.9	61.7
2010 starting cohort	62.8	65.8	53.3	68.3	72.4	73.4	68.9	61.4	59.0	69.7
Males										
All 2-year institutions										
2000 starting cohort	28.7	30.0	23.1	27.9	30.1	—	—	28.3	—	22.9
2002 starting cohort	27.2	28.6	21.3	27.0	28.7	—	—	23.7	—	22.5
2003 starting cohort	27.2	28.5	20.6	26.8	29.4	—	—	22.4	—	22.6
2004 starting cohort	25.7	27.3	19.1	22.6	27.9	—	—	23.6	—	30.1
2005 starting cohort	25.3	27.0	18.6	21.8	28.4	—	—	23.4	—	29.4
2006 starting cohort	26.3	27.2	20.3	25.4	30.5	—	—	22.6	—	27.4
2007 starting cohort	26.2	27.0	20.3	26.6	29.3	—	—	23.7	—	27.1
2008 starting cohort	27.4	27.7	22.7	29.1	30.3	30.9	23.8	23.0	28.8	30.5
2009 starting cohort	27.3	27.9	22.1	30.2	30.9	31.7	21.6	23.7	24.5	31.5
2010 starting cohort	26.2	27.6	19.4	27.7	31.5	31.5	31.8	21.4	22.3	33.2
Public institutions										
2000 starting cohort	22.2	24.2	16.5	15.4	22.6	—	—	19.3	—	20.4
2002 starting cohort	20.9	23.2	13.1	15.2	21.8	—	—	16.9	—	21.4
2003 starting cohort	20.8	23.0	12.5	15.2	22.7	—	—	16.4	—	21.3
2004 starting cohort	19.6	21.8	11.5	13.8	22.6	—	—	17.5	—	27.8
2005 starting cohort	19.9	22.1	12.0	14.6	23.5	—	—	18.7	—	27.4
2006 starting cohort	19.8	22.2	12.2	14.7	23.7	—	—	16.3	—	22.5
2007 starting cohort	19.8	22.2	11.9	15.1	23.6	—	—	18.6	—	22.1
2008 starting cohort	19.6	22.1	12.0	14.9	24.3	25.1	15.2	15.2	16.7	28.1
2009 starting cohort	19.4	22.0	11.4	14.8	24.4	25.4	12.4	16.0	16.8	29.9
2010 starting cohort	19.0	21.9	10.7	15.1	24.6	25.4	14.6	14.1	16.2	30.2
Nonprofit institutions										
2000 starting cohort	49.5	49.3	31.7	54.3	62.5	—	—	64.5	—	42.6
2002 starting cohort	51.1	58.8	33.0	42.9	56.0	—	—	21.7	—	35.3
2003 starting cohort	49.6	57.0	31.4	42.4	48.1	—	—	16.8	—	51.6
2004 starting cohort	43.2	46.4	38.3	36.4	40.3	—	—	17.5	—	52.0
2005 starting cohort	44.5	49.1	38.7	42.9	43.7	—	—	10.4	—	47.7
2006 starting cohort	51.3	52.6	45.1	45.6	54.0	—	—	21.8	—	68.2
2007 starting cohort	50.1	56.4	45.5	41.1	49.3	—	—	10.3	—	58.1
2008 starting cohort	49.8	53.8	47.3	49.4	45.4	46.3	‡	14.6	46.7	52.1
2009 starting cohort	53.6	57.5	51.0	58.2	47.4	47.7	‡	22.4	56.1	45.1
2010 starting cohort	46.2	49.4	42.5	52.1	47.6	48.8	‡	19.8	27.0	44.0

See notes at end of table.

Table 326.20. Graduation rate from first institution attended within 150 percent of normal time for first-time, full-time degree/certificate-seeking students at 2-year postsecondary institutions, by race/ethnicity, sex, and control of institution: Selected cohort entry years, 2000 through 2010—Continued

Sex, control of institution, and cohort entry year	Percent graduating with a certificate or associate's degree within 150 percent of normal time									
	Total	White	Black	Hispanic	Asian/Pacific Islander			American Indian/ Alaska Native	Two or more races	Nonresident alien
					Total	Asian	Pacific Islander			
1	2	3	4	5	6	7	8	9	10	11
For-profit institutions										
2000 starting cohort	59.3	63.7	45.6	58.2	63.1	—	—	55.9	—	55.0
2002 starting cohort	56.6	62.0	45.9	56.1	59.7	—	—	58.4	—	61.9
2003 starting cohort	58.0	63.7	45.7	56.9	62.0	—	—	59.5	—	36.7
2004 starting cohort	58.1	65.4	44.6	55.4	64.3	—	—	59.6	—	69.4
2005 starting cohort	57.7	64.8	43.1	57.5	65.7	—	—	56.3	—	56.3
2006 starting cohort	56.5	62.2	42.3	57.6	69.7	—	—	57.5	—	63.8
2007 starting cohort	58.4	65.1	45.0	59.5	66.8	—	—	56.7	—	67.9
2008 starting cohort	58.9	63.9	48.2	63.1	67.7	68.1	65.1	54.6	58.2	54.6
2009 starting cohort	59.8	63.7	49.3	64.6	67.7	68.7	59.2	59.4	55.2	59.9
2010 starting cohort	60.8	65.9	49.4	63.4	71.2	72.8	65.5	59.4	57.4	66.4
Females										
All 2-year institutions										
2000 starting cohort	32.1	33.0	28.1	31.8	36.3	—	—	30.0	—	28.3
2002 starting cohort	30.9	32.0	26.1	33.4	33.9	—	—	28.2	—	30.4
2003 starting cohort	30.7	31.2	26.3	32.7	33.9	—	—	28.4	—	31.5
2004 starting cohort	29.6	30.5	25.2	29.0	32.6	—	—	28.8	—	35.3
2005 starting cohort	29.3	29.9	25.2	28.6	34.6	—	—	25.9	—	34.8
2006 starting cohort	31.5	31.2	26.9	34.5	37.4	—	—	25.7	—	32.5
2007 starting cohort	32.7	31.5	28.5	37.9	37.0	—	—	26.8	—	34.4
2008 starting cohort	34.4	32.3	30.9	39.4	38.3	39.6	24.3	27.9	36.2	36.7
2009 starting cohort	34.1	32.3	29.4	40.9	39.3	40.4	28.0	27.3	34.9	37.6
2010 starting cohort	32.2	31.1	26.7	38.2	39.4	38.9	43.2	26.0	28.8	39.0
Public institutions										
2000 starting cohort	24.8	27.1	18.8	17.9	28.4	—	—	19.9	—	26.2
2002 starting cohort	22.8	25.8	13.2	17.8	25.9	—	—	20.2	—	29.2
2003 starting cohort	22.2	25.1	12.8	17.3	27.1	—	—	19.0	—	30.0
2004 starting cohort	21.0	24.0	11.5	16.0	26.1	—	—	17.9	—	32.8
2005 starting cohort	21.2	23.8	12.1	16.4	28.2	—	—	17.8	—	32.2
2006 starting cohort	20.9	23.9	11.8	16.2	27.3	—	—	17.5	—	27.3
2007 starting cohort	20.7	23.6	11.7	16.7	27.1	—	—	16.4	—	28.7
2008 starting cohort	20.7	23.5	11.7	16.5	28.3	29.6	15.2	15.6	17.3	32.9
2009 starting cohort	20.2	23.1	11.2	16.8	28.1	29.6	11.4	15.8	19.8	35.3
2010 starting cohort	20.0	23.0	10.8	17.2	29.0	30.0	16.7	15.7	18.6	35.0
Nonprofit institutions										
2000 starting cohort	50.7	50.0	43.1	58.3	60.1	—	—	60.2	—	43.8
2002 starting cohort	47.3	51.4	39.2	48.9	44.3	—	—	19.3	—	55.0
2003 starting cohort	48.5	55.0	38.8	37.5	51.4	—	—	18.7	—	75.4
2004 starting cohort	45.4	51.1	36.3	35.1	34.3	—	—	21.0	—	57.4
2005 starting cohort	51.3	54.9	44.9	49.6	40.1	—	—	18.0	—	55.2
2006 starting cohort	54.0	56.7	47.7	48.5	48.8	—	—	23.2	—	70.4
2007 starting cohort	51.8	55.8	41.6	49.5	52.2	—	—	18.9	—	69.9
2008 starting cohort	59.9	63.2	55.8	67.7	56.8	57.7	‡	31.5	58.3	66.8
2009 starting cohort	66.6	70.8	63.4	72.5	63.2	62.7	‡	34.5	70.3	54.5
2010 starting cohort	57.7	60.0	55.0	66.8	54.5	54.5	‡	17.3	45.5	58.7
For-profit institutions										
2000 starting cohort	58.9	62.6	48.6	61.8	65.3	—	—	63.8	—	55.7
2002 starting cohort	57.4	60.3	50.8	61.7	63.3	—	—	58.0	—	56.7
2003 starting cohort	56.8	60.4	49.4	61.9	52.1	—	—	59.0	—	36.4
2004 starting cohort	58.3	63.4	49.9	61.9	66.2	—	—	58.7	—	72.3
2005 starting cohort	57.7	61.6	49.4	63.3	65.8	—	—	55.7	—	58.6
2006 starting cohort	59.3	63.2	48.8	65.1	73.7	—	—	57.4	—	67.0
2007 starting cohort	61.6	64.9	51.4	67.4	70.0	—	—	60.0	—	67.5
2008 starting cohort	63.2	64.2	54.7	70.3	71.2	71.4	67.3	64.0	57.1	67.6
2009 starting cohort	64.5	66.0	54.7	70.9	72.7	73.4	67.0	61.5	61.9	62.8
2010 starting cohort	63.8	65.8	55.0	70.7	73.1	73.8	71.0	62.6	59.8	72.7

—Not available.
‡Reporting standards not met (too few cases).
NOTE: Data are for 2-year degree-granting postsecondary institutions participating in Title IV federal financial aid programs. Graduation rates refer to students receiving associate's degrees or certificates from their initial institutions of attendance only. Totals include data for persons whose race/ethnicity was not reported. Race categories exclude persons of Hispanic ethnicity. Some data have been revised from previously published figures.
SOURCE: U.S. Department of Education, National Center for Education Statistics, Integrated Postsecondary Education Data System (IPEDS), Fall 2001 and Spring 2002 through Spring 2014, Graduation Rates component. (This table was prepared November 2014.)

Table 326.30. Retention of first-time degree-seeking undergraduates at degree-granting postsecondary institutions, by attendance status, level and control of institution, and percentage of applications accepted: 2006 to 2013

Attendance status, level, control, and percent of applications accepted	First-time degree-seekers (adjusted entry cohort),[1] by entry year							Students from adjusted cohort returning in the following year							Percent of first-time undergraduates retained						
	2006	2007	2008	2009	2010	2011	2012	2007	2008	2009	2010	2011	2012	2013	2006 to 2007	2007 to 2008	2008 to 2009	2009 to 2010	2010 to 2011	2011 to 2012	2012 to 2013
1	2	3	4	5	6	7	8	9	10	11	12	13	14	15	16	17	18	19	20	21	22
Full-time students																					
All institutions	2,171,714	2,269,712	2,296,305	2,386,597	2,341,321	2,270,919	2,223,481	1,542,175	1,619,269	1,647,198	1,714,013	1,679,620	1,630,899	1,621,301	71.0	71.3	71.7	71.8	71.7	71.8	72.9
Public institutions	1,524,044	1,603,819	1,654,779	1,743,668	1,698,663	1,665,771	1,637,612	1,072,644	1,132,790	1,167,180	1,229,276	1,192,769	1,170,408	1,168,799	70.4	70.6	70.5	70.5	70.2	70.3	71.4
Nonprofit institutions	466,139	477,369	476,153	478,708	487,864	484,498	483,953	369,084	375,721	378,111	381,423	389,217	386,716	388,539	79.2	78.7	79.4	79.7	79.8	79.8	80.3
For-profit institutions	181,531	188,524	165,373	164,221	154,794	120,650	101,916	100,447	110,758	101,907	103,314	97,634	73,775	63,963	55.3	58.8	61.6	62.9	63.1	61.1	62.8
4-year institutions	1,458,731	1,505,161	1,511,976	1,465,669	1,461,703	1,472,550	1,466,842	1,115,529	1,152,921	1,176,973	1,153,975	1,152,644	1,160,025	1,167,016	76.5	76.6	77.8	78.7	78.9	78.8	79.6
Public institutions	912,401	936,000	973,089	945,951	941,098	958,009	957,853	711,490	732,384	765,163	751,623	746,633	758,805	765,747	78.0	78.2	78.6	79.5	79.3	79.2	79.9
Open admissions	62,724	60,815	81,559	47,943	43,261	41,327	35,041	38,839	38,724	52,988	30,079	26,633	25,148	21,189	61.9	63.7	65.0	62.7	61.6	60.9	60.5
90 percent or more accepted	68,835	66,114	58,002	60,147	74,731	49,819	47,775	49,274	46,731	39,851	43,654	54,244	35,005	33,969	71.6	70.7	68.7	72.6	72.6	70.3	71.1
75.0 to 89.9 percent accepted	244,177	237,913	213,388	213,441	205,404	230,328	226,673	185,457	180,320	164,522	164,136	157,956	176,662	174,316	76.0	75.8	77.1	76.9	76.9	76.7	76.9
50.0 to 74.9 percent accepted	417,093	439,824	473,007	468,817	469,055	450,981	469,245	336,177	357,137	382,663	380,679	379,466	363,040	381,496	80.6	81.2	80.9	81.2	80.9	80.5	81.3
25.0 to 49.9 percent accepted	103,118	107,824	127,960	134,042	131,782	170,541	164,067	88,888	90,141	108,638	114,472	112,015	145,642	141,590	86.2	83.6	84.9	85.4	85.0	85.4	86.3
Less than 25.0 percent accepted	7,716	10,223	13,479	14,326	13,996	9,468	8,843	7,045	9,477	12,792	13,653	13,296	9,014	8,357	91.3	92.7	94.9	95.3	95.0	95.2	94.5
Information not available	8,738	13,287	5,694	7,235	2,869	5,545	6,209	5,765	10,071	3,928	5,230	2,323	4,232	4,669	66.0	75.8	69.0	72.3	81.0	76.3	75.2
Nonprofit institutions	457,566	468,955	468,220	470,748	476,912	473,800	476,215	363,760	370,740	373,352	376,726	382,520	380,279	383,984	79.5	79.1	79.7	80.0	80.2	80.3	80.6
Open admissions	26,679	26,571	24,220	22,613	22,861	21,962	22,493	16,116	15,227	16,499	14,349	14,330	13,835	14,351	60.4	57.3	68.1	63.5	62.7	63.0	63.8
90 percent or more accepted	13,684	16,008	16,738	15,066	13,922	13,393	12,348	9,549	11,249	11,899	10,898	9,720	9,174	8,516	69.8	70.3	71.1	72.3	69.8	68.5	69.0
75.0 to 89.9 percent accepted	102,218	93,360	81,056	80,332	80,816	79,225	79,817	78,495	71,066	61,765	62,246	62,865	61,606	62,184	76.8	76.1	76.2	77.5	77.8	77.8	77.9
50.0 to 74.9 percent accepted	190,079	196,121	210,894	218,136	224,992	219,751	220,080	148,781	152,948	164,566	170,310	176,699	171,851	173,261	78.3	78.0	78.0	78.1	78.5	78.2	78.7
25.0 to 49.9 percent accepted	93,560	100,121	98,546	98,239	92,996	93,743	95,784	81,880	86,755	84,760	84,926	79,847	80,260	81,876	87.5	86.7	86.0	86.4	85.9	85.6	85.5
Less than 25.0 percent accepted	26,696	28,631	32,190	32,980	38,926	44,290	44,735	25,639	27,621	30,570	31,790	37,386	42,698	43,215	96.0	96.5	95.0	96.4	96.0	96.4	96.6
Information not available	4,650	8,143	4,576	3,382	2,399	1,436	958	3,300	5,874	3,333	2,207	1,673	855	581	71.0	72.1	72.8	65.3	69.7	59.5	60.6
For-profit institutions	88,764	100,206	70,667	48,970	43,693	40,741	32,774	40,279	49,797	38,458	25,626	23,491	20,941	17,285	45.4	49.7	54.4	52.3	53.8	51.4	52.7
Open admissions	45,273	46,801	20,894	16,997	16,350	20,661	16,811	18,735	22,723	12,459	9,329	8,990	10,758	8,331	41.4	48.6	59.6	54.9	55.0	52.1	49.6
90 percent or more accepted	6,285	5,347	4,632	3,713	2,900	5,234	3,337	3,454	2,764	2,465	1,301	1,524	2,426	1,650	55.0	51.7	53.2	35.0	52.6	46.4	49.4
75.0 to 89.9 percent accepted	3,703	6,157	6,384	3,224	2,428	2,860	1,880	2,081	3,129	3,085	1,549	1,284	1,354	1,224	56.2	50.8	48.3	48.0	52.9	47.3	65.1
50.0 to 74.9 percent accepted	12,845	19,724	8,874	15,929	10,122	4,854	6,245	6,536	10,249	5,602	8,243	5,443	2,691	3,608	50.9	52.0	63.1	51.7	53.8	55.4	57.8
25.0 to 49.9 percent accepted	18,142	18,118	28,288	6,098	7,214	6,860	2,908	8,036	8,672	14,094	3,423	3,942	3,547	1,554	44.3	47.9	49.8	56.1	54.6	51.7	53.4
Less than 25.0 percent accepted	0	0	0	0	0	0	0	0	0	0	0	0	0	0	†	†	†	†	†	†	†
Information not available	2,516	4,059	1,595	3,009	4,679	272	1,593	1,437	2,260	753	1,781	2,308	165	918	57.1	55.7	47.2	59.2	49.3	60.7	57.6
2-year institutions	712,983	764,551	784,329	920,928	879,618	798,369	756,639	426,646	466,348	470,225	560,038	526,976	470,874	454,285	59.8	61.0	60.0	60.8	59.9	59.0	60.0
Public institutions	611,643	667,819	681,680	797,717	757,565	707,762	679,759	361,154	400,406	402,017	477,653	446,136	411,603	403,052	59.0	60.0	59.0	59.9	58.9	58.2	59.3
Nonprofit institutions	8,573	8,414	7,993	7,960	10,952	10,698	7,738	5,324	4,981	4,759	4,697	6,131	6,697	4,555	62.1	60.0	60.0	61.1	58.8	60.2	58.9
For-profit institutions	92,767	88,318	94,706	115,251	111,101	79,909	69,142	60,168	60,961	63,449	77,688	74,143	52,834	46,678	64.9	69.0	67.0	67.4	66.7	66.1	67.5
Part-time students																					
All institutions	463,234	532,827	519,619	551,181	545,227	532,000	516,025	191,586	219,857	210,836	231,593	228,460	224,512	222,420	41.4	41.3	40.6	42.0	41.9	42.2	43.1
Public institutions	419,006	475,209	477,242	502,825	497,707	494,287	483,211	171,746	194,321	192,225	211,093	211,585	209,121	209,110	41.0	40.9	40.3	42.0	42.3	42.3	43.3
Nonprofit institutions	14,585	14,414	11,213	10,369	9,861	9,757	9,935	7,018	6,523	5,477	4,899	4,360	4,384	3,996	48.1	45.3	48.8	47.2	44.2	44.9	40.2
For-profit institutions	29,643	43,204	31,164	37,987	37,659	27,956	22,879	12,822	19,013	13,134	15,601	13,515	11,007	9,314	43.3	44.0	42.1	41.1	35.9	39.4	40.7
4-year institutions	82,367	95,410	97,051	73,376	69,350	58,104	53,825	38,257	43,441	45,678	32,720	29,048	25,327	23,701	46.4	45.5	47.1	44.6	41.9	43.6	44.0
Public institutions	48,353	48,190	63,932	34,504	29,922	28,594	27,517	23,631	23,006	31,910	17,240	15,361	14,235	13,803	48.9	47.7	49.9	50.0	51.3	49.8	50.2
Open admissions	20,223	20,645	38,295	9,470	6,318	6,291	5,553	8,298	9,122	17,982	3,852	2,626	2,443	1,991	41.0	44.2	47.0	40.7	41.6	38.8	35.9
90 percent or more accepted	3,745	3,450	2,707	3,735	4,930	2,263	2,223	1,909	1,667	1,205	1,861	2,784	998	1,005	51.0	48.3	44.5	49.8	50.5	44.1	45.2
75.0 to 89.9 percent accepted	8,969	8,145	7,476	6,504	5,650	5,993	5,226	3,818	4,196	3,872	3,277	3,106	2,886	2,595	46.8	46.9	51.8	50.4	50.5	51.8	49.7
50.0 to 74.9 percent accepted	11,599	12,236	11,969	11,496	10,667	10,801	10,671	6,766	6,245	6,649	6,131	5,699	5,802	5,840	58.3	51.0	55.6	53.3	53.4	53.7	54.7
25.0 to 49.9 percent accepted	3,373	3,023	3,084	3,125	2,262	2,854	2,965	2,223	1,866	1,992	2,023	1,330	1,681	1,844	65.9	61.7	64.6	64.7	58.8	58.9	62.2
Less than 25.0 percent accepted	65	44	42	44	43	41	49	50	34	34	35	35	27	38	76.9	77.3	81.0	79.5	81.4	65.9	77.6
Information not available	379	647	359	130	52	240	941	189	254	176	61	31	114	560	49.9	39.3	49.0	46.9	59.6	47.5	59.5

See notes at end of table.

Table 326.30. Retention of first-time degree-seeking undergraduates at degree-granting postsecondary institutions, by attendance status, level and control of institution, and percentage of applications accepted: 2006 to 2013—Continued

Attendance status, level, control, and percent of applications accepted	First-time degree-seekers (adjusted entry cohort),[1] by entry year							Students from adjusted cohort returning in the following year							Percent of first-time undergraduates retained						
	2006	2007	2008	2009	2010	2011	2012	2007	2008	2009	2010	2011	2012	2013	2006 to 2007	2007 to 2008	2008 to 2009	2009 to 2010	2010 to 2011	2011 to 2012	2012 to 2013
1	2	3	4	5	6	7	8	9	10	11	12	13	14	15	16	17	18	19	20	21	22
Nonprofit institutions	12,828	12,886	9,883	9,609	9,110	8,802	9,195	6,045	5,614	4,772	4,499	3,992	3,870	3,628	47.1	43.6	48.3	46.8	43.8	44.0	39.5
Open admissions	5,446	5,330	3,369	3,821	3,949	4,220	4,433	2,579	2,306	1,504	1,693	1,614	1,636	1,400	47.4	43.3	44.6	44.3	40.9	38.8	31.6
90 percent or more accepted	523	1,272	971	393	478	843	915	237	434	421	199	180	357	377	45.3	34.1	43.4	50.6	37.7	42.3	41.2
75.0 to 89.9 percent accepted	2,459	2,132	1,307	1,177	951	1,254	1,177	1,047	895	633	558	456	671	521	42.6	42.0	48.4	47.4	47.9	53.5	44.3
50.0 to 74.9 percent accepted	3,131	2,899	2,016	3,256	2,955	1,868	1,829	1,406	1,307	1,029	1,531	1,333	844	865	44.9	45.1	51.0	47.0	45.1	45.2	47.3
25.0 to 49.9 percent accepted	853	917	1,963	712	647	466	584	452	478	1,016	366	319	240	278	53.0	52.1	51.8	51.4	49.3	51.5	47.6
Less than 25.0 percent accepted	112	94	78	93	84	116	126	86	84	70	78	67	104	106	76.8	89.4	89.7	83.9	79.8	89.7	84.1
Information not available	304	242	179	157	46	35	131	238	110	99	74	23	18	81	78.3	45.5	55.3	47.1	50.0	51.4	61.8
For-profit institutions	21,186	34,334	23,236	29,263	30,318	20,708	17,113	8,581	14,821	8,996	10,981	9,695	7,222	6,270	40.5	43.2	38.7	37.5	32.0	34.9	36.6
Open admissions	10,515	20,602	10,933	10,996	13,052	10,632	9,561	4,105	9,896	4,296	4,333	4,767	4,251	3,909	39.0	48.0	39.3	39.4	36.5	40.0	40.9
90 percent or more accepted	2,212	1,616	3,518	1,375	2,549	2,246	360	639	735	1,037	379	569	643	137	28.9	45.5	29.5	27.6	22.3	28.6	38.1
75.0 to 89.9 percent accepted	2,838	2,702	2,057	3,151	2,407	4,145	854	1,342	959	697	1,093	527	1,106	250	47.3	35.5	33.9	34.7	21.9	26.7	29.3
50.0 to 74.9 percent accepted	2,774	4,360	3,686	4,661	6,237	525	1,819	1,134	1,399	1,707	2,283	1,996	221	594	40.9	32.1	46.3	49.0	32.0	42.1	32.7
25.0 to 49.9 percent accepted	2,033	3,185	2,584	1,099	1,826	2,933	2,537	627	951	1,116	342	583	936	727	30.8	29.9	43.2	31.1	31.9	31.9	28.7
Less than 25.0 percent accepted	0	170	48	0	0	0	0	0	67	22	0	0	0	0	†	39.4	45.8	†	†	†	†
Information not available	814	1,699	410	7,981	4,247	227	1,982	734	814	121	2,551	1,253	65	653	90.2	47.9	29.5	32.0	29.5	28.6	32.9
2-year institutions	380,867	437,417	422,568	477,305	475,877	473,896	462,200	153,329	176,416	165,158	198,873	199,412	199,185	198,719	40.3	40.3	39.1	41.6	41.9	42.0	43.0
Public institutions	370,653	427,019	413,310	468,321	467,785	465,693	455,694	148,115	171,315	160,315	193,853	195,224	194,886	195,307	40.0	40.1	38.8	41.4	41.7	41.8	42.9
Nonprofit institutions	1,757	1,528	1,330	760	751	955	740	973	909	705	400	368	514	368	55.4	59.5	53.0	52.6	49.0	53.8	49.7
For-profit institutions	8,457	8,870	7,928	8,724	7,341	7,248	5,766	4,241	4,192	4,138	4,620	3,820	3,785	3,044	50.1	47.3	52.2	53.0	52.0	52.2	52.8

†Not applicable.
[1] Adjusted student counts exclude students who died or were totally and permanently disabled, served in the armed forces (including those called to active duty), served with a foreign aid service of the federal government (e.g., Peace Corps), or served on official church missions.

SOURCE: U.S. Department of Education, National Center for Education Statistics, Integrated Postsecondary Education Data System (IPEDS), Spring 2008 through Spring 2014, Enrollment component; and IPEDS Fall 2006 through Fall 2012, Institutional Characteristics component. (This table was prepared November 2014.)

Table 326.40. Percentage distribution of first-time postsecondary students starting at 2- and 4-year institutions during the 2003–04 academic year, by highest degree attained, enrollment status, and selected characteristics: Spring 2009

[Standard errors appear in parentheses]

| Selected characteristic | Students starting at 2-year institutions — Highest degree attained ||||| | Students starting at 4-year institutions — Highest degree attained ||||| |
| | Total, any degree[1] | Certificate | Associate's | Bachelor's[2] | No degree, still enrolled | No degree, not enrolled | Total, any degree[1] | Certificate | Associate's | Bachelor's[2] | No degree, still enrolled | No degree, not enrolled |
1	2	3	4	5	6	7	8	9	10	11	12	13
Total	35.1 (0.86)	9.5 (0.68)	15.0 (0.63)	10.6 (0.63)	18.5 (0.98)	46.4 (1.01)	64.2 (1.18)	1.7 (0.24)	4.6 (0.49)	58.0 (1.34)	12.2 (0.60)	23.6 (0.97)
Sex												
Male	33.3 (1.54)	9.4 (1.19)	13.7 (1.00)	10.3 (0.79)	19.1 (1.64)	47.6 (1.54)	61.4 (1.40)	1.2 (0.29)	5.1 (0.72)	55.1 (1.54)	13.9 (0.86)	24.8 (1.18)
Female	36.5 (1.18)	9.6 (0.90)	16.0 (0.92)	10.9 (0.83)	18.1 (0.93)	45.4 (1.37)	66.5 (1.45)	2.1 (0.34)	4.2 (0.51)	60.2 (1.58)	10.9 (0.71)	22.6 (1.24)
Age when first enrolled												
18 years old or younger	39.4 (1.63)	6.1 (0.78)	15.5 (1.24)	17.9 (1.36)	20.6 (1.70)	40.0 (1.58)	69.1 (1.27)	1.6 (0.29)	3.7 (0.45)	63.8 (1.41)	11.2 (0.76)	19.8 (1.07)
19 years old	37.7 (2.04)	8.9 (2.01)	16.2 (1.46)	12.6 (1.21)	17.7 (1.57)	44.6 (1.75)	65.1 (1.43)	1.0 (0.24)	4.2 (0.63)	59.9 (1.51)	12.3 (0.92)	22.6 (1.16)
20 to 23 years old	29.1 (1.94)	10.3 (1.38)	14.6 (1.68)	4.1 (0.69)	21.9 (1.92)	49.0 (2.10)	41.9 (3.78)	4.1! (1.62)	8.4 (1.74)	29.4 (3.71)	17.8 (2.91)	40.3 (3.49)
24 to 29 years old	28.8 (4.04)	15.6 (3.98)	10.8 (1.98)	2.5 (0.74)	17.2 (2.62)	53.9 (4.05)	32.7 (5.77)	‡ (†)	9.4! (4.28)	20.4 (5.06)	18.8 (4.87)	48.6 (5.81)
30 years old or over	31.7 (2.43)	14.4 (2.08)	15.0 (1.89)	‡ (†)	10.4 (1.97)	57.9 (2.65)	33.7 (7.09)	3.9! (1.84)	13.4! (5.05)	16.4! (6.14)	14.8 (3.97)	51.4 (7.32)
Race/ethnicity												
White	38.9 (1.16)	9.8 (1.0)	16.6 (0.82)	12.5 (0.85)	16.2 (1.21)	44.9 (1.31)	68.9 (1.04)	1.5 (0.31)	4.8 (0.54)	62.6 (1.31)	9.8 (0.58)	21.4 (0.94)
Black	28.1 (2.60)	11.3 (1.66)	11.4 (2.12)	5.3 (1.10)	22.0 (2.04)	50.0 (2.79)	46.9 (3.16)	2.2 (0.91)	4.2! (1.48)	40.5 (3.03)	19.6 (2.21)	33.6 (3.08)
Hispanic	28.3 (2.18)	8.2 (1.67)	12.7 (1.51)	7.4 (1.10)	18.8 (2.03)	52.9 (2.58)	48.8 (3.24)	2.2! (0.83)	5.1 (1.39)	41.5 (2.96)	18.6 (2.36)	32.5 (3.34)
Asian/Pacific Islander	38.3 (4.50)	6.5! (2.29)	14.6 (2.91)	17.2 (3.50)	29.0 (4.58)	32.7 (3.51)	72.8 (3.21)	1.4! (0.67)	2.1! (0.94)	69.3 (3.22)	11.9 (2.23)	15.2 (2.59)
American Indian/Alaska Native	32.1 (9.62)	‡ (†)	‡ (†)	‡ (†)	28.4! (10.89)	39.6 (10.68)	51.5 (9.53)	‡ (†)	‡ (†)	39.3 (9.11)	19.3! (8.63)	29.3! (10.85)
Two or more races	33.9 (5.51)	9.0! (3.65)	14.6! (4.39)	10.3 (2.87)	21.4 (4.98)	44.7 (5.50)	57.1 (5.42)	‡ (†)	4.0! (1.83)	50.4 (5.57)	19.2 (4.71)	23.6 (4.32)
Highest education level of parents												
High school diploma or less	32.0 (1.42)	11.0 (1.30)	14.3 (1.05)	6.7 (0.72)	17.1 (1.18)	50.9 (1.51)	49.9 (2.12)	2.9 (0.83)	6.6 (0.97)	40.4 (2.01)	15.4 (1.33)	34.7 (1.98)
Some college/vocational	38.3 (2.24)	9.6 (1.48)	17.6 (1.17)	11.1 (1.07)	18.0 (1.70)	43.8 (2.06)	59.1 (1.90)	2.3! (0.76)	7.0 (1.08)	49.8 (2.11)	13.4 (1.24)	27.5 (1.84)
Bachelor's degree	39.4 (1.91)	8.2 (1.60)	14.1 (1.87)	17.2 (1.74)	20.6 (2.09)	40.0 (2.53)	70.1 (1.60)	1.2 (0.28)	3.4 (0.58)	65.6 (1.62)	11.0 (0.87)	18.9 (1.41)
Advanced (higher than bachelor's) degree	37.2 (3.03)	6.2 (1.70)	13.7 (1.81)	17.2 (2.09)	22.4 (2.56)	40.4 (3.74)	75.8 (1.44)	0.6! (0.24)	2.1 (0.39)	73.1 (1.51)	9.2 (0.78)	15.0 (1.35)
Dependency status when first enrolled												
Dependent	39.4 (1.26)	7.5 (0.76)	16.7 (0.85)	15.2 (0.88)	19.6 (1.19)	41.0 (1.15)	68.3 (1.06)	1.4 (0.22)	4.2 (0.45)	62.7 (1.22)	11.6 (0.63)	20.1 (0.90)
Independent	28.3 (1.44)	12.8 (1.26)	12.3 (1.13)	3.3 (0.60)	16.8 (1.42)	54.9 (1.75)	31.4 (3.08)	3.7 (1.10)	7.5 (1.92)	20.2 (2.84)	17.3 (2.61)	51.3 (3.25)
Dependent student family income in 2002												
Less than $25,000	34.6 (2.35)	8.4 (1.48)	14.5 (1.54)	11.7 (1.73)	18.0 (1.91)	47.4 (2.43)	52.7 (2.28)	2.8! (1.09)	5.0 (1.00)	44.9 (2.40)	15.9 (1.63)	31.4 (2.38)
$25,000 to $44,999	36.0 (2.12)	7.3 (1.36)	16.4 (1.75)	12.3 (1.60)	19.0 (2.24)	45.0 (2.67)	62.7 (2.31)	1.9 (0.53)	5.4 (1.03)	55.3 (2.50)	13.1 (1.69)	24.2 (1.97)
$45,000 to $69,999	41.3 (2.13)	7.1 (1.29)	17.6 (1.59)	16.6 (1.58)	22.0 (1.92)	36.7 (1.86)	67.1 (1.94)	1.5 (0.34)	5.1 (0.77)	60.6 (2.00)	12.8 (1.27)	20.1 (1.86)
$70,000 to $99,999	43.1 (3.50)	7.6! (3.67)	16.3 (2.58)	19.1 (2.14)	18.4 (2.75)	38.5 (2.76)	71.9 (1.64)	0.9! (0.30)	4.4 (0.88)	66.7 (1.85)	9.4 (0.83)	18.7 (1.37)
$100,000 or more	45.0 (3.56)	6.6 (1.77)	19.6 (3.74)	18.8 (2.40)	20.5 (3.25)	34.4 (3.61)	80.0 (1.30)	0.7! (0.29)	1.9 (0.37)	77.5 (1.38)	8.5 (0.94)	11.4 (0.99)
Timing of postsecondary enrollment												
Delayed entry	29.1 (1.25)	11.0 (1.11)	13.2 (1.02)	4.9 (0.63)	17.2 (1.26)	53.7 (1.44)	36.6 (2.80)	3.8 (1.01)	7.9 (1.54)	24.9 (2.53)	17.8 (2.06)	45.6 (2.75)
Did not delay entry[3]	41.0 (1.36)	7.8 (0.86)	17.0 (0.99)	16.2 (1.00)	20.1 (1.44)	38.8 (1.16)	69.2 (1.05)	1.3 (0.21)	4.0 (0.40)	64.0 (1.17)	11.1 (0.61)	19.6 (0.91)
Intensity of enrollment through 2009												
Always full-time	44.9 (1.66)	11.4 (1.50)	18.0 (1.42)	15.5 (1.11)	10.1 (0.87)	44.9 (1.65)	73.7 (1.15)	1.2 (0.26)	3.8 (0.55)	68.7 (1.41)	6.7 (0.46)	19.6 (1.03)
Always part-time	13.9 (2.80)	8.4! (2.79)	5.5 (1.12)	‡ (†)	13.3 (1.79)	72.8 (2.68)	12.5! (4.93)	‡ (†)	‡ (†)	‡ (†)	13.8! (4.23)	73.6 (6.59)
Mixed	36.6 (1.32)	8.7 (0.83)	16.6 (1.10)	11.4 (0.99)	26.1 (1.34)	37.2 (1.69)	48.3 (1.59)	2.7 (0.47)	6.1 (0.72)	39.5 (1.60)	23.3 (1.39)	28.4 (1.42)
Remedial course taken in 2003–04												
No	35.4 (0.95)	10.0 (0.84)	14.5 (0.81)	10.9 (0.78)	17.6 (0.99)	47.0 (1.21)	65.2 (1.23)	1.8 (0.28)	4.4 (0.53)	59.0 (1.43)	11.5 (0.62)	23.4 (1.05)
Yes	34.3 (2.10)	8.3 (1.62)	16.2 (1.37)	9.8 (0.98)	21.0 (1.70)	44.7 (1.92)	59.6 (1.98)	1.2 (0.32)	5.4 (0.92)	53.0 (2.13)	15.7 (1.44)	24.6 (1.81)

See notes at end of table.

Table 326.40. Percentage distribution of first-time postsecondary students starting at 2- and 4-year institutions during the 2003–04 academic year, by highest degree attained, enrollment status, and selected characteristics: Spring 2009—Continued

[Standard errors appear in parentheses]

Selected characteristic	Students starting at 2-year institutions						Students starting at 4-year institutions					
	Highest degree attained				No degree, still enrolled	No degree, not enrolled	Highest degree attained				No degree, still enrolled	No degree, not enrolled
	Total, any degree[1]	Certificate	Associate's	Bachelor's[2]			Total, any degree[1]	Certificate	Associate's	Bachelor's[2]		
1	2	3	4	5	6	7	8	9	10	11	12	13
Highest degree expected in 2003–04												
No degree or certificate	‡ (†)	‡ (†)	‡ (†)	# (†)	‡ (†)	87.3 (4.75)	‡ (†)	‡ (†)	‡ (†)	‡ (†)	‡ (†)	‡ (†)
Certificate	44.8 (5.47)	42.8 (5.28)	‡ (†)	‡ (†)	6.9 (2.02)	48.3 (5.60)	41.2 ! (18.43)	‡ (†)	‡ (†)	‡ (†)	‡ (5.09)	‡ (†)
Associate's degree	34.6 (2.38)	13.9 (2.05)	19.3 (1.86)	1.4 ! (0.49)	12.3 (1.69)	53.1 (2.80)	43.7 (8.43)	16.2 ! (5.50)	21.3 ! (7.06)	6.1 ! (2.93)	12.8 ! (5.09)	43.5 (7.70)
Bachelor's degree[4]	32.7 (1.81)	8.0 (1.49)	15.4 (1.02)	9.3 (1.03)	18.1 (1.50)	49.3 (1.60)	55.2 (2.02)	2.2 (0.52)	6.8 (1.02)	46.2 (2.07)	15.1 (1.37)	29.7 (1.59)
Master's degree[4]	38.2 (1.72)	7.0 (1.32)	14.8 (1.21)	16.4 (1.19)	22.7 (1.63)	39.1 (1.66)	66.7 (1.42)	1.0 (0.25)	4.1 (0.62)	61.7 (1.42)	11.2 (0.77)	22.1 (1.32)
Doctoral/first-professional degree[4]	34.7 (2.30)	4.8 (0.93)	13.8 (2.02)	16.0 (1.65)	22.4 (2.54)	42.9 (3.25)	70.6 (1.57)	1.3 (0.36)	1.9 (0.36)	67.4 (1.69)	11.0 (0.95)	18.3 (1.35)
Work intensity (including work-study) in 2003–04												
Did not work	34.7 (1.79)	11.2 (1.57)	15.8 (1.20)	7.7 (0.85)	19.9 (1.80)	45.3 (2.16)	69.9 (1.35)	0.8 (0.18)	3.4 (0.55)	65.8 (1.47)	10.9 (0.92)	19.1 (1.08)
Worked part time	39.9 (2.08)	7.9 (1.20)	17.4 (1.00)	14.6 (1.04)	17.2 (1.28)	42.8 (1.70)	66.2 (1.42)	1.7 (0.31)	5.2 (0.69)	59.3 (1.44)	12.1 (0.85)	21.7 (1.21)
Worked full time	28.6 (1.96)	10.6 (1.63)	10.9 (1.08)	7.2 (0.94)	19.3 (1.53)	52.1 (2.10)	40.1 (2.93)	4.1 (1.22)	5.9 (1.20)	30.1 (2.60)	16.5 (1.77)	43.4 (2.86)
Control of first institution												
Public	34.4 (0.95)	8.5 (0.68)	14.4 (0.61)	11.6 (0.68)	19.6 (1.03)	46.0 (1.00)	64.8 (1.22)	1.6 (0.23)	3.8 (0.45)	59.5 (1.32)	12.9 (0.73)	22.2 (0.98)
Private, nonprofit	46.2 (8.52)	13.3 ! (6.56)	21.5 ! (6.76)	11.3 ! (4.99)	10.4 ! (3.32)	43.4 (8.28)	69.9 (1.45)	1.5 (0.37)	3.8 (0.95)	64.6 (1.89)	11.1 (1.02)	19.0 (1.18)
Private, for profit	39.5 (3.70)	19.6 (4.78)	19.5 (3.51)	‡ (†)	9.6 (2.61)	50.9 (4.64)	33.9 (4.37)	‡ (†)	14.6 (3.45)	15.7 (3.78)	11.3 (2.44)	54.8 (3.82)
Income quartile in 2003–04[5]												
Lowest quartile	30.6 (1.45)	9.4 (1.27)	13.0 (1.14)	8.3 (0.84)	18.4 (1.46)	51.0 (1.78)	49.5 (1.91)	2.7 (0.73)	4.6 (0.74)	42.2 (2.15)	16.2 (1.37)	34.3 (1.75)
Second quartile	37.1 (1.58)	10.5 (1.56)	15.8 (1.26)	10.8 (0.97)	19.7 (1.58)	43.2 (1.86)	60.5 (2.04)	2.4 (0.51)	6.5 (1.10)	51.6 (2.20)	13.5 (1.16)	26.0 (1.82)
Third quartile	36.3 (2.51)	9.6 (1.71)	15.0 (1.35)	11.6 (1.53)	18.7 (1.64)	45.0 (2.18)	67.2 (1.58)	1.3 (0.31)	4.9 (0.80)	61.0 (1.85)	11.2 (0.88)	21.6 (1.55)
Highest quartile	38.6 (2.51)	8.1 (1.49)	17.3 (1.96)	13.2 (1.65)	16.5 (2.30)	45.0 (3.20)	76.8 (1.37)	0.6 ! (0.25)	2.4 (0.46)	73.8 (1.42)	8.7 (0.80)	14.4 (1.18)

†Not applicable.

#Rounds to zero.

!Interpret data with caution. The coefficient of variation (CV) for this estimate is between 30 and 50 percent.

‡Reporting standards not met. Either there are too few cases for a reliable estimate or the coefficient of variation (CV) is 50 percent or greater.

[1]Includes a small percentage of students who had attained a degree and were still enrolled. Includes recipients of degrees not shown separately.

[2]Includes a small percentage of students who had attained an advanced degree.

[3]Includes students with a standard high school diploma who enrolled in postsecondary education in the same year as their graduation.

[4]Students starting at 2-year institutions include students whose goal was to transfer to a 4-year institution.

[5]Indicates the income quartile of the student, based on the student's total income in 2002 for independent students or the parents' total income in 2002 for dependent students. Income quartiles were determined separately for dependent and independent students based on percentile rankings and then combined into one variable.

NOTE: Race categories exclude persons of Hispanic ethnicity. Detail may not sum to totals because of rounding.

SOURCE: U.S. Department of Education, National Center for Education Statistics, 2004/09 Beginning Postsecondary Students Longitudinal Study (BPS:04/09). (This table was prepared November 2011.)

Table 327.10. Average scores and standard deviations on Graduate Record Examination (GRE) general and subject tests: 1965 through 2013

[Standard deviations appear in square brackets]

Academic year ending	Number of GRE takers	GRE takers as a percent of bachelor's degrees[1]	General test sections — Verbal	Quantitative	Analytical reasoning[3]	Analytical writing[3]	Subject tests[2] — Biochemistry, cell and molecular biology	Biology	Chemistry	Computer science	Education	Engineering	Literature	Mathematics	Physics	Psychology
1	2	3	4	5	6	7	8	9	10	11	12	13	14	15	16	17
			Former scale (200–800)[4]													
1965	93,792	18.7	530 [124]	533 [137]	†	†	†	617 [117]	628 [114]	†	481 [86]	618 [108]	591 [95]	—	—	556 [91]
1966	123,960	23.8	520 [124]	528 [133]	†	†	†	610 [115]	618 [110]	†	474 [87]	609 [106]	588 [94]	—	—	552 [91]
1967	151,134	27.0	519 [125]	528 [134]	†	†	†	613 [114]	615 [104]	†	476 [90]	603 [104]	582 [91]	—	—	553 [93]
1968	182,432	28.8	520 [124]	527 [135]	†	†	†	614 [114]	617 [104]	†	478 [87]	601 [105]	572 [91]	—	—	547 [93]
1969	206,113	28.3	515 [124]	524 [132]	†	†	†	613 [112]	613 [104]	†	477 [88]	591 [103]	569 [89]	—	—	543 [89]
1970	265,359	33.5	503 [123]	516 [132]	†	†	†	603 [111]	613 [113]	†	462 [92]	586 [110]	556 [90]	—	—	532 [91]
1971	298,600	35.0	497 [125]	512 [134]	†	†	†	603 [114]	618 [117]	†	457 [95]	587 [115]	546 [91]	—	—	530 [92]
1972	293,506	33.1	494 [126]	508 [136]	†	†	†	606 [115]	624 [124]	†	446 [93]	594 [119]	544 [96]	—	—	528 [92]
1973	290,104	31.5	497 [125]	512 [135]	†	†	†	619 [110]	630 [114]	†	459 [96]	593 [114]	545 [96]	—	—	529 [92]
1974	301,070	31.8	492 [126]	509 [137]	†	†	†	624 [110]	634 [115]	†	452 [93]	591 [121]	547 [99]	—	—	530 [95]
1975	298,335	32.3	493 [125]	508 [137]	†	†	†	—	—	†	—	—	—	—	—	—
1976	299,292	32.3	492 [127]	510 [138]	†	†	†	627 [112]	627 [107]	†	454 [93]	594 [119]	539 [101]	—	—	531 [93]
1977	287,715	31.3	490 [129]	514 [139]	†	†	†	625 [113]	630 [109]	†	453 [93]	592 [115]	532 [101]	—	—	532 [95]
1978	286,383	31.1	484 [128]	518 [135]	†	†	†	622 [113]	624 [114]	†	452 [91]	594 [114]	530 [102]	—	—	529 [97]
1979	282,482	30.7	476 [130]	517 [135]	†	†	†	621 [117]	623 [104]	†	451 [89]	592 [115]	525 [102]	—	—	530 [97]
1980	272,281	29.3	474 [131]	522 [136]	†	†	†	619 [115]	618 [105]	†	449 [90]	590 [116]	521 [105]	—	—	534 [98]
1981	262,855	28.1	473 [128]	523 [136]	†	†	†	617 [115]	615 [103]	†	453 [90]	590 [116]	520 [99]	—	—	532 [97]
1982	256,381	26.9	469 [130]	533 [137]	498 [126]	†	†	616 [114]	616 [105]	†	456 [89]	593 [115]	521 [100]	—	—	532 [97]
1983	263,674	27.2	473 [131]	541 [138]	504 [128]	†	†	623 [115]	620 [105]	†	459 [90]	599 [114]	527 [98]	—	—	542 [95]
1984	265,221	27.2	475 [130]	541 [139]	512 [129]	†	†	622 [115]	619 [102]	†	461 [90]	604 [114]	530 [97]	—	—	543 [96]
1985	271,972	27.8	474 [126]	545 [140]	516 [129]	†	†	619 [114]	621 [101]	†	459 [89]	615 [120]	531 [95]	—	—	541 [95]
1986	279,428	28.3	475 [126]	552 [140]	520 [129]	†	†	612 [114]	628 [106]	†	464 [87]	616 [119]	527 [96]	—	—	542 [97]
1987	293,560	29.6	477 [126]	550 [140]	521 [128]	†	†	616 [116]	629 [104]	†	465 [86]	619 [119]	526 [95]	—	—	536 [95]
1988	303,703	30.5	483 [123]	557 [140]	528 [128]	†	†	615 [116]	631 [108]	†	467 [85]	622 [120]	525 [94]	—	—	537 [94]
1989	326,096	32.0	484 [125]	560 [142]	530 [129]	†	†	612 [114]	642 [117]	†	465 [87]	626 [116]	528 [91]	—	—	538 [95]
1990	344,572	32.8	486 [123]	562 [143]	534 [128]	†	†	612 [114]	662 [123]	†	461 [84]	617 [111]	523 [92]	—	—	537 [95]
1991	379,882	34.7	485 [122]	562 [141]	536 [129]	†	†	609 [113]	660 [123]	†	457 [85]	611 [111]	523 [93]	—	—	535 [95]
1992	411,528	36.2	483 [120]	561 [140]	537 [129]	†	†	605 [113]	654 [128]	†	462 [82]	610 [117]	525 [92]	—	—	536 [95]
1993	400,246	34.4	481 [117]	557 [140]	541 [129]	†	—	606 [114]	662 [133]	†	462 [80]	602 [115]	516 [94]	—	—	536 [97]
1994	399,395[5]	34.2	479 [116]	553 [139]	545 [129]	†	—	620 [116]	627 [113]	†	493[6] [104]	601 [115]	517 [95]	—	—	538 [96]
1995	389,539[5]	33.6	477 [115]	553 [140]	544 [131]	†	—	622 [116]	675 [138]	†	488[6] [102]	596 [113]	513 [96]	—	—	544 [98]
1996	376,013[5]	32.3	473 [114]	558 [139]	549 [131]	†	—	614 [114]	678 [135]	†	489[6] [104]	604 [119]	512 [97]	—	—	547 [99]
1997	376,062[5]	32.1	472 [113]	562 [139]	548 [129]	†	—	620 [115]	684 [143]	†	487[6] [103]	602 [114]	525 [100]	—	—	554 [99]
1998	364,554[5]	30.8	471 [113]	569 [141]	543 [133]	†	—	628 [113]	686 [137]	†	477[6] [100]	609 [118]	530 [100]	—	—	563 [100]
1999	396,350	33.0	468 [114]	565 [143]	542 [133]	†	—	626 [114]	684 [137]	—	†	604 [115]	527 [100]	—	—	559 [99]

See notes at end of table.

Table 327.10. Average scores and standard deviations on Graduate Record Examination (GRE) general and subject tests: 1965 through 2013—Continued

[Standard deviations appear in square brackets]

Academic year ending	Number of GRE takers	GRE takers as a percent of bachelor's degrees[1]	General test sections				Subject tests[2]									
			Verbal	Quantitative	Analytical reasoning[3]	Analytical writing[3]	Biochemistry, cell and molecular biology	Biology	Chemistry	Computer science	Education	Engineering	Literature	Mathematics	Physics	Psychology
1	2	3	4	5	6	7	8	9	10	11	12	13	14	15	16	17
2007[7]	387,422	31.3	465 [116]	578 [147]	562 [141]	† [†]	— [†]	629 [114]	686 [133]	— [†]	† [†]	— [†]	530 [99]	— [†]	— [†]	563 [98]
2001	433,109	34.8	— [†]	— [†]	— [†]	† [†]	— [†]	— [†]	— [†]	— [†]	† [†]	— [†]	— [†]	— [†]	— [†]	— [†]
2002	536,523	41.5	473 [123]	597 [151]	571 [139]	† [†]	— [†]	— [†]	— [†]	— [†]	† [†]	† [†]	— [†]	— [†]	— [†]	— [†]
2003[9]	440,982	32.7	470 [121]	598 [148]	† [†]	4.2 [1.0]	517 [100]	635 [114]	682 [125]	712 [97]	† [†]	† [†]	538 [98]	620 [131]	669 [151]	580 [101]
2004[8,9,10]	446,661	31.9	469 [120]	597 [148]	† [†]	4.2 [1.0]	517 [101]	643 [115]	675 [120]	715 [93]	† [†]	† [†]	537 [97]	621 [130]	665 [148]	586 [101]
2005[8,9,10]	474,594	33.0	467 [118]	591 [148]	†	4.2 [0.9]	518 [100]	647 [117]	675 [117]	715 [91]	† [†]	† [†]	540 [97]	623 [130]	672 [151]	592 [101]
2006[8,10,11]	506,633	34.1	465 [117]	584 [149]	†	4.1 [0.9]	519 [99]	650 [118]	677 [116]	717 [92]	† [†]	† [†]	541 [97]	627 [129]	678 [153]	598 [101]
2007[8,10,11]	556,729	36.5	462 [119]	584 [151]	†	4.0 [0.9]	521 [97]	650 [120]	689 [115]	715 [91]	† [†]	† [†]	542 [98]	636 [130]	686 [155]	600 [101]
2008[8,10,11]	540,441	34.6	457 [121]	586 [152]	†	3.9 [0.9]	525 [97]	651 [120]	694 [116]	712 [92]	† [†]	† [†]	541 [98]	640 [131]	692 [156]	603 [101]
2009[8,10,11]	597,171	37.3	456 [120]	590 [150]	†	3.8 [0.9]	523 [97]	650 [120]	699 [115]	708 [91]	† [†]	† [†]	541 [97]	648 [134]	692 [156]	605 [103]
2010[8]	630,212	38.2	— [†]	— [†]	†	—	525 [97]	651 [121]	700 [115]	702 [96]	† [†]	† [†]	542 [98]	650 [134]	692 [157]	609 [103]
Revised scale (130-170)[4]																
2011[8]	700,713	40.8	151[12] [8.5]	151[12] [8.7]	†	3.7[12] [0.9]	525 [97]	651 [122]	703 [114]	698 [99]	† [†]	† [†]	547 [98]	655 [135]	689 [156]	612 [103]
2012[8]	585,959	32.7	151[12] [8.4]	151[12] [8.8]	†	3.6[12] [0.9]	526 [95]	658 [123]	703 [115]	693 [100]	† [†]	† [†]	549 [99]	657 [136]	696 [158]	616 [102]
2013[8]	662,493	36.0	151[12] [8.4]	151[12] [8.8]	†	3.6[12] [0.9]	524 [94]	664 [121]	700 [114]	— [†]	† [†]	† [†]	551 [98]	658 [136]	702 [156]	616 [102]

—Not available.

†Not applicable.

[1] GRE takers include examinees from inside and outside of the United States, while the bachelor's degrees include only those conferred by U.S. institutions.

[2] The range of scores is different for the various subject tests, from as low as 200 to as high as 990. The education subject test was administered for the final time in April 1998. The engineering subject test was administered for the final time in April 2001.

[3] The analytical reasoning section of the GRE, a multiple-choice test, was discontinued in September 2002 and replaced by the analytical writing section, an essay-based test. Scores for the analytical writing section range from 0 to 6, in half-point increments.

[4] Prior to 2011, GRE scores for the verbal and quantitative sections ranged from 200 to 800, in 10-point increments, as did scores for the analytical reasoning section until it was replaced by the analytical writing section in 2002. On August 1, 2011, the GRE revised general test was introduced. Scores for the revised verbal reasoning and quantitative reasoning sections range from 130 to 170, in 1-point increments. In the revised general test, the score scale for the analytical writing section continues to range from 0 to 6, in half-point increments.

[5] Total includes examinees who received no score on one or more general test measures.

[6] Data reported for 1994 through 1998 are from the revised education test.

[7] Subject test score data reflect the 3-year average for all examinees who tested between October 1 three years prior to the reported test year and September 30 of the reported test year. These data are not directly comparable with data for most other years.

[8] Subject test score data reflect the 3-year average for all examinees who tested between July 1 three years prior to the reported test year and June 30 of the reported test year. These data are not directly comparable with previous years, except for 1999 and 2000.

[9] Analytical writing test score data reflect the average for all examinees who tested between October 1, 2002, and June 30 of the reported test year.

[10] Verbal and quantitative test score data reflect the 3-year average for all examinees who tested between July 1 three years prior to the reported test year and June 30 of the reported test year. These data are not directly comparable with previous years.

[11] Analytical writing test score data reflect the 3-year average for all examinees who tested between July 1 three years prior to the reported test year and June 30 of the reported test year.

[12] For all three sections of the revised general test, 2011 scores are based on the performance of all examinees who tested between August 1, 2011, and April 30, 2012; 2012 scores are based on the performance of all examinees who tested between August 1, 2011, and April 30, 2013; and 2013 scores are based on the performance of all examinees who tested between August 1, 2011, and April 30, 2014. These scores are not comparable with scores from previous years.

NOTE: GRE data include test takers from both within and outside of the United States.
SOURCE: Graduate Record Examination Board, *Examinee and Score Trends for the GRE General Test, 1964–65 through 1985–86; A Summary of Data Collected From Graduate Record Examinations Test-Takers During 1986–87; Guide to the Use of Scores, 1987–88 through 2014–15; GRE Volumes by Country, 2000–2013;* and *Interpreting Your GRE Scores, 2005–06 through 2011–12.* U.S. Department of Education, National Center for Education Statistics, Higher Education General Information Survey (HEGIS), "Degrees and Other Formal Awards Conferred" surveys, 1964–65 through 1985–86; Integrated Postsecondary Education Data System (IPEDS), "Completions Survey" (IPEDS-C:87–99); and IPEDS Fall 2000 through Fall 2013, Completions component. (This table was prepared March 2015.)

Table 329.10. On-campus crimes, arrests, and referrals for disciplinary action at degree-granting postsecondary institutions, by location of incident, control and level of institution, and type of incident: 2001 through 2012

Control and level of institution and type of incident	2001	2002	2003	2004	2005	2006	2007	2008	2009	2010	2011	2012 Total	2012 In residence halls	2012 At other locations
1	2	3	4	5	6	7	8	9	10	11	12	13	14	15
All institutions														
Selected crimes against persons and property	41,596	42,521	43,064	43,555	42,710	44,492	41,829	40,296	34,054	32,097	30,678	29,527	14,589	14,938
Murder[1]	17	20	9	15	11	8	44	12	16	15	16	11	5	6
Negligent manslaughter[2]	2	0	1	0	2	0	3	3	0	1	1	1	1	0
Sex offenses—forcible[3]	2,201	2,327	2,595	2,667	2,674	2,670	2,694	2,639	2,544	2,927	3,387	3,885	2,792	1,093
Sex offenses—nonforcible[4]	461	261	60	27	42	43	40	35	65	33	47	44	19	25
Robbery[5]	1,663	1,802	1,625	1,550	1,551	1,547	1,561	1,576	1,409	1,392	1,304	1,362	232	1,130
Aggravated assault[6]	2,947	2,804	2,832	2,721	2,656	2,817	2,604	2,495	2,327	2,221	2,270	2,403	803	1,600
Burglary[7]	26,904	28,038	28,639	29,480	29,256	31,260	29,488	28,737	23,083	21,335	19,610	18,099	10,288	7,811
Motor vehicle theft[8]	6,221	6,181	6,285	6,062	5,531	5,231	4,619	4,104	3,977	3,441	3,402	3,033	10	3,023
Arson[9]	1,180	1,088	1,018	1,033	987	916	776	695	633	732	641	689	439	250
Weapons-, drug-, and liquor-related arrests and referrals														
Arrests[10]	40,348	43,407	44,581	47,939	49,024	50,187	50,558	50,639	50,066	51,519	54,439	51,387	25,762	25,625
Illegal weapons possession	1,073	1,142	1,094	1,263	1,316	1,316	1,318	1,190	1,077	1,112	1,033	1,031	268	763
Drug law violations	11,854	12,041	12,467	12,775	13,707	13,952	14,135	15,146	15,871	18,589	20,788	20,842	10,792	10,050
Liquor law violations	27,421	30,224	31,020	33,901	34,001	34,919	35,105	34,303	33,118	31,818	32,618	29,514	14,702	14,812
Referrals for disciplinary action[10]	155,201	167,319	184,915	196,775	202,816	218,040	216,600	217,526	220,987	230,269	250,079	248,882	223,334	25,548
Illegal weapons possession	1,277	1,287	1,566	1,799	1,882	1,871	1,658	1,455	1,275	1,314	1,298	1,405	919	486
Drug law violations	23,900	26,038	25,753	25,762	25,356	27,251	28,476	32,469	36,344	42,022	51,706	54,009	45,467	8,542
Liquor law violations	130,024	139,994	157,596	169,214	175,578	188,918	186,466	183,602	183,368	186,933	197,075	193,468	176,948	16,520
Public 4-year														
Selected crimes against persons and property	18,710	19,563	19,789	19,984	19,582	20,648	19,579	18,695	15,975	15,503	14,725	14,206	7,066	7,140
Murder[1]	9	9	5	8	4	5	42	9	8	9	10	6	5	1
Negligent manslaughter[2]	2	0	1	0	1	0	2	1	0	0	1	1	1	0
Sex offenses—forcible[3]	1,245	1,278	1,358	1,482	1,398	1,400	1,425	1,317	1,214	1,461	1,645	1,877	1,313	564
Sex offenses—nonforcible[4]	207	113	28	16	25	15	23	12	40	15	17	16	9	7
Robbery[5]	584	659	669	612	696	680	722	750	647	662	616	652	156	496
Aggravated assault[6]	1,434	1,320	1,381	1,269	1,280	1,338	1,258	1,182	1,134	1,076	1,083	1,184	437	747
Burglary[7]	11,520	12,523	12,634	13,026	12,935	14,027	13,371	12,970	10,708	10,219	9,386	8,659	4,864	3,795
Motor vehicle theft[8]	3,072	3,092	3,116	2,964	2,667	2,662	2,266	2,027	1,824	1,604	1,610	1,399	10	1,389
Arson[9]	637	569	597	607	576	521	470	427	400	457	357	412	271	141
Weapons-, drug-, and liquor-related arrests and referrals														
Arrests[10]	31,077	33,831	34,657	36,746	38,051	39,900	39,570	40,607	40,780	41,992	44,999	42,116	21,176	20,940
Illegal weapons possession	692	745	697	811	878	859	825	759	659	669	633	630	192	438
Drug law violations	9,125	9,238	9,389	9,620	10,606	10,850	10,693	11,714	12,186	14,362	16,362	16,398	8,701	7,697
Liquor law violations	21,260	23,848	24,571	26,315	26,567	28,191	28,052	28,134	27,935	26,961	28,004	25,088	12,283	12,805
Referrals for disciplinary action[10]	79,152	84,636	94,365	100,588	100,211	107,289	106,148	104,585	108,756	116,029	129,718	129,585	117,419	12,166
Illegal weapons possession	678	675	847	1,001	1,097	972	867	792	669	664	615	650	457	193
Drug law violations	13,179	13,943	13,811	13,658	13,020	13,798	14,458	16,656	18,260	21,451	27,356	28,869	24,523	4,346
Liquor law violations	65,295	70,018	79,707	85,929	86,094	92,519	90,823	87,137	89,827	93,914	101,747	100,066	92,439	7,627
Nonprofit 4-year														
Selected crimes against persons and property	14,844	14,859	15,179	15,523	15,574	16,864	15,452	14,892	11,964	11,202	10,751	10,738	6,565	4,173
Murder[1]	5	9	2	4	5	3	2	1	6	5	3	2	0	2
Negligent manslaughter[2]	0	0	0	0	1	0	1	0	0	0	0	0	0	0
Sex offenses—forcible[3]	820	914	1,048	1,026	1,088	1,080	1,065	1,083	1,102	1,225	1,432	1,710	1,389	321
Sex offenses—nonforcible[4]	113	81	14	5	6	10	8	16	11	8	13	10	8	2
Robbery[5]	649	735	538	577	500	502	460	437	366	319	324	366	50	316
Aggravated assault[6]	882	900	773	838	744	834	768	754	661	641	631	647	269	378
Burglary[7]	10,471	10,561	11,066	11,426	11,657	13,051	11,941	11,551	8,810	8,138	7,426	7,071	4,688	2,383
Motor vehicle theft[8]	1,471	1,273	1,385	1,316	1,248	1,077	984	859	834	641	705	704	0	704
Arson[9]	433	386	353	331	325	307	223	191	174	225	217	228	161	67
Weapons-, drug-, and liquor-related arrests and referrals														
Arrests[10]	6,329	6,548	6,856	7,722	7,406	6,134	6,732	6,112	5,777	5,459	5,452	5,559	3,121	2,438
Illegal weapons possession	167	162	166	184	150	146	178	158	148	137	131	126	48	78
Drug law violations	1,628	1,723	1,869	1,751	1,691	1,650	1,804	1,883	2,080	2,248	2,428	2,436	1,554	882
Liquor law violations	4,534	4,663	4,821	5,787	5,565	4,338	4,750	4,071	3,549	3,074	2,893	2,997	1,519	1,478
Referrals for disciplinary action[10]	71,293	77,641	85,184	90,749	96,646	103,484	103,254	105,289	103,457	104,939	110,647	110,448	98,671	11,777
Illegal weapons possession	443	424	537	608	590	622	545	457	358	393	421	494	356	138
Drug law violations	9,688	11,100	10,885	10,903	11,208	12,114	12,685	14,157	15,845	17,841	21,244	22,198	18,957	3,241
Liquor law violations	61,162	66,117	73,762	79,238	84,848	90,748	90,024	90,675	87,254	86,705	88,982	87,756	79,358	8,398
For-profit 4-year														
Selected crimes against persons and property	505	592	720	718	829	641	612	574	525	561	511	439	107	332
Murder[1]	0	0	0	0	0	0	0	0	0	1	0	0	0	0
Negligent manslaughter[2]	0	0	0	0	0	0	0	0	0	0	0	0	0	0
Sex offenses—forcible[3]	4	4	8	5	4	12	12	9	9	22	30	21	13	8
Sex offenses—nonforcible[4]	13	1	2	0	1	0	2	0	1	1	0	3	0	3
Robbery[5]	64	71	43	46	43	25	31	38	86	70	81	69	1	68
Aggravated assault[6]	23	45	41	38	59	31	31	63	43	51	48	54	17	37
Burglary[7]	347	376	542	524	607	489	446	385	299	350	272	220	75	145
Motor vehicle theft[8]	52	94	80	100	110	78	89	79	85	65	77	71	0	71
Arson[9]	2	1	4	5	5	6	1	0	2	2	2	1	1	0
Weapons-, drug-, and liquor-related arrests and referrals														
Arrests[10]	11	17	11	41	28	52	28	40	54	165	173	131	72	59
Illegal weapons possession	2	3	2	5	2	5	3	8	6	13	12	12	2	10
Drug law violations	4	9	4	12	16	14	16	14	22	66	46	54	23	31
Liquor law violations	5	5	5	24	10	33	9	18	26	86	115	65	47	18
Referrals for disciplinary action[10]	316	399	465	298	529	513	519	566	882	760	988	861	760	101
Illegal weapons possession	11	25	24	11	42	13	11	13	23	9	23	33	21	12
Drug law violations	92	133	130	99	128	138	132	159	231	221	349	314	261	53
Liquor law violations	213	241	311	188	359	362	376	394	628	530	616	514	478	36

See notes at end of table.

Table 329.10. On-campus crimes, arrests, and referrals for disciplinary action at degree-granting postsecondary institutions, by location of incident, control and level of institution, and type of incident: 2001 through 2012—Continued

Control and level of institution and type of incident	\multicolumn{11}{c}{Number of incidents — Total, in residence halls and at other locations}											2012		
	2001	2002	2003	2004	2005	2006	2007	2008	2009	2010	2011	Total	In residence halls	At other locations
1	2	3	4	5	6	7	8	9	10	11	12	13	14	15
Public 2-year														
Selected crimes against persons and property	6,817	6,860	6,637	6,637	5,981	5,669	5,381	5,464	4,984	4,396	4,270	3,786	806	2,980
Murder[1]	2	1	2	3	2	0	0	2	2	1	2	3	0	3
Negligent manslaughter[2]	0	0	0	0	0	0	0	0	0	1	0	0	0	0
Sex offenses—forcible[3]	118	118	160	142	175	167	181	210	205	210	262	258	72	186
Sex offenses—nonforcible[4]	119	61	14	6	10	16	7	12	8	17	14	14	2	12
Robbery[5]	245	234	230	213	248	284	279	285	251	298	264	245	23	222
Aggravated assault[6]	545	503	589	497	501	546	462	401	431	409	417	441	77	364
Burglary[7]	4,132	4,158	3,973	4,068	3,541	3,261	3,202	3,430	2,920	2,398	2,327	1,995	626	1,369
Motor vehicle theft[8]	1,552	1,661	1,607	1,620	1,428	1,319	1,174	1,059	1,109	1,028	921	782	0	782
Arson[9]	104	124	62	88	76	76	76	70	54	43	60	48	6	42
Weapons-, drug-, and liquor-related arrests and referrals														
Arrests[10]	2,660	2,844	2,950	3,270	3,416	3,993	4,124	3,764	3,335	3,811	3,740	3,505	1,347	2,158
Illegal weapons possession	198	221	220	255	278	300	304	258	256	282	251	251	21	230
Drug law violations	989	996	1,141	1,312	1,326	1,378	1,563	1,490	1,507	1,866	1,904	1,910	490	1,420
Liquor law violations	1,473	1,627	1,589	1,703	1,812	2,315	2,257	2,016	1,572	1,663	1,585	1,344	836	508
Referrals for disciplinary action[10]	3,529	3,744	4,036	4,371	4,688	5,897	5,987	6,425	7,241	8,017	8,198	7,520	6,094	1,426
Illegal weapons possession	127	146	145	167	133	238	218	183	210	242	228	217	82	135
Drug law violations	761	692	679	858	819	908	1,006	1,302	1,745	2,336	2,580	2,441	1,588	853
Liquor law violations	2,641	2,906	3,212	3,346	3,736	4,751	4,763	4,940	5,286	5,439	5,390	4,862	4,424	438
Nonprofit 2-year														
Selected crimes against persons and property	248	230	189	166	314	250	258	272	147	120	148	108	43	65
Murder[1]	1	0	0	0	0	0	0	0	0	0	0	0	0	0
Negligent manslaughter[2]	0	0	0	0	0	0	0	1	0	0	0	0	0	0
Sex offenses—forcible[3]	2	7	6	3	8	3	9	16	8	7	11	8	4	4
Sex offenses—nonforcible[4]	2	2	0	0	0	1	0	0	0	0	0	0	0	0
Robbery[5]	54	56	64	22	9	7	2	13	9	5	1	2	1	1
Aggravated assault[6]	23	17	12	17	22	35	52	66	5	9	53	46	3	43
Burglary[7]	142	123	83	111	266	187	178	160	120	95	74	48	35	13
Motor vehicle theft[8]	23	21	23	13	7	14	14	9	4	2	7	4	0	4
Arson[9]	1	4	1	0	2	3	3	7	1	2	2	0	0	0
Weapons-, drug-, and liquor-related arrests and referrals														
Arrests[10]	108	39	23	48	76	67	59	93	58	49	52	52	35	17
Illegal weapons possession	1	2	3	2	5	3	4	3	4	6	5	5	1	4
Drug law violations	21	10	16	16	32	34	27	33	35	18	34	31	20	11
Liquor law violations	86	27	4	30	39	30	28	57	19	25	13	16	14	2
Referrals for disciplinary action[10]	624	569	552	447	514	537	519	413	348	377	360	300	277	23
Illegal weapons possession	2	3	6	5	12	19	10	6	7	4	1	6	3	3
Drug law violations	91	65	52	58	47	74	73	85	100	105	109	103	92	11
Liquor law violations	531	501	494	384	455	444	436	322	241	268	250	191	182	9
For-profit 2-year														
Selected crimes against persons and property	472	417	550	527	430	420	547	399	459	315	273	250	2	248
Murder[1]	0	1	0	0	0	0	0	0	0	0	0	0	0	0
Negligent manslaughter[2]	0	0	0	0	0	0	0	1	0	0	0	0	0	0
Sex offenses—forcible[3]	12	6	15	9	1	8	2	4	6	2	7	11	1	10
Sex offenses—nonforcible[4]	7	3	2	0	0	1	0	0	1	1	0	1	0	1
Robbery[5]	67	47	81	80	55	49	67	53	50	38	18	28	1	27
Aggravated assault[6]	40	19	36	62	50	33	33	29	53	35	38	31	0	31
Burglary[7]	292	297	341	325	250	245	350	241	226	135	125	106	0	106
Motor vehicle theft[8]	51	40	74	49	71	81	92	71	121	101	82	73	0	73
Arson[9]	3	4	1	2	3	3	3	0	2	3	3	0	0	0
Weapons-, drug-, and liquor-related arrests and referrals														
Arrests[10]	163	128	84	112	47	41	45	23	62	43	23	24	11	13
Illegal weapons possession	13	9	6	6	3	3	4	4	4	5	1	7	4	3
Drug law violations	87	65	48	64	36	26	32	12	41	29	14	13	4	9
Liquor law violations	63	54	30	42	8	12	9	7	17	9	8	4	3	1
Referrals for disciplinary action[10]	287	330	313	322	228	320	173	248	303	147	168	168	113	55
Illegal weapons possession	16	14	7	7	8	7	7	4	8	2	10	5	0	5
Drug law violations	89	105	196	186	134	219	122	110	163	68	68	84	46	38
Liquor law violations	182	211	110	129	86	94	44	134	132	77	90	79	67	12

[1]Excludes suicides, fetal deaths, traffic fatalities, accidental deaths, and justifiable homicide (such as the killing of a felon by a law enforcement officer in the line of duty).
[2]Killing of another person through gross negligence (excludes traffic fatalities).
[3]Any sexual act directed against another person forcibly and/or against that person's will.
[4]Includes only statutory rape or incest.
[5]Taking or attempting to take anything of value using actual or threatened force or violence.
[6]Attack upon a person for the purpose of inflicting severe or aggravated bodily injury.
[7]Unlawful entry of a structure to commit a felony or theft.
[8]Theft or attempted theft of a motor vehicle.
[9]Willful or malicious burning or attempt to burn a dwelling house, public building, motor vehicle, or personal property of another.
[10]If an individual is both arrested and referred to college officials for disciplinary action for a single offense, only the arrest is counted.

NOTE: Data are for degree-granting institutions, which are institutions that grant associate's or higher degrees and participate in Title IV federal financial aid programs. Some institutions that report Clery data—specifically, non-degree-granting institutions and institutions outside of the 50 states and the District of Columbia—are excluded from this table. Crimes, arrests, and referrals include incidents involving students, staff, and on-campus guests. Excludes off-campus crimes and arrests even if they involve college students or staff. Some data have been revised from previously published figures.
SOURCE: U.S. Department of Education, Office of Postsecondary Education, Campus Safety and Security Reporting System, 2001 through 2012; and National Center for Education Statistics, Integrated Postsecondary Education Data System (IPEDS), Spring 2002 through Spring 2013, Enrollment component. (This table was prepared September 2014.)

Table 329.20. On-campus crimes, arrests, and referrals for disciplinary action per 10,000 full-time-equivalent (FTE) students at degree-granting postsecondary institutions, by whether institution has residence halls, control and level of institution, and type of incident: 2001 through 2012

Control and level of institution and type of incident	Number of incidents per 10,000 full-time-equivalent (FTE) students[1]													
	Total, institutions with and without residence halls											2012		
	2001	2002	2003	2004	2005	2006	2007	2008	2009	2010	2011	Total	Institutions with residence halls	Institutions without residence halls
1	2	3	4	5	6	7	8	9	10	11	12	13	14	15
All institutions														
Selected crimes against persons and property	35.619	34.649	34.040	33.580	32.864	33.347	30.568	28.987	22.922	20.877	20.011	19.437	25.605	7.121
Murder[2]	0.015	0.016	0.007	0.012	0.008	0.006	0.032	0.009	0.011	0.010	0.010	0.007	0.010	0.002
Negligent manslaughter[3]	0.002	0.000	0.001	0.000	0.002	0.000	0.002	0.002	0.000	0.001	0.001	0.001	0.001	0.000
Sex offenses—forcible[4]	1.885	1.896	2.051	2.056	2.058	2.001	1.969	1.898	1.712	1.904	2.209	2.557	3.632	0.412
Sex offenses—nonforcible[5]	0.395	0.213	0.047	0.021	0.032	0.032	0.029	0.025	0.044	0.021	0.031	0.029	0.031	0.026
Robbery[6]	1.424	1.468	1.284	1.195	1.193	1.159	1.141	1.134	0.948	0.905	0.851	0.897	1.002	0.686
Aggravated assault[7]	2.524	2.285	2.239	2.098	2.044	2.111	1.903	1.795	1.566	1.445	1.481	1.582	1.940	0.866
Burglary[8]	23.038	22.847	22.638	22.728	22.511	23.429	21.549	20.672	15.538	13.877	12.792	11.914	16.298	3.162
Motor vehicle theft[9]	5.327	5.037	4.968	4.674	4.256	3.921	3.375	2.952	2.677	2.238	2.219	1.997	2.049	1.892
Arson[10]	1.010	0.887	0.805	0.796	0.759	0.687	0.567	0.500	0.426	0.476	0.418	0.454	0.643	0.075
Weapons-, drug-, and liquor-related arrests and referrals														
Arrests[11]	34.550	35.371	35.239	36.960	37.722	37.615	36.947	36.428	33.700	33.509	35.511	33.826	48.928	3.675
Illegal weapons possession	0.919	0.931	0.865	0.974	1.013	0.986	0.963	0.856	0.725	0.723	0.674	0.679	0.814	0.408
Drug law violations	10.151	9.812	9.854	9.849	10.547	10.457	10.330	10.895	10.683	12.091	13.560	13.720	19.340	2.497
Liquor law violations	23.481	24.629	24.520	26.137	26.163	26.172	25.654	24.676	22.292	20.695	21.277	19.428	28.774	0.769
Referrals for disciplinary action[11]	132.899	136.344	146.165	151.708	156.060	163.421	158.288	156.479	148.751	149.773	163.128	163.830	244.325	3.120
Illegal weapons possession	1.093	1.049	1.238	1.387	1.448	1.402	1.212	1.047	0.858	0.855	0.847	0.925	1.273	0.231
Drug law violations	20.466	21.218	20.356	19.862	19.511	20.425	20.810	23.357	24.464	27.332	33.728	35.552	52.652	1.412
Liquor law violations	111.340	114.077	124.571	130.459	135.101	141.594	136.267	132.076	123.429	121.586	128.553	127.353	190.400	1.477
Public 4-year														
Selected crimes against persons and property	36.191	36.334	35.725	35.522	34.295	35.532	32.837	30.531	24.898	23.446	21.924	21.071	22.480	6.789
Murder[2]	0.017	0.017	0.009	0.014	0.007	0.009	0.070	0.015	0.012	0.014	0.015	0.009	0.010	0.000
Negligent manslaughter[3]	0.004	0.000	0.002	0.000	0.002	0.000	0.003	0.002	0.000	0.000	0.001	0.001	0.002	0.000
Sex offenses—forcible[4]	2.408	2.374	2.452	2.634	2.448	2.409	2.390	2.151	1.892	2.210	2.449	2.784	3.025	0.347
Sex offenses—nonforcible[5]	0.400	0.210	0.051	0.028	0.044	0.026	0.039	0.020	0.062	0.023	0.025	0.024	0.026	0.000
Robbery[6]	1.130	1.224	1.208	1.088	1.219	1.170	1.211	1.225	1.008	1.001	0.917	0.967	1.005	0.578
Aggravated assault[7]	2.774	2.452	2.493	2.256	2.242	2.302	2.110	1.930	1.767	1.627	1.612	1.756	1.869	0.611
Burglary[8]	22.283	23.259	22.808	23.154	22.654	24.138	22.425	21.181	16.689	15.455	13.975	12.844	13.754	3.618
Motor vehicle theft[9]	5.942	5.743	5.625	5.269	4.671	4.581	3.800	3.310	2.843	2.426	2.397	2.075	2.122	1.602
Arson[10]	1.232	1.057	1.078	1.079	1.009	0.897	0.788	0.697	0.623	0.691	0.532	0.611	0.668	0.033
Weapons-, drug-, and liquor-related arrests and referrals														
Arrests[11]	60.113	62.833	62.566	65.318	66.641	68.662	66.366	66.315	63.558	63.508	66.999	62.469	68.237	3.998
Illegal weapons possession	1.339	1.384	1.258	1.442	1.538	1.478	1.384	1.240	1.027	1.012	0.942	0.934	0.999	0.281
Drug law violations	17.651	17.158	16.950	17.100	18.575	18.671	17.934	19.130	18.993	21.721	24.362	24.322	26.502	2.230
Liquor law violations	41.123	44.292	44.358	46.776	46.529	48.513	47.048	45.945	43.539	40.775	41.695	37.212	40.736	1.487
Referrals for disciplinary action[11]	153.104	157.192	170.355	178.800	175.506	184.628	178.029	170.797	169.504	175.480	193.138	192.208	210.926	2.461
Illegal weapons possession	1.311	1.254	1.529	1.779	1.921	1.673	1.454	1.293	1.043	1.004	0.916	0.964	1.045	0.149
Drug law violations	25.492	25.896	24.933	24.278	22.803	23.744	24.249	27.201	28.459	32.442	40.731	42.820	46.930	1.156
Liquor law violations	126.301	130.043	143.893	152.743	150.782	159.211	152.326	142.303	140.001	142.034	151.492	148.424	162.951	1.156
Nonprofit 4-year														
Selected crimes against persons and property	57.358	55.445	54.891	54.728	54.165	57.681	52.039	49.315	38.658	35.185	33.136	32.503	34.919	7.026
Murder[2]	0.019	0.034	0.007	0.014	0.017	0.010	0.007	0.003	0.019	0.016	0.009	0.006	0.007	0.000
Negligent manslaughter[3]	0.000	0.000	0.000	0.000	0.003	0.000	0.003	0.000	0.000	0.000	0.000	0.000	0.000	0.000
Sex offenses—forcible[4]	3.169	3.410	3.790	3.617	3.784	3.694	3.587	3.586	3.561	3.848	4.414	5.176	5.644	0.245
Sex offenses—nonforcible[5]	0.437	0.302	0.051	0.018	0.021	0.034	0.027	0.053	0.036	0.025	0.040	0.030	0.030	0.035
Robbery[6]	2.508	2.743	1.946	2.034	1.739	1.717	1.549	1.447	1.183	1.002	0.999	1.108	1.104	1.154
Aggravated assault[7]	3.408	3.358	2.795	2.954	2.588	2.853	2.586	2.497	2.136	2.013	1.945	1.958	2.101	0.454
Burglary[8]	40.460	39.407	40.017	40.284	40.542	44.639	40.214	38.251	28.467	25.561	22.888	21.404	23.062	3.915
Motor vehicle theft[9]	5.684	4.750	5.008	4.640	4.340	3.684	3.314	2.845	2.695	2.013	2.173	2.131	2.230	1.084
Arson[10]	1.673	1.440	1.277	1.167	1.130	1.050	0.751	0.632	0.562	0.707	0.669	0.690	0.742	0.140
Weapons-, drug-, and liquor-related arrests and referrals														
Arrests[11]	24.456	24.433	24.793	27.225	25.758	20.981	22.672	20.240	18.667	17.146	16.804	16.827	18.160	2.761
Illegal weapons possession	0.645	0.604	0.600	0.649	0.522	0.499	0.599	0.523	0.478	0.430	0.404	0.381	0.411	0.070
Drug law violations	6.291	6.429	6.759	6.173	5.881	5.644	6.075	6.236	6.721	7.061	7.483	7.374	7.894	1.888
Liquor law violations	17.520	17.399	17.434	20.403	19.355	14.838	15.997	13.481	11.467	9.655	8.917	9.072	9.856	0.804
Referrals for disciplinary action[11]	275.480	289.709	308.044	319.945	336.127	353.954	347.734	348.663	334.288	329.608	341.027	334.320	364.229	18.841
Illegal weapons possession	1.712	1.582	1.942	2.144	2.052	2.127	1.835	1.513	1.157	1.234	1.298	1.495	1.624	0.140
Drug law violations	37.435	41.418	39.363	38.440	38.981	41.434	42.720	46.881	51.198	56.038	65.477	67.192	73.373	1.992
Liquor law violations	236.333	246.708	266.740	279.362	295.095	310.392	303.179	300.269	281.934	272.336	274.253	265.633	289.231	16.709
For-profit 4-year														
Selected crimes against persons and property	19.109	17.840	17.605	13.650	17.049	9.552	8.095	10.320	7.288	6.545	6.253	5.574	10.085	4.445
Murder[2]	0.000	0.000	0.000	0.000	0.000	0.000	0.000	0.000	0.000	0.000	0.012	0.000	0.000	0.000
Negligent manslaughter[3]	0.000	0.000	0.000	0.000	0.000	0.000	0.000	0.000	0.000	0.000	0.000	0.000	0.000	0.000
Sex offenses—forcible[4]	0.151	0.121	0.196	0.095	0.082	0.179	0.159	0.162	0.125	0.257	0.367	0.267	0.888	0.111
Sex offenses—nonforcible[5]	0.492	0.030	0.049	0.000	0.021	0.000	0.026	0.000	0.014	0.012	0.000	0.038	0.000	0.048
Robbery[6]	2.422	2.140	1.051	0.875	0.884	0.373	0.410	0.683	1.194	0.817	0.991	0.876	0.444	0.984
Aggravated assault[7]	0.870	1.356	1.003	0.722	1.213	0.462	0.410	1.133	0.597	0.595	0.587	0.686	1.586	0.460
Burglary[8]	13.130	11.331	13.253	9.962	12.484	7.287	5.899	6.922	4.151	4.083	3.328	2.793	6.596	1.842
Motor vehicle theft[9]	1.968	2.833	1.956	1.901	2.262	1.162	1.177	1.420	1.180	0.758	0.942	0.902	0.507	1.000
Arson[10]	0.076	0.030	0.098	0.095	0.103	0.089	0.013	0.000	0.028	0.023	0.024	0.013	0.063	0.000
Weapons-, drug-, and liquor-related arrests and referrals														
Arrests[11]	0.416	0.512	0.269	0.779	0.576	0.775	0.370	0.719	0.750	1.925	2.117	1.663	5.582	0.683
Illegal weapons possession	0.076	0.090	0.049	0.095	0.041	0.075	0.040	0.144	0.083	0.152	0.147	0.152	0.317	0.111
Drug law violations	0.151	0.271	0.098	0.228	0.329	0.209	0.212	0.252	0.305	0.770	0.563	0.686	1.839	0.397
Liquor law violations	0.189	0.151	0.122	0.456	0.206	0.492	0.119	0.324	0.361	1.003	1.407	0.825	3.425	0.175
Referrals for disciplinary action[11]	11.957	12.024	11.370	5.665	10.880	7.645	6.865	10.177	12.244	8.866	12.090	10.933	52.138	0.619
Illegal weapons possession	0.416	0.753	0.587	0.209	0.864	0.194	0.145	0.234	0.319	0.105	0.281	0.419	1.522	0.143
Drug law violations	3.481	4.008	3.179	1.882	2.632	2.057	1.746	2.859	3.207	2.578	4.271	3.987	18.775	0.286
Liquor law violations	8.060	7.263	7.605	3.574	7.383	5.395	4.973	7.084	8.718	6.183	7.538	6.527	31.841	0.191

See notes at end of table.

Table 329.20. On-campus crimes, arrests, and referrals for disciplinary action per 10,000 full-time-equivalent (FTE) students at degree-granting postsecondary institutions, by whether institution has residence halls, control and level of institution, and type of incident: 2001 through 2012—Continued

	Number of incidents per 10,000 full-time-equivalent (FTE) students[1]													
	Total, institutions with and without residence halls											2012		
Control and level of institution and type of incident	2001	2002	2003	2004	2005	2006	2007	2008	2009	2010	2011	Total	Institutions with residence halls	Institutions without residence halls
1	2	3	4	5	6	7	8	9	10	11	12	13	14	15
Public 2-year														
Selected crimes against persons and property	19.867	18.834	18.044	17.903	16.389	15.423	14.388	13.991	11.735	10.190	10.261	9.427	17.299	7.496
Murder[2]	0.006	0.003	0.005	0.008	0.005	0.000	0.000	0.005	0.005	0.002	0.005	0.007	0.025	0.003
Negligent manslaughter[3]	0.000	0.000	0.000	0.000	0.000	0.000	0.000	0.000	0.000	0.002	0.000	0.000	0.000	0.000
Sex offenses—forcible[4]	0.344	0.324	0.435	0.383	0.480	0.454	0.484	0.538	0.483	0.487	0.630	0.642	1.239	0.496
Sex offenses—nonforcible[5]	0.347	0.167	0.038	0.016	0.027	0.044	0.019	0.018	0.028	0.019	0.041	0.035	0.076	0.025
Robbery[6]	0.714	0.642	0.625	0.575	0.680	0.773	0.746	0.730	0.591	0.691	0.634	0.610	0.670	0.595
Aggravated assault[7]	1.588	1.381	1.601	1.341	1.373	1.485	1.235	1.027	1.015	0.948	1.002	1.098	1.922	0.896
Burglary[8]	12.042	11.416	10.801	10.974	9.703	8.872	8.561	8.783	6.875	5.559	5.592	4.967	12.051	3.230
Motor vehicle theft[9]	4.523	4.560	4.369	4.370	3.913	3.588	3.139	2.712	2.611	2.383	2.213	1.947	1.113	2.152
Arson[10]	0.303	0.340	0.169	0.237	0.208	0.207	0.203	0.179	0.127	0.100	0.144	0.120	0.202	0.099
Weapons-, drug-, and liquor-related arrests and referrals														
Arrests[11]	7.752	7.808	8.020	8.821	9.360	10.863	11.027	9.638	7.852	8.834	8.987	8.727	25.671	4.573
Illegal weapons possession	0.577	0.607	0.598	0.688	0.762	0.816	0.813	0.661	0.603	0.654	0.603	0.625	0.923	0.552
Drug law violations	2.882	2.735	3.102	3.539	3.633	3.749	4.179	3.815	3.548	4.326	4.575	4.756	11.090	3.203
Liquor law violations	4.293	4.467	4.320	4.594	4.965	6.298	6.035	5.162	3.701	3.855	3.809	3.346	13.657	0.818
Referrals for disciplinary action[11]	10.284	10.279	10.973	11.791	12.846	16.043	16.008	16.451	17.049	18.584	19.699	18.724	84.953	2.486
Illegal weapons possession	0.370	0.401	0.394	0.450	0.364	0.648	0.583	0.469	0.494	0.561	0.548	0.540	1.606	0.279
Drug law violations	2.218	1.900	1.846	2.314	2.244	2.470	2.690	3.334	4.109	5.415	6.200	6.078	24.090	1.662
Liquor law violations	7.697	7.978	8.732	9.026	10.237	12.926	12.735	12.649	12.446	12.608	12.952	12.106	59.257	0.546
Nonprofit 2-year														
Selected crimes against persons and property	63.955	58.903	51.594	48.535	91.263	81.948	103.819	99.299	55.894	48.495	44.912	34.597	61.512	24.863
Murder[2]	0.258	0.000	0.000	0.000	0.000	0.000	0.000	0.000	0.365	0.000	0.000	0.000	0.000	0.000
Negligent manslaughter[3]	0.000	0.000	0.000	0.000	0.000	0.000	0.000	0.000	0.000	0.000	0.000	0.000	0.000	0.000
Sex offenses—forcible[4]	0.516	1.793	1.638	0.877	2.325	0.983	3.622	5.841	3.042	2.829	3.338	2.563	4.825	1.745
Sex offenses—nonforcible[5]	0.516	0.512	0.000	0.000	0.000	0.328	0.000	0.000	0.000	0.000	0.000	0.000	0.000	0.000
Robbery[6]	13.926	14.342	17.471	6.432	2.616	2.295	0.805	4.746	3.422	2.021	0.303	0.641	1.206	0.436
Aggravated assault[7]	5.931	4.354	3.276	4.970	6.394	11.473	20.925	24.095	1.901	3.637	16.084	14.736	7.237	17.447
Burglary[8]	36.620	31.500	22.658	32.454	77.312	61.297	71.627	58.411	45.627	38.392	22.456	15.376	45.833	4.362
Motor vehicle theft[9]	5.931	5.378	6.279	3.801	2.035	4.589	5.634	3.286	1.521	0.808	2.124	1.281	2.412	0.872
Arson[10]	0.258	1.024	0.273	0.000	0.581	0.983	1.207	2.555	0.380	0.808	0.607	0.000	0.000	0.000
Weapons-, drug-, and liquor-related arrests and referrals														
Arrests[11]	27.852	9.988	6.279	14.034	22.089	21.962	23.741	33.952	22.053	19.802	15.780	16.658	48.245	5.234
Illegal weapons possession	0.258	0.512	0.819	0.585	1.453	0.983	1.610	1.095	1.521	2.425	1.517	1.602	4.825	0.436
Drug law violations	5.416	2.561	4.368	4.678	9.301	11.145	10.865	12.047	13.308	7.274	10.318	9.930	25.329	4.362
Liquor law violations	22.178	6.915	1.092	8.771	11.335	9.834	11.267	20.809	7.224	10.103	3.945	5.125	18.092	0.436
Referrals for disciplinary action[11]	160.920	145.722	150.688	130.694	149.393	176.025	208.845	150.774	132.319	152.354	109.247	96.101	360.632	0.436
Illegal weapons possession	0.516	0.768	1.638	1.462	3.488	6.228	4.024	2.190	2.662	1.616	0.303	1.922	7.237	0.000
Drug law violations	23.468	16.647	14.195	16.958	13.660	24.257	29.375	31.031	38.023	42.433	33.077	32.995	124.231	0.000
Liquor law violations	136.937	128.307	134.855	112.274	132.244	145.540	175.446	117.553	91.635	108.305	75.866	61.185	229.164	0.436
For-profit 2-year														
Selected crimes against persons and property	25.385	21.447	24.700	21.845	17.851	18.237	23.658	14.826	13.060	8.225	7.634	8.043	6.418	8.102
Murder[2]	0.000	0.051	0.000	0.000	0.000	0.000	0.000	0.000	0.000	0.000	0.000	0.000	0.000	0.000
Negligent manslaughter[3]	0.000	0.000	0.000	0.000	0.000	0.000	0.000	0.037	0.000	0.000	0.000	0.000	0.000	0.000
Sex offenses—forcible[4]	0.645	0.309	0.674	0.373	0.042	0.347	0.087	0.149	0.171	0.052	0.196	0.354	0.917	0.333
Sex offenses—nonforcible[5]	0.376	0.154	0.090	0.000	0.000	0.043	0.000	0.000	0.028	0.026	0.000	0.032	0.000	0.033
Robbery[6]	3.603	2.417	3.638	3.316	2.283	2.128	2.898	1.969	1.423	0.992	0.503	0.901	2.751	0.834
Aggravated assault[7]	2.151	0.977	1.617	2.570	2.076	1.433	1.427	1.078	1.508	0.914	1.063	0.997	0.000	1.034
Burglary[8]	15.704	15.275	15.314	13.472	10.378	10.638	15.138	8.955	6.430	3.525	3.495	3.410	1.834	3.468
Motor vehicle theft[9]	2.743	2.057	3.323	2.031	2.947	3.517	3.979	2.638	3.443	2.637	2.293	2.349	0.917	2.401
Arson[10]	0.161	0.206	0.045	0.083	0.125	0.130	0.130	0.000	0.057	0.078	0.084	0.000	0.000	0.000
Weapons-, drug-, and liquor-related arrests and referrals														
Arrests[11]	8.766	6.583	3.772	4.643	1.951	1.780	1.946	0.855	1.764	1.123	0.643	0.772	11.002	0.400
Illegal weapons possession	0.699	0.463	0.269	0.249	0.125	0.130	0.173	0.149	0.114	0.131	0.028	0.225	4.584	0.067
Drug law violations	4.679	3.343	2.156	2.653	1.495	1.129	1.384	0.446	1.167	0.757	0.391	0.418	3.667	0.300
Liquor law violations	3.388	2.777	1.347	1.741	0.332	0.521	0.389	0.260	0.484	0.235	0.224	0.129	2.751	0.033
Referrals for disciplinary action[11]	15.435	16.972	14.057	13.348	9.465	13.895	7.482	9.215	8.621	3.839	4.698	5.405	106.354	1.734
Illegal weapons possession	0.861	0.720	0.314	0.290	0.332	0.304	0.303	0.149	0.228	0.052	0.280	0.161	0.000	0.167
Drug law violations	4.787	5.400	8.802	7.710	5.563	9.509	5.277	4.087	4.638	1.776	1.901	2.703	44.925	1.167
Liquor law violations	9.788	10.852	4.940	5.347	3.570	4.082	1.903	4.979	3.756	2.011	2.517	2.542	61.428	0.400

[1]Although crimes, arrests, and referrals include incidents involving students, staff, and campus guests, they are expressed as a ratio to FTE students because comprehensive FTE counts of all these groups are not available.
[2]Excludes suicides, fetal deaths, traffic fatalities, accidental deaths, and justifiable homicide (such as the killing of a felon by a law enforcement officer in the line of duty).
[3]Killing of another person through gross negligence (excludes traffic fatalities).
[4]Any sexual act directed against another person forcibly and/or against that person's will.
[5]Includes only statutory rape or incest.
[6]Taking or attempting to take anything of value using actual or threatened force or violence.
[7]Attack upon a person for the purpose of inflicting severe or aggravated bodily injury.
[8]Unlawful entry of a structure to commit a felony or theft.
[9]Theft or attempted theft of a motor vehicle.
[10]Willful or malicious burning or attempt to burn a dwelling house, public building, motor vehicle, or personal property of another.

[11]If an individual is both arrested and referred to college officials for disciplinary action for a single offense, only the arrest is counted.
NOTE: Data are for degree-granting institutions, which are institutions that grant associate's or higher degrees and participate in Title IV federal financial aid programs. Some institutions that report Clery data—specifically, non-degree-granting institutions and institutions outside of the 50 states and the District of Columbia—are excluded from this table. Crimes, arrests, and referrals include incidents involving students, staff, and on-campus guests. Excludes off-campus crimes and arrests even if they involve college students or staff. Detail may not sum to totals because of rounding. Some data have been revised from previously published figures.
SOURCE: U.S. Department of Education, Office of Postsecondary Education, Campus Safety and Security Reporting System, 2001 through 2012; and National Center for Education Statistics, Integrated Postsecondary Education Data System (IPEDS), Spring 2002 through Spring 2013, Enrollment component. (This table was prepared September 2014.)

Table 329.30. On-campus hate crimes at degree-granting postsecondary institutions, by level and control of institution, type of crime, and category of bias motivating the crime: 2009 through 2012

Type of crime and category of bias motivating the crime[1]	Total, 2009	Total, 2010	2011 Total	2011 4-year Public	2011 4-year Non-profit	2011 4-year For-profit	2011 2-year Public	2011 2-year Non-profit	2011 2-year For-profit	2012 Total	2012 4-year Public	2012 4-year Non-profit	2012 4-year For-profit	2012 2-year Public	2012 2-year Non-profit	2012 2-year For-profit
1	2	3	4	5	6	7	8	9	10	11	12	13	14	15	16	17
All on-campus hate crimes	672	928	763	332	290	9	130	2	0	791	334	300	14	137	2	4
Murder[2]	0	0	0	0	0	0	0	0	0	0	0	0	0	0	0	0
Negligent manslaughter[3]	0	0	0	0	0	0	0	0	0	0	0	0	0	0	0	0
Sex offenses–forcible[4]	11	7	9	1	7	0	1	0	0	4	1	1	0	2	0	0
Race	0	0	0	0	0	0	0	0	0	1	0	0	0	0	0	0
Ethnicity	0	0	0	0	0	0	0	0	0	0	0	0	0	0	0	0
Religion	0	0	2	1	1	0	0	0	0	0	0	0	0	0	0	0
Sexual orientation	0	4	1	0	1	0	0	0	0	2	1	0	0	1	0	0
Gender	3	3	6	0	5	0	1	0	0	1	0	1	0	0	0	0
Disability	8	0	0	0	0	0	0	0	0	0	0	0	0	0	0	0
Sex offenses–nonforcible[5]	0	0	0	0	0	0	0	0	0	0	0	0	0	0	0	0
Robbery[6]	5	2	2	0	1	0	1	0	0	5	2	0	0	3	0	0
Race	3	1	1	0	1	0	0	0	0	4	2	0	0	2	0	0
Ethnicity	0	1	0	0	0	0	0	0	0	0	0	0	0	0	0	0
Religion	0	0	0	0	0	0	0	0	0	0	0	0	0	0	0	0
Sexual orientation	2	0	1	0	0	0	1	0	0	0	0	0	0	0	0	0
Gender	0	0	0	0	0	0	0	0	0	0	0	0	0	0	0	0
Disability	0	0	0	0	0	0	0	0	0	1	0	0	0	1	0	0
Aggravated assault[7]	9	17	13	8	3	0	2	0	0	14	6	4	1	3	0	0
Race	3	6	5	4	1	0	0	0	0	6	3	1	0	2	0	0
Ethnicity	1	1	0	0	0	0	0	0	0	0	0	0	0	0	0	0
Religion	0	1	2	0	2	0	0	0	0	1	1	0	0	0	0	0
Sexual orientation	4	9	6	4	0	0	2	0	0	5	2	2	1	0	0	0
Gender	1	0	0	0	0	0	0	0	0	1	0	0	0	1	0	0
Disability	0	0	0	0	0	0	0	0	0	1	0	1	0	0	0	0
Burglary[8]	8	11	8	4	2	0	2	0	0	5	0	0	0	4	0	1
Race	4	7	4	3	0	0	1	0	0	0	0	0	0	0	0	0
Ethnicity	2	0	0	0	0	0	0	0	0	0	0	0	0	0	0	0
Religion	0	0	2	0	1	0	1	0	0	1	0	0	0	0	0	1
Sexual orientation	1	2	1	1	0	0	0	0	0	0	0	0	0	0	0	0
Gender	1	1	1	0	1	0	0	0	0	4	0	0	0	4	0	0
Disability	0	1	0	0	0	0	0	0	0	0	0	0	0	0	0	0
Motor vehicle theft[9]	0	0	0	0	0	0	0	0	0	0	0	0	0	0	0	0
Arson[10]	0	0	1	0	0	0	1	0	0	0	0	0	0	0	0	0
Race	0	0	0	0	0	0	0	0	0	0	0	0	0	0	0	0
Ethnicity	0	0	0	0	0	0	0	0	0	0	0	0	0	0	0	0
Religion	0	0	0	0	0	0	0	0	0	0	0	0	0	0	0	0
Sexual orientation	0	0	1	0	0	0	1	0	0	0	0	0	0	0	0	0
Gender	0	0	0	0	0	0	0	0	0	0	0	0	0	0	0	0
Disability	0	0	0	0	0	0	0	0	0	0	0	0	0	0	0	0
Simple assault[11]	58	67	67	35	15	1	16	0	0	79	42	20	2	12	1	2
Race	23	25	22	12	5	1	4	0	0	35	19	11	1	2	0	2
Ethnicity	5	5	10	5	3	0	2	0	0	5	2	1	0	2	0	0
Religion	1	4	8	4	1	0	3	0	0	9	6	2	0	1	0	0
Sexual orientation	18	23	16	10	4	0	2	0	0	22	13	5	1	3	0	0
Gender	7	9	8	3	1	0	4	0	0	5	2	1	0	1	1	0
Disability	4	1	3	1	1	0	1	0	0	3	0	0	0	3	0	0
Larceny[12]	10	9	15	2	7	1	4	1	0	11	2	4	1	2	1	1
Race	0	1	2	0	2	0	0	0	0	2	0	1	0	1	0	0
Ethnicity	3	3	3	0	2	0	1	0	0	2	0	1	0	0	1	0
Religion	1	1	2	0	2	0	0	0	0	3	2	0	0	0	1	0
Sexual orientation	2	1	3	0	3	0	0	0	0	3	0	2	0	0	0	1
Gender	4	3	3	2	0	0	1	1	0	1	0	0	1	0	0	0
Disability	0	0	2	0	0	0	1	0	1	0	0	0	0	0	0	0
Intimidation[13]	175	260	282	121	110	4	46	1	0	261	91	117	7	46	0	0
Race	58	79	111	54	37	1	19	0	0	118	44	47	2	25	0	0
Ethnicity	23	17	22	9	10	1	2	0	0	23	6	13	2	2	0	0
Religion	20	38	24	17	5	1	1	0	0	29	12	14	1	2	0	0
Sexual orientation	57	87	91	35	42	1	13	0	0	66	25	27	0	14	0	0
Gender	13	37	31	6	15	0	9	1	0	21	1	15	2	3	0	0
Disability	4	2	3	0	1	0	2	0	0	4	3	1	0	0	0	0
Destruction, damage, and vandalism[14]	396	555	366	161	145	3	57	0	0	412	190	154	3	65	0	0
Race	174	257	168	80	52	2	34	0	0	189	93	56	1	39	0	0
Ethnicity	28	43	30	16	11	0	3	0	0	32	20	7	1	4	0	0
Religion	72	103	57	23	22	0	12	0	0	73	21	43	1	8	0	0
Sexual orientation	109	135	104	40	57	0	7	0	0	104	47	46	0	11	0	0
Gender	13	17	7	2	3	1	1	0	0	14	9	2	0	3	0	0
Disability	0	0	0	0	0	0	0	0	0	0	0	0	0	0	0	0

[1]Bias categories correspond to characteristics against which the bias is directed (i.e., race, ethnicity, religion, sexual orientation, gender, or disability).

[2]Excludes suicides, fetal deaths, traffic fatalities, accidental deaths, and justifiable homicide (such as the killing of a felon by a law enforcement officer in the line of duty).

[3]Killing of another person through gross negligence (excludes traffic fatalities).

[4]Any sexual act directed against another person forcibly and/or against that person's will.

[5]Includes only statutory rape or incest.

[6]Taking or attempting to take anything of value using actual or threatened force or violence.

[7]Attack upon a person for the purpose of inflicting severe or aggravated bodily injury.

[8]Unlawful entry of a structure to commit a felony or theft.

[9]Theft or attempted theft of a motor vehicle.

[10]Willful or malicious burning or attempt to burn a dwelling house, public building, motor vehicle, or personal property of another.

[11]A physical attack by one person upon another where neither the offender displays a weapon, nor the victim suffers obvious severe or aggravated bodily injury involving apparent broken bones, loss of teeth, possible internal injury, severe laceration, or loss of consciousness.

[12]The unlawful taking, carrying, leading, or riding away of property from the possession of another.

[13]Placing another person in reasonable fear of bodily harm through the use of threatening words and/or other conduct, but without displaying a weapon or subjecting the victim to actual physical attack.

[14]Willfully or maliciously destroying, damaging, defacing, or otherwise injuring real or personal property without the consent of the owner or the person having custody or control of it.

NOTE: Data are for degree-granting institutions, which are institutions that grant associate's or higher degrees and participate in Title IV federal financial aid programs. Some institutions that report Clery data–specifically, non-degree-granting institutions and institutions outside of the 50 states and the District of Columbia–are excluded from this table. A hate crime is a criminal offense that is motivated, in whole or in part, by the perpetrator's bias against a group of people based on their race, ethnicity, religion, sexual orientation, gender, or disability. Includes on-campus incidents involving students, staff, and on-campus guests. Excludes off-campus crimes and arrests even if they involve college students or staff.

SOURCE: U.S. Department of Education, Office of Postsecondary Education, Campus Safety and Security Reporting System, 2009 through 2012. (This table was prepared November 2014.)

Table 330.10. Average undergraduate tuition and fees and room and board rates charged for full-time students in degree-granting postsecondary institutions, by level and control of institution: 1963–64 through 2013–14

	Constant 2013–14 dollars[1]												Current dollars												
	Total tuition, fees, room, and board			Tuition and required fees[2]			Dormitory rooms			Board[3]			Total tuition, fees, room, and board			Tuition and required fees[2]			Dormitory rooms			Board[3]		
Year and control of institution	All institutions	4-year	2-year	All institutions	4-year	2-year	All institutions	4-year	2-year	All institutions	4-year	2-year	All institutions	4-year	2-year	All institutions	4-year	2-year	All institutions	4-year	2-year	All institutions	4-year	2-year
1	2	3	4	5	6	7	8	9	10	11	12	13	14	15	16	17	18	19	20	21	22	23	24	25
All institutions																								
1963–64	$9,507	$9,798	$5,908	$3,872	$4,210	$1,305	$2,151	$2,122	$1,593	$3,484	$3,466	$3,010	$1,248	$1,286	$775	$508	$553	$171	$282	$279	$209	$457	$455	$395
1964–65[†]	9,651	9,971	6,328	3,987	4,364	1,409	2,224	2,191	1,787	3,440	3,416	3,132	1,283	1,325	841	530	580	187	296	291	238	457	454	416
1965–66	9,748	10,126	6,513	4,089	4,466	1,494	2,287	2,265	1,904	3,422	3,395	3,115	1,324	1,375	884	549	607	203	311	308	258	465	461	423
1966–67	9,837	10,274	6,608	4,097	4,571	1,530	2,345	2,335	1,998	3,395	3,368	3,080	1,378	1,439	926	574	640	214	328	327	280	476	472	431
1967–68	9,777	10,276	6,797	4,059	4,578	1,604	2,363	2,357	2,082	3,355	3,340	3,112	1,415	1,487	984	588	663	232	342	341	301	486	483	450
1968–69	9,609	10,180	6,937	3,928	4,501	1,650	2,373	2,372	2,153	3,307	3,306	3,134	1,459	1,545	1,053	596	683	250	360	360	327	502	502	476
1969–70	9,704	10,415	6,776	4,013	4,696	1,539	2,421	2,438	2,158	3,270	3,282	3,079	1,560	1,674	1,089	645	755	247	389	392	347	526	528	495
1970–71	9,775	10,554	6,627	4,013	4,811	1,475	2,477	2,496	2,185	3,229	3,245	2,966	1,653	1,784	1,120	688	814	249	419	422	369	546	549	501
1971–72	9,881	10,721	6,691	4,133	4,941	1,432	2,540	2,560	2,232	3,208	3,219	3,026	1,730	1,878	1,172	724	865	251	445	448	391	562	564	530
1972–73	10,069	11,146	7,003	4,168	5,216	1,574	2,677	2,703	2,277	3,203	3,227	3,152	1,834	2,031	1,276	759	950	287	488	492	415	587	588	574
1973–74	9,590	10,569	6,846	4,010	4,962	1,655	2,497	2,519	2,165	3,084	3,088	3,025	1,903	2,097	1,358	796	985	328	495	500	430	612	613	600
1974–75	8,997	9,920	6,494	3,672	4,573	1,486	2,396	2,417	2,088	2,929	2,930	2,920	1,983	2,187	1,432	809	1,008	328	528	533	460	646	646	644
1975–76	8,911	9,977	6,243	3,513	4,547	1,259	2,410	2,441	2,008	2,988	2,989	2,975	2,103	2,355	1,473	829	1,073	297	569	576	474	705	706	702
1976–77	9,109	10,316	6,397	3,693	4,878	1,383	2,416	2,445	2,013	2,994	2,993	3,001	2,275	2,577	1,598	924	1,218	346	603	611	503	748	748	750
1977–78	9,044	10,223	6,390	3,693	4,845	1,419	2,421	2,453	1,969	2,930	2,925	3,003	2,411	2,725	1,703	984	1,291	378	645	654	525	781	780	801
1978–79	8,873	10,007	6,270	3,679	4,791	1,409	2,360	2,386	1,972	2,833	2,830	2,889	2,587	2,917	1,828	1,073	1,397	411	688	696	575	826	825	842
1979–80	8,502	9,585	5,991	3,519	4,579	1,365	2,273	2,298	1,901	2,709	2,708	2,725	2,809	3,167	1,979	1,163	1,513	451	751	759	628	895	895	900
1980–81	8,412	9,492	6,049	3,495	4,553	1,426	2,268	2,294	1,911	2,649	2,644	2,730	3,101	3,499	2,230	1,289	1,679	526	836	846	705	976	975	1,000
1981–82	8,712	9,864	6,181	3,637	4,762	1,472	2,372	2,400	1,979	2,704	2,702	2,790	3,489	3,951	2,476	1,457	1,907	590	950	961	793	1,083	1,082	1,094
1982–83	9,291	10,548	6,618	3,892	5,122	1,615	2,546	2,580	2,091	2,842	2,846	2,790	3,877	4,406	2,713	1,626	2,139	675	1,064	1,078	873	1,187	1,189	1,165
1983–84	9,620	10,959	6,590	4,115	5,410	1,686	2,643	2,683	2,115	2,861	2,866	2,789	4,167	4,747	2,854	1,783	2,344	730	1,145	1,162	916	1,239	1,242	1,208
1984–85	10,136	11,464	7,063	4,410	5,704	1,824	2,815	2,848	2,350	2,911	2,912	2,889	4,563	5,160	3,179	1,985	2,567	821	1,267	1,282	1,058	1,310	1,311	1,301
1985–86[4]	10,547	11,885	7,270	4,709	6,012	1,918	2,890	2,925	2,390	2,948	2,947	2,862	4,885	5,504	3,367	2,181	2,784	888	1,338	1,355	1,107	1,365	1,365	1,372
1986–87	10,956	12,598	6,961	4,884	6,246	1,895	2,967	3,013	2,185	3,145	3,159	2,881	5,206	5,964	3,295	2,312	3,042	897	1,405	1,427	1,034	1,489	1,495	1,364
1987–88	11,145	12,722	6,618	4,986	6,492	1,641	3,017	3,075	2,063	3,142	3,155	2,914	5,494	6,272	3,263	2,458	3,201	809	1,488	1,516	1,017	1,549	1,555	1,437
1988–89	11,378	13,039	6,927	5,152	6,732	1,899	3,053	3,119	2,103	3,173	3,188	2,925	5,869	6,725	3,573	2,658	3,472	979	1,575	1,609	1,085	1,636	1,644	1,509
1989–90	11,486	13,345	6,856	5,254	7,032	1,809	3,031	3,099	2,044	3,201	3,214	3,002	6,207	7,212	3,705	2,839	3,800	978	1,638	1,675	1,105	1,730	1,737	1,622
1990–91	11,513	13,337	6,896	5,292	7,034	1,908	3,059	3,126	2,075	3,162	3,177	2,913	6,562	7,602	3,930	3,016	4,009	1,087	1,743	1,782	1,182	1,802	1,811	1,660
1991–92	12,032	14,005	6,957	5,586	7,455	2,022	3,186	3,266	2,058	3,260	3,283	2,877	7,077	8,258	4,092	3,286	4,385	1,189	1,874	1,921	1,210	1,918	1,931	1,692
1992–93	12,286	14,438	6,936	5,798	7,834	2,103	3,196	3,282	2,044	3,291	3,321	2,789	7,452	8,758	4,207	3,517	4,752	1,276	1,939	1,991	1,240	1,996	2,015	1,692
1993–94	12,745	14,939	7,149	6,150	8,226	2,248	3,306	3,392	2,141	3,289	3,321	2,761	7,931	9,296	4,449	3,827	5,119	1,399	2,057	2,111	1,332	2,047	2,067	1,718
1994–95	12,975	15,197	7,238	6,318	8,422	2,324	3,351	3,436	2,181	3,305	3,339	2,733	8,306	9,728	4,633	4,044	5,391	1,488	2,145	2,200	1,396	2,116	2,138	1,750
1995–96	13,384	15,710	7,186	6,597	8,799	2,315	3,443	3,525	2,240	3,344	3,385	2,631	8,800	10,330	4,725	4,338	5,786	1,522	2,264	2,318	1,473	2,199	2,226	1,730
1996–97	13,612	16,029	7,238	6,749	9,047	2,282	3,497	3,581	2,251	3,366	3,402	2,705	9,206	10,841	4,895	4,564	6,118	1,543	2,365	2,422	1,522	2,276	2,301	1,830
1997–98	13,928	16,383	7,543	6,907	9,226	2,464	3,550	3,642	2,321	3,470	3,515	2,760	9,588	11,277	5,192	4,755	6,351	1,695	2,444	2,507	1,598	2,389	2,419	1,900
1998–99	14,388	16,977	7,555	7,159	9,600	2,446	3,652	3,749	2,308	3,578	3,627	2,784	10,076	11,888	5,291	5,013	6,723	1,725	2,557	2,626	1,616	2,506	2,540	1,950
1999–2000	14,476	17,140	7,522	7,248	9,772	2,398	3,728	3,818	2,459	3,501	3,550	2,665	10,430	12,349	5,420	5,222	7,040	1,728	2,686	2,751	1,771	2,523	2,558	1,920
2000–01	14,520	17,341	7,335	7,216	9,892	2,279	3,786	3,882	2,390	3,517	3,567	2,667	10,820	12,922	5,466	5,377	7,372	1,698	2,821	2,893	1,781	2,621	2,658	1,987
2001–02	15,006	17,985	7,540	7,446	10,267	2,373	3,931	4,035	2,437	3,630	3,683	2,730	11,380	13,639	5,718	5,646	7,786	1,800	2,981	3,060	1,848	2,753	2,793	2,070
2002–03	15,501	18,630	8,067	7,744	10,720	2,456	4,102	4,210	2,680	3,654	3,700	2,931	12,014	14,439	6,252	6,002	8,309	1,903	3,179	3,263	2,077	2,832	2,867	2,272
2003–04	16,355	19,578	8,466	8,344	11,400	2,746	4,242	4,354	2,788	3,770	3,824	2,932	12,953	15,505	6,705	6,608	9,029	2,174	3,359	3,448	2,208	2,986	3,028	2,322
2004–05	16,927	20,237	8,697	8,730	11,897	2,866	4,378	4,489	2,885	3,799	3,851	2,946	13,793	16,510	7,095	7,122	9,706	2,338	3,572	3,662	2,354	3,100	3,142	2,404
2005–06	17,279	20,606	8,544	8,896	12,137	2,854	4,499	4,611	2,847	3,805	3,858	2,843	14,634	17,451	7,236	7,601	10,279	2,417	3,810	3,905	2,411	3,222	3,268	2,408
2006–07	17,821	21,261	8,593	9,314	12,582	2,873	4,625	4,738	2,909	3,882	3,941	2,812	15,483	18,471	7,466	8,092	10,931	2,496	4,019	4,116	2,527	3,372	3,424	2,443
2007–08	18,014	21,490	8,943	9,416	12,712	2,796	4,677	4,791	2,925	3,922	3,987	2,756	16,231	19,363	7,637	8,483	11,454	2,519	4,214	4,317	2,635	3,534	3,592	2,483
2008–09	18,709	22,340	9,017	9,734	13,185	2,866	4,866	4,988	3,043	4,109	4,167	3,108	17,092	20,409	8,238	8,893	12,045	2,618	4,446	4,557	2,780	3,754	3,807	2,839
2009–10	19,134	22,903	9,259	9,903	13,448	3,169	5,050	5,187	3,246	4,181	4,268	2,845	17,650	21,126	8,541	9,135	12,404	2,923	4,658	4,785	2,994	3,857	3,937	2,624
2010–11	19,636	23,460	9,425	10,176	13,758	3,252	5,184	5,335	3,267	4,276	4,367	2,906	18,476	22,074	8,868	9,575	12,945	3,060	4,878	5,024	3,074	4,023	4,109	2,735
2011–12	20,032	23,759	9,651	10,510	14,013	3,350	5,250	5,394	3,305	4,272	4,352	2,996	19,401	23,011	9,347	10,179	13,572	3,244	5,085	5,224	3,201	4,138	4,215	2,901
2012–13	20,551	24,245	9,723	10,849	14,321	3,374	5,379	5,518	3,392	4,323	4,405	2,957	20,234	23,872	9,574	10,683	14,101	3,322	5,296	5,433	3,340	4,256	4,338	2,912
2013–14	21,003	24,706	9,888	11,074	14,561	3,370	5,520	5,654	3,540	4,409	4,492	2,979	21,003	24,706	9,888	11,074	14,561	3,370	5,520	5,654	3,540	4,409	4,492	2,979

See notes at end of table.

Table 330.10. Average undergraduate tuition and fees and room and board rates charged for full-time students in degree-granting postsecondary institutions, by level and control of institution: 1963–64 through 2013–14—Continued

Columns 2–13 are in **Constant 2013–14 dollars[1]**; columns 14–25 are in **Current dollars**. Under each dollar basis the groups are: Total tuition, fees, room, and board; Tuition and required fees[2]; Dormitory rooms; Board[3].

Year and control of institution	Total tuition, fees, room, and board			Tuition and required fees[2]			Dormitory rooms			Board[3]			Total tuition, fees, room, and board			Tuition and required fees[2]			Dormitory rooms			Board[3]		
	All institutions	4-year	2-year	All institutions	4-year	2-year	All institutions	4-year	2-year	All institutions	4-year	2-year	All institutions	4-year	2-year	All institutions	4-year	2-year	All institutions	4-year	2-year	All institutions	4-year	2-year
1	2	3	4	5	6	7	8	9	10	11	12	13	14	15	16	17	18	19	20	21	22	23	24	25
Public institutions																								
1963–64	6,951	7,075	4,800	1,783	1,854	739	1,903	1,931	1,310	3,266	3,290	2,750	912	929	630	234	243	97	250	253	172	429	432	361
1964–65	7,009	7,155	4,800	1,828	1,924	745	1,964	1,992	1,339	3,217	3,239	2,716	932	951	638	243	256	99	261	265	178	428	431	361
1965–66	7,127	7,332	4,934	1,893	2,047	803	2,022	2,050	1,429	3,212	3,236	2,703	968	996	670	257	278	109	275	278	194	436	439	367
1966–67	7,243	7,487	5,068	1,963	2,158	864	2,079	2,104	1,520	3,201	3,225	2,684	1,015	1,049	710	275	302	121	291	295	213	448	452	376
1967–68	7,293	7,521	5,451	1,955	2,142	995	2,144	2,165	1,679	3,194	3,213	2,777	1,055	1,089	789	283	310	144	310	313	243	462	465	402
1968–69	7,322	7,529	5,817	1,943	2,115	1,120	2,201	2,220	1,831	3,178	3,194	2,866	1,112	1,143	883	295	321	170	334	337	278	482	485	435
1969–70	7,443	7,700	5,915	2,009	2,229	1,107	2,276	2,298	1,916	3,158	3,173	2,892	1,197	1,238	951	323	358	178	366	369	308	508	510	465
1970–71	7,548	7,843	5,903	2,076	2,329	1,106	2,350	2,337	1,999	3,121	3,142	2,798	1,276	1,326	998	351	394	187	397	401	338	528	531	473
1971–72	7,691	8,021	6,127	2,147	2,443	1,096	2,431	2,454	2,090	3,113	3,125	2,941	1,347	1,405	1,073	376	428	192	426	430	366	545	547	515
1972–73	7,972	8,527	6,573	2,234	2,759	1,279	2,587	2,614	2,185	3,151	3,154	3,107	1,452	1,553	1,197	407	503	233	471	476	398	574	575	566
1973–74	7,635	8,043	6,420	2,207	2,588	1,381	2,411	2,437	2,061	3,016	3,019	2,978	1,515	1,596	1,274	438	514	274	479	483	409	598	599	591
1974–75	7,083	7,470	6,075	1,960	2,325	1,257	2,292	2,319	1,924	2,831	2,826	2,894	1,561	1,647	1,339	432	512	277	505	511	424	624	623	638
1975–76	7,046	7,540	5,872	1,835	2,297	1,038	2,302	2,338	1,873	2,909	2,905	2,962	1,663	1,780	1,386	433	542	245	543	552	442	687	686	699
1976–77	7,162	7,747	5,967	1,916	2,468	1,135	2,332	2,369	1,861	2,914	2,909	2,972	1,789	1,935	1,491	479	617	283	582	592	465	728	727	742
1977–78	7,081	7,645	5,963	1,919	2,456	1,150	2,329	2,368	1,823	2,833	2,821	2,991	1,888	2,038	1,590	512	655	306	621	631	486	755	752	797
1978–79	6,838	7,357	5,800	1,862	2,359	1,123	2,246	2,278	1,807	2,730	2,720	2,870	1,994	2,145	1,691	543	688	327	655	664	527	796	793	837
1979–80	6,552	7,044	5,513	1,766	2,232	1,074	2,164	2,195	1,737	2,623	2,617	2,703	2,165	2,327	1,822	583	738	355	715	725	574	867	865	893
1980–81	6,438	6,918	5,498	1,722	2,180	1,061	2,166	2,200	1,741	2,549	2,538	2,697	2,373	2,550	2,027	635	804	391	799	811	642	940	936	994
1981–82	6,648	7,168	5,553	1,782	2,271	1,085	2,271	2,311	1,756	2,595	2,586	2,712	2,663	2,871	2,224	714	909	434	909	925	703	1,039	1,036	1,086
1982–83	7,049	7,650	5,720	1,911	2,469	1,132	2,418	2,467	1,808	2,720	2,715	2,781	2,945	3,196	2,390	798	1,031	473	1,010	1,030	755	1,136	1,134	1,162
1983–84	7,286	7,925	5,849	2,058	2,650	1,219	2,509	2,562	1,848	2,719	2,714	2,782	3,156	3,433	2,534	891	1,148	528	1,087	1,110	801	1,178	1,175	1,205
1984–85	7,571	8,179	6,236	2,157	2,728	1,297	2,657	2,703	2,045	2,758	2,748	2,893	3,408	3,682	2,807	971	1,228	584	1,196	1,217	921	1,241	1,237	1,302
1985–86[4]	7,711	8,332	6,437	2,256	2,845	1,384	2,681	2,727	2,073	2,774	2,759	2,980	3,571	3,859	2,981	1,045	1,318	641	1,242	1,263	960	1,285	1,278	1,380
1986–87	8,038	8,740	6,313	2,337	2,986	1,395	2,748	2,794	2,068	2,953	2,954	2,851	3,805	4,138	2,989	1,106	1,414	660	1,301	1,323	979	1,398	1,401	1,349
1987–88	8,215	8,931	6,218	2,471	3,118	1,432	2,795	2,859	1,912	2,948	2,954	2,874	4,050	4,403	3,066	1,218	1,537	706	1,378	1,410	943	1,454	1,456	1,417
1988–89	8,287	9,070	6,171	2,491	3,192	1,415	2,824	2,900	1,870	2,972	2,978	2,885	4,274	4,678	3,183	1,285	1,646	730	1,457	1,496	965	1,533	1,536	1,488
1989–90	8,334	9,207	6,105	2,509	3,293	1,399	2,800	2,882	1,780	3,025	3,032	2,926	4,504	4,975	3,299	1,356	1,780	756	1,513	1,557	962	1,635	1,638	1,581
1990–91	8,346	9,198	6,084	2,551	3,313	1,446	2,828	2,906	1,841	2,967	2,979	2,796	4,757	5,243	3,467	1,454	1,888	824	1,612	1,657	1,050	1,691	1,698	1,594
1991–92	8,736	9,679	6,159	2,768	3,599	1,592	2,943	3,034	1,826	3,026	3,046	2,741	5,138	5,693	3,623	1,628	2,117	936	1,731	1,785	1,074	1,780	1,792	1,612
1992–93	8,867	9,924	6,263	2,937	3,873	1,690	2,895	2,994	1,823	3,035	3,056	2,750	5,379	6,020	3,799	1,782	2,349	1,025	1,756	1,816	1,106	1,841	1,854	1,668
1993–94	9,151	10,229	6,421	3,121	4,076	1,807	3,009	3,108	1,912	3,021	3,045	2,702	5,694	6,365	3,996	1,942	2,537	1,125	1,873	1,934	1,190	1,880	1,895	1,681
1994–95	9,318	10,420	6,462	3,213	4,188	1,863	3,061	3,160	1,924	3,044	3,073	2,675	5,965	6,670	4,137	2,057	2,681	1,192	1,959	2,023	1,232	1,949	1,967	1,712
1995–96	9,514	10,667	6,413	3,313	4,331	1,885	3,129	3,226	1,972	3,072	3,110	2,556	6,256	7,014	4,217	2,179	2,848	1,239	2,057	2,121	1,297	2,020	2,045	1,681
1996–97	9,655	10,845	6,512	3,359	4,417	1,887	3,176	3,273	1,980	3,121	3,155	2,645	6,530	7,334	4,404	2,271	2,987	1,276	2,148	2,214	1,339	2,111	2,133	1,789
1997–98	9,898	11,147	6,551	3,429	4,517	1,909	3,232	3,342	2,035	3,236	3,288	2,607	6,813	7,673	4,509	2,360	3,110	1,314	2,225	2,301	1,401	2,228	2,263	1,795
1998–99	10,148	11,462	6,575	3,470	4,611	1,894	3,327	3,440	2,071	3,352	3,411	2,610	7,107	8,027	4,604	2,430	3,229	1,327	2,330	2,409	1,450	2,347	2,389	1,828
1999–2000	10,143	11,484	6,565	3,475	4,648	1,871	3,386	3,496	2,150	3,282	3,340	2,545	7,308	8,274	4,730	2,504	3,349	1,348	2,440	2,519	1,549	2,364	2,406	1,834
2000–01	10,180	11,613	6,494	3,438	4,698	1,788	3,447	3,562	2,148	3,295	3,353	2,558	7,586	8,653	4,839	2,562	3,501	1,333	2,569	2,654	1,600	2,455	2,499	1,906
2001–02	10,577	12,126	6,774	3,561	4,925	1,819	3,591	3,714	2,271	3,426	3,487	2,684	8,022	9,196	5,137	2,700	3,735	1,380	2,723	2,816	1,722	2,598	2,645	2,036
2002–03	10,969	12,628	7,227	3,745	5,221	1,913	3,780	3,908	2,521	3,444	3,500	2,793	8,502	9,787	5,601	2,903	4,046	1,483	2,930	3,029	1,954	2,669	2,712	2,164
2003–04	11,675	13,478	7,591	4,190	5,791	2,149	3,922	4,056	2,638	3,563	3,631	2,805	9,247	10,674	6,012	3,319	4,587	1,702	3,106	3,212	2,089	2,822	2,876	2,221
2004–05	12,091	14,005	7,815	4,448	6,161	2,266	4,050	4,190	2,665	3,593	3,653	2,884	9,864	11,426	6,375	3,629	5,027	1,849	3,304	3,418	2,174	2,931	2,981	2,353
2005–06	12,344	14,297	7,665	4,574	6,318	2,285	4,186	4,327	2,658	3,584	3,652	2,751	10,454	12,108	6,492	3,874	5,351	1,935	3,545	3,664	2,251	3,035	3,093	2,306
2006–07	12,718	14,730	7,844	4,721	6,522	2,322	4,324	4,464	2,771	3,672	3,744	2,751	11,049	12,797	6,815	4,102	5,666	2,018	3,757	3,878	2,407	3,191	3,253	2,390
2007–08	12,845	14,904	7,742	4,762	6,596	2,287	4,386	4,530	2,781	3,697	3,778	2,674	11,573	13,429	6,975	4,291	5,943	2,061	3,952	4,082	2,506	3,331	3,404	2,409
2008–09	13,416	15,611	8,284	4,939	6,909	2,338	4,586	4,741	2,916	3,891	3,962	3,030	12,256	14,262	7,568	4,512	6,312	2,136	4,190	4,331	2,664	3,554	3,619	2,769
2009–10	13,898	16,301	8,356	5,164	7,282	2,475	4,771	4,948	3,094	3,963	4,071	2,787	12,819	15,036	7,708	4,763	6,717	2,283	4,401	4,564	2,854	3,655	3,755	2,571
2010–11	14,418	16,919	8,586	5,394	7,580	2,594	4,938	5,135	3,141	4,087	4,205	2,851	13,566	15,920	8,079	5,075	7,132	2,441	4,646	4,832	2,955	3,846	3,956	2,683
2011–12	14,826	17,332	8,897	5,744	7,964	2,737	5,007	5,195	3,201	4,074	4,174	2,959	14,359	16,787	8,617	5,563	7,713	2,651	4,849	5,031	3,100	3,946	4,042	2,866
2012–13	15,256	17,747	9,068	5,991	8,196	2,836	5,141	5,323	3,298	4,124	4,228	2,934	15,022	17,474	8,928	5,899	8,070	2,792	5,062	5,241	3,247	4,061	4,163	2,889
2013–14	15,640	18,110	9,282	6,122	8,312	2,882	5,304	5,479	3,447	4,214	4,319	2,953	15,640	18,110	9,282	6,122	8,312	2,882	5,304	5,479	3,447	4,214	4,319	2,953

See notes at end of table.

Table 330.10. Average undergraduate tuition and fees and room and board rates charged for full-time students in degree-granting postsecondary institutions, by level and control of institution: 1963–64 through 2013–14—Continued

Year and control of institution	Constant 2013–14 dollars[1]												Current dollars											
	Total tuition, fees, room, and board			Tuition and required fees[2]			Dormitory rooms			Board[3]			Total tuition, fees, room, and board			Tuition and required fees[2]			Dormitory rooms			Board[3]		
	All institutions	4-year	2-year	All institutions	4-year	2-year	All institutions	4-year	2-year	All institutions	4-year	2-year	All institutions	4-year	2-year	All institutions	4-year	2-year	All institutions	4-year	2-year	All institutions	4-year	2-year
1	2	3	4	5	6	7	8	9	10	11	12	13	14	15	16	17	18	19	20	21	22	23	24	25
Private nonprofit and for-profit institutions																								
1963–64	13,827	13,787	10,003	7,710	7,701	4,891	2,407	2,382	1,859	3,710	3,704	3,253	1,815	1,810	1,313	1,012	1,011	642	316	313	244	487	486	427
1964–65	14,346	14,415	10,946	8,185	8,252	5,281	2,490	2,486	2,174	3,671	3,678	3,491	1,907	1,916	1,455	1,088	1,097	702	331	330	289	488	489	464
1965–66	14,765	14,816	11,466	8,498	8,559	5,655	2,622	2,607	2,327	3,645	3,649	3,483	2,005	2,012	1,557	1,154	1,162	768	356	354	316	495	496	473
1966–67	15,161	15,195	11,985	8,801	8,861	6,032	2,748	2,723	2,477	3,612	3,612	3,476	2,124	2,129	1,679	1,233	1,241	845	385	382	347	506	506	487
1967–68	15,235	15,362	12,174	8,961	9,100	6,163	2,708	2,697	2,529	3,565	3,565	3,482	2,205	2,223	1,762	1,297	1,317	892	392	390	366	516	516	504
1968–69	15,290	15,522	12,359	9,111	9,336	6,298	2,661	2,665	2,576	3,518	3,521	3,485	2,321	2,356	1,876	1,383	1,417	956	404	405	391	534	534	529
1969–70	15,721	15,916	12,397	9,535	9,715	6,560	2,700	2,709	2,569	3,486	3,492	3,396	2,527	2,559	1,993	1,533	1,562	1,034	434	436	413	560	561	546
1970–71	16,142	16,292	12,439	9,961	10,092	6,560	2,735	2,745	2,567	3,446	3,455	3,312	2,729	2,754	2,103	1,684	1,706	1,109	462	464	434	583	584	560
1971–72	16,572	16,665	12,482	10,392	10,462	6,692	2,772	2,785	2,564	3,410	3,419	3,226	2,902	2,919	2,186	1,820	1,832	1,172	486	488	449	597	599	565
1972–73	16,665	16,967	12,476	10,418	10,694	6,702	2,870	2,891	2,508	3,377	3,383	3,266	3,036	3,091	2,273	1,898	1,948	1,221	523	527	457	615	616	595
1973–74	15,936	16,236	12,145	10,024	10,303	6,566	2,681	2,696	2,434	3,232	3,237	3,145	3,162	3,222	2,410	1,989	2,045	1,303	532	535	483	641	642	624
1974–75	15,371	15,444	11,755	9,604	9,665	6,202	2,622	2,626	2,559	3,144	3,153	2,994	3,388	3,404	2,591	2,117	2,130	1,367	578	579	564	693	695	660
1975–76	15,440	15,544	11,486	9,708	9,708	6,046	2,650	2,663	2,423	3,164	3,173	3,017	3,644	3,669	2,971	2,272	2,291	1,427	625	629	572	747	749	712
1976–77	15,637	15,921	11,894	9,875	10,145	6,373	2,598	2,608	2,431	3,165	3,169	3,089	3,906	3,977	2,971	2,467	2,534	1,592	649	651	607	790	791	772
1977–78	15,600	15,906	11,809	9,843	10,130	6,398	2,619	2,634	2,369	3,138	3,143	3,042	4,158	4,240	3,148	2,624	2,700	1,706	698	702	631	836	838	811
1978–79	15,485	15,811	11,626	9,836	10,146	6,280	2,599	2,611	2,401	3,049	3,054	2,945	4,514	4,609	3,389	2,867	2,958	1,831	758	761	700	889	890	858
1979–80	14,868	15,171	11,354	9,474	9,761	6,240	2,504	2,515	2,319	2,891	2,896	2,794	4,912	5,013	3,751	3,130	3,225	2,062	827	831	766	955	957	923
1980–81	14,837	15,172	11,671	9,488	9,810	6,545	2,489	2,497	2,364	2,860	2,865	2,763	5,470	5,594	4,303	3,498	3,617	2,413	918	921	871	1,054	1,056	1,019
1981–82	15,394	15,804	11,850	9,871	10,270	6,503	2,591	2,593	2,553	2,935	2,941	2,794	6,166	6,330	4,746	3,953	4,113	2,605	1,038	1,039	1,022	1,175	1,178	1,119
1982–83	16,566	17,059	12,842	10,626	11,105	7,201	2,828	2,828	2,818	3,112	3,126	2,822	6,920	7,126	5,364	4,439	4,639	3,008	1,181	1,181	1,177	1,300	1,306	1,179
1983–84	17,333	17,913	12,861	11,198	11,757	7,154	2,949	2,953	2,892	3,186	3,203	2,814	7,508	7,759	5,571	4,851	5,093	3,099	1,279	1,279	1,253	1,380	1,387	1,219
1984–85	18,221	18,773	13,781	11,806	12,343	7,742	3,168	3,168	3,164	3,247	3,263	2,875	8,202	8,451	6,203	5,315	5,556	3,485	1,426	1,426	1,424	1,462	1,469	1,294
1985–86[4]	19,184	19,926	14,061	12,500	13,216	7,999	3,354	3,361	3,239	3,330	3,349	2,893	8,885	9,228	6,512	5,789	6,121	3,672	1,553	1,557	1,500	1,542	1,551	1,340
1986–87	20,440	21,207	13,485	13,341	14,065	7,781	3,503	3,535	2,674	3,595	3,607	3,029	9,676	10,039	6,384	6,316	6,658	3,684	1,658	1,673	1,266	1,702	1,708	1,434
1987–88	21,321	21,621	14,356	14,115	14,444	8,440	3,545	3,570	2,800	3,601	3,616	3,117	10,512	10,659	7,078	6,988	7,116	4,161	1,748	1,760	1,380	1,775	1,783	1,537
1988–89	21,694	22,246	15,446	14,465	14,971	9,340	3,584	3,613	2,986	3,644	3,663	3,120	11,189	11,474	7,967	7,461	7,722	4,817	1,849	1,863	1,540	1,880	1,889	1,609
1989–90	22,240	22,731	16,044	15,076	15,537	9,616	3,559	3,581	3,078	3,605	3,614	3,351	12,018	12,284	8,670	8,147	8,396	5,196	1,923	1,935	1,663	1,948	1,953	1,811
1990–91	22,651	23,225	16,321	15,392	15,936	9,773	3,620	3,645	3,059	3,639	3,645	3,489	12,910	13,237	9,302	8,772	9,083	5,570	2,063	2,077	1,744	2,074	2,077	1,989
1991–92	23,618	24,239	16,376	16,014	16,592	9,783	3,776	3,810	3,040	3,828	3,837	3,553	13,892	14,258	9,632	9,419	9,759	5,754	2,221	2,241	1,788	2,252	2,257	2,090
1992–93	24,125	24,744	16,327	16,390	16,970	9,989	3,871	3,893	3,248	3,864	3,881	3,090	14,634	15,009	9,903	9,942	10,294	6,059	2,348	2,362	1,970	2,344	2,344	1,875
1993–94	24,901	25,557	16,723	16,988	17,600	10,236	4,001	4,028	3,321	3,911	3,929	3,166	15,496	15,904	10,406	10,572	10,952	6,370	2,490	2,506	2,067	2,434	2,445	1,970
1994–95	25,318	25,935	17,450	17,357	17,935	10,801	4,042	4,063	3,489	3,919	3,937	3,160	16,207	16,602	11,170	11,111	11,481	6,914	2,587	2,601	2,233	2,509	2,520	2,023
1995–96	26,171	26,784	17,586	18,043	18,620	10,789	4,164	4,184	3,606	3,964	3,980	3,191	17,208	17,612	11,563	11,864	12,243	7,094	2,738	2,751	2,371	2,606	2,617	2,098
1996–97	26,673	27,269	17,676	18,480	19,047	10,700	4,255	4,272	3,752	3,938	3,951	3,225	18,039	18,442	11,954	12,498	12,881	7,236	2,878	2,889	2,537	2,663	2,672	2,181
1997–98	26,899	27,703	17,771	18,596	19,385	10,844	4,291	4,306	3,882	4,012	4,012	4,045	18,516	19,070	12,921	12,881	13,344	7,464	2,954	2,964	2,672	2,762	2,761	2,785
1998–99	27,658	28,459	19,020	19,176	19,953	11,215	4,391	4,414	3,686	4,092	4,091	4,119	19,368	19,929	13,319	13,428	13,973	7,854	3,075	3,091	2,581	2,865	2,865	2,884
1999–2000	28,055	28,781	19,494	19,570	20,286	11,416	4,492	4,499	4,257	3,993	3,993	3,820	20,213	20,737	14,045	14,100	14,616	8,225	3,236	3,242	3,067	2,877	2,879	2,753
2000–01	28,682	29,330	20,005	20,130	20,761	12,167	4,539	4,552	4,034	4,014	4,017	3,804	21,373	21,856	14,907	15,000	15,470	9,067	3,382	3,392	3,006	2,991	2,993	2,833
2001–02	29,555	30,191	20,868	20,758	21,376	13,287	4,704	4,716	4,109	4,093	4,099	3,472	22,413	22,896	15,825	15,742	16,211	10,076	3,567	3,576	3,116	3,104	3,109	2,633
2002–03	30,115	30,692	22,906	21,138	21,710	13,742	4,841	4,857	4,170	4,136	4,125	4,993	23,340	23,787	17,753	16,383	16,826	10,651	3,752	3,764	3,232	3,209	3,197	3,870
2003–04	31,091	31,654	21,862	21,862	22,428	14,578	4,981	4,990	4,521	4,247	4,235	5,596	24,624	25,070	19,558	17,315	17,763	11,545	3,945	3,952	3,581	3,364	3,354	4,432
2004–05	31,645	32,188	24,879	22,252	22,804	14,859	5,121	5,114	5,486	4,272	4,270	4,535	25,817	26,260	20,297	18,154	18,604	12,122	4,178	4,173	4,475	3,485	3,483	3,700
2005–06	31,772	32,274	25,273	22,272	22,779	14,701	5,195	5,200	4,928	4,304	4,295	5,645	26,908	27,333	21,404	18,862	19,292	12,450	4,400	4,404	4,173	3,645	3,637	4,781
2006–07	32,734	33,286	23,347	23,075	23,616	14,627	5,302	5,309	4,773	4,357	4,360	3,947	28,439	28,919	20,284	20,048	20,517	12,708	4,606	4,613	4,147	3,785	3,788	3,429
2007–08	33,038	33,548	24,068	23,276	23,782	14,569	5,331	5,336	4,977	4,431	4,430	4,522	29,767	30,226	21,685	20,972	21,427	13,126	4,808	4,808	4,484	3,992	3,991	4,074
2008–09	33,718	34,232	24,876	23,611	24,121	14,846	5,501	5,508	4,966	4,607	4,604	5,064	30,804	31,273	22,726	21,570	22,036	13,562	5,025	5,032	4,537	4,209	4,206	4,627
2009–10	33,977	34,525	26,521	23,595	24,143	16,113	5,689	5,690	5,249	4,693	4,693	4,759	31,341	31,847	24,463	21,764	22,269	13,687	5,248	5,248	5,211	4,329	4,329	4,390
2010–11	33,876	34,559	24,546	23,425	24,547	14,547	5,742	5,749	5,221	4,709	4,709	4,756	31,875	32,518	23,101	22,042	22,677	13,607	5,403	5,410	4,939	4,431	4,431	4,445
2011–12	34,134	34,772	24,372	23,594	24,227	14,416	5,805	5,810	5,298	4,735	4,735	4,620	33,058	33,677	23,605	22,850	23,464	13,961	5,622	5,627	5,169	4,586	4,586	4,475
2012–13	35,022	35,622	23,693	24,318	24,908	14,349	5,922	5,928	5,253	4,782	4,785	4,040	34,483	35,074	23,328	23,943	24,525	14,129	5,831	5,837	5,222	4,709	4,712	3,977
2013–14	35,987	36,589	23,860	25,101	25,696	14,168	6,021	6,026	5,493	4,865	4,867	4,199	35,987	36,589	23,860	25,101	25,696	14,168	6,021	6,026	5,493	4,865	4,867	4,199

See notes at end of table.

Table 330.10. Average undergraduate tuition and fees and room and board rates charged for full-time students in degree-granting postsecondary institutions, by level and control of institution: 1963–64 through 2013–14—Continued

Year and control of institution	Constant 2013–14 dollars[1]												Current dollars												
	Total tuition, fees, room, and board			Tuition and required fees[2]			Dormitory rooms			Board[3]			Total tuition, fees, room, and board			Tuition and required fees[2]			Dormitory rooms			Board[3]		
	All institutions	4-year	2-year	All institutions	4-year	2-year	All institutions	4-year	2-year	All institutions	4-year	2-year	All institutions	4-year	2-year	All institutions	4-year	2-year	All institutions	4-year	2-year	All institutions	4-year	2-year
1	2	3	4	5	6	7	8	9	10	11	12	13	14	15	16	17	18	19	20	21	22	23	24	25
Nonprofit																								
1999–2000	29,132	29,468	16,222	20,695	21,001	9,567	4,447	4,470	2,936	3,990	3,996	3,720	20,989	21,231	11,688	14,911	15,131	6,893	3,204	3,221	2,115	2,875	2,879	2,680
2000–01	29,435	29,751	15,723	20,929	21,218	9,351	4,492	4,516	2,695	4,014	4,017	3,677	21,934	22,170	11,717	15,596	15,811	6,968	3,347	3,365	2,008	2,991	2,993	2,740
2001–02	30,433	30,667	17,102	21,678	21,894	10,716	4,662	4,674	3,038	4,093	4,099	3,349	23,080	23,257	12,970	16,440	16,604	8,126	3,536	3,544	2,304	3,104	3,109	2,540
2002–03	31,323	31,542	18,634	22,397	22,602	11,492	4,803	4,814	3,414	4,122	4,125	3,727	24,276	24,446	14,442	17,359	17,517	8,907	3,723	3,731	2,646	3,195	3,197	2,889
2003–04	32,431	32,643	19,658	23,269	23,465	12,104	4,933	4,943	3,603	4,229	4,235	3,951	25,685	25,853	15,569	18,429	18,584	9,587	3,907	3,915	2,853	3,349	3,354	3,129
2004–05	33,197	33,408	19,497	23,900	24,088	12,147	5,041	5,049	3,591	4,256	4,270	3,760	27,083	27,255	15,906	19,498	19,652	9,910	4,113	4,119	2,929	3,472	3,483	3,067
2005–06	33,676	33,880	19,281	24,286	24,480	12,183	5,095	5,105	3,562	4,294	4,295	3,536	28,520	28,692	16,329	20,568	20,732	10,318	4,315	4,323	3,017	3,637	3,637	2,994
2006–07	34,720	34,899	20,351	25,140	25,316	12,587	5,217	5,222	4,116	4,363	4,360	3,648	30,165	30,320	17,681	21,841	21,994	10,936	4,532	4,537	3,576	3,791	3,788	3,169
2007–08	35,429	35,572	20,929	25,751	25,892	13,084	5,245	5,250	4,213	4,433	4,430	3,632	31,921	32,050	18,857	23,201	23,328	11,789	4,725	4,730	3,796	3,994	3,991	3,272
2008–09	36,865	37,002	22,189	26,820	26,967	13,795	5,426	5,431	4,257	4,620	4,604	4,137	33,679	33,804	20,271	24,502	24,636	12,603	4,957	4,962	3,889	4,221	4,206	3,779
2009–10	37,857	37,990	22,502	27,532	27,683	13,699	5,609	5,614	4,463	4,717	4,693	4,340	34,920	35,042	20,756	25,396	25,535	12,636	5,173	5,178	4,116	4,351	4,329	4,004
2010–11	38,583	38,703	21,353	28,101	28,250	13,464	5,737	5,744	4,230	4,745	4,709	3,660	36,304	36,416	20,092	26,441	26,581	12,668	5,398	5,404	3,980	4,465	4,431	3,444
2011–12	38,931	39,066	23,672	28,336	28,514	14,536	5,811	5,816	4,420	4,785	4,735	4,715	37,705	37,835	22,926	27,443	27,616	14,078	5,628	5,633	4,281	4,634	4,586	4,567
2012–13	39,785	39,916	22,455	29,015	29,195	13,961	5,930	5,936	4,474	4,840	4,785	4,020	39,173	39,302	22,110	28,569	28,746	13,747	5,839	5,844	4,405	4,766	4,712	3,958
2013–14	40,614	40,708	23,002	29,648	29,799	14,002	6,037	6,042	4,808	4,929	4,867	4,192	40,614	40,708	23,002	29,648	29,799	14,002	6,037	6,042	4,808	4,929	4,867	4,192
For-profit																								
1999–2000	22,379	22,967	21,837	12,085	12,021	12,166	5,894	6,428	5,429	4,401	4,518	4,242	16,124	16,547	15,734	8,707	8,661	8,766	4,247	4,631	3,912	3,171	3,255	3,056
2000–01	23,736	24,451	22,896	13,678	13,971	13,346	6,048	6,657	5,307	4,010	3,823	4,242	17,688	18,220	17,061	10,192	10,411	9,945	4,507	4,960	3,955	2,988	2,849	3,161
2001–02	24,495	26,072	22,359	14,320	14,596	14,016	6,104	7,116	4,720	4,071	4,360	3,623	18,576	19,772	16,956	10,860	11,069	10,629	4,629	5,396	3,578	3,087	3,307	2,748
2002–03	25,410	25,856	25,036	14,593	14,718	14,359	5,907	6,946	4,554	4,911	4,192	6,123	19,694	20,039	19,404	11,310	11,407	11,129	4,578	5,384	3,530	3,806	3,249	4,746
2003–04	27,553	27,630	28,246	15,503	15,654	15,182	6,429	7,265	5,040	5,621	4,710	8,024	21,822	21,883	22,371	12,278	12,398	12,024	5,092	5,754	3,992	4,451	3,730	6,355
2004–05	28,313	28,701	27,399	15,979	16,177	15,453	6,932	7,187	6,312	5,402	5,338	5,634	23,098	23,415	22,353	13,036	13,197	12,607	5,655	5,863	5,149	4,407	4,355	4,596
2005–06	27,816	27,424	30,311	15,630	15,722	15,301	7,185	7,657	5,640	5,001	4,045	5,370	23,557	23,225	25,670	13,237	13,315	12,959	6,085	6,485	4,776	4,235	3,426	7,935
2006–07	27,630	28,441	24,460	16,434	16,797	15,061	7,142	7,640	5,140	4,055	4,005	4,259	24,005	24,710	21,250	14,277	14,593	13,085	6,205	6,638	4,466	3,523	3,479	3,700
2007–08	27,465	27,840	26,106	15,992	16,254	14,831	7,154	7,526	5,439	4,319	4,060	5,836	24,745	25,083	23,522	14,409	14,644	13,363	6,445	6,781	4,901	3,892	3,658	5,258
2008–09	26,623	26,760	27,002	15,662	15,787	15,024	6,799	7,051	5,363	4,162	3,922	6,616	24,322	24,447	24,669	14,309	14,423	13,725	6,212	6,441	4,899	3,802	3,583	6,044
2009–10	26,147	25,894	28,157	15,209	14,928	16,404	6,767	6,865	6,161	4,171	4,102	5,592	24,118	23,885	25,973	14,029	13,769	15,132	6,242	6,332	5,683	3,847	3,783	5,158
2010–11	24,424	24,311	27,405	14,601	14,588	14,658	5,803	5,823	5,661	4,021	3,900	7,086	22,982	22,875	25,787	13,739	13,727	13,792	5,460	5,479	5,327	3,783	3,669	6,668
2011–12	23,719	23,669	24,249	14,198	14,158	14,397	5,739	5,731	5,810	3,783	3,779	4,042	22,972	22,923	23,486	13,751	13,712	13,944	5,558	5,551	5,663	3,663	3,660	3,915
2012–13	23,519	23,444	24,366	13,982	13,903	14,415	5,828	5,835	5,751	3,710	3,706	4,200	23,083	23,083	23,991	13,766	13,689	14,193	5,738	5,745	5,663	3,653	3,649	4,135
2013–14	23,135	23,045	24,346	13,787	13,712	14,193	5,803	5,795	5,891	3,544	3,538	4,261	23,135	23,045	24,346	13,787	13,712	14,193	5,803	5,795	5,891	3,544	3,538	4,261

[1]Constant dollars based on the Consumer Price Index, prepared by the Bureau of Labor Statistics, U.S. Department of Labor, adjusted to a school-year basis.
[2]For public institutions, in-state tuition and required fees are used.
[3]Data for 1986–87 and later years reflect a basis of 20 meals per week, while data for earlier years are for meals served 7 days a week (the number of meals per day was not specified). Because of this revision in data collection and tabulation procedures, data are not entirely comparable with figures for previous years. In particular, data on board rates are somewhat higher than in earlier years because they reflect the basis of 20 meals per week rather than meals served 7 days a week. Since many institutions serve fewer than 3 meals each day, the 1986–87 and later data reflect a more accurate accounting of total board costs.
[4]Room and board data are estimated.
NOTE: Data are for the entire academic year and are average charges for full-time students. Tuition and fees were weighted by the number of full-time-equivalent undergraduates, but were not adjusted to reflect student residency. Room and board are based on full-time students. Data through 1995–96 are for institutions of higher education, while later data are for degree-granting institutions.

Degree-granting institutions grant associate's or higher degrees and participate in Title IV federal financial aid programs. The degree-granting classification is very similar to the earlier higher education classification, but it includes more 2-year colleges and excludes a few higher education institutions that did not grant degrees. Because of their low response rate, data for private 2-year colleges must be interpreted with caution. Some data have been revised from previously published figures. Detail may not sum to totals because of rounding.
SOURCE: U.S. Department of Education, National Center for Education Statistics, Projections of Education Statistics to 1986–87; Higher Education General Information Survey (HEGIS), "Institutional Characteristics of Colleges and Universities" surveys, 1969–70 through 1985–86; "Fall Enrollment in Higher Education" surveys, 1963 through 1985; Integrated Postsecondary Education Data System (IPEDS-IC:86–99); "Fall Enrollment Survey" (IPEDS-EF-86–99) and "Institutional Characteristics Survey" (IPEDS:86–99); IPEDS Spring 2001 through Spring 2014, Enrollment component; and IPEDS Fall 2000 through Fall 2013, Institutional Characteristics component. (This table was prepared December 2014.)

Table 330.20. Average undergraduate tuition and fees and room and board rates charged for full-time students in degree-granting postsecondary institutions, by control and level of institution and state or jurisdiction: 2012–13 and 2013–14

[In current dollars]

State or jurisdiction	Public 4-year In-state, 2012-13 Total	Tuition and required fees	Public 4-year In-state, 2013-14 Total	Tuition and required fees	Room	Board	Out-of-state tuition and required fees, 2013-14	Private 4-year 2012-13 Total	Tuition and required fees	Private 4-year 2013-14 Total	Tuition and required fees	Room	Board	Public 2-year In-state, 2012-13	In-state, 2013-14	Out-of-state, 2013-14
1	2	3	4	5	6	7	8	9	10	11	12	13	14	15	16	17
United States	$17,474	$8,070	$18,110	$8,312	$5,479	$4,319	$22,603	$35,074	$24,525	$36,589	$25,696	$6,026	$4,867	$2,792	$2,882	$7,003
Alabama	16,546	8,073	17,247	8,503	4,932	3,812	21,389	22,486	13,983	22,974	14,201	4,503	4,271	4,048	4,108	7,855
Alaska	15,415	6,317	15,697	6,141	5,618	3,938	18,458	30,418	21,496	30,261	20,943	4,271	5,047	3,972	4,652	4,569
Arizona	19,064	9,694	19,784	9,906	6,417	3,461	22,878	20,394	11,650	20,196	11,462	4,732	4,002	1,842	1,949	7,994
Arkansas	13,936	6,604	14,653	6,894	4,285	3,474	16,266	25,267	18,004	26,475	19,104	3,752	3,619	2,633	2,812	4,905
California	21,029	8,892	21,283	8,903	6,821	5,559	30,663	40,599	28,345	41,891	29,678	6,930	5,283	1,225	1,233	6,593
Colorado	18,052	7,656	18,979	8,228	5,518	5,232	26,233	30,907	19,967	31,473	20,359	6,172	4,943	3,004	3,160	9,261
Connecticut	20,655	9,517	21,642	10,128	6,213	5,301	28,337	48,262	35,336	48,718	35,407	7,331	5,980	3,596	3,824	11,287
Delaware	21,940	10,929	22,685	11,278	6,839	4,568	27,162	23,701	12,943	24,221	13,444	5,156	5,621	3,242	3,380	7,910
District of Columbia	†	7,244	†	7,255	†	†	14,535	48,440	35,524	49,894	36,723	8,682	4,489	†	†	†
Florida	14,170	4,377	14,372	4,423	5,676	4,273	17,077	30,123	20,155	31,288	20,971	5,634	4,684	2,486	2,513	9,362
Georgia	15,331	6,325	16,062	6,614	5,636	3,812	23,730	33,177	22,456	34,659	23,521	6,037	5,100	2,652	2,926	7,816
Hawaii	16,987	7,731	18,027	8,216	4,965	4,847	25,021	25,808	14,287	27,266	15,073	5,270	6,923	2,484	2,608	7,360
Idaho	13,476	5,980	13,819	6,315	3,494	4,009	18,875	11,544	6,752	14,163	6,736	2,451	4,976	2,915	2,963	7,355
Illinois	22,222	11,882	23,096	12,520	5,999	4,577	27,623	37,097	26,299	38,629	27,504	6,417	4,709	3,192	3,306	9,417
Indiana	17,758	8,269	18,253	8,443	5,122	4,687	27,001	36,368	26,794	37,964	28,035	5,053	4,877	3,455	3,605	7,632
Iowa	16,358	7,832	16,534	7,839	4,211	4,484	23,568	22,258	15,426	24,517	17,492	3,446	3,579	4,099	4,253	5,356
Kansas	13,901	6,970	14,634	7,387	3,631	3,616	18,642	28,525	20,852	27,963	20,122	3,670	4,170	2,621	2,890	4,116
Kentucky	16,581	8,416	17,281	8,715	4,289	4,277	19,979	28,654	20,639	29,527	21,271	4,171	4,085	3,391	3,487	12,125
Louisiana	14,245	5,817	15,240	6,585	5,125	3,530	19,985	39,088	28,691	41,044	30,257	6,035	4,752	2,837	3,178	6,463
Maine	18,676	9,295	19,123	9,368	4,582	5,174	24,791	42,745	31,558	44,057	32,534	5,814	5,709	3,409	3,545	6,254
Maryland	18,094	8,051	18,881	8,320	5,932	4,629	20,772	44,819	32,580	47,023	34,316	7,193	5,514	3,500	3,550	8,453
Massachusetts	21,094	10,632	21,817	10,702	6,628	4,487	25,461	49,871	36,795	51,484	38,009	7,751	5,723	4,186	4,216	9,561
Michigan	19,865	11,027	20,415	11,295	4,677	4,443	32,042	26,381	18,135	27,836	19,372	4,150	4,313	2,736	2,922	6,116
Minnesota	17,998	10,291	18,389	10,355	4,211	3,823	16,915	35,409	26,499	36,247	27,104	4,821	4,322	5,362	5,387	6,203
Mississippi	13,583	6,147	14,414	6,612	4,386	3,416	15,980	20,881	14,592	21,699	15,042	3,486	3,171	2,276	2,409	4,467
Missouri	16,236	7,815	16,787	7,998	4,985	3,804	19,319	27,615	19,020	28,415	19,523	4,828	4,065	2,716	2,850	5,470
Montana	13,572	6,267	14,082	6,323	3,574	4,185	20,797	27,320	19,737	28,733	20,868	3,676	4,189	3,151	3,202	8,417
Nebraska	15,291	7,023	15,637	7,081	4,480	4,076	16,734	27,212	19,478	27,884	19,832	4,208	3,843	2,594	2,670	3,612
Nevada	15,944	4,953	16,036	5,029	5,302	5,705	19,616	37,710	16,108	30,745	16,169	8,983	5,592	2,700	2,700	9,345
New Hampshire	24,705	14,435	25,248	14,469	6,241	4,538	25,357	42,310	30,202	43,490	31,029	7,428	5,032	7,218	7,230	15,717
New Jersey	23,773	11,955	24,246	12,266	7,388	4,592	25,637	42,831	31,195	44,239	32,010	7,008	5,221	3,782	3,929	6,868
New Mexico	13,225	5,483	14,106	5,973	4,259	3,874	14,647	25,144	16,256	27,468	17,657	5,689	4,122	1,399	1,443	4,642
New York	18,397	6,556	19,757	6,892	8,237	4,627	17,082	45,338	32,438	47,055	33,825	7,948	5,282	4,331	4,507	8,148
North Carolina	14,514	6,223	15,197	6,578	4,945	3,674	20,410	36,194	26,336	37,542	27,284	5,313	4,945	2,212	2,304	8,255
North Dakota	13,210	6,572	13,714	6,824	2,765	4,125	16,753	17,743	12,318	18,123	12,408	2,612	3,104	4,048	3,978	8,157
Ohio	19,453	9,301	20,000	9,443	5,805	4,752	21,939	35,367	25,756	36,856	26,917	5,070	4,869	3,480	3,544	7,313
Oklahoma	13,005	5,882	13,496	6,043	4,107	3,346	17,009	29,230	20,572	29,990	21,411	4,413	4,166	2,904	3,062	7,461
Oregon	18,526	8,294	19,153	8,616	6,107	4,431	26,144	40,655	30,195	42,385	31,599	5,564	5,222	3,752	3,935	8,038
Pennsylvania	21,637	12,184	22,771	12,607	5,871	4,293	23,571	44,407	32,949	46,239	34,313	6,500	5,426	4,133	4,352	11,424
Rhode Island	21,582	10,817	21,761	10,809	6,820	4,133	26,763	46,114	33,940	46,706	35,036	6,752	4,918	3,950	3,944	10,576
South Carolina	18,655	10,691	19,504	11,066	5,076	3,361	27,040	29,165	20,990	30,169	21,769	4,247	4,154	3,820	3,928	8,063
South Dakota	13,858	7,413	14,430	7,735	3,202	3,493	10,201	25,796	18,843	27,523	20,114	3,520	3,889	5,066	4,800	4,822
Tennessee	15,416	7,472	16,265	7,958	4,548	3,759	23,290	31,135	22,046	31,709	22,561	5,087	4,061	3,526	3,637	14,092
Texas	15,940	7,402	16,211	7,476	4,628	4,107	20,420	34,861	25,174	36,292	26,382	5,482	4,428	1,815	1,898	5,248
Utah	12,076	5,375	12,802	5,656	2,931	4,216	17,441	15,330	7,758	15,365	7,765	3,836	3,763	3,170	3,342	10,594
Vermont	23,290	13,524	24,073	13,952	6,362	3,759	33,700	46,255	35,130	47,909	36,449	6,189	5,271	5,452	5,668	11,236
Virginia	18,843	9,866	19,847	10,531	5,207	4,109	28,578	30,483	21,524	31,828	22,280	4,759	4,789	3,910	4,095	8,824
Washington	18,925	8,856	19,286	8,766	5,500	5,019	27,714	40,293	30,133	41,865	31,599	5,453	4,812	3,957	4,026	7,108
West Virginia	14,126	5,599	14,835	5,998	4,707	4,130	17,270	19,120	10,721	19,697	11,050	4,122	4,524	3,135	3,403	8,357
Wisconsin	15,446	8,339	15,722	8,406	4,309	3,007	20,183	34,199	25,500	35,654	26,637	4,884	4,134	4,073	4,233	6,945
Wyoming	12,479	3,642	12,949	3,756	4,027	5,166	11,532	13,562	13,562	†	16,620	†	†	2,420	2,579	6,353

†Not applicable.
NOTE: Data are for the entire academic year and are average charges for full-time students. In-state tuition and fees were weighted by the number of full-time-equivalent undergraduates, but were not adjusted to reflect the number of students who were state residents. Out-of-state tuition and fees were weighted by the number of first-time freshmen attending the institution in fall 2012 from out of state. Institutional room and board rates are weighted by the number of full-time students. Degree-granting institutions grant associate's or higher degrees and participate in Title IV federal financial aid programs. Some data have been revised from previously published figures. Detail may not sum to totals because of rounding.
SOURCE: U.S. Department of Education, National Center for Education Statistics, Integrated Postsecondary Education Data System (IPEDS), Fall 2012 and Fall 2013, Institutional Characteristics component; and Spring 2013 and Spring 2014, Enrollment component. (This table was prepared March 2015.)

Table 330.30. Average undergraduate tuition, fees, room, and board rates for full-time students in degree-granting postsecondary institutions, by percentile of charges and control and level of institution: Selected years, 2000–01 through 2013–14

	Current dollars										Constant 2013–14 dollars				
	Tuition, fees, room, and board					Tuition and required fees					Tuition and required fees				
Control and level of institution, and year	10th percentile	25th percentile	Median (50th percentile)	75th percentile	90th percentile	10th percentile	25th percentile	Median (50th percentile)	75th percentile	90th percentile	10th percentile	25th percentile	Median (50th percentile)	75th percentile	90th percentile
1	2	3	4	5	6	7	8	9	10	11	12	13	14	15	16
Public institutions[1]															
2000–01	$5,741	$6,880	$8,279	$9,617	$11,384	$612	$1,480	$2,403	$3,444	$4,583	$821	$1,986	$3,225	$4,622	$6,150
2005–06	7,700	9,623	11,348	13,543	16,264	990	2,070	3,329	5,322	6,972	1,169	2,444	3,931	6,284	8,232
2010–11	9,889	12,856	15,234	17,860	21,593	1,230	2,626	4,632	7,115	9,420	1,307	2,791	4,923	7,562	10,011
2011–12	10,730	13,650	16,401	18,801	22,697	1,408	2,910	5,187	7,657	10,164	1,454	3,005	5,356	7,906	10,495
2012–13	11,283	14,426	17,012	19,481	23,298	1,536	3,048	5,576	8,132	10,514	1,560	3,096	5,663	8,259	10,678
2013–14	11,820	14,954	17,668	20,167	23,948	1,560	3,217	5,963	8,506	10,918	1,560	3,217	5,963	8,506	10,918
Public 4-year[1]															
2000–01	6,503	7,347	8,468	9,816	11,611	2,118	2,520	3,314	4,094	5,085	2,842	3,382	4,447	5,494	6,824
2005–06	8,863	10,219	11,596	13,830	16,443	3,094	3,822	5,084	6,458	8,097	3,653	4,513	6,003	7,625	9,561
2010–11	12,048	13,604	15,823	18,419	22,191	4,336	5,091	6,779	8,689	11,029	4,608	5,411	7,205	9,234	11,721
2011–12	12,675	14,478	16,882	19,018	23,024	4,703	5,765	7,183	9,478	12,612	4,856	5,952	7,417	9,786	13,022
2012–13	13,324	15,102	17,561	19,713	23,686	4,982	6,180	7,554	9,769	12,692	5,060	6,277	7,672	9,922	12,890
2013–14	13,785	15,656	18,239	20,415	24,232	5,086	6,343	7,816	10,037	12,864	5,086	6,343	7,816	10,037	12,864
Public 2-year[1]															
2000–01	3,321	3,804	4,627	5,750	6,871	310	724	1,387	1,799	2,460	416	972	1,861	2,414	3,301
2005–06	4,380	4,822	6,234	7,567	8,993	691	1,109	1,920	2,589	3,100	816	1,309	2,267	3,057	3,660
2010–11	5,347	6,327	7,339	9,370	11,312	700	1,412	2,537	3,315	3,840	744	1,501	2,696	3,523	4,081
2011–12	5,770	6,703	7,831	9,767	11,567	960	1,592	2,701	3,542	4,132	991	1,644	2,789	3,657	4,266
2012–13	5,812	6,536	8,291	10,282	12,464	1,183	1,627	2,804	3,717	4,352	1,201	1,652	2,848	3,775	4,420
2013–14	6,144	6,952	8,764	10,729	13,369	1,178	1,560	2,954	3,826	4,550	1,178	1,560	2,954	3,826	4,550
Private nonprofit institutions															
2000–01	13,514	17,552	22,493	27,430	32,659	7,800	11,730	15,540	19,600	24,532	10,467	15,741	20,854	26,302	32,921
2005–06	18,243	23,258	29,497	35,918	41,707	9,981	15,375	21,070	26,265	31,690	11,785	18,155	24,879	31,013	37,419
2010–11	23,143	29,884	38,063	47,061	52,235	11,930	19,625	26,920	34,536	40,082	12,679	20,857	28,610	36,704	42,598
2011–12	24,435	31,398	39,540	49,762	54,258	11,860	20,180	28,128	36,190	41,576	12,246	20,836	29,043	37,367	42,928
2012–13	24,955	32,582	41,412	51,744	56,419	12,048	21,152	29,312	37,830	43,204	12,236	21,482	29,770	38,421	43,879
2013–14	26,280	34,023	43,047	53,665	58,615	12,550	22,080	30,390	39,120	44,848	12,550	22,080	30,390	39,120	44,848
Nonprofit 4-year															
2000–01	13,972	17,714	22,554	27,476	32,659	8,450	11,920	15,746	19,730	24,532	11,340	15,996	21,130	26,477	32,921
2005–06	18,350	23,322	29,598	36,028	41,774	10,300	15,560	21,190	26,500	31,690	12,162	18,373	25,021	31,291	37,419
2010–11	23,548	30,042	38,129	47,061	52,235	12,220	19,854	27,100	34,580	40,082	12,987	21,100	28,801	36,751	42,598
2011–12	24,552	31,460	39,596	49,762	54,258	12,242	20,582	28,310	36,420	41,576	12,640	21,251	29,231	37,604	42,928
2012–13	25,183	32,668	41,476	51,750	56,419	12,464	21,496	29,460	38,000	43,204	12,659	21,832	29,920	38,594	43,879
2013–14	26,663	34,095	43,236	53,667	58,615	12,700	22,252	30,579	39,330	44,848	12,700	22,252	30,579	39,330	44,848
Nonprofit 2-year															
2000–01	6,850	6,850	9,995	14,209	20,240	2,430	4,825	7,250	8,266	11,100	3,261	6,475	9,729	11,093	14,896
2005–06	8,030	15,680	16,830	20,829	28,643	4,218	8,640	9,940	12,270	14,472	4,981	10,202	11,737	14,488	17,088
2010–11	10,393	19,718	21,186	27,386	30,758	3,840	9,730	12,000	14,640	18,965	4,081	10,341	12,753	15,559	20,156
2011–12	19,325	20,300	22,303	28,506	32,679	7,036	10,904	14,531	16,131	19,880	7,265	11,259	15,004	16,656	20,527
2012–13	20,135	22,399	24,480	28,882	30,114	7,124	11,640	14,944	16,162	19,220	7,235	11,822	15,177	16,414	19,520
2013–14	21,148	23,815	25,400	29,677	31,200	3,060	10,500	15,533	16,345	20,660	3,060	10,500	15,533	16,345	20,660
Private for-profit institutions															
2000–01	13,396	15,778	19,403	21,400	21,845	6,900	8,202	9,644	12,090	14,600	9,260	11,007	12,942	16,224	19,593
2005–06	17,278	19,098	25,589	26,499	31,903	7,632	10,011	12,450	14,335	17,740	9,012	11,821	14,701	16,926	20,947
2010–11	16,097	16,097	17,484	26,175	31,639	10,194	10,194	13,520	15,750	18,048	10,834	10,834	14,369	16,739	19,181
2011–12	15,827	15,827	15,827	25,518	31,639	9,763	11,415	12,822	15,374	18,048	10,081	11,786	13,239	15,874	18,635
2012–13	16,115	16,115	16,115	22,612	32,239	9,936	11,202	12,685	16,156	18,650	10,091	11,377	12,883	16,408	18,941
2013–14	16,466	16,466	16,745	28,348	34,316	10,312	10,878	13,049	16,156	18,313	10,312	10,878	13,049	16,156	18,313
For-profit 4-year															
2000–01	13,396	15,818	20,417	21,400	21,400	7,206	8,305	9,675	12,800	15,090	9,670	11,145	12,983	17,177	20,250
2005–06	17,383	19,098	25,589	26,499	31,903	7,632	10,418	12,900	14,450	17,735	9,012	12,301	15,232	17,062	20,941
2010–11	16,097	16,097	17,484	26,175	31,639	10,194	10,194	13,560	16,500	18,048	10,834	10,834	14,411	17,536	19,181
2011–12	15,827	15,827	15,827	25,518	31,639	9,648	11,415	12,682	15,660	18,050	9,962	11,786	13,094	16,169	18,637
2012–13	16,115	16,115	16,115	21,697	32,239	9,936	11,202	12,110	16,156	18,650	10,091	11,377	12,299	16,408	18,941
2013–14	16,466	16,466	16,745	28,348	34,316	10,312	10,878	12,435	16,360	18,748	10,312	10,878	12,435	16,360	18,748
For-profit 2-year															
2000–01	15,778	15,778	19,403	21,845	21,845	6,025	7,365	9,644	12,000	14,255	8,085	9,884	12,942	16,103	19,130
2005–06	13,010	18,281	43,425	43,425	43,425	7,870	9,285	11,550	14,196	19,425	9,293	10,964	13,638	16,762	22,937
2010–11	23,687	23,687	25,161	25,161	25,161	10,075	12,049	13,418	15,263	17,918	10,707	12,805	14,260	16,221	19,043
2011–12	22,788	22,788	25,172	25,172	25,172	10,600	12,094	13,494	14,994	17,620	10,945	12,487	13,933	15,482	18,193
2012–13	23,600	23,600	23,600	25,866	25,866	10,425	12,314	13,240	15,552	18,048	10,588	12,506	13,447	15,795	18,330
2013–14	24,023	24,023	26,295	26,295	26,295	10,360	12,307	13,620	15,356	18,000	10,360	12,307	13,620	15,356	18,000

[1]Average undergraduate tuition and fees are based on in-state students only.
NOTE: Data are for the entire academic year and are average charges for full-time students. Student charges were weighted by the number of full-time-equivalent undergraduates, but were not adjusted to reflect student residency. Degree-granting institutions grant associate's or higher degrees and participate in Title IV federal financial aid programs. Some data have been revised from previously published figures.

SOURCE: U.S. Department of Education, National Center for Education Statistics, Integrated Postsecondary Education Data System (IPEDS), Fall 2000 through Fall 2013, Institutional Characteristics component; and Spring 2001 through Spring 2014, Enrollment component. (This table was prepared March 2015.)

Table 330.40. Average total cost of attendance for first-time, full-time undergraduate students in degree-granting postsecondary institutions, by control and level of institution, living arrangement, and component of student costs: 2009–10 through 2013–14

Level of institution, living arrangement, and component of student costs	2009–10 All institutions	2009–10 Public, in-state	2009–10 Private Nonprofit	2009–10 Private For-profit	2010–11 All institutions	2010–11 Public, in-state	2010–11 Private Nonprofit	2010–11 Private For-profit	2011–12 All institutions	2011–12 Public, in-state	2011–12 Private Nonprofit	2011–12 Private For-profit	2012–13 All institutions	2012–13 Public, in-state	2012–13 Private Nonprofit	2012–13 Private For-profit	2013–14 All institutions	2013–14 Public, in-state	2013–14 Private Nonprofit	2013–14 Private For-profit
1	2	3	4	5	6	7	8	9	10	11	12	13	14	15	16	17	18	19	20	21
									Current dollars											
4-year institutions																				
Average total cost, by living arrangement																				
On campus	$26,283	$19,219	$38,254	$28,916	$27,648	$20,068	$39,811	$32,132	$28,457	$20,997	$41,375	$29,887	$29,506	$21,712	$42,883	$29,820	$30,320	$22,192	$44,366	$29,945
Off campus, living with family	19,091	11,950	30,500	19,318	20,137	12,587	31,758	22,488	20,705	13,344	32,982	21,526	21,340	13,651	34,085	22,010	21,736	13,691	35,193	22,139
Off campus, not living with family	28,829	20,724	38,824	28,836	29,267	21,442	40,234	31,245	29,322	22,261	41,413	28,840	30,069	22,748	42,455	29,318	30,694	23,046	43,805	29,407
Component of student costs																				
Tuition and required fees	13,734	6,773	25,676	12,873	14,654	7,195	26,772	15,388	15,077	7,703	27,931	14,609	15,734	8,033	29,024	14,940	16,243	8,254	30,127	14,967
Books and supplies	1,192	1,165	1,182	1,389	1,223	1,196	1,219	1,561	1,237	1,230	1,230	1,373	1,249	1,240	1,240	1,444	1,260	1,255	1,252	1,391
Room, board, and other expenses																				
On campus: Room and board	8,583	8,155	9,114	10,082	8,913	8,498	9,456	9,304	9,255	8,839	9,824	9,660	9,600	9,187	10,181	9,242	9,905	9,459	10,530	9,646
On campus: Other	2,774	3,126	2,282	4,573	2,858	3,179	2,363	5,879	2,889	3,225	2,389	4,245	2,923	3,253	2,439	4,194	2,912	3,224	2,457	3,941
Off campus, living with family: Other	4,165	4,012	3,642	5,057	4,260	4,196	3,767	5,539	4,391	4,411	3,821	5,544	4,356	4,379	3,821	5,627	4,233	4,182	3,813	5,781
Off campus, not living with family: Room and board	8,862	8,722	8,164	8,997	8,866	9,014	8,299	8,888	8,572	9,206	8,327	7,898	8,640	9,318	8,300	7,881	8,795	9,535	8,475	7,947
Off campus, not living with family: Other	5,041	4,065	3,801	5,578	4,524	4,037	3,944	5,408	4,437	4,122	3,925	4,960	4,446	4,157	3,892	5,054	4,396	4,003	3,951	5,101
2-year institutions																				
Average total cost, by living arrangement																				
On campus	$14,351	$11,886	$23,352	$27,721	$13,831	$12,345	$25,868	$28,435	$14,049	$12,796	$26,246	$27,873	$14,457	$13,257	$27,471	$27,934	$14,780	$13,576	$28,291	$28,064
Off campus, living with family	9,731	7,581	16,639	18,982	9,044	7,842	18,947	19,292	9,115	8,129	19,066	19,810	9,291	8,384	19,825	20,032	9,426	8,527	20,550	19,946
Off campus, not living with family	17,063	14,758	24,969	26,556	16,477	15,140	27,044	27,329	16,562	15,567	27,528	27,015	16,889	15,886	29,760	28,025	17,067	16,089	30,053	27,866
Component of student costs																				
Tuition and required fees	4,705	2,619	12,326	13,511	3,919	2,745	13,917	13,758	3,912	2,940	14,007	14,298	3,982	3,090	14,359	14,420	4,085	3,201	14,734	14,364
Books and supplies	1,259	1,241	1,205	1,371	1,301	1,295	1,239	1,377	1,315	1,311	1,332	1,368	1,351	1,353	1,305	1,324	1,366	1,372	1,390	1,270
Room, board, and other expenses																				
On campus: Room and board	5,481	5,171	7,096	8,729	5,648	5,368	7,796	9,365	5,913	5,630	8,011	9,417	6,111	5,817	8,529	9,285	6,304	6,001	8,820	9,509
On campus: Other	2,906	2,856	2,726	4,111	2,964	2,937	2,916	3,935	2,910	2,915	2,896	2,789	3,014	2,997	3,278	2,906	3,024	3,002	3,347	2,921
Off campus, living with family: Other	3,767	3,721	3,108	4,101	3,824	3,802	3,791	4,157	3,888	3,878	3,726	4,143	3,958	3,941	4,161	4,289	3,974	3,955	4,426	4,312
Off campus, not living with family: Room and board	7,334	7,240	8,095	7,588	7,477	7,403	7,525	7,948	7,514	7,524	7,680	7,390	7,676	7,626	8,983	7,968	7,730	7,675	8,852	8,091
Off campus, not living with family: Other	3,765	3,659	3,343	4,087	3,780	3,697	4,363	4,246	3,822	3,792	4,508	3,959	3,880	3,817	5,113	4,314	3,885	3,841	5,077	4,141
									Constant 2013–14 dollars[1]											
4-year institutions																				
Average total cost, by living arrangement																				
On campus	$28,494	$20,836	$41,472	$31,348	$29,384	$21,328	$42,310	$34,149	$29,383	$21,680	$42,720	$30,859	$29,967	$22,052	$43,553	$30,286	$30,320	$22,192	$44,366	$29,945
Off campus, living with family	20,697	12,955	33,065	20,943	21,401	13,377	33,751	23,900	21,378	13,778	34,055	22,227	21,673	13,865	34,617	22,354	21,736	13,691	35,193	22,139
Off campus, not living with family	31,254	22,467	42,089	31,262	31,104	22,788	42,760	33,207	30,276	22,985	42,760	29,778	30,539	23,104	43,118	29,776	30,694	23,046	43,805	29,407
2-year institutions																				
Average total cost, by living arrangement																				
On campus	$15,558	$12,886	$25,317	$30,053	$14,699	$13,120	$27,492	$30,220	$14,506	$13,212	$27,100	$28,779	$14,683	$13,464	$27,900	$28,371	$14,780	$13,576	$28,291	$28,064
Off campus, living with family	10,550	8,218	18,038	20,579	9,611	8,334	20,137	20,503	9,411	8,393	19,686	20,454	9,436	8,515	20,134	20,345	9,426	8,527	20,550	19,946
Off campus, not living with family	18,498	16,000	27,069	28,790	17,511	16,090	28,742	29,045	17,101	16,073	28,423	27,894	17,153	16,134	30,225	28,462	17,067	16,089	30,053	27,866

[1]Constant dollars based on the Consumer Price Index, prepared by the Bureau of Labor Statistics, U.S. Department of Labor, adjusted to a school-year basis.

NOTE: Excludes students who previously attended another postsecondary institution or who began their studies on a part-time basis. Tuition and fees at public institutions are the lower of either in-district or in-state tuition and fees. Data illustrating the average total cost of attendance for all students are weighted by the number of students at the institution receiving Title IV aid. Detail may not sum to totals because of rounding. Some data have been revised from previously published figures.

SOURCE: U.S. Department of Education, National Center for Education Statistics, Integrated Postsecondary Education Data System (IPEDS), Spring 2010 through Spring 2011 and Winter 2011–12 through Winter 2013–14, Student Financial Aid component; and Fall 2009 through Fall 2014, Institutional Characteristics component. (This table was prepared January 2015.)

Table 330.50. Average graduate tuition and required fees in degree-granting postsecondary institutions, by control of institution and percentile of charges: 1989–90 through 2013–14

Year	Total	Public institutions[1]	Private institutions			Public institutions,[1] by percentile			Nonprofit institutions, by percentile		
			Total	Nonprofit	For-profit	25th percentile	Median (50th percentile)	75th percentile	25th percentile	Median (50th percentile)	75th percentile
1	2	3	4	5	6	7	8	9	10	11	12
Current dollars											
1989–90	$4,135	$1,999	$7,881	—	—	—	—	—	—	—	—
1990–91	4,488	2,206	8,507	—	—	—	—	—	—	—	—
1991–92	5,116	2,524	9,592	—	—	—	—	—	—	—	—
1992–93	5,475	2,791	10,008	—	—	—	—	—	—	—	—
1993–94	5,973	3,050	10,790	—	—	—	—	—	—	—	—
1994–95	6,247	3,250	11,338	—	—	—	—	—	—	—	—
1995–96	6,741	3,449	12,083	—	—	—	—	—	—	—	—
1996–97	7,111	3,607	12,537	—	—	—	—	—	—	—	—
1997–98	7,246	3,744	12,774	—	—	—	—	—	—	—	—
1998–99	7,685	3,897	13,299	—	—	—	—	—	—	—	—
1999–2000	8,069	4,042	13,821	$14,123	$9,611	$2,640	$3,637	$5,163	$7,998	$12,870	$20,487
2000–01	8,429	4,243	14,420	14,457	13,229	2,931	3,822	5,347	8,276	13,200	21,369
2001–02	8,857	4,496	15,165	15,232	13,414	3,226	4,119	5,596	8,583	14,157	22,054
2002–03	9,226	4,842	14,983	15,676	9,644	3,395	4,452	5,927	8,690	14,140	22,700
2003–04	10,312	5,544	16,209	16,807	12,542	3,795	5,103	7,063	9,072	15,030	25,600
2004–05	11,004	6,080	16,751	17,551	13,133	4,236	5,663	7,616	9,300	16,060	26,140
2005–06	11,621	6,493	17,244	18,171	13,432	4,608	6,209	7,977	9,745	16,222	26,958
2006–07	12,312	6,894	18,108	19,033	14,421	4,909	6,594	8,341	10,346	17,057	29,118
2007–08	13,002	7,415	18,878	19,896	14,713	5,176	6,990	9,288	10,705	17,647	30,247
2008–09	13,647	7,999	19,230	20,485	14,418	5,612	7,376	9,912	11,290	18,270	30,514
2009–10	14,542	8,763	20,078	21,317	14,512	6,074	7,983	10,658	12,290	19,460	31,730
2010–11	15,017	9,238	20,397	21,993	13,811	6,550	8,788	10,937	12,510	19,586	33,215
2011–12	15,845	9,978	21,230	22,899	14,285	7,506	9,440	11,954	12,936	20,625	34,680
2012–13	16,435	10,408	21,955	23,698	14,418	7,706	9,900	12,590	13,030	21,352	36,820
2013–14	16,946	10,725	22,607	24,467	14,210	7,791	10,242	12,779	13,567	22,018	36,660
Constant 2013–14 dollars											
1989–90	$7,652	$3,699	$14,584	—	—	—	—	—	—	—	—
1990–91	7,874	3,871	14,926	—	—	—	—	—	—	—	—
1991–92	8,698	4,291	16,307	—	—	—	—	—	—	—	—
1992–93	9,026	4,601	16,499	—	—	—	—	—	—	—	—
1993–94	9,598	4,901	17,339	—	—	—	—	—	—	—	—
1994–95	9,759	5,078	17,713	—	—	—	—	—	—	—	—
1995–96	10,252	5,245	18,376	—	—	—	—	—	—	—	—
1996–97	10,515	5,333	18,538	—	—	—	—	—	—	—	—
1997–98	10,526	5,439	18,557	—	—	—	—	—	—	—	—
1998–99	10,974	5,564	18,991	—	—	—	—	—	—	—	—
1999–2000	11,199	5,610	19,182	$19,602	$13,340	$3,664	$5,048	$7,166	$11,101	$17,863	$28,435
2000–01	11,312	5,694	19,351	19,400	17,753	3,933	5,129	7,175	11,106	17,714	28,676
2001–02	11,679	5,928	19,997	20,086	17,687	4,254	5,431	7,379	11,318	18,668	29,081
2002–03	11,903	6,247	19,332	20,226	12,444	4,380	5,744	7,647	11,212	18,244	29,289
2003–04	13,020	7,000	20,466	21,221	15,837	4,792	6,443	8,918	11,455	18,977	32,323
2004–05	13,489	7,452	20,533	21,513	16,098	5,192	6,941	9,335	11,399	19,686	32,041
2005–06	13,722	7,667	20,361	21,456	15,860	5,441	7,331	9,419	11,507	19,155	31,831
2006–07	14,171	7,935	20,842	21,908	16,599	5,650	7,590	9,601	11,908	19,633	33,515
2007–08	14,431	8,230	20,952	22,083	16,330	5,745	7,758	10,309	11,881	19,586	33,571
2008–09	14,938	8,755	21,049	22,424	15,782	6,143	8,074	10,850	12,358	19,998	33,401
2009–10	15,765	9,500	21,767	23,110	15,733	6,585	8,655	11,555	13,324	21,097	34,399
2010–11	15,990	9,818	21,677	23,374	14,678	6,961	9,340	11,624	13,295	20,816	35,300
2011–12	16,360	10,303	21,920	23,643	14,750	7,750	9,747	12,343	13,357	21,296	35,808
2012–13	16,692	10,570	22,298	24,068	14,643	7,826	10,055	12,787	13,234	21,686	37,395
2013–14	16,946	10,725	22,607	24,467	14,210	7,791	10,242	12,779	13,567	22,018	36,660

—Not available.
[1]Data are based on in-state tuition only.
NOTE: Average graduate student tuition weighted by fall full-time-equivalent graduate enrollment. Excludes doctoral students in professional practice programs. Data through 1995–96 are for institutions of higher education, while later data are for degree-granting institutions. Degree-granting institutions grant associate's or higher degrees and participate in Title IV federal financial aid programs. The degree-granting classification is very similar to the earlier higher education classification, but it includes more 2-year colleges and excludes a few higher education institutions that did not grant degrees. Some data have been revised from previously published figures.
SOURCE: U.S. Department of Education, National Center for Education Statistics, Integrated Postsecondary Education Data System (IPEDS), "Fall Enrollment Survey" (IPEDS-EF:89–99); "Completions Survey" (IPEDS-C:90–99); "Institutional Characteristics Survey" (IPEDS-IC:89–99); IPEDS Fall 2000 through Fall 2013, Institutional Characteristics component; and IPEDS Spring 2001 through Spring 2014, Enrollment component. (This table was prepared March 2015.)

Table 331.10. Percentage of undergraduates receiving financial aid, by type and source of aid and selected student characteristics: 2011–12
[Standard errors appear in parentheses]

Selected student characteristic	Number of undergraduates[1] (in thousands)	Any aid — Total[2]	Any aid — Federal[3]	Any aid — Nonfederal	Grants — Total	Grants — Federal	Grants — Nonfederal	Loans — Total[4]	Loans — Federal[4]	Loans — Nonfederal	Work study — Total[5]
1	2	3	4	5	6	7	8	9	10	11	12
All undergraduates	23,055	70.7 (0.56)	59.4 (0.51)	40.4 (0.44)	59.1 (0.45)	41.5 (0.36)	36.3 (0.42)	41.9 (0.14)	40.3 (0.10)	6.5 (0.14)	5.9 (0.14)
Sex											
Male	9,921	68.4 (0.72)	56.7 (0.73)	39.8 (0.55)	55.1 (0.57)	36.7 (0.55)	35.6 (0.53)	39.0 (0.35)	37.3 (0.35)	6.4 (0.18)	6.0 (0.22)
Female	13,135	72.5 (0.53)	61.5 (0.46)	40.9 (0.47)	62.1 (0.46)	45.1 (0.36)	36.7 (0.45)	44.1 (0.22)	42.6 (0.22)	6.5 (0.17)	5.9 (0.15)
Race/ethnicity											
White	13,345	68.1 (0.59)	55.3 (0.53)	40.0 (0.49)	54.5 (0.47)	33.7 (0.38)	35.9 (0.48)	41.9 (0.34)	40.2 (0.32)	6.8 (0.19)	6.0 (0.17)
Black	3,709	81.0 (0.81)	75.2 (0.87)	36.8 (0.78)	71.4 (0.72)	62.1 (0.80)	32.2 (0.72)	52.3 (0.84)	51.0 (0.82)	6.5 (0.34)	5.1 (0.27)
Hispanic	3,696	72.3 (0.85)	61.9 (0.91)	43.0 (0.89)	64.0 (0.81)	50.1 (0.81)	38.9 (0.90)	35.6 (0.83)	34.2 (0.84)	5.6 (0.27)	5.3 (0.30)
Asian	1,292	60.8 (1.64)	46.3 (1.45)	44.2 (1.46)	53.0 (1.49)	33.4 (1.22)	41.2 (1.36)	28.4 (1.12)	27.0 (1.06)	5.0 (0.49)	9.0 (0.66)
Pacific Islander	119	68.3 (3.58)	56.7 (3.66)	37.4 (3.05)	55.1 (3.32)	39.3 (3.23)	34.9 (3.14)	37.9 (3.28)	37.3 (3.22)	4.6 (1.02)	4.5 ! (1.46)
American Indian/Alaska Native	209	76.3 (3.13)	69.0 (3.23)	40.9 (3.05)	67.6 (3.18)	55.3 (3.10)	37.6 (3.02)	43.0 (3.17)	41.9 (3.12)	5.1 (0.91)	4.7 (1.15)
Two or more races	686	74.8 (1.48)	63.6 (1.43)	46.7 (1.76)	63.9 (1.59)	45.7 (1.45)	41.9 (1.75)	46.1 (1.46)	44.1 (1.40)	8.4 (0.84)	7.2 (0.68)
Age											
15 to 23 years old	12,956	72.1 (0.49)	59.2 (0.41)	48.2 (0.47)	60.9 (0.42)	38.0 (0.29)	44.4 (0.47)	42.8 (0.28)	41.1 (0.25)	7.4 (0.15)	9.0 (0.21)
24 to 29 years old	4,253	70.4 (1.05)	61.9 (1.09)	31.8 (0.76)	59.0 (0.89)	49.1 (0.83)	27.1 (0.70)	41.6 (0.68)	39.9 (0.64)	5.8 (0.30)	2.4 (0.18)
30 years old or over	5,846	67.9 (0.89)	58.2 (0.92)	29.5 (0.64)	55.1 (0.76)	43.7 (0.77)	25.0 (0.60)	40.4 (0.52)	39.1 (0.51)	4.9 (0.25)	1.6 (0.13)
Marital status											
Not married[6]	18,507	71.9 (0.50)	60.6 (0.41)	43.0 (0.46)	60.9 (0.43)	42.2 (0.30)	38.8 (0.44)	43.5 (0.17)	41.9 (0.15)	7.0 (0.14)	7.0 (0.17)
Married	4,087	63.9 (1.21)	52.2 (1.28)	30.0 (0.71)	49.4 (0.92)	35.5 (1.00)	26.0 (0.68)	33.8 (0.75)	32.4 (0.70)	4.3 (0.32)	1.4 (0.14)
Separated	461	82.0 (1.72)	76.6 (1.91)	30.8 (1.62)	74.2 (1.92)	67.1 (2.07)	26.3 (1.72)	50.8 (2.09)	50.0 (2.07)	5.3 (0.88)	1.6 (0.47)
Attendance status[7]											
Full-time, full-year	8,864	84.4 (0.36)	72.8 (0.51)	56.9 (0.46)	72.4 (0.41)	47.4 (0.50)	52.6 (0.45)	56.7 (0.53)	55.5 (0.54)	9.2 (0.22)	11.9 (0.25)
Part-time or part-year	14,192	62.1 (1.05)	51.1 (1.10)	30.1 (0.60)	50.8 (0.87)	37.8 (0.85)	26.1 (0.56)	32.7 (0.48)	30.9 (0.45)	4.8 (0.17)	2.2 (0.12)
Dependency status and family income											
Dependent	11,231	71.6 (0.49)	58.2 (0.40)	49.9 (0.50)	59.6 (0.44)	34.9 (0.30)	46.1 (0.50)	43.4 (0.31)	41.7 (0.29)	7.8 (0.17)	9.8 (0.22)
Less than $20,000	1,775	88.3 (0.68)	83.5 (0.79)	53.2 (1.01)	87.0 (0.67)	82.1 (0.78)	50.8 (1.00)	45.5 (0.84)	44.3 (0.84)	4.9 (0.35)	10.7 (0.56)
$20,000–$39,999	2,011	81.5 (0.88)	74.1 (0.92)	54.7 (0.99)	79.1 (0.92)	70.9 (0.92)	52.0 (1.03)	42.8 (0.80)	41.6 (0.82)	5.6 (0.35)	11.6 (0.54)
$40,000–$59,999	1,389	79.7 (0.89)	70.0 (0.96)	57.5 (1.06)	72.1 (0.97)	54.7 (0.91)	54.3 (1.07)	51.0 (0.96)	49.9 (0.99)	8.5 (0.50)	11.2 (0.53)
$60,000–$79,999	1,535	65.7 (1.06)	49.6 (1.07)	49.0 (0.97)	48.3 (1.00)	14.2 (0.62)	44.3 (1.01)	46.0 (1.02)	43.9 (0.97)	9.8 (0.62)	11.2 (0.59)
$80,000–$99,999	1,339	61.6 (1.29)	45.0 (0.95)	44.5 (1.22)	40.4 (1.17)	2.7 (0.28)	39.6 (1.17)	43.9 (0.91)	41.4 (0.89)	10.2 (0.62)	9.3 (0.65)
$100,000 or more	3,183	59.5 (0.79)	38.7 (0.64)	31.4 (0.74)	40.2 (0.74)	0.7 (0.09)	39.9 (0.74)	38.0 (0.63)	35.9 (0.59)	8.5 (0.34)	7.6 (0.37)
Independent	11,825	69.9 (0.81)	60.6 (0.85)	35.2 (0.55)	58.6 (0.67)	47.7 (0.68)	26.9 (0.52)	40.5 (0.33)	39.0 (0.30)	5.2 (0.20)	2.3 (0.10)
Less than $10,000	3,561	78.6 (0.72)	71.6 (0.74)	32.1 (0.93)	73.5 (0.76)	66.5 (0.76)	30.3 (0.76)	46.7 (0.72)	45.1 (0.73)	5.8 (0.30)	4.4 (0.25)
$10,000–$19,999	2,349	77.0 (1.09)	71.1 (1.05)	30.4 (1.06)	71.2 (1.14)	65.5 (1.12)	27.0 (0.83)	46.9 (0.86)	45.6 (0.87)	5.7 (0.35)	2.3 (0.23)
$20,000–$29,999	1,702	71.4 (1.14)	62.9 (1.41)	30.2 (1.11)	56.6 (1.14)	45.7 (1.20)	25.7 (1.04)	42.3 (0.90)	40.6 (0.91)	5.7 (0.41)	1.8 (0.24)
$30,000–$49,999	1,895	65.5 (1.23)	53.6 (1.36)	26.6 (0.94)	48.7 (1.17)	34.0 (0.98)	25.8 (1.13)	36.8 (0.91)	35.1 (0.92)	5.1 (0.34)	0.8 (0.13)
$50,000 or more	2,318	51.8 (1.73)	37.1 (1.54)	24.8 (1.01)	32.3 (1.08)	13.7 (0.75)	23.2 (0.88)	26.2 (1.25)	25.2 (1.14)	3.7 (0.37)	0.6 (0.12)
Housing status[8]											
School-owned	2,800	85.3 (0.52)	69.6 (0.59)	71.8 (0.63)	74.5 (0.59)	35.5 (0.60)	68.1 (0.64)	63.0 (0.64)	61.4 (0.62)	11.6 (0.39)	23.0 (0.63)
Off-campus, not with parents	10,619	68.1 (0.88)	57.4 (0.87)	34.4 (0.59)	56.1 (0.69)	42.1 (0.67)	30.0 (0.54)	39.1 (0.41)	37.5 (0.39)	5.8 (0.19)	3.1 (0.15)
With parents	7,734	68.3 (0.74)	57.8 (0.69)	36.9 (0.69)	57.7 (0.69)	43.2 (0.65)	33.1 (0.67)	36.5 (0.53)	35.0 (0.53)	5.2 (0.24)	3.6 (0.19)

!Interpret data with caution. The coefficient of variation (CV) for this estimate is between 30 and 50 percent.
[1]Numbers of undergraduates may not equal figures reported in other tables, since these data are based on a sample survey of students who enrolled at any time during the school year. Includes all postsecondary institutions.
[2]Includes students who reported they were awarded aid, but did not specify the source or type of aid.
[3]Includes Department of Veterans Affairs and Department of Defense benefits.
[4]Includes Parent Loans for Undergraduate Students (PLUS).
[5]Details on federal and nonfederal work-study participants are not available.
[6]Includes students who were single, divorced, or widowed.
[7]Full-time, full-year includes students enrolled full time for 9 or more months. Part-time or part-year includes students enrolled part time for 9 or more months and students enrolled less than 9 months either part time or full time.
[8]Excludes students attending more than one institution.
NOTE: Detail may not sum to totals because of rounding and because some students receive multiple types of aid and from different sources. Data include undergraduates in degree-granting and non-degree-granting institutions. Data exclude Puerto Rico. Race categories exclude persons of Hispanic ethnicity. In 2012, no students were reported in the "Other" race category.
SOURCE: U.S. Department of Education, National Center for Education Statistics, 2011–12 National Postsecondary Student Aid Study (NPSAS:12). (This table was prepared January 2014.)

Table 331.20. Full-time, first-time degree/certificate-seeking undergraduate students enrolled in degree-granting postsecondary institutions, by participation and average amount awarded in financial aid programs, and control and level of institution: 2000–01 through 2012–13

Control and level of institution, and year	Number enrolled	Number receiving financial aid	Percent receiving aid	Percent of enrolled students in student aid programs				Average award for students in aid programs[1]							
								Current dollars				Constant 2013–14 dollars			
				Federal grants	State/local grants	Institutional grants	Student loans[2]	Federal grants	State/local grants	Institutional grants	Student loans[2]	Federal grants	State/local grants	Institutional grants	Student loans[2]
1	2	3	4	5	6	7	8	9	10	11	12	13	14	15	16
All institutions															
2000–01	1,976,600	1,390,527	70.3	31.6	31.2	31.1	40.1	$2,486	$2,039	$4,740	$3,764	$3,337	$2,736	$6,360	$5,051
2001–02	2,050,016	1,481,592	72.3	33.3	32.5	31.5	40.7	2,739	2,057	4,918	3,970	3,612	2,712	6,485	5,235
2002–03	2,135,613	1,553,024	72.7	34.1	30.9	31.5	41.4	2,947	2,189	5,267	4,331	3,802	2,824	6,796	5,588
2003–04	2,178,517	1,610,967	73.9	34.6	31.2	31.9	43.1	2,934	2,226	5,648	4,193	3,704	2,811	7,132	5,295
2004–05	2,260,590	1,689,910	74.8	35.2	31.3	31.7	44.0	2,939	2,343	5,958	4,463	3,603	2,872	7,303	5,470
2005–06	2,309,543	1,731,315	75.0	33.7	30.8	32.7	44.6	2,959	2,441	6,213	4,831	3,494	2,882	7,336	5,705
2006–07	2,427,043	1,766,257	72.8	32.1	30.0	32.2	43.5	3,125	2,526	6,593	5,014	3,597	2,907	7,588	5,771
2007–08	2,532,955	1,914,567	75.6	35.4	30.6	33.6	45.6	3,376	2,580	6,791	6,009	3,747	2,864	7,538	6,669
2008–09	2,542,748	1,974,063	77.6	36.4	31.7	34.6	46.6	3,927	2,706	7,518	6,723	4,298	2,962	8,230	7,359
2009–10	2,855,241	2,323,706	81.4	46.2	28.6	33.3	51.2	4,693	2,771	7,693	7,019	5,088	3,004	8,340	7,609
2010–11	2,648,101	2,179,582	82.3	47.8	31.0	35.8	50.1	4,758	2,843	8,393	6,624	5,057	3,021	8,920	7,039
2011–12	2,571,120	2,140,556	83.3	47.6	30.8	37.9	51.2	4,424	2,912	8,767	6,641	4,568	3,007	9,052	6,857
2012–13	2,511,146	2,077,316	82.7	45.5	31.2	39.8	49.4	4,452	3,052	9,220	6,899	4,522	3,100	9,364	7,007
Public															
2000–01	1,333,236	872,109	65.4	30.0	33.5	22.7	30.7	2,408	1,707	2,275	3,050	3,231	2,290	3,052	4,093
2005–06	1,510,268	1,066,041	70.6	31.1	34.8	25.1	34.2	2,926	2,226	3,162	3,866	3,455	2,629	3,734	4,565
2006–07	1,568,395	1,096,808	69.9	30.9	34.9	25.2	34.2	3,099	2,318	3,316	4,081	3,567	2,668	3,817	4,697
2007–08	1,648,583	1,173,222	71.2	32.6	35.8	25.9	34.7	3,368	2,351	3,530	4,803	3,738	2,609	3,918	5,331
2008–09	1,701,017	1,245,890	73.2	33.6	36.8	26.5	36.2	3,886	2,485	3,780	5,590	4,253	2,720	4,137	6,119
2009–10	1,804,745	1,383,660	76.7	41.1	35.6	26.3	38.6	4,698	2,555	3,903	5,682	5,093	2,770	4,231	6,160
2010–11	1,802,335	1,421,369	78.9	46.0	35.9	27.2	40.2	4,765	2,676	4,160	5,780	5,064	2,845	4,421	6,143
2011–12	1,766,428	1,418,651	80.3	46.8	35.7	29.6	42.5	4,400	2,772	4,439	5,909	4,543	2,862	4,583	6,101
2012–13	1,736,952	1,390,827	80.1	45.0	36.2	31.1	41.4	4,427	2,916	4,693	6,127	4,496	2,962	4,766	6,223
4-year															
2000–01	804,793	573,430	71.3	26.6	36.5	29.6	40.7	2,569	2,068	2,616	3,212	3,448	2,775	3,511	4,310
2005–06	906,948	695,017	76.6	26.6	36.8	34.2	44.4	3,071	2,752	3,573	4,166	3,626	3,250	4,219	4,919
2006–07	949,162	716,323	75.5	26.6	36.7	34.2	43.8	3,365	2,848	3,759	4,433	3,873	3,278	4,326	5,102
2007–08	976,830	753,643	77.2	28.0	37.4	36.2	45.2	3,675	2,963	3,956	5,190	4,079	3,289	4,391	5,761
2008–09	1,007,672	791,177	78.5	28.1	37.6	37.2	46.6	4,191	3,158	4,215	6,038	4,588	3,456	4,614	6,609
2009–10	1,021,273	833,194	81.6	34.4	37.4	38.9	50.1	4,966	3,302	4,345	6,065	5,384	3,580	4,710	6,575
2010–11	1,039,126	858,424	82.6	38.9	38.2	39.6	51.5	4,983	3,469	4,634	6,127	5,296	3,687	4,925	6,511
2011–12	1,059,837	878,933	82.9	39.1	37.1	42.1	52.6	4,472	3,531	4,895	6,326	4,617	3,646	5,055	6,532
2012–13	1,056,185	872,769	82.6	37.8	37.3	43.8	50.9	4,508	3,670	5,165	6,579	4,579	3,727	5,245	6,682
2-year															
2000–01	528,443	298,679	56.5	35.2	28.8	12.1	15.3	2,222	1,009	1,004	2,396	2,982	1,355	1,347	3,215
2005–06	603,320	371,024	61.5	38.0	31.9	11.3	19.0	2,774	1,314	1,297	2,812	3,275	1,552	1,531	3,321
2006–07	619,233	380,485	61.4	37.5	32.2	11.6	19.6	2,810	1,393	1,311	2,877	3,234	1,603	1,509	3,312
2007–08	671,753	419,579	62.5	39.1	33.4	10.8	19.4	3,048	1,354	1,458	3,488	3,383	1,503	1,619	3,872
2008–09	693,345	454,713	65.6	41.5	35.5	11.0	21.1	3,584	1,448	1,637	4,150	3,924	1,585	1,792	4,543
2009–10	783,472	550,466	70.3	49.7	33.3	9.9	23.7	4,455	1,461	1,647	4,629	4,830	1,584	1,785	5,018
2010–11	763,209	562,945	73.8	55.7	32.8	10.3	24.9	4,557	1,418	1,677	4,802	4,843	1,507	1,782	5,103
2011–12	706,591	539,718	76.4	58.2	33.4	10.9	27.5	4,327	1,508	1,789	4,711	4,467	1,557	1,848	4,864
2012–13	680,767	518,058	76.1	56.3	34.4	11.4	26.8	4,342	1,648	1,891	4,797	4,410	1,674	1,921	4,872
Private nonprofit															
2000–01	439,369	363,044	82.6	28.4	31.8	68.1	57.7	2,879	2,998	7,368	4,019	3,863	4,023	9,887	5,394
2005–06	471,069	401,908	85.3	26.5	31.3	73.8	59.8	3,426	3,117	9,932	5,270	4,046	3,681	11,728	6,222
2006–07	477,698	407,247	85.3	26.2	30.5	73.9	59.3	3,704	3,321	10,724	5,544	4,263	3,822	12,344	6,382
2007–08	494,088	424,943	86.0	27.3	30.0	74.4	60.2	3,928	3,386	11,465	6,615	4,360	3,758	12,725	7,120
2008–09	496,594	433,231	87.2	27.5	30.2	76.7	60.5	4,446	3,527	12,691	7,618	4,867	3,860	13,892	8,339
2009–10	501,227	445,500	88.9	33.1	27.8	78.4	63.0	5,059	3,642	13,642	7,445	5,485	3,949	14,790	8,071
2010–11	517,831	462,840	89.4	36.4	27.1	78.4	64.3	5,076	3,556	14,324	7,296	5,395	3,779	15,224	7,754
2011–12	512,754	457,227	89.2	34.9	27.0	79.4	63.3	4,656	3,538	15,067	7,480	4,807	3,653	15,557	7,723
2012–13	515,423	459,216	89.1	33.8	26.1	79.9	62.0	4,668	3,671	15,948	7,886	4,741	3,729	16,197	8,009

See notes at end of table.

Table 331.20. Full-time, first-time degree/certificate-seeking undergraduate students enrolled in degree-granting postsecondary institutions, by participation and average amount awarded in financial aid programs, and control and level of institution: 2000–01 through 2012–13—Continued

Control and level of institution, and year	Number enrolled	Number receiving financial aid	Percent receiving aid	Percent of enrolled students in student aid programs				Average award for students in aid programs[1] — Current dollars				Average award — Constant 2013–14 dollars			
				Federal grants	State/local grants	Institutional grants	Student loans[2]	Federal grants	State/local grants	Institutional grants	Student loans[2]	Federal grants	State/local grants	Institutional grants	Student loans[2]
1	2	3	4	5	6	7	8	9	10	11	12	13	14	15	16
4-year															
2000–01	419,499	347,638	82.9	27.4	32.2	70.1	58.1	2,930	3,001	7,458	4,000	3,933	4,028	10,008	5,367
2005–06	460,832	393,429	85.4	26.0	31.2	74.6	59.8	3,437	3,121	10,002	5,264	4,059	3,685	11,811	6,216
2006–07	468,969	400,044	85.3	25.8	30.4	74.4	59.4	3,729	3,329	10,797	5,558	4,292	3,832	12,428	6,398
2007–08	484,021	416,405	86.0	26.7	30.0	75.1	60.3	3,960	3,391	11,539	6,435	4,395	3,764	12,807	7,142
2008–09	487,034	424,917	87.2	26.9	30.1	77.4	60.6	4,484	3,526	12,772	7,647	4,909	3,860	13,980	8,371
2009–10	491,140	436,485	88.9	32.4	27.7	79.2	63.1	5,092	3,656	13,737	7,471	5,520	3,964	14,893	8,099
2010–11	504,715	451,012	89.4	35.4	27.7	79.6	64.3	5,105	3,574	14,414	7,305	5,425	3,798	15,319	7,764
2011–12	499,901	445,144	89.0	33.9	27.0	80.6	63.2	4,683	3,554	15,178	7,493	4,835	3,670	15,672	7,736
2012–13	505,099	449,905	89.1	33.1	26.0	80.8	62.0	4,698	3,678	16,058	7,905	4,771	3,736	16,309	8,028
2-year															
2000–01	19,870	15,406	77.5	49.2	23.9	25.7	49.5	2,269	2,892	2,168	4,509	3,045	3,881	2,909	6,051
2005–06	10,237	8,479	82.8	51.6	36.1	38.5	55.9	3,176	2,974	3,799	5,531	3,751	3,511	4,486	6,531
2006–07	8,729	7,203	82.5	47.6	37.2	44.0	53.5	2,992	2,963	4,122	4,715	3,444	3,410	4,745	5,427
2007–08	10,067	8,538	84.8	53.3	31.6	37.7	54.1	3,161	3,138	4,364	5,323	3,509	3,483	4,844	5,908
2008–09	9,560	8,314	87.0	59.3	32.1	37.5	58.1	3,564	3,554	4,194	6,081	3,902	3,890	4,591	6,656
2009–10	10,087	9,015	89.4	66.9	29.1	41.5	58.6	4,294	3,000	4,798	6,078	4,656	3,252	5,201	6,589
2010–11	13,116	11,828	90.2	73.3	26.8	29.8	64.3	4,553	2,835	5,059	6,944	4,838	3,013	5,377	7,380
2011–12	12,853	12,083	94.0	76.3	24.3	31.8	65.5	4,180	2,830	4,075	7,014	4,316	2,922	4,208	7,242
2012–13	10,324	9,311	90.2	67.1	30.3	37.6	60.6	3,939	3,374	4,347	6,971	4,001	3,427	4,415	7,080
Private for-profit															
2000–01	203,995	155,374	76.2	49.3	15.2	6.2	63.5	2,312	2,494	1,540	5,517	3,103	3,346	2,066	7,404
2005–06	328,206	263,366	80.2	55.6	11.4	8.8	70.4	2,725	2,796	1,423	6,454	3,218	3,301	1,680	7,620
2006–07	380,950	262,202	68.8	44.8	9.3	8.4	61.7	2,776	2,474	1,545	6,506	3,195	2,847	1,778	7,489
2007–08	390,284	316,402	81.1	57.8	9.5	14.9	72.9	3,066	2,996	1,154	8,010	3,403	3,326	1,281	8,890
2008–09	345,137	294,942	85.5	63.4	9.1	14.0	77.7	3,710	3,194	1,677	8,323	4,061	3,497	1,835	9,111
2009–10	549,269	494,546	90.0	74.8	6.3	15.2	81.5	4,538	3,275	1,218	8,800	4,920	3,550	1,321	9,540
2010–11	327,935	295,373	90.1	75.7	9.0	15.5	82.0	4,494	3,028	1,884	8,064	4,776	3,219	2,002	8,570
2011–12	291,938	264,678	90.7	75.3	8.4	15.3	82.3	4,327	2,992	2,102	7,797	4,468	3,089	2,170	8,051
2012–13	258,771	227,273	87.8	71.9	7.8	18.2	77.4	4,357	3,158	2,350	8,098	4,425	3,207	2,387	8,224
4-year															
2000–01	81,075	51,739	63.8	36.1	11.9	8.3	57.7	2,295	2,889	1,616	5,749	3,080	3,877	2,168	7,714
2005–06	157,705	116,237	73.7	46.8	8.9	10.9	67.2	2,490	2,945	1,641	7,046	2,941	3,477	1,938	8,320
2006–07	229,746	127,215	55.4	32.5	5.7	8.4	52.0	2,608	2,622	1,878	6,989	3,001	3,018	2,162	8,044
2007–08	210,468	159,991	76.0	51.5	7.2	20.4	68.7	3,030	2,922	1,235	8,799	3,363	3,243	1,371	9,766
2008–09	125,211	107,014	85.5	57.8	11.7	21.5	77.9	3,554	3,172	2,324	9,356	3,891	3,472	2,543	10,241
2009–10	241,369	222,795	92.3	75.9	6.6	23.7	86.6	4,578	2,899	1,379	9,667	4,963	3,143	1,495	10,480
2010–11	112,706	102,000	90.5	73.6	11.3	23.6	82.9	4,733	2,950	2,805	8,561	5,030	3,135	2,981	9,099
2011–12	112,969	102,357	90.6	75.5	10.7	22.4	82.7	4,692	2,994	2,860	8,231	4,845	3,091	2,953	8,499
2012–13	100,541	89,411	88.9	73.5	9.7	26.9	79.1	4,664	2,941	3,040	8,300	4,737	2,987	3,087	8,430
2-year															
2000–01	122,920	103,635	84.3	58.0	17.3	4.8	67.3	2,319	2,314	1,453	5,387	3,112	3,105	1,949	7,229
2005–06	170,501	147,129	86.3	63.6	13.7	6.8	73.4	2,885	2,706	1,098	5,951	3,406	3,195	1,297	7,027
2006–07	151,204	134,987	89.3	63.4	14.7	8.3	76.4	2,906	2,386	1,029	6,007	3,345	2,746	1,185	6,914
2007–08	179,816	156,411	87.0	65.0	12.3	8.4	77.9	3,100	3,047	924	7,195	3,440	3,382	1,025	7,986
2008–09	219,926	187,928	85.5	66.6	7.6	9.8	77.5	3,787	3,215	865	7,733	4,146	3,519	946	8,465
2009–10	307,900	271,751	88.3	74.0	6.1	8.5	77.5	4,506	3,596	865	8,040	4,885	3,898	938	8,717
2010–11	215,229	193,373	89.8	76.8	7.8	11.3	81.5	4,374	3,088	875	7,799	4,649	3,282	930	8,289
2011–12	178,969	162,321	90.7	75.2	6.9	10.8	82.0	4,095	2,990	1,108	7,521	4,229	3,088	1,144	7,766
2012–13	158,230	137,862	87.1	70.9	6.6	12.7	76.2	4,155	3,359	1,421	7,964	4,220	3,412	1,443	8,088

[1] Average amounts for students participating in indicated programs.
[2] Includes only loans made directly to students. Does not include Parent Loans for Undergraduate Students (PLUS) and other loans made directly to parents.

NOTE: Degree-granting institutions grant associate's or higher degrees and participate in Title IV federal financial aid programs. Some data have been revised from previously published figures.

SOURCE: U.S. Department of Education, National Center for Education Statistics, Integrated Postsecondary Education Data System (IPEDS), Spring 2011, Spring 2002 through Spring 2011, Winter 2011–12, and Winter 2012–13, Student Financial Aid component. (This table was prepared January 2015.)

Table 331.30. Average amount of grant and scholarship aid and average net price for first-time, full-time students receiving Title IV aid, by control and level of institution and income level: 2009–10 through 2012–13

Current dollars

Level of institution and income level	2009–10 All institutions	2009–10 Public	2009–10 Private Nonprofit	2009–10 Private For-profit	2010–11 All institutions	2010–11 Public	2010–11 Private Nonprofit	2010–11 Private For-profit	2011–12 All institutions	2011–12 Public	2011–12 Private Nonprofit	2011–12 Private For-profit
	2	3	4	5	6	7	8	9	10	11	12	13
4-year institutions												
Grant and scholarship aid[1]												
All income levels	$9,050	$5,980	$15,560	$4,420	$9,620	$6,380	$16,240	$4,710	$9,730	$6,270	$16,930	$4,850
$0 to $30,000	10,290	9,080	17,460	5,110	10,820	9,480	17,480	5,350	10,690	9,230	18,110	5,300
$30,001 to $48,000	11,170	8,330	18,710	4,530	11,750	8,760	19,350	4,940	11,870	8,580	20,150	5,060
$48,001 to $75,000	9,140	4,910	16,810	2,430	9,700	5,350	17,680	3,030	9,870	5,230	18,490	3,260
$75,001 to $110,000	7,150	2,270	14,650	1,220	7,640	2,410	15,590	1,330	7,960	2,460	16,380	1,620
$110,001 or more	6,300	1,590	11,560	1,020	6,910	1,590	12,460	1,040	7,280	1,630	13,210	1,870
Net price[2]												
All income levels	15,900	11,070	21,780	22,590	16,290	11,470	22,500	22,700	16,890	12,350	23,450	21,430
$0 to $30,000	12,570	7,720	15,970	21,770	12,820	8,060	16,950	22,240	13,340	9,180	17,660	20,940
$30,001 to $48,000	13,110	9,260	17,200	23,590	13,420	9,680	17,930	23,350	14,060	10,820	18,620	22,370
$48,001 to $75,000	16,610	13,290	20,270	26,710	16,870	13,650	20,920	26,350	17,540	14,630	21,590	25,300
$75,001 to $110,000	19,860	16,410	23,900	29,830	20,440	17,120	24,590	29,110	21,040	17,920	25,170	28,180
$110,001 or more	24,080	17,880	30,210	32,910	25,010	18,760	31,020	31,480	25,660	19,550	31,740	30,380
2-year institutions												
Grant and scholarship aid[1]												
All income levels	4,460	4,540	5,180	4,090	4,630	4,680	5,920	4,320	4,490	4,530	5,820	4,120
$0 to $30,000	5,250	5,450	5,540	4,590	5,390	5,510	6,160	4,860	5,250	5,350	6,120	4,690
$30,001 to $48,000	4,380	4,520	5,080	3,670	4,630	4,730	6,020	4,020	4,370	4,510	6,190	3,570
$48,001 to $75,000	2,240	2,250	4,150	1,960	2,480	2,470	5,750	2,210	2,400	2,380	5,280	2,050
$75,001 to $110,000	800	750	3,240	830	880	830	5,590	610	780	730	4,850	560
$110,001 or more	610	600	2,940	470	660	610	6,130	290	530	460	3,790	500
Net price[2]												
All income levels	8,930	6,290	16,270	18,360	8,950	6,540	16,830	18,960	9,130	7,000	17,790	19,330
$0 to $30,000	8,560	5,380	16,500	18,240	8,490	5,650	16,380	18,880	8,610	6,220	17,350	19,190
$30,001 to $48,000	8,720	6,330	16,620	19,070	8,910	6,520	17,470	19,780	9,590	7,080	18,750	20,190
$48,001 to $75,000	10,690	8,810	18,650	21,290	10,680	8,920	19,230	22,000	10,840	9,300	20,020	22,340
$75,001 to $110,000	12,230	10,630	20,760	23,020	12,400	10,790	20,670	24,060	12,500	11,160	20,900	24,060
$110,001 or more	12,760	10,820	20,930	24,620	12,930	11,020	21,790	25,020	12,860	11,370	21,840	25,060

Level of institution and income level	2012–13 All institutions	2012–13 Public	2012–13 Private Nonprofit	2012–13 Private For-profit
	14	15	16	17
4-year institutions				
Grant and scholarship aid[1]				
All income levels	$10,320	$6,560	$17,900	$5,090
$0 to $30,000	11,420	9,650	19,190	5,490
$30,001 to $48,000	12,450	8,910	21,180	5,420
$48,001 to $75,000	10,630	5,670	19,670	3,600
$75,001 to $110,000	8,520	2,710	17,440	2,130
$110,001 or more	7,660	1,760	14,030	2,200
Net price[2]				
All income levels	17,250	12,700	24,060	21,410
$0 to $30,000	13,500	9,390	18,190	21,050
$30,001 to $48,000	14,120	11,010	19,050	21,930
$48,001 to $75,000	17,710	14,790	21,970	24,780
$75,001 to $110,000	21,250	18,170	25,490	27,550
$110,001 or more	26,070	20,010	32,350	29,950
2-year institutions				
Grant and scholarship aid[1]				
All income levels	4,600	4,620	6,010	4,310
$0 to $30,000	5,390	5,490	6,060	4,010
$30,001 to $48,000	4,620	4,660	6,580	4,010
$48,001 to $75,000	2,560	2,530	6,340	2,320
$75,001 to $110,000	830	770	4,920	850
$110,001 or more	620	530	5,580	680
Net price[2]				
All income levels	9,080	7,110	18,420	19,960
$0 to $30,000	8,630	6,280	18,160	19,840
$30,001 to $48,000	8,900	7,130	19,240	20,990
$48,001 to $75,000	10,720	9,390	20,150	22,630
$75,001 to $110,000	12,570	11,350	22,190	24,450
$110,001 or more	12,920	11,600	22,630	24,750

Constant 2013–14 dollars[3]

Level of institution and income level	2009–10 All institutions	2009–10 Public	2009–10 Private Nonprofit	2009–10 Private For-profit	2010–11 All institutions	2010–11 Public	2010–11 Private Nonprofit	2010–11 Private For-profit	2011–12 All institutions	2011–12 Public	2011–12 Private Nonprofit	2011–12 Private For-profit	2012–13 All institutions	2012–13 Public	2012–13 Private Nonprofit	2012–13 Private For-profit
	2	3	4	5	6	7	8	9	10	11	12	13	14	15	16	17
4-year institutions																
Grant and scholarship aid[1]																
All income levels	$9,810	$6,480	$16,870	$4,790	$10,230	$6,780	$17,260	$5,000	$10,040	$6,470	$17,480	$5,010	$10,480	$6,660	$18,180	$5,170
$0 to $30,000	11,160	9,840	18,920	5,540	11,490	10,080	18,580	5,690	11,040	9,530	18,700	5,480	11,600	9,800	19,490	5,580
$30,001 to $48,000	12,110	9,040	20,290	4,910	12,490	9,310	20,570	5,250	12,260	8,860	20,810	5,220	12,640	9,050	21,510	5,510
$48,001 to $75,000	9,910	5,330	18,230	2,630	10,310	5,680	18,790	3,220	10,190	5,400	19,090	3,370	10,800	5,760	19,980	3,650
$75,001 to $110,000	7,760	2,460	15,890	1,320	8,120	2,560	16,570	1,410	8,220	2,540	16,910	1,670	8,660	2,760	17,720	2,160
$110,001 or more	6,830	1,720	12,540	1,100	7,350	1,690	13,240	1,110	7,520	1,690	13,630	1,930	7,780	1,790	14,250	2,230
Net price[2]																
All income levels	17,240	12,010	23,620	24,490	17,310	12,190	23,910	24,130	17,440	12,750	24,210	22,130	17,510	12,890	24,430	21,740
$0 to $30,000	13,630	8,370	17,320	23,600	13,630	8,560	18,010	23,640	13,770	9,470	18,240	21,620	13,710	9,530	18,480	21,380
$30,001 to $48,000	14,210	10,030	18,650	25,580	14,260	10,290	19,060	24,810	14,510	11,170	19,230	23,090	14,340	11,180	19,340	22,280
$48,001 to $75,000	18,010	14,410	21,970	28,950	17,930	14,500	22,230	28,000	18,110	15,110	22,290	26,120	17,980	15,020	22,310	25,170
$75,001 to $110,000	21,530	17,790	25,910	32,340	21,730	18,200	26,130	30,940	21,730	18,500	25,990	29,090	21,580	18,450	25,890	27,980
$110,001 or more	26,110	19,380	32,750	35,680	26,580	19,940	32,960	33,460	26,490	20,190	32,770	31,370	26,480	20,330	32,860	30,420

See notes at end of table.

Table 331.30. Average amount of grant and scholarship aid and average net price for first-time, full-time students receiving Title IV aid, by control and level of institution and income level: 2009–10 through 2012–13—Continued

Level of institution and income level	2009–10				2010–11				2011–12				2012–13			
	All institutions	Public	Private		All institutions	Public	Private		All institutions	Public	Private		All institutions	Public	Private	
			Nonprofit	For-profit			Nonprofit	For-profit			Nonprofit	For-profit			Nonprofit	For-profit
1	2	3	4	5	6	7	8	9	10	11	12	13	14	15	16	17
2-year institutions																
Grant and scholarship aid[1]																
All income levels	4,830	4,920	5,620	4,440	4,920	4,970	6,290	4,590	4,630	4,680	6,010	4,250	4,670	4,690	6,110	4,380
$0 to $30,000	5,690	5,910	6,010	4,980	5,730	5,860	6,540	5,160	5,420	5,530	6,320	4,850	5,470	5,580	6,160	4,880
$30,001 to $48,000	4,750	4,900	5,500	3,970	4,920	5,030	6,400	4,270	4,520	4,660	6,390	3,690	4,690	4,740	6,690	4,080
$48,001 to $75,000	2,430	2,440	4,500	2,130	2,630	2,620	6,110	2,350	2,470	2,460	5,450	2,120	2,600	2,570	6,440	2,350
$75,001 to $110,000	870	810	3,510	900	930	890	5,940	650	810	750	5,010	580	850	780	5,000	860
$110,001 or more	670	650	3,190	510	700	640	6,520	310	540	480	3,920	520	630	540	5,670	690
Net price[2]																
All income levels	9,680	6,820	17,640	19,900	9,510	6,950	17,880	20,150	9,430	7,230	18,370	19,960	9,220	7,220	18,700	20,270
$0 to $30,000	9,280	5,830	17,880	19,770	9,020	6,010	17,410	20,060	8,890	6,420	17,910	19,810	8,770	6,380	18,440	20,150
$30,001 to $48,000	9,450	6,860	18,020	20,670	9,470	6,930	18,560	21,030	9,900	7,310	19,360	20,840	9,040	7,240	19,540	21,320
$48,001 to $75,000	11,590	9,560	20,220	23,090	11,350	9,480	20,440	23,450	11,190	9,610	20,670	23,060	10,890	9,540	20,460	22,990
$75,001 to $110,000	13,260	11,520	22,500	24,960	13,180	11,460	21,970	25,570	12,910	11,520	21,580	24,840	12,760	11,520	22,540	24,830
$110,001 or more	13,840	11,730	22,690	26,690	13,740	11,720	23,160	26,590	13,280	11,740	22,550	25,870	13,130	11,780	22,980	25,140

[1]Grant and scholarship aid consists of federal Title IV grants, as well as other grant or scholarship aid from the federal government, state or local governments, or institutional sources. Title IV grants include Federal Pell Grants, Federal Supplemental Educational Opportunity Grants (FSEOGs), Academic Competitiveness Grants (ACGs), National Science and Mathematics Access to Retain Talent Grants (National SMART Grants), and Teacher Education Assistance for College and Higher Education (TEACH) Grants. The average amount of grant and scholarship aid by income level was calculated based on all students who received any type of Title IV aid, even those students who received zero Title IV aid in the form of grants and received Title IV aid only in the form of work-study aid or loan aid.

[2]Net price is the total cost of attendance minus grant and scholarship aid from the federal government, state or local governments, or institutional sources. However, average net price by income level was calculated based on all students who received any type of Title IV aid, even those who received zero Title IV aid in the form of grants and received Title IV aid only in the form of work-study aid or loan aid.

[3]Constant dollars based on the Consumer Price Index, prepared by the Bureau of Labor Statistics, U.S. Department of Labor, adjusted to a school-year basis.
NOTE: Excludes students who previously attended another postsecondary institution or who began their studies on a part-time basis. Includes only first-time, full-time students who paid the in-state or in-district tuition rate (if they attended public institutions) and who received Title IV aid. Excludes the approximately 17 percent of students who did not receive any Title IV aid. Title IV aid includes grant aid, work-study aid, and loan aid. Data are weighted by the number of students at the institution receiving Title IV aid. Some data have been revised from previously published figures.
SOURCE: U.S. Department of Education, National Center for Education Statistics, Integrated Postsecondary Education Data System (IPEDS), Spring 2010 through Spring 2011, Winter 2011–12, and Winter 2012–13, Student Financial Aid component. (This table was prepared January 2015.)

Table 331.35. Percentage of full-time, full-year undergraduates receiving financial aid, and average annual amount received, by source of aid and selected student characteristics: Selected years, 1999–2000 through 2011–12

[Standard errors appear in parentheses. Amounts in constant 2013–14 dollars]

Year and selected student characteristic	Number enrolled (in thousands)	Any aid						Grants				Loans[1]	
		Percent receiving			Average amount			Percent receiving		Average amount		Percent receiving	Average amount
		Total[2]	Federal[3]	Nonfederal	Total[2]	Federal[3]	Nonfederal	Total	Pell	Total	Pell		
1	2	3	4	5	6	7	8	9	10	11	12	13	14
1999–2000													
Total	6,145	71.9 (0.59)	56.7 (0.44)	52.3 (0.67)	$11,750 (138)	$8,280 (80)	$7,170 (132)	58.5 (0.60)	28.3 (0.43)	$7,080 (112)	$3,170 (21)	45.6 (0.44)	$8,370 (82)
Sex													
Male	2,687	69.1 (0.74)	53.9 (0.65)	49.7 (0.79)	11,730 (214)	8,390 (117)	7,200 (205)	53.9 (0.83)	24.5 (0.59)	7,050 (171)	3,110 (29)	43.8 (0.67)	8,550 (143)
Female	3,458	74.0 (0.73)	59.0 (0.62)	54.3 (0.86)	11,770 (158)	8,200 (93)	7,140 (134)	62.1 (0.75)	31.3 (0.61)	7,100 (118)	3,210 (28)	46.9 (0.64)	8,240 (102)
Race/ethnicity													
White	4,335	69.9 (0.73)	53.1 (0.59)	52.2 (0.73)	11,870 (186)	8,330 (103)	7,430 (170)	55.2 (0.70)	21.5 (0.53)	7,120 (143)	3,000 (30)	45.3 (0.61)	8,580 (112)
Black	675	88.0 (1.16)	78.6 (1.49)	54.7 (2.09)	11,580 (400)	8,620 (238)	6,150 (348)	76.2 (1.24)	55.7 (1.38)	6,640 (209)	3,410 (47)	59.2 (2.36)	7,640 (264)
Hispanic	500	77.1 (1.41)	65.6 (1.84)	53.1 (2.20)	10,740 (419)	7,780 (292)	5,980 (329)	66.7 (1.76)	45.4 (2.10)	6,420 (259)	3,320 (53)	42.7 (1.99)	8,200 (268)
Asian	372	60.3 (1.65)	47.8 (1.79)	47.9 (1.55)	12,340 (781)	8,120 (304)	7,430 (716)	53.0 (1.67)	31.7 (1.62)	8,200 (645)	3,460 (85)	33.0 (2.03)	7,860 (293)
Pacific Islander	41	62.3 (6.39)	56.0 (5.70)	48.8 (5.63)	12,130 (1,129)	7,290 (622)	7,110 (1,069)	53.1 (6.29)	31.9 (5.85)	7,280 (837)	3,110 (261)	30.7 (5.58)	8,550 (1,190)
American Indian/Alaska Native	42	81.5 (4.72)	75.0 (5.05)	61.7 (6.64)	12,110 (1,003)	7,590 (761)	6,760 (962)	78.7 (4.73)	50.8 (7.04)	7,420 (671)	3,510 (174)	44.6 (7.94)	7,740 (760)
Two or more races	93	75.6 (3.00)	60.6 (3.36)	57.1 (3.44)	12,370 (669)	7,940 (402)	7,940 (552)	62.0 (3.22)	34.2 (3.30)	8,380 (596)	3,320 (180)	43.8 (2.76)	8,150 (366)
Other	86	61.9 (3.54)	45.2 (3.64)	46.9 (4.04)	11,180 (1,013)	7,410 (470)	7,610 (1,006)	51.4 (4.32)	26.0 (3.70)	7,720 (815)	3,010 (225)	29.8 (4.02)	8,210 (361)
Dependency status and family income													
Dependent	4,612	70.2 (0.65)	53.4 (0.52)	53.7 (0.75)	12,170 (164)	7,970 (93)	7,980 (165)	56.2 (0.70)	21.1 (0.52)	7,730 (136)	2,950 (26)	45.6 (0.50)	8,280 (103)
Low-income[4]	990	85.4 (0.90)	78.1 (1.03)	65.2 (1.43)	12,460 (222)	7,990 (123)	6,750 (194)	82.3 (0.94)	70.4 (1.12)	7,950 (151)	3,370 (28)	50.5 (1.27)	6,980 (142)
Middle-income[4]	2,383	70.6 (0.85)	53.4 (0.79)	54.7 (1.01)	12,300 (248)	7,600 (111)	8,440 (244)	54.3 (1.00)	11.6 (0.47)	7,680 (232)	1,880 (48)	49.8 (0.80)	8,160 (119)
High-income[4]	1,238	57.3 (1.10)	33.7 (0.77)	42.6 (1.07)	11,510 (225)	9,020 (257)	8,360 (182)	38.8 (1.08)	‡ (†)	7,500 (180)	‡ (†)	33.5 (0.72)	10,180 (265)
Independent[4]	1,533	76.9 (0.88)	66.8 (0.80)	48.1 (1.11)	10,620 (193)	9,040 (127)	4,420 (140)	65.5 (0.84)	50.0 (0.72)	5,390 (111)	3,460 (33)	45.6 (1.17)	8,640 (103)
2003–04													
Total	7,562	75.3 (0.62)	60.3 (0.49)	54.9 (0.63)	$12,330 (117)	$8,850 (76)	$7,180 (149)	62.2 (0.58)	31.4 (0.31)	$7,160 (127)	$3,840 (23)	48.6 (0.42)	$8,840 (90)
Sex													
Male	3,340	72.8 (0.89)	57.2 (0.83)	53.8 (0.78)	12,470 (155)	9,000 (104)	7,290 (164)	58.6 (0.82)	28.0 (0.62)	7,130 (144)	3,760 (34)	46.8 (0.77)	9,140 (128)
Female	4,222	77.3 (0.56)	62.7 (0.51)	55.8 (0.70)	12,220 (136)	8,740 (81)	7,090 (170)	65.0 (0.61)	34.2 (0.46)	7,180 (140)	3,900 (26)	50.0 (0.45)	8,610 (93)
Race/ethnicity													
White	5,137	73.3 (0.86)	56.3 (0.79)	55.2 (0.81)	12,280 (149)	8,820 (87)	7,310 (162)	59.0 (0.79)	23.9 (0.54)	7,000 (149)	3,660 (35)	48.4 (0.68)	9,010 (97)
Black	895	88.7 (0.90)	81.3 (1.08)	55.5 (1.68)	12,840 (277)	9,400 (187)	6,750 (250)	79.0 (1.27)	61.5 (1.64)	7,330 (231)	4,090 (35)	59.2 (1.90)	8,370 (226)
Hispanic	718	78.8 (1.09)	67.8 (1.21)	55.0 (1.32)	11,940 (260)	8,500 (162)	6,630 (258)	68.1 (1.15)	46.7 (1.17)	7,280 (185)	4,090 (56)	46.3 (1.19)	8,510 (227)
Asian	459	65.1 (1.55)	51.4 (1.46)	50.6 (1.70)	12,570 (308)	8,130 (225)	7,910 (265)	54.5 (1.74)	30.6 (1.40)	8,670 (259)	4,070 (72)	35.7 (1.28)	8,280 (294)
Pacific Islander	34	71.1 (5.10)	61.5 (4.79)	46.2 (4.95)	12,000 (1,175)	8,570 (875)	7,070 (1,145)	53.0 (5.12)	43.4 (4.85)	7,360 (774)	4,090 (288)	45.0 (5.02)	9,280 (1,066)
American Indian/Alaska Native	59	81.1 (5.18)	66.2 (6.31)	64.5 (4.42)	11,400 (788)	8,680 (458)	5,430 (944)	73.8 (5.79)	43.4 (4.64)	6,860 (742)	3,690 (195)	46.5 (5.70)	8,000 (530)
Two or more races	156	77.1 (2.12)	61.6 (2.12)	55.9 (2.11)	12,550 (512)	9,180 (360)	7,190 (440)	63.8 (2.18)	31.5 (2.39)	7,060 (374)	3,840 (111)	49.3 (2.34)	9,350 (486)
Other	104	72.2 (2.56)	56.6 (2.71)	53.2 (2.58)	11,450 (622)	8,610 (415)	6,370 (568)	61.7 (2.89)	35.5 (2.94)	6,580 (398)	3,930 (137)	42.9 (2.65)	8,710 (549)
Dependency status and family income													
Dependent	5,574	73.3 (0.79)	56.3 (0.68)	57.2 (0.74)	12,750 (147)	8,480 (81)	7,980 (164)	59.6 (0.74)	23.6 (0.39)	7,740 (158)	3,610 (26)	47.5 (0.62)	8,970 (102)
Low-income[4]	1,250	87.9 (0.70)	77.8 (0.80)	66.6 (1.00)	13,560 (257)	9,080 (119)	7,280 (245)	84.8 (0.80)	70.8 (0.92)	8,890 (209)	4,270 (24)	51.0 (0.91)	7,330 (165)
Middle-income[4]	2,886	72.7 (1.01)	55.4 (0.89)	58.0 (0.97)	12,480 (173)	7,940 (105)	8,060 (182)	57.2 (0.88)	14.8 (0.42)	7,130 (179)	2,270 (34)	50.4 (0.80)	8,980 (124)
High-income[4]	1,438	61.6 (0.98)	39.3 (0.82)	47.4 (0.91)	12,380 (216)	8,990 (152)	8,640 (214)	42.5 (1.02)	‡ (†)	7,360 (213)	‡ (†)	38.8 (0.83)	10,830 (189)
Independent[4]	1,988	80.9 (0.77)	71.5 (0.79)	48.5 (0.91)	11,250 (133)	9,650 (114)	4,540 (125)	69.4 (0.79)	53.5 (0.82)	5,780 (85)	4,130 (30)	51.6 (0.85)	8,480 (113)
2007–08													
Total	7,527	80.1 (0.28)	63.9 (0.31)	63.7 (0.36)	$14,410 (109)	$9,070 (56)	$9,030 (98)	64.6 (0.37)	32.7 (0.29)	$8,050 (79)	$3,610 (16)	54.8 (0.32)	$10,560 (86)
Sex													
Male	3,277	77.1 (0.44)	60.0 (0.47)	61.8 (0.49)	14,520 (157)	9,220 (102)	9,170 (122)	60.8 (0.54)	27.7 (0.42)	8,110 (105)	3,570 (25)	52.1 (0.56)	10,780 (130)
Female	4,249	82.4 (0.36)	66.9 (0.42)	65.2 (0.47)	14,340 (128)	8,970 (62)	8,920 (124)	67.6 (0.47)	36.6 (0.41)	8,010 (94)	3,630 (23)	56.9 (0.43)	10,410 (96)
Race/ethnicity													
White	4,963	78.1 (0.39)	59.6 (0.44)	63.2 (0.46)	14,420 (140)	8,970 (78)	9,350 (127)	61.1 (0.51)	24.1 (0.37)	7,940 (101)	3,430 (23)	54.0 (0.45)	10,850 (108)
Black	899	92.1 (0.58)	83.9 (0.86)	67.8 (0.85)	15,050 (184)	9,960 (123)	8,120 (180)	79.6 (0.92)	61.5 (1.06)	7,880 (156)	3,840 (41)	70.3 (0.84)	9,880 (166)
Hispanic	844	84.3 (0.71)	71.8 (0.88)	65.8 (0.91)	13,690 (216)	8,680 (120)	8,060 (199)	72.0 (0.85)	50.5 (1.02)	7,800 (136)	3,710 (37)	52.0 (0.92)	10,350 (229)
Asian	489	69.5 (1.35)	53.7 (1.33)	57.6 (1.47)	14,140 (316)	8,300 (200)	9,340 (279)	57.0 (1.61)	32.2 (1.21)	9,810 (267)	3,820 (48)	38.6 (1.29)	9,680 (275)
Pacific Islander	45	81.4 (3.79)	67.3 (4.93)	64.1 (4.44)	15,000 (996)	9,970 (792)	8,650 (814)	69.0 (4.14)	36.1 (4.59)	6,990 (578)	3,500 (233)	53.8 (4.44)	12,390 (772)
American Indian/Alaska Native	50	85.9 (3.32)	71.3 (3.81)	61.8 (4.53)	15,060 (872)	9,970 (578)	7,080 (716)	76.3 (3.20)	48.3 (4.15)	7,430 (663)	3,650 (186)	48.7 (4.70)	8,990 (664)
Two or more races	199	83.4 (1.31)	68.1 (1.72)	67.1 (2.01)	12,180 (437)	9,560 (257)	9,410 (389)	67.9 (1.66)	37.6 (1.87)	9,180 (372)	3,700 (96)	59.1 (1.92)	8,940 (379)
Other	17	79.8 (5.18)	72.9 (5.30)	50.9 (6.42)	13,900 (1,377)	8,750 (660)	9,270 (1,293)	67.3 (5.59)	51.9 (5.87)	8,390 (1,234)	3,490 (265)	54.7 (5.64)	8,140 (823)

See notes at end of table.

Table 331.35. Percentage of full-time, full-year undergraduates receiving financial aid, and average annual amount received, by source of aid and selected student characteristics: Selected years, 1999–2000 through 2011–12—Continued

[Standard errors appear in parentheses. Amounts in constant 2013–14 dollars]

Year and selected student characteristic	Number enrolled (in thousands)	Any aid — Percent receiving Total²	Any aid — Percent receiving Federal³	Any aid — Percent receiving Nonfederal	Any aid — Average amount Total²	Any aid — Average amount Federal³	Any aid — Average amount Nonfederal	Grants — Percent receiving Total	Grants — Percent receiving Pell	Grants — Average amount Total	Grants — Average amount Pell	Loans¹ — Percent receiving	Loans¹ — Average amount
1	2	3	4	5	6	7	8	9	10	11	12	13	14
Dependency status and family income													
Dependent	5,675	78.0 (0.34)	59.5 (0.37)	65.1 (0.40)	14,870 (133)	8,770 (72)	9,830 (115)	62.7 (0.44)	25.2 (0.27)	8,810 (97)	3,530 (19)	51.9 (0.38)	10,790 (108)
Low-income⁴	1,203	92.3 (0.49)	85.9 (0.59)	74.9 (0.62)	15,330 (176)	9,210 (87)	8,320 (145)	89.2 (0.57)	80.9 (0.66)	9,880 (123)	4,140 (18)	56.7 (0.75)	8,350 (158)
Middle-income⁴	2,825	79.3 (0.41)	59.4 (0.50)	67.1 (0.48)	14,790 (163)	8,230 (94)	10,200 (148)	61.6 (0.50)	16.1 (0.33)	8,380 (129)	2,240 (31)	56.0 (0.50)	10,790 (122)
High-income⁴	1,647	65.5 (0.66)	40.3 (0.65)	54.4 (0.76)	14,570 (232)	9,440 (210)	10,550 (180)	45.2 (0.84)	‡ (†)	8,280 (166)	‡ (†)	41.4 (0.68)	13,210 (224)
Independent	1,851	86.4 (0.47)	77.4 (0.59)	59.6 (0.74)	13,140 (133)	9,790 (85)	6,340 (113)	70.5 (0.64)	55.8 (0.64)	5,960 (78)	3,710 (29)	63.6 (0.74)	10,000 (109)
2011–12 Total	8,864 (†)	84.4 (0.36)	72.8 (0.51)	56.9 (0.46)	16,010 (110)	11,170 (78)	9,460 (114)	72.4 (0.41)	47.1 (0.50)	9,530 (95)	4,570 (17)	56.7 (0.53)	10,420 (77)
Sex													
Male	3,868	82.3 (0.50)	70.1 (0.65)	56.2 (0.61)	16,220 (173)	11,350 (112)	9,600 (179)	68.9 (0.58)	42.9 (0.60)	9,720 (154)	4,540 (25)	53.9 (0.70)	10,510 (116)
Female	4,996	86.0 (0.42)	74.9 (0.60)	57.5 (0.53)	15,860 (138)	11,040 (90)	9,350 (145)	75.1 (0.46)	50.4 (0.62)	9,400 (113)	4,580 (22)	58.8 (0.58)	10,360 (97)
Race/ethnicity⁵													
White	5,369	82.6 (0.45)	68.5 (0.63)	57.0 (0.50)	15,880 (151)	11,110 (105)	9,670 (143)	68.8 (0.52)	37.8 (0.57)	9,360 (119)	4,380 (25)	56.4 (0.67)	10,620 (102)
Black	1,209	94.0 (0.54)	90.7 (0.70)	52.8 (1.24)	16,640 (265)	12,280 (162)	8,530 (310)	84.6 (0.72)	73.5 (1.07)	8,880 (197)	4,780 (27)	71.9 (1.12)	10,320 (172)
Hispanic	1,274	88.3 (0.74)	79.1 (0.91)	60.4 (1.12)	15,210 (320)	10,520 (162)	8,470 (329)	79.9 (0.84)	62.7 (0.94)	9,580 (276)	4,740 (36)	51.2 (1.09)	9,760 (186)
Asian	603	71.4 (1.77)	58.5 (1.82)	56.4 (1.60)	16,760 (553)	9,830 (256)	11,040 (529)	63.3 (1.71)	40.8 (1.60)	12,120 (458)	4,710 (66)	38.4 (1.59)	9,790 (413)
Pacific Islander	42	82.1 (3.87)	73.1 (5.20)	55.0 (4.22)	18,400 (1,713)	12,300 (900)	11,460 (1,931)	67.3 (4.42)	44.6 (4.76)	12,350 (1,760)	4,980 (152)	50.7 (5.38)	11,100 (1,209)
American Indian/Alaska Native	67	93.0 (2.55)	86.4 (2.44)	57.1 (3.82)	15,240 (1,024)	10,310 (530)	9,220 (1,166)	85.4 (3.24)	69.5 (3.37)	9,650 (810)	4,600 (172)	62.3 (3.60)	8,260 (627)
Two or more races	301	85.8 (1.46)	76.3 (1.76)	59.6 (2.14)	17,620 (562)	11,870 (304)	10,160 (592)	73.1 (1.71)	49.4 (1.94)	10,400 (429)	4,690 (86)	59.3 (2.06)	11,250 (365)
Age													
15 to 23	6,650	82.7 (0.39)	68.6 (0.54)	62.4 (0.46)	16,720 (130)	10,800 (93)	10,290 (128)	70.9 (0.43)	39.7 (0.44)	10,680 (115)	4,540 (19)	54.0 (0.53)	10,640 (102)
24 to 29	1,048	87.5 (0.76)	83.1 (0.91)	43.4 (1.01)	14,580 (248)	12,150 (170)	6,140 (366)	76.7 (0.95)	68.6 (1.11)	6,770 (208)	4,630 (38)	61.9 (1.20)	10,020 (127)
30 or over	1,165	91.1 (0.72)	87.2 (0.80)	37.8 (1.14)	13,590 (248)	12,000 (150)	5,070 (242)	77.0 (0.90)	70.3 (1.01)	5,990 (129)	4,610 (37)	67.3 (1.08)	9,770 (126)
Marital status													
Not married⁶	7,920	84.0 (0.37)	71.6 (0.53)	59.1 (0.47)	16,400 (114)	11,160 (82)	9,760 (119)	72.5 (0.41)	45.3 (0.50)	9,930 (101)	4,580 (18)	56.4 (0.54)	10,540 (84)
Married	828	86.9 (0.76)	80.6 (1.06)	38.4 (1.18)	12,790 (262)	11,140 (184)	5,550 (346)	69.5 (1.15)	59.5 (1.28)	6,190 (193)	4,430 (48)	57.3 (1.16)	9,570 (173)
Separated	117	97.2 (1.02)	95.9 (1.25)	37.5 (2.73)	13,560 (534)	11,730 (369)	5,130 (843)	88.6 (2.00)	85.0 (2.35)	6,210 (313)	4,790 (76)	71.4 (2.68)	9,240 (324)
Dependency status and family income													
Dependent	6,141	82.3 (0.39)	67.7 (0.56)	63.3 (0.46)	16,990 (136)	10,850 (98)	10,480 (129)	69.9 (0.43)	37.0 (0.43)	10,920 (121)	4,480 (21)	54.3 (0.55)	10,780 (108)
Low-income⁴	1,361	94.2 (0.58)	90.6 (0.73)	67.9 (0.94)	17,170 (232)	10,870 (121)	9,320 (277)	93.6 (0.61)	89.2 (0.76)	11,740 (212)	5,380 (16)	56.1 (0.89)	8,310 (136)
Middle-income⁴	3,045	83.2 (0.50)	69.0 (0.68)	65.8 (0.64)	17,030 (189)	10,430 (115)	10,590 (176)	70.1 (0.59)	34.6 (0.55)	10,600 (167)	3,440 (167)	58.2 (0.70)	10,700 (132)
High-income⁴	1,735	71.3 (0.73)	47.4 (0.89)	55.4 (0.81)	16,720 (310)	11,850 (261)	11,380 (288)	50.9 (0.83)	0.4 (0.07)	10,510 (279)	3,410 (436)	46.1 (0.92)	13,330 (250)
Independent	2,723	89.2 (0.54)	84.3 (0.64)	42.5 (0.80)	13,980 (171)	11,760 (107)	6,010 (229)	78.1 (0.67)	70.0 (0.79)	6,740 (122)	4,680 (26)	62.0 (0.86)	9,710 (92)
Housing status													
School-owned	2,219	88.2 (0.50)	72.9 (0.66)	76.3 (0.59)	22,940 (259)	12,740 (166)	14,330 (257)	78.1 (0.59)	35.9 (0.67)	14,860 (265)	4,520 (37)	65.9 (0.75)	11,780 (145)
Off-campus, not with parents	3,222	84.4 (0.63)	74.6 (0.73)	48.9 (0.73)	13,920 (174)	11,140 (116)	7,040 (178)	71.6 (0.63)	53.0 (0.77)	7,420 (127)	4,590 (28)	56.1 (0.74)	10,150 (128)
With parents	2,502	82.7 (0.69)	72.0 (0.85)	52.0 (0.86)	12,780 (173)	9,860 (102)	6,670 (200)	71.2 (0.73)	52.1 (0.87)	7,580 (145)	4,610 (32)	49.4 (0.88)	9,470 (136)
Attended more than one institution	921	79.9 (0.74)	68.2 (0.94)	51.5 (0.87)	14,410 (231)	11,020 (148)	7,770 (244)	64.9 (0.90)	40.0 (0.86)	8,070 (188)	4,440 (40)	56.3 (1.00)	9,810 (151)

—Not available.
†Not applicable.
‡Reporting standards not met. Either there are too few cases for a reliable estimate or the coefficient of variation (CV) is 50 percent or greater.
¹Includes Parent Loans for Undergraduate Students (PLUS).
²Includes students who reported they were awarded aid but did not specify the source of aid.
³Includes Department of Veterans Affairs and Department of Defense benefits.
⁴Low-income students have family incomes below the 25th percentile, middle-income students have family incomes from the 25th to the 75th percentile, and high-income students have family incomes above the 75th percentile.
⁵The 2012 questionnaire did not offer students the option of choosing an "Other" race category.

⁶Includes students who were single, divorced, or widowed.
NOTE: Full-time, full-year undergraduates are those who were enrolled full time for 9 or more months at one or more institutions. Data include undergraduates in degree-granting and non-degree-granting institutions. Constant dollars based on the Consumer Price Index, prepared by the Bureau of Labor Statistics, U.S. Department of Labor, adjusted to an academic-year basis. Detail may not sum to totals because of rounding and because some students receive multiple types of aid and aid from different sources. Data exclude Puerto Rico. Race categories exclude persons of Hispanic ethnicity.
SOURCE: U.S. Department of Education, National Center for Education Statistics, 1999–2000, 2003–04, 2007–08, and 2011–12 National Postsecondary Student Aid Study (NPSAS:2000, NPSAS:04, NPSAS:08, and NPSAS:12). (This table was prepared June 2015.)

Table 331.37. Percentage of part-time or part-year undergraduates receiving financial aid, and average annual amount received, by source of aid and selected student characteristics: Selected years, 1999–2000 through 2011–12

[Standard errors appear in parentheses. Amounts in constant 2013–14 dollars]

Year and selected student characteristic	Number enrolled (in thousands)	Any aid — Percent receiving: Total	Federal[3]	Nonfederal	Any aid — Average amount: Total[2]	Federal[3]	Nonfederal	Grants — Percent receiving: Total	Pell	Grants — Average amount: Total	Pell	Loans[1] — Percent receiving	Loans[1] — Average amount
	2	3	4	5	6	7	8	9	10	11	12	13	14
1999–2000													
Total	(—)	44.2 (0.66)	29.3 (0.34)	27.5 (0.72)	$5,220 (92)	$5,400 (66)	$2,640 (79)	35.3 (0.62)	17.9 (0.25)	$2,720 (47)	$2,080 (22)	18.6 (0.28)	$6,360 (88)
Sex													
Male	4,467	41.5 (0.91)	26.7 (0.60)	26.1 (0.80)	5,370 (176)	5,660 (150)	2,750 (118)	31.6 (0.79)	14.3 (0.48)	2,720 (67)	2,040 (42)	17.5 (0.66)	6,500 (170)
Female	5,719	46.4 (0.80)	31.4 (0.62)	28.7 (0.80)	5,120 (93)	5,220 (65)	2,560 (92)	38.2 (0.72)	20.8 (0.44)	2,730 (59)	2,100 (24)	19.4 (0.49)	6,250 (92)
Race/ethnicity													
White	6,682	41.9 (0.56)	26.7 (0.37)	26.9 (0.52)	5,260 (84)	5,470 (73)	2,770 (83)	32.6 (0.49)	14.4 (0.33)	2,720 (58)	1,970 (28)	18.1 (0.32)	6,380 (106)
Black	1,349	59.9 (2.01)	43.2 (1.52)	33.2 (2.84)	4,980 (261)	5,190 (179)	2,250 (195)	49.8 (2.26)	32.0 (1.30)	2,600 (108)	2,150 (47)	23.8 (1.46)	6,300 (196)
Hispanic	1,189	46.2 (1.92)	32.3 (1.52)	28.1 (1.66)	5,090 (224)	5,380 (237)	2,190 (148)	38.4 (1.55)	22.9 (1.16)	2,620 (99)	2,240 (66)	18.7 (1.35)	6,180 (302)
Asian	494	31.8 (2.19)	21.3 (1.69)	21.6 (1.69)	6,050 (497)	5,920 (518)	3,080 (340)	26.4 (1.90)	15.3 (1.25)	3,630 (306)	2,570 (147)	13.2 (1.61)	6,410 (532)
Pacific Islander	86	33.9 (5.65)	28.4 (5.17)	19.4 (3.47)	5,350 (678)	5,080 (797)	1,920! (604)	26.4 (4.13)	18.6 (3.88)	2,650 (378)	1,930 (110)	13.3 (3.33)	7,110 (1,043)
American Indian/Alaska Native	114	49.0 (4.71)	33.3 (4.13)	27.8 (3.76)	4,300 (425)	4,370 (408)	2,340 (408)	40.4 (4.34)	23.5 (3.88)	2,790 (331)	2,010 (110)	16.1 (2.69)	4,780 (425)
Two or more races	170	42.1 (3.26)	28.6 (2.70)	25.8 (2.43)	5,360 (488)	4,940 (293)	3,260 (455)	33.7 (3.17)	17.9 (2.46)	3,020 (375)	2,020 (200)	15.7 (1.61)	7,030 (550)
Other	103	35.9 (3.91)	23.7 (3.57)	24.5 (3.03)	6,810 (891)	5,750 (628)	4,430 (979)	28.7 (3.38)	15.4 (2.94)	3,180 (403)	2,120 (215)	17.2 (2.74)	8,110 (1,178)
Dependency status and family income													
Dependent	3,472	43.5 (0.82)	31.6 (0.65)	27.1 (0.67)	6,360 (155)	5,410 (85)	3,910 (177)	32.6 (0.69)	15.3 (0.50)	3,670 (133)	2,110 (47)	23.2 (0.55)	6,200 (108)
Low-income[4]	895	61.1 (1.17)	52.2 (1.38)	35.5 (1.30)	6,020 (219)	4,960 (148)	3,080 (174)	57.3 (1.13)	46.1 (1.37)	3,590 (150)	2,340 (52)	27.3 (1.08)	5,380 (191)
Middle-income[4]	1,798	40.4 (1.12)	27.1 (0.93)	25.9 (0.75)	6,300 (229)	5,470 (142)	4,090 (239)	26.8 (0.90)	6.6 (0.54)	3,560 (198)	1,320 (50)	23.5 (0.77)	6,200 (156)
High-income[4]	779	30.6 (1.56)	18.1 (1.12)	20.1 (1.16)	7,330 (367)	6,700 (306)	5,100 (453)	17.7 (1.15)	‡ (†)	4,380 (363)	† (†)	17.8 (1.16)	7,670 (331)
Independent	6,714	44.6 (0.82)	28.2 (0.39)	27.8 (0.93)	4,640 (106)	5,390 (80)	2,000 (68)	36.7 (0.79)	19.3 (0.30)	2,290 (37)	2,070 (23)	16.2 (0.38)	6,470 (116)
2003–04													
Total	(—)	54.0 (0.82)	38.1 (0.81)	31.6 (0.59)	$5,770 (79)	$5,520 (80)	$3,200 (78)	43.1 (0.76)	23.5 (0.65)	$3,060 (43)	$2,380 (28)	24.5 (0.24)	$6,400 (94)
Sex													
Male	4,661	50.6 (1.05)	34.1 (0.91)	30.5 (0.73)	6,010 (127)	5,820 (107)	3,450 (116)	37.9 (0.92)	17.4 (0.63)	3,130 (64)	2,370 (36)	22.5 (0.48)	6,820 (163)
Female	6,646	56.3 (0.78)	40.9 (0.85)	32.3 (0.63)	5,620 (77)	5,340 (87)	3,040 (82)	46.8 (0.76)	27.8 (0.76)	3,030 (49)	2,380 (31)	25.9 (0.35)	6,140 (79)
Race/ethnicity													
White	6,841	51.5 (1.09)	33.8 (1.11)	31.7 (0.67)	5,700 (106)	5,600 (88)	3,280 (97)	40.0 (0.95)	18.3 (0.81)	2,970 (54)	2,260 (29)	23.6 (0.57)	6,540 (117)
Black	1,778	68.9 (0.94)	55.8 (1.09)	34.2 (1.06)	5,850 (196)	5,530 (192)	2,770 (111)	57.8 (0.91)	41.0 (0.93)	3,090 (77)	2,450 (50)	33.2 (1.60)	5,870 (133)
Hispanic	1,559	53.0 (1.24)	40.8 (1.10)	29.6 (1.15)	5,660 (151)	5,170 (119)	3,030 (140)	44.0 (1.17)	28.7 (0.97)	3,130 (81)	2,490 (37)	22.6 (0.94)	6,260 (200)
Asian	570	39.4 (2.05)	25.7 (1.65)	26.8 (1.67)	5,830 (284)	5,670 (225)	3,680 (275)	31.2 (1.86)	15.2 (1.13)	3,880 (221)	2,790 (119)	14.8 (1.23)	7,180 (416)
Pacific Islander	66	39.5 (5.31)	26.9 (4.62)	26.1 (4.75)	4,680 (855)	4,970 (567)	2,560 (797)	30.6 (4.95)	16.4 (3.80)	3,120 (526)	2,340 (291)	14.5 (3.44)	7,880 (1,303)
American Indian/Alaska Native	116	59.2 (3.54)	40.5 (3.38)	34.8 (3.02)	5,820 (411)	4,640 (352)	2,560 (293)	51.1 (3.38)	26.0 (3.39)	2,870 (284)	2,400 (135)	21.8 (3.00)	5,310 (676)
Two or more races	233	51.7 (1.97)	38.9 (2.03)	29.8 (1.98)	4,680 (434)	5,820 (293)	4,510 (478)	41.7 (2.15)	25.8 (2.09)	3,540 (271)	2,260 (127)	24.7 (1.96)	7,490 (461)
Other	143	61.6 (3.04)	48.2 (3.00)	35.7 (2.44)	6,400 (347)	5,810 (331)	3,190 (307)	48.3 (3.04)	30.2 (2.79)	3,260 (178)	2,680 (131)	28.8 (2.65)	6,750 (428)
Dependency status and family income													
Dependent	3,943	50.2 (1.05)	37.3 (0.89)	31.0 (0.78)	6,830 (163)	5,450 (106)	4,510 (155)	37.9 (0.94)	19.3 (0.67)	3,930 (95)	2,440 (37)	26.6 (0.58)	6,620 (173)
Low-income[4]	1,069	67.0 (1.17)	56.6 (1.09)	37.7 (1.09)	6,480 (164)	5,130 (105)	3,820 (158)	62.5 (1.17)	50.4 (1.02)	4,110 (102)	2,750 (37)	27.9 (0.82)	5,560 (175)
Middle-income[4]	2,018	48.4 (1.02)	34.6 (0.88)	30.9 (0.88)	6,740 (201)	5,400 (145)	4,520 (192)	32.4 (0.89)	11.1 (0.57)	3,590 (116)	1,690 (44)	29.4 (0.80)	6,570 (201)
High-income[4]	855	33.2 (1.72)	19.7 (1.13)	22.6 (1.30)	8,050 (354)	6,780 (291)	5,910 (349)	20.0 (1.22)	‡ (†)	4,490 (295)	‡ (†)	18.5 (1.08)	8,790 (355)
Independent	7,364	56.0 (0.86)	38.6 (0.90)	31.9 (0.62)	5,260 (65)	5,560 (95)	2,520 (57)	45.9 (0.80)	25.8 (0.74)	2,680 (34)	2,350 (32)	23.4 (0.34)	6,270 (80)
2007–08													
Total	(—)	56.6 (0.47)	38.9 (0.31)	37.8 (0.47)	$6,530 (83)	$5,840 (59)	$3,780 (76)	43.0 (0.48)	23.8 (0.30)	$2,970 (44)	$2,140 (17)	30.1 (0.22)	$7,230 (87)
Sex													
Male	5,539	51.3 (0.66)	32.7 (0.57)	35.0 (0.64)	6,540 (129)	6,040 (136)	3,930 (98)	37.1 (0.64)	17.3 (0.41)	3,040 (63)	2,120 (31)	25.4 (0.55)	7,450 (158)
Female	7,445	60.6 (0.56)	43.4 (0.47)	39.9 (0.55)	6,530 (91)	5,730 (59)	3,690 (85)	47.4 (0.56)	28.7 (0.45)	2,930 (49)	2,140 (20)	33.7 (0.42)	7,100 (96)
Race/ethnicity													
White	7,723	54.0 (0.60)	35.3 (0.45)	37.0 (0.54)	6,550 (110)	5,880 (86)	3,960 (103)	39.3 (0.56)	18.9 (0.38)	2,980 (54)	2,060 (25)	29.3 (0.44)	7,250 (123)
Black	2,093	69.0 (1.00)	54.1 (1.10)	42.1 (0.89)	6,780 (135)	5,840 (91)	3,600 (119)	55.6 (0.97)	39.3 (0.92)	3,200 (59)	2,200 (36)	40.6 (1.13)	7,070 (141)
Hispanic	1,874	59.1 (1.07)	41.0 (0.91)	39.5 (1.15)	6,100 (186)	5,700 (157)	3,210 (136)	47.5 (1.11)	29.0 (0.83)	2,830 (84)	2,180 (38)	27.2 (0.91)	7,310 (203)
Asian	731	41.2 (1.54)	25.2 (1.25)	29.9 (1.37)	6,700 (370)	5,890 (333)	4,260 (340)	32.6 (1.32)	16.3 (1.06)	3,920 (309)	2,370 (87)	17.3 (1.16)	7,310 (364)
Pacific Islander	104	54.8 (4.74)	33.5 (4.88)	35.2 (4.17)	5,640 (511)	5,680 (557)	3,380 (460)	43.8 (4.67)	25.0 (4.76)	2,630 (340)	2,070 (165)	24.8 (4.56)	6,960 (739)
American Indian/Alaska Native	122	64.0 (3.87)	47.5 (3.74)	42.4 (3.91)	5,530 (608)	5,020 (619)	2,720 (285)	53.8 (3.82)	30.9 (3.84)	2,650 (369)	2,250 (123)	30.6 (3.99)	5,330 (615)
Two or more races	293	57.3 (2.28)	43.8 (2.08)	37.2 (2.08)	7,480 (317)	6,320 (261)	4,080 (331)	43.1 (2.12)	26.5 (1.72)	3,410 (217)	2,150 (77)	29.9 (1.98)	7,540 (333)
Other	43	57.8 (5.95)	37.0 (4.66)	38.1 (5.90)	6,170 (891)	5,470 (645)	4,060 (1,176)	42.0 (5.75)	23.4 (3.36)	2,340 (233)	2,200 (163)	29.5 (4.75)	8,490 (1,182)

See notes at end of table.

Table 331.37. Percentage of part-time or part-year undergraduates receiving financial aid, and average annual amount received, by source of aid and selected student characteristics: Selected years, 1999–2000 through 2011–12—Continued

[Standard errors appear in parentheses. Amounts in constant 2013–14 dollars]

Year and selected student characteristic	Number enrolled (in thousands)	Any aid — Percent receiving — Total[2]	Federal[3]	Nonfederal	Any aid — Average amount — Total[2]	Federal[3]	Nonfederal	Grants — Percent receiving — Total	Pell	Grants — Average amount — Total	Pell	Loans[1] — Percent receiving	Loans[1] — Average amount
1	2	3	4	5	6	7	8	9	10	11	12	13	14
Dependency status and family income													
Dependent	4,852	52.6 (0.66)	35.9 (0.52)	36.8 (0.59)	7,340 (166)	5,780 (115)	4,850 (148)	37.0 (0.61)	18.0 (0.39)	3,810 (102)	2,250 (27)	29.2 (0.51)	7,720 (167)
Low-income[4]	1,265	67.5 (1.16)	55.7 (1.16)	42.6 (1.03)	6,510 (161)	5,260 (136)	3,440 (109)	60.4 (1.09)	49.2 (1.07)	3,670 (82)	2,540 (28)	30.8 (1.12)	6,360 (186)
Middle-income[4]	2,575	49.8 (0.84)	31.7 (0.67)	36.5 (0.77)	7,530 (205)	5,840 (166)	5,210 (179)	31.3 (0.76)	9.7 (0.41)	3,710 (139)	1,540 (42)	30.6 (0.64)	7,810 (218)
High-income[4]	1,012	40.9 (1.11)	22.0 (0.94)	30.5 (0.95)	8,480 (330)	7,170 (339)	6,210 (312)	22.4 (0.89)	‡ (†)	4,650 (286)	‡ (†)	23.8 (0.91)	9,580 (330)
Independent	8,132	59.0 (0.59)	40.6 (0.41)	38.4 (0.58)	6,110 (68)	5,880 (56)	3,170 (66)	46.6 (0.58)	27.3 (0.38)	2,570 (32)	2,090 (20)	30.7 (0.29)	6,950 (85)
2011–12													
Total	14,192 (—)	62.1 (1.05)	51.1 (1.10)	30.1 (0.60)	6,980 (72)	6,550 (65)	3,300 (89)	50.8 (0.87)	37.6 (0.85)	3,540 (47)	2,720 (22)	32.7 (0.48)	6,780 (57)
Sex													
Male	6,053	59.4 (1.28)	48.1 (1.40)	29.3 (0.72)	6,980 (109)	6,610 (88)	3,300 (107)	46.3 (1.02)	32.4 (1.07)	3,470 (66)	2,650 (29)	29.6 (0.72)	6,760 (88)
Female	8,139	64.2 (0.97)	53.3 (0.96)	30.7 (0.65)	6,980 (87)	6,510 (75)	3,290 (111)	54.1 (0.86)	41.4 (0.79)	3,590 (59)	2,760 (27)	35.1 (0.45)	6,780 (68)
Race/ethnicity[5]													
White	7,977	58.3 (1.10)	46.5 (1.15)	28.7 (0.62)	7,110 (98)	6,700 (79)	3,580 (114)	45.0 (0.88)	30.6 (0.84)	3,570 (66)	2,670 (25)	32.2 (0.64)	6,800 (79)
Black	2,500	74.8 (1.18)	67.7 (1.29)	29.1 (0.94)	7,270 (125)	6,650 (131)	3,230 (169)	65.0 (1.05)	56.3 (1.19)	3,510 (84)	2,730 (39)	42.8 (0.91)	6,680 (109)
Hispanic	2,422	63.9 (1.35)	52.8 (1.44)	33.9 (1.14)	6,230 (145)	5,980 (134)	2,450 (118)	55.7 (1.29)	43.3 (1.27)	3,300 (74)	2,770 (37)	27.4 (1.04)	6,720 (127)
Asian	688	51.5 (2.42)	35.7 (2.11)	33.5 (1.97)	6,970 (363)	6,460 (334)	3,840 (370)	44.0 (2.24)	26.7 (1.83)	4,340 (283)	2,980 (110)	19.5 (1.53)	7,440 (530)
Pacific Islander	77	60.8 (5.54)	48.7 (5.57)	27.8 (3.98)	6,560 (545)	6,680 (484)	2,650 (461)	48.4 (4.83)	36.4 (4.84)	3,240 (319)	2,790 (185)	30.9 (4.47)	7,370 (644)
American Indian/Alaska Native	142	68.4 (4.29)	60.8 (4.35)	33.3 (3.82)	6,820 (555)	6,310 (431)	2,490 (396)	59.1 (4.21)	46.7 (3.92)	3,480 (315)	2,740 (146)	33.9 (3.63)	6,430 (411)
Two or more races	386	66.3 (2.20)	53.7 (2.10)	36.7 (2.38)	7,250 (285)	6,640 (245)	3,400 (306)	56.7 (2.35)	42.0 (2.03)	3,690 (176)	2,660 (86)	35.8 (1.86)	6,620 (286)
Age													
15 to 23	6,306	60.8 (1.09)	49.2 (1.08)	33.2 (0.72)	7,140 (120)	6,140 (85)	3,990 (140)	50.3 (0.92)	35.7 (0.82)	4,150 (86)	2,800 (27)	30.9 (0.53)	6,630 (111)
24 to 29	3,205	64.8 (1.47)	55.0 (1.57)	28.0 (0.94)	6,760 (113)	6,640 (101)	2,580 (117)	53.3 (1.27)	42.4 (1.24)	3,030 (89)	2,620 (32)	34.9 (0.93)	6,660 (85)
30 or over	4,681	62.1 (1.16)	51.0 (1.23)	27.4 (0.71)	6,930 (88)	7,000 (102)	2,670 (105)	49.7 (0.98)	36.8 (1.02)	3,080 (62)	2,690 (31)	33.7 (0.71)	7,040 (79)
Marital status													
Not married[6]	10,588	62.9 (1.00)	52.4 (1.01)	30.8 (0.66)	7,080 (87)	6,450 (68)	3,500 (104)	52.1 (0.89)	39.4 (0.80)	3,690 (54)	2,740 (21)	33.9 (0.45)	6,730 (69)
Married	3,260	58.1 (1.51)	45.0 (1.60)	27.9 (0.81)	6,590 (133)	6,870 (137)	2,640 (133)	44.3 (1.16)	29.1 (1.24)	3,010 (82)	2,580 (44)	27.8 (0.95)	6,950 (100)
Separated	344	76.9 (2.18)	70.1 (2.43)	28.5 (1.92)	7,240 (256)	6,850 (256)	2,700 (274)	69.3 (2.29)	60.9 (2.42)	3,260 (113)	2,840 (89)	43.8 (2.44)	6,700 (218)
Dependency status and family income													
Dependent	5,090	58.7 (1.10)	46.8 (1.03)	33.8 (0.81)	7,280 (139)	6,090 (101)	4,200 (153)	47.2 (0.94)	31.8 (0.78)	4,370 (99)	2,810 (29)	30.3 (0.58)	6,820 (131)
Low-income[4]	1,342	77.9 (1.22)	71.1 (1.35)	38.4 (1.35)	6,590 (143)	5,480 (113)	3,220 (158)	75.5 (1.19)	69.1 (1.33)	4,300 (92)	3,100 (37)	31.8 (1.01)	5,470 (125)
Middle-income[4]	2,676	56.5 (1.16)	43.6 (1.11)	34.7 (0.97)	7,410 (179)	6,130 (116)	4,340 (189)	43.2 (1.06)	25.7 (0.79)	4,220 (138)	2,400 (41)	32.0 (0.70)	6,930 (157)
High-income[4]	1,071	40.1 (1.78)	24.4 (1.15)	25.8 (1.43)	8,540 (401)	8,160 (384)	5,560 (452)	21.8 (1.30)	0.5 ! (0.20)	5,470 (504)	‡ (†)	24.1 (1.16)	8,660 (376)
Independent	9,102	64.1 (1.16)	53.5 (1.26)	28.1 (0.66)	6,830 (71)	6,770 (83)	2,690 (88)	52.7 (0.99)	40.8 (1.04)	3,120 (44)	2,680 (25)	34.1 (0.58)	6,750 (53)
Housing status													
School-owned	582	74.4 (1.83)	56.8 (1.95)	54.4 (1.86)	13,030 (483)	9,230 (396)	8,170 (410)	60.7 (1.88)	31.6 (1.50)	7,780 (395)	2,840 (85)	51.9 (2.07)	8,840 (380)
Off-campus, not with parents	7,397	60.9 (1.33)	50.0 (1.38)	28.1 (0.68)	6,680 (78)	6,520 (81)	2,880 (93)	49.3 (1.07)	37.1 (1.07)	3,240 (50)	2,700 (26)	31.7 (0.66)	6,660 (69)
With parents	5,232	61.5 (1.20)	51.0 (1.19)	29.6 (0.94)	6,370 (123)	6,040 (97)	2,820 (160)	51.2 (1.12)	38.7 (1.11)	3,330 (82)	2,690 (36)	30.3 (0.75)	6,400 (96)
Attended more than one institution	982	67.6 (1.07)	57.0 (1.18)	33.3 (1.10)	8,080 (173)	7,520 (166)	3,500 (157)	53.0 (1.19)	38.8 (1.18)	3,860 (112)	2,950 (54)	42.0 (1.26)	7,350 (138)

—Not available.
†Not applicable.
!Interpret data with caution. The coefficient of variation (CV) for this estimate is between 30 and 50 percent.
‡Reporting standards not met. Either there are too few cases for a reliable estimate or the coefficient of variation (CV) is 50 percent or greater.
[1]Includes Parent Loans for Undergraduate Students (PLUS).
[2]Includes students who reported they were awarded aid but did not specify the source of aid.
[3]Includes Department of Veterans Affairs and Department of Defense benefits.
[4]Low-income students have family incomes below the 25th percentile, middle-income students have family incomes between the 25th and the 75th percentile, and high-income students have family incomes above the 75th percentile.
[5]The 2012 questionnaire did not offer students the option of choosing an "Other" race category.

[6]Includes students who were single, divorced, or widowed.
NOTE: Part-time or part-year undergraduates include those who were enrolled part time for 9 or more months and those who were enrolled less than 9 months either part time or full time. Data include undergraduates in degree-granting and non-degree-granting institutions. Constant dollars based on the Consumer Price Index, prepared by the Bureau of Labor Statistics, U.S. Department of Labor, adjusted to an academic-year basis. Detail may not sum to totals because of rounding and because some students receive multiple types of aid and aid from different sources. Data exclude Puerto Rico. Race categories exclude persons of Hispanic ethnicity.
SOURCE: U.S. Department of Education, National Center for Education Statistics, 1999–2000, 2003–04, 2007–08, and 2011–12 National Postsecondary Student Aid Study (NPSAS:2000, NPSAS:04, NPSAS:08, and NPSAS:12). (This table was prepared June 2015.)

Table 331.40. Average amount of financial aid awarded to full-time, full-year undergraduates, by type and source of aid and selected student characteristics: 2011–12

[In current dollars. Standard errors appear in parentheses]

Selected student characteristic	Any aid Total[1]	Any aid Federal[2]	Any aid Nonfederal	Grants Total	Grants Federal	Grants Nonfederal	Loans Total[3]	Loans Federal[3]	Loans Nonfederal	Work study Total[4]
1	2	3	4	5	6	7	8	9	10	11
All full-time, full-year undergraduates	$15,510 (106)	$10,820 (75)	$9,160 (110)	$9,230 (92)	$4,580 (20)	$8,590 (115)	$10,090 (75)	$9,160 (69)	$6,980 (187)	$2,250 (48)
Sex										
Male	15,710 (168)	11,000 (109)	9,300 (174)	9,420 (149)	4,550 (27)	8,750 (178)	10,180 (112)	9,240 (98)	6,910 (255)	2,300 (59)
Female	15,360 (134)	10,690 (88)	9,060 (141)	9,100 (109)	4,590 (26)	8,480 (140)	10,030 (94)	9,100 (91)	7,040 (275)	2,200 (57)
Race/ethnicity										
White	15,380 (146)	10,760 (101)	9,370 (138)	9,060 (115)	4,370 (27)	8,670 (144)	10,280 (99)	9,250 (97)	7,230 (181)	2,200 (67)
Black	16,120 (257)	11,890 (157)	8,270 (300)	8,600 (191)	4,780 (30)	7,850 (313)	9,990 (167)	9,320 (157)	6,360 (406)	2,320 (86)
Hispanic	14,730 (310)	10,190 (157)	8,200 (319)	9,280 (267)	4,750 (40)	7,920 (340)	9,450 (180)	8,670 (163)	6,330 (338)	2,350 (87)
Asian	16,230 (536)	9,520 (248)	10,690 (512)	11,740 (444)	4,780 (82)	10,310 (498)	9,480 (400)	8,500 (303)	7,500 (1,734)	2,350 (119)
Pacific Islander	17,820 (1,659)	11,910 (872)	11,100 (1,870)	11,960 (1,704)	4,990 (164)	11,100 (1,983)	10,750 (1,171)	10,240 (1,057)	‡ (†)	‡ (†)
American Indian/Alaska Native	14,760 (992)	9,980 (514)	8,930 (1,129)	9,350 (785)	4,970 (260)	8,490 (1,048)	8,000 (607)	7,300 (487)	6,620 ! (2,584)	‡ (†)
Two or more races	17,060 (544)	11,490 (295)	9,840 (573)	10,070 (416)	4,750 (94)	9,110 (536)	10,890 (353)	9,750 (300)	6,710 (955)	2,120 (153)
Age										
15 to 23 years old	16,190 (126)	10,460 (90)	9,960 (124)	10,340 (112)	4,570 (22)	9,380 (124)	10,300 (99)	9,320 (94)	6,900 (215)	2,220 (50)
24 to 29 years old	14,120 (240)	11,770 (165)	5,950 (355)	6,550 (202)	4,600 (39)	5,000 (389)	9,700 (123)	8,770 (82)	7,790 (482)	2,530 (159)
30 years old or over	13,160 (210)	11,620 (145)	4,910 (234)	5,800 (125)	4,570 (39)	4,000 (266)	9,460 (122)	8,760 (86)	6,750 (367)	2,550 (157)
Marital status										
Not married[5]	15,890 (111)	10,810 (79)	9,460 (115)	9,620 (97)	4,600 (20)	8,880 (117)	10,200 (81)	9,230 (75)	6,980 (197)	2,240 (47)
Married	12,390 (254)	10,790 (178)	5,380 (335)	5,990 (187)	4,400 (50)	4,680 (380)	9,270 (168)	8,610 (114)	6,800 (619)	2,630 (339)
Separated	13,130 (517)	11,360 (358)	4,970 (817)	6,010 (303)	4,750 (80)	4,070 (857)	8,950 (314)	8,260 (222)	8,150 (1,369)	‡ (†)
Dependency status and family income										
Dependent	16,460 (132)	10,500 (95)	10,150 (125)	10,580 (117)	4,520 (24)	9,570 (128)	10,440 (105)	9,450 (101)	6,840 (219)	2,210 (52)
Less than $20,000	16,380 (272)	10,530 (137)	8,800 (328)	11,150 (255)	5,460 (28)	8,560 (330)	8,010 (149)	7,590 (143)	5,180 (426)	2,140 (78)
$20,000–$39,999	17,000 (284)	10,440 (134)	9,450 (278)	11,530 (239)	5,010 (31)	9,250 (284)	8,350 (148)	7,880 (145)	4,610 (347)	2,250 (99)
$40,000–$59,999	16,700 (313)	9,770 (161)	9,930 (293)	10,030 (265)	2,980 (50)	9,330 (278)	9,700 (215)	8,930 (185)	5,330 (397)	2,250 (112)
$60,000–$79,999	16,080 (387)	9,870 (221)	10,330 (353)	9,690 (356)	2,090 (70)	9,680 (378)	9,660 (245)	9,460 (216)	6,680 (373)	2,160 (95)
$80,000–$99,999	16,180 (398)	10,460 (277)	10,690 (388)	9,880 (382)	2,350 (184)	9,880 (387)	11,620 (267)	10,360 (268)	6,950 (425)	2,110 (87)
$100,000 or more	16,310 (276)	11,380 (241)	11,160 (253)	10,300 (243)	2,900 (327)	10,300 (244)	12,810 (240)	11,360 (229)	8,530 (517)	2,280 (84)
Independent	13,540 (166)	11,390 (104)	5,820 (222)	6,520 (118)	4,640 (28)	5,010 (239)	9,410 (89)	9,180 (60)	7,350 (299)	2,480 (99)
Less than $10,000	14,400 (255)	11,600 (148)	6,210 (333)	7,510 (185)	5,070 (31)	5,490 (340)	9,180 (134)	8,600 (96)	7,560 (552)	2,330 (106)
$10,000–$19,999	13,700 (282)	11,590 (195)	5,580 (369)	6,160 (188)	4,440 (53)	4,760 (404)	9,440 (137)	8,650 (104)	7,170 (388)	2,700 (279)
$20,000–$29,999	12,670 (295)	11,120 (210)	4,840 (380)	5,550 (189)	3,920 (69)	3,920 (412)	9,080 (207)	8,440 (159)	6,550 (489)	3,230 (384)
$30,000–$49,999	12,920 (409)	11,390 (262)	5,820 (743)	5,750 (374)	4,320 (65)	4,940 (798)	9,650 (217)	8,810 (134)	7,440 (837)	1,920 (257)
$50,000 or more	11,770 (359)	10,420 (240)	5,940 (534)	4,690 (363)	2,750 (97)	4,820 (573)	10,410 (292)	9,330 (166)	7,890 (1,159)	‡ (†)
Housing status										
School-owned	22,220 (251)	12,340 (160)	13,880 (249)	14,390 (257)	4,690 (44)	13,060 (259)	11,410 (140)	10,190 (145)	7,690 (269)	2,140 (67)
Off-campus, not with parents	13,480 (169)	10,780 (113)	6,820 (172)	7,190 (123)	4,550 (28)	6,230 (191)	9,830 (124)	8,990 (110)	6,580 (268)	2,410 (69)
With parents	12,380 (167)	9,550 (98)	6,460 (193)	7,340 (141)	4,580 (36)	5,900 (197)	9,170 (132)	8,360 (100)	6,900 (439)	2,490 (92)
Attended more than one institution	13,960 (224)	10,670 (143)	7,530 (237)	7,810 (182)	4,430 (45)	7,010 (237)	9,500 (146)	8,750 (122)	6,170 (339)	2,050 (90)

†Not applicable.
!Interpret data with caution. The coefficient of variation (CV) for this estimate is between 30 and 50 percent.
‡Reporting standards not met (too few cases for a reliable estimate).
[1]Includes students who reported they were awarded aid, but did not specify the source or type of aid.
[2]Includes Department of Veterans Affairs and Department of Defense benefits.
[3]Includes Parent Loans for Undergraduate Students (PLUS).
[4]Details on federal and nonfederal work-study participants are not available.
[5]Includes students who were single, divorced, or widowed.
NOTE: Aid averages are for those students who received the specified type of aid. Detail may not sum to totals because of rounding and because some students receive multiple types of aid and aid from different sources. Full-time, full-year undergraduates were enrolled full time for 9 or more months at one or more institutions. Data include undergraduates in degree-granting and non-degree-granting institutions. Data exclude Puerto Rico. Race categories exclude persons of Hispanic ethnicity.
SOURCE: U.S. Department of Education, National Center for Education Statistics, 2011–12 National Postsecondary Student Aid Study (NPSAS:12). (This table was prepared January 2014.)

Table 331.45. Average amount of financial aid awarded to part-time or part-year undergraduates, by type and source of aid and selected student characteristics: 2011–12

[In current dollars. Standard errors appear in parentheses]

Selected student characteristic	Any aid			Grants			Loans			Work study
	Total[1]	Federal[2]	Nonfederal	Total	Federal	Nonfederal	Total[3]	Federal[3]	Nonfederal	Total[4]
1	2	3	4	5	6	7	8	9	10	11
All part-time or part-year undergraduates	$6,760 (70)	$6,340 (63)	$3,190 (86)	$3,430 (45)	$2,680 (22)	$2,790 (86)	$6,560 (55)	$6,270 (47)	$4,420 (131)	$2,350 (82)
Sex										
Male	6,760 (105)	6,400 (86)	3,200 (104)	3,360 (64)	2,620 (28)	2,770 (107)	6,550 (86)	6,240 (76)	4,480 (191)	2,600 (157)
Female	6,760 (84)	6,300 (73)	3,190 (107)	3,470 (57)	2,710 (27)	2,810 (111)	6,570 (66)	6,280 (56)	4,370 (163)	2,160 (107)
Race/ethnicity										
White	6,880 (95)	6,490 (77)	3,470 (111)	3,460 (64)	2,630 (25)	3,030 (113)	6,590 (76)	6,280 (65)	4,740 (190)	2,310 (112)
Black	7,040 (121)	6,440 (126)	3,130 (164)	3,400 (81)	2,690 (38)	2,810 (189)	6,470 (106)	6,210 (103)	3,850 (202)	2,210 (254)
Hispanic	6,040 (140)	5,790 (130)	2,370 (114)	3,200 (71)	2,740 (39)	1,970 (104)	6,510 (123)	6,200 (107)	4,150 (238)	2,910 (246)
Asian	6,750 (352)	6,260 (323)	3,720 (358)	4,200 (274)	2,920 (107)	3,480 (356)	7,210 (514)	7,000 (514)	3,980 (516)	2,040 (205)
Pacific Islander	6,350 (528)	6,470 (469)	2,560 (447)	3,140 (309)	2,740 (185)	2,060 (457)	7,140 (623)	6,840 (586)	‡ (†)	‡ (†)
American Indian/Alaska Native	6,610 (537)	6,110 (417)	2,410 (384)	3,370 (305)	2,720 (154)	2,240 (359)	6,230 (399)	6,030 (375)	‡ (†)	‡ (†)
Two or more races	7,020 (276)	6,430 (237)	3,290 (296)	3,570 (170)	2,610 (83)	2,880 (285)	6,410 (277)	6,140 (238)	4,400 (758)	1,870 (309)
Age										
15 to 23 years old	6,920 (116)	5,950 (83)	3,860 (136)	4,020 (84)	2,760 (27)	3,540 (135)	6,420 (107)	6,110 (101)	4,370 (173)	2,290 (101)
24 to 29 years old	6,540 (110)	6,430 (98)	2,500 (113)	2,930 (58)	2,580 (32)	1,950 (98)	6,450 (82)	6,110 (73)	4,670 (223)	2,640 (239)
30 years old or over	6,710 (85)	6,780 (98)	2,590 (102)	2,990 (60)	2,650 (31)	2,140 (112)	6,820 (76)	6,570 (67)	4,310 (270)	2,300 (198)
Marital status										
Not married[5]	6,860 (85)	6,240 (66)	3,390 (101)	3,580 (52)	2,700 (21)	2,970 (100)	6,520 (66)	6,200 (57)	4,520 (150)	2,300 (80)
Married	6,380 (129)	6,660 (133)	2,550 (129)	2,910 (79)	2,550 (44)	2,240 (132)	6,730 (97)	6,560 (87)	3,930 (248)	2,820 (404)
Separated	7,010 (248)	6,630 (248)	2,610 (265)	3,150 (110)	2,800 (87)	1,950 (251)	6,490 (211)	6,110 (200)	4,570 (585)	‡ (†)
Dependency status and family income										
Dependent	7,050 (135)	5,900 (98)	4,070 (149)	4,240 (96)	2,770 (30)	3,730 (146)	6,600 (127)	6,270 (118)	4,430 (198)	2,230 (105)
Less than $20,000	6,530 (171)	5,420 (131)	3,140 (180)	4,190 (106)	3,080 (45)	2,930 (190)	5,270 (136)	5,080 (136)	3,640 (255)	2,050 (343)
$20,000–$39,999	6,690 (215)	5,360 (124)	3,640 (334)	4,340 (188)	2,930 (45)	3,380 (340)	5,660 (166)	5,410 (158)	3,880 (418)	1,910 (177)
$40,000–$59,999	6,990 (260)	5,740 (194)	3,530 (220)	3,560 (156)	2,020 (53)	3,230 (211)	6,790 (252)	6,440 (254)	3,650 (388)	2,160 (261)
$60,000–$79,999	7,070 (344)	6,210 (258)	4,270 (299)	3,910 (262)	1,620 (118)	3,930 (289)	6,760 (288)	6,480 (257)	4,110 (405)	2,290 (280)
$80,000–$99,999	7,260 (352)	6,280 (272)	4,960 (328)	4,310 (324)	1,760 (244)	4,310 (343)	7,060 (298)	6,420 (271)	5,770 (554)	2,170 (248)
$100,000 or more	8,280 (374)	7,810 (344)	5,440 (392)	5,220 (425)	4,390 (605)	5,160 (433)	8,380 (345)	8,070 (351)	5,310 (551)	2,830 (268)
Independent	6,610 (69)	6,560 (80)	2,600 (85)	3,030 (42)	2,640 (25)	2,140 (88)	6,540 (51)	6,260 (42)	4,410 (169)	2,530 (145)
Less than $10,000	6,800 (110)	6,430 (101)	2,710 (135)	3,330 (59)	2,860 (31)	2,200 (139)	6,010 (75)	5,690 (66)	4,620 (235)	2,280 (177)
$10,000–$19,999	6,990 (131)	6,590 (137)	2,580 (137)	3,090 (68)	2,580 (40)	2,050 (152)	6,490 (95)	6,190 (91)	4,480 (218)	2,710 (319)
$20,000–$29,999	6,610 (143)	6,520 (160)	2,500 (161)	2,910 (80)	2,560 (51)	1,970 (147)	6,580 (131)	6,300 (111)	4,250 (372)	2,490 (613)
$30,000–$49,999	6,370 (152)	6,610 (135)	2,470 (150)	2,820 (97)	2,610 (51)	1,970 (140)	6,950 (128)	6,720 (118)	4,540 (548)	3,600 (530)
$50,000 or more	6,000 (172)	6,770 (192)	2,650 (137)	2,420 (108)	1,700 (63)	2,400 (138)	7,350 (135)	7,180 (132)	3,940 (318)	2,750 (709)
Housing status										
School-owned	12,620 (468)	8,940 (383)	7,910 (397)	7,540 (382)	2,870 (81)	7,420 (428)	8,560 (368)	7,880 (353)	6,350 (709)	1,700 (143)
Off-campus, not with parents	6,460 (76)	6,320 (79)	2,790 (91)	3,140 (48)	2,650 (26)	2,340 (98)	6,450 (67)	6,180 (59)	4,430 (188)	2,550 (165)
With parents	6,170 (120)	5,850 (94)	2,730 (155)	3,220 (80)	2,660 (36)	2,380 (149)	6,200 (93)	5,960 (76)	4,010 (200)	2,610 (156)
Attended more than one institution	7,830 (167)	7,290 (161)	3,390 (152)	3,740 (108)	2,900 (53)	2,960 (163)	7,110 (133)	6,760 (129)	4,220 (255)	2,180 (223)

†Not applicable.
‡Reporting standards not met (too few cases for a reliable estimate).
[1]Includes students who reported they were awarded aid, but did not specify the source or type of aid.
[2]Includes Department of Veterans Affairs and Department of Defense benefits.
[3]Includes Parent Loans for Undergraduate Students (PLUS).
[4]Details on federal and nonfederal work-study participants are not available.
[5]Includes students who were single, divorced, or widowed.

NOTE: Aid averages are for those students who received the specified type of aid. Detail may not sum to totals because of rounding and because some students receive multiple types of aid and aid from different sources. Part-time or part-year undergraduates include students enrolled part time for 9 or more months and students enrolled less than 9 months either part time or full time. Data include undergraduates in degree-granting and non-degree-granting institutions. Data exclude Puerto Rico. Race categories exclude persons of Hispanic ethnicity.
SOURCE: U.S. Department of Education, National Center for Education Statistics, 2011–12 National Postsecondary Student Aid Study (NPSAS:12). (This table was prepared January 2014.)

Table 331.50. Amount borrowed, aid status, and sources of aid for full-time and part-time undergraduates, by control and level of institution: 2007–08 and 2011–12

[Standard errors appear in parentheses]

Control and level of institution	Number of undergraduates[1] (in thousands)	Cumulative amount borrowed for undergraduate education[2] — In current dollars	Cumulative amount borrowed — In constant 2013–14 dollars[3]	Nonaided	Any aid[4,5]	Federal[5]	State	Institutional	Other[4]
1	2	3	4	5	6	7	8	9	10
2007–08									
Full-time, full-year students									
All institutions	7,527 (—)	$15,270 (128)	$16,940 (142)	19.9 (0.28)	80.1 (0.28)	63.9 (0.31)	28.3 (0.39)	34.5 (0.47)	32.9 (0.32)
Public	5,159 (—)	13,170 (117)	14,620 (130)	24.6 (0.33)	75.4 (0.33)	58.7 (0.36)	29.8 (0.42)	27.1 (0.39)	26.5 (0.32)
4-year doctoral	2,522 (—)	14,720 (169)	16,330 (188)	22.2 (0.40)	77.8 (0.40)	59.6 (0.48)	30.6 (0.61)	33.6 (0.59)	30.8 (0.43)
Other 4-year	1,031 (—)	13,510 (203)	14,990 (225)	17.5 (0.59)	82.5 (0.59)	67.6 (0.68)	34.6 (0.96)	25.5 (0.91)	29.6 (0.68)
2-year	1,584 (—)	8,710 (176)	9,670 (196)	33.1 (0.69)	66.9 (0.69)	51.4 (0.73)	25.8 (0.76)	18.1 (0.71)	17.6 (0.56)
Less-than-2-year	22 (—)	10,000 (996)	11,100 (1,106)	30.9 (3.87)	69.1 (3.87)	58.6 (3.84)	17.1 (4.00)	‡ (†)	21.6 (3.23)
Private, nonprofit	1,672 (—)	19,610 (335)	21,760 (372)	10.5 (0.57)	89.5 (0.57)	71.2 (0.62)	32.0 (1.05)	68.5 (1.58)	43.7 (0.70)
4-year doctoral	844 (—)	20,980 (479)	23,290 (531)	14.5 (0.93)	85.5 (0.93)	67.1 (1.12)	27.5 (0.94)	66.2 (1.84)	42.0 (1.01)
Other 4-year	814 (—)	18,430 (456)	20,450 (506)	6.4 (0.74)	93.6 (0.74)	75.1 (1.12)	36.5 (1.99)	71.7 (2.48)	45.6 (1.07)
Less-than-4-year	14 (—)	13,970 (1,706)	15,510 (1,893)	8.0 ! (2.79)	92.0 (2.79)	84.4 (3.65)	35.4 ! (11.44)	23.3 ! (8.37)	31.2 (6.68)
Private, for-profit	695 (—)	16,170 (390)	17,940 (432)	7.4 (0.70)	92.6 (0.70)	84.6 (1.24)	8.0 (1.06)	7.9 (1.61)	54.8 (1.29)
2-year and above	599 (—)	17,160 (456)	19,040 (506)	7.6 (0.79)	92.4 (0.79)	84.2 (1.41)	8.4 (1.21)	7.9 (1.86)	57.2 (1.44)
Less-than-2-year	96 (—)	9,910 (220)	11,000 (244)	6.4 (0.82)	93.6 (0.82)	87.4 (1.74)	5.5 ! (1.82)	8.0 (1.69)	40.0 (1.49)
Part-time or part-year students									
All institutions	12,984 (—)	$12,820 (117)	$14,230 (130)	43.4 (0.47)	56.6 (0.47)	38.9 (0.31)	10.5 (0.23)	12.0 (0.36)	24.0 (0.35)
Public	10,386 (—)	11,810 (114)	13,110 (127)	50.8 (0.54)	49.2 (0.54)	30.3 (0.36)	10.6 (0.25)	10.6 (0.33)	19.0 (0.31)
4-year doctoral	1,683 (—)	16,390 (250)	18,190 (277)	35.8 (0.73)	64.2 (0.73)	44.0 (0.74)	15.9 (0.57)	16.6 (0.59)	26.7 (0.77)
Other 4-year	1,150 (—)	13,710 (287)	15,220 (319)	40.0 (1.02)	60.0 (1.02)	42.9 (0.95)	11.2 (0.56)	7.4 (0.42)	25.3 (0.96)
2-year	7,477 (—)	9,360 (152)	10,390 (169)	55.8 (0.68)	44.3 (0.68)	25.2 (0.42)	9.4 (0.32)	9.8 (0.44)	16.4 (0.36)
Less-than-2-year	76 (—)	8,140 (574)	9,030 (637)	53.3 (2.17)	46.7 (2.17)	31.4 (1.91)	9.9 ! (3.86)	4.0 ! (1.25)	15.5 (1.43)
Private, nonprofit	1,109 (—)	18,880 (365)	20,950 (405)	23.5 (0.92)	76.5 (0.92)	53.7 (0.86)	15.1 (0.83)	29.1 (1.22)	41.9 (0.97)
4-year doctoral	455 (—)	20,610 (584)	22,880 (648)	24.8 (1.38)	75.2 (1.38)	48.9 (1.82)	12.2 (0.88)	31.3 (2.06)	43.6 (1.46)
Other 4-year	599 (—)	18,130 (501)	20,120 (556)	22.2 (1.32)	77.8 (1.32)	56.4 (1.50)	17.2 (1.26)	29.1 (1.54)	41.8 (1.49)
Less-than-4-year	54 (—)	13,220 (1,901)	14,670 (2,110)	27.7 (4.93)	72.4 (4.93)	63.0 (3.97)	16.6 ! (6.35)	9.9 ! (4.11)	27.9 (2.67)
Private, for-profit	1,489 (—)	12,580 (336)	13,970 (372)	6.6 (0.56)	93.4 (0.56)	87.8 (0.72)	6.3 (0.68)	9.0 (1.80)	45.2 (1.66)
2-year and above	1,169 (—)	13,500 (410)	14,980 (455)	5.2 (0.70)	94.8 (0.70)	89.9 (0.88)	6.9 (0.81)	9.3 (2.21)	47.6 (2.03)
Less-than-2-year	319 (—)	8,980 (203)	9,960 (226)	11.8 (0.84)	88.2 (0.84)	80.0 (1.21)	4.1 (0.93)	7.8 (2.05)	36.5 (1.46)
2011–12									
Full-time, full-year students									
All institutions	8,864 (—)	$18,960 (146)	$19,580 (150)	15.6 (0.36)	84.4 (0.36)	72.8 (0.51)	24.0 (0.43)	33.9 (0.48)	28.1 (0.36)
Public	5,997 (—)	16,550 (165)	17,080 (170)	19.6 (0.47)	80.4 (0.47)	68.4 (0.61)	26.5 (0.58)	26.2 (0.59)	24.3 (0.36)
4-year doctoral	2,893 (—)	18,080 (196)	18,670 (203)	16.1 (0.46)	83.9 (0.46)	70.9 (0.47)	30.6 (0.68)	33.2 (0.90)	28.1 (0.49)
Other 4-year	969 (—)	16,980 (347)	17,530 (358)	16.5 (0.93)	83.5 (0.93)	72.7 (1.34)	30.2 (1.36)	22.9 (1.33)	27.5 (0.90)
2-year	2,104 (—)	12,740 (416)	13,150 (430)	25.5 (1.03)	74.5 (1.03)	63.0 (1.24)	19.3 (0.98)	18.5 (0.97)	17.8 (0.57)
Less-than-2-year	31 (—)	12,740 (3,005)	13,150 (3,103)	28.4 (4.50)	71.6 (4.50)	67.8 (4.72)	18.2 ! (6.85)	‡ (†)	18.9 (4.08)
Private, nonprofit	1,875 (—)	21,780 (425)	22,490 (439)	8.4 (0.55)	91.6 (0.55)	76.1 (0.75)	25.3 (0.87)	73.7 (0.97)	39.6 (0.96)
4-year doctoral	990 (—)	22,190 (756)	22,910 (781)	9.6 (0.84)	90.4 (0.84)	74.3 (0.94)	23.3 (1.29)	74.5 (1.29)	38.9 (1.50)
Other 4-year	849 (—)	21,500 (466)	22,200 (481)	6.9 (0.68)	93.1 (0.68)	78.0 (1.20)	28.0 (1.24)	74.3 (1.38)	40.5 (1.08)
Less-than-4-year	36 (—)	17,230 (1,985)	17,790 (2,049)	9.8 (4.12)	90.2 (4.12)	78.1 (5.04)	19.5 ! (7.60)	34.5 ! (11.90)	38.4 (4.24)
Private, for-profit	992 (—)	23,830 (303)	24,600 (313)	5.2 (0.46)	94.8 (0.46)	93.1 (0.51)	6.9 (0.70)	4.8 (0.72)	29.2 (0.89)
2-year and above	859 (—)	25,440 (351)	26,270 (363)	5.4 (0.53)	94.6 (0.53)	92.8 (0.59)	7.5 (0.78)	5.4 (0.83)	30.7 (0.96)
Less-than-2-year	133 (—)	13,080 (356)	13,500 (367)	4.1 (0.75)	95.9 (0.75)	95.2 (0.79)	‡ (†)	‡ (†)	19.3 (2.30)
Part-time or part-year students									
All institutions	14,192 (—)	$16,350 (186)	$16,880 (192)	37.9 (1.05)	62.1 (1.05)	51.1 (1.10)	10.1 (0.36)	12.1 (0.52)	16.4 (0.34)
Public	10,929 (—)	14,870 (202)	15,350 (208)	44.0 (1.18)	56.0 (1.18)	44.5 (1.22)	10.8 (0.41)	11.8 (0.64)	13.4 (0.36)
4-year doctoral	1,875 (—)	20,940 (368)	21,630 (380)	33.9 (1.04)	66.1 (1.04)	53.4 (0.81)	14.8 (0.60)	13.9 (0.88)	20.7 (0.73)
Other 4-year	1,477 (—)	15,890 (452)	16,400 (467)	40.5 (1.46)	59.5 (1.46)	49.7 (1.66)	11.7 (0.75)	7.0 (0.80)	16.9 (0.94)
2-year	7,521 (—)	12,080 (248)	12,470 (256)	47.3 (1.36)	52.7 (1.36)	41.2 (1.39)	9.6 (0.53)	12.3 (0.88)	10.9 (0.39)
Less-than-2-year	56 (—)	11,420 (2,303)	11,790 (2,377)	29.8 (4.21)	70.2 (4.21)	60.3 (4.47)	19.7 (5.84)	3.1 ! (1.37)	9.2 (2.44)
Private, nonprofit	1,135 (—)	23,120 (850)	23,870 (878)	22.6 (1.47)	77.4 (1.47)	61.0 (1.61)	13.5 (1.28)	30.2 (1.95)	28.7 (1.58)
4-year doctoral	557 (—)	24,890 (1,518)	25,700 (1,567)	24.0 (1.87)	76.0 (1.87)	57.9 (2.12)	9.5 (1.49)	30.1 (2.15)	28.1 (2.61)
Other 4-year	527 (—)	22,300 (946)	23,030 (977)	20.8 (2.42)	79.2 (2.42)	64.0 (2.54)	18.6 (2.12)	32.3 (3.36)	30.2 (2.14)
Less-than-4-year	51 (—)	12,630 (1,266)	13,040 (1,308)	25.7 (4.47)	74.3 (4.47)	64.3 (3.22)	‡ (†)	‡ (†)	18.2 (4.18)
Private, for-profit	2,128 (—)	17,450 (245)	18,020 (253)	14.6 (1.02)	85.4 (1.02)	79.7 (0.83)	4.2 (0.52)	3.7 (0.71)	25.3 (1.09)
2-year and above	1,790 (—)	18,680 (281)	19,280 (290)	14.7 (1.20)	85.3 (1.20)	78.8 (0.97)	4.2 (0.49)	3.6 (0.68)	27.0 (1.22)
Less-than-2-year	337 (—)	11,170 (344)	11,530 (355)	14.1 (1.39)	85.9 (1.39)	84.6 (1.40)	‡ (†)	‡ (†)	16.3 (1.71)

—Not available.
†Not applicable.
!Interpret data with caution. The coefficient of variation (CV) for this estimate is between 30 and 50 percent.
‡Reporting standards not met. The coefficient of variation (CV) for this estimate is 50 percent or greater.
[1]Numbers of undergraduates may not equal figures reported in other tables, since these data are based on a sample survey of students who enrolled at any time during the academic year.
[2]Includes only those students who borrowed to finance their undergraduate education. Excludes loans from family sources.

[3]Constant dollars based on the Consumer Price Index, prepared by the Bureau of Labor Statistics, U.S. Department of Labor, adjusted to a school-year basis.
[4]Includes students who reported that they were awarded aid, but did not specify the source of the aid.
[5]Includes Department of Veterans Affairs and Department of Defense benefits.
NOTE: Excludes students whose attendance status was not reported. Detail may not sum to totals because of rounding and because some students receive multiple types of aid and aid from different sources. Data exclude Puerto Rico. Some data have been revised from previously published figures.
SOURCE: U.S. Department of Education, National Center for Education Statistics, 2007–08 and 2011–12 National Postsecondary Student Aid Study (NPSAS:08 and NPSAS:12). (This table was prepared July 2014.)

Table 331.60. Percentage of full-time, full-year undergraduates receiving financial aid, by type and source of aid and control and level of institution: Selected years, 1992–93 through 2011–12

[Standard errors appear in parentheses]

Control and level of institution	Any aid Total[2]	Any aid Federal[3]	Any aid Nonfederal	Grants Total	Grants Federal	Grants Nonfederal	Loans Total[4]	Loans Federal[4]	Loans Nonfederal	Work study[1] Total	Work study[1] Federal
1	2	3	4	5	6	7	8	9	10	11	12
1992–93, all institutions	58.2 (0.50)	45.0 (0.50)	37.9 (0.58)	48.3 (0.51)	28.6 (0.47)	34.9 (0.51)	34.0 (0.61)	33.1 (0.61)	2.7 (0.22)	10.3 (0.38)	6.8 (0.30)
Public	52.4 (0.67)	39.8 (0.60)	32.7 (0.69)	42.8 (0.58)	27.4 (0.50)	29.6 (0.64)	27.1 (0.57)	26.3 (0.54)	2.0 (0.27)	6.8 (0.36)	4.2 (0.23)
4-year doctoral	54.0 (0.94)	39.1 (0.80)	34.7 (0.82)	42.2 (0.80)	23.6 (0.65)	31.2 (0.79)	33.1 (0.86)	32.3 (0.86)	2.4 (0.29)	7.1 (0.50)	4.3 (0.34)
Other 4-year	56.5 (1.07)	45.4 (1.19)	36.7 (1.27)	45.4 (1.29)	31.1 (1.24)	32.4 (1.32)	34.4 (0.98)	33.4 (0.93)	2.8 (0.69)	9.7 (0.77)	5.6 (0.57)
2-year	47.2 (1.93)	36.0 (1.70)	27.0 (1.62)	41.9 (1.68)	29.9 (1.43)	25.7 (1.65)	12.7 (1.23)	12.3 (1.17)	0.7 ! (0.28)	4.1 (0.79)	3.0 (0.54)
Less-than-2-year	35.4 (3.60)	31.6 (4.08)	15.7 (4.47)	30.3 (2.53)	26.6 (2.91)	13.3 ! (4.75)	3.0 ! (1.30)	3.0 ! (1.30)	‡ (†)	‡ (†)	‡ (†)
Private, nonprofit	69.5 (1.38)	52.3 (1.24)	58.9 (1.49)	62.0 (1.36)	25.8 (1.59)	55.9 (1.47)	47.6 (1.33)	45.9 (1.40)	5.1 (0.47)	22.5 (1.10)	16.1 (1.00)
4-year doctoral	63.5 (1.65)	44.3 (1.37)	54.7 (1.76)	56.0 (1.61)	17.0 (0.97)	52.7 (1.68)	41.7 (1.27)	39.8 (1.27)	6.1 (0.74)	18.9 (1.33)	13.2 (1.40)
Other 4-year	75.4 (1.91)	59.4 (2.08)	64.3 (2.46)	68.4 (2.11)	33.0 (2.79)	60.6 (2.81)	53.8 (1.88)	52.4 (1.99)	4.3 (0.80)	27.7 (1.75)	20.1 (1.58)
Less-than-4-year	70.7 (3.80)	59.5 (4.15)	44.4 (6.26)	56.6 (4.50)	40.9 (3.70)	39.2 (6.82)	43.5 (5.33)	41.7 (5.08)	2.8 ! (1.17)	4.1 ! (1.90)	2.3 ! (1.00)
Private, for-profit	77.0 (2.18)	72.0 (2.17)	16.8 (2.32)	56.2 (1.75)	49.9 (1.71)	13.6 (2.41)	55.4 (4.82)	55.1 (4.79)	2.2 ! (0.91)	1.9 ! (0.78)	0.7 ! (0.25)
2-year and above	82.2 (4.50)	76.5 (4.35)	24.1 (4.65)	50.3 (4.06)	40.5 (2.52)	21.0 (5.02)	68.5 (5.41)	68.5 (5.41)	‡ (†)	3.6 ! (1.62)	1.4 ! (0.54)
Less-than-2-year	73.2 (2.46)	68.8 (2.64)	11.5 (2.49)	60.4 (2.46)	56.7 (2.31)	8.3 ! (2.53)	46.0 (5.63)	45.4 (5.56)	1.5 ! (0.53)	‡ (†)	0.2 ! (0.09)
1999–2000, all institutions	71.9 (0.59)	56.7 (0.44)	52.3 (0.67)	58.5 (0.60)	29.0 (0.44)	49.0 (0.69)	45.6 (0.44)	44.5 (0.41)	6.8 (0.31)	11.6 (0.46)	8.9 (0.36)
Public	66.9 (0.73)	51.6 (0.51)	46.4 (0.86)	52.8 (0.68)	29.3 (0.43)	43.0 (0.81)	37.9 (0.50)	36.9 (0.46)	4.4 (0.30)	7.5 (0.47)	5.6 (0.38)
4-year doctoral	71.1 (0.79)	54.4 (0.68)	49.7 (0.77)	53.3 (0.87)	25.1 (0.74)	45.6 (0.68)	49.0 (0.73)	47.9 (0.69)	5.6 (0.41)	8.7 (0.51)	6.1 (0.42)
Other 4-year	75.7 (1.29)	63.0 (1.43)	50.6 (2.13)	57.5 (1.38)	33.7 (1.53)	46.6 (2.10)	51.5 (1.66)	50.7 (1.66)	4.7 (0.45)	11.0 (1.33)	8.1 (1.12)
2-year	55.7 (1.47)	40.5 (1.08)	39.5 (1.51)	49.2 (1.34)	31.9 (0.97)	37.3 (1.49)	14.9 (0.75)	13.9 (0.62)	2.5 (0.40)	3.8 (0.69)	3.5 (0.68)
Less-than-2-year	58.4 (6.03)	45.0 (6.96)	35.0 (5.14)	48.4 (7.50)	39.7 (7.40)	26.4 (6.54)	4.7 ! (2.14)	4.7 ! (2.13)	‡ (†)	‡ (†)	# (†)
Private, nonprofit	84.0 (0.77)	67.3 (0.75)	73.5 (1.37)	74.9 (1.13)	24.2 (1.24)	71.1 (1.42)	62.6 (0.83)	61.2 (0.83)	14.2 (0.89)	25.8 (1.27)	19.8 (1.05)
4-year doctoral	79.0 (1.03)	62.7 (1.22)	71.0 (1.27)	70.4 (1.19)	20.6 (1.22)	68.2 (1.33)	60.0 (1.16)	58.4 (1.19)	16.0 (1.08)	25.7 (1.16)	21.7 (1.05)
Other 4-year	88.7 (1.08)	72.2 (1.31)	76.3 (2.29)	78.9 (1.63)	26.3 (1.80)	74.1 (2.28)	67.4 (1.41)	66.0 (1.45)	13.4 (1.20)	26.7 (2.24)	19.0 (1.55)
Less-than-4-year	77.2 (4.01)	53.3 (2.88)	64.0 (5.11)	72.7 (4.37)	37.0 (3.48)	62.5 (5.62)	27.4 (2.59)	27.3 (2.60)	3.1 (0.62)	13.7 (2.56)	10.0 (2.71)
Private, for-profit	89.9 (1.11)	87.0 (1.39)	33.4 (3.08)	63.5 (2.14)	52.9 (2.59)	26.6 (3.88)	82.7 (1.49)	82.0 (1.50)	7.8 (1.62)	2.1 (0.87)	1.9 ! (0.86)
2-year and above	88.6 (1.50)	85.7 (1.77)	37.5 (4.17)	60.8 (2.81)	47.3 (3.29)	32.6 (3.88)	82.9 (2.19)	82.2 (2.19)	6.9 (2.04)	2.2 (1.17)	2.5 ! (1.15)
Less-than-2-year	93.7 (1.32)	91.1 (1.88)	20.8 (2.75)	71.9 (2.96)	69.8 (2.97)	8.6 (2.27)	81.9 (3.65)	81.5 (3.64)	10.4 (1.93)	2.9 (†)	‡ (0.18)
2007–08, all institutions	80.1 (0.28)	63.9 (0.31)	63.7 (0.36)	64.6 (0.37)	33.1 (0.29)	53.6 (0.41)	54.8 (0.32)	51.0 (0.32)	20.5 (0.31)	13.8 (0.29)	10.6 (0.23)
Public	75.4 (0.33)	58.7 (0.36)	58.0 (0.39)	59.2 (0.38)	32.3 (0.29)	49.6 (0.40)	46.2 (0.34)	42.7 (0.33)	14.2 (0.25)	9.5 (0.25)	7.1 (0.22)
4-year doctoral	77.8 (0.40)	59.6 (0.48)	62.8 (0.49)	59.9 (0.55)	27.8 (0.38)	53.8 (0.53)	54.7 (0.50)	50.8 (0.50)	17.4 (0.38)	10.2 (0.35)	7.6 (0.32)
Other 4-year	82.5 (0.59)	67.6 (0.68)	62.7 (0.80)	63.2 (0.81)	35.2 (0.66)	52.7 (0.85)	57.5 (0.72)	54.4 (0.72)	16.4 (0.61)	11.5 (0.60)	8.7 (0.45)
2-year	66.9 (0.69)	51.4 (0.73)	47.5 (0.79)	55.5 (0.63)	37.3 (0.65)	41.3 (0.76)	25.5 (0.59)	22.3 (0.57)	7.8 (0.37)	7.1 (0.36)	5.5 (0.29)
Less-than-2-year	69.1 (3.87)	58.6 (3.84)	33.0 (4.74)	56.6 (3.58)	50.0 (3.97)	16.1 (2.88)	26.5 (4.79)	23.6 (4.33)	10.7 (2.75)	# (†)	# (†)
Private, nonprofit	89.5 (0.57)	71.2 (0.62)	83.2 (0.79)	80.9 (0.85)	27.4 (0.67)	77.5 (1.02)	68.1 (0.66)	64.3 (0.61)	30.4 (0.74)	32.2 (1.08)	25.0 (0.86)
4-year doctoral	85.5 (0.93)	67.1 (1.12)	79.4 (1.11)	76.5 (1.18)	23.6 (0.82)	73.6 (1.38)	64.2 (1.21)	60.0 (1.22)	29.7 (1.02)	30.3 (1.10)	24.5 (1.04)
Other 4-year	93.6 (0.74)	75.1 (1.12)	87.5 (1.06)	85.8 (1.11)	31.0 (1.18)	82.1 (1.40)	72.3 (1.18)	68.8 (1.21)	31.2 (1.06)	34.7 (1.88)	26.0 (1.45)
Less-than-4-year	92.0 (2.79)	84.4 (3.65)	61.8 (10.16)	61.3 (4.96)	45.3 (5.77)	48.2 (9.77)	60.2 (7.26)	56.8 (7.31)	26.0 ! (7.94)	5.8 (1.50)	4.7 ! (1.63)
Private, for-profit	92.6 (0.70)	84.6 (1.24)	59.8 (1.60)	65.5 (1.48)	53.0 (1.50)	25.8 (1.66)	86.5 (1.19)	81.2 (1.29)	43.1 (1.67)	1.8 (0.29)	1.6 (0.28)
2-year and above	92.4 (0.79)	84.2 (1.41)	61.7 (1.82)	64.7 (1.69)	50.7 (1.70)	27.8 (1.90)	86.4 (1.36)	81.3 (1.46)	44.1 (1.92)	2.0 (0.34)	1.8 (0.33)
Less-than-2-year	93.6 (0.82)	87.4 (1.74)	47.6 (2.52)	70.8 (2.12)	67.6 (2.14)	13.5 (2.33)	87.2 (1.70)	80.7 (2.44)	36.9 (1.61)	0.7 ! (0.27)	‡ (†)
2011–12, all institutions	84.4 (0.36)	72.8 (0.51)	56.9 (0.46)	72.4 (0.41)	47.4 (0.50)	52.6 (0.45)	56.7 (0.53)	55.5 (0.54)	9.2 (0.22)	11.9 (0.25)	10.5 (0.24)
Public	80.4 (0.47)	68.4 (0.61)	53.3 (0.58)	67.3 (0.49)	46.1 (0.59)	49.7 (0.56)	48.5 (0.57)	47.4 (0.57)	6.3 (0.19)	6.9 (0.24)	6.2 (0.23)
4-year doctoral	83.9 (0.46)	70.9 (0.47)	61.2 (0.63)	67.8 (0.51)	41.1 (0.40)	56.8 (0.61)	61.6 (0.44)	60.4 (0.43)	8.6 (0.31)	8.3 (0.37)	7.4 (0.37)
Other 4-year	83.5 (0.93)	72.7 (1.34)	54.1 (1.23)	69.2 (0.99)	48.3 (1.10)	50.1 (1.32)	55.5 (1.49)	54.3 (1.51)	7.4 (0.60)	9.3 (0.70)	8.6 (0.61)
2-year	74.5 (1.03)	63.0 (1.24)	42.5 (1.14)	65.7 (1.09)	51.6 (1.30)	40.2 (1.15)	27.5 (0.99)	26.6 (1.00)	2.7 (0.24)	3.9 (0.28)	3.4 (0.28)
Less-than-2-year	71.6 (4.50)	67.8 (4.72)	33.5 (5.54)	68.6 (4.05)	63.7 (4.54)	27.2 (3.90)	20.5 (5.20)	20.5 (5.20)	‡ (†)	1.0 ! (0.46)	‡ (†)
Private, nonprofit	91.6 (0.55)	76.1 (0.75)	83.1 (0.77)	85.4 (0.77)	37.6 (0.80)	80.3 (0.85)	68.4 (0.90)	66.7 (0.88)	15.3 (0.65)	33.1 (0.85)	29.2 (0.81)
4-year doctoral	90.4 (0.84)	74.3 (0.94)	82.9 (1.13)	82.9 (1.17)	34.9 (0.80)	80.4 (1.21)	66.7 (1.08)	65.3 (1.05)	15.0 (0.92)	33.2 (1.27)	30.0 (1.26)
Other 4-year	93.1 (0.68)	78.0 (1.20)	84.2 (0.98)	87.2 (0.92)	40.3 (1.10)	81.3 (1.15)	70.7 (1.41)	68.7 (1.44)	15.8 (0.91)	33.9 (1.22)	29.1 (1.14)
Less-than-4-year	90.2 (4.12)	78.1 (5.04)	60.2 (7.07)	77.8 (6.09)	48.5 (6.54)	51.1 (8.78)	61.2 (5.71)	59.0 (7.42)	12.2 (2.62)	‡ (†)	‡ (†)
Private, for-profit	94.8 (0.46)	93.1 (0.51)	29.3 (1.05)	78.6 (0.76)	73.9 (0.82)	17.4 (0.94)	84.1 (0.85)	83.4 (0.89)	14.8 (0.75)	1.9 (0.21)	1.8 (0.20)
2-year and above	94.6 (0.53)	92.8 (0.59)	30.7 (1.16)	77.4 (0.86)	72.2 (0.92)	18.9 (1.05)	84.2 (0.85)	83.4 (0.89)	15.0 (0.82)	2.1 (0.24)	2.1 (0.23)
Less-than-2-year	95.9 (0.75)	95.2 (0.79)	20.3 (2.64)	86.2 (1.54)	85.4 (1.63)	7.5 (1.82)	83.8 (3.56)	83.0 (3.52)	13.5 (1.58)	‡ (†)	‡ (†)

†Not applicable.
#Rounds to zero.
!Interpret data with caution. The coefficient of variation (CV) for this estimate is between 30 and 50 percent.
‡Reporting standards not met. The coefficient of variation (CV) for this estimate is 50 percent or greater.
[1]Details on nonfederal work-study participants are not available.
[2]Includes students who reported they were awarded aid, but did not specify the source of aid.
[3]Includes Department of Veterans Affairs and Department of Defense benefits.
[4]Includes Parent Loans for Undergraduate Students (PLUS).

NOTE: Excludes students whose attendance status was not reported. Detail may not sum to totals because of rounding and because some students receive multiple types of aid and aid from different sources. Data exclude Puerto Rico. Some data have been revised from previously published figures.

SOURCE: U.S. Department of Education, National Center for Education Statistics, 1992–93, 1999–2000, 2007–08, and 2011–12 National Postsecondary Student Aid Study (NPSAS:93, NPSAS:2000, NPSAS:08, and NPSAS:12). (This table was prepared August 2014.)

Table 331.70. Average amount of financial aid awarded to full-time, full-year undergraduates, by type and source of aid and control and level of institution: Selected years, 1992–93 through 2011–12

[Standard errors appear in parentheses]

Current dollars

Control and level of institution	Any aid			Grants			Loans			Work study[1]	
	Total[2]	Federal[3]	Nonfederal	Total[4]	Federal	Nonfederal	Total[5]	Federal[5]	Nonfederal	Total	Federal
1	2	3	4	5	6	7	8	9	10	11	12
1992–93, all institutions	**$5,600** (80)	**$4,320** (54)	**$3,390** (85)	**$3,520** (63)	**$2,000** (17)	**$3,250** (85)	**$3,860** (59)	**$3,750** (54)	**$2,640** (133)	**$1,360** (34)	**$1,280** (38)
Public	4,030 (39)	3,740 (40)	1,860 (34)	2,420 (28)	1,900 (18)	1,740 (34)	3,350 (42)	3,290 (40)	2,020 (133)	1,380 (48)	1,350 (52)
4-year doctoral	4,720 (60)	4,390 (49)	2,330 (55)	2,750 (45)	1,970 (26)	2,230 (55)	3,660 (46)	3,590 (43)	2,150 (142)	1,440 (57)	1,360 (55)
Other 4-year	4,240 (92)	3,850 (92)	1,710 (47)	1,960 (48)	1,960 (28)	1,530 (52)	3,200 (65)	3,120 (71)	2,150 (198)	1,240 (59)	1,360 (69)
2-year	2,720 (88)	2,640 (87)	1,170 (84)	1,940 (59)	1,760 (42)	1,120 (88)	2,500 (125)	2,530 (112)	‡	1,260 (59)	1,260 (69)
Less-than-2-year	2,250 (198)	1,950 (192)	1,100 ! (476)	1,930 (154)	1,760 (60)	880 (154)	3,310 (472)	3,120 (621)	‡	1,500 (179)	1,490 (155)
Private, nonprofit	9,040 (184)	5,280 (94)	5,880 (206)	6,010 (183)	2,320 (39)	5,600 (171)	4,360 (86)	4,140 (67)	3,350 (274)	1,320 (44)	1,230 (48)
4-year doctoral	10,160 (250)	5,650 (147)	7,060 (225)	6,940 (201)	2,420 (74)	6,590 (200)	4,910 (140)	4,560 (106)	3,750 (411)	1,520 (64)	1,360 (79)
Other 4-year	8,460 (253)	5,120 (130)	5,100 (276)	5,500 (275)	2,290 (56)	4,970 (233)	4,000 (115)	3,880 (103)	2,750 (272)	1,190 (48)	1,140 (51)
Less-than-4-year	4,910 (507)	3,980 (258)	2,490 (434)	2,890 (431)	2,140 (149)	1,940 (427)	3,520 (260)	3,410 (257)	‡	‡	‡
Private, for-profit	5,460 (321)	5,130 (301)	2,590 (377)	2,290 (116)	1,950 (47)	2,320 (452)	4,910 (276)	4,840 (254)	2,410 (373)	‡	‡
2-year and above	6,670 (296)	6,130 (251)	2,820 (528)	2,780 (265)	2,060 (93)	2,670 (582)	5,590 (291)	5,480 (260)	‡	‡	‡
Less-than-2-year	4,480 (425)	4,330 (416)	2,240 (533)	2,010 (95)	1,890 (68)	1,680 (532)	4,180 (383)	4,150 (372)	‡	‡	‡
1995–96, all institutions	**$6,880** (159)	**$5,250** (61)	**$4,000** (163)	**$3,990** (138)	**$2,000** (23)	**$3,710** (162)	**$4,830** (61)	**$4,770** (58)	**$2,790** (232)	**$1,410** (40)	**$1,350** (37)
Public	5,160 (105)	4,670 (77)	2,410 (74)	2,740 (68)	1,920 (23)	2,110 (74)	4,390 (87)	4,370 (81)	2,440 (476)	1,390 (63)	1,350 (63)
4-year doctoral	6,230 (124)	5,490 (122)	3,050 (82)	3,250 (107)	1,920 (35)	2,790 (105)	4,910 (149)	4,850 (140)	2,750 (500)	1,330 (100)	1,290 (89)
Other 4-year	5,440 (235)	4,790 (166)	2,170 (81)	2,720 (81)	1,970 (25)	1,870 (60)	4,100 (139)	4,090 (137)	‡	1,450 (56)	1,380 (58)
2-year	3,110 (162)	3,110 (101)	1,530 (213)	2,020 (106)	1,900 (53)	1,100 (140)	3,140 (162)	3,210 (137)	‡	1,430 (254)	1,410 (234)
Less-than-2-year	2,440 ! (887)	2,040 (267)	2,120 ! (897)	2,190 (485)	1,650 (127)	2,360 ! (882)	2,870 (441)	2,870 (441)	‡	‡	‡
Private, nonprofit	10,870 (388)	6,470 (137)	6,740 (331)	6,640 (312)	2,280 (75)	6,230 (305)	5,600 (128)	5,470 (126)	3,210 (328)	1,430 (52)	1,350 (45)
4-year doctoral	13,130 (727)	7,160 (176)	8,720 (735)	8,370 (674)	2,350 (63)	8,000 (641)	6,260 (188)	6,120 (160)	3,610 (933)	1,660 (84)	1,550 (63)
Other 4-year	10,220 (453)	6,310 (179)	6,040 (357)	6,090 (349)	2,280 (106)	5,590 (345)	5,340 (162)	5,120 (160)	‡	1,320 (40)	1,250 (39)
Less-than-4-year	5,310 (229)	4,150 (229)	3,050 (201)	3,230 (364)	2,060 (159)	2,780 (340)	4,520 (189)	4,480 (181)	‡	1,260 (81)	1,210 (241)
Private, for-profit	6,150 (137)	5,540 (162)	3,010 (188)	2,470 (123)	1,940 (30)	2,350 (211)	4,940 (237)	4,920 (212)	2,300 (210)	‡	‡
2-year and above	6,850 (235)	6,110 (310)	3,340 (157)	2,880 (264)	2,010 (40)	2,860 (148)	5,330 (164)	5,250 (200)	‡	‡	‡
Less-than-2-year	5,520 (337)	5,020 (318)	2,700 (284)	2,120 (67)	1,880 (43)	1,520 (264)	4,550 (525)	4,570 (443)	2,080 (160)	‡	‡
1999–2000, all institutions	**$8,470** (100)	**$5,970** (58)	**$5,160** (95)	**$5,100** (81)	**$2,520** (19)	**$4,590** (92)	**$6,030** (59)	**$5,430** (51)	**$4,870** (155)	**$1,680** (37)	**$1,570** (39)
Public	6,140 (90)	5,260 (60)	2,990 (61)	3,520 (55)	2,490 (22)	2,630 (53)	5,180 (72)	4,870 (55)	3,820 (194)	1,720 (56)	1,630 (69)
4-year doctoral	7,410 (84)	6,180 (65)	3,840 (85)	4,170 (77)	2,530 (33)	3,480 (80)	5,620 (81)	5,300 (68)	3,850 (209)	1,780 (45)	1,680 (42)
Other 4-year	6,190 (175)	5,280 (136)	2,690 (105)	3,270 (91)	2,430 (28)	2,290 (60)	4,770 (179)	4,520 (147)	3,540 (426)	1,670 (148)	1,580 (194)
2-year	3,990 (135)	3,670 (96)	2,140 (84)	2,800 (91)	2,490 (45)	1,560 (80)	4,190 (198)	3,750 (122)	4,090 (841)	1,650 (118)	1,580 (105)
Less-than-2-year	3,490 (383)	3,050 (387)	1,900 (296)	2,930 (234)	2,410 (167)	1,750 (357)	5,090 (950)	5,040 (975)	‡	‡	‡
Private, nonprofit	14,050 (307)	7,280 (104)	9,390 (238)	8,710 (235)	2,490 (52)	8,280 (218)	7,460 (117)	6,300 (93)	5,750 (211)	1,620 (41)	1,500 (33)
4-year doctoral	16,060 (359)	7,890 (149)	10,910 (326)	10,140 (302)	2,860 (81)	9,600 (283)	8,240 (156)	6,700 (131)	6,430 (237)	1,810 (51)	1,700 (51)
Other 4-year	12,930 (424)	6,930 (162)	8,480 (318)	7,880 (317)	2,530 (70)	7,490 (291)	6,910 (166)	6,020 (149)	5,070 (312)	1,490 (69)	1,330 (47)
Less-than-4-year	7,700 (780)	5,540 (645)	4,680 (485)	5,070 (459)	2,640 (196)	4,340 (550)	6,010 (186)	5,380 (176)	5,590 (1,440)	950 (96)	850 (63)
Private, for-profit	8,730 (285)	7,440 (240)	4,120 (296)	3,380 (144)	2,490 (77)	3,110 (285)	6,590 (285)	6,070 (266)	5,970 (474)	‡	‡
2-year and above	9,430 (381)	7,920 (315)	4,190 (375)	3,730 (197)	2,550 (109)	3,240 (321)	7,030 (367)	6,530 (345)	6,620 (663)	‡	‡
Less-than-2-year	6,730 (354)	6,080 (330)	3,700 (556)	2,490 (64)	1,880 (63)	1,570 (385)	5,240 (355)	4,670 (319)	4,660 (800)	‡	‡
2003–04, all institutions	**$9,760** (93)	**$7,010** (60)	**$5,690** (118)	**$5,670** (101)	**$3,230** (22)	**$4,950** (125)	**$7,000** (72)	**$6,060** (57)	**$6,100** (138)	**$1,940** (36)	**$1,790** (37)
Public	7,400 (95)	6,260 (90)	3,620 (45)	4,230 (64)	3,190 (31)	3,110 (49)	6,060 (72)	5,520 (64)	5,100 (114)	1,860 (45)	1,860 (51)
4-year doctoral	8,970 (109)	7,360 (99)	4,500 (70)	4,890 (64)	3,220 (39)	3,930 (63)	6,760 (100)	6,150 (81)	5,510 (160)	2,070 (64)	1,900 (66)
Other 4-year	7,870 (183)	6,440 (146)	3,560 (84)	4,230 (118)	3,150 (64)	2,900 (91)	5,870 (127)	5,280 (112)	5,260 (227)	1,930 (86)	1,820 (100)
2-year	4,690 (130)	4,420 (143)	2,140 (84)	3,330 (64)	3,180 (45)	1,810 (86)	4,170 (146)	3,850 (147)	3,700 (207)	2,010 (100)	1,830 (109)
Less-than-2-year	4,770 (389)	4,490 (368)	2,920 (250)	3,180 (206)	2,800 (157)	2,500 (243)	5,260 (621)	4,740 (402)	4,230 (802)	2,460 ! (1,180)	†
Private, nonprofit	16,250 (258)	8,480 (127)	10,270 (234)	9,620 (261)	3,390 (49)	8,860 (250)	8,800 (178)	7,040 (135)	7,430 (273)	1,810 (52)	1,670 (51)
4-year doctoral	17,650 (367)	9,000 (204)	11,590 (383)	10,660 (465)	3,460 (101)	9,950 (466)	9,790 (272)	7,600 (190)	8,220 (333)	2,120 (78)	1,980 (75)
Other 4-year	15,650 (352)	8,260 (161)	9,580 (303)	9,130 (295)	3,340 (57)	8,280 (283)	8,270 (219)	6,740 (161)	6,920 (391)	1,620 (56)	1,470 (52)
Less-than-4-year	8,910 (647)	6,240 (375)	5,160 (534)	5,720 (547)	3,560 (333)	4,600 (607)	6,200 (584)	5,630 (470)	4,460 (774)	1,580 ! (549)	1,570 ! (557)
Private, for-profit	10,480 (328)	8,550 (222)	5,070 (285)	4,300 (167)	3,230 (72)	3,880 (317)	7,640 (267)	6,580 (190)	5,730 (275)	2,730 (328)	2,660 (328)
2-year and above	11,380 (433)	9,100 (297)	5,330 (349)	4,660 (222)	3,370 (101)	4,030 (369)	8,140 (351)	6,950 (253)	6,050 (308)	2,890 (361)	2,780 (361)
Less-than-2-year	7,810 (139)	6,880 (93)	3,980 (157)	3,210 (102)	2,850 (58)	3,010 (185)	6,050 (140)	5,350 (112)	4,560 (205)	1,760 (129)	1,570 (108)

See notes at end of table.

Table 331.70. Average amount of financial aid awarded to full-time, full-year undergraduates, by type and source of aid and control and level of institution: Selected years, 1992–93 through 2011–12—Continued

[Standard errors appear in parentheses]

Control and level of institution	Any aid			Grants			Loans			Work study[1]	
	Total[2]	Federal[3]	Nonfederal	Total[4]	Federal	Nonfederal	Total[5]	Federal[5]	Nonfederal	Total	Federal
1	2	3	4	5	6	7	8	9	10	11	12
2007–08, all institutions	$12,990 (98)	$8,170 (51)	$8,130 (89)	$7,250 (71)	$3,680 (19)	$6,470 (79)	$9,520 (77)	$7,080 (56)	$7,800 (112)	$2,270 (26)	$2,160 (30)
Public	9,680 (62)	7,250 (51)	5,240 (50)	5,420 (40)	3,670 (18)	5,170 (43)	7,990 (60)	6,470 (58)	6,520 (108)	2,430 (37)	2,360 (44)
4-year doctoral	11,670 (96)	8,320 (82)	6,550 (83)	6,410 (71)	3,780 (33)	5,170 (67)	8,870 (90)	7,100 (83)	7,130 (156)	2,440 (42)	2,290 (46)
Other 4-year	10,040 (136)	7,430 (110)	5,200 (95)	5,420 (88)	3,690 (32)	4,040 (99)	7,690 (123)	6,240 (95)	6,300 (204)	2,280 (69)	2,110 (81)
2-year	5,750 (68)	5,160 (68)	2,510 (45)	3,750 (44)	3,530 (29)	1,860 (29)	5,450 (91)	4,600 (73)	4,670 (150)	2,560 (107)	2,760 (122)
Less-than-2-year	6,210 (528)	5,200 (441)	3,750 (477)	3,610 (212)	3,320 (153)	2,390 (351)	6,910 (500)	5,550 (387)	4,920 (284)	‡ (†)	‡ (†)
Private, nonprofit	21,640 (307)	10,020 (158)	14,700 (221)	12,470 (186)	4,090 (51)	11,570 (176)	12,320 (207)	8,350 (164)	9,930 (224)	2,090 (35)	1,930 (35)
4-year doctoral	22,880 (388)	10,380 (192)	15,850 (289)	13,170 (250)	4,280 (82)	12,320 (231)	13,420 (253)	8,840 (213)	11,140 (351)	2,230 (52)	2,080 (55)
Other 4-year	20,620 (447)	9,720 (224)	13,710 (341)	11,880 (268)	3,920 (60)	10,940 (263)	11,330 (313)	7,920 (223)	8,750 (263)	1,970 (40)	1,780 (43)
Less-than-4-year	12,530 (1,097)	8,340 (1,134)	7,270 (1,107)	6,970 (1,588)	4,710 (935)	4,440 (1,230)	11,310 (613)	8,000 (1,208)	8,740 (1,011)	‡ (†)	‡ (†)
Private, for-profit	12,890 (294)	9,160 (176)	6,990 (269)	4,050 (96)	3,200 (60)	3,720 (201)	10,260 (233)	7,040 (133)	7,340 (307)	3,650 (392)	3,840 (385)
2-year and above	13,270 (340)	9,270 (203)	7,220 (303)	4,130 (113)	3,180 (73)	3,810 (216)	10,600 (269)	7,140 (153)	7,610 (350)	3,760 (402)	3,940 (386)
Less-than-2-year	10,540 (234)	8,510 (188)	5,100 (250)	3,590 (86)	3,270 (52)	2,470 (381)	8,150 (215)	6,380 (166)	5,320 (212)	‡ (†)	‡ (†)
2011–12, all institutions	$15,510 (106)	$10,820 (75)	$9,160 (110)	$9,230 (92)	$4,580 (20)	$8,590 (115)	$10,090 (75)	$9,160 (69)	$6,980 (187)	$2,250 (48)	$2,180 (37)
Public	11,420 (93)	9,400 (71)	5,170 (75)	6,610 (62)	4,560 (22)	4,730 (75)	8,860 (87)	8,300 (81)	5,790 (237)	2,330 (60)	2,290 (60)
4-year doctoral	14,130 (125)	11,000 (106)	6,610 (108)	7,880 (101)	4,610 (27)	6,070 (112)	9,750 (112)	9,040 (109)	6,400 (289)	2,410 (80)	2,320 (79)
Other 4-year	11,730 (229)	9,800 (150)	6,440 (170)	6,440 (133)	4,410 (49)	4,410 (155)	8,790 (186)	8,210 (152)	5,630 (483)	2,020 (106)	2,050 (112)
2-year	7,120 (117)	6,740 (91)	2,480 (76)	4,910 (76)	4,460 (41)	2,320 (74)	6,060 (78)	6,060 (79)	3,380 (208)	2,460 (130)	2,460 (146)
Less-than-2-year	7,300 (989)	6,360 (1,018)	2,740 (813)	5,050 (458)	4,510 (464)	2,170 ! (676)	7,060 (950)	7,060 (939)	‡ (†)	‡ (†)	‡ (†)
Private, nonprofit	27,250 (300)	13,300 (217)	17,870 (265)	17,780 (264)	4,710 (46)	16,720 (266)	12,550 (200)	10,930 (190)	8,460 (437)	2,150 (67)	2,050 (44)
4-year doctoral	29,080 (456)	13,700 (355)	19,410 (383)	19,380 (410)	4,690 (81)	18,260 (396)	13,120 (356)	11,420 (330)	8,700 (728)	2,280 (65)	2,220 (60)
Other 4-year	25,630 (384)	12,870 (216)	16,400 (355)	16,370 (336)	4,720 (46)	15,210 (348)	11,960 (167)	10,430 (172)	8,200 (385)	1,980 (130)	1,830 (69)
Less-than-4-year	16,190 (2,359)	12,830 (1,038)	7,610 ! (2,474)	7,410 (1,336)	4,870 (140)	6,670 ! (2,156)	11,600 (1,621)	10,330 (1,239)	8,170 ! (3,055)	2,750 (478)	2,790 (508)
Private, for-profit	15,070 (214)	13,300 (173)	6,480 (205)	5,270 (85)	4,600 (49)	4,600 (257)	10,610 (139)	9,440 (107)	7,170 (211)	3,690 (272)	3,760 (291)
2-year and above	15,520 (219)	13,660 (181)	6,530 (218)	5,310 (85)	4,580 (40)	4,580 (267)	10,960 (151)	9,740 (117)	7,350 (222)	3,750 (281)	3,830 (299)
Less-than-2-year	12,170 (633)	10,990 (483)	5,960 (551)	5,050 (268)	4,670 (230)	4,880 (532)	8,370 (313)	7,510 (211)	5,810 (675)	‡ (†)	‡ (†)
Constant 2013–14 dollars[6]											
All institutions											
1992–93	$9,240 (132)	$7,130 (89)	$5,590 (139)	$5,810 (103)	$3,290 (28)	$5,350 (140)	$6,370 (97)	$6,190 (90)	$4,350 (219)	$2,250 (56)	$2,110 (63)
1995–96	10,460 (242)	7,980 (93)	6,080 (248)	6,060 (210)	3,050 (35)	5,640 (247)	7,350 (93)	7,260 (88)	4,240 (353)	2,140 (61)	2,050 (56)
1999–2000	11,750 (138)	8,280 (80)	7,170 (132)	7,080 (112)	3,500 (26)	6,380 (128)	7,530 (82)	7,660 (70)	6,760 (215)	2,330 (51)	2,170 (55)
2003–04	12,330 (117)	8,850 (76)	7,180 (149)	7,160 (127)	4,080 (28)	6,230 (158)	8,840 (90)	7,700 (72)	7,700 (175)	2,440 (45)	2,260 (47)
2007–08	14,410 (109)	9,070 (56)	9,030 (98)	8,050 (79)	4,080 (21)	7,180 (88)	10,560 (86)	7,860 (62)	8,660 (124)	2,520 (28)	2,390 (33)
2011–12	16,010 (110)	11,170 (78)	9,460 (114)	9,530 (95)	4,730 (20)	8,870 (119)	10,420 (77)	9,460 (71)	7,210 (193)	2,320 (49)	2,250 (38)

†Not applicable.

!Interpret data with caution. The coefficient of variation (CV) for this estimate is between 30 and 50 percent.

‡Reporting standards not met. Either there are too few cases for a reliable estimate or the coefficient of variation (CV) is 50 percent or greater.

[1]Details on nonfederal work-study participants are not available.

[2]Includes students who reported that they were awarded aid, but did not specify the source or type of aid.

[3]Includes Department of Veterans Affairs and Department of Defense benefits.

[4]Indicates all grants, scholarships, or tuition waivers received from federal, state, institutional, or private sources, including employers.

[5]Includes Parent Loans for Undergraduate Students (PLUS).

[6]Constant dollars based on the Consumer Price Index, prepared by the Bureau of Labor Statistics, U.S. Department of Labor, adjusted to a school-year basis.

NOTE: Aid averages are for those students who received the specified type of aid. Full-time, full-year students were enrolled full time for 9 or more months from July 1 through June 30. Data exclude Puerto Rico. Some data have been revised from previously published figures.

SOURCE: U.S. Department of Education, National Center for Education Statistics, 1992–93, 1995–96, 1999–2000, 2003–04, 2007–08, and 2011–12 National Postsecondary Student Aid Study (NPSAS:93, NPSAS:96, NPSAS:2000, NPSAS:04, NPSAS:08, and NPSAS:12). (This table was prepared August 2014.)

Table 331.80.   Percentage of part-time or part-year undergraduates receiving financial aid, by type and source of aid and control and level of institution: Selected years, 1992–93 through 2011–12

[Standard errors appear in parentheses]

Control and level of institution	Any aid Total[2]	Any aid Federal[3]	Any aid Nonfederal	Grants Total	Grants Federal	Grants Nonfederal	Loans Total[4]	Loans Federal[4]	Loans Nonfederal	Work study[1] Total	Work study Federal
1	2	3	4	5	6	7	8	9	10	11	12
1992–93, all institutions	37.3 (0.49)	24.7 (0.34)	16.5 (0.45)	32.0 (0.40)	18.3 (0.26)	19.3 (0.43)	13.9 (0.36)	13.5 (0.37)	0.8 (0.10)	2.1 (0.10)	1.2 (0.07)
Public.	31.7 (0.49)	19.9 (0.29)	14.5 (0.48)	27.6 (0.44)	15.3 (0.24)	17.2 (0.50)	9.6 (0.26)	9.2 (0.27)	0.6 (0.11)	1.7 (0.10)	0.9 (0.08)
4-year doctoral	40.5 (0.72)	27.8 (0.74)	19.5 (0.67)	31.2 (0.81)	17.0 (0.69)	20.7 (0.73)	21.8 (0.76)	21.4 (0.75)	1.1 (0.19)	3.6 (0.27)	2.1 (0.22)
Other 4-year	39.5 (1.06)	28.5 (1.13)	19.1 (1.05)	33.8 (0.78)	22.0 (0.92)	20.1 (0.87)	16.8 (0.85)	16.3 (0.81)	1.3! (0.40)	3.1 (0.40)	1.5 (0.26)
2-year	28.6 (0.65)	16.6 (0.44)	12.7 (0.64)	25.9 (0.56)	13.7 (0.32)	16.2 (0.66)	5.8 (0.34)	5.5 (0.33)	0.4 (0.10)	1.1 (0.12)	0.6 (0.10)
Less-than-2-year	21.2 (1.69)	15.1 (1.09)	6.9 (1.48)	19.4 (1.62)	13.8 (1.06)	8.0 (1.85)	0.7! (0.31)	0.7! (0.31)	# (†)	‡ (†)	‡ (†)
Private, nonprofit.	54.6 (1.33)	32.5 (1.43)	34.5 (1.43)	48.2 (1.19)	19.9 (1.23)	38.8 (1.16)	25.0 (1.26)	24.4 (1.25)	1.9 (0.19)	6.0 (0.69)	3.9 (0.51)
4-year doctoral	51.4 (1.88)	28.5 (1.31)	33.0 (1.98)	44.3 (1.97)	12.6 (0.88)	43.0 (2.14)	24.7 (1.95)	23.8 (1.95)	2.7 (0.52)	5.4 (0.98)	3.1 (0.69)
Other 4-year	56.8 (4.06)	34.1 (2.31)	36.9 (1.79)	50.8 (1.73)	21.7 (2.10)	31.3 (1.85)	26.3 (1.96)	25.8 (1.95)	1.6 (0.29)	7.7 (1.18)	5.0 (0.81)
Less-than-4-year	52.7 (2.20)	34.5 (2.94)	28.4 (3.54)	46.0 (3.73)	26.5 (2.29)	11.3 (3.79)	21.2 (2.96)	20.7 (3.00)	1.2! (0.41)	‡ (†)	‡ (†)
Private, for-profit	70.9 (4.57)	64.3 (2.02)	11.9 (1.31)	55.0 (1.31)	48.4 (0.95)	7.1 (1.41)	43.2 (3.57)	42.8 (3.52)	1.5! (0.57)	0.8 (0.20)	0.3 (0.08)
2-year and above	63.7 (1.80)	54.1 (3.69)	14.7 (3.04)	44.9 (2.97)	33.3 (1.26)	11.6 (3.61)	47.7 (4.16)	47.5 (4.10)	‡ (†)	1.2! (0.37)	0.5! (0.24)
Less-than-2-year	75.5 (1.80)	70.9 (1.73)	10.2 (1.75)	61.5 (1.37)	58.1 (1.11)	3.4 (1.45)	40.3 (4.97)	39.7 (4.93)	1.8! (0.63)	0.5! (0.23)	0.2! (0.08)
1999–2000, all institutions	44.2 (0.66)	29.3 (0.34)	27.5 (0.72)	35.3 (0.62)	18.2 (0.25)	25.2 (0.68)	18.6 (0.28)	17.9 (0.27)	2.1 (0.13)	1.9 (0.09)	1.4 (0.08)
Public.	38.9 (0.77)	23.9 (0.36)	25.4 (0.80)	31.4 (0.70)	15.5 (0.26)	23.4 (0.76)	12.6 (0.24)	12.0 (0.22)	1.3 (0.12)	1.5 (0.11)	1.1 (0.09)
4-year doctoral	51.8 (0.73)	37.8 (0.77)	30.6 (0.84)	36.1 (0.70)	18.1 (0.71)	27.3 (0.73)	33.0 (0.81)	31.8 (0.72)	3.4 (0.47)	3.3 (0.30)	2.1 (0.27)
Other 4-year	53.0 (1.18)	39.2 (1.27)	30.4 (1.23)	40.0 (1.20)	22.2 (1.10)	28.2 (1.22)	30.4 (1.06)	29.5 (1.08)	2.6 (0.35)	3.3 (0.52)	2.7 (0.45)
2-year	33.4 (1.07)	18.0 (0.43)	23.4 (1.10)	28.9 (1.01)	13.8 (0.37)	21.8 (1.05)	4.8 (0.14)	4.4 (0.11)	0.6 (0.09)	0.8 (0.10)	0.6 (0.08)
Less-than-2-year	36.9 (2.46)	19.7 (3.00)	22.6 (1.47)	28.4 (2.64)	16.7 (2.68)	14.6 (2.36)	†	†	†	1.6! (0.50)	0.9! (0.37)
Private, nonprofit.	65.5 (0.86)	44.9 (1.29)	49.2 (1.35)	54.3 (1.02)	20.5 (1.30)	46.9 (1.48)	37.6 (1.17)	36.4 (1.13)	6.5 (0.57)	6.4 (0.36)	4.3 (0.29)
4-year doctoral	61.2 (1.65)	42.4 (1.75)	49.1 (1.92)	50.9 (1.68)	16.5 (1.49)	46.7 (1.81)	37.4 (2.00)	36.5 (2.04)	8.2 (1.48)	7.2 (0.87)	5.3 (0.73)
Other 4-year	67.8 (1.19)	45.9 (2.08)	50.3 (2.19)	55.7 (1.56)	20.6 (1.73)	48.1 (2.49)	39.4 (1.93)	37.9 (1.81)	6.2 (0.65)	6.3 (0.51)	4.0 (0.42)
Less-than-4-year	64.0 (4.98)	46.2 (5.18)	39.8 (6.19)	56.8 (4.67)	36.0 (4.62)	37.0 (6.29)	22.9 (2.57)	22.3 (2.48)	2.0! (0.72)	4.1! (1.40)	3.1! (1.09)
Private, for-profit	87.3 (1.08)	83.0 (1.08)	21.9 (1.98)	60.3 (1.59)	54.7 (1.70)	14.6 (1.64)	75.3 (1.61)	74.3 (1.55)	6.5 (0.83)	†	†
2-year and above	86.0 (1.60)	83.0 (1.69)	25.5 (3.00)	56.5 (2.60)	48.0 (2.56)	19.3 (2.38)	77.9 (2.46)	77.1 (2.38)	6.6 (1.29)	†	†
Less-than-2-year	89.1 (1.77)	85.2 (1.66)	17.2 (2.78)	65.3 (2.27)	63.3 (2.20)	8.5 (2.21)	72.0 (3.97)	70.7 (3.96)	6.4 (1.14)	†	†
2007–08, all institutions	56.6 (0.47)	38.9 (0.31)	37.8 (0.47)	43.0 (0.48)	23.9 (0.30)	28.4 (0.46)	30.1 (0.22)	26.2 (0.18)	11.6 (0.28)	3.4 (0.16)	2.6 (0.11)
Public.	49.2 (0.54)	30.3 (0.36)	33.3 (0.46)	38.0 (0.54)	19.1 (0.31)	27.7 (0.46)	19.6 (0.21)	15.9 (0.17)	6.6 (0.17)	2.9 (0.17)	2.2 (0.10)
4-year doctoral	64.2 (0.73)	44.0 (0.74)	45.0 (0.71)	43.1 (0.61)	19.7 (0.57)	34.3 (0.61)	42.6 (0.81)	36.8 (0.76)	14.0 (0.56)	4.5 (0.30)	3.4 (0.26)
Other 4-year	60.0 (1.02)	42.9 (0.95)	36.0 (1.08)	42.2 (0.77)	25.0 (0.75)	26.8 (0.84)	35.1 (0.95)	29.8 (0.83)	10.8 (0.64)	3.2 (0.29)	2.4 (0.27)
2-year	44.3 (0.68)	25.2 (0.42)	30.4 (0.58)	36.2 (0.69)	18.0 (0.38)	26.4 (0.60)	12.1 (0.20)	9.1 (0.13)	4.3 (0.18)	2.5 (0.22)	2.0 (0.13)
Less-than-2-year	46.7 (2.17)	31.4 (1.91)	26.5 (4.22)	38.5 (1.87)	27.6 (1.43)	15.8 (2.14)	14.6 (1.79)	11.3 (1.91)	5.7 (1.24)	# (†)	# (†)
Private, nonprofit.	76.5 (0.92)	53.7 (0.86)	60.6 (1.05)	59.1 (1.08)	22.3 (0.87)	50.4 (1.14)	51.5 (0.83)	46.9 (0.87)	20.2 (0.77)	9.5 (0.75)	7.1 (0.66)
4-year doctoral	75.2 (1.38)	48.9 (1.82)	62.3 (1.70)	58.3 (1.67)	18.8 (1.02)	51.6 (1.90)	49.9 (1.60)	43.5 (1.92)	21.4 (1.24)	10.9 (1.45)	8.1 (1.22)
Other 4-year	77.8 (1.32)	56.4 (1.50)	60.8 (1.39)	60.5 (1.41)	23.6 (1.28)	51.7 (1.46)	52.7 (1.47)	49.3 (1.50)	19.2 (1.19)	9.1 (0.85)	6.8 (0.77)
Less-than-4-year	72.4 (4.93)	63.0 (3.97)	44.5 (5.84)	49.8 (4.95)	37.7 (6.05)	25.4 (4.39)	51.7 (4.57)	48.3 (5.29)	20.9 (3.05)	2.0! (0.74)	1.5! (0.51)
Private, for-profit	93.4 (0.56)	87.8 (0.72)	51.9 (1.75)	66.0 (1.01)	58.8 (1.16)	17.6 (1.80)	87.9 (0.75)	82.6 (0.84)	40.1 (1.69)	2.0 (0.35)	1.7 (0.51)
2-year and above	94.8 (0.70)	89.9 (0.88)	53.9 (2.16)	66.5 (1.25)	58.2 (1.44)	18.9 (2.23)	90.3 (0.82)	86.0 (0.97)	41.7 (2.06)	2.5 (0.44)	2.1 (0.35)
Less-than-2-year	88.2 (0.84)	80.0 (1.21)	44.2 (2.01)	64.3 (1.33)	60.8 (1.21)	13.1 (2.20)	79.1 (1.69)	69.9 (1.87)	34.2 (1.65)	†	†
2011–12, all institutions	62.1 (1.05)	51.1 (1.10)	30.1 (0.60)	50.8 (0.87)	37.8 (0.85)	26.1 (0.56)	32.7 (0.48)	30.9 (0.45)	4.8 (0.17)	2.2 (0.12)	2.0 (0.12)
Public.	56.0 (1.18)	44.5 (1.22)	28.9 (0.67)	46.5 (0.93)	33.6 (0.90)	26.3 (0.64)	23.6 (0.45)	22.2 (0.43)	2.9 (0.13)	1.7 (0.11)	1.6 (0.11)
4-year doctoral	66.1 (1.04)	53.4 (0.81)	36.8 (1.02)	47.7 (1.05)	30.9 (0.65)	31.2 (1.02)	47.3 (0.60)	44.3 (0.61)	7.0 (0.41)	2.7 (0.26)	2.5 (0.26)
Other 4-year	59.5 (1.46)	49.7 (1.66)	27.0 (1.13)	46.2 (1.23)	35.7 (1.21)	23.1 (0.98)	30.8 (1.17)	28.5 (1.16)	4.5 (0.53)	2.5 (0.36)	2.4 (0.33)
2-year	52.7 (1.36)	41.2 (1.39)	27.4 (0.86)	46.1 (1.08)	33.7 (1.09)	25.8 (0.83)	16.4 (0.47)	15.4 (0.42)	1.6 (0.13)	1.3 (0.14)	1.3 (0.14)
Less-than-2-year	70.2 (4.21)	60.3 (4.47)	28.4 (5.72)	63.7 (4.42)	54.0 (4.26)	19.4 (4.26)	22.9 (3.99)	20.8 (4.28)	10.5 (1.01)	# (†)	# (†)
Private, nonprofit.	77.4 (1.47)	57.9 (1.87)	60.6 (2.65)	57.4 (1.91)	34.9 (1.51)	43.2 (2.13)	53.6 (1.60)	49.8 (1.59)	10.2 (1.62)	8.9 (0.86)	7.1 (0.76)
4-year doctoral	76.0 (1.87)	57.9 (2.12)	51.5 (3.34)	57.4 (2.68)	29.3 (1.78)	43.2 (2.63)	52.6 (2.12)	48.5 (1.99)	10.2 (1.52)	9.7 (1.26)	6.9 (0.96)
Other 4-year	79.2 (2.42)	64.0 (2.54)	56.6 (3.34)	63.9 (2.81)	38.7 (2.60)	50.8 (2.94)	55.6 (2.61)	52.0 (2.45)	11.0 (2.85)	8.9 (1.15)	7.8 (1.15)
Less-than-4-year	74.3 (4.47)	64.3 (3.22)	44.5 (6.12)	67.7 (4.68)	57.9 (2.94)	38.7 (2.94)	45.0 (4.55)	40.8 (3.99)	8.5 (0.64)	†	†
Private, for-profit	85.4 (1.02)	79.7 (0.83)	24.7 (1.17)	67.2 (1.33)	60.8 (1.08)	14.5 (1.26)	68.2 (0.69)	65.7 (0.51)	11.5 (0.51)	1.0 (0.13)	0.9 (0.14)
2-year and above	85.3 (1.20)	78.8 (0.97)	25.5 (1.30)	65.9 (1.56)	58.6 (1.24)	15.6 (1.45)	67.3 (0.78)	64.5 (0.56)	11.3 (0.68)	1.2 (0.15)	1.1 (0.16)
Less-than-2-year	85.9 (1.39)	84.6 (1.40)	20.7 (3.40)	74.2 (1.66)	72.3 (1.58)	8.6 (2.47)	73.3 (1.16)	71.6 (1.35)	12.5 (1.71)	0.2! (0.08)	0.2! (0.07)

†Not applicable.
#Rounds to zero.
!Interpret data with caution. The coefficient of variation (CV) for this estimate is between 30 and 50 percent.
‡Reporting standards not met. Either there are too few cases for a reliable estimate or the coefficient of variation (CV) is 50 percent or greater.
[1]Details on nonfederal work-study participants are not available.
[2]Includes students who reported they were awarded aid, but did not specify the source of aid.
[3]Includes Department of Veterans Affairs and Department of Defense benefits.
[4]Includes Parent Loans for Undergraduate Students (PLUS).
NOTE: Excludes students whose attendance status was not reported. Detail may not sum to totals because of rounding and because some students receive multiple types of aid and aid from different sources. Data exclude Puerto Rico. Some data have been revised from previously published figures.
SOURCE: U.S. Department of Education, National Center for Education Statistics, 1992–93, 1999–2000, 2007–08, and 2011–12 National Postsecondary Student Aid Study (NPSAS:93, NPSAS:2000, NPSAS:08, and NPSAS:12). (This table was prepared August 2014.)

Table 331.90. Percentage of full-time and part-time undergraduates receiving federal aid, by aid program and control and level of institution: 2007–08 and 2011–12

[Standard errors appear in parentheses]

Control and level of institution	Number of undergraduates[1] (in thousands)		Percent receiving federal aid														
					Selected Title IV programs[2]												
			Any federal aid		Any Title IV aid		Pell		SEOG[3]		CWS[4]		Perkins[5]		Stafford[6]		PLUS[7]
1	2		3		4		5		6		7		8		9		10
2007–08																	
Full-time, full-year students																	
All institutions	7,527	(—)	63.9	(0.31)	62.9	(0.31)	32.7	(0.29)	8.9	(0.20)	10.6	(0.23)	6.0	(0.17)	50.2	(0.32)	7.5	(0.20)
Public	5,159	(—)	58.7	(0.36)	57.6	(0.36)	32.0	(0.29)	6.8	(0.18)	7.1	(0.22)	4.1	(0.15)	41.9	(0.33)	6.1	(0.21)
4-year doctoral	2,522	(—)	59.6	(0.48)	58.7	(0.48)	27.3	(0.37)	6.5	(0.23)	7.6	(0.32)	6.1	(0.27)	49.7	(0.49)	9.3	(0.39)
Other 4-year	1,031	(—)	67.6	(0.68)	66.6	(0.70)	34.9	(0.66)	7.9	(0.37)	8.7	(0.45)	5.0	(0.42)	53.8	(0.72)	6.4	(0.40)
2-year	1,584	(—)	51.4	(0.73)	49.9	(0.75)	37.2	(0.65)	6.6	(0.36)	5.5	(0.29)	0.4	(0.08)	22.1	(0.58)	1.1	(0.12)
Less-than-2-year	22	(—)	58.6	(3.84)	57.1	(4.15)	49.7	(4.14)	‡	(†)	#	(†)	#	(†)	23.6	(4.33)	‡	(†)
Private, nonprofit	1,672	(—)	71.2	(0.62)	70.4	(0.62)	26.6	(0.65)	13.1	(0.51)	25.0	(0.86)	13.8	(0.63)	62.9	(0.65)	12.2	(0.59)
4-year doctoral	844	(—)	67.1	(1.12)	66.1	(1.14)	22.2	(0.79)	11.7	(0.60)	24.5	(1.04)	16.3	(1.02)	58.4	(1.28)	12.3	(0.69)
Other 4-year	814	(—)	75.1	(1.12)	74.7	(1.12)	30.8	(1.19)	14.5	(0.80)	26.0	(1.45)	11.5	(0.80)	67.7	(1.23)	12.2	(0.93)
Less-than-4-year	14	(—)	84.4	(3.65)	82.8	(4.17)	43.3	(6.07)	12.6 !	(5.08)	4.7 !	(1.63)	‡	(†)	56.2	(7.28)	‡	(†)
Private, for-profit	695	(—)	84.6	(1.24)	83.9	(1.36)	52.9	(1.48)	13.6	(1.27)	1.6	(0.28)	1.0	(0.19)	81.0	(1.30)	5.8	(0.63)
2-year and above	599	(—)	84.2	(1.41)	83.4	(1.55)	50.5	(1.69)	12.2	(1.45)	1.8	(0.33)	1.1	(0.22)	81.2	(1.46)	4.9	(0.69)
Less-than-2-year	96	(—)	87.4	(1.74)	87.1	(1.84)	67.5	(2.15)	22.3	(2.49)	‡	(†)	‡	(†)	79.8	(2.50)	11.3	(1.16)
Part-time or part-year students																	
All institutions	12,984	(—)	38.9	(0.31)	37.3	(0.30)	23.8	(0.30)	4.3	(0.23)	2.6	(0.11)	0.9	(0.05)	26.0	(0.18)	1.6	(0.10)
Public	10,386	(—)	30.3	(0.36)	28.6	(0.34)	19.0	(0.31)	2.1	(0.11)	2.2	(0.10)	0.6	(0.04)	15.7	(0.16)	0.9	(0.06)
Private, nonprofit	1,109	(—)	53.7	(0.86)	51.4	(0.86)	22.1	(0.85)	5.9	(0.51)	7.1	(0.66)	3.6	(0.49)	46.3	(0.86)	3.6	(0.44)
Private, for-profit	1,489	(—)	87.8	(0.72)	87.3	(0.72)	58.6	(1.15)	18.6	(1.68)	1.7	(0.35)	0.9	(0.13)	82.4	(0.84)	5.3	(0.59)
2011–12																	
Full-time, full-year students																	
All institutions	8,864	(—)	72.8	(0.51)	71.4	(0.54)	47.1	(0.50)	9.0	(0.24)	10.5	(0.24)	4.2	(0.18)	55.1	(0.54)	9.1	(0.23)
Public	5,997	(—)	68.4	(0.61)	67.1	(0.64)	45.8	(0.59)	6.6	(0.26)	6.2	(0.23)	2.7	(0.15)	47.1	(0.57)	7.1	(0.28)
4-year doctoral	2,893	(—)	70.9	(0.47)	70.1	(0.48)	40.8	(0.39)	7.1	(0.39)	7.4	(0.37)	4.3	(0.30)	60.0	(0.43)	11.4	(0.45)
Other 4-year	969	(—)	72.7	(1.34)	71.4	(1.43)	48.1	(1.07)	6.5	(0.52)	8.6	(0.61)	2.8	(0.35)	54.0	(1.53)	8.1	(0.67)
2-year	2,104	(—)	63.0	(1.24)	61.0	(1.29)	51.4	(1.30)	5.9	(0.40)	3.4	(0.28)	0.3	(0.06)	26.5	(0.99)	1.0	(0.11)
Less-than-2-year	31	(—)	67.8	(4.72)	66.4	(5.20)	62.4	(5.04)	‡	(†)	‡	(†)	#	(†)	19.7	(4.83)	‡	(†)
Private, nonprofit	1,875	(—)	76.1	(0.75)	74.9	(0.75)	37.2	(0.64)	12.2	(0.60)	29.2	(0.81)	10.6	(0.61)	66.0	(0.90)	16.5	(0.67)
4-year doctoral	990	(—)	74.3	(0.94)	73.4	(0.96)	34.5	(0.77)	11.0	(0.89)	30.0	(1.26)	13.3	(0.97)	64.4	(1.08)	16.7	(1.10)
Other 4-year	849	(—)	78.0	(1.20)	76.7	(1.17)	39.8	(1.11)	13.6	(0.74)	29.1	(1.14)	8.0	(0.69)	68.2	(1.48)	16.2	(0.76)
Less-than-4-year	36	(—)	78.1	(5.04)	74.6	(5.35)	48.5	(6.54)	13.1 !	(5.38)	‡	(†)	‡	(†)	59.0	(7.42)	13.9	(3.36)
Private, for-profit	992	(—)	93.1	(0.51)	90.4	(0.52)	73.8	(0.81)	17.8	(0.87)	1.8	(0.20)	1.4	(0.23)	83.2	(0.90)	7.1	(0.44)
2-year and above	859	(—)	92.8	(0.59)	89.7	(0.59)	72.1	(0.91)	15.7	(0.81)	2.1	(0.23)	1.6	(0.27)	83.3	(0.91)	7.3	(0.48)
Less-than-2-year	133	(—)	95.2	(0.79)	95.1	(0.80)	85.0	(1.46)	31.4	(4.40)	‡	(†)	‡	(†)	82.9	(3.51)	5.9	(0.77)
Part-time or part-year students																	
All institutions	14,192	(—)	51.1	(1.10)	48.4	(1.09)	37.6	(0.85)	4.4	(0.19)	2.0	(0.12)	0.9	(0.08)	30.7	(0.44)	1.6	(0.10)
Public	10,929	(—)	44.5	(1.22)	42.4	(1.13)	33.4	(0.89)	2.6	(0.14)	1.6	(0.11)	0.5	(0.05)	22.1	(0.43)	1.0	(0.08)
4-year doctoral	1,875	(—)	53.4	(0.81)	51.2	(0.75)	30.6	(0.65)	2.9	(0.32)	2.5	(0.26)	2.1	(0.26)	44.0	(0.63)	4.1	(0.32)
Other 4-year	1,477	(—)	49.7	(1.66)	47.2	(1.51)	35.4	(1.18)	2.6	(0.36)	2.4	(0.33)	0.9	(0.26)	28.3	(1.16)	1.7	(0.40)
2-year	7,521	(—)	41.2	(1.39)	39.1	(1.31)	33.6	(1.08)	2.5	(0.17)	1.3	(0.14)	0.1	(0.02)	15.4	(0.41)	0.1	(0.02)
Less-than-2-year	56	(—)	60.3	(4.47)	59.6	(4.47)	53.9	(4.11)	‡	(†)	#	(†)	#	(†)	20.7	(4.33)	‡	(†)
Private, nonprofit	1,135	(—)	61.0	(1.61)	56.5	(1.99)	34.8	(1.51)	6.8	(0.66)	7.1	(0.76)	1.9	(0.30)	49.5	(1.57)	4.3	(0.51)
4-year doctoral	557	(—)	57.9	(2.12)	53.3	(2.19)	29.1	(1.77)	4.2	(0.73)	6.9	(0.96)	2.4	(0.47)	48.3	(2.08)	3.9	(0.65)
Other 4-year	527	(—)	64.0	(2.54)	59.1	(2.91)	38.6	(2.59)	8.2	(1.21)	7.8	(1.15)	1.6	(0.41)	51.6	(2.42)	4.9	(0.96)
Less-than-4-year	51	(—)	64.3	(3.22)	64.2	(3.18)	57.9	(2.94)	21.0	(5.35)	‡	(†)	‡	(†)	40.6	(3.92)	2.0 !	(0.81)
Private, for-profit	2,128	(—)	79.7	(0.83)	75.2	(1.16)	60.5	(1.09)	12.8	(0.83)	0.9	(0.14)	2.0	(0.47)	65.3	(0.47)	3.4	(0.32)
2-year and above	1,790	(—)	78.8	(0.97)	73.6	(1.35)	58.4	(1.25)	11.8	(0.84)	1.1	(0.16)	2.4	(0.56)	64.1	(0.51)	3.2	(0.33)
Less-than-2-year	337	(—)	84.6	(1.40)	83.6	(1.33)	71.9	(1.60)	18.1	(2.38)	0.2 !	(0.07)	‡	(†)	71.5	(1.36)	4.2	(0.84)

—Not available.
†Not applicable.
#Rounds to zero.
!Interpret data with caution. The coefficient of variation (CV) for this estimate is between 30 and 50 percent.
‡Reporting standards not met. The coefficient of variation (CV) for this estimate is 50 percent or greater.
[1]Numbers of undergraduates may not equal figures reported in other tables, since these data are based on a sample survey of students who enrolled at any point during the year.
[2]Title IV of the Higher Education Act.
[3]Supplemental Educational Opportunity Grants.

[4]College Work Study. Prior to October 17, 1986, private for-profit institutions were prohibited by law from spending CWS funds for on-campus work. Includes persons who participated in the program but had no earnings.
[5]Formerly National Direct Student Loans (NDSL).
[6]Formerly Guaranteed Student Loans (GSL).
[7]Parent Loans for Undergraduate Students.
NOTE: Excludes students whose attendance status was not reported. Detail may not sum to totals because of rounding and because some students receive multiple types of aid and aid from different sources. Data exclude Puerto Rico. Some data have been revised from previously published figures.
SOURCE: U.S. Department of Education, National Center for Education Statistics, 2007–08 and 2011–12 National Postsecondary Student Aid Study (NPSAS:08 and NPSAS:12). (This table was prepared July 2014.)

Table 331.95. Percentage of undergraduate students ages 18 to 24 in their 4th (senior) year or above who ever received federal loans, nonfederal loans, or Parent Loans for Undergraduates (PLUS), and average cumulative amount borrowed, by selected student characteristics and control and level of institution: 1989–90, 1999–2000, and 2011–12

[Standard errors appear in parentheses]

Selected student characteristic or control and level of institution	1989–90					1999–2000			2011–12		
	Federal loans to students[2]			Parent PLUS loans[4]	Total[1]	Federal loans to students[2]	Parent PLUS loans[4]	Total[1]	Federal loans to students[2]	Nonfederal loans	Parent PLUS loans[4]
	Total[1]	Stafford loans[3]	Perkins loans								
1	2	3	4	5	6	7	8	9	10	11	12
Percent of students with loans											
Total	50.5 (0.81)	38.0 (0.77)	13.0 (0.65)	4.1 (0.22)	60.2 (0.66)	58.1 (0.69)	12.4 (0.51)	67.7 (0.74)	64.3 (0.71)	29.0 (0.73)	19.9 (0.70)
Sex											
Male	51.8 (1.24)	37.9 (1.18)	12.6 (0.76)	3.8 (0.29)	58.2 (0.98)	55.8 (0.99)	12.4 (0.56)	67.2 (1.14)	63.4 (1.10)	29.2 (1.09)	19.9 (1.07)
Female	49.3 (0.90)	37.9 (0.88)	13.1 (0.72)	4.4 (0.30)	61.8 (0.87)	59.9 (0.88)	12.3 (0.70)	68.0 (1.01)	65.1 (1.05)	28.9 (0.96)	19.9 (0.91)
Race/ethnicity											
White	49.5 (0.97)	36.8 (0.92)	11.9 (0.64)	4.2 (0.27)	58.9 (0.79)	56.9 (0.82)	12.4 (0.57)	65.5 (0.87)	62.1 (0.81)	29.6 (0.92)	19.9 (0.88)
Black	68.9 (2.24)	57.1 (2.16)	23.2 (2.42)	7.0 (1.06)	76.8 (2.53)	74.5 (2.49)	15.5 (1.47)	90.3 (1.34)	88.1 (1.74)	31.3 (3.03)	30.4 (2.25)
Hispanic	57.3 (3.71)	42.3 (4.17)	15.9 (1.65)	4.3 (0.99)	67.4 (2.28)	64.3 (1.88)	14.0 (1.79)	72.3 (1.93)	70.2 (1.98)	28.4 (2.19)	19.3 (2.06)
Asian[5]	40.5 (1.78)	27.5 (2.30)	13.4 (2.68)	‡ (†)	50.6 (2.16)	49.5 (2.22)	7.5 (1.29)	50.8 (2.88)	45.2 (2.72)	21.4 (2.76)	9.9 (1.58)
Pacific Islander	‡ (†)	— (†)	‡ (†)	‡	55.3 (9.93)	55.3 (9.93)	14.2 ! (5.01)	‡ (†)	‡ (†)	‡ (†)	‡ (†)
American Indian/Alaska Native	‡ (†)	— (†)	— (†)	—	46.9 (9.93)	38.7 (9.01)	‡ (†)	‡ (†)	‡ (†)	‡ (†)	‡ (†)
Two or more races	— (†)	— (†)	— (†)	—	50.1 (4.67)	48.5 (4.93)	9.4 ! (2.91)	77.9 (3.68)	76.4 (3.84)	36.1 (4.68)	20.2 (4.44)
Dependency status											
Dependent	47.5 (0.96)	35.6 (0.93)	11.7 (0.56)	4.4 (0.25)	59.6 (0.74)	57.4 (0.75)	13.7 (0.60)	66.5 (0.79)	63.4 (0.78)	29.2 (0.79)	21.0 (0.80)
Independent	59.6 (1.51)	45.0 (1.30)	16.7 (1.28)	3.4 (0.36)	62.4 (1.33)	60.7 (1.30)	7.4 (0.59)	73.1 (1.82)	69.0 (1.85)	28.3 (1.99)	14.7 (1.50)
Public institutions											
4-year doctoral	49.5 (1.41)	36.4 (1.32)	11.8 (1.07)	3.5 (0.30)	57.4 (1.13)	55.2 (1.15)	11.2 (0.62)	64.6 (0.89)	61.9 (0.88)	25.0 (0.87)	16.5 (0.83)
Other 4-year	49.6 (2.01)	34.5 (1.92)	11.5 (0.76)	3.5 (0.52)	58.6 (1.81)	57.1 (1.81)	9.0 (1.33)	64.9 (2.05)	60.1 (1.96)	27.1 (1.94)	16.5 (1.55)
2-year	‡ (†)	‡ (†)	‡ (†)	‡	46.2 (4.35)	42.6 (4.16)	5.4 (1.41)	‡	‡	‡	‡
Private nonprofit institutions											
4-year doctoral	50.5 (1.76)	42.7 (1.98)	20.7 (1.35)	5.2 (0.48)	63.1 (1.71)	61.2 (1.69)	17.5 (1.26)	74.1 (2.82)	69.2 (2.69)	36.9 (2.87)	29.0 (3.14)
Other 4-year	61.8 (1.81)	51.7 (1.59)	14.9 (1.72)	7.4 (0.76)	72.3 (1.86)	70.2 (1.94)	17.7 (1.80)	74.2 (2.69)	71.8 (2.73)	38.2 (2.28)	25.9 (2.16)
Private for-profit institutions											
2-year and above	‡ (†)	‡ (†)	‡ (†)	‡ (†)	86.2 (3.62)	84.9 (3.76)	28.4 (5.58)	85.4 (3.16)	84.3 (3.43)	38.0 (3.73)	38.6 (4.07)
Average cumulative loan amount for students with loans (constant 2013–14 dollars)[6]											
Total	$15,200 ($320)	$11,800 ($210)	$4,500 ($150)	$9,000 ($260)	$22,100 ($200)	$19,400 ($150)	$19,300 ($760)	$26,300 ($410)	$20,900 ($230)	$14,900 ($740)	$28,200 ($1,250)
Sex											
Male	15,700 (350)	12,100 (260)	4,300 (220)	9,600 (400)	22,000 (300)	19,500 (180)	20,000 (990)	26,600 (660)	20,600 (320)	16,400 (1,260)	29,500 (2,120)
Female	14,700 (410)	11,600 (230)	4,600 (170)	8,600 (430)	22,200 (300)	19,300 (220)	18,700 (1,010)	26,000 (490)	21,100 (300)	13,600 (800)	27,000 (1,450)
Race/ethnicity											
White	15,900 (330)	12,100 (260)	4,300 (130)	9,400 (250)	22,000 (270)	19,100 (170)	20,000 (910)	26,200 (490)	20,300 (270)	15,400 (780)	28,500 (1,610)
Black	12,000 (720)	12,100 (490)	5,500 (620)	‡ (†)	25,400 (770)	22,900 (670)	15,100 (1,380)	30,900 (1,170)	26,400 (670)	14,900 (2,210)	26,200 (3,310)
Hispanic	10,300 (990)	10,100 (580)	4,000 (290)	‡ (†)	21,300 (880)	18,600 (590)	18,000 (1,790)	25,100 (1,100)	20,200 (700)	14,000 (2,240)	24,700 (3,460)
Asian[5]	13,300 (850)	9,500 (550)	4,400 (720)	‡ (†)	19,500 (570)	18,000 (540)	15,500 (3,400)	20,600 (1,190)	18,200 (760)	10,300 (1,970)	29,100 (3,640)
Pacific Islander	‡ (†)	‡ (†)	‡ (†)	‡ (†)	18,700 (2,690)	16,400 (1,800)	‡ (†)	‡ (†)	‡ (†)	‡ (†)	‡ (†)
American Indian/Alaska Native	‡ (†)	‡ (†)	‡ (†)	— (†)	22,700 (3,800)	22,100 (2,960)	‡ (†)	‡ (†)	‡ (†)	15,800 ! (1,200)	‡ (†)
Two or more races	— (†)	— (†)	— (†)	— (†)	23,900 (1,650)	21,100 (1,390)	‡ (†)	26,300 (2,960)	19,400 (1,200)	15,800 ! (5,260)	‡ (†)
Dependency status											
Dependent	15,500 (330)	11,600 (200)	4,500 (170)	9,200 (300)	21,900 (220)	18,900 (150)	20,000 (830)	26,000 (450)	20,300 (240)	15,100 (790)	28,100 (1,110)
Independent	14,400 (550)	12,400 (350)	4,300 (180)	8,200 (510)	22,800 (530)	20,800 (470)	14,800 (1,230)	27,400 (930)	23,300 (720)	13,900 (1,710)	28,500 (6,280)
Public institutions											
4-year doctoral	13,600 (520)	11,100 (290)	4,000 (240)	9,200 (420)	21,000 (300)	19,000 (240)	16,400 (790)	24,000 (440)	20,100 (310)	12,200 (680)	23,000 (1,100)
Other 4-year	10,200 (400)	9,400 (610)	3,600 (240)	7,700 (580)	19,800 (540)	17,900 (460)	12,700 (710)	21,600 (840)	18,500 (610)	10,600 (1,210)	20,100 (1,780)
2-year	‡ (†)	‡ (†)	‡ (†)	‡ (†)	12,400 (1,280)	11,900 (1,160)	‡ (†)	‡ (†)	‡ (†)	‡ (†)	‡ (†)

See notes at end of table.

Table 331.95. Percentage of undergraduate students ages 18 to 24 in their 4th (senior) year or above who ever received federal loans, nonfederal loans, or Parent Loans for Undergraduates (PLUS), and average cumulative amount borrowed, by selected student characteristics and control and level of institution: 1989–90, 1999–2000, and 2011–12—Continued

[Standard errors appear in parentheses]

Selected student characteristic or control and level of institution	1989–90				1999–2000			2011–12			
	Federal loans to students[2]			Parent PLUS loans[4]	Total[1]	Federal loans to students[2]	Parent PLUS loans[4]	Total[1]	Federal loans to students[2]	Nonfederal loans	Parent PLUS loans[4]
	Total[1]	Stafford loans[3]	Perkins loans								
1	2	3	4	5	6	7	8	9	10	11	12
Private nonprofit institutions											
4-year doctoral	23,600 (410)	14,300 (320)	5,700 (300)	9,800 (540)	27,600 (670)	22,400 (480)	27,900 (1,710)	31,300 (1,880)	23,000 (710)	19,800 (3,170)	42,300 (4,940)
Other 4-year	19,800 (980)	13,900 (450)	5,800 (480)	9,200 (690)	25,900 (690)	21,500 (380)	24,000 (2,120)	32,500 (1,320)	22,700 (590)	20,400 (2,360)	30,600 (2,150)
Private for-profit institutions											
2-year and above	‡ (†)	‡ (†)	‡ (†)	‡	24,000 (1,780)	19,900 (1,940)	18,900 (4,820)	40,200 (2,050)	32,200 (1,270)	18,900 (3,490)	34,100 (4,140)

—Not available.
†Not applicable.
!Interpret data with caution. The coefficient of variation (CV) for this estimate is between 30 and 50 percent.
‡Reporting standards not met. Either there are too few cases for a reliable estimate or the coefficient of variation (CV) is 50 percent or greater.
[1]For 1989–90 data, total borrowed includes loans from family and friends. For 1999–2000 and 2011–12 data, total borrowed excludes loans from family and friends.
[2]Includes Stafford loans and Perkins loans only.
[3]Cumulative Stafford loan amounts shown in the table include federal subsidized and unsubsidized Stafford loans as well as any Supplemental Loans for Students (SLS) received in prior years. The SLS program was an unsubsidized student loan program limited to independent students and some dependent students with special circumstances. Beginning in 1993–94, the SLS program was replaced by unsubsidized Stafford loans, which are available to both independent and dependent students regardless of need. Subsidized Stafford loans are only available to students with demonstrated financial need. Stafford Loans were avail-

able through both the William D. Ford Federal Direct Loan Program and the Federal Family Education Loan Program (FFELP) until FFELP was discontinued in 2010. Since then, Stafford Loans have been referred to as Direct Loans.
[4]Parent PLUS loans are taken out by parents of dependent students and are used towards the students' undergraduate education. Parent PLUS Loans were available through both the William D. Ford Federal Direct Loan Program and the Federal Family Education Loan Program (FFELP) until FFELP was discontinued in 2010. Since then, Parent PLUS Loans have been referred to as Direct PLUS Loans.
[5]Includes Pacific Islanders in 1989–90.
[6]Average loan amounts were calculated only for students who took out a loan (or whose parents took out a PLUS loan on their behalf). Constant dollars based on the Consumer Price Index, prepared by the Bureau of Labor Statistics, U.S. Department of Labor, adjusted to a school-year basis.
NOTE: Data exclude Puerto Rico. Some data have been revised from previously published figures.
SOURCE: U.S. Department of Education, National Center for Education Statistics, 1989–90, 1999–2000, and 2011–12 National Postsecondary Student Aid Study (NPSAS:90, NPSAS:2000, and NPSAS:12). (This table was prepared August 2014.)

Table 332.10. Amount borrowed, aid status, and sources of aid for full-time, full-year postbaccalaureate students, by level of study and control and level of institution: Selected years, 1992–93 through 2011–12

[Standard errors appear in parentheses]

Level of study, control and level of institution	Cumulative borrowing for undergraduate and graduate education[1]			Aid status (percent of students)					
	Percent who borrowed	Average amount for those who borrowed		Nonaided	Source of aid				
		Current dollars	Constant 2013–14 dollars[4]		Any aid[2]	Federal[3]	State	Institutional	Employer
1	2	3	4	5	6	7	8	9	10
1992–93, all institutions	— (†)	— (†)	— (†)	30.7 (1.43)	69.3 (1.43)	44.3 (1.42)	6.9 (0.64)	40.6 (2.02)	5.3 (0.59)
Master's degree	— (†)	— (†)	— (†)	35.5 (2.54)	64.5 (2.54)	33.8 (1.91)	5.8 (0.79)	42.4 (2.97)	8.3 (1.01)
Public	— (†)	— (†)	— (†)	32.7 (2.40)	67.3 (2.40)	33.9 (2.04)	7.8 (1.10)	44.1 (2.68)	7.6 (1.24)
4-year doctoral	— (†)	— (†)	— (†)	32.4 (2.59)	67.6 (2.59)	32.4 (2.23)	6.7 (0.96)	46.4 (3.19)	7.7 (1.28)
Other 4-year	— (†)	— (†)	— (†)	34.6 (4.38)	65.4 (4.38)	42.5 (5.30)	14.4 (4.13)	30.5 (3.67)	6.8 (2.66)
Private	— (†)	— (†)	— (†)	39.2 (4.74)	60.8 (4.74)	33.7 (3.62)	3.2 (0.89)	40.2 (6.34)	9.4 (1.88)
4-year doctoral	— (†)	— (†)	— (†)	37.4 (4.70)	62.6 (4.70)	34.2 (4.09)	2.9 (1.00)	42.9 (6.75)	8.9 (1.88)
Other 4-year	— (†)	— (†)	— (†)	50.5 (10.60)	49.5 (10.60)	30.5 (7.06)	5.1 (2.98)	22.8 (9.39)	12.1 (6.81)
Doctor's degree	— (†)	— (†)	— (†)	30.1 (2.32)	69.9 (2.32)	28.3 (2.14)	4.4 (0.71)	51.6 (2.70)	3.0 (0.79)
Public	— (†)	— (†)	— (†)	29.9 (2.99)	70.1 (2.99)	22.3 (2.26)	6.5 (1.14)	55.5 (3.01)	3.9 (1.00)
Private	— (†)	— (†)	— (†)	30.4 (3.27)	69.6 (3.27)	37.8 (3.54)	1.1 (0.73)	45.5 (3.52)	1.7 (1.19)
First-professional	— (†)	— (†)	— (†)	22.6 (0.96)	77.4 (0.96)	68.2 (1.54)	9.9 (1.34)	37.0 (1.81)	2.3 (0.52)
Public	— (†)	— (†)	— (†)	20.4 (1.02)	79.6 (1.02)	72.5 (1.29)	13.4 (1.75)	37.7 (1.67)	2.3 (0.59)
Private	— (†)	— (†)	— (†)	24.6 (1.66)	75.4 (1.66)	64.2 (2.42)	6.8 (1.19)	36.4 (3.29)	2.3 (0.70)
Other graduate	— (†)	— (†)	— (†)	38.3 (6.82)	61.7 (6.82)	42.1 (4.26)	6.6 (1.81)	23.0 (4.05)	6.0 (2.98)
1999–2000, all institutions	69.4 (0.74)	$41,924 (863)	$58,190 (1,198)	18.3 (0.66)	81.7 (0.66)	52.5 (0.76)	6.0 (0.60)	49.7 (1.03)	6.0 (0.57)
Master's degree	68.3 (1.12)	31,933 (1,097)	44,320 (1,523)	20.6 (1.15)	79.4 (1.15)	50.6 (1.23)	5.1 (0.66)	45.4 (1.61)	9.2 (1.03)
Public	63.2 (1.60)	28,072 (1,079)	38,960 (1,497)	22.3 (1.52)	77.7 (1.52)	44.8 (1.82)	7.3 (1.14)	49.8 (2.16)	7.0 (1.04)
4-year doctoral	62.5 (1.56)	27,512 (1,234)	38,180 (1,712)	20.2 (1.46)	79.8 (1.46)	43.3 (1.71)	7.0 (1.31)	54.3 (2.02)	7.3 (1.20)
Other 4-year	70.9 (6.04)	31,921 (2,822)	44,300 (3,917)	29.9 (5.08)	70.1 (5.08)	54.7 (6.88)	10.2 ! (3.32)	27.4 (6.85)	5.1 ! (1.79)
Private	74.4 (1.55)	35,893 (1,855)	49,820 (2,575)	18.6 (1.59)	81.4 (1.59)	57.8 (1.88)	2.5 (0.63)	40.2 (2.63)	11.8 (1.89)
4-year doctoral	73.3 (1.76)	38,421 (2,521)	53,330 (3,499)	17.1 (1.93)	82.9 (1.93)	58.3 (2.36)	2.9 ! (0.90)	50.5 (3.22)	8.3 (1.31)
Other[5]	76.9 (3.74)	30,769 (1,850)	42,710 (2,568)	21.8 (2.75)	78.2 (2.75)	56.6 (4.41)	‡ (†)	18.1 (3.91)	19.1 (5.24)
Doctor's degree	56.8 (1.95)	38,991 (3,421)	54,120 (4,748)	12.0 (1.38)	88.0 (1.38)	29.6 (2.80)	2.6 (0.54)	77.4 (1.65)	5.4 (0.64)
Public	54.5 (1.92)	33,595 (1,564)	46,630 (2,171)	11.4 (1.38)	88.6 (1.38)	26.1 (1.86)	3.2 (0.75)	80.0 (1.59)	7.3 (0.88)
Private	60.5 (3.62)	46,679 (7,288)	64,790 (10,116)	13.0 (2.80)	87.0 (2.80)	35.2 (6.26)	‡ (†)	73.2 (3.22)	2.3 (0.55)
First-professional	85.1 (1.14)	60,857 (1,713)	84,470 (2,378)	13.4 (1.18)	86.6 (1.18)	77.1 (1.29)	9.9 (1.65)	41.4 (2.40)	1.7 ! (0.53)
Public	86.8 (1.70)	52,792 (1,954)	73,270 (2,712)	13.8 (1.82)	86.2 (1.82)	78.3 (2.13)	12.7 (2.57)	38.9 (2.84)	1.8 ! (0.87)
Private	83.6 (1.63)	67,821 (3,213)	94,130 (4,460)	13.1 (1.49)	86.9 (1.49)	76.1 (1.84)	7.5 (2.11)	43.4 (3.65)	1.7 ! (0.66)
Other graduate	57.5 (3.81)	27,835 (2,036)	38,630 (2,826)	39.3 (3.68)	60.7 (3.68)	44.9 (3.72)	8.1 (2.37)	25.3 (3.22)	2.8 ! (1.20)
2007–08, all institutions	71.3 (1.04)	$55,106 (993)	$61,160 (1,102)	13.1 (0.80)	86.9 (0.80)	56.6 (1.18)	3.8 (0.28)	43.9 (1.17)	11.6 (0.93)
Master's degree	71.8 (1.77)	43,253 (1,374)	48,010 (1,525)	15.6 (1.34)	84.4 (1.34)	55.5 (1.93)	2.9 (0.40)	35.5 (1.48)	16.3 (1.76)
Public	66.5 (1.79)	37,772 (1,473)	41,920 (1,635)	13.3 (1.27)	86.7 (1.27)	50.7 (1.91)	4.1 (0.83)	52.2 (2.40)	13.4 (1.49)
4-year doctoral	65.1 (1.95)	38,451 (1,644)	42,680 (1,825)	12.1 (1.34)	87.9 (1.34)	50.1 (2.07)	4.2 (0.93)	56.0 (2.62)	14.5 (1.68)
Other 4-year	77.1 (4.81)	33,441 (2,285)	37,120 (2,536)	22.7 (3.92)	77.3 (3.92)	55.6 (5.96)	‡ (†)	23.5 (4.89)	5.1 ! (1.92)
Private	75.5 (2.58)	46,587 (1,974)	51,710 (2,191)	17.2 (1.96)	82.8 (1.96)	58.8 (2.81)	2.0 (0.35)	24.0 (1.59)	18.3 (2.79)
4-year doctoral	71.4 (1.85)	46,510 (1,654)	51,620 (1,836)	19.1 (1.45)	80.9 (1.45)	55.1 (1.51)	2.4 (0.50)	36.0 (2.46)	14.4 (1.17)
Other[5]	80.8 (5.13)	46,675 (3,671)	51,800 (4,075)	14.8 (3.91)	85.2 (3.91)	63.6 (5.96)	1.6 (0.43)	8.4 (1.44)	23.4 (6.23)
Doctor's degree	59.8 (1.73)	55,199 (2,108)	61,260 (2,340)	7.1 (0.88)	92.9 (0.88)	38.4 (2.18)	2.9 (0.41)	70.7 (3.03)	7.9 (0.79)
Public	52.3 (2.17)	44,192 (1,604)	49,050 (1,780)	7.9 (1.48)	92.1 (1.48)	29.7 (1.80)	3.6 (0.65)	81.1 (1.89)	7.7 (0.93)
Private	67.8 (2.41)	64,125 (3,123)	71,170 (3,467)	6.2 (1.08)	93.8 (1.08)	47.6 (3.43)	2.2 ! (0.65)	59.8 (5.02)	8.0 (1.36)
First-professional	84.9 (1.29)	81,400 (1,782)	90,350 (1,977)	11.5 (1.12)	88.5 (1.12)	81.7 (1.35)	7.5 (0.83)	35.7 (1.89)	4.6 (0.75)
Public	84.4 (1.96)	73,227 (2,717)	81,270 (3,016)	11.5 (1.65)	88.5 (1.65)	81.8 (2.12)	10.6 (1.46)	34.0 (2.67)	4.9 (1.44)
Private	85.4 (1.57)	87,799 (2,183)	97,450 (2,423)	11.5 (1.46)	88.5 (1.46)	81.5 (1.67)	5.1 (0.85)	37.0 (2.56)	4.4 (0.72)
Other graduate	62.4 (6.48)	43,740 (3,904)	48,550 (4,333)	30.8 (6.54)	69.2 (6.54)	51.0 (6.62)	‡ (†)	25.5 (5.78)	6.2 ! (2.33)
2011–12, all institutions	73.3 (0.90)	$74,710 (996)	$77,140 (1,029)	13.9 (0.77)	86.1 (0.77)	62.3 (0.93)	2.4 (0.34)	42.2 (1.19)	10.2 (0.48)
Master's degree	73.5 (1.45)	58,590 (1,142)	60,500 (1,179)	17.4 (1.28)	82.6 (1.28)	63.0 (1.44)	1.8 (0.35)	35.1 (1.53)	8.8 (0.70)
Public	71.8 (2.24)	50,200 (1,816)	51,830 (1,875)	16.2 (1.84)	83.8 (1.84)	58.2 (2.41)	3.7 (0.80)	45.6 (2.35)	10.3 (1.17)
4-year doctoral	70.7 (2.41)	50,620 (2,015)	52,270 (2,080)	16.3 (2.03)	83.7 (2.03)	57.0 (2.60)	4.0 (0.89)	47.1 (2.56)	10.8 (1.28)
Other 4-year	82.2 (3.71)	46,900 (2,538)	48,430 (2,621)	15.4 (4.13)	84.6 (4.13)	69.5 (5.18)	‡ (†)	31.2 (3.46)	5.9 (1.68)
Private	74.8 (1.95)	64,510 (1,456)	66,610 (1,503)	18.2 (1.80)	81.8 (1.80)	66.5 (2.13)	0.4 ! (0.19)	27.5 (2.09)	7.8 (0.88)
4-year doctoral	70.1 (2.41)	67,130 (2,165)	69,310 (2,235)	19.6 (2.06)	80.4 (2.06)	59.5 (2.45)	‡ (†)	35.2 (2.96)	7.8 (1.23)
Other[5]	81.8 (3.20)	61,140 (1,816)	63,130 (1,875)	16.1 (3.09)	83.9 (3.09)	77.0 (3.66)	‡ (†)	15.9 (2.70)	7.6 (1.04)
Doctor's degree—research/scholarship	50.5 (1.42)	65,090 (2,343)	67,210 (2,420)	6.6 (0.73)	93.4 (0.73)	27.8 (1.19)	1.5 ! (0.49)	79.8 (1.27)	24.0 (1.25)
Public	47.9 (2.23)	55,500 (2,291)	57,310 (2,366)	5.9 (1.04)	94.1 (1.04)	24.2 (1.41)	2.1 ! (0.78)	87.2 (1.59)	27.0 (1.93)
Private	54.0 (1.86)	76,180 (4,351)	78,660 (4,493)	7.5 (1.07)	92.5 (1.07)	32.3 (2.30)	‡ (†)	70.1 (2.28)	20.1 (1.06)
Doctor's degree—professional practice and other[6]	88.3 (0.90)	110,570 (1,848)	114,170 (1,908)	9.3 (0.88)	90.7 (0.88)	84.4 (1.03)	4.5 (0.96)	35.1 (1.66)	4.4 (0.51)
Public	88.3 (1.00)	102,220 (2,726)	105,540 (2,815)	8.9 (1.09)	91.1 (1.09)	84.4 (1.31)	8.1 (2.27)	40.6 (2.21)	5.4 (0.82)
Private	88.3 (1.28)	116,000 (2,490)	119,770 (2,571)	9.6 (1.22)	90.4 (1.22)	84.4 (1.50)	2.2 (0.53)	31.5 (2.19)	3.7 (0.62)
Other graduate	74.9 (6.28)	57,540 (5,456)	59,410 (5,633)	29.1 (6.46)	70.9 (6.46)	61.4 (7.24)	‡ (†)	16.9 (4.78)	5.5 ! (2.47)

—Not available.
†Not applicable.
!Interpret data with caution. The coefficient of variation (CV) for this estimate is between 30 and 50 percent.
‡Reporting standards not met. Either there are too few cases for a reliable estimate or the coefficient of variation (CV) is 50 percent or greater.
[1]Includes all loans ever taken out for both graduate and undergraduate education. Does not include Parent Loans for Undergraduate Students (PLUS) or loans from families and friends.
[2]Includes students who reported they were awarded aid, but did not specify the source of aid.
[3]Includes Department of Veterans Affairs and Department of Defense benefits.
[4]Constant dollars based on the Consumer Price Index, prepared by the Bureau of Labor Statistics, U.S. Department of Labor, adjusted to a school-year basis.

[5]Includes nonprofit 4-year nondoctoral institutions and for-profit 2-year-and-above institutions.
[6]Professional practice doctor's degrees include most degrees formerly classified as first-professional (such as M.D., D.D.S., and J.D.). "Other" doctor's degrees are those that are neither research/scholarship degrees nor professional practice degrees.
NOTE: Excludes students whose attendance status was not reported. Total includes some students whose level of study or control of institution was unknown. Detail may not sum to totals because of rounding and because some students receive multiple types of aid and aid from different sources. Data exclude Puerto Rico. Some data have been revised from previously published figures.
SOURCE: U.S. Department of Education, National Center for Education Statistics, 1992–93, 1999–2000, 2007–08, and 2011–12 National Postsecondary Student Aid Study (NPSAS:93, NPSAS:2000, NPSAS:08, and NPSAS:12). (This table was prepared August 2014.)

Table 332.20. Amount borrowed, aid status, and sources of aid for part-time or part-year postbaccalaureate students, by level of study and control and level of institution: Selected years, 1992–93 through 2011–12

[Standard errors appear in parentheses]

Level of study, control and level of institution	Cumulative borrowing for undergraduate and graduate education[1]: Percent who borrowed	Cumulative borrowing: Average amount for those who borrowed: Current dollars	Cumulative borrowing: Average amount for those who borrowed: Constant 2013–14 dollars[4]	Aid status (percent of students): Nonaided	Aid status: Any aid[2]	Aid status: Source of aid: Federal[3]	Source of aid: State	Source of aid: Institutional	Source of aid: Employer
1	2	3	4	5	6	7	8	9	10
1992–93, all institutions	**— (†)**	**— (†)**	**— (†)**	**63.2 (0.81)**	**36.8 (0.81)**	**10.8 (0.53)**	**1.9 (0.14)**	**12.7 (0.53)**	**16.7 (0.71)**
Master's degree	— (†)	— (†)	— (†)	62.5 (0.85)	37.5 (0.85)	10.5 (0.61)	1.6 (0.18)	11.1 (0.70)	18.7 (0.91)
Public	— (†)	— (†)	— (†)	66.4 (1.00)	33.6 (1.00)	10.1 (0.57)	2.5 (0.30)	11.7 (0.77)	14.6 (0.83)
4-year doctoral	— (†)	— (†)	— (†)	62.2 (1.25)	37.8 (1.25)	11.9 (0.81)	2.5 (0.48)	15.3 (1.11)	14.6 (1.06)
Other 4-year	— (†)	— (†)	— (†)	73.7 (1.39)	26.3 (1.39)	6.9 (0.76)	2.4 (0.55)	5.5 (1.11)	14.4 (1.09)
Private	— (†)	— (†)	— (†)	57.0 (1.56)	43.0 (1.56)	11.1 (1.06)	0.4 (0.12)	10.3 (1.04)	24.5 (1.46)
4-year doctoral	— (†)	— (†)	— (†)	55.2 (1.91)	44.8 (1.91)	12.1 (1.15)	0.3 (0.16)	12.1 (1.57)	25.1 (1.72)
Other 4-year	— (†)	— (†)	— (†)	60.4 (2.84)	39.6 (2.84)	9.1 (1.73)	0.6 (0.28)	6.9 (1.33)	23.3 (2.36)
Doctor's degree	— (†)	— (†)	— (†)	51.7 (2.56)	48.3 (2.56)	8.7 (1.18)	3.5 (0.79)	32.9 (2.46)	12.0 (1.49)
Public	— (†)	— (†)	— (†)	51.6 (3.09)	48.4 (3.09)	8.5 (1.38)	4.4 (1.25)	33.0 (3.05)	12.9 (1.89)
Private	— (†)	— (†)	— (†)	51.8 (5.53)	48.2 (5.53)	8.9 (2.49)	1.6 (0.68)	32.6 (4.51)	10.2 (2.47)
First-professional	— (†)	— (†)	— (†)	41.4 (3.04)	58.6 (3.04)	44.9 (3.13)	3.3 (0.71)	25.7 (2.07)	6.1 (1.34)
Public	— (†)	— (†)	— (†)	48.3 (4.43)	51.7 (4.43)	42.8 (3.96)	3.6 (1.11)	22.2 (3.35)	5.0 (1.61)
Private	— (†)	— (†)	— (†)	37.4 (3.43)	62.6 (3.43)	46.1 (3.92)	3.2 (0.91)	27.8 (2.44)	6.7 (1.81)
Other graduate	— (†)	— (†)	— (†)	73.0 (1.42)	27.0 (1.42)	7.6 (0.76)	1.7 (0.42)	8.4 (0.85)	13.4 (1.00)
1999–2000, all institutions	**55.7 (0.78)**	**$22,060 (408)**	**$30,620 (570)**	**51.3 (0.72)**	**48.7 (0.72)**	**19.2 (0.50)**	**1.7 (0.21)**	**16.0 (0.51)**	**20.2 (0.66)**
Master's degree	56.9 (0.90)	20,800 (400)	28,870 (550)	48.8 (0.83)	51.2 (0.83)	20.6 (0.66)	1.4 (0.26)	14.1 (0.59)	23.2 (0.81)
Public	55.9 (1.22)	18,029 (499)	25,020 (690)	53.0 (1.19)	47.0 (1.19)	16.9 (0.82)	2.0 (0.38)	15.3 (0.95)	20.7 (1.32)
4-year doctoral	56.3 (1.53)	18,640 (686)	25,870 (950)	49.6 (1.56)	50.4 (1.56)	18.2 (1.21)	2.1 (0.51)	18.1 (1.22)	21.4 (1.62)
Other 4-year	54.5 (2.19)	16,320 (649)	22,650 (900)	60.8 (1.96)	39.2 (1.96)	14.2 (1.45)	2.0 (0.50)	9.5 (1.52)	18.5 (2.28)
Private	58.2 (1.24)	24,180 (666)	33,560 (920)	43.5 (1.26)	56.5 (1.26)	25.2 (1.05)	0.6 ! (0.23)	12.6 (0.94)	26.5 (1.15)
4-year doctoral	57.6 (1.62)	25,615 (918)	35,550 (1,270)	42.3 (1.43)	57.7 (1.43)	25.2 (1.38)	0.9 ! (0.34)	14.8 (1.12)	25.5 (1.23)
Other[5]	59.4 (2.15)	21,609 (1,068)	29,990 (1,480)	45.9 (2.26)	54.1 (2.26)	25.3 (1.96)	‡ (†)	8.4 (1.63)	28.3 (2.23)
Doctor's degree	53.1 (1.73)	28,145 (1,966)	39,060 (2,730)	45.5 (1.81)	54.5 (1.81)	15.0 (1.41)	0.9 (0.17)	37.3 (1.66)	14.0 (1.35)
Public	48.6 (1.86)	25,053 (1,478)	34,770 (2,050)	46.7 (2.34)	53.3 (2.34)	13.1 (1.17)	1.4 (0.25)	40.5 (2.04)	12.1 (1.46)
Private	62.5 (3.81)	33,255 (4,031)	46,160 (5,590)	42.9 (2.95)	57.1 (2.95)	19.3 (3.46)	# (†)	30.6 (2.65)	18.1 (3.16)
First-professional	77.2 (4.07)	47,476 (3,827)	65,890 (5,310)	24.4 (3.17)	75.6 (3.17)	55.4 (4.94)	5.0 ! (1.80)	28.0 (2.97)	11.0 (2.09)
Public	78.6 (6.98)	40,594 (3,682)	56,340 (5,110)	27.3 (6.84)	72.7 (6.84)	54.4 (8.28)	4.8 ! (2.30)	21.7 (6.36)	8.0 ! (3.85)
Private	76.7 (4.80)	50,552 (5,236)	70,160 (7,270)	23.2 (3.14)	76.8 (3.14)	55.9 (6.37)	5.0 ! (2.46)	30.7 (2.91)	12.3 (2.85)
Other graduate	48.7 (2.02)	15,806 (711)	21,940 (990)	67.0 (1.77)	33.0 (1.77)	9.8 (1.25)	2.2 (0.47)	10.2 (1.07)	15.3 (1.31)
2007–08, all institutions	**66.9 (0.76)**	**$36,284 (840)**	**$40,270 (932)**	**33.2 (0.85)**	**66.8 (0.85)**	**32.0 (0.71)**	**1.9 (0.50)**	**18.7 (0.65)**	**27.2 (0.93)**
Master's degree	67.3 (1.08)	34,105 (906)	37,850 (1005)	31.0 (1.10)	69.0 (1.10)	34.4 (0.98)	2.0 ! (0.68)	15.9 (0.71)	29.8 (1.22)
Public	65.2 (1.30)	30,879 (702)	34,270 (779)	34.3 (1.39)	65.7 (1.39)	29.7 (0.94)	1.7 (0.37)	18.0 (0.92)	27.8 (1.43)
4-year doctoral	65.4 (1.38)	31,437 (816)	34,890 (905)	32.3 (1.60)	67.7 (1.60)	29.7 (1.17)	1.8 (0.47)	20.3 (1.15)	29.4 (1.71)
Other 4-year	64.7 (3.08)	29,077 (1,639)	32,270 (1,819)	40.6 (2.99)	59.4 (2.99)	29.7 (2.67)	1.2 ! (0.48)	10.4 (1.40)	22.7 (2.56)
Private	69.5 (1.57)	37,176 (1,517)	41,260 (1,684)	27.7 (1.59)	72.3 (1.59)	39.1 (1.49)	‡ (†)	13.8 (1.12)	31.7 (1.85)
4-year doctoral	66.6 (1.37)	37,232 (909)	41,320 (1,009)	29.0 (1.52)	71.0 (1.52)	34.1 (1.53)	1.5 (0.40)	15.9 (1.27)	32.9 (1.20)
Other[5]	74.1 (3.29)	37,092 (3,292)	41,170 (3,654)	25.6 (3.25)	74.4 (3.25)	47.2 (2.91)	‡ (†)	10.4 (1.68)	29.9 (4.50)
Doctor's degree	64.8 (3.47)	52,083 (5,396)	57,810 (5,989)	20.1 (1.92)	79.9 (1.92)	32.0 (4.96)	1.5 (0.33)	48.4 (3.16)	19.2 (1.73)
Public	54.8 (1.94)	36,794 (1,355)	40,840 (1,504)	23.2 (1.57)	76.8 (1.57)	18.0 (1.21)	2.2 (0.42)	60.2 (1.77)	19.6 (1.43)
Private	77.9 (5.58)	66,365 (9,120)	73,660 (10,123)	16.0 (3.95)	84.0 (3.95)	50.5 (9.18)	‡ (†)	32.7 (5.18)	18.6 (4.11)
First-professional	82.7 (2.34)	64,525 (3,850)	71,620 (4,273)	14.4 (2.54)	85.6 (2.54)	64.0 (4.52)	3.0 ! (1.36)	31.7 (3.39)	16.5 (2.21)
Public	78.2 (4.97)	63,521 (5,656)	70,500 (6,277)	11.7 (4.96)	88.3 (4.96)	65.4 (7.23)	6.3 ! (2.74)	32.9 (5.87)	16.3 (3.79)
Private	85.1 (2.51)	65,013 (5,405)	72,160 (5,999)	15.9 (3.09)	84.1 (3.09)	63.3 (6.18)	‡ (†)	31.1 (4.56)	16.7 (2.86)
Other graduate	64.0 (2.69)	28,951 (1,970)	32,130 (2,187)	56.1 (3.07)	43.9 (3.07)	16.1 (1.59)	1.2 (0.32)	7.5 (1.09)	23.4 (2.79)
2011–12, all institutions	**63.6 (0.90)**	**$49,410 (968)**	**$51,020 (1,000)**	**39.1 (0.99)**	**60.9 (0.99)**	**35.8 (0.66)**	**1.0 (0.14)**	**18.0 (0.76)**	**17.0 (0.88)**
Master's degree	65.1 (1.13)	45,860 (1,055)	47,350 (1,089)	37.5 (1.29)	62.5 (1.29)	39.4 (0.88)	0.9 (0.18)	16.1 (0.89)	17.3 (1.13)
Public	61.5 (1.63)	40,340 (1,364)	41,650 (1,409)	42.9 (1.51)	57.1 (1.51)	34.3 (1.28)	1.6 (0.33)	17.0 (1.17)	14.7 (1.02)
4-year doctoral	60.2 (1.87)	40,870 (1,584)	42,200 (1,636)	41.5 (1.74)	58.5 (1.74)	34.1 (1.47)	1.8 (0.39)	18.6 (1.38)	15.6 (1.15)
Other 4-year	68.2 (2.74)	38,070 (2,079)	39,310 (2,146)	49.8 (2.32)	50.2 (2.32)	35.4 (2.04)	‡ (†)	9.0 (1.31)	10.3 (1.66)
Private	68.3 (1.73)	50,210 (1,536)	51,840 (1,586)	32.7 (1.94)	67.3 (1.94)	43.9 (1.31)	‡ (†)	15.3 (1.31)	19.5 (1.91)
4-year doctoral	63.6 (2.49)	49,510 (1,979)	51,120 (2,043)	34.3 (2.07)	65.7 (2.07)	37.9 (1.65)	‡ (†)	15.9 (1.77)	21.2 (2.02)
Other 4-year	74.4 (1.75)	51,000 (2,306)	52,660 (2,381)	30.6 (3.63)	69.4 (3.63)	51.7 (2.22)	‡ (†)	14.4 (2.05)	17.3 (3.39)
Doctor's degree—research/scholarship	57.7 (1.52)	66,220 (2,390)	68,370 (2,468)	29.1 (1.67)	70.9 (1.67)	25.6 (1.54)	1.2 (0.21)	43.4 (2.01)	20.9 (1.35)
Public	50.2 (1.96)	51,810 (2,294)	53,500 (2,369)	30.1 (2.12)	69.9 (2.12)	16.6 (1.62)	1.3 (0.25)	51.6 (2.40)	23.6 (1.77)
Private	72.8 (1.72)	86,290 (3,951)	89,100 (4,079)	26.9 (2.56)	73.1 (2.56)	43.7 (2.76)	0.8 ! (0.38)	26.9 (2.44)	15.5 (1.78)
Doctor's degree—professional practice and other[6]	69.4 (3.45)	100,780 (4,860)	104,060 (5,018)	31.5 (3.09)	68.5 (3.09)	48.7 (3.68)	2.0 (0.59)	19.3 (2.20)	12.1 (1.83)
Public	61.6 (4.88)	79,230 (5,498)	81,810 (5,677)	41.7 (4.51)	58.3 (4.51)	38.1 (4.14)	3.6 ! (1.32)	23.3 (3.59)	12.6 (2.94)
Private	74.7 (4.23)	112,960 (6,242)	116,630 (6,445)	24.5 (3.48)	75.5 (3.48)	56.0 (5.04)	‡ (†)	16.6 (2.60)	11.8 (2.64)
Other graduate	56.0 (2.72)	39,690 (2,498)	40,980 (2,579)	59.4 (2.66)	40.6 (2.66)	16.5 (1.63)	1.1 ! (0.33)	11.5 (2.13)	14.6 (1.91)

—Not available.
†Not applicable.
#Rounds to zero.
!Interpret data with caution. The coefficient of variation (CV) for this estimate is between 30 and 50 percent.
‡Reporting standards not met. The coefficient of variation (CV) for this estimate is 50 percent or greater.
[1]Includes all loans ever taken out for both graduate and undergraduate education. Does not include Parent Loans for Undergraduate Students (PLUS) or loans from families or friends.
[2]Includes students who reported they were awarded aid, but did not specify the source of aid.
[3]Includes Department of Veterans Affairs and Department of Defense benefits.
[4]Constant dollars based on the Consumer Price Index, prepared by the Bureau of Labor Statistics, U.S. Department of Labor, adjusted to a school-year basis.
[5]Includes nonprofit 4-year nondoctoral institutions and for-profit 2-year-and-above institutions.
[6]Professional practice doctor's degrees include most degrees formerly classified as first-professional (such as M.D., D.D.S., and J.D). "Other" doctor's degrees are those that are neither research/scholarship degrees nor professional practice degrees.

NOTE: Excludes students whose attendance status was not reported. Total includes some students whose level of study or control of institution was unknown. Detail may not sum to totals because of rounding and because some students receive multiple types of aid and aid from different sources. Data exclude Puerto Rico. Some data have been revised from previously published figures.

SOURCE: U.S. Department of Education, National Center for Education Statistics, 1992–93, 1999–2000, 2007–08, and 2011–12 National Postsecondary Student Aid Study (NPSAS:93, NPSAS:2000, NPSAS:08, and NPSAS:12). (This table was prepared August 2014.)

Table 332.30. Percentage of full-time, full-year postbaccalaureate students receiving financial aid, by type of aid, level of study, and control and level of institution: Selected years, 1992–93 through 2011–12

[Standard errors appear in parentheses]

Level of study, control and level of institution	Number of students[1] (in thousands)		Percent receiving aid								
			Any aid[2]	Fellowship grants	Tuition waivers	Assistantships[3]	Employer (includes college staff)	Loans		
								Any loans	Stafford[4]	Perkins[5]
1	2		3	4	5	6	7	8	9	10
1992–93, all institutions	672	(—)	69.3 (1.43)	[6] (†)	12.4 (1.00)	14.3 (1.32)	5.3 (0.59)	43.3 (1.36)	41.1 (1.40)	9.0 (0.89)
Master's degree	281	(—)	64.5 (2.54)	[6] (†)	15.7 (1.53)	18.1 (2.01)	8.3 (1.01)	32.3 (1.80)	30.5 (1.84)	5.0 (0.89)
Public	162	(—)	67.3 (2.40)	[6] (†)	20.6 (2.40)	22.4 (1.83)	7.6 (1.24)	32.1 (1.96)	30.9 (1.99)	4.0 (0.87)
4-year doctoral	139	(—)	67.6 (2.59)	[6] (†)	23.4 (2.76)	23.6 (2.25)	7.7 (1.28)	30.6 (2.15)	29.6 (2.16)	3.3 (0.85)
Other 4-year	24	(—)	65.4 (4.38)	[6] (†)	4.4 ! (2.12)	15.8 (3.11)	6.8 ! (2.66)	40.4 (5.65)	38.4 (5.72)	8.3 ! (3.50)
Private	118	(—)	60.8 (4.74)	[6] (†)	8.9 (1.74)	12.2 ! (4.44)	9.4 (1.88)	32.7 (3.39)	29.9 (3.42)	6.4 (1.50)
4-year doctoral	103	(—)	62.6 (4.70)	[6] (†)	9.5 (1.92)	13.6 ! (4.86)	8.9 (1.88)	33.3 (3.97)	30.8 (4.04)	6.7 (1.66)
Other 4-year	16	(—)	49.5 (10.60)	[6] (†)	‡ (†)	‡ (†)	‡ (†)	28.7 (5.35)	24.6 (5.32)	‡ (†)
Doctor's degree	120	(—)	69.9 (2.32)	[6] (†)	19.4 (1.91)	27.0 (2.36)	3.0 (0.79)	25.8 (2.33)	23.9 (2.16)	3.5 (0.71)
Public	74	(—)	70.1 (2.99)	[6] (†)	23.1 (2.78)	31.6 (2.31)	3.9 (1.00)	20.6 (2.04)	18.9 (2.07)	2.9 (0.85)
Private	46	(—)	69.6 (3.27)	[6] (†)	13.6 (2.50)	19.9 (3.74)	‡ (†)	34.1 (4.20)	31.9 (3.67)	4.3 (1.16)
First-professional	210	(—)	77.4 (0.96)	[6] (†)	5.6 (0.99)	4.3 (0.69)	2.3 (0.52)	67.8 (1.49)	65.6 (1.47)	19.3 (1.65)
Public	101	(—)	79.6 (1.02)	[6] (†)	5.4 (1.11)	4.2 (0.53)	2.3 (0.59)	71.9 (1.30)	70.0 (1.19)	23.3 (2.25)
Private	110	(—)	75.4 (1.66)	[6] (†)	5.8 (1.40)	4.4 (1.24)	2.3 ! (0.70)	64.0 (2.33)	61.5 (2.35)	15.7 (1.92)
Other graduate	61	(—)	61.7 (6.82)	[6] (†)	7.6 (1.65)	6.2 (1.62)	6.0 ! (2.98)	43.3 (4.26)	39.3 (4.04)	2.6 ! (0.87)
1999–2000, all institutions	873	(—)	81.7 (0.66)	20.5 (0.97)	11.9 (0.49)	24.0 (0.92)	6.0 (0.57)	52.4 (0.77)	50.6 (0.80)	8.3 (0.64)
Master's degree	406	(—)	79.4 (1.15)	16.8 (1.12)	11.5 (0.87)	21.9 (1.37)	9.2 (1.03)	50.5 (1.26)	48.9 (1.35)	5.8 (0.54)
Public	222	(—)	77.7 (1.52)	15.5 (1.45)	18.3 (1.46)	30.5 (1.89)	7.0 (1.04)	43.5 (1.82)	42.3 (1.91)	2.8 (0.57)
4-year doctoral	179	(—)	79.8 (1.46)	16.4 (1.64)	19.6 (1.59)	34.0 (2.06)	7.3 (1.20)	41.8 (1.68)	41.2 (1.66)	3.0 (0.67)
Other 4-year	37	(—)	70.1 (5.08)	11.2 (3.31)	14.6 ! (4.91)	14.1 ! (4.31)	5.1 ! (1.79)	54.4 (6.55)	53.1 (6.84)	‡ (†)
Private	184	(—)	81.4 (1.59)	18.3 (1.76)	3.2 (0.75)	11.6 (1.64)	11.8 (1.89)	59.1 (1.61)	56.8 (2.08)	9.5 (1.18)
4-year doctoral	125	(—)	82.9 (1.93)	23.9 (2.29)	4.1 (1.05)	13.9 (1.70)	8.3 (1.31)	60.7 (2.14)	57.4 (2.61)	11.9 (1.64)
Other[7]	58	(—)	78.2 (2.75)	6.3 ! (2.12)	1.4 ! (0.53)	‡ (†)	19.1 (5.24)	55.5 (4.49)	55.5 (4.49)	4.3 ! (1.52)
Doctor's degree	184	(—)	88.0 (1.38)	37.7 (1.43)	23.3 (1.40)	54.8 (3.13)	5.4 (0.64)	28.9 (2.89)	27.3 (2.84)	‡ (†)
Public	113	(—)	88.6 (1.38)	30.0 (1.28)	34.9 (1.66)	62.8 (1.80)	7.3 (0.88)	25.8 (1.96)	24.0 (1.89)	1.1 ! (0.37)
Private	71	(—)	87.0 (2.80)	49.8 (3.31)	5.1 (1.10)	42.1 (6.85)	2.3 (0.55)	33.7 (6.36)	32.4 (6.32)	‡ (†)
First-professional	222	(—)	86.6 (1.18)	17.3 (2.25)	4.3 (0.80)	6.9 (0.99)	1.7 ! (0.53)	77.9 (1.35)	75.5 (1.38)	17.5 (1.85)
Public	101	(—)	86.2 (1.82)	12.3 (1.72)	7.6 (1.52)	7.0 (1.51)	1.8 ! (0.87)	78.5 (2.17)	77.1 (2.16)	18.7 (2.22)
Private	121	(—)	86.9 (1.49)	21.4 (3.78)	1.6 ! (0.60)	6.8 (1.51)	1.7 ! (0.66)	77.3 (1.85)	74.2 (1.97)	16.5 (2.88)
Other graduate	61	(—)	60.7 (3.68)	5.5 (1.57)	8.5 (1.93)	7.1 (1.96)	2.8 ! (1.20)	42.7 (3.71)	42.5 (3.69)	3.4 ! (1.45)
2007–08, all institutions	1,139	(—)	86.9 (0.80)	23.6 (0.87)	12.2 (0.62)	25.1 (0.87)	11.6 (0.93)	58.4 (1.21)	55.2 (1.18)	6.1 (0.38)
Master's degree	592	(—)	84.4 (1.34)	17.8 (1.04)	10.7 (0.90)	19.3 (1.01)	16.3 (1.76)	59.5 (2.03)	54.9 (1.93)	4.4 (0.50)
Public	242	(—)	86.7 (1.27)	20.0 (1.83)	21.1 (1.99)	35.3 (1.78)	13.4 (1.49)	53.4 (1.87)	50.2 (1.88)	4.7 (0.96)
4-year doctoral	213	(—)	87.9 (1.34)	21.9 (2.03)	23.1 (2.18)	37.4 (1.98)	14.5 (1.68)	52.4 (2.02)	49.5 (2.05)	4.5 (1.01)
Other 4-year	28	(—)	77.3 (3.92)	5.2 ! (2.19)	6.0 ! (2.38)	19.8 (4.57)	5.1 ! (1.92)	61.1 (5.94)	55.6 (5.96)	6.2 ! (2.87)
Private	350	(—)	82.8 (1.96)	16.2 (1.33)	3.5 (0.61)	8.2 (0.74)	18.3 (2.89)	63.7 (2.89)	58.1 (2.79)	4.2 (0.54)
4-year doctoral	197	(—)	80.9 (1.45)	25.6 (2.19)	3.8 (0.63)	13.0 (1.18)	14.4 (1.17)	58.0 (1.52)	54.0 (1.51)	7.1 (0.95)
Other 4-year	153	(—)	85.2 (3.91)	4.1 (0.85)	3.2 ! (1.14)	2.0 (0.51)	23.4 (6.23)	71.0 (6.08)	63.5 (5.96)	‡ (†)
Doctor's degree	280	(—)	92.9 (0.88)	35.2 (1.91)	25.4 (1.70)	53.1 (2.55)	7.9 (0.79)	37.3 (2.32)	35.4 (2.23)	2.6 (0.46)
Public	143	(—)	92.1 (1.48)	30.8 (2.40)	39.2 (2.33)	66.4 (2.70)	7.7 (0.93)	29.1 (1.71)	27.8 (1.71)	2.5 (0.60)
Private	136	(—)	93.8 (1.08)	39.8 (3.42)	10.9 (1.91)	39.1 (3.41)	8.0 (1.36)	46.0 (3.85)	43.4 (3.74)	2.8 (0.69)
First-professional	235	(—)	88.5 (1.12)	26.2 (1.78)	1.7 (0.42)	7.9 (0.78)	4.6 (0.75)	81.8 (1.38)	80.4 (1.41)	14.6 (1.26)
Public	104	(—)	88.5 (1.65)	22.1 (2.16)	3.2 (0.90)	9.4 (1.39)	4.9 (1.44)	81.7 (2.25)	80.6 (2.26)	14.7 (2.04)
Private	131	(—)	88.5 (1.46)	29.4 (2.57)	0.5 ! (0.18)	6.7 (0.93)	4.4 (0.72)	81.9 (1.62)	80.2 (1.70)	14.6 (1.66)
Other graduate	33	(—)	69.2 (6.54)	10.4 ! (3.71)	3.2 ! (1.27)	16.0 ! (5.08)	6.2 ! (2.33)	49.3 (6.72)	47.4 (6.58)	4.7 ! (2.12)
2011–12, all institutions	1,391	(—)	86.1 (0.77)	26.3 (1.06)	10.0 (0.60)	20.7 (0.79)	10.2 (0.48)	61.6 (0.90)	60.0 (0.91)	3.9 (0.39)
Master's degree	777	(—)	82.6 (1.28)	21.5 (1.36)	7.4 (0.73)	15.9 (1.13)	8.8 (0.70)	62.6 (1.43)	60.8 (1.40)	3.1 (0.47)
Public	329	(—)	83.8 (1.84)	24.0 (2.28)	12.1 (1.40)	24.6 (1.98)	10.3 (1.17)	57.5 (2.27)	56.2 (2.31)	3.8 (0.83)
4-year doctoral	297	(—)	83.7 (2.03)	25.5 (2.49)	12.5 (1.57)	25.0 (2.17)	10.8 (1.28)	56.2 (2.43)	54.8 (2.48)	4.0 (0.91)
Other 4-year	32	(—)	84.6 (4.13)	10.1 (2.79)	7.5 (2.05)	21.1 (2.80)	5.9 (1.68)	69.5 (5.14)	69.0 (5.14)	1.5 ! (0.65)
Private	448	(—)	81.8 (1.80)	19.6 (1.76)	4.0 (0.71)	9.6 (1.33)	7.8 (0.88)	66.4 (1.99)	64.3 (2.00)	2.7 (0.47)
4-year doctoral	269	(—)	80.4 (2.06)	25.3 (2.64)	5.2 (1.04)	13.1 (1.69)	7.8 (1.23)	61.0 (2.15)	57.9 (2.35)	4.3 (0.76)
Other 4-year	180	(—)	83.9 (3.09)	11.0 (2.25)	2.1 ! (0.76)	4.3 ! (1.88)	7.6 (1.04)	74.5 (3.59)	73.8 (3.45)	‡ (†)
Doctor's degree—research/ scholarship	235	(—)	93.4 (0.73)	42.6 (1.58)	28.1 (1.56)	62.2 (1.29)	24.0 (1.25)	25.4 (1.20)	23.9 (1.13)	1.2 ! (0.38)
Public	133	(—)	94.1 (1.04)	39.8 (2.10)	33.3 (2.32)	72.7 (1.65)	27.0 (1.93)	22.2 (1.49)	20.9 (1.46)	1.1 ! (0.46)
Private	102	(—)	92.5 (1.07)	46.3 (2.46)	21.3 (2.16)	48.5 (1.96)	20.1 (1.06)	29.5 (2.23)	27.8 (2.06)	1.3 ! (0.58)
Doctor's degree—professional practice and other[8]	342	(—)	90.7 (0.88)	28.5 (1.55)	4.7 (0.70)	4.0 (0.48)	4.4 (0.51)	84.2 (1.05)	82.9 (1.00)	7.6 (1.10)
Public	135	(—)	91.1 (1.09)	32.3 (2.24)	7.5 (1.38)	5.5 (0.92)	5.4 (0.82)	83.9 (1.23)	83.3 (1.25)	7.5 (1.17)
Private	207	(—)	90.4 (1.22)	25.9 (2.11)	2.8 (0.73)	3.0 (0.53)	3.7 (0.62)	84.4 (1.51)	82.7 (1.45)	7.7 (1.64)
Other graduate	37	(—)	70.9 (6.46)	6.6 ! (2.45)	‡ (†)	10.7 ! (3.85)	5.5 ! (2.47)	61.7 (7.20)	58.9 (7.45)	2.3 ! (1.10)

—Not available.
†Not applicable.
!Interpret data with caution. The coefficient of variation (CV) for this estimate is between 30 and 50 percent.
‡Reporting standards not met. Either there are too few cases for a reliable estimate or the coefficient of variation (CV) is 50 percent or greater.
[1]Numbers of full-time, full-year postbaccalaureate students may not equal figures reported in other tables, since these data are based on a sample survey of all postbaccalaureate students who enrolled at any time during the school year.
[2]Includes students who reported they were awarded aid, but did not specify the source of aid.
[3]Includes students who received teaching or research assistantships and/or participated in work-study programs.
[4]Formerly Guaranteed Student Loans (GSL).
[5]Formerly National Direct Student Loans (NDSL). Includes subsidized amounts only.

[6]Fellowship estimates for 1992–93 were based primarily on information provided by institutions and are not comparable to data for 1999–2000 and later years, which were based on information provided by both students and institutions.
[7]Includes nonprofit 4-year nondoctoral institutions and for-profit 2-year-and-above institutions.
[8]Professional practice doctor's degrees include most degrees formerly classified as first-professional (such as M.D., D.D.S., and J.D). "Other" doctor's degrees are those that are neither research/scholarship degrees nor professional practice degrees.
NOTE: Excludes students whose attendance status was not reported. Total includes some students whose level of study or control of institution was unknown. Detail may not sum to totals because of rounding and because some students receive aid from multiple sources. Data exclude Puerto Rico. Some data have been revised from previously published figures.
SOURCE: U.S. Department of Education, National Center for Education Statistics, 1992–93, 1999–2000, 2007–08, and 2011–12 National Postsecondary Student Aid Study (NPSAS:93, NPSAS:2000, NPSAS:08, and NPSAS:12). (This table was prepared August 2014.)

Table 332.40. Percentage of part-time or part-year postbaccalaureate students receiving financial aid, by type of aid, level of study, and control and level of institution: Selected years, 1992–93 through 2011–12

[Standard errors appear in parentheses]

Level of study, control and level of institution	Number of students[1] (in thousands)		Percent receiving aid										Loans					
			Any aid[2]		Fellowship grants		Tuition waivers		Assistantships[3]		Employer (includes college staff)		Any loans		Stafford[4]		Perkins[5]	
1	2		3		4		5		6		7		8		9		10	
1992–93, all institutions	**1,975**	**(—)**	**36.8**	**(0.81)**	**[6]**	**(†)**	**5.1**	**(0.38)**	**4.2**	**(0.27)**	**16.7**	**(0.71)**	**10.5**	**(0.52)**	**9.4**	**(0.48)**	**1.0**	**(0.13)**
Master's degree	1,319	(—)	37.5	(0.85)	[6]	(†)	4.6	(0.48)	3.8	(0.37)	18.7	(0.91)	10.3	(0.62)	9.2	(0.54)	0.9	(0.15)
Public	772	(—)	33.6	(1.00)	[6]	(†)	4.9	(0.49)	5.2	(0.46)	14.6	(0.83)	9.8	(0.65)	8.9	(0.55)	1.2	(0.23)
4-year doctoral	488	(—)	37.8	(1.25)	[6]	(†)	6.5	(0.66)	6.7	(0.70)	14.6	(1.06)	11.8	(0.90)	10.7	(0.74)	1.5	(0.33)
Other 4-year	284	(—)	26.3	(1.39)	[6]	(†)	2.2	(0.59)	2.6	(0.62)	14.4	(1.09)	6.5	(0.76)	6.0	(0.76)	0.6 !	(0.21)
Private	547	(—)	43.0	(1.56)	[6]	(†)	4.2	(0.69)	1.8 !	(0.60)	24.5	(1.46)	10.9	(1.03)	9.6	(0.89)	0.5 !	(0.18)
4-year doctoral	357	(—)	44.8	(1.91)	[6]	(†)	4.4	(0.89)	2.5 !	(0.82)	25.1	(1.72)	11.9	(1.16)	10.5	(0.99)	0.6 !	(0.26)
Other 4-year	191	(—)	39.6	(2.84)	[6]	(†)	3.8	(1.11)	0.7 !	(0.31)	23.3	(2.36)	9.1	(1.60)	7.9	(1.33)	‡	(†)
Doctor's degree	148	(—)	48.3	(2.56)	[6]	(†)	12.7	(2.19)	16.8	(1.75)	12.0	(1.49)	7.3	(1.16)	6.9	(1.20)	0.8 !	(0.35)
Public	97	(—)	48.4	(3.09)	[6]	(†)	15.0	(2.91)	16.6	(2.11)	12.9	(1.89)	7.1	(1.20)	6.5	(1.20)	‡	(†)
Private	51	(—)	48.2	(5.53)	[6]	(†)	8.3	(2.05)	17.0	(4.31)	10.2	(2.47)	7.6 !	(2.76)	7.5 !	(2.79)	‡	(†)
First-professional	64	(—)	58.6	(3.04)	[6]	(†)	5.9	(1.41)	3.1	(0.92)	6.1	(1.34)	45.6	(3.35)	42.0	(3.20)	6.2	(0.84)
Public	24	(—)	51.7	(4.43)	[6]	(†)	6.8	(1.65)	6.1 !	(2.23)	5.0 !	(1.61)	42.4	(3.99)	41.4	(3.86)	8.5	(1.77)
Private	40	(—)	62.6	(3.43)	[6]	(†)	5.4 !	(1.77)	1.4 !	(0.50)	6.7	(1.81)	47.5	(4.28)	42.3	(3.94)	4.9	(0.96)
Other graduate	414	(—)	27.0	(1.42)	[6]	(†)	3.4	(0.55)	1.6	(0.32)	13.4	(1.00)	7.1	(0.68)	5.9	(0.59)	‡	(†)
1999–2000, all institutions	**1,724**	**(—)**	**48.7**	**(0.72)**	**4.9**	**(0.27)**	**5.8**	**(0.33)**	**5.4**	**(0.34)**	**20.2**	**(0.66)**	**19.1**	**(0.51)**	**18.1**	**(0.47)**	**0.9**	**(0.13)**
Master's degree	1,131	(—)	51.2	(0.83)	4.5	(0.37)	5.0	(0.32)	4.7	(0.36)	23.2	(0.81)	20.4	(0.68)	19.3	(0.63)	0.7	(0.14)
Public	633	(—)	47.0	(1.19)	3.8	(0.52)	6.4	(0.55)	6.2	(0.56)	20.7	(1.32)	16.9	(0.86)	15.8	(0.79)	0.7	(0.16)
4-year doctoral	436	(—)	50.4	(1.56)	4.2	(0.48)	7.4	(0.71)	8.0	(0.79)	21.4	(1.62)	17.8	(1.24)	16.7	(1.18)	0.5 !	(0.17)
Other 4-year	188	(—)	39.2	(1.96)	3.2 !	(1.41)	4.2	(0.93)	2.3	(0.46)	18.5	(2.28)	14.4	(1.47)	13.6	(1.49)	1.2 !	(0.41)
Private	498	(—)	56.5	(1.26)	5.3	(0.55)	3.2	(0.41)	2.8	(0.50)	26.5	(1.15)	24.9	(1.05)	23.8	(1.04)	0.8 !	(0.29)
4-year doctoral	322	(—)	57.7	(1.43)	6.5	(0.68)	3.5	(0.55)	3.3	(0.52)	25.5	(1.23)	24.7	(1.25)	23.5	(1.26)	0.8 !	(0.33)
Other[7]	176	(—)	54.1	(2.26)	3.1	(0.93)	2.6	(0.62)	1.9 !	(0.92)	28.3	(2.23)	25.3	(2.00)	24.2	(2.03)	‡	(†)
Doctor's degree	159	(—)	54.5	(1.81)	10.8	(0.95)	15.0	(1.24)	20.9	(1.60)	14.0	(1.35)	14.7	(1.34)	14.1	(1.37)	‡	(†)
Public	108	(—)	53.3	(2.34)	8.8	(0.85)	19.5	(1.34)	25.7	(1.98)	12.1	(1.46)	12.6	(1.13)	12.0	(1.12)	‡	(†)
Private	51	(—)	57.1	(2.95)	15.1	(2.49)	5.5	(1.60)	10.8	(1.83)	18.1	(3.16)	19.2	(3.16)	18.5	(3.29)	‡	(†)
First-professional	72	(—)	75.6	(3.17)	10.2	(2.70)	5.3 !	(1.62)	‡	(†)	11.0	(2.09)	57.7	(4.43)	54.8	(5.09)	6.8 !	(2.70)
Public	22	(—)	72.7	(6.84)	8.5 !	(3.72)	‡	(†)	‡	(†)	8.0 !	(3.85)	57.4	(8.37)	54.4	(8.28)	4.7 !	(1.93)
Private	50	(—)	76.8	(3.14)	11.0 !	(3.67)	6.0 !	(2.17)	2.7 !	(1.34)	12.3	(2.85)	57.8	(5.44)	54.9	(6.63)	7.8 !	(3.72)
Other graduate	363	(—)	33.0	(1.77)	2.6	(0.44)	4.4	(0.80)	1.3	(0.33)	15.3	(1.31)	9.5	(1.09)	8.9	(1.09)	0.4 !	(0.18)
2007–08, all institutions	**2,337**	**(—)**	**66.8**	**(0.85)**	**6.6**	**(0.50)**	**6.8**	**(0.34)**	**9.7**	**(0.38)**	**27.2**	**(0.93)**	**34.6**	**(0.70)**	**30.5**	**(0.65)**	**0.9**	**(0.09)**
Master's degree	1,646	(—)	69.0	(1.10)	5.5	(0.45)	5.6	(0.40)	7.5	(0.40)	29.8	(1.22)	36.8	(0.97)	32.7	(0.93)	0.9	(0.12)
Public	829	(—)	65.7	(1.39)	4.4	(0.53)	7.2	(0.69)	10.6	(0.72)	27.8	(1.43)	32.8	(1.16)	27.8	(0.90)	1.0	(0.16)
4-year doctoral	631	(—)	67.7	(1.60)	4.9	(0.64)	8.4	(0.81)	12.0	(0.94)	29.4	(1.71)	32.3	(1.36)	28.0	(1.16)	1.0	(0.18)
Other 4-year	198	(—)	59.4	(2.99)	3.0 !	(0.97)	3.6 !	(1.18)	6.0	(1.17)	22.7	(2.56)	34.5	(2.98)	27.2	(2.63)	1.2 !	(0.37)
Private	818	(—)	72.3	(1.59)	6.5	(0.74)	4.0	(0.51)	4.3	(0.43)	31.7	(1.85)	40.9	(1.42)	37.6	(1.41)	0.8	(0.19)
4-year doctoral	509	(—)	71.0	(1.52)	8.0	(0.95)	3.8	(0.52)	5.5	(0.57)	32.9	(1.20)	36.5	(1.33)	32.8	(1.24)	1.1	(0.29)
Other[7]	309	(—)	74.4	(3.25)	4.0	(0.79)	4.4	(1.00)	2.4	(0.57)	29.9	(4.50)	48.3	(2.89)	45.5	(2.86)	0.2 !	(0.12)
Doctor's degree	270	(—)	79.9	(1.92)	17.1	(2.09)	16.4	(1.78)	34.0	(3.40)	19.2	(1.73)	33.3	(4.81)	30.4	(5.07)	0.5 !	(0.25)
Public	154	(—)	76.8	(1.57)	16.8	(1.67)	24.2	(1.52)	47.2	(2.02)	19.6	(1.43)	18.9	(1.26)	15.9	(1.15)	‡	(†)
Private	116	(—)	84.0	(3.95)	17.5	(4.59)	6.0 !	(2.03)	16.4	(4.27)	18.6	(4.11)	52.4	(8.69)	49.6	(9.37)	‡	(†)
First-professional	58	(—)	85.6	(2.54)	20.5	(3.99)	6.5 !	(2.52)	10.3	(2.01)	16.5	(2.21)	68.5	(3.89)	62.9	(4.62)	4.1 !	(1.48)
Public	20	(—)	88.3	(4.96)	13.8	(3.97)	11.0 !	(4.26)	18.5	(4.72)	16.3	(3.79)	68.4	(5.79)	62.7	(7.17)	7.9 !	(3.25)
Private	38	(—)	84.1	(3.09)	24.0	(5.43)	‡	(†)	6.0	(1.69)	16.7	(2.86)	68.6	(5.46)	63.0	(6.20)	‡	(†)
Other graduate	363	(—)	43.9	(3.07)	1.5	(0.37)	4.9	(0.97)	1.5	(0.41)	23.4	(2.79)	20.0	(2.10)	15.5	(1.58)	0.5 !	(0.25)
2011–12, all institutions	**2,291**	**(—)**	**60.9**	**(0.99)**	**8.6**	**(0.55)**	**6.7**	**(0.56)**	**6.4**	**(0.43)**	**17.0**	**(0.88)**	**35.0**	**(0.61)**	**32.7**	**(0.60)**	**0.8**	**(0.17)**
Master's degree	1,715	(—)	62.5	(1.29)	7.6	(0.61)	5.6	(0.62)	4.8	(0.47)	17.3	(1.13)	38.1	(0.83)	36.0	(0.83)	0.7	(0.17)
Public	800	(—)	57.1	(1.51)	7.2	(0.83)	5.8	(0.72)	7.5	(0.85)	14.7	(1.02)	33.7	(1.19)	31.2	(1.12)	1.2 !	(0.37)
4-year doctoral	664	(—)	58.5	(1.74)	8.1	(1.00)	6.2	(0.84)	7.9	(1.02)	15.6	(1.15)	33.4	(1.36)	31.1	(1.29)	1.2 !	(0.43)
Other 4-year	136	(—)	50.2	(2.32)	2.7	(0.76)	3.8	(1.07)	5.3	(1.06)	10.3	(1.66)	35.0	(2.15)	31.7	(2.10)	‡	(†)
Private	914	(—)	67.3	(1.94)	8.0	(0.92)	5.5	(0.91)	2.5	(0.55)	19.5	(1.91)	41.9	(1.32)	40.1	(1.30)	0.2 !	(0.08)
4-year doctoral	515	(—)	65.7	(2.07)	10.1	(1.49)	3.7	(0.91)	2.7	(0.72)	21.2	(2.02)	37.9	(1.67)	35.4	(1.72)	‡	(†)
Other 4-year	399	(—)	69.4	(3.63)	5.2	(0.93)	7.8	(1.71)	2.1 !	(0.95)	17.3	(3.39)	47.2	(2.03)	46.1	(1.92)	‡	(†)
Doctor's degree—research/ scholarship	198	(—)	70.9	(1.67)	18.1	(1.31)	20.0	(1.27)	30.4	(1.98)	20.9	(1.35)	24.4	(1.46)	22.4	(1.44)	0.3 !	(0.10)
Public	133	(—)	69.9	(2.12)	20.0	(1.76)	25.2	(1.78)	39.4	(2.56)	23.6	(1.77)	14.7	(1.34)	13.5	(1.28)	0.4 !	(0.15)
Private	66	(—)	73.1	(2.56)	14.2	(1.34)	9.6	(1.24)	12.2	(1.77)	15.5	(1.78)	44.0	(2.68)	40.5	(2.75)	‡	(†)
Doctor's degree—professional practice and other[8]	100	(—)	68.5	(3.09)	13.8	(1.88)	4.6	(0.98)	2.3 !	(0.79)	12.1	(1.83)	51.5	(3.52)	47.3	(3.67)	4.7 !	(2.12)
Public	41	(—)	58.3	(4.51)	16.0	(2.83)	7.3	(1.96)	3.8 !	(1.75)	12.6	(2.94)	40.3	(4.01)	37.4	(4.10)	3.0 !	(1.32)
Private	59	(—)	75.5	(3.48)	12.3	(2.41)	2.7 !	(1.02)	1.3 !	(0.50)	11.8	(2.64)	59.1	(4.83)	54.1	(5.03)	‡	(†)
Other graduate	278	(—)	40.6	(2.66)	6.5	(1.57)	4.6 !	(1.47)	0.7 !	(0.34)	14.6	(1.91)	17.9	(1.76)	14.9	(1.64)	‡	(†)

—Not available.
†Not applicable.
!Interpret data with caution. The coefficient of variation (CV) for this estimate is between 30 and 50 percent.
‡Reporting standards not met. The coefficient of variation (CV) for this estimate is 50 percent or greater.
[1]Numbers of part-time or part-year postbaccalaureate students may not equal figures reported in other tables, since these data are based on a sample survey of all postbaccalaureate students enrolled at any time during the school year.
[2]Includes students who reported they were awarded aid, but did not specify the source of aid.
[3]Includes students who received teaching or research assistantships and/or participated in work-study programs.
[4]Formerly Guaranteed Student Loans (GSL).
[5]Formerly National Direct Student Loans (NDSL). Includes subsidized amounts only.
[6]Fellowship estimates for 1992–93 were based primarily on information provided by institutions and are not comparable to data for 1999–2000 and later years, which were based on information provided by both students and institutions.
[7]Includes nonprofit 4-year nondoctoral institutions and for-profit 2-year-and-above institutions.
[8]Professional practice doctor's degrees include most degrees formerly classified as first-professional (such as M.D., D.D.S., and J.D). "Other" doctor's degrees are those that are neither research/scholarship degrees nor professional practice degrees.
NOTE: Excludes students whose attendance status was not reported. Total includes some students whose level of study or control of institution was unknown. Detail may not sum to totals because of rounding and because some students receive aid from multiple sources. Data exclude Puerto Rico. Some data have been revised from previously published figures.
SOURCE: U.S. Department of Education, National Center for Education Statistics, 1992–93, 1999–2000, 2007–08, and 2011–12 National Postsecondary Student Aid Study (NPSAS:93, NPSAS:2000, NPSAS:08, and NPSAS:12). (This table was prepared August 2014.)

Table 332.50. Number of postsecondary students who entered the student loan repayment phase, number of students who defaulted, and student loan cohort default rates, by 2-year or 3-year default period and level and control of institution: Fiscal years 2009 through 2011

Fiscal year and level and control of institution	For student loan cohorts over a 2-year period			For student loan cohorts over a 3-year period		
	Number entering repayment phase in given fiscal year[1]	Number defaulting by end of next fiscal year[2]	2-year default rate[3,4]	Number entering repayment phase in given fiscal year[1]	Number defaulting by end of second following fiscal year[2]	3-year default rate[4,5]
1	2	3	4	5	6	7
Fiscal year 2009						
All institutions[6]	3,628,846	320,194	8.8	3,629,109	489,040	13.4
Public	1,778,903	128,121	7.2	1,778,645	196,032	11.0
Private nonprofit	825,221	38,718	4.6	835,492	63,047	7.5
Private for-profit	1,015,855	152,862	15.0	1,006,190	229,315	22.7
Less-than-2-year institutions	142,632	19,385	13.6	140,742	29,940	21.3
Public	7,548	749	9.9	7,401	1,202	16.2
Private nonprofit	4,148	605	14.5	4,106	950	23.1
Private for-profit	130,936	18,031	13.7	129,235	27,788	21.5
2-year institutions	824,841	106,634	12.9	814,256	161,448	19.8
Public	520,256	62,234	11.9	518,299	94,945	18.3
Private nonprofit	15,039	1,507	10.0	16,244	2,357	14.5
Private for-profit	289,546	42,893	14.8	279,713	64,146	22.9
4-year institutions	2,652,506	193,682	7.3	2,665,329	297,006	11.1
Public	1,251,099	65,138	5.2	1,252,945	99,885	7.9
Private nonprofit	806,034	36,606	4.5	815,142	59,740	7.3
Private for-profit	595,373	91,938	15.4	597,242	137,381	23.0
Fiscal year 2010						
All institutions[6]	4,100,778	374,940	9.1	4,082,570	600,545	14.7
Public	1,928,054	161,815	8.3	1,922,773	250,661	13.0
Private nonprofit	882,005	46,481	5.2	879,269	72,347	8.2
Private for-profit	1,281,215	166,364	12.9	1,270,965	277,088	21.8
Less-than-2-year institutions	179,650	21,274	11.8	178,904	37,223	20.8
Public	8,261	831	10.0	7,963	1,315	16.5
Private nonprofit	4,953	676	13.6	5,020	1,097	21.8
Private for-profit	166,436	19,767	11.8	165,921	34,811	20.9
2-year institutions	966,842	124,136	12.8	950,143	199,922	21.0
Public	604,872	81,120	13.4	599,467	125,764	20.9
Private nonprofit	18,384	1,573	8.5	16,217	2,305	14.2
Private for-profit	343,586	41,443	12.0	334,459	71,853	21.4
4-year institutions	2,944,782	229,250	7.8	2,943,960	362,951	12.3
Public	1,314,921	79,864	6.0	1,315,343	123,582	9.3
Private nonprofit	858,668	44,232	5.1	858,032	68,945	8.0
Private for-profit	771,193	105,154	13.6	770,585	170,424	22.1
Fiscal year 2011						
All institutions[6]	4,739,481	475,538	10.0	4,732,793	650,727	13.7
Public	2,253,463	218,418	9.6	2,252,334	292,012	12.9
Private nonprofit	967,956	51,153	5.2	969,156	70,186	7.2
Private for-profit	1,507,562	205,681	13.6	1,500,812	288,126	19.1
Less-than-2-year institutions	211,988	29,576	14.0	202,526	41,526	20.5
Public	8,779	824	9.3	8,750	1,196	13.6
Private nonprofit	5,219	734	14.0	6,567	1,644	25.0
Private for-profit	197,990	28,018	14.1	187,209	38,686	20.6
2-year institutions	1,179,508	172,265	14.6	1,174,583	237,571	20.2
Public	774,772	116,966	15.0	767,073	158,104	20.6
Private nonprofit	17,458	1,445	8.2	16,861	2,026	12.0
Private for-profit	387,278	53,854	13.9	390,649	77,441	19.8
4-year institutions	3,337,485	273,411	8.2	3,345,193	371,227	11.1
Public	1,469,912	100,628	6.8	1,476,511	132,712	8.9
Private nonprofit	945,279	48,974	5.1	945,728	66,516	7.0
Private for-profit	922,294	123,809	13.4	922,954	171,999	18.6

[1]The repayment phase is the period when student loans must be repaid; it generally begins 6 months after a student leaves an institution. Students who enter the repayment phase during a particular federal fiscal year (October 1 through September 30) make up the cohort for that fiscal year. For example, members of the fiscal year (FY) 2009 cohort entered the repayment phase any time from October 1, 2008, through September 30, 2009.
[2]Default occurs when a borrower fails to make a payment for 270 days.
[3]The 2-year cohort default rate is the percentage of borrowers entering repayment during one fiscal year and defaulting by the end of the next fiscal year. For example, the 2-year cohort default rate for FY 2009 is the percentage of borrowers who entered repayment during FY 2009 (any time from October 1, 2008, through September 30, 2009) and who defaulted by the end of FY 2010 (September 30, 2010).
[4]For purposes of computing default rates, if an individual or entity affiliated with the institution makes a payment to prevent a borrower's default on a loan, the borrower is still considered in default.
[5]The 3-year cohort default rate is the percentage of borrowers entering repayment during the specified fiscal year and defaulting by the end of the second fiscal year that follows. For example, the 3-year cohort default rate for FY 2009 is the percentage of borrowers who entered

repayment during FY 2009 (any time from October 1, 2008, through September 30, 2009) and who defaulted by the end of FY 2011 (September 30, 2011).
[6]Includes borrowers from foreign and unclassified schools, which account for less than 1 percent of borrowers and are not included elsewhere.
NOTE: Data are for certain loans under the Federal Family Education Loan (FFEL) Program and the William D. Ford Federal Direct Loan Program (commonly referred to as the Direct Loan Program). Includes Federal Stafford Loans. Does not include PLUS loans, Federal Insured Student Loans (FISLs), or Federal Perkins Loans. For more details, see http://ifap.ed.gov/Default Management/guide/attachments/CDRGuideCh2Pt1CDRCalculation.pdf. Beginning with the 2011 cohort, the Office of Federal Student Aid (OFSA) is publishing only 3-year default rates. The 2-year default rates shown in this table are no longer available online; therefore, no source for the 2-year rates can be provided.
SOURCE: U.S. Department of Education, Office of Federal Student Aid, Direct Loan and Federal Family Education Loan Programs, Cohort Default Rate Database; retrieved October 13, 2014, from http://www2.ed.gov/offices/OSFAP/defaultmanagement/schooltyperates.pdf. (This table was prepared October 2014.)

Table 333.10. Revenues of public degree-granting postsecondary institutions, by source of revenue and level of institution: 2006–07 through 2012–13

Level of institution and year	Total revenues	Tuition and fees[1]	Grants and contracts — Federal	State	Local and private	Sales and services of auxiliary enterprises[1]	Sales and services of hospitals	Independent operations	Other operating revenues[2]
1	2	3	4	5	6	7	8	9	10
In thousands of current dollars									
All levels									
2006–07............	$268,556,045	$44,773,470	$30,779,946	$7,613,614	$8,176,011	$20,398,261	$22,575,459	$688,024	$13,765,596
2007–08............	273,109,306	48,070,012	25,522,915	7,831,530	8,699,329	20,488,319	25,183,379	1,174,836	14,108,986
2008–09............	267,385,180	51,840,367	26,092,100	7,403,141	9,600,416	21,358,319	27,301,883	1,036,660	14,165,654
2009–10............	303,329,538	55,930,482	28,397,667	6,904,221	9,620,133	22,173,700	29,236,931	1,343,230	14,814,344
2010–11............	323,817,821	60,240,671	29,808,728	7,020,373	10,062,621	23,606,433	31,105,677	1,330,334	15,804,536
2011–12............	317,306,882	65,386,643	29,170,906	6,830,610	10,143,900	24,275,773	33,508,840	1,356,396	16,287,670
2012–13............	327,932,633	68,095,088	28,430,717	6,687,856	10,779,776	24,666,058	34,940,780	1,359,043	17,336,700
4-year									
2006–07............	221,882,332	37,205,630	26,027,591	5,530,987	7,586,434	18,520,922	22,575,459	688,024	13,057,589
2007–08............	223,566,529	40,083,063	23,518,933	5,715,188	8,106,887	18,507,934	25,183,379	1,174,836	13,135,633
2008–09............	216,432,317	43,478,018	24,178,064	5,526,583	9,031,844	19,391,219	27,301,883	1,036,660	13,291,611
2009–10............	248,104,870	46,943,248	26,272,013	5,301,243	9,062,160	20,099,137	29,236,931	1,343,230	13,894,006
2010–11............	265,941,566	51,018,362	27,643,131	5,480,388	9,495,263	21,507,520	31,105,677	1,330,334	14,876,568
2011–12............	261,153,808	55,979,010	27,238,924	5,352,808	9,573,172	22,239,682	33,508,840	1,356,396	15,337,305
2012–13............	272,356,474	58,627,864	26,601,896	5,196,508	10,251,194	22,714,712	34,940,780	1,359,043	16,456,904
2-year									
2006–07............	46,673,713	7,567,840	4,752,356	2,082,627	589,578	1,877,338	0	0	708,007
2007–08............	49,542,777	7,986,949	2,003,982	2,116,343	592,442	1,980,385	0	0	973,353
2008–09............	50,952,862	8,362,349	1,914,036	1,876,558	568,572	1,967,100	0	0	874,043
2009–10............	55,224,668	8,987,234	2,125,654	1,602,978	557,973	2,074,563	0	0	920,338
2010–11............	57,876,255	9,222,309	2,165,597	1,539,985	567,358	2,098,913	0	0	927,968
2011–12............	56,153,074	9,407,634	1,931,982	1,477,802	570,728	2,036,091	0	0	950,365
2012–13............	55,576,159	9,467,224	1,828,820	1,491,347	528,582	1,951,346	0	0	879,795
Percentage distribution									
All levels									
2006–07............	100.00	16.67	11.46	2.84	3.04	7.60	8.41	0.26	5.13
2007–08............	100.00	17.60	9.35	2.87	3.19	7.50	9.22	0.43	5.17
2008–09............	100.00	19.39	9.76	2.77	3.59	7.99	10.21	0.39	5.30
2009–10............	100.00	18.44	9.36	2.28	3.17	7.31	9.64	0.44	4.88
2010–11............	100.00	18.60	9.21	2.17	3.11	7.29	9.61	0.41	4.88
2011–12............	100.00	20.61	9.19	2.15	3.20	7.65	10.56	0.43	5.13
2012–13............	100.00	20.76	8.67	2.04	3.29	7.52	10.65	0.41	5.29
4-year									
2006–07............	100.00	16.77	11.73	2.49	3.42	8.35	10.17	0.31	5.88
2007–08............	100.00	17.93	10.52	2.56	3.63	8.28	11.26	0.53	5.88
2008–09............	100.00	20.09	11.17	2.55	4.17	8.96	12.61	0.48	6.14
2009–10............	100.00	18.92	10.59	2.14	3.65	8.10	11.78	0.54	5.60
2010–11............	100.00	19.18	10.39	2.06	3.57	8.09	11.70	0.50	5.59
2011–12............	100.00	21.44	10.43	2.05	3.67	8.52	12.83	0.52	5.87
2012–13............	100.00	21.53	9.77	1.91	3.76	8.34	12.83	0.50	6.04
2-year									
2006–07............	100.00	16.21	10.18	4.46	1.26	4.02	0.00	0.00	1.52
2007–08............	100.00	16.12	4.04	4.27	1.20	4.00	0.00	0.00	1.96
2008–09............	100.00	16.41	3.76	3.68	1.12	3.86	0.00	0.00	1.72
2009–10............	100.00	16.27	3.85	2.90	1.01	3.76	0.00	0.00	1.67
2010–11............	100.00	15.93	3.74	2.66	0.98	3.63	0.00	0.00	1.60
2011–12............	100.00	16.75	3.44	2.63	1.02	3.63	0.00	0.00	1.69
2012–13............	100.00	17.03	3.29	2.68	0.95	3.51	0.00	0.00	1.58
Revenue per full-time-equivalent student in constant 2013–14 dollars[3]									
All levels									
2006–07............	$32,526	$5,423	$3,728	$922	$990	$2,471	$2,734	$83	$1,667
2007–08............	31,122	5,478	2,908	892	991	2,335	2,870	134	1,608
2008–09............	29,088	5,640	2,839	805	1,044	2,324	2,970	113	1,541
2009–10............	30,600	5,642	2,865	696	970	2,237	2,949	136	1,494
2010–11............	31,233	5,810	2,875	677	971	2,277	3,000	128	1,524
2011–12............	29,907	6,163	2,749	644	956	2,288	3,158	128	1,535
2012–13............	30,894	6,415	2,678	630	1,016	2,324	3,292	128	1,633
4-year									
2006–07............	43,846	7,352	5,143	1,093	1,499	3,660	4,461	136	2,580
2007–08............	41,396	7,422	4,355	1,058	1,501	3,427	4,663	218	2,432
2008–09............	38,587	7,752	4,311	985	1,610	3,457	4,868	185	2,370
2009–10............	41,686	7,887	4,414	891	1,523	3,377	4,912	226	2,334
2010–11............	42,593	8,171	4,427	878	1,521	3,445	4,982	213	2,383
2011–12............	40,042	8,583	4,176	821	1,468	3,410	5,138	208	2,352
2012–13............	40,892	8,802	3,994	780	1,539	3,410	5,246	204	2,471
2-year									
2006–07............	14,603	2,368	1,487	652	184	587	0	0	222
2007–08............	14,681	2,367	594	627	176	587	0	0	288
2008–09............	14,220	2,334	534	524	159	549	0	0	244
2009–10............	13,942	2,269	537	405	141	524	0	0	232
2010–11............	14,034	2,236	525	373	138	509	0	0	225
2011–12............	13,737	2,301	473	362	140	498	0	0	232
2012–13............	14,054	2,394	462	377	134	493	0	0	222

See notes at end of table.

Table 333.10. Revenues of public degree-granting postsecondary institutions, by source of revenue and level of institution: 2006–07 through 2012–13—Continued

Level of institution and year	Nonoperating revenue									Other revenues and additions			
	Appropriations			Nonoperating grants			Gifts	Investment income	Other	Capital appropriations	Capital grants and gifts	Additions to permanent endowments	Other
	Federal	State	Local	Federal	State	Local							
1	11	12	13	14	15	16	17	18	19	20	21	22	23
In thousands of current dollars													
All levels													
2006–07	$1,910,169	$63,204,939	$8,818,685	$2,859,223	$1,291,896	$129,138	$5,589,156	$15,588,573	$3,950,191	$7,332,387	$3,509,682	$1,039,425	$4,562,199
2007–08	1,849,775	68,375,062	9,319,219	10,022,315	1,909,570	177,555	6,070,499	5,278,643	2,251,324	7,578,049	3,090,589	1,133,783	4,973,618
2008–09	2,010,843	65,486,232	9,787,019	12,760,716	2,720,449	265,789	5,893,912	-9,487,915	3,011,240	7,038,658	2,938,605	843,528	5,317,562
2009–10	2,152,228	62,456,235	9,954,504	20,740,102	3,123,358	231,104	5,876,450	10,046,610	5,210,022	6,041,010	3,780,012	869,950	4,427,245
2010–11	1,946,965	63,015,552	10,023,205	24,366,180	3,404,970	228,045	6,286,802	14,185,059	5,623,707	5,640,026	3,744,845	965,007	5,408,083
2011–12	1,835,767	58,789,643	10,214,576	23,205,569	3,559,749	232,167	6,540,837	6,171,056	4,191,861	5,544,504	3,724,320	825,587	5,510,507
2012–13	1,747,391	58,634,067	10,725,798	22,393,312	3,830,396	279,760	7,117,638	11,298,624	4,990,501	5,195,685	3,614,091	928,928	4,880,426
4-year													
2006–07	1,786,143	49,216,667	446,923	1,625,932	705,405	71,908	5,332,020	14,616,593	3,365,017	5,064,705	3,161,015	1,016,329	4,281,040
2007–08	1,776,452	53,268,648	453,280	5,177,569	1,201,394	103,824	5,798,732	4,430,479	1,770,108	5,637,968	2,762,277	1,120,806	4,639,141
2008–09	1,934,958	50,863,465	484,689	6,425,434	1,729,985	131,427	5,635,304	-9,958,068	2,601,770	4,987,773	2,554,107	830,264	4,975,326
2009–10	2,006,623	48,721,670	431,615	10,318,977	2,088,155	134,608	5,646,279	9,666,292	4,595,894	4,003,617	3,312,753	853,705	4,172,713
2010–11	1,853,109	48,977,437	507,010	11,849,748	2,320,005	130,451	6,061,073	13,771,423	4,783,422	3,880,567	3,249,730	943,748	5,156,596
2011–12	1,715,489	45,755,610	517,219	11,264,322	2,398,688	130,598	6,274,473	5,994,816	3,491,418	3,884,832	3,357,088	815,973	4,967,146
2012–13	1,634,057	45,842,103	551,917	11,126,358	2,516,165	153,773	6,864,121	11,126,073	4,356,413	3,619,996	3,260,502	899,534	4,256,561
2-year													
2006–07	124,026	13,988,272	8,371,762	1,233,292	586,491	57,230	257,136	971,979	585,175	2,267,682	348,667	23,096	281,159
2007–08	73,324	15,106,414	8,865,938	4,844,746	708,176	73,731	271,766	848,164	481,216	1,940,082	328,312	12,978	334,477
2008–09	75,885	14,622,766	9,302,330	6,335,282	990,464	134,362	258,608	470,153	409,470	2,050,885	384,498	13,263	342,236
2009–10	145,606	13,734,565	9,522,890	10,421,125	1,035,203	96,496	230,170	380,318	614,128	2,037,393	467,258	16,245	254,532
2010–11	93,856	14,038,114	9,516,195	12,516,431	1,084,965	97,594	225,730	413,636	840,284	1,759,459	495,115	21,258	251,487
2011–12	120,279	13,034,033	9,697,357	11,941,246	1,161,061	101,569	266,364	176,240	700,443	1,659,672	367,232	9,614	543,362
2012–13	113,334	12,791,964	10,173,882	11,266,954	1,314,232	125,987	253,517	172,551	634,088	1,575,688	353,588	29,394	623,866
Percentage distribution													
All levels													
2006–07	0.71	23.54	3.28	1.06	0.48	0.05	2.08	5.80	1.47	2.73	1.31	0.39	1.70
2007–08	0.68	25.04	3.41	3.67	0.70	0.07	2.22	1.93	0.82	2.77	1.13	0.42	1.82
2008–09	0.75	24.49	3.66	4.77	1.02	0.10	2.20	-3.55	1.13	2.63	1.10	0.32	1.99
2009–10	0.71	20.59	3.28	6.84	1.03	0.08	1.94	3.31	1.72	1.99	1.25	0.29	1.46
2010–11	0.60	19.46	3.10	7.52	1.05	0.07	1.94	4.38	1.74	1.74	1.16	0.30	1.67
2011–12	0.58	18.53	3.22	7.31	1.12	0.07	2.06	1.94	1.32	1.75	1.17	0.26	1.74
2012–13	0.53	17.88	3.27	6.83	1.17	0.09	2.17	3.45	1.52	1.58	1.10	0.28	1.49
4-year													
2006–07	0.80	22.18	0.20	0.73	0.32	0.03	2.40	6.59	1.52	2.28	1.42	0.46	1.93
2007–08	0.79	23.83	0.20	2.32	0.54	0.05	2.59	1.98	0.79	2.52	1.24	0.50	2.08
2008–09	0.89	23.50	0.22	2.97	0.80	0.06	2.60	-4.60	1.20	2.30	1.18	0.38	2.30
2009–10	0.81	19.64	0.17	4.16	0.84	0.05	2.28	3.90	1.85	1.61	1.34	0.34	1.68
2010–11	0.70	18.42	0.19	4.46	0.87	0.05	2.28	5.18	1.80	1.46	1.22	0.35	1.94
2011–12	0.66	17.52	0.20	4.31	0.92	0.05	2.40	2.30	1.34	1.49	1.29	0.31	1.90
2012–13	0.60	16.83	0.20	4.09	0.92	0.06	2.52	4.09	1.60	1.33	1.20	0.33	1.56
2-year													
2006–07	0.27	29.97	17.94	2.64	1.26	0.12	0.55	2.08	1.25	4.86	0.75	0.05	0.60
2007–08	0.15	30.49	17.90	9.78	1.43	0.15	0.55	1.71	0.97	3.92	0.66	0.03	0.68
2008–09	0.15	28.70	18.26	12.43	1.94	0.26	0.51	0.92	0.80	4.03	0.75	0.03	0.67
2009–10	0.26	24.87	17.24	18.87	1.87	0.17	0.42	0.69	1.11	3.69	0.85	0.03	0.46
2010–11	0.16	24.26	16.44	21.63	1.87	0.17	0.39	0.71	1.45	3.04	0.86	0.04	0.43
2011–12	0.21	23.21	17.27	21.27	2.07	0.18	0.47	0.31	1.25	2.96	0.65	0.02	0.97
2012–13	0.20	23.02	18.31	20.27	2.36	0.23	0.46	0.31	1.14	2.84	0.64	0.05	1.12
Revenue per full-time-equivalent student in constant 2013–14 dollars[3]													
All levels													
2006–07	$231	$7,655	$1,068	$346	$156	$16	$677	$1,888	$478	$888	$425	$126	$553
2007–08	211	7,792	1,062	1,142	218	20	692	602	257	864	352	129	567
2008–09	219	7,124	1,065	1,388	296	29	641	-1,032	328	766	320	92	578
2009–10	217	6,301	1,004	2,092	315	23	593	1,013	526	609	381	88	447
2010–11	188	6,078	967	2,350	328	22	606	1,368	542	544	361	93	522
2011–12	173	5,541	963	2,187	336	22	616	582	395	523	351	78	519
2012–13	165	5,524	1,010	2,110	361	26	671	1,064	470	489	340	88	460
4-year													
2006–07	353	9,726	88	321	139	14	1,054	2,888	665	1,001	625	201	846
2007–08	329	9,863	84	959	222	19	1,074	820	328	1,044	511	208	859
2008–09	345	9,068	86	1,146	308	23	1,005	-1,775	464	889	455	148	887
2009–10	337	8,186	73	1,734	351	23	949	1,624	772	673	557	143	701
2010–11	297	7,844	81	1,898	372	21	971	2,206	766	622	520	151	826
2011–12	263	7,016	79	1,727	368	20	962	919	535	596	515	125	762
2012–13	245	6,883	83	1,671	378	23	1,031	1,670	654	544	490	135	639
2-year													
2006–07	39	4,377	2,619	386	184	18	80	304	183	710	109	7	88
2007–08	22	4,476	2,627	1,436	210	22	81	251	143	575	97	4	99
2008–09	21	4,081	2,596	1,768	276	37	72	131	114	572	107	4	96
2009–10	37	3,467	2,404	2,631	261	24	58	96	155	514	118	4	64
2010–11	23	3,404	2,307	3,035	263	24	55	100	204	427	120	5	61
2011–12	29	3,189	2,372	2,921	284	25	65	43	171	406	90	2	133
2012–13	29	3,235	2,573	2,849	332	32	64	44	160	398	89	7	158

[1]After deducting discounts and allowances.
[2]Includes sales and services of educational activities.
[3]Constant dollars based on the Consumer Price Index, prepared by the Bureau of Labor Statistics, U.S. Department of Labor, adjusted to a school-year basis.
NOTE: Degree-granting institutions grant associate's or higher degrees and participate in Title IV federal financial aid programs. Includes data for public institutions reporting data according to either the Governmental Accounting Standards Board (GASB) or the Financial Accounting Standards Board (FASB) questionnaire. Detail may not sum to totals because of rounding.
SOURCE: U.S. Department of Education, National Center for Education Statistics, Integrated Postsecondary Education Data System (IPEDS), Spring 2007 through Spring 2014, Finance and Enrollment components. (This table was prepared January 2015.)

Table 333.20. Revenues of public degree-granting postsecondary institutions, by source of revenue and state or jurisdiction: 2012–13

[In thousands of current dollars]

State or jurisdiction	Total revenues	Operating revenue							Nonoperating revenue[1]			Other revenues and additions
		Total	Tuition and fees[2]	Federal grants and contracts	State, local, and private grants and contracts	Sales and services of auxiliary enterprises[2]	Sales and services of hospitals	Independent operations and other[3]	Total	State appropriations	Local appropriations	
1	2	3	4	5	6	7	8	9	10	11	12	13
United States......	$327,932,633	$192,296,017	$68,095,088	$28,430,717	$17,467,631	$24,666,058	$34,940,780	$18,695,743	$121,017,487	$58,634,067	$10,725,798	$14,619,130
Alabama......................	6,873,908	4,676,097	1,537,881	665,855	244,652	392,669	1,525,475	309,565	2,084,780	1,289,898	1,337	113,032
Alaska........................	1,074,808	398,997	129,045	124,980	81,039	41,639	0	22,292	498,788	377,504	10,031	177,024
Arizona.......................	5,601,910	2,936,309	1,656,475	575,196	177,471	380,347	0	146,821	2,598,081	772,257	763,521	67,520
Arkansas....................	3,720,787	2,327,134	470,622	241,160	200,539	252,483	886,577	275,753	1,346,358	759,693	30,714	47,296
California....................	44,779,628	25,871,534	6,321,216	3,629,998	2,362,886	1,940,032	7,429,845	4,187,558	16,656,440	7,353,389	2,870,210	2,251,653
Colorado....................	5,637,979	4,689,736	1,792,470	908,962	542,275	508,746	561,249	376,034	809,403	30,479	84,923	138,839
Connecticut................	3,069,149	1,732,051	603,443	172,748	96,997	274,951	304,861	279,052	1,185,345	926,224	0	151,753
Delaware....................	1,333,327	809,517	443,232	140,148	44,219	137,989	0	43,929	513,370	236,730	0	10,440
District of Columbia......	165,210	56,442	29,414	13,327	9,950	661	0	3,090	88,809	75,405	0	19,960
Florida.......................	10,520,522	5,321,652	2,289,055	1,079,917	999,049	768,736	0	184,896	4,824,910	2,765,668	0	373,960
Georgia......................	7,870,675	4,456,367	1,853,232	797,247	567,072	814,399	185,045	239,371	3,001,508	1,887,336	69	412,799
Hawaii........................	1,576,969	798,169	243,009	347,834	69,639	85,589	0	52,099	613,116	372,872	0	165,684
Idaho.........................	1,263,122	651,172	314,100	115,315	57,328	121,324	0	43,105	566,671	334,283	26,483	45,278
Illinois.......................	12,345,250	6,077,507	2,436,756	865,063	421,893	892,821	675,818	785,156	5,998,214	1,830,155	1,028,222	269,530
Indiana.......................	6,720,526	4,230,584	2,205,556	576,799	289,142	757,616	0	401,471	2,407,263	1,393,030	8,241	82,680
Iowa..........................	5,164,897	3,739,928	887,046	541,718	146,786	487,133	1,356,530	320,715	1,309,720	752,635	117,353	115,249
Kansas.......................	3,419,968	1,930,113	804,302	336,410	219,666	336,940	0	232,794	1,389,483	743,076	255,347	100,373
Kentucky....................	5,291,995	3,472,209	977,383	412,577	217,501	313,301	1,139,203	412,244	1,680,595	920,031	19,349	139,191
Louisiana...................	3,985,874	2,509,918	864,738	311,532	451,688	362,397	337,874	181,689	1,355,485	874,193	0	120,471
Maine........................	885,026	483,104	219,955	62,024	56,591	90,931	0	53,602	380,604	251,703	0	21,317
Maryland....................	6,458,002	3,808,158	1,576,944	752,043	432,843	675,622	0	370,707	2,294,531	1,426,571	318,138	355,313
Massachusetts	4,800,266	3,052,620	1,269,990	381,863	243,726	463,163	0	693,879	1,494,867	1,042,983	0	252,780
Michigan	14,817,212	10,049,608	3,730,049	1,474,022	469,336	1,079,795	2,786,063	510,343	4,402,963	1,551,995	511,749	364,640
Minnesota..................	5,298,932	2,932,816	1,290,654	500,660	339,005	615,603	0	186,895	2,076,937	1,099,848	0	289,178
Mississippi	4,046,857	2,313,424	570,630	320,370	180,862	278,869	813,262	149,432	1,563,269	905,656	63,053	170,164
Missouri.....................	4,898,353	3,136,016	1,077,950	256,781	175,121	777,235	705,836	143,093	1,695,826	841,745	148,724	66,511
Montana.....................	992,157	656,460	287,630	158,417	35,166	87,138	0	88,108	321,164	193,116	8,622	14,533
Nebraska....................	2,503,592	1,287,636	421,947	225,302	197,580	311,861	27,392	103,554	1,066,703	631,041	134,270	149,252
Nevada......................	1,474,459	764,875	350,169	151,051	71,846	91,162	0	100,646	702,540	464,295	0	7,044
New Hampshire...........	1,042,622	750,075	392,293	76,158	54,956	198,053	0	28,616	206,855	94,372	0	85,692
New Jersey.................	5,636,445	3,301,867	1,956,875	348,193	252,687	575,479	0	168,634	2,228,366	1,127,237	194,041	106,212
New Mexico................	3,312,433	1,865,746	280,882	384,351	166,007	123,627	646,086	264,793	1,394,065	711,375	128,028	52,622
New York....................	15,490,768	7,847,928	2,500,582	778,365	1,203,418	641,884	2,538,562	185,117	6,915,047	3,549,146	802,810	727,792
North Carolina.............	10,667,584	4,500,331	1,653,429	832,589	328,271	1,476,575	0	209,466	5,683,548	3,549,146	206,763	483,705
North Dakota..............	1,155,107	686,227	285,907	140,101	60,278	114,628	0	85,312	398,576	312,859	3,025	70,304
Ohio..........................	13,025,768	8,954,332	3,538,492	752,546	546,018	1,125,848	2,674,429	316,999	3,773,805	1,875,678	151,995	297,632
Oklahoma...................	4,121,624	2,438,353	826,756	277,203	288,063	483,587	66,254	496,491	1,551,552	899,841	56,133	131,719
Oregon.......................	5,941,762	4,219,736	1,159,385	658,823	165,943	489,040	1,509,144	237,401	1,576,757	471,202	219,987	145,269
Pennsylvania	13,503,970	10,295,403	3,912,369	1,333,060	352,713	989,303	2,799,175	908,782	3,103,350	1,216,803	113,607	105,218
Rhode Island..............	762,531	516,474	279,382	82,265	18,223	105,945	0	30,659	207,110	141,512	0	38,947
South Carolina............	4,217,034	2,881,186	1,356,767	421,301	388,380	420,917	0	293,822	1,182,288	506,615	62,217	153,560
South Dakota..............	796,691	495,080	223,345	106,171	45,239	67,673	0	52,653	266,908	168,873	0	34,702
Tennessee..................	4,398,447	2,184,537	1,042,417	307,985	267,542	296,294	0	270,299	1,974,171	1,032,518	5,684	239,739
Texas........................	31,830,906	14,180,679	4,780,008	2,084,094	2,094,765	1,307,991	2,067,004	1,846,817	13,992,263	4,891,792	1,539,448	3,657,963
Utah..........................	5,055,326	3,693,349	712,244	401,920	142,756	214,464	1,422,544	799,420	1,189,560	697,252	0	172,417
Vermont.....................	865,372	683,629	357,548	125,655	69,805	103,247	3,018	24,355	162,597	67,725	0	19,146
Virginia......................	9,894,251	6,246,127	2,407,167	882,938	216,093	1,235,559	1,189,867	314,504	3,037,175	1,608,217	3,698	610,950
Washington................	8,515,256	5,930,569	1,788,615	1,282,000	675,936	559,932	1,162,389	461,634	2,203,003	1,060,355	0	381,684
West Virginia..............	1,900,281	1,148,270	546,394	133,418	189,092	225,805	0	53,561	626,526	439,393	719	125,486
Wisconsin..................	6,597,064	3,719,329	1,357,482	728,592	468,323	450,138	0	714,794	2,529,265	986,520	789,097	348,470
Wyoming....................	918,522	301,595	80,969	58,929	68,468	59,507	0	33,722	520,304	358,988	48,190	96,623
U.S. Service Academies.............	1,691,507	285,041	827	94,738	2,789	59,410	127,276	0	1,366,653	0	0	39,814
Other jurisdictions.	1,725,824	445,627	112,164	182,225	39,465	11,726	65,478	34,570	1,267,178	954,953	43,362	13,020
American Samoa........	20,181	10,848	4,149	6,224	0	163	0	311	9,333	1,830	0	0
Federated States of Micronesia............	23,089	6,332	1,592	1,404	1,101	1,760	0	476	16,757	0	0	0
Guam.........................	136,518	62,700	14,096	35,396	2,966	2,525	0	7,718	72,716	32,661	16,156	1,102
Marshall Islands	14,157	3,201	473	1,331	0	657	0	740	10,956	2,901	0	0
Northern Marianas.......	18,880	12,078	29,414	8,883	0	1,163	0	10	6,802	4,474	0	0
Palau.........................	11,290	4,718	2,722	1,750	0	81	0	164	6,572	2,411	0	0
Puerto Rico.................	1,425,049	308,415	72,890	109,671	33,210	2,347	65,478	24,820	1,108,708	910,675	2,319	7,926
U.S. Virgin Islands........	76,661	37,335	14,220	17,566	2,189	3,030	0	330	35,334	0	24,887	3,992

[1]Includes other categories not separately shown.
[2]After deducting discounts and allowances.
[3]Includes sales and services of educational activities.
NOTE: Degree-granting institutions grant associate's or higher degrees and participate in Title IV federal financial aid programs. Includes data for public institutions reporting data according to either the Governmental Accounting Standards Board (GASB) or the Financial Accounting Standards Board (FASB) questionnaire. Detail may not sum to totals because of rounding.
SOURCE: U.S. Department of Education, National Center for Education Statistics, Integrated Postsecondary Education Data System (IPEDS), Spring 2014, Finance component. (This table was prepared January 2015.)

Table 333.25. Revenues of public degree-granting postsecondary institutions, by source of revenue and state or jurisdiction: 2011–12
[In thousands of current dollars]

State or jurisdiction	Total revenues	Operating revenue Total	Tuition and fees[2]	Federal grants and contracts	State, local, and private grants and contracts	Sales and services of auxiliary enterprises[2]	Sales and services of hospitals	Independent operations and other[3]	Nonoperating revenue[1] Total	State appropriations	Local appropriations	Other revenues and additions
1	2	3	4	5	6	7	8	9	10	11	12	13
United States......	$317,306,882	$186,960,737	$65,386,643	$29,170,906	$16,974,510	$24,275,773	$33,508,840	$17,644,066	$114,741,226	$58,789,643	$10,214,576	$15,604,918
Alabama..................	6,898,551	4,470,826	1,445,641	638,664	234,802	377,327	1,430,697	343,695	2,266,648	1,332,025	1,277	161,078
Alaska.....................	984,645	323,106	124,504	63,452	75,364	40,611	0	19,175	494,218	358,441	10,031	167,322
Arizona...................	5,417,482	2,794,932	1,548,148	577,593	174,917	338,428	0	155,846	2,524,426	783,210	749,180	98,124
Arkansas................	3,746,046	2,299,638	441,167	298,138	187,638	246,418	876,544	249,734	1,338,735	755,308	31,131	107,673
California................	43,273,373	25,008,634	6,064,944	3,799,698	2,422,968	1,892,987	6,817,495	4,010,541	15,543,874	7,397,375	2,561,870	2,720,866
Colorado................	5,481,511	4,543,086	1,708,897	949,988	558,591	490,576	478,461	356,573	748,878	30,648	78,374	189,547
Connecticut............	3,112,449	1,705,133	590,081	173,699	98,321	270,590	289,388	283,054	1,117,577	892,046	0	289,739
Delaware...............	1,133,613	784,390	423,082	145,096	40,460	128,887	0	46,863	320,566	222,253	0	28,658
District of Columbia......	167,230	56,749	27,050	13,854	12,207	377	0	3,260	84,445	67,362	0	26,036
Florida...................	10,622,365	5,055,543	2,097,380	1,084,379	940,208	771,409	0	162,165	5,205,271	3,037,050	0	361,551
Georgia..................	7,664,812	4,299,845	1,780,346	776,296	529,480	800,241	196,911	216,571	2,979,565	1,847,730	44	385,401
Hawaii...................	1,584,602	780,940	238,172	346,662	60,956	87,631	0	47,518	616,659	375,754	0	187,003
Idaho....................	1,282,864	660,724	322,712	120,035	51,578	121,301	0	45,097	581,949	308,986	20,559	40,191
Illinois...................	11,780,728	5,996,283	2,393,531	888,551	394,977	910,618	655,563	753,043	5,582,666	1,815,619	1,015,855	201,779
Indiana..................	6,604,271	4,142,356	2,141,648	609,029	262,448	724,944	0	404,288	2,376,556	1,415,835	9,012	85,359
Iowa.....................	5,034,055	3,699,260	843,756	577,340	143,341	470,520	1,319,642	344,661	1,250,437	709,408	114,880	84,357
Kansas..................	3,320,431	1,898,469	758,127	370,136	188,492	307,221	0	274,493	1,323,151	719,033	233,851	98,812
Kentucky...............	5,148,333	3,425,174	954,277	438,238	245,000	300,764	1,084,839	402,057	1,623,158	969,989	17,501	100,000
Louisiana..............	4,000,467	2,386,961	791,720	333,795	442,797	340,265	287,764	190,621	1,463,053	944,649	0	150,453
Maine....................	919,695	493,225	216,316	67,108	68,063	92,353	0	49,385	374,279	255,518	0	52,191
Maryland...............	6,381,736	3,731,747	1,548,101	784,837	413,076	649,640	0	336,091	2,242,606	1,411,746	310,463	407,383
Massachusetts............	4,648,600	2,903,740	1,186,789	407,861	241,733	428,542	0	638,816	1,454,496	1,046,090	0	290,364
Michigan...............	13,321,669	9,614,780	3,564,224	1,469,930	418,510	1,072,373	2,601,803	487,939	3,401,418	1,490,701	523,771	305,471
Minnesota.............	5,053,633	2,918,488	1,265,215	513,955	348,166	597,554	0	193,597	1,937,790	1,095,626	0	197,354
Mississippi............	4,008,102	2,237,835	548,043	384,546	174,346	267,205	704,269	159,426	1,612,497	939,075	59,716	157,771
Missouri...............	4,736,828	3,021,550	1,023,031	265,314	187,060	734,490	656,903	154,752	1,623,104	836,519	146,266	92,174
Montana................	1,018,626	661,181	279,324	173,977	34,181	86,022	15,484	72,191	325,884	192,386	8,404	31,562
Nebraska..............	2,351,516	1,248,587	404,450	245,921	175,016	286,557	25,752	110,892	1,008,319	616,412	127,737	94,609
Nevada.................	1,362,281	694,960	335,187	141,148	65,159	91,760	0	61,706	643,010	466,961	0	24,312
New Hampshire...........	939,405	724,302	371,385	65,790	64,294	198,475	0	24,358	174,129	80,192	0	40,975
New Jersey................	7,319,457	4,631,023	2,025,314	497,186	410,975	585,610	920,868	191,069	2,531,469	1,495,920	194,452	156,965
New Mexico............	3,203,410	1,822,786	273,385	385,027	157,246	120,755	624,117	262,256	1,301,481	675,069	126,890	79,143
New York...............	15,687,238	7,840,647	2,410,166	795,823	1,048,339	927,283	2,459,479	199,557	7,120,420	4,248,791	797,232	726,171
North Carolina.........	10,263,991	4,289,664	1,539,459	823,784	309,500	1,427,382	974	188,566	5,330,955	3,387,420	200,980	643,372
North Dakota............	1,115,052	691,468	275,366	164,278	58,833	113,007	0	79,984	365,624	276,228	2,686	57,960
Ohio.....................	12,202,046	8,689,965	3,427,072	791,674	502,995	1,116,246	2,550,550	301,429	3,278,851	1,861,830	158,190	233,230
Oklahoma..............	4,042,219	2,363,087	771,736	269,595	292,237	456,635	67,631	505,254	1,533,106	898,544	50,986	146,025
Oregon..................	5,722,757	4,105,013	1,122,000	675,695	172,101	459,727	1,442,402	233,088	1,493,524	583,336	210,454	124,220
Pennsylvania..........	12,076,791	9,495,751	3,841,626	1,300,138	330,584	984,355	2,412,708	626,339	2,480,199	1,189,943	111,524	100,840
Rhode Island...........	780,754	522,339	264,236	87,381	38,536	102,825	0	29,361	209,791	141,208	0	48,624
South Carolina.........	4,063,314	2,755,593	1,304,733	416,150	360,754	398,300	0	275,654	1,155,894	465,402	62,126	151,828
South Dakota..........	800,354	512,259	214,192	125,186	43,018	66,209	0	63,654	247,252	159,652	0	40,843
Tennessee.............	4,297,676	2,151,942	992,372	332,362	257,387	299,677	0	270,145	1,903,832	1,002,136	5,655	241,901
Texas...................	30,178,634	13,571,633	4,655,347	2,082,244	2,023,194	1,259,078	1,922,484	1,629,287	12,954,728	5,022,641	1,452,266	3,652,272
Utah.....................	5,016,569	3,455,190	674,688	433,497	141,904	195,995	1,267,170	741,935	1,107,769	677,217	0	453,610
Vermont................	760,959	645,422	348,332	127,751	43,807	102,133	0	23,398	105,702	67,894	0	9,835
Virginia.................	9,215,536	6,003,793	2,302,342	850,969	199,854	1,171,606	1,173,193	305,829	2,562,990	1,441,710	5,141	648,753
Washington............	7,678,762	5,557,323	1,615,340	1,289,869	623,460	522,263	1,097,525	408,867	1,881,491	1,074,462	0	239,948
West Virginia..........	1,922,218	1,128,696	517,199	146,773	185,225	221,689	0	57,811	625,209	429,716	874	168,313
Wisconsin..............	6,404,192	3,558,863	1,294,046	712,773	452,724	482,556	0	616,764	2,393,871	943,010	769,923	451,458
Wyoming...............	804,486	281,495	78,962	45,014	62,851	59,262	0	35,405	494,402	333,566	45,274	28,589
U.S. Service Academies...........	1,750,547	304,344	1,480	92,709	4,838	77,093	128,223	0	1,423,303	0	0	22,900
Other jurisdictions.	1,833,704	585,614	122,708	239,686	76,116	14,326	86,819	45,959	1,240,687	891,770	40,258	7,403
American Samoa........	25,002	14,919	4,208	10,036	0	669	0	6	10,083	1,948	0	0
Federated States of Micronesia............	23,179	6,283	612	2,180	1,206	1,874	0	412	16,896	0	0	0
Guam.....................	147,097	68,274	15,693	34,233	3,322	2,559	0	12,467	77,719	34,197	14,569	1,104
Marshall Islands	18,067	2,157	534	0	250	1,012	0	362	15,909	2,875	0	0
Northern Marianas.......	19,824	13,279	2,527	9,473	0	1,265	0	16	6,545	3,749	0	0
Palau.....................	11,310	4,528	3,092	1,081	0	139	0	216	6,781	2,654	0	0
Puerto Rico...............	1,508,112	434,319	81,275	162,460	68,421	3,216	86,819	32,128	1,071,487	846,348	2	2,307
U.S. Virgin Islands........	81,113	41,854	14,768	20,223	2,917	3,593	0	354	35,267	0	25,687	3,992

[1]Includes other categories not separately shown.
[2]After deducting discounts and allowances.
[3]Includes sales and services of educational activities.
NOTE: Degree-granting institutions grant associate's or higher degrees and participate in Title IV federal financial aid programs. Includes data for public institutions reporting data according to either the Governmental Accounting Standards Board (GASB) or the Financial

Accounting Standards Board (FASB) questionnaire. Detail may not sum to totals because of rounding.
SOURCE: U.S. Department of Education, National Center for Education Statistics, Integrated Postsecondary Education Data System (IPEDS), Spring 2013, Finance component. (This table was prepared January 2014.)

Table 333.30. Appropriations from state and local governments for public degree-granting postsecondary institutions, by state or jurisdiction: Selected years, 1990–91 through 2012–13

[In thousands of current dollars]

State or jurisdiction	State appropriations						Local appropriations					
	1990–91	2000–01	2009–10	2010–11	2011–12	2012–13	1990–91	2000–01	2009–10	2010–11	2011–12	2012–13
1	2	3	4	5	6	7	8	9	10	11	12	13
United States	$35,898,653	$56,268,990	$62,456,235	$63,015,552	$58,789,643	$58,634,067	$3,159,789	$5,582,287	$9,954,504	$10,023,205	$10,214,576	$10,725,798
Alabama	708,191	991,302	1,289,317	1,281,923	1,332,025	1,289,898	6,796	4,829	1,124	1,204	1,277	1,337
Alaska	168,395	190,650	334,826	346,644	358,441	377,504	260	10,340	8,993	9,681	10,031	10,031
Arizona	591,656	903,196	1,011,599	1,006,196	783,210	772,257	149,337	310,762	734,888	746,962	749,180	763,521
Arkansas	315,372	583,794	753,337	753,573	755,308	759,693	216	9,496	30,776	30,375	31,131	30,714
California	5,313,052	7,891,669	8,849,101	9,338,728	7,397,375	7,353,389	771,160	1,764,717	2,447,042	2,490,105	2,561,870	2,870,210
Colorado	423,710	655,037	31,950	33,667	30,648	30,479	22,400	36,840	96,324	82,141	78,374	84,923
Connecticut	363,427	664,356	992,343	1,018,015	892,046	926,224	0	0	0	0	0	0
Delaware	115,729	193,695	219,409	214,445	222,253	236,730	0	0	0	0	0	0
District of Columbia ...	0	3,019	62,070	66,420	67,362	75,405	73,495	46,933	0	0	0	0
Florida	1,638,218	2,656,376	3,075,209	3,243,232	3,037,050	2,765,668	1,850	2	0	0	0	0
Georgia	915,303	1,826,961	1,770,643	1,938,523	1,847,730	1,887,336	25,705	21,615	0	23	44	69
Hawaii	304,131	395,884	366,836	359,077	375,754	372,872	0	0	0	0	0	0
Idaho	177,918	290,746	324,563	312,809	308,986	334,283	6,161	11,148	12,900	13,398	20,559	26,483
Illinois	1,296,895	1,760,300	1,779,108	1,789,707	1,815,619	1,830,155	284,635	520,136	967,455	1,001,566	1,015,855	1,028,222
Indiana	886,124	1,257,919	1,435,079	1,431,488	1,415,835	1,393,030	1,507	6,190	6,932	7,951	9,012	8,241
Iowa	544,945	813,805	781,895	731,485	709,408	752,635	21,624	36,129	99,099	107,022	114,880	117,353
Kansas	437,413	664,201	731,725	741,285	719,033	743,076	87,026	160,873	229,963	228,630	233,851	255,347
Kentucky	617,915	939,047	967,970	971,263	969,989	920,031	4,682	14,930	16,437	18,261	17,501	19,349
Louisiana	566,798	834,643	1,030,152	1,018,696	944,649	874,193	1,462	517	0	0	0	0
Maine	174,737	212,144	245,705	252,786	255,518	251,703	0	0	0	0	0	0
Maryland	724,223	999,723	1,276,246	1,392,864	1,411,746	1,426,571	117,913	185,034	328,704	319,337	310,463	318,138
Massachusetts	471,368	1,038,998	899,748	1,034,211	1,046,090	1,042,983	0	0	0	0	0	0
Michigan	1,326,884	1,991,098	1,786,389	1,713,747	1,490,701	1,551,995	159,202	288,112	596,436	551,945	523,771	511,749
Minnesota	744,381	1,174,797	1,242,407	1,206,301	1,095,626	1,099,848	2,040	0	0	0	0	0
Mississippi	365,574	758,242	895,859	868,311	939,075	905,656	25,670	38,167	57,730	58,179	59,716	63,053
Missouri	563,430	945,746	992,722	904,594	836,519	841,745	38,097	101,562	146,283	148,970	146,266	148,724
Montana	110,199	137,341	174,784	173,250	192,386	193,116	3,310	4,069	8,105	8,151	8,404	8,622
Nebraska	318,482	514,235	629,652	621,957	616,412	631,041	36,569	19,892	122,263	120,979	127,737	134,270
Nevada	161,581	333,117	388,082	539,712	466,961	464,295	0	0	0	0	0	0
New Hampshire	71,226	96,157	130,868	131,878	80,192	94,372	6	0	0	7	0	0
New Jersey	854,989	1,246,554	1,549,086	1,495,505	1,495,920	1,127,237	145,010	172,667	211,947	211,638	194,452	194,041
New Mexico	307,083	538,822	773,235	724,046	675,069	711,375	34,364	60,183	119,340	120,930	126,890	128,028
New York	2,313,128	4,461,671	4,350,324	4,247,113	4,248,791	4,311,984	372,650	431,415	757,504	762,484	797,232	802,810
North Carolina	1,351,111	2,221,600	3,375,984	3,434,423	3,387,420	3,549,146	62,785	113,448	194,949	196,168	200,980	206,763
North Dakota	129,986	188,047	267,744	268,488	276,228	312,859	9	21	185	2,459	2,686	3,025
Ohio	1,360,141	1,922,571	1,884,232	1,888,347	1,861,830	1,875,678	63,899	101,647	145,807	163,891	158,190	151,995
Oklahoma	473,898	754,540	928,324	924,623	898,544	899,841	12,822	28,367	48,197	49,857	50,986	56,133
Oregon	377,476	640,347	666,799	537,918	583,336	471,202	118,499	106,436	203,681	206,762	210,454	219,987
Pennsylvania	962,121	1,331,544	1,420,760	1,401,316	1,189,943	1,216,803	62,794	94,338	118,747	117,967	111,524	113,607
Rhode Island	113,614	157,137	137,159	137,071	141,208	141,512	0	0	0	0	0	0
South Carolina	578,794	853,139	604,283	480,329	465,402	506,615	18,670	36,060	61,419	62,799	62,126	62,217
South Dakota	81,859	129,680	163,817	157,444	159,652	168,873	0	0	0	0	0	0
Tennessee	663,536	969,316	1,089,782	1,250,509	1,002,136	1,032,518	1,779	3,824	5,184	5,327	5,655	5,684
Texas	2,627,916	4,236,852	5,445,771	5,179,075	5,022,641	4,891,792	210,934	439,342	1,384,512	1,377,390	1,452,266	1,539,448
Utah	304,738	531,975	658,038	661,823	677,217	697,252	0	0	0	0	0	0
Vermont	40,997	53,605	76,575	72,466	67,894	67,725	4	0	0	0	0	0
Virginia	886,208	1,395,308	1,433,589	1,516,128	1,441,710	1,608,217	973	1,570	2,289	3,737	5,141	3,698
Washington	828,700	1,200,392	1,367,777	1,329,108	1,074,462	1,060,355	2,470	0	0	0	0	0
West Virginia	263,269	382,269	393,821	395,050	429,716	439,393	574	503	451	316	874	719
Wisconsin	841,192	1,186,415	1,099,243	1,151,462	943,010	986,520	197,712	379,648	739,123	757,773	769,923	789,097
Wyoming	120,623	149,009	300,301	326,523	333,566	358,988	12,721	20,525	49,716	38,818	45,274	48,190
U.S. Service Academies	0	0	0	0	0	0	0	0	0	0	0	0
Other jurisdictions.	337,393	709,473	901,837	883,692	891,770	954,953	12,724	20,612	50,593	46,944	40,258	43,362
American Samoa	0	0	0	0	1,948	1,830	0	0	0	0	0	0
Federated States of Micronesia	0	40	0	0	0	0	0	3,327	0	0	0	0
Guam	28,283	29,122	33,072	31,936	34,197	32,661	10,028	12,826	16,516	15,700	14,569	16,156
Marshall Islands	0	1,924	2,000	2,000	2,875	2,901	0	0	0	0	0	0
Northern Marianas	0	9,055	5,323	4,385	3,749	4,474	0	0	0	0	0	0
Palau	644	2,345	2,310	2,039	2,654	2,411	0	0	0	0	0	0
Puerto Rico	277,295	647,623	859,133	843,332	846,348	910,675	2,375	4,459	2,651	1,824	2	2,319
U.S. Virgin Islands	31,170	19,365	0	0	0	0	320	0	31,427	29,420	25,687	24,887

NOTE: Data for 1990–91 are for institutions of higher education, while later data are for degree-granting institutions. Degree-granting institutions grant associate's or higher degrees and participate in Title IV federal financial aid programs. The degree-granting classification is very similar to the earlier higher education classification, but it includes more 2-year colleges and excludes a few higher education institutions that did not grant degrees. Includes data for public institutions reporting data according to either the Govern-mental Accounting Standards Board (GASB) or the Financial Accounting Standards Board (FASB) questionnaire. Detail may not sum to totals because of rounding.
SOURCE: U.S. Department of Education, National Center for Education Statistics, Integrated Postsecondary Education Data System (IPEDS), "Finance Survey" (IPEDS-F:FY91); and Spring 2002 through Spring 2014, Finance component. (This table was prepared January 2015.)

Table 333.40. Total revenue of private nonprofit degree-granting postsecondary institutions, by source of funds and level of institution: 1999–2000 through 2012–13

Level of institution and year	Total	Student tuition and fees (net of allowances)	Federal appropriations, grants, and contracts[1]	State and local appropriations, grants, and contracts	Private gifts, grants, and contracts — Total	Private grants and contracts	Private gifts and contributions from affiliated entities	Investment return (gain or loss)	Educational activities	Auxiliary enterprises (net of allowances)	Hospitals	Other
1	2	3	4	5	6	7	8	9	10	11	12	13
					In thousands of current dollars							
All levels												
1999–2000	$120,625,806	$29,651,812	$12,191,827	$1,697,979	$16,488,984	—	—	$37,763,518	$2,865,606	$8,317,607	$7,208,600	$4,439,874
2000–01	82,174,492	31,318,106	13,378,019	1,684,425	15,859,313	—	—	-3,602,326	3,468,680	8,742,610	7,126,343	4,199,323
2001–02	84,346,652	33,499,121	14,790,235	1,796,930	15,394,353	—	—	-6,545,330	3,220,868	9,317,922	8,083,935	4,788,618
2002–03	105,672,753	36,019,267	16,625,072	1,988,977	14,380,351	—	—	9,340,400	3,056,259	9,833,972	8,942,047	5,486,409
2003–04	134,230,762	38,505,631	18,335,784	1,941,273	15,847,571	—	—	30,896,917	3,290,420	10,325,606	9,657,753	5,429,805
2004–05	140,150,716	41,394,424	19,699,204	1,957,921	16,738,916	—	—	30,431,521	3,595,559	10,823,963	10,377,808	5,131,401
2005–06	152,744,665	44,263,227	19,683,291	2,075,850	18,346,525	—	—	35,634,520	3,716,409	11,610,762	11,536,658	5,877,423
2006–07	182,381,275	47,481,431	20,193,637	2,165,371	20,193,231	—	—	55,907,662	4,105,289	12,291,973	12,636,904	7,405,779
2007–08	139,250,857	50,736,003	20,204,523	2,385,888	20,991,936	—	—	6,446,982	4,849,728	12,928,521	13,299,928	7,407,348
2008–09	69,064,329	53,707,913	21,023,733	2,391,285	17,671,730	—	—	-64,205,252	4,791,466	13,559,084	14,802,999	5,321,371
2009–10	168,689,242	56,355,862	22,913,792	2,193,084	18,017,260	$4,189,573	$13,827,687	28,425,581	4,821,825	14,080,329	16,541,461	5,340,047
2010–11	207,236,345	60,047,027	24,334,677	2,165,996	22,100,617	4,379,206	17,721,411	53,571,921	4,992,000	14,797,598	17,521,091	7,705,419
2011–12	161,868,611	63,021,108	24,147,119	1,964,938	21,617,966	4,446,490	17,171,476	4,544,786	5,082,882	15,499,433	18,667,425	7,322,955
2012–13	202,084,062	65,595,255	23,714,629	1,938,964	22,336,587	4,834,524	17,502,063	38,537,742	5,534,688	15,957,898	19,011,711	9,456,589
4–year												
1999–2000	119,708,625	29,257,523	12,133,829	1,673,707	16,346,616	—	—	37,698,219	2,837,784	8,261,507	7,208,600	4,290,841
2000–01	81,568,928	30,996,381	13,318,572	1,659,505	15,788,869	—	—	-3,623,323	3,452,731	8,703,316	7,125,648	4,147,227
2001–02	83,764,907	33,165,965	14,708,582	1,771,383	15,328,974	—	—	-6,547,915	3,206,440	9,263,171	8,083,935	4,784,371
2002–03	105,064,157	35,676,736	16,515,854	1,957,729	14,319,622	—	—	9,338,684	3,041,307	9,779,275	8,942,047	5,492,904
2003–04	133,594,668	38,181,648	18,236,313	1,903,374	15,789,672	—	—	30,854,091	3,277,767	10,287,215	9,657,753	5,406,836
2004–05	139,528,763	41,045,608	19,622,002	1,931,021	16,671,017	—	—	30,408,545	3,581,869	10,784,161	10,377,808	5,106,733
2005–06	152,150,193	43,944,766	19,607,858	2,045,814	18,288,085	—	—	35,603,805	3,699,630	11,573,115	11,536,658	5,850,463
2006–07	181,853,949	47,211,041	20,137,112	2,144,350	20,143,850	—	—	55,857,220	4,097,001	12,253,297	12,636,904	7,373,173
2007–08	138,749,560	50,431,352	20,143,833	2,361,511	20,938,774	—	—	6,459,197	4,838,649	12,890,431	13,299,928	7,385,886
2008–09	68,617,694	53,408,932	20,964,805	2,370,216	17,625,407	—	—	-64,173,065	4,785,951	13,522,267	14,802,999	5,310,181
2009–10	168,169,978	56,056,932	22,843,558	2,179,072	17,966,413	4,185,606	13,780,807	28,404,786	4,814,426	14,044,652	16,541,461	5,318,679
2010–11	206,577,102	59,582,471	24,274,070	2,150,455	22,061,064	4,376,380	17,684,684	53,555,533	4,987,562	14,762,886	17,521,091	7,681,969
2011–12	161,272,285	62,582,114	24,098,850	1,953,324	21,579,107	4,443,977	17,135,131	4,539,625	5,079,876	15,471,108	18,667,425	7,300,856
2012–13	201,568,379	65,246,827	23,668,765	1,925,440	22,294,772	4,832,217	17,462,555	38,524,192	5,531,823	15,928,400	19,011,711	9,436,448
2–year												
1999–2000	917,181	394,289	57,998	24,272	142,368	—	—	65,299	27,822	56,100	0	149,033
2000–01	605,564	321,724	59,446	24,920	70,444	—	—	20,996	15,949	39,294	694	52,096
2001–02	581,745	333,156	81,653	25,547	65,379	—	—	2,585	14,429	54,750	0	4,246
2002–03	608,596	342,531	109,217	31,247	60,729	—	—	1,716	14,953	54,697	0	-6,495
2003–04	636,094	323,983	99,471	37,900	57,900	—	—	42,826	12,653	38,391	0	22,969
2004–05	621,953	348,815	77,202	26,900	67,899	—	—	22,976	13,690	39,802	0	24,668
2005–06	594,473	318,460	75,433	30,036	58,441	—	—	30,716	16,778	37,648	0	26,960
2006–07	527,327	270,389	56,525	21,021	49,381	—	—	50,442	8,288	38,675	0	32,606
2007–08	501,297	304,651	60,689	24,377	53,162	—	—	-12,214	11,080	38,091	0	21,462
2008–09	446,635	298,981	58,927	21,069	46,323	—	—	-32,187	5,515	36,816	0	11,191
2009–10	519,264	298,930	70,235	14,012	50,847	3,967	46,880	20,795	7,400	35,677	0	21,368
2010–11	659,244	464,556	60,607	15,541	39,553	2,825	36,727	16,388	4,437	34,712	0	23,450
2011–12	596,326	438,994	48,269	11,614	38,858	2,513	36,345	5,161	3,007	28,325	0	22,099
2012–13	515,683	348,427	45,863	13,524	41,815	2,307	39,508	13,550	2,865	29,498	0	20,140
					Percentage distribution							
All levels												
1999–2000	100.00	24.58	10.11	1.41	13.67	—	—	31.31	2.38	6.90	5.98	3.68
2000–01	100.00	38.11	16.28	2.05	19.30	—	—	-4.38	4.22	10.64	8.67	5.11
2001–02	100.00	39.72	17.54	2.13	18.25	—	—	-7.76	3.82	11.05	9.58	5.68
2002–03	100.00	34.09	15.73	1.88	13.61	—	—	8.84	2.89	9.31	8.46	5.19
2003–04	100.00	28.69	13.66	1.45	11.81	—	—	23.02	2.45	7.69	7.19	4.05
2004–05	100.00	29.54	14.06	1.40	11.94	—	—	21.71	2.57	7.72	7.40	3.66
2005–06	100.00	28.98	12.89	1.36	12.01	—	—	23.33	2.43	7.60	7.55	3.85
2006–07	100.00	26.03	11.07	1.19	11.07	—	—	30.65	2.25	6.74	6.93	4.06
2007–08	100.00	36.43	14.51	1.71	15.07	—	—	4.63	3.48	9.28	9.55	5.32
2008–09	100.00	77.77	30.44	3.46	25.59	—	—	-92.96	6.94	19.63	21.43	7.70
2009–10	100.00	33.41	13.58	1.30	10.68	2.48	8.20	16.85	2.86	8.35	9.81	3.17
2010–11	100.00	28.98	11.74	1.05	10.66	2.11	8.55	25.85	2.41	7.14	8.45	3.72
2011–12	100.00	38.93	14.92	1.21	13.36	2.75	10.61	2.81	3.14	9.58	11.53	4.52
2012–13	100.00	32.46	11.74	0.96	11.05	2.39	8.66	19.07	2.74	7.90	9.41	4.68
4–year												
1999–2000	100.00	24.44	10.14	1.40	13.66	—	—	31.49	2.37	6.90	6.02	3.58
2000–01	100.00	38.00	16.33	2.03	19.36	—	—	-4.44	4.23	10.67	8.74	5.08
2001–02	100.00	39.59	17.56	2.11	18.30	—	—	-7.82	3.83	11.06	9.65	5.71
2002–03	100.00	33.96	15.72	1.86	13.63	—	—	8.89	2.89	9.31	8.51	5.23
2003–04	100.00	28.58	13.65	1.42	11.82	—	—	23.10	2.45	7.70	7.23	4.05
2004–05	100.00	29.42	14.06	1.38	11.95	—	—	21.79	2.57	7.73	7.44	3.66
2005–06	100.00	28.88	12.89	1.34	12.02	—	—	23.40	2.43	7.61	7.58	3.85
2006–07	100.00	25.96	11.07	1.18	11.08	—	—	30.72	2.25	6.74	6.95	4.05
2007–08	100.00	36.35	14.52	1.70	15.09	—	—	4.66	3.49	9.29	9.59	5.32
2008–09	100.00	77.84	30.55	3.45	25.69	—	—	-93.52	6.97	19.71	21.57	7.74
2009–10	100.00	33.33	13.58	1.30	10.68	2.49	8.19	16.89	2.86	8.35	9.84	3.16
2010–11	100.00	28.84	11.75	1.04	10.68	2.12	8.56	25.93	2.41	7.15	8.48	3.72
2011–12	100.00	38.81	14.94	1.21	13.38	2.76	10.62	2.81	3.15	9.59	11.58	4.53
2012–13	100.00	32.37	11.74	0.96	11.06	2.40	8.66	19.11	2.74	7.90	9.43	4.68

See notes at end of table.

Table 333.40. Total revenue of private nonprofit degree-granting postsecondary institutions, by source of funds and level of institution: 1999–2000 through 2012–13—Continued

Level of institution and year	Total	Student tuition and fees (net of allowances)	Federal appropriations, grants, and contracts[1]	State and local appropriations, grants, and contracts	Private gifts, grants, and contracts			Investment return (gain or loss)	Educational activities	Auxiliary enterprises (net of allowances)	Hospitals	Other
					Total	Private grants and contracts	Private gifts and contributions from affiliated entities					
1	2	3	4	5	6	7	8	9	10	11	12	13
2-year												
1999–2000	100.00	42.99	6.32	2.65	15.52	—	—	7.12	3.03	6.12	0.00	16.25
2000–01	100.00	53.13	9.82	4.12	11.63	—	—	3.47	2.63	6.49	0.11	8.60
2001–02	100.00	57.27	14.04	4.39	11.24	—	—	0.44	2.48	9.41	0.00	0.73
2002–03	100.00	56.28	17.95	5.13	9.98	—	—	0.28	2.46	8.99	0.00	-1.07
2003–04	100.00	50.93	15.64	5.96	9.10	—	—	6.73	1.99	6.04	0.00	3.61
2004–05	100.00	56.08	12.41	4.33	10.92	—	—	3.69	2.20	6.40	0.00	3.97
2005–06	100.00	53.57	12.69	5.05	9.83	—	—	5.17	2.82	6.33	0.00	4.54
2006–07	100.00	51.28	10.72	3.99	9.36	—	—	9.57	1.57	7.33	0.00	6.18
2007–08	100.00	60.77	12.11	4.86	10.60	—	—	-2.44	2.21	7.60	0.00	4.28
2008–09	100.00	66.94	13.19	4.72	10.37	—	—	-7.21	1.23	8.24	0.00	2.51
2009–10	100.00	57.57	13.53	2.70	9.79	0.76	9.03	4.00	1.43	6.87	0.00	4.12
2010–11	100.00	70.47	9.19	2.36	6.00	0.43	5.57	2.49	0.67	5.27	0.00	3.56
2011–12	100.00	73.62	8.09	1.95	6.52	0.42	6.09	0.87	0.50	4.75	0.00	3.71
2012–13	100.00	67.57	8.89	2.62	8.11	0.45	7.66	2.63	0.56	5.72	0.00	3.91
Revenue per full-time-equivalent student in constant 2013–14 dollars[2]												
All levels												
1999–2000	$65,942	$16,210	$6,665	$928	$9,014	—	—	$20,644	$1,567	$4,547	$3,941	$2,427
2000–01	42,589	16,232	6,934	873	8,220	—	—	-1,867	1,798	4,531	3,693	2,176
2001–02	42,032	16,694	7,370	895	7,671	—	—	-3,262	1,605	4,643	4,028	2,386
2002–03	49,862	16,996	7,845	939	6,785	—	—	4,407	1,442	4,640	4,219	2,589
2003–04	60,502	17,356	8,264	875	7,143	—	—	13,926	1,483	4,654	4,353	2,447
2004–05	59,868	17,682	8,415	836	7,150	—	—	12,999	1,536	4,624	4,433	2,192
2005–06	61,998	17,966	7,989	843	7,447	—	—	14,464	1,508	4,713	4,683	2,386
2006–07	70,886	18,455	7,849	842	7,849	—	—	21,730	1,596	4,778	4,912	2,878
2007–08	50,912	18,550	7,387	872	7,675	—	—	2,357	1,773	4,727	4,863	2,708
2008–09	24,523	19,071	7,465	849	6,275	—	—	-22,798	1,701	4,815	5,256	1,890
2009–10	57,846	19,325	7,857	752	6,178	$1,437	$4,742	9,748	1,653	4,828	5,672	1,831
2010–11	67,036	19,424	7,872	701	7,149	1,417	5,732	17,329	1,615	4,787	5,668	2,493
2011–12	50,423	19,632	7,522	612	6,734	1,385	5,349	1,416	1,583	4,828	5,815	2,281
2012–13	61,202	19,866	7,182	587	6,765	1,464	5,301	11,671	1,676	4,833	5,758	2,864
4-year												
1999–2000	66,843	16,337	6,775	935	9,128	—	—	21,050	1,585	4,613	4,025	2,396
2000–01	42,935	16,316	7,011	874	8,311	—	—	-1,907	1,817	4,581	3,751	2,183
2001–02	42,366	16,774	7,439	896	7,753	—	—	-3,312	1,622	4,685	4,089	2,420
2002–03	50,241	17,061	7,898	936	6,848	—	—	4,466	1,454	4,676	4,276	2,627
2003–04	60,984	17,429	8,325	869	7,208	—	—	14,084	1,496	4,696	4,409	2,468
2004–05	60,326	17,746	8,484	835	7,208	—	—	13,147	1,549	4,663	4,487	2,208
2005–06	62,428	18,031	8,045	839	7,504	—	—	14,608	1,518	4,748	4,734	2,400
2006–07	71,294	18,509	7,895	841	7,897	—	—	21,898	1,606	4,804	4,954	2,891
2007–08	51,183	18,604	7,431	871	7,724	—	—	2,383	1,785	4,755	4,906	2,725
2008–09	24,572	19,126	7,507	849	6,312	—	—	-22,980	1,714	4,842	5,301	1,902
2009–10	58,142	19,381	7,898	753	6,212	1,447	4,764	9,820	1,665	4,856	5,719	1,839
2010–11	67,539	19,480	7,936	703	7,213	1,431	5,782	17,510	1,631	4,827	5,728	2,512
2011–12	50,736	19,688	7,581	615	6,789	1,398	5,391	1,428	1,598	4,867	5,873	2,297
2012–13	61,559	19,926	7,228	588	6,809	1,476	5,333	11,765	1,689	4,865	5,806	2,882
2-year												
1999–2000	23,900	10,274	1,511	632	3,710	—	—	1,702	725	1,462	0	3,884
2000–01	20,417	10,847	2,004	840	2,375	—	—	708	538	1,325	23	1,756
2001–02	19,694	11,279	2,764	865	2,213	—	—	88	488	1,854	0	144
2002–03	21,655	12,188	3,886	1,112	2,161	—	—	61	532	1,946	0	-231
2003–04	22,743	11,584	3,557	1,355	2,070	—	—	1,531	452	1,373	0	821
2004–05	22,140	12,417	2,748	958	2,417	—	—	818	487	1,417	0	878
2005–06	22,440	12,021	2,847	1,134	2,206	—	—	1,159	633	1,421	0	1,018
2006–07	23,848	12,228	2,556	951	2,233	—	—	2,281	375	1,749	0	1,475
2007–08	20,615	12,528	2,496	1,002	2,186	—	—	-502	456	1,566	0	883
2008–09	18,831	12,606	2,484	888	1,953	—	—	-1,357	233	1,552	0	472
2009–10	21,835	12,570	2,953	589	2,138	167	1,971	874	311	1,500	0	899
2010–11	20,101	14,165	1,848	474	1,206	86	1,120	500	135	1,058	0	715
2011–12	18,926	13,933	1,532	369	1,233	80	1,153	164	95	899	0	701
2012–13	18,735	12,659	1,666	491	1,519	84	1,435	492	104	1,072	0	732

—Not available.
[1]Includes independent operations.
[2]Constant dollars based on the Consumer Price Index, prepared by the Bureau of Labor Statistics, U.S. Department of Labor, adjusted to a school-year basis.
NOTE: Degree-granting institutions grant associate's or higher degrees and participate in Title IV federal financial aid programs. Detail may not sum to totals because of rounding.

SOURCE: U.S. Department of Education, National Center for Education Statistics, Integrated Postsecondary Education Data System (IPEDS), "Fall Enrollment Survey" (IPEDS-EF:99); and Spring 2001 through Spring 2014, Enrollment and Finance components. (This table was prepared January 2015.)

Table 333.50. Total revenue of private nonprofit degree-granting postsecondary institutions, by source of funds and classification of institution: 2012–13

Classification of institution	Total	Student tuition and fees (net of allowances)	Federal appropriations, grants, and contracts[1]	State and local appropriations, grants, and contracts	Private grants and contracts	Private gifts and contributions from affiliated entities	Investment return (gain or loss)	Educational activities	Auxiliary enterprises (net of allowances)	Hospitals	Other
1	2	3	4	5	6	7	8	9	10	11	12
In thousands of current dollars											
Total	$202,084,062	$65,595,255	$23,714,629	$1,938,964	$4,834,524	$17,502,063	$38,537,742	$5,534,688	$15,957,898	$19,011,711	$9,456,589
4-year	201,568,379	65,246,827	23,668,765	1,925,440	4,832,217	17,462,555	38,524,192	5,531,823	15,928,400	19,011,711	9,436,448
Research university, very high[2]	97,581,867	14,212,716	18,185,555	896,133	3,287,663	8,127,553	23,447,562	4,081,708	4,340,008	15,008,297	5,994,673
Research university, high[3]	14,358,222	6,202,481	1,189,029	152,757	203,057	1,369,033	1,970,691	624,195	1,497,163	447,955	701,862
Doctoral/research[4]	9,059,885	5,818,095	216,545	77,368	92,152	620,460	992,907	63,779	961,691	0	216,887
Master's[5]	32,220,691	20,600,185	993,166	301,467	158,978	2,180,275	2,875,898	153,443	4,115,711	118,696	722,872
Baccalaureate[6]	28,925,929	11,818,296	777,335	158,522	193,778	3,564,962	7,391,967	142,884	4,202,361	1,470	674,354
Special-focus institutions[7]	19,421,785	6,595,055	2,307,135	339,192	896,590	1,600,272	1,845,166	465,814	811,466	3,435,293	1,125,802
Art, music, or design	2,466,054	1,544,807	29,754	14,037	23,550	218,906	318,458	29,169	236,182	0	51,191
Business and management	771,222	532,538	24,393	8,256	828	42,435	77,544	5,987	73,382	0	5,858
Engineering or technology	224,129	107,555	4,123	768	122	18,164	62,374	1,296	25,421	0	4,306
Law	694,152	541,859	9,177	3,444	5,373	31,974	75,769	841	15,102	0	10,613
Medical or other health	12,634,150	3,047,050	2,099,611	302,094	831,899	593,403	774,988	402,581	245,193	3,435,293	902,037
Theological	2,181,695	612,236	41,140	4,436	30,421	658,691	508,021	12,807	187,673	0	126,270
Tribal[8]	113,918	8,303	84,982	2,033	1,312	722	576	865	2,539	0	12,585
Other special focus	336,466	200,707	13,954	4,124	3,085	35,976	27,437	12,267	25,974	0	12,941
2-year	515,683	348,427	45,863	13,524	2,307	39,508	13,550	2,865	29,498	0	20,140
Associate's of arts	495,287	347,609	32,781	12,928	1,832	38,823	13,495	2,865	29,313	0	15,642
Tribal[8]	20,396	818	13,082	596	475	685	56	0	185	0	4,498
Percentage distribution											
Total	100.00	32.46	11.74	0.96	2.39	8.66	19.07	2.74	7.90	9.41	4.68
4-year	100.00	32.37	11.74	0.96	2.40	8.66	19.11	2.74	7.90	9.43	4.68
Research university, very high[2]	100.00	14.56	18.64	0.92	3.37	8.33	24.03	4.18	4.45	15.38	6.14
Research university, high[3]	100.00	43.20	8.28	1.06	1.41	9.53	13.73	4.35	10.43	3.12	4.89
Doctoral/research[4]	100.00	64.22	2.39	0.85	1.02	6.85	10.96	0.70	10.61	0.00	2.39
Master's[5]	100.00	63.93	3.08	0.94	0.49	6.77	8.93	0.48	12.77	0.37	2.24
Baccalaureate[6]	100.00	40.86	2.69	0.55	0.67	12.32	25.55	0.49	14.53	0.01	2.33
Special-focus institutions[7]	100.00	33.96	11.88	1.75	4.62	8.24	9.50	2.40	4.18	17.69	5.80
Art, music, or design	100.00	62.64	1.21	0.57	0.95	8.88	12.91	1.18	9.58	0.00	2.08
Business and management	100.00	69.05	3.16	1.07	0.11	5.50	10.05	0.78	9.52	0.00	0.76
Engineering or technology	100.00	47.99	1.84	0.34	0.05	8.10	27.83	0.58	11.34	0.00	1.92
Law	100.00	78.06	1.32	0.50	0.77	4.61	10.92	0.12	2.18	0.00	1.53
Medical or other health	100.00	24.12	16.62	2.39	6.58	4.70	6.13	3.19	1.94	27.19	7.14
Theological	100.00	28.06	1.89	0.20	1.39	30.19	23.29	0.59	8.60	0.00	5.79
Tribal[8]	100.00	7.29	74.60	1.78	1.15	0.63	0.51	0.76	2.23	0.00	11.05
Other special focus	100.00	59.65	4.15	1.23	0.92	10.69	8.15	3.65	7.72	0.00	3.85
2-year	100.00	67.57	8.89	2.62	0.45	7.66	2.63	0.56	5.72	0.00	3.91
Associate's of arts	100.00	70.18	6.62	2.61	0.37	7.84	2.72	0.58	5.92	0.00	3.16
Tribal[8]	100.00	4.01	64.14	2.92	2.33	3.36	0.27	0.00	0.91	0.00	22.05
Revenue per full-time-equivalent student in current dollars											
Total	$60,261	$19,560	$7,072	$578	$1,442	$5,219	$11,492	$1,650	$4,759	$5,669	$2,820
4-year	60,612	19,620	7,117	579	1,453	5,251	11,584	1,663	4,790	5,717	2,838
Research university, very high[2]	194,561	28,338	36,259	1,787	6,555	16,205	46,750	8,138	8,653	29,924	11,952
Research university, high[3]	51,577	22,280	4,271	549	729	4,918	7,079	2,242	5,378	1,609	2,521
Doctoral/research[4]	34,384	22,081	822	294	350	2,355	3,768	242	3,650	0	823
Master's[5]	26,047	16,653	803	244	129	1,763	2,325	124	3,327	96	584
Baccalaureate[6]	39,329	16,069	1,057	216	263	4,847	10,050	194	5,714	2	917
Special-focus institutions[7]	62,727	21,300	7,451	1,095	2,896	5,168	5,959	1,504	2,621	11,095	3,636
Art, music, or design	42,773	26,794	516	243	408	3,797	5,524	506	4,096	0	888
Business and management	24,025	16,589	760	257	26	1,322	2,416	187	2,286	0	182
Engineering or technology	14,721	7,064	271	50	8	1,193	4,097	85	1,670	0	283
Law	42,164	32,914	557	209	326	1,942	4,602	51	917	0	645
Medical or other health	118,232	28,515	19,648	2,827	7,785	5,553	7,252	3,767	2,295	32,148	8,441
Theological	30,616	8,592	577	62	427	9,243	7,129	180	2,634	0	1,772
Tribal[8]	41,230	3,005	30,757	736	475	261	209	313	919	0	4,555
Other special focus	46,091	27,494	1,911	565	423	4,928	3,759	1,680	3,558	0	1,773
2-year	18,447	12,464	1,641	484	83	1,413	485	102	1,055	0	720
Associate's of arts	18,076	12,686	1,196	472	67	1,417	493	105	1,070	0	571
Tribal[8]	36,749	1,474	23,571	1,074	857	1,235	100	0	333	0	8,105

[1]Includes independent operations.
[2]Research universities with a very high level of research activity.
[3]Research universities with a high level of research activity.
[4]Includes institutions that award at least 20 doctor's degrees per year, but did not have high levels of research activity.
[5]Master's institutions award at least 50 master's degrees per year.
[6]Baccalaureate institutions primarily emphasize undergraduate education. Also includes institutions classified as 4-year under the IPEDS system, which had been classified as 2-year in the Carnegie classification system because they primarily award associate's degrees.
[7]Special-focus 4-year institutions award degrees primarily in single fields of study, such as medicine, business, fine arts, theology, and engineering.

[8]Tribally controlled colleges are located on reservations and are members of the American Indian Higher Education Consortium.
NOTE: Relative levels of research activity for research universities were determined by an analysis of research and development expenditures, science and engineering research staffing, and doctoral degrees conferred, by field. Further information on the Carnegie 2005 classification system used in this table may be obtained from http://carnegieclassifications.iu.edu/. Degree-granting institutions grant associate's or higher degrees and participate in Title IV federal financial aid programs. Detail may not sum to totals because of rounding.
SOURCE: U.S. Department of Education, National Center for Education Statistics, Integrated Postsecondary Education Data System (IPEDS), Spring 2013, Enrollment component; and Spring 2014, Finance component. (This table was prepared January 2015.)

Table 333.55. Total revenue of private for-profit degree-granting postsecondary institutions, by source of funds and level of institution: Selected years, 1999–2000 through 2012–13

Level of institution and year	Total	Student tuition and fees (net of allowances)	Federal appropriations, grants, and contracts	State and local appropriations, grants, and contracts	Private gifts, grants, and contracts	Investment income and gains (losses)	Educational activities	Auxiliary enterprises (net of allowances)	Other
1	2	3	4	5	6	7	8	9	10
In thousands of current dollars									
All levels									
1999–2000	$4,321,985	$3,721,032	$198,923	$71,904	$2,151	$18,537	$70,672	$156,613	$82,153
2007–08	16,083,784	14,029,958	959,684	67,926	4,755	64,848	289,640	351,900	315,073
2008–09	19,373,779	16,740,041	1,407,615	130,378	80,345	38,707	368,034	395,728	212,930
2009–10	24,684,829	22,374,050	1,951,202	114,075	38,299	40,115	435,519	485,216	-753,647
2010–11	28,221,419	25,155,815	1,583,146	157,269	31,272	32,859	402,384	542,589	316,084
2011–12	26,922,879	24,035,276	1,527,947	102,568	9,386	36,726	352,468	511,364	347,145
2012–13	24,780,997	22,483,997	1,092,117	96,650	14,700	58,267	312,065	484,747	238,453
4-year									
1999–2000	2,381,042	2,050,136	103,865	39,460	1,109	10,340	33,764	102,103	40,266
2007–08	12,174,363	10,751,121	644,062	30,688	2,638	50,771	246,419	269,771	178,894
2008–09	14,766,008	12,954,629	897,503	80,021	71,601	35,461	327,474	297,764	101,555
2009–10	18,983,250	17,321,210	1,226,115	69,168	35,634	35,949	376,427	372,285	-453,538
2010–11	21,689,815	19,480,318	1,113,185	118,033	29,118	28,976	346,786	405,572	167,828
2011–12	21,204,816	18,942,669	1,143,845	70,872	7,298	30,546	308,909	404,301	296,375
2012–13	19,574,783	17,783,754	809,567	64,261	12,233	49,224	265,836	395,722	194,187
2-year									
1999–2000	1,940,943	1,670,896	95,058	32,444	1,042	8,197	36,908	54,510	41,888
2007–08	3,909,421	3,278,837	315,622	37,238	2,117	14,077	43,222	82,129	136,178
2008–09	4,607,770	3,785,412	510,112	50,358	8,745	3,246	40,560	97,964	111,374
2009–10	5,701,579	5,052,841	725,087	44,907	2,664	4,166	59,092	112,930	-300,108
2010–11	6,531,603	5,675,497	469,961	39,236	2,154	3,882	55,599	137,018	148,256
2011–12	5,718,063	5,092,607	384,102	31,696	2,087	6,180	43,558	107,063	50,770
2012–13	5,206,214	4,700,243	282,550	32,390	2,467	9,043	46,230	89,025	44,266
Percentage distribution									
All levels									
1999–2000	100.00	86.10	4.60	1.66	0.05	0.43	1.64	3.62	1.90
2007–08	100.00	87.23	5.97	0.42	0.03	0.40	1.80	2.19	1.96
2008–09	100.00	86.41	7.27	0.67	0.41	0.20	1.90	2.04	1.10
2009–10	100.00	90.64	7.90	0.46	0.16	0.16	1.76	1.97	-3.05
2010–11	100.00	89.14	5.61	0.56	0.11	0.12	1.43	1.92	1.12
2011–12	100.00	89.27	5.68	0.38	0.03	0.14	1.31	1.90	1.29
2012–13	100.00	90.73	4.41	0.39	0.06	0.24	1.26	1.96	0.96
4-year									
1999–2000	100.00	86.10	4.36	1.66	0.05	0.43	1.42	4.29	1.69
2007–08	100.00	88.31	5.29	0.25	0.02	0.42	2.02	2.22	1.47
2008–09	100.00	87.73	6.08	0.54	0.48	0.24	2.22	2.02	0.69
2009–10	100.00	91.24	6.46	0.36	0.19	0.19	1.98	1.96	-2.39
2010–11	100.00	89.81	5.13	0.54	0.13	0.13	1.60	1.87	0.77
2011–12	100.00	89.33	5.39	0.33	0.03	0.14	1.46	1.91	1.40
2012–13	100.00	90.85	4.14	0.33	0.06	0.25	1.36	2.02	0.99
2-year									
1999–2000	100.00	86.09	4.90	1.67	0.05	0.42	1.90	2.81	2.16
2007–08	100.00	83.87	8.07	0.95	0.05	0.36	1.11	2.10	3.48
2008–09	100.00	82.15	11.07	1.09	0.19	0.07	0.88	2.13	2.42
2009–10	100.00	88.62	12.72	0.79	0.05	0.07	1.04	1.98	-5.26
2010–11	100.00	86.89	7.20	0.60	0.03	0.06	0.85	2.10	2.27
2011–12	100.00	89.06	6.72	0.55	0.04	0.11	0.76	1.87	0.89
2012–13	100.00	90.28	5.43	0.62	0.05	0.17	0.89	1.71	0.85
Revenue per full-time-equivalent student in constant 2013–14 dollars[1]									
All levels									
1999–2000	$15,596	$13,428	$718	$259	$8	$67	$255	$565	$296
2007–08	17,322	15,110	1,034	73	5	70	312	379	339
2008–09	16,650	14,387	1,210	112	69	33	316	340	183
2009–10	16,660	15,100	1,317	77	26	27	294	327	-509
2010–11	18,205	16,228	1,021	101	20	21	260	350	204
2011–12	17,264	15,413	980	66	6	24	226	328	223
2012–13	17,783	16,135	784	69	11	42	224	348	171
4-year									
1999–2000	15,830	13,630	691	262	7	69	224	679	268
2007–08	17,126	15,124	906	43	4	71	347	379	252
2008–09	16,495	14,471	1,003	89	80	40	366	333	113
2009–10	16,665	15,206	1,076	61	31	32	330	327	-398
2010–11	18,379	16,507	943	100	25	25	294	344	142
2011–12	17,424	15,565	940	58	6	25	254	332	244
2012–13	17,955	16,313	743	59	11	45	244	363	178
2-year									
1999–2000	15,319	13,188	750	256	8	65	291	430	331
2007–08	17,962	15,065	1,450	171	10	65	199	377	626
2008–09	17,169	14,105	1,901	188	33	12	151	365	415
2009–10	16,643	14,749	2,117	131	8	12	172	330	-876
2010–11	17,650	15,337	1,270	106	6	10	150	370	401
2011–12	16,696	14,870	1,122	93	6	18	127	313	148
2012–13	17,164	15,496	932	107	8	30	152	294	146

[1]Constant dollars based on the Consumer Price Index, prepared by the Bureau of Labor Statistics, U.S. Department of Labor, adjusted to a school-year basis.
NOTE: Degree-granting institutions grant associate's or higher degrees and participate in Title IV federal financial aid programs. Detail may not sum to totals because of rounding.

SOURCE: U.S. Department of Education, National Center for Education Statistics, Integrated Postsecondary Education Data System (IPEDS), "Fall Enrollment Survey" (IPEDS-EF:99); and Spring 2002 through Spring 2014, Enrollment and Finance components. (This table was prepared January 2015.)

Table 333.60. Total revenue of private for-profit degree-granting postsecondary institutions, by source of funds and classification of institution: 2012–13

Classification of institution	Total	Student tuition and fees (net of allowances)	Federal appropriations, grants, and contracts	State and local appropriations, grants, and contracts	Private gifts, grants, and contracts	Investment income and gains (losses)	Educational activities	Auxiliary enterprises (net of allowances)	Other
1	2	3	4	5	6	7	8	9	10
In thousands of current dollars									
Total...........................	$24,780,997	$22,483,997	$1,092,117	$96,650	$14,700	$58,267	$312,065	$484,747	$238,453
4-year...........................	19,574,783	17,783,754	809,567	64,261	12,233	49,224	265,836	395,722	194,187
Doctoral/research[1].............	3,631,956	3,394,862	27,661	215	0	18,615	149,891	3,556	37,156
Master's[2].........................	4,948,753	4,773,684	27,987	1,598	0	3,297	48,609	81,237	12,341
Baccalaureate[3]...................	2,368,788	2,098,860	166,537	10,232	9,849	2,858	19,939	49,421	11,091
Special-focus institutions[4].....	8,625,286	7,516,348	587,382	52,216	2,383	24,454	47,397	261,507	133,599
Art, music, or design	2,520,306	1,945,422	343,404	37,720	163	4,322	67	154,574	34,633
Business and management	3,488,663	3,150,291	204,464	9,352	1,589	3,909	31,205	68,014	19,840
Engineering or technology	1,425,437	1,366,803	22,628	4,706	117	5,265	4,169	15,134	6,616
Law...............................	228,935	223,488	4,730	0	81	6	387	61	182
Medical or other health	800,895	755,153	12,156	438	434	9,295	7,782	6,182	9,455
Theological.......................	114,779	34,517	0	0	0	1,625	124	16,005	62,509
Other special focus	46,269	40,674	0	0	0	32	3,664	1,535	364
2-year...........................	5,206,214	4,700,243	282,550	32,390	2,467	9,043	46,230	89,025	44,266
Percentage distribution									
Total...........................	100.00	90.73	4.41	0.39	0.06	0.24	1.26	1.96	0.96
4-year...........................	100.00	90.85	4.14	0.33	0.06	0.25	1.36	2.02	0.99
Doctoral/research[1].............	100.00	93.47	0.76	0.01	0.00	0.51	4.13	0.10	1.02
Master's[2].........................	100.00	96.46	0.57	0.03	0.00	0.07	0.98	1.64	0.25
Baccalaureate[3]...................	100.00	88.60	7.03	0.43	0.42	0.12	0.84	2.09	0.47
Special-focus institutions[4].....	100.00	87.14	6.81	0.61	0.03	0.28	0.55	3.03	1.55
Art, music, or design	100.00	77.19	13.63	1.50	0.01	0.17	#	6.13	1.37
Business and management	100.00	90.30	5.86	0.27	0.05	0.11	0.89	1.95	0.57
Engineering or technology	100.00	95.89	1.59	0.33	0.01	0.37	0.29	1.06	0.46
Law...............................	100.00	97.62	2.07	0.00	0.04	#	0.17	0.03	0.08
Medical or other health	100.00	94.29	1.52	0.05	0.05	1.16	0.97	0.77	1.18
Theological.......................	100.00	30.07	0.00	0.00	0.00	1.42	0.11	13.94	54.46
Other special focus	100.00	87.91	0.00	0.00	0.00	0.07	7.92	3.32	0.79
2-year...........................	100.00	90.28	5.43	0.62	0.05	0.17	0.89	1.71	0.85
Revenue per full-time-equivalent student in current dollars									
Total...........................	$17,510	$15,887	$772	$68	$10	$41	$220	$343	$168
4-year...........................	17,679	16,062	731	58	11	44	240	357	175
Doctoral/research[1].............	11,141	10,414	85	1	0	57	460	11	114
Master's[2].........................	15,867	15,306	90	5	#	11	156	260	40
Baccalaureate[3]...................	19,365	17,158	1,361	84	81	23	163	404	91
Special-focus institutions[4].....	24,857	21,661	1,693	150	7	70	137	754	385
Art, music, or design	27,692	21,375	3,773	414	2	47	1	1,698	381
Business and management	22,979	20,750	1,347	62	10	26	206	448	131
Engineering or technology	23,819	22,839	378	79	2	88	70	253	111
Law...............................	34,640	33,816	716	0	12	1	59	9	28
Medical or other health	24,938	23,514	379	14	14	289	242	193	294
Theological.......................	36,140	10,868	0	0	0	512	39	5,039	19,682
Other special focus	19,167	16,849	0	0	0	13	1,518	636	151
2-year...........................	16,900	15,258	917	105	8	29	150	289	144
Revenue per full-time-equivalent student in constant 2013–14 dollars[5]									
Total...........................	$17,783	$16,135	$784	$69	$11	$42	$224	$348	$171
4-year...........................	17,955	16,313	743	59	11	45	244	363	178
Doctoral/research[1].............	11,315	10,576	86	1	0	58	467	11	116
Master's[2].........................	16,115	15,545	91	5	#	11	158	265	40
Baccalaureate[3]...................	19,667	17,426	1,383	85	82	24	166	410	92
Special-focus institutions[4].....	25,246	22,000	1,719	153	7	72	139	765	391
Art, music, or design	28,125	21,709	3,832	421	2	48	1	1,725	386
Business and management	23,338	21,074	1,368	63	11	26	209	455	133
Engineering or technology	24,191	23,196	384	80	2	89	71	257	112
Law...............................	35,181	34,344	727	0	12	1	59	9	28
Medical or other health	25,328	23,881	384	14	14	294	246	196	299
Theological.......................	36,704	11,038	0	0	0	520	40	5,118	19,989
Other special focus	19,467	17,112	0	0	0	13	1,541	646	153
2-year...........................	17,164	15,496	932	107	8	30	152	294	146

#Rounds to zero.
[1]Includes institutions that award at least 20 doctor's degrees per year, but did not have high levels of research activity.
[2]Master's institutions award at least 50 master's degrees per year.
[3]Baccalaureate institutions primarily emphasize undergraduate education. Also includes institutions classified as 4-year under the IPEDS system, which had been classified as 2-year in the Carnegie classification system because they primarily award associate's degrees.
[4]Special-focus 4-year institutions award degrees primarily in single fields of study, such as medicine, business, fine arts, theology, and engineering.

[5]Constant dollars based on the Consumer Price Index, prepared by the Bureau of Labor Statistics, U.S. Department of Labor, adjusted to a school-year basis.
NOTE: Degree-granting institutions grant associate's or higher degrees and participate in Title IV federal financial aid. Further information on the Carnegie 2005 classification system used in this table may be obtained from http://carnegieclassifications.iu.edu/. Detail may not sum to totals because of rounding.
SOURCE: U.S. Department of Education, National Center for Education Statistics, Integrated Postsecondary Education Data System (IPEDS), Spring 2013, Enrollment component; and Spring 2014, Finance component. (This table was prepared January 2015.)

Table 333.70. Revenue received from the federal government by the 120 degree-granting postsecondary institutions receiving the largest amounts, by control and rank order: 2012–13

Institution	Control[1]	Rank order	Revenue from the federal government[2] (in thousands)	Institution	Control[1]	Rank order	Revenue from the federal government[2] (in thousands)
1	2	3	4	1	2	3	4
United States (all institutions)	†	†	$78,737,208				
120 institutions receiving the largest amounts	†	†	46,149,338				
Johns Hopkins University (MD)	2	1	2,326,399	Icahn School of Medicine at Mount Sinai (NY)	2	61	278,748
California Institute of Technology	2	2	1,718,069	Purdue University, Main Campus (IN)	1	62	277,486
University of Chicago (IL)	2	3	1,573,706	University of California, Irvine	1	63	261,504
Massachusetts Institute of Technology	2	4	1,354,832	Virginia Polytechnic Institute and State University	1	64	253,406
University of Washington, Seattle Campus	1	5	1,103,484	University of Kentucky	1	65	250,045
Stanford University (CA)	2	6	1,017,022	Boston University (MA)	2	66	248,729
New York University	2	7	943,400	Princeton University (NJ)	2	67	248,237
Weill Cornell Medical College (NY)	2	8	897,738	University of Maryland, Baltimore	1	68	247,653
University of Michigan, Ann Arbor	1	9	896,789	University of Miami (FL)	2	69	247,045
University of Pennsylvania	2	10	794,636	University of Virginia, Main Campus	1	70	244,070
Columbia University in the City of New York	2	11	788,254	Ivy Tech Community College (IN)	1	71	232,730
University of Utah	1	12	777,010	University of South Florida, Main Campus	1	72	232,405
University of California, San Diego	1	13	734,178	University of New Mexico, Main Campus	1	73	226,419
University of Pittsburgh, Pittsburgh Campus (PA)	1	14	666,065	Indiana University-Purdue University, Indianapolis	1	74	222,358
University of North Carolina at Chapel Hill	1	15	665,055	University of Massachusetts Medical School, Worcester	1	75	220,665
Harvard University (MA)	2	16	653,373	Iowa State University	1	76	217,513
University of California, San Francisco	1	17	652,409	Colorado State University, Fort Collins	1	77	216,102
University of California, Los Angeles	1	18	652,037	Yeshiva University (NY)	2	78	204,250
University of Southern California	2	19	642,255	George Washington University (DC)	2	79	204,103
University of Wisconsin, Madison	1	20	570,491	Oregon State University	1	80	203,760
University of Minnesota, Twin Cities	1	21	549,062	University of Texas Southwestern Medical Center	1	81	203,336
Yale University (CT)	2	22	535,767	Florida State University	1	82	195,772
Duke University (NC)	2	23	535,382	University of Kansas	1	83	194,181
United States Air Force Academy (CO)	1	24	527,430	Miami-Dade College (FL)	1	84	193,831
Pennsylvania State University, Main Campus	1	25	522,696	University of Texas Health Science Center at Houston	1	85	181,028
Georgia Institute of Technology, Main Campus	1	26	516,034	North Carolina State University at Raleigh	1	86	179,561
Vanderbilt University (TN)	2	27	502,511	Stony Brook University (NY)	1	87	178,251
University of Texas at Austin	1	28	484,330	Virginia Commonwealth University	1	88	176,357
Washington University in St. Louis (MO)	2	29	470,152	Utah State University	1	89	175,557
University of Illinois at Urbana, Champaign	1	30	465,798	Washington State University	1	90	173,498
University of Arizona	1	31	449,427	University of California, Santa Barbara	1	91	172,100
United States Naval Academy (MD)	1	32	441,879	University of Cincinnati, Main Campus (OH)	1	92	170,759
Emory University (GA)	2	33	440,934	University of Missouri, Columbia	1	93	170,167
University of Florida	1	34	439,763	Wake Forest University (NC)	2	94	169,893
University of California, Davis	1	35	430,265	University of Central Florida	1	95	168,608
University of Oklahoma Health Sciences Center	1	36	409,849	Tulane University of Louisiana	2	96	157,401
University of California, Berkeley	1	37	407,751	University of Georgia	1	97	153,752
Ohio State University, Main Campus	1	38	406,232	Florida International University	1	98	152,902
Northwestern University (IL)	2	39	405,984	University of Nebraska, Lincoln	1	99	152,840
University of Maryland, College Park	1	40	374,649	Wayne State University (MI)	1	100	150,633
University of Connecticut	1	41	362,731	Indiana University, Bloomington	1	101	149,474
Carnegie Mellon University (PA)	2	42	362,255	Louisiana State University and Ag. & Mech. College	1	102	148,162
Michigan State University	1	43	351,990	Georgetown University (DC)	2	103	148,060
University of Alabama at Birmingham	1	44	340,914	University of South Carolina, Columbia	1	104	147,633
University of Colorado, Boulder	1	45	338,039	University at Buffalo (NY)	1	105	146,045
Cornell University (NY)	2	46	336,216	Brown University (RI)	2	106	145,583
Case Western Reserve University (OH)	2	47	332,550	Mississippi State University	1	107	140,042
Arizona State University, Tempe	1	48	328,567	Medical University of South Carolina	1	108	137,867
Texas A & M University, College Station	1	49	325,824	University of Texas Medical Branch	1	109	137,227
Howard University (DC)	2	50	324,416	State University of New York at Albany	1	110	133,184
University of Tennessee, Knoxville	1	51	323,508	New Mexico State University, Main Campus	1	111	129,212
Baylor College of Medicine (TX)	2	52	322,062	Kansas State University	1	112	128,732
University of Iowa	1	53	321,134	University of Massachusetts, Amherst	1	113	128,571
University of Illinois at Chicago	1	54	317,371	Medical College of Wisconsin	2	114	125,202
United States Military Academy (NY)	1	55	315,085	Tufts University (MA)	2	115	124,959
University of Hawaii at Manoa	1	56	311,104	University of California, Santa Cruz	1	116	124,404
University of Colorado, Denver	1	57	310,943	Temple University (PA)	1	117	124,101
Rutgers University, New Brunswick (NJ)	1	58	306,581	University of Vermont	1	118	122,350
University of Rochester (NY)	2	59	301,015	Dartmouth College (NH)	2	119	121,966
Oregon Health & Science University	1	60	281,903	University of Houston (TX)	1	120	121,608

†Not applicable.
[1]Publicly controlled institutions are identified by a "1"; private nonprofit, by a "2"; and private for-profit, by a "3."
[2]Includes federal appropriations; operating, nonoperating, unrestricted, and restricted federal contracts and grants; and revenue for independent operations. Independent operations generally include only the revenues associated with major federally funded research and development centers. Pell grants are included for public institutions and may also be included for private nonprofit institutions that do not treat Pell grants as pass-through trans-

actions. Data for public, private nonprofit, and private for profit institutions are only roughly comparable because they were collected using different survey instruments.
NOTE: Degree-granting institutions grant associate's or higher degrees and participate in Title IV federal financial aid programs.
SOURCE: U.S. Department of Education, National Center for Education Statistics, Integrated Postsecondary Education Data System (IPEDS), Spring 2014, Finance component. (This table was prepared May 2015.)

Table 333.80. Voluntary support for degree-granting postsecondary institutions, by source and purpose of support: Selected years, 1949–50 through 2012–13

Year	Total voluntary support, in millions of constant 2013–14 dollars[1]	In millions of current dollars										Voluntary support as a percent of total expenditures[2]
		Total voluntary support	Sources						Purpose		
			Alumni	Nonalumni individuals	Corporations	Foundations	Religious organizations	Other	Current operations	Capital purposes	
1	2	3	4	5	6	7	8	9	10	11	12
1949–50	$2,381	$240	$60	$60	$28	$60	$16	$16	$101	$139	10.7
1959–60	6,517	815	191	194	130	163	80	57	385	430	14.6
1965–66	10,604	1,440	310	350	230	357	108	85	675	765	11.5
1970–71	11,002	1,860	458	495	259	418	104	126	1,050	810	8.0
1975–76	10,211	2,410	588	569	379	549	130	195	1,480	930	6.2
1980–81	11,474	4,230	1,049	1,007	778	922	140	334	2,590	1,640	6.6
1985–86	15,979	7,400	1,825	1,781	1,702	1,363	211	518	4,022	3,378	7.6
1989–90	18,135	9,800	2,540	2,230	2,170	1,920	240	700	5,440	4,360	7.3
1990–91	17,897	10,200	2,680	2,310	2,230	2,030	240	710	5,830	4,370	7.0
1993–94	19,846	12,350	3,410	2,800	2,510	2,540	240	850	6,710	5,640	7.1
1994–95	19,918	12,750	3,600	2,940	2,560	2,460	250	940	7,230	5,520	7.0
1995–96	21,672	14,250	4,040	3,400	2,800	2,815	255	940	7,850	6,400	7.5
1996–97	23,658	16,000	4,650	3,850	3,050	3,200	250	1,000	8,500	7,500	8.0
1997–98	26,730	18,400	5,500	4,500	3,250	3,800	300	1,050	9,000	9,400	8.8
1998–99	29,131	20,400	5,930	4,810	3,610	4,530	330	1,190	9,900	10,500	9.3
1999–2000	32,200	23,200	6,800	5,420	4,150	5,080	370	1,380	11,270	11,930	9.8
2000–01	32,475	24,200	6,830	5,200	4,350	6,000	370	1,450	12,200	12,000	9.3
2001–02	31,515	23,900	5,900	5,400	4,370	6,300	360	1,570	12,400	11,500	8.5
2002–03	30,450	23,600	6,570	4,280	4,250	6,600	360	1,540	12,900	10,700	7.8
2003–04	30,808	24,400	6,700	5,200	4,400	6,200	350	1,550	13,600	10,800	7.7
2004–05	31,379	25,600	7,100	5,000	4,400	7,000	370	1,730	14,200	11,400	7.6
2005–06	33,062	28,000	8,400	5,700	4,600	7,100	375	1,825	15,000	13,000	7.9
2006–07	34,243	29,750	8,270	5,650	4,800	8,500	380	2,150	16,100	13,650	7.9
2007–08	35,073	31,600	8,700	6,120	4,900	9,100	380	2,400	17,070	14,530	7.7
2008–09	30,485	27,850	7,130	4,995	4,620	8,235	325	2,545	16,955	10,895	6.5
2009–10	30,355	28,000	7,100	4,920	4,730	8,400	305	2,545	17,000	11,000	6.3
2010–11	32,202	30,300	7,800	5,650	5,020	8,675	305	2,850	17,800	12,500	6.4
2011–12	32,008	31,000	7,700	5,825	5,250	9,150	275	2,800	18,900	12,100	6.3
2012–13	34,328	33,800	9,000	6,200	5,100	10,000	300	3,200	20,200	13,600	6.8

[1]Constant dollars based on the Consumer Price Index, prepared by the Bureau of Labor statistics, U.S. Department of Labor, adjusted to a school-year basis.
[2]Total expenditures include current-fund expenditures and additions to plant value through 1995–96.
NOTE: Data rounding is consistent with the original source material. Voluntary support data are from the Council for Aid to Education, while the percentage of total expenditures is based on total expenditures reported through the Integrated Postsecondary Education Data System.

SOURCE: Council for Aid to Education, *Voluntary Support of Education*, selected years, 1949–50 through 2012–13. U.S. Department of Education, National Center for Education Statistics, Higher Education General Information Survey (HEGIS), 1965–66 through 1985–86; *Financial Statistics of Institutions of Higher Education*, 1949–50 and 1959–60; Integrated Postsecondary Education Data System (IPEDS), "Finance Survey" (IPEDS-F:FY87–99); and IPEDS Spring 2001 through Spring 2014, Finance component. (This table was prepared April 2015.)

Table 333.90. Endowment funds of the 120 degree-granting postsecondary institutions with the largest endowments, by rank order: Fiscal year 2013

Institution	Rank order, end of FY[1]	Market value of endowment — Beginning of FY (in thousands)	End of FY (in thousands)	Percent change[2]
1	2	3	4	5
United States (all institutions)	†	$424,625,337	$466,659,158	9.9
120 institutions with the largest amounts	†	315,119,508	344,895,467	9.4
Harvard University (MA)	1	30,745,534	32,689,489	6.3
Yale University (CT)	2	19,264,289	20,708,793	7.5
University of Texas System Office	3	17,070,515	19,740,283	15.6
Princeton University (NJ)	4	17,404,002	18,786,132	7.9
Stanford University (CA)	5	17,035,804	18,688,868	9.7
Massachusetts Institute of Technology	6	10,149,564	10,857,976	7.0
University of Michigan, Ann Arbor	7	7,586,547	8,272,366	9.0
Columbia University in the City of New York (NY)	8	7,654,152	8,197,880	7.1
Texas A & M University, College Station	9	7,032,204	8,072,055	14.8
University of Pennsylvania	10	6,754,658	7,741,396	14.6
University of Notre Dame (IN)	11	6,444,599	6,959,051	8.0
University of California System Admin. Central Office	12	5,990,577	6,402,600	6.9
Northwestern University (IL)	13	5,574,319	6,283,130	12.7
Emory University (GA)	14	5,774,500	6,115,582	5.9
Duke University (NC)	15	5,555,196	6,040,973	8.7
University of Chicago (IL)	16	5,701,419	5,886,968	3.3
Washington University in St. Louis (MO)	17	5,303,196	5,749,297	8.4
University of Virginia, Main Campus	18	4,734,895	5,106,876	7.9
Rice University (TX)	19	4,448,069	4,895,299	10.1
Cornell University (NY)	20	3,850,426	4,133,842	7.4
University of Southern California	21	3,488,933	3,868,355	10.9
Dartmouth College (NH)	22	3,486,383	3,733,596	7.1
Vanderbilt University (TN)	23	3,360,036	3,635,343	8.2
Ohio State University, Main Campus	24	2,348,193	3,130,942	33.3
University of Texas at Austin	25	2,861,389	3,012,895	5.3
New York University	26	2,800,399	2,980,027	6.4
University of Pittsburgh, Pittsburgh Campus (PA)	27	2,600,314	2,956,739	13.7
Johns Hopkins University (MD)	28	2,593,316	2,918,546	12.5
Brown University (RI)	29	2,525,091	2,669,948	5.7
University of Minnesota, Twin Cities	30	2,365,693	2,610,544	10.4
University of Washington, Seattle Campus	31	2,206,040	2,432,421	10.3
University of North Carolina at Chapel Hill	32	2,157,237	2,344,280	8.7
University of Wisconsin, Madison	33	2,068,495	2,295,273	11.0
Purdue University, Main Campus (IN)	34	1,861,079	2,189,202	17.6
University of Richmond (VA)	35	1,868,910	2,025,996	8.4
Michigan State University	36	1,760,708	2,007,498	14.0
California Institute of Technology	37	1,813,842	1,960,435	8.1
Pennsylvania State University, Main Campus	38	1,772,921	1,924,143	8.5
Williams College (MA)	39	1,728,549	1,902,112	10.0
Boston College (MA)	40	1,632,635	1,868,699	14.5
Amherst College (MA)	41	1,640,666	1,823,748	11.2
Pomona College (CA)	42	1,679,640	1,823,441	8.6
University of Rochester (NY)	43	1,581,773	1,730,829	9.4
Georgia Institute of Technology, Main Campus	44	1,608,248	1,714,876	6.6
Case Western Reserve University (OH)	45	1,600,013	1,678,563	4.9
Swarthmore College (PA)	46	1,498,775	1,634,685	9.1
Wellesley College (MA)	47	1,468,582	1,576,337	7.3
Smith College (MA)	48	1,409,755	1,557,427	10.5
Grinnell College (IA)	49	1,383,856	1,553,629	12.3
Tufts University (MA)	50	1,351,166	1,440,527	6.6
University of California, Los Angeles	51	1,222,823	1,411,797	15.5
University of California, Berkeley	52	1,254,517	1,411,707	12.5
Boston University (MA)	53	1,190,512	1,403,061	17.9
George Washington University (DC)	54	1,305,892	1,375,202	5.3
University of Florida	55	1,127,419	1,360,073	20.6
Washington and Lee University (VA)	56	1,261,553	1,345,356	6.6
University of Kansas	57	1,202,585	1,310,655	9.0
Georgetown University (DC)	58	1,140,486	1,286,322	12.8
Southern Methodist University (TX)	59	1,162,415	1,268,079	9.1
Texas Christian University	60	1,110,868	1,256,030	13.1

Institution	Rank order, end of FY[1]	Market value of endowment — Beginning of FY (in thousands)	End of FY (in thousands)	Percent change[2]
1	2	3	4	5
University of Delaware	61	1,087,873	1,171,166	7.7
Weill Cornell Medical College (NY)	62	1,096,528	1,138,386	3.8
Soka University of America (CA)	63	1,035,512	1,117,424	7.9
Lehigh University (PA)	64	1,035,593	1,103,449	6.6
University of Iowa	65	981,104	1,094,803	11.6
Carnegie Mellon University (PA)	66	979,230	1,066,149	8.9
Wake Forest University (NC)	67	1,025,069	1,061,638	3.6
Baylor University (TX)	68	964,161	1,061,157	10.1
University of Kentucky	69	947,383	1,054,448	11.3
Brigham Young University, Provo (UT)	70	957,010	1,053,241	10.1
Syracuse University (NY)	71	940,056	1,053,214	12.0
University of Illinois at Urbana-Champaign	72	996,226	1,050,492	5.4
University of Cincinnati, Main Campus (OH)	73	834,929	1,044,198	25.1
Bowdoin College (ME)	74	902,364	1,038,640	15.1
Yeshiva University (NY)	75	931,914	1,034,254	11.0
Tulane University of Louisiana	76	946,176	1,031,661	9.0
Trinity University (TX)	77	915,918	1,013,929	10.7
Berea College (KY)	78	942,618	1,012,401	7.4
Middlebury College (VT)	79	879,690	972,992	10.6
Saint Louis University, Main Campus (MO)	80	852,842	956,014	12.1
Princeton Theological Seminary (NJ)	81	866,930	941,110	8.6
University of Tulsa (OK)	82	802,455	893,055	11.3
Juilliard School (NY)	83	787,698	882,012	12.0
University of Texas Southwestern Medical Center	84	836,413	878,855	5.1
Vassar College (NY)	85	804,912	868,741	7.9
Berry College (GA)	86	821,977	861,107	4.8
University of Oklahoma, Norman Campus	87	784,834	845,635	7.7
Baylor College of Medicine (TX)	88	751,378	844,261	12.4
Indiana University, Bloomington	89	772,185	835,123	8.2
University of Arkansas	90	770,550	819,814	6.4
University of Miami (FL)	91	678,694	777,947	14.6
Washington State University	92	737,428	777,644	5.5
Hamilton College (NY)	93	693,919	773,828	11.5
North Carolina State University at Raleigh	94	635,326	769,404	21.1
Brandeis University (MA)	95	674,522	766,205	13.6
University of California, San Francisco	96	655,924	766,144	16.8
Oberlin College (OH)	97	708,238	765,804	8.1
Colgate University (NY)	98	687,474	760,825	10.7
Santa Clara University (CA)	99	688,118	760,218	10.5
University of Louisville (KY)	100	721,104	757,336	5.0
Lafayette College (PA)	101	681,536	749,031	9.9
Pepperdine University (CA)	102	607,953	715,660	17.7
Bryn Mawr College (PA)	103	641,173	710,168	10.8
Indiana University, Purdue University, Indianapolis	104	634,979	709,877	11.8
Rutgers University, New Brunswick (NJ)	105	645,556	703,701	9.0
Carleton College (MN)	106	645,654	700,540	8.5
College of William and Mary (VA)	107	644,233	697,724	8.3
Macalester College (MN)	108	625,068	694,311	11.1
University of Missouri, Columbia	109	624,382	692,853	11.0
Denison University (OH)	110	644,201	691,740	7.4
Wesleyan University (CT)	111	616,195	688,643	11.8
Rochester Institute of Technology (NY)	112	628,128	669,132	6.5
Cooper Union for the Advancement of Science and Art (NY)	113	640,536	668,546	4.4
Bucknell University (PA)	114	599,216	666,563	11.2
University of Tennessee, Knoxville	115	665,833	662,942	-0.4
Colorado College	116	507,013	656,658	29.5
Virginia Polytechnic Institute and State U.	117	588,300	653,700	11.1
Colby College (ME)	118	599,557	649,992	8.4
University of Utah	119	577,505	642,219	11.2
Mount Holyoke College (MA)	120	594,045	638,552	7.5

†Not applicable.
[1]Institutions ranked by size of endowment at end of 2013 fiscal year.
[2]Change in market value of endowment. Includes growth from gifts and returns on investments, as well as reductions from expenditures and withdrawals.

NOTE: Degree-granting institutions grant associate's or higher degrees and participate in Title IV federal financial aid programs.
SOURCE: U.S. Department of Education, National Center for Education Statistics, Integrated Postsecondary Education Data System (IPEDS), Spring 2014, Finance component. (This table was prepared April 2015.)

Table 334.10. Expenditures of public degree-granting postsecondary institutions, by purpose of expenditure and level of institution: 2006–07 through 2012–13

Level of institution and year	Total expenditures	Instruction Total[1]	Instruction Salaries and wages	Research	Public service	Academic support	Student services	Institutional support	Operation and maintenance of plant	Depreciation	Scholarships and fellowships[2]	Auxiliary enterprises	Hospitals	Independent operations	Interest	Other
1	2	3	4	5	6	7	8	9	10	11	12	13	14	15	16	17
									In thousands of current dollars							
All levels																
2006–07	$238,828,801	$67,188,249	$45,998,524	$23,893,564	$10,148,312	$16,306,542	$11,377,541	$19,962,037	$15,806,925	$10,772,442	$8,956,265	$18,501,797	$22,111,404	$784,684	$3,819,104	$9,199,935
2007–08[3]	261,045,829	71,807,253	48,691,508	25,331,167	10,800,588	17,871,280	12,205,110	22,145,030	17,032,966	12,814,049	9,664,173	19,533,181	23,974,721	931,838	4,301,708	12,632,765
2008–09[3]	273,030,301	75,078,714	51,151,501	26,651,018	11,244,501	18,805,325	12,939,434	23,078,908	17,839,601	13,719,465	11,104,773	20,588,239	25,944,900	1,177,848	2,972,642	11,884,935
2009–10[3]	281,368,314	76,292,102	51,812,151	28,077,991	11,506,354	18,878,483	13,137,932	22,685,634	18,052,279	14,306,697	15,435,492	20,457,106	26,674,882	1,236,092	5,061,939	9,565,330
2010–11[3]	296,114,046	79,373,704	53,573,417	29,357,793	11,865,709	19,338,463	13,566,425	23,863,660	18,847,081	15,413,378	17,604,651	21,715,258	27,894,885	1,153,975	5,628,124	10,490,939
2011–12[3]	305,534,191	80,898,639	54,360,626	29,655,988	11,943,858	20,301,350	14,160,344	24,154,135	19,180,861	16,469,939	16,620,812	22,190,775	30,899,227	1,204,016	6,136,311	11,717,934
2012–13[3]	311,424,709	82,946,384	55,555,811	29,860,945	11,905,234	21,259,036	14,688,802	25,269,318	19,717,247	17,436,827	16,221,476	22,490,098	31,838,319	1,224,309	6,364,472	10,202,242
4-year																
2006–07	196,121,062	50,755,304	34,541,885	23,875,451	9,455,605	13,151,359	7,430,739	14,046,030	12,031,682	9,140,557	6,031,919	16,308,351	22,111,404	784,684	3,129,141	7,868,836
2007–08[3]	215,474,080	54,371,328	36,618,879	25,312,279	10,055,606	14,471,795	8,051,799	15,812,151	13,047,228	10,959,500	6,467,362	17,296,774	23,974,721	931,838	3,523,683	11,198,015
2008–09[3]	225,363,128	57,265,615	38,666,432	26,629,400	10,499,031	15,300,115	8,612,795	16,505,969	13,805,143	11,719,734	7,156,258	18,293,456	25,944,900	1,177,848	2,354,694	10,098,170
2009–10[3]	230,216,045	58,268,076	39,035,682	28,057,280	10,752,578	15,355,204	8,755,313	16,348,654	13,675,766	12,311,891	9,092,603	18,120,806	26,674,882	1,236,092	4,091,219	7,475,682
2010–11[3]	241,754,071	60,607,823	40,407,972	29,336,607	11,099,605	15,720,410	9,112,980	17,294,034	14,260,755	13,184,265	10,103,136	19,321,726	27,894,885	1,153,975	4,502,944	8,160,925
2011–12[3]	251,503,636	62,238,557	41,349,288	29,635,707	11,184,077	16,652,094	9,634,329	17,439,517	14,705,781	14,105,698	9,739,168	19,819,696	30,899,227	1,204,016	4,777,487	9,468,280
2012–13[3]	257,543,514	64,142,742	42,541,275	29,842,594	11,178,539	17,528,570	10,103,438	18,349,595	15,212,898	14,870,558	9,819,766	20,191,850	31,838,319	1,224,309	5,071,595	8,168,742
2-year																
2006–07	42,707,739	16,432,945	11,456,639	18,113	692,707	3,155,183	3,946,803	5,916,007	3,775,243	1,631,885	2,924,346	2,193,446	0	0	689,963	1,331,099
2007–08[3]	45,571,749	17,435,926	12,072,630	18,887	744,982	3,399,485	4,153,311	6,332,879	3,985,738	1,854,549	3,196,811	2,236,407	0	0	778,025	1,434,749
2008–09[3]	47,667,173	17,813,099	12,485,070	21,617	745,470	3,505,209	4,326,639	6,572,940	4,034,457	1,999,732	3,948,515	2,294,783	0	0	617,948	1,786,764
2009–10[3]	51,152,269	18,024,027	12,776,469	20,711	753,776	3,523,280	4,382,619	6,336,980	4,376,513	1,994,806	6,342,889	2,336,300	0	0	970,721	2,089,648
2010–11[3]	54,359,975	18,765,881	13,165,446	21,187	766,104	3,618,052	4,453,445	6,569,626	4,586,326	2,229,112	7,501,515	2,393,532	0	0	1,125,180	2,330,014
2011–12[3]	54,030,554	18,660,082	13,011,338	20,281	759,781	3,649,257	4,526,015	6,714,618	4,475,080	2,364,242	6,881,643	2,371,079	0	0	1,358,824	2,249,654
2012–13[3]	53,881,195	18,803,642	13,014,536	18,351	726,695	3,730,467	4,585,363	6,919,723	4,504,349	2,566,269	6,401,710	2,298,249	0	0	1,292,877	2,033,500
									Percentage distribution							
All levels																
2006–07	100.00	28.13	19.26	10.00	4.25	6.83	4.76	8.36	6.62	4.51	3.75	7.75	9.26	0.33	1.60	3.85
2007–08[3]	100.00	27.51	18.65	9.70	4.14	6.85	4.68	8.48	6.52	4.91	3.70	7.48	9.18	0.36	1.65	4.84
2008–09[3]	100.00	27.50	18.73	9.76	4.12	6.89	4.74	8.45	6.53	5.02	4.07	7.54	9.50	0.43	1.09	4.35
2009–10[3]	100.00	27.11	18.41	9.98	4.09	6.71	4.67	8.06	6.42	5.08	5.49	7.27	9.48	0.44	1.80	3.40
2010–11[3]	100.00	26.81	18.09	9.91	4.01	6.53	4.58	8.06	6.36	5.21	5.95	7.33	9.42	0.39	1.90	3.54
2011–12[3]	100.00	26.48	17.79	9.71	3.91	6.64	4.63	7.91	6.28	5.39	5.44	7.26	10.11	0.39	2.01	3.84
2012–13[3]	100.00	26.63	17.84	9.59	3.82	6.83	4.72	8.11	6.33	5.60	5.21	7.22	10.22	0.39	2.04	3.28
4-year																
2006–07	100.00	25.88	17.61	12.17	4.82	6.71	3.79	7.16	6.13	4.66	3.08	8.32	11.27	0.40	1.60	4.01
2007–08[3]	100.00	25.23	16.99	11.75	4.67	6.72	3.74	7.34	6.06	5.09	3.00	8.03	11.13	0.43	1.64	5.20
2008–09[3]	100.00	25.41	17.16	11.82	4.66	6.79	3.82	7.32	6.13	5.20	3.18	8.12	11.51	0.52	1.04	4.48
2009–10[3]	100.00	25.31	16.96	12.19	4.67	6.67	3.80	7.10	5.94	5.35	3.95	7.87	11.59	0.54	1.78	3.25
2010–11[3]	100.00	25.07	16.71	12.13	4.59	6.50	3.77	7.15	5.90	5.45	4.18	7.99	11.54	0.48	1.86	3.38
2011–12[3]	100.00	24.75	16.44	11.78	4.45	6.62	3.83	6.93	5.85	5.61	3.87	7.88	12.29	0.48	1.90	3.76
2012–13[3]	100.00	24.91	16.52	11.59	4.34	6.81	3.92	7.12	5.91	5.77	3.81	7.84	12.36	0.48	1.97	3.17
2-year																
2006–07	100.00	38.48	26.83	0.04	1.62	7.39	9.24	13.85	8.84	3.82	6.85	5.14	0.00	0.00	1.62	3.12
2007–08[3]	100.00	38.26	26.49	0.04	1.63	7.46	9.11	13.90	8.75	4.07	7.01	4.91	0.00	0.00	1.71	3.15
2008–09[3]	100.00	37.37	26.19	0.05	1.56	7.35	9.08	13.79	8.46	4.20	8.28	4.81	0.00	0.00	1.30	3.75
2009–10[3]	100.00	35.24	24.98	0.04	1.47	6.89	8.57	12.39	8.56	3.90	12.40	4.57	0.00	0.00	1.90	4.09
2010–11[3]	100.00	34.52	24.22	0.04	1.41	6.66	8.19	12.09	8.44	4.10	13.80	4.40	0.00	0.00	2.07	4.29
2011–12[3]	100.00	34.54	24.08	0.04	1.41	6.75	8.38	12.43	8.28	4.38	12.74	4.39	0.00	0.00	2.51	4.16
2012–13[3]	100.00	34.90	24.15	0.03	1.35	6.92	8.51	12.84	8.36	4.76	11.88	4.27	0.00	0.00	2.40	3.77

See notes at end of table.

Table 334.10. Expenditures of public degree-granting postsecondary institutions, by purpose of expenditure and level of institution: 2006–07 through 2012–13—Continued

| Level of institution and year | Total expenditures | Instruction | | Research | Public service | Academic support | Student services | Institutional support | Operation and maintenance of plant | Depreciation | Scholarships and fellowships[2] | Auxiliary enterprises | Hospitals | Independent operations | Interest | Other |
		Total[1]	Salaries and wages													
1	2	3	4	5	6	7	8	9	10	11	12	13	14	15	16	17
						Expenditures per full-time-equivalent student in current dollars										
All levels																
2006–07	$25,130	$7,070	$4,840	$2,514	$1,068	$1,716	$1,197	$2,100	$1,663	$1,134	$942	$1,947	$2,327	$83	$402	$968
2007–08[3]	26,802	7,373	4,999	2,601	1,109	1,835	1,253	2,274	1,749	1,316	992	2,006	2,462	96	442	1,297
2008–09[3]	27,135	7,462	5,084	2,649	1,118	1,869	1,286	2,294	1,773	1,364	1,104	2,046	2,579	117	295	1,181
2009–10[3]	26,874	7,099	4,821	2,613	1,071	1,757	1,223	2,111	1,630	1,331	1,436	1,904	2,482	115	471	890
2010–11[3]	26,182	7,204	4,862	2,664	1,077	1,755	1,231	2,166	1,710	1,399	1,598	1,971	2,532	105	511	952
2011–12[3]	27,891	7,385	4,962	2,707	1,090	1,853	1,293	2,205	1,751	1,503	1,517	2,026	2,821	110	560	1,070
2012–13[3]	28,887	7,694	5,153	2,770	1,104	1,972	1,363	2,344	1,829	1,617	1,505	2,086	2,953	114	590	946
4-year																
2006–07	33,670	8,714	5,930	4,099	1,623	2,258	1,276	2,411	2,066	1,569	1,036	2,800	3,796	135	537	1,351
2007–08[3]	35,947	9,071	6,109	4,223	1,678	2,414	1,343	2,638	2,177	1,828	1,079	2,886	4,000	155	588	1,868
2008–09[3]	36,707	9,327	6,298	4,337	1,710	2,492	1,403	2,688	2,249	1,909	1,166	2,980	4,226	192	384	1,645
2009–10[3]	35,679	9,030	6,050	4,348	1,666	2,380	1,357	2,534	2,119	1,908	1,409	2,808	4,134	192	634	1,159
2010–11[3]	36,432	9,133	6,089	4,421	1,673	2,369	1,373	2,606	2,184	1,987	1,523	2,912	4,204	174	679	1,230
2011–12[3]	37,348	9,242	6,140	4,401	1,661	2,473	1,431	2,590	2,184	2,095	1,446	2,943	4,588	179	709	1,406
2012–13[3]	38,073	9,482	6,289	4,412	1,653	2,591	1,494	2,713	2,249	2,198	1,452	2,985	4,707	181	750	1,208
2-year																
2006–07	11,609	4,467	3,114	5	188	858	1,073	1,608	1,026	444	795	596	0	0	188	362
2007–08[3]	12,167	4,655	3,223	5	199	908	1,109	1,691	1,064	495	854	597	0	0	208	383
2008–09[3]	12,153	4,542	3,183	6	190	894	1,103	1,676	1,029	510	1,007	585	0	0	158	456
2009–10[3]	11,912	4,197	2,975	5	176	820	1,021	1,476	1,019	465	1,477	544	0	0	226	487
2010–11[3]	12,403	4,282	3,004	5	175	825	1,016	1,499	1,046	509	1,712	546	0	0	257	532
2011–12[3]	12,802	4,421	3,083	5	180	865	1,072	1,591	1,060	560	1,630	562	0	0	322	533
2012–13[3]	13,416	4,682	3,240	5	181	929	1,142	1,723	1,122	639	1,594	572	0	0	322	506
						Expenditures per full-time-equivalent student in constant 2013–14 dollars[4]										
All levels																
2006–07	$28,926	$8,137	$5,571	$2,894	$1,229	$1,975	$1,378	$2,418	$1,914	$1,305	$1,085	$2,241	$2,678	$95	$463	$1,114
2007–08[3]	29,748	8,183	5,549	2,887	1,231	2,037	1,391	2,524	1,941	1,460	1,101	2,226	2,732	106	490	1,440
2008–09[3]	29,702	8,168	5,565	2,899	1,223	2,046	1,408	2,511	1,941	1,493	1,208	2,240	2,822	128	323	1,293
2009–10[3]	28,384	7,696	5,227	2,832	1,161	1,904	1,325	2,289	1,821	1,443	1,557	2,064	2,691	125	511	965
2010–11[3]	28,561	7,656	5,167	2,832	1,144	1,865	1,309	2,302	1,818	1,487	1,698	2,094	2,691	111	543	1,012
2011–12[3]	28,798	7,625	5,124	2,795	1,126	1,913	1,335	2,277	1,808	1,552	1,567	2,092	2,912	113	578	1,104
2012–13[3]	29,338	7,814	5,234	2,813	1,122	2,003	1,384	2,381	1,858	1,643	1,528	2,119	2,999	115	600	961
4-year																
2006–07	38,755	10,030	6,826	4,718	1,868	2,599	1,468	2,776	2,378	1,806	1,192	3,223	4,369	155	618	1,555
2007–08[3]	39,897	10,067	6,780	4,687	1,862	2,680	1,491	2,928	2,416	2,029	1,197	3,203	4,439	173	652	2,073
2008–09[3]	40,180	10,210	6,894	4,748	1,872	2,728	1,536	2,943	2,461	2,089	1,276	3,262	4,626	210	420	1,800
2009–10[3]	38,680	9,790	6,559	4,714	1,807	2,580	1,471	2,747	2,298	2,069	1,528	3,045	4,482	208	687	1,256
2010–11[3]	38,719	9,707	6,472	4,698	1,778	2,518	1,460	2,770	2,284	2,112	1,618	3,095	4,468	185	721	1,307
2011–12[3]	38,562	9,543	6,340	4,544	1,715	2,553	1,477	2,674	2,255	2,163	1,493	3,039	4,738	185	733	1,452
2012–13[3]	38,668	9,630	6,387	4,481	1,678	2,632	1,517	2,755	2,284	2,233	1,474	3,032	4,780	184	761	1,226
2-year																
2006–07	13,362	5,142	3,585	6	217	987	1,235	1,851	1,181	511	915	686	0	0	216	416
2007–08[3]	13,504	5,167	3,577	6	221	1,007	1,231	1,877	1,181	550	947	663	0	0	231	425
2008–09[3]	13,303	4,971	3,484	6	208	978	1,207	1,834	1,126	558	1,102	640	0	0	172	499
2009–10[3]	12,914	4,550	3,226	5	190	889	1,106	1,600	1,105	504	1,601	590	0	0	245	528
2010–11[3]	13,181	4,550	3,192	5	186	877	1,080	1,593	1,112	541	1,819	580	0	0	273	565
2011–12[3]	13,218	4,565	3,183	5	186	893	1,107	1,643	1,095	578	1,684	580	0	0	332	550
2012–13[3]	13,625	4,755	3,291	5	184	943	1,160	1,750	1,139	649	1,619	581	0	0	327	514

[1]Includes other categories not separately shown.

[2]Excludes discounts and allowances.

[3]All expenditures reported by institutions for operation and maintenance of plant have been aggregated in the operation and maintenance of plant category, even in cases where they originally were reported by purpose. Similarly, all expenditures reported by institutions for depreciation have been aggregated in the depreciation category, even in cases where they originally were reported by purpose. In addition, all expenditures reported by institutions for interest have been aggregated in the interest category, even in cases where they originally were reported by purpose.

[4]Constant dollars based on the Consumer Price Index, prepared by the Bureau of Labor Statistics, U.S. Department of Labor, adjusted to a school-year basis.

NOTE: Degree-granting institutions grant associate's or higher degrees and participate in Title IV federal financial aid programs. Includes data for public institutions reporting data according to either the Governmental Accounting Standards Board (GASB) or the Financial Accounting Standards Board (FASB) questionnaire. Detail may not sum to totals because of rounding.

SOURCE: U.S. Department of Education, National Center for Education Statistics, Integrated Postsecondary Education Data System (IPEDS), Spring 2007 through Spring 2014, Finance and Enrollment components. (This table was prepared January 2015.)

Table 334.20. Expenditures of public degree-granting postsecondary institutions, by level of institution, purpose of expenditure, and state or jurisdiction: 2009–10 through 2012–13

[In thousands of current dollars]

State or jurisdiction	Total expenditures, 2009–10	Total expenditures, 2010–11	Total expenditures, 2011–12			2012–13					
			All institutions	4-year institutions	2-year institutions	All institutions		4-year institutions		2-year institutions	
						Total[1]	Instruction[2]	Total[1]	Instruction[2]	Total[1]	Instruction[2]
1	2	3	4	5	6	7	8	9	10	11	12
United States...............	$281,368,314	$296,114,046	$305,534,191	$251,503,636	$54,030,554	$311,424,709	$82,946,384	$257,543,514	$64,142,742	$53,881,195	$18,803,642
Alabama........................	6,324,853	6,649,467	6,249,322	5,505,628	743,694	6,499,646	1,484,289	5,761,237	1,210,975	738,409	273,314
Alaska...........................	780,028	800,218	829,978	806,882	23,096	845,578	224,790	809,679	212,485	35,899	12,305
Arizona.........................	4,721,129	4,968,606	5,126,746	3,711,078	1,415,668	5,372,323	1,555,735	3,908,951	1,089,240	1,463,372	466,495
Arkansas.......................	3,268,738	3,454,422	3,592,033	3,079,753	512,279	3,614,017	742,613	3,115,538	581,911	498,479	160,703
California.......................	39,702,048	42,790,625	45,496,484	34,205,136	11,291,348	45,915,560	10,849,433	34,830,021	7,566,285	11,085,538	3,283,149
Colorado.......................	4,516,268	4,837,724	5,149,199	4,593,560	555,639	5,342,995	1,541,508	4,756,073	1,325,455	586,922	216,052
Connecticut...................	2,814,866	2,974,554	2,931,898	2,476,931	454,966	3,030,961	845,284	2,565,900	663,966	465,062	181,317
Delaware.......................	967,381	1,032,228	1,128,190	976,509	151,681	1,121,660	425,831	965,973	356,721	155,687	69,110
District of Columbia	109,469	152,640	147,034	147,034	0	141,338	47,739	141,338	47,739	0	0
Florida..........................	9,721,394	10,413,803	10,559,827	10,047,373	512,454	10,659,595	3,107,105	10,272,223	3,001,908	387,372	105,196
Georgia.........................	6,426,195	7,028,610	7,293,926	6,090,473	1,203,453	7,409,996	1,949,309	6,310,205	1,558,758	1,099,791	390,551
Hawaii..........................	1,406,821	1,523,301	1,609,315	1,364,952	244,363	1,647,129	446,357	1,395,933	332,636	251,196	113,721
Idaho...........................	1,070,934	1,116,296	1,216,909	951,754	265,155	1,182,070	351,189	974,156	283,798	207,914	67,391
Illinois..........................	9,954,173	10,302,240	10,888,678	7,958,821	2,929,857	11,603,379	3,373,084	8,567,709	2,396,050	3,035,670	977,034
Indiana.........................	5,739,211	5,959,191	6,098,731	5,438,638	660,093	6,227,063	2,142,564	5,587,045	1,934,163	640,018	208,401
Iowa............................	4,169,366	4,332,274	4,726,859	3,842,076	884,783	4,846,304	981,476	3,957,757	646,002	888,547	335,474
Kansas.........................	2,916,446	3,053,391	3,214,748	2,490,979	723,769	3,306,016	1,021,286	2,562,868	770,535	743,148	250,751
Kentucky.......................	4,723,961	4,889,725	5,136,705	4,423,207	713,498	5,180,174	1,177,883	4,454,346	931,670	725,828	246,213
Louisiana.......................	4,143,613	4,163,519	4,204,018	3,688,602	515,416	4,151,993	1,096,889	3,656,295	913,757	495,698	183,133
Maine...........................	807,827	837,119	844,272	722,060	122,212	847,717	236,554	725,066	187,615	122,652	48,939
Maryland.......................	5,489,313	5,627,221	5,829,195	4,472,795	1,356,400	5,979,533	1,658,119	4,623,170	1,170,993	1,356,363	487,126
Massachusetts...............	3,941,641	4,224,820	4,297,014	3,490,312	806,702	4,442,564	1,239,779	3,610,605	926,914	831,958	312,865
Michigan	12,411,095	12,793,640	13,384,789	11,447,703	1,937,086	13,788,962	3,422,599	11,940,315	2,769,449	1,848,647	653,150
Minnesota.....................	4,782,817	4,841,837	4,810,022	3,798,676	1,011,346	5,019,669	1,437,377	3,976,182	1,011,067	1,043,487	426,310
Mississippi....................	3,591,772	3,717,313	3,815,187	2,909,603	905,584	3,855,187	892,777	2,976,363	591,741	878,824	301,036
Missouri........................	4,220,808	4,370,406	4,563,353	3,777,389	785,964	4,619,674	1,267,632	3,823,178	976,168	796,496	291,464
Montana........................	933,785	961,380	980,626	852,199	128,427	992,536	254,602	866,457	221,953	126,079	32,649
Nebraska	2,005,277	2,119,516	2,176,505	1,788,005	388,500	2,226,961	655,888	1,838,167	508,003	388,794	147,885
Nevada	1,423,657	1,452,203	1,374,536	1,307,944	66,592	1,442,757	496,725	1,375,441	470,306	67,316	26,419
New Hampshire..............	837,543	916,009	894,369	764,722	129,647	901,393	266,816	769,683	222,929	131,710	43,887
New Jersey....................	6,679,185	6,818,023	7,080,758	5,766,819	1,313,939	5,474,962	1,866,896	4,147,457	1,416,674	1,327,505	450,222
New Mexico...................	3,094,887	3,195,659	3,150,710	2,545,009	605,701	3,252,357	618,286	2,643,255	423,188	609,102	195,098
New York.......................	14,564,719	15,481,165	16,037,336	12,848,763	3,188,573	15,844,606	4,607,393	12,689,386	3,315,856	3,155,220	1,291,538
North Carolina................	9,061,392	9,639,567	9,556,563	7,417,647	2,138,916	9,964,777	3,173,886	7,766,190	2,272,448	2,198,588	901,438
North Dakota	960,204	993,822	1,041,219	950,491	90,728	1,068,159	373,922	977,140	339,900	91,019	34,022
Ohio............................	11,191,776	11,618,185	11,808,439	10,182,544	1,625,895	12,192,587	3,214,787	10,636,363	2,660,002	1,556,224	554,786
Oklahoma......................	3,565,946	3,722,869	3,859,699	3,377,425	482,275	3,924,755	1,097,434	3,432,762	909,757	491,994	187,677
Oregon.........................	4,989,706	5,312,294	5,531,213	4,341,196	1,190,017	5,744,633	1,234,968	4,529,658	842,727	1,214,975	392,241
Pennsylvania..................	10,880,853	11,287,473	11,823,354	10,615,217	1,208,137	12,176,869	2,924,435	10,975,980	2,493,983	1,200,889	430,452
Rhode Island	663,552	683,831	717,329	600,406	116,924	719,733	196,387	603,025	145,218	116,707	51,170
South Carolina................	3,537,943	3,715,311	3,827,663	3,010,114	817,549	4,030,358	1,287,972	3,202,729	999,258	827,629	288,714
South Dakota.................	686,412	707,073	739,971	663,378	76,594	744,419	220,804	669,445	192,477	74,974	28,327
Tennessee....................	3,781,861	3,980,862	4,156,217	3,492,606	663,611	4,193,989	1,450,849	3,522,799	1,201,450	671,191	249,398
Texas	25,080,639	26,346,922	26,413,997	21,789,774	4,624,223	27,655,846	6,922,926	22,880,541	5,330,044	4,775,306	1,592,883
Utah............................	3,940,464	4,248,983	4,461,853	4,260,114	201,739	4,744,745	782,163	4,539,033	698,046	205,712	84,117
Vermont	761,182	793,941	799,662	762,660	37,002	843,550	218,327	806,021	208,071	37,529	10,256
Virginia.........................	7,329,410	7,878,109	8,367,116	7,254,946	1,112,170	8,757,065	2,336,347	7,615,345	1,871,968	1,141,720	464,378
Washington....................	6,874,560	7,312,805	7,402,548	6,055,036	1,347,512	7,740,652	2,172,021	6,429,794	1,653,874	1,310,858	518,147
West Virginia..................	1,672,009	1,738,447	1,813,682	1,651,111	162,572	1,761,432	518,208	1,600,198	468,912	161,234	49,297
Wisconsin......................	5,757,793	5,974,368	5,942,717	4,629,546	1,313,171	6,044,715	1,848,358	4,704,511	1,222,453	1,340,203	625,905
Wyoming.......................	671,896	706,750	752,127	478,492	273,635	744,748	229,095	469,004	137,558	275,744	91,537
U.S. Service Academies	1,699,493	1,653,288	1,679,549	1,679,549	†	1,585,003	457,684	1,585,003	457,684	†	†
Other jurisdictions......	1,776,740	1,698,347	1,727,062	1,625,469	101,592	1,684,136	496,123	1,591,208	463,020	92,928	33,103
American Samoa..............	13,243	15,942	15,097	15,097	0	14,449	4,558	14,449	4,558	0	0
Federated States of Micronesia	23,128	21,048	23,134	0	23,134	22,472	7,583	0	0	22,472	7,583
Guam...........................	115,262	125,565	136,515	99,800	36,715	129,808	30,277	96,962	18,224	32,846	12,052
Marshall Islands..............	12,681	17,259	18,381	0	18,381	13,552	3,042	0	0	13,552	3,042
Northern Marianas	14,619	20,214	18,085	18,085	0	18,031	7,979	18,031	7,979	0	0
Palau...........................	5,416	4,856	9,023	0	9,023	10,384	4,177	0	0	10,384	4,177
Puerto Rico....................	1,506,865	1,406,063	1,418,143	1,403,804	14,339	1,393,668	424,018	1,379,994	417,770	13,674	6,248
U.S. Virgin Islands	85,525	87,400	88,683	88,683	0	81,772	14,489	81,772	14,489	0	0

†Not applicable.
[1]Includes other categories not separately shown.
[2]Excludes expenditures for operations and maintenance, interest, and depreciation, which are included in the total.
NOTE: Degree-granting institutions grant associate's or higher degrees and participate in Title IV federal financial aid programs. Includes data for public institutions reporting data according to either the Governmental Accounting Standards Board (GASB) or the Financial Accounting Standards Board (FASB) questionnaire. All expenditures reported by institutions for operation and maintenance of plant have been aggregated in the operation and maintenance of plant category, even in cases where they originally were reported by pur-

pose. Similarly, all expenditures reported by institutions for depreciation have been aggregated in the depreciation category, even in cases where they originally were reported by purpose. In addition, all expenditures reported by institutions for interest have been aggregated in the interest category, even in cases where they originally were reported by purpose. Detail may not sum to totals because of rounding.
SOURCE: U.S. Department of Education, National Center for Education Statistics, Integrated Postsecondary Education Data System (IPEDS), Spring 2011 through Spring 2014, Finance component. (This table was prepared January 2015.)

Table 334.30. Total expenditures of private nonprofit degree-granting postsecondary institutions, by purpose and level of institution: 1999–2000 through 2012–13

Level of institution and year	Total	Instruction	Research	Public service	Academic support	Student services	Institutional support	Auxiliary enterprises[1]	Net grant aid to students[2]	Hospitals	Independent operations	Other
1	2	3	4	5	6	7	8	9	10	11	12	13
						In thousands of current dollars						
All levels												
1999–2000	$80,613,037	$26,012,599	$8,381,926	$1,446,958	$6,510,951	$5,688,499	$10,585,850	$8,300,021	$1,180,882	$7,355,110	$2,753,679	$2,396,563
2000–01	85,625,016	27,607,324	9,025,739	1,473,292	7,368,263	6,117,195	11,434,074	9,010,853	1,176,160	7,255,376	3,134,609	2,022,132
2001–02	92,192,297	29,689,041	10,035,480	1,665,884	7,802,637	6,573,185	12,068,120	9,515,829	1,188,690	7,633,043	3,397,979	2,622,409
2002–03	99,748,076	32,062,218	11,079,532	1,878,380	8,156,688	7,096,223	13,157,744	9,936,478	1,173,845	7,586,208	3,879,736	3,741,024
2003–04	104,317,870	33,909,179	12,039,531	1,972,351	8,759,743	7,544,021	13,951,408	10,508,719	1,101,738	8,374,128	4,222,980	1,934,070
2004–05	110,394,127	36,258,473	12,812,857	2,000,437	9,342,064	8,191,737	14,690,328	10,944,342	1,069,591	9,180,775	4,223,779	1,679,741
2005–06	116,817,913	38,465,058	13,242,343	1,941,519	10,217,274	8,965,704	15,667,101	11,741,258	708,158	9,645,428	4,203,523	2,020,548
2006–07	124,557,725	41,223,483	13,704,450	2,036,588	10,882,028	9,591,334	16,831,353	12,451,087	728,139	10,400,055	4,680,393	2,028,816
2007–08	133,503,539	44,226,329	14,474,367	2,182,676	11,884,345	10,363,476	18,364,513	13,319,602	721,487	10,754,966	4,887,609	2,324,170
2008–09	141,349,229	46,452,942	15,262,667	2,298,526	12,579,759	11,012,204	19,400,981	13,707,921	757,852	11,930,840	5,158,480	2,787,056
2009–10	145,141,785	47,486,299	16,155,474	2,089,745	12,939,489	11,416,177	19,433,113	13,887,042	832,078	13,174,405	5,154,851	2,573,113
2010–11	152,509,741	49,692,506	17,378,300	2,255,102	13,609,316	12,239,151	20,234,530	14,457,573	772,177	14,239,347	5,376,016	2,255,722
2011–12	159,873,305	52,214,210	17,430,156	2,334,489	14,186,675	12,881,771	21,153,637	14,948,085	845,319	15,483,513	5,450,073	2,945,376
2012–13	165,573,669	54,257,906	17,514,795	2,318,128	14,922,229	13,685,488	21,857,624	15,330,575	851,647	16,701,193	5,436,746	2,697,338
4-year												
1999–2000	79,699,659	25,744,199	8,376,568	1,438,544	6,476,338	5,590,978	10,398,914	8,228,409	1,162,570	7,355,110	2,752,019	2,176,011
2000–01	85,048,123	27,413,897	9,019,966	1,467,325	7,333,851	6,036,478	11,292,310	8,957,973	1,160,660	7,253,479	3,133,099	1,979,086
2001–02	91,612,337	29,492,583	10,035,394	1,658,781	7,768,870	6,497,127	11,914,149	9,470,557	1,173,725	7,632,942	3,396,831	2,571,376
2002–03	99,137,236	31,866,310	11,079,332	1,871,274	8,122,181	7,014,149	12,996,836	9,876,937	1,161,441	7,586,208	3,854,471	3,708,098
2003–04	103,733,257	33,712,542	12,039,080	1,964,898	8,726,505	7,466,472	13,774,084	10,464,984	1,084,880	8,374,128	4,221,611	1,904,075
2004–05	109,789,731	36,051,084	12,812,326	1,993,767	9,307,600	8,101,214	14,516,197	10,899,456	1,051,216	9,180,775	4,223,779	1,652,317
2005–06	116,247,359	38,249,125	13,241,769	1,931,804	10,177,381	8,894,330	15,524,004	11,696,510	699,462	9,645,428	4,203,523	1,984,024
2006–07	124,061,478	41,056,590	13,703,502	2,028,364	10,850,270	9,522,535	16,693,987	12,414,609	714,398	10,400,055	4,680,393	1,996,775
2007–08	132,967,352	44,041,162	14,473,394	2,176,695	11,847,922	10,286,780	18,216,170	13,281,694	711,903	10,754,966	4,887,609	2,289,058
2008–09	140,852,609	46,286,662	15,262,322	2,294,914	12,538,248	10,943,745	19,258,651	13,670,550	750,687	11,930,840	5,158,480	2,757,510
2009–10	144,651,140	47,320,761	16,154,889	2,084,704	12,896,579	11,347,049	19,297,756	13,852,640	824,895	13,174,405	5,154,851	2,542,611
2010–11	151,886,926	49,483,331	17,378,015	2,252,753	13,555,980	12,152,861	20,068,168	14,427,590	770,812	14,239,347	5,376,016	2,182,053
2011–12	159,287,851	52,010,324	17,429,483	2,332,440	14,135,313	12,796,288	21,003,182	14,924,473	843,247	15,483,513	5,450,073	2,879,516
2012–13	165,073,451	54,076,793	17,514,466	2,316,357	14,883,058	13,617,897	21,719,080	15,304,071	846,965	16,701,193	5,436,746	2,656,826
2-year												
1999–2000	913,378	268,400	5,358	8,415	34,612	97,521	186,936	71,612	18,311	0	1,660	220,553
2000–01	576,893	193,428	5,772	5,967	34,412	80,717	141,764	52,880	15,500	1,896	1,510	43,046
2001–02	579,960	196,459	86	7,102	33,767	76,058	153,971	45,271	14,965	100	1,147	51,033
2002–03	610,840	195,909	200	7,106	34,506	82,074	160,908	59,541	12,404	0	25,265	32,926
2003–04	584,612	196,637	451	7,453	33,238	77,549	177,324	43,735	16,859	0	1,369	29,995
2004–05	604,395	207,389	532	6,670	34,464	90,523	174,131	44,886	18,375	0	0	27,425
2005–06	570,554	215,934	574	9,715	39,893	71,374	143,096	44,748	8,696	0	0	36,524
2006–07	496,247	166,893	947	8,224	31,758	68,799	137,366	36,478	13,741	0	0	32,041
2007–08	536,187	185,167	973	5,982	36,423	76,696	148,343	37,908	9,584	0	0	35,112
2008–09	496,620	166,280	345	3,612	41,511	68,459	142,330	37,372	7,165	0	0	29,546
2009–10	490,645	165,538	585	5,041	42,909	69,129	135,357	34,402	7,183	0	0	30,502
2010–11	622,815	209,176	285	2,349	53,336	86,290	166,362	29,983	1,365	0	0	73,669
2011–12	585,454	203,885	673	2,049	51,363	85,483	150,455	23,613	2,072	0	0	65,861
2012–13	500,218	181,113	329	1,771	39,171	67,591	138,543	26,505	4,682	0	0	40,512
						Percentage distribution						
All levels												
1999–2000	100.00	32.27	10.40	1.79	8.08	7.06	13.13	10.30	1.46	9.12	3.42	2.97
2000–01	100.00	32.24	10.54	1.72	8.61	7.14	13.35	10.52	1.37	8.47	3.66	2.36
2001–02	100.00	32.20	10.89	1.81	8.46	7.13	13.09	10.32	1.29	8.28	3.69	2.84
2002–03	100.00	32.14	11.11	1.88	8.18	7.11	13.19	9.96	1.18	7.61	3.89	3.75
2003–04	100.00	32.51	11.54	1.89	8.40	7.23	13.37	10.07	1.06	8.03	4.05	1.85
2004–05	100.00	32.84	11.61	1.81	8.46	7.42	13.31	9.91	0.97	8.32	3.83	1.52
2005–06	100.00	32.93	11.34	1.66	8.75	7.67	13.41	10.05	0.61	8.26	3.60	1.73
2006–07	100.00	33.10	11.00	1.64	8.74	7.70	13.51	10.00	0.58	8.35	3.76	1.63
2007–08	100.00	33.13	10.84	1.63	8.90	7.76	13.76	9.98	0.54	8.06	3.66	1.74
2008–09	100.00	32.86	10.80	1.63	8.90	7.79	13.73	9.70	0.54	8.44	3.65	1.97
2009–10	100.00	32.72	11.13	1.44	8.92	7.87	13.39	9.57	0.57	9.08	3.55	1.77
2010–11	100.00	32.58	11.39	1.48	8.92	8.03	13.27	9.48	0.51	9.34	3.53	1.48
2011–12	100.00	32.66	10.90	1.46	8.87	8.06	13.23	9.35	0.53	9.68	3.41	1.84
2012–13	100.00	32.77	10.58	1.40	9.01	8.27	13.20	9.26	0.51	10.09	3.28	1.63
4-year												
1999–2000	100.00	32.30	10.51	1.80	8.13	7.02	13.05	10.32	1.46	9.23	3.45	2.73
2000–01	100.00	32.23	10.61	1.73	8.62	7.10	13.28	10.53	1.36	8.53	3.68	2.33
2001–02	100.00	32.19	10.95	1.81	8.48	7.09	13.00	10.34	1.28	8.33	3.71	2.81
2002–03	100.00	32.14	11.18	1.89	8.19	7.08	13.11	9.96	1.17	7.65	3.89	3.74
2003–04	100.00	32.50	11.61	1.89	8.41	7.20	13.28	10.09	1.05	8.07	4.07	1.84
2004–05	100.00	32.84	11.67	1.82	8.48	7.38	13.22	9.93	0.96	8.36	3.85	1.50
2005–06	100.00	32.90	11.39	1.66	8.75	7.65	13.35	10.06	0.60	8.30	3.62	1.71
2006–07	100.00	33.09	11.05	1.63	8.75	7.68	13.46	10.01	0.58	8.38	3.77	1.61
2007–08	100.00	33.12	10.88	1.64	8.91	7.74	13.70	9.99	0.54	8.09	3.68	1.72
2008–09	100.00	32.86	10.84	1.63	8.90	7.77	13.67	9.71	0.53	8.47	3.66	1.96
2009–10	100.00	32.71	11.17	1.44	8.92	7.84	13.34	9.58	0.57	9.11	3.56	1.76
2010–11	100.00	32.58	11.44	1.48	8.93	8.00	13.21	9.50	0.51	9.37	3.54	1.44
2011–12	100.00	32.65	10.94	1.46	8.87	8.03	13.19	9.37	0.53	9.72	3.42	1.81
2012–13	100.00	32.76	10.61	1.40	9.02	8.25	13.16	9.27	0.51	10.12	3.29	1.61

See notes at end of table.

Table 334.30. Total expenditures of private nonprofit degree-granting postsecondary institutions, by purpose and level of institution: 1999–2000 through 2012–13—Continued

Level of institution and year	Total	Instruction	Research	Public service	Academic support	Student services	Institutional support	Auxiliary enterprises[1]	Net grant aid to students[2]	Hospitals	Independent operations	Other
1	2	3	4	5	6	7	8	9	10	11	12	13
2-year												
1999–2000	100.00	29.39	0.59	0.92	3.79	10.68	20.47	7.84	2.00	0.00	0.18	24.15
2000–01	100.00	33.53	1.00	1.03	5.96	13.99	24.57	9.17	2.69	0.33	0.26	7.46
2001–02	100.00	33.87	0.01	1.22	5.82	13.11	26.55	7.81	2.58	0.02	0.20	8.80
2002–03	100.00	32.07	0.03	1.16	5.65	13.44	26.34	9.75	2.03	0.00	4.14	5.39
2003–04	100.00	33.64	0.08	1.27	5.69	13.27	30.33	7.48	2.88	0.00	0.23	5.13
2004–05	100.00	34.31	0.09	1.10	5.70	14.98	28.81	7.43	3.04	0.00	0.00	4.54
2005–06	100.00	37.85	0.10	1.70	6.99	12.51	25.08	7.84	1.52	0.00	0.00	6.40
2006–07	100.00	33.63	0.19	1.66	6.40	13.86	27.68	7.35	2.77	0.00	0.00	6.46
2007–08	100.00	34.53	0.18	1.12	6.79	14.30	27.67	7.07	1.79	0.00	0.00	6.55
2008–09	100.00	33.48	0.07	0.73	8.36	13.78	28.66	7.53	1.44	0.00	0.00	5.95
2009–10	100.00	33.74	0.12	1.03	8.75	14.09	27.59	7.01	1.46	0.00	0.00	6.22
2010–11	100.00	33.59	0.05	0.38	8.56	13.85	26.71	4.81	0.22	0.00	0.00	11.83
2011–12	100.00	34.83	0.11	0.35	8.77	14.60	25.70	4.03	0.35	0.00	0.00	11.25
2012–13	100.00	36.21	0.07	0.35	7.83	13.51	27.70	5.30	0.94	0.00	0.00	8.10
	Expenditure per full-time-equivalent student in constant 2013–14 dollars[3]											
All levels												
1999–2000	$43,390	$14,001	$4,512	$779	$3,505	$3,062	$5,698	$4,468	$636	$3,959	$1,482	$1,290
2000–01	44,378	14,308	4,678	764	3,819	3,170	5,926	4,670	610	3,760	1,625	1,048
2001–02	45,942	14,795	5,001	830	3,888	3,276	6,014	4,742	592	3,804	1,693	1,307
2002–03	47,067	15,129	5,228	886	3,849	3,348	6,209	4,689	554	3,580	1,831	1,765
2003–04	47,020	15,284	5,427	889	3,948	3,400	6,288	4,737	497	3,775	1,903	872
2004–05	47,157	15,488	5,473	855	3,991	3,499	6,275	4,675	457	3,922	1,804	718
2005–06	47,415	15,613	5,375	788	4,147	3,639	6,359	4,766	287	3,915	1,706	820
2006–07	48,412	16,022	5,327	792	4,230	3,728	6,542	4,839	283	4,042	1,819	789
2007–08	48,810	16,170	5,292	798	4,345	3,789	6,714	4,870	264	3,932	1,787	850
2008–09	50,191	16,495	5,419	816	4,467	3,910	6,889	4,867	269	4,236	1,832	990
2009–10	49,771	16,284	5,540	717	4,437	3,915	6,664	4,762	285	4,518	1,768	882
2010–11	49,333	16,074	5,621	729	4,402	3,959	6,545	4,677	250	4,606	1,739	730
2011–12	49,802	16,265	5,430	727	4,419	4,013	6,590	4,656	263	4,823	1,698	918
2012–13	50,145	16,432	5,304	702	4,519	4,145	6,620	4,643	258	5,058	1,647	817
4-year												
1999–2000	44,502	14,375	4,677	803	3,616	3,122	5,807	4,595	649	4,107	1,537	1,215
2000–01	44,767	14,430	4,748	772	3,860	3,177	5,944	4,715	611	3,818	1,649	1,042
2001–02	46,335	14,917	5,076	839	3,929	3,286	6,026	4,790	594	3,861	1,718	1,301
2002–03	47,407	15,238	5,298	895	3,884	3,354	6,215	4,723	555	3,628	1,843	1,773
2003–04	47,354	15,390	5,496	897	3,984	3,408	6,288	4,777	495	3,823	1,927	869
2004–05	47,468	15,587	5,539	862	4,024	3,503	6,276	4,712	455	3,969	1,826	714
2005–06	47,697	15,694	5,433	793	4,176	3,649	6,370	4,799	287	3,958	1,725	814
2006–07	48,637	16,096	5,372	795	4,254	3,733	6,545	4,867	280	4,077	1,835	783
2007–08	49,050	16,246	5,339	803	4,371	3,795	6,720	4,899	263	3,967	1,803	844
2008–09	50,439	16,575	5,465	822	4,490	3,919	6,896	4,895	269	4,272	1,847	987
2009–10	50,011	16,360	5,585	721	4,459	3,923	6,672	4,789	285	4,555	1,782	879
2010–11	49,659	16,178	5,682	737	4,432	3,973	6,561	4,717	252	4,655	1,758	713
2011–12	50,111	16,362	5,483	734	4,447	4,026	6,608	4,695	265	4,871	1,715	906
2012–13	50,413	16,515	5,349	707	4,545	4,159	6,633	4,674	259	5,101	1,660	811
2-year												
1999–2000	23,801	6,994	140	219	902	2,541	4,871	1,866	477	0	43	5,747
2000–01	19,450	6,521	195	201	1,160	2,721	4,780	1,783	523	64	51	1,451
2001–02	19,634	6,651	3	240	1,143	2,575	5,213	1,533	507	3	39	1,728
2002–03	21,735	6,971	7	253	1,228	2,920	5,726	2,119	441	0	899	1,172
2003–04	20,910	7,033	16	267	1,189	2,774	6,342	1,564	603	0	49	1,073
2004–05	21,515	7,382	19	237	1,227	3,222	6,199	1,598	654	0	0	976
2005–06	21,537	8,151	22	367	1,506	2,694	5,402	1,689	328	0	0	1,379
2006–07	22,443	7,548	43	372	1,436	3,111	6,212	1,650	621	0	0	1,449
2007–08	22,050	7,615	40	246	1,498	3,154	6,100	1,559	394	0	0	1,444
2008–09	20,938	7,011	15	152	1,750	2,886	6,001	1,576	302	0	0	1,246
2009–10	20,631	6,961	25	212	1,804	2,907	5,692	1,447	302	0	0	1,283
2010–11	18,990	6,378	9	72	1,626	2,631	5,072	914	42	0	0	2,246
2011–12	18,581	6,471	21	65	1,630	2,713	4,775	749	66	0	0	2,090
2012–13	18,173	6,580	12	64	1,423	2,456	5,033	963	170	0	0	1,472

[1]Essentially self-supporting operations of institutions that furnish a service to students, faculty, or staff, such as residence halls and food services.
[2]Excludes tuition, fee, and auxiliary enterprise allowances and agency transactions, such as student awards made from contributed funds or grant funds. These exclusions account for the majority of total student grants.
[3]Constant dollars based on the Consumer Price Index, prepared by the Bureau of Labor Statistics, U.S. Department of Labor, adjusted to a school-year basis.

NOTE: Degree-granting institutions grant associate's or higher degrees and participate in Title IV federal financial aid programs. Detail may not sum to totals because of rounding.
SOURCE: U.S. Department of Education, National Center for Education Statistics, Integrated Postsecondary Education Data System (IPEDS), Spring 2001 through Spring 2013, Enrollment component; and Spring 2002 through Spring 2014, Finance component. (This table was prepared January 2015.)

Table 334.40. Total expenditures of private nonprofit degree-granting postsecondary institutions, by purpose and classification of institution: 2012–13

Classification of institution	Total	Instruction	Research	Public service	Academic support	Student services	Institutional support	Auxiliary enterprises[1]	Net grant aid to students[2]	Hospitals	Independent operations	Other
1	2	3	4	5	6	7	8	9	10	11	12	13
					In thousands of current dollars							
Total	$165,573,669	$54,257,906	$17,514,795	$2,318,128	$14,922,229	$13,685,488	$21,857,624	$15,330,575	$851,647	$16,701,193	$5,436,746	$2,697,338
4-year	165,073,451	54,076,793	17,514,466	2,316,357	14,883,058	13,617,897	21,719,080	15,304,071	846,965	16,701,193	5,436,746	2,656,826
Research university, very high[3]	77,727,786	23,619,190	14,104,247	775,566	5,644,723	2,920,855	6,746,775	4,809,955	553,519	12,913,604	4,308,046	1,331,306
Research university, high[4]	11,989,460	4,380,373	1,025,723	183,100	1,807,361	910,119	1,605,593	1,482,458	21,756	482,076	55,308	35,594
Doctoral/research[5]	7,792,328	3,133,292	235,704	119,823	905,085	956,381	1,371,928	1,004,415	9,018	0	16,799	39,884
Master's[6]	27,899,988	10,757,871	280,484	274,848	2,835,324	4,332,735	5,245,213	3,621,347	85,796	90,318	125,200	250,852
Baccalaureate[7]	22,418,857	7,943,777	256,488	220,123	1,961,821	3,566,289	4,293,642	3,614,596	123,828	6,335	60,403	371,554
Special-focus institutions[8]	17,245,033	4,242,291	1,611,821	742,897	1,728,743	931,518	2,455,929	771,300	53,049	3,208,859	870,990	627,636
Art, music, or design	2,107,018	873,024	727	24,208	259,436	218,316	443,084	217,623	7,751	0	10,704	52,145
Business and management	672,376	233,656	6,167	955	80,303	99,293	148,963	64,104	178	0	0	38,757
Engineering or technology	201,052	82,258	2,751	7	14,210	33,736	47,744	15,991	2,300	0	42	2,014
Law	614,252	265,816	6,745	15,996	92,361	76,296	134,504	15,549	1,118	0	229	5,638
Medical or other health	11,440,386	2,066,874	1,585,584	615,586	1,073,424	296,959	1,095,102	241,708	9,395	3,208,859	849,018	397,877
Theological	1,810,083	569,628	6,491	57,862	175,758	164,747	489,180	191,424	30,233	0	10,997	113,764
Tribal[9]	108,452	33,091	882	11,671	5,660	16,602	22,132	2,292	1,247	0	0	14,874
Other special focus	291,415	117,944	2,474	16,612	27,591	25,569	75,221	22,609	827	0	0	2,568
2-year	500,218	181,113	329	1,771	39,171	67,591	138,543	26,505	4,682	0	0	40,512
Associate's of arts	482,000	178,150	86	1,522	38,109	65,985	133,230	25,937	663	0	0	38,318
Tribal[9]	18,218	2,964	244	249	1,063	1,606	5,313	568	4,019	0	0	2,193
					Percentage distribution							
Total	100.00	32.77	10.58	1.40	9.01	8.27	13.20	9.26	0.51	10.09	3.28	1.63
4-year	100.00	32.76	10.61	1.40	9.02	8.25	13.16	9.27	0.51	10.12	3.29	1.61
Research university, very high[3]	100.00	30.39	18.15	1.00	7.26	3.76	8.68	6.19	0.71	16.61	5.54	1.71
Research university, high[4]	100.00	36.54	8.56	1.53	15.07	7.59	13.39	12.36	0.18	4.02	0.46	0.30
Doctoral/research[5]	100.00	40.21	3.02	1.54	11.62	12.27	17.61	12.89	0.12	0.00	0.22	0.51
Master's[6]	100.00	38.56	1.01	0.99	10.16	15.53	18.80	12.98	0.31	0.32	0.45	0.90
Baccalaureate[7]	100.00	35.43	1.14	0.98	8.75	15.91	19.15	16.12	0.55	0.03	0.27	1.66
Special-focus institutions[8]	100.00	24.60	9.35	4.31	10.02	5.40	14.24	4.47	0.31	18.61	5.05	3.64
Art, music, or design	100.00	41.43	0.03	1.15	12.31	10.36	21.03	10.33	0.37	0.00	0.51	2.47
Business and management	100.00	34.75	0.92	0.14	11.94	14.77	22.15	9.53	0.03	0.00	0.00	5.76
Engineering or technology	100.00	40.91	1.37	#	7.07	16.78	23.75	7.95	1.14	0.00	0.02	1.00
Law	100.00	43.27	1.10	2.60	15.04	12.42	21.90	2.53	0.18	0.00	0.04	0.92
Medical or other health	100.00	18.07	13.86	5.38	9.38	2.60	9.57	2.11	0.08	28.05	7.42	3.48
Theological	100.00	31.47	0.36	3.20	9.71	9.10	27.03	10.58	1.67	0.00	0.61	6.29
Tribal[9]	100.00	30.51	0.81	10.76	5.22	15.31	20.41	2.11	1.15	0.00	0.00	13.71
Other special focus	100.00	40.47	0.85	5.70	9.47	8.77	25.81	7.76	0.28	0.00	0.00	0.88
2-year	100.00	36.21	0.07	0.35	7.83	13.51	27.70	5.30	0.94	0.00	0.00	8.10
Associate's of arts	100.00	36.96	0.02	0.32	7.91	13.69	27.64	5.38	0.14	0.00	0.00	7.95
Tribal[9]	100.00	16.27	1.34	1.37	5.83	8.82	29.17	3.12	22.06	0.00	0.00	12.04
					Expenditure per full-time-equivalent student in current dollars							
Total	$49,373	$16,180	$5,223	$691	$4,450	$4,081	$6,518	$4,572	$254	$4,980	$1,621	$804
4-year	49,638	16,261	5,267	697	4,475	4,095	6,531	4,602	255	5,022	1,635	799
Research university, very high[3]	154,975	47,092	28,121	1,546	11,255	5,824	13,452	9,590	1,104	25,747	8,589	2,654
Research university, high[4]	43,068	15,735	3,685	658	6,492	3,269	5,768	5,325	78	1,732	199	128
Doctoral/research[5]	29,574	11,892	895	455	3,435	3,630	5,207	3,812	34	0	64	151
Master's[6]	22,554	8,697	227	222	2,292	3,503	4,240	2,928	69	73	101	203
Baccalaureate[7]	30,482	10,801	349	299	2,667	4,849	5,838	4,915	168	9	82	505
Special-focus institutions[8]	55,696	13,701	5,206	2,399	5,583	3,009	7,932	2,491	171	10,364	2,813	2,027
Art, music, or design	36,545	15,142	13	420	4,500	3,787	7,685	3,775	134	0	186	904
Business and management	20,946	7,279	192	30	2,502	3,093	4,640	1,997	6	0	0	1,207
Engineering or technology	13,205	5,403	181	#	933	2,216	3,136	1,050	151	0	3	132
Law	37,311	16,146	410	972	5,610	4,634	8,170	944	68	0	14	342
Medical or other health	107,061	19,342	14,838	5,761	10,045	2,779	10,248	2,262	88	30,029	7,945	3,723
Theological	25,401	7,994	91	812	2,466	2,312	6,865	2,686	424	0	154	1,596
Tribal[9]	39,251	11,977	319	4,224	2,048	6,009	8,010	830	451	0	0	5,383
Other special focus	39,920	16,157	339	2,276	3,780	3,503	10,304	3,097	113	0	0	352
2-year	17,894	6,479	12	63	1,401	2,418	4,956	948	167	0	0	1,449
Associate's of arts	17,591	6,502	3	56	1,391	2,408	4,862	947	24	0	0	1,398
Tribal[9]	32,825	5,340	439	449	1,915	2,894	9,574	1,023	7,241	0	0	3,952

#Rounds to zero.
[1]Essentially self-supporting operations of institutions that furnish a service to students, faculty, or staff, such as residence halls and food services.
[2]Excludes tuition, fee, and auxiliary enterprise allowances and agency transactions, such as student awards made from contributed funds or grant funds. These exclusions account for the majority of total student grants.
[3]Research universities with a very high level of research activity.
[4]Research universities with a high level of research activity.
[5]Includes institutions that award at least 20 doctor's degrees per year, but did not have high levels of research activity.
[6]Master's institutions award at least 50 master's degrees per year.
[7]Baccalaureate institutions primarily emphasize undergraduate education. Also includes institutions classified as 4-year under the IPEDS system, which had been classified as 2-year in the Carnegie classification system because they primarily award associate's degrees.

[8]Special-focus 4-year institutions award degrees primarily in single fields of study, such as medicine, business, fine arts, theology, and engineering.
[9]Tribally controlled colleges are located on reservations and are members of the American Indian Higher Education Consortium.
NOTE: Relative levels of research activity for research universities were determined by an analysis of research and development expenditures, science and engineering research staffing, and doctoral degrees conferred, by field. Further information on the Carnegie 2005 classification system used in this table may be obtained from http://carnegieclassifications.iu.edu/. Degree-granting institutions grant associate's or higher degrees and participate in Title IV federal financial aid programs. Detail may not sum to totals because of rounding.
SOURCE: U.S. Department of Education, National Center for Education Statistics, Integrated Postsecondary Education Data System (IPEDS), Spring 2013, Enrollment component; and Spring 2014, Finance component. (This table was prepared January 2015.)

Table 334.50. Total expenditures of private for-profit degree-granting postsecondary institutions, by purpose and level of institution: 1999–2000 through 2012–13

Year and level of institution	Total	Instruction	Research and public service	Student services, academic and institutional support	Auxiliary enterprises[1]	Net grant aid to students[2]	Other
1	2	3	4	5	6	7	8
	In thousands of current dollars						
All levels							
1999–2000	$3,846,246	$1,171,732	$24,738	$2,041,594	$144,305	$26,278	$437,599
2000–01	4,235,781	1,310,054	22,896	2,337,151	181,243	43,788	340,649
2001–02	5,087,292	1,517,389	16,632	2,977,225	213,195	23,283	339,567
2002–03	6,110,378	1,747,725	17,987	3,670,218	240,380	36,031	398,037
2003–04	7,364,012	1,883,733	8,606	4,592,730	249,472	56,467	573,004
2004–05	8,830,792	2,313,895	7,583	5,693,200	269,883	54,819	491,411
2005–06	10,208,845	2,586,870	8,445	6,569,329	276,587	66,569	701,044
2006–07	12,152,366	2,884,481	6,087	7,760,044	332,887	68,300	1,100,568
2007–08	13,940,442	3,238,406	9,547	9,322,781	421,714	82,072	865,922
2008–09	16,364,360	3,871,127	9,939	11,004,500	396,704	44,440	1,037,650
2009–10	19,973,659	4,750,829	13,257	13,086,981	466,042	120,215	1,536,334
2010–11	22,585,686	5,656,557	19,327	14,851,333	486,343	87,947	1,484,179
2011–12	23,036,898	5,609,659	42,657	15,340,710	489,409	54,579	1,499,885
2012–13	21,940,185	5,424,430	27,729	14,357,843	464,188	53,555	1,612,440
4–year							
1999–2000	2,022,622	595,976	4,393	1,104,001	92,071	11,805	214,377
2000–01	2,414,655	726,328	4,878	1,385,095	113,371	18,519	166,465
2001–02	3,046,929	883,899	3,192	1,842,373	134,740	8,229	174,495
2002–03	3,754,727	1,030,470	5,339	2,337,388	153,528	14,813	213,190
2003–04	4,821,864	1,143,050	3,705	3,108,697	168,069	32,603	365,740
2004–05	5,989,792	1,430,196	3,513	4,110,514	180,036	38,639	226,894
2005–06	7,218,830	1,680,603	4,065	4,985,531	179,064	54,291	315,276
2006–07	8,837,598	1,857,765	4,303	5,909,914	228,624	56,930	780,063
2007–08	10,424,536	2,149,651	7,534	7,335,592	312,834	71,324	547,602
2008–09	12,399,217	2,580,208	7,629	8,832,095	276,200	33,417	669,669
2009–10	15,286,549	3,259,657	10,726	10,587,709	337,501	72,265	1,018,691
2010–11	17,139,103	3,925,914	15,582	12,033,229	343,230	75,599	745,548
2011–12	17,730,800	4,000,492	37,912	12,403,955	349,405	51,818	887,218
2012–13	16,779,710	3,897,632	24,432	11,443,167	356,202	46,446	1,011,832
2–year							
1999–2000	1,823,624	575,756	20,345	937,593	52,234	14,473	223,223
2000–01	1,821,126	583,727	18,019	952,056	67,872	25,269	174,184
2001–02	2,040,363	633,490	13,440	1,134,853	78,455	15,054	174,184
2002–03	2,355,650	717,255	12,648	1,332,830	86,853	21,218	184,846
2003–04	2,542,148	740,683	4,901	1,484,033	81,403	23,864	207,264
2004–05	2,840,999	883,699	4,070	1,582,687	89,846	16,181	264,517
2005–06	2,990,015	906,267	4,381	1,583,798	97,523	12,278	385,768
2006–07	3,314,768	1,026,716	1,784	1,850,129	104,264	11,370	320,505
2007–08	3,515,906	1,088,755	2,014	1,987,189	108,880	10,747	318,320
2008–09	3,965,143	1,290,919	2,310	2,172,405	120,504	11,023	367,981
2009–10	4,687,110	1,491,172	2,531	2,499,272	128,542	47,950	517,643
2010–11	5,446,582	1,730,642	3,744	2,818,104	143,113	12,347	738,631
2011–12	5,306,098	1,609,167	4,745	2,936,755	140,004	2,761	612,667
2012–13	5,160,475	1,526,798	3,297	2,914,676	107,986	7,109	600,609
	Percentage distribution						
All levels							
1999–2000	100.00	30.46	0.64	53.08	3.75	0.68	11.38
2000–01	100.00	30.93	0.54	55.18	4.28	1.03	8.04
2001–02	100.00	29.83	0.33	58.52	4.19	0.46	6.67
2002–03	100.00	28.60	0.29	60.07	3.93	0.59	6.51
2003–04	100.00	25.58	0.12	62.37	3.39	0.77	7.78
2004–05	100.00	26.20	0.09	64.47	3.06	0.62	5.56
2005–06	100.00	25.34	0.08	64.35	2.71	0.65	6.87
2006–07	100.00	23.74	0.05	63.86	2.74	0.56	9.06
2007–08	100.00	23.23	0.07	66.88	3.03	0.59	6.21
2008–09	100.00	23.66	0.06	67.25	2.42	0.27	6.34
2009–10	100.00	23.79	0.07	65.52	2.33	0.60	7.69
2010–11	100.00	25.04	0.09	65.76	2.15	0.39	6.57
2011–12	100.00	24.35	0.19	66.59	2.12	0.24	6.51
2012–13	100.00	24.72	0.13	65.44	2.12	0.24	7.35
4–year							
1999–2000	100.00	29.47	0.22	54.58	4.55	0.58	10.60
2000–01	100.00	30.08	0.20	57.36	4.70	0.77	6.89
2001–02	100.00	29.01	0.10	60.47	4.42	0.27	5.73
2002–03	100.00	27.44	0.14	62.25	4.09	0.39	5.68
2003–04	100.00	23.71	0.08	64.47	3.49	0.68	7.59
2004–05	100.00	23.88	0.06	68.63	3.01	0.65	3.79
2005–06	100.00	23.28	0.06	69.06	2.48	0.75	4.37
2006–07	100.00	21.02	0.05	66.87	2.59	0.64	8.83
2007–08	100.00	20.62	0.07	70.37	3.00	0.68	5.25
2008–09	100.00	20.81	0.06	71.23	2.23	0.27	5.40
2009–10	100.00	21.32	0.07	69.26	2.21	0.47	6.66
2010–11	100.00	22.91	0.09	70.21	2.00	0.44	4.35
2011–12	100.00	22.56	0.21	69.96	1.97	0.29	5.00
2012–13	100.00	23.23	0.15	68.20	2.12	0.28	6.03

See notes at end of table.

Table 334.50. Total expenditures of private for-profit degree-granting postsecondary institutions, by purpose and level of institution: 1999–2000 through 2012–13—Continued

Year and level of institution	Total	Instruction	Research and public service	Student services, academic and institutional support	Auxiliary enterprises[1]	Net grant aid to students[2]	Other
1	2	3	4	5	6	7	8
2-year							
1999–2000	100.00	31.57	1.12	51.41	2.86	0.79	12.24
2000–01	100.00	32.05	0.99	52.28	3.73	1.39	9.56
2001–02	100.00	31.05	0.66	55.62	3.85	0.74	8.09
2002–03	100.00	30.45	0.54	56.58	3.69	0.90	7.85
2003–04	100.00	29.14	0.19	58.38	3.20	0.94	8.15
2004–05	100.00	31.11	0.14	55.71	3.16	0.57	9.31
2005–06	100.00	30.31	0.15	52.97	3.26	0.41	12.90
2006–07	100.00	30.97	0.05	55.81	3.15	0.34	9.67
2007–08	100.00	30.97	0.06	56.52	3.10	0.31	9.05
2008–09	100.00	32.56	0.06	54.79	3.04	0.28	9.28
2009–10	100.00	31.81	0.05	53.32	2.74	1.02	11.04
2010–11	100.00	31.77	0.07	51.74	2.63	0.23	13.56
2011–12	100.00	30.33	0.09	55.35	2.64	0.05	11.55
2012–13	100.00	29.59	0.06	56.48	2.09	0.14	11.64
Total expenditures per full-time-equivalent student in constant 2013–14 dollars[3]							
All levels							
1999–2000	$13,880	$4,228	$89	$7,367	$521	$95	$1,579
2000–01	14,468	4,475	78	7,983	619	150	1,164
2001–02	14,694	4,383	48	8,599	616	67	981
2002–03	14,582	4,171	43	8,759	574	86	950
2003–04	14,370	3,676	17	8,962	487	110	1,118
2004–05	13,735	3,599	12	8,855	420	85	764
2005–06	13,386	3,392	11	8,614	363	87	919
2006–07	14,825	3,519	7	9,467	406	83	1,343
2007–08	15,013	3,488	10	10,040	454	88	933
2008–09	14,064	3,327	9	9,457	341	38	892
2009–10	13,480	3,206	9	8,832	315	81	1,037
2010–11	14,570	3,649	12	9,580	314	57	957
2011–12	14,772	3,597	27	9,837	314	35	962
2012–13	15,745	3,893	20	10,303	333	38	1,157
4-year							
1999–2000	13,447	3,962	29	7,340	612	78	1,425
2000–01	14,209	4,274	29	8,151	667	109	980
2001–02	14,532	4,216	15	8,787	643	39	832
2002–03	14,014	3,846	20	8,724	573	55	796
2003–04	14,256	3,380	11	9,191	497	96	1,081
2004–05	13,260	3,166	8	9,100	399	86	502
2005–06	12,867	2,996	7	8,887	319	97	562
2006–07	14,447	3,037	7	9,661	374	93	1,275
2007–08	14,664	3,024	11	10,319	440	100	770
2008–09	13,851	2,882	9	9,866	309	37	748
2009–10	13,420	2,862	9	9,295	296	63	894
2010–11	14,523	3,327	13	10,197	291	64	632
2011–12	14,569	3,287	31	10,192	287	43	729
2012–13	15,392	3,575	22	10,497	327	43	928
2-year							
1999–2000	14,393	4,544	161	7,400	412	114	1,762
2000–01	14,826	4,752	147	7,751	553	206	1,418
2001–02	14,944	4,640	98	8,312	575	110	1,209
2002–03	15,587	4,746	84	8,819	575	140	1,223
2003–04	14,592	4,252	28	8,518	467	137	1,190
2004–05	14,856	4,621	21	8,276	470	85	1,383
2005–06	14,829	4,495	22	7,855	484	61	1,913
2006–07	15,939	4,937	9	8,896	501	55	1,541
2007–08	16,154	5,002	9	9,130	500	49	1,463
2008–09	14,775	4,810	9	8,095	449	41	1,371
2009–10	13,682	4,353	7	7,295	375	140	1,511
2010–11	14,718	4,677	10	7,615	387	33	1,996
2011–12	15,494	4,699	14	8,575	409	8	1,789
2012–13	17,013	5,034	11	9,609	356	23	1,980

[1]Essentially self-supporting operations of institutions that furnish a service to students, faculty, or staff, such as residence halls and food services.
[2]Excludes tuition and fee allowances and agency transactions, such as student awards made from contributed funds or grant funds.
[3]Constant dollars based on the Consumer Price Index, prepared by the Bureau of Labor Statistics, U.S. Department of Labor, adjusted to a school-year basis.

NOTE: Degree-granting institutions grant associate's or higher degrees and participate in Title IV federal financial aid programs. Detail may not sum to totals because of rounding.
SOURCE: U.S. Department of Education, National Center for Education Statistics, Integrated Postsecondary Education Data System (IPEDS), "Fall Enrollment Survey" (IPEDS-EF:99), and Spring 2001 through Spring 2014, Enrollment and Finance components. (This table was prepared January 2015.)

Table 334.60. Total expenditures of private for-profit degree-granting postsecondary institutions, by purpose and classification of institution: 2012–13

Classification of institution	Total	Instruction	Research and public service	Student services, academic and institutional support	Auxiliary enterprises[1]	Net grant aid to students[2]	Other
1	2	3	4	5	6	7	8
In thousands of current dollars							
Total	$21,940,185	$5,424,430	$27,729	$14,357,843	$464,188	$53,555	$1,612,440
4-year	16,779,710	3,897,632	24,432	11,443,167	356,202	46,446	1,011,832
Doctoral/research[3]	2,891,360	536,192	8,469	2,085,730	4,585	0	256,385
Master's[4]	4,037,333	840,502	1,915	2,885,379	51,990	0	257,547
Baccalaureate[5]	2,004,548	668,393	730	1,210,158	42,351	680	82,235
Special-focus institutions[6]	7,846,469	1,852,544	13,318	5,261,900	257,276	45,766	415,664
Art, music, or design	2,334,050	556,835	163	1,475,845	145,222	3,462	152,521
Business and management	3,148,125	697,748	10,041	2,246,962	57,116	23,974	112,285
Engineering or technology	1,320,826	301,073	2	991,448	13,234	613	14,455
Law	204,211	48,043	1,492	108,886	511	17,224	28,053
Medical or other health	680,093	209,485	504	397,715	26,842	492	45,056
Theological	112,365	22,536	1,116	19,381	12,965	0	56,367
Other special focus	46,800	16,824	0	21,664	1,386	0	6,927
2-year	5,160,475	1,526,798	3,297	2,914,676	107,986	7,109	600,609
Percentage distribution							
Total	100.00	24.72	0.13	65.44	2.12	0.24	7.35
4-year	100.00	23.23	0.15	68.20	2.12	0.28	6.03
Doctoral/research[3]	100.00	18.54	0.29	72.14	0.16	0.00	8.87
Master's[4]	100.00	20.82	0.05	71.47	1.29	0.00	6.38
Baccalaureate[5]	100.00	33.34	0.04	60.37	2.11	0.03	4.10
Special-focus institutions[6]	100.00	23.61	0.17	67.06	3.28	0.58	5.30
Art, music, or design	100.00	23.86	0.01	63.23	6.22	0.15	6.53
Business and management	100.00	22.16	0.32	71.37	1.81	0.76	3.57
Engineering or technology	100.00	22.79	#	75.06	1.00	0.05	1.09
Law	100.00	23.53	0.73	53.32	0.25	8.43	13.74
Medical or other health	100.00	30.80	0.07	58.48	3.95	0.07	6.62
Theological	100.00	20.06	0.99	17.25	11.54	0.00	50.16
Other special focus	100.00	35.95	0.00	46.29	2.96	0.00	14.80
2-year	100.00	29.59	0.06	56.48	2.09	0.14	11.64
Expenditure per full-time-equivalent student in current dollars							
Total	$15,502	$3,833	$20	$10,145	$328	$38	$1,139
4-year	15,155	3,520	22	10,335	322	42	914
Doctoral/research[3]	8,869	1,645	26	6,398	14	0	786
Master's[4]	12,945	2,695	6	9,251	167	0	826
Baccalaureate[5]	16,387	5,464	6	9,893	346	6	672
Special-focus institutions[6]	22,613	5,339	38	15,164	741	132	1,198
Art, music, or design	25,646	6,118	2	16,216	1,596	38	1,676
Business and management	20,736	4,596	66	14,800	376	158	740
Engineering or technology	22,071	5,031	#	16,567	221	10	242
Law	30,899	7,269	226	16,475	77	2,606	4,245
Medical or other health	21,177	6,523	16	12,384	836	15	1,403
Theological	35,379	7,096	352	6,102	4,082	0	17,748
Other special focus	19,387	6,969	0	8,974	574	0	2,870
2-year	16,752	4,956	11	9,461	351	23	1,950
Expenditure per full-time-equivalent student in constant 2013–14 dollars[7]							
Total	$15,745	$3,893	$20	$10,303	$333	$38	$1,157
4-year	15,392	3,575	22	10,497	327	43	928
Doctoral/research[3]	9,008	1,670	26	6,498	14	0	799
Master's[4]	13,147	2,737	6	9,396	169	0	839
Baccalaureate[5]	16,643	5,549	6	10,048	352	6	683
Special-focus institutions[6]	22,966	5,422	39	15,401	753	134	1,217
Art, music, or design	26,046	6,214	2	16,469	1,621	39	1,702
Business and management	21,060	4,668	67	15,031	382	160	751
Engineering or technology	22,416	5,109	#	16,826	225	10	245
Law	31,382	7,383	229	16,733	79	2,647	4,311
Medical or other health	21,508	6,625	16	12,578	849	16	1,425
Theological	35,932	7,206	357	6,197	4,146	0	18,025
Other special focus	19,690	7,078	0	9,114	583	0	2,914
2-year	17,013	5,034	11	9,609	356	23	1,980

#Rounds to zero.
[1]Essentially self-supporting operations of institutions that furnish a service to students, faculty, or staff, such as residence halls and food services.
[2]Excludes tuition, fee, and auxiliary enterprise allowances and agency transactions, such as student awards made from contributed funds or grant funds.
[3]Includes institutions that award at least 20 doctor's degrees per year, but did not have high levels of research activity.
[4]Master's institutions award at least 50 master's degrees per year.
[5]Baccalaureate institutions primarily emphasize undergraduate education. Also includes institutions classified as 4-year under the IPEDS system, which had been classified as 2-year in the Carnegie classification system because they primarily award associate's degrees.

[6]Special focus 4-year institutions award degrees primarily in single fields of study, such as medicine, business, fine arts, theology, and engineering.
[7]Constant dollars based on the Consumer Price Index, prepared by the Bureau of Labor Statistics, U.S. Department of Labor, adjusted to a school-year basis.
NOTE: Degree-granting institutions grant associate's or higher degrees and participate in Title IV federal financial aid programs. Further information on the Carnegie 2005 classification system used in this table may be obtained from http://carnegieclassifications.iu.edu/. Detail may not sum to totals because of rounding.
SOURCE: U.S. Department of Education, National Center for Education Statistics, Integrated Postsecondary Education Data System (IPEDS), Spring 2013, Enrollment component; and Spring 2014, Finance component. (This table was prepared January 2015.)

Table 334.70. Total expenditures of private nonprofit and for-profit degree-granting postsecondary institutions, by state or jurisdiction: Selected years, 1999–2000 through 2012–13

[In thousands of current dollars]

State or jurisdiction	Nonprofit institutions						For-profit institutions					
	1999–2000	2004–05	2009–10	2010–11	2011–12	2012–13	1999–2000	2004–05	2009–10	2010–11	2011–12	2012–13
1	2	3	4	5	6	7	8	9	10	11	12	13
United States ...	$80,613,037	$110,394,127	$145,141,785	$152,509,741	$159,873,305	$165,573,669	$3,846,246	$8,830,792	$19,973,659	$22,585,686	$23,036,898	$21,940,185
Alabama	393,465	459,250	561,968	583,205	604,992	629,327	88,190	60,629	139,366	244,943	218,687	235,259
Alaska	19,042	21,076	16,249	18,319	17,245	20,965	3,559	3,986	19,302	41,245	53,164	59,584
Arizona	143,698	147,825	176,443	212,911	237,638	251,981	278,286	1,095,783	3,412,261	3,623,551	3,419,611	3,003,342
Arkansas	230,860	239,357	289,868	322,896	341,827	353,657	5,828	11,574	31,263	27,834	29,152	23,245
California	7,871,651	10,728,872	13,925,287	14,557,205	15,355,141	15,815,988	666,020	1,243,346	2,552,449	2,952,470	3,016,592	3,016,715
Colorado	376,887	524,349	627,123	659,716	692,467	776,700	154,801	320,550	661,384	736,387	739,248	719,598
Connecticut	2,094,981	2,882,963	3,975,262	4,127,051	4,337,333	4,557,470	18,110	41,931	59,726	80,628	95,498	118,571
Delaware	52,533	87,617	132,851	141,186	150,054	148,481	†	†	4,042	4,957	5,191	4,480
District of Columbia ..	2,267,409	2,824,081	3,687,042	3,724,430	3,929,951	3,976,868	59,375	127,859	66,677	77,469	68,746	70,981
Florida	2,031,623	3,067,443	4,592,898	5,071,442	5,356,148	5,570,552	315,721	781,280	1,825,704	1,982,163	2,038,395	2,083,657
Georgia	2,635,438	3,442,374	4,497,299	4,796,550	5,346,024	5,530,320	106,794	261,219	675,496	783,834	811,908	707,447
Hawaii	209,135	195,152	210,680	231,683	251,071	262,526	9,422	24,996	34,299	41,754	46,358	51,477
Idaho	118,150	164,694	228,589	242,764	261,954	300,184	5,932	13,073	32,602	51,944	50,751	36,771
Illinois	5,668,566	7,113,842	9,512,165	10,095,051	10,532,731	11,212,425	166,956	620,678	1,100,032	1,054,104	1,542,922	1,274,607
Indiana	1,343,315	1,796,767	2,251,554	2,360,297	2,502,296	2,557,015	89,932	211,310	591,600	726,450	730,138	613,850
Iowa	740,760	921,320	1,156,393	1,188,889	1,248,348	1,261,785	34,311	146,688	1,002,405	1,269,406	1,189,547	1,165,192
Kansas	208,729	265,476	364,286	381,327	414,219	444,498	9,156	11,213	47,645	57,986	58,226	84,242
Kentucky	400,513	470,392	597,495	637,466	683,702	728,838	55,010	114,564	242,672	285,217	288,146	269,760
Louisiana	746,629	940,075	1,089,736	1,137,685	1,192,748	1,202,971	31,675	70,241	111,844	104,007	110,097	106,710
Maine	316,114	422,938	552,463	592,174	619,223	640,969	7,137	5,648	12,409	14,411	13,111	13,023
Maryland	2,205,880	3,497,182	4,792,089	5,069,546	5,278,869	5,535,099	5,354	41,717	115,071	118,794	107,983	100,249
Massachusetts	7,591,344	10,799,206	13,862,598	14,533,360	15,252,538	15,940,319	34,893	64,126	118,526	130,488	127,099	120,182
Michigan	995,384	1,327,051	1,638,367	1,680,792	1,751,050	1,731,507	25,340	55,391	120,070	142,261	151,906	163,271
Minnesota	1,004,427	1,297,457	1,622,869	1,664,254	1,729,682	1,757,253	123,571	325,758	928,396	1,092,542	1,179,028	1,168,273
Mississippi	150,123	178,142	225,484	234,795	248,970	257,215	†	8,369	21,061	26,002	29,899	32,917
Missouri	2,144,299	3,128,635	3,958,548	4,203,742	4,377,146	4,479,649	100,307	196,447	331,391	426,479	432,200	342,705
Montana	69,426	91,446	116,161	132,829	107,390	111,276	†	†	†	†	†	†
Nebraska	387,569	557,724	709,182	731,588	744,788	733,066	12,051	25,524	42,559	42,926	43,275	39,015
Nevada	7,006	9,637	73,701	85,024	98,835	130,845	29,278	104,949	143,358	156,577	152,954	149,537
New Hampshire	589,823	883,914	1,085,570	1,115,169	1,179,386	1,289,111	21,831	41,599	36,737	47,598	44,532	42,598
New Jersey	1,362,090	1,873,156	2,591,234	2,681,051	2,747,352	2,803,276	61,109	85,429	126,833	137,408	125,946	141,366
New Mexico	54,280	54,076	30,447	31,564	32,930	34,809	25,806	35,073	83,708	104,193	111,639	110,443
New York	12,519,671	17,680,799	23,511,385	24,664,171	25,903,697	26,742,737	326,329	624,764	762,214	876,944	871,255	899,389
North Carolina	3,530,337	4,808,306	6,452,783	6,890,504	7,001,839	7,263,282	4,041	38,078	186,514	242,098	261,901	286,151
North Dakota	56,000	88,860	87,938	93,751	114,109	118,499	1,145	7,885	20,198	18,456	15,292	12,964
Ohio	2,211,035	3,017,764	3,582,655	3,732,414	3,803,772	3,900,304	122,531	232,685	564,498	636,245	658,160	564,238
Oklahoma	338,276	392,427	523,630	550,897	583,898	601,224	32,527	72,537	110,336	129,544	145,509	139,022
Oregon	456,683	550,322	734,883	790,331	832,852	879,799	23,175	86,156	120,490	131,966	134,421	134,361
Pennsylvania	7,590,629	9,960,675	13,154,197	13,800,521	14,460,608	14,638,232	306,135	530,515	842,052	935,748	861,247	863,594
Rhode Island	828,715	1,237,106	1,564,624	1,596,480	1,702,209	1,727,591	4,519	10,073	†	†	†	†
South Carolina	408,127	563,952	680,369	717,448	739,911	744,752	6,627	18,374	226,848	273,395	289,770	289,924
South Dakota	69,555	99,575	119,974	125,637	125,509	132,514	18,061	23,477	41,594	47,972	51,505	50,760
Tennessee	1,971,564	3,140,336	4,500,016	4,801,285	4,918,450	5,120,422	50,921	142,256	331,287	346,050	340,537	342,166
Texas	2,490,597	3,379,710	4,376,280	4,665,642	4,806,456	5,043,913	172,327	343,221	803,401	851,581	847,702	823,269
Utah	648,035	867,956	1,012,997	1,061,194	1,177,439	1,370,858	36,348	62,880	144,226	206,186	211,978	116,470
Vermont	347,293	510,623	717,199	754,383	782,385	792,944	24,841	24,914	17,126	16,242	16,288	13,159
Virginia	944,905	1,311,743	1,841,075	1,737,579	1,923,966	2,015,158	65,804	258,642	614,287	678,326	663,162	670,139
Washington	600,315	778,678	988,571	1,034,761	1,073,689	1,104,511	51,134	104,107	161,645	178,364	163,426	159,308
West Virginia	170,653	181,181	211,877	222,031	179,112	186,523	17,926	28,634	165,043	214,223	259,876	315,675
Wisconsin	999,502	1,410,625	1,929,430	2,024,751	2,119,356	2,141,821	16,333	36,044	131,140	170,376	172,703	156,315
Wyoming	†	†	†	†	†	1,643	19,766	34,596	39,869	45,942	40,220	34,218
Other jurisdictions..	431,216	615,990	742,820	793,439	855,651	845,821	56,116	70,535	116,452	260,512	258,693	263,553
Guam	†	1,535	2,551	2,215	1,756	1,639	†	†	†	†	†	†
Puerto Rico	431,216	614,455	740,269	791,224	853,895	844,183	56,116	70,535	116,452	260,512	258,693	263,553

†Not applicable.
NOTE: Degree-granting institutions grant associate's or higher degrees and participate in Title IV federal financial aid programs. Detail may not sum to totals because of rounding.

SOURCE: U.S. Department of Education, National Center for Education Statistics, Integrated Postsecondary Education Data System (IPEDS), Spring 2001 through Spring 2014, Finance component. (This table was prepared April 2015.)

CHAPTER 4
Federal Funds for Education and Related Activities

This chapter provides information on federal support for education. The tables include detailed data on funding by specific federal agencies, funding for different levels of education and types of education-related activities, and funding for specific programs. Preceding the tables is a brief chronology of federal education legislation enacted since 1787, which provides historical context for the education funding data.

The data in this chapter primarily reflect outlays and appropriations of federal agencies. The data are compiled from budget information prepared by federal agencies. In contrast, most of the federal revenue data reported in other chapters are compiled by educational institutions or state education agencies and reported to the federal government through standardized survey forms. Tabulations based on institution- or state-reported revenue data differ substantially from federal budget reports because of numerous variations in methodology and definitions. Federal dollars are not necessarily spent by recipient institutions in the same year in which they are appropriated. In some cases, institutions cannot identify the source of federal revenues because they flow through state agencies. Some types of revenues, such as tuition and fees, are reported as revenues from students even though they may be supported by federal student aid programs. Some institutions that receive federal education funds (e.g., Department of Defense overseas and domestic schools, state education agencies, Head Start programs, and federal libraries) are not included in regular surveys, censuses, and administrative data collections conducted by the National Center for Education Statistics (NCES). Thus, the federal programs data tabulated in this chapter are not comparable with figures reported in other chapters. Readers should also be careful about comparing the data on obligations shown in table 402.10 with the data on outlays and appropriations appearing in other tables in this chapter.

Federal Education Funding

Federal on-budget funding (federal appropriations) for education increased an estimated 401 percent from fiscal year (FY) 1965 to FY 2013, after adjustment for inflation (table D, table 401.10, and figure 20). From FY 1965 to FY 1975, federal on-budget funding for education increased by 152 percent. From FY 1975 to FY 1985, there was a decrease of 16 percent. Thereafter, federal on-budget funding for education generally increased. From FY 1990 to FY 2000, after adjustment for inflation, federal on-budget funding for education increased by 30 percent. From FY 2000 to FY 2013, it increased by an estimated 60 percent.

Table D. Federal on-budget funding for education, by category: Selected fiscal years, 1965 through 2013

[In billions of constant fiscal year (FY) 2014 dollars]

Year	Total	Elementary/ secondary	Post- secondary	Other education	Research at educational institutions
1965	$37.2	$13.5	$8.3	$2.6	$12.7
1975	93.5	42.6	30.7	6.5	13.7
1980	94.5	43.9	30.4	4.2	15.9
1985	78.6	34.1	22.5	4.2	17.8
1990	89.6	38.2	23.7	5.9	21.9
1995	106.1	49.8	26.1	7.0	23.2
2000	116.7	59.5	20.4	7.4	29.4
2005	176.2	82.2	46.0	8.2	39.8
2010	196.0	92.7	53.7	10.0	39.6
2013	186.2	80.4	63.8	9.9	32.2 [1]

[1] For FY 2013, research at educational institutions is estimated by the National Science Foundation.
NOTE: Detail may not sum to totals because of rounding.
SOURCE: U.S. Department of Education, Budget Service and National Center for Education Statistics, unpublished tabulations. U.S. Office of Management and Budget, *Budget of the U.S. Government, Appendix,* various FYs. National Science Foundation, *Federal Funds for Research and Development,* various FYs.

Between FY 1990 and FY 2000, after adjustment for inflation, federal on-budget funding increased for three of the four major categories reported: elementary and secondary education (by 56 percent), other education (by 27 percent), and research at educational institutions (by 34 percent) (table D, table 401.10, and figure 20). During the same period, funding for postsecondary education decreased by 14 percent. From FY 2000 to FY 2013, after adjustment for inflation, federal on-budget funding showed a net increase of 35 percent for elementary and secondary education, 213 percent for postsecondary education, 33 percent for other education, and an estimated 10 percent for research at educational institutions. In FY 2009, federal on-budget funding for elementary and secondary education was at a record-high level ($186.9 billion in FY 2014 dollars) due to funds from the American Recovery and Reinvestment Act of 2009 (ARRA) (table 401.10).[1] For FY 2014, federal program funds totaled $80.1 billion for elementary and secondary education, $57.0 billion for postsecondary education, $9.5 billion for other education programs, and an estimated $32.9 billion for research at educational institutions (tables 401.10 and 401.30).

---

[1] Throughout this chapter, all education funds from ARRA are included in FY 2009. Most of these funds had a 2-year availability, meaning that they were available for the Department of Education to obligate during FY 2009 and FY 2010.

After adjustment for inflation, off-budget support (federal support for education not tied to appropriations) and nonfederal funds generated by federal legislation (e.g., private loans, grants, and aid) showed an increase of 135 percent between FY 1990 ($19.4 billion in FY 2014 dollars) and FY 2000 ($45.6 billion in FY 2014 dollars) (table 401.10). In FY 2013, these same funds totaled $103.3 billion in FY 2014 dollars, an increase of 126 percent over FY 2000. In FY 2014, these funds totaled $100.1 billion.

In FY 2013, federal on-budget funds for education totaled an estimated $183.4 billion in current dollars (figure 21 and table 401.20). The U.S. Department of Education provided 50 percent ($91.1 billion) of this total. Funds exceeding $3 billion also came from the U.S. Department of Health and Human Services ($28.8 billion), the U.S. Department of Agriculture ($23.3 billion), the U.S. Department of Veterans Affairs ($11.7 billion), the U.S. Department of Defense ($7.1 billion), the U.S. Department of Labor ($5.3 billion), and the National Science Foundation ($5.3 billion).

Chronology of Federal Education Legislation

A capsule view of the history of federal education activities is provided in the following list of selected legislation:

1787 *Northwest Ordinance* authorized land grants for the establishment of educational institutions.

1802 *An Act Fixing the Military Peace Establishment of the United States* established the U.S. Military Academy. (The U.S. Naval Academy was established in 1845 by the Secretary of the Navy.)

1862 *First Morrill Act* authorized public land grants to the states for the establishment and maintenance of agricultural and mechanical colleges.

1867 *Department of Education Act* authorized the establishment of the U.S. Department of Education.[2]

1876 *Appropriation Act*, U.S. Department of the Treasury, established the U.S. Coast Guard Academy.

1890 *Second Morrill Act* provided for money grants for support of instruction in the agricultural and mechanical colleges.

1911 *State Marine School Act* authorized federal funds to be used for the benefit of any nautical school in any of 11 specified state seaport cities.

1917 *Smith-Hughes Act* provided for grants to states for support of vocational education.

---

[2]The U.S. Department of Education as established in 1867 was later known as the Office of Education. In 1980, under Public Law 96-88, it became a cabinet-level department. Therefore, for purposes of consistency, it is referred to as the "U.S. Department of Education" even in those tables covering years when it was officially the Office of Education.

1918 *Vocational Rehabilitation Act* provided for grants for rehabilitation through training of World War I veterans.

1920 *Smith-Bankhead Act* authorized grants to states for vocational rehabilitation programs.

1935 *Bankhead-Jones Act* (Public Law 74-182) authorized grants to states for agricultural experiment stations.

Agricultural Adjustment Act (Public Law 74-320) authorized 30 percent of the annual customs receipts to be used to encourage the exportation and domestic consumption of agricultural commodities. Commodities purchased under this authorization began to be used in school lunch programs in 1936. The National School Lunch Act of 1946 continued and expanded this assistance.

1936 *An Act to Further the Development and Maintenance of an Adequate and Well-Balanced American Merchant Marine* (Public Law 74-415) established the U.S. Merchant Marine Academy.

1937 *National Cancer Institute Act* established the Public Health Service fellowship program.

1941 *Amendment to Lanham Act of 1940* authorized federal aid for construction, maintenance, and operation of schools in federally impacted areas. Such assistance was continued under Public Law 815 and Public Law 874, 81st Congress, in 1950.

1943 *Vocational Rehabilitation Act* (Public Law 78-16) provided assistance to veterans with disabilities.

School Lunch Indemnity Plan (Public Law 78-129) provided funds for local lunch food purchases.

1944 *Servicemen's Readjustment Act* (Public Law 78-346), known as the GI Bill, provided assistance for the education of veterans.

Surplus Property Act (Public Law 78-457) authorized transfer of surplus property to educational institutions.

1946 *National School Lunch Act* (Public Law 79-396) authorized assistance through grants-in-aid and other means to states to assist in providing adequate foods and facilities for the establishment, maintenance, operation, and expansion of nonprofit school lunch programs.

George-Barden Act (Public Law 80-402) expanded federal support of vocational education.

1948 *United States Information and Educational Exchange Act* (Public Law 80-402) provided for the interchange of people, knowledge, and skills between the United States and other countries.

1949 *Federal Property and Administrative Services Act* (Public Law 81-152) provided for donation of surplus property to educational institutions and for other public purposes.

1950 *Financial Assistance for Local Educational Agencies Affected by Federal Activities* (Public Law 81-815 and Public Law 81-874) provided assistance for construction (Public Law 815) and operation (Public Law 874) of schools in federally affected areas.

Housing Act (Public Law 81-475) authorized loans for construction of college housing facilities.

1954 *An Act for the Establishment of the United States Air Force Academy and Other Purposes* (Public Law 83-325) established the U.S. Air Force Academy.

Educational Research Act (Public Law 83-531) authorized cooperative arrangements with universities, colleges, and state educational agencies for educational research.

School Milk Program Act (Public Law 83-597) provided funds for purchase of milk for school lunch programs.

1956 *Library Services Act* (Public Law 84-597) provided grants to states for extension and improvement of rural public library services.

1957 *Practical Nurse Training Act* (Public Law 84-911) provided grants to states for practical nurse training.

1958 *National Defense Education Act* (Public Law 85-864) provided assistance to state and local school systems for instruction in science, mathematics, modern foreign languages, and other critical subjects; state statistical services; guidance, counseling, and testing services and training institutes; higher education student loans and fellowships as well as foreign language study and training; experimentation and dissemination of information on more effective use of television, motion pictures, and related media for educational purposes; and vocational education for technical occupations necessary to the national defense.

Education of Mentally Retarded Children Act (Public Law 85-926) authorized federal assistance for training teachers of the disabled.

Captioned Films for the Deaf Act (Public Law 85-905) authorized a loan service of captioned films for the deaf.

1961 *Area Redevelopment Act* (Public Law 87-27) included provisions for training or retraining of people in redevelopment areas.

1962 *Manpower Development and Training Act* (Public Law 87-415) provided training in new and improved skills for the unemployed and underemployed.

Migration and Refugee Assistance Act of 1962 (Public Law 87-510) authorized loans, advances, and grants for education and training of refugees.

1963 *Health Professions Educational Assistance Act of 1963* (Public Law 88-129) provided funds to expand teaching facilities and for loans to students in the health professions.

Vocational Education Act of 1963 (Part of Public Law 88-210) increased federal support of vocational education schools; vocational work-study programs; and research, training, and demonstrations in vocational education.

Higher Education Facilities Act of 1963 (Public Law 88-204) authorized grants and loans for classrooms, libraries, and laboratories in public community colleges and technical institutes, as well as undergraduate and graduate facilities in other institutions of higher education.

1964 *Civil Rights Act of 1964* (Public Law 88-352) authorized the Commissioner of Education to arrange for support for institutions of higher education and school districts to provide inservice programs for assisting instructional staff in dealing with problems caused by desegregation.

Economic Opportunity Act of 1964 (Public Law 88-452) authorized grants for college work-study programs for students from low-income families; established a Job Corps program and authorized support for work-training programs to provide education and vocational training and work experience opportunities in welfare programs; authorized support of education and training activities and of community action programs, including Head Start, Follow Through, and Upward Bound; and authorized the establishment of Volunteers in Service to America (VISTA).

1965 *Elementary and Secondary Education Act of 1965* (Public Law 89-10) authorized grants for elementary and secondary school programs for children of low-income families; school library resources, textbooks, and other instructional materials for school children; supplementary educational centers and services; strengthening state education agencies; and educational research and research training.

Health Professions Educational Assistance Amendments of 1965 (Public Law 89-290) authorized scholarships to aid needy students in the health professions.

Higher Education Act of 1965 (Public Law 89-329) provided grants for university community service programs, college library assistance, library training and research, strengthening developing institutions, teacher training programs, and undergraduate instructional equipment. Authorized insured student loans, established a National Teacher Corps, and provided for graduate teacher training fellowships.

National Foundation on the Arts and the Humanities Act (Public Law 89-209) authorized grants and loans for projects in the creative and performing arts and for research, training, and scholarly publications in the humanities.

National Technical Institute for the Deaf Act (Public Law 89-36) provided for the establishment, construction, equipping, and operation of a residential school for postsecondary education and technical training of the deaf.

School Assistance in Disaster Areas Act (Public Law 89-313) provided for assistance to local education agencies to help meet exceptional costs resulting from a major disaster.

1966 *International Education Act* (Public Law 89-698) provided grants to institutions of higher education for the establishment, strengthening, and operation of centers for research and training in international studies and the international aspects of other fields of study.

National Sea Grant College and Program Act (Public Law 89-688) authorized the establishment and operation of Sea Grant Colleges and programs by initiating and supporting programs of education and research in the various fields relating to the development of marine resources.

Adult Education Act (Public Law 89-750) authorized grants to states for the encouragement and expansion of educational programs for adults, including training of teachers of adults and demonstrations in adult education (previously part of Economic Opportunity Act of 1964).

Model Secondary School for the Deaf Act (Public Law 89-694) authorized the establishment and operation, by Gallaudet College, of a model secondary school for the deaf.

1967 *Education Professions Development Act* (Public Law 90-35) amended the Higher Education Act of 1965 for the purpose of improving the quality of teaching and to help meet critical shortages of adequately trained educational personnel.

Public Broadcasting Act of 1967 (Public Law 90-129) established a Corporation for Public Broadcasting to assume major responsibility in channeling federal funds to noncommercial radio and television stations, program production groups, and educational television networks; conduct research, demonstration, or training in matters related to noncommercial broadcasting; and award grants for construction of educational radio and television facilities.

1968 *Elementary and Secondary Education Amendments of 1968* (Public Law 90-247) modified existing programs and authorized support of regional centers for education of children with disabilities, model centers and services for deaf-blind children, recruitment of personnel and dissemination of information on education of children with disabilities; technical assistance in education to rural areas; support of dropout prevention projects; and support of bilingual education programs.

Handicapped Children's Early Education Assistance Act (Public Law 90-538) authorized preschool and early education programs for children with disabilities.

Vocational Education Amendments of 1968 (Public Law 90-576) modified existing programs and provided for a National Advisory Council on Vocational Education and collection and dissemination of information for programs administered by the Commissioner of Education.

1970 *Elementary and Secondary Education Assistance Programs, Extension* (Public Law 91-230) authorized comprehensive planning and evaluation grants to state and local education agencies; provided for the establishment of a National Commission on School Finance.

National Commission on Libraries and Information Services Act (Public Law 91-345) established a National Commission on Libraries and Information Science to effectively utilize the nation's educational resources.

Office of Education Appropriation Act (Public Law 91-380) provided emergency school assistance to desegregating local education agencies.

Environmental Education Act (Public Law 91-516) established an Office of Environmental Education to develop curriculum and initiate and maintain environmental education programs at the elementary/secondary levels; disseminate information; provide training programs for teachers and other educational, public, community, labor, and industrial leaders and employees; provide community education programs; and distribute material dealing with the environment and ecology.

Drug Abuse Education Act of 1970 (Public Law 91-527) provided for development, demonstration, and evaluation of curricula on the problems of drug abuse.

1971 *Comprehensive Health Manpower Training Act of 1971* (Public Law 92-257) amended Title VII of the Public Health Service Act, increasing and expanding provisions for health manpower training and training facilities.

1972 *Drug Abuse Office and Treatment Act of 1972* (Public Law 92-255) established a Special Action Office for Drug Abuse Prevention to provide overall planning and policy for all federal drug-abuse prevention functions; a National Advisory Council for Drug Abuse Prevention; community assistance grants for community mental health centers for treatment and rehabilitation of people with drug-abuse problems; and, in December 1974, a National Institute on Drug Abuse.

Education Amendments of 1972 (Public Law 92-318) established the Education Division in the U.S. Department of Health, Education, and Welfare and the National Institute of Education; general aid for institutions of higher education; federal matching grants for state Student Incentive Grants; a National Commission on Financing Postsecondary Education; State Advisory Councils on Community Colleges; a Bureau of Occupational and Adult Education and State Grants for the design, establishment, and conduct of postsecondary occupational education; and a bureau-level Office of Indian Education. Amended current U.S. Department of Education programs to increase their effectiveness and better meet special needs. Prohibited sex bias in admission to vocational, professional, and graduate schools, and public institutions of undergraduate higher education.

1973 *Older Americans Comprehensive Services Amendment of 1973* (Public Law 93-29) made available to older citizens comprehensive programs of health, education, and social services.

Comprehensive Employment and Training Act of 1973 (Public Law 93-203) provided for opportunities for employment and training to unemployed and underemployed people. Extended and expanded provisions in the Manpower Development and Training Act of 1962, Title I of the Economic Opportunity Act of 1962, Title I of the Economic Opportunity Act of 1964, and the Emergency Employment Act of 1971 as in effect prior to June 30, 1973.

1974 *Education Amendments of 1974* (Public Law 93-380) provided for the consolidation of certain programs; and established a National Center for Education Statistics.

Juvenile Justice and Delinquency Prevention Act of 1974 (Public Law 93-415) provided for technical assistance, staff training, centralized research, and resources to develop and implement programs to keep students in elementary and secondary schools; and established, in the U.S. Department of Justice, a National Institute for Juvenile Justice and Delinquency Prevention.

1975 *Indian Self-Determination and Education Assistance Act* (Public Law 93-638) provided for increased participation of American Indians in the establishment and conduct of their education programs and services.

Harry S Truman Memorial Scholarship Act (Public Law 93-642) established the Harry S Truman Scholarship Foundation and created a perpetual education scholarship fund for young Americans to prepare for and pursue careers in public service.

Education for All Handicapped Children Act (Public Law 94-142) provided that all children with disabilities have available to them a free appropriate education designed to meet their unique needs.

1976 *Educational Broadcasting Facilities and Telecommunications Demonstration Act of 1976* (Public Law 94-309) established a telecommunications demonstration program to promote the development of nonbroadcast telecommunications facilities and services for the transmission, distribution, and delivery of health, education, and public or social service information.

1977 *Youth Employment and Demonstration Projects Act of 1977* (Public Law 95-93) established a youth employment training program including, among other activities, promoting education-to-work transition, literacy training and bilingual training, and attainment of certificates of high school equivalency.

Career Education Incentive Act (Public Law 95-207) authorized the establishment of a career education program for elementary and secondary schools.

1978 *Tribally Controlled Community College Assistance Act of 1978* (Public Law 95-471) provided federal funds for the operation and improvement of tribally controlled community colleges for American Indian/Alaska Native students.

Middle Income Student Assistance Act (Public Law 95-566) modified the provisions for student financial assistance programs to allow middle-income as well as low-income students attending college or other postsecondary institutions to qualify for federal education assistance.

1979 *Department of Education Organization Act* (Public Law 96-88) established a U.S. Department of Education containing functions from the Education Division of the U.S. Department of Health, Education, and Welfare (HEW) along with other selected education programs from HEW, the U.S. Department of Justice, U.S. Department of Labor, and the National Science Foundation.

1980 *Asbestos School Hazard Detection and Control Act of 1980* (Public Law 96-270) established a program for inspection of schools for detection of hazardous asbestos materials and provided loans to assist educational agencies to contain or remove and replace such materials.

1981 *Education Consolidation and Improvement Act of 1981* (Part of Public Law 97-35) consolidated 42 programs into 7 programs to be funded under the elementary and secondary block grant authority.

1983 *Student Loan Consolidation and Technical Amendments Act of 1983* (Public Law 98-79) established an 8 percent interest rate for Guaranteed Student Loans and an extended Family Contribution Schedule.

Challenge Grant Amendments of 1983 (Public Law 98-95) amended Title III of the Higher Education Act of 1965, and added authorization of the Challenge Grant program. The Challenge Grant program provides funds to eligible institutions on a matching basis as an incentive to seek alternative sources of funding.

Education of the Handicapped Act Amendments of 1983 (Public Law 98-199) added the Architectural Barrier amendment (providing funds for altering existing buildings and equipment to make them accessible to those with physical disabilities) and clarified participation of children with disabilities in private schools.

1984 *Education for Economic Security Act* (Public Law 98-377) added new science and mathematics programs for elementary, secondary, and postsecondary education. The new programs included magnet schools, excellence in education, and equal access.

Carl D. Perkins Vocational Education Act (Public Law 98-524) continued federal assistance for vocational education through FY 1989. The act replaced the Vocational Education Act of 1963. It provided aid to the states to make vocational education programs accessible to all people, including disabled and disadvantaged, single parents and homemakers, and the incarcerated.

Human Services Reauthorization Act (Public Law 98-558) created a Carl D. Perkins scholarship program, a National Talented Teachers Fellowship program, a Federal Merit Scholarships program, and a Leadership in Educational Administration program.

1985 *Montgomery GI Bill—Active Duty* (Public Law 98-525), brought about a new GI Bill for individuals who initially entered active military duty on or after July 1, 1985.

Montgomery GI Bill—Selected Reserve (Public Law 98-525), established an education program for members of the Selected Reserve (which includes the National Guard) who enlist, reenlist, or extend an enlistment after June 30, 1985, for a 6-year period.

1986 *Handicapped Children's Protection Act of 1986* (Public Law 99-372) allowed parents of children with disabilities to collect attorneys' fees in cases brought under the Education of the Handicapped Act and provided that the Education of the Handicapped Act does not preempt other laws, such as Section 504 of the Rehabilitation Act.

Drug-Free Schools and Communities Act of 1986 (Part of Public Law 99-570) established programs for drug abuse education and prevention, coordinated with related community efforts and resources, through the use of federal financial assistance.

1988 *Augustus F. Hawkins-Robert T. Stafford Elementary and Secondary School Improvement Amendments of 1988* (Public Law 100-297) reauthorized through 1993 major elementary and secondary education programs, including Chapter 1, Chapter 2, Bilingual Education, Math-Science Education, Magnet Schools, Impact Aid, Indian Education, Adult Education, and other smaller education programs.

Stewart B. McKinney Homeless Assistance Amendments Act of 1988 (Public Law 100-628) extended for 2 additional years programs providing assistance to the homeless, including literacy training for homeless adults and education for homeless youths.

Tax Reform Technical Amendments (Public Law 100-647) authorized an Education Savings Bond for the purpose of postsecondary educational expenses. The bill grants tax exclusion for interest earned on regular series EE savings bonds.

1989 *Childhood Education and Development Act of 1989* (Part of Public Law 101-239) authorized the appropriations to expand Head Start programs and programs carried out under the Elementary and Secondary Education Act of 1965 to include child care services.

1990 *Excellence in Mathematics, Science and Engineering Education Act of 1990* (Public Law 101-589) created a national mathematics and science clearinghouse and created several other mathematics, science, and engineering education programs.

Student Right-To-Know and Campus Security Act (Public Law 101-542) required institutions of higher education receiving federal financial assistance to provide certain information about graduation rates of student-athletes and about campus crime statistics and security policies. (The 1990 campus crime and security legislation, along with later acts that amended it, is generally referred to as "the Clery Act.")

Americans with Disabilities Act of 1990 (Public Law 101-336) prohibited discrimination against people with disabilities.

National and Community Service Act of 1990 (Public Law 101-610) increased school and college-based community service opportunities and authorized the President's Points of Light Foundation.

1991 *National Literacy Act of 1991* (Public Law 102-73) established the National Institute for Literacy, the National Institute Board, and the Interagency Task Force on Literacy. Amended various federal laws to establish and extend various literacy programs.

High-Performance Computing Act of 1991 (Public Law 102-194) directed the President to implement a National High-Performance Computing Program. Provided for (1) establishment of a National Research and Education Network; (2) standards and guidelines for high-performance networks; and (3) the responsibility of certain federal departments and agencies with regard to the Network.

Veterans' Educational Assistance Amendments of 1991 (Public Law 102-127) restored certain educational benefits available to reserve and active-duty personnel under the Montgomery GI Bill to students whose courses of studies were interrupted by the Persian Gulf War.

Civil Rights Act of 1991 (Public Law 102-166) amended the Civil Rights Act of 1964, the Age Discrimination in Employment Act of 1967, and the Americans with Disabilities Act of 1990, with regard to employment discrimination. Established the Technical Assistance Training Institute.

1992 *Ready-To-Learn Act* (Public Law 102-545) amended the General Education Provisions Act to establish Ready-To-Learn Television programs to support educational programming and support materials for preschool and elementary school children and their parents, child care providers, and educators.

1993 *Student Loan Reform Act* (Public Law 103-66) reformed the student aid process by phasing in a system of direct lending designed to provide savings for taxpayers and students. Allows students to choose among a variety of repayment options, including income contingency.

National Service Trust Act (Public Law 103-82) amended the National and Community Service Act of 1990 to establish a Corporation for National Service. In addition, provided education grants up to $4,725 per year for 2 years to people age 17 or older who perform community service before, during, or after postsecondary education.

NAEP Assessment Authorization (Public Law 103-33) authorized use of the National Assessment of Educational Progress (NAEP) for state-by-state comparisons.

1994 *Goals 2000: Educate America Act* (Public Law 103-227) established a new federal partnership through a system of grants to states and local communities to reform the nation's education system. The Act formalized the national education goals and established the National Education Goals Panel.

School-To-Work Opportunities Act of 1994 (Public Law 103-239) established a national framework within which states and communities can develop School-To-Work Opportunities systems to prepare young people for first jobs and continuing education. The Act also provided money to states and communities to develop a system of programs that include work-based learning, school-based learning, and connecting activities components.

Safe Schools Act of 1994 (Part of Public Law 103-227) authorized the award of competitive grants to local educational agencies with serious crime to implement violence prevention activities such as conflict resolution and peer mediation.

1996 *Contract With America: Unfunded Mandates* (Public Law 104-4) ended the imposition, in the absence of full consideration by Congress, of federal mandates on state, local, and tribal governments without adequate funding, in a manner that may displace other essential governmental priorities; and ensured that the federal government pays the costs incurred by those governments in complying with certain requirements under federal statutes and regulations.

1997 *The Taxpayer Relief Act of 1997* (Public Law 105-34) enacted the Hope Scholarship and Life-Long Learning Tax Credit provisions into law.

Emergency Student Loan Consolidation Act of 1997 (Public Law 105-78) amended the Higher Education Act of 1965 to provide for improved student loan consolidation services.

1998 *Workforce Investment Act of 1998* (Public Law 105-220) enacted the Adult Education and Family Literacy Act, and substantially revised and extended, through FY 2003, the Rehabilitation Act of 1973.

Jeanne Clery Disclosure of Campus Security Policy and Campus Crime Statistics Act (Public Law 105-244) expanded crime categories that must be reported by postsecondary institutions.

Omnibus Consolidated and Emergency Supplemental Appropriations Act, 1999 (Public Law 105-277) enacted the Reading Excellence Act, to promote the ability of children to read independently by the third grade; and earmarked funds to help states and school districts reduce class sizes in the early grades.

Charter School Expansion Act (Public Law 105-278) amended the charter school program, enacted in 1994 as Title X, Part C of the Elementary and Secondary Education Act of 1965.

Carl D. Perkins Vocational and Applied Technology Education Amendments of 1998 (Public Law 105-332) revised, in its entirety, the Carl D. Perkins Vocational and Applied Technology Education Act, and reauthorized the Act through FY 2003.

Assistive Technology Act of 1998 (Public Law 105-394) replaced the Technology-Related Assistance for Individuals with Disabilities Act of 1988 with a new Act, authorized through FY 2004, to address the assistive-technology needs of individuals with disabilities.

1999 *Education Flexibility Partnership Act of 1999* (Public Law 106-25) authorized the Secretary of Education to allow all states to participate in the Education Flexibility Partnership program.

District of Columbia College Access Act of 1999 (Public Law 106-98) established a program to afford high school graduates from the District of Columbia the benefits of in-state tuition at state colleges and universities outside the District of Columbia.

2000 *The National Defense Authorization Act for Fiscal Year 2001* (Public Law 106-398) included, as Title XVIII, the Impact Aid Reauthorization Act of 2000, which extended the Impact Aid programs through FY 2003.

College Scholarship Fraud Prevention Act of 2000 (Public Law 106-420) enhanced federal penalties for offenses involving scholarship fraud; required an annual scholarship fraud report by the Attorney General, the Secretary of Education, and the Federal Trade Commission (FTC); and required the Secretary of Education, in conjunction with the FTC, to maintain a scholarship fraud awareness website.

Consolidated Appropriations Act 2001 (Public Law 106-554) created a new program of assistance for school repair and renovation, and amended the Elementary and Secondary Education Act of 1965 to authorize credit enhancement initiatives to help charter schools obtain, construct, or repair facilities; reauthorized the Even Start program; and enacted the "Children's Internet Protection Act."

2001 *50th Anniversary of Brown v. the Board of Education* (Public Law 107-41) established a commission for the purpose of encouraging and providing for the commemoration of the 50th anniversary of the 1954 Supreme Court decision *Brown* v. *Board of Education*.

2002 *No Child Left Behind Act of 2001* (Public Law 107-110) provided for the comprehensive reauthorization of the Elementary and Secondary Education Act of 1965, incorporating specific proposals in such areas as testing, accountability, parental choice, and early reading.

Education Sciences Reform Act (Public Law 107-279) established the Institute of Education Sciences within the U.S. Department of Education to carry out a coordinated, focused agenda of high-quality research, statistics, and evaluation that is relevant to the educational challenges of the nation.

The Higher Education Relief Opportunities for Students Act of 2001 (Public Law 107-122) provided the Secretary of Education with waiver authority over student financial aid programs under Title IV of the Higher Education Act of 1965, to deal with student and family situations resulting from the September 11, 2001, terrorist attacks.

Established fixed interest rates for student and parent borrowers (Public Law 107-139) under Title IV of the Higher Education Act of 1965.

2003 *The Higher Education Relief Opportunities for Students Act of 2003* (Public Law 108-76) provided the Secretary of Education with waiver authority over student financial aid programs under Title IV of the Higher Education Act of 1965, to deal with student and family situations resulting from wars or national emergencies.

2004 *Assistive Technology Act of 2004* (Public Law 108-364) reauthorized the Assistive Technology program, administered by the Department of Education.

Taxpayer-Teacher Protection Act of 2004 (Public Law 108-409) temporarily stopped excessive special allowance payments to certain lenders under the Federal Family Education Loan (FFEL) Program and increased the amount of loans that can be forgiven for certain borrowers who are highly qualified mathematics, science, and special education teachers who serve in high-poverty schools for 5 years.

Individuals with Disabilities Education Improvement Act of 2004 (Public Law 108-446) provided a comprehensive reauthorization of the Individuals with Disabilities Education Act.

2005 *Student Grant Hurricane and Disaster Relief Act* (Public Law 109-67) authorized the Secretary of Education to waive certain repayment requirements for students receiving campus-based federal grant assistance if they were residing in, employed in, or attending an institution of higher education located in a major disaster area, or their attendance was interrupted because of the disaster.

Natural Disaster Student Aid Fairness Act (Public Law 109-86) authorized the Secretary of Education during FY 2006 to reallocate campus-based student aid funds to institutions of higher learning in Louisiana, Mississippi, Alabama, and Texas, or institutions that had accepted students displaced by Hurricane Katrina or Rita. The law also waived requirements for matching funds that are normally imposed on institutions and students.

Hurricane Education Recovery Act (HERA) (Public Law 109-148, provision in the Defense Department Appropriations Act for FY 2006) provided funds for states affected by Hurricane Katrina to restart school operations, provide temporary emergency aid for displaced students, and assist homeless youth. The law also permitted the Secretary of Education to extend deadlines under the Individuals with Disabilities Education Act for those affected by Katrina or Rita.

2006 *Higher Education Reconciliation Act of 2005* (Public Law 109-171) made various amendments to programs of student financial assistance under Title IV of the Higher Education Act of 1965.

Public Law 109-211 reauthorized the "ED-FLEX" program (under the Education Flexibility Partnership Act of 1999), under which the Secretary of Education permits states to waive certain requirements of federal statutes and regulations if they meet certain conditions.

Carl D. Perkins Career and Technical Education Improvement Act of 2006 (Public Law 109-270) reauthorized the vocational and technical education programs under the Perkins Act through 2012.

2007 *America COMPETES Act* (or *"America Creating Opportunities to Meaningfully Promote Excellence in Technology, Education, and Science Act"*) (Public Law 110-69) created new STEM (science, technology, engineering, and mathematics) education programs in various agencies, including the Department of Education.

College Cost Reduction and Access Act of 2007 (Public Law 110-84) reduced interest rates on student loans and made other amendments to the Higher Education Act of 1965 to make college more accessible and affordable.

Permanent extension of the *Higher Education Relief Opportunities for Students Act of 2003 (HEROES Act)* (Public Law 110-93) gave the Secretary of Education authority to waive or modify any statutory or regulatory provision applicable to the student financial assistance programs under Title IV of the Higher Education Act of 1965 as deemed necessary in connection with a war or other military operation or national emergency.

2008 *Ensuring Continued Access to Student Loans Act of 2008* (Public Law 110-227) provided various authorities to the Department of Education, among other provisions, to help ensure that college students and their parents continue to have access to loans in the tight credit market.

Higher Education Opportunity Act (Public Law 110-315) provided a comprehensive reauthorization of the Higher Education Act of 1965.

2009 *American Recovery and Reinvestment Act of 2009* (Public Law 111-5) provided about $100 billion to state education systems and supplemental appropriations for several Department of Education programs.

Public Law 111-39 made miscellaneous and technical amendments to the Higher Education Act of 1965.

2010 *Health Care and Education Reconciliation Act of 2010* (Public Law 111-152) included, as Title II, the "SAFRA Act" (also known as the "Student Aid and Fiscal Responsibility Act"). The SAFRA Act ended the federal government's role in subsidizing financial institutions that make student loans through the Federal Family Education Loan (FFEL) Program under Part B of Title IV of the Higher Education Act of

1965 (HEA), and correspondingly expanded the Federal Direct Student Loan Program administered by the Department of Education under Part D of Title IV of the HEA.

Public Law 111-226 provided an additional $10 billion to states and school districts, through an "Education Jobs Fund" modeled closely on the State Fiscal Stabilization Fund created by the 2009 Recovery Act, to hire (or avoid laying off) teachers and other educators.

2013 *The Bipartisan Student Loan Certainty Act of 2013* (Public Law 113-28) amended the Higher Education Act of 1965 (HEA) to govern the interest rates on the various categories of student loans under Title IV of the HEA.

Violence Against Women Reauthorization Act of 2013 (Public Law 113-4) amended the Clery Act, increasing the responsibility of postsecondary institutions to prevent, address, and report crimes on campus.

2014 *Workforce Innovation and Opportunity Act* (Public Law 113-128) amended the Workforce Investment Act of 1998 to strengthen the U.S. workforce development system through innovation in, and alignment and improvement of, employment, training, and education programs in the United States, and to promote individual and national economic growth, and for other purposes.

Public Law 113-174 extended the National Advisory Committee on Institutional Quality and Integrity and the Advisory Committee on Student Financial Assistance for 1 year.

Figure 20. Federal on-budget funds for education, by level or other educational purpose: Selected years, 1965 through 2014

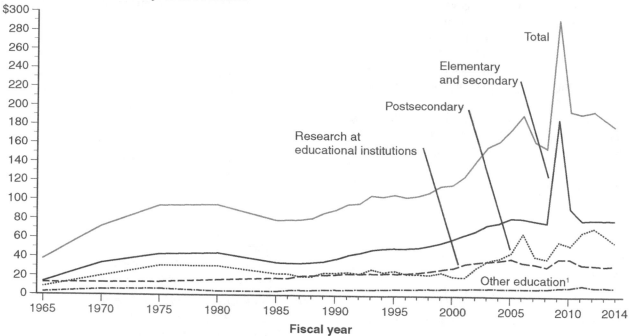

Billions of constant fiscal year 2014 dollars

[1]Other education includes libraries, museums, cultural activities, and miscellaneous research.

NOTE: The increase in postsecondary expenditures in 2006 resulted primarily from an accounting adjustment. Amounts for 2009 include funds from the American Recovery and Reinvestment Act of 2009 (ARRA). Data for research at educational institutions are estimated for 2013 and 2014.

SOURCE: U.S. Department of Education, Budget Service, unpublished tabulations. U.S. Department of Education, National Center for Education Statistics, unpublished tabulations. U.S. Office of Management and Budget, *Budget of the U.S. Government, Appendix*, fiscal years 1967 through 2015. National Science Foundation, *Federal Funds for Research and Development*, fiscal years 1967 through 2014.

Figure 21. Percentage of federal on-budget funds for education, by agency: Fiscal year 2013

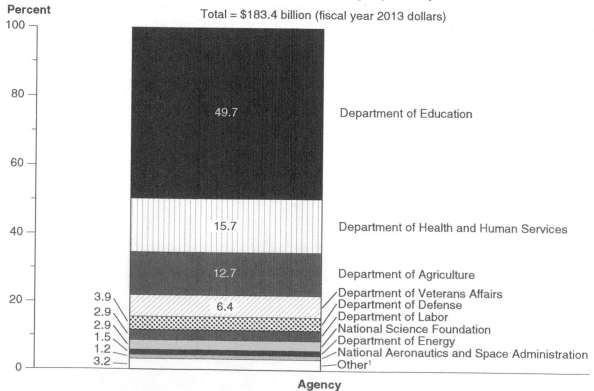

Percent

Total = $183.4 billion (fiscal year 2013 dollars)

[1]In addition to the nine agencies shown in this figure, other agencies provide smaller amounts of funding for education.

NOTE: On-budget funds are tied to federal appropriations for education programs. Includes estimated data. Detail may not sum to totals because of rounding.

SOURCE: U.S. Department of Education, National Center for Education Statistics, unpublished tabulations. U.S. Office of Management and Budget, *Budget of the U.S. Government, Appendix*, fiscal year 2014. National Science Foundation, *Federal Funds for Research and Development*, fiscal year 2013.

Table 401.10. Federal support and estimated federal tax expenditures for education, by category: Selected fiscal years, 1965 through 2014

[In millions of dollars]

Fiscal year	Total on-budget support, off-budget support, and nonfederal funds generated by federal legislation	On-budget support[1] — Total	Elementary and secondary	Post-secondary	Other education[3]	Research at educational institutions	Off-budget support and nonfederal funds — Total	Off-budget support — Direct Loan Program[4]	Nonfederal funds — Federal Family Education Loan Program[5]	Perkins Loans[6]	Income Contingent Loans[7]	Leveraging Educational Assistance Partnerships[8]	Supplemental Educational Opportunity Grants[9]	Work-Study Aid[10]	Estimated federal tax expenditures for education[2]
1	2	3	4	5	6	7	8	9	10	11	12	13	14	15	16
Current dollars															
1965	$5,354.7	$5,331.0	$1,942.6	$1,197.5	$374.7	$1,816.3	$23.7	†	†	$16.1	†	†	†	$7.6	—
1970	13,359.1	12,526.5	5,830.4	3,447.7	964.7	2,283.6	832.6	†	$770.0	21.0	†	$20.0	†	41.6	$8,605.0
1975	24,691.5	23,288.1	10,617.2	7,644.0	1,608.5	3,418.4	1,403.4	†	1,233.0	35.7	†	†	†	114.7	13,320.0
1980	39,349.5	34,493.5	16,027.7	11,115.9	1,548.7	5,801.2	4,856.0	†	4,598.0	31.8	†	76.8	†	149.4	—
1985	47,753.4	39,027.9	16,901.3	11,174.4	2,107.6	8,844.6	8,725.5	†	8,467.0	21.4	†	76.0	†	161.1	19,105.0
1986	48,357.3	39,962.9	17,049.9	11,283.6	2,620.0	9,009.4	8,394.4	†	8,142.0	20.2	†	72.7	†	159.5	20,425.0
1987	50,724.6	41,194.7	17,535.7	10,300.0	2,820.4	10,538.6	9,529.8	†	9,272.0	20.9	$0.6	76.0	†	160.4	20,830.0
1988	54,078.7	43,454.4	18,564.3	10,657.5	2,981.6	11,250.5	10,624.3	†	10,380.0	20.6	0.5	72.8	$22.0	150.4	17,025.0
1989	59,537.4	48,269.6	19,809.5	13,269.9	3,180.3	12,009.8	11,267.8	†	10,938.0	20.4	0.5	71.9	†	215.0	17,755.0
1990	62,811.5	51,624.3	21,984.4	13,650.9	3,383.0	12,606.0	11,187.2	†	10,826.0	15.0	0.5	59.2	48.8	237.7	19,040.0
1991	70,375.6	57,599.5	25,418.0	14,707.4	3,698.6	13,775.4	12,776.1	†	12,372.0	17.3	0.5	63.5	87.7	235.0	18,995.0
1992	74,481.1	60,483.1	27,926.9	14,387.4	3,992.0	14,176.9	13,998.0	†	13,568.0	17.3	0.5	72.0	97.2	242.9	19,950.0
1993	84,741.5	67,740.6	30,834.3	17,844.0	4,107.2	14,955.1	17,000.8	†	16,524.0	29.3	†	72.4	184.6	190.5	21,010.0
1994	92,781.5	68,254.2	32,304.4	16,177.1	4,483.7	15,289.1	24,527.3	$813.0	23,214.0	52.7	†	72.4	184.6	190.5	22,630.0
1995	95,810.8	71,639.5	33,623.8	17,618.1	4,719.7	15,677.9	24,171.2	5,161.0	18,519.0	52.7	†	63.4	184.6	190.5	24,600.0
1996	96,833.0	71,327.4	34,391.5	15,775.5	4,828.0	16,332.3	25,505.6	8,357.0	16,711.0	31.1	†	31.4	184.6	190.5	26,340.0
1997	103,259.8	73,731.8	35,478.9	15,959.4	5,021.2	17,272.4	29,528.0	9,838.0	19,163.0	52.7	†	50.0	194.3	239.7	28,125.0
1998	107,810.5	76,909.2	37,486.2	15,799.6	5,148.5	18,475.0	30,901.3	10,400.1	20,002.5	45.0	†	25.0	195.9	234.4	29,540.0
1999	113,417.2	82,863.6	39,937.9	17,651.2	5,318.0	19,956.5	30,553.6	9,953.0	20,107.0	33.3	†	33.3	199.7	239.4	37,360.0
2000	119,541.6	85,944.2	43,790.8	15,008.7	5,484.6	21,660.1	33,597.4	10,347.0	22,711.0	33.3	†	50.0	184.0	256.4	39,475.0
2001	130,668.5	94,846.5	48,530.1	14,938.3	5,880.0	25,498.1	35,822.0	10,635.0	24,694.0	25.0	†	80.0	192.0	204.0	41,460.0
2002	150,034.5	109,211.5	52,754.1	22,964.2	6,297.7	27,195.5	40,823.0	11,689.0	28,606.0	25.0	†	104.0	202.0	207.0	—
2003	170,671.5	124,374.5	59,274.2	29,499.7	6,532.5	29,068.1	46,297.0	11,969.0	33,791.0	33.0	†	103.0	244.0	199.0	—
2004	185,176.7	132,420.7	62,653.2	32,433.0	6,576.8	30,757.7	52,756.0	12,840.0	39,266.0	33.0	†	102.0	246.0	271.0	—
2005	204,702.2	147,873.2	68,957.7	38,587.3	6,908.5	33,419.7	56,829.0	12,930.0	43,284.0	0.0	†	101.0	205.0	268.0	—
2006[11]	226,978.7	166,495.7	70,948.2	57,757.7	7,074.5	30,715.2	60,483.0	12,677.0	47,307.0	0.0	†	100.0	205.0	194.0	—
2007	210,536.0	145,698.0	70,735.9	37,465.3	7,214.9	30,281.9	64,838.0	13,022.0	51,320.0	0.0	†	100.0	201.0	191.0	—
2008	220,336.9	144,338.9	71,272.6	36,386.3	7,882.2	28,797.8	75,998.0	18,213.0	57,296.0	0.0	†	98.0	201.0	190.0	—
2009[12]	368,349.6	271,297.6	172,660.8	53,085.4	8,853.7	36,697.7	97,052.0	29,738.0	66,778.0	0.0	†	98.0	201.0	237.0	—
2010	288,009.7	183,199.7	86,681.8	50,197.8	9,326.7	36,993.3	104,810.0	84,703.0	19,618.0	0.0	†	98.0	201.0	190.0	—
2011	292,976.2	183,669.9	76,118.9	64,400.2	11,133.7	32,017.1	109,306.3	108,926.3	0.0	0.0	†	0.0	195.0	185.0	—
2012	294,677.2	189,846.6	78,227.1	70,053.8	9,389.5	32,176.2	104,830.6	104,450.6	0.0	0.0	†	0.0	195.0	185.0[13]	—
2013	285,034.3	183,367.5	79,131.2	62,784.2	9,727.8	31,724.3[13]	101,666.8	101,255.9	0.0	0.0	†	0.0	230.4[13]	180.5[13]	—
2014	279,429.8	179,342.4	80,072.3	56,953.7	9,454.9	32,861.6[13]	100,087.4	99,647.2	0.0	0.0	†	0.0	244.9[13]	195.2[13]	—
Constant fiscal year 2014 dollars[14]															
1965	$37,324.5	$37,159.2	$13,540.5	$8,347.1	$2,611.5	$12,660.1	$165.3	†	†	$112.3	†	†	†	$53.0	—
1970	76,151.7	71,405.7	33,235.7	19,653.1	5,499.3	13,017.6	4,746.0	†	$4,389.3	119.6	†	$80.3	†	237.1	$34,550.9
1975	99,141.4	93,506.6	42,630.2	30,692.4	6,458.4	13,725.6	5,634.8	†	4,950.8	143.2	†	†	†	460.5	36,475.8
1980	107,755.7	94,457.9	43,890.6	30,440.0	4,241.1	15,886.2	13,297.7	†	12,591.3	87.0	†	210.3	†	409.1	—
1985	96,208.9	78,629.6	34,051.2	22,513.1	4,246.2	17,819.2	17,579.3	†	17,058.5	43.1	†	153.1	†	324.6	38,490.9
1986	95,401.5	78,840.6	33,636.9	22,260.8	5,168.9	17,774.1	16,560.9	†	16,062.9	39.9	†	143.4	†	314.7	40,295.4
1987	97,288.0	79,010.1	33,632.9	19,755.0	5,409.4	20,212.7	18,277.9	†	17,783.4	40.1	$1.1	145.8	†	307.6	39,951.2
1988	100,328.6	80,616.0	34,441.2	19,771.7	5,531.4	20,871.7	19,710.1	†	19,256.8	38.3	0.9	135.1	†	279.0	31,584.5
1989	106,369.5	86,238.3	35,391.7	23,708.0	5,682.0	21,456.7	20,131.1	†	19,541.8	36.4	1.0	128.5	$39.3	384.1	31,721.1

See notes at end of table.

Table 401.10. Federal support and estimated federal tax expenditures for education, by category: Selected fiscal years, 1965 through 2014—Continued

[In millions of dollars]

Fiscal year	Total on-budget support, off-budget support, and nonfederal funds generated by federal legislation	On-budget support[1]					Off-budget support and nonfederal funds generated by federal legislation								Estimated federal tax expenditures for education[2]
		Total	Elementary and secondary	Post-secondary	Other education[3]	Research at educational institutions	Off-budget support			Nonfederal funds					
							Total	Direct Loan Program[4]	Federal Family Education Loan Program[5]	Perkins Loans[6]	Income Contingent Loans[7]	Leveraging Educational Assistance Partnerships[8]	Supplemental Educational Opportunity Grants[9]	Work-Study Aid[10]	
1	2	3	4	5	6	7	8	9	10	11	12	13	14	15	16
1990	108,998.9	89,585.4	38,150.2	23,688.9	5,870.7	21,875.7	19,413.5	†	18,786.7	26.1	0.9	102.7	84.7	412.5	33,040.7
1991	116,717.5	95,528.5	42,155.7	24,392.2	6,134.1	22,846.5	21,189.1	†	20,518.9	28.8	0.8	105.4	145.5	389.7	31,503.1
1992	119,057.6	96,681.8	44,641.0	22,998.1	6,381.1	22,661.6	21,375.8	†	21,688.4	27.7	0.9	115.1	155.4	388.3	31,890.0
1993	131,554.0	105,161.6	47,867.7	27,701.3	6,376.1	23,216.5	26,392.4	†	25,652.1	45.4	†	112.4	286.6	295.8	32,616.3
1994	141,459.1	105,063.6	49,252.8	24,664.3	6,836.1	23,310.5	37,395.4	$1,239.5	35,393.2	80.3	†	110.4	281.5	290.5	34,502.8
1995	141,939.4	106,130.8	49,812.2	26,100.5	6,992.0	23,226.1	35,808.6	7,645.8	27,435.1	78.0	†	93.9	273.5	282.3	36,443.8
1996	140,511.6	103,501.2	49,904.6	22,891.4	7,005.8	23,699.4	37,010.5	12,126.6	24,248.9	45.1	†	45.6	267.9	276.4	38,221.2
1997	146,845.5	104,853.8	50,454.4	22,695.8	7,140.6	24,563.0	41,991.7	13,990.6	27,251.6	74.9	†	71.1	262.5	340.9	39,996.5
1998	151,939.7	108,389.9	52,830.1	22,266.7	7,255.9	26,037.2	43,549.9	14,657.1	28,190.0	63.4	†	35.2	273.8	330.3	41,631.4
1999	157,847.9	115,325.1	55,583.4	24,566.0	7,401.3	27,774.3	42,522.8	13,852.0	27,983.8	46.3	†	34.8	272.6	333.2	51,995.6
2000	162,343.2	116,716.3	59,470.0	20,382.6	7,443.3	29,415.5	45,626.9	14,051.7	30,842.6	45.2	†	67.9	271.2	348.2	53,608.9
2001	172,835.6	125,453.7	64,190.8	19,758.9	7,777.5	33,726.4	47,381.9	14,066.9	32,662.8	33.1	†	105.8	243.4	269.8	54,839.3
2002	195,207.1	142,093.1	68,637.4	29,878.3	8,193.8	35,383.6	53,114.1	15,208.3	37,218.7	32.5	†	135.3	249.8	269.3	—
2003	215,957.8	157,376.3	75,002.2	37,327.2	8,265.8	36,781.1	58,581.5	15,144.9	42,757.2	41.8	†	130.3	255.6	251.8	—
2004	228,333.3	163,282.2	77,255.0	39,991.7	8,109.6	37,925.9	65,051.1	15,832.4	48,417.2	40.7	†	125.8	300.9	334.2	—
2005	243,961.4	176,233.3	82,182.9	45,987.8	8,233.5	39,829.2	67,728.1	15,409.8	51,585.3	0.0	†	120.4	293.2	319.4	—
2006[11]	261,498.9	191,817.3	81,738.5	66,541.9	8,150.4	35,386.6	69,681.6	14,605.0	54,501.7	0.0	†	115.2	236.2	223.5	—
2007	236,318.1	163,540.1	79,398.2	42,053.3	8,098.4	33,990.2	72,778.0	14,616.7	57,604.6	0.0	†	112.2	230.1	214.4	—
2008	238,968.7	156,544.3	77,299.4	39,463.1	8,548.7	31,233.0	82,424.4	19,753.1	62,141.0	0.0	†	106.3	218.0	206.1	—
2009[12]	398,738.4	293,679.6	186,905.3	57,464.9	9,584.1	39,725.2	105,058.8	32,191.4	72,287.2	0.0	†	106.1	217.6	256.1	—
2010	308,104.0	195,981.5	92,729.6	53,700.1	9,977.4	39,574.3	112,122.6	90,612.7	20,986.7	0.0	†	104.8	215.0	203.3	—
2011	307,372.3	192,694.9	79,859.1	67,564.7	11,680.8	33,580.4	114,677.3	114,278.7	0.0	0.0	†	0.0	204.6	194.1	—
2012	303,451.4	195,499.4	80,556.4	72,139.7	9,669.0	33,134.2	107,952.0	107,560.7	0.0	0.0	†	0.0	200.8	190.5	—
2013	289,473.3	186,223.2	80,363.6	63,762.0	9,879.3	32,218.4[13]	103,250.1	102,832.8	0.0	0.0	†	0.0	234.0[13]	183.3[13]	—
2014	279,429.8	179,342.4	80,072.3	56,953.7	9,454.9	32,861.6[13]	100,087.4	99,647.2	0.0	0.0	†	0.0	244.9[13]	195.2[13]	—

—Not available.
†Not applicable.
[1]On-budget support includes federal funds for education programs tied to appropriations. Excludes federal support for medical education benefits under Medicare in the U.S. Department of Health and Human Services. Benefits excluded because data before fiscal year (FY) 1990 are not available. This program existed since Medicare began, but was not available as a separate budget item until FY 1990. Excluded amounts range from an estimated $4,440,000,000 in FY 1990 to an estimated $11,330,000,000 in FY 2014.
[2]Losses of tax revenue attributable to provisions of the federal income tax laws that allow a special exclusion, exemption, or deduction from gross income or provide a special credit, preferential rate of tax, or a deferral of tax liability affecting individual or corporate income tax liabilities.
[3]Other education includes libraries, museums, cultural activities, and miscellaneous research.
[4]The William D. Ford Federal Direct Loan Program (commonly referred to as the Direct Loan Program) provides students with the same benefits they were eligible to receive under the Federal Family Education Loan (FFEL) Program, but provides loans to students through federal capital rather than through private lenders.
[5]The Federal Family Education Loan (FFEL) Program, formerly known as the Guaranteed Student Loan Program, provided student loans guaranteed by the federal government and disbursed to borrowers. After June 30, 2010, no new FFEL loans have been originated; all new loans are originated through the Direct Loan Program.
[6]Student loans created from institutional matching funds (since 1993 one-third of federal capital contributions). Excludes repayments of outstanding loans.
[7]Student loans created from institutional matching funds (one-ninth of federal contributions). This was a demonstration project that involved only 10 institutions and had unsubsidized interest rates. Program repealed in fiscal year 1992.

[8]Formerly the State Student Incentive Grant Program. Starting in fiscal year 2000, amounts under $30.0 million have required dollar-for-dollar state matching contributions, while amounts over $30.0 million have required two-to-one state matching contributions.
[9]Institutions award grants to undergraduate students, and the federal share of such grants may not exceed 75 percent of the total grant.
[10]Employer contributions to student earnings are generally one-third of federal allocation.
[11]The increase in postsecondary expenditures in 2006 resulted primarily from an accounting adjustment.
[12]All education funds from the American Recovery and Reinvestment Act of 2009 (ARRA) are included in the FY 2009 row of this table. Most of these funds had a 2-year availability, meaning that they were available for the Department of Education to obligate during FY 2009 and FY 2010.
[13]Estimated.
[14]Data adjusted by the federal budget composite deflator, as reported in the U.S. Office of Management and Budget's *Budget of the U.S. Government, Historical Tables, Fiscal Year 2015.*
NOTE: To the extent possible, federal education funds data represent outlays rather than obligations. Some data have been revised from previously published figures. Detail may not sum to totals because of rounding.
SOURCE: U.S. Department of Education, Budget Service, unpublished tabulations. U.S. Department of Education, National Center for Education Statistics, unpublished tabulations. U.S. Office of Management and Budget, *Budget of the U.S. Government, Appendix,* fiscal years 1967 through 2015. National Science Foundation, *Federal Funds for Research and Development,* fiscal years 1967 through 2014. (This table was prepared February 2015.)

Table 401.20. Federal on-budget funds for education, by agency: Selected fiscal years, 1970 through 2013
[In thousands of dollars]

Agency	1970	1980	1990	2000	2005	2009[1,2]	2010[1]	2011[1]	2012[1]	2013[1,3]
1	2	3	4	5	6	7	8	9	10	11
					Current dollars					
Total	$12,526,499	$34,493,502	$51,624,342	$85,944,203	$147,873,199	$271,297,567	$183,199,676	$183,669,874	$189,846,616	$183,367,513
Department of Education[2]	4,625,224	13,137,785	23,198,575	34,106,697	72,893,301	187,733,247	91,893,199	93,777,295	99,129,939	91,130,762
Department of Agriculture	960,910	4,562,467	6,260,843	11,080,031	13,817,553	16,603,791	19,260,881	20,241,295	22,120,982	23,254,398
Department of Commerce	13,990	135,561	53,835	114,575	243,948	263,000	303,000	242,778	205,085	227,530
Department of Defense	821,388	1,560,301	3,605,509	4,525,030	7,986,654	6,894,895	7,686,288	7,617,359	7,400,880	7,082,019
Department of Energy	551,527	1,605,558	2,561,950	3,577,004	4,339,879	3,747,800	3,402,600	2,994,903	2,983,055	2,704,198
Department of Health and Human Services	1,796,854	5,613,930	7,956,011	17,670,857	26,107,860	31,860,858	31,962,136	28,356,790	28,598,226	28,807,625
Department of Homeland Security	†	†	†	†	624,860	508,920	540,229	2,046,558	333,217	375,432
	†	†	118	1,400	1,100	200	400	1,600	300	4,400
Department of Housing and Urban Development	114,709	5,314	630,537	959,802	1,254,533	1,010,559	1,039,367	1,037,621	968,460	924,470
Department of the Interior	190,975	440,547	99,775	278,927	608,148	186,215	205,692	203,988	217,850	221,291
Department of Justice	15,728	60,721	†	†	†	†	†	†	†	†
Department of Labor	424,494	1,862,738	2,511,380	4,696,100	5,764,500	6,073,300	6,826,000	6,121,000	5,802,000	5,347,004
Department of State	59,742	25,188	51,225	388,349	533,309	676,520	778,180	741,670	725,222	824,879
Department of Transportation	27,534	54,712	76,186	117,054	126,900	138,433	165,246	141,935	189,620	200,400
Department of the Treasury	18	1,247,463	41,715	83,000	†	†	†	†	†	†
Department of Veterans Affairs	1,032,918	2,351,233	757,476	1,577,374	4,293,624	4,763,479	8,802,944	10,293,752	10,603,821	11,697,551
Other agencies and programs										
ACTION	88,034	2,833	8,472	†	†	†	†	†	†	†
Agency for International Development	37,838	176,770	249,786	332,500	602,100	642,225	557,900	621,900	629,900	634,069
Appalachian Regional Commission	†	19,032	93	7,243	8,542	6,106	5,070	11,902	11,124	13,070
Barry Goldwater Scholarship and Excellence in Education Foundation	†	†	1,033	3,000	3,000	3,000	4,000	3,000	4,000	4,000
Corporation for National and Community Service	†	†	†	386,000	472,000	401,000	965,000	983,000	750,251	754,843
Environmental Protection Agency	19,446	41,083	87,481	98,900	83,400	52,900	54,700	79,200	87,200	74,200
Estimated education share of federal aid to the District of Columbia	33,019	81,847	104,940	127,127	154,962	157,465	159,670	155,643	151,381	217,160
Federal Emergency Management Agency	290	1,946	215	14,894	†	†	†	†	†	†
General Services Administration	14,775	34,800	2,883	†	3,000	2,000	2,000	1,000	1,200	1,500
Harry S Truman Scholarship fund	†	-1,895	4,305	3,000	6,000	8,000	8,000	8,284	8,500	9,550
Institute of American Indian and Alaska Native Culture and Arts Development	†	†	191	2,000	†	†	†	†	†	†
Institute of Museum and Library Services	†	†	†	166,000	250,000	265,000	265,000	274,000	242,605	231,954
James Madison Memorial Fellowship Foundation	†	†	†	7,000	2,000	2,000	2,000	†	2,000	2,000
Japanese-United States Friendship Commission	†	2,294	2,299	3,000	3,000	2,000	2,000	3,700	3,700	3,700
Library of Congress	29,478	151,871	189,827	299,000	430,000	468,000	516,000	521,000	521,000	470,202
National Aeronautics and Space Administration	258,366	255,511	1,093,303	2,077,830	2,763,120	1,754,100	1,585,500	1,430,761	2,289,837	2,189,841
National Archives and Records Administration	†	†	77,997	121,879	276,000	329,000	339,000	349,000	339,000	373,000
National Commission on Libraries and Information Science	†	2,090	2,000	2,000	1,000	1,000	†	†	†	†
National Endowment for the Arts	340	5,220	5,577	10,048	10,976	12,918	14,413	13,495	16,595	13,910
National Endowment for the Humanities	8,459	142,586	141,048	100,014	117,825	134,533	142,654	131,135	136,100	114,171
National Science Foundation	295,628	808,392	1,588,891	2,955,244	3,993,216	6,464,300	5,560,700	5,127,990	5,250,856	5,337,402
Nuclear Regulatory Commission	†	32,590	42,328	12,200	15,100	8,200	14,500	14,000	8,600	4,100
Office of Economic Opportunity	1,092,410	†	†	†	†	†	†	†	†	†
Smithsonian Institution	2,461	5,153	5,779	25,764	45,890	61,104	63,107	67,322	65,109	65,483
U.S. Arms Control and Disarmament Agency	100	661	25	†	†	†	†	†	†	†
United States Information Agency	8,423	66,210	201,547	†	†	†	†	†	†	†
United States Institute of Peace	†	†	7,621	13,000	28,000	49,000	58,000	47,000	44,000	47,000
Other agencies	1,421	990	885	300	7,900	13,500	14,300	6,000	5,000	4,400

See notes at end of table.

Table 401.20. Federal on-budget funds for education, by agency: Selected fiscal years, 1970 through 2013—Continued

[In thousands of dollars]

Agency	1970	1980	1990[1]	2000[1]	2005[1]	2009[1,2]	2010[1]	2011[1]	2012[1]	2013[1,3]
1	2	3	4	5	6	7	8	9	10	11
					Constant fiscal year 2014 dollars[4]					
Total	$71,405,662	$94,457,920	$89,585,364	$116,716,346	$176,233,335	$293,679,616	$195,981,469	$192,694,940	$195,499,393	$186,223,222
Department of Education[2]	26,365,482	35,976,859	40,257,226	46,318,529	86,873,278	203,221,240	98,304,564	98,385,270	102,081,582	92,550,005
Department of Agriculture[2]	5,477,541	12,493,981	10,864,640	15,047,213	16,467,578	17,973,603	20,604,708	21,235,900	22,779,645	23,616,555
Department of Commerce	79,748	371,224	93,422	155,598	290,734	284,698	324,140	254,707	211,192	231,073
Department of Defense	4,682,214	4,272,770	6,256,755	6,145,275	9,518,389	7,463,724	8,222,558	7,991,656	7,621,245	7,192,312
Department of Energy	3,143,907	4,396,703	4,445,834	4,857,743	5,172,211	4,056,994	3,639,999	3,142,065	3,071,877	2,746,312
Department of Health and Human Services	10,242,730	15,373,335	13,806,319	23,997,884	31,115,004	34,489,379	34,192,126	29,750,170	29,449,752	29,256,266
Department of Homeland Security	†	†	†	†	744,700	550,906	577,921	2,147,120	343,139	381,279
Department of Housing and Urban Development	653,884	14,552	205	1,901	1,311	217	428	1,679	309	4,469
Department of the Interior	1,088,628	1,206,406	1,094,192	1,303,457	1,495,136	1,093,930	1,111,883	1,088,607	997,296	938,867
Department of Justice	89,655	166,280	173,143	378,796	724,783	201,578	220,043	214,012	224,337	224,737
Department of Labor	2,419,772	5,100,971	4,358,078	6,377,529	6,870,055	6,574,347	7,302,248	6,421,770	5,974,757	5,430,277
Department of State	340,551	68,975	88,892	527,397	635,591	732,333	832,473	778,114	746,816	837,725
Department of Transportation	156,954	149,825	132,208	158,965	151,238	149,854	176,775	148,909	195,266	203,521
Department of the Treasury	103	3,416,086	72,389	112,718	†	†	†	†	†	†
Department of Veterans Affairs	5,888,013	6,438,679	1,314,472	2,142,149	5,117,085	5,156,466	9,417,123	10,799,561	10,919,555	11,879,725
Other agencies and programs										
ACTION	†	7,758	14,702	†	†	†	†	†	†	†
Agency for International Development	501,826	484,072	433,462	451,551	717,575	695,209	596,825	652,459	648,656	643,944
Appalachian Regional Commission	215,691	52,118	161	9,836	10,180	6,610	5,424	12,487	11,456	13,274
Barry Goldwater Scholarship and Excellence in Education Foundation	†	†	1,793	4,074	3,575	3,248	4,279	3,147	4,119	4,062
Corporation for National and Community Service	†	†	†	524,206	562,523	434,083	1,032,328	1,031,302	772,590	766,599
Environmental Protection Agency	110,849	112,503	151,809	134,311	99,395	57,264	58,516	83,092	89,796	75,356
Estimated education share of federal aid to the District of Columbia	188,220	224,132	182,106	172,645	184,682	170,456	170,810	163,291	155,888	220,542
Federal Emergency Management Agency	1,653	5,329	373	20,227	†	†	†	†	†	†
General Services Administration	84,223	95,297	†	†	†	†	†	†	†	†
Harry S Truman Scholarship fund	†	-5,189	5,003	4,074	3,575	2,165	2,140	1,049	1,236	1,523
Institute of American Indian and Alaska Native Culture and Arts Development	†	†	7,471	2,716	7,151	8,660	8,558	8,691	8,753	9,699
Institute of Museum and Library Services	†	†	†	225,436	297,947	286,863	283,489	287,464	249,829	235,566
James Madison Memorial Fellowship Foundation	†	†	331	9,506	2,384	2,165	2,140	2,098	2,060	2,031
Japanese-United States Friendship Commission	†	6,282	3,990	4,074	3,575	2,165	2,140	3,882	3,810	3,758
Library of Congress	168,035	415,888	329,413	406,056	512,468	506,610	552,001	546,601	536,513	477,525
National Aeronautics and Space Administration	1,472,781	699,698	1,897,244	2,821,793	3,293,050	1,898,813	1,696,120	1,501,065	2,358,018	2,223,945
National Archives and Records Administration	†	†	134,309	165,518	328,933	356,143	362,652	366,149	349,094	378,809
National Commission on Libraries and Information Science	1,938	5,723	5,694	2,716	1,192	†	†	†	†	†
National Endowment for the Arts	48,219	14,295	9,678	13,645	13,081	13,984	15,419	14,158	17,089	14,127
National Endowment for the Humanities	†	390,461	244,765	135,824	140,422	145,632	152,606	137,578	140,152	115,949
National Science Foundation	1,685,189	2,213,722	2,757,253	4,013,363	4,759,062	6,997,605	5,948,669	5,379,966	5,407,208	5,420,525
Nuclear Regulatory Commission	†	89,245	73,453	16,568	17,996	8,877	15,512	14,688	8,856	4,164
Office of Economic Opportunity	6,227,140	†	†	†	†	†	†	†	†	†
Smithsonian Institution	14,029	14,111	10,028	34,989	54,691	66,145	67,510	70,630	67,048	66,503
U.S. Arms Control and Disarmament Agency	570	1,810	43	†	†	†	†	†	†	†
United States Information Agency	48,014	181,311	349,751	†	†	†	†	†	†	†
United States Institute of Peace	†	†	13,225	17,655	33,370	53,043	62,047	49,309	45,310	47,732
Other agencies	8,100	2,711	1,536	407	9,415	14,614	15,298	6,295	5,149	4,469

†Not applicable.

[1] Excludes federal support for medical education benefits under Medicare in the U.S. Department of Health and Human Services. Benefits excluded from total because data before fiscal year (FY) 1990 are not available. This program existed since Medicare began, but was not available as a separate budget item until FY 1990. Excluded amounts are estimated as follows: $4,440,000,000 in FY 1990, $8,020,000,000 in FY 2000, $8,290,000,000 in FY 2005, $8,800,000,000 in FY 2009, $9,080,000,000 in FY 2010, $9,200,000,000 in FY 2011, $9,800,000,000 in FY 2012, and $10,000,000,000 in FY 2013.

[2] All education funds from the American Recovery and Reinvestment Act of 2009 (ARRA) are included in the Department of Education amount for FY 2009. Most of these funds had a 2-year availability, meaning that they were available for the Department of Education to obligate during FY 2009 and FY 2010.

[3] Estimated.

[4] Data adjusted by the federal budget composite deflator, as reported in the U.S. Office of Management and Budget's Budget of the U.S. Government, Historical Tables, Fiscal Year 2015.

NOTE: To the extent possible, amounts reported represent outlays rather than obligations. Negative amounts occur when program receipts exceed outlays. Starting in FY 2010, amounts for the U.S. Department of Education are appropriations, not outlays. Some data have been revised from previously published figures. Detail may not sum to totals because of rounding.

SOURCE: U.S. Department of Education, National Center for Education Statistics, unpublished tabulations. U.S. Office of Management and Budget, Budget of the U.S. Government, Appendix, fiscal years 1972 through 2014. National Science Foundation, Federal Funds for Research and Development, fiscal years 1970 to 2013. (This table was prepared December 2014.)

Table 401.30. Federal on-budget funds for education, by level/educational purpose, agency, and program: Selected fiscal years, 1970 through 2014
[In thousands of current dollars]

Level/educational purpose, agency, and program	1970	1980	1990[1]	1995[1]	2000[1]	2005[1]	2010[1]	2011[1]	2012[1]	2013[1,2]	2014[1,2]
1	2	3	4	5	6	7	8	9	10	11	12
Total	$12,526,499	$34,493,502	$51,624,342	$71,639,520	$85,944,203	$147,873,199	$183,199,676	$183,669,874	$189,846,616	$183,367,513	$179,342,408
Elementary/secondary education	5,830,442	16,027,686	21,984,361	33,623,809	43,790,783	68,957,711	86,681,807	76,118,858	78,227,148	79,131,192	80,072,257
Department of Education[2]	2,719,204	6,629,095	9,681,313	14,029,000	20,039,563	37,477,594	49,621,475	38,652,240	38,600,066	38,705,852	37,771,972
Education for the disadvantaged	1,339,014	3,204,664	4,494,111	6,808,000	8,529,111	14,635,566	15,864,666	15,515,444	15,741,703	15,590,733	15,552,693
Impact aid program[4]	656,372	690,170	816,366	808,000	877,101	1,262,174	1,276,183	1,273,631	1,291,186	1,299,088	1,286,603
School improvement programs[5]	288,304	788,918	1,189,158	1,397,000	2,549,971	7,918,091	16,999,862	6,738,485	6,327,886	6,543,628	5,883,351
Indian education	†	93,365	69,451	71,000	65,285	121,911	127,282	127,027	130,779	131,579	123,939
English Language Acquisition	21,250	169,540	188,919	225,000	362,662	667,485	750,000	733,530	732,144	736,624	723,400
Special education	79,090	821,777	1,616,623	3,177,000	4,948,977	10,940,312	12,587,035	12,526,672	12,640,709	12,661,256	12,497,300
Vocational and adult education	335,174	860,661	1,306,685	1,482,000	1,462,977	1,967,086	2,016,447	1,797,451	1,735,659	1,742,944	1,702,686
Education Reform—Goals 2000[6]	†	†	†	61,000	1,243,479	-35,031	†	†	†	†	†
Hurricane Education Recovery	†	†	†	†	†	†	†	†	†	†	†
Department of Agriculture	760,477	4,064,497	5,528,950	8,201,294	10,051,278	12,577,265	17,875,561	18,843,607	20,849,143	21,781,420	21,895,211
Child nutrition programs[7]	299,131	3,377,056	4,977,075	7,644,789	9,554,028	11,901,943	16,383,421	17,290,601	19,504,343	20,487,229	20,487,299
McGovern-Dole International Food for Education and Child Nutrition Program[8]	†	†	†	†	†	86,000	210,000	343,500	196,400	197,126	197,000
Agricultural Marketing Service—commodities[9]	341,597	388,000	350,441	400,000	400,000	399,322	1,100,000	1,006,000	952,000	903,000	1,032,000
Special Milk Program	83,800	159,293	18,707	(7)	(7)	(7)	(7)	(7)	(7)	(7)	(7)
Estimated education share of Forest Service permanent appropriations	35,949	140,148	182,727	156,505	97,250	190,000	182,140	203,506	196,400	194,065	178,912
Department of Commerce	†	54,816	†	†	†	†	†	†	†	†	†
Local public works program—school facilities[10]	†	54,816	†	†	†	†	†	†	†	†	†
Department of Defense	143,100	370,846	1,097,876	1,295,547	1,485,611	1,786,253	1,981,321	2,047,825	2,132,046	2,220,611	2,262,093
Junior Reserve Officers Training Corps (JROTC)	12,100	32,000	39,300	155,600	210,432	315,122	359,689	377,526	391,682	407,335	450,229
Overseas dependents schools	131,000	338,846	864,958	855,772	904,829	1,060,920	1,186,560	1,193,636	1,235,707	1,262,545	1,235,335
Domestic schools[4]	†	†	193,618	284,175	370,350	410,211	435,072	476,663	504,657	550,731	576,529
Department of Energy	200	77,633	15,563	12,646	†	†	†	†	†	†	†
Energy conservation for school buildings[11]	†	77,240	15,213	10,746	†	†	†	†	†	†	†
Pre-engineering program	200	393	350	1,900	†	†	†	†	†	†	†
Department of Health and Human Services	167,333	1,077,000	2,396,793	5,116,559	6,011,036	8,003,348	8,547,000	8,871,364	9,298,710	9,428,300	10,900,500
Head Start[12]	†	735,000	1,447,758	3,534,000	5,267,000	6,842,348	7,234,000	7,559,164	7,969,210	8,107,000	9,621,000
Payments to states for Aid to Families with Dependent Children (AFDC) work programs[13]	†	†	459,221	953,000	15,000	—	†	†	†	†	†
Social Security student benefits[14]	167,333	342,000	489,814	529,559	729,036	1,161,000	1,313,000	1,312,200	1,329,500	1,321,300	1,279,500
Department of Homeland Security	†	†	†	†	†	500	505	504	454	364	462
Tuition assistance for educational accreditation—Coast Guard personnel[15]	†	†	†	†	†	500	505	504	454	364	462
Department of the Interior	140,705	318,170	445,267	493,124	725,423	938,506	781,075	815,877	782,335	760,793	765,705
Mineral Leasing Act and other funds											
Payments to states—estimated education share	12,294	62,636	123,811	18,750	24,610	60,290	23,000	24,380	26,450	24,770	23,800
Payments to counties—estimated education share	16,359	48,953	102,522	37,490	53,500	79,686	50,000	53,000	58,000	53,970	51,900
Indian Education											
Bureau of Indian Education schools	95,850	178,112	192,841	411,524	466,905	517,647	580,492	583,572	631,477	597,412	622,382
Johnson-O'Malley assistance[16]	16,080	28,081	25,556	24,359	17,387	16,510	13,589	13,415	13,304	12,615	14,338
Education construction	†	†	†	1,000	161,021	263,373	112,994	140,509	52,104	71,026	52,285
Education expenses for children of employees, Yellowstone National Park	122	388	538	†	2,000	1,000	1,000	1,000	1,000	1,000	1,000
Department of Justice	8,237	23,890	65,997	128,850	224,800	554,500	137,529	140,525	149,587	160,684	151,630
Advanced occupational education	†	†	†	†	†	†	137,529	140,525	149,587	160,684	151,630
Vocational training expenses for prisoners in federal prisons	2,720	4,966	2,066	3,000	1,000	0	†	†	†	†	†
Inmate programs[17]	5,517	18,924	63,931	125,850	223,800	554,500	†	†	†	†	†

See notes at end of table.

Table 401.30. Federal on-budget funds for education, by level/educational purpose, agency, and program: Selected fiscal years, 1970 through 2014—Continued

[In thousands of current dollars]

Level/educational purpose, agency, and program	1970	1980	1990[1]	1995[1]	2000[1]	2005[1]	2010[1]	2011[1]	2012[1]	2013[1,2]	2014[1,2]
1	2	3	4	5	6	7	8	9	10	11	12
Department of Labor	420,927	1,849,800	2,505,487	3,957,800	4,683,200	5,654,000	6,826,000	6,121,000	5,802,000	5,347,004	5,564,123
Job Corps	†	469,800	739,376	1,029,000	1,256,000	1,521,000	1,850,000	1,660,000	1,789,000	1,650,004	1,691,123
Training programs—estimated funds for education programs[18]	420,927	1,380,000	1,766,111	2,928,800	3,427,200	4,133,000	4,976,000	4,461,000	4,013,000	3,697,000	3,873,000
Department of Transportation	45	60	46	62	188	†	†	†	†	†	†
Tuition assistance for educational accreditation—Coast Guard personnel[15]	45	60	46	62	188	†	†	†	†	†	†
Department of the Treasury	†	935,903	†	†	†	†	†	†	†	†	†
Estimated education share of general revenue sharing[19]											
State[20]	†	525,019	†	†	†	†	†	†	†	†	†
Local	†	410,884	†	†	†	†	†	†	†	†	†
Department of Veterans Affairs	338,910	545,786	155,351	311,768	445,052	1,815,000	760,500	472,000	488,769	534,796	573,975
Noncollegiate and job training programs[21]	281,640	439,993	12,848	298,132	438,635	1,815,000	760,500	472,000	488,769	534,796	573,975
Vocational rehabilitation for disabled veterans[22]	41,700	87,980	136,780	5,961	6,417	†	†	†	†	†	†
Dependents education[23]	15,570	17,813	5,723	7,675	†	†	†	†	†	†	†
Service members occupational conversion training act of 1992	†	†	†	†	†	†	†	†	†	†	†
Other agencies											
Appalachian Regional Commission	33,161	9,157	93	2,173	2,588	2,962	986	2,290	962	1,689	3,163
National Endowment for the Arts	†	4,989	4,641	7,117	6,002	8,470	11,530	12,125	10,450	10,427	10,924
Arts in education	†	4,989	4,641	7,117	6,002	8,470	11,530	12,125	10,450	10,427	10,924
National Endowment for the Humanities	20	330	404	997	812	603	125	75	100	333	181
Office of Economic Opportunity	1,072,375	†	†	†	†	†	†	†	†	†	†
Head Start[24]	325,700	†	†	†	†	†	†	†	†	†	†
Other elementary and secondary programs[25]	42,809	†	†	†	†	†	†	†	†	†	†
Job Corps[26]	144,000	†	†	†	†	†	†	†	†	†	†
Youth Corps and other training programs[26]	553,368	†	†	†	†	†	†	†	†	†	†
Volunteers in Service to America (VISTA)[27]	6,498	†	†	†	†	†	†	†	†	†	†
Other programs											
Estimated education share of federal aid to the District of Columbia	25,748	65,714	86,579	66,871	115,230	138,710	138,200	139,426	112,526	178,919	172,318
Postsecondary education[3]	**$3,447,697**	**$11,115,882**	**$13,650,915**	**$17,618,137**	**$15,008,715**	**$38,587,287**	**$50,197,838**	**$64,400,219**	**$70,053,827**	**$62,784,231**	**$56,953,714**
Department of Education[3]	1,187,962	5,682,242	11,175,978	14,234,000	10,727,315	31,420,023	36,539,655	49,260,330	54,470,178	46,131,422	38,981,641
Student financial assistance	†	3,682,789	5,920,328	7,047,000	9,060,317	15,209,515	25,959,478	43,753,247	43,324,872	37,319,312	31,092,464
Direct Loan Program[28]	†	†	†	840,000	-2,862,240	3,020,992	3,481,859	2,781,709	6,917,373	3,273,880	2,871,258
Federal Family Education Loan Program[29]	2,323	1,407,977	4,372,446	5,190,000	2,707,473	10,777,470	3,932,994	-91,796	1,498,353	2,787,755	2,269,320
Higher education	1,029,131	399,787	659,492	871,000	1,530,779	2,053,288	2,740,665	2,388,946	2,297,656	2,302,753	2,322,592
Facilities—loans and insurance	114,199	-19,031	19,219	-6,000	-2,174	-1,464	-8,360	-4,607	-8,513	-129	-156
College housing loans[30]	774	14,082	-57,167	-46,000	-41,886	-33,521	-16,725	-13,265	-16,725	-1,176	-1,176
Educational activities overseas	†	3,561	82	†	150	169	23,330	23,289	32,160	21,424	20,227
Historically Black Colleges and Universities Capital Financing, Program Account	†	†	†	†	†	†	†	†	†	†	†
Gallaudet College and Howard University	38,559	176,829	230,327	292,000	291,060	339,823	357,977	357,261	359,580	361,781	340,821
National Technical Institute for the Deaf	2,976	16,248	31,251	46,000	43,836	53,751	68,437	65,546	65,422	65,822	66,291
Hurricane Katrina, aid to institutions	†	†	†	†	†	†	†	†	†	†	†
Department of Agriculture	†	10,453	31,273	33,373	30,676	61,957	80,697	81,658	81,658	79,089	84,439
Agriculture Extension Service, Second Morrill Act payments to agricultural and mechanical colleges and Tuskegee Institute	†	10,453	31,273	33,373	30,676	61,957	80,697	81,658	81,658	79,089	84,439
Department of Commerce	8,277	29,971	3,312	3,487	3,800	—	—	—	—	—	—
Sea Grant Program[31]	6,160	3,123	3,312	3,487	3,800	—	—	—	—	—	—
Merchant Marine Academy[32]	2,117	14,809	†	†	†	†	†	—	—	—	—
State marine schools[32]	†	12,039	†	†	†	†	†	†	†	†	†

See notes at end of table.

Table 401.30. Federal on-budget funds for education, by level/educational purpose, agency, and program: Selected fiscal years, 1970 through 2014—Continued
[In thousands of current dollars]

Level/educational purpose, agency, and program	1970	1980	1990[1]	1995[1]	2000[1]	2005[1]	2010[1]	2011[1]	2012[1]	2013[1,2]	2014[1,2]
	2	3	4	5	6	7	8	9	10	11	12
Department of Defense	322,100	545,000	635,769	729,500	1,147,759	1,858,301	2,550,667	2,297,234	2,407,629	2,420,958	2,435,322
Tuition assistance for military personnel	57,500	—	95,300	127,000	263,303	608,109	669,892	567,412	590,626	564,604	524,745
Service academies	78,700	106,100	120,613	163,300	212,678	300,760	402,640	348,836	375,250	372,726	372,734
Senior Reserve Officers Training Corps (SROTC)	108,100	—	193,056	219,400	363,461	537,525	885,500	851,910	844,498	843,018	885,703
Professional development education[33]	77,800	—	226,800	219,800	308,317	411,907	592,635	529,076	597,255	640,610	652,140
Department of Energy	3,000	57,701	25,502	28,027	†	†	†	†	†	†	†
University laboratory cooperative program	3,000	2,800	9,402	8,552	†	†	†	†	†	†	†
Teacher development projects	†	1,400	†	†	†	†	†	†	†	†	†
Energy conservation for buildings—higher education[11]	†	53,501	7,459	7,381	†	†	†	†	†	†	†
Minority honors vocational training	†	†	†	†	†	†	†	†	†	†	†
Honors research program	†	†	6,472	2,221	†	†	†	†	†	†	†
Students and teachers	†	†	2,169	9,873	†	†	†	†	†	†	†
Department of Health and Human Services	981,483	2,412,058	578,542	796,035	954,190	1,433,516	1,278,936	1,367,895	1,331,410	1,295,616	1,339,545
Health professions training programs[34]	353,029	460,736	230,600	298,302	340,361	581,661	406,000	498,000	459,000	438,039	469,236
Indian health manpower	†	7,187	9,508	27,000	16,000	27,000	46,000	41,000	41,000	41,000	41,000
National Health Service Corps scholarships	†	70,667	4,759	78,206	33,300	45,000	41,000	46,400	42,940	39,868	42,600
National Institutes of Health training grants[35]	†	176,388	241,356	380,502	550,220	756,014	775,186	771,766	777,761	766,000	776,000
National Institute of Occupational Safety and Health training grants[36]	8,088	12,899	10,461	11,660	14,198	23,841	10,750	10,729	10,709	10,709	10,709
Alcohol, drug abuse, and mental health training programs[37]	118,366	122,103	81,353	†	†	†	†	†	†	†	†
Health teaching facilities[38]	†	3,078	505	365	110	†	†	†	†	†	†
Social Security postsecondary students' benefits[39]	502,000	1,559,000	†	†	†	†	†	†	†	†	†
Department of Homeland Security	†	†	†	†	†	36,400	45,824	49,604	48,592	43,468	36,518
Coast Guard Academy[15]	†	†	†	†	†	16,400	26,326	27,581	26,803	24,359	25,766
Postgraduate training for Coast Guard officers[40]	†	†	†	†	†	8,700	4,645	4,883	5,891	6,198	5,416
Tuition assistance to Coast Guard military personnel[15]	†	†	†	†	†	11,300	14,853	17,140	15,898	12,911	5,336
Department of Housing and Urban Development[30]	114,199	†	†	†	†	†	†	†	†	†	†
College housing loans[30]	114,199	†	†	†	†	†	†	†	†	†	†
Department of the Interior	31,749	80,202	135,480	159,054	187,179	249,227	174,092	112,970	120,720	107,477	109,534
Shared revenues, Mineral Leasing Act and other receipts—estimated education share	6,949	35,403	69,980	82,810	98,740	146,235	16,250	20,430	29,900	20,310	19,500
Indian programs											
Continuing education	9,380	16,909	34,911	43,907	57,576	76,271	126,791	61,603	61,435	58,832	61,887
Higher education scholarships	15,420	27,890	30,589	32,337	30,863	26,721	31,051	30,937	29,385	28,335	28,147
Department of State	30,850	†	2,167	3,000	319,000	424,000	657,660	620,050	601,770	605,641	584,124
Educational exchange[41]	30,850	†	†	†	319,000	424,000	657,660	620,050	601,770	605,641	584,124
Mutual educational and cultural exchange activities	30,454	†	†	†	303,000	402,000	635,000	599,550	583,200	586,957	562,659
International educational exchange activities	396	†	†	†	16,000	22,000	22,660	20,500	18,570	18,684	21,465
Russian, Eurasian, and East European Research and Training	†	†	2,167	3,000	†	†	†	†	†	†	†
Department of Transportation	11,197	12,530	46,025	59,257	60,300	73,000	95,000	77,000	118,000	130,000	98,400
Merchant Marine Academy[22]	†	†	20,926	30,850	34,000	61,000	79,000	61,000	101,000	109,000	81,300
State marine schools[22]	†	†	8,269	8,980	7,000	12,000	16,000	16,000	17,000	21,000	17,100
Coast Guard Academy[15]	9,342	10,000	12,074	13,500	15,500	†	†	†	†	†	†
Postgraduate training for Coast Guard officers[40]	1,655	2,230	4,173	5,513	2,500	†	†	†	†	†	†
Tuition assistance to Coast Guard military personnel[15]	200	300	582	414	1,300	†	†	†	†	†	†
Department of the Treasury	†	296,750	†	†	†	†	†	†	†	†	†
General revenue sharing—estimated state share to higher education[19,20]	†	296,750	†	†	†	†	†	†	†	†	†
Department of Veterans Affairs	693,490	1,803,847	599,825	1,010,114	1,132,322	2,478,624	8,042,444	9,821,752	10,115,052	11,162,755	12,231,739
Vietnam-era veterans	638,260	1,579,974	46,998	†	†	†	†	†	†	†	†
College student support	†	1,560,081	39,458	†	†	†	†	†	†	†	†
Work-study	†	19,893	7,540	†	†	†	†	†	†	†	†

See notes at end of table.

Table 401.30. Federal on-budget funds for education, by level/educational purpose, agency, and program: Selected fiscal years, 1970 through 2014—Continued

[In thousands of current dollars]

Level/educational purpose, agency, and program	1970	1980	1990[1]	1995[1]	2000[1]	2005[1]	2010[1]	2011[1]	2012[1]	2013[1,2]	2014[1,2]
1	2	3	4	5	6	7	8	9	10	11	12
Service persons college support	18,900	46,617	8,911	†	†	†	†	†	†	†	†
Post-Vietnam veterans	†	922	161,475	33,596	3,958	1,136	894	1,343	932	848	764
All-volunteer-force educational assistance	†	†	269,947	868,394	984,068	2,070,996	1,854,917	1,587,376	1,086,585	885,715	746,887
Veterans	†	†	183,765	760,390	876,434	1,887,239	1,659,694	1,385,943	931,756	726,697	591,750
Reservists	†	†	86,182	108,004	107,634	183,757	195,223	201,433	154,829	159,018	155,137
Post 9-11 GI Bill[46]	0	†	†	†	†	†	5,542,843	7,656,490	8,476,227	9,716,174	10,901,760
Veteran dependents' education	36,330	176,334	100,494	95,124	131,296	388,719	507,294	462,877	455,318	486,705	523,778
Payments to state education agencies	†	†	12,000	13,000	13,000	17,773	18,342	18,342	19,000	19,000	19,000
Reserve Education Assistance Program (REAP)[43]	†	†	†	†	†	†	136,496	95,324	76,990	54,313	39,550
Other agencies											
Appalachian Regional Commission	4,105	1,751	—	2,741	2,286	4,407	2,464	6,098	6,653	4,443	7,471
National Endowment for the Humanities	3,349	56,451	50,938	56,481	28,395	29,253	47,949	40,168	45,000	39,399	39,824
National Science Foundation	42,000	64,583	161,884	211,800	389,000	490,000	646,000	636,060	653,590	709,720	950,250
Science and engineering education programs	37,000	64,583	161,884	211,800	389,000	490,000	646,000	636,060	653,590	709,720	950,250
Sea Grant Program[31]	5,000	†	†	†	†	†	†	†	†	†	†
United States Information Agency[44]	8,423	51,095	181,172	260,800	†	†	†	†	†	†	†
Educational and cultural affairs[41]	†	49,546	35,862	13,600	†	†	†	†	†	†	†
Educational and cultural exchange programs[45]	†	†	145,307	247,200	†	†	†	†	†	†	†
Educational exchange activities, international	†	1,549	3	†	†	†	†	†	†	†	†
Information center and library activities	8,423	†	†	†	†	†	†	†	†	†	†
Other programs											
Barry Goldwater Scholarship and Excellence in Education Foundation	†	†	1,033	3,000	3,000	3,000	4,000	3,000	4,000	4,000	4,000
Estimated education share of federal aid to the District of Columbia[46]	†	13,143	14,637	9,468	11,493	14,578	20,450	15,115	37,875	37,193	37,538
Harry S Truman Scholarship fund	5,513	-1,895	2,883	3,000	3,000	3,000	2,000	1,000	1,200	1,500	†
Institute of American Indian and Alaska Native Culture and Arts Development	†	†	4,305	13,000	2,000	6,000	8,000	8,284	8,500	9,550	11,369
James Madison Memorial Fellowship Foundation	†	†	191	2,000	7,000	2,000	2,000	2,000	2,000	2,000	2,000
Other education	**$964,719**	**$1,548,730**	**$3,383,031**	**$4,719,655**	**$5,484,571**	**$6,908,504**	**$9,326,725**	**$11,133,686**	**$9,389,458**	**$9,727,789**	**$9,454,871**
Department of Education[3]	630,235	747,706	2,251,801	2,861,000	3,223,355	3,538,862	5,073,063	5,255,939	5,466,031	5,696,191	5,420,115
Administration	47,456	187,317	328,293	404,000	458,054	548,842	1,531,232	1,755,384	1,928,821	2,048,098	1,971,955
Libraries[47]	108,284	129,127	137,264	117,000	†	†	†	†	†	†	†
Rehabilitative services and disability research	473,091	426,886	1,780,360	2,333,000	2,755,468	2,973,346	3,506,861	3,474,718	3,511,281	3,622,925	3,422,749
American Printing House for the Blind	1,404	4,349	5,736	7,000	9,368	16,538	24,600	24,551	24,505	24,655	24,456
Trust funds and contributions	0	27	148	0	465	136	10,370	1,286	1,424	513	955
Department of Agriculture	135,637	271,112	352,511	422,878	444,477	468,631	567,423	552,030	547,081	549,989	535,935
Extension Service	131,734	263,584	337,907	405,371	424,174	445,631	543,423	530,030	526,081	528,989	509,935
National Agricultural Library	3,903	7,528	14,604	17,507	20,303	23,000	24,000	22,000	21,000	21,000	26,000
Department of Commerce	1,226	2,479	†	†	†	†	†	†	†	†	†
Maritime Administration	†	†	†	†	†	†	†	†	†	†	†
Training for private sector employees[32]	1,226	2,479	†	†	†	†	†	†	†	†	†
Department of Health and Human Services	24,273	37,819	77,962	138,000	214,000	313,000	340,000	337,000	337,639	339,705	382,252
National Library of Medicine	24,273	37,819	77,962	138,000	214,000	313,000	340,000	337,000	337,639	339,705	382,252
Department of Homeland Security	†	†	†	†	†	278,243	341,100	1,892,000	215,471	258,000	259,000
Federal Law Enforcement Training Center[48]	†	†	†	†	†	159,000	323,000	311,000	271,000	258,000	259,000
Estimated disaster relief[49]	†	†	†	†	†	119,243	18,100	1,581,000	-55,529	—	—
Department of Justice	5,546	27,642	26,920	36,296	34,727	26,148	33,563	33,563	33,563	30,207	31,001
Federal Bureau of Investigation National Academy	2,066	7,234	6,028	12,831	22,479	15,619	19,443	19,443	19,443	21,268	21,732
Federal Bureau of Investigation Field Police Academy	2,500	7,715	10,548	11,140	11,962	10,456	14,120	14,120	14,120	8,939	9,270
Narcotics and dangerous drug training	980	2,416	850	325	286	73	†	†	†	†	†
National Institute of Corrections	†	10,277	9,494	12,000	†	†	†	†	†	†	†

See notes at end of table.

Table 401.30. Federal on-budget funds for education, by level/educational purpose, agency, and program: Selected fiscal years, 1970 through 2014—Continued

[In thousands of current dollars]

Level/educational purpose, agency, and program	1970	1980	1990[1]	1995[1]	2000[1]	2005[1]	2010[1]	2011[1]	2012[1]	2013[1,2]	2014[1,2]
1	2	3	4	5	6	7	8	9	10	11	12
Department of State	20,672	25,000	47,539	51,648	69,349	109,309	120,520	121,620	123,452	219,238	217,431
Foreign Service Institute	15,857	25,000	47,539	51,648	69,349	109,309	120,520	121,620	123,452	219,238	217,431
Center for Cultural and Technical Interchange[41]	4,815	†	†	†	†	†	†	†	†	†	†
Department of Transportation	3,964	10,212	1,507	650	700	1,100	146	135	120	—	—
Highways training and education grants	2,418	3,412	—	—	—	—	—	—	—	—	—
Maritime Administration											
Training for private sector employees[30]	1,546	500	1,507	650	700	1,100	146	135	120	—	—
Urban mass transportation—managerial training grants	—	—	—	—	—	—	—	—	—	—	—
Federal Aviation Administration											
Air traffic controllers second career program	—	6,300	—	—	—	†	†	†	†	†	†
Department of the Treasury	18	14,584	41,488	48,000	83,000	†	†	†	†	†	†
Federal Law Enforcement Training Center[48]	18	14,584	41,488	48,000	83,000	†	†	†	†	†	†
Other agencies											
ACTION[50]	†	2,833	8,472	†	†	†	†	†	†	†	†
Estimated education funds	†	2,833	8,472	†	†	†	†	†	†	†	†
Agency for International Development	88,034	99,707	170,371	260,408	299,000	574,000	542,700	599,500	598,800	602,369	562,659
Education and human resources	61,570	80,518	142,801	248,408	299,000	574,000	542,700	599,500	598,800	602,369	562,659
American schools and hospitals abroad	26,464	19,189	27,570	12,000	†	†	†	†	†	†	†
Appalachian Regional Commission	572	8,124	†	5,709	2,369	1,173	1,620	3,514	3,510	6,938	2,439
Corporation for National and Community Service[50]	†	†	†	214,600	386,000	472,000	965,000	983,000	750,251	754,843	760,264
Federal Emergency Management Agency[51]	290	281	215	170,400	14,894	†	†	†	†	†	†
Estimated architect/engineer student development program	40	31	200	—	—	†	†	†	†	†	†
Estimated other training programs[52]	250	250	15	—	—	†	†	†	†	†	†
Estimated disaster relief[49]	—	—	—	170,400	14,894	†	†	†	†	†	†
General Services Administration	14,775	34,800	†	†	†	†	†	†	†	†	†
Libraries and other archival activities[53]	14,775	34,800	†	†	†	†	†	†	†	†	†
Institute of Museum and Library Services[47]	†	†	†	†	166,000	250,000	265,000	274,000	242,605	231,954	225,813
Japanese-United States Friendship Commission	†	2,294	2,299	2,000	3,000	3,000	2,000	3,700	3,700	3,700	4,000
Library of Congress	29,478	151,871	189,827	241,000	299,000	430,000	516,000	521,000	521,000	470,202	485,757
Salaries and expenses	20,700	102,364	148,985	198,000	247,000	383,000	439,000	446,000	442,000	422,625	433,830
Books for the blind and the physically handicapped	6,195	31,436	37,473	39,000	46,000	47,000	77,000	75,000	79,000	47,577	51,927
Special foreign currency program	2,273	3,492	10	4,000	6,000	†	†	†	†	†	†
Furniture and furnishings	310	14,579	3,359	—	—	—	†	†	†	†	†
National Aeronautics and Space Administration	350	882	3,300	5,923	6,800	†	†	†	†	†	†
Aerospace education services project	350	882	3,300	5,923	6,800	†	†	†	†	†	†
National Archives and Records Administration	†	†	77,397	105,172	121,879	276,000	339,000	349,000	339,000	373,000	370,706
Libraries and other archival activities[53]	†	†	77,397	105,172	121,879	276,000	339,000	349,000	339,000	373,000	370,706
National Commission on Libraries and Information Science[54]	†	2,090	3,281	1,000	2,000	1,000	†	†	†	†	†
National Endowment for the Arts	340	231	936	2,304	4,046	2,506	2,883	1,370	6,145	3,483	4,502
National Endowment for the Humanities	5,090	85,805	89,706	94,249	70,807	87,969	94,580	90,891	91,000	74,439	77,528
Smithsonian Institution	2,461	5,153	5,779	9,961	25,764	45,890	63,107	67,322	65,109	65,483	66,593
Museum programs and related research	2,261	3,254	690	3,190	18,000	32,000	52,000	56,000	54,000	54,313	55,979
National Gallery of Art extension service	200	426	474	771	764	890	107	119	122	115	114
Woodrow Wilson International Center for Scholars	†	1,473	4,615	6,000	7,000	13,000	11,000	11,203	10,987	11,055	10,500

See notes at end of table.

Table 401.30. Federal on-budget funds for education, by level/educational purpose, agency, and program: Selected fiscal years, 1970 through 2014—Continued
[In thousands of current dollars]

Level/educational purpose, agency, and program	1970	1980	1990¹	1995¹	2000¹	2005¹	2010¹	2011¹	2012¹	2013¹²	2014¹²
1	2	3	4	5	6	7	8	9	10	11	12
U.S. Information Agency—Center for Cultural and Technical Interchange⁴¹	†	15,115	20,375	34,000	†	†	†	†	†	†	†
United States Institute of Peace	†	†	7,621	12,000	13,000	28,000	58,000	47,000	44,000	47,000	48,000
Other programs											
Estimated education share of federal aid for the District of Columbia	1,758	2,990	3,724	2,457	404	1,674	1,020	1,102	980	1,048	876
Research programs at universities and related institutions⁵⁵	$2,283,641	$5,801,204	$12,606,035	$15,677,919	$21,660,134	$33,419,698	$36,993,306	$32,017,112	$32,176,184	$31,724,301	$32,861,567
Department of Education⁵⁶	87,823	78,742	89,483	279,000	116,464	456,822	659,006	608,786	593,664	$597,297	$576,935
Department of Agriculture	64,796	216,405	348,109	434,544	553,600	709,700	737,200	764,000	643,100	843,900	804,800
Department of Commerce	4,487	48,295	50,523	85,442	110,775	243,948	303,000	242,778	205,085	227,530	287,503
Department of Defense	356,188	644,455	1,871,864	1,853,955	1,891,710	4,342,100	3,154,300	3,272,300	2,861,205	2,440,450	2,574,093
Department of Energy	548,327	1,470,224	2,520,885	2,651,641	3,577,004	4,339,879	3,402,600	2,994,903	2,983,055	2,704,198	3,159,495
Department of Health and Human Services	623,765	2,087,053	4,902,714	6,418,969	10,491,641	16,357,996	21,796,200	17,780,531	17,630,467	17,744,004	17,891,104
Department of Homeland Security	†	†	†	†	†	309,717	152,800	104,450	68,700	73,600	72,500
Department of Housing and Urban Development	510	5,314	118	1,613	1,400	1,100	400	1,600	300	4,400	1,600
Department of the Interior	18,521	42,175	49,790	50,618	47,200	66,800	84,200	108,774	65,405	56,200	64,700
Department of Justice	1,945	9,189	6,858	7,204	19,400	27,500	34,600	29,900	34,700	30,400	30,400
Department of Labor	3,567	12,938	5,893	10,114	12,900	110,500	†	†	†	†	†
Department of State	8,220	188	1,519	23	†	†	†	†	†	†	†
Department of Transportation	12,328	31,910	28,608	75,847	55,866	52,800	70,100	64,800	71,500	70,400	73,600
Department of the Treasury	†	226	227	1,496	†	†	†	†	†	†	†
Department of Veterans Affairs	518	1,600	2,300	2,500	†	†	†	†	†	†	†
Agency for International Development	†	77,063	79,415	30,172	33,500	28,100	15,200	22,400	31,100	31,700	32,300
Environmental Protection Agency	19,446	41,083	87,481	125,721	98,900	83,400	54,700	79,200	87,200	74,200	79,900
Federal Emergency Management Agency	†	1,665	†	†	†	†	†	†	†	†	†
National Aeronautics and Space Administration	258,016	254,629	1,090,003	1,751,977	2,071,030	2,763,120	1,585,500	1,430,761	2,289,837	2,189,841	2,159,858
National Science Foundation	253,628	743,809	1,427,007	1,874,395	2,566,244	3,503,216	4,914,700	4,491,930	4,597,266	4,627,682	5,038,779
Nuclear Regulatory Commission	†	32,590	42,328	22,188	12,200	15,100	14,500	14,000	8,600	4,100	7,200
Office of Economic Opportunity	20,035	†	†	†	†	†	†	†	†	†	†
U.S. Arms Control and Disarmament Agency	100	661	25	†	†	†	†	†	†	†	†
Other agencies	1,421	990	885	500	300	7,900	14,300	6,000	5,000	4,400	6,800

See notes at end of table.

Table 401.30. Federal on-budget funds for education, by level/educational purpose, agency, and program: Selected fiscal years, 1970 through 2014—Continued

—Not available.

†Not applicable.

[1]Excludes federal support for medical education benefits under Medicare in the U.S. Department of Health and Human Services. Benefits excluded from total because data before fiscal year (FY) 1990 are not available. This program existed since Medicare began, but was not available as a separate budget item until FY 1990. Excluded amounts are estimated as follows: $4,440,000,000 in FY 1990, $7,510,000,000 in FY 1995, $8,020,000,000 in FY 2000, $8,290,000,000 in FY 2005, $9,080,000,000 in FY 2010, $9,200,000,000 in FY 2011, $9,800,000,000 in FY 2012, $10,000,000,000 in FY 2013, and $11,330,000,000 in FY 2014.

[2]Data for research programs at universities and related institutions are estimated.

[3]The U.S. Department of Education was created in May 1980. It formerly was the Office of Education in the U.S. Department of Health, Education, and Welfare.

[4]Arranges for the education of children who reside on federal property when no suitable local school district can or will provide for the education of these children.

[5]Includes many programs, such as No Child Left Behind, 21st Century Community Learning Centers, Class Size Reduction, Charter Schools, Safe and Drug-Free Schools, and Innovative programs.

[6]Included the School-To-Work Opportunities program, which initiated a national system to be administered jointly by the U.S. Departments of Education and Labor. Programs in the Education Reform program were transferred to the school improvement programs or discontinued in FY 2002. Amounts after FY 2002 reflect balances that are spending out from prior-year appropriations.

[7]Starting in FY 1994, the Special Milk Program has been included in the child nutrition programs.

[8]The Farm Security and Rural Investment Act of 2002 (Public Law 107-171) carries out preschool and school feeding programs in foreign countries to help reduce the incidence of hunger and malnutrition, and improve literacy and primary education.

[9]These commodities are purchased under Section 32 of the Act of August 24, 1935, for use in the child nutrition programs.

[10]Assisted in the construction of public facilities, such as vocational schools, through grants or loans. No funds have been appropriated for this program since FY 1977, and it was completely phased out in FY 1984.

[11]Established in 1979, with funds first appropriated in FY 1990.

[12]Formerly in the Office of Economic Opportunity. In FY 1972, funds were transferred to the U.S. Department of Health, Education, and Welfare, Office of Child Development.

[13]Created by the Family Support Act of 1988 to provide funds for the Job Opportunities and Basic Skills Training program. Later incorporated into the Temporary Assistance for Needy Families program.

[14]After age 18, benefits terminate at the end of the school term or in 3 months, whichever comes first.

[15]Transferred from the U.S. Department of Transportation to the U.S. Department of Homeland Security in March 2003.

[16]Provides funding for supplemental programs for eligible American Indian students in public schools.

[17]Finances the cost of academic, social, and occupational education courses for inmates in federal prisons.

[18]Some of the work and training programs were in the Office of Economic Opportunity and were transferred to the U.S. Department of Labor in FYs 1971 and 1972. From FY 1994 through FY 2001, included the School-to-Work Opportunities program, which was administered jointly by the U.S. Departments of Education and Labor.

[19]Established in FY 1972 and closed in FY 1986.

[20]The states' share of revenue-sharing funds could not be spent on education in FYs 1981 through 1986.

[21]Provided educational assistance allowances in order to restore lost educational opportunities to those individuals whose careers were interrupted or impeded by reason of active military service between January 31, 1955, and January 1, 1977.

[22]This program is in Readjustment Benefits program, Chapter 31, and covers the costs of subsistence, tuition, books, supplies, and equipment for disabled veterans requiring vocational rehabilitation.

[23]This program is in Readjustment Benefits program, Chapter 35, and provides benefits to children and spouses of veterans.

[24]Head Start program funds were transferred to the U.S. Department of Health, Education, and Welfare, Office of Child Development, in FY 1972.

[25]Most of these programs were transferred to the U.S. Department of Health, Education, and Welfare, Office of Education, in FY 1972.

[26]Transferred to the U.S. Department of Labor in FYs 1971 and 1972.

[27]Transferred to the ACTION Agency in FY 1972.

[28]Under the William D. Ford Federal Direct Loan Program (commonly referred to as the Direct Loan Program), the federal government uses Treasury funds to provide loan capital directly to schools, which then disburse loan funds to students.

[29]The Federal Family Education Loan (FFEL) Program eliminated the authorization to originate new FFEL loans after June 30, 2010; all new loans are originated through the Direct Loan Program. The FFEL Program made loan capital available for students and their families through private lenders. State and private nonprofit guaranty agencies administer the federal guarantee FFEL lenders against losses related to borrower default. These agencies also collect on defaulted loans and provide other services to lenders.

[30]Transferred from the U.S. Department of Housing and Urban Development to the U.S. Department of Health, Education, and Welfare, Office of Education, in FY 1979.

[31]Transferred from the National Science Foundation to the U.S. Department of Commerce in October 1970.

[32]Transferred from the U.S. Department of Commerce to the U.S. Department of Transportation in FY 1981.

[33]Includes special education programs (military and civilian); legal education program; flight training; advanced degree program; college degree program (officers); and Armed Forces Health Professions Scholarship program.

[34]Does not include higher education assistance loans.

[35]Alcohol, drug abuse, and mental health training programs are included starting in FY 1992.

[36]From 2008 onward, funding came from Harwood Training Grants.

[37]Beginning in FY 1992, data were included in the National Institutes of Health training grants program.

[38]This program closed in FY 2004.

[39]Postsecondary student benefits were ended by the Omnibus Budget Reconciliation Act of 1981 (Public Law 97-35) and were completely phased out by August 1985.

[40]Includes flight training. Transferred to the U.S. Department of Homeland Security in March 2003.

[41]Transferred from the U.S. Department of State to the United States Information Agency in 1977, then transferred back to the U.S. Department of State in FY 1998.

[42]Chapter 33 was enacted in the Post 9-11 Veterans Educational Assistance Act of 2008 (Public Law 110-252).

[43]Part of the Ronald W. Reagan National Defense Authorization Act for FY 2005 (Public Law 108-375), enacted October 28, 2004. The Reserve Education Assistance Program (REAP) provides educational assistance to members of the National Guard and Reserves who serve on active duty in support of a contingency operation under federal authority on or after September 11, 2001.

[44]Abolished in FY 1998, with functions transferred to the U.S. Department of State and the newly created Broadcasting Board of Governors.

[45]Included in the Educational and Cultural Affairs program in FYs 1980 through 1983, and became an independent program in FY 1984.

[46]Includes funding for D.C. College Tuition Assistance Grant (DC TAG), D.C. Adoption Scholarship Program, Robert C. Byrd Honors Scholarship Program, United States Senate Youth Program (USSYP), Advanced Placement Test Fee Program, the Early College Grant, and the College Access Challenge Grant.

[47]Transferred from U.S. Department of Education to the Institute of Museum and Library Services in FY 1997.

[48]Transferred to the U.S. Department of Homeland Security in FY 2003.

[49]The disaster relief program repairs and replaces damaged and destroyed school buildings. This program was transferred from the Federal Emergency Management Agency to the U.S. Department of Homeland Security in FY 2003.

[50]The National Service Trust Act of 1993 established the Corporation for National and Community Service. In 1993, ACTION became part of this agency.

[51]The Federal Emergency Management Agency was created in 1979, representing a combination of five existing agencies. The funds for the Federal Emergency Management Agency in FY 1970 to FY 1975 were in other agencies. This agency was transferred to the U.S. Department of Homeland Security in March 2003.

[52]These programs include the Fall-Out Shelter Analysis, Blast Protection Design through FY 1992. Starting in FY 1993, earthquake training and safety for teachers and administrators for grades 1 through 12 are included.

[53]Transferred from the General Services Administration to the National Archives and Records Administration in April 1985.

[54]The Consolidated Appropriations Act of 2008 (Public Law 110-161) transferred the National Commission on Libraries and Information Science to the Institute of Museum and Library Services starting in FY 2008.

[55]Includes federal obligations for research and development centers and R&D plant administered by colleges and universities. FY 2013 and FY 2014 data are estimated, except the U.S Department of Education data, which are actual numbers.

[56]FY 1970 includes outlays for the Research and Training program. FY 1980 includes outlays for the National Institute of Education program. FY 1990 through FY 2000 amounts are outlays for the Office of Educational Research and Improvement. Amounts for FY 2005 and later years are for the Institute of Education Sciences; these amounts are outlays for years prior to FY 2010 and appropriations for later years.

NOTE: To the extent possible, amounts reported represent outlays rather than obligations. Negative amounts occur when program receipts exceed outlays. Starting in FY 2010, amounts for the U.S. Department of Education are appropriations, not outlays. Some data have been revised from previously published figures. Detail may not sum to totals because of rounding.

SOURCE: U.S. Department of Education, Budget Service, unpublished tabulations. U.S. Office of Management and Budget, *Budget of the U.S. Government, Appendix*, fiscal years 1972 through 2015. National Science Foundation, *Federal Funds for Research and Development*, fiscal years 1970 through 2014. (This table was prepared October 2014.)

Table 401.60. U.S. Department of Education appropriations for major programs, by state or jurisdiction: Fiscal year 2013
[In thousands of current dollars]

State or jurisdiction	Total	Grants for the disadvantaged[1]	Block grants to states for school improvement[2]	School assistance in federally affected areas[3]	Career/technical and adult education[4]	Special education[5]	Language assistance[6]	American Indian education	Student financial assistance[7]	Rehabilitation services[8]
1	2	3	4	5	6	7	8	9	10	11
Total, 50 states and D.C.[9]	$70,478,278	$14,036,475	$3,950,449	$1,198,400	$1,568,961	$11,466,667	$637,077	$100,381	$34,439,972	$3,079,895
Total, 50 states, D.C., other activities, and other jurisdictions	73,011,140	14,686,340	4,171,808	1,215,949	1,628,400	11,747,756	693,848	100,381	35,485,800	3,280,858
Alabama	1,197,378	225,529	67,264	2,849	28,511	183,331	3,669	1,530	626,093	58,601
Alaska	328,128	46,353	20,860	143,520	5,222	37,679	1,055	12,383	48,585	12,470
Arizona	2,604,471	329,674	73,003	178,406	33,715	191,061	15,354	10,437	1,707,657	65,164
Arkansas	707,172	157,668	44,691	517	16,885	114,882	3,100	260	327,380	41,789
California	8,258,783	1,727,173	437,003	66,849	199,244	1,243,469	149,276	5,691	4,120,669	309,410
Colorado	1,032,056	152,054	47,203	20,232	20,863	156,977	8,662	651	582,369	43,045
Connecticut	638,478	112,738	37,097	4,418	13,904	134,498	5,676	30	301,350	28,767
Delaware	193,911	44,783	20,798	43	6,123	35,732	1,199	0	69,781	15,453
District of Columbia	293,139	45,653	20,376	914	5,473	18,619	894	0	185,805	15,405
Florida	4,183,475	751,054	186,315	6,969	93,166	636,612	40,731	107	2,319,225	149,295
Georgia	2,345,569	506,861	119,072	22,650	52,119	332,064	13,805	0	1,193,408	105,589
Hawaii	284,777	50,528	20,950	51,574	7,324	40,667	3,402	0	95,044	15,289
Idaho	370,714	59,646	23,312	6,067	8,236	56,569	1,812	424	195,334	19,314
Illinois	3,038,820	653,520	167,136	16,173	59,122	512,416	26,786	192	1,487,346	116,130
Indiana	1,509,319	262,763	71,344	115	33,202	261,255	8,194	0	808,465	63,981
Iowa	1,073,529	88,449	34,660	194	15,475	123,446	3,288	286	779,159	28,572
Kansas	630,618	111,858	36,242	27,554	13,851	109,225	4,080	1,022	296,474	30,311
Kentucky	1,027,998	226,133	65,599	942	26,444	164,854	3,567	0	491,635	48,824
Louisiana	1,095,774	293,035	85,675	8,724	29,901	190,941	2,986	918	446,744	36,849
Maine	283,707	51,870	23,575	2,068	6,939	56,324	695	158	123,173	18,906
Maryland	1,023,323	190,390	56,851	6,576	23,866	203,109	9,244	80	482,440	50,767
Massachusetts	1,238,895	215,360	67,755	249	27,111	285,760	12,566	86	564,180	65,829
Michigan	2,403,871	537,523	150,097	4,221	48,204	401,596	10,182	2,418	1,143,792	105,838
Minnesota	1,187,677	152,797	55,279	20,792	22,403	193,649	8,068	3,589	677,604	53,497
Mississippi	833,333	184,137	59,588	2,287	19,403	121,512	1,574	459	397,524	46,849
Missouri	1,360,914	235,151	73,554	20,952	29,680	228,553	4,987	76	700,823	67,137
Montana	270,460	45,562	25,894	44,061	6,162	38,351	529	3,532	91,336	15,034
Nebraska	406,656	73,022	25,709	18,188	9,117	75,542	2,695	875	179,703	21,805
Nevada	404,647	105,776	26,102	3,422	14,083	72,433	8,049	731	155,791	18,260
New Hampshire	236,203	41,800	23,005	6	6,851	48,535	963	0	101,071	13,973
New Jersey	1,551,217	290,966	88,267	11,556	35,935	364,046	20,524	33	676,779	63,112
New Mexico	643,517	117,062	34,717	97,744	12,066	92,256	4,009	7,855	251,167	26,641
New York	4,722,091	1,127,026	298,902	34,491	91,963	774,432	55,430	1,797	2,182,001	156,051
North Carolina	1,970,355	400,326	101,542	16,934	49,186	331,303	13,580	3,560	944,016	109,907
North Dakota	194,119	33,887	21,325	26,973	5,189	29,179	571	1,878	62,707	12,410
Ohio	2,522,382	578,184	152,772	1,592	58,126	439,256	9,419	0	1,165,919	117,113
Oklahoma	877,708	154,913	56,040	37,881	21,006	148,582	4,585	23,995	384,791	45,915
Oregon	873,095	162,663	43,656	3,560	17,739	130,249	7,379	1,867	464,763	41,218
Pennsylvania	2,513,309	560,204	155,377	854	58,240	431,124	13,715	0	1,175,143	118,652
Rhode Island	276,849	49,299	20,844	1,575	7,429	45,110	2,296	0	135,232	15,063
South Carolina	1,013,574	214,796	56,292	1,817	25,141	180,391	3,886	18	472,014	59,220
South Dakota	291,848	43,888	21,660	52,561	5,398	34,872	853	3,729	116,353	12,533
Tennessee	1,354,151	274,366	76,155	4,021	32,891	238,461	5,051	0	660,562	62,643
Texas	5,777,246	1,417,811	346,290	103,083	137,876	986,501	98,364	510	2,436,412	250,398
Utah	742,873	90,701	29,722	8,618	14,585	111,964	4,204	1,357	441,803	39,920
Vermont	166,592	34,285	20,430	7	5,106	28,284	500	217	59,366	18,397
Virginia	1,514,080	230,231	70,573	40,010	35,970	285,405	11,432	11	763,923	76,525
Washington	1,190,137	227,582	66,612	45,358	28,763	225,488	16,399	4,104	518,422	57,408
West Virginia	524,272	94,138	34,691	13	12,046	77,371	653	0	262,478	42,882
Wisconsin	1,127,445	220,873	68,068	13,289	26,710	213,006	6,642	2,612	515,827	60,418
Wyoming	167,623	34,415	20,504	14,932	4,994	29,727	500	904	50,334	11,314
Other activities/jurisdictions										
Indian Tribe Set-Aside	272,296	96,451	22,124	0	13,306	98,091	5,000	0	0	37,325
Other nonstate allocations	294,642	45,255	66,644	16,529	12,625	23,693	45,100	0	0	84,796
American Samoa	32,903	10,939	4,679	0	560	6,889	1,225	0	7,139	1,471
Freely Associated States[10]	26,836	0	0	0	166	6,579	0	0	20,091	0
Guam	54,779	11,632	7,093	38	1,022	15,411	1,193	0	17,106	1,285
Northern Marianas	20,360	4,289	2,983	0	668	5,239	999	0	4,881	1,301
Puerto Rico	1,791,972	467,547	112,583	847	30,025	115,540	3,201	0	989,948	72,279
U.S. Virgin Islands	39,074	13,751	5,253	135	1,068	9,647	52	0	6,663	2,506

[1]Title I grants. Includes Grants to Local Education Agencies (Basic, Concentration, Targeted, and Education Finance Incentive Grants); School Turnaround Grants; Migrant Education Grants; and Neglected and Delinquent Children Grants.
[2]Title VI grants. Includes Improving Teacher Quality State Grants; Mathematics and Science Partnerships; 21st Century Community Learning Centers; Assessing Achievement, including No Child Left Behind; Rural and Low-Income Schools Program; Small, Rural School Achievement Program; and Homeless Children and Youth Education.
[3]Includes Impact Aid—Basic Support Payments; Impact Aid—Payments for Children with Disabilities; and Impact Aid—Construction.
[4]Includes Career and Technical Education State Grants; Adult Basic and Literacy Education State Grants; and English Literacy and Civics Education State Grants.
[5]Includes Special Education—Grants to States; Preschool Grants; and Grants for Infants and Families.
[6]Includes English Learner Education.

[7]Includes Pell Grants; Federal Supplemental Educational Opportunity Grants; Federal Work-Study; College Access Challenge Grant; and Student Loan Program interest subsidies.
[8]Includes Vocational Rehabilitation State Grants; Client Assistance State Grants; Protection and Advocacy of Individual Rights; Supported Employment State Grants; Independent Living State Grants; Centers for Independent Living; Services for Older Blind Individuals; Assistive Technology State Grant Program; and Protection and Advocacy for Assistive Technology.
[9]Total excludes other activities and other jurisdictions.
[10]Includes the Marshall Islands, the Federated States of Micronesia, and Palau.
NOTE: Data reflect revisions to figures in the Budget of the United States Government, Fiscal Year 2015. Detail may not sum to totals because of rounding.
SOURCE: U.S. Department of Education, Budget Service, October 6, 2014, from http://www2.ed.gov/about/overview/budget/statetables/index.html; and unpublished tabulations. (This table was prepared October 2014.)

Table 401.70. Appropriations for Title I and selected other programs under the No Child Left Behind Act of 2001, by program and state or jurisdiction: Fiscal years 2013 and 2014

[In thousands of current dollars]

State or jurisdiction	Title I total, 2013	Title I, 2014				Turn-around Grants	Assessing Achievement, 2014	Improving Teacher Quality State Grants, 2014
		Total	Grants to local education agencies[1]	State agency programs				
				Neglected and Delinquent	Migrant			
1	2	3	4	5	6	7	8	9
Total, 50 states and D.C.[2]	$14,036,475	$14,670,761	$13,796,419	$45,801	$364,751	$463,789	$359,992	$2,196,200
Total, 50 states, D.C., other activities, and other jurisdictions	14,686,340	15,306,917	14,378,796	47,614	374,751	505,756	378,000	2,348,898
Alabama	225,529	231,483	221,466	678	2,038	7,301	6,138	36,401
Alaska	46,353	47,015	38,380	274	6,895	1,467	3,511	10,864
Arizona	329,674	343,741	325,037	1,541	6,506	10,658	7,566	35,624
Arkansas	157,668	169,704	158,732	437	5,218	5,317	4,992	22,098
California	1,727,173	1,879,397	1,689,214	1,565	128,658	59,960	28,691	255,264
Colorado	152,054	165,061	152,377	458	6,965	5,261	6,479	25,582
Connecticut	112,738	120,110	115,076	1,220	0	3,814	5,287	21,636
Delaware	44,783	46,329	44,036	555	289	1,448	3,567	10,864
District of Columbia	45,653	44,788	43,228	168	0	1,392	3,272	10,864
Florida	751,054	828,405	777,790	1,489	22,495	26,631	14,361	103,321
Georgia	506,861	534,297	508,022	1,594	7,809	16,872	10,018	60,114
Hawaii	50,528	56,130	53,163	361	794	1,812	3,834	10,864
Idaho	59,646	64,157	58,158	422	3,532	2,045	4,211	10,899
Illinois	653,520	671,485	646,908	1,203	1,887	21,488	11,571	93,923
Indiana	262,763	274,461	259,785	527	5,437	8,712	7,490	38,966
Iowa	88,449	89,682	84,913	349	1,591	2,829	5,040	17,870
Kansas	111,858	121,697	106,047	368	11,413	3,871	5,018	18,313
Kentucky	226,133	237,193	221,318	1,058	7,310	7,508	5,848	35,960
Louisiana	293,035	305,595	291,923	1,700	2,443	9,529	6,101	52,193
Maine	51,870	55,009	51,908	209	1,156	1,735	3,756	10,864
Maryland	190,390	205,842	197,275	1,435	500	6,632	6,766	33,300
Massachusetts	215,360	224,142	213,005	2,397	1,591	7,148	6,963	41,942
Michigan	537,523	547,089	521,188	795	8,459	16,647	9,444	91,567
Minnesota	152,797	152,302	145,020	418	2,046	4,817	6,590	31,295
Mississippi	184,137	194,567	186,626	905	1,024	6,012	5,077	34,127
Missouri	235,151	248,856	238,060	1,539	1,499	7,758	6,934	39,564
Montana	45,562	47,324	44,750	110	995	1,469	3,627	10,864
Nebraska	73,022	78,641	70,737	370	5,032	2,503	4,288	11,141
Nevada	105,776	119,842	115,346	397	234	3,865	4,863	11,474
New Hampshire	41,800	45,043	42,952	539	144	1,408	3,792	10,864
New Jersey	290,966	320,160	306,501	1,641	1,938	10,079	8,737	52,350
New Mexico	117,062	115,290	110,471	336	910	3,573	4,421	18,091
New York	1,127,026	1,136,001	1,087,574	2,780	9,764	35,884	14,816	188,531
North Carolina	400,326	433,586	413,385	732	5,567	13,902	9,448	49,995
North Dakota	33,887	34,704	33,277	103	231	1,093	3,439	10,864
Ohio	578,184	589,653	567,409	1,030	2,621	18,593	10,549	86,106
Oklahoma	154,913	162,053	155,106	351	1,515	5,081	5,630	26,302
Oregon	162,663	163,660	146,982	1,371	10,121	5,185	5,418	22,199
Pennsylvania	560,204	578,222	550,543	510	8,946	18,222	10,706	93,787
Rhode Island	49,299	50,567	48,499	494	0	1,573	3,614	10,864
South Carolina	214,796	223,916	214,667	1,559	554	7,136	6,034	28,601
South Dakota	43,888	44,507	42,116	163	827	1,401	3,570	10,864
Tennessee	274,366	286,771	276,465	542	568	9,196	7,207	38,950
Texas	1,417,811	1,424,442	1,319,477	2,108	58,218	44,639	22,656	187,495
Utah	90,701	94,371	88,478	1,038	1,823	3,033	5,477	14,983
Vermont	34,285	35,503	33,553	206	626	1,118	3,355	10,864
Virginia	230,231	243,176	233,413	1,275	784	7,704	8,211	40,841
Washington	227,582	239,255	215,320	1,454	14,921	7,560	7,436	37,519
West Virginia	94,138	92,171	88,259	996	0	2,916	4,077	19,693
Wisconsin	220,873	217,322	208,484	1,353	627	6,858	6,712	37,811
Wyoming	34,415	36,043	33,999	679	230	1,135	3,383	10,864
Other activities/jurisdictions								
Indian Tribe Set-Aside	96,451	95,688	92,597	0	0	3,091	1,845	11,686
Other nonstate allocations	45,255	45,462	8,984	1,190	10,000	25,288	8,949	58,722
American Samoa	10,939	11,221	10,859	0	0	362	359	2,671
Guam	11,632	16,769	16,228	0	0	542	809	4,494
Northern Marianas	4,289	7,171	6,939	0	0	232	262	1,643
Puerto Rico	467,547	447,436	434,644	623	0	12,169	5,369	70,605
U.S. Virgin Islands	13,751	12,409	12,125	0	0	284	415	2,877

[1]Includes Basic, Concentration, Targeted, and Education Finance Incentive Grants.
[2]Total excludes other activities and other jurisdictions.
NOTE: Detail may not sum to totals because of rounding. Estimates for fiscal year 2014 are preliminary.

SOURCE: U.S. Department of Education, Budget Service, Elementary, Secondary, and Vocational Education Analysis Division, retrieved October 6, 2014, from http://www2.ed.gov/about/overview/budget/statetables/15stbyprogram.pdf. (This table was prepared October 2014.)

Table 402.10. Federal obligations for research, development, and R&D plant, by category of obligation, performers, and fields of science: Fiscal years 2006 through 2014

[In millions]

Category of obligation, performers, and fields of science	Actual							Estimated		Percent change, 2013 to 2014
	2006	2007	2008	2009	2010	2011	2012	2013	2014	
1	2	3	4	5	6	7	8	9	10	11
	Current dollars									
Total obligations for research, development, and R&D plant.....	$112,270.7	$129,431.1	$129,049.4	$144,760.5	$146,967.8	$139,661.5	$140,635.8	$134,546.5	$134,042.3	-0.4
Research and development obligations....	110,145.8	127,262.7	127,105.6	141,092.5	140,354.5	135,490.8	138,485.1	132,435.7	130,846.5	-1.2
Performers										
Federal intramural[1].............................	25,563.2	29,932.5	29,637.9	31,546.4	30,911.8	35,144.7	34,367.8	32,677.6	32,513.8	-0.5
Industrial firms.................................	44,152.9	55,342.3	56,337.6	59,749.3	59,867.8	53,550.2	58,910.1	55,175.7	53,152.0	-3.7
Federally funded research and development centers (FFRDCs) administered by industrial firms	1,421.9	2,691.6	4,119.9	4,067.1	3,946.2	4,424.5	3,611.7	3,647.2	3,184.6	-12.7
Universities and colleges	24,336.3	25,547.8	26,026.5	31,557.7	31,192.3	27,680.3	27,509.5	27,394.7	28,159.9	2.8
FFRDCs[2] administered by universities and colleges.................	5,439.1	4,171.2	1,988.6	3,402.7	3,370.5	3,437.8	3,694.2	3,350.8	3,581.4	6.9
Other nonprofit institutions...................	6,000.1	5,984.4	5,965.0	7,049.7	7,245.3	6,636.6	6,347.0	6,316.6	6,351.2	0.5
FFRDCs[2] administered by nonprofit institutions.....................	1,816.0	2,520.3	2,083.0	2,730.7	2,784.1	2,923.7	2,752.2	2,614.3	2,696.9	3.2
State and local governments.................	619.6	362.0	389.0	392.0	426.7	716.2	453.2	483.9	450.3	-6.9
Foreign...	796.7	710.6	558.1	596.9	609.9	976.8	839.5	774.7	756.5	-2.4
Research obligations.........................	53,535.7	54,093.5	53,893.6	63,694.3	63,728.0	58,023.7	61,946.9	61,616.7	64,199.4	4.2
Performers										
Federal intramural[1].............................	12,261.6	11,816.4	11,921.7	13,321.2	13,280.9	12,663.4	14,295.0	14,561.5	14,900.0	2.3
Industrial firms.................................	6,436.3	6,074.2	5,782.4	6,280.2	6,625.5	6,037.4	7,794.0	7,164.0	7,864.8	9.8
FFRDCs[2] administered by industrial firms............................	947.9	1,863.0	2,929.7	3,070.5	2,960.1	2,984.4	2,678.7	2,644.1	2,787.6	5.4
Universities and colleges.................	22,809.4	23,966.9	24,323.2	30,168.8	29,607.8	26,253.2	26,289.9	26,308.6	27,203.2	3.4
FFRDCs[2] administered by universities and colleges	3,783.0	2,942.4	1,623.1	2,148.1	2,151.6	2,224.4	2,856.9	2,831.6	3,007.9	6.2
Other nonprofit institutions...................	5,448.9	5,416.7	5,397.5	6,500.7	6,687.0	5,760.8	5,812.9	5,918.1	6,015.7	1.7
FFRDCs[2] administered by nonprofit institutions.....................	1,028.6	1,283.0	1,205.7	1,462.0	1,633.6	1,447.7	1,457.0	1,422.0	1,657.8	16.6
State and local governments.............	417.9	297.6	338.8	343.6	352.8	282.2	352.2	388.3	380.5	-2.0
Foreign.......................................	402.1	433.3	371.5	399.3	428.6	370.2	410.3	378.6	381.9	0.9
Fields of science										
Life sciences.................................	27,927.7	29,463.6	28,918.8	33,267.1	33,909.1	29,408.6	30,966.7	31,162.4	31,458.2	0.9
Psychology..................................	1,747.3	1,837.9	1,740.8	2,086.3	2,155.6	1,886.8	2,086.6	2,101.9	2,144.5	2.0
Physical sciences...........................	5,351.1	5,136.1	5,072.6	5,821.1	5,870.8	5,426.6	6,407.5	6,478.2	6,791.0	4.8
Environmental sciences	3,430.6	3,170.5	2,984.6	3,751.1	3,338.9	3,207.2	3,884.3	3,946.7	4,100.7	3.9
Mathematics and computer sciences...	2,814.9	2,945.7	3,047.3	3,611.8	3,411.8	3,374.3	3,527.5	3,643.1	3,931.8	7.9
Engineering.................................	8,678.7	8,989.7	8,975.5	10,285.0	11,081.2	10,057.2	11,403.4	10,635.6	11,274.5	6.0
Social sciences.............................	1,123.9	1,147.1	977.0	1,159.2	1,197.3	1,262.4	1,124.5	1,031.7	1,212.6	17.5
Other sciences..............................	2,461.3	1,403.1	2,177.1	3,712.7	2,763.2	3,400.5	2,546.3	2,617.0	3,286.2	25.6
Development obligations	56,610.1	73,169.2	73,211.9	77,398.2	76,626.5	77,467.1	76,538.3	70,819.0	66,647.1	-5.9
Performers										
Federal intramural[1].............................	13,301.6	18,116.1	17,716.1	18,225.2	17,630.9	22,481.3	20,072.8	18,116.1	17,613.9	-2.8
Industrial firms.................................	37,716.6	49,268.1	50,555.2	53,467.0	53,242.3	47,512.8	51,116.1	48,011.7	45,287.1	-5.7
FFRDCs[2] administered by industrial firms............................	474.0	828.6	1,190.2	996.6	986.1	1,440.1	933.0	1,003.1	397.0	-60.4
Universities and colleges.................	1,526.9	1,580.9	1,703.3	1,389.0	1,584.5	1,427.1	1,219.6	1,086.1	956.6	-11.9
FFRDCs[2] administered by universities and colleges	1,656.1	1,228.8	365.5	1,254.6	1,218.9	1,213.3	837.3	519.2	573.5	10.5
Other nonprofit institutions	551.2	567.7	567.5	549.0	558.3	875.8	534.1	398.6	335.4	-15.8
FFRDCs[2] administered by nonprofit institutions.....................	787.4	1,237.3	877.3	1,268.7	1,150.4	1,476.0	1,295.2	1,192.3	1,039.1	-12.8
State and local governments.............	201.7	64.4	50.2	48.4	73.9	434.0	101.0	95.7	69.8	-27.0
Foreign.......................................	394.6	277.3	186.6	197.6	181.3	606.6	429.2	396.2	374.6	-5.4
R&D plant obligations	2,124.9	2,168.4	1,943.8	3,668.0	6,613.3	4,170.7	2,150.7	2,110.8	3,195.8	51.4
Performers										
Federal intramural[1].............................	662.8	593.4	494.0	804.7	1,953.3	846.5	486.2	631.0	936.5	48.4
Industrial firms.................................	265.8	401.4	449.0	396.3	1,751.2	2,030.0	460.5	429.4	878.6	104.6
FFRDCs[2] administered by industrial firms............................	82.7	27.6	175.6	127.7	167.7	118.3	51.8	44.4	34.7	-21.8
Universities and colleges	262.5	265.6	210.2	607.0	1,532.6	286.0	372.5	338.6	398.9	17.8
FFRDCs[2] administered by universities and colleges	519.3	498.4	334.4	706.5	491.4	242.9	248.1	264.6	348.0	31.5
Other nonprofit institutions	127.3	79.7	23.7	154.4	245.9	141.3	200.8	209.8	281.2	34.0
FFRDCs[2] administered by nonprofit institutions.....................	201.6	296.2	253.8	868.2	465.3	491.0	323.1	184.5	309.7	67.8
State and local governments.................	2.6	#	#	1.2	2.0	0.2	#	#	#	#
Foreign...	0.3	6.1	3.1	2.0	4.0	14.6	7.6	8.4	8.2	-2.1

See notes at end of table.

Table 402.10. Federal obligations for research, development, and R&D plant, by category of obligation, performers, and fields of science: Fiscal years 2006 through 2014—Continued

[In millions]

Category of obligation, performers, and fields of science	Actual							Estimated		Percent change, 2013 to 2014
	2006	2007	2008	2009	2010	2011	2012	2013	2014	
1	2	3	4	5	6	7	8	9	10	11
	Constant fiscal year 2014 dollars[3]									
Total obligations for research, development, and R&D plant.....	$129,564.3	$145,511.0	$140,182.8	$156,934.9	$157,469.7	$146,754.9	$145,051.2	$136,549.2	$134,042.3	-1.8
Research and development obligations....	127,112.1	143,073.2	138,071.3	152,958.4	150,383.8	142,372.4	142,832.9	134,407.0	130,846.5	-2.6
Performers										
Federal intramural[1]...............	29,500.8	33,651.2	32,194.8	34,199.5	33,120.7	36,929.7	35,446.8	33,164.0	32,513.8	-2.0
Industrial firms........................	50,954.0	62,217.8	61,198.0	64,774.2	64,145.8	56,270.0	60,759.6	55,997.0	53,152.0	-5.1
Federally funded research and development centers (FFRDCs) administered by industrial firms	1,640.9	3,026.0	4,475.3	4,409.1	4,228.2	4,649.2	3,725.1	3,701.5	3,184.6	-14.0
Universities and colleges	28,084.9	28,721.7	28,271.9	34,211.7	33,421.2	29,086.2	28,373.2	27,802.5	28,159.9	1.3
FFRDCs[2] administered by universities and colleges..................	6,276.9	4,689.4	2,160.2	3,688.9	3,611.3	3,612.4	3,810.2	3,400.7	3,581.4	5.3
Other nonprofit institutions	6,924.3	6,727.9	6,479.6	7,642.6	7,763.0	6,973.7	6,546.3	6,410.6	6,351.2	-0.9
FFRDCs[2] administered by nonprofit institutions.....................	2,095.7	2,833.4	2,262.7	2,960.4	2,983.0	3,072.2	2,838.6	2,653.2	2,696.9	1.6
State and local governments.................	715.0	407.0	422.6	425.0	457.2	752.6	467.4	491.1	450.3	-8.3
Foreign..........................	919.4	798.9	606.2	647.1	653.5	1,026.4	865.9	786.2	756.5	-3.8
Research obligations.............................	61,782.0	60,813.8	58,543.1	69,051.0	68,281.8	60,970.7	63,891.8	62,533.9	64,199.4	2.7
Performers										
Federal intramural[1]	14,150.3	13,284.4	12,950.2	14,441.5	14,229.9	13,306.6	14,743.8	14,778.2	14,900.0	0.8
Industrial firms..........................	7,427.7	6,828.8	6,281.3	6,808.4	7,098.9	6,344.0	8,038.7	7,270.6	7,864.8	8.2
FFRDCs[2] administered by industrial firms.....................	1,093.9	2,094.5	3,182.5	3,328.7	3,171.6	3,136.0	2,762.8	2,683.5	2,787.6	3.9
Universities and colleges....................	26,322.8	26,944.4	26,421.6	32,706.0	31,723.5	27,586.6	27,115.3	26,700.2	27,203.2	1.9
FFRDCs[2] administered by universities and colleges	4,365.7	3,307.9	1,763.1	2,328.8	2,305.3	2,337.4	2,946.6	2,873.7	3,007.9	4.7
Other nonprofit institutions	6,288.2	6,089.6	5,863.2	7,047.4	7,164.8	6,053.4	5,995.4	6,006.2	6,015.7	0.2
FFRDCs[2] administered by nonprofit institutions.....................	1,187.0	1,442.4	1,309.7	1,585.0	1,750.3	1,521.2	1,502.7	1,443.2	1,657.8	14.9
State and local governments..............	482.3	334.6	368.0	372.5	378.0	296.5	363.3	394.1	380.5	-3.4
Foreign..........................	464.0	487.1	403.6	432.9	459.2	389.0	423.2	384.2	381.9	-0.6
Fields of science										
Life sciences.............................	32,229.5	33,124.0	31,413.7	36,064.9	36,332.1	30,902.3	31,938.9	31,626.2	31,458.2	-0.5
Psychology.............................	2,016.4	2,066.2	1,891.0	2,261.8	2,309.6	1,982.6	2,152.1	2,133.2	2,144.5	0.5
Physical sciences	6,175.4	5,774.2	5,510.2	6,310.7	6,290.3	5,702.2	6,608.7	6,574.6	6,791.0	3.3
Environmental sciences	3,959.0	3,564.4	3,242.1	4,066.6	3,577.5	3,370.1	4,006.3	4,005.4	4,100.7	2.4
Mathematics and computer sciences...	3,248.5	3,311.7	3,310.2	3,915.6	3,655.6	3,545.7	3,638.2	3,697.3	3,931.8	6.3
Engineering.............................	10,015.5	10,106.5	9,749.8	11,150.0	11,873.0	10,568.0	11,761.4	10,793.9	11,274.5	4.5
Social sciences...........................	1,297.0	1,289.6	1,061.3	1,256.7	1,282.9	1,326.5	1,159.8	1,047.1	1,212.6	15.8
Other sciences..........................	2,840.4	1,577.4	2,364.9	4,024.9	2,960.6	3,573.2	2,626.2	2,656.0	3,286.2	23.7
Development obligations	65,330.0	82,259.4	79,528.1	83,907.4	82,102.0	81,401.7	78,941.3	71,873.1	66,647.1	-7.3
Performers										
Federal intramural[1]	15,350.5	20,366.8	19,244.5	19,757.9	18,890.7	23,623.1	20,703.0	18,385.8	17,613.9	-4.2
Industrial firms..........................	43,526.3	55,388.9	54,916.7	57,963.6	57,046.8	49,926.0	52,720.9	48,726.3	45,287.1	-7.1
FFRDCs[2] administered by industrial firms.....................	547.0	931.5	1,292.9	1,080.4	1,056.6	1,513.2	962.3	1,018.0	397.0	-61.0
Universities and colleges....................	1,762.1	1,777.3	1,850.2	1,505.8	1,697.7	1,499.6	1,257.9	1,102.3	956.6	-13.2
FFRDCs[2] administered by universities and colleges	1,911.2	1,381.5	397.0	1,360.1	1,306.0	1,274.9	863.6	526.9	573.5	8.8
Other nonprofit institutions	636.1	638.2	616.5	595.2	598.2	920.3	550.9	404.5	335.4	-17.1
FFRDCs[2] administered by nonprofit institutions.........................	908.7	1,391.0	953.0	1,375.4	1,232.6	1,551.0	1,335.9	1,210.0	1,039.1	-14.1
State and local governments...............	232.8	72.4	54.5	52.5	79.2	456.0	104.2	97.1	69.8	-28.1
Foreign	455.4	311.8	202.7	214.2	194.3	637.4	442.7	402.1	374.6	-6.8
R&D plant obligations...........................	2,452.2	2,437.8	2,111.5	3,976.5	7,085.9	4,382.5	2,218.2	2,142.2	3,195.8	49.2
Performers										
Federal intramural[1]	764.9	667.1	536.6	872.4	2,092.9	889.5	501.5	640.4	936.5	46.2
Industrial firms..........................	306.7	451.3	487.7	429.6	1,876.3	2,133.1	475.0	435.8	878.6	101.6
FFRDCs[2] administered by industrial firms.....................	95.4	31.0	190.7	138.4	179.7	124.3	53.4	45.1	34.7	-23.0
Universities and colleges	302.9	298.6	228.3	658.0	1,642.1	300.5	384.2	343.6	398.9	16.1
FFRDCs[2] administered by universities and colleges	599.3	560.3	363.2	765.9	526.5	255.2	255.9	268.5	348.0	29.6
Other nonprofit institutions	146.9	89.6	25.7	167.4	263.5	148.5	207.1	212.9	281.2	32.1
FFRDCs[2] administered by nonprofit institutions.........................	232.7	333.0	275.7	941.2	498.5	515.9	333.2	187.2	309.7	65.4
State and local governments..................	3.0	#	#	1.3	2.1	0.2	#	#	#	#
Foreign..........................	0.3	6.9	3.4	2.2	4.3	15.3	7.8	8.5	8.2	-3.8

#Rounds to zero.
[1]Includes costs associated with the administration of intramural and extramural programs by federal personnel as well as actual intramural performance.
[2]Federally funded research and development centers.
[3]Data adjusted by the federal budget composite deflator reported in U.S. Office of Management and Budget, *Budget of the U.S. Government, Historical Tables, Fiscal Year 2015.*

NOTE: Some data have been revised from previously published figures. Detail may not sum to totals because of rounding. Totals do not include the U.S. Department of Homeland Security.
SOURCE: National Science Foundation, National Center for Science and Engineering Statistics, Survey of Federal Funds for Research and Development, 2006 through 2014, retrieved November 4, 2014, from http://www.nsf.gov/statistics/nsf14316/content.cfm?pub_id=4418&id=2. (This table was prepared November 2014.)

CHAPTER 5
Outcomes of Education

This chapter contains tables comparing educational attainment and workforce characteristics. The data show labor force status, income levels, and occupations of high school dropouts and high school and college graduates. Most of these tables are based on data from the U.S. Census Bureau and the U.S. Bureau of Labor Statistics. Population characteristics are provided for many of the measures to allow for comparisons among various demographic groups. While most of the tables in this chapter focus on labor market outcomes, the chapter ends with a few tables on adults' attitudes, skills, and participation in continuing education.

Statistics related to outcomes of education appear in other sections of the *Digest*. For example, statistics on educational attainment of the entire population are in chapter 1. More detailed data on the numbers of high school and college graduates can be found in chapters 2 and 3. Chapter 3 contains trend data on the percentage of high school completers going to college. Chapter 6 includes international comparisons of employment rates by educational attainment. Additional data on earnings by educational attainment may be obtained from the U.S. Census Bureau's Current Population Reports, Series P-60. The U.S. Bureau of Labor Statistics has a series of publications dealing with the educational characteristics of the labor force. Further information on survey methodologies can be found in Appendix A: Guide to Sources and in the publications cited in the table source notes.

Labor Force

The labor force participation rate—that is, the percentage of people either employed or actively seeking employment—was generally higher for adults with higher levels of educational attainment than for those with less education. Among 25- to 64-year-old adults, 86 percent of those with a bachelor's or higher degree participated in the labor force in 2013, compared with 73 percent of those who had completed only high school and 61 percent of those who had not completed high school (table 501.10). Within each education level, the labor force participation rate also varied by race/ethnicity. For 25- to 64-year-olds who had completed only high school, the 2013 labor force participation rate was highest for Hispanics (77 percent), followed by Asians (74 percent), then Whites (73 percent), then Blacks (68 percent), and then American Indians/Alaska Natives (62 percent). For 25- to 64-year-olds with a bachelor's or higher degree in 2013, the labor force participation rate was highest for Blacks (88 percent), followed by Hispanics (87 percent),

then Whites (86 percent), and then Asians (83 percent). The labor force participation rate for American Indians/Alaska Natives with a bachelor's or higher degree (82 percent) was lower than the rates for Blacks, Hispanics, and Whites, but not measurably different from the rate for Asians.

The unemployment rate—that is, the percentage of people in the labor force who are not employed and who have made specific efforts to find employment sometime during the prior 4 weeks—was generally higher for people with lower levels of educational attainment than for those with more education. In 2014, the unemployment rate for 25- to 64-year-old adults who had not completed high school was 11 percent, compared with 7 percent for those who had completed only high school and 3 percent for those with a bachelor's or higher degree (table 501.80). Within each education level, the unemployment rates for 16- to 19-year-olds and 20- to 24-year-olds tended to be higher than the unemployment rate for 25- to 64-year-olds. For example, among 20- to 24-year-olds who had not completed high school and were not enrolled in school, the 2014 unemployment rate was 25 percent, compared with 11 percent for 25- to 64-year-olds with the same level of educational attainment. Among adults in the 25- to 34-year-old age group, the 2014 unemployment rate was 14 percent for those who had not completed high school, 10 percent for high school completers, and 4 percent for those with a bachelor's or higher degree (table 501.80 and figure 22).

The employment to population ratio—that is, the percentage of the population that is employed—was generally higher for people with higher levels of educational attainment than for those with less education. Among 25- to 34-year-olds, for example, 84 percent of those with a bachelor's or higher degree were employed in 2014, compared with 68 percent of those who had completed only high school and 58 percent of those who had not completed high school (table 501.50 and figure 23).

The relative difficulties that high school dropouts encounter in entering the job market are highlighted by comparing the labor force participation and employment rates of recent high school dropouts with those of recent high school completers. In October 2013, about 43 percent of 2012–13 dropouts participated in the labor force (i.e., were either employed or looking for work), with 31 percent employed and 12 percent looking for work (table 504.20 and figure 24). In contrast, the labor force participation rate was 74 percent for 2012–13 high school completers who were not enrolled in college, with 51 percent employed and 23 percent looking for work (table 504.10 and figure 24).

Earnings

Median annual earnings were generally higher for adults with higher levels of educational attainment than for those with lower levels of educational attainment. Among full-time year-round workers age 25 and over, both males and females who had more education generally earned more than people of the same sex who had less education. In 2013, for example, males whose highest level of educational attainment was a bachelor's degree earned 67 percent more than males whose highest level of attainment was high school completion, and females who had attained a bachelor's degree earned 65 percent more than females who had only completed high school (table E, table 502.20, and figure 25).

Among full-time year-round workers age 25 and over, the earnings of females were lower than the earnings of males overall, as well as by education level. For example, median 2013 earnings for full-time year-round workers with a bachelor's degree were 32 percent higher for males than for females. Among those who had only completed high school, median 2013 earnings were 31 percent higher for males than for females.

From 1995 to 2013, net percentage changes in earnings (after adjustment for inflation) varied by highest level of educational attainment and sex. In constant 2013 dollars, the median annual earnings of male full-time year-round workers age 25 and over who had started but not completed high school decreased 10 percent from 1995 ($33,920) to 2013 ($30,570), and the median earnings of those who had completed high school decreased 11 percent from 1995 ($45,120) to 2013 ($40,290). For males with a bachelor's degree, median annual earnings in constant 2013 dollars decreased 3 percent from 1995 ($69,210) to 2013 ($67,240). In constant 2013 dollars, the median annual earnings of female full-time year-round workers who had started but not completed high school decreased 8 percent from 1995 ($24,190) to 2013 ($22,250), and the median earnings of those who had completed high school decreased 2 percent from 1995 ($31,290) to 2013 ($30,800). For females with a bachelor's degree, median annual earnings in constant 2013 dollars increased 4 percent from 1995 ($49,000) to 2013 ($50,750).

Table E. Median annual earnings of full-time year-round workers 25 years old and over, by selected levels of educational attainment and sex: Selected years, 1995 through 2013

[In constant 2013 dollars]

Sex and year	Some high school, no completion	High school completion	Bachelor's degree
Males			
1995	$33,920	$45,120	$69,210
2000	33,960	46,410	76,220
2005	32,440	43,310	71,610
2013	30,570	40,290	67,240
Females			
1995	24,190	31,290	49,000
2000	24,250	33,790	54,680
2005	24,010	31,360	50,310
2013	22,250	30,800	50,750

SOURCE: U.S. Department of Commerce, Census Bureau, Current Population Reports, Series P-60, *Money Income in the United States*, 1995 and 2000; and Current Population Survey (CPS), 2005 and 2013 Annual Social and Economic Supplement.

In 2009, the median annual salary of bachelor's degree recipients employed full time 1 year after graduation was $39,100 in constant 2013 dollars (table 505.50 and figure 26). Full-time median annual salaries varied by degree field, however. In 2009, graduates employed full time 1 year after receiving bachelor's degrees in engineering had the highest median annual salary ($58,600 in constant 2013 dollars), followed by those with degrees in the health professions ($49,900) and mathematics/computer science ($48,900), and then those with degrees in business/management ($43,400). Among the lowest full-time median annual salaries were those earned by graduates with degrees in the humanities ($31,500) and psychology ($31,900).

Overall, the inflation-adjusted median annual salary of graduates employed full time 1 year after receiving their bachelor's degree was 7 percent lower in 2009 than in 2001. However, the change in median annual salary from 2001 to 2009 varied by degree field, ranging from an increase of 7 percent for graduates with degrees in the health professions to a decrease of 19 percent for those with degrees in mathematics/computer science and a decrease of 16 percent for those with degrees in the humanities. Although the overall median annual salary of graduates employed full time 1 year after graduation decreased from 2001 to 2009, it had previously increased 13 percent from 1991 to 2001. From 1991 to 2009, there was a net increase of 5 percent in the overall median salary.

In 2013, 25- to 29-year-olds with a bachelor's or higher degree had median annual earnings of $45,280 (table 505.10). Median annual earnings varied by bachelor's degree field. For example, 25- to 29-year-olds with a bachelor's degree in computer engineering had median annual earnings of $74,880, while those with a bachelor's degree in theology and religious vocations had median annual earnings of $32,880.

Figure 22. Unemployment rates of persons 25 to 34 years old, by highest level of educational attainment: Selected years, 1990 through 2014

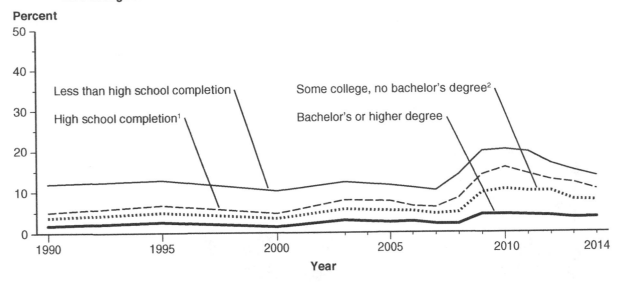

¹Includes equivalency credentials, such as the GED credential.
²Includes persons with no college degree as well as those with an associate's degree.
NOTE: The unemployment rate is the percentage of persons in the civilian labor force who are not working and who made specific efforts to find employment sometime during the prior 4 weeks. The civilian labor force consists of all civilians who are employed or seeking employment.
SOURCE: U.S. Department of Labor, Bureau of Labor Statistics, Office of Employment and Unemployment Statistics, unpublished annual average data from the Current Population Survey (CPS), selected years, 1990 through 2014.

Figure 23. Employment to population ratios of persons 25 to 34 years old, by highest level of educational attainment: Selected years, 1990 through 2014

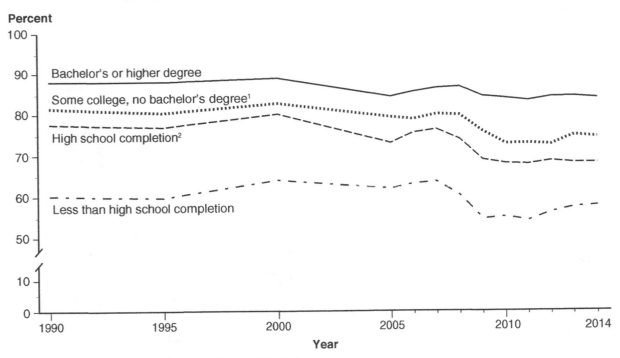

¹Includes persons with no college degree as well as those with an associate's degree.
²Includes equivalency credentials, such as the GED credential.
NOTE: The employment to population ratio is the number of persons employed as a percentage of the civilian population.
SOURCE: U.S. Department of Labor, Bureau of Labor Statistics, Office of Employment and Unemployment Statistics, unpublished annual average data from the Current Population Survey (CPS), selected years, 1990 through 2014.

Figure 24. Percentage distribution of 2012–13 high school dropouts and high school completers not enrolled in college, by labor force status: October 2013

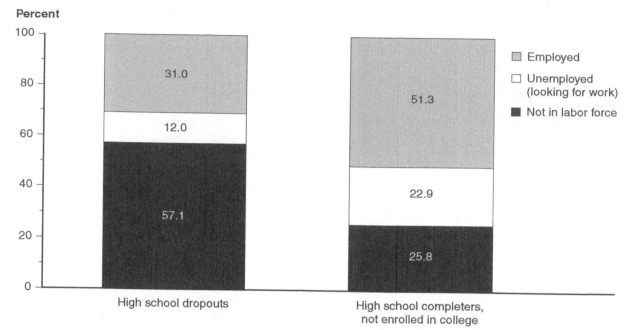

Percent

NOTE: Dropouts are persons who have not completed high school and are not enrolled in school. High school completers include recipients of equivalency credentials as well as diploma recipients. Detail may not sum to totals because of rounding.
SOURCE: U.S. Department of Commerce, Census Bureau, Current Population Survey (CPS), October 2013.

Figure 25. Median annual earnings of full-time year-round workers 25 years old and over, by highest level of educational attainment and sex: 2013

[In current dollars]

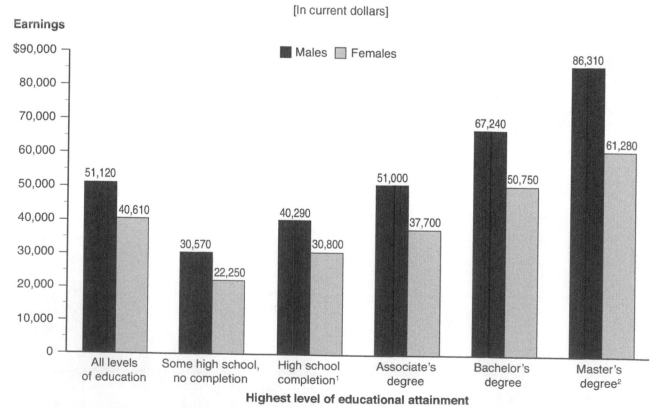

[1]Includes equivalency credentials, such as the GED credential.
[2]Includes only persons whose highest level of education is a master's degree. Doctor's and professional degree recipients are not included.
SOURCE: U.S. Department of Commerce, Census Bureau, Current Population Survey (CPS), 2014 Annual Social and Economic Supplement, retrieved November 24, 2014, from http://www.census.gov/hhes/www/cpstables/032014/perinc/pinc03_000.htm.

Figure 26. Median annual salaries of bachelor's degree recipients employed full time 1 year after graduation, by field of study: 1991, 2001, and 2009

[In constant 2013 dollars]

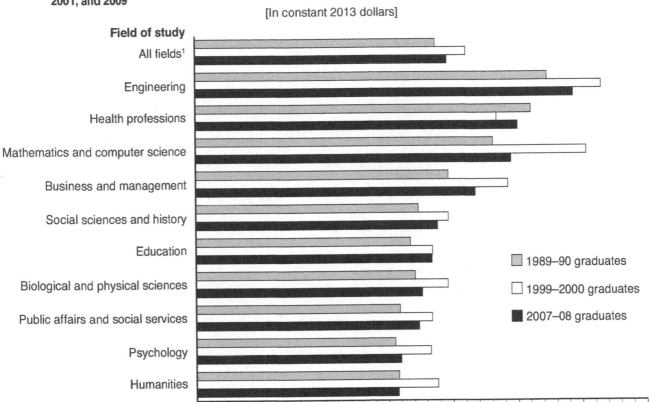

[1]Includes graduates in other fields not separately shown.
SOURCE: U.S. Department of Education, National Center for Education Statistics, "Recent College Graduates" survey, 1991; and 2000/01 and 2008/09 Baccalaureate and Beyond Longitudinal Study (B&B:2000/01 and B&B:08/09).

Table 501.10. Labor force participation, employment, and unemployment of persons 25 to 64 years old, by sex, race/ethnicity, age group, and educational attainment: 2011, 2012, and 2013

[Standard errors appear in parentheses]

Sex, race/ethnicity, age group, and educational attainment	Labor force participation rate[1] 2011	2012	2013	Number of participants (in thousands) 2013	Employment to population ratio[2] 2011	2012	2013	Number employed (in thousands) 2013	Unemployment rate[3] 2011	2012	2013	Number unemployed (in thousands) 2013
	2	3	4	5	6	7	8	9	10	11	12	13
All persons 25 to 64 years old, all education levels	77.5 (0.04)	77.5 (0.04)	77.2 (0.04)	128,013 (76.3)	70.8 (0.04)	71.5 (0.04)	71.9 (0.04)	119,077 (71.8)	8.6 (0.03)	7.8 (0.03)	7.0 (0.03)	8,936 (38.2)
Less than high school completion	61.0 (0.13)	60.7 (0.14)	60.7 (0.14)	12,014 (48.9)	51.4 (0.14)	52.1 (0.14)	53.0 (0.16)	10,486 (47.0)	15.7 (0.14)	14.1 (0.14)	12.7 (0.14)	1,528 (17.0)
High school completion[4]	73.6 (0.09)	73.2 (0.09)	72.8 (0.09)	31,916 (83.3)	65.5 (0.10)	65.9 (0.09)	66.2 (0.09)	29,027 (76.2)	10.9 (0.09)	10.0 (0.07)	9.1 (0.06)	2,889 (20.0)
Some college, no degree	78.3 (0.10)	78.0 (0.09)	77.5 (0.09)	27,836 (62.6)	70.7 (0.11)	71.2 (0.10)	71.5 (0.09)	25,700 (59.8)	9.7 (0.07)	8.7 (0.07)	7.7 (0.07)	2,136 (19.9)
Associate's degree	82.4 (0.12)	82.2 (0.13)	82.0 (0.13)	12,008 (43.4)	76.7 (0.15)	76.7 (0.15)	77.2 (0.15)	11,307 (41.6)	6.9 (0.09)	6.6 (0.09)	5.8 (0.07)	701 (10.9)
Bachelor's or higher degree	85.8 (0.06)	86.1 (0.06)	86.0 (0.05)	44,239 (115.1)	81.9 (0.07)	82.5 (0.07)	82.7 (0.06)	42,557 (111.9)	4.5 (0.04)	4.2 (0.04)	3.8 (0.03)	1,682 (15.8)
Sex												
Male, all education levels	82.8 (0.05)	82.9 (0.05)	82.7 (0.05)	67,480 (49.3)	75.5 (0.06)	76.4 (0.05)	76.8 (0.06)	62,729 (53.0)	8.8 (0.05)	7.9 (0.04)	7.0 (0.04)	4,751 (28.0)
Less than high school completion	70.1 (0.16)	69.7 (0.19)	69.8 (0.18)	7,534 (34.7)	59.7 (0.19)	60.7 (0.20)	61.7 (0.21)	6,666 (34.1)	14.8 (0.17)	13.0 (0.14)	11.5 (0.16)	868 (12.1)
High school completion[4]	79.3 (0.11)	79.2 (0.11)	78.7 (0.10)	18,327 (51.7)	70.3 (0.13)	71.0 (0.12)	71.4 (0.12)	16,643 (49.6)	11.3 (0.11)	10.4 (0.10)	9.2 (0.09)	1,685 (16.5)
Some college, no degree	83.0 (0.13)	83.0 (0.10)	82.6 (0.13)	14,297 (44.3)	75.1 (0.15)	76.1 (0.13)	76.5 (0.14)	13,233 (42.0)	9.5 (0.11)	8.3 (0.09)	7.4 (0.11)	1,064 (15.9)
Associate's degree	86.6 (0.17)	86.6 (0.16)	86.4 (0.16)	5,381 (27.1)	80.8 (0.22)	81.0 (0.18)	81.5 (0.20)	5,071 (26.6)	7.0 (0.14)	6.5 (0.11)	5.8 (0.13)	310 (7.3)
Bachelor's or higher degree	91.1 (0.07)	91.5 (0.06)	91.4 (0.06)	21,941 (58.4)	87.1 (0.09)	87.8 (0.08)	87.9 (0.07)	21,116 (26.6)	4.4 (0.05)	4.0 (0.04)	3.8 (0.05)	825 (11.1)
Female, all education levels	72.3 (0.06)	72.2 (0.06)	72.0 (0.06)	60,533 (50.9)	66.3 (0.06)	66.7 (0.07)	67.0 (0.06)	56,348 (51.6)	8.4 (0.05)	7.7 (0.04)	6.9 (0.04)	4,186 (27.4)
Less than high school completion	50.1 (0.21)	49.8 (0.23)	49.8 (0.21)	4,480 (25.3)	41.5 (0.22)	41.8 (0.23)	42.5 (0.22)	3,820 (23.9)	17.1 (0.29)	15.9 (0.26)	14.7 (0.25)	660 (11.8)
High school completion[4]	67.2 (0.14)	66.5 (0.14)	66.1 (0.13)	13,589 (48.1)	60.2 (0.15)	60.1 (0.15)	60.2 (0.14)	12,385 (44.3)	10.4 (0.11)	9.6 (0.10)	8.9 (0.11)	1,205 (15.8)
Some college, no degree	73.9 (0.12)	73.4 (0.14)	72.7 (0.13)	13,539 (43.3)	66.7 (0.13)	66.7 (0.15)	66.9 (0.13)	12,467 (41.9)	9.8 (0.09)	9.1 (0.10)	7.9 (0.09)	1,072 (12.8)
Associate's degree	79.1 (0.16)	78.9 (0.16)	78.7 (0.17)	6,627 (32.1)	73.6 (0.18)	73.3 (0.20)	73.6 (0.18)	6,236 (31.0)	6.9 (0.12)	6.7 (0.13)	5.9 (0.11)	391 (7.6)
Bachelor's or higher degree	81.0 (0.08)	81.3 (0.09)	81.2 (0.08)	22,298 (72.4)	77.3 (0.10)	77.8 (0.11)	78.1 (0.10)	21,441 (70.8)	4.7 (0.06)	4.3 (0.05)	3.8 (0.05)	857 (10.4)
Race/ethnicity												
White, all education levels	78.5 (0.05)	78.5 (0.05)	78.2 (0.05)	82,804 (50.7)	72.8 (0.05)	73.4 (0.06)	73.7 (0.05)	78,017 (49.3)	7.3 (0.04)	6.5 (0.04)	5.8 (0.03)	4,786 (27.6)
Less than high school completion	55.2 (0.24)	54.3 (0.23)	54.3 (0.23)	3,729 (24.1)	45.5 (0.25)	45.7 (0.21)	46.6 (0.23)	3,199 (20.0)	17.6 (0.24)	15.8 (0.20)	14.2 (0.24)	530 (10.4)
High school completion[4]	73.9 (0.11)	73.5 (0.11)	72.9 (0.11)	20,312 (54.5)	66.7 (0.12)	67.1 (0.12)	67.2 (0.11)	18,717 (51.9)	9.6 (0.09)	8.7 (0.08)	7.9 (0.07)	1,595 (14.3)
Some college, no degree	78.1 (0.12)	78.0 (0.10)	77.4 (0.10)	18,123 (43.0)	71.5 (0.13)	71.8 (0.13)	72.4 (0.10)	16,953 (40.4)	8.5 (0.08)	7.3 (0.09)	6.5 (0.07)	1,170 (13.0)
Associate's degree	82.7 (0.13)	82.5 (0.16)	82.0 (0.15)	8,439 (33.6)	77.3 (0.16)	77.8 (0.19)	77.8 (0.17)	8,009 (31.8)	6.0 (0.10)	5.8 (0.12)	5.1 (0.10)	430 (8.5)
Bachelor's or higher degree	85.8 (0.07)	86.1 (0.07)	86.1 (0.06)	32,201 (78.3)	82.4 (0.07)	83.0 (0.08)	83.2 (0.06)	31,139 (77.1)	4.0 (0.04)	3.7 (0.04)	3.3 (0.04)	1,062 (13.2)
Black, all education levels	73.1 (0.14)	72.9 (0.13)	72.9 (0.12)	14,722 (32.7)	62.5 (0.14)	62.9 (0.15)	63.9 (0.12)	12,908 (31.3)	14.4 (0.13)	13.6 (0.11)	12.3 (0.11)	1,814 (16.5)
Less than high school completion	48.1 (0.44)	47.3 (0.43)	47.8 (0.40)	1,283 (13.9)	35.2 (0.37)	34.9 (0.39)	35.8 (0.39)	961 (11.6)	26.7 (0.43)	26.2 (0.48)	25.1 (0.52)	322 (7.9)
High school completion[4]	69.0 (0.26)	68.3 (0.26)	68.1 (0.20)	4,317 (28.9)	57.1 (0.28)	57.1 (0.24)	58.0 (0.23)	3,674 (26.1)	17.2 (0.28)	16.4 (0.22)	14.9 (0.24)	643 (11.5)
Some college, no degree	77.1 (0.24)	76.8 (0.24)	76.4 (0.22)	4,142 (22.7)	65.8 (0.27)	66.2 (0.30)	67.4 (0.26)	3,651 (21.4)	14.6 (0.22)	13.7 (0.26)	11.8 (0.21)	490 (9.3)
Associate's degree	82.0 (0.46)	81.9 (0.40)	82.6 (0.41)	1,401 (17.3)	73.0 (0.51)	73.3 (0.46)	75.0 (0.48)	1,272 (16.3)	11.0 (0.39)	10.5 (0.32)	9.2 (0.32)	129 (4.8)
Bachelor's or higher degree	88.5 (0.24)	88.5 (0.20)	88.1 (0.18)	3,579 (29.4)	82.1 (0.32)	82.7 (0.27)	82.4 (0.22)	3,349 (29.1)	7.3 (0.22)	6.5 (0.19)	6.4 (0.16)	230 (5.9)
Hispanic, all education levels	77.1 (0.10)	77.3 (0.09)	76.9 (0.11)	20,232 (31.7)	69.2 (0.12)	70.3 (0.11)	70.7 (0.13)	18,605 (36.6)	10.1 (0.10)	9.1 (0.09)	8.0 (0.09)	1,627 (16.9)
Less than high school completion	70.0 (0.18)	70.1 (0.18)	69.8 (0.21)	6,118 (33.4)	61.4 (0.20)	62.6 (0.22)	63.3 (0.25)	5,549 (33.7)	12.3 (0.19)	10.7 (0.19)	9.3 (0.17)	569 (10.0)
High school completion[4]	77.1 (0.23)	77.3 (0.20)	76.8 (0.23)	5,585 (29.3)	68.7 (0.27)	69.6 (0.21)	70.1 (0.25)	5,096 (28.6)	10.9 (0.19)	10.0 (0.16)	8.8 (0.15)	489 (8.3)
Some college, no degree	81.4 (0.26)	80.8 (0.23)	80.1 (0.25)	3,882 (26.0)	73.5 (0.31)	73.4 (0.28)	73.5 (0.28)	3,562 (26.4)	9.7 (0.23)	9.1 (0.19)	8.2 (0.20)	320 (7.5)
Associate's degree	83.1 (0.41)	83.7 (0.38)	83.4 (0.41)	1,335 (17.0)	76.3 (0.46)	77.5 (0.38)	78.2 (0.44)	1,248 (16.3)	8.2 (0.36)	7.4 (0.27)	6.3 (0.28)	84 (3.8)
Bachelor's or higher degree	86.7 (0.21)	87.1 (0.23)	86.8 (0.22)	3,315 (30.4)	81.8 (0.26)	82.4 (0.26)	82.5 (0.26)	3,151 (29.7)	5.6 (0.20)	5.4 (0.16)	5.0 (0.17)	165 (5.9)
Asian, all education levels	78.7 (0.18)	78.4 (0.16)	78.6 (0.15)	7,256 (18.2)	73.3 (0.18)	73.5 (0.18)	74.3 (0.17)	6,857 (19.9)	6.9 (0.12)	6.2 (0.12)	5.5 (0.10)	399 (7.0)
Less than high school completion	64.4 (0.59)	64.5 (0.52)	63.8 (0.50)	651 (10.0)	57.7 (0.62)	58.5 (0.50)	57.8 (0.49)	591 (9.6)	10.4 (0.47)	9.3 (0.43)	9.3 (0.45)	60 (3.1)
High school completion[4]	75.1 (0.49)	74.3 (0.49)	73.8 (0.43)	978 (12.8)	67.9 (0.56)	68.8 (0.56)	68.8 (0.48)	912 (12.6)	9.4 (0.36)	8.6 (0.37)	6.8 (0.31)	66 (3.1)
Some college, no degree	78.7 (0.52)	78.0 (0.48)	78.2 (0.49)	906 (12.8)	71.5 (0.55)	71.3 (0.49)	72.6 (0.51)	841 (11.4)	9.2 (0.36)	8.6 (0.39)	7.2 (0.32)	65 (3.3)
Associate's degree	79.1 (0.66)	76.4 (0.68)	79.1 (0.56)	537 (9.0)	73.4 (0.73)	71.3 (0.70)	74.3 (0.61)	505 (8.8)	7.2 (0.32)	6.6 (0.41)	6.1 (0.43)	33 (2.4)
Bachelor's or higher degree	82.8 (0.23)	82.7 (0.21)	82.8 (0.22)	4,183 (22.3)	78.5 (0.24)	79.0 (0.21)	79.4 (0.24)	4,009 (22.7)	5.2 (0.16)	4.5 (0.13)	4.2 (0.11)	174 (4.5)
American Indian/Alaska Native, all education levels	66.6 (0.62)	66.2 (0.56)	65.1 (0.58)	695 (9.7)	57.0 (0.65)	57.2 (0.60)	56.7 (0.60)	605 (9.3)	14.5 (0.50)	13.7 (0.44)	12.9 (0.45)	89 (3.3)
Less than high school completion	44.9 (1.46)	44.0 (1.21)	45.8 (1.50)	78 (3.5)	32.7 (1.41)	33.0 (1.13)	35.3 (1.47)	60 (3.3)	27.2 (2.22)	24.9 (1.88)	22.9 (1.59)	18 (1.3)
High school completion[4]	63.1 (1.08)	64.7 (0.96)	62.5 (0.84)	216 (5.5)	52.4 (1.08)	52.4 (1.03)	52.4 (0.97)	182 (5.4)	17.0 (0.91)	16.0 (0.94)	16.1 (0.96)	35 (2.1)
Some college, no degree	71.9 (1.01)	68.5 (1.14)	67.2 (0.98)	199 (5.1)	59.0 (1.12)	59.1 (1.13)	59.1 (1.05)	175 (4.7)	14.1 (0.78)	13.8 (0.85)	12.0 (0.77)	24 (1.7)
Associate's degree	74.1 (1.70)	75.0 (1.75)	74.8 (1.55)	74 (2.9)	67.3 (1.69)	67.4 (1.69)	68.3 (1.64)	68 (2.8)	10.0 (1.23)	10.0 (1.04)	8.6 (1.18)	6 (0.9)
Bachelor's or higher degree	82.5 (0.93)	84.4 (1.13)	82.1 (1.25)	127 (4.2)	77.3 (1.11)	79.9 (1.16)	78.0 (1.35)	121 (4.2)	6.3 (0.77)	5.2 (0.65)	5.0 (0.71)	6 (0.9)

See notes at end of table.

Table 501.10.   Labor force participation, employment, and unemployment of persons 25 to 64 years old, by sex, race/ethnicity, age group, and educational attainment: 2011, 2012, and 2013—Continued

[Standard errors appear in parentheses]

Sex, race/ethnicity, age group, and educational attainment	Labor force participation				Employment				Unemployment			
	Labor force participation rate[1]			Number of participants (in thousands)	Employment to population ratio[2]			Number employed (in thousands)	Unemployment rate[3]			Number unemployed (in thousands)
	2011	2012	2013	2013	2011	2012	2013	2013	2011	2012	2013	2013
1	2	3	4	5	6	7	8	9	10	11	12	13
Age group												
25 to 34, all education levels	**81.8** (0.08)	**82.0** (0.06)	**81.8** (0.08)	**34,486** (46.8)	**73.2** (0.08)	**74.1** (0.07)	**74.6** (0.09)	**31,480** (47.1)	**10.6** (0.08)	**9.7** (0.06)	**8.7** (0.06)	**3,007** (19.6)
Less than high school completion	66.0 (0.31)	65.5 (0.29)	65.3 (0.30)	3,179 (27.3)	53.2 (0.32)	53.7 (0.32)	54.4 (0.30)	2,648 (24.9)	19.5 (0.28)	18.0 (0.31)	16.7 (0.26)	531 (9.1)
High school completion[4]	78.1 (0.19)	78.0 (0.17)	77.1 (0.18)	7,806 (40.2)	66.8 (0.20)	67.2 (0.17)	67.5 (0.21)	6,828 (38.7)	14.5 (0.20)	13.9 (0.15)	12.5 (0.15)	978 (12.1)
Some college, no degree	82.2 (0.17)	82.1 (0.17)	81.8 (0.19)	7,916 (35.7)	72.1 (0.20)	72.9 (0.20)	73.8 (0.20)	7,140 (35.0)	12.3 (0.17)	11.2 (0.15)	9.8 (0.14)	776 (11.1)
Associate's degree	86.3 (0.25)	86.7 (0.22)	86.6 (0.21)	3,167 (22.7)	79.4 (0.28)	80.1 (0.26)	80.8 (0.23)	2,953 (21.7)	8.0 (0.20)	7.7 (0.22)	6.7 (0.15)	214 (5.0)
Bachelor's or higher degree	89.3 (0.11)	89.7 (0.10)	89.6 (0.11)	12,418 (50.3)	84.9 (0.13)	85.8 (0.11)	85.9 (0.11)	11,911 (49.7)	4.9 (0.10)	4.3 (0.08)	4.1 (0.06)	507 (7.9)
35 to 44, all education levels	**82.5** (0.08)	**82.5** (0.08)	**82.1** (0.08)	**33,386** (40.1)	**75.7** (0.09)	**76.3** (0.09)	**76.6** (0.09)	**31,136** (42.5)	**8.2** (0.07)	**7.5** (0.06)	**6.7** (0.06)	**2,250** (21.4)
Less than high school completion	68.5 (0.29)	68.4 (0.24)	68.0 (0.28)	3,447 (24.8)	58.2 (0.29)	59.3 (0.26)	59.8 (0.31)	3,034 (23.7)	15.1 (0.27)	13.4 (0.22)	12.0 (0.27)	412 (9.7)
High school completion[4]	79.3 (0.18)	79.0 (0.18)	78.4 (0.18)	7,821 (36.2)	70.4 (0.20)	70.9 (0.18)	71.1 (0.20)	7,090 (34.6)	11.2 (0.15)	10.3 (0.16)	9.3 (0.15)	731 (12.0)
Some college, no degree	83.6 (0.15)	83.1 (0.18)	82.3 (0.17)	7,031 (29.2)	76.0 (0.19)	76.1 (0.23)	76.0 (0.20)	6,490 (28.9)	9.2 (0.15)	8.5 (0.15)	7.7 (0.14)	541 (10.0)
Associate's degree	86.9 (0.23)	86.5 (0.24)	86.1 (0.23)	3,171 (20.1)	81.1 (0.27)	80.8 (0.27)	81.2 (0.30)	2,990 (19.9)	6.7 (0.19)	6.6 (0.22)	5.7 (0.21)	181 (6.8)
Bachelor's or higher degree	88.7 (0.10)	89.1 (0.11)	89.1 (0.10)	11,917 (47.0)	85.3 (0.12)	85.8 (0.12)	86.2 (0.11)	11,533 (45.2)	3.8 (0.08)	3.7 (0.08)	3.2 (0.06)	385 (7.5)
45 to 54, all education levels	**80.4** (0.07)	**80.3** (0.07)	**80.0** (0.07)	**34,872** (41.6)	**74.0** (0.08)	**74.6** (0.08)	**75.0** (0.08)	**32,678** (39.8)	**7.9** (0.06)	**7.0** (0.05)	**6.3** (0.05)	**2,194** (18.9)
Less than high school completion	62.1 (0.26)	61.9 (0.26)	62.1 (0.29)	3,297 (26.1)	53.2 (0.29)	53.8 (0.27)	55.0 (0.30)	2,919 (24.1)	14.4 (0.25)	13.0 (0.22)	11.5 (0.23)	378 (8.3)
High school completion[4]	77.4 (0.14)	76.9 (0.16)	76.4 (0.14)	9,567 (34.4)	69.9 (0.15)	70.3 (0.17)	70.5 (0.15)	8,829 (32.9)	9.7 (0.13)	8.6 (0.10)	7.7 (0.09)	738 (9.1)
Some college, no degree	81.4 (0.17)	81.258 (0.13)	80.9 (0.18)	7,376 (33.9)	74.6 (0.18)	75.3 (0.16)	75.7 (0.19)	6,900 (32.7)	8.4 (0.11)	7.3 (0.11)	6.5 (0.11)	477 (8.2)
Associate's degree	85.4 (0.21)	84.6 (0.21)	84.7 (0.22)	3,340 (22.4)	79.9 (0.26)	79.5 (0.27)	80.3 (0.22)	3,167 (21.0)	6.4 (0.16)	6.0 (0.17)	5.2 (0.13)	173 (4.8)
Bachelor's or higher degree	89.3 (0.10)	89.4 (0.12)	89.0 (0.11)	11,291 (41.8)	85.4 (0.11)	85.9 (0.14)	85.7 (0.13)	10,863 (40.7)	4.4 (0.07)	4.0 (0.07)	3.8 (0.08)	428 (8.8)
55 to 64, all education levels	**64.0** (0.09)	**64.1** (0.08)	**64.3** (0.08)	**25,268** (32.5)	**59.3** (0.09)	**59.9** (0.08)	**60.5** (0.09)	**23,782** (34.1)	**7.5** (0.06)	**6.6** (0.06)	**5.9** (0.06)	**1,486** (15.2)
Less than high school completion	45.4 (0.28)	45.5 (0.26)	46.0 (0.26)	2,091 (14.6)	39.7 (0.29)	40.5 (0.26)	41.5 (0.27)	1,885 (15.1)	12.7 (0.30)	10.8 (0.24)	9.9 (0.25)	206 (5.2)
High school completion[4]	59.2 (0.16)	59.3 (0.15)	59.8 (0.15)	6,722 (29.6)	54.3 (0.16)	54.9 (0.15)	55.8 (0.15)	6,281 (27.5)	8.2 (0.14)	7.4 (0.11)	6.6 (0.12)	442 (8.8)
Some college, no degree	64.7 (0.23)	64.4 (0.19)	64.1 (0.17)	5,513 (24.6)	59.2 (0.22)	59.8 (0.20)	60.1 (0.19)	5,171 (23.7)	8.4 (0.14)	7.2 (0.12)	7.2 (0.13)	342 (7.2)
Associate's degree	69.1 (0.29)	69.2 (0.31)	69.1 (0.28)	2,330 (17.0)	64.4 (0.32)	65.0 (0.34)	65.2 (0.30)	2,197 (16.4)	6.7 (0.20)	6.2 (0.19)	5.7 (0.18)	134 (4.3)
Bachelor's or higher degree	74.4 (0.14)	74.5 (0.15)	74.6 (0.14)	8,612 (29.1)	70.5 (0.15)	71.0 (0.16)	71.5 (0.14)	8,249 (29.1)	5.2 (0.08)	4.8 (0.08)	4.2 (0.07)	363 (6.4)

[1]Percentage of the civilian population who are employed or seeking employment.
[2]Number of persons employed as a percentage of the civilian population.
[3]The percentage of persons in the civilian labor force who are not working and who made specific efforts to find employment sometime during the prior 4 weeks.
[4]Includes equivalency credentials, such as the GED credential.

NOTE: Race categories exclude persons of Hispanic ethnicity. Totals include racial/ethnic groups not separately shown. Standard errors were computed using replicate weights.
SOURCE: U.S. Department of Commerce, Census Bureau, American Community Survey (ACS), 2011, 2012, and 2013, unpublished tabulations. (This table was prepared February 2015.)

Table 501.20. Labor force participation, employment, and unemployment of persons 16 to 24 years old who are not enrolled in school, by age group, sex, race/ethnicity, and educational attainment: 2011, 2012, and 2013

[Standard errors appear in parentheses]

Age group, sex, race/ethnicity, and educational attainment	Labor force participation rate[1] 2011	Labor force participation rate[1] 2012	Labor force participation rate[1] 2013	Number of participants (in thousands) 2013	Employment to population ratio[2] 2011	Employment to population ratio[2] 2012	Employment to population ratio[2] 2013	Number employed (in thousands) 2013	Unemployment rate[3] 2011	Unemployment rate[3] 2012	Unemployment rate[3] 2013	Number unemployed (in thousands) 2013
1	2	3	4	5	6	7	8	9	10	11	12	13
16 to 19 years old												
All persons, all education levels	62.7 (0.43)	64.1 (0.39)	64.3 (0.40)	1,585 (16.2)	41.7 (0.42)	43.5 (0.41)	45.5 (0.39)	1,122 (13.8)	33.5 (0.52)	32.1 (0.50)	29.2 (0.48)	463 (8.9)
Less than high school completion[4]	47.2 (0.75)	47.9 (0.72)	47.1 (0.81)	339 (8.9)	26.6 (0.71)	27.6 (0.63)	28.4 (0.76)	204 (6.8)	43.6 (1.12)	42.5 (1.06)	39.7 (1.19)	134 (5.3)
High school completion[4]	70.0 (0.47)	70.3 (0.53)	70.2 (0.52)	1,004 (14.0)	47.9 (0.53)	48.6 (0.54)	50.3 (0.53)	719 (11.1)	31.6 (0.61)	30.8 (0.61)	28.4 (0.57)	285 (7.3)
At least some college	74.7 (1.13)	77.1 (1.03)	76.4 (1.09)	242 (7.5)	57.9 (1.22)	61.0 (1.22)	62.7 (1.09)	199 (6.6)	22.5 (1.35)	20.8 (1.12)	18.0 (0.92)	44 (2.6)
Male, all education levels	64.4 (0.58)	66.0 (0.52)	66.9 (0.61)	923 (12.9)	42.0 (0.55)	44.9 (0.49)	46.6 (0.55)	642 (10.7)	34.9 (0.60)	32.0 (0.59)	30.4 (0.56)	281 (6.3)
Less than high school completion[4]	50.9 (1.04)	51.2 (1.09)	50.1 (1.13)	212 (7.6)	28.9 (0.97)	30.1 (0.90)	30.1 (0.96)	127 (5.5)	43.2 (1.36)	41.2 (1.30)	40.0 (1.37)	85 (4.1)
High school completion[4]	71.6 (0.59)	72.5 (0.63)	73.9 (0.71)	592 (11.2)	47.9 (0.71)	50.7 (0.65)	52.1 (0.66)	418 (5.8)	33.1 (0.78)	30.1 (0.75)	29.5 (0.72)	175 (5.7)
At least some college	75.8 (1.54)	77.2 (1.43)	76.6 (1.68)	119 (4.8)	59.0 (1.79)	60.2 (1.58)	62.6 (1.74)	97 (4.1)	22.3 (1.79)	22.1 (1.75)	18.2 (1.42)	22 (2.0)
Female, all education levels	60.4 (0.65)	61.5 (0.66)	60.9 (0.56)	662 (10.2)	41.3 (0.62)	41.6 (0.65)	44.1 (0.65)	480 (9.6)	31.6 (0.75)	32.3 (0.82)	27.5 (0.75)	182 (5.2)
Less than high school completion[4]	41.4 (1.04)	43.0 (1.05)	42.7 (1.16)	127 (4.7)	23.1 (0.90)	23.8 (0.89)	26.0 (1.04)	77 (3.6)	44.3 (1.46)	44.7 (1.70)	39.1 (1.76)	50 (3.0)
High school completion[4]	68.0 (0.77)	67.2 (0.78)	65.5 (0.87)	411 (8.9)	48.0 (0.78)	45.9 (0.92)	48.0 (0.87)	301 (7.9)	29.4 (0.90)	31.8 (1.03)	26.8 (0.88)	110 (4.0)
At least some college	73.6 (1.59)	77.0 (1.34)	76.3 (1.33)	123 (5.2)	57.0 (1.91)	62.0 (1.56)	62.7 (1.68)	101 (4.8)	22.6 (1.78)	19.5 (1.57)	17.8 (1.48)	22 (1.9)
White, all education levels	67.4 (0.55)	68.8 (0.51)	68.5 (0.57)	808 (9.2)	47.4 (0.55)	50.4 (0.58)	51.4 (0.53)	607 (8.2)	29.7 (0.66)	26.7 (0.57)	24.9 (0.58)	201 (5.3)
Less than high school completion[4]	47.5 (1.24)	49.6 (1.07)	49.5 (1.19)	151 (5.0)	28.3 (1.00)	29.1 (1.01)	31.2 (1.00)	95 (3.8)	40.5 (1.52)	41.3 (1.47)	36.9 (1.64)	56 (3.2)
High school completion[4]	74.9 (0.63)	74.8 (0.64)	74.1 (0.66)	532 (8.5)	53.4 (0.67)	56.3 (0.71)	56.1 (0.66)	403 (7.3)	28.7 (0.73)	24.8 (0.70)	24.3 (0.62)	129 (3.8)
At least some college	79.8 (1.30)	81.8 (1.20)	79.5 (1.30)	126 (4.6)	65.0 (1.91)	68.5 (1.36)	69.2 (1.22)	110 (4.1)	18.6 (1.66)	16.2 (1.27)	13.0 (1.18)	16 (1.7)
Black, all education levels	51.4 (1.03)	55.6 (1.12)	55.7 (0.82)	245 (5.8)	26.1 (0.90)	27.6 (1.02)	30.4 (0.97)	134 (5.1)	49.3 (1.31)	50.3 (1.39)	45.5 (1.55)	111 (4.5)
Less than high school completion[4]	35.4 (1.56)	35.4 (1.75)	36.0 (1.65)	51 (2.9)	12.0 (1.16)	12.6 (1.25)	14.1 (1.41)	20 (2.2)	66.2 (2.75)	64.4 (2.97)	61.0 (3.33)	31 (2.2)
High school completion[4]	60.5 (1.34)	63.2 (1.36)	64.0 (1.34)	155 (5.1)	33.0 (1.26)	31.8 (1.47)	35.9 (1.63)	87 (4.2)	45.5 (1.63)	49.6 (1.85)	43.9 (1.90)	68 (3.7)
At least some college	63.3 (3.03)	75.8 (2.88)	68.6 (2.20)	40 (3.1)	42.9 (3.34)	50.1 (2.69)	46.7 (2.78)	27 (2.6)	32.2 (3.71)	33.9 (2.90)	31.9 (3.60)	13 (1.7)
Hispanic, all education levels	63.4 (0.71)	61.9 (0.72)	63.3 (0.88)	425 (9.4)	43.9 (0.87)	42.1 (0.67)	46.0 (0.83)	308 (8.0)	30.8 (1.10)	32.0 (0.96)	27.4 (0.96)	116 (4.8)
Less than high school completion[4]	54.4 (1.09)	52.8 (1.48)	51.9 (1.66)	115 (6.0)	34.7 (1.23)	34.7 (1.27)	34.1 (1.60)	75 (4.8)	36.2 (1.86)	34.2 (1.79)	34.3 (1.97)	39 (2.9)
High school completion[4]	66.6 (1.11)	67.6 (1.05)	67.6 (1.19)	254 (6.9)	44.8 (1.43)	50.0 (1.11)	50.0 (1.13)	188 (5.8)	32.7 (1.58)	28.3 (1.33)	26.0 (1.18)	66 (3.6)
At least some college	73.6 (2.12)	71.2 (2.70)	75.9 (2.13)	56 (3.4)	54.7 (2.58)	56.1 (2.83)	61.4 (2.61)	45 (3.0)	25.6 (2.85)	21.2 (2.42)	19.1 (2.27)	11 (1.4)
Asian, all education levels	55.1 (3.11)	57.5 (3.08)	49.6 (3.11)	24 (1.8)	38.2 (2.84)	48.3 (3.36)	34.5 (2.34)	16 (1.4)	30.6 (3.20)	16.0 (2.76)	30.5 (3.48)	7 (1.0)
Less than high school completion[4]	36.7 (5.19)	34.6 (5.69)	29.3 (3.44)	5 (0.7)	21.3 (4.16)	27.4 (5.25)	20.3 (3.55)	‡ (†)	41.9 (9.67)	20.5 (5.60)	30.8 (7.86)	‡ (†)
High school completion[4]	61.0 (3.85)	57.4 (4.12)	57.4 (4.60)	12 (1.4)	42.0 (3.76)	56.0 (4.27)	35.2 (3.77)	7 (1.0)	31.1 (4.27)	14.3 (3.29)	38.7 (5.59)	5 (0.9)
At least some college	61.7 (8.02)	61.8 (7.32)	67.4 (5.89)	7 (1.1)	49.9 (6.86)	49.6 (8.50)	56.7 (5.60)	6 (0.9)	19.1 ! (6.74)	19.8 (8.49)	15.9 ! (5.22)	‡ (†)
American Indian/Alaska Native, all education levels	47.8 (3.08)	56.1 (3.26)	53.2 (3.11)	17 (1.3)	23.3 (2.78)	28.3 (3.43)	34.1 (3.22)	11 (1.2)	51.1 (4.89)	49.6 (5.04)	35.8 (4.24)	6 (0.8)
Less than high school completion[4]	37.8 (4.83)	45.7 (5.02)	42.0 (4.72)	6 (0.9)	17.3 (3.90)	17.3 (3.98)	26.3 (4.69)	3 (0.8)	54.3 (8.63)	62.1 (8.22)	37.5 (7.65)	2 (0.4)
High school completion[4]	55.3 (4.38)	63.6 (4.40)	61.8 (4.20)	10 (1.1)	27.3 (4.55)	36.4 (4.67)	40.1 (5.21)	6 (1.0)	50.6 (6.87)	42.7 (5.70)	35.1 (6.01)	3 (0.7)
At least some college	49.3 (9.42)	66.7 (7.65)	58.2 (8.60)	‡ (†)	27.6 ! (8.42)	38.3 (8.74)	38.0 (8.31)	‡ (†)	†	42.6 (11.01)	†	‡ (†)
20 to 24 years old												
All persons, all education levels	79.9 (0.13)	80.5 (0.13)	80.7 (0.15)	10,513 (34.8)	65.1 (0.17)	66.6 (0.18)	67.9 (0.19)	8,846 (34.2)	18.6 (0.18)	17.3 (0.18)	15.9 (0.18)	1,667 (19.6)
Less than high school completion[4]	64.5 (0.42)	64.2 (0.47)	63.3 (0.51)	1,260 (17.7)	45.5 (0.46)	45.3 (0.44)	46.7 (0.53)	930 (15.3)	29.5 (0.57)	29.5 (0.58)	26.2 (0.50)	330 (7.3)
High school completion[4]	77.9 (0.23)	78.4 (0.24)	78.5 (0.27)	4,161 (28.6)	62.4 (0.28)	62.4 (0.30)	63.6 (0.34)	3,374 (27.0)	20.4 (0.30)	20.4 (0.30)	18.9 (0.28)	787 (12.5)
Some college, no degree	85.1 (0.30)	85.3 (0.27)	85.8 (0.31)	2,783 (18.8)	72.7 (0.44)	71.6 (0.36)	74.0 (0.34)	2,401 (18.0)	14.7 (0.44)	14.7 (0.33)	13.7 (0.27)	383 (7.8)
Associate's degree	90.1 (0.54)	89.4 (0.60)	90.8 (0.43)	586 (10.1)	81.2 (0.79)	81.2 (0.72)	82.9 (0.54)	535 (9.5)	9.8 (0.71)	9.2 (0.53)	8.7 (0.53)	51 (3.3)
Bachelor's or higher degree	93.4 (0.25)	93.8 (0.25)	93.6 (0.21)	1,722 (17.7)	87.0 (0.40)	87.1 (0.35)	87.1 (0.27)	1,606 (17.2)	7.8 (0.31)	7.2 (0.27)	6.7 (0.25)	116 (4.5)

See notes at end of table.

Table 501.20. Labor force participation, employment, and unemployment of persons 16 to 24 years old who are not enrolled in school, by age group, sex, race/ethnicity, and educational attainment: 2011, 2012, and 2013—Continued

[Standard errors appear in parentheses]

Age group, sex, race/ethnicity, and educational attainment	Labor force participation rate[1] 2011	2012	2013	Number of participants (in thousands) 2013	Employment to population ratio[2] 2011	2012	2013	Number employed (in thousands) 2013	Unemployment rate[3] 2011	2012	2013	Number unemployed (in thousands) 2013
1	2	3	4	5	6	7	8	9	10	11	12	13
Male, all education levels	**82.6 (0.19)**	**83.0 (0.17)**	**82.9 (0.18)**	**5,807 (26.5)**	**66.6 (0.25)**	**67.8 (0.24)**	**69.1 (0.24)**	**4,844 (25.0)**	**19.4 (0.23)**	**18.2 (0.23)**	**16.6 (0.23)**	**963 (14.4)**
Less than high school completion	71.0 (0.47)	69.7 (0.57)	68.4 (0.62)	823 (13.9)	52.1 (0.53)	50.7 (0.65)	52.0 (0.68)	626 (12.1)	26.6 (0.62)	27.1 (0.74)	24.0 (0.61)	197 (5.7)
High school completion[4]	81.9 (0.27)	81.9 (0.27)	81.8 (0.30)	2,530 (21.0)	63.6 (0.36)	66.3 (0.39)	66.3 (0.40)	2,051 (19.4)	22.3 (0.39)	20.5 (0.38)	19.0 (0.40)	480 (9.9)
Some college, no degree	87.6 (0.42)	88.2 (0.31)	88.4 (0.37)	1,448 (13.2)	73.4 (0.60)	74.7 (0.45)	75.6 (0.49)	1,238 (12.8)	16.2 (0.52)	15.2 (0.41)	14.5 (0.40)	209 (6.1)
Associate's degree	92.3 (0.68)	92.2 (0.70)	93.2 (0.59)	284 (7.2)	83.9 (0.95)	82.8 (1.02)	85.3 (0.88)	260 (6.7)	9.1 (0.81)	10.2 (0.85)	8.5 (0.77)	24 (2.3)
Bachelor's or higher degree	93.8 (0.44)	94.9 (0.30)	94.1 (0.34)	722 (11.1)	85.7 (0.62)	87.0 (0.50)	87.3 (0.49)	670 (11.0)	8.6 (0.48)	8.4 (0.39)	7.2 (0.42)	52 (3.1)
Female, all education levels	**76.7 (0.21)**	**77.7 (0.21)**	**78.2 (0.22)**	**4,706 (23.0)**	**63.3 (0.26)**	**65.1 (0.27)**	**66.5 (0.26)**	**4,002 (21.7)**	**17.5 (0.26)**	**16.2 (0.24)**	**15.0 (0.22)**	**704 (11.1)**
Less than high school completion	54.8 (0.71)	56.0 (0.81)	55.5 (0.76)	437 (9.1)	35.5 (0.73)	37.0 (0.74)	38.6 (0.73)	304 (7.7)	35.2 (1.06)	33.9 (1.07)	30.4 (0.90)	133 (4.6)
High school completion[4]	72.5 (0.43)	73.6 (0.39)	73.9 (0.45)	1,631 (19.2)	57.3 (0.48)	58.6 (0.48)	59.9 (0.51)	1,324 (17.4)	21.0 (0.44)	20.4 (0.46)	18.8 (0.42)	307 (7.5)
Some college, no degree	82.6 (0.43)	82.3 (0.42)	83.1 (0.46)	1,336 (14.2)	69.8 (0.53)	70.7 (0.54)	72.3 (0.51)	1,163 (13.5)	15.4 (0.48)	14.0 (0.47)	13.0 (0.40)	173 (5.7)
Associate's degree	88.4 (0.78)	87.0 (0.89)	88.6 (0.72)	302 (7.4)	79.7 (1.11)	79.7 (1.01)	80.7 (0.84)	275 (7.1)	9.7 (1.02)	8.3 (0.65)	8.9 (0.74)	27 (2.4)
Bachelor's or higher degree	93.1 (0.34)	93.0 (0.32)	93.0 (0.31)	1,000 (12.3)	86.5 (0.47)	87.0 (0.41)	87.1 (0.42)	936 (12.0)	7.2 (0.34)	6.4 (0.33)	6.3 (0.32)	63 (3.3)
White, all education levels	**83.4 (0.22)**	**84.1 (0.17)**	**84.0 (0.19)**	**5,947 (25.9)**	**70.5 (0.26)**	**72.4 (0.20)**	**73.0 (0.25)**	**5,163 (25.8)**	**15.4 (0.21)**	**14.0 (0.20)**	**13.2 (0.21)**	**784 (13.1)**
Less than high school completion	63.6 (0.83)	64.6 (0.80)	64.1 (0.70)	471 (9.0)	42.4 (0.67)	45.0 (0.70)	46.6 (0.78)	342 (7.7)	33.4 (0.77)	30.2 (1.00)	27.4 (0.81)	129 (4.5)
High school completion[4]	80.4 (0.36)	81.1 (0.34)	81.0 (0.34)	2,259 (20.0)	65.1 (0.37)	66.6 (0.39)	67.4 (0.44)	1,882 (18.7)	19.0 (0.35)	17.8 (0.35)	16.7 (0.37)	378 (9.1)
Some college, no degree	86.9 (0.33)	86.7 (0.35)	87.1 (0.38)	1,573 (15.3)	75.7 (0.49)	76.7 (0.45)	77.1 (0.50)	1,393 (15.4)	12.9 (0.40)	11.6 (0.38)	11.4 (0.38)	180 (6.1)
Associate's degree	91.7 (0.59)	91.5 (0.61)	92.2 (0.55)	399 (9.0)	84.9 (0.79)	84.5 (0.78)	85.8 (0.69)	371 (8.5)	7.5 (0.70)	7.7 (0.59)	6.9 (0.55)	27 (2.3)
Bachelor's or higher degree	94.9 (0.30)	95.6 (0.24)	94.9 (0.25)	1,245 (14.4)	88.7 (0.48)	89.9 (0.31)	89.6 (0.32)	1,175 (14.1)	6.6 (0.36)	6.0 (0.27)	5.6 (0.28)	70 (3.6)
Black, all education levels	**71.9 (0.43)**	**73.0 (0.45)**	**74.0 (0.48)**	**1,538 (15.0)**	**48.8 (0.51)**	**50.4 (0.61)**	**53.8 (0.52)**	**1,117 (13.3)**	**32.1 (0.56)**	**30.9 (0.61)**	**27.4 (0.55)**	**421 (9.7)**
Less than high school completion	51.3 (1.08)	53.3 (1.09)	51.3 (1.09)	198 (6.9)	23.7 (0.94)	25.6 (0.95)	27.4 (1.04)	106 (5.0)	53.8 (1.54)	52.1 (1.60)	46.6 (1.43)	92 (3.9)
High school completion[4]	71.4 (0.64)	71.1 (0.61)	73.2 (0.69)	681 (12.5)	46.1 (0.86)	47.7 (0.76)	51.3 (0.71)	478 (10.2)	35.4 (0.90)	32.9 (0.81)	29.9 (0.72)	203 (6.0)
Some college, no degree	81.8 (0.81)	84.0 (0.72)	84.7 (0.69)	469 (9.3)	62.8 (0.96)	63.0 (1.08)	66.1 (0.90)	366 (8.4)	23.3 (1.02)	25.0 (1.01)	22.0 (0.91)	103 (4.7)
Associate's degree	88.9 (1.79)	86.3 (1.98)	89.7 (1.66)	63 (3.4)	74.1 (2.46)	73.0 (2.75)	77.1 (2.23)	54 (3.2)	16.6 (2.59)	15.4 (2.47)	14.1 (2.21)	9 (1.4)
Bachelor's or higher degree	94.7 (0.93)	92.9 (1.03)	92.9 (1.08)	128 (5.4)	82.1 (1.38)	81.1 (1.46)	83.0 (1.51)	114 (5.0)	13.3 (1.41)	13.3 (1.37)	10.7 (1.24)	14 (1.7)
Hispanic, all education levels	**77.9 (0.26)**	**77.8 (0.32)**	**78.3 (0.34)**	**2,355 (19.2)**	**63.9 (0.37)**	**64.5 (0.38)**	**66.6 (0.44)**	**2,002 (17.8)**	**18.0 (0.35)**	**17.1 (0.38)**	**15.0 (0.38)**	**353 (9.6)**
Less than high school completion	71.6 (0.65)	69.4 (0.72)	69.2 (0.79)	533 (12.4)	58.2 (0.74)	55.0 (0.83)	57.1 (0.88)	439 (11.1)	18.7 (0.69)	20.7 (0.81)	17.5 (0.74)	93 (4.4)
High school completion[4]	77.8 (0.48)	78.3 (0.51)	78.0 (0.48)	1,006 (11.5)	63.0 (0.59)	64.3 (0.60)	65.3 (0.64)	843 (11.8)	19.0 (0.55)	17.9 (0.57)	16.2 (0.51)	163 (5.1)
Some college, no degree	80.3 (0.68)	83.4 (0.54)	84.7 (0.69)	566 (10.3)	68.9 (0.93)	71.2 (0.73)	74.1 (0.81)	495 (9.4)	18.0 (0.79)	14.6 (0.67)	12.5 (0.69)	71 (4.3)
Associate's degree	86.3 (1.69)	84.0 (1.80)	87.6 (1.34)	95 (4.2)	73.7 (2.36)	74.5 (1.90)	76.7 (1.81)	83 (4.2)	13.2 (2.02)	11.4 (1.66)	12.5 (1.66)	12 (1.6)
Bachelor's or higher degree	90.3 (1.06)	91.2 (0.85)	91.7 (0.89)	156 (5.6)	81.4 (1.51)	81.7 (1.31)	83.3 (1.13)	142 (5.5)	9.8 (1.30)	10.4 (0.94)	9.1 (0.94)	14 (1.5)
Asian, all education levels	**80.3 (0.87)**	**78.9 (0.73)**	**77.3 (0.77)**	**294 (5.9)**	**68.9 (1.12)**	**68.3 (0.97)**	**68.4 (0.94)**	**260 (5.5)**	**14.2 (1.03)**	**13.4 (0.83)**	**11.5 (0.79)**	**34 (2.5)**
Less than high school completion	72.1 (2.63)	61.2 (3.18)	60.2 (3.95)	18 (1.6)	49.3 (2.95)	50.7 (3.53)	50.7 (3.99)	15 (1.5)	24.3 (3.30)	19.5 (3.45)	15.8 (3.50)	‡ (†)
High school completion[4]	78.1 (2.03)	78.9 (1.75)	71.8 (1.68)	65 (3.3)	65.0 (2.36)	65.6 (2.13)	61.4 (2.19)	55 (3.1)	16.7 (1.99)	16.9 (1.93)	14.4 (1.85)	9 (1.2)
Some college, no degree	80.3 (1.68)	80.0 (2.00)	75.3 (2.27)	57 (2.8)	69.6 (2.23)	68.2 (2.29)	67.3 (2.31)	51 (2.5)	13.4 (2.02)	14.8 (1.70)	10.6 (1.40)	6 (0.9)
Associate's degree	86.3 (3.13)	81.2 (3.87)	80.7 (4.04)	14 (1.4)	80.4 (3.48)	71.8 (4.44)	70.7 (5.08)	13 (1.3)	6.8 ! (2.38)	11.5 (3.42)	12.3 (3.61)	‡ (†)
Bachelor's or higher degree	83.3 (1.50)	82.7 (1.23)	83.8 (1.03)	139 (5.0)	73.4 (1.85)	74.5 (1.42)	75.5 (1.20)	125 (4.7)	11.9 (1.30)	10.0 (1.07)	9.9 (1.01)	14 (1.5)
American Indian/Alaska Native, all education levels	**65.9 (1.51)**	**71.8 (1.39)**	**67.9 (1.75)**	**83 (3.9)**	**48.2 (1.93)**	**50.6 (1.72)**	**48.0 (1.72)**	**59 (3.1)**	**26.9 (2.17)**	**29.5 (1.82)**	**29.3 (1.94)**	**24 (2.0)**
Less than high school completion	51.6 (3.44)	55.9 (3.41)	52.5 (3.50)	14 (1.3)	30.6 (3.27)	32.1 (3.53)	30.6 (3.32)	8 (1.0)	40.7 (4.85)	42.5 (4.49)	41.8 (5.16)	6 (0.9)
High school completion[4]	68.3 (2.13)	73.0 (1.68)	65.4 (2.44)	38 (2.1)	51.4 (3.02)	50.3 (2.25)	45.2 (2.58)	26 (2.0)	24.7 (3.23)	31.0 (2.44)	30.8 (3.13)	12 (1.4)
Some college, no degree	71.9 (3.25)	79.0 (2.84)	79.8 (2.32)	24 (2.1)	52.8 (4.15)	61.2 (3.13)	60.7 (3.32)	18 (1.8)	‡ (†)	22.5 (2.76)	23.9 (3.62)	6 (1.0)
Associate's degree	84.0 (6.15)	86.3 (5.12)	89.8 (5.17)	3 (0.8)	72.5 (8.45)	76.3 (7.99)	83.0 (6.10)	3 (0.8)	‡ (†)	‡ (†)	‡ (†)	‡ (†)
Bachelor's or higher degree	82.0 (8.14)	89.7 (4.84)	87.7 (4.03)	5 (1.0)	77.9 (8.00)	72.4 (10.74)	66.7 (7.86)	4 (0.8)	‡ (†)	‡ (†)	23.9 ! (9.08)	‡ (†)

†Not applicable.
!Interpret data with caution. The coefficient of variation (CV) for this estimate is between 30 and 50 percent.
‡Reporting standards not met. Either there are too few cases for a reliable estimate or the coefficient of variation (CV) is 50 percent or greater.
[1]Percentage of the civilian population who are employed or seeking employment.
[2]Number of persons employed as a percentage of the civilian population.
[3]The percentage of persons in the civilian labor force who are not working and who made specific efforts to find employment sometime during the prior 4 weeks.
[4]Includes equivalency credentials, such as the GED credential.
NOTE: Table excludes persons enrolled in school. Race categories exclude persons of Hispanic ethnicity. Totals include racial/ethnic groups not separately shown. Standard errors were computed using replicate weights.
SOURCE: U.S. Department of Commerce, Census Bureau, American Community Survey (ACS), 2011, 2012, and 2013, unpublished tabulations. (This table was prepared February 2015.)

Table 501.30. Number and percentage of persons 16 to 24 years old who were neither enrolled in school nor working, by educational attainment, age group, family poverty status, and race/ethnicity: 2014

[Standard errors appear in parentheses]

Age group, family poverty status, and race/ethnicity	All 16- to 24-year-olds (in thousands)	Neither enrolled in school nor working						
		Number (in thousands)	Percentage distribution	Percent, by educational attainment				
				Total	Less than high school completion	High school completion[1]	Some college, no bachelor's degree[2]	Bachelor's or higher degree
1	2	3	4	5	6	7	8	9
Total, 16 to 24 years old	38,950 (26.3)	5,497 (133.4)	100.0 (†)	14.1 (0.34)	10.9 (0.50)	28.7 (0.90)	8.9 (0.51)	8.9 (1.10)
White	21,642 (53.7)	2,586 (98.6)	47.0 (1.26)	12.0 (0.45)	8.3 (0.59)	26.9 (1.35)	7.9 (0.62)	7.0 (1.12)
Black	5,507 (38.8)	1,163 (62.9)	21.2 (1.06)	21.1 (1.14)	16.6 (1.62)	34.5 (2.38)	15.4 (1.88)	11.3 ! (4.20)
Hispanic	8,309 (9.5)	1,333 (61.4)	24.2 (1.00)	16.0 (0.74)	14.3 (1.14)	28.0 (1.59)	9.3 (1.04)	10.1 (2.97)
Asian	1,984 (37.4)	180 (24.8)	3.3 (0.44)	9.1 (1.25)	5.2 (1.40)	20.4 (4.39)	4.9 (1.42)	18.4 (5.08)
Pacific Islander	126 (25.0)	‡ (†)	0.2 ! (0.05)	6.9 ! (2.65)	‡ (†)	‡ (†)	‡ (†)	‡ (†)
American Indian/Alaska Native	391 (65.0)	115 (27.3)	2.1 (0.49)	29.5 (4.40)	19.7 (5.33)	49.4 (6.95)	16.8 ! (7.44)	‡ (†)
Two or more races	991 (48.5)	111 (17.1)	2.0 (0.31)	11.2 (1.73)	6.5 ! (2.17)	31.9 (5.46)	‡ (†)	‡ (†)
Family poverty status								
Poor[3]	7,170 (170.8)	1,959 (88.5)	100.0 (†)	27.3 (1.07)	22.3 (1.60)	49.4 (2.05)	17.0 (1.70)	14.6 (3.55)
White	3,075 (133.6)	728 (55.1)	37.2 (2.17)	23.7 (1.61)	21.4 (3.16)	45.5 (3.41)	14.5 (2.37)	11.6 ! (4.06)
Black	1,758 (90.6)	615 (55.1)	31.4 (2.33)	35.0 (2.34)	27.9 (3.29)	49.5 (3.93)	28.3 (4.46)	‡ (†)
Hispanic	1,768 (73.7)	481 (36.0)	24.6 (1.65)	27.2 (1.78)	21.0 (2.73)	50.5 (3.90)	15.0 (3.09)	‡ (†)
Asian	313 (38.7)	‡ (†)	2.4 (0.70)	15.1 (4.11)	‡ (†)	‡ (†)	‡ (†)	‡ (†)
Pacific Islander	‡ (†)	‡ (†)	‡ (†)	‡ (†)	‡ (†)	‡ (†)	‡ (†)	‡ (†)
American Indian/Alaska Native	105 ! (32.9)	‡ (†)	2.7 ! (0.85)	49.7 (7.65)	20.9 ! (9.80)	‡ (†)	‡ (†)	‡ (†)
Two or more races	142 (21.2)	‡ (†)	1.7 (0.48)	22.9 (5.63)	‡ (†)	‡ (†)	‡ (†)	‡ (†)
Nonpoor[3]	31,780 (173.5)	3,538 (114.8)	100.0 (†)	11.1 (0.35)	8.1 (0.48)	23.2 (0.90)	7.3 (0.54)	8.0 (1.08)
White	18,567 (139.7)	1,858 (86.8)	52.5 (1.62)	10.0 (0.45)	6.5 (0.54)	23.3 (1.31)	6.7 (0.67)	6.4 (1.08)
Black	3,750 (97.3)	548 (48.7)	15.5 (1.29)	14.6 (1.22)	10.0 (1.76)	25.9 (2.61)	11.3 (1.97)	8.6 ! (3.72)
Hispanic	6,540 (73.9)	852 (51.1)	24.1 (1.30)	13.0 (0.77)	11.9 (1.17)	21.8 (1.65)	8.3 (1.04)	8.0 ! (2.87)
Asian	1,671 (53.7)	132 (22.1)	3.7 (0.61)	7.9 (1.26)	4.4 ! (1.41)	13.7 ! (4.32)	4.2 ! (1.41)	22.9 (6.19)
Pacific Islander	117 (25.0)	‡ (†)	0.2 ! (0.07)	5.2 ! (2.32)	‡ (†)	‡ (†)	‡ (†)	‡ (†)
American Indian/Alaska Native	286 (41.5)	63 (16.0)	1.8 (0.45)	22.1 (4.67)	18.8 ! (8.23)	36.8 (8.70)	‡ (†)	‡ (†)
Two or more races	849 (48.3)	78 (15.0)	2.2 (0.41)	9.2 (1.78)	6.7 ! (2.41)	25.3 (5.29)	‡ (†)	‡ (†)
Total, 16 to 19 years old	16,679 (7.3)	1,314 (59.9)	100.0 (†)	7.9 (0.36)	5.6 (0.34)	22.5 (1.45)	5.6 (0.99)	‡ (†)
White	9,197 (30.1)	630 (41.0)	47.9 (2.28)	6.8 (0.45)	4.7 (0.41)	19.6 (1.89)	6.6 (1.40)	‡ (†)
Black	2,304 (23.5)	220 (26.7)	16.8 (1.87)	9.6 (1.14)	7.5 (1.03)	23.9 (4.41)	4.2 ! (1.92)	‡ (†)
Hispanic	3,657 (3.1)	371 (32.6)	28.2 (2.06)	10.1 (0.89)	7.5 (0.89)	28.0 (3.03)	5.8 (1.72)	‡ (†)
Asian	800 (32.7)	‡ (†)	1.9 ! (0.57)	3.1 (0.91)	2.7 ! (1.18)	10.7 ! (4.45)	‡ (†)	‡ (†)
Pacific Islander	62 (14.3)	‡ (†)	0.4 ! (0.19)	8.3 ! (3.94)	‡ (†)	‡ (†)	‡ (†)	‡ (†)
American Indian/Alaska Native	157 (33.1)	‡ (†)	‡ (†)	17.3 ! (6.14)	12.2 ! (5.11)	‡ (†)	‡ (†)	‡ (†)
Two or more races	502 (34.0)	‡ (†)	2.7 (0.74)	7.1 (1.92)	3.5 ! (1.44)	27.8 ! (8.78)	‡ (†)	‡ (†)
Poor[3]	2,752 (88.8)	439 (39.0)	33.4 (2.32)	15.9 (1.34)	11.3 (1.25)	37.4 (4.16)	14.7 ! (4.49)	‡ (†)
Nonpoor[3]	13,927 (90.4)	875 (46.1)	66.6 (2.32)	6.3 (0.33)	4.4 (0.33)	18.8 (1.47)	4.4 (0.82)	‡ (†)
Total, 20 to 24 years old	22,271 (26.0)	4,183 (119.6)	100.0 (†)	18.8 (0.54)	45.8 (2.42)	30.9 (1.10)	9.7 (0.59)	9.0 (1.13)
White	12,445 (44.1)	1,956 (90.6)	46.8 (1.45)	15.7 (0.72)	49.9 (4.16)	29.4 (1.74)	8.2 (0.74)	7.1 (1.14)
Black	3,203 (29.1)	943 (53.4)	22.5 (1.21)	29.4 (1.63)	61.6 (4.91)	37.6 (2.75)	17.8 (2.11)	11.9 ! (4.42)
Hispanic	4,652 (8.6)	962 (50.4)	23.0 (1.08)	20.7 (1.09)	36.6 (3.24)	28.0 (1.87)	10.3 (1.25)	10.0 (2.99)
Asian	1,184 (39.9)	155 (24.7)	3.7 (0.57)	13.1 (2.07)	‡ (†)	25.3 (6.26)	6.2 (1.85)	18.8 (5.15)
Pacific Islander	64 ! (19.4)	‡ (†)	0.1 ! (0.04)	‡ (†)	‡ (†)	‡ (†)	‡ (†)	‡ (†)
American Indian/Alaska Native	234 (37.8)	88 (17.6)	2.1 (0.42)	37.8 (6.54)	‡ (†)	52.1 (7.83)	‡ (†)	‡ (†)
Two or more races	489 (33.2)	75 (13.9)	1.8 (0.33)	15.4 (2.84)	‡ (†)	34.2 (6.30)	‡ (†)	‡ (†)
Poor[3]	4,418 (128.1)	1,521 (75.4)	36.3 (1.59)	34.4 (1.49)	55.3 (3.88)	53.1 (2.20)	17.4 (1.88)	14.6 (3.55)
Nonpoor[3]	17,853 (130.4)	2,663 (106.6)	63.7 (1.59)	14.9 (0.57)	40.1 (3.01)	24.7 (1.19)	8.0 (0.64)	8.2 (1.10)

†Not applicable.

!Interpret data with caution. The coefficient of variation (CV) for this estimate is between 30 and 50 percent.

‡Reporting standards not met. Either there are too few cases for a reliable estimate or the coefficient of variation (CV) is 50 percent or greater.

[1]Includes equivalency credentials, such as the GED credential.

[2]Includes persons with no college degree as well as those with an associate's degree.

[3]Poor is defined to include families with incomes below the poverty threshold. Nonpoor is defined to include families with incomes at or above the poverty threshold. For information about how the Census Bureau determines who is in poverty, see http://www.census.gov/hhes/www/poverty/about/overview/measure.html.

NOTE: Race categories exclude persons of Hispanic ethnicity. Standard errors were computed using replicate weights. Detail may not sum to totals because of rounding.

SOURCE: U.S. Department of Commerce, Census Bureau, Current Population Survey (CPS), March 2014, unpublished data. (This table was prepared February 2015.)

Table 501.40. Percentage distribution of 25- to 34-year-olds with various levels of educational attainment, by labor force status, sex, race/ethnicity, and U.S. nativity and citizenship status: 2013

[Standard errors appear in parentheses]

Sex, race/ethnicity, and U.S. nativity and citizenship status	All 25- to 34-year-olds — In labor force, Employed	Unemployed (seeking employment)	Not in labor force	Less than high school completion — In labor force, Employed	Unemployed (seeking employment)	Not in labor force	High school completion[1] — In labor force, Employed	Unemployed (seeking employment)	Not in labor force	Some college, no bachelor's degree[2] — In labor force, Employed	Unemployed (seeking employment)	Not in labor force	Bachelor's or higher degree — In labor force, Employed	Unemployed (seeking employment)	Not in labor force
1	2	3	4	5	6	7	8	9	10	11	12	13	14	15	16
Total	74.6 (0.09)	7.1 (0.06)	18.2 (0.08)	54.4 (0.30)	10.9 (0.18)	34.7 (0.30)	67.5 (0.21)	9.7 (0.12)	22.9 (0.18)	75.7 (0.15)	7.4 (0.09)	16.9 (0.14)	85.9 (0.11)	3.7 (0.06)	10.4 (0.11)
Sex															
Male	79.2 (0.13)	7.6 (0.08)	13.2 (0.11)	64.8 (0.36)	10.5 (0.24)	24.7 (0.30)	73.3 (0.28)	10.1 (0.16)	16.7 (0.22)	80.8 (0.25)	7.6 (0.15)	11.6 (0.20)	89.9 (0.16)	3.9 (0.10)	6.3 (0.12)
Female	70.0 (0.12)	6.7 (0.07)	23.3 (0.12)	40.4 (0.45)	11.5 (0.33)	48.2 (0.49)	59.6 (0.33)	9.1 (0.21)	31.3 (0.30)	71.0 (0.20)	7.3 (0.13)	21.7 (0.19)	82.9 (0.17)	3.5 (0.07)	13.6 (0.15)
Race/ethnicity															
White	77.9 (0.11)	6.0 (0.06)	16.1 (0.10)	49.0 (0.57)	12.6 (0.35)	38.3 (0.59)	72.5 (0.25)	8.9 (0.15)	21.8 (0.25)	77.3 (0.17)	6.2 (0.11)	16.5 (0.17)	87.9 (0.13)	3.1 (0.07)	9.0 (0.12)
Black	65.7 (0.30)	12.7 (0.21)	21.6 (0.24)	34.6 (0.84)	18.5 (0.60)	46.8 (0.88)	57.5 (0.58)	15.2 (0.46)	27.2 (0.45)	71.5 (0.48)	12.2 (0.30)	16.3 (0.37)	86.3 (0.38)	6.3 (0.30)	7.4 (0.28)
Hispanic	72.2 (0.30)	7.2 (0.12)	20.7 (0.17)	63.9 (0.39)	7.6 (0.21)	28.5 (0.37)	70.9 (0.38)	7.8 (0.21)	21.3 (0.34)	75.9 (0.39)	7.2 (0.24)	16.9 (0.34)	83.7 (0.47)	4.9 (0.29)	11.4 (0.39)
Asian	74.2 (0.39)	4.8 (0.12)	21.0 (0.17)	59.1 (1.46)	7.2 (0.99)	33.7 (1.37)	70.7 (1.10)	6.7 (0.64)	24.1 (1.03)	75.9 (0.77)	6.6 (0.43)	21.0 (0.74)	76.9 (0.48)	3.8 (0.18)	19.4 (0.44)
Pacific Islander	65.7 (2.26)	10.9 (1.63)	23.4 (1.91)	39.7 (6.39)	12.4 (5.77)	47.9 (7.45)	63.7 (3.77)	10.7 (2.61)	25.6 (3.21)	71.0 (2.98)	8.0 (2.13)	21.0 (2.82)	74.7 (4.94)	17.3 (5.17)	8.1 (2.34)
American Indian/Alaska Native[3]	57.9 (1.21)	11.4 (0.64)	30.7 (1.07)	31.3 (2.70)	17.3 (1.94)	51.4 (2.76)	54.1 (1.95)	12.8 (1.11)	33.1 (1.81)	64.1 (1.71)	10.0 (0.94)	25.9 (1.66)	85.0 (2.06)	4.2 ‡ (1.35)	10.8 (1.61)
American Indian	57.5 (1.20)	11.6 (0.71)	30.9 (1.08)	29.3 (2.71)	17.3 (2.01)	53.4 (2.79)	54.6 (2.08)	13.2 (1.24)	32.3 (1.78)	62.7 (1.86)	10.1 (0.95)	27.2 (1.84)	85.5 (2.40)	4.8 ‡ (1.64)	9.7 ‡ (1.98)
Alaska Native	54.5 (5.01)	13.8 (3.19)	31.6 (4.97)	32.1 ‡ (10.46)	12.8 ‡ (5.80)	55.1 (10.33)	52.0 (6.78)	16.6 ‡ (5.26)	31.4 (8.22)	71.7 (7.32)	11.3 ‡ (4.11)	17.0 ‡ (6.70)	83.2 (†)	‡ (†)	11.8 ‡ (0.83)
Two or more races	70.9 (0.61)	9.1 (0.42)	20.0 (0.51)	37.1 (2.92)	20.4 (2.73)	42.5 (2.87)	60.5 (1.55)	11.2 (0.88)	28.3 (1.34)	70.9 (1.23)	10.0 (0.77)	19.1 (0.96)	83.2 (0.87)	4.9 (0.52)	11.8 (0.63)
Race/ethnicity by sex															
Male															
White	82.0 (0.15)	6.8 (0.09)	11.2 (0.13)	57.3 (0.66)	13.6 (0.51)	29.1 (0.69)	75.2 (0.30)	9.6 (0.19)	15.2 (0.28)	83.2 (0.27)	6.5 (0.17)	10.3 (0.22)	91.1 (0.17)	3.5 (0.11)	5.4 (0.14)
Black	62.5 (0.48)	13.1 (0.33)	24.3 (0.42)	31.3 (1.19)	16.6 (0.81)	52.1 (1.30)	55.9 (0.79)	15.5 (0.60)	28.7 (0.66)	71.4 (0.72)	12.6 (0.45)	16.0 (0.58)	87.3 (0.73)	6.0 (0.50)	6.7 (0.54)
Hispanic	81.5 (0.27)	6.9 (0.17)	11.7 (0.21)	79.4 (0.43)	6.6 (0.27)	14.0 (0.34)	80.7 (0.48)	7.5 (0.28)	11.8 (0.40)	82.2 (0.52)	6.9 (0.49)	10.8 (0.66)	87.5 (0.73)	5.6 (0.54)	6.9 (0.50)
Asian	83.0 (0.48)	4.9 (0.17)	12.1 (0.21)	70.8 (2.17)	8.4 (1.10)	20.7 (1.87)	78.7 (1.38)	8.5 (1.10)	12.8 (1.38)	79.1 (1.15)	7.0 ‡ (2.53)	13.9 (4.07)	86.8 (0.53)	3.2 (0.27)	10.0 (0.46)
Pacific Islander	75.9 (2.83)	9.5 (1.91)	14.6 (2.27)	62.7 (8.83)	‡ (†)	‡ (†)	53.0 (4.16)	16.0 (2.94)	31.0 (3.45)	69.2 (2.27)	9.6 (2.53)	21.2 (1.88)	87.9 (10.06)	5.4 ‡ (2.37)	6.7 ‡ (2.24)
American Indian/Alaska Native[3]	58.3 (1.33)	14.0 (0.94)	27.7 (1.18)	33.5 (3.41)	22.5 (3.24)	44.1 (3.21)	53.4 (2.29)	16.0 (1.68)	30.6 (2.05)	67.5 (2.42)	9.9 (1.40)	22.7 (1.88)	88.8 (3.25)	‡ (†)	‡ (†)
American Indian	58.0 (1.42)	13.9 (0.98)	28.1 (1.18)	31.8 (3.83)	22.2 (3.28)	46.1 (3.28)	54.0 (2.77)	16.0 (1.68)	30.0 (2.77)	74.2 (12.05)	10.3 (1.39)	15.8 (2.10)	88.8 (3.55)	‡ (†)	‡ (†)
Alaska Native	55.3 (5.72)	19.3 (4.49)	25.4 (4.33)	‡ (3.68)	‡ (3.54)	60.5 (10.14)	54.0 (8.34)	27.5 (8.09)	18.6 (5.30)	74.6 (1.53)	‡ (1.06)	15.8 (1.16)	85.9 (1.28)	5.5 (0.99)	8.6 (0.91)
Two or more races	73.3 (0.95)	9.7 (0.52)	17.0 (0.80)	44.4 (3.68)	19.4 (3.54)	36.2 (3.95)	64.0 (2.00)	12.4 (1.22)	23.6 (1.70)	74.6 (1.53)	9.6 (1.06)	15.8 (1.16)	85.9 (1.28)	5.5 (0.99)	8.6 (0.91)
Female															
White	73.8 (0.14)	5.2 (0.08)	21.0 (0.10)	37.7 (0.84)	11.3 (0.59)	51.0 (0.86)	60.6 (0.42)	7.9 (0.25)	31.5 (0.42)	71.6 (0.60)	5.9 (0.15)	22.6 (0.24)	85.4 (0.19)	2.8 (0.09)	11.8 (0.17)
Black	68.6 (0.37)	12.3 (0.27)	19.2 (0.34)	39.0 (1.04)	21.1 (1.04)	39.9 (1.16)	60.6 (0.87)	14.9 (0.64)	25.4 (0.74)	71.6 (0.60)	11.8 (0.44)	16.6 (0.51)	85.7 (0.52)	6.4 (0.40)	7.8 (0.42)
Hispanic	61.9 (0.37)	7.5 (0.17)	30.6 (0.27)	42.4 (0.67)	9.0 (0.36)	48.6 (0.69)	58.1 (0.60)	8.2 (0.33)	33.6 (0.61)	70.2 (0.56)	7.5 (0.33)	22.4 (0.51)	80.9 (0.58)	4.4 (0.26)	14.6 (0.57)
Asian	66.3 (0.57)	4.8 (0.25)	28.9 (0.52)	48.3 (2.51)	6.1 (1.29)	45.6 (2.35)	59.9 (1.70)	5.0 (0.71)	35.1 (1.67)	63.9 (0.99)	5.8 (0.49)	26.2 (0.66)	68.2 (0.53)	4.3 (0.26)	27.5 (0.64)
Pacific Islander	55.8 (3.24)	12.3 (2.32)	31.9 (2.74)	28.3 (3.94)	9.9 (2.35)	62.7 (11.56)	47.0 (6.16)	11.7 (4.33)	41.4 (5.11)	63.9 (5.12)	8.8 (3.31)	27.3 (4.85)	73.0 (5.94)	17.1 ‡ (5.95)	9.9 (2.86)
American Indian/Alaska Native[3]	57.4 (1.62)	8.9 (0.81)	33.7 (1.61)	26.1 (3.42)	10.6 (2.51)	63.3 (3.82)	55.4 (2.82)	9.1 (1.44)	35.6 (2.93)	58.9 (2.66)	10.3 (1.27)	29.7 (2.27)	82.8 (2.72)	3.4 ‡ (1.45)	13.8 (2.53)
American Indian	56.9 (1.64)	9.4 (0.89)	33.7 (1.65)	26.1 (3.42)	‡ (†)	61.8 (4.13)	55.4 (2.83)	9.9 (1.61)	34.1 (2.57)	58.9 (2.83)	10.3 (1.39)	30.8 (2.57)	83.0 (3.38)	4.1 ‡ (1.78)	12.9 (3.14)
Alaska Native	53.7 (8.88)	7.9 ‡ (2.69)	38.4 (9.23)	31.8 (†)	‡ (†)	‡ (†)	49.7 (14.39)	‡ (†)	‡ (†)	69.5 (8.58)	12.0 (5.86)	18.5 (8.83)	81.2 ‡ (1.33)	‡ (†)	14.4 (1.23)
Two or more races	68.7 (0.99)	8.6 (0.52)	22.8 (0.85)	27.5 (4.28)	21.8 (3.65)	50.7 (4.31)	55.8 (2.42)	9.6 (1.31)	34.7 (2.22)	67.7 (1.62)	10.3 (1.06)	21.9 (1.32)	81.2 (1.33)	4.5 (0.58)	14.4 (1.23)
Nativity															
Hispanic															
Born within United States[4]	71.9 (0.31)	8.4 (0.18)	19.6 (0.23)	51.1 (0.80)	12.5 (0.53)	36.4 (0.83)	68.9 (0.54)	9.4 (0.30)	21.7 (0.48)	75.8 (0.45)	7.8 (0.27)	16.4 (0.44)	85.7 (0.56)	4.9 (0.35)	9.4 (0.39)
Born outside United States[4]	72.4 (0.46)	5.7 (0.16)	21.9 (0.27)	68.9 (0.45)	5.7 (0.23)	25.4 (0.41)	73.0 (0.52)	6.0 (0.30)	20.9 (0.54)	76.2 (0.63)	5.8 (0.45)	18.1 (0.58)	79.3 (0.93)	4.9 (0.46)	15.8 (0.80)
Asian															
Born within United States[4]	81.3 (0.55)	5.1 (0.36)	13.6 (0.44)	53.0 (3.70)	4.7 (1.37)	42.2 (3.93)	75.0 (2.07)	6.2 (0.98)	18.8 (1.88)	78.0 (1.18)	7.1 (0.79)	14.9 (1.18)	85.3 (0.68)	4.0 (0.36)	10.7 (0.54)
Born outside United States[4]	71.1 (0.46)	4.7 (0.20)	24.2 (0.43)	60.4 (1.71)	7.8 (1.15)	31.8 (1.69)	66.6 (1.36)	6.9 (0.81)	26.5 (1.21)	68.9 (0.99)	6.2 (0.48)	24.9 (0.99)	73.4 (0.56)	3.7 (0.21)	22.9 (0.53)
Citizenship status															
U.S.-born citizen	75.3 (0.10)	7.4 (0.05)	17.3 (0.09)	45.3 (0.41)	14.3 (0.27)	40.4 (0.41)	66.7 (0.23)	10.3 (0.13)	23.1 (0.21)	76.1 (0.16)	7.5 (0.10)	16.4 (0.16)	88.1 (0.11)	3.5 (0.06)	8.4 (0.10)
Naturalized citizen	78.2 (0.36)	6.0 (0.21)	15.8 (0.31)	66.4 (1.49)	7.5 (0.86)	26.0 (1.35)	74.2 (0.91)	7.1 (0.57)	18.7 (0.83)	77.6 (0.66)	5.7 (0.40)	16.7 (0.52)	83.5 (0.52)	5.4 (0.30)	11.1 (0.44)
Noncitizen	69.2 (0.25)	5.7 (0.14)	25.1 (0.24)	67.6 (0.46)	5.9 (0.22)	26.5 (0.44)	70.4 (0.60)	6.6 (0.29)	23.0 (0.57)	68.9 (0.71)	7.2 (0.42)	23.9 (0.64)	70.2 (0.52)	3.7 (0.15)	26.0 (0.49)

†Not applicable.
‡Reporting standards not met. Either there are too few cases for a reliable estimate or the coefficient of variation (CV) is 50 percent or greater.
Interpret data with caution. The coefficient of variation (CV) for this estimate is between 30 and 50 percent.

[1]Data are for all persons with high school completion as their highest level of education, including those with equivalency credentials, such as the GED credential.
[2]Includes persons with no college degree as well as those with an associate's degree.
[3]Includes persons reporting American Indian alone, persons reporting Alaska Native alone, and persons from American Indian and/or Alaska Native tribes specified or not specified.

[4]United States refers to the 50 states, the District of Columbia, Puerto Rico, American Samoa, Guam, the U.S. Virgin Islands, and the Northern Marianas. Children born abroad to U.S. citizen parents are also counted as born within the United States.
NOTE: Estimates are for the entire population in the indicated age range, including persons living in households and persons living in group quarters (such as college residence halls, residential treatment centers, military barracks, and correctional facilities). The labor force consists of all employed persons plus those seeking employment. Standard errors were computed using replicate weights. Detail may not sum to totals because of rounding. Race categories exclude persons of Hispanic ethnicity.
SOURCE: U.S. Department of Commerce, Census Bureau, American Community Survey (ACS), 2013. (This table was prepared February 2015.)

Table 501.50. Employment to population ratios of persons 16 to 64 years old, by age group and highest level of educational attainment: Selected years, 1975 through 2014

[Standard errors appear in parentheses]

Age group and highest level of educational attainment	1975	1980	1985	1990	1995	2000	2004	2005	2008	2009	2010	2011	2012	2013	2014
1	2	3	4	5	6	7	8	9	10	11	12	13	14	15	16
16 to 19 years old, all education levels[1]	— (†)	— (†)	— (†)	60.8 (2.03)	58.0 (2.13)	62.6 (2.09)	56.7 (1.67)	53.7 (1.40)	53.5 (1.41)	46.6 (1.36)	43.2 (1.30)	44.8 (1.40)	45.8 (1.43)	46.3 (1.40)	51.0 (1.67)
Less than high school completion	— (†)	— (†)	— (†)	44.2 (3.08)	44.0 (3.13)	52.2 (3.19)	42.9 (2.46)	39.4 (2.01)	37.5 (1.90)	31.1 (1.89)	29.4 (1.83)	31.1 (2.21)	28.5 (2.05)	32.6 (2.03)	39.7 (2.63)
High school completion[2]	— (†)	— (†)	— (†)	74.2 (2.54)	70.1 (2.99)	70.1 (2.92)	67.8 (2.36)	65.0 (2.04)	64.3 (1.96)	53.6 (1.72)	51.1 (1.84)	50.3 (2.01)	53.6 (1.90)	52.7 (2.15)	58.5 (2.22)
At least some college	— (†)	— (†)	— (†)	76.8 (9.32)	71.6 (6.38)	78.2 (6.22)	72.0 (5.04)	66.6 (4.54)	65.3 (3.89)	65.4 (3.70)	57.5 (3.99)	61.5 (3.63)	64.3 (4.07)	63.5 (3.96)	60.5 (5.27)
20 to 24 years old, all education levels[1]	— (†)	— (†)	— (†)	75.6 (0.90)	73.7 (0.93)	77.4 (0.93)	73.0 (0.69)	73.2 (0.66)	73.4 (0.60)	68.3 (0.66)	65.5 (0.72)	67.0 (0.59)	68.7 (0.67)	68.5 (0.72)	69.4 (0.74)
Less than high school completion	— (†)	— (†)	— (†)	54.4 (2.29)	52.7 (2.41)	60.8 (2.43)	59.5 (1.69)	55.7 (1.27)	55.1 (1.73)	50.6 (1.60)	44.4 (1.58)	46.8 (1.71)	47.7 (1.95)	46.8 (1.88)	46.6 (2.62)
High school completion[2]	— (†)	— (†)	— (†)	76.6 (1.26)	72.2 (1.46)	76.5 (1.46)	70.6 (1.09)	72.3 (0.91)	69.8 (0.97)	63.9 (1.03)	61.5 (1.01)	62.9 (1.07)	64.2 (0.99)	63.5 (1.16)	63.7 (1.31)
Some college, no bachelor's degree[3]	— (†)	— (†)	— (†)	85.6 (1.69)	83.6 (1.52)	86.6 (1.49)	80.1 (1.26)	80.3 (1.19)	81.8 (1.09)	74.9 (1.32)	73.2 (1.01)	73.2 (1.01)	75.3 (1.19)	75.0 (1.15)	75.0 (1.29)
Bachelor's or higher degree	— (†)	— (†)	— (†)	93.3 (1.57)	90.9 (1.76)	87.8 (2.07)	87.8 (1.38)	89.3 (1.16)	89.6 (1.21)	87.2 (1.26)	86.5 (1.37)	85.2 (1.41)	87.3 (1.16)	86.6 (1.46)	88.1 (1.47)
25 to 64 years old, all education levels	65.8 (0.33)	70.2 (0.30)	71.6 (0.30)	75.0 (0.29)	75.5 (0.28)	77.7 (0.27)	74.8 (0.20)	75.0 (0.19)	75.5 (0.16)	72.2 (0.19)	71.5 (0.19)	71.2 (0.19)	71.7 (0.18)	72.1 (0.19)	72.3 (0.26)
Less than high school completion	55.3 (0.62)	55.5 (0.66)	53.1 (0.74)	54.9 (0.80)	53.8 (0.85)	57.8 (0.91)	56.5 (0.64)	57.2 (0.51)	56.2 (0.51)	52.5 (0.57)	52.1 (0.60)	51.1 (0.56)	52.9 (0.60)	53.2 (0.60)	54.9 (0.78)
High school completion[2]	65.7 (0.53)	70.4 (0.48)	70.7 (0.48)	74.4 (0.46)	73.3 (0.49)	75.5 (0.49)	71.5 (0.36)	71.5 (0.34)	71.6 (0.28)	67.8 (0.33)	67.0 (0.36)	66.2 (0.39)	66.5 (0.35)	66.7 (0.38)	67.0 (0.44)
Some college, no bachelor's degree[3]	71.7 (0.86)	76.1 (0.70)	77.8 (0.66)	80.2 (0.60)	79.5 (0.51)	80.7 (0.50)	77.2 (0.36)	77.7 (0.33)	77.5 (0.31)	73.9 (0.33)	72.7 (0.30)	72.2 (0.30)	72.2 (0.30)	73.1 (0.31)	72.6 (0.44)
Bachelor's or higher degree	82.5 (0.68)	84.5 (0.55)	85.6 (0.51)	86.7 (0.47)	86.5 (0.44)	86.4 (0.42)	83.4 (0.31)	83.7 (0.26)	84.4 (0.27)	82.2 (0.25)	81.6 (0.24)	81.5 (0.26)	82.1 (0.24)	81.9 (0.26)	82.0 (0.34)
25 to 34 years old, all education levels	67.7 (0.59)	74.5 (0.49)	76.2 (0.48)	76.2 (0.47)	78.5 (0.48)	81.6 (0.49)	76.8 (0.38)	76.8 (0.31)	78.1 (0.31)	74.2 (0.36)	73.2 (0.34)	73.0 (0.35)	73.8 (0.31)	74.6 (0.33)	74.5 (0.43)
Less than high school completion	52.9 (1.43)	58.3 (1.46)	57.0 (1.54)	60.3 (1.50)	59.8 (1.59)	64.1 (1.76)	62.2 (1.19)	62.0 (0.95)	60.4 (0.93)	54.6 (1.07)	55.1 (0.95)	54.2 (1.17)	56.2 (1.14)	57.4 (1.03)	57.8 (1.37)
High school completion[2]	65.5 (0.92)	72.0 (0.81)	74.3 (0.78)	77.7 (0.74)	77.0 (0.84)	80.2 (0.91)	73.8 (0.73)	73.1 (0.60)	74.0 (0.60)	69.0 (0.66)	68.1 (0.72)	67.9 (0.67)	68.7 (0.75)	68.2 (0.68)	68.2 (0.73)
Some college, no bachelor's degree[3]	71.7 (1.33)	77.8 (1.01)	80.1 (0.97)	81.6 (0.96)	80.5 (0.87)	82.8 (0.90)	77.6 (0.70)	79.4 (0.54)	79.9 (0.52)	75.9 (0.60)	72.9 (0.57)	73.0 (0.62)	72.7 (0.68)	73.1 (0.64)	77.3 (0.68)
Bachelor's or higher degree	82.0 (1.04)	85.4 (0.82)	86.6 (0.79)	88.1 (0.76)	88.1 (0.75)	89.0 (0.73)	85.2 (0.57)	84.4 (0.52)	86.8 (0.46)	84.5 (0.49)	84.0 (0.49)	83.4 (0.45)	84.3 (0.45)	84.4 (0.45)	84.0 (0.59)
35 to 44 years old, all education levels	70.3 (0.66)	76.5 (0.58)	78.1 (0.54)	81.6 (0.48)	80.2 (0.46)	81.8 (0.45)	79.0 (0.34)	79.9 (0.26)	80.1 (0.30)	76.7 (0.29)	76.0 (0.30)	76.0 (0.35)	76.9 (0.35)	77.0 (0.35)	77.1 (0.40)
Less than high school completion	61.4 (1.31)	63.4 (1.39)	60.0 (1.58)	62.5 (1.69)	58.6 (1.66)	64.8 (1.64)	63.5 (1.17)	64.9 (0.93)	64.3 (1.05)	60.2 (1.01)	58.2 (1.13)	57.5 (1.04)	59.6 (1.13)	61.6 (1.03)	61.3 (1.25)
High school completion[2]	69.6 (1.02)	76.6 (0.90)	76.6 (0.88)	80.0 (0.80)	78.6 (0.82)	81.0 (0.79)	76.9 (0.63)	78.0 (0.52)	76.9 (0.57)	72.6 (0.63)	72.4 (0.64)	71.8 (0.64)	72.1 (0.68)	72.6 (0.66)	72.6 (0.80)
Some college, no bachelor's degree[3]	74.5 (1.74)	80.9 (1.33)	81.6 (1.15)	85.0 (0.93)	83.3 (0.81)	84.4 (0.80)	81.8 (0.63)	82.0 (0.48)	82.4 (0.58)	78.5 (0.53)	76.9 (0.53)	76.9 (0.62)	78.2 (0.61)	77.0 (0.64)	77.3 (0.68)
Bachelor's or higher degree	84.5 (1.31)	87.1 (1.00)	88.8 (0.80)	89.5 (0.72)	88.5 (0.71)	87.6 (0.74)	85.3 (0.55)	85.9 (0.41)	86.4 (0.40)	84.8 (0.42)	84.7 (0.39)	84.8 (0.43)	85.0 (0.41)	84.8 (0.43)	85.0 (0.57)
45 to 54 years old, all education levels	68.4 (0.65)	71.7 (0.65)	73.5 (0.67)	77.6 (0.62)	78.8 (0.55)	81.2 (0.50)	78.3 (0.36)	78.4 (0.32)	78.4 (0.33)	75.2 (0.34)	74.7 (0.35)	74.3 (0.32)	74.6 (0.30)	74.9 (0.30)	76.2 (0.43)
Less than high school completion	59.8 (1.14)	58.7 (1.24)	58.7 (1.52)	60.7 (1.63)	58.4 (1.79)	60.3 (1.89)	56.4 (1.33)	59.0 (1.04)	56.0 (1.02)	54.0 (1.13)	52.5 (1.05)	51.7 (0.84)	54.7 (1.06)	53.3 (1.04)	59.4 (1.50)
High school completion[2]	68.8 (1.03)	72.0 (1.02)	77.5 (1.03)	77.5 (0.97)	78.2 (1.01)	78.2 (0.95)	75.8 (0.66)	75.1 (0.64)	75.4 (0.57)	71.6 (0.53)	71.0 (0.56)	70.1 (0.58)	70.4 (0.62)	70.1 (0.60)	70.7 (0.84)
Some college, no bachelor's degree[3]	74.7 (1.81)	76.5 (1.72)	79.2 (1.63)	81.9 (1.38)	81.7 (1.03)	83.4 (0.91)	80.5 (0.65)	80.4 (0.57)	80.2 (0.51)	77.3 (0.58)	77.3 (0.55)	76.6 (0.53)	76.2 (0.53)	77.4 (0.53)	77.4 (0.76)
Bachelor's or higher degree	87.1 (1.36)	87.3 (1.21)	87.9 (1.16)	89.4 (0.97)	89.5 (0.78)	89.7 (0.71)	86.3 (0.54)	87.5 (0.45)	88.1 (0.45)	85.2 (0.45)	84.4 (0.45)	84.9 (0.45)	84.7 (0.48)	84.7 (0.47)	85.9 (0.54)
55 to 64 years old, all education levels	54.6 (0.77)	52.1 (0.73)	52.1 (0.77)	53.4 (0.81)	55.0 (0.82)	58.1 (0.79)	60.4 (0.51)	60.8 (0.48)	62.8 (0.41)	60.8 (0.42)	60.6 (0.41)	60.2 (0.43)	60.6 (0.41)	61.3 (0.43)	60.9 (0.52)
Less than high school completion	48.5 (1.11)	41.8 (1.16)	41.8 (1.29)	39.5 (1.46)	40.4 (1.67)	40.4 (1.84)	39.9 (1.38)	39.4 (1.13)	41.0 (1.24)	38.2 (1.19)	40.0 (1.19)	39.1 (1.15)	39.1 (1.08)	38.5 (1.32)	39.6 (1.34)
High school completion[2]	56.5 (1.32)	52.5 (1.19)	54.0 (1.22)	54.0 (1.29)	55.3 (1.34)	55.4 (1.34)	55.3 (0.90)	57.8 (0.79)	57.8 (0.69)	55.8 (0.73)	55.1 (0.71)	54.4 (0.81)	54.6 (0.75)	56.3 (0.74)	57.6 (0.90)
Some college, no bachelor's degree[3]	62.6 (2.48)	58.9 (2.08)	60.4 (2.21)	60.4 (2.12)	62.0 (1.74)	62.4 (1.64)	64.0 (1.00)	64.8 (0.90)	64.8 (0.80)	61.6 (0.74)	61.8 (0.76)	61.2 (0.78)	61.2 (0.70)	62.3 (0.72)	60.5 (0.99)
Bachelor's or higher degree	72.6 (2.34)	71.9 (1.96)	71.3 (1.83)	70.5 (1.79)	70.0 (1.72)	71.9 (1.49)	73.2 (0.87)	73.5 (0.74)	74.0 (0.68)	72.7 (0.63)	72.0 (0.65)	71.8 (0.71)	73.1 (0.66)	72.4 (0.67)	71.7 (0.90)

—Not available.
†Not applicable.
[1]Data for 16- to 19-year-olds and 20- to 24-year-olds exclude persons enrolled in school.
[2]Includes equivalency credentials, such as the General Educational Development (GED) credential.
[3]Includes persons with no college degree as well as those with an associate's degree.

NOTE: For each age group, the employment to population ratio is the number of persons in that age group who are employed as a percentage of the civilian population in that age group.
SOURCE: U.S. Department of Labor, Bureau of Labor Statistics, Office of Employment and Unemployment Statistics, unpublished annual average data from the Current Population Survey (CPS), selected years, 1975 through 2014. (This table was prepared November 2014.)

Table 501.60. Employment to population ratios of males 16 to 64 years old, by age group and highest level of educational attainment: Selected years, 1975 through 2014

[Standard errors appear in parentheses]

Age group and highest level of educational attainment	1975	1980	1985	1990	1995	2000	2004	2005	2008	2009	2010	2011	2012	2013	2014
1	2	3	4	5	6	7	8	9	10	11	12	13	14	15	16
16 to 19 years old, all education levels[1]	(†)	(†)	(†)	65.3 (2.82)	63.6 (2.87)	69.2 (2.70)	61.0 (2.20)	56.2 (2.10)	58.7 (1.72)	45.8 (1.77)	44.0 (1.72)	47.0 (1.94)	48.1 (2.00)	48.1 (1.92)	51.9 (2.37)
Less than high school completion	(†)	(†)	(†)	51.5 (4.20)	50.6 (4.26)	63.1 (4.09)	49.4 (3.27)	47.0 (3.07)	45.8 (2.44)	34.0 (2.70)	31.5 (2.64)	37.4 (3.03)	34.7 (3.25)	33.9 (2.63)	43.6 (3.64)
High school completion[2]	(†)	(†)	(†)	78.7 (3.51)	76.1 (3.87)	74.4 (3.77)	71.4 (3.04)	63.1 (2.88)	67.1 (2.47)	51.1 (2.35)	51.0 (2.37)	51.2 (2.84)	52.5 (2.51)	55.8 (2.86)	58.1 (3.28)
At least some college	(†)	(†)	(†)	83.1 (13.41)	75.9 (8.99)	77.0 (9.81)	72.4 (7.16)	70.4 (5.98)	74.3 (4.67)	62.9 (5.37)	61.4 (6.00)	60.2 (5.67)	64.2 (5.72)	65.9 (5.64)	57.6 (8.04)
20 to 24 years old, all education levels[1]	(†)	(†)	(†)	83.5 (1.10)	81.2 (1.16)	83.3 (1.16)	80.9 (0.83)	78.9 (0.86)	79.1 (0.68)	70.6 (0.86)	68.4 (0.97)	69.5 (0.84)	72.1 (0.96)	71.4 (0.95)	72.4 (1.04)
Less than high school completion	(†)	(†)	(†)	70.0 (2.84)	69.3 (2.99)	72.1 (2.93)	71.4 (2.03)	69.5 (1.80)	68.2 (2.11)	59.2 (2.28)	52.9 (2.06)	57.3 (2.43)	56.6 (2.42)	57.0 (2.54)	58.3 (3.16)
High school completion[2]	(†)	(†)	(†)	84.6 (1.50)	81.1 (1.73)	82.7 (1.78)	76.3 (1.35)	78.0 (1.21)	76.9 (1.05)	66.9 (1.38)	66.0 (1.31)	66.2 (1.31)	68.0 (1.43)	67.3 (1.47)	66.6 (1.77)
Some college, no bachelor's degree[3]	(†)	(†)	(†)	91.8 (1.98)	87.5 (1.97)	92.6 (1.65)	85.5 (1.54)	84.6 (1.43)	85.2 (1.38)	77.7 (1.69)	74.8 (1.71)	75.2 (1.66)	80.5 (1.59)	77.9 (1.51)	78.6 (1.82)
Bachelor's or higher degree	(†)	(†)	(†)	94.9 (2.07)	91.1 (2.70)	89.1 (3.07)	90.1 (2.00)	90.6 (1.82)	92.4 (1.51)	86.4 (1.94)	86.3 (2.04)	84.7 (2.16)	88.7 (1.77)	86.1 (2.11)	90.6 (1.93)
25 to 64 years old, all education levels	84.6 (0.36)	85.0 (0.34)	83.1 (0.36)	84.5 (0.34)	83.0 (0.34)	84.6 (0.33)	83.0 (0.24)	81.9 (0.25)	81.6 (0.22)	77.0 (0.25)	76.3 (0.27)	76.3 (0.27)	77.4 (0.25)	78.2 (0.27)	78.2 (0.35)
Less than high school completion	74.3 (0.77)	72.4 (0.84)	67.6 (0.98)	67.9 (1.04)	64.2 (1.13)	69.6 (1.17)	70.9 (0.79)	69.7 (0.70)	66.6 (0.78)	61.6 (0.80)	61.2 (0.93)	61.0 (0.81)	63.0 (0.77)	64.0 (0.75)	66.3 (1.04)
High school completion[2]	87.2 (0.56)	87.0 (0.54)	83.5 (0.58)	85.1 (0.55)	81.9 (0.61)	82.9 (0.61)	82.0 (0.43)	78.6 (0.44)	78.3 (0.42)	72.1 (0.49)	71.7 (0.50)	71.8 (0.50)	72.6 (0.45)	73.1 (0.51)	73.6 (0.59)
Some college, no bachelor's degree[3]	88.8 (0.83)	88.3 (0.73)	87.1 (0.75)	87.9 (0.70)	86.1 (0.63)	86.1 (0.63)	83.3 (0.47)	83.7 (0.44)	82.9 (0.42)	78.1 (0.41)	76.6 (0.42)	75.9 (0.45)	77.3 (0.43)	78.3 (0.46)	77.5 (0.59)
Bachelor's or higher degree	93.8 (0.55)	93.6 (0.48)	92.4 (0.50)	92.5 (0.48)	91.4 (0.48)	91.8 (0.47)	89.1 (0.36)	89.4 (0.35)	90.0 (0.31)	87.6 (0.34)	86.9 (0.33)	86.9 (0.35)	87.5 (0.33)	88.0 (0.33)	87.7 (0.42)
25 to 34 years old, all education levels	87.4 (0.59)	88.1 (0.52)	86.9 (0.54)	87.9 (0.52)	87.1 (0.55)	89.4 (0.55)	85.0 (0.44)	84.6 (0.40)	84.6 (0.41)	79.1 (0.46)	78.4 (0.48)	78.5 (0.51)	80.1 (0.48)	81.3 (0.46)	80.9 (0.56)
Less than high school completion[3]	76.2 (1.78)	76.3 (1.80)	75.1 (1.87)	75.6 (1.77)	73.7 (1.91)	78.4 (2.04)	77.8 (1.35)	78.1 (1.23)	73.5 (1.40)	66.2 (1.45)	66.6 (1.42)	66.3 (1.47)	70.1 (1.51)	70.2 (1.32)	73.1 (1.88)
High school completion[2]	88.4 (0.93)	88.4 (0.86)	86.1 (0.98)	88.6 (0.80)	86.6 (0.94)	89.1 (0.98)	81.8 (0.86)	81.7 (0.77)	81.7 (0.83)	73.4 (0.87)	73.0 (0.85)	74.3 (0.91)	76.5 (0.90)	77.3 (0.82)	77.2 (0.93)
Some college, no bachelor's degree[3]	87.7 (1.31)	88.5 (1.06)	89.7 (1.04)	89.7 (1.08)	89.6 (0.98)	90.7 (1.02)	83.1 (0.90)	86.4 (0.82)	86.3 (0.73)	81.4 (0.82)	78.7 (0.83)	77.5 (0.90)	78.2 (0.97)	80.7 (0.95)	79.1 (1.25)
Bachelor's or higher degree	93.5 (0.87)	93.4 (0.76)	92.2 (0.62)	93.1 (0.83)	93.0 (0.83)	93.6 (0.82)	90.8 (0.68)	89.6 (0.66)	91.7 (0.62)	89.5 (0.68)	89.2 (0.74)	89.0 (0.70)	89.3 (0.67)	89.8 (0.57)	88.8 (0.78)
35 to 44 years old, all education levels	90.1 (0.61)	91.1 (0.55)	89.1 (0.57)	90.2 (0.52)	86.8 (0.55)	88.8 (0.52)	86.9 (0.40)	87.2 (0.37)	87.1 (0.41)	82.7 (0.41)	82.3 (0.42)	82.4 (0.43)	83.3 (0.43)	84.7 (0.47)	83.8 (0.56)
Less than high school completion	81.6 (1.48)	80.1 (1.65)	74.6 (1.99)	73.9 (2.13)	66.7 (2.15)	76.5 (2.00)	73.6 (1.42)	75.9 (1.26)	73.3 (1.40)	69.4 (1.47)	69.5 (1.61)	70.9 (1.59)	70.6 (1.47)	74.8 (1.38)	73.9 (1.75)
High school completion[2]	91.3 (0.95)	92.3 (0.85)	88.6 (1.00)	89.1 (0.91)	85.9 (0.98)	87.1 (0.93)	82.8 (0.78)	83.7 (0.71)	83.3 (0.76)	77.6 (0.80)	77.6 (0.92)	76.8 (0.83)	78.2 (0.97)	79.4 (0.88)	78.2 (1.17)
Some college, no bachelor's degree[3]	93.8 (1.34)	93.8 (1.13)	90.2 (1.25)	92.6 (0.97)	88.8 (0.99)	90.2 (0.95)	87.8 (0.78)	89.4 (0.84)	89.0 (0.71)	83.9 (0.74)	82.7 (0.73)	83.1 (0.86)	83.9 (0.76)	84.6 (0.78)	83.9 (1.04)
Bachelor's or higher degree	97.0 (0.77)	97.1 (0.65)	96.3 (0.62)	96.3 (0.59)	95.1 (0.68)	95.1 (0.67)	93.7 (0.53)	94.6 (0.45)	94.9 (0.41)	92.3 (0.56)	91.9 (0.55)	91.4 (0.51)	92.2 (0.51)	92.9 (0.48)	92.4 (0.75)
45 to 54 years old, all education levels	86.6 (0.68)	87.4 (0.67)	85.8 (0.76)	87.1 (0.70)	84.9 (0.68)	86.5 (0.62)	85.8 (0.43)	83.9 (0.45)	83.7 (0.43)	78.8 (0.44)	78.3 (0.50)	78.9 (0.45)	79.9 (0.44)	79.7 (0.38)	81.8 (0.61)
Less than high school completion	78.2 (1.34)	79.6 (1.42)	73.2 (1.90)	74.3 (2.05)	66.4 (2.41)	66.5 (2.52)	64.6 (1.76)	69.9 (1.55)	65.5 (1.49)	61.4 (1.50)	58.8 (1.48)	58.6 (1.25)	62.5 (1.45)	61.1 (1.33)	67.3 (1.96)
High school completion[2]	90.3 (1.01)	89.3 (1.08)	87.3 (1.18)	87.5 (1.15)	82.1 (1.35)	84.6 (1.21)	80.6 (0.87)	80.7 (0.86)	80.4 (0.81)	74.2 (0.80)	74.6 (0.91)	75.4 (0.78)	75.2 (0.88)	74.2 (0.78)	76.4 (1.12)
Some college, no bachelor's degree[3]	91.0 (1.66)	89.4 (1.78)	89.3 (1.76)	88.9 (1.58)	87.2 (1.29)	86.4 (1.18)	84.3 (0.86)	84.5 (0.84)	85.6 (0.64)	80.1 (0.84)	79.4 (0.80)	79.4 (0.81)	81.9 (0.74)	82.1 (0.69)	83.5 (0.95)
Bachelor's or higher degree	95.6 (1.02)	96.0 (0.88)	94.8 (1.00)	95.2 (0.88)	93.8 (0.80)	94.6 (0.72)	91.1 (0.62)	92.2 (0.53)	93.5 (0.46)	90.2 (0.58)	89.4 (0.58)	90.5 (0.53)	90.2 (0.60)	90.7 (0.51)	91.4 (0.65)
55 to 64 years old, all education levels	71.3 (1.00)	69.7 (0.98)	64.6 (1.05)	64.0 (1.12)	63.2 (1.13)	64.9 (1.09)	69.8 (0.68)	67.3 (0.66)	68.0 (0.54)	65.2 (0.59)	64.4 (0.61)	64.1 (0.61)	65.1 (0.58)	66.0 (0.54)	65.7 (0.76)
Less than high school completion	64.5 (1.51)	58.3 (1.65)	53.4 (1.85)	49.6 (2.13)	46.9 (2.46)	51.2 (2.71)	49.2 (1.99)	48.8 (1.70)	48.3 (1.60)	44.3 (1.75)	45.0 (1.81)	45.2 (1.68)	44.6 (1.48)	45.5 (1.73)	48.4 (1.96)
High school completion[2]	74.9 (1.73)	74.6 (1.61)	66.1 (1.80)	66.0 (1.89)	62.7 (1.99)	61.0 (1.97)	61.5 (1.32)	61.8 (1.15)	62.9 (1.10)	59.3 (1.19)	58.5 (1.12)	58.2 (1.12)	59.1 (1.05)	61.1 (1.04)	62.6 (1.34)
Some college, no bachelor's degree[3]	80.8 (2.87)	77.2 (2.53)	67.5 (3.01)	67.7 (2.93)	67.8 (2.41)	66.6 (2.31)	68.8 (1.41)	69.6 (1.31)	67.9 (1.10)	64.5 (1.06)	63.9 (1.11)	63.0 (1.08)	64.3 (1.11)	64.9 (1.02)	63.3 (1.29)
Bachelor's or higher degree	84.1 (2.52)	83.8 (2.04)	80.7 (1.98)	77.9 (2.03)	74.9 (2.04)	77.0 (1.82)	78.1 (1.08)	78.6 (0.89)	78.6 (0.81)	77.4 (0.83)	76.2 (0.82)	76.3 (0.84)	77.7 (0.85)	77.8 (0.91)	77.2 (1.18)

—Not available.
†Not applicable.
[1]Data for 16- to 19-year-olds and 20- to 24-year-olds exclude persons enrolled in school.
[2]Includes equivalency credentials, such as the General Educational Development (GED) credential.
[3]Includes persons with no college degree as well as those with an associate's degree.

NOTE: For each age group, the employment to population ratio of males is the number of males in that age group who are employed as a percentage of the male civilian population in that age group.
SOURCE: U.S. Department of Labor, Bureau of Labor Statistics, Office of Employment and Unemployment Statistics, unpublished annual average data from the Current Population Survey (CPS), selected years, 1975 through 2014. (This table was prepared November 2014.)

Table 501.70. Employment to population ratios of females 16 to 64 years old, by age group and highest level of educational attainment: Selected years, 1975 through 2014

[Standard errors appear in parentheses]

Age group and highest level of educational attainment	1975	1980	1985	1990	1995	2000	2004	2005	2008	2009	2010	2011	2012	2013	2014
1	2	3	4	5	6	7	8	9	10	11	12	13	14	15	16
16 to 19 years old, all education levels[1]	—	(†)	(†)	56.6 (2.72)	52.2 (2.93)	55.1 (2.98)	51.5 (2.38)	51.0 (1.88)	47.3 (2.14)	47.7 (1.81)	42.3 (1.88)	42.3 (2.14)	43.1 (2.03)	44.3 (1.90)	50.0 (2.39)
Less than high school completion	—	(†)	(†)	36.0 (4.13)	36.5 (4.23)	38.9 (4.42)	34.7 (3.39)	30.3 (2.72)	25.9 (2.84)	27.3 (2.57)	26.8 (2.75)	23.5 (2.92)	22.6 (2.88)	31.0 (3.10)	34.5 (3.67)
High school completion[2]	—	(†)	(†)	70.5 (3.38)	64.1 (4.22)	65.2 (4.22)	63.6 (3.42)	67.0 (2.60)	61.2 (2.94)	56.7 (2.54)	51.2 (2.99)	49.1 (2.91)	55.2 (2.97)	48.9 (2.96)	59.0 (3.35)
At least some college	—	(†)	(†)	73.1 (11.73)	68.3 (8.37)	79.1 (7.56)	71.7 (6.65)	63.6 (6.23)	55.9 (5.75)	67.6 (4.82)	54.4 (5.29)	62.5 (5.31)	64.3 (5.68)	61.7 (4.61)	63.0 (7.14)
20 to 24 years old, all education levels[1]	—	(†)	(†)	68.2 (1.29)	66.3 (1.34)	71.5 (1.35)	69.4 (0.98)	67.0 (1.01)	67.2 (0.97)	65.8 (0.94)	62.4 (1.01)	64.1 (0.92)	65.0 (0.94)	65.2 (1.01)	66.3 (1.06)
Less than high school completion	—	(†)	(†)	36.7 (3.08)	33.6 (3.18)	46.2 (3.57)	43.8 (2.47)	38.5 (2.20)	37.5 (2.47)	38.6 (2.32)	33.3 (2.50)	33.2 (2.31)	36.2 (2.84)	33.4 (2.55)	30.5 (3.57)
High school completion[2]	—	(†)	(†)	68.8 (1.84)	62.2 (2.19)	70.0 (2.15)	63.5 (1.64)	65.0 (1.47)	60.8 (1.55)	59.9 (1.53)	55.6 (1.43)	58.5 (1.77)	59.2 (1.55)	58.4 (1.78)	60.2 (1.86)
Some college, no bachelor's degree[3]	—	(†)	(†)	80.9 (2.39)	80.3 (2.12)	81.4 (2.23)	74.7 (1.84)	76.6 (1.72)	78.7 (1.56)	72.4 (1.67)	72.4 (1.65)	71.2 (1.47)	70.6 (1.64)	72.9 (1.64)	71.6 (1.89)
Bachelor's or higher degree	—	(†)	(†)	92.0 (2.12)	90.8 (2.19)	86.9 (2.61)	86.3 (1.76)	88.4 (1.53)	87.8 (1.55)	87.7 (1.60)	86.7 (1.67)	85.5 (1.81)	86.4 (1.53)	87.0 (1.64)	86.3 (1.96)
25 to 64 years old, all education levels	48.5 (0.46)	56.5 (0.44)	60.8 (0.43)	66.0 (0.42)	68.3 (0.40)	71.2 (0.39)	69.3 (0.28)	68.4 (0.23)	69.6 (0.23)	67.6 (0.24)	66.9 (0.23)	66.2 (0.24)	66.3 (0.25)	66.4 (0.23)	66.6 (0.32)
Less than high school completion	37.7 (0.80)	39.8 (0.86)	39.1 (0.97)	41.8 (1.06)	43.2 (1.15)	45.8 (1.24)	44.8 (0.89)	43.4 (0.72)	43.8 (0.74)	41.9 (0.67)	41.6 (0.81)	39.7 (0.71)	41.6 (0.89)	40.6 (0.82)	41.5 (0.89)
High school completion[2]	50.1 (0.70)	58.2 (0.65)	60.8 (0.65)	65.6 (0.64)	65.7 (0.69)	68.6 (0.70)	63.5 (0.52)	64.2 (0.44)	64.7 (0.43)	63.2 (0.42)	61.9 (0.44)	60.1 (0.51)	60.0 (0.49)	59.8 (0.47)	59.7 (0.58)
Some college, no bachelor's degree[3]	53.8 (1.30)	63.7 (1.07)	69.0 (0.98)	73.2 (0.88)	73.8 (0.71)	76.0 (0.70)	74.1 (0.49)	72.8 (0.42)	73.0 (0.43)	70.4 (0.44)	69.4 (0.45)	69.1 (0.37)	67.9 (0.43)	68.6 (0.46)	68.3 (0.58)
Bachelor's or higher degree	65.6 (1.29)	71.8 (1.01)	76.7 (0.88)	79.8 (0.78)	80.8 (0.71)	80.8 (0.66)	80.0 (0.44)	78.1 (0.40)	79.1 (0.40)	77.3 (0.38)	76.9 (0.36)	76.6 (0.39)	77.2 (0.38)	76.6 (0.40)	77.1 (0.47)
25 to 34 years old, all education levels	49.3 (0.83)	61.6 (0.73)	65.9 (0.72)	69.6 (0.70)	70.2 (0.71)	74.1 (0.74)	69.1 (0.55)	69.0 (0.48)	71.7 (0.47)	69.3 (0.51)	68.0 (0.44)	67.5 (0.42)	67.7 (0.44)	68.0 (0.45)	68.2 (0.55)
Less than high school completion	33.7 (1.74)	42.3 (1.91)	38.7 (2.05)	42.5 (2.12)	43.5 (2.25)	47.6 (2.56)	42.8 (1.73)	42.7 (1.44)	42.4 (1.37)	39.5 (1.50)	40.2 (1.35)	37.5 (1.55)	38.9 (1.69)	40.7 (1.49)	40.2 (1.86)
High school completion[2]	48.1 (1.22)	59.4 (1.12)	63.9 (1.11)	67.5 (1.11)	67.2 (1.27)	70.7 (1.43)	64.6 (1.10)	62.5 (0.99)	64.3 (0.92)	63.2 (0.98)	61.4 (1.14)	59.5 (0.94)	59.1 (1.05)	57.1 (1.07)	56.3 (1.19)
Some college, no bachelor's degree[3]	53.6 (2.06)	66.3 (1.58)	71.0 (1.46)	74.5 (1.40)	73.0 (1.26)	76.3 (1.31)	72.6 (0.98)	73.0 (0.81)	74.4 (0.81)	70.8 (0.86)	67.7 (0.80)	69.1 (0.79)	67.7 (0.90)	69.7 (0.84)	70.3 (0.91)
Bachelor's or higher degree	66.3 (1.88)	75.5 (1.42)	80.6 (1.26)	83.2 (1.18)	83.4 (1.16)	84.7 (1.11)	80.3 (0.83)	80.1 (0.72)	82.8 (0.66)	80.7 (0.73)	79.9 (0.63)	78.8 (0.60)	80.3 (0.63)	80.1 (0.67)	80.2 (0.77)
35 to 44 years old, all education levels	51.9 (0.95)	62.8 (0.87)	67.7 (0.80)	73.3 (0.72)	73.8 (0.68)	75.1 (0.67)	72.3 (0.50)	72.8 (0.38)	73.3 (0.40)	70.9 (0.42)	69.9 (0.42)	69.8 (0.48)	70.7 (0.48)	69.6 (0.47)	70.7 (0.57)
Less than high school completion	42.8 (1.76)	48.2 (1.90)	46.4 (2.13)	51.0 (2.35)	49.7 (2.33)	52.5 (2.35)	51.2 (1.72)	51.5 (1.33)	53.1 (1.57)	48.9 (1.47)	44.8 (1.54)	42.5 (1.41)	47.0 (1.49)	45.8 (1.52)	45.6 (1.61)
High school completion[2]	53.9 (1.38)	64.7 (1.28)	67.8 (1.22)	72.7 (1.13)	71.7 (1.19)	74.7 (1.18)	70.7 (0.93)	71.6 (0.74)	69.6 (0.78)	66.9 (0.94)	66.3 (0.87)	65.8 (0.87)	64.9 (1.02)	64.8 (0.92)	66.8 (1.07)
Some college, no bachelor's degree[3]	55.1 (2.67)	67.8 (2.14)	73.6 (1.73)	77.9 (1.44)	78.5 (1.16)	79.4 (1.16)	76.9 (0.88)	76.1 (0.67)	76.9 (0.81)	74.0 (0.79)	72.2 (0.74)	71.8 (0.87)	73.4 (0.85)	70.3 (0.90)	71.7 (1.06)
Bachelor's or higher degree	63.2 (2.73)	73.0 (1.97)	78.5 (1.53)	81.2 (1.30)	81.5 (1.19)	80.2 (1.20)	77.3 (0.86)	78.1 (0.66)	78.9 (0.63)	78.1 (0.61)	78.3 (0.59)	78.9 (0.68)	78.8 (0.64)	78.0 (0.71)	79.0 (0.80)
45 to 54 years old, all education levels	51.5 (0.93)	57.1 (0.94)	62.1 (0.98)	68.6 (0.92)	72.9 (0.80)	76.0 (0.73)	74.7 (0.50)	73.2 (0.40)	73.2 (0.46)	71.8 (0.46)	71.3 (0.44)	70.0 (0.44)	69.6 (0.42)	70.3 (0.41)	70.8 (0.58)
Less than high school completion	41.5 (1.55)	43.9 (1.71)	44.3 (2.06)	47.6 (2.22)	50.6 (2.43)	52.3 (2.57)	47.6 (1.83)	47.8 (1.40)	44.6 (1.30)	45.5 (1.47)	45.2 (1.61)	44.1 (1.25)	45.8 (1.53)	43.8 (1.52)	49.6 (2.11)
High school completion[2]	53.8 (1.37)	60.2 (1.37)	64.2 (1.41)	69.9 (1.35)	71.1 (1.46)	72.9 (1.33)	71.4 (0.92)	69.5 (0.83)	70.1 (0.80)	68.8 (0.85)	67.1 (0.72)	64.4 (0.89)	65.5 (0.82)	65.7 (0.84)	64.8 (1.17)
Some college, no bachelor's degree[3]	58.1 (2.78)	64.7 (2.56)	69.7 (2.45)	75.2 (2.08)	76.9 (1.46)	80.6 (1.28)	77.2 (0.90)	76.9 (0.72)	75.9 (0.74)	75.0 (0.73)	75.5 (0.77)	74.4 (0.71)	71.4 (0.77)	73.6 (0.78)	72.6 (1.03)
Bachelor's or higher degree	72.2 (2.87)	72.3 (2.55)	77.3 (2.24)	81.8 (1.76)	83.8 (1.36)	84.5 (1.17)	81.4 (0.83)	82.8 (0.72)	83.0 (0.73)	80.5 (0.69)	79.7 (0.69)	79.6 (0.68)	79.6 (0.72)	79.2 (0.71)	80.6 (0.83)
55 to 64 years old, all education levels	39.7 (0.99)	40.5 (0.94)	44.0 (0.99)	44.0 (1.05)	47.5 (1.08)	51.9 (1.06)	57.2 (0.68)	54.8 (0.61)	58.1 (0.55)	56.7 (0.55)	57.1 (0.53)	56.4 (0.51)	56.5 (0.57)	57.1 (0.57)	56.4 (0.63)
Less than high school completion	33.5 (1.39)	31.2 (1.41)	30.5 (1.60)	30.3 (2.07)	30.9 (2.07)	30.9 (2.26)	31.1 (1.74)	30.5 (1.33)	34.1 (1.70)	32.1 (1.47)	35.1 (1.54)	33.6 (1.46)	34.0 (1.57)	32.1 (1.57)	30.4 (1.69)
High school completion[2]	42.6 (1.65)	45.8 (1.48)	45.7 (1.48)	45.7 (1.60)	47.5 (1.66)	51.3 (1.69)	50.6 (1.14)	50.5 (0.95)	53.8 (0.90)	52.9 (0.97)	52.2 (0.92)	51.1 (0.95)	50.6 (0.97)	52.0 (0.93)	52.9 (1.09)
Some college, no bachelor's degree[3]	45.9 (3.37)	48.2 (2.87)	54.1 (2.95)	54.1 (2.81)	57.0 (2.32)	58.8 (2.17)	60.0 (1.32)	60.9 (1.06)	62.0 (1.04)	59.1 (1.02)	59.9 (1.08)	59.6 (1.08)	58.7 (1.01)	60.2 (1.03)	58.2 (1.19)
Bachelor's or higher degree	57.8 (3.72)	54.0 (3.27)	55.1 (3.18)	58.6 (2.98)	61.9 (2.81)	65.1 (2.28)	67.1 (1.30)	67.5 (1.22)	68.7 (1.04)	67.5 (0.96)	67.5 (0.98)	67.0 (1.04)	68.3 (1.03)	67.2 (0.93)	66.6 (1.25)

—Not available.
†Not applicable.
[1]Data for 16- to 19-year-olds and 20- to 24-year-olds exclude persons enrolled in school.
[2]Includes equivalency credentials, such as the General Educational Development (GED) credential.
[3]Includes persons with no college degree as well as those with an associate's degree.

NOTE: For each age group, the employment to population ratio of females is the number of females who are employed as a percentage of the female civilian population in that age group.
SOURCE: U.S. Department of Labor, Bureau of Labor Statistics, Office of Employment and Unemployment Statistics, unpublished annual average data from the Current Population Survey (CPS), selected years, 1975 through 2014. (This table was prepared November 2014.)

Table 501.80. Unemployment rates of persons 16 to 64 years old, by age group and highest level of educational attainment: Selected years, 1975 through 2014

[Standard errors appear in parentheses]

Age group and highest level of educational attainment	1975	1980	1985	1990	1995	2000	2004	2005	2008	2009	2010	2011	2012	2013	2014
1	2	3	4	5	6	7	8	9	10	11	12	13	14	15	16
16 to 19 years old, all education levels[1]	—	(†)	(†)	17.0 (1.83)	21.0 (2.06)	17.2 (1.89)	20.9 (1.63)	22.8 (1.39)	20.9 (1.36)	30.3 (1.58)	31.9 (1.59)	28.8 (1.62)	30.6 (1.57)	29.4 (1.57)	22.9 (1.83)
Less than high school completion	—	(†)	(†)	26.2 (3.54)	30.3 (3.67)	21.4 (3.23)	27.5 (2.90)	30.3 (2.34)	30.8 (2.40)	38.9 (3.05)	41.7 (3.14)	35.1 (3.42)	41.1 (3.01)	36.3 (2.70)	22.9 (3.38)
High school completion[2]	—	(†)	(†)	11.7 (2.05)	15.1 (2.59)	15.3 (2.54)	17.6 (2.13)	19.1 (2.02)	17.2 (1.62)	29.1 (1.80)	29.6 (2.08)	28.9 (2.18)	28.7 (2.00)	29.2 (2.12)	25.0 (2.32)
At least some college	—	(†)	(†)	‡ (†)	12.4 ‡ (5.19)	‡ !	12.6 ! (4.13)	15.8 (3.54)	11.3 (2.99)	18.1 (3.68)	18.1 (3.65)	16.2 (3.55)	19.6 (3.83)	16.2 (3.32)	15.1 (4.16)
20 to 24 years old, all education levels[1]	—	(†)	(†)	8.2 (0.63)	10.7 (0.72)	9.2 (0.70)	11.6 (0.55)	10.9 (0.48)	10.7 (0.43)	17.0 (0.62)	18.8 (0.66)	18.1 (0.60)	15.5 (0.55)	15.2 (0.62)	14.9 (0.70)
Less than high school completion	—	(†)	(†)	17.4 (2.15)	19.5 (2.37)	16.6 (2.18)	16.0 (1.50)	18.9 (1.24)	19.2 (1.66)	29.0 (1.69)	32.3 (1.80)	30.1 (1.95)	27.6 (2.12)	29.2 (2.27)	25.3 (2.75)
High school completion	—	(†)	(†)	7.8 (0.88)	12.0 (1.18)	10.0 (1.12)	13.4 (0.91)	12.0 (0.73)	13.0 (0.70)	20.3 (1.05)	22.3 (0.95)	21.6 (1.02)	18.3 (0.96)	17.5 (0.91)	18.9 (1.18)
Some college, no bachelor's degree[3]	—	(†)	(†)	4.8 (1.09)	7.3 (1.13)	5.2 (1.02)	8.6 (0.95)	7.3 (0.76)	6.8 (0.67)	12.1 (0.94)	14.2 (1.07)	14.0 (0.98)	12.7 (0.89)	12.2 (1.02)	12.2 (1.16)
Bachelor's or higher degree	—	(†)	(†)	3.1 ! (1.12)	4.1 ! (1.26)	5.0 (1.43)	6.7 (1.09)	5.4 (0.91)	4.5 (0.78)	7.9 (1.02)	7.9 (1.15)	8.7 (1.05)	6.0 (0.95)	7.0 (1.09)	6.7 (1.09)
25 to 64 years old, all education levels	6.8 (0.21)	5.0 (0.17)	6.1 (0.18)	3.6 (0.14)	4.8 (0.15)	3.3 (0.13)	5.1 (0.11)	4.4 (0.09)	4.4 (0.09)	8.1 (0.12)	9.1 (0.13)	8.3 (0.12)	7.4 (0.11)	6.6 (0.12)	5.8 (0.14)
Less than high school completion	10.5 (0.49)	8.4 (0.48)	11.4 (0.61)	7.7 (0.55)	10.0 (0.66)	7.9 (0.63)	10.5 (0.50)	10.1 (0.44)	10.1 (0.44)	15.8 (0.54)	16.8 (0.54)	16.2 (0.55)	14.3 (0.49)	12.7 (0.46)	10.6 (0.63)
High school completion[2]	6.8 (0.34)	5.1 (0.27)	6.9 (0.31)	3.8 (0.23)	5.2 (0.28)	3.8 (0.25)	5.9 (0.22)	5.5 (0.17)	5.8 (0.18)	10.4 (0.21)	12.1 (0.26)	10.9 (0.27)	9.2 (0.25)	8.7 (0.27)	7.4 (0.29)
Some college, no bachelor's degree[3]	5.5 (0.50)	4.3 (0.38)	4.7 (0.37)	3.1 (0.29)	4.5 (0.29)	3.0 (0.24)	4.9 (0.21)	4.2 (0.17)	4.2 (0.17)	8.0 (0.22)	8.8 (0.23)	8.1 (0.20)	7.9 (0.24)	6.5 (0.21)	6.1 (0.27)
Bachelor's or higher degree	2.4 (0.30)	1.9 (0.23)	2.4 (0.24)	1.7 (0.19)	2.5 (0.21)	1.5 (0.16)	2.9 (0.15)	2.3 (0.13)	2.1 (0.11)	4.3 (0.15)	4.7 (0.15)	4.4 (0.15)	4.1 (0.14)	3.8 (0.13)	3.4 (0.16)
25 to 34 years old, all education levels	8.6 (0.41)	6.8 (0.32)	7.3 (0.33)	4.8 (0.27)	5.8 (0.30)	4.0 (0.27)	6.4 (0.24)	5.8 (0.18)	5.9 (0.21)	10.1 (0.27)	10.8 (0.28)	10.0 (0.28)	9.2 (0.26)	8.0 (0.23)	7.4 (0.30)
Less than high school completion	17.2 (1.36)	13.7 (1.24)	15.5 (1.38)	12.0 (1.21)	12.9 (1.32)	10.3 (1.33)	12.4 (0.97)	11.6 (0.69)	14.2 (0.93)	19.9 (1.05)	20.3 (1.02)	19.7 (1.18)	16.8 (1.09)	15.1 (0.97)	13.7 (1.24)
High school completion[2]	9.4 (0.67)	7.9 (0.55)	9.1 (0.57)	5.1 (0.44)	6.8 (0.56)	4.8 (0.54)	7.9 (0.50)	7.7 (0.41)	8.5 (0.49)	14.1 (0.57)	15.9 (0.62)	14.3 (0.55)	12.8 (0.57)	12.1 (0.57)	10.5 (0.68)
Some college, no bachelor's degree[3]	6.7 (0.85)	6.0 (0.64)	5.4 (0.60)	3.8 (0.51)	5.0 (0.52)	3.6 (0.49)	6.4 (0.45)	5.4 (0.36)	5.0 (0.33)	9.8 (0.46)	10.6 (0.44)	10.1 (0.46)	10.1 (0.51)	8.0 (0.42)	7.8 (0.52)
Bachelor's or higher degree	2.9 (0.50)	2.5 (0.39)	2.8 (0.41)	1.9 (0.34)	2.7 (0.40)	1.6 (0.31)	2.9 (0.29)	2.6 (0.26)	2.2 (0.21)	4.5 (0.28)	4.5 (0.28)	4.3 (0.31)	4.1 (0.28)	3.6 (0.25)	3.7 (0.30)
35 to 44 years old, all education levels	6.4 (0.41)	4.3 (0.31)	5.6 (0.33)	3.3 (0.24)	4.6 (0.27)	3.5 (0.23)	5.3 (0.21)	4.2 (0.14)	4.3 (0.17)	7.9 (0.18)	9.2 (0.24)	8.2 (0.23)	7.1 (0.22)	6.4 (0.19)	5.7 (0.24)
Less than high school completion	11.2 (1.02)	9.0 (1.00)	12.4 (1.29)	10.5 (1.17)	10.5 (1.28)	8.4 (1.14)	11.1 (0.90)	8.7 (0.63)	9.1 (0.79)	15.3 (0.87)	17.8 (1.07)	15.9 (1.04)	14.1 (1.09)	11.5 (0.80)	11.5 (1.08)
High school completion[2]	5.7 (0.60)	4.2 (0.48)	6.1 (0.55)	3.7 (0.41)	5.1 (0.48)	3.9 (0.43)	6.1 (0.40)	5.2 (0.31)	6.0 (0.35)	10.6 (0.44)	11.9 (0.51)	11.3 (0.44)	9.1 (0.48)	8.5 (0.50)	7.4 (0.48)
Some college, no bachelor's degree[3]	4.6 (0.95)	3.1 (0.64)	4.8 (0.69)	2.8 (0.47)	4.7 (0.49)	3.1 (0.41)	4.9 (0.38)	3.9 (0.25)	3.8 (0.27)	7.2 (0.36)	7.5 (0.42)	7.4 (0.39)	7.4 (0.44)	6.7 (0.40)	6.1 (0.49)
Bachelor's or higher degree	2.3 (0.59)	1.6 (0.41)	2.2 (0.39)	1.6 (0.31)	2.2 (0.34)	1.8 (0.31)	2.8 (0.27)	2.0 (0.20)	1.9 (0.17)	4.2 (0.29)	4.6 (0.26)	4.6 (0.29)	3.6 (0.26)	3.6 (0.23)	2.8 (0.30)
45 to 54 years old, all education levels	5.9 (0.39)	3.9 (0.32)	5.4 (0.39)	2.5 (0.26)	3.9 (0.29)	2.4 (0.22)	4.3 (0.20)	3.9 (0.16)	3.9 (0.16)	7.4 (0.21)	8.4 (0.22)	7.5 (0.20)	6.8 (0.18)	6.0 (0.18)	4.9 (0.24)
Less than high school completion	8.5 (0.81)	6.6 (0.78)	10.2 (1.16)	4.7 (0.88)	7.9 (1.24)	6.1 (1.16)	9.1 (0.99)	7.0 (0.66)	8.9 (0.74)	13.6 (0.95)	15.6 (0.98)	16.3 (0.92)	13.5 (0.92)	12.3 (0.94)	8.0 (0.95)
High school completion[2]	5.6 (0.60)	3.4 (0.48)	5.4 (0.60)	2.3 (0.39)	4.0 (0.53)	2.7 (0.42)	4.9 (0.37)	4.6 (0.33)	4.7 (0.34)	8.8 (0.42)	11.0 (0.43)	9.3 (0.42)	7.8 (0.36)	7.8 (0.40)	6.1 (0.50)
Some college, no bachelor's degree[3]	4.7 (1.00)	3.0 (0.78)	3.2 (0.79)	2.6 (0.62)	3.9 (0.56)	2.4 (0.40)	4.0 (0.35)	3.7 (0.30)	4.0 (0.32)	7.5 (0.39)	7.6 (0.40)	7.1 (0.35)	6.9 (0.36)	5.2 (0.36)	4.8 (0.44)
Bachelor's or higher degree	2.0 ! (0.61)	1.3 ! (0.44)	2.1 (0.54)	1.4 (0.38)	2.4 (0.41)	1.3 (0.28)	3.0 (0.28)	2.5 (0.25)	1.9 (0.18)	4.3 (0.29)	4.8 (0.30)	4.0 (0.27)	3.9 (0.27)	3.8 (0.26)	3.2 (0.29)
55 to 64 years old, all education levels	5.5 (0.46)	3.2 (0.35)	4.6 (0.44)	2.8 (0.36)	3.9 (0.42)	2.8 (0.35)	4.0 (0.26)	3.7 (0.20)	3.3 (0.18)	6.7 (0.25)	7.3 (0.25)	6.9 (0.25)	6.6 (0.23)	5.7 (0.23)	5.2 (0.28)
Less than high school completion	7.1 (0.79)	5.2 (0.78)	7.1 (1.01)	3.9 (0.90)	6.7 (1.35)	5.2 (1.28)	7.0 (1.10)	7.5 (0.90)	5.6 (0.77)	12.7 (1.25)	10.1 (0.99)	10.0 (1.02)	11.5 (1.05)	11.2 (1.19)	8.2 (1.21)
High school completion[2]	5.1 (0.76)	2.7 (0.51)	4.5 (0.69)	3.0 (0.59)	3.4 (0.65)	3.1 (0.62)	4.4 (0.49)	4.3 (0.39)	3.4 (0.35)	7.8 (0.50)	9.3 (0.56)	8.4 (0.58)	7.1 (0.50)	6.4 (0.47)	5.6 (0.53)
Some college, no bachelor's degree[3]	4.1 ! (1.26)	2.0 ! (0.77)	3.0 ! (1.00)	2.2 ! (0.82)	3.2 (0.80)	2.8 (0.70)	3.6 (0.48)	3.5 (0.37)	3.7 (0.37)	7.0 (0.50)	7.7 (0.52)	7.3 (0.52)	7.1 (0.44)	5.8 (0.40)	5.5 (0.54)
Bachelor's or higher degree	1.5 ! (0.75)	‡ ! (†)	2.2 ! (0.70)	1.8 ! (0.62)	3.3 (0.79)	1.4 ! (0.46)	3.0 (0.39)	2.3 (0.26)	2.4 (0.26)	4.3 (0.33)	5.0 (0.34)	4.9 (0.35)	4.8 (0.38)	4.2 (0.29)	4.0 (0.39)

—Not available.
†Not applicable.
!Interpret data with caution. The coefficient of variation (CV) for this estimate is between 30 and 50 percent.
‡Reporting standards not met. The coefficient of variation (CV) for this estimate is 50 percent or greater.
[1]Data for 16- to 19-year-olds and 20- to 24-year-olds exclude persons enrolled in school.
[2]Includes equivalency credentials, such as the General Educational Development (GED) credential.
[3]Includes persons with no college degree as well as those with an associate's degree.

NOTE: The unemployment rate is the percentage of persons in the civilian labor force who are not working and who made specific efforts to find employment sometime during the prior 4 weeks. The civilian labor force consists of all civilians who are employed or seeking employment. Some data have been revised from previously published figures.
SOURCE: U.S. Department of Labor, Bureau of Labor Statistics, Office of Employment and Unemployment Statistics, unpublished annual average data from the Current Population Survey (CPS), selected years, 1975 through 2014. (This table was prepared November 2014.)

Table 501.85. Unemployment rates of males 16 to 64 years old, by age group and highest level of educational attainment: Selected years, 1975 through 2014

[Standard errors appear in parentheses]

Age group and highest level of educational attainment	1975	1980	1985	1990	1995	2000	2004	2005	2008	2009	2010	2011	2012	2013	2014
1	2	3	4	5	6	7	8	9	10	11	12	13	14	15	16
16 to 19 years old, all education levels[1]	—	(†)	(†)	18.9 (2.58)	21.3 (2.71)	16.0 (2.36)	21.4 (2.10)	25.2 (1.83)	22.3 (1.79)	35.1 (2.08)	35.6 (2.07)	31.2 (2.10)	31.4 (2.05)	29.7 (2.00)	24.4 (2.40)
Less than high school completion	—	(†)	(†)	27.9 (4.45)	30.6 (4.60)	17.6 (3.69)	26.3 (3.52)	29.9 (2.88)	30.7 (2.87)	41.2 (3.89)	44.7 (4.07)	32.0 (4.05)	37.1 (3.82)	36.1 (3.57)	23.1 (4.25)
High school completion[2]	—	(†)	(†)	12.1 (2.96)	14.4 (3.38)	15.0 (3.30)	17.8 (2.77)	23.4 (2.77)	18.9 (2.43)	34.4 (2.46)	33.0 (2.59)	32.7 (2.96)	31.8 (2.68)	28.8 (2.70)	26.7 (3.29)
At least some college	—	(†)	(†)	‡! (†)	‡! (†)	‡! (†)	19.0! (6.64)	12.7! (4.34)	9.1! (3.09)	22.4 (5.43)	19.0 (5.64)	21.4 (5.91)	20.2 (5.03)	17.5 (4.79)	17.7! (7.00)
20 to 24 years old, all education levels[1]	—	(†)	(†)	8.4 (0.86)	11.1 (0.97)	9.4 (0.94)	12.0 (0.73)	11.4 (0.61)	11.5 (0.58)	19.8 (0.85)	21.4 (0.88)	19.7 (0.81)	16.6 (0.83)	16.5 (0.80)	17.0 (0.92)
Less than high school completion	—	(†)	(†)	16.9 (2.53)	17.4 (2.68)	16.5 (2.61)	14.7 (1.74)	16.1 (1.37)	18.2 (1.89)	29.2 (2.06)	32.4 (2.20)	27.0 (2.23)	27.8 (2.48)	26.4 (2.72)	23.6 (3.04)
High school completion[2]	—	(†)	(†)	7.4 (1.15)	11.6 (1.48)	9.6 (1.45)	12.4 (1.17)	12.4 (0.97)	13.3 (0.85)	22.7 (1.31)	23.7 (1.25)	22.9 (1.31)	19.0 (1.28)	19.0 (1.24)	21.1 (1.60)
Some college, no bachelor's degree[3]	—	(†)	(†)	4.6! (1.54)	8.0 (1.65)	4.8 (1.36)	8.2 (1.24)	7.8 (1.04)	7.1 (0.97)	13.7 (1.39)	16.4 (1.58)	15.2 (1.46)	12.0 (1.23)	12.8 (1.36)	13.8 (1.56)
Bachelor's or higher degree	—	(†)	(†)	‡! (†)	5.6! (2.22)	5.5! (2.32)	8.0 (1.84)	6.8 (1.54)	4.7 (1.19)	10.1 (1.71)	9.8 (1.82)	10.8 (1.82)	6.6 (1.54)	8.5 (1.89)	7.3 (1.71)
25 to 64 years old, all education levels	6.5 (0.26)	4.9 (0.22)	6.1 (0.24)	3.6 (0.19)	5.1 (0.21)	3.3 (0.18)	5.4 (0.15)	4.7 (0.14)	4.9 (0.13)	9.5 (0.18)	10.5 (0.19)	9.2 (0.18)	8.0 (0.16)	6.9 (0.16)	5.9 (0.19)
Less than high school completion	10.3 (0.59)	8.2 (0.58)	11.2 (0.76)	7.3 (0.68)	10.9 (0.86)	7.1 (0.75)	9.4 (0.59)	7.9 (0.44)	10.9 (0.60)	16.5 (0.72)	17.8 (0.79)	16.7 (0.70)	13.6 (0.59)	11.9 (0.58)	9.4 (0.70)
High school completion[2]	6.6 (0.43)	5.3 (0.37)	7.2 (0.43)	3.8 (0.32)	5.7 (0.40)	3.9 (0.34)	6.0 (0.31)	6.0 (0.25)	6.3 (0.24)	12.4 (0.31)	13.8 (0.39)	12.2 (0.38)	10.1 (0.33)	9.2 (0.37)	7.8 (0.37)
Some college, no bachelor's degree[3]	5.0 (0.59)	4.4 (0.49)	4.5 (0.49)	3.0 (0.38)	4.4 (0.39)	3.1 (0.34)	5.4 (0.30)	4.3 (0.27)	4.2 (0.25)	9.3 (0.31)	10.2 (0.35)	8.7 (0.33)	8.2 (0.34)	6.5 (0.30)	5.9 (0.37)
Bachelor's or higher degree	2.1 (0.34)	1.7 (0.26)	2.4 (0.30)	1.8 (0.25)	2.6 (0.28)	1.6 (0.22)	3.0 (0.20)	2.5 (0.19)	2.0 (0.15)	4.7 (0.23)	5.1 (0.22)	4.6 (0.20)	4.3 (0.20)	3.7 (0.18)	3.4 (0.25)
25 to 34 years old, all education levels	8.3 (0.50)	6.8 (0.41)	7.3 (0.43)	4.5 (0.35)	5.9 (0.40)	4.2 (0.37)	6.9 (0.33)	6.0 (0.27)	6.5 (0.28)	11.9 (0.40)	12.6 (0.40)	11.3 (0.38)	10.0 (0.38)	8.4 (0.31)	7.5 (0.41)
Less than high school completion	17.3 (1.65)	13.4 (1.53)	10.3 (1.60)	10.3 (1.36)	12.5 (1.57)	8.8 (1.51)	10.9 (1.09)	9.7 (0.84)	14.8 (1.18)	19.2 (1.27)	20.7 (1.36)	19.2 (1.30)	14.3 (1.17)	13.2 (1.19)	10.8 (1.37)
High school completion[2]	9.0 (0.85)	8.2 (0.75)	9.5 (0.77)	4.6 (0.55)	6.6 (0.72)	4.9 (0.70)	8.1 (0.65)	7.8 (0.52)	8.5 (0.64)	16.1 (0.77)	17.8 (0.77)	15.2 (0.74)	13.5 (0.70)	11.8 (0.69)	10.1 (0.81)
Some college, no bachelor's degree[3]	6.6 (1.03)	6.0 (0.81)	4.9 (0.76)	3.6 (0.68)	4.6 (0.70)	3.8 (0.69)	7.5 (0.67)	5.6 (0.57)	5.0 (0.48)	11.3 (0.68)	11.8 (0.69)	11.2 (0.71)	11.1 (0.75)	8.5 (0.63)	7.8 (0.76)
Bachelor's or higher degree	2.6 (0.57)	2.4 (0.48)	2.8 (0.54)	1.9 (0.46)	2.8 (0.55)	1.8 (0.46)	3.2 (0.42)	2.7 (0.36)	2.1 (0.30)	5.1 (0.52)	4.8 (0.45)	4.5 (0.47)	4.2 (0.45)	3.9 (0.40)	3.8 (0.51)
35 to 44 years old, all education levels	6.0 (0.50)	4.1 (0.39)	5.7 (0.44)	3.2 (0.32)	4.9 (0.37)	3.4 (0.31)	5.6 (0.29)	4.4 (0.20)	4.7 (0.24)	9.2 (0.30)	10.1 (0.33)	8.9 (0.32)	7.6 (0.31)	6.3 (0.29)	5.7 (0.33)
Less than high school completion	10.8 (1.24)	8.4 (1.22)	12.3 (1.63)	7.9 (1.46)	11.8 (1.69)	6.3 (1.27)	9.9 (1.06)	7.8 (0.76)	9.9 (1.05)	16.5 (1.23)	18.4 (1.42)	15.8 (1.34)	13.5 (1.13)	10.3 (0.97)	9.8 (1.22)
High school completion[2]	5.8 (0.80)	4.2 (0.65)	6.5 (0.79)	3.4 (0.56)	5.6 (0.68)	4.2 (0.58)	7.0 (0.56)	5.7 (0.46)	6.4 (0.45)	12.2 (0.62)	12.9 (0.71)	12.4 (0.66)	9.7 (0.66)	8.8 (0.63)	8.2 (0.68)
Some college, no bachelor's degree[3]	3.3! (1.01)	2.9 (0.81)	5.3 (0.96)	2.8 (0.63)	4.8 (0.69)	2.9 (0.56)	5.3 (0.55)	4.1 (0.38)	4.1 (0.43)	8.3 (0.62)	9.9 (0.63)	7.4 (0.64)	7.4 (0.64)	6.1 (0.58)	5.5 (0.69)
Bachelor's or higher degree	1.9! (0.61)	1.3! (0.44)	2.2 (0.49)	1.7 (0.41)	2.0 (0.43)	1.7 (0.42)	2.8 (0.37)	2.1 (0.27)	1.7 (0.24)	4.6 (0.40)	4.6 (0.38)	4.7 (0.39)	4.1 (0.40)	3.1 (0.33)	2.6 (0.43)
45 to 54 years old, all education levels	5.5 (0.48)	3.7 (0.40)	5.4 (0.51)	2.7 (0.36)	4.6 (0.42)	2.5 (0.30)	4.4 (0.27)	4.1 (0.25)	4.3 (0.23)	8.6 (0.31)	9.9 (0.32)	8.2 (0.30)	7.0 (0.22)	6.5 (0.26)	4.9 (0.33)
Less than high school completion	8.3 (0.97)	6.1 (0.92)	10.9 (1.48)	4.7 (1.12)	9.4 (1.74)	6.9 (1.60)	8.4 (1.22)	6.3 (0.81)	9.7 (0.97)	14.1 (1.24)	16.8 (1.29)	16.6 (1.15)	13.7 (1.12)	12.3 (1.23)	8.7 (1.17)
High school completion[2]	4.9 (0.76)	3.3 (0.64)	5.5 (0.84)	2.8 (0.61)	5.5 (0.87)	2.4 (0.55)	5.4 (0.53)	5.1 (0.51)	5.4 (0.47)	10.7 (0.59)	12.6 (0.67)	8.7 (0.56)	8.7 (0.51)	8.0 (0.58)	6.2 (0.65)
Some college, no bachelor's degree[3]	4.4 (1.21)	3.5! (1.11)	2.6! (0.94)	2.5! (0.82)	4.0 (0.79)	2.6 (0.58)	3.8 (0.50)	3.8 (0.47)	3.9 (0.45)	8.6 (0.64)	9.5 (0.63)	8.1 (0.56)	6.3 (0.49)	5.0 (0.47)	4.3 (0.48)
Bachelor's or higher degree	1.8! (0.67)	1.1! (0.47)	2.0! (0.63)	1.4! (0.49)	2.7 (0.55)	1.3 (0.38)	2.8 (0.37)	2.7 (0.38)	1.9 (0.28)	4.8 (0.43)	5.3 (0.42)	3.9 (0.37)	3.8 (0.34)	3.7 (0.33)	3.1 (0.39)
55 to 64 years old, all education levels	5.5 (0.58)	3.6 (0.46)	4.7 (0.57)	3.3 (0.51)	4.3 (0.59)	3.2 (0.49)	4.3 (0.36)	3.9 (0.30)	3.4 (0.25)	7.6 (0.36)	8.6 (0.37)	7.9 (0.34)	7.1 (0.33)	6.1 (0.32)	5.6 (0.37)
Less than high school completion	6.9 (0.96)	5.9 (1.01)	4.6 (1.28)	4.6 (1.24)	7.7 (1.84)	5.5! (1.67)	6.3 (1.33)	6.7 (1.01)	5.7 (1.06)	14.8 (1.75)	11.6 (1.48)	13.4 (1.53)	12.1 (1.27)	11.7 (1.56)	7.2 (1.50)
High school completion[2]	5.5 (1.02)	2.8 (0.70)	3.7 (0.96)	3.7 (0.91)	3.6 (0.95)	3.5 (0.93)	5.0 (0.73)	5.2 (0.63)	4.0 (0.48)	9.4 (0.78)	11.1 (0.88)	10.2 (0.80)	7.7 (0.68)	6.7 (0.64)	6.5 (0.76)
Some college, no bachelor's degree[3]	3.1! (1.39)	2.5! (1.06)	3.6! (1.43)	‡! (†)	3.7! (1.16)	3.4! (1.06)	4.2 (0.72)	3.3 (0.52)	3.5 (0.51)	8.5 (0.80)	9.2 (0.77)	7.5 (0.65)	8.0 (0.70)	6.2 (0.62)	5.9 (0.80)
Bachelor's or higher degree	‡! (†)	(†)	2.2! (0.80)	2.1! (0.78)	3.6 (1.00)	1.7! (0.63)	3.3 (0.52)	2.6 (0.41)	2.4 (0.34)	4.3 (0.47)	5.8 (0.48)	5.3 (0.47)	5.2 (0.55)	4.4 (0.42)	4.3 (0.53)

—Not available.
†Not applicable.
!Interpret data with caution. The coefficient of variation (CV) for this estimate is between 30 and 50 percent.
‡Reporting standards not met. The coefficient of variation (CV) for this estimate is 50 percent or greater.
[1]Data for 16- to 19-year-olds and 20- to 24-year-olds exclude persons enrolled in school.
[2]Includes equivalency credentials, such as the General Educational Development (GED) credential.
[3]Includes persons with no college degree as well as those with an associate's degree.

NOTE: The unemployment rate is the percentage of persons in the civilian labor force who are not working and who made specific efforts to find employment sometime during the prior 4 weeks. The civilian labor force consists of all civilians who are employed or seeking employment.
SOURCE: U.S. Department of Labor, Bureau of Labor Statistics, Office of Employment and Unemployment Statistics, unpublished annual average data from the Current Population Survey (CPS), selected years, 1975 through 2014. (This table was prepared November 2014.)

Table 501.90. Unemployment rates of females 16 to 64 years old, by age group and highest level of educational attainment: Selected years, 1975 through 2014

[Standard errors appear in parentheses]

Age group and highest level of educational attainment	1975	1980	1985	1990	1995	2000	2004	2005	2008	2009	2010	2011	2012	2013	2014
1	2	3	4	5	6	7	8	9	10	11	12	13	14	15	16
16 to 19 years old, all education levels[1]	(†)	(†)	(†)	14.7 (2.39)	20.6 (2.93)	18.9 (2.85)	20.1 (2.38)	19.7 (1.86)	18.8 (2.01)	23.8 (2.10)	26.9 (2.14)	25.5 (2.45)	29.6 (2.48)	28.9 (2.31)	20.9 (2.54)
Less than high school completion	—	—	—	23.4 (5.31)	29.7 (5.57)	27.9 (5.53)	29.5 (4.63)	31.0 (3.88)	30.9 (4.44)	34.9 (4.60)	36.4 (4.75)	40.4 (5.78)	46.2 (5.08)	36.5 (4.27)	22.5 (4.49)
High school completion[2]	—	—	—	11.3 (2.64)	16.0 (3.69)	15.7 (3.66)	17.4 (3.07)	14.2 (2.34)	15.0 (2.09)	22.2 (2.59)	24.9 (3.03)	23.8 (2.91)	24.5 (3.01)	29.6 (3.16)	22.9 (3.54)
At least some college	(†)	(†)	(†)	‡ (†)	‡ (†)	‡ (†)	‡ (†)	18.3 (5.47)	14.2 ! (5.49)	14.0 (4.16)	17.3 (4.41)	11.8 ! (4.28)	18.7 ! (5.62)	15.2 (3.92)	12.9 ! (4.87)
20 to 24 years old, all education levels[1]	(†)	(†)	(†)	7.8 (0.86)	10.2 (1.00)	8.9 (0.96)	11.0 (0.77)	10.3 (0.73)	9.7 (0.63)	13.5 (0.78)	15.6 (0.86)	16.0 (0.75)	14.1 (0.79)	13.4 (0.85)	12.4 (0.89)
Less than high school completion	(†)	(†)	(†)	18.6 (3.70)	24.3 (4.34)	17.0 (3.60)	18.5 (2.63)	24.5 (2.79)	21.6 (3.02)	28.4 (2.94)	32.2 (3.38)	36.3 (3.46)	27.3 (3.57)	34.9 (3.85)	29.3 (5.22)
High school completion[2]	—	—	—	8.1 (1.26)	12.7 (1.78)	10.6 (1.63)	12.6 (1.33)	11.5 (1.14)	12.5 (1.17)	16.6 (1.37)	19.9 (1.46)	19.5 (1.43)	17.1 (1.31)	15.1 (1.44)	15.8 (1.72)
Some college, no bachelor's degree[3]	—	—	—	4.9 (1.43)	6.7 (1.43)	5.7 (1.42)	9.1 (1.34)	6.8 (1.01)	6.5 (0.94)	10.5 (1.18)	12.1 (1.33)	12.8 (1.27)	13.4 (1.28)	11.5 (1.36)	10.6 (1.41)
Bachelor's or higher degree	—	—	—	3.5 ! (1.47)	3.1 ! (1.35)	4.6 ! (1.70)	5.9 (1.26)	4.4 (1.05)	4.4 (1.01)	6.1 (1.13)	6.3 (1.29)	7.2 (1.27)	5.6 (1.14)	5.6 (1.01)	6.3 (1.38)
25 to 64 years old, all education levels[1]	7.3 (0.33)	5.0 (0.25)	6.0 (0.26)	3.7 (0.20)	4.4 (0.21)	3.2 (0.18)	4.7 (0.15)	4.2 (0.12)	4.0 (0.12)	6.6 (0.12)	7.5 (0.15)	7.2 (0.17)	6.8 (0.15)	6.3 (0.15)	5.7 (0.19)
Less than high school completion	10.8 (0.79)	8.9 (0.76)	11.7 (0.96)	8.3 (0.88)	8.6 (0.95)	9.1 (1.00)	12.2 (0.83)	10.9 (0.65)	8.5 (0.62)	14.5 (0.72)	15.0 (0.71)	15.2 (0.74)	15.4 (0.83)	14.1 (0.84)	12.7 (0.98)
High school completion[2]	7.1 (0.49)	5.0 (0.37)	6.5 (0.41)	3.9 (0.32)	4.6 (0.36)	3.6 (0.33)	5.2 (0.29)	4.8 (0.23)	5.1 (0.27)	7.9 (0.26)	9.8 (0.30)	9.1 (0.36)	8.1 (0.31)	8.1 (0.35)	6.8 (0.42)
Some college, no bachelor's degree[3]	6.3 (0.84)	4.1 (0.54)	4.8 (0.53)	3.2 (0.40)	4.5 (0.38)	2.9 (0.31)	4.3 (0.26)	4.0 (0.22)	4.2 (0.21)	6.7 (0.27)	7.5 (0.27)	7.5 (0.27)	7.7 (0.30)	6.4 (0.29)	6.3 (0.36)
Bachelor's or higher degree	3.1 (0.57)	2.2 (0.39)	2.5 (0.36)	1.6 (0.27)	2.4 (0.30)	1.4 (0.22)	2.9 (0.21)	2.2 (0.17)	2.1 (0.15)	4.0 (0.19)	4.3 (0.19)	4.3 (0.21)	3.8 (0.19)	3.8 (0.19)	3.4 (0.22)
25 to 34 years old, all education levels[1]	9.1 (0.65)	6.8 (0.47)	7.3 (0.47)	5.1 (0.39)	5.7 (0.42)	3.9 (0.37)	5.7 (0.32)	5.6 (0.27)	5.3 (0.29)	8.0 (0.28)	8.7 (0.33)	8.6 (0.33)	8.2 (0.32)	7.5 (0.32)	7.3 (0.36)
Less than high school completion[2]	17.0 (2.18)	14.2 (1.93)	18.5 (2.37)	15.1 (2.17)	13.7 (2.20)	12.9 (2.33)	15.6 (1.78)	15.7 (1.36)	12.8 (1.53)	21.5 (1.79)	19.5 (1.52)	20.8 (1.84)	22.0 (1.99)	19.3 (1.65)	19.1 (2.42)
High school completion[2]	10.0 (1.01)	7.6 (0.76)	8.6 (0.78)	5.7 (0.65)	6.9 (0.81)	4.8 (0.78)	7.5 (0.73)	7.6 (0.62)	8.7 (0.67)	10.8 (0.67)	12.6 (0.86)	12.9 (0.78)	11.6 (0.82)	12.5 (0.88)	11.1 (1.04)
Some college, no bachelor's degree[3]	6.9 (1.38)	5.9 (0.94)	6.0 (0.88)	4.0 (0.72)	5.4 (0.73)	3.5 (0.63)	5.2 (0.56)	5.1 (0.46)	5.1 (0.45)	8.2 (0.56)	9.3 (0.57)	9.0 (0.61)	9.1 (0.59)	7.4 (0.57)	7.7 (0.68)
Bachelor's or higher degree	3.5 (0.88)	2.6 (0.60)	2.7 (0.57)	2.0 (0.47)	2.6 (0.53)	1.4 (0.39)	2.7 (0.38)	2.5 (0.31)	2.3 (0.37)	4.1 (0.37)	4.3 (0.37)	4.1 (0.35)	3.9 (0.38)	3.3 (0.33)	3.6 (0.38)
35 to 44 years old, all education levels[1]	7.1 (0.66)	4.7 (0.47)	5.4 (0.46)	3.5 (0.34)	4.3 (0.36)	3.7 (0.33)	4.9 (0.26)	3.9 (0.20)	3.8 (0.22)	6.4 (0.25)	8.2 (0.29)	7.4 (0.30)	6.5 (0.29)	6.6 (0.27)	5.6 (0.34)
Less than high school completion[2]	11.9 (1.65)	10.0 (1.56)	12.7 (1.95)	8.9 (1.79)	8.4 (1.75)	11.3 (1.94)	13.1 (1.51)	10.1 (1.02)	7.7 (1.03)	13.0 (1.33)	16.7 (1.32)	16.1 (1.51)	15.2 (1.29)	13.6 (1.57)	14.9 (1.99)
High school completion[2]	5.7 (0.85)	4.1 (0.65)	5.7 (0.72)	4.0 (0.57)	4.5 (0.63)	3.6 (0.58)	5.1 (0.52)	4.5 (0.40)	5.3 (0.50)	8.4 (0.63)	10.5 (0.67)	9.6 (0.66)	8.3 (0.71)	8.1 (0.70)	6.2 (0.68)
Some college, no bachelor's degree[3]	6.8 (1.76)	3.3 (0.97)	4.3 (0.91)	2.8 (0.64)	4.7 (0.66)	3.3 (0.57)	4.6 (0.49)	3.7 (0.36)	3.6 (0.35)	6.2 (0.46)	8.5 (0.51)	7.6 (0.56)	7.4 (0.54)	7.3 (0.53)	6.7 (0.70)
Bachelor's or higher degree	3.5 ! (1.29)	2.3 ! (0.76)	2.2 (0.61)	1.4 ! (0.42)	2.4 (0.52)	1.8 (0.44)	2.8 (0.38)	1.9 (0.26)	2.1 (0.35)	3.7 (0.35)	4.5 (0.41)	4.5 (0.41)	3.1 (0.31)	4.0 (0.35)	3.0 (0.40)
45 to 54 years old, all education levels[1]	6.5 (0.62)	4.1 (0.49)	5.3 (0.56)	2.3 (0.35)	3.1 (0.36)	2.4 (0.30)	4.2 (0.26)	3.6 (0.19)	3.5 (0.20)	6.1 (0.23)	6.8 (0.27)	6.7 (0.29)	6.5 (0.28)	5.6 (0.25)	4.9 (0.32)
Less than high school completion[2]	9.0 (1.33)	7.6 (1.32)	9.2 (1.71)	4.7 (1.33)	5.8 (1.55)	5.1 ! (1.52)	10.1 (1.52)	8.2 (1.08)	7.3 (1.06)	12.7 (1.38)	13.6 (1.41)	15.8 (1.50)	13.1 (1.49)	12.1 (1.43)	6.7 (1.32)
High school completion[2]	6.3 (0.88)	3.6 (0.66)	5.4 (0.30)	1.8 (0.46)	2.7 (0.57)	3.0 (0.59)	4.3 (0.48)	4.0 (0.39)	3.7 (0.41)	6.6 (0.50)	5.9 (0.56)	8.0 (0.62)	6.7 (0.48)	6.4 (0.45)	6.1 (0.69)
Some college, no bachelor's degree[3]	5.3 ! (1.61)	2.3 ! (0.99)	4.0 ! (1.23)	2.7 ! (0.89)	3.7 (0.73)	2.2 (0.52)	3.9 (0.46)	3.6 (0.41)	4.2 (0.40)	6.5 (0.47)	5.9 (0.43)	6.2 (0.43)	7.5 (0.57)	5.4 (0.44)	5.3 (0.64)
Bachelor's or higher degree	2.6 ! (1.18)	1.9 ! (0.90)	2.4 ! (0.92)	1.3 ! (0.56)	2.1 (0.52)	1.3 ! (0.39)	3.2 (0.41)	2.2 (0.33)	1.9 (0.24)	3.8 (0.34)	4.3 (0.36)	4.1 (0.40)	4.1 (0.38)	3.9 (0.38)	3.3 (0.40)
55 to 64 years old, all education levels[1]	5.4 (0.71)	2.5 (0.47)	4.5 (0.63)	2.2 (0.47)	3.3 (0.55)	2.4 (0.45)	3.6 (0.34)	3.4 (0.29)	3.2 (0.24)	5.6 (0.33)	6.0 (0.32)	5.9 (0.34)	6.0 (0.31)	5.4 (0.33)	4.7 (0.38)
Less than high school completion	7.3 (1.28)	3.7 (1.06)	6.7 (1.49)	2.9 ! (1.17)	5.3 ! (1.78)	4.8 ! (1.84)	8.1 (1.76)	8.6 (1.51)	5.6 (1.10)	9.7 (1.45)	8.0 (1.36)	4.8 (1.05)	10.8 (1.78)	10.5 (1.69)	9.8 (2.00)
High school completion[2]	4.6 (1.05)	2.6 (0.69)	4.5 (0.93)	2.2 ! (0.68)	3.2 (0.84)	2.8 (0.77)	3.8 (0.60)	3.3 (0.46)	2.9 (0.45)	6.3 (0.64)	7.5 (0.58)	6.7 (0.65)	6.5 (0.69)	6.0 (0.64)	4.6 (0.65)
Some college, no bachelor's degree[3]	5.6 ! (2.23)	‡ (†)	‡ (†)	2.4 ! (1.15)	2.8 ! (1.00)	2.2 ! (0.84)	3.1 (0.59)	3.7 (0.54)	3.9 (0.51)	5.5 (0.63)	6.3 (0.55)	7.1 (0.66)	6.3 (0.58)	5.5 (0.50)	5.1 (0.68)
Bachelor's or higher degree	‡ (†)	‡ (†)	‡ (†)	‡ (†)	2.6 ! (1.16)	‡ (†)	2.6 (0.53)	1.9 (0.39)	2.3 (0.36)	4.3 (0.50)	4.1 (0.49)	4.4 (0.52)	4.4 (0.51)	4.0 (0.44)	3.6 (0.59)

—Not available.
†Not applicable.
!Interpret data with caution. The coefficient of variation (CV) for this estimate is between 30 and 50 percent.
‡Reporting standards not met. The coefficient of variation (CV) for this estimate is 50 percent or greater.
[1]Data for 16- to 19-year-olds and 20- to 24-year-olds exclude persons enrolled in school.
[2]Includes equivalency credentials, such as the General Educational Development (GED) credential.
[3]Includes persons with no college degree as well as those with an associate's degree.

NOTE: The unemployment rate is the percentage of persons in the civilian labor force who are not working and who made specific efforts to find employment sometime during the prior 4 weeks. The civilian labor force consists of all civilians who are employed or seeking employment. Some data have been revised from previously published figures.
SOURCE: U.S. Department of Labor, Bureau of Labor Statistics, Office of Employment and Unemployment Statistics, unpublished annual average data from the Current Population Survey (CPS), selected years, 1975 through 2014. (This table was prepared November 2014.)

Table 502.10. Occupation of employed persons 25 years old and over, by highest level of educational attainment and sex: 2013

[Standard errors appear in parentheses]

Sex and occupation	Total employed (in thousands)	Percentage distribution, by highest level of educational attainment				College		
		Total	Less than high school completion	High school completion (includes equivalency)	Some college, no degree	Associate's degree	Bachelor's degree	Master's or higher degree
1	2	3	4	5	6	7	8	9
All persons	**125,872** (230.1)	**100.0**	**7.8** (0.09)	**26.7** (0.14)	**16.6** (0.12)	**11.1** (0.10)	**23.9** (0.14)	**13.8** (0.11)
Management, professional, and related	51,609 (222.7)	100.0	1.3 (0.06)	10.4 (0.16)	11.4 (0.16)	10.8 (0.16)	36.9 (0.25)	29.3 (0.23)
Management, business, and financial operations	21,883 (160.5)	100.0	2.1 (0.11)	15.5 (0.28)	14.8 (0.28)	9.1 (0.22)	38.8 (0.38)	19.7 (0.31)
Professional and related	29,726 (182.5)	100.0	0.7 (0.05)	6.5 (0.17)	8.8 (0.19)	12.0 (0.22)	35.6 (0.32)	36.4 (0.32)
Education, training, and library	7,954 (100.8)	100.0	0.6 (0.10)	6.2 (0.31)	6.8 (0.33)	5.6 (0.30)	34.2 (0.61)	46.6 (0.65)
Preschool and kindergarten teachers	612 (28.6)	100.0	‡ (†)	14.5 (1.65)	16.2 (1.72)	11.9 (1.51)	38.9 (2.28)	17.6 (1.78)
Elementary and middle school teachers	2,900 (61.8)	100.0	0.4! (0.14)	2.1 (0.31)	2.9 (0.36)	2.5 (0.34)	42.1 (1.06)	49.9 (1.07)
Secondary school teachers	1,015 (36.7)	100.0	# (†)	2.0 (0.50)	2.1 (0.52)	1.2! (0.39)	40.8 (1.78)	53.9 (1.81)
Special education teachers	364 (22.0)	100.0	# (†)	3.0! (1.04)	3.0! (1.04)	3.6! (1.12)	36.5 (2.92)	53.6 (3.02)
Postsecondary teachers	1,208 (40.0)	100.0	‡ (†)	1.4 (0.39)	1.4 (0.39)	3.0 (0.57)	13.6 (1.14)	80.6 (1.31)
Other education, training, and library workers	1,855 (49.5)	100.0	1.5 (0.33)	16.0 (0.98)	16.5 (1.00)	12.8 (0.90)	29.8 (1.23)	23.3 (1.13)
Service occupations	20,093 (154.6)	100.0	16.2 (0.30)	37.5 (0.39)	19.9 (0.33)	11.7 (0.26)	12.1 (0.27)	2.5 (0.13)
Sales and office occupations	27,665 (177.2)	100.0	4.1 (0.14)	31.8 (0.32)	23.1 (0.29)	12.3 (0.23)	23.7 (0.30)	5.0 (0.15)
Natural resources, construction, and maintenance	11,626 (120.6)	100.0	19.6 (0.43)	42.4 (0.53)	17.2 (0.40)	12.0 (0.35)	7.5 (0.28)	1.3 (0.12)
Production, transportation, and material moving	14,879 (135.2)	100.0	16.6 (0.35)	47.2 (0.47)	18.0 (0.36)	8.6 (0.27)	8.2 (0.26)	1.4 (0.11)
Males	**67,163** (154.4)	**100.0**	**9.4** (0.13)	**28.4** (0.20)	**16.3** (0.16)	**9.6** (0.13)	**23.1** (0.18)	**13.2** (0.15)
Management, professional, and related	25,221 (154.1)	100.0	1.6 (0.09)	10.9 (0.22)	11.6 (0.23)	8.4 (0.20)	37.2 (0.35)	30.3 (0.33)
Management, business, and financial operations	12,439 (118.0)	100.0	2.5 (0.16)	16.3 (0.38)	14.5 (0.36)	8.0 (0.28)	38.4 (0.50)	20.3 (0.41)
Professional and related	12,782 (119.4)	100.0	0.6 (0.08)	5.7 (0.23)	8.8 (0.28)	8.9 (0.29)	36.1 (0.48)	39.9 (0.49)
Education, training, and library	2,064 (51.1)	100.0	0.4! (0.16)	2.8 (0.41)	4.2 (0.50)	3.4 (0.45)	32.5 (1.17)	56.6 (1.24)
Service occupations	8,674 (100.9)	100.0	17.1 (0.46)	34.9 (0.58)	20.1 (0.49)	10.2 (0.37)	14.9 (0.43)	2.8 (0.20)
Sales and office occupations	10,506 (109.8)	100.0	4.4 (0.23)	28.6 (0.50)	21.4 (0.45)	10.2 (0.34)	29.2 (0.50)	6.3 (0.27)
Natural resources, construction, and maintenance	11,115 (112.5)	100.0	19.4 (0.43)	43.0 (0.53)	17.2 (0.41)	12.0 (0.35)	7.2 (0.28)	1.2 (0.12)
Production, transportation, and material moving	11,647 (114.8)	100.0	15.7 (0.38)	47.7 (0.53)	18.3 (0.41)	8.8 (0.30)	8.2 (0.29)	1.4 (0.12)
Females	**58,710** (159.7)	**100.0**	**5.9** (0.11)	**24.7** (0.20)	**17.0** (0.17)	**12.9** (0.15)	**25.0** (0.20)	**14.6** (0.16)
Management, professional, and related	26,388 (150.9)	100.0	1.0 (0.07)	9.8 (0.20)	11.1 (0.21)	13.0 (0.23)	36.7 (0.33)	28.4 (0.31)
Management, business, and financial operations	9,444 (101.3)	100.0	1.5 (0.14)	14.6 (0.40)	15.2 (0.41)	10.5 (0.35)	39.4 (0.55)	18.9 (0.44)
Professional and related	16,944 (129.4)	100.0	0.7 (0.07)	7.2 (0.22)	8.9 (0.24)	14.4 (0.30)	35.2 (0.40)	33.6 (0.40)
Education, training, and library	5,890 (81.7)	100.0	0.6 (0.11)	7.4 (0.38)	7.7 (0.38)	6.4 (0.35)	34.8 (0.68)	43.0 (0.71)
Service occupations	11,420 (110.1)	100.0	15.5 (0.37)	39.5 (0.50)	19.8 (0.41)	12.9 (0.34)	10.0 (0.31)	2.3 (0.16)
Sales and office occupations	17,159 (130.0)	100.0	3.9 (0.16)	33.7 (0.40)	24.2 (0.36)	13.7 (0.29)	20.3 (0.34)	4.3 (0.17)
Natural resources, construction, and maintenance	510 (24.8)	100.0	22.2 (2.02)	30.6 (2.25)	16.9 (1.83)	12.0 (1.58)	15.3 (1.75)	3.3 (0.88)
Production, transportation, and material moving	3,232 (61.5)	100.0	20.2 (0.78)	45.5 (0.96)	16.7 (0.72)	7.8 (0.52)	8.4 (0.54)	1.5 (0.24)

†Not applicable.
#Rounds to zero.
!Interpret data with caution. The coefficient of variation (CV) for this estimate is between 30 and 50 percent.
‡Reporting standards not met. The coefficient of variation (CV) for this estimate is 50 percent or greater.

NOTE: Detail may not sum to totals because of rounding.
SOURCE: U.S. Department of Labor, Bureau of Labor Statistics, Office of Employment and Unemployment Statistics, unpublished 2013 annual average data from the Current Population Survey (CPS). (This table was prepared August 2014.)

Table 502.20. Median annual earnings, number, and percentage of full-time year-round workers 25 years old and over, by highest level of educational attainment and sex: 1990 through 2013

[Standard errors appear in parentheses]

Values are in current dollars. Columns 2–6 fall under "Elementary/secondary"; columns 7–12 under "College"; columns 9–12 under "Bachelor's or higher degree[4]".

Sex and year	Total	Less than 9th grade	Some high school, no completion[1]	High school completion (includes equivalency)[2]	Some college, no degree[3]	Associate's degree	Total (college)	Bachelor's degree[5]	Master's degree	Professional degree	Doctor's degree
1	2	3	4	5	6	7	8	9	10	11	12
Males											
1990	$30,730 (—)	$17,390 (—)	$20,900 (—)	$26,650 (—)	$31,730 (—)	$33,820[6] (†)	$42,670 (—)	$39,240 (—)	$49,730[6] (†)	$74,000[6] (†)	$57,190[6] (†)
1991	31,610 (—)	17,620 (—)	21,400 (—)	26,780 (—)	31,660 (—)	33,430 (—)	45,140 (—)	40,910 (—)	49,970 (—)	76,220 (—)	57,420 (—)
1992	32,060 (120)	17,290 (—)	21,270 (—)	27,280 (—)	32,100 (—)	33,690 (—)	45,800 (—)	41,360 (304)	51,870 (—)	80,550 (—)	63,150 (—)
1993	32,360 (124)	16,860 (—)	21,750 (204)	27,370 (—)	32,080 (—)	— (—)	47,740 (—)	42,760 (536)	53,500 (—)	75,010 (—)	61,920 (—)
1994	33,440 (246)	17,530 (453)	22,050 (319)	28,040 (322)	32,280 (300)	35,790 (430)	49,230 (707)	43,660 (633)	53,500 (854)	75,010 (3,040)	61,920 (1,619)
1995	34,550 (275)	18,350 (545)	22,190 (342)	29,510 (358)	33,880 (517)	35,200 (535)	50,480 (312)	45,270 (510)	55,220 (973)	79,670 (2,582)	65,340 (2,188)
1996	35,620 (150)	17,960 (594)	22,730 (414)	30,710 (184)	34,850 (456)	37,130 (435)	51,440 (303)	45,850 (458)	60,510 (945)	85,960 (3,317)	71,230 (3,362)
1997	36,680 (149)	19,290 (629)	24,730 (466)	31,220 (171)	35,950 (293)	38,020 (774)	53,450 (755)	48,620 (851)	61,690 (771)	85,010 (4,253)	76,230 (3,611)
1998	37,910 (291)	19,380 (600)	23,960 (547)	31,480 (169)	36,930 (291)	40,270 (539)	56,520 (421)	51,410 (349)	62,240 (847)	94,740 (12,105)	75,080 (2,507)
1999	40,330 (144)	20,430 (444)	25,040 (535)	33,180 (388)	39,220 (581)	41,640 (459)	60,200 (439)	52,990 (722)	66,240 (690)	100,000! (37,836)	81,690 (3,953)
2000	41,060 (156)	20,790 (376)	25,100 (436)	34,300 (457)	40,340 (312)	41,950 (460)	61,870 (303)	56,330 (573)	68,320 (1,506)	99,410 (20,832)	80,250 (2,446)
2001	41,620 (104)	21,360 (235)	26,210 (251)	34,720 (299)	41,050 (214)	42,780 (561)	62,220 (279)	55,930 (335)	70,900 (687)	100,000 (—)	86,970 (3,013)
2002	41,150 (100)	20,920 (213)	25,900 (207)	33,210 (311)	40,850 (195)	42,860 (673)	61,700 (201)	56,080 (385)	67,280 (1,294)	100,000 (—)	83,310 (2,076)
2003	41,940 (89)	21,220 (227)	26,470 (280)	35,410 (168)	41,350 (182)	42,870 (719)	62,080 (187)	56,500 (365)	70,640 (562)	100,000 (—)	87,130 (2,528)
2004	42,090 (—)	21,660 (191)	26,280 (234)	35,730 (148)	41,900 (175)	44,400 (931)	62,800 (798)	57,220 (393)	71,530 (490)	100,000 (—)	82,400 (2,423)
2005	43,320 (367)	22,330 (220)	27,190 (237)	36,300 (141)	42,420 (323)	47,180 (367)	66,170 (356)	60,020 (653)	75,030 (1,229)	100,000 (—)	85,860 (3,061)
2006	45,760 (134)	22,710 (398)	27,650 (573)	37,030 (164)	43,830 (812)	47,070 (390)	66,930 (346)	60,910 (235)	75,430 (859)	100,000 (—)	100,000 (—)
2007	47,000 (130)	23,380 (544)	29,320 (590)	37,860 (406)	44,900 (585)	49,040 (801)	70,400 (241)	62,090 (236)	76,280 (416)	100,000 (—)	92,090 (1,894)
2008	49,000 (339)	24,260 (631)	29,680 (458)	39,010 (399)	45,820 (276)	50,150 (344)	72,220 (236)	65,800 (388)	80,960 (468)	123,240 (2,539)	100,000 (—)
2009	49,990 (201)	23,950 (394)	28,020 (542)	39,480 (379)	47,100 (347)	50,300 (238)	71,470 (239)	62,440 (707)	79,340 (1,568)	— (—)	100,740 (519)
2010	50,360 (93)	24,450 (597)	29,440 (684)	40,060 (237)	46,430 (348)	50,280 (245)	71,780 (267)	63,740 (1,115)	80,960 (453)	115,300 (4,891)	101,220 (653)
2011	50,660 (25)	25,220 (23)	30,420 (300)	40,450 (87)	47,070 (78)	50,930 (212)	73,850 (490)	66,200 (25)	83,030 (755)	119,470 (1,917)	100,770 (192)
2012	50,950 (144)	25,130 (440)	30,330 (430)	40,350 (194)	47,190 (407)	50,960 (329)	75,320 (565)	66,150 (570)	85,120 (1,412)	116,350 (5,632)	106,470 (4,656)
2013	51,120 (149)	26,160 (531)	30,570 (551)	40,290 (227)	47,650 (739)	51,000 (493)	76,110 (485)	67,240 (992)	86,310 (1,429)	126,730 (8,647)	105,280 (4,631)
Females											
1990	21,370 (—)	12,250 (—)	14,430 (—)	18,320 (—)	22,230 (—)	25,000[6] (†)	30,380 (—)	28,020 (—)	34,950[6] (†)	46,740[6] (†)	43,300[6] (†)
1991	22,040 (—)	12,070 (—)	14,460 (—)	18,840 (—)	22,140 (—)	25,620 (—)	31,310 (—)	29,080 (—)	36,040 (—)	46,260 (—)	45,790 (—)
1992	23,140 (159)	12,960 (—)	14,560 (—)	19,430 (176)	23,160 (—)	25,880 (—)	32,300 (—)	30,330 (294)	38,610 (—)	50,210 (—)	51,120 (—)
1993	23,630 (166)	12,420 (—)	15,390 (—)	19,960 (173)	23,060 (—)	25,940 (295)	34,310 (—)	31,200 (310)	39,460 (—)	50,620 (2,154)	— (—)
1994	24,400 (165)	12,430 (427)	15,130 (328)	20,370 (158)	23,510 (327)	— (—)	35,380 (280)	31,740 (314)	— (606)	— (—)	— (2,888)
1995	24,880 (160)	13,580 (490)	15,830 (293)	20,460 (162)	24,000 (274)	27,310 (428)	35,260 (313)	32,050 (273)	40,260 (556)	50,000 (2,532)	48,140 (2,373)
1996	25,810 (131)	14,410 (559)	16,950 (333)	21,180 (143)	25,170 (267)	28,080 (526)	36,460 (296)	33,530 (437)	41,900 (564)	57,620 (3,635)	56,270 (3,300)
1997	26,970 (134)	14,160 (492)	16,700 (335)	22,080 (148)	26,340 (291)	28,810 (660)	38,040 (481)	35,380 (295)	44,950 (837)	61,050 (4,737)	53,040 (3,626)
1998	27,960 (199)	14,470 (429)	16,480 (322)	22,780 (254)	27,420 (271)	29,920 (513)	39,790 (408)	36,560 (305)	45,280 (760)	57,570 (1,705)	57,800 (1,881)
1999	28,840 (216)	15,100 (492)	17,020 (298)	23,060 (279)	27,760 (369)	30,920 (318)	41,750 (275)	37,990 (614)	48,100 (862)	59,900 (4,479)	60,080 (3,130)
2000	30,330 (138)	15,800 (327)	17,920 (434)	24,970 (236)	28,700 (364)	31,070 (307)	42,710 (439)	40,420 (284)	50,140 (735)	58,960 (3,552)	57,090 (2,490)
2001	31,360 (91)	16,690 (255)	19,160 (359)	25,300 (132)	30,140 (186)	32,150 (231)	44,780 (367)	40,990 (231)	50,670 (328)	61,750 (3,976)	62,120 (1,779)
2002	31,010 (83)	16,510 (297)	19,310 (360)	25,180 (121)	29,400 (299)	31,630 (211)	43,250 (568)	40,850 (173)	48,890 (595)	57,020 (2,421)	65,720 (2,155)
2003	31,570 (85)	16,910 (256)	18,940 (327)	26,070 (118)	30,140 (176)	32,250 (241)	45,240 (291)	41,330 (454)	50,160 (454)	66,490 (3,469)	67,210 (2,144)
2004	31,990 (80)	17,020 (241)	19,160 (319)	26,030 (116)	30,820 (135)	33,480 (489)	45,910 (229)	41,680 (172)	51,320 (263)	75,040 (2,436)	68,880 (912)
2005	33,080 (242)	16,140 (250)	20,130 (274)	26,290 (134)	31,400 (165)	33,940 (497)	46,950 (232)	42,170 (179)	51,410 (283)	80,460 (2,774)	66,850 (2,490)
2006	35,100 (113)	18,130 (408)	20,130 (270)	26,740 (136)	31,950 (165)	35,160 (376)	49,570 (441)	45,410 (259)	55,430 (561)	76,240 (2,488)	70,520 (1,779)
2007	36,090 (105)	18,260 (461)	20,400 (292)	27,240 (133)	32,840 (415)	36,330 (283)	50,400 (158)	45,770 (262)	57,510 (412)	71,100 (910)	68,990 (2,155)
2008	36,700 (109)	18,630 (494)	20,410 (295)	28,380 (283)	32,630 (355)	36,760 (243)	51,410 (145)	47,030 (237)	57,510 (745)	71,300 (2,859)	74,030 (2,144)
2009	37,260 (107)	18,480 (451)	21,230 (301)	29,150 (273)	34,090 (483)	37,270 (310)	51,880 (169)	46,830 (260)	61,070 (304)	83,910 (3,210)	76,580 (912)
2010	38,290 (272)	18,240 (592)	20,880 (334)	29,860 (260)	33,400 (410)	37,770 (588)	51,940 (159)	47,440 (336)	59,100 (1,021)	76,740 (2,723)	77,390 (2,174)
2011	38,910 (216)	20,100 (250)	21,110 (131)	30,010 (145)	34,590 (512)	39,290 (40)	52,140 (88)	49,110 (103)	60,300 (533)	80,720 (135)	77,460 (21)
2012	39,980 (294)	20,060 (514)	21,390 (285)	30,410 (165)	35,060 (452)	37,320 (455)	53,690 (888)	50,170 (290)	60,930 (464)	94,470 (6,655)	77,900 (3,616)
2013	40,610 (134)	19,840 (502)	22,250 (544)	30,800 (173)	35,240 (312)	37,700 (751)	55,720 (416)	50,750 (341)	61,280 (561)	85,400 (6,196)	75,090 (3,515)

See notes at end of table.

Table 502.20. Median annual earnings, number, and percentage of full-time year-round workers 25 years old and over, by highest level of educational attainment and sex: 1990 through 2013—Continued

[Standard errors appear in parentheses]

Constant 2013 dollars[7]

Columns 3–6 are grouped under **Elementary/secondary**; columns 7–12 are grouped under **College**. Columns 8–12 are grouped under **Bachelor's or higher degree[4]**.

Sex and year (1)	Total (2)	Less than 9th grade (3)	Some high school, no completion[1] (4)	High school completion (includes equivalency)[2] (5)	Some college, no degree[3] (6)	Associate's degree (7)	College Total (8)	Bachelor's degree[5] (9)	Master's degree (10)	Professional degree[4] (11)	Doctor's degree (12)
Males											
1990	$54,790 (—)	$31,010 (—)	$37,260 (—)	$47,510 (—)	$56,570 (—)	$57,850[6] (†)	$76,070 (—)	$69,950 (—)	$85,080[6] (†)	$126,590[6] (†)	$97,830[6] (†)
1991	54,080 (—)	30,150 (—)	36,610 (—)	45,810 (—)	54,170 (—)	55,520 (—)	77,220 (—)	69,980 (—)	82,990 (—)	126,580 (—)	95,360 (—)
1992	53,240 (199)	28,720 (—)	35,330 (—)	45,300 (291)	53,310 (—)	54,320 (—)	76,060 (—)	68,680 (505)	83,630 (—)	129,880 (—)	101,830 (—)
1993	52,180 (200)	27,190 (—)	35,070 (—)	44,130 (329)	51,720 (—)	‡ (—)	76,980 (—)	68,940 (864)	‡ (—)	‡ (—)	‡ (—)
1994	52,570 (387)	27,560 (712)	34,660 (502)	44,080 (506)	50,750 (472)	56,280 (676)	77,400 (1,112)	68,650 (995)	84,110 (1,343)	117,980 (4,779)	97,350 (2,545)
1995	52,820 (420)	28,060 (833)	33,920 (523)	45,120 (547)	51,800 (790)	53,820 (818)	77,180 (477)	69,210 (780)	84,420 (1,488)	121,800 (3,948)	99,890 (3,345)
1996	52,900 (223)	26,670 (882)	33,740 (615)	45,600 (273)	51,750 (677)	55,140 (646)	76,380 (450)	68,080 (680)	89,860 (1,403)	127,660 (4,926)	105,770 (4,993)
1997	53,250 (216)	28,010 (913)	35,900 (676)	45,320 (248)	52,180 (425)	55,200 (1,124)	77,590 (1,096)	70,580 (1,235)	89,560 (1,119)	123,410 (6,174)	110,670 (5,242)
1998	54,180 (416)	27,700 (858)	34,250 (782)	44,990 (242)	52,800 (416)	57,570 (770)	80,800 (602)	73,480 (499)	88,970 (1,211)	135,420 (17,303)	107,320 (3,584)
1999	56,410 (201)	28,570 (621)	35,010 (748)	46,410 (543)	54,850 (813)	58,230 (642)	84,190 (614)	74,100 (1,010)	92,640 (965)	139,860 ! (52,916)	114,240 (5,529)
2000	55,560 (211)	28,130 (509)	33,960 (590)	46,410 (618)	54,580 (422)	56,760 (622)	83,710 (410)	76,220 (775)	92,440 (2,038)	134,510 (28,187)	108,580 (3,310)
2001	54,750 (137)	28,100 (309)	34,480 (330)	45,680 (393)	54,000 (282)	56,280 (738)	81,860 (367)	73,580 (441)	93,280 (904)	131,560 (—)	114,410 (3,964)
2002	53,300 (130)	27,090 (276)	33,550 (268)	43,010 (403)	52,910 (253)	55,510 (872)	79,910 (260)	72,630 (499)	87,140 (1,676)	129,520 (—)	107,890 (2,689)
2003	53,110 (114)	26,870 (287)	33,520 (355)	44,840 (213)	52,360 (230)	54,290 (910)	78,610 (237)	71,550 (462)	89,450 (712)	126,630 (—)	110,330 (3,201)
2004	51,910 (110)	26,720 (236)	32,410 (289)	44,070 (183)	51,680 (216)	54,770 (1,148)	77,460 (984)	70,580 (485)	88,230 (604)	123,350 (—)	101,640 (2,989)
2005	51,680 (438)	26,640 (262)	32,440 (283)	43,310 (168)	50,610 (385)	56,290 (438)	78,940 (425)	71,610 (779)	89,510 (1,466)	119,300 (3,871)	102,440 (3,652)
2006	52,890 (155)	26,240 (460)	31,960 (662)	42,800 (190)	50,660 (938)	54,400 (451)	77,360 (400)	70,390 (272)	87,180 (993)	115,580 (5,398)	115,580 (—)
2007	52,820 (146)	26,270 (611)	32,940 (663)	42,540 (456)	50,460 (657)	55,110 (900)	79,110 (271)	69,770 (265)	85,720 (467)	112,370 (6,877)	103,480 (—)
2008	53,080 (367)	26,250 (683)	32,120 (496)	42,220 (432)	49,590 (299)	54,270 (372)	78,150 (255)	71,210 (420)	87,620 (506)	108,220 (—)	108,220 (2,128)
2009	54,300 (218)	26,010 (428)	30,430 (589)	42,880 (412)	51,150 (377)	54,630 (258)	77,620 (260)	67,820 (768)	86,170 (1,703)	133,850 (2,758)	109,410 (564)
2010	53,810 (99)	26,130 (638)	31,450 (731)	42,800 (253)	49,620 (372)	53,730 (262)	76,700 (285)	68,110 (1,191)	86,510 (484)	123,200 (5,226)	108,160 (698)
2011	52,470 (26)	26,130 (24)	31,510 (311)	41,900 (90)	48,760 (81)	52,750 (220)	76,500 (508)	68,570 (26)	86,000 (782)	123,760 (1,986)	104,380 (199)
2012	51,710 (146)	25,500 (447)	30,780 (436)	40,950 (197)	47,890 (413)	51,720 (334)	76,440 (573)	67,130 (578)	86,380 (1,433)	118,080 (5,715)	108,040 (4,725)
2013	51,120 (149)	26,160 (531)	30,570 (551)	40,290 (227)	47,650 (739)	51,000 (493)	76,110 (485)	67,240 (992)	86,310 (1,429)	126,730 (8,647)	105,280 (4,631)
Females											
1990	$38,100 (—)	$21,840 (—)	$25,720 (—)	$32,660 (—)	$39,620 (—)	$42,770[6] (†)	$54,150 (—)	$49,950 (—)	$59,790[6] (†)	$79,960[6] (†)	$74,080[6] (†)
1991	37,710 (—)	20,640 (—)	24,730 (—)	32,220 (—)	37,880 (—)	42,550 (—)	53,560 (—)	49,750 (—)	59,850 (—)	76,820 (—)	76,040 (—)
1992	38,430 (264)	21,520 (—)	24,180 (—)	32,260 (292)	38,460 (—)	‡ (—)	53,650 (—)	50,360 (488)	‡ (—)	‡ (—)	‡ (—)
1993	38,100 (268)	20,020 (—)	24,810 (—)	32,180 (279)	37,180 (—)	41,740 (—)	55,320 (—)	50,300 (500)	62,260 (—)	80,960 (—)	76,190 (—)
1994	38,360 (259)	19,540 (671)	23,790 (516)	32,030 (248)	36,970 (514)	40,780 (464)	55,620 (440)	49,900 (494)	62,030 (953)	79,580 (3,387)	80,370 (4,541)
1995	38,030 (245)	20,760 (749)	24,190 (448)	31,290 (248)	36,690 (419)	41,760 (654)	53,910 (479)	49,000 (417)	61,560 (850)	76,440 (3,871)	73,600 (3,628)
1996	38,330 (195)	21,410 (830)	25,180 (495)	31,450 (215)	37,370 (397)	41,700 (781)	54,150 (440)	49,790 (649)	62,220 (838)	85,570 (5,398)	83,560 (4,901)
1997	39,160 (195)	20,560 (714)	24,240 (486)	32,030 (215)	38,230 (422)	41,830 (958)	51,830 (698)	51,560 (428)	65,250 (1,215)	88,630 (6,877)	77,000 (5,264)
1998	39,960 (284)	20,680 (613)	23,560 (460)	32,560 (363)	39,200 (387)	42,770 (733)	55,220 (583)	52,260 (436)	64,730 (1,086)	82,290 (2,437)	82,620 (2,689)
1999	40,340 (302)	21,120 (688)	23,800 (417)	32,250 (390)	38,820 (516)	43,240 (445)	58,390 (385)	53,140 (859)	67,270 (1,206)	83,780 (6,264)	84,020 (4,377)
2000	41,030 (187)	21,380 (442)	24,250 (587)	33,790 (319)	38,830 (493)	42,040 (415)	57,780 (594)	54,680 (384)	67,840 (995)	79,770 (4,806)	77,240 (4,058)
2001	41,250 (120)	21,960 (335)	25,200 (472)	33,290 (174)	40,020 (245)	42,300 (304)	58,910 (483)	53,930 (304)	66,660 (432)	81,240 (5,231)	81,730 (2,931)
2002	40,160 (107)	21,380 (385)	25,010 (466)	32,610 (157)	38,080 (387)	40,960 (273)	56,010 (736)	52,910 (224)	63,320 (771)	73,850 (3,136)	85,110 (2,937)
2003	39,970 (108)	21,410 (324)	23,980 (414)	33,020 (149)	38,170 (223)	40,840 (305)	57,130 (368)	52,330 (258)	63,520 (575)	84,350 (4,393)	85,110 (3,118)
2004	39,460 (99)	21,000 (297)	23,640 (393)	32,110 (143)	38,010 (167)	41,300 (603)	56,630 (282)	51,410 (212)	63,300 (324)	92,550 (3,005)	84,950 (3,022)
2005	39,460 (289)	19,260 (298)	24,070 (327)	31,360 (160)	37,460 (197)	40,490 (593)	56,010 (277)	50,310 (214)	61,340 (338)	95,990 (3,309)	79,760 (2,971)
2006	40,560 (131)	20,960 (472)	23,270 (312)	30,900 (157)	36,930 (191)	40,640 (435)	57,290 (510)	52,480 (299)	60,610 (648)	88,120 (2,876)	81,500 (2,056)
2007	40,550 (118)	20,520 (518)	22,920 (328)	30,610 (149)	36,900 (466)	40,830 (318)	56,630 (178)	51,440 (294)	62,280 (463)	79,900 (1,023)	77,530 (2,422)
2008	39,710 (118)	20,170 (535)	22,080 (319)	30,710 (306)	35,310 (384)	39,780 (263)	55,630 (157)	50,890 (256)	62,240 (806)	77,160 (3,094)	80,110 (2,320)
2009	40,470 (116)	20,070 (490)	23,050 (327)	31,660 (296)	37,020 (525)	40,470 (337)	56,340 (184)	50,860 (282)	66,320 (330)	91,130 (3,486)	83,170 (990)
2010	40,920 (291)	19,490 (633)	22,310 (357)	31,900 (278)	35,690 (438)	40,360 (628)	55,500 (170)	50,870 (359)	63,150 (1,091)	82,000 (2,910)	82,700 (2,323)
2011	40,300 (224)	20,820 (259)	21,870 (136)	31,090 (150)	35,830 (530)	40,690 (41)	54,000 (91)	50,870 (107)	62,470 (552)	83,610 (140)	80,230 (22)
2012	40,570 (298)	20,360 (522)	21,700 (289)	30,860 (167)	35,580 (459)	37,870 (462)	54,480 (901)	50,920 (294)	61,830 (471)	95,870 (6,754)	79,060 (3,670)
2013	40,610 (134)	19,840 (502)	22,250 (544)	30,800 (173)	35,240 (312)	37,700 (751)	55,720 (416)	50,750 (341)	61,280 (561)	85,400 (6,196)	75,090 (3,515)

See notes at end of table.

Table 502.20. Median annual earnings, number, and percentage of full-time year-round workers 25 years old and over, by highest level of educational attainment and sex: 1990 through 2013—Continued

[Standard errors appear in parentheses]

Number of persons with earnings who worked full time, year round (in thousands)

Sex and year	Total	Elementary/secondary — Less than 9th grade	Elementary/secondary — Some high school, no completion[1]	Elementary/secondary — High school completion (includes equivalency)[2]	Some college, no degree[3]	Associate's degree	College — Total	College — Bachelor's degree[5]	College — Master's degree	College — Professional degree[4]	College — Doctor's degree
1	2	3	4	5	6	7	8	9	10	11	12
Males											
1990	44,406 (268.6)	2,250 (73.9)	3,315 (89.3)	16,394 (188.0)	9,113 (144.6)	[6] (†)	13,334 (171.8)	7,569 (132.6)	[6] (†)	[6] (†)	[6] (†)
1991	44,199 (268.3)	1,807 (66.5)	3,083 (86.2)	15,025 (181.1)	8,034 (136.4)	2,899 (83.6)	13,350 (171.9)	8,456 (139.7)	3,073 (86.1)	1,147 (53.0)	674 (40.7)
1992	44,752 (269.1)	1,815 (66.5)	3,009 (85.2)	14,722 (179.5)	8,067 (136.6)	3,203 (87.8)	13,937 (175.2)	8,719 (141.7)	3,178 (87.5)	1,295 (56.3)	745 (42.8)
1993	45,873 (270.6)	1,790 (66.0)	3,083 (86.2)	14,604 (178.9)	8,493 (140.0)	3,557 (92.4)	14,346 (177.5)	9,178 (145.1)	3,131 (86.8)	1,231 (54.9)	808 (44.5)
1994	47,566 (303.0)	1,895 (69.2)	3,057 (87.6)	15,109 (188.5)	8,783 (146.2)	3,735 (96.6)	14,987 (187.8)	9,636 (152.8)	3,225 (89.9)	1,258 (56.4)	868 (46.9)
1995	48,500 (306.1)	1,946 (72.8)	3,335 (94.9)	15,331 (195.6)	8,908 (152.3)	3,926 (102.8)	15,054 (194.0)	9,597 (157.8)	3,395 (95.7)	1,208 (57.5)	853 (48.4)
1996	49,764 (301.1)	2,041 (69.2)	3,441 (89.6)	15,840 (186.5)	9,173 (144.2)	3,931 (95.6)	15,339 (183.7)	9,898 (149.6)	3,272 (87.4)	1,277 (54.8)	893 (45.9)
1997	50,807 (299.0)	1,914 (67.0)	3,548 (90.9)	16,225 (187.8)	9,170 (143.9)	4,086 (97.4)	15,864 (185.9)	10,349 (152.4)	3,228 (86.7)	1,321 (55.8)	966 (47.7)
1998	52,381 (306.4)	1,870 (66.3)	3,613 (91.7)	16,442 (189.7)	9,375 (145.7)	4,347 (100.4)	16,733 (191.2)	11,058 (157.6)	3,414 (89.2)	1,264 (54.6)	998 (48.5)
1999	53,062 (307.8)	1,993 (68.4)	3,295 (87.7)	16,589 (190.5)	9,684 (148.0)	4,359 (100.6)	17,142 (193.3)	11,142 (158.2)	3,725 (93.1)	1,267 (54.6)	1,008 (48.8)
2000	54,065 (309.7)	1,968 (68.0)	3,354 (88.4)	16,834 (191.7)	9,792 (148.8)	4,729 (104.7)	17,387 (194.6)	11,395 (159.9)	3,680 (92.6)	1,274 (54.8)	1,038 (49.5)
2001	54,013 (224.8)	2,207 (51.4)	3,503 (64.5)	16,314 (135.4)	9,494 (104.9)	4,714 (74.7)	17,780 (140.9)	11,479 (114.8)	3,961 (68.5)	1,298 (39.5)	1,041 (35.4)
2002	54,108 (225.0)	2,154 (50.7)	3,680 (66.1)	16,005 (134.2)	9,603 (105.5)	4,399 (72.2)	18,267 (142.0)	11,829 (116.5)	4,065 (69.4)	1,308 (39.6)	1,065 (35.4)
2003	54,253 (225.2)	2,209 (51.4)	3,369 (63.3)	16,285 (135.3)	9,340 (104.1)	4,696 (74.5)	18,354 (143.0)	11,846 (116.6)	4,124 (69.9)	1,348 (40.2)	1,037 (35.3)
2004	55,655 (227.0)	2,427 (53.8)	3,468 (64.2)	17,067 (138.3)	9,257 (103.6)	4,913 (76.2)	18,338 (142.9)	11,701 (115.9)	4,243 (70.9)	1,305 (39.6)	1,088 (36.1)
2005	56,717 (228.7)	2,425 (53.8)	3,652 (65.9)	17,266 (139.0)	9,532 (105.1)	5,022 (77.0)	18,820 (144.7)	12,032 (117.4)	4,275 (71.2)	1,369 (40.5)	1,144 (37.1)
2006	58,109 (230.6)	2,361 (53.1)	3,872 (67.8)	17,369 (139.4)	9,493 (104.9)	5,110 (77.7)	19,903 (148.4)	12,764 (120.7)	4,542 (73.3)	1,425 (41.3)	1,172 (37.5)
2007	58,147 (230.7)	2,142 (50.6)	3,451 (64.0)	17,224 (138.9)	9,867 (106.8)	5,244 (78.7)	20,218 (149.5)	12,962 (121.6)	4,800 (75.3)	1,332 (40.0)	1,125 (36.7)
2008	55,655 (227.2)	1,982 (48.7)	3,118 (60.9)	16,195 (135.0)	9,515 (105.0)	5,020 (77.0)	19,825 (148.1)	12,609 (120.0)	4,709 (74.6)	1,388 (40.8)	1,119 (36.7)
2009	52,445 (222.5)	1,561 (43.2)	2,795 (57.7)	15,258 (131.3)	8,609 (100.1)	4,828 (75.5)	19,395 (146.7)	12,290 (118.6)	4,575 (73.6)	1,319 (39.8)	1,212 (38.1)
2010	52,890 (223.2)	1,600 (43.8)	2,615 (55.9)	15,104 (130.7)	8,541 (99.7)	5,042 (77.2)	19,990 (148.7)	12,836 (121.1)	4,670 (74.3)	1,237 (38.5)	1,246 (38.7)
2011	54,279 (225.2)	1,848 (47.0)	2,715 (56.9)	15,335 (131.6)	8,752 (100.9)	5,206 (78.4)	20,423 (150.1)	13,013 (121.8)	4,839 (75.6)	1,300 (39.5)	1,271 (39.0)
2012	55,208 (226.6)	1,793 (46.3)	2,671 (56.4)	15,295 (131.4)	8,974 (102.1)	5,423 (80.0)	21,052 (152.2)	13,315 (123.2)	5,003 (76.9)	1,301 (39.5)	1,433 (41.4)
2013	56,703 (289.3)	1,944 (61.0)	2,910 (74.5)	16,034 (170.0)	8,960 (129.0)	5,605 (102.8)	21,249 (193.4)	13,378 (156.2)	5,146 (98.6)	1,249 (49.0)	1,476 (53.2)
Females											
1990	28,636 (234.7)	847 (45.6)	1,861 (67.3)	11,810 (162.8)	6,462 (123.1)	[6] (†)	7,655 (133.3)	4,704 (105.8)	[6] (†)	[6] (†)	[6] (†)
1991	29,474 (237.1)	733 (42.4)	1,819 (66.5)	10,959 (157.4)	5,633 (115.3)	2,523 (78.1)	7,807 (134.6)	5,263 (111.6)	2,025 (70.1)	312 (27.7)	206 (22.5)
1992	30,346 (239.6)	734 (42.4)	1,659 (63.6)	11,039 (157.9)	5,904 (117.9)	2,655 (80.1)	8,355 (138.9)	5,604 (115.0)	2,192 (72.9)	334 (28.7)	225 (23.5)
1993	30,683 (240.5)	765 (43.3)	1,576 (62.0)	10,513 (154.4)	6,279 (121.4)	3,067 (86.7)	8,483 (139.9)	5,735 (116.3)	2,166 (72.5)	323 (28.2)	260 (25.3)
1994	31,379 (259.2)	696 (42.0)	1,675 (65.1)	10,785 (161.2)	6,256 (124.2)	3,210 (89.0)	8,756 (146.0)	5,901 (120.8)	2,174 (74.0)	398 (31.8)	283 (26.8)
1995	32,673 (268.2)	774 (46.1)	1,763 (69.3)	11,064 (168.6)	6,329 (129.5)	3,336 (94.7)	9,406 (156.3)	6,434 (130.5)	2,268 (78.5)	421 (34.0)	283 (27.9)
1996	33,549 (259.0)	750 (42.1)	1,751 (64.1)	11,363 (159.7)	6,582 (122.9)	3,468 (89.9)	9,636 (147.7)	6,689 (123.9)	2,213 (72.0)	413 (31.2)	322 (27.6)
1997	34,624 (260.1)	791 (43.2)	1,765 (64.4)	11,475 (160.1)	6,628 (123.2)	3,538 (90.7)	10,427 (153.0)	7,173 (128.0)	2,448 (75.7)	488 (34.0)	318 (27.4)
1998	35,628 (265.4)	814 (43.8)	1,878 (66.4)	11,613 (161.3)	7,070 (127.3)	3,527 (90.7)	10,725 (155.4)	7,288 (129.2)	2,639 (78.6)	468 (33.3)	329 (27.9)
1999	37,091 (269.7)	886 (45.7)	1,883 (66.5)	11,824 (162.7)	7,453 (130.6)	3,804 (94.1)	11,242 (158.9)	7,607 (131.9)	2,818 (81.2)	470 (33.3)	346 (28.6)
2000	37,762 (271.6)	930 (46.8)	1,950 (67.7)	11,789 (162.5)	7,391 (130.0)	4,118 (97.8)	11,584 (161.1)	7,899 (134.3)	2,823 (81.2)	509 (34.7)	353 (28.9)
2001	38,228 (197.0)	927 (33.4)	1,869 (47.3)	11,690 (115.8)	7,283 (92.3)	4,190 (70.5)	12,269 (118.5)	8,257 (98.1)	3,089 (60.6)	531 (25.3)	392 (21.7)
2002	38,510 (197.6)	858 (32.1)	1,841 (46.9)	11,687 (115.8)	7,354 (92.7)	4,285 (71.2)	12,484 (119.5)	8,229 (97.9)	3,281 (62.5)	572 (26.2)	402 (22.0)
2003	38,681 (197.9)	882 (32.6)	1,739 (45.6)	11,587 (115.3)	7,341 (92.6)	4,397 (72.2)	12,735 (120.6)	8,330 (98.5)	3,376 (63.4)	567 (26.1)	462 (23.6)
2004	39,072 (198.7)	917 (33.2)	1,797 (46.4)	11,392 (114.4)	7,330 (92.6)	4,505 (73.0)	13,131 (122.4)	8,664 (100.4)	3,451 (64.0)	564 (26.0)	452 (23.3)
2005	40,021 (200.6)	902 (32.9)	1,740 (45.6)	11,419 (114.5)	7,452 (93.3)	4,751 (74.9)	13,758 (125.1)	9,074 (102.6)	3,591 (65.3)	657 (28.1)	437 (22.9)
2006	41,311 (203.2)	934 (33.5)	1,802 (46.4)	11,652 (115.6)	7,613 (94.3)	4,760 (75.0)	14,549 (128.4)	9,645 (105.7)	3,746 (66.7)	662 (28.2)	497 (24.5)
2007	42,196 (204.9)	823 (31.5)	1,649 (44.4)	11,447 (114.7)	7,916 (96.1)	4,891 (76.0)	15,469 (132.1)	9,931 (107.2)	3,889 (72.1)	666 (28.3)	484 (24.1)
2008	40,979 (202.5)	814 (31.3)	1,568 (43.3)	10,851 (111.8)	7,456 (93.3)	4,955 (76.5)	15,335 (131.6)	9,856 (106.8)	4,176 (70.3)	753 (30.1)	550 (25.7)
2009	40,376 (201.4)	776 (30.5)	1,519 (42.7)	10,467 (109.9)	7,164 (91.6)	4,924 (76.3)	15,526 (132.4)	10,066 (107.9)	4,261 (71.0)	606 (27.0)	592 (26.7)
2010	40,196 (201.0)	732 (29.7)	1,371 (40.5)	10,117 (108.1)	7,150 (91.5)	4,999 (76.8)	15,826 (133.5)	9,903 (107.0)	4,576 (73.6)	622 (27.4)	725 (29.5)
2011	40,885 (202.4)	779 (30.6)	1,380 (40.7)	10,040 (107.7)	6,989 (90.5)	5,131 (77.8)	16,566 (136.4)	10,537 (110.2)	4,700 (74.6)	635 (27.6)	694 (28.9)
2012	41,319 (203.2)	690 (28.8)	1,351 (40.3)	9,870 (106.8)	6,899 (89.9)	5,246 (78.7)	17,263 (139.0)	10,961 (112.3)	4,887 (76.0)	670 (28.4)	745 (29.9)
2013	42,021 (258.8)	788 (38.9)	1,309 (50.1)	9,990 (135.9)	7,070 (115.1)	5,253 (99.6)	17,611 (177.5)	11,124 (143.1)	4,963 (96.9)	793 (39.1)	732 (37.5)

See notes at end of table.

Table 502.20. Median annual earnings, number, and percentage of full-time year-round workers 25 years old and over, by highest level of educational attainment and sex: 1990 through 2013—Continued

[Standard errors appear in parentheses]

Percent of persons with earnings who worked full time, year round[8]

Sex and year	Elementary/secondary					College						
	Total	Less than 9th grade	Some high school, no completion[1]	High school completion (includes equivalency)[2]	Some college, no degree[3]	Associate's degree	Bachelor's or higher degree[4]					
							Total	Bachelor's degree[5]	Master's degree	Professional degree	Doctor's degree
1	2	3	4	5	6	7	8	9	10	11	12
Males											
1996	78.2 (0.25)	64.5 (1.31)	66.9 (1.01)	77.2 (0.45)	78.8 (0.58)	83.8 (0.83)	82.9 (0.43)	83.2 (0.53)	80.6 (0.95)	85.4 (1.40)	85.1 (1.69)
1997	81.6 (0.24)	63.9 (1.35)	69.5 (0.99)	78.7 (0.44)	79.5 (0.58)	81.7 (0.84)	83.3 (0.42)	83.9 (0.51)	80.8 (0.96)	85.4 (1.38)	83.4 (1.68)
1998	81.0 (0.24)	66.8 (1.37)	73.5 (0.97)	80.3 (0.43)	81.0 (0.56)	85.3 (0.76)	84.6 (0.39)	85.9 (0.47)	81.6 (0.92)	86.0 (1.39)	80.0 (1.74)
1999	81.1 (0.24)	70.3 (1.32)	71.5 (1.02)	80.3 (0.43)	81.3 (0.55)	84.2 (0.78)	84.7 (0.39)	85.3 (0.48)	83.5 (0.86)	85.6 (1.40)	81.8 (1.69)
2000	81.7 (0.23)	69.7 (1.33)	71.8 (1.01)	80.9 (0.42)	82.2 (0.54)	86.6 (0.71)	84.8 (0.39)	85.6 (0.47)	82.8 (0.87)	85.8 (1.39)	82.5 (1.65)
2001	80.1 (0.17)	69.7 (0.90)	70.9 (0.71)	79.4 (0.31)	80.2 (0.40)	84.1 (0.54)	83.3 (0.28)	83.6 (0.35)	82.4 (0.60)	84.6 (1.01)	82.2 (1.18)
2002	79.4 (0.17)	70.1 (0.91)	71.3 (0.69)	77.8 (0.32)	78.8 (0.41)	81.4 (0.58)	83.9 (0.27)	84.4 (0.34)	82.2 (0.60)	85.7 (0.99)	82.8 (1.16)
2003	79.5 (0.17)	71.5 (0.89)	70.1 (0.73)	78.7 (0.31)	78.8 (0.41)	82.1 (0.56)	83.1 (0.28)	84.0 (0.34)	81.1 (0.60)	84.4 (1.00)	80.3 (1.22)
2004	80.0 (0.17)	74.7 (0.84)	71.2 (0.71)	79.1 (0.30)	79.3 (0.41)	83.6 (0.53)	83.0 (0.28)	83.1 (0.35)	83.1 (0.58)	83.3 (1.03)	81.7 (1.16)
2005	80.3 (0.16)	74.0 (0.84)	73.8 (0.69)	79.5 (0.30)	80.0 (0.40)	82.5 (0.54)	82.9 (0.27)	83.0 (0.34)	82.7 (0.58)	83.7 (1.00)	82.4 (1.12)
2006	81.1 (0.16)	73.6 (0.85)	72.9 (0.67)	79.6 (0.30)	80.1 (0.40)	85.3 (0.50)	84.7 (0.26)	85.2 (0.32)	83.5 (0.55)	85.9 (0.94)	83.4 (1.09)
2007	80.5 (0.16)	71.1 (0.91)	70.8 (0.72)	79.4 (0.30)	79.5 (0.40)	83.3 (0.52)	84.5 (0.26)	85.1 (0.32)	83.5 (0.54)	83.1 (1.03)	83.5 (1.11)
2008	77.0 (0.17)	66.3 (0.95)	64.6 (0.76)	74.6 (0.32)	76.5 (0.42)	79.4 (0.56)	82.6 (0.27)	83.2 (0.33)	80.9 (0.57)	82.4 (1.02)	83.1 (1.12)
2009	73.9 (0.18)	56.2 (1.03)	61.8 (0.79)	70.1 (0.34)	73.4 (0.45)	77.9 (0.58)	80.8 (0.28)	79.9 (0.35)	82.0 (0.56)	85.1 (0.99)	81.2 (1.11)
2010	74.8 (0.18)	58.8 (1.04)	61.6 (0.82)	71.9 (0.34)	72.9 (0.45)	78.2 (0.56)	81.4 (0.27)	81.8 (0.34)	80.0 (0.58)	81.4 (1.10)	82.2 (1.08)
2011	76.6 (0.17)	67.2 (0.98)	64.2 (0.81)	74.2 (0.33)	75.2 (0.44)	78.0 (0.56)	82.0 (0.27)	82.1 (0.33)	82.3 (0.55)	81.6 (1.07)	81.0 (1.09)
2012	76.5 (0.17)	65.4 (1.00)	64.4 (0.82)	74.5 (0.33)	73.7 (0.44)	78.8 (0.54)	82.1 (0.26)	82.5 (0.33)	80.8 (0.55)	84.4 (1.01)	81.4 (1.02)
2013	78.1 (0.21)	69.3 (1.21)	68.9 (0.99)	76.5 (0.41)	76.2 (0.55)	79.6 (0.67)	82.4 (0.33)	82.6 (0.41)	82.5 (0.67)	83.2 (1.34)	79.7 (1.30)
Females											
1996	60.7 (0.32)	47.9 (1.94)	49.4 (1.29)	60.0 (0.55)	62.0 (0.73)	63.7 (1.00)	63.5 (0.60)	63.4 (0.72)	62.4 (1.25)	68.4 (2.91)	70.0 (3.29)
1997	61.7 (0.32)	48.7 (1.91)	49.3 (1.29)	61.0 (0.55)	61.9 (0.72)	64.3 (0.99)	65.4 (0.58)	64.6 (0.70)	65.7 (1.20)	73.6 (2.63)	72.1 (3.29)
1998	62.5 (0.31)	51.8 (1.94)	53.1 (1.29)	61.9 (0.55)	63.3 (0.70)	64.9 (1.00)	65.0 (0.57)	64.0 (0.69)	66.2 (1.15)	71.9 (2.71)	68.5 (3.26)
1999	63.7 (0.31)	53.0 (1.88)	54.0 (1.30)	63.0 (0.54)	64.8 (0.69)	65.1 (0.96)	66.2 (0.56)	65.9 (0.68)	66.5 (1.12)	68.4 (2.73)	68.2 (3.18)
2000	64.6 (0.30)	53.5 (1.84)	56.5 (1.30)	64.1 (0.54)	65.3 (0.69)	66.6 (0.92)	66.5 (0.55)	66.7 (0.67)	64.9 (1.11)	70.6 (2.61)	71.5 (3.13)
2001	64.3 (0.22)	54.0 (1.32)	55.3 (0.94)	63.5 (0.39)	65.1 (0.49)	65.8 (0.65)	66.6 (0.38)	66.6 (0.47)	65.6 (0.76)	70.3 (1.83)	70.9 (2.12)
2002	64.1 (0.22)	52.6 (1.36)	55.5 (0.95)	63.2 (0.39)	65.0 (0.49)	65.6 (0.65)	66.5 (0.37)	65.9 (0.47)	66.1 (0.74)	74.3 (1.73)	73.8 (2.07)
2003	64.4 (0.21)	56.5 (1.38)	53.8 (0.96)	64.4 (0.39)	64.2 (0.49)	65.6 (0.64)	66.4 (0.37)	65.8 (0.46)	66.3 (0.73)	72.3 (1.75)	71.9 (1.95)
2004	64.5 (0.21)	56.3 (1.35)	56.1 (0.96)	64.5 (0.40)	64.2 (0.49)	64.6 (0.63)	66.7 (0.37)	66.3 (0.45)	66.3 (0.72)	71.5 (1.77)	71.2 (1.97)
2005	65.3 (0.21)	56.5 (1.36)	54.5 (0.97)	65.1 (0.40)	63.5 (0.49)	67.2 (0.61)	68.2 (0.36)	68.0 (0.44)	68.3 (0.70)	71.2 (1.64)	67.3 (2.02)
2006	66.2 (0.21)	58.5 (1.35)	56.0 (0.96)	65.6 (0.39)	65.9 (0.48)	67.3 (0.61)	68.6 (0.35)	68.4 (0.43)	67.5 (0.69)	73.6 (1.61)	74.0 (1.86)
2007	66.7 (0.21)	56.8 (1.43)	55.3 (1.00)	65.7 (0.39)	66.7 (0.48)	67.3 (0.60)	69.3 (0.34)	68.4 (0.42)	70.6 (0.63)	74.1 (1.60)	71.2 (1.91)
2008	64.4 (0.21)	51.6 (1.38)	52.8 (1.01)	64.2 (0.40)	64.7 (0.48)	65.5 (0.60)	67.9 (0.34)	67.8 (0.43)	66.9 (0.65)	74.0 (1.51)	70.0 (1.80)
2009	64.3 (0.21)	52.0 (1.42)	54.5 (1.04)	62.4 (0.41)	63.9 (0.50)	64.5 (0.60)	68.0 (0.34)	68.3 (0.42)	67.5 (0.65)	66.4 (1.72)	68.3 (1.74)
2010	64.4 (0.21)	51.7 (1.46)	52.4 (1.07)	62.6 (0.42)	63.3 (0.50)	64.3 (0.60)	68.5 (0.34)	67.7 (0.42)	68.5 (0.62)	73.9 (1.66)	76.3 (1.51)
2011	65.0 (0.21)	52.2 (1.42)	49.1 (1.04)	63.0 (0.42)	62.9 (0.50)	66.3 (0.59)	69.6 (0.33)	69.4 (0.41)	69.0 (0.62)	72.8 (1.65)	73.6 (1.58)
2012	64.8 (0.21)	50.0 (1.48)	51.1 (1.07)	62.3 (0.42)	61.7 (0.50)	64.7 (0.58)	70.0 (0.32)	70.6 (0.40)	68.0 (0.60)	73.2 (1.61)	73.9 (1.52)
2013	65.6 (0.26)	56.0 (1.84)	52.3 (1.07)	63.8 (0.46)	63.4 (0.62)	65.1 (0.79)	69.6 (0.40)	70.4 (0.50)	67.4 (0.82)	73.9 (1.86)	69.4 (1.97)

—Not available.
†Not applicable.
‡Interpret data with caution. The coefficient of variation (CV) for this estimate is between 30 and 50 percent.
[1]Includes 1 to 3 years of high school for 1990.
[2]Includes 4 years of high school for 1990.
[3]Includes 1 to 3 years of college and associate's degrees for 1990.
[4]Includes 4 or more years of college for 1990.
[5]Includes 4 years of college for 1990.
[6]Not reported separately for 1990.

[7]Constant dollars based on the Consumer Price Index, prepared by the Bureau of Labor Statistics, U.S. Department of Labor.
[8]Data not available for 1990 through 1995.
NOTE: Detail may not sum to totals because of rounding.
SOURCE: U.S. Department of Commerce, Census Bureau, Current Population Reports, Series P-60, Money Income of Households, Families, and Persons in the United States, through 1994; Series P-60, Money Income in the United States, 1995 through 2002; Current Population Survey (CPS), 2004 through 2014 Annual Social and Economic Supplement, retrieved November 24, 2014, from http://www.census.gov/hhes/www/cpstables/032014/perinc/pinc03_000.htm. (This table was prepared November 2014.)

Table 502.30. Median annual earnings of full-time year-round workers 25 to 34 years old and full-time year-round workers as a percentage of the labor force, by sex, race/ethnicity, and educational attainment: Selected years, 1995 through 2013

[Amounts in constant 2013 dollars. Standard errors appear in parentheses]

Sex, race/ethnicity, and educational attainment	1995	2000	2003	2005	2007	2008	2009	2010	2011	2012	2013
1	2	3	4	5	6	7	8	9	10	11	12
Total, all full-time year-round workers 25 to 34 years old											
Median annual earnings, all education levels	$38,220 (212)	$40,580 (129)	$40,440 (123)	$39,340 (1,075)	$39,320 (#)	$38,940 (831)	$41,220 (1,073)	$39,930 (827)	$39,310 (97)	$38,550 (887)	$40,000 (#)
Less than high school completion	24,230 (385)	24,490 (532)	25,250 (267)	24,500 (765)	24,630 (695)	23,120 (756)	22,630 (784)	22,490 (840)	23,680 (854)	23,250 (826)	23,940 (714)
High school completion[1]	31,780 (303)	33,820 (238)	33,380 (213)	33,270 (1,118)	32,540 (704)	32,430 (5)	32,490 (16)	31,950 (32)	31,020 (25)	30,400 (15)	30,000 (2)
Some college, no degree	35,530 (662)	39,030 (508)	37,880 (246)	37,430 (765)	36,930 (866)	34,580 (469)	36,020 (1,243)	35,150 (922)	33,130 (518)	33,330 (729)	34,080 (1,166)
Associate's degree	37,930 (622)	40,400 (383)	40,400 (364)	40,520 (1,027)	39,100 (154)	38,880 (787)	38,980 (1,046)	39,510 (1,100)	38,350 (1,501)	36,240 (1,471)	37,540 (2,123)
Bachelor's or higher degree	50,410 (860)	54,100 (280)	54,360 (766)	52,330 (1,059)	53,760 (1,444)	54,040 (15)	54,120 (35)	52,060 (1,073)	51,780 (353)	50,690 (16)	50,000 (1,277)
Bachelor's degree	47,330 (385)	53,990 (400)	50,640 (265)	48,670 (1,315)	50,360 (890)	49,770 (937)	48,850 (294)	48,070 (663)	46,570 (650)	47,590 (906)	48,530 (1,709)
Master's or higher degree	60,600 (1,114)	64,820 (2,002)	63,020 (609)	59,570 (54)	62,550 (2,208)	59,450 (743)	64,300 (2,196)	58,390 (1,059)	61,340 (1,556)	60,500 (1,150)	59,570 (447)
Percent,[2] all education levels	63.6 (0.44)	68.4 (0.32)	66.3 (0.39)	66.6 (0.37)	67.8 (0.36)	64.6 (0.41)	61.0 (0.41)	61.9 (0.42)	63.3 (0.41)	64.2 (0.44)	65.1 (0.49)
Less than high school completion	49.6 (1.37)	59.4 (1.02)	56.4 (1.02)	60.0 (1.32)	56.5 (1.26)	50.2 (1.32)	47.0 (1.25)	44.9 (1.52)	48.1 (1.43)	48.6 (1.38)	53.3 (1.72)
High school completion[1]	62.8 (0.79)	67.2 (0.59)	66.3 (0.62)	66.9 (0.75)	67.0 (0.71)	61.7 (0.75)	55.3 (0.74)	57.0 (0.80)	59.1 (0.78)	60.3 (0.80)	61.7 (1.07)
Some college, no degree	61.5 (0.99)	67.8 (0.71)	63.1 (0.75)	63.5 (0.83)	64.8 (0.92)	62.9 (0.79)	58.7 (0.91)	58.1 (0.92)	59.0 (0.99)	59.2 (1.00)	59.0 (1.10)
Associate's degree	67.4 (1.41)	70.9 (1.01)	68.5 (1.05)	67.8 (1.16)	67.8 (1.23)	66.3 (1.30)	65.1 (1.18)	63.6 (1.29)	65.4 (1.17)	64.8 (1.18)	67.5 (1.51)
Bachelor's or higher degree	70.4 (0.79)	72.3 (0.55)	71.0 (0.67)	70.2 (0.67)	73.5 (0.59)	71.6 (0.56)	69.4 (0.63)	71.4 (0.59)	71.4 (0.62)	72.8 (0.62)	72.1 (0.71)
Bachelor's degree	70.5 (0.90)	73.1 (0.62)	71.1 (0.64)	70.9 (0.76)	73.2 (0.70)	71.6 (0.70)	69.1 (0.77)	71.2 (0.71)	71.1 (0.72)	72.9 (0.75)	71.9 (0.84)
Master's or higher degree	69.8 (1.65)	69.6 (1.18)	70.7 (1.08)	68.2 (1.27)	74.4 (1.21)	71.5 (1.05)	70.0 (1.10)	71.7 (1.23)	72.2 (1.25)	72.5 (1.20)	72.6 (1.32)
Male											
Median annual earnings, all education levels	41,180 (281)	43,280 (207)	43,010 (550)	41,750 (#)	42,630 (99)	43,270 (1)	43,430 (#)	42,600 (31)	41,340 (33)	40,580 (1)	40,000 (349)
Less than high school completion	27,150 (717)	26,950 (336)	25,300 (326)	26,140 (1,038)	25,830 (563)	25,940 (846)	24,600 (1,058)	25,640 (828)	25,850 (1,097)	24,960 (992)	24,390 (386)
High school completion[1]	36,600 (601)	38,980 (640)	37,870 (357)	35,650 (49)	34,640 (1,049)	34,580 (715)	35,710 (1,225)	35,040 (894)	33,600 (856)	33,310 (731)	31,710 (478)
Some college, no degree	39,660 (547)	43,030 (363)	41,780 (1,158)	41,640 (314)	41,210 (1,541)	39,190 (1,428)	41,990 (966)	40,470 (983)	38,000 (1,237)	38,220 (854)	38,340 (1,415)
Associate's degree	39,430 (1,013)	47,320 (739)	44,280 (750)	46,370 (1,850)	44,640 (373)	43,570 (1,720)	45,270 (1,670)	42,640 (459)	43,340 (1,793)	44,280 (2,782)	41,750 (2,427)
Bachelor's or higher degree	56,830 (881)	62,120 (560)	60,480 (1,400)	59,610 (1,903)	57,940 (1,101)	59,350 (414)	59,110 (596)	56,360 (1,901)	56,310 (1,072)	55,640 (521)	56,950 (2,144)
Bachelor's degree	53,470 (707)	60,570 (811)	56,540 (523)	53,640 (1,282)	56,050 (52)	57,240 (1,756)	54,810 (1,394)	53,180 (162)	51,540 (125)	50,700 (593)	51,940 (1,256)
Master's or higher degree	67,670 (2,169)	74,260 (2,010)	75,040 (1,900)	65,590 (3,979)	69,310 (3,378)	69,600 (1,902)	75,190 (3,151)	68,550 (1,497)	70,420 (2,434)	65,950 (2,396)	66,770 (2,526)
Percent,[2] all education levels	69.7 (0.57)	75.1 (0.40)	71.9 (0.42)	72.5 (0.48)	72.2 (0.51)	68.5 (0.57)	62.8 (0.58)	64.5 (0.56)	67.4 (0.57)	68.4 (0.53)	69.5 (0.62)
Less than high school completion	54.3 (1.71)	67.8 (1.22)	63.9 (1.22)	66.7 (1.54)	61.1 (1.51)	55.7 (1.54)	49.2 (1.71)	47.4 (1.81)	55.5 (1.74)	54.1 (1.88)	59.9 (2.06)
High school completion[1]	69.3 (1.00)	73.6 (0.73)	72.3 (0.76)	73.5 (0.91)	71.9 (0.94)	64.8 (0.95)	57.4 (1.01)	60.6 (1.01)	63.8 (1.00)	65.5 (1.00)	67.0 (1.27)
Some college, no degree	68.5 (1.31)	76.1 (0.91)	68.1 (1.01)	70.7 (1.13)	71.1 (1.31)	68.2 (1.12)	62.7 (1.31)	62.0 (1.17)	64.2 (1.33)	64.3 (1.41)	63.9 (1.56)
Associate's degree	78.6 (1.81)	80.9 (1.31)	75.9 (1.38)	75.1 (1.67)	73.4 (1.70)	73.2 (1.82)	70.1 (1.65)	68.6 (1.77)	71.6 (1.61)	71.8 (1.70)	76.3 (2.03)
Bachelor's or higher degree	75.9 (1.04)	78.0 (0.72)	76.5 (0.74)	74.6 (0.93)	77.7 (0.94)	76.6 (0.90)	71.8 (0.94)	75.0 (0.80)	75.3 (0.84)	77.1 (0.87)	76.3 (1.01)
Bachelor's degree	76.4 (1.19)	78.8 (0.81)	76.7 (0.86)	74.5 (1.01)	78.0 (1.07)	76.3 (1.10)	70.6 (1.15)	75.4 (0.91)	74.7 (0.98)	77.3 (0.94)	74.8 (1.34)
Master's or higher degree	74.6 (2.11)	75.3 (1.58)	75.8 (1.47)	75.1 (2.00)	76.8 (1.93)	77.2 (1.50)	75.6 (1.61)	74.0 (1.88)	77.3 (1.63)	76.4 (1.82)	78.0 (1.83)
Female											
Median annual earnings, all education levels	33,330 (274)	37,490 (322)	37,940 (184)	35,740 (35)	37,010 (435)	36,760 (515)	37,920 (226)	37,270 (36)	36,200 (21)	35,510 (798)	36,930 (788)
Less than high school completion	19,780 (771)	20,260 (566)	22,650 (841)	20,040 (762)	20,020 (907)	17,870 (757)	20,590 (629)	18,990 (704)	19,610 (487)	18,160 (784)	19,910 (578)
High school completion[1]	26,920 (454)	29,640 (324)	30,280 (445)	28,510 (194)	27,000 (1,085)	26,950 (130)	27,090 (27)	26,680 (67)	26,830 (759)	25,350 (9)	24,980 (136)
Some college, no degree	30,560 (442)	33,780 (330)	32,770 (399)	33,300 (474)	33,600 (807)	31,320 (945)	31,700 (1,063)	31,520 (1,084)	29,970 (1,133)	29,780 (636)	29,740 (1,023)
Associate's degree	36,600 (1,364)	36,040 (485)	36,680 (895)	34,980 (426)	34,820 (1,167)	35,160 (1,065)	33,550 (1,310)	37,030 (912)	33,220 (1,383)	32,070 (983)	32,430 (1,529)
Bachelor's or higher degree	45,510 (643)	48,700 (337)	50,090 (409)	47,440 (125)	48,210 (1,075)	48,630 (28)	48,810 (26)	46,990 (1,255)	46,500 (59)	47,530 (704)	46,810 (1,023)
Bachelor's degree	42,650 (924)	47,200 (377)	46,540 (375)	44,740 (1,091)	44,770 (104)	45,050 (589)	43,580 (1,263)	42,410 (1,207)	43,580 (1,381)	43,580 (1,254)	44,620 (482)
Master's or higher degree	52,810 (1,458)	56,250 (1,133)	56,290 (791)	56,000 (2,194)	56,380 (1,697)	54,960 (1,576)	58,630 (2,294)	53,240 (95)	53,300 (1,608)	54,300 (1,479)	53,910 (1,457)
Percent,[2] all education levels	56.6 (0.67)	60.7 (0.49)	59.7 (0.50)	59.6 (0.57)	62.7 (0.57)	60.0 (0.51)	58.9 (0.53)	58.7 (0.53)	58.6 (0.52)	59.3 (0.63)	59.9 (0.76)
Less than high school completion	41.3 (2.24)	45.3 (1.68)	41.8 (1.74)	45.9 (1.83)	45.9 (2.22)	38.6 (1.91)	42.7 (2.03)	39.4 (2.22)	34.1 (2.03)	37.8 (1.96)	41.1 (2.70)
High school completion[1]	54.4 (1.23)	58.5 (0.96)	57.9 (1.00)	57.0 (1.11)	59.4 (1.13)	56.6 (1.11)	51.8 (1.12)	51.1 (1.19)	51.6 (1.19)	51.9 (1.24)	52.4 (1.64)
Some college, no degree	53.9 (1.46)	59.2 (1.08)	57.7 (1.11)	55.7 (1.19)	57.9 (1.22)	56.6 (1.26)	54.1 (1.28)	53.6 (1.29)	53.3 (1.33)	53.3 (1.22)	53.4 (1.69)
Associate's degree	57.6 (2.05)	62.7 (1.45)	61.3 (1.56)	60.8 (1.57)	62.7 (1.75)	60.1 (1.68)	60.8 (1.65)	59.1 (1.67)	59.5 (1.75)	58.8 (1.69)	59.6 (2.13)
Bachelor's or higher degree	64.7 (1.17)	66.8 (0.82)	65.7 (0.81)	66.0 (0.99)	69.9 (0.76)	67.2 (0.71)	67.2 (0.82)	68.0 (0.77)	68.0 (0.84)	68.9 (0.90)	68.9 (0.98)
Bachelor's degree	64.9 (1.32)	67.6 (0.93)	65.6 (0.95)	67.4 (1.18)	68.7 (0.92)	67.3 (0.88)	67.9 (1.03)	67.8 (0.94)	67.8 (1.06)	68.5 (1.13)	69.1 (1.16)
Master's or higher degree	63.9 (2.57)	64.2 (1.71)	66.1 (1.55)	62.6 (1.76)	72.6 (1.52)	67.1 (1.44)	65.7 (1.58)	70.0 (1.63)	68.6 (1.76)	69.7 (1.71)	68.5 (1.79)

See notes at end of table.

Table 502.30. Median annual earnings of full-time year-round workers 25 to 34 years old and full-time year-round workers as a percentage of the labor force, by sex, race/ethnicity, and educational attainment: Selected years, 1995 through 2013—Continued

[Amounts in constant 2013 dollars. Standard errors appear in parentheses]

Sex, race/ethnicity, and educational attainment	1995	2000	2003	2005	2007	2008	2009	2010	2011	2012	2013
1	2	3	4	5	6	7	8	9	10	11	12
White											
Median annual earnings, all education levels	39,730 (240)	44,270 (380)	44,270 (195)	41,750 (92)	44,910 (1,336)	43,270 (1)	43,430 (#)	42,690 (24)	41,410 (150)	41,560 (1,248)	41,960 (328)
Less than high school completion	26,860 (1,072)	28,130 (558)	29,060 (854)	27,380 (1,561)	26,910 (1,616)	27,690 (1,396)	26,780 (1,065)	26,700 (423)	28,710 (1,224)	24,990 (1,094)	30,000 (1,975)
High school completion[1]	33,600 (378)	37,360 (500)	36,490 (713)	35,690 (43)	33,690 (20)	33,710 (737)	34,680 (772)	34,140 (913)	33,080 (641)	32,800 (701)	31,670 (625)
Some college, no degree	36,690 (692)	40,460 (347)	39,010 (308)	38,030 (404)	39,230 (844)	35,730 (1,230)	37,990 (210)	37,200 (810)	35,950 (1,140)	35,440 (1,129)	34,970 (793)
Associate's degree	39,630 (771)	42,880 (418)	43,020 (1,396)	41,330 (445)	41,310 (1,484)	42,240 (1,086)	43,270 (1,595)	42,380 (802)	40,940 (1,381)	39,200 (1,895)	39,980 (14)
Bachelor's or higher degree	51,910 (912)	54,110 (309)	54,400 (855)	53,230 (899)	53,870 (1,066)	54,030 (23)	54,120 (39)	52,920 (848)	51,410 (92)	50,680 (19)	50,000 (1,479)
Bachelor's degree	48,910 (475)	54,020 (356)	51,740 (320)	48,880 (1,069)	50,450 (67)	50,740 (1,208)	48,860 (859)	48,860 (1,208)	48,610 (1,203)	48,130 (1,076)	49,710 (2,013)
Master's or higher degree	60,760 (1,058)	64,720 (2,224)	62,860 (795)	59,570 (60)	61,400 (937)	59,300 (354)	62,520 (1,844)	58,030 (917)	60,830 (1,665)	57,780 (2,510)	58,780 (822)
Percent,[2] all education levels	64.5 (0.52)	68.2 (0.39)	66.1 (0.41)	66.9 (0.49)	68.3 (0.47)	65.7 (0.54)	62.5 (0.52)	63.3 (0.52)	65.6 (0.54)	66.0 (0.54)	66.3 (0.68)
Less than high school completion	48.6 (2.03)	55.2 (1.76)	52.2 (1.88)	58.7 (2.29)	51.8 (2.28)	44.3 (2.56)	41.0 (2.43)	39.5 (2.78)	41.2 (2.70)	45.0 (2.44)	47.3 (3.27)
High school completion[1]	62.7 (0.94)	66.2 (0.75)	64.9 (0.80)	66.6 (0.92)	66.9 (0.89)	61.9 (1.04)	55.9 (1.04)	57.1 (1.08)	60.8 (1.15)	61.7 (1.10)	62.4 (1.41)
Some college, no degree	62.3 (1.18)	67.6 (0.88)	62.3 (0.95)	64.2 (1.02)	63.7 (1.18)	63.2 (1.02)	59.0 (1.14)	57.0 (1.20)	60.7 (1.25)	59.2 (1.39)	60.5 (1.53)
Associate's degree	66.7 (1.63)	68.2 (1.23)	67.9 (1.26)	66.9 (1.41)	69.6 (1.51)	66.3 (1.59)	65.4 (1.54)	63.9 (1.60)	65.7 (1.29)	66.2 (1.45)	66.9 (1.85)
Bachelor's or higher degree	70.5 (0.87)	72.2 (0.63)	70.5 (0.65)	69.8 (0.79)	72.8 (0.65)	71.5 (0.66)	69.5 (0.77)	71.7 (0.69)	72.4 (0.76)	72.8 (0.74)	71.9 (0.91)
Bachelor's degree	70.6 (0.99)	72.9 (0.72)	70.0 (0.75)	70.1 (0.92)	72.7 (0.77)	71.5 (0.82)	69.4 (0.90)	71.5 (0.79)	72.2 (0.84)	73.2 (0.87)	72.0 (1.03)
Master's or higher degree	70.3 (1.84)	69.9 (1.36)	72.0 (1.26)	68.8 (1.56)	73.3 (1.48)	71.5 (1.32)	69.5 (1.43)	72.3 (1.47)	72.8 (1.44)	71.9 (1.38)	71.7 (1.76)
Black											
Median annual earnings, all education levels	32,040 (551)	33,810 (356)	35,420 (970)	34,070 (1,207)	33,630 (44)	32,460 (1,409)	32,560 (131)	33,750 (765)	33,020 (753)	32,260 (474)	33,290 (1,686)
Less than high school completion	21,120 (1,662)	22,420 (1,049)	22,630 (1,185)	24,320 (1,412)	21,100 (2,054)	19,550 (1,459)	24,110 (3,806)	21,660 (1,973)	20,140 (759)	21,400 (1,720)	20,480 (1,279)
High school completion[1]	27,450 (881)	29,570 (489)	31,620 (449)	27,380 (1,204)	29,020 (1,473)	28,070 (1,314)	27,100 (941)	26,700 (781)	26,190 (1,085)	26,820 (1,349)	25,010 (1,348)
Some college, no degree	33,590 (1,299)	35,090 (702)	33,830 (678)	34,630 (1,670)	33,560 (169)	32,100 (477)	31,510 (1,677)	31,270 (415)	30,370 (600)	30,440 (1,310)	31,670 (1,510)
Associate's degree	33,510 (1,384)	33,680 (964)	35,130 (2,083)	36,210 (1,503)	33,100 (817)	33,230 (2,288)	30,110 (2,072)	33,570 (2,310)	34,850 (2,498)	32,060 (2,569)	34,180 (4,409)
Bachelor's or higher degree	41,860 (1,430)	46,760 (1,265)	50,390 (556)	46,200 (1,730)	44,700 (1,233)	47,930 (925)	48,400 (929)	43,830 (1,529)	43,000 (1,859)	44,730 (1,976)	44,590 (754)
Bachelor's degree	39,700 (1,301)	44,300 (1,936)	50,390 (1,258)	42,070 (2,565)	43,820 (1,283)	43,270 (971)	43,270 (1,687)	42,190 (526)	42,040 (1,019)	44,040 (833)	39,930 (3,025)
Master's or higher degree	50,620 (1,907)	54,630 (2,512)	62,700 (3,257)	51,370 (3,622)	50,500 (2,626)	56,760 (4,196)	57,660 (2,912)	52,460 (6,362)	51,780 (1,073)	55,460 (2,242)	54,510 (5,774)
Percent,[2] all education levels	62.4 (1.30)	69.7 (1.28)	66.1 (1.36)	64.5 (1.19)	65.0 (1.21)	60.5 (1.12)	57.4 (1.13)	57.7 (1.26)	55.7 (1.33)	58.5 (1.23)	59.6 (1.51)
Less than high school completion	42.4 (4.02)	48.8 (4.46)	43.4 (4.92)	40.3 (3.98)	43.9 (4.11)	38.3 (3.96)	38.1 (4.26)	30.5 (3.73)	30.3 (3.80)	27.5 (4.20)	40.9 (5.90)
High school completion[1]	60.7 (2.11)	68.3 (2.16)	65.0 (2.30)	64.0 (2.01)	60.4 (2.11)	57.8 (1.83)	48.9 (1.93)	53.6 (2.03)	50.8 (2.16)	51.4 (2.22)	51.2 (2.64)
Some college, no degree	62.2 (2.51)	69.8 (2.57)	63.6 (2.72)	59.3 (2.65)	65.5 (2.78)	60.0 (2.13)	57.7 (2.21)	56.2 (2.42)	50.8 (2.40)	58.0 (2.18)	54.6 (2.94)
Associate's degree	69.2 (4.29)	78.0 (3.79)	69.5 (4.44)	72.2 (3.57)	57.9 (3.78)	58.6 (3.75)	63.2 (3.58)	61.5 (3.25)	69.0 (3.32)	58.9 (3.34)	64.2 (4.19)
Bachelor's or higher degree	77.3 (2.85)	78.6 (2.58)	78.5 (2.54)	79.0 (1.94)	82.0 (1.95)	73.5 (2.15)	73.5 (2.05)	72.4 (2.11)	69.1 (2.13)	76.2 (2.12)	78.2 (2.27)
Bachelor's degree	76.1 (3.15)	79.4 (2.80)	80.1 (2.80)	79.9 (2.14)	82.5 (2.44)	72.2 (2.49)	73.1 (2.46)	71.1 (2.70)	68.5 (2.41)	75.1 (2.47)	74.3 (2.99)
Master's or higher degree	84.0 (6.41)	74.9 (6.52)	72.9 (5.84)	76.5 (3.95)	80.5 (3.78)	77.2 (3.80)	74.7 (3.60)	76.5 (3.65)	70.6 (4.32)	79.3 (3.96)	88.6 (3.30)
Hispanic											
Median annual earnings, all education levels	28,640 (668)	30,300 (452)	30,380 (463)	29,800 (10)	30,320 (756)	31,330 (1,150)	31,310 (1,377)	32,010 (631)	31,020 (22)	30,340 (44)	29,640 (121)
Less than high school completion	22,730 (616)	23,000 (475)	24,930 (548)	23,720 (74)	23,120 (806)	21,630 (568)	21,600 (81)	21,280 (277)	22,440 (972)	22,760 (1,185)	22,810 (1,771)
High school completion[1]	28,790 (1,195)	31,060 (807)	30,300 (803)	28,560 (1,039)	28,990 (931)	28,990 (1,584)	27,940 (863)	29,740 (965)	28,940 (1,332)	27,980 (775)	28,270 (1,120)
Some college, no degree	29,830 (1,361)	35,780 (953)	37,670 (913)	37,380 (1,700)	34,730 (1,079)	34,480 (1,836)	35,040 (997)	33,890 (1,469)	31,050 (808)	32,240 (1,376)	29,890 (1,060)
Associate's degree	36,320 (2,183)	40,060 (1,718)	39,300 (947)	39,300 (1,938)	33,680 (1,461)	34,490 (1,943)	33,370 (1,584)	36,200 (1,400)	35,920 (1,499)	33,830 (1,762)	32,600 (2,268)
Bachelor's or higher degree	45,540 (1,773)	49,160 (1,741)	46,960 (2,076)	48,580 (2,234)	48,650 (1,775)	48,300 (1,778)	49,490 (1,631)	47,110 (2,110)	42,660 (1,817)	45,310 (582)	45,820 (1,476)
Bachelor's degree	42,900 (2,043)	47,360 (1,298)	45,320 (1,039)	47,070 (828)	44,940 (2,343)	44,930 (2,290)	48,150 (1,057)	44,560 (3,221)	41,020 (308)	43,300 (2,071)	44,960 (1,461)
Master's or higher degree	63,800 (8,604)	51,630 (3,165)	57,560 (4,388)	60,000 (4,200)	65,040 (3,019)	56,190 (3,564)	57,470 (4,308)	52,160 (3,820)	52,700 (2,586)	50,730 (4,102)	49,540 (5,565)
Percent,[2] all education levels	60.5 (1.32)	68.7 (1.14)	66.7 (1.11)	68.1 (0.82)	67.9 (0.86)	63.3 (0.93)	58.2 (0.96)	59.4 (0.85)	61.4 (0.89)	61.8 (0.87)	64.7 (1.04)
Less than high school completion	53.5 (2.27)	64.4 (2.00)	61.5 (1.91)	64.9 (1.67)	61.1 (1.72)	55.2 (1.80)	51.8 (1.67)	50.4 (1.77)	54.9 (1.69)	54.4 (1.81)	58.9 (2.15)
High school completion[1]	66.0 (2.31)	70.5 (2.00)	71.5 (1.95)	71.3 (1.40)	72.1 (1.31)	64.3 (1.40)	58.2 (1.57)	59.0 (1.64)	61.5 (1.49)	63.3 (1.53)	66.9 (1.78)
Some college, no degree	58.4 (3.18)	69.5 (2.89)	66.1 (2.74)	66.6 (1.93)	67.9 (2.06)	66.8 (2.02)	61.1 (2.28)	64.5 (1.85)	63.0 (2.09)	61.7 (2.13)	58.2 (2.44)
Associate's degree	67.0 (5.34)	79.0 (3.95)	70.0 (4.49)	70.0 (2.63)	65.6 (3.15)	66.8 (2.68)	66.2 (3.03)	65.1 (2.70)	65.3 (3.06)	65.2 (2.90)	73.5 (2.81)
Bachelor's or higher degree	66.9 (3.73)	70.1 (3.27)	69.8 (3.08)	69.5 (2.11)	73.5 (1.92)	71.0 (2.06)	64.4 (2.12)	68.1 (2.10)	68.4 (1.84)	68.4 (1.96)	71.1 (2.00)
Bachelor's degree	66.3 (4.12)	71.1 (3.57)	70.1 (3.43)	69.3 (2.40)	71.6 (2.15)	71.5 (2.28)	64.2 (2.23)	68.1 (2.29)	68.6 (2.13)	67.6 (2.21)	72.2 (2.27)
Master's or higher degree	69.8 (8.84)	65.5 (8.05)	68.8 (7.00)	70.4 (4.19)	80.2 (3.55)	68.7 (4.10)	65.3 (4.32)	68.2 (3.89)	67.1 (3.97)	71.3 (4.09)	67.5 (4.31)

See notes at end of table.

Table 502.30. Median annual earnings of full-time year-round workers 25 to 34 years old and full-time year-round workers as a percentage of the labor force, by sex, race/ethnicity, and educational attainment: Selected years, 1995 through 2013—Continued

[Amounts in constant 2013 dollars. Standard errors appear in parentheses]

Sex, race/ethnicity, and educational attainment	1995	2000	2003	2005	2007	2008	2009	2010	2011	2012	2013
1	2	3	4	5	6	7	8	9	10	11	12
Asian[3]											
Median annual earnings, all education levels	38,660 (1,076)	48,510 (822)	50,130 (999)	47,540 (1,935)	50,260 (2,055)	53,630 (755)	53,420 (801)	48,850 (2,736)	50,970 (2,719)	54,620 (2,536)	50,440 (1,979)
Less than high school completion[1]	‡ (†)	24,880 (2,231)	‡ (†)	32,080 (1,684)	‡ (†)	‡ (†)	‡ (†)	‡ (†)	‡ (†)	‡ (†)	‡ (†)
High school completion[1]	30,340 (2,220)	33,810 (1,224)	31,300 (1,583)	35,390 (2,484)	31,330 (2,868)	30,250 (2,671)	28,090 (2,197)	31,200 (1,840)	25,830 (1,332)	29,960 (828)	27,940 (2,521)
Some college, no degree	28,310 (2,662)	38,910 (2,014)	37,350 (737)	40,590 (5,034)	39,120 (2,704)	35,630 (4,627)	41,240 (3,565)	37,110 (1,525)	31,990 (1,862)	33,690 (2,673)	34,680 (4,713)
Associate's degree	30,570 (1,874)	39,910 (1,994)	37,520 (†)	39,460	39,460 (5,115)	34,180 (2,721)	39,400 (4,153)	38,340 (2,867)	35,820 (6,747)	43,730 (3,208)	31,590 (3,009)
Bachelor's or higher degree	50,290 (2,167)	66,710 (1,380)	64,980 (2,324)	59,640 (1,086)	61,740 (5,117)	64,430 (911)	64,370 (1,522)	63,940 (1,154)	63,280 (2,448)	65,160 (1,699)	59,910 (2,381)
Bachelor's degree	46,090 (972)	60,660 (2,444)	61,730 (2,811)	59,620 (3,877)	55,380 (1,923)	59,110 (2,262)	54,080 (1,219)	57,700 (4,237)	53,110 (3,433)	60,150 (1,953)	58,140 (2,721)
Master's or higher degree	58,010 (5,553)	77,390 (5,938)	76,050 (5,720)	64,920 (4,761)	72,760 (2,444)	74,940 (3,041)	76,010 (3,266)	72,960 (5,240)	75,830 (4,623)	70,740 (1,992)	74,650 (5,310)
Percent,[2] all education levels	63.4 (2.98)	68.5 (1.78)	68.1 (1.88)	64.8 (1.57)	71.2 (1.63)	68.8 (1.72)	66.7 (1.51)	65.1 (1.46)	65.1 (1.73)	67.9 (1.57)	66.0 (1.79)
Less than high school completion[1]	46.6 (9.98)	61.6 (3.31)	42.0 (9.48)	49.4 (7.62)	58.3 (8.93)	33.1 (8.96)	52.4 (11.87)	46.6 (11.24)	56.2 (6.80)	50.9 (7.17)	53.3 (9.35)
High school completion[1]	66.9 (7.05)	68.9 (4.59)	73.7 (4.80)	62.5 (4.82)	68.5 (4.09)	63.0 (4.17)	59.3 (4.15)	55.9 (3.97)	53.7 (4.47)	64.6 (3.35)	62.4 (5.45)
Some college, no degree	51.8 (8.46)	63.4 (4.59)	60.6 (5.57)	66.5 (4.65)	73.4 (4.48)	63.8 (4.70)	57.4 (5.03)	58.2 (4.93)	58.3 (4.37)	51.7 (4.31)	57.2 (5.79)
Associate's degree	77.1 (8.01)	72.2 (5.92)	70.6 (6.66)	66.3 (5.93)	70.6 (5.49)	78.4 (5.36)	70.3 (4.25)	56.5 (5.57)	55.1 (5.88)	60.6 (5.79)	69.3 (5.81)
Bachelor's or higher degree	65.6 (4.18)	69.9 (2.35)	69.9 (2.35)	66.0 (2.07)	72.4 (2.04)	71.9 (1.93)	70.5 (1.84)	71.1 (1.89)	70.4 (2.08)	72.9 (1.80)	68.5 (2.24)
Bachelor's degree	68.0 (5.27)	70.8 (2.87)	71.8 (2.96)	68.7 (2.69)	71.6 (2.40)	72.7 (2.48)	69.7 (2.46)	72.2 (2.22)	69.6 (2.59)	73.7 (2.31)	67.6 (3.04)
Master's or higher degree	62.0 (6.80)	67.9 (4.11)	66.9 (3.82)	61.3 (3.08)	73.6 (3.25)	70.9 (2.79)	71.6 (3.17)	69.4 (3.15)	71.8 (3.20)	71.7 (2.85)	70.0 (3.51)
Median annual earnings for other race groups, all education levels											
Pacific Islander[4]	[3]	[3]	46,660 (5,323)	36,040 (3,845)	38,620 (3,636)	37,750 (5,029)	31,540 (5,654)	36,590 (1,405)	35,460 (2,662)	32,560 (4,976)	39,000 (4,350)
American Indian/Alaska Native[4]	30,310 (3,035)	33,800 (1,481)	32,920 (2,376)	35,190 (2,031)	34,480 (1,961)	31,160 (2,483)	32,580 (4,282)	33,640 (3,379)	30,340 (1,735)	33,370 (2,755)	32,220 (6,558)
Two or more races[4]	— (†)	— (†)	37,960 (1,324)	40,560 (1,701)	36,430 (3,460)	36,280 (3,047)	36,480 (2,923)	37,170 (1,487)	38,010 (1,705)	36,090 (1,537)	36,580 (3,362)
Percent[2] for other race groups, all education levels											
Pacific Islander[4]	[3]	[3]	61.8 (7.75)	53.7 (6.81)	70.2 (5.06)	58.6 (4.76)	46.9 (7.15)	62.2 (6.71)	56.9 (5.50)	69.4 (6.03)	77.2 (6.48)
American Indian/Alaska Native[4]	46.9 (8.10)	57.6 (4.94)	58.8 (5.83)	60.2 (4.01)	64.3 (4.58)	52.7 (4.28)	59.8 (4.30)	52.9 (4.14)	52.2 (4.58)	55.8 (5.05)	59.4 (5.26)
Two or more races[4]	— (†)	— (†)	64.5 (4.34)	61.9 (3.46)	59.5 (3.21)	59.5 (2.89)	50.2 (2.95)	60.2 (2.87)	58.1 (2.93)	59.0 (2.94)	61.0 (3.73)

—Not available.
†Not applicable.
#Rounds to zero.
‡Reporting standards not met (too few cases for a reliable estimate).
[1]Includes equivalency credentials, such as the General Educational Development (GED) credential.
[2]Full-time year-round workers as a percentage of the population ages 25 through 34 who reported working or looking for work in the given year.
[3]For 1995 and 2000, data for Asians and Pacific Islanders were not reported separately; therefore, Pacific Islanders are included with Asians for 1995 and 2000.

[4]For Pacific Islanders, American Indians/Alaska Natives, and persons of two or more races, data by educational attainment are omitted because these data did not meet reporting standards. All data shown for these three race categories are for persons of all education levels.
NOTE: Beginning in 2005, standard errors were computed using replicate weights, which produced more precise values than the generalized variance function methodology used in prior years. Race categories exclude persons of Hispanic ethnicity. Constant dollars based on the Consumer Price Index, prepared by the Bureau of Labor Statistics, U.S. Department of Labor.
SOURCE: U.S. Department of Commerce, Census Bureau, Current Population Survey (CPS), March 1996 through March 2014. (This table was prepared November 2014.)

Table 502.40. Annual earnings and median earnings of persons 25 years old and over, by highest level of educational attainment and sex: 2013

[Standard errors appear in parentheses]

Sex and earnings	Total	Elementary/secondary			Some college, no degree	College					
		Less than 9th grade	Some high school, no completion	High school completion (includes equivalency)		Associate's degree	Bachelor's or higher degree				
							Total	Bachelor's degree	Master's degree	Professional degree	Doctor's degree
1	2	3	4	5	6	7	8	9	10	11	12
Number of persons (in thousands)..........	209,287 (260.3)	9,913 (137.9)	14,545 (165.4)	62,240 (305.6)	34,919 (245.0)	20,790 (195.1)	66,879 (312.8)	42,256 (264.8)	17,772 (181.6)	3,148 (78.8)	3,703 (85.4)
With earnings..........	136,641 (351.6)	4,213 (91.0)	6,726 (114.4)	36,603 (249.8)	22,917 (203.9)	15,110 (168.4)	51,072 (284.9)	31,999 (236.1)	13,594 (160.3)	2,574 (71.3)	2,906 (75.8)
For persons with earnings											
Percentage distribution, by total annual earnings[1]	100.0 (†)	100.0 (†)	100.0 (†)	100.0 (†)	100.0 (†)	100.0 (†)	100.0 (†)	100.0 (†)	100.0 (†)	100.0 (†)	100.0 (†)
$1 to $4,999 or loss[2].......	4.8 (0.08)	6.1 (0.52)	8.5 (0.48)	5.4 (0.17)	5.7 (0.22)	4.7 (0.24)	3.4 (0.11)	3.6 (0.15)	3.4 (0.22)	2.6 (0.44)	1.9 (0.36)
$5,000 to $9,999..........	5.0 (0.08)	9.9 (0.65)	10.4 (0.53)	6.0 (0.18)	5.9 (0.22)	4.9 (0.25)	2.7 (0.10)	3.0 (0.15)	2.5 (0.19)	0.8 ! (0.25)	1.8 (0.35)
$10,000 to $14,999........	6.3 (0.09)	14.9 (0.78)	12.1 (0.56)	8.2 (0.20)	7.0 (0.24)	5.6 (0.26)	3.3 (0.11)	3.6 (0.15)	3.0 (0.21)	2.4 (0.43)	2.0 (0.37)
$15,000 to $19,999........	7.2 (0.10)	17.6 (0.83)	13.4 (0.59)	9.4 (0.22)	8.3 (0.26)	6.7 (0.29)	3.5 (0.11)	4.1 (0.16)	2.6 (0.19)	1.3 (0.32)	2.4 (0.40)
$20,000 to $24,999........	8.1 (0.10)	16.5 (0.81)	14.5 (0.61)	11.4 (0.23)	8.1 (0.26)	8.1 (0.31)	4.2 (0.13)	4.8 (0.17)	3.4 (0.22)	2.4 (0.43)	2.1 (0.38)
$25,000 to $29,999........	6.9 (0.10)	9.4 (0.63)	9.6 (0.51)	8.6 (0.21)	8.3 (0.26)	7.7 (0.31)	4.1 (0.12)	5.0 (0.17)	3.2 (0.22)	1.7 (0.36)	1.8 (0.35)
$30,000 to $34,999........	7.6 (0.10)	7.7 (0.58)	7.4 (0.45)	10.2 (0.22)	8.9 (0.27)	8.5 (0.32)	5.0 (0.14)	6.0 (0.19)	3.5 (0.22)	3.1 (0.48)	2.8 (0.43)
$35,000 to $39,999........	6.3 (0.09)	4.2 (0.44)	4.7 (0.37)	7.5 (0.19)	7.7 (0.25)	7.1 (0.30)	4.9 (0.14)	5.8 (0.19)	3.8 (0.23)	1.7 (0.36)	3.1 (0.45)
$40,000 to $49,999........	11.7 (0.12)	5.8 (0.51)	8.5 (0.48)	11.6 (0.24)	12.8 (0.31)	14.7 (0.41)	11.3 (0.20)	12.4 (0.26)	10.7 (0.38)	5.9 (0.65)	6.3 (0.64)
$50,000 to $74,999........	18.1 (0.15)	5.3 (0.49)	7.5 (0.45)	14.3 (0.26)	16.5 (0.35)	19.7 (0.46)	23.6 (0.27)	23.8 (0.34)	24.9 (0.52)	17.8 (1.07)	20.1 (1.05)
$75,000 to $99,999........	8.2 (0.10)	1.9 (0.30)	2.0 (0.24)	4.6 (0.15)	5.8 (0.22)	7.1 (0.30)	13.5 (0.21)	12.4 (0.26)	16.2 (0.45)	12.7 (0.93)	14.5 (0.92)
$100,000 or more........	9.9 (0.11)	0.7 (0.18)	1.4 (0.20)	2.8 (0.12)	4.9 (0.20)	5.3 (0.26)	20.5 (0.25)	15.5 (0.29)	22.7 (0.51)	47.6 (1.39)	41.3 (1.29)
Median annual earnings[1].	$37,330 (176)	$20,310 (290)	$21,420 (255)	$30,290 (168)	$32,450 (392)	$36,890 (357)	$56,240 (373)	$50,740 (230)	$61,880 (387)	$91,370 (5,040)	$81,740 (2,804)
Number of males (in thousands)..........	100,592 (197.7)	4,945 (97.4)	7,403 (118.0)	30,718 (215.1)	16,457 (169.0)	8,973 (129.0)	32,095 (218.3)	20,099 (183.6)	7,846 (121.2)	1,821 (59.9)	2,329 (67.6)
With earnings..........	72,562 (246.4)	2,806 (74.0)	4,223 (90.3)	20,950 (186.6)	11,758 (145.9)	7,038 (115.2)	25,787 (202.2)	16,200 (167.8)	6,235 (108.8)	1,501 (54.4)	1,851 (60.4)
For males with earnings											
Percentage distribution, by total annual earnings[1].	100.1 (†)	100.1 (†)	100.0 (†)	100.0 (†)	100.0 (†)	100.0 (†)	100.0 (†)	100.0 (†)	100.0 (†)	100.0 (†)	100.0 (†)
$1 to $4,999 or loss[2].......	3.4 (0.10)	4.8 (0.57)	5.8 (0.51)	4.0 (0.19)	4.0 (0.26)	3.1 (0.29)	2.2 (0.13)	2.2 (0.16)	2.7 (0.29)	1.4 ! (0.43)	1.6 (0.41)
$5,000 to $9,999..........	3.8 (0.10)	7.1 (0.68)	7.9 (0.59)	4.5 (0.20)	4.4 (0.27)	3.3 (0.30)	2.2 (0.13)	2.4 (0.17)	1.9 (0.25)	0.5 ! (0.27)	2.0 (0.46)
$10,000 to $14,999........	4.7 (0.11)	10.7 (0.83)	8.6 (0.61)	6.2 (0.24)	4.8 (0.28)	3.9 (0.33)	2.3 (0.13)	2.6 (0.18)	2.0 (0.25)	2.1 (0.53)	1.4 (0.39)
$15,000 to $19,999........	5.9 (0.12)	16.4 (0.99)	11.2 (0.69)	7.3 (0.25)	6.2 (0.32)	4.7 (0.36)	2.8 (0.14)	3.2 (0.20)	2.1 (0.25)	1.2 ! (0.40)	2.7 (0.53)
$20,000 to $24,999........	7.1 (0.13)	18.2 (1.03)	15.2 (0.78)	9.7 (0.29)	6.2 (0.31)	6.5 (0.41)	3.0 (0.15)	3.4 (0.20)	2.4 (0.27)	1.9 (0.49)	1.8 (0.44)
$25,000 to $29,999........	6.2 (0.13)	10.0 (0.80)	10.7 (0.67)	7.6 (0.26)	7.3 (0.34)	5.9 (0.40)	3.4 (0.16)	4.2 (0.22)	2.6 (0.27)	1.3 ! (0.42)	1.2 (0.36)
$30,000 to $34,999........	7.1 (0.13)	9.3 (0.78)	8.2 (0.60)	10.4 (0.30)	7.7 (0.35)	6.9 (0.43)	3.7 (0.17)	4.6 (0.23)	2.4 (0.28)	2.7 (0.59)	2.1 (0.47)
$35,000 to $39,999........	6.0 (0.12)	5.2 (0.59)	5.9 (0.51)	8.1 (0.27)	7.3 (0.34)	5.5 (0.38)	4.0 (0.17)	4.9 (0.24)	2.7 (0.29)	1.4 ! (0.43)	2.6 (0.52)
$40,000 to $49,999........	11.7 (0.17)	7.4 (0.70)	11.5 (0.69)	12.9 (0.33)	13.8 (0.45)	15.8 (0.61)	9.0 (0.25)	10.5 (0.34)	7.1 (0.46)	4.8 (0.78)	5.5 (0.75)
$50,000 to $74,999........	20.1 (0.21)	7.2 (0.69)	10.1 (0.65)	18.8 (0.38)	21.7 (0.54)	24.7 (0.73)	22.1 (0.37)	24.3 (0.48)	20.0 (0.72)	15.3 (1.31)	15.5 (1.19)
$75,000 to $99,999........	10.3 (0.16)	2.7 (0.43)	3.1 (0.37)	6.6 (0.24)	8.7 (0.37)	10.9 (0.53)	15.9 (0.32)	15.5 (0.40)	18.3 (0.69)	11.7 (1.17)	14.2 (1.15)
$100,000 or more........	13.8 (0.18)	1.0 (0.27)	1.8 (0.29)	4.0 (0.19)	7.7 (0.35)	8.7 (0.47)	29.4 (0.40)	22.1 (0.46)	35.9 (0.86)	55.5 (1.81)	49.6 (1.64)
Median annual earnings[1].	$43,620 (715)	$22,030 (298)	$25,390 (392)	$35,160 (380)	$40,900 (374)	$45,670 (656)	$69,790 (1,267)	$61,130 (458)	$79,870 (2,166)	$111,510 (8,853)	$97,400 (5,794)

See notes at end of table.

Table 502.40. Annual earnings and median earnings of persons 25 years old and over, by highest level of educational attainment and sex: 2013—Continued

[Standard errors appear in parentheses]

| Sex and earnings | Total | Elementary/secondary | | | College | | | Bachelor's or higher degree | | | | |
| | | Less than 9th grade | Some high school, no completion | High school completion (includes equivalency) | Some college, no degree | Associate's degree | Total | Bachelor's degree | Master's degree | Professional degree | Doctor's degree |
1	2	3	4	5	6	7	8	9	10	11	12
Number of females (in thousands)	**108,695** (167.7)	**4,968** (97.6)	**7,142** (116.0)	**31,522** (217.0)	**18,462** (177.3)	**11,818** (146.2)	**34,784** (223.9)	**22,157** (190.8)	**9,926** (135.1)	**1,327** (51.2)	**1,374** (52.1)
With earnings	64,079 (249.7)	1,407 (52.7)	2,503 (70.0)	15,653 (165.4)	11,160 (142.5)	8,072 (122.8)	25,285 (200.7)	15,798 (166.0)	7,359 (117.6)	1,073 (46.1)	1,055 (45.7)
For females with earnings											
Percentage distribution, by total annual earnings[1]											
Total	100.0 (†)	100.0 (†)	99.8 (†)	100.0 (†)	100.0 (†)	100.0 (†)	100.0 (†)	100.0 (†)	100.0 (†)	100.0 (†)	100.1 (†)
$1 to $4,999 or loss[2]	6.3 (0.14)	8.6 (1.06)	12.9 (0.95)	7.2 (0.29)	7.5 (0.35)	6.1 (0.38)	4.6 (0.19)	5.0 (0.25)	4.0 (0.32)	4.3 (0.87)	2.5 (0.67)
$5,000 to $9,999	6.2 (0.14)	15.5 (1.36)	14.7 (1.00)	8.1 (0.31)	7.4 (0.35)	6.3 (0.38)	3.2 (0.16)	3.6 (0.21)	2.9 (0.28)	1.2 ! (0.47)	1.4 ! (0.52)
$10,000 to $14,999	8.1 (0.15)	23.2 (1.59)	18.1 (1.09)	10.9 (0.35)	9.3 (0.39)	7.0 (0.40)	4.3 (0.18)	4.6 (0.24)	3.8 (0.32)	2.8 (0.71)	3.0 (0.75)
$15,000 to $19,999	8.6 (0.16)	20.1 (1.51)	17.0 (1.06)	12.3 (0.37)	10.4 (0.41)	8.4 (0.44)	4.2 (0.18)	5.0 (0.25)	3.1 (0.29)	1.5 ! (0.52)	1.9 ! (0.59)
$20,000 to $24,999	9.2 (0.16)	13.2 (1.28)	13.3 (0.96)	13.7 (0.39)	10.2 (0.40)	9.4 (0.46)	5.4 (0.20)	6.3 (0.27)	4.3 (0.33)	3.0 (0.73)	2.7 (0.70)
$25,000 to $29,999	7.6 (0.15)	8.2 (1.03)	7.6 (0.75)	10.0 (0.34)	9.3 (0.39)	9.3 (0.46)	4.9 (0.19)	5.8 (0.26)	3.7 (0.31)	2.1 (0.62)	2.8 (0.72)
$30,000 to $34,999	8.3 (0.15)	4.6 (0.79)	6.1 (0.68)	10.0 (0.34)	10.3 (0.41)	9.8 (0.47)	6.2 (0.21)	7.4 (0.29)	4.5 (0.34)	3.5 (0.80)	4.2 (0.87)
$35,000 to $39,999	6.6 (0.14)	2.2 (0.55)	2.8 (0.47)	6.8 (0.28)	8.1 (0.37)	8.5 (0.44)	5.9 (0.21)	6.8 (0.28)	4.8 (0.35)	2.1 (0.61)	3.9 (0.84)
$40,000 to $49,999	11.7 (0.18)	2.5 (0.59)	3.5 (0.52)	9.8 (0.34)	11.6 (0.43)	13.8 (0.54)	13.6 (0.30)	14.3 (0.39)	13.8 (0.57)	7.4 (1.13)	7.8 (1.17)
$50,000 to $74,999	15.9 (0.20)	1.6 (0.48)	3.2 (0.50)	8.3 (0.31)	11.0 (0.42)	15.3 (0.57)	25.1 (0.39)	23.3 (0.48)	29.1 (0.75)	21.5 (1.77)	28.1 (1.96)
$75,000 to $99,999	5.8 (0.13)	‡ (†)	‡ (†)	1.8 (0.15)	2.8 (0.22)	3.8 (0.30)	11.2 (0.28)	9.2 (0.32)	14.4 (0.58)	14.1 (1.50)	15.2 (1.56)
$100,000 or more	5.5 (0.13)	# (†)	0.6 ! (0.22)	1.1 (0.12)	2.0 (0.19)	2.4 (0.24)	11.5 (0.28)	8.7 (0.32)	11.6 (0.53)	36.5 (2.08)	26.7 (1.93)
Median annual earnings[1]	$31,520 (140)	$15,610 (506)	$16,140 (434)	$23,800 (383)	$27,090 (363)	$31,250 (326)	$47,180 (399)	$42,090 (308)	$52,090 (422)	$75,420 (3,177)	$66,760 (2,160)

†Not applicable.
#Rounds to zero.
!Interpret data with caution. The coefficient of variation (CV) for this estimate is between 30 and 50 percent.
‡Reporting standards not met. The coefficient of variation (CV) for this estimate is 50 percent or greater.
[1]Excludes persons without earnings.

[2]A negative amount (a net loss) may be reported by self-employed persons.
NOTE: Detail may not sum to totals because of rounding.
SOURCE: U.S. Department of Commerce, Census Bureau, Current Population Survey (CPS), 2014 Annual Social and Economic Supplement, retrieved December 2, 2014, from http://www.census.gov/hhes/www/cpstables/032014/perinc/pinc03_000.htm. (This table was prepared December 2014.)

Table 503.10. Percentage of high school students age 16 and over who were employed, by age group, sex, race/ethnicity, family income, nativity, and hours worked per week: Selected years, 1970 through 2013

[Standard errors appear in parentheses]

Year	Total	Age group		Sex		Race/ethnicity			Family income[1]			Nativity	
		16 and 17 years old	18 years old and over	Male	Female	White	Black	Hispanic	Low income	Middle income	High income	U.S.-born	Foreign-born
1	2	3	4	5	6	7	8	9	10	11	12	13	14
Percent employed[2]													
1970	31.9 (0.88)	30.8 (0.93)	39.7 (2.55)	35.2 (1.24)	28.3 (1.22)	— (†)	— (†)	— (†)	22.0 (2.51)	31.5 (1.12)	35.9 (1.64)	— (†)	— (†)
1975	33.2 (0.85)	32.9 (0.91)	34.9 (2.40)	35.0 (1.19)	31.2 (1.22)	38.0 (1.00)	13.9 (1.63)	21.8 (3.59)	18.4 (2.22)	31.8 (1.10)	40.4 (1.59)	—	—
1980	35.6 (0.87)	34.9 (0.94)	39.6 (2.28)	36.9 (1.22)	34.2 (1.24)	41.2 (1.03)	15.0 (1.64)	24.1 (3.65)	19.4 (2.10)	35.2 (1.15)	42.3 (1.59)	—	—
1985	31.6 (0.93)	30.8 (1.00)	36.1 (2.47)	32.1 (1.29)	31.0 (1.33)	37.9 (1.15)	15.0 (1.85)	17.6 (2.63)	14.7 (1.85)	31.0 (1.23)	41.1 (1.81)	—	—
1990	32.3 (0.98)	31.2 (1.08)	37.1 (2.33)	33.1 (1.37)	31.3 (1.39)	37.8 (1.24)	17.3 (2.05)	26.4 (2.86)	21.4 (2.16)	33.1 (1.29)	36.8 (1.97)	—	—
1995	33.6 (0.92)	32.7 (1.02)	37.5 (2.19)	33.1 (1.26)	34.2 (1.35)	40.8 (1.18)	18.0 (1.91)	22.2 (2.41)	17.4 (1.82)	34.4 (1.23)	42.1 (1.88)	34.9 (0.97)	20.1 (2.65)
2000	34.1 (0.93)	33.3 (1.03)	37.7 (2.15)	33.2 (1.28)	35.1 (1.36)	41.3 (1.20)	21.3 (2.14)	20.9 (2.18)	22.0 (2.11)	34.1 (1.22)	40.7 (1.85)	35.1 (0.99)	24.4 (2.74)
2001	32.4 (0.86)	31.1 (0.95)	37.8 (1.99)	30.6 (1.17)	34.5 (1.27)	38.9 (1.11)	18.7 (1.85)	23.6 (2.23)	21.4 (2.04)	33.3 (1.12)	36.1 (1.70)	33.3 (0.90)	23.0 (2.64)
2002	30.6 (0.84)	29.2 (0.93)	35.9 (1.92)	28.0 (1.13)	33.4 (1.24)	37.5 (1.11)	16.9 (1.81)	21.1 (1.94)	18.4 (1.83)	31.4 (1.11)	35.3 (1.64)	31.6 (0.89)	21.3 (2.34)
2003	27.0 (0.79)	25.3 (0.86)	34.6 (1.97)	26.7 (1.09)	27.3 (1.15)	33.3 (1.07)	15.2 (1.68)	18.8 (1.82)	14.3 (1.64)	27.8 (1.05)	31.8 (1.57)	28.0 (0.84)	17.7 (2.17)
2004	27.2 (0.80)	25.6 (0.87)	34.7 (2.03)	26.2 (1.09)	28.3 (1.17)	32.9 (1.08)	15.1 (1.71)	21.2 (1.92)	12.0 (1.55)	27.5 (1.05)	34.4 (1.64)	27.8 (0.85)	20.8 (2.43)
2005	26.4 (0.77)	25.2 (0.84)	32.2 (1.95)	25.3 (1.05)	27.6 (1.14)	31.8 (1.05)	13.7 (1.63)	19.4 (1.78)	14.8 (1.61)	26.9 (1.03)	31.7 (1.55)	26.8 (0.81)	21.7 (2.49)
2006	27.6 (0.79)	26.0 (0.86)	34.1 (1.87)	26.5 (1.08)	28.8 (1.16)	33.6 (1.08)	20.1 (1.85)	17.5 (1.72)	17.8 (1.72)	27.5 (1.04)	33.5 (1.59)	27.9 (0.82)	23.9 (2.64)
2007	26.2 (0.78)	24.8 (0.85)	32.2 (1.87)	25.0 (1.06)	27.6 (1.14)	31.3 (1.06)	15.1 (1.68)	21.1 (1.83)	17.3 (1.74)	25.9 (1.01)	32.1 (1.62)	26.0 (0.81)	28.5 (2.64)
2008	22.6 (0.74)	21.0 (0.80)	29.5 (1.83)	20.0 (0.99)	25.4 (1.10)	27.7 (1.04)	15.5 (1.69)	15.1 (1.54)	13.5 (1.54)	22.6 (0.96)	28.4 (1.59)	23.1 (0.78)	18.0 (2.35)
2009	17.0 (0.67)	15.2 (0.72)	23.8 (1.65)	16.0 (0.91)	18.1 (0.98)	21.5 (0.96)	10.5 (1.43)	11.9 (1.39)	9.7 (1.33)	16.3 (0.85)	23.5 (1.51)	17.0 (0.70)	16.9 (2.32)
2010[3]	16.2 (0.55)	15.0 (0.59)	20.8 (1.52)	14.0 (0.78)	18.5 (0.86)	20.9 (0.86)	9.6 (1.28)	10.4 (1.18)	8.5 (1.01)	16.5 (0.80)	20.9 (1.31)	16.4 (0.60)	13.4 (2.20)
2011[3]	16.9 (0.67)	16.4 (0.77)	18.7 (1.28)	14.7 (0.76)	19.4 (1.09)	22.2 (1.07)	10.2 (1.43)	11.3 (1.11)	10.2 (1.29)	17.5 (0.83)	19.6 (1.39)	17.3 (0.74)	12.4 (1.91)
2012[3]	18.0 (0.71)	16.0 (0.75)	24.5 (1.88)	16.6 (0.83)	19.4 (1.13)	23.2 (0.97)	12.7 (2.17)	11.4 (1.23)	13.0 (1.42)	16.4 (0.88)	24.9 (1.55)	18.6 (0.76)	12.0 (2.01)
2013[3]	17.9 (0.65)	15.8 (0.69)	24.7 (1.73)	17.6 (0.89)	18.3 (0.94)	23.3 (0.99)	11.8 (1.42)	14.0 (1.19)	9.7 (1.26)	16.9 (0.90)	25.4 (1.69)	17.8 (0.66)	19.0 (2.67)
Percent working less than 15 hours per week[4]													
1970	13.6 (0.64)	14.5 (0.71)	7.5 (1.37)	12.3 (0.85)	14.9 (0.97)	— (†)	— (†)	— (†)	9.9 (1.81)	12.6 (0.80)	16.8 (1.28)	— (†)	— (†)
1975	13.4 (0.62)	14.0 (0.67)	8.8 (1.43)	12.5 (0.82)	14.3 (0.92)	15.5 (0.75)	5.3 (1.05)	6.6 ! (2.15)	6.8 (1.44)	12.3 (0.78)	17.4 (1.23)	—	—
1980	14.0 (0.63)	14.9 (0.70)	8.9 (1.33)	13.7 (0.87)	14.2 (0.91)	16.4 (0.77)	4.6 (0.96)	9.4 (2.49)	7.7 (1.41)	13.2 (0.82)	17.7 (1.23)	—	—
1985	12.3 (0.65)	12.8 (0.72)	9.5 (1.51)	11.7 (0.89)	12.9 (0.96)	15.2 (0.85)	6.2 (1.25)	3.0 ! (1.18)	3.6 (0.97)	11.8 (0.86)	17.5 (1.40)	—	—
1990	11.7 (0.67)	12.9 (0.78)	6.8 (1.21)	11.3 (0.92)	12.2 (0.98)	14.7 (0.90)	6.0 (1.28)	4.8 (1.39)	5.9 (1.24)	11.5 (0.88)	15.6 (1.48)	—	—
1995	11.9 (0.63)	13.1 (0.73)	6.8 (1.14)	11.1 (0.84)	12.9 (0.96)	14.8 (0.85)	6.5 (1.22)	6.5 (1.42)	4.4 (0.98)	11.3 (0.82)	18.1 (1.47)	12.6 (0.68)	5.1 (1.46)
2000	11.9 (0.64)	12.9 (0.73)	7.8 (1.19)	11.2 (0.86)	12.6 (0.94)	15.4 (0.88)	6.3 (1.27)	3.7 (1.01)	5.4 (1.15)	11.3 (0.82)	16.5 (1.40)	12.6 (0.68)	5.2 (1.42)
2001	11.6 (0.59)	12.6 (0.68)	7.7 (1.10)	9.8 (0.75)	13.7 (0.91)	15.0 (0.82)	4.3 (0.96)	6.1 (1.26)	5.7 (1.15)	10.8 (0.74)	16.4 (1.31)	12.2 (0.63)	5.5 (1.43)
2002	11.1 (0.57)	12.1 (0.66)	7.2 (1.04)	9.7 (0.74)	12.7 (0.87)	15.0 (0.82)	4.5 (1.00)	3.6 (0.89)	6.0 (1.12)	10.0 (0.72)	16.1 (1.26)	11.9 (0.62)	4.1 (1.13)
2003	9.6 (0.52)	10.0 (0.59)	7.8 (1.11)	9.0 (0.70)	10.2 (0.78)	12.4 (0.75)	4.5 (0.96)	5.5 (1.06)	4.8 (1.00)	9.1 (0.67)	13.1 (1.14)	10.2 (0.57)	3.7 (1.07)
2004	10.4 (0.55)	10.9 (0.62)	8.4 (1.18)	9.9 (0.74)	11.0 (0.82)	14.0 (0.80)	4.9 (1.03)	4.4 (0.96)	3.5 (0.87)	8.5 (0.66)	18.1 (1.33)	11.0 (0.59)	5.2 (1.33)
2005	10.1 (0.53)	10.7 (0.60)	7.2 (1.08)	8.9 (0.69)	11.4 (0.81)	13.4 (0.77)	3.7 (0.89)	5.0 (0.99)	3.7 (0.85)	9.9 (0.69)	13.9 (1.16)	10.6 (0.56)	4.6 (1.26)
2006	9.9 (0.53)	10.7 (0.61)	6.4 (0.97)	8.8 (0.69)	11.0 (0.80)	12.8 (0.76)	5.2 (1.03)	4.2 (0.91)	3.7 (0.85)	9.2 (0.67)	14.7 (1.25)	10.5 (0.56)	3.0 ! (1.06)
2007	10.6 (0.54)	11.4 (0.63)	7.0 (1.02)	9.5 (0.72)	11.7 (0.82)	14.2 (0.80)	3.0 (0.80)	6.0 (1.06)	6.1 (1.10)	9.6 (0.68)	15.3 (1.20)	11.1 (0.58)	5.7 (1.36)
2008	9.2 (0.51)	9.9 (0.59)	6.1 (0.96)	8.1 (0.68)	10.3 (0.77)	12.4 (0.77)	3.2 (0.82)	4.1 (0.85)	3.1 (0.78)	9.1 (0.66)	13.0 (1.18)	9.6 (0.54)	4.6 (1.28)
2009	7.6 (0.47)	8.0 (0.54)	6.2 (0.94)	6.8 (0.62)	8.4 (0.71)	10.1 (0.71)	3.6 (0.86)	4.7 (0.91)	3.6 (0.83)	6.9 (0.58)	11.8 (1.15)	7.8 (0.50)	5.2 (1.38)
2010[3]	7.3 (0.42)	7.5 (0.49)	6.8 (0.94)	6.3 (0.50)	8.4 (0.69)	9.5 (0.65)	4.1 (0.82)	4.5 (0.79)	3.0 (0.63)	7.1 (0.54)	10.9 (1.01)	7.7 (0.45)	3.4 ! (1.21)
2011[3]	7.3 (0.40)	8.1 (0.50)	4.4 (0.71)	5.8 (0.51)	9.0 (0.66)	11.0 (0.66)	2.2 (0.60)	2.7 (0.54)	3.7 (0.81)	7.0 (0.55)	10.2 (0.94)	7.7 (0.44)	2.8 ! (0.98)
2012[3]	8.2 (0.46)	8.5 (0.53)	7.3 (0.95)	7.1 (0.57)	9.4 (0.73)	12.2 (0.73)	3.7 (0.92)	2.4 (0.58)	4.2 (0.89)	7.2 (0.53)	13.3 (1.27)	8.8 (0.50)	2.4 ! (0.75)
2013[3]	7.9 (0.50)	8.2 (0.54)	6.8 (0.99)	6.9 (0.61)	8.9 (0.77)	12.2 (0.81)	2.6 (0.71)	3.4 (0.62)	2.9 (0.78)	7.0 (0.54)	13.1 (1.38)	8.1 (0.50)	5.5 ! (1.75)
Percent working 15 or more hours per week[4]													
1970	17.5 (0.71)	15.6 (0.73)	30.8 (2.41)	22.1 (1.08)	12.6 (0.90)	— (†)	— (†)	— (†)	10.6 (1.87)	18.4 (0.93)	18.1 (1.32)	— (†)	— (†)
1975	19.2 (0.71)	18.2 (0.75)	25.7 (2.20)	21.7 (1.03)	16.4 (0.97)	21.8 (0.85)	8.3 (1.30)	14.7 (3.08)	11.3 (1.81)	19.0 (0.93)	23.1 (1.34)	—	—
1980	20.5 (0.73)	19.0 (0.77)	29.4 (2.12)	22.1 (1.05)	18.9 (1.02)	23.5 (0.89)	10.1 (1.39)	14.3 (2.99)	11.4 (1.69)	21.0 (0.98)	23.1 (1.36)	—	—
1985	18.4 (0.77)	17.5 (0.81)	25.5 (2.24)	19.5 (1.09)	17.3 (1.09)	21.7 (0.97)	8.4 (1.44)	13.7 (2.37)	10.0 (1.57)	18.4 (1.03)	22.6 (1.54)	—	—
1990	19.7 (0.83)	17.5 (0.88)	29.1 (2.19)	21.0 (1.19)	18.3 (1.16)	22.1 (1.06)	10.6 (1.67)	21.5 (2.66)	15.0 (1.88)	20.8 (1.11)	20.2 (1.64)	—	—
1995	20.5 (0.79)	18.4 (0.84)	29.7 (2.07)	20.8 (1.09)	20.2 (1.14)	24.5 (1.03)	10.9 (1.55)	15.1 (2.07)	12.7 (1.60)	21.9 (1.07)	22.5 (1.59)	21.1 (0.83)	14.9 (2.35)

See notes at end of table.

Table 503.10. Percentage of high school students age 16 and over who were employed, by age group, sex, race/ethnicity, family income, nativity, and hours worked per week: Selected years, 1970 through 2013—Continued

[Standard errors appear in parentheses]

Year	Total	Age group		Sex		Race/ethnicity			Family income[1]			Nativity	
		16 and 17 years old	18 years old and over	Male	Female	White	Black	Hispanic	Low income	Middle income	High income	U.S.-born	Foreign-born
1	2	3	4	5	6	7	8	9	10	11	12	13	14
2000	21.1 (0.80)	19.2 (0.86)	28.8 (2.01)	21.1 (1.11)	21.0 (1.16)	24.6 (1.05)	13.8 (1.80)	16.3 (1.98)	15.6 (1.85)	21.5 (1.06)	23.1 (1.59)	21.3 (0.84)	19.0 (2.50)
2001	19.4 (0.73)	17.1 (0.77)	28.3 (1.85)	19.6 (1.01)	19.1 (1.05)	22.2 (0.95)	13.4 (1.62)	17.0 (1.97)	14.6 (1.76)	20.9 (0.97)	18.4 (1.37)	19.6 (0.76)	16.9 (2.35)
2002	18.5 (0.71)	16.1 (0.75)	27.9 (1.80)	17.5 (0.95)	19.7 (1.04)	21.4 (0.94)	11.9 (1.57)	16.8 (1.78)	12.3 (1.55)	20.7 (0.97)	17.4 (1.30)	18.7 (0.75)	16.5 (2.12)
2003	16.4 (0.66)	14.3 (0.69)	25.9 (1.82)	16.8 (0.92)	16.0 (0.94)	19.5 (0.90)	10.4 (1.42)	13.1 (1.57)	9.1 (1.35)	17.6 (0.89)	17.7 (1.29)	16.7 (0.70)	13.6 (1.95)
2004	16.0 (0.66)	13.8 (0.68)	26.2 (1.88)	15.5 (0.90)	16.6 (0.97)	17.8 (0.88)	10.2 (1.45)	16.6 (1.75)	8.1 (1.30)	18.3 (0.91)	15.2 (1.24)	16.1 (0.69)	15.2 (2.15)
2005	15.2 (0.63)	13.4 (0.66)	23.5 (1.77)	15.5 (0.88)	14.8 (0.90)	17.0 (0.84)	9.6 (1.40)	13.6 (1.55)	10.8 (1.40)	15.9 (0.85)	16.1 (1.23)	15.1 (0.66)	16.5 (2.24)
2006	17.0 (0.66)	14.4 (0.69)	27.0 (1.75)	16.8 (0.91)	17.1 (0.96)	19.5 (0.90)	14.5 (1.63)	13.3 (1.54)	13.8 (1.55)	17.7 (0.89)	17.3 (1.27)	16.6 (0.68)	20.8 (2.51)
2007	15.0 (0.63)	12.8 (0.66)	24.2 (1.72)	14.8 (0.87)	15.2 (0.92)	16.2 (0.85)	11.4 (1.49)	14.9 (1.59)	10.9 (1.44)	15.6 (0.83)	15.8 (1.27)	14.3 (0.65)	22.2 (2.43)
2008	12.8 (0.59)	10.3 (0.60)	22.7 (1.68)	11.4 (0.79)	14.1 (0.88)	14.3 (0.82)	11.9 (1.51)	10.6 (1.32)	9.9 (1.34)	12.8 (0.77)	14.4 (1.23)	12.7 (0.62)	13.0 (2.06)
2009	8.7 (0.50)	6.4 (0.49)	17.3 (1.47)	8.4 (0.69)	9.1 (0.73)	10.4 (0.71)	6.5 (1.15)	7.2 (1.11)	5.9 (1.06)	8.9 (0.66)	9.9 (1.07)	8.4 (0.52)	11.7 (1.99)
2010[3]	8.3 (0.45)	6.9 (0.47)	13.4 (1.24)	7.2 (0.62)	9.4 (0.70)	10.5 (0.67)	5.3 (1.01)	5.6 (0.84)	5.3 (0.88)	9.0 (0.58)	8.7 (1.16)	8.1 (0.46)	9.6 (1.83)
2011[3]	9.0 (0.52)	7.7 (0.56)	13.6 (1.10)	8.4 (0.63)	9.8 (0.78)	10.5 (0.77)	7.4 (1.30)	8.4 (1.06)	6.3 (1.10)	10.0 (0.69)	8.5 (0.94)	9.0 (0.55)	9.6 (1.84)
2012[3]	8.9 (0.55)	6.7 (0.51)	16.5 (1.62)	8.4 (0.62)	9.5 (0.84)	10.0 (0.69)	8.2 (1.97)	3.4 (1.04)	8.3 (1.22)	8.7 (0.68)	9.9 (1.30)	8.9 (0.59)	9.6 (1.76)
2013[3]	9.7 (0.56)	7.3 (0.53)	17.4 (1.57)	10.3 (0.85)	9.1 (0.67)	10.6 (0.81)	9.1 (1.37)	10.6 (1.10)	6.7 (1.19)	9.7 (0.82)	11.7 (1.12)	9.4 (0.60)	13.4 (2.15)

—Not available.
†Not applicable.
‡Interpret data with caution. The coefficient of variation (CV) for this estimate is between 30 and 50 percent.
[1] Low income refers to the bottom 20 percent of all family incomes; high income refers to the top 20 percent of all family incomes; and middle income refers to the 60 percent in between.
[2] Percent employed includes those who were employed but not at work during the survey week.
[3] Beginning in 2010, standard errors were computed using replicate weights, which produced more precise values than the generalized variance function methodology used in prior years.

[4] Hours worked per week refers to the number of hours the respondent worked at all jobs during the survey week. The estimates of the percentage of high school students age 16 and over who worked less than 15 hours per week or 15 or more hours per week exclude those who were employed but not at work during the survey week. Therefore, detail may not sum to total percentage employed.
NOTE: Race categories exclude persons of Hispanic ethnicity. Totals include racial/ethnic groups not shown separately.
SOURCE: U.S. Department of Commerce, Census Bureau, Current Population Survey (CPS), October, 1970 through 2013. (This table was prepared August 2014.)

Table 503.20. Percentage of college students 16 to 24 years old who were employed, by attendance status, hours worked per week, and control and level of institution: Selected years, October 1970 through 2013

[Standard errors appear in parentheses]

Control and level of institution and year	Full-time students				Part-time students			
	Percent employed[2]	Hours worked per week[1]			Percent employed[2]	Hours worked per week[1]		
		Less than 20 hours	20 to 34 hours	35 or more hours		Less than 20 hours	20 to 34 hours	35 or more hours
1	2	3	4	5	6	7	8	9
Total, all institutions								
1970	33.8 (0.88)	19.0 (0.73)	10.4 (0.57)	3.7 (0.35)	82.1 (1.81)	5.0 (1.03)	15.9 (1.72)	60.1 (2.31)
1975	35.3 (0.83)	18.0 (0.67)	12.0 (0.56)	4.6 (0.36)	80.8 (1.55)	6.0 (0.94)	19.4 (1.56)	52.6 (1.97)
1980	40.0 (0.84)	21.3 (0.70)	14.0 (0.59)	3.9 (0.33)	84.7 (1.38)	7.9 (1.04)	22.5 (1.60)	52.7 (1.91)
1985	44.2 (0.88)	21.7 (0.73)	17.3 (0.67)	4.3 (0.36)	85.9 (1.41)	5.7 (0.94)	26.9 (1.80)	52.7 (1.91)
1990	45.7 (0.89)	20.6 (0.73)	19.3 (0.71)	4.8 (0.38)	83.7 (1.50)	4.0 (0.80)	26.0 (1.78)	52.2 (2.03)
1991	47.2 (0.88)	20.9 (0.72)	19.8 (0.70)	5.6 (0.41)	85.9 (1.45)	8.2 (1.15)	25.4 (1.82)	51.0 (2.09)
1992	47.2 (0.87)	20.3 (0.70)	20.3 (0.70)	5.5 (0.40)	83.4 (1.50)	7.5 (1.06)	27.2 (1.79)	47.8 (2.01)
1993	46.3 (0.89)	20.8 (0.72)	19.5 (0.71)	5.1 (0.39)	84.6 (1.43)	8.5 (1.10)	31.4 (1.84)	43.7 (1.96)
1994	48.6 (0.87)	20.1 (0.70)	21.7 (0.72)	5.8 (0.41)	86.3 (1.28)	9.8 (1.10)	31.1 (1.72)	43.8 (1.84)
1995	47.2 (0.87)	19.1 (0.69)	20.3 (0.70)	6.5 (0.43)	82.9 (1.45)	8.6 (1.08)	30.4 (1.77)	42.3 (1.90)
1996	49.2 (0.88)	18.2 (0.68)	22.3 (0.74)	7.0 (0.45)	84.8 (1.47)	8.3 (1.13)	27.5 (1.83)	48.0 (2.05)
1997	47.8 (0.86)	18.3 (0.67)	21.4 (0.71)	7.4 (0.45)	84.4 (1.46)	9.4 (1.17)	26.2 (1.77)	47.7 (2.01)
1998	50.2 (0.86)	20.2 (0.69)	20.6 (0.70)	8.0 (0.47)	84.1 (1.45)	7.0 (1.01)	26.8 (1.76)	49.3 (1.98)
1999	50.4 (0.86)	19.0 (0.68)	22.3 (0.72)	7.8 (0.46)	82.3 (1.55)	6.2 (0.98)	28.8 (1.85)	45.9 (2.03)
2000	52.0 (0.86)	20.1 (0.69)	21.7 (0.71)	8.9 (0.49)	84.9 (1.38)	8.6 (1.08)	27.8 (1.73)	47.5 (1.93)
2001	47.1 (0.80)	17.4 (0.61)	20.6 (0.65)	7.9 (0.43)	84.4 (1.29)	8.0 (0.97)	25.8 (1.56)	48.9 (1.78)
2002	47.8 (0.78)	17.3 (0.59)	20.9 (0.64)	8.5 (0.44)	78.9 (1.51)	8.7 (1.04)	25.3 (1.61)	43.4 (1.84)
2003	47.7 (0.78)	17.1 (0.59)	20.7 (0.63)	8.8 (0.44)	79.0 (1.44)	7.8 (0.95)	27.2 (1.58)	42.8 (1.75)
2004	49.0 (0.76)	17.7 (0.58)	21.6 (0.62)	8.6 (0.43)	81.5 (1.44)	8.5 (1.04)	27.4 (1.66)	44.1 (1.84)
2005	49.1 (0.75)	17.8 (0.58)	21.1 (0.61)	9.0 (0.43)	85.0 (1.30)	10.2 (1.10)	27.1 (1.62)	47.1 (1.82)
2006	46.5 (0.76)	15.1 (0.55)	22.0 (0.63)	8.1 (0.42)	81.0 (1.41)	7.3 (0.94)	27.6 (1.61)	45.5 (1.80)
2007	45.5 (0.74)	15.4 (0.54)	20.7 (0.60)	8.7 (0.42)	81.2 (1.39)	6.8 (0.90)	27.2 (1.59)	45.9 (1.78)
2008	45.3 (0.72)	15.6 (0.53)	20.1 (0.58)	8.7 (0.41)	79.4 (1.51)	9.3 (1.09)	24.7 (1.61)	44.4 (1.86)
2009	40.6 (0.69)	15.6 (0.51)	17.6 (0.54)	6.2 (0.34)	76.2 (1.57)	10.1 (1.11)	27.5 (1.65)	36.9 (1.78)
2010[3]	39.8 (1.01)	14.9 (0.57)	17.2 (0.77)	6.6 (0.46)	73.4 (2.03)	10.7 (1.24)	28.3 (1.92)	32.8 (2.19)
2011[3]	41.3 (0.94)	15.8 (0.67)	17.4 (0.66)	7.0 (0.44)	75.5 (1.93)	9.7 (1.21)	28.4 (1.99)	35.5 (2.16)
2012[3]	41.0 (0.83)	15.1 (0.72)	17.8 (0.71)	7.2 (0.44)	71.7 (2.07)	9.0 (1.27)	29.5 (2.09)	32.1 (2.07)
2013[3]	39.5 (1.00)	14.0 (0.67)	18.5 (0.77)	6.6 (0.50)	75.7 (2.06)	10.5 (1.44)	28.7 (1.76)	35.4 (2.11)
Public 4-year institutions								
1990	43.0 (1.18)	19.8 (0.95)	18.6 (0.93)	3.7 (0.45)	87.4 (2.25)	4.2 ! (1.37)	27.9 (3.05)	54.7 (3.39)
1995	48.8 (1.16)	19.4 (0.92)	22.6 (0.97)	5.6 (0.53)	86.7 (2.08)	9.6 (1.80)	30.8 (2.83)	45.0 (3.05)
2000	50.5 (1.15)	19.1 (0.90)	21.5 (0.94)	9.0 (0.66)	87.3 (1.91)	8.5 (1.60)	26.4 (2.53)	50.9 (2.87)
2005	49.6 (0.99)	17.8 (0.76)	22.7 (0.83)	8.0 (0.54)	86.3 (1.90)	9.0 (1.58)	26.8 (2.45)	49.7 (2.76)
2008	44.1 (0.96)	15.1 (0.70)	19.2 (0.76)	8.8 (0.55)	83.9 (2.25)	9.3 (1.78)	24.7 (2.64)	49.5 (3.06)
2009	40.6 (0.91)	14.7 (0.66)	18.7 (0.73)	5.8 (0.44)	78.7 (2.45)	11.1 (1.88)	25.7 (2.61)	39.8 (2.92)
2010[3]	40.8 (1.27)	15.2 (0.88)	18.0 (0.93)	6.6 (0.64)	70.4 (3.58)	10.5 (2.04)	26.9 (2.82)	32.1 (3.59)
2011[3]	41.0 (1.20)	15.0 (0.91)	17.6 (0.85)	7.4 (0.63)	77.5 (3.27)	7.8 (1.65)	28.4 (3.18)	39.7 (3.29)
2012[3]	41.0 (1.13)	14.9 (0.95)	18.6 (0.99)	6.7 (0.57)	77.6 (3.20)	9.9 (2.41)	28.0 (3.44)	38.8 (3.36)
2013[3]	40.1 (1.31)	13.9 (0.88)	19.2 (0.98)	6.6 (0.63)	78.8 (2.88)	9.8 (1.94)	26.6 (2.80)	41.1 (3.84)
Private 4-year institutions								
1990	38.1 (1.89)	24.0 (1.66)	9.9 (1.17)	3.5 (0.72)	89.9 (4.27)	‡ (†)	31.9 (6.62)	53.1 (7.09)
1995	38.6 (1.78)	21.6 (1.51)	10.7 (1.13)	4.6 (0.77)	80.1 (4.85)	14.9 (4.32)	26.8 (5.38)	36.5 (5.84)
2000	45.8 (1.88)	23.6 (1.60)	14.9 (1.34)	5.4 (0.85)	78.0 (5.36)	‡ (†)	18.5 (5.02)	52.6 (6.46)
2005	42.3 (1.64)	20.1 (1.33)	13.8 (1.15)	7.0 (0.85)	88.5 (3.32)	10.6 ! (3.20)	34.5 (4.94)	43.2 (5.15)
2008	38.0 (1.68)	18.5 (1.35)	12.4 (1.14)	5.6 (0.80)	84.4 (4.44)	‡ (†)	21.4 (5.01)	55.3 (6.08)
2009	35.2 (1.64)	18.6 (1.33)	10.7 (1.06)	5.1 (0.76)	93.9 (2.89)	7.5 ! (3.17)	22.1 (5.00)	62.4 (5.84)
2010[3]	35.6 (2.37)	15.7 (1.63)	12.2 (1.52)	6.0 (1.08)	78.6 (7.00)	‡ (†)	23.4 ! (7.49)	45.6 (9.01)
2011[3]	36.3 (2.07)	20.0 (1.61)	10.1 (1.34)	4.5 (0.82)	79.4 (6.01)	‡ (†)	34.2 (7.03)	38.2 (7.67)
2012[3]	40.4 (2.39)	19.9 (1.80)	12.2 (1.40)	6.7 (1.13)	84.4 (5.35)	9.5 ! (4.53)	33.9 (6.58)	36.9 (7.38)
2013[3]	34.0 (2.27)	14.9 (1.55)	12.8 (1.33)	5.6 (1.13)	86.9 (4.71)	21.9 (6.40)	29.8 (7.01)	35.2 (6.56)
Public 2-year institutions								
1990	61.2 (1.94)	19.1 (1.57)	31.2 (1.85)	9.2 (1.15)	81.5 (2.17)	4.1 (1.12)	24.9 (2.42)	51.1 (2.80)
1995	52.9 (1.97)	15.6 (1.43)	25.3 (1.72)	10.9 (1.23)	81.1 (2.21)	6.1 (1.35)	32.5 (2.64)	40.5 (2.77)
2000	63.9 (1.79)	20.6 (1.51)	29.9 (1.71)	11.9 (1.21)	85.5 (2.09)	9.9 (1.77)	30.0 (2.72)	44.9 (2.95)
2005	54.2 (1.69)	15.6 (1.23)	24.2 (1.46)	13.4 (1.16)	82.0 (2.20)	10.8 (1.77)	25.8 (2.50)	44.8 (2.84)
2008	52.9 (1.43)	14.6 (1.01)	26.9 (1.27)	10.7 (0.89)	74.8 (2.29)	9.7 (1.56)	25.9 (2.31)	37.8 (2.56)
2009	45.4 (1.45)	16.0 (1.07)	20.5 (1.18)	7.8 (0.78)	71.8 (2.36)	10.3 (1.60)	30.6 (2.42)	29.4 (2.39)
2010[3]	40.6 (1.90)	14.0 (1.20)	19.1 (1.50)	6.8 (0.78)	74.7 (2.51)	11.6 (1.93)	30.1 (2.86)	31.0 (3.08)
2011[3]	45.6 (2.00)	14.7 (1.45)	22.1 (1.47)	8.1 (1.01)	73.6 (2.58)	11.3 (1.73)	27.5 (3.12)	32.4 (3.21)
2012[3]	41.2 (1.76)	12.0 (1.17)	19.8 (1.44)	8.4 (0.95)	66.1 (2.98)	8.3 (1.60)	30.0 (2.70)	26.9 (2.79)
2013[3]	41.8 (1.89)	13.8 (1.37)	20.5 (1.55)	7.1 (1.05)	71.1 (3.02)	8.8 (1.92)	29.8 (2.85)	31.2 (3.09)

†Not applicable.
!Interpret data with caution. The coefficient of variation (CV) for this estimate is between 30 and 50 percent.
‡Reporting standards not met. Either there are too few cases for a reliable estimate or the coefficient of variation (CV) is 50 percent or greater.
[1]Excludes those who were employed but not at work during the survey week; therefore, detail may not sum to total percentage employed. "Hours worked per week" refers to the number of hours worked at all jobs during the survey week.

[2]Includes those who were employed but not at work during the survey week.
[3]Beginning in 2010, standard errors were computed using replicate weights, which produced more precise values than the generalized variance function methodology used in prior years.
NOTE: Students were classified as full time if they were taking at least 12 hours of classes (or at least 9 hours of graduate classes) during an average school week and as part time if they were taking fewer hours.
SOURCE: U.S. Department of Commerce, Census Bureau, Current Population Survey (CPS), October, selected years, 1970 through 2013. (This table was prepared August 2014.)

Table 503.30. Percentage of college students 16 to 24 years old who were employed, by attendance status, hours worked per week, and selected characteristics: October 2011 through 2013

[Standard errors appear in parentheses]

Year and selected characteristic	Full-time students				Part-time students			
	Percent employed[1]	Hours worked per week[2]			Percent employed[1]	Hours worked per week[2]		
		Less than 20 hours	20 to 34 hours	35 or more hours		Less than 20 hours	20 to 34 hours	35 or more hours
1	2	3	4	5	6	7	8	9
2011								
Total	41.3 (0.94)	15.8 (0.67)	17.4 (0.66)	7.0 (0.44)	75.5 (1.93)	9.7 (1.21)	28.4 (1.99)	35.5 (2.16)
Sex								
Male	38.0 (1.29)	13.1 (0.84)	17.0 (1.02)	7.0 (0.64)	77.3 (2.72)	8.0 (1.63)	27.8 (2.89)	39.9 (3.19)
Female	44.1 (1.32)	18.3 (0.98)	17.7 (0.90)	7.0 (0.63)	73.7 (2.66)	11.3 (1.87)	28.9 (2.65)	31.1 (2.90)
2012								
Total	41.0 (0.83)	15.1 (0.72)	17.8 (0.71)	7.2 (0.44)	71.7 (2.07)	9.0 (1.27)	29.5 (2.09)	32.1 (2.07)
Sex								
Male	39.1 (1.27)	13.0 (0.93)	17.0 (1.08)	7.9 (0.69)	74.0 (2.68)	7.9 (2.04)	30.9 (3.08)	35.1 (3.26)
Female	42.7 (1.19)	17.0 (0.98)	18.4 (0.98)	6.5 (0.57)	69.9 (2.61)	9.9 (1.72)	28.3 (2.60)	29.5 (2.46)
Level and control of institution								
2-year	41.5 (1.71)	12.4 (1.14)	19.6 (1.35)	8.5 (0.90)	66.4 (2.86)	8.4 (1.55)	29.7 (2.63)	27.5 (2.72)
Public	41.2 (1.76)	12.0 (1.17)	19.8 (1.44)	8.4 (0.95)	66.1 (2.98)	8.3 (1.60)	30.0 (2.70)	26.9 (2.79)
Private	46.4 (6.27)	18.0 (4.60)	17.2 (4.92)	9.5 ! (3.52)	‡ (†)	‡ (†)	‡ (†)	‡ (†)
4-year	40.9 (1.00)	16.1 (0.87)	17.1 (0.84)	6.7 (0.53)	79.0 (2.76)	9.8 (2.15)	29.2 (3.06)	38.4 (3.01)
Public	41.0 (1.13)	14.9 (0.95)	18.6 (0.99)	6.7 (0.57)	77.6 (3.20)	9.9 (2.41)	28.0 (3.44)	38.8 (3.36)
Private	40.4 (2.39)	19.9 (1.80)	12.2 (1.40)	6.7 (1.13)	84.4 (5.35)	9.5 ! (4.53)	33.9 (6.58)	36.9 (7.38)
2013								
Total	39.5 (1.00)	14.0 (0.67)	18.5 (0.77)	6.6 (0.50)	75.7 (2.06)	10.5 (1.44)	28.7 (1.76)	35.4 (2.11)
Sex								
Male	35.9 (1.36)	12.2 (0.94)	16.6 (1.05)	6.6 (0.78)	70.9 (3.16)	7.4 (1.95)	28.8 (2.84)	33.9 (2.98)
Female	42.7 (1.31)	15.6 (0.99)	20.2 (0.97)	6.6 (0.67)	79.4 (2.50)	12.9 (1.93)	28.6 (2.49)	36.5 (2.93)
Race/ethnicity								
White	42.9 (1.24)	16.7 (0.88)	19.3 (0.96)	6.3 (0.63)	79.1 (2.56)	13.9 (2.24)	28.6 (2.48)	35.6 (2.73)
Black	35.0 (3.34)	8.7 (1.74)	19.5 (2.54)	6.7 (1.38)	75.1 (5.08)	‡ (†)	30.6 (5.90)	38.7 (6.40)
Hispanic	38.5 (2.47)	9.6 (1.46)	20.3 (1.94)	8.3 (1.44)	72.7 (4.16)	9.3 (2.58)	30.7 (3.97)	32.0 (4.34)
Asian	25.2 (2.76)	10.9 (1.74)	9.4 (2.01)	4.4 ! (1.35)	69.6 (9.05)	‡ (†)	21.2 ! (7.16)	43.1 (9.20)
Pacific Islander	‡ (†)	‡ (†)	‡ (†)	‡ (†)	‡ (†)	‡ (†)	‡ (†)	‡ (†)
American Indian/Alaska Native	‡ (†)	‡ (†)	‡ (†)	‡ (†)	‡ (†)	‡ (†)	‡ (†)	‡ (†)
Two or more races	40.9 (6.84)	15.8 (4.70)	16.3 ! (4.96)	8.8 ! (3.84)	‡ (†)	‡ (†)	‡ (†)	‡ (†)
Level and control of institution								
2-year	42.0 (1.84)	13.6 (1.32)	20.7 (1.52)	7.3 (1.01)	71.3 (2.90)	9.0 (1.92)	30.0 (2.75)	31.0 (2.99)
Public	41.8 (1.89)	13.8 (1.37)	20.5 (1.55)	7.1 (1.05)	71.1 (3.02)	8.8 (1.92)	29.8 (2.85)	31.2 (3.09)
Private	45.1 (8.22)	10.1 ! (4.13)	24.5 (6.99)	10.5 ! (5.01)	‡ (†)	‡ (†)	‡ (†)	‡ (†)
4-year	38.7 (1.15)	14.1 (0.76)	17.8 (0.87)	6.3 (0.53)	80.4 (2.59)	12.2 (2.03)	27.2 (2.45)	39.9 (3.29)
Public	40.1 (1.31)	13.9 (0.88)	19.2 (0.98)	6.6 (0.63)	78.8 (2.88)	9.8 (1.94)	26.6 (2.80)	41.1 (3.84)
Private	34.0 (2.27)	14.9 (1.55)	12.8 (1.33)	5.6 (1.13)	86.9 (4.71)	21.9 (6.40)	29.8 (7.01)	35.2 (6.56)
Student enrollment level								
Undergraduate	39.3 (1.01)	14.0 (0.69)	18.8 (0.80)	6.1 (0.50)	75.0 (2.26)	10.2 (1.48)	29.9 (1.75)	33.8 (2.15)
Sex								
Male	35.1 (1.35)	12.3 (0.94)	16.2 (1.07)	6.0 (0.79)	69.6 (3.48)	7.8 (2.07)	29.8 (3.07)	31.1 (3.25)
Female	43.0 (1.37)	15.4 (1.05)	21.1 (1.04)	6.2 (0.66)	79.5 (2.80)	12.2 (2.02)	29.9 (2.59)	36.1 (3.01)
Race/ethnicity								
White	43.0 (1.29)	16.6 (0.95)	19.9 (1.01)	5.9 (0.65)	79.4 (2.82)	13.1 (2.26)	30.4 (2.64)	34.9 (2.86)
Black	34.1 (3.08)	8.9 (1.80)	18.9 (2.16)	6.3 (1.46)	73.7 (5.26)	1.7 ! (0.84)	32.3 (6.15)	36.7 (6.23)
Hispanic	37.2 (2.42)	9.3 (1.49)	20.1 (1.96)	7.6 (1.31)	72.0 (4.43)	10.0 (2.73)	30.0 (4.06)	31.3 (4.35)
Asian	25.8 (3.10)	11.6 (1.95)	10.1 (2.28)	4.1 ! (1.46)	63.0 (10.70)	‡ (†)	26.3 ! (8.74)	32.8 (9.53)
Pacific Islander	‡ (†)	‡ (†)	‡ (†)	‡ (†)	‡ (†)	‡ (†)	‡ (†)	‡ (†)
American Indian/Alaska Native	‡ (†)	‡ (†)	‡ (†)	‡ (†)	‡ (†)	‡ (†)	‡ (†)	‡ (†)
Two or more races	38.6 (7.19)	15.2 ! (4.69)	15.7 ! (5.22)	‡ (†)	‡ (†)	‡ (†)	‡ (†)	‡ (†)
Level and control of institution								
2-year	41.7 (1.87)	13.5 (1.33)	21.0 (1.53)	6.9 (0.94)	70.9 (3.01)	8.3 (1.86)	30.8 (2.75)	30.5 (3.01)
Public	41.5 (1.91)	13.5 (1.38)	21.0 (1.56)	6.9 (0.97)	70.7 (3.08)	8.4 (1.90)	30.2 (2.85)	30.7 (3.10)
Private	47.2 (8.95)	11.9 ! (4.99)	27.3 (7.89)	‡ (†)	‡ (†)	‡ (†)	‡ (†)	‡ (†)
4-year	38.4 (1.19)	14.1 (0.82)	18.0 (0.90)	5.8 (0.55)	79.7 (2.96)	12.4 (2.30)	28.8 (2.58)	37.7 (3.48)
Public	39.5 (1.32)	13.7 (0.91)	19.3 (1.01)	6.2 (0.66)	78.4 (3.16)	10.0 (2.20)	27.8 (2.89)	39.6 (4.04)
Private	34.3 (2.41)	15.9 (1.83)	13.3 (1.44)	4.3 (1.00)	86.1 (5.24)	23.8 ! (7.75)	33.6 (8.25)	28.7 (6.87)
Graduate	42.0 (3.40)	14.5 (2.62)	15.2 (2.61)	11.6 (2.45)	81.6 (5.15)	13.2 ! (4.01)	18.9 (5.51)	48.0 (6.18)

†Not applicable.
!Interpret data with caution. The coefficient of variation (CV) for this estimate is between 30 and 50 percent.
‡Reporting standards not met. Either there are too few cases for a reliable estimate or the coefficient of variation (CV) is 50 percent or greater.
[1]Includes those who were employed but not at work during the survey week.

[2]Excludes those who were employed but not at work during the survey week; therefore, detail may not sum to total percentage employed. "Hours worked per week" refers to the number of hours worked at all jobs during the survey week.
NOTE: Students were classified as full time if they were taking at least 12 hours of classes (or at least 9 hours of graduate classes) during an average school week and as part time if they were taking fewer hours. Race categories exclude persons of Hispanic ethnicity.
SOURCE: U.S. Department of Commerce, Census Bureau, Current Population Survey (CPS), October, 2011 through 2013. (This table was prepared August 2014.)

Table 504.10. Labor force status of 2011, 2012, and 2013 high school completers, by college enrollment status, sex, and race/ethnicity: October 2011, 2012, and 2013

[Standard errors appear in parentheses]

College enrollment status, sex, and race/ethnicity	Total number of high school completers (in thousands)	Percent of high school completers — Separately for those enrolled in college vs. those not enrolled	Percent of high school completers — For all high school completers	Percentage distribution of all high school completers — Employed	Unemployed (seeking employment)	Not in labor force	Labor force participation rate of all high school completers[1]	High school completers in civilian labor force[2] — Number (in thousands) — Total, all completers in labor force	Employed	Unemployed (seeking employment)	Unemployment rate	High school completers not in labor force (in thousands)
1	2	3	4	5	6	7	8	9	10	11	12	13
2011 high school completers[3]												
Total	3,079 (88.3)	† (†)	100.0 (†)	35.2 (1.40)	12.9 (1.12)	51.9 (1.60)	48.1 (1.60)	1,482 (58.7)	1,084 (50.0)	398 (34.8)	26.8 (2.01)	1,597 (73.3)
Male	1,611 (60.6)	† (†)	52.3 (1.30)	34.2 (2.00)	16.0 (1.62)	49.8 (2.40)	50.2 (2.40)	808 (46.2)	551 (36.3)	258 (27.3)	31.9 (2.67)	802 (51.6)
Female	1,468 (58.4)	† (†)	47.7 (1.30)	36.3 (2.22)	9.5 (1.32)	54.1 (2.28)	45.9 (2.28)	674 (40.4)	534 (37.3)	140 (19.7)	20.8 (2.69)	795 (48.6)
White	1,747 (60.6)	† (†)	56.7 (1.38)	42.7 (1.85)	10.2 (1.25)	47.1 (2.15)	52.9 (2.15)	925 (46.9)	746 (39.7)	179 (22.4)	19.3 (2.08)	822 (49.5)
Black	464 (36.1)	† (†)	15.1 (1.08)	23.1 (3.76)	17.5 (3.65)	59.4 (4.49)	40.6 (4.49)	189 (25.6)	107 (20.8)	‡ (†)	43.2 (7.23)	275 (29.2)
Hispanic	623 (42.0)	† (†)	20.2 (1.20)	28.4 (3.25)	15.9 (2.72)	55.7 (3.60)	44.3 (3.60)	276 (29.2)	177 (23.6)	99 (18.0)	35.9 (5.33)	347 (32.0)
Enrolled in college, 2011	2,101 (77.2)	100.0 (†)	68.2 (1.45)	30.4 (1.69)	8.2 (1.17)	61.4 (1.92)	38.6 (1.92)	810 (49.2)	638 (42.1)	172 (25.1)	21.2 (2.68)	1,291 (63.1)
Male	1,041 (55.6)	49.6 (1.70)	33.8 (1.44)	26.2 (2.33)	10.1 (1.96)	63.7 (2.86)	36.3 (2.86)	378 (35.7)	273 (27.2)	106 (21.6)	27.9 (4.47)	663 (46.2)
Female	1,060 (49.1)	50.4 (1.70)	34.4 (1.29)	34.5 (2.57)	6.3 (1.15)	59.2 (2.62)	40.8 (2.62)	432 (34.3)	365 (32.4)	‡ (†)	15.3 (2.73)	628 (40.0)
2-year	798 (49.2)	38.0 (1.89)	25.9 (1.49)	37.9 (3.07)	11.8 (2.32)	50.3 (3.30)	49.7 (3.30)	397 (36.0)	303 (30.0)	94 (19.8)	23.7 (4.21)	401 (35.9)
4-year	1,303 (62.2)	62.0 (1.89)	42.3 (1.44)	25.7 (2.08)	6.0 (1.23)	68.3 (2.14)	31.7 (2.14)	413 (33.8)	336 (32.2)	78 (15.9)	18.9 (3.67)	890 (51.2)
Full-time students	1,930 (74.2)	91.9 (1.11)	62.7 (1.42)	27.0 (1.71)	7.9 (1.20)	65.1 (1.95)	34.9 (1.95)	674 (44.0)	522 (36.8)	152 (24.0)	22.6 (3.02)	1,256 (63.0)
Part-time students	170 (24.1)	8.1 (1.11)	5.5 (0.78)	68.3 (6.42)	11.4 ! (4.38)	20.3 (4.97)	79.7 (4.97)	136 (20.8)	116 (18.8)	‡ (†)	14.3 ! (5.53)	‡ (†)
White	1,193 (52.9)	56.8 (1.73)	38.7 (1.43)	37.4 (2.27)	6.4 (1.33)	56.2 (2.69)	43.8 (2.69)	522 (40.1)	446 (33.1)	‡ (†)	14.6 (2.66)	670 (43.0)
Black	312 (31.6)	14.8 (1.44)	10.1 (0.96)	19.9 (4.50)	7.7 ! (3.02)	72.4 (4.76)	27.6 (4.76)	86 (17.2)	‡ (†)	‡ (†)	28.0 ! (10.19)	226 (26.9)
Hispanic	415 (33.9)	19.7 (1.39)	13.5 (1.02)	24.9 (3.96)	12.5 (3.31)	62.6 (4.45)	37.4 (4.45)	155 (22.3)	103 (18.5)	‡ (†)	33.5 (7.70)	260 (28.0)
Not enrolled in college, 2011	978 (51.1)	100.0 (†)	31.8 (1.45)	45.6 (2.88)	23.1 (2.58)	31.3 (2.74)	68.7 (2.74)	672 (42.5)	446 (34.7)	226 (27.9)	33.6 (3.40)	306 (32.3)
Male	569 (38.2)	58.2 (2.65)	18.5 (1.20)	48.8 (3.94)	26.7 (3.33)	24.5 (3.42)	75.5 (3.42)	430 (34.3)	278 (27.4)	152 (22.5)	35.4 (4.17)	139 (21.7)
Female	409 (34.4)	41.8 (2.65)	13.3 (1.03)	41.1 (4.39)	18.0 (3.43)	40.8 (4.77)	59.2 (4.77)	242 (24.5)	168 (21.8)	74 (13.9)	30.5 (5.11)	167 (26.5)
White	554 (37.4)	56.7 (2.58)	18.0 (1.14)	54.1 (3.72)	18.5 (2.97)	27.4 (3.32)	72.6 (3.32)	402 (31.6)	300 (26.6)	103 (18.4)	25.5 (3.89)	152 (21.7)
Black	152 (21.3)	15.6 (2.01)	5.0 (0.69)	29.7 (6.97)	37.6 (7.13)	32.6 (7.91)	67.4 (7.91)	103 (19.8)	‡ (†)	‡ (†)	55.9 (8.44)	‡ (†)
Hispanic	208 (26.8)	21.3 (2.38)	6.8 (0.84)	35.4 (6.04)	22.6 (5.12)	42.0 (6.75)	58.0 (6.75)	121 (19.4)	74 (15.0)	‡ (†)	39.0 (7.47)	‡ (†)
2012 high school completers[3]												
Total	3,203 (96.2)	† (†)	100.0 (†)	36.3 (1.53)	12.6 (1.15)	51.2 (1.61)	48.8 (1.61)	1,563 (67.9)	1,161 (57.7)	402 (38.9)	25.7 (2.13)	1,639 (73.1)
Male	1,622 (70.1)	† (†)	50.6 (1.25)	33.7 (2.21)	14.5 (1.75)	51.8 (2.29)	48.2 (2.29)	783 (49.3)	547 (42.8)	235 (29.5)	30.0 (3.29)	840 (52.7)
Female	1,581 (54.0)	† (†)	49.4 (1.25)	38.8 (1.92)	10.6 (1.29)	50.6 (2.16)	49.4 (2.16)	781 (42.2)	614 (36.0)	167 (21.1)	21.4 (2.31)	800 (44.7)
White	1,820 (62.8)	† (†)	56.8 (1.52)	42.5 (2.07)	10.9 (1.31)	46.6 (2.02)	53.4 (2.02)	971 (49.9)	774 (46.1)	198 (24.8)	20.3 (2.35)	849 (46.7)
Black	413 (33.9)	† (†)	12.9 (0.98)	26.4 (4.59)	23.2 (4.11)	50.4 (4.88)	49.6 (4.88)	205 (26.1)	109 (19.8)	96 (19.3)	46.8 (7.23)	208 (26.4)
Hispanic	697 (54.9)	† (†)	21.8 (1.41)	32.1 (3.10)	10.2 (2.13)	57.6 (3.29)	42.4 (3.29)	296 (28.7)	224 (25.2)	‡ (†)	24.2 (4.60)	402 (42.7)
Enrolled in college, 2012	2,121 (76.4)	100.0 (†)	66.2 (1.59)	31.5 (1.66)	6.8 (0.92)	61.8 (1.84)	38.2 (1.84)	811 (46.7)	667 (41.0)	143 (20.0)	17.7 (2.18)	1,310 (63.9)
Male	994 (53.3)	46.9 (1.66)	31.0 (1.31)	27.4 (2.39)	7.0 (1.37)	65.6 (2.58)	34.4 (2.58)	342 (29.7)	272 (27.0)	‡ (†)	20.4 (3.65)	652 (45.6)
Female	1,127 (49.9)	53.1 (1.66)	35.2 (1.41)	35.1 (2.19)	6.5 (1.20)	58.4 (2.43)	41.6 (2.43)	469 (32.6)	395 (29.0)	‡ (†)	15.7 (2.60)	658 (42.0)
2-year	921 (57.7)	43.4 (2.07)	28.8 (1.57)	39.9 (3.10)	8.0 (1.57)	52.1 (3.22)	47.9 (3.22)	441 (35.2)	367 (32.0)	‡ (†)	16.7 (3.09)	480 (47.1)
4-year	1,200 (58.3)	56.6 (2.07)	37.5 (1.60)	25.0 (1.92)	5.8 (1.14)	69.2 (2.17)	30.8 (2.17)	370 (31.8)	300 (27.6)	‡ (†)	18.8 (3.32)	830 (47.5)
Full-time students	1,863 (71.3)	87.8 (1.31)	58.2 (1.61)	28.1 (1.74)	5.8 (0.87)	66.1 (1.89)	33.9 (1.89)	632 (41.6)	523 (36.6)	109 (16.8)	17.2 (2.34)	1,231 (60.3)
Part-time students	258 (29.7)	12.2 (1.31)	8.1 (0.90)	55.9 (5.63)	13.4 (3.98)	30.8 (5.73)	69.2 (5.73)	179 (25.8)	144 (22.3)	‡ (†)	19.3 (5.36)	‡ (†)

See notes at end of table.

Table 504.10. Labor force status of 2011, 2012, and 2013 high school completers, by college enrollment status, sex, and race/ethnicity: October 2011, 2012, and 2013—Continued

[Standard errors appear in parentheses]

College enrollment status, sex, and race/ethnicity	Total number of high school completers (in thousands)	Percent of high school completers — Separately for those enrolled in college vs. those not enrolled	Percent of high school completers — For all high school completers	Percentage distribution of all high school completers — Employed	Percentage distribution — Unemployed (seeking employment)	Percentage distribution — Not in labor force	Labor force participation rate of all high school completers[1]	HS completers in civilian labor force[2] — Number — Total, all completers in labor force	Number — Employed	Number — Unemployed (seeking employment)	Unemployment rate	High school completers not in labor force (in thousands)
1	2	3	4	5	6	7	8	9	10	11	12	13
White	1,196 (52.7)	56.4 (1.88)	37.3 (1.50)	35.0 (2.32)	6.6 (1.16)	58.3 (2.46)	41.7 (2.46)	498 (35.5)	419 (32.1)	79 (14.3)	15.9 (2.61)	698 (44.0)
Black	233 (30.4)	11.0 (1.38)	7.3 (0.93)	24.4 (5.79)	10.8 ! (4.25)	64.7 (6.27)	35.3 (6.27)	‡ (†)	‡ (†)	‡ (†)	‡ (†)	151 (24.1)
Hispanic	490 (43.3)	23.1 (1.71)	15.3 (1.16)	31.7 (3.98)	4.7 ! (1.83)	63.6 (4.00)	36.4 (4.00)	178 (22.7)	155 (22.0)	‡ (†)	12.9 ! (4.91)	312 (36.1)
Not enrolled in college, 2012	1,082 (63.3)	100.0 (†)	33.8 (1.59)	45.7 (2.52)	23.9 (2.62)	30.4 (2.69)	69.6 (2.69)	753 (53.4)	494 (40.9)	259 (31.4)	34.4 (3.24)	329 (34.5)
Male	628 (45.9)	58.1 (2.47)	19.6 (1.22)	43.8 (3.64)	26.3 (3.63)	29.8 (3.64)	70.2 (3.64)	441 (39.1)	275 (31.1)	166 (25.0)	37.5 (4.55)	187 (27.0)
Female	454 (37.3)	41.9 (2.47)	14.2 (1.09)	48.2 (3.92)	20.5 (3.35)	31.3 (3.78)	68.7 (3.78)	312 (29.8)	219 (25.1)	93 (16.5)	29.9 (4.50)	142 (21.3)
White	624 (42.3)	57.7 (2.63)	19.5 (1.21)	56.9 (3.29)	18.9 (2.69)	24.2 (3.11)	75.8 (3.11)	473 (39.3)	355 (34.3)	118 (17.9)	25.0 (3.32)	151 (20.9)
Black	180 (22.0)	16.6 (1.84)	5.6 (0.66)	28.8 (6.82)	39.2 (7.43)	31.9 (7.23)	68.1 (7.23)	122 (19.9)	‡ (†)	‡ (†)	57.6 (9.06)	‡ (†)
Hispanic	207 (28.4)	19.1 (2.25)	6.5 (0.85)	33.2 (6.32)	23.4 (5.69)	43.4 (5.64)	56.6 (5.64)	117 (18.0)	‡ (†)	‡ (†)	41.4 (9.35)	90 (18.2)
2013 high school completers[3] — Total	2,977 (84.4)	† (†)	100.0 (†)	35.4 (1.58)	12.3 (1.25)	52.2 (1.64)	47.8 (1.64)	1,422 (69.5)	1,054 (60.7)	367 (39.0)	25.8 (2.38)	1,556 (58.3)
Male	1,524 (62.9)	† (†)	51.2 (1.43)	35.5 (2.24)	14.5 (1.80)	50.0 (2.46)	50.0 (2.46)	763 (49.7)	542 (40.6)	221 (29.4)	29.0 (3.16)	762 (48.0)
Female	1,453 (57.0)	† (†)	48.8 (1.43)	35.3 (2.41)	10.1 (1.49)	54.6 (2.43)	45.4 (2.43)	659 (46.4)	513 (42.7)	146 (22.3)	22.2 (3.13)	794 (43.8)
White	1,737 (63.0)	† (†)	58.3 (1.61)	39.0 (2.08)	11.2 (1.63)	49.8 (2.15)	50.2 (2.15)	872 (51.7)	677 (44.7)	195 (29.8)	22.4 (2.97)	865 (45.7)
Black	378 (36.2)	† (†)	12.7 (1.13)	33.6 (5.31)	14.8 (3.39)	51.7 (5.48)	48.3 (5.48)	183 (27.2)	127 (23.5)	‡ (†)	30.6 (6.64)	195 (27.7)
Hispanic	571 (42.6)	† (†)	19.2 (1.32)	31.1 (3.71)	14.3 (2.81)	54.6 (4.00)	45.4 (4.00)	260 (30.4)	178 (25.3)	‡ (†)	31.5 (5.53)	312 (32.4)
Enrolled in college, 2013	1,962 (74.1)	100.0 (†)	65.9 (1.58)	27.2 (1.86)	6.9 (1.11)	65.9 (1.86)	34.1 (1.86)	669 (47.1)	534 (43.0)	135 (22.8)	20.2 (3.11)	1,293 (56.7)
Male	968 (53.9)	49.4 (1.90)	32.5 (1.48)	24.4 (2.71)	9.3 (1.90)	66.3 (3.01)	33.7 (3.01)	326 (34.7)	236 (28.7)	90 (19.5)	27.5 (4.99)	642 (45.6)
Female	994 (51.0)	50.6 (1.90)	33.4 (1.48)	29.9 (2.62)	4.6 (1.23)	65.5 (2.61)	34.5 (2.61)	343 (31.9)	297 (30.3)	‡ (†)	13.2 (3.47)	651 (41.3)
2-year	709 (48.8)	36.1 (2.07)	23.8 (1.44)	33.8 (3.35)	11.4 (2.40)	54.8 (3.62)	45.2 (3.62)	320 (36.3)	240 (30.5)	‡ (†)	25.2 (4.79)	389 (33.9)
4-year	1,253 (62.3)	63.9 (2.07)	42.1 (1.76)	23.5 (2.17)	4.3 (1.07)	72.2 (2.24)	27.8 (2.24)	348 (33.8)	294 (31.3)	‡ (†)	15.6 (3.66)	904 (51.5)
Full-time students	1,820 (70.6)	92.8 (1.11)	61.1 (1.60)	25.1 (1.82)	5.9 (1.12)	69.0 (1.94)	31.0 (1.94)	564 (44.7)	458 (38.9)	107 (21.4)	18.9 (3.32)	1,256 (54.6)
Part-time students	141 (22.8)	7.2 (1.11)	4.8 (0.75)	53.7 (7.40)	20.1 (5.38)	26.2 (6.13)	73.8 (6.13)	104 (19.8)	76 (16.5)	‡ (†)	27.2 (7.29)	‡ (†)
White	1,196 (52.8)	60.9 (2.02)	40.2 (1.52)	30.9 (2.36)	5.6 (1.47)	63.5 (2.38)	36.5 (2.38)	436 (33.8)	369 (32.0)	‡ (†)	15.4 (3.84)	759 (44.5)
Black	215 (29.5)	10.9 (1.38)	7.2 (0.95)	24.5 (7.01)	7.8 ! (3.43)	67.6 (7.27)	32.4 (7.27)	‡ (†)	‡ (†)	‡ (†)	‡ (†)	145 (24.9)
Hispanic	342 (35.3)	17.4 (1.61)	11.5 (1.12)	22.3 (3.85)	11.1 (3.17)	66.7 (4.52)	33.3 (4.52)	114 (19.6)	‡ (†)	‡ (†)	33.2 (7.94)	228 (28.0)
Not enrolled in college, 2013	1,016 (54.1)	100.0 (†)	34.1 (1.58)	51.3 (3.14)	22.9 (2.84)	25.8 (2.90)	74.2 (2.90)	753 (51.3)	521 (43.2)	232 (31.5)	30.9 (3.53)	262 (31.6)
Male	556 (39.2)	54.8 (2.55)	18.7 (1.22)	54.9 (3.73)	23.6 (3.60)	21.5 (3.43)	78.5 (3.43)	437 (34.6)	305 (27.9)	131 (22.3)	30.1 (4.18)	119 (21.3)
Female	459 (35.8)	45.2 (2.55)	15.4 (1.13)	46.9 (4.79)	22.0 (3.77)	31.2 (4.56)	68.8 (4.56)	316 (33.1)	215 (28.7)	101 (18.7)	31.9 (5.18)	143 (23.3)
White	542 (39.1)	53.3 (2.80)	18.2 (1.24)	56.9 (3.88)	23.7 (3.62)	19.4 (3.27)	80.6 (3.27)	436 (39.1)	308 (32.3)	128 (22.2)	29.4 (4.21)	105 (17.8)
Black	164 (26.1)	16.1 (2.32)	5.5 (0.86)	45.4 (8.24)	23.9 (6.59)	30.7 (7.76)	69.3 (7.76)	114 (22.4)	‡ (†)	‡ (†)	34.5 (9.08)	‡ (†)
Hispanic	229 (24.8)	22.6 (2.22)	7.7 (0.82)	44.3 (6.65)	19.2 (5.20)	36.5 (6.68)	63.5 (6.68)	146 (21.4)	102 (18.6)	‡ (†)	30.2 (7.57)	‡ (†)

†Not applicable.
‡Reporting standards not met (too few cases for a reliable estimate).
!Interpret data with caution. The coefficient of variation (CV) for this estimate is between 30 and 50 percent.
[1]The labor force participation rate is the percentage of persons who are either employed or seeking employment.
[2]The unemployment rate is the percentage of persons in the labor force who are unemployed plus those seeking employment and who made specific efforts to find employment sometime during the prior 4 weeks.
[3]Includes 16- to 24-year-olds who completed high school between October of the previous year and October of the given year. Includes recipients of equivalency credentials as well as diploma recipients.
NOTE: Data are for October of given year. Data are based on sample surveys of the civilian noninstitutional population. Percentages are only shown when the base is 75,000 or greater. Standard errors were computed using replicate weights. Totals include race categories not separately shown. Race categories exclude persons of Hispanic ethnicity. Detail may not sum to totals because of rounding. (This table was prepared May 2015.)
SOURCE: U.S. Department of Commerce, Census Bureau, Current Population Survey (CPS), October 2011, 2012, and 2013.

Table 504.20. Labor force status of high school dropouts, by sex and race/ethnicity: Selected years, October 1980 through 2013

[Standard errors appear in parentheses]

Year, sex, and race/ethnicity	Number of dropouts (in thousands)	Percent of all dropouts	Percentage distribution of dropouts — Employed	Percentage distribution of dropouts — Unemployed (seeking employment)	Percentage distribution of dropouts — Not in labor force	Labor force participation rate of dropouts[1]	Dropouts in civilian labor force[2] — Number (in thousands) — Total	Dropouts in civilian labor force[2] — Number (in thousands) — Unemployed (seeking employment)	Unemployment rate	Dropouts not in labor force (in thousands)
1	2	3	4	5	6	7	8	9	10	11
Estimates for individual years										
All dropouts										
1980................	738 (44.0)	100.0 (†)	43.8 (2.97)	20.0 (2.37)	36.2 (2.87)	63.8 (2.87)	471 (35.2)	148 (19.5)	31.4 (3.44)	267 (26.5)
1990................	412 (36.0)	100.0 (†)	46.3 (4.37)	21.6 (3.57)	32.2 (4.09)	67.8 (4.09)	279 (29.7)	89 (16.6)	31.8 (4.90)	132 (20.4)
2000................	515 (28.5)	100.0 (†)	48.7 (2.77)	19.2 (3.01)	32.0 (2.59)	68.0 (2.59)	350 (23.5)	99 (17.2)	28.1 (4.16)	165 (16.2)
2005................	407 (35.3)	100.0 (†)	38.3 (4.22)	18.9 (3.42)	42.8 (3.32)	57.2 (4.30)	233 (26.7)	77 (15.4)	32.9 (5.42)	174 (17.9)
2010[3]............	340 (29.0)	100.0 (†)	30.9 (4.24)	23.0 (4.29)	46.1 (4.78)	53.9 (4.78)	183 (21.5)	78 (16.0)	42.7 (6.67)	157 (21.9)
2012[3]............	370 (37.1)	100.0 (†)	23.8 (4.56)	23.4 (4.69)	52.8 (5.64)	47.2 (5.64)	174 (27.0)	‡ (†)	49.6 (7.82)	195 (28.8)
2013[3]............	529 (45.1)	100.0 (†)	31.0 (3.87)	12.0 (2.33)	57.1 (4.13)	42.9 (4.13)	227 (29.7)	‡ (†)	27.9 (5.06)	302 (33.2)
3-year moving averages[4]										
All dropouts										
1980................	748 (44.3)	100.0 (†)	44.4 (1.70)	19.9 (1.38)	35.7 (1.27)	64.3 (1.64)	481 (35.6)	149 (19.9)	30.9 (1.99)	267 (20.5)
1990................	413 (36.1)	100.0 (†)	43.5 (2.50)	21.5 (2.08)	35.0 (1.86)	65.0 (2.41)	268 (29.1)	89 (16.8)	33.1 (2.96)	144 (16.5)
2000................	515 (41.8)	100.0 (†)	44.1 (2.33)	19.0 (1.85)	36.9 (1.75)	63.1 (2.27)	325 (33.2)	98 (18.3)	30.1 (2.72)	190 (19.7)
2005................	449 (37.1)	100.0 (†)	36.8 (2.30)	17.7 (1.83)	45.5 (1.84)	54.5 (2.38)	245 (27.4)	79 (15.7)	32.5 (3.04)	205 (19.4)
2010................	365 (33.4)	100.0 (†)	28.7 (2.39)	23.7 (2.26)	47.6 (2.04)	52.4 (2.64)	191 (24.2)	87 (16.4)	45.2 (3.65)	174 (17.8)
2012................	424 (36.0)	100.0 (†)	29.8 (2.25)	18.0 (1.89)	52.3 (1.90)	47.7 (2.45)	202 (24.9)	76 (15.3)	37.7 (3.46)	221 (20.1)
2013................	449 (37.1)	100.0 (†)	28.0 (2.62)	16.7 (2.19)	55.3 (2.25)	44.7 (2.90)	201 (24.8)	75 (15.2)	37.3 (4.25)	249 (21.3)
Male										
1980................	393 (31.6)	52.6 (1.69)	55.5 (2.31)	19.5 (1.84)	25.0 (2.01)	75.0 (2.01)	295 (27.4)	77 (14.0)	25.9 (2.35)	98 (15.8)
1990................	216 (25.7)	52.3 (2.48)	50.9 (3.44)	25.2 (2.98)	23.9 (2.93)	76.1 (2.93)	164 (22.4)	55 (12.9)	33.1 (3.71)	52 (12.6)
2000................	279 (30.3)	54.1 (2.30)	49.8 (3.14)	19.6 (2.49)	30.7 (2.90)	69.3 (2.90)	193 (25.2)	55 (13.4)	28.2 (3.39)	85 (16.8)
2005................	254 (27.4)	56.5 (2.33)	40.0 (3.06)	19.0 (2.45)	41.0 (3.07)	59.0 (3.07)	150 (21.1)	48 (12.0)	32.2 (3.80)	104 (17.6)
2010................	196 (24.1)	53.6 (2.60)	32.1 (3.32)	22.4 (2.97)	45.5 (3.54)	54.5 (3.54)	107 (17.8)	44 (11.4)	41.2 (4.74)	89 (16.3)
2012................	227 (25.9)	53.5 (2.41)	35.3 (3.16)	15.5 (2.39)	49.2 (3.30)	50.8 (3.30)	115 (18.5)	35 (10.2)	30.6 (4.27)	111 (18.2)
2013................	238 (26.6)	53.1 (2.87)	32.4 (3.69)	15.3 (2.84)	52.3 (3.94)	47.7 (3.94)	114 (18.4)	‡ (†)	32.1 (5.34)	125 (19.2)
Female										
1980................	354 (29.1)	47.4 (1.63)	32.1 (2.21)	20.4 (1.91)	47.5 (2.37)	52.5 (2.37)	186 (21.1)	72 (13.1)	38.9 (3.19)	168 (20.0)
1990................	197 (23.7)	47.7 (2.40)	35.4 (3.33)	17.4 (2.64)	47.2 (3.48)	52.8 (3.48)	104 (17.2)	34 (9.9)	33.0 (4.51)	93 (16.3)
2000................	236 (27.0)	45.9 (2.23)	37.4 (3.19)	18.3 (2.55)	44.3 (3.28)	55.7 (3.28)	132 (20.1)	43 (11.6)	32.9 (4.15)	105 (18.0)
2005................	196 (23.3)	43.5 (2.25)	32.6 (3.23)	16.0 (2.52)	51.4 (3.44)	48.6 (3.44)	95 (16.2)	31 (9.3)	32.9 (4.64)	101 (16.7)
2010................	169 (21.7)	46.4 (2.51)	24.9 (3.20)	25.1 (3.21)	50.0 (3.70)	50.0 (3.70)	85 (15.3)	43 (10.9)	50.2 (5.23)	85 (15.3)
2012................	197 (23.4)	46.5 (2.33)	23.3 (2.90)	20.8 (2.78)	55.9 (3.41)	44.1 (3.41)	87 (15.5)	41 (10.7)	47.1 (5.16)	110 (17.5)
2013................	211 (24.2)	46.9 (2.78)	23.1 (3.42)	18.2 (3.13)	58.8 (4.00)	41.2 (4.00)	87 (15.5)	‡ (†)	44.0 (6.28)	124 (18.6)
White										
1980................	494 (36.0)	66.0 (1.62)	50.9 (2.11)	17.6 (1.61)	31.5 (1.52)	68.5 (1.96)	338 (29.8)	87 (15.2)	25.7 (2.24)	156 (15.7)
1990................	240 (27.5)	58.0 (2.49)	51.4 (3.31)	19.3 (2.63)	29.3 (2.33)	70.7 (3.02)	170 (23.1)	46 (12.1)	27.3 (3.53)	70 (11.5)
2000................	279 (30.8)	54.1 (2.34)	48.3 (3.19)	18.7 (2.50)	33.0 (2.32)	67.0 (3.00)	187 (25.2)	52 (13.4)	27.8 (3.51)	92 (13.7)
2005................	215 (25.7)	48.0 (2.38)	41.6 (3.40)	14.2 (2.42)	44.2 (2.64)	55.8 (3.42)	120 (19.2)	31 ! (9.7)	25.5 (4.04)	95 (13.2)
2010................	164 (22.4)	45.0 (2.63)	32.7 (3.70)	20.8 (3.22)	46.4 (3.04)	53.6 (3.93)	88 (16.4)	34 ! (10.3)	38.9 (5.28)	76 (11.8)
2012................	180 (23.5)	42.4 (2.43)	31.5 (3.50)	13.1 (2.56)	55.4 (2.90)	44.6 (3.75)	80 (15.7)	24 ! (8.6)	29.5 (5.17)	100 (13.5)
2013................	179 (23.4)	39.9 (2.86)	30.8 (4.27)	10.6 (2.86)	58.6 (3.52)	41.4 (4.56)	74 (15.1)	‡ (†)	25.6 (6.31)	105 (13.9)
Black										
1980................	154 (21.3)	20.6 (1.47)	21.0 (3.27)	28.3 (3.62)	50.6 (4.01)	49.4 (4.01)	76 (15.0)	44 (11.4)	57.4 (5.65)	78 (15.2)
1990................	96 (18.5)	23.3 (2.27)	27.1 (4.93)	29.0 (5.04)	43.9 (5.51)	56.1 (5.51)	54 (13.8)	28 ! (10.0)	51.7 (7.41)	42 (12.3)
2000................	102 (19.7)	19.8 (1.98)	28.0 (5.03)	22.2 (4.65)	49.8 (5.60)	50.2 (5.60)	51 (14.0)	‡ (†)	44.2 (7.85)	51 (13.9)
2005................	88 (17.4)	19.5 (2.01)	21.5 (4.71)	27.7 (5.13)	50.9 (5.73)	49.1 (5.73)	43 (12.2)	‡ (†)	56.3 (8.11)	45 (12.4)
2010................	70 (15.6)	19.3 (2.22)	22.4 (5.33)	30.4 (5.88)	47.2 (6.38)	52.8 (6.38)	37 ! (11.3)	‡ (†)	57.5 (8.69)	33 ! (10.7)
2012................	90 (17.6)	21.2 (2.13)	20.0 (4.54)	23.7 (4.82)	56.3 (5.62)	43.7 (5.62)	39 (11.6)	‡ (†)	54.2 (8.54)	50 (13.2)
2013................	99 (18.4)	22.0 (2.57)	11.1 ! (4.16)	23.4 (5.60)	65.5 (6.29)	34.5 (6.29)	‡ (†)	‡ (†)	‡ (†)	65 (14.9)
Hispanic										
1980................	84 (18.7)	11.3 (1.36)	48.2 (6.40)	19.5 (5.07)	32.3 (5.99)	67.7 (5.99)	57 (15.4)	‡ (†)	28.8 (7.05)	27 ! (10.6)
1990................	66 (15.3)	15.9 (1.96)	39.3 (6.56)	19.9 (5.36)	40.8 (6.60)	59.2 (6.60)	39 ! (11.8)	‡ (†)	33.5 (8.24)	27 ! (9.8)
2000................	113 (20.8)	21.9 (2.06)	50.4 (5.32)	17.7 (4.06)	31.9 (4.96)	68.1 (4.96)	77 (17.1)	‡ (†)	26.0 (5.66)	36 ! (11.7)
2005................	125 (20.8)	27.9 (2.27)	39.2 (4.68)	16.1 (3.52)	44.7 (4.77)	55.3 (4.77)	69 (15.4)	‡ (†)	29.1 (5.86)	56 (13.9)
2010................	102 (18.8)	28.0 (2.52)	25.8 (4.64)	24.3 (4.55)	49.9 (5.30)	50.1 (5.30)	51 (13.3)	25 ! (9.3)	48.4 (7.49)	51 (13.3)
2012................	123 (20.5)	29.0 (2.37)	31.3 (4.49)	18.8 (3.78)	49.9 (4.84)	50.1 (4.84)	62 (14.6)	‡ (†)	37.5 (6.62)	61 (14.5)
2013................	135 (21.5)	30.0 (2.84)	32.5 (5.30)	18.3 (4.38)	49.2 (5.66)	50.8 (5.66)	68 (15.4)	‡ (†)	36.0 (7.63)	66 (15.1)

†Not applicable.
!Interpret data with caution. The coefficient of variation (CV) for this estimate is between 30 and 50 percent.
‡Reporting standards not met. Either there are too few cases for a reliable estimate or the coefficient of variation (CV) is 50 percent or greater.
[1]The labor force participation rate is the percentage of persons who are either employed or seeking employment.
[2]The labor force includes all employed persons plus those seeking employment. The unemployment rate is the percentage of persons in the labor force who are not working and who made specific efforts to find employment sometime during the prior 4 weeks.
[3]Beginning in 2010, standard errors for the individual year estimates were computed using replicate weights in order to produce more precise values. This methodology can only be used for these estimates. For all other estimates in the table, standard errors were computed using generalized variance function methodology.

[4]A 3-year moving average is the arithmetic average of the year indicated, the year immediately preceding, and the year immediately following. For example, the estimates shown for 2000 reflect an average of 1999, 2000, and 2001. Use of a moving average increases the sample size, thereby reducing the size of sampling errors and producing more stable estimates. For the final year of available data, a 2-year moving average is used; thus, the estimates for 2013 reflect the average of 2012 and 2013.
NOTE: Data are based on sample surveys of the civilian noninstitutional population. Data are for October of a given year. Dropouts are considered persons 16 to 24 years old who dropped out of school in the 12-month period ending in October of years shown. Includes dropouts from any grade, including a small number from elementary and middle schools. Percentages are only shown when the base is 75,000 or greater. Totals include race categories not separately shown. Race categories exclude persons of Hispanic ethnicity. Detail may not sum to totals because of rounding.
SOURCE: U.S. Department of Commerce, Census Bureau, Current Population Survey (CPS), selected years, October 1979 through 2013. (This table was prepared May 2015.)

Table 504.30. Among special education students out of high school up to 8 years, percentage attending and completing postsecondary education, living independently, and working competitively, by type of disability: 2007 and 2009

[Standard errors appear in parentheses]

Year, postsecondary status and institution type, and living and employment status	All disabilities[1]	Specific learning disabilities	Speech or language impairments	Intellectual disability	Emotional disturbance	Hearing impairments	Orthopedic impairments	Other health impairments[2]	Visual impairments	Multiple disabilities	Deaf-blindness	Autism	Traumatic brain injury
1	2	3	4	5	6	7	8	9	10	11	12	13	14
2007 (out of high school up to 6 years)													
Ever attended institution													
Any postsecondary	55.0 (2.62)	60.9 (3.88)	63.0 (3.77)	28.2 (3.65)	44.6 (4.36)	70.9 (4.61)	59.8 (4.59)	56.9 (4.14)	70.8 (5.23)	31.3 (5.28)	48.8 (6.83)	46.6 (5.25)	56.2 (7.49)
4-year	14.7 (1.87)	15.6 (2.89)	29.8 (3.57)	6.2! (1.96)	7.7! (2.34)	31.4 (4.71)	22.5 (3.91)	19.5 (3.31)	42.8 (5.70)	8.0! (3.08)	18.2 (5.28)	15.7! (3.82)	15.7! (5.49)
2-year	37.3 (2.55)	40.8 (3.91)	41.0 (3.84)	21.2 (3.32)	30.0 (4.02)	44.9 (5.05)	45.5 (4.66)	44.6 (4.16)	47.0 (5.74)	17.2 (4.29)	29.1 (6.21)	32.6 (4.93)	33.5 (7.12)
Vocational/technical	28.3 (2.37)	31.4 (3.69)	20.3 (3.14)	16.0 (2.97)	27.5 (3.92)	37.8 (4.92)	21.5 (3.84)	28.1 (3.76)	21.2 (4.71)	14.8 (4.04)	18.9 (5.35)	21.8 (4.35)	33.2 (7.11)
Graduation rate, by type of institution[3]													
Any postsecondary	38.4 (4.41)	37.5 (6.13)	48.4 (6.64)	40.0 (10.17)	41.1 (7.55)	38.9 (8.80)	35.7 (7.55)	33.8 (6.09)	49.7 (9.35)	32.1! (10.55)	‡ (†)	35.3 (10.36)	50.4 (12.59)
4-year	29.4 (8.30)	‡ (†)	39.8! (12.46)	‡ (†)	‡ (†)	37.2! (13.80)	35.7! (16.18)	‡ (†)	58.7 (13.84)	‡ (†)	‡ (†)	‡ (†)	‡ (†)
2-year	29.7 (4.83)	29.4 (6.81)	40.2 (7.79)	28.1! (11.70)	26.7! (8.47)	30.6! (10.78)	23.1! (8.41)	32.6 (6.63)	42.9 (11.33)	‡ (†)	‡ (†)	33.0! (13.39)	24.8! (12.11)
Vocational/technical	54.6 (7.22)	55.1 (9.66)	69.8 (10.43)	50.3! (15.09)	56.5 (11.38)	33.0! (14.56)	44.4 (11.95)	47.1 (11.65)	50.9! (19.67)	‡ (†)	‡ (†)	49.2! (15.05)	‡ (†)
Living independently[4]	35.7 (2.53)	40.6 (3.91)	30.4 (3.60)	21.2 (3.32)	34.4 (4.17)	28.5 (4.60)	14.0 (3.26)	30.8 (3.86)	31.3 (5.35)	10.6! (3.51)	13.7! (4.69)	11.8 (3.39)	24.8 (6.52)
Competitively employed[5]													
Currently	61.1 (2.86)	70.4 (4.12)	61.4 (4.17)	31.6 (4.22)	53.2 (4.94)	49.4 (5.85)	26.2 (4.36)	60.3 (4.51)	34.4 (5.98)	31.6 (6.13)	15.0! (5.46)	32.7 (5.63)	32.6 (7.47)
In the past 2 years	78.6 (2.27)	85.9 (2.92)	78.8 (3.30)	49.8 (4.32)	78.9 (3.77)	70.3 (4.93)	42.8 (4.62)	78.8 (3.54)	54.6 (5.97)	41.0 (5.99)	26.4 (6.17)	44.1 (5.40)	63.6 (7.50)
2009 (out of high school up to 8 years)													
Ever attended institution													
Any postsecondary	59.2 (2.64)	65.3 (3.93)	67.0 (3.62)	29.5 (3.62)	53.0 (4.53)	74.8 (4.24)	62.0 (4.42)	65.2 (4.05)	70.7 (5.01)	33.2 (5.09)	56.8 (7.09)	44.2 (4.66)	60.4 (7.40)
4-year	18.4 (2.08)	20.9 (3.36)	30.9 (3.56)	6.2! (1.92)	11.0 (2.84)	34.7 (4.66)	23.5 (3.87)	19.1 (3.34)	41.5 (5.43)	7.3! (2.82)	23.7 (6.09)	17.4 (3.56)	18.5! (5.87)
2-year	44.4 (2.67)	49.7 (4.13)	46.5 (3.86)	19.7 (3.16)	38.0 (4.40)	53.4 (4.88)	50.9 (4.57)	53.2 (4.25)	51.2 (5.51)	21.7 (4.45)	36.9 (6.91)	32.2 (4.39)	42.1 (7.47)
Vocational/technical	31.3 (2.49)	34.1 (3.92)	28.5 (3.48)	17.2 (2.99)	33.0 (4.27)	40.3 (4.79)	26.5 (4.03)	33.1 (4.00)	25.6 (4.81)	17.6 (4.11)	21.6 (5.89)	22.1 (3.90)	34.5 (7.20)
Currently attending institution													
Any postsecondary	15.1 (1.93)	17.3 (3.13)	20.1 (3.09)	‡ (†)	12.9 (3.04)	25.0 (4.23)	23.3 (3.87)	16.1 (3.13)	25.0 (4.79)	8.2! (2.99)	24.5 (6.19)	14.0 (3.26)	14.6! (5.34)
4-year	5.2 (1.20)	5.9! (1.95)	10.6 (2.38)	‡ (†)	3.9! (1.76)	15.0 (3.51)	8.0! (2.47)	3.1! (1.48)	15.1 (3.94)	‡ (†)	9.1! (4.11)	5.3! (2.12)	‡ (†)
2-year	9.0 (1.54)	10.3 (2.52)	8.3 (2.14)	‡ (†)	8.6 (2.56)	11.6 (3.15)	13.2 (3.10)	10.9 (2.67)	8.9! (3.16)	‡ (†)	16.7! (5.34)	8.2! (2.59)	9.2! (4.38)
Vocational/technical	2.2! (0.79)	‡ (†)	2.7! (1.24)	‡ (†)	‡ (†)	‡ (†)	5.5! (2.09)	2.9! (1.43)	‡ (†)	‡ (†)	‡ (†)	‡ (†)	‡ (†)
Graduation rate, by type of institution[3]													
Any postsecondary	47.6 (3.92)	47.8 (5.49)	53.5 (5.35)	39.8 (8.45)	45.9 (6.45)	58.7 (6.67)	45.3 (6.40)	44.8 (5.64)	58.4 (7.24)	58.9 (9.71)	‡ (†)	50.7 (8.15)	61.8 (10.33)
4-year	45.3 (7.28)	47.7 (10.07)	60.1 (8.80)	‡ (†)	‡ (†)	49.5 (9.93)	48.8 (11.86)	30.6! (9.72)	63.1 (10.01)	‡ (†)	‡ (†)	59.0 (12.15)	‡ (†)
2-year	37.2 (4.46)	38.2 (6.16)	39.2 (6.35)	28.2! (9.90)	33.3 (7.61)	42.5 (8.53)	32.9 (7.24)	35.1 (6.12)	45.9 (9.06)	44.3 (12.86)	‡ (†)	43.3 (10.61)	35.7! (11.88)
Vocational/technical	54.6 (5.96)	52.7 (8.29)	64.3 (8.39)	51.2 (12.94)	62.5 (8.67)	63.8 (10.75)	50.7 (10.12)	58.7 (8.28)	47.3 (12.97)	46.5 (12.73)	‡ (†)	53.2 (12.43)	73.9 (14.00)
Living independently[4]	44.7 (2.68)	51.0 (4.15)	38.7 (3.75)	25.7 (3.48)	44.3 (4.52)	40.3 (4.79)	24.9 (3.95)	39.2 (4.17)	41.4 (5.43)	11.2! (3.41)	20.5 (5.79)	7.1! (2.42)	24.0 (6.48)
Competitively employed[5]													
Currently	53.1 (2.82)	62.4 (4.27)	58.5 (3.93)	25.7 (3.60)	40.9 (4.65)	47.4 (5.14)	26.4 (4.03)	53.8 (4.48)	34.1 (5.36)	21.5 (4.63)	23.1 (6.19)	24.2 (4.07)	41.7 (7.52)
In the past 2 years	70.1 (2.52)	78.1 (3.51)	77.2 (3.28)	38.7 (3.98)	68.6 (4.31)	65.0 (4.81)	40.2 (4.53)	72.2 (3.92)	47.2 (5.61)	32.1 (5.15)	34.9 (6.96)	33.9 (4.54)	53.3 (7.64)

†Not applicable.
!Interpret data with caution. The coefficient of variation (CV) for this estimate is between 30 and 50 percent.
‡Reporting standards not met. The coefficient of variation (CV) for this estimate is 50 percent or greater.
[1]Includes disability categories not shown separately.
[2]Other health impairments include having limited strength, vitality, or alertness that is due to chronic or acute health problems (such as a heart condition, rheumatic fever, asthma, hemophilia, and leukemia) and that adversely affects educational performance.
[3]Among students who had ever attended the type of institution specified, the percentage who received a diploma, certificate, or license.
[4]Living independently includes living alone, with a spouse or roommate, in a college dormitory, in Job Corps housing, or in military housing as a service member.

[5]Competitively employed refers to those receiving more than minimum wage and working in an environment where the majority of workers are not disabled.
NOTE: Data based on students who had been out of high school up to 6 years in 2007 and up to 8 years in 2009 and had attended special or regular schools in the 1999–2000 or 2000–01 school year. Apparent discrepancies in attendance and graduation percentages between 2007 and 2009 may be due to inconsistent reporting by respondents and smaller numbers of respondents for the 2009 survey wave. Some data have been revised from previously published figures.
SOURCE: U.S. Department of Education, Institute of Education Sciences, National Center for Special Education Research, National Longitudinal Transition Study-2 (NLTS2), Waves 4 and 5, 2007 and 2009, unpublished tabulations. (This table was prepared July 2010.)

Table 505.10. Number, percentage distribution, unemployment rates, and median earnings of 25- to 29-year-old bachelor's degree holders and percentage of degree holders among all 25- to 29-year-olds, by field of study: 2009 and 2013

[Standard errors appear in parentheses]

Field of study	2009					2013				
	25- to 29-year-old bachelor's degree holders				Percent of all 25- to 29-year-olds with degree in specific field	Number, in thousands	25- to 29-year-old bachelor's degree holders			Percent of all 25- to 29-year-olds with degree in specific field
	Number, in thousands	Percentage distribution	Unemployment rate	Median annual earnings (in current dollars)			Percentage distribution	Unemployment rate	Median annual earnings (in current dollars)	
1	2	3	4	5	6	7	8	9	10	11
Total, all bachelor's degrees	6,418 (30.8)	100.0 (†)	5.2 (0.12)	$44,880 (547)	29.9 (0.14)	6,830 (34.1)	100.0 (†)	4.5 (0.09)	$45,280 (677)	32.0 (0.16)
Agriculture	59 (2.9)	0.9 (0.04)	2.2! (0.85)	38,970 (995)	0.3 (0.01)	61 (3.1)	0.9 (0.04)	1.7! (0.67)	40,260 (1,677)	0.3 (0.01)
Architecture	45 (2.3)	0.7 (0.04)	9.6 (1.58)	45,950 (1,186)	0.2 (0.01)	51 (3.1)	0.7 (0.05)	7.2 (2.01)	45,040 (1,682)	0.2 (0.01)
Area, ethnic, and civilization studies	27 (2.1)	0.4 (0.03)	7.3 (2.10)	39,930 (1,495)	0.1 (0.01)	29 (2.1)	0.4 (0.03)	6.9 (1.94)	40,740 (3,948)	0.1 (0.01)
Arts, fine and commercial										
Fine arts	250 (6.5)	3.9 (0.10)	8.8 (0.79)	35,870 (889)	1.2 (0.03)	284 (8.0)	4.2 (0.12)	5.7 (0.51)	36,070 (983)	1.3 (0.04)
Commercial art and graphic design	96 (4.9)	1.5 (0.08)	9.2 (1.22)	39,940 (535)	0.4 (0.02)	109 (4.5)	1.6 (0.07)	7.0 (1.12)	41,020 (1,123)	0.5 (0.02)
Business										
Business, general	224 (6.6)	3.5 (0.10)	5.2 (0.63)	45,910 (1,110)	1.0 (0.03)	252 (6.3)	3.7 (0.09)	4.9 (0.66)	48,790 (1,621)	1.2 (0.03)
Accounting	184 (5.9)	2.9 (0.09)	4.4 (0.63)	52,840 (1,428)	0.9 (0.03)	200 (5.5)	2.9 (0.08)	4.1 (0.65)	54,650 (518)	0.9 (0.03)
Business management and administration	372 (8.7)	5.8 (0.13)	5.9 (0.46)	43,900 (1,237)	1.7 (0.04)	330 (8.0)	4.8 (0.12)	5.0 (0.52)	45,260 (441)	1.5 (0.04)
Marketing and marketing research	196 (6.3)	3.0 (0.10)	5.7 (0.67)	44,740 (134)	0.9 (0.03)	203 (6.6)	3.0 (0.10)	4.5 (0.74)	46,190 (1,393)	0.9 (0.03)
Finance	168 (5.2)	2.6 (0.08)	4.8 (0.74)	51,390 (891)	0.8 (0.02)	163 (5.2)	2.4 (0.08)	3.2 (0.55)	53,060 (1,549)	0.8 (0.02)
Management information systems and statistics	27 (2.0)	0.4 (0.03)	5.8 (1.66)	55,350 (2,569)	0.1 (0.01)	21 (1.7)	0.3 (0.02)	2.5! (1.18)	50,240 (2,181)	0.1 (0.01)
Business, other and medical administration	121 (5.2)	1.9 (0.08)	4.9 (0.88)	45,040 (1,434)	0.6 (0.02)	145 (4.8)	2.1 (0.07)	5.5 (0.77)	44,660 (927)	0.7 (0.02)
Communications and communications technologies	384 (8.8)	6.0 (0.13)	5.4 (0.51)	39,900 (62)	1.8 (0.04)	398 (8.1)	5.8 (0.12)	5.1 (0.50)	42,310 (1,056)	1.9 (0.04)
Computer and information systems	259 (6.2)	4.0 (0.09)	5.2 (0.64)	59,030 (947)	1.2 (0.03)	227 (5.3)	3.3 (0.08)	3.5 (0.53)	60,270 (1,058)	1.1 (0.03)
Construction/electrical/transportation technologies	34 (2.2)	0.5 (0.03)	4.1 (1.19)	49,950 (2,248)	0.2 (0.01)	38 (2.7)	0.6 (0.04)	1.4! (0.58)	60,060 (677)	0.2 (0.02)
Criminal justice and fire protection	133 (4.5)	2.1 (0.07)	4.2 (0.72)	39,900 (453)	0.6 (0.02)	155 (4.9)	2.3 (0.07)	5.0 (0.70)	39,720 (625)	0.7 (0.02)
Education										
General education	143 (4.8)	2.2 (0.08)	3.3 (0.63)	39,180 (537)	0.7 (0.02)	160 (5.7)	2.3 (0.08)	3.3 (0.65)	39,920 (1,085)	0.7 (0.03)
Early childhood education	41 (2.5)	0.6 (0.04)	2.8! (1.00)	35,230 (889)	0.2 (0.01)	36 (2.4)	0.5 (0.03)	4.5! (1.76)	34,750 (1,366)	0.2 (0.01)
Elementary education	192 (5.2)	3.0 (0.08)	3.2 (0.49)	35,980 (896)	0.9 (0.02)	157 (5.3)	2.3 (0.08)	3.8 (0.64)	36,200 (394)	0.7 (0.02)
Secondary teacher education	21 (1.5)	0.3 (0.02)	3.8! (1.86)	38,480 (958)	0.1 (0.01)	20 (2.2)	0.3 (0.03)	‡ (†)	38,850 (1,413)	0.1 (0.01)
Education, other	180 (5.0)	2.8 (0.08)	3.2 (0.59)	37,970 (824)	0.8 (0.02)	185 (6.2)	2.7 (0.09)	3.1 (0.49)	38,280 (1,192)	0.9 (0.03)
Engineering and engineering-related fields										
General engineering	55 (3.2)	0.9 (0.05)	6.0 (1.25)	59,780 (1,395)	0.3 (0.01)	69 (4.1)	1.0 (0.06)	2.2 (0.60)	63,050 (1,840)	0.3 (0.02)
Chemical engineering	30 (2.1)	0.5 (0.03)	3.6! (1.65)	64,930 (3,706)	0.1 (0.01)	32 (2.2)	0.5 (0.03)	3.9! (1.28)	70,500 (1,465)	0.2 (0.01)
Civil engineering	42 (2.3)	0.7 (0.03)	4.2 (1.13)	57,840 (1,793)	0.2 (0.01)	54 (2.9)	0.8 (0.04)	5.7 (1.19)	59,000 (1,166)	0.3 (0.01)
Computer engineering	55 (2.5)	0.9 (0.04)	4.9 (1.19)	59,900 (1,524)	0.3 (0.01)	52 (3.2)	0.8 (0.05)	7.2 (1.63)	74,880 (2,137)	0.2 (0.01)
Electrical engineering	95 (3.3)	1.5 (0.05)	4.3 (0.90)	63,580 (1,522)	0.4 (0.02)	101 (4.2)	1.5 (0.06)	3.3 (0.75)	70,350 (1,320)	0.5 (0.02)
Mechanical engineering	84 (3.7)	1.3 (0.06)	5.0 (0.92)	61,590 (1,699)	0.4 (0.02)	92 (4.0)	1.3 (0.06)	3.2 (0.91)	68,500 (1,608)	0.4 (0.02)
Engineering, other	74 (3.7)	1.2 (0.06)	4.3 (0.93)	58,870 (931)	0.3 (0.02)	79 (3.8)	1.2 (0.06)	3.7 (0.86)	64,860 (2,687)	0.3 (0.02)
Engineering technologies	38 (2.8)	0.6 (0.04)	7.0 (1.59)	54,240 (1,871)	0.2 (0.01)	44 (2.8)	0.6 (0.04)	5.3 (1.43)	55,800 (1,287)	0.2 (0.01)
English language and literature	200 (5.3)	3.1 (0.08)	5.7 (0.77)	37,960 (1,050)	0.9 (0.02)	203 (5.9)	3.0 (0.09)	4.5 (0.60)	39,230 (1,416)	0.9 (0.03)
Family and consumer sciences	62 (2.8)	1.0 (0.05)	2.4 (0.65)	35,920 (2,415)	0.3 (0.01)	57 (3.0)	0.8 (0.04)	3.1! (1.04)	35,160 (1,020)	0.3 (0.01)
Health professions										
General medical and health services	183 (5.2)	2.9 (0.08)	3.3 (0.60)	49,880 (1,305)	0.9 (0.02)	245 (6.8)	3.6 (0.10)	3.1 (0.51)	48,250 (1,351)	1.1 (0.03)
Nursing	164 (5.2)	2.6 (0.08)	1.5 (0.34)	52,890 (1,753)	0.8 (0.02)	233 (7.2)	3.4 (0.10)	1.5 (0.31)	55,360 (859)	1.1 (0.03)
History	133 (4.3)	2.1 (0.07)	7.4 (0.90)	39,640 (737)	0.6 (0.02)	150 (4.5)	2.2 (0.07)	4.9 (0.61)	40,000 (133)	0.7 (0.02)
Liberal arts and humanities	117 (4.4)	1.8 (0.07)	7.1 (0.88)	38,890 (1,374)	0.5 (0.02)	90 (3.9)	1.3 (0.06)	7.1 (1.18)	38,060 (1,974)	0.4 (0.02)
Linguistics and comparative language and literature	68 (3.3)	1.1 (0.05)	5.6 (1.18)	39,910 (795)	0.3 (0.02)	65 (3.5)	1.0 (0.05)	3.5 (0.93)	41,280 (1,440)	0.3 (0.02)
Mathematics	70 (3.2)	1.1 (0.05)	4.7 (1.33)	49,540 (909)	0.3 (0.01)	78 (3.5)	1.1 (0.05)	3.8 (0.87)	47,250 (2,017)	0.4 (0.02)
Multi/interdisciplinary studies	121 (4.3)	1.9 (0.07)	5.8 (0.92)	42,980 (1,946)	0.6 (0.02)	76 (3.7)	1.1 (0.05)	4.6 (0.93)	40,270 (1,397)	0.4 (0.02)
Natural sciences										
Biology	354 (6.8)	5.5 (0.10)	4.5 (0.52)	42,300 (879)	1.6 (0.03)	400 (7.3)	5.9 (0.10)	4.5 (0.46)	45,180 (474)	1.9 (0.03)
Environmental science	42 (2.5)	0.7 (0.04)	7.5 (1.71)	39,220 (603)	0.2 (0.01)	41 (2.6)	0.6 (0.04)	7.9 (1.87)	38,500 (2,252)	0.2 (0.01)
Physical sciences	104 (4.2)	1.6 (0.06)	4.2 (0.81)	44,170 (433)	0.5 (0.02)	187 (6.0)	2.7 (0.09)	4.8 (0.73)	44,280 (1,547)	0.9 (0.03)

See notes at end of table.

Table 505.10. Number, percentage distribution, unemployment rates, and median earnings of 25- to 29-year-old bachelor's degree holders and percentage of degree holders among all 25- to 29-year-olds, by field of study: 2009 and 2013—Continued

[Standard errors appear in parentheses]

Field of study	2009					2013				
	25- to 29-year-old bachelor's degree holders				Percent of all 25- to 29-year-olds with degree in specific field	25- to 29-year-old bachelor's degree holders				Percent of all 25- to 29-year-olds with degree in specific field
	Number, in thousands	Percentage distribution	Unemployment rate	Median annual earnings (in current dollars)		Number, in thousands	Percentage distribution	Unemployment rate	Median annual earnings (in current dollars)	
1	2	3	4	5	6	7	8	9	10	11
Physical fitness, parks, recreation and leisure	96 (3.9)	1.5 (0.06)	5.9 (0.93)	39,380 (350)	0.4 (0.02)	114 (4.5)	1.7 (0.06)	3.5 (0.70)	40,220 (1,387)	0.5 (0.02)
Philosophy and religious studies	57 (3.0)	0.9 (0.05)	8.1 (1.51)	40,970 (1,387)	0.3 (0.01)	47 (2.9)	0.7 (0.04)	5.0 (1.16)	40,200 (1,766)	0.2 (0.01)
Psychology	371 (7.6)	5.8 (0.12)	5.0 (0.50)	39,890 (765)	1.7 (0.04)	405 (8.5)	5.9 (0.12)	6.2 (0.56)	38,180 (981)	1.9 (0.04)
Public administration and public policy	14 (1.7)	0.2 (0.03)	‡ (†)	52,150 (4,290)	0.1 (0.01)	13 (1.6)	0.2 (0.02)	‡ (†)	45,070 (4,535)	0.1 (0.01)
Social sciences										
Anthropology and archeology	33 (2.1)	0.5 (0.03)	5.6 ! (1.91)	33,260 (2,555)	0.2 (0.01)	38 (2.4)	0.6 (0.03)	4.4 ! (1.38)	40,040 (1,012)	0.2 (0.01)
Economics	126 (4.5)	2.0 (0.07)	5.1 (0.80)	58,980 (3,144)	0.6 (0.02)	139 (4.4)	2.0 (0.07)	4.8 (0.77)	55,760 (2,898)	0.6 (0.02)
Geography	21 (1.7)	0.3 (0.03)	5.8 ! (2.11)	40,170 (1,216)	0.1 (0.01)	19 (1.9)	0.3 (0.03)	5.7 ! (2.29)	39,910 (2,976)	0.1 (0.01)
International relations	20 (1.6)	0.3 (0.02)	7.4 (2.18)	45,320 (2,964)	0.1 (0.01)	26 (2.1)	0.4 (0.03)	5.3 ! (1.83)	49,570 (3,055)	0.1 (0.01)
Political science and government	167 (5.2)	2.6 (0.08)	6.6 (0.85)	47,480 (1,034)	0.8 (0.02)	176 (4.6)	2.6 (0.06)	6.4 (0.71)	46,200 (1,502)	0.8 (0.02)
Sociology	113 (3.9)	1.8 (0.06)	5.3 (0.94)	38,620 (1,585)	0.5 (0.02)	114 (4.1)	1.7 (0.06)	5.2 (0.91)	39,920 (679)	0.5 (0.02)
Miscellaneous social sciences	32 (2.4)	0.5 (0.04)	6.6 ! (2.21)	39,900 (526)	0.2 (0.01)	41 (3.2)	0.6 (0.05)	4.9 ! (1.53)	39,860 (1,047)	0.2 (0.01)
Social work and human services	67 (3.9)	1.0 (0.06)	4.0 (0.92)	34,950 (1,081)	0.3 (0.02)	72 (3.7)	1.1 (0.05)	4.2 (0.90)	35,140 (857)	0.3 (0.02)
Theology and religious vocations	32 (2.4)	0.5 (0.04)	3.7 ! (1.20)	35,300 (962)	0.1 (0.01)	32 (2.4)	0.5 (0.04)	2.6 ! (1.25)	32,880 (2,213)	0.2 (0.01)
Other fields	22 (2.2)	0.3 (0.03)	7.2 ! (2.59)	42,760 (3,817)	0.1 (0.01)	24 (2.1)	0.4 (0.03)	8.9 (2.61)	38,740 (3,321)	0.1 (0.01)

†Not applicable.
!Interpret data with caution. The coefficient of variation (CV) for this estimate is between 30 and 50 percent.
‡Reporting standards not met. Either there are too few cases for a reliable estimate or the coefficient of variation (CV) is 50 percent or greater.

NOTE: The first bachelor's degree major reported by respondents was used to classify their field of study, even though they were able to report a second bachelor's degree major and may possess advanced degrees in other fields. Detail may not sum to totals because of rounding. Some data have been revised from previously published figures.
SOURCE: U.S. Department of Commerce, Census Bureau, 2009 and 2013 American Community Survey (ACS) Public Use Microdata Sample (PUMS) data. (This table was prepared May 2015.)

Table 505.20. Unemployment rate of 25- to 34-year-olds with a bachelor's or higher degree, by undergraduate field of study, sex, race/ethnicity, and U.S. nativity and citizenship status: 2013

[Standard errors appear in parentheses]

Sex, race/ethnicity, and U.S. nativity and citizenship status	Total, all fields	STEM total	Bachelor's degree in a science, technology, engineering, or mathematics (STEM) field								Bachelor's degree in a non-STEM field			
			Agriculture/ natural resources	Architecture	Computer and information sciences	Engineering/ engineering technologies	Biology/ biomedical sciences	Mathematics/ statistics	Physical/ social sciences	Health studies	Non-STEM total	Business	Education	All other fields of study
1	2	3	4	5	6	7	8	9	10	11	12	13	14	15
Total[1]	4.0 (0.06)	3.7 (0.10)	3.0 (0.48)	5.7 (1.18)	3.1 (0.31)	3.2 (0.23)	3.7 (0.31)	3.7 (0.67)	4.8 (0.20)	2.6 (0.22)	4.3 (0.09)	4.1 (0.16)	2.9 (0.22)	4.7 (0.13)
Sex														
Male	4.1 (0.10)	3.5 (0.14)	3.0 (0.70)	5.0 (1.34)	2.6 (0.33)	3.0 (0.24)	4.0 (0.53)	4.4 (1.03)	4.7 (0.34)	2.2 (0.40)	4.5 (0.16)	3.8 (0.20)	2.5 (0.46)	5.3 (0.23)
Female	4.0 (0.08)	3.9 (0.14)	3.1 (0.64)	6.7‡ (2.22)	4.9 (0.88)	4.2 (0.62)	3.5 (0.38)	2.8 (0.71)	4.9 (0.30)	2.7 (0.25)	4.1 (0.12)	4.5 (0.23)	3.0 (0.24)	4.3 (0.19)
Race/ethnicity														
White	3.4 (0.08)	3.2 (0.13)	3.3 (0.56)	4.1 (1.06)	2.6 (0.37)	2.8 (0.29)	3.2 (0.39)	3.3 (0.72)	4.0 (0.24)	2.0 (0.25)	3.5 (0.09)	3.1 (0.20)	2.6 (0.22)	4.0 (0.15)
Black	6.7 (0.32)	5.8 (0.50)	‡	9.8! (4.76)	5.3 (1.38)	6.6 (1.45)	5.3 (1.24)	†	7.1 (0.85)	3.0 (0.71)	7.3 (0.46)	7.8 (0.75)	5.0 (1.09)	7.4 (0.74)
Hispanic	5.5 (0.32)	5.3 (0.50)	‡	9.3! (4.47)	3.5! (1.16)	4.9 (0.93)	5.3 (1.52)	†	6.7 (0.92)	4.1 (1.00)	5.6 (0.38)	4.9 (0.56)	3.9 (0.91)	6.5 (0.54)
Asian	4.7 (0.23)	3.7 (0.24)	†	†	3.2 (0.55)	2.8 (0.36)	4.1 (0.82)	2.5! (0.98)	4.7 (0.67)	4.4 (0.82)	6.3 (0.49)	6.3 (0.64)	4.6! (1.48)	6.4 (0.71)
Pacific Islander	18.6 (5.44)	†									21.1! (6.76)			
American Indian/Alaska Native[2]	5.7! (1.50)	6.3! (2.70)									3.7! (1.65)			
American Indian	5.3! (1.80)	7.0! (3.23)									4.2! (1.99)			
Alaska Native	‡	†												
Two or more races	5.5 (0.57)	6.4 (0.98)					5.7! (2.04)		9.5 (1.90)	3.5! (1.46)	4.9 (0.64)	4.3 (1.04)		5.6 (0.96)
Race/ethnicity by sex														
Male														
White	3.6 (0.12)	3.2 (0.17)	3.6 (0.81)	4.3! (1.37)	2.3 (0.39)	2.7 (0.34)	3.3 (0.60)	3.5 (1.02)	4.1 (0.39)	1.9 (0.46)	3.9 (0.16)	3.3 (0.24)	2.2 (0.47)	4.7 (0.24)
Black	6.3 (0.52)	6.0 (0.83)			7.5 (1.94)	7.1 (1.77)	6.8! (2.58)		4.5 (0.92)	†	6.5 (0.65)	6.3 (0.98)	5.8 (1.37)	7.1 (1.02)
Hispanic	5.9 (0.57)	5.8 (0.74)			2.8! (0.99)	4.2 (1.03)	8.9! (3.55)		9.2 (1.77)	†	6.1 (0.71)	4.2 (0.73)	3.7 (0.99)	7.6 (0.98)
Asian	3.5 (0.29)	2.6 (0.29)			1.8! (0.58)	2.1 (0.36)	3.9! (1.22)	3.7! (1.65)	3.9 (0.91)	2.8! (1.34)	5.7 (0.66)	5.4 (0.82)	4.8! (1.67)	6.3 (1.10)
Pacific Islander	5.7! (2.51)										†			
American Indian/Alaska Native[2]	†													
American Indian	‡													
Alaska Native	†													
Two or more races	5.9 (1.06)	6.0 (1.62)		†	†	4.5! (1.99)	7.1! (2.83)		10.6! (4.14)		5.8 (1.17)			7.4 (1.62)
Female														
White	3.2 (0.10)	3.1 (0.18)	3.0 (0.72)		4.5 (1.31)	2.9 (0.67)	3.1 (0.43)	2.9 (0.86)	4.0 (0.29)	2.0 (0.29)	3.2 (0.13)	2.9 (0.27)	2.7 (0.26)	3.5 (0.19)
Black	7.0 (0.43)	5.7 (0.63)			†	5.1! (2.44)	4.7 (1.35)		8.3 (1.14)	3.0 (0.76)	7.8 (0.62)	8.8 (1.07)	5.8 (1.37)	7.5 (0.97)
Hispanic	5.1 (0.34)	5.0 (0.67)			†	8.1! (2.95)	3.2! (1.23)		5.4 (1.05)	4.3 (1.20)	5.3 (0.40)	5.7 (0.76)	3.7 (0.99)	5.5 (0.61)
Asian	5.9 (0.36)	5.3 (0.42)			6.7 (1.45)	5.0 (0.94)	4.3 (1.02)		5.5 (0.99)	5.0 (0.95)	6.7 (0.66)	7.1 (1.00)	4.8! (1.67)	6.5 (0.93)
Pacific Islander	18.9! (6.46)										33.5! (9.63)			
American Indian/Alaska Native[2]	3.9! (1.66)													
American Indian	4.8! (2.02)													
Alaska Native	‡													
Two or more races	5.2 (0.68)	6.9 (1.40)			†	†			8.8 (2.43)	4.5! (1.82)	4.1 (0.80)	4.3! (1.41)		4.3 (1.10)
Nativity														
Hispanic														
U.S.-born citizen[3]	5.4 (0.39)	5.5 (0.65)			3.2! (1.25)	5.0 (1.36)	5.4! (1.88)	†	6.9 (1.14)	3.8! (1.16)	5.3 (0.41)	4.6 (0.67)	3.5 (0.84)	5.3 (0.63)
Foreign-born	5.8 (0.55)	4.9 (0.72)			3.8! (1.86)	4.9 (1.37)	5.0! (2.19)	†	6.2 (1.63)	5.1! (2.10)	6.4 (0.83)	5.7 (1.24)	†	7.4 (1.13)
Asian														
U.S.-born[3]	4.5 (0.41)	3.7 (0.49)		14.9! (7.40)	6.2! (2.24)	4.1 (1.14)	3.0 (0.89)	†	4.1 (1.00)	1.9! (0.83)	5.3 (0.72)	6.5 (1.06)	†	6.2 (0.63)
Foreign-born	4.8 (0.27)	3.7 (0.28)			2.8 (0.57)	2.6 (0.37)	5.0 (1.16)	†	5.2 (0.92)	5.5 (1.00)	7.0 (0.66)	6.3 (0.88)	5.2! (1.95)	8.5 (1.08)
Citizenship status														
U.S.-born citizen	3.8 (0.07)	3.6 (0.11)	3.1 (0.51)	4.1 (1.04)	3.2 (0.38)	3.3 (0.26)	3.4 (0.34)	4.2 (0.82)	4.6 (0.23)	2.1 (0.21)	3.9 (0.09)	3.6 (0.16)	2.7 (0.20)	4.4 (0.14)
Naturalized citizen	6.0 (0.34)	5.5 (0.41)	†	†	3.2 (0.76)	5.4 (0.84)	6.9 (1.27)	†	6.2 (0.90)	4.8 (0.99)	6.2 (0.50)	6.2 (0.80)	3.8 (1.12)	7.2 (0.75)
Noncitizen	5.1 (0.25)	3.6 (0.26)	2.6! (1.29)	12.3! (4.07)	3.0 (0.59)	2.5 (0.37)	3.4 (0.83)	†	5.9 (0.88)	5.3 (1.07)	7.8 (0.54)	7.6 (0.74)	7.1 (2.45)	8.1 (0.86)

†Not applicable.
!Interpret data with caution. The coefficient of variation (CV) for this estimate is between 30 and 50 percent.
‡Reporting standards not met. Either there are too few cases for a reliable estimate or the coefficient of variation (CV) is 50 percent or greater.
[1]Total includes other racial/ethnic groups not shown separately.
[2]Includes persons reporting American Indian alone, persons reporting Alaska Native alone, and persons from American Indian and/or Alaska Native tribes specified or not specified.
[3]Includes those born in the 50 states, the District of Columbia, Puerto Rico, American Samoa, Guam, the U.S. Virgin Islands, and the Northern Marianas, as well as those born abroad to U.S.-citizen parents.
NOTE: The unemployment rate is the percentage of labor force participants who are not employed but are actively seeking and the labor force consists of persons who are employed as well as persons who are not employed but are looking for work. (It does not include those who are neither employed nor looking for work.) Estimates are for the entire population of bachelor's degree holders in the indicated age range, including persons living in households and persons living in group quarters (such as college residence halls, residential treatment centers, military barracks, and correctional facilities). The first bachelor's degree major reported by respondents was used to classify their field of study, even though they were able to report a second bachelor's degree major and may possess advanced degrees in other fields. STEM fields, as defined here, consist of the fields specified in columns 4 through 11. Data were assembled based on major field aggregations, except that management of STEM activities was counted as a STEM field instead of a business field. Race categories exclude persons of Hispanic ethnicity.
SOURCE: U.S. Department of Commerce, Census Bureau, American Community Survey (ACS), 2013. (This table was prepared May 2015.)

Table 505.30. Among employed 25- to 34-year-olds with a bachelor's degree in a science, technology, engineering, or mathematics (STEM) field, percentage with STEM and non-STEM occupations, by sex, race/ethnicity, and U.S. nativity and citizenship status: 2013

[Standard errors appear in parentheses]

Sex, race/ethnicity, and U.S. nativity and citizenship status	Total all occupation types	Science, technology, engineering, or mathematics (STEM) occupation					Non-STEM occupation								
		STEM total	Computer scientists and mathematicians	Engineers and architects	Life, physical and social scientists	Medical professionals	Non-STEM total	Healthcare support workers	Agriculture and forestry workers	Business workers/ managers	Educators	Legal professionals	Human/ protective services workers	Military personnel	Other
1	2	3	4	5	6	7	8	9	10	11	12	13	14	15	16
Total[1]	100.0 (†)	46.9 (0.30)	12.0 (0.21)	8.8 (0.16)	5.0 (0.12)	21.1 (0.21)	53.1 (0.30)	1.3 (0.06)	0.2 (0.02)	20.3 (0.28)	9.0 (0.17)	1.7 (0.08)	4.5 (0.12)	0.5 (0.04)	15.6 (0.21)
Sex															
Male	100.0 (†)	47.7 (0.41)	18.8 (0.36)	14.1 (0.26)	4.7 (0.14)	10.1 (0.23)	52.3 (0.41)	0.7 (0.06)	0.2 (0.03)	22.6 (0.34)	7.4 (0.20)	1.7 (0.11)	3.2 (0.15)	0.8 (0.07)	15.6 (0.29)
Female	100.0 (†)	46.1 (0.41)	5.2 (0.17)	3.5 (0.16)	5.3 (0.20)	32.0 (0.34)	53.9 (0.41)	2.0 (0.10)	0.1 (0.03)	18.0 (0.39)	10.6 (0.25)	1.7 (0.10)	5.8 (0.20)	0.1 (0.02)	15.6 (0.33)
Race/ethnicity															
White	100.0 (†)	46.2 (0.36)	8.9 (0.22)	9.5 (0.21)	5.3 (0.16)	22.5 (0.30)	53.8 (0.36)	1.3 (0.08)	0.2 (0.03)	21.1 (0.35)	9.1 (0.21)	1.9 (0.10)	4.6 (0.14)	0.5 (0.05)	15.1 (0.26)
Black	100.0 (†)	36.1 (1.05)	7.2 (0.58)	4.5 (0.49)	2.6 (0.37)	21.7 (1.04)	63.9 (1.05)	2.3 (0.32)	(†)	20.2 (1.01)	8.7 (0.67)	1.3 (0.24)	9.1 (0.59)	0.5 ! (0.17)	21.8 (1.19)
Hispanic	100.0 (†)	36.2 (0.83)	7.4 (0.52)	7.3 (0.61)	4.2 (0.42)	17.3 (0.65)	63.8 (0.83)	1.4 (0.23)	0.5 ! (0.19)	21.3 (0.89)	9.8 (0.57)	1.5 (0.21)	6.9 (0.51)	0.5 ! (0.16)	22.0 (0.82)
Asian	100.0 (†)	60.3 (0.65)	28.1 (0.70)	9.3 (0.42)	5.5 (0.31)	17.6 (0.45)	39.7 (0.65)	1.0 (0.15)	(†)	17.2 (0.54)	8.1 (0.35)	1.1 (0.14)	1.2 (0.13)	0.1 (0.06)	10.8 (0.40)
Pacific Islander	100.0 (†)	22.4 (7.22)	‡ (†)	‡ (†)	5.3 ! (2.44)	14.9 ! (5.45)	77.6 (7.22)	‡ (†)	(†)	11.3 ! (5.31)	15.7 (6.89)	‡ (†)	13.6 ! (6.35)	‡ (†)	23.6 ! (7.18)
American Indian/Alaska Native[2]	100.0 (†)	26.6 (5.10)	‡ (†)	‡ (†)	6.1 ! (2.86)	13.6 (3.20)	73.4 (5.10)	‡ (†)	(†)	21.9 (5.54)	8.6 ! (2.88)	‡ (†)	6.2 ! (2.26)	‡ (†)	34.4 (6.00)
American Indian	100.0 (†)	27.7 (6.16)	‡ (†)	‡ (†)	(†)	14.7 (3.71)	72.3 (6.16)	‡ (†)	(†)	25.5 (6.78)	6.6 ! (2.91)	‡ (†)	6.7 ! (2.54)	‡ (†)	30.5 (6.19)
Alaska Native	100.0 (†)	‡ (†)	‡ (†)	‡ (†)	(†)	(†)	‡ (†)	‡ (†)	(†)	(†)	(†)	‡ (†)	(†)	‡ (†)	(†)
Two or more races	100.0 (†)	45.2 (1.92)	11.9 (1.21)	7.6 (0.84)	6.4 (0.85)	19.4 (1.53)	54.8 (1.92)	1.9 (0.48)	(†)	18.6 (1.37)	9.2 (1.16)	2.0 (0.55)	4.6 (0.92)	0.7 ! (0.27)	17.7 (1.64)
Race/ethnicity by sex															
Male															
White	100.0 (†)	45.8 (0.49)	14.9 (0.39)	15.8 (0.33)	5.0 (0.20)	10.1 (0.31)	54.2 (0.49)	0.6 (0.07)	0.3 (0.05)	24.8 (0.47)	7.1 (0.22)	2.0 (0.16)	3.3 (0.19)	0.9 (0.09)	15.1 (0.34)
Black	100.0 (†)	30.8 (1.66)	11.6 (1.21)	7.2 (0.99)	2.5 (0.60)	9.4 (1.11)	69.2 (1.66)	1.5 (0.43)	(†)	22.7 (1.79)	7.6 (1.28)	1.1 (0.30)	8.0 (0.92)	1.3 ! (0.46)	27.1 (1.83)
Hispanic	100.0 (†)	36.6 (1.30)	12.8 (1.07)	12.1 (1.03)	3.6 (0.46)	8.1 (0.87)	63.4 (1.30)	0.6 ! (0.21)	0.4 ! (0.17)	21.9 (1.49)	8.2 (0.78)	1.0 (0.25)	4.8 (0.69)	0.9 ! (0.32)	25.5 (1.43)
Asian	100.0 (†)	63.3 (0.76)	35.7 (0.87)	11.8 (0.58)	5.2 (0.39)	10.7 (0.52)	36.7 (0.76)	0.6 (0.13)	(†)	16.7 (0.69)	7.8 (0.48)	1.0 (0.18)	1.0 (0.17)	0.3 ! (0.10)	9.3 (0.50)
Pacific Islander	100.0 (†)	16.7 (7.77)	‡ (†)	‡ (†)	‡ (†)	‡ (†)	83.3 (7.77)	‡ (†)	(†)	15.1 ! (6.83)	‡ (†)	‡ (†)	7.8 ! (3.64)	‡ (†)	44.4 (8.03)
American Indian/Alaska Native[2]	100.0 (†)	23.3 (6.91)	‡ (†)	‡ (†)	‡ (†)	‡ (†)	76.7 (6.91)	‡ (†)	(†)	21.5 (5.55)	‡ (†)	‡ (†)	9.9 ! (4.63)	‡ (†)	40.3 (9.26)
American Indian	100.0 (†)	21.6 (7.91)	‡ (†)	‡ (†)	‡ (†)	‡ (†)	78.4 (7.91)	‡ (†)	(†)	25.1 (6.97)	‡ (†)	‡ (†)	‡ (†)	‡ (†)	‡ (†)
Alaska Native	100.0 (†)	‡ (†)	‡ (†)	‡ (†)	‡ (†)	‡ (†)	‡ (†)	‡ (†)	(†)	(†)	‡ (†)	‡ (†)	‡ (†)	‡ (†)	‡ (†)
Two or more races	100.0 (†)	47.6 (2.58)	19.6 (2.20)	12.6 (1.74)	4.0 (0.91)	11.5 (1.67)	52.4 (2.58)	‡ (†)	(†)	19.0 (1.83)	7.6 (1.46)	1.6 ! (0.66)	3.2 ! (1.09)	1.2 ! (0.53)	18.9 (2.60)
Female															
White	100.0 (†)	46.5 (0.50)	3.1 (0.16)	3.3 (0.18)	5.6 (0.25)	34.6 (0.47)	53.5 (0.50)	1.9 (0.14)	0.1 (0.03)	17.6 (0.48)	11.0 (0.31)	1.8 (0.11)	5.8 (0.25)	0.1 (0.03)	15.2 (0.39)
Black	100.0 (†)	39.5 (1.30)	4.4 (0.60)	2.8 (0.50)	2.7 (0.46)	29.5 (1.27)	60.5 (1.30)	2.8 (0.44)	(†)	18.6 (1.31)	9.4 (0.73)	1.4 (0.30)	9.8 (0.79)	‡ (†)	18.4 (1.43)
Hispanic	100.0 (†)	35.8 (1.23)	2.6 (0.40)	3.1 (0.47)	4.7 (0.62)	25.4 (1.06)	64.2 (1.23)	2.1 (0.35)	(†)	20.7 (1.15)	11.2 (0.78)	1.8 (0.33)	8.7 (0.80)	‡ (†)	19.0 (1.07)
Asian	100.0 (†)	56.1 (1.13)	17.2 (0.75)	5.6 (0.47)	5.9 (0.49)	27.3 (0.87)	43.9 (1.13)	1.7 (0.30)	(†)	17.9 (0.89)	8.6 (0.58)	1.3 (0.25)	1.4 (0.25)	‡ (†)	13.1 (0.75)
Pacific Islander	100.0 (†)	16.7 (7.77)	‡ (†)	‡ (†)	‡ (†)	11.7 (5.83)	83.3 (7.77)	‡ (†)	(†)	15.1 (6.83)	15.1 (7.34)	‡ (†)	‡ (†)	‡ (†)	25.7 ! (8.14)
American Indian/Alaska Native[2]	100.0 (†)	30.2 (7.29)	‡ (†)	‡ (†)	‡ (†)	20.6 (5.89)	69.8 (7.29)	‡ (†)	(†)	22.3 (8.96)	16.1 (5.49)	‡ (†)	‡ (†)	‡ (†)	23.5 ! (7.60)
American Indian	100.0 (†)	34.0 (8.73)	‡ (†)	‡ (†)	‡ (†)	22.9 (6.72)	66.0 (8.73)	‡ (†)	(†)	25.9 ! (10.42)	11.9 ! (5.68)	‡ (†)	‡ (†)	‡ (†)	20.5 ! (7.83)
Alaska Native	100.0 (†)	‡ (†)	‡ (†)	‡ (†)	‡ (†)	‡ (†)	‡ (†)	‡ (†)	(†)	(†)	‡ (†)	‡ (†)	‡ (†)	‡ (†)	‡ (†)
Two or more races	100.0 (†)	43.0 (2.68)	4.8 (1.06)	2.9 (0.66)	8.6 (1.51)	26.8 (2.57)	57.0 (2.68)	2.9 (0.86)	(†)	18.3 (2.06)	10.7 (1.67)	2.4 ! (0.80)	5.8 (1.26)	‡ (†)	16.7 (2.06)
Nativity															
Hispanic[3] U.S.-born[3]	100.0 (†)	37.4 (1.01)	6.6 (0.59)	6.7 (0.68)	4.5 (0.58)	19.6 (0.82)	62.6 (1.01)	1.6 (0.33)	(†)	21.2 (1.01)	10.0 (0.73)	1.6 (0.28)	8.5 (0.71)	0.7 ! (0.23)	18.6 (0.79)
Foreign-born	100.0 (†)	33.7 (1.65)	8.9 (1.10)	8.7 (1.05)	3.5 (0.51)	12.7 (1.25)	66.3 (1.65)	1.0 ! (0.32)	0.6 ! (0.30)	21.4 (1.52)	9.4 (0.92)	1.1 (0.39)	3.7 (0.64)	‡ (†)	28.9 (1.77)
Asian[3] U.S.-born[3]	100.0 (†)	51.4 (1.39)	11.5 (0.81)	7.1 (0.64)	5.1 (0.61)	27.6 (1.20)	48.6 (1.39)	1.3 (0.30)	(†)	22.3 (1.17)	6.0 (0.49)	2.5 (0.44)	2.3 (0.43)	0.5 ! (0.18)	13.7 (0.87)
Foreign-born	100.0 (†)	63.5 (0.73)	33.9 (0.88)	10.0 (0.50)	5.6 (0.36)	14.0 (0.55)	36.5 (0.73)	0.9 (0.16)	(†)	15.4 (0.58)	8.9 (0.42)	0.7 (0.11)	0.8 (0.13)	‡ (†)	9.9 (0.48)
Citizenship status															
U.S.-born citizen	100.0 (†)	44.6 (0.31)	8.4 (0.19)	8.6 (0.20)	4.8 (0.14)	22.8 (0.27)	55.4 (0.31)	1.4 (0.07)	0.2 (0.03)	21.1 (0.29)	8.8 (0.18)	1.9 (0.10)	5.4 (0.15)	0.6 (0.05)	16.0 (0.24)
Naturalized citizen	100.0 (†)	52.7 (1.08)	13.2 (0.74)	9.2 (0.55)	4.1 (0.41)	26.2 (0.91)	47.3 (1.08)	1.6 (0.29)	(†)	19.7 (0.92)	5.7 (0.41)	1.6 (0.26)	2.8 (0.30)	0.2 ! (0.07)	15.6 (0.80)
Noncitizen	100.0 (†)	56.5 (0.80)	31.4 (0.85)	9.6 (0.48)	6.9 (0.39)	8.6 (0.44)	43.5 (0.80)	0.9 (0.16)	(†)	16.6 (0.63)	11.4 (0.51)	0.5 (0.12)	0.8 (0.15)	‡ (†)	13.2 (0.53)

†Not applicable.

!Interpret data with caution. The coefficient of variation (CV) for this estimate is between 30 and 50 percent.

‡Reporting standards not met. Either there are too few cases for a reliable estimate or the coefficient of variation (CV) is 50 percent or greater.

[1]Total includes other racial/ethnic groups not shown separately.

[2]Includes persons reporting American Indian alone, persons reporting Alaska Native alone, and persons from American Indian and/or Alaska Native tribes specified or not specified.

[3]Includes those born in the 50 states, the District of Columbia, Puerto Rico, American Samoa, Guam, the U.S. Virgin Islands, and the Northern Marianas, as well as those born abroad to U.S.-citizen parents.

NOTE: Estimates include persons in the indicated age range who live in households as well as those who live in group quarters (such as college residence halls, residential treatment centers, military barracks, and correctional facilities). This table includes only employed persons who have a bachelor's degree in a STEM field of study. The first bachelor's degree major reported by respondents was used to classify their field of study, even though they were able to report a second bachelor's degree major and may possess advanced degrees in other fields. Aggregated occupation classifications were used to assemble the data, except that managers of STEM activities were counted as practitioners of STEM occupations instead of "Business workers/ managers." Detail may not sum to totals because of rounding. Race categories exclude persons of Hispanic ethnicity. SOURCE: U.S. Department of Commerce, Census Bureau, American Community Survey (ACS), 2013. (This table was prepared February 2015.)

Table 505.31. Among employed 25- to 34-year-olds with a bachelor's degree in a science, technology, engineering, or mathematics (STEM) field, percentage with STEM and non-STEM occupations, by sex, race/ethnicity, nativity, and U.S. nativity and citizenship status: 2012

[Standard errors appear in parentheses]

Sex, race/ethnicity, nativity, and citizenship status	Total, all occupation types	Science, technology, engineering, or mathematics (STEM) occupation					Non-STEM occupation								
		STEM total	Computer scientists and mathematicians	Engineers/ architects	Life, physical, and social scientists	Medical professionals	Non-STEM total	Healthcare support workers	Agriculture and forestry workers	Business workers/ managers	Educators	Legal professionals	Human/ protective services workers	Military personnel	Other
1	2	3	4	5	6	7	8	9	10	11	12	13	14	15	16
Total[1]	100.0	48.0 (0.35)	13.0 (0.22)	8.9 (0.16)	5.3 (0.15)	20.9 (0.26)	52.0 (0.35)	1.5 (0.08)	0.2 (0.03)	18.9 (0.29)	8.7 (0.17)	1.7 (0.08)	5.0 (0.17)	0.4 (0.04)	15.5 (0.23)
Sex															
Male	100.0	49.4 (0.41)	20.3 (0.32)	14.4 (0.29)	5.1 (0.19)	9.7 (0.26)	50.6 (0.41)	0.7 (0.08)	0.2 (0.05)	21.5 (0.41)	7.4 (0.21)	1.6 (0.11)	3.3 (0.17)	0.7 (0.08)	15.1 (0.34)
Female	100.0	46.7 (0.44)	5.8 (0.23)	3.3 (0.14)	5.5 (0.20)	32.1 (0.39)	53.3 (0.44)	2.3 (0.13)	0.1 ! (0.03)	16.3 (0.35)	10.0 (0.23)	1.8 (0.11)	6.8 (0.25)	0.1 (0.03)	16.0 (0.29)
Race/ethnicity															
White	100.0	47.3 (0.37)	9.5 (0.23)	9.3 (0.24)	5.7 (0.18)	22.8 (0.28)	52.7 (0.37)	1.4 (0.10)	0.2 (0.04)	19.7 (0.34)	8.7 (0.19)	1.9 (0.10)	5.1 (0.19)	0.5 (0.06)	15.3 (0.29)
Black	100.0	36.3 (1.27)	9.2 (0.75)	5.3 (0.49)	2.6 (0.43)	19.3 (0.98)	63.7 (1.27)	2.6 (0.40)	†	19.7 (0.91)	8.3 (0.64)	1.8 (0.30)	10.8 (0.81)	0.2 ! (0.09)	20.3 (0.95)
Hispanic	100.0	37.2 (0.97)	8.4 (0.75)	8.1 (0.60)	4.2 (0.34)	16.5 (0.76)	62.8 (0.97)	1.6 (0.24)	0.3 ! (0.14)	17.9 (0.85)	9.9 (0.68)	1.6 (0.25)	6.6 (0.62)	0.4 ! (0.15)	24.6 (1.02)
Asian	100.0	61.5 (0.79)	29.9 (0.72)	9.3 (0.52)	5.3 (0.33)	17.0 (0.53)	38.5 (0.79)	1.2 (0.19)	†	16.3 (0.62)	8.2 (0.44)	1.3 (0.18)	1.4 (0.18)	†	9.9 (0.44)
Pacific Islander	100.0	26.9 (8.01)	11.4 ! (4.28)	†	†	16.2 ! (6.60)	73.1 (8.01)	†	†	38.2 (10.86)	10.2 ! (3.62)	#	12.0 ! (4.33)	†	16.5 ! (6.73)
American Indian/Alaska Native[2]	100.0	38.9 (5.46)	8.2 ! (3.94)	†	4.7 ! (2.30)	19.4 (4.35)	61.1 (5.46)	‡	‡	19.8 (4.74)	11.7 ! (4.15)	#	13.7 ! (4.84)	‡	18.0 (4.70)
American Indian	100.0	38.2 (5.69)	‡	†	‡	22.3 (4.94)	61.8 (5.69)	‡	†	19.7 (4.96)	‡	#	‡	‡	15.3 ! (4.96)
Alaska Native	‡	‡	‡	†	†	‡	‡	†	†	‡	‡	†	‡	†	‡
Two or more races	100.0	45.9 (2.56)	12.8 (1.36)	9.1 (1.54)	5.0 (0.89)	19.0 (1.55)	54.1 (2.56)	1.0 ! (0.31)	†	16.9 (1.62)	10.6 (1.30)	2.3 ! (0.70)	5.8 (1.31)	†	16.5 (1.59)
Race/ethnicity by sex															
Male															
White	100.0	47.3 (0.51)	15.9 (0.38)	15.7 (0.43)	5.6 (0.22)	10.0 (0.28)	52.7 (0.51)	0.7 (0.10)	0.3 (0.07)	23.1 (0.46)	7.3 (0.27)	1.8 (0.14)	3.4 (0.19)	0.9 (0.10)	15.2 (0.42)
Black	100.0	37.4 (1.95)	16.6 (1.48)	9.3 (1.14)	2.4 (0.62)	9.1 (1.21)	62.6 (1.95)	0.7 ! (0.29)	†	23.7 (1.64)	7.7 (1.02)	1.4 (0.41)	7.9 (1.00)	‡	21.0 (1.69)
Hispanic	100.0	39.7 (1.70)	13.7 (1.46)	13.3 (1.04)	4.2 (0.59)	8.5 (0.85)	60.3 (1.70)	0.6 ! (0.22)	†	20.0 (1.50)	7.3 (0.74)	1.5 (0.38)	5.0 (0.82)	0.8 ! (0.30)	24.9 (1.43)
Asian	100.0	63.9 (0.97)	37.5 (0.94)	12.2 (0.72)	4.7 (0.38)	9.6 (0.53)	36.1 (0.97)	0.7 (0.16)	†	16.8 (0.84)	7.9 (0.52)	1.0 (0.21)	0.9 (0.20)	†	8.5 (0.60)
Pacific Islander	100.0	‡	‡	‡	‡	‡	‡	†	†	‡	‡	#	‡	†	‡
American Indian/Alaska Native[2]	100.0	37.9 (8.05)	20.2 ! (7.37)	‡	‡	‡	62.1 (8.05)	‡	†	18.6 ! (7.54)	‡	#	‡	†	23.4 ! (7.87)
American Indian	100.0	35.7 (8.85)	‡	‡	‡	‡	64.3 (8.85)	‡	†	19.9 ! (8.42)	‡	#	‡	†	20.0 ! (8.99)
Alaska Native	‡	‡	‡	‡	†	†	‡	†	†	‡	†	†	‡	†	‡
Two or more races	100.0	47.6 (3.27)	19.9 (2.37)	14.6 (2.63)	4.8 (1.35)	8.3 (1.37)	52.4 (3.27)	1.8 ! (0.60)	†	19.0 (2.79)	7.5 (1.65)	‡	4.1 ! (1.34)	†	17.6 (2.41)
Female															
White	100.0	47.4 (0.46)	3.4 (0.23)	3.1 (0.16)	5.9 (0.23)	35.0 (0.41)	52.6 (0.46)	2.1 (0.15)	0.1 ! (0.03)	16.4 (0.41)	10.0 (0.27)	1.9 (0.15)	6.8 (0.29)	0.1 ! (0.04)	15.3 (0.34)
Black	100.0	35.6 (1.58)	4.3 (0.59)	2.6 (0.50)	2.7 (0.53)	26.0 (1.30)	64.4 (1.58)	3.8 (0.61)	†	17.1 (1.09)	8.6 (0.90)	2.0 (0.44)	12.7 (1.09)	†	19.9 (1.20)
Hispanic	100.0	34.5 (1.27)	2.9 (0.40)	2.7 (0.42)	4.1 (0.50)	24.8 (1.33)	65.5 (1.27)	2.6 (0.44)	†	15.7 (1.04)	12.7 (1.11)	1.7 (0.35)	8.2 (0.77)	#	24.3 (1.54)
Asian	100.0	58.1 (1.15)	19.1 (0.92)	5.2 (0.52)	6.2 (0.56)	27.6 (0.87)	41.9 (1.15)	2.0 (0.38)	†	15.6 (0.78)	8.5 (0.67)	1.7 (0.27)	2.0 (0.31)	†	12.0 (0.70)
Pacific Islander	100.0	‡	‡	‡	‡	‡	‡	†	†	‡	‡	#	‡	†	‡
American Indian/Alaska Native[2]	100.0	39.8 (6.71)	‡	‡	‡	33.1 (7.30)	60.2 (6.71)	‡	†	20.9 (6.60)	10.6 ! (4.12)	#	13.7 ! (6.26)	†	12.5 ! (5.42)
American Indian	100.0	40.5 (7.06)	‡	‡	‡	35.8 (7.70)	59.5 (7.06)	‡	†	19.5 ! (6.43)	11.5 ! (4.39)	#	14.9 ! (6.76)	†	11.0 ! (5.06)
Alaska Native	‡	‡	‡	†	†	‡	‡	†	†	‡	‡	†	‡	†	‡
Two or more races	100.0	44.3 (3.48)	6.0 (1.41)	3.9 (1.16)	5.2 (1.00)	29.2 (2.62)	55.7 (3.48)	‡	†	14.8 (2.10)	13.5 (2.13)	2.3 ! (0.90)	7.4 (1.89)	†	15.4 (2.14)
Nativity															
Hispanic															
U.S.-born[3]	100.0	40.8 (1.35)	8.6 (0.95)	8.2 (0.76)	4.3 (0.42)	19.7 (1.01)	59.2 (1.35)	1.5 (0.27)	†	17.4 (1.15)	9.8 (0.77)	1.6 (0.34)	7.8 (0.79)	0.5 ! (0.18)	20.4 (1.11)
Foreign-born	100.0	29.4 (1.80)	7.8 (1.14)	7.8 (0.96)	3.9 (0.71)	9.8 (1.02)	70.6 (1.80)	1.7 (0.41)	†	18.8 (1.47)	10.2 (1.33)	1.4 ! (0.52)	4.0 (0.68)	‡	33.7 (2.10)
Asian															
U.S.-born[3]	100.0	52.5 (1.65)	12.9 (0.94)	9.3 (0.94)	4.5 (0.57)	25.7 (1.19)	47.5 (1.65)	1.5 (0.37)	#	20.4 (1.22)	6.0 (0.63)	3.7 (0.63)	2.5 (0.52)	†	13.2 (1.07)
Foreign-born	100.0	64.4 (0.93)	35.3 (0.93)	9.3 (0.62)	5.5 (0.38)	14.3 (0.57)	35.6 (0.93)	1.2 (0.21)	†	15.0 (0.72)	8.9 (0.52)	0.6 (0.10)	1.0 (0.19)	†	8.9 (0.48)
Citizenship status															
U.S.-born citizen	100.0	46.0 (0.39)	9.3 (0.21)	8.8 (0.20)	5.0 (0.16)	22.8 (0.30)	54.0 (0.39)	1.5 (0.09)	0.2 (0.03)	19.5 (0.32)	8.4 (0.17)	2.0 (0.09)	5.9 (0.20)	0.5 (0.05)	16.1 (0.27)
Naturalized citizen	100.0	51.1 (1.08)	14.7 (0.85)	9.1 (0.66)	4.4 (0.43)	22.9 (0.87)	48.9 (1.08)	1.8 (0.27)	†	20.1 (0.94)	5.3 (0.53)	1.8 (0.28)	3.2 (0.41)	0.4 (0.12)	16.4 (0.75)
Noncitizen	100.0	57.3 (0.96)	31.8 (0.77)	9.0 (0.56)	6.8 (0.44)	9.7 (0.51)	42.7 (0.96)	1.2 (0.18)	0.2 ! (0.07)	15.1 (0.72)	12.2 (0.59)	0.5 (0.11)	2.3 (0.22)	#	12.3 (0.50)

†Not applicable.

#Rounds to zero.

!Interpret data with caution. The coefficient of variation (CV) for this estimate is between 30 and 50 percent.

‡Reporting standards not met. Either there are too few cases for a reliable estimate or the coefficient of variation (CV) is 50 percent or greater.

[1]Total includes other racial/ethnic groups not shown separately.

[2]Includes persons reporting American Indian alone, persons reporting Alaska Native alone, persons reporting American Indian and/or Alaska Native tribes specified or not specified.

[3]Includes those born in the 50 states, the District of Columbia, Puerto Rico, American Samoa, Guam, the U.S. Virgin Islands, and the Northern Marianas, as well as those born abroad to U.S.-citizen parents.

NOTE: Estimates include persons in the indicated age range who live in households as well as those who live in group quarters (such as college residence halls, residential treatment centers, military barracks, and correctional facilities). This table includes only employed persons who have a bachelor's degree in a STEM field of study. The first bachelor's degree major reported by respondents was used to classify their field of study, even though they were able to report a second bachelor's degree major and may possess advanced degrees in other fields. Aggregated occupation classifications were used to assemble the data, except that managers of STEM activities were counted as practitioners of STEM occupations instead of "Business workers/ managers." Detail may not sum to totals because of rounding. Race categories exclude persons of Hispanic ethnicity. SOURCE: U.S. Department of Commerce, Census Bureau, American Community Survey (ACS), 2012. (This table was prepared April 2014.)

Table 505.40. Percentage distribution of recipients of bachelor's degrees in various fields of study 1 year after graduation, by time to completion, enrollment and employment status, and occupation: 2001 and 2009

[Standard errors appear in parentheses]

Time to completion, enrollment and employment status, and occupation	1999–2000 graduates in 2001, total	2007–08 graduates in 2009 — Total[1]	Engineering	Biological and physical sciences	Mathematics and computer science	Social sciences	History	Humanities	Health professions	Business and management	Education[2]	Psychology	Public affairs and social services
1	2	3	4	5	6	7	8	9	10	11	12	13	14
Total graduates	100.0 (†)	100.0 (†)	100.0 (†)	100.0 (†)	100.0 (†)	100.0 (†)	100.0 (†)	100.0 (†)	100.0 (†)	100.0 (†)	100.0 (†)	100.0 (†)	100.0 (†)
Time between high school graduation and degree completion													
4 years or less	32.7 (0.83)	40.3 (0.64)	35.5 (2.68)	56.2 (2.24)	36.3 (3.27)	53.4 (2.08)	44.1 (3.78)	50.4 (2.02)	28.9 (2.01)	37.5 (1.53)	32.5 (1.65)	48.9 (2.17)	29.1 (3.42)
More than 4, up to 5 years	22.9 (0.58)	20.7 (0.51)	31.0 (2.58)	17.8 (1.74)	16.9 (2.62)	19.2 (1.62)	20.4 (2.81)	20.7 (1.57)	18.1 (1.41)	17.4 (1.09)	25.5 (1.59)	19.5 (1.73)	16.0 (2.85)
More than 5, up to 6 years	10.8 (0.48)	9.5 (0.35)	11.2 (1.69)	9.8 (1.59)	8.4 (1.79)	7.6 (1.09)	12.2 (2.87)	7.9 (1.01)	8.9 (1.14)	8.0 (0.79)	13.2 (1.34)	7.7 (1.10)	10.4 (2.12)
More than 6, up to 10 years	14.8 (0.59)	13.4 (0.42)	11.1 (1.64)	8.9 (1.21)	13.8 (2.25)	11.9 (1.21)	12.4 (2.87)	12.6 (1.40)	16.3 (1.64)	14.1 (1.01)	13.8 (1.32)	11.8 (1.54)	19.0 (3.09)
More than 10 years	18.8 (0.59)	16.0 (0.52)	11.2 (1.89)	7.3 (1.24)	24.6 (2.58)	7.8 (1.05)	10.9 (2.55)	8.3 (1.02)	27.8 (2.13)	23.1 (1.25)	15.0 (1.41)	12.1 (1.61)	25.5 (2.74)
Enrollment status													
Enrolled	20.8 (0.51)	21.7 (0.47)	22.8 (1.98)	40.9 (2.33)	19.9 (2.58)	23.5 (1.65)	38.1 (3.99)	23.6 (1.48)	23.5 (1.93)	13.9 (1.01)	19.9 (1.36)	36.6 (2.15)	24.3 (3.28)
Not enrolled	79.2 (0.51)	78.3 (0.47)	77.2 (1.98)	59.1 (2.33)	80.1 (2.58)	76.5 (1.65)	61.9 (3.99)	76.4 (1.48)	76.5 (1.93)	86.1 (1.01)	80.1 (1.36)	63.4 (2.15)	75.7 (3.28)
Employment status													
Employed	87.4 (0.46)	83.8 (0.49)	88.4 (1.54)	69.6 (1.92)	88.9 (1.88)	78.9 (1.72)	74.9 (3.93)	79.4 (1.58)	86.6 (1.64)	88.1 (0.95)	90.2 (1.12)	79.7 (1.91)	81.2 (2.92)
Full time	76.5 (0.52)	65.0 (0.62)	76.1 (2.12)	49.0 (2.38)	75.1 (2.67)	61.2 (1.94)	46.1 (4.35)	47.6 (2.12)	68.5 (1.86)	76.7 (1.18)	70.7 (1.74)	46.6 (2.40)	69.8 (3.44)
Part time	10.9 (0.40)	18.8 (0.48)	12.3 (1.88)	20.7 (1.84)	13.8 (2.11)	17.6 (1.72)	28.8 (3.66)	31.9 (1.72)	18.0 (1.59)	11.4 (0.92)	19.4 (1.54)	33.1 (2.33)	11.4 (2.15)
Unemployed[3]	6.1 (0.33)	9.2 (0.38)	6.7 (1.15)	7.2 (1.06)	5.8 (1.28)	11.3 (1.32)	14.5 (3.24)	11.8 (1.32)	6.4 (1.07)	8.5 (0.83)	5.1 (0.76)	10.2 (1.42)	13.5 (2.63)
Not in labor force[4]	6.4 (0.35)	7.0 (0.31)	4.9 (1.08)	23.1 (1.99)	5.3 (1.51)	9.9 (1.32)	10.6 (2.39)	8.8 (1.03)	7.0 (1.27)	3.4 (0.51)	4.7 (0.91)	10.0 (1.44)	5.2 (1.52)
Unemployment rate (labor force participants only)[5]	6.5 (—)	9.9 (—)	7.0 (—)	9.4 (—)	6.1 (—)	12.5 (—)	16.2 (—)	12.9 (—)	6.9 (—)	8.8 (—)	5.4 (—)	11.3 (—)	14.3 (—)
Total employed	100.0 (†)	100.0 (†)	100.0 (†)	100.0 (†)	100.0 (†)	100.0 (†)	100.0 (†)	100.0 (†)	100.0 (†)	100.0 (†)	100.0 (†)	100.0 (†)	100.0 (†)
Occupation													
Administrative/clerical	4.5 (0.28)	2.6 (0.21)	‡ (†)	1.9 ! (0.61)	‡ (†)	4.1 (0.88)	4.6 ! (2.17)	4.9 (1.01)	‡ (†)	2.6 (0.51)	‡ (†)	2.9 (0.65)	5.8 ! (2.10)
Arts/communications	4.2 (0.30)	4.5 (0.32)	2.3 ! (1.09)	‡ (†)	1.6 ! (0.65)	3.0 ! (0.92)	‡ (†)	14.4 (1.54)	‡ (†)	1.3 (0.37)	1.0 ! (0.35)	‡ (†)	‡ (†)
Business — Management	12.5 (0.47)	8.4 (0.41)	10.8 (2.08)	3.2 ! (0.96)	3.4 ! (1.24)	9.5 (1.45)	5.0 ! (1.83)	4.8 (0.99)	5.1 (1.10)	14.5 (1.08)	1.6 (0.45)	6.9 (1.43)	11.1 (2.98)
Business — Nonmanagement	15.1 (0.58)	21.1 (0.61)	7.0 (1.54)	10.5 (1.63)	17.0 (2.82)	26.3 (2.05)	19.5 (3.67)	15.8 (1.93)	6.4 (1.14)	43.5 (1.76)	4.0 (0.76)	16.8 (1.98)	11.6 (2.91)
Computer information systems/mathematics[6]	6.8 (0.34)	4.6 (0.27)	7.0 (1.19)	‡ (†)	50.6 (3.28)	3.0 (0.89)	‡ (†)	1.0 ! (0.39)	‡ (†)	4.6 (0.69)	0.6 ! (0.27)	1.8 ! (0.77)	‡ (†)
Construction/trade/transportation	3.1 (0.26)	3.3 (0.23)	5.0 (1.22)	2.5 (0.72)	2.0 ! (0.70)	2.2 (0.61)	5.1 ! (2.51)	4.2 (1.01)	‡ (†)	4.2 (0.59)	0.9 ! (0.31)	1.7 (0.50)	‡ (†)
Education	18.1 (0.52)	15.6 (0.43)	5.2 (1.26)	16.3 (2.12)	12.5 (2.01)	11.4 (1.45)	27.9 (3.49)	19.1 (1.74)	3.5 (0.72)	3.1 (0.55)	78.7 (1.61)	12.7 (1.41)	13.1 (2.69)
Engineering/engineering technician/science	8.4 (0.33)	6.2 (0.30)	55.6 (3.02)	28.8 (2.39)	2.2 ! (0.93)	1.0 ! (0.38)	‡ (†)	0.8 ! (0.32)	‡ (†)	1.3 (0.35)	0.2 ! (0.09)	1.7 ! (0.74)	# (†)
Health professions	7.8 (0.26)	8.6 (0.30)	1.1 ! (0.53)	13.5 (1.62)	‡ (†)	3.3 (0.84)	3.7 ! (1.68)	2.4 ! (0.78)	74.4 (2.00)	1.2 (0.32)	1.2 ! (0.48)	7.0 (1.38)	2.3 ! (1.06)
Military/protective service	2.4 (0.20)	2.9 (0.24)	1.6 ! (0.72)	2.9 ! (0.89)	2.3 ! (1.12)	6.3 (1.08)	6.5 ! (2.23)	0.9 ! (0.39)	1.9 ! (0.68)	2.4 (0.46)	0.8 ! (0.35)	1.8 ! (0.69)	7.0 ! (2.79)
Sales	6.8 (0.31)	7.9 (0.40)	2.1 (0.61)	7.4 (1.78)	1.6 ! (0.70)	7.4 (1.29)	8.9 ! (3.28)	9.8 (1.34)	‡ (†)	12.9 (1.12)	1.7 (0.44)	7.4 (1.37)	5.5 ! (2.21)
Other occupations	10.2 (0.42)	14.3 (0.43)	2.0 ! (0.65)	10.9 (1.65)	4.3 ! (1.40)	22.4 (2.16)	13.0 (2.53)	21.8 (1.77)	4.6 (0.87)	8.8 (1.08)	9.2 (1.22)	38.5 (2.19)	42.4 (4.03)

—Not available.
†Not applicable.
#Rounds to zero.
!Interpret data with caution. The coefficient of variation (CV) for this estimate is between 30 and 50 percent. The coefficient of variation (CV) for this estimate is 50 percent or greater.
‡Reporting standards not met.
[1]Includes graduates in other fields not separately shown.
[2]Includes graduates who have not finished all requirements for teaching certification or were previously qualified to teach.
[3]Percentage of all graduates who are not employed, but are looking for work.
[4]Percentage of all graduates who are neither employed nor looking for work.

[5]The labor force is made up of persons who are employed and persons who are not employed but are looking for work. (It does not include those who are neither employed nor looking for work.) The unemployment rate is the percentage of labor force participants who are not employed but are actively seeking work.
[6]For 2001, does not include mathematics professions.
NOTE: Data exclude bachelor's degree recipients from U.S. Service Academies, deceased graduates, and graduates living at foreign addresses at the time of the survey. Detail may not sum to totals because of rounding.
SOURCE: U.S. Department of Education, National Center for Education Statistics, 2000/01 and 2008/09 Baccalaureate and Beyond Longitudinal Study (B&B:2000/01 and B&B:08/09). (This table was prepared August 2011.)

Table 505.50. Percentage, selected employment characteristics, and annual salaries of bachelor's degree recipients employed full time 1 year after graduation, by field of study: 1991, 2001, and 2009

[Standard errors appear in parentheses]

Selected employment characteristic and annual salary	All fields of study[1]	Engineering	Biological and physical sciences[2]	Mathematics and computer science[2]	Social sciences and history	Humanities	Health professions	Business and management	Education[3]	Psychology	Public affairs and social services
1	2	3	4	5	6	7	8	9	10	11	12
Employment characteristics											
Percent of recipients employed full time											
1989–90 recipients in June 1991	73.8 (0.36)	85.2 (0.95)	50.6 (1.72)	71.2 (1.30)	66.2 (0.94)	59.2 (1.32)	80.9 (1.35)	83.2 (0.57)	77.0 (0.74)	59.8 (1.64)	77.0 (2.06)
1999–2000 recipients in July 2001	76.5 (0.52)	86.0 (1.77)	58.6 (2.04)	83.7 (2.06)	68.3 (1.88)	67.5 (1.65)	74.8 (1.50)	85.5 (1.27)	84.0 (1.29)	64.0 (2.64)	85.1 (2.25)
2007–08 recipients in June 2009	65.0 (0.62)	76.1 (2.12)	49.0 (2.38)	75.1 (2.67)	58.0 (1.81)	50.4 (1.82)	68.5 (1.86)	77.2 (1.20)	70.6 (1.75)	46.6 (2.40)	69.8 (3.44)
Percent of full-time employees looking for a different job[4]											
1989–90 recipients in June 1991	21.5 (0.35)	12.9 (1.05)	21.0 (1.95)	16.6 (1.08)	24.5 (1.20)	25.8 (1.44)	9.2 (1.10)	20.7 (0.78)	25.5 (0.92)	21.8 (1.57)	26.8 (2.36)
1999–2000 recipients in July 2001	24.6 (0.66)	19.2 (2.30)	22.9 (2.64)	18.3 (2.36)	27.1 (2.06)	28.3 (2.13)	20.9 (1.93)	24.4 (1.51)	17.4 (1.45)	23.9 (2.54)	25.8 (2.80)
2007–08 recipients in June 2009	31.2 (0.74)	20.2 (2.53)	28.5 (3.47)	27.7 (3.37)	35.3 (2.47)	39.2 (2.56)	21.8 (2.40)	32.0 (1.61)	23.6 (1.78)	37.3 (2.99)	30.4 (4.86)
Percent of full-time employees in job closely related to field of study											
1989–90 recipients in June 1991	52.5 (0.55)	57.5 (1.24)	49.4 (2.31)	66.4 (1.34)	20.2 (1.12)	32.2 (2.07)	88.2 (2.10)	49.8 (0.79)	79.2 (0.89)	40.3 (2.13)	57.6 (2.56)
1999–2000 recipients in July 2001	56.1 (0.65)	70.0 (3.35)	48.6 (3.00)	72.7 (2.58)	28.7 (2.03)	41.5 (2.16)	77.5 (2.45)	58.7 (1.67)	84.3 (1.68)	40.1 (3.65)	61.2 (3.11)
2007–08 recipients in June 2009	49.7 (0.78)	61.3 (2.86)	49.0 (3.36)	61.9 (3.57)	21.6 (2.07)	27.6 (2.56)	81.7 (2.10)	49.3 (1.76)	82.0 (1.68)	26.6 (3.04)	57.2 (4.93)
Annual salaries of full-time employees[5]											
Average salary, in current dollars											
1989–90 recipients in June 1991	$23,600 (180)	$30,900 (390)	$21,100 (410)	$27,200 (400)	$22,100 (330)	$19,100 (350)	$31,500 (860)	$24,700 (330)	$19,100 (140)	$19,200 (310)	$20,900 (470)
1999–2000 recipients in July 2001	35,400 (300)	47,900 (840)	31,000 (710)	47,400 (1,080)	33,000 (700)	30,100 (690)	39,400 (1,110)	41,000 (860)	27,600 (370)	28,800 (990)	30,400 (1,030)
2007–08 recipients in June 2009	40,100 (340)	53,900 (1,080)	34,600 (1,220)	48,800 (1,570)	36,600 (980)	31,100 (780)	49,100 (1,290)	44,200 (890)	33,000 (490)	30,600 (910)	35,000 (1,700)
Average salary, in constant 2013 dollars											
1989–90 recipients in June 1991	$40,400 (310)	$52,900 (670)	$36,000 (710)	$46,500 (680)	$37,800 (570)	$32,600 (610)	$53,800 (1,470)	$42,300 (560)	$32,700 (230)	$32,800 (540)	$35,700 (800)
1999–2000 recipients in July 2001	46,600 (390)	63,100 (1,100)	40,800 (940)	62,400 (1,420)	43,400 (930)	39,600 (910)	51,900 (1,460)	54,000 (1,130)	36,300 (480)	37,900 (1,300)	40,000 (1,360)
2007–08 recipients in June 2009	43,500 (370)	58,500 (1,180)	37,600 (1,320)	53,000 (1,710)	39,700 (1,070)	33,800 (840)	53,400 (1,400)	47,900 (970)	35,800 (530)	33,200 (990)	38,000 (1,850)
Percent change in average salary, in constant 2013 dollars											
1991 to 2009	7.6	10.6	4.4	14.1	5.1	3.5	-0.8	13.2	9.5	1.5	6.6
1991 to 2001	15.2	19.2	13.2	34.3	14.7	21.4	-3.6	27.4	11.2	15.8	12.1
2001 to 2009	-6.6	-7.2	-7.7	-15.0	-8.4	-14.7	2.8	-11.1	-1.5	-12.4	-4.9
Median salary, in current dollars											
1989–90 recipients in June 1991	$21,800 (210)	$31,900 (470)	$20,000 (430)	$27,000 (510)	$20,300 (250)	$18,500 (360)	$30,400 (760)	$23,000 (300)	$19,500 (220)	$18,100 (320)	$18,600 (410)
1999–2000 recipients in July 2001	32,000 (90)	47,800 (880)	29,800 (470)	46,100 (1,990)	29,900 (360)	28,600 (700)	35,500 (770)	36,800 (700)	27,900 (410)	27,700 (1,180)	27,900 (710)
2007–08 recipients in June 2009	36,000 (220)	54,000 (900)	32,500 (1,570)	45,000 (1,830)	34,600 (920)	29,000 (1,060)	45,900 (920)	40,000 (300)	33,800 (570)	29,300 (1,040)	32,000 (1,430)
Median salary, in constant 2013 dollars											
1989–90 recipients in June 1991	$37,300 (350)	$54,500 (810)	$34,100 (730)	$46,100 (880)	$34,600 (430)	$31,600 (610)	$52,000 (1,300)	$39,300 (510)	$33,400 (380)	$31,000 (550)	$31,800 (700)
1999–2000 recipients in July 2001	42,000 (120)	62,900 (1,160)	39,200 (620)	60,600 (2,610)	39,300 (470)	37,600 (920)	46,700 (1,020)	48,400 (920)	36,800 (550)	36,500 (1,550)	36,700 (940)
2007–08 recipients in June 2009	39,100 (240)	58,600 (980)	35,200 (1,710)	48,900 (1,990)	37,600 (990)	31,500 (1,150)	49,900 (1,000)	43,400 (320)	36,700 (620)	31,900 (1,130)	34,700 (1,550)
Percent change in median salary, in constant 2013 dollars											
1991 to 2009	4.9	7.5	3.2	6.0	8.5	-0.3	-4.1	10.5	10.0	2.8	9.2
1991 to 2001	12.8	15.4	14.9	31.5	13.5	19.1	-10.2	23.2	10.1	17.9	15.4
2001 to 2009	-7.0	-6.8	-10.1	-19.4	-4.5	-16.3	6.9	-10.3	-0.1	-12.7	-5.4

—Not available.

[1]Includes graduates in other fields not separately shown.

[2]For 1991, physical sciences not included in column 4 with biological sciences; instead, they are included in column 5 with mathematics and computer science.

[3]Most educators work 9- to 10-month contracts.

[4]In 1991, respondents were asked whether they were "looking for a different principal job." In 2001 and 2009, they were asked whether they were "looking for a different job" (instead of "a different principal job").

[5]In all years, reported salaries of full-time workers under $1,000 were excluded from the tabulations. In addition, salaries reported as above $500,000 were set to $500,000 in 2001, and salaries reported as above $250,000 were set to $250,000 in 2009. In all years, only a tiny fraction of reported full-time salaries were either below $1,000 or above $250,000. NOTE: Data exclude bachelor's degree recipients from U.S. Service Academies, deceased graduates, and graduates living at foreign addresses at the time of the survey. Constant dollars based on the Consumer Price Index, prepared by the Bureau of Labor Statistics, U.S. Department of Labor. Some data have been revised from previously published figures. SOURCE: U.S. Department of Education, National Center for Education Statistics, "Recent College Graduates" survey, 1991; and 2000/01 and 2008/09 Baccalaureate and Beyond Longitudinal Study (B&B:2000/01 and B&B:08/09). (This table was prepared November 2014.)

Table 506.10. Percentage of 1972 high school seniors, 1992 high school seniors, and 2004 high school seniors who felt that certain life values were "very important," by sex: Selected years, 1972 through 2004

[Standard errors appear in parentheses]

Year and sex	Being successful in work	Finding steady work	Having lots of money	Being a leader in the community	Helping others in the community	Correcting inequalities	Having children	Having a happy family life	Giving my children better opportunities	Living close to parents or relatives	Moving from area	Having strong friendships	Having leisure time
1	2	3	4	5	6	7	8	9	10	11	12	13	14
1972 seniors													
In 1972													
Total	84.5 (0.35)	78.2 (0.39)	17.9 (0.36)	11.4 (0.29)	— (†)	27.1 (0.41)	— (†)	82.1 (0.36)	67.7 (0.44)	8.0 (0.25)	14.3 (0.33)	79.1 (0.37)	— (†)
Male	86.4 (0.47)	82.3 (0.52)	25.8 (0.58)	14.9 (0.47)	— (†)	23.0 (0.55)	— (†)	79.0 (0.55)	67.4 (0.62)	7.4 (0.34)	14.0 (0.46)	80.5 (0.52)	— (†)
Female	82.6 (0.51)	74.1 (0.58)	10.1 (0.38)	7.9 (0.34)	— (†)	31.2 (0.60)	— (†)	85.2 (0.47)	67.9 (0.61)	8.7 (0.37)	14.7 (0.47)	77.6 (0.53)	— (†)
In 1974													
Total	77.2 (0.40)	66.9 (0.44)	13.1 (0.31)	6.1 (0.21)	— (†)	16.6 (0.34)	— (†)	84.8 (0.34)	59.4 (0.45)	9.9 (0.28)	7.6 (0.25)	75.4 (0.40)	57.9 (0.46)
Male	80.3 (0.54)	74.4 (0.59)	17.6 (0.51)	8.2 (0.35)	— (†)	15.8 (0.47)	— (†)	82.7 (0.51)	58.8 (0.65)	8.0 (0.36)	7.9 (0.36)	76.2 (0.57)	60.6 (0.65)
Female	74.2 (0.58)	59.7 (0.64)	8.6 (0.36)	4.1 (0.25)	— (†)	17.3 (0.48)	— (†)	86.9 (0.44)	60.0 (0.63)	11.8 (0.42)	7.3 (0.34)	74.7 (0.56)	55.4 (0.65)
In 1976													
Total	74.5 (0.41)	70.4 (0.43)	13.0 (0.31)	6.2 (0.22)	— (†)	16.1 (0.34)	— (†)	85.1 (0.34)	57.9 (0.46)	9.3 (0.27)	6.4 (0.23)	74.3 (0.41)	62.6 (0.45)
Male	79.8 (0.55)	79.3 (0.55)	17.1 (0.50)	8.7 (0.36)	— (†)	15.6 (0.48)	— (†)	84.2 (0.50)	58.8 (0.65)	7.2 (0.34)	6.6 (0.33)	76.4 (0.57)	65.1 (0.64)
Female	69.3 (0.61)	61.6 (0.64)	9.0 (0.37)	3.8 (0.24)	— (†)	16.5 (0.48)	— (†)	85.9 (0.46)	57.1 (0.64)	11.4 (0.42)	6.3 (0.32)	72.3 (0.58)	60.0 (0.64)
1992 seniors													
In 1992													
Total	88.8 (0.44)	88.5 (0.41)	37.1 (0.63)	— (†)	33.8 (0.63)	20.2 (0.55)	44.6 (0.65)	79.0 (0.57)	76.0 (0.56)	16.6 (0.46)	20.6 (0.55)	80.0 (0.52)	64.0 (0.64)
Male	88.3 (0.69)	87.8 (0.59)	45.6 (0.98)	— (†)	27.9 (0.93)	17.1 (0.72)	39.5 (0.96)	75.8 (0.89)	74.6 (0.83)	14.9 (0.60)	20.9 (0.83)	79.8 (0.70)	66.3 (0.95)
Female	89.3 (0.53)	89.2 (0.56)	28.6 (0.79)	— (†)	39.7 (0.86)	23.3 (0.83)	49.7 (0.87)	82.1 (0.72)	77.3 (0.75)	18.2 (0.68)	20.3 (0.71)	80.3 (0.77)	61.7 (0.84)
In 1994													
Total	89.7 (0.38)	89.7 (0.40)	36.9 (0.63)	— (†)	— (†)	— (†)	— (†)	—	91.3 (0.34)	— (†)	— (†)	86.2 (0.44)	— (†)
Male	89.6 (0.55)	89.1 (0.61)	41.3 (0.94)	— (†)	— (†)	— (†)	— (†)	—	91.1 (0.52)	— (†)	— (†)	87.2 (0.58)	— (†)
Female	89.7 (0.52)	90.3 (0.52)	32.5 (0.86)	— (†)	— (†)	— (†)	— (†)	—	91.5 (0.43)	— (†)	— (†)	85.1 (0.65)	— (†)
2004 seniors													
In 2004													
Total	91.3 (0.33)	87.3 (0.40)	35.1 (0.58)	— (†)	41.7 (0.57)	19.7 (0.46)	49.3 (0.55)	81.0 (0.46)	82.5 (0.45)	24.5 (0.50)	18.3 (0.45)	85.5 (0.41)	69.0 (0.55)
Male	89.7 (0.49)	85.6 (0.55)	42.7 (0.80)	— (†)	35.2 (0.77)	18.1 (0.60)	45.4 (0.75)	80.1 (0.63)	82.1 (0.64)	22.3 (0.65)	18.6 (0.63)	84.9 (0.56)	70.2 (0.69)
Female	92.9 (0.40)	89.0 (0.49)	27.6 (0.69)	— (†)	48.1 (0.74)	21.2 (0.67)	53.2 (0.78)	81.9 (0.64)	82.9 (0.58)	26.6 (0.74)	17.9 (0.59)	86.1 (0.57)	67.8 (0.74)

—Not available.
†Not applicable.
SOURCE: U.S. Department of Education, National Center for Education Statistics, National Longitudinal Study of the High School Class of 1972, "Base Year" (NLS:72), "Second Follow-up" (NLS:72/74), and "Third Follow-up" (NLS:72/76); National Education Longitudinal Study of 1988, "Second Follow-up, Student Survey, 1992" (NELS:88/92) and "Third Follow-up, 1994" (NELS:88/94); and Education Longitudinal Study of 2002, "First Follow-up" (ELS:02/04). (This table was prepared October 2011.)

Table 507.10. Literacy skills of adults, by type of literacy, proficiency levels, and selected characteristics: 1992 and 2003

[Standard errors appear in parentheses]

Selected characteristic	Prose literacy[1] Average score 1992	2003	Prose — Below Basic 2003	Basic	Intermediate	Proficient	Document literacy[2] Average score 1992	2003	Document — Below Basic 2003	Basic	Intermediate	Proficient	Quantitative literacy[3] Average score 1992	2003	Quantitative — Below Basic 2003	Basic	Intermediate	Proficient
1	2	3	4	5	6	7	8	9	10	11	12	13	14	15	16	17	18	19
Total	276 (1.1)	275 (1.3)	14 (0.6)	29 (0.6)	44 (0.7)	13 (0.5)	271 (1.1)	271 (1.2)	12 (0.5)	22 (0.5)	53 (0.7)	13 (0.6)	275 (1.1)	283 (1.2)	22 (0.6)	33 (0.5)	33 (0.5)	13 (0.5)
Sex																		
Male	276 (1.2)	272 (1.5)	15 (0.6)	29 (0.7)	43 (0.7)	13 (0.6)	274 (1.2)	269 (1.5)	14 (0.6)	23 (0.5)	51 (0.8)	13 (0.6)	283 (1.4)	286 (1.3)	21 (0.6)	31 (0.5)	33 (0.5)	16 (0.6)
Female	277 (1.3)	277 (1.4)	12 (0.6)	29 (0.6)	46 (0.8)	14 (0.8)	268 (1.2)	272 (1.2)	11 (0.6)	22 (0.6)	54 (0.8)	13 (0.6)	269 (1.2)	279 (1.3)	22 (0.8)	35 (0.7)	32 (0.7)	11 (0.6)
Age																		
16 to 18 years old	270 (2.3)	267 (2.8)	11 (1.7)	37 (2.5)	48 (2.7)	5 (1.4)	270 (2.2)	268 (2.9)	11 (1.4)	24 (1.8)	56 (2.4)	9 (1.7)	264 (2.5)	267 (3.1)	28 (2.3)	38 (2.1)	28 (2.1)	6 (1.3)
19 to 24 years old	280 (2.0)	276 (2.4)	11 (1.1)	29 (1.3)	48 (1.5)	12 (1.1)	282 (2.2)	277 (2.5)	9 (1.1)	20 (1.1)	58 (1.1)	13 (1.5)	277 (2.2)	279 (2.3)	21 (1.4)	36 (1.3)	33 (1.4)	10 (1.1)
25 to 39 years old	288 (1.3)	283 (1.7)	12 (0.6)	25 (0.7)	45 (0.7)	18 (0.8)	286 (1.2)	282 (1.8)	8 (0.7)	19 (0.7)	56 (1.1)	17 (1.1)	286 (1.3)	292 (1.9)	17 (0.8)	31 (0.8)	35 (0.8)	17 (0.9)
40 to 54 years old	293 (1.4)	282 (2.3)	11 (0.9)	27 (1.1)	47 (1.1)	15 (1.1)	284 (1.9)	277 (1.8)	10 (0.7)	20 (0.8)	54 (1.2)	15 (0.9)	292 (1.8)	289 (1.9)	19 (0.9)	32 (0.8)	34 (0.8)	16 (0.8)
55 to 64 years old	269 (1.4)	278 (1.9)	13 (0.8)	27 (0.9)	44 (1.1)	15 (0.8)	258 (1.4)	258 (2.1)	12 (0.9)	23 (0.9)	54 (1.2)	12 (1.1)	272 (1.8)	289 (1.9)	19 (1.0)	30 (1.0)	34 (0.9)	17 (0.8)
65 years old and older	235 (1.7)	248 (2.0)	23 (1.3)	38 (1.2)	34 (1.4)	4 (0.6)	221 (2.2)	235 (2.0)	27 (1.5)	33 (1.0)	38 (1.4)	3 (0.4)	235 (2.7)	257 (2.2)	34 (1.6)	37 (1.2)	24 (1.2)	5 (0.6)
Race/ethnicity																		
White	287 (1.2)	288 (1.5)	7 (0.5)	25 (0.8)	51 (0.9)	17 (0.9)	281 (1.2)	282 (1.5)	8 (0.5)	19 (0.7)	58 (1.0)	15 (1.0)	288 (1.1)	297 (1.3)	13 (0.7)	32 (0.7)	39 (0.8)	17 (0.8)
Black	237 (1.4)	243 (1.8)	24 (1.4)	43 (1.2)	31 (1.4)	2 (0.4)	230 (1.4)	238 (2.1)	24 (1.7)	35 (1.4)	40 (1.9)	2 (0.5)	222 (1.6)	238 (2.2)	47 (1.8)	36 (1.8)	15 (1.1)	4 (0.4)
Hispanic	234 (4.0)	216 (3.5)	44 (1.8)	30 (1.0)	23 (1.1)	4 (0.4)	238 (1.8)	224 (3.6)	36 (1.6)	26 (0.8)	33 (1.2)	5 (0.5)	233 (2.3)	233 (3.2)	50 (1.7)	29 (0.9)	17 (0.9)	4 (0.5)
Asian/Pacific Islander	255 (6.1)	271 (4.0)	14 (2.0)	32 (2.2)	42 (2.5)	12 (1.8)	259 (6.1)	272 (5.0)	11 (2.2)	22 (2.1)	54 (3.0)	13 (2.3)	268 (7.8)	285 (5.1)	19 (3.0)	34 (2.9)	35 (2.8)	12 (2.5)
Highest level of education																		
Still in high school	268 (2.5)	262 (3.7)	14 (2.5)	37 (2.8)	45 (3.1)	4! (1.5)	270 (2.4)	265 (4.3)	13 (2.3)	24 (2.2)	54 (3.0)	9 (1.9)	263 (3.2)	261 (4.2)	31 (2.9)	38 (2.5)	25 (2.3)	5 (1.4)
Less than high school completion	216 (1.4)	207 (2.4)	50 (1.4)	33 (1.0)	16 (0.9)	1 (0.2)	211 (1.5)	208 (2.6)	45 (1.4)	29 (0.7)	25 (1.0)	2 (0.3)	209 (2.1)	211 (2.2)	64 (1.3)	25 (0.8)	10 (0.7)	1 (0.2)
GED/high school equivalency	265 (2.2)	260 (2.1)	10 (1.8)	45 (2.9)	43 (3.0)	3! (1.1)	259 (2.3)	257 (2.5)	13 (2.3)	30 (2.3)	53 (2.8)	4! (1.2)	265 (2.3)	265 (3.1)	26 (3.1)	43 (3.1)	28 (2.9)	3! (1.2)
High school graduate	268 (1.0)	262 (1.3)	13 (1.0)	39 (1.2)	44 (1.3)	4 (0.6)	261 (1.4)	258 (1.5)	13 (1.0)	29 (1.0)	52 (1.4)	5 (0.7)	267 (1.4)	269 (1.6)	24 (1.4)	42 (1.3)	29 (2.3)	5 (0.7)
Vocational/trade/business	278 (2.1)	268 (2.7)	10 (1.8)	36 (2.6)	49 (2.7)	5! (1.5)	273 (2.0)	267 (2.5)	9 (2.3)	26 (2.3)	59 (2.7)	7 (1.7)	280 (2.2)	279 (2.2)	18 (2.0)	41 (2.0)	35 (2.4)	6 (1.4)
Some college	292 (1.6)	282 (1.6)	5 (0.7)	35 (1.4)	56 (1.7)	11 (1.4)	288 (1.9)	280 (1.7)	5 (0.8)	19 (1.3)	65 (1.8)	10 (1.5)	295 (1.7)	294 (1.7)	10 (1.2)	36 (1.8)	43 (1.8)	11 (1.5)
Associate's degree	306 (1.9)	298 (2.4)	4 (0.7)	20 (1.5)	56 (2.0)	19 (2.0)	301 (1.9)	291 (2.0)	5 (0.7)	15 (1.5)	66 (2.0)	16 (2.2)	305 (2.0)	305 (2.1)	7 (1.1)	30 (1.9)	45 (1.5)	18 (2.1)
Bachelor's degree	325 (1.9)	314 (2.1)	3 (0.5)	14 (1.0)	53 (1.7)	31 (1.8)	317 (1.9)	303 (2.2)	2! (0.6)	11 (1.2)	62 (2.5)	25 (2.7)	323 (1.8)	323 (1.8)	4 (0.6)	22 (1.5)	43 (2.1)	31 (1.9)
Graduate studies/degree	340 (2.0)	327 (2.8)	3! (0.4)	10 (1.2)	48 (2.3)	41 (2.6)	328 (1.9)	311 (2.1)	2! (0.4)	9 (1.1)	59 (2.6)	31 (2.8)	336 (2.1)	332 (2.1)	3 (0.6)	18 (1.5)	43 (2.1)	36 (2.6)
Employment																		
Full-time	290 (1.3)	285 (1.5)	— (†)	— (†)	— (†)	— (†)	286 (1.2)	281 (1.2)	— (†)	— (†)	— (†)	— (†)	292 (1.3)	296 (1.1)	— (†)	— (†)	— (†)	— (†)
Part-time	285 (1.7)	281 (2.2)	— (†)	— (†)	— (†)	— (†)	279 (1.8)	277 (2.2)	— (†)	— (†)	— (†)	— (†)	281 (1.7)	287 (2.2)	— (†)	— (†)	— (†)	— (†)
Unemployed	263 (2.3)	269 (2.8)	— (†)	— (†)	— (†)	— (†)	261 (2.2)	265 (0.3)	— (†)	— (†)	— (†)	— (†)	261 (3.2)	270 (3.6)	— (†)	— (†)	— (†)	— (†)
Not in labor force	252 (1.4)	255 (1.7)	— (†)	— (†)	— (†)	— (†)	244 (1.5)	250 (1.9)	— (†)	— (†)	— (†)	— (†)	247 (1.9)	261 (1.8)	— (†)	— (†)	— (†)	— (†)
Language spoken before starting school																		
English only	282 (1.2)	283 (1.4)	9 (0.5)	27 (0.7)	49 (0.8)	15 (0.7)	275 (1.2)	276 (1.3)	9 (0.5)	21 (0.6)	56 (0.8)	13 (0.7)	280 (1.2)	289 (1.2)	18 (0.6)	33 (0.6)	35 (0.6)	15 (0.6)
English and Spanish	255 (2.9)	262 (3.1)	14 (2.1)	38 (2.2)	42 (2.4)	6 (1.3)	253 (3.6)	259 (3.4)	12 (2.5)	29 (3.0)	54 (3.8)	5! (1.8)	247 (4.6)	261 (3.8)	31 (3.3)	39 (2.6)	26 (2.8)	4! (1.3)
English and other language	273 (4.0)	278 (3.8)	7 (1.8)	35 (2.8)	51 (3.1)	9 (2.5)	260 (4.5)	268 (3.2)	10 (2.0)	25 (2.3)	57 (2.9)	8 (2.0)	271 (5.6)	289 (4.1)	15 (2.7)	38 (2.7)	34 (3.0)	14 (2.6)
Spanish	205 (2.9)	188 (3.8)	61 (1.8)	25 (1.1)	13 (0.9)	1! (0.3)	216 (2.4)	199 (4.2)	49 (2.0)	25 (1.0)	23 (1.3)	3 (0.4)	212 (3.3)	211 (4.6)	62 (2.2)	25 (1.7)	11 (1.1)	2 (0.5)
Other language	239 (3.4)	249 (4.6)	26 (2.2)	33 (2.3)	34 (2.3)	7 (1.3)	241 (3.7)	257 (4.2)	20 (1.9)	24 (1.3)	46 (1.9)	10 (1.2)	246 (4.3)	246 (4.3)	28 (2.3)	33 (1.7)	29 (1.5)	10 (1.5)

—Not available.
†Not applicable.
!Interpret data with caution. The coefficient of variation (CV) for this estimate is between 30 and 50 percent.

[1]Prose literacy refers to the knowledge and skills needed to search, comprehend, and use information from continuous texts. Adults at the Below Basic level, rated 0 to 209, range from being nonliterate in English to being able to locate easily identifiable information in short, commonplace prose texts. At the Basic level, rated 210 to 264, adults are able to read and understand moderately dense, less commonplace prose texts as well as summarize, make simple inferences, determine cause and effect, and recognize the author's purpose. At the Proficient level, rated 340 to 500, adults are able to read lengthy, complex, abstract prose texts as well as synthesize information and make complex inferences.

[2]Document literacy refers to the knowledge and skills needed to search, comprehend, and use information from noncontinuous texts in various formats. Adults at the Below Basic level, rated 0 to 204, range from being nonliterate in English to being able to locate easily identifiable information and follow instructions in simple documents (e.g., charts or forms). At the Basic level, rated 205 to 249, adults are able to read and understand information in simple documents. At the Intermediate level, rated 250 to 334, adults are able to make simple inferences about the information. At the Proficient level, rated 350 to 500, adults are able to integrate, synthesize, and analyze multiple pieces of information located in complex documents.

[3]Quantitative literacy refers to the knowledge and skills required to identify and perform computations, either alone or sequentially, using numbers embedded in printed materials. Adults at the Below Basic level, rated 0 to 234, range from being nonliterate in English to being able to locate numbers and use them to perform simple quantitative operations (primarily addition) when the mathematical information is very concrete and familiar. At the Basic level, rated 235 to 289, adults are able to locate easily identifiable quantitative information and use it to solve simple, one-step problems when the arithmetic operation is specified or easily inferred. At the Intermediate level, rated 290 to 349, adults are able to locate less familiar quantitative information and use it to solve problems when the arithmetic operation is not specified or easily inferred. At the Proficient level, rated 350 to 500, adults are able to locate more abstract quantitative information and use it to solve multistep problems when the arithmetic operations are not easily inferred and the problems are more complex.

NOTE: Adults are defined as people age 16 and older living in households or prisons. Adults who could not be interviewed due to language spoken or cognitive or mental disabilities (3 percent in 2003 and 4 percent in 1992) are excluded from this table. Race categories exclude persons of Hispanic ethnicity. Totals include racial/ethnic groups not separately shown. Detail may not sum to totals because of rounding.

SOURCE: U.S. Department of Education, National Center for Education Statistics, 1992 National Adult Literacy Survey (NALS) and 2003 National Assessment of Adult Literacy (NAAL), A First Look at the Literacy of America's Adults in the 21st Century, and supplemental data retrieved July 6, 2006, from http://nces.ed.gov/naal/Excel/2006470_DataTable.xls. (This table was prepared July 2006.)

Table 507.20. Participants in state-administered adult basic education, secondary education, and English as a second language programs, by type of program and state or jurisdiction: Selected fiscal years, 2000 through 2012

State or jurisdiction	2000, total	2005, total	2010, total	2011 Total	2011 Adult basic education	2011 Adult secondary education	2011 English as a second language	2012 Total	2012 Adult basic education	2012 Adult secondary education	2012 English as a second language
1	2	3	4	5	6	7	8	9	10	11	12
United States	2,629,643	2,543,953	1,990,118	1,792,527	847,792	212,390	732,345	1,690,211	819,465	193,979	676,767
Alabama	23,666	19,827	24,339	23,338	17,628	4,199	1,511	24,375	18,323	4,021	2,031
Alaska............................	5,312	3,791	3,176	2,928	1,875	278	775	2,986	1,914	276	796
Arizona	31,136	26,881	18,552	17,719	10,540	1,251	5,928	17,554	10,110	1,218	6,226
Arkansas........................	38,867	37,102	27,603	25,406	16,104	5,028	4,274	22,462	14,053	4,123	4,286
California	473,050	591,893	392,918	354,066	95,891	32,266	225,909	302,169	85,347	31,079	185,743
Colorado	13,818	15,011	12,873	10,812	3,661	1,087	6,064	10,579	3,952	1,069	5,558
Connecticut....................	30,844	31,958	25,924	24,120	7,030	5,836	11,254	18,024	6,611	5,375	6,038
Delaware........................	4,342	6,329	4,961	4,922	3,068	592	1,262	4,899	2,926	621	1,352
District of Columbia	3,667	3,646	3,808	3,145	1,546	171	1,428	3,356	1,570	189	1,597
Florida............................	404,912	348,119	239,653	168,664	74,624	21,400	72,640	147,474	66,360	16,213	64,901
Georgia..........................	108,004	95,434	64,668	60,235	41,878	5,267	13,090	55,747	38,816	3,995	12,936
Hawaii............................	10,525	7,461	9,058	8,654	3,746	2,283	2,625	6,677	2,995	1,524	2,158
Idaho..............................	10,506	7,744	6,675	6,329	3,897	489	1,943	5,633	3,286	406	1,941
Illinois............................	122,043	118,296	96,620	91,697	26,456	13,715	51,526	85,698	29,072	9,122	47,504
Indiana...........................	42,135	43,498	28,571	28,791	19,687	4,647	4,457	30,440	21,553	4,668	4,219
Iowa...............................	20,161	11,989	11,167	10,921	4,948	1,926	4,047	9,244	4,137	1,703	3,404
Kansas...........................	11,248	9,475	8,100	7,642	3,864	898	2,880	9,560	5,113	1,237	3,210
Kentucky	31,050	30,931	38,654	39,487	26,640	9,070	3,777	37,909	25,106	8,683	4,120
Louisiana........................	30,929	29,367	27,270	26,747	21,730	3,279	1,738	24,421	19,728	3,014	1,679
Maine..............................	12,430	8,151	6,776	6,433	3,682	1,481	1,270	6,373	3,634	1,358	1,381
Maryland.........................	22,702	27,055	32,833	31,094	14,102	3,899	13,093	31,029	13,921	3,270	13,838
Massachusetts.................	24,053	21,448	20,314	21,369	4,800	3,668	12,901	19,726	4,773	3,462	11,491
Michigan.........................	56,096	34,768	25,745	28,614	17,335	2,697	8,582	29,533	18,505	2,746	8,282
Minnesota.......................	42,039	47,174	46,009	43,449	18,052	5,806	19,591	43,844	18,662	5,801	19,381
Mississippi......................	37,947	25,675	16,854	16,403	13,900	2,252	251	14,799	12,612	1,931	256
Missouri..........................	41,089	37,052	31,397	28,307	19,289	3,261	5,757	27,888	19,122	2,936	5,830
Montana..........................	4,892	3,291	3,494	3,353	2,442	734	177	2,755	1,975	600	180
Nebraska.........................	7,917	10,226	8,485	7,946	4,017	788	3,141	7,260	3,577	755	2,928
Nevada	22,992	9,981	8,673	7,358	1,163	316	5,879	8,524	1,758	392	6,374
New Hampshire	5,962	5,804	5,740	5,389	1,560	1,614	2,215	4,959	1,520	1,200	2,239
New Jersey......................	44,317	40,889	30,976	27,263	9,819	1,015	16,429	28,788	11,113	1,350	16,325
New Mexico.....................	23,243	24,132	21,466	18,854	10,466	1,588	6,800	19,364	10,399	1,668	7,297
New York.........................	176,239	157,486	122,833	115,699	44,938	7,011	63,750	115,032	46,482	6,251	62,299
North Carolina	107,504	109,047	115,312	105,080	61,911	19,769	23,400	109,973	63,657	19,985	26,331
North Dakota	2,124	2,063	1,581	1,653	832	369	452	2,006	1,001	497	508
Ohio...............................	65,579	50,869	41,692	39,877	28,624	4,935	6,318	37,172	26,258	4,182	6,732
Oklahoma........................	20,101	20,447	18,329	16,241	11,024	1,737	3,480	16,524	11,132	1,551	3,841
Oregon............................	25,228	21,668	20,851	18,848	9,018	2,218	7,612	18,171	8,764	2,008	7,399
Pennsylvania...................	49,369	54,274	30,577	24,310	14,294	3,050	6,966	24,388	14,404	3,069	6,915
Rhode Island	5,592	6,697	6,012	6,345	2,715	447	3,183	5,781	2,534	402	2,845
South Carolina.................	94,452	65,901	49,484	47,237	35,716	6,982	4,539	44,526	32,058	7,597	4,871
South Dakota...................	5,637	3,517	2,423	2,395	1,374	471	550	2,433	1,395	418	620
Tennessee	40,615	48,924	28,170	27,694	21,242	3,187	3,265	26,955	20,411	2,992	3,552
Texas..............................	111,585	119,867	99,333	91,710	41,624	3,211	46,875	91,906	43,274	2,941	45,691
Utah...............................	30,714	29,320	24,686	21,005	13,121	2,202	5,682	20,665	12,714	2,012	5,939
Vermont	1,146	2,015	1,590	2,188	1,406	404	378	2,097	1,223	579	295
Virginia...........................	35,261	29,222	28,220	24,898	10,507	3,721	10,670	24,163	10,352	2,684	11,127
Washington......................	53,460	50,386	61,392	55,176	24,585	4,041	26,550	53,425	23,226	3,688	26,511
West Virginia....................	13,072	9,444	9,785	9,199	7,091	1,802	306	9,088	6,923	1,869	296
Wisconsin........................	27,304	26,029	21,523	18,829	10,815	3,396	4,618	19,108	9,613	4,579	4,916
Wyoming.........................	2,767	2,379	2,973	2,688	1,515	636	537	2,749	1,501	670	578
Other jurisdictions ...	44,785	37,328	22,045	25,914	5,421	19,579	1,276	17,894	3,764	12,513	1,617
American Samoa..............	662	838	225	132	0	34	98	161	0	47	114
Federated States of Micronesia	0	0	0	0	0	0	0	0	0	0	0
Guam..............................	1,092	1,062	539	873	713	58	102	730	588	51	91
Marshall Islands...............	335	0	0	0	0	0	0	0	0	0	0
Northern Marianas	680	740	607	455	93	305	57	332	49	233	50
Palau..............................	132	206	56	76	0	76	0	95	0	95	0
Puerto Rico.....................	41,043	33,463	20,464	24,378	4,261	19,098	1,019	16,281	2,849	12,078	1,354
U.S. Virgin Islands	841	1,019	154	—	354	8	—	295	278	9	8

—Not available.

NOTE: Adult basic education provides instruction in basic skills for adults 16 and over functioning at literacy levels below the secondary level. Adult secondary education provides instruction at the high school level for adults who are seeking to pass the GED or obtain an adult high school creden-

tial. English as a second language instruction is for adults who lack proficiency in English and who seek to improve their literacy and competence in English.
SOURCE: U.S. Department of Education, Office of Vocational and Adult Education (OVAE), OVAE National Reporting System, retrieved November 21, 2014, from http://wdcrobcolp01.ed.gov/CFAPPS/OVAE/NRS/reports/index.cfm. (This table was prepared November 2014.)

Table 507.30. Participation of employed persons, 17 years old and over, in career-related adult education during the previous 12 months, by selected characteristics of participants: 1995, 1999, and 2005

[Standard errors appear in parentheses]

Characteristic of employed person	1995 — Percent of adults participating in career- or job-related courses	1995 — Number of career- or job-related courses taken, per employed adult	1999 — Percent of adults participating in career- or job-related courses	1999 — Number of career- or job-related courses taken, per employed adult	2005 — Employed persons, in thousands	2005 — In career- or job-related courses[1]	2005 — In apprenticeship programs	2005 — In personal interest courses	2005 — In informal learning activities for personal interest	2005 — Number of career- or job-related courses taken[1], In thousands	2005 — Per employed adult
	2	3	4	5	6	7	8	9	10	11	12
Total	31.1 (0.54)	0.8 (0.02)	30.5 (1.14)	0.7 (0.03)	133,386 (1,508.1)	38.8 (0.83)	1.4 (0.24)	21.8 (0.94)	73.5 (1.01)	108,443	0.8 (0.03)
Sex											
Male	29.0 (0.72)	0.7 (0.02)	28.3 (1.15)	0.6 (0.03)	71,754 (934.7)	31.7 (1.22)	2.0 (0.37)	18.5 (1.30)	73.4 (1.52)	44,512	0.6 (0.03)
Female	33.4 (0.83)	0.9 (0.03)	32.9 (1.14)	0.8 (0.03)	61,632 (1,219.3)	47.1 (1.43)	0.8 (0.23)	25.8 (1.23)	73.6 (1.37)	63,931	1.0 (0.05)
Age											
17 through 24 years old	18.6 (1.01)	0.4 (0.02)	19.1 (1.91)	0.4 (0.06)	15,027 (1,030.4)	26.4 (3.01)	3.0 ! (1.03)	25.2 (3.37)	71.4 (3.15)	8,024	0.5 (0.09)
25 through 29 years old	31.2 (1.46)	0.8 (0.05)	34.3 (2.44)	0.8 (0.08)	14,555 (918.4)	36.1 (2.94)	3.1 ! (1.12)	24.5 (3.66)	70.9 (4.49)	9,493	0.7 (0.06)
30 through 34 years old	31.6 (1.30)	0.8 (0.04)	34.4 (2.50)	0.8 (0.08)	15,250 (977.2)	41.0 (3.06)	2.7 ! (1.10)	23.7 (2.63)	74.0 (2.54)	12,681	0.8 (0.07)
35 through 39 years old	35.1 (1.02)	0.9 (0.03)	29.2 (2.15)	0.7 (0.07)	15,286 (922.4)	41.7 (4.16)	1.0 ! (0.46)	21.6 (3.15)	77.7 (3.00)	13,807	0.9 (0.14)
40 through 44 years old	36.6 (1.29)	0.9 (0.04)	36.4 (2.44)	0.8 (0.07)	18,141 (946.3)	39.8 (2.73)	‡ (†)	23.3 (2.60)	71.2 (3.15)	15,586	0.9 (0.07)
45 through 49 years old	39.6 (1.94)	1.0 (0.06)	30.4 (2.42)	0.7 (0.06)	18,149 (842.5)	45.0 (2.15)	0.7 ! (0.29)	19.0 (2.09)	73.5 (2.68)	16,809	0.9 (0.06)
50 through 54 years old	34.4 (1.69)	0.9 (0.04)	34.7 (2.57)	0.8 (0.07)	14,624 (732.1)	42.6 (2.49)	0.7 ! (0.32)	19.5 (1.92)	76.3 (2.27)	14,881	1.0 (0.10)
55 through 59 years old	26.7 (1.86)	0.7 (0.06)	30.3 (2.83)	0.6 (0.08)	10,522 (676.0)	44.7 (2.98)	‡ (†)	18.3 (1.93)	73.0 (2.95)	9,901	0.9 (0.09)
60 through 64 years old	21.1 (2.41)	0.5 (0.06)	27.2 (3.80)	0.7 (0.15)	6,021 (498.8)	38.9 (3.97)	‡ (†)	23.4 (3.52)	73.0 (4.22)	4,919	0.8 (0.10)
65 years old and over	13.7 (1.86)	0.4 (0.06)	20.3 (4.21)	0.4 (0.08)	5,812 (493.3)	21.6 (3.48)	# (†)	17.4 (3.13)	74.2 (3.75)	2,343	0.4 (0.07)
65 through 69	13.1 (2.28)	0.4 (0.08)	— (†)	— (†)	3,385 (415.5)	19.1 (4.05)	# (†)	20.9 (4.88)	75.4 (5.18)	1,102	0.3 (0.08)
70 and over	14.6 (2.85)	0.4 (0.09)	— (†)	— (†)	2,427 (282.3)	25.1 (5.81)	# (†)	12.6 (2.93)	72.6 (6.11)	1,241	0.5 (0.14)
Race/ethnicity											
White	33.2 (0.61)	0.8 (0.02)	32.8 (0.98)	0.6 (0.03)	94,881 (1,538.6)	41.3 (0.93)	1.2 (0.25)	22.2 (1.11)	75.3 (1.17)	82,511	0.9 (0.03)
Black	26.2 (1.46)	0.7 (0.04)	28.1 (2.34)	1.0 (0.07)	13,773 (533.2)	39.2 (3.82)	1.7 ! (0.83)	23.5 (3.04)	66.9 (3.02)	10,311	0.7 (0.11)
Hispanic	18.1 (1.00)	0.4 (0.02)	16.4 (1.83)	0.5 (0.05)	15,741 (681.1)	25.0 (2.66)	2.9 (0.85)	16.2 (2.31)	65.8 (3.39)	8,786	0.6 (0.11)
Asian	— (†)	— (†)	— (†)	— (†)	3,770 (520.7)	36.9 (7.00)	‡ (†)	32.3 (7.26)	81.1 (5.88)	2,207	0.6 (0.12)
Pacific Islander	— (†)	— (†)	— (†)	— (†)	‡ (†)	‡ (†)	‡ (†)	‡ (†)	‡ (†)	‡	‡ (†)
Asian/Pacific Islander	25.5 (2.69)	0.6 (0.07)	32.8 (4.84)	0.4 ! (0.15)	‡ (†)	— (†)	— (†)	‡ (†)	‡ (†)	—	— (†)
American Indian/Alaska Native	34.0 (6.32)	0.9 (0.20)	29.5 ! (11.52)	‡ (†)	‡ (†)	‡ (†)	‡ (†)	‡ (†)	‡ (†)	‡	‡ (†)
Two or more races	— (†)	— (†)	— (†)	‡ (†)	3,786 (562.7)	39.1 (6.85)	‡ (†)	22.6 (6.34)	77.6 (8.40)	3,083	0.8 (0.15)
Other races	25.3 (2.99)	0.7 (0.09)	— (†)	— (†)	‡ (†)	‡ (†)	‡ (†)	‡ (†)	‡ (†)	‡	‡ (†)
Highest level of education completed											
Less than high school completion	8.8 (1.05)	0.1 (0.02)	7.9 (2.29)	0.4 (0.05)	16,627 (838.2)	10.4 (2.11)	2.4 ! (0.90)	8.8 (1.54)	57.0 (3.76)	2,592	0.2 (0.03)
8th grade or less	6.1 ! (2.00)	0.1 ! (0.04)	— (†)	— (†)	5,016 (599.7)	2.7 (1.12)	‡ (†)	3.8 ! (1.71)	46.7 (7.11)	197	# (†)
9th through 12th grade, no completion	10.0 (1.27)	0.2 (0.02)	— (†)	— (†)	11,610 (792.8)	13.7 (2.99)	‡ (†)	11.0 (2.06)	61.5 (4.05)	2,396	0.2 (0.04)
High school completion	20.9 (0.79)	0.4 (0.02)	21.4 (1.45)	0.8 (0.03)	34,121 (1,147.2)	24.7 (1.76)	1.3 ! (0.46)	17.1 (1.89)	63.4 (2.55)	16,640	0.5 (0.05)
Some vocational/technical	32.3 (2.50)	0.8 (0.07)	28.7 (5.76)	0.9 (0.17)	3,744 (393.1)	48.2 (5.92)	‡ (†)	25.5 (4.61)	74.0 (5.54)	3,802	1.0 (0.17)
Some college	29.9 (0.91)	0.7 (0.03)	29.0 (1.78)	0.7 (0.06)	24,479 (1,067.7)	39.9 (2.36)	1.9 ! (0.69)	25.2 (2.50)	79.8 (2.04)	18,437	0.8 (0.05)
Associate's degree	39.2 (1.58)	1.0 (0.05)	39.7 (3.07)	0.9 (0.09)	9,943 (730.7)	50.4 (3.71)	2.3 ! (0.84)	19.1 (2.86)	78.4 (3.88)	14,224	1.4 (0.21)
Bachelor's degree	44.6 (1.33)	1.2 (0.04)	43.8 (2.01)	1.0 (0.06)	26,475 (902.7)	53.1 (1.88)	‡ (†)	29.0 (1.77)	78.7 (1.94)	28,099	1.1 (0.06)
Some graduate work (or study)	50.2 (1.63)	1.4 (0.05)	46.8 (4.17)	1.2 (0.14)	17,998 (735.4)	61.1 (2.16)	‡ (†)	28.6 (2.01)	88.8 (1.16)	24,649	1.4 (0.07)
No degree	44.3 (3.18)	1.2 (0.10)	54.2 (4.94)	1.2 (0.14)	2,125 (227.9)	53.8 (5.79)	‡ (†)	39.3 (6.05)	75.0 (5.64)	2,412	1.1 (0.16)
Master's	50.5 (1.99)	1.4 (0.06)	45.3 (2.97)	1.1 (0.11)	11,330 (614.7)	62.7 (2.98)	‡ (†)	28.2 (2.27)	90.5 (1.40)	15,394	1.4 (0.09)
Doctor's	40.4 (6.42)	1.0 (0.16)	34.4 (4.79)	0.7 (0.12)	1,600 (227.2)	49.0 (5.80)	‡ (†)	28.8 (4.76)	87.8 (4.35)	2,204	1.4 (0.36)
Professional	67.6 (3.89)	2.0 (0.15)	67.6 (6.98)	1.9 (0.31)	2,943 (382.7)	66.5 (6.39)	‡ (†)	22.1 (5.05)	92.9 (2.21)	4,639	1.6 (0.21)

See notes at end of table.

Table 507.30. Participation of employed persons, 17 years old and over, in career-related adult education during the previous 12 months, by selected characteristics of participants: 1995, 1999, and 2005—Continued

[Standard errors appear in parentheses]

Characteristic of employed person	1995		1999		2005						
	Percent of adults participating in career- or job-related courses	Number of career- or job-related courses taken, per employed adult	Percent of adults participating in career- or job-related courses	Number of career- or job-related courses taken, per employed adult	Employed persons, in thousands	Percent of adults participating				Number of career- or job-related courses taken[1]	
						In career- or job-related courses[1]	In apprenticeship programs	In personal interest courses	In informal learning activities for personal interest	In thousands	Per employed adult
1	2	3	4	5	6	7	8	9	10	11	12
Locale[2]											
City	(†)	(†)	(†)	(†)	39,283 (1,391.3)	39.6 (1.67)	2.2 (0.60)	23.1 (1.43)	74.0 (1.77)	34,327	0.9 (0.05)
Suburban	(†)	(†)	(†)	(†)	48,452 (1,555.0)	41.1 (1.87)	1.2 (0.32)	23.3 (1.38)	74.2 (1.49)	39,802	0.8 (0.04)
Town	(†)	(†)	(†)	(†)	17,616 (1,060.7)	36.0 (2.64)	‡ (†)	19.6 (2.83)	71.7 (3.02)	12,947	0.7 (0.07)
Rural	(†)	(†)	(†)	(†)	27,847 (885.2)	35.4 (2.14)	1.4 ! (0.58)	19.0 (2.19)	72.7 (2.22)	21,135	0.8 (0.06)
Occupation											
Executive, administrative, or managerial occupations.	42.9 (1.49)	1.2 (0.05)	40.6 (2.06)	1.0 (0.07)	14,596 (707.6)	53.6 (2.79)	‡ (†)	29.5 (2.89)	77.7 (2.87)	16,567	1.1 (0.09)
Engineers, surveyors, and architects.	44.2 (4.46)	1.1 (0.12)	52.1 (6.96)	1.0 (0.16)	1,987 (244.9)	56.3 (5.68)	‡ (†)	30.5 (6.36)	81.0 (4.73)	2,323	1.2 (0.16)
Natural scientists and mathematicians	59.7 (3.97)	1.7 (0.15)	46.0 (6.61)	0.8 (0.14)	4,130 (445.4)	51.5 (5.64)	‡ (†)	31.2 (4.83)	85.3 (5.44)	3,693	0.9 (0.11)
Social scientists and workers, religious workers, and lawyers	59.5 (2.61)	1.8 (0.11)	56.9 (5.66)	1.7 (0.24)	4,697 (480.9)	66.8 (4.48)	‡ (†)	28.3 (3.81)	88.6 (2.95)	7,822	1.7 (0.29)
Teachers, elementary/secondary	53.9 (2.23)	1.5 (0.08)	52.1 (3.53)	1.2 (0.11)	7,085 (568.5)	67.7 (4.16)	‡ (†)	31.5 (3.93)	83.0 (2.79)	12,233	1.7 (0.13)
Teachers, postsecondary and counselors, librarians, and archivists.	41.6 (4.57)	1.0 (0.15)	35.6 (5.85)	0.7 (0.14)	2,393 (420.9)	53.1 (8.63)	‡ (†)	17.7 (4.91)	90.9 (3.97)	2,122	0.9 (0.09)
Health diagnosing and treating practitioners.	68.6 (5.85)	2.0 (0.23)	65.2 (11.99)	1.5 ! (0.50)	978 (208.8)	78.9 (7.10)	‡ (†)	27.4 ! (9.60)	86.6 (5.37)	1,951	2.0 (0.25)
Registered nurses, pharmacists, dieticians, therapists, and physician's assistants.	72.8 (3.02)	2.2 (0.14)	72.2 (5.04)	1.8 (0.21)	2,794 (238.8)	79.7 (4.60)	‡ (†)	29.4 (4.17)	84.3 (3.70)	4,984	1.8 (0.15)
Writers, artists, entertainers, and athletes.	23.4 (2.89)	0.5 (0.07)	30.6 (6.21)	0.6 (0.18)	2,969 (405.2)	29.9 (5.69)	‡ (†)	31.8 (6.15)	88.9 (4.39)	1,865	0.6 (0.15)
Health technologists and technicians	50.0 (4.08)	1.4 (0.12)	41.8 (6.00)	1.0 (0.19)	3,060 (436.7)	70.6 (7.31)	‡ (†)	27.8 (6.48)	77.5 (6.40)	4,473	1.5 (0.18)
Technologists and technicians, except health.	43.8 (2.67)	1.1 (0.10)	37.6 (4.87)	1.0 (0.15)	1,774 (336.5)	29.4 (8.10)	‡ (†)	5.3 ! (2.02)	75.2 (8.98)	1,015	0.6 (0.17)
Marketing and sales occupations	25.2 (1.26)	0.6 (0.03)	21.1 (2.27)	0.4 (0.06)	14,845 (971.9)	32.3 (3.17)	‡ (†)	20.8 (2.64)	70.5 (3.53)	7,724	0.5 (0.05)
Administrative support occupations, including clerical	30.8 (1.15)	0.7 (0.03)	27.4 (2.02)	0.6 (0.05)	21,167 (1,179.4)	36.1 (2.95)	0.8 ! (0.40)	28.2 (2.28)	72.9 (2.37)	15,443	0.7 (0.10)
Service occupations	22.6 (1.25)	0.6 (0.04)	21.0 (2.15)	0.5 (0.07)	17,180 (1,033.7)	33.7 (3.13)	1.1 ! (0.36)	16.2 (2.31)	69.0 (2.74)	13,029	0.8 (0.10)
Agriculture, forestry, and fishing occupations	12.4 (2.47)	0.3 (0.07)	12.2 ! (4.09)	0.2 ! (0.07)	2,522 (423.8)	22.4 ! (7.61)	‡ (†)	23.0 ! (11.03)	62.9 (11.04)	960	0.4 ! (0.12)
Mechanics and repairers.	29.1 (2.62)	0.7 (0.08)	15.0 (3.40)	0.3 (0.09)	5,241 (521.6)	28.3 (4.47)	4.0 ! (1.44)	12.6 (3.24)	69.3 (4.36)	2,669	0.5 (0.09)
Construction and extractive occupations.	18.6 (2.33)	0.3 (0.04)	13.2 (3.16)	0.2 (0.06)	6,827 (647.1)	12.4 (3.04)	5.3 ! (2.26)	7.8 (1.88)	69.0 (5.25)	2,323	0.3 ! (0.13)
Precision production[3]	25.6 (4.04)	0.6 (0.12)	18.3 ! (6.52)	0.4 ! (0.12)	10,483 (839.3)	23.5 (3.79)	‡ (†)	14.0 (3.34)	64.9 (3.74)	4,904	0.5 (0.07)
Production workers	14.8 (1.13)	0.3 (0.02)	23.0 (3.17)	0.5 (0.08)	— (†)	— (†)	— (†)	— (†)	— (†)	—	— (†)

See notes at end of table.

Table 507.30. Participation of employed persons, 17 years old and over, in career-related adult education during the previous 12 months, by selected characteristics of participants: 1995, 1999, and 2005—Continued

[Standard errors appear in parentheses]

Characteristic of employed person	1995		1999		2005						Number of career- or job-related courses taken[1]	
	Percent of adults participating in career- or job-related courses	Number of career- or job-related courses taken, per employed adult	Percent of adults participating in career- or job-related courses	Number of career- or job-related courses taken, per employed adult	Employed persons, in thousands	Percent of adults participating					In thousands	Per employed adult
						In career- or job-related courses[1]	In apprenticeship programs	In personal interest courses	In informal learning activities for personal interest			
1	2	3	4	5	6	7	8	9	10		11	12
Transportation and material moving...........	15.8 (1.83)	0.3 (0.04)	18.4 (3.62)	0.3 (0.06)	7,858 (742.5)	15.2 (2.81)	‡ (†)	10.5 (3.10)	62.5 (5.32)		1,935	0.2 (0.05)
Handlers, equipment cleaners, helpers, and laborers	11.7 (2.77)	0.2 (0.06)	‡ (†)	‡ (†)	— (†)	— (†)	‡ (†)	— (†)	— (†)		—	— (†)
Miscellaneous occupations.	38.8 (3.50)	1.0 (0.11)	14.2 ! (4.62)	0.3 ! (0.08)	801 (189.4)	17.2 ! (6.87)	‡ (†)	8.7 ! (4.31)	48.3 (13.96)		409	‡ (†)
Annual household income												
$10,000 or less...............	12.6 (1.31)	0.2 (0.03)	9.5 ! (3.09)	0.2 ! (0.05)	4,425 (444.8)	16.7 (4.35)	‡ (†)	26.2 ! (7.96)	69.7 (5.72)		1,556	0.4 ! (0.12)
$5,000 or less..............	8.7 (1.91)	0.1 (0.03)	— (†)	— (†)	1,635 (252.7)	19.1 (6.52)	‡ (†)	22.9 ! (7.91)	60.9 (8.84)		850	‡ (†)
$5,001 to $10,000.......	15.1 (1.62)	0.3 (0.04)	— (†)	— (†)	2,791 (454.1)	15.3 (5.68)	‡ (†)	28.1 ! (12.27)	74.8 (6.88)		706	0.3 ! (0.10)
$10,001 to $15,000........	15.1 (1.71)	0.4 (0.04)	8.3 (1.88)	0.1 (0.03)	4,814 (633.4)	22.2 (5.77)	‡ (†)	17.3 ! (5.25)	64.5 (7.57)		2,189	0.5 (0.12)
$15,001 to $20,000........	20.1 (1.36)	0.4 (0.03)	16.3 (2.75)	0.3 (0.05)	4,515 (398.8)	18.2 (3.09)	5.7 ! (2.71)	11.5 (1.96)	60.4 (5.11)		1,322	0.3 (0.05)
$20,001 to $25,000........	20.4 (1.52)	0.5 (0.05)	18.8 (2.79)	0.4 (0.08)	5,593 (490.2)	23.8 (4.02)	1.1 ! (0.51)	13.3 (3.21)	71.5 (4.11)		2,817	0.5 (0.10)
$25,001 to $30,000........	24.7 (1.34)	0.5 (0.03)	22.2 (2.73)	0.5 (0.07)	7,444 (680.4)	31.4 (4.88)	‡ (0.65)	16.7 (3.77)	73.5 (3.91)		4,322	0.6 (0.11)
$30,001 to $40,000........	30.2 (1.13)	0.8 (0.03)	26.6 (2.82)	0.6 (0.07)	13,123 (928.5)	35.1 (3.45)	1.5 ! (0.72)	21.7 (3.71)	69.1 (3.55)		8,224	0.6 (0.06)
$40,001 to $50,000........	34.7 (1.30)	0.8 (0.04)	32.3 (2.34)	0.7 (0.07)	13,647 (1,058.4)	31.5 (3.01)	1.8 ! (0.72)	20.1 (3.32)	73.5 (2.78)		10,072	0.7 (0.10)
$50,001 to $75,000........	40.0 (1.18)	1.0 (0.04)	36.6 (1.86)	0.9 (0.06)	33,665 (1,430.4)	42.7 (1.80)	1.2 ! (0.51)	20.9 (2.10)	71.3 (2.55)		28,991	0.9 (0.06)
More than $75,000........	45.2 (1.40)	1.3 (0.04)	42.5 (1.79)	1.0 (0.06)	46,160 (1,263.3)	48.1 (1.57)	1.3 ! (0.39)	26.0 (1.37)	79.2 (1.55)		48,951	1.1 (0.05)

—Not available.
†Not applicable.
#Rounds to zero.
!Interpret data with caution. The coefficient of variation (CV) for this estimate is between 30 and 50 percent.
‡Reporting standards not met. The coefficient of variation (CV) for this estimate is 50 percent or greater.
[1]The 2005 estimates on participation in career- or job-related courses were based on responses to multiple questions. Specifically, respondents were first asked what courses they had taken, and then whether each course was career- or job-related. In contrast, 1995 and 1999 respondents were asked a single, general question about whether they had participated in any career- or job-related courses. Therefore, 2005 results may not be comparable to results from the earlier years.

[2]Detail may not sum to totals due to missing locale information.
[3]For 2005, figures include "Production workers" occupations data.
NOTE: Data do not include persons enrolled in high school or below. Race categories exclude persons of Hispanic ethnicity. Detail may not sum to totals because of rounding.
SOURCE: U.S. Department of Education, National Center for Education Statistics, Adult Education Survey (AE-NHES:1995, AE-NHES:1999, and AE-NHES:2005) of the National Household Education Surveys Program. (This table was prepared October 2010.)

Table 507.40. Participation rate of persons, 17 years old and over, in adult education during the previous 12 months, by selected characteristics of participants: Selected years, 1991 through 2005

[Standard errors appear in parentheses]

Columns 2–6: **Percent taking any program, class, or course.** Columns 7–12: **Percent taking specific programs, classes, or courses, 2005.** Column 13: **Percent doing informal learning activities for personal interest, 2005.**

Characteristic of participant	1991	1995	1999	2001	2005	Basic skills/ General Educational Development (GED) classes	English as a second language (ESL) classes	Part-time post-secondary education[1]	Career- or job-related courses	Apprenticeship programs	Personal-interest courses	Informal learning activities for personal interest, 2005
1	2	3	4	5	6	7	8	9	10	11	12	13
Total	33.0 (0.68)	40.2 (0.48)	44.5 (0.77)	46.4 (0.55)	44.4 (0.74)	1.3 (0.22)	0.9 (0.17)	5.0 (0.29)	27.0 (0.63)	1.2 (0.18)	21.4 (0.71)	70.5 (0.79)
Sex												
Male	32.6 (1.09)	38.2 (0.65)	41.7 (1.15)	43.1 (0.83)	41.0 (1.20)	1.4 (0.41)	0.9! (0.29)	5.0 (0.44)	24.5 (0.99)	1.7 (0.31)	18.3 (1.08)	70.8 (1.10)
Female	33.2 (0.97)	42.1 (0.59)	47.1 (1.02)	49.5 (0.78)	47.5 (1.01)	1.2 (0.19)	0.9 (0.15)	5.1 (0.37)	29.2 (0.95)	0.7 (0.15)	24.2 (0.88)	70.2 (1.03)
Age												
17 to 24 years old	37.8 (1.46)	47.0 (1.12)	49.9 (2.34)	52.8 (2.04)	52.8 (2.79)	6.0 (1.48)	1.7! (0.61)	11.5 (1.34)	21.3 (2.22)	2.7 (0.76)	26.3 (2.60)	69.2 (2.54)
25 to 29 years old	40.0 (2.33)	49.6 (1.31)	56.5 (2.53)	52.9 (2.60)	51.6 (3.82)	1.8 (0.48)	3.3! (1.48)	9.1 (1.50)	29.5 (2.48)	3.2! (1.06)	20.9 (2.78)	66.8 (3.75)
30 to 34 years old	37.6 (2.88)	47.3 (1.41)	56.2 (2.57)	53.7 (2.18)	52.7 (2.52)	1.9! (0.66)	1.6 (0.64)	8.4 (1.28)	33.8 (2.71)	2.5! (0.89)	23.2 (2.23)	73.8 (2.22)
35 to 39 years old	42.1 (2.71)	47.7 (1.15)	50.1 (2.43)	54.0 (1.71)	48.6 (3.21)	0.4! (0.16)	0.7 (0.26)	6.1 (0.90)	32.6 (3.29)	0.9! (0.36)	20.7 (2.67)	75.5 (2.69)
40 to 44 years old	49.2 (3.28)	50.9 (1.15)	50.5 (2.43)	53.5 (1.88)	48.9 (2.43)	0.8! (0.31)	0.6 (0.23)	4.7 (0.77)	34.8 (2.30)	0.9! (0.42)	23.4 (2.29)	71.6 (2.62)
45 to 49 years old	40.0 (2.43)	48.7 (1.66)	49.8 (2.69)	55.4 (2.02)	49.0 (2.09)	† (†)	0.6 (0.25)	3.2 (0.48)	37.7 (1.83)	0.5! (0.23)	19.3 (1.88)	71.5 (2.52)
50 to 54 years old	40.0 (3.31)	42.5 (1.38)	47.2 (2.51)	51.1 (2.22)	46.6 (2.36)	† (†)	0.3! (0.15)	4.5 (0.75)	35.2 (2.25)	0.6! (0.28)	20.3 (1.64)	75.6 (1.89)
55 to 59 years old	26.8 (3.74)	32.2 (1.66)	38.0 (2.60)	44.1 (1.98)	42.2 (2.78)	† (†)	† (†)	1.9 (0.43)	31.9 (2.39)	† (†)	18.0 (1.63)	69.5 (2.56)
60 to 64 years old	29.0 (1.90)	23.7 (1.89)	31.4 (2.83)	30.8 (2.18)	37.9 (3.00)	† (†)	† (†)	0.9! (0.36)	20.9 (2.07)	† (†)	24.1 (2.40)	71.4 (3.04)
65 to 69 years old	17.4 (2.97)	18.1 (1.46)	25.4 (2.54)	20.5 (1.74)	26.2 (2.67)	† (†)	† (†)	0.5! (0.22)	8.1 (1.36)	† (†)	20.9 (2.41)	67.6 (2.52)
70 years old and over	8.6 (1.25)	13.8 (1.09)	15.0 (1.38)	21.7 (1.37)	21.5 (1.44)	† (†)	† (†)	‡ (†)	4.0 (0.78)	† (†)	17.9 (1.33)	62.9 (1.82)
Racial/ethnic group												
White	34.1 (0.82)	41.5 (0.54)	44.4 (0.89)	47.4 (0.59)	45.6 (0.84)	0.9 (0.23)	0.2! (0.08)	4.9 (0.35)	29.1 (0.70)	0.9 (0.17)	22.1 (0.87)	73.0 (0.92)
Black	25.9 (2.23)	37.0 (1.45)	46.3 (2.30)	43.3 (1.50)	46.4 (2.81)	1.9 (0.49)	† (†)	5.4 (0.97)	27.0 (2.53)	1.5! (0.73)	23.7 (2.11)	65.3 (2.02)
Hispanic	31.4 (2.63)	33.7 (1.18)	41.3 (2.51)	41.7 (2.28)	37.8 (2.43)	2.6 (0.72)	5.6 (1.22)	5.7 (1.55)	16.9 (1.72)	2.2 (0.63)	15.4 (1.75)	57.5 (2.86)
Asian	— (†)	— (†)	— (†)	— (†)	48.3 (5.39)	† (†)	2.6! (1.03)	7.6! (2.62)	27.2 (4.70)	† (†)	26.5 (5.06)	81.1 (4.10)
Pacific Islander	— (†)	— (†)	— (†)	— (†)	‡ (†)	‡ (†)	‡ (†)	‡ (†)	‡ (†)	‡ (†)	‡ (†)	‡ (†)
Asian/Pacific Islander	35.9 (5.55)	39.7 (2.92)	51.1 (4.63)	49.5 (3.81)	36.3 (10.17)	† (†)	† (†)	4.4! (1.82)	23.0! (8.51)	† (†)	13.0! (6.16)	70.6 (9.18)
American Indian/Alaska Native	29.3! (11.55)	38.8 (4.85)	36.3 (9.16)	50.2 (8.28)	39.4 (4.94)	5.1! (2.17)	† (†)	3.2! (1.07)	23.8 (4.06)	1.3! (0.59)	21.0 (4.13)	77.6 (5.28)
Two or more races	—	—	—	—	—	—	—	—	—	—	—	—
Highest level of education completed												
8th grade or less	7.7 (1.44)	10.0 (1.10)	14.7 (2.92)	19.7 (2.84)	15.5 (2.47)	1.9 (0.57)	4.3! (1.70)	† (†)	1.7! (0.55)	† (†)	7.3 (1.24)	38.1 (3.27)
9th through 12th grade, no completion	15.8 (2.25)	20.2 (1.38)	25.6 (2.55)	25.5 (1.53)	27.2 (2.40)	7.9 (1.69)	1.1 (0.41)	2.1 (0.57)	7.6 (1.44)	1.5! (0.61)	12.5 (1.53)	55.7 (2.52)
High school completion	24.1 (1.10)	30.7 (0.84)	34.8 (1.37)	33.9 (1.07)	33.0 (1.62)	0.5! (0.24)	0.7! (0.24)	2.5 (0.36)	17.2 (1.18)	1.1! (0.35)	16.8 (1.27)	63.6 (1.93)
Some vocational/technical	34.2 (3.80)	41.9 (2.16)	41.1 (3.97)	50.7 (3.51)	43.3 (4.30)	† (†)	† (†)	4.5! (1.42)	28.3 (3.71)	1.4! (0.47)	23.2 (3.09)	77.6 (3.98)
Some college	41.4 (1.67)	49.3 (0.92)	51.1 (1.76)	57.4 (1.29)	51.1 (1.79)	† (†)	1.1! (0.51)	8.6 (1.06)	28.8 (1.54)	1.9! (0.66)	26.8 (1.80)	79.8 (1.52)
Associate's degree	49.2 (5.82)	56.1 (1.85)	56.6 (2.93)	62.5 (2.15)	56.5 (3.64)	† (†)	0.4! (0.17)	6.6 (1.42)	40.8 (3.27)	0.4! (0.17)	20.1 (2.48)	75.9 (3.70)
Bachelor's degree	51.1 (2.46)	56.9 (1.20)	60.3 (1.84)	64.5 (1.39)	59.8 (1.56)	† (†)	† (†)	6.3 (0.82)	44.1 (1.61)	† (†)	28.6 (1.55)	79.3 (1.72)
Some graduate work (or study)	55.1 (2.90)	59.9 (1.55)	63.6 (1.96)	68.9 (1.64)	66.3 (1.99)	† (†)	† (†)	8.7 (0.86)	49.3 (2.15)	† (†)	30.7 (1.77)	88.0 (1.06)
No degree	— (†)	62.2 (2.67)	64.7 (4.39)	64.2 (3.54)	65.3 (4.84)	† (†)	† (†)	8.7 (2.55)	40.5 (4.68)	† (†)	38.7 (4.81)	88.2 (4.34)
Master's	— (†)	59.1 (1.88)	65.7 (2.64)	70.7 (2.10)	67.5 (2.59)	† (†)	† (†)	14.5 (1.31)	50.5 (2.81)	† (†)	30.6 (2.04)	88.8 (1.33)
Doctor's	— (†)	54.0 (6.99)	53.1 (4.73)	63.7 (3.98)	58.0 (4.94)	† (†)	† (†)	8.9 (3.14)	51.4 (4.53)	† (†)	31.4 (3.95)	90.3 (3.26)
Professional	— (†)	65.9 (3.91)	72.5 (5.75)	72.8 (3.79)	68.2 (5.77)	† (†)	† (†)	10.1! (3.14)	59.0 (6.35)	† (†)	23.9 (4.35)	91.6 (2.15)
Urbanicity												
City	— (†)	— (†)	— (†)	— (†)	45.8 (1.46)	1.4 (0.31)	1.6 (0.38)	5.7 (0.59)	26.7 (1.24)	1.8 (0.43)	22.5 (1.10)	69.2 (1.39)
Suburban	— (†)	— (†)	— (†)	— (†)	46.9 (1.33)	0.9 (0.23)	0.9! (0.36)	5.8 (0.55)	29.7 (1.26)	0.9 (0.22)	23.4 (1.16)	73.4 (1.28)
Town	— (†)	— (†)	— (†)	— (†)	41.8 (2.33)	2.7! (1.16)	0.4! (0.14)	4.2 (0.87)	25.6 (1.74)	0.5! (0.21)	18.5 (1.96)	70.5 (2.43)
Rural	— (†)	— (†)	— (†)	— (†)	39.5 (2.04)	0.8 (0.22)	‡ (†)	3.3 (0.59)	24.2 (1.38)	1.2! (0.40)	18.3 (1.76)	67.6 (1.76)
Labor force status												
In labor force	40.7 (0.96)	49.8 (0.69)	52.1 (0.94)	— (†)	52.3 (0.93)	1.4 (0.32)	0.8 (0.19)	6.4 (0.39)	37.1 (0.83)	1.5 (0.24)	21.9 (0.91)	73.0 (0.94)
Employed	42.0 (1.00)	50.7 (0.53)	52.5 (0.96)	— (†)	53.4 (0.94)	1.1 (0.31)	0.7 (0.20)	6.5 (0.39)	38.8 (0.83)	1.4 (0.24)	21.8 (0.94)	73.5 (1.01)
Unemployed	26.0 (3.24)	36.6 (1.91)	44.9 (4.60)	— (†)	37.8 (4.26)	5.8 (1.60)	1.9! (0.79)	5.2 (1.37)	13.5 (2.16)	‡ (†)	22.1 (3.99)	66.7 (3.80)
Not in labor force	15.7 (0.91)	21.3 (0.69)	24.9 (1.17)	— (†)	27.6 (1.18)	1.1 (0.24)	1.3 (0.36)	2.3 (0.45)	5.7 (0.55)	0.6! (0.22)	20.5 (0.97)	65.2 (1.27)

See notes at end of table.

[1] Part-time postsecondary education.

Table 507.40. Participation rate of persons, 17 years old and over, in adult education during the previous 12 months, by selected characteristics of participants: Selected years, 1991 through 2005—Continued

[Standard errors appear in parentheses]

Characteristic of participant	Percent taking any program, class, or course					Percent taking specific programs, classes, or courses, 2005						Percent doing informal learning activities for personal interest, 2005
	1991	1995	1999	2001	2005	Basic skills/General Educational Development (GED) classes	English as a second language (ESL) classes	Part-time postsecondary education[1]	Career- or job-related courses	Apprenticeship programs	Personal-interest courses	
1	2	3	4	5	6	7	8	9	10	11	12	13
Occupation												
Executive, administrative, or managerial occupations	49.3 (3.45)	55.8 (1.92)	57.0 (2.11)	66.2 (1.61)	64.1 (2.73)	‡ (†)	‡ (†)	6.0 (1.10)	51.8 (2.82)	‡ (†)	28.8 (2.89)	78.6 (2.71)
Engineers, surveyors, and architects	62.6 (7.85)	65.5 (4.18)	79.8 (6.01)	68.1 (4.46)	71.2 (5.68)	‡ (†)	‡ (†)	9.3! (3.21)	55.6 (5.60)	‡ (†)	31.4 (6.19)	81.1 (4.63)
Natural scientists and mathematicians	48.2 (9.86)	72.3 (3.52)	60.5 (6.74)	74.0 (4.46)	69.1 (4.63)	‡ (†)	‡ (†)	9.2 (2.49)	49.6 (5.27)	‡ (†)	30.2 (4.53)	85.5 (5.16)
Social scientists and workers, religious workers, and lawyers	55.6 (6.01)	76.6 (2.61)	79.3 (4.35)	83.5 (3.05)	77.7 (4.11)	‡ (†)	‡ (†)	12.8 (3.16)	64.3 (4.42)	‡ (†)	29.2 (3.52)	89.4 (2.78)
Teachers: college, university, postsecondary institutions	56.0 (4.20)	54.8 (4.64)	66.5 (5.61)	79.9 (2.95)	79.7 (2.59)	‡ (†)	‡ (†)	8.3! (3.16)	65.0 (3.99)	‡ (†)	31.7 (3.78)	83.8 (2.62)
Teachers: elementary/secondary	45.5 (8.31)	76.7 (1.98)	78.4 (3.11)	69.4 (4.60)	61.3 (6.96)	‡ (†)	‡ (†)	‡ (†)	49.0 (8.50)	‡ (†)	19.5 (4.98)	91.7 (3.58)
Health diagnosing and treating practitioners	67.1 (13.73)	71.1 (5.78)	79.8 (9.02)	78.5 (6.38)	88.8 (5.59)	‡ (†)	‡ (†)	15.4 (2.47)	79.5 (6.59)	‡ (†)	31.9 (9.15)	84.5 (5.63)
Registered nurses, pharmacists, dieticians, therapists, and physician's assistants	59.6 (6.69)	86.7 (2.47)	85.4 (4.10)	82.7 (3.83)	85.4 (4.05)	‡ (†)	‡ (†)	7.9 (2.17)	78.2 (4.89)	‡ (†)	27.4 (3.73)	83.1 (3.92)
Writers, artists, entertainers, and athletes	42.9 (6.63)	49.9 (4.37)	50.0 (6.93)	46.8 (6.03)	52.5 (6.59)	‡ (†)	‡ (†)	5.4! (2.16)	27.8 (5.02)	‡ (†)	35.3 (6.42)	88.2 (3.89)
Health technologists and technicians	68.6 (10.03)	74.8 (3.64)	66.9 (6.16)	85.6 (3.25)	72.1 (8.37)	‡ (†)	‡ (†)	6.0! (2.11)	63.2 (8.67)	‡ (†)	24.6 (5.91)	75.6 (7.26)
Technologists and technicians, except health and engineering	53.0 (6.49)	64.3 (2.84)	59.6 (5.07)	70.2 (3.32)	33.8 (8.53)	‡ (†)	‡ (†)	7.1! (3.19)	29.1 (7.68)	‡ (†)	6.2! (2.14)	76.0 (8.80)
Marketing and sales occupations	34.4 (2.38)	44.2 (1.34)	44.4 (2.73)	51.1 (2.10)	45.7 (3.00)	1.7! (0.59)	‡ (†)	4.5 (0.88)	30.2 (2.77)	‡ (†)	21.5 (2.43)	68.9 (3.37)
Administrative support occupations, including clerical	29.9 (1.74)	51.7 (1.25)	50.1 (2.29)	58.7 (1.72)	54.6 (2.70)	1.1! (0.53)	‡ (†)	6.6 (0.98)	33.5 (2.70)	1.4! (0.57)	27.7 (2.18)	73.8 (2.33)
Service occupations	25.2 (1.82)	46.5 (1.38)	50.9 (2.74)	49.3 (2.24)	44.7 (2.47)	1.6 (0.39)	1.9! (0.88)	6.8 (1.42)	28.5 (2.64)	‡ (†)	17.5 (2.10)	65.4 (2.71)
Agriculture, forestry, and fishing occupations	14.3! (5.19)	26.4 (3.55)	34.3 (7.16)	46.4 (6.80)	44.4 (9.02)	‡ (†)	‡ (†)	‡ (†)	20.3! (6.92)	‡ (†)	21.6! (10.05)	64.0 (10.03)
Mechanics and repairers	32.1 (4.72)	47.6 (2.70)	42.2 (5.44)	35.1 (3.40)	40.1 (5.10)	‡ (†)	‡ (†)	6.0! (1.89)	27.4 (4.26)	3.8! (1.38)	12.7 (3.18)	69.3 (4.27)
Construction and extractive occupations	21.9 (3.38)	38.0 (2.45)	34.5 (4.78)	32.3 (3.19)	27.6 (3.73)	‡ (†)	‡ (†)	‡ (†)	12.3 (2.54)	‡ (†)	11.4 (2.72)	72.3 (4.48)
Precision production[2]	31.2 (6.09)	43.2 (4.32)	38.3 (8.48)	35.1 (6.19)	33.0 (3.98)	‡ (†)	1.1! (0.49)	3.2! (1.08)	22.2 (3.41)	5.2! (1.89)	13.3 (2.99)	63.9 (3.46)
Production workers	21.1 (2.31)	30.7 (1.29)	38.0 (3.47)	39.4 (2.82)	— (†)	— (†)	0.4! (0.16)	4.2! (1.42)	— (†)	— (†)	— (†)	— (†)
Transportation, material moving,	20.7 (4.69)	28.4 (2.32)	33.3 (4.25)	30.4 (3.29)	34.6 (5.27)	‡ (†)	‡ (†)	— (†)	14.7 (2.63)	— (†)	11.2 (2.85)	60.8 (4.98)
Handler, equipment, cleaners, helpers, and laborers	20.8 (3.49)	25.1 (2.70)	19.6 (4.56)	18.2 (3.20)	— (†)	— (†)	‡ (†)	‡ (†)	— (†)	3.2! (1.57)	— (†)	— (†)
Miscellaneous occupations	— (†)	56.6 (3.61)	43.0 (7.98)	64.9 (7.07)	39.2 (11.25)	‡ (†)	‡ (†)	‡ (†)	15.7! (5.81)	‡ (†)	7.8! (3.63)	52.2 (12.32)
Annual household income												
$5,000 or less	13.6 (1.70)	21.3 (1.59)	21.0 (3.22)	25.1 (2.92)	35.9 (4.83)	‡ (†)	‡ (†)	3.6! (1.52)	13.7 (4.00)	‡ (†)	17.2 (3.59)	52.9 (4.97)
$5,001 to $10,000	17.5 (2.14)	23.9 (1.37)	24.5 (3.99)	28.0 (2.74)	29.6 (4.49)	2.4! (0.92)	1.5! (0.71)	1.7! (0.81)	8.4 (2.11)	‡ (†)	21.8 (4.75)	61.0 (3.75)
$10,001 to $15,000	22.8 (2.60)	26.7 (1.61)	22.8 (2.45)	28.6 (2.30)	25.0 (3.41)	2.4 (0.69)	0.8! (0.33)	3.3! (1.17)	11.3 (2.52)	‡ (†)	15.5 (3.14)	58.6 (4.43)
$15,001 to $20,000	21.9 (2.35)	31.8 (1.55)	31.4 (2.75)	30.2 (2.48)	24.3 (2.54)	1.0! (0.38)	‡ (†)	3.3! (1.19)	10.1 (1.37)	2.6! (1.20)	12.9 (2.00)	61.1 (3.17)
$20,001 to $25,000	26.7 (3.20)	31.4 (1.27)	35.8 (2.81)	28.2 (2.27)	28.2 (2.51)	1.7! (0.78)	1.9! (0.62)	4.4 (1.26)	12.8 (2.04)	1.1! (0.50)	13.6 (1.88)	63.2 (3.11)
$25,001 to $30,000	32.1 (2.51)	37.9 (1.47)	36.7 (2.61)	38.3 (2.43)	38.6 (3.63)	‡ (†)	1.3! (0.61)	6.8! (2.09)	20.2 (3.37)	‡ (†)	18.4 (2.52)	71.0 (3.38)
$30,001 to $40,000	35.6 (1.84)	42.7 (0.86)	45.2 (2.05)	44.6 (1.54)	42.7 (2.65)	1.9! (0.65)	1.0! (0.49)	3.7 (0.68)	22.8 (2.27)	1.1! (0.39)	23.0 (2.49)	68.7 (2.36)
$40,001 to $50,000	44.8 (1.84)	46.8 (1.39)	44.6 (2.31)	49.1 (1.93)	41.4 (2.92)	1.6! (0.53)	‡ (†)	2.9 (0.55)	22.4 (2.00)	1.5! (0.56)	20.5 (2.47)	71.9 (2.62)
$50,001 to $75,000	46.6 (2.03)	52.0 (0.94)	49.1 (1.93)	55.7 (1.48)	47.7 (1.74)	0.4! (0.19)	‡ (†)	5.8 (0.69)	33.0 (1.37)	0.9! (0.36)	20.5 (1.67)	70.6 (2.15)
More than $75,000	48.7 (3.15)	58.0 (1.27)	55.1 (1.80)	— (†)	— (†)	‡ (†)	‡ (†)	— (†)	— (†)	— (†)	— (†)	— (†)
$75,001 to $100,000	— (†)	— (†)	56.9 (1.66)	59.7 (1.91)	56.4 (2.28)	‡ (†)	‡ (†)	7.5 (0.89)	38.6 (2.26)	1.8! (0.64)	25.3 (1.51)	75.0 (1.97)
More than $100,000	— (†)	— (†)	— (†)	59.3 (1.82)	58.4 (2.11)	‡ (†)	‡ (†)	6.1 (0.70)	39.4 (1.80)	‡ (†)	28.2 (1.62)	81.2 (1.68)

—Not available.
†Not applicable.
!Interpret data with caution. The coefficient of variation (CV) for this estimate is between 30 and 50 percent.
‡Reporting standards not met. Either there are too few cases for a reliable estimate or the coefficient of variation (CV) is 50 percent or greater.
[1]Includes college and university degree programs, post-degree certificate programs, and vocational certificate programs.

[2]For 2005, figures include "Production workers" occupations data.
NOTE: Adult education is defined as all education activities, except full-time enrollment in higher education credential programs. Data do not include persons enrolled in high school or below. Race categories exclude persons of Hispanic ethnicity.
SOURCE: U.S. Department of Education, National Center for Education Statistics, Adult Education Survey (AE-NHES:1991, AE-NHES:1995, AE-NHES:1999, and AE-NHES:2005) and Adult Education and Lifelong Learning Survey (AELL-NHES:2001) of the National Household Education Surveys Program. (This table was prepared November 2010.)

CHAPTER 6
International Comparisons of Education

This chapter offers a broad perspective on education across the nations of the world. It also provides an international context for examining the condition of education in the United States. Insights into the educational practices and outcomes of the United States are obtained by comparing them with those of other education systems. Most of the education systems represent countries; however, some of the tables in this chapter also include data for subnational entities with separate education systems, such as Hong Kong. The National Center for Education Statistics (NCES) carries out a variety of activities in order to provide statistical data for international comparisons of education.

This chapter presents data drawn from materials prepared by the United Nations Educational, Scientific, and Cultural Organization (UNESCO); the Organization for Economic Cooperation and Development (OECD); and the International Association for the Evaluation of Educational Achievement (IEA). Basic summary data on enrollments and enrollment ratios, teachers, educational attainment, and finances were synthesized from data published by OECD in the Online Education Database and the annual *Education at a Glance* report, as well as from data collected by UNESCO. Even though these tabulations are carefully prepared, international data users should be cautioned about the many problems of definition and reporting involved in the collection of data about the education systems of the world, which vary greatly in structure from country to country (see the UNESCO entry on page 897 at the end of Appendix A: Guide to Sources).

Also presented in this chapter are data from two international assessments of student achievement that are carried out under the aegis of IEA and supported by NCES. The Trends in International Mathematics and Science Study (TIMSS), formerly known as the Third International Mathematics and Science Study, assesses the mathematics and science knowledge and skills of fourth- and eighth-graders every 4 years. The Progress in International Reading Literacy Study (PIRLS) measures the reading knowledge and skills of fourth-graders every 5 years.

This chapter includes additional information from the Program for International Student Assessment (PISA), an OECD assessment supported by NCES. PISA provides performance scores of 15-year-olds in the areas of reading, mathematics, and science literacy; it also measures general, or cross-curricular, competencies such as learning strategies. While PISA focuses on OECD countries, data from some non-OECD education systems are also provided.

Further information on survey methodologies is in Appendix A: Guide to Sources and in the publications cited in the table source notes.

Population

Among the reporting OECD countries, Mexico had the largest percentage of its population made up of young people ages 5 to 14 (19 percent) in 2011, followed by Israel (18 percent) and Turkey (17 percent) (table 601.30). OECD countries with small percentages of people in this age group included the Czech Republic, Germany, Greece, Italy, Japan, and Slovenia (all at 9 percent), and Austria, Estonia, Hungary, Poland, Portugal, the Slovak Republic, Spain, and Switzerland (all at 10 percent). In the United States, the proportion of 5- to 14-year-olds was 13 percent, which was higher than in most of the other OECD countries.

Enrollments

In 2012, about 1.5 billion students were enrolled in schools around the world (table 601.10). Of these students, 706 million were in elementary-level programs, 552 million were in secondary programs, and 196 million were in postsecondary programs.

From 2000 to 2012, enrollment changes varied from region to region. Changes in elementary enrollment ranged from increases of 56 percent in Africa and 35 percent in Oceania to decreases of 11 percent in Europe, 7 percent in Central and South America (including Latin America and the Caribbean), 3 percent in Northern America (including Bermuda, Canada, Greenland, St. Pierre and Miquelon, and the United States), and less than 1 percent in Asia (table F, table 601.10, and figure 27). Over the same period, secondary enrollment increased by 75 percent in Africa, 31 percent in Asia, 10 percent in Central and South America, 6 percent in Northern America, and 3 percent in Oceania but decreased by 20 percent in Europe. At the postsecondary level, enrollments increased in all major areas of the world from 2000 to 2012. Postsecondary enrollment rose by 155 percent in Asia, 103 percent in Central and South America, 92 percent in Africa, 58 percent in Oceania, 55 percent in Northern America, and 27 percent in Europe.

Table F. Population and enrollment at different levels in major areas of the world: 2000 and 2012

[In millions]

Area of the world	Population	Enrollment		
		Elementary	Secondary	Postsecondary
World total				
2000.................	6,090.3	655.6	449.9	99.5
2012.................	7,020.8	705.7	552.4	196.1
Africa				
2000.................	803.5	108.4	38.4	6.1
2012.................	1,073.1	168.9	67.0	11.7
Asia				
2000.................	3,694.6	404.8	257.5	41.0
2012.................	4,223.7	403.9	338.3	104.7
Europe				
2000.................	730.6	41.7	70.5	25.6
2012.................	741.2	37.2	56.2	32.5
Central and South America				
2000.................	517.8	70.0	55.1	11.4
2012.................	598.6	65.0	60.7	23.1
Northern America				
2000.................	313.4	27.4	25.1	14.4
2012.................	348.3	26.6	26.7	22.4
Oceania				
2000.................	30.4	3.1	3.4	1.0
2012.................	35.8	4.2	3.5	1.7

SOURCE: United Nations Educational, Scientific, and Cultural Organization, unpublished tabulations, and U.S. Department of Commerce, Census Bureau, International Data Base.

In 2012, the reporting OECD country with the highest proportion of 18- to 21-year-olds enrolled in postsecondary education was the Republic of Korea (68 percent), followed by Greece and the United States (both at 49 percent), Belgium (46 percent), and Ireland and Slovenia (both at 44 percent) (table 601.40). Also in 2012, the reporting OECD country with the highest proportion of 22- to 25-year-olds enrolled in postsecondary education was Slovenia (39 percent), followed by Denmark (38 percent), and Finland and the Republic of Korea (both at 37 percent). The United States' proportion of enrolled 22- to 25-year-olds was 28 percent. Postsecondary enrollment varied among countries due partially to differences in how postsecondary education is defined and the age at which postsecondary education begins. For example, programs classified as postsecondary education in some countries may be classified as long-duration secondary education in other countries.

Achievement

Mathematics and Science at Grades 4 and 8

The 2011 Trends in International Mathematics and Science Study (TIMSS) assessed students' mathematics and science performance at grade 4 in 45 countries and at grade 8 in 38 countries. A number of subnational entities also participated in TIMSS as separate education systems. Examples of subnational participants include the cities of Hong Kong and Taipei, several U.S. states and Canadian provinces, Northern Ireland and England within the United Kingdom, and the Flemish community in Belgium. Results for individ-

ual U.S. states are based on public school students only, while U.S. national results are based on both public and private school students. TIMSS assessments are curriculum based and measure what students have actually learned against the subject matter that is expected to be taught by the end of grades 4 and 8, as described in the TIMSS mathematics and science frameworks, which guide assessment development. At both grades, TIMSS scores are reported on a scale of 0 to 1,000, with the scale average set at 500.

In 2011, the average mathematics scores of U.S. fourth-graders (541) and eighth-graders (509) were higher than the TIMSS scale average of 500 (tables 602.20 and 602.30). The average U.S. fourth-grade mathematics score was higher than the average score in 37 of the 44 other countries participating at grade 4, lower than the average score in 3 countries, and not measurably different from the average score in the remaining 4 countries (table 602.20). The 3 countries that outperformed the United States in fourth-grade mathematics were Singapore, the Republic of Korea, and Japan. At grade 8, the average U.S. mathematics score was higher than the average score in 27 of the 37 other participating countries in 2011, lower than the average score in 4 countries, and not measurably different from the average score in the remaining 6 countries (table 602.30). The 4 countries that outperformed the United States in eighth-grade mathematics were the Republic of Korea, Singapore, Japan, and the Russian Federation.

Of the two U.S. states that participated in the 2011 TIMSS as separate education systems at grade 4, one state—North Carolina—had an average score for public schools that was higher than both the TIMSS scale average and the U.S. national average in mathematics (table 602.20). Public schools in the other state, Florida, had an average fourth-grade mathematics score that was higher than the TIMSS scale average but not measurably different from the U.S. national average. Of the nine U.S. states that participated separately at grade 8, four states—Massachusetts, Minnesota, North Carolina, and Indiana—had public school average scores that were higher than both the TIMSS scale average and the U.S. national average in mathematics (table 602.30). The public schools in three states—Colorado, Connecticut, and Florida—had average eighth-grade mathematics scores that were higher than the TIMSS scale average but not measurably different from the U.S. national average. The average eighth-grade score for public schools in California was not measurably different from the TIMSS scale average but was lower than the U.S. national average, while Alabama's public school average was lower than both the TIMSS scale average and the U.S. national average in mathematics.

The average science scores of both U.S. fourth-graders (544) and U.S. eighth-graders (525) were higher than the TIMSS scale average of 500 in 2011 (tables 602.20 and 602.30). The average U.S. fourth-grade science score was higher than the average score in 39 of the 44 other countries participating at grade 4 and lower than the average score in 5 countries (table 602.20). The 5 countries that outperformed the United States in fourth-grade science were the

Republic of Korea, Singapore, Finland, Japan, and the Russian Federation. At grade 8, the average U.S. science score was higher than the average score in 28 of the 37 other participating countries in 2011, lower than the average score in 6 countries, and not measurably different from the average score in the remaining 3 countries (table 602.30). The 6 countries that outperformed the United States in eighth-grade science were Singapore, the Republic of Korea, Japan, Finland, Slovenia, and the Russian Federation.

Public schools in both Florida and North Carolina, which were the two U.S. states participating in the 2011 TIMSS at grade 4, had average fourth-grade science scores that were higher than the TIMSS scale average but not measurably different from the U.S. national average (table 602.20). Of the nine U.S. states that participated at grade 8, three states—Massachusetts, Minnesota, and Colorado—had public school average scores that were higher than both the TIMSS scale average and the U.S. national average in science (table 602.30). Public schools in four states—Indiana, Connecticut, North Carolina, and Florida—had average eighth-grade science scores that were higher than the TIMSS scale average but not measurably different from the U.S. national average. The average eighth-grade score for public schools in California was not measurably different from the TIMSS scale average but was lower than the U.S. national average, while Alabama's public school average was lower than both the TIMSS scale average and the U.S. national average in science.

Reading Literacy at Grade 4

The Progress in International Reading Literacy Study (PIRLS) has conducted international assessments of fourth-grade reading literacy in 2001, 2006, and 2011. In 2011, PIRLS participants consisted of 40 countries as well as a number of subnational education systems. Examples of subnational participants include the cities of Hong Kong and Taipei, the public school system of the U.S. state of Florida, several Canadian provinces, Northern Ireland and England within the United Kingdom, and the Flemish community in Belgium. PIRLS scores are reported on a scale from 0 to 1,000, with the scale average set at 500.

On the 2011 PIRLS, U.S. fourth-graders had an average reading literacy score of 556 (table 602.10). The U.S. average score in 2011 was 14 points higher than in 2001 and 16 points higher than in 2006. In all 3 assessment years, the U.S. average score was higher than the PIRLS scale average.

In 2011, the average reading literacy score of fourth-graders in the United States was higher than the average score in 33 of the 39 other participating countries, lower than the average score in 3 countries, and not measurably different from the average in the remaining 3 countries. The 3 countries that outperformed the United States on the 2011 PIRLS were the Russian Federation, Finland, and Singapore. Public school students in Florida scored higher than both the PIRLS scale average and the U.S. national average.

In the United States, the 2011 average reading literacy score for females (562) was higher than the average score for males (551). In 34 of the 39 other participating countries, the average score for females was also higher than the average score for males, while there was no measurable difference between females' and males' average scores in the remaining 5 countries.

Reading, Mathematics, and Science Literacy at Age 15

The Program for International Student Assessment (PISA) assesses 15-year-old students' application of reading, mathematics, and science literacy to problems within a real-life context. In 2012, PISA assessed students in the 34 OECD countries as well as in a number of other education systems. Some subnational entities participated as separate education systems, including the U.S. states of Connecticut, Florida, and Massachusetts. Results for individual U.S. states are based on public school students only, while U.S. national results are based on both public and private school students. PISA scores are reported on a scale of 0 to 1,000.

On the 2012 PISA assessment, U.S. 15-year-olds' average score in reading literacy was 498, which was not measurably different from the OECD average of 496 (table 602.50). The average reading literacy score in the United States was lower than the average score in 13 of the 33 other OECD countries, higher than the average score in 10 of the other OECD countries, and not measurably different from the average score in 10 of the OECD countries. The average reading literacy scores of public school students in Massachusetts (527) and Connecticut (521) were higher than both the U.S. average and the OECD average, while the average score in Florida (492) was not measurably different from either the U.S. average or the OECD average. In all participating education systems, females outperformed males in reading (table 602.40). The U.S. gender gap in reading (31 points) was smaller than the OECD average gap (38 points) and smaller than the gaps in 14 of the OECD countries.

In mathematics literacy, U.S. 15-year-olds' average score of 481 on the 2012 PISA assessment was lower than the OECD average score of 494 (table 602.60). The average mathematics literacy score in the United States was lower than the average in 21 of the 33 other OECD countries, higher than the average in 5 OECD countries, and not measurably different from the average in 7 OECD countries. The average mathematics literacy score of public school students in Massachusetts (514) was higher than both the U.S. average and the OECD average, while the average score in Connecticut (506) was higher than the U.S. average but not measurably different from the OECD average. The average score in Florida (467) was lower than both the U.S. average and the OECD average. In 25 of the OECD countries, males outperformed females in mathematics literacy (table 602.40). In the United States, however, the average score of males (484) was not measurably different from that of females (479).

In science literacy, U.S. 15-year-olds' average score of 497 was not measurably different from the OECD average score of 501 (table 602.70). The average science literacy score in the United States was lower than the average in 15 OECD countries, higher than the average in 8 OECD countries, and not measurably different from the average in 10 OECD countries. The average science literacy scores of public school students in Massachusetts (527) and Connecticut (521) were higher than both the U.S. average and the OECD average. The average score in Florida (485) was not measurably different from the U.S. average but was lower than the OECD average.

Educational Attainment

In 2012, the percentage of 25- to 64-year-olds who had completed high school varied among reporting OECD countries (table 603.10). The OECD country reporting the highest percentage of 25- to 64-year-olds who had completed high school was the Czech Republic (92 percent), followed by the Slovak Republic (also at 92 percent, when rounded to the nearest whole number). High school completers made up 89 to 90 percent of 25- to 64-year-olds in 4 OECD countries—Canada (89 percent), the United States (89 percent), Estonia (90 percent), and Poland (90 percent)—and 10 OECD countries reported percentages between 80 and 88 percent. The OECD country reporting the lowest percentage of high school completers among 25- to 64-year-olds was Turkey (34 percent), followed by Mexico (37 percent) and Portugal (38 percent).

In 2012, the OECD country reporting the highest percentage of 25- to 64-year-olds with a bachelor's or higher degree was Norway (36 percent), followed by the United States and Israel (both at 33 percent) (table 603.20). An additional 16 OECD countries reported that 24 to 32 percent of their 25- to 64-year-olds had a bachelor's or higher degree. The OECD country reporting the lowest percentage of 25- to 64-year-olds with a bachelor's or higher degree was Austria (13 percent), followed by Slovenia (about 15 percent) and then Turkey and Italy (both at 15 percent).

Among younger adults (25 to 34 years old) in OECD countries, the percentage with a bachelor's or higher degree also varied in 2012 (table 603.20 and figure 28). The OECD country reporting the highest percentage of younger adults with a bachelor's or higher degree was Norway (44 percent). More than 30 percent of younger adults had a bachelor's or higher degree in 17 additional countries, including the United States (34 percent). The OECD country reporting the lowest percentage of younger adults with a bachelor's or higher degree in 2012 was Austria (18 percent).

Degrees

In 29 of the 32 reporting OECD countries, more than half of all bachelor's and higher degrees were awarded to women in 2012 (table 603.60). However, the proportion of degrees awarded to women varied by field. For example, 30 of the 32 countries reported that at least 70 percent of education degrees at the bachelor's or higher level were awarded to women. In contrast, women received less than 25 percent of the computer science degrees in 24 of the 31 countries reporting data on degrees awarded in this field.

The percentages of bachelor's degrees that were awarded in mathematics and science fields—including natural sciences, mathematics and computer science, and engineering—varied across the 31 OECD countries that reported these data in 2011 (table 603.70). Only one of the reporting OECD countries awarded more than 30 percent of its bachelor's degrees in mathematics and science fields: the Republic of Korea (34 percent). Two countries awarded 15 percent or less of their bachelor's degrees in mathematics and science fields: the Netherlands (13 percent) and Norway (15 percent). In 2011, the United States awarded 16 percent of its bachelor's degrees in mathematics and science fields, a lower percentage than most other reporting countries.

The percentages of graduate degrees awarded in mathematics and science fields varied widely across the 31 OECD countries that reported these data in 2011 (table 603.80). Five of the reporting OECD countries awarded more than 30 percent of their graduate degrees in mathematics and science fields: Japan (47 percent), Sweden (43 percent), Germany (35 percent), Austria (33 percent), and Greece (32 percent). Six OECD countries awarded less than 15 percent of their graduate degrees in mathematics and science fields: Chile (8 percent), Poland (11 percent), Mexico (12 percent), the United States (13 percent), and Hungary and the Netherlands (both at 14 percent).

Finances

In 2011, expenditures per full-time-equivalent (FTE) student at the combined elementary and secondary level of education were over $11,000 (in current U.S. dollars) in 5 of the 32 OECD countries that reported finance data for this level of education (table 605.10). Specifically, Luxembourg spent $19,600 per elementary/secondary student; Switzerland spent $14,600; Norway spent $13,200; Austria spent $12,500; and the United States spent $11,800. At the higher education level, 7 of 31 reporting countries had expenditures of over $17,000 per FTE student in 2011: the United States ($26,000), Switzerland ($22,900), Denmark ($21,300), Sweden ($20,800), Norway ($18,800), Finland ($18,000), and the Netherlands ($17,500). These expenditures were adjusted to U.S. dollars using the purchasing-power-parity (PPP) index. This index is considered more stable and comparable than indexes using currency exchange rates.

A comparison of public direct expenditures on education as a percentage of gross domestic product (GDP) in reporting OECD countries shows that public investment in education in 2011 ranged from 3.6 percent in Japan to 7.5 percent in Denmark (table 605.20 and figure 29). Among reporting OECD countries, the average public direct expenditure on education in 2011 was 5.3 percent of GDP. In the United States, the public direct expenditure on education as a percentage of GDP was 4.7 percent.

Figure 27. Percentage change in enrollment, by major areas of the world and level of education: 2000 to 2012

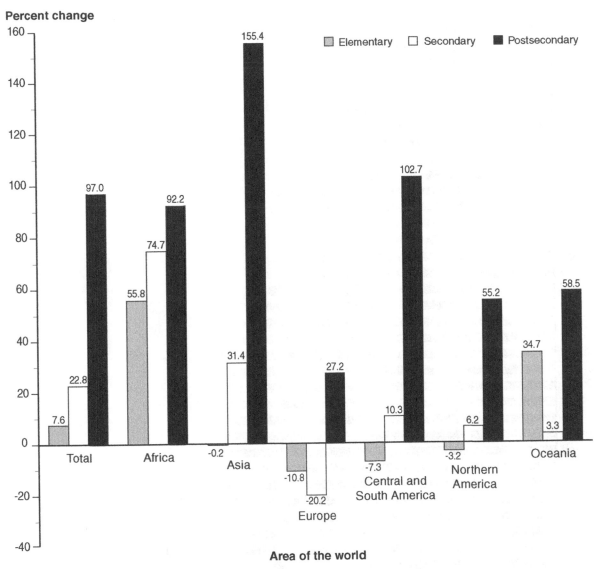

NOTE: Europe includes all countries of the former Union of Soviet Socialist Republics (U.S.S.R.) except Armenia, Azerbaijan, Georgia, Kazakhstan, Kyrgyzstan, Tajikistan, Turkmenistan, and Uzbekistan, which are included in Asia. Turkey, the Arab states, and Israel are also included in Asia. Central and South America includes Latin America and the Caribbean. Northern America includes Bermuda, Canada, Greenland, St. Pierre and Miquelon, and the United States of America. Data include imputed values for nonrespondent countries.
SOURCE: United Nations Educational, Scientific, and Cultural Organization (UNESCO), previously unpublished tabulations (January 2015).

Figure 28. Percentage of the population 25 to 34 years old with a bachelor's or higher degree, by OECD country: 2012

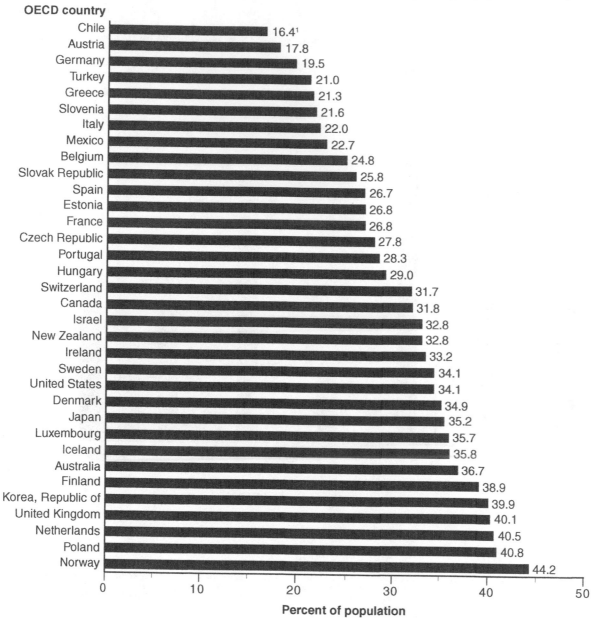

OECD country

Chile	16.4[1]
Austria	17.8
Germany	19.5
Turkey	21.0
Greece	21.3
Slovenia	21.6
Italy	22.0
Mexico	22.7
Belgium	24.8
Slovak Republic	25.8
Spain	26.7
Estonia	26.8
France	26.8
Czech Republic	27.8
Portugal	28.3
Hungary	29.0
Switzerland	31.7
Canada	31.8
Israel	32.8
New Zealand	32.8
Ireland	33.2
Sweden	34.1
United States	34.1
Denmark	34.9
Japan	35.2
Luxembourg	35.7
Iceland	35.8
Australia	36.7
Finland	38.9
Korea, Republic of	39.9
United Kingdom	40.1
Netherlands	40.5
Poland	40.8
Norway	44.2

Percent of population

[1]Data for Chile are from 2011.
NOTE: Refers to degrees classified by OECD as International Standard Classification of Education (ISCED) level 5A (first and second award) or level 6. ISCED 5A, first award, corresponds to the bachelor's degree in the United States; ISCED 5A, second award, corresponds to master's and first-professional degrees in the United States; and ISCED 6 corresponds to doctor's degrees.
SOURCE: Organization for Economic Cooperation and Development (OECD), *Education at a Glance, 2014*.

Figure 29. Public direct expenditures on education institutions as a percentage of gross domestic product (GDP), by OECD country: 2011

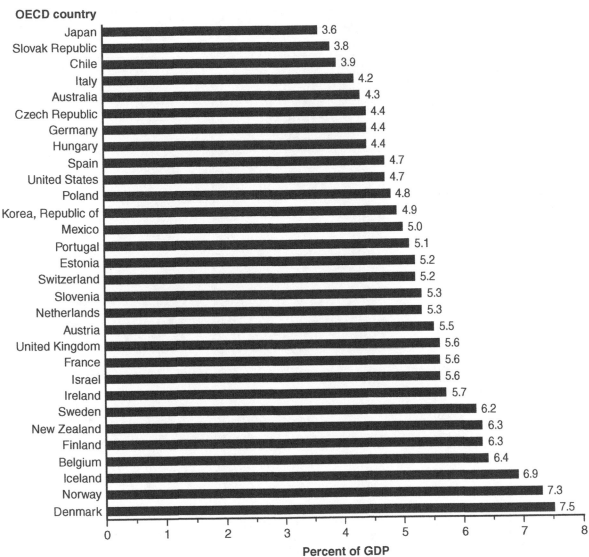

OECD country

Country	Percent of GDP
Japan	3.6
Slovak Republic	3.8
Chile	3.9
Italy	4.2
Australia	4.3
Czech Republic	4.4
Germany	4.4
Hungary	4.4
Spain	4.7
United States	4.7
Poland	4.8
Korea, Republic of	4.9
Mexico	5.0
Portugal	5.1
Estonia	5.2
Switzerland	5.2
Slovenia	5.3
Netherlands	5.3
Austria	5.5
United Kingdom	5.6
France	5.6
Israel	5.6
Ireland	5.7
Sweden	6.2
New Zealand	6.3
Finland	6.3
Belgium	6.4
Iceland	6.9
Norway	7.3
Denmark	7.5

Percent of GDP

NOTE: Includes amounts spent directly by governments to hire educational personnel and to procure other resources, as well as amounts provided by governments to public or private institutions.
SOURCE: Organization for Economic Cooperation and Development (OECD), *Education at a Glance, 2014.*

Table 601.10. Population, school enrollment, and number of teachers, by major areas of the world and level of education: Selected years, 1980 through 2012

[In thousands]

Year and selected characteristic	World total[1]	Major areas of the world					
		Africa	Asia[1,2]	Europe[2]	Central and South America[3]	Northern America[3]	Oceania
1	2	3	4	5	6	7	8
1980							
Population, all ages[4]	4,450,930	478,544	2,644,088	695,225	358,609	251,929	22,534
Enrollment, all levels	858,346	76,926	494,035	134,519	87,117	60,542	—
First level[5]	524,410	60,306	334,104	47,664	56,794	22,893	2,649
Second level[6]	284,202	14,915	146,933	69,985	25,528	24,695	—
Third level[7]	49,734	1,705	12,998	16,870	4,795	12,955	411
Teachers, all levels	38,943	—	19,248	—	—	—	276
First level[5]	18,484	1,657	10,711	2,498	1,871	—	134
Second level[6]	16,573	603	7,402	—	—	—	112
Third level[7]	3,886	—	1,135	—	382	815	31
1990							
Population, all ages[4]	5,287,869	630,169	3,190,508	722,638	440,609	277,533	26,412
Enrollment, all levels	976,827	106,051	562,119	132,711	108,612	61,543	5,790
First level[5]	576,069	77,084	361,509	45,197	65,042	24,629	2,607
Second level[6]	333,215	26,128	177,832	68,828	36,327	21,534	2,566
Third level[7]	67,543	2,839	22,778	18,686	7,243	15,380	617
Teachers, all levels	47,486	3,674	24,504	—	—	3,938	314
First level[5]	22,131	2,313	13,063	2,607	2,400	1,608	139
Second level[6]	20,336	1,220	9,728	—	—	1,340	134
Third level[7]	5,019	141	1,713	1,532	601	991	41
1995							
Population, all ages[4]	5,699,768	712,602	3,452,081	730,000	480,608	296,092	28,385
Enrollment, all levels	1,086,479	125,625	630,611	136,971	120,335	65,901	7,035
First level[5]	619,539	90,578	387,406	44,748	67,551	26,243	3,014
Second level[6]	387,868	30,912	214,757	71,120	44,619	23,595	2,864
Third level[7]	79,072	4,136	28,447	21,103	8,165	16,063	1,158
Teachers, all levels	52,145	4,264	26,978	10,538	5,781	4,208	—
First level[5]	23,831	2,602	14,067	2,762	2,628	1,622	150
Second level[6]	22,617	1,459	10,934	6,102	2,453	1,503	—
Third level[7]	5,697	202	1,978	1,674	699	1,083	—
2000							
Population, all ages[4]	6,090,319	803,528	3,694,628	730,598	517,756	313,388	30,421
Enrollment, all levels	1,205,000	152,856	703,352	137,738	136,527	66,968	7,559
First level[5]	655,589	108,437	404,844	41,703	70,040	27,435	3,131
Second level[6]	449,883	38,357	257,494	70,458	55,072	25,117	3,384
Third level[7]	99,528	6,062	41,014	25,577	11,415	14,416	1,044
Teachers, all levels	56,619	4,972	29,319	10,695	6,579	4,648	—
First level[5]	24,928	2,889	14,571	2,730	2,777	1,806	155
Second level[6]	25,017	1,804	12,309	6,092	2,934	1,682	—
Third level[7]	6,675	278	2,439	1,873	869	1,161	—
2005							
Population, all ages[4]	6,474,229	907,745	3,920,235	733,119	552,438	328,033	32,659
Enrollment, all levels	1,324,516	192,515	772,798	135,516	143,401	72,389	7,898
First level[5]	677,948	135,425	405,287	38,474	68,840	26,780	3,142
Second level[6]	507,363	48,597	304,872	64,896	58,497	27,039	3,462
Third level[7]	139,205	8,493	62,639	32,145	16,063	18,570	1,295
Teachers, all levels	64,309	6,010	34,422	10,693	7,741	5,007	—
First level[5]	26,896	3,513	15,733	2,663	2,966	1,865	—
Second level[6]	28,315	2,153	14,822	5,801	3,553	1,774	—
Third level[7]	9,098	344	3,867	2,229	1,222	1,368	—
2012							
Population, all ages[4]	7,020,760	1,073,075	4,223,675	741,226	598,608	348,347	35,830
Enrollment, all levels	1,454,218	247,546	846,954	125,939	148,822	75,588	9,369
First level[5]	705,696	168,891	403,884	37,197	64,955	26,552	4,218
Second level[6]	552,444	67,005	338,328	56,218	60,728	26,670	3,496
Third level[7]	196,077	11,650	104,742	32,524	23,139	22,367	1,655
Teachers, all levels	73,196	8,155	40,361	10,248	8,659	5,298	—
First level[5]	29,136	4,599	16,773	2,641	3,120	1,815	—
Second level[6]	32,343	3,105	18,140	5,229	3,884	1,781	—
Third level[7]	11,717	451	5,447	2,378	1,655	1,701	—

—Not available.

[1]Enrollment and teacher data for the world total and Asia exclude Taiwan.

[2]Europe includes all countries of the former Union of Soviet Socialist Republics (U.S.S.R.) except Armenia, Azerbaijan, Georgia, Kazakhstan, Kyrgyzstan, Tajikistan, Turkmenistan, and Uzbekistan, which are included in Asia. Asia also includes Turkey, the Arab states (with the exception of those located in Africa), and Israel.

[3]Central and South America includes Latin America and the Caribbean. Northern America includes Bermuda, Canada, Greenland, St. Pierre and Miquelon, and the United States.

[4]Estimate of midyear population.

[5]First-level enrollment generally consists of elementary school, grades 1–6.

[6]Second-level enrollment includes general education, teacher training (at the second level), and technical and vocational education. This level generally corresponds to secondary education in the United States, grades 7–12.

[7]Third-level enrollment includes college and university enrollment, and technical and vocational education beyond the secondary school level.

NOTE: Detail may not sum to totals because of rounding. Data include imputed values for nonrespondent countries. Enrollment and teacher data exclude several island countries or territories with small populations (less than 150,000). Some data have been revised from previously published figures.

SOURCE: United Nations Educational, Scientific, and Cultural Organization (UNESCO), unpublished tabulations. U.S. Department of Commerce, Census Bureau, International Data Base, retrieved January 16, 2015, from http://www.census.gov/population/international/data/idb/informationGateway.php. (This table was prepared March 2015.)

Table 601.20. Selected population and enrollment statistics for countries with populations of at least 10 million in 2012, by continent and country: Selected years, 1990 through 2012

Continent and country[1]	Midyear population (in millions)			Persons per square kilometer 2012	First level[2]					Second level[3]					Third level[4]				
					Enrollment (in thousands)		Gross enrollment ratio[5]			Enrollment (in thousands)		Gross enrollment ratio[5]			Enrollment (in thousands)		Gross enrollment ratio[5]		
	1991	2000	2012	2012	1999–2000	2011–12	1990–91	1999–2000	2011–12	1999–2000	2011–12	1990–91	1999–2000	2011–12	1999–2000	2011–12	1990–91	1999–2000	2011–12
1	2	3	4	5	6	7	8	9	10	11	12	13	14	15	16	17	18	19	20
World total[6]	5,371	6,090	7,021	53	654,745	705,103[7]	99	98	108[7]	449,070	551,686[7]	52	59	73[7]	99,180	195,557[7]	14	19	32[7]
Africa																			
Algeria[8]	26	31	37	16	4,843	3,452	100	103	117	2,994	—	61	62	—	—	1,210	11	—	31
Angola	10	13	18	15	—	—	92	—	85	355	676	12	15	26	—	—	1	—	5
Burkina Faso	9	12	17	63	852	2,344	33	45	85	190	—	7	10	26	—	69	1	1	5
Cameroon	12	16	22	46	2,237[9]	3,849	101	83[9]	111	700	1,713	28	27	50	66	—	3	5[7]	—
Chad	6	8	11	9	914	2,091	54	64	95	137	458	8[10]	11	23	6	—	1[11,12]	1	—
Congo, Democratic Republic of the	41	52	74	33	—	12,005	70	77	111	—	3,894	21[13]	—	43	—	511	2	—	8
Cote d'Ivoire	13	17	22	69	1,943	2,921	67	77	94	—	—	22	—	—	—	81	—	—	4
Egypt[8]	56	65	84	84	7,947[7]	10,820	94	101[7]	113	8,028[7]	7,850	76	86[7]	86	—	2,301	16[14,15]	—	30
Ethiopia	49	64	91	91	5,847	14,532	33	55	—	1,195	4,849	14	14	38	68	693	1[11]	1	—
Ghana[8]	16	19	25	108	2,561	4,062	75	86	110	1,057	2,216	36	41	58	—	295	1	—	12
Guinea	7	8	11	44	790	1,600	37	57	91	—	657	10	—	38	—	101	1	—	10
Kenya[8]	24	31	43	76	5,035	—	95	96	—	1,909	1,405	24[10]	39	38	89	90	2[11]	3	4
Madagascar	12	16	22	38	2,208	4,403	103	100	145	487	—	18[10]	32	—	32	—	3	2	—
Malawi	10	12	16	174	2,695	3,688	68	138	141	258[7]	761	8	4	34	4	97	1	#	7
Mali	9	11	15	13	1,017	2,114	26	62	88	1,541	2,554	7	38	69	20	—	1	2[11]	—
Morocco[8]	24	28	32	72	3,670	4,017	67	92	116	124	728	35	6	26	276	22	11	9	2
Mozambique[8]	13	18	24	30	2,544	5,359	67	74	105	106[7]	389	8	7[7]	16	12	—	#[12]	1	—
Niger	8	11	16	13	579	2,051	29	34	71	4,104	—	7	24	—	9	72	7	#	7
Nigeria[8]	99	124	169	185	19,151	—	91	98	134	130	535	25	11	32	—	—	4[11,16]	1	—
Rwanda[8]	7	8	12	474	1,432	2,395	70	111	84	250	—	8	16	—	—	—	#[17]	—	—
Senegal	8	9	13	67	1,108	1,783	59	68	102	—	—	16	—	—	—	—	3[18]	—	—
Somalia	6	8	10	16	—	—	—	—	—	—	—	—	—	—	—	—	—	—	—
South Africa	39	45	49	40	7,445	7,004	122	107	102	4,142	4,844	74	84	102	727	—	13[18]	—	15
South Sudan	5	6	11	17	—	—	—	—	93	—	—	—	—	—	—	—	—	—	—
Sudan[8]	22	27	34	18	—	—	53	68	110	—	2,118	24	—	35	—	551	3[11]	7[7]	—
Tanzania	26	33	47	53	4,382	8,247	70	116	93	1,104[7]	—	5	75[7]	—	180	166	#[13]	—	4
Tunisia	8	10	11	69	1,414	1,047	113	129	110	547	—	45	16	—	56	357	9	3	35
Uganda[8]	17	23	34	171	6,559	—	74[19,20]	84	110	844	—	13[10,20]	—	—	25[7]	—	1	—	—
Zambia	8	10	14	19	1,590	6,924	99	101	104	—	—	24	—	—	—	94	2	2[7]	—
Zimbabwe	10	12	13	33	2,461	3,135	116	—	101	—	—	50	43	—	—	—	5	—	6
Asia																			
Afghanistan[8]	14	22	30	47	749	5,768	27	21	104	—	2,416	9	—	54	—	—	2	—	—
Bangladesh	114	132	161	1,238	—	—	72	—	124	10,329	12,187	19	48	54	727	—	4	5	—
Cambodia	10	12	15	85	2,248	2,195	121	106	128	351	—	32	17	—	22	—	1	2	—
China	1,164	1,264	1,343	140	113,613	99,540	125	—	128	81,488	95,004	49	58	89	7,364	32,586	3	8	27
India	854	1,006	1,205	405	28,509	30,784	97	96	109	71,031	21,446	44[10]	46	—	9,404	28,526	6	10	25
Indonesia	185	214	249	137	8,288	5,747	115	110	106	14,720	7,118	44	56	83	3,126	6,234	9[13]	15	32
Iran	60	69	79	52	3,639	—	112	101	—	9,955	—	55	79	86	1,405	4,405	10[14]	19	55
Iraq	17	23	31	71	—	—	111	96	106	1,224	—	47[10]	37	37	289	—	12[17]	12	—
Japan	124	127	127	349	7,529	6,924	100	101	102	8,782	7,283	97	102	102	3,982	3,885	30[13]	49	61
Kazakhstan	17	16	18	7	1,208	1,008	87	99	105	2,003	1,643	98	96	98	370	652	40	29	45
Korea, Democratic People's Republic of	21	23	25	204	—	—	—	—	—	—	—	—	—	—	—	—	—	—	—
Korea, Republic of	43	47	49	504	4,030	2,959	105	102	103	3,959	3,783	90	99	97	3,003	3,357	39	79	98

See notes at end of table.

Table 601.20. Selected population and enrollment statistics for countries with populations of at least 10 million in 2012, by continent and country: Selected years, 1990 through 2012—Continued

Continent and country[1]	Midyear population (in millions)			Persons per square kilometer, 2012	First level[2]					Second level[3]					Third level[4]				
	1991	2000	2012	2012	Enrollment (in thousands)		Gross enrollment ratio[5]			Enrollment (in thousands)		Gross enrollment ratio[5]			Enrollment (in thousands)		Gross enrollment ratio[5]		
					1999–2000	2011–12	1990–91	1999–2000	2011–12	1999–2000	2011–12	1990–91	1999–2000	2011–12	1999–2000	2011–12	1990–91	1999–2000	2011–12
1	2	3	4	5	6	7	8	9	10	11	12	13	14	15	16	17	18	19	20
Malaysia	18	23	29	89	3,026	—	94	98	—	2,205	—	56	66	—	549	—	7	26	—
Myanmar[8]	41	47	55	84	4,858	—	106	98	—	2,268	3,015	23	36	66	—	—	4[13]	—	—
Nepal[8]	19	25	30	209	3,780[9]	4,783	108	126[9]	139	1,348	—	33	37	37	94	—	5	4	10
Pakistan	122	152	190	247	13,987[21]	18,119	61[22]	70[21]	93	—	10,372	23	—	—	—	1,817	3	—	10
Philippines	67	81	104	348	12,708	—	111	110	103	—	—	73	—	—	—	—	28	—	—
Saudi Arabia	16	21	27	12	—	3,436	73	—	98	—	3,169[7]	44	—	114[7]	404	1,206	12	23	51
Sri Lanka[8]	17	19	21	332	2,775	1,752	106	108	122	—	2,590	74	—	99	—	271	5[13,23]	—	17
Syria	13	16	23	123	—	2,553	108	108	—	1,069	2,876	52	44	74	—	—	18	—	—
Taiwan	20	22	23	720	—	—	100	—	—	—	—	—	—	—	—	—	—	—	—
Thailand	57	63	67	132	6,101	5,005	99	98	95	5,658	4,786	30	—	87	1,900	2,430	19[12]	35	51
Turkey	58	67	80	104	6,562	6,430	99	103	100	—	7,758	47	73	86	—	4,354	13	13	69
Uzbekistan	21	25	28	67	2,602	—	81	99	—	3,566	—	99	88	—	305	—	30	13	—
Vietnam	69	79	92	295	10,063	7,101	103	107	105	—	—	32	—	—	732	2,261	2	9	25
Yemen	13	17	25	47	—	3,685	79[16]	—	97	—	1,675	23[16]	—	47	—	—	4[13]	—	—
Europe																			
Belgium	10	10	10	345	774	744	101	105	103	1,058	794	103	145	107	356	478	40	58	71
Czech Republic	10	10	11	137	645	477	96	103	100	958	777	91	89	97	254	440	16[24]	28	64
France[25]	59	61	66	103	3,885	4,156	108	104	107	5,929	5,920	99	106	110	2,015	2,296	40	57	58
Germany	80	82	81	233	3,656	2,937	101	103	100	8,307	7,393	98	96	101	—	2,939	34	—	62
Greece	10	11	11	82	645	—	98	96	—	739	—	93	89	—	422	—	36	51	—
Italy[8]	57	58	61	208	2,836	—	103	103	106	4,404	—	83	93	—	1,770	1,926	32	49	62
Netherlands[8]	15	16	17	494	1,279	1,277	102	109	101	1,379	1,550	120	123	130	488	794	40	53	77
Poland[8]	38	39	38	126	3,319	2,187	98	99	106	3,988	2,611	81	100	98	1,580	2,007	22	50	73
Portugal	10	10	11	118	811	704	123	122	106	831	734	67	105	113	374	390	23	48	69
Romania[8]	23	22	22	95	1,189	807	91	93	94	2,226	1,714	92	81	95	453	—	10	24	—
Russian Federation	148	147	143	9	6,138	5,515	109	103	101	—	9,165	93	111	95	6,331	7,983	52	55	76
Spain[8]	39	41	47	94	2,540	2,817	109	106	103	3,246	3,296	104	99	131	1,829	1,966[7]	37	59	85[7]
Ukraine[8]	52	49	45	77	2,079	1,584	89	109	106	5,204	2,899	93	99	98	1,812	2,391	47	49	80
United Kingdom[8]	58	59	63	261	4,632	4,524	104	101	109	5,315	4,849	85	102	95	2,024	2,496	30	58	62
North America																			
Canada	28	31	34	4	2,456	—	103	100	—	2,519	—	101	102	—	1,212	—	95	59	—
Cuba	11	11	11	101	1,046	803	98	101	99	790	784	89	82	90	159	503	21	22	62
Dominican Republic	7	8	10	209	1,364	1,284	—	113	103	654	906	—	59	76	—	—	—	—	—
Guatemala	9	11	14	132	1,909	—	78	104	104	504	—	23[13]	38	—	—	—	8[12]	—	—
Mexico	86	100	117	60	14,766	14,957	114	106	105	9,094	12,139	53	70	86	1,963	3,161	15	19	29
United States	253	282	314	34	24,973	24,382	102	101	98	22,594	24,122	93	92	94	13,203	20,994	75	68	94
South America																			
Argentina	34	37	42	15	4,728	—	106	114	—	3,428	—	71	87	—	1,767[7]	—	38[13]	53[7]	—
Bolivia	7	8	10	10	1,492	—	95	112	—	877[7]	—	37	78[7]	—	279	—	21	35	—
Brazil	152	174	199	24	20,212	16,135	106	106	101	—	23,134	38	—	89	2,781	7,241	11[26]	—	—
Chile	13	15	17	23	1,799	1,504	100	100	101	1,391	1,444	73	82	89	452	1,119	21[13]	37	74
Colombia	34	39	45	44	5,221	4,742	102	119	107	3,569	4,903	50[13]	72	93	934	1,958	13	24	45

See notes at end of table.

Table 601.20. Selected population and enrollment statistics for countries with populations of at least 10 million in 2012, by continent and country: Selected years, 1990 through 2012—Continued

Continent and country[1]	Midyear population (in millions)			Persons per square kilometer	First level[2] Enrollment (in thousands)		First level Gross enrollment ratio[5]			Second level[3] Enrollment (in thousands)		Second level Gross enrollment ratio[5]			Third level[4] Enrollment (in thousands)		Third level Gross enrollment ratio[5]		
	1991	2000	2012	2012	1999–2000	2011–12	1990–91	1999–2000	2011–12	1999–2000	2011–12	1990–91	1999–2000	2011–12	1999–2000	2011–12	1990–91	1999–2000	2011–12
1	2	3	4	5	6	7	8	9	10	11	12	13	14	15	16	17	18	19	20
Ecuador	10	12	15	55	1,925	2,118	116	113	114	917	1,531	55	59	87	—	—	20	—	—
Peru	22	26	30	23	4,338	3,479	118	122	100	2,374	2,611	67	85	90	—	—	30	—	—
Venezuela	20	23	28	32	3,328	3,486	96	101	102	1,543	2,354	35	60	85	668	—	29	28	—
Oceania																			
Australia[8]	17	19	22	3	1,906	2,083	108	100	105	2,589	2,377	82	161	136	845	1,364	35[27]	65	86

—Not available.
#Rounds to zero.
[1]Selection based on total population for midyear 2012.
[2]First-level enrollment consists of elementary school, typically corresponding to grades 1–6 in the United States.
[3]Second-level enrollment includes general education, teacher training (at the second level), and technical and vocational education.
[4]Third-level enrollment includes college and university enrollment and technical and vocational education beyond the secondary school level.
[5]Data represent the total enrollment of all ages in the school level divided by the population of the specific age groups that correspond to the school level. Adjustments have been made for the varying lengths of first- and second-level programs. Ratios may exceed 100 because some countries have many students from outside the normal age range.
[6]Enrollment totals and ratios exclude the Democratic People's Republic of Korea (North Korea).
[7]Estimated by the United Nations Educational, Scientific, and Cultural Organization (UNESCO) Institute for Statistics.
[8]Classification or data coverage of levels has been revised. Data by level may not be comparable over time.
[9]Policy change in 1999–2000: introduction of free universal primary education.
[10]General education enrollment only. Excludes teacher training and vocational education enrollments.
[11]Excludes nonuniversity institutions (such as teacher training colleges and technical colleges) and excludes distance-learning universities.
[12]Data for 1992–93.
[13]Data for 1991–92.

[14]Excludes private institutions.
[15]Data refer to universities and exclude Al Azhar.
[16]Data for 1993–94.
[17]Data for 1985–86.
[18]Not including the former Independent States of Transkei, Bophuthatswana, Venda, and Ciskei.
[19]Estimated.
[20]Data refer to government aided and maintained schools only.
[21]National estimation.
[22]Includes preprimary education.
[23]Excludes some nonuniversity institutions.
[24]Includes full-time students only.
[25]Data include both former East and West Germany.
[26]Excludes enrollments in programs formerly classified as doctoral.
[27]Data do not include Vocational Education and Training (VET) institutes.
NOTE: Data do not include adult education or special education provided outside regular schools. Some data have been revised from previously published figures.
SOURCE: United Nations Educational, Scientific, and Cultural Organization (UNESCO), Statistical Yearbook, 1999, unpublished tabulations; and tabulations from the UNESCO Institute for Statistics Online Data Center, retrieved February 18, 2015, from http://data.uis.unesco.org/ U.S. Department of Commerce, Census Bureau, International Data Base, retrieved February 18, 2015, from http://www.census.gov/population/international/data/idb/informationGateway.php. (This table was prepared March 2015.)

Table 601.30. School-age populations as a percentage of total population, by age group and country: Selected years, 1985 through 2011

Country	5- to 14-year-olds as a percent of total population												15- to 19-year-olds as a percent of total population											
	1985[1]	1990[1]	1995[1]	1999	2004	2005	2006	2007	2008	2009	2010	2011	1985[2]	1990[2]	1995[2]	1999	2004	2005	2006	2007	2008	2009	2010	2011
1	2	3	4	5	6	7	8	9	10	11	12	13	14	15	16	17	18	19	20	21	22	23	24	25
OECD average[3]	—	—	—	13	13	13	12	12	12	12	12	12	—	—	—	7	7	7	7	7	7	7	6	6
Australia	14	13	13	14	14	13	13	13	13	13	12	12	7	6	6	7	7	7	7	7	7	7	6	7
Austria	11	11	11	—	11	11	11	11	11	10	11	10	7	6	6	7	6	7	6	6	7	6	7	6
Belgium	11	11	11	12	12	12	12	11	11	11	11	12	6	5	5	6	6	6	6	6	6	6	6	6
Canada	13	12	12	14	13	12	12	12	12	11	11	11	6	5	5	7	6	7	6	7	7	7	7	7
Chile	—	—	—	—	18	18	17	16	15	15	15	15	—	—	—	7	9	9	9	9	9	9	9	8
Czech Republic	(4)	(4)	12	12	11	10	10	10	9	9	9	9	(4)	(4)	6	7	7	6	6	6	6	6	6	6
Denmark	12	10	10	12	13	13	13	13	12	12	12	12	6	6	6	5	5	6	6	6	6	7	6	6
Estonia	(4)	(4)	11	—	—	11	10	10	10	9	9	10	(4)	(4)	6	6	—	8	8	8	7	7	7	6
Finland	11	12	11	13	12	12	12	12	11	11	11	11	6	5	5	6	6	6	6	6	6	6	6	6
France	13	12	12	13	12	12	12	12	12	11	12	12	6	6	5	7	6	7	6	6	6	6	6	6
Germany[5]	9	9	10	11	10	10	10	10	9	9	9	9	6	4	4	6	6	6	6	6	6	5	5	5
Greece	—	—	11	11	10	10	10	10	9	9	9	9	—	5	6	7	6	6	5	5	5	5	5	5
Hungary	16	15	14	16	11	11	11	10	10	10	10	10	7	7	7	8	7	7	7	7	7	7	6	6
Iceland	18	18	15	15	15	15	15	14	14	14	14	14	7	7	8	8	8	7	7	7	8	7	7	7
Ireland	10	10	11	12	14	14	13	13	13	13	13	14	8	8	6	6	6	6	6	6	6	6	6	6
Israel	13	10	—	10	18	18	18	18	18	18	18	18	—	—	—	—	8	8	8	8	8	8	8	8
Italy	14	12	9	10	10	9	9	9	9	9	9	9	6	6	5	5	5	5	5	5	5	5	5	5
Japan	14	12	10	10	9	9	9	9	9	9	9	9	6	7	6	6	5	5	5	5	5	5	5	5
Korea, Republic of	—	—	14	14	14	14	14	13	13	12	12	11	5	7	7	8	7	7	7	7	6	6	6	7
Luxembourg	10	10	11	12	13	13	13	12	12	12	11	12	5	4	4	6	6	6	6	6	6	6	6	6
Mexico	—	—	—	—	22	21	21	21	21	20	20	19	—	5	5	6	10	10	10	10	10	10	10	10
Netherlands	12	11	11	12	12	12	12	11	11	10	12	12	7	5	6	6	7	6	6	6	6	6	6	6
New Zealand	15	13	13	15	15	15	14	14	14	14	13	12	7	6	5	6	6	7	8	7	8	7	7	7
Norway	13	11	11	13	14	13	13	13	13	14	13	12	6	6	5	6	8	8	8	8	8	7	7	7
Poland	—	—	—	—	12	12	12	11	11	10	10	10	—	—	—	—	8	8	8	7	7	7	7	7
Portugal	(4)	(4)	—	—	10	10	10	10	10	10	10	10	(4)	(4)	—	—	6	6	6	6	6	6	6	6
Slovak Republic	(4)	(4)	—	—	13	12	12	11	11	10	10	10	(4)	(4)	—	—	8	8	8	8	7	7	7	7
Slovenia	(4)	(4)	—	—	—	10	10	10	9	9	9	9	(4)	(4)	—	—	—	6	6	6	6	6	6	6
Spain	15	13	10	10	10	9	9	9	9	9	10	10	7	7	6	7	6	5	5	5	5	5	5	5
Sweden	11	10	11	13	13	12	12	11	11	11	11	11	5	5	5	6	6	6	6	5	5	5	5	5
Switzerland	11	10	10	12	11	11	11	11	11	10	10	10	6	5	5	6	6	6	6	6	6	6	6	6
Turkey	21	21	20	21	19	19	19	19	18	18	18	17	9	9	9	11	9	9	9	9	9	9	9	9
United Kingdom	11	11	12	13	13	12	12	12	12	11	11	11	6	5	6	6	7	7	7	7	7	7	6	6
United States	13	13	13	15	14	14	14	13	13	13	13	13	6	5	7	7	7	7	7	7	7	7	7	7
Other reporting countries																								
Brazil	—	—	—	—	20	19	19	18	18	17	17	16	—	(4)	—	—	10	10	10	8	9	9	9	9
Russian Federation	(4)	(4)	14	14	11	10	10	10	9	9	9	10	(4)	(4)	—	—	9	9	8	8	7	7	6	6

—Not available.
[1]Data are for the 5- to 13-year-old population.
[2]Data are for the 14- to 17-year-old population.
[3]Refers to the mean of the data values for all reporting Organization for Economic Cooperation and Development (OECD) countries, to which each country reporting data contributes equally. The average includes all current OECD countries for which a given year's data are available, even if they were not members of OECD in that year. However, if data were reported for less than 75 percent of the countries, the average for that year is omitted.
[4]Country did not exist in its current form in the given year.
[5]Data for 1985 are for the former West Germany.
SOURCE: Organization for Economic Cooperation and Development (OECD), *Education at a Glance*, selected years, 1987 through 2001; and Online Education Database, retrieved July 21, 2014, from http://stats.oecd.org/Index.aspx. (This table was prepared July 2014.)

Table 601.35. Percentage of 3- and 4-year-olds and 5- to 14-year-olds enrolled in school, by country: 2000 through 2012

Country	Percent of 3- and 4-year-olds enrolled		Percent of 5- to 14-year-olds enrolled												
	2011	2012	2000	2001	2002	2003	2004	2005	2006	2007	2008	2009	2010	2011	2012
1	2	3	4	5	6	7	8	9	10	11	12	13	14	15	16
OECD average[1]	74.1	76.2	97.8	98.1	98.3	98.0	98.0	98.2	98.3	98.5	98.7	98.5	98.8	98.6	98.4
Australia	40.0	46.6	100.0	100.1	99.3	98.2	98.5	99.1	99.6	99.3	99.3	99.3	99.2	99.4	101.1
Austria	76.1	77.8	98.2	98.7	98.9	98.5	98.5	98.4	98.1	98.3	98.5	98.4	98.4	98.2	98.2
Belgium	98.6	98.6	99.1	100.2	100.1	100.3	100.4 [2]	99.6 [2]	99.4	99.3	99.1	98.9	98.6	98.5	98.5
Canada	24.1 [3]	—	97.1	97.2	—	—	—	—	—	—	—	98.7	98.8	98.9	—
Chile	59.3	62.1	93.6	—	92.1	90.8	89.5	88.3	91.2	96.1	96.1	93.2	95.1	94.3	93.9
Czech Republic	72.0	70.3	99.8	99.8	99.3	99.8	99.7	99.8	99.9	99.8	98.7	98.7	98.1	97.7	98.6
Denmark	94.1	97.5	99.2	97.2	99.1	99.1	98.0	97.1	97.4	98.0	97.6	97.6	99.1	99.4	99.3
Estonia	88.1	88.9	—	—	—	—	—	104.6	102.2	100.4	100.4	100.0	96.4	95.7	95.2
Finland	53.1	55.1	91.6	93.5	94.4	94.6	95.1	95.1	95.1	95.3	95.5	95.5	95.5	95.7	95.7
France	98.7	99.1	99.8	101.0	101.1	101.4	101.6	101.3	101.0	100.9	100.7	99.8	99.6	99.4	99.1
Germany	92.7	93.3	99.4	100.1	97.5	97.6	97.9	98.3	98.8	99.2	99.3	99.4	99.4	98.5	99.4
Greece	27.2	25.6	99.8	98.1	96.3	96.7	97.2	97.5	98.1	97.7	98.9	100.1	100.7	100.0	99.2
Hungary	83.6	83.6	99.9	99.4	100.3	100.4	100.5	100.3	100.3	99.8	99.6	98.9	98.5	98.1	97.6
Iceland	96.1	96.1	98.5	98.9	98.5	98.8	98.8	98.9	98.8	98.3	98.5	98.2	98.5	98.6	98.8
Ireland	69.9	69.1	100.5	100.6	101.4	100.4	100.9	101.1	101.2	102.6	101.5	101.7	102.1	101.1	100.9
Israel	89.9	89.1	96.6	96.9	96.1	96.8	96.6	96.0	95.8	96.1	95.7	96.2	97.8	96.8	97.8
Italy	94.3	94.2	99.7	99.4	101.7	101.9	101.6	101.2	100.7	100.3	100.3	99.8	99.5	99.0	98.6
Japan	84.7	85.9	101.2	101.0	100.8	100.7	100.7	100.7	100.7	100.5	100.7	101.0	101.5	101.1	101.3
Korea, Republic of ..	82.4	86.3	92.3	92.6	92.7	93.2	93.5	94.1	94.9	95.7	95.1	95.7	99.7	99.1	98.8
Luxembourg	83.4	85.4	95.3	92.2	93.4	96.7	96.4	96.7	96.2	95.9	95.8	95.6	95.8	96.0	97.9
Mexico	72.4	63.3	94.8	95.0	95.7	96.9	97.7	99.9	100.9	102.1	103.4	104.6	106.1	107.7	100.2
Netherlands	93.2	91.4	99.4	99.3	99.3	99.7	99.6	99.0	99.6	99.5	99.6	99.5	99.5	99.8	99.8
New Zealand	90.0	90.7	99.0	99.3	99.5	100.1	100.5	100.9	101.0	99.7	100.2	100.6	100.9	101.0	100.7
Norway	96.1	96.1	97.4	97.6	97.9	98.1	98.3	98.4	98.8	99.2	99.5	99.5	99.5	99.6	99.5
Poland	56.8	58.0	93.6	94.3	94.4	94.2	94.5	94.6	94.5	94.5	94.0	94.1	94.9	95.3	95.5
Portugal	81.6	84.9	105.2	107.0	106.0	105.3	104.1	103.9	103.8	104.2	104.1	103.1	102.4	102.1	102.1
Slovak Republic	66.5	67.5	—	97.9	98.1	97.3	97.3	97.1	96.8	96.8	96.6	96.1	95.8	95.5	94.5
Slovenia	85.8	87.1	—	—	—	—	—	96.5	96.4	96.2	96.8	97.1	97.1	97.1	97.4
Spain	98.7	96.1	104.4	103.6	103.8	102.5	101.8	101.4	101.0	100.7	100.4	100.1	99.5	99.0	97.8
Sweden	93.0	93.4	97.8	98.1	98.2	98.6	99.1	99.5	98.8	100.3	99.3	98.7	98.5	97.4	99.0
Switzerland	22.1	21.6	98.8	98.7	98.6	99.3	99.6	99.6	100.3	100.4	100.2	100.0	100.1	99.5	99.3
Turkey	11.6	12.0	80.2	83.5	—	82.0	81.2	81.8	82.9	84.3	91.9	91.3	94.1	94.9	95.2
United Kingdom	91.4	95.5	98.9	98.7	98.9	100.5	100.4	101.0	100.7	99.3	101.5	101.4	103.1	100.7	98.0
United States	52.4	53.5	99.3	102.1	96.9	97.1	97.3	97.7	98.0	98.3	98.6	97.1	96.8	96.2	97.3
Other reporting countries															
Brazil	46.5	49.3	89.8	91.3	91.8	—	93.0	93.1	—	91.7	95.6	96.5	96.2	94.9	94.8
Russian Federation	73.3	73.4	—	83.3	84.6	94.2	90.4	81.5	—	—	93.8	93.5	93.1	92.1	92.7

—Not available.
[1]Refers to the mean of the data values for all reporting Organization for Economic Cooperation and Development (OECD) countries, to which each country reporting data contributes equally. The average includes all current OECD countries for which a given year's data are available, even if they were not members of OECD in that year.
[2]Excludes the German-speaking Community of Belgium.
[3]Data are for 2010.
NOTE: For each country, this table shows the number of persons in each age group who are enrolled in that country as a percentage of that country's total population in the speci-

fied age group. However, some of a country's population may be enrolled in a different country, and some persons enrolled in the country may be residents of a different country. Enrollment rates may be underestimated for countries such as Luxembourg that are net exporters of students and may be overestimated for countries that are net importers. If a country enrolls many residents of other countries, the country's total population in the specified age group can be smaller than the total number enrolled, resulting in enrollment estimates exceeding 100 percent.
SOURCE: Organization for Economic Cooperation and Development (OECD), Education at a Glance, 2002 through 2014. (This table was prepared August 2014.)

Table 601.40. Percentage of the population enrolled in secondary and postsecondary education, by age group and country: Selected years, 2002 through 2012

| Country | Secondary education, 2012 | | | | | | | Postsecondary education (total tertiary education) | | | | | | | | | | | | |
| | 16 years old | 17 years old | 18 to 21 years old: Total | 18 years old | 19 years old | 20 years old | 21 years old | 22 years old and older | 18 to 21 yrs: 2002 | 2005 | 2011 | 2012 | 22 to 25 yrs: 2002 | 2005 | 2011 | 2012 | 26 to 29 yrs: 2002 | 2005 | 2011 | 2012 |
1	2	3	4	5	6	7	8	9	10	11	12	13	14	15	16	17	18	19	20	21
OECD average[1]	**93**	**88**	**25**	**56**	**27**	**13**	**8**	**1**	**26**	**28**	**31**	**32**	**21**	**23**	**26**	**27**	**9**	**10**	**12**	**12**
Australia	96	82	25	41	25	20	15	3	35	34	37	39	20	21	25	25	10	10	11	11
Austria	90	75	19	44	19	8	4	#	15	16	21	22	18	20	27	27	9	9	11	11
Belgium	101	99	23	48	23	14	10	4	42	43	46	46	18	19	24	23	5	6	7	7
Canada	—	—	—	—	—	—	—	—	—	—	35	37	—	—	20	20	—	—	8	8
Chile	89	86	12	31	10	4	2	#	—	—	39	39	—	—	30	30	—	—	12	12
Czech Republic	98	96	35	86	43	10	4	#	20	23	28	28	16	21	28	28	6	6	8	8
Denmark	95	90	50	86	58	33	24	2	10	10	15	16	29	34	40	38	16	20	20	20
Estonia	96	92	27	80	23	10	6	#	—	32	31	31	—	22	26	26	—	12	11	11
Finland	94	94	40	93	33	19	17	4	21	24	22	21	39	40	37	37	19	20	20	20
France	92	85	19	43	20	8	4	#	35	36	38	39	20	20	21	21	5	5	5	5
Germany	95	89	38	77	43	24	15	#	12	13	19	20	20	23	27	27	12	13	15	15
Greece	96	96	11	20	12	9	5	#	46	65	48	49	24	18	27	29	11	8	55[2]	42
Hungary	98	99	32	76	34	14	8	1	24	29	28	28	18	23	24	28	12	16	8	8
Iceland	96	90	54	83	73	37	25	3	10	12	14	14	24	28	32	32	12	16	17	18
Ireland	101	88	13	45	4	1	1	#	36	38	41	44	11	13	12	14	5	5	—	—
Israel	93	89	5	17	2	1	#	#	10	12	13	13	26	25	27	27	17	15	20	20
Italy	92	86	26	75	21	8	4	#	24	29	27	27	21	23	25	25	8	6	9	9
Japan	97	92	1	3	1	#	—	#	—	—	—	—	—	—	—	—	—	—	—	—
Korea, Republic of	97	93	2	6	#	#	#	#	56	65	68	68	32	32	37	37	7	7	7	8
Luxembourg	88	80	38	69	42	27	14	#	—	—	—	—	—	—	—	—	—	—	—	—
Mexico	62	50	13	19	27	3	1	2	15	16	21	21	7	9	11	11	3	3	3	3
Netherlands	99	91	40	66	44	30	19	2	28	29	36	36	22	24	31	31	6	7	11	11
New Zealand	97	84	13	29	12	8	6	1	30	34	37	37	17	23	22	22	8	11	11	11
Norway	95	93	38	88	39	19	9	#	17	19	21	21	27	30	30	29	13	14	14	13
Poland	96	95	36	92	42	12	6	#	27	31	35	35	26	30	31	32	7	6	6	6
Portugal	96	92	26	52	28	15	9	1	25	27	34	34	20	21	20	22	8	8	7	8
Slovak Republic	93	90	32	82	40	9	9	#	21	22	25	26	13	16	24	25	4	5	6	6
Slovenia	97	95	31	87	24	11	9	1	—	37	44	44	—	35	37	39	—	11	10	10
Spain	97	90	25	45	28	18	12	1	35	34	38	40	24	22	26	26	8	9	10	10
Sweden	99	98	36	94	25	14	13	2	17	17	18	18	28	32	28	28	13	16	16	15
Switzerland	89	86	39	77	48	23	11	#	10	12	15	15	18	20	25	25	9	10	12	12
Turkey	72	59	6	23	—	—	—	—	—	20	33	35	—	11	27	27	—	4	11	11
United Kingdom	94	85	16	34	15	9	7	1	30	28	33	34	12	13	13	13	6	7	7	6
United States	93	82	8	30	5	#	#	#	46	45	50	49	25	23	29	28	11	11	14	14
Other reporting countries																				
Brazil	90	84	29	54	30	18	13	2	3	10	15	15	10	9	15	16	5	5	9	9
Russian Federation	69	54	6	17	6	3	1	#	42	41	49	52	10	26	20	20	5	9	9	9

—Not available.
#Rounds to zero.
[1]Refers to the mean of the data values for all reporting Organization for Economic Cooperation and Development (OECD) countries, to which each country reporting data contributes equally. The average includes all current OECD countries for which a given year's data are available, even if they were not members of OECD in that year.
[2]Data are for the population 26 to 28 years old.
NOTE: Data refer to programs classified as International Standard Classification of Education (ISCED) level 3, level 5A (first and second award), level 5B, and level 6. ISCED level 3 corresponds to secondary education in the United States. ISCED levels 5A (first and second award), 5B, and 6 together make up total tertiary education, which corresponds to 2-year and 4-year college undergraduate and graduate programs in the United States. Excludes enrollment in ISCED level 4, which is nontertiary education that corresponds to enrollment in programs of less than 2 years after high school in the United States. Includes both full-time and part-time students. Some increases in enrollment rates may be due to more complete reporting by countries. Enrollment rates may not be directly comparable across countries due to differing definitions of postsecondary (tertiary) education and the age at which it begins. Differences in reference dates between enrollment and population data can result in enrollment rates that exceed 100 percent. Postsecondary data for Luxembourg are not shown because tertiary students generally study for no more than 1 year in Luxembourg and must complete their studies in other countries.
SOURCE: Organization for Economic Cooperation and Development (OECD), Online Education Database, retrieved January 5, 2015, from http://stats.oecd.org/Index.aspx. (This table was prepared January 2015.)

Table 601.50. Pupil/teacher ratios in public and private elementary and secondary schools, by level of education and country: Selected years, 2000 through 2012

Country	Elementary school							Junior high school (lower secondary)							Senior high school (upper secondary)						
	2000	2005	2008	2009	2010	2011	2012	2000	2005	2008	2009	2010	2011	2012	2000	2005	2008	2009	2010	2011	2012
1	2	3	4	5	6	7	8	9	10	11	12	13	14	15	16	17	18	19	20	21	22
OECD average[1]	17.7	17.0	16.4	16.0	15.9	15.4	15.2	—	14.0	13.7	13.5	13.6	13.3	13.3	13.7	13.5	13.3	13.4	13.6	13.7	13.5
Australia	17.3	16.2	15.8	15.8	15.7	15.6	15.5	—	10.6	9.9	9.6	9.3	9.1	9.0	—	12.1[2][3]	12.0[2][3]	12.0[2][3]	12.0[2][3]	12.0[2][3]	12.0[2][3]
Austria	—	14.1	12.9	12.6	12.2	12.1	12.0	—	—	8.1[5]	8.1[5]	8.1[5]	8.1[5]	8.2[5]	9.7[3][6]	11.3	10.8[5][6]	10.2[5][6]	10.1[5][6]	10.1[5][6]	9.8
Belgium	15.0[4]	12.8	12.6[5]	12.5[5]	12.4[5]	12.4[5]	12.5[5]	—	9.4	8.1[5]	8.1[5]	8.1[5]	8.1[5]	8.2[5]	19.5	9.9[6]	10.8[5][6]	10.2[5][6]	10.1[5][6]	10.1[5][6]	10.1[5][6]
Canada	18.1	—	24.1	22.4	24.6	23.1	22.1	18.1	25.9	24.1	22.4	25.1	23.6	22.4	—	26.6	25.2	24.7	26.1	25.4	24.0
Chile	—	25.9	24.1	22.4	24.6	23.1	22.1	—	25.9	24.1	22.4	25.1	23.6	22.1	—	26.6	25.2	24.7	26.1	25.4	24.0
Czech Republic	19.7	17.5	18.1	18.4	18.7	18.7	18.9	14.7	13.5	11.8	11.5	11.2	11.1	11.1	11.5	12.8	12.2	12.2	12.1	11.7	11.3
Denmark	10.4	—	—	—	—	—	—	11.4	11.9[7]	10.1[7]	9.9[7]	11.5[7]	10.1[7]	11.9[7]	14.4	—	12.4[6]	16.8[6]	16.6[6]	13.7	9.9
Estonia	16.9	15.9	16.4	16.2	16.2	13.2	13.1	10.7	10.0	16.0	15.7	14.9	10.1	9.9	17.0[6][8]	18.0[6][8]	15.9[6]	16.6[6]	17.1[6]	16.3[6]	14.1[6]
Finland	19.8	15.9	14.4	13.6	14.0	13.7	13.6	10.7	10.0	10.6	10.1	9.8	9.3	9.9	17.0[6][8]	18.0[6][8]	15.9[6]	16.6[6]	17.1[6]	16.3[6]	16.1[6]
France	19.8	19.4	19.9[5]	19.7[5]	18.7[5]	18.4[5]	18.9[5]	14.7	14.2	14.6[5]	14.9[5]	15.0[5]	14.8[5]	15.5[5]	10.4	10.3	9.4[5]	9.6[5]	9.7[5]	10.0[5]	9.9[5]
Germany	19.8	18.8	18.0	17.4	16.7	16.3	16.0	15.7	15.5	15.0	15.1	14.9	14.2	14.0	13.9	14.0	14.0	13.9	13.2	13.8	13.7
Greece	13.4	11.1	10.6	10.7	10.8	10.7	9.4	10.8	7.9	10.9	10.8	10.7	10.5	10.6	10.5	8.8	12.3	12.8	12.5	12.4	12.5
Hungary	10.9	10.6	10.6	10.7	10.8	10.5	10.6	10.9	10.4	10.0[7]	9.9[7]	10.3[7]	10.6	10.6	11.4[6]	12.2	10.6[6]	10.9[6]	11.3	11.5[6]	11.5[6]
Iceland	—	17.9	17.8	15.9	15.9	15.7	16.2	12.7[7]	11.3[7]	10.0[7]	9.9[7]	10.3[7]	10.6	10.6	9.7	10.8[6]	12.8[3][6]	12.6[3][6]	14.4[3][6]	14.4[3][6]	15.0[3][6]
Ireland	21.5	17.9	17.8	15.9	15.9	15.7	16.2	—	11.3[7]	14.6[5]	14.9[5]	15.0[5]	14.8[5]	15.5[5]	15.9[3][6]	15.5[3][6]	12.8[3][6]	12.6[3][6]	14.4[3][6]	14.4[3][6]	15.0[3][6]
Israel	—	17.3	16.3	17.0	20.6[9]	15.9[9]	15.2	10.4	10.1	12.2	13.7	12.8[9]	13.6[9]	13.6[9]	10.2	13.4	10.9	10.8	11.0	11.3[9]	11.0
Italy	11.0	10.6	10.6[9]	10.7[9]	11.3[9]	11.7[9]	12.1[9]	10.4	10.1	9.7[9]	10.0[9]	11.9[9]	11.5[9]	11.8[9]	10.2	13.4	11.8[9]	11.8[9]	12.1[9]	12.8[9]	13.0[6]
Japan	20.9	19.4	18.8	18.6	18.4	18.1	17.7	16.8	15.1	14.7	14.5	14.4	14.2	14.1	14.0	13.0[6]	12.3[6]	12.2[6]	12.2[6]	12.6[6]	12.1[6]
Korea, Republic of	32.1	28.0	24.1	22.5	21.1	19.6	18.4	21.5	20.8	20.2	19.9	19.7	18.8	18.1	20.9	16.0	16.5	16.7	16.5	15.8	15.4
Luxembourg	15.9[9]	—	12.1[9]	11.6	10.1	9.9	9.2	—	—	9.1[9]	9.2[9]	10.1	9.9	10.7	9.2[3][9]	9.0[3][9]	9.1[3][9]	9.1[3]	9.1[3]	9.6[3]	7.6
Mexico	27.2	28.3	28.0	28.1	28.1	28.1	28.0	34.8	33.7	33.9	33.0	32.7	31.9	31.9	26.5	25.8	25.8[3][9]	26.1[3][9]	26.9	26.8	26.9
Netherlands	16.8[4]	15.9[4]	15.8[4][9]	15.8[4][9]	15.7[4][9]	15.8	15.8	19.9	16.8	16.2[9]	16.3	16.3	16.3	15.6	17.1[3]	16.2[3]	15.8[3][9]	16.1[3][9]	16.5[3][9]	18.2	18.6
New Zealand	20.6	18.1	17.1	16.3	16.2	16.3	16.4	9.9	16.8	16.2[9]	16.3	16.3	16.3	16.4	13.1	12.9	12.8	12.8	14.4	13.9	13.7
Norway	12.4	11.7	10.8[9]	10.7[9]	10.5[9]	10.4[9]	10.3	9.9	—	10.1[9]	9.9[9]	9.9[9]	10.0[9]	10.4	9.7	—	9.9[6]	9.4[6]	9.4[9]	9.7[6][9]	9.6[6]
Poland	12.7	11.7	10.5	10.2	10.0	11.0	11.0	11.5	12.7	12.9	12.9	12.7	10.0	9.9	16.9	12.9	12.2	12.0	12.1	11.1	10.9
Portugal	12.1	10.8	11.3	11.3	10.9	11.2	11.9	10.4	8.2	8.1	7.6	7.9	8.2	9.6	7.9	8.0	7.3[6]	7.6[6]	7.2[6]	7.3[6]	7.6[6]
Slovak Republic	18.3	18.9	18.6	17.7	17.1	16.9	16.8	13.5	14.1	14.5	14.0	13.6	13.1	12.8	12.8	14.3	13.7[6]	14.3[6]	14.3[6]	14.3[6]	13.9
Slovenia	15.0	15.0	15.8	16.7	16.2	16.0	15.9	—	11.1	8.9	7.9	8.0	7.9	7.9	11.9[3]	8.1	8.7	9.3	9.6	9.8	14.1[6]
Spain	14.9	14.3	13.1	13.3	13.2	13.2	13.4	—	12.5	10.3	10.1	10.1	10.3	10.6	—	8.1	8.7	9.3	9.6	9.8	9.9
Sweden	12.8	12.2	12.2	12.1	11.7	11.3	11.8	12.8	12.0	11.4	11.3	11.4	11.3	11.3	15.2	14.0	14.7	13.2	13.1	13.0	13.2
Switzerland[8]	—	14.6	15.4	15.4	14.9	—	—	—	11.7	12.1	12.0	11.8	†	—	14.0	10.5[2]	10.4[2]	10.4[2]	10.3[2]	10.6[2]	†
Turkey	30.5	25.8	24.4	22.9	21.7	21.0	20.1	17.6[2]	†	15.0	16.1	17.1	15.2	14.2	12.5[2]	16.2	17.0	16.9	17.6	17.8	16.2
United Kingdom[6]	21.2	20.7	20.2	19.9	19.8	19.9	21.1	16.3	17.0	15.0	16.1	17.1	15.2	14.2	14.1	11.8[2][6]	12.4[6]	12.3[6]	15.2[6]	17.3	17.1
United States	15.8	14.9	15.0	14.8	14.5	15.3	15.3	16.3	15.1	14.8	14.3	14.0	15.2	15.3	—	16.0	15.6	15.1	15.0	15.3	15.3
Other reporting countries																					
Brazil	—	22.9	24.5	24.0	23.4	22.5	21.7	—	18.1	21.2	21.0	20.4	19.8	19.1	—	17.6	18.4	18.1	17.3	16.9	16.8
Russian Federation[7]	—	—	17.3[9]	17.9[9]	19.2[9]	20.0[9]	20.1[9]	—	—	—	—	—	—	8.9[9]	—	11.2[6][10]	8.7[3][6][11]	8.7[3][6][11]	11.3[3][6][11]	8.7[3][6][11]	15.3[9]

—Not available.

†Not applicable. This level of education does not exist within the national education structure; students in the age group normally associated with this education level are reported in other levels.

[1]Refers to the mean of the data values for all reporting Organization for Economic Cooperation and Development (OECD) countries, to which each country reporting data contributes equally. The average includes all current OECD countries for which a given year's data are available, even if they were not members of OECD in that year. However, if data were reported for less than 75 percent of the countries, the average for that year is omitted.

[2]Includes only general programs.

[3]Includes junior high school data.

[4]Includes preprimary data.

[5]Excludes independent private institutions.

[6]Includes postsecondary non-higher-education.

[7]Includes elementary school data.

[8]Includes occupation-specific education corresponding to that offered at the vocational associate's degree level in the United States.

[9]Public schools only.

[10]Excludes part-time personnel in public institutions.

[11]Excludes general programs.

NOTE: The pupil/teacher ratio is the number of full-time-equivalent students divided by the number of full-time-equivalent teachers, including teachers for students with disabilities and other special teachers. In this table, elementary school corresponds to International Standard Classification of Education 1997 (ISCED:97) level 1 (U.S. grades 1 through 6), junior high school corresponds to ISCED:97 level 2 (U.S. grades 7 through 9), and senior high school corresponds to ISCED:97 level 3 (U.S. grades 10 through 12).

SOURCE: Organization for Economic Cooperation and Development (OECD), Online Education Database; and Education at a Glance, 2002 through 2014. (This table was prepared August 2014.)

Table 601.60. Teachers' statutory teaching and total working time and average class size in public elementary and secondary schools, by level of education and country: 2012

Country	Number of weeks teaching			Number of days teaching			Net teaching time in hours			Total working time in hours			Average class size	
	Elementary school	Junior high school (lower secondary)	Senior high school (upper secondary)[1]	Elementary school	Junior high school (lower secondary)	Senior high school (upper secondary)[1]	Elementary school	Junior high school (lower secondary)	Senior high school (upper secondary)[1]	Elementary school	Junior high school (lower secondary)	Senior high school (upper secondary)[1]	Elementary school	Junior high school (lower secondary)
1	2	3	4	5	6	7	8	9	10	11	12	13	14	15
OECD average[2]	38	38	37	183	182	180	782	694	655	1,200	1,173	1,142	21	24
Australia[3]	40	40	40	197	197	195	871	809	801	1,211	1,234	1,234	23	23
Austria[3]	38	38	38	180	180	180	779	607	589	†	†	†	18	21
Belgium (Flemish)[3]	37	37	37	176	174	174	748	652	609	915	†	†	—	—
Belgium (French)[3]	37	37	37	181	181	181	721	661	601	†	†	†	21	—
Canada[3]	37	37	37	183	183	183	802	747	751	1,223	1,224	1,229	—	—
Chile[4]	38	38	38	179	179	179	1,103	1,103	1,103	1,839	1,839	1,839	29	31
Czech Republic[3]	39	39	39	188	188	188	827	620	592	†	†	†	20	21
Denmark[5]	†	†	†	†	†	†	659	659	369	†	†	†	21	21
England[5]	38	38	38	189	189	189	680	692	692	1,259	1,259	1,259	—	—
Estonia[4]	35	35	35	172	172	172	619	619	568	1,540	1,540	1,540	17	16
Finland[6]	38	38	38	187	187	187	673	589	547	787	703	642	19	20
France[3]	36	36	36	144	†	†	924	648	648	972	†	†	23	25
Germany[3]	40	40	40	193	193	193	804	755	718	†	†	†	21	25
Greece[3]	35	31	31	171	152	152	569	415	415	1,140	1,170	1,170	17	22
Hungary[6]	37	37	37	183	183	183	604	604	604	—	—	—	21	21
Iceland[3]	37	37	35	180	180	170	624	624	544	1,650	1,650	1,720	19	20
Ireland[3]	37	33	33	183	167	167	915	735	735	1,079	778	778	24	—
Israel[3]	38	37	37	182	175	175	838	629	558	1,219	924	781	28	29
Italy[3]	39	39	39	171	171	171	752	616	616	†	†	†	19	22
Japan[5]	40	40	39	200	200	196	731	602	510	†	†	†	28	33
Korea, Republic of[6]	38	38	38	190	190	190	694	568	549	†	†	†	25	34
Luxembourg[3]	36	36	36	176	176	176	810	739	739	990	828	828	15	19
Mexico[3]	42	42	36	200	200	171	800	1,047	838	800	1,167	971	20	27
Netherlands[4]	40	—	—	195	—	—	930	750	750	†	†	†	—	—
New Zealand[3]	39	39	38	195	193	190	935	848	760	1,560	1,255	950	—	—
Norway[3]	38	38	38	190	190	190	741	663	523	1,300	1,225	1,150	†	†
Poland[5]	38	38	37	184	182	180	633	561	558	—	—	—	19	23
Portugal[4]	37	37	37	168	168	168	756	616	616	1,027	926	926	21	22
Scotland[4]	38	38	38	190	190	190	855	855	855	1,045	1,045	1,045	—	—
Slovak Republic[3]	38	38	38	184	184	184	819	635	607	—	—	—	17	20
Slovenia[3]	40	40	40	190	190	190	627	627	570	†	†	†	19	20
Spain[3]	37	37	36	176	176	171	880	713	693	1,140	1,140	1,140	20	24
Sweden[3]	†	†	†	†	†	†	—	—	—	1,360	1,360	1,360	—	—
Switzerland	—	—	—	—	—	—	—	—	—	—	—	—	—	—
Turkey[3]	38	38	38	180	180	180	720	504	567	980	836	921	24	29
United Kingdom	—	—	—	—	—	—	—	—	—	—	—	—	26	20
United States[5]	36	36	36	180	180	180	1,131	1,085	1,076	1,362	1,366	1,365	22	28
Other reporting countries														
Brazil	42	42	42	203	203	203	—	—	—	†	†	†	25	29
China	—	—	—	—	—	—	—	—	—	†	†	†	38	52
Indonesia	44	44	44	251	163	163	1,255	734	734	—	—	—	24	36
Russian Federation[5]	34	35	35	170	210	210	561	483	483	†	†	†	18	18

—Not available.

†Not applicable according to the Organization for Economic Cooperation and Development (OECD).

[1]General programs only.

[2]Refers to the mean of the data values for all reporting OECD countries, to which each country or country component reporting data contributes equally.

[3]Typical teaching time reported.

[4]Maximum teaching time reported.

[5]Actual teaching time reported.

[6]Minimum teaching time reported.

NOTE: In this table, elementary school corresponds to International Standard Classification of Education 1997 (ISCED:97) level 1 (U.S. grades 1 through 6), junior high school corresponds to ISCED:97 level 2 (U.S. grades 7 through 9), and senior high school corresponds to ISCED:97 level 3 (U.S. grades 10 through 12).

SOURCE: Organization for Economic Cooperation and Development (OECD), *Education at a Glance*, 2014. (This table was prepared August 2014.)

Table 602.10. Average reading literacy scale scores of fourth-graders and percentage whose schools emphasize reading skills and strategies at or before second grade or at third grade, by sex and country or other education system: 2001, 2006, and 2011

[Standard errors appear in parentheses]

Country or other education system[1]	Average reading literacy scale score[2] 2001		2006		2011 Total		2011 Male		2011 Female		Percent of fourth-graders in 2011, by grade at which reading skills and strategies emphasized[3] At or before second grade		At third grade	
1	2		3		4		5		6		7		8	
PIRLS average[4]	500	(†)	500	(†)	500	(†)	504	(0.5)	520	(0.5)	28	(0.5)	68	(0.5)
Australia	—	(†)	—	(†)	527	(2.2)	519	(2.7)	536	(2.7)	73	(4.0)	27	(4.0)
Austria	—	(†)	538	(2.2)	529	(2.0)	525	(2.3)	533	(2.2)	29	(4.2)	71	(4.2)
Azerbaijan[5]	—	(†)	—	(†)	462 [6]	(3.3)	456 [6]	(3.5)	470 [6]	(3.6)	19	(3.6)	79	(3.8)
Belgium (French)-BEL	—	(†)	500	(2.6)	506 [6,7]	(2.9)	504 [6,7]	(3.1)	509 [6,7]	(3.1)	29	(5.0)	70	(5.1)
Bulgaria	550	(3.8)	547	(4.4)	532	(4.1)	524	(4.3)	539	(4.5)	25	(3.5)	74	(3.6)
Canada	—	(†)	—	(†)	548 [6]	(1.6)	542 [6]	(2.1)	555 [6]	(1.7)	55	(2.7)	44	(2.7)
Chinese Taipei-CHN	—	(†)	535	(2.0)	553	(1.9)	546	(2.1)	561	(2.1)	17	(3.0)	80	(3.0)
Colombia	422	(4.4)	—	(†)	448	(4.1)	448	(4.6)	447	(4.6)	13	(3.3)	81	(3.6)
Croatia	—	(†)	—	(†)	553 [6]	(1.9)	546 [6]	(2.2)	560 [6]	(2.1)	31	(4.1)	68	(4.2)
Czech Republic	537	(2.3)	—	(†)	545	(2.2)	542	(2.5)	549	(2.5)	24	(3.8)	74	(4.0)
Denmark	—	(†)	546	(2.3)	554 [6]	(1.7)	548 [6]	(2.1)	560 [6]	(1.9)	21	(2.4)	79	(2.4)
England-GBR	553 [4,5]	(3.4)	539	(2.6)	552 [7]	(2.6)	540 [7]	(3.1)	563 [7]	(3.0)	84	(3.3)	15	(3.2)
Finland	—	(†)	—	(†)	568	(1.9)	558	(2.2)	578	(2.3)	10	(2.6)	87	(2.8)
France	525	(2.4)	522	(2.1)	520	(2.6)	518	(2.4)	522	(3.4)	18	(3.3)	81	(3.4)
Georgia[5]	—	(†)	471 [6,8]	(3.1)	488 [8]	(3.1)	477 [8]	(4.0)	499 [8]	(2.7)	20	(2.8)	79	(2.9)
Germany	539	(1.9)	548	(2.2)	541	(2.2)	537	(2.7)	545	(2.3)	30	(3.4)	69	(3.3)
Hong Kong-CHN	528	(3.1)	564	(2.4)	571 [9]	(2.3)	563 [9]	(2.5)	579 [9]	(2.3)	16	(3.5)	81	(3.8)
Hungary	543	(2.2)	551	(3.0)	539	(2.9)	532	(3.2)	547	(3.2)	28	(4.1)	71	(4.0)
Indonesia	—	(†)	405	(4.1)	428	(4.2)	419	(4.3)	437	(4.5)	‡	(†)	88	(3.2)
Iran, Islamic Republic of	414	(4.2)	421	(3.1)	457	(2.8)	448	(4.3)	467	(4.3)	7	(1.6)	85	(2.4)
Ireland	—	(†)	—	(†)	552	(2.3)	544	(3.0)	559	(2.9)	40	(4.0)	60	(4.0)
Israel	509 [10]	(2.8)	512 [10]	(3.3)	541 [9]	(2.7)	538 [9]	(3.4)	544 [9]	(3.1)	59	(4.7)	41	(4.7)
Italy	541	(2.4)	551	(2.9)	541	(2.2)	540	(2.7)	543	(2.4)	15	(2.5)	84	(2.5)
Lithuania	543 [8]	(2.6)	537 [8]	(1.6)	528 [6,8]	(2.0)	520 [6,8]	(2.4)	537 [6,8]	(2.4)	23	(3.3)	76	(3.4)
Malta	—	(†)	—	(†)	477	(1.4)	468	(2.0)	486	(1.9)	14	(0.1)	86	(0.1)
Morocco	350 [11]	(9.6)	323	(5.9)	310 [12]	(3.9)	296 [12]	(4.6)	326 [12]	(4.0)	‡	(†)	48	(4.0)
Netherlands	554 [7]	(2.5)	547 [7]	(1.5)	546 [7]	(1.9)	543 [7]	(2.2)	549 [7]	(2.1)	22 [13]	(4.4)	78 [13]	(4.4)
New Zealand	529	(3.6)	532	(2.0)	531	(1.9)	521	(2.7)	541	(2.2)	73	(3.6)	27	(3.6)
Northern Ireland-GBR	—	(†)	—	(†)	558 [7]	(2.4)	550 [7]	(3.2)	567 [7]	(2.5)	55 [13]	(4.6)	45 [13]	(4.6)
Norway	499	(2.9)	498 [13]	(2.6)	507 [11]	(1.9)	500 [11]	(2.7)	514 [11]	(2.2)	14	(3.4)	83	(3.9)
Oman	—	(†)	—	(†)	391 [14]	(2.8)	371 [14]	(3.4)	411 [14]	(3.0)	4	(0.9)	86	(2.0)
Poland	—	(†)	519	(2.4)	526	(2.1)	519	(2.7)	533	(2.5)	6 !	(2.1)	94	(2.1)
Portugal	—	(†)	—	(†)	541	(2.6)	534	(2.8)	548	(3.0)	25	(4.1)	75	(4.1)
Qatar	—	(†)	353	(1.1)	425 [6]	(3.5)	411 [6]	(4.2)	441 [6]	(4.7)	24	(3.0)	66	(3.4)
Romania	512	(4.6)	489	(5.0)	502	(4.3)	495	(4.3)	510	(4.8)	14	(3.4)	85	(3.5)
Russian Federation	528 [6]	(4.4)	565 [6]	(3.4)	568	(2.7)	559	(3.1)	578	(2.8)	50	(3.7)	50	(3.7)
Saudi Arabia	—	(†)	—	(†)	430	(4.4)	402	(8.2)	456	(3.1)	7	(1.7)	78	(3.5)
Singapore	528	(5.2)	558	(2.9)	567 [6]	(3.3)	559 [6]	(3.6)	576 [6]	(3.5)	46	(#)	54	(#)
Slovak Republic	518	(2.8)	531	(2.8)	535	(2.8)	530	(2.8)	540	(3.1)	24	(3.2)	76	(3.3)
Slovenia	502	(2.0)	522	(2.1)	530	(2.0)	523	(2.7)	539	(2.2)	8	(1.8)	87	(2.4)
Spain	—	(†)	513	(2.5)	513	(2.3)	511	(2.8)	516	(2.5)	29	(3.2)	71	(3.2)
Sweden	561	(2.2)	549	(2.3)	542	(2.1)	535	(2.5)	549	(2.4)	37 [13]	(4.5)	63 [13]	(4.5)
Trinidad and Tobago	—	(†)	436	(4.9)	471	(3.8)	456	(4.3)	487	(4.5)	32	(3.8)	66	(4.0)
United Arab Emirates	—	(†)	—	(†)	439	(2.2)	425	(3.5)	452	(3.0)	15	(1.3)	68	(2.2)
United States	542 [6,7]	(3.8)	540 [7]	(3.5)	556 [6]	(1.5)	551 [6]	(1.7)	562 [6]	(1.9)	75 [13]	(2.7)	24 [13]	(2.7)
Benchmarking education systems														
Abu Dhabi-UAE	—	(†)	—	(†)	424	(4.7)	406	(6.3)	442	(5.5)	11	(2.6)	61	(4.4)
Alberta-CAN	—	(†)	560 [6]	(2.4)	548 [6]	(2.9)	543 [6]	(3.1)	553 [6]	(3.1)	52	(4.5)	48	(4.5)
Andalusia-ESP	—	(†)	—	(†)	515	(2.3)	511	(2.8)	519	(2.4)	26	(3.6)	74	(3.6)
Dubai-UAE	—	(†)	—	(†)	476	(2.0)	470	(3.5)	483	(3.9)	28	(0.3)	66	(0.3)
Florida-USA[15]	—	(†)	—	(†)	569 [8,10]	(2.9)	561 [8,10]	(3.0)	576 [8,10]	(3.4)	82 [13]	(4.7)	18 [13]	(4.7)
Maltese-MLT	—	(†)	—	(†)	457	(1.5)	445	(2.2)	470	(2.0)	14	(0.1)	86	(0.1)
Ontario-CAN	548 [6]	(3.3)	555 [6]	(2.7)	552 [6]	(2.6)	546 [6]	(2.8)	558 [6]	(3.3)	75	(4.0)	25	(4.0)
Quebec-CAN	537	(3.0)	533	(2.8)	538	(2.1)	531	(2.4)	544	(2.6)	23	(3.9)	75	(4.1)

—Not available.

†Not applicable.

#Rounds to zero.

!Interpret data with caution. The coefficient of variation (CV) for this estimate is between 30 and 50 percent.

‡Reporting standards not met. The coefficient of variation (CV) for this estimate is 50 percent or greater.

[1]Most of the education systems represent complete countries, but some represent subnational entities such as U.S. states, Canadian provinces, and England (which is part of the United Kingdom). The name of each subnational entity appears in italics and includes as a suffix the three-letter International Organization for Standardization (ISO) abbreviation for its complete country. Examples include *Florida-USA*, *Ontario-CAN*, and *England-GBR*.

[2]Progress in International Reading Literacy Study (PIRLS) scores are reported on a scale from 0 to 1,000, with the scale average set at 500 and the standard deviation set at 100.

[3]Based on principals' reports of the earliest grade at which each of 11 reading skills and strategies first receive a major emphasis in instruction. A school is counted as emphasizing reading skills and strategies at a certain grade (or before) only if its principal reported that all 11 skills and strategies are emphasized at that grade (or before). A small percentage of fourth-graders (1 percent in the United States) are not shown because their schools first emphasized reading skills and strategies at fourth grade or later.

[4]The PIRLS average includes only education systems that are members of the International Association for the Evaluation of Educational Achievement (IAE), which develops and implements PIRLS at the international level. "Benchmarking" education systems are not members of the IEA and are therefore not included in the average.

[5]Exclusion rates for Azerbaijan and Georgia are slightly underestimated as some conflict zones were not covered and no official statistics were available for 2011.

[6]National Defined Population covers 90 percent to 95 percent of National Target Population.

[7]Met guidelines for sample participation rates only after replacement schools were included.

[8]National Target Population does not include all of the International Target Population.

[9]National Defined Population covers less than 90 percent of National Target Population.

[10]National Defined Population covers less than 80 percent of National Target Population.

[11]Nearly satisfied guidelines for sample participation rates after replacement schools were included.

[12]The TIMSS & PIRLS International Study Center has reservations about the reliability of the average achievement score because the percentage of students with achievement too low for estimation exceeds 25 percent.

[13]Data are available for at least 70 percent but less than 85 percent of students.

[14]The TIMSS & PIRLS International Study Center has reservations about the reliability of the average achievement score because the percentage of students with achievement too low for estimation exceeds 15 percent, though it is less than 25 percent.

[15]All data for Florida are based on public schools only.

SOURCE: International Association for the Evaluation of Educational Achievement (IEA), Progress in International Reading Literacy Study (PIRLS), 2001, 2006, and 2011. (This table was prepared February 2013).

Table 602.20. Average fourth-grade scores and annual instructional time in mathematics and science, by country or other education system: 2011
[Standard errors appear in parentheses]

Country or other education system[1]	Total instructional hours per year		Mathematics							Science					
			Average score[2]		Instructional time in mathematics				Average score[2]		Instructional time in science			
					Hours per year		As a percent of total instructional hours				Hours per year		As a percent of total instructional hours	
1	2		3		4		5		6		7		8	
TIMSS average[3]	897	(2.0)	500	(†)	162	(0.5)	18	(0.1)	500	(†)	85	(0.5)	10	(0.1)
Armenia	851[4]	(17.1)	452	(3.5)	139[4]	(1.7)	16	(0.2)	416	(3.8)	54[5]	(0.6)	6	(0.1)
Australia	1,008	(6.9)	516	(2.9)	230[5]	(5.8)	23	(0.6)	516	(2.8)	65[5]	(2.3)	6	(0.2)
Austria	808	(6.9)	508	(2.6)	146	(2.1)	18	(0.3)	532	(2.8)	96	(2.3)	12	(0.3)
Azerbaijan[6,7]	804	(27.7)	463	(5.8)	130	(3.3)	18	(0.7)	438	(5.6)	61	(1.4)	8	(0.3)
Bahrain	964	(10.8)	436	(3.3)	131[4]	(4.4)	14	(0.4)	449	(3.5)	85[4]	(2.7)	9	(0.3)
Belgium (Flemish)-BEL	1,010[4]	(16.8)	549	(1.9)	224[4]	(4.1)	21	(0.3)	509	(2.0)	—	(†)	—	(†)
Chile	1,228[4]	(22.6)	462	(2.3)	231[5]	(6.7)	19	(0.6)	480	(2.4)	161[5]	(6.4)	13	(0.5)
Chinese Taipei-CHN	989[4]	(13.4)	591	(2.0)	133	(3.9)	12	(0.4)	552	(2.2)	90	(2.3)	9	(0.3)
Croatia[6]	776	(19.4)	490	(1.9)	134	(2.3)	18	(0.4)	516	(2.1)	95	(2.4)	13	(0.4)
Czech Republic	782	(8.2)	511	(2.4)	163	(3.0)	21	(0.4)	536	(2.5)	60	(2.2)	8	(0.3)
Denmark[6]	863[4]	(9.4)	537	(2.6)	124[5]	(2.0)	15	(0.3)	528	(2.8)	62[5]	(1.9)	7	(0.2)
England-GBR	970[4]	(8.3)	542	(3.5)	188[5]	(3.3)	19	(0.4)	529	(2.9)	76[5]	(3.2)	8	(0.3)
Finland	779	(9.8)	545	(2.3)	139	(2.5)	18	(0.4)	570	(2.6)	98	(1.9)	13	(0.4)
Georgia[7,8]	748[4]	(18.7)	450	(3.7)	148[4]	(3.9)	21	(0.6)	455	(3.8)	110[4]	(2.7)	16	(0.4)
Germany	863[4]	(11.2)	528	(2.2)	163[4]	(3.1)	19	(0.3)	528	(2.9)	75[5]	(3.5)	8	(0.4)
Hong Kong-CHN[6]	1,059[4]	(11.2)	602	(3.4)	158[4]	(3.0)	15	(0.3)	535	(3.8)	88[4]	(4.2)	8	(0.4)
Hungary	760	(12.2)	515	(3.4)	148	(3.3)	20	(0.5)	534	(3.7)	72	(2.2)	10	(0.3)
Iran, Islamic Republic of	727	(11.2)	431	(3.5)	146	(3.9)	20	(0.4)	453	(3.7)	106	(3.2)	14	(0.4)
Ireland	854	(#)	527	(2.6)	150	(2.8)	18	(0.3)	516	(3.4)	63	(6.6)	7	(0.8)
Italy	1,085	(12.6)	508	(2.6)	214	(3.9)	20	(0.4)	524	(2.7)	78[4]	(1.8)	7	(0.2)
Japan	891	(3.7)	585	(1.7)	150	(1.6)	17	(0.1)	559	(1.9)	91	(0.8)	10	(0.1)
Kazakhstan[6]	779	(10.6)	501	(4.5)	140	(2.7)	18	(0.4)	495	(5.1)	57	(1.3)	8	(0.2)
Korea, Republic of	789	(11.4)	605	(1.9)	121	(3.0)	15	(0.4)	587	(2.0)	92	(2.5)	12	(0.4)
Kuwait[8]	928[4]	(23.1)	342[9]	(3.4)	120[4]	(4.9)	13	(0.4)	347[10]	(4.7)	85[5]	(5.8)	11	(0.6)
Lithuania[6,8]	649	(9.0)	534	(2.4)	133	(2.6)	21	(0.5)	515	(2.4)	60	(1.5)	9	(0.3)
Malta	891[4]	(0.2)	496	(1.3)	183[4]	(0.1)	21	(#)	446	(1.9)	39[4]	(0.1)	4	(#)
Morocco	1,040[4]	(23.6)	335[9]	(4.0)	174[5]	(3.5)	17	(0.4)	264[9]	(4.5)	44[5]	(5.5)	5	(0.6)
Netherlands[11]	1,074[5]	(9.9)	540	(1.7)	195[5]	(7.0)	18	(0.5)	531	(2.2)	42[5]	(2.4)	4	(0.2)
New Zealand	925	(3.9)	486	(2.6)	168	(2.4)	18	(0.3)	497	(2.3)	52[5]	(3.0)	6	(0.3)
Northern Ireland-GBR[11]	970[4]	(11.0)	562	(2.9)	232[5]	(6.1)	24	(0.6)	517	(2.6)	72[5]	(3.9)	8	(0.4)
Norway[12]	817	(10.7)	495	(2.8)	157	(4.1)	19	(0.6)	494	(2.3)	55	(2.2)	7	(0.3)
Oman	999[5]	(17.4)	385[10]	(2.9)	170[5]	(3.1)	17	(0.3)	377	(4.3)	120[5]	(2.4)	12	(0.2)
Poland	764[4]	(13.5)	481	(2.2)	157[4]	(3.0)	21	(0.5)	505	(2.6)	64[4]	(3.1)	8	(0.4)
Portugal	940[4]	(13.1)	532	(3.4)	250[4]	(4.3)	27	(0.4)	522	(3.9)	162[4]	(4.1)	17	(0.8)
Qatar[6]	1,068	(9.1)	413	(3.5)	185	(6.3)	17	(0.6)	394	(4.3)	135	(6.8)	13	(0.6)
Romania	796	(17.9)	482	(5.8)	148	(3.9)	19	(0.5)	505	(5.9)	56	(6.2)	7	(0.8)
Russian Federation	660[4]	(8.0)	542	(3.7)	104	(1.0)	16	(0.2)	552	(3.5)	49	(0.7)	8	(0.2)
Saudi Arabia	977[4]	(19.4)	410	(5.3)	147[4]	(6.6)	15	(0.5)	429	(5.4)	82[4]	(4.2)	8	(0.5)
Serbia[6]	778	(18.5)	516	(3.0)	153	(2.1)	20	(0.5)	516	(3.1)	72	(5.0)	10	(0.9)
Singapore[6]	1,012	(#)	606	(3.2)	208	(3.2)	21	(0.3)	583	(3.4)	96	(2.1)	9	(0.2)
Slovak Republic	780	(8.8)	507	(3.8)	147	(1.4)	19	(0.1)	532	(3.8)	101	(4.3)	13	(0.6)
Slovenia	684	(#)	513	(2.2)	169	(2.6)	25	(0.4)	520	(2.7)	101	(1.2)	15	(0.2)
Spain	884[4]	(9.7)	482	(2.9)	167[4]	(2.3)	19	(0.2)	505	(3.0)	145[4]	(2.6)	16	(0.3)
Sweden	849[4]	(11.3)	504	(2.0)	138[5]	(3.8)	17	(0.5)	533	(2.7)	75[5]	(3.0)	9	(0.4)
Thailand	1,201[4]	(20.9)	458	(4.8)	167	(5.2)	14	(0.6)	472	(5.6)	109	(4.9)	9	(0.5)
Tunisia	963[4]	(22.9)	359[10]	(3.9)	175[4]	(2.9)	19	(0.3)	346[10]	(5.3)	93[4]	(5.4)	10	(0.6)
Turkey	900	(19.3)	469	(4.7)	126	(2.5)	15	(0.4)	463	(4.5)	94	(1.8)	11	(0.3)
United Arab Emirates	1,025[4]	(8.5)	434	(2.0)	154[5]	(2.4)	15	(0.2)	428	(2.5)	108[5]	(3.0)	11	(0.3)
United States[6]	1,078	(7.3)	541	(1.8)	206[4]	(4.6)	19	(0.5)	544	(2.1)	105[4]	(3.1)	10	(0.3)
Yemen	831[4]	(14.1)	248[9]	(6.0)	135[4]	(6.4)	16	(0.7)	209[9]	(7.3)	91[4]	(5.6)	11	(0.6)
Benchmarking education systems														
Abu Dhabi-UAE	1,033[4]	(18.1)	417	(4.6)	150[5]	(4.3)	15	(0.4)	411	(4.9)	110[5]	(6.8)	11	(0.6)
Alberta-CAN[6]	1,006	(8.8)	507	(2.5)	169[5]	(3.2)	17	(0.4)	541	(2.4)	130[5]	(4.1)	13	(0.6)
Dubai-UAE	993[4]	(0.7)	468	(1.6)	158[5]	(2.3)	16	(0.2)	461	(2.3)	99[5]	(1.6)	10	(0.2)
Florida-USA[8,13,14]	1,073[4]	(19.7)	545	(2.9)	217[5]	(8.8)	20	(0.9)	545	(3.7)	99[5]	(9.6)	10	(0.8)
North Carolina-USA[6,8,14]	1,113[4]	(22.9)	554	(4.2)	221[4]	(13.5)	20	(1.2)	538	(4.6)	113[5]	(6.0)	10	(0.8)
Ontario-CAN	969	(7.4)	518	(3.1)	201[4]	(4.1)	21	(0.5)	528	(3.0)	94[4]	(3.2)	9	(0.4)
Quebec-CAN	916	(5.1)	533	(2.4)	229	(5.0)	25	(0.6)	516	(2.7)	92[4]	(1.7)	10	(0.2)
											50		5	

—Not available.
†Not applicable.
#Rounds to zero.
[1]Most of the education systems represent complete countries, but some represent subnational entities such as U.S. states, Canadian provinces, and England (which is part of the United Kingdom). The name of each subnational entity appears in italics and includes as a suffix the three-letter International Organization for Standardization (ISO) abbreviation for its complete country. Examples include *Florida-USA*, *Ontario-CAN*, and *England-GBR*.
[2]Trends in International Mathematics and Science Study (TIMSS) scores are reported on a scale from 0 to 1,000, with the scale average set at 500 and the standard deviation set at 100.
[3]The TIMSS average includes only education systems that are members of the International Association for the Evaluation of Educational Achievement (IAE), which develops and implements TIMSS at the international level. "Benchmarking" education systems are not members of the IEA and are therefore not included in the average.
[4]Data are available for at least 70 percent but less than 85 percent of students.
[5]Data are available for at least 50 percent but less than 70 percent of students.
[6]National Defined Population covers 90 to 95 percent of National Target Population.
[7]Exclusion rates for Azerbaijan and Georgia are slightly underestimated as some conflict zones were not covered and no official statistics were available.
[8]National Target Population does not include all of the International Target Population defined by TIMSS.
[9]The TIMSS & PIRLS International Study Center has reservations about the reliability of the average achievement score because the percentage of students with achievement too low for estimation exceeds 25 percent.

[10]The TIMSS & PIRLS International Study Center has reservations about the reliability of the average achievement score because the percentage of students with achievement too low for estimation exceeds 15 percent, though it is less than 25 percent.
[11]Met guidelines for sample participation rates only after replacement schools were included.
[12]Nearly satisfied guidelines for sample participation rates after replacement schools were included.
[13]National Defined Population covers less than 90 percent of National Target Population (but at least 77 percent).
[14]All U.S. state data are based on public school students only.
NOTE: Countries were required to sample students in the grade that corresponded to the end of 4 years of formal schooling, providing that the mean age at the time of testing was at least 9.5 years. Instructional times shown in this table are actual or implemented times (as opposed to intended times prescribed by the curriculum). Principals reported total instructional hours per day and school days per year. Total instructional hours per year were calculated by multiplying the number of school days per year by the number of instructional hours per day. Teachers reported instructional hours per week in mathematics and science. Instructional hours per year in mathematics and science were calculated by dividing weekly instructional hours by the number of school days per week and then multiplying by the number of school days per year.
SOURCE: International Association for the Evaluation of Educational Achievement (IEA), Trends in International Mathematics and Science Study (TIMSS), 2011; *TIMSS 2011 International Results in Mathematics*, by Ina V.S. Mullis et al.; and *TIMSS 2011 International Results in Science*, by Michael O. Martin et al. (This table was prepared December 2012.)

Table 602.30. Average eighth-grade scores and annual instructional time in mathematics and science, by country or other education system: 2011

[Standard errors appear in parentheses]

Country or other education system[1]	Total instructional hours per year		Mathematics						Science					
					Instructional time in mathematics						Instructional time in science[3]			
			Average score[2]		Hours per year		As a percent of total instructional hours		Average score[2]		Hours per year		As a percent of total instructional hours	
1	2		3		4		5		6		7		8	
TIMSS average[4]	1,031	(2.3)	500	(†)	138	(0.5)	14	(0.1)	500	(†)	158	(0.8)	11	(0.1)
Armenia	979 [5]	(12.8)	467	(2.7)	143 [5]	(3.0)	15	(0.2)	437	(3.1)	240 [6]	(4.9)	‡	(†)
Australia	1,039	(7.2)	505	(5.1)	143 [6]	(3.5)	14	(0.3)	519	(4.8)	131 [6]	(4.5)	12	(0.4)
Bahrain	1,019	(1.1)	409 [7]	(2.0)	142 [5]	(2.5)	14	(0.3)	452	(2.0)	130 [5]	(2.8)	13	(0.3)
Chile	1,245 [5]	(23.5)	416	(2.6)	193 [5]	(4.5)	15	(0.3)	461	(2.5)	134 [5]	(3.8)	11	(0.3)
Chinese Taipei-CHN	1,153	(11.7)	609	(3.2)	166	(2.4)	15	(0.2)	564	(2.3)	157	(2.7)	14	(0.3)
England-GBR[8]	992 [5]	(8.4)	507	(5.5)	116 [5]	(2.1)	11	(0.3)	533	(4.9)	102 [6]	(3.1)	10	(0.4)
Finland	934	(11.7)	514	(2.5)	105	(1.8)	11	(0.2)	552	(2.5)	190 [5]	(6.0)	‡	(†)
Georgia[9,10]	833 [5]	(10.8)	431	(3.8)	123 [5]	(3.3)	15	(0.5)	420	(3.0)	198 [5]	(6.8)	‡	(†)
Ghana	1,153 [5]	(18.9)	331 [11]	(4.3)	165 [5]	(6.8)	14	(0.6)	306 [7]	(5.2)	148 [5]	(6.1)	13	(0.4)
Hong Kong-CHN	1,026 [5]	(11.3)	586	(3.8)	138 [5]	(2.9)	13	(0.3)	535	(3.4)	103 [5]	(4.6)	10	(0.4)
Hungary	836	(12.2)	505	(3.5)	119	(1.9)	15	(0.3)	522	(3.1)	236	(4.8)	28 !	(13.1)
Indonesia	1,494 [5]	(40.9)	386 [7]	(4.3)	173 [5]	(7.9)	12	(0.6)	406	(4.5)	190 [5]	(12.2)	10	(0.5)
Iran, Islamic Republic of	994	(15.9)	415 [7]	(4.3)	124	(3.3)	13	(0.3)	474	(4.0)	120	(3.6)	12	(0.4)
Israel[12]	1,108 [5]	(14.1)	516	(4.1)	165 [5]	(3.0)	15	(0.2)	516	(4.0)	132	(3.9)	12	(0.4)
Italy	1,085	(9.4)	498	(2.4)	155	(2.5)	14	(0.2)	501	(2.5)	73	(1.0)	7	(0.1)
Japan	1,016	(6.7)	570	(2.6)	108	(1.4)	11	(0.1)	558	(2.4)	128	(1.7)	12	(0.3)
Jordan	1,041	(11.9)	406 [7]	(3.7)	130	(3.8)	13	(0.4)	449	(4.0)	134	(3.1)	13	(0.4)
Kazakhstan	920	(9.9)	487	(4.0)	117	(3.2)	13	(0.4)	490	(4.3)	244	(4.8)	27 !	(11.0)
Korea, Republic of	1,006	(12.1)	613	(2.9)	137	(1.8)	13	(0.2)	560	(2.0)	126	(2.5)	11	(0.2)
Lebanon	1,028 [5]	(12.7)	449	(3.7)	178 [5]	(3.9)	17	(0.4)	406	(4.9)	‡	(†)	‡	(†)
Lithuania[9]	898	(13.9)	502	(2.5)	132	(2.7)	15	(0.4)	514	(2.6)	251 [5]	(5.2)	‡	(†)
Macedonia, Republic of	1,023 [5]	(21.4)	426 [7]	(5.2)	122 [6]	(4.6)	13	(0.6)	407	(5.4)	334 [6]	(14.7)	‡	(†)
Malaysia	1,198 [5]	(13.7)	440	(5.4)	123 [5]	(3.4)	10	(0.3)	426	(6.3)	126	(3.6)	10	(0.3)
Morocco	1,303 [5]	(24.9)	371 [11]	(2.0)	148 [5]	(2.1)	12	(0.2)	376	(2.2)	144 [5]	(2.0)	‡	(†)
New Zealand	959	(4.4)	488	(5.5)	141	(1.8)	15	(0.2)	512	(4.6)	130 [5]	(2.6)	14	(0.3)
Norway	880	(6.3)	475	(2.4)	125	(3.4)	14	(0.4)	494	(2.6)	101	(3.3)	11	(0.4)
Oman	1,044 [5]	(17.7)	366 [7]	(2.8)	161 [5]	(5.1)	16	(0.4)	420	(3.2)	161 [6]	(3.8)	16	(0.3)
Palestinian National Authority	918	(7.3)	404 [7]	(3.5)	134	(4.0)	15	(0.4)	420	(3.2)	107	(3.4)	12	(0.4)
Qatar	1,054	(1.3)	410 [7]	(3.1)	162	(3.6)	15	(0.4)	419	(3.4)	131	(6.9)	12	(0.5)
Romania	984	(15.5)	458	(4.0)	145	(3.7)	15	(0.3)	465	(3.5)	281	(10.1)	‡	(†)
Russian Federation[13]	882	(8.7)	539	(3.6)	142	(2.0)	16	(0.3)	542	(3.2)	208	(1.6)	24 !	(8.8)
Saudi Arabia	1,050 [5]	(20.9)	394 [7]	(4.6)	134 [5]	(5.4)	13	(0.4)	436	(3.9)	124 [5]	(6.8)	12	(0.5)
Singapore[13]	1,106	(#)	611	(3.8)	138	(1.7)	13	(0.2)	590	(4.3)	115	(2.1)	11	(0.2)
Slovenia	798	(#)	505	(2.2)	121	(1.5)	15	(0.2)	543	(2.7)	251	(4.6)	31	(4.6)
Sweden	969 [5]	(13.4)	484	(1.9)	97 [6]	(2.2)	10	(0.3)	509	(2.5)	94 [6]	(3.1)	9	(0.4)
Syrian Arab Republic	811	(14.2)	380 [7]	(4.5)	118 [5]	(4.7)	15	(0.5)	426	(3.9)	150 [5]	(7.5)	‡	(†)
Thailand	1,270 [5]	(15.1)	427	(4.3)	129	(4.3)	10	(0.3)	451	(3.9)	119	(2.9)	9	(0.3)
Tunisia	1,299 [5]	(25.4)	425	(2.8)	131 [5]	(3.0)	10	(0.2)	439	(2.5)	64 [5]	(1.9)	5	(0.1)
Turkey	889	(16.7)	452	(3.9)	117	(1.8)	14	(0.3)	483	(3.4)	99	(1.1)	12	(0.2)
Ukraine	901	(10.7)	479	(3.9)	132	(3.5)	15	(0.4)	501	(3.4)	239	(4.0)	27 !	(11.4)
United Arab Emirates	1,046 [5]	(8.0)	456	(2.1)	157 [5]	(2.9)	15	(0.3)	465	(2.4)	115 [6]	(2.7)	11	(0.3)
United States[13]	1,114	(6.6)	509	(2.6)	157 [6]	(3.2)	14	(0.3)	525	(2.6)	139 [14]	(2.4)	13 [14]	(0.2)
Benchmarking education systems														
Abu Dhabi-UAE	1,045 [5]	(16.6)	449	(3.7)	158 [5]	(5.8)	15	(0.5)	461	(4.0)	111 [6]	(4.8)	11	(0.5)
Alabama-USA[9,15]	1,135 [5]	(16.0)	466	(5.9)	166 [6]	(8.9)	15	(0.9)	485	(6.2)	167 [6]	(6.0)	15	(0.5)
Alberta-CAN[13]	1,031	(10.0)	505	(2.6)	156	(4.2)	19	(0.4)	546	(2.4)	145 [5]	(4.0)	10	(0.4)
California-USA[9,13,15]	1,040 [5]	(15.2)	493	(4.9)	172 [6]	(8.0)	17	(0.7)	499	(4.6)	‡	(†)	14	(0.7)
Colorado-USA[9,15]	1,148	(17.0)	518	(4.9)	173 [5]	(8.6)	15	(0.8)	542	(4.4)	138 [6]	(6.0)	12	(0.5)

See notes at end of table.

Table 602.30. Average eighth-grade scores and annual instructional time in mathematics and science, by country or other education system: 2011—Continued

[Standard errors appear in parentheses]

Country or other education system[1]	Total instructional hours per year	Mathematics			Science		
		Average score[2]	Instructional time in mathematics		Average score[2]	Instructional time in science[3]	
			Hours per year	As a percent of total instructional hours		Hours per year	As a percent of total instructional hours
1	2	3	4	5	6	7	8
Connecticut-USA[9,13,15]	1,071 (19.3)	518 (4.8)	144 [5] (4.4)	14 (0.5)	532 (4.6)	139 [6] (6.2)	13 (0.6)
Dubai-UAE	1,022 [5] (1.5)	478 (2.1)	155 [5] (3.6)	15 (0.3)	485 (2.5)	125 [6] (3.6)	11 (0.3)
Florida-USA[9,13,15]	1,119 [5] (17.0)	513 (6.4)	144 [6] (7.4)	13 (0.7)	530 (7.3)	‡ (†)	13 (0.8)
Indiana-USA[9,13,15]	1,133 [5] (14.9)	522 (5.1)	149 [6] (6.9)	13 (0.7)	533 (4.8)	132 [6] (6.5)	12 (0.6)
Massachusetts-USA[9,13,15]	1,087 (13.6)	561 (5.3)	154 [5] (5.4)	14 (0.6)	567 (5.1)	156 [6] (6.1)	15 (0.6)
Minnesota-USA[9,15]	1,043 (14.8)	545 (4.6)	142 [5] (7.5)	14 (0.7)	553 (4.6)	140 [6] (8.3)	14 (0.9)
North Carolina-USA[9,12,15]	1,159 (16.0)	537 (6.8)	185 [6] (9.7)	16 (0.8)	532 (6.3)	‡ (†)	16 (1.2)
Ontario-CAN[13]	971 [5] (7.5)	512 (2.5)	181 [5] (3.9)	16 (0.5)	521 (2.5)	96 [5] (3.5)	11 (0.3)
Quebec-CAN	913 (3.3)	532 (2.3)	147 (4.1)	15 (0.5)	520 (2.5)	102 [5] (3.0)	14 (0.4)

†Not applicable.
#Rounds to zero.
!Interpret data with caution. The coefficient of variation (CV) for this estimate is between 30 and 50 percent.
‡Reporting standards not met. Either data are available for less than 50 percent of the students or the coefficient of variation (CV) is 50 percent or greater.
[1]Most of the education systems represent complete countries, but some represent subnational entities such as U.S. states, Canadian provinces, and England (which is part of the United Kingdom). The name of each subnational entity appears in italics and includes as a suffix the three-letter International Organization for Standardization (ISO) abbreviation for its complete country. Examples include *Florida-USA*, *Ontario-CAN*, and *England-GBR*.
[2]Trends in International Mathematics and Science Study (TIMSS) scores are reported on a scale from 0 to 1,000, with the scale average set at 500 and the standard deviation set at 100.
[3]General/integrated science instructional time is shown for the 27 participating countries that teach science as a general or integrated subject at the eighth grade. For the 15 participating countries that teach the sciences as separate subjects (biology, chemistry, etc.) at the eighth grade, total instructional time across science subjects is shown.
[4]The TIMSS average includes only education systems that are members of the International Association for the Evaluation of Educational Achievement (IAE), which develops and implements TIMSS at the international level. "Benchmarking" education systems are not members of the IEA and are therefore not included in the average.
[5]Data are available for at least 70 percent but less than 85 percent of students.
[6]Data are available for at least 50 percent but less than 70 percent of students.
[7]The TIMSS & PIRLS International Study Center has reservations about the reliability of the average achievement score because the percentage of students with achievement too low for estimation exceeds 15 percent, though it is less than 25 percent.
[8]Nearly satisfied guidelines for sample participation rate after replacement schools were included.

[9]National Target Population does not include all of the International Target Population defined by TIMSS.
[10]Exclusion rates for Georgia are slightly underestimated as some conflict zones were not covered and no official statistics were available.
[11]The TIMSS & PIRLS International Study Center has reservations about the reliability of the average achievement score because the percentage of students with achievement too low for estimation exceeds 25 percent.
[12]National Defined Population covers less than 90 percent of National Target Population (but at least 77 percent).
[13]National Defined Population covers 90 to 95 percent of National Target Population.
[14]Data are for 2007 and are from *TIMSS 2007 International Results in Science*. Met guidelines for sample participation rates only after replacement schools were included. Data are available for at least 50 percent but less than 70 percent of students.
[15]All U.S. state data are based on public school students only.
NOTE: Countries were required to sample students in the grade that corresponded to the end of 8 years of formal schooling, providing that the mean age at the time of testing was at least 13.5 years. Instructional times shown in this table are actual or implemented times (as opposed to intended times prescribed by the curriculum). Principals reported total instructional hours per day and school days per year. Total instructional hours per year were calculated by multiplying the number of school days per year by the number of instructional hours per day. Teachers reported instructional hours per week in mathematics and science. Instructional hours per year in mathematics and science were calculated by dividing weekly instructional hours by the number of school days per week and then multiplying by the number of school days per year.
SOURCE: International Association for the Evaluation of Educational Achievement (IEA), Trends in International Mathematics and Science Study (TIMSS), 2011; *TIMSS 2011 International Results in Mathematics*, by Ina V.S. Mullis et al.; and *TIMSS 2011 International Results in Science*, by Michael O. Martin et al. (This table was prepared December 2012.)

Table 602.40. Average reading literacy, mathematics literacy, and science literacy scores of 15-year-old students, by sex and country or other education system: 2009 and 2012

[Standard errors appear in parentheses]

Country or other education system	Reading literacy				Mathematics literacy				Science literacy			
	2009	2012			2009	2012			2009	2012		
		Total	Male	Female		Total	Male	Female		Total	Male	Female
1	2	3	4	5	6	7	8	9	10	11	12	13
OECD average[1]	**493 (0.5)**	**496 (0.5)**	**478 (0.6)**	**515 (0.5)**	**496 (0.5)**	**494 (0.5)**	**499 (0.6)**	**489 (0.5)**	**501 (0.5)**	**501 (0.5)**	**502 (0.6)**	**500 (0.5)**
Australia	515 (2.3)	512 (1.6)	495 (2.3)	530 (2.0)	514 (2.5)	504 (1.6)	510 (2.4)	498 (2.0)	527 (2.5)	521 (1.8)	524 (2.5)	519 (2.1)
Austria	470 (2.9)	490 (2.8)	471 (4.0)	508 (3.4)	496 (2.7)	506 (2.7)	517 (3.9)	494 (3.3)	494 (3.2)	506 (2.7)	510 (3.9)	501 (3.4)
Belgium	506 (2.3)	509 (2.3)	493 (3.0)	525 (2.7)	515 (2.3)	515 (2.1)	520 (2.9)	509 (2.6)	507 (2.5)	505 (2.2)	507 (3.0)	503 (2.6)
Canada	524 (1.5)	523 (1.9)	506 (2.3)	541 (2.1)	527 (1.6)	518 (1.8)	523 (2.1)	513 (2.1)	529 (1.6)	525 (1.9)	527 (2.4)	524 (2.0)
Chile	449 (3.1)	441 (2.9)	430 (3.8)	452 (2.9)	421 (3.1)	423 (3.1)	436 (3.8)	411 (3.1)	447 (2.9)	445 (2.9)	448 (3.7)	442 (2.9)
Czech Republic	478 (2.9)	493 (2.9)	474 (3.3)	513 (3.4)	493 (2.8)	499 (2.9)	505 (3.7)	493 (3.6)	500 (3.0)	508 (3.0)	509 (3.7)	508 (3.5)
Denmark	495 (2.1)	496 (2.6)	481 (3.3)	512 (2.6)	503 (2.6)	500 (2.3)	507 (2.9)	493 (2.3)	499 (2.5)	498 (2.7)	504 (3.5)	493 (2.5)
Estonia	501 (2.6)	516 (2.0)	494 (2.4)	538 (2.3)	512 (2.6)	521 (2.0)	523 (2.6)	518 (2.2)	528 (2.7)	541 (1.9)	540 (2.5)	543 (2.3)
Finland	536 (2.3)	524 (2.4)	494 (3.1)	556 (2.4)	541 (2.2)	519 (1.9)	517 (2.6)	520 (2.2)	554 (2.3)	545 (2.2)	537 (3.0)	554 (2.3)
France	496 (3.4)	505 (2.8)	483 (3.8)	527 (3.0)	497 (3.1)	495 (2.5)	499 (3.4)	491 (2.5)	498 (3.6)	499 (2.6)	498 (3.8)	500 (2.4)
Germany	497 (2.7)	508 (2.8)	486 (2.9)	530 (3.1)	513 (2.9)	514 (2.9)	520 (3.0)	507 (3.4)	520 (2.8)	524 (3.0)	524 (3.1)	524 (3.5)
Greece	483 (4.3)	477 (3.3)	452 (4.1)	502 (3.1)	466 (3.9)	453 (2.5)	457 (3.3)	449 (2.6)	470 (4.0)	467 (3.1)	460 (3.8)	473 (3.0)
Hungary	494 (3.2)	488 (3.2)	468 (3.9)	508 (3.3)	490 (3.5)	477 (3.2)	482 (3.7)	473 (3.6)	503 (3.1)	494 (2.9)	496 (3.4)	493 (3.3)
Iceland	500 (1.4)	483 (1.8)	457 (2.4)	508 (2.5)	507 (1.4)	493 (1.7)	490 (2.3)	496 (2.3)	496 (1.4)	478 (2.1)	477 (2.7)	480 (2.9)
Ireland	496 (3.0)	523 (2.6)	509 (3.5)	538 (3.0)	487 (2.5)	501 (2.2)	509 (3.3)	494 (2.6)	508 (3.3)	522 (2.5)	524 (3.4)	520 (3.1)
Israel	474 (3.6)	486 (5.0)	463 (8.2)	507 (3.9)	447 (3.3)	466 (4.7)	472 (7.8)	461 (3.5)	455 (3.1)	470 (5.0)	470 (7.9)	470 (4.0)
Italy	486 (1.6)	490 (2.0)	471 (2.5)	510 (2.3)	483 (1.9)	485 (2.0)	494 (2.4)	476 (2.2)	489 (1.8)	494 (1.9)	495 (2.2)	492 (2.4)
Japan	520 (3.5)	538 (3.7)	527 (4.7)	551 (3.6)	529 (3.3)	536 (3.6)	545 (4.6)	527 (3.6)	539 (3.4)	547 (3.6)	552 (4.7)	541 (3.5)
Korea, Republic of	539 (3.5)	536 (3.9)	525 (5.0)	548 (4.5)	546 (4.0)	554 (4.6)	562 (5.8)	544 (5.1)	538 (3.4)	538 (3.7)	539 (4.7)	536 (4.2)
Luxembourg	472 (1.3)	488 (1.5)	473 (1.9)	503 (1.8)	489 (1.2)	490 (1.1)	502 (1.5)	477 (1.4)	484 (1.2)	491 (1.3)	499 (1.7)	483 (1.7)
Mexico	425 (2.0)	424 (1.5)	411 (1.7)	435 (1.6)	419 (1.8)	413 (1.4)	420 (1.6)	406 (1.4)	416 (1.8)	415 (1.3)	418 (1.5)	412 (1.3)
Netherlands	508 (5.1)	511 (3.5)	498 (4.0)	525 (3.5)	526 (4.7)	523 (3.5)	528 (3.6)	518 (3.9)	522 (5.4)	522 (3.5)	524 (3.7)	520 (3.9)
New Zealand	521 (2.4)	512 (2.4)	495 (3.3)	530 (3.5)	519 (2.3)	500 (2.2)	507 (3.2)	492 (2.9)	532 (2.6)	516 (2.1)	518 (3.2)	513 (3.3)
Norway	503 (2.6)	504 (3.2)	481 (3.3)	528 (3.9)	498 (2.4)	489 (2.7)	490 (2.8)	488 (3.4)	500 (2.6)	495 (3.1)	493 (3.2)	496 (3.7)
Poland	500 (2.6)	518 (3.1)	497 (3.7)	539 (3.1)	495 (2.8)	518 (3.6)	520 (4.3)	516 (3.8)	508 (2.4)	526 (3.1)	524 (3.7)	527 (3.2)
Portugal	489 (3.1)	488 (3.8)	468 (4.2)	508 (3.7)	487 (2.9)	487 (3.8)	493 (4.1)	481 (3.9)	493 (2.9)	489 (3.7)	488 (4.1)	490 (3.8)
Slovak Republic	477 (2.5)	463 (4.2)	444 (4.6)	483 (5.1)	497 (3.1)	482 (3.4)	486 (4.1)	477 (4.1)	490 (3.0)	471 (3.6)	475 (4.3)	467 (4.2)
Slovenia	483 (1.0)	481 (1.2)	454 (1.7)	510 (1.8)	501 (1.2)	501 (1.2)	503 (2.0)	499 (2.0)	512 (1.1)	514 (1.3)	510 (1.9)	519 (1.9)
Spain	481 (2.0)	488 (1.9)	474 (2.3)	503 (1.9)	483 (2.1)	484 (1.9)	492 (2.4)	476 (2.0)	488 (2.1)	496 (1.8)	500 (2.3)	493 (1.9)
Sweden	497 (2.9)	483 (3.0)	458 (4.0)	509 (2.8)	494 (2.9)	478 (2.3)	477 (3.0)	480 (2.4)	495 (2.7)	485 (3.0)	481 (3.9)	489 (2.8)
Switzerland	501 (2.4)	509 (2.6)	491 (3.1)	527 (2.5)	534 (3.3)	531 (3.0)	537 (3.5)	524 (3.1)	517 (2.8)	515 (2.7)	518 (3.3)	512 (2.7)
Turkey	464 (3.5)	475 (4.2)	453 (4.6)	499 (4.3)	445 (4.4)	448 (4.8)	452 (5.1)	444 (5.7)	454 (3.6)	463 (3.9)	458 (4.5)	469 (4.3)
United Kingdom	494 (2.3)	499 (3.5)	487 (4.5)	512 (3.8)	492 (2.4)	494 (3.3)	500 (4.2)	488 (3.8)	514 (2.5)	514 (3.4)	521 (4.5)	508 (3.7)
United States	500 (3.7)	498 (3.7)	482 (4.1)	513 (3.8)	487 (3.6)	481 (3.6)	484 (3.8)	479 (3.9)	502 (3.6)	497 (3.8)	497 (4.1)	498 (4.0)
Non-OECD education systems												
Albania	385 (4.0)	394 (3.2)	387 (3.8)	401 (3.7)	377 (4.0)	394 (2.0)	394 (2.6)	395 (2.6)	391 (3.9)	397 (2.4)	394 (3.0)	401 (2.9)
Argentina	398 (4.6)	396 (3.7)	377 (4.5)	414 (3.6)	388 (4.1)	388 (3.5)	396 (4.2)	382 (3.4)	401 (4.6)	406 (3.9)	402 (4.5)	409 (4.0)
Brazil	412 (2.7)	410 (2.1)	394 (2.4)	425 (2.2)	386 (2.4)	391 (2.1)	401 (2.2)	383 (2.3)	405 (2.4)	405 (2.1)	406 (2.3)	404 (2.3)
Bulgaria	429 (6.7)	436 (6.0)	403 (6.3)	472 (5.6)	428 (5.9)	439 (4.0)	438 (4.7)	440 (4.2)	439 (5.9)	446 (4.8)	437 (5.6)	457 (4.6)
Chinese Taipei	— (†)	523 (3.0)	507 (4.3)	539 (4.3)	— (†)	560 (3.3)	563 (5.4)	557 (5.7)	— (†)	523 (2.3)	524 (3.9)	523 (4.0)
Colombia	413 (3.7)	403 (3.4)	394 (3.9)	412 (3.8)	381 (3.2)	376 (2.9)	390 (3.4)	364 (3.2)	402 (3.6)	399 (3.1)	408 (3.4)	390 (3.6)
Connecticut-USA[2]	— (†)	521 (6.5)	510 (7.1)	532 (6.7)	— (†)	506 (6.2)	513 (6.9)	499 (6.3)	— (†)	521 (5.7)	528 (6.2)	514 (6.1)
Costa Rica	— (†)	441 (3.5)	427 (3.9)	452 (3.5)	— (†)	407 (3.0)	420 (3.6)	396 (3.1)	— (†)	429 (2.9)	436 (3.5)	424 (3.2)
Croatia	476 (2.9)	485 (3.3)	461 (4.1)	509 (3.3)	460 (3.1)	471 (3.5)	477 (4.4)	465 (3.7)	486 (2.8)	491 (3.1)	490 (3.9)	493 (3.3)
Cyprus	— (†)	449 (1.2)	418 (1.9)	481 (1.9)	— (†)	440 (1.1)	440 (1.5)	440 (1.6)	— (†)	438 (1.2)	431 (1.8)	444 (1.7)
Florida-USA[2]	— (†)	492 (6.1)	481 (7.0)	503 (5.9)	— (†)	467 (5.8)	474 (6.3)	460 (6.0)	— (†)	485 (6.4)	491 (7.4)	478 (6.2)
Hong Kong-China	533 (2.1)	545 (2.8)	533 (3.8)	558 (3.3)	555 (2.7)	561 (3.2)	568 (4.6)	553 (3.9)	549 (2.8)	555 (2.6)	558 (3.6)	551 (3.1)
Indonesia	402 (3.7)	396 (4.2)	382 (4.8)	410 (4.3)	371 (3.7)	375 (4.0)	377 (4.4)	373 (4.3)	383 (3.8)	382 (3.8)	380 (4.1)	383 (4.1)
Jordan	405 (3.3)	399 (3.6)	361 (5.5)	436 (3.1)	387 (3.7)	386 (3.1)	375 (5.4)	396 (3.1)	415 (3.5)	409 (3.1)	388 (5.4)	430 (2.9)
Kazakhstan	390 (3.1)	393 (2.7)	374 (3.4)	411 (2.6)	405 (3.0)	432 (3.0)	432 (3.4)	432 (3.3)	400 (3.1)	425 (3.0)	420 (3.4)	429 (3.2)
Latvia	484 (3.0)	489 (2.4)	462 (3.3)	516 (2.7)	482 (3.1)	491 (2.8)	489 (3.4)	493 (3.2)	494 (3.1)	502 (2.8)	495 (3.6)	510 (2.8)
Liechtenstein	499 (2.8)	516 (4.1)	504 (6.2)	529 (5.8)	536 (4.1)	535 (4.0)	546 (6.0)	523 (5.8)	520 (3.4)	525 (3.5)	533 (5.8)	516 (5.7)
Lithuania	468 (2.4)	477 (2.5)	450 (2.8)	505 (2.6)	477 (2.6)	479 (2.6)	479 (2.8)	479 (3.0)	491 (2.9)	496 (2.6)	488 (3.0)	503 (2.6)
Macao-China	487 (0.9)	509 (0.9)	492 (1.4)	527 (1.1)	525 (0.9)	538 (1.0)	540 (1.4)	537 (1.3)	511 (1.0)	521 (0.8)	520 (1.3)	521 (1.2)
Malaysia	— (†)	398 (3.3)	377 (3.9)	418 (3.3)	— (†)	421 (3.2)	416 (3.7)	424 (3.7)	— (†)	420 (3.0)	414 (3.8)	425 (3.1)
Montenegro, Republic of	408 (1.7)	422 (1.2)	391 (2.3)	453 (1.5)	403 (2.0)	410 (1.1)	410 (1.6)	410 (1.6)	401 (2.0)	410 (1.1)	402 (1.6)	419 (1.6)
Peru	370 (4.0)	384 (4.3)	373 (4.0)	395 (5.4)	365 (4.0)	368 (3.7)	378 (3.6)	359 (4.8)	369 (3.5)	373 (3.6)	376 (3.5)	370 (4.6)
Massachusetts-USA[2]	— (†)	527 (6.1)	511 (6.2)	542 (6.6)	— (†)	514 (6.2)	518 (6.3)	509 (7.1)	— (†)	527 (6.0)	529 (6.1)	526 (6.8)
Qatar	372 (0.8)	388 (0.8)	354 (1.1)	424 (1.2)	368 (0.7)	376 (0.8)	369 (1.1)	385 (0.9)	379 (0.9)	384 (0.7)	367 (1.2)	402 (1.1)
Romania	424 (4.1)	438 (4.0)	417 (4.5)	457 (4.2)	427 (3.4)	445 (3.8)	447 (4.3)	443 (4.0)	428 (3.4)	439 (3.3)	436 (3.7)	441 (3.5)
Russian Federation	459 (3.3)	475 (3.0)	455 (3.5)	495 (3.2)	468 (3.3)	482 (3.0)	481 (3.7)	483 (3.1)	478 (3.3)	486 (2.9)	484 (3.5)	489 (2.9)
Serbia, Republic of	442 (2.4)	446 (3.4)	423 (3.9)	469 (3.8)	442 (2.9)	449 (3.4)	453 (4.1)	444 (3.7)	443 (2.4)	445 (3.4)	443 (4.0)	447 (3.8)
Shanghai-China	556 (2.4)	570 (2.9)	557 (3.3)	581 (2.8)	600 (2.8)	613 (3.3)	616 (4.0)	610 (3.4)	575 (2.3)	580 (3.0)	583 (3.5)	578 (3.1)
Singapore	526 (1.1)	542 (1.4)	527 (1.9)	559 (1.9)	562 (1.4)	573 (1.3)	572 (1.9)	575 (1.8)	542 (1.4)	551 (1.5)	551 (2.1)	552 (1.9)
Thailand	421 (2.6)	441 (3.1)	410 (3.6)	465 (3.3)	419 (3.2)	427 (3.4)	419 (3.6)	433 (4.1)	425 (3.0)	444 (2.9)	433 (3.3)	452 (3.4)
Tunisia	404 (2.9)	404 (4.5)	388 (5.0)	418 (4.4)	371 (3.0)	388 (3.9)	396 (4.3)	381 (4.0)	401 (2.7)	398 (3.5)	399 (3.9)	398 (3.6)
United Arab Emirates	— (†)	442 (2.5)	413 (3.9)	469 (3.2)	— (†)	434 (2.4)	432 (3.8)	436 (3.0)	— (†)	448 (2.8)	434 (4.1)	462 (3.7)
Uruguay	426 (2.6)	411 (3.2)	392 (3.9)	428 (3.2)	427 (2.6)	409 (2.8)	415 (3.5)	404 (2.9)	427 (2.6)	416 (2.8)	415 (3.4)	416 (3.1)
Vietnam	— (†)	508 (4.4)	492 (5.0)	523 (4.0)	— (†)	511 (4.8)	517 (5.6)	507 (4.7)	— (†)	528 (4.3)	529 (5.0)	528 (4.1)

—Not available.
†Not applicable.
[1]Refers to the mean of the data values for all Organization for Economic Cooperation and Development (OECD) countries, to which each country contributes equally regardless of the absolute size of the student population of each country.
[2]Results are for public school students only.
NOTE: Program for International Student Assessment (PISA) scores are reported on a scale from 0 to 1,000.
SOURCE: Organization for Economic Cooperation and Development (OECD), Program for International Student Assessment (PISA), 2009 and 2012. (This table was prepared July 2014.)

Table 602.50. Average reading literacy scores of 15-year-old students and percentage attaining reading literacy proficiency levels, by country or other education system: 2012

[Standard errors appear in parentheses]

Country or other education system	Average reading literacy score	Percentage attaining reading literacy proficiency levels[1]							At or above level 5		
		Below level 2				At level 2	At level 3	At level 4	Total at or above level 5	At level 5	At level 6
		Total below level 2	Below level 1b	At level 1b	At level 1a						
1	2	3	4	5	6	7	8	9	10	11	12
OECD average[2]	496 (0.5)	18.0 (0.18)	1.3 (0.05)	4.4 (0.08)	12.3 (0.13)	23.5 (0.16)	29.1 (0.17)	21.0 (0.16)	8.4 (0.12)	7.3 (0.10)	1.1 (0.04)
Australia	512 (1.6)	14.2 (0.46)	0.9 (0.11)	3.1 (0.21)	10.2 (0.42)	21.6 (0.47)	29.1 (0.53)	23.3 (0.51)	11.7 (0.54)	9.8 (0.46)	1.9 (0.19)
Austria	490 (2.8)	19.5 (1.07)	0.8 (0.24)	4.8 (0.64)	13.8 (0.84)	24.2 (0.89)	29.6 (0.92)	21.2 (0.94)	5.5 (0.61)	5.2 (0.59)	0.3 (0.10)
Belgium	509 (2.3)	16.2 (0.77)	1.6 (0.31)	4.1 (0.40)	10.4 (0.55)	20.4 (0.62)	27.3 (0.70)	24.4 (0.71)	12.3 (0.55)	10.4 (0.54)	1.4 (0.17)
Canada	523 (1.9)	10.9 (0.45)	0.5 (0.09)	2.4 (0.19)	8.0 (0.36)	19.4 (0.55)	31.0 (0.72)	25.8 (0.59)	12.9 (0.62)	10.8 (0.53)	2.1 (0.17)
Chile	441 (2.9)	33.0 (1.67)	1.0 (0.19)	8.1 (0.79)	23.9 (1.08)	35.1 (1.08)	24.3 (1.06)	6.9 (0.62)	0.6 (0.10)	0.6 (0.11)	‡ (†)
Czech Republic	493 (2.9)	16.9 (1.21)	0.6 ! (0.27)	3.5 (0.56)	12.7 (0.94)	26.4 (1.30)	31.3 (1.23)	19.4 (1.13)	6.1 (0.55)	5.3 (0.49)	0.8 (0.16)
Denmark	496 (2.6)	14.6 (1.07)	0.8 ! (0.30)	3.1 (0.39)	10.7 (0.77)	25.8 (0.92)	33.6 (0.85)	20.5 (0.86)	5.4 (0.62)	5.1 (0.58)	0.4 ! (0.12)
Estonia	516 (2.0)	9.1 (0.65)	‡ (†)	1.3 (0.28)	7.7 (0.61)	22.7 (0.94)	35.0 (1.06)	24.9 (1.08)	8.3 (0.72)	7.5 (0.71)	0.9 (0.18)
Finland	524 (2.4)	11.3 (0.71)	0.7 (0.16)	2.4 (0.38)	8.2 (0.57)	19.1 (0.81)	29.3 (0.70)	26.8 (0.84)	13.5 (0.64)	11.3 (0.60)	2.2 (0.26)
France	505 (2.8)	18.9 (0.98)	2.1 (0.40)	4.9 (0.43)	11.9 (0.70)	18.9 (0.85)	26.3 (0.84)	23.0 (0.67)	12.9 (0.85)	10.6 (0.62)	2.3 (0.41)
Germany	508 (2.8)	14.5 (0.91)	0.5 ! (0.18)	3.3 (0.40)	10.7 (0.67)	22.1 (0.93)	29.9 (0.86)	24.6 (0.88)	8.9 (0.70)	8.3 (0.64)	0.7 ! (0.23)
Greece	477 (3.3)	22.6 (1.24)	2.6 (0.40)	5.9 (0.60)	14.2 (0.83)	25.1 (1.06)	30.0 (1.02)	17.2 (1.19)	5.1 (0.61)	4.6 (0.59)	0.5 (0.13)
Hungary	488 (3.2)	19.7 (1.22)	0.7 ! (0.24)	5.2 (0.64)	13.8 (0.88)	24.3 (1.17)	29.9 (1.00)	20.4 (1.05)	5.6 (0.75)	5.3 (0.68)	0.4 ! (0.13)
Iceland	483 (1.8)	21.0 (0.72)	2.3 (0.33)	5.4 (0.47)	13.3 (0.63)	24.7 (0.92)	29.9 (1.09)	18.6 (1.12)	5.8 (0.51)	5.2 (0.41)	0.6 ! (0.21)
Ireland	523 (2.6)	9.6 (0.88)	0.3 ! (0.13)	1.9 (0.35)	7.5 (0.69)	19.6 (1.19)	33.4 (1.17)	26.0 (0.90)	11.4 (0.65)	10.1 (0.67)	1.3 (0.35)
Israel	486 (5.0)	23.6 (1.64)	3.8 (0.59)	6.9 (0.74)	12.9 (0.96)	20.8 (0.87)	25.3 (0.81)	20.6 (1.03)	9.6 (0.84)	8.1 (0.77)	1.5 (0.30)
Italy	490 (2.0)	19.5 (0.67)	1.6 (0.15)	5.2 (0.29)	12.7 (0.48)	23.7 (0.57)	29.7 (0.53)	20.5 (0.62)	6.7 (0.35)	6.1 (0.33)	0.6 (0.07)
Japan	538 (3.7)	9.8 (0.92)	0.6 (0.16)	2.4 (0.37)	6.7 (0.67)	16.6 (0.89)	26.7 (0.98)	28.4 (1.08)	18.5 (1.27)	14.6 (0.99)	3.9 (0.59)
Korea, Republic of	536 (3.9)	7.6 (0.89)	0.4 (0.13)	1.7 (0.39)	5.5 (0.60)	16.4 (0.94)	30.8 (1.00)	31.0 (1.06)	14.1 (1.24)	12.6 (1.05)	1.6 (0.32)
Luxembourg	488 (1.5)	22.2 (0.74)	2.0 (0.21)	6.3 (0.33)	13.8 (0.81)	23.4 (0.71)	25.8 (0.64)	19.7 (0.64)	8.9 (0.39)	7.5 (0.35)	1.4 (0.20)
Mexico	424 (1.5)	41.1 (0.90)	2.6 (0.22)	11.0 (0.53)	27.5 (0.70)	34.5 (0.62)	19.6 (0.54)	4.5 (0.25)	0.4 (0.09)	0.4 (0.08)	‡ (†)
Netherlands	511 (3.5)	14.0 (1.23)	‡ (†)	2.8 (0.49)	10.3 (0.93)	21.0 (1.27)	29.2 (1.32)	26.1 (1.36)	9.8 (0.82)	9.0 (0.72)	0.8 (0.19)
New Zealand	512 (2.4)	16.3 (0.83)	1.3 (0.28)	4.0 (0.46)	11.0 (0.67)	20.8 (0.76)	26.3 (1.06)	22.7 (1.06)	14.0 (0.77)	10.9 (0.62)	3.0 (0.37)
Norway	504 (3.2)	16.2 (1.03)	1.7 (0.31)	3.7 (0.36)	10.8 (0.69)	21.9 (1.03)	29.4 (1.35)	22.3 (1.21)	10.2 (0.74)	8.5 (0.61)	1.7 (0.31)
Poland	518 (3.1)	10.6 (0.80)	0.3 ! (0.11)	2.1 (0.35)	8.1 (0.74)	21.4 (0.90)	32.0 (0.89)	26.0 (0.96)	10.0 (0.93)	8.6 (0.76)	1.4 (0.37)
Portugal	488 (3.8)	18.8 (1.42)	1.3 (0.30)	5.1 (0.53)	12.3 (0.98)	25.5 (1.16)	30.2 (1.46)	19.7 (1.07)	5.8 (0.61)	5.3 (0.57)	0.5 ! (0.15)
Slovak Republic	463 (4.2)	28.2 (1.78)	4.1 (0.77)	7.9 (0.80)	16.2 (1.06)	25.0 (1.08)	26.8 (1.38)	15.7 (0.96)	4.4 (0.68)	4.1 (0.60)	‡ (†)
Slovenia	481 (1.2)	21.1 (0.68)	1.2 (0.14)	4.9 (0.37)	15.0 (0.71)	27.2 (0.94)	28.4 (0.94)	18.2 (0.63)	5.0 (0.43)	4.7 (0.45)	0.3 ! (0.12)
Spain	488 (1.9)	18.3 (0.76)	1.3 (0.17)	4.4 (0.38)	12.6 (0.47)	25.8 (0.81)	31.2 (0.68)	19.2 (0.62)	5.5 (0.30)	5.0 (0.30)	0.5 (0.10)
Sweden	483 (3.0)	22.7 (1.15)	2.9 (0.39)	6.0 (0.64)	13.9 (0.72)	23.5 (0.88)	27.3 (0.73)	18.6 (0.93)	7.9 (0.64)	6.7 (0.53)	1.2 (0.20)
Switzerland	509 (2.6)	13.7 (0.76)	0.5 (0.14)	2.9 (0.34)	10.3 (0.59)	21.9 (0.86)	31.5 (0.71)	23.8 (0.84)	9.1 (0.68)	8.2 (0.60)	1.0 (0.25)
Turkey	475 (4.2)	21.6 (1.43)	0.6 (0.15)	4.5 (0.57)	16.6 (1.07)	30.8 (1.39)	28.7 (1.34)	14.5 (1.39)	4.3 (0.85)	4.1 (0.79)	‡ (†)
United Kingdom	499 (3.5)	16.6 (1.30)	1.5 (0.27)	4.0 (0.54)	11.2 (0.79)	23.5 (1.01)	29.9 (1.08)	21.3 (1.14)	8.8 (0.74)	7.5 (0.59)	0.3 ! (0.13)
United States	498 (3.7)	16.6 (1.26)	0.8 ! (0.24)	3.6 (0.49)	12.3 (0.89)	24.9 (0.99)	30.5 (0.88)	20.1 (1.08)	7.9 (0.67)	6.9 (0.59)	1.0 (0.22)

See notes at end of table.

Table 602.50. Average reading literacy scores of 15-year-old students and percentage attaining reading literacy proficiency levels, by country or other education system: 2012—Continued

[Standard errors appear in parentheses]

Country or other education system	Average reading literacy score	Percentage attaining reading literacy proficiency levels[1]									
		Below level 2				At level 2	At level 3	At level 4	At or above level 5		
		Total below level 2	Below level 1b	At level 1b	At level 1a				Total at or above level 5	At level 5	At level 6
1	2	3	4	5	6	7	8	9	10	11	12
Non-OECD education systems											
Albania	394 (3.2)	52.3 (1.28)	12.0 (0.84)	15.9 (1.00)	24.4 (1.23)	24.7 (1.01)	15.9 (0.73)	5.9 (0.61)	1.2 (0.25)	1.1 (0.24)	‡ (†)
Argentina	396 (3.7)	53.6 (1.73)	8.1 (0.80)	17.7 (1.20)	27.7 (1.34)	27.3 (1.12)	14.6 (0.91)	4.0 (0.57)	0.5 (0.14)	0.5 ! (0.15)	‡ (†)
Brazil	410 (2.1)	49.2 (1.13)	4.0 (0.36)	14.8 (0.64)	30.4 (0.79)	30.1 (0.77)	15.8 (0.63)	4.4 (0.37)	0.5 (0.12)	0.5 (0.12)	‡ (†)
Bulgaria	436 (6.0)	39.4 (2.21)	8.0 (1.07)	12.8 (1.15)	18.6 (1.10)	22.2 (1.16)	21.4 (1.10)	12.7 (1.03)	4.3 (0.64)	3.8 (0.56)	0.5 ! (0.18)
Chinese Taipei	523 (3.0)	11.5 (0.87)	0.6 (0.15)	2.5 (0.32)	8.4 (0.65)	18.1 (0.83)	29.9 (0.92)	28.7 (1.01)	11.8 (0.84)	10.4 (0.73)	1.4 (0.32)
Colombia	403 (3.4)	51.4 (1.78)	5.0 (0.76)	15.4 (0.98)	31.0 (1.29)	30.5 (1.22)	14.5 (0.91)	3.2 (0.50)	0.3 ! (0.13)	0.3 ! (0.12)	‡ (†)
Connecticut-USA[3]	521 (6.5)	13.2 (1.76)	‡ (†)	3.2 (0.87)	9.7 (1.26)	19.6 (1.49)	28.2 (1.32)	24.4 (1.83)	14.5 (1.68)	11.7 (1.38)	2.9 (0.54)
Costa Rica	441 (3.5)	32.4 (1.81)	0.8 ! (0.24)	7.3 (1.02)	24.3 (1.25)	38.1 (1.40)	22.9 (1.42)	6.0 (0.78)	0.6 ! (0.19)	0.6 ! (0.19)	‡ (†)
Croatia	485 (3.3)	18.7 (1.29)	0.7 ! (0.25)	4.0 (0.59)	13.9 (0.97)	27.8 (1.07)	31.2 (1.24)	17.8 (1.09)	4.4 (0.69)	4.2 (0.66)	0.2 ! (0.11)
Cyprus	449 (1.2)	32.8 (0.67)	6.1 (0.32)	9.7 (0.44)	17.0 (0.61)	25.1 (0.78)	24.9 (0.75)	13.2 (0.64)	4.0 (0.32)	3.5 (0.34)	0.5 (0.12)
Florida-USA[3]	492 (6.1)	17.5 (2.00)	0.7 ! (0.31)	3.6 (0.75)	13.2 (1.46)	25.8 (1.56)	30.9 (1.50)	20.4 (2.06)	5.5 (1.02)	4.9 (1.00)	‡ (†)
Hong Kong-China	545 (2.8)	6.8 (0.72)	0.2 ! (0.09)	1.3 (0.24)	5.3 (0.61)	14.3 (0.79)	29.2 (1.21)	32.9 (1.39)	16.8 (1.16)	14.9 (1.00)	1.9 (0.39)
Indonesia	396 (4.2)	55.2 (2.18)	4.1 (0.81)	16.3 (1.28)	34.8 (1.56)	31.6 (1.54)	11.5 (1.28)	1.5 ! (0.53)	‡ (†)	‡ (†)	‡ (†)
Jordan	399 (3.6)	50.7 (1.57)	7.5 (0.84)	14.9 (0.79)	28.3 (1.01)	30.8 (1.14)	15.5 (0.83)	2.9 (0.63)	‡ (†)	‡ (†)	‡ (†)
Kazakhstan	393 (2.7)	57.1 (1.56)	4.2 (0.47)	17.3 (1.24)	35.6 (1.15)	31.3 (1.12)	10.4 (0.87)	1.2 (0.24)	‡ (†)	‡ (†)	0.3 ! (0.11)
Latvia	489 (2.4)	17.0 (1.14)	0.7 ! (0.24)	3.7 (0.54)	12.6 (0.96)	26.7 (1.31)	33.1 (1.05)	19.1 (0.88)	4.2 (0.55)	3.9 (0.56)	0.3 ! (0.11)
Liechtenstein	516 (4.1)	12.4 (1.88)	# (†)	‡ (†)	10.5 (1.85)	22.4 (3.44)	28.6 (4.53)	25.7 (2.44)	10.9 (2.89)	10.4 (2.44)	0.2 ! (0.07)
Lithuania	477 (2.5)	21.2 (1.18)	1.0 (0.19)	4.6 (0.49)	15.6 (1.06)	28.1 (1.13)	31.1 (0.94)	16.3 (0.78)	3.3 (0.37)	3.1 (0.35)	0.6 ! (0.21)
Macao-China	509 (0.9)	11.5 (0.42)	0.3 ! (0.11)	2.1 (0.22)	9.0 (0.42)	23.3 (0.58)	34.3 (0.67)	24.0 (0.60)	7.0 (0.41)	6.4 (0.48)	‡ (†)
Malaysia	398 (3.3)	52.7 (1.71)	5.8 (0.59)	16.4 (1.03)	30.5 (0.99)	31.0 (1.09)	13.6 (1.11)	2.5 (0.45)	‡ (†)	‡ (†)	‡ (†)
Massachusetts-USA[3]	527 (6.1)	11.5 (1.37)	‡ (†)	2.3 (0.55)	8.6 (1.19)	18.5 (1.76)	29.8 (1.52)	24.2 (1.82)	16.1 (1.98)	12.9 (1.59)	3.2 (0.86)
Montenegro, Republic of	422 (1.2)	43.3 (0.75)	4.4 (0.53)	13.2 (0.62)	25.7 (0.94)	29.2 (0.77)	19.9 (0.76)	6.6 (0.53)	1.0 (0.19)	0.9 (0.19)	‡ (†)
Peru	384 (4.3)	59.9 (1.95)	9.8 (0.87)	20.6 (1.11)	29.5 (0.98)	24.9 (1.02)	11.4 (0.96)	3.3 (0.61)	0.5 ! (0.21)	0.5 ! (0.21)	‡ (†)
Qatar	388 (0.8)	57.1 (0.42)	13.6 (0.32)	18.9 (0.48)	24.6 (0.44)	21.9 (0.50)	13.5 (0.43)	5.8 (0.21)	1.6 (0.14)	1.4 (0.13)	0.2 (0.05)
Romania	438 (4.0)	37.3 (1.87)	2.5 (0.38)	10.3 (0.82)	24.4 (1.28)	30.6 (1.12)	21.8 (1.17)	8.7 (0.88)	1.6 (0.38)	1.5 (0.35)	‡ (†)
Russian Federation	475 (3.0)	22.3 (1.29)	1.1 (0.18)	5.2 (0.49)	16.0 (1.03)	29.5 (1.08)	28.3 (1.05)	15.3 (0.93)	4.6 (0.58)	4.2 (0.51)	0.5 (0.12)
Serbia, Republic of	446 (3.4)	33.1 (1.66)	2.6 (0.40)	9.3 (0.73)	21.3 (1.09)	30.8 (1.20)	23.3 (1.15)	10.5 (0.81)	2.2 (0.41)	2.0 (0.39)	0.2 ! (0.08)
Shanghai-China	570 (2.9)	2.9 (0.39)	‡ (†)	0.3 ! (0.11)	2.5 (0.34)	11.0 (0.85)	25.3 (0.85)	35.7 (1.07)	25.1 (1.19)	21.3 (0.98)	3.8 (0.65)
Singapore	542 (1.4)	9.9 (0.42)	0.5 (0.12)	1.9 (0.27)	7.5 (0.41)	16.7 (0.65)	25.4 (0.66)	26.8 (0.79)	21.2 (0.60)	16.2 (0.73)	5.0 (0.43)
Thailand	441 (3.1)	33.0 (1.40)	1.2 (0.29)	7.7 (0.77)	24.1 (0.98)	36.0 (1.12)	23.5 (1.13)	6.7 (0.79)	0.8 (0.22)	0.8 (0.21)	‡ (†)
Tunisia	404 (4.5)	49.3 (2.24)	6.2 (0.91)	15.5 (1.20)	27.6 (1.31)	31.4 (1.43)	15.6 (1.15)	3.5 (0.69)	‡ (†)	‡ (†)	‡ (†)
United Arab Emirates	442 (2.5)	35.5 (1.08)	3.3 (0.34)	10.4 (0.65)	21.8 (0.72)	28.6 (0.72)	24.0 (0.77)	9.7 (0.58)	2.2 (0.29)	2.1 (0.28)	0.2 ! (0.06)
Uruguay	411 (3.2)	47.0 (1.42)	6.4 (0.70)	14.7 (0.84)	25.9 (0.88)	28.9 (1.00)	17.4 (0.71)	5.7 (0.62)	0.9 (0.27)	0.9 (0.26)	‡ (†)
Vietnam	508 (4.4)	9.4 (1.43)	‡ (†)	1.5 ! (0.48)	7.8 (1.10)	23.7 (1.40)	39.0 (1.47)	23.4 (1.47)	4.5 (0.81)	4.2 (0.71)	0.4 ! (0.16)

†Not applicable.
#Rounds to zero.
!Interpret data with caution. The coefficient of variation (CV) for this estimate is between 30 and 50 percent.
‡Reporting standards not met. Either there are too few cases for a reliable estimate or the coefficient of variation (CV) is 50 percent or greater.
[1]To reach a particular proficiency level, a student must correctly answer a majority of items at that level. Students were classified into reading literacy levels according to their scores. Exact cut scores are as follows: below level 1b (a score less than or equal to 262.04); level 1b (a score greater than 262.04 and less than or equal to 334.75); level 1a (a score greater than 334.75 and less than or equal to 407.47); level 2 (a score greater than 407.47 and less than or equal to 480.18); level 3 (a score greater than 480.18 and less than or equal to 552.89); level 4 (a score greater than 552.89 and less than or equal to 625.61); level 5 (a score greater than 625.61 and less than or equal to 698.32); and level 6 (a score greater than 698.32).
[2]Refers to the mean of the data values for all Organization for Economic Cooperation and Development (OECD) countries, to which each country contributes equally, regardless of the absolute size of the student population of each country.
[3]Results are for public school students only.
NOTE: Program for International Student Assessment (PISA) scores are reported on a scale from 0 to 1,000. Detail may not sum to totals because of rounding.
SOURCE: Organization for Economic Cooperation and Development (OECD), Program for International Student Assessment (PISA), 2012. (This table was prepared November 2013.)

Table 602.60. Average mathematics literacy scores of 15-year-old students and percentage attaining mathematics literacy proficiency levels, by country or other education system: 2012

[Standard errors appear in parentheses]

Country or other education system	Average mathematics literacy score	Percentage attaining mathematics literacy proficiency levels [1]						At or above level 5		
		Below level 2			At level 2	At level 3	At level 4	Total at or above level 5	At level 5	At level 6
		Total below level 2	Below level 1	At level 1						
1	2	3	4	5	6	7	8	9	10	11
OECD average [2]	494 (0.5)	23.0 (0.17)	8.0 (0.12)	15.0 (0.13)	22.5 (0.15)	23.7 (0.15)	18.1 (0.14)	12.7 (0.14)	9.3 (0.11)	3.3 (0.08)
Australia	504 (1.6)	19.7 (0.60)	6.1 (0.35)	13.5 (0.57)	21.9 (0.76)	24.6 (0.65)	19.0 (0.50)	14.8 (0.64)	10.5 (0.43)	4.3 (0.36)
Austria	506 (2.7)	18.7 (0.96)	5.7 (0.59)	13.0 (0.74)	21.9 (0.87)	24.2 (0.84)	21.0 (0.90)	14.3 (0.95)	11.0 (0.75)	3.3 (0.41)
Belgium	515 (2.1)	19.0 (0.82)	7.0 (0.58)	12.0 (0.52)	18.4 (0.58)	22.4 (0.70)	20.6 (0.63)	19.5 (0.76)	13.4 (0.73)	6.1 (0.43)
Canada	518 (1.8)	13.8 (0.55)	3.6 (0.29)	10.2 (0.45)	21.0 (0.64)	26.4 (0.63)	22.4 (0.49)	16.4 (0.64)	12.1 (0.47)	4.3 (0.29)
Chile	423 (3.1)	51.5 (1.67)	22.0 (1.35)	29.5 (1.01)	25.3 (1.00)	15.4 (0.78)	6.2 (0.60)	1.6 (0.22)	1.5 (0.21)	0.1 ! (0.04)
Czech Republic	499 (2.9)	21.0 (1.20)	6.8 (0.76)	14.2 (0.97)	21.7 (0.83)	24.8 (1.07)	19.7 (0.90)	12.9 (0.82)	9.6 (0.66)	3.2 (0.31)
Denmark	500 (2.3)	16.8 (0.98)	4.4 (0.49)	12.5 (0.70)	24.4 (0.97)	29.0 (1.03)	19.8 (0.69)	10.0 (0.66)	8.3 (0.57)	1.7 (0.32)
Estonia	521 (2.0)	10.5 (0.63)	2.0 (0.26)	8.6 (0.57)	22.0 (0.84)	29.4 (0.79)	23.4 (0.91)	14.6 (0.76)	11.0 (0.67)	3.6 (0.37)
Finland	519 (1.9)	12.3 (0.67)	3.3 (0.39)	8.9 (0.49)	20.5 (0.66)	28.8 (0.78)	23.2 (0.78)	15.3 (0.74)	11.7 (0.60)	3.5 (0.30)
France	495 (2.5)	22.4 (0.87)	8.7 (0.72)	13.6 (0.76)	22.1 (0.95)	23.8 (0.82)	18.9 (0.79)	12.9 (0.77)	9.8 (0.55)	3.1 (0.40)
Germany	514 (2.9)	17.7 (1.03)	5.5 (0.65)	12.2 (0.81)	19.4 (0.81)	23.7 (0.79)	21.7 (0.73)	17.5 (0.94)	12.8 (0.71)	4.7 (0.49)
Greece	453 (2.5)	35.7 (1.34)	14.5 (0.92)	21.2 (0.85)	27.2 (1.02)	22.1 (0.86)	11.2 (0.79)	3.9 (0.43)	3.3 (0.43)	0.6 (0.15)
Hungary	477 (3.2)	28.1 (1.31)	9.9 (0.77)	18.2 (1.04)	25.3 (1.21)	23.0 (1.02)	14.4 (0.86)	9.3 (1.12)	7.1 (0.73)	2.1 (0.51)
Iceland	493 (1.7)	21.5 (0.74)	7.5 (0.54)	14.0 (0.83)	23.6 (0.89)	25.7 (0.95)	18.1 (0.79)	11.2 (0.69)	8.9 (0.61)	2.3 (0.35)
Ireland	501 (2.2)	16.9 (0.99)	4.8 (0.55)	12.1 (0.70)	23.9 (0.72)	28.2 (0.87)	20.3 (0.76)	10.7 (0.54)	8.5 (0.51)	2.2 (0.23)
Israel	466 (4.7)	33.5 (1.68)	15.9 (1.23)	17.6 (0.93)	21.6 (0.93)	21.0 (0.87)	14.6 (0.88)	9.4 (0.99)	7.2 (0.74)	2.2 (0.39)
Italy	485 (2.0)	24.7 (0.76)	8.5 (0.39)	16.1 (0.51)	24.1 (0.55)	24.6 (0.62)	16.7 (0.48)	9.9 (0.57)	7.8 (0.44)	2.2 (0.25)
Japan	536 (3.6)	11.1 (0.98)	3.2 (0.49)	7.9 (0.69)	16.9 (0.85)	24.7 (1.00)	23.7 (0.89)	23.7 (1.46)	16.0 (0.89)	7.6 (0.84)
Korea, Republic of	554 (4.6)	9.1 (0.95)	2.7 (0.46)	6.4 (0.62)	14.7 (0.85)	21.4 (0.99)	23.9 (1.23)	30.9 (1.83)	18.8 (0.92)	12.1 (1.26)
Luxembourg	490 (1.1)	24.3 (0.54)	8.8 (0.54)	15.5 (0.54)	22.3 (0.72)	23.6 (0.72)	18.5 (0.58)	11.2 (0.42)	8.6 (0.38)	2.6 (0.25)
Mexico	413 (1.4)	54.7 (0.82)	22.8 (0.68)	31.9 (0.58)	27.8 (0.53)	13.1 (0.41)	3.7 (0.23)	0.6 (0.08)	0.6 (0.07)	‡ (†)
Netherlands	523 (3.5)	14.8 (1.28)	3.8 (0.57)	11.0 (0.93)	17.9 (1.08)	24.2 (1.19)	23.8 (1.11)	19.3 (1.21)	14.9 (0.99)	4.4 (0.56)
New Zealand	500 (2.2)	22.6 (0.80)	7.5 (0.58)	15.1 (0.66)	21.6 (0.83)	22.7 (0.76)	18.1 (0.84)	15.0 (0.88)	10.5 (0.75)	4.5 (0.40)
Norway	489 (2.7)	22.3 (1.06)	7.2 (0.78)	15.1 (0.88)	24.3 (0.84)	25.7 (1.01)	18.3 (0.96)	9.4 (0.67)	7.3 (0.56)	2.1 (0.30)
Poland	518 (3.6)	14.4 (0.89)	3.3 (0.38)	11.1 (0.77)	22.1 (0.93)	25.5 (0.94)	21.3 (1.12)	16.7 (1.33)	11.7 (0.78)	5.0 (0.80)
Portugal	487 (3.8)	24.9 (1.52)	8.9 (0.79)	16.0 (0.98)	22.8 (0.88)	24.0 (0.84)	17.7 (0.88)	10.6 (0.79)	8.5 (0.73)	2.1 (0.33)
Slovak Republic	482 (3.4)	27.5 (1.28)	11.1 (1.03)	16.4 (0.94)	23.1 (1.10)	22.1 (1.09)	16.4 (1.08)	11.0 (0.94)	7.8 (0.64)	3.1 (0.55)
Slovenia	501 (1.2)	20.1 (0.65)	5.1 (0.48)	15.0 (0.69)	23.6 (0.95)	23.9 (0.96)	18.7 (0.80)	13.7 (0.55)	10.3 (0.64)	3.4 (0.43)
Spain	484 (1.9)	23.6 (0.85)	7.8 (0.50)	15.8 (0.57)	24.9 (0.65)	26.0 (0.59)	17.6 (0.56)	8.0 (0.43)	6.7 (0.42)	1.3 (0.15)
Sweden	478 (2.3)	27.1 (1.12)	9.5 (0.68)	17.5 (0.76)	24.7 (0.92)	23.9 (0.78)	16.3 (0.69)	8.0 (0.52)	6.5 (0.49)	1.6 (0.25)
Switzerland	531 (3.0)	12.4 (0.70)	3.6 (0.35)	8.9 (0.59)	17.8 (1.06)	24.5 (1.02)	23.9 (0.80)	21.4 (1.19)	14.6 (0.78)	6.8 (0.69)
Turkey	448 (4.8)	42.0 (1.93)	15.5 (1.08)	26.5 (1.28)	25.5 (1.16)	16.5 (1.05)	10.1 (1.09)	5.9 (1.13)	4.7 (0.81)	1.2 ! (0.46)
United Kingdom	494 (3.3)	21.8 (1.30)	7.8 (0.77)	14.0 (0.76)	23.2 (0.81)	24.8 (0.85)	18.4 (0.78)	11.8 (0.81)	9.0 (0.63)	2.9 (0.42)
United States	481 (3.6)	25.8 (1.39)	8.0 (0.73)	17.9 (0.98)	26.3 (0.84)	23.3 (0.93)	15.8 (0.91)	8.8 (0.78)	6.6 (0.61)	2.2 (0.34)

See notes at end of table.

Table 602.60. Average mathematics literacy scores of 15-year-old students and percentage attaining mathematics literacy proficiency levels, by country or other education system: 2012—Continued

[Standard errors appear in parentheses]

Country or other education system	Average mathematics literacy score	Percentage attaining mathematics literacy proficiency levels[1]								
		Below level 2			At level 2	At level 3	At level 4	At or above level 5		
		Total below level 2	Below level 1	At level 1				Total at or above level 5	At level 5	At level 6
1	2	3	4	5	6	7	8	9	10	11
Non-OECD education systems										
Albania	394 (2.0)	60.7 (0.95)	32.5 (1.03)	28.1 (0.97)	22.9 (0.91)	12.0 (0.92)	3.6 (0.35)	0.8 (0.19)	0.8 (0.20)	‡ (†)
Argentina	388 (3.5)	66.5 (2.03)	34.9 (1.95)	31.6 (1.22)	22.2 (1.36)	9.2 (0.88)	1.8 (0.35)	0.3! (0.10)	0.3! (0.10)	‡ (†)
Brazil	391 (2.1)	67.1 (1.03)	35.2 (0.93)	31.9 (0.70)	20.4 (0.67)	8.9 (0.47)	2.9 (0.35)	0.8 (0.20)	0.7 (0.19)	‡ (†)
Bulgaria	439 (4.0)	43.8 (1.78)	20.0 (1.45)	23.8 (0.95)	24.4 (1.12)	17.9 (0.91)	9.9 (0.83)	4.1 (0.62)	3.4 (0.50)	0.7 (0.19)
Chinese Taipei	560 (3.3)	12.8 (0.84)	4.5 (0.53)	8.3 (0.61)	13.1 (0.61)	17.1 (0.65)	19.7 (0.75)	37.2 (1.24)	19.2 (0.89)	18.0 (1.00)
Colombia	376 (2.9)	73.8 (1.43)	41.6 (1.71)	32.2 (1.05)	17.8 (0.90)	6.4 (0.61)	1.6 (0.28)	0.3! (0.11)	0.3! (0.10)	‡ (†)
Connecticut-USA[3]	506 (6.2)	20.6 (2.14)	6.8 (1.18)	13.8 (1.33)	20.0 (1.28)	24.3 (1.36)	18.6 (1.79)	16.4 (1.91)	11.5 (1.46)	4.9 (0.83)
Costa Rica	407 (3.0)	59.9 (1.87)	23.6 (1.68)	36.2 (1.22)	26.8 (1.29)	10.1 (0.99)	2.6 (0.46)	0.6! (0.19)	0.5! (0.16)	‡ (†)
Croatia	471 (3.5)	29.9 (1.36)	9.5 (0.74)	20.4 (1.02)	26.7 (0.95)	22.9 (1.12)	13.5 (0.80)	7.0 (1.15)	5.4 (0.76)	1.6! (0.51)
Cyprus	440 (1.1)	42.0 (0.63)	19.0 (0.58)	23.0 (0.65)	25.5 (0.62)	19.2 (0.58)	9.6 (0.44)	3.7 (0.27)	3.1 (0.25)	0.6! (0.20)
Florida-USA[3]	467 (5.8)	30.4 (2.65)	9.7 (1.44)	20.6 (1.87)	27.9 (1.42)	23.0 (1.64)	13.0 (1.34)	5.8 (1.18)	4.9 (1.04)	0.9! (0.39)
Hong Kong-China	561 (3.2)	8.5 (0.79)	2.6 (0.36)	5.9 (0.61)	12.0 (0.77)	19.7 (0.97)	26.1 (1.09)	33.7 (1.35)	21.4 (0.96)	12.3 (0.95)
Indonesia	375 (4.0)	75.7 (2.05)	42.3 (2.14)	33.4 (1.59)	16.8 (1.12)	5.7 (0.90)	1.5! (0.54)	‡ (†)	‡ (†)	‡ (†)
Jordan	386 (3.1)	68.6 (1.50)	36.5 (1.59)	32.1 (0.95)	21.0 (1.04)	8.1 (0.63)	1.8 (0.33)	‡ (†)	‡ (†)	‡ (†)
Kazakhstan	432 (3.0)	45.2 (1.70)	14.5 (0.90)	30.7 (1.40)	31.5 (0.95)	16.9 (1.11)	5.4 (0.79)	0.9! (0.29)	0.9! (0.27)	‡ (†)
Latvia	491 (2.8)	19.9 (1.13)	4.8 (0.53)	15.1 (0.96)	26.6 (1.29)	27.8 (0.92)	17.6 (0.90)	8.0 (0.78)	6.5 (0.65)	1.5 (0.28)
Liechtenstein	535 (4.0)	14.1 (2.02)	3.5! (1.31)	10.6 (1.81)	15.2 (2.52)	22.7 (2.81)	23.2 (3.01)	24.8 (2.55)	17.4 (3.17)	7.4 (1.86)
Lithuania	479 (2.6)	26.0 (1.18)	8.7 (0.68)	17.3 (0.89)	25.9 (0.80)	24.6 (1.01)	15.4 (0.70)	8.1 (0.60)	6.6 (0.49)	1.4 (0.24)
Macao-China	538 (1.0)	10.8 (0.49)	3.2 (0.29)	7.6 (0.53)	16.4 (0.71)	24.0 (0.69)	24.4 (0.87)	24.3 (0.56)	16.8 (0.63)	7.6 (0.35)
Malaysia	421 (3.2)	51.8 (1.68)	23.0 (1.19)	28.8 (1.12)	26.0 (0.95)	14.9 (0.93)	6.0 (0.69)	1.3 (0.30)	1.2 (0.28)	0.1! (0.05)
Massachusetts-USA[3]	514 (6.2)	17.8 (1.46)	5.3 (0.83)	12.5 (1.17)	20.4 (1.61)	24.3 (1.49)	18.9 (1.18)	18.5 (2.47)	12.7 (1.61)	5.8 (1.11)
Montenegro, Republic of	410 (1.1)	56.6 (1.02)	27.5 (0.64)	29.1 (1.14)	24.2 (1.06)	13.1 (0.73)	4.9 (0.48)	1.0 (0.20)	0.9 (0.20)	‡ (†)
Peru	368 (3.7)	74.6 (1.75)	47.0 (1.79)	27.6 (0.88)	16.1 (1.00)	6.7 (0.68)	2.1 (0.38)	0.6! (0.21)	0.5! (0.20)	‡ (†)
Qatar	376 (0.8)	69.6 (0.46)	47.0 (0.42)	22.6 (0.53)	15.2 (0.39)	8.8 (0.34)	4.5 (0.28)	2.0 (0.21)	1.7 (0.20)	0.3 (0.07)
Romania	445 (3.8)	40.8 (1.93)	14.0 (1.15)	26.8 (1.23)	28.3 (1.09)	19.2 (1.07)	8.4 (0.81)	3.2 (0.61)	2.6 (0.45)	0.6! (0.27)
Russian Federation	482 (3.0)	24.0 (1.13)	7.5 (0.70)	16.5 (0.80)	26.6 (0.99)	26.0 (0.97)	15.7 (0.78)	7.8 (0.85)	6.3 (0.64)	1.5 (0.31)
Serbia, Republic of	449 (3.4)	38.9 (1.54)	15.5 (1.16)	23.4 (0.93)	26.5 (1.12)	19.5 (1.03)	10.5 (0.69)	4.6 (0.71)	3.5 (0.52)	1.1 (0.31)
Shanghai-China	613 (3.3)	3.8 (0.55)	0.8 (0.21)	2.9 (0.46)	7.5 (0.64)	13.1 (0.77)	20.2 (0.83)	55.4 (1.37)	24.6 (1.04)	30.8 (1.24)
Singapore	573 (1.3)	8.3 (0.48)	2.2 (0.23)	6.1 (0.40)	12.2 (0.68)	17.5 (0.66)	22.0 (0.62)	40.0 (0.71)	21.0 (0.58)	19.0 (0.51)
Thailand	427 (3.4)	49.7 (1.74)	19.1 (1.07)	30.6 (1.20)	27.3 (1.00)	14.5 (1.15)	5.8 (0.74)	2.6 (0.51)	2.0 (0.38)	0.5! (0.19)
Tunisia	388 (3.9)	67.7 (1.83)	36.5 (1.88)	31.3 (1.09)	21.1 (1.17)	3.0 (0.79)	2.3 (0.68)	0.8! (0.37)	0.7! (0.32)	‡ (†)
United Arab Emirates	434 (2.4)	46.3 (1.22)	20.5 (0.92)	25.8 (0.81)	24.9 (0.69)	16.9 (0.64)	8.5 (0.54)	3.5 (0.29)	2.9 (0.25)	0.5 (0.11)
Uruguay	409 (2.8)	55.8 (1.31)	29.2 (1.20)	26.5 (0.76)	23.0 (0.93)	14.4 (0.87)	5.4 (0.60)	1.4 (0.32)	1.3 (0.28)	‡ (†)
Vietnam	511 (4.8)	14.2 (1.75)	3.6 (0.80)	10.6 (1.26)	22.8 (1.28)	28.4 (1.52)	21.3 (1.22)	13.3 (1.47)	9.8 (0.99)	3.5 (0.75)

†Not applicable.
!Interpret data with caution. The coefficient of variation (CV) for this estimate is between 30 and 50 percent.
‡Reporting standards not met. Either there are too few cases for a reliable estimate or the coefficient of variation (CV) is 50 percent or greater.
[1]To reach a particular proficiency level, a student must correctly answer a majority of items at that level. Students were classified into mathematics literacy levels according to their scores. Exact cut scores are as follows: below level 1 (a score less than or equal to 357.77); level 1 (a score greater than 357.77 and less than or equal to 420.07); level 2 (a score greater than 420.07 and less than or equal to 482.38); level 3 (a score greater than 482.38 and less than or equal to 544.68); level 4 (a score greater than 544.68 and

less than or equal to 606.99); level 5 (a score greater than 606.99 and less than or equal to 669.30); and level 6 (a score greater than 669.30).
[2]Refers to the mean of the data values for all Organization for Economic Cooperation and Development (OECD) countries, to which each country contributes equally, regardless of the absolute size of the student population of each country.
[3]Results are for public school students only.
NOTE: Program for International Student Assessment (PISA) scores are reported on a scale from 0 to 1,000. Detail may not sum to totals because of rounding.
SOURCE: Organization for Economic Cooperation and Development (OECD), Program for International Student Assessment (PISA), 2012. (This table was prepared November 2013.)

Table 602.70. Average science literacy scores of 15-year-old students and percentage attaining science literacy proficiency levels, by country or other education system: 2012

[Standard errors appear in parentheses]

Country or other education system	Average science literacy score	Percentage attaining science literacy proficiency levels[1]								
		Below level 2			At level 2	At level 3	At level 4	At or above level 5		
		Total below level 2	Below level 1	At level 1				Total at or above level 5	At level 5	At level 6
1	2	3	4	5	6	7	8	9	10	11
OECD average[2]	501 (0.5)	17.8 (0.17)	4.8 (0.09)	13.0 (0.14)	24.5 (0.16)	28.8 (0.17)	20.5 (0.15)	8.4 (0.11)	7.2 (0.10)	1.1 (0.04)
Australia	521 (1.8)	13.6 (0.48)	3.4 (0.25)	10.2 (0.41)	21.5 (0.47)	28.5 (0.68)	22.8 (0.63)	13.6 (0.55)	10.9 (0.47)	2.6 (0.25)
Austria	506 (2.7)	15.8 (1.00)	3.6 (0.54)	12.2 (0.92)	24.3 (1.05)	30.1 (0.85)	21.9 (0.81)	7.9 (0.70)	7.0 (0.62)	0.8 (0.20)
Belgium	505 (2.2)	17.7 (0.86)	5.9 (0.53)	11.8 (0.58)	21.5 (0.63)	28.7 (0.71)	23.0 (0.66)	9.1 (0.43)	8.1 (0.42)	0.9 (0.16)
Canada	525 (1.9)	10.4 (0.47)	2.4 (0.24)	8.0 (0.38)	21.0 (0.65)	32.0 (0.54)	25.3 (0.58)	11.3 (0.55)	9.5 (0.47)	1.8 (0.20)
Chile	445 (2.9)	34.5 (1.58)	8.1 (0.80)	26.3 (1.11)	34.6 (1.06)	22.4 (0.96)	7.5 (0.60)	1.0 (0.15)	1.0 (0.15)	# (†)
Czech Republic	508 (3.0)	13.8 (1.13)	3.3 (0.62)	10.5 (1.03)	24.7 (0.99)	31.7 (1.23)	22.2 (0.96)	7.6 (0.58)	6.7 (0.53)	0.9 (0.18)
Denmark	498 (2.7)	16.7 (0.97)	4.7 (0.55)	12.0 (0.69)	25.7 (0.80)	31.3 (0.90)	19.6 (0.79)	6.8 (0.70)	6.1 (0.67)	0.7 (0.17)
Estonia	541 (1.9)	5.0 (0.45)	0.5 (0.14)	4.5 (0.43)	19.0 (0.87)	34.5 (0.87)	28.7 (0.96)	12.8 (0.73)	11.1 (0.66)	1.7 (0.25)
Finland	545 (2.2)	7.7 (0.58)	1.8 (0.28)	5.9 (0.48)	16.8 (0.69)	29.6 (0.77)	28.8 (0.73)	17.1 (0.66)	13.9 (0.62)	3.2 (0.38)
France	499 (2.6)	18.7 (1.01)	6.1 (0.67)	12.6 (0.71)	22.9 (1.08)	29.2 (1.12)	21.3 (0.87)	7.9 (0.77)	6.9 (0.68)	1.0 (0.21)
Germany	524 (3.0)	12.2 (0.90)	2.9 (0.46)	9.3 (0.73)	20.5 (0.82)	28.9 (0.89)	26.2 (1.05)	12.2 (0.95)	10.6 (0.80)	1.6 (0.28)
Greece	467 (3.1)	25.5 (1.47)	7.4 (0.70)	18.1 (1.14)	31.0 (1.10)	28.8 (1.02)	12.2 (0.81)	2.5 (0.40)	2.3 (0.40)	‡ (†)
Hungary	494 (2.9)	18.0 (1.14)	4.1 (0.61)	14.0 (1.04)	26.4 (1.08)	30.9 (1.16)	18.7 (0.98)	5.9 (0.75)	5.5 (0.73)	0.5! (0.18)
Iceland	478 (2.1)	24.0 (0.78)	8.0 (0.56)	16.0 (0.72)	27.5 (0.87)	27.2 (0.86)	16.2 (0.74)	5.2 (0.61)	4.6 (0.60)	0.6 (0.17)
Ireland	522 (2.5)	11.1 (0.88)	2.6 (0.40)	8.5 (0.76)	22.0 (1.15)	31.1 (1.03)	25.0 (0.94)	10.7 (0.58)	9.3 (0.63)	1.5 (0.25)
Israel	470 (5.0)	28.9 (1.67)	11.2 (1.08)	17.7 (0.93)	24.8 (0.93)	24.4 (1.19)	16.1 (1.12)	5.8 (0.65)	5.2 (0.58)	0.6! (0.22)
Italy	494 (1.9)	18.7 (0.68)	4.9 (0.35)	13.8 (0.52)	26.0 (0.58)	30.1 (0.66)	19.1 (0.59)	6.1 (0.41)	5.5 (0.37)	0.6 (0.08)
Japan	547 (3.6)	8.5 (0.88)	2.0 (0.39)	6.4 (0.61)	16.3 (0.79)	27.5 (0.92)	29.5 (1.06)	18.2 (1.21)	14.8 (0.93)	3.4 (0.49)
Korea, Republic of	538 (3.7)	6.6 (0.77)	1.2 (0.25)	5.5 (0.60)	18.0 (1.02)	33.6 (1.11)	30.1 (1.24)	11.7 (1.13)	10.6 (0.93)	1.1! (0.39)
Luxembourg	491 (1.3)	22.2 (0.63)	7.2 (0.42)	15.1 (0.67)	24.2 (0.63)	26.2 (0.60)	19.2 (0.53)	8.2 (0.54)	7.0 (0.49)	1.2 (0.17)
Mexico	415 (1.3)	47.0 (0.81)	12.6 (0.52)	34.4 (0.58)	37.0 (0.59)	13.8 (0.52)	2.1 (0.16)	0.1! (0.04)	0.1! (0.04)	‡ (†)
Netherlands	522 (3.5)	13.1 (1.12)	3.1 (0.53)	10.1 (0.83)	20.1 (1.35)	29.1 (1.28)	25.8 (1.24)	11.8 (1.06)	10.5 (0.98)	1.3 (0.28)
New Zealand	516 (2.1)	16.3 (0.86)	4.7 (0.39)	11.6 (0.76)	21.7 (0.94)	26.4 (0.95)	22.3 (0.85)	13.4 (0.69)	10.7 (0.62)	2.7 (0.25)
Norway	495 (3.1)	19.6 (1.10)	6.0 (0.63)	13.6 (0.71)	24.8 (0.80)	28.9 (0.91)	19.0 (0.79)	7.5 (0.57)	6.4 (0.56)	1.1 (0.24)
Poland	526 (3.1)	9.0 (0.75)	1.3 (0.32)	7.7 (0.70)	22.5 (0.98)	33.1 (0.92)	24.5 (0.96)	10.8 (1.01)	9.1 (0.76)	1.7 (0.35)
Portugal	489 (3.7)	19.0 (1.44)	4.7 (0.66)	14.3 (1.09)	27.3 (0.96)	31.4 (1.25)	17.8 (1.06)	4.5 (0.55)	4.2 (0.55)	0.3! (0.11)
Slovak Republic	471 (3.6)	26.9 (1.58)	9.2 (0.95)	17.6 (1.14)	27.0 (1.30)	26.2 (1.62)	15.0 (1.02)	4.9 (0.72)	4.3 (0.58)	0.6! (0.25)
Slovenia	514 (1.3)	12.9 (0.56)	2.4 (0.19)	10.4 (0.55)	24.5 (1.00)	30.0 (1.02)	23.0 (0.92)	9.6 (0.72)	8.4 (0.71)	1.2 (0.24)
Spain	496 (1.8)	15.7 (0.71)	3.7 (0.33)	12.0 (0.51)	27.3 (0.64)	32.8 (0.60)	19.4 (0.53)	4.8 (0.29)	4.5 (0.26)	0.3 (0.08)
Sweden	485 (3.0)	22.2 (1.11)	7.3 (0.62)	15.0 (0.80)	26.2 (0.84)	28.0 (0.84)	17.2 (0.77)	6.3 (0.50)	5.6 (0.45)	0.7 (0.14)
Switzerland	515 (2.7)	12.8 (0.72)	3.0 (0.31)	9.8 (0.62)	22.8 (0.82)	31.3 (0.74)	23.7 (0.86)	9.3 (0.77)	8.3 (0.70)	1.0 (0.22)
Turkey	463 (3.9)	26.4 (1.50)	4.4 (0.50)	21.9 (1.27)	35.4 (1.43)	25.1 (1.28)	11.3 (1.28)	1.8 (0.36)	1.8 (0.34)	‡ (†)
United Kingdom	514 (3.4)	15.0 (1.07)	4.3 (0.48)	10.7 (0.86)	22.4 (1.00)	28.4 (0.98)	23.0 (0.91)	11.2 (0.79)	9.3 (0.70)	1.8 (0.34)
United States	497 (3.8)	18.1 (1.33)	4.2 (0.54)	14.0 (1.08)	26.7 (1.08)	28.9 (1.07)	18.8 (1.07)	7.5 (0.74)	6.3 (0.64)	1.1 (0.20)

See notes at end of table.

Table 602.70. Average science literacy scores of 15-year-old students and percentage attaining science literacy proficiency levels, by country or other education system: 2012—Continued

[Standard errors appear in parentheses]

Country or other education system	Average science literacy score	Percentage attaining science literacy proficiency levels[1]								
		Below level 2			At level 2	At level 3	At level 4	At or above level 5		
		Total below level 2	Below level 1	At level 1				Total at or above level 5	At level 5	At level 6
1	2	3	4	5	6	7	8	9	10	11
Non-OECD education systems										
Albania	397 (2.4)	53.1 (1.20)	23.5 (1.04)	29.6 (0.94)	28.5 (1.19)	14.4 (0.78)	3.6 (0.41)	0.4! (0.13)	0.4! (0.14)	‡ (†)
Argentina	406 (3.9)	50.9 (2.21)	19.8 (1.39)	31.0 (1.46)	31.1 (1.33)	14.8 (1.20)	3.0 (0.43)	0.2! (0.10)	0.2! (0.10)	‡ (†)
Brazil	405 (2.1)	53.7 (1.14)	18.6 (0.78)	35.1 (0.79)	30.7 (0.78)	12.5 (0.68)	2.8 (0.37)	0.3! (0.10)	0.3! (0.10)	‡ (†)
Bulgaria	446 (4.8)	36.9 (2.02)	14.4 (1.34)	22.5 (1.15)	26.3 (1.07)	22.5 (1.09)	11.2 (0.84)	3.1 (0.58)	2.8 (0.50)	0.3! (0.12)
Chinese Taipei	523 (2.3)	9.8 (0.77)	1.6 (0.25)	8.2 (0.64)	20.8 (0.89)	33.7 (0.97)	27.3 (1.00)	8.3 (0.61)	7.8 (0.56)	0.6 (0.13)
Colombia	399 (3.1)	56.2 (1.61)	19.8 (1.36)	36.3 (1.10)	30.8 (1.08)	11.0 (0.83)	1.9 (0.25)	‡ (†)	‡ (†)	‡ (†)
Connecticut-USA[3]	521 (5.7)	13.5 (1.70)	3.3 (0.82)	10.2 (1.36)	21.4 (1.58)	29.4 (1.69)	22.8 (1.46)	12.9 (1.34)	10.7 (1.13)	2.2 (0.60)
Costa Rica	429 (2.9)	39.3 (1.75)	8.6 (0.79)	30.7 (1.30)	39.2 (1.25)	17.8 (1.12)	3.4 (0.57)	0.2! (0.10)	0.2! (0.11)	‡ (†)
Croatia	491 (3.1)	17.3 (0.93)	3.2 (0.38)	14.0 (0.74)	29.1 (0.99)	31.4 (1.19)	17.6 (1.16)	4.6 (0.79)	4.3 (0.75)	‡ (†)
Cyprus	438 (1.2)	38.0 (0.67)	14.4 (0.47)	23.7 (0.66)	30.3 (0.89)	21.3 (0.73)	8.4 (0.43)	2.0 (0.29)	1.8 (0.29)	0.2! (0.08)
Florida-USA[3]	485 (6.4)	21.3 (2.15)	5.1 (0.96)	16.1 (1.61)	28.4 (1.61)	28.2 (2.00)	16.6 (1.64)	5.5 (1.05)	4.9 (1.01)	‡ (†)
Hong Kong-China	555 (2.6)	5.6 (0.62)	1.2 (0.23)	4.4 (0.52)	13.0 (0.72)	29.8 (1.06)	34.9 (0.99)	16.7 (1.05)	14.9 (0.91)	1.8 (0.36)
Indonesia	382 (3.8)	66.6 (2.20)	24.7 (1.96)	41.9 (1.42)	26.3 (1.54)	6.5 (1.02)	‡ (†)	‡ (†)	‡ (†)	‡ (†)
Jordan	409 (3.1)	49.6 (1.55)	18.2 (1.21)	31.4 (0.96)	32.2 (1.04)	15.0 (0.86)	3.0 (0.57)	‡ (†)	0.2! (†)	‡ (†)
Kazakhstan	425 (3.0)	41.9 (1.83)	11.3 (0.99)	30.7 (1.49)	36.8 (1.16)	17.8 (1.19)	3.3 (0.45)	0.2! (0.09)	0.2! (0.09)	‡ (†)
Latvia	502 (2.8)	12.4 (0.96)	1.8 (0.39)	10.5 (0.90)	28.2 (1.20)	35.1 (1.02)	20.0 (1.05)	4.4 (0.51)	4.0 (0.47)	0.3! (0.13)
Liechtenstein	525 (3.5)	10.4 (1.96)	‡ (†)	9.6 (1.94)	22.0 (3.94)	30.8 (3.79)	26.7 (2.58)	10.1 (1.80)	9.1 (1.47)	‡ (†)
Lithuania	496 (2.6)	16.1 (1.08)	3.4 (0.48)	12.7 (0.84)	27.6 (1.00)	32.9 (1.08)	18.3 (0.88)	5.1 (0.49)	4.7 (0.47)	0.4 (0.09)
Macao-China	521 (0.8)	8.8 (0.46)	1.4 (0.20)	7.4 (0.49)	22.2 (0.60)	36.2 (0.81)	26.2 (0.73)	6.7 (0.36)	6.2 (0.35)	0.4 (0.10)
Malaysia	420 (3.0)	45.5 (1.55)	14.5 (1.13)	31.0 (1.21)	33.9 (1.10)	16.5 (1.07)	3.7 (0.54)	0.3! (0.12)	0.3! (0.13)	‡ (†)
Massachusetts-USA[3]	527 (6.0)	11.5 (1.18)	2.6 (0.65)	8.9 (1.03)	21.2 (1.96)	29.4 (1.50)	23.8 (1.84)	14.2 (1.94)	11.3 (1.48)	2.9 (0.73)
Montenegro, Republic of	410 (1.1)	50.7 (0.72)	18.7 (0.74)	32.0 (0.98)	29.7 (0.94)	15.4 (0.76)	3.8 (0.47)	0.4! (0.14)	0.4! (0.14)	‡ (†)
Peru	373 (3.6)	68.5 (1.95)	31.5 (1.61)	37.0 (1.26)	23.5 (1.29)	7.0 (0.85)	1.0 (0.28)	‡ (†)	‡ (†)	‡ (†)
Qatar	384 (0.7)	62.6 (0.53)	34.6 (0.38)	28.0 (0.58)	19.6 (0.71)	11.2 (0.39)	5.1 (0.40)	1.5 (0.12)	1.3 (0.11)	0.1 (0.04)
Romania	439 (3.3)	37.3 (1.64)	8.7 (0.77)	28.7 (1.32)	34.6 (1.23)	21.0 (1.12)	6.2 (0.77)	0.9! (0.29)	0.9 (0.26)	‡ (†)
Russian Federation	486 (2.9)	18.8 (1.15)	3.6 (0.39)	15.1 (0.96)	30.1 (1.08)	31.2 (0.89)	15.7 (0.98)	4.3 (0.59)	3.9 (0.51)	0.3! (0.16)
Serbia, Republic of	445 (3.4)	35.0 (1.81)	10.3 (0.99)	24.7 (1.15)	32.4 (1.21)	22.8 (1.06)	8.1 (0.63)	1.7 (0.36)	1.6 (0.35)	‡ (†)
Shanghai-China	580 (3.0)	2.7 (0.41)	0.3! (0.11)	2.4 (0.36)	10.0 (0.86)	24.6 (0.87)	35.5 (1.11)	27.2 (1.32)	23.0 (1.09)	4.2 (0.57)
Singapore	551 (1.5)	9.6 (0.51)	2.2 (0.27)	7.4 (0.48)	16.7 (0.73)	24.0 (0.73)	27.0 (0.87)	22.7 (0.81)	16.9 (0.94)	5.8 (0.41)
Thailand	444 (2.9)	33.6 (1.56)	7.0 (0.64)	26.6 (1.33)	37.5 (1.07)	21.6 (1.14)	6.4 (0.74)	0.9 (0.27)	0.9! (0.27)	‡ (†)
Tunisia	398 (3.5)	55.3 (1.87)	21.3 (1.45)	34.0 (1.07)	31.1 (1.36)	11.7 (1.00)	1.8 (0.49)	‡ (†)	‡ (†)	‡ (†)
United Arab Emirates	448 (2.8)	35.2 (1.30)	11.3 (0.76)	23.8 (0.99)	29.9 (0.83)	22.3 (0.88)	10.1 (0.60)	2.5 (0.27)	2.3 (0.25)	0.3 (0.07)
Uruguay	416 (2.8)	46.9 (1.25)	19.7 (1.06)	27.2 (0.92)	29.3 (1.00)	17.1 (0.95)	5.6 (0.53)	1.0 (0.25)	1.0 (0.24)	‡ (†)
Vietnam	528 (4.3)	6.7 (1.09)	0.9! (0.26)	5.8 (0.90)	20.7 (1.40)	37.5 (1.48)	27.0 (1.50)	8.1 (1.09)	7.1 (0.90)	1.0! (0.32)

†Not applicable.
#Rounds to zero.
!Interpret data with caution. The coefficient of variation (CV) for this estimate is between 30 and 50 percent.
‡Reporting standards not met. Either there are too few cases for a reliable estimate or the coefficient of variation (CV) is 50 percent or greater.
[1]To reach a particular proficiency level, a student must correctly answer a majority of items at that level. Students were classified into science literacy levels according to their scores. Exact cut scores are as follows: below level 1 (a score less than or equal to 334.94); level 1 (a score greater than 334.94 and less than or equal to 409.54); level 2 (a score greater than 409.54 and less than or equal to 484.14); level 3 (a score greater than 484.14 and less than or equal to 558.73) and

less than or equal to 633.33); level 5 (a score greater than 633.33 and less than or equal to 707.93); and level 6 (a score greater than 707.93).
[2]Refers to the mean of the data values for all Organization for Economic Cooperation and Development (OECD) countries, to which each country contributes equally, regardless of the absolute size of the student population of each country.
[3]Results are for public school students only.
NOTE: Program for International Student Assessment (PISA) scores are reported on a scale from 0 to 1,000. Detail may not sum to totals because of rounding.
SOURCE: Organization for Economic Cooperation and Development (OECD), Program for International Student Assessment (PISA), 2012. (This table was prepared November 2013.)

Table 603.10. Percentage of the population 25 to 64 years old who completed high school, by age group and country: Selected years, 2001 through 2012

[Standard errors appear in parentheses]

Country	2001 Total, 25 to 64 years old	2001 25 to 34 years old	2005 Total, 25 to 64 years old	2005 25 to 34 years old	2011 Total, 25 to 64 years old	2011 25 to 34 years old	2012 Total, 25 to 64 years old	2012 25 to 34 years old	2012 35 to 44 years old	2012 45 to 54 years old	2012 55 to 64 years old
1	2	3	4	5	6	7	8	9	10	11	12
OECD average[1]	64.2	74.0	72.8	82.6	74.4 (0.04)	81.9 (0.07)	75.7 (0.03)	82.7 (0.07)	79.4 (0.06)	73.7 (0.07)	65.2 (0.08)
Australia	58.9	70.7	65.0	78.6	74.1 (0.25)	84.4 (0.41)	76.4 (0.25)	86.6 (0.41)	80.9 (0.45)	70.9 (0.51)	63.5 (0.59)
Austria[2,3]	75.7	83.3	80.6	87.5	82.5 (0.26)	88.2 (0.44)	83.1 (0.24)	88.6 (0.50)	86.3 (0.45)	82.8 (0.41)	73.8 (0.55)
Belgium[2]	58.5	75.3	66.1	80.9	71.3 (0.19)	81.9 (0.35)	71.6 (0.19)	81.9 (0.35)	78.8 (0.35)	68.9 (0.38)	56.3 (0.43)
Canada	81.9	89.3	85.2	90.8	88.8 (0.13)	92.5 (0.19)	89.1 (0.13)	92.2 (0.19)	91.9 (0.19)	88.1 (0.22)	84.0 (0.26)
Chile[4]	—	—	50.0	64.3	57.5 (0.16)	76.6 (0.27)	— (†)	— (†)	— (†)	— (†)	— (†)
Czech Republic	86.2	92.5	89.9	93.9	92.3 (0.07)	94.3 (0.14)	92.5 (0.07)	93.7 (0.15)	95.4 (0.12)	93.3 (0.15)	87.0 (0.17)
Denmark	80.2	86.3	81.0	87.4	76.9 (0.17)	80.3 (0.38)	77.9 (0.16)	81.7 (0.36)	82.3 (0.30)	77.3 (0.29)	70.5 (0.35)
Estonia	—	—	89.1	87.4	88.9 (0.29)	85.7 (0.71)	89.8 (0.41)	86.4 (0.95)	90.2 (0.77)	94.2 (0.62)	88.3 (0.83)
Finland	73.8	86.8	78.8	89.4	83.7 (0.18)	90.2 (0.31)	84.8 (0.18)	90.0 (0.32)	89.7 (0.31)	86.9 (0.32)	74.0 (0.40)
France[5]	63.9	78.4	66.3	81.1	71.6 (0.09)	83.3 (0.16)	72.5 (0.09)	83.3 (0.16)	79.5 (0.16)	68.6 (0.17)	59.1 (0.19)
Germany	82.6	85.5	83.1	84.1	86.3 (0.12)	86.8 (0.21)	86.3 (0.12)	86.8 (0.32)	86.7 (0.31)	87.1 (0.27)	84.4 (0.31)
Greece	51.4	72.6	57.1	73.6	67.1 (0.12)	80.1 (0.22)	68.5 (0.13)	82.5 (0.23)	74.5 (0.24)	64.8 (0.26)	49.6 (0.28)
Hungary	70.2	80.9	76.4	85.0	81.8 (0.27)	87.3 (0.32)	82.1 (0.10)	87.5 (0.18)	83.6 (0.19)	82.0 (0.21)	74.9 (0.21)
Iceland	56.9	61.2	62.9	69.0	70.7 (0.48)	74.7 (0.90)	71.0 (0.48)	75.0 (0.87)	75.4 (0.91)	71.0 (0.94)	61.4 (1.12)
Ireland	57.6	73.4	64.5	81.1	73.4 (0.13)	85.0 (0.20)	74.6 (0.13)	85.9 (0.19)	80.2 (0.21)	69.9 (0.27)	55.1 (0.32)
Israel	—	—	79.2	85.7	83.0 (0.15)	89.7 (0.23)	84.5 (0.15)	90.3 (0.23)	86.1 (0.28)	81.1 (0.35)	77.4 (0.41)
Italy	43.3	57.5	50.1	65.9	56.0 (0.14)	71.3 (0.36)	57.2 (0.14)	71.8 (0.37)	62.0 (0.29)	52.7 (0.28)	42.4 (0.28)
Japan	83.1	93.6	—	—	— (†)	— (†)	— (†)	— (†)	— (†)	— (†)	— (†)
Korea, Republic of	68.0	94.6	75.5	97.3	81.4 (0.20)	98.0 (0.14)	82.4 (0.20)	98.2 (0.14)	96.4 (0.19)	78.1 (0.42)	47.6 (0.63)
Luxembourg	52.7	59.4	65.9	76.5	77.3 (0.40)	83.4 (0.76)	78.3 (0.31)	86.1 (0.58)	80.4 (0.60)	75.7 (0.59)	68.6 (0.67)
Mexico	21.6	25.4	21.3	24.0	36.3 (0.06)	44.0 (0.12)	37.3 (0.06)	45.8 (0.12)	37.2 (0.12)	34.6 (0.13)	24.9 (0.15)
Netherlands[2,5]	65.0	74.0	71.8	81.3	72.3 (0.09)	81.7 (0.18)	73.4 (0.09)	83.3 (0.17)	78.1 (0.17)	71.5 (0.16)	61.4 (0.20)
New Zealand	75.7	81.8	78.7	85.2	74.1 (0.36)	80.4 (0.71)	74.1 (0.37)	80.0 (0.72)	77.9 (0.67)	73.0 (0.70)	64.0 (0.82)
Norway[2]	85.2	93.4	77.2	83.5	81.9 (0.16)	83.8 (0.33)	82.1 (0.16)	82.1 (0.36)	85.5 (0.29)	78.7 (0.34)	81.6 (0.33)
Poland	45.9	51.7	51.4	62.5	89.1 (0.06)	94.1 (0.10)	89.6 (0.06)	94.4 (0.10)	92.4 (0.12)	90.3 (0.12)	81.2 (0.15)
Portugal	19.9	32.5	26.5	42.8	35.0 (0.16)	55.7 (0.39)	37.6 (0.17)	57.9 (0.39)	43.3 (0.35)	27.2 (0.28)	19.8 (0.26)
Slovak Republic	85.1	93.7	85.7	93.0	91.3 (0.23)	94.1 (0.46)	91.7 (0.23)	94.1 (0.41)	94.5 (0.39)	91.7 (0.44)	85.7 (0.55)
Slovenia	—	—	80.3	91.2	84.5 (0.19)	94.0 (0.27)	85.0 (0.19)	94.2 (0.27)	88.7 (0.37)	82.7 (0.38)	74.4 (0.45)
Spain	40.0	57.1	48.8	63.9	54.0 (0.29)	64.8 (0.59)	54.6 (0.08)	64.2 (0.17)	62.0 (0.15)	51.4 (0.15)	35.3 (0.16)
Sweden	80.6	90.7	83.6	90.6	87.0 (0.08)	90.9 (0.14)	87.5 (0.08)	90.8 (0.14)	91.7 (0.13)	87.7 (0.15)	79.5 (0.18)
Switzerland	87.4	91.8	83.0	87.9	85.6 (0.12)	89.1 (0.24)	86.3 (0.13)	89.4 (0.28)	87.6 (0.23)	85.9 (0.23)	81.9 (0.27)
Turkey	24.3	30.2	27.2	35.7	32.1 (0.09)	43.5 (0.18)	33.9 (0.09)	45.9 (0.18)	32.0 (0.17)	25.3 (0.17)	20.7 (0.19)
United Kingdom[3,5]	63.0	68.0	66.7	72.9	76.8 (0.09)	84.3 (0.17)	78.1 (0.09)	84.8 (0.16)	81.4 (0.16)	75.8 (0.18)	69.1 (0.20)
United States	87.7	88.1	87.8	86.7	89.3 (0.13)	89.0 (0.25)	89.3 (0.16)	89.3 (0.29)	89.0 (0.24)	89.1 (0.26)	89.9 (0.23)
Other reporting countries											
Brazil[4]	—	—	29.5	38.0	43.3 (0.11)	56.7 (0.19)	44.9 (0.11)	58.9 (0.19)	45.5 (0.21)	38.5 (0.22)	27.1 (0.25)
Russian Federation[6]	88.0	91.0	—	—	94.1 (0.05)	94.0 (0.10)	94.3 (0.05)	94.4 (0.10)	95.2 (0.10)	95.8 (0.09)	91.6 (0.15)

—Not available.
†Not applicable.
[1]Refers to the mean of the data values for all reporting Organization for Economic Cooperation and Development (OECD) countries, to which each country reporting data contributes equally. The average includes all current OECD countries for which a given year's data are available, even if they were not members of OECD in that year.
[2]Data from 2000 reported for 2001.
[3]Data in 2005 columns include some International Standard Classification of Education (ISCED) 3C short secondary programs.
[4]Data from 2004 reported for 2005.

[5]Data in 2001 columns include some short secondary (ISCED 3C) programs.
[6]Data from 2002 reported for 2001.
NOTE: Data in this table refer to degrees classified as International Standard Classification of Education (ISCED) level 3. ISCED level 3 corresponds to high school completion in the United States. ISCED 3C short programs do not correspond to high school completion; these short programs are excluded from this table except where otherwise noted. Standard errors are not available for 2001 and 2005.
SOURCE: Organization for Economic Cooperation and Development (OECD), *Education at a Glance*, 2002, 2007, 2013, and 2014. (This table was prepared November 2014.)

Table 603.20. Percentage of the population 25 to 64 years old who attained selected levels of postsecondary education, by age group and country: 2001 and 2012

[Standard errors appear in parentheses]

Country	Total, any postsecondary degree 2001 Total, 25 to 64	2001 25 to 34	2012 Total, 25 to 64	2012 25 to 34	2012 Vocational degree[1] Total, 25 to 64	Voc. 25 to 34	Voc. 35 to 44	Voc. 45 to 54	Voc. 55 to 64	2012 Bachelor's or higher degree[2] Total, 25 to 64	Bach. 25 to 34	Bach. 35 to 44	Bach. 45 to 54	Bach. 55 to 64
	2	3	4	5	6	7	8	9	10	11	12	13	14	15
OECD average[3]	**22.6**	**27.3**	**32.2 (0.04)**	**39.2 (0.09)**	**9.8 (0.03)**	**10.0 (0.06)**	**10.8 (0.06)**	**10.2 (0.06)**	**8.6 (0.06)**	**23.5 (0.04)**	**30.3 (0.08)**	**25.9 (0.08)**	**20.1 (0.07)**	**16.9 (0.07)**
Australia	29.0	33.5	41.3 (0.27)	47.2 (0.56)	11.5 (0.17)	10.5 (0.33)	12.8 (0.34)	12.3 (0.36)	10.1 (0.35)	29.8 (0.25)	36.7 (0.53)	32.2 (0.50)	25.2 (0.47)	23.0 (0.50)
Austria	14.1	14.3	20.0 (0.23)	23.0 (0.50)	7.3 (0.14)	5.2 (0.29)	7.1 (0.28)	8.2 (0.29)	8.5 (0.30)	12.7 (0.21)	17.8 (0.47)	14.4 (0.46)	10.3 (0.33)	8.2 (0.37)
Belgium	27.6	37.5	35.3 (0.20)	43.0 (0.45)	16.9 (0.16)	18.2 (0.35)	19.5 (0.34)	16.4 (0.30)	13.4 (0.29)	18.4 (0.17)	24.8 (0.39)	20.7 (0.35)	16.0 (0.30)	12.0 (0.28)
Canada	41.6	50.5	52.6 (0.23)	57.3 (0.40)	24.9 (0.16)	25.5 (0.32)	26.6 (0.32)	25.2 (0.28)	22.0 (0.28)	27.7 (0.23)	31.8 (0.41)	32.4 (0.41)	24.4 (0.34)	22.5 (0.34)
Chile[4,5]	10.1	12.3	17.8 (0.12)	22.5 (0.26)	5.8 (0.07)	6.1 (0.15)	7.0 (0.16)	6.0 (0.14)	3.7 (0.13)	12.0 (0.10)	16.4 (0.23)	12.0 (0.20)	9.5 (0.18)	9.4 (0.21)
Czech Republic[6]	11.1	11.3	19.3 (0.11)	27.8 (0.28)	5.6 (0.09)	5.3 (0.21)	6.4 (0.19)	5.5 (0.16)	— (†)	13.7 (0.11)	22.5 (0.28)	12.2 (0.22)	12.1 (0.18)	7.2 (0.17)
Denmark	26.8	27.5	34.8 (0.19)	40.2 (0.46)	12.6 (0.45)	13.1 (0.98)	12.0 (0.83)	13.3 (0.85)	12.1 (0.88)	22.2 (0.18)	34.9 (0.45)	32.4 (0.37)	23.9 (0.31)	23.7 (0.33)
Estonia	—	38.2	37.3 (0.69)	39.8 (1.46)	13.5 (0.17)	0.9 (0.98)	14.8 (0.37)	20.7 (0.38)	16.6 (0.34)	23.8 (0.64)	26.8 (1.37)	32.7 (1.25)	20.6 (1.16)	23.4 (1.18)
Finland	32.3	38.2	39.7 (0.24)	39.7 (0.52)	11.9 (0.17)	16.1 (0.10)	15.5 (0.37)	9.6 (0.38)	6.7 (0.34)	27.8 (0.22)	38.9 (0.51)	32.7 (0.48)	26.6 (0.38)	14.8 (0.32)
France	23.0	34.2	30.9 (0.09)	42.9 (0.21)	12.0 (0.06)	16.1 (0.16)	15.5 (0.14)	9.6 (0.11)	6.7 (0.09)	18.9 (0.08)	26.8 (0.19)	22.1 (0.16)	14.3 (0.13)	12.9 (0.13)
Germany	23.2	21.8	28.1 (0.08)	29.0 (0.19)	11.1 (0.06)	9.5 (0.11)	10.9 (0.12)	12.4 (0.11)	11.2 (0.12)	17.0 (0.07)	19.5 (0.16)	18.6 (0.15)	15.3 (0.12)	15.2 (0.14)
Greece	17.8	24.0	26.7 (0.12)	34.7 (0.29)	8.8 (0.08)	13.5 (0.21)	8.2 (0.15)	8.1 (0.15)	5.2 (‡)	17.9 (0.11)	21.3 (0.25)	18.9 (0.21)	16.2 (0.20)	14.8 (0.20)
Hungary	14.1	14.7	22.0 (0.11)	30.4 (0.26)	0.7 (0.02)	1.5 (0.07)	0.8 (0.05)	0.8 (0.07)	0.5 (0.07)	21.3 (0.11)	29.0 (0.25)	21.6 (0.21)	18.9 (0.21)	15.3 (0.18)
Iceland	24.8	26.6	35.2 (0.50)	38.4 (0.98)	4.1 (0.21)	2.6 (0.32)	4.7 (0.45)	4.5 (0.43)	4.5 (0.48)	31.1 (0.49)	35.8 (0.97)	37.0 (1.02)	29.8 (0.94)	20.4 (0.92)
Ireland	35.6	47.8	39.7 (0.14)	49.2 (0.28)	14.8 (0.10)	16.0 (0.20)	17.8 (0.20)	13.4 (0.20)	10.2 (0.20)	24.9 (0.12)	33.2 (0.26)	28.3 (0.24)	19.0 (0.23)	14.7 (0.23)
Israel	10.0	—	46.4 (0.20)	44.5 (0.38)	13.9 (0.14)	11.7 (0.25)	14.2 (0.29)	14.5 (0.30)	16.2 (0.32)	32.5 (0.18)	32.8 (0.35)	35.6 (0.37)	30.4 (0.37)	30.4 (0.38)
Italy	10.0	11.8	15.7 (0.08)	22.3 (0.21)	0.3 (0.03)	0.2 (†)	0.4 (†)	0.5 (†)	0.3 (†)	15.4 (0.08)	22.0 (0.21)	17.0 (0.16)	11.8 (0.14)	11.1 (0.15)
Japan	33.8	47.7	46.6 (0.19)	58.6 (0.19)	20.2 (0.15)	23.4 (0.35)	24.8 (0.33)	20.3 (0.34)	12.8 (0.30)	26.4 (0.17)	35.2 (0.39)	26.7 (0.33)	25.8 (0.37)	19.3 (0.36)
Korea, Republic of	24.2	39.5	41.7 (0.25)	65.7 (0.46)	13.3 (0.17)	25.8 (0.43)	16.5 (0.31)	6.3 (0.43)	2.4 (0.16)	28.4 (0.23)	39.9 (0.47)	35.7 (0.44)	22.8 (0.40)	11.2 (0.40)
Luxembourg	18.1	23.4	39.1 (0.36)	49.9 (0.83)	13.1 (0.25)	14.1 (0.58)	15.2 (0.54)	12.1 (0.45)	9.8 (0.43)	26.1 (0.33)	35.7 (0.80)	29.8 (0.69)	19.8 (0.55)	16.6 (0.54)
Mexico	15.0	17.9	18.1 (#)	24.1 (0.23)	1.2 (#)	1.4 (#)	1.1 (#)	1.2 (#)	0.9 (#)	16.9 (#)	22.7 (†)	14.8 (†)	15.3 (#)	11.6 (#)
Netherlands	23.2	26.5	34.4 (0.10)	43.0 (0.89)	2.8 (0.03)	2.6 (0.07)	3.2 (0.07)	2.9 (0.06)	2.4 (0.06)	31.6 (0.09)	40.5 (0.84)	33.7 (0.73)	27.9 (0.65)	25.4 (0.65)
New Zealand	29.2	28.5	40.6 (0.41)	46.9 (0.46)	15.3 (0.30)	14.1 (0.62)	14.5 (0.57)	16.0 (0.58)	16.7 (0.63)	25.4 (0.21)	32.8 (0.46)	28.0 (0.41)	21.8 (0.39)	17.9 (0.38)
Norway	30.2	37.9	45.0 (0.21)	45.0 (0.46)	2.4 (0.06)	0.8 (0.08)	2.3 (0.12)	3.0 (0.14)	3.4 (0.15)	42.6 (0.21)	44.2 (0.46)	41.2 (0.41)	31.6 (0.39)	26.6 (0.38)
Poland	11.9	15.2	24.5 (0.09)	40.8 (0.21)	— (†)	— (†)	— (†)	—	—	24.5 (0.09)	40.8 (0.21)	26.4 (0.19)	16.5 (0.15)	12.6 (0.13)
Portugal[6]	9.0	13.7	18.5 (0.13)	28.3 (0.36)	1.3 (†)	1.2 (†)	1.1 (†)	1.5 (†)	1.4 (†)	18.5 (0.13)	28.3 (0.36)	20.3 (0.28)	13.6 (0.22)	11.1 (0.20)
Slovak Republic	10.9	11.9	19.0 (0.32)	27.0 (0.77)	1.3 (0.09)	1.2 (0.19)	1.2 (0.19)	1.2 (0.19)	9.2 (0.30)	17.6 (0.32)	25.8 (0.63)	16.0 (0.45)	14.8 (0.57)	12.3 (0.52)
Slovenia	—	—	26.4 (0.24)	35.4 (0.55)	11.7 (0.18)	13.8 (0.40)	12.9 (0.39)	11.2 (0.32)	4.2 (0.30)	14.7 (0.19)	21.6 (0.48)	17.6 (0.45)	11.8 (0.33)	8.0 (0.28)
Spain	23.6	35.5	32.3 (0.08)	39.3 (0.18)	9.7 (0.05)	12.5 (0.12)	12.1 (0.10)	8.2 (0.08)	4.2 (0.07)	22.7 (0.07)	26.7 (0.16)	26.6 (0.14)	20.2 (0.12)	14.8 (0.12)
Sweden	31.6	36.9	35.7 (0.11)	43.5 (0.24)	9.1 (0.07)	9.4 (0.14)	8.5 (0.13)	9.0 (0.13)	9.7 (0.13)	26.6 (0.10)	34.1 (0.21)	31.6 (0.21)	21.5 (0.19)	19.0 (0.18)
Switzerland	25.4	25.6	36.6 (0.18)	40.6 (0.46)	10.8 (0.12)	9.0 (0.25)	12.2 (0.23)	12.0 (0.23)	9.5 (0.22)	25.8 (0.17)	31.7 (0.44)	28.8 (0.31)	23.0 (0.29)	19.2 (0.29)
Turkey[4,6]	8.9	10.2	15.3 (0.07)	21.0 (0.15)	—	—	—	—	—	15.3 (0.07)	21.0 (0.15)	14.8 (0.13)	9.9 (0.12)	10.3 (0.14)
United Kingdom	26.0	30.0	41.0 (0.11)	47.9 (0.23)	10.0 (0.06)	7.7 (0.12)	10.5 (0.13)	11.4 (0.13)	10.3 (0.13)	31.0 (0.10)	40.1 (0.22)	34.6 (0.20)	25.7 (0.18)	22.3 (0.18)
United States	37.3	39.1	43.1 (0.24)	44.0 (0.42)	10.4 (0.12)	9.9 (0.20)	10.8 (0.25)	10.4 (0.22)	10.6 (0.28)	32.6 (0.22)	34.1 (0.43)	34.7 (0.41)	30.5 (0.38)	31.2 (0.41)
Other reporting countries														
Brazil[4,6]	7.7	6.7	13.0 (0.07)	14.5 (0.12)	—	—	—	—	—	13.0 (0.07)	14.5 (0.12)	12.9 (0.13)	13.1 (0.14)	10.2 (0.16)
China[4,7]	4.6	6.1	3.6	—	—	—	—	—	—	—	—	—	—	—
Russian Federation[8]	54.0	55.5	53.5	57.0	25.7	21.5	25.8	28.0	28.4	27.7	35.5	28.7	24.4	20.8

—Not available.
†Not applicable.
#Rounds to zero.
‡Reporting standards not met (too few cases for a reliable estimate).
[1] The vocational degree data in this table refer to degrees classified as International Standard Classification of Education (ISCED) level 5B. ISCED level 5B corresponds to the associate's degree in the United States.
[2] The data for bachelor's degree or higher in this table refer to degrees classified as ISCED level 5A (first and second award) and as level 6. ISCED 5A, first award, corresponds to the bachelor's degree in the United States; ISCED 5A, second award, corresponds to master's and first-professional degrees in the United States; and ISCED 6 corresponds to doctor's degrees.
[3] Refers to the mean of the data values for all reporting Organization for Economic Cooperation and Development (OECD) countries, to which each country reporting data contributes equally. The average includes all current OECD countries for which a given year's data are available, even if they were not members of OECD in that year.
[4] Data from 2000 reported for 2001.
[5] Data from 2011 reported for 2012.
[6] Columns for bachelor's or higher degree include vocational degree data.
[7] Data from 2010 reported for 2012.
[8] Data from 2002 reported for 2001.
NOTE: Standard errors are not available for 2001.
SOURCE: Organization for Economic Cooperation and Development (OECD), *Education at a Glance*, 2002 and 2014. (This table was prepared November 2014.)

Table 603.30. Percentage of the population 25 to 64 years old who attained a bachelor's or higher level degree, by age group and country: Selected years, 1999 through 2012

[Standard errors appear in parentheses]

Country	1999 Total, 25 to 64 years old	1999 25 to 34 years old	2001 Total, 25 to 64 years old	2001 25 to 34 years old	2005 Total, 25 to 64 years old	2005 25 to 34 years old	2008 Total, 25 to 64 years old	2008 25 to 34 years old	2009 Total, 25 to 64 years old	2009 25 to 34 years old	2010 Total, 25 to 64 years old	2010 25 to 34 years old	2012 Total, 25 to 64 years old	2012 25 to 34 years old
1	2	3	4	5	6	7	8	9	10	11	12	13	14	15
OECD average[1]	14.0	16.5	15.1	18.2	18.8	23.9	20.8	26.6	21.4 (0.03)	27.7 (0.08)	22.0 (0.04)	28.5 (0.09)	23.5 (0.04)	30.3 (0.08)
Australia	17.7	20.1	19.2	23.9	22.7	29.2	25.5	31.9	26.8 (0.29)	34.6 (0.62)	26.9 (0.41)	34.2 (0.81)	29.8 (0.25)	36.7 (0.53)
Austria[2]	6.1	6.8	6.8	6.9	9.1	11.6	10.7	13.5	11.4 (0.10)	15.3 (0.25)	12.0 (0.25)	15.4 (0.49)	12.7 (0.21)	17.8 (0.47)
Belgium	12.0	16.0	12.7	17.8	13.8	19.1	16.4	22.8	17.5 (0.16)	24.2 (0.38)	17.2 (0.16)	23.3 (0.37)	18.4 (0.17)	24.8 (0.39)
Canada	19.1	23.1	20.4	25.1	23.3	28.2	25.2	29.8	25.4 (0.16)	30.1 (0.34)	26.4 (0.22)	30.7 (0.42)	27.7 (0.23)	31.8 (0.41)
Chile[2,3]	8.2	9.6	9.0	10.7	—	—	15.7	22.3	16.4 (0.15)	24.0 (0.30)	16.5 (0.15)	25.4 (0.30)	12.0 (0.10)	16.4 (0.23)
Czech Republic[4]	10.8	10.9	11.1	11.3	13.1	14.2	14.5	17.7	15.5 (0.10)	20.2 (0.23)	16.8 (0.10)	22.6 (0.25)	19.3 (0.11)	27.8 (0.28)
Denmark	—	—	21.5	21.7	26.0	30.7	27.5	34.9	27.1 (0.18)	36.2 (0.60)	27.0 (0.17)	31.4 (0.48)	29.2 (0.18)	34.9 (0.45)
Estonia	—	—	—	—	22.2	24.1	22.3	23.5	22.7 (0.41)	21.7 (0.87)	21.9 (0.71)	23.8 (1.59)	24.6 (0.64)	26.8 (1.37)
Finland	13.9	15.6	14.8	18.0	18.1	26.6	21.5	32.9	22.6 (0.13)	36.0 (0.34)	23.5 (0.21)	36.7 (0.52)	26.2 (0.22)	38.9 (0.51)
France	11.0	15.3	11.9	17.5	14.8	22.3	16.4	23.7	17.3 (0.08)	25.7 (0.20)	17.5 (0.08)	26.0 (0.19)	18.9 (0.08)	26.8 (0.19)
Germany	13.0	12.9	13.5	13.5	14.8	15.1	16.4	17.5	17.1 (0.06)	18.9 (0.14)	17.0 (0.07)	18.9 (0.16)	17.0 (0.07)	19.5 (0.16)
Greece	12.2	16.6	12.4	16.6	14.5	17.0	16.8	18.6	16.9 (0.09)	19.3 (0.21)	17.5 (0.29)	20.0 (0.51)	17.9 (0.11)	21.3 (0.25)
Hungary[5]	13.5	13.7	14.1	14.7	16.9	19.1	18.7	22.9	19.4 (0.10)	24.1 (0.23)	19.6 (0.10)	24.7 (0.24)	21.3 (0.11)	29.0 (0.25)
Iceland	17.8	22.3	18.8	21.1	25.9	32.5	27.9	30.6	28.8 (0.48)	33.4 (0.96)	28.7 (0.48)	34.0 (0.98)	31.1 (0.49)	35.8 (0.97)
Ireland[2]	10.6	16.1	14.0	19.8	18.4	26.2	22.2	30.6	20.9 (0.11)	28.8 (0.23)	21.8 (0.11)	29.7 (0.24)	24.9 (0.12)	33.2 (0.26)
Israel[5]	—	—	—	—	29.8	34.8	28.8	28.9	29.4 (0.18)	29.5 (0.35)	30.5 (0.18)	31.8 (0.35)	32.5 (0.18)	32.8 (0.35)
Italy[6]	9.3	10.0	10.0	11.8	11.7	15.5	14.0	19.6	14.1 (0.06)	19.9 (0.15)	14.4 (0.07)	20.5 (0.19)	15.4 (0.08)	22.0 (0.21)
Japan	18.3	23.0	19.2	24.3	22.3	27.9	24.3	30.9	24.6 (0.11)	31.8 (0.27)	25.3 (0.18)	33.0 (0.38)	26.4 (0.17)	35.2 (0.39)
Korea, Republic of	16.9	23.2	17.5	25.0	22.7	31.7	25.6	34.5	27.1 (0.23)	37.6 (0.47)	27.5 (0.23)	39.0 (0.47)	28.4 (0.23)	39.9 (0.47)
Luxembourg	11.7	13.1	11.4	15.1	17.0	23.8	20.0	27.9	20.2 (0.39)	24.1 (0.93)	20.8 (0.39)	26.1 (0.96)	26.1 (0.33)	35.7 (0.80)
Mexico	11.9	14.1	13.3	15.3	13.8	17.0	14.9	18.5	15.9 (0.05)	20.2 (0.10)	16.2 (#)	20.6 (#)	16.9 (#)	22.7 (#)
Netherlands	20.1	22.7	20.9	24.1	28.3	33.8	29.8	37.5	30.0 (0.09)	37.6 (0.22)	29.8 (0.10)	38.4 (0.23)	31.6 (0.09)	40.5 (0.23)
New Zealand	13.1	15.6	13.9	16.9	19.7	26.2	25.1	33.6	23.2 (0.41)	30.8 (0.96)	24.3 (0.36)	31.5 (0.83)	25.3 (0.36)	32.8 (0.84)
Norway[2,4]	25.3	30.6	27.6	35.4	30.3	38.9	33.6	43.8	34.5 (0.20)	45.5 (0.45)	35.2 (0.20)	46.2 (0.45)	36.2 (0.21)	44.2 (0.46)
Poland[2,4]	11.3	12.3	11.9	15.2	16.9	25.5	19.6	32.1	21.2 (0.12)	35.4 (0.29)	22.9 (0.09)	37.4 (0.21)	24.5 (0.09)	40.8 (0.21)
Portugal[6]	7.1	9.3	6.6	10.6	12.8	19.1	14.3	23.2	14.7 (0.24)	23.3 (0.32)	15.4 (0.15)	24.8 (0.28)	18.5 (0.13)	28.3 (0.36)
Slovak Republic	—	—	10.3	11.2	12.8	15.4	14.0	17.8	15.0 (0.15)	19.7 (0.34)	16.6 (0.16)	23.5 (0.28)	17.6 (0.32)	25.8 (0.76)
Slovenia	—	—	—	—	10.6	15.2	11.8	18.4	12.6 (0.17)	18.7 (0.42)	13.1 (0.17)	19.2 (0.43)	14.7 (0.19)	21.6 (0.48)
Spain	14.8	22.1	16.9	23.9	19.9	27.0	20.0	25.7	20.1 (0.07)	25.0 (0.15)	21.5 (0.07)	26.9 (0.15)	22.7 (0.07)	26.7 (0.16)
Sweden	13.1	11.1	16.9	19.7	20.6	28.4	23.4	32.4	24.3 (0.11)	33.9 (0.26)	25.4 (0.10)	34.0 (0.22)	26.6 (0.10)	34.1 (0.23)
Switzerland	14.5	16.6	15.8	15.9	19.0	21.9	23.3	28.8	24.7 (0.24)	30.5 (0.56)	24.3 (0.15)	30.6 (0.37)	25.8 (0.17)	31.7 (0.44)
Turkey[4]	7.1	7.6	8.9	10.2	9.7	11.8	12.0	15.5	12.7 (0.07)	16.6 (0.13)	13.1 (0.07)	17.4 (0.13)	15.3 (0.07)	21.0 (0.15)
United Kingdom	16.6	18.8	18.0	21.0	20.8	26.9	23.6	30.7	26.9 (0.09)	36.3 (0.21)	28.0 (0.19)	37.9 (0.45)	31.0 (0.10)	40.1 (0.22)
United States	27.5	28.7	28.3	29.9	29.6	30.3	31.5	32.3	31.4 (0.16)	32.1 (0.32)	31.7 (0.22)	32.8 (0.36)	32.6 (0.22)	34.1 (0.43)
Other reporting countries														
Brazil[2,4]	7.5	6.5	7.6	6.6	—	—	10.8	11.0	10.9 (0.07)	11.6 (0.12)	(†)	(†)	13.0 (0.07)	14.5 (0.12)
Russian Federation[7]	—	—	20.8	21.3	—	—	—	—	(†)	(†)	(†)	(†)	27.7 (—)	35.5 (—)

—Not available.
†Not applicable.
#Rounds to zero.

[1]Refers to the mean of the data values for all reporting Organization for Economic Cooperation and Development (OECD) countries, to which each country reporting data contributes equally. The average includes all current OECD countries for which a given year's data are available, even if they were not members of OECD in that year.
[2]Data from 1998 reported for 1999.
[3]Data from 2000 reported for 2001. Data from 2011 reported for 2012.
[4]Data include vocational degrees.
[5]Data for 1999 and 2001 include vocational degrees.
[6]Data for 2005 to 2012 include vocational degrees.
[7]Data from 2002 are reported for 2001.

NOTE: Data in this table refer to degrees classified as International Standard Classification of Education (ISCED) level 5A (first and second award) and as level 6. ISCED 5A, first award, corresponds to the bachelor's degree in the United States; ISCED 5A, second award, corresponds to master's and first-professional degrees in the United States; and ISCED 6 corresponds to doctor's degrees. Standard errors are not available for years prior to 2009.
SOURCE: Organization for Economic Cooperation and Development (OECD), Education at a Glance, 2001 through 2014. (This table was prepared December 2014.)

Table 603.40. Percentage of the population 25 to 64 years old who attained a postsecondary vocational degree, by age group and country: Selected years, 1999 through 2012

[Standard errors appear in parentheses]

Country	1999 Total, 25 to 64	1999 25 to 34	2001 Total, 25 to 64	2001 25 to 34	2005 Total, 25 to 64	2005 25 to 34	2008 Total, 25 to 64	2008 25 to 34	2009 Total, 25 to 64	2009 25 to 34	2010 Total, 25 to 64	2010 25 to 34	2012 Total, 25 to 64	2012 25 to 34
1	2	3	4	5	6	7	8	9	10	11	12	13	14	15
OECD average[1]	8.4	10.5	8.9	10.8	8.6	9.6	9.7	10.4	10.4 (0.03)	11.0 (0.07)	10.2 (0.04)	10.9 (0.07)	9.8 (0.03)	10.0 (0.06)
Australia	9.0	8.8	9.7	9.7	9.0	8.9	10.1	9.8	10.1 (0.20)	10.2 (0.39)	10.7 (0.29)	10.2 (0.52)	11.5 (0.17)	10.5 (0.33)
Austria[2]	4.7	5.8	7.3	7.4	8.7	8.1	7.4	5.9	7.6 (0.08)	5.8 (0.16)	7.3 (0.19)	5.4 (0.29)	7.3 (0.14)	5.2 (0.29)
Belgium	13.9	17.9	14.9	19.7	17.3	21.5	15.9	19.5	15.9 (0.15)	18.3 (0.34)	17.8 (0.16)	20.5 (0.36)	16.9 (0.16)	18.2 (0.35)
Canada	20.2	23.7	21.2	25.4	22.8	25.6	23.6	26.1	24.1 (0.16)	26.0 (0.32)	24.2 (0.17)	25.8 (0.38)	24.9 (0.16)	25.5 (0.32)
Chile[2,3,4,5]	0.9	1.4	1.0	1.6	2.8	4.1	8.5	11.5	8.0 (0.11)	11.0 (0.22)	10.3 (0.13)	13.1 (0.23)	5.8 (0.07)	6.1 (0.15)
Denmark	—	—	5.3	5.8	7.6	9.1	7.0	8.2	7.2 (0.11)	8.5 (0.35)	6.3 (0.10)	6.2 (0.25)	5.6 (0.09)	5.3 (0.21)
Estonia	—	—	—	—	11.1	8.7	12.0	12.3	13.2 (0.33)	14.8 (0.75)	13.3 (0.55)	14.0 (1.24)	12.6 (0.45)	13.1 (0.98)
Finland	17.4	21.8	17.5	20.2	16.6	11.0	15.0	5.4	14.7 (0.11)	3.4 (0.13)	14.7 (0.18)	2.5 (0.17)	13.5 (0.17)	0.9 (0.10)
France	10.5	15.6	11.2	16.7	10.0	17.0	11.1	16.9	11.6 (0.07)	17.5 (0.18)	11.5 (0.06)	16.9 (0.16)	11.9 (0.06)	16.1 (0.16)
Germany	9.9	8.6	9.7	8.2	9.7	7.4	9.0	6.5	9.3 (0.05)	6.8 (0.09)	9.6 (0.05)	7.2 (0.10)	11.1 (0.06)	9.5 (0.11)
Greece	5.5	8.6	5.4	7.4	6.7	8.4	6.6	9.6	6.7 (0.06)	10.1 (0.16)	7.2 (0.16)	10.9 (0.34)	8.8 (0.08)	13.5 (0.21)
Hungary	—	—	—	—	0.2	0.5	#	1.0	# (†)	1.0 (#)	0.6 (0.02)	1.4 (0.06)	0.7 (0.02)	1.5 (0.07)
Iceland	4.6	5.3	6.0	5.5	4.7	3.3	3.4	2.2	3.9 (0.21)	2.5 (0.31)	3.8 (0.20)	2.2 (0.30)	4.1 (0.21)	2.6 (0.32)
Ireland[2]	10.5	13.4	21.6	28.1	10.6	14.4	11.7	14.5	14.9 (0.10)	18.7 (0.20)	15.6 (0.10)	18.4 (0.20)	14.8 (0.10)	16.0 (0.20)
Israel	—	—	—	—	16.0	15.1	15.1	13.4	15.5 (0.14)	13.4 (0.26)	15.0 (0.14)	12.4 (0.25)	13.9 (0.14)	11.7 (0.25)
Italy	13.4	22.1	14.6	23.4	0.5	0.6	#	#	# (†)	# (†)	# (†)	# (†)	0.3 (0.15)	0.2 (—)
Japan	5.8	11.9	6.7	14.5	17.7	25.3	18.5	24.1	19.1 (0.10)	23.9 (0.25)	19.5 (0.16)	23.7 (0.34)	20.2 (0.15)	23.4 (0.35)
Korea, Republic of	6.6	8.1	6.7	8.3	8.9	19.3	10.9	23.3	11.6 (0.16)	25.5 (0.42)	12.2 (0.17)	26.0 (0.43)	13.3 (0.17)	25.8 (0.43)
Luxembourg	1.3	2.2	1.7	2.7	9.6	13.2	7.7	10.8	14.6 (0.34)	20.4 (0.87)	14.7 (0.34)	18.1 (0.84)	13.1 (0.25)	14.1 (0.58)
Mexico	—	—	—	—	1.1	1.2	1.1	1.2	1.1 (0.01)	1.2 (0.03)	1.1 (#)	1.3 (#)	1.2 (#)	1.4 (#)
Netherlands	2.5	2.4	2.3	2.4	1.8	1.6	2.4	2.4	2.8 (0.03)	2.5 (0.07)	2.5 (0.03)	2.4 (0.07)	2.8 (0.03)	2.6 (0.07)
New Zealand	13.9	10.4	15.3	11.6	7.4	4.6	14.9	13.9	16.9 (0.36)	15.9 (0.76)	16.4 (0.31)	14.9 (0.64)	15.3 (0.30)	14.1 (0.62)
Norway	2.0	2.2	2.6	2.6	2.4	1.9	2.4	1.8	2.2 (0.06)	1.4 (0.11)	2.1 (0.06)	1.0 (0.09)	2.4 (0.06)	0.8 (0.08)
Portugal	2.7	3.0	2.4	3.1	—	—	—	—	†	†	†	†	†	†
Slovak Republic	—	—	0.6	0.6	0.8	0.9	0.8	0.6	0.8 (0.04)	0.9 (0.08)	0.7 (0.04)	0.6 (0.05)	1.3 (0.09)	1.2 (0.19)
Slovenia	6.2	11.4	6.7	11.6	9.6	12.8	10.8	13.0	10.8 (0.16)	11.7 (0.35)	10.6 (0.16)	12.2 (0.36)	11.7 (0.18)	13.8 (0.40)
Spain	15.6	20.7	14.7	17.1	8.3	9.1	9.2	12.8	9.5 (0.05)	13.2 (0.11)	9.2 (0.05)	12.2 (0.11)	9.7 (0.05)	12.5 (0.12)
Sweden	9.1	9.3	9.6	9.7	9.1	9.7	8.6	8.4	8.7 (0.07)	8.5 (0.15)	8.8 (0.06)	8.2 (0.13)	9.1 (0.07)	9.4 (0.14)
Switzerland	8.2	8.4	8.0	9.0	9.7	9.1	10.4	9.7	10.3 (0.17)	9.4 (0.36)	10.8 (0.11)	9.9 (0.24)	10.8 (0.12)	9.0 (0.25)
United Kingdom	8.3	8.7	9.0	9.2	8.8	8.1	9.0	7.7	10.0 (0.06)	8.5 (0.12)	10.2 (0.13)	8.1 (0.25)	10.0 (0.06)	7.7 (0.12)
United States	—	—	—	—	9.4	9.0	9.6	9.6	9.8 (0.08)	8.9 (0.15)	10.0 (0.12)	9.5 (0.22)	10.4 (0.12)	9.9 (0.20)
Other reporting countries														
Russian Federation[6]	—	—	33.5	34.2	—	—	—	—	—	—	†	†	25.7 (—)	21.5 (—)

—Not available.
†Not applicable.
#Rounds to zero.
[1] Refers to the mean of the data values for all reporting Organization for Economic Cooperation and Development (OECD) countries, to which each country reporting data contributes equally. The average includes all current OECD countries for which a given year's data are available, even if they were not members of OECD in that year.
[2] Data from 1998 reported for 1999.
[3] Data from 2000 reported for 2001.
[4] Data from 2004 reported for 2005.
[5] Data from 2011 reported for 2012.
[6] Data from 2002 reported for 2001.

NOTE: Data in this table refer to degrees classified as International Standard Classification of Education (ISCED) level 5B. ISCED level 5B corresponds to the associate's degree in the United States. Data for the Czech Republic, Poland, and Turkey are not shown because these countries do not separate tertiary degrees at this level. Standard errors are not available for years prior to 2009.
SOURCE: Organization for Economic Cooperation and Development (OECD), Education at a Glance, 2001 through 2014. (This table was prepared December 2014.)

Table 603.50. Number of bachelor's degree recipients per 100 persons at the typical minimum age of graduation, by sex and country: Selected years, 2005 through 2012

Country	Typical age of graduation,[1] 2012	Total							Male							Female						
		2005	2007	2008	2009	2010	2011	2012	2005	2007	2008	2009	2010	2011	2012	2005	2007	2008	2009	2010	2011	2012
1	2	3	4	5	6	7	8	9	10	11	12	13	14	15	16	17	18	19	20	21	22	23
OECD average[2]	—	34.7	37.5	39.1	38.9	39.8	39.7	40.8	27.5	30.0	31.0	31.0	31.5	31.8	32.7	42.3	45.3	47.5	47.1	48.5	48.0	49.3
Australia	23	59.9	60.7	58.9	58.5	58.6	59.0	63.4	47.9	48.6	47.0	46.9	46.5	47.0	50.6	72.5	73.4	71.4	70.8	71.4	71.8	76.7
Austria	22–25	20.4	22.4	25.8	30.3	30.7	33.7	36.4	19.0	20.8	22.7	25.9	26.3	28.5	29.7	21.8	24.0	29.1	34.7	35.2	39.0	43.3
Belgium (Flemish)[3]	21	18.4	35.4	27.0	—	—	—	—	17.0	35.4	24.4	—	—	—	—	19.8	38.2	29.6	—	—	—	—
Canada	22	33.6	35.2	39.5	38.9	38.6	37.6	35.1	25.2	26.5	29.1	29.3	29.1	28.5	26.8	42.2	44.3	50.6	49.0	48.6	47.2	43.9
Chile	23–26	11.5	14.5	14.7	17.6	18.1	18.5	19.0	9.7	11.9	11.7	13.2	14.9	15.5	16.1	13.4	17.3	17.8	22.1	21.5	21.6	21.9
Czech Republic	22–26	26.0	36.4	39.2	39.7	42.3	42.8	45.2	22.6	31.0	32.2	30.4	31.1	30.8	32.9	29.5	42.1	46.6	49.7	54.4	55.5	57.9
Denmark	24–26	52.9	50.9	50.3	48.3	50.7	50.6	49.3	37.2	38.3	38.3	35.3	37.5	38.3	37.1	69.2	63.9	62.6	61.7	64.3	63.3	62.0
Estonia	22–24	28.5	27.3	23.8	22.9	22.3	23.8	22.1	17.6	17.6	14.9	13.7	14.0	15.4	15.1	39.5	37.3	32.8	32.7	31.6	32.6	29.4
Finland[4]	24	53.8	58.8	79.8	42.3	46.4	50.3	52.0	38.8	41.3	55.3	28.7	33.1	36.4	38.4	69.7	77.4	105.6	56.6	60.3	65.0	66.3
France	19–24	—	33.8	33.9	33.0	—	—	—	—	30.2	30.3	29.8	—	—	—	37.5	37.6	37.6	36.3	—	—	—
Germany	24–27	20.5	23.2	25.5	28.9	30.4	31.0	30.5	20.0	22.0	24.0	27.4	28.7	29.6	29.0	21.1	24.4	27.0	30.5	32.2	32.5	32.0
Greece	23–24	23.9	21.7	26.6	—	25.4	27.3	26.7	16.3	14.7	18.3	—	17.5	18.6	18.7	32.2	29.4	35.5	—	34.0	36.7	35.5
Hungary	21–24	41.5	38.8	37.6	39.0	38.4	32.8	29.9	29.0	26.2	25.2	27.1	28.0	25.0	23.0	54.5	51.8	50.4	51.2	49.1	41.0	37.2
Iceland	23–25	56.3	62.8	55.9	50.7	65.4	—	57.7	33.6	38.0	34.1	30.7	40.1	—	38.8	80.5	88.0	78.9	72.2	91.3	—	77.9
Ireland	21	40.7	44.8	46.0	47.1	52.2	46.8	48.3	33.3	36.4	36.9	38.5	45.3	40.0	40.7	48.0	53.4	55.2	55.4	58.9	53.5	56.1
Israel	26–29	32.9	36.1	36.3	36.4	36.8	38.5	41.1	25.7	29.1	29.6	30.8	30.6	31.8	33.6	40.2	43.1	43.1	42.0	43.1	45.3	48.7
Italy	23–25	44.8	38.7	35.8	34.6	33.6	34.3	33.1	37.3	31.6	29.5	28.5	26.9	27.3	25.9	52.7	46.1	42.3	40.9	40.6	41.6	40.6
Japan	21–23	36.9	38.8	40.6	41.5	41.3	44.8	46.3	41.3	42.9	44.9	46.1	45.4	49.1	50.1	32.2	34.4	36.0	36.7	37.1	40.2	42.3
Korea, Republic of	22–26	35.5	42.9	48.7	50.0	50.7	49.9	49.0	34.8	42.7	49.0	51.0	50.9	49.2	47.3	36.2	43.2	48.5	48.8	50.4	50.7	51.1
Mexico	23	15.2	18.2	17.8	19.0	19.5	20.9	21.3	14.5	16.8	16.2	17.4	17.7	19.3	20.0	15.9	19.7	19.3	20.7	21.2	22.4	22.6
Netherlands	23	47.2	47.8	46.0	45.6	44.7	45.3	49.2	40.2	41.7	39.8	39.4	38.6	38.5	42.2	54.3	54.1	52.3	51.9	52.2	52.2	56.2
New Zealand	21–23	49.0	53.8	50.0	50.7	47.3	51.0	54.8	36.6	41.6	37.6	38.9	36.7	37.6	40.2	62.0	66.0	63.0	63.1	58.6	65.1	70.6
Norway	22–25	42.1	45.0	46.1	44.3	46.1	46.1	44.3	28.8	31.8	33.9	32.0	33.7	33.4	32.5	55.8	58.7	58.8	57.3	58.8	59.3	56.5
Poland	23–25	45.0	46.6	48.2	49.4	56.9	60.6	55.7	32.8	34.4	35.0	34.4	40.5	42.9	36.0	57.6	59.2	61.9	63.3	73.8	79.1	71.6
Portugal	22	33.7	46.0	50.4	44.3	44.6	42.9	44.4	21.7	35.0	40.3	35.9	34.5	34.2	36.0	46.0	57.4	60.9	53.1	55.2	52.1	53.0
Slovak Republic	21–23	30.1	37.9	57.6	61.7	50.9	48.6	46.3	25.6	26.8	38.7	42.8	35.2	33.9	32.7	34.8	49.6	77.3	81.5	67.3	63.6	60.5
Slovenia	23–26	21.6	21.1	22.6	27.9	34.7	38.1	45.6	14.3	13.9	14.4	17.2	21.7	25.2	31.1	29.4	29.0	31.7	39.6	49.2	52.1	61.4
Spain	20–22	35.0	34.7	35.5	37.4	39.5	45.1	43.1	27.1	26.6	27.3	28.8	30.7	35.7	35.7	43.3	43.3	44.2	46.4	48.5	54.9	51.0
Sweden	25	44.0	42.2	40.9	38.1	35.7	38.5	35.1	30.8	29.1	27.9	25.8	23.6	25.0	23.8	57.6	55.8	54.7	51.0	48.6	52.7	50.6
Switzerland	24–26	25.0	28.9	30.6	29.2	28.8	28.0	28.7	26.1	28.7	29.2	27.0	26.7	25.4	26.4	23.9	29.2	32.0	31.5	31.0	30.7	31.2
Turkey	23–24	11.3	17.0	19.5	20.8	23.1	22.7	27.1	11.8	17.9	20.6	22.4	24.9	23.9	27.4	10.7	15.9	18.4	19.2	21.2	21.4	26.8
United Kingdom	20–24	39.8	39.0	40.2	39.9	41.9	43.4	45.5	34.1	32.9	33.5	33.8	35.6	36.6	38.5	45.7	45.4	47.2	46.3	48.6	50.6	52.8
United States	21	34.2	36.5	37.3	37.8	38.2	38.8	38.8	28.1	30.1	31.0	31.4	31.8	32.4	32.4	40.7	43.4	43.9	44.5	45.0	45.4	45.3
Other reporting countries																						
Brazil	22	17.5	22.7	25.6	24.9	23.1	25.9	26.9	13.3	18.4	19.9	17.9	16.9	19.0	19.2	21.6	27.0	31.3	32.0	29.4	32.8	35.1
Russian Federation	22–24	45.9	48.6	52.7	51.8	55.1	58.6	60.3	—	—	—	—	—	—	46.4	—	—	—	—	—	—	74.6

—Not available.

[1] The typical age of graduation is based on full-time attendance and normal progression through the education system (without repeating coursework, taking time off, etc.); this age varies across countries because of differences in their education systems and differences in program duration. In countries where the typical duration of bachelor's degree programs varies, an age span is shown. For example, if a typical program duration can be as little as 3 years or as much as 6 years, then the first age in the span represents those who graduate after 3 years, while the final age represents those who graduate after 6 years. The typical age of graduation is presented for the most recent year of data and may differ from previous years; please see previously published volumes of the Digest of Education Statistics for the typical age in previous years.
[2] Refers to the mean of the data values for all reporting Organization for Economic Cooperation and Development (OECD) countries, to which each country reporting data contributes equally. The average includes all current OECD countries for which a given year's data are available, even if they were not members of OECD in that year.
[3] Reference year for typical age of graduation is 2008.
[4] Structural changes in the Finnish higher education system accounted for much of the increase in Finnish degree recipients in 2008, as well as the decrease in 2009. Students had a strong incentive to complete their degrees in 2008. Students who did not complete their degrees in 2008 may have had to spend extra time or take additional courses in order to meet new requirements that went into effect in 2009.

NOTE: Data in this table refer to degrees classified by OECD as International Standard Classification of Education (ISCED) level 5A, first award. This level corresponds to the bachelor's degree in the United States. The recipients-per-100-persons ratio relates the number of people of all ages earning bachelor's degrees in a particular year to the number of people in the population at the typical minimum age of graduation. Some countries have two types of awards that correspond to the bachelor's degree (with different typical minimum ages of graduation). The typical minimum age for an award that requires 3 to 5 years for completion would be based on graduation after 3 years, and the typical minimum age for an award that requires 5 to 6 years would be based on graduation after 5 years. The recipients-per-100-persons ratio is the sum of all persons earning the two different award types, divided by the sum of all persons at the minimum graduation age for each of the award types. Data for Luxembourg are not shown because students generally attend no more than 1 year of higher education in Luxembourg and must complete their degrees in other countries.
SOURCE: Organization for Economic Cooperation and Development (OECD), Education at a Glance, 2006 through 2014; and Online Education Database, retrieved November 26, 2014, from http://stats.oecd.org/Index.aspx. (This table was prepared December 2014.)

Table 603.60. Percentage of bachelor's and higher degrees awarded to women, by field of study and country: 2012

Country	All fields[1]	Education	Humanities and arts	Health and welfare	Social sciences, business, and law	Personal, transport, environmental protection, and security services	Engineering, manufacturing, and construction	Sciences, mathematics, and computer science Total	Life sciences	Physical sciences	Mathematics and statistics	Computer science	Agriculture
1	2	3	4	5	6	7	8	9	10	11	12	13	14
OECD average[2]	58.0	77.2	65.8	74.9	58.1	52.7	27.0	41.3	63.0	43.2	46.1	20.0	54.9
Australia[3]	57.6	75.4	64.2	75.0	55.6	54.9	24.2	38.1	55.4	48.4	38.9	20.3	56.8
Austria	55.3	80.4	68.4	67.8	57.7	41.7	24.9	36.3	69.1	31.9	36.9	15.7	63.7
Belgium	55.3	75.9	64.8	66.7	59.6	39.2	25.6	34.8	53.2	32.7	40.0	9.8	57.4
Canada[3]	59.6	75.3	63.8	82.4	57.9	59.2	23.4	48.6	61.4	43.4	41.1	19.0	58.1
Chile	56.3	70.1	60.9	69.9	51.8	48.9	27.2	30.1	54.5	39.7	34.3	11.2	47.6
Czech Republic	61.1	80.7	71.2	80.2	67.6	47.8	27.7	38.0	72.0	46.4	53.5	12.2	59.5
Denmark	59.2	73.1	66.2	80.0	54.9	28.7	32.6	39.7	65.2	42.3	47.3	26.8	69.9
Estonia	65.8	91.0	75.6	84.0	71.3	62.9	33.2	47.9	74.9	50.6	72.2	23.1	58.7
Finland	61.0	82.1	73.6	84.9	64.9	69.5	22.1	43.2	73.2	46.3	46.6	23.9	54.8
France[3]	55.8	78.4	70.9	62.4	60.6	46.6	31.1	38.0	63.6	39.0	36.7	16.6	58.0
Germany	54.5	73.3	72.7	69.9	54.7	52.8	22.1	43.8	66.8	41.9	59.2	16.7	55.3
Greece	—	—	—	—	—	—	—	—	—	—	—	—	—
Hungary	62.3	82.2	69.7	74.7	68.4	59.5	22.2	40.6	67.5	46.5	50.9	17.2	47.7
Iceland	64.8	83.8	62.6	85.9	63.6	79.8	32.6	39.2	60.2	44.3	35.0	13.1	72.7
Ireland	57.2	76.2	61.7	80.3	53.9	52.6	20.6	42.4	42.4	42.4	42.4	42.3	43.5
Israel	58.8	82.2	62.0	78.9	56.8	79.0	28.1	43.3	62.0	37.7	37.6	26.1	55.2
Italy	62.2	87.8	75.1	68.7	59.3	50.7	39.7	54.7	71.5	41.9	54.3	25.5	48.0
Japan	42.2	59.4	69.0	58.3	35.3	90.9	11.3	25.6	—	—	—	24.0	39.6
Korea, Republic of	47.9	70.7	67.0	65.6	45.2	37.3	24.2	40.1	48.7	44.0	55.9	39.4	36.0
Mexico	54.3	72.2	58.0	66.7	59.1	24.9	28.7	47.1	59.0	41.0	45.5	—	—
Netherlands	56.6	79.1	58.6	75.0	53.8	51.8	21.0	25.8	60.6	26.7	32.2	12.8	54.9
New Zealand	61.8	83.2	65.5	78.2	57.7	48.9	30.9	43.5	62.5	41.6	43.4	19.8	59.6
Norway	61.0	74.2	57.4	83.1	57.6	43.0	26.1	36.1	66.2	39.8	34.5	13.2	62.4
Poland	65.8	81.6	76.2	75.9	68.9	55.6	33.9	44.8	72.5	67.4	64.0	15.6	55.5
Portugal	60.5	81.4	60.0	79.0	62.8	51.1	31.1	56.2	72.3	48.7	62.8	22.4	58.7
Slovak Republic	63.9	77.8	68.7	82.7	69.3	42.1	31.3	43.1	71.6	54.7	44.2	12.8	50.8
Slovenia	63.7	84.8	74.6	80.3	69.3	56.0	31.1	43.8	75.0	41.4	61.6	15.0	62.3
Spain	57.5	72.2	62.9	74.2	58.7	49.0	31.4	42.4	62.0	49.4	50.2	17.0	49.7
Sweden	62.5	81.4	61.9	81.6	60.5	54.0	29.9	43.1	60.0	43.2	37.9	29.4	58.9
Switzerland	51.2	73.4	61.8	69.4	48.8	54.9	19.2	35.4	52.4	35.2	28.9	8.6	66.4
Turkey	48.4	57.5	58.6	60.6	45.4	35.3	31.6	53.9	71.0	50.3	58.2	29.3	37.0
United Kingdom	55.7	76.8	62.3	74.2	54.9	63.0	22.8	37.7	49.6	42.6	41.7	19.0	66.8
United States	57.6	77.5	59.0	79.5	54.4	54.4	22.2	43.1	58.1	38.7	41.6	21.1	52.0
Other reporting countries													
Argentina[3]	61.3	77.4	70.4	72.7	61.4	45.5	36.2	50.6	71.4	55.1	70.0	26.9	43.3
Brazil	62.9	77.2	52.6	77.4	58.2	67.8	30.6	40.2	72.6	45.8	46.1	16.6	42.6
China	49.2	—	—	—	—	—	—	—	—	—	—	—	—
Indonesia	47.9	—	—	—	—	—	—	—	—	—	—	—	—
Russian Federation[4]	60.5	—	—	—	—	—	—	—	—	—	—	—	—
Saudi Arabia	63.5	54.1	74.8	53.6	57.9	61.5	6.7	69.1	81.4	77.0	75.8	44.7	11.5
South Africa	58.7	72.4	61.8	72.5	58.7	82.8	28.9	49.6	64.0	48.2	39.0	36.6	46.3

—Not available.
[1]May contain fields not shown in this table.
[2]Refers to the mean of the data values for all reporting Organization for Economic Cooperation and Development (OECD) countries, to which each country reporting data contributes equally.
[3]Data are for 2011 instead of 2012.
[4]Data exclude International Standard Classification of Education 1997 (ISCED:97) level 6 (corresponding to doctor's degrees in the United States).

NOTE: Data in this table refer to degrees classified as ISCED:97 level 5A (first and second award) or level 6. ISCED:97 level 5A, first award, corresponds to the bachelor's degree in the United States; ISCED:97 level 5A, second award, corresponds to master's and first-professional degrees in the United States; and ISCED:97 level 6 corresponds to doctor's degrees. Data for Luxembourg are not shown because students generally attend no more than 1 year of higher education in Luxembourg and must complete their degrees in other countries.
SOURCE: Organization for Economic Cooperation and Development (OECD), *Education at a Glance, 2014*. (This table was prepared August 2014.)

Table 603.70. Percentage of bachelor's degrees awarded in mathematics, science, and engineering, by field of study and country: Selected years, 1990 through 2011

Country	All mathematics, science, and engineering degrees[1]							Natural sciences[2]							Mathematics and computer science[3]							Engineering, manufacturing, and construction						
	1990	1995	2000	2005	2009	2010	2011	1990	1995	2000	2005	2009	2010	2011	1990	1995	2000	2005	2009	2010	2011	1990	1995	2000	2005	2009	2010	2011
1	2	3	4	5	6	7	8	9	10	11	12	13	14	15	16	17	18	19	20	21	22	23	24	25	26	27	28	29
OECD average[4]	—	—	22.7	22.7	21.0	21.0	21.5	—	—	5.7	4.8	4.6	4.6	4.7	—	—	4.1	5.3	4.2	4.1	4.1	—	—	13.6	12.8	12.3	12.6	12.9
Australia	19.6	19.3	21.1	21.1	18.2	17.0	17.2	—	9.9	7.6	5.9	6.3	5.9	5.9	—	3.8	5.1	8.2	4.8	4.2	4.2	—	5.6	8.5	7.0	7.1	6.9	7.1
Austria	—	21.1	25.7	26.8	24.9	25.1	24.2	5.3	6.0	5.0	5.4	5.0	5.7	5.9	5.2	5.3	3.4	7.2	6.8	5.4	4.9	9.0	9.9	17.3	14.2	13.1	14.0	13.4
Belgium	—	—	23.6	24.7	19.3	20.0	20.9	—	—	6.4	5.7	4.3	3.7	3.8	—	—	2.3	5.2	1.7	1.7	1.6	—	—	14.9	13.8	13.3	14.6	15.5
Canada	16.4	16.7	20.0	20.7	20.3	20.0	19.7	6.0	6.5	8.1	6.5	9.3	9.1	9.3	4.2	3.8	4.3	5.9	3.4	3.4	3.1	6.2	6.4	7.6	8.2	7.6	7.4	7.3
Chile	—	—	—	22.9	18.9	18.2	17.8	—	—	—	3.2	1.5	1.5	1.5	—	—	—	2.6	2.6	2.2	2.3	—	—	—	17.2	14.8	14.5	14.1
Czech Republic	(5)	—	29.5	26.7	24.0	21.7	19.8	(5)	—	4.2	3.9	4.1	4.1	4.0	(5)	—	8.4	3.8	5.5	5.1	5.0	(5)	—	16.9	19.0	14.4	12.4	10.8
Denmark	—	—	10.5	16.3	17.5	16.4	17.3	4.4	2.5	6.8	2.4	3.0	3.1	3.0	—	—	3.1	3.1	2.8	3.1	3.7	21.7	17.0	—	10.8	11.7	10.2	10.6
Estonia	(5)	—	32.2	23.8	20.1	21.1	21.6	(5)	—	3.9	6.3	4.6	4.9	5.1	(5)	—	3.3	6.2	5.1	5.3	5.3	(5)	—	24.9	11.3	10.4	11.0	11.2
Finland	33.5	37.2	30.1	26.0	26.1	27.4	27.4	4.1	4.0	12.2	6.5	6.0	5.7	6.0	5.9	6.9	5.5	5.6	5.8	4.4	4.0	23.4	26.3	12.5	14.0	14.4	17.3	17.4
France	—	—	—	—	—	—	—	—	—	—	—	—	—	—	—	—	—	—	—	—	—	—	—	—	—	—	—	—
Germany	31.3	31.6	31.7	31.3	28.2	29.0	29.7	7.2	6.7	6.4	6.3	7.8	8.1	8.0	3.5	5.2	4.9	8.1	8.0	7.6	7.5	20.5	19.7	20.3	16.9	12.4	13.3	14.2
Greece	—	—	—	25.9	26.1	26.1	25.3	—	—	—	8.3	8.0	5.9	5.8	—	—	—	8.4	8.4	7.4	7.4	—	—	—	9.2	9.7	12.8	12.0
Hungary	—	—	12.6	11.0	17.1	18.9	19.9	—	—	1.1	1.2	2.8	3.7	3.6	—	—	1.2	2.4	4.5	4.2	3.8	—	—	10.4	7.4	8.7	10.9	12.5
Iceland	—	—	16.5	14.1	15.2	16.6	—	—	—	6.0	5.0	3.4	3.5	—	—	—	4.0	3.5	3.2	3.0	—	—	—	6.5	5.5	8.6	10.1	—
Ireland	34.1	32.3	29.3	17.7	19.4	21.6	22.3	14.1	16.9	11.5	3.5	5.9	5.7	6.0	6.3	4.7	7.2	4.4	3.5	4.4	5.1	13.7	10.7	10.6	9.9	9.9	11.6	11.2
Israel	19.7	19.5	19.0	26.7	21.3	21.0	20.7	7.6	6.8	3.1	5.1	5.0	4.6	4.1	3.9	3.8	6.8	7.5	4.2	4.5	4.3	8.3	8.9	9.1	14.1	12.1	11.9	12.3
Italy	19.5	—	27.5	23.9	22.6	22.9	22.4	7.6	6.8	5.9	4.8	5.0	5.2	5.1	—	—	3.2	2.2	2.2	2.3	2.1	—	—	18.4	16.9	15.4	15.5	15.2
Japan	12.9	16.8	22.3	20.8	19.5	16.1	19.1	2.4	3.4	—	—	5.0	5.1	5.0	—	4.5	4.3	5.4	5.7	5.3	5.1	8.3	8.9	18.9	17.4	16.3	16.1	15.8
Korea, Republic of	—	—	36.9	37.0	34.7	34.4	34.4	6.3	—	6.3	5.2	5.0	5.1	5.0	6.3	—	6.7	9.3	7.4	3.7	3.5	21.0	19.3	26.3	26.3	24.0	23.9	24.2
Mexico	—	15.0	23.0	27.3	25.9	25.6	26.9	6.7	2.2	2.2	2.6	2.8	2.7	2.5	—	—	6.7	9.4	7.5	3.7	3.5	—	—	14.1	15.3	15.6	19.2	20.9
Netherlands	21.1	—	16.2	14.9	13.5	13.4	13.4	7.1	—	3.2	2.5	1.2	1.3	1.5	1.6	1.6	1.9	4.6	4.6	4.6	4.1	12.4	—	11.1	7.7	7.7	7.7	7.9
New Zealand	19.5	—	17.8	19.9	21.1	22.1	20.6	8.2	—	11.2	6.7	8.0	8.3	7.9	5.5	—	1.9	7.6	6.0	6.0	5.7	5.8	—	4.7	5.6	7.0	7.7	7.0
Norway	12.9	—	11.6	13.7	14.2	15.0	15.4	2.1	3.1	0.7	0.8	1.9	2.1	2.1	0.6	0.5	3.4	4.7	3.0	3.1	3.4	10.2	3.2	7.5	8.2	9.3	9.8	9.9
Poland	—	—	11.6	17.7	19.0	19.2	20.9	—	—	2.7	2.3	3.7	3.9	3.4	—	—	2.0	5.3	4.7	4.5	4.4	—	13.2	6.9	10.1	10.7	10.8	13.1
Portugal	—	15.0	17.5	25.6	24.8	22.0	23.1	6.7	2.2	1.7	6.0	3.8	3.5	3.9	4.7	2.8	3.6	6.2	2.4	1.9	1.9	8.1	8.3	12.2	13.4	18.6	16.6	17.4
Slovak Republic	(5)	—	21.9	24.6	18.9	19.7	19.4	(5)	—	2.0	3.7	3.3	3.5	3.2	(5)	—	4.6	4.4	3.8	4.2	4.5	(5)	—	15.3	7.7	11.8	11.9	11.7
Slovenia	(5)	—	17.7	17.7	15.8	19.9	23.2	(5)	—	2.7	4.1	3.2	3.4	4.0	(5)	—	2.0	2.0	2.1	2.7	4.3	(5)	—	13.1	11.6	10.6	13.7	14.9
Spain	15.0	18.2	22.7	24.1	24.3	22.1	26.0	5.7	4.3	5.3	4.2	3.3	3.4	3.6	2.6	4.5	4.3	4.0	5.3	5.1	3.9	6.7	9.4	13.1	14.7	15.7	15.7	18.6
Sweden	24.0	26.4	27.7	26.9	22.9	22.1	21.1	4.1	3.9	3.7	3.6	3.7	3.2	2.8	4.7	5.5	3.7	4.0	2.6	2.6	2.6	15.2	17.0	20.3	19.2	16.6	16.5	15.7
Switzerland	23.0	22.3	25.1	24.2	20.4	18.5	19.7	5.1	10.4	6.6	5.8	6.4	6.7	5.5	3.7	3.7	1.8	4.7	3.0	2.7	2.8	8.1	8.3	12.2	12.7	11.6	10.8	11.4
Turkey	20.6	20.9	24.1	22.3	18.1	15.7	17.5	4.6	5.1	7.4	6.1	5.3	4.2	5.7	2.1	2.7	3.6	4.1	3.6	3.1	3.3	13.8	13.1	13.1	12.0	9.2	8.4	8.5
United Kingdom	—	—	28.5	26.0	24.3	24.3	24.2	—	—	12.5	9.2	9.5	9.3	9.4	—	—	5.8	8.3	6.0	5.9	5.8	—	—	10.2	8.4	8.8	9.1	9.0
United States	16.9	—	17.1	16.7	15.7	16.0	16.2	5.1	—	6.6	5.8	6.4	6.7	6.7	4.0	3.3	3.9	4.8	3.3	3.4	3.5	7.8	6.7	6.6	6.2	5.9	6.0	6.0
Other reporting countries																												
Brazil	(5)	—	—	11.4	11.0	10.1	10.4	(5)	—	—	3.2	2.9	1.8	2.1	(5)	—	—	3.5	2.9	2.5	2.3	(5)	—	—	4.8	5.2	5.7	6.0
Russian Federation	—	—	—	—	24.3	24.4	23.0	—	—	—	—	1.5	1.5	1.3	(5)	—	—	—	5.2	5.7	5.1	(5)	—	—	—	17.6	17.2	16.7

—Not available.

[1]Includes life sciences, physical sciences, mathematics/statistics, computer science, and engineering, manufacturing, and construction.

[2]Includes life sciences and physical sciences.

[3]Includes mathematics/statistics and computer science.

[4]Refers to the mean of the data values for all reporting Organization for Economic Cooperation and Development (OECD) countries, to which each country reporting data contributes equally. The average includes all current OECD countries for which a given year's data are available, even if they were not members of OECD in that year. However, if data were reported for less than 75 percent of the countries, the average for that year is omitted.

[5]Country did not exist in its current form in the given year.
NOTE: Data in this table refer to degrees classified as International Standard Classification of Education 1997 (ISCED-97) level 5A, first award. This level corresponds to the bachelor's degree in the United States. Data for Luxembourg are not shown because students generally attend no more than 1 year of higher education in Luxembourg and must complete their degrees in other countries. Detail may not sum to totals because of rounding.
SOURCE: Organization for Economic Cooperation and Development (OECD), Online Education Database, July 21, 2014, from http://stats.oecd.org/Index.aspx; and unpublished tabulations. (This table was prepared July 2014.)

Table 603.80. Percentage of graduate degrees awarded in mathematics, science, and engineering, by field of study and country: Selected years, 1990 through 2011

Country	All mathematics, science, and engineering degrees[1]							Natural sciences[2]							Mathematics and computer science[3]							Engineering, manufacturing, and construction						
	1990	1996	2000	2005	2009	2010	2011	1990	1996	2000	2005	2009	2010	2011	1990	1996	2000	2005	2009	2010	2011	1990	1996	2000	2005	2009	2010	2011
1	2	3	4	5	6	7	8	9	10	11	12	13	14	15	16	17	18	19	20	21	22	23	24	25	26	27	28	29
OECD average[4]	—	—	27.9	24.3	22.6	23.2	23.4	—	—	10.1	8.3	6.9	6.6	6.6	—	—	5.3	4.9	4.2	4.4	4.6	—	—	12.9	11.4	11.7	12.4	12.5
Australia	—	14.0	15.2	20.0	18.9	18.8	19.8	—	5.4	4.0	3.1	3.0	3.0	3.1	—	3.8	4.9	8.7	7.6	7.1	7.7	—	4.7	6.3	8.1	8.3	8.7	9.0
Austria	37.7	38.8	39.2	38.6	33.4	31.8	33.4	12.3	17.5	16.7	15.0	7.6	6.4	6.8	4.6	4.7	4.7	6.6	10.8	9.4	8.8	20.8	16.6	17.7	16.9	14.9	16.0	17.8
Belgium	—	—	19.7	18.7	21.2	22.1	21.4	—	7.7	7.4	5.0	5.7	5.3	5.2	—	3.5	4.1	4.0	3.2	2.5	3.7	—	11.2	7.0	9.8	12.3	14.3	13.7
Canada	20.0	22.3	22.4	18.8	26.0	26.0	23.9	7.8	7.7	7.4	5.0	10.1	10.1	9.3	3.4	3.5	4.1	4.0	4.1	4.1	2.2	8.8	11.2	10.9	9.8	11.9	11.9	10.9
Chile	—	—	—	8.5	7.9	10.5	8.2	—	—	—	2.2	2.1	2.8	2.0	—	—	—	1.6	2.2	2.2	2.0	—	—	—	4.6	3.6	5.5	4.0
Czech Republic	[5]22.2	12.3	21.0	26.1	26.9	29.4	27.3	[5]4.8	3.1	5.3	8.3	6.5	6.2	5.8	[5]4.8	1.5	7.9	5.6	3.9	5.7	5.1	[5]11.6	7.8	7.7	12.3	16.5	19.0	17.3
Denmark	—	—	27.8	23.4	23.3	24.5	25.2	—	—	9.8	7.5	5.7	5.5	5.1	—	—	2.5	9.2	7.9	9.0	8.6	—	—	15.4	6.7	9.7	10.0	11.6
Estonia	[5]30.6	—	28.7	23.9	27.3	28.0	28.8	[5]14.7	—	11.3	10.0	8.3	9.3	8.6	[5]5.4	4.0	2.4	4.1	5.7	6.5	6.7	[5]10.5	12.7	14.9	8.9	13.3	12.3	13.5
Finland	—	28.3	28.7	30.5	34.3	39.8	28.4	—	—	13.5	11.6	11.0	13.5	6.3	—	—	5.6	4.0	6.7	3.7	6.3	—	—	7.3	14.8	24.8	30.8	17.3
France	30.6	—	26.4	28.4	28.0	—	—	14.7	11.6	13.5	12.5	11.0	—	—	5.4	4.0	5.6	7.0	6.7	—	—	10.5	12.7	7.3	8.9	10.3	—	—
Germany	33.2	38.6	38.1	30.9	32.2	33.1	34.8	23.5	25.5	24.9	14.8	14.7	14.4	13.7	2.3	3.5	3.7	4.8	6.1	7.3	7.2	7.4	9.5	9.5	11.3	11.4	11.5	13.8
Greece	—	—	9.9	42.8	—	31.9	32.2	—	—	1.7	22.3	2.8	6.8	7.2	—	—	0.7	5.3	1.2	13.1	11.9	—	—	7.5	15.2	6.0	11.9	13.0
Hungary	—	—	9.9	6.4	10.0	9.5	14.1	—	—	1.7	1.8	2.8	2.6	4.2	—	—	#	1.7	0.9	1.3	1.5	—	—	7.5	2.9	6.0	5.6	8.4
Iceland	—	—	35.9	23.0	12.7	14.0	14.1	—	—	19.4	9.5	4.6	5.8	5.2	—	—	#	3.0	0.9	0.9	1.7	—	—	16.5	10.5	7.2	7.3	7.2
Ireland	34.5	23.1	28.1	16.8	16.3	17.3	18.9	19.5	10.9	6.9	4.1	5.1	3.4	4.3	5.8	3.0	15.2	6.3	6.2	7.1	7.2	9.3	9.2	6.0	6.4	5.1	6.8	6.7
Israel	28.9	18.6	18.1	17.9	18.4	16.7	15.4	—	—	9.2	8.9	8.8	8.2	7.5	—	—	2.8	3.2	3.2	3.0	2.7	—	—	6.1	5.9	6.3	5.5	5.2
Italy	22.6	16.7	11.7	15.9	18.4	16.7	21.2	13.8	12.7	0.3	3.5	8.8	8.2	5.2	—	—	2.8	3.5	2.1	2.1	2.1	15.4	21.2	5.7	8.9	7.4	4.7	13.8
Japan	33.4	38.3	54.4	50.9	46.8	46.4	46.6	8.0	—	9.2	8.9	8.8	9.7	7.5	2.1	1.9	5.7	2.0	1.4	1.6	1.7	45.1	44.4	41.9	38.0	34.7	34.5	34.8
Korea, Republic of	—	—	48.4	43.9	46.6	24.1	26.0	9.5	10.2	8.5	9.5	4.7	4.7	3.4	—	—	5.7	3.2	2.3	1.5	3.4	—	—	34.3	32.4	18.1	17.8	19.1
Mexico	—	—	22.0	14.7	12.1	12.7	11.8	—	—	8.5	3.3	2.3	5.8	3.3	—	—	5.7	3.0	2.3	2.3	1.3	—	—	8.2	8.2	6.9	6.5	7.2
Netherlands	—	18.6	—	21.3	15.1	15.5	14.4	17.7	4.4	11.6	7.2	4.0	4.2	4.0	1.5	3.7	1.4	5.2	3.2	3.0	2.7	9.7	10.6	—	11.9	7.9	8.3	7.7
New Zealand	22.6	16.7	20.5	16.6	20.1	20.2	22.1	13.8	12.7	11.6	7.2	9.6	9.7	4.7	4.7	1.1	1.4	5.2	4.6	4.1	9.5	3.0	3.0	7.5	4.2	5.9	6.4	7.9
Norway	33.4	38.3	22.0	25.8	19.1	19.8	21.6	17.7	4.4	14.9	7.8	4.7	4.7	5.1	2.1	1.9	5.7	11.9	2.3	1.6	3.4	23.3	27.7	2.5	3.5	6.5	6.5	6.4
Poland	—	—	—	9.1	11.5	11.4	11.3	—	—	—	—	—	—	—	—	—	—	—	2.3	2.0	2.0	—	—	—	—	11.9	11.9	6.4
Portugal	—	—	—	33.8	32.7	31.3	26.8	—	—	—	12.0	7.2	7.2	6.7	—	—	4.7	10.0	2.3	2.0	2.0	—	—	20.9	11.9	23.2	22.1	18.1
Slovak Republic	[5]	[5]	38.1	36.8	25.4	22.5	21.6	[5]	[5]	12.6	10.8	5.3	4.9	4.3	[5]1.4	[5]	—	4.2	3.7	3.6	4.0	[5]	—	20.9	21.8	16.5	14.2	13.8
Slovenia	26.9	36.0	—	24.2	18.2	22.9	17.0	[5]	[5]	—	6.4	6.1	2.4	4.0	[5]1.4	[5]	—	4.2	2.4	2.5	2.9	[5]5.7	—	—	13.6	9.7	10.9	10.1
Spain	26.9	36.0	40.5	23.7	32.0	23.2	22.6	19.7	24.8	14.3	8.0	12.3	9.7	10.2	1.4	5.9	4.0	2.8	8.3	5.5	6.0	19.9	17.1	22.2	12.9	18.5	25.6	8.6
Sweden	48.5	32.3	42.7	32.0	29.5	25.2	27.4	22.0	25.8	11.7	8.0	8.3	5.6	10.2	9.2	5.9	4.0	3.4	5.2	5.5	5.6	19.9	17.1	22.2	16.9	18.5	25.6	27.4
Switzerland	30.2	40.1	42.7	32.0	29.5	25.2	25.6	22.0	25.8	11.7	11.7	12.5	10.6	10.5	1.7	4.1	19.5	3.4	3.9	2.9	2.9	6.5	10.1	11.6	16.9	13.1	11.8	12.2
Turkey	24.0	—	25.7	21.4	18.3	16.5	25.9	7.6	—	7.6	6.7	5.3	5.0	10.2	3.3	—	3.0	5.7	3.4	5.6	3.4	13.2	—	15.2	9.2	9.9	9.8	11.6
United Kingdom	—	—	21.7	20.3	20.4	21.4	21.9	—	—	7.4	5.5	5.8	5.6	5.6	—	—	5.0	5.7	4.8	5.3	5.6	—	—	9.2	9.0	9.8	10.6	10.8
United States	14.5	13.8	13.0	13.5	13.1	13.0	13.3	4.2	4.0	3.4	3.3	3.4	3.5	3.4	3.4	3.2	3.4	3.5	3.2	3.1	3.2	6.9	6.7	6.2	6.7	6.5	6.4	6.7

—Not available.
#Rounds to zero.
[1]Includes life sciences, physical sciences, mathematics/statistics, computer science, and engineering, manufacturing, and construction.
[2]Includes life sciences and physical sciences.
[3]Includes mathematics/statistics and computer science.
[4]Refers to the mean of the data values for all reporting Organization for Economic Cooperation and Development (OECD) countries, to which each country reporting data contributes equally. The average includes all current OECD countries for which a given year's data are available, even if they were not members of OECD in that year. However, if data are available, even if they were not members of OECD in that year. However, if data were reported for less than 75 percent of the countries that were members of OECD in that year. However, if data were reported for less than 75 percent of the countries, the average for that year is omitted.
[5]Country did not exist in its current form in the given year.

NOTE: Data in this table refer to degrees classified as International Standard Classification of Education 1997 (ISCED:97) level 5A, second award, and as ISCED:97 level 6. ISCED:97 level 5A, second award, corresponds to master's degrees. Data for Luxembourg and first-professional degrees in the United States, and ISCED:97 level 6 corresponds to doctor's degrees. Data for Luxembourg are not shown because students generally attend no more than 1 year of higher education in Luxembourg and must complete their degrees in other countries. Detail may not sum to totals because of rounding.

SOURCE: Organization for Economic Cooperation and Development (OECD), Online Education Database, retrieved July 21, 2014, from http://stats.oecd.org/Index.aspx; and unpublished tabulations. (This table was prepared July 2014.)

Table 603.90. Employment to population ratios of 25- to 64-year-olds, by sex, highest level of educational attainment, and country: 2012

Country	Total population, 25 to 64 years old				Male				Female			
	All levels of education	Less than high school completion	High school completion	Associate's or higher degree	All levels of education	Less than high school completion	High school completion	Associate's or higher degree	All levels of education	Less than high school completion	High school completion	Associate's or higher degree
1	2	3	4	5	6	7	8	9	10	11	12	13
OECD average[1]	72.7	55.1	73.6	83.2	80.0	65.4	80.7	87.9	65.5	45.5	65.8	78.6
Australia	78.8	66.2	80.5	84.4	86.6	77.6	87.8	90.6	71.0	56.4	70.8	79.4
Austria	76.3	56.0	78.2	87.4	81.9	64.7	82.1	90.5	70.8	51.2	74.0	83.6
Belgium	70.0	47.6	73.5	84.6	75.7	57.5	79.8	87.2	64.4	36.9	66.5	82.3
Canada	76.4	56.2	74.8	81.7	80.5	64.9	79.9	85.0	72.3	45.3	68.3	79.0
Chile[2]	68.4	60.0	70.3	84.3	86.1	83.7	86.2	91.7	53.0	40.0	56.1	77.8
Czech Republic	74.7	40.4	75.9	83.6	83.7	48.6	84.3	91.2	65.5	36.1	66.8	76.0
Denmark	77.5	61.4	78.7	86.4	80.6	67.1	81.5	89.2	74.4	55.5	75.0	84.3
Estonia	74.9	50.6	74.5	82.2	78.2	54.6	79.5	86.4	71.9	44.5	68.9	79.8
Finland	75.5	55.2	74.6	84.4	77.1	59.0	76.9	86.9	74.0	49.8	71.8	82.5
France	71.9	55.5	73.5	84.4	76.6	63.1	77.5	87.6	67.5	48.6	69.2	81.7
Germany	78.1	57.5	78.2	87.9	83.6	67.6	82.7	91.3	72.5	50.1	73.6	83.8
Greece	58.0	47.3	57.6	71.2	68.4	60.7	69.5	75.9	47.5	34.0	45.6	66.4
Hungary	65.3	38.8	67.9	79.7	71.8	47.9	73.1	86.4	59.1	32.3	62.0	74.8
Iceland	83.5	73.0	84.9	90.6	86.7	78.2	88.4	92.0	80.3	68.4	79.5	89.7
Ireland	65.8	44.1	65.4	80.0	71.1	52.5	72.3	84.4	60.6	33.8	58.3	76.5
Israel	74.0	47.2	71.7	84.9	79.6	63.2	76.7	89.0	68.6	30.1	65.9	81.6
Italy	63.6	50.9	71.1	78.7	74.8	66.7	80.4	84.0	52.7	34.2	61.8	74.6
Japan	76.5	—	73.6	79.8	88.5	—	85.4	92.0	64.5	—	61.9	67.4
Korea, Republic of	72.5	65.3	70.9	77.1	85.8	77.4	84.1	89.9	58.9	57.6	57.4	61.2
Luxembourg	75.0	63.0	71.9	84.8	82.6	73.1	79.3	90.1	67.2	54.3	64.6	78.5
Mexico	68.6	64.1	71.9	80.5	88.8	88.4	90.5	88.3	50.9	43.8	56.3	71.9
Netherlands	78.1	62.2	80.0	87.6	84.0	74.3	84.6	89.9	72.1	51.2	75.4	85.2
New Zealand	79.0	68.3	81.3	83.9	85.6	76.5	88.0	89.4	72.8	60.9	72.7	79.8
Norway	81.8	65.2	81.2	90.3	84.5	69.2	85.2	91.7	79.0	61.0	76.1	89.1
Poland	67.4	39.8	65.4	84.7	74.8	49.6	74.3	89.1	60.2	30.2	55.4	81.5
Portugal	69.1	63.2	76.0	81.8	72.7	69.0	77.8	82.2	65.6	56.8	74.4	81.5
Slovak Republic	68.8	30.7	70.3	80.1	76.7	36.0	78.2	85.9	61.0	27.3	61.4	75.6
Slovenia	71.0	47.2	70.7	85.1	74.7	56.1	74.5	87.4	67.1	39.3	65.7	83.5
Spain	61.9	49.1	65.7	77.1	67.6	57.1	71.5	80.7	56.1	40.4	60.1	73.9
Sweden	82.5	64.0	82.6	88.7	85.2	72.9	85.9	89.7	79.6	52.3	78.6	88.0
Switzerland	83.0	68.5	82.3	89.3	89.6	77.8	88.5	93.7	76.3	62.2	76.8	83.1
Turkey	57.0	51.2	61.7	76.2	78.1	75.4	81.2	84.2	32.7	27.1	30.8	64.6
United Kingdom	76.1	56.8	78.8	84.1	82.5	66.4	84.0	89.0	69.9	48.7	73.0	79.3
United States	71.4	52.9	67.5	80.1	76.7	63.0	73.1	84.9	66.2	41.6	61.8	76.0
Other reporting countries												
Brazil	72.6	66.8	77.3	85.7	86.1	83.2	89.3	92.2	60.2	50.3	66.8	81.3
Russian Federation	77.1	49.5	73.2	83.0	82.6	57.2	80.2	88.6	72.2	40.5	64.6	79.2

—Not available.

[1]Refers to the mean of the data values for all reporting Organization for Economic Cooperation and Development (OECD) countries, to which each country reporting data contributes equally.

[2]Data are for 2011 instead of 2012.

NOTE: The "high school completion" columns include International Standard Classification of Education 1997 (ISCED:97) levels 3 and 4, with the exception of ISCED:97 level 3C short programs. (ISCED:97 level 3C short programs do not correspond to high school completion in the United States and are included in the "less than high school completion" columns in this table.) ISCED:97 level 5B corresponds to the associate's degree in the United States in this table. Also included in the "associate's or higher degree" columns are the following higher level degrees: ISCED:97 level 5A, first award, which corresponds to the bachelor's degree in the United States; ISCED:97 level 5A, second award, which corresponds to master's and first-professional degrees in the United States; and ISCED:97 level 6, which corresponds to doctor's degrees. For each country, the employment to population ratio of 25- to 64-year-olds is the number of persons in this age group who are employed as a percentage of the total civilian population in this age group.

SOURCE: Organization for Economic Cooperation and Development (OECD), *Education at a Glance, 2014.* (This table was prepared August 2014.)

Table 605.10. Gross domestic product per capita and public and private education expenditures per full-time-equivalent (FTE) student, by level of education and country: Selected years, 2005 through 2011

Country	Gross domestic product per capita					Elementary and secondary education expenditures per FTE student					Higher education expenditures per FTE student				
	2005	2008	2009	2010	2011	2005	2008	2009	2010	2011	2005	2008	2009	2010	2011
1	2	3	4	5	6	7	8	9	10	11	12	13	14	15	16
						Current dollars									
OECD average[1]	$28,772	$33,886	$33,206	$33,471	$35,276	$6,751	$8,180	$8,632	$8,501	$8,789	$11,342	$13,391	$13,707	$13,211	$13,619
Australia	33,983	39,532	39,971	40,801	43,208	7,142	7,814	9,139	9,603	9,383	14,579	15,043	16,074	15,142	16,267
Austria	34,107	39,849	38,834	40,411	42,978	9,436	10,994	11,681	11,693	12,509	14,775	15,043	14,257	15,007	14,895
Belgium	32,077	36,879	36,698	37,878	40,093	7,306	9,706	9,783	10,123	10,722	11,960	15,020	15,443	15,179	15,420
Canada	—	38,522	40,136	37,480	—	7,774[2]	8,997[2]	9,774[2]	10,078[2]	—	22,810[3,4]	20,903[3]	22,475[3]	23,226[3]	—
Chile	12,635	14,106	14,578	15,107	17,312	2,099	2,245	2,635	2,935	3,203	6,873	6,829	6,829	6,863	7,101
Czech Republic	20,280	25,845	25,614	25,364	27,046	4,098	5,236	5,615	5,532	6,128	6,649	8,318	8,237	7,635	9,392
Denmark[5]	33,626	39,494	38,299	40,600	41,843	8,997	10,429	11,094	11,404	10,230	14,959	17,634	18,556	18,977	21,254
Estonia	16,660	21,802	19,789	20,093	23,088	3,736	6,054	6,149	5,984	6,055	3,869	6,022[4]	6,373	6,501	7,868
Finland	30,468	37,795	35,848	36,030	38,611	6,610	8,068	8,314	8,591	9,180	12,285	15,402	16,569	16,714	18,002
France	29,644	34,233	33,724	34,395	36,391	7,456	8,559	8,861	9,070	9,329	10,995	14,079	14,642	15,067	15,375
Germany	30,496	37,171	36,048	37,661	40,990	7,039	7,859	8,534	—	9,521	12,446	15,390	15,711	—	16,723
Greece	25,472	29,920	29,381	27,539	26,622	5,493[2]	—	—	—	—	6,130	7,327	8,518	8,745	9,210
Hungary[3]	17,014	20,700	20,154	20,625	22,413	4,027	4,626	4,506	4,555	4,527	9,474[5]	10,429	9,939	8,728	8,612
Iceland	35,571	39,029	36,718	35,509	38,224	8,815	8,915[3]	9,615[3]	9,638[3]	9,830[3]	10,468	16,284[3]	16,420[3]	16,008[3]	16,095[3]
Ireland	38,061	42,644	39,750	41,000	42,943	6,411	9,745	9,309	8,592	9,326	10,919	12,568	11,214	10,730	11,554
Israel	21,474	27,690	27,454	26,552	30,168	5,041	5,780	5,464	5,692	6,277	8,026[3]	9,553	9,562	9,580	9,990
Italy	27,750	33,271	32,397	32,110	33,870	7,410[3]	9,071[3]	8,943[3]	8,489[3]	8,534[3]	12,326	14,890	15,957	16,015	16,446
Japan[5]	30,290	33,902	32,324	35,238	34,967	7,343	8,301	8,502	9,168	9,102	7,606	9,081	9,513	9,972	9,927
Korea, Republic of	21,342	26,877	27,171	28,829	29,035	5,638	6,723	8,122	7,396	7,652	—	—	—	—	—
Luxembourg	69,984	89,732	82,972	84,672	88,668	15,930[2,3]	16,909	18,018	19,050	19,600	—	—	—	—	—
Mexico	11,299	15,190	14,397	15,195	17,125	2,025	2,284	2,339	2,464	2,765	6,402	7,504	8,020	7,872	7,889
Netherlands	34,724	42,887	41,089	41,682	43,150	7,045	9,251	10,030	10,075	10,268	13,883	17,245	17,849	17,161	17,549
New Zealand	24,882	29,231	29,204	29,629	31,487	5,659	6,496	7,556	7,681	8,831	10,262	10,526	10,619	10,418	10,582
Norway	47,620	43,659	54,708	44,825	46,696	9,975	12,070	12,971	13,067	13,219	15,552	18,942	19,269	18,512	18,840
Poland[3]	13,573	18,062	18,910	20,034	21,753	3,165	4,682	5,167	5,693	6,066	5,593	7,063	7,776	8,866	9,659
Portugal[3]	19,967	24,962	24,935	25,519	25,672	5,646	6,276	7,288	7,419	7,282	8,787	10,373	10,481	10,578	9,640
Slovak Republic[6]	15,881	23,205	22,620	23,194	25,130	2,740	4,006	4,781	5,066	5,105	5,783	6,560	6,758	6,904	8,177
Slovenia	23,043	29,241	27,150	26,649	28,156	7,065	8,555	8,670	8,505	8,867	8,573	9,263	9,311	9,693	10,413
Spain	27,270	33,173	32,146	31,574	32,157	6,411	8,522	8,818	8,479	8,476	10,089	13,366	13,614	13,373	13,173
Sweden	32,770	39,321	37,192	39,251	41,761	7,861	9,524	9,709	10,044	10,548	15,946	20,014	19,961	19,562	20,818
Switzerland[8]	35,500	45,517	44,773	48,962	51,582	10,721	13,775	13,411	13,510	14,623	21,734	21,648	21,577	21,893	22,882
Turkey	—	14,963	14,442	15,775	17,781	—	—	—	2,020	2,501	—	—	—	—	8,193
United Kingdom	31,580	36,817	34,483	35,299	33,886	6,888	9,169	9,602	9,980	9,738	13,506	15,310	16,338	15,862	14,223
United States	41,674	46,901	45,087	46,548	49,321	9,771	11,107	11,818	11,826	11,841	23,435	27,499	27,066	25,576	26,021

See notes at end of table.

Table 605.10. Gross domestic product per capita and public and private education expenditures per full-time-equivalent (FTE) student, by level of education and country: Selected years, 2005 through 2011—Continued

Constant 2013 dollars

Country	Gross domestic product per capita					Elementary and secondary education expenditures per FTE student					Higher education expenditures per FTE student				
	2005	2008	2009	2010	2011	2005	2008	2009	2010	2011	2005	2008	2009	2010	2011
1	2	3	4	5	6	7	8	9	10	11	12	13	14	15	16
OECD average[1]	$34,322	$36,665	$36,057	$35,759	$36,534	$8,053	$8,850	$9,373	$9,082	$9,102	$13,529	$14,489	$14,884	$14,114	$14,104
Australia	40,537	42,774	43,403	43,590	44,748	8,519	8,454	9,924	10,473	9,717	17,391	16,276	17,454	16,177	16,847
Austria	40,685	43,116	42,168	43,172	44,510	11,256	11,895	12,684	12,492	12,955	17,625	16,277	15,482	16,033	15,426
Belgium	38,263	39,903	39,849	40,466	41,522	8,715	10,501	10,623	10,815	11,105	14,267	16,252	16,769	16,216	15,970
Canada	—	41,680	43,582	40,042	—	9,273[2]	9,734[2]	10,613[2]	10,766[2]	—	27,209[3,4]	22,617[3]	24,405[3]	24,813[3]	—
Chile	15,072	15,263	15,829	16,139	17,929	2,504	2,429	2,861	3,136	3,317	8,198	7,389	7,415	7,332	7,354
Czech Republic	24,192	27,964	27,814	27,097	28,010	4,888	5,666	6,098	5,910	6,347	7,931	9,000	8,944	8,157	9,727
Denmark[5]	40,112	42,733	41,587	43,375	43,334	10,732	11,284	12,047	12,183	10,595	17,844	19,080	20,149	20,274	22,011
Estonia	19,873	23,590	21,488	21,466	23,911	4,457	6,550	6,677	6,393	6,271	4,615	6,516[4]	6,920	6,945	8,148
Finland	36,345	40,894	38,926	38,492	39,987	7,885	8,730	9,028	9,178	9,507	14,654	16,665	17,991	17,856	18,643
France	35,362	37,040	36,619	36,745	37,688	8,895	9,261	9,622	9,689	9,662	13,116	15,233	15,899	16,097	15,923
Germany	36,377	40,219	39,143	40,234	42,451	8,396	8,503	9,267	—	9,860	14,846	16,652	17,060	—	17,319
Greece	30,385	32,373	31,904	29,421	27,571	6,553[2]	—	—	—	—	7,313	—	—	—	—
Hungary[3]	20,296	22,397	21,885	22,035	23,212	4,803	5,006	4,893	4,866	4,689	7,449	7,928	9,249	9,343	9,538
Iceland	42,431	42,229	39,871	37,936	39,587	10,515	10,544	10,108	9,179	9,658	11,302[5]	11,285	10,792	9,324	8,919
Ireland	45,401	46,141	43,163	43,802	44,473	7,647	9,646[3]	10,441[3]	10,296[3]	10,180[3]	12,487	17,619[3]	17,830[3]	17,102[3]	16,669[3]
Israel	25,616	29,961	29,812	28,367	31,243	6,013	6,254	5,933	6,081	6,501	13,025	13,599	12,177	11,463	11,966
Italy	33,102	35,999	35,179	34,304	35,077	8,839[3]	9,815[3]	9,711[3]	9,069[3]	8,838[3]	9,574[3]	10,337	10,382	10,234	10,346
Japan[5]	36,132	36,682	35,100	37,646	36,213	8,760	8,981	9,231	9,794	9,427	14,703	16,111	17,327	17,109	17,082
Korea, Republic of	25,458	29,080	29,504	30,799	30,070	6,726	7,274	8,820	7,902	7,924	9,073	9,826	10,330	10,653	10,280
Luxembourg	83,482	97,090	90,096	90,458	91,829	19,003[2,3]	18,296	19,565	20,352	20,298					
Mexico	13,478	16,435	15,634	16,233	17,735	2,416	2,471	2,540	2,632	2,863	7,637	8,119	8,709	8,410	8,170
Netherlands	41,421	46,404	44,617	44,530	44,688	8,404	10,010	10,892	10,764	10,634	16,560	18,659	19,382	18,334	18,175
New Zealand	29,680	31,628	31,712	31,654	32,609	6,751	7,028	8,205	8,206	9,146	12,241	11,389	11,531	11,130	10,959
Norway	56,805	47,239	59,405	47,889	48,360	11,899	13,060	14,084	13,960	13,690	18,552	20,495	20,923	19,777	19,512
Poland[3]	16,191	19,543	20,534	21,403	22,528	3,775	5,065	5,610	6,082	6,282	6,671	7,642	8,444	9,472	10,003
Portugal[3]	23,818	27,009	27,076	27,263	26,587	6,735	6,790	7,914	7,926	7,541	10,482	11,223	11,380	11,301	9,983
Slovak Republic[6]	18,944	25,108	24,562	24,779	26,025	3,268	4,335	5,191	5,413	5,287	6,899	7,098	7,338	7,375	8,469
Slovenia	27,488	31,638	29,481	28,470	29,159	8,427	9,257	9,415	9,086	9,183	10,226	10,022	10,111	10,355	10,785
Spain	32,530	35,893	34,906	33,731	33,303	7,647	9,221	9,575	9,058	8,778	12,035	14,462	14,783	14,287	13,642
Sweden	39,090	42,546	40,385	41,934	43,250	9,378	10,305	10,543	10,731	10,924	19,022	21,655	21,675	20,899	21,560
Switzerland[3]	42,346	49,249	48,617	52,308	53,421	12,788	14,905	14,562	14,434	15,145	25,926	23,423	23,430	23,389	23,697
Turkey	—	16,189	15,682	16,853	18,415	—	—	—	2,158	2,590	—	—	—	—	8,485
United Kingdom	37,671	39,836	37,444	37,711	35,094	8,217	9,921	10,427	10,662	10,085	16,111	16,565	17,741	16,946	14,730
United States	49,712	50,747	48,959	49,729	51,079	11,655	12,018	12,832	12,634	12,263	27,955	29,754	29,390	27,324	26,949

—Not available.
[1] Refers to the mean of the data values for all reporting Organization for Economic Cooperation and Development (OECD) countries, to which each country reporting data contributes equally. The average includes all current OECD countries for which a given year's data are available, even if they were not members of OECD in that year.
[2] Includes preprimary education.
[3] Public institutions only.
[4] Excludes occupation-specific education corresponding to that offered at the vocational associate's degree level in the United States.
[5] Postsecondary non-higher-education included in both secondary and higher education.
[6] Occupation-specific education corresponding to that offered at the vocational associate's degree level in the United States is included under elementary and secondary education instead of under higher education.

NOTE: Includes all expenditures by public and private education institutions (such as administration, instruction, ancillary services for students and families, and research and development) unless otherwise noted. Expenditures for International Standard Classification of Education (ISCED) level 4 (postsecondary non-higher-education) are included in elementary and secondary education unless otherwise noted. Data for Canada, France, Greece, Italy, Luxembourg, Portugal, and the United States do not include postsecondary non-higher-education. Data adjusted to U.S. dollars using the purchasing power parity (PPP) index. Constant dollars based on the Consumer Price Index, prepared by the Bureau of Labor Statistics, U.S. Department of Labor.
SOURCE: Organization for Economic Cooperation and Development (OECD), Education at a Glance, 2008 through 2014. (This table was prepared August 2014.)

Table 605.20. Public and private direct expenditures on education institutions as a percentage of gross domestic product, by level of education and country: Selected years, 1995 through 2011

	All institutions (including preprimary education and subsidies to households, not separately shown)								Elementary and secondary institutions (excludes preprimary unless otherwise noted)								Higher education institutions							
	Public direct expenditures					Direct expenditures, 2011			Public direct expenditures					Direct expenditures, 2011			Public direct expenditures					Direct expenditures, 2011		
Country	1995	2000[1]	2005[1]	2009[1]	2010[1]	Public[1]	Private	Total	1995	2001[1]	2005[1]	2009[1]	2010[1]	Public[1]	Private	Total	1995	2001[1]	2005[1]	2009[1]	2010[1]	Public[1]	Private	Total
1	2	3	4	5	6	7	8	9	10	11	12	13	14	15	16	17	18	19	20	21	22	23	24	25
OECD average[2]	4.9	4.9	5.0	5.4	5.4	5.3	0.9	6.1	3.5	3.4	3.5	3.7	3.7	3.6	0.3	3.8	0.9	1.0	1.0	1.1	1.1	1.1	0.5	1.6
Australia	4.5	4.6	4.3	4.5	4.6	4.3	1.5	5.8	3.2	3.7	3.4	3.6	3.7	3.5	0.6	4.1	1.2	0.8	0.8	0.7	0.8	0.7	0.9	1.6
Austria	5.3	5.4[3]	5.2	5.7	5.6	5.5	0.2	5.7	3.8	3.7[3]	3.5	3.8	3.5	3.5	0.1	3.6	0.9	1.2[3]	1.2	1.4	1.5	1.4	0.1	1.5
Belgium	5.0	5.1	6.4	6.4	6.4	6.4	0.2	6.6	3.4	3.4[4]	3.9	4.3	4.3	4.3	0.1	4.4	0.9	1.2[4]	1.2	1.4	1.4	1.3	0.1	1.4
Canada	5.8	5.1	4.8	5.0	5.2	—	—	—	4.0	3.3[5]	3.9[5,6]	3.4[6]	3.6[6]	—	—	—	1.5	1.6[5]	1.5[5]	1.5	1.6	—	—	—
Chile	—	4.2	3.3	4.1	4.3	3.9	2.5	6.4	—	3.2	2.7	3.3	2.9	2.7	0.7	3.4	—	0.6	0.3	0.3	0.8	0.7	1.7	2.4
Czech Republic	4.8	4.2	4.1	4.2	4.1	4.4	0.6	5.0	3.4	2.8[4]	2.7	2.6	2.6	2.6	0.3	2.9	0.7	0.8[4]	0.8	1.0	1.0	1.2	0.3	1.4
Denmark	6.5	6.4[3]	6.8	7.5	7.6	7.5	0.4	7.9	4.2	4.1[3]	4.4	4.7	4.7	4.3	0.1	4.4	1.3	1.5[3,7]	1.6[7]	1.8[7]	1.8[7]	1.8[7]	0.1[7]	1.9[7]
Estonia	—	—	4.7	5.9	5.6	5.2	0.3	5.5	—	—	3.3	4.1	3.9	3.3	#	3.4	—	—	—	—	—	1.4	0.3	1.7
Finland	6.6	5.5	5.9	6.3	6.4	6.3	0.1	6.5	4.2	3.5	3.8	4.1	4.1	4.1	#	4.1	1.7	1.7	1.7	1.8	1.9	1.9	0.1	1.9
France	5.8	5.7	5.6	5.8	5.8	5.6	0.5	6.1	4.1	4.0	3.8	3.8	3.8	3.7	0.3	3.9	1.0	1.0	1.1	1.3	1.3	1.3	0.2	1.5
Germany	4.5	4.3	4.2	4.5	—	4.4	0.7	5.1	2.9	2.9	2.8	2.9	—	2.8	0.4	3.1	1.0	1.0	0.9	1.1	—	1.1	0.2	1.3
Greece	3.7	3.7[3]	4.0	—	—	—	—	—	2.8	2.7[3,6]	2.5[6]	—	—	—	—	—	0.8	0.9[3]	1.4	1.0	0.8	—	—	—
Hungary	4.9	4.4	5.1	4.8	4.6	4.4	0.7	—	3.3	2.8	3.3	3.0	2.8	2.6	0.2	—	0.8	0.9	0.9	1.0	1.1	1.0	0.1	1.2
Iceland	4.5	5.7[3]	7.2	7.3	7.0	6.9	0.5	7.7	3.4	4.6[3]	5.2	5.0	4.7	4.7	0.2	4.9	0.7	0.8[3]	1.1[7]	1.3	1.3	1.1	0.3	1.5
Ireland	4.7	4.1	4.3	6.0	6.0	5.7	0.5	6.2	3.3	2.9[4]	3.3	4.6	4.6	4.4	0.4	4.6	0.9	1.2[4]	1.0	1.4	—	1.2	0.5	1.7
Israel	4.5	6.6	6.2	5.9	5.9	5.6	1.7	7.3	—	4.5	4.2	3.8	4.0	3.8	0.4	4.2	—	1.1	1.0	1.0	1.0	0.9	0.8	1.7
Italy	3.6	4.5	4.3	4.5	4.3	4.2	0.4	4.6	3.2	3.2	3.2	3.3	3.1	3.0	0.1	3.1	0.7	0.7	0.6	0.7	0.8	0.8	0.2	1.0
Japan	3.6	3.5	3.4	3.6	3.6	3.6	1.6	5.1	2.8	2.7	2.6	2.7	2.8	2.7	0.2	2.9	0.4	0.5[7]	0.5[7]	0.5[7]	0.5[7]	0.5[7]	1.0[7]	1.6[7]
Korea, Republic of	4.3	4.3	4.3	4.9	4.8	4.9	2.8	7.6	3.0	3.3	3.4	3.6	3.4	3.4	0.8	4.1	0.3	0.6	0.6	0.7	0.7	0.7	1.9	2.6
Luxembourg	—	—	—	—	—	—	—	—	4.2	—	3.7[6]	3.2	3.4	3.3	0.1	3.4	0.1	—	—	—	—	—	—	—
Mexico	4.6	4.7	5.3	5.0	5.1	5.0	1.1	6.2	3.4	3.3	3.7	3.3	3.4	3.3	0.6	4.0	0.8	0.8	0.9	1.0	1.0	0.9	0.4	1.3
Netherlands	4.6	4.3	4.6	5.3	5.4	5.3	0.9	6.2	3.0	3.0	3.3	3.7	3.7	3.6	0.4	4.0	1.1	1.0	1.0	1.1	1.3	1.3	0.5	1.8
New Zealand	5.3	5.8	5.2	6.1	6.0	6.3	1.2	7.5	3.6	4.6	4.0	4.5	4.4	4.8	0.6	5.4	1.1	0.9	0.9	1.3	1.3	1.0	0.5	1.5
Norway	6.8	5.8	5.7	6.1	7.5	7.3	0.2	7.5	4.1	3.6	3.8	4.2	5.1	4.9	0.2	5.1	1.5	1.2	1.3	1.3	1.6	1.6	0.1	1.7
Poland	5.2	5.2[3]	5.4	5.0	5.0	4.8	0.7	5.5	3.3	3.7[3]	3.7	3.5	3.4	3.2	0.2	3.4	0.8	0.8[3]	1.2	1.1	1.0	1.0	0.4	1.3
Portugal	5.4	5.6[3]	5.3	5.5	5.4	5.1	0.4	5.5	4.1	4.1[3]	3.8	4.0	3.9	3.7	#	3.7	1.0	1.0[3]	0.9	1.0[7,8]	0.7[8]	1.0	0.2[8]	1.4
Slovak Republic	4.6	4.0[3]	3.7	4.1	4.0	3.8	0.5	4.4	—	2.7[3,4,8]	2.5[8]	2.7[8]	2.8[8]	2.5	0.3	2.8	—	0.7[3,4,8]	0.7[8]	1.1	1.1	0.8[8]	0.3	1.0[8]
Slovenia	—	—	5.9	5.3	5.2	5.3	0.7	5.9	—	—	3.9	3.6	3.6	3.5	0.3	3.8	—	—	1.0	1.1	1.1	1.1	0.3	1.3
Spain	4.8	4.3	4.1	4.9	4.8	4.7	0.8	5.5	3.5	3.1	2.7	3.1	3.0	2.9	#	3.2	0.8	0.9	0.9	1.1	1.1	1.0	0.2	1.3
Sweden	6.6	6.3	6.2	6.6	6.3	6.2	0.2	6.3	4.4	4.4	4.2	4.2	4.0	3.9	0.5	3.9	1.6	1.5[4]	1.5	1.6	1.6	1.6	—	1.7
Switzerland	5.5	5.3[3]	5.6	5.5	5.2	5.2	0.4	5.6	4.1	3.8[3]	3.9	3.8	3.6	3.6	—	4.0	1.1	1.2	1.4	1.4	1.3	1.3	—	1.3
Turkey	2.2	3.4[3]	—	—	—	—	—	—	1.4	2.4[3]	—	—	2.5	—	—	—	0.8	1.0[3]	—	—	—	—	—	—
United Kingdom	4.6	4.5	5.0	5.3	5.9	5.6	0.8	6.4	3.8	3.4	3.8	4.5	4.8	4.4	0.4	4.7	0.7	0.7	0.9	0.6	0.7	0.9	0.3	1.2
United States	5.0	4.6	4.9	5.3	5.1	4.7	2.2	6.9	3.5	3.5[5]	3.6	3.8	3.7	3.4	0.3	3.7	1.1	0.8[5]	1.0	1.1	1.0	0.9	1.8	2.7
Other reporting countries																								
Brazil	—	—	4.4	5.5	5.6	5.9	—	—	—	—	3.3	4.3	4.3	4.4	—	4.4	—	—	0.8	0.8	0.9	0.9	—	—
Russian Federation	3.4	3.0[3]	3.8	4.7	4.1	3.9	0.7	4.6	1.9	1.7	1.9	2.3	2.0	2.0	0.1	2.1	0.7	0.5	0.8	1.2	1.0	0.9	0.5	1.4

—Not available.
#Rounds to zero.
[1]Unless otherwise noted, includes public subsidies to households for payments to education institutions and direct expenditures on education institutions from international sources.
[2]Refers to the mean of the data values for all reporting Organization for Economic Cooperation and Development (OECD) countries, to which each country reporting data contributes equally. The average includes all current OECD countries for which a given year's data are available, even if they were not members of OECD in that year.
[3]Public subsidies to households not included in public expenditures.
[4]Direct expenditures on education institutions from international sources exceed 1.5 percent of all public expenditures.
[5]Postsecondary non-higher-education included in higher education.
[6]Preprimary education (for children ages 3 and older) included in elementary and secondary education.
[7]Postsecondary non-higher-education included in both secondary and higher education.
[8]Occupation-specific education corresponding to that offered at the vocational associate's degree level in the United States is included in secondary education.

NOTE: Public direct expenditures on education include both amounts spent directly by governments to hire education personnel and to procure other resources, and amounts provided by governments to public or private institutions. Private direct expenditures exclude public subsidies that are used for payments to education institutions. Postsecondary non-higher-education is included in elementary and secondary education unless otherwise noted. Data for "all institutions" include expenditures that could not be reported by level of education. Detail may not sum to totals because of rounding.

SOURCE: Organization for Economic Cooperation and Development (OECD), Online Education Database; and Education at a Glance, 2008 through 2014. U.S. Department of Education, National Center for Education Statistics, International Education Statistics, International Education Indicators: A Time Series Perspective, 1985–1995 (NCES 2000-021). (This table was prepared August 2014.)

CHAPTER 7
Libraries and Internet Use

This chapter presents statistics on elementary and secondary school libraries, college and university libraries (including institution-level information for the 60 largest college libraries in the country), and public libraries. It contains data on library collections, staff, and expenditures, as well as library usage. The chapter ends with a table on internet usage among persons of various racial/ethnic groups, age groups, educational attainment levels, and income levels. Tables on the use of technology and distance education in elementary and secondary schools and in postsecondary institutions can be found in chapters 2 and 3.

Libraries

Among public schools that had a library in 2011–12, the average number of library staff per school was 1.8, including 0.9 certified library/media specialists (table 701.10). On average, public school libraries had larger numbers of books on a per student basis in 2011–12 (2,188 per 100 students) than in 1999–2000 (1,803 per 100 students), 2003–04 (1,891 per 100 students), and 2007–08 (2,015 per 100 students). In 2011–12, public elementary school libraries had larger holdings than public secondary school libraries on a per student basis (2,570 books per 100 students, compared with 1,474 books per 100 students).

At degree-granting postsecondary institutions, library operating expenditures per full-time-equivalent (FTE) student were 1 percent higher in 2001–02 than in 1991–92, after adjustment for inflation (table 701.40). From 2001–02 to 2011–12, library operating expenditures per FTE student dropped 25 percent in inflation-adjusted dollars. Overall, there was a net decrease of 24 percent in library operating expenditures per FTE student between 1991–92 and 2011–12. In 2011–12, library operating expenditures per FTE student averaged $441 (in current dollars) across all degree-granting institutions. The amount varied widely by institution control, however. Library operating expenditures averaged $372 per FTE student attending a public institution in 2011–12, compared with $844 per FTE student attending a private nonprofit institution, and $78 per FTE student attending a private for-profit institution. In 2011–12, the

average number of volumes per FTE student also differed for public institutions (61 volumes), private nonprofit institutions (128 volumes), and private for-profit institutions (4 volumes). Across all degree-granting institutions, the average number of volumes per FTE student in 2011–12 was 69, which was 4 percent less than in 1991–92. The calculations of library operating expenditures and number of volumes per FTE student include both institutions with libraries and those without libraries. In 2011–12, there were libraries at 81 percent of degree-granting institutions overall, 95 percent of public institutions, 88 percent of private nonprofit institutions, and 55 percent of private for-profit institutions.

In 2012, there were 9,082 public libraries in the United States with a total of 784 million books and serial volumes (table 701.60). The annual number of visits per capita—that is, per resident of the areas served by the libraries—was 4.9, the annual number of reference transactions per capita was 0.9, and the annual number of uses of public-access internet computers per capita was 1.1.

Computer and Internet Use

In 2013, 71 percent of the U.S. population age 3 and over used the Internet (table 702.10). Comparing the White, Black, and Hispanic populations age 3 and over, the percentage of internet users was highest among Whites (75 percent), followed by Blacks (64 percent), and then Hispanics (61 percent). The percentage of internet users in the population age 3 and over was generally higher for those with higher family income levels. For example, 72 percent of people with family incomes from $40,000 to $49,999 used the Internet, compared to 85 percent of people with family incomes of $100,000 or more. Among persons age 25 and over, the percentage of internet users tended to be higher for those with higher levels of educational attainment. For example, 54 percent of persons who had not completed high school used the Internet, compared with 64 percent of those who had completed only a high school diploma or equivalent and 89 percent of those with a bachelor's or higher degree.

Table 701.10. Selected statistics on public school libraries/media centers, by level of school: Selected years, 1999–2000 through 2011–12

[Standard errors appear in parentheses]

Selected statistic	1999–2000	2003–04	2007–08 Total	Elementary	Secondary	Combined elementary/ secondary	2011–12 Total	Elementary	Secondary	Combined elementary/ secondary
	2	3	4	5	6	7	8	9	10	11
Number of schools with libraries/media centers	77,300 (421)	78,300 (548)	81,900 (634)	59,700 (492)	17,800 (414)	4,400 (239)	81,200 (510)	58,000 (418)	17,100 (357)	6,100 (373)
Average number of staff per library/media center	1.89 (0.018)	1.76	1.72 (0.017)	1.65 (0.019)	2.04 (0.039)	1.42 (0.057)	1.77 (0.017)	1.72 (0.020)	1.93 (0.027)	1.76 (0.056)
Certified library/media specialists	0.81 (0.007)	0.79 (0.009)	0.78 (0.011)	0.73 (0.013)	0.98 (0.019)	0.66 (0.033)	0.90 (0.012)	0.88 (0.014)	0.99 (0.017)	0.88 (0.031)
Full-time	0.65 (0.006)	0.65 (0.009)	0.66 (0.011)	0.61 (0.012)	0.88 (0.018)	0.49 (0.032)	0.71 (0.010)	0.67 (0.012)	0.84 (0.017)	0.69 (0.029)
Part-time	0.16 (0.006)	0.14 (0.007)	0.13 (0.007)	0.13 (0.010)	0.10 (0.009)	0.18 (0.020)	0.20 (0.008)	0.21 (0.010)	0.15 (0.010)	0.19 (0.020)
Other professional staff	0.17 (0.007)	0.19 (0.008)	0.22 (0.010)	0.22 (0.013)	0.21 (0.021)	0.18 (0.027)	0.19 (0.007)	0.18 (0.009)	0.17 (0.014)	0.27 (0.026)
Full-time	0.12 (0.005)	0.13 (0.007)	0.13 (0.008)	0.13 (0.009)	0.14 (0.017)	0.15 (0.022)	0.12 (0.006)	0.11 (0.007)	0.13 (0.013)	0.16 (0.022)
Part-time	0.06 (0.004)	0.05 (0.005)	0.08 (0.007)	0.08 (0.009)	0.07 (0.013)	0.08 (0.017)	0.07 (0.005)	0.07 (0.007)	0.05 (0.005)	0.11 (0.014)
Other paid employees	0.91 (0.014)	0.78 (0.011)	0.72 (0.013)	0.70 (0.016)	0.86 (0.027)	0.51 (0.036)	0.68 (0.011)	0.66 (0.012)	0.76 (0.021)	0.61 (0.040)
Full-time	0.49 (0.008)	0.46 (0.009)	0.43 (0.013)	0.39 (0.016)	0.60 (0.022)	0.27 (0.028)	0.40 (0.008)	0.37 (0.009)	0.52 (0.017)	0.39 (0.031)
Part-time	0.41 (0.014)	0.33 (0.012)	0.29 (0.011)	0.31 (0.014)	0.26 (0.018)	0.24 (0.028)	0.28 (0.009)	0.29 (0.012)	0.24 (0.012)	0.22 (0.027)
Percent of libraries/media centers with certain media equipment										
Automated catalog	72.8 (0.69)	82.7 (0.66)	87.2 (0.71)	87.5 (0.94)	90.6 (1.08)	69.8 (2.88)	88.3 (0.49)	89.1 (0.60)	90.3 (0.78)	74.4 (2.16)
Automated circulation system	74.4 (0.65)	86.9 (0.61)	89.5 (0.68)	89.9 (0.87)	92.6 (0.98)	72.4 (3.15)	90.3 (0.47)	91.7 (0.59)	90.1 (0.75)	77.8 (2.17)
Media retrieval system[1]	—	—	34.9 (1.05)	35.9 (1.33)	35.1 (1.66)	20.6 (2.32)	32.5 (0.76)	33.6 (0.99)	32.3 (0.91)	22.4 (1.92)
Connection to Internet	90.1 (0.57)	95.1 (0.35)	96.7 (0.40)	96.5 (0.51)	98.6 (0.51)	91.6 (1.90)	95.9 (0.34)	96.2 (0.46)	97.3 (0.49)	89.6 (1.82)
Digital video disc (DVD) player/video cassette recorder (VCR)	—	87.8 (0.60)	87.2 (0.77)	86.7 (1.02)	89.6 (1.00)	84.5 (2.20)	83.2 (0.76)	82.8 (0.98)	86.7 (0.76)	77.7 (2.00)
Disability assistance technologies, such as TDD	—	11.9 (0.50)	23.9 (1.05)	23.0 (1.33)	26.4 (1.34)	25.9 (2.76)	31.0 (0.75)	29.9 (0.94)	34.3 (1.02)	31.9 (1.95)
Percent of libraries/media centers with certain services										
Students permitted to check out laptops	—	—	27.5 (1.02)	26.9 (1.27)	29.8 (1.34)	26.1 (2.57)	40.2 (0.69)	39.3 (0.85)	42.4 (1.08)	41.8 (2.67)
Staff permitted to check out laptops	—	—	45.9 (1.07)	45.2 (1.35)	50.1 (1.50)	38.5 (2.85)	54.3 (0.85)	53.9 (0.99)	55.5 (1.23)	54.2 (2.43)
Number of library computer workstations per 100 students	—	2.3 (0.04)	2.6 (0.05)	2.5 (0.07)	2.9 (0.06)	3.0 (0.17)	3.1 (0.05)	2.8 (0.06)	3.6 (0.08)	3.3 (0.23)
Number of holdings per 100 students at the end of the school year[2]										
Books (number of volumes)	1,803 (19.7)	1,891 (45.1)	2,015 (30.5)	2,316 (40.2)	1,432 (36.6)	2,439 (132.3)	2,188 (42.4)	2,570 (58.5)	1,474 (24.7)	2,066 (87.3)
Audio and video materials	59 (0.9)	80 (3.7)	90 (3.8)	93 (5.6)	81 (5.2)	107 (13.3)	81 (2.4)	85 (3.3)	71 (2.9)	97 (8.3)
Number of additions per 100 students during the school year[2]										
Books (number of volumes)	—	99.3 (2.08)	95.3 (2.21)	113.3 (3.26)	62.1 (2.67)	103.4 (7.41)	89.4 (3.47)	104.8 (5.45)	58.9 (2.08)	92.5 (6.54)
Audio and video materials	—	5.1 (0.19)	5.4 (0.49)	5.9 (0.77)	4.5 (0.41)	5.7 (0.84)	4.3 (0.37)	3.8 (0.32)	4.2 (0.70)	8.2 ! (3.28)
Expenditures for library/media materials per pupil[2] in current dollars										
Total[3]	$23.37 (0.438)	$16.24 (0.322)	$16.11 (0.461)	$16.18 (0.591)	$15.90 (0.647)	$17.00 (1.216)	$16.00 (0.691)	$16.48 (1.099)	$14.80 (0.584)	$17.26 (1.215)
Books	9.97 (0.153)	10.99 (0.299)	11.40 (0.291)	11.99 (0.389)	10.26 (0.504)	12.10 (1.094)	10.28 (0.343)	10.73 (0.480)	9.41 (0.526)	10.27 (0.830)
Audio and video materials	1.66 (0.032)	1.14 (0.045)	1.08 (0.055)	1.06 (0.088)	1.11 (0.054)	1.16 (0.152)	0.84 (0.072)	0.80 (0.113)	0.89 (0.062)	0.89 (0.131)
Current serial subscriptions	1.26 (0.016)	1.38 (0.025)	—	—	—	—	—	—	—	—
Electronic subscriptions	0.81 (0.018)	0.88 (0.033)	— (†)	— (†)	— (†)	— (†)	— (†)	— (†)	— (†)	— (†)
Expenditures for library/media materials per pupil[2] in constant 2012–13 dollars[4]										
Total[3]	$31.94 (0.599)	$20.19 (0.400)	$17.60 (0.503)	$17.68 (0.645)	$17.38 (0.707)	$18.57 (1.329)	$16.27 (0.703)	$16.76 (1.117)	$15.04 (0.593)	$17.54 (1.235)
Books	13.62 (0.209)	13.66 (0.371)	12.46 (0.319)	13.10 (0.425)	11.22 (0.551)	13.23 (1.196)	10.45 (0.349)	10.91 (0.488)	9.57 (0.534)	10.44 (0.844)
Audio and video materials	2.27 (0.044)	1.42 (0.055)	1.18 (0.061)	1.16 (0.096)	1.21 (0.059)	1.27 (0.166)	0.85 (0.074)	0.81 (0.115)	0.91 (0.063)	0.91 (0.133)
Current serial subscriptions	1.72 (0.022)	1.72 (0.031)	—	—	—	—	—	—	—	—
Electronic subscriptions	1.11 (0.025)	1.10 (0.041)	— (†)	— (†)	— (†)	— (†)	— (†)	— (†)	— (†)	— (†)

—Not available.
†Not applicable.
!Interpret data with caution. The coefficient of variation (CV) for this estimate is between 30 percent and 50 percent.
[1]Centralized video distribution equipment with a scheduling and control server that telecasts video to classrooms.
[2]Holdings, additions, and expenditures are from the prior school year, while enrollment counts are from the current school year.
[3]Includes other expenditures not separately shown.
[4]Constant dollars based on the Consumer Price Index, prepared by the Bureau of Labor Statistics, U.S. Department of Labor, adjusted to a school-year basis.
NOTE: Detail may not sum to totals because of rounding.
SOURCE: U.S. Department of Education, National Center for Education Statistics, Schools and Staffing Survey (SASS), "Public School Library Media Center Questionnaire," 1999–2000, 2003–04, 2007–08, and 2011–12; and "Charter School Questionnaire," 1999–2000. (This table was prepared December 2013.)

Table 701.20. Selected statistics on public school libraries/media centers, by level and enrollment size of school: 2011–12

[Standard errors appear in parentheses]

Selected statistic	All public school libraries/media centers	Elementary school enrollment size					Total	Secondary school enrollment size			
		Total	Less than 150	150 to 499	500 to 749	750 or more		Less than 500	500 to 749	750 to 1,499	1,500 or more
1	2	3	4	5	6	7	8	9	10	11	12
Number of schools with libraries/media centers	81,200 (510)	58,000 (418)	3,000 (308)	29,700 (658)	16,600 (591)	8,600 (426)	17,100 (357)	6,400 (289)	3,100 (170)	4,600 (188)	3,000 (160)
Average number of staff per library/media center	1.77 (0.017)	1.72 (0.020)	1.76 (0.226)	1.66 (0.022)	1.75 (0.032)	1.87 (0.040)	1.93 (0.027)	1.58 (0.041)	1.76 (0.050)	2.07 (0.045)	2.63 (0.062)
Certified library/media specialists	0.90 (0.012)	0.88 (0.014)	0.90 (0.176)	0.86 (0.016)	0.88 (0.019)	0.92 (0.024)	0.99 (0.017)	0.78 (0.029)	0.95 (0.029)	1.10 (0.024)	1.32 (0.039)
Full-time	0.71 (0.010)	0.67 (0.012)	0.47 (0.171)	0.61 (0.015)	0.74 (0.016)	0.81 (0.022)	0.84 (0.017)	0.59 (0.029)	0.81 (0.025)	0.99 (0.021)	1.21 (0.037)
Part-time	0.20 (0.008)	0.21 (0.010)	0.44 (0.054)	0.26 (0.014)	0.14 (0.014)	0.11 (0.017)	0.15 (0.010)	0.19 (0.018)	0.15 (0.025)	0.11 (0.019)	0.12 (0.018)
Other professional staff	0.19 (0.007)	0.18 (0.009)	0.27 (0.081)	0.18 (0.020)	0.18 (0.020)	0.16 (0.019)	0.17 (0.014)	0.21 (0.027)	0.19 (0.030)	0.14 (0.015)	0.14 (0.019)
Full-time	0.12 (0.006)	0.11 (0.007)	0.19 (0.076)	0.10 (0.010)	0.09 (0.011)	0.13 (0.020)	0.13 (0.013)	0.14 (0.025)	0.12 (0.030)	0.11 (0.014)	0.13 (0.019)
Part-time	0.07 (0.005)	0.07 (0.007)	0.08 (0.034)	0.08 (0.010)	0.09 (0.016)	0.03 ! (0.009)	0.05 (0.005)	0.07 (0.013)	0.07 (0.017)	0.02 (0.006)	0.02 ! (0.005)
Other paid employees	0.68 (0.011)	0.66 (0.012)	0.59 (0.063)	0.61 (0.026)	0.69 (0.016)	0.79 (0.035)	0.76 (0.021)	0.59 (0.032)	0.62 (0.036)	0.84 (0.032)	1.16 (0.049)
Full-time	0.40 (0.008)	0.37 (0.009)	0.29 (0.048)	0.32 (0.017)	0.39 (0.017)	0.51 (0.027)	0.52 (0.017)	0.35 (0.024)	0.39 (0.030)	0.61 (0.028)	0.87 (0.044)
Part-time	0.28 (0.009)	0.29 (0.012)	0.30 (0.061)	0.29 (0.015)	0.30 (0.022)	0.28 (0.029)	0.24 (0.012)	0.24 (0.020)	0.23 (0.026)	0.22 (0.024)	0.29 (0.027)
Percent of libraries/media centers with certain media equipment											
Automated catalog	88.3 (0.49)	89.1 (0.60)	75.2 (4.05)	88.0 (0.97)	90.0 (1.14)	96.2 (0.81)	90.3 (0.78)	80.4 (1.72)	93.3 (1.72)	97.2 (0.73)	97.1 (0.82)
Automated circulation system	90.3 (0.47)	91.7 (0.59)	77.0 (4.30)	91.4 (0.80)	93.0 (1.07)	95.7 (0.97)	90.1 (0.75)	81.2 (1.60)	94.1 (1.62)	96.2 (0.94)	95.3 (1.00)
Media retrieval system[1]	32.5 (0.76)	33.6 (0.99)	15.9 (3.35)	27.3 (1.48)	39.2 (1.77)	51.1 (2.24)	32.3 (0.91)	25.2 (1.89)	36.8 (2.56)	38.7 (1.99)	32.7 (2.19)
Connection to Internet	95.9 (0.34)	96.2 (0.46)	88.6 (3.28)	95.7 (0.66)	97.3 (0.79)	98.5 (0.64)	97.3 (0.49)	93.9 (1.18)	98.4 (0.67)	99.4 (0.33)	100.0 (†)
Digital video disc (DVD) player/video cassette recorder (VCR)	83.2 (0.76)	82.8 (0.98)	66.0 (5.70)	83.1 (1.49)	84.3 (2.02)	84.6 (2.02)	86.7 (0.76)	83.9 (1.50)	89.5 (1.82)	88.4 (1.23)	87.0 (1.88)
Disability assistance technologies, such as TDD	31.0 (0.75)	29.9 (0.94)	20.7 (3.54)	26.8 (1.33)	33.2 (2.00)	37.4 (2.25)	34.3 (1.02)	30.8 (2.29)	34.6 (2.53)	36.8 (2.17)	37.6 (2.67)
Percent of libraries/media centers with certain services											
Students permitted to check out laptops	40.2 (0.69)	39.3 (0.85)	31.7 (4.21)	38.5 (1.52)	39.7 (2.01)	44.1 (2.02)	42.4 (1.08)	42.7 (2.07)	40.3 (2.72)	44.3 (2.12)	40.9 (2.77)
Staff permitted to check out laptops	54.3 (0.85)	53.9 (0.99)	38.9 (4.84)	51.8 (1.65)	57.5 (1.89)	59.6 (2.20)	55.5 (1.23)	52.6 (2.24)	55.6 (2.76)	58.1 (2.31)	57.8 (2.37)
Number of library computer workstations per 100 students	3.1 (0.05)	2.8 (0.06)	12.0 (1.49)	3.7 (0.13)	2.3 (0.09)	2.1 (0.07)	3.6 (0.08)	7.2 (0.35)	4.4 (0.16)	3.5 (0.09)	2.6 (0.12)
Number of holdings per 100 students at the end of the school year[2]											
Books (number of volumes)	2,188 (42.4)	2,570 (58.5)	9,505 (1472.0)	3,273 (115.0)	2,366 (101.2)	1,692 (53.5)	1,474 (24.7)	3,252 (98.6)	1,908 (74.2)	1,338 (21.2)	976 (20.9)
Audio and video materials	81 (2.4)	85 (3.3)	201 (58.1)	100 (6.6)	80 (4.5)	67 (5.9)	71 (2.9)	131 (8.7)	83 (7.3)	73 (5.4)	50 (4.0)
Number of additions per 100 students during the school year[2]											
Books (number of volumes)	89.4 (3.47)	104.8 (5.45)	423.0 ! (83.50)	126.3 (6.91)	99.5 (12.14)	73.4 (4.29)	58.9 (2.08)	124.0 (9.17)	77.5 (5.52)	50.0 (2.54)	43.0 (3.70)
Audio and video materials	4.3 (0.37)	3.8 (0.32)	10.6 ! (4.33)	4.7 (0.50)	3.2 (0.29)	3.2 (0.79)	4.2 (0.70)	5.8 (0.66)	4.3 (0.55)	3.5 (0.67)	4.5 ! (1.50)
Total expenditures for library/media materials per pupil[2,3]	$16.00 (0.691)	$16.48 (1.099)	$46.34 (7.286)	$20.40 (1.625)	$15.81 (2.409)	$11.31 (0.649)	$14.80 (0.584)	$27.69 (2.135)	$18.59 (2.051)	$13.48 (0.571)	$11.26 (1.169)
Books	10.28 (0.343)	10.73 (0.480)	32.08 (5.256)	12.82 (0.566)	9.83 (1.001)	8.47 (0.505)	9.41 (0.526)	16.28 (1.284)	12.55 (2.077)	8.06 (0.451)	7.70 (1.025)
Audio and video materials	0.84 (0.072)	0.80 (0.113)	1.02 (0.257)	0.80 (0.074)	1.00 (0.294)	0.56 (0.064)	0.89 (0.062)	1.50 (0.238)	0.79 (0.072)	0.88 (0.080)	0.77 (0.113)

†Not applicable.
!Interpret data with caution. The coefficient of variation (CV) for this estimate is between 30 percent and 50 percent.
[1]Centralized video distribution equipment with a scheduling and control server that telecasts video to classrooms.
[2]Holdings, additions, and expenditures are from the prior school year, while enrollment counts are from the current school year.
[3]Includes other expenditures not separately shown.

NOTE: Total includes combined elementary/secondary schools not separately shown. Detail may not sum to totals because of rounding.
SOURCE: U.S. Department of Education, National Center for Education Statistics, Schools and Staffing Survey (SASS), "Public School Library Media Center Questionnaire," 2011–12. (This table was prepared December 2013.)

Table 701.30. Selected statistics on public school libraries/media centers, by state: 2011–12

[Standard errors appear in parentheses]

State	Percent of libraries/media centers offering selected services/equipment							Average number of staff per library/media center[2]	Books (number of volumes) held at end of year per 100 students[3]	Books (number of volumes) acquired during year per 100 students[3]	Total expenditure for materials per student[3]	Number of library computer workstations per 100 students
	Automated catalog	Automated circulation system	Laptops for student use outside of library/media center	Laptops for staff use outside of library/media center	Media retrieval system[1]	Connection to the Internet	DVD player/VCR					
1	2	3	4	5	6	7	8	9	10	11	12	13
United States	88.3 (0.49)	90.3 (0.47)	40.2 (0.69)	54.3 (0.85)	32.5 (0.76)	95.9 (0.34)	83.2 (0.76)	1.8 (0.02)	2,188 (42.4)	89 (3.5)	$16.00 (0.691)	3.1 (0.05)
Alabama	96.0 (1.59)	98.5 (0.74)	46.7 (4.48)	59.9 (3.98)	29.6 (3.44)	97.2 (1.38)	95.4 (1.47)	1.6 (0.05)	2,114 (117.4)	48 (4.0)	7.31 (0.630)	2.4 (0.13)
Alaska	63.1 (5.91)	58.0 (6.01)	50.6 (5.32)	46.2 (5.49)	10.0! (3.22)	79.7 (6.31)	69.9 (6.51)	1.2 (0.11)	5,077 (351.4)	190 (29.7)	25.19 (3.742)	5.9 (0.66)
Arizona	77.5 (5.11)	78.5 (4.74)	33.0 (4.44)	51.4 (5.49)	35.2 (3.89)	88.7 (3.97)	78.8 (4.58)	1.5 (0.09)	1,988 (97.3)	57 (7.8)	9.60 (1.505)	2.7 (0.15)
Arkansas	97.4 (1.15)	97.4 (1.15)	29.5 (3.73)	48.1 (5.16)	30.6 (3.94)	100.0 (†)	94.2 (2.46)	1.8 (0.10)	1,880 (102.6)	96 (9.5)	16.00 (1.328)	2.7 (0.27)
California	78.5 (3.00)	82.5 (2.27)	20.8 (2.96)	40.7 (4.08)	13.1 (2.55)	93.6 (1.77)	58.9 (4.36)	1.5 (0.05)	2,065 (161.6)	75 (13.4)	10.25 (2.611)	2.2 (0.17)
Colorado	93.2 (3.07)	88.9 (3.73)	52.7 (4.25)	64.5 (4.58)	34.7 (4.91)	98.2 (0.90)	91.1 (2.64)	1.8 (0.10)	2,101 (137.0)	89 (8.4)	11.23 (1.648)	4.3 (0.30)
Connecticut	84.5 (4.76)	84.1 (4.79)	46.5 (7.41)	61.1 (6.05)	21.5 (4.98)	96.9 (2.11)	86.6 (3.83)	2.0 (0.08)	2,405 (105.1)	111 (29.0)	17.01 (1.330)	4.8 (0.46)
Delaware	95.1 (1.69)	97.1 (1.57)	41.6 (5.58)	48.6 (5.83)	24.4 (5.13)	98.2 (1.45)	81.4 (4.88)	1.2 (0.07)	2,835 (752.6)	61 (6.0)	9.41 (0.690)	3.0 (0.25)
District of Columbia	93.9 (2.05)	91.4 (2.67)	40.5 (4.01)	70.2 (4.51)	73.9 (3.17)	97.4 (0.94)	89.6 (2.88)	1.6 (0.05)	1,904 (114.0)	68 (5.9)	10.98 (1.115)	2.6 (0.11)
Georgia	96.3 (1.26)	98.2 (0.78)	51.2 (4.92)	78.7 (3.79)	73.1 (4.13)	99.3 (0.37)	97.6 (1.38)	2.0 (0.06)	1,909 (81.2)	85 (7.8)	13.06 (0.806)	2.3 (0.16)
Hawaii	75.5 (5.06)	85.6 (3.70)	9.9 (2.35)	22.1 (4.21)	24.5 (4.39)	97.4 (1.81)	81.5 (6.08)	1.6 (0.12)	2,378 (179.4)	64 (6.9)	8.45 (0.954)	3.0 (0.22)
Idaho	80.3 (3.31)	81.6 (3.25)	39.4 (4.92)	48.1 (4.94)	15.2 (2.39)	94.9 (2.41)	79.9 (4.00)	2.1 (0.21)	2,453 (206.1)	110 (17.5)	20.31 (3.342)	3.6 (0.27)
Indiana	89.7 (3.52)	88.9 (4.46)	33.2 (4.58)	50.2 (5.73)	31.7 (5.41)	96.9 (1.75)	89.6 (3.38)	2.0 (0.09)	2,486 (142.5)	84 (7.5)	14.54 (1.057)	2.9 (0.27)
Iowa	94.5 (2.53)	95.8 (1.94)	59.5 (4.38)	66.3 (4.73)	26.5 (5.18)	98.0 (1.26)	86.4 (3.45)	2.3 (0.09)	2,603 (143.2)	101 (9.8)	14.44 (1.345)	5.8 (0.59)
Kansas	92.0 (4.50)	99.2 (0.40)	58.0 (4.86)	58.2 (5.34)	28.3 (4.63)	93.9 (3.36)	97.7 (1.27)	2.0 (0.09)	3,564 (259.0)	101 (14.2)	22.42 (5.432)	4.2 (0.43)
Kentucky	91.0 (2.31)	93.0 (2.16)	34.2 (4.76)	51.3 (4.59)	56.3 (4.89)	95.0 (2.02)	92.5 (3.27)	1.5 (0.08)	2,026 (192.1)	96 (18.6)	17.68 (1.388)	3.5 (0.14)
Louisiana	83.9 (4.21)	86.9 (3.53)	48.4 (5.33)	66.8 (5.40)	31.5 (5.98)	98.1 (1.48)	85.9 (4.22)	1.4 (0.11)	1,951 (119.4)	74 (8.4)	23.54 (4.543)	3.1 (0.31)
Maine	85.6 (4.05)	88.6 (3.44)	48.1 (4.85)	53.1 (4.18)	11.3 (3.20)	84.7 (3.91)	75.8 (4.94)	1.7 (0.10)	3,393 (283.8)	109 (9.9)	22.60 (1.615)	2.6 (0.22)
Maryland	68.1 ‡ (4.03)	70.9 (4.42)	33.6 (4.95)	42.6 (5.18)	20.0 (4.09)	96.8 (1.82)	84.5 (3.77)	1.3 (0.10)	1,664 (121.0)	61 (7.5)	13.79 (2.749)	3.4 (0.26)
Massachusetts	83.6 (10.18)	87.1 (10.49)	39.9 (3.62)	51.3 (5.93)	45.9 (7.31)	95.8 (2.70)	80.8 (3.40)	1.8 (0.24)	2,085 (117.9)	58 (5.1)	10.13 (1.086)	4.5 (0.30)
Michigan	86.3 (2.85)	92.1 (2.41)	39.8 (3.67)	57.6 (4.04)	34.4 (3.13)	94.4 (0.98)	86.3 (2.82)	1.7 (0.07)	2,760 (139.9)	105 (7.8)	16.40 (2.140)	5.4 (0.35)
Minnesota	91.5 (2.33)	95.5 (1.67)	57.3 (3.97)	86.1 (2.53)	55.4 (3.83)	98.5 (1.01)	81.3 (2.74)	1.6 (0.06)	1,862 (110.5)	106 (10.1)	15.85 (1.164)	3.2 (0.18)
Mississippi	71.9 (5.72)	80.5 (3.66)	45.1 (5.00)	52.7 (4.42)	20.1 (3.43)	96.6 (1.43)	89.5 (3.43)	2.0 (0.09)			13.03 (1.871)	1.9 (0.15)
Missouri	93.8 (1.87)	97.3 (1.37)	34.8 (3.06)	44.1 (3.32)	19.8 (2.78)	98.2 (1.40)	89.2 (2.91)	1.9 (0.09)	2,624 (93.4)	106 (6.2)	21.23 (0.896)	4.4 (0.20)
Montana	77.6 (6.74)	87.9 (4.59)	34.8 (6.14)	50.6 (7.14)	17.0! (5.97)	96.2 (2.31)	93.3 (2.57)	1.8 (0.09)	3,570 (325.3)	118 (9.4)	21.51 (2.129)	6.1 (0.73)
Nebraska	90.0 (2.94)	96.3 (2.83)	35.3 (5.04)	71.8 (4.32)	33.6 (4.96)	95.0 (2.14)	92.5 (2.55)	2.1 (0.11)	3,629 (430.3)	137 (18.6)	21.64 (1.246)	5.8 (0.44)
Nevada	89.4 (3.12)	98.3 (0.96)	28.6 (4.31)	41.2 (4.77)	34.4 (3.34)	97.4 (1.78)	65.2 (5.29)	1.8 (0.07)	1,674 (65.0)	74 (5.5)	10.23 (0.490)	1.9 (0.13)
New Hampshire	91.3 (4.46)	94.4 (4.05)	58.4 (7.08)	66.7 (6.26)	7.9! (3.66)	100.0 (†)	96.1 (2.84)	1.8 (0.12)	2,134 (124.6)	81 (5.5)	21.78 (1.383)	3.7 (0.31)
New Jersey	85.7 (3.03)	86.5 (2.85)	46.5 (4.19)	45.4 (4.10)	20.7 (3.29)	96.0 (2.08)	79.9 (3.22)	1.4 (0.06)	2,172 (121.3)	68 (8.2)	15.47 (1.072)	3.1 (0.19)
New Mexico	87.3 (2.75)	86.3 (2.33)	36.4 (8.56)	65.2 (5.93)	37.6 (7.31)	95.8 (2.70)	83.7 (6.05)	1.8 (0.24)	3,057 (631.5)	95 (16.1)	19.25 (1.274)	2.5 ‡ (1.21)
New York	94.2 (2.24)	93.8 (1.67)	38.3 (3.90)	45.8 (4.46)	21.2 (3.23)	98.1 (1.23)	81.3 (2.94)	2.0 (0.06)	1,898 (97.3)	101 (7.8)	15.85 (1.164)	3.2 (0.18)
North Carolina	95.9 (2.17)	95.5 (1.67)	57.3 (4.17)	86.1 (2.53)	55.4 (3.83)	98.5 (0.98)	83.6 (2.74)	1.6 (0.06)	1,940 (97.3)	88 (10.1)	24.28 (1.378)	3.5 (0.26)
North Dakota	77.6 (5.81)	80.5 (3.66)	45.1 (5.00)	52.7 (4.42)	20.1 (3.43)	96.6 (1.43)	75.6 (3.99)	2.0 (0.09)	3,728 (230.1)	172 (16.8)		4.8 (0.61)
Ohio	91.1 (2.26)	94.1 (2.23)	45.5 (3.69)	48.5 (3.52)	42.0 (4.60)	94.4 (1.88)	81.5 (3.43)	1.8 (0.07)	1,889 (75.4)	64 (4.0)	9.06 (0.500)	3.3 (0.20)
Oklahoma	84.1 (4.75)	86.4 (4.26)	46.3 (5.72)	50.4 (5.42)	26.7 (5.71)	94.1 (2.45)	87.7 (3.89)	1.9 (0.10)	2,676 (229.2)	133 (33.8)	15.91 (2.051)	3.0 (0.22)
Oregon	90.0 (3.18)	93.3 (1.71)	35.3 (5.04)	50.4 (5.10)	28.7 (5.09)	97.5 (1.54)	74.4 (5.11)	1.8 (0.10)	2,569 (116.8)	77 (10.6)	11.28 (1.628)	4.0 (0.42)
Pennsylvania	89.4 (3.12)	91.0 (2.86)	39.5 (4.85)	46.3 (4.96)	19.9 (3.71)	92.1 (3.19)	75.7 (4.33)	1.8 (0.08)	2,302 (181.0)	81 (10.1)	16.68 (1.792)	3.3 (0.22)
Rhode Island	72.9 (5.12)	76.7 (4.20)	26.0 (5.81)	22.9 (5.38)	5.1! (2.06)	94.3 (3.60)	72.4 (7.05)	1.7 (0.11)	1,993 (110.8)	62 (9.1)	9.22 (0.978)	3.3 (0.40)
South Carolina	95.2 (2.02)	97.2 (1.55)	49.1 (4.63)	79.0 (3.80)	85.0 (3.67)	100.0 (†)	96.1 (3.67)	1.8 (0.07)	2,246 (401.6)	79 (5.9)	15.47 (1.105)	3.0 (0.24)
South Dakota	75.1 (4.80)	69.3 (5.65)	46.3 (5.49)	51.9 (6.10)	21.6 (4.22)	84.2 (5.62)	77.5 (5.53)	1.7 (0.11)	3,370 (329.1)	81 (9.3)	22.94 (1.947)	3.5 (0.45)
Tennessee	92.3 (1.98)	98.1 (0.90)	48.3 (5.01)	57.9 (4.83)	28.0 (3.68)	98.1 (1.23)	90.5 (3.57)	1.7 (0.08)	1,756 (60.8)	81 ‡ (23.0)	11.96 (1.448)	3.5 (0.21)
Texas	93.2 (1.98)	96.8 (1.28)	42.1 (3.37)	59.2 (3.89)	32.9 (3.57)	96.9 (1.41)	90.5 (2.07)	1.7 (0.06)	2,261 (250.8)	113 (12.2)	23.54 (4.438)	2.3 (0.10)
Utah	86.1 (5.81)	85.8 (5.81)	28.0 (5.07)	34.2 (5.33)	44.5 (5.72)	84.8 (5.15)	84.8 (5.98)	1.7 (0.13)	1,652 (90.6)	85 (12.2)	10.03 (0.862)	2.1 (0.18)
Vermont	84.5 (4.69)	80.6 (4.24)	58.5 (5.72)	64.5 (4.95)	11.2 (2.48)	93.1 (2.97)	90.1 (4.12)	1.8 (0.09)	4,010 (145.6)	155 (9.1)	32.89 (1.796)	4.8 (0.48)
Virginia	95.7 (2.26)	97.3 (1.38)	60.8 (3.91)	74.7 (4.14)	49.5 (4.90)	96.3 (1.33)	90.1 (3.92)	1.9 (0.09)	2,018 (78.8)	122 (24.9)	18.86 (3.017)	3.1 (0.50)
Washington	92.2 (2.67)	94.9 (2.49)	29.0 (4.20)	47.9 (4.47)	28.1 (4.08)	96.3 (2.48)	84.1 (3.53)	1.9 (0.11)	2,325 (107.8)	82 (9.4)	9.46 (0.680)	3.9 (0.27)
West Virginia	69.0 (4.92)	74.9 (5.24)	32.1 (4.40)	47.5 (5.04)	22.0 (2.80)	92.8 (3.28)	68.6 (5.32)	1.0 (0.07)	1,923 (109.9)	110 (32.3)	15.04 (0.674)	4.5 (0.80)
Wisconsin	96.0 (2.31)	97.9 (1.07)	50.4 (4.28)	63.0 (4.58)	27.2 (3.97)	98.6 (1.35)	95.7 (2.36)	2.4 (0.09)	3,125 (149.7)	159 (8.7)	37.93 (2.217)	5.2 (0.41)
Wyoming	95.5 (4.10)	95.5 (4.10)	56.8 (5.80)	51.1 (4.62)	19.3 (5.06)	98.7 (0.80)	81.2 (5.71)	1.8 (0.10)	3,714 (330.4)	211 (33.4)	32.02 (5.222)	4.8 (0.67)

†Not applicable.
!Interpret data with caution. The coefficient of variation (CV) for this estimate is between 30 percent and 50 percent.
‡Reporting standards not met. Either the response rate is under 50 percent or there are too few cases for a reliable estimate.
[1]Centralized video distribution equipment with a scheduling and control server that telecasts video to classrooms.
[2]Includes professional and nonprofessional staff.
[3]Books held, books acquired, and expenditures are from the prior school year, while enrollment counts are from the current school year.

SOURCE: U.S. Department of Education, National Center for Education Statistics, Schools and Staffing Survey (SASS), "Public School Library Media Center Questionnaire," 2011–12. (This table was prepared December 2013.)

Table 701.40. Collections, staff, and operating expenditures of degree-granting postsecondary institution libraries: Selected years, 1981–82 through 2011–12

Collections, staff, and operating expenditures	1981–82	1987–88	1991–92	1997–98	2001–02	2005–06	2007–08	2009–10	2011–12 Total	Public	Private nonprofit	Private for-profit
1	2	3	4	5	6	7	8	9	10	11	12	13
Number of libraries	3,104	3,438	3,274	3,658	3,568	3,617	3,827	3,689	3,793	1,560	1,461	772
Percentage of institutions with libraries	—	—	—	90.0	85.0	84.6	87.9	82.1	80.6	94.6	88.4	55.0
Number of circulation transactions (in thousands)	—	—	—	216,067	189,248	187,236	178,766	176,736	154,409	99,897	51,930	2,582
Number of circulation transactions per full-time equivalent (FTE) student	—	—	—	20	16	14	13	11	10	9	16	2
Enrollment (in thousands)												
Total enrollment[1]	12,372	12,767	14,359	14,502	15,928	17,487	18,248	20,428	20,994	15,110	3,927	1,957
Full-time-equivalent (FTE) enrollment[1]	9,015	9,230	10,361	10,615	11,766	13,201	13,783	15,496	15,886	10,949	3,321	1,616
Collections (in thousands)												
Number of volumes at end of year	567,826	718,504	749,429	878,906	954,030	1,015,658	1,052,531	1,076,027	1,099,951	669,521	424,671	5,760
Number of volumes added during year	19,507	21,907	20,982	24,551	24,574	22,241	23,990	27,164	27,605	17,134	9,984	488
Number of serial subscriptions at end of year[2]	4,890	6,416	6,966	10,908	9,855	16,361	25,342	25,041	—	—	—	—
Microform units at end of year	—	—	—	1,062,082	1,143,678	1,166,295	1,157,365	1,124,941	1,044,521	705,525	337,405	1,591
E-books at end of year	—	—	—	—	10,318	64,366	102,502	158,652	252,599	136,181	102,413	14,006
Number of volumes per FTE student	63	78	72	83	81	77	76	69	69	61	128	4
Full-time-equivalent (FTE) library staff												
Total staff in regular positions[3]	58,476	67,251	67,166	68,337	69,526	69,615	69,328	66,562	65,242	39,776	23,770	1,696
Librarians and professional staff	23,816	25,115	26,341	30,041	32,053	33,265	34,520	34,147	34,423	19,601	13,382	1,440
Other paid staff	34,660	40,733	40,421	38,026	37,473	36,350	34,808	32,415	30,819	20,175	10,388	256
Contributed services	—	1,403	404	270	—	—	—	—	—	—	—	—
Student assistants	—	33,821	29,075	28,373	25,305	23,976	24,110	22,382	20,509	11,288	8,498	724
FTE student enrollment per FTE staff member	154	137	154	155	169	190	199	233	243	275	140	953
Library operating expenditures[4]												
Total operating expenditures (in thousands of current dollars)	$1,943,769	$2,770,075	$3,648,654	$4,592,657	$5,416,716	$6,234,192	$6,785,542	$6,829,108	$7,008,114	$4,077,793	$2,803,864	$126,457
Salaries and wages	914,379[5]	1,451,551	1,889,368	2,314,380	2,753,404	3,102,561	3,342,082	3,401,649	3,443,831	2,060,066	1,308,607	75,158
Student hourly wages	100,847	[6]	[6]	[6]	[6]	[6]	[6]	[6]	[6]	[6]	[6]	[6]
Fringe benefits	167,515	—	—	—	—	—	—	—	—	—	—	—
Furniture/equipment	—	—	—	57,013	—	—	—	—	—	—	—	—
Computer hardware/software	—	—	—	164,379	155,791	153,002	158,698	142,652	143,660	90,583	51,050	2,028
Bibliographic utilities/networks/consortia	—	—	—	89,618	92,242	106,268	113,427	117,838	123,650	71,925	50,694	1,031
Information resources	591,550	925,425	1,240,419	1,643,914	1,990,989	2,375,485	2,663,082	2,680,298	2,790,039	1,572,279	1,172,378	45,383
Books and serial backfiles—paper	—	—	—	514,048	563,007	572,228	611,192	515,942	503,851	248,460	244,454	10,938
Books and serial backfiles—electronic	—	—	—	28,061	44,792	93,778	133,586	152,359	180,570	100,553	74,724	5,292
Current serials—paper	—	—	—	849,399	926,105	830,137	699,906	536,357	487,265	272,219	207,707	7,339
Current serials—electronic	—	—	—	125,470	297,657	691,585	1,004,393	1,249,726	1,436,671	856,062	562,111	18,498
Audiovisual materials	—	—	23,879	30,623	37,041	39,029	43,849	55,659	37,022	19,486	15,609	1,926
Document delivery/interlibrary loan	—	—	—	19,309	22,913	26,513	30,496	33,679	32,490	20,069	11,768	652
Preservation	30,351	34,144	43,126	42,919	46,499	41,102	41,591	31,212	26,838	14,382	12,392	63
Other collection expenditures	561,199	891,281	1,173,414	34,086	52,976	81,113	98,069	105,364	85,334	41,047	43,612	675
Other library operating expenditures	169,478	393,099	518,867	323,354	424,290	496,877	508,253	486,672	506,934	282,941	221,136	2,857
Operating expenditures per full-time-equivalent (FTE) student												
In current dollars	216	300	352	433	460	472	492	441	441	372	844	78
In constant 2012–13 dollars[7]	530	599	590	619	598	549	538	470	448	379	858	80
Information resource expenditures per FTE student												
In current dollars	66	100	120	155	169	180	193	173	176	144	353	28
In constant 2012–13 dollars[7]	161	200	200	222	220	209	211	185	179	146	359	29
Operating expenditures (percentage distribution)	100.0	100.0	100.0	100.0	100.0	100.0	100.0	100.0	100.0	100.0	100.0	100.0
Salaries and wages	47.0	52.4	51.8	50.4	50.8	49.8	49.3	49.8	49.1	50.5	46.7	59.4
Student hourly wages	5.2	[6]	[6]	[6]	[6]	[6]	[6]	[6]	[6]	[6]	[6]	[6]
Fringe benefits	8.6	—	—	—	—	—	—	—	—	—	—	—
Preservation	1.6	1.2	1.2	0.9	0.9	0.7	0.6	0.5	0.4	0.4	0.4	0.1
Information resources	28.9	32.2	32.8	34.9	35.9	37.4	38.6	38.8	39.4	38.2	41.4	35.8
Other[8]	8.7	14.2	14.2	13.8	12.4	12.1	11.5	10.9	11.0	10.9	11.5	4.7
Library operating expenditures as a percent of total institutional expenditures for educational and general purposes	3.5	3.2	3.0	—	—	—	—	—	—	—	—	—

—Not available.
[1] Fall enrollment for the academic year specified.
[2] For 1997–98 and later years, includes microform and electronic serials.
[3] Excludes student assistants.
[4] Excludes capital outlay.
[5] Includes salary equivalents of contributed services staff.
[6] Included under salaries and wages.
[7] Constant dollars based on the Consumer Price Index, prepared by the Bureau of Labor Statistics, U.S. Department of Labor, adjusted to a school-year basis.
[8] Includes furniture/equipment, computer hardware/software, and bibliographic utilities/networks/consortia as well as expenditures classified as "other library operating expenditures."

NOTE: Data through 1995 are for institutions of higher education, while later data are for degree-granting institutions. Degree-granting institutions grant associate's or higher degrees and participate in Title IV federal financial aid programs. The degree-granting classification is very similar to the earlier higher education classification, but it includes more 2-year colleges and excludes a few higher education institutions that did not grant degrees. Detail may not sum to totals because of rounding.
SOURCE: U.S. Department of Education, National Center for Education Statistics, *Library Statistics of Colleges and Universities*, 1981–82; Integrated Postsecondary Education Data System (IPEDS), "Academic Libraries Survey" (IPEDS-L:88–98), "Fall Enrollment Survey" (IPEDS-EF:87–98), and IPEDS Spring 2002 through Spring 2012, Enrollment component; Academic Libraries Survey (ALS), 2000 through 2012. (This table was prepared May 2014.)

Table 701.50. Collections, staff, operating expenditures, public service hours, and reference services of the 60 largest college and university libraries: Fiscal year 2012

Institution	Rank order, by number of volumes	Number of volumes at end of year (in thousands)	Number of e-books at end of year	Full-time-equivalent staff		Operating expenditures (in thousands of current dollars)		Public service hours per typical week	Gate count per typical week[1]	Annual reference information services to individuals[2]
				Total	Librarians	Total	Salaries and wages			
1	2	3	4	5	6	7	8	9	10	11
Harvard University (MA)	1	17,225	402,473	1,073	400	$134,533	$83,834	168	27,194 [3]	187,903
Yale University (CT)	2	13,504	1,090,187	600	163	81,221	35,235	111	27,194 [3]	31,783
University of Illinois at Urbana-Champaign	3	12,937	645,398	437	77	43,703	20,744	152	93,818	110,973
University of California, Berkeley	4	11,537	1,097,969	434	74	47,325	24,022	77	39,081 [3]	70,986
University of Michigan, Ann Arbor	5	11,458	1,926,938	690	186	63,828	32,553	168	114,557	211,469
University of Chicago (IL)	6	11,397	1,251,085	309	68	36,112	13,450	148	28,732	16,610
Columbia University in the City of New York	7	11,291	1,329,421	526	162	57,422	26,244	107	84,930	58,489
University of Texas at Austin	8	10,185	752,892	489	104	43,968	20,476	120	101,797	119,058
University of California, Los Angeles	9	9,981	1,288,821	527	133	50,171	27,406	96	81,905	113,725
Indiana University, Bloomington	10	9,276	1,363,894	395	90	33,371	15,259	101	64,700	138,542
Stanford University (CA)	11	9,025	841,538	653	153	69,922	31,704	105	20,491 [3]	105,636
University of Wisconsin, Madison	12	7,841	656,536	533	202	38,018	18,778	148	103,845	650
Tarrant County College District (TX)	13	7,828	83,036	73	24	3,878	2,723	84	26,583	—
Cornell University (NY)	14	7,684	903,397	468	110	45,471	21,917	145	73,193	62,429
Princeton University (NJ)	15	7,486	322,690	382	87	50,222	20,476	120	8,508	19,018
University of Washington, Seattle Campus	16	7,375	460,477	385	122	36,649	17,592	135	135,000	56,062
University of Minnesota, Twin Cities	17	6,918	484,151	355	87	39,526	17,992	107	45,000	46,021
Michigan State University	18	6,702	2,715,914	236	70	27,496	10,389	140	37,453	50,633
University of Pittsburgh, Main Campus (PA)	19	6,663	988,230	319	118	31,800	11,881	118	39,081 [3]	80,695
Duke University (NC)	20	6,540	875,488	321	114	41,043	17,127	149	95,437	80,518
University of Colorado at Boulder	21	6,510	675,723	232	62	24,263	10,114	128	66,545	57,345
University of North Carolina at Chapel Hill	22	6,437	996,453	409	130	38,135	18,921	146	90,160	84,345
University of Pennsylvania	23	6,108	1,100,111	416	137	41,535	19,601	116	31,779	6,500
Ohio State University, Main Campus	24	6,050	526,075	449	75	43,185	17,349	168	128,852	27,876
University of Arizona	25	6,030	1,184,441	194	51	23,350	8,410	142	38,585	17,247
University of Florida	26	5,611	815,537	301	90	28,657	13,434	138	53,235	44,945
Rutgers University, New Brunswick (NJ)	27	5,478	595,141	272	56	25,958	14,493	115	60,618	25,656
Pennsylvania State University, Main Campus	28	5,351	316,913	539	143	50,972	25,757	148	139,775	85,211
University of Iowa	29	5,310	772,023	221	66	24,728	9,883	116	34,623	52,416
University of Virginia, Main Campus	30	5,247	460,840	344	97	33,796	16,775	149	76,921	76,853
University of California, Davis	31	5,204	582,966	185	54	18,506	8,783	102	34,482	78,595
New York University	32	5,196	1,101,383	465	68	51,534	21,977	126	65,163	132,850
Northwestern University (IL)	33	5,140	139,418	362	111	32,029	14,629	122	21,560	23,444
University of Oklahoma, Norman Campus	34	5,139	1,168,077	142	34	17,000	4,727	117	26,456	21,693
University of Georgia	35	4,947	555,015	283	76	24,101	10,262	109	61,786	42,991
University of Southern California	36	4,845	877,824	329	84	66,405	17,589	159	53,335	110,159
Brown University (RI)	37	4,724	979,523	172	48	21,368	8,709	112	27,890	11,568
Texas A&M University, College Station	38	4,531	1,073,198	321	78	35,350	12,945	145	63,798	44,988
Arizona State University	39	4,531	403,504	288	73	25,459	9,795	149	39,081 [3]	42,726
University of South Carolina, Columbia	40	4,460	206,886	265	71	21,752	7,785	111	38,470	85,215
Johns Hopkins University (MD)	41	4,396	985,644	271	29	37,396	13,445	120	34,500	28,667
University of Cincinnati, Main Campus (OH)	42	4,336	1,243,527	188	44	21,019	8,588	106	33,229	119,451
Tulane University of Louisiana	43	4,320	927,113	172	55	17,813	6,275	118	20,000	21,633
Auburn University (AL)	44	4,318	821,083	106	29	12,762	4,502	146	28,066	98,072
University of Kansas	45	4,285	404,676	249	59	20,282	9,362	140	42,000	91,236
Miami University-Oxford (OH)	46	4,225	595,932	121	44	9,654	4,533	168	29,976	12,947
University at Buffalo (NY)	47	4,119	726,127	173	52	19,414	9,663	168	48,000	35,367
University of Maryland, College Park	48	4,094	599,198	250	80	29,353	11,724	138	58,461	386,001
University of Utah	49	4,068	334,463	322	79	25,130	12,508	142	55,008	165,837
University of Kentucky	50	4,023	588,428	238	74	21,285	8,741	140	51,632	29,825
University of Alabama	51	3,974	855,794	200	64	19,417	7,290	135	35,307	29,854
Brigham Young University (UT)	52	3,946	526,051	352	61	26,686	11,771	101	72,336	57,917
Washington University in St. Louis (MO)	53	3,890	590,299	245	97	32,570	10,042	120	28,000	52,905
Emory University (GA)	54	3,878	555,313	287	97	37,737	14,269	106	35,117	8,935
Syracuse University (NY)	55	3,815	942,224	207	59	19,271	8,613	136	34,993	21,395
Louisiana State University and Agricultural & Mechanical College	56	3,802	402,264	124	43	15,718	—	99	34,772	28,978
University of Notre Dame (IN)	57	3,796	466,168	249	77	26,934	10,880	147	26,544	20,612
Vanderbilt University (TN)	58	3,720	606,267	196	61	23,624	9,181	147	40,417	18,507
North Carolina State University at Raleigh	59	3,653	514,635	280	103	27,504	12,395	146	44,540	32,916
Temple University (PA)	60	3,573	635,008	196	55	23,382	8,263	145	80,009	73,889

—Not available.
[1]The number of entries into the library in an average week. A single person can be counted more than once.
[2]Includes both in-person and virtual services.

[3]Imputed.
SOURCE: U.S. Department of Education, National Center for Education Statistics, Academic Libraries Survey (ALS), fiscal year 2012. (This table was prepared March 2014.)

Table 701.60. Public libraries, books and serial volumes, and per capita usage of selected library services per year, by state: Fiscal years 2011 and 2012

State	Number of public libraries[1]		In thousands		Per capita[2]		Number of library visits[3]		Circulation (number of materials lent)		Reference transactions[4]		Uses of public-access internet computers	
	2011	2012	2011	2012	2011	2012	2011	2012	2011	2012	2011	2012	2011	2012
1	2	3	4	5	6	7	8	9	10	11	12	13	14	15
United States	8,956	9,082	791,183	783,882	2.6	2.6	5.1	4.9	8.1	8.0	1.0	0.9	1.1	1.1
Alabama	212	219	9,766	9,671	2.1	2.1	3.7	3.6	4.4	4.5	0.9	0.9	0.9	1.0
Alaska	72	77	2,271	2,354	3.2	3.6	4.7	5.1	6.4	7.1	0.6	0.7	1.3	1.6
Arizona	90	91	9,601	8,399	1.5	1.3	4.4	4.3	7.9	7.8	0.6	0.7	0.9	1.0
Arkansas	55	56	6,611	6,501	2.5	2.5	4.1	4.1	5.7	5.4	0.9	0.8	1.3	0.8
California	182	183	70,531	68,912	1.9	1.8	4.5	4.3	6.5	6.1	0.7	0.6	0.9	0.9
Colorado	114	115	11,454	11,367	2.3	2.2	6.6	6.5	13.0	13.1	1.0	0.9	1.4	1.4
Connecticut	183	183	14,610	14,522	4.3	4.3	6.9	6.9	9.8	9.7	1.1	1.1	1.5	1.5
Delaware	21	21	1,657	1,697	1.8	1.9	4.9	5.1	6.0	7.0	0.5	0.5	0.8	0.9
District of Columbia	1	1	1,466	1,334	2.4	2.1	4.3	4.0	5.0	5.3	1.4	1.5	1.5	1.3
Florida	77	79	32,483	32,481	1.7	1.7	4.5	4.3	6.8	6.6	1.7	1.6	1.1	1.0
Georgia	61	61	16,660	16,637	1.6	1.6	3.4	3.2	4.5	4.2	1.0	0.9	1.3	1.3
Hawaii	1	1	3,375	3,394	2.5	2.5	3.6	3.9	5.1	5.0	0.5	0.5	0.4	0.4
Idaho	101	101	4,358	4,350	3.1	3.1	6.4	6.8	10.9	10.9	0.9	0.9	1.3	1.3
Illinois	621	622	44,091	43,846	3.8	3.7	7.1	6.6	10.4	10.3	1.2	1.2	1.4	1.3
Indiana	238	237	24,342	24,321	4.3	4.0	6.7	6.3	13.6	12.7	1.0	0.9	1.5	1.3
Iowa	531	533	12,183	12,105	4.0	4.1	6.6	6.5	9.8	9.7	0.6	0.6	1.3	1.3
Kansas	311	321	9,517	9,473	3.9	3.8	6.2	6.0	11.0	10.7	0.9	0.8	1.8	1.6
Kentucky	118	119	8,953	8,803	2.1	2.0	4.6	4.5	6.9	6.8	0.8	0.9	1.1	1.1
Louisiana	68	68	11,876	11,934	2.6	2.6	3.6	3.7	4.4	4.5	0.9	0.9	1.5	1.4
Maine	214	229	5,855	5,964	5.1	5.2	6.1	6.2	8.3	8.4	0.5	0.6	1.1	1.2
Maryland	24	24	12,953	13,022	2.3	2.3	5.4	5.1	10.2	10.0	1.4	1.5	1.1	1.2
Massachusetts	359	359	32,576	32,668	5.0	5.0	6.4	6.5	9.9	9.9	0.8	0.8	1.2	1.2
Michigan	389	389	34,080	33,728	3.5	3.4	5.9	5.7	9.2	8.9	1.0	1.0	1.4	1.2
Minnesota	138	138	15,457	15,164	2.9	2.8	5.2	4.9	11.1	10.5	0.7	0.6	1.3	1.2
Mississippi	50	51	5,698	5,734	1.9	1.9	3.4	3.2	2.9	2.8	0.6	0.5	0.9	0.9
Missouri	147	147	16,961	17,220	3.1	3.2	5.7	5.6	9.9	10.0	1.0	0.7	1.2	1.2
Montana	81	82	2,781	2,700	2.8	2.7	4.7	4.7	7.6	7.6	0.5	0.5	1.4	1.6
Nebraska	216	265	5,733	5,949	4.0	4.1	6.0	6.0	9.7	9.4	0.7	0.6	1.6	1.6
Nevada	22	22	4,523	4,441	1.7	1.6	4.1	4.1	7.1	7.4	0.7	0.7	0.9	0.9
New Hampshire	221	218	5,965	5,874	6.0	6.0	8.0	7.7	11.7	11.6	0.8	0.8	1.0	1.2
New Jersey	281	297	28,671	29,075	3.3	3.3	5.6	5.5	7.2	7.1	1.0	0.9	1.2	1.2
New Mexico	82	85	4,508	4,271	2.8	2.6	5.0	4.5	6.3	5.7	0.7	0.6	1.2	1.2
New York	756	756	71,909	70,074	3.8	3.6	6.1	5.9	8.6	8.2	1.4	1.6	1.2	1.2
North Carolina	77	77	16,620	16,519	1.7	1.7	4.3	4.2	5.7	5.7	1.2	1.1	1.0	0.9
North Dakota	76	75	2,349	2,294	3.9	3.7	3.9	3.8	6.6	6.7	0.6	0.6	0.9	1.0
Ohio	251	251	44,570	44,120	3.9	3.8	7.7	7.6	16.6	16.4	1.8	1.8	1.8	1.8
Oklahoma	117	118	7,394	7,441	2.4	2.4	4.5	4.7	7.2	7.1	0.9	1.0	1.3	1.3
Oregon	126	128	9,910	9,926	2.7	2.7	6.5	6.3	17.2	17.2	0.7	0.7	0.7	0.7
Pennsylvania	456	456	27,363	26,694	2.2	2.2	3.9	3.8	5.5	5.6	0.7	0.6	0.7	0.7
Rhode Island	48	48	4,585	4,428	4.4	4.2	5.8	5.8	7.5	7.1	0.7	0.7	1.4	1.4
South Carolina	42	42	9,480	9,343	2.0	2.0	3.9	3.9	5.7	5.6	1.1	0.7	1.1	1.0
South Dakota	103	112	2,887	2,988	4.1	4.0	5.6	5.3	8.8	8.9	0.6	0.6	1.5	1.9
Tennessee	185	185	11,445	11,525	1.8	1.8	3.3	3.4	4.1	4.2	0.6	0.6	0.9	0.9
Texas	553	551	41,284	40,707	1.8	1.7	3.3	3.2	5.1	5.5	0.7	0.6	0.8	0.8
Utah	72	72	6,800	6,964	2.5	2.5	7.1	6.8	13.8	13.5	1.2	1.2	1.3	1.2
Vermont	159	163	2,874	2,881	5.3	4.9	7.0	6.5	8.9	7.8	0.9	0.9	1.6	1.5
Virginia	91	91	18,723	18,332	2.4	2.3	5.3	5.0	9.9	9.7	1.0	0.9	1.1	1.3
Washington	61	61	13,972	14,842	2.1	2.2	6.7	6.4	12.9	12.1	0.8	0.8	1.4	1.6
West Virginia	97	97	5,356	5,140	3.0	2.8	3.2	3.2	4.0	3.6	0.4	0.4	0.8	0.7
Wisconsin	382	382	19,648	19,265	3.5	3.4	6.3	6.3	11.3	11.1	0.9	0.8	1.3	1.2
Wyoming	23	23	2,450	2,488	4.3	4.4	6.8	6.4	9.2	8.8	0.9	0.9	1.7	1.7

[1]"Number of public libraries" refers to the number of administrative entities that are legally established under local or state law to provide public library service to the population of a local jurisdiction. A public library (administrative entity) may have a single outlet that provides direct service to the public, or it may have multiple service outlets. Outlets can be central libraries, branch libraries, bookmobiles, or books-by-mail-only outlets. In 2011, there were a total of 17,110 service outlets; in 2012, there were 17,219 service outlets.
[2]Per capita (or per person) data are based on unduplicated populations of the areas served by public libraries.
[3]Includes only the number of physical visits (entering the library for any purpose). The survey does not collect data on the number of online visits.

[4]A reference transaction is an information contact that involves the knowledge, use, recommendations, interpretation, or instruction in the use of one or more information sources by a member of the library staff.
NOTE: Data include imputations for nonresponse. Detail may not sum to totals because of rounding.
SOURCE: Institute of Museum and Library Services, Public Libraries Survey, fiscal years 2011 and 2012, retrieved March 2, 2015, from http://www.imls.gov/research/public_libraries_in_the_united_states_survey.aspx. (This table was prepared April 2015.)

Table 702.10. Number and percentage of persons age 3 and over using the Internet and percentage distribution by means of internet access from home and main reason for not having high-speed access, by selected age groups and other characteristics of all users and of students: 2013

[Standard errors appear in parentheses]

Selected age group or other characteristic	Total population (in thousands)	Persons using the Internet anywhere — Number (in thousands)	Persons using the Internet anywhere — Percent of population	Among internet users, percent using the Internet from home	Percentage distribution of home internet users, by means of access from home — A regular "dial-up" telephone	High speed (i.e., faster than dial-up)[1]	Percentage distribution of persons with no internet access at home or no high-speed access at home, by main reason for not having high-speed access — Don't need it, not interested	Too expensive	Can use it somewhere else	Not available in area	No computer or computer inadequate	Other reasons[2]
1	2	3	4	5	6	7	8	9	10	11	12	13
Total, all persons age 3 and over	299,216 (52.0)	213,708 (725.5)	71.4 (0.24)	91.5 (0.18)	1.0 (0.07)	99.0 (0.07)	41.1 (0.64)	33.6 (0.69)	3.2 (0.27)	2.2 (0.21)	11.9 (0.50)	7.9 (0.36)
Sex												
Male	145,897 (37.9)	103,462 (412.0)	70.9 (0.29)	91.8 (0.22)	1.0 (0.08)	99.0 (0.08)	40.8 (0.75)	33.9 (0.76)	3.3 (0.33)	2.4 (0.23)	11.9 (0.54)	7.8 (0.40)
Female	153,319 (36.9)	110,246 (441.5)	71.9 (0.29)	91.2 (0.20)	1.1 (0.08)	98.9 (0.08)	41.5 (0.67)	33.4 (0.72)	3.0 (0.26)	2.1 (0.22)	11.9 (0.54)	8.0 (0.41)
Race/ethnicity												
White	188,805 (111.9)	142,313 (487.0)	75.4 (0.25)	93.7 (0.17)	1.1 (0.08)	98.9 (0.08)	47.9 (0.84)	25.6 (0.77)	2.8 (0.26)	3.2 (0.34)	11.3 (0.60)	9.2 (0.49)
Black	35,918 (175.0)	22,996 (273.2)	64.0 (0.74)	83.8 (0.82)	1.2 (0.23)	98.8 (0.23)	35.9 (1.54)	40.5 (1.57)	3.1 (0.51)	0.8 ! (0.27)	12.8 (1.08)	6.9 (0.82)
Hispanic	50,425 (34.5)	30,771 (340.8)	61.0 (0.67)	85.8 (0.58)	0.8 (0.19)	99.2 (0.19)	33.1 (1.20)	43.6 (1.48)	3.3 (0.68)	1.3 ! (0.42)	12.7 (1.09)	6.0 (0.70)
Other[3]	24,068 (176.2)	17,627 (219.7)	73.2 (0.76)	93.7 (0.48)	0.7 (0.19)	99.3 (0.19)	34.2 (2.24)	39.1 (2.67)	5.4 (1.33)	2.1 ! (0.86)	10.7 (1.76)	8.6 (1.31)
Age												
3 and 4	8,147 (52.0)	2,773 (92.4)	34.0 (1.14)	91.5 (1.19)	1.3 ! (0.56)	98.7 (0.56)	24.8 (2.44)	49.4 (2.74)	6.4 (1.41)	3.0 ! (0.90)	10.8 (1.81)	5.5 (1.04)
5 to 9	20,570 (0.0)	10,795 (168.5)	52.5 (0.82)	91.7 (0.62)	0.7 (0.19)	99.3 (0.19)	24.1 (1.63)	50.1 (1.77)	4.1 (0.72)	2.1 (0.49)	12.3 (1.34)	7.4 (1.14)
10 to 15	24,743 (0.0)	17,657 (163.7)	71.4 (0.64)	92.2 (0.48)	0.8 (0.17)	99.2 (0.17)	26.0 (1.53)	47.4 (1.76)	3.3 (0.71)	3.7 (0.68)	10.6 (1.11)	9.0 (1.14)
16 to 19	16,795 (0.0)	14,205 (108.2)	84.6 (0.64)	91.8 (0.52)	0.9 (0.19)	99.1 (0.19)	28.4 (2.18)	46.2 (2.38)	2.4 ! (0.72)	3.7 (0.80)	12.3 (1.71)	7.0 (1.25)
20 to 24	22,066 (0.0)	18,563 (135.5)	84.1 (0.61)	89.4 (0.54)	0.6 (0.15)	99.4 (0.15)	27.6 (1.82)	44.8 (1.99)	4.8 (0.83)	2.8 ! (0.85)	12.5 (1.30)	7.4 (1.05)
25 to 29	20,877 (0.0)	17,266 (125.9)	82.7 (0.60)	90.3 (0.50)	0.6 (0.18)	99.4 (0.18)	30.0 (1.73)	45.2 (1.94)	5.6 (0.94)	2.0 (0.48)	10.4 (1.29)	6.8 (0.94)
30 to 39	39,842 (0.0)	32,998 (178.5)	82.8 (0.45)	91.9 (0.35)	0.7 (0.13)	99.3 (0.13)	27.6 (1.36)	46.3 (1.51)	4.2 (0.74)	2.3 (0.38)	11.9 (0.98)	7.7 (0.73)
40 to 49	41,357 (0.0)	33,604 (165.7)	81.3 (0.40)	93.5 (0.30)	0.7 (0.10)	99.3 (0.10)	33.9 (1.41)	39.0 (1.41)	3.7 (0.57)	2.9 (0.54)	12.4 (1.00)	8.1 (0.83)
50 to 59	43,244 (78.2)	31,295 (199.9)	72.4 (0.44)	91.7 (0.35)	1.3 (0.15)	98.7 (0.15)	44.1 (1.12)	31.2 (1.25)	2.8 (0.36)	2.9 (0.44)	11.9 (0.79)	7.1 (0.63)
60 to 69	32,588 (124.6)	21,651 (177.5)	66.4 (0.52)	91.6 (0.44)	2.0 (0.21)	98.0 (0.21)	50.9 (1.23)	22.5 (1.03)	2.7 (0.39)	1.8 (0.35)	13.3 (0.93)	8.8 (0.75)
70 or older	28,987 (84.0)	12,899 (179.9)	44.5 (0.62)	87.6 (0.58)	2.3 (0.30)	97.7 (0.30)	66.8 (1.08)	11.4 (0.78)	1.0 (0.17)	0.7 (0.15)	11.4 (0.68)	8.7 (0.57)
Educational attainment of persons age 25 and over												
Less than high school	39,330 (419.3)	21,063 (286.4)	53.6 (0.62)	85.1 (0.56)	1.2 (0.18)	98.8 (0.18)	43.0 (0.98)	33.3 (1.14)	1.5 (0.27)	1.8 (0.25)	13.3 (0.84)	7.1 (0.55)
High school diploma or equivalent	72,679 (611.1)	46,166 (493.1)	63.5 (0.43)	87.9 (0.32)	1.5 (0.14)	98.5 (0.14)	45.3 (0.78)	30.5 (0.74)	2.3 (0.27)	2.0 (0.22)	12.3 (0.57)	7.6 (0.45)
Some college	46,159 (450.2)	38,219 (443.2)	82.8 (0.41)	91.9 (0.31)	1.2 (0.12)	98.8 (0.12)	41.1 (1.29)	33.1 (1.20)	4.5 (0.51)	2.1 (0.40)	10.7 (0.82)	8.6 (0.73)
Associate's degree	22,427 (304.9)	18,752 (279.0)	83.6 (0.52)	92.8 (0.40)	1.0 (0.15)	99.0 (0.15)	44.0 (1.86)	28.7 (1.28)	4.8 (0.92)	3.5 (0.70)	11.6 (1.21)	7.4 (0.88)
Bachelor's or higher degree	69,248 (549.2)	61,627 (496.6)	89.0 (0.25)	95.4 (0.21)	0.7 (0.09)	99.3 (0.09)	44.8 (1.67)	25.6 (1.63)	6.4 (0.80)	2.8 (0.57)	9.2 (0.92)	11.1 (0.95)
Bachelor's degree	45,322 (410.7)	39,977 (364.6)	88.2 (0.32)	95.1 (0.25)	0.8 (0.11)	99.3 (0.11)	44.1 (1.67)	26.9 (1.91)	6.7 (0.86)	2.8 (0.63)	8.6 (1.01)	10.9 (1.05)
Master's or higher degree	23,927 (391.2)	21,650 (368.0)	90.5 (0.40)	96.0 (0.31)	0.6 (0.11)	99.4 (0.11)	46.6 (2.32)	22.4 (1.92)	5.7 (1.29)	3.0 (0.85)	10.7 (1.71)	11.7 (1.87)
Family income												
Less than $10,000	20,430 (594.5)	10,937 (377.5)	53.5 (1.04)	75.1 (1.20)	1.8 (0.43)	98.2 (0.43)	32.3 (1.51)	45.1 (1.71)	2.2 (0.47)	1.5 (0.37)	12.1 (1.02)	6.8 (0.88)
$10,000 to $19,999	31,314 (608.2)	16,419 (468.8)	52.4 (0.81)	81.1 (0.84)	2.1 (0.34)	97.9 (0.34)	42.0 (1.39)	34.9 (1.44)	1.5 (0.35)	1.4 (0.39)	12.3 (0.99)	8.0 (0.88)
$20,000 to $29,999	33,039 (617.8)	19,913 (466.5)	60.3 (0.80)	85.2 (0.64)	2.1 (0.35)	97.8 (0.35)	43.1 (1.41)	33.8 (1.43)	2.5 (0.45)	1.4 (0.38)	12.5 (1.06)	6.6 (0.76)
$30,000 to $39,999	32,893 (634.2)	21,155 (445.8)	64.3 (0.68)	86.1 (0.61)	1.2 (0.23)	98.8 (0.23)	42.8 (1.60)	31.7 (1.55)	3.0 (0.64)	1.9 (0.46)	12.3 (1.09)	8.3 (0.93)
$40,000 to $49,999	24,764 (509.1)	17,766 (422.9)	71.7 (0.75)	92.4 (0.64)	0.8 (0.18)	99.2 (0.18)	44.5 (2.55)	29.4 (2.41)	2.8 (0.75)	2.0 ! (0.71)	12.6 (1.85)	8.7 (1.53)
$50,000 to $74,999	56,781 (699.1)	43,490 (577.0)	76.6 (0.47)	94.1 (0.32)	1.2 (0.18)	98.8 (0.18)	40.7 (2.06)	28.4 (1.91)	6.4 (1.01)	4.3 (0.81)	11.5 (1.56)	8.8 (0.99)
$75,000 to $99,999	36,007 (582.6)	29,429 (479.6)	81.7 (0.52)	96.3 (0.31)	0.6 (0.13)	99.4 (0.13)	44.3 (3.17)	25.9 (2.63)	7.3 (1.90)	7.0 (1.67)	6.7 (1.69)	8.8 (1.93)
$100,000 or more	63,988 (816.4)	54,598 (740.2)	85.3 (0.39)	97.3 (0.20)	0.5 (0.10)	99.5 (0.10)	46.7 (3.37)	20.0 (3.12)	6.5 (1.66)	5.1 (1.69)	10.0 (2.01)	11.8 (2.06)
Total school-age population (all 5- to 15-year-olds)	45,313 (0.0)	28,452 (271.1)	62.8 (0.60)	92.0 (0.42)	0.8 (0.15)	99.2 (0.15)	25.1 (1.24)	48.7 (1.40)	3.7 (0.61)	2.9 (0.52)	11.4 (1.01)	8.2 (0.94)
Age												
5 to 9 years old	20,570 (0.0)	10,795 (168.3)	52.5 (0.82)	91.7 (0.62)	0.7 (0.19)	99.3 (0.19)	24.1 (1.63)	50.1 (1.77)	4.1 (0.72)	2.1 (0.49)	12.3 (1.34)	7.4 (1.14)
10 to 15 years old	24,743 (0.0)	17,657 (163.7)	71.4 (0.66)	92.2 (0.48)	0.8 (0.17)	99.2 (0.17)	26.0 (1.53)	47.4 (1.76)	3.3 (0.71)	3.7 (0.68)	10.6 (1.11)	9.0 (1.14)
Sex												
Male school-age population	23,146 (0.0)	14,519 (169.9)	62.7 (0.73)	92.2 (0.56)	0.8 (0.19)	99.2 (0.19)	24.9 (1.52)	48.3 (1.85)	4.2 (0.93)	2.9 (0.52)	11.6 (1.24)	8.1 (1.12)
5 to 9 years old	10,508 (0.0)	5,416 (115.8)	51.5 (1.10)	91.6 (0.88)	0.7 ! (0.25)	99.3 (0.25)	23.4 (2.23)	49.7 (2.17)	4.6 (1.05)	1.9 (0.54)	13.1 (1.70)	7.3 (1.40)
10 to 15 years old	12,638 (0.0)	9,103 (102.3)	72.0 (0.81)	92.5 (0.62)	0.9 (0.24)	99.1 (0.24)	26.3 (1.97)	47.0 (2.52)	3.8 (1.04)	3.9 (0.78)	10.1 (1.45)	8.9 (1.42)
Female school-age population	22,167 (0.0)	13,933 (166.1)	62.9 (0.75)	91.8 (0.52)	0.7 ! (0.18)	99.3 (0.18)	25.2 (1.65)	49.2 (1.67)	3.1 (0.60)	3.0 (0.68)	11.2 (1.15)	8.3 (1.07)
5 to 9 years old	10,062 (0.0)	5,379 (102.1)	53.5 (1.01)	91.7 (0.82)	0.7 ! (0.27)	99.3 (0.27)	24.8 (2.19)	50.5 (2.58)	3.6 (0.93)	2.3 (0.65)	11.4 (1.72)	7.4 (1.53)
10 to 15 years old	12,105 (0.0)	8,554 (118.3)	70.7 (0.98)	91.8 (0.65)	0.7 ! (0.22)	99.3 (0.22)	25.6 (2.28)	47.9 (2.31)	2.7 (0.74)	3.6 (0.95)	11.0 (1.43)	9.2 (1.50)

See notes at end of table.

Table 702.10. Number and percentage of persons age 3 and over using the Internet and percentage distribution by means of internet access from home and main reason for not having high-speed access, by selected age groups and other characteristics of all users and of students: 2013—Continued

[Standard errors appear in parentheses]

Selected age group or other characteristic	Total population (in thousands)	Persons using the Internet anywhere — Number (in thousands)	Persons using the Internet anywhere — Percent of population	Among internet users, percent using the Internet from home	Home internet users by means of access — A regular "dial-up" telephone	High speed (i.e., faster than dial-up)[1]	No high-speed access — Don't need it, not interested	Too expensive	Can use it somewhere else	Not available in area	No computer or computer inadequate	Other reasons[2]
1	2	3	4	5	6	7	8	9	10	11	12	13
Race/ethnicity												
White school-age population......	24,016 (51.2)	16,262 (189.4)	67.7 (0.77)	95.8 (0.41)	0.8! (0.18)	99.2 (0.18)	27.4 (2.38)	41.2 (2.83)	2.6 (0.73)	5.6 (1.23)	11.0 (1.71)	12.4 (2.06)
5 to 9 years old......	10,626 (40.3)	6,119 (117.6)	57.6 (1.10)	95.5 (0.63)	0.9! (0.29)	99.1 (0.29)	27.1 (3.01)	42.9 (3.36)	3.0! (1.02)	3.0! (0.96)	12.2 (2.11)	11.9 (2.45)
10 to 15 years old......	13,390 (49.4)	10,143 (102.5)	75.8 (0.90)	95.9 (0.45)	0.7 (0.18)	99.2 (0.18)	27.7 (2.78)	39.5 (3.36)	2.1! (0.69)	8.1 (1.77)	9.8 (2.03)	12.8 (2.39)
Black school-age population......	6,221 (55.5)	3,499 (102.5)	56.2 (1.64)	82.6 (1.96)	0.8! (0.41)	99.2 (0.41)	22.1 (2.74)	57.0 (3.31)	3.7 (1.10)	‡ (†)	10.6 (2.29)	5.8 (1.54)
5 to 9 years old......	2,842 (29.9)	1,320 (63.3)	46.4 (2.19)	83.3 (2.72)	‡ (†)	99.7 (0.26)	18.5 (3.35)	58.5 (4.10)	5.6! (1.75)	‡ (†)	11.2 (2.91)	5.5 (1.64)
10 to 15 years old......	3,379 (41.8)	2,179 (67.9)	64.5 (1.97)	82.2 (2.11)	‡ (†)	98.8 (0.64)	24.8 (3.27)	55.9 (3.88)	2.3! (1.11)	2.0! (0.79)	10.1 (2.37)	6.1! (1.88)
Hispanic school-age population......	10,810 (0.0)	5,944 (141.9)	55.0 (1.31)	86.3 (1.16)	0.9! (0.36)	99.1 (0.36)	25.0 (1.90)	49.0 (2.23)	4.3 (1.12)	‡ (†)	13.0 (1.68)	6.8 (1.33)
5 to 9 years old......	5,131 (0.0)	2,307 (90.4)	45.0 (1.76)	85.6 (1.92)	‡ (†)	99.4 (0.35)	23.8 (2.46)	50.9 (2.91)	4.2 (1.24)	1.9! (0.78)	13.8 (2.33)	5.3 (1.35)
10 to 15 years old......	5,679 (0.0)	3,636 (85.0)	64.0 (1.50)	86.7 (1.19)	1.0! (0.45)	99.0 (0.45)	26.1 (2.58)	47.0 (2.73)	4.3! (1.38)	2.2! (0.95)	12.2 (1.87)	8.2 (1.95)
Family income												
Less than $10,000......	3,465 (168.6)	1,559 (110.8)	45.0 (2.28)	69.6 (3.29)	‡ (†)	98.5 (1.00)	17.1 (2.29)	63.9 (3.13)	2.4! (0.82)	2.0! (0.78)	9.0 (1.72)	5.6! (1.69)
$10,000 to $19,999......	4,983 (202.3)	2,491 (154.8)	50.0 (2.09)	83.9 (1.99)	1.3! (0.65)	98.7 (0.65)	22.6 (2.35)	51.7 (3.28)	1.9! (0.78)	2.2! (0.98)	9.7 (1.94)	11.9 (2.32)
$20,000 to $29,999......	4,837 (196.3)	2,603 (149.1)	53.8 (1.74)	88.5 (1.40)	1.6! (0.74)	98.4 (0.74)	25.6 (3.06)	47.8 (3.61)	3.9 (1.13)	‡ (†)	14.6 (2.82)	6.5 (1.80)
$30,000 to $39,999......	4,728 (183.6)	2,667 (120.1)	56.4 (1.78)	85.8 (1.64)	‡ (†)	99.5 (0.35)	25.8 (3.99)	45.0 (3.57)	5.7! (1.96)	3.3! (1.29)	11.4 (2.40)	8.7 (2.45)
$40,000 to $49,999......	3,627 (147.7)	2,264 (120.1)	62.4 (1.80)	92.9 (1.62)	‡ (†)	99.1 (0.54)	35.3 (5.90)	37.6 (5.78)	‡ (†)	‡ (†)	16.0! (5.19)	‡ (†)
$50,000 to $74,999......	8,279 (221.3)	5,469 (187.8)	66.1 (1.37)	93.9 (1.07)	1.6! (0.53)	98.4 (0.53)	29.8 (4.23)	39.8 (4.58)	5.0! (2.00)	7.9! (2.70)	12.0 (3.53)	5.5 (1.64)
$75,000 to $99,999......	5,291 (220.7)	3,791 (155.5)	71.7 (1.42)	98.4 (0.48)	‡ (†)	99.9 (0.07)	32.9 (7.16)	32.8 (7.66)	8.4! (3.77)	‡ (†)	‡ (†)	13.5! (6.39)
$100,000 or more......	10,103 (242.0)	7,609 (215.8)	75.3 (1.10)	97.7 (0.38)	‡ (†)	100.0 (0.01)	37.5 (7.71)	26.8 (7.71)	‡ (†)	‡ (†)	13.3! (6.43)	13.8! (4.94)
Total, all 16- to 24-year-old students[4]	11,784 (223.2)	10,230 (212.0)	86.8 (0.76)	92.9 (0.61)	0.8 (0.25)	99.2 (0.25)	31.0 (3.19)	44.9 (3.07)	3.1 (0.91)	2.4 (0.72)	10.1 (1.82)	8.5 (1.73)
School level												
High school......	4,352 (120.6)	3,553 (116.6)	81.6 (1.32)	91.8 (0.99)	0.7! (0.35)	99.3 (0.35)	29.5 (4.07)	50.8 (4.20)	‡ (†)	‡ (†)	11.8 (2.71)	5.5! (1.89)
College......	7,432 (192.3)	6,677 (182.6)	89.8 (0.78)	93.4 (0.77)	0.9! (0.32)	99.1 (0.32)	32.4 (4.29)	39.7 (4.04)	5.2! (1.62)	‡ (†)	8.6 (2.27)	11.2 (2.73)
Sex												
Male......	5,584 (132.7)	4,793 (132.1)	85.8 (1.11)	91.7 (0.97)	0.7! (0.27)	99.3 (0.27)	35.4 (4.35)	45.6 (3.93)	2.5! (1.01)	2.2! (1.08)	8.7 (2.39)	5.5! (1.91)
High school......	2,256 (82.5)	1,838 (80.6)	81.5 (1.75)	91.4 (1.43)	‡ (†)	99.9 (0.05)	34.3 (5.74)	52.7 (5.40)	# (†)	‡ (†)	8.3 (3.11)	7.3! (2.89)
College......	3,329 (118.0)	2,955 (115.4)	88.8 (1.22)	92.0 (1.18)	1.1! (0.43)	98.9 (0.43)	36.5 (5.46)	39.0 (4.93)	4.8! (1.92)	2.7! (0.90)	9.2! (3.35)	11.5 (2.78)
Female......	6,200 (150.3)	5,437 (139.9)	87.7 (0.99)	93.9 (0.70)	1.0! (0.35)	99.0 (0.35)	26.5 (4.08)	44.2 (4.04)	3.6! (1.57)	‡ (†)	11.4 (2.66)	7.5! (3.14)
High school......	2,096 (88.0)	1,715 (82.5)	81.8 (1.86)	93.0 (1.34)	1.5! (0.72)	98.5 (0.72)	24.4 (5.35)	48.8 (5.78)	5.6! (2.71)	‡ (†)	15.5 (4.35)	‡ (†)
College......	4,104 (128.8)	3,722 (121.5)	90.7 (1.00)	94.6 (0.90)	0.7! (0.36)	99.3 (0.36)	28.4 (5.57)	40.3 (5.47)	‡ (†)	‡ (†)	8.0! (3.09)	15.0 (4.22)
Race/ethnicity												
White[3]......	6,531 (154.0)	5,809 (149.8)	89.0 (0.86)	95.2 (0.59)	‡ (†)	99.5 (0.25)	33.3 (4.48)	38.5 (4.82)	5.5! (1.72)	‡ (†)	9.9 (2.82)	10.5 (3.09)
High school......	2,245 (85.0)	1,913 (76.6)	85.2 (1.58)	94.0 (1.09)	‡ (†)	99.3 (0.37)	37.1 (6.66)	44.9 (6.56)	‡ (†)	‡ (†)	7.2! (3.37)	15.3! (4.89)
College......	4,286 (135.8)	3,896 (134.7)	90.9 (0.92)	95.8 (0.71)	‡ (†)	99.6 (0.30)	29.9 (6.47)	32.8 (6.46)	‡ (†)	‡ (†)	12.3 (4.04)	14.4 (5.35)
Black[3]......	1,602 (87.5)	1,313 (80.5)	81.9 (2.16)	90.6 (1.83)	2.4! (1.14)	97.6 (1.14)	21.5 (5.16)	47.4 (6.61)	‡ (†)	‡ (†)	12.8 (4.94)	18.2! (8.28)
High school......	675 (51.4)	519 (48.9)	76.9 (3.54)	91.0 (2.90)	‡ (†)	97.3 (2.01)	15.2! (5.82)	57.4 (9.55)	# (†)	‡ (†)	16.6! (7.68)	3.7! (1.70)
College......	928 (69.4)	794 (65.0)	85.6 (2.93)	90.4 (2.38)	‡ (†)	97.8 (1.31)	28.0 (8.13)	37.0 (8.79)	‡ (†)	‡ (†)	10.7! (3.22)	‡ (†)
Hispanic......	2,452 (92.4)	2,047 (89.7)	83.5 (2.04)	86.9 (1.71)	‡ (†)	99.0 (0.54)	32.3 (5.49)	50.3 (5.87)	‡ (†)	‡ (†)	14.1! (4.95)	‡ (†)
High school......	1,014 (63.6)	758 (56.9)	74.7 (3.64)	85.6 (2.88)	‡ (†)	99.3 (...)	30.8 (6.76)	52.2 (7.30)	‡ (†)	‡ (†)	‡ (†)	‡ (†)
College......	1,437 (71.9)	1,289 (67.4)	89.7 (1.96)	87.7 (2.12)	‡ (†)	98.5 (0.84)	33.8 (6.91)	48.4 (7.86)	‡ (†)	‡ (†)	‡ (†)	‡ (†)
Family income												
Less than $10,000......	958 (85.2)	767 (84.7)	80.1 (3.18)	81.0 (3.93)	‡ (†)	98.0 (1.28)	22.5 (6.64)	50.7 (7.10)	‡ (†)	‡ (†)	16.4 (4.92)	7.9! (3.58)
$10,000 to $19,999......	1,151 (84.9)	906 (71.9)	78.7 (2.59)	84.9 (2.78)	‡ (†)	99.9 (0.11)	24.6 (6.52)	53.6 (7.11)	‡ (†)	‡ (†)	8.3! (3.44)	9.6! (3.66)
$20,000 to $29,999......	1,117 (88.8)	968 (78.1)	86.6 (2.37)	89.9 (1.99)	‡ (†)	96.9 (1.91)	27.0 (7.44)	55.6 (8.30)	‡ (†)	‡ (†)	9.8 (4.57)	‡ (†)
$30,000 to $39,999......	1,088 (74.9)	916 (67.4)	84.2 (2.58)	89.1 (2.32)	‡ (†)	98.8 (1.09)	38.9 (8.72)	32.2 (7.19)	‡ (†)	‡ (†)	11.2! (5.13)	‡ (†)
$40,000 to $49,999......	922 (69.9)	792 (65.9)	86.0 (2.69)	93.3 (1.81)	‡ (†)	100.0 (0.00)	41.8 (9.60)	39.6 (9.84)	‡ (†)	‡ (†)	‡ (†)	‡ (†)
$50,000 to $74,999......	2,349 (117.4)	2,090 (110.5)	89.0 (1.58)	94.2 (1.34)	‡ (†)	99.3 (0.35)	26.7! (9.25)	32.5 (8.41)	11.3! (5.23)	‡ (†)	12.5! (5.79)	11.5! (5.01)
$75,000 to $99,999......	1,378 (86.3)	1,240 (82.4)	90.0 (2.06)	97.1 (1.12)	‡ (†)	99.4 (0.46)	‡ (†)	‡ (†)	‡ (†)	‡ (†)	‡ (†)	‡ (†)
$100,000 or more......	2,822 (129.4)	2,551 (118.0)	90.4 (1.29)	98.4 (0.55)	‡ (†)	99.7 (0.32)	‡ (†)	‡ (†)	‡ (†)	‡ (†)	‡ (†)	‡ (†)

†Not applicable.
#Rounds to zero.
!Interpret data with caution. The coefficient of variation (CV) for this estimate is between 30 and 50 percent.
‡Reporting standards not met. Either there are too few cases for a reliable estimate or the coefficient of variation (CV) is 50 percent or greater.
[1]Includes DSL, cable, modem, satellite, wireless, mobile phone or PDA, fiber optics or other broadband, and other.
[2]Includes "Privacy or security concerns" and "Other reason."
[3]Includes all other races and Two or more races.
[4]Includes only those 16- to 24-year-olds who are enrolled in school.
NOTE: Race categories exclude persons of Hispanic ethnicity. Detail may not sum to totals because of rounding.
SOURCE: U.S. Department of Commerce, Census Bureau, Current Population Survey (CPS), July 2013. (This table was prepared May 2015.)

APPENDIX A
Guide to Sources

The information presented in the *Digest of Education Statistics* was obtained from many sources, including federal and state agencies, private research organizations, and professional associations. The data were collected using many research methods, including surveys of a universe (such as all colleges) or of a sample, compilations of administrative records, and statistical projections. Brief descriptions of the information sources, data collections, and data collection methods that were used to produce this report are presented below, grouped by sponsoring organization. Additional details about many of these and other datasets can be found on the Department of Education's Data Inventory website (http://datainventory.ed.gov/).

National Center for Education Statistics (NCES)

Baccalaureate and Beyond Longitudinal Study

The Baccalaureate and Beyond Longitudinal Study (B&B) is based on the National Postsecondary Student Aid Study (NPSAS) and provides information concerning education and work experience after completing a bachelor's degree. A special emphasis of B&B is on those entering teaching. B&B provides cross-sectional information 1 year after bachelor's degree completion (comparable to the information that was provided in the Recent College Graduates study), while at the same time providing longitudinal data concerning entry into and progress through graduate-level education and the workforce, income, and debt repayment. This information has not been available through follow-ups involving high school cohorts or even college-entry cohorts, because these cohorts have limited numbers who actually complete a bachelor's degree and continue their graduate education. Also, these cohorts are not representative of all bachelor's degree recipients.

B&B followed NPSAS baccalaureate degree completers for a 10-year period after completion, beginning with NPSAS:93. About 11,000 students who completed their degrees in the 1992–93 academic year were included in the first B&B cohort (B&B:93). The first follow-up of this cohort (B&B:93/94) occurred 1 year later. In addition to collecting student data, B&B:93/94 collected postsecondary transcripts covering the undergraduate period, which pro-

vided complete information on progress and persistence at the undergraduate level. The second follow-up of this cohort (B&B:93/97) took place in spring 1997 and gathered information on employment history, family formation, and enrollment in graduate programs. The third follow-up (B&B:93/03) occurred in 2003 and provided information concerning graduate study and long-term employment experiences after degree completion.

The second B&B cohort (B&B:2000), which was associated with NPSAS:2000, included 11,700 students who completed their degrees in the 1999–2000 academic year. The first and only follow-up survey of this cohort was conducted in 2001 (B&B:2000/01) and focused on time to degree completion, participation in postbaccalaureate education and employment, and the activities of newly qualified teachers.

The third B&B cohort (B&B:08), which is associated with NPSAS:08, included 18,000 students who completed their degrees in the 2007–08 academic year. The first follow-up took place in 2009 (B&B:08/09), and the second follow-up took place in 2012 (B&B:08/12). The report *Baccalaureate and Beyond: A First Look at the Employment Experiences and Lives of College Graduates, 4 Years On (B&B:08/12)* (NCES 2014-141) presents findings based on data from the second follow-up. It examines bachelor's degree recipients' labor market experiences and enrollment in additional postsecondary degree programs through the 4th year after graduation. In addition, *2008/12 Baccalaureate and Beyond Longitudinal Study (B&B:08/12) Data File Documentation* (NCES 2015-141) is available. It describes the universe, methods, and data collection procedures used in the second follow-up. A third and final follow-up (B&B:08/18) to the third B&B cohort is planned for 2018.

Further information on B&B may be obtained from

Aurora D'Amico
Ted Socha
Sample Surveys Division
Longitudinal Surveys Branch
National Center for Education Statistics
550 12th Street SW
Washington, DC 20202
aurora.damico@ed.gov
ted.socha@ed.gov
http://nces.ed.gov/surveys/b&b

Beginning Postsecondary Students Longitudinal Study

The Beginning Postsecondary Students Longitudinal Study (BPS) provides information on persistence, progress, and attainment for 6 years after initial time of entry into postsecondary education. BPS includes traditional and nontraditional (e.g., older) students and is representative of all beginning students in postsecondary education in a given year. Initially, these individuals are surveyed in the National Postsecondary Student Aid Study (NPSAS) during the year in which they first begin their postsecondary education. These same students are surveyed again 2 and 5 years later through the BPS. By starting with a cohort that has already entered postsecondary education and following it for 6 years, the BPS can determine to what extent students who start postsecondary education at various ages differ in their progress, persistence, and attainment, as well as their entry into the workforce. The first BPS was conducted in 1989–90, with follow-ups in 1992 (BPS:90/92) and 1994 (BPS:90/94). The second BPS was conducted in 1995–96, with follow-ups in 1998 (BPS:96/98) and 2001 (BPS:96/01). The third BPS was conducted in 2003–04, with follow-ups in 2006 (BPS:04/06) and 2009 (BPS:04/09). A fourth BPS was conducted in 2012, with a follow-up in 2014 and one planned for 2017.

Further information on BPS may be obtained from

Aurora D'Amico
Sean Simone
Sample Surveys Division
Longitudinal Surveys Branch
National Center for Education Statistics
550 12th Street SW
Washington, DC 20202
aurora.damico@ed.gov
sean.simone@ed.gov
http://nces.ed.gov/surveys/bps

Common Core of Data

The Common Core of Data (CCD) is NCES's primary database on public elementary and secondary education in the United States. It is a comprehensive, annual, national statistical database of all public elementary and secondary schools and school districts containing data designed to be comparable across all states. This database can be used to select samples for other NCES surveys and provide basic information and descriptive statistics on public elementary and secondary schools and schooling in general.

The CCD collects statistical information annually from approximately 100,000 public elementary and secondary schools and approximately 18,000 public school districts (including supervisory unions and regional education service agencies) in the 50 states, the District of Columbia, Department of Defense (DoD) dependents schools, the Bureau of Indian Education (BIE), Puerto Rico, American Samoa, Guam, the Northern Mariana Islands, and the U.S.

Virgin Islands. Three categories of information are collected in the CCD survey: general descriptive information on schools and school districts; data on students and staff; and fiscal data. The general school and district descriptive information includes name, address, phone number, and type of locale; the data on students and staff include selected demographic characteristics; and the fiscal data pertain to revenues and current expenditures.

The ED*Facts* data collection system is the primary collection tool for the CCD. NCES works collaboratively with the Department of Education's Performance Information Management Service to develop the CCD collection procedures and data definitions. Coordinators from state education agencies (SEAs) submit the CCD data at different levels (school, agency, and state) to the ED*Facts* collection system. Prior to submitting CCD files to ED*Facts*, SEAs must collect and compile information from their respective local education agencies (LEAs) through established administrative records systems within their state or jurisdiction.

Once SEAs have completed their submissions, the CCD survey staff analyzes and verifies the data for quality assurance. Even though the CCD is a universe collection and thus not subject to sampling errors, nonsampling errors can occur. The two potential sources of nonsampling errors are nonresponse and inaccurate reporting. NCES attempts to minimize nonsampling errors through the use of annual training of SEA coordinators, extensive quality reviews, and survey editing procedures. In addition, each year, SEAs are given the opportunity to revise their state-level aggregates from the previous survey cycle.

The CCD survey consists of five components: The Public Elementary/Secondary School Universe Survey, the Local Education Agency (School District) Universe Survey, the State Nonfiscal Survey of Public Elementary/Secondary Education, the National Public Education Financial Survey (NPEFS), and the School District Finance Survey (F-33).

Public Elementary/Secondary School Universe Survey

The Public Elementary/Secondary School Universe Survey includes all public schools providing education services to prekindergarten, kindergarten, grade 1–12, and ungraded students. For school year (SY) 2012–13, the survey included records for each public elementary and secondary school in the 50 states, the District of Columbia, Guam, Puerto Rico, the Northern Mariana Islands, the U.S. Virgin Islands, and the Bureau of Indian Education (BIE). The DoD dependents schools (overseas and domestic) and American Samoa did not report data for SY 2012–13.

The Public Elementary/Secondary School Universe Survey includes data for the following variables: NCES school ID number, state school ID number, name of the school, name of the agency that operates the school, mailing address, physical location address, phone number, school type, operational status, locale code, latitude, longitude, county number, county name, full-time-equivalent (FTE) classroom teacher count, low/high grade span offered, congressional district code, school level, students eligible for free lunch, students eligible for reduced-price lunch, total students eligible for free and reduced-price lunch, and student totals and detail (by grade, by race/ethnicity, and by sex). The survey also contains flags indicating whether a school is Title I eligible, schoolwide Title I eligible, a magnet school, a charter school, a shared-time school, or a BIE school, as well as which grades are offered at the school.

Local Education Agency (School District) Universe Survey

The coverage of the Local Education Agency Universe Survey includes all school districts and administrative units providing education services to prekindergarten, kindergarten, grade 1–12, and ungraded students. The Local Education Agency Universe Survey includes records for the 50 states, the District of Columbia, Puerto Rico, the Bureau of Indian Education (BIE), American Samoa, Guam, the Northern Mariana Islands, the U.S. Virgin Islands, and the DoD dependents schools (overseas and domestic).

The Local Education Agency Universe Survey includes the following variables: NCES agency ID number, state agency ID number, agency name, phone number, mailing address, physical location address, agency type code, supervisory union number, American National Standards Institute (ANSI) state and county code, county name, core based statistical area (CBSA) code, metropolitan/micropolitan code, metropolitan status code, district locale code, congressional district code, operational status code, BIE agency status, low/high grade span offered, agency charter status, number of schools, number of full-time-equivalent teachers, number of ungraded students, number of PK–12 students, number of special education/Individualized Education Program students, number of English language learner students, instructional staff fields, support staff fields, and a flag indicating whether student counts by race/ethnicity were reported by five or seven racial/ethnic categories.

State Nonfiscal Survey of Public Elementary/ Secondary Education

The State Nonfiscal Survey of Public Elementary/Secondary Education for the 2012–13 school year provides state-level, aggregate information about students and staff in public elementary and secondary education. It includes data from the 50 states, the District of Columbia, Puerto Rico, the U.S. Virgin Islands, the Northern Mariana Islands, Guam, and American Samoa. The DoD dependents schools (overseas and domestic) and the BIE are also included in the survey universe. This survey covers public school student membership by grade, race/ethnicity, and state or jurisdiction and covers number of staff in public schools by category and state or jurisdiction. Beginning with the 2006–07 school year, the number of diploma recipients and other high school completers are no longer included in the State Nonfiscal Survey of Public Elementary/Secondary Education file. These data are now published in the public-use CCD State Dropout and Completion Data File.

National Public Education Financial Survey

The purpose of the National Public Education Financial Survey (NPEFS) is to provide district, state, and federal policymakers, researchers, and other interested users with descriptive information about revenues and expenditures for public elementary and secondary education. The data collected are useful to (1) chief officers of state education agencies; (2) policymakers in the executive and legislative branches of federal and state governments; (3) education policy and public policy researchers; and (4) the public, journalists, and others.

Data for NPEFS are collected from state education agencies (SEAs) in the 50 states, the District of Columbia, Puerto Rico, American Samoa, Guam, the Northern Mariana Islands, and the U.S. Virgin Islands. The data file is organized by state or jurisdiction and contains revenue data by funding source; expenditure data by function (the activity being supported by the expenditure) and object (the category of expenditure); average daily attendance data; and total student membership data from the State Nonfiscal Survey of Public Elementary/Secondary Education.

School District Finance Survey

The purpose of the School District Finance Survey (F-33) is to provide finance data for all LEAs that provide free public elementary and secondary education in the United States. National and state totals are not included (national- and state-level figures are presented, however, in the National Public Education Financial Survey.

NCES partners with the U.S. Census Bureau in the collection of school district finance data. The Census Bureau distributes Census Form F-33, Annual Survey of School System Finances, to all SEAs, and representatives from the SEAs collect and edit data from their LEAs and submit data to the Census Bureau. The Census Bureau then produces two data files: one for distribution and reporting by NCES and the other for distribution and reporting by the Census Bureau. The files include variables for revenues by source, expenditures by function and object, indebtedness, assets, and student membership counts, as well as identification variables.

Teacher Compensation Survey

The Teacher Compensation Survey (TCS) is a research and development effort designed to assess the feasibility of collecting and publishing teacher-level data from the administrative records residing in state education agencies. Twenty-three states participated in the TCS for SY 2008–09. Participating states provided data on salaries, years of teaching experience, highest degree earned, race/ethnicity, and gender for each public school teacher.

The following text table lists the CCD file versions used in the current edition of the *Digest of Education Statistics*:

Table G. Common Core of Data (CCD) file versions used in the current edition of the *Digest of Education Statistics*: 1986–87 through 2012–13

Year	State Nonfiscal Survey of Public Elementary and Secondary Education	NCES CCD State Dropout and Completion Data	National Public Education Financial Survey	Local Education Agency Universe Survey	School District Finance Survey	Public Elementary/ Secondary School Universe File
1986–87 (FY 1987)	v.1c	†	v.1b-Revised	v.1	†	v.1
1987–88 (FY 1988)	v.1c	†	v.1b-Revised	v.1	†	v.1
1988–89 (FY 1989)	v.1c	†	v.1b-Revised	v.1	†	v.1
1989–90 (FY 1990)	v.1c	†	v.1b-Revised	v.1	v.1a-Final[1]	v.1
1990–91 (FY 1991)	v.1c	†	v.1b-Revised	v.1	†	v.1
1991–92 (FY 1992)	v.1c	†	v.1b-Revised	v.1	v.1a-Final[1]	Revised
1992–93 (FY 1993)	v.1c	†	v.1b-Revised	v.1	†	v.1
1993–94 (FY 1994)	v.1b	†	v.1b-Revised	v.1	†	Revised
1994–95 (FY 1995)	v.1b	†	v.1b-Revised	v.1	†	Revised
1995–96 (FY 1996)	v.1b	†	v.1b-Revised	Revised	v.1d-Revised[1]	Revised
1996–97 (FY 1997)	v.1c	†	v.1b-Revised	v.1	v.1b-Revised[1]	v.1
1997–98 (FY 1998)	v.1c	†	v.1b-Revised	v.1	v.1a-Final[1]	v.1
1998–99 (FY 1999)	v.1b	†	v.1b-Revised	v.1	v.1e-Revised[1]	v.1
1999–2000 (FY 2000)	v.1b	†	v.1b-Revised	v.1b	v.1d-Revised[1]	v.1c
2000–01 (FY 2001)	v.1c	†	v.1b-Revised	v.1a	v.1d-Revised[1]	v.1b
2001–02 (FY 2002)	v.1c	†	v.1c-Revised	v.1a	v.1c-Revised[1]	v.1a
2002–03 (FY 2003)	v.1b	†	v.1b-Revised	v.1a	v.1b-Revised[1]	v.1a
2003–04 (FY 2004)	v.1b	†	v.1b-Revised	v.1b	v.1b-Revised[1]	v.1a
2004–05 (FY 2005)	v.1f	†	v.1b-Revised	v.1c	v.1c-Revised[1]	v.1b
2005–06 (FY 2006)	v.1b	v.1b	v.1b-Revised	v.1a	v.1a-Final[1]	v.1a
2006–07 (FY 2007)	v.1c	v.1a	v.1b-Revised	v.1c	v.1a-Final[1]	v.1c
2007–08 (FY 2008)	v.1b	v.1a	v.1a-Final	v.1b	v.1a-Final[1]	v.1b
2008–09 (FY 2009)	v.1c	v.1a	v.1b-Revised	v.1a	v.1a-Final[1]	v.1b
2009–10 (FY 2010)	v.1b	v.1a	v.1a-Provisional	v.2a	v.1a[1]	v.2a
2010–11 (FY 2011)	v.1a	—	v.1a-Preliminary	v.2a	v.1a-Provisional[1]	v.2a
2011–12 (FY 2012)	v.1a	—	v.1a-Provisional	v.1a	v.1a-Provisional[1]	v.1a
2012–13	v.1a	—	—	v.1a	—	v.1a

—Not available.

†Not applicable. Survey not conducted.

[1]Data not used in current edition of *Digest of Education Statistics*.

NOTE: Preliminary data have been edited but are subject to further NCES quality control procedures. Provisional data have undergone all NCES data quality control procedures. NCES releases a final data file after a publication using provisional data has been released. If NCES receives revised data from states or discovers errors in the final data file, a revised data file is released.

SOURCE: U.S. Department of Education, National Center for Education Statistics, Common Core of Data (CCD), retrieved June 19, 2015, from http://nces.ed.gov/ccd/ccddata.asp. (This table was prepared June 2015.)

Further information on the nonfiscal CCD data may be obtained from

Patrick Keaton
Administrative Data Division
Elementary and Secondary Branch
National Center for Education Statistics
550 12th Street SW
Washington, DC 20202
patrick.keaton@ed.gov
http://nces.ed.gov/ccd

Further information on the fiscal CCD data may be obtained from

Stephen Cornman
Administrative Data Division
Elementary and Secondary Branch
National Center for Education Statistics
550 12th Street SW
Washington, DC 20202
stephen.cornman@ed.gov
http://nces.ed.gov/ccd

Early Childhood Longitudinal Study, Birth Cohort

The Early Childhood Longitudinal Study, Birth Cohort (ECLS-B) was designed to provide decisionmakers, researchers, child care providers, teachers, and parents with nationally representative information about children's early learning experiences and their transition to child care and school. From the time the ECLS-B children were infants until they entered kindergarten, their cognitive and physical development was measured using standardized assessments, and information about their care and learning experiences at home, in early care and education settings, and at school was collected through interviews with adults in the children's lives.

Data were collected from a sample of about 10,700 children born in the United States in 2001, representing a population of approximately 4 million. The children participating in the study came from diverse socioeconomic and racial/ethnic backgrounds, with oversamples of Chinese, other Asian and Pacific Islander, and American Indian/Alaska Native children. There were also oversamples of twins and of children born with moderately low and very low birthweight. Children, their parents (including nonresident and resident fathers), their child care and early education providers, and their kindergarten teachers provided information on children's cognitive, social, emotional, and physical development. Information was also collected about the children's experiences across multiple settings (e.g., home, child care, and school).

Information about the ECLS-B children was collected when they were approximately 9 months old (2001–02), 2 years old (2003–04), and 4 years old/preschool age (2005–06). Additionally, in the fall of 2006, data were collected from all participating sample children, approximately 75 percent of whom were in kindergarten or higher. In the fall of 2007, data were collected from the approximately 25 percent of participating sample children who had not yet entered kindergarten or higher in the previous collection, as well as children who were repeating kindergarten in the 2007–08 school year.

In every round of data collection, children participated in assessment activities and parent respondents (usually the mothers of the children) were asked about themselves, their families, and their children. Resident fathers were asked about themselves and their role in the ECLS-B children's lives in the 9-month, 2-year, and preschool collections. Similar information was collected from nonresident biological fathers in the 9-month and 2-year collections. In addition, beginning when the children were 2 years old, their child care and early education providers were asked to provide information about their own experience and training and their setting's learning environment. At 2 years and at preschool, observations were conducted in the regular nonparental care and education arrangements of a subsample of children in order to obtain information about the quality of the arrangements. When the ECLS-B children were in kindergarten, their teachers were asked to provide information about the children's early learning experiences and the school and classroom environments. Also, the before- and after-school care and education providers of children in kindergarten were asked to provide information about their own experience, their training, and their setting's learning environment. School-level data, taken from other NCES datasets (the Common Core of Data and the Private School Universe Survey) and residential ZIP codes collected at each wave are also available.

Further information on the ECLS-B may be obtained from

Gail Mulligan
Sample Surveys Division
Longitudinal Surveys Branch
National Center for Education Statistics
550 12th Street SW
Washington, DC 20202
ecls@ed.gov
http://nces.ed.gov/ecls/birth.asp

Early Childhood Longitudinal Study, Kindergarten Class of 1998–99

The Early Childhood Longitudinal Study, Kindergarten Class of 1998–99 (ECLS-K) was designed to provide detailed information on children's school experiences throughout elementary school and into middle school. The study began in the fall of 1998. A nationally representative sample of about 21,300 children enrolled in 940 kindergarten programs during the 1998–99 school year was selected to participate in the ECLS-K. The children attended both public and private kindergartens and full- and part-day programs. The sample included children from different racial/ethnic and socioeco-

nomic backgrounds and oversamples of Asian and Pacific Islander children and private school kindergartners.

In the kindergarten year (1998–99), base-year data were collected in the fall and spring. In the first-grade year (1999–2000), data were collected again in the fall and spring. In the 3rd-grade (2002), 5th-grade (2004), and 8th-grade (2007) years, data were collected in the spring. The fall 1999 collection drew from a 30 percent subsample of schools; all other collections drew from the full sample of schools.

From kindergarten to 5th grade, the ECLS-K included a direct child cognitive assessment that was administered one on one with each child in the study. The assessment used a computer-assisted personal interview (CAPI) approach and a two-stage adaptive testing methodology. In the 8th grade, a two-stage adaptive paper-and-pencil assessment was administered in small groups. In kindergarten and first grade, the assessment included three cognitive domains—reading, mathematics, and general knowledge. General knowledge was replaced by science in the 3rd, 5th, and 8th grades. Children's height and weight were measured at each data collection point, and a direct measure of children's psychomotor development was administered in the fall of the kindergarten year only. In addition to these measures, the ECLS-K collected information about children's social skills and academic achievement through teacher reports in every grade and through student reports in the 3rd, 5th, and 8th grades.

A computer-assisted telephone interview with the children's parents/guardians was conducted at each data collection point. Parents/guardians were asked to provide key information about the children in the ECLS-K sample on subjects such as family structure (e.g., household members and composition), family demographics (e.g., family members' age, relation to the child being studied, and race/ethnicity), parent involvement, home educational activities (e.g., reading to the child), child health, parental education and employment status, and the social skills and behaviors of their children.

Data on the schools that children attended and their classrooms were collected through self-administered questionnaires completed by school administrators and classroom teachers. Administrators provided information about the school population, programs, and policies. At the classroom level, data were collected from the teachers on the composition of the classroom, teaching practices, curriculum, and teacher qualifications and experience. In addition, special education teachers and related services staff provided reports on the services received by children with an Individualized Education Program (IEP).

Further information on the ECLS-K may be obtained from

Gail Mulligan
Sample Surveys Division
Longitudinal Surveys Branch
National Center for Education Statistics
550 12th Street SW
Washington, DC 20202
ecls@ed.gov
http://nces.ed.gov/ecls/kindergarten.asp

Early Childhood Longitudinal Study, Kindergarten Class of 2010–11

The Early Childhood Longitudinal Study, Kindergarten Class of 2010–11 (ECLS-K:2011) is providing detailed information on the school achievement and experiences of students throughout their elementary school years. The students participating in the ECLS-K:2011 are being followed longitudinally from the kindergarten year (the 2010–11 school year) through the spring of 2016, when most of them are expected to be in 5th grade. This sample of students is designed to be nationally representative of all students who were enrolled in kindergarten or who were of kindergarten age and being educated in an ungraded classroom or school in the United States in the 2010–11 school year, including those in public and private schools, those who attended full-day and part-day programs, those who were in kindergarten for the first time, and those who were kindergarten repeaters. Students who attended early learning centers or institutions that offered education only through kindergarten are included in the study sample and represented in the cohort.

The ECLS-K:2011 places emphasis on measuring students' experiences within multiple contexts and development in multiple domains. The design of the study includes the collection of information from the students, their parents/guardians, their teachers, and their schools. Information was collected from their before- and after-school care providers in the kindergarten year.

A nationally representative sample of approximately 18,170 children from about 1,310 schools participated in the base-year administration of the ECLS-K:2011 in the 2010–11 school year. The sample included children from different racial/ethnic and socioeconomic backgrounds. Asian/Pacific Islander students were oversampled to ensure that the sample included enough students of this race/ethnicity to make accurate estimates for the group as a whole. Eight data collections have been conducted to date: fall and spring of the children's kindergarten year (the base year), fall 2011 and spring 2012 (the 1st-grade year), fall 2012 and spring 2013 (the 2nd-grade year), spring 2014 (the 3rd-grade year), and spring 2015 (the 4th-grade year). The final data collection is planned for the spring of 2016. Although the study refers to later rounds of data collection by the grade the majority of children are expected to be in (that is, the modal grade for children who were in kindergarten in the 2010–11 school year), children are included in subsequent data collections regardless of their grade level.

A total of approximately 780 of the 1,310 originally sampled schools participated during the base year of the study. This translates to a weighted unit response rate (weighted by the base weight) of 63 percent for the base year. In the base year, the weighted child assessment unit response rate was 87 percent for the fall data collection and 85 percent for the spring collection, and the weighted parent unit response rate was 74 percent for the fall collection and 67 percent for the spring collection.

Fall and spring data collections were conducted in the 2011–12 school year, when the majority of the children were in the 1st grade. The fall collection was conducted within a 33 percent subsample of the full base-year sample, and the spring collection was conducted within the full base-year sample. The weighted child assessment unit response rate was 89 percent for the fall data collection and 88 percent for the spring collection, and the weighted parent unit response rate was 87 percent for the fall data collection and 76 percent for the spring data collection.

In the 2012–13 data collection (when the majority of the children were in the 2nd grade) the weighted child assessment unit response rate was 84.0 percent in the fall and 83.4 percent in the spring.

Further information on ECLS-K:2011 may be obtained from

Gail Mulligan
Sample Surveys Division
Longitudinal Surveys Branch
National Center for Education Statistics
550 12th Street SW
Washington, DC 20202
ecls@ed.gov
http://nces.ed.gov/ecls/kindergarten2011.asp

EDFacts

EDFacts is a centralized data collection through which state education agencies submit K–12 education data to the U.S. Department of Education (ED). All data in EDFacts are organized into "data groups" and reported to ED using defined file specifications. Depending on the data group, state education agencies may submit aggregate counts for the state as a whole or detailed counts for individual schools or school districts. EDFacts does not collect student-level records. The entities that are required to report EDFacts data vary by data group but may include the 50 states, the District of Columbia, the Department of Defense (DoD) dependents schools, the Bureau of Indian Education, Puerto Rico, American Samoa, Guam, the Northern Mariana Islands, and the U.S. Virgin islands. More information about EDFacts file specifications and data groups can be found at http://www.ed.gov/EDFacts.

EDFacts is a universe collection and is not subject to sampling error, but nonsampling errors such as nonresponse and inaccurate reporting may occur. The U.S. Department of Education attempts to minimize nonsampling errors by training data submission coordinators and reviewing the quality of state data submissions. However, anomalies may still be present in the data.

Differences in state data collection systems may limit the comparability of EDFacts data across states and across time. To build EDFacts files, state education agencies rely on data that were reported by their schools and school districts. The systems used to collect these data are evolving rapidly and differ from state to state.

In some cases, ED*Facts* data may not align with data reported on state education agency websites. States may update their websites on schedules different from those they use to report data to ED. Furthermore, ED may use methods for protecting the privacy of individuals represented within the data that could be different from the methods used by an individual state.

ED*Facts* firearm incidents data are collected in data group 601 within file 094. ED*Facts* collects this data group on behalf of the Office of Safe and Healthy Students in the Office of Elementary and Secondary Education. The definition for this data group is "The number of incidents involving students who brought or possessed firearms at school." The reporting period is the entire school year. Data group 601 collects separate counts for incidents involving handguns, rifles/shotguns, other firearms, and multiple weapon types. The counts reported here exclude the "other firearms" category. For more information about this data group, please see file specification 094 for the relevant school year, available at http://www2.ed.gov/about/inits/ed/edfacts/file-specifications.html.

For more information about ED*Facts*, contact

ED*Facts*
Administrative Data Division
Elementary/Secondary Branch
National Center for Education Statistics
550 12th Street SW
Washington, DC 20202
EDFacts@ed.gov
http://www2.ed.gov/about/inits/ed/edfacts/index.html

Education Longitudinal Study of 2002

The Education Longitudinal Study of 2002 (ELS:2002) is a longitudinal survey that is monitoring the transitions of a national probability sample of 10th-graders in public, Catholic, and other private schools. Survey waves follow both students and high school dropouts and monitor the transition of the cohort to postsecondary education, the labor force, and family formation.

In the base year of the study, of 1,200 eligible contacted schools, 750 participated, for an overall weighted school participation rate of approximately 68 percent (62 percent unweighted). Of 17,600 selected eligible students, 15,400 participated, for an overall weighted student response rate of approximately 87 percent. (School and student weighted response rates reflect use of the base weight [design weight] and do not include nonresponse adjustments.) Information for the study is obtained not just from students and their school records, but also from the students' parents, their teachers, their librarians, and the administrators of their schools.

The first follow-up was conducted in 2004, when most sample members were high school seniors. Base-year students who remained in their base schools were resurveyed and tested in mathematics. Sample freshening was conducted to make the study representative of spring 2004 high school seniors nationwide. Students who were not still at their base

schools were all administered a questionnaire. The first follow-up weighted student response rate was 89 percent.

The second follow-up, conducted in 2006, continued to follow the sample of students into postsecondary education, the workforce, or both. The weighted student response rate for this follow-up was 82 percent. The third follow-up, which had a weighted student response rate of 78 percent, was conducted in 2012; the data were released in January 2014.

The postsecondary transcript data collection was conducted in 2013–14. Postsecondary transcripts were requested for each of the ELS:2002 sample members who reported attending an IPEDS postsecondary institution. Transcripts were obtained for 11,623 of 12,549 eligible sample members for a weighted response rate of 77 percent. For more information on the postsecondary transcript data collection, see *Education Longitudinal Study of 2002 (ELS:2002): A First Look at the Postsecondary Transcripts of 2002 High School Sophomores* (NCES 2015-034).

Further information on ELS:2002 may be obtained from

Elise Christopher
Sample Surveys Division
Longitudinal Surveys Branch
National Center for Education Statistics
550 12th Street SW
Washington, DC 20202
elise.christopher@ed.gov
http://nces.ed.gov/surveys/els2002

Fast Response Survey System

The Fast Response Survey System (FRSS) was established in 1975 to collect issue-oriented data quickly, with a minimal burden on respondents. The FRSS, whose surveys collect and report data on key education issues at the elementary and secondary levels, was designed to meet the data needs of Department of Education analysts, planners, and decisionmakers when information could not be collected quickly through NCES's large recurring surveys. Findings from FRSS surveys have been included in congressional reports, testimony to congressional subcommittees, NCES reports, and other Department of Education reports. The findings are also often used by state and local education officials.

Data collected through FRSS surveys are representative at the national level, drawing from a sample that is appropriate for each study. The FRSS collects data from state education agencies and national samples of other educational organizations and participants, including local education agencies, public and private elementary and secondary schools, elementary and secondary school teachers and principals, and public libraries and school libraries. To ensure a minimal burden on respondents, the surveys are generally limited to three pages of questions, with a response burden of about 30 minutes per respondent. Sample sizes are relatively small (usually about 1,000 to 1,500 respondents per survey) so that data collection can be completed quickly.

Further information on the FRSS may be obtained from

John Ralph
Annual Reports and Information Staff
National Center for Education Statistics
550 12th Street SW
Washington, DC 20202
john.ralph@ed.gov
http://nces.ed.gov/surveys/frss

Condition of Public School Facilities

Condition of Public School Facilities: 1999 (NCES 2000-032) is a report that presents national data about the condition of public schools in 1999. It provides results from the survey "Condition of Public School Facilities, 1999" (FRSS 73), which was conducted by NCES using its Fast Response Survey System (FRSS). The survey collected information about the condition of school facilities and the costs of bringing them into good condition; school plans for repairs, renovations, and replacements; the age of public schools; and overcrowding and practices used to address overcrowding. The results presented in this report are based on questionnaire data for 900 public elementary and secondary schools in the United States. The responses were weighted to produce national estimates that represent all regular public schools in the United States.

In 2013, NCES conducted "Condition of Public School Facilities: 2012–13" (FRSS 105), an FRSS survey covering most of the same topics. The First Look report *Condition of America's Public School Facilities: 2012–13* (NCES 2014-022) is based on results from this FRSS survey.

Further information on these FRSS reports and surveys may be obtained from

John Ralph
Annual Reports and Information Staff
National Center for Education Statistics
550 12th Street SW
Washington, DC 20202
john.ralph@ed.gov
http://nces.ed.gov/surveys/frss

Public School Principals Report on Their School Facilities: Fall 2005

This report (NCES 2007-007) presents information on the extent of the match between the enrollment and the capacity of the school buildings, environmental factors that can affect the use of classrooms and school buildings, the extent and ways in which schools use portable buildings and the reasons for using them, the availability of dedicated rooms for particular subject areas (such as science labs or music rooms), and the cleanliness and maintenance of student restrooms.

Results from the FRSS survey "Public School Principals' Perceptions of Their School Facilities: Fall 2005" (FRSS 88) form the basis of the report. The survey was mailed to school principals, who were asked to complete it themselves. The

sample included 1,205 public schools in the 50 states and the District of Columbia. The sample was selected from the 2002–03 Common Core of Data (CCD) Public Elementary/Secondary School Universe File, the most current available at the time of selection. Of the 1,205 schools surveyed, 47 were determined to be ineligible. Of the remaining 1,158 schools, responses were received from 1,045. Data have been weighted to yield national estimates of public elementary/secondary schools. The unweighted response rate was 90 percent, and the weighted response rate was 91 percent.

Further information on this report may be obtained from

John Ralph
Annual Reports and Information Staff
National Center for Education Statistics
550 12th Street SW
Washington, DC 20202
john.ralph@ed.gov
http://nces.ed.gov/surveys/frss

Internet Access in U.S. Public Schools and Classrooms, 1994–2005

This report (NCES 2007-020) is based on data collected in the FRSS survey "Internet Access in U.S. Public Schools, Fall 2005" (FRSS 90). The survey was designed to assess the federal government's commitment to assist every school and classroom in connecting to the Internet by the year 2000.

In 1994, NCES began surveying approximately 1,000 public schools each year regarding their access to the Internet, access in classrooms, and, since 1996, their type of internet connections. Later administrations of this survey were expanded to cover emerging issues. The 2003 survey (FRSS 86) was designed to update the questions in the 2002 survey (FRSS 83) and covered the following topics: school connectivity, student access to computers and the Internet, school websites, technologies and procedures to prevent student access to inappropriate websites, and teacher professional development on how to incorporate the Internet into the curriculum.

In 2005, respondents were asked about the number of instructional computers with access to the Internet, the types of internet connections, technologies and procedures used to prevent student access to inappropriate material on the Internet, and the availability of handheld and laptop computers for students and teachers. Respondents also provided information on teacher professional development in integrating the use of the Internet into the curriculum and using the Internet to provide opportunities and information for teaching and learning.

Use of Educational Technology in Public Schools

In 2008, the NCES survey on educational technology use in public schools was redesigned and expanded to a set of three surveys (i.e., a school-, district-, and teacher-level survey). The three surveys provide complementary information and together cover a broader range of topics than would be possible with one survey alone. The set of surveys collected data on availability and use of a range of educational technology resources, such as district and school networks, computers, devices that enhance the capabilities of computers for instruction, and computer software. They also collected information on leadership and staff support for educational technology within districts and schools.

Educational Technology in U.S. Public Schools, Fall 2008 (NCES 2010-034) is based on the school-level survey, "Education Technology in U.S. Public Schools: Fall 2008" (FRSS 92); *Educational Technology in Public School Districts: Fall 2008* (NCES 2010-003) is based on the district-level school technology survey, "Educational Technology in Public School Districts: Fall 2008" (FRSS 93); and *Teachers' Use of Educational Technology in U.S. Public Schools: 2009* (NCES 2010-040) is based on the teacher-level school technology survey, "Teachers' Use of Educational Technology in U.S. Public Schools" (FRSS 95).

Further information on internet access and technology use in public schools and classrooms may be obtained from

John Ralph
Annual Reports and Information Staff
National Center for Education Statistics
550 12th Street SW
Washington, DC 20202
john.ralph@ed.gov
http://nces.ed.gov/surveys/frss

Distance Education for Public Elementary and Secondary School Students

The report *Technology-Based Distance Education Courses for Public Elementary and Secondary School Students: 2002–03 and 2004–05* (NCES 2008-008) presented data collected in the FRSS survey "Distance Education Courses for Public Elementary and Secondary School Students: 2004–05" (FRSS 89, 2005). The report included national estimates of the prevalence and characteristics of technology-based distance education courses in public schools nationwide in school year 2004–05. The report also compared those data with the baseline data that were collected in the FRSS survey "Distance Education Courses for Public School Elementary and Secondary Students: 2002–03" (FRSS 84, 2003) and provided longitudinal analysis of change in the districts that responded to both the 2002–03 and 2004–05 surveys.

Distance education courses were defined as credit-granting courses offered to elementary and secondary school students enrolled in the district in which the teacher and student were in different locations. These courses could be delivered via audio, video (live or prerecorded), or Internet or other computer technologies.

Distance Education Courses for Public Elementary and Secondary School Students: 2009–10 (NCES 2012–008) presents national estimates about student enrollment in distance education courses in public school districts. The esti-

mates are based on a district survey ("Distance Education Courses for Public Elementary and Secondary School Students: 2009–10," FRSS 98, 2010) about distance education courses offered by the district or by any of the schools in the district during the 12-month 2009–10 school year. Distance education courses were defined as courses offered to elementary and secondary school students regularly enrolled in the district that were (1) credit granting; (2) technology delivered; and (3) had the instructor in a different location than the students and/or had course content developed in, or delivered from, a different location than that of the students.

Further information on FRSS reports on distance education may be obtained from

John Ralph
Annual Reports and Information Staff
National Center for Education Statistics
550 12th Street SW
Washington, DC 20202
john.ralph@ed.gov
http://nces.ed.gov/surveys/frss

School Safety and Discipline

The FRSS survey "School Safety and Discipline: 2013–14" (FRSS 106, 2014) collected nationally representative data on public school safety and discipline for the 2013–14 school year. The topics covered included specific safety and discipline plans and practices, training for classroom teachers and aides related to school safety and discipline issues, security personnel, frequency of specific discipline problems, and number of incidents of various offenses.

The survey was mailed to approximately 1,600 regular public schools in the 50 states and the District of Columbia. Recipients were informed that the survey was designed to be completed by the person most knowledgeable about safety and discipline at the school. The unweighted survey response rate was 86 percent, and the weighted response rate using the initial base weights was 85 percent. The survey weights were adjusted for questionnaire nonresponse, and the data were then weighted to yield national estimates that represent all eligible regular public schools in the United States. The report *Public School Safety and Discipline: 2013–14* (NCES 2015-051) presents selected findings from the survey.

Further information on this FRSS survey may be obtained from

John Ralph
Annual Reports and Information Staff
National Center for Education Statistics
550 12th Street SW
Washington, DC 20202
john.ralph@ed.gov
http://nces.ed.gov/surveys/frss

Federal Support for Education

NCES prepares an annual compilation of federal funds for education for the *Digest of Education Statistics*. Data for U.S. Department of Education programs come from the *Budget of the United States Government*. Budget offices of other federal agencies provide information for all other federal program support except for research funds, which are obligations reported by the National Science Foundation in *Federal Funds for Research and Development*. Some data are estimated, based on reports from the federal agencies contacted and the *Budget of the United States Government*.

Except for money spent on research, outlays are used to report program funds to the extent possible. Some *Digest of Education Statistics* tables report program funds as obligations, as noted in the title of the table. Some federal program funds not commonly recognized as education assistance are also included in the totals reported. For example, portions of federal funds paid to some states and counties as shared revenues resulting from the sale of timber and minerals from public lands have been estimated as funds used for education purposes. Parts of the funds received by states (in 1980) and localities (in all years) under the General Revenue Sharing Program are also included, as are portions of federal funds received by the District of Columbia. The share of these funds allocated to education is assumed to be equal to the share of general funds expended for elementary and secondary education by states and localities in the same year, as reported by the U.S. Census Bureau in its annual publication, *Government Finances*.

The share of federal funds assigned to education for the District of Columbia is assumed to be equal to the share of the city's general fund expenditures for each level of education.

For the job training programs conducted by the Department of Labor, only estimated sums spent on classroom training have been reported as educational program support.

During the 1970s, the Office of Management and Budget (OMB) prepared an annual analysis of federal education program support. These were published in the *Budget of the United States Government, Special Analyses*. The information presented in this report is not, however, a continuation of the OMB series. A number of differences in the two series should be noted. OMB required all federal agencies to report outlays for education-related programs using a standardized form, thereby assuring agency compliance in reporting. The scope of education programs reported in the *Digest of Education Statistics* differs from the scope of programs reported in the OMB reports. Off-budget items such as the annual volume of guaranteed student loans were not included in OMB's reports. Finally, while some mention is made of an annual estimate of federal tax expenditures, OMB did not include them in its annual analysis of federal education support. Estimated federal tax expenditures for education are the difference between current federal tax receipts and what these receipts would be without existing education deductions to income allowed by federal tax provisions.

Recipients' data are estimated based on *Estimating Federal Funds for Education: A New Approach Applied to Fiscal Year 1980* (Miller, V., and Noell, J., 1982, Journal of Education Finance); *Federal Support for Education*, various years; and the *Catalog of Federal Domestic Assistance* (http://www.cfda.gov). The recipients' data are estimated and tend to undercount institutions of higher education, students, and local education agencies. This is because some of the federal programs have more than one recipient receiving funds. In these cases, the recipients were put into a "mixed recipients" category, because there was no way to disaggregate the amount each recipient received.

Further information on federal support for education may be obtained from

Tom Snyder
Annual Reports and Information Staff
National Center for Education Statistics
550 12th Street SW
Washington, DC 20202
tom.snyder@ed.gov
http://nces.ed.gov/surveys/AnnualReports/federal.asp

High School and Beyond Longitudinal Study

The High School and Beyond Longitudinal Study (HS&B) is a nationally representative sample survey of individuals who were high school sophomores and seniors in 1980. As a large-scale, longitudinal survey, its primary purpose is to observe the educational and occupational plans and activities of young people as they pass through the American educational system and take on their adult roles. The study contributes to the understanding of the development of young adults and the factors that determine individual education and career outcomes. The availability of this longitudinal data encourages research in such areas as the strength of secondary school curricula, the quality and effectiveness of secondary and postsecondary schooling, the demand for postsecondary education, problems of financing postsecondary education, and the adequacy of postsecondary alternatives open to high school students.

The HS&B survey gathered data on the education, work, and family experiences of young adults for the pivotal years during and immediately following high school. The student questionnaire covered school experiences, activities, attitudes, plans, selected background characteristics, and language proficiency. Parents were asked about their educational aspirations for their children and plans for how their education would be financed. Teachers were surveyed regarding their assessments of their students' futures. The survey also collected detailed information, from complete high school transcripts, on courses taken and grades achieved.

The base-year survey (conducted in 1980) was a probability sample of 1,015 high schools with a target number of 36 sophomores and 36 seniors in each school. A total of 58,270 students participated in the base-year survey. Substitutions were made for nonparticipating schools—but not for students—in those strata where it was possible. Overall, 1,120 schools were selected in the original sample and 810 of these schools participated in the survey. An additional 200 schools were drawn in a replacement sample. Student refusals and absences resulted in an 82 percent completion rate for the survey.

Several small groups in the population were oversampled to allow for special study of certain types of schools and students. Students completed questionnaires and took a battery of cognitive tests. In addition, a sample of parents of sophomores and seniors (about 3,600 for each cohort) was surveyed.

HS&B first follow-up activities took place in the spring of 1982. The sample for the first follow-up survey included approximately 30,000 individuals who were sophomores in 1980. The completion rate for sample members eligible for on-campus survey administration was about 96 percent. About 89 percent of the students who left school between the base-year and first follow-up surveys (e.g., dropouts, transfer students, and early graduates) completed the first follow-up sophomore questionnaire.

As part of the first follow-up survey of HS&B, transcripts were requested in fall 1982 for an 18,150-member subsample of the sophomore cohort. Of the 15,940 transcripts actually obtained, 12,120 transcripts represented students that had graduated in 1982 and thus were eligible for use in the overall curriculum analysis presented in this publication. All courses in each transcript were assigned a 6-digit code based on the Classification of Secondary School Courses (a coding system developed to standardize course descriptions; see http://nces.ed.gov/surveys/hst/courses.asp). Credits earned in each course are expressed in Carnegie units. (The Carnegie unit is a standard of measurement that represents one credit for the completion of a 1-year course. To receive credit for a course, the student must have received a passing grade—"pass," "D," or higher.) Students who transferred from public to private schools or from private to public schools between their sophomore and senior years were eliminated from public/private analyses.

In designing the senior cohort first follow-up survey, one of the goals was to reduce the size of the retained sample while still keeping sufficient numbers of various racial/ethnic groups to allow important policy analyses. A total of about 11,230 (93.6 percent) of the 12,000 individuals subsampled completed the questionnaire. Information was obtained about the respondents' school and employment experiences, family status, and attitudes and plans.

The samples for the second follow-up, which took place in spring 1984, consisted of about 12,000 members of the senior cohort and about 15,000 members of the sophomore cohort. The completion rate for the senior cohort was 91 percent, and the completion rate for the sophomore cohort was 92 percent.

HS&B third follow-up data collection activities were performed in spring 1986. Both the sophomore and senior cohort samples for this round of data collection were the same as those used for the second follow-up survey. The completion rates for the sophomore and senior cohort samples were 91 percent and 88 percent, respectively.

HS&B fourth follow-up data collection activities were performed in 1992 but only covered the 1980 sophomore class. These activities included examining aspects of these students' early adult years, such as enrollment in postsecondary education, experience in the labor market, marriage and child rearing, and voting behavior.

An NCES series of technical reports and data file user's manuals, available electronically, provides additional information on the survey methodology.

Further information on HS&B may be obtained from

Aurora D'Amico
Sample Surveys Division
Longitudinal Surveys Branch
National Center for Education Statistics
550 12th Street SW
Washington, DC 20202
aurora.damico@ed.gov
http://nces.ed.gov/surveys/hsb

High School Longitudinal Study of 2009

The High School Longitudinal Study of 2009 (HSLS:09) is a nationally representative, longitudinal study of approximately 21,000 9th-grade students in 944 schools who will be followed through their secondary and postsecondary years. The study focuses on understanding students' trajectories from the beginning of high school into postsecondary education, the workforce, and beyond. The HSLS:09 questionnaire is focused on, but not limited to, information on science, technology, engineering, and mathematics (STEM) education and careers. It is designed to provide data on mathematics and science education, the changing high school environment, and postsecondary education. This study features a new student assessment in algebra skills, reasoning, and problem solving and includes surveys of students, their parents, math and science teachers, and school administrators, as well as a new survey of school counselors.

The HSLS:09 base year took place in the 2009–10 school year, with a randomly selected sample of fall-term 9th-graders in more than 900 public and private high schools that had both a 9th and an 11th grade. Students took a mathematics assessment and survey online. Students' parents, principals, and mathematics and science teachers and the school's lead counselor completed surveys on the phone or online.

The HSLS:09 student questionnaire includes interest and motivation items for measuring key factors predicting choice of postsecondary paths, including majors and eventual careers. This study explores the roles of different factors in the development of a student's commitment to attend college and then take the steps necessary to succeed in college (the right courses, courses in specific sequences, etc.). Questionnaires in this study have asked more questions of students and parents regarding reasons for selecting specific colleges (e.g., academic programs, financial aid and access prices, and campus environment).

The first follow-up of HSLS:09 occurred in the spring of 2012, when most sample members were in the 11th grade. Data files and documentation for the first follow-up were released in fall 2013 and are available on the NCES website.

A between-round postsecondary status update survey took place in the spring of students' expected graduation year (2013). It asked respondents about college applications, acceptances, and rejections, as well as their actual college choices. In the fall of 2013 and the spring of 2014, high school transcripts were collected and coded.

A full second follow-up is planned for 2016, when most sample members will be 3 years beyond high school graduation. Additional follow-ups are planned, to at least age 30.

Further information on HSLS:09 may be obtained from

Elise Christopher
Sample Surveys Division
Longitudinal Surveys Branch
National Center for Education Statistics
550 12th Street SW
Washington, DC 20202
hsls09@ed.gov
http://nces.ed.gov/surveys/hsls09

High School Transcript Studies

High school transcript studies have been conducted since 1982 in conjunction with major NCES data collections. The studies collect information that is contained in a student's high school record—courses taken while attending secondary school, information on credits earned, when specific courses were taken, and final grades.

A high school transcript study was conducted in 2004 as part of the Education Longitudinal Study of 2002 (ELS:2002/2004). A total of 1,550 schools participated in the request for transcripts, for an unweighted participation rate of approximately 79 percent. Transcript information was received on 14,920 members of the student sample (not just graduates), for an unweighted response rate of 91 percent.

Similar studies were conducted of the coursetaking patterns of 1982, 1987, 1990, 1992, 1994, 1998, 2000, 2005, and 2009 high school graduates. The 1982 data are based on approximately 12,000 transcripts collected by the High School and Beyond Longitudinal Study (HS&B). The 1987 data are based on approximately 25,000 transcripts from 430 schools obtained as part of the 1987 NAEP High School Transcript Study, a scope comparable to that of the NAEP transcript studies conducted in 1990, 1994, 1998, and 2000. The 1992 data are based on approximately 15,000 transcripts collected by the National Education Longitudinal Study of 1988 (NELS:88/92). The 2005 data, from the 2005 NAEP High School Transcript Study, come from a sample of over 26,000 transcripts from 640 public schools and 80 private schools. The 2009 data are from the 2009 NAEP High School Transcript Study, which collected transcripts from a nationally representative sample of 37,700 high school graduates from about 610 public schools and 130 private schools.

Because the 1982 HS&B transcript study used a different method for identifying students with disabilities than was used in NAEP transcript studies after 1982, and in order to make the statistical summaries as comparable as possible, all the counts and percentages in this report are restricted to students whose records indicate that they had not participated in a special education program. This restriction lowers the number of 1990 graduates represented in the tables to 20,870.

Further information on NAEP high school transcript studies may be obtained from

Elise Christopher
Sample Surveys Division
Longitudinal Surveys Branch
National Center for Education Statistics
550 12th Street SW
Washington, DC 20202
elise.christopher@ed.gov
http://nces.ed.gov/surveys/hst

Further information on all other high school transcript studies may be obtained from

Carl Schmitt
Administrative Data Division
Elementary and Secondary Branch
National Center for Education Statistics
550 12th Street SW
Washington, DC 20202
carl.schmitt@ed.gov
http://nces.ed.gov/surveys/hst

Integrated Postsecondary Education Data System

The Integrated Postsecondary Education Data System (IPEDS) surveys approximately 7,500 postsecondary institutions, including universities and colleges, as well as institutions offering technical and vocational education beyond the high school level. IPEDS, an annual universe collection that began in 1986, replaced the Higher Education General Information Survey (HEGIS). In order to present data in a timely manner, *Digest of Education Statistics* tables use "provisional" IPEDS data for the most recent years. These data have been fully reviewed, edited, and imputed, but do not incorporate data revisions submitted by institutions after the close of data collection. Tables are revised with these institutional revisions on a periodic basis.

IPEDS consists of interrelated survey components that provide information on postsecondary institutions, student enrollment, programs offered, degrees and certificates conferred, and both the human and financial resources involved in the provision of institutionally based postsecondary education. Prior to 2000, the IPEDS survey had the following subject-matter components: Graduation Rates; Fall Enrollment; Institutional Characteristics; Completions; Salaries, Tenure, and Fringe Benefits of Full-Time Faculty; Fall

Staff; Finance; and Academic Libraries (in 2000, the Academic Libraries component became a survey separate from IPEDS). Since 2000, IPEDS survey components occurring in a particular collection year have been organized into three seasonal collection periods: fall, winter, and spring. The Institutional Characteristics and Completions components first took place during the fall 2000 collection; the Employees by Assigned Position (EAP), Salaries, and Fall Staff components first took place during the winter 2001–02 collection; and the Enrollment, Student Financial Aid, Finance, and Graduation Rates components first took place during the spring 2001 collection. In the winter 2005–06 data collection, the EAP, Fall Staff, and Salaries components were merged into the Human Resources component. During the 2007–08 collection year, the Enrollment component was broken into two separate components: 12-Month Enrollment (taking place in the fall collection) and Fall Enrollment (taking place in the spring collection). In the 2011–12 IPEDS data collection year, the Student Financial Aid component was moved to the winter data collection to aid in the timing of the net price of attendance calculations displayed on the College Navigator (http://nces.ed.gov/collegenavigator). In the 2012–13 IPEDS data collection year, the Human Resources component was moved from the winter data collection to the spring data collection, and in the 2013–14 data collection year, the Graduation Rates and Graduation Rates 200% components were moved from the spring data collection to the winter data collection.

Beginning in 2008–09, the first-professional degree category was combined with the doctor's degree category. However, some degrees formerly identified as first-professional that take more than two full-time-equivalent academic years to complete, such as those in Theology (M.Div, M.H.L./Rav), are included in the Master's degree category. Doctor's degrees were broken out into three distinct categories: research/scholarship, professional practice, and other doctor's degrees.

IPEDS race/ethnicity data collection also changed in 2008–09. The "Asian" race category is now separate from a "Native Hawaiian or Other Pacific Islander" category, and a new category of "Two or more races" was added.

The degree-granting institutions portion of IPEDS is a census of colleges that award associate's or higher degrees and are eligible to participate in Title IV financial aid programs. Prior to 1993, data from technical and vocational institutions were collected through a sample survey. Beginning in 1993, all data are gathered in a census of all postsecondary institutions. Beginning in 1997, the survey was restricted to institutions participating in Title IV programs. The tabulations developed for editions of the *Digest of Education Statistics* from 1993 forward are based on lists of all institutions and are not subject to sampling errors.

The classification of institutions offering college and university education changed as of 1996. Prior to 1996, institutions that had courses leading to an associate's or higher degree or that had courses accepted for credit toward those degrees were considered higher education institutions. Higher education institutions were accredited by an agency or association that was recognized by the U.S. Department of Education or were recognized directly by the Secretary of Education. The newer standard includes institutions that award associate's or higher degrees and that are eligible to participate in Title IV federal financial aid programs. Tables that contain any data according to this standard are titled "degree-granting" institutions. Time-series tables may contain data from both series, and they are noted accordingly. The impact of this change on data collected in 1996 was not large. For example, tables on faculty salaries and benefits were only affected to a very small extent. Also, degrees awarded at the bachelor's level or higher were not heavily affected. The largest impact was on private 2-year college enrollment. In contrast, most of the data on public 4-year colleges were affected to a minimal extent. The impact on enrollment in public 2-year colleges was noticeable in certain states, such as Arizona, Arkansas, Georgia, Louisiana, and Washington, but was relatively small at the national level. Overall, total enrollment for all institutions was about one-half of a percent higher in 1996 for degree-granting institutions than for higher education institutions.

Prior to the establishment of IPEDS in 1986, HEGIS acquired and maintained statistical data on the characteristics and operations of institutions of higher education. Implemented in 1966, HEGIS was an annual universe survey of institutions accredited at the college level by an agency recognized by the Secretary of the U.S. Department of Education. These institutions were listed in NCES's *Education Directory, Colleges and Universities.*

HEGIS surveys collected information on institutional characteristics, faculty salaries, finances, enrollment, and degrees. Since these surveys, like IPEDS, were distributed to all higher education institutions, the data presented are not subject to sampling error. However, they are subject to nonsampling error, the sources of which varied with the survey instrument.

The NCES Taskforce for IPEDS Redesign recognized that there were issues related to the consistency of data definitions as well as the accuracy, reliability, and validity of other quality measures within and across surveys. The IPEDS redesign in 2000 provided institution-specific web-based data forms. While the new system shortened data processing time and provided better data consistency, it did not address the accuracy of the data provided by institutions.

Beginning in 2003–04 with the Prior Year Data Revision System, prior-year data have been available to institutions entering current data. This allows institutions to make changes to their prior-year entries either by adjusting the data or by providing missing data. These revisions allow the evaluation of the data's accuracy by looking at the changes made.

NCES conducted a study (NCES 2005-175) of the 2002–03 data that were revised in 2003–04 to determine the accuracy of the imputations, track the institutions that submitted revised data, and analyze the revised data they submitted. When institutions made changes to their data, it was assumed that the revised data were the "true" data. The data were analyzed for the number and type of institutions making changes, the type of changes, the magnitude of the changes, and the impact on published data.

Because NCES imputes for missing data, imputation procedures were also addressed by the Redesign Taskforce. For the 2003–04 assessment, differences between revised values and values that were imputed in the original files were compared (i.e., revised value minus imputed value). These differences were then used to provide an assessment of the effectiveness of imputation procedures. The size of the differences also provides an indication of the accuracy of imputation procedures. To assess the overall impact of changes on aggregate IPEDS estimates, published tables for each component were reconstructed using the revised 2002–03 data. These reconstructed tables were then compared to the published tables to determine the magnitude of aggregate bias and the direction of this bias.

Since fall 2000 and spring 2001, IPEDS data collections have been web-based. Data have been provided by "keyholders," institutional representatives appointed by campus chief executives, who are responsible for ensuring that survey data submitted by the institution are correct and complete. Because Title IV institutions are the primary focus of IPEDS and because these institutions are required to respond to IPEDS, response rates for Title IV institutions have been high (data on specific components are cited below). More details on the accuracy and reliability of IPEDS data can be found in the *Integrated Postsecondary Education Data System Data Quality Study* (NCES 2005-175).

Further information on IPEDS may be obtained from

Richard Reeves
Administrative Data Division
Postsecondary Branch
National Center for Education Statistics
550 12th Street SW
Washington, DC 20202
richard.reeves@ed.gov
http://nces.ed.gov/ipeds

Fall (12-Month Enrollment)

The 12-month period during which data are collected is July 1 through June 30. Data are collected by race/ethnicity, gender, and level of study (undergraduate or postbaccalaureate) and include unduplicated headcounts and instructional activity (contact or credit hours). These data are also used to calculate a full-time-equivalent (FTE) enrollment based on instructional activity. FTE enrollment is useful for gauging the size of the educational enterprise at the institution. Prior to the 2007–08 IPEDS data collection, the data collected in the 12-Month Enrollment component were part of the Fall Enrollment component, which is conducted during the spring data collection period. However, to improve the timeliness of the data, a separate 12-Month Enrollment survey component was developed in 2007. These data are now collected in the fall for the previous academic year. Of the 7,387 Title IV entities that were expected to respond to the 12-Month Enrollment com-

ponent of the fall 2013 data collection, 7,386 responded, for a response rate of 100.0 percent.

Further information on the IPEDS 12-Month Enrollment component may be obtained from

Bao Le
Administrative Data Division
Postsecondary Branch
National Center for Education Statistics
550 12th Street SW
Washington, DC 20202
bao.le@ed.gov
http://nces.ed.gov/ipeds

Fall (Completions)

This survey was part of the HEGIS series throughout its existence. However, the degree classification taxonomy was revised in 1970–71, 1982–83, 1991–92, 2002–03, and 2009–10. Collection of degree data has been maintained through IPEDS.

Degrees-conferred trend tables arranged by the 2009–10 classification are included in the *Digest of Education Statistics* to provide consistent data from 1970–71 through the most recent year. Data in this edition on associate's and other formal awards below the baccalaureate degree, by field of study, cannot be made comparable with figures from years prior to 1982–83. The nonresponse rate does not appear to be a significant source of nonsampling error for this survey. The response rate over the years has been high; for the fall 2013 Completions component, it was about 100.0 percent. Because of the high response rate, there was no need to conduct a nonresponse bias analysis. Imputation methods for the fall 2013 Completions component are discussed in *Postsecondary Institutions and Cost of Attendance in 2013–14; Degrees and Other Awards Conferred, 2012–13; and 12-Month Enrollment, 2012–13* (NCES 2014-066rev).

The *Integrated Postsecondary Education Data System Data Quality Study* (NCES 2005-175) indicated that most Title IV institutions supplying revised data on completions in 2003–04 were able to supply missing data for the prior year. The small differences between imputed data for the prior year and the revised actual data supplied by the institution indicated that the imputed values produced by NCES were acceptable.

Further information on the IPEDS Completions component may be obtained from

Andrew Mary
Administrative Data Division
Postsecondary Branch
National Center for Education Statistics
550 12th Street SW
Washington, DC 20202
andrew.mary@ed.gov
http://nces.ed.gov/ipeds

Fall (Institutional Characteristics)

This survey collects the basic information necessary to classify institutions, including control, level, and types of programs offered, as well as information on tuition, fees, and room and board charges. Beginning in 2000, the survey collected institutional pricing data from institutions with first-time, full-time, degree/certificate-seeking undergraduate students. Unduplicated full-year enrollment counts and instructional activity are now collected in the 12-Month Enrollment survey. Beginning in 2008–09, the student financial aid data collected include greater detail. The overall unweighted response rate was 100.0 percent for Title IV degree-granting institutions for 2009 data. In the fall 2013 data collection, the response rate for the Institutional Characteristics component among all Title IV entities was 100.0 percent: Of the 7,477 Title IV entities expected to respond to this component, all responded. Data from six institutions that responded to the Institutional Characteristics component contained item nonresponse, however; thus, these missing items were imputed. Imputation methods for the fall 2013 Institutional Characteristics component are discussed in the 2013–14 *Integrated Postsecondary Education Data System (IPEDS) Methodology Report* (NCES 2014-067). The *Integrated Postsecondary Education Data System Data Quality Study* (NCES 2005-175) looked at tuition and price in Title IV institutions. Only 8 percent of institutions in 2002–03 and 2003–04 reported the same data to IPEDS and Thomson Peterson consistently across all selected data items. Differences in wordings or survey items may account for some of these inconsistencies.

Further information on the IPEDS Institutional Characteristics component may be obtained from

Stefanie McDonald
Chris Cody
Administrative Data Division
Postsecondary Branch
National Center for Education Statistics
550 12th Street SW
Washington, DC 20202
srmcdonald@air.org
ccody@air.org
http://nces.ed.gov/ipeds

Winter (Student Financial Aid)

This component was part of the spring data collection from IPEDS data collection years 2000–01 to 2010–11, but it moved to the winter data collection starting with the 2011–12 IPEDS data collection year. This move will aid in the timing of the net price of attendance calculations displayed on College Navigator (http://nces.ed.gov/collegenavigator).

Financial aid data are collected for undergraduate students. Data are collected regarding federal grants, state and local government grants, institutional grants, and loans. The collected data include the number of students receiving each type of financial assistance and the average amount of aid received by type of aid. Beginning in 2008–09, student financial aid data collected includes greater detail on types of aid offered.

In the winter 2013–14 data collection, the Student Financial Aid component collected data on the number of undergraduate students awarded aid and the amount of aid awarded, with particular emphasis on first-time, full-time degree- and certificate-seeking undergraduate students awarded financial aid for the 2012–13 academic year. Of the 7,082 Title IV institutions expected to respond to the Student Financial Aid component, 7,079 Title IV institutions responded, resulting in a response rate of about 100.0 percent.

Further information on the IPEDS Student Financial Aid component may be obtained from

Stefanie McDonald
Chris Cody
Administrative Data Division
Postsecondary Branch
National Center for Education Statistics
550 12th Street SW
Washington, DC 20202
srmcdonald@air.org
ccody@air.org
http://nces.ed.gov/ipeds

Winter (Graduation Rates and Graduation Rates 200 Percent)

In IPEDS data collection years 2012–13 and earlier, the Graduation Rates and 200 Percent Graduation Rates components were collected during the spring collection. In the IPEDS 2013–14 data collection year, however, the Graduation Rates and 200 Percent Graduation Rates collections were moved to the winter data collection.

The 2013–14 Graduation Rates component collected counts of full-time, first-time degree- and certificate-seeking undergraduate students beginning their postsecondary education in the specified cohort year and their completion status as of August 31, 2013 (150 percent of normal program completion time) at the same institution where the students started. Four-year institutions used 2007 as the cohort year, while less-than-4-year institutions used 2010 as the cohort year. The response rate for this component was about 100.0 percent.

The 2013–14 200 Percent Graduation Rates component collected counts of full-time, first-time degree- and certificate-seeking undergraduate students beginning their postsecondary education in the specified cohort year and their completion status as of August 31, 2013 (200 percent of normal program completion time) at the same institution where the students started. Four-year institutions used 2005 as the cohort year, while less-than-4-year institutions used 2009 as the cohort year. The response rate for this component was 100.0 percent.

Further information on the IPEDS Graduation Rates and 200 Percent Graduation Rates components may be obtained from

Gigi Jones
Administrative Data Division
Postsecondary Branch
National Center for Education Statistics
550 12th Street SW
Washington, DC 20202
gigi.jones@ed.gov
http://nces.ed.gov/ipeds/

Spring (Fall Enrollment)

This survey has been part of the HEGIS and IPEDS series since 1966. Response rates for this survey have been relatively high, generally exceeding 85 percent. Beginning in 2000, with web-based data collection, higher response rates were attained. In the spring 2014 data collection, where the Fall Enrollment component covered fall 2013, the response rate was 99.9 percent. Data collection procedures for the Fall Enrollment component of the spring 2014 data collection are presented in *Enrollment in Postsecondary Institutions, Fall 2013; Financial Statistics, Fiscal Year 2013; and Employees in Postsecondary Institutions, Fall 2013* (NCES 2015-012).

Beginning with the fall 1986 survey and the introduction of IPEDS (see above), the survey was redesigned. The survey allows (in alternating years) for the collection of age and residence data. Beginning in 2000, the survey collected instructional activity and unduplicated headcount data, which are needed to compute a standardized, full-time-equivalent (FTE) enrollment statistic for the entire academic year. As of 2007–08, the timeliness of the instructional activity data has been improved by collecting these data in the fall as part of the 12-Month Enrollment component instead of in the spring as part of the Fall Enrollment component.

The *Integrated Postsecondary Education Data System Data Quality Study* (NCES 2005-175) showed that public institutions made the majority of changes to enrollment data during the 2004 revision period. The majority of changes were made to unduplicated headcount data, with the net differences between the original data and the revised data at about 1 percent. Part-time students in general and enrollment in private not-for-profit institutions were often underestimated. The fewest changes by institutions were to Classification of Instructional Programs (CIP) code data. (The CIP is a taxonomic coding scheme that contains titles and descriptions of primarily postsecondary instructional programs.)

Further information on the IPEDS Fall Enrollment component may be obtained from

Bao Le
Administrative Data Division
Postsecondary Branch
National Center for Education Statistics
550 12th Street SW
Washington, DC 20202
bao.le@ed.gov
http://nces.ed.gov/ipeds

Spring (Finance)

This survey was part of the HEGIS series and has been continued under IPEDS. Substantial changes were made in the financial survey instruments in fiscal year (FY) 1976, FY 1982, FY 1987, FY 1997, and FY 2002. While these changes were significant, considerable effort has been made to present only comparable information on trends in this report and to note inconsistencies. The FY 1976 survey instrument contained numerous revisions to earlier survey forms, which made direct comparisons of line items very difficult. Beginning in FY 1982, Pell Grant data were collected in the categories of federal restricted grant and contract revenues and restricted scholarship and fellowship expenditures. The introduction of IPEDS in the FY 1987 survey included several important changes to the survey instrument and data processing procedures. Beginning in FY 1997, data for private institutions were collected using new financial concepts consistent with Financial Accounting Standards Board (FASB) reporting standards, which provide a more comprehensive view of college finance activities. The data for public institutions continued to be collected using the older survey form. The data for public and private institutions were no longer comparable and, as a result, no longer presented together in analysis tables. In FY 2001, public institutions had the option of either continuing to report using Government Accounting Standards Board (GASB) standards or using the new FASB reporting standards. Beginning in FY 2002, public institutions had three options: the original GASB standards, the FASB standards, or the new GASB Statement 35 standards (GASB35).

Possible sources of nonsampling error in the financial statistics include nonresponse, imputation, and misclassification. The unweighted response rate has been about 85 to 90 percent for most of the historic years presented in the *Digest of Education Statistics*; however, in more recent years, response rates have been much higher because Title IV institutions are required to respond. Beginning with 2002, the IPEDS data collection was a full-scale web-based collection, which offered features that improved the quality and timeliness of the data. The ability of IPEDS to tailor online data entry forms for each institution based on characteristics such as institutional control, level of institution, and calendar system, and the institutions' ability to submit their data online, were two such features that improved response.

The response rate for the FY 2013 Finance survey component was 99.9 percent. Data collection procedures for the FY 2013 survey are discussed in *Enrollment in Postsecondary Institutions, Fall 2013; Financial Statistics, Fiscal Year 2013; and Employees in Postsecondary Institutions, Fall 2013: First Look (Provisional Data)* (NCES 2015-012).

The *Integrated Postsecondary Education Data System Data Quality Study* (NCES 2005-175) found that only a small percentage (2.9 percent, or 168) of postsecondary institutions either revised 2002–03 data or submitted data for items they previously left unreported. Though relatively few institutions made changes, the changes made were relatively large—greater than 10 percent of the original data. With a few exceptions, these changes, large as they were, did not greatly affect the aggregate totals.

Further information on the IPEDS Finance component may be obtained from

Bao Le
Administrative Data Division
Postsecondary Branch
National Center for Education Statistics
550 12th Street SW
Washington, DC 20202
bao.le@ed.gov
http://nces.ed.gov/ipeds

Spring (Human Resources)

The Human Resources component was part of the IPEDS winter data collection from data collection years 2000–01 to 2011–12. For the 2012–13 data collection year, the Human Resources component was moved to the spring 2013 data collection, in order to give institutions more time to prepare their survey responses (the spring and winter collections begin on the same date, but the reporting deadline for the spring collection is several weeks later than the reporting deadline for the winter collection).

IPEDS Collection Years 2012–13 and Later

In 2012–13, new occupational categories replaced the primary function/occupational activity categories previously used in the IPEDS Human Resources component. This change was required in order to align the IPEDS Human Resources categories with the 2010 Standard Occupational Classification (SOC) system. In tandem with the change in 2012–13 from using primary function/occupational activity categories to using the new occupational categories, the sections making up the IPEDS Human Resources component (which previously had been Employees by Assigned Position, Fall Staff, and Salaries) were changed to Full-Time Instructional Staff, Full-time Noninstructional Staff, Salaries, Part-Time Staff, and New Hires.

The webpage "Changes to the 2012–13 IPEDS Data Collection and Changes to Occupational Categories for the 2012–13 Human Resources Data Collection" (http://nces.ed.gov/ipeds/surveys/datacollection2012-13.asp) provides information on the redesigned IPEDS Human Resources component. "Resources for Implementing Changes to the IPEDS Human Resources (HR) Survey Component Due to Updated 2010 Standard Occupational Classification (SOC) System" (http://nces.ed.gov/ipeds/resource/soc.asp) is a webpage containing additional information, including notes comparing the new classifications with the old ("Comparison of New IPEDS Occupational Categories with Previous Categories"), a crosswalk from the new IPEDS occupational categories to the 2010 SOC occupational categories ("New IPEDS Occupational Categories and 2010 SOC"), answers to frequently asked questions, and a link to current IPEDS Human Resources survey screens.

In the 2012–13 collection year, the response rate for the (spring 2013) Human Resources component was 99.9 percent. Data collection procedures for this component are pre-

sented in *Enrollment in Postsecondary Institutions, Fall 2012; Financial Statistics, Fiscal Year 2012; Graduation Rates, Selected Cohorts, 2004–09; and Employees in Postsecondary Institutions, Fall 2012: First Look (Provisional Data)* (NCES 2013-183). In the 2013–14 collection year, the response rate for the (spring 2014) Human Resources component was also 99.9 percent. Data collection procedures for this component are presented in *Enrollment in Postsecondary Institutions, Fall 2013; Financial Statistics, Fiscal Year 2013; and Employees in Postsecondary Institutions, Fall 2013: First Look (Provisional Data)* (NCES 2015-012).

IPEDS Collection Years Prior to 2012–13

In collection years before 2001–02, IPEDS conducted a Fall Staff survey and a Salaries survey; in the 2001–02 collection year, the Employees by Assigned Position survey was added to IPEDS. In the 2005–06 collection year, these three surveys became sections of the IPEDS "Human Resources" component.

Data gathered by the Employees by Assigned Position section categorized all employees by full- or part-time status, faculty status, and primary function/occupational activity. Institutions with M.D. or D.O. programs were required to report their medical school employees separately. A response to the EAP was required of all 6,858 Title IV institutions and administrative offices in the United States and other jurisdictions for winter 2008–09, and 6,845, or 99.8 percent unweighted, responded. Of the 6,970 Title IV institutions and administrative offices required to respond to the winter 2009–10 EAP, 6,964, or 99.9 percent, responded. And of the 7,256 Title IV institutions and administrative offices required to respond to the EAP for winter 2010–11, 7,252, or 99.9 percent, responded.

The main functions/occupational activities of the EAP section were primarily instruction, instruction combined with research and/or public service, primarily research, primarily public service, executive/administrative/managerial, other professionals (support/service), graduate assistants, technical and paraprofessionals, clerical and secretarial, skilled crafts, and service/maintenance.

All full-time instructional faculty classified in the EAP full-time non-medical school part as either (1) primarily instruction or (2) instruction combined with research and/or public service were included in the Salaries section, unless they were exempt.

The Fall Staff section categorized all staff on the institution's payroll as of November 1 of the collection year by employment status (full time or part time), primary function/occupational activity, gender, and race/ethnicity. These data elements were collected from degree-granting and non-degree-granting institutions; however, additional data elements were collected from degree-granting institutions and related administrative offices with 15 or more full-time staff. These elements include faculty status, contract length/teaching period, academic rank, salary class intervals, and newly hired full-time permanent staff.

The Fall Staff section, which was required only in odd-numbered reporting years, was not required during the 2008–09 Human Resources data collection. However, of the 6,858 Title IV institutions and administrative offices in the United States and other jurisdictions, 3,295, or 48.0 percent unweighted, did provide data in the Fall Staff section that year. During the 2009–10 Human Resources data collection, when all 6,970 Title IV institutions and administrative offices were required to respond to the Fall Staff section, 6,964, or 99.9 percent, did so. A response to the Fall Staff section of the 2010–11 Human Resources collection was optional, and 3,364 Title IV institutions and administrative offices responded that year (a response rate of 46.3 percent).

The *Integrated Postsecondary Education Data System Data Quality Study* (NCES 2005-175) found that for 2003–04 employee data items, changes were made by 1.2 percent (77) of the institutions that responded. All institutions making changes made changes that resulted in different employee counts. For both institutional and aggregate differences, however, the changes had little impact on the original employee count submissions. A large number of institutions reported different staff data to IPEDS and Thomson Peterson; however, the magnitude of the differences was small—usually no more than 17 faculty members for any faculty variable.

The Salaries section collected data for full-time instructional faculty (except those in medical schools in the EAP section, described above) on the institution's payroll as of November 1 of the collection year by contract length/teaching period, gender, and academic rank. The reporting of data by faculty status in the Salaries section was required from 4-year degree-granting institutions and above only. Salary outlays and fringe benefits were also collected for full-time instructional staff on 9/10- and 11/12-month contracts/teaching periods. This section was applicable to degree-granting institutions unless exempt.

Between 1966–67 and 1985–86, this survey differed from other HEGIS surveys in that imputations were not made for nonrespondents. Thus, there is some possibility that the salary averages presented in this report may differ from the results of a complete enumeration of all colleges and universities. Beginning with the surveys for 1987–88, the IPEDS data tabulation procedures included imputations for survey nonrespondents. The unweighted response rate for the 2008–09 Salaries survey section was 99.9 percent. The response rate for the 2009–10 Salaries section was 100.0 percent (4,453 of the 4,455 required institutions responded), and the response rate for 2010–11 was 99.9 percent (4,561 of the 4,565 required institutions responded). Imputation methods for the 2010–11 Salaries survey section are discussed in *Employees in Postsecondary Institutions, Fall 2010, and Salaries of Full-Time Instructional Staff, 2010–11* (NCES 2012-276).

Although data from this survey are not subject to sampling error, sources of nonsampling error may include computational errors and misclassification in reporting and processing. The electronic reporting system does allow corrections to prior-year reported or missing data, and this should help with these problems. Also, NCES reviews indi-vidual institutions' data for internal and longitudinal consistency and contacts institutions to check inconsistent data.

The *Integrated Postsecondary Education Data System Data Quality Study* (NCES 2005-175) found that only 1.3 percent of the responding Title IV institutions in 2003–04 made changes to their salaries data. The differences between the imputed data and the revised data were small and found to have little impact on the published data.

Further information on the Human Resources component may be obtained from

Moussa Ezzeddine
Administrative Data Division
Postsecondary Branch
National Center for Education Statistics
550 12th Street SW
Washington, DC 20202
moussa.ezzeddine@ed.gov

Library Statistics

In the past, NCES collected library data through the Public Libraries Survey (PLS), the State Library Agencies (StLA) Survey, the Academic Libraries Survey (ALS), and the Library Media Centers (LMC) Survey. On October 1, 2007, the administration of the Public Libraries Survey (PLS) and the State Library Agencies (StLA) Survey was transferred to the Institute of Museum and Library Services (IMLS) (see below).

NCES administered the Academic Libraries Survey (ALS) on a 3-year cycle between 1966 and 1988. From 1988 through 1999, ALS was a component of the Integrated Postsecondary Education Data System (IPEDS) and was on a 2-year cycle. Beginning in the year 2000, ALS began collecting data independent from the IPEDS data collection, but it remained on a 2-year cycle. ALS provided data on approximately 3,700 academic libraries. In aggregate, these data provided an overview of the status of academic libraries nationally and statewide. The survey collected data on the libraries in the entire universe of degree-granting institutions. Beginning with the collection of FY 2000 data, ALS changed to web-based data collection. ALS produced descriptive statistics on academic libraries in postsecondary institutions in the 50 states, the District of Columbia, and the outlying areas. *Academic Libraries: 2012* (NCES 2014-038) presented tabulations for the 2012 survey, the most recent administration of ALS for which data are available. ALS will again be a component of IPEDS beginning in the 2014–15 IPEDS data collection year (Spring 2015 collection).

School library data were collected on the School and Principal Surveys of the 1990–91 Schools and Staffing Survey (SASS). The School Library Media Centers (LMC) Survey became a component of SASS with the 1993–94 administration of the survey. Thus, readers should refer to the section on the Schools and Staffing Survey, below, regarding data on school libraries. Data for the 2011–12 School Library Media Centers (LMC) Survey are available on the NCES website at http://nces.ed.gov/surveys/sass/index.asp.

Further information on library statistics may be obtained from

Tai Phan
Administrative Data Division
National Center for Education Statistics
550 12th Street SW
Washington, DC 20202
tai.phan@ed.gov
http://nces.ed.gov/surveys/libraries

National Adult Literacy Survey

The National Adult Literacy Survey (NALS), funded by the U.S. Department of Education and 12 states, was created in 1992 as a new measure of literacy. The aim of the survey was to profile the English literacy of adults in the United States based on their performance across a wide array of tasks that reflect the types of materials and demands they encounter in their daily lives.

To gather information on adults' literacy skills, trained staff interviewed a nationally representative sample of nearly 13,600 individuals ages 16 and older during the first 8 months of 1992. These participants had been randomly selected to represent the adult population in the country as a whole. Black and Hispanic households were oversampled to ensure reliable estimates of literacy proficiencies and to permit analyses of the performance of these subpopulations. In addition, some 1,100 inmates from 80 federal and state prisons were interviewed to gather information on the proficiencies of the prison population. In total, nearly 26,000 adults were surveyed.

Each survey participant was asked to spend approximately an hour responding to a series of diverse literacy tasks, as well as to questions about his or her demographic characteristics, educational background, reading practices, and other areas related to literacy. Based on their responses to the survey tasks, adults received proficiency scores along three scales that reflect varying degrees of skill in prose, document, and quantitative literacy. The results of the 1992 survey were first published in *Adult Literacy in America: A First Look at the Findings of the National Adult Literacy Survey* (NCES 93-275), in September 1993. See the section on the National Assessment of Adult Literacy (below) for information on later adult literacy surveys.

Further information on NALS may be obtained from

Sheida White
Assessments Division
National Assessment Branch
National Center for Education Statistics
550 12th Street SW
Washington, DC 20202
sheida.white@ed.gov
http://nces.ed.gov/naal/nals_products.asp

National Assessment of Adult Literacy

The 2003 National Assessment of Adult Literacy (NAAL) was conducted to measure both English literacy and health literacy. The assessment was administered to 19,000 adults (including 1,200 prison inmates) age 16 and over in all 50 states and the District of Columbia. Components of the assessment included a background questionnaire; a prison component that assesses the literacy skills of adults in federal and state prisons; the State Assessment of Adult Literacy (SAAL), a voluntary survey given in conjunction with NAAL; a health literacy component; the Fluency Addition to NAAL (FAN), an oral reading assessment; and the Adult Literacy Supplemental Assessment (ALSA). ALSA is an alternative to main NAAL for those with very low scores on seven core screening questions. NAAL assesses literacy directly through the completion of tasks that cover quantitative literacy, document literacy, and prose literacy. Results were reported using the following achievement levels: *Below Basic, Basic, Intermediate,* and *Proficient.*

Results from NAAL and NALS can be compared. NALS offers a snapshot of the condition of literacy of the U.S. population as a whole and among key population subgroups in 1992. NAAL provides an updated picture of adult literacy skills in 2003, revealing changes in literacy over the intervening decade.

Further information on NAAL may be obtained from

Sheida White
Assessments Division
National Assessment Branch
National Center for Education Statistics
550 12th Street SW
Washington, DC 20202
sheida.white@ed.gov
http://nces.ed.gov/naal

National Assessment of Educational Progress

The National Assessment of Educational Progress (NAEP) is a series of cross-sectional studies initially implemented in 1969 to assess the educational achievement of U.S. students and monitor changes in those achievements. In the main national NAEP, a nationally representative sample of students is assessed at grades 4, 8, and 12 in various academic subjects. The assessments are based on frameworks developed by the National Assessment Governing Board (NAGB). Assessment items include both multiple-choice and constructed-response (requiring written answers) items. Results are reported in two ways: by average score and by achievement level. Average scores are reported for the nation, for participating states and jurisdictions, and for subgroups of the population. Percentages of students performing at or above three achievement levels (*Basic, Proficient,* and *Advanced*) are also reported for these groups.

From 1990 until 2001, main NAEP was conducted for states and other jurisdictions that chose to participate. In 2002, under the provisions of the No Child Left Behind Act of 2001, all states began to participate in main NAEP, and an aggregate of all state samples replaced the separate national sample.

Results are available for the mathematics assessments administered in 2000, 2003, 2005, 2007, 2009, 2011, 2013, and 2015. In 2005, NAGB called for the development of a new mathematics framework. The revisions made to the mathematics framework for the 2005 assessment were intended to reflect recent curricular emphases and better assess the specific objectives for students at each grade level.

The revised mathematics framework focuses on two dimensions: mathematical content and cognitive demand. By considering these two dimensions for each item in the assessment, the framework ensures that NAEP assesses an appropriate balance of content, as well as a variety of ways of knowing and doing mathematics.

Since the 2005 changes to the mathematics framework were minimal for grades 4 and 8, comparisons over time can be made between assessments conducted before and after the framework's implementation for these grades. The changes that the 2005 framework made to the grade 12 assessment, however, were too drastic to allow grade 12 results from before and after implementation to be directly compared. These changes included adding more questions on algebra, data analysis, and probability to reflect changes in high school mathematics standards and coursework; merging the measurement and geometry content areas; and changing the reporting scale from 0–500 to 0–300. For more information regarding the 2005 mathematics framework revisions, see http://nces.ed.gov/nationsreportcard/mathematics/frameworkcomparison.asp.

Results are available for the reading assessments administered in 2000, 2002, 2003, 2005, 2007, 2009, 2011, 2013, and 2015. In 2009, a new framework was developed for the 4th-, 8th-, and 12th-grade NAEP reading assessments.

Both a content alignment study and a reading trend or bridge study were conducted to determine if the new assessment was comparable to the prior assessment. Overall, the results of the special analyses suggested that the assessments were similar in terms of their item and scale characteristics and the results they produced for important demographic groups of students. Thus, it was determined that the results of the 2009 reading assessment could still be compared to those from earlier assessment years, thereby maintaining the trend lines first established in 1992. For more information regarding the 2009 reading framework revisions, see http://nces.ed.gov/nationsreportcard/reading/whatmeasure.asp.

In spring 2013, NAEP released results from the NAEP 2012 economics assessment in *The Nation's Report Card: Economics 2012* (NCES 2013-453). First administered in 2006, the NAEP economics assessment measures 12th-graders' understanding of a wide range of topics in three main content areas: market economy, national economy, and international economy. The 2012 assessment is based on a nationally representative sample of nearly 11,000 12th-graders.

In *The Nation's Report Card: A First Look—2013 Mathematics and Reading* (NCES 2014-451), NAEP released the results of the 2013 mathematics and reading assessments. Results can also be accessed using the interactive graphics and downloadable data available at the new online Nation's Report Card website (http://nationsreportcard.gov/reading_math_2013/#/).

The online interactive report *The Nation's Report Card: 2014 U.S. History, Geography, and Civics at Grade 8* (NCES 2015-112) provides grade 8 results for the 2014 NAEP U.S. history, geography, and civics assessments. Trend results for previous assessment years in these three subjects, as well as information on school and student participation rates and sample tasks and student responses are also presented.

In addition to conducting the main assessments, NAEP also conducts the long-term trend assessments and trial urban district assessments. Long-term trend assessments provide an opportunity to observe educational progress in reading and mathematics of 9-, 13-, and 17-year-olds since the early 1970s. The long-term trend reading assessment measures students' reading comprehension skills using an array of passages that vary by text types and length. The assessment was designed to measure students' ability to locate specific information in the text provided; make inferences across a passage to provide an explanation; and identify the main idea in the text.

The NAEP long-term trend assessment in mathematics measures knowledge of mathematical facts; ability to carry out computations using paper and pencil; knowledge of basic formulas, such as those applied in geometric settings; and ability to apply mathematics to skills of daily life, such as those involving time and money.

The Nation's Report Card: Trends in Academic Progress 2012 (NCES 2013-456) provides the results of 12 long-term trend reading assessments dating back to 1971 and 11 long-term trend mathematics assessments dating back to 1973.

The NAEP Trial Urban District Assessment (TUDA) focuses attention on urban education and measures educational progress within participating large urban districts. TUDA mathematics and reading assessments are based on the same mathematics and reading assessments used to report national and state results. TUDA reading results were first reported for 6 urban districts in 2002, and TUDA mathematics results were first reported for 10 urban districts in 2003.

The Nation's Report Card: A First Look—2013 Mathematics and Reading Trial Urban District Assessment (NCES 2014-466) provides the results of the 2013 mathematics and reading TUDA, which measured the reading and mathematics progress of 4th- and 8th-graders from 21 urban school districts. Results from the 2013 mathematics and reading TUDA can also be accessed using the interactive graphics and downloadable data available at the online TUDA website (http://nationsreportcard.gov/reading_math_tuda_2013/#/).

Further information on NAEP may be obtained from

Daniel McGrath
Assessments Division
 Reporting and Dissemination Branch
National Center for Education Statistics
550 12th Street SW
Washington, DC 20202
daniel.mcgrath@ed.gov
http://nces.ed.gov/nationsreportcard

National Education Longitudinal Study of 1988

The National Education Longitudinal Study of 1988 (NELS:88) was the third major secondary school student longitudinal study conducted by NCES. The two studies that preceded NELS:88—the National Longitudinal Study of the High School Class of 1972 (NLS:72) and the High School and Beyond Longitudinal Study (HS&B) in 1980—surveyed high school seniors (and sophomores in HS&B) through high school, postsecondary education, and work and family formation experiences. Unlike its predecessors, NELS:88 began with a cohort of 8th-grade students. In 1988, some 25,000 8th-graders, their parents, their teachers, and their school principals were surveyed. Follow-ups were conducted in 1990 and 1992, when a majority of these students were in the 10th and 12th grades, respectively, and then 2 years after their scheduled high school graduation, in 1994. A fourth follow-up was conducted in 2000.

NELS:88 was designed to provide trend data about critical transitions experienced by young people as they develop, attend school, and embark on their careers. It complements and strengthens state and local efforts by furnishing new information on how school policies, teacher practices, and family involvement affect student educational outcomes (i.e., academic achievement, persistence in school, and participation in postsecondary education). For the base year, NELS:88 included a multifaceted student questionnaire, four cognitive tests, a parent questionnaire, a teacher questionnaire, and a school questionnaire.

In 1990, when most of the students were in 10th grade, students, school dropouts, their teachers, and their school principals were surveyed. (Parents were not surveyed in the 1990 follow-up.) In 1992, when most of the students were in 12th grade, the second follow-up conducted surveys of students, dropouts, parents, teachers, and school principals. Also, information from the students' transcripts was collected. The 1994 survey data were collected when most sample members had completed high school. The primary goals of the 1994 survey were (1) to provide data for trend comparisons with NLS:72 and HS&B; (2) to address issues of employment and postsecondary access and choice; and (3) to ascertain how many dropouts had returned to school and by what route. The 2000 follow-up examined the educational and labor market outcomes of the 1988 cohort at a time of transition. Most had been out of high school 8 years; many had completed their postsecondary educations, were embarking on first or even second careers, and were starting families.

Further information on NELS:88 may be obtained from

Elise Christopher
Sample Surveys Division
Longitudinal Surveys Branch
National Center for Education Statistics
550 12th Street SW
Washington, DC 20202
elise.christopher@ed.gov
http://nces.ed.gov/surveys/nels88

National Household Education Surveys Program

The National Household Education Surveys Program (NHES) is a data collection system that is designed to address a wide range of education-related issues. Surveys have been conducted in 1991, 1993, 1995, 1996, 1999, 2001, 2003, 2005, 2007, and 2012. NHES targets specific populations for detailed data collection. It is intended to provide more detailed data on the topics and populations of interest than are collected through supplements to other household surveys.

The topics addressed by NHES:1991 were early childhood education and adult education. About 60,000 households were screened for NHES:1991. In the Early Childhood Education Survey, about 14,000 parents/guardians of 3- to 8-year-olds completed interviews about their children's early educational experiences. Included in this component were participation in nonparental care/education; care arrangements and school; and family, household, and child characteristics. In the NHES:1991 Adult Education Survey, about 9,800 people 16 years of age and older, identified as having participated in an adult education activity in the previous 12 months, were questioned about their activities. Data were collected on programs and up to four courses, including the subject matter, duration, sponsorship, purpose, and cost. Information on the household and the adult's background and current employment was also collected.

In NHES:1993, nearly 64,000 households were screened. Approximately 11,000 parents of 3- to 7-year-olds completed interviews for the School Readiness Survey. Topics included the developmental characteristics of preschoolers; school adjustment and teacher feedback to parents for kindergartners and primary students; center-based program participation; early school experiences; home activities with family members; and health status. In the School Safety and Discipline Survey, about 12,700 parents of children in grades 3 to 12 and about 6,500 youth in grades 6 to 12 were interviewed about their school experiences. Topics included the school learning environment, discipline policy, safety at school, victimization, the availability and use of alcohol/drugs, and alcohol/drug education. Peer norms for behavior in school and substance use were also included in this topical component. Extensive family and household background information was collected, as well as characteristics of the school attended by the child.

In NHES:1995, the Early Childhood Program Participation Survey and the Adult Education Survey were similar to those fielded in 1991. In the Early Childhood component, about 14,000 parents of children from birth to 3rd grade were interviewed out of 16,000 sampled, for a completion rate of 90.4 percent. In the Adult Education Survey, about 24,000 adults were sampled and 82.3 percent (20,000) completed the interview.

NHES:1996 covered parent and family involvement in education and civic involvement. Data on homeschooling and school choice also were collected. The 1996 survey screened about 56,000 households. For the Parent and Family Involvement in Education Survey, nearly 21,000 parents of children in grades 3 to 12 were interviewed. For the Civic Involvement Survey, about 8,000 youth in grades 6 to 12, about 9,000 parents, and about 2,000 adults were interviewed. The 1996 survey also addressed public library use. Adults in almost 55,000 households were interviewed to support state-level estimates of household public library use.

NHES:1999 collected end-of-decade estimates of key indicators from the surveys conducted throughout the 1990s. Approximately 60,000 households were screened for a total of about 31,000 interviews with parents of children from birth through grade 12 (including about 6,900 infants, toddlers, and preschoolers) and adults age 16 or older not enrolled in grade 12 or below. Key indicators included participation of children in nonparental care and early childhood programs, school experiences, parent/family involvement in education at home and at school, youth community service activities, plans for future education, and adult participation in educational activities and community service.

NHES:2001 included two surveys that were largely repeats of similar surveys included in earlier NHES collections. The Early Childhood Program Participation Survey was similar in content to the Early Childhood Program Participation Survey fielded as part of NHES:1995, and the Adult Education and Lifelong Learning Survey was similar in content to the Adult Education Survey of NHES:1995. The Before- and After-School Programs and Activities Survey, while containing items fielded in earlier NHES collections, had a number of new items that collected information about what school-age children were doing during the time they spent in child care or in other activities, what parents were looking for in care arrangements and activities, and parent evaluations of care arrangements and activities. Parents of approximately 6,700 children from birth through age 6 who were not yet in kindergarten completed Early Childhood Program Participation Survey interviews. Nearly 10,900 adults completed Adult Education and Lifelong Learning Survey interviews, and parents of nearly 9,600 children in kindergarten through grade 8 completed Before- and After-School Programs and Activities Survey interviews.

NHES:2003 included two surveys: the Parent and Family Involvement in Education Survey and the Adult Education for Work-Related Reasons Survey (the first administration). Whereas previous adult education surveys were more general in scope, this survey had a narrower focus on occupation-related adult education programs. It collected in-depth information about training and education in which adults participated specifically for work-related reasons, either to prepare for work or a career or to maintain or improve work-related skills and knowledge they already had. The Parent and Family Involvement Survey expanded on the first survey fielded on this topic in 1996. In 2003, screeners were completed with 32,050 households. About 12,700 of the 16,000 sampled adults completed the Adult Education for Work-Related Reasons Survey, for a weighted response rate of 76 percent. For the Parent and Family Involvement in Education Survey, inter-

views were completed by the parents of about 12,400 of the 14,900 sampled children in kindergarten through grade 12, yielding a weighted unit response rate of 83 percent.

NHES:2005 included surveys that covered adult education, early childhood program participation, and after-school programs and activities. Data were collected from about 8,900 adults for the Adult Education Survey, from parents of about 7,200 children for the Early Childhood Program Participation Survey, and from parents of nearly 11,700 children for the After-School Programs and Activities Survey. These surveys were substantially similar to the surveys conducted in 2001, with the exceptions that the Adult Education Survey addressed a new topic—informal learning activities for personal interest—and the Early Childhood Program Participation Survey and After-School Programs and Activities Survey did not collect information about before-school care for school-age children.

NHES:2007 fielded the Parent and Family Involvement in Education Survey and the School Readiness Survey. These surveys were similar in design and content to surveys included in the 2003 and 1993 collections, respectively. New features added to the Parent and Family Involvement Survey were questions about supplemental education services provided by schools and school districts (including use of and satisfaction with such services), as well as questions that would efficiently identify the school attended by the sampled students. New features added to the School Readiness Survey were questions that collected details about TV programs watched by the sampled children. For the Parent and Family Involvement Survey, interviews were completed with parents of 10,680 sampled children in kindergarten through grade 12, including 10,370 students enrolled in public or private schools and 310 homeschooled children. For the School Readiness Survey, interviews were completed with parents of 2,630 sampled children ages 3 to 6 and not yet in kindergarten. Parents who were interviewed about children in kindergarten through 2nd grade for the Parent and Family Involvement Survey were also asked some questions about these children's school readiness.

The 2007 and earlier administrations of NHES used a random-digit-dial sample of landline phones and computer-assisted telephone interviewing to conduct interviews. However, due to declining response rates for all telephone surveys and the increase in households that only or mostly use a cell phone instead of a landline, the data collection method was changed to an address-based sample survey for NHES:2012. Because of this change in survey mode, readers should use caution when comparing NHES:2012 estimates to those of prior NHES administrations.

NHES:2012 included the Parent and Family Involvement in Education Survey and the Early Childhood Program Participation Survey. The Parent and Family Involvement in Education Survey gathered data on students who were enrolled in kindergarten through grade 12 or who were homeschooled at equivalent grade levels. Survey questions that pertained to students enrolled in kindergarten through grade 12 requested information on various aspects of parent involvement in education (such as help with homework, family activities, and parent involvement at school) and survey questions pertaining to homeschooled students requested information on the student's homeschooling experiences, the sources of the curriculum, and the reasons for homeschooling.

The 2012 Parent and Family Involvement in Education Survey questionnaires were completed for 17,563 (397 homeschooled and 17,166 enrolled) children, for a weighted unit response rate of 78.4 percent. The overall estimated unit response rate (the product of the screener unit response rate of 73.8 percent and the Parent and Family Involvement in Education Survey unit response rate) was 57.8 percent.

The 2012 Early Childhood Program Participation Survey collected data on the early care and education arrangements and early learning of children from birth through the age of 5 who were not yet enrolled in kindergarten. Questionnaires were completed for 7,893 children, for a weighted unit response rate of 78.7 percent. The overall estimated weighted unit response rate (the product of the screener weighted unit response rate of 73.8 percent and the Early Childhood Program Participation Survey unit weighted response rate) was 58.1 percent.

Data for the 2012 NHES Parent and Family Involvement in Education Survey are available in the First Look report, *Parent and Family Involvement in Education, From the National Household Education Surveys Program of 2012* (NCES 2013-028). Data for the 2012 NHES Early Childhood Program Participation Survey are available in the First Look report *Early Childhood Program Participation, From the National Household Education Surveys Program of 2012* (NCES 2013-029).

Further information on NHES may be obtained from

Andrew Zukerberg
Gail Mulligan
Sample Surveys Division
National Center for Education Statistics
550 12th Street SW
Washington, DC 20202
andrew.zukerberg@ed.gov
gail.mulligan@ed.gov
http://nces.ed.gov/nhes

National Longitudinal Study of the High School Class of 1972

The National Longitudinal Study of the High School Class of 1972 (NLS:72) began with the collection of base-year survey data from a sample of about 19,000 high school seniors in the spring of 1972. Five follow-up surveys of these students were conducted in 1973, 1974, 1976, 1979, and 1986. NLS:72 was designed to provide the education community with information on the transitions of young adults from high school through postsecondary education and the workplace.

In addition to the follow-ups, a number of supplemental data collection efforts were made. For example, a Postsec-

ondary Education Transcript Study (PETS) was conducted in 1984; in 1986, the fifth follow-up included a supplement for those who became teachers.

The sample design for NLS:72 was a stratified, two-stage probability sample of 12th-grade students from all schools, public and private, in the 50 states and the District of Columbia during the 1971–72 school year. During the first stage of sampling, about 1,070 schools were selected for participation in the base-year survey. As many as 18 students were selected at random from each of the sample schools. The sizes of both the school and student samples were increased during the first follow-up survey. Beginning with the first follow-up and continuing through the fourth follow-up, about 1,300 schools participated in the survey and slightly fewer than 23,500 students were sampled. The unweighted response rates for each of the different rounds of data collection were 80 percent or higher.

Sample retention rates across the survey years were quite high. For example, of the individuals responding to the base-year questionnaire, the percentages who responded to the first, second, third, and fourth follow-up questionnaires were about 94, 93, 89, and 83 percent, respectively. The fifth follow-up took its sample from students who had participated in at least one of the prior surveys. In all, 91.7 percent of participants had responded to at least five of the six surveys, and 62.1 percent had responded to all six.

Further information on NLS:72 may be obtained from

Aurora D'Amico
Sample Surveys Division
Longitudinal Surveys Branch
National Center for Education Statistics
550 12th Street SW
Washington, DC 20202
aurora.damico@ed.gov
http://nces.ed.gov/surveys/nls72

National Postsecondary Student Aid Study

The National Postsecondary Student Aid Study (NPSAS) is a comprehensive nationwide study of how students and their families pay for postsecondary education. Data gathered from the study are used to help guide future federal student financial aid policy. The study covers nationally representative samples of undergraduates, graduates, and first-professional students in the 50 states, the District of Columbia, and Puerto Rico, including students attending less-than-2-year institutions, community colleges, 4-year colleges, and universities. Participants include students who do not receive aid and those who do receive financial aid. Since NPSAS identifies nationally representative samples of student subpopulations of interest to policymakers and obtains baseline data for longitudinal study of these subpopulations, data from the study provide the base-year sample for the Beginning Postsecondary Students (BPS) longitudinal study and the Baccalaureate and Beyond (B&B) longitudinal study.

Originally, NPSAS was conducted every 3 years. Beginning with the 1999–2000 study (NPSAS:2000), NPSAS has been conducted every 4 years. NPSAS:08 included a new set of instrument items to obtain baseline measures of the awareness of two new federal grants introduced in 2006: the Academic Competitiveness Grant (ACG) and the National Science and Mathematics Access to Retain Talent (SMART) grant.

The first NPSAS (NPSAS:87) was conducted during the 1986–87 school year. Data were gathered from about 1,100 colleges, universities, and other postsecondary institutions; 60,000 students; and 14,000 parents. These data provided information on the cost of postsecondary education, the distribution of financial aid, and the characteristics of both aided and nonaided students and their families.

For NPSAS:93, information on 77,000 undergraduates and graduate students enrolled during the school year was collected at 1,000 postsecondary institutions. The sample included students who were enrolled at any time between July 1, 1992, and June 30, 1993. About 66,000 students and a subsample of their parents were interviewed by telephone. NPSAS:96 contained information on more than 48,000 undergraduate and graduate students from about 1,000 postsecondary institutions who were enrolled at any time during the 1995–96 school year. NPSAS:2000 included nearly 62,000 students (50,000 undergraduates and almost 12,000 graduate students) from 1,000 postsecondary institutions. NPSAS:04 collected data on about 80,000 undergraduates and 11,000 graduate students from 1,400 postsecondary institutions. For NPSAS:08, about 114,000 undergraduate students and 14,000 graduate students who were enrolled in postsecondary education during the 2007–08 school year were selected from more than 1,730 postsecondary institutions.

NPSAS:12 sampled about 95,000 undergraduates and 16,000 graduate students from approximately 1,500 postsecondary institutions. Public access to the data is available online through PowerStats (http://nces.ed.gov/datalab/).

Further information on NPSAS may be obtained from

Aurora D'Amico
Tracy Hunt-White
Sample Surveys Division
Longitudinal Surveys Branch
National Center for Education Statistics
550 12th Street SW
Washington, DC 20202
aurora.damico@ed.gov
tracy.hunt-white@ed.gov
http://nces.ed.gov/npsas

National Study of Postsecondary Faculty

The National Study of Postsecondary Faculty (NSOPF) was designed to provide data about faculty to postsecondary researchers, planners, and policymakers. NSOPF is the most comprehensive study of faculty in postsecondary education institutions ever undertaken.

The first cycle of NSOPF (NSOPF:88) was conducted by NCES with support from the National Endowment for the Humanities (NEH) in 1987–88 with a sample of 480 colleges and universities, over 3,000 department chairpersons, and over 11,000 instructional faculty. The second cycle of NSOPF (NSOPF:93) was conducted by NCES with support from NEH and the National Science Foundation in 1992–93. NSOPF:93 was limited to surveys of institutions and faculty, but with a substantially expanded sample of 970 colleges and universities and 31,350 faculty and instructional staff. The third cycle, NSPOF:99, included 960 degree-granting postsecondary institutions and approximately 18,000 faculty and instructional staff. The fourth cycle of NSOPF was conducted in 2003–04 and included 1,080 degree-granting postsecondary institutions and approximately 26,000 faculty and instructional staff.

There are no plans to repeat the study. Rather, NCES plans to provide technical assistance to state postsecondary data systems and to encourage the development of robust connections between faculty and student data systems so that key questions concerning faculty, instruction, and student outcomes—such as persistence and completion—can be addressed.

Further information on NSOPF may be obtained from

Aurora D'Amico
Sample Surveys Division
Longitudinal Surveys Branch
National Center for Education Statistics
550 12th Street SW
Washington, DC 20202
aurora.damico@ed.gov
http://nces.ed.gov/surveys/nsopf

Principal Follow-up Survey

The Principal Follow-up Survey (PFS), first conducted in school year 2008–09, is a component of the 2011–12 Schools and Staffing Survey (SASS). The 2012–13 PFS was administered in order to provide attrition rates for principals in K–12 public and private schools. The goal was to assess how many of those who worked as a principal in the 2011–12 school year still worked as a principal in the same school in the 2012–13 school year, how many had moved to become a principal in another school, and how many no longer worked as a principal. The PFS sample included all schools whose principals had completed SASS principal questionnaires. Schools that had returned a completed 2011–12 SASS principal questionnaire were mailed the PFS form in March 2013.

Further information on the PFS may be obtained from

Chelsea Owens
Sample Surveys Division
Cross-Sectional Surveys Branch
National Center for Education Statistics
550 12th Street SW
Washington, DC 20202
chelsea.owens@ed.gov
http://nces.ed.gov/surveys/sass/

Private School Universe Survey

The purposes of the Private School Universe Survey (PSS) data collection activities are (1) to build an accurate and complete list of private schools to serve as a sampling frame for NCES sample surveys of private schools and (2) to report data on the total number of private schools, teachers, and students in the survey universe. Begun in 1989 under the U.S. Census Bureau, the PSS has been conducted every 2 years, and data for the 1989–90, 1991–92, 1993–94, 1995–96, 1997–98, 1999–2000, 2001–02, 2003–04, 2005–06, 2007–08, 2009–10, and 2011–12 school years have been released. A First Look report of the 2011–12 PSS data, *Characteristics of Private Schools in the United States: Results From the 2011–12 Private School Universe Survey* (NCES 2013-316) was published in July 2013.

The PSS produces data similar to that of the Common Core of Data for public schools, and can be used for public-private comparisons. The data are useful for a variety of policy- and research-relevant issues, such as the growth of religiously affiliated schools, the number of private high school graduates, the length of the school year for various private schools, and the number of private school students and teachers.

The target population for this universe survey is all private schools in the United States that meet the PSS criteria of a private school (i.e., the private school is an institution that provides instruction for any of grades K through 12, has one or more teachers to give instruction, is not administered by a public agency, and is not operated in a private home).

The survey universe is composed of schools identified from a variety of sources. The main source is a list frame initially developed for the 1989–90 PSS. The list is updated regularly by matching it with lists provided by nationwide private school associations, state departments of education, and other national guides and sources that list private schools. The other source is an area frame search in approximately 124 geographic areas, conducted by the U.S. Census Bureau.

Of the 40,302 schools included in the 2009–10 sample, 10,229 were found ineligible for the survey. Those not responding numbered 1,856, and those responding numbered 28,217. The unweighted response rate for the 2009–10 PSS survey was 93.8 percent.

Of the 39,325 schools included in the 2011–12 sample, 10,030 cases were considered as out-of-scope (not eligible for the PSS). A total of 26,983 private schools completed a PSS interview (15.8 percent completed online), while 2,312 schools refused to participate, resulting in an unweighted response rate of 92.1 percent.

Further information on the PSS may be obtained from

Steve Broughman
Sample Surveys Division
Cross-Sectional Surveys Branch
National Center for Education Statistics
550 12th Street SW
Washington, DC 20202
stephen.broughman@ed.gov
http://nces.ed.gov/surveys/pss

Projections of Education Statistics

Since 1964, NCES has published projections of key statistics for elementary and secondary schools and institutions of higher education. The latest report is titled *Projections of Education Statistics to 2022* (NCES 2014-051). The *Projections of Education Statistics* series uses projection models for elementary and secondary enrollment, high school graduates, elementary and secondary teachers, expenditures for public elementary and secondary education, enrollment in postsecondary degree-granting institutions, and postsecondary degrees conferred to develop national and state projections. These models are described more fully in the report's appendix on projection methodology.

Differences between the reported and projected values are, of course, almost inevitable. An evaluation of past projections revealed that, at the elementary and secondary level, projections of enrollments have been quite accurate: mean absolute percentage differences for enrollment ranged from 0.3 to 1.3 percent for projections from 1 to 5 years in the future, while those for teachers were less than 3 percent. At the higher education level, projections of enrollment have been fairly accurate: mean absolute percentage differences were 5 percent or less for projections from 1 to 5 years into the future.

Further information on *Projections of Education Statistics* may be obtained from

William Hussar
Annual Reports and Information
National Center for Education Statistics
550 12th Street SW
Washington, DC 20202
william.hussar@ed.gov
http://nces.ed.gov/annuals

Recent College Graduates Study

Between 1976 and 1991, NCES conducted periodic surveys of baccalaureate and master's degree recipients 1 year after graduation with the Recent College Graduates (RCG) Study. The RCG Study—which has been replaced by the Baccalaureate and Beyond Longitudinal Study (B&B) (see listing above)—concentrated on those graduates entering the teaching profession. The study linked respondents' major field of study with outcomes such as whether the respondent entered the labor force or was seeking additional education. Labor force data collected included employment status (unemployed, employed part time, or employed full time), occupation, salary, career potential, relation to major field of study, and need for a college degree. To obtain accurate results on teachers, graduates with a major in education were oversampled. The last two studies oversampled education majors and increased the sampling of graduates with majors in other fields.

For each of the selected institutions, a list of graduates by major field of study was obtained, and a sample of graduates was drawn by major field of study. Graduates in certain major fields of study (e.g., education, mathematics, and physical sciences) were sampled at higher rates than were graduates in other fields. Roughly 1 year after graduation, the sample of graduates was located, contacted by mail or telephone, and asked to respond to the questionnaire.

The locating process was more detailed than that in most surveys. Nonresponse rates were directly related to the time, effort, and resources used in locating graduates, rather than to graduates' refusals to participate. Despite the difficulties in locating graduates, RCG response rates are comparable to studies that do not face problems locating their sample membership.

The 1976 study of 1974–75 college graduates was the first, and smallest, of the series. The sample consisted of about 210 institutions, of which 200 (96 percent) responded. Of the approximately 5,850 graduates in the sample, 4,350 responded, for a response rate of 79 percent.

The 1981 study was somewhat larger than the 1976 study, covering about 300 institutions and 15,850 graduates. Responses were obtained from 280 institutions, for an institutional response rate of 95 percent, and from 9,310 graduates (about 720 others were found not to meet eligibility requirements), for a response rate of 74 percent.

The 1985 study sampled about 400 colleges and 18,740 graduates, of whom 17,850 were found to be eligible. Responses were obtained from 13,200 graduates, for a response rate of 78 percent. The response rate for colleges was 98 percent. The 1987 study sampled 21,960 graduates. Responses were received from 16,880, for a response rate of nearly 80 percent.

The 1991 study sampled about 18,140 graduates of 400 bachelor's and master's degree-granting institutions, including 16,170 bachelor's degree recipients and 1,960 master's degree recipients receiving diplomas between July 1, 1989, and June 30, 1990. Random samples of graduates were selected from lists stratified by field of study. Graduates in education, mathematics, and the physical sciences were sampled at a higher rate, as were graduates of various racial/ethnic groups, to provide a sufficient number of these graduates for analysis purposes. The graduates included in the sample were selected in proportion to the institution's number of graduates. The unweighted institutional response rate was 95 percent, and the unweighted graduate response rate was 83 percent.

Further information on the RCG Study may be obtained from

Aurora D'Amico
Sample Surveys Division
Longitudinal Surveys Branch
National Center for Education Statistics
550 12th Street SW
Washington, DC 20202
aurora.damico@ed.gov
http://nces.ed.gov/surveys/b&b

School Survey on Crime and Safety

The most recent School Survey on Crime and Safety (SSOCS) was conducted by NCES in spring/summer of the 2009–10 school year. SSOCS focuses on incidents of specific crimes/offenses and a variety of specific discipline issues in public schools. It also covers characteristics of school policies, school violence prevention programs and policies, and school characteristics that have been associated with school crime. The survey was conducted with a nationally representative sample of regular public elementary, middle, and high schools in the 50 states and the District of Columbia. Special education, alternative, and vocational schools; schools in the other jurisdictions; and schools that taught only prekindergarten, kindergarten, or adult education were not included in the sample.

The sampling frame for the 2010 SSOCS was constructed from the 2007–08 Public Elementary/Secondary School Universe File of the Common Core of Data, an annual collection of data on all public K–12 schools and school districts. The sample was stratified by instructional level, type of locale (urbanicity), and enrollment size. The sample of schools in each instructional level was allocated to each of the 16 cells formed by the cross-classification of the four categories of enrollment size and four types of locale. The sample was allocated to each subgroup in proportion to the sum of the square roots of the total student enrollment in each school in that stratum. The effective sample size within each stratum was then inflated to account for nonresponse. Once the final sample sizes were determined for each of the 64 strata, the subgroups were sorted by region and racial/ethnic composition of enrollment, and an initial sample of 3,476 schools was selected. Of those schools, 2,648 completed the survey. In February 2010, questionnaires were mailed to school principals, who were asked to complete the survey or to have it completed by the person at the school most knowledgeable about discipline issues.

SSOCS will be administered again in the spring of the 2015–16 school year.

Further information about SSOCS may be obtained from

Rachel Hansen
Sample Surveys Division
Cross-Sectional Surveys Branch
National Center for Education Statistics
550 12th Street SW
Washington, DC 20202
rachel.hansen@ed.gov
http://nces.ed.gov/surveys/ssocs

Schools and Staffing Survey

The Schools and Staffing Survey (SASS) is a set of related questionnaires that collect descriptive data on the context of public and private elementary and secondary education. Data reported by districts, schools, principals, and teachers provide a variety of statistics on the condition of education in the United States that may be used by policymakers and the general public. The SASS system covers a wide range of topics, including teacher demand, teacher and principal characteristics, teachers' and principals' perceptions of school climate and problems in their schools, teacher and principal compensation, district hiring and retention practices, general conditions in schools, and basic characteristics of the student population.

SASS data are collected through a mail questionnaire with telephone and in-person field follow-up. SASS has been conducted by the Census Bureau for NCES since the first administration of the survey, which was conducted during the 1987–88 school year. Subsequent SASS administrations were conducted in 1990–91, 1993–94, 1999–2000, 2003–04, 2007–08, and 2011–12.

SASS is designed to produce national, regional, and state estimates for public elementary and secondary schools, school districts, principals, teachers, and school library media centers and national and regional estimates for public charter schools, as well as principals, teachers, and school library media centers within these schools. For private schools, the sample supports national, regional, and affiliation estimates for schools, principals, and teachers.

From its inception, SASS has had four core components: school questionnaires, teacher questionnaires, principal questionnaires, and school district (prior to 1999–2000, "teacher demand and shortage") questionnaires. A fifth component, school library media center questionnaires, was introduced in the 1993–94 administration and has been included in every subsequent administration of SASS. School library data were also collected in the 1990–91 administration of the survey through the school and principal questionnaires.

School questionnaires used in SASS include the Public and Private School Questionnaires; teacher questionnaires include the Public and Private School Teacher Questionnaires; principal questionnaires include the Public and Private School Principal (or School Administrator) Questionnaires; and school district questionnaires include the School District (or Teacher Demand and Shortage) Questionnaires.

Although the four core questionnaires and the school library media questionnaires have remained relatively stable over the various administrations of SASS, the survey has changed to accommodate emerging issues in elementary and secondary education. Some questionnaire items have been added, some have been deleted, and some have been reworded.

During the 1990–91 SASS cycle, NCES worked with the Office of Indian Education to add an Indian School Questionnaire to SASS, and it remained a part of SASS through 2007–08. The Indian School Questionnaire explores the same school-level issues that the Public and Private School Questionnaires explore, allowing comparisons among the three types of schools. The 1990–91, 1993–94, 1999–2000, 2003–04, and 2007–08 administrations of SASS obtained data on Bureau of Indian Education (BIE) schools (schools funded or operated by the BIE), but the 2011–12 administration did not obtain BIE data. SASS estimates for all survey years presented in this report exclude BIE schools, and as a result, estimates in this report may differ from those in previously published reports.

School library media center questionnaires were administered in public, private, and BIE schools as part of the 1993–1994 and 1999–2000 SASS. During the 2003–04 administration of SASS, only library media centers in public schools were surveyed, and in 2007–08 only library media centers in public schools and BIE and BIE-funded schools were surveyed. The 2011–12 survey collected data only on school library media centers in traditional public schools and in public charter schools. School library questions focused on facilities, services and policies, staffing, technology, information literacy, collections and expenditures, and media equipment. New or revised topics included access to online licensed databases, resource availability, and additional elements on information literacy. The Student Records and Library Media Specialist/Librarian Questionnaires were administered only in 1993–94.

As part of the 1999–2000 SASS, the Charter School Questionnaire was sent to the universe of charter schools in operation in 1998–99. In 2003–04 and in subsequent administrations of SASS, there was no separate questionnaire for charter schools—charter schools were included in the public school sample instead. Another change in the 2003–04 administration of SASS was a revised data collection procedure using a primary in-person contact within the school intended to reduce the field follow-up phase.

The SASS teacher surveys collect information on the characteristics of teachers, such as their age, race/ethnicity, years of teaching experience, average number of hours per week spent on teaching activities, base salary, average class size, and highest degree earned. These teacher-reported data may be combined with related information on their school's characteristics, such as school type (e.g., public traditional, public charter, Catholic, private other religious, and private nonsectarian), community type, and school enrollment size. The teacher questionnaires also ask for information on teacher opinions regarding the school and teaching environment. In 1993–94, about 53,000 public school teachers and 10,400 private school teachers were sampled. In 1999–2000, about 56,300 public school teachers, 4,400 public charter school teachers, and 10,800 private school teachers were sampled. In 2003–04, about 52,500 public school teachers and 10,000 private school teachers were sampled. In 2007–08, about 48,400 public school teachers and 8,200 private school teachers were sampled. In 2011–12, about 51,100 public school teachers and 7,100 private school teachers were sampled. Weighted overall response rates in 2011–12 were 61.8 percent for public school teachers and 50.1 percent for private school teachers.

The SASS principal surveys focus on such topics as age, race/ethnicity, sex, average annual salary, years of experience, highest degree attained, perceived influence on decisions made at the school, and hours spent per week on all school activities. These data on principals can be placed in the context of other SASS data, such as the type of the principal's school (e.g., public traditional, public charter, Catholic, other religious, or nonsectarian), enrollment, and percentage of students eligible for free or reduced price lunch. In 2003–04, about 10,200 public school principals were sampled, and in 2007–08, about 9,800 public school principals were sampled. In 2011–12, about 11,000 public school principals and 3,000 private school principals were sampled. Weighted response rates in 2011–12 for public school principals and private school principals were 72.7 percent and 64.7 percent, respectively.

The SASS 2011–12 sample of schools was confined to the 50 states and the District of Columbia and excludes the other jurisdictions, the Department of Defense overseas schools, the BIE schools, and schools that do not offer teacher-provided classroom instruction in grades 1–12 or the ungraded equivalent. The SASS 2011–12 sample included 10,250 traditional public schools, 750 public charter schools, and 3,000 private schools.

The public school sample for the 2011–12 SASS was based on an adjusted public school universe file from the 2009–10 Common Core of Data, a database of all the nation's public school districts and public schools. The private school sample for the 2011–12 SASS was selected from the 2009–10 Private School Universe Survey (PSS), as updated for the 2011–12 PSS. This update collected membership lists from private school associations and religious denominations, as well as private school lists from state education departments. The 2011–12 SASS private school frame was further augmented by the inclusion of additional schools that were identified through the 2009–10 PSS area frame data collection.

The NCES data product *2011–12 Schools and Staffing Survey (SASS) Restricted-Use Data Files* (NCES 2014-356) is available. (Information on how to obtain a restricted-use data license is located at http://nces.ed.gov/pubsearch/licenses.asp.) This DVD contains eight files (Public School District, Public School Principal, Public School, Public School Teacher, Public School Library Media Center, Private School Principal, Private School, and Private School Teacher) in multiple formats. It also contains a six-volume User's Manual, which includes a codebook for each file.

Further information on SASS may be obtained from

Amy Ho
Sample Surveys Division
Cross-Sectional Surveys Branch
National Center for Education Statistics
550 12th Street SW
Washington, DC 20202
amy.ho@ed.gov
http://nces.ed.gov/surveys/sass

Teacher Follow-up Survey

The Teacher Follow-up Survey (TFS) is a follow-up survey of selected elementary and secondary school teachers who participate in the NCES Schools and Staffing Survey (SASS). Its purpose is to determine how many teachers remain at the same school, move to another school, or leave the profession in the year following a SASS administration.

It is administered to elementary and secondary teachers in the 50 states and the District of Columbia. The TFS uses two questionnaires, one for teachers who left teaching since the previous SASS administration and another for those who are still teaching either in the same school as last year or in a different school. The objective of the TFS is to focus on the characteristics of each group in order to answer questions about teacher mobility and attrition.

The 2008–09 TFS is different from any previous TFS administration in that it also serves as the second wave of a longitudinal study of first-year teachers. Because of this, the 2008–09 TFS consists of four questionnaires. Two are for respondents who were first-year public school teachers in the 2007–08 SASS and two are for the remainder of the sample.

The 2012–13 TFS sample was made up of teachers who had taken the 2011–12 SASS survey. The 2012–13 TFS sample contained about 5,800 public school teachers and 1,200 private school teachers. The weighted overall response rate using the initial basic weight for private school teachers was notably low (39.7 percent), resulting in a decision to exclude private school teachers from the 2012–13 TFS data files. The weighted overall response rate for public school teachers was 49.9 percent (50.3 percent for current and 45.6 percent for former teachers). Further information about the 2012–13 TFS, including the analysis of unit nonresponse bias, is available in the First Look report *Teacher Attrition and Mobility: Results From the 2012–13 Teacher Follow-up Survey* (NCES 2014-077).

Further information on the TFS may be obtained from

Chelsea Owens
Sample Surveys Division
Cross-Sectional Surveys Branch
National Center for Education Statistics
550 12th Street SW
Washington, DC 20202
chelsea.owens@ed.gov
http://nces.ed.gov/surveys/sass/

Other Department of Education Agencies

National Center for Special Education Research

The National Center for Special Education Research (NCSER) was created as part of the reauthorization of the Individuals with Disabilities Education Act (IDEA). NCSER sponsors a program of special education research designed to expand the knowledge and understanding of infants, toddlers, and children with disabilities. NCSER funds programs of research that address its mission. In order to determine which programs work, as well as how, why, and in what settings they work, NCSER sponsors research on the needs of infants, toddlers, and children with disabilities and evaluates the effectiveness of services provided through IDEA.

Further information on NCSER may be obtained from

Joan McLaughlin
Commissioner
National Center for Special Education Research
555 New Jersey Avenue NW
Washington, DC 20208
joan.mclaughlin@ed.gov
http://ies.ed.gov/ncser/help/webmail/

The National Longitudinal Transition Study-2

Funded by NCSER, the National Longitudinal Transition Study-2 (NLTS-2) is a follow-up of the original National Longitudinal Transition Study conducted from 1985 through 1993. NLTS-2 began in 2001 with a sample of special education students who were ages 13 through 16 and in at least 7th grade on December 1, 2000. The study was designed to provide a national picture of these youths' experiences and achievements as they transition into adulthood. Data were collected from parents, youth, and schools by survey, telephone interviews, student assessments, and transcripts.

NLTS-2 was designed to align with the original NLTS by including many of the same questions and data items, thus allowing comparisons between the NLTS and NLTS-2 youths' experiences. NLTS-2 also included items that have been collected in other national databases to permit comparisons between NLTS-2 youth and the general youth population. Data are currently available for Waves 1 through 5.

Further information on NLTS-2 may be obtained from

Jacquelyn Buckley
Office of the Commissioner
National Center for Special Education Research
555 New Jersey Avenue NW
Washington, DC 20208
jacquelyn.buckley@ed.gov
http://www.nlts2.org/

Office for Civil Rights

Civil Rights Data Collection

The U.S. Department of Education's Office for Civil Rights (OCR) has surveyed the nation's public elementary and secondary schools since 1968. The survey was first known as the OCR Elementary and Secondary School (E&S) Survey; in 2004, it was renamed the Civil Rights Data Collection (CRDC). The survey provides information about the enrollment of students in public schools in every state and about some education services provided to those students. These data are reported by race/ethnicity, sex, and disability.

Data in the survey are collected pursuant to 34 C.F.R. Section 100.6(b) of the Department of Education regulation implementing Title VI of the Civil Rights Act of 1964. The requirements are also incorporated by reference in Department regulations implementing Title IX of the Education

Amendments of 1972, Section 504 of the Rehabilitation Act of 1973, and the Age Discrimination Act of 1975. School, district, state, and national data are currently available. Data from individual public schools and districts are used to generate projected national and state data.

The CRDC has generally been conducted biennially in each of the 50 states plus the District of Columbia. The 2009–10 CRDC was collected from a sample of approximately 7,000 school districts and over 72,000 schools in those districts. It was made up of two parts: part 1 contained beginning-of-year "snapshot" data and part 2 contained cumulative, or end-of-year, data.

The 2011–12 CRDC survey, which collected data from approximately 16,500 school districts and 97,000 schools, was the first CRDC survey since 2000 that included data from every public school district and school in the nation. Data from the 2011–12 CRDC are currently available. The 2013–14 CRDC survey also collected information from a universe of every public school district and school in the nation.

Further information on the Civil Rights Data Collection may be obtained from

Office for Civil Rights
U.S. Department of Education
400 Maryland Avenue SW
Washington, DC 20202
http://www.ed.gov/about/offices/list/ocr/data.html

Office of Special Education Programs

Annual Report to Congress on the Implementation of the Individuals with Disabilities Education Act

The Individuals with Disabilities Education Act (IDEA) is a law ensuring services to children with disabilities throughout the nation. IDEA governs how states and public agencies provide early intervention, special education, and related services to more than 6.5 million eligible infants, toddlers, children, and youth with disabilities.

IDEA, formerly the Education of the Handicapped Act (EHA), requires the Secretary of Education to transmit to Congress annually a report describing the progress made in serving the nation's children with disabilities. This annual report contains information on children served by public schools under the provisions of Part B of IDEA and on children served in state-operated programs for persons with disabilities under Chapter I of the Elementary and Secondary Education Act.

Statistics on children receiving special education and related services in various settings and school personnel providing such services are reported in an annual submission of data to the Office of Special Education Programs (OSEP) by the 50 states, the District of Columbia, the Bureau of Indian Education schools, Puerto Rico, American Samoa, Guam, the Northern Mariana Islands, the U.S. Virgin Islands, the Federated States of Micronesia, Palau, and the Marshall

Islands. The child count information is based on the number of children with disabilities receiving special education and related services on December 1 of each year. Count information is available from http://www.ideadata.org.

Since all participants in programs for persons with disabilities are reported to OSEP, the data are not subject to sampling error. However, nonsampling error can arise from a variety of sources. Some states only produce counts of students receiving special education services by disability category because Part B of the EHA requires it. In those states that typically produce counts of students receiving special education services by disability category without regard to EHA requirements, definitions and labeling practices vary.

Further information on this annual report to Congress may be obtained from

Office of Special Education Programs
Office of Special Education and Rehabilitative Services
U.S. Department of Education
400 Maryland Avenue SW
Washington, DC 20202-7100
http://www.ed.gov/about/reports/annual/osep/index.html
http://idea.ed.gov/
http://www.ideadata.org

Office of Career, Technical, and Adult Education, Division of Adult Education and Literacy

Enrollment Data for State-Administered Adult Education Programs

The Division of Adult Education and Literacy (DAEL) promotes programs that help American adults get the basic skills they need to be productive workers, family members, and citizens. The major areas of support are Adult Basic Education, Adult Secondary Education, and English Language Acquisition. These programs emphasize basic skills such as reading, writing, math, English language competency, and problem solving. Each year, DAEL reports enrollment numbers in state-administered adult education programs for these major areas of support for all 50 states, the District of Columbia, American Samoa, the Federated States of Micronesia, Guam, the Marshall Islands, the Northern Mariana Islands, Palau, Puerto Rico, and the U.S. Virgin Islands.

Further information on DAEL may be obtained from

Office of Career, Technical, and Adult Education
Division of Adult Education and Literacy
U.S. Department of Education
400 Maryland Avenue SW
Washington, DC 20202
http://www.ed.gov/about/offices/list/ovae/pi/AdultEd/

Other Governmental Agencies and Programs

Bureau of Economic Analysis

National Income and Product Accounts

The National Income and Product Accounts (NIPAs), produced by the Bureau of Economic Analysis, represent measures of economic activity in the United States, including production, income distribution, and personal savings. NIPAs also include data on employee compensation and wages. These estimations were first calculated in the early 1930s to help the government design economic policies to combat the Great Depression. Most of the NIPA series are published quarterly, with annual reviews of estimates from the three most recent years conducted in the summer.

Revisions to the NIPAs have been made over the years to create a more comprehensive economic picture of the United States. For example, in 1976, consumption of fixed capital (CFC) estimates shifted to a current-cost basis. In 1991, NIPAs began to use gross domestic product (GDP), instead of gross national product (GNP), as the primary measure of U.S. production. (At that time, virtually all other countries were already using GDP as their primary measure of production.) In the 2003 comprehensive revision, a more complete and accurate measure of insurance services was adopted. The incorporation of a new classification system for personal consumption expenditures (PCE) was among the changes contained in the 2009 comprehensive revision. The comprehensive revision of 2013 included the treatment of research and development expenditures by business, government, and nonprofit institutions serving households as fixed investment.

NIPA is slowly being integrated with other federal account systems, such as the federal account system of the Bureau of Labor Statistics.

Further information on NIPAs may be obtained from

U.S. Department of Commerce
Bureau of Economic Analysis
www.bea.gov

Bureau of Labor Statistics

Consumer Price Indexes

The Consumer Price Index (CPI) represents changes in prices of all goods and services purchased for consumption by urban households. Indexes are available for two population groups: a CPI for All Urban Consumers (CPI-U) and a CPI for Urban Wage Earners and Clerical Workers (CPI-W). Unless otherwise specified, data are adjusted for inflation using the CPI-U. These values are generally adjusted to a school-year basis by averaging the July through June figures. Price indexes are available for the United States, the four Census regions, size of city, cross-classifications of regions and size classes, and 26 local areas. The major uses of the CPI include as an economic indicator, as a deflator of other economic series, and as a means of adjusting income.

Also available is the Consumer Price Index research series using current methods (CPI-U-RS), which presents an estimate of the CPI-U from 1978 to the present that incorporates most of the improvements that the Bureau of Labor Statistics has made over that time span into the entire series. The historical price index series of the CPI-U does not reflect these changes, though these changes do make the present and future CPI more accurate. The limitations of the CPI-U-RS include considerable uncertainty surrounding the magnitude of the adjustments and the several improvements in the CPI that have not been incorporated into the CPI-U-RS for various reasons. Nonetheless, the CPI-U-RS can serve as a valuable proxy for researchers needing a historical estimate of inflation using current methods. This series has not been used in NCES tables.

Further information on consumer price indexes may be obtained from

Bureau of Labor Statistics
U.S. Department of Labor
2 Massachusetts Avenue NE
Washington, DC 20212
http://www.bls.gov/cpi

Employment and Unemployment Surveys

Statistics on the employment and unemployment status of the population and related data are compiled by the Bureau of Labor Statistics (BLS) using data from the Current Population Survey (CPS) (see below) and other surveys. The CPS, a monthly household survey conducted by the U.S. Census Bureau for the Bureau of Labor Statistics, provides a comprehensive body of information on the employment and unemployment experience of the nation's population, classified by age, sex, race, and various other characteristics.

Further information on unemployment surveys may be obtained from

Bureau of Labor Statistics
U.S. Department of Labor
2 Massachusetts Avenue NE
Washington, DC 20212
cpsinfo@bls.gov
http://www.bls.gov/bls/employment.htm

Census Bureau

American Community Survey

The Census Bureau introduced the American Community Survey (ACS) in 1996. Fully implemented in 2005, it provides a large monthly sample of demographic, socioeconomic, and housing data comparable in content to the Long Forms of the Decennial Census up to and including the 2000 long form. Aggregated over time, these data serve as a replacement for the Long Form of the Decennial Census. The survey includes questions mandated by federal law, federal regulations, and court decisions.

Since 2011, the survey has been mailed to approximately 295,000 addresses in the United States and Puerto Rico each month, or about 3.5 million addresses annually. A larger proportion of addresses in small governmental units (e.g., American Indian reservations, small counties, and towns) also receive the survey. The monthly sample size is designed to approximate the ratio used in the 2000 Census, which requires more intensive distribution in these areas. The ACS covers the U.S. resident population, which includes the entire civilian, noninstitutionalized population; incarcerated persons; institutionalized persons; and the active duty military who are in the United States. In 2006, the ACS began interviewing residents in group quarter facilities. Institutionalized group quarters include adult and juvenile correctional facilities, nursing facilities, and other health care facilities. Noninstitutionalized group quarters include college and university housing, military barracks, and other noninstitutional facilities such as workers and religious group quarters and temporary shelters for the homeless.

National-level data from the ACS are available from 2000 onward. The ACS produces 1-year estimates for jurisdictions with populations of 65,000 and over, 3-year estimates for jurisdictions with populations of 20,000 or over, and 5-year estimates for jurisdictions with smaller populations. For example, the 2013 1-year estimates used data collected between January 1, 2013, and December 31, 2013; the 2013 3-year estimates used data collected between January 1, 2011, and December 31, 2013; and the 2013 5-year estimates used data collected between January 1, 2009, and December 31, 2013.

Further information about the ACS is available at http://www.census.gov/acs/www/.

Annual Survey of State and Local Government Finances

The Census Bureau conducts an Annual Survey of State and Local Government Finances as authorized by law under Title 13, United States Code, Section 182. Periodic surveys of government finances have been conducted since 1902 and annually since 1952. This survey covers the entire range of government finance activities: revenue, expenditure, debt, and assets. Revenues and expenditures comprise actual receipts and payments of a government and its agencies, including government-operated enterprises, utilities, and public trust funds. The expenditure-reporting categories comprise all amounts of money paid out by a government and its agencies, with the exception of amounts for debt retirement and for loan, investment, agency, and private trust transactions.

Most of the federal government statistics are based on figures that appear in *The Budget of the United States Government.* Since the classification used by the Census Bureau for reporting state and local government finance statistics differs in a number of important respects from the classification used in the U.S. budget, it was necessary to adjust the federal data. For this report, federal budget expenditures include interest accrued, but not paid, during the fiscal year; Census data on interest are on a disbursement basis.

State government finances are based primarily on the Census Bureau Annual Survey of State and Local Government Finances. Census analysts compile figures from official records and reports of the state governments for most of the state financial data. States differ in the ways they administer activities; they may fund such activities directly, or they may disburse the money to a lower level government or government agency. Therefore, caution is advised when attempting to make a direct comparison between states on their state fiscal aid data.

The sample of local governments is drawn from the periodic (years ending in "2" and "7") Census of Governments and consists of certain local governments sampled with certainty plus a sample below the certainty level. Finance data for all school districts are collected on an annual basis and released through the NCES Common Core of Data system. A new sample is usually selected every 5 years (years ending in "4" and "9"), the most recent one being in fiscal year 2009.

The statistics in Government Finances that are based wholly or partly on data from the sample are subject to sampling error. State government finance data are not subject to sampling error. Estimates of major U.S. totals for local governments are subject to a computed sampling variability of less than one-half of 1 percent. The estimates are also subject to the inaccuracies in classification, response, and processing that would occur if a complete census had been conducted under the same conditions as the sample.

Further information on government finances may be obtained from

Governments Division
Census Bureau
U.S. Department of Commerce
4600 Silver Hill Road
Washington, DC 20233

Local government
govs.finstaff@census.gov

State government
govs.public.finance.analysis.b.@census.gov
http://www.census.gov/govs

Census of Population—Education in the United States

Some NCES tables are based on a part of the decennial census that consisted of questions asked of a 1 in 6 sample of people and housing units in the United States. This sample was asked more detailed questions about income, occupation, and housing costs, as well as questions about general demographic information. This decennial Long Form is no longer conducted and has been replaced by the American Community Survey (ACS).

School enrollment. People classified as enrolled in school reported attending a "regular" public or private school or college. They were asked whether the institution they attended was public or private and what level of school they were enrolled in.

Educational attainment. Data for educational attainment were tabulated for people ages 15 and older and classified according to the highest grade completed or the highest degree received. Instructions were also given to include the level of the previous grade attended or the highest degree received for people currently enrolled in school.

Poverty status. To determine poverty status, answers to income questions were used to make comparisons to the appropriate poverty threshold. All people except those who were institutionalized, people in military group quarters and college dormitories, and unrelated people under age 15 were considered. If the total income of each family or unrelated individual in the sample was below the corresponding cutoff, that family or individual was classified as "below the poverty level."

Further information on the 1990 and 2000 Census of Population may be obtained from

Population Division
Census Bureau
U.S. Department of Commerce
4600 Silver Hill Road
Washington, DC 20233
http://www.census.gov/main/www/cen1990.html
http://www.census.gov/main/www/cen2000.html

Current Population Survey

The Current Population Survey (CPS) is a monthly survey of about 60,000 households conducted by the U.S. Census Bureau for the Bureau of Labor Statistics. The CPS is the primary source of information of labor force statistics for the U.S. noninstitutionalized population (e.g., it excludes military personnel and their families living on bases and inmates of correctional institutions). In addition, supplemental questionnaires are used to provide further information about the U.S. population. Specifically, in October, detailed questions regarding school enrollment and school characteristics are asked. In March, detailed questions regarding income are asked.

The current sample design, introduced in July 2001, includes about 72,000 households. Each month about 58,900 of the 72,000 households are eligible for interview, and of those, 7 to 10 percent are not interviewed because of temporary absence or unavailability. Information is obtained each month from those in the household who are 15 years of age and older, and demographic data are collected for children 0–14 years of age. In addition, supplemental questions regarding school enrollment are asked about eligible household members ages 3 and older in the October survey. Prior to July 2001, data were collected in the CPS from about 50,000 dwelling units. The samples are initially selected based on the decennial census files and are periodically updated to reflect new housing construction.

A major redesign of the CPS was implemented in January 1994 to improve the quality of the data collected. Survey questions were revised, new questions were added, and computer-assisted interviewing methods were used for the survey data collection. Further information about the redesign is available in *Current Population Survey, October 1995: (School Enrollment Supplement) Technical Documentation* at http://www.census.gov/prod/techdoc/cps/cpsoct95.pdf.

Caution should be used when comparing data from 1994 through 2001 with data from 1993 and earlier. Data from 1994 through 2001 reflect 1990 census-based population controls, while data from 1993 and earlier reflect 1980 or earlier census-based population controls. Changes in population controls generally have relatively little impact on summary measures such as means, medians, and percentage distributions. They can have a significant impact on population counts. For example, use of the 1990 census-based population controls resulted in about a 1 percent increase in the civilian noninstitutional population and in the number of families and households. Thus, estimates of levels for data collected in 1994 and later years will differ from those for earlier years by more than what could be attributed to actual changes in the population. These differences could be disproportionately greater for certain subpopulation groups than for the total population.

Beginning in 2003, race/ethnicity questions expanded to include information on people of two or more races. Native Hawaiian/Pacific Islander data are collected separately from Asian data. The questions have also been worded to make it clear that self-reported data on race/ethnicity should reflect the race/ethnicity with which the responder identifies, rather than what may be written in official documentation.

The estimation procedure employed for monthly CPS data involves inflating weighted sample results to independent estimates of characteristics of the civilian noninstitutional population in the United States by age, sex, and race. These independent estimates are based on statistics from decennial censuses; statistics on births, deaths, immigration, and emigration; and statistics on the population in the armed services. Generalized standard error tables are provided in the Current Population Reports; methods for deriving standard errors can be found within the CPS technical documentation at http://www.census.gov/cps/methodology/techdocs.html. The CPS data are subject to both nonsampling and sampling errors.

Prior to 2009, standard errors were estimated using the generalized variance function. The generalized variance function is a simple model that expresses the variance as a function of the expected value of a survey estimate. Beginning with March 2009 CPS data, standard errors were estimated using replicate weight methodology. Those interested in using CPS household-level supplement replicate weights to calculate variances may refer to *Estimating Current Population Survey (CPS) Household-Level Supplement Variances Using Replicate Weights* at http://thedataweb.rm.census.gov/pub/cps/supps/HH-level Use of the Public Use Replicate Weight File.doc.

Further information on the CPS may be obtained from

Education and Social Stratification Branch
Population Division
Census Bureau
U.S. Department of Commerce
4600 Silver Hill Road
Washington, DC 20233
http://www.census.gov/cps

Dropouts

Each October, the Current Population Survey (CPS) includes supplemental questions on the enrollment status of the population ages 3 years and over as part of the monthly basic survey on labor force participation. In addition to gathering the information on school enrollment, with the limitations on accuracy as noted below under "School Enrollment," the survey data permit calculations of dropout rates. Both status and event dropout rates are tabulated from the October CPS. Event rates describe the proportion of students who leave school each year without completing a high school program. Status rates provide cumulative data on dropouts among all young adults within a specified age range. Status rates are higher than event rates because they include all dropouts ages 16 through 24, regardless of when they last attended school.

In addition to other survey limitations, dropout rates may be affected by survey coverage and exclusion of the institutionalized population. The incarcerated population has grown more rapidly and has a higher dropout rate than the general population. Dropout rates for the total population might be higher than those for the noninstitutionalized population if the prison and jail populations were included in the dropout rate calculations. On the other hand, if military personnel, who tend to be high school graduates, were included, it might offset some or all of the impact from the theoretical inclusion of the jail and prison populations.

Another area of concern with tabulations involving young people in household surveys is the relatively low coverage ratio compared to older age groups. CPS undercoverage results from missed housing units and missed people within sample households. Overall CPS undercoverage for October 2013 is estimated to be about 15 percent. CPS coverage varies with age, sex, and race. Generally, coverage is larger for females than for males and larger for non-Blacks than for Blacks. This differential coverage is a general problem for most household-based surveys. Further information on CPS methodology may be found in the technical documentation at http://www.census.gov/cps.

Further information on the calculation of dropouts and dropout rates may be obtained from *Trends in High School Dropout and Completion Rates in the United States: 1972–2012* (NCES 2015-015) at http://nces.ed.gov/pubs2015/2015015.pdf or by contacting

Joel McFarland
Annual Reports and Information Staff
National Center for Education Statistics
550 12th Street SW
Washington, DC 20202
joel.mcfarland@ed.gov

Educational Attainment

Reports documenting educational attainment are produced by the Census Bureau using March Current Population Survey (CPS) supplement (Annual Social and Economic Supplement [ASEC]) results. The sample size for the 2013 ASEC supplement (including basic CPS) was about 99,000 households. The results were released in *Educational Attainment in the United States: 2013*; the tables may be downloaded at http://www.census.gov/hhes/socdemo/education/data/cps/ 2013/tables.html. The sample size for the 2014 ASEC supplement (including basic CPS) was about 98,000 households. The results were released in *Educational Attainment in the United States: 2014*; the tables may be downloaded at http://www.census.gov/hhes/socdemo/education/data/cps/2014/ tables.html. In addition to the general constraints of CPS, some data indicate that the respondents have a tendency to overestimate the educational level of members of their household. Some inaccuracy is due to a lack of the respondent's knowledge of the exact educational attainment of each household member and the hesitancy to acknowledge anything less than a high school education. Another cause of nonsampling variability is the change in the numbers in the armed services over the years.

Further information on educational attainment data from CPS may be obtained from

Education and Social Stratification Branch
Census Bureau
U.S. Department of Commerce
4600 Silver Hill Road
Washington, DC 20233
http://www.census.gov/hhes/socdemo/education

School Enrollment

Each October, the Current Population Survey (CPS) includes supplemental questions on the enrollment status of the population ages 3 years and over. Prior to 2001, the October supplement consisted of approximately 47,000 interviewed households. Beginning with the October 2001 supplement, the sample was expanded by 9,000 to a total of approximately 56,000 interviewed households. The main sources of nonsampling variability in the responses to the supplement are those inherent in the survey instrument. The question of current enrollment may not be answered accurately for various reasons. Some respondents may not know current grade information for every student in the household, a problem especially prevalent for households with members in college or in nursery school. Confusion over college credits or hours taken by a student may make it difficult to determine the year in which the student is enrolled. Problems may occur with the definition of nursery school (a group or class organized to provide educational experiences for children) where respondents' interpretations of "educational experiences" vary.

For the October 2013 basic CPS, the household-level nonresponse rate was 9.86 percent. The person-level nonresponse rate for the school enrollment supplement was an additional 8.0 percent. Since the basic CPS nonresponse rate is a household-level rate and the school enrollment supplement nonresponse rate is a person-level rate, these rates cannot be combined to derive an overall nonresponse rate. Nonresponding households may have fewer persons than interviewed ones, so combining these rates may lead to an overestimate of the true overall nonresponse rate for persons for the school enrollment supplement.

Further information on CPS methodology may be obtained from http://www.census.gov/cps.

Further information on the CPS School Enrollment Supplement may be obtained from

Education and Social Stratification Branch
Census Bureau
U.S. Department of Commerce
4600 Silver Hill Road
Washington, DC 20233
http://www.census.gov/hhes/school/index.html

Decennial Census, Population Estimates, and Population Projections

The decennial census is a universe survey mandated by the U.S. Constitution. It is a questionnaire sent to every household in the country, and it is composed of seven questions about the household and its members (name, sex, age, relationship, Hispanic origin, race, and whether the housing unit is owned or rented). The Census Bureau also produces annual estimates of the resident population by demographic characteristics (age, sex, race, and Hispanic origin) for the nation, states, and counties, as well as national and state projections for the resident population. The reference date for population estimates is July 1 of the given year. With each new issue of July 1 estimates, the Census Bureau revises estimates for each year back to the last census. Previously published estimates are superseded and archived.

Census respondents self-report race and ethnicity. The race questions on the 1990 and 2000 censuses differed in some significant ways. In 1990, the respondent was instructed to select the one race "that the respondent considers himself/herself to be," whereas in 2000, the respondent could select one or more races that the person considered himself or herself to be. American Indian, Eskimo, and Aleut were three separate race categories in 1990; in 2000, the American Indian and Alaska Native categories were combined, with an option to write in a tribal affiliation. This write-in option was provided only for the American Indian category in 1990. There was a combined Asian and Pacific Islander race category in 1990, but the groups were separated into two categories in 2000.

The census question on ethnicity asks whether the respondent is of Hispanic origin, regardless of the race option(s) selected; thus, persons of Hispanic origin may be of any race. In the 2000 census, respondents were first asked, "Is this person Spanish/Hispanic/Latino?" and then given the following options: No, not Spanish/Hispanic/Latino; Yes, Puerto Rican; Yes, Mexican, Mexican American, Chicano; Yes, Cuban; and Yes, other Spanish/Hispanic/Latino (with space to print the specific group). In the 2010 census, respondents were asked "Is this person of Hispanic,

Latino, or Spanish origin?" The options given were No, not of Hispanic, Latino, or Spanish origin; Yes, Mexican, Mexican Am., Chicano; Yes, Puerto Rican; Yes, Cuban; and Yes, another other Hispanic, Latino, or Spanish origin—along with instructions to print "Argentinean, Colombian, Dominican, Nicaraguan, Salvadoran, Spaniard, and so on" in a specific box.

The 2000 and 2010 censuses each asked the respondent "What is this person's race?" and allowed the respondent to select one or more options. The options provided were largely the same in both the 2000 and 2010 censuses: White; Black, African American, or Negro; American Indian or Alaska Native (with space to print the name of enrolled or principal tribe); Asian Indian; Japanese; Native Hawaiian; Chinese; Korean; Guamanian or Chamorro; Filipino; Vietnamese; Samoan; Other Asian; Other Pacific Islander; and Some other race. The last three options included space to print the specific race. Two significant differences between the 2000 and 2010 census questions on race were that no race examples were provided for the "Other Asian" and "Other Pacific Islander" responses in 2000, whereas the race examples of "Hmong, Laotian, Thai, Pakistani, Cambodian, and so on" and "Fijian, Tongan, and so on," were provided for the "Other Asian" and "Other Pacific Islander" responses, respectively, in 2010.

The census population estimates program modified the enumerated population from the 2010 census to produce the population estimates base for 2010 and onward. As part of the modification, the Census Bureau recoded the "Some other race" responses from the 2010 census to one or more of the five OMB race categories used in the estimates program (for more information, see http://www.census.gov/popest/methodology/2012-nat-st-co-meth.pdf).

Further information on the decennial census may be obtained from http://www.census.gov.

Centers for Disease Control and Prevention

National Health Interview Survey

The National Health Interview Survey (NHIS) is the principal source of information on the health of the civilian noninstitutionalized population of the United States and is one of the major data collection programs of the National Center for Health Statistics (NCHS), which is part of the Centers for Disease Control and Prevention (CDC). The main objective of the NHIS is to monitor the health of the U.S. population through the collection and analysis of data on a broad range of health topics. A major strength of this survey lies in its ability to display these health characteristics by many demographic and socioeconomic characteristics.

The NHIS covers the civilian noninstitutionalized population residing in the United States at the time of the interview. The NHIS is a cross-sectional household interview survey. Sampling and interviewing are continuous throughout each year. The sampling plan follows a multistage area probability design that permits the representative sampling of households and noninstitutional group quarters (e.g., college dormitories). The sampling plan is redesigned after every decennial census. The current sampling plan was implemented in 2006. It is similar in many ways to the previous sampling plan, which was in place from 1995 to 2005. The first stage of the current sampling plan consists of a sample of 428 primary sampling units (PSUs) drawn from approximately 1,900 geographically defined PSUs that cover the 50 states and the District of Columbia. A PSU consists of a county, a small group of contiguous counties, or a metropolitan statistical area.

The revised NHIS questionnaire, implemented since 1997, contains Core questions and Supplements. The Core questions remain largely unchanged from year to year and allow for trends analysis and for data from more than one year to be pooled to increase sample size for analytic purposes. The Core contains four major components: Household, Family, Sample Adult, and Sample Child.

The Household component collects limited demographic information on all of the individuals living in a particular house. The Family component verifies and collects additional demographic information on each member from each family in the house and collects data on topics including health status and limitations, injuries, healthcare access and utilization, health insurance, and income and assets. The Family Core component allows the NHIS to serve as a sampling frame for additional integrated surveys as needed.

Data are collected through a personal household interview conducted by interviewers employed and trained by the U.S. Bureau of the Census according to procedures specified by the NCHS.

Further information on the NHIS may be obtained from

Information Dissemination Staff
National Center for Health Statistics
Centers for Disease Control and Prevention
3311 Toledo Road, Room 5407
Hyattsville, MD 20782-2003
(800) 232-4636
nhis@cdc.gov
http://www.cdc.gov/nchs/nhis.htm

Morbidity and Mortality Weekly Report: Summary of Notifiable Diseases

The Summary of Notifiable Diseases, a publication of the Morbidity and Mortality Weekly Report (MMWR), contains the official statistics, in tabular and graphic form, for the reported occurrence of nationally notifiable infectious diseases in the United States. These statistics are collected and compiled from reports sent by state health departments and territories to the National Notifiable Diseases Surveillance System (NNDSS), which is operated by the Centers for Disease Control and Prevention (CDC) in collaboration with the Council of State and Territorial Epidemiologists.

For more information on the MMWR: Summary of Notifiable Diseases, see

http://www.cdc.gov/mmwr/mmwr_nd/.

National Vital Statistics System

The National Vital Statistics System (NVSS) is the method by which data on births, deaths, marriages, and divorces are provided to the National Center for Health Statistics (NCHS), part of the Centers for Disease Control and Prevention (CDC). The data are provided to NCHS through the Vital Statistics Cooperative Program (VSCP). In 1984 and earlier years, the VSCP included varying numbers of states that provided data based on a 100 percent sample of their birth certificates. Data for states not in the VSCP were based on a 50 percent sample of birth certificates filed in those states. Population data used to compile birth rates are based on special estimation procedures and are not actual counts.

Race and Hispanic ethnicity are reported separately in the NVSS. Data are available for non-Hispanic Whites and non-Hispanic Blacks for 1990 and later; however, for 1980 and 1985, data for Whites and Blacks may include persons of Hispanic ethnicity. For all years, Asian/Pacific Islander and American Indian/Alaska Native categories include persons of Hispanic ethnicity.

For more information on the NCHS and the NVSS, see

http://www.cdc.gov/nchs/nvss.htm.

School-Associated Violent Deaths Study

The School-Associated Violent Deaths Study (SAVD) is an epidemiological study developed by the Centers for Disease Control and Prevention in conjunction with the U.S. Department of Education and the U.S. Department of Justice. SAVD seeks to describe the epidemiology of school-associated violent deaths, identify common features of these deaths, estimate the rate of school-associated violent death in the United States, and identify potential risk factors for these deaths. The study includes descriptive data on all school-associated violent deaths in the United States, including all homicides, suicides, or legal intervention in which the fatal injury occurred on the campus of a functioning elementary or secondary school; while the victim was on the way to or from regular sessions at such a school; or while attending or on the way to or from an official school-sponsored event. Victims of such incidents include nonstudents, as well as students and staff members. SAVD includes descriptive information about the school, event, victim(s), and offender(s). The SAVD study has collected data from July 1, 1992, through the present.

SAVD uses a four-step process to identify and collect data on school-associated violent deaths. Cases are initially identified through a search of the LexisNexis newspaper and media database. Then law enforcement officials are contacted to confirm the details of the case and to determine if the event meets the case definition. Once a case is confirmed, a law enforcement official and a school official are interviewed regarding details about the school, event, victim(s), and offender(s). A copy of the full law enforcement report is also sought for each case. The information obtained on schools includes school demographics, attendance/absentee rates, suspensions/expulsions and mobility, school history of weapon-carrying incidents, security measures, violence prevention activities, school response to the event, and school policies about weapon carrying. Event information includes the location of injury, the context of injury (while classes were being held, during break, etc.), motives for injury, method of injury, and school and community events happening around the time period. Information obtained on victim(s) and offender(s) includes demographics, circumstances of the event (date/time, alcohol or drug use, number of persons involved), types and origins of weapons, criminal history, psychological risk factors, school-related problems, extracurricular activities, and family history, including structure and stressors.

One hundred and five school-associated violent deaths were identified from July 1, 1992, to June 30, 1994 (Kachur et al., 1996, School-Associated Violent Deaths in the United States, 1992 to 1994, *Journal of the American Medical Association, 275:* 1729–1733). A more recent report from this data collection identified 253 school-associated violent deaths between July 1, 1994, and June 30, 1999 (Anderson et al., 2001, School-Associated Violent Deaths in the United States, 1994–1999, *Journal of the American Medical Association, 286:* 2695–2702). Other publications from this study have described how the number of events change during the school year (Centers for Disease Control and Prevention, 2001, Temporal Variations in School-Associated Student Homicide and Suicide Events—United States, 1992–1999, *Morbidity and Mortality Weekly Report, 50:* 657–660), the source of the firearms used in these events (Reza et al., 2003, Source of Firearms Used by Students in School-Associated Violent Deaths—United States, 1992–1999, *Morbidity and Mortality Weekly Report, 52:* 169–172), and suicides that were associated with schools (Kauffman et al., 2004, School-Associated Suicides—United States, 1994–1999, *Morbidity and Mortality Weekly Report, 53:* 476–478). The most recent publication describes trends in school-associated homicide from July 1, 1992, to June 30, 2006 (Centers for Disease Control and Prevention, 2008, School-Associated Student Homicides—United States, 1992–2006, *Morbidity and Mortality Weekly Report 2008, 57:* 33–36). The interviews conducted on cases between July 1, 1994, and June 30, 1999, achieved a response rate of 97 percent for police officials and 78 percent for school officials. For several reasons, all data for years from 1999 to the present are flagged as preliminary. For some recent data, the interviews with school and law enforcement officials to verify case details have not been completed. The details learned during the interviews can occasionally change the classification of a case. Also, new cases may be identified because of the expansion of the scope of the media files used for case identification. Sometimes other cases not identified during earlier data years using the independent case finding efforts (which focus on nonmedia sources of information) will be discovered. Also, other cases may occasionally be identified while the law enforcement and school interviews are being conducted to verify known cases.

Further information on SAVD may be obtained from

Jeff Hall
Division of Violence Prevention
National Center for Injury Prevention and Control
Centers for Disease Control and Prevention
4770 Buford Highway NE
Mailstop F63
Atlanta, GA 30341-3742
(770) 488-4648
dzu4@cdc.gov

Web-based Injury Statistics Query and Reporting System Fatal

WISQARS Fatal provides mortality data related to injury. The mortality data reported in WISQARS Fatal come from death certificate data reported to the National Center for Health Statistics (NCHS), Centers for Disease Control and Prevention. Data include causes of death reported by attending physicians, medical examiners, and coroners and demographic information about decedents reported by funeral directors, who obtain that information from family members and other informants. NCHS collects, compiles, verifies, and prepares these data for release to the public. The data provide information about unintentional injury, homicide, and suicide as leading causes of death, how common these causes of death are, and whom they affect. These data are intended for a broad audience—the public, the media, public health practitioners and researchers, and public health officials—to increase their knowledge of injury.

WISQARS Fatal mortality reports provide tables of the total numbers of injury-related deaths and the death rates per 100,000 U.S. population. The reports list deaths according to cause (mechanism) and intent (manner) of injury by state, race, Hispanic origin, sex, and age groupings.

Further information on WISQARS Fatal may be obtained from

National Center for Injury Prevention and Control
Mailstop K65
4770 Buford Highway NE
Atlanta, GA 30341-3724
(770) 488-1506
ohcinfo@cdc.gov
www.cdc.gov/info
http://www.cdc.gov/injury/wisqars/fatal_help/data_sources.html

Youth Risk Behavior Surveillance System

The Youth Risk Behavior Surveillance System (YRBSS) is an epidemiological surveillance system developed by the Centers for Disease Control and Prevention (CDC) to monitor the prevalence of youth behaviors that most influence health.

The YRBSS focuses on priority health-risk behaviors established during youth that result in the most significant mortality, morbidity, disability, and social problems during both youth and adulthood. The YRBSS includes a national school-based Youth Risk Behavior Survey (YRBS), as well as surveys conducted in states and large urban school districts.

The national YRBS uses a three-stage cluster sampling design to produce a nationally representative sample of students in grades 9–12 in the United States. The target population consisted of all public and private school students in grades 9–12 in the 50 states and the District of Columbia. The first-stage sampling frame included selecting primary sampling units (PSUs) from strata formed on the basis of urbanization and the relative percentage of Black and Hispanic students in the PSU. These PSUs are either counties; subareas of large counties; or groups of smaller, adjacent counties. At the second stage, schools were selected with probability proportional to school enrollment size.

The final stage of sampling consisted of randomly selecting, in each chosen school and in each of grades 9–12, one or two classrooms from either a required subject, such as English or social studies, or a required period, such as homeroom or second period. All students in selected classes were eligible to participate. In surveys conducted before 2013, three strategies were used to oversample Black and Hispanic students: (1) larger sampling rates were used to select PSUs that are in high-Black and high-Hispanic strata; (2) a modified measure of size was used that increased the probability of selecting schools with a disproportionately high minority enrollment; and (3) two classes per grade, rather than one, were selected in schools with a high percentage of combined Black, Hispanic, Asian/Pacific Islander, or American Indian/Alaska Native enrollment. In 2013, only selection of two classes per grade was needed to achieve an adequate precision with minimum variance. Approximately 16,300 students participated in the 1993 survey, 10,900 students participated in the 1995 survey, 16,300 students participated in the 1997 survey, 15,300 students participated in the 1999 survey, 13,600 students participated in the 2001 survey, 15,200 students participated in the 2003 survey, 13,900 students participated in the 2005 survey, 14,000 students participated in the 2007 survey, 16,400 students participated in the 2009 survey, 15,400 participated in the 2011 survey, and 13,600 participated in the 2013 survey.

The overall response rate was 70 percent for the 1993 survey, 60 percent for the 1995 survey, 69 percent for the 1997 survey, 66 percent for the 1999 survey, 63 percent for the 2001 survey, 67 percent for the 2003 survey, 67 percent for the 2005 survey, 68 percent for the 2007 survey, 71 percent for the 2009 survey, 71 percent for the 2011 survey, and 68 percent for the 2013 survey. NCES standards call for response rates of 85 percent or better for cross-sectional surveys, and bias analyses are required by NCES when that percentage is not achieved. For YRBS data, a full nonresponse bias analysis has not been done because the data necessary to do the analysis are not available. The weights were developed to adjust for nonresponse and the oversampling of Black and Hispanic students in the sample. The final weights were constructed so that only weighted proportions of students (not weighted counts of students) in each grade matched national population projections.

State-level data were downloaded from the Youth Online: Comprehensive Results web page (http://nccd.cdc.gov/Youth Online/). Each state and district school-based YRBS employs a two-stage, cluster sample design to produce representative samples of students in grades 9–12 in their jurisdiction. All except a few state samples, and all district samples, include only public schools, and each district sample includes only schools in the funded school district (e.g., San Diego Unified School District) rather than in the entire city (e.g., greater San Diego area).

In the first sampling stage in all except a few states and districts, schools are selected with probability proportional to school enrollment size. In the second sampling stage, intact classes of a required subject or intact classes during a required period (e.g., second period) are selected randomly. All students in sampled classes are eligible to participate. Certain states and districts modify these procedures to meet their individual needs. For example, in a given state or district, all schools, rather than a sample of schools, might be selected to participate. State and local surveys that have a scientifically selected sample, appropriate documentation, and an overall response rate greater than or equal to 60 percent are weighted. The overall response rate reflects the school response rate multiplied by the student response rate. These three criteria are used to ensure that the data from those surveys can be considered representative of students in grades 9–12 in that jurisdiction. A weight is applied to each record to adjust for student nonresponse and the distribution of students by grade, sex, and race/ethnicity in each jurisdiction. Therefore, weighted estimates are representative of all students in grades 9–12 attending schools in each jurisdiction. Surveys that do not have an overall response rate of greater than or equal to 60 percent and that do not have appropriate documentation are not weighted and are not included in this report.

In 2013, a total of 42 states and 21 districts had weighted data. Not all of the districts were contained in the 42 states. For example, California was not one of the 42 states that obtained weighted data, but it contained several districts that did. For more information on the location of the districts, please see http://www.cdc.gov/healthyyouth/yrbs/participation.htm. In sites with weighted data, the student sample sizes for the state and district YRBS ranged from 1,107 to 53,785. School response rates ranged from 70 to 100 percent, student response rates ranged from 60 to 94 percent, and overall response rates ranged from 60 to 87 percent.

Readers should note that reports of these data published by the CDC and in this report do not include percentages where the denominator includes less than 100 unweighted cases.

In 1999, in accordance with changes to the Office of Management and Budget's standards for the classification of federal data on race and ethnicity, the YRBS item on race/ethnicity was modified. The version of the race and ethnicity question used in 1993, 1995, and 1997 was

How do you describe yourself?
   a. White—not Hispanic
   b. Black—not Hispanic
   c. Hispanic or Latino
   d. Asian or Pacific Islander
   e. American Indian or Alaskan Native
   f. Other

The version used in 1999, 2001, 2003, and in the 2005, 2007, and 2009 state and local district surveys was

How do you describe yourself? (Select one or more responses.)
   a. American Indian or Alaska Native
   b. Asian
   c. Black or African American
   d. Hispanic or Latino
   e. Native Hawaiian or Other Pacific Islander
   f. White

In the 2005 national survey and in all 2007, 2009, 2011, and 2013 surveys, race/ethnicity was computed from two questions: (1) "Are you Hispanic or Latino?" (response options were "yes" and "no"), and (2) "What is your race?" (response options were "American Indian or Alaska Native," "Asian," "Black or African American," "Native Hawaiian or Other Pacific Islander," or "White"). For the second question, students could select more than one response option. For this report, students were classified as "Hispanic" if they answered "yes" to the first question, regardless of how they answered the second question. Students who answered "no" to the first question and selected more than one race/ethnicity in the second category were classified as "More than one race." Students who answered "no" to the first question and selected only one race/ethnicity were classified as that race/ethnicity. Race/ethnicity was classified as missing for students who did not answer the first question and for students who answered "no" to the first question but did not answer the second question.

CDC has conducted two studies to understand the effect of changing the race/ethnicity item on the YRBS. Brener, Kann, and McManus (*Public Opinion Quarterly, 67*:227–226, 2003) found that allowing students to select more than one response to a single race/ethnicity question on the YRBS had only a minimal effect on reported race/ethnicity among high school students. Eaton, Brener, Kann, and Pittman (*Journal of Adolescent Health, 41*: 488–494, 2007) found that self-reported race/ethnicity was similar regardless of whether the single-question or a two-question format was used.

Further information on the YRBSS may be obtained from

Laura Kann
Division of Adolescent and School Health
National Center for HIV/AIDS, Viral Hepatitis, STD,
   and TB Prevention
Centers for Disease Control and Prevention
Mailstop E-75
1600 Clifton Road NE
Atlanta, GA 30329
(404) 718-8132
lkk1@cdc.gov
http://www.cdc.gov/yrbs

Department of Justice

Bureau of Justice Statistics

A division of the U.S. Department of Justice Office of Justice Programs, the Bureau of Justice Statistics (BJS) collects, analyzes, publishes, and disseminates statistical information on crime, criminal offenders, victims of crime, and the operations of the justice system at all levels of government and internationally. It also provides technical and financial support to state governments for development of criminal justice statistics and information systems on crime and justice.

For information on the BJS, see www.ojp.usdoj.gov/bjs/.

National Crime Victimization Survey

The National Crime Victimization Survey (NCVS), administered for the U.S. Bureau of Justice Statistics (BJS) by the U.S. Census Bureau, is the nation's primary source of information on crime and the victims of crime. Initiated in 1972 and redesigned in 1992, the NCVS collects detailed information on the frequency and nature of the crimes of rape, sexual assault, robbery, aggravated and simple assault, theft, household burglary, and motor vehicle theft experienced by Americans and American households each year. The survey measures both crimes reported to police and crimes not reported to the police.

NCVS estimates presented may differ from those in previous published reports. This is because a small number of victimizations, referred to as series victimizations, are included using a new counting strategy. High-frequency repeat victimizations, or series victimizations, are six or more similar but separate victimizations that occur with such frequency that the victim is unable to recall each individual event or describe each event in detail. As part of ongoing research efforts associated with the redesign of the NCVS, BJS investigated ways to include high-frequency repeat victimizations, or series victimizations, in estimates of criminal victimization. Including series victimizations results in more accurate estimates of victimization. BJS has decided to include series victimizations using the victim's estimates of the number of times the victimizations occurred over the past 6 months, capping the number of victimizations within each series at a maximum of 10. This strategy for counting series victimizations balances the desire to estimate national rates and account for the experiences of persons who have been subjected to repeat victimizations against the desire to minimize the estimation errors that can occur when repeat victimizations are reported. Including series victimizations in national rates results in rather large increases in the level of violent victimization; however, trends in violence are generally similar regardless of whether series victimizations are included. For more information on the new counting strategy and supporting research, see *Methods for Counting High-Frequency Repeat Victimizations in the National Crime Victimization Survey* at http://bjs.ojp.usdoj.gov/content/pub/pdf/mchfrv.pdf.

Readers should note that in 2003, in accordance with changes to the Office of Management and Budget's standards for the classification of federal data on race and ethnicity, the NCVS item on race/ethnicity was modified. A question on Hispanic origin is now followed by a new question on race. The new question about race allows the respondent to choose more than one race and delineates Asian as a separate category from Native Hawaiian or Other Pacific Islander. An analysis conducted by the Demographic Surveys Division at the U.S. Census Bureau showed that the new race question had very little impact on the aggregate racial distribution of the NCVS respondents, with one exception: There was a 1.6 percentage point decrease in the percentage of respondents who reported themselves as White. Due to changes in race/ethnicity categories, comparisons of race/ethnicity across years should be made with caution.

There were changes in the sample design and survey methodology in the 2006 NCVS that may have affected survey estimates. Caution should be used when comparing the 2006 estimates to estimates of other years. Data from 2007 onward are comparable to earlier years. Analyses of the 2007 estimates indicate that the program changes made in 2006 had relatively small effects on NCVS estimates. For more information on the 2006 NCVS data, see *Criminal Victimization, 2006,* at http://bjs.ojp.usdoj.gov/content/pub/pdf/cv06.pdf, the technical notes at http://bjs.ojp.usdoj.gov/content/pub/pdf/cv06tn.pdf, and *Criminal Victimization, 2007,* at http://bjs.ojp.usdoj.gov/content/pub/pdf/cv07.pdf.

The number of NCVS-eligible households in the sample in 2013 was about 107,400. Households were selected using a stratified, multistage cluster design. In the first stage, the primary sampling units (PSUs), consisting of counties or groups of counties, were selected. In the second stage, smaller areas, called Enumeration Districts (EDs), were selected from each sampled PSU. Finally, from selected EDs, clusters of four households, called segments, were selected for interview. At each stage, the selection was done proportionate to population size in order to create a self-weighting sample. The final sample was augmented to account for households constructed after the decennial Census. Within each sampled household, the U.S. Census Bureau interviewer attempts to interview all household members age 12 and older to determine whether they had been victimized by the measured crimes during the 6 months preceding the interview.

The first NCVS interview with a housing unit is conducted in person. Subsequent interviews are conducted by telephone, if possible. About 80,000 persons age 12 and older are interviewed each 6 months. Households remain in the sample for 3 years and are interviewed seven times at 6-month intervals. Since the survey's inception, the initial interview at each sample unit has been used only to bound future interviews to establish a time frame to avoid duplication of crimes uncovered in these subsequent interviews. Beginning in 2006, data from the initial interview have been adjusted to account for the effects of bounding and have been included in the survey estimates. After a household has been interviewed its seventh time, it is replaced by a new sample household. In 2013, the household response rate was about 84 percent and the completion rate for persons within households was about 88 percent. Weights were developed to permit estimates for the total U.S. population 12 years and older.

Further information on the NCVS may be obtained from

Rachel E. Morgan
Victimization Statistics Branch
Bureau of Justice Statistics
rachel.morgan@usdoj.gov
http://www.bjs.gov/

School Crime Supplement

Created as a supplement to the NCVS and co-designed by the National Center for Education Statistics and Bureau of Justice Statistics, the School Crime Supplement (SCS) survey has been conducted in 1989, 1995, and biennially since 1999 to collect additional information about school-related victimizations on a national level. This report includes data from the 1995, 1999, 2001, 2003, 2005, 2007, 2009, 2011, and 2013 collections. The 1989 data are not included in this report as a result of methodological changes to the NCVS and SCS. The SCS was designed to assist policymakers, as well as academic researchers and practitioners at federal, state, and local levels, to make informed decisions concerning crime in schools. The survey asks students a number of key questions about their experiences with and perceptions of crime and violence that occurred inside their school, on school grounds, on the school bus, or on the way to or from school. Students are asked additional questions about security measures used by their school, students' participation in after-school activities, students' perceptions of school rules, the presence of weapons and gangs in school, the presence of hate-related words and graffiti in school, student reports of bullying and reports of rejection at school, and the availability of drugs and alcohol in school. Students are also asked attitudinal questions relating to fear of victimization and avoidance behavior at school.

The SCS survey was conducted for a 6-month period from January through June in all households selected for the NCVS (see discussion above for information about the NCVS sampling design and changes to the race/ethnicity variable beginning in 2003). Within these households, the eligible respondents for the SCS were those household members who had attended school at any time during the 6 months preceding the interview, were enrolled in grades 6–12, and were not home schooled. In 2007, the questionnaire was changed and household members who attended school sometime during the school year of the interview were included. The age range of students covered in this report is 12–18 years of age. Eligible respondents were asked the supplemental questions in the SCS only after completing their entire NCVS interview. It should be noted that the first or unbounded NCVS interview has always been

included in analysis of the SCS data and may result in the reporting of events outside of the requested reference period.

The prevalence of victimization for 1995, 1999, 2001, 2003, 2005, 2007, 2009, 2011, and 2013 was calculated by using NCVS incident variables appended to the SCS data files of the same year. The NCVS type of crime variable was used to classify victimizations of students in the SCS as serious violent, violent, or theft. The NCVS variables asking where the incident happened (at school) and what the victim was doing when it happened (attending school or on the way to or from school) were used to ascertain whether the incident happened at school. Only incidents that occurred inside the United States are included.

In 2001, the SCS survey instrument was modified from previous collections. First, in 1995 and 1999, "at school" was defined for respondents as in the school building, on the school grounds, or on a school bus. In 2001, the definition for "at school" was changed to mean in the school building, on school property, on a school bus, or going to and from school. This change was made to the 2001 questionnaire in order to be consistent with the definition of "at school" as it is constructed in the NCVS and was also used as the definition in subsequent SCS collections. Cognitive interviews conducted by the U.S. Census Bureau on the 1999 SCS suggested that modifications to the definition of "at school" would not have a substantial impact on the estimates.

A total of about 9,700 students participated in the 1995 SCS, 8,400 in 1999, 8,400 in 2001, 7,200 in 2003, 6,300 in 2005, 5,600 in 2007, 5,000 in 2009, 6,500 in 2011, and 5,700 in 2013. In the 2013 SCS, the household completion rate was 86 percent.

In the 1995, 1999, 2001, 2003, 2005, 2007, 2009, and 2011 SCS, the household completion rates were 95 percent, 94 percent, 93 percent, 92 percent, 91 percent, 90 percent, 92 percent, and 91 percent, respectively, and the student completion rates were 78 percent, 78 percent, 77 percent, 70 percent, 62 percent, 58 percent, 56 percent, and 63 percent, respectively. For the 2013 SCS, the student completion rate was 60 percent. The overall unweighted SCS unit response rate (calculated by multiplying the household completion rate by the student completion rate) was about 74 percent in 1995, 73 percent in 1999, 72 percent in 2001, 64 percent in 2003, 56 percent in 2005, 53 percent in 2007, 51 percent in 2009, 57 percent in 2011, and 51 percent in 2013.

There are two types of nonresponse: unit and item nonresponse. NCES requires that any stage of data collection within a survey that has a unit base-weighted response rate of less than 85 percent be evaluated for the potential magnitude of unit nonresponse bias before the data or any analysis using the data may be released (U.S. Department of Education 2003). Due to the low unit response rate in 2005, 2007, 2009, 2011, and 2013, a unit nonresponse bias analysis was done. Unit response rates indicate how many sampled units have completed interviews. Because interviews with students could only be completed after households had responded to the NCVS, the unit completion rate for the SCS reflects both the household interview completion rate and the student interview completion rate. Nonresponse can greatly affect the strength and application of survey data by leading to an increase in variance as a result of a reduction in the actual size of the sample and can produce bias if the nonrespondents have characteristics of interest that are different from the respondents.

In order for response bias to occur, respondents must have different response rates and responses to particular survey variables. The magnitude of unit nonresponse bias is determined by the response rate and the differences between respondents and nonrespondents on key survey variables. Although the bias analysis cannot measure response bias since the SCS is a sample survey and it is not known how the population would have responded, the SCS sampling frame has four key student or school characteristic variables for which data are known for respondents and nonrespondents: sex, race/ethnicity, household income, and urbanicity, all of which are associated with student victimization. To the extent that there are differential responses by respondents in these groups, nonresponse bias is a concern.

In 2005, the analysis of unit nonresponse bias found evidence of bias for the race, household income, and urbanicity variables. White (non-Hispanic) and Other (non-Hispanic) respondents had higher response rates than Black (non-Hispanic) and Hispanic respondents. Respondents from households with an income of $35,000–$49,999 and $50,000 or more had higher response rates than those from households with incomes of less than $7,500, $7,500–$14,999, $15,000–$24,999 and $25,000–$34,999. Respondents who live in urban areas had lower response rates than those who live in rural or suburban areas. Although the extent of nonresponse bias cannot be determined, weighting adjustments, which corrected for differential response rates, should have reduced the problem.

In 2007, the analysis of unit nonresponse bias found evidence of bias by the race/ethnicity and household income variables. Hispanic respondents had lower response rates than other races/ethnicities.

Respondents from households with an income of $25,000 or more had higher response rates than those from households with incomes of less than $25,000. However, when responding students are compared to the eligible NCVS sample, there were no measurable differences between the responding students and the eligible students, suggesting that the nonresponse bias has little impact on the overall estimates.

In 2009, the analysis of unit nonresponse bias found evidence of potential bias for the race/ethnicity and urbanicity variables. White students and students of other races/ethnicities had higher response rates than did Black and Hispanic respondents. Respondents from households located in rural areas had higher response rates than those from households located in urban areas. However, when responding students are compared to the eligible NCVS sample, there were no measurable differences between the responding students and the eligible students, suggesting that the nonresponse bias has little impact on the overall estimates.

In 2011, the analysis of unit nonresponse bias found evidence of potential bias for the age variable. Respondents 12 to 17 years old had higher response rates than did 18-year-old respondents in the NCVS and SCS interviews. Weighting the data adjusts for unequal selection probabilities and for the effects of nonresponse. The weighting adjustments that correct for differential response rates are created by region, age, race, and sex, and should have reduced the effect of nonresponse.

In 2013, the analysis of unit nonresponse bias found evidence of potential bias for the age variable in the SCS respondent sample. Students age 14 and those from the western region showed percentage bias exceeding 5 percent; however, both subgroups had the highest response rate out of their respective categories. All other subgroups evaluated showed less than 1 percent nonresponse bias and had between 0.3 and 2.6 percent difference between the response population and the eligible population.

Response rates for most SCS survey items in all survey years were high—typically over 97 percent of all eligible respondents, meaning there is little potential for item nonresponse bias for most items in the survey. Weights were developed to compensate for differential probabilities of selection and nonresponse. The weighted data permit inferences about the eligible student population who were enrolled in schools in all SCS data years.

Further information about the SCS may be obtained from

Rachel Hansen
Sample Surveys Division
Cross-Sectional Surveys Branch
National Center for Education Statistics
550 12th Street SW
Washington, DC 20202
(202) 502-7486
rachel.hansen@ed.gov
http://nces.ed.gov/programs/crime

Federal Bureau of Investigation

The Federal Bureau of Investigation (FBI) collects statistics on crimes from law enforcement agencies throughout the country through the Uniform Crime Reporting (UCR) Program. The UCR Program was conceived in 1929 by the International Association of Chiefs of Police to meet a need for reliable, uniform crime statistics for the nation. In 1930, the FBI was tasked with collecting, publishing, and archiving those statistics. Today, several annual statistical publications, such as the comprehensive *Crime in the United States*, are produced from data provided by nearly 17,000 law enforcement agencies across the United States. *Crime in the United States* (CIUS) is an annual publication in which the FBI compiles volume and rate of crime offenses for the nation, the states, and individual agencies. This report also includes arrest, clearance, and law enforcement employee data.

For more information on the UCR Program, see http://www.fbi.gov/about-us/cjis/ucr/ucr.

Supplementary Homicide Reports

Supplementary Homicide Reports (SHR) are a part of the Uniform Crime Reporting (UCR) program of the Federal Bureau of Investigation (FBI). These reports provide incident-level information on criminal homicides, including situation type (e.g., number of victims, number of offenders, and whether offenders are known); the age, sex, and race of victims and offenders; weapon used; circumstances of the incident; and the relationship of the victim to the offender. The data are provided monthly to the FBI by local law enforcement agencies participating in the UCR program. The data include murders and nonnegligent manslaughters in the United States from January 1980 to December 2012; that is, negligent manslaughters and justifiable homicides have been eliminated from the data. Based on law enforcement agency reports, the FBI estimates that 625,919 murders (including nonnegligent manslaughters) were committed from 1980 to 2011. Agencies provided detailed information on 590,954 of these homicide victims. SHR estimates in this report have been revised from those in previously published reports.

About 90 percent of homicides are included in the SHR program. However, adjustments can be made to the weights to correct for missing victim reports. Estimates from the SHR program used in this report were generated by the Bureau of Justice Statistics (BJS). The SHR data were weighted to compensate for the average annual 10 percent of homicides that were not reported to the SHR. The development of the set of annual weights is a three-step process.

Each year the FBI's annual *Crime in the United States* report presents a national estimate of murder victims in the United States and estimates of the number of murder victims in each of the 50 states and the District of Columbia. The first stage weight uses the FBI's annual estimates of murder victims in each state and the number of murder victims from that state found in the annual SHR database.

Specifically, the first stage weight for victims in state S in year Y is

$$\frac{\text{FBI's estimate of murder victims in state S}_{(\text{year Y})}}{\text{Number of murder victims in the SHR file from state S}_{(\text{year Y})}}$$

For complete reporting states, this first stage weight is equal to 1. For partial reporting states, this weight is greater than 1. For states with a first stage weight greater than 2—that is, the state-reported SHR data for less than half of the FBI's estimated number of murder victims in the state—the first stage weight is set to 1.

The second stage weight uses the FBI's annual national estimates of murder victims in the United States and the sum of the first stage weights for each state. The second stage weight for victims in all states in year Y is

$$\frac{\text{FBI's estimate of murder victims in the United States}_{(\text{year Y})}}{\text{Sum of the first stage weights of all states}_{(\text{year Y})}}$$

The third step in the process is to calculate the final annual victim-level SHR weight. The weight used to develop national estimates of the attributes of murder victims is

$$\text{SHR weight}_{(\text{year Y})} = (\text{First stage weight}_{(\text{year Y})}) \times (\text{Second stage weight}_{(\text{year Y})})$$

Conceptually, the first stage weight uses a state's own reported SHR records to represent all murder victims in that state, as long as at least 50 percent of the estimated number of murder victims in that state have a record in the SHR. The sum of the first stage weights then equals the sum of the total number of all murder victims in states with at least 50 percent SHR coverage and the simple count of those victims from the other reporting states. The second stage weight is used to inflate the first stage weights so that the weight derived from the product of the first and second stage weights represents all murder victims in that year in the United States. The difference between the sum of the first stage weights and the FBI's annual national estimate of murder victims is the unreported murder victims in states with less than 50 percent SHR coverage and the murder victims in states that report no data to the SHR in that year. The second stage weight compensates for this difference by assuming that the attributes of the nonreported victims are similar to the attributes of weighted murder victims in that year's SHR database.

The weighting procedure outlined above assumes that the characteristics of unreported homicide incidents are similar to the characteristics of reported incidents. There is no comprehensive way to assess the validity of this assumption. There is one exception to this weighting process. Some states did not report any data in some years. For example, Florida reported no incidents to the SHR program for the years 1988 through 2012. The annual national weights, however, attempt to compensate for those few instances in which entire states did not report any data.

Further information on the SHR program may be obtained from

Communications Unit
Criminal Justice Information Services Division
Federal Bureau of Investigation
Module D3
1000 Custer Hollow Road
Clarksburg, WV 26306
(304) 625-4995
cjis_comm@leo.gov

Department of Defense

Defense Manpower Data Center

The Statistical Information Analysis Division of the Defense Manpower Data Center (DMDC) maintains the largest archive of personnel, manpower, and training data in the Department of Defense (DoD). The DMDC's statistical activities include the personnel survey program, an enlistment testing program to support screening of military applicants, and a client support program to provide statistical support to the Office of the Secretary of Defense. The DMDC collects DoD contract information in support of national economic tables and the Small Business Competitiveness Demonstration Program; it also produces statistics on DoD purchases from educational and nonprofit institutions and from state and local governments.

For more information on the DMDC, see

http://www.dhra.mil/website/locations/map_page_dmdc.shtml.

Institute of Museum and Library Statistics

On October 1, 2007, the administration of the Public Libraries Survey (PLS) and the State Library Agencies (StLA) Survey was transferred from the National Center for Education Statistics to the Institute of Museum and Library Statistics (IMLS).

IMLS Library Statistics

Public library statistics are collected annually using the PLS and disseminated annually through the Federal-State Cooperative System (FSCS) for Public Library Data. Descriptive statistics are produced for over 9,000 public libraries. The PLS includes information about staffing; operating income and expenditures; type of governance; type of administrative structure; size of collection; and service measures such as reference transactions, public service hours, interlibrary loans, circulation, and library visits. In the FSCS, respondents supply the information electronically, and data are edited and tabulated in machine-readable form.

The respondents are public libraries identified in the 50 states and the District of Columbia by state library agencies. At the state level, FSCS is administered by State Data Coordinators, who are appointed by the Chief Officer of each State Library Agency. The State Data Coordinator collects the requested data from local public libraries. All 50 states and the District of Columbia submit data for individual public libraries, which are aggregated to state and national levels.

From 1994 through 2006, NCES conducted the StLA Survey for the 50 states and the District of Columbia. A state library agency is the official agency of a state that is charged by state law with the extension and development of public library services throughout the state and that has adequate authority under state law to administer state plans in accordance with the provisions of the Library Services and Technology Act (LSTA) of 2003. The StLA Survey collected data on services, collections, staffing, revenue, and expenditures.

Further information on the Public Library Survey and State Library Agency Survey can be obtained from

Institute of Museum and Library Services
Office of Policy, Planning, Research, and Communication
Research and Statistics Division
1800 M Street NW, 9th Floor
Washington, DC 20036-5802
imlsinfo@imls.gov
http://www.imls.gov/

My Brother's Keeper Initiative

Established by President Obama in 2014, the My Brother's Keeper Initiative is an interagency effort to improve measurably the expected educational and life outcomes for and address the persistent opportunity gaps faced by boys and young men of color. The Initiative established a Task Force to develop a coordinated federal effort to identify the public and private efforts that are working and how to expand upon them.

The My Brother's Keeper Task Force and the Federal Interagency Forum on Child and Family Statistics have collected federal statistics on a number of national level indicators to provide an initial snapshot of young people's well-being across multiple domains, including health, nutrition, poverty, education, economic opportunity, criminal justice and more. A selection of these data may be accessed at http://mbk.ed.gov/data/.

Further information about the My Brother's Keeper Initiative may be obtained from

https://www.whitehouse.gov/my-brothers-keeper
http://mbk.ed.gov/
http://mbk.ed.gov/data/

National Institute on Drug Abuse

Monitoring the Future Survey

The National Institute on Drug Abuse of the U.S. Department of Health and Human Services is the primary supporter of the long-term study entitled "Monitoring the Future: A Continuing Study of American Youth," conducted by the University of Michigan Institute for Social Research. One component of the study deals with student drug abuse. Results of the national sample survey have been published annually since 1975. With the exception of 1975, when about 9,400 students participated in the survey, the annual samples comprise roughly 16,000 students in 150 public and private schools. Students complete self-administered questionnaires given to them in their classrooms by University of Michigan personnel. Each year, 8th-, 10th-, and 12th-graders are surveyed (12th-graders since 1975, and 8th- and 10th-graders since 1991). The 8th- and 10th-grade surveys are anonymous, while the 12th-grade survey is confidential. The 10th-grade samples involve about 17,000 students in 140 schools each year, while the 8th-grade samples have approximately 18,000 students in about 150 schools. In all, approximately 50,000 students from about 420 public and private secondary schools are surveyed annually. Approximately 88.4 percent of 8th-grade students, 87.2 percent of 10th-grade students, and 84.7 percent of 12th-grade students surveyed participated in the study in 2010. Beginning with the class of 1976, a randomly selected sample from each senior class has been followed in the years after high school on a continuing basis.

Understandably, there is some reluctance to admit illegal activities. Also, students who are out of school on the day of the survey are nonrespondents, and the survey does not include high school dropouts. The inclusion of absentees and dropouts would tend to increase the proportion of individuals who had used drugs. A 1983 study found that the inclusion of absentees could increase some of the drug usage estimates by as much as 2.7 percentage points. (Details on that study and its methodology were published in *Drug Use Among American High School Students, College Students, and Other Young Adults*, by L.D. Johnston, P.M. O'Malley, and J.G. Bachman, available from the National Clearinghouse on Drug Abuse Information, 5600 Fishers Lane, Rockville, MD 20857.)

The 2014 Monitoring the Future survey encompassed about 41,600 8th-, 10th-, and 12th-grade students in 377 secondary schools nationwide. The first published results were presented in *Monitoring the Future, National Results on Drug Use, 1975–2014: Overview, Key Findings on Adolescent Drug Use,* at http://www.monitoringthefuture.org/pubs/monographs/mtf-overview2014.pdf.

Further information on the Monitoring the Future drug abuse survey may be obtained from

National Institute on Drug Abuse
Division of Epidemiology, Services and
 Prevention Research (DESPR)
6001 Executive Boulevard
Bethesda, MD 20892
mtfinformation@umich.edu
http://www.monitoringthefuture.org

National Science Foundation

Survey of Federal Funds for Research and Development

The annual federal funds survey is the primary source of information about federal funding for research and development in the United States. It is used by policymakers in the executive and legislative branches of the federal government in determining policies, laws, and regulations affecting science; it is also used by those who follow science trends in every sector of the economy, including university administrators and professors, economic and political analysts, research and development managers inside and outside the government, the science press, and leading members of the science community in the United States and around the world.

The survey is completed by the 15 federal departments and their 72 subagencies and 12 independent agencies that conduct research and development programs. The sample is obtained from information in the President's budget submitted to Congress.

Federal funds data, as collected, span 3 government fiscal years: the fiscal year just completed, the current fiscal year, and the next fiscal year. Actual data are collected for the year just completed; estimates are obtained for the current fiscal year and the next fiscal year.

The data are collected and managed online; this system was designed to help improve survey reporting by offering respondents direct online reporting and editing.

The federal funds survey has an unweighted response rate of 100 percent with no known item nonresponse. The information included in this survey has been stable since fiscal year 1973, when federal obligations for research to universities and colleges by agency and detailed science and engineering fields were added to the survey.

Further information on federal funds for research and development may be obtained from

Michael Yamaner
Research and Development Statistics Program
National Center for Science and Engineering Statistics
National Science Foundation
4201 Wilson Boulevard, Suite 965
Arlington, VA 22230
myamaner@nsf.gov
http://www.nsf.gov/statistics

Survey of Earned Doctorates

The Survey of Earned Doctorates (SED) has collected basic statistics from the universe of doctoral recipients in the United States each year since 1958. It is supported by six federal agencies: the National Science Foundation, in conjunction with the U.S. Department of Education; the National Endowment for the Humanities; the U.S. Department of Agriculture; the National Institutes of Health; and the National Aeronautics and Space Administration.

With the assistance of institutional coordinators at each doctorate-awarding institution, a survey form is distributed to each person completing the requirements for a research doctorate. Of the 52,760 persons receiving research doctorates granted in 2013, 92 percent responded to the survey. The survey questionnaire obtains information on sex, race/ethnicity, marital status, citizenship, disabilities, dependents, specialty field of doctorate, educational institutions attended, time spent in completion of doctorate, financial support, education debt, postgraduation plans, and educational attainment of parents.

Further information on the Survey of Earned Doctorates may be obtained from

Lynn Milan
Project Officer
Human Resources Statistics Program
National Center for Science and Engineering Statistics
National Science Foundation
4201 Wilson Boulevard
Arlington, VA 22230
lmilan@nsf.gov
http://www.nsf.gov/statistics/srvydoctorates

Survey of Graduate Students and Postdoctorates in Science and Engineering

The Survey of Graduate Students and Postdoctorates in Science and Engineering, also known as the graduate student survey (GSS), is an annual survey of all U.S. academic institutions granting research-based master's degrees or doctorates in science, engineering, or selected health fields. Sponsored by the National Science Foundation and the National Institutes of Health, the survey provides data on the number and characteristics of graduate students, postdoctoral researchers, and doctorate-holding nonfaculty researchers in selected health fields. Results are used to assess shifts in graduate enrollment and postdoctorate appointments and trends in financial support.

Data collection for the 2013 GSS began in fall 2013. The 2013 survey universe consisted of 364 doctorate-granting and 200 master's-granting institutions, for a total of 564 institutions. There were 680 schools affiliated with these institutions: 480 at doctorate-granting institutions and 200 at master's-granting institutions.

New procedures to improve coverage of GSS-eligible units were introduced in the 2007 survey cycle and were continued in subsequent cycles. Increased emphasis was given to updating the unit list by providing an exhaustive list of GSS-eligible programs within existing GSS fields. In previous years, only a representative list was provided for each GSS field, which may have resulted in not reporting all eligible units. The set of GSS-eligible fields was also modified. Due to these changes, data for 2007 and later years are not directly comparable with data from previous years.

Further information on the Survey of Graduate Students and Postdoctorates in Science and Engineering may be obtained from

Kelly Kang
Project Officer
Human Resources Statistics Program
National Center for Science and Engineering Statistics
National Science Foundation
4201 Wilson Boulevard, Suite 965
Arlington, VA 22230
kkang@nsf.gov
http://www.nsf.gov/statistics/srvygradpostdoc/

Substance Abuse and Mental Health Services Administration

National Survey on Drug Use and Health

Conducted by the federal government since 1971 (annually since 1991), the National Survey on Drug Use and Health (NSDUH) is a survey of the civilian, noninstitutionalized population of the United States age 12 or older. It is the primary source of information on the prevalence, patterns, and consequences of alcohol, tobacco, and illegal drug use and abuse. The survey collects data by administering questionnaires to a representative sample of the population (since 1999, the NSDUH interview has been carried out using computer-assisted interviewing). NSDUH collects information from residents of households, noninstitutional group quarters, and civilians living on military bases. The main results of the NSDUH present national estimates of rates of use, numbers of users, and other measures related to illicit drugs, alcohol, and tobacco products.

Prior to 2002, the survey was called the National Household Survey on Drug Abuse (NHSDA). The 2002 update of the survey's name coincided with improvements to the survey. In light of these improvements, NSDUH data from 2002 and later should not be compared with NHSDA data from 2001 and earlier as a method of assessing changes in substance use over time.

The 2005 NSDUH was the first in a coordinated 5-year sample design providing estimates for all 50 states and the District of Columbia for the years 2005 through 2009. Because the 2005 design enables estimates to be developed by state, states may be viewed as the first level of stratification, as well as a reporting variable.

In the 2013 NSDUH, screening was completed at 160,325 addresses, and 67,838 completed interviews were obtained. The survey was conducted from January through December 2013. Weighted response rates for household screening and for interviewing were 83.9 and 71.7 percent, respectively.

Further information on the NSDUH may be obtained from

SAMHSA, Center for Behavioral Health Statistics and Quality
1 Choke Cherry Road, Room 2-1049
Rockville, MD 20857
http://www.samhsa.gov/data/

Other Organization Sources

ACT

ACT assessment

The ACT assessment is designed to measure educational development in the areas of English, mathematics, social studies, and natural sciences. The ACT assessment is taken by college-bound high school students and by all graduating seniors in Colorado and Illinois. The test results are used to predict how well students might perform in college.

Prior to the 1984–85 school year, national norms were based on a 10 percent sample of the students taking the test. Since then, national norms have been based on the test scores of all students taking the test. Beginning with 1984–85, these norms have been based on the most recent ACT scores available from students scheduled to graduate in the spring of the year. Duplicate test records are no longer used to produce national figures.

Separate ACT standard scores are computed for English, mathematics, science reasoning, and, as of October 1989, reading. ACT standard scores are reported for each subject area on a scale from 1 to 36. In 2014, the national composite score (the simple average of the four ACT standard scores) was 21.0, with a standard deviation of 5.4. The tests emphasize reasoning, analysis, problem solving, and the integration of learning from various sources, as well as the application of these proficiencies to the kinds of tasks college students are expected to perform.

It should be noted that graduating students who take the ACT assessment are not necessarily representative of graduating students nationally. Students who live in the Midwest, Rocky Mountains, Plains, and South are overrepresented among ACT-tested students as compared to graduating students nationally. Students in these areas often aspire to public colleges and universities, which in these jurisdictions require the ACT assessment more often than the SAT test.

Further information on the ACT may be obtained from

ACT
500 ACT Drive
P.O. Box 168
Iowa City, IA 52243-0168
http://www.act.org

The College Board

Advanced Placement Exam

The Advanced Placement (AP) program is a curriculum sponsored by the College Board that offers high school students the opportunity to take college-level courses in a high school setting. A student taking an AP course in high school can earn college credit for participation by attaining a certain minimum score on the AP exam in that subject area.

The AP program offers 35 courses in 20 subject areas. Although nearly 60 percent of U.S. high schools in the United States offer AP courses, the College Board does not require students to take an AP course before taking an AP exam. AP exams are offered once a year in May. Most of the exams take 2 to 3 hours to complete. The scores for all AP exams range from 1 to 5, with 5 being the highest score. Over 90 percent of the nation's colleges and universities have an AP policy granting incoming students credit, placement, or both, for qualifying AP exam scores.

SAT

The Admissions Testing Program of the College Board is made up of a number of college admissions tests, including the Preliminary Scholastic Assessment Test (PSAT) and the Scholastic Assessment Test, now known as the SAT. High school students participate in the testing program as sophomores, juniors, or seniors—some more than once during these three years. If they have taken the tests more than once, only the most recent scores are tabulated. The PSAT and SAT report subscores in the areas of mathematics and verbal ability.

Each year, over 2 million students take the SAT examination. SAT results are not representative of high school students or college-bound students nationally, however, since the sample is self-selected (i.e., taken by students who need the results to apply to a particular college or university). In addition, public colleges in many states—particularly those in the Midwest, parts of the South, and the West—require ACT scores rather than SAT scores; thus, the proportion of students taking the SAT in these states is very low and is inappropriate for comparison. The current version of the SAT, which includes a writing component, was first administered in March 2005; a redesigned SAT is planned for March 2016.

Further information on AP and the SAT may be obtained from

The College Board National Office
250 Vesey Street
New York, NY 10281
http://www.collegeboard.org/

Commonfund Institute

Higher Education Price Index

Commonfund Institute took over management of the Higher Education Price Index (HEPI) in 2005 from Research Associates of Washington, which originated the index in 1961. HEPI is an inflation index designed specifically to track the main cost drivers in higher education. It measures the average relative level of prices in a fixed basket of goods and services purchased each year by colleges and universities through current fund educational and general expenditures, excluding research.

The main components of HEPI are professional salaries and fringe benefits of faculty, administrators, and other professional service personnel; nonprofessional wages, salaries, and fringe benefits for clerical, technical, service, and other nonprofessional personnel; contracted services such as data processing, communication, transportation, supplies and materials, and equipment; library acquisitions; and utilities. These represent the major items purchased for current operations by colleges and universities. Prices for these items are obtained from salary surveys conducted by the American Association of University Professors, the College and University Personnel Association, and the Bureau of Labor Statistics (BLS), as well as from price series of components of BLS's Consumer Price Index (CPI) and Producer Price Index (PPI). Since 2009, data have been consistently drawn from the July–June academic fiscal year. Prior to 2009, data were collected from years with varying endpoints.

HEPI measures price levels from a designated reference year in which budget weights are assigned. This base year is FY 1983 and is assigned a price value of 100.0 for index compilation. An index value of 115.0, for example, represents a 15 percent price increase over 1983 values.

Further information on HEPI may be obtained from

Commonfund Institute
15 Old Danbury Road
Wilton, CT 06897
http://www.commonfund.org

Council for Aid to Education

Survey of Voluntary Support of Education

The Council for Aid to Education, Inc. (CAE) is a non-profit corporation funded by contributions from businesses. CAE largely provides consulting and research services to corporations and information on voluntary support services to education institutions. Each year, CAE conducts a survey of colleges and universities and private elementary and secondary schools to obtain information on the amounts, sources, and purposes of private gifts, grants, and bequests received during the academic year.

The annual Voluntary Support of Education (VSE) survey consistently captures about 85 percent of the total voluntary support to colleges and universities in the United States. Institutional reports of voluntary support data from the VSE survey are more comprehensive and detailed than the related data in the Integrated Postsecondary Education Data System (IPEDS) Finance survey conducted by NCES.

The VSE survey is conducted online. All accredited institutions of higher education are eligible to participate, and about a quarter of these institutions fill out a survey each year. CAE reviews the survey forms for internal consistency, queries institutions whose data appear out of line with national trends or their own historical data, and makes an effort to clean the data before preparing a computerized database of the results.

Individual institutions and several state systems of higher education use the VSE data to monitor and analyze their fundraising results. CAE uses the data to develop national estimates of giving to education and to report in detail on private support of education. The results from the VSE survey are available to subscribers online and are also published in the annual report *Voluntary Support of Education*, which may be purchased from CAE.

Further information on the VSE survey may be obtained from

Ann Kaplan
Council for Aid to Education
215 Lexington Avenue
16th Floor
New York, NY 10016-6023
vse@cae.org
http://www.cae.org

Council of Chief State School Officers

State Education Indicators

The Council of Chief State School Officers (CCSSO) is a nonpartisan, nationwide, nonprofit organization of the public officials who head departments of public education in the 50 states, the District of Columbia, the Department of Defense dependents schools, the Bureau of Indian Education, Puerto Rico, American Samoa, Guam, the Northern Mariana Islands, and the U.S. Virgin Islands. The CCSSO State Education Indicators project provides leadership in developing a system of state-by-state indicators of the condition of K–12 education. Indicator activities include collecting and reporting statistical indicators by state, tracking state policy changes, assisting with accountability systems, and conducting analysis of trends in education. *Key State Education Policies on PK–12 Education* is one of the publications issued by the State Education Indicators project. It is intended to inform policymakers and educators about the current status of key education policies that define and shape elementary and secondary education in the nation's public schools. State education staff reported on current policies through a survey, and CCSSO staff collected additional assessment information through state websites.

Further information on CCSSO publications may be obtained from

State Education Indicators Program
Standards, Assessment, and Accountability
Council of Chief State School Officers
1 Massachusetts Avenue NW
Suite 700
Washington, DC 20001-1431
http://www.ccsso.org

Editorial Projects in Education

Education Week

Editorial Projects in Education is an independent, nonprofit publisher of *Education Week* and other print and online products on K–12 education.

Further information on Editorial Projects in Education publications may be obtained from

Editorial Projects in Education, Inc.
Suite 100
6935 Arlington Road
Bethesda, MD 20814-5233
http://www.edweek.org/info/about

Education Commission of the States

StateNotes

Education Commission of the States (ECS) regularly issues compilations, comparisons, and summaries of state policies—enacted or pending—on a number of education issues, including high school graduation requirements and school term information. ECS monitors state education activities for changes in education policies and updates ECS state information accordingly.

Further information on ECS StateNotes may be obtained from

Education Commission of the States
700 Broadway, #810
Denver, CO 80203-3442
ecs@ecs.org
http://www.ecs.org

GED Testing Service

GED Testing Service is a joint venture, begun in 2011, between the American Council on Education (ACE) and Pearson. A GED credential documents high school-level academic skills. The test was first administered to World War II veterans in 1942 and was subsequently administered to civilians beginning in 1947. The first four generations of the GED test were the original GED test released in 1942, the 1978 series, the 1988 series, and the 2002 series. In 2014, a new test was implemented. Differences and similarities between the 2014 GED test and the 2002 series test are available at http://www.gedtestingservice.com/uploads/files/2487f6e1ca5659684cbe1f8b16f564d0.pdf.

The annual *GED Testing Program Statistical Report* looks at those who take the GED, test performance statistics, and historical information on the GED testing program.

Attempting to make comparisons in GED testing across jurisdictions is problematic, since each jurisdiction manages its own GED testing program. As such, each jurisdiction develops its own policies, which would be reflected in its testing program outcomes, such as pass rates.

Further information on the GED may be obtained from

GED Testing Service
1919 M Street NW
Suite 600
Washington, DC 20036
http://www.gedtestingservice.com/ged-testing-service

Graduate Record Examinations Board

GRE tests

Graduate Record Examinations (GRE) tests are taken by individuals applying to graduate or professional school. GRE offers two types of tests, the revised General Test and Subject Tests. The revised General Test, which is mainly taken on computer, measures verbal, quantitative, and analytical writing skills. The analytical writing section (which replaced the analytical reasoning section on the general GRE in October 2002) consists of two analytical writing tasks. The Subject Tests measure achievement in biochemistry, cell and molecular biology, biology, chemistry, literature in English, mathematics, physics, and psychology. Each graduate institution or division of the institution determines which GRE tests are required for admission.

Individuals may take GRE tests more than once. Score reports only reflect scores earned within the past 5-year period.

Further information on the GRE may be obtained from

GRE-ETS
Educational Testing Service
P.O. Box 6000
Princeton, NJ 08541
http://www.ets.org/gre

Institute of International Education

Open Doors

Each year, the Institute of International Education (IIE) conducts a survey of the number of foreign students studying in American colleges and universities and U.S. students studying abroad. The results of these surveys are reported in the publication *Open Doors*. All of the regionally accredited institutions in NCES's Integrated Postsecondary Education Data System (IPEDS) are surveyed by IIE. The foreign student enrollment data presented in the *Digest of Education Statistics* are drawn from IIE surveys that ask U.S. institutions for information on enrollment of foreign students, as well as student characteristics such as country of origin. For the 2012–13 survey, 58.8 percent of the 2,816 institutions surveyed reported data. For 2013–14, 62.0 percent of the 2,814 institutions surveyed reported data.

Surveys on the flows of U.S. college students studying abroad have been conducted since 1985–86. Surveys are sent to U.S. institutions asking them to provide information on the number and characteristics of the students to whom they awarded credit for study abroad during the previous academic year. For the 2011–12 academic year, data were obtained from 1,068, or 62.3 percent, of the 1,713 institutions surveyed; for the 2012–13 academic year, data were obtained from 1,119, or 64.1 percent, of the 1,746 institutions surveyed.

Additional information may be obtained from the publication *Open Doors* or by contacting

Sharon Witherell
Institute of International Education–Public Affairs
809 United Nations Plaza
New York, NY 10017
switherell@iie.org
http://www.iie.org/en/Research-and-Publications/Open-Doors

International Association for the Evaluation of Educational Achievement

The International Association for the Evaluation of Educational Achievement (IEA) is composed of governmental research centers and national research institutions around the world whose aim is to investigate education problems common among countries. Since its inception in 1958, the IEA has conducted more than 30 research studies of cross-national achievement. The regular cycle of studies encompasses learning in basic school subjects. Examples are the Trends in International Mathematics and Science Study (TIMSS) and the Progress in International Reading Literacy Study (PIRLS). IEA projects also include studies of particular interest to IEA members, such as the TIMSS 1999 Video Study of Mathematics and Science Teaching, the Civic Education Study, and studies on information technology in education.

The international bodies that coordinate international assessments vary in the labels they apply to participating education systems, most of which are countries. IEA differentiates between IEA members, which IEA refers to as "countries" in all cases, and "benchmarking participants." IEA members include countries such as the United States and Ireland, as well as subnational entities such as England and Scotland (which are both part of the United Kingdom), the Flemish community of Belgium, and Hong Kong (a Special Administrative Region of China). IEA benchmarking participants are all subnational entities and include Canadian provinces, U.S. states, and Dubai in the United Arab Emirates (among others). Benchmarking participants, like the participating countries, are given the opportunity to assess the comparative international standing of their students' achievement and to view their curriculum and instruction in an international context.

Some IEA studies, such as TIMSS and PIRLS, include an assessment portion as well as contextual questionnaires to collect information about students' home and school experiences. The TIMSS and PIRLS scales, including the scale averages and standard deviations, are designed to remain constant from assessment to assessment so that education systems (including countries and subnational education systems) can compare their scores over time, as well as compare their scores directly with the scores of other education systems. Although each scale was created to have a mean of 500 and a standard deviation of 100, the subject matter and the level of difficulty of items necessarily differ by grade, subject, and domain/dimension. Therefore, direct comparisons between scores across grades, subjects, and different domain/dimension types should not be made.

Further information on the International Association for the Evaluation of Educational Achievement may be obtained from http://www.iea.nl.

Trends in International Mathematics and Science Study

The Trends in International Mathematics and Science Study (TIMSS, formerly known as the Third International Mathematics and Science Study) provides data on the mathematics and science achievement of U.S. 4th- and 8th-graders compared with that of their peers in other countries. TIMSS collects information through mathematics and science assessments and questionnaires. The questionnaires request information to help provide a context for student performance. They focus on such topics as students' attitudes and beliefs about learning mathematics and science, what students do as part of their mathematics and science lessons, students' completion of homework, and their lives both in and outside of school; teachers' perceptions of their preparedness for teaching mathematics and science, teaching assignments, class size and organization, instructional content and practices, collaboration with other teachers, and participation in professional development activities; and principals' viewpoints on policy and budget responsibilities, curriculum and instruction issues, and student behavior. The questionnaires also elicit information on the organization of schools and courses. The assessments and questionnaires are designed to specifications in a guiding framework. The TIMSS framework describes the mathematics and science content to be assessed and provides grade-specific objectives, an overview of the assessment design, and guidelines for item development.

TIMSS is on a 4-year cycle. Data collections occurred in 1995, 1999 (8th grade only), 2003, 2007, and 2011. TIMSS 2015 is the sixth administration of TIMSS since 1995. It consists of five assessments: 4th-grade mathematics; numeracy (a less difficult version of 4th-grade mathematics, newly developed for 2015); 8th-grade mathematics; 4th-grade science; and 8th-grade science. In addition to the 4th- and 8th-grade assessments, TIMSS 2015 includes the third administration of TIMSS Advanced since 1995. TIMSS Advanced assesses final-year (12th-grade) secondary students' achievement in advanced mathematics and physics. The study also collects policy-relevant information about students, curriculum emphasis, technology use, and teacher preparation and training.

Progress in International Reading Literacy Study

The Progress in International Reading Literacy Study (PIRLS) provides data on the reading literacy of U.S. 4th-graders compared with that of their peers in other countries. PIRLS is on a 5-year cycle: PIRLS data collections have been conducted in 2001, 2006, and 2011. In 2011, a total of 57 education systems, including 48 IEA members and 9 benchmarking participants, participated in the survey. The next PIRLS data collection is scheduled for 2016.

PIRLS collects information through a reading literacy assessment and questionnaires that help to provide a context for student performance. Questionnaires are administered to collect information about students' home and school experiences in learning to read. A student questionnaire addresses students' attitudes toward reading and their reading habits. In addition, questionnaires are given to students' teachers and school principals to gather information about students' school experiences in developing reading literacy. In countries other than the United States, a parent questionnaire is also administered. The assessments and questionnaires are designed to specifications in a guiding framework. The PIRLS framework describes the reading content to be assessed and provides objectives specific to 4th grade, an overview of the assessment design, and guidelines for item development.

TIMSS and PIRLS Sampling and Response Rates

As is done in all participating countries and other education systems, representative samples of students in the United States are selected. The sample design that was employed by TIMSS and PIRLS in 2011 is generally referred to as a two-stage stratified cluster sample. In the first stage of sampling, individual schools were selected with a probability proportionate to size (PPS) approach, which means that the probability is proportional to the estimated number of students enrolled in the target grade. In the second stage of sampling, intact classrooms were selected within sampled schools.

TIMSS and PIRLS guidelines call for a minimum of 150 schools to be sampled, with a minimum of 4,000 students assessed. The basic sample design of one classroom per school was designed to yield a total sample of approximately 4,500 students per population.

About 23,000 students in almost 900 schools across the United States participated in the 2011 TIMSS, joining 600,000 other student participants around the world. Because PIRLS was also administered at grade 4 in spring 2011, TIMSS and PIRLS in the United States were administered in the same schools to the extent feasible. Students took either TIMSS or PIRLS on the day of the assessments. About 13,000 U.S. students participated in PIRLS in 2011, joining 300,000 other student participants around the world. Accommodations were not provided for students with disabilities or students who were unable to read or speak the language of the test. These students were excluded from the sample. The IEA requirement is that the overall exclusion rate, which includes exclusions of schools and students, should not exceed more than 5 percent of the national desired target population.

In order to minimize the potential for response biases, the IEA developed participation or response rate standards that apply to all participating education systems and govern whether or not an education system's data are included in the TIMSS or PIRLS international datasets and the way in which its statistics are presented in the international reports. These standards were set using composites of response rates at the school, classroom, and student and teacher levels. Response rates were calculated with and without the inclusion of substitute schools that were selected to replace schools refusing to participate. In TIMSS 2011 at grade 4 in the United States, the weighted school participation rate was 79 percent before the use of substitute schools and 84 percent after the use of replacement schools; the weighted student response rate was 95 percent. In TIMSS 2011 at grade 8 in the United States, the weighted school participation rate was 87 percent before the use of substitute schools and 87 percent after the use of replacement schools; the weighted student response rate was 94 percent. In the 2011 PIRLS administered in the United States, the weighted school participation rate was 80 percent before the use of substitute schools and 85 percent after the use of replacement schools; the weighted student response rate was 96 percent.

Further information on the TIMSS study may be obtained from

Stephen Provasnik
Assessments Division
International Assessment Branch
National Center for Education Statistics
550 12th Street SW
Washington, DC 20202
(202) 502-7480
stephen.provasnik@ed.gov
http://nces.ed.gov/timss
http://www.iea.nl/timss_2011.html

Further information on the PIRLS study may be obtained from

Sheila Thompson
Assessments Division
International Assessment Branch
National Center for Education Statistics
550 12th Street SW
Washington, DC 20202
(202) 502-7425
sheila.thompson@ed.gov
http://nces.ed.gov/surveys/pirls/
http://www.iea.nl/pirls_2011.html

National Association of State Directors of Teacher Education and Certification

NASDTEC Manual/KnowledgeBase

The National Association of State Directors of Teacher Education and Certification (NASDTEC) was organized in 1928 to represent professional standards boards and commissions and state departments of education that are responsible for the preparation, licensure, and discipline of educational personnel. Currently, NASDTEC's membership includes all 50 states, the District of Columbia, the U.S. Department of Defense Education Activity, U.S. territories, and Canadian provinces and territories.

The NASDTEC Manual on the Preparation and Certification of Educational Personnel was printed between 1984 and 2004, when it was replaced by an online publication, KnowledgeBase. KnowledgeBase is an expanded version of the Manual and is the most comprehensive source of state-by-state information pertaining to the certification requirements and preparation of teachers and other school personnel in the United States and Canada.

Further information on KnowledgeBase may be obtained from

Phillip S. Rogers
Executive Director
NASDTEC
1629 K Street NW
Suite 300
Washington, DC 20006
philrogers@nasdtec.com
http://www.nasdtec.net/

National Catholic Educational Association

The United States Catholic Elementary and Secondary Schools

The National Catholic Educational Association (NCEA) has been providing leadership and service to Catholic education since 1904. NCEA began to publish *The United States Catholic Elementary and Secondary Schools: Annual Statistical Report on Schools, Enrollment and Staffing* in 1970 because of the lack of educational data on the private sector. The report is based on data gathered by all of the archdiocesan and diocesan offices of education in the United States. These data enable NCEA to present information on school enrollment and staffing patterns for prekindergarten through grade 12. The first part of the report presents data concerning the context of American education, while the following segment focuses on statistical data of Catholic schools. Statistics include enrollment by grade level, race/ethnicity, and affiliation.

Further information on *The United States Catholic Elementary and Secondary Schools: Annual Statistical Report on Schools, Enrollment, and Staffing* may be obtained from

Sister Dale McDonald
National Catholic Educational Association
1005 North Glebe Road
Suite 525
Arlington, VA 22201
mcdonald@ncea.org
http://www.ncea.org

National Education Association

Estimates of School Statistics

The National Education Association (NEA) publishes *Estimates of School Statistics* annually as part of the report *Rankings of the States & Estimates of School Statistics*. *Estimates of School Statistics* presents projections of public school enrollment, employment and personnel compensation, and finances, as reported by individual state departments of education. The state-level data in these estimates allow broad assessments of trends in the above areas. These data should be looked at with the understanding that the state-level data do not necessarily reflect the varying conditions within a state on education issues.

Data in *Estimates of School Statistics* are provided by state and District of Columbia departments of education and by other, mostly governmental, sources. Surveys are sent to the departments of education requesting estimated data for the current year and revisions to 4 years of historical data, as necessary. Twice a year, NEA submits current-year estimates on more than 35 education statistics to state departments of education for verification or revision. The estimates are generated using regression analyses and are used only if the states do not provide current data.

Further information on *Estimates of School Statistics* may be obtained from

NEA Rankings & Estimates Team—NEA Research
1201 16th Street NW
Washington, DC 20036
http://www.nea.org

Organization for Economic Cooperation and Development

The Organization for Economic Cooperation and Development (OECD) publishes analyses of national policies and survey data in education, training, and economics in OECD and partner countries. Newer studies include student survey data on financial literacy and on digital literacy.

Education at a Glance

To highlight current education issues and create a set of comparative education indicators that represent key features of education systems, OECD initiated the Indicators of Education Systems (INES) project and charged the Centre for Educational Research and Innovation (CERI) with developing the cross-national indicators for it. The development of these indicators involved representatives of the OECD countries and the OECD Secretariat. Improvements in data quality and comparability among OECD countries have resulted from the country-to-country interaction sponsored through the INES project. The most recent publication in this series is *Education at a Glance 2014: OECD Indicators (EAG)*.

The 2014 *EAG* featured data on the 34 OECD countries (Australia, Austria, Belgium, Canada, Chile, the Czech Republic, Denmark, Estonia, Finland, France, Germany, Greece, Hungary, Iceland, Ireland, Israel, Italy, Japan, the Republic of Korea, Luxembourg, Mexico, the Netherlands, New Zealand, Norway, Poland, Portugal, the Slovak Republic, Slovenia, Spain, Sweden, Switzerland, Turkey, the United Kingdom, and the United States); two partner countries that participate in INES (Brazil and the Russian Federation); and the other partner countries that do not participate in INES (Argentina, China, Colombia, India, Indonesia, Latvia, Saudi Arabia, and South Africa).

The *OECD Handbook for Internationally Comparative Education Statistics: Concepts, Standards, Definitions, and Classifications* provides countries with specific guidance on how to prepare information for OECD education surveys; facilitates countries' understanding of OECD indicators and their use in policy analysis; and provides a reference for collecting and assimilating educational data. Chapter 7 of the *OECD Handbook for Internationally Comparative Education Statistics* contains a discussion of data quality issues. Users should examine footnotes carefully to recognize some of the data limitations.

Further information on international education statistics may be obtained from

Andreas Schleicher
Director for the Directorate of Education and Skills and Special
   Advisor on Education Policy to the OECD's Secretary General
OECD Directorate for Education nd Skills
2, rue André Pascal
75775 Paris CEDEX 16
France
andreas.schleicher@oecd.org
http://www.oecd.org

Program for International Student Assessment

The Program for International Student Assessment (PISA) is a system of international assessments organized by the Organization for Economic Cooperation and Development (OECD), an intergovernmental organization of industrialized countries, that focuses on 15-year-olds' capabilities in reading literacy, mathematics literacy, and science literacy. PISA also includes measures of general, or cross-curricular, competencies such as learning strategies. PISA emphasizes functional skills that students have acquired as they near the end of compulsory schooling.

PISA is a 2-hour paper-and-pencil exam. Assessment items include a combination of multiple-choice questions and open-ended questions that require students to develop their own response. PISA scores are reported on a scale that ranges from 0 to 1,000, with the OECD mean set at 500 and a standard deviation set at 100. In 2012, mathematics, science, and reading literacy were assessed primarily through a paper-and-pencil exam, and problem-solving was administered using a computer-based exam. Education systems could also participate in optional pencil-and-paper financial literacy assessments and computer-based mathematics and reading assessments. In each education system, the assessment is translated into the primary language of instruction; in the United States, all materials are written in English.

To implement PISA, each of the participating education systems scientifically draws a nationally representative sample of 15-year-olds, regardless of grade level. In the United States, about 6,100 students from 161 public and private schools took the PISA 2012 assessment. In the U.S. state education systems, about 1,700 students at 50 schools in Connecticut, about 1,900 students at 54 schools in Florida, and about 1,700 students at 49 schools in Massachusetts took the 2012 assessment. PISA 2012 was only administered at public schools in the U.S. state education systems.

The intent of PISA reporting is to provide an overall description of performance in reading literacy, mathematics literacy, and science literacy every 3 years, and to provide a more detailed look at each domain in the years when it is the major focus. These cycles will allow education systems to compare changes in trends for each of the three subject areas over time. In the first cycle, PISA 2000, reading literacy was the major focus, occupying roughly two-thirds of assessment time. For 2003, PISA focused on mathematics literacy as well as the ability of students to solve problems in real-life settings. In 2006, PISA focused on science literacy; in 2009, it focused on reading literacy again; and in 2012, it focused on mathematics literacy. PISA 2015 focuses on science, as it did in 2006.

In 2000, 43 education systems participated in PISA. In 2003, 41 education systems participated; in 2006, 57 education systems (30 OECD member countries and 27 nonmember countries or education systems) participated; and in 2009, 65 education systems (34 OECD member countries and 31 nonmember countries or education systems) participated. (An additional nine education systems administered PISA 2009 in 2010.) In PISA 2012, the most recent administration for which results are available, 65 education systems (34 OECD member countries and 31 nonmember countries or education systems), as well as the U.S. states of Connecticut, Florida, and Massachusetts, participated. PISA 2015 is assessing students' mathematics, reading, and science literacy in more than 70 countries and educational jurisdictions. The survey also includes a collaborative problem-solving assessment and an optional financial literacy assessment. U.S. 15-year-old students are participating in this optional assessment.

Further information on PISA may be obtained from

Holly Xie
Dana Kelly
Assessments Division
International Assessment Branch
National Center for Education Statistics
550 12th Street SW
Washington, DC 20202
holly.xie@ed.gov
dana.kelly@ed.gov
http://nces.ed.gov/surveys/pisa

School Bus Fleet

School Bus Fleet magazine is a trade publication serving more than 28,000 school transportation professionals in the United States and Canada that provides information on the management and maintenance of school bus fleets operated by public school districts, private schools, Head Start agencies, and child care centers. The readership includes public operators and contract service providers.

Further information on School Bus Fleet magazine may be obtained from

School Bus Fleet
3520 Challenger Street
Torrance, CA 90503
info@schoolbusfleet.com
http://www.schoolbusfleet.com/

School Transportation News

School Transportation News is a monthly news and feature magazine covering the field of pupil transportation. The publication focuses on school bus and school vehicle safety and reports on transportation-related legislation and environmental issues touching on school transportation. The School Transportation News website offers a detailed history of school transportation services in the United States.

Further information about School Transportation News may be obtained from

School Transportation News
P.O. Box 789
Redondo Beach, CA 90277
http://stnonline.com/

United Nations Educational, Scientific, and Cultural Organization

Statistical Yearbook and Global Education Digest

The United Nations Educational, Scientific, and Cultural Organization (UNESCO) conducts annual surveys of education statistics of its member countries. Data from official surveys are supplemented by information obtained by UNESCO through other publications and sources. Each year, more than 200 countries reply to the UNESCO surveys. In some cases, estimates are made by UNESCO for particular items, such as world and continent totals. While great efforts are made to make them as comparable as possible, the data still reflect the vast differences among the countries of the world in the structure of education. While there is some agreement about the reporting of primary and secondary data, tertiary-level data (i.e., postsecondary education data) present numerous substantive problems. Some countries report only university enrollment, while other countries report all postsecondary enrollment, including enrollment in vocational and technical schools and correspondence programs. A very high proportion of some countries' tertiary-level students attend institutions in other countries. The member countries that provide data to UNESCO are responsible for their validity. Thus, data for particular countries are subject to nonsampling error and perhaps sampling error as well. Users should examine footnotes carefully to recognize some of the data limitations. UNESCO publishes the data in reports such as the *Statistical Yearbook* and the *Global Education Digest*.

Further information on the *Statistical Yearbook* and the *Global Education Digest* may be obtained from

UNESCO Institute for Statistics
Publications
C.P. 6128 Succursale Centre-ville
Montreal, Quebec, H3C 3J7
Canada
http://www.uis.unesco.org

APPENDIX B
Definitions

Academic support This category of college expenditures includes expenditures for support services that are an integral part of the institution's primary missions of instruction, research, or public service. It also includes expenditures for libraries, galleries, audio/visual services, academic computing support, ancillary support, academic administration, personnel development, and course and curriculum development.

Achievement gap Occurs when one group of students outperforms another group, and the difference in average scores for the two groups is statistically significant (that is, larger than the margin of error).

Achievement levels, NAEP Specific achievement levels for each subject area and grade to provide a context for interpreting student performance. At this time they are being used on a trial basis.

Basic—denotes partial mastery of the knowledge and skills that are fundamental for *proficient* work at a given grade.

Proficient—represents solid academic performance. Students reaching this level have demonstrated competency over challenging subject matter.

Advanced—signifies superior performance.

Achievement test An examination that measures the extent to which a person has acquired certain information or mastered certain skills, usually as a result of specific instruction.

ACT The ACT (formerly the American College Testing Program) assessment program measures educational development and readiness to pursue college-level coursework in English, mathematics, natural science, and social studies. Student performance on the tests does not reflect innate ability and is influenced by a student's educational preparedness.

Administrative support staff Staff whose activities are concerned with support of teaching and administrative duties of the office of the principal or department chairpersons, including clerical staff and secretaries.

Advanced Placement (AP) A program of tertiary-level courses and examinations, taught by specially qualified teachers, that provides opportunities for secondary school students to earn undergraduate credits for first-year university courses. The schools and teachers offering AP programs must meet College Board requirements and are monitored.

Agriculture Courses designed to improve competencies in agricultural occupations. Included is the study of agricultural production, supplies, mechanization and products, agricultural science, forestry, and related services.

Alternative school A public elementary/secondary school that serves students whose needs cannot be met in a regular, special education, or vocational school; may provide nontraditional education; and may serve as an adjunct to a regular school. Although alternative schools fall outside the categories of regular, special education, and vocational education, they may provide similar services or curriculum. Some examples of alternative schools are schools for potential dropouts; residential treatment centers for substance abuse (if they provide elementary or secondary education); schools for chronic truants; and schools for students with behavioral problems.

Appropriation (federal funds) Budget authority provided through the congressional appropriation process that permits federal agencies to incur obligations and to make payments.

Appropriation (institutional revenues) An amount (other than a grant or contract) received from or made available to an institution through an act of a legislative body.

Associate's degree A degree granted for the successful completion of a sub-baccalaureate program of studies, usually requiring at least 2 years (or equivalent) of full-time college-level study. This includes degrees granted in a cooperative or work-study program.

Autocorrelation Correlation of the error terms from different observations of the same variable. Also called Serial correlation.

Auxiliary enterprises This category includes those essentially self-supporting operations which exist to furnish a service to students, faculty, or staff, and which charge a fee that is directly related to, although not necessarily equal to, the cost of the service. Examples are residence halls, food services, college stores, and intercollegiate athletics.

Average daily attendance (ADA) The aggregate attendance of a school during a reporting period (normally a school year) divided by the number of days school is in session during this period. Only days on which the pupils are under the guidance and direction of teachers should be considered days in session.

Average daily membership (ADM) The aggregate membership of a school during a reporting period (normally a school year) divided by the number of days school is in session during this period. Only days on which the pupils are under the guidance and direction of teachers should be considered as days in session. The average daily membership for groups of schools having varying lengths of terms is the average of the average daily memberships obtained for the individual schools. Membership includes all pupils who are enrolled, even if they do not actually attend.

Averaged freshman graduation rate (AFGR) A measure of the percentage of the incoming high school freshman class that graduates 4 years later. It is calculated by taking the number of graduates with a regular diploma and dividing that number by the estimated count of incoming freshman 4 years earlier, as reported through the NCES Common Core of Data (CCD). The estimated count of incoming freshman is the sum of the number of 8th-graders 5 years earlier, the number of 9th-graders 4 years earlier (when current seniors were freshman), and the number of 10th-graders 3 years earlier, divided by 3. The purpose of this averaging is to account for the high rate of grade retention in the freshman year, which adds 9th-grade repeaters from the previous year to the number of students in the incoming freshman class each year. Ungraded students are allocated to individual grades proportional to each state's enrollment in those grades. The AFGR treats students who transfer out of a school or district in the same way as it treats students from that school or district who drop out.

Bachelor's degree A degree granted for the successful completion of a baccalaureate program of studies, usually requiring at least 4 years (or equivalent) of full-time college-level study. This includes degrees granted in a cooperative or work-study program.

Books Nonperiodical printed publications bound in hard or soft covers, or in loose-leaf format, of at least 49 pages, exclusive of the cover pages; juvenile nonperiodical publications of any length found in hard or soft covers.

Breusch-Godfrey serial correlation LM test A statistic testing the independence of errors in least-squares regression against alternatives of first-order and higher degrees of serial correlation. The test belongs to a class of asymptotic tests known as the Lagrange multiplier (LM) tests.

Budget authority (BA) Authority provided by law to enter into obligations that will result in immediate or future outlays. It may be classified by the period of availability (1-year, multiple-year, no-year), by the timing of congressional action (current or permanent), or by the manner of determining the amount available (definite or indefinite).

Business Program of instruction that prepares individuals for a variety of activities in planning, organizing, directing, and controlling business office systems and procedures.

Capital outlay Funds for the acquisition of land and buildings; building construction, remodeling, and additions; the initial installation or extension of service systems and other built-in equipment; and site improvement. The category also encompasses architectural and engineering services including the development of blueprints.

Career/technical education (CTE) In high school, encompasses occupational education, which teaches skills required in specific occupations or occupational clusters, as well as nonoccupational CTE, which includes family and consumer sciences education (i.e., courses that prepare students for roles outside the paid labor market) and general labor market preparation (i.e., courses that teach general employment skills such as word processing and introductory technology skills).

Carnegie unit The number of credits a secondary student received for a course taken every day, one period per day, for a full year; a factor used to standardize all credits indicated on secondary school transcripts across studies.

Catholic school A private school over which a Roman Catholic church group exercises some control or provides some form of subsidy. Catholic schools for the most part include those operated or supported by a parish, a group of parishes, a diocese, or a Catholic religious order.

Central cities The largest cities, with 50,000 or more inhabitants, in a Metropolitan Statistical Area (MSA). Additional cities within the metropolitan area can also be classified as "central cities" if they meet certain employment, population, and employment/residence ratio requirements.

Certificate A formal award certifying the satisfactory completion of a postsecondary education program. Certificates can be awarded at any level of postsecondary education and include awards below the associate's degree level.

Charter school A school providing free public elementary and/or secondary education to eligible students under a specific charter granted by the state legislature or other appropriate authority, and designated by such authority to be a charter school.

City school See Locale codes.

Class size The membership of a class at a given date.

Classification of Instructional Programs (CIP) The CIP is a taxonomic coding scheme that contains titles and descriptions of primarily postsecondary instructional programs. It was developed to facilitate NCES' collection and reporting of postsecondary degree completions by major field of study using standard classifications that capture the majority of reportable program activity. It was originally published in 1980 and was revised in 1985, 1990, 2000, and 2010.

Classification of Secondary School Courses (CSSC) A modification of the Classification of Instructional Programs used for classifying high school courses. The CSSC contains over 2,200 course codes that help compare the thousands of high school transcripts collected from different schools.

Classroom teacher A staff member assigned the professional activities of instructing pupils in self-contained classes or courses, or in classroom situations; usually expressed in full-time equivalents.

Coefficient of variation (CV) Represents the ratio of the standard error to the estimate. For example, a CV of 30 percent indicates that the standard error of the estimate is equal to 30 percent of the estimate's value. The CV is used to compare the amount of variation relative to the magnitude of the estimate. A CV of 30 percent or greater indicates that an estimate should be interpreted with caution. For a discussion of standard errors, see Appendix A: Guide to Sources.

Cohort A group of individuals that have a statistical factor in common, for example, year of birth.

Cohort-component method A method for estimating and projecting a population that is distinguished by its ability to preserve knowledge of an age distribution of a population (which may be of a single sex, race, and Hispanic origin) over time.

College A postsecondary school that offers general or liberal arts education, usually leading to an associate's, bachelor's, master's, or doctor's degree. Junior colleges and community colleges are included under this terminology.

Combined school A school that encompasses instruction at both the elementary and the secondary levels; includes schools starting with grade 6 or below and ending with grade 9 or above.

Combined school (2007–08 Schools and Staffing Survey) A school with at least one grade lower than 7 and at least one grade higher than 8; schools with only ungraded classes are included with combined schools.

Combined Statistical Area (CSA) A combination of Core Based Statistical Areas (see below), each of which contains a core with a substantial population nucleus as well as adjacent communities having a high degree of economic and social integration with that core. A CSA is a region with social and economic ties as measured by commuting, but at lower levels than are found within each component area. CSAs represent larger regions that reflect broader social and economic interactions, such as wholesaling, commodity distribution, and weekend recreation activities.

Computer science A group of instructional programs that describes computer and information sciences, including computer programming, data processing, and information systems.

Constant dollars Dollar amounts that have been adjusted by means of price and cost indexes to eliminate inflationary factors and allow direct comparison across years.

Consumer Price Index (CPI) This price index measures the average change in the cost of a fixed market basket of goods and services purchased by consumers. Indexes vary for specific areas or regions, periods of time, major groups of consumer expenditures, and population groups. The CPI reflects spending patterns for two population groups: (1) all urban consumers and urban wage earners and (2) clerical workers. CPIs are calculated for both the calendar year and the school year using the U.S. All Items CPI for All Urban Consumers (CPI-U). The calendar year CPI is the same as the annual CPI-U. The school year CPI is calculated by adding the monthly CPI-U figures, beginning with July of the first year and ending with June of the following year, and then dividing that figure by 12.

Consumption That portion of income which is spent on the purchase of goods and services rather than being saved.

Control of institutions A classification of institutions of elementary/secondary or postsecondary education by whether the institution is operated by publicly elected or appointed officials and derives its primary support from public funds (public control) or is operated by privately elected or appointed officials and derives its major source of funds from private sources (private control).

Core Based Statistical Area (CBSA) A population nucleus and the nearby communities having a high degree of economic and social integration with that nucleus. Each CBSA includes at least one urban area of 10,000 or more people and one or more counties. In addition to a "central county" (or counties), additional "outlying counties" are included in the CBSA if they meet specified requirements of commuting to or from the central counties.

Credit The unit of value, awarded for the successful completion of certain courses, intended to indicate the quantity of course instruction in relation to the total requirements for a diploma, certificate, or degree. Credits are frequently expressed in terms such as "Carnegie units" "semester credit hours" and "quarter credit hours."

Current dollars Dollar amounts that have not been adjusted to compensate for inflation.

Current expenditures (elementary/secondary) The expenditures for operating local public schools, excluding capital outlay and interest on school debt. These expenditures include such items as salaries for school personnel, benefits, student transportation, school books and materials, and energy costs. Beginning in 1980–81, expenditures for state administration are excluded.

Instruction expenditures Includes expenditures for activities related to the interaction between teacher and students. Includes salaries and benefits for teachers and instructional aides, textbooks, supplies, and purchased services such as instruction via television, webinars, and other online instruction. Also included are tuition expenditures to other local education agencies.

Administration expenditures Includes expenditures for school administration (i.e., the office of the principal, full-time department chairpersons, and graduation expenses), general administration (the superintendent and board of education and their immediate staff), and other support services expenditures.

Transportation Includes expenditures for vehicle operation, monitoring, and vehicle servicing and maintenance.

Food services Includes all expenditures associated with providing food to students and staff in a school or school district. The services include preparing and serving regular and incidental meals or snacks in connection with school activities, as well as the delivery of food to schools.

Enterprise operations Includes expenditures for activities that are financed, at least in part, by user charges, similar to a private business. These include operations funded by sales of products or services, together with amounts for direct program support made by state education agencies for local school districts.

Current expenditures per pupil in average daily attendance Current expenditures for the regular school term divided by the average daily attendance of full-time pupils (or full-time equivalency of pupils) during the term. See also Current expenditures and Average daily attendance.

Current-fund expenditures (postsecondary education) Money spent to meet current operating costs, including salaries, wages, utilities, student services, public services, research libraries, scholarships and fellowships, auxiliary enterprises, hospitals, and independent operations; excludes loans, capital expenditures, and investments.

Current-fund revenues (postsecondary education) Money received during the current fiscal year from revenue which can be used to pay obligations currently due, and surpluses reappropriated for the current fiscal year.

Deaf-blindness See Disabilities, children with.

Deafness See Disabilities, children with.

Default rate The percentage of loans that are in delinquency and have not been repaid according to the terms of the loan. According to the federal government, a federal student loan is in default if there has been no payment on the loan in 270 days. The Department of Education calculates a *3-year cohort* default rate, which is the percentage of students who entered repayment in a given fiscal year (from October 1 to September 30) and then defaulted within the following 2 fiscal years. For example, the 3-year cohort default rate for fiscal year (FY) 2009 is the percentage of borrowers who entered repayment during FY 2009 (any time from October 1, 2008, through September 30, 2009) and who defaulted by the end of FY 2011 (September 30, 2011).

Degree An award conferred by a college, university, or other postsecondary education institution as official recognition for the successful completion of a program of studies. Refers specifically to associate's or higher degrees conferred by degree-granting institutions. See also Associate's degree, Bachelor's degree, Master's degree, and Doctor's degree.

Degree/certificate-seeking student A student enrolled in courses for credit and recognized by the institution as seeking a degree, certificate, or other formal award. High school students also enrolled in postsecondary courses for credit are not considered degree/certificate-seeking. See also Degree and Certificate.

Degree-granting institutions Postsecondary institutions that are eligible for Title IV federal financial aid programs and grant an associate's or higher degree. For an institution to be eligible to participate in Title IV financial aid programs it must offer a program of at least 300 clock hours in length, have accreditation recognized by the U.S. Department of Education, have been in business for at least 2 years, and have signed a participation agreement with the Department.

Degrees of freedom The number of free or linearly independent sample observations used in the calculation of a statistic. In a time series regression with t time periods and k independent variables including a constant term, there would be t minus k degrees of freedom.

Department of Defense (DoD) dependents schools Schools that are operated by the Department of Defense Education Activity (a civilian agency of the U.S. Department of Defense) and provide comprehensive prekindergarten through 12th-grade educational programs on military installations both within the United States and overseas.

Dependency status A designation of whether postsecondary students are financially dependent on their parents or financially independent of their parents. Undergraduates are assumed to be dependent unless they meet one of the following criteria: are age 24 or older, are married or have legal dependents other than a spouse, are veterans, are orphans or wards of the court, or provide documentation that they self-supporting.

Dependent variable A mathematical variable whose value is determined by that of one or more other variables in a function. In regression analysis, when a random variable, *y*, is expressed as a function of variables *x1, x2, ... xk*, plus a stochastic term, then *y* is known as the "dependent variable."

Disabilities, children with Those children evaluated as having any of the following impairments and who, by reason thereof, receive special education and related services under the Individuals with Disabilities Education Act (IDEA) according to an Individualized Education Program (IEP), Individualized Family Service Plan (IFSP), or a services plan.

Autism Having a developmental disability significantly affecting verbal and nonverbal communication and social interaction, generally evident before age 3, that adversely affects educational performance. Other characteristics often associated with autism are engagement in repetitive activities and stereotyped movements, resistance to environmental change or change in daily routines, and unusual responses to sensory experiences. A child is not considered autistic if the child's educational performance is adversely affected primarily because of an emotional disturbance.

Deaf-blindness Having concomitant hearing and visual impairments which cause such severe communication and other developmental and educational problems that the student cannot be accommodated in special education programs solely for deaf or blind students.

Developmental delay Having developmental delays, as defined at the state level, and as measured by appropriate diagnostic instruments and procedures in one or more of the following cognitive areas: physical development, cognitive development, communication development, social or emotional development, or adaptive development.

Emotional disturbance Exhibiting one or more of the following characteristics over a long period of time, to a marked degree, and adversely affecting educational performance: an inability to learn which cannot be explained by intellectual, sensory, or health factors; an inability to build or maintain satisfactory interpersonal relationships with peers and teachers; inappropriate types of behavior or feelings under normal circumstances; a general pervasive mood of unhappiness or depression; or a tendency to develop physical symptoms or fears associated with personal or school problems. This term does not include children who are socially maladjusted, unless they also display one or more of the listed characteristics.

Hearing impairment Having a hearing impairment, whether permanent or fluctuating, which adversely affects the student's educational performance. It also includes a hearing impairment which is so severe that the student is impaired in processing linguistic information through hearing (with or without amplification) and which adversely affects educational performance.

Intellectual disability Having significantly subaverage general intellectual functioning, existing concurrently with defects in adaptive behavior and manifested during the developmental period, which adversely affects the child's educational performance.

Multiple disabilities Having concomitant impairments (such as intellectually disabled-blind, intellectually disabled-orthopedically impaired, etc.), the combination of which causes such severe educational problems that the student cannot be accommodated in special education programs solely for one of the impairments. Term does not include deaf-blind students.

Orthopedic impairment Having a severe orthopedic impairment which adversely affects a student's educational performance. The term includes impairment resulting from congenital anomaly, disease, or other causes.

Other health impairment Having limited strength, vitality, or alertness due to chronic or acute health problems, such as a heart condition, tuberculosis, rheumatic fever, nephritis, asthma, sickle cell anemia, hemophilia, epilepsy, lead poisoning, leukemia, or diabetes which adversely affect the student's educational performance.

Specific learning disability Having a disorder in one or more of the basic psychological processes involved in understanding or in using spoken or written language, which may manifest itself in an imperfect ability to listen, think, speak, read, write, spell, or do mathematical calculations. The term includes such conditions as perceptual disabilities, brain injury, minimal brain dysfunction, dyslexia, and developmental aphasia. The term does not include children who have learning problems which are primarily the result of visual, hearing, motor, or intellectual disabilities, or of environmental, cultural, or economic disadvantage.

Speech or language impairment Having a communication disorder, such as stuttering, impaired articulation, language impairment, or voice impairment, which adversely affects the student's educational performance.

Traumatic brain injury Having an acquired injury to the brain caused by an external physical force, resulting in total or partial functional disability or psychosocial impairment or both, that adversely affects the student's educational performance. The term applies to open or closed head injuries resulting in impairments in one or more areas, such as cognition; language; memory; attention; reasoning; abstract thinking; judgment; problem-solving; sensory, perceptual, and motor abilities; psychosocial behavior; physical functions; information processing; and speech. The term does not apply to brain injuries that are congenital or degenerative or to brain injuries induced by birth trauma.

Visual impairment Having a visual impairment which, even with correction, adversely affects the student's educational performance. The term includes partially seeing and blind children.

Discipline divisions Degree programs that include break-outs to the 6-digit level of the Classification of Instructional Programs (CIP). See also Fields of study.

Disposable personal income Current income received by people less their contributions for social insurance, personal tax, and nontax payments. It is the income available to people for spending and saving. Nontax payments include passport fees, fines and penalties, donations, and tuitions and fees paid to schools and hospitals operated mainly by the government. See also Personal income.

Distance education Education that uses one or more technologies to deliver instruction to students who are separated from the instructor and to support regular and substantive interaction between the students and the instructor synchronously or asynchronously. Technologies used for instruction may include the following: Internet; one-way and two-way transmissions through open broadcasts, closed circuit, cable, microwave, broadband lines, fiber optics, and satellite or wireless communication devices; audio conferencing; and DVDs and CD-ROMs, if used in a course in conjunction with the technologies listed above.

Doctor's degree The highest award a student can earn for graduate study. Includes such degrees as the Doctor of Education (Ed.D.); the Doctor of Juridical Science (S.J.D.); the Doctor of Public Health (Dr.P.H.); and the Doctor of Philosophy (Ph.D.) in any field, such as agronomy, food technology, education, engineering, public administration, ophthalmology, or radiology. The doctor's degree classification encompasses three main subcategories—research/scholarship degrees, professional practice degrees, and other degrees—which are described below.

Doctor's degree—research/scholarship A Ph.D. or other doctor's degree that requires advanced work beyond the master's level, including the preparation and defense of a dissertation based on original research, or the planning and execution of an original project demonstrating substantial artistic or scholarly achievement. Examples of this type of degree may include the following and others, as designated by the awarding institution: the Ed.D. (in education), D.M.A. (in musical arts), D.B.A. (in business administration), D.Sc. (in science), D.A. (in arts), or D.M (in medicine).

Doctor's degree—professional practice A doctor's degree that is conferred upon completion of a program providing the knowledge and skills for the recognition, credential, or license required for professional practice. The degree is awarded after a period of study such that the total time to the degree, including both preprofessional and professional preparation, equals at least 6 full-time-equivalent academic years. Some doctor's degrees of this type were formerly classified as first-professional degrees. Examples of this type of degree may include the following and others, as designated by the awarding insti-

tution: the D.C. or D.C.M. (in chiropractic); D.D.S. or D.M.D. (in dentistry); L.L.B. or J.D. (in law); M.D. (in medicine); O.D. (in optometry); D.O. (in osteopathic medicine); Pharm.D. (in pharmacy); D.P.M., Pod.D., or D.P. (in podiatry); or D.V.M. (in veterinary medicine).

Doctor's degree—other A doctor's degree that does not meet the definition of either a doctor's degree—research/scholarship or a doctor's degree—professional practice.

Double exponential smoothing A method that takes a single smoothed average component of demand and smoothes it a second time to allow for estimation of a trend effect.

Dropout The term is used to describe both the event of leaving school before completing high school and the status of an individual who is not in school and who is not a high school completer. High school completers include both graduates of school programs as well as those completing high school through equivalency programs such as the General Educational Development (GED) program. Transferring from a public school to a private school, for example, is not regarded as a dropout event. A person who drops out of school may later return and graduate but is called a "dropout" at the time he or she leaves school. Measures to describe these behaviors include the event dropout rate (or the closely related school persistence rate), the status dropout rate, and the high school completion rate.

Durbin-Watson statistic A statistic testing the independence of errors in least squares regression against the alternative of first-order serial correlation. The statistic is a simple linear transformation of the first-order serial correlation of residuals and, although its distribution is unknown, it is tested by bounding statistics that follow R. L. Anderson's distribution.

Early childhood school Early childhood program schools serve students in prekindergarten, kindergarten, transitional (or readiness) kindergarten, and/or transitional first (or prefirst) grade.

Econometrics The quantitative examination of economic trends and relationships using statistical techniques, and the development, examination, and refinement of those techniques.

Education specialist/professional diploma A certificate of advanced graduate studies that advance educators in their instructional and leadership skills beyond a master's degree level of competence.

Educational and general expenditures The sum of current funds expenditures on instruction, research, public service, academic support, student services, institutional support, operation and maintenance of plant, and awards from restricted and unrestricted funds.

Educational attainment The highest grade of regular school attended and completed.

Educational attainment (Current Population Survey) This measure uses March CPS data to estimate the percentage of civilian, noninstitutionalized people who have achieved certain levels of educational attainment. Estimates of educational attainment do not differentiate between those who graduated from public schools, those who graduated from private schools, and those who earned a GED; these estimates also include individuals who earned their credential or completed their highest level of education outside of the United States.

1972–1991 During this period, an individual's educational attainment was considered to be his or her last fully completed year of school. Individuals who completed 12 years of schooling were deemed to be high school graduates, as were those who began but did not complete the first year of college. Respondents who completed 16 or more years of schooling were counted as college graduates.

1992–present Beginning in 1992, CPS asked respondents to report their highest level of school completed or their highest degree received. This change means that some data collected before 1992 are not strictly comparable with data collected from 1992 onward and that care must be taken when making comparisons across years. The revised survey question emphasizes credentials received rather than the last grade level attended or completed. The new categories include the following:

- High school graduate, high school diploma, or the equivalent (e.g., GED)
- Some college but no degree
- Associate's degree in college, occupational/vocational program
- Associate's degree in college, academic program (e.g., A.A., A.S., A.A.S.)
- Bachelor's degree (e.g., B.A., A.B., B.S.)
- Master's degree (e.g., M.A., M.S., M.Eng., M.Ed., M.S.W., M.B.A.)
- Professional school degree (e.g., M.D., D.D.S., D.V.M., LL.B., J.D.)
- Doctor's degree (e.g., Ph.D., Ed.D.)

Elementary education/programs Learning experiences concerned with the knowledge, skills, appreciations, attitudes, and behavioral characteristics which are considered to be needed by all pupils in terms of their awareness of life within our culture and the world of work, and which normally may be achieved during the elementary school years (usually kindergarten through grade 8 or kindergarten through grade 6), as defined by applicable state laws and regulations.

Elementary school A school classified as elementary by state and local practice and composed of any span of grades not above grade 8.

Elementary/secondary school Includes only schools that are part of state and local school systems, and also most nonprofit private elementary/secondary schools, both religiously affiliated and nonsectarian. Includes regular, alternative, vocational, and special education schools. U.S. totals exclude federal schools for American Indians, and federal schools on military posts and other federal installations.

Emotional disturbance See Disabilities, children with.

Employees in degree-granting institutions Persons employed by degree-granting institutions, who are classified into the following occupational categories in this publication:

Executive/administrative/managerial staff Employees whose assignments require management of the institution or of a customarily recognized department or subdivision thereof. These employees perform work that is directly related to management policies or general business operations and that requires them to exercise discretion and independent judgment.

Faculty (instruction/research/public service) Employees whose principal activities are for the purpose of providing instruction or teaching, research, or public service. These employees may hold such titles as professor, associate professor, assistant professor, instructor, or lecturer. Graduate assistants are not included in this category.

Graduate assistants Graduate-level students who are employed on a part-time basis for the primary purpose of assisting in classroom or laboratory instruction or in the conduct of research.

Nonprofessional staff Employees whose primary activities can be classified as one of the following: technical and paraprofessional work (which generally requires less formal training and experience than required for professional status); clerical and secretarial work; skilled crafts work; or service/maintenance work.

Other professional staff Employees who perform academic support, student service, and institutional support and who need either a degree at the bachelor's or higher level or experience of such kind and amount as to provide a comparable background.

Professional staff Employees who are classified as executive/administrative/managerial staff, faculty, graduate assistants, or other professional staff.

Employment Includes civilian, noninstitutional people who (1) worked during any part of the survey week as paid employees; worked in their own business, profession, or farm; or worked 15 hours or more as unpaid workers in a family-owned enterprise; or (2) were not working but had jobs or businesses from which they were temporarily absent due to illness, bad weather, vacation, labor-management dispute, or personal reasons whether or not they were seeking another job.

Employment (Current Population Survey) According to the October Current Population Survey (CPS), employed persons are persons age 16 or older who, during the reference week, (1) did any work at all (at least 1 hour) as paid employees or (2) were not working but had jobs or businesses from which they were temporarily absent because of vacation, illness, bad weather, child care problems, maternity or paternity leave, labor-management dispute, job training, or other family or personal reasons, whether or not they were paid for the time off or were seeking other jobs.

Employment status A classification of individuals as employed (either full or part time), unemployed (looking for work or on layoff), or not in the labor force (due to being retired, having unpaid employment, or some other reason).

Endowment A trust fund set aside to provide a perpetual source of revenue from the proceeds of the endowment investments. Endowment funds are often created by donations from benefactors of an institution, who may designate the use of the endowment revenue. Normally, institutions or their representatives manage the investments, but they are not permitted to spend the endowment fund itself, only the proceeds from the investments. Typical uses of endowments would be an endowed chair for a particular department or for a scholarship fund. Endowment totals tabulated in this book also include funds functioning as endowments, such as funds left over from the previous year and placed with the endowment investments by the institution. These funds may be withdrawn by the institution and spent as current funds at any time. Endowments are evaluated by two different measures, book value and market value. Book value is the purchase price of the endowment investment. Market value is the current worth of the endowment investment. Thus, the book value of a stock held in an endowment fund would be the purchase price of the stock. The market value of the stock would be its selling price as of a given day.

Engineering Instructional programs that describe the mathematical and natural science knowledge gained by study, experience, and practice and applied with judgment to develop ways to utilize the materials and forces of nature economically. Includes programs that prepare individuals to support and assist engineers and similar professionals.

English A group of instructional programs that describes the English language arts, including composition, creative writing, and the study of literature.

English language learner (ELL) An individual who, due to any of the reasons listed below, has sufficient difficulty speaking, reading, writing, or understanding the English language to be denied the opportunity to learn successfully in classrooms where the language of instruction is English or to participate fully in the larger U.S. society. Such an individual (1) was not born in the United States or has a native language other than English; (2) comes from environments where a language other than English is dominant; or (3) is an American Indian or Alaska Native and comes from environments where a language other than English has had a significant impact on the individual's level of English language proficiency.

Enrollment The total number of students registered in a given school unit at a given time, generally in the fall of a year. At the postsecondary level, separate counts are also available for full-time and part-time students, as well as full-time-equivalent enrollment. See also Full-time enrollment, Full-time-equivalent (FTE) enrollment, and Part-time enrollment.

Estimate A numerical value obtained from a statistical sample and assigned to a population parameter. The particular value yielded by an estimator in a given set of circumstances or the rule by which such particular values are calculated.

Estimating equation An equation involving observed quantities and an unknown that serves to estimate the latter.

Estimation Estimation is concerned with inference about the numerical value of unknown population values from incomplete data, such as a sample. If a single figure is calculated for each unknown parameter, the process is called point estimation. If an interval is calculated within which the parameter is likely, in some sense, to lie, the process is called interval estimation.

Executive/administrative/managerial staff See Employees in degree-granting institutions.

Expenditures, Total For elementary/secondary schools, these include all charges for current outlays plus capital outlays and interest on school debt. For degree-granting institutions, these include current outlays plus capital outlays. For government, these include charges net of recoveries and other correcting transactions other than for retirement of debt, investment in securities, extension of credit, or as agency transactions. Government expenditures include only external transactions, such as the provision of perquisites or other payments in kind. Aggregates for groups of governments exclude intergovernmental transactions among the governments.

Expenditures per pupil Charges incurred for a particular period of time divided by a student unit of measure, such as average daily attendance or fall enrollment.

Exponential smoothing A method used in time series analysis to smooth or to predict a series. There are various forms, but all are based on the supposition that more remote history has less importance than more recent history.

Extracurricular activities Activities that are not part of the required curriculum and that take place outside of the regular course of study. They include both school-sponsored (e.g., varsity athletics, drama, and debate clubs) and community-sponsored (e.g., hobby clubs and youth organizations like the Junior Chamber of Commerce or Boy Scouts) activities.

Faculty (instruction/research/public service) See Employees in degree-granting institutions.

Family A group of two or more people (one of whom is the householder) related by birth, marriage, or adoption and residing together. All such people (including related subfamily members) are considered as members of one family.

Family income Includes all monetary income from all sources (including jobs, businesses, interest, rent, and social security payments) over a 12-month period. The income of nonrelatives living in the household is excluded, but the income of all family members age 15 or older (age 14 or older in years prior to 1989), including those temporarily living outside of the household, is included. In the October CPS, family income is determined from a single question asked of the household respondent.

Federal funds Amounts collected and used by the federal government for the general purposes of the government. The major federal fund is the general fund, which is derived from general taxes and borrowing. Other types of federal fund accounts include special funds (earmarked for a specific purpose other than a business-like activity), public enterprise funds (earmarked for a business-like activity conducted primarily with the public), and intragovernmental funds (earmarked for a business-like activity conducted primarily within the government).

Federal sources (postsecondary degree-granting institutions) Includes federal appropriations, grants, and contracts, and federally-funded research and development centers (FFRDCs). Federally subsidized student loans are not included.

Fields of study The primary field of concentration in postsecondary certificates and degrees. In the Integrated Postsecondary Education Data System (IPEDS), refers to degree programs that are broken out only to the 2-digit level of the Classification of Instructional Programs (CIP). See also Discipline divisions.

Financial aid Grants, loans, assistantships, scholarships, fellowships, tuition waivers, tuition discounts, veteran's benefits, employer aid (tuition reimbursement), and other monies (other than from relatives or friends) provided to students to help them meet expenses. Except where designated, includes Title IV subsidized and unsubsidized loans made directly to students.

First-order serial correlation When errors in one time period are correlated directly with errors in the ensuing time period.

First-professional degree NCES no longer uses this classification. Most degrees formerly classified as first-professional (such as M.D., D.D.S., Pharm.D., D.V.M., and J.D.) are now classified as doctor's degrees—professional practice. However, master's of divinity degrees are now classified as master's degrees.

First-time student (undergraduate) A student who has no prior postsecondary experience (except as noted below) attending any institution for the first time at the undergraduate level. Includes students enrolled in the fall term who attended college for the first time in the prior summer term, and students who entered with advanced standing (college credits earned before graduation from high school).

Fiscal year A period of 12 months for which accounting records are compiled. Institutions and states may designate their own accounting period, though most states use a July 1 through June 30 accounting year. The yearly accounting period for the federal government begins on October 1 and ends on the following September 30. The fiscal year is designated by the calendar year in which it ends; e.g., fiscal year 2006 begins on October 1, 2005, and ends on September 30, 2006. (From fiscal year 1844 to fiscal year 1976, the federal fiscal year began on July 1 and ended on the following June 30.)

Forecast An estimate of the future based on rational study and analysis of available pertinent data, as opposed to subjective prediction.

Forecasting Assessing the magnitude that a quantity will assume at some future point in time, as distinct from "estimation," which attempts to assess the magnitude of an already existent quantity.

Foreign languages A group of instructional programs that describes the structure and use of language that is common or indigenous to people of a given community or nation, geographical area, or cultural traditions. Programs cover such features as sound, literature, syntax, phonology, semantics, sentences, prose, and verse, as well as the development of skills and attitudes used in communicating and evaluating thoughts and feelings through oral and written language.

For-profit institution A private institution in which the individual(s) or agency in control receives compensation other than wages, rent, or other expenses for the assumption of risk.

Free or reduced-price lunch See National School Lunch Program.

Full-time enrollment The number of students enrolled in postsecondary education courses with total credit load equal to at least 75 percent of the normal full-time course load. At the undergraduate level, full-time enrollment typically includes students who have a credit load of 12 or more semester or quarter credits. At the postbaccalaureate level, full-time enrollment includes students who typically have a credit load of 9 or more semester or quarter credits, as well as other students who are considered full time by their institutions.

Full-time-equivalent (FTE) enrollment For postsecondary institutions, enrollment of full-time students, plus the full-time equivalent of part-time students. The full-time equivalent of the part-time students is estimated using different factors depending on the type and control of institution and level of student.

Full-time-equivalent (FTE) staff Full-time staff, plus the full-time equivalent of the part-time staff.

Full-time-equivalent teacher See Instructional staff.

Full-time instructional faculty Those members of the instruction/research staff who are employed full time as defined by the institution, including faculty with released time for research and faculty on sabbatical leave. Full-time counts exclude faculty who are employed to teach less than two semesters, three quarters, two trimesters, or two 4-month sessions; replacements for faculty on sabbatical leave or those on leave without pay; faculty for preclinical and clinical medicine; faculty who are donating their services; faculty who are members of military organizations and paid on a different pay scale from civilian employees; those academic officers whose primary duties are administrative; and graduate students who assist in the instruction of courses.

Full-time worker In educational institutions, an employee whose position requires being on the job on school days throughout the school year for at least the number of hours the schools are in session. For higher education, a member of an educational institution's staff who is employed full time, as defined by the institution.

Function A mathematical correspondence that assigns exactly one element of one set to each element of the same or another set. A variable that depends on and varies with another.

Functional form A mathematical statement of the relationship among the variables in a model.

General administration support services Includes salary, benefits, supplies, and contractual fees for boards of education staff and executive administration. Excludes state administration.

General Educational Development (GED) program Academic instruction to prepare people to take the high school equivalency examination. See also GED recipient.

GED certificate This award is received following successful completion of the General Educational Development (GED) test. The GED program—sponsored by the GED Testing Service (a joint venture of the American Council on Education and Pearson)—enables individuals to demonstrate that they have acquired a level of learning comparable to that of high school graduates. See also High school equivalency certificate.

GED recipient A person who has obtained certification of high school equivalency by meeting state requirements and passing an approved exam, which is intended to provide an appraisal of the person's achievement or performance in the broad subject matter areas usually required for high school graduation.

General program A program of studies designed to prepare students for the common activities of a citizen, family member, and worker. A general program of studies may include instruction in both academic and vocational areas.

Geographic region One of the four regions of the United States used by the U.S. Census Bureau, as follows:

Northeast
Connecticut (CT)
Maine (ME)
Massachusetts (MA)
New Hampshire (NH)
New Jersey (NJ)
New York (NY)
Pennsylvania (PA)
Rhode Island (RI)
Vermont (VT)

Midwest
Illinois (IL)
Indiana (IN)
Iowa (IA)
Kansas (KS)
Michigan (MI)
Minnesota (MN)
Missouri (MO)
Nebraska (NE)
North Dakota (ND)
Ohio (OH)
South Dakota (SD)
Wisconsin (WI)

South
Alabama (AL)
Arkansas (AR)
Delaware (DE)
District of Columbia (DC)
Florida (FL)
Georgia (GA)
Kentucky (KY)
Louisiana (LA)
Maryland (MD)
Mississippi (MS)
North Carolina (NC)
Oklahoma (OK)
South Carolina (SC)
Tennessee (TN)
Texas (TX)
Virginia (VA)
West Virginia (WV)

West
Alaska (AK)
Arizona (AZ)
California (CA)
Colorado (CO)
Hawaii (HI)
Idaho (ID)
Montana (MT)
Nevada (NV)
New Mexico (NM)
Oregon (OR)
Utah (UT)
Washington (WA)
Wyoming (WY)

Government appropriation An amount (other than a grant or contract) received from or made available to an institution through an act of a legislative body.

Government grant or contract Revenues received by a postsecondary institution from a government agency for a specific research project or other program. Examples are research projects, training programs, and student financial assistance.

Graduate An individual who has received formal recognition for the successful completion of a prescribed program of studies.

Graduate assistants See Employees in degree-granting institutions.

Graduate enrollment The number of students who are working towards a master's or doctor's degree and students who are in postbaccalaureate classes but not in degree programs.

Graduate Record Examination (GRE) Multiple-choice examinations administered by the Educational Testing Service and taken by college students who are intending to attend certain graduate schools. There are two types of testing available: (1) the general exam which measures critical thinking, analytical writing, verbal reasoning, and quantitative reasoning skills, and (2) the subject test which is offered in eight specific subjects and gauges undergraduate achievement in a specific field. The subject tests are intended for those who have majored in or have extensive background in that specific area.

Graduation Formal recognition given to an individual for the successful completion of a prescribed program of studies.

Gross domestic product (GDP) The total national output of goods and services valued at market prices. GDP can be viewed in terms of expenditure categories which include purchases of goods and services by consumers and government, gross private domestic investment, and net exports of goods and services. The goods and services included are largely those bought for final use (excluding illegal transactions) in the market economy. A number of inclusions, however, represent imputed values, the most important of which is rental value of owner-occupied housing.

Group quarters Living arrangements where people live or stay in a group situation that is owned or managed by an entity or organization providing housing and/or services for the residents. Group quarters include such places as college residence halls, residential treatment centers, skilled nursing facilities, group homes, military barracks, correctional facilities, and workers' dormitories.

> ***Noninstitutionalized group quarters*** Include college and university housing, military quarters, facilities for workers and religious groups, and temporary shelters for the homeless.

> ***Institutionalized group quarters*** Include adult and juvenile correctional facilities, nursing facilities, and other health care facilities.

Handicapped See Disabilities, children with.

Head Start A local public or private nonprofit or for-profit entity authorized by the Department of Health and Human Services' Administration for Children and Families to operate a Head Start program to serve children age 3 to compulsory school age, pursuant to section 641(b) and (d) of the Head Start Act.

Hearing impairment See Disabilities, children with.

High school A secondary school offering the final years of high school work necessary for graduation. A high school is usually either a 3-year school that includes grades 10, 11, and 12 or a 4-year school that includes grades 9, 10, 11, and 12.

High school (2007–08 Schools and Staffing Survey) A school with no grade lower than 7 and at least one grade higher than 8.

High school completer An individual who has been awarded a high school diploma or an equivalent credential, including a General Educational Development (GED) certificate.

High school diploma A formal document regulated by the state certifying the successful completion of a prescribed secondary school program of studies. In some states or communities, high school diplomas are differentiated by type, such as an academic diploma, a general diploma, or a vocational diploma.

High school equivalency certificate A formal document certifying that an individual has met the state requirements for high school graduation equivalency by obtaining satisfactory scores on an approved examination and meeting other performance requirements (if any) set by a state education agency or other appropriate body. One particular version of this certificate is the General Educational Development (GED) test. The GED test is a comprehensive test used primarily to appraise the educational development of students who have not completed their formal high school education and who may earn a high school equivalency certificate by achieving satisfactory scores. GEDs are awarded by the states or other agencies, and the test is developed and distributed by the GED Testing Service (a joint venture of the American Council on Education and Pearson).

High school program A program of studies designed to prepare students for employment and postsecondary education. Three types of programs are often distinguished—academic, vocational, and general. An academic program is designed to prepare students for continued study at a college or university. A vocational program is designed to prepare students for employment in one or more semiskilled, skilled, or technical occupations. A general program is designed to provide students with the understanding and competence to function effectively in a free society and usually represents a mixture of academic and vocational components.

Higher education Study beyond secondary school at an institution that offers programs terminating in an associate's, bachelor's, or higher degree.

Higher education institutions (basic classification and Carnegie classification) See Postsecondary institutions (basic classification by level) and Postsecondary institutions (Carnegie classification of degree-granting institutions).

Higher Education Price Index A price index which measures average changes in the prices of goods and services purchased by colleges and universities through current-fund education and general expenditures (excluding expenditures for sponsored research and auxiliary enterprises).

Hispanic serving institutions Pursuant to 302 (d) of Public Law 102-325 (20 U.S.C. 1059c), most recently amended December 20, 1993, in 2(a)(7) of Public Law 103-208, where Hispanic serving institutions are defined as those with full-time-equivalent undergraduate enrollment of Hispanic students at 25 percent or more.

Historically black colleges and universities Accredited institutions of higher education established prior to 1964 with the principal mission of educating black Americans. Federal regulations (20 USC 1061 (2)) allow for certain exceptions of the founding date.

Hours worked per week According to the October CPS, the number of hours a respondent worked in all jobs in the week prior to the survey interview.

Household All the people who occupy a housing unit. A house, an apartment, a mobile home, a group of rooms, or a single room is regarded as a housing unit when it is occupied or intended for occupancy as separate living quarters, that is, when the occupants do not live and eat with any other people in the structure, and there is direct access from the outside or through a common hall.

Housing unit A house, an apartment, a mobile home, a group of rooms, or a single room that is occupied as separate living quarters.

Income tax Taxes levied on net income, that is, on gross income less certain deductions permitted by law. These taxes can be levied on individuals or on corporations or unincorporated businesses where the income is taxed distinctly from individual income.

Independent operations A group of self-supporting activities under control of a college or university. For purposes of financial surveys conducted by the National Center for Education Statistics, this category is composed principally of federally funded research and development centers (FFRDC).

Independent variable In regression analysis, a random variable, *y*, is expressed as a function of variables $x1, x2, ... xk$, plus a stochastic term; the *x*'s are known as "independent variables."

Individuals with Disabilities Education Act (IDEA) IDEA is a federal law enacted in 1990 and reauthorized in 1997 and 2004. IDEA requires services to children with disabilities throughout the nation. IDEA governs how states and public agencies provide early intervention, special education, and related services to eligible infants, toddlers, children, and youth with disabilities. Infants and toddlers with disabilities (birth–age 2) and their families receive early intervention services under IDEA, Part C. Children and youth (ages 3–21) receive special education and related services under IDEA, Part B.

Inflation A rise in the general level of prices of goods and services in an economy over a period of time, which gener-

ally corresponds to a decline in the real value of money or a loss of purchasing power. See also Constant dollars and Purchasing Power Parity indexes.

Institutional support The category of higher education expenditures that includes day-to-day operational support for colleges, excluding expenditures for physical plant operations. Examples of institutional support include general administrative services, executive direction and planning, legal and fiscal operations, and community relations.

Instruction (colleges and universities) That functional category including expenditures of the colleges, schools, departments, and other instructional divisions of higher education institutions and expenditures for departmental research and public service which are not separately budgeted; includes expenditures for both credit and noncredit activities. Excludes expenditures for academic administration where the primary function is administration (e.g., academic deans).

Instruction (elementary and secondary) Instruction encompasses all activities dealing directly with the interaction between teachers and students. Teaching may be provided for students in a school classroom, in another location such as a home or hospital, and in other learning situations such as those involving co-curricular activities. Instruction may be provided through some other approved medium, such as the Internet, television, radio, telephone, and correspondence.

Instructional staff Full-time-equivalent number of positions, not the number of different individuals occupying the positions during the school year. In local schools, includes all public elementary and secondary (junior and senior high) day-school positions that are in the nature of teaching or in the improvement of the teaching-learning situation; includes consultants or supervisors of instruction, principals, teachers, guidance personnel, librarians, psychological personnel, and other instructional staff, and excludes administrative staff, attendance personnel, clerical personnel, and junior college staff.

Instructional support services Includes salary, benefits, supplies, and contractual fees for staff providing instructional improvement, educational media (library and audiovisual), and other instructional support services.

Intellectual disability See Disabilities, children with.

Interest on debt Includes expenditures for long-term debt service interest payments (i.e., those longer than 1 year).

International baccalaureate (IB) A recognized international program of primary, middle, and secondary studies leading to the International Baccalaureate (IB) Diploma. This diploma (or certificate) is recognized in Europe and elsewhere as qualifying holders for direct access to university studies. Schools offering the IB program are approved by the International Baccalaureate Organization (IBO) and their regional office and may use IBO instructional materials, local school materials, or a combination.

International finance data Include data on public and private expenditures for educational institutions. Educational institutions directly provide instructional programs (i.e., teaching) to individuals in an organized group setting or through distance education. Business enterprises or other institutions that provide short-term courses of training or instruction to individuals on a "one-to-one" basis are not included. Where noted, international finance data may also include publicly subsidized spending on education-related purchases, such as school books, living costs, and transportation.

Public expenditures Corresponds to the nonrepayable current and capital expenditures of all levels of the government directly related to education. Expenditures that are not directly related to education (e.g., cultures, sports, youth activities) are, in principle, not included. Expenditures on education by other ministries or equivalent institutions (e.g., Health and Agriculture) are included. Public subsidies for students' living expenses are excluded to ensure international comparability of the data.

Private expenditures Refers to expenditures funded by private sources (i.e., households and other private entities). "Households" means students and their families. "Other private entities" includes private business firms and nonprofit organizations, including religious organizations, charitable organizations, and business and labor associations. Private expenditures are composed of school fees, the cost of materials (such as textbooks and teaching equipment), transportation costs (if organized by the school), the cost of meals (if provided by the school), boarding fees, and expenditures by employers on initial vocational training.

Current expenditures Includes final consumption expenditures (e.g., compensation of employees, consumption of intermediate goods and services, consumption of fixed capital, and military expenditures); property income paid; subsidies; and other current transfers paid.

Capital expenditures Includes spending to acquire and improve fixed capital assets, land, intangible assets, government stocks, and nonmilitary, nonfinancial assets, as well as spending to finance net capital transfers.

International Standard Classification of Education (ISCED) Used to compare educational systems in different countries. ISCED is the standard used by many countries to report education statistics to the United Nations Educational, Scientific, and Cultural Organization (UNESCO) and the Organization for Economic Cooperation and Development (OECD). ISCED divides educational systems into the following seven categories, based on six levels of education.

ISCED Level 0 Education preceding the first level (early childhood education) usually begins at age 3, 4, or 5 (sometimes earlier) and lasts from 1 to 3 years, when it is provided. In the United States, this level includes nursery school and kindergarten.

ISCED Level 1 Education at the first level (primary or elementary education) usually begins at age 5, 6, or 7 and continues for about 4 to 6 years. For the United States, the first level starts with 1st grade and ends with 6th grade.

ISCED Level 2 Education at the second level (lower secondary education) typically begins at about age 11 or 12 and continues for about 2 to 6 years. For the United States, the second level starts with 7th grade and typically ends with 9th grade. Education at the lower secondary level continues the basic programs of the first level, although teaching is typically more subject focused, often using more specialized teachers who conduct classes in their field of specialization. The main criterion for distinguishing lower secondary education from primary education is whether programs begin to be organized in a more subject-oriented pattern, using more specialized teachers conducting classes in their field of specialization. If there is no clear breakpoint for this organizational change, lower secondary education is considered to begin at the end of 6 years of primary education. In countries with no clear division between lower secondary and upper secondary education, and where lower secondary education lasts for more than 3 years, only the first 3 years following primary education are counted as lower secondary education.

ISCED Level 3 Education at the third level (upper secondary education) typically begins at age 15 or 16 and lasts for approximately 3 years. In the United States, the third level starts with 10th grade and ends with 12th grade. Upper secondary education is the final stage of secondary education in most OECD countries. Instruction is often organized along subject-matter lines, in contrast to the lower secondary level, and teachers typically must have a higher level, or more subject-specific, qualification. There are substantial differences in the typical duration of programs both across and between countries, ranging from 2 to 5 years of schooling. The main criteria for classifications are (1) national boundaries between lower and upper secondary education and (2) admission into educational programs, which usually requires the completion of lower secondary education or a combination of basic education and life experience that demonstrates the ability to handle the subject matter in upper secondary schools.

ISCED Level 4 Education at the fourth level (postsecondary nontertiary education) straddles the boundary between secondary and postsecondary education. This program of study, which is primarily vocational in nature, is generally taken after the completion of secondary school and typically lasts from 6 months to 2 years. Although the content of these programs may not be significantly more advanced than upper secondary programs, these programs serve to broaden the knowledge of participants who have already gained an upper secondary qualification.

ISCED Level 5 Education at the fifth level (first stage of tertiary education) includes programs with more advanced content than those offered at the two previous levels. Entry into programs at the fifth level normally requires successful completion of either of the two previous levels.

ISCED Level 5A Tertiary-type A programs provide an education that is largely theoretical and is intended to provide sufficient qualifications for gaining entry into advanced research programs and professions with high skill requirements. Entry into these programs normally requires the successful completion of an upper secondary education; admission is competitive in most cases. The minimum cumulative theoretical duration at this level is 3 years of full-time enrollment. In the United States, tertiary-type A programs include first university programs that last approximately 4 years and lead to the award of a bachelor's degree and second university programs that lead to a master's degree or a first-professional degree such as an M.D., a J.D., or a D.V.M.

ISCED Level 5B Tertiary-type B programs are typically shorter than tertiary-type A programs and focus on practical, technical, or occupational skills for direct entry into the labor market, although they may cover some theoretical foundations in the respective programs. They have a minimum duration of 2 years of full-time enrollment at the tertiary level. In the United States, such programs are often provided at community colleges and lead to an associate's degree.

ISCED Level 6 Education at the sixth level (advanced research qualification) is provided in graduate and professional schools that generally require a university degree or diploma as a minimum condition for admission. Programs at this level lead to the award of an advanced, postgraduate degree, such as a Ph.D. The theoretical duration of these programs is 3 years of full-time enrollment in most countries (for a cumulative total of at least 7 years at levels five and six), although the length of the actual enrollment is often longer. Programs at this level are devoted to advanced study and original research.

Interpolation See Linear interpolation.

Junior high school A separately organized and administered secondary school intermediate between the elementary and senior high schools. A junior high school is usually either a 3-year school that includes grades 7, 8, and 9 or a 2-year school that includes grades 7 and 8.

Labor force People employed (either full time or part time) as civilians, unemployed but looking for work, or in the armed services during the survey week. The "civilian labor force" comprises all civilians classified as employed or unemployed. See also Unemployed.

Lag An event occurring at time $t + k$ ($k > 0$) is said to lag behind an event occurring at time t, the extent of the lag being k. An event occurring k time periods before another may be regarded as having a negative lag.

Land-grant colleges The First Morrill Act of 1862 facilitated the establishment of colleges through grants of land or funds in lieu of land. The Second Morrill Act in 1890 provided for money grants and for the establishment of land-grant colleges and universities for blacks in those states with dual systems of higher education.

Lead time When forecasting a statistic, the number of time periods since the last time period of actual data for that statistic used in producing the forecast.

Level of school A classification of elementary/secondary schools by instructional level. Includes elementary schools, secondary schools, and combined elementary and secondary schools. See also Elementary school, Secondary school, and Combined elementary and secondary school.

Limited-English proficient Refers to an individual who was not born in the United States and whose native language is a language other than English, or who comes from an environment where a language other than English has had a significant impact on the individual's level of English language proficiency. It may also refer to an individual who is migratory, whose native language is a language other than English, and who comes from an environment where a language other than English is dominant; and whose difficulties in speaking, reading, writing, or understanding the English language may be sufficient to deny the individual the ability to meet the state's proficient level of achievement on state assessments as specified under the No Child Left Behind Act, the ability to successfully achieve in classrooms where the language of instruction is English, or the opportunity to participate fully in society. See also English language learner.

Linear interpolation A method that allows the prediction of an unknown value if any two particular values on the same scale are known and the rate of change is assumed constant.

Local education agency (LEA) See School district.

Locale codes A classification system to describe a type of location. The "Metro-Centric" locale codes, developed in the 1980s, classified all schools and school districts based on their county's proximity to a Metropolitan Statistical Area (MSA) and their specific location's population size and density. In 2006, the "Urban-Centric" locale codes were introduced. These locale codes are based on an address's proximity to an urbanized area. For more information see http://nces.ed.gov/ccd/rural_locales.asp.

Pre-2006 Metro-Centric Locale Codes

Large City: A central city of a consolidated metropolitan statistical area (CMSA) or MSA, with the city having a population greater than or equal to 250,000.

Mid-size City: A central city of a CMSA or MSA, with the city having a population less than 250,000.

Urban Fringe of a Large City: Any territory within a CMSA or MSA of a Large City and defined as urban by the Census Bureau.

Urban Fringe of a Mid-size City: Any territory within a CMSA or MSA of a Mid-size City and defined as urban by the Census Bureau.

Large Town: An incorporated place or Census-designated place with a population greater than or equal to 25,000 and located outside a CMSA or MSA.

Small Town: An incorporated place or Census-designated place with a population less than 25,000 and greater than or equal to 2,500 and located outside a CMSA or MSA.

Rural, Outside MSA: Any territory designated as rural by the Census Bureau that is outside a CMSA or MSA of a Large or Mid-size City.

Rural, Inside MSA: Any territory designated as rural by the Census Bureau that is within a CMSA or MSA of a Large or Mid-size City.

2006 Urban-Centric Locale Codes

City, Large: Territory inside an urbanized area and inside a principal city with population of 250,000 or more.

City, Midsize: Territory inside an urbanized area and inside a principal city with population less than 250,000 and greater than or equal to 100,000.

City, Small: Territory inside an urbanized area and inside a principal city with population less than 100,000.

Suburb, Large: Territory outside a principal city and inside an urbanized area with population of 250,000 or more.

Suburb, Midsize: Territory outside a principal city and inside an urbanized area with population less than 250,000 and greater than or equal to 100,000.

Suburb, Small: Territory outside a principal city and inside an urbanized area with population less than 100,000.

Town, Fringe: Territory inside an urban cluster that is less than or equal to 10 miles from an urbanized area.

Town, Distant: Territory inside an urban cluster that is more than 10 miles and less than or equal to 35 miles from an urbanized area.

Town, Remote: Territory inside an urban cluster that is more than 35 miles from an urbanized area.

Rural, Fringe: Census-defined rural territory that is less than or equal to 5 miles from an urbanized area, as well as rural territory that is less than or equal to 2.5 miles from an urban cluster.

Rural, Distant: Census-defined rural territory that is more than 5 miles but less than or equal to 25 miles from an urbanized area, as well as rural territory that is more than 2.5 miles but less than or equal to 10 miles from an urban cluster.

Rural, Remote: Census-defined rural territory that is more than 25 miles from an urbanized area and is also more than 10 miles from an urban cluster.

Magnet school or program A special school or program designed to reduce, prevent, or eliminate racial isolation and/or to provide an academic or social focus on a particular theme.

Mandatory transfer A transfer of current funds that must be made in order to fulfill a binding legal obligation of a post-secondary institution. Included under mandatory transfers are debt service provisions relating to academic and administrative buildings, including (1) amounts set aside for debt retirement and interest and (2) required provisions for renewal and replacement of buildings to the extent these are not financed from other funds.

Margin of error The range of potential true or actual values for a sample survey estimate. The margin of error depends on several factors such as the amount of variation in the responses, the size and representativeness of the sample, and the size of the subgroup for which the estimate is computed. The magnitude of the margin of error is represented by the standard error of the estimate.

Master's degree A degree awarded for successful completion of a program generally requiring 1 or 2 years of full-time college-level study beyond the bachelor's degree. One type of master's degree, including the Master of Arts degree, or M.A., and the Master of Science degree, or M.S., is awarded in the liberal arts and sciences for advanced scholarship in a subject field or discipline and demonstrated ability to perform scholarly research. A second type of master's degree is awarded for the completion of a professionally oriented program, for example, an M.Ed. in education, an M.B.A. in business administration, an M.F.A. in fine arts, an M.M. in music, an M.S.W. in social work, and an M.P.A. in public administration. Some master's degrees—such as divinity degrees (M.Div. or M.H.L./Rav), which were formerly classified as "first-professional"—may require more than 2 years of full-time study beyond the bachelor's degree.

Mathematics A group of instructional programs that describes the science of numbers and their operations, interrelations, combinations, generalizations, and abstractions and of space configurations and their structure, measurement, transformations, and generalizations.

Mean absolute percentage error (MAPE) The average value of the absolute value of errors expressed in percentage terms.

Mean test score The score obtained by dividing the sum of the scores of all individuals in a group by the number of individuals in that group for which scores are available.

Median earnings The amount which divides the income distribution into two equal groups, half having income above that amount and half having income below that amount. Earnings include all wage and salary income. Unlike mean earnings, median earnings either do not change or change very little in response to extreme observations.

Middle school A school with no grade lower than 5 and no higher than 8.

Migration Geographic mobility involving a change of usual residence between clearly defined geographic units, that is, between counties, states, or regions.

Minimum-competency testing Measuring the acquisition of competence or skills to or beyond a certain specified standard.

Model A system of postulates, data, and inferences presented as a mathematical description of a phenomenon, such as an actual system or process. The actual phenomenon is represented by the model in order to explain, predict, and control it.

Montessori school A school that provides instruction using Montessori teaching methods.

Multiple disabilities See Disabilities, children with.

National Assessment of Educational Progress (NAEP) See Appendix A: Guide to Sources.

National School Lunch Program Established by President Truman in 1946, the program is a federally assisted meal program operated in public and private nonprofit schools and residential child care centers. To be eligible for free lunch, a student must be from a household with an income at or below 130 percent of the federal poverty guideline; to be eligible for reduced-price lunch, a student must be from a household with an income between 130 percent and 185 percent of the federal poverty guideline.

Newly qualified teacher People who: (1) first became eligible for a teaching license during the period of the study referenced or who were teaching at the time of survey, but were not certified or eligible for a teaching license; and (2) had never held full-time, regular teaching positions (as opposed to substitute) prior to completing the requirements for the degree which brought them into the survey.

Non-degree-granting institutions Postsecondary institutions that participate in Title IV federal financial aid programs but do not offer accredited 4-year or 2-year degree programs. Includes some institutions transitioning to higher level program offerings, though still classified at a lower level.

Nonprofessional staff See Employees in degree-granting institutions.

Nonprofit institution A private institution in which the individual(s) or agency in control receives no compensation other than wages, rent, or other expenses for the assumption of risk. Nonprofit institutions may be either independent nonprofit (i.e., having no religious affiliation) or religiously affiliated.

Nonresident alien A person who is not a citizen of the United States and who is in this country on a temporary basis and does not have the right to remain indefinitely.

Nonsectarian school Nonsectarian schools do not have a religious orientation or purpose and are categorized as regular, special program emphasis, or special education schools. See also Regular school, Special program emphasis school, and Special education school.

Nonsupervisory instructional staff People such as curriculum specialists, counselors, librarians, remedial specialists, and others possessing education certification, but not responsible for day-to-day teaching of the same group of pupils.

Nursery school An instructional program for groups of children during the year or years preceding kindergarten, which provides educational experiences under the direction of teachers. See also Prekindergarten and Preschool.

Obligations Amounts of orders placed, contracts awarded, services received, or similar legally binding commitments made by federal agencies during a given period that will require outlays during the same or some future period.

Occupational home economics Courses of instruction emphasizing the acquisition of competencies needed for getting and holding a job or preparing for advancement in an occupational area using home economics knowledge and skills.

Occupied housing unit Separate living quarters with occupants currently inhabiting the unit. See also Housing unit.

Off-budget federal entities Organizational entities, federally owned in whole or in part, whose transactions belong in the budget under current budget accounting concepts, but that have been excluded from the budget totals under provisions of law. An example of an off-budget federal entity is the Federal Financing Bank, which provides student loans under the Direct Loan Program.

On-budget funding Federal funding for education programs that is tied to appropriations. On-budget funding does not include the Direct Loan Program, under which student loans are provided by the Federal Financing Bank, an off-budget federal entity. See also Off-budget federal entities.

Operation and maintenance services Includes salary, benefits, supplies, and contractual fees for supervision of operations and maintenance, operating buildings (heating, lighting, ventilating, repair, and replacement), care and upkeep of grounds and equipment, vehicle operations and maintenance (other than student transportation), security, and other operations and maintenance services.

Ordinary least squares (OLS) The estimator that minimizes the sum of squared residuals.

Organization for Economic Cooperation and Development (OECD) An intergovernmental organization of industrialized countries that serves as a forum for member countries to cooperate in research and policy development on social and economic topics of common interest. In addition to member countries, partner countries contribute to the OECD's work in a sustained and comprehensive manner.

Orthopedic impairment See Disabilities, children with.

Other foreign languages and literatures Any instructional program in foreign languages and literatures not listed in the table, including language groups and individual languages, such as the non-Semitic African languages, Native American languages, the Celtic languages, Pacific language groups, the Ural-Altaic languages, Basque, and others.

Other health impairment See Disabilities, children with.

Other professional staff See Employees in degree-granting institutions.

Other religious school Other religious schools have a religious orientation or purpose, but are not Roman Catholic. Other religious schools are categorized according to religious association membership as Conservative Christian, other affiliated, or unaffiliated.

Other support services Includes salary, benefits, supplies, and contractual fees for business support services, central support services, and other support services not otherwise classified.

Other support services staff All staff not reported in other categories. This group includes media personnel, social workers, bus drivers, security, cafeteria workers, and other staff.

Outlays The value of checks issued, interest accrued on the public debt, or other payments made, net of refunds and reimbursements.

Parameter A quantity that describes a statistical population.

Part-time enrollment The number of students enrolled in postsecondary education courses with a total credit load less than 75 percent of the normal full-time credit load. At the undergraduate level, part-time enrollment typically includes students who have a credit load of less than 12 semester or quarter credits. At the postbaccalaureate level, part-time enrollment typically includes students who have a credit load of less than 9 semester or quarter credits.

Pass-through transaction A payment that a postsecondary institution applies directly to a student's account. The payment "passes through" the institution for the student's benefit. Most private institutions treat Pell grants as pass-through transactions. At these institutions, any Pell grant funds that are applied to a student's tuition are reported as tuition revenues. In contrast, the vast majority of public institutions report Pell grants both as federal revenues and as allowances that reduce tuition revenues.

Personal income Current income received by people from all sources, minus their personal contributions for social insurance. Classified as "people" are individuals (including owners of unincorporated firms), nonprofit institutions serving individuals, private trust funds, and private noninsured welfare funds. Personal income includes transfers (payments not resulting from current production) from government and business such as social security benefits and military pensions, but excludes transfers among people.

Physical plant assets Includes the values of land, buildings, and equipment owned, rented, or utilized by colleges. Does not include those plant values which are a part of endowment or other capital fund investments in real estate; excludes construction in progress.

Postbaccalaureate enrollment The number of students working towards advanced degrees and of students enrolled in graduate-level classes but not enrolled in degree programs. See also Graduate enrollment.

Postsecondary education The provision of formal instructional programs with a curriculum designed primarily for students who have completed the requirements for a high school diploma or equivalent. This includes programs of an academic, vocational, and continuing professional education purpose, and excludes avocational and adult basic education programs.

Postsecondary institutions (basic classification by level)

4-year institution An institution offering at least a 4-year program of college-level studies wholly or principally creditable toward a baccalaureate degree.

2-year institution An institution offering at least a 2-year program of college-level studies which terminates in an associate degree or is principally creditable toward a baccalaureate degree. Data prior to 1996 include some institutions that have a less-than-2-year program, but were designated as institutions of higher education in the Higher Education General Information Survey.

Less-than-2-year institution An institution that offers programs of less than 2 years' duration below the baccalaureate level. Includes occupational and vocational schools with programs that do not exceed 1,800 contact hours.

Postsecondary institutions (2005 Carnegie classification of degree-granting institutions)

Doctorate-granting Characterized by a significant level and breadth of activity in commitment to doctoral-level education as measured by the number of doctorate recipients and the diversity in doctoral-level program offerings. These institutions are assigned to one of the three subcategories listed below based on level of research activity (for more information on the research activity index used to assign institutions to the subcategories, see http://carnegieclassifications.iu.edu:

Research university, very high Characterized by a very high level of research activity.

Research university, high Characterized by a high level of research activity.

Doctoral/research university Awarding at least 20 doctor's degrees per year, but not having a high level of research activity.

Master's Characterized by diverse postbaccalaureate programs but not engaged in significant doctoral-level education.

Baccalaureate Characterized by primary emphasis on general undergraduate, baccalaureate-level education. Not significantly engaged in postbaccalaureate education.

Special focus Baccalaureate or postbaccalaureate institution emphasizing one area (plus closely related specialties), such as business or engineering. The programmatic emphasis is measured by the percentage of degrees granted in the program area.

Associate's Institutions conferring at least 90 percent of their degrees and awards for work below the bachelor's level. In NCES tables, excludes all institutions offering any 4-year programs leading to a bachelor's degree.

Tribal Colleges and universities that are members of the American Indian Higher Education Consortium, as identified in IPEDS Institutional Characteristics.

Poverty The U.S. Census Bureau uses a set of money income thresholds that vary by family size and composition. A family, along with each individual in it, is considered poor if the family's total income is less than that family's threshold. The poverty thresholds do not vary geographically and are adjusted annually for inflation using the Consumer Price Index. The official poverty definition counts money income before taxes and does not include capital gains and noncash benefits (such as public housing, Medicaid, and food stamps).

Prekindergarten Preprimary education for children typically ages 3–4 who have not yet entered kindergarten. It may offer a program of general education or special education and may be part of a collaborative effort with Head Start.

Preschool An instructional program enrolling children generally younger than 5 years of age and organized to provide children with educational experiences under professionally qualified teachers during the year or years immediately preceding kindergarten (or prior to entry into elementary school when there is no kindergarten). See also Nursery school and Prekindergarten.

Primary school A school with at least one grade lower than 5 and no grade higher than 8.

Private institution An institution that is controlled by an individual or agency other than a state, a subdivision of a state, or the federal government, which is usually supported primarily by other than public funds, and the operation of whose program rests with other than publicly elected or appointed officials.

Private nonprofit institution An institution in which the individual(s) or agency in control receives no compensation other than wages, rent, or other expenses for the assumption of risk. These include both independent nonprofit institutions and those affiliated with a religious organization.

Private for-profit institution An institution in which the individual(s) or agency in control receives compensation other than wages, rent, or other expenses for the assumption of risk (e.g., proprietary schools).

Private school Private elementary/secondary schools surveyed by the Private School Universe Survey (PSS) are assigned to one of three major categories (Catholic, other religious, or nonsectarian) and, within each major category, one of three subcategories based on the school's religious affiliation provided by respondents.

Catholic Schools categorized according to governance, provided by Catholic school respondents, into parochial, diocesan, and private schools.

Other religious Schools that have a religious orientation or purpose but are not Roman Catholic. Other religious schools are categorized according to religious association membership, provided by respondents, into Conservative Christian, other affiliated, and unaffiliated schools. Conservative Christian schools are those "Other religious" schools with membership in at least one of four associations: Accelerated Christian Education, American Association of Christian Schools, Association of Christian Schools International, and Oral Roberts University Education Fellowship. Affiliated schools are those "Other religious" schools not classified as Conservative Christian with membership in at least 1 of 11 associations— Association of Christian Teachers and Schools, Christian Schools International, Evangelical Lutheran Education

Association, Friends Council on Education, General Conference of the Seventh-Day Adventist Church, Islamic School League of America, National Association of Episcopal Schools, National Christian School Association, National Society for Hebrew Day Schools, Solomon Schechter Day Schools, and Southern Baptist Association of Christian Schools—or indicating membership in "other religious school associations." Unaffiliated schools are those "Other religious" schools that have a religious orientation or purpose but are not classified as Conservative Christian or affiliated.

Nonsectarian Schools that do not have a religious orientation or purpose and are categorized according to program emphasis, provided by respondents, into regular, special emphasis, and special education schools. Regular schools are those that have a regular elementary/secondary or early childhood program emphasis. Special emphasis schools are those that have a Montessori, vocational/technical, alternative, or special program emphasis. Special education schools are those that have a special education program emphasis.

Professional staff See Employees in degree-granting institutions.

Program for International Student Assessment (PISA) A system of international assessments organized by the OECD that focuses on 15-year-olds' capabilities in reading literacy, mathematics literacy, and science literacy. PISA also includes measures of general, or cross-curricular, competencies such as learning strategies. The measures emphasize functional skills that students have acquired as they near the end of mandatory schooling. PISA was administered for the first time in 2000, when 43 countries participated. Forty-one countries participated in the 2003 administration of PISA; 57 jurisdictions (30 OECD members and 27 nonmembers) participated in 2006; and 65 jurisdictions (34 OECD members and 31 nonmembers) participated in 2009.

Projection In relation to a time series, an estimate of future values based on a current trend.

Property tax The sum of money collected from a tax levied against the value of property.

Proprietary (for profit) institution A private institution in which the individual(s) or agency in control receives compensation other than wages, rent, or other expenses for the assumption of risk.

Public school or institution A school or institution controlled and operated by publicly elected or appointed officials and deriving its primary support from public funds.

Pupil/teacher ratio The enrollment of pupils at a given period of time, divided by the full-time-equivalent number of classroom teachers serving these pupils during the same period.

Purchasing Power Parity (PPP) indexes PPP exchange rates, or indexes, are the currency exchange rates that equalize the purchasing power of different currencies, meaning that when a given sum of money is converted into different currencies at the PPP exchange rates, it will buy the same basket of goods and services in all countries. PPP indexes are the rates of currency conversion that eliminate the difference in price levels among countries. Thus, when expenditures on gross domestic product (GDP) for different countries are converted into a common currency by means of PPP indexes, they are expressed at the same set of international prices, so that comparisons among countries reflect only differences in the volume of goods and services purchased.

R^2 The coefficient of determination; the square of the correlation coefficient between the dependent variable and its ordinary least squares (OLS) estimate.

Racial/ethnic group Classification indicating general racial or ethnic heritage. Race/ethnicity data are based on the *Hispanic* ethnic category and the race categories listed below (five single-race categories, plus the *Two or more races* category). Race categories exclude persons of Hispanic ethnicity unless otherwise noted.

White A person having origins in any of the original peoples of Europe, the Middle East, or North Africa.

Black or African American A person having origins in any of the black racial groups of Africa. Used interchangeably with the shortened term *Black*.

Hispanic or Latino A person of Cuban, Mexican, Puerto Rican, South or Central American, or other Spanish culture or origin, regardless of race. Used interchangeably with the shortened term *Hispanic*.

Asian A person having origins in any of the original peoples of the Far East, Southeast Asia, or the Indian subcontinent, including, for example, Cambodia, China, India, Japan, Korea, Malaysia, Pakistan, the Philippine Islands, Thailand, and Vietnam. Prior to 2010–11, the Common Core of Data (CCD) combined Asian and Pacific Islander categories.

Native Hawaiian or Other Pacific Islander A person having origins in any of the original peoples of Hawaii, Guam, Samoa, or other Pacific Islands. Prior to 2010–11, the Common Core of Data (CCD) combined Asian and Pacific Islander categories. Used interchangeably with the shortened term *Pacific Islander*.

American Indian or Alaska Native A person having origins in any of the original peoples of North and South America (including Central America), and who maintains tribal affiliation or community attachment.

Two or more races A person identifying himself or herself as of two or more of the following race groups: White, Black, Asian, Native Hawaiian or Other Pacific Islander, or American Indian or Alaska Native. Some, but not all, reporting districts use this category. "Two or more races" was introduced in the 2000 Census and became a regular category for data collection in the Current Population Survey (CPS) in 2003. The category is sometimes excluded from a historical series of data with constant categories. It is sometimes included within the category "Other."

Region See Geographic region.

Regression analysis A statistical technique for investigating and modeling the relationship between variables.

Regular school A public elementary/secondary or charter school providing instruction and education services that does not focus primarily on special education, vocational/technical education, or alternative education.

Related children Related children in a family include own children and all other children in the household who are related to the householder by birth, marriage, or adoption.

Remedial education Instruction for a student lacking those reading, writing, or math skills necessary to perform college-level work at the level required by the attended institution.

Resident population Includes civilian population and armed forces personnel residing within the United States; excludes armed forces personnel residing overseas.

Revenue All funds received from external sources, net of refunds, and correcting transactions. Noncash transactions, such as receipt of services, commodities, or other receipts in kind are excluded, as are funds received from the issuance of debt, liquidation of investments, and nonroutine sale of property.

Revenue receipts Additions to assets that do not incur an obligation that must be met at some future date and do not represent exchanges of property for money. Assets must be available for expenditures.

Rho A measure of the correlation coefficient between errors in time period t and time period t minus 1.

Rural school See Locale codes.

Salary The total amount regularly paid or stipulated to be paid to an individual, before deductions, for personal services rendered while on the payroll of a business or organization.

Sales and services Revenues derived from the sales of goods or services that are incidental to the conduct of instruction, research, or public service. Examples include film rentals, scientific and literary publications, testing services, university presses, and dairy products.

Sales tax Tax imposed upon the sale and consumption of goods and services. It can be imposed either as a general tax on the retail price of all goods and services sold or as a tax on the sale of selected goods and services.

SAT An examination administered by the Educational Testing Service and used to predict the facility with which an individual will progress in learning college-level academic subjects. It was formerly called the Scholastic Assessment Test.

Scholarships and fellowships This category of college expenditures applies only to money given in the form of outright grants and trainee stipends to individuals enrolled in formal coursework, either for credit or not. Aid to students in the form of tuition or fee remissions is included. College work-study funds are excluded and are reported under the program in which the student is working.

School A division of the school system consisting of students in one or more grades or other identifiable groups and organized to give instruction of a defined type. One school may share a building with another school or one school may be housed in several buildings. Excludes schools that have closed or are planned for the future.

School administration support services Includes salary, benefits, supplies, and contractual fees for the office of the principal, full-time department chairpersons, and graduation expenses.

School climate The social system and culture of the school, including the organizational structure of the school and values and expectations within it.

School district An education agency at the local level that exists primarily to operate public schools or to contract for public school services. Synonyms are "local basic administrative unit" and "local education agency."

Science The body of related courses concerned with knowledge of the physical and biological world and with the processes of discovering and validating this knowledge.

Secondary enrollment The total number of students registered in a school beginning with the next grade following an elementary or middle school (usually 7, 8, or 9) and ending with or below grade 12 at a given time.

Secondary instructional level The general level of instruction provided for pupils in secondary schools (generally covering grades 7 through 12 or 9 through 12) and any instruction of a comparable nature and difficulty provided for adults and youth beyond the age of compulsory school attendance.

Secondary school A school comprising any span of grades beginning with the next grade following an elementary or middle school (usually 7, 8, or 9) and ending with or below grade 12. Both junior high schools and senior high schools are included.

Senior high school A secondary school offering the final years of high school work necessary for graduation.

Serial correlation Correlation of the error terms from different observations of the same variable. Also called Autocorrelation.

Serial volumes Publications issued in successive parts, usually at regular intervals, and as a rule, intended to be continued indefinitely. Serials include periodicals, newspapers, annuals, memoirs, proceedings, and transactions of societies.

Social studies A group of instructional programs that describes the substantive portions of behavior, past and present activities, interactions, and organizations of people associated together for religious, benevolent, cultural, scientific, political, patriotic, or other purposes.

Socioeconomic status (SES) The SES index is a composite of often equally weighted, standardized components, such as father's education, mother's education, family income, father's occupation, and household items. The terms high, middle, and low SES refer to ranges of the weighted SES composite index distribution.

Special education Direct instructional activities or special learning experiences designed primarily for students identified as having exceptionalities in one or more aspects of the cognitive process or as being underachievers in relation to general level or model of their overall abilities. Such services usually are directed at students with the following conditions: (1) physically handicapped; (2) emotionally disabled; (3) culturally different, including compensatory education; (4) intellectually disabled; and (5) students with learning disabilities. Programs for the mentally gifted and talented are also included in some special education programs. See also Disabilities, children with.

Special education school A public elementary/secondary school that focuses primarily on special education for children with disabilities and that adapts curriculum, materials, or instruction for students served. See also Disabilities, children with.

Special program emphasis school A science/mathematics school, a performing arts high school, a foreign language immersion school, and a talented/gifted school are examples of schools that offer a special program emphasis.

Specific learning disability See Disabilities, children with.

Speech or language impairment See Disabilities, children with.

Standard error of estimate An expression for the standard deviation of the observed values about a regression line. An estimate of the variation likely to be encountered in making predictions from the regression equation.

Standardized test A test composed of a systematic sampling of behavior, administered and scored according to specific instructions, capable of being interpreted in terms of adequate norms, and for which there are data on reliability and validity.

Standardized test performance The weighted distributions of composite scores from standardized tests used to group students according to performance.

Status dropout rate The percentage of individuals within a given age range who are not enrolled in school and lack a high school credential, irrespective of when they dropped out.

Status dropout rate (Current Population Survey) The percentage of civilian, noninstitutionalized young people ages 16–24 who are not in school and have not earned a high school credential (either a diploma or equivalency credential such as a General Educational Development [GED] certificate). The numerator of the status dropout rate for a given year is the number of individuals ages 16–24 who, as of October of that year, have not completed a high school credential and are not currently enrolled in school. The denominator is the total number of individuals ages 16–24 in the United States in October of that year. Status dropout rates count as dropouts individuals who never attended school and immigrants who did not complete the equivalent of a high school education in their home country.

Status dropout rate (American Community Survey) Similar to the status dropout rate (Current Population Survey), except that institutionalized persons, incarcerated persons, and active duty military personnel living in barracks in the United States may be included in this calculation.

STEM fields Science, Technology, Engineering, and Mathematics (STEM) fields of study that are considered to be of particular relevance to advanced societies. For the purposes of *The Condition of Education 2015*, STEM fields include agriculture and natural resources, architecture, biology and biomedical sciences, computer and information sciences, engineering and engineering technologies, health studies, mathematics and statistics, and physical and social sciences. STEM occupations include computer scientists and mathematicians; engineers and architects; life, physical, and social scientists; medical professionals; and managers of STEM activities.

Student An individual for whom instruction is provided in an educational program under the jurisdiction of a school, school system, or other education institution. No distinction is made between the terms "student" and "pupil," though "student" may refer to one receiving instruction at any level while "pupil" refers only to one attending school at the elementary or secondary level. A student may receive instruction in a school facility or in another location, such as at home or in a hospital. Instruction may be provided by direct student-teacher interaction or by some other approved medium such as television, radio, telephone, and correspondence.

Student membership Student membership is an annual head-count of students enrolled in school on October 1 or the school day closest to that date. The Common Core of Data (CCD) allows a student to be reported for only a single school or agency. For example, a vocational school (identified as a "shared time" school) may provide classes for students from a number of districts and show no membership.

Student support services Includes salary, benefits, supplies, and contractual fees for staff providing attendance and social work, guidance, health, psychological services, speech pathology, audiology, and other support to students.

Study abroad population U.S. citizens and permanent residents, enrolled for a degree at an accredited higher education institution in the United States, who received academic credit for study abroad from their home institutions upon their return. Students studying abroad without receiving academic credit are not included, nor are U.S. students enrolled for a degree overseas.

Subject-matter club Organizations that are formed around a shared interest in a particular area of study and whose primary activities promote that interest. Examples of such organizations are math, science, business, and history clubs.

Supervisory staff Principals, assistant principals, and supervisors of instruction; does not include superintendents or assistant superintendents.

Tax base The collective value of objects, assets, and income components against which a tax is levied.

Tax expenditures Losses of tax revenue attributable to provisions of the federal income tax laws that allow a special exclusion, exemption, or deduction from gross income or provide a special credit, preferential rate of tax, or a deferral of tax liability affecting individual or corporate income tax liabilities.

Teacher see Instructional staff.

Technical education A program of vocational instruction that ordinarily includes the study of the sciences and mathematics underlying a technology, as well as the methods, skills, and materials commonly used and the services performed in the technology. Technical education prepares individuals for positions—such as draftsman or lab technician—in the occupational area between the skilled craftsman and the professional person.

Three-year moving average An arithmetic average of the year indicated, the year immediately preceding, and the year immediately following. Use of a 3-year moving average increases the sample size, thereby reducing the size of sampling errors and producing more stable estimates.

Time series A set of ordered observations on a quantitative characteristic of an individual or collective phenomenon taken at different points in time. Usually the observations are successive and equally spaced in time.

Time series analysis The branch of quantitative forecasting in which data for one variable are examined for patterns of trend, seasonality, and cycle.

Title I school A school designated under appropriate state and federal regulations as a high-poverty school that is eligible for participation in programs authorized by Title I of the Reauthorization of the Elementary and Secondary Education Act, P.L. 107-110.

Title IV Refers to a section of the Higher Education Act of 1965 that covers the administration of the federal student financial aid program.

Title IV eligible institution A postsecondary institution that meets the criteria for participating in federal student financial aid programs. An eligible institution must be any of the following: (1) an institution of higher education (with public or private, nonprofit control), (2) a proprietary institution (with private for-profit control), and (3) a postsecondary vocational institution (with public or private, nonprofit control). In addition, it must have acceptable legal authorization, acceptable accreditation and admission standards, eligible academic program(s), administrative capability, and financial responsibility.

Total expenditure per pupil in average daily attendance Includes all expenditures allocable to per pupil costs divided by average daily attendance. These allocable expenditures include current expenditures for regular school programs, interest on school debt, and capital outlay. Beginning in 1980–81, expenditures for state administration are excluded and expenditures for other programs (summer schools and designated subsidies for community colleges and private schools) are included.

Town school See Locale codes.

Trade and industrial occupations The branch of vocational education which is concerned with preparing people for initial employment or with updating or retraining workers in a wide range of trade and industrial occupations. Such occupations are skilled or semiskilled and are concerned with layout designing, producing, processing, assembling, testing, maintaining, servicing, or repairing any product or commodity.

Traditional public school Publicly funded schools other than public charter schools. See also Public school or institution and Charter school.

Transcript An official list of all courses taken by a student at a school or college showing the final grade received for each course, with definitions of the various grades given at the institution.

Trust funds Amounts collected and used by the federal government for carrying out specific purposes and programs according to terms of a trust agreement or statute, such as the social security and unemployment trust funds. Trust fund receipts that are not anticipated to be used in the immediate future are generally invested in interest-bearing government securities and earn interest for the trust fund.

Tuition and fees A payment or charge for instruction or compensation for services, privileges, or the use of equipment, books, or other goods. Tuition may be charged per term, per course, or per credit.

Type of school A classification of public elementary and secondary schools that includes the following categories: regular schools, special education schools, vocational schools, and alternative schools. See also Regular school, Special education school, Vocational school, and Alternative school.

Unadjusted dollars See Current dollars.

Unclassified students Students who are not candidates for a degree or other formal award, although they are taking higher education courses for credit in regular classes with other students.

Undergraduate students Students registered at an institution of postsecondary education who are working in a baccalaureate degree program or other formal program below the baccalaureate, such as an associate's degree, vocational, or technical program.

Unemployed Civilians who had no employment but were available for work and: (1) had engaged in any specific job seeking activity within the past 4 weeks; (2) were waiting to be called back to a job from which they had been laid off; or (3) were waiting to report to a new wage or salary job within 30 days.

Ungraded student (elementary/secondary) A student who has been assigned to a school or program that does not have standard grade designations.

Urban fringe school See Locale codes.

U.S. Service Academies These institutions of higher education are controlled by the U.S. Department of Defense and the U.S. Department of Transportation. The 5 institutions counted in the NCES surveys of degree-granting institutions include: the U.S. Air Force Academy, U.S. Coast Guard Academy, U.S. Merchant Marine Academy, U.S. Military Academy, and the U.S. Naval Academy.

Variable A quantity that may assume any one of a set of values.

Visual and performing arts A group of instructional programs that generally describes the historic development, aesthetic qualities, and creative processes of the visual and performing arts.

Visual impairment See Disabilities, children with.

Vocational education Organized educational programs, services, and activities which are directly related to the preparation of individuals for paid or unpaid employment, or for additional preparation for a career, requiring other than a baccalaureate or advanced degree.

Vocational school A public school that focuses primarily on providing formal preparation for semiskilled, skilled, technical, or professional occupations for high school–age students who have opted to develop or expand their employment opportunities, often in lieu of preparing for college entry.

Years out In forecasting by year, the number of years since the last year of actual data for that statistic used in producing the forecast.

APPENDIX C
Index of Table Numbers